The

AMERICAN HERITAGE®

D0010286

desk dictionary

FIFTH
EDITION

Houghton Mifflin Harcourt
BOSTON   NEW YORK

Visit our website at www.ahdictionary.com
or www.youareyourwords.com

Library of Congress Cataloging-in-Publication Data

The American heritage desk dictionary. -- 5th ed.
    p. cm.
  Previous ed.: 2003.
  ISBN 978-0-547-70813-3
  1. English language--Dictionaries. 2. English language--United States--Dictionaries.
  PE1628.A62286 2012
  423--dc23

                                                                    2011051290

Manufactured in the United States of America

3 4 5 6 7 8 9 10 - DOC - 16 15 14 13

Table of Contents

Tables and Charts

Editorial and Production Staff

GUIDE TO THE DICTIONARY

Main Entries. Entries are listed in alphabetical order without taking into account spaces or hyphens. Two or more entries with identical spellings but different origins are distinguished by superscript numbers. For example: **ground¹, ground², groundbreaking, ground floor, groundhog, groundless.** A pair of boldface guidewords at the top of each page shows the first and last main entries on that page. Thus **feedback** and **femur** and all of the entries that fall alphabetically between them are entered and defined on page 311. Entry words of more than one syllable are divided by centered dots. Syllable dots are omitted for parts of compound words that are also main entries in the Dictionary; for example, see **Conestoga wagon** (p. 181), where **Conestoga** has syllable dots but **wagon** does not.

Variant Forms. If a word has two or more different spellings, the definition appears at the spelling that is most frequently used. The variant spellings are shown in boldface type after the main entry. The word "or" separates two forms used with approximately equal frequency; "also" introduces a less frequent variant. Variant forms are listed separately when they fall more than ten entries away from the main entry.

Inflected Forms. Inflected forms regarded as being irregular or those offering possible spelling problems are entered in boldface type, often in shortened form. The following regular inflections are also entered: degrees of adjectives and adverbs, and regular plurals if irregular plurals are shown. Pronunciations are given only if they differ significantly from the base form of the word:

> **good** (gŏod) ►*adj.* **bet·ter** (bĕt′ər), **best** (bĕst) **1.** Being . . .
> **com·pute** (kəm-pyōōt′) ►*v.* **-put·ed, -put·ing 1.** To . . .
> **ax·is** (ăk′sĭs) ►*n., pl.* **ax·es** (ăk′sēz′) **1.** A . . .

The inflected forms of verbs are given in the following order: past tense, past participle (if it differs from the past tense), and present participle.

Irregular inflected forms are listed separately when they fall more than ten entries away from the main entry.

Verbs. Verbal definitions indicate transitivity or intransitivity by their wording. In the following examples, **bloom** is defined intransitively and **shuck** transitively:

> **bloom** (blōom) ►*v.* **1.** To bear flowers.
> **shuck** (shŭk) ►*v.* **1.** To remove the husk or shell from: *shuck corn.*

Parentheses are used in certain transitive definitions to indicate a usual or typical direct object:

> **de·clas·si·fy** (dē-klăs′ə-fī′) ►*v.* To remove official security classification from (a document).

Parentheses are also used around a final preposition to indicate that a verb can be used either transitively or intransitively in that sense:

> **kink** (kĭngk) ►*v.* To form a kink (in).

Labels. The following labels, set in italics, indicate that an entry word or a definition is limited to a particular level or style of usage: *Nonstandard* is applied to forms and usages that educated speakers and writers consider unacceptable (e.g., **ain't**); *Informal* indicates a term whose acceptability is limited to conversation and informal writing (e.g., **boondoggle**); *Slang* indicates a style of language that is distinguished by a striving for rhetorical effect through the use of extravagant, often facetious coinages or figures of speech (e.g., **twerp**); and *Offensive* is reserved for words and expressions considered insulting and derogatory. Other, usually abbreviated, labels, such as *Geol.* and *Electron.*, identify the special area of knowledge to which an entry word or a definition applies, while such labels as *Scots* and *Chiefly Brit.* identify an entry as a form that is used chiefly in another part of the English-speaking world.

Undefined Forms. At the end of many entries additional boldface words appear without definitions. They are closely and clearly related in basic meaning to the entry word but may have different grammatical functions.

Etymologies. Etymologies appear in square brackets following the definitions. The symbol < is used to mean "from" and is often an indication that transitional stages have been omitted in order to give a concise history of the word. A word or word element printed in small capitals is an entry in the Dictionary and should be referred to for more etymological information. Linguistic forms that are not Modern English words appear in italics. A question mark indicates that the origin is unknown.

Abbreviations. Common abbreviations used in this Dictionary, such as *adj., pl., var.,* and *e.g.,* are main entries. Additional abbreviations and symbols are listed on page vii.

Additional Abbreviations in This Dictionary

At. no.	Atomic number	p.	past
b.	born	part.	participle
c.	circa (about)	perh.	perhaps
comp.	comparative	pers.	person
d.	died	poss.	possibly
dim.	diminutive	pr.	present
gen.	generally	prob.	probably
imit.	imitative	superl.	superlative
imper.	imperative	t.	tense
indic.	indicative	ult.	ultimately
orig.	origin, originally	var.	variant

Language Abbreviations Used in Etymologies

Afr.	Afrikaans	ME	Middle English
Am.Sp.	American Spanish	Med.Gk.	Medieval Greek
Ar.	Arabic	Med.Lat.	Medieval Latin
Aram.	Aramaic	MFlem.	Middle Flemish
Balt.	Baltic	MHGer.	Middle High German
Celt.	Celtic	MLGer.	Middle Low German
Chin.	Chinese	Mod.	Modern
Dan.	Danish	MPers.	Middle Persian
dial.	dialectal	NLat.	New Latin
Du.	Dutch	Norw.	Norwegian
E.	English	O	Old (in combination)
Egypt.	Egyptian	OE	Old English
Finn.	Finnish	OHGer.	Old High German
Flem.	Flemish	ONFr.	Old North French
Fr.	French	Penn.Du.	Pennsylvania Dutch
Gael.	Gaelic	Pers.	Persian
Ger.	German	Pol.	Polish
Gk.	Greek	Port.	Portuguese
Heb.	Hebrew	Prov.	Provençal
Hung.	Hungarian	Rom.	Romanian
Icel.	Icelandic	Russ.	Russian
Ir.	Irish	Sc.	Scots
Ital.	Italian	Scand.	Scandinavian
J.	Japanese	Sc.Gael.	Scottish Gaelic
Lat.	Latin	Skt.	Sanskrit
LGer.	Low German	Slav.	Slavic
LGk.	Late Greek	Sp.	Spanish
LHeb.	Late Hebrew	Swed.	Swedish
LLat.	Late Latin	Turk.	Turkish
MDu.	Middle Dutch	VLat.	Vulgar Latin

*	unattested	<	derived from
+	combined with	?	origin unknown

Pronunciation Key

Symbols	Examples	Symbols	Examples
ă	pat	ōō	boot
ā	pay	ou	out
âr	care	p	pop
ä	father	r	roar
b	bib	s	sauce
ch	church	sh	ship, dish
d	deed, milled	t	tight, stopped
ĕ	pet	th	thin
ē	bee	*th*	this
f	fife, phase, rough	ŭ	cut
g	gag	ûr	urge, term, firm, word,
h	hat		heard
hw	which	v	valve
ĭ	pit	w	with
ī	pie, by	y	yes
îr	pier	z	zebra, xylem
j	judge	zh	vision, pleasure, garage
k	kick, cat, pique	ə	about, item, edible,
l	lid, needle (nēd′l)		gallop, circus*
m	mum	ər	butter
n	no, sudden (sŭd′n)		
ng	thing	**Foreign**	
ŏ	pot	œ	French feu
ō	toe		German schön
ô	caught, for, paw,	ü	French tu
	horrid, hoarse		German über
ôr	core	KH	German ich
oi	noise		Scottish loch
ŏŏ	took	N	French bon
ŏŏr	lure		

Primary stress (′)   **bi·ol·o·gy** (bī-ŏl′ə-jē)**

Secondary stress (′)   **bi·o·log·i·cal** (bī′ə-lŏj′ĭ-kəl)**

   *The symbol (ə) is called a *schwa*. It represents a vowel that receives the weakest level of stress within a word. The schwa sound varies, sometimes according to the vowel it is representing and often according to the sounds surrounding it.

   **Stress, the relative degree of emphasis with which the syllables of a word (or phrase) are spoken, is indicated in three different ways. The strongest, or primary, stress is marked with a bold mark (′). An intermediate, or secondary, level of stress is marked with a similar but lighter mark (′). An unmarked syllable has the weakest stress in the word. Words of one syllable show no stress mark, since there is no other stress level to which the syllable is compared.

A

a¹ or **A** (ā) ►*n., pl.* **a's** or **A's** also **as** or **As 1.** The 1st letter of the English alphabet. **2.** The best in quality or rank. **3.** *Mus.* The 6th tone in the scale of C major. **4. A** A type of blood in the ABO system.

a² (ə; ā *when stressed*) ►*indef.art.* **1.** One: *a region; a person.* **2.** Any: *not a drop to drink.* [ME, var. of *an,* AN.]

a³ (ə) ►*prep.* Per: *once a day.* [< OE *an,* in.]

a⁴ ►*abbr.* **1.** acceleration **2.** are (measurement)

A ►*abbr.* **1.** across **2.** alto **3.** ampere **4.** or **Å** angstrom **5.** answer **6.** area

a. ►*abbr.* **1.** acre **2.** adjective **3.** *Lat.* anno (in the year) **4.** *Lat.* annus (year) **5.** anode

a–¹ or **an–** ►*pref.* Without; not: *amoral.* [Gk.]

a–² ►*pref.* **1.** On; in: *abed.* **2.** In the direction of: *astern.* **3.** In a specified state: *aflutter.* [< OE < *an,* on.]

AA ►*abbr.* **1.** Alcoholics Anonymous **2.** antiaircraft **3.** Associate in Arts

AAE ►*abbr.* African American English

AANWR ►*abbr.* Alaskan Arctic National Wildlife Refuge

aard·vark (ärd′värk′) ►*n.* A burrowing African mammal having large ears, a long tubular snout, and strong digging claws. [Obsolete Afr. : *aarde,* earth + *vark,* pig.]

Aaron, Henry Louis "Hank." b. 1934. Amer. baseball player.

Hank Aaron
photographed in 1975

AAVE ►*abbr.* African American Vernacular English

AB¹ (ā′bē′) ►*n.* A type of blood in the ABO system.

AB² ►*abbr.* **1.** airman basic **2.** Alberta **3.** *Lat.* Artium Baccalaureus (Bachelor of Arts)

ab– ►*pref.* Away from: *aboral.* [Lat.]

ABA ►*abbr.* **1.** American Bar Association **2.** American Basketball Association

a·back (ə-băk′) ►*adv.* By surprise: *I was taken aback by her retort.*

ab·a·cus (ăb′ə-kəs, ə-băk′əs) ►*n., pl.* **-cus·es** or **-ci** (ăb′ə-sī′, ə-băk′ī′) A manual computing device consisting of a frame holding parallel rods strung with movable counters. [< Gk. *abax,* counting board, perh. of Semitic orig.]

a·baft (ə-băft′) *Naut.* ►*prep.* Toward the stern

from. ►*adv.* Toward the stern. [A–² + < OE *bæftan,* behind.]

ab·a·lo·ne (ăb′ə-lō′nē) ►*n.* A large, edible marine gastropod having an ear-shaped shell. [Am.Sp. *abulón.*]

a·ban·don (ə-băn′dən) ►*v.* **1.** To forsake; desert. **2.** To give up completely: *abandoned the ship.* **3.** To quit: *abandoned the search.* ►*n.* A complete surrender to feeling or impulse. [< OFr. *abandoner* < *a bandon,* in one's power.] —**a·ban′don·ment** *n.*

a·ban·doned (ə-băn′dənd) ►*adj.* **1.** Deserted; forsaken. **2.** Recklessly unrestrained.

a·base (ə-bās′) ►*v.* **a·based, a·bas·ing** To humble or degrade. See Synonyms at **debase.** [< LLat. *bassus,* low.] —**a·base′ment** *n.*

a·bash (ə-băsh′) ►*v.* To make ashamed; disconcert. See Synonyms at **embarrass.** [< OFr. *esbahir,* be abashed.] —**a·bash′ment** *n.*

a·bate (ə-bāt′) ►*v.* **a·bat·ed, a·bat·ing 1.** To reduce in amount, degree, or intensity; lessen: *abated pollution.* **2.** *Law* **a.** To make void: *abated the lawsuit.* **b.** To reduce for some period of time: *abated taxes for three years.* [< OFr. *abattre,* beat down.] —**a·bate′ment** *n.*

ab·at·toir (ăb′ə-twär′) ►*n.* A slaughterhouse. [< OFr. *abattre,* beat down.]

Abb. ►*abbr.* **1.** abbess **2.** abbot

ab·ba·cy (ăb′ə-sē) ►*n., pl.* **-cies** The office, term, or jurisdiction of an abbot. [< LLat. *abbātia.*]

ab·bess (ăb′ĭs) ►*n.* The superior of a convent.

ab·bey (ăb′ē) ►*n., pl.* **-beys 1.** A monastery supervised by an abbot. **2.** A convent supervised by an abbess. **3.** A church that is or once was part of a monastery or convent. [< LLat. *abbātia.*]

ab·bot (ăb′ət) ►*n.* The superior of a monastery. [< Aram. *'abbā,* my father.]

abbr. or **abbrev.** ►*abbr.* abbreviation

ab·bre·vi·ate (ə-brē′vē-āt′) ►*v.* **-at·ed, -at·ing** To make shorter. See Synonyms at **shorten.** [< LLat. *abbreviāre.*] —**ab·bre′vi·a′tor** *n.*

ab·bre·vi·a·tion (ə-brē′vē-ā′shən) ►*n.* **1.** The act or product of shortening. **2.** A shortened form of a word or phrase.

ABC (ā′bē-sē′) ►*n.* often **ABCs 1.** The alphabet: *learned her ABCs.* **2.** The rudiments of reading and writing.

ab·di·cate (ăb′dĭ-kāt′) ►*v.* **-cat·ed, -cat·ing** To relinquish (power or responsibility) formally. [Lat. *abdicāre,* disclaim.] —**ab′di·ca′tion** *n.* —**ab′di·ca′tor** *n.*

ab·do·men (ăb′də-mən) ►*n.* **1.** The part of the body that lies between the thorax and the pelvis; belly. **2.** The posterior segment of the body in arthropods. [Lat. *abdōmen.*] —**ab·dom′i·nal** (ăb-dŏm′ə-nəl) *adj.*

ab·duct (ăb-dŭkt′) ►*v.* **1.** To carry off by force; kidnap. **2.** *Physiol.* To draw away from the body's midline or from an adjacent part. [Lat. *abdūcere,* lead away.] —**ab·duc′tion** *n.* —**ab·duc′tor** *n.*

a·beam (ə-bēm′) ►*adv.* At right angles to the keel of a ship.

a·bed (ə-bĕd′) ►*adv.* In bed.

A·bel (ā′bəl) In the Bible, the son of Adam and Eve; slain by Cain.

Ab·e·lard (ăb′ə-lärd′) also **A·bé·lard** (ä-bā-lär′), **Peter** 1079–1142. French theologian and philosopher; secretly married Héloise.

Ab·e·na·ki (ä′bə-nä′kē, ăb′ə-năk′ē) or **Ab·na·ki** (äb-nä′kē, ăb-) ►*n., pl.* **-ki** or **-kis 1.** A member of a group of Native American peoples of N New England and S Quebec. **2.** Either or both of the two Algonquian languages of the Abenaki.

ab·er·ra·tion (ăb′ə-rā′shən) ►*n.* **1.** A deviation from the normal, proper, or expected course. **2.** A defect of focus, such as blurring in an image. [< Lat. *aberrāre*, stray away.] —**ab′er·rant** (ăb′ər-ənt, ă-bĕr′-) *adj.*

a·bet (ə-bĕt′) ►*v.* **a·bet·ted, a·bet·ting** To encourage or assist, esp. in wrongdoing. [< OFr. *abeter*, entice : *a-*, to + *beter*, to bait.] —**a·bet′ment** *n.* —**a·bet′tor, a·bet′ter** *n.*

a·bey·ance (ə-bā′əns) ►*n.* The condition of being temporarily set aside; suspension. [< OFr. *abeance*, desire < *abaer*, gape at.]

ab·hor (ăb-hôr′) ►*v.* **-horred, -hor·ring** To regard with loathing; detest. [< Lat. *abhorrēre*, shrink from.] —**ab·hor′rer** *n.*

ab·hor·rence (ăb-hôr′əns, -hŏr′-) ►*n.* A feeling of repugnance or loathing. —**ab·hor′rent** *adj.* —**ab·hor′rent·ly** *adv.*

a·bide (ə-bīd′) ►*v.* **a·bode** (ə-bōd′) or **a·bid·ed, a·bid·ing 1.** To put up with; tolerate. **2.** To remain; endure. **3.** To dwell; reside. —*idiom:* **abide by** To comply with: *abide by the rules.* [< OE *ābīdan.*] —**a·bid′er** *n.*

a·bid·ing (ə-bī′dĭng) ►*adj.* Lasting; enduring.

Ab·i·djan (ăb′ĭ-jän′) The de facto capital of Côte d'Ivoire, in the S part.

a·bil·i·ty (ə-bĭl′ĭ-tē) ►*n., pl.* **-ties 1.** The quality of being able to do something: *I have the ability to run a mile.* **2.** A skill or talent. **3.** The quality of being suitable for or receptive to a specified treatment: *a plastic with the ability to be molded at low temperatures.* [< Lat. *habilis,* ABLE.]

ab·ject (ăb′jĕkt′) ►*adj.* **1.** Contemptible; despicable: *abject cowardice.* **2.** Miserable; wretched: *abject poverty.* [< Lat. *abicere, abiect-,* cast away.] —**ab′ject·ly** *adv.* —**ab·jec′tion** *n.*

ab·jure (ăb-jŏŏr′) ►*v.* **-jured, -jur·ing 1.** To renounce under oath. **2.** To recant solemnly; repudiate. [< Lat. *abiūrāre.*] —**ab′ju·ra′tion** *n.*

ab·la·tion (ă-blā′shən) ►*n.* **1.** Amputation of a body part. **2.** Reduction or dissipation, as by melting. [< Lat. *ablātus,* p.part. of *auferre,* carry off.]

ab·la·tive (ăb′lə-tĭv) ►*adj.* Of or being a grammatical case indicating separation, direction away from, and sometimes manner or agency. ►*n.* The ablative case. [< Lat. *ablātus,* carried off; see ABLATION.]

a·blaze (ə-blāz′) ►*adj.* **1.** Being on fire; blazing. **2.** Bright with color. **3.** Fervent or excited. —**a·blaze′** *adv.*

a·ble (ā′bəl) ►*adj.* **a·bler, a·blest 1.** Having sufficient ability or resources to do something: *a singer able to reach high notes.* **2.** Highly capable or talented. [< Lat. *habilis* < *habēre,* to handle.] —**a′bly** (ā′blē) *adv.*

–able or **–ible** ►*suff.* **1.** Susceptible, capable, or worthy of (an action): *debatable.* **2.** Inclined or given to: *changeable.* [< Lat. *-ābilis, -ibilis.*]

a·ble-bod·ied (ā′bəl-bŏd′ēd) ►*adj.* Physically strong and healthy.

a·ble·ism (ā′bə-lĭz′əm) ►*n.* Discrimination or prejudice against people with disabilities, esp. physical disabilities. —**a′ble·ist** *adj. & n.*

able seaman ►*n.* An experienced seaman certified to perform all routine duties at sea.

a·bloom (ə-blōōm′) ►*adj.* Being in bloom.

ab·lu·tion (ă-blōō′shən) ►*n.* A washing or cleansing of the body, esp. in a ritual manner. [< Lat. *abluere,* wash away.]

ABM ►*abbr.* antiballistic missile

Ab·na·ki (äb-nä′kē, ăb-) ►*n.* Var. of **Abenaki.**

ab·ne·ga·tion (ăb′nĭ-gā′shən) ►*n.* Self-denial; renunciation. [< Lat. *abnegāre,* refuse.]

ab·nor·mal (ăb-nôr′məl) ►*adj.* Not typical or normal; deviant. —**ab′nor·mal′i·ty** (ăb′nôr-măl′ĭ-tē) *n.* —**ab·nor′mal·ly** *adv.*

abnormal psychology ►*n.* The study of mental and emotional disorders or of mental phenomena such as altered levels of consciousness.

a·board (ə-bôrd′) ►*adv.* On board a ship, train, aircraft, or other passenger vehicle. ►*prep.* On board of; on; in.

a·bode (ə-bōd′) ►*v.* P.t. and p.part. of **abide.** ►*n.* A dwelling place; home. [ME *abod* < *abiden,* ABIDE.]

a·bol·ish (ə-bŏl′ĭsh) ►*v.* To do away with; annul: *abolished the tax.* [< Lat. *abolēre.*] —**a·bol′ish·er** *n.* —**a·bol′ish·ment** *n.*

ab·o·li·tion (ăb′ə-lĭsh′ən) ►*n.* **1.** The act of abolishing. **2.** Abolishment of slavery.

ab·o·li·tion·ism (ăb′ə-lĭsh′ə-nĭz′əm) ►*n.* Advocacy of the abolition of slavery. —**ab′o·li′tion·ist** *n.*

A-bomb (ā′bŏm′) ►*n.* See **atomic bomb.**

a·bom·i·na·ble (ə-bŏm′ə-nə-bəl) ►*adj.* **1.** Utterly detestable; loathsome. **2.** Thoroughly unpleasant or disagreeable: *abominable weather.* —**a·bom′i·na·bly** *adv.*

abominable snowman ►*n.* A hairy humanlike animal purported to inhabit the snows of the high Himalaya Mountains.

a·bom·i·nate (ə-bŏm′ə-nāt′) ►*v.* **-nat·ed, -nat·ing** To detest thoroughly; abhor. [Lat. *abōminārī,* deprecate as a bad omen.] —**a·bom′i·na′tion** *n.* —**a·bom′i·na′tor** *n.*

ab·o·rig·i·nal (ăb′ə-rĭj′ə-nəl) ►*adj.* **1.** Existing from the beginning. See Usage Note at **native. 2.** Of or relating to aborigines. **3.** often **Aboriginal** Relating to any of the indigenous peoples of Australia. ►*n.* An aborigine. —**ab′o·rig′i·nal·ly** *adv.*

ab·o·rig·i·ne (ăb′ə-rĭj′ə-nē) ►*n.* **1.** A member of the earliest known population of a region. See Usage Note at **native. 2.** often **Aborigine** A member of any of the indigenous peoples of Australia. [< Lat. *aborīginēs,* original inhabitants.]

a·born·ing (ə-bôr′nĭng) ►*adv.* While coming into being or getting under way.

a·bort (ə-bôrt′) ►*v.* **1a.** To terminate (a pregnancy) by abortion. **b.** To cause the expulsion of (an embryo or fetus) by abortion. **c.** To undergo the abortion of (an embryo or fetus). **d.** To miscarry. **2.** To terminate before completion: *abort a takeoff.* ►*n.* The act of terminating before completion. [< Lat. *aborīrī, abort-,* miscarry.] —**a·bor′tive** *adj.*

a·bor·ti·fa·cient (ə-bôr′tə-fā′shənt) ►*adj.* Causing abortion. ►*n.* A substance or device used to induce abortion.

a·bor·tion (ə-bôr′shən) ►*n.* **1.** Induced termination of a pregnancy with destruction of the

embryo or fetus. **2.** See **miscarriage** (sense 1).
3. The premature ending or abandonment of an
undertaking. —**a·bor′tion·ist** *n.*

ABO system (ā′bē′ō′) ►*n.* A system of classifying blood into four major types, A, B,
AB, and O, for determining compatibility in
transfusions.

a·bound (ə-bound′) ►*v.* **1.** To be great in number or amount. **2.** To have something in great
numbers or amounts. See Synonyms at **teem.**
[< Lat. *abundāre,* overflow : AB– + *unda,* wave.]

a·bout (ə-bout′) ►*adv.* **1.** Approximately: *The
movies lasts about two hours.* **2.** Almost: *The job
is about done.* **3.** To a reversed position: *turned
about.* **4.** All around. **5.** In the vicinity. ►*prep.* **1.**
On all sides of. **2.** In the vicinity of. **3.** Relating
to; concerning: *a book about snakes.* **4.** On the
point of: *about to go.* [< OE *onbūtan.*]

a·bout-face (ə-bout′fās′) ►*n.* A sudden change
to the opposite direction, attitude, or viewpoint. —**a·bout′-face′** *v.*

a·bove (ə-bŭv′) ►*adv.* **1.** On high; overhead:
the clouds above. **2.** In or to a higher place. **3.**
In an earlier part of a text. ►*prep.* **1.** Over or
higher than: *above the timberline.* **2.** Superior
to: *put principles above expediency.* **3.** Upstream
of. **4.** North of: *Minnesota is above Iowa.* ►*n.*
An earlier part of a given text. ►*adj.* Appearing
earlier in the same text. —*idiom:* **above all**
Exceeding all other factors in importance. [<
OE *abufan.*]

a·bove·board (ə-bŭv′bôrd′) ►*adv. & adj.* Without deceit or trickery. [Orig. a gambling term.]

a·bove·men·tioned (ə-bŭv′mĕn′shənd) ►*adj.*
Mentioned previously. ►*n.* The one or ones
mentioned previously.

ab·ra·ca·dab·ra (ăb′rə-kə-dăb′rə) ►*n.* **1.** A
magical charm believed to ward off disease or
disaster. **2.** Gibberish. [LLat.]

a·brade (ə-brād′) ►*v.* **a·brad·ed, a·brad·ing**
To wear away by friction; erode. [Lat. *abrādere,*
scrape off.] —**a·bra′sion** (ə-brā′zhən) *n.*

A·bra·ham (ā′brə-hăm′) In the Bible, the first
patriarch of the Hebrew people.

a·bra·sive (ə-brā′sĭv, -zĭv) ►*adj.* **1.** Causing
abrasion: *an abrasive cleanser.* **2.** Harsh or irritating in manner. ►*n.* A substance that abrades.
—**a·bra′sive·ly** *adv.* —**a·bra′sive·ness** *n.*

a·breast (ə-brĕst′) ►*adv.* **1.** Side by side. **2.** Up to
date: *abreast of developments.*

a·bridge (ə-brĭj′) ►*v.* **a·bridged, a·bridg·ing**
1. To reduce the length of (a text); condense.
See Synonyms at **shorten. 2.** To limit; curtail.
[< LLat. *abbreviāre,* abbreviate.] —**a·bridg′-
ment, a·bridge′ment** *n.*

a·broad (ə-brôd′) ►*adv. & adj.* **1.** In or to a
foreign country, esp. overseas. **2.** Away from
home. **3.** In wide circulation; at large.

ab·ro·gate (ăb′rə-gāt′) ►*v.* **-gat·ed, -gat·ing**
To abolish or annul, esp. by authority. [Lat.
abrogāre.] —**ab′ro·ga′tion** *n.*

a·brupt (ə-brŭpt′) ►*adj.* **1.** Unexpectedly
sudden. **2.** Curt; brusque: *an abrupt retort.*
3. Jerky; disconnected. **4.** Steeply inclined.
See Synonyms at **steep¹.** [< Lat. *abrumpere,
abrupt-,* break off.] —**a·brupt′ly** *adv.* —**a·
brupt′ness** *n.*

ABS ►*abbr.* antilock braking system

ab·scess (ăb′sĕs) ►*n.* A collection of pus surrounded by an inflamed area. ►*v.* To form an
abscess. [< Lat. *abscēdere, abscess-,* go away.]

ab·scis·sa (ăb-sĭs′ə) ►*n., pl.* **-scis·sas** or **-scis·
sae** (-sĭs′ē) *Symbol* **x** The coordinate representing the position of a point along a line
perpendicular to the *y*-axis in a plane Cartesian
coordinate system. [NLat. *(linea) abscissa,* cut-
off (line).]

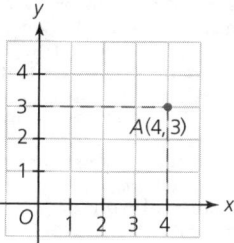

abscissa
The coordinates for *A* are (4,3);
the abscissa is 4 and the ordinate is 3.

ab·scis·sion (ăb-sĭzh′ən) ►*n.* **1.** The act of
cutting off. **2.** The shedding of leaves, flowers,
or fruits.

ab·scond (ăb-skŏnd′) ►*v.* To leave secretly and
hide, often to avoid the law. [Lat. *abscondere,*
hide away.] —**ab·scond′er** *n.*

ab·sence (ăb′səns) ►*n.* **1.** The state or a period
of being away. **2.** Lack; want: *an absence of
leadership.*

ab·sent (ăb′sənt) ►*adj.* **1.** Not present. **2.** Not
existent; lacking. **3.** Absent-minded; inattentive: *an absent nod.* ►*v.* (ăb-sĕnt′) To keep
(oneself) away. ►*prep.* Without. [< Lat. *absēns,*
pr.part. of *abesse,* be away.] —**ab′sent·ly** *adv.*

ab·sen·tee (ăb′sən-tē′) ►*n.* One that is absent.
►*adj.* Not in residence: *absentee landlords.* ►*adv.*
As an absentee voter.

absentee ballot ►*n.* A ballot marked and
mailed in advance by a voter away from the
place where he or she is registered.

ab·sen·tee·ism (ăb′sən-tē′ĭz′əm) ►*n.* Habitual
absence, esp. from work or duty.

ab·sent-mind·ed (ăb′sənt-mīn′dĭd) ►*adj.* Deep
in thought and heedless of present circumstances or activities; preoccupied. —**ab′sent-
mind′ed·ly** *adv.* —**ab′sent-mind′ed·ness** *n.*

ab·sinthe also **ab·sinth** (ăb′sĭnth) ►*n.* A strong,
bitter liqueur flavored with wormwood. [< Gk.
apsinthion, wormwood.]

ab·so·lute (ăb′sə-lōōt′) ►*adj.* **1a.** Unqualified
in extent or degree; total: *absolute silence.* **b.**
Not limited by restrictions or exceptions: *an
absolute right.* **c.** Being fully such; utter: *an absolute fool.* **2.** Not mixed; pure: *absolute oxygen.*
See Synonyms at **pure. 3.** Certain; positive:
absolute proof. **4.** *Phys.* **a.** Relating to measurements or units of measurement derived from
fundamental units of length, mass, and time.
b. Relating to a temperature scale whose zero
is absolute zero. ►*n.* Something that is absolute.
[< Lat. *absolvere, absolūt-,* loosen.] —**ab′so·
lute′ly** *adv.* —**ab′so·lute′ness** *n.*

absolute pitch ►*n.* **1.** The precise pitch of an
isolated tone as established by its rate of vibration. **2.** *Mus.* The ability to identify any pitch
heard or sing any pitch named.

absolute value ►*n.* The numerical value of a
real number without regard to its sign.

absolute zero ►*n.* The theoretical temperature at which substances possess no thermal energy, equal to 0 K, −273.15°C, or −459.67°F.

ab·so·lu·tion (ăb'sə-lōō'shən) ►*n.* **1.** The act of absolving. **2.** The formal remission of sin imparted by a priest, as in the sacrament of penance. [< Lat. *absolvere*, absolve.]

ab·so·lut·ism (ăb'sə-lōō'tĭz'əm) ►*n.* **1.** A form of government in which all power is vested in a single ruler or other authority. **2.** An absolute doctrine, principle, or standard. —**ab'so·lut'ist** *n.*

ab·solve (əb-zŏlv', -sŏlv') ►*v.* **-solved, -solv·ing 1.** To pronounce clear of guilt or blame. **2.** To relieve of a requirement or obligation. **3.** To grant absolution to. [< Lat. *absolvere.*] —**ab·solv'a·ble** *adj.* —**ab·solv'er** *n.*

ab·sorb (əb-zôrb', -sôrb') ►*v.* **1.** To take (something) in through or as through pores or interstices. **2.** To occupy completely; engross. See Synonyms at **engross. 3.** *Phys.* To retain (e.g., sound) wholly, without reflection or transmission. **4.** To assimilate into a larger whole. **5.** To take on: *absorb a cost.* **6.** To use up; consume: *absorbed all of our resources.* [< Lat. *absorbēre.*] —**ab·sorb'a·ble** *adj.* —**ab·sorb'er** *n.* —**ab·sorb'ing·ly** *adv.*

ab·sor·bent (əb-zôr'bənt, -sôr'-) ►*adj.* Capable of absorbing. —**ab·sor'ben·cy** *n.*

ab·sorp·tion (əb-zôrp'shən, -sôrp'-) ►*n.* **1.** The act or process of absorbing. **2.** A state of mental concentration. —**ab·sorp'tive** (-tĭv) *adj.* —**ab'sorp·tiv'i·ty** *n.*

ab·stain (ăb-stān') ►*v.* **1.** To keep oneself from doing, engaging in, or partaking of something. See Synonyms at **refrain**[1]. **2.** To refrain from voting. [< Lat. *abstinēre*, hold back.] —**ab·stain'er** *n.*

ab·ste·mi·ous (ăb-stē'mē-əs) ►*adj.* **1.** Eating and drinking in moderation. **2.** Marked by abstinence or moderation. [< Lat. *abstēmius.*] —**ab·ste'mi·ous·ly** *adv.*

ab·sten·tion (ăb-stĕn'shən) ►*n.* **1.** The act or habit of abstaining. **2.** An abstaining vote or voter. [< Lat. *abstinēre, abstent-*, hold back.]

ab·sti·nence (ăb'stə-nəns) ►*n.* The act or practice of refraining from indulging an appetite or desire, esp. for alcoholic drink or sexual intercourse. —**ab'sti·nent** *adj.*

ab·stract (ăb-străkt', ăb'străkt') ►*adj.* **1.** Considered apart from concrete existence: *an abstract concept.* **2.** Not applied or practical. **3.** Difficult to understand; abstruse. **4.** Denoting something that is immaterial, conceptual, or nonspecific, as an idea or quality. **5.** Having an artistic content that depends on intrinsic form rather than on narrative content or pictorial representation: *abstract painting.* ►*n.* (ăb'străkt') **1.** A summary or condensation. **2.** Something abstract. ►*v.* (ăb-străkt') **1.** To take away; remove. **2.** To remove without permission; steal. **3.** (ăb'străkt') To summarize. [< Lat. *abstrahere, abstract-*, draw away.] —**ab·stract'ly** *adv.* —**ab·stract'ness** *n.*

ab·stract·ed (ăb-străk'tĭd) ►*adj.* **1.** Removed; apart. **2.** Not engaged with what is going on around one; preoccupied. —**ab·stract'ed·ly** *adv.*

ab·strac·tion (ăb-străk'shən) ►*n.* **1a.** The act or the process of abstracting. **b.** An abstract idea or term. **2.** Preoccupation; absent-mindedness.

3. An abstract work of art.

ab·struse (ăb-strōōs') ►*adj.* Difficult to understand. [< Lat. *abstrūdere, abstrūs-*, hide away.] —**ab·struse'ly** *adv.* —**ab·struse'ness** *n.*

ab·surd (əb-sûrd', -zûrd') ►*adj.* **1.** Ridiculously incongruous or unreasonable. See Synonyms at **foolish. 2.** Relating to or manifesting the view that neither human life nor the universe has order or value. [Lat. *absurdus.*] —**ab·surd'i·ty, ab·surd'ness** *n.* —**ab·surd'ly** *adv.*

A·bu Dha·bi (ä'bōō dä'bē) A sheikdom and the capital of the United Arab Emirates, in E Arabia on the Persian Gulf.

A·bu·ja (ä-bōō'jä) The capital of Nigeria, in the center of the country.

a·bu·li·a (ə-bōō'lē-ə, -byōō'-) ►*n.* Loss or impairment of the ability to make decisions. [< A−[1] + Gk. *boulē*, will.] —**a·bu'lic** *adj.*

a·bun·dant (ə-bŭn'dənt) ►*adj.* **1.** Existing in large amounts: *abundant crops.* See Synonyms at **plentiful. 2.** Abounding: *a river abundant in fish.* [< Lat. *abundāre*, ABOUND.] —**a·bun'dance** *n.* —**a·bun'dant·ly** *adv.*

a·buse (ə-byōōz') ►*v.* **a·bused, a·bus·ing 1.** To use wrongly or improperly. **2.** To hurt or injure by maltreatment. **3.** To rape or molest. **4.** To insult; revile. ►*n.* (ə-byōōs') **1a.** Misuse: *drug abuse.* **b.** Rough treatment or use. **2.** Physical maltreatment. **3.** Insulting or coarse language. [< Lat. *abūtī, abūs-*.] —**a·bus'er** *n.* —**a·bu'sive** *adj.* —**a·bu'sive·ly** *adv.*

a·but (ə-bŭt') ►*v.* **a·but·ted, a·but·ting 1.** To have a common boundary; lie adjacent. **2.** To border upon. [< OFr. *abouter.*] —**a·but'ter** *n.*

a·but·ment (ə-bŭt'mənt) ►*n.* **1.** The act of abutting. **2.** Something that abuts. **3.** A supporting structure, as at the end of a bridge.

a·bys·mal (ə-bĭz'məl) ►*adj.* **1.** Very profound; limitless. **2.** Very bad: *an abysmal performance.* —**a·bys'mal·ly** *adv.*

a·byss (ə-bĭs') ►*n.* **1.** An immeasurably deep chasm, depth, or void. **2a.** In the book of Genesis, the chaos out of which earth and sky were formed. **b.** Hell. [< Gk. *abussos*, bottomless.]

Ab·ys·sin·i·a (ăb'ĭ-sĭn'ē-ə) See **Ethiopia.** —**Ab'ys·sin'i·an** *adj. & n.*

AC ►*abbr.* **1.** or **a/c** air conditioning **2.** alternating current **3.** area code

a/c ►*abbr.* account current

a·ca·cia (ə-kā'shə) ►*n.* **1.** Any of various often spiny trees or shrubs having feathery leaves and heads or spikes of small flowers. **2.** See **gum arabic.** [< Gk. *akakia.*]

ac·a·deme (ăk'ə-dēm') ►*n.* Academia.

ac·a·de·mi·a (ăk'ə-dē'mē-ə) ►*n.* The academic life or environment.

ac·a·dem·ic (ăk'ə-dĕm'ĭk) ►*adj.* **1.** Of or relating to a school or college. **2a.** Relating to studies that rely on reading and involve abstract thought rather than being primarily practical or technical. **b.** Relating to scholarly performance: *a student's academic average.* **3.** Having little practical use or value, as by being overly detailed, unengaging, or theoretical. **4.** Having no important consequence or relevancy. ►*n.* A member of a college or university faculty. —**ac'a·dem'i·cal·ly** *adv.*

ac·a·de·mi·cian (ăk'ə-də-mĭsh'ən, ə-kăd'ə-) ►*n.* **1.** An academic. **2.** A member of an academy or learned society.

ac·a·dem·i·cism (ăk'ə-dĕm'ĭ-sĭz'əm) also **a·**

cad·e·mism (ə-kăd′ə-mĭz′əm) ►*n.* Traditional formalism, esp. when reflected in art.

ac·a·dem·ics (ăk′ə-dĕm′ĭks) ►*n. (takes pl. v.)* College or university studies.

a·cad·e·my (ə-kăd′ə-mē) ►*n., pl.* -mies 1. A school for special instruction. 2. A secondary or college-preparatory school, esp. a private one. 3a. Academia. b. A society of scholars, scientists, or artists. [< Gk. *Akadēmia,* school where Plato taught.]

A·ca·di·a (ə-kā′dē-ə) A region and former French colony of E Canada and E ME. —**A·ca′di·an** *adj. & n.*

a·can·thus (ə-kăn′thəs) ►*n., pl.* -thus·es or -thi (-thī′) 1. Any of various Mediterranean shrubs with large, segmented, thistlelike leaves. 2. *Archit.* A design patterned after acanthus leaves. [< Gk. *akantha,* thorn.]

a cap·pel·la (ä′ kə-pĕl′ə) ►*adv. Mus.* Without instrumental accompaniment. [Ital., chapel style.]

ac·cede (ăk-sēd′) ►*v.* -ced·ed, -ced·ing 1. To give one's consent; agree. 2. To come into an office or dignity: *accede to the throne.* [< Lat. *accēdere,* go near.] —**ac·ced′ence** *n.*

ac·cel·er·an·do (ä-chĕl′ə-rän′dō) ►*adv. & adj. Mus.* Gradually accelerating in tempo. [Ital.]

ac·cel·er·ant (ăk-sĕl′ər-ənt) ►*n.* A substance used as a catalyst, as in spreading an intentionally set fire.

ac·cel·er·ate (ăk-sĕl′ə-rāt′) ►*v.* -at·ed, -at·ing 1. To make or become faster. 2. To cause to occur sooner than expected. 3. To cause to develop or progress more quickly. [Lat. *accelerāre.*] —**ac·cel′er·a′tion** *n.* —**ac·cel′er·a′tive** *adj.*

ac·cel·er·a·tor (ăk-sĕl′ə-rā′tər) ►*n.* 1. A device, esp. the gas pedal of a motor vehicle, for increasing speed. 2. *Chem.* A substance that increases the speed of a reaction. 3. *Phys.* A particle accelerator.

ac·cel·er·om·e·ter (ăk-sĕl′ə-rŏm′ĭ-tər) ►*n.* An instrument used to measure acceleration.

ac·cent (ăk′sĕnt′) ►*n.* 1. Vocal emphasis given to a particular syllable, word, or phrase. 2. A characteristic manner of speech or pronunciation: *a British accent.* 3. A mark placed over a letter to indicate vocal stress or phonetic quality: *an acute accent.* 4. Rhythmical stress in a line of verse. 5. A distinctive quality, as of decorative style. 6. Particular importance or interest. See Synonyms at **emphasis.** ►*v.* To stress or emphasize. [< Lat. *accentus,* accentuation.]

ac·cen·tu·ate (ăk-sĕn′chōō-āt′) ►*v.* -at·ed, -at·ing To stress; accent.

ac·cept ►*v.* 1. To receive willingly: *accepted a glass of water.* 2. To admit to a group or place. 3. To regard as proper or true: *accept a new theory.* 4. To answer affirmatively: *accept an invitation.* 5. To consent to pay, as by a signed agreement. 6. To take payment in the form of: *does not accept checks.* 7. *Med.* To receive without immunological rejection. [< Lat. *accipere,* take on, receive.]

ac·cept·a·ble (ăk-sĕp′tə-bəl) ►*adj.* 1. Adequate; satisfactory: *an acceptable excuse.* See Synonyms at **sufficient.** 2. Satisfactory but not superior; passable. —**ac·cept′a·bil′i·ty** *n.* —**ac·cept′a·bly** *adv.*

ac·cep·tance (ăk-sĕp′təns) ►*n.* 1. The act or process of accepting. 2. The state of being accepted or acceptable. 3. A formal agreement to pay a draft or bill of exchange.

ac·cept·ed (ăk-sĕp′tĭd) ►*adj.* Widely encountered, used, or recognized.

ac·cep·tor (ăk-sĕp′tər) ►*n. Chem.* An atom that incorporates electrons to form a bond with another atom.

ac·cess (ăk′sĕs) ►*n.* 1. A means of approaching, entering, exiting, communicating with, or making use of. 2. The ability or right to approach, enter, exit, communicate with, or make use of: *has access to classified material.* 3. An outburst: *an access of rage.* ►*v.* To obtain access to, esp. by computer. [< Lat. *accēdere, access-,* come toward.]

ac·ces·si·ble (ăk-sĕs′ə-bəl) ►*adj.* Easily approached, entered, or obtained. —**ac·ces′si·bil′i·ty** *n.* —**ac·ces′si·bly** *adv.*

ac·ces·sion (ăk-sĕsh′ən) ►*n.* 1. The attainment of a dignity or rank. 2a. Something acquired or added. b. An increase by means of something added. —**ac·ces′sion·al** *adj.*

ac·ces·so·ry (ăk-sĕs′ə-rē) ►*n., pl.* -ries 1a. A supplementary item; adjunct. b. Something nonessential but desirable. 2. *Law* One who knowingly assists a lawbreaker in the commission of a crime but does not actually participate in that crime. ►*adj.* Supplementary; adjunct.

ac·ci·dent (ăk′sĭ-dənt) ►*n.* 1a. An unexpected, undesirable event. b. An unforeseen incident. 2. Chance; fortuity: *discovered the secret by accident.* 3. *Philos.* An attribute that is not essential to the nature of something. [< Lat. *accidere,* happen.]

ac·ci·den·tal (ăk′sĭ-dĕn′tl) ►*adj.* Occurring unexpectedly, unintentionally, or by chance. ►*n. Mus.* A sharp, flat, or natural not indicated in the key signature. —**ac′ci·den′tal·ly** *adv.*

ac·cip·i·ter (ăk-sĭp′ĭ-tər) ►*n.* Any of several hawks with short wings and a long tail. [Lat.]

ac·claim (ə-klām′) ►*v.* To praise openly and enthusiastically; applaud. ►*n.* Enthusiastic applause; acclamation. [< Lat. *acclāmāre,* shout at.] —**ac·claim′er** *n.*

ac·cla·ma·tion (ăk′lə-mā′shən) ►*n.* 1. A show of enthusiastic approval. 2. An oral vote, esp. a vote of approval taken without formal ballot. —**ac·clam′a·to′ry** (ə-klăm′ə-tôr′ē) *adj.*

ac·cli·mate (ăk′lə-māt′, ə-klī′mĭt) ►*v.* -mat·ed, -mat·ing To make or become accustomed to a new environment or situation; adapt. See Synonyms at **harden.** [Fr. *acclimater.*] —**ac′cli·ma′tion** *n.*

ac·cli·ma·tize (ə-klī′mə-tīz′) ►*v.* -tized, -tiz·ing To acclimate. See Synonyms at **harden.** —**ac·cli′ma·ti·za′tion** *n.*

ac·cliv·i·ty (ə-klĭv′ĭ-tē) ►*n., pl.* -ties An upward slope. [< Lat. *acclīvis,* uphill : *ad-,* ad- + *clīvus,* slope.]

ac·co·lade (ăk′ə-lād′, -läd′) ►*n.* 1. High praise. 2. A special acknowledgment or award. [< OFr. *acoler,* to embrace.]

ac·com·mo·date (ə-kŏm′ə-dāt′) ►*v.* -dat·ed, -dat·ing 1a. To have enough space for: *constructed a parking lot that accommodates over 2,000 cars.* b. To provide lodging for: *a hotel that accommodated the wedding guests.* 2. To take into consideration; allow for. 3a. To do a favor for. See Synonyms at **oblige.** b. To provide or allow for: *accommodate the needs of both groups.* 4. To make suitable; adjust. See Synonyms at

adapt. [Lat. *accommodāre*, make fit.]

ac·com·mo·dat·ing (ə-kŏm′ə-dā′tĭng) ►*adj.* Helpful and obliging.

ac·com·mo·da·tion (ə-kŏm′ə-dā′shən) ►*n.* **1.** The act of accommodating or the state of being accommodated. **2.** Something that meets a need. **3. accommodations** Room and board.

ac·com·pa·ni·ment (ə-kŭm′pə-nē-mənt, ə-kŭmp′nē-) ►*n.* **1.** *Mus.* A part that supports another, often solo, part. **2.** Something that accompanies or complements.

ac·com·pa·nist (ə-kŭm′pə-nĭst, ə-kŭmp′nĭst) ►*n. Mus.* One who plays or sings an accompaniment.

ac·com·pa·ny (ə-kŭm′pə-nē, ə-kŭmp′nē) ►*v.* **-nied, -ny·ing** **1.** To go with as a companion. **2.** To add to; supplement. **3.** To occur with: *dark clouds that were accompanied by rain.* **4.** *Mus.* To perform an accompaniment to. [< OFr. *acompagnier*.]

ac·com·plice (ə-kŏm′plĭs) ►*n.* One who participates in the commission of a crime without being the principal actor. [< Lat. *complex*, closely connected.]

ac·com·plish (ə-kŏm′plĭsh) ►*v.* **1.** To succeed in doing; achieve. **2.** To finish; complete. [< OFr. *acomplir* < Lat. *complēre*, COMPLETE.] —**ac·com′plish·er** *n.*

ac·com·plished (ə-kŏm′plĭsht) ►*adj.* **1.** Skilled; expert: *an accomplished pianist.* **2.** Definite: *an accomplished fact.*

ac·com·plish·ment (ə-kŏm′plĭsh-mənt) ►*n.* **1.** The act of accomplishing or state of being accomplished. **2.** Something completed successfully; achievement. **3.** An acquired skill. **4.** Social poise and grace.

ac·cord (ə-kôrd′) ►*v.* **1.** To grant or bestow. **2.** To be in agreement or harmony. ►*n.* **1.** Agreement; harmony. **2.** A settlement or understanding, esp. between nations. **3.** Free or spontaneous choice: *signed up on my own accord.* [< Lat. *cor, cord-,* heart.]

ac·cor·dance (ə-kôr′dns) ►*n.* Agreement: *in accordance with your instructions.*

ac·cord·ing·ly (ə-kôr′dĭng-lē) ►*adv.* **1.** In accordance; correspondingly. **2.** So; consequently.

ac·cord·ing to (ə-kôr′dĭng) ►*prep.* **1.** As stated or indicated by: *according to law.* **2.** In keeping with: *according to custom.* **3.** As determined by: *a list arranged according to the alphabet.*

ac·cor·di·on (ə-kôr′dē-ən) ►*n.* A portable musical instrument with a small keyboard and free metal reeds that sound when air is forced past them by pleated bellows. [Ger. *Akkordion* < OFr. *acorder,* ACCORD.] —**ac·cor′di·on·ist** *n.*

ac·cost (ə-kôst′, -kŏst′) ►*v.* To approach and speak to aggressively or insistently, as with a demand. [< Med.Lat. *accostāre,* adjoin.]

ac·count (ə-kount′) ►*n.* **1a.** A narrative or record of events. **b.** A reason given for an action or event. **c.** A basis or ground: *no reason to worry on that account.* **2a.** A business arrangement, as with a bank or store, in which money is kept, exchanged, or owed. **b.** A detailed record, esp. of financial transactions. **3.** A private access to a computer system or online service, usu. requiring a password. **4.** Worth or importance. **5.** Profit; advantage: *turned her skills to good account.* ►*v.* To consider as being; regard. —*phrasal verb:* **account for** To provide or constitute a reason for; explain.

—*idioms:* **on account of** Because of. **take into account** To take into consideration. [< OFr. *aconter,* reckon < Lat. *computāre,* COUNT[1].]

ac·count·a·ble (ə-koun′tə-bəl) ►*adj.* Responsible; answerable. —**ac·count′a·bil′i·ty, ac·count′a·ble·ness** *n.* —**ac·count′a·bly** *adv.*

ac·coun·tant (ə-koun′tənt) ►*n.* One trained in accounting. —**ac·coun′tan·cy** *n.*

ac·count·ing (ə-koun′tĭng) ►*n.* The bookkeeping methods used to record business transactions and prepare financial statements.

ac·cou·tre or **ac·cou·ter** (ə-kōō′tər) ►*v.* **-tred, -tre·ing** or **-tered, -ter·ing** To outfit and equip, as for military duty. [< OFr. *acoustrer.*] —**ac·cou′tre·ments** *n.* (ə-kōō′trə-mənts)

Ac·cra (ăk′rə, ə-krä′) The capital of Ghana, in the SE part on the Gulf of Guinea.

ac·cred·it (ə-krĕd′ĭt) ►*v.* **1.** To attribute to; credit. **2.** To supply with credentials. See Synonyms at **authorize. 3.** To certify as meeting a prescribed standard. [Fr. *accréditer.*] —**ac·cred′i·ta′tion** *n.*

ac·cre·tion (ə-krē′shən) ►*n.* **1.** Growth or increase in size by gradual external addition, fusion, or inclusion. **2.** Something contributing to such growth or increase. [< Lat. *accrēscere, accrēt-,* grow.] —**ac·cre′tion·ar′y, ac·cre′tive** *adj.*

ac·crue (ə-krōō′) ►*v.* **-crued, -cru·ing** **1.** To come to one as a gain: *benefits that accrue from scientific research.* **2.** To increase or accumulate over time: *interest accruing in a bank account.* [< Lat. *accrēscere,* grow.] —**ac·cru′al** *n.*

ac·cul·tur·a·tion (ə-kŭl′chə-rā′shən) ►*n.* The modification of the culture of a group or individual by contact with a different culture. —**ac·cul′tur·ate′** *v.*

ac·cu·mu·late (ə-kyōōm′yə-lāt′) ►*v.* **-lat·ed, -lat·ing** To gather or pile up; amass. [Lat. *accumulāre* < *cumulus,* heap.] —**ac·cu′mu·la′tion** *n.* —**ac·cu′mu·la′tor** *n.*

ac·cu·ra·cy (ăk′yər-ə-sē) ►*n.* **1.** Conformity to fact. **2.** Precision; exactness.

ac·cu·rate (ăk′yər-ĭt) ►*adj.* **1.** Conforming exactly to fact; errorless. **2.** Capable of providing a correct reading or measurement: *an accurate scale.* **3.** Performing with precision; meticulous: *an accurate proofreader.* [< Lat. *accūrāre,* attend to carefully.] —**ac′cu·rate·ly** *adv.* —**ac′cu·rate·ness** *n.*

ac·curs·ed (ə-kûr′sĭd, ə-kûrst′) also **ac·curst** (ə-kûrst′) ►*adj.* **1.** Abominable; hateful: *this accursed mud.* **2.** Being under a curse; doomed. —**ac·curs′ed·ly** *adv.*

ac·cu·sa·tive (ə-kyōō′zə-tĭv) ►*adj.* Of, relating to, or being the grammatical case that is the direct object of a verb or the object of certain prepositions. ►*n.* The accusative case.

ac·cuse (ə-kyōōz′) ►*v.* **-cused, -cus·ing** **1.** To charge with an error or offense. **2.** To bring charges against. [< Lat. *accūsāre.*] —**ac′cu·sa′tion** (ăk′yōō-zā′shən) *n.* —**ac·cus′er** *n.* —**ac·cus′ing·ly** *adv.*

ac·cused (ə-kyōōzd′) ►*n., pl.* **accused** The defendant in a criminal case.

ac·cus·tom (ə-kŭs′təm) ►*v.* **-tomed, -tom·ing** To familiarize, as by habit or frequent use: *accustom oneself to working late.* [< OFr. *acostumer.*]

ac·cus·tomed (ə-kŭs′təmd) ►*adj.* **1.** Being in the habit of: *I am accustomed to sleeping late.*

2. Usual; customary. See Synonyms at **usual.**

ace (ās) ►*n.* **1.** A playing card, die, or domino having one spot or pip. **2.** In racket games, a serve that one's opponent fails to return. **3.** A fighter pilot who has destroyed five or more enemy aircraft. **4.** An expert in a given field. ►*adj.* Top-notch; first-rate. ►*v.* **aced, ac·ing 1.** To serve an ace against. **2.** To perform with distinction on: *aced the exam; aced the interview.* **3.** *Slang* To triumph over; defeat. —*idioms:* **ace in the hole** A hidden advantage. **within an ace of** Very near to. [< Lat. *as,* unit.]

a·cer·bic (ə-sûr′bĭk) also **a·cerb** (ə-sûrb′) ►*adj.* **1.** Sour or bitter tasting; acid. See Synonyms at **bitter, sour. 2.** Sharp or biting, as in character or expression. [< Lat. *acerbus.*] —**a·cer′bi·cal·ly** *adv.*

a·cer·bi·ty (ə-sûr′bĭ-tē) ►*n.,* pl. **-ties** Bitterness, acidness.

a·cet·a·min·o·phen (ə-sē′tə-mĭn′ə-fən) ►*n.* A crystalline compound, $C_8H_9NO_2$, used in medicine to relieve pain and fever.

ac·e·tate (ăs′ĭ-tāt′) ►*n.* **1.** A salt or ester of acetic acid. **2.** Cellulose acetate or a product, esp. fibers, derived from it.

a·ce·tic (ə-sē′tĭk) ►*adj.* Relating to or containing acetic acid or vinegar. [< Lat. *acētum,* vinegar.]

acetic acid ►*n.* A clear, colorless organic acid, $C_2H_4O_2$, with a distinctive pungent odor, that is the chief acid of vinegar.

ac·e·tone (ăs′ĭ-tōn′) ►*n.* A colorless, volatile, highly flammable liquid, C_3H_6O, used as an organic solvent.

a·ce·tyl·cho·line (ə-sēt′l-kō′lēn′) ►*n.* A white crystalline compound, $C_7H_{17}NO_3$, that mediates transmission of nerve impulses across synapses.

a·cet·y·lene (ə-sēt′l-ēn′, -ən) ►*n.* A colorless, highly flammable or explosive gas, C_2H_2, used for metal welding and cutting.

a·ce·tyl·sal·i·cyl·ic acid (ə-sēt′l-săl′ĭ-sĭl′ĭk) ►*n.* See **aspirin** (sense 1).

ache (āk) ►*v.* **ached, ach·ing 1.** To suffer a dull, sustained pain. **2.** To yearn painfully. ►*n.* **1.** A dull, steady pain. See Synonyms at **pain. 2.** A longing or yearning. [< OE *acan.*] —**ach′y** *adj.*

a·chene (ā-kēn′) ►*n.* A small, dry, one-seeded fruit with a thin wall. [NLat. *achenium* : A⁻¹ + Gk. *khainein,* yawn.]

a·chieve (ə-chēv′) ►*v.* **a·chieved, a·chiev·ing 1.** To perform successfully; accomplish: *achieve a task.* **2.** To attain with effort: *achieve fame.* [< OFr. *achever* < *(venir) a chief,* (come) to a head.] —**a·chiev′a·ble** *adj.* —**a·chiev′er** *n.*

a·chieve·ment (ə-chēv′mənt) ►*n.* **1.** The act of achieving. **2.** Something accomplished successfully. See Synonyms at **feat.**

A·chil·les (ə-kĭl′ēz) ►*n.* Gk. Myth. The hero of Homer's *Iliad,* who slew Hector.

Achilles' heel ►*n.* A seemingly small but crucial weakness. [From Achilles's being vulnerable only in one heel.]

Achilles tendon ►*n.* The large tendon connecting the heel bone to the calf muscle.

ach·ro·mat·ic (ăk′rə-măt′ĭk) ►*adj.* **1.** Designating a color, such as black or white, that has no hue. **2.** Refracting light without spectral color separation. **3.** *Mus.* Having only the diatonic tones of the scale. —**ach′ro·mat′i·cal·ly** *adv.* —**a·chro′ma·tism** (ā-krō′mə-tĭz′əm) *n.*

ac·id (ăs′ĭd) ►*n.* **1.** *Chem.* Any of a large class of

sour-tasting substances whose aqueous solutions turn blue litmus red and react with bases, alkalis, or certain metals to form salts. **2.** A sour-tasting substance. **3.** *Slang* See **LSD.** ►*adj.* **1.** *Chem.* **a.** Of an acid. **b.** Having a high concentration of acid. **c.** Having a pH of less than 7. **2.** Having a sour taste. See Synonyms at **sour. 3.** Biting; sarcastic: *an acid wit.* [< Lat. *acidus,* sour < *acēre,* be sharp.] —**a·cid′ic** (ə-sĭd′ĭk) *adj.* —**a·cid′i·ty** *n.* —**ac′id·ly** *adv.*

a·cid·i·fy (ə-sĭd′ə-fī′) ►*v.* **-fied, -fy·ing** To make or become acid. —**a·cid′i·fi·ca′tion** *n.* —**a·cid′i·fi′er** *n.*

ac·i·do·sis (ăs′ĭ-dō′sĭs) ►*n.* An abnormal increase in the acidity of the body's fluids. —**ac′i·dot′ic** (-dŏt′ĭk) *adj.*

acid rain ►*n.* Acid precipitation falling as rain.

acid reflux ►*n.* See **heartburn.**

acid rock ►*n.* Rock music having a heavy repetitive beat and lyrics that suggest psychedelic experiences.

acid test ►*n.* A decisive or critical test.

a·cid·u·late (ə-sĭj′ə-lāt′) ►*v.* **-lat·ed, -lat·ing** To make or become slightly acid.

a·cid·u·lous (ə-sĭj′ə-ləs) ►*adj.* Slightly sour in taste or in manner. [< Lat. *acidulus* < *acidus,* ACID.]

ac·knowl·edge (ăk-nŏl′ĭj) ►*v.* **-edged, -edg·ing 1.** To admit the existence or truth of. **2a.** To express recognition of: *acknowledge a friend's smile.* **b.** To express thanks or gratitude for. **3.** To report the receipt of. **4.** *Law* To accept or certify as legally binding. [Prob. blend of ME *knowlechen,* acknowledge, and *aknouen,* recognize.] —**ac·knowl′edge·a·ble** *adj.* —**ac·knowl′edg·ment, ac·knowl′edge·ment** *n.*

ACLU ►*abbr.* American Civil Liberties Union

ac·me (ăk′mē) ►*n.* The highest point, as of perfection. [Gk. *akmē.*]

ac·ne (ăk′nē) ►*n.* An inflammatory disease of the oil glands and hair follicles of the skin, marked by pimples, esp. on the face. [Poss. < Gk. *akmē,* point; see ACME.] —**ac′ned** *adj.*

ac·o·lyte (ăk′ə-līt′) ►*n.* **1.** One who assists the celebrant in the performance of liturgical rites. **2.** A devoted follower. [< Gk. *akolouthos,* attendant.]

A·con·ca·gua (ăk′ən-kä′gwə, ä′kən-) A mountain, about 6,962 m (22,841 ft), in the Andes of W Argentina; highest peak of the Western Hemisphere.

ac·o·nite (ăk′ə-nīt′) ►*n.* **1.** Any of various usu. poisonous plants with hooded flowers. **2.** The dried leaves and roots of some these plants, formerly used medicinally. [< Gk. *akoniton.*]

a·corn (ā′kôrn′, -kərn) ►*n.* The fruit of an oak, consisting of a nut set in a woody, cuplike base. [< OE *æcern.*]

acorn squash ►*n.* A type of squash shaped somewhat like an acorn with a ridged rind and yellow to orange flesh.

a·cous·tic (ə-kōō′stĭk) also **a·cous·ti·cal** (-stĭ-kəl) ►*adj.* **1.** Of or relating to sound, the sense of hearing, or the science of sound. **2a.** Designed to aid in hearing. **b.** Designed to absorb sound: *acoustic tile.* **3.** *Mus.* Not electronically produced or modified: *an acoustic guitar.* [Gk. *akoustikos* < *akouein,* hear.] —**a·cous′ti·cal·ly** *adv.*

a·cous·tics (ə-kōō′stĭks) ►*n.* **1.** *(takes sing. v.)* The scientific study of sound. **2.** *(takes pl. v.)*

The total effect of sound, esp. as produced in an enclosed space.

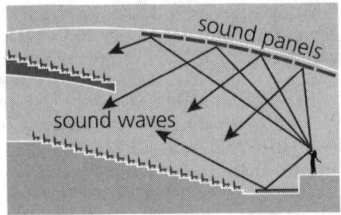

acoustics
Sound waves from a stage are deflected by sound panels and distributed throughout an auditorium.

ac·quaint (ə-kwānt′) ▸*v.* To make familiar: *acquainted myself with the controls.* [< Med.Lat. *adcognitāre*, make known to.]

ac·quain·tance (ə-kwān′təns) ▸*n.* **1.** Knowledge of a person less intimate than friendship. **2.** A person whom one knows. **3.** Personal knowledge or information. —**ac·quain′tance·ship′** *n.*

ac·qui·esce (ăk′wē-ĕs′) ▸*v.* **-esced, -esc·ing** To consent or comply without protest. [Lat. *acquiēscere*.] —**ac′qui·es′cence** *n.* —**ac′qui·es′cent** *adj.* —**ac′qui·es′cent·ly** *adv.*

   Usage: *Acquiesce* usu. takes the preposition *in* (*acquiesced in the ruling*) but sometimes takes *to* (*acquiesced to her parents' wishes*).

ac·quire (ə-kwīr′) ▸*v.* **-quired, -quir·ing 1.** To gain possession of. **2.** To get by one's own efforts: *acquire proficiency in math.* **3.** To gain through experience; come by. [< Lat. *acquīrere, acquīsit-*, add to.] —**ac·quir′a·ble** *adj.* —**ac·quire′ment** *n.*

ac·quired (ə-kwīrd′) ▸*adj.* **1.** Developing after birth; not congenital. **2.** Caused by exposure to something. **3.** Gained by one's own efforts.

acquired immune deficiency syndrome ▸*n.* See **AIDS**.

ac·qui·si·tion (ăk′wĭ-zĭsh′ən) ▸*n.* **1.** The act of acquiring. **2.** Something acquired.

ac·quis·i·tive (ə-kwĭz′ĭ-tĭv) ▸*adj.* Eager to gain and possess; grasping. —**ac·quis′i·tive·ly** *adv.*

ac·quit (ə-kwĭt′) ▸*v.* **-quit·ted, -quit·ting 1.** *Law* To find not guilty of a criminal offense. **2.** To conduct (oneself) in a specified manner. [< OFr. *aquiter*.] —**ac·quit′tal** *n.*

a·cre (ā′kər) ▸*n.* See table at **measurement**. [< OE *æcer*, field.]

a·cre·age (ā′kər-ĭj) ▸*n.* Land area in acres.

ac·rid (ăk′rĭd) ▸*adj.* **1.** Unpleasantly sharp or bitter to the taste or smell. See Synonyms at **bitter. 2.** Caustic in language or tone. [< Lat. *ācer*, bitter.] —**a·crid′i·ty** (ə-krĭd′ĭ-tē), **ac′rid·ness** *n.* —**ac′rid·ly** *adv.*

ac·ri·mo·ny (ăk′rə-mō′nē) ▸*n.* Bitter, ill-natured animosity, esp. in speech or behavior. [< Lat. *ācer*, sharp.] —**ac′ri·mo′ni·ous** *adj.* —**ac′ri·mo′ni·ous·ly** *adv.*

acro– or **acr–** ▸*pref.* **1.** Height; summit: *acrophobia.* **2.** Beginning: *acronym.* [< Gk. *akros*, extreme.]

ac·ro·bat (ăk′rə-băt′) ▸*n.* One skilled in feats of agility in gymnastics. [< Gk. *akrobatē* : ACRO– + *bainein*, bat-, walk.] —**ac′ro·bat′ic** *adj.* —**ac′ro·bat′i·cal·ly** *adv.*

ac·ro·bat·ics (ăk′rə-băt′ĭks) ▸*n.* **1.** (*takes sing. v.*) The gymnastic moves of an acrobat. **2.** (*takes pl. v.*) A display of spectacular agility.

ac·ro·nym (ăk′rə-nĭm′) ▸*n.* A word formed from the initial letters of a name, esp. when pronounced as a single word, such as *AIDS* for acquired *i*mmune *d*eficiency *s*yndrome.

ac·ro·pho·bi·a (ăk′rə-fō′bē-ə) ▸*n.* An abnormal fear of high places.

a·crop·o·lis (ə-krŏp′ə-lĭs) ▸*n.* The fortified height or citadel of an ancient Greek city. [Gk. *akropolis* : ACRO– + *polis*, city.]

a·cross (ə-krôs′, -krŏs′) ▸*prep.* **1.** On, at, to, or from the other side of. **2.** Into contact with: *came across an old friend.* ▸*adv.* **1.** From one side to the other: *The footbridge swayed when I ran across.* **2.** Crosswise; crossed. **3.** In such a way as to be comprehensible or successful: *got my point across.* [< AN *an croiz*, crosswise.]

a·cross-the-board (ə-krôs′thə-bôrd′, -krŏs′-) ▸*adj.* Including all categories or members.

a·cros·tic (ə-krô′stĭk, -krŏs′tĭk) ▸*n.* A poem or series of lines in which certain letters, usu. the first in each line, form a name, motto, or message when read in sequence. [< Gk. *akrostikhis* : ACRO– + *stikhos*, line.] —**a·cros′tic** *adj.*

a·cryl·ic (ə-krĭl′ĭk) ▸*n.* **1.** An acrylic resin. **2.** A paint containing acrylic resin. **3.** Any of numerous synthetic fibers used in sweaters, knits, and carpets. [*acrolein*, an aldehyde + –YL + –IC.] —**a·cryl′ic** *adj.*

acrylic fiber ▸*n.* Any of numerous synthetic fibers used in sweaters, knits, and carpets.

acrylic resin ▸*n.* Any of numerous thermoplastics used to produce paints, synthetic rubbers, and lightweight plastics.

act (ăkt) ▸*n.* **1.** The process of doing something. **2a.** Something done; a deed. **b.** Something done that has legal significance: *a criminal act.* **3.** *Law* A statute or other law formally adopted by a legislature. **4.** A formal written record of transactions. **5.** One of the major divisions of a play or opera. **6.** A manifestation of insincerity; pose: *put on an act.* ▸*v.* **1.** To perform in a dramatic role. **2.** To behave; conduct oneself. **3.** To seem to be. **4.** To carry out an action. **5.** To substitute for another. **6.** To produce an effect. —*phrasal verb:* **act up 1.** To misbehave. **2.** To malfunction. **3.** To become troublesome after a period of quiescence: *My arthritis is acting up.* —*idiom:* **get (one's) act together** *Slang* To get organized. [< Lat. *agere, āct-*, do.]

ACTH (ā′sē′tē-āch′) ▸*n.* A hormone that stimulates the secretion of cortisone and other hormones by the adrenal cortex. [*a(dreno)c(ortico)-t(ropic) h(ormone)*.]

ac·tin (ăk′tĭn) ▸*n.* A muscle protein that acts with myosin to produce muscle contraction. [Lat. *agere, āct-*, ACT + –IN.]

act·ing (ăk′tĭng) ▸*adj.* Temporarily assuming the duties or authority of another. See Synonyms at **temporary.** ▸*n.* The occupation of or performance as an actor or actress.

ac·ti·nide (ăk′tə-nīd′) ▸*n.* Any of a series of chemically similar radioactive elements with atomic numbers ranging from 89 (actinium) through 103 (lawrencium).

ac·ti·nism (ăk′tə-nĭz′əm) ▸*n.* The intrinsic property in radiation that produces photochemical activity. —**ac·tin′ic** (-tĭn′ĭk) *adj.*

ac·tin·i·um (ăk-tĭn′ē-əm) ▸*n.* *Symbol* **Ac** A radioactive metallic element found in uranium ores and used as a source of alpha rays. At. no. 89. See table at **element.** [< Gk. *aktis*, ray.]

ac·tin·o·my·cin (ăk-tĭn′ō-mī′sĭn, ăk′tə-nō-) ►*n.* Any of various red, often toxic antibiotics obtained from soil bacteria.

ac·tion (ăk′shən) ►*n.* **1.** The state or process of acting or doing. **2.** Something done; a deed or act. **3.** Habitual or vigorous activity; energy. **4.** often **actions** Behavior or conduct. **5.** A lawsuit. **6.** Combat. **7.** Important or exciting work or activity. **8a.** A movement or a series of movements. **b.** Manner of movement: *a gearshift with smooth action.* **9.** The plot of a story or play. **10.** The operating parts of a mechanism.

ac·tion·a·ble (ăk′shə-nə-bəl) ►*adj.* **1.** Giving cause for legal action: *an actionable statement.* **2.** Relating to information that allows action to be taken. —**ac′tion·a·bly** *adv.*

ac·ti·vate (ăk′tə-vāt′) ►*v.* **-vat·ed, -vat·ing 1.** To make active. **2.** To organize or create (e.g., a military unit). **3.** To treat (sewage) with aeration and bacteria. **4.** *Phys.* To make radioactive. —**ac′ti·va′tion** *n.* —**ac′ti·va′tor** *n.*

ac·ti·vat·ed charcoal (ăk′tə-vā′tĭd) ►*n.* Highly absorbent carbon obtained by heating granulated charcoal to exhaust contained gases.

ac·tive (ăk′tĭv) ►*adj.* **1.** Being in motion. **2.** Capable of functioning; working. **3.** Marked by energetic activity; busy. **4.** Involving or requiring physical exertion and energy. **5.** Being in action; not passive: *an active volcano.* **6a.** Marked by or involving direct participation: *an active interest in politics.* **b.** Currently in use or effect: *an active membership.* **7.** *Gram.* Of or being a verb form or voice used to indicate that the subject of the sentence is performing or causing the action. —**ac′tive·ly** *adv.*

active immunity ►*n.* Immunity resulting from the production of antibodies in response to an antigen.

ac·tiv·ism (ăk′tə-vĭz′əm) ►*n.* The use of direct, often confrontational action, in opposition to or support of a cause. —**ac′tiv·ist** *adj. & n.*

ac·tiv·i·ty (ăk-tĭv′ĭ-tē) ►*n., pl.* **-ties 1.** The state of being active. **2.** Energetic action; liveliness. **3a.** A pursuit or pastime. **b.** An educational procedure to stimulate learning through actual experience. **4.** A physiological process.

act of God ►*n.* A violent or destructive natural event, such as a lightning strike or an earthquake.

ac·tor (ăk′tər) ►*n.* **1.** A theatrical performer. **2.** A participant. **3.** *Law* **a.** One, such as an administrator, who acts for another. **b.** In civil law, the plaintiff in an action.

ac·tress (ăk′trĭs) ►*n.* A woman who is an actor. See Usage Note at **–ess.**

Acts of the Apostles (ăkts) ►*pl.n.* (takes sing. v.) See table at **Bible.**

ac·tu·al (ăk′chōō-əl) ►*adj.* **1.** Existing in fact; real. **2.** Existing or acting at the present moment; current. [< Lat. *agere, āct-,* ACT.] —**ac′tu·al·ly** *adv.*

ac·tu·al·i·ty (ăk′chōō-ăl′ĭ-tē) ►*n., pl.* **-ties** The state or fact of being actual; reality. See Synonyms at **existence.**

ac·tu·al·ize (ăk′chōō-ə-līz′) ►*v.* **-ized, -iz·ing** To realize in action; make real. —**ac′tu·al·i·za′tion** *n.*

ac·tu·ar·y (ăk′chōō-ĕr′ē) ►*n., pl.* **-ies** A stat-

istician who computes insurance risks and premiums. [< Lat. *ācta,* records < *agere,* ACT.] —**ac′tu·ar′i·al** (-âr′ē-əl) *adj.*

ac·tu·ate (ăk′chōō-āt′) ►*v.* **-at·ed, -at·ing** To put into motion or action. [Med.Lat. *āctuāre, āctuāt-* < Lat. *agere,* ACT.] —**ac′tu·a′tion** *n.* —**ac′tu·a′tor** *n.*

a·cu·i·ty (ə-kyōō′ĭ-tē) ►*n.* Acuteness of vision or of perception; keenness. [< Lat. *acūtus,* ACUTE.]

ac·u·men (ăk′yə-mən, ə-kyōō′-) ►*n.* Accuracy and keenness of judgment or insight. [Lat. *acūmen* < *acus,* needle.]

ac·u·pres·sure (ăk′yə-prĕsh′ər) ►*n.* See **shiatsu.** [ACU(PUNCTURE) + PRESSURE.]

ac·u·punc·ture (ăk′yōō-pŭngk′chər) ►*n.* A Chinese medical procedure in which specific body areas are pierced with fine needles for pain relief or other therapeutic purposes. [Lat. *acus,* needle + PUNCTURE.] —**ac′u·punc′ture** *v.* —**ac′u·punc′tur·ist** *n.*

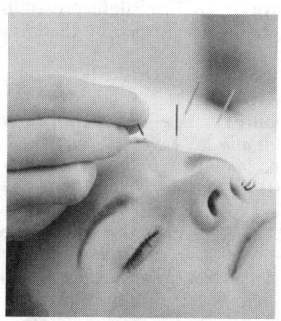
acupuncture

a·cute (ə-kyōōt′) ►*adj.* **1.** Having a sharp point. **2.** Keenly perceptive or discerning. **3.** Sensitive: *acute vision.* **4.** Crucial: *an acute lack of research funds.* **5.** Extremely sharp or severe: *acute pain.* **6.** *Med.* Having a rapid onset and following a short but severe course: *acute disease.* **7.** Designating angles less than 90°. [< Lat. *acuere, acūt-,* sharpen < *acus,* needle.] —**a·cute′ly** *adv.* —**a·cute′ness** *n.*

acute accent ►*n.* A mark (′) written over a letter to indicate syllable stress or the length or quality of a vowel sound.

acute care ►*n.* Short-term medical treatment, usu. in a hospital, for acute illness or injury.

ACV ►*abbr.* actual cash value

ad (ăd) ►*n.* An advertisement.

AD ►*abbr.* **1.** active duty **2.** or **AD** anno Domini **3.** athletic director

ad– ►*pref.* Toward; to; near: *adrenal.* [< Lat. *ad,* to.]

ad·age (ăd′ĭj) ►*n.* A short proverb; saying. [< Lat. *adagium.*]

a·da·gio (ə-dä′jō, -jē-ō′) ►*adv. & adj. Mus.* In a slow tempo. [Ital.]

Ad·am (ăd′əm) In the Bible, the first man and the husband of Eve.

ad·a·mant (ăd′ə-mənt) ►*adj.* Not willing to change one's opinion, purpose, or principles; unyielding. ►*n.* A legendary stone of impenetrable hardness. [< Gk. *adamas,* hard steel.]

Ad·ams (ăd′əmz), **Abigail Smith** 1744–1818. First lady of the US (1797–1801) and noted correspondent.

Adams, John 1735–1826. The first vice president (1789–97) and second president (1797–1801) of the US.

Adams, John Quincy 1767–1848. The sixth US president (1825–29).

John Adams   **John Quincy Adams**

Adams, Samuel 1722–1803. Amer. Revolutionary leader.

Adam's apple ►*n.* The slight projection at the front of the throat formed by the largest cartilage of the larynx.

a·dapt (ə-dăpt′) ►*v.* To make or become suitable for a specific use. [< Lat. *adaptāre*, fit to.] —**a·dapt′a·bil′i·ty** *n.* —**a·dapt′a·ble** *adj.* —**a·dapt′ive** *adj.*
    Syns: accommodate, adjust, conform, fit *v.*

ad·ap·ta·tion (ăd′ăp-tā′shən) ►*n.* **1a.** The act or process of adapting. **b.** The state of being adapted. **2.** A composition recast into a new form: *The play is an adaptation of a short novel.* **3.** *Biol.* An alteration or adjustment in characteristics, often occurring through natural selection, by which a species or individual becomes better able to function in its environment. —**ad′ap·ta′tion·al** *adj.*

a·dapt·er also **a·dap·tor** (ə-dăp′tər) ►*n.* One that adapts, such as a device used to effect compatibility between different parts of a system or apparatus.

A·dar (ä-där′) ►*n.* The 12th month of the Jewish calendar. See table at **calendar.** [Heb. *ădār.*]

Adar She·ni (shä-nē′) ►*n.* An intercalary month in the Jewish calendar. See table at **calendar.** [Heb. *ădār šēnî*, second Adar.]

ADC ►*abbr.* **1.** aide-de-camp **2.** Aid to Dependent Children

add (ăd) ►*v.* **1.** To join or combine (numbers) to form a sum. **2.** To join so as to increase in size, quantity, value, or scope: *added 12 inches to the deck.* **3.** To say or write further. —*phrasal verb:* **add up** To be reasonable or plausible: *an excuse that didn't add up.* —*idiom:* **add up to** To constitute; amount to. [< Lat. *addere:* AD– + *dare*, give.] —**add′a·ble, add′i·ble** *adj.*

ADD ►*abbr.* attention deficit disorder

Ad·dams (ăd′əmz), **Jane** 1860–1935. Amer. social reformer and pacifist.

ad·dend (ăd′ĕnd′) ►*n.* Any of a set of numbers to be added. [Short for ADDENDUM.]

ad·den·dum (ə-dĕn′dəm) ►*n.,* pl. **-da** (-də) Something added or to be added, esp. a supplement to a book. [Lat. < *addere*, ADD.]

add·er[1] (ăd′ər) ►*n.* One that adds, esp. a device that performs arithmetic addition.

ad·der[2] (ăd′ər) ►*n.* **1.** Any of several venomous snakes, esp. a viper. **2.** Any of several nonvenomous snakes, such as the milk snake, popularly believed to be harmful. [< OE *nædre.*]

ad·dict (ə-dĭkt′) ►*v.* **1.** To cause to become physiologically or psychologically dependent: *He is addicted to gambling.* **2.** To occupy (oneself) with something habitually: *She is addicted to surfing the Internet.* ►*n.* (ăd′ĭkt) **1.** One who is addicted, as to narcotics. **2.** A devoted fan: *a comic book addict.* [Lat. *addīcere, addict-*, bind over to.] —**ad·dic′tion** *n.* —**ad·dic′tive** *adj.*

add-in (ăd′ĭn′) ►*n.* **1.** Something designed for use in conjunction with another. **2.** *Comp.* See **plug-in.**

Ad·dis Ab·a·ba (ăd′ĭs äb′ə-bə, ä′dĭs ä′bə-bä′) The capital of Ethiopia, in the central part.

ad·di·tion (ə-dĭsh′ən) ►*n.* **1.** The act or process of adding. **2.** Something added, such as a room to a building. —*idiom:* **in addition** Also; as well as. See Usage Note at **together.** —**ad·di′tion·al** *adj.* —**ad·di′tion·al·ly** *adv.*

ad·di·tive (ăd′ĭ-tĭv) ►*n.* A substance added in small amounts to something else to improve or strengthen it. ►*adj.* Relating to addition.

ad·dle (ăd′l) ►*v.* **-dled, -dling** **1.** To make or become confused. See Synonyms at **befuddle.** **2.** To become rotten. [< OE *adel*, filth.]

add-on (ăd′ŏn′, -ôn′) ►*n.* **1.** One thing added as a supplement to another. **2.** *Comp.* **a.** See **plug-in. b.** A hardware device added to a computer to increase its capabilities.

ad·dress (ə-drĕs′) ►*v.* **1.** To speak to. **2.** To direct to the attention of. **3.** To mark with a destination. **4.** To direct one's efforts or attention to. ►*n.* (ə-drĕs′, ăd′rĕs′) **1.** The directions on a deliverable item indicating destination. **2.** The location at which an organization or person may be found. **3.** *Comp.* **a.** A number assigned to a specific memory location. **b.** A name or character sequence that designates an e-mail account or website. **4.** A formal spoken or written communication. [< OFr. *adresser*, direct to.]

ad·dress·ee (ăd′rĕ-sē′, ə-drĕs′ē′) ►*n.* The one to whom something is addressed.

ad·duce (ə-dōōs′, -dyōōs′) ►*v.* **-duced, -ducing** To cite as an example or means of proof in an argument. [Lat. *addūcere*, bring to.]

–ade ►*suff.* A sweetened beverage of: *lemonade.* [< OFr. < Lat. *-ātus*, -ate.]

A·den (äd′n, ād′n) **1.** A former British colony and protectorate of S Arabia, part of Southern Yemen (now Yemen) since 1967. **2.** A city of S Yemen on the **Gulf of Aden,** an arm of the Arabian Sea between Yemen and Somalia.

Ad·en·au·er (ăd′n-ou′ər, äd′-), **Konrad** 1876–1967. German politician; first chancellor of West Germany (1949–63).

ad·e·nine (ăd′n-ēn′, -ĭn) ►*n.* A purine base, $C_5H_5N_5$, that is a constituent of DNA and RNA. [Gk. *adēn*, gland + –INE[2].]

ad·e·noid (ăd′n-oid′) ►*n.* One of two masses of lymphoid tissue at the back of the nose above the throat. [Gk. *adēn*, gland + –OID.] —**ad′e·noid′** *adj.*

ad·e·noi·dal (ăd′n-oid′l) ►*adj.* **1.** Of the adenoids. **2.** Nasal; stuffy: *an adenoidal voice.*

a·dept (ə-dĕpt′) ►*adj.* Very skilled; expert. [< Lat. *adipīscī, adept-*, attain to.] —**ad′ept′** (ăd′ĕpt′) *n.* —**a·dept′ly** *adv.*

ad·e·quate (ăd′ĭ-kwĭt) ►*adj.* Sufficient to satisfy a requirement. See Synonyms at **sufficient.** [< Lat. *adaequāre*, make equal to.] —**ad′e·qua·cy** (-kwə-sē) *n.* —**ad′e·quate·ly** *adv.*

ADHD ►*abbr.* attention deficit hyperactivity disorder

ad·here (ăd-hîr′) ►*v.* **-hered, -her·ing 1.** To stick fast, as by suction or glue. **2.** To be a devoted follower. **3.** To carry something out without deviation: *We will adhere to our plan.* [< Lat. *adhaerēre*, stick to.] —**ad·her′ence** *n.* —**ad·her′ent** *adj. & n.*

ad·he·sion (ăd-hē′zhən) ►*n.* **1.** The act or state of adhering. **2.** Attachment or devotion; loyalty. **3.** *Med.* A condition in which normally separate bodily tissues grow together.

ad·he·sive (ăd-hē′sĭv, -zĭv) ►*adj.* **1.** Tending to adhere; sticky. **2.** Gummed so as to adhere. —**ad·he′sive** *n.* —**ad·he′sive·ly** *adv.*

ad hoc (ăd hŏk′, hōk′) ►*adv.* For only the specific case or situation at hand. ►*adj.* Improvised; impromptu. [Lat., for this.]

ad hom·i·nem (hŏm′ə-něm′) ►*adj.* **1.** Attacking an opponent's character to avoid discussing the issues. **2.** Appealing to the emotions rather than to logic or reason. [Lat., to the man.] —**ad hom′i·nem** *adv.*

ad·i·a·bat·ic (ăd′ē-ə-băt′ĭk, ā′dī-) ►*adj.* Relating to a reversible process occurring without gain or loss of heat. [< Gk. *adiabatos*, impassable : A-¹ + *diabatos*, passable (*dia-*, across + *bainein, bat-*, go).]

a·dieu (ə-dyōō′, -dōō′) ►*interj.* Used to express farewell. ►*n., pl.* **a·dieus** or **a·dieux** (ə-dyōōz′, -dōōz′) A farewell. [< OFr.]

ad in·fi·ni·tum (ăd ĭn′fə-nī′təm) ►*adv. & adj.* To infinity; having no end. [Lat. *ad īnfīnītum.*]

a·di·os (ä′dē-ōs′) ►*interj.* Used to express farewell. [Sp. *adiós.*]

ad·i·pose (ăd′ə-pōs′) ►*adj.* Relating to animal fat; fatty. [< Lat. *adeps, adip-*, fat.]

Ad·i·ron·dack Mountains (ăd′ə-rŏn′dăk′) A group of mountains in NE NY rising to 1,629 m (5,344 ft).

adj. ►*abbr.* **1.** adjective **2.** adjunct **3. Adj.** adjutant

ad·ja·cent (ə-jā′sənt) ►*adj.* **1.** Close to; lying near: *adjacent cities.* **2.** Next to; adjoining: *adjacent garden plots.* [< Lat. *adiacēre*, lie near to.] —**ad·ja′cen·cy** *n.*

ad·jec·tive (ăj′ĭk-tĭv) ►*n.* The part of speech that modifies a noun or other substantive by limiting, qualifying, or specifying. [< Lat. *adicere, adiect-*, add to.] —**ad′jec·ti′val** (-tī′vəl) *adj.* —**ad′jec·ti′val·ly** *adv.*

ad·join (ə-join′) ►*v.* **1.** To be next to. **2.** To attach. [< Lat. *adiungere*, join to : AD– + *iungere*, join.]

ad·journ (ə-jûrn′) ►*v.* **1.** To suspend until a later time. **2.** To move from one place to another: *After the meal, we adjourned to the living room.* [< OFr. *ajourner* < LLat. *diurnum*, day.] —**ad·journ′ment** *n.*

ad·judge (ə-jŭj′) ►*v.* **-judged, -judg·ing 1.** To determine or award by law. **2.** To regard; deem: *was adjudged incompetent.* [< Lat. *adiūdicāre.*]

ad·ju·di·cate (ə-jōō′dĭ-kāt′) ►*v.* **-cat·ed, -cat·ing 1.** To make a decision (in a legal case or proceeding). **2.** To act as a judge of (e.g., a contest). [Lat. *adiūdicāre.*] —**ad·ju′di·ca′tion** *n.* —**ad·ju′di·ca′tor** *n.*

ad·junct (ăj′ŭngkt′) ►*n.* One attached to another in a dependent or subordinate position. [< Lat. *adiungere, adiūnct-*, ADJOIN.] —**ad·junc′tive** *adj.*

ad·jure (ə-jŏŏr′) ►*v.* **-jured, -jur·ing 1.** To command or enjoin solemnly, as under oath. **2.** To appeal to or entreat earnestly. [< Lat. *adiūrāre*, swear to.] —**ad′ju·ra′tion** (ăj′ə-rā′shən) *n.*

ad·just (ə-jŭst′) ►*v.* **1.** To move or change (something) so as to be in a more effective arrangement or desired condition: *adjusted the hearing aid.* **2.** To change so as to be suitable to or conform with something else: *adjusted the schedule.* See Synonyms at **adapt. 3.** To settle (an insurance claim).

ad·ju·tant (ăj′ə-tənt) ►*n.* **1.** A staff officer who helps a commanding officer with administration. **2.** An assistant. [< Lat. *adiūtāre*, give help to.] —**ad′ju·tan·cy** *n.*

ad lib (ăd lĭb′) ►*adv.* In an unrestrained manner; spontaneously. [< Lat. *ad libitum*, at pleasure.]

ad-lib (ăd-lĭb′) ►*v.* **-libbed, -lib·bing** To improvise and deliver extemporaneously. ►*n.* (ăd′lĭb′) Words, music, or actions uttered or performed extemporaneously. —**ad′-lib′** *adj.* —**ad-lib′ber** *n.*

ad loc. ►*abbr. Lat.* ad locum (to, or at, the place)

ad·min·is·ter (ăd-mĭn′ĭ-stər) ►*v.* **1.** To direct; manage. **2a.** To give or apply in a formal way: *administer the last rites.* **b.** To apply as a remedy: *administer a sedative.* **3.** To mete out; dispense: *administer justice.* **4.** To tender (an oath). [< Lat. *administrāre.*] —**ad·min′is·trant** *adj. & n.*

ad·min·is·tra·tion (ăd-mĭn′ĭ-strā′shən) ►*n.* **1.** The act or process of administering, esp. the management of a government or large institution. **2.** The activity of a sovereign state in the exercise of its powers or duties. **3.** often **Administration** The executive branch of a government. **4.** Those who manage an institution, esp. a school or college. —**ad·min′is·tra′tive** (-strā′tĭv, -strə-) *adj.*

ad·min·is·tra·tor (ăd-mĭn′ĭ-strā′tər) ►*n.* **1.** One who administers. **2.** One appointed to manage an estate.

ad·mi·ra·ble (ăd′mər-ə-bəl) ►*adj.* Deserving admiration. —**ad′mi·ra·bly** *adv.*

ad·mi·ral (ăd′mər-əl) ►*n.* **1.** The commander in chief of a fleet. **2.** A rank, as in the US Navy, above vice admiral and below fleet admiral. [< Ar. ′*amīr al-* . . . ., high commander of the . . . .]

ad·mi·ral·ty (ăd′mər-əl-tē) ►*n., pl.* **-ties 1a.** A court exercising jurisdiction over all maritime cases. **b.** Maritime law. **2. Admiralty** The department of the British government that once had control over all naval affairs.

ad·mire (ăd-mīr′) ►*v.* **-mired, -mir·ing 1.** To regard with pleasure, wonder, and approval. **2.** To esteem or respect. **3.** *Archaic* To marvel at. [< Lat. *admīrārī*, to wonder at.] —**ad′mi·ra′tion** (ăd′mə-rā′shən) *n.* —**ad·mir′er** *n.* —**ad·mir′ing·ly** *adv.*

ad·mis·si·ble (ăd-mĭs′ə-bəl) ►*adj.* **1.** Capable of being accepted; allowable: *admissible evidence.* **2.** Worthy of admission. —**ad·mis′si·bil′i·ty** *n.*

ad·mis·sion (ăd-mĭsh′ən) ►*n.* **1.** The act of admitting. **2.** Right to enter; access. **3.** The price required for entering; entrance fee. **4.** The people admitted, as to an institution: *hospital admissions.* **5a.** A confession; disclosure. **b.** *Law* A statement against one's personal interests that can be used as evidence. —**ad·mis′sive** (-mĭs′ĭv) *adj.*

ad·mit (ăd-mĭt′) ▸v. **-mit·ted, -mit·ting 1.** To grant as true or valid; concede. **2.** To allow; permit. **3.** To disclose; confess. **4a.** To grant the right to enter: *a ticket that admits two.* **b.** To permit to enter: *a window that admits light.* [< Lat. *admittere.*] —**ad·mit′tance** (-mĭt′ns) *n.*

ad·mit·ted·ly (ăd-mĭt′ĭd-lē) ▸adv. By general admission; confessedly.

ad·mix·ture (ăd-mĭks′chər) ▸n. **1.** The act of mixing. **2.** A mixture. **3.** Something added in mixing. —**ad·mix′** *v.*

ad·mon·ish (ăd-mŏn′ĭsh) ▸v. **1.** To counsel against something to be avoided or warn that something is dangerous. **2.** To remind of an obligation. **3.** To reprove gently but earnestly. [< Lat. *admonēre* : AD– + *monēre,* warn.] —**ad·mon′ish·ment, ad′mo·ni′tion** (ăd′mə-nĭsh′ən) *n.*

ad·mon·i·to·ry (ăd-mŏn′ĭ-tôr′ē) ▸adj. Expressing admonition.

ad nau·se·am (ăd nô′zē-əm) ▸adv. To a disgusting or absurd degree. [Lat., to nausea.]

a·do (ə-dōō′) ▸n. Fuss; bother; trouble. [< ME *at do,* to do.]

a·do·be (ə-dō′bē) ▸n. **1.** A sun-dried, unburned brick of clay mixed with straw or dung. **2.** A structure built of adobe brick. [< Ar. *aṭ-ṭūba,* the brick.]

ad·o·les·cence (ăd′l-ĕs′əns) ▸n. The period of physical and psychological development from the onset of puberty to maturity. [< Lat. *adolēscere,* grow up.] —**ad′o·les′cent** *adj. & n.*

A·don·is (ə-dŏn′ĭs, -dō′nĭs) ▸n. **1.** *Gk. Myth.* A beautiful youth loved by Aphrodite. **2.** often **adonis** A handsome young man.

a·dopt (ə-dŏpt′) ▸v. **1.** To take on the legal responsibilities as parent of (a child that is not one's biological child). **2.** To take and follow (a course of action) by choice or assent. **3.** To take up and make one's own. [< Lat. *adoptāre,* opt for.] —**a·dopt′a·ble** *adj.* —**a·dopt′er** *n.* —**a·dop′tion** *n.*

a·dop·tee (ə-dŏp′tē) ▸n. One, such as a child, that is or has been adopted.

a·dop·tive (ə-dŏp′tĭv) ▸adj. **1.** Of or relating to adoption. **2.** Related by adoption. —**a·dop′tive·ly** *adv.*

a·dor·a·ble (ə-dôr′ə-bəl) ▸adj. **1.** Delightful, lovable, and charming. **2.** Worthy of adoration. —**a·dor′a·bly** *adv.*

a·dore (ə-dôr′) ▸v. **a·dored, a·dor·ing 1.** To worship as God or a god. **2.** To regard with deep or rapturous love. **3.** To like very much. [< Lat. *adōrāre,* pray to.] —**ad·o·ra′tion** (ăd′ə-rā′shən) *n.* —**a·dor′er** *n.* —**a·dor′ing·ly** *adv.*

a·dorn (ə-dôrn′) ▸v. **1.** To lend beauty to. **2.** To decorate; embellish. [< Lat. *adōrnāre.*] —**a·dorn′ment** *n.*

ad·re·nal (ə-drē′nəl) ▸adj. **1.** At, near, or on the kidneys. **2.** Of or relating to the adrenal glands or their secretions.

adrenal gland ▸n. Either of two small endocrine glands, one located above each kidney.

a·dren·a·line (ə-drĕn′ə-lĭn) ▸n. Epinephrine.

A·dri·at·ic Sea (ā′drē-ăt′ĭk) An arm of the Mediterranean between Italy and the Balkan Peninsula.

a·drift (ə-drĭft′) ▸adv. & adj. **1.** Drifting or floating freely; not anchored. **2.** Without direction or purpose.

a·droit (ə-droit′) ▸adj. Quick and skillful in

body or mind; deft. [Fr.] —**a·droit′ly** *adv.* —**a·droit′ness** *n.*

ad·sorb (ăd-zôrb′, -sôrb′) ▸v. To take up and hold (liquid or gas) on the surface of a solid. [AD– + Lat. *sorbēre,* suck.] —**ad·sorb′a·ble** *adj.* —**ad·sorp′tion** (-zôrp′shən, -sôrp′-) *n.* —**ad·sorp′tive** *adj.*

ad·u·late (ăj′ə-lāt′) ▸v. **-lat·ed, -lat·ing** To praise or admire excessively; fawn on. [< Lat. *adūlārī,* to flatter.] —**ad′u·la′tion** *n.* —**ad′u·la·to′ry** (-lə-tôr′ē) *adj.*

a·dult (ə-dŭlt′, ăd′ŭlt) ▸n. One that has attained maturity or legal age. ▸adj. **1.** Fully developed; mature. **2.** For or befitting adults: *adult education.* [< Lat. *adolēscere,* adult-, grow up.] —**a·dult′hood′** *n.*

a·dul·ter·ate (ə-dŭl′tə-rāt′) ▸v. **-at·ed, -at·ing** To make impure by adding improper or inferior ingredients. [Lat. *adulterāre,* pollute.] —**a·dul′ter·ant** *adj. & n.* —**a·dul′ter·a′tion** *n.* —**a·dul′ter·a′tor** *n.*

a·dul·ter·y (ə-dŭl′tə-rē, -trē) ▸n., pl. **-ies** Consensual sexual intercourse between a married person and a person other than the spouse. [< Lat. *adulter,* adulterer.] —**a·dul′ter·er** *n.* —**a·dul′ter·ess** (-trĭs, -tər-ĭs) *n.* —**a·dul′ter·ous** *adj.*

ad·um·brate (ăd′əm-brāt′, ə-dŭm′-) ▸v. **-brat·ed, -brat·ing 1.** To give a sketchy outline of. **2.** To foreshadow. **3.** To disclose partially. **4.** To overshadow. [Lat. *adumbrāre,* shade in.] —**ad′um·bra′tion** *n.*

adv. ▸abbr. **1.** adverb **2.** *Lat.* adversus (against)

ad·vance (ăd-văns′) ▸v. **-vanced, -vanc·ing 1.** To move or bring forward. **2.** To put forward; suggest. **3a.** To aid the progress of. **b.** To make progress; proceed. **4.** To raise or rise in rank, amount, or value. **5.** To cause to occur sooner. **6.** To pay (money or interest) before due. **7.** To lend, esp. on credit. ▸n. **1.** The act or process of moving or going forward. **2.** Improvement; progress. **3.** An increase of price or value. **4. advances** Opening approaches made to secure acquaintance, favor, or an agreement. **5.** Payment of money before due. ▸adj. **1.** Made or given ahead of time: *an advance payment.* **2.** Going before or in front. —*idioms:* **in advance** Ahead of time; beforehand. **in advance of** Ahead of. [< Lat. *ab ante,* from before.] —**ad·vanc′er** *n.*

Syns: forward, foster, further, promote **Ant:** *retard v.*

ad·vanced (ăd-vănst′) ▸adj. **1.** Highly developed or complex. **2.** At a higher level than others: *an advanced text in physics.* **3.** Progressive: *advanced teaching methods.* **4.** Far along in course or time: *an advanced stage of illness.*

advance directive ▸n. A legal document in which one gives directions about one's medical care in the event that one becomes incapable of doing so.

ad·vance·ment (ăd-văns′mənt) ▸n. **1.** The act of advancing. **2.** Development; progress: *the advancement of knowledge.* **3.** A promotion.

ad·van·tage (ăd-văn′tĭj) ▸n. **1.** A beneficial factor or combination of factors. **2.** Benefit or profit; gain. **3.** A relatively favorable position. **4.** The first point scored in tennis after deuce. ▸v. **-taged, -tag·ing** To afford profit or gain to; benefit. —*idiom:* **take advantage of 1.** To put to good use. **2.** To exploit. [< OFr.

avantage < Lat. *ab ante,* from before.] **—ad·van·ta′geous** (-văn-tā′jəs) *adj.* **—ad′van·ta′geous·ly** *adv.*

ad·vec·tion (ăd-věk′shən) ►*n.* **1.** The transfer of an atmospheric property (e.g., temperature) by the motion of the air. **2.** The horizontal movement of water, as in a current. [< Lat. *advehere, advect-,* carry toward.]

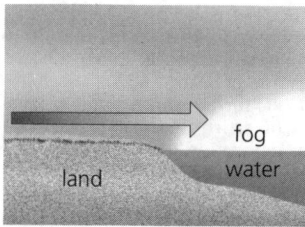

advection
Advection of heat in warm moist air over a cool surface of water causes fog.

ad·vent (ăd′věnt′) ►*n.* **1.** The coming or arrival, esp. of something important: *the advent of the computer.* **2.** also **Advent** Christianity **a.** The period of preparation for Christmas, beginning on the fourth Sunday before Christmas. **b.** The birth of Jesus. [< Lat. *advenīre, advent-,* come to.]

ad·ven·ti·tious (ăd′věn-tĭsh′əs) ►*adj.* Arising from an external cause or factor. [< Lat. *adventus,* ADVENT.] **—ad′ven·ti′tious·ly** *adv.*

ad·ven·ture (ăd-věn′chər) ►*n.* **1a.** An enterprise of a hazardous nature. **b.** An undertaking of a questionable nature, esp. intervention in another state's affairs. **2.** An unusual or exciting experience. ►*v.* **-tured, -tur·ing 1.** To hazard or risk. **2.** To take risks. [< Lat. *advenīre, advent-,* come to; see ADVENT.]

ad·ven·tur·er (ăd-věn′chər-ər) ►*n.* **1.** One that seeks adventure. **2.** A soldier of fortune. **3.** A financial speculator. **4.** One who attempts to gain wealth and social position by unscrupulous means.

ad·ven·ture·some (ăd-věn′chər-səm) ►*adj.* Daring. See Synonyms at **adventurous.**

ad·ven·tur·ess (ăd-věn′chər-ĭs) ►*n.* A woman who seeks social and financial advancement by unscrupulous means. See Usage Note at **–ess.**

ad·ven·tur·ous (ăd-věn′chər-əs) ►*adj.* **1.** Inclined to undertake new and daring enterprises. **2.** Hazardous; risky. **—ad·ven′tur·ous·ly** *adv.* **—ad·ven′tur·ous·ness** *n.*

Syns: *adventuresome, audacious, daredevil, daring, venturesome* **adj.**

ad·verb (ăd′vûrb) ►*n.* The part of speech that modifies a verb, an adjective, or another adverb. [< Lat. *adverbium.*] **—ad·ver′bi·al** *adj.* **—ad·ver′bi·al·ly** *adv.*

ad·ver·sar·y (ăd′vər-sĕr′ē) ►*n., pl.* **-ies** An opponent; enemy. **—ad′ver·sar′i·al** (-sâr′ē-əl) *adj.*

ad·verse (ăd-vûrs′, ăd′vûrs′) ►*adj.* **1.** Acting or serving to oppose; antagonistic: *adverse criticism.* **2.** Harmful or unfavorable: *adverse circumstances.* [< Lat. *advertere, advers-,* turn toward.] **—ad·verse′ly** *adv.*

ad·ver·si·ty (ăd-vûr′sĭ-tē) ►*n., pl.* **-ties** Great hardship or affliction; misfortune.

ad·vert (ăd-vûrt′) ►*v.* To call attention; refer: *advert to a problem.* [< Lat. *advertere,* turn toward.]

ad·ver·tise (ăd′vər-tīz′) ►*v.* **-tised, -tis·ing 1.** To make public announcement of, esp. to promote sales: *advertise a new product.* See Synonyms at **announce. 2.** To make known. **3.** To warn or notify. **—ad′ver·tis′er** *n.*

ad·ver·tise·ment (ăd′vər-tīz′mənt, ăd-vûr′tĭs-, -tĭz-) ►*n.* **1.** The act of advertising. **2.** A notice designed to attract public attention or patronage.

ad·ver·tis·ing (ăd′vər-tī′zĭng) ►*n.* **1.** The business of designing, preparing, and disseminating advertisements. **2.** Advertisements collectively.

ad·vice (ăd-vīs′) ►*n.* Opinion about a course of action; counsel. [< OFr. *avis : a,* to + Lat. *vidēre, vīs-,* see.]

Syns: *counsel, recommendation* **n.**

ad·vis·a·ble (ăd-vī′zə-bəl) ►*adj.* Worthy of being recommended or suggested; prudent. **—ad·vis′a·bil′i·ty** *n.* **—ad·vis′a·bly** *adv.*

ad·vise (ăd-vīz′) ►*v.* **-vised, -vis·ing 1.** To offer advice to; counsel: *advised her to study abroad.* **2.** To recommend; suggest: *advised patience.* **3.** To inform; notify: *advised him that the meeting was over.* [< OFr. *aviser < avis,* ADVICE.] **—ad·vis′er, ad·vi′sor** *n.*

ad·vis·ed·ly (ăd-vī′zĭd-lē) ►*adv.* With careful consideration; deliberately.

ad·vise·ment (ăd-vīz′mənt) ►*n.* Careful consideration.

ad·vi·so·ry (ăd-vī′zə-rē) ►*adj.* **1.** Empowered to advise: *an advisory committee.* **2.** Containing advice, esp. a warning. ►*n., pl.* **-ries** A report giving information, esp. a warning.

ad·vo·ca·cy (ăd′və-kə-sē) ►*n.* The act of arguing in favor of something, such as a cause.

ad·vo·cate (ăd′və-kāt′) ►*v.* **-cat·ed, -cat·ing** To speak, plead, or argue in favor of. ►*n.* (-kĭt) **1.** One that argues for a cause. **2.** One that pleads in another's behalf. **3.** A lawyer. [< Lat. *advocāre,* call to.] **—ad′vo·ca′tor** *n.*

adz or **adze** (ădz) ►*n.* An axlike tool with a curved blade at right angles to the handle, used for dressing wood. [< OE *adesa.*]

Ae·ge·an Sea (ĭ-jē′ən) An arm of the Mediterranean off SE Europe between Greece and Turkey.

ae·gis also **e·gis** (ē′jĭs) ►*n.* **1.** Protection. **2.** Sponsorship; patronage. **3.** *Gk. Myth.* The shield of Zeus, later an attribute of Athena. [< Gk. *aigis.*]

Ae·ne·as (ĭ-nē′əs) ►*n. Gk. & Rom. Myth.* Trojan hero of Virgil's epic poem, the *Aeneid.*

ae·on (ē′ŏn′, ē′ən) ►*n.* Var. of **eon.**

aer·ate (âr′āt) ►*v.* **-at·ed, -at·ing 1.** To supply with air or expose to the circulation of air: *aerate soil.* **2.** To oxygenate (blood) by respiration. **3.** To charge (liquid) with a gas, esp. with carbon dioxide. **—aer·a′tion** *n.* **—aer′a′tor** *n.*

aer·i·al (âr′ē-əl) ►*adj.* **1.** Of, in, or caused by the air. **2.** Lofty. **3.** Airy. **4.** Of, for, or by means of aircraft: *aerial photography.* **5.** *Bot.* Growing above the ground or water: *aerial roots.* ►*n.* A radio antenna, esp. one extending into the air.

aer·i·al·ist (âr′ē-ə-lĭst) ►*n.* An acrobat who performs in the air, as on a trapeze.

aer·ie or **aer·y** also **ey·rie, eyrie** (âr′ē, îr′ē) ►*n., pl.* **-ies** A nest, as of an eagle, built on a high place. [< Lat. *ārea,* open space.]

aero– or **aer–** ►*pref.* **1a.** Air; atmosphere: *aero-pause.* **b.** Gas: *aerosol.* **2.** Aviation: *aeronautics.* [< Gk. *aēr,* air.]

aer·obe (âr′ōb′) ►*n.* An organism, such as a bacterium, requiring oxygen to live. [< AERO– + Gk. *bios,* life.]

aer·o·bic (â-rō′bĭk) ►*adj.* **1.** Occurring or living only in the presence of oxygen. **2.** Relating to aerobics. —**aer·o′bi·cal·ly** *adv.*

aer·o·bics (â-rō′bĭks) ►*n.* *(takes sing. or pl. v.)* An exercise regimen designed to strengthen the cardiovascular system.

aer·o·dy·nam·ic (âr′ō-dī-năm′ĭk) ►*adj.* **1.** Of or relating to aerodynamics. **2.** Styled with rounded edges to reduce wind drag. —**aer′o·dy·nam′i·cal·ly** *adv.*

aer·o·dy·nam·ics (âr′ō-dī-năm′ĭks) ►*n.* *(takes sing. v.)* The dynamics of bodies moving relative to gases, esp. the interaction of moving objects with the atmosphere.

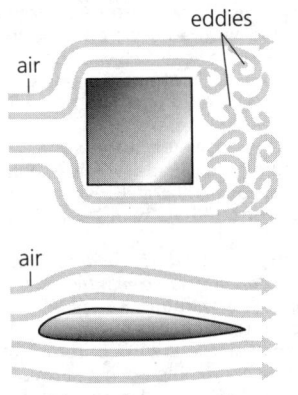

aerodynamics
top: high drag on a less aerodynamic shape
bottom: low drag on a more aerodynamic shape

aer·o·gel (âr′ə-jĕl′) ►*n.* A highly porous solid formed from a gel in which the liquid is replaced with a gas.

aer·om·e·ter (â-rŏm′ĭ-tər) ►*n.* An instrument for determining the weight and density of a gas.

aer·o·naut (âr′ə-nôt′) ►*n.* A pilot or navigator of a lighter-than-air craft, such as a balloon. [AERO– + Gk. *nautēs,* sailor.]

aer·o·nau·tics (âr′ə-nô′tĭks) ►*n.* *(takes sing. v.)* **1.** The design and construction of aircraft. **2.** Aircraft navigation. —**aer′o·nau′tic, aer′o·nau′ti·cal** *adj.*

aer·o·plane (âr′ə-plān′) ►*n. Chiefly Brit.* Var. of **airplane.**

aer·o·pon·ics (âr′ə-pŏn′ĭks) ►*n.* *(takes sing. v.)* A technique for growing plants without soil by misting the roots with nutrient-laden water. [AERO– + (HYDRO)PONICS.]

aer·o·sol (âr′ə-sôl′, -sŏl′) ►*n.* **1.** A gaseous suspension of fine solid or liquid particles. **2a.** A substance packaged under pressure for release as a spray of fine particles. **b.** An aerosol can. [AERO– + SOL(UTION).]

aerosol can ►*n.* A usu. handheld container from which an aerosol is released.

aer·o·space (âr′ō-spās′) ►*adj.* **1.** Relating to Earth's atmosphere and the space beyond. **2.** Relating to the science or technology of flight.

aer·y (âr′ē, îr′ē) ►*n.* Var. of **aerie.**

Aes·chy·lus (ĕs′kə-ləs, ē′skə-) 525–456 BC. Greek tragic dramatist. —**Aes′chy·le′an** (-lē′-ən) *adj.*

Ae·sop (ē′səp, -sŏp′) 6th cent. BC. Greek storyteller. —**Ae·so′pi·an** (ē-sō′pē-ən) *adj.*

aes·thete or **es·thete** (ĕs′thēt) ►*n.* One who cultivates a superior sensitivity to beauty, esp. in art. [< AESTHETIC.]

aes·thet·ic or **es·thet·ic** (ĕs-thĕt′ĭk) ►*adj.* **1.** Relating to aesthetics. **2.** Of or concerning the appreciation of beauty. **3.** Artistic: *The play was an aesthetic success.* ►*n.* A guiding principle in matters of artistic beauty. [< Gk. *aisthētikos,* of sense perception.] —**aes·thet′i·cal·ly** *adv.*

aes·thet·i·cism or **es·thet·i·cism** (ĕs-thĕt′ĭ-sĭz′əm) ►*n.* **1.** The doctrine that beauty is the basic principle from which all others are derived. **2.** Devotion to the beautiful.

aes·thet·ics or **es·thet·ics** (ĕs-thĕt′ĭks) ►*n.* *(takes sing. v.)* The branch of philosophy that deals with the nature and expression of beauty, as in the fine arts.

aès·ti·vate (ĕs′tə-vāt′) ►*v.* Var. of **estivate.**

AFAIK ►*abbr.* as far as I know

a·far (ə-fär′) ►*adv.* From, at, or to a great distance: *traveled afar.* ►*n.* A great distance: *tales from afar.*

AFB ►*abbr.* air force base

AFDC ►*abbr.* Aid to Families with Dependent Children

af·fa·ble (ăf′ə-bəl) ►*adj.* Easy and pleasant to speak to; amiable. [< Lat. *affārī,* speak to.] —**af′fa·bil′i·ty** *n.* —**af′fa·bly** *adv.*

af·fair (ə-fâr′) ►*n.* **1a.** Something done or experienced; occurrence; event. **b.** A matter of personal concern. **c.** A social function: *a posh affair.* **2. affairs** Matters of personal or professional business. **3.** A sexual relationship between two people, esp. when at least one of them is married or in another committed romantic relationship. [< OFr. *a faire,* to do.]

af·fect[1] (ə-fĕkt′) ►*v.* **1.** To influence or change. **2.** To touch the emotions of. ►*n.* (ăf′ĕkt′) Feeling or emotion, esp. as expressed physically. [Lat. *afficere, affect-,* do to.]
 Usage: Affect[1] and *effect* have no senses in common. As a verb *affect*[1] is most commonly used in the sense of "to influence" (*how smoking affects health*). *Effect* means "to bring about or execute" (*layoffs designed to effect savings*).

af·fect[2] (ə-fĕkt′) ►*v.* **1.** To put on a false or pretentious show of: *affected a British accent.* **2.** To fancy; like: *affects dramatic clothes.* [< Lat. *affectāre,* strive for < *afficere,* AFFECT[1].]

af·fec·ta·tion (ăf′ĕk-tā′shən) ►*n.* **1.** A mannerism that is assumed rather than natural, esp. to impress others. **2.** Behavior characterized by such mannerisms.

af·fect·ed (ə-fĕk′tĭd) ►*adj.* **1.** Assumed or simulated to impress others. **2.** Behaving artificially to make an impression. [< AFFECT[2].] —**af·fect′ed·ly** *adv.*

af·fect·ing (ə-fĕk′tĭng) ►*adj.* Inspiring strong emotion; moving. —**af·fect′ing·ly** *adv.*

af·fec·tion (ə-fĕk′shən) ►*n.* A tender feeling toward another; fondness. —**af·fec′tion·ate** (-shə-nĭt) *adj.* —**af·fec′tion·ate·ly** *adv.*

af·fec·tive (ə-fĕk′tĭv) ►*adj. Psychol.* Influenced by or resulting from the emotions.

af·fer·ent (ăf′ər-ənt) ►*adj.* Carrying inward to a central organ or section. [< Lat. *afferre,* bring to : AD– + *ferre,* bring.]

af·fi·ance (ə-fī′əns) ►*v.* **-anced, -anc·ing** To pledge to marry; betroth. [< Med.Lat. *affidāre,* trust to : AD– + Lat. *fidus,* faithful.]

af·fi·da·vit (ăf′ĭ-dā′vĭt) ►*n.* A written declaration made under oath before an authorized officer. [< Med.Lat. *affidāre,* to pledge; see AFFIANCE.]

af·fil·i·ate (ə-fĭl′ē-āt′) ►*v.* **-at·ed, -at·ing** To accept as a member, associate, or branch. ►*n.* (-ē-ĭt, -āt′) An associate or subordinate member: *network affiliates.* [< Lat. *filius,* son.] —**af·fil′i·a′tion** *n.*

af·fin·i·ty (ə-fĭn′ĭ-tē) ►*n., pl.* **-ties 1.** A natural attraction or feeling of kinship. **2.** A natural tendency or ability to use or do something. **3.** Relationship by marriage. **4.** An inherent similarity. [< Lat. *affinis,* related by marriage : AD– + *finis,* boundary.]

af·firm (ə-fûrm′) ►*v.* **1.** To declare positively; assert to be true. **2.** To declare support for or belief in. **3.** *Law* To rule (a court decision) to have been correct. [< Lat. *affirmāre,* strengthen.] —**af·firm′a·ble** *adj.* —**af·fir′mant** *adj. & n.* —**af′fir·ma′tion** (ăf′ər-mā′shən) *n.*

af·fir·ma·tive (ə-fûr′mə-tĭv) ►*adj.* **1.** Giving assent; confirming. **2.** Positive; optimistic: *an affirmative outlook.* ►*n.* **1.** A word or statement of assent. **2.** The side in a debate that upholds the proposition. —**af·fir′ma·tive·ly** *adv.*

affirmative action ►*n.* A policy that seeks to redress past discrimination by ensuring equal opportunity, as in education and employment.

af·fix (ə-fĭks′) ►*v.* **1.** To secure; attach: *affix a label.* **2.** To add or append: *affix a postscript.* ►*n.* (ăf′ĭks′) **1.** Something affixed. **2.** A word element, such as a prefix or suffix, that is attached to a base, stem, or root. [< Lat. *affigere, affix-,* fasten to.]

af·flict (ə-flĭkt′) ►*v.* To cause grievous suffering to. [< Lat. *afflīgere, afflīct-,* strike down.] —**af·flic′tive** *adj.*
   Syns: agonize, rack, torment, torture **v.**

af·flic·tion (ə-flĭk′shən) ►*n.* **1.** A condition of distress. See Synonyms at **trial. 2.** A cause of distress. See Synonyms at **burden.**

af·flu·ence (ăf′lōō-əns) ►*n.* **1.** Wealth; prosperity. **2.** A great quantity; abundance.

af·flu·ent (ăf′lōō-ənt) ►*adj.* **1.** Wealthy. See Synonyms at **rich. 2.** Manifesting or requiring wealth: *affluent homes.* ►*n.* A stream; tributary. [< Lat. *affluere,* overflow with.] —**af′flu·ent·ly** *adv.*

af·ford (ə-fôrd′) ►*v.* **1.** To have the financial means for. **2.** To be able to spare or give up. **3.** To provide: *a tree that affords ample shade.* [< OE *geforthian,* carry through.] —**af·ford′a·bil′i·ty** *n.* —**af·ford′a·ble** *adj.* —**af·ford′a·bly** *adv.*

af·fray (ə-frā′) ►*n.* A noisy quarrel or brawl. [< OFr. *esfraier,* frighten.]

af·front (ə-frŭnt′) ►*v.* **1.** To insult intentionally. **2.** To confront. ►*n.* An insult. [< OFr. *front,* face; see FRONT.]

Af·ghan (ăf′găn′) ►*n.* **1.** A native or inhabitant of Afghanistan. **2. afghan** A coverlet knitted or crocheted in geometric designs. **3.** An Afghan hound. [Pers. *afghān,* an Afghan.] —**Af′ghan** *adj.*

Afghan hound ►*n.* A large slender dog having

long hair and drooping ears, orig. bred as a hunting dog.

af·ghan·i (ăf-găn′ē, -gä′nē) ►*n., pl.* **-is** See table at **currency.** [Pashto *afghānī.*]

Af·ghan·i·stan (ăf-găn′ĭ-stăn′) A landlocked country of SW-central Asia E of Iran. Cap. Kabul.

a·fi·cio·na·do (ə-fĭsh′ē-ə-nä′dō) ►*n., pl.* **-dos** A fan; devotee. [Sp., ult. < Lat. *affectiō,* liking.]

a·field (ə-fēld′) ►*adv.* **1.** Off the usual or desired track. **2.** Away from one's home or usual environment. **3.** To or on a field.

a·fire (ə-fīr′) ►*adv. & adj.* On fire.

AFL ►*abbr.* **1.** American Federation of Labor **2.** American Football League

a·flame (ə-flām′) ►*adv. & adj.* On fire.

af·la·tox·in (ăf′lə-tŏk′sĭn) ►*n.* A toxic compound that is produced by certain molds and contaminates stored food. [NLat. *A(spergillus) flā(vus),* mold species + TOXIN.]

AFL-CIO ►*abbr.* American Federation of Labor and Congress of Industrial Organizations

a·float (ə-flōt′) ►*adv. & adj.* **1.** Floating. **2.** At sea. **3.** Awash; flooded. **4.** Financially sound.

a·flut·ter (ə-flŭt′ər) ►*adj.* **1.** Fluttering: *with flags aflutter.* **2.** Nervous and excited.

a·foot (ə-fŏŏt′) ►*adv. & adj.* **1.** On foot. **2.** In progress: *plans afoot to resign.*

a·fore·men·tioned (ə-fôr′mĕn′shənd) ►*adj.* Mentioned previously. [< OE *onforan,* before.]

a·fore·said (ə-fôr′sĕd′) ►*adj.* Spoken of earlier. [< OE *onforan,* before.]

a·fore·thought (ə-fôr′thôt′) ►*adj.* Premeditated: *malice aforethought.*

a for·ti·o·ri (ä fôr′tē-ôr′ē, ä) ►*adv.* For a still stronger reason; all the more. [Lat.]

a·foul of (ə-foul′) ►*prep.* In or into collision, entanglement, or conflict with.

Afr. ►*abbr.* **1a.** Africa **b.** African **2.** Afrikaans

a·fraid (ə-frād′) ►*adj.* **1.** Filled with fear: *afraid of snakes.* **2.** Averse; opposed: *not afraid of hard work.* **3.** Regretful: *I'm afraid you're wrong.* [< OFr. *esfraier,* frighten.]

A-frame (ā′frām′) ►*n.* A structure with steeply angled sides in the shape of the letter A.

a·fresh (ə-frĕsh′) ►*adv.* Once more; anew; again.

Af·ri·ca (ăf′rĭ-kə) The second-largest continent, S of Europe between the Atlantic and Indian Oceans.

Af·ri·can (ăf′rĭ-kən) ►*adj.* Of or relating to Africa or its peoples, languages, or cultures. ►*n.* **1.** A native or inhabitant of Africa. **2.** A person of African ancestry.

Af·ri·ca·na (ăf′rĭ-kä′nə, -kăn′ə, -kä′nə) ►*n.* (*takes pl. v.*) Materials relating to the history or culture of African peoples.

African American ►*n.* A black American of African ancestry. —**Af′ri·can-A·mer′i·can** *adj.*

Af·ri·can·ized honeybee (ăf′rĭ-kə-nīzd′) ►*n.* A hybrid strain of honeybee that has a tendency to sting with great frequency.

African violet ►*n.* Any of various East African herbs having showy violet, blue, pink, or white flowers and grown as house plants.

Af·ri·kaans (ăf′rĭ-käns′, -känz′) ►*n.* A language that developed from 17th-cent. Dutch and is an official language of South Africa.

Af·ri·ka·ner (ăf′rĭ-kä′nər) ►*n.* An Afrikaans-speaking South African of European and esp. Dutch ancestry.

Af·ro (ăf′rō) ►*n., pl.* **-ros** A rounded, thick, tightly curled hairstyle. ►*adj.* African in style or origin.

Afro– ►*pref.* African: *Afro-Asiatic.*

Af·ro-A·mer·i·can (ăf′rō-ə-měr′ĭ-kən) ►*adj.* African-American.

Af·ro-A·si·at·ic (ăf′rō-ā′zhē-ăt′ĭk, -zē-) ►*n.* A family of languages spoken in N Africa and SW Asia. —**Af′ro-A′si·at′ic** *adj.*

Af·ro·cen·tric (ăf′rō-sĕn′trĭk) ►*adj.* Centered or focused on Africa or African peoples. —**Af′ro·cen′trism** *n.* —**Af′ro·cen′trist** *adj. & n.*

Af·ro·pop (ăf′rō-pŏp′) ►*n.* Popular music that combines various African music styles with elements of Western popular music.

aft (ăft) ►*adv. & adj.* At, in, or toward a ship's stern or the rear of an aircraft. [< OE *æftan,* behind.]

AFT ►*abbr.* American Federation of Teachers

af·ter (ăf′tər) ►*prep.* **1.** Behind in place or order: *Z comes after Y.* **2.** In pursuit of. **3.** Concerning: *asked after you.* **4.** At a later time than: *come after dinner.* **5.** In the style of: *satires after Horace.* **6.** With the same name as: *named after her mother.* ►*adv.* **1.** Behind. **2.** Afterward: *three hours after.* ►*adj.* **1.** Later: *in after years.* **2.** *Naut.* Nearer the stern. ►*conj.* Following the time that: *I saw them after I arrived.* —**idiom:** **after all 1.** In spite of everything. **2.** Ultimately. [< OE *æfter.*]

af·ter·birth (ăf′tər-bûrth′) ►*n.* The placenta and fetal membranes expelled from the uterus following birth.

af·ter·burn·er (ăf′tər-bûr′nər) ►*n.* A device for augmenting jet engine thrust by burning additional fuel with the hot exhaust gases.

af·ter·ef·fect (ăf′tər-ĭ-fĕkt′) ►*n.* A delayed or prolonged response to a stimulus.

af·ter·glow (ăf′tər-glō′) ►*n.* **1.** The light emitted after removal of a source of energy. **2.** A lingering pleasantness.

af·ter-hours (ăf′tər-ourz′) ►*adj.* Occurring or operating after the usual closing time.

af·ter·im·age (ăf′tər-ĭm′ĭj) ►*n.* A visual image persisting after the visual stimulus has ceased.

af·ter·life (ăf′tər-līf′) ►*n.* A life or existence believed to follow death.

af·ter·math (ăf′tər-măth′) ►*n.* **1.** A consequence, esp. of a disaster or misfortune. **2.** A period of time after a disastrous event: *in the aftermath of war.* [AFTER + OE *mǣth,* mowing.]

af·ter·noon (ăf′tər-nōōn′) ►*n.* The part of day from noon until dinnertime or sunset.

af·ter·school (ăf′tər-skōōl′) ►*adj.* Of or being a program providing care for children following school classes. —**af′ter·school′** *n.*

af·ter-shave (ăf′tər-shāv′) ►*n.* A usu. fragrant lotion for use after shaving.

af·ter·shock (ăf′tər-shŏk′) ►*n.* **1.** A quake of lesser magnitude following a large earthquake. **2.** A subsequent shock or trauma.

af·ter·taste (ăf′tər-tāst′) ►*n.* **1.** A taste remaining after the original stimulus is gone. **2.** A lingering emotion or feeling.

af·ter·thought (ăf′tər-thôt′) ►*n.* An idea that occurs to one after an event or decision.

af·ter·ward (ăf′tər-wərd) also **af·ter·wards** (-wərdz) ►*adv.* At a later time; subsequently.

af·ter·word (ăf′tər-wûrd′) ►*n.* See **epilogue** (sense 2).

af·ter·world (ăf′tər-wûrld′) ►*n.* A world believed to exist for those in the afterlife.

AG ►*abbr.* **1.** adjutant general **2.** attorney general

a·gain (ə-gĕn′) ►*adv.* **1.** Once more; anew: *Try again.* **2.** To a previous place, position, or state: *never went back again.* **3.** Furthermore. **4.** On the other hand. [< OE *ongeagn,* against.]

a·gainst (ə-gĕnst′) ►*prep.* **1.** In a direction opposite to: *row against the current.* **2.** So as to come into forcible contact with: *waves dashing against the shore.* **3.** Resting or pressing on: *leaned against the tree.* **4.** In opposition to. **5.** Contrary to: *against all advice.* **6.** In competition with: *raced against me.* **7.** As a safeguard from: *protection against the cold.* [< OE *ongeagn.*]

Ag·a·mem·non (ăg′ə-měm′nŏn′) ►*n. Gk. Myth.* King of Mycenae and leader of the Greeks in the Trojan War.

A·ga·na (ä-gä′nyä) The capital of Guam, on the W coast of the island.

a·gape¹ (ə-gāp′, ə-găp′) ►*adv. & adj.* **1.** With the mouth wide open, as in wonder. **2.** Wide open.

a·ga·pe² (ä-gä′pā, ä′gə-pā′) ►*n.* **1.** In Christianity, love as revealed in Jesus, seen as spiritual and selfless. **2.** Love that is spiritual, not sexual, in its nature. [Gk. *agapē.*]

a·gar (ä′gär′, ä′gär′) also **a·gar-a·gar** (ä′gär-ä′gär′, ä′gär-ä′-) ►*n.* A gelatinous material prepared from certain marine algae and used in bacterial culture media and for thickening foods. [Malay *agar-agar.*]

ag·ate (ăg′ĭt) ►*n.* **1.** A variety of chalcedony with colored bands. **2.** A marble made of agate or a glass imitation. [< Gk. *akhatēs.*]

a·ga·ve (ə-gä′vē, ə-gā′-) ►*n.* Any of numerous tropical American plants with tough sword-shaped leaves. [< Gk. *agauos,* noble.]

age (āj) ►*n.* **1a.** The length of time that one has existed. **b.** The time of life when a person can assume certain civil and personal rights and responsibilities: *under age; of age.* **c.** A stage of life. **d.** Old age: *hair white with age.* **2.** often **Age a.** A distinctive period in human history. **b.** A period in the history of the earth: *the Ice Age.* **3.** **ages** *Informal* A long time: *left ages ago.* ►*v.* **aged, ag·ing 1.** To grow older or more mature. **2.** To bring or come to a desired ripeness. [< OFr. *aage* < Lat. *aetās.*]

–age ►*suff.* **1a.** Collection; mass: *sewerage.* **b.** Amount: *footage* **2.** Relationship; connection: *parentage.* **3.** Condition; state: *vagabondage.* **4a.** An action: *blockage.* **b.** Result of an action: *breakage.* **5.** Residence or place of: *vicarage.* **6.** Charge or fee: *dockage.* [< Lat. *-āticum.*]

ag·ed (ā′jĭd) ►*adj.* **1.** Advanced in years; old. **2.** (ājd) Of the age of: *aged three.* **3.** (ājd) Of a desired ripeness or maturity: *aged cheese.* ►*n.* Elderly people. Used with *the.*

age·ism also **ag·ism** (ā′jĭz′əm) ►*n.* Discrimination based on age, esp. against the elderly. —**age′ist** *adj. & n.*

age·less (āj′lĭs) ►*adj.* **1.** Seeming never to grow old. **2.** Existing forever; eternal. —**age′less·ly** *adv.* —**age′less·ness** *n.*

a·gen·cy (ā′jən-sē) ►*n., pl.* **-cies 1.** Action; operation. **2.** A mode of acting; means. **3.** A business with agents that negotiate deals for clients: *a talent agency.* **4.** An administrative division of a government.

a·gen·da (ə-jĕn′də) ►*n.* **1.** A list of things to be discussed in a meeting. **2.** A program of things to be done or considered. [< Lat. *agere,* do.]

a·gent (ā′jənt) ►*n.* **1.** One that acts or has the power to act. **2.** One that acts for or represents another: *an insurance agent.* **3.** A means of doing something; instrument. **4.** Something that causes a change: *a chemical agent.* **5.** A member of a government agency: *an FBI agent.* **6.** A spy. [< Lat. *agere,* do.]

Agent Orange ►*n.* A herbicide used in the Vietnam War to defoliate areas of forest.

a·gent pro·vo·ca·teur (ä-zhäɴ′ prô-vô′-kä-tœr′) ►*n., pl.* **a·gents pro·vo·ca·teurs** (ä-zhäɴ′ prô-vô′kä-tœr′) One who infiltrates an organization in order to incite its members to commit illegal acts. [Fr.]

age-old (āj′ōld′) ►*adj.* Very old or ancient.

ag·er·a·tum (ăj′ə-rā′təm) ►*n.* Any of a genus of tropical New World plants having showy colorful flower heads. [< Gk. *agēratos,* ageless.]

age spot ►*n.* See **liver spot.**

ag·gie (ăg′ē) ►*n. Games* A playing marble. [AG(ATE) + –IE.]

ag·glom·er·ate (ə-glŏm′ə-rāt′) ►*v.* **-at·ed, -at·ing** To form or collect into a rounded mass. ►*n.* (-ər-ĭt) A jumbled mass; heap. [Lat. *agglomerāre.*] —**ag·glom′er·a′tion** *n.*

ag·glu·ti·nate (ə-glōōt′n-āt′) ►*v.* **-nat·ed, -nat·ing 1.** To join; adhere. **2.** To cause (red blood cells or bacteria) to clump together. [Lat. *agglūtināre,* glue to.] —**ag·glu′ti·na′tion** *n.* —**ag·glu′ti·na′tive** *adj.*

ag·gran·dize (ə-grăn′dīz′, ăg′rən-) ►*v.* **-dized, -diz·ing 1.** To make greater; increase. **2.** To exaggerate. [< OFr. *agrandir.*] —**ag·gran′dize·ment** (ə-grăn′dīz-mənt, -dīz′-) *n.*

ag·gra·vate (ăg′rə-vāt′) ►*v.* **-vat·ed, -vat·ing 1.** To make worse or more troublesome: *aggravate a medical condition.* **2.** To exasperate; provoke. See Synonyms at **annoy.** [Lat. *aggravāre.*] —**ag′gra·va′tion** *n.* —**ag′gra·va′tor** *n.*

ag·gre·gate (ăg′rĭ-gĭt) ►*adj.* **1.** Amounting to a whole; total. **2.** Composed of a mixture of minerals separable by mechanical means. ►*n.* **1.** A whole considered with respect to its constituent parts. **2.** The mineral materials used in making concrete. ►*v.* (-gāt′) **-gat·ed, -gat·ing 1.** To gather into a mass or whole. **2.** To collect (content from different sources on the Internet) into one webpage or newsreader. [< Lat. *aggregāre,* add to.] —**ag′gre·ga′tion** *n.* —**ag′gre·ga′tive** *adj.*

ag·gre·ga·tor (ăg′rĭ-gā′tər) ►*n.* **1.** One that aggregates. **2.** A software program or website that collects web feeds, allowing the viewing of content from different sources in one place.

ag·gres·sion (ə-grĕsh′ən) ►*n.* **1.** The initiation of unprovoked hostilities. **2.** The launching of attacks. **3.** Hostile behavior. [< Lat. *aggredī, aggress-,* to attack.]

ag·gres·sive (ə-grĕs′ĭv) ►*adj.* **1.** Characterized by aggression: *aggressive behavior.* **2.** Inclined to hostile behavior: *an aggressive regime.* **3.** Bold and enterprising: *an aggressive sales campaign.* **4.** Relating to an investment that seeks above-average returns by taking above-average risks. **5.** Relating to or characterized by intensive medical treatment. —**ag·gres′sive·ly** *adv.*

—**ag·gres′sive·ness** *n.* —**ag·gres′sor** *n.*

ag·grieve (ə-grēv′) ►*v.* **-grieved, -griev·ing 1.** To distress; afflict. **2.** To injure; wrong. [< Lat. *aggravāre,* make worse.]

a·ghast (ə-găst′) ►*adj.* Struck by terror or amazement. [< OE *gǣstan,* frighten.]

ag·ile (ăj′əl, -īl′) ►*adj.* **1.** Quick, light, and easy in movement; nimble. **2.** Mentally alert: *an agile mind.* [< Lat. *agilis < agere,* do.] —**ag′ile·ly** *adv.* —**a·gil′i·ty** (ə-jĭl′ĭ-tē), **ag′ile·ness** *n.*

ag·ing (ā′jĭng) ►*n.* The process of growing old or maturing.

ag·ism (ā′jĭz′əm) ►*n.* Var. of **ageism.**

ag·i·tate (ăj′ĭ-tāt′) ►*v.* **-tat·ed, -tat·ing 1.** To move with violence or sudden force. **2.** To upset; disturb. **3.** To stir up public interest in a cause. [Lat. *agitāre < agere,* do.] —**ag′i·tat·ed·ly** *adv.* —**ag′i·ta′tion** *n.*
  Syns: *churn, convulse, rock, shake* **v.**

ag·i·ta·tor (ăj′ĭ-tā′tər) ►*n.* **1.** One who agitates, esp. in political struggles. **2.** An apparatus that shakes or stirs, as in a washing machine.

a·gleam (ə-glēm′) ►*adv. & adj.* Brightly shining.

a·glit·ter (ə-glĭt′ər) ►*adv. & adj.* Glittering; sparkling.

a·glow (ə-glō′) ►*adv. & adj.* Glowing.

ag·nos·tic (ăg-nŏs′tĭk) ►*n.* **1a.** One who believes it is impossible to know whether God exists. **b.** One who is skeptical or uncertain about the existence of God. **2.** One who is doubtful or noncommital about something. [< A⁻¹ + Gk. *gnōsis,* knowledge.] —**ag·nos′tic** *adj.* —**ag·nos′ti·cism** (-tĭ-sĭz′əm) *n.*

Ag·nus De·i (ăg′nəs dē′ī′, än′yŏos dā′ē) *Christianity* ►*n.* **1.** Lamb of God; an emblem of Jesus; Jesus. **2a.** A liturgical prayer. **b.** A musical setting for this prayer. [LLat. *Agnus Deī.*]

a·go (ə-gō′) ►*adv. & adj.* **1.** Gone by; past: *two years ago.* **2.** In the past: *It happened ages ago.* [< OE *āgān,* go away.]

a·gog (ə-gŏg′) ►*adv. & adj.* Full of eager excitement. [< OFr. *en gogue,* in merriment.]

ag·o·nist (ăg′ə-nĭst) ►*n.* **1.** A drug or other chemical that combines with a cell receptor to produce a reaction typical of a substance found in the body. **2.** A contracting muscle that is counteracted by an antagonist. [< Gk. *agōn,* contest; see AGONY.]

ag·o·nize (ăg′ə-nīz′) ►*v.* **-nized, -niz·ing** To suffer or cause to suffer great anguish or extreme pain. See Synonyms at **afflict.** —**ag′o·niz′ing·ly** *adv.*

ag·o·ny (ăg′ə-nē) ►*n., pl.* **-nies 1.** Intense physical or mental pain. **2.** An intense emotion: *an agony of doubt.* **3.** The struggle that precedes death. [< Gk. *agōn,* struggle < *agein,* drive.]

ag·o·ra (ăg′ər-ə) ►*n., pl.* **-ras** or **-rae** (-ə-rē′) A place of congregation, esp. an ancient Greek marketplace. [Gk.]

ag·o·ra·pho·bi·a (ăg′ər-ə-fō′bē-ə, ə-gôr′ə-) ►*n.* An abnormal fear of open or public places. [< Gk. *agora,* market place.] —**ag′o·ra·pho′bic** (-fō′bĭk, -fŏb′ĭk) *adj. & n.*

a·grar·i·an (ə-grâr′ē-ən) ►*adj.* **1.** Relating to agriculture: *an agrarian economy.* **2.** Relating to land and its ownership. ►*n.* One who favors equitable distribution of land. [< Lat. *ager, agr-,* field.]

a·grar·i·an·ism (ə-grâr′ē-ə-nĭz′əm) ►*n.* A movement for the distribution of land in an equitable manner and for agrarian reform.

a·gree (ə-grē′) ►*v.* **1a.** To come into or be in accord. **b.** To express consent; concur: *agreed to her suggestion.* **c.** To come to an understanding, as by negotiating: *agreed on the price.* **2.** To be compatible or consistent: *The copy agrees with the original.* **3.** To be pleasing or healthful: *Spicy food does not agree with me.* **4.** *Gram.* To correspond in gender, number, case, or person. [< OFr. *agreer.*]

a·gree·a·ble (ə-grē′ə-bəl) ►*adj.* **1.** To one's liking; pleasing: *agreeable weather.* **2.** Suitable; conformable. **3.** Ready to consent or submit. —**a·gree′a·ble·ness** *n.* —**a·gree′a·bly** *adv.*

a·gree·ment (ə-grē′mənt) ►*n.* **1.** Harmony of opinion; accord. **2.** An arrangement between parties, usu. resulting from a discussion, regarding a course of action. **3.** *Law* A properly executed and legally binding compact. **4.** *Gram.* Correspondence in gender, number, case, or person between words.

Syns: *bargain, compact, covenant, deal, pact* **n.**

ag·ri·busi·ness (ăg′rə-bĭz′nĭs) ►*n.* Farming as a large-scale business operation.

ag·ri·cul·ture (ăg′rĭ-kŭl′chər) ►*n.* The cultivation of the soil and raising of livestock; farming. [< Lat. *agricultūra.*] —**ag′ri·cul′tur·al** *adj.* —**ag′ri·cul′tur·al·ist** *n.*

a·gron·o·my (ə-grŏn′ə-mē) ►*n.* Application of soil and plant sciences to farming. [Gk. *agros,* field + –NOMY.] —**ag′ro·nom′ic** (ăg′rə-nŏm′-ĭk), **ag′ro·nom′i·cal** *adj.* —**a·gron′o·mist** *n.*

a·ground (ə-ground′) ►*adv. & adj.* Stranded on a shore, reef, or in shallow water.

a·gue (ā′gyo͞o) ►*n.* A condition characterized by alternating chills and sweating, esp. associated with malaria. [< OFr. *(fievre) ague,* sharp (fever) < Lat. *acūtus,* ACUTE.] —**a′gu·ish** *adj.*

ah (ä) ►*interj.* Used to express various emotions, such as satisfaction, surprise, or pain.

A.h. ►*abbr.* ampere-hour

a·ha (ä-hä′) ►*interj.* Used to express surprise, pleasure, or triumph.

A·hab (ā′hăb′) 9th cent. BC. A king of Israel and the husband of Jezebel.

a·head (ə-hĕd′) ►*adv.* **1.** At or to the front. **2a.** In advance; before: *Pay ahead.* **b.** In or into the future: *planned ahead.* **3.** Forward: *The train moved ahead slowly.* —**idioms: be ahead** To be winning or in a superior position. **get ahead** To attain success.

a·hem (ə-hĕm′) ►*interj.* Used to attract attention or to express doubt or warning.

–aholic ►*suff.* One that is compulsively in need of: *workaholic.* [< (ALC)OHOLIC.]

a·hoy (ə-hoi′) ►*interj. Naut.* Used to hail a ship or person or to attract attention.

A·hu·ra Maz·da (ä-hŏŏr′ə măz′də) ►*n.* The chief deity of Zoroastrianism; Ohrmazd. [< Avestan (ancient Iranian language), the Wise Lord : *ahurō,* lord + *mazdā,* wise.]

AI ►*abbr.* **1.** Amnesty International **2.** artificial insemination **3.** artificial intelligence

aid (ād) ►*v.* To help; support. ►*n.* **1.** Assistance. **2.** Something that provides help or support: *sent medical aid to the area ravaged by the storm.* **3a.** An assistant. **b.** A device that assists: *visual aids such as slides.* [< Lat. *adiuvāre,* give help to.] —**aid′er** *n.*

aide (ād) ►*n.* **1.** A helper. **2.** An aide-de-camp. [Fr. < *aider,* AID.]

aide-de-camp (ād′dĭ-kămp′) ►*n., pl.* **aides-de-camp** A military officer acting as an assistant to a superior officer. [Fr.]

AIDS (ādz) ►*n.* A severe immunological disorder caused by HIV that increases susceptibility to certain infections and cancers and is usu. transmitted by exposure to infected blood and semen. [A(CQUIRED) I(MMUNE) D(EFICIENCY) S(YNDROME).]

AIDS-related complex (ādz′rĭ-lā′tĭd) ►*n. Abbr.* **ARC** A combination of symptoms, including fever, lymphadenopathy, and susceptibility to certain infections in some people infected with HIV before they are diagnosed with AIDS.

ai·grette or **ai·gret** (ā-grĕt′, ā′grĕt′) ►*n.* An ornamental tuft of plumes, esp. the tail feathers of an egret. [< OFr., EGRET.]

ai·ki·do (ī′kē-dō′, ī-kē′dō) ►*n.* A Japanese art of self-defense that employs holds, locks, and principles of nonresistance. [Jap. *aikidō.*]

ail (āl) ►*v.* **1.** To feel ill or have pain. **2.** To make ill or cause pain. [< OE *eglian.*]

ai·lan·thus (ā-lăn′thəs) ►*n.* Any of several Asian trees, esp. the tree-of-heaven. [< Ambonese (Austronesian) *ai lanto.*]

ai·le·ron (ā′lə-rŏn′) ►*n.* A movable flap on the wings of an airplane that controls rolling and banking. [< Lat. *āla,* wing.]

Ai·ley (ā′lē, ī′-), **Alvin, Jr.** 1931–89. Amer. choreographer.

ail·ment (āl′mənt) ►*n.* A mild illness.

aim (ām) ►*v.* **1.** To direct (e.g., a weapon or remark) toward an intended target. **2.** To determine a course: *aim for a better life.* **3.** To propose to do something; intend: *aims to run in the race.* ►*n.* **1a.** The act of aiming. **b.** Skill at hitting a target: *a good aim.* **2.** The line of fire of an aimed weapon. **3.** A purpose or intention. [< Lat. *aestimāre,* to estimate.]

Syns: *direct, level, point, train* **v.**

aim·less (ām′lĭs) ►*adj.* Without direction or purpose. —**aim′less·ly** *adv.* —**aim′less·ness** *n.*

ain't (ānt) *Nonstandard* **1.** Am not. **2.** Used also as a contraction for *are not, is not, has not,* and *have not.*

Ai·nu (ī′no͞o) ►*n., pl.* **Ainu** or **-nus 1.** A member of an indigenous people inhabiting the northernmost islands of Japan. **2.** The language of the Ainu.

air (âr) ►*n.* **1a.** A colorless, odorless, tasteless, gaseous mixture, mainly nitrogen (78%) and oxygen (21%). **b.** The earth's atmosphere. **2.** The sky; firmament. **3.** A breeze or wind. **4.** Aircraft: *send troops by air.* **5a.** Public utterance; vent: *gave air to their grievances.* **b.** The medium of broadcast radio or television. **6a.** A manner of behaving that conveys an impression. **b.** A distinctive quality or appearance; aura: *an air of mystery.* **7. airs** Affected behavior; affectation. **8.** *Mus.* A melody or tune. ►*v.* **1.** To expose to air; ventilate. **2.** To give vent to publicly: *aired my complaints.* **3.** To broadcast on television or radio. —**idioms: in the air** Abroad; prevalent: *Excitement was in the air.* **up in the air** Not yet decided; uncertain. [< Gk. *aēr.*]

air·bag (âr′băg′) ►*n.* A bag recessed in an automobile interior and inflated upon impact in a crash to prevent passenger injury.

air·borne (âr′bôrn′) ►*adj.* **1.** Carried by or through the air: *airborne pollen.* **2.** In flight.

air brake ►*n.* A brake, esp. on a motor vehicle, that is operated by compressed air.

air·brush (âr′brŭsh′) ►*n.* An atomizer using compressed air to spray a liquid, such as paint, on a surface. —**air′brush** *v.*

air conditioner ►*n.* An apparatus for lowering the temperature and humidity of an enclosed space. —**air′-con·di′tion** *v.* —**air conditioning** *n.*

air·craft (âr′krăft′) ►*n., pl.* **aircraft** A machine, such as an airplane or helicopter, capable of atmospheric flight.

aircraft carrier ►*n.* A large naval vessel designed as a mobile air base.

air·date (âr′dāt′) ►*n.* The date a program is scheduled for broadcast.

air·drop (âr′drŏp′) ►*n.* A delivery, as of supplies, by parachute from aircraft. —**air′drop′** *v.*

Aire·dale terrier (âr′dāl′) ►*n.* A large terrier with a wiry tan coat marked with black. [After *Airedale*, a valley of north-central England.]

air·fare (âr′fâr′) ►*n.* Fare for travel by aircraft.

air·field (âr′fēld′) ►*n.* **1.** A runway or landing strip. **2.** An airport.

air·foil (âr′foil′) ►*n.* An aircraft part or surface, such as a wing, that controls stability, direction, lift, thrust, or propulsion.

air force ►*n.* The aviation branch of a country's armed forces.

air gun ►*n.* A gun discharged by compressed air.

air·head[1] (âr′hĕd′) ►*n. Slang* A silly, stupid person.

air·head[2] (âr′hĕd′) ►*n.* An area of hostile territory secured by paratroops. [AIR + (BEACH)-HEAD.]

air lane ►*n.* A regular route of travel for aircraft.

air·lift (âr′lĭft′) ►*n.* A system of transportation by aircraft when surface routes are blocked. —**air′lift′** *v.*

air·line (âr′līn′) ►*n.* A business providing air transportation for passengers and freight.

air·lin·er (âr′lī′nər) ►*n.* A large passenger airplane.

air·lock (âr′lŏk′) ►*n.* An airtight chamber, usu. located between two regions of unequal pressure, in which air pressure can be regulated.

air·mail (âr′māl′) ►*n.* **1.** The system of conveying mail by aircraft. **2.** Mail conveyed by aircraft. ►*v.* To send (e.g., a letter) by air. —**air′mail′** *adj.*

air·man (âr′mən) ►*n.* **1.** Any of the three lowest ranks in the US Air Force. **2.** An aviator.

air mass ►*n.* A large body of air with only small horizontal variations of temperature, pressure, and moisture.

air mile ►*n.* A nautical mile.

air·plane (âr′plān′) ►*n.* A self-propelled winged vehicle heavier than air and capable of flight.

air·play (âr′plā′) ►*n.* Broadcast time given to the playing of a song, movie, or other recording.

air·port (âr′pôrt′) ►*n.* A place where aircraft can take off and land, with accommodations for passengers and cargo.

air·pow·er or **air power** (âr′pou′ər) ►*n.* The strategic strength of a country's air force.

air raid ►*n.* An attack by military aircraft.

air rifle ►*n.* A low-powered rifle, such as a BB gun, that uses manually compressed air to fire small pellets.

air sac ►*n.* **1.** Any of several air-filled spaces in the body of a bird that are part of the respiratory system. **2.** See **alveolus** (sense 2).

air·ship (âr′shĭp′) ►*n.* A self-propelled lighter-than-air craft with directional control surfaces.

air·sick (âr′sĭk′) ►*adj.* Suffering nausea from the motion of air flight. —**air′sick′ness** *n.*

air·space or **air space** (âr′spās′) ►*n.* The portion of the atmosphere above a particular land area, esp. above a nation.

air·speed (âr′spēd′) ►*n.* The speed of an aircraft relative to the air.

air·strip (âr′strĭp′) ►*n.* An aircraft runway without airport facilities.

air·tight (âr′tīt′) ►*adj.* **1.** Impermeable by air. **2.** Solid; sound: *an airtight excuse.*

air·time (âr′tīm′) ►*n.* **1.** The time that a radio or television station is broadcasting. **2.** The scheduled time of a broadcast. **3.** The amount of time that a cell phone is connected to a network.

air-to-air (âr′tə-âr′) ►*adj.* Operating or fired between aircraft in flight: *air-to-air missiles.*

air·waves (âr′wāvz′) ►*pl.n.* **1.** The medium of radio waves, esp. as used by broadcast radio and television. **2.** Electromagnetic frequencies allocated for wireless broadcasting or communication.

air·way (âr′wā′) ►*n.* **1a.** A passageway or shaft in which air circulates. **b.** The upper passages of the respiratory system by which air reaches the lungs. **2a.** often **airways** An airline. **b.** A regular route of travel for aircraft.

air·wor·thy (âr′wûr′thē) ►*adj.* **-thi·er, -thi·est** Fit to fly. —**air′wor′thi·ness** *n.*

air·y (âr′ē) ►*adj.* **-i·er, -i·est 1a.** Open to the air; breezy: *airy bungalows.* **b.** Extensive in area or height; spacious: *an airy room.* **2.** High in the air; lofty: *airy skyscrapers.* **3.** Like air, esp.: **a.** Immaterial: *an airy apparition.* **b.** Light; delicate: *an airy dress.* **4.** Speculative and impractical. **5.** Haughty; affected. **6.** Lighthearted; merry. —**air′i·ly** *adv.* —**air′i·ness** *n.*

Syns: filmy, gauzy, gossamer, sheer adj.

aisle (īl) ►*n.* **1.** A passageway between rows of seats, as in a theater or airplane. **2.** A part of a church separated from the nave by a row of pillars or columns. **3.** A passageway for inside traffic, as in a store. [< Lat. *āla*, wing.]

a·jar (ə-jär′) ►*adv. & adj.* Partially opened: *left the door ajar.* [ME *on char*, in turning.]

AK ►*abbr.* Alaska

AKA ►*abbr.* also known as

Ak·bar (ăk′bär) "the Great." 1542–1605. Mughal emperor of India (1556–1605).

A·ki·hi·to (ä′kē-hē′tō) b. 1933. Emperor of Japan (assumed the throne 1989).

a·kim·bo (ə-kĭm′bō) ►*adv. & adj.* With hands on hips and elbows bowed outward. [ME *in kenebowe* (perh. orig., in jug handles : *kene*, jug + *bowe*, bow, bend).]

a·kin (ə-kĭn′) ►*adj.* **1.** Of the same kin; related by blood. **2.** Similar in quality or character; analogous. **3.** *Ling.* Cognate.

A·ki·ta (ä-kē′tə) ►*n.* A large dog developed in Japan for hunting. [After *Akita* prefecture in NW Honshu, Japan.]

Ak·kad (ăk′ăd′, ä′käd′) **1.** An ancient region of Mesopotamia in N Babylonia. **2.** An ancient city of Mesopotamia and capital of the Akkadian empire.

Ak·ka·di·an (ə-kā′dē-ən) ►*n.* **1.** A native of

ancient Akkad. **2.** The Semitic language of Mesopotamia. —**Ak·ka'di·an** *adj.*

AL ►*abbr.* **1.** Alabama **2.** American League

–al¹ ►*suff.* Of, relating to, or characterized by: *parental.* [< Lat. *-ālis.*]

–al² ►*suff.* Action; process: *retrieval.* [< Lat. *-ālia.*]

a·la (ā'lə) ►*n., pl.* **a·lae** (ā'lē) A winglike structure or part. [Lat. *āla,* wing.]

à la also **a la** (ä' lä, ä' lə) ►*prep.* In the style or manner of: *a poem à la Ogden Nash.* [< Fr. *à la mode de.*]

Al·a·bam·a (ăl'ə-băm'ə) A state of the SE US. Cap. Montgomery. —**Al'a·ba'mi·an** (-bā'mē-ən), **Al'a·bam'an** *adj. & n.*

al·a·bas·ter (ăl'ə-băs'tər) ►*n.* **1.** A translucent white or tinted gypsum. **2.** A translucent, often banded variety of calcite. [< Gk. *alabastros.*]

à la carte also **a la carte** (ä'lə kärt') ►*adv. & adj.* With a separate price for each item on the menu. [Fr., by the menu.]

a·lac·ri·ty (ə-lăk'rĭ-tē) ►*n.* **1.** Cheerful willingness; eagerness. **2.** Speed or quickness. [< Lat. *alacer,* lively.] —**a·lac'ri·tous** *adj.*

Al·a·mo (ăl'ə-mō') A mission in San Antonio, TX; besieged and taken by Mexico (1836) during the Texas Revolution.

à la mode (ä'lə mōd') ►*adj.* **1.** In the prevailing fashion. **2.** Served with ice cream: *apple pie à la mode.* [Fr.]

Al·a·ric (ăl'ər-ĭk) AD 370?–410. King of the Visigoths (395–410).

a·larm (ə-lärm') ►*n.* **1.** Sudden fear or concern caused by the realization of danger or an impending setback. **2.** A warning of danger. **3.** A device that signals a warning: *a fire alarm.* **4.** The sounding mechanism of an alarm clock. **5.** A call to arms. ►*v.* **1.** To frighten. **2.** To warn. **3.** To equip with or protect by an alarm: *The doors are alarmed at night.* [< OItal. *all' arme,* to arms.] —**a·larm'ing·ly** *adv.*

a·larm·ist (ə-lär'mĭst) ►*n.* One who needlessly alarms others. —**a·larm'ism** *n.*

a·las (ə-lăs') ►*interj.* Used to express sorrow, regret, or grief. [< OFr. *helas.*]

A·las·ka (ə-lăs'kə) A state of the US in extreme NW North America. Cap. Juneau. —**A·las'-kan** *adj. & n.*

Alaska Native ►*n.* A member of any of the aboriginal people of Alaska, including Native American and Eskimo peoples.

alb (ălb) ►*n.* A long white linen robe worn by a priest or minister during church services. [< Lat. *albus,* white.]

al·ba·core (ăl'bə-kôr') ►*n., pl.* **al·ba·core** or **-cores** A large tuna that is commercially important as a source of canned fish. [< Ar. *al-bakūra.*]

Al·ba·ni·a (ăl-bā'nē-ə, -bān'yə) A country of SE Europe on the Adriatic Sea. Cap. Tiranë.

Al·ba·ni·an (ăl-bā'nē-ən, -bān'yən) ►*n.* **1.** A native or inhabitant of Albania. **2.** The Indo-European language of the Albanians. —**Al·ba'ni·an** *adj.*

Al·ba·ny (ôl'bə-nē) The capital of NY, in the E part on the Hudson R.

al·ba·tross (ăl'bə-trôs', -trŏs') ►*n., pl.* **-tross** or **-tross·es** **1.** Any of several large web-footed seabirds. **2.** A source of worry or distress. [< Ar. *al-ġaṭṭās,* sea eagle.]

al·be·do (ăl-bē'dō) ►*n., pl.* **-dos** **1.** The reflecting power of a surface, as of a planet. **2.** The white tissue inside a citrus fruit rind. [LLat. *albēdō,* whiteness.]

Al·bee (ôl'bē, ŏl'-), **Edward Franklin** b. 1928. Amer. playwright.

al·be·it (ôl-bē'ĭt, ăl-) ►*conj.* Even though; although: *clear albeit cold weather.* [ME, although it be.]

Al·bert (ăl'bərt), Prince. 1819–61. German-born consort (1840–61) of Queen Victoria.

Albert, Lake A lake of E-central Africa located on the Dem. Rep. of the Congo–Uganda border.

Al·ber·ta (ăl-bûr'tə) A province of W Canada between British Columbia and Saskatchewan. Cap. Edmonton. —**Al·ber'tan** *adj. & n.*

Al·ber·tus Mag·nus (ăl-bûr'təs măg'nəs), Saint. 1206?–80. German religious philosopher.

al·bi·no (ăl-bī'nō) ►*n., pl.* **-nos** A person or animal lacking normal pigmentation, esp. one having abnormally white skin and hair and pink eyes. [Port. < Lat. *albus,* white.] —**al'bi·nism** (ăl'bə-nĭz'əm) *n.*

Al·bright (ôl'brīt), **Madeleine Korbel** b. 1937. Czechoslovakian-born Amer. diplomat.

al·bum (ăl'bəm) ►*n.* **1a.** A book with blank pages for preserving collections, as of stamps or autographs. **b.** A collection of personal photographs arranged for private viewing, as in a book or on a computer. **2a.** A set of phonograph records in one binding. **b.** A recording of different musical pieces, esp. a phonograph record. [Lat., blank tablet < *albus,* white.]

al·bu·men (ăl-byōō'mən) ►*n.* **1.** The white of an egg, mainly albumin dissolved in water. **2.** See **albumin.** [Lat. *albūmen* < *albus,* white.]

al·bu·min (ăl-byōō'mĭn) ►*n.* A class of proteins found in egg white, blood serum, milk, and many other animal and plant tissues. —**al·bu'mi·nous** *adj.*

Al·bu·quer·que (ăl'bə-kûr'kē) A city of central NM SW of Santa Fe.

Al·ca·traz (ăl'kə-trăz') A rocky island of N CA in San Francisco Bay; site of a prison until 1963.

al·ca·zar (ăl-kăz'ər, ăl'kə-zär') ►*n.* A Spanish palace or fortress. [< Ar. *al-qaṣr,* castle.]

al·che·my (ăl'kə-mē) ►*n.* **1.** A medieval chemical philosophy concerned primarily with the transmutation of base metals into gold. **2.** A seemingly magical power. [< Ar. *al-kīmiyā',* chemistry.] —**al·chem'i·cal** (ăl-kĕm'-ĭ-kəl), **al·chem'ic** *adj.* —**al·chem'i·cal·ly** *adv.* —**al'chem·ist** *n.*

Al·ci·bi·a·des (ăl'sə-bī'ə-dēz') 450?–404 BC. Athenian politician and general.

al·co·hol (ăl'kə-hôl', -hŏl') ►*n.* **1.** Any of a series of organic compounds with the general formula $C_nH_{2n+1}OH$. **2.** A colorless flammable liquid, C_2H_5OH, obtained by fermentation of sugars and starches and used as a solvent, in drugs, and in intoxicating beverages; ethanol. **3.** Intoxicating liquor containing alcohol. [< Ar. *al-kuḥl,* antimony powder.]

al·co·hol·ic (ăl'kə-hô'lĭk, -hŏl'ĭk) ►*adj.* **1.** Of, containing, or resulting from alcohol. **2.** Suffering from alcoholism. ►*n.* A person who suffers from alcoholism.

al·co·hol·ism (ăl'kə-hô-lĭz'əm, -hŏ-) ►*n.* A disorder characterized by the excessive consumption of and dependence on alcoholic beverages.

Al·cott (ôl′kət, -kŏt), **Louisa May** 1832–88. Amer. writer.

Louisa May Alcott

al·cove (ăl′kōv′) ▸n. A small recessed extension of a room. [< Ar. *al-qubba*, vault.]

al·de·hyde (ăl′də-hīd′) ▸n. Any of a class of highly reactive organic chemical compounds obtained by oxidation of alcohols. [< NLat., *al(cohol) dehyd(rogenatum)*, dehydrogenized alcohol.]

Al·den (ôl′dən), **John** 1599?–1687. Amer. Pilgrim colonist.

al·der (ôl′dər) ▸n. A deciduous shrub or tree having toothed leaves and woody, conelike catkins. [< OE *alor.*]

al·der·man (ôl′dər-mən) ▸n. A member of a municipal legislative body. [< OE *ealdorman*, nobleman < *eald*, old.]

ale (āl) ▸n. A fermented alcoholic beverage with malt and hops, similar to beer. [< OE *ealu.*]

a·le·a·to·ry (ā′lē-ə-tôr′ē) ▸adj. Dependent on chance. [< Lat. *ālea*, dice.]

a·lee (ə-lē′) ▸adv. *Naut.* Away from the wind.

A·lem·bert (ăl′əm-bâr′, ä-läɴ-bĕr′), **Jean Le Rond d'** 1717–83. French mathematician and philosopher.

a·lem·bic (ə-lĕm′bĭk) ▸n. An apparatus formerly used for distilling. [< Ar. *al-'anbīq.*]

a·lert (ə-lûrt′) ▸adj. **1.** Vigilantly attentive; watchful. See Synonyms at **careful. 2.** Mentally perceptive; quick. **3.** Brisk or lively. ▸n. **1.** A signal that warns of attack or danger. **2.** A period of watchfulness or preparation for action. ▸v. To notify of approaching danger; warn. —*idiom:* **on the alert** Watchful for danger or opportunity. [< Ital. *all'erta*, on the watch.] —**a·lert′ness** *n.*

A·leut (ə-lōōt′, ăl′ē-ōōt′) ▸n., *pl.* **Aleut** or **A·leuts 1.** A member of a Native American people inhabiting the Aleutian Islands and coastal areas of SW Alaska. **2.** Either or both of the two languages of the Aleut. See Usage Note at **Native American.** —**A·leu′tian** (ə-lōō′-shən) *adj. & n.*

Aleutian Islands A chain of volcanic islands of SW AK curving about 1,850 km (1,150 mi) W from the mainland and separating the Bering Sea from the Pacific.

Al·ex·an·der I¹ (ăl′ĭg-zăn′dər) 1777–1825. Czar of Russia (1801–25).

Alexander I² 1876–1903. King of Serbia (1889–1903).

Alexander I³ 1888–1934. King of Yugoslavia (1921–34).

Alexander II 1818–81. Czar of Russia (1855–81); emancipated the serfs (1861).

Alexander III "the Great." 356–323 bc. King of Macedon (336–323) and conqueror of Asia Minor, Syria, Egypt, Babylonia, and Persia.

Alexander Archipelago A group of more than 1,000 islands in SE AK.

Al·ex·an·dri·a (ăl′ĭg-zăn′drē-ə) A city of N Egypt on the Mediterranean Sea on the W tip of the Nile Delta.

Al·ex·an·dri·an (ăl′ĭg-zăn′drē-ən) ▸adj. **1.** Relating to Alexander the Great. **2.** Relating to Alexandria, Egypt. **3.** Relating to a learned school of Hellenistic literature, science, and philosophy at Alexandria in the last three centuries bc.

al·ex·an·drine (ăl′ĭg-zăn′drĭn) ▸n. **1.** A line of English verse composed in iambic hexameter. **2.** A line of French verse consisting of 12 syllables. [< OFr. < *Alexandre*, a romance about Alexander the Great.]

a·lex·i·a (ə-lĕk′sē-ə) ▸n. Loss of the ability to read, usu. caused by brain lesions. [< A⁻¹ + Gk. *lexis*, speech.]

al·fal·fa (ăl-făl′fə) ▸n. A cloverlike perennial herb widely cultivated for forage. [< Ar. *al-faṣfaṣa.*]

Al·fon·so XIII (ăl-fŏn′sō) 1886–1941. King of Spain (1886–1931).

Al·fred (ăl′frĭd) "the Great." 849–899. King of the West Saxons (871–899).

al·fres·co (ăl-frĕs′kō) ▸adv. & adj. In the fresh air; outdoors. [Ital. *al fresco.*]

al·ga (ăl′gə) ▸n., *pl.* **-gae** (-jē) Any of various chiefly aquatic photosynthetic organisms, ranging from single-celled forms to the giant kelp. [Lat., seaweed.] —**al′gal** *adj.*

al·ge·bra (ăl′jə-brə) ▸n. A branch of mathematics in which symbols represent numbers or members of a specified set and express general relationships that hold for all members in the set. [< Ar. *al-jabr.*] —**al′ge·bra′ic** (-brā′ĭk) *adj.*

Al·ge·ri·a (ăl-jîr′ē-ə) A country of NW Africa on the Mediterranean Sea E of Morocco and W of Tunisia and Libya. Cap. Algiers. —**Al·ge′ri·an** *adj. & n.*

–algia ▸suff. Pain: *neuralgia.* [Gk. < *algos*, pain.]

Al·giers (ăl-jîrz′) The capital of Algeria, in the N on the Mediterranean Sea.

Al·gon·qui·an (ăl-gŏng′kwē-ən, -kē-ən) also **Al·gon·ki·an** (-kē-ən) ▸n., *pl.* **-an** or **-ans 1.** A family of North American Indian languages spoken or formerly spoken in an area from Labrador to the Carolinas between the Atlantic coast and the Rocky Mountains. **2.** A member of a people traditionally speaking an Algonquian language. —**Al·gon′qui·an** *adj.*

Al·gon·quin (ăl-gŏng′kwĭn, ăl-gŏng′kĭn) ▸n., *pl.* **-quin** or **-quins 1a.** A member of any of various Native American peoples inhabiting the Ottawa R. valley of Quebec and Ontario. **b.** Any of the varieties of Ojibwa spoken by these peoples. **2a.** A member of an Algonquian people. **b.** An Algonquian language. —**Al·gon′quin** *adj.*

al·go·rithm (ăl′gə-rĭth′əm) ▸n. A step-by-step problem-solving procedure. [Ult. after Muhammad ibn-Musa al-*Khwarizmi.*] —**al′go·rith′mic** *adj.*

A·li (ä-lē′), **Muhammad** Orig. Cassius Marcellus Clay. b. 1942. Amer. prizefighter.

Muhammad Ali
photographed in 2005

a·li·as (ā′lē-əs) ►*n.* **1.** An assumed name. **2.** *Comp.* An alternate name or address, esp. an e-mail address that forwards incoming e-mail to another address. ►*adv.* Also known as; otherwise. [Lat. *aliās*, otherwise.]

al·i·bi (ăl′ə-bī′) ►*n., pl.* **-bis 1.** *Law* A form of defense whereby a defendant attempts to prove that he or she was elsewhere when the crime was committed. **2.** An excuse. [Lat., elsewhere.]

a·li·en (ā′lē-ən, āl′yən) ►*adj.* **1.** Owing political allegiance to another country; foreign. **2.** Belonging to a very different place or society. See Synonyms at **foreign. 3.** Dissimilar or opposed: *ideas alien to her nature.* ►*n.* **1.** An unnaturalized foreign resident of a country. **2.** A person from a very different group or place. **3.** An outsider. **4.** A creature from outer space. [< Lat. *aliēnus.*]

al·ien·a·ble (āl′yə-nə-bəl, ā′lē-ə-) ►*adj.* *Law* Transferrable to the ownership of another. —**al′ien·a·bil′i·ty** *n.*

al·ien·ate (āl′yə-nāt′, ā′lē-ə-) ►*v.* **-at·ed, -at·ing 1.** To make unfriendly or hostile; estrange. **2.** *Law* To transfer (property or a right) to the ownership of another. —**al′ien·a′tor** *n.*

al·ien·a·tion (āl′yə-nā′shən, ā′lē-ə-) ►*n.* **1.** The act of alienating or the condition of being alienated. **2.** Emotional isolation or dissociation. **3.** The act of transferring property or title to another.

a·light¹ (ə-līt′) ►*v.* **a·light·ed** or **a·lit** (ə-līt′), **a·light·ing 1.** To come down and settle, as after flight. **2.** To dismount. [< OE *ālīhtan.*]

a·light² (ə-līt′) ►*adj.* **1.** Burning; lighted. **2.** Illuminated. —**a·light′** *adv.*

a·lign (ə-līn′) ►*v.* **a·ligned, a·lign·ing 1.** To arrange or be arranged in a straight line. **2.** To adjust (e.g., parts of a mechanism) to produce a proper orientation. **3.** To ally (oneself) with one side of an argument or cause. [< OFr. *ligne,* LINE¹.] —**a·lign′ment** *n.*

a·like (ə-līk′) ►*adj.* Having close resemblance; similar. ►*adv.* In the same manner or to the same degree. [< OE *gelīc.*] —**a·like′ness** *n.*

al·i·ment (ăl′ə-mənt) ►*n.* **1.** Something that nourishes; food. **2.** Support. [< Lat. *alere,* nourish.]

al·i·men·ta·ry (ăl′ə-měn′tə-rē, -trē) ►*adj.* **1.** Relating to food, nutrition, or digestion. **2.** Providing nourishment.

alimentary canal ►*n.* See **digestive tract.**

al·i·mo·ny (ăl′ə-mō′nē) ►*n., pl.* **-nies** *Law* An allowance for support usu. made under court order to a divorced person by the former spouse. [Lat. *alimōnia,* sustenance.]

al·i·phat·ic (ăl′ə-făt′ĭk) ►*adj.* Relating to a group of organic chemical compounds in which the carbon atoms are linked in open chains. [< Gk. *aleiphar, aleiphat-,* oil.]

al·i·quot (ăl′ĭ-kwŏt′) *Math.* ►*adj.* Relating to an exact divisor or factor, esp. of an integer. ►*n.* An aliquot part. [Lat. *aliquot,* a number of.]

a·lit·er·ate (ā-lĭt′ər-ĭt) ►*adj.* Able to read but not interested in reading. —**a·lit′er·a·cy** *n.*

a·live (ə-līv′) ►*adj.* **1.** Having life; living. See Synonyms at **living. 2.** In existence or operation. **3.** Full of living things. **4.** Animated; lively. —**idiom: alive to** Aware of; alert to.

a·liz·a·rin (ə-lĭz′ər-ĭn) ►*n.* An orange-red crystalline compound, $C_{14}H_8O_4$, used in dyes. [Prob. < Ar. *al-'uṣāra,* juice.]

al·ka·li (ăl′kə-lī′) ►*n., pl.* **-lis** or **-lies 1.** A carbonate or hydroxide of an alkali metal, the aqueous solution of which is basic in reactions. **2.** Any of various soluble mineral salts found in natural water and arid soils. **3.** A substance having highly basic properties; a strong base. [< Ar. *al-qily,* ashes, lye.]

alkali metal ►*n.* Any of a group of highly reactive metallic elements, including lithium, sodium, potassium, rubidium, cesium, and francium.

al·ka·line (ăl′kə-lĭn, -līn′) ►*adj.* **1.** Relating to or containing an alkali. **2.** Having a pH greater than 7. **3.** Having a relatively low concentration of hydrogen ions. —**al′ka·lin′i·ty** (-lĭn′ĭ-tē) *n.*

al·ka·line-earth metal (ăl′kə-lĭn-ûrth′, -līn′-) ►*n.* Any of a group of metallic elements, esp. calcium, strontium, magnesium, and barium, but usu. including beryllium and radium.

al·ka·lize (ăl′kə-līz′) also **al·ka·lin·ize** (-lə-nīz′) ►*v.* **-lized, -liz·ing** also **-ized, -iz·ing** To make alkaline or become an alkali. —**al′ka·li·za′tion** *n.*

al·ka·loid (ăl′kə-loid′) ►*n.* Any of various organic compounds containing nitrogen, occurring in many vascular plants, and including nicotine, quinine, cocaine, and caffeine. —**al′ka·loi′dal** *adj.*

al·ka·lo·sis (ăl′kə-lō′sĭs) ►*n.* Abnormally high alkalinity of the blood and body fluids.

al·kyd (ăl′kĭd) ►*n.* A widely used durable synthetic resin. [Ult. < ALCOHOL + (ACI)D.]

all (ôl) ►*adj.* **1.** Being the total number, amount, or quantity: *All the windows are open. Deal all the cards.* See Synonyms at **whole. 2.** Constituting or being the total. **3.** The utmost possible. **4.** Every: *all kinds of trouble.* **5.** Any whatsoever: *beyond all doubt.* ►*n.* Everything one has: *They gave their all.* ►*pron.* **1.** The total number; totality: *All the kittens are black.* **2.** Everyone; everything: *justice for all.* ►*adv.* **1a.** Wholly; completely: *directions that were all wrong.* **b.** So much: *I am all the better for that experience.* **c.** Used as an intensive: *Then he got all mad and left.* **2.** Each; apiece: *a score of five all.* —**idioms: all along** From the beginning. **all but** Nearly; almost: *all but crying with relief.*

all in Tired; exhausted. **all in all 1.** Everything considered. **2.** Used in poker as a declaration that one is staking all of one's chips. **be all** *Informal* To say: *He's all, "Why did you do that?"* [< OE *eall.*]

Al·lah (ä′lə, ə-lä′) ►*n.* God, esp. in Islam. [Ar. *Allāh* : *al-*, the + *'ilāh*, god.]

all-A·mer·i·can (ôl′ə-mĕr′ĭ-kən) ►*adj.* **1.** Representative of the people of the US; typically American. **2.** *Sports* Chosen as the best amateur in the US at a particular position or event. —**All′-A·mer′i·can** *n.*

all-a·round (ôl′ə-round′) also **all-round** (ôl′-round′) ►*adj.* **1.** In all or most respects: *We had an all-around good time.* **2.** Comprehensive: *a good all-around education.* **3.** Versatile: *an all-around athlete.*

al·lay (ə-lā′) ►*v.* **1.** To calm or pacify (an emotion): *allayed their fears.* **2.** To reduce the intensity of; relieve: *allay skin irritation.* [< OE *ālecgan*, to lay aside.]

all clear ►*n.* A signal, usu. by siren, that an air raid is over or a danger has passed.

al·lege (ə-lĕj′) ►*v.* **-leged, -leg·ing 1.** To assert to be true; affirm: *alleged her innocence of the charges.* **2.** To assert prior to a final determination: *The indictment alleges that he took bribes.* **3.** To state (e.g., a plea) in support or denial of a claim or accusation: *alleges temporary insanity.* [< LLat. *exlītigāre*, to clear : EX– + Lat. *lītigāre*, LITIGATE.] —**al′le·ga′tion** (ăl′ĭ-gā′shən) *n.* —**al·lege′a·ble** *adj.* —**al·leg′er** *n.*

al·leged (ə-lĕjd′, ə-lĕj′ĭd) ►*adj.* Represented as existing or as being as described but not so proved; supposed: *an alleged traitor.* —**al·leg′ed·ly** (ə-lĕj′ĭd-lē) *adv.*

Al·le·ghe·ny Mountains (ăl′ĭ-gā′nē) also **Al·le·ghe·nies** (-nēz) A range forming the W part of the Appalachian Mts. and extending from N PA to SW VA.

Allegheny River A river rising in N-central PA and flowing about 523 km (325 mi) to Pittsburgh, where it forms the Ohio R.

al·le·giance (ə-lē′jəns) ►*n.* Loyalty or the obligation of loyalty, as to a nation, sovereign, or cause. See Synonyms at **fidelity.** [< OFr. *lige*, LIEGE.]

al·le·go·ry (ăl′ĭ-gôr′ē) ►*n., pl.* **-ries 1.** The use of characters or events to represent ideas or principles in a story, play, or picture. **2.** A story, play, or picture in which such representation occurs. **3.** A symbolic representation. [< Gk. *allēgorein*, interpret.] —**al′le·gor′ic, al′le·gor′i·cal** *adj.* —**al′le·gor′i·cal·ly** *adv.* —**al′le·go′rist** *n.*

al·le·gret·to (ăl′ĭ-grĕt′ō) ►*adv. & adj. Mus.* In a moderately quick tempo. [Ital.]

al·le·gro (ə-lĕg′rō, ə-lā′grō) ►*adv. & adj. Mus.* In a quick, lively tempo. [< Lat. *alacer*, lively.]

al·lele (ə-lēl′) ►*n.* Any of the alternative forms of a gene or other homologous DNA sequence. [Ger. *Allel.*] —**al·le′lic** (-lē′lĭk, -lĕl′ĭk) *adj.*

al·le·lop·a·thy (ə-lē-lŏp′ə-thē, ăl′ə-) ►*n.* The inhibition of growth of one plant by a chemical released by another plant. [Gk. *allēlōn*, reciprocally + -PATHY.] —**al·le′lo·path′ic** (-lē′lə-păth′ĭk, -lĕl′ə-) *adj.*

al·le·lu·ia (ăl′ə-loō′yə) ►*interj.* Hallelujah.

Al·len (ăl′ən) ►*n.* **1.** Of or relating to a bolt or screw with a head having a hexagonal socket: *an Allen bolt; an Allen screw.* **2.** Of or relating to a usu. L-shaped wrench or screwdriver that

fits such a socket. [Orig. a trademark.]

Allen, Ethan 1738–89. Amer. Revolutionary soldier.

Al·len·de Gos·sens (ä-yĕn′dä gō′sĕns), **Salvador** 1908–73. Chilean president (1970–73); died during a coup d'état.

al·ler·gen (ăl′ər-jən) ►*n.* A substance that causes an allergy. —**al′ler·gen′ic** (-jĕn′ĭk) *adj.*

al·ler·gist (ăl′ər-jĭst) ►*n.* A physician specializing in treating allergies.

al·ler·gy (ăl′ər-jē) ►*n., pl.* **-gies** An abnormally high sensitivity to certain substances, such as pollens, foods, or microorganisms. [< ALLO– + Gk. *ergon*, action.] —**al·ler′gic** (ə-lûr′jĭk) *adj.*

al·le·vi·ate (ə-lē′vē-āt′) ►*v.* **-at·ed, -at·ing 1.** To make more bearable: *alleviate pain.* **2.** To lessen or reduce: *alleviate unemployment.* [LLat. *alleviāre*, lighten.] —**al·le′vi·a′tion** *n.*

al·ley (ăl′ē) ►*n., pl.* **-leys 1.** A narrow street or passageway between or behind buildings. **2.** A straight, narrow course or track. —*idiom:* **up (one's) alley** Compatible with one's interests or qualifications. [< OFr. *aller*, to walk < Lat. *ambulāre.*]

alley cat ►*n.* A homeless or stray cat.

al·ley·way (ăl′ē-wā′) ►*n.* A narrow passage between buildings.

al·li·ance (ə-lī′əns) ►*n.* **1a.** A close, formal association of nations or other groups. **b.** A formal agreement establishing such an association. **2.** A connection based on kinship, marriage, or common interest. **3.** Close similarity in nature or type.

al·lied (ə-līd′, ăl′īd′) ►*adj.* **1.** Joined in an alliance. **2.** Of a similar nature; related: *city planning and allied studies.*

al·li·ga·tor (ăl′ĭ-gā′tər) ►*n.* **1.** A large amphibious reptile having sharp teeth, powerful jaws, and a broader, shorter snout than the related crocodile. **2.** Leather made from the hide of one of these reptiles. [< Sp. *el lagarto*, the lizard.]

alligator pear ►*n.* See **avocado.**

all-im·por·tant (ôl′ĭm-pôr′tnt) ►*adj.* Of the greatest importance; crucial.

al·lit·er·a·tion (ə-lĭt′ə-rā′shən) ►*n.* The repetition of identical or similar sounds at the beginning of words or in stressed syllables, as in *"on scrolls of silver snowy sentences"* (Hart Crane). [< AD– + Lat. *littera*, letter.] —**al·lit′er·ate** *v.* —**al·lit′er·a′tive** *adj.* —**al·lit′er·a·tive·ly** *adv.*

allo– ►*pref.* Other; different: *allophone.* [Gk. < *allos*, other.]

al·lo·cate (ăl′ə-kāt′) ►*v.* **-cat·ed, -cat·ing 1.** To set apart; designate. **2.** To distribute; allot: *allocate rations.* [Med.Lat. *allocāre.*] —**al′lo·ca·ble** (-kə-bəl) *adj.* —**al′lo·ca′tion** *n.*

   Syns: *appropriate, assign, designate, earmark* v.

al·lo·morph (ăl′ə-môrf′) ►*n.* Any of the variant forms of a morpheme. —**al′lo·mor′phic** *adj.* —**al′lo·mor′phism** *n.*

al·lo·phone (ăl′ə-fōn′) ►*n.* A predictable phonetic variant of a phoneme. —**al′lo·phon′ic** (-fŏn′ĭk) *adj.*

al·lot (ə-lŏt′) ►*v.* **-lot·ted, -lot·ting 1.** To parcel out; distribute by lot. **2.** To assign as a portion; allocate. [< OFr. *aloter.*] —**al·lot′ment** *n.* —**al·lot′ter** *n.*

al·lot·ro·py (ə-lŏt′rə-pē) ►*n.* The existence of two or more crystalline or molecular structural forms of an element that have different chemical or physical attributes. —**al′lo·trope** (ăl′ə-trōp′) *n.* —**al′lo·trop′ic** (-trŏp′ĭk, -trō′pĭk), **al′lo·trop′i·cal** *adj.*

all-out (ôl′out′) ▸*adj.* Using all available means or resources: *an all-out sprint.*

all over ▸*adv.* **1.** Over the whole area. **2.** Everywhere: *searched all over for my keys.* **3.** In all respects. —**all′-o′ver** *adj.*

al·low (ə-lou′) ▸*v.* **1.** To let do or happen; permit: *Smoking is not allowed here.* **2.** To permit the presence of: *Dogs are allowed in the park.* **3.** To make provision for: *The schedule allows time for a break.* **4.** To grant as a discount. **5.** *Regional* To admit; grant: *I allowed he was right.* —*phrasal verbs:* **allow for** To make a provision for: *allow for bad weather.* **allow of** To admit: *a poem allowing of several interpretations.* [< OFr. *allouer.*] —**al·low′a·ble** *adj.* —**al·low′a·bly** *adv.*

al·low·ance (ə-lou′əns) ▸*n.* **1.** The act of allowing or an amount allowed. **2.** Something, such as money, given at regular intervals or for a specific purpose. **3.** A small amount of money regularly given to a child, often as payment for chores. **4.** A price reduction. **5.** A consideration for circumstances: *an allowance for breakage.*

al·low·ed·ly (ə-lou′ĭd-lē) ▸*adv.* By general admission; admittedly.

al·loy (ăl′oi′, ə-loi′) ▸*n.* **1.** A homogeneous mixture of two or more metals: *Brass is an alloy of zinc and copper.* **2.** Something added that lowers value or purity. [< Lat. *alligāre,* bind to.] —**al·loy′** *v.*

all-pur·pose (ôl′pûr′pəs) ▸*adj.* Having many uses.

all right ▸*adj.* **1.** In satisfactory order. **2.** Correct: *Your answers are all right.* **3.** Heatlhy or untroubled: *I am feeling all right again.* **4.** Average; mediocre. ▸*adv.* **1.** In a satisfactory way; adequately. **2.** Very well; yes. **3.** Without a doubt: *It's cold, all right.*

all-round (ôl′round′) ▸*adj.* Var. of **all-around.**

All Saints′ Day ▸*n.* November 1, a Christian feast honoring all the saints.

All Souls′ Day ▸*n. Rom. Cath. Ch.* November 2, the day on which prayers are offered for the souls in purgatory.

all·spice (ôl′spīs′) ▸*n.* The dried, nearly ripe berries of a tropical American evergreen tree, used as a spice.

all-ter·rain vehicle (ôl′tə-rān′) ▸*n.* A small cabless motor vehicle having three or more wheels for use over rugged terrain.

all-star (ôl′stär′) ▸*adj.* Made up wholly of star performers.

all-time (ôl′tīm′) ▸*adj.* Unsurpassed by any others: *an all-time broad jump record.*

all told ▸*adv.* With everything considered; in all.

al·lude (ə-lōōd′) ▸*v.* **-lud·ed, -lud·ing** To make an indirect reference. [Lat. *allūdere,* play with.]

al·lure (ə-lōōr′) ▸*v.* **-lured, -lur·ing** To attract with something desirable; entice. ▸*n.* The power to attract; enticement. [< OFr. *alurer.*] —**al·lure′ment** *n.* —**al·lur′ing·ly** *adv.*

al·lu·sion (ə-lōō′zhən) ▸*n.* **1.** The act of alluding; indirect reference. **2.** An indirect reference: *an allusion to classical mythology in a poem.* [< LLat. *allūsiō, allūsiōn-,* a playing with.] —**al·lu′sive** (-sĭv) *adj.* —**al·lu′sive·ly** *adv.*

al·lu·vi·on (ə-lōō′vē-ən) ▸*n.* **1.** See **alluvium.**

2. The flow of water against a shore or bank. [Lat. *alluviō, alluviōn-* < *alluere,* to wash against; see ALLUVIUM.]

al·lu·vi·um (ə-lōō′vē-əm) ▸*n., pl.* **-vi·ums** or **-vi·a** (-vē-ə) Sediment deposited by flowing water, as in a riverbed or delta. [< Lat. *alluere,* wash against : AD– + *luere,* wash.] —**al·lu′vi·al** *adj.*

al·ly (ə-lī′, ăl′ī) ▸*v.* **-lied, -ly·ing 1.** To unite in a formal relationship, as by treaty or contract. **2.** To join with another or others out of mutual interest. ▸*n., pl.* **-lies** One allied with another, esp. by treaty or contract. [< Lat. *alligāre,* bind to.]

al·ma ma·ter or **Al·ma Ma·ter** (ăl′mə mä′tər, äl′mə) ▸*n.* **1.** The school that one has attended. **2.** The anthem of a school or college. [Lat. *alma māter,* nourishing mother.]

al·ma·nac (ôl′mə-năk′, ăl′-) ▸*n.* An annual publication in calendar form with weather forecasts, astronomical information, tide tables, and other information. [Ult. < Ar., al-manāḫ.]

Al·ma·ty (äl′mə-tē′) A city of SE Kazakhstan near the Chinese border.

al·might·y (ôl-mī′tē) ▸*adj.* Omnipotent; all-powerful. [< OE *ealmihtig :* *eall,* all + *miht,* MIGHT[1].] —**al·might′i·ly** *adv.*

al·mond (ä′mənd, äl′-, ôl′-, ăm′ənd) ▸*n.* **1.** A deciduous tree having pink flowers and leathery fruits. **2.** The kernel of this tree, eaten or used for flavoring. [< LLat. *amandula.*]

al·most (ôl′mōst′, ôl-mōst′) ▸*adv.* Slightly short of; not quite: *almost time to go; was almost asleep.* [< OE *ealmǣst.*]

alms (ämz) ▸*pl.n.* Money or goods given as charity to the poor. [< Gk. *eleēmosunē* < *eleos,* pity.]

alms·house (ämz′hous′) ▸*n.* A poorhouse.

al·oe (ăl′ō) ▸*n.* **1.** Any of various chiefly African plants having rosettes of succulent, often spiny-margined leaves. **2. aloes** *(takes sing. v.)* A laxative obtained from the juice of a certain aloe. [< Gk. *aloē.*]

aloe ver·a (věr′ə, vîr′ə) ▸*n.* **1.** An aloe having fleshy serrated leaves and yellow flowers. **2.** The gel obtained from its leaves, widely used in cosmetics. [Lat. *aloē,* ALOE + *vērus,* true.]

a·loft (ə-lôft′, -lŏft′) ▸*adv.* **1.** In or into a high place. **2.** *Naut.* At or toward the upper rigging. [< ON *ā lopt,* in the air.]

a·lo·ha (ə-lō′ə, ä-lō′hä′) ▸*interj.* Used as a greeting or farewell. [Hawaiian.]

a·lone (ə-lōn′) ▸*adj.* **1.** Apart from others; solitary. **2.** Without anyone or anything else; only. **3.** Separate from all others of the same class. **4.** Without equal; unique. [ME.] —**a·lone′** *adv.* —**a·lone′ness** *n.*

a·long (ə-lông′, -lŏng′) ▸*prep.* **1.** Over the length of: *walked along the path.* **2.** On a course parallel and close to. **3.** In accordance with: *The vote split along party lines.* ▸*adv.* **1.** Forward; onward: *moving along.* **2.** As company: *Bring your friend along.* **3.** In accompaniment; together. See Usage Note at **together. 4.** With one; at hand: *had my camera along.* **5.** Advanced to some degree: *getting along in years.* [< OE *andlang.*]

a·long·shore (ə-lông′shôr′, -lŏng′-) ▸*adv.* Along, near, or by the shore.

a·long·side (ə-lông′sīd′, -lŏng′-) ▸*adv.* Along, near, at, or to the side. ▸*prep.* By the side of; side by side with.

a·loof (ə-lōōf′) ►*adj.* Distant or reserved in manner or social relations. ►*adv.* Apart. [A⁻² + *luff,* windward side of a ship.] —**a·loof′ly** *adv.* —**a·loof′ness** *n.*

al·o·pe·cia (ăl′ə-pē′shə, -shē-ə) ►*n.* Loss of hair, esp. as a result of disease. [Lat. *alōpecia,* fox-mange, ult. < Gk. *alōpēx,* fox.]

a·loud (ə-loud′) ►*adv.* **1.** Using the voice; orally: *Read this passage aloud.* **2.** In a loud tone; loudly: *crying aloud for help.*

al·pac·a (ăl-păk′ə) ►*n., pl.* **-a** or **-as 1.** A domesticated South American mammal related to the llama and having fine long wool. **2a.** The silky wool of this mammal. **b.** Cloth made from alpaca. [Am.Sp.]

al·pen·horn (ăl′pən-hôrn′) ►*n.* A long curved wooden horn used by herders in the Alps to call cows to pasture. [Ger.]

alpenhorn

al·pha (ăl′fə) ►*n.* **1.** The 1st letter of the Greek alphabet. **2.** The first in a series. [Gk., of Phoenician orig.]

al·pha·bet (ăl′fə-bĕt′) ►*n.* **1.** The letters of a language, arranged in a customary order. **2.** A set of basic parts or elements. [< Gk. *alpha,* ALPHA + *bēta,* BETA.]

al·pha·bet·i·cal (ăl′fə-bĕt′ĭ-kəl) also **al·pha·bet·ic** (-bĕt′ĭk) ►*adj.* **1.** Arranged in the customary order of the letters of a language. **2.** Relating to or expressed by an alphabet. —**al′pha·bet′i·cal·ly** *adv.*

al·pha·bet·ize (ăl′fə-bĭ-tīz′) ►*v.* **-ized, -iz·ing** To arrange in alphabetical order. —**al′pha·bet′i·za′tion** *n.* —**al′pha·bet·iz′er** *n.*

alpha helix ►*n.* A protein structure characterized by a single, spiral chain of amino acids stabilized by hydrogen bonds.

al·pha·nu·mer·ic (ăl′fə-nōō-mĕr′ĭk, -nyōō-) also **al·pha·mer·ic** (-fə-mĕr′ĭk) ►*adj.* Consisting of both letters and numbers, sometimes with punctuation marks or other symbols.

alpha particle ►*n.* A positively charged particle, indistinguishable from a helium atom nucleus, consisting of two protons and two neutrons.

alpha ray ►*n.* A narrow beam of alpha particles.

alpha wave also **alpha rhythm** ►*n.* A pattern of regular electrical oscillations in the brain that occur at a frequency of 8 to 13 hertz when a person is awake and relaxed.

al·pine (ăl′pīn′) ►*adj.* **1. Alpine** Relating to the Alps or their inhabitants. **2.** Of or relating to high mountains.

Alps (ălps) A mountain system of S-central Europe.

al-Qae·da (ăl-kā′də, -kī′də, -kä-ē′də) ►*n.* An international organization that attempts to advance Islamic fundamentalism and disrupt the influence of Western nations through violence. [< Ar. *al-qā'ida,* the base.]

al·read·y (ôl-rĕd′ē) ►*adv.* **1.** By this or a specified time; before: *It was already dark at 5:00.* **2.** So soon: *Are you going already?* [ME *alredi : all,* ALL + *redi,* READY.]

al·right (ôl-rīt′) ►*adv.* Nonstandard All right.

Al·sace (ăl-săs′, -sās′) A region and former province of E France W of the Rhine R.

Al·sa·tian (ăl-sā′shən) ►*adj.* Of Alsace. ►*n.* **1.** A native or inhabitant of Alsace. **2.** *Chiefly Brit.* A German shepherd.

al·so (ôl′sō) ►*adv.* **1.** In addition; besides. **2.** Likewise; too: *If you will stay, I will also.* ►*conj.* And in addition. [< OE *ealswā.*]

al·so-ran (ôl′sō-răn′) ►*n.* **1.** A horse that does not win, place, or show in a race. **2.** A loser in a competition.

alt. ►*abbr.* **1.** alternate **2.** altitude

Al·ta·ic (ăl-tā′ĭk) ►*n.* A putative language family of Europe and Asia that includes the Turkic, Tungusic, and Mongolian subfamilies. —**Al·ta′ic** *adj.*

al·tar (ôl′tər) ►*n.* An elevated place or structure before or upon which religious ceremonies may be performed. [< Lat. *altāre.*]

al·tar·piece (ôl′tər-pēs′) ►*n.* A piece of artwork, such as a painting or carving, that is placed above and behind an altar.

al·ter (ôl′tər) ►*v.* **1.** To change; modify: *altered my will.* **2.** To adjust (a garment) for a better fit. **3.** To castrate or spay (an animal). [< Med. Lat. *alterāre,* make other.] —**al′ter·a·ble** *adj.* —**al′ter·a′tion** *n.*

al·ter·cate (ôl′tər-kāt′) ►*v.* **-cat·ed, -cat·ing** To argue or dispute vehemently. [Lat. *altercārī* < *alter,* another.] —**al′ter·ca′tion** *n.*

alter ego ►*n.* **1.** Another side of oneself. **2.** An intimate friend. [Lat., other I.]

al·ter·nate (ôl′tər-nāt′, ăl′-) ►*v.* **-nat·ed, -nat·ing 1.** To perform or occur in successive turns. **2.** To pass back and forth from one state, action, or place to another. ►*adj.* (-nĭt) **1.** Happening or following in turns: *alternate seasons of the year.* **2.** Designating or relating to every other one of a series: *alternate lines.* **3.** Substitute: *an alternate plan.* ►*n.* (-nĭt) **1.** A substitute. **2.** An alternative. [< Lat. *alternus,* by turns.] —**al′ter·nate·ly** *adv.* —**al′ter·na′tion** *n.*

al·ter·nat·ing current (ôl′tər-nā′tĭng, ăl′-) ►*n.* An electric current that reverses direction at regular intervals.

al·ter·na·tive (ôl-tûr′nə-tĭv, ăl-) ►*n.* **1a.** One of a number of possible choices. **b.** A choice that is mutually exclusive with another. **2.** A situation presenting a choice between two mutually exclusive possibilities. ►*adj.* **1.** Allowing or necessitating a choice between two or more things. **2.** Existing outside traditional or established institutions or systems: *an alternative lifestyle; alternative energy.* —**al·ter′na·tive·ly** *adv.*

alternative medicine ►*n.* Any of various health care practices that do not follow generally accepted medical methods.

alternative school ►*n.* A school that is nontraditional, esp. in ideals or curriculum.

al·ter·na·tor (ôl′tər-nā′tər, ăl′-) ►*n.* An electric generator that produces alternating current.

al·though also **al·tho** (ôl-thō′) ►*conj.* **1.** Regardless of the fact that; even though. **2.** But;

however: *He says he has a dog, although I've never seen it.* [ME.]

　Usage: *Although* is usu. placed at the beginning of its clause, whereas *though* may occur there or elsewhere and is more commonly used to link words or phrases, as in *wiser though poorer.*

al·tim·e·ter (ăl-tĭm′ĭ-tər) ►*n.* An instrument for determining elevation. [Lat. *altus*, high + –METER.] —**al·tim′e·try** *n.*

al·ti·pla·no (äl′tĭ-plä′nō) ►*n., pl.* **-nos** A high mountain plateau, as in Bolivia and Peru. [< Lat. *altus*, high + *plānum*, plain.]

al·ti·tude (ăl′tĭ-tōod′, -tyōod′) ►*n.* **1.** The height of a thing above a reference level, esp. above sea level. See Synonyms at **elevation. 2.** often **altitudes** A high region. **3.** The angular distance above the observer's horizon of a celestial object. **4.** The perpendicular distance from the base of a geometric figure to the opposite vertex, parallel side, or parallel surface. [< Lat. *altus*, high.] —**al′ti·tu′di·nal** *adj.*

Alt key (ôlt) ►*n.* A key on a computer keyboard pressed in combination with another key to execute an alternate operation.

al·to (ăl′tō) ►*n., pl.* **-tos** *Mus.* **1.** A low female singing voice; contralto. **2.** The range between soprano and tenor. **3.** A singer, voice, or instrument having this range. [< Lat. *altus*, high.]

al·to·geth·er (ôl′tə-gĕth′ər) ►*adv.* **1.** Entirely. **2.** With all included or counted: *Altogether the bill came to $60.* **3.** With everything considered: *Altogether, I'm sorry it happened.* [ME *al togeder.*]

al·tru·ism (ăl′trōo-ĭz′əm) ►*n.* Unselfish concern for the welfare of others; selflessness. [Fr. *altruisme*, ult. < Lat. *alter*, other.] —**al′tru·ist** *n.* —**al′tru·is′tic** *adj.* —**al′tru·is′ti·cal·ly** *adv.*

al·um¹ (ăl′əm) ►*n.* Any of various double sulfates of a trivalent metal and a univalent metal, esp. aluminum potassium sulfate, used as hardeners and purifiers. [< Lat. *alūmen.*]

a·lum² (ə-lŭm′) ►*n. Informal* An alumna or alumnus.

a·lu·mi·na (ə-lōo′mə-nə) ►*n.* Any of several forms of aluminum oxide, Al_2O_3, occurring naturally as corundum, in bauxite, and with various impurities as ruby, sapphire, and emery. [< Lat. *alūmen*, alum.]

al·u·min·i·um (ăl′yə-mĭn′ē-əm) ►*n. Chiefly Brit.* Var. of **aluminum.**

a·lu·mi·nize (ə-lōo′mə-nīz′) ►*v.* **-nized, -niz·ing** To coat or cover with aluminum.

a·lu·mi·nous (ə-lōo′mə-nəs) ►*adj.* Relating to or containing aluminum or alum.

a·lu·mi·num (ə-lōo′mə-nəm) ►*n. Symbol* **Al** A silvery-white, ductile metallic element used to form many hard, light, corrosion-resistant alloys. At. no. 13. See table at **element.** [< ALUMINA.]

a·lum·na (ə-lŭm′nə) ►*n., pl.* **-nae** (-nē′) A woman graduate of a school, college, or university. [Lat., female pupil.]

a·lum·nus (ə-lŭm′nəs) ►*n., pl.* **-ni** (-nī′) A male graduate of a school, college, or university. [Lat., male pupil.]

al·ve·o·lus (ăl-vē′ə-ləs) ►*n., pl.* **-li** (-lī′) **1.** A tooth socket in the jawbone. **2.** A tiny, capillary-rich sac in the lungs where the exchange of oxygen and carbon dioxide takes place. [Lat., small cavity.]

al·ways (ôl′wāz, -wĭz) ►*adv.* **1.** At all times; invariably. **2.** For all time; forever: *will always be friends.* **3.** At any time; in any event. [< OE *ealne weg.*]

a·lys·sum (ə-lĭs′əm) ►*n.* Any of various chiefly Mediterranean weeds or ornamentals in the mustard family, having racemes of white or yellow flowers. [< Gk. *alusson*, plant believed to cure rabies.]

Alz·hei·mer's disease (älts′hī-mərz, ălts′-) ►*n.* A degenerative disease of the brain, seen primarily in elderly people and associated with the development of abnormal tissues and protein deposits in the cerebral cortex, and characterized by memory failure and the progressive loss of mental capacity. [After Alois *Alzheimer* (1864–1915), German neurologist.]

am (ăm) ►*v.* 1st pers. sing. pr. indic. of **be.** [< OE *eom.*]

AM ►*abbr.* **1.** airmail **2.** amplitude modulation **3.** or **AM** ante meridiem **4.** *Lat.* artium magister (Master of Arts)

　Usage: Although *12* AM denotes midnight, and *12* PM denotes noon, using the phrases *12 noon* and *12 midnight* will avoid confusion.

Am. ►*abbr.* **1.** America **2.** American

AMA ►*abbr.* American Medical Association

a·mal·gam (ə-măl′gəm) ►*n.* **1.** An alloy of mercury with other metals, as with tin or silver. **2.** A combination of diverse elements. [< Med. Lat. *amalgama.*]

a·mal·ga·mate (ə-măl′gə-māt′) ►*v.* **-mat·ed, -mat·ing** To form into an integrated whole; unite. —**a·mal′ga·ma′tion** *n.*

a·man·u·en·sis (ə-măn′yōo-ĕn′sĭs) ►*n., pl.* **-ses** (-sēz) One employed to take dictation or copy manuscript. [Lat. *āmanuēnsis.*]

am·a·ranth (ăm′ə-rănth′) ►*n.* **1a.** Any of various plants having dense clusters of tiny flowers. **b.** The small edible seeds of several of these species. **2.** An imaginary flower that never fades. [< Gk. *amarantos*, unfading.] —**am′a·ran′thine** *adj.*

am·a·ryl·lis (ăm′ə-rĭl′ĭs) ►*n.* A tropical American bulbous plant grown as an ornamental for its large lilylike flowers. [< Gk. *Amarullis*, name of a shepherdess.]

a·mass (ə-măs′) ►*v.* To accumulate. [< OFr. *amasser.*] —**a·mass′ment** *n.*

am·a·teur (ăm′ə-tûr′, -chŏor′, -tyŏor′) ►*n.* **1.** One who engages in an activity or study as a pastime and not as a profession. **2.** One lacking expertise. [< Lat. *amātor*, lover.] —**am′a·teur′ish** *adj.* —**am′a·teur′ish·ly** *adv.* —**am′a·teur·ism** *n.*

am·a·to·ry (ăm′ə-tôr′ē) ►*adj.* Relating to love, esp. romantic love. [< Lat. *amāre*, to love.]

a·maze (ə-māz′) ►*v.* **a·mazed, a·maz·ing** To affect with great wonder; astonish. [< OE *āmasian*, bewilder.] —**a·maz′ed·ly** (-mā′zĭd-lē) *adv.* —**a·maze′ment** *n.* —**a·maz′ing·ly** *adv.*

Am·a·zon (ăm′ə-zŏn′) ►*n.* **1.** *Gk. Myth.* A member of a nation of women warriors. **2.** often **amazon** A tall, aggressive, strong-willed woman.

Am·a·zo·ni·an (ăm′ə-zō′nē-ən) ►*adj.* **1.** Relating to the Amazon R. **2.** Relating to an Amazon.

Amazon River The world's second-longest river, flowing about 6,600 km (4,100 mi) from Peru across N Brazil to a wide delta on the Atlantic.

am·bas·sa·dor (ăm-băs′ə-dər) ►*n.* A diplomat of the highest rank accredited as representative in residence by one government to another. [< Lat. *ambactus*, servant.] —**am·bas′sa·do′ri·al** (-dôr′ē-əl) *adj.* —**am·bas′sa·dor·ship′** *n.*

am·ber (ăm′bər) ►*n.* **1.** A hard, translucent, brownish-yellow fossil resin, used esp. for making jewelry. **2.** A brownish yellow. [< Ar. *'anbar*, ambergris.] —**am′ber** *adj.*

Amber Alert ►*n.* A message about a recently missing or abducted person, posted on electronic signs or broadcast to enlist the public's help in finding the person. [After *Amber* Hagerman (1987–96).]

am·ber·gris (ăm′bər-grĭs′, -grēs′) ►*n.* A waxy, grayish substance formed in the intestines of sperm whales, formerly used in perfumes. [< OFr. *ambre gris*.]

ambi- ►*pref.* Both: *ambivalence*. [Lat., around.]

am·bi·ance *also* **am·bi·ence** (ăm′bē-əns) ►*n.* The special atmosphere of a particular environment. [< Lat. *ambiēns*, AMBIENT.]

am·bi·dex·trous (ăm′bĭ-děk′strəs) ►*adj.* Able to use both hands with equal facility. [< Med. Lat. *ambidexter* : AMBI– + Lat. *dexter*, right.] —**am′bi·dex·ter′i·ty** (-stěr′ĭ-tē) *n.* —**am′bi·dex′trous·ly** *adv.*

am·bi·ent (ăm′bē-ənt) ►*adj.* Surrounding; encircling. [< Lat. *ambīre*, go around.]

am·big·u·ous (ăm-bĭg′yōō-əs) ►*adj.* **1.** Open to more than one interpretation. **2.** Doubtful or uncertain. [< Lat. *ambiguus* : AMBI– + *agere*, drive.] —**am′bi·gu′i·ty** (-bĭ-gyōō′ĭ-tē) *n.* —**am·big′u·ous·ly** *adv.*

am·bit (ăm′bĭt) ►*n.* **1.** An external boundary; circuit. **2.** Sphere or scope. See Synonyms at **range.** [Lat. *ambitus* < *ambīre*, go around.]

am·bi·tion (ăm-bĭsh′ən) ►*n.* A strong desire to achieve something. The object or goal desired. [< Lat. *ambīre*, solicit.]

am·bi·tious (ăm-bĭsh′əs) ►*adj.* **1.** Full of or motivated by ambition. **2.** Challenging: *an ambitious schedule.* —**am·bi′tious·ly** *adv.* —**am·bi′tious·ness** *n.*

am·biv·a·lence (ăm-bĭv′ə-ləns) ►*n.* The coexistence of opposing feelings toward a person, object, or idea. —**am·biv′a·lent** *adj.* —**am·biv′a·lent·ly** *adv.*

am·ble (ăm′bəl) ►*v.* **-bled, -bling** To walk slowly or leisurely; stroll. [< Lat. *ambulāre*, walk.] —**am′ble** *n.* —**am′bler** *n.*

am·bro·sia (ăm-brō′zhə) ►*n.* **1.** *Gk. & Rom. Myth.* The food of the gods. **2.** Something with a delicious flavor or fragrance. [< Gk. *ambrotos*, immortal.] —**am·bro′sial** *adj.*

am·bu·lance (ăm′byə-ləns) ►*n.* A specially equipped vehicle used to transport the sick or injured. [< Fr. *ambulant*, AMBULANT.]

am·bu·lant (ăm′byə-lənt) ►*adj.* Moving or walking about. [< Lat. *ambulāre*, walk.]

am·bu·la·to·ry (ăm′byə-lə-tôr′ē) ►*adj.* **1.** Relating to or adapted for walking. **2.** Capable of walking; not bedridden. **3.** Moving about. ►*n.,* *pl.* **-ries** A covered place for walking, as in a cloister. [< Lat. *ambulāre*, walk.]

am·bush (ăm′bŏosh) ►*n.* **1.** The act of lying in wait to attack by surprise. **2.** A sudden attack made from a concealed position. ►*v.* To attack from a concealed position. [< OFr. *embuschier,* to ambush.]

Syns: bushwhack, waylay **n.**

a·me·ba (ə-mē′bə) ►*n.* Var. of amoeba.

a·me·lio·rate (ə-mēl′yə-rāt′) ►*v.* **-rat·ed, -rat·ing** To make or become better; improve. [Alteration of MELIORATE.] —**a·me′lio·ra′tion** *n.*

a·men (ā-měn′, ä-) ►*interj.* Used at the end of a prayer or to express approval. [< Heb. *ʾāmēn,* verily.]

a·me·na·ble (ə-mē′nə-bəl, -měn′ə-) ►*adj.* Obedient; compliant. [< OFr. *mener,* to lead.] —**a·me′na·bly** *adv.*

a·mend (ə-měnd′) ►*v.* **1.** To improve. **2.** To remove the errors in; correct. **3.** To alter (e.g., a law) formally by adding, deleting, or rephrasing. [< Lat. *ēmendāre.*]

a·mend·ment (ə-měnd′mənt) ►*n.* **1.** Improvement. **2.** Correction. **3a.** Formal revision, as of a bill or constitution. **b.** A statement of such a revision: *read the 19th Amendment.*

a·mends (ə-měndz′) ►*pl.n.* (takes sing. or pl. v.) Recompense for grievance or injury.

a·men·i·ty (ə-měn′ĭ-tē, -mē′nĭ-) ►*n.,* *pl.* **-ties** **1.** Pleasantness; agreeableness. **2.** Something that contributes to comfort. **3.** A feature that increases attractiveness or value. **4. amenities** Social courtesies; pleasantries. [< Lat. *amoenus,* pleasant.]

Syns: comfort, convenience **n.**

a·men·or·rhe·a (ā-měn′ə-rē′ə) ►*n.* Abnormal suppression or absence of menstruation. [A–[1] + Gk. *mēn,* month + –RRHEA.] —**a·men′or·rhe′ic** *adj.*

Amer. ►*abbr.* **1.** America **2.** American

Am·er·a·sian (ăm′ə-rā′zhən, -shən) ►*n.* A person of American and Asian ancestry. —**Am′er·a′sian** *adj.*

a·merce (ə-mûrs′) ►*v.* **a·merced, a·merc·ing** To punish by fine or other penalty. [< AN *amercier.*]

A·mer·i·ca (ə-měr′ĭ-kə) **1.** The United States. **2.** Also **the Americas** The landmasses and islands of North America, Central America, and South America.

A·mer·i·can (ə-měr′ĭ-kən) ►*adj.* **1.** Of or relating to the US. **2.** Of or relating to America or the Americas. ►*n.* **1.** A citizen of the US. **2.** A native or inhabitant of America or the Americas.

A·mer·i·ca·na (ə-měr′ə-kä′nə, -kăn′ə, -kā′nə) ►*n.* (takes sing. or pl. v.) Materials relating to American history, folklore, or geography.

American English ►*n.* The English language as used in the US.

American Indian ►*n.* A member of any of the peoples indigenous to the Americas except the Eskimos, Aleuts, and Inuits. See Usage Note at **Native American.**

A·mer·i·can·ism (ə-měr′ĭ-kə-nĭz′əm) ►*n.* **1.** A custom or trait originating in the US. **2.** A word, phrase, or idiom characteristic of American English.

A·mer·i·can·ize (ə-měr′ĭ-kə-nīz′) ►*v.* **-ized, -iz·ing** **1.** To make or become American, as in culture or method. **2.** To bring under American control. —**A·mer′i·can·i·za′tion** *n.*

American Samoa An unincorp. territory of the US in the S Pacific NE of Fiji. Cap. Pago Pago.

American Sign Language ►*n.* An American system of communication for the hearing-impaired that uses manual signs.

American Spanish ►*n.* The Spanish language

as used in the Western Hemisphere.

a·me·ri·ci·um (ăm′ə-rĭsh′ē-əm) ►*n. Symbol* **Am** A white metallic radioactive element used as a radiation source in research. At. no. 95. See table at **element.** [AMERICA.]

Am·er·in·di·an (ăm′ə-rĭn′dē-ən) also **Am·er·ind** (ăm′ə-rĭnd′) ►*n.* An American Indian. See Usage Note at **Native American.** —**Am′er·in′di·an, Am′er·ind′** *adj.*

am·e·thyst (ăm′ə-thĭst) ►*n.* **1.** A purple or violet variety of transparent quartz used as a gemstone. **2.** A moderate to grayish reddish purple. [< Gk. *amethustos.*]

Amex ►*abbr.* American Stock Exchange

Am·har·ic (ăm-hăr′ĭk, äm-hä′rĭk) ►*n.* A Semitic language, the official language of Ethiopia.

a·mi·a·ble (ā′mē-ə-bəl) ►*adj.* Friendly; good-natured. [< LLat. *amīcābilis,* AMICABLE.] —**a′-mi·a·bil′i·ty** *n.* —**a′mi·a·bly** *adv.*

am·i·ca·ble (ăm′ĭ-kə-bəl) ►*adj.* Friendly; peaceable. [< Lat. *amīcus,* friend.] —**am′i·ca·bil′i·ty** *n.* —**am′i·ca·bly** *adv.*

a·mid (ə-mĭd′) also **a·midst** (ə-mĭdst′) ►*prep.* Surrounded by; in the middle of.

a·mid·ships (ə-mĭd′shĭps′) also **a·mid·ship** (-shĭp′) ►*adv. Naut.* Midway between the bow and the stern.

a·mi·go (ə-mē′gō) ►*n., pl.* **-gos** A friend. [Sp. < Lat. *amīcus.*]

A·min Da·da (ä-mēn′ dä-dä′), **Idi** 1925?–2003. Ugandan dictator (1971–79).

a·mine (ə-mēn′, ăm′ēn) ►*n.* Any of a group of organic compounds derived from ammonia by replacing one or more hydrogen atoms by a hydrocarbon group. [AM(MONIUM) + –INE².]

a·mi·no acid (ə-mē′nō, ăm′ə-nō′) ►*n.* Any of a class of organic compounds including the 20 compounds that can be joined to form proteins.

A·mish (ä′mĭsh, ăm′ĭsh) ►*n.* A member of an Anabaptist sect formed in the 1600s and now active esp. in PA, OH, and IN. [After Jacob Amman, 17th-century Mennonite bishop.] —**A′mish** *adj.*

a·miss (ə-mĭs′) ►*adv.* In an improper, defective, unfortunate, or mistaken way. ►*adj.* Out of proper order. [Prob. < ON *ā mis.*]

am·i·ty (ăm′ĭ-tē) ►*n., pl.* **-ties** Peaceful relations, as between nations. [< OFr. *amitie* < Lat. *amīcus,* friend.]

Am·man (ä-män′) The capital of Jordan, in the NW part.

am·me·ter (ăm′mē′tər) ►*n.* An instrument that measures electric current. [AM(PERE) + –METER.]

am·mo (ăm′ō) ►*n. Informal* Ammunition.

am·mo·nia (ə-mōn′yə) ►*n.* **1.** A colorless, pungent gas, NH₃, used to manufacture fertilizers and a wide variety of nitrogen-containing chemicals. **2.** See **ammonium hydroxide.** [< Lat. *(sal) ammōniacus,* (salt) of Amen, an Egyptian god.]

am·mon·ite (ăm′ə-nīt′) ►*n.* An extinct cephalopod mollusk typically having a thick, coiled shell. [< Lat. *(cornū) Ammōnis,* (horn) of Amen (Egypt. god), ammonite.]

am·mo·ni·um (ə-mō′nē-əm) ►*n.* The chemical ion NH₄+. [AMMON(IA) + –IUM.]

ammonium chloride ►*n.* A white crystalline compound, NH₄Cl, used in dry cells and as an expectorant.

ammonium hydroxide ►*n.* A basic, aqueous solution of ammonia, NH₄OH, used as a household cleanser and in other products.

am·mu·ni·tion (ăm′yə-nĭsh′ən) ►*n.* **1.** Projectiles that can be fired from guns or otherwise propelled. **2.** Explosive or destructive materials used in war. **3.** A means of offense or defense. [< OFr. *(la) munition,* MUNITIONS.]

am·ne·sia (ăm-nē′zhə) ►*n.* Loss of memory. [Gk. *amnēsia* : A⁻¹ + *mimnēskein,* remember.] —**am·ne′si·ac′** (-zē-ăk′, -zhē-ăk′), **am·ne′sic** (-zĭk, -sĭk) *n. & adj.*

am·nes·ty (ăm′nĭ-stē) ►*n., pl.* **-ties** A general pardon, esp. for political offenses. [< Gk. *amnēstia* : A⁻¹ + *mimnēskein,* remember.]

am·ni·o·cen·te·sis (ăm′nē-ō-sĕn-tē′sĭs) ►*n., pl.* **-ses** (-sēz) A procedure in which a small sample of fluid is drawn out of the uterus, then analyzed to determine genetic abnormalities in, or the sex of, a fetus. [AMNION + Gk. *kentēsis,* pricking.]

am·ni·on (ăm′nē-ən) ►*n., pl.* **-ni·ons** or **-ni·a** (-nē-ə) A membranous sac filled with a serous fluid that encloses the embryo or fetus of a mammal, bird, or reptile. [Gk. *amniōn.*] —**am′-ni·ot′ic** (-ŏt′ĭk), **am′ni·on′ic** (-ŏn′ĭk) *adj.*

a·moe·ba also **a·me·ba** (ə-mē′bə) ►*n., pl.* **-bas** or **-bae** (-bē) An aquatic or parasitic protozoan consisting essentially of an amorphous mass of protoplasm with a flexible outer membrane. [< Gk. *amoibē,* change.] —**a·moe′bic** *adj.*

a·mok (ə-mŭk′, ə-mŏk′) ►*adv.* Var. of **amuck.**

a·mong (ə-mŭng′) also **a·mongst** (ə-mŭngst′) ►*prep.* **1.** In the midst of; surrounded by. **2.** In the group or class of. **3.** With portions to each of: *Distribute this among you.* **4.** Each with the other. See Usage Note at **between.** [< OE *āmang.*]

a·mon·til·la·do (ə-mŏn′tl-ä′dō) ►*n., pl.* **-dos** A pale dry sherry. [Sp. *(vino) amontillado,* (wine) made in Montilla, Spain.]

a·mor·al (ā-môr′əl, -mŏr′-) ►*adj.* **1.** Neither moral nor immoral. **2.** Lacking moral sensibility; not caring about right and wrong. —**a·mor′al·ism** *n.* —**a′mo·ral′i·ty** (ā′mô-răl′ĭ-tē, -mə-) *n.* —**a·mor′al·ly** *adv.*

am·o·rous (ăm′ər-əs) ►*adj.* **1.** Full of or strongly disposed to romantic love. **2.** Showing or expressing romantic or sexual love. [< Lat. *amor,* love.] —**am′or·ous·ly** *adv.* —**am′or·ous·ness** *n.*

a·mor·phous (ə-môr′fəs) ►*adj.* **1.** Lacking definite organization or form. **2.** *Chem.* Lacking distinct crystalline structure. [< Gk. *amorphos.*]

am·or·tize (ăm′ər-tīz′, ə-môr′-) ►*v.* **-tized, -tiz·ing** To liquidate (a debt) by installment payments. [< OFr. *amortir.*] —**am′or·tiz′a·ble** *adj.* —**am′or·ti·za′tion** *n.*

A·mos (ā′məs) ►*n. Bible* **1.** A Hebrew prophet of the 8th cent. BC. **2.** See table at **Bible.**

a·mount (ə-mount′) ►*n.* The total quantity or number. ►*v.* **1.** To add up in number. **2.** To add up in effect. **3.** To be equivalent. [< OFr. *amont,* upward.]

a·mour (ə-mŏor′) ►*n.* A love affair, esp. an illicit one. [< OFr. < Lat. *amor,* love.]

a·mour-pro·pre (ä-mŏor-prôp′rə) ►*n.* Self-respect. [Fr.]

a·mox·i·cil·lin (ə-mŏk′sĭ-sĭl′ĭn) ►*n.* An oral antibiotic that is derived from penicillin and has antibacterial properties similar to ampicillin. [AM(INE) + OX(Y)– + (PEN)ICILLIN.]

amp (ămp) ►*n.* **1.** An ampere. **2.** An amplifier, esp. one used to amplify music.

am·per·age (ăm′pər-ĭj, ăm′pîr′-) ►*n.* The strength of an electric current expressed in amperes.

am·pere (ăm′pîr′) ►*n.* A unit of electric current strength equal to a flow of one coulomb per second. [After André Marie AMPÈRE.]

Am·père (ăm′pîr, än-pĕr′), **André Marie** 1775–1836. French physicist and mathematician.

am·per·sand (ăm′pər-sănd′) ►*n.* The character (&) representing the word *and*. [Contraction of *and per se and*, & (the sign) by itself (equals) and.]

am·phet·a·mine (ăm-fĕt′ə-mēn′, -mĭn) ►*n.* A colorless, volatile liquid, $C_9H_{13}N$, or one of its derivatives, used primarily as a central nervous system stimulant. [*a(lpha) m(ethyl) ph(enyl) et(hyl) amine.*]

am·phib·i·an (ăm-fĭb′ē-ən) ►*n.* **1.** A vertebrate that hatches as an aquatic larva with gills, then transforms into an adult having lungs. **2.** An aircraft that can take off and land on land or water. **3.** A vehicle that can operate on land and in water. [< Gk. *amphibios,* AMPHIBIOUS.]

am·phib·i·ous (ăm-fĭb′ē-əs) ►*adj.* **1.** Able to live on land and in water. **2.** Able to operate on land and in water. [< Gk. *amphibios* : *amphi-,* both + *bios,* life.]

am·phi·bole (ăm′fə-bōl′) ►*n.* Any of a group of silicate minerals containing various combinations of sodium, calcium, magnesium, iron, and aluminum. [< Gk. *amphibolos,* doubtful.] —**am′phi·bol′ic** (-bŏl′ĭk) *adj.*

am·phi·the·a·ter (ăm′fə-thē′ə-tər) ►*n.* A round or oval structure having tiers of seats rising gradually outward from a central arena. [< Gk. *amphitheatron.*]

am·pho·ra (ăm′fər-ə) ►*n., pl.* **-pho·rae** (-fə-rē′) or **-pho·ras** A two-handled jar with a narrow neck of ancient Greece and Rome. [< Gk. *amphoreus* : *amphi-,* both + *pherein,* carry.]

am·pi·cil·lin (ăm′pĭ-sĭl′ĭn) ►*n.* A type of penicillin having a broad antibacterial spectrum and used to treat a variety of infections. [Blend of AMINE and PENICILLIN.]

am·ple (ăm′pəl) ►*adj.* **-pler, -plest 1.** Of great size, amount, extent, or capacity. See Synonyms at **spacious. 2.** Sufficient for a purpose. See Synonyms at **plentiful.** [< Lat. *amplus.*] —**am′ple·ness** *n.* —**am′ply** *adv.*

am·pli·fi·er (ăm′plə-fī′ər) ►*n.* **1.** One that amplifies. **2.** A device that increases the magnitude of an electrical signal.

am·pli·fy (ăm′plə-fī′) ►*v.* **-fied, -fy·ing 1.** To make greater; increase. **2.** To add to; make complete. **3.** To exaggerate. **4.** To increase the magnitude of a variable quantity, esp. of voltage, power, or current. [< Lat. *amplificāre.*] —**am′pli·fi·ca′tion** *n.*

am·pli·tude (ăm′plĭ-tōōd′, -tyōōd′) ►*n.* **1.** Largeness; magnitude. **2.** Fullness; copiousness. **3.** *Phys.* The maximum absolute value of a periodically varying quantity. [< Lat. *amplus,* large.]

amplitude modulation ►*n.* The encoding of a carrier wave by varying its amplitude in accordance with an input signal.

am·pule also **am·poule** (ăm′pōōl, -pyōōl) ►*n.* A small sealed vial, esp. one containing a hypodermic injection solution. [< Lat. *ampulla,* dim. of *amphora,* AMPHORA.]

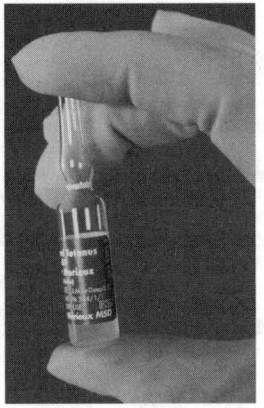

ampule

am·pu·tate (ăm′pyōō-tāt′) ►*v.* **-tat·ed, -tat·ing** To cut off (an appendage), esp. by surgery. [Lat. *amputāre,* cut around.] —**am′pu·ta′tion** *n.* —**am′pu·ta′tor** *n.*

am·pu·tee (ăm′pyōō-tē′) ►*n.* A person who has had one or more limbs amputated.

Am·ster·dam (ăm′stər-dăm′) The constitutional capital of the Netherlands, in the W part.

AMT ►*abbr.* alternative minimum tax

amu ►*abbr.* atomic mass unit

a·muck (ə-mŭk′) also **a·mok** (ə-mŭk′, ə-mŏk′) ►*adv.* **1.** In a frenzy to do violence or kill: *rioters running amuck.* **2.** In a jumbled or confused state: *The plans went amuck.* [Malay *amok.*]

A·mu Dar·ya (ä′mōō där′yə, ə-mōō′ dŭr-yä′) A river of central Asia flowing about 2,575 km (1,600 mi) westward to the S Aral Sea.

am·u·let (ăm′yə-lĭt) ►*n.* An object worn, esp. around the neck, as a charm against evil or injury. [Lat. *amulētum.*]

A·mur (ä-mōōr′) A river of NE Asia flowing about 4,400 km (2,730 mi) mainly along the border between China and Russia.

a·muse (ə-myōōz′) ►*v.* **a·mused, a·mus·ing 1.** To occupy in an entertaining fashion. **2.** To cause to laugh. [< OFr. *amuser,* stupefy.] —**a·mus′a·ble** *adj.* —**a·muse′ment** *n.*

am·y·lase (ăm′ə-lās′) ►*n.* Any of a group of enzymes that convert starch to sugar. [Lat. *amyl(um),* starch + -ASE.]

an (ən; ăn *when stressed*) ►*indef.art.* The form of *a* used before words beginning with a vowel sound: *an elephant; an hour.* [< OE *ān,* one.]

an. ►*abbr. Lat.* **1.** anno (in the year) **2.** ante (before)

an– ►*pref.* Var. of **a–**¹.

–an ►*suff.* **1.** Of or resembling: *Lutheran.* **2.** One relating to or characterized by: *librarian.* [< Lat. *-ānus,* adj. and n. suff.]

ana– ►*pref.* Upward; up: *anabolism.* [< Gk. *ana,* up.]

–ana or **–iana** ►*suff.* A collection of items relating to a specified person or place: *Americana.* [< Lat. *-āna,* neuter pl. adj. and n. suff.]

An·a·bap·tist (ăn′ə-băp′tĭst) ►*n.* A member of a radical Protestant movement founded in the

1500s. [< LGk. *anabaptizein*, baptize again.] —**An′a·bap′tism** *n.*

a·nab·o·lism (ə-năb′ə-lĭz′əm) ►*n.* Metabolic activity in which complex substances are synthesized from simpler substances. [ANA– + (META)BOLISM.] —**an′a·bol′ic** (ăn′ə-bŏl′ĭk) *adj.*

a·nach·ro·nism (ə-năk′rə-nĭz′əm) ►*n.* **1.** Representation of something as existing or happening outside its historical order. **2.** One that is out of its proper or chronological order. [< Gk. *ana-*, back + *khronos*, time.] —**a·nach′- ro·nis′tic, a·nach′ro·nous** (-nəs) *adj.* —**a· nach′ro·nis′ti·cal·ly, a·nach′ro·nous·ly** *adv.*

an·a·con·da (ăn′ə-kŏn′də) ►*n.* A large nonvenomous snake of tropical South America that suffocates its prey in its coils. [Perh. < Sinhalese *henakandayā*, whip snake.]

an·aer·obe (ăn′ə-rōb′, ăn-âr′ōb′) ►*n.* An organism, such as a bacterium, that can live in the absence of atmospheric oxygen. —**an′aer· o′bic** *adj.* —**an′aer·o′bi·cal·ly** *adv.*

an·aes·the·sia (ăn′ĭs-thē′zhə) ►*n.* Var. of **anesthesia.**

an·a·gram (ăn′ə-grăm′) ►*n.* A word or phrase formed by reordering the letters of another word or phrase, such as *satin* to *stain.* [< Gk. *anagrammatizein*, rearrange letters : ANA– + *gramma*, letter.]

a·nal (ā′nəl) ►*adj.* **1.** Of or near the anus. **2.** Relating to the second stage of psychosexual development in psychoanalytic theory. —**a′- nal·ly** *adv.*

an·al·ge·si·a (ăn′əl-jē′zē-ə, -zhə) ►*n.* A deadening of the sense of pain without loss of consciousness. [Gk. *analgēsia.*]

an·al·ge·sic (ăn′əl-jē′zĭk, -sĭk) ►*n.* A medication that reduces or eliminates pain. —**an′al· ge′sic** *adj.*

an·a·log also **an·a·logue** (ăn′ə-lôg′, -lŏg′) ►*n.* Something that is analogous. ►*adj.* Of or relating to the representation of data by continuously variable physical quantities: *an analog clock.*

a·nal·o·gous (ə-năl′ə-gəs) ►*adj.* **1.** Similar or alike in such a way as to permit the drawing of an analogy. **2.** *Biol.* Similar in function but not in structure and evolutionary origin. —**a· nal′o·gous·ly** *adv.*

a·nal·o·gy (ə-năl′ə-jē) ►*n., pl.* -**gies 1a.** Similarity in some respects between things otherwise dissimilar. **b.** A comparison based on such similarity. **2.** *Biol.* Correspondence in function between organs of dissimilar evolution. **3.** An inference that if two things are alike in some respects they must be alike in others. [< Gk. *analogos*, proportionate.]

a·nal·y·sis (ə-năl′ĭ-sĭs) ►*n., pl.* -**ses** (-sēz′) **1.** The separation of a whole into its parts for study. **2.** A statement of the results of such a study. **3.** Psychoanalysis. [< Gk. *analusis*, a dissolving.] —**an′a·lyst** (ăn′ə-lĭst) *n.*

an·a·lyt·ic (ăn′ə-lĭt′ĭk) or **an·a·lyt·i·cal** (-ĭ-kəl) ►*adj.* **1.** Relating to analysis. **2.** Reasoning or acting from a perception of the parts and interrelations of a subject. **3.** Expert in or using analysis, esp. in thinking. See Synonyms at **logical.** [< Gk. *analutikos.*] —**an′a·lyt′i· cal·ly** *adv.*

an·a·lyze (ăn′ə-līz′) ►*v.* -**lyzed, -lyz·ing 1.** To make an analysis of. **2.** To psychoanalyze. [< Gk. *analusis*, analysis.]

Syns: *anatomize, dissect* **v.**

an·a·pest (ăn′ə-pĕst′) ►*n.* A metrical foot composed of two short or unaccented syllables followed by one long or accented one. [< Gk. *anapaistos.*] —**an′a·pes′tic** *adj.*

an·ar·chism (ăn′ər-kĭz′əm) ►*n.* **1.** The theory that all forms of government are oppressive and should be abolished. **2.** Terrorism against the state. —**an′ar·chist** *n.* —**an′ar·chis′tic** *adj.*

an·ar·chy (ăn′ər-kē) ►*n., pl.* -**chies 1.** Absence of governmental authority or law. **2.** Disorder and confusion. [< Gk. *anarkhos*, without a ruler.] —**an·ar′chic** (ăn-är′kĭk), **an·ar′chi·cal** *adj.* —**an·ar′chi·cal·ly** *adv.*

a·nath·e·ma (ə-năth′ə-mə) ►*n., pl.* -**mas 1.** A formal ecclesiastical ban or excommunication. **2.** One that is greatly reviled or shunned. [< Gk. *anathēma*, an accursed thing.]

An·a·to·li·a (ăn′ə-tō′lē-ə, -tōl′yə) The Asian part of Turkey; usu. considered synonymous with Asia Minor.

An·a·to·li·an (ăn′ə-tō′lē-ən) ►*n.* **1.** A native or inhabitant of Anatolia. **2.** An extinct group of Indo-European languages of ancient Anatolia, including Hittite. —**An′a·to′li·an** *adj.*

a·nat·o·mize (ə-năt′ə-mīz′) ►*v.* -**mized, -miz· ing 1.** To dissect (an organism) for study. **2.** To analyze. See Synonyms at **analyze.**

a·nat·o·my (ə-năt′ə-mē) ►*n., pl.* -**mies 1.** The structure of an organism or organ. **2.** The science of the structure of organisms and their parts. **3.** A detailed analysis. [< Gk. *anatomē*, a cutting up.] —**an′a·tom′ic** (ăn′ə-tŏm′ĭk), **an′a·tom′i·cal** *adj.* —**an′a·tom′i·cal·ly** *adv.* —**a·nat′o·mist** *n.*

–ance ►*suff.* **1.** State or condition: *repentance.* **2.** Action: *utterance.* [ME < Lat. *-antia*, n. suff.]

an·ces·tor (ăn′sĕs′tər) ►*n.* **1.** A person from whom one is remotely descended; forebear. **2.** A forerunner or predecessor. **3.** *Biol.* The organism from which later kinds evolved. [< Lat. *antecessor*, predecessor.] —**an·ces′tral** *adj.* —**an·ces′tral·ly** *adv.*

Syns: *forebear, forefather, progenitor* **Ant:** *descendant* **n.**

an·ces·try (ăn′sĕs′trē) ►*n., pl.* -**tries 1.** Descent or lineage. **2.** Ancestors collectively.

an·chor (ăng′kər) ►*n.* **1.** A heavy object attached to a vessel and cast overboard to keep the vessel in place. **2.** A source of security or stability. **3.** *Sports* An athlete who performs the last stage of a relay race. **4.** An anchorperson. ►*v.* **1.** To hold fast by or as if by an anchor. See Synonyms at **fasten. 2.** *Sports* To serve as an anchor for (a team). **3.** To narrate or coordinate (a newscast). [< Gk. *ankura.*]

an·chor·age (ăng′kər-ĭj) ►*n.* A place for anchoring ships.

Anchorage A city of S AK SSW of Fairbanks.

an·cho·rite (ăng′kə-rīt′) ►*n.* A religious hermit. [< LGk. *anakhōrētēs*, one who withdraws.]

an·chor·man (ăng′kər-măn′) ►*n.* **1.** A man who anchors a newscast. **2.** See **anchor** (sense 3).

an·chor·per·son (ăng′kər-pûr′sən) ►*n.* An anchorman or anchorwoman.

an·chor·wom·an (ăng′kər-wŏŏm′ən) ►*n.* A woman who anchors a newscast.

an·cho·vy (ăn′chō′vē) ►*n., pl.* -**vy** or -**vies**

A small, edible, herringlike marine fish. [Sp. *anchova.*]

an·cien ré·gime (än-syän′ rä-zhēm′) ►*n.* **1.** The political and social system that existed in France before the Revolution of 1789. **2.** A former or outmoded sociopolitical system. [Fr., old regime.]

an·cient (ān′shənt) ►*adj.* **1.** Of great age; very old. **2.** Relating to times long past, esp. before the fall of Rome (A.D. 476). ►*n.* **1.** A very old person. **2. ancients** The peoples of classical antiquity. [< Lat. *ante,* before.] —**an′cient·ly** *adv.*

an·cil·lar·y (ăn′sə-lĕr′ē) ►*adj.* **1.** Subordinate. **2.** Auxiliary; helping. [< Lat. *ancilla,* maid-servant.]

–ancy ►*suff.* Condition or quality: *buoyancy.* [Lat. *-antia.*]

and (ənd, ən; ănd *when stressed*) ►*conj.* **1.** Together with or along with; as well as. **2.** Added to; plus. ►*n.* An addition: *no ifs, ands, or buts.* [< OE.]

  Usage: The use of *and* or *but* to begin a sentence has a long and respectable history in English, occurring in writers from Shakespeare to Virginia Woolf.

An·da·lu·sia (ăn′də-lōō′zhə, -zhē-ə) A region of S Spain on the Mediterranean. —**An′da·lu′sian** *adj. & n.*

An·da·man Islands (ăn′də-mən) A group of Indian islands in the E part of the Bay of Bengal S of Myanmar; separated from the Malay Peninsula by the **Andaman Sea.**

an·dan·te (än-dän′tā) ►*adv. & adj. Mus.* In a moderately slow tempo. [Ital. < *andare,* walk.]

An·der·sen (ăn′dər-sən), **Hans Christian** 1805–75. Danish writer.

Anderson (ăn′dər-sən), **Marian** 1902–93. Amer. contralto.

An·des (ăn′dēz) A mountain system of W South America extending from Venezuela to Tierra del Fuego. —**An′de·an** *adj. & n.*

and·i·ron (ănd′ī′ərn) ►*n.* One of a pair of metal supports for logs in a fireplace. [< OFr. *andier.*]

and/or (ănd′ôr′) ►*conj.* Used to indicate that either or both of the items connected by it are involved.

An·dor·ra (ăn-dôr′ə, -dôr′ə) A tiny country of SW Europe between France and Spain in the E Pyrenees. Cap. Andorra la Vella. —**An·dor′ran** *adj. & n.*

An·drew (ăn′drōō), Saint. fl. 1st cent. A.D. One of the 12 Apostles.

andro– or **andr–** ►*pref.* Male; masculine: *androgen.* [< Gk. *anēr, andr-.*]

an·dro·gen (ăn′drə-jən) ►*n.* Any of various hormones, such as testosterone, that control and maintain masculine characteristics. —**an′dro·gen′ic** (-jĕn′ĭk) *adj.*

an·drog·y·nous (ăn-drŏj′ə-nəs) ►*adj.* **1.** *Biol.* Having both female and male characteristics; hermaphroditic. **2.** Being neither distinguishably masculine nor feminine. [ANDRO– + Gk. *gunē,* woman.] —**an·drog′y·nous·ly** *adv.* —**an·drog′y·ny** *n.*

an·droid (ăn′droid′) ►*n.* A mobile robot or automaton, esp. one that resembles a human.

–andry ►*suff.* Kind or number of husbands: *polyandry.* [< Gk. *anēr, andr-,* man.]

–ane ►*suff.* A saturated hydrocarbon: *propane.* [Alteration of –ENE.]

an·ec·dote (ăn′ĭk-dōt′) ►*n.* A short account of an interesting or humorous incident. [< Gk. *anekdotos,* unpublished : A–¹ + *ek-,* out + *didonai,* give.] —**an′ec·dot′al** *adj.*

an·e·cho·ic (ăn′ĕ-kō′ĭk) ►*adj.* Neither having nor producing echoes.

a·ne·mi·a (ə-nē′mē-ə) ►*n.* A pathological deficiency in the oxygen-carrying component of the blood. —**a·ne′mic** *adj.*

an·e·mom·e·ter (ăn′ə-mŏm′ĭ-tər) ►*n.* An instrument for measuring wind speed. [< Gk. *anemos,* wind.]

a·nem·o·ne (ə-nĕm′ə-nē) ►*n.* **1.** A perennial plant having lobed leaves and large white or colored flowers. **2.** A sea anemone. [< Gk. *anemōnē.*]

a·nent (ə-nĕnt′) ►*prep.* Regarding; concerning. [< OE *onefn,* near.]

an·er·oid barometer (ăn′ə-roid′) ►*n.* A barometer in which changes in atmospheric pressure are indicated by the relative bulges of a thin metal disk covering a partially evacuated chamber. [A–¹ + Gk. *nēron,* water.]

an·es·the·sia also **an·aes·the·sia** (ăn′ĭs-thē′zhə) ►*n.* Total or partial loss of physical sensation caused by disease or an anesthetic. [< Gk. *anaisthēsia,* lack of sensation.]

an·es·the·si·ol·o·gy also **an·aes·the·si·ol·o·gy** (ăn′ĭs-thē′zē-ŏl′ə-jē) ►*n.* The medical study and application of anesthetics. —**an′es·the′si·ol′o·gist** *n.*

an·es·thet·ic also **an·aes·thet·ic** (ăn′ĭs-thĕt′ĭk) ►*adj.* Causing anesthesia. ►*n.* An agent or substance that induces anesthesia. —**an′es·thet′i·cal·ly** *adv.*

a·nes·the·tize also **a·naes·the·tize** (ə-nĕs′thĭ-tīz′) ►*v.* **-tized, -tiz·ing** To induce anesthesia in. —**an·es′the·tist** *n.* —**an·es′the·ti·za′tion** *n.*

an·eu·rysm also **an·eu·rism** (ăn′yə-rĭz′əm) ►*n.* A pathological, blood-filled dilatation of a blood vessel. [< Gk. *aneurusma.*]

a·new (ə-nōō′, -nyōō′) ►*adv.* **1.** Once more; again. **2.** In a new and different way.

an·gel (ān′jəl) ►*n.* **1.** In many religions, a usu. benevolent celestial being that acts as an intermediary between heaven and earth. **2.** A good, kind person. **3.** *Informal* A financial backer of an enterprise, esp. a dramatic production. [< Gk. *angelos,* messenger.] —**an·gel′ic** (ăn-jĕl′ĭk), **an·gel′i·cal** *adj.*

an·gel·fish (ān′jəl-fĭsh′) ►*n., pl.* **-fish** or **-fish·es** A brightly colored tropical fish having a laterally compressed body.

an·gel·i·ca (ăn-jĕl′ĭ-kə) ►*n.* An herb in the parsley family, whose roots and fruits are used in flavoring. [Med.Lat. *(herba) angelica,* angelic (herb).]

An·gel·i·co (ăn-jĕl′ĭ-kō′), **Fra.** 1400?–55. Italian Dominican friar and painter.

an·ger (ăng′gər) ►*n.* A strong feeling of displeasure, resentment, or hostility. ►*v.* To make or become angry. [< ON *angr,* grief.]

an·gi·na (ăn-jī′nə) ►*n.* **1.** Angina pectoris. **2.** A condition in which spasmodic attacks of suffocating pain occur. [< Gk. *ankhonē,* a strangling.]

angina pec·to·ris (pĕk′tər-ĭs) ►*n.* Severe paroxysmal pain in the chest associated with an insufficient supply of blood to the heart. [NLat., angina of the chest.]

an·gi·o·gen·e·sis (ăn′jē-ō-jĕn′ĭ-sĭs) ►*n.* The formation of new blood vessels. [Gk. *angeion,* vessel + –GENESIS.] —**an′gi·o·gen′ic** *adj.*

an·gi·o·gram (ăn′jē-ə-grăm′) ►*n.* An x-ray of the blood vessels following the injection of a radiopaque substance. [Gk. *angeion,* vessel + –GRAM.]

an·gi·o·plas·ty (ăn′jē-ə-plăs′tē) ►*n., pl.* **-ties** The repair of a blood vessel by surgical reconstruction or by use of an inflatable catheter to widen a partly-blocked passage. [Gk. *angeion,* vessel + E. *-plasty,* surgical repair.]

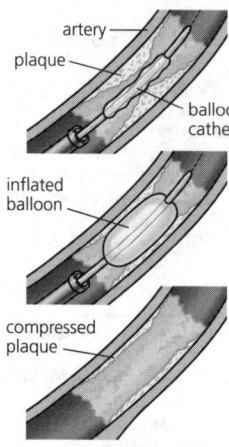

angioplasty
balloon angioplasty

an·gi·o·sperm (ăn′jē-ə-spûrm′) ►*n.* A seed-bearing plant whose ovules are enclosed in an ovary; a flowering plant. [Gk. *angeion,* vessel + SPERM.]

an·gle¹ (ăng′gəl) ►*v.* **-gled, -gling** **1.** To fish with a hook and line. **2.** To try to get something by using schemes or tricks. [< OE *angul,* fishhook.] —**an′gler** *n.*

an·gle² (ăng′gəl) ►*n.* **1.** *Math.* **a.** The figure formed by two lines diverging from a common point. **b.** The figure formed by two planes diverging from a common line. **c.** The space between such lines or surfaces. **2.** A corner, as of a building. **3a.** The place or direction from which an object is seen. **b.** A point of view. **4.** *Slang* A devious method; scheme. ►*v.* **-gled, -gling** To move or turn at an angle. [< Lat. *angulus.*]

An·gle (ăng′gəl) ►*n.* A member of a Germanic people that migrated to England from S Jutland in the 5th cent. A.D. and formed part of the Anglo-Saxon peoples.

an·gle·worm (ăng′gəl-wûrm′) ►*n.* A worm, such as an earthworm, used as bait in fishing.

An·gli·can (ăng′glĭ-kən) ►*adj.* Relating to the Church of England or to the churches in communion with it. —**An′gli·can** *n.* —**An′gli·can·ism** *n.*

An·gli·cism (ăng′glĭ-sĭz′əm) ►*n.* A word, phrase, or idiom peculiar to the English language, esp. as spoken in England.

An·gli·cize (ăng′glĭ-sīz′) ►*v.* **-cized, -ciz·ing** To make or become English. —**An′gli·ci·za′-tion** *n.*

An·glo (ăng′glō) ►*n., pl.* **-glos** An English-speaking person, esp. a white North American. —**An′glo** *adj.*

Anglo– ►*pref.* England; English: *Anglophile.* [< LLat. *Anglī,* the Angles.]

An·glo-A·mer·i·can (ăng′glō-ə-mĕr′ĭ-kən) ►*n.* An American of English ancestry. ►*adj.* Relating to England and the US.

An·glo·cen·tric (ăng′glō-sĕn′trĭk) ►*adj.* Centered or focused on England or the English. —**An′glo·cen′trism** *n.* —**An′glo·cen′trist** *adj. & n.*

An·glo-Nor·man (ăng′glō-nôr′mən) ►*n.* **1.** A Norman settler in England after 1066. **2.** The dialect of Old French used by the Anglo-Normans. —**An′glo-Nor′man** *adj.*

An·glo·phile (ăng′glə-fīl′) also **An·glo·phil** (-fĭl) ►*n.* One who admires England and its culture. —**An′glo·phil′i·a** (-fĭl′ē-ə) *n.*

An·glo·phobe (ăng′glə-fōb′) ►*n.* One who dislikes England or its culture. —**An′glo·pho′bi·a** *n.* —**An′glo·pho′bic** *adj.*

An·glo·phone (ăn′glə-fōn′) ►*n.* An English-speaking person, esp. in a region of linguistic diversity.

An·glo-Sax·on (ăng′glō-săk′sən) ►*n.* **1.** A member of one of the Germanic peoples who migrated to Britain in the 5th and 6th cent. **2.** See **Old English. 3.** A person of English ancestry. —**An′glo-Sax′on** *adj.*

An·go·la (ăng-gō′lə, ăn-) A country of SW Africa bordering on the Atlantic Ocean. Cap. Luanda. —**An·go′lan** *adj. & n.*

An·go·ra (ăng-gôr′ə) ►*n.* **1.** A cat, goat, or rabbit with long silky hair. **2.** often **angora** A yarn or fabric that is made from the hair of the Angora goat or rabbit. [After *Angora* (Ankara), Turkey.]

an·gry (ăng′grē) ►*adj.* **-gri·er, -gri·est 1.** Feeling or showing anger. **2.** Resulting from anger: *an angry silence.* **3.** Having a menacing aspect: *angry clouds.* **4.** Inflamed and painful.
   Syns: furious, indignant, irate, ireful, mad, wrathful adj.

angst (ängkst) ►*n.* A feeling of anxiety or apprehension. [Ger.]

ang·strom or **ång·strom** (ăng′strəm) ►*n.* A unit of length equal to one hundred-millionth (10^{-8}) of a centimeter. [After Anders Jonas *Ångström* (1814–74).]

An·guil·la (ăng-gwĭl′ə, ăn-) An island of the British West Indies in the N Leeward Is.

an·guish (ăng′gwĭsh) ►*n.* Agonizing physical or mental pain; torment. ►*v.* To cause or suffer anguish. [< Lat. *angustiae,* distress.]

an·gu·lar (ăng′gyə-lər) ►*adj.* **1.** Having an angle or angles. **2.** Measured by an angle. **3.** Bony and lean; gaunt. —**an′gu·lar′i·ty** (-lăr′ĭ-tē) *n.* —**an′gu·lar·ly** *adv.*

an·he·do·ni·a (ăn′hē-dō′nē-ə) ►*n.* The inability to experience pleasure, as seen in certain mood disorders. [Gk. *an-,* AN- + *hēdonē,* pleasure.]

an·hy·dride (ăn-hī′drīd′) ►*n.* A chemical compound formed from another by the removal of water. [ANHYDR(OUS) + –IDE.]

an·hy·drous (ăn-hī′drəs) ►*adj.* Without water. [< Gk. *anudros :* AN- + *hudōr,* water.]

an·i·line also **an·i·lin** (ăn′ə-lĭn) ►*n.* A colorless, oily, poisonous benzene derivative, C_6H_7N. [< *anil,* indigo.] —**an′i·line** *adj.*

an·i·mad·vert (ăn′ə-măd-vûrt′) ►*v.* To comment critically, usu. with disapproval. [< Lat.

animadvertere, direct the mind to.] —**an′i·mad·ver′sion** *n.*

an·i·mal (ăn′ə-məl) ►*n.* **1.** An organism of the kingdom Animalia, differing from plants in certain typical characteristics such as capacity for locomotion. **2.** An animal other than a human. **3.** A brutish person. ►*adj.* **1.** Of or relating to animals. **2.** Relating to physical as distinct from rational or spiritual nature: *animal instincts.* [Lat. < *anima*, spirit.]

animal husbandry ►*n.* The care and breeding of domestic animals.

an·i·mate (ăn′ə-māt′) ►*v.* -**mat·ed, -mat·ing 1.** To give life to. **2.** To impart interest to. **3.** To fill with spirit. **4.** To produce (e.g., a cartoon) with the illusion of motion. ►*adj.* (ăn′ə-mĭt) **1.** Possessing life; living. See Synonyms at **living. 2.** Relating to animal life. [Lat. *animāre* < *anima*, spirit.] —**an′i·ma′tion** (-mā′shən) *n.*

an·i·mat·ed (ăn′ə-mā′tĭd) ►*adj.* **1.** Spirited; lively. **2.** Designed so as to appear alive and moving. —**an′i·mat′ed·ly** *adv.*

a·ni·ma·to (ä′nē-mä′tō) ►*adv. & adj. Mus.* In an animated or lively manner. [Ital. < Lat. *animāre,* ANIMATE.]

an·i·ma·tor (ăn′ə-mā′tər) ►*n.* One that animates, esp. an artist or technician who produces animated cartoons.

an·i·me (ăn′ə-mā′) ►*n.* A style of animation marked by colorful art, futuristic settings, and violence. [Jap. < ANIMATION.]

an·i·mism (ăn′ə-mĭz′əm) ►*n.* The belief that natural phenomena or inanimate objects possess spirits. [< Lat. *anima*, spirit.] —**an′i·mist** *n.* —**an′i·mis′tic** *adj.*

an·i·mos·i·ty (ăn′ə-mŏs′ĭ-tē) ►*n., pl.* -**ties** Bitter hostility or open enmity. [< Lat. *animōsus,* bold.]

an·i·mus (ăn′ə-məs) ►*n.* **1.** Animosity. **2.** An attitude; disposition. [Lat., spirit.]

an·i·on (ăn′ī′ən) ►*n.* A negatively charged ion, esp. one that migrates to an anode. [< Gk. *anienai*, go up.] —**an′i·on′ic** (-ŏn′ĭk) *adj.* —**an′i·on′i·cal·ly** *adv.*

an·ise (ăn′ĭs) ►*n.* **1.** An annual aromatic Mediterranean herb in the parsley family used as flavoring. **2.** Aniseed. [< Gk. *anison.*]

an·i·seed (ăn′ĭ-sēd′) ►*n.* The seedlike fruit of the anise.

an·i·sette (ăn′ĭ-sĕt′, -zĕt′) ►*n.* A liqueur flavored with anise. [Fr.]

An·jou¹ (ăn′jōō′, äN-zhōō′) A historical region and former province of NW France in the Loire R. valley.

An·jou² (ăn′zhōō, -jōō) ►*n.* A variety of pear with green skin.

An·ka·ra (ăng′kər-ə, äng′-) The capital of Turkey, in the W-central part.

ankh (ăngk) ►*n.* A cross shaped like a T with a loop at the top. [Egypt. *'nḫ*, life.]

an·kle (ăng′kəl) ►*n.* **1.** The joint between the foot and the leg. **2.** The slender section of the leg above the foot. [ME *ancle.*]

an·kle·bone (ăng′kəl-bōn′) ►*n.* See **talus.**

an·klet (ăng′klĭt) ►*n.* **1.** An ornament worn around the ankle. **2.** A sock that reaches just above the ankle.

Ann (ăn), **Cape** A peninsula of NE MA projecting into the Atlantic.

an·nals (ăn′əlz) ►*pl.n.* **1.** A chronological record of the events of successive years. **2.** A descriptive account or record; history. [< Lat. *annus,* year.] —**an′nal·ist** *n.* —**an′nal·is′tic** *adj.*

An·nap·o·lis (ə-năp′ə-lĭs) The capital of MD, in the central part on an inlet of Chesapeake Bay SSE of Baltimore.

Ann Arbor A city of SE MI W of Detroit.

Anne (ăn) 1665–1714. Queen of Great Britain and Ireland (1702–14).

an·neal (ə-nēl′) ►*v.* **1.** To heat (glass or metal) and slowly cool it to toughen and reduce brittleness. **2.** To strengthen or harden. [< OE *onǣlan.*]

an·ne·lid (ăn′ə-lĭd) ►*n.* Any of various worms with cylindrical segmented bodies, including the earthworm. [< Lat. *ānellus,* small ring.]

an·nex (ə-nĕks′) ►*v.* **1.** To add, esp. to a larger thing. **2.** To incorporate (territory) into a larger existing political unit. ►*n.* (ăn′ĕks′) A building that is near or added on to a larger one. [< Lat. *annectere, annex-,* connect to.] —**an′nex·a′tion** *n.*

an·ni·hi·late (ə-nī′ə-lāt′) ►*v.* -**lat·ed, -lat·ing** To destroy completely. [LLat. *annihilāre.*] —**an·ni′hi·la′tion** *n.*

an·ni·ver·sa·ry (ăn′ə-vûr′sə-rē) ►*n., pl.* -**ries** The annually recurring date of a past event. [< Lat. *anniversārius,* returning yearly.]

an·no Dom·i·ni (ăn′ō dŏm′ə-nī′, -nē) ►*adv.* In a specified year of the Christian era. [Med.Lat., in the year of the Lord.]

an·no·tate (ăn′ō-tāt′) ►*v.* -**tat·ed, -tat·ing** To furnish (a literary work) with commentary or explanatory notes. [Lat. *annotāre,* note down.] —**an′no·ta′tion** *n.* —**an′no·ta′tive** *adj.* —**an′no·ta′tor** *n.*

an·nounce (ə-nouns′) ►*v.* -**nounced, -nounc·ing 1.** To make known publicly. **2.** To proclaim the arrival of. **3.** To serve as an announcer (for). [< Lat. *annūntiāre,* report to.] —**an·nounce′ment** *n.*

Syns: advertise, broadcast, declare, proclaim, promulgate, publish **v.**

an·nounc·er (ə-noun′sər) ►*n.* One that announces, esp. a person who introduces programs, reads announcements, or provides commentary on television or radio.

an·noy (ə-noi′) ►*v.* To bother or irritate. [< VLat. **inodiāre,* make odious.] —**an·noy′ing·ly** *adv.*

Syns: aggravate, bother, irk, irritate, peeve, rile, vex **v.**

an·noy·ance (ə-noi′əns) ►*n.* **1.** The act of annoying or the state of being annoyed. **2.** A cause of vexation; nuisance.

an·nu·al (ăn′yōō-əl) ►*adj.* **1.** Recurring or done every year; yearly. **2.** Determined by a year: *an annual income.* **3.** *Bot.* Living or growing for only one year or season. ►*n.* **1.** A periodical that is published yearly; yearbook. **2.** *Bot.* An annual plant. [< Lat. *annus,* year.] —**an′nu·al·ly** *adv.*

annual ring ►*n.* A growth ring formed during a single year.

an·nu·i·tant (ə-nōō′ĭ-tənt, -nyōō′-) ►*n.* One that receives an annuity.

an·nu·i·ty (ə-nōō′ĭ-tē, -nyōō′-) ►*n., pl.* -**ties 1.** The annual payment of an allowance or income. **2.** An investment on which one receives fixed payments for a lifetime or for a specified period. [< Lat. *annuus,* yearly.]

an·nul (ə-nŭl′) ►*v.* -**nulled, -nul·ling** To declare

invalid, as a marriage or a law; nullify. [< LLat. *annullāre*.] —**an·nul′ment** *n.*

an·nu·lar (ăn′yə-lər) ►*adj.* Ring-shaped.

an·nu·lus (ăn′yə-ləs) ►*n., pl.* **-lus·es** or **-li** (-lī′) A ringlike figure, part, structure, or marking. [Lat. *ānulus*, ring.]

an·nun·ci·a·tion (ə-nŭn′sē-ā′shən) ►*n.* **1.** The act of announcing. **2.** An announcement. **3. Annunciation** *Christianity* The angel Gabriel's announcement to the Virgin Mary of the Incarnation. —**an·nun′ci·ate′** (-āt′) *v.*

an·ode (ăn′ōd′) ►*n.* **1.** A positively charged electrode on a device that receives electrical current. **2.** A negatively charged electrode on a device that supplies electrical current. [Gk. *anodos*, a way up.]

an·o·dize (ăn′ə-dīz′) ►*v.* **-dized, -diz·ing** To coat (a metal) electrolytically with an oxide.

an·o·dyne (ăn′ə-dīn′) ►*n.* **1.** A medicine that relieves pain. **2.** A source of comfort. [< Gk. *anōdunos*, free from pain : AN– + *odunē*, pain.] —**an′o·dyne** *adj.*

a·noint (ə-noint′) ►*v.* **1.** To apply oil or ointment to, esp. in a religious ceremony. **2.** To choose by or as if by divine intervention. [< Lat. *inunguere*.] —**a·noint′ment** *n.*

a·no·le (ə-nō′lē) ►*n.* Any of a genus of chiefly tropical American lizards having the ability to change color. [Of Cariban orig.]

a·nom·a·ly (ə-nŏm′ə-lē) ►*n., pl.* **-lies 1.** Deviation from the normal order, form, or rule. **2.** One that is peculiar, abnormal, or difficult to classify. [< Gk. *anōmalos*, uneven.] —**a·nom′a·lis′tic** (-lĭs′tĭk) *adj.* —**a·nom′a·lous** *adj.*

a·non (ə-nŏn′) ►*adv.* **1.** In a short time; soon. **2.** *Archaic* At once; forthwith. [< OE *on ān.*]

anon. ►*abbr.* anonymous

a·non·y·mous (ə-nŏn′ə-məs) ►*adj.* Having an unknown or unacknowledged name, authorship, or agency. [< Gk. *anōnumos*, nameless.] —**an′o·nym′i·ty** (ăn′ə-nĭm′ĭ-tē) *n.* —**a·non′y·mous·ly** *adv.*

a·noph·e·les (ə-nŏf′ə-lēz′) ►*n.* A mosquito that transmits malaria to humans. [< Gk. *anōphelēs*, useless.]

an·o·rak (ăn′ə-răk′) ►*n.* A parka. [Inuit *annoraaq.*]

anorak

an·o·rec·tic (ăn′ə-rĕk′tĭk) ►*adj.* **1.** Marked by or causing loss of appetite. **2.** Of or afflicted with anorexia nervosa. [< Gk. *anorektos.*] —**an′o·rec′tic** *n.*

an·o·rex·i·a (ăn′ə-rĕk′sē-ə) ►*n.* **1.** Loss of appetite, esp. as a result of disease. **2.** Anorexia nervosa. [Gk.]

anorexia ner·vo·sa (nûr-vō′sə) ►*n.* A psychophysiological disorder usu. occurring in young women, marked by an abnormal fear of becoming obese. [NLat., nervous anorexia.]

an·o·rex·ic (ăn′ə-rĕk′sĭk) ►*adj.* **1.** Afflicted with anorexia nervosa. **2.** Anorectic. —**an′o·rex′ic** *n.*

an·oth·er (ə-nŭth′ər) ►*adj.* **1.** One more; an additional: *another cup of coffee.* **2.** Distinctly different: *tried another method.* **3.** Some other: *costumes from another era.* ►*pron.* **1.** An additional or different one. **2.** One of an undetermined number.

A·nou·ilh (ä-nōō′ē), **Jean** 1910–87. French playwright.

ANSI ►*abbr.* American National Standards Institute

an·swer (ăn′sər) ►*n.* **1.** A spoken or written reply, as to a question. **2.** A solution, as to a problem. **3.** An act in response. ►*v.* **1.** To reply (to). **2.** To be liable or accountable. **3.** To suffice. See Synonyms at **satisfy. 4.** To correspond (to); match. [< OE *andswaru.*] —**an′swer·a·ble** *adj.* —**an′swer·a·bly** *adv.*

an·swer·ing machine (ăn′sər-ĭng) ►*n.* An electronic device for answering one's telephone and recording callers' messages.

ant (ănt) ►*n.* Any of various social insects usu. having wings only in the males and fertile females and living in complexly organized colonies. [< OE *æmete.*]

ant. ►*abbr.* antonym

Ant. ►*abbr.* Antarctica

ant– ►*pref.* Var. of **anti–.**

–ant ►*suff.* **1a.** Performing or promoting an action: *conversant.* **b.** In a state or condition: *expectant.* **2.** One that performs or promotes an action: *stimulant.* [< Lat. *-āns, -ant-*, pres. part. suff.]

ant·ac·id (ănt-ăs′ĭd) ►*adj.* Counteracting acidity, esp. of the stomach. ►*n.* A substance, such as sodium bicarbonate, that neutralizes acid.

an·tag·o·nism (ăn-tăg′ə-nĭz′əm) ►*n.* **1.** Hostility; enmity. **2.** The condition of being an opposing force.

an·tag·o·nist (ăn-tăg′ə-nĭst) ►*n.* **1.** One who opposes; adversary. **2.** The principal character in opposition to the protagonist or hero of a narrative or drama. **3.** A chemical substance that interferes with the physiological action of another. **4.** *Physiol.* A muscle that counteracts the action of another muscle, the agonist. —**an·tag′o·nis′tic** *adj.* —**an·tag′o·nis′ti·cal·ly** *adv.*

an·tag·o·nize (ăn-tăg′ə-nīz′) ►*v.* **-nized, -niz·ing** To provoke hostility in. [Gk. *antagōnizesthai*, struggle against : ANTI– + *agōn*, contest; see AGONY.]

An·ta·na·na·ri·vo (ăn′tə-năn′ə-rē′vō, än′-tə-nä′nə-) The capital of Madagascar, in the E-central part.

Ant·arc·ti·ca (ănt-ärk′tĭ-kə, -är′tĭ-kə) An ice-covered continent centered asymmetrically centered on the South Pole. —**Ant·arc′tic** *adj.*

Antarctic Circle The parallel of latitude (approx. 66°33′ S) that separates the South Temperate and South Frigid zones.

An·tar·es (ăn-târ′ēz, -tăr′-) ►*n.* The brightest star in the constellation Scorpio.

an·te (ăn′tē) ►*n.* **1.** The stake each poker player puts into the pool before receiving a hand or before receiving new cards. **2.** A price to be paid, esp. as one's share. ►*v.* **-ted** or **-teed, -te·ing 1.** To put up (one's stake) in poker. **2.** To pay (one's share). [< Lat., before.]

ante– ►*pref.* **1.** Earlier: *antedate.* **2.** In front of: *anteroom.* [Lat.]

ant·eat·er (ănt′ē′tər) ►*n.* Any of several tropical American mammals that lack teeth and feed on ants and termites.

an·te·bel·lum (ăn′tē-bĕl′əm) ►*adj.* Of the period before the American Civil War. [Lat. *ante bellum,* before the war.]

an·te·ce·dent (ăn′tĭ-sēd′nt) ►*adj.* Going before; preceding. ►*n.* **1.** One that precedes. **2.** A preceding occurrence or cause. **3. antecedents** One's ancestors. **4.** *Gram.* The word, phrase, or clause to which a pronoun refers. [< Lat. *antecēdere,* go before.] —**an′te·ce′dence** *n.*

an·te·cham·ber (ăn′tē-chām′bər) ►*n.* An anteroom.

an·te·date (ăn′tĭ-dāt′) ►*v.* **-dat·ed, -dat·ing 1.** To precede in time. **2.** To give a date earlier than the actual one.

an·te·di·lu·vi·an (ăn′tĭ-də-lōō′vē-ən) ►*adj.* **1.** *Bible* Occurring before the Flood. **2.** Extremely old or old-fashioned. [< ANTE– + Lat. *dīluvium,* flood (< *dīluere,* wash away; see DILUTE).] —**an′te·di·lu′vi·an** *n.*

an·te·lope (ăn′tl-ōp′) ►*n., pl.* **-lope** or **-lopes 1.** Any of various swift-running ruminant mammals native to Africa and Eurasia and having unbranched horns. **2.** The pronghorn. [< LGk. *antholops.*]

an·te me·rid·i·em (ăn′tē mə-rĭd′ē-əm) ►*adv. & adj.* Before noon. See Usage Note at **AM.** [Lat.]

an·ten·na (ăn-tĕn′ə) ►*n., pl.* **-ten·nae** (-tĕn′ē) **1.** One of the paired, flexible sensory organs on the head of an insect, myriapod, or crustacean. **2.** *pl.* **-nas** An apparatus for sending or receiving electromagnetic waves. [< Lat., sail yard.]

an·te·pe·nul·ti·mate (ăn′tē-pĭ-nŭl′tə-mĭt) ►*adj.* Coming third from the end of a series. [< LLat. *antepaenultimus* : Lat. *ante-,* ante- + *paenultimus,* penultimate.]

an·te·ri·or (ăn-tîr′ē-ər) ►*adj.* **1.** Placed before or in front. **2.** Prior in time. [Lat.]

an·te·room (ăn′tē-rōōm′, -rōōm′) ►*n.* An outer room that opens into another room.

an·them (ăn′thəm) ►*n.* **1.** A hymn of praise or loyalty. **2.** A sacred choral composition. **3.** A popular song felt to sum up the attitudes associated with a period or social group. [< LGk. *antiphōnos,* sounding in answer.]

an·ther (ăn′thər) ►*n.* The pollen-bearing part of a stamen. [Ult. < Gk. *anthos,* flower.]

ant·hill (ănt′hĭl′) ►*n.* A mound of earth formed by ants or termites in digging a nest.

an·thol·o·gy (ăn-thŏl′ə-jē) ►*n., pl.* **-gies** A collection of selected writings. [< Gk. *anthologia,* gathering of flowers.] —**an·thol′o·gist** *n.* —**an·thol′o·gize′** *v.*

An·tho·ny (ăn′thə-nē), Saint. AD 251?–356? Egyptian ascetic monk considered the founder of Christian monasticism.

Anthony, Susan Brownell 1820–1906. Amer. reformer and suffragist.

Susan B. Anthony

an·thra·cite (ăn′thrə-sīt′) ►*n.* A dense shiny coal that has a high carbon content. [Prob. < Gk. *anthrakitis,* a kind of coal.] —**an′thra·cit′ic** (-sĭt′ĭk) *adj.*

an·thrax (ăn′thrăks′) ►*n.* An infectious, usu. fatal bacterial disease esp. of cattle and sheep, marked by skin ulcers and transmissible to humans. [< Gk., carbuncle.]

anthropo– ►*pref.* Human: *anthropoid.* [< Gk. *anthrōpos,* human being.]

an·thro·po·cen·tric (ăn′thrə-pə-sĕn′trĭk) ►*adj.* Interpreting reality in terms of human values and experience. —**an′thro·po·cen′trism** *n.*

an·thro·po·gen·ic (ăn′thrə-pə-jĕn′ĭk) ►*adj.* **1.** Relating to the origin and development of humans. **2.** Caused by humans. —**an′thro·po·gen′i·cal·ly** *adv.*

an·thro·poid (ăn′thrə-poid′) ►*n.* A member of the group of primates that includes monkeys and apes, including humans. ►*adj.* **1.** Of or belonging to this group. **2.** Resembling a human.

an·thro·pol·o·gy (ăn′thrə-pŏl′ə-jē) ►*n.* The scientific study of the origin, development, and cultural behavior of humans. —**an′thro·po·log′i·cal** (-pə-lŏj′ĭ-kəl), **an′thro·po·log′ic** (-ĭk) *adj.* —**an′thro·pol′o·gist** *n.*

an·thro·po·mor·phism (ăn′thrə-pə-môr′fĭz′-əm) ►*n.* Attribution of human characteristics to animals, inanimate objects, or natural phenomena. —**an′thro·po·mor′phic** *adj.* —**an′-thro·po·mor′phize** *v.*

an·ti (ăn′tī, -tē) ►*n., pl.* **-tis** One who is opposed. [< ANTI–.] —**an′ti** *adj. & prep.*

anti– or **ant–** ►*pref.* **1a.** Opposite: *antiparticle.* **b.** Opposed to: *antinuclear.* **c.** Counteracting: *antibody.* **2.** Inverse: *antilogarithm.* [< Gk. *anti,* opposite.]

an·ti·a·bor·tion (ăn′tē-ə-bôr′shən, ăn′tī-) ►*adj.* Opposed to abortion. —**an′ti·a·bor′tion·ist** *n.*

an·ti·bal·lis·tic missile (ăn′tĭ-bə-lĭs′tĭk, ăn′tī-) ►*n.* A defensive missile designed to intercept and destroy a ballistic missile in flight.

an·ti·bi·ot·ic (ăn′tĭ-bī-ŏt′ĭk, ăn′tī-) ►*n.* A substance, such as penicillin or erythromycin, that destroys or inhibits the growth of microorganisms and is used to treat infectious diseases and conditions. —**an′ti·bi·ot′ic** *adj.*

an·ti·bod·y (ăn′tĭ-bŏd′ē) ►*n.* A protein produced in the blood as an immune response to a specific antigen.

an·tic (ăn′tĭk) ►*n.* A ludicrous act or gesture.

[Ital. *antico*, ancient.] —**an′tic** *adj.*

an·ti·choice (ăn′tē-chois′, ăn′tī-) ►*adj.* Opposed to the right of women to choose or reject abortion.

An·ti·christ (ăn′tĭ-krīst′, ăn′tī-) ►*n. Bible* The great enemy of Christ expected to appear in the last days before Christ's return.

an·tic·i·pate (ăn-tĭs′ə-pāt′) ►*v.* -**pat·ed, -pat·ing 1.** To foresee. **2.** To look forward to; expect. **3.** To act in advance to prevent; forestall. [Lat. *anticipāre*, take before.] —**an·tic′i·pa′tion** *n.* —**an·tic′i·pa′tor** *n.* —**an·tic′i·pa·to′ry** (-pə-tôr′ē) *adj.*

an·ti·cler·i·cal (ăn′tē-klĕr′ĭ-kəl, ăn′tī-) ►*adj.* Opposed to the influence of the church in public life. —**an′ti·cler′i·cal·ism** *n.*

an·ti·cli·max (ăn′tē-klī′măks′, ăn′tī-) ►*n.* **1.** A decline viewed in disappointing contrast to previous events. **2.** Something commonplace that concludes a series of significant events. —**an′ti·cli·mac′tic** *adj.*

an·ti·cy·clone (ăn′tē-sī′klōn′, ăn′tī-) ►*n.* A system of winds spiraling outward from a high-pressure center. —**an′ti·cy·clon′ic** (-klŏn′-ĭk) *adj.*

an·ti·de·pres·sant (ăn′tē-dĭ-prĕs′ənt, ăn′tī-) ►*n.* A drug used to treat mental depression. —**an′ti·de·pres′sive** *adj.*

an·ti·dote (ăn′tĭ-dōt′) ►*n.* **1.** An agent that counteracts a poison. **2.** Something that relieves or counteracts. [< Gk. *antidoton* : ANTI–, anti- + *didonai*, do-, give.] —**an′ti·dot′al** *adj.*

Usage: Antidote may be followed by *to, for,* or *against: an antidote to boredom; an antidote for snakebite; an antidote against inflation.*

An·tie·tam (ăn-tē′təm) A creek of N-central MD emptying into the Potomac R.; site of a Civil War battle (1862).

an·ti·freeze (ăn′tĭ-frēz′) ►*n.* A substance, such as ethylene glycol, mixed into a liquid to lower its freezing point.

an·ti·gen (ăn′tĭ-jən) ►*n.* A substance, such as a toxin, bacterium, or foreign cell, that when introduced into the body stimulates the production of an antibody. —**an′ti·gen′ic** (-jĕn′-ĭk) *adj.* —**an′ti·ge·nic′i·ty** (-jə-nĭs′ĭ-tē) *n.*

An·ti·gua and Barbuda (ăn-tē′gə) A country in the N Leeward Is. of the Caribbean Sea, comprising the islands of **Antigua,** Barbuda, and Redonda. Cap. St. John's. —**An·ti′guan** *adj. & n.*

an·ti·he·ro also **an·ti-he·ro** (ăn′tē-hîr′ō, ăn′tī-) ►*n., pl.* -**roes** A main character in a fiction or drama who lacks traditional heroic qualities. —**an′ti·her·o′ic** (-hĭ-rō′ĭk) *adj.*

an·ti·her·o·ine or **an·ti-her·o·ine** (ăn′tē-hĕr′-ō-ĭn, ăn′tī-) ►*n.* An antihero who is a woman or girl.

an·ti·his·ta·mine (ăn′tē-hĭs′tə-mēn′, -mĭn) ►*n.* A drug used to counteract the physiological effects of histamine production in allergic reactions and colds.

an·ti·knock (ăn′tĭ-nŏk′) ►*n.* A substance added to gasoline to reduce engine knock.

An·til·les (ăn-tĭl′ēz) The islands of the West Indies except for the Bahamas, separating the Caribbean Sea from the Atlantic and divided into the **Greater Antilles** to the N and the **Lesser Antilles** to the E.

an·ti·lock (ăn′tē-lŏk′, ăn′tī-) ►*adj.* Of or being a motor vehicle braking system in which wheel speeds are electronically adjusted to prevent locking.

an·ti·log (ăn′tē-lôg′, -lŏg′, ăn′tī-) ►*n.* An antilogarithm.

an·ti·log·a·rithm (ăn′tē-lô′gə-rĭ*th*′əm, -lŏg′-ə-, ăn′tī-) ►*n.* The number for which a given logarithm stands; e.g., if log *x* equals *y,* then *x* is the antilogarithm of *y.*

an·ti·ma·cas·sar (ăn′tē-mə-kăs′ər) ►*n.* A protective covering for the back of a chair or sofa. [ANTI– + *Macassar*, a brand of hair oil.]

an·ti·mat·ter (ăn′tĭ-măt′ər, ăn′tī-) ►*n.* A form of matter identical to physical matter except that it is composed of antiparticles.

an·ti·mo·ny (ăn′tə-mō′nē) ►*n. Symbol* **Sb** A metallic element used in a wide variety of alloys, esp. with lead in battery plates, and in paints, semiconductors, and ceramics. At. no. 51. See table at **element.** [< Med.Lat. *antimonium.*]

an·ti·neu·tron (ăn′tē-nōō′trŏn′, -nyōō′-, ăn′-

---

an′ti·air′craft′ *adj. & n.*
an′ti·al·ler′gic *adj.*
an′ti-A·mer′i·can *adj.*
an′ti·anx·i′e·ty *adj.*
an′ti·bac·te′ri·al *adj. & n.*
an′ti·can′cer *adj.*
an′ti·cap′i·tal·ist *n. & adj.*
an′ti·Cath′o·lic *adj. & n.*
an′ti·co·ag′u·lant *n. & adj.*
an′ti·co·lo′ni·al *adj. & n.*
an′ti·co·lo′ni·al·ism *n.*
an′ti·com′mu·nism *n.*
an′ti·com′mu·nist *n. & adj.*
an′ti·con·vul′sant *n.*
an′ti·cor·ro′sive *adj. & n.*
an′ti·crime′ *adj.*
an′ti·dem′o·crat′ic *adj.*
an′ti·di′ar·rhe′al *n. & adj.*
an′ti·es·tab′lish·ment *n.*
an′ti·fas′cism *n.*
an′ti·fas′cist *n. & adj.*
an′ti·fem′i·nism *n.*
an′ti·fem′i·nist *adj. & n.*
an′ti·fun′gal *adj. & n.*

an′ti·im·pe′ri·al·ism *n.*
an′ti·im·pe′ri·al·ist *adj. & n.*
an′ti·in·fec′tive *adj. & n.*
an′ti·in·flam′ma·to′ry
   adj. & n.
an′ti·in·tel·lec′tu·al *adj.*
   & n.
an′ti·in·tel·lec′tu·al·ism *n.*
an′ti·i′so·la′tion·ist *n.*
an′ti·la′bor *adj.*
an′ti·lib′er·al *adj. & n.*
an′ti·ma·lar′i·al *adj.*
an′ti·mi·cro′bi·al *adj.*
an′ti·mil′i·ta·rism *n.*
an′ti·mi·tot′ic *adj. & n.*
an′ti·mon′ar·chist *n.*
an′ti·mo·nop′o·lis′tic
   adj.
an′ti·nar·cot′ic *n. & adj.*
an′ti·na′tion·al·ist *n.*
an′ti·pac′i·fist *n.*
an′ti·par′a·sit′ic *adj. & n.*
an′ti·pole′ *n.*
an′ti·pol·lu′tion *adj.*

an′ti·pov′er·ty *adj.*
an′ti·Prot′es·tant *n. & adj.*
an′ti·rad′i·cal *adj. & n.*
an′ti·ra′tion·al *adj.*
an′ti·re·lig′ious *adj.*
an′ti·ret′ro·vi′ral *adj. & n.*
an′ti·rev′o·lu′tion·ar′y
   adj. & n.
an′ti·scor·bu′tic *adj. & n.*
an′ti·slav′er·y *adj. & n.*
an′ti·spas·mod′ic *adj.*
   & n.
an′ti·stat′ic *adj. & n.*
an′ti·sub′ma·rine′ *adj.*
an′ti·take′o′ver *adj.*
an′ti·tank′ *adj.*
an′ti·ter′ror·ism *n.*
an′ti·ter′ror·ist *adj.*
an′ti·tu′mor *adj.*
an′ti·viv′i·sec′tion *adj.*
an′ti·viv′i·sec′tion·ist *n.*
an′ti·war′ *adj.*
an′ti-Zi′on·ist *adj. & n.*

tī-) ►*n.* The antiparticle of the neutron.

an·ti·nov·el (ăn′tē-nŏv′əl, ăn′tī-) ►*n.* A fictional work that lacks traditional elements of the novel, such as coherent plot structure or realistic character development.

an·ti·nu·cle·ar (ăn′tē-no͞o′klē-ər, -nyo͞o′-, ăn′-tī-) ►*adj.* Opposing the production or use of nuclear power or nuclear weaponry.

An·ti·och (ăn′tē-ŏk′) An ancient town of Phrygia in SW Turkey.

an·ti·ox·i·dant (ăn′tē-ŏk′sĭ-dənt, ăn′tī-) ►*n.* **1.** A substance that inhibits oxidation. **2.** A substance, such as vitamin E, thought to protect body cells from the damaging effects of oxidation.

an·ti·par·ti·cle (ăn′tē-pär′tĭ-kəl, ăn′tī-) ►*n.* A subatomic particle, such as a positron or antiproton, having the same mass, lifetime, and spin as the particle to which it corresponds but having the opposite electric charge and magnetic properties.

an·ti·pas·to (än′tē-päs′tō) ►*n.,* *pl.* **-tos** or **-ti** (-tē) An appetizer usu. of assorted meats, cheeses, and vegetables. [Ital.]

an·tip·a·thy (ăn-tĭp′ə-thē) ►*n.,* *pl.* **-thies 1.** Extreme dislike; aversion or repugnance. **2.** A feeling of aversion. [< Gk. *antipathēs,* of opposite feelings.]

an·ti·per·son·nel (ăn′tē-pûr′sə-nĕl′, ăn′tī-) ►*adj.* Designed to cause death or injury rather than material damage.

an·ti·per·spi·rant (ăn′tē-pûr′spər-ənt, ăn′-tī-) ►*n.* A preparation applied to the skin to decrease perspiration.

an·ti·phon (ăn′tə-fŏn′) ►*n.* A devotional composition sung responsively as part of a liturgy. [LLat. *antiphōna,* ANTHEM.] —**an·tiph′o·nal** (-tĭf′ə-nəl) *adj.*

an·tiph·o·ny (ăn-tĭf′ə-nē) ►*n.,* *pl.* **-nies 1.** Responsive or antiphonal singing. **2.** An exchange, as of ideas or opinions.

an·ti·pode (ăn′tĭ-pōd′) ►*n.* A direct opposite. —**an·tip′o·dal** (-tĭp′ə-dəl) *adj.*

an·tip·o·des (ăn-tĭp′ə-dēz′) ►*pl.n.* **1.** Two places on diametrically opposite sides of the earth. **2.** *(takes sing. or pl. v.)* One that is the exact opposite of another. [< Gk. : ANTI– + *pous, pod-,* foot.]

an·ti·pope (ăn′tĭ-pōp′) ►*n.* One claiming to be pope in opposition to the one chosen by church law.

an·ti·pro·ton (ăn′tē-prō′tŏn′, ăn′tī-) ►*n.* The antiparticle of the proton.

an·ti·psy·chot·ic (ăn′tē-sī-kŏt′ĭk, ăn′tī-) ►*adj.* Counteracting the symptoms of psychosis.

an·ti·py·ret·ic (ăn′tē-pī-rĕt′ĭk, ăn′tī-) ►*adj.* Reducing fever. ►*n.* A medication that reduces fever. —**an′ti·py·re′sis** (-rē′sĭs) *n.*

an·ti·quar·i·an (ăn′tĭ-kwâr′ē-ən) ►*n.* One who studies, collects, or deals in antiquities. —**an′·ti·quar′i·an** *adj.*

an·ti·quark (ăn′tē-kwôrk′, ăn′tī-) ►*n.* The antiparticle of a quark.

an·ti·quar·y (ăn′tĭ-kwĕr′ē) ►*n.,* *pl.* **-ies** An antiquarian.

an·ti·quate (ăn′tĭ-kwāt′) ►*v.* **-quat·ed, -quat·ing** To make obsolete. —**an′ti·qua′tion** *n.*

an·tique (ăn-tēk′) ►*adj.* Belonging to or made in an earlier period. ►*n.* An object that is considered valuable because of its age and artistry. ►*v.* **-tiqued, -tiqu·ing** To give the appearance

of an antique to. [< Lat. *antīquus.*]

an·tiq·ui·ty (ăn-tĭk′wĭ-tē) ►*n.,* *pl.* **-ties 1.** Ancient times, esp. those before the Middle Ages. **2.** The quality of being old or ancient: *a carving of great antiquity.* **3.** often **antiquities** Something dating from ancient times.

an·ti·re·jec·tion (ăn′tē-rĭ-jĕk′shən, ăn′tī-) ►*adj.* Preventing rejection of a transplanted tissue or organ.

an·ti·sat·el·lite (ăn′tē-săt′l-īt, ăn′tī-) ►*adj.* Directed against enemy satellites.

an·ti·Sem·ite (ăn′tē-sĕm′īt′, ăn′tī-) ►*n.* One who is prejudiced against Jews. —**an′ti·Se·mit′ic** (-sə-mĭt′ĭk) *adj.* —**an′ti·Sem′i·tism** (-sĕm′ĭ-tĭz′əm) *n.*

an·ti·sep·sis (ăn′tĭ-sĕp′sĭs) ►*n.* Destruction of disease-causing microorganisms to prevent infection.

an·ti·sep·tic (ăn′tĭ-sĕp′tĭk) ►*adj.* **1.** Relating to or producing antisepsis. **2.** Thoroughly clean; aseptic. —**an′ti·sep′tic** *n.*

an·ti·se·rum (ăn′tĭ-sîr′əm) ►*n.,* *pl.* **-se·rums** or **-se·ra** (-sî′rə) Serum containing antibodies that are specific for one or more antigens.

an·ti·smok·ing (ăn′tē-smō′kĭng, ăn′tī-) ►*adj.* Opposed to or prohibiting the smoking of tobacco, esp. in public.

an·ti·so·cial (ăn′tē-sō′shəl, ăn′tī-) ►*adj.* **1.** Shunning others; not sociable. **2.** Disruptive of the established social order.

an·ti·theft (ăn′tē-thĕft′, ăn′tī-) ►*adj.* Designed to prevent theft.

an·tith·e·sis (ăn-tĭth′ĭ-sĭs) ►*n.,* *pl.* **-ses** (-sēz′) **1.** Direct contrast; opposition. **2.** The direct opposite. **3.** The juxtaposition of contrasting ideas in parallel grammatical structures. [< Gk.] —**an′ti·thet′i·cal** (ăn′tĭ-thĕt′ĭ-kəl), **an′·ti·thet′ic** *adj.*

an·ti·tox·in (ăn′tē-tŏk′sĭn) ►*n.* An antibody formed in response to and capable of neutralizing a specific biological toxin.

an·ti·trust (ăn′tē-trŭst′, ăn′tī-) ►*adj.* Opposing or regulating business monopolies, such as trusts or cartels.

an·ti·tus·sive (ăn′tē-tŭs′ĭv, ăn′tī-) ►*adj.* Relieving or suppressing coughing. [< ANTI- + Lat. *tussis,* cough.] —**an′ti·tus′sive** *n.*

an·ti·vi·ral (ăn′tē-vī′rəl, ăn′tī-) ►*adj.* **1.** Destroying or inhibiting viral growth and reproduction. **2.** *Comp.* Designed to inactivate a virus. ►*n.* An antiviral drug.

an·ti·vi·rus (ăn′tē-vī′rəs, ăn′tī-) ►*adj.* Of or relating to software designed to find and remove computer viruses.

ant·ler (ănt′lər) ►*n.* One of a pair of branched bony growths on the head of a deer. [< OFr. *antoillier.*] —**ant′lered** *adj.*

ant·li·on (ănt′lī′ən) ►*n.* The large-jawed larva of an insect resembling a dragonfly, which digs holes to trap ants for food.

an·to·nym (ăn′tə-nĭm′) ►*n.* A word meaning the opposite of another word. —**an′to·nym′ic** *adj.* —**an·ton′y·mous** (ăn-tŏn′ə-məs) *adj.* —**an·ton′y·my** *n.*

ant·sy (ănt′sē) ►*adj.* **-si·er, -si·est** *Slang* Restless or fidgety.

Ant·werp (ănt′twərp) A city of N Belgium N of Brussels.

a·nus (ā′nəs) ►*n.,* *pl.* **a·nus·es** The excretory opening at the lower end of the digestive tract. [< Lat. *ānus.*]

an·vil (ăn′vĭl) ►*n.* **1.** A heavy block of iron or steel with a smooth flat top on which metals are shaped by hammering. **2.** *Anat.* See **incus.** [< OE *anfilt.*]

anx·i·e·ty (ăng-zī′ĭ-tē) ►*n., pl.* **-ties** Uneasiness, apprehension, or fear resulting from anticipation of an unpleasant event. [< Lat. *ānxius,* ANXIOUS.]

anx·ious (ăngk′shəs, ăng′-) ►*adj.* **1.** Uneasy and apprehensive; worried. **2.** *Informal* Eager; desirous: *was anxious to see the new show.* [< Lat. *ānxius < angere,* to torment.] —**anx′ious·ly** *adv.* —**anx′ious·ness** *n.*

an·y (ĕn′ē) ►*adj.* One, some, every, or all without specification: *Take any book you want. Are there any messages for me? Any child would love that.* See Usage Note at **every.** ►*pron. (takes sing. or pl. v.)* Any one or more persons, things, or quantities. ►*adv.* To any degree; at all: *didn't feel any better.* [< OE *ǣnig.*]

an·y·bod·y (ĕn′ē-bŏd′ē, -bŭd′ē) ►*pron.* Anyone. ►*n.* An important person: *Everybody who is anybody was there.*

an·y·how (ĕn′ē-hou′) ►*adv.* **1.** In whatever way or manner. **2.** Haphazardly. **3a.** In any case; at least. **b.** Nevertheless.

an·y·more (ĕn′ē-môr′) ►*adv.* **1a.** Any longer; still: *Do they make this model anymore?* **b.** From now on: *promised not to quarrel anymore.* **2.** *Regional* Nowadays.
    Usage: The word *anymore* is widely used to mean "nowadays," esp. in the South Midland and Midwestern states and the Western states that received settlers from those areas.

an·y·one (ĕn′ē-wŭn′, -wən) ►*pron.* Any person.

an·y·place (ĕn′ē-plās′) ►*adv.* To, in, or at any place; anywhere.

an·y·thing (ĕn′ē-thĭng′) ►*pron.* Any object or matter at all. —*idiom:* **anything but** By no means: *anything but happy to do it.*

an·y·time (ĕn′ē-tīm′) ►*adv.* At any time.

an·y·way (ĕn′ē-wā′) ►*adv.* **1.** In any manner whatever. **2.** Nevertheless: *It was raining but they played the game anyway.*

an·y·where (ĕn′ē-wâr′, -hwâr′) ►*adv.* **1.** To, in, or at any place. **2.** To any extent at all.

ao dai (ou′ dī, ô′) ►*n., pl.* **ao dais** A knee-length jacket with sides slit up to the hips, traditionally worn over loose trousers by Vietnamese women. [Vietnamese *áo dài.*]

ao dai

A-one also **A-1** (ā′wŭn′) ►*adj. Informal* First-class; excellent.

a·or·ta (ā-ôr′tə) ►*n., pl.* **-tas** or **-tae** (-tē) The main trunk of the systemic arteries, carrying blood to all bodily organs except the lungs. [< Gk. *aortē.*] —**a·or′tal, a·or′tic** *adj.*

a·ou·dad (ä′ŏŏ-dăd′, ou′dăd′) ►*n.* A wild sheep of N Africa. [< Berber *audad.*]

AP ►*abbr.* **1.** accounts payable **2.** advanced placement **3.** American plan **4.** antipersonnel **5.** Associated Press

a·pace (ə-pās′) ►*adv.* At a rapid pace; swiftly. [< OFr. *a pas.*]

A·pach·e (ə-păch′ē) ►*n., pl.* **-e** or **-es 1.** A member of a Native American people of the SW US and N Mexico, now mainly in Arizona, New Mexico, and Oklahoma. **2.** Any of the Athabaskan languages of the Apache.

a·part (ə-pärt′) ►*adv.* **1.** Separately or at a distance in place, position, or time. **2.** In or into pieces: *split apart.* **3.** One from another: *I can't tell the twins apart.* [< OFr. *a part.*] —**a·part′ness** *n.*

a·part·heid (ə-pärt′hīt′, -hāt′) ►*n.* A formerly official policy of racial segregation practiced in the Republic of South Africa. [Afr.]

a·part·ment (ə-pärt′mənt) ►*n.* **1.** A room or suite designed as a residence. **2.** An apartment building. [< Ital. *appartamento.*]

apartment building ►*n.* A building divided into apartments.

ap·a·thy (ăp′ə-thē) ►*n.* **1.** Lack of interest or concern, esp. in important matters. **2.** Lack of emotion; impassiveness. [< Gk. *apathēs,* without feeling.] —**ap′a·thet′ic** (-thĕt′ĭk) *adj.*

a·pat·o·saur·us (ə-păt′ə-sôr′əs) or **a·pat·o·saur** (ə-păt′ə-sôr′) ►*n.* A large herbivorous dinosaur of the Jurassic Period. [Gk. *apatē,* untruth, lie + *sauros,* lizard.]

APB ►*abbr.* all points bulletin

ape (āp) ►*n.* **1a.** One of a group of tailless Old World primates including the chimpanzees, gorillas, gibbons, orangutans, and humans. **b.** A monkey. **2.** A mimic. ►*v.* **aped, ap·ing** To mimic. [< OE *apa.*]

Ap·en·nines (ăp′ə-nīnz′) A mountain system extending from NW Italy S to the Strait of Messina.

a·pé·ri·tif (ä-pĕr′ĭ-tēf′) ►*n.* An alcoholic drink taken as an appetizer. [< Lat. *aperīre, apert-,* to open.]

ap·er·ture (ăp′ər-chər) ►*n.* **1.** An opening, such as a hole or slit. **2.** A usu. adjustable opening in an optical instrument, such as a camera, that limits the amount of light passing through a lens. [< Lat. *aperīre, apert-,* to open.] —**ap′er·tur′al** *adj.*

a·pex (ā′pĕks) ►*n., pl.* **-es** or **a·pi·ces** (ā′pĭ-sēz′, ăp′ĭ-) The highest point; peak. [Lat.]

Ap·gar score (ăp′gär) ►*n.* A system of assessing the physical condition of a newborn infant. [After Virginia *Apgar* (1909–74).]

a·pha·sia (ə-fā′zhə) ►*n.* Partial or total loss of the ability to speak or comprehend spoken or written language, resulting from brain damage. [Gk.] —**a·pha′si·ac′** (-zē-ăk′) *n.* —**a·pha′sic** (-zĭk, -sĭk) *adj. & n.*

a·phe·li·on (ə-fē′lē-ən, ə-fēl′yən) ►*n., pl.* **-li·a** (-lē-ə) The point on the orbit of a celestial body that is farthest from the sun. [Gk. *apo-,* away from + Gk. *hēlios,* sun.]

a·phid (ā′fĭd, ăf′ĭd) ►*n.* Any of various small, soft-bodied insects that feed by sucking sap from plants. [NLat. *Aphis, Aphid-,* type genus.]

aph·o·rism (ăf′ə-rĭz′əm) ►*n.* **1.** A maxim; adage. **2.** A brief statement of a principle. [< Gk. *aphorismos.*] **—aph′o·ris′tic** *adj.*

aph·ro·di·si·ac (ăf′rə-dē′zē-ăk′, -dĭz′ē-) ►*adj.* Arousing or intensifying sexual desire. ►*n.* Something having an aphrodisiac effect. [< Gk. *Aphroditē,* Aphrodite.]

Aph·ro·di·te (ăf′rə-dī′tē) ►*n. Gk. Myth.* The goddess of love and beauty.

API ►*abbr.* **1.** application programming interface **2.** Asian and Pacific Islander

A·pi·a (ə-pē′ə, ä′pē-ä′) The capital of Samoa, on the N coast of Upolu I. in the S Pacific.

a·pi·ar·y (ā′pē-ĕr′ē) ►*n., pl.* **-ies** A place where bees are raised for their honey. [< Lat. *apis,* bee.] **—a′pi·a·rist** (-ə-rĭst) *n.*

a·pi·ces (ā′pĭ-sēz′, ăp′ĭ-) ►*n.* Pl. of **apex.**

a·pi·cul·ture (ā′pĭ-kŭl′chər) ►*n.* The raising of bees. [< Lat. *apis,* bee.] **—a′pi·cul′tur·al** *adj.* **—a′pi·cul′tur·ist** *n.*

a·piece (ə-pēs′) ►*adv.* To or for each one: *The apples cost a dollar apiece.*

a·plomb (ə-plŏm′, ə-plŭm′) ►*n.* Self-confidence; poise. [< OFr. *a plomb,* perpendicular.]

ap·ne·a (ăp′nē-ə, ăp-nē′ə) ►*n.* Temporary absence or voluntary cessation of breathing. [< Gk. *apnoia,* without breathing.]

APO ►*abbr.* Army Post Office

a·poc·a·lypse (ə-pŏk′ə-lĭps′) ►*n.* **1. Apocalypse** *Bible* The Book of Revelation. **2.** Great devastation; doom. [< Gk. *apokalupsis,* revelation.] **—a·poc′a·lyp′tic, a·poc′a·lyp′ti·cal** *adj.* **—a·poc′a·lyp′ti·cal·ly** *adv.*

A·poc·ry·pha (ə-pŏk′rə-fə) ►*n. (takes sing. or pl. v.)* **1.** *Bible* The books of the Septuagint that are included in the Vulgate but considered uncanonical by some. See table at **Bible. 2. apocrypha** Writings of questionable authenticity. [< Gk. *apokruphos,* hidden away.]

a·poc·ry·phal (ə-pŏk′rə-fəl) ►*adj.* **1.** Of questionable authorship or authenticity. **2.** Erroneous; fictitious. **3. Apocryphal** *Bible* Of the Apocrypha. **—a·poc′ry·phal·ly** *adv.*

ap·o·gee (ăp′ə-jē) ►*n.* **1.** The point in the orbit of the moon or of an artificial satellite most distant from the center of the earth. **2.** The farthest or highest point; apex. [< Gk. *apogaios,* far from earth.]

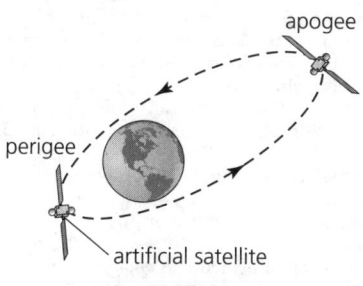

apogee

perigee

artificial satellite

apogee

a·po·lit·i·cal (ā′pə-lĭt′ĭ-kəl) ►*adj.* **1.** Having no interest in politics. **2.** Politically unimportant. **—a′po·lit′i·cal·ly** *adv.*

A·pol·lo (ə-pŏl′ō) ►*n.* **1.** *Gk. Myth.* The god of prophecy, music, medicine, and poetry. **2.**

apollo *pl.* **-los** A beautiful young man.

a·pol·o·get·ic (ə-pŏl′ə-jĕt′ĭk) also **a·pol·o·get·i·cal** (-ĭ-kəl) ►*adj.* Making an apology. ►*n.* A formal defense or apology. **—a·pol′o·get′i·cal·ly** *adv.*

ap·o·lo·gi·a (ăp′ə-lō′jē-ə, -jə) ►*n.* A formal defense or justification. [< Gk.] **—a·pol′o·gist** (ə-pŏl′ə-jĭst) *n.*

a·pol·o·gize (ə-pŏl′ə-jīz′) ►*v.* **-gized, -giz·ing** **1.** To make an apology. **2.** To make a formal defense or justification.

a·pol·o·gy (ə-pŏl′ə-jē) ►*n., pl.* **-gies 1.** A statement expressing regret or asking pardon for a fault or offense. **2.** A formal justification or defense. [< Gk. *apologia.*]

ap·o·plex·y (ăp′ə-plĕk′sē) ►*n.* **1.** Sudden impairment of neurological function, esp. resulting from a cerebral hemorrhage; stroke. **2.** A fit of extreme anger; rage. [< Gk. *apoplēxia.*] **—ap′o·plec′tic** *adj.* **—ap′o·plec′ti·cal·ly** *adv.*

a·pos·ta·sy (ə-pŏs′tə-sē) ►*n., pl.* **-sies** Abandonment of one's religious faith, political party, or cause. [< Gk. *apostasis,* revolt : *apo-,* away + *histanai,* place.] **—a·pos′tate** (-tāt′) *n. & adj.* **—a·pos′ta·tize** (-tə-tīz′) *v.*

a pos·te·ri·o·ri (ä′ pŏ-stîr′ē-ôr′ē, -ôr′ī, ā′) ►*adj.* Reasoning from particular facts to general principles; empirical. [Med.Lat., from the subsequent.]

a·pos·tle (ə-pŏs′əl) ►*n.* **1. Apostle** One of the 12 disciples chosen by Jesus to preach the gospel. **2.** One who pioneers a cause. [< Gk. *apostolos,* messenger.]

ap·os·tol·ic (ăp′ə-stŏl′ĭk) ►*adj.* **1.** Relating to an apostle. **2.** Relating to the teaching of the 12 Apostles. **3.** Papal.

a·pos·tro·phe¹ (ə-pŏs′trə-fē) ►*n.* The sign (′) used to indicate the omission of a letter or letters from a word, the possessive case, and the plurals of numbers, letters, and abbreviations. [< Gk. *apostrophos.*]

a·pos·tro·phe² (ə-pŏs′trə-fē) ►*n.* A rhetorical device in which a speaker or writer addresses an absent person, an abstraction, or an inanimate object. [< Gk. *apostrophē.*] **—ap′os·troph′ic** (ăp′ə-strŏf′ĭk) *adj.* **—a·pos′tro·phize** *v.*

a·poth·e·car·y (ə-pŏth′ĭ-kĕr′ē) ►*n., pl.* **-ies 1.** A druggist; pharmacist. See **pharmacy** (sense 2). [< Gk. *apothēkē,* storehouse.]

ap·o·thegm (ăp′ə-thĕm′) ►*n.* A proverb; maxim. [Gk. *apophthegma < apophthengesthai,* speak plainly.] **—ap′o·theg·mat′ic** (-thĕg-măt′ĭk) *adj.*

ap·o·them (ăp′ə-thĕm′) ►*n.* The perpendicular distance from the center of a regular polygon to any of its sides. [*apo-,* off + Gk. *thema,* something set down.]

a·poth·e·o·sis (ə-pŏth′ē-ō′sĭs, ăp′ə-thē′ə-sĭs) ►*n., pl.* **-ses** (-sēz′) **1.** Exaltation to divine rank or stature; deification. **2.** An exalted or glorified example. [< Gk. *apotheoun,* deify.] **—a·poth′e·o·size′** *v.*

app (ăp) ►*n. Informal* A computer application.

Ap·pa·la·chi·a (ăp′ə-lā′chē-ə, -chə, -lăch′ē-ə, -lăch′ə) A region of the central and S Appalachian Mts.

Ap·pa·la·chi·an Mountains (ăp′ə-lā′chē-ən, -chən, -lăch′ē-ən, -lăch′ən) A mountain system of E North America extending SW from SE Canada to central AL.

ap·pall (ə-pôl′) ►*v.* To fill with horror or dismay.

[< OFr. *apalir*, grow pallid, faint.] —**ap·pall'-ing·ly** *adv.*

Ap·pa·loo·sa (ăp'ə-lōō'sə) ►*n.* A breed of horse typically having a spotted coat. [Perh. after the *Palouse* River of ID and WA.]

ap·pa·rat·us (ăp'ə-răt'əs, -rā'təs) ►*n., pl.* **-us** or **-us·es 1.** A mechanical device or set of devices, esp. for a particular purpose. See Synonyms at **equipment. 2.** An organization; system. [< Lat. *apparāre*, prepare.]

ap·par·el (ə-păr'əl) ►*n.* Clothing, esp. outer garments. ►*v.* **-eled, -el·ing** or **-elled, -el·ling** To clothe or dress. [< OFr. *apareillier*, prepare.]

ap·par·ent (ə-păr'ənt, -pâr'-) ►*adj.* **1.** Readily seen; visible. **2.** Readily understood; obvious. **3.** Appearing as such but not necessarily so. [< Lat. *appārēre*, appear.] —**ap·par'ent·ly** *adv.*
    Syns: *clear, clear-cut, distinct, evident, manifest, obvious, patent, plain* **adj.**

ap·pa·ri·tion (ăp'ə-rĭsh'ən) ►*n.* **1.** A ghost. **2.** A sudden or unusual sight. [< Lat. *appārēre*, appear.] —**ap'pa·ri'tion·al** *adj.*

ap·peal (ə-pēl') ►*n.* **1.** An earnest request. **2.** An application to a higher authority: *an appeal to reason.* **3.** *Law* **a.** The transfer of a case from a lower to a higher court for a new hearing. **b.** A request for a new hearing. **4.** The power of attracting interest: *a city with appeal for tourists.* ►*v.* **1.** To make an earnest request, as for help. **2.** *Law* To make or apply for an appeal. **3.** To be attractive. [< Lat. *appellāre*, entreat.] —**ap·peal'a·ble** *adj.* —**ap·peal'er** *n.* —**ap·peal'ing·ly** *adv.*

ap·pear (ə-pîr') ►*v.* **1.** To become visible. **2.** To come into existence. **3.** To seem. **4.** To seem likely. **5.** To come before the public. **6.** *Law* To present oneself before a court. [< Lat. *appārēre.*]

ap·pear·ance (ə-pîr'əns) ►*n.* **1.** The act of appearing. **2.** Outward aspect: *an untidy appearance.* **3.** A pretense: *keeping up appearances.*

ap·pease (ə-pēz') ►*v.* **-peased, -peas·ing 1.** To pacify (an enemy), esp. by granting concessions. **2.** To satisfy or relieve. [< OFr. *apesier.*] —**ap·peas'a·ble** *adj.* —**ap·pease'ment** *n.*

ap·pel·lant (ə-pĕl'ənt) ►*adj.* Appellate. ►*n.* One who appeals a court decision.

ap·pel·late (ə-pĕl'ĭt) ►*adj.* Relating to the process of judicial appeal. [< Lat. *appellāre*, entreat.]

ap·pel·la·tion (ăp'ə-lā'shən) ►*n.* **1.** A name or title. **2.** A legally protected name for a regional variety of wine. [< Lat. *appellāre*, entreat.]

ap·pend (ə-pĕnd') ►*v.* **1.** To add as a supplement. **2.** To attach. [Lat. *appendere*, hang upon.]

ap·pend·age (ə-pĕn'dĭj) ►*n.* **1.** Something attached to a larger entity. **2.** *Biol.* A subordinate external body part or organ, such as an arm or tail.

ap·pen·dec·to·my (ăp'ən-dĕk'tə-mē) ►*n., pl.* **-mies** Surgical removal of the vermiform appendix.

ap·pen·di·ci·tis (ə-pĕn'dĭ-sī'tĭs) ►*n.* Inflammation of the vermiform appendix.

ap·pen·dix (ə-pĕn'dĭks) ►*n., pl.* **-di·ces** (-dĭ-sēz') or **-dix·es 1.** Supplementary material at the end of a book. **2.** *Anat.* The vermiform appendix. [Lat. < *appendere*, hang upon.]

ap·per·tain (ăp'ər-tān') ►*v.* To belong as a part. [< LLat. *appertinēre*, pertain.]

ap·pe·tite (ăp'ĭ-tīt') ►*n.* **1.** A desire for food or drink. **2.** A strong wish or urge. [< Lat. *appetere*, strive after.] —**ap'pe·ti'tive** *adj.*

ap·pe·tiz·er (ăp'ĭ-tī'zər) ►*n.* A food or drink served before a meal.

ap·pe·tiz·ing (ăp'ĭ-tī'zĭng) ►*adj.* Stimulating the appetite. —**ap'pe·tiz'ing·ly** *adv.*

ap·plaud (ə-plôd') ►*v.* To express approval (of), esp. by clapping hands. —**ap·plaud'a·ble** *adj.* —**ap·plaud'er** *n.*

ap·plause (ə-plôz') ►*n.* Approval expressed esp. by the clapping of hands. [< Lat. *applaudere*, *applaus-*, applaud.]

ap·ple (ăp'əl) ►*n.* **1.** A deciduous tree having white or pink flowers. **2.** The firm, edible, usu. rounded fruit of this tree. —*idiom:* apple of (one's) eye One that is treasured: *Her grandson is the apple of her eye.* [< OE *æppel.*]

ap·ple·jack (ăp'əl-jăk') ►*n.* Brandy distilled from hard cider.

ap·ple·sauce (ăp'əl-sôs') ►*n.* Apples stewed to a pulp.

ap·plet (ăp'lĭt) ►*n.* A small computer program that is downloaded from the Internet to run on a webpage. [APPL(ICATION) + -ET.]

ap·pli·ance (ə-plī'əns) ►*n.* A device, esp. one operated by gas or electricity, designed for household use. [< APPLY.]

ap·pli·ca·ble (ăp'lĭ-kə-bəl, ə-plĭk'ə-) ►*adj.* That can be applied; appropriate. —**ap'pli·ca·bil'i·ty** *n.* —**ap'pli·ca·bly** *adv.*

ap·pli·cant (ăp'lĭ-kənt) ►*n.* One who applies.

ap·pli·ca·tion (ăp'lĭ-kā'shən) ►*n.* **1.** The act of applying. **2.** Something applied. **3.** The act of putting something to a special use. **4.** The capacity of being usable; relevance. **5.** Close attention; diligence: *shows application to her work.* **6a.** A request, as for employment. **b.** The form on which such a request is made. **7.** *Comp.* A computer program designed for a specific task.

ap·pli·ca·tor (ăp'lĭ-kā'tər) ►*n.* An instrument for applying something, such as glue.

ap·plied (ə-plīd') ►*adj.* Put into practice; used: *applied physics.*

ap·pli·qué (ăp'lĭ-kā') ►*n.* A decoration, as in needlework, cut from one material and affixed to the surface of another. [< Fr. *appliquer*, APPLY.] —**ap'pli·qué'** *v.*

ap·ply (ə-plī') ►*v.* **-plied, -ply·ing 1.** To bring into contact with something. **2.** To adapt for a special use. **3.** To put into action: *applied the brakes.* **4.** To devote (oneself or one's efforts) to something. **5.** To be relevant. **6.** To request or seek assistance, employment, or admission. [< Lat. *applicāre*, affix to.]

ap·point (ə-point') ►*v.* **1.** To select for an office or position. **2.** To fix or set by authority. **3.** To furnish; equip. [< OFr. *apointier*, arrange.]
    Syns: *designate, name, nominate, tap* **v.**

ap·point·ee (ə-poin'tē', ăp'oin-) ►*n.* One who is appointed to an office or position.

ap·poin·tive (ə-poin'tĭv) ►*adj.* Relating to or filled by appointment: *an appointive office.*

ap·point·ment (ə-point'mənt) ►*n.* **1.** The act of appointing. **2.** The office or position to which one has been appointed. **3.** An arrangement for a meeting. **4. appointments** Furnishings; equipment.

Ap·po·mat·tox (ăp'ə-măt'əks) A town of S-central VA E of Lynchburg; site of Confederate surrender that ended the Civil War (1865).

ap·por·tion (ə-pôr′shən) ►*v.* To divide and assign by a plan; allot. [< OFr. *apportioner*.] —**ap·por′tion·ment** *n.*

ap·po·site (ăp′ə-zĭt) ►*adj.* Appropriate; relevant. [< Lat. *appōnere, apposit-*, place near to.] —**ap′po·site·ly** *adv.*

ap·po·si·tion (ăp′ə-zĭsh′ən) ►*n.* **1.** *Gram.* A construction in which a noun or noun phrase is placed with another as an explanatory equivalent, e.g., *Copley* and *the painter* in *The painter Copley was born in Boston.* **2.** Placement side by side. —**ap′po·si′tion·al** *adj.*

ap·pos·i·tive (ə-pŏz′ĭ-tĭv) ►*adj.* Being in apposition. —**ap·pos′i·tive** *n.*

ap·praise (ə-prāz′) ►*v.* **-praised, -prais·ing** **1.** To estimate the price or value of: *appraise real estate.* **2.** To make a considered judgment about: *appraise a threat.* [< LLat. *appretiāre*.] —**ap·prais′a·ble** *adj.* —**ap·prais′al** *n.* —**ap·praise′ment** *n.* —**ap·prais′er** *n.*

ap·pre·cia·ble (ə-prē′shə-bəl) ►*adj.* Possible to estimate, measure, or perceive. —**ap·pre′cia·bly** *adv.*

ap·pre·ci·ate (ə-prē′shē-āt′) ►*v.* **-at·ed, -at·ing** **1.** To recognize the quality or magnitude of. **2.** To be fully aware of; realize. **3.** To be thankful for. **4.** To increase in value. [LLat. *appretiāre*, appraise.] —**ap·pre′ci·a′tion** *n.* —**ap·pre′ci·a′tor** *n.*

ap·pre·cia·tive (ə-prē′shə-tĭv, -shē-ā′tĭv) ►*adj.* Capable of or showing appreciation. —**ap·pre′cia·tive·ly** *adv.*

ap·pre·hend (ăp′rĭ-hĕnd′) ►*v.* **1.** To arrest. **2.** To understand. **3.** To perceive. [< Lat. *apprehendere*, to grasp.] —**ap′pre·hen′sion** *n.*

ap·pre·hen·sive (ăp′rĭ-hĕn′sĭv) ►*adj.* Fearful about the future; uneasy: *was apprehensive about the airplane flight.* —**ap′pre·hen′sive·ly** *adv.*

ap·pren·tice (ə-prĕn′tĭs) ►*n.* **1.** One who is indentured to work under a skilled master in order to learn a trade. **2.** A beginner. ►*v.* **-ticed, -tic·ing** To place or take on as an apprentice. [< Lat. *apprehendere*, seize.] —**ap·pren′tice·ship′** *n.*

ap·prise (ə-prīz′) ►*v.* **-prised, -pris·ing** To give notice to; inform. [< OFr. *aprendre*, APPRE-HEND.]

ap·proach (ə-prōch′) ►*v.* **1.** To come near or nearer (to). **2.** To come close to, as in appearance; approximate. **3.** To make a proposal or overtures to. **4.** To begin to deal with: *approached the task with dread.* ►*n.* **1.** The act of approaching. **2.** A way of dealing with something. **3.** A way of reaching something. [< LLat. *appropiāre*.] —**ap·proach′a·ble** *adj.*

ap·pro·ba·tion (ăp′rə-bā′shən) ►*n.* Approval; praise. [< Lat. *approbāre*, approve.]

ap·pro·pri·ate (ə-prō′prē-ĭt) ►*adj.* Suited to a particular condition or use; fitting. ►*v.* (-āt′) **-at·ed, -at·ing** **1.** To set apart for a specific use. See Synonyms at **allocate.** **2.** To take possession of, often without permission. [< LLat. *appropriāre*, make one's own.] —**ap·pro′pri·ate·ly** *adv.* —**ap·pro′pri·ate·ness** *n.* —**ap·pro′pri·a′tor** *n.*

Syns: *arrogate, commandeer, confiscate* **v.**

ap·pro·pri·a·tion (ə-prō′prē-ā′shən) ►*n.* **1.** The act of appropriating. **2.** Something appropriated, esp. public funds set aside for a purpose.

ap·prov·al (ə-prōō′vəl) ►*n.* **1.** Favorable regard:

He expressed his approval of the painting. **2.** The act of officially approving something: *The mayor gave her approval to the project.* —**idiom: on approval** For inspection by a customer with no obligation to buy.

ap·prove (ə-prōōv′) ►*v.* **-proved, -prov·ing** **1a.** To consider right or good. **b.** To express approval. **2.** To consent to formally; authorize. [< Lat. *approbāre*.]

ap·prox·i·mate (ə-prŏk′sə-mĭt) ►*adj.* **1.** Almost exact or correct. **2.** Very similar. ►*v.* (-māt′) **-mat·ed, -mat·ing** To come close to; be nearly the same as. [< LLat. *approximāre*, go near to.] —**ap·prox′i·mate·ly** *adv.* —**ap·prox′i·ma′tion** *n.*

ap·pur·te·nance (ə-pûr′tn-əns) ►*n.* **1.** Something associated with another, more important thing; an accessory. **2. appurtenances** Equipment used for a specific task. [< LLat. *appertinēre*, PERTAIN.] —**ap·pur′te·nant** *adj.*

APR ►*abbr.* annual percentage rate

a·pri·cot (ăp′rĭ-kŏt′, ā′prĭ-) ►*n.* **1.** A deciduous tree having clusters of white flowers. **2.** Its edible, yellow-orange, peachlike fruit. [Ult. < Lat. *praecoquus*, ripe early.]

A·pril (ā′prəl) ►*n.* The 4th month of the Gregorian calendar. See table at **calendar.** [< Lat. *aprīlis*.]

April Fools' Day ►*n.* April 1, marked by the playing of practical jokes.

a pri·o·ri (ä′ prē-ôr′ē) ►*adj.* **1.** From a known or assumed cause to a necessarily related effect; deductive. **2.** Based on theory rather than on experiment. [Med.Lat., from the former.] —**a′ pri·o′ri** *adv.*

a·pron (ā′prən) ►*n.* **1.** A garment worn over the front of the body to protect clothing. **2.** The paved strip around airport hangars and terminal buildings. **3.** The part of a theater stage in front of the curtain. [< OFr. *naperon*, small tablecloth.]

ap·ro·pos (ăp′rə-pō′) ►*adj.* Appropriate; pertinent. ►*adv.* **1.** Appropriately; opportunely. **2.** Incidentally. ►*prep.* With regard to. [Fr. *à propos*, to the purpose.]

apropos of ►*prep.* With reference to.

apse (ăps) ►*n.* A semicircular or polygonal projection of a church. [Var. of APSIS.]

ap·sis (ăp′sĭs) ►*n., pl.* **-si·des** (-sĭ-dēz′) The nearest or farthest orbital point of a celestial body from a center of attraction. [< Gk. *hapsis*, arch.]

apt (ăpt) ►*adj.* **1.** Exactly suitable; appropriate. **2.** Liable; likely: *The river is apt to flood in spring.* **3.** Quick to learn or understand: *an apt student.* [< Lat. *aptus* < *apere*, fasten.] —**apt′ly** *adv.* —**apt′ness** *n.*

apt. ►*abbr.* apartment

ap·ti·tude (ăp′tĭ-tōōd′, -tyōōd′) ►*n.* **1.** A natural ability, as for learning; talent. **2.** Suitability. [< Lat. *aptus*, APT.]

A·qa·ba (ä′kə-bə), **Gulf of** An arm of the Red Sea between the Sinai Peninsula and NW Saudi Arabia.

aq·ua (ăk′wə, ä′kwə) ►*n., pl.* **aq·uae** (ăk′wē, ä′kwī′) or **aq·uas** **1.** Water. **2.** An aqueous solution. **3.** A light blue-green to green-blue. [< Lat.] —**aq′ua** *adj.*

aq·ua·cul·ture (ăk′wə-kŭl′chər, ä′kwə-) ►*n.* The cultivation of fish or shellfish for food. —**aq′ua·cul′tur·ist** *n.*

aq·ua·ma·rine (ăk′wə-mə-rēn′, ä′kwə-) ►*n.*
1. A transparent blue-green beryl, used as a
gemstone. **2.** A pale to light greenish blue. [Lat.
aqua marīna, sea water.]

aq·ua·naut (ăk′wə-nôt′, ä′kwə-) ►*n.* A scuba
diver who works or takes part in scientific
research in underwater installations. [Lat. *aqua,*
water + Gk. *nautēs,* sailor.]

aqua re·gi·a (rē′jē-ə) ►*n.* A corrosive mixture
of hydrochloric and nitric acids, used for testing metals and dissolving platinum and gold.
[NLat., royal water.]

a·quar·i·um (ə-kwâr′ē-əm) ►*n., pl.* **-i·ums** or
-i·a (-ē-ə) **1.** A water-filled enclosure in which
living aquatic animals and plants are kept. **2.** A
place for the public exhibition of live aquatic
animals and plants. [Ult. < Lat. *aqua,* water.]

A·quar·i·us (ə-kwâr′ē-əs) ►*n.* **1.** A constellation
in the equatorial region of the Southern Hemisphere. **2.** The 11th sign of the zodiac. **—A·**
quar′i·an *adj. & n.*

a·quat·ic (ə-kwăt′ĭk, ə-kwŏt′-) ►*adj.* **1.** Living
or growing in, on, or near the water. **2.** Taking
place in or on the water: *an aquatic sport.* **—a·**
quat′i·cal·ly *adv.*

aq·ua·tint (ăk′wə-tĭnt′, ä′kwə-) ►*n.* **1.** A process of etching capable of producing tonal variations in the resulting print. **2.** An etching so
made. [< Ital. *acquatinta* : Lat. *aqua,* water +
tinta, dyed.]

a·qua·vit (ä′kwə-vēt′) ►*n.* A strong clear liquor
flavored with caraway seed. [Swed., Dan., and
Norw. *akvavit,* AQUA VITAE.]

aqua vi·tae (vī′tē) ►*n.* A strong liquor such as
brandy. [< Med.Lat. *aqua vītae* : Lat. *aqua,* water
+ Lat. *vīta,* life.]

aq·ue·duct (ăk′wĭ-dŭkt′) ►*n.* **1.** A conduit for
transporting water from a remote source. **2.**
A bridgelike structure supporting a conduit or
canal passing over a river or low ground. [Lat.
aquaeductus : *aqua,* water + *ductus,* DUCT.]

a·que·ous (ä′kwē-əs, ăk′wē-) ►*adj.* Relating to,
containing, or dissolved in water; watery. [<
Lat. *aqua,* water.]

aqueous humor ►*n. Anat.* The clear, watery
fluid in the chamber of the eye between the
cornea and the lens.

aq·ui·fer (ăk′wə-fər, ä′kwə-) ►*n.* An underground layer of earth, gravel, or porous stone
that yields water.

aq·ui·line (ăk′wə-līn′, -lĭn) ►*adj.* **1.** Of or like an
eagle. **2.** Curved like an eagle's beak: *an aquiline
nose.* [< Lat. *aquila,* eagle.]

A·qui·nas (ə-kwī′nəs), Saint **Thomas** 1225–74.
Italian Dominican theologian and philosopher.

Aq·ui·taine (ăk′wĭ-tān′) A historical region of
SW France on the Bay of Biscay.

Ar The symbol for **argon.**

AR ►*abbr.* **1.** accounts receivable **2.** Arkansas

Ar. ►*abbr.* Arabic

-ar ►*suff.* Of, relating to, or resembling: *polar.* [<
Lat. *-āris,* alteration of *-ālis, -al.*]

Ar·ab (ăr′əb) ►*n.* **1.** A member of a Semitic
people of Arabia whose language and Islamic
religion spread throughout the Middle East and
N Africa from the 7th cent. **2.** A member of an
Arabic-speaking people. **—Ar′ab** *adj.*

Arab. ►*abbr.* Arabic

ar·a·besque (ăr′ə-běsk′) ►*n.* **1.** A ballet position executed while standing on one leg. **2.** A
complex design of interwined floral, foliate,

and geometric figures. **3.** A short, whimsical
composition esp. for the piano. [< Ital. *arabesco,*
in Arabian fashion.]

arabesque

A·ra·bi·a (ə-rā′bē-ə) also **A·ra·bi·an Peninsula**
(-bē-ən) A peninsula of SW Asia between the
Red Sea and the Persian Gulf. **—A·ra′bi·an**
adj. & n.

Arabian Sea The NW part of the Indian Ocean
between Arabia and W India.

Ar·a·bic (ăr′ə-bĭk) ►*adj.* Of or relating to Arabia,
the Arabs, their language, or their culture. ►*n.*
The Semitic language of the Arabs, spoken in
the Middle East and N Africa.

Arabic numeral ►*n.* One of the numerical symbols 1, 2, 3, 4, 5, 6, 7, 8, 9, or 0.

ar·a·ble (ăr′ə-bəl) ►*adj.* Fit for cultivation. [<
Lat. *arāre,* to plow.] **—ar′a·bil′i·ty** *n.*

a·rach·nid (ə-răk′nĭd) ►*n.* Any of various eight-
legged arthropods such as spiders, scorpions,
mites, and ticks. [< Gk. *arakhnē,* spider.] **—a·**
rach′ni·dan *adj. & n.*

Ar·a·fat (ăr′ə-făt′, är′ə-fät′), **Yasir** 1929–2004.
Leader of the Palestine Liberation Organization; president of the Palestinian Authority
(1996–2004).

Ar·a·gon (ăr′ə-gŏn′) A region and former kingdom of NE Spain. **—Ar′a·go·nese′** (-gə-nēz′,
-nēs′) *adj. & n.*

Ar·al Sea (ăr′əl) An inland sea between S
Kazakhstan and NW Uzbekistan.

Ar·a·ma·ic (ăr′ə-mā′ĭk) ►*n.* The Semitic language of the ancient Arameans, now widely
used by non-Aramean peoples throughout
southwest Asia. **—Ar′a·ma′ic** *adj.*

Ar·an Islands (ăr′ən) Three small islands of W
Ireland at the entrance to Galway Bay.

A·rap·a·ho (ə-răp′ə-hō′) ►*n., pl.* **-ho** or **-hos 1.**
A member of a Native American people for-
merly of E Colorado and SE Wyoming, now in
Oklahoma and Wyoming. **2.** The Algonquian
language of the Arapaho.

Ar·a·rat (ăr′ə-răt′), **Mount** A massif of extreme
E Turkey; traditional resting place of Noah's
ark.

Ar·a·wak (ăr′ə-wäk′) ►*n., pl.* **-wak** or **-waks 1.**
A member of an American Indian people for-
merly inhabiting parts of the West Indies, now
chiefly in Guiana. **2.** The Arawakan language
of the Arawak.

Ar·a·wa·kan (ăr′ə-wä′kən) ►*n., pl.* **-kan** or
-kans 1. A family of South American Indian
languages spoken in the Amazon Basin, NE
South America, and formerly the Greater

Antilles. **2.** A member of an Arawakan-speaking people. —**Ar′a·wa′kan** *adj.*

ar·bi·ter (är′bĭ-tər) ►*n.* One having the power to judge or decide. [< Lat.]

ar·bi·trage (är′bĭ-träzh′) ►*n.* The purchase of assets on one market for resale on another to profit from a price discrepancy. [< OFr. *arbitration.*] —**ar′bi·trage′** *v.* —**ar′bi·tra·geur′** *n.*

ar·bit·ra·ment (är-bĭt′rə-mənt) ►*n.* **1.** The act of arbitrating; arbitration. **2.** The judgment of an arbiter. [< OFr. *arbitrer,* ARBITRATE.]

ar·bi·trar·y (är′bĭ-trĕr′ē) ►*adj.* **1.** Determined by chance, whim, or impulse. **2.** Not limited by law; despotic. [< Lat. *arbiter,* judge.] —**ar′bi·trar′i·ly** (-trâr′ə-lē) *adv.* —**ar′bi·trar′i·ness** *n.*

ar·bi·trate (är′bĭ-trāt′) ►*v.* **-trat·ed, -trat·ing** **1.** To judge or decide as an arbitrator. **2.** To submit (a dispute) to an arbitrator for settlement. [Lat. *arbitrārī* < *arbiter,* judge.] —**ar′bi·tra′tion** *n.*

ar·bi·tra·tor (är′bĭ-trā′tər) ►*n.* A person chosen to settle a dispute.

ar·bor (är′bər) ►*n.* A shady resting place in a garden or park. [< OFr. *erbier,* garden.]

ar·bo·re·al (är-bôr′ē-əl) ►*adj.* **1.** Of or like a tree. **2.** Living in trees. [< Lat. *arbor,* tree.]

ar·bo·re·tum (är′bə-rē′təm) ►*n., pl.* **-tums** or **-ta** (-tə) A place for the study and exhibition of trees. [< Lat. *arbor,* tree.]

ar·bor·vi·tae also **ar·bor vi·tae** (är′bər-vī′tē) ►*n.* Any of several evergreen trees having scalelike leaves and small cones. [Lat. *arbor,* tree + *vīta,* life.]

ar·bo·vi·rus (är′bə-vī′rəs) ►*n.* Any of a large group of viruses that cause encephalitis and yellow fever. [*ar(thropod-)bo(rne) virus.*]

arc (ärk) ►*n.* **1.** Something that is shaped like a curve or an arch. **2.** *Math.* A segment of a circle. **3.** A luminous electric discharge, as between two electrodes. ►*v.* **arced** (ärkt), **arc·ing** (är′kĭng) To move in or form an arc. [< Lat. *arcus.*]

ARC ►*abbr.* **1.** AIDS-related complex **2.** American Red Cross

ar·cade (är-kād′) ►*n.* **1.** A series of arches supported by columns. **2.** A roofed passageway, esp. one with shops on one or both sides. **3.** A commercial establishment featuring rows of mechanical or electronic games. [< Ital. *arcata* < Lat. *arcus,* arch.]

Ar·ca·di·a (är-kā′dē-ə) also **Ar·ca·dy** (är′kə-dē) A region of ancient Greece proverbial for its simple pastoral life. —**Ar·ca′di·an** *adj. & n.*

ar·ca·na (är-kā′nə) ►*pl.n.* Arcane knowledge or detail.

ar·cane (är-kān′) ►*adj.* Known to only a few; esoteric. See Synonyms at **mysterious.** [Lat. *arcānus* < *arca,* chest.]

arch¹ (ärch) ►*n.* **1.** A usu. curved structure forming the upper edge of an open space and supporting the weight above it. **2.** A structure, such as a monument, that is shaped like an inverted U. **3.** Something that is curved like an arch. ►*v.* **1.** To provide with an arch. **2.** To form or cause to form an arch. [< Lat. *arcus.*] —**arched** *adj.*

arch² (ärch) ►*adj.* **1.** Chief; principal: *their arch foe.* **2.** Mischievous: *an arch glance.* [< ARCH–.] —**arch′ly** *adv.* —**arch′ness** *n.*

arch. ►*abbr.* **1.** archaic **2.** archipelago **3.** architecture

arch– ►*pref.* **1.** Chief; highest: *archbishop.* **2.** Extreme: *archconservative.* [< Gk. *arkhi-.*]

–arch ►*suff.* Ruler; leader: *matriarch.* [< Gk. *arkhos,* ruler.]

ar·chae·ol·o·gy or **ar·che·ol·o·gy** (är′kē-ŏl′ə-jē) ►*n.* The systematic study of past human life and culture by the examination of remaining material evidence. [< Gk. *arkhaiologia,* antiquarian lore.] —**ar′chae·o·log′i·cal** (-ə-lŏj′ĭ-kəl), **ar′chae·o·log′ic** *adj.* —**ar′chae·ol′o·gist** *n.*

ar·chae·on or **Ar·chae·on** (är′kē-ŏn′) ►*n., pl.* **-chae·a** (-kē-ə) Any of various single-celled prokaryotes genetically distinct from bacteria, often living in extreme environmental conditions. [Gk. *arkhaion,* neut. sing. of *arkhaios,* ancient.]

ar·cha·ic (är-kā′ĭk) ►*adj.* **1.** Belonging to an earlier time. **2.** No longer current; antiquated. **3.** Relating to words and language once in regular use but now rare and suggestive of an earlier style or period. [Gk. *arkhaikos* < *arkhē,* beginning.] —**ar·cha′i·cal·ly** *adv.*

ar·cha·ism (är′kē-ĭz′əm, -kā-) ►*n.* An archaic word, phrase, or style. —**ar′cha·ist** *n.*

arch·an·gel (ärk′ān′jəl) ►*n.* A spritual being ranking above an ordinary angel.

arch·bish·op (ärch-bĭsh′əp) ►*n.* A bishop of the highest rank. —**arch·bish′op·ric** *n.*

arch·dea·con (ärch-dē′kən) ►*n.* A church official, as in the Anglican Church, in charge of temporal and other affairs in a diocese. —**arch·dea′con·ate** (-kə-nĭt) *n.*

arch·di·o·cese (ärch-dī′ə-sĭs, -sēs′, -sēz′) ►*n.* The district under an archbishop's jurisdiction. —**arch′di·oc′e·san** (-ŏs′ĭ-sən) *adj.*

arch·duch·ess (ärch-dŭch′ĭs) ►*n.* A royal princess, esp. of imperial Austria.

arch·duke (ärch-dook′, -dyook′) ►*n.* A royal prince, esp. of imperial Austria.

arch·en·e·my (ärch-ĕn′ə-mē) ►*n.* A principal enemy.

ar·che·ol·o·gy (är′kē-ŏl′ə-jē) ►*n.* Var. of **archaeology.**

arch·er (är′chər) ►*n.* One who shoots with a bow and arrow. [< LLat. *arcārius* < Lat. *arcus,* bow.] —**arch′er·y** *n.*

arch·er·fish (är′chər-fĭsh′) ►*n.* Any of various freshwater fish that prey on insects by spitting a jet of water to knock them off vegetation above the water surface.

ar·che·type (är′kĭ-tīp′) ►*n.* **1.** An original model or type after which other similar things are patterned; prototype. **2.** An ideal example of a type. [< Gk. *arkhetupos,* original.] —**ar′che·typ′al** (-tī′pəl), **ar′che·typ′ic** (-tĭp′ĭk), **ar′che·typ′i·cal** *adj.*

arch·fiend (ärch-fēnd′) ►*n.* **1.** A principal fiend. **2. Archfiend** Satan.

ar·chi·e·pis·co·pal (är′kē-ĭ-pĭs′kə-pəl) ►*adj.* Relating to an archbishop.

ar·chi·man·drite (är′kə-măn′drīt′) ►*n. Eastern Orthodox Ch.* A celibate priest ranking below a bishop. [< LGk. *arkhimandritēs.*]

Ar·chi·me·des (är′kə-mē′dēz) 287?–212 BC. Greek mathematician, engineer, and physicist. —**Ar′chi·me′de·an** *adj.*

ar·chi·pel·a·go (är′kə-pĕl′ə-gō′) ►*n., pl.* **-goes** or **-gos 1.** A large group of islands. **2.** A sea containing a large group of islands. [Ital. *Arci-pelago*, the Aegean Sea.] —**ar'chi·pe·lag'ic** (-pə-lăj'ĭk) *adj.*

ar·chi·tect (är'kĭ-tĕkt') ►*n.* **1.** One who designs buildings or other large structures. **2.** One that plans or devises. **3.** One who designs or organizes complex systems. [< Gk. *arkhitektōn*, master builder : *arkhi-*, chief + *tektōn*, builder.]

ar·chi·tec·ton·ics (är'kĭ-tĕk-tŏn'ĭks) ►*n. (takes sing. v.)* **1.** The science of architecture. **2.** Structural design, as in a musical work. —**ar'chi·tec·ton'ic** *adj.*

ar·chi·tec·ture (är'kĭ-tĕk'chər) ►*n.* **1.** The art and science of designing and erecting buildings. **2.** A style and method of design and construction: *Byzantine architecture.* **3.** Orderly arrangement of parts; structure. —**ar'chi·tec'tur·al** *adj.*

ar·chi·trave (är'kĭ-trāv') ►*n.* **1.** In classical architecture, the lowest part of an entablature, resting on top of a column. **2.** The molding around a door or window. [< OItal.]

ar·chive (är'kīv') ►*n.* **1.** often **archives** A place or collection containing documents of historical interest. **2.** *Comp.* **a.** A storage area, usu. on magnetic tape, for files not in active use. **b.** A file containing data compressed for ease of storage or transfer. [< Gk. *arkheion*, town hall.] —**ar·chi'val** *adj.* —**ar'chive** *v.*

ar·chi·vist (är'kə-vĭst, -kī'-) ►*n.* One who is in charge of archives.

arch·ri·val (ärch'rī'vəl) ►*n.* A principal rival.

arch·way (ärch'wā') ►*n.* **1.** A passageway under an arch. **2.** An arch over a passageway.

–archy ►*suff.* Rule; government: *oligarchy.*

arc lamp ►*n.* An electric light in which a current traverses a gas between two incandescent electrodes.

arc·tic (ärk'tĭk, är'tĭk) ►*adj.* Extremely cold; frigid. See Synonyms at **cold.** [< Gk. *arktikos* < *arktos*, bear, Ursa Major.]

Arctic A region between the North Pole and the N timberlines of North America and Eurasia. —**Arctic** *adj.*

Arctic Archipelago A group of islands of N Canada in the Arctic between North America and Greenland.

Arctic Circle The parallel of latitude (approx. 66°33' N) that separates the North Temperate and North Frigid zones.

Arctic Ocean The waters around the North Pole between North America and Eurasia.

–ard or **–art** ►*suff.* One who habitually or excessively is in a certain state or performs a certain action: *drunkard.* [< OFr.]

Ar·dennes (är-dĕn') A wooded plateau region of N France, SE Belgium, and N Luxembourg.

ar·dent (är'dnt) ►*adj.* Characterized by warmth of feeling; passionate. [< Lat. *ārdēre*, burn.] —**ar'den·cy** *n.* —**ar'dent·ly** *adv.*

ar·dor (är'dər) ►*n.* **1.** Fiery intensity of feeling. **2.** Intense heat. [< Lat. *ārdor.*]

ar·du·ous (är'jōō-əs) ►*adj.* Full of hardships. [< Lat. *arduus*, steep.] —**ar'du·ous·ly** *adv.*

are¹ (är) ►*v.* 2nd pers. sing. and pl. and 1st and 3rd pers. pl. pr. indic. of **be.**

are² (âr, är) ►*n.* A unit of area equal to 100 square meters. [< Lat. *ārea*, open space.]

ar·e·a (âr'ē-ə) ►*n.* **1.** A portion of the space on a surface; region. **2.** A distinct part or section: *a storage area.* **3.** A division of experience or knowledge; field. **4.** *Math.* The extent of a planar region or of the surface of a solid. [< Lat. *ārea*, open space.]

area code ►*n.* A number used to distinguish broad geographic areas of telephone service, esp. a 3-digit number used in the US, Canada, and the Caribbean.

ar·e·a·way (âr'ē-ə-wā') ►*n.* A small sunken area allowing access or light and air to basement doors or windows.

a·re·na (ə-rē'nə) ►*n.* **1.** A building for the presentation of sports events and spectacles. **2.** A sphere of activity: *the political arena.* [Lat. *arēna*, sand, sandy place.]

arena theater ►*n.* A theater in which the stage is at the center of the auditorium.

aren't (ärnt, är'ənt) Are not.

Ar·es (âr'ēz) ►*n. Gk. Myth.* The god of war.

Ar·gen·ti·na (är'jən-tē'nə) A country of SE South America E of Chile extending to S Tierra del Fuego, an island it shares with Chile. Cap. Buenos Aires. —**Ar'gen·tine'** (-tēn', -tīn'), **Ar'gen·tin'e·an** (-tĭn'ē-ən) *adj. & n.*

Ar·go·lis (är'gə-lĭs) An ancient region of S Greece in the NE Peloponnesus.

ar·gon (är'gŏn') ►*n. Symbol* **Ar** A colorless, odorless, inert gaseous element constituting approx. one percent of Earth's atmosphere and used in electric light bulbs, fluorescent tubes, and welding. At. no. 18. See table at **element.** [< Gk. *argos*, inert : A-¹ + *ergon*, work.]

Ar·gonne (är-gŏn', är'gŏn) A wooded hilly region of NE France between the Meuse and Aisne Rivers.

ar·go·sy (är'gə-sē) ►*n., pl.* **-sies 1.** A large merchant ship. **2.** A fleet of ships. [< Ital. *ragusea*, vessel of Ragusa, Croatia.]

ar·got (är'gō, -gət) ►*n.* The specialized vocabulary of a group: *thieves' argot.* [Fr.]

ar·gu·a·ble (är'gyōō-ə-bəl) ►*adj.* **1.** Open to argument. **2.** Defensible in argument; plausible. —**ar'gu·a·bly** *adv.*

ar·gue (är'gyōō) ►*v.* **-gued, -gu·ing 1.** To put forth reasons for or against; debate. **2.** To maintain by reasoning; contend. **3.** To give evidence of. **4.** To quarrel; dispute. [< Lat. *arguere*, make clear.] —**ar'gu·er** *n.*

ar·gu·ment (är'gyə-mənt) ►*n.* **1.** A discussion of differing points of view; debate. **2.** A quarrel; dispute. **3a.** A course of reasoning aimed at demonstrating truth or falsehood. **b.** A persuasive reason: *The low rates are an argument for buying now.*

ar·gu·men·ta·tion (är'gyə-mĕn-tā'shən) ►*n.* The presentation and elaboration of an argument.

ar·gu·men·ta·tive (är'gyə-mĕn'tə-tĭv) ►*adj.* **1.** Given to arguing; disputatious. **2.** Of or marked by argument. —**ar'gu·men'ta·tive·ness** *n.*

Syns: *contentious, disputatious, quarrelsome, scrappy* **adj.**

ar·gyle also **ar·gyll** (är'gīl') ►*n.* **1.** A knitting pattern of varicolored, diamond-shaped areas on a solid background. **2.** A sock knit in this pattern. [After Clan Campbell of County *Argyll*, Scotland.]

a·ri·a (ä'rē-ə) ►*n.* A solo vocal piece with instrumental accompaniment, as in an opera. [Ital. < Gk. *aēr*, air.]

–arian ►*suff.* Believer in; advocate of: *utilitarian.* [< Lat. *-ārius.*]

a·ri·a·ry (ä′rē-ä′rē) ►*n., pl.* **-ries** See table at **currency.** [Malagasy.]

ar·id (ăr′ĭd) ►*adj.* **1.** Lacking in rainfall; dry. **2.** Lifeless; dull. [Lat. *āridus.*] —**a·rid′i·ty** (ə-rĭd′ĭ-tē), **ar′id·ness** *n.*

Ar·ies (âr′ēz, âr′ē-ēz′) ►*n.* **1.** A constellation in the Northern Hemisphere. **2.** The 1st sign of the zodiac. [< Lat. *ariēs,* ram.]

a·right (ə-rīt′) ►*adv.* Properly; correctly.

ar·il (ăr′əl) ►*n.* A fleshy, usu. brightly colored cover of a seed. [Med.Lat. *arillus,* grape seed.]

a·rise (ə-rīz′) ►*v.* **a·rose** (ə-rōz′), **a·ris·en** (ə-rĭz′ən), **a·ris·ing** **1.** To get up; rise. **2.** To move upward; ascend. **3.** To originate. **4.** To result or proceed. See Synonyms at **stem¹.** [< OE *ārīsan.*]

Ar·is·ti·des (ăr′ĭ-stī′dēz) "the Just." 530?–468? BC. Athenian general and political leader.

ar·is·toc·ra·cy (ăr′ĭ-stŏk′rə-sē) ►*n., pl.* **-cies 1.** A hereditary ruling class. **2.** Government by the nobility or by a privileged upper class. **3.** A group or class considered superior to others. [< Gk. *aristos,* best.] —**a·ris′to·crat′** (ə-rĭs′tə-krăt′, ăr′ĭs-) *n.* —**a·ris′to·crat′ic** *adj.*

Ar·is·toph·a·nes (ăr′ĭ-stŏf′ə-nēz) 448?–388? BC. Athenian playwright.

Ar·is·tot·le (ăr′ĭ-stŏt′l) 384–322 BC. Greek philosopher.

a·rith·me·tic (ə-rĭth′mĭ-tĭk) ►*n.* The branch of mathematics dealing with real or complex numbers under addition, subtraction, multiplication, and division. ►*adj.* **ar·ith·met·ic** (ăr′ĭth-mĕt′ĭk) also **ar·ith·met·i·cal** (-ĭ-kəl) **1.** Relating to arithmetic. **2.** Increasing or decreasing at a fixed rate: *arithmetic progression.* [< Gk. *arithmētikē (tekhnē),* (the art) of counting.] —**ar′ith·met′i·cal·ly** *adv.*

arithmetic mean ►*n.* The value obtained by dividing the sum of a set of quantities by the number of quantities in the set.

–arium ►*suff.* A place or device containing or associated with: *planetarium.* [Lat., neuter of *-ārius,* -ary.]

A·ri·us (ə-rī′əs, ăr′ē-, âr′-) AD 256?–336. Greek Christian theologian.

A·ri·zo·na (ăr′ĭ-zō′nə) A state of the SW US on the Mexican border. Cap. Phoenix. —**Ar′i·zo′nan** *adj. & n.*

ark (ärk) ►*n.* **1.** often **Ark** *Bible* The chest containing the Ten Commandments, carried by the Hebrews during their desert wanderings. **2.** often **Ark** *Judaism* The Holy Ark. **3.** *Bible* The boat built by Noah for the Flood. **4.** A shelter or refuge. [< Lat. *arca,* chest.]

Ar·kan·sas (är′kən-sô′) A state of the S-central US Cap. Little Rock. —**Ar·kan′san** (-kăn′zən) *adj. & n.*

Ar·kan·sas River (är′kən-sô′, är-kăn′zəs) A river of the S-central US rising in the Rocky Mts. in central CO and flowing about 2,350 km (1,450 mi) to the Mississippi R. in SE AR.

Ark·wright (ärk′rīt′), Sir **Richard** 1732–92. British inventor and manufacturer.

Ar·ling·ton (är′lĭng-tən) **1.** A city of N TX between Dallas and Fort Worth. **2.** A county and unincorp. city of N VA across the Potomac R. from Washington DC.

arm¹ (ärm) ►*n.* **1.** An upper limb of the human body. **2.** A part similar to a human arm. **3.** A narrow extension: *an arm of the sea.* See Synonyms at **branch. 4.** An administrative

or functional branch. —*idiom:* **with open arms** In a warm, friendly manner. [< OE *earm.*] —**armed** *adj.*

arm² (ärm) ►*n.* **1.** A weapon. **2.** A branch of a military force. **3. arms a.** Warfare: *a call to arms.* **b.** Military service. **4. arms** Heraldic bearings or insignia. ►*v.* **1.** To equip with weapons. **2.** To prepare for or as if for war. **3.** To prepare (a weapon or electronic system) for use. —*idiom:* **up in arms** Angry; indignant. [< Lat. *arma,* weapons.] —**armed** *adj.*

ARM ►*n.* adjustable-rate mortgage

ar·ma·da (är-mä′də, -mä′-) ►*n.* A fleet of warships. [Sp. < Lat. *armāre,* to arm.]

ar·ma·dil·lo (är′mə-dĭl′ō) ►*n., pl.* **-los** A burrowing mammal of South America and S North America having bony, armorlike plates. [Sp., dim. of *armado,* armored.]

Ar·ma·ged·don (är′mə-gĕd′n) ►*n.* **1.** *Bible* The site of the gathering of armies for battle before the end of the world. **2.** A catastrophic confrontation.

ar·ma·ment (är′mə-mənt) ►*n.* **1.** The weapons and supplies of a military unit. **2.** often **armaments** All the military forces and equipment of a country. [< Lat. *arma.*]

ar·ma·ture (är′mə-chŏor′, -chər) ►*n.* **1.** *Elect.* **a.** The rotating part of a dynamo, consisting of copper wire wound around an iron core. **b.** The moving part of an electromagnetic device such as a relay, buzzer, or loudspeaker. **c.** A piece of soft iron connecting the poles of a magnet. **2.** *Biol.* A protective covering or part. **3.** A supporting framework. [< Lat. *armāre,* to arm.]

arm·band (ärm′bănd′) ►*n.* A band worn esp. on the upper arm for ornament or identification.

arm·chair (ärm′châr′) ►*n.* A chair with sides to support the arms or elbows. ►*adj.* Taking interest in a subject without being personally involved in it: *an armchair adventurer.*

armed forces ►*pl.n.* The military forces of a country.

Ar·me·ni·a (är-mē′nē-ə, -mēn′yə) A country of W Asia S of Georgia. Cap. Yerevan.

Ar·me·ni·an (är-mē′nē-ən, -mēn′yən) ►*n.* **1.** A native or inhabitant of Armenia. **2.** The Indo-European language of the Armenians. —**Ar·me′ni·an** *adj.*

arm·ful (ärm′fŏol′) ►*n.* The amount that an arm or arms can hold.

arm·hole (ärm′hōl′) ►*n.* An opening in a garment for an arm.

ar·mi·stice (är′mĭ-stĭs) ►*n.* A temporary cessation of fighting by mutual consent; truce. [< NLat. *armistitium* : Lat. *arma,* arms + Lat. *-stitium,* a stopping.]

arm·let (ärm′lĭt) ►*n.* A band that is worn esp. on the upper arm for ornament or for identification.

ar·moire (ärm-wär′) ►*n.* A large, often ornate cabinet or wardrobe. [Fr. < Lat. *armārium,* chest.]

ar·mor (är′mər) ►*n.* **1.** A protective or defensive covering for the body. **2a.** Metal plates covering a military vehicle or ship. **b.** The armored vehicles of an army. ►*v.* To cover with armor. [< Lat. *armātūra,* ARMATURE.] —**ar′mored** *adj.*

ar·mo·ri·al (är-môr′ē-əl) ►*adj.* Of or relating to heraldry or heraldic arms.

ar·mor·y (är′mə-rē) ►*n., pl.* **-ies 1.** A storehouse

for arms and military equipment. **2.** An arms factory.

arm·pit (ärm′pĭt′) ►*n.* The hollow under the upper part of the arm at the shoulder.

arm·rest (ärm′rĕst′) ►*n.* A support for the arm.

Arm·strong (ärm′strông), **Louis** "Satchmo." 1901–71. Amer. jazz musician.

Armstrong, Neil Alden 1930–2012. Amer. astronaut; first to walk on the moon (1969).

Neil Armstrong
photographed in 1969

arm-twist·ing (ärm′twĭs′tĭng) ►*n. Informal* The use of personal or political pressure to persuade or to gain support.

ar·my (är′mē) ►*n., pl.* **-mies 1.** A large body of people organized for warfare. **2.** A large group of people organized for a cause: *an army of volunteers.* **3.** A multitude. [< Lat. *armāta* < *armāre,* to arm.]

army ant ►*n.* A tropical ant that hunts live prey in columns or swarms.

ar·ni·ca (är′nĭ-kə) ►*n.* **1.** A perennial herb having yellow flowers. **2.** A tincture of dried arnica flower heads used on bruises and sprains. [NLat. *Arnica,* genus name.]

Ar·no (är′nō) A river of central Italy rising in the N Apennines and flowing about 240 km (150 mi) to the Ligurian Sea.

Ar·nold (är′nəld), **Benedict** 1741–1801. Amer. Revolutionary general and traitor.

Arnold, Matthew 1822–88. British poet and critic.

a·ro·ma (ə-rō′mə) ►*n.* **1.** A quality that can be perceived by the olfactory sense. See Synonyms at **smell. 2.** A usu. pleasant characteristic odor, as of a plant, spice, or food. See Synonyms at **fragrance.** [< Gk. *arōma,* aromatic herb.] —**ar′o·mat′ic** (ăr′ə-măt′ĭk) *adj.*

a·rose (ə-rōz′) ►*v.* P.t. of **arise.**

a·round (ə-round′) ►*adv.* **1a.** On or to all sides: *toys that were lying around.* **b.** In all directions. **2.** In a circle. **3.** In circumference. **4.** In the opposite direction: *wheeled around.* **5.** From one place to another: *wander around.* **6.** Nearby. **7.** Approximately: *a sack of flour that weighed around 30 pounds.* ►*prep.* **1.** On all sides of. **2a.** About the circumference of. **b.** So as to encircle or surround. **3a.** Here and there within: *walked around the city.* **b.** Near. **4.** On or to the farther side of: *around the corner.* **5.** So as to bypass or avoid. **6.** Approximately at: *left around seven.*

a·rouse (ə-rouz′) ►*v.* **a·roused, a·rous·ing**

1. To awaken from or as if from sleep. **2.** To stir up; excite: *aroused her curiosity.* [< ROUSE.] —**a·rous′al** *n.*

ar·peg·gi·o (är-pĕj′ē-ō′, -pĕj′ō) ►*n., pl.* **-os 1.** The playing of the tones of a chord in rapid succession rather than simultaneously. **2.** A chord played or sung in this manner. [Ital. < *arpa,* harp.]

ARR ►*abbr.* arrival

ar·raign (ə-rān′) ►*v.* **1.** To call (an accused person) before a court to answer a charge. **2.** To denounce. [< VLat. **adratiōnāre,* call to account.] —**ar·raign′ment** *n.*

ar·range (ə-rānj′) ►*v.* **-ranged, -rang·ing 1.** To put into a specific order or relation. **2.** To plan: *arrange a picnic.* **3.** To agree about; settle. **4.** To reset (music) for other instruments or voices. [< OFr. *arengier.*] —**ar·range′ment** *n.* —**ar·rang′er** *n.*
   Syns: marshal, order, organize, sort, systematize **Ant:** *disarrange* **v.**

ar·rant (ăr′ənt) ►*adj.* Utter; thoroughgoing: *an arrant fool.* [Var. of ERRANT.]

ar·ras (ăr′əs) ►*n.* **1.** A tapestry. **2.** A curtain or wall hanging. [ME, after *Arras,* France.]

ar·ray (ə-rā′) ►*v.* **1.** To place in an orderly arrangement. **2.** To dress in finery; adorn. ►*n.* **1.** An orderly arrangement. **2.** An impressively large number. **3.** Splendid attire; finery. **4.** *Math.* An arrangement of quantities in rows and columns. **5.** *Comp.* A group of memory elements accessed by one or more indices. [< VLat. **arrēdāre.*]

ar·rears (ə-rîrz′) ►*pl.n.* **1.** An overdue debt. **2.** The state of being behind in fulfilling obligations: *an account in arrears.* [< OFr. *arere,* behind.] —**ar·rear′age** *n.*

ar·rest (ə-rĕst′) ►*v.* **1.** To stop; check. **2.** To seize and hold by legal authority. **3.** To capture; engage: *arrested my attention.* ►*n.* **1.** The act of stopping or the condition of being stopped. **2a.** The act of detaining in legal custody. **b.** The state of being so detained: *under arrest.* [< OFr. *arester* : AD– + RE– + Lat. *stāre,* stand.] —**ar·rest′er, ar·res′tor** *n.*

ar·rest·ing (ə-rĕs′tĭng) ►*adj.* Attracting and holding the attention; striking.

ar·rhyth·mi·a (ə-rĭth′mē-ə) ►*n.* Irregularity in the force or rhythm of the heartbeat.

ar·ri·val (ə-rī′vəl) ►*n.* **1.** The act of arriving. **2.** One that arrives or has arrived.

ar·rive (ə-rīv′) ►*v.* **-rived, -riv·ing 1.** To reach a destination. **2.** To come eventually: *The day of reckoning has arrived.* **3.** To achieve success or recognition. [< OFr. *ariver.*]

ar·ro·gant (ăr′ə-gənt) ►*adj.* Unpleasantly or disdainfully self-important; haughty. [< Lat. *arrogāre,* arrogate.] —**ar′ro·gance** *n.* —**ar′ro·gant·ly** *adv.*

ar·ro·gate (ăr′ə-gāt′) ►*v.* **-gat·ed, -gat·ing** To take or claim for oneself unjustly. See Synonyms at **appropriate.** [Lat. *arrogāre.*] —**ar′ro·ga′tion** *n.* —**ar′ro·ga′tive** *adj.*

ar·row (ăr′ō) ►*n.* **1.** A straight thin shaft with a pointed head and often stabilizing vanes, meant to be shot from a bow. **2.** Something shaped like an arrow. [< OE *arwe.*]

ar·row·head (ăr′ō-hĕd′) ►*n.* The pointed, removable striking tip of an arrow.

ar·row·root (ăr′ō-rōōt′, ăr′ō-rŏŏt′) ►*n.* **1.** An edible starch that is obtained from the rhizomes of a tropical American plant. **2.** This plant or its rhizome. [< Arawak *aru-aru*, meal of meals.]

ar·roy·o (ə-roi′ō) ►*n., pl.* **-os** A deep gully cut by an intermittent stream. [Sp.]

ar·se·nal (är′sə-nəl) ►*n.* **1.** A place for the storage, manufacture, or repair of arms and ammunition. **2.** A stock or supply, esp. of weapons. [< Ar. *dār-aṣ-ṣinā'a*, place of manufacture.]

ar·se·nic (är′sə-nĭk) ►*n. Symbol* **As** A highly poisonous metallic element used in insecticides, weed killers, semiconductors, and various alloys. At. no. 33. See table at **element.** [< Gk. *arsenikon*, a yellow substance, of Iranian orig.]

ar·son (är′sən) ►*n.* The crime of willfully setting fire to buildings or other property. [< LLat. *ārsiō* < Lat. *ārdēre*, to burn.] —**ar′son·ist** *n.*

art¹ (ärt) ►*n.* **1a.** The use of the imagination in the effort to produce beautiful objects, as by arranging forms, sounds, or words. **b.** Such activity in the visual arts. **c.** Products of this activity, considered as a group. **2.** A field or category of art, such as music, ballet, or literature. **3.** A craft or trade and its methods. **4.** Contrivance; cunning. [< Lat. *ars, art-*.]

art² (ərt; ärt *when stressed*) ►*v.* Archaic 2nd pers. sing. pr. indic. of **be.**

art. ►*abbr.* article

–art ►*suff.* Var. of **–ard.**

art dec·o (dĕk′ō) ►*n.* A decorative style of the period 1925–40, marked by geometric designs and bold colors. [< *Exposition Internationale des Arts Décoratifs et Industriels Modernes*, held in 1925 in Paris.]

ar·te·fact (är′tə-făkt′) ►*n.* Var. of **artifact.**

Ar·te·mis (är′tə-mĭs) ►*n. Gk. Myth.* The virgin goddess of the hunt and the moon. [Gk.]

ar·te·ri·o·scle·ro·sis (är-tîr′ē-ō-sklə-rō′sĭs) ►*n.* A chronic disease in which thickening and hardening of the arterial walls impair blood circulation. —**ar·te′ri·o·scle·rot′ic** (-rŏt′ĭk) *adj.*

ar·ter·y (är′tə-rē) ►*n., pl.* **-ies** **1.** Any of a branching system of muscular tubes that carry blood away from the heart. **2.** A major transportation route into which local routes flow. [< Gk. *artēria*.] —**ar·te′ri·al** (-tîr′ē-əl) *adj.*

ar·te·sian well (är-tē′zhən) ►*n.* A deep well in which water rises to the surface by internal hydrostatic pressure. [Fr. *(puit) artésien*, (well) of Artois, France.]

art·ful (ärt′fəl) ►*adj.* **1.** Exhibiting art or skill. **2.** Deceitful; cunning; crafty. —**art′ful·ly** *adv.* —**art′ful·ness** *n.*

ar·thri·tis (är-thrī′tĭs) ►*n.* Inflammation of a joint or joints. —**ar·thrit′ic** (-thrĭt′ĭk) *adj.*

arthro– *or* **arthr–** ►*pref.* Joint: *arthropod.* [< Gk. *arthron*, joint.]

ar·thro·pod (är′thrə-pŏd′) ►*n.* An invertebrate, such as an insect, crustacean, or arachnid, that has an exoskeleton, a segmented body, and paired, jointed limbs.

ar·thros·co·py (är-thrŏs′kə-pē) ►*n., pl.* **-pies** Endoscopic examination of a joint, such as the knee. —**ar′thro·scop′ic** (-skŏp′ĭk) *adj.*

Ar·thur (är′thər) ►*n.* A legendary British hero, said to have been king of the Britons in the 6th cent. AD, who held court at Camelot. —**Ar·thu′ri·an** (-thŏŏr′ē-ən) *adj.*

Arthur, Chester Alan 1829–86. The 21st US president (1881–85).

Chester A. Arthur
1881 portrait

ar·ti·choke (är′tĭ-chōk′) ►*n.* **1.** A thistlelike plant having large heads of bluish flowers. **2.** The edible, unopened flower head of this plant. [Ult. < Ar. *al-ḥaršūf*.]

ar·ti·cle (är′tĭ-kəl) ►*n.* **1.** An individual element of a class; item. **2.** A section in a written document. **3.** A nonfictional composition or essay in a publication. **4.** *Gram.* Any of a class of words, such as *a* or *the*, used to signal nouns and to specify their application. [< Lat. *articulus*, dim. of *artus*, joint.]

ar·tic·u·lar (är-tĭk′yə-lər) ►*adj.* Of a joint or joints. [< Lat. *articulus*, small joint.]

ar·tic·u·late (är-tĭk′yə-lĭt) ►*adj.* **1.** Endowed with speech. **2.** Composed of meaningful syllables or words. **3.** Using or characterized by clear, expressive language. **4.** *Biol.* Jointed. ►*v.* (är-tĭk′yə-lāt′) **-lat·ed, -lat·ing** **1.** To pronounce distinctly; enunciate. **2.** To utter (a speech sound). **3.** To express in words. **4.** To fit together; unify. **5.** *Biol.* To unite by or form a joint. [< Lat. *articulāre*, divide into joints.] —**ar·tic′u·late·ly** *adv.* —**ar·tic′u·la′tion** *n.* —**ar·tic′u·la′tor** *n.*

ar·ti·fact *also* **ar·te·fact** (är′tə-făkt′) ►*n.* **1.** An object, such as a tool, made by human craft. **2.** A phenomenon that arises as a product, esp. an unintended product, of human activity. [Lat. *ars*, art + *factum*, something made.]

ar·ti·fice (är′tə-fĭs) ►*n.* **1.** A crafty expedient; stratagem. **2.** Deception; trickery. **3.** Cleverness; ingenuity. [< Lat. *artificium*.]

ar·ti·fi·cial (är′tə-fĭsh′əl) ►*adj.* **1.** Made by humans rather than occurring in nature. **2.** Made in imitation of something natural. **3.** Not genuine: *an artificial smile.* [< Lat. *artificium*, artifice.] —**ar′ti·fi′ci·al·i·ty** (-ē-ăl′ĭ-tē) *n.* —**ar′ti·fi′cial·ly** *adv.*

artificial insemination ►*n.* Introduction of semen into the vagina or uterus without sexual contact.

artificial intelligence ►*n.* The ability of a computer to perform activities normally thought to require intelligence.

artificial respiration ►*n.* A procedure to restore respiration in a person who has stopped breathing by forcing air into and out of the lungs.

ar·til·ler·y (är-tĭl′ə-rē) ►*n.* **1.** Large-caliber weapons, such as cannons, operated by crews. **2.** Troops armed with artillery. [< OFr. *artillier*, equip.]

ar·ti·san (är′tĭ-zən, -sən) ►*n.* A skilled manual worker. [< Ital. *artigiano* < Lat. *ars*, art.] —**ar·**

tis′·i·nal (är-tĭz′ə-nəl, -tĭs′-, är′tĭ-zə-, -sə-) *n.* —**ar′ti·san·ship′** *n.*

art·ist (är′tĭst) ►*n.* **1.** One who practices any of the fine or performing arts, as painting or music. **2.** One whose work shows skill. —**ar·tis′tic** *adj.* —**ar·tis′ti·cal·ly** *adv.*

ar·tiste (är-tēst′) ►*n.* A public performer, esp. a singer or dancer. [Fr., artist.]

art·ist·ry (är′tĭ-strē) ►*n.* Artistic ability, quality, or craft.

art·less (ärt′lĭs) ►*adj.* **1.** Without cunning; guileless. **2.** Simple; natural. **3.** Lacking art; crude. —**art′less·ly** *adv.* —**art′less·ness** *n.*

art·y (är′tē) or **art·sy** (ärt′sē) ►*adj.* **-i·er, -i·est** or **-si·er, -si·est** *Informal* Affectedly artistic. —**art′i·ly** *adv.* —**art′i·ness** *n.*

A·ru·ba (ə-rōō′bə) An island and autonomous territory of the Netherlands in the Lesser Antilles N of the Venezuela coast. Cap. Oranjestad.

a·ru·gu·la (ə-rōō′gə-lə) ►*n.* A Mediterranean plant having yellowish flowers and leaves that are used in salads. [Ital. dial. < Lat. ērūca.]

ar·um (âr′əm, ăr′-) ►*n.* Any of several Eurasian plants having arrowhead-shaped leaves. [< Gk. aron.]

–ary ►*suff.* Of or relating to: *reactionary.* [< Lat. -ārius, adj. and n. suff.]

Ar·y·an (âr′ē-ən, ăr′-) ►*n.* **1.** See **Indo-Iranian**. **2.** A member of the people who spoke Proto-Indo-European. **3.** A member of a people speaking an Indo-European language. **4.** In Nazism, a non-Jewish Caucasian, esp. one of Nordic type. [< Skt. ārya-, compatriot, Aryan.] —**Ar′y·an** *adj.*

as (ăz; əz *when unstressed*) ►*adv.* **1.** To the same extent or degree; equally. **2.** For instance: *large carnivores, as the bear or lion.* ►*conj.* **1.** To the same degree or quantity that: *as sweet as sugar.* See Usage Note at **like²**. **2.** In the same way that: *Think as I think.* **3.** At the same time that; while. **4.** Since; because. **5.** Though: *Trite as it sounds, it's true.* **6.** *Informal* That: *I don't know as I can.* ►*pron.* That; which; who: *I received the same grade as you did.* ►*prep.* **1.** In the role, capacity, or function of: *acting as a mediator.* **2.** In a manner similar to; the same as. —**idioms: as is** *Informal* Just the way it is. **as it were** In a manner of speaking. [< OE *eallswā.*]

Usage: Use a comma before *as* to express a causal relation, as in *She won't be coming, as we didn't invite her.* To express a time relation, do not use a comma before *as: She was finishing the painting as I walked into the room.* In using a clause that starts with *as* at the beginning of a sentence, make clear whether *as* is used to mean "because" or "at the same time that." E.g., *As they were leaving, John walked to the door* may mean that John walked to the door either because they were leaving or at the same time that they were leaving.

as·a·fet·i·da (ăs′ə-fĕt′ĭ-də) ►*n.* A strong-smelling resin derived from certain plants in the parsley family, used as a seasoning and in medicines. [< Med.Lat. asa foetida.]

ASAP ►*abbr.* as soon as possible

as·bes·tos (ăs-bĕs′təs, ăz-) ►*n.* An incombustible, chemical-resistant, fibrous mineral formerly used for fireproofing and electrical insulation. [< Gk. asbestos, unquenchable.]

as·bes·to·sis (ăs′bĕs-tō′sĭs, ăz′-) ►*n.* A progressive lung disease that is caused by prolonged inhalation of asbestos particles.

ASCAP ►*abbr.* American Society of Composers, Authors, and Publishers

as·cend (ə-sĕnd′) ►*v.* **1a.** To go or move upward; rise. **b.** To climb: *ascend the stairs.* **2.** To slope upward: *The road ascends the ridge.* **3.** To succeed to; occupy: *ascended the throne.* [< Lat. ascendere.]

as·cen·dan·cy also **as·cen·den·cy** (ə-sĕn′dən-sē) ►*n.* Decisive advantage; domination.

as·cen·dant also **as·cen·dent** (ə-sĕn′dənt) ►*adj.* **1.** Inclining or moving upward. **2.** Dominant; superior. ►*n.* The position or state of being dominant.

as·cen·sion (ə-sĕn′shən) ►*n.* **1.** The act or process of ascending. **2. Ascension** *Christianity* The bodily rising of Jesus into heaven on the 40th day after his Resurrection.

as·cent (ə-sĕnt′) ►*n.* **1.** The act of rising upward. **2.** An upward slope.

as·cer·tain (ăs′ər-tān′) ►*v.* To discover through investigation. See Synonyms at **discover**. [< OFr. acertener < certain, CERTAIN.] —**as′cer·tain′a·ble** *adj.*

as·cet·ic (ə-sĕt′ĭk) ►*n.* One who leads a life of austerity, esp. for religious reasons. [< Gk. askētēs, hermit.] —**as·cet′ic** *adj.* —**as·cet′i·cism** (-ĭ-sĭz′əm) *n.*

ASCII (ăs′kē) ►*n.* A standard for assigning numerical values to letters of the Roman alphabet and typographic characters. [*A(merican) S(tandard) C(ode for) I(nformation) I(nterchange).)*]

a·scor·bic acid (ə-skôr′bĭk) ►*n.* A vitamin, $C_6H_8O_6$, found in citrus fruits and leafy green vegetables and used to prevent scurvy. [A⁻¹ + SCORB(UT)IC.]

as·cot (ăs′kət) ►*n.* A broad scarf knotted so that its ends are laid flat upon each other. [< Ascot, England.]

as·cribe (ə-skrīb′) ►*v.* **-cribed, -crib·ing** To attribute to a specified cause, source, or origin. [< Lat. ascribere.] —**as·crib′a·ble** *adj.* —**as·crip′tion** (-skrĭp′shən) *n.*

–ase ►*suff.* Enzyme: *amylase.* [< diastase, an amylase found in germinating grains.]

a·sep·tic (ə-sĕp′tĭk, ā-) ►*adj.* Free of pathogenic microorganisms. —**a·sep′sis** *n.*

a·sex·u·al (ā-sĕk′shōō-əl) ►*adj.* **1.** Having no sex or sex organs. **2.** Not involving sex organs or the union of sex cells. **3.** Lacking desire for sex. —**a·sex′u·al·ly** *adv.*

as for ►*prep.* With regard to.

ash¹ (ăsh) ►*n.* **1.** The grayish powdery residue left when something is burned. **2.** *Geol.* A grayish powdery material ejected by erupting volcanoes. **3. ashes** Ruins. **4. ashes** Human remains, esp. after cremation. [< OE æsce.]

ash² (ăsh) ►*n.* **1.** A deciduous timber tree with compound leaves. **2.** The strong elastic wood of this tree. [< OE æsc.]

a·shamed (ə-shāmd′) ►*adj.* **1.** Feeling shame. **2.** Feeling inferior or embarrassed. **3.** Reluctant through fear of shame: *ashamed to tell.* [< OE āsceamian, feel shame.] —**a·sham′ed·ly** (-shā′mĭd-lē) *adv.*

A·shan·ti (ə-shăn′tē, ə-shän′-) ►*n., pl.* **-ti** or **-tis 1.** A member of a people of central Ghana. **2.** The Twi language of the Ashanti.

Ashe (ăsh), **Arthur Robert, Jr.** 1943–93. Amer. tennis player.

ash·en (ăsh′ən) ►*adj.* **1.** Consisting of ashes. **2.**

Resembling ashes, esp. in color; pale.

Ash·ga·bat (ăsh′gä-bät′) The capital of Turkmenistan, in the S-central part.

Ash·ke·naz·i (äsh′kə-nä′zē) ►*n., pl.* **-naz·im** (-näz′ĭm, -nä′zĭm) A descendant of the Yiddish-speaking Jews of E and central Europe.

ash·lar (ăsh′lər) ►*n.* **1.** A squared block of building stone. **2.** Masonry of such stones. [< OFr. *aisselier,* board.]

a·shore (ə-shôr′) ►*adv.* To or on the shore.

ash·ram (äsh′rəm) ►*n.* A residence of a Hindu religious community and its guru. [Skt. *āśramaḥ.*]

ash·tray (ăsh′trā′) ►*n.* A receptacle for tobacco ashes and cigarette butts.

Ash Wednesday ►*n.* The 7th Wednesday before Easter and the 1st day of Lent.

ash·y (ăsh′ē) ►*adj.* **-i·er, -i·est 1.** Of or covered with ashes. **2.** Ashen; pale.

A·sia (ā′zhə) The largest continent, occupying the E part of the Eurasian landmass and its adjacent islands and separated from Europe by the Ural Mts.

Asia Minor A peninsula of W Asia between the Black and Mediterranean Seas.

A·sian (ā′zhən, -shən) ►*adj.* Of or relating to Asia or its peoples, languages, or cultures. ►*n.* **1.** A native or inhabitant of Asia. **2.** A person of Asian ancestry.

Asian American ►*n.* A US citizen or resident of Asian ancestry. —**A′sian-A·mer′i·can** *adj.*

A·si·at·ic (ā′zhē-ăt′ĭk, -shē-, -zē-) ►*adj.* Asian. ►*n. Often Offensive* An Asian.

a·side (ə-sīd′) ►*adv.* **1.** To one side. **2.** Out of one's thoughts or mind. **3.** Apart. **4.** In reserve; away. ►*n.* Dialogue supposedly not heard by the other actors in a play.

aside from ►*prep.* Excluding; except for.

As·i·mov (ăz′ĭ-môv′, -mŏv′), **Isaac** 1920–92. Russian-born Amer. scientist and writer.

as·i·nine (ăs′ə-nīn′) ►*adj.* Stupid; silly. [Lat. *asinīnus < asinus,* ass.]

ask (ăsk) ►*v.* **1.** To put a question to. **2.** To seek an answer to. **3.** To inquire. **4.** To request. **5.** To expect or demand. **6.** To invite. [< OE *āscian.*]

a·skance (ə-skăns′) ►*adv.* **1.** With disapproval or distrust. **2.** With a sideways glance; obliquely. [?]

a·skew (ə-skyōō′) ►*adv. & adj.* To one side; awry.

ASL ►*abbr.* American Sign Language

a·slant (ə-slănt′) ►*adv. & adj.* Obliquely.

a·sleep (ə-slēp′) ►*adj.* **1.** Sleeping. **2.** Inactive; dormant. **3.** Numb. —**a·sleep′** *adv.*

As·ma·ra (ăz-mä′rə) The capital of Eritrea, in the W part.

a·so·cial (ā-sō′shəl) ►*adj.* **1.** Averse to the society of others. **2.** Unwilling to conform to normal social behavior; antisocial.

as of ►*prep.* On; at: *payable as of May 1.*

asp (ăsp) ►*n.* Any of several venomous African or Eurasian snakes. [< Gk. *aspis.*]

as·par·a·gus (ə-spăr′ə-gəs) ►*n.* A perennial plant having edible young shoots and fernlike foliage. [< Gk. *asparagos.*]

ASPCA ►*abbr.* American Society for the Prevention of Cruelty to Animals

as·pect (ăs′pĕkt) ►*n.* **1.** An appearance; air. **2.** An element; facet. **3.** A position facing a given direction. **4.** *Gram.* A category of the verb designating the duration or type of action. [< Lat.

aspicere, look at : AD– + *specere,* look.]

as·pen (ăs′pən) ►*n.* A poplar tree having leaves that flutter readily in even a light breeze. [< OE *æspe.*]

as·per·i·ty (ă-spĕr′ĭ-tē) ►*n.* **1.** Roughness; harshness. **2.** Ill temper. [< Lat. *asper,* rough.]

as·per·sion (ə-spûr′zhən, -shən) ►*n.* A slanderous remark. [< Lat. *aspergere,* scatter.]

as·phalt (ăs′fôlt′) ►*n.* A brownish-black solid or semisolid mixture of bitumens used in paving, roofing, and waterproofing. [< Gk. *asphaltos,* pitch.] —**as·phal′tic** *adj.*

as·pho·del (ăs′fə-dĕl′) ►*n.* A Mediterranean plant having clusters of white, pink, or yellow flowers. [< Gk. *asphodelos.*]

as·phyx·i·a (ăs-fĭk′sē-ə) ►*n.* Lack of oxygen accompanied by an increase of carbon dioxide in the blood, leading to unconsciousness or death. [< Gk. *asphuxia,* stopping of the pulse.]

as·phyx·i·ant (ăs-fĭk′sē-ənt) ►*n.* Something, esp. a toxic gas, that induces asphyxia.

as·phyx·i·ate (ăs-fĭk′sē-āt′) ►*v.* **-at·ed, -at·ing** To suffocate; smother. —**as·phyx′i·a′tion** *n.* —**as·phyx′i·a′tor** *n.*

as·pic (ăs′pĭk) ►*n.* A clear jelly made of meat, fish, or vegetable stock and gelatin. [Fr., asp (from its color).]

as·pi·dis·tra (ăs′pĭ-dĭs′trə) ►*n.* A popular houseplant having large evergreen leaves. [< Gk. *aspis, aspid-,* shield.]

as·pi·rant (ăs′pər-ənt, ə-spīr′-) ►*n.* One who aspires, as to advancement.

as·pi·rate (ăs′pə-rāt′) ►*v.* **-rat·ed, -rat·ing 1.** *Ling.* To pronounce (a speech sound) with an audible release of breath, as in the *h* of *hit* or the *p* of *pit.* **2.** To inhale. **3.** *Med.* To remove with a suction device. [Lat. *aspīrāre,* breathe on.] —**as′pi·rate** (-pər-ĭt) *n.*

as·pi·ra·tion (ăs′pə-rā′shən) ►*n.* **1a.** A desire for achievement. **b.** An object of such desire. **2.** The removal of fluids or gases from the body by suction. **3.** The pronunciation of an aspirated speech sound. **4.** The act of inhaling.

as·pi·ra·tor (ăs′pə-rā′tər) ►*n.* A device for removing substances, such as mucus or serum, from a body cavity by suction.

as·pire (ə-spīr′) ►*v.* **-pired, -pir·ing** To have a great ambition; desire. [< Lat. *aspīrāre,* desire.] —**as·pir′er** *n.* —**as·pir′ing·ly** *adv.*

as·pi·rin (ăs′pər-ĭn, -prĭn) ►*n.* **1.** A white crystalline compound derived from salicylic acid and used to relieve pain and reduce fever and inflammation. **2.** A tablet of aspirin. [Originally a trademark.]

ass (ăs) ►*n.* **1.** Any of several hoofed, long-eared mammals resembling and closely related to the horse. **2.** A vain, silly, or stupid person. [< OE *assa,* ult. < Lat. *asinus.*]

as·sail (ə-sāl′) ►*v.* To attack violently. [< Lat. *assilīre,* jump on.] —**as·sail′a·ble** *adj.* —**as·sail′ant** *n.* —**as·sail′er** *n.*

as·sas·sin (ə-săs′ĭn) ►*n.* A murderer, esp. of a prominent person. [< Ar. *ḥaššāšīn,* pl. of *ḥaššāš,* hashish user.]

as·sas·si·nate (ə-săs′ə-nāt′) ►*v.* **-nat·ed, -nat·ing 1.** To murder by surprise attack, as for political reasons. **2.** To destroy (a rival's character). —**as·sas′si·na′tion** *n.*

as·sault (ə-sôlt′) ►*n.* **1.** A violent physical or verbal attack. **2.** An unlawful threat or attempt to do bodily injury to another. **3.** The crime of rape. [< Lat. *assilīre, assult-*, jump on.] —**as·sault'** *v.* —**as·sault'er** *n.* —**as·saul'tive** *adj.*

assault and battery ►*n. Law* A physical assault involving bodily contact with the victim.

assault weapon ►*n.* A weapon designed for use in close combat.

as·say (ăs'ā', ă-sā') ►*n.* Analysis of a substance, esp. of an ore or drug, to determine its composition. ►*v.* (ă-sā', ăs'ā') **1.** To subject to or undergo an assay. **2.** To evaluate; assess. **3.** To attempt. [< OFr. *assai*, ESSAY.] —**as·say'a·ble** *adj.* —**as·say'er** *n.*

as·sem·blage (ə-sĕm'blĭj) ►*n.* **1.** The act of assembling or the state of being assembled. **2.** A collection of persons or things. **3.** A fitting together of parts, as in a machine. **4.** A sculptural arrangement of miscellaneous objects.

as·sem·ble (ə-sĕm'bəl) ►*v.* **-bled, -bling 1.** To bring or gather together. See Synonyms at **call. 2.** To fit together the parts of. [< OFr. *assembler*.]

as·sem·bler (ə-sĕm'blər) ►*n.* **1.** One that assembles. **2.** A program that produces executable machine code from symbolic assembly language.

as·sem·bly (ə-sĕm'blē) ►*n., pl.* **-blies 1.** The act of assembling or the state of being assembled. **2.** A group of persons gathered together for a common purpose. **3. Assembly** The lower house of a legislature. **4a.** The putting together of parts to make a product. **b.** A set of parts so assembled. **5.** *Comp.* The automatic translation of symbolic code into machine code.

assembly language ►*n.* A programming language closely resembling binary machine code.

assembly line ►*n.* An arrangement of workers and tools in which the product passes from operation to operation until completed.

as·sent (ə-sĕnt') ►*v.* To agree; concur. [< Lat. *assentārī.*] —**as·sent'** *n.* —**as·sent'er, as·sen'tor** *n.*

as·sert (ə-sûrt') ►*v.* **1.** To state positively; affirm. **2.** To defend or maintain. **3.** To put (oneself) forward boldly or forcefully. [Lat. *asserere*.] —**as·ser'tive** *adj.* —**as·ser'tive·ly** *adv.* —**as·ser'tive·ness** *n.*

as·ser·tion (ə-sûr'shən) ►*n.* A positive, often unsupported declaration.

as·sess (ə-sĕs') ►*v.* **1.** To make a judgment about. **2.** To evaluate, esp. for taxation. **3.** To set the amount of (a tax or fine). **4.** To charge with a tax or fine. [< Lat. *assidēre, assess-*, assist as judge : AD– + *sedēre*, sit.] —**as·sess'a·ble** *adj.* —**as·sess'ment** *n.* —**as·ses'sor** *n.*

as·set (ăs'ĕt') ►*n.* **1.** A useful or valuable quality, person, or thing. **2. assets** All properties, such as cash or stock, that may cover the liabilities of a person or business. [< AN *asez*, enough.]

as·sev·er·ate (ə-sĕv'ə-rāt') ►*v.* **-at·ed, -at·ing** To declare positively; assert. [Lat. *assevērāre*.] —**as·sev·er·a'tion** *n.*

as·sid·u·ous (ə-sĭj'ōo-əs) ►*adj.* Constant in application or attention; diligent. [< Lat. *assidēre*, attend to; see ASSESS.] —**as·si·du'i·ty** (ăs'ĭ-dōo'ĭ-tē, -dyōo'-) *n.* —**as·sid'u·ous·ly** *adv.* —**as·sid'u·ous·ness** *n.*

as·sign (ə-sīn') ►*v.* **1.** To select for a duty; appoint. **2.** To specify; designate. See Synonyms at **allocate. 3.** To give out as a task; allot: *assigned homework to the class.* **4.** To ascribe; attribute. **5.** *Law* To transfer (e.g., property)

from one to another. ►*n. Law* One to whom something has been assigned. [< Lat. *assignāre*.] —**as·sign'a·bil'i·ty** *n.* —**as·sign'a·ble** *adj.* —**as·sign'er** *n.*

as·sig·na·tion (ăs'ĭg-nā'shən) ►*n.* An appointment for a meeting between lovers.

as·sign·ment (ə-sīn'mənt) ►*n.* **1.** The act of assigning. **2.** Something assigned.

as·sim·i·late (ə-sĭm'ə-lāt') ►*v.* **-lat·ed, -lat·ing 1.** To take in and understand. **2.** To make or become similar. **3.** To take in, digest, and transform (food) into living tissue. [< Lat. *assimilāre*, make similar.] —**as·sim'i·la·ble** (-lə-bəl) *adj.* —**as·sim'i·la'tion** *n.* —**as·sim'i·la'tor** *n.*

As·sin·i·boin (ə-sĭn'ə-boin') ►*n., pl.* **-boin** or **-boins 1.** A member of a Native American people of N Montana and adjacent regions of Canada, now located in Montana, Alberta, and Saskatchewan. **2.** Their Siouan language.

as·sist (ə-sĭst') ►*v.* To help; support. ►*n.* An act of giving aid; help. [< Lat. *assistere* : AD– + *sistere*, stand.] —**as·sis'tance** *n.*

as·sis·tant (ə-sĭs'tənt) ►*n.* One that assists; helper. ►*adj.* **1.** Subordinate. **2.** Auxiliary.

as·sist·ed living (ə-sĭs'tĭd) ►*n.* A living arrangement in which people with special needs, esp. seniors, live in a facility that provides help with everyday tasks.

as·size (ə-sīz') ►*n.* **1.** A session or a decree of a court. **2. assizes** One of the periodic court sessions formerly held in the counties of England and Wales. [< Lat. *assidēre*, sit beside : AD– + *sedēre*, sit.]

assn. ►*abbr.* association

assoc. ►*abbr.* **1.** associate **2.** association

as·so·ci·ate (ə-sō'sē-āt', -shē-) ►*v.* **-at·ed, -at·ing 1.** To join or connect in a relationship. **2.** To connect in the mind or imagination. ►*n.* (-ĭt, -āt') **1.** A partner; colleague. **2.** A companion; comrade. ►*adj.* (-ĭt, -āt') Joined in equal or nearly equal status: *an associate editor.* [< Lat. *associāre*, join to.]

as·so·ci·a·tion (ə-sō'sē-ā'shən, -shē-) ►*n.* **1.** The act of associating or the state of being associated. **2.** An organized body of people; society. **3.** An emotion, idea, or sensation linked to a person, object, or idea. —**as·so'ci·a'tion·al** *adj.*

association football ►*n. Chiefly Brit.* Soccer.

as·so·ci·a·tive (ə-sō'shə-tĭv, -sē-ə-tĭv, -sē-ā'tĭv, -shē-) ►*adj.* **1.** Of or causing association. **2.** *Math.* Independent of the grouping of elements. —**as·so'ci·a'tive·ly** *adv.*

as·so·nance (ăs'ə-nəns) ►*n.* Resemblance esp. of the vowel sounds in words. [< Lat. *assonāre*, respond to.] —**as'so·nant** *adj. & n.* —**as'so·nan'tal** (-năn'tl) *adj.*

as·sort (ə-sôrt') ►*v.* To separate into groups according to kind; classify. [< OFr. *assorter*.] —**as·sor'ta·tive** *adj.* —**as·sort'er** *n.*

as·sort·ed (ə-sôr'tĭd) ►*adj.* Of different kinds; various: *assorted sizes.*

as·sort·ment (ə-sôrt'mənt) ►*n.* **1.** A collection of various kinds; variety. **2.** The act of assorting.

asst. ►*abbr.* assistant

as·suage (ə-swāj') ►*v.* **-suaged, -suag·ing 1.** To make less severe; ease. **2.** To satisfy or appease. [< OFr. *assuagier* < Lat. *suavis*, sweet.]

as·sume (ə-sōom') ►*v.* **-sumed, -sum·ing 1.** To take upon oneself. **2.** To take on; adopt. **3.** To take for granted; suppose. [< Lat. *assūmere*, take to.] —**as·sum′a·ble** *adj.* —**as·sum′a·bly** *adv.*

as·sumed (ə-soōmd′) ▸*adj.* **1.** Feigned; pretended. **2.** Taken for granted; supposed. —**as·sum′ed·ly** (-soō′mĭd-lē) *adv.*

as·sum·ing (ə-soō′mĭng) ▸*adj.* Presumptuous; arrogant. ▸*conj.* Supposing.

as·sump·tion (ə-sŭmp′shən) ▸*n.* **1.** The act of assuming. **2.** Something accepted as true without proof; supposition. **3. Assumption** *Christianity* The bodily taking up of the Virgin Mary into heaven after her death.

as·sur·ance (ə-shoōr′əns) ▸*n.* **1.** The act of assuring. **2.** Freedom from doubt; certainty. **3.** Self-confidence. **4.** *Chiefly Brit.* Insurance, esp. life insurance.

as·sure (ə-shoōr′) ▸*v.* **-sured, -sur·ing** **1.** To inform positively. **2.** To cause to feel sure. **3.** To make certain; ensure. **4.** *Chiefly Brit.* To insure, as against loss. [< VLat. *assēcūrāre*, make sure.] —**as·sur′er** *n.*

as·sured (ə-shoōrd′) ▸*adj.* **1.** Certain; guaranteed. **2.** Confident; sure. —**as·sur′ed·ly** (-ĭd-lē) *adv.* —**as·sur′ed·ness** *n.*

As·syr·i·a (ə-sîr′ē-ə) An ancient empire and civilization of W Asia in the upper valley of the Tigris R.

As·syr·i·an (ə-sîr′ē-ən) ▸*adj.* Of or relating to Assyria. ▸*n.* **1.** A native or inhabitant of Assyria. **2.** See **Akkadian** (sense 2).

A·staire (ə-stâr′), **Fred** 1899–1987. Amer. dancer, singer, and actor.

as·ta·tine (ăs′tə-tēn′, -tĭn) ▸*n. Symbol* **At** A highly unstable radioactive element used in medicine as a radioactive tracer. At. no. 85. See table at **element.** [< Gk. *astatos*, unstable.]

as·ter (ăs′tər) ▸*n.* Any of various plants having daisylike flower heads with white, pink, or violet rays and a usu. yellow disk. [< Gk. *astēr*, star.]

as·ter·isk (ăs′tə-rĭsk′) ▸*n.* A star-shaped figure (*) used in printing to indicate an omission or a reference to a footnote. [< Gk. *asteriskos*, dim. of *astēr*, star.]

a·stern (ə-stûrn′) ▸*adv. & adj.* **1.** Behind a vessel. **2.** At or to the stern of a vessel.

as·ter·oid (ăs′tə-roid′) ▸*n.* Any of numerous small celestial bodies that revolve around the sun chiefly between Mars and Jupiter. [< Gk. *astēr*, star.]

asth·ma (ăz′mə, ăs′-) ▸*n.* A respiratory disease, often arising from allergies, marked by labored breathing, chest constriction, and coughing. [< Gk.] —**asth·mat′ic** (-măt′ĭk) *adj. & n.*

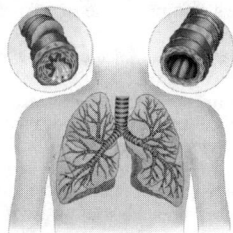

asthma
left: inflamed bronchial tube with contracted muscles and mucus discharge
right: normal bronchial tube

a·stig·ma·tism (ə-stĭg′mə-tĭz′əm) ▸*n.* A visual defect in which the shape of the cornea or another part of the eye prevents light rays from focusing clearly on the retina. [A-¹ + Gk. *stigma*, mark.] —**as′tig·mat′ic** (ăs′tĭg-măt′-ĭk) *adj. & n.*

a·stir (ə-stûr′) ▸*adj.* Moving about.

a·ston·ish (ə-stŏn′ĭsh) ▸*v.* To fill with sudden wonder or amazement. [< OFr. *estoner*.] —**a·ston′ish·ing·ly** *adv.* —**a·ston′ish·ment** *n.*

As·tor (ăs′tər), **John Jacob** 1763–1848. German-born Amer. fur trader and capitalist.

a·stound (ə-stound′) ▸*v.* To astonish and bewilder. [< ME *astoned*, astonished.] —**a·stound′ing** *adj.* —**a·stound′ing·ly** *adv.*

a·strad·dle (ə-străd′l) ▸*adv. & prep.* Astride.

as·tra·khan (ăs′trə-kăn′, -kən) ▸*n.* A curly, wavy fur that is made from the skins of young lambs.

As·tra·khan (ăs′trə-kăn′, ä-strä-кнän′) A city of SW Russia on the Volga R. delta.

as·tral (ăs′trəl) ▸*adj.* Of or resembling the stars. [< Gk. *astron*, star.]

a·stray (ə-strā′) ▸*adv.* **1.** Away from the correct direction or route. **2.** Into wrong or evil ways. [< OFr. *estraier*, STRAY.] —**a·stray′** *adj.*

a·stride (ə-strīd′) ▸*adv. & prep.* With a leg on each side (of).

as·trin·gent (ə-strĭn′jənt) ▸*adj.* **1.** *Med.* Tending to draw together or constrict living tissues; styptic. **2.** Sharp; harsh: *made astringent remarks.* ▸*n.* An astringent agent or drug. [< Lat. *astringere*, bind together.] —**as·trin′gen·cy** *n.* —**as·trin′gent·ly** *adv.*

astro– or **astr–** ▸*pref.* **1.** Star: *astrophysics.* **2.** Outer space: *astronaut.* [< Gk., *astron*, star.]

as·tro·labe (ăs′trə-lāb′) ▸*n.* A medieval instrument used to determine the altitude of a celestial body. [< Gk. *(organon) astrolabon*, (instrument) for taking the stars.]

as·trol·o·gy (ə-strŏl′ə-jē) ▸*n.* The study of the positions and motions of celestial bodies in the belief that they influence the course of human affairs. —**as·trol′o·ger** *n.* —**as′tro·log′i·cal** (ăs′trə-lŏj′ĭ-kəl), **as′tro·log′ic** *adj.*

as·tro·naut (ăs′trə-nôt′) ▸*n.* A person who is trained to pilot or otherwise participate in the flight of a spacecraft. [ASTRO– + Gk. *nautēs*, sailor.]

as·tro·nau·tics (ăs′trə-nô′tĭks) ▸*n.* (*takes sing. or pl. v.*) The science and technology of space flight. —**as′tro·nau′tic, as′tro·nau′ti·cal** *adj.*

as·tro·nom·i·cal (ăs′trə-nŏm′ĭ-kəl) also **as·tro·nom·ic** (-nŏm′ĭk) ▸*adj.* **1.** Of or relating to astronomy. **2.** Colossal; immense. —**as′tro·nom′i·cal·ly** *adv.*

astronomical unit ▸*n.* A unit of length that is equal to the mean distance from Earth to the sun, approx. 150 million km (93 million mi).

as·tron·o·my (ə-strŏn′ə-mē) ▸*n.* The scientific study of matter and phenomena in the universe, especially in outer space. —**as·tron′o·mer** *n.*

as·tro·phys·ics (ăs′trō-fĭz′ĭks) ▸*n.* (*takes sing. v.*) The branch of applied physics that deals with astronomical phenomena. —**as′tro·phys′i·cal** *adj.* —**as′tro·phys′i·cist** (-fĭz′ĭ-sĭst) *n.*

As·tro·Turf (ăs′trō-tûrf′) A trademark for an artificial grasslike ground covering.

as·tute (ə-stōōt′, ə-styōōt′) ▸*adj.* Having or showing keen judgment: *an astute observation.* [Lat. *astūtus* < *astus,* craft.] —**as·tute′ly** *adv.* —**as·tute′ness** *n.*

A·sun·ción (ä-sōōn′syōn′) The capital of Paraguay, in the S part.

a·sun·der (ə-sŭn′dər) ▸*adv.* **1.** Into separate parts, pieces, or groups. **2.** Apart in position or direction. [< OE *on sundran.*]

as well as ▸*conj.* And in addition: *big as well as strong.* ▸*prep.* In addition to.

a·sy·lum (ə-sī′ləm) ▸*n.* **1.** Protection granted by a government to a political refugee from another country. **2.** A place of safety; refuge. **3.** An institution for the care of ill or needy people, esp. those with mental impairments. [< Gk. *asulos,* inviolable.]

a·sym·met·ric (ā′sĭ-mĕt′rĭk) also **a·sym·met·ri·cal** (-rĭ-kəl) ▸*adj.* Not symmetrical. —**a′·sym·met′ri·cal·ly** *adv.* —**a·sym′me·try** *n.*

a·symp·to·mat·ic (ā′sĭmp-tə-măt′ĭk) ▸*adj.* Not causing or exhibiting symptoms of disease. —**a′symp·to·mat′i·cal·ly** *adv.*

as·ymp·tote (ăs′ĭm-tōt′, -ĭmp-) ▸*n.* A line whose distance to a given curve tends to zero. [< Gk. *asumptōtos,* not intersecting.] —**as′·ymp·tot′ic** (-tŏt′ĭk), **as′ymp·tot′i·cal** *adj.*

at (ăt; ət *when unstressed*) ▸*prep.* **1.** In or near the position or area occupied by: *at the market.* **2.** To or toward the direction or goal of: *aimed at the target.* **3.** In the state or condition of: *at peace.* **4.** In the activity or field of: *good at math; at work.* **5.** On, near, or by the time or age of: *at three o'clock.* **6.** Because of: *rejoice at a victory.* [< OE *æt.*]

at·a·vism (ăt′ə-vĭz′əm) ▸*n.* The reappearance of a characteristic in an organism after several generations of absence. [< Lat. *atavus,* ancestor.] —**at′a·vis′tic** *adj.* —**at′a·vis′ti·cal·ly** *adv.*

ate (āt) ▸*v.* P.t. of **eat.**

–ate[1] ▸*suff.* **1a.** Having: *nervate.* **b.** Characterized by: *affectionate.* **c.** Resembling: *palmate.* **2.** Rank; office: *pastorate.* **3.** To act upon in a specified manner: *acidulate.* **4.** Product of an action or process: *distillate.* [< Lat. *-ātus,* p.part. suff.]

–ate[2] ▸*suff.* **1.** A derivative of a specified chemical compound or element: *silicate.* **2.** A salt or ester of a specified acid: *acetate.* [NLat. *-ātum* < Lat. *-ātus,* p.part. suff.]

at·el·ier (ăt′l-yā′) ▸*n.* A workshop or studio, esp. for an artist. [< OFr. *astelier.*]

Ath·a·bas·ca River (ăth′ə-băs′kə) A river rising in the Rocky Mts. of SW Alberta, Canada, and flowing about 1,230 km (765 mi) to **Lake Athabasca** on the Saskatchewan border.

Ath·a·bas·kan or **Ath·a·bas·can** (ăth′ə-băs′kən) also **Ath·a·pas·can** (-păs′-) ▸*n.* **1.** A group of related Native American languages including Navajo, Apache, and languages of NW Canada. **2.** A member of an Athabaskan-speaking people.

a·the·ism (ā′thē-ĭz′əm) ▸*n.* Disbelief in or denial of the existence of God. [< Gk. *atheos,* without a god.] —**a′the·ist** *n.* —**a′the·is′tic** *adj.*

A·the·na (ə-thē′nə) also **A·the·ne** (-nē) ▸*n.* Gk. *Myth.* The goddess of wisdom, the practical arts, and warfare.

ath·e·nae·um also **ath·e·ne·um** (ăth′ə-nē′əm) ▸*n.* **1.** An institution for the promotion of learning. **2.** A library. [< Gk. *Athēnaion,* temple of Athena.]

Ath·ens (ăth′ənz) The capital of Greece, in the E part near the Saronic Gulf; reached the height of its power and cultural achievements in the 5th cent. BC. —**A·the′ni·an** (ə-thē′nē-ən) *adj.* & *n.*

ath·er·o·scle·ro·sis (ăth′ə-rō-sklə-rō′sĭs) ▸*n.* A form of arteriosclerosis in which plaque containing cholesterol and lipids is deposited on the inner walls of the arteries. [< Lat. *athērōma,* kind of tumor.]

a·thirst (ə-thûrst′) ▸*adj.* Strongly desirous; eager: *athirst for freedom.*

ath·lete (ăth′lēt′) ▸*n.* One who participates esp. in competitive sports. [< Gk. *athlētēs* < *athlein,* compete.]

ath·lete's foot (ăth′lēts) ▸*n.* A contagious fungal infection of the skin usu. affecting the feet, characterized by itching, cracking, and scaling.

ath·let·ic (ăth-lĕt′ĭk) ▸*adj.* **1.** Of or for athletics or athletes. **2.** Physically strong. —**ath·let′i·cal·ly** *adv.* —**ath·let′i·cism** (-lĕt′ĭ-sĭz′əm) *n.*

ath·let·ics (ăth-lĕt′ĭks) ▸*n. (takes sing. or pl. v.)* **1.** Athletic activities. **2.** A system of training and practice for such activities.

athletic supporter ▸*n.* A jockstrap.

a·thwart (ə-thwôrt′) ▸*prep.* From one side to the other of; across. ▸*adv.* From side to side; crosswise.

a·tilt (ə-tĭlt′) ▸*adv.* & *adj.* In a tilted position.

–ation ▸*suff.* **1a.** Action or process: *strangulation.* **b.** The result of an action or process: *acculturation.* **2.** State, condition, or quality of: *moderation.* [< Lat. *-ātiō,* n. suff.]

–ative ▸*suff.* Relating to or characterized by: *talkative.* [< Lat. *-ātīvus* < *-ātus,* –ATE[1].]

At·lan·ta (ăt-lăn′tə) The capital of GA, in the NW part. —**At·lan′tan** *n.*

At·lan·tic City (ăt-lăn′tĭk) A coastal city of SE NJ.

Atlantic Ocean The second-largest ocean, divided into the **North Atlantic** and the **South Atlantic** and extending from the Arctic in the N to the Antarctic in the S between the Americas and Europe and Africa.

At·lan·tis (ăt-lăn′tĭs) ▸*n.* A legendary sunken island in the Atlantic Ocean W of Gibraltar.

at·las (ăt′ləs) ▸*n.* A book of maps. [After ATLAS, often depicted holding the world on his shoulders on the frontispiece of early atlases.]

Atlas ▸*n.* Gk. *Myth.* A Titan condemned by Zeus to hold up the heavens.

Atlas Mountains A system of ranges and plateaus of NW Africa.

at·la·tl (ät-lät′l) ▸*n.* A device used to increase the effective length of the arm in throwing a spear. [Nahuatl.]

ATM (ā′tē′-ĕm) ▸*n.* An electronic machine in a public place, connected to a data system and related equipment and activated by a bank customer to obtain cash withdrawals and other banking services. [*a(utomatic) t(eller) m(achine)* or *a(utomated) t(eller) m(achine).*]

at·mos·phere (ăt′mə-sfîr′) ▸*n.* **1.** The mass of gases enveloping a celestial body, esp. Earth. **2.** *Phys.* A unit of pressure equal to the air pressure at sea level. **3.** Surroundings; environment. **4.** A dominant tone or attitude: *an atmosphere of distrust.* [Gk. *atmos,* vapor + Lat. *sphaera,* sphere.] —**at′mos·pher′ic** (-sfĕr′ĭk) *adj.*

exosphere

thermosphere

mesosphere

stratosphere

troposphere

atmosphere

at·mos·pher·ics (ăt′mə-sfĕr′ĭks) ►*n. (takes sing. v.)* Radio interference that is produced by electromagnetic radiation from natural phenomena.

at. no. ►*abbr.* atomic number

a·toll (ăt′ôl′, -ŏl′, ä′tôl′, ā′tŏl′) ►*n.* A ringlike coral island or chain of islets that encloses a lagoon. [Perh. < Tamil *aṭar*, be close together.]

at·om (ăt′əm) ►*n.* **1.** A unit of matter, the smallest unit of an element, having all the characteristics of that element and consisting of a dense, positively charged nucleus surrounded by a system of electrons. **2.** An extremely small part, quantity, or amount. [< Gk. *atomos*, indivisible.]

a·tom·ic (ə-tŏm′ĭk) ►*adj.* **1.** Of or relating to an atom. **2.** Of or employing nuclear energy: *an atomic submarine.* **3.** Very small; infinitesimal. —**a·tom′i·cal·ly** *adv.*

atomic bomb ►*n.* An explosive weapon of great destructive power derived from the rapid release of energy in the fission of heavy atomic nuclei.

atomic energy ►*n.* See **nuclear energy.**

atomic number ►*n.* The number of protons in an atomic nucleus.

atomic weight ►*n.* The average mass of an atom of an element, usu. given relative to carbon 12, which is assigned a mass of 12.

at·om·ize (ăt′ə-mīz′) ►*v.* **-ized, -iz·ing 1.** To reduce to fine or minute particles, as in a spray. **2.** To fragment; disintegrate. —**at′om·i·za′tion** *n.*

at·om·iz·er (ăt′ə-mī′zər) ►*n.* A device for producing a fine spray of a liquid.

atom smasher ►*n.* See **particle accelerator.**

a·ton·al (ā-tōn′əl) ►*adj. Mus.* Lacking a traditional key or tonality. —**a′to·nal′i·ty** (-tō-năl′ĭ-tē) *n.* —**a·ton′al·ly** *adv.*

a·tone (ə-tōn′) ►*v.* **a·toned, a·ton·ing** To make amends (for). [< ME *at one*, of one mind.]

a·tone·ment (ə-tōn′mənt) ►*n.* **1.** Reparation made for an injury or wrong. **2.** *Theol.* Reconciliation with God.

a·top (ə-tŏp′) ►*prep.* On top of. ►*adv.* To, on, or at the top.

–ator ►*suff.* One that acts in a specified manner: *radiator.* [Lat. *-ātor.*]

–atory ►*suff.* **1a.** Of or relating to: *reconciliatory.* **b.** Tending to: *derogatory.* **2.** One that is connected with: *observatory.* [< Lat. *-ātōrius.*]

ATP (ā′tē′pē′) ►*n.* A nucleotide that supplies energy to cells. [*a(denosine) t(ri)p(hosphate)* (blend of ADENINE and RIBOSE).]

a·tri·um (ā′trē-əm) ►*n., pl.* **a·tri·a** (ā′trē-ə) or **-ums 1a.** A usu. skylighted central area in a building, esp. a public building. **b.** An open central court in an ancient Roman house. **2.** A body cavity or chamber, esp. either of the upper chambers of the heart; auricle. [Lat. *ātrium.*]

a·tro·cious (ə-trō′shəs) ►*adj.* **1.** Extremely evil, savage, or cruel: *an atrocious crime.* **2.** Exceptionally bad; abominable: *atrocious decor.* [< Lat. *atrōx,* cruel.] —**a·tro′cious·ly** *adv.* —**a·tro′cious·ness** *n.*

a·troc·i·ty (ə-trŏs′ĭ-tē) ►*n., pl.* **-ties 1.** Something that is atrocious, esp. a cruel act inflicted by an armed force on civilians or prisoners. **2.** The state of being atrocious. **3.** Atrocious behavior.

at·ro·phy (ăt′rə-fē) ►*n., pl.* **-phies** A wasting or shrinking of a bodily organ, tissue, or part. ►*v.* **-phied, -phy·ing** To waste or cause to waste away. [< Gk. *atrophos,* without food.] —**a·troph′ic** (ā-trŏf′ĭk) *adj.*

at·ro·pine (ăt′rə-pēn′, -pĭn) also **at·ro·pin** (-pĭn) ►*n.* A poisonous, bitter, crystalline alkaloid, $C_{17}H_{23}NO_3$, obtained from belladonna and used to dilate the pupil of the eye. [< NLat. *Atropa,* belladonna.]

at sign ►*n.* The symbol (@) for the word *at,* used esp. in e-mail addresses to separate the username from the domain name.

at·tach (ə-tăch′) ►*v.* **1.** To fasten or become fastened; connect. **2.** To bind by ties of affection or loyalty. **3.** To affix or append: *attached conditions to the contract.* **4.** To seize by legal writ. [< OFr. *attachier.*] —**at·tach′a·ble** *adj.*

at·ta·ché (ăt′ə-shā′, ă-tă-) ►*n.* One who is assigned to a diplomatic mission to serve in a particular capacity: *a cultural attaché.* [Fr., one attached.]

attaché case ►*n.* A slim briefcase with flat sides.

at·tach·ment (ə-tăch′mənt) ►*n.* **1.** The act of attaching or the condition of being attached. **2.** Something, such as a tie or band, that attaches one thing to another. **3.** A bond of affection or loyalty. **4.** A supplementary part, as of an appliance; accessory. **5.** *Law* **a.** Legal seizure of property. **b.** The writ ordering this.

at·tack (ə-tăk′) ►*v.* **1.** To set upon with violent force. **2.** To criticize strongly. **3.** To start work on with vigor. **4.** To affect harmfully: *a disease that attacked the nervous system.* **5.** *Sports* To make an energetic offensive move. ►*n.* **1.** The act of attacking; assault. **2.** An expression of strong or hostile criticism. **3.** The onset of a disease, esp. a chronic disease. **4.** *Sports* An energetic offensive move. [< OFr. *attaquer.*] —**at·tack′er** *n.*

at·tain (ə-tān′) ►*v.* **1.** To accomplish; achieve. **2.** To arrive at. [< Lat. *attingere,* reach to, touch.] —**at·tain′a·bil′i·ty** *n.* —**at·tain′a·ble** *adj.* —**at·tain′ment** *n.*

at·tain·der (ə-tān′dər) ►*n.* Formerly, the loss of all civil rights by a person who was sentenced for a capital offense. [< OFr. *ataindre,* to convict.]

at·tar (ăt′ər) ►*n.* A fragrant oil obtained from flowers. [< Ar. *'aṭir,* aromatic.]

at·tempt (ə-tĕmpt′) ►*v.* To make an effort to do, perform, or achieve; try. ►*n.* **1.** An effort; try. **2.** An attack: *an attempt on one's life.* [< Lat. *attemptāre,* try to.] —**at·tempt′a·ble** *adj.*

at·tend (ə-tĕnd′) ►*v.* **1.** To be present (at). **2.** To accompany. **3.** To take care (of). See Synonyms at **tend**². **4.** To take charge of; manage. **5.** To pay attention (to); heed. [< Lat. *attendere,* stretch toward, heed.]

at·ten·dance (ə-tĕn′dəns) ►*n.* **1.** The act of attending. **2.** The number of persons present. **3.** The frequency with which a person is present.

at·ten·dant (ə-tĕn′dənt) ►*n.* **1.** One who attends or waits on another. **2.** One who is present. ►*adj.* Accompanying; consequent: *attendant conditions.*

at·ten·tion (ə-tĕn′shən) ►*n.* **1.** The act of dealing with someone or something: *a wound that needs attention.* **2. attentions** Acts indicating interest: *the attentions of an unwanted suitor.* **3.** An erect military posture assumed on command. —**at·ten′tive** *adj.* —**at·ten′tive·ly** *adv.* —**at·ten′tive·ness** *n.*

attention deficit disorder ►*n.* See **attention deficit hyperactivity disorder.**

attention deficit hyperactivity disorder ►*n.* A syndrome, usu. diagnosed in childhood, marked by persistent impulsiveness and inattention, with or without hyperactivity.

at·ten·u·ate (ə-tĕn′yo͞o-āt′) ►*v.* **-at·ed, -at·ing** **1.** To make or become thin or small. **2.** To weaken. **3.** To rarefy or dilute. [Lat. *attenuāre,* make thin.] —**at·ten′u·a′tion** *n.*

at·test (ə-tĕst′) ►*v.* **1.** To affirm to be correct, true, or genuine, esp. by affixing one's signature as witness. **2.** To supply evidence of: *actions that attested their bravery.* See Synonyms at **indicate**. **3.** To bear witness: *attested to their good faith.* [Lat. *attestārī,* be witness to.] —**at′tes·ta′tion** (ăt′ĕs-tā′shən) *n.* —**at·test′er, at·tes′tor** *n.*

at·tic (ăt′ĭk) ►*n.* A story or room directly below the roof of a building. [Ult. < ATTIC.]

Attic ►*adj.* Of ancient Attica or Athens. ►*n.* A dialect of ancient Greek.

At·ti·ca (ăt′ĭ-kə) An ancient region of E-central Greece around Athens.

At·ti·la (ăt′l-ə, ə-tĭl′ə) AD 406?–453. King of the Huns (433?–453).

at·tire (ə-tīr′) ►*v.* **-tired, -tir·ing** To dress or clothe. ►*n.* Clothing or array; apparel. [< OFr. *atirier,* arrange in ranks.]

at·ti·tude (ăt′ĭ-to͞od′, -tyo͞od′) ►*n.* **1.** A state of mind or a feeling; disposition: *an attitude of friendliness.* **2a.** A position of the body or manner of carrying oneself: *stood in a belligerent attitude.* See Synonyms at **posture**. **b.** A position in which a ballet dancer stands on one leg with the other raised and bent at the knee. **3a.** The orientation of an aircraft's axes esp. with respect to the horizon. **b.** The orientation of a spacecraft relative to its direction of motion. [< LLat. *aptitūdō,* fitness.] —**at′ti·tu′di·nal** *adj.*

at·tor·ney (ə-tûr′nē) ►*n., pl.* **-neys** A person appointed or empowered to represent another

in legal matters. [< OFr. *atorner,* assign to.] —**at·tor′ney·ship′** *n.*

attorney-at-law (ə-tûr′nē-ət-lô′) ►*n., pl.* **attorneys-at-law** An attorney.

attorney general ►*n., pl.* **attorneys general** or **attorney generals** The chief law officer and counsel of a state or nation's government.

at·tract (ə-trăkt′) ►*v.* **1.** To cause to draw near or adhere. **2.** To arouse the interest, admiration, or attention of. [< Lat. *attrahere, attract-,* draw toward.] —**at·tract′a·ble** *adj.* —**at·trac′tive** *adj.* —**at·trac′tive·ness** *n.*

at·trac·tant (ə-trăk′tənt) ►*n.* A substance, such as a pheromone, that attracts insects or other animals.

at·trac·tion (ə-trăk′shən) ►*n.* **1.** The act or power of attracting. **2.** Allure; charm. **3.** A feature or characteristic that attracts. **4.** A public spectacle or entertainment. **5.** *Phys.* A gravitational, magnetic, or electric force tending to draw two particles or bodies together.

at·trib·ute (ə-trĭb′yo͞ot) ►*v.* **-ut·ed, -ut·ing** To regard as arising from a particular cause, source, or agent; ascribe: *attributed the traffic to the concert at the stadium.* ►*n.* **at·tri·bute** (ăt′rə-byo͞ot′) **1.** A distinctive feature of or object associated with someone or something. **2.** *Gram.* An attributive. [Lat. *attribuere,* allot to.] —**at·trib′ut·a·ble** *adj.* —**at·trib′ut·er, at·trib′u·tor** *n.* —**at′tri·bu′tion** (ăt′rə-byo͞o′shən) *n.*

at·trib·u·tive (ə-trĭb′yə-tĭv) ►*n.* A word or word group, such as an adjective, that is adjacent to the noun it modifies without a linking verb; e.g., *pale* in *the pale moon.* ►*adj.* **1.** Of or being an attributive. **2.** Of or like an attribute. —**at·trib′u·tive·ly** *adv.*

at·trit (ə-trĭt′) ►*v.* **-trit·ted, -trit·ting** To weaken or destroy by attrition. [< ATTRITION.]

at·tri·tion (ə-trĭsh′ən) ►*n.* **1.** A rubbing away or wearing down by friction. **2.** A gradual diminution in number or strength because of stress or military action: *a war of attrition.* **3.** A gradual, natural reduction in membership or personnel, as through resignation or death. [< Lat. *atterere, attrit-,* rub against.]

At·tucks (ăt′əks), **Crispus** 1723?–70. Amer. patriot; killed in the Boston Massacre.

At·tu Island (ăt′o͞o′) An island of SW AK, the westernmost of the Aleutians.

at·tune (ə-to͞on′, -tyo͞on′) ►*v.* **-tuned, -tun·ing** **1.** To bring into harmony. **2.** To tune.

Atty. ►*abbr.* attorney

Atty. Gen. ►*abbr.* Attorney General

ATV ►*abbr.* all-terrain vehicle

at. wt. ►*abbr.* atomic weight

a·typ·i·cal (ā-tĭp′ĭ-kəl) ►*adj.* Not typical; unusual or irregular. —**a·typ′i·cal·ly** *adv.*

au·burn (ô′bərn) ►*n.* A reddish brown. [< Med. Lat. *alburnus,* whitish.] —**au′burn** *adj.*

Auck·land (ôk′lənd) A city of New Zealand, on NW North I.

au cou·rant (ō′ ko͞o-räN′) ►*adj.* **1.** Up-to-date. **2.** Knowledgeable. [Fr.]

auc·tion (ôk′shən) ►*n.* A public sale in which property or items are sold to the highest bidder. ►*v.* To sell at an auction. [< Lat. *augēre,* increase.] —**auc′tion·eer′** (-shə-nîr′) *n. & v.*

au·da·cious (ô-dā′shəs) ►*adj.* **1.** Fearlessly daring. See Synonyms at **adventurous**. **2.** Unrestrained by propriety; insolent. [< Lat. *audēre,* dare.] —**au·da′cious·ly** *adv.* —**au·da′cious·ness** *n.* —**au·dac′i·ty** (-dăs′ĭ-tē) *n.*

Au·den (ôd′n), **W(ystan) H(ugh)** 1907–73. British-born Amer. writer and critic.

au·di·al (ô′dē-əl) ►*adj.* Of or relating to the sense of hearing; aural. [AUDI(O)– + –AL[1].] —**au′di·al·ly** *adv.*

au·di·ble (ô′də-bəl) ►*adj.* That is or can be heard. [< Lat. *audīre*, hear.] —**au′di·bil′i·ty** *n.* —**au′di·bly** *adv.*

au·di·ence (ô′dē-əns) ►*n.* **1.** A gathering of spectators or listeners. **2.** All those reached by printed matter or a radio or television broadcast. **3.** A formal hearing or conference: *a papal audience.* [< Lat. *audīre*, hear.]

au·di·o (ô′dē-ō′) ►*adj.* Of or relating to sound, esp. recorded, transmitted, or reproduced sound. ►*n., pl.* -**di·os** Recorded or reproduced sound. [< AUDIO–.]

audio– ►*pref.* **1.** Hearing: *audiology.* **2.** Sound: *audiophile.* [< Lat. *audīre*, hear.]

au·di·o·book (ô′dē-ō-bŏok′) ►*n.* An audio recording consisting of a book or other material read aloud.

au·di·o·cas·sette (ô′dē-ō-kə-sĕt′) ►*n.* A cassette containing audiotape.

audio frequency ►*n.* A range of frequencies, usu. from 15 hertz to 20,000 hertz, characteristic of signals audible to the normal human ear.

au·di·ol·o·gy (ô′dē-ŏl′ə-jē) ►*n.* The study of hearing, esp. hearing defects and their treatment. —**au′di·o·log′i·cal** (-ə-lŏj′ĭ-kəl) *adj.* —**au′di·ol′o·gist** *n.*

au·di·o·phile (ô′dē-ə-fīl′) ►*n.* One who has an ardent interest in high-fidelity sound reproduction.

au·di·o·tape (ô′dē-ō-tāp′) ►*n.* A magnetic tape used to record sound for later playback. ►*v.* -**taped, -tap·ing** To record (sound) on magnetic tape.

au·di·o·vis·u·al (ô′dē-ō-vĭzh′ōō-əl) ►*adj.* Conveying information using both audio and visual media. ►*n.* Audio-visual materials, esp. ones used in presentations or demonstrations.

au·dit (ô′dĭt) ►*n.* A formal examination or verification of financial accounts. ►*v.* **1.** To formally examine or verify the financial accounts of: *audit a tax return.* **2.** To attend (a college course) without receiving academic credit. [< Lat. *audīre, audīt-,* hear.]

au·di·tion (ô-dĭsh′ən) ►*n.* A hearing, esp. a trial performance of an actor, dancer, or musician, to obtain a particular role or position. ►*v.* **1.** To take part in an audition. **2.** To evaluate (a performer) in an audition. [< Lat. *audīre, audīt-,* hear.]

au·di·tor (ô′dĭ-tər) ►*n.* **1.** One who audits accounts. **2.** One who audits a college course. **3.** One who hears; listener.

au·di·to·ri·um (ô′dĭ-tôr′ē-əm) ►*n.* **1.** A large room to accommodate an audience. **2.** A building for public gatherings or entertainments.

au·di·to·ry (ô′dĭ-tôr′ē) ►*adj.* Relating to the sense, the organs, or the experience of hearing.

Au·du·bon (ô′də-bŏn′, -bən), **John James** 1785–1851. Haitian-born Amer. ornithologist and artist.

auf Wie·der·seh·en (ouf vē′dər-zā′ən) ►*interj.* Farewell. [Ger.]

au·ger (ô′gər) ►*n.* A tool for boring holes in wood, ice, or the earth. [< OE *nafogār.*]

aught[1] also **ought** (ôt) ►*pron.* Anything whatever. [< OE *āuht.*]

aught[2] also **ought** (ôt) ►*n.* The digit zero. [< *a naught.*]

aug·ment (ôg-mĕnt′) ►*v.* To make or become greater in size, extent, or quantity; increase. [< Lat. *augēre,* to increase.] —**aug′men·ta′tion** *n.*

au gra·tin (ō grät′n, grăt′n) ►*adj.* Baked with a topping of bread crumbs and grated cheese. [Fr.]

Augs·burg (ôgz′bûrg′, ouks′bŏork′) A city of S Germany WNW of Munich.

au·gur (ô′gər) ►*n.* A seer; soothsayer. ►*v.* **1.** To predict, esp. from signs or omens. See Synonyms at **foretell. 2.** To serve as a sign or omen (of). [< Lat.]

au·gu·ry (ô′gyə-rē) ►*n., pl.* -**ries 1.** The art or practice of auguring. **2.** An omen.

au·gust (ô-gŭst′) ►*adj.* Inspiring awe, reverence, or admiration; majestic. [Lat. *augustus.*] —**au·gust′ly** *adv.* —**au·gust′ness** *n.*

August ►*n.* The 8th month of the Gregorian calendar. See table at **calendar.** [After AUGUSTUS.]

Au·gus·ta (ô-gŭs′tə, ə-) The capital of ME, in the SW part NNE of Portland.

Au·gus·tine (ô′gə-stēn′, ô-gŭs′tĭn), Saint. AD 354–430. Early Christian church father and philosopher.

Au·gus·tus (ô-gŭs′təs) also **Oc·ta·vi·an** (ŏk-tā′vē-ən) 63 BC–AD 14. 1st emperor of Rome (27 BC–AD 14); defeated Mark Antony and Cleopatra in 31 BC.

au jus (ō zhōōs′, zhü′) ►*adj.* Served with the natural juices or gravy. [Fr.]

auk (ôk) ►*n.* A diving seabird of northern regions, having a chunky body, short wings, and webbed feet. [< ON *ālka.*]

auld lang syne (ôld′ lăng zīn′, sīn′) ►*n.* The good old days long past. [Sc., old long since.]

Aung San Suu Kyi (ông′ sän′ sōo′ chē′) b. 1945. Burmese political leader.

Aung San Suu Kyi
photographed in 2007

aunt (ănt, änt) ►*n.* **1.** The sister of one's father or mother. **2.** The wife of a sibling of one's mother or father. [< Lat. *amita,* paternal aunt.]

au pair (ō pâr′) ►*n.* A young foreigner who works for a family for room and board and in order to learn the language. [Fr.]

au·ra (ôr′ə) ►*n., pl.* -**ras** or -**rae** (ôr′ē) **1.** An invisible emanation said to issue from a person or object. **2.** A distinctive quality that seems to surround a person or thing; atmosphere. [< Gk., breath.]

au·ral¹ (ôr′əl) ►*adj.* Of or perceived by the ear. [< Lat. *auris*, ear.] —**au′ral·ly** *adv.*

au·ral² (ôr′əl) ►*adj.* Of or relating to an aura.

Au·re·lian (ô-rēl′yən, ô-rē′lē-ən) AD 215?–275. Roman emperor (AD 270–275).

au·re·ole (ôr′ē-ōl′) also **au·re·o·la** (ô-rē′ə-lə) ►*n.* **1.** A halo. **2.** See **corona** (sense 1). [< Lat. *aureolus*, golden.]

au re·voir (ō′ rə-vwär′) ►*interj.* Farewell. [Fr.]

au·ri·cle (ôr′ĭ-kəl) ►*n.* **1.** *Anat.* **a.** The outer projecting portion of the ear. **b.** See **atrium** (sense 2). **2.** *Biol.* An earlobe-shaped part or appendage. [< Lat. *auricula*, dim. of *auris*, ear.] —**au′ri·cled** (-kəld) *adj.*

au·ric·u·lar (ô-rĭk′yə-lər) ►*adj.* **1.** Aural. **2.** Received by or spoken into the ear. **3.** Shaped like an ear or earlobe. **4.** Of or relating to an auricle of the heart.

au·ro·ra (ə-rôr′ə) ►*n.* **1.** Streamers or bands of light that sometimes appear in the night skies of northern or southern regions of the earth, likely caused by charged particles entering the earth's magnetic field. **2.** The dawn. [< Lat. *aurōra*, dawn.] —**au·ro′ral** *adj.*

Aurora¹ ►*n. Rom. Myth.* The goddess of the dawn.

aurora aus·tra·lis (ô-strā′lĭs) ►*n.* An aurora occurring in southern regions of the earth. [NLat., southern dawn.]

aurora bo·re·al·is (bôr′ē-ăl′ĭs) ►*n.* An aurora occurring in northern regions of the earth. [NLat., northern dawn.]

aus·cul·ta·tion (ô′skəl-tā′shən) ►*n.* Diagnostic monitoring of the sounds made by internal bodily organs. [< Lat. *auscultāre*, listen to.]

aus·pice (ô′spĭs) ►*n., pl.* **aus·pic·es** (ô′spĭ-sĭz, -sēz′) **1.** also **auspices** Protection or support; patronage. **2.** A sign, portent, or omen. [Lat. *auspicium* < *auspex*, bird augur.]

aus·pi·cious (ô-spĭsh′əs) ►*adj.* Showing signs of a favorable outcome. —**aus·pi′cious·ly** *adv.*

Aus·ten (ô′stən), **Jane** 1775–1817. British writer.

aus·tere (ô-stîr′) ►*adj.* **-ter·er, -ter·est 1.** Severe or stern; somber: *an austere Puritan minister.* **2.** Strict or severe in discipline; ascetic: *a nomad's austere life.* **3.** Without adornment; bare: *austere living quarters.* [< Gk. *austēros*, harsh.] —**aus·tere′ly** *adv.* —**aus·ter′i·ty** (-stĕr′ĭ-tē) *n.*

Aus·tin (ô′stən, ŏs′tən) The capital of TX, in the S-central part.

Austin, Stephen Fuller 1793–1836. Amer. colonizer and political leader in TX.

aus·tral (ô′strəl) ►*adj.* Southern. [< Lat. *auster*, south.]

Aus·tral·a·sia (ô′strə-lā′zhə) **1.** The islands of the S Pacific, including Australia, New Zealand, and New Guinea. **2.** Oceania. —**Aus′tral·a′sian** *adj. & n.*

Aus·tra·lia (ô-strāl′yə) **1.** The world's smallest continent, SE of Asia between the Pacific and Indian Oceans. **2.** A commonwealth comprising the continent of Australia, the island state of Tasmania, and several external territories and dependencies. Cap. Canberra.

Aus·tra·lian (ô-strāl′yən) ►*adj.* Of or relating to Australia. ►*n.* **1.** A native or inhabitant of Aus-

tralia. **2a.** A member of an aboriginal people of Australia. **b.** Any of the aboriginal languages of Australia.

Australian Alps A chain of mountain ranges of SE Australia.

Aus·tra·loid (ô′strə-loid′) ►*adj. Anthro.* Of or being a human racial classification traditionally distinguished by dark skin and dark curly hair and including peoples indigenous to Australia and parts of SE Asia. Not in scientific use. See Usage Note at **Negroid.** —**Aus′tra·loid′** *n.*

Aus·tri·a (ô′strē-ə) A landlocked country of central Europe W of Slovakia and Hungary. Cap. Vienna. —**Aus′tri·an** *adj. & n.*

Aus·tri·a-Hun·ga·ry (ô′strē-ə-hŭng′gə-rē) A former dual monarchy (1867–1918) of central Europe. —**Aus′tro-Hun·gar′i·an** *adj. & n.*

Aus·tro-A·si·at·ic (ô′strō-ā′zhē-ăt′ĭk, -shē-, -zē-) ►*n.* A family of languages of SE Asia once dominant in NE India and Indochina. —**Aus′-tro-A′si·at′ic** *adj.*

Aus·tro·ne·sia (ô′strō-nē′zhə) The islands of the Pacific, including Indonesia, Melanesia, Micronesia, and Polynesia.

Aus·tro·ne·sian (ô′strō-nē′zhən, -shən) ►*adj.* Of or relating to Austronesia or its peoples, languages, or cultures. ►*n.* A family of languages that includes the Indonesian, Malay, Melanesian, Micronesian, and Polynesian subfamilies.

aut- ►*pref.* Var. of **auto-.**

au·tar·chy (ô′tär′kē) ►*n., pl.* **-chies** Autocracy. [< Gk. *autarkhos*, self-governing.] —**au′tarch** *n.* —**au·tar′chic** *adj.*

au·then·tic (ô thĕn′tĭk) ►*adj.* **1.** Worthy of trust, reliance, or belief. **2.** Being so in fact; not fraudulent or counterfeit: *an authentic medieval sword.* [< Gk. *authentēs*, author.] —**au·then′ti·cal·ly** *adv.* —**au′then·tic′i·ty** (-tĭs′ĭ-tē) *n.*
    Syns: *bona fide, genuine, real, true* **Ant:** *counterfeit* *adj.*

au·then·ti·cate (ô-thĕn′tĭ-kāt′) ►*v.* **-cat·ed, -cat·ing** To prove or establish as being genuine. —**au·then′ti·ca′tion** *n.*

au·thor (ô′thər) ►*n.* **1a.** The writer of a literary work. **b.** A person who writes as a profession. **2.** A person who creates something. [< Lat. *auctor* < *augēre*, create.] —**au′thor** *v.* —**au·thor′i·al** (ô-thôr′ē-əl, -thôr′-) *adj.* —**au′thor·ship′** *n.*

au·thor·i·tar·i·an (ə-thôr′ĭ-târ′ē-ən, -thôr′-, ô-) ►*adj.* Marked by or favoring absolute obedience to authority. See Synonyms at **dictatorial.** —**au·thor′i·tar′i·an** *n.* —**au·thor′i·tar′i·an·ism** *n.*

au·thor·i·ta·tive (ə-thôr′ĭ-tā′tĭv, -thôr′-, ô-) ►*adj.* **1.** Having or arising from proper authority; official. **2.** Having or showing expert knowledge. —**au·thor′i·ta′tive·ly** *adv.* —**au·thor′i·ta′tive·ness** *n.*

au·thor·i·ty (ə-thôr′ĭ-tē, -thôr′-, ô-) ►*n., pl.* **-ties 1a.** The right and power to enforce laws, exact obedience, command, determine, or judge. **b.** One that is invested with this right and power, esp. a government or government official. **2.** Authorization. **3.** One that is an accepted source of expert information. **4.** Firm self-assurance; confidence.

au·thor·i·za·tion (ô′thər-ĭ-zā′shən) ►*n.* **1.** The act of authorizing. **2.** Something that authorizes. See Synonyms at **permission.**

au·thor·ize (ô′thə-rīz′) ►*v.* **-ized, -iz·ing 1.** To

grant authority or power to. **2.** To give permission for; sanction. **3.** To justify.

Syns: *accredit, commission, empower, license v.*

au·tism (ô′tĭz′əm) ►*n.* A developmental disorder marked by severe deficits in social interaction, a limited range of activities and interests, and often the presence of repetitive behaviors. —**au·tis′tic** (-tĭs′tĭk) *adj. & n.*

au·to (ô′tō) ►*n., pl.* -**tos** An automobile.

auto– or **aut–** ►*pref.* **1.** Self; same: *autobiography.* **2.** Automatic: *autopilot.* [< Gk. *autos,* self.]

au·to·bahn (ô′tə-bän′, ou′tō-) ►*n.* An expressway in Germany. [Ger. : *Auto,* automobile + MHGer. *ban,* road.]

au·to·bi·og·ra·phy (ô′tō-bī-ŏg′rə-fē) ►*n., pl.* -**phies** The biography of a person written by that person. —**au′to·bi·og′ra·pher** *n.* —**au′to·bi′o·graph′ic** (-bī′ə-grăf′ĭk), **au′to·bi′o·graph′i·cal** *adj.*

au·toch·tho·nous (ô-tŏk′thə-nəs) ►*adj.* Originating where found; indigenous; native. [< Gk. *autokhthōn* : AUTO– + *khthōn,* earth.]

au·toc·ra·cy (ô-tŏk′rə-sē) ►*n., pl.* -**cies** Government by a single person having unlimited power. —**au′to·crat′** *n.* —**au′to·crat′ic, au′to·crat′i·cal** *adj.*

au·to·di·dact (ô′tō-dī′dăkt′) ►*n.* A self-taught person. [< Gk. *autodidaktos,* self-taught.] —**au′to·di·dac′tic** *adj.*

au·to·graph (ô′tə-grăf′) ►*n.* **1.** A person's own signature. **2.** A manuscript in the author's handwriting. ►*v.* To write one's signature on.

au·to·im·mune (ô′tō-ĭ-myoōn′) ►*adj.* Of or relating to an immune response by the body against one of its own cells or tissues. —**au′to·im·mu′ni·ty** *n.*

au·to·mate (ô′tə-māt′) ►*v.* -**mat·ed, -mat·ing** **1.** To convert to automatic operation. **2.** To operate by automation.

au·to·mat·ed teller machine (ô′tə-mā′tĭd) ►*n.* See **ATM.**

au·to·mat·ic (ô′tə-măt′ĭk) ►*adj.* **1.** Acting or operating with little or no external influence or control. **2.** Involuntary; reflex. **3.** Responding or behaving in a mechanical way. **4.** Capable of firing continuously until ammunition is exhausted. ►*n.* A machine or device, esp. a firearm or an automobile transmission, that is automatic. [< Gk. *automatikos* : AUTO– + *-matos,* willing.] —**au′to·mat′i·cal·ly** *adv.*

automatic pilot ►*n.* A navigational mechanism, as on an aircraft, that automatically maintains a preset course; autopilot.

automatic teller machine ►*n.* See **ATM.**

au·to·ma·tion (ô′tə-mā′shən) ►*n.* The automatic operation or control of equipment, a process, or a system.

au·tom·a·tism (ô-tŏm′ə-tĭz′əm) ►*n.* The state, quality, or action of being automatic.

au·tom·a·tize (ô-tŏm′ə-tīz′) ►*v.* -**tized, -tiz·ing** To make automatic. —**au·tom′a·ti·za′tion** *n.*

au·tom·a·ton (ô-tŏm′ə-tən, -tŏn′) ►*n., pl.* -**tons** or -**ta** (-tə) **1.** An automatic machine or mechanism, esp. a robot. **2.** One that behaves or responds in an automatic or mechanical way. [< Gk. *automatos,* AUTOMATIC.]

au·to·mo·bile (ô′tə-mō-bēl′, -mō′bēl′) ►*n.* A land vehicle, esp. a four-wheeled passenger car powered by an internal-combustion engine.

au·to·mo·tive (ô′tə-mō′tĭv) ►*adj.* **1.** Moving by

itself; self-propelled. **2.** Of or relating to self-propelled vehicles, esp. automobiles.

au·to·nom·ic nervous system (ô′tə-nŏm′ĭk) ►*n.* The part of the vertebrate nervous system that regulates involuntary action, as of the intestines, heart, and glands.

au·ton·o·mous (ô-tŏn′ə-məs) ►*adj.* **1.** Not controlled by others; independent. **2.** Self-governing, esp. with regard to internal affairs. [< Gk. *autonomos,* self-ruling.] —**au·ton′o·my** *n.*

au·to·pi·lot (ô′tō-pī′lət) ►*n.* Automatic pilot.

au·top·sy (ô′tŏp′sē, ô′təp-) ►*n., pl.* -**sies** Examination of a dead body to find the cause of death; postmortem. [Gk. *autopsia,* seeing for oneself.] —**au′top′sist** *n.*

au·to·some (ô′tə-sōm′) ►*n.* A chromosome that is not a sex chromosome.

au·to·sug·ges·tion (ô′tō-səg-jĕs′chən) ►*n. Psychol.* The process by which a person induces self-acceptance of an opinion, belief, or plan of action.

au·to·troph (ô′tə-trŏf′, -trōf′) ►*n.* An organism capable of synthesizing its own food from inorganic substances. [AUTO– + Gk. *trophē,* food.] —**au′to·troph′ic** *adj.*

au·tumn (ô′təm) ►*n.* **1.** The season between summer and winter; fall. **2.** A period of maturity verging on decline. [< Lat. *autumnus.*] —**au·tum′nal** (-tŭm′nəl) *adj.*

Au·vergne (ō-vûrn′, -věrn′) A historical region and former province of central France.

aux. ►*abbr.* **1.** auxiliary **2.** auxiliary verb

aux·il·ia·ry (ôg-zĭl′yə-rē, -zĭl′ə-rē) ►*adj.* **1.** Giving assistance or support; helping. **2.** Subsidiary; supplementary. **3.** Held in or used as a reserve. ►*n., pl.* -**ries 1.** One that acts in a supporting capacity. **2.** An auxiliary verb. [< Lat. *auxilium,* help.]

auxiliary verb ►*n.* A verb, such as *have, can,* or *will,* that comes first in a verb phrase and helps form the mood, voice, aspect, and tense of the main verb.

aux·in (ôk′sĭn) ►*n.* Any of several plant growth hormones. [< Gk. *auxein,* grow.]

Av (äv, ôv) ►*n.* The 5th month of the Jewish calendar. See table at **calendar.** [Heb. *ăb.*]

AV ►*abbr.* **1.** or **A/V** ad valorem **2.** or **A/V** audiovisual **3.** Authorized Version

av. ►*abbr.* **1.** average **2.** avoirdupois

a·vail (ə-vāl′) ►*v.* To be of use or advantage (to); help. ►*n.* Use, benefit, or advantage: *labored to no avail.* [< Lat. *valēre,* be strong, be worth.]

a·vail·a·ble (ə-vā′lə-bəl) ►*adj.* **1.** At hand; accessible. **2.** Capable of being used or gotten; obtainable. —**a·vail′a·bil′i·ty** *n.*

av·a·lanche (ăv′ə-lănch′) ►*n.* **1.** A slide of a large mass, esp. of snow, down a mountainside. **2.** A massive amount: *an avalanche of mail.* [Fr.]

a·vant-garde (ä′vänt-gärd′, ăv′änt-) ►*n.* A group that creates or promotes innovative ideas or techniques in a given field, esp. in the arts. [Fr., vanguard.] —**a′vant-garde′** *adj.*

av·a·rice (ăv′ə-rĭs) ►*n.* Extreme desire for wealth; greed. [< Lat. *avārus,* greedy.] —**av′a·ri′cious** (-ə-rĭsh′əs) *adj.*

a·vast (ə-văst′) ►*interj. Naut.* Used as a command to stop or desist. [< MDu. *hou vast,* hold fast.]

av·a·tar (ăv′ə-tär′) ►*n.* **1.** *Hinduism* One that is regarded as an incarnation, esp. of Vishnu.

2. An embodiment or exemplar; archetype. **3.** An image representing a user on an electronic network. [Skt. *avatāraḥ*.]

avatar
Vishnu as Matsya *(top)* and as Varaha *(bottom)*

a·vaunt (ə-vônt′, ə-vänt′) ►*adv.* Hence; away. [< Lat. *ab ante*, forward.]

avdp. ►*abbr.* avoirdupois

Ave. ►*abbr.* avenue

a·venge (ə-vĕnj′) ►*v.* **a·venged, a·veng·ing 1.** To take revenge for: *avenge a murder.* **2.** To take vengeance on behalf of: *avenged his father.* [< Lat. *vindicāre*, to claim.] —**a·veng′er** *n.*

av·e·nue (ăv′ə-nōō′, -nyōō′) ►*n.* **1.** A wide street or thoroughfare. **2.** A means of access or approach: *new avenues of trade.* [< Lat. *advenīre*, come to; see ADVENT.]

a·ver (ə-vûr′) ►*v.* **a·verred, a·ver·ring** To assert positively; declare. [< VLat. **adverāre*, state as true.] —**a·ver′ment** *n.*

av·er·age (ăv′ər-ĭj, ăv′rĭj) ►*n.* **1a.** A number that typifies a set of numbers of which it is a function. **b.** See **arithmetic mean. 2.** A relative level, proportion, or degree that indicates position or achievement. ►*adj.* **1.** Of or constituting a mathematical average. **2.** Intermediate between extremes, as on a scale. **3.** Usual; ordinary: *a poll of average people.* ►*v.* **-aged, -ag·ing 1.** To calculate the average of. **2.** To do or have an average of: *averaged ten pages an hour.* [< ME *averay*, charge above the cost of freight, ult. < Ar. *'awārīya*, damaged goods.]

A·ver·ro·ës or **A·ver·rho·ës** (ə-vĕr′ō-ēz′, ăv′ə-rō′ēz) also **Ibn Rushd** (ĭb′ən rŏŏsht′) 1126–98. Spanish-Arab philosopher.

a·verse (ə-vûrs′) ►*adj.* Strongly disinclined; reluctant. [< Lat. *āvertere*, *āvers-*, turn away.] —**a·verse′ly** *adv.*

a·ver·sion (ə-vûr′zhən, -shən) ►*n.* **1.** A fixed, intense dislike; repugnance. **2.** The cause or object of such a feeling.

a·vert (ə-vûrt′) ►*v.* **1.** To turn away: *averted one's eyes.* **2.** To ward off; prevent. [< Lat.

āvertere.] —**a·vert′i·ble, a·vert′a·ble** *adj.*

A·ves·ta (ə-vĕs′tə) ►*n.* The sacred writings of the Zoroastrian religion.

avg. ►*abbr.* average

a·vi·an (ā′vē-ən) ►*adj.* Of or characteristic of birds. [< Lat. *avis*, bird.]

a·vi·ar·y (ā′vē-ĕr′ē) ►*n., pl.* **-ies** A large enclosure for holding birds, as in a zoo. [< Lat. *avis*, bird.]

a·vi·a·tion (ā′vē-ā′shən, ăv′ē-) ►*n.* **1.** The operation of aircraft. **2.** The design, development, and production of aircraft. [< Lat. *avis*, bird.]

a·vi·a·tor (ā′vē-ā′tər, ăv′ē-) ►*n.* One who operates an aircraft; pilot.

a·vi·a·trix (ā′vē-ā′trĭks, ăv′ē-) ►*n.* A woman who operates an aircraft.

Av·i·cen·na (ăv′ĭ-sĕn′ə) also **Ibn Si·na** (ĭb′ən sē′nə) 980–1037. Persian physician.

av·id (ăv′ĭd) ►*adj.* **1.** Passionate; enthusiastic: *an avid sports fan.* **2.** Having an ardent desire or craving; eager: *avid for adventure.* [Lat. *avidus.*] —**a·vid′i·ty** (ə-vĭd′ĭ-tē) —**av′id·ly** *adv.*

a·vi·on·ics (ā′vē-ŏn′ĭks, ăv′ē-) ►*n. (takes sing. v.)* The science and technology of electronics as applied to aeronautics and astronautics. —**a′vi·on′ic** *adj.*

av·o·ca·do (ăv′ə-kä′dō, ä′və-) ►*n., pl.* **-dos 1.** A tropical American tree having pear-shaped fruit with leathery skin and yellowish-green flesh. **2.** The edible fruit of this tree. [< Nahuatl *ahuacatl.*]

av·o·ca·tion (ăv′ō-kā′shən) ►*n.* An activity taken up in addition to one's regular work, usu. for enjoyment; hobby. [< Lat. *āvocāre*, call away.] —**av′o·ca′tion·al** *adj.*

av·o·cet (ăv′ə-sĕt′) ►*n.* A long-legged shorebird with a long slender beak. [< Ital. *avocetta.*]

A·vo·ga·dro's number (ä′vō-gä′drōz) ►*n.* The number of items in a mole, approx. 6.0221 × 10^{23}. [After Amedeo *Avogadro* (1776–1856).]

a·void (ə-void′) ►*v.* **1.** To stay clear of; evade; shun: *avoid the pothole.* **2.** To keep from happening; prevent: *avoided disaster.* **3.** To refrain from: *avoiding red meat.* [< AN *avoider*, empty out.] —**a·void′a·ble** *adj.* —**a·void′a·bly** *adv.* —**a·void′ance** *n.* —**a·void′er** *n.*

av·oir·du·pois weight (ăv′ər-də-poiz′) ►*n.* A system of weights and measures based on one pound containing 16 ounces or 7,000 grains and equal to 453.59 grams. [< OFr. *aver de peis*, goods of weight.]

a·vouch (ə-vouch′) ►*v.* **1.** To affirm. **2.** To vouch for. [< Lat. *advocāre*, summon.]

a·vow (ə-vou′) ►*v.* **1.** To acknowledge openly; confess: *avow guilt.* **2.** To assert: *avowed the words to be true.* [< Lat. *advocāre*, summon.] —**a·vow′al** *n.* —**a·vowed′** *adj.* —**a·vow′ed·ly** (-ĭd-lē) *adv.*

a·vun·cu·lar (ə-vŭng′kyə-lər) ►*adj.* Of or like an uncle. [< Lat. *avunculus*, maternal uncle.]

a·wait (ə-wāt′) ►*v.* **1.** To wait (for). **2.** To be in store (for): *Success awaits him. A busy day awaits.* [< ONFr. *awaitier.*]

a·wake (ə-wāk′) ►*v.* **a·woke** (ə-wōk′), **a·waked** or **a·wok·en** (ə-wō′kən), **a·wak·ing 1.** To rouse or become roused from sleep. **2.** To stir up (e.g., desire). **3.** To become aware: *awoke to reality.* ►*adj.* **1.** Not asleep. **2.** Fully alert. [< OE *āwacan.*]

a·wak·en (ə-wā′kən) ►*v.* To awake. [< OE *āwæcnian.*] —**a·wak′en·ing** *adj. & n.*

a·ward (ə-wôrd′) ►*v.* **1.** To grant as merited or due: *awarded prizes to the winners.* **2.** To grant an amount or other benefit legally due: *awarded damages to the plaintiff.* ►*n.* **1.** Something awarded; prize. **2.** An amount or other benefit granted. [< AN *awarder,* decide (a legal case).]

a·ware (ə-wâr′) ►*adj.* **1.** Having knowledge of a particular fact. **2.** Attentive and mindful. [< OE *gewær.*] —**a·ware′ness** *n.*

a·wash (ə-wŏsh′, -wôsh′) ►*adj. & adv.* **1.** Level with or washed by waves. **2.** Flooded. **3.** Afloat.

a·way (ə-wā′) ►*adv.* **1.** From a particular thing or place: *ran away from the lion.* **2.** At or to a distance in space or time: *away off on the horizon.* **3.** In or to a different place or direction: *glanced away.* **4.** Out of existence: *music fading away.* **5.** From one's presence or possession: *gave the tickets away.* **6.** Continuously; steadily: *worked away.* **7.** At will; freely: *Fire away!* ►*adj.* **1.** Absent: *The neighbors are away.* **2.** Distant, as in space or time: *miles away.* **3.** Played on an opponent's home grounds: *an away game.* [< OE *aweg.*]

awe (ô) ►*n.* An emotion of reverent wonder, often tinged with fear. ►*v.* **awed, aw·ing** To inspire or fill with awe. [< ON *agi.*]

a·weigh (ə-wā′) ►*adj.* Hanging clear of the bottom. Used of an anchor.

awe·some (ô′səm) ►*adj.* **1.** Inspiring awe. **2.** *Slang* Superb. —**awe′some·ly** *adv.*

awe·struck (ô′strŭk′) ►*adj.* Full of awe.

aw·ful (ô′fəl) ►*adj.* **1.** Very bad or unpleasant; terrible. **2.** Commanding, inspiring, or filled with awe. **3.** Formidable: *an awful burden.* —**aw′ful·ly** *adv.* —**aw′ful·ness** *n.*

a·while (ə-wīl′, ə-hwīl′) ►*adv.* For a short time.

awk·ward (ôk′wərd) ►*adj.* **1.** Lacking grace or dexterity; clumsy or ungainly. **2.** Hard to handle or manage; unwieldy: *an awkward bundle.* **3.** Uncomfortable; inconvenient: *an awkward pose; an awkward time.* **4.** Causing embarrassment: *an awkward remark.* [ME *awkeward,* in the wrong direction.] —**awk′ward·ly** *adv.* —**awk′ward·ness** *n.*

awl (ôl) ►*n.* A pointed tool for making holes, as in wood or leather. [< OE *æl.*]

awn (ôn) ►*n.* A slender bristle on the spikelets of many grasses. [< ON *ögn* and OE *agen,* ear of grain.] —**awned** *adj.*

awn·ing (ô′nĭng) ►*n.* A rooflike structure, as over a window or storefront, used to provide shade or shelter. [?]

a·woke (ə-wōk′) ►*v.* P.t. of **awake.**

a·wok·en (ə-wō′kən) ►*v.* P.part. of **awake.**

AWOL (ā′wôl′) ►*adj. & adv.* Absent without leave. ►*n.* One who is absent without leave, esp. from military service.

a·wry (ə-rī′) ►*adv.* **1.** Wrong; amiss: *Our plans went awry.* **2.** Askew. —**a·wry′** *adj.*

ax also **axe** (ăks) ►*n., pl.* **ax·es** (ăk′sĭz) **1.** A chopping tool with a bladed head mounted on a handle. **2.** *Informal* A sudden termination, as of employment. ►*v.* **axed, ax·ing 1.** To use an ax on in order to chop or fell. **2.** To remove ruthlessly or suddenly. —*idiom:* **ax to grind** A selfish or subjective aim: *claimed disinterest but had an ax to grind.* [< OE *æx.*]

ax·i·al (ăk′sē-əl) ►*adj.* **1.** Of, relating to, or forming an axis. **2.** Located on, around, or along an axis. —**ax′i·al·ly** *adv.*

ax·il·la (ăk-sĭl′ə) ►*n., pl.* **-il·lae** (-sĭl′ē) **1.** The armpit. **2.** An analogous structure, as under a bird's wing. [Lat.]

ax·i·om (ăk′sē-əm) ►*n.* **1.** A self-evident or universally recognized truth; maxim. **2.** A principle that is accepted as true without proof; postulate. [< Gk. *axiōma* < *axios,* worthy.] —**ax′i·o·mat′ic** *adj.*

ax·is (ăk′sĭs) ►*n., pl.* **ax·es** (ăk′sēz′) **1.** A straight line about which an object rotates or can be conceived to rotate. **2.** *Math.* **a.** A line, ray, or line segment with respect to which a figure or object is symmetric. **b.** A reference line from which distances or angles are measured in a coordinate system. **3.** A center line to which parts of a structure or body may be referred. **4.** *Bot.* The main stem or central part about which plant parts, as branches, are arranged. **5.** An alliance of powers, such as nations, to promote mutual interests. [< Lat.]

ax·le (ăk′səl) ►*n.* A supporting shaft on which a wheel or a set of wheels revolves. [< ON *öxull.*]

ax·le·tree (ăk′səl-trē′) ►*n.* A crossbar, as on a cart, with terminal spindles on which the wheels revolve.

ax·on (ăk′sŏn′) ►*n.* The usu. long extension of a nerve cell that conducts impulses away from the cell body. [Gk. *axōn,* axis.]

a·ya (ä′yä′) ►*n., pl.* **a·yat** (ä-yät′) A verse of the Koran. [Ar. *āya,* sign, aya.]

a·ya·tol·lah (ī′ə-tō′lə) ►*n. Islam* A Shiite scholar regarded as having religious and administrative authority. [< Ar. *āyatu llāh,* sign of god.]

aye¹ also **ay** (ī) ►*n.* An affirmative vote or voter. ►*adv.* Yes. [Perh. < AYE² + YEA.]

aye² also **ay** (ā) ►*adv. Archaic* Always; ever: *for aye.* [< ON *ei.*]

Ay·ma·ra (ī′mä-rä′, ī′mə-) ►*n., pl.* **-ra** or **-ras 1.** A member of a South American Indian people inhabiting parts of highland Bolivia and Peru. **2.** Their language. —**Ay′ma·ran′** *adj.*

AZ ►*abbr.* Arizona

a·zal·ea (ə-zāl′yə) ►*n.* Any of a genus of shrubs cultivated for their showy, variously colored flowers. [< Gk. *azaleos,* dry.]

A·zer·bai·jan (ăz′ər-bī-jän′, ä′zər-) A country of Transcaucasia N of Iran, formerly a kingdom that extended into NW Iran. Cap. Baku. —**A′zer·bai·ja′ni** *adj. & n.*

az·i·muth (ăz′ə-məth) ►*n.* The horizontal angular distance measured clockwise from a reference direction, usu. due north, to another point such as the point on the horizon appearing to lie directly below a celestial body. [< Ar. *as-sumūt,* pl. of *as-samt,* the way, bearing.]

A·zores (ā′zôrz, ə-zôrz′) A group of Portuguese volcanic islands in the N Atlantic about 1,450 km (900 mi) W of mainland Portugal. —**A·zor′e·an, A·zor′i·an** *adj. & n.*

A·zov (ăz′ôf, ä′zôf, ə-zôf′), **Sea of** The N arm of the Black Sea between Russia and Ukraine.

Az·tec (ăz′tĕk′) ►*n.* **1.** A member of a people of central Mexico whose empire was at its height at the time of the Spanish conquest in the early 1500s. **2.** The Nahuatl language of the Aztecs. —**Az′tec′, Az′tec′an** *adj.*

az·ure (ăzh′ər) ►*n.* A bright blue, as of a clear sky. [< Ar. *al-lāzaward,* lapis lazuli.] —**az′ure** *adj.*

B

b or **B** (bē) ▸*n., pl.* **b's** or **B's** also **bs** or **Bs 1.** The 2nd letter of the English alphabet. **2.** The second best in quality or rank. **3.** *Mus.* The 7th tone in the scale of C major. **4. B** A type of blood in the ABO system.
B ▸*abbr.* **1.** baryon number **2.** *Baseball* base **3.** *Mus.* bass **4.** billion **5.** bishop (chess)
b. ▸*abbr.* born
BA ▸*abbr.* **1.** Bachelor of Arts **2.** bathroom
baa (bă, bä) ▸*v.* **baaed, baa·ing** To bleat, as a sheep or goat. [Imit.] **—baa** *n.*
Ba·al (bā′əl) ▸*n., pl.* **-als** or **-al·im** (-ə-lĭm) Any of various fertility and nature gods of the ancient Semitic, non-Hebrew peoples.
ba·ba gha·nouj or **ba·ba ghan·ouj** or **ba·ba ga·noosh** (bä′bə gə-nōōsh′, -nōōzh′) ▸*n.* A purée of roasted eggplant, tahini, garlic, and lemon juice. [Egypt. Ar. *bābā ġannūj.*]
Bab·bitt (băb′ĭt) ▸*n.* A smug, provincial member of the American middle class. [After the main character in the novel *Babbitt* by Sinclair Lewis.] **—Bab′bitt·ry** *n.*
bab·ble (băb′əl) ▸*v.* **-bled, -bling 1.** To utter meaningless words or sounds. **2.** To talk foolishly; chatter. **3.** To make a continuous low, murmuring sound. [ME *babelen.*] **—bab′ble** *n.* **—bab′bler** *n.*
babe (bāb) ▸*n.* **1.** A baby. **2.** An innocent or naive person. **3.** *Slang* A young, attractive woman. [ME.]
ba·bel (băb′əl, bā′bəl) ▸*n.* A confusion of sounds or voices. [After BABEL.]
Ba·bel (bā′bəl, băb′əl) In the Bible, a city (now thought to be Babylon) in Shinar.
ba·boon (bă-bōōn′) ▸*n.* **1.** Any of several large African and Asian monkeys having an elongated, doglike muzzle. **2.** *Slang* A lout; oaf. [< OFr. *babuin.*]
ba·bush·ka (bə-bōōsh′kə) ▸*n.* A woman's head scarf, folded triangularly and tied under the chin. [Russ., grandmother.]
ba·by (bā′bē) ▸*n., pl.* **-bies 1a.** A very young child; infant. **b.** An unborn child; fetus. **c.** The youngest member of a family or group. **2.** One who behaves in an infantile way. **3.** *Slang* A lover or sweetheart. **4.** *Slang* An object of personal concern: *The project is your baby.* ▸*v.* **-bied, -by·ing** To treat overindulgently; pamper. [ME.] **—ba′by·hood**′ *n.* **—ba′by·ish** *adj.*
baby boom ▸*n.* A sudden, large, sustained increase in the birthrate, esp. the one in the US and Canada after World War II through the early 1960s. **—ba′by-boom**′ *adj.* **—ba′by-boom′er** *n.*
baby carriage ▸*n.* A four-wheeled, often hooded carriage for pushing an infant.
Bab·y·lon (băb′ə-lən, -lŏn′) The capital of ancient Babylonia, on the Euphrates R.
Bab·y·lo·ni·a (băb′ə-lō′nē-ə) An ancient empire of Mesopotamia in the Euphrates R. valley.
Bab·y·lo·ni·an (băb′ə-lō′nē-ən) ▸*adj.* Of Babylonia or Babylon. ▸*n.* **1.** A native or inhabitant of Babylon or Babylonia. **2.** The form of Akkadian used in Babylonia.
ba·by's breath (bā′bēz) ▸*n.* A plant having panicles of numerous small white flowers.

ba·by·sit (bā′bē-sĭt′) ▸*v.* To take care of a child or children, as when the parents are away. **—ba′by·sit′ter** *n.*
bac·ca·lau·re·ate (băk′ə-lôr′ē-ĭt) ▸*n.* **1.** A bachelor's degree. **2.** A farewell address delivered to a graduating class. [Med.Lat. *baccalaureātus.*]
bac·ca·rat (bä′kə-rä′, băk′ə-) ▸*n.* A card game in which the objective is to hold cards totaling closest to nine. [Fr. *baccara.*]
bac·cha·nal (băk′ə-năl′, -näl′) ▸*n.* **1.** A drunken or riotous celebration. **2.** A reveler. [< Lat. *bacchānālis,* of Bacchus.]
Bac·cha·na·lia (băk′ə-nāl′yə, -nä′lē-ə) ▸*n.* **1.** The ancient Roman festival in honor of Bacchus. **2. bacchanalia** A drunken festivity. [Lat. *bacchānālia.*] **—Bac′cha·na′lian** *adj. & n.*
Bac·chus (băk′əs) ▸*n. Gk. & Rom. Myth.* See **Dionysus. —Bac′chic** *adj.*
Bach (bäкн, bäk), **Johann Sebastian** 1685–1750. German composer and organist.
bach·e·lor (băch′ə-lər, băch′lər) ▸*n.* **1.** A man who has never married. **2.** A person who holds a bachelor's degree. [Ult. < Med.Lat. *baccalārius,* tenant farmer.] **—bach′e·lor·hood**′, **bach′e·lor·dom** *n.*
bach·e·lor's button (băch′ə-lərz, băch′lərz) ▸*n.* See **cornflower.**
bachelor's degree ▸*n.* A college or university degree signifying completion of the undergraduate curriculum.
ba·cil·lus (bə-sĭl′əs) ▸*n., pl.* **-cil·li** (-sĭl′ī′) Any of various rod-shaped aerobic bacteria. [LLat., little rod.] **—bac′il·lar′y** (băs′ə-lěr′ē), **ba·cil′·lar** *adj.*
bac·i·tra·cin (băs′ĭ-trā′sĭn) ▸*n.* A topical antibiotic obtained from bacteria and used to treat certain bacterial infections. [< BACI(LLUS) + Margaret *Tracy,* in whose blood it was first isolated.]
back (băk) ▸*n.* **1a.** The posterior portion of the trunk of the human body between the neck and the pelvis. **b.** The analogous dorsal region in other animals. **2a.** The backbone or spine. **b.** A part that supports or fits the human back: *the back of a chair.* **3.** The part farthest from the front; the rear. **4.** The reverse side, as of a coin. **5.** *Sports* A player who takes a position behind the frontline. ▸*v.* **1.** To move or cause to move backward. **2.** To support or sustain: *back a political cause.* ▸*adj.* **1.** At the rear. **2.** Distant; remote. **3.** Of a past date; not current: *a back issue of a periodical.* **4.** In arrears: *back pay.* ▸*adv.* **1.** To or toward the rear; backward. **2.** To or toward a former place, state, or time. **3.** In reserve or concealment. **4.** In check: *Barriers held the crowd back.* **5.** In reply or return. **—*phrasal verbs:* back down** To withdraw, as from a confrontation. **back off** To retreat, as from a position or commitment. **back out** To withdraw from something before completion. **back up 1.** To accumulate in a clogged state. **2.** To assist, support, or corroborate. **3.** *Comp.* To make a backup of. [< OE *bæc.*] **—back′less** *adj.*
back·ache (băk′āk′) ▸*n.* A pain in the back.
back·beat (băk′bēt′) ▸*n.* A sharp rhythmic beat, characteristic of rock music.

back·bench (băk′běnch′) ►*n. Chiefly Brit.* The rear benches in the House of Commons where junior members of Parliament sit. —**back· bench′er** *n.*

back·bite (băk′bīt′) ►*v.* To speak spitefully or slanderously about a person who is not present. —**back′bit′er** *n.*

back·board (băk′bôrd′) ►*n.* **1.** A board placed under or behind something to provide support. **2.** *Basketball* The elevated board from which the basket projects.

backboard

back·bone (băk′bōn′) ►*n.* **1.** The vertebrate spine. **2.** A main support: *the backbone of a policy.* **3.** Strength of character.

back·break·ing (băk′brā′kĭng) ►*adj.* Demanding great exertion; arduous.

back·court (băk′kôrt′) ►*n. Sports* The part of a court farthest from the net, goal, or front wall.

back·date (băk′dāt′) ►*v.* To supply (e.g., a check) with a date earlier than the actual date.

back·door (băk′dôr′) ►*adj.* **1.** Secret or surreptitious; clandestine. **2.** Devious or underhanded.

back·drop (băk′drŏp′) ►*n.* **1.** A painted cloth hung at the back of a stage set. **2.** A setting; background.

back·er (băk′ər) ►*n.* One that backs a person, group, or enterprise: *a financial backer.*

back·field (băk′fēld′) ►*n.* **1.** *Football* The players stationed behind the line of scrimmage. **2.** The primarily defensive players in soccer, field hockey, and rugby.

back·fire (băk′fīr′) ►*n.* **1.** An explosion of prematurely ignited fuel or of unburned exhaust in an engine. **2.** A fire started to extinguish or control a larger fire. ►*v.* **1.** To explode in a backfire. **2.** To produce an unexpected, undesired result.

back·for·ma·tion (băk′fôr-mā′shən) ►*n.* **1.** A new word created by removing an actual or supposed affix from an already existing word, as *laze* from *lazy.* **2.** This process.

back·gam·mon (băk′găm′ən) ►*n.* A board game for two persons, with moves determined by throws of dice.

back·ground (băk′ground′) ►*n.* **1.** The area or surface against which something is seen or depicted. **2.** A setting or context. **3.** A state of relative obscurity. **4.** One's total experience, training, and education. **5.** The cultural or social environment in which one was brought up or has lived: *students from many different backgrounds.*

back·hand (băk′hănd′) ►*n.* **1.** *Sports* A stroke, as of a racket, made with the back of the dominant hand facing forward. **2.** Handwriting having letters that slant to the left. ►*adj.* Backhanded. —**back′hand′** *v. & adv.*

back·hand·ed (băk′hăn′dĭd) ►*adj.* **1.** *Sports*

Backhand. **2.** Oblique or roundabout: *a backhanded compliment.* —**back′hand′ed·ly** *adv.*

back·hoe (băk′hō′) ►*n.* An excavator with a boom that is drawn backward to the machine.

back·ing (băk′ĭng) ►*n.* **1.** Something forming a back: *the backing of a carpet.* **2a.** Support or aid. **b.** Approval or endorsement.

back·lash (băk′lăsh′) ►*n.* **1.** A sudden or violent backward whipping motion. **2.** A hostile reaction, esp. to a social or political movement. —**back′lash′** *v.*

back·light (băk′līt′) ►*v.* To light (a subject or a scene) from behind. —**back′light′** *n.*

back·log (băk′lŏg′, -lôg′) ►*n.* **1.** A reserve supply or source. **2.** An accumulation, esp. of unfinished work or unfilled orders.

back·pack (băk′păk′) ►*n.* **1.** A knapsack that is worn on the back. **2.** An apparatus designed to be used while carried on the back. ►*v.* To hike with a backpack. —**back′pack′er** *n.*

back·ped·al (băk′pěd′l) ►*v.* **1.** To pedal backward, as in braking. **2.** To back off.

back·rest (băk′rěst′) ►*n.* A support for the back.

back seat ►*n.* **1.** A seat in the back, esp. of a vehicle. **2.** A subordinate position.

back-seat driver (băk′sēt′) ►*n.* A person who gives unsolicited direction or advice, esp. a passenger in a car.

back·side (băk′sīd′) ►*n. Informal* The buttocks.

back·slash (băk′slăsh′) ►*n.* A backward virgule (\).

back·slide (băk′slīd′) ►*v.* To revert to bad habits or behavior that is criminal or immoral. —**back′slid′er** *n.*

back·space (băk′spās′) ►*v.* To move the cursor on a computer screen back one or more spaces. ►*n.* The key used for backspacing.

back·spin (băk′spĭn′) ►*n.* A spin that tends to slow, stop, or reverse the linear motion of an object, esp. of a ball.

back·stage (băk′stāj′) ►*adv.* In or toward the area behind the stage in a theater. ►*adj.* (băk′- stāj′) **1.** Relating to the area behind the stage in a theater. **2.** Concealed from the public; private.

back·stairs (băk′stârz′) ►*adj.* Furtively carried on; clandestine: *backstairs gossip.*

back·stop (băk′stŏp′) ►*n.* **1.** A screen or fence used to stop a ball from going beyond the playing area. **2.** *Baseball* A catcher.

back·stretch (băk′strěch′) ►*n.* The part of an oval racecourse farthest from the spectators and opposite the homestretch.

back·stroke (băk′strōk′) ►*n.* **1.** A swimming stroke executed with the swimmer lying face up in the water. **2.** A backhanded stroke. —**back′stroke′** *v.*

back·swept (băk′swěpt′) ►*adj.* Brushed or angled backward: *a backswept hairstyle.*

back talk ►*n.* Insolent or impudent retorts.

back·track (băk′trăk′) ►*v.* **1.** To retrace one's route. **2.** To reverse one's position.

back·up (băk′ŭp′) ►*n.* **1a.** A reserve or substitute. **b.** *Comp.* A copy of a program or file stored separately from the original. **2a.** Support or backing. **b.** *Mus.* A background accompaniment. **3.** An overflow or accumulation caused by clogging. ►*adj.* Extra; standby.

back·ward (băk′wərd) ►*adj.* **1.** Directed or facing toward the back. **2.** Reversed. **3.** Behind in

progress or development. ►*adv.* or **back·wards** (-wərdz) **1.** To or toward the back. **2.** With the back leading. **3.** In a reverse manner. **4.** Toward a worse or less advanced condition. —**idiom: bend (or lean) over backward** To do one's utmost. —**back′ward·ly** *adv.* —**back′ward· ness** *n.*
   Usage: The adverb forms *backward* and *backwards* are interchangeable: *stepped backward; a mirror facing backwards.* Only *backward* is an adjective: *a backward view.*

back·wash (băk′wŏsh′, -wôsh′) ►*n.* **1.** A backward flow. **2.** An aftermath.

back·wa·ter (băk′wô′tər, -wŏt′ər) ►*n.* **1.** Water that stagnates or flows backward, as at the edge of a current. **2.** A place that is backward or isolated.

back·woods (băk′wŏŏdz′) ►*pl.n. (takes sing. or pl. v.)* **1.** Heavily wooded, thinly settled areas. **2.** An isolated and uncultured place. —**back′- woods′man** *n.*

ba·con (bā′kən) ►*n.* The salted and smoked meat from the back and sides of a pig. [< OFr.]

Bacon¹, Francis 1561–1626. English philosopher, essayist, and politician.

Bacon², Francis 1909–92. Irish-born British painter.

Bacon, Roger 1214?–92. English friar, scientist, and philosopher.

bac·te·ri·a (băk-tîr′′ē-ə) ►*n.* Pl. of **bacterium.**

bac·te·ri·cide (băk-tîr′ĭ-sīd′) ►*n.* An agent that kills bacteria. —**bac·te′ri·cid′al** *adj.*

bac·te·ri·ol·o·gy (băk-tîr′ē-ŏl′ə-jē) ►*n.* The scientific study of bacteria. —**bac·te′ri·o·log′ic** (-ə-lŏj′ĭk), **bac·te′ri·o·log′i·cal** *adj.* —**bac· te′ri·ol′o·gist** *n.*

bac·te·ri·o·phage (băk-tîr′ē-ə-fāj′) ►*n.* A virus that destroys certain bacteria.

bac·te·ri·um (băk-tîr′ē-əm) ►*n., pl.* **-te·ri·a** (-tîr′ē-ə) Any of various single-celled microorganisms that lack a nucleus, some of which cause disease in plants or animals. [< Gk. *baktērion,* little rod.] —**bac·te′ri·al** *adj.* —**bac· te′ri·al·ly** *adv.*

Bac·tri·a (băk′trē-ə) An ancient country of SW Asia. —**Bac′tri·an** *adj. & n.*

bad (băd) ►*adj.* **worse** (wûrs), **worst** (wûrst) **1.** Not achieving an adequate standard; poor: *a bad movie.* **2.** Evil; sinful. **3.** Vulgar or obscene: *bad language.* **4.** Disobedient or naughty: *bad children.* **5.** Unpleasant or disturbing: *bad news.* **6.** Unfavorable: *a bad review.* **7.** Not fresh; spoiled: *bad meat.* **8.** Detrimental: *bad habits.* **9.** Being so far behind in repayment as to be considered a loss: *bad loans.* **10.** Severe; intense: *a bad cold.* **11.** Being in poor health or condition: *I feel bad today.* **12.** Sorry; regretful: *I feel bad about how I've treated you.* **13. bad· der, bad·dest** *Slang* Very good; great. ►*n.* Something bad: *Take the good with the bad.* ►*adv. Informal* Badly. [ME *badde.*] —**bad′ly** *adv.* —**bad′ness** *n.*
   Usage: The use of *bad* as an adverb, while common in informal speech, is widely regarded as unacceptable in formal writing. Formal usage requires *His tooth ached badly* (not *bad*).

bad blood ►*n.* Enmity or bitterness between persons or groups.

bad breath ►*n.* Stale or foul-smelling breath.

bade (băd, bād) ►*v.* P.t. of **bid.**

badge (băj) ►*n.* A device or emblem worn as

an insignia of rank, office, or honor. [< Norman Fr. *bage.*]

badg·er (băj′ər) ►*n.* A carnivorous burrowing mammal with long front claws and a heavy grizzled coat. ►*v.* To pester persistently. [Perh. < BADGE.]

bad·i·nage (băd′n-äzh′) ►*n.* Light, playful banter. [Fr. < *badin,* joker.]

bad·min·ton (băd′mĭn′tən) ►*n.* A sport played by volleying a shuttlecock over a net with long-handled rackets. [After *Badminton,* the Duke of Beaufort's country seat in western England.]

bad-mouth (băd′mouth′, -mouth′) ►*v. Slang* To criticize or disparage, often unfairly.

Baf·fin Bay (băf′ĭn) An ice-clogged body of water between NE Canada and Greenland.

Baffin Island An island of E Nunavut, Canada, W of Greenland.

baf·fle (băf′əl) ►*v.* **-fled, -fling** To frustrate; stymie. ►*n.* A barrier designed to check or regulate the flow of a liquid, gas, sound, or light. [Perh. < Fr. *bafouer,* to ridicule.] —**baf′fle·ment** *n.*

bag (băg) ►*n.* **1a.** A nonrigid container, as of paper, plastic, or leather. **b.** A handbag; purse. **c.** A suitcase. **2.** An object that resembles a pouch. **3.** An amount of game taken at one time. **4.** *Baseball* A base. **5.** *Slang* An area of interest or skill: *Cooking is not my bag.* ►*v.* **bagged, bag·ging 1.** To put into a bag. **2a.** To hang loosely. **b.** To bulge out. **3.** To capture or kill as game. —**idiom: in the bag** Assured of a successful outcome. [< ON *baggi.*] —**bag′ful** *n.*

bag·a·telle (băg′ə-tĕl′) ►*n.* **1.** A trifle. **2.** A short piece of verse or music. [Fr. < Ital. dial. *bagata,* little property.]

ba·gel (bā′gəl) ►*n.* A ring-shaped roll with a tough chewy texture. [Yiddish *beygl.*]

bag·gage (băg′ĭj) ►*n.* **1.** The bags and belongings of a traveler; luggage. **2.** The movable supplies of an army. [< OFr. *bague,* bundle.]

bag·gy (băg′ē) ►*adj.* **-gi·er, -gi·est** Bulging or hanging loosely: *baggy trousers.* —**bag′gi· ly** *adv.*

Bagh·dad or **Bag·dad** (băg′dăd′) The capital of Iraq, in the center on the Tigris R.

bag·pipe (băg′pīp′) ►*n.* often **bagpipes** A wind instrument having an inflatable bag, a double-reed melody pipe, and one or more drone pipes. —**bag′pipe′** *v.* —**bag′pip′er** *n.*

ba·guette (bă-gĕt′) ►*n.* **1.** A gem cut in a narrow rectangle. **2.** A narrow loaf of French bread. [Fr., small rod.]

Ba·ha·mas (bə-hä′məz, -hä′-) also **Ba·ha·ma Islands** (-mə) An island country in the Atlantic E of FL and Cuba. Cap. Nassau. —**Ba·ha′mi· an** (-hä′mē-ən, -hä′-), **Ba·ha′man** *adj. & n.*

Bah·rain or **Bah·rein** (bä-rān′) An island country in the Persian Gulf between Qatar and Saudi Arabia. Cap. Manama. —**Bah·rain′i** *adj. & n.*

baht (bät) ►*n., pl.* **bahts** or **baht** See table at **currency.** [Thai *bāt.*]

Bai·kal (bī-kôl′, -kŏl′), **Lake** A deep lake of S-central Russia.

bail¹ (bāl) ►*n.* **1.** Security, usu. money, supplied as a guarantee that an arrested person will appear for trial. **2.** Release from imprisonment obtained by bail. ►*v.* To secure the release of by paying bail. —**phrasal verb: bail out** *Informal* To extricate from trouble. [< Lat. *bāiulus,* carrier.] —**bail′er** *n.*

bail² (bāl) ►*v.* **1.** To remove (water) from a boat by repeatedly filling a container and emptying it over the side. **2.** To empty (a boat) of water by bailing. —*phrasal verb:* **bail out 1.** To parachute from an aircraft. **2.** To abandon a project or enterprise. [< OFr. *baille*, bucket.] —**bail′er** *n.*

bail³ (bāl) ►*n.* The arched, hooplike handle of a container, such as a pail. [ME *beil.*]

bail·iff (bā′lĭf) ►*n.* **1.** A court attendant with duties such as the maintenance of order during a trial. **2.** An official who assists a British sheriff by executing writs and arrests. **3.** *Chiefly Brit.* An overseer of an estate. [< OFr. *baillis*, steward.]

bail·i·wick (bā′lə-wĭk′) ►*n.* **1.** One's specific area of interest, skill, or authority. See Synonyms at **field. 2.** The office or district of a bailiff. [ME *bailliwik*, bailiff's village.]

bail·or (bā′lər, bā-lôr′) ►*n.* One who bails property to another.

bairn (bârn) ►*n.* *Scots* A child. [< OE *bearn.*]

bait (bāt) ►*n.* **1.** Food or other lure used to catch fish or trap animals. **2.** An enticement; lure. ►*v.* **1.** To place bait in (a trap) or on (a fishhook). **2.** To entice; lure. **3.** To set dogs upon (a chained animal) for sport. **4.** To taunt or verbally torment (someone), as with persistent insults or ridicule. **5.** To tease. [< ON *beita*, food, to hunt with dogs.] —**bait′er** *n.*

bait and switch ►*n.* **1.** A sales tactic in which a bargain-priced item is used to attract customers who are then encouraged to purchase a more expensive similar item. **2.** A deception based on a false claim or enticement.

baize (bāz) ►*n.* A thick feltlike cloth used chiefly to cover gaming tables. [< Lat. *badius*, bay-colored.]

Ba·ja California (bä′hä) A peninsula of W Mexico extending SSE between the Pacific and the Gulf of California.

bake (bāk) ►*v.* **baked, bak·ing 1.** To cook (food) with dry heat, esp. in an oven. **2.** To harden or dry in or as if in an oven: *bake bricks.* ►*n.* The act or process of baking. [< OE *bacan.*] —**bak′er** *n.*

Ba·ke·lite (bā′kə-līt′, bāk′līt′) A trademark for any of a group of synthetic resins and plastics that are found in a variety of manufactured articles.

Ba·ker (bā′kər), **Josephine** 1906–75. Amer.-born French jazz dancer and singer.

bak·er's dozen (bā′kərz) ►*n.* A group of 13. [From adding an extra roll to avoid the possibility of 12 weighing light.]

bak·er·y (bā′kə-rē) ►*n., pl.* -**ies** A place where bread, cake, and pastries are baked or sold.

bak·ing powder (bā′kĭng) ►*n.* A mixture of baking soda, starch, and cream of tartar, used as a leavening agent in baking.

baking soda ►*n.* A white crystalline compound, $NaHCO_3$, used esp. in baking powder, effervescent beverages, pharmaceuticals, and fire extinguishers.

ba·kla·va (bä′klə-vä′) ►*n.* A dessert made of paper-thin layers of pastry, chopped nuts, and honey. [Turk.]

bak·sheesh (băk′shēsh′, băk-shēsh′) ►*n., pl.* -**sheesh** A gratuity or bribe paid to expedite service, esp. in some Near Eastern countries. [Pers. *bakhshish.*]

Ba·ku (bä-kōō′) The capital of Azerbaijan, in the E part on the Caspian Sea.

bal·a·lai·ka (băl′ə-lī′kə) ►*n.* A musical instrument with a triangular body, fretted neck, and three strings. [Russ. *balalaĭka.*]

bal·ance (băl′əns) ►*n.* **1.** A weighing device, esp. one consisting of a rigid beam suspended at its center and brought into equilibrium by adding known weights at one end while the unknown weight hangs from the other. **2a.** A state of equilibrium. **b.** An influence or force tending to produce equilibrium. **3.** A harmonious arrangement or proportion of parts. **4.** *Accounting* **a.** Equality of totals in the debit and credit sides of an account. **b.** A difference between such totals. **5.** Something left over; remainder. **6.** *Math.* Equality of symbolic quantities on each side of an equation. ►*v.* -**anced,** -**anc·ing 1.** To weigh in or as if in a balance. **2.** To bring into or be in a state of equilibrium. **3.** To counterbalance. **4.** *Accounting* To compute the difference between the debits and credits of (an account). —*idioms:* **in the balance** With the result or outcome still uncertain. **on balance** Taking everything into consideration. [< Lat. *bilānx*, having two scales.]

balance beam ►*n.* A horizontal raised beam used in gymnastics for balancing exercises.

balance beam
Evgenia Zafeiraki at the 2007 World Artistic Gymnastics Championships

balance sheet ►*n.* A statement of the assets and liabilities of a business or institution.

balance wheel ►*n.* A wheel that regulates rate of mechanical movement, as in a watch.

Bal·an·chine (băl′ən-chēn′), **George** 1904–83. Russian-born Amer. ballet director and choreographer.

bal·bo·a (băl-bō′ə) ►*n.* See table at **currency.** [After Vasco Núñez de BALBOA.]

Balboa, Vasco Núñez de 1475–1517. Spanish explorer.

bal·co·ny (băl′kə-nē) ►*n., pl.* -**nies 1.** A platform that projects from the wall of a building and is surrounded by a railing. **2.** A gallery that projects over the main floor in a theater or auditorium. [Ital. *balcone.*]

bald (bôld) ►*adj.* -**er,** -**est 1.** Lacking hair on the head. **2.** Lacking a natural or usual covering; bare. **3.** *Zool.* Having white feathers or markings on the head. **4.** Plain; blunt: *the bald* *truth.* **5.** Lacking tread, as a tire. [ME *balled.*] —**bald′ly** *adv.* —**bald′ness** *n.*

bal·da·chin (bôl′də-kĭn, băl′-) also **bal·da·chi·no** (băl′də-kē′nō) ►*n., pl.* **-chins** also **-chi·nos** A canopy over an altar, throne, or dais. [< OItal. *Baldacco,* Baghdad.]

bald eagle ►*n.* A North American eagle with a dark body and white head and tail.

bal·der·dash (bôl′dər-dăsh′) ►*n.* Nonsense. [?]

bald-faced (bôld′fāst′) ►*adj.* Blatant; brazen: *a bald-faced lie.*

bal·dric (bôl′drĭk) ►*n.* A belt worn across the chest to support a sword or bugle. [< OFr. *baudre* and MHGer. *balderich.*]

Bald·win (bôld′wĭn), **James Arthur** 1924–87. Amer. writer and essayist.

James Baldwin
photographed in the 1980s

bale (bāl) ►*n.* A large, tightly bound package of material, such as hay. ►*v.* **baled, bal·ing** To bind in bales. [ME.] —**bal′er** *n.*

Bal·e·ar·ic Islands (băl′ē-ăr′ĭk) An archipelago in the W Mediterranean Sea off the E coast of Spain.

ba·leen (bə-lēn′) ►*n.* See **whalebone** (sense 1). [< Lat. *balaena,* whale.]

baleen whale ►*n.* A usu. large cetacean having two blowholes and whalebone plates instead of teeth.

bale·ful (bāl′fəl) ►*adj.* **1.** Portending evil; ominous. **2.** Malignant in effect. [*bale,* evil + –FUL.] —**bale′ful·ly** *adv.* —**bale′ful·ness** *n.*

Ba·li (bä′lē) An island of S Indonesia in the Lesser Sundas E of Java.

Ba·li·nese (bä′lə-nēz′, -nēs′) ►*n., pl.* **-nese 1.** A native or inhabitant of Bali. **2.** The Indonesian language of Bali. —**Ba′li·nese′** *adj.*

balk (bôk) ►*v.* **1.** To stop short and refuse to move forward. **2.** To refuse to proceed, as out of doubt or moral principle. **3.** *Baseball* To make an illegal motion before pitching, entitling any base runner to advance. ►*n.* **1.** A hindrance, check, or defeat. **2.** *Baseball* An act of balking. [< OE *balca,* ridge.] —**balk′er** *n.* —**balk′y** *adj.*

Bal·kan Mountains (bôl′kən) A mountain system of SE Europe extending about 560 km (350 mi) from E Serbia through central Bulgaria to the Black Sea.

Balkan Peninsula A peninsula of SE Europe bounded by the Black Sea, the Sea of Marmara, and the Aegean, Mediterranean, Ionian, and Adriatic Seas. —**Bal′kan** *adj.*

Balkans (bôl′kənz) **1.** The Balkan Peninsula. **2.** The Balkan Mountains.

Bal·khash (băl-käsh′, -кнäsh′), **Lake** A shallow lake of SE Kazakhstan.

ball¹ (bôl) ►*n.* **1.** A spherical or almost spherical object or body. **2a.** Any of various round or oblong objects used in sports and games. **b.** A game played with such an object. **c.** A pitched baseball that does not pass through the strike zone and is not swung at by the batter. **3.** A usu. round projectile. **4.** A rounded part, esp. of the body: *the ball of the foot.* ►*v.* To form or become formed into a ball. —*phrasal verb:* **ball up** To confuse; bungle. —*idiom:* **on the ball** *Informal* Alert or efficient. [ME.]

ball² (bôl) ►*n.* **1.** A formal gathering for social dancing. **2.** *Slang* An extremely enjoyable time: *had a ball on our trip.* [< Gk. *ballizein,* to dance.]

bal·lad (băl′əd) ►*n.* **1a.** A narrative poem, often of folk origin and intended to be sung, consisting of simple stanzas and usu. having a refrain. **b.** The music for such a poem. **2.** A slow, usu. romantic song. [< OProv. *balada,* dancing song.] —**bal′lad·eer′** *n.* —**bal′lad·ry** *n.*

bal·last (băl′əst) ►*n.* **1.** Heavy material placed in the hold of a ship or the gondola of a balloon to enhance stability. **2.** Coarse gravel or crushed rock laid to form a roadbed. ►*v.* To provide with ballast. [Of Scand. orig.]

ball bearing ►*n.* **1.** A friction-reducing bearing, as for a rotating shaft, in which the moving and stationary parts are separated by hard metal balls revolving freely in a lubricated track. **2.** A hard ball used in such a bearing.

bal·le·ri·na (băl′ə-rē′nə) ►*n.* A female ballet dancer. [Ital. < *ballare,* to dance.]

bal·let (bă-lā′, băl′ā′) ►*n.* **1.** A classical dance form characterized by elaborate formal technique. **2.** A choreographed production of this dance form accompanied by music. [< Ital. *ballare,* to dance.]

bal·let·o·mane (bă-lĕt′ə-mān′) ►*n.* An admirer of ballet. [Fr. < *ballet,* BALLET.]

ball game ►*n.* **1.** A game or sport played with a ball. **2.** *Slang* A particular situation, esp. one that is highly competitive.

ballistic missile ►*n.* A projectile that assumes a free-falling trajectory after a self-powered ascent.

bal·lis·tics (bə-lĭs′tĭks) ►*n.* (takes sing. v.) **1.** The study of the dynamics or flight characteristics of projectiles. **2a.** The study of the firing of firearms. **b.** The study of the flight characteristics and effects of ammunition. [< Gk. *ballein,* to throw.] —**bal·lis′tic** *adj.* —**bal·lis′ti·cal·ly** *adv.*

bal·loon (bə-lōōn′) ►*n.* **1.** An inflatable toy rubber bag. **2.** A flexible bag inflated with gas or hot air that is lighter than the surrounding air, causing it to rise and float in the atmosphere. **3.** An outline containing the words or thoughts of a cartoon character. **4.** *Med.* An inflatable device that is inserted into a body cavity or structure and distended with air or gas for therapeutic purposes. ►*v.* **1.** To ride in a balloon. **2.** To expand or cause to expand like a balloon. **3.** To increase rapidly. [< Ital. dial. *ballone,* big ball.] —**bal·loon′ist** *n.*

bal·lot (băl′ət) ►*n.* **1.** A paper or card used to cast a vote. **2.** The act or method of voting. **3.** A list of candidates for office; ticket. ►*v.* To cast a ballot. [< Ital. *balla*, ball.]

ball·park (bôl′pärk′) ►*n.* **1.** A park or stadium in which ball games are played. **2.** *Slang* The approximately proper range, as of an estimate. —**ball′park′** *adj.*

ball·point pen (bôl′point′) ►*n.* A pen having a small, freely revolving ball as its writing point.

ball·room (bôl′rōōm′, -rŏŏm′) ►*n.* A large room for dancing.

bal·ly·hoo (băl′ē-hōō′) ►*n., pl.* **-hoos 1.** Sensational promotion or publicity. **2.** Clamor; uproar. ►*v.* To promote by sensational methods. [?]

balm (bäm) ►*n.* **1.** Any of several aromatic plants, esp. one used as a seasoning or for tea. **2.** An aromatic salve or oil. **3.** Something that soothes or heals. [< Lat. *balsamum*, balsam.]

balm·y (bä′mē) ►*adj.* **-i·er, -i·est 1.** Having the quality or fragrance of balm. **2.** Mild and pleasant: *a balmy breeze.* **3.** *Slang* Eccentric or crazy. —**balm′i·ly** *adv.* —**balm′i·ness** *n.*

ba·lo·ney¹ (bə-lō′nē) ►*n.* Var. of **bologna.**

ba·lo·ney² (bə-lō′nē) ►*n. Slang* Nonsense. [Prob. var. of BOLOGNA.]

bal·sa (bôl′sə) ►*n.* **1.** A tropical American tree having very light, soft, buoyant wood. **2.** The wood of this tree. [Sp.]

bal·sam (bôl′səm) ►*n.* **1.** An aromatic resin obtained from various trees or plants. **2.** A tree, esp. the balsam fir, yielding balsam. **3.** See **impatiens.** [< Gk. *balsamon.*]

balsam fir ►*n.* A North American evergreen tree that is used for pulpwood.

bal·sam·ic vinegar (bôl-săm′ĭk) ►*n.* Any of various aromatic vinegars, esp. a dark sweet aged Italian variety. [< *balsamic,* restorative (translation of Ital. *aceto balsamico*).]

Balt (bôlt) ►*n.* A member of a Baltic-speaking people.

Bal·tic (bôl′tĭk) ►*adj.* **1.** Of the Baltic Sea. **2.** Of the branch of Indo-European that includes Latvian and Lithuanian. ►*n.* The Baltic language branch.

Baltic Sea An arm of the Atlantic in N Europe.

Baltic States Estonia, Latvia, and Lithuania, on the E coast of the Baltic Sea.

Bal·ti·more (bôl′tə-môr′) A city of N MD on an arm of Chesapeake Bay NE of Washington DC.

Baltimore oriole ►*n.* A North American songbird having bright orange plumage in the male and olive brown plumage in the female.

bal·us·ter (băl′ə-stər) ►*n.* One of the upright supports of a handrail. [< Ital. *balaustro.*]

bal·us·trade (băl′ə-strād′) ►*n.* A handrail and the row of balusters or posts that support it. [< Ital. *balaustrata.*]

Bal·zac (bôl′zăk′, bäl-zäk′), **Honoré de** 1799–1850. French writer.

Ba·ma·ko (bä′mə-kō′) The capital of Mali, in the SW on the Niger R.

bam·boo (băm-bōō′) ►*n., pl.* **-boos 1.** Any of various tall, usu. woody, temperate or tropical grasses. **2.** The hard hollow stems of any of these grasses, used in construction and crafts. [Malay *bambu.*]

bam·boo·zle (băm-bōō′zəl) ►*v.* **-zled, -zling** *Informal* **1.** To trick or deceive; hoodwink.

2. To confuse; bewilder. [?] —**bam·boo′zle·ment** *n.*

ban (băn) ►*v.* **banned, ban·ning a.** To prohibit, esp. by official decree: *ban smoking; ban pesticides.* **b.** To refuse to allow (someone) to do something or go somewhere; exclude: *The player was banned to the sidelines.* ►*n.* A prohibition imposed by law or official decree. [< OE *bannan,* summon, and ON *banna,* prohibit.]

ba·nal (bə-năl′, bā′nəl, bə-näl′) ►*adj.* Completely ordinary; trite. [< OFr., held in common.] —**ba·nal′i·ty** (-năl′ĭ-tē) *n.* —**ba·nal′ly** *adv.*

ba·nan·a (bə-năn′ə) ►*n.* **1.** Any of several treelike tropical or subtropical plants having large leaves and hanging clusters of edible fruit. **2.** The elongated fruit of these plants, having yellowish to reddish skin and white pulpy flesh. [Of African orig.]

band¹ (bănd) ►*n.* **1.** A thin strip of flexible material used to encircle and bind together. **2.** A strip or stripe of a contrasting color or material. **3.** A simple ring, esp. a wedding ring. **4.** *Phys.* A range or interval, esp. of radio wavelengths or frequencies. ►*v.* **1.** To bind with or as if with a band. **2.** To tag (e.g., birds) with a band. [< OFr. *bande.*]

band² (bănd) ►*n.* **1.** A group of people or animals. **2.** A group of musicians who perform together. ►*v.* To assemble or unite in a group: *band together for safety.* [< OFr.]

band·age (băn′dĭj) ►*n.* A strip of material used to protect or support a wound or other injury. ►*v.* **-aged, -ag·ing** To apply a bandage to. [< OFr. *bande,* strip.]

Band-Aid (bănd′ād′) A trademark for an adhesive bandage with a gauze pad in the center, used to protect minor wounds.

ban·dan·na or **ban·dan·a** (băn-dăn′ə) ►*n.* A large handkerchief, usu. patterned and brightly colored. [< Hindi *bāndhnā,* to tie.]

bandanna

Ban·dar Se·ri Be·ga·wan (bŭn′dər sĕr′ē bə-gä′wən) The capital of Brunei, on the N coast of Borneo.

band·box (bănd′bŏks′) ►*n.* A round box used to hold small articles of clothing.

ban·di·coot (băn′dĭ-kōōt′) ►*n.* **1.** A large rat of SE Asia. **2.** A ratlike Australian marsupial. [Telugu *bantikoku : banti,* ball + *kokku,* long beak.]

ban·dit (băn′dĭt) ►*n.* **1.** A robber, esp. one who is armed. **2.** One who cheats or exploits others. [Ital. *bandito.*] —**ban′dit·ry** *n.*

ban·do·leer or **ban·do·lier** (băn′də-lîr′) ►*n.* A

military belt for carrying cartridges that is worn across the chest. [< Sp. *bandolera.*]

band saw ►*n.* A power saw having a toothed metal band driven around pulleys.

band·stand (bănd'stănd') ►*n.* A usu. outdoor platform for musical performers.

Ban·dung (bän'dŏŏng') A city of Indonesia in W Java SE of Jakarta. Pop. 1,462,637.

band·wag·on (bănd'wăg'ən) ►*n.* **1.** A decorated wagon used to transport musicians in a parade. **2.** *Informal* A cause or trend that attracts increasing numbers of followers.

band·width (bănd'wĭdth', -wĭth') ►*n. Comp.* The amount of data that can be passed along a communications channel in a given period of time.

ban·dy (băn'dē) ►*v.* **-died, -dy·ing 1.** To toss back and forth. **2.** To discuss in a casual or frivolous manner. ►*adj.* Bowed in an outward curve: *bandy legs.* [?]

bane (bān) ►*n.* **1.** A cause of harm or ruin. **2.** A source of persistent annoyance. [< OE *bana.*] —**bane'ful** *adj.*

bang[1] (băng) ►*n.* **1.** A sudden loud noise, blow, or thump. **2.** *Slang* A sense of excitement; thrill. **3.** *Informal* A sudden burst of action: *The campaign started off with a bang.* ►*v.* **1.** To strike heavily; bump. **2.** To handle noisily or violently. **3.** To make a loud, explosive noise. ►*adv.* Exactly; precisely: *hit bang on the target.* [Prob. < ON *bang,* a hammering.]

bang[2] (băng) ►*n.* often **bangs** Hair cut straight across the forehead. [< BANG[1], suddenly, abruptly.]

Ban·ga·lore (băng'gə-lôr') See **Bengaluru.**

Bang·kok (băng'kŏk') The capital of Thailand, in the SW.

Bang·la·desh (bäng'glə-dĕsh', băng'-) A country of South Asia between India and Myanmar on the Bay of Bengal. Cap. Dhaka. —**Bang'la·desh'i** *adj. & n.*

ban·gle (băng'gəl) ►*n.* **1.** A rigid bracelet or anklet, esp. one with no clasp. **2.** An ornament that hangs from a bracelet or anklet. [Hindi *baṅgrī,* glass bracelet.]

Ban·gui (bäng-gē', bän-) The capital of Central African Republic, in the S part on the Ubangi R.

bang-up (băng'ŭp') ►*adj. Informal* Very good; excellent.

ban·ian (băn'yən) ►*n.* Var. of **banyan.**

ban·ish (băn'ĭsh) ►*v.* **1.** To force to leave a country or place by official decree; exile. **2.** To drive away; expel. [< OFr. *banir.*] —**ban'ish·ment** *n.*

ban·is·ter also **ban·nis·ter** (băn'ĭ-stər) ►*n.* **1.** A handrail, esp. on a staircase. **2.** A baluster. [Var. of BALUSTER.]

ban·jo (băn'jō) ►*n., pl.* **-jos** or **-joes** *Mus.* A usu. fretted stringed instrument having a hollow circular body with a stretched diaphragm of vellum. [Prob. of African orig.] —**ban'jo·ist** *n.*

Ban·jul (bän'jōōl') The capital of Gambia, at the mouth of the Gambia R.

bank[1] (băngk) ►*n.* **1.** A piled-up mass, as of snow or clouds; heap. **2.** A steep natural incline. **3.** often **banks a.** The slope of land adjoining a body of water, esp. adjoining a river, lake, or channel. **b.** A large elevated area of a sea floor. **4.** Lateral tilting, as of an aircraft or vehicle in turning. ►*v.* **1.** To border or protect with a bank. **2.** To pile up; amass: *banked earth along the wall.* **3.** To cover (a fire) with ashes or fuel for continued low burning. **4.** To construct with a slope rising to the outside edge. **5.** To tilt (e.g., an aircraft) in turning. [Of Scand. orig.]

bank[2] (băngk) ►*n.* **1a.** A business establishment authorized to perform financial transactions, such as receiving or lending money. **b.** The offices in which a bank is located. **2.** The funds held by a dealer or banker in certain games esp. gambling games. **3.** A supply for future or emergency use: *a blood bank.* **4.** A place of storage: *a computer's memory bank.* ►*v.* **1.** To deposit in a bank. **2.** To transact business with a bank. **3.** To operate a bank. —***phrasal verb*: bank on** To count on; rely on. [< OItal. *banca,* moneychanger's table.] —**bank'a·ble** *adj.* —**bank'er** *n.* —**bank'ing** *n.*

bank[3] (băngk) ►*n.* **1.** A set of similar things arranged in a row: *a bank of elevators.* **2.** *Naut.* **a.** A bench for rowers in a galley. **b.** A row of oars in a galley. ►*v.* To arrange in a row. [< LLat. *bancus,* bench.]

bank·book (băngk'bŏŏk') ►*n.* A booklet held by a depositor in which deposits and withdrawals are entered by the bank; passbook.

bank·card (băngk'kärd') ►*n.* A card issued by a bank authorizing the holder to receive bank services and often functioning as a debit card.

bank holiday ►*n.* A day on which banks are legally closed.

Ban Ki Moon or **Ban Ki-moon** (bän' gē' mōŏn', kē') Born 1944. South Korean diplomat; secretary-general of the United Nations (assumed office 2007).

bank·note (băngk'nōt') ►*n.* **1.** A promissory note issued by a central bank. **2.** A piece of paper currency.

bank·roll (băngk'rōl') ►*n.* **1.** A roll of paper money. **2.** *Informal* One's ready cash. ►*v. Informal* To underwrite the expense of.

bank·rupt (băngk'rŭpt', -rəpt) ►*adj.* **1a.** Having been legally declared insolvent. **b.** Financially ruined; impoverished. **2.** Lacking in quality or resources; depleted. ►*v.* To cause to become financially bankrupt. [< Ital. *bancarotta,* bankruptcy : *banca,* bank + *rotta,* broken.] —**bank'rupt·cy** *n.*

ban·ner (băn'ər) ►*n.* **1.** A piece of cloth attached to a staff and used as a standard by a monarch, army, or knight. **2.** A flag. **3.** A headline spanning the width of a newspaper page. ►*adj.* Outstanding: *a banner crop.* [< OFr. *baniere.*]

ban·nis·ter (băn'ĭ-stər) ►*n.* Var. of **banister.**

Bannister, Sir Roger. b. 1929. British runner; first person to run the mile in under four minutes (1954).

ban·nock (băn'ək) ►*n.* **1.** A flat, usu. unleavened bread made of oatmeal or barley flour. **2.** *Chiefly New England* Thin cornbread baked on a griddle. [< OE *bannuc,* of Celt. orig.]

banns (bănz) ►*pl.n.* An announcement, esp. in a church, of an intended marriage. [< OE *gebann,* proclamation.]

ban·quet (băng'kwĭt) ►*n.* **1.** An elaborate, sumptuous feast. **2.** A ceremonial dinner honoring a particular guest or occasion. ►*v.* To honor at or partake of a banquet. [< OFr. *banc,* bench.] —**ban'quet·er** *n.*

ban·quette (băng-kĕt') ►*n.* **1.** A platform lining a trench or parapet for soldiers when firing.

2. A long upholstered bench along a wall. [< Prov. *banqueta*.]

ban·shee (băn′shē) ►*n.* A female spirit in Gaelic folklore believed to presage a death in a family by wailing. [Ir.Gael. *bean sídhe*.]

ban·tam (băn′təm) ►*n.* **1.** Any of various breeds of small domestic fowl that are often miniatures of larger breeds. **2.** A small but aggressive and spirited person. ►*adj.* **1.** Small; tiny. **2.** Aggressive and spirited. [After *Bantam*, Indonesia.]

ban·tam·weight (băn′təm-wāt′) ►*n.* A boxer weighing from 113 to 118 lbs., between a flyweight and a featherweight.

ban·ter (băn′tər) ►*n.* Good-humored, playful, or teasing conversation. ►*v.* To exchange good-humored, playful, or teasing remarks. [?]

Ban·tu (băn′tōō) ►*n., pl.* **-tu** or **-tus 1.** A large group of related languages spoken in central, E-central, and S Africa, including Swahili, Zulu, and Xhosa. **2.** A member of a Bantu-speaking people. —**Ban′tu** *adj.*

ban·yan also **ban·ian** (băn′yən) ►*n.* A tropical fig tree having many aerial roots that descend from the branches and develop new trunks. [Short for *banyan tree*, merchant's tree < Skt. *vāṇijaḥ*, merchant.]

ban·zai (bän-zī′) ►*n.* A Japanese battle cry or patriotic cheer. [J., ten thousand years.]

ba·o·bab (bā′ō-băb′, bä′-) ►*n.* A tropical African tree with edible gourdlike fruits and a broad trunk that stores water. [Prob. < Ar. dial. *būḥibab*, fruit of many seeds : Ar. *'ab*, father, source + *ḥibāb*, pl. of *ḥabb*, seed.]

bap·tism (băp′tĭz′əm) ►*n.* **1a.** A rite of initiation into Christianity, marked by immersion of the body in water or application of water to the head. **b.** Any of various initiatory ceremonies in other traditions. **2.** A first act or experience, esp. a difficult one that may impart new insights. [< Gk. *baptismos*.] —**bap·tis′mal** *adj.*

Bap·tist (băp′tĭst) ►*n.* **1.** A member of an evangelical Protestant church that practices voluntary adult baptism. **2. baptist** One that baptizes. —**Bap′tist** *adj.*

bap·tis·ter·y also **bap·tis·try** (băp′tĭ-strē) ►*n., pl.* **-ies** also **-tries 1.** A part of a church or a separate building used for baptizing. **2.** A font used for baptism.

bap·tize (băp-tīz′, băp′tīz′) ►*v.* **-tized, -tiz·ing 1.** To administer baptism (to). **2a.** To cleanse or purify. **b.** To initiate. **3.** To give a Christian name to a person; christen. [< Gk. *baptein*, to dip.] —**bap·tiz′er** *n.*

bar (bär) ►*n.* **1.** A relatively long, straight, rigid piece of solid material. **2.** A solid oblong block of a substance, such as soap, candy, or gold. **3.** An obstacle. **4.** A narrow marking, as a stripe or band. **5.** *Law* The nullification or prevention of a claim or action. **6.** The railing in a courtroom in front of which the judges, lawyers, and defendants sit. **7.** *Law* **a.** Attorneys considered as a group. Used with *the.* **b.** The legal profession. **8.** *Mus.* A vertical line drawn through a staff to mark off a measure. **9a.** A counter at which food and esp. drinks are served: *an oyster bar.* **b.** A place having such a counter. **10.** Var. of **barre.** ►*v.* **barred, bar·ring 1.** To fasten securely with a bar. **2.** To shut in or out with bars. **3.** To obstruct. **4a.** To forbid; prohibit: *bars the dumping of waste.* **b.** To exclude: *was barred from the club.* ►*prep.* Except for;

excluding: *my best student, bar none.* —*idiom:* **behind bars** In prison. [< OFr. *barre*.]

Ba·rab·bas (bə-răb′əs) In the New Testament, the prisoner whose release, instead of that of Jesus, was demanded by the multitude.

barb (bärb) ►*n.* **1.** A sharp backward-pointing projection, as on an arrow or fishhook. **2.** A cutting remark. **3.** A parallel filament projecting from the main shaft of a feather. **4.** *Bot.* A hooked bristle or hairlike projection. **5.** See **barbel.** ►*v.* To provide with a barb. [< Lat. *barba*, beard.] —**barbed** *adj.*

Bar·ba·dos (bär-bā′dōs′, -dōz′) An island country in the E West Indies. Cap. Bridgetown. —**Bar·ba′di·an** *adj. & n.*

bar·bar·i·an (bär-bâr′ē-ən) ►*n.* **1.** A member of a people considered uncivilized or culturally inferior by members of another people. **2.** A cruel or brutal person. **3.** An insensitive, uncultured person. See Synonyms at **boor.** [< Lat. *barbarus*, BARBAROUS.] —**bar·bar′i·an** *adj.* —**bar·bar′i·an·ism** *n.*

bar·bar·ic (bär-băr′ĭk) ►*adj.* **1.** Of or typical of barbarians. **2.** Marked by crudeness in taste, style, or manner. **3.** Brutal or cruel.

bar·ba·rism (bär′bə-rĭz′əm) ►*n.* Brutality or cruelty.

bar·ba·rous (bär′bər-əs) ►*adj.* **1.** Considered to be primitive in culture or customs. **2.** Lacking refinement; coarse. **3.** Marked by cruelty. [< Gk. *barbaros*, foreign.] —**bar′ba·rize′** *v.* —**bar′ba·rous·ly** *adv.* —**bar′ba·rous·ness, bar·bar′i·ty** (-băr′ĭ-tē) *n.*

Bar·ba·ry (bär′bə-rē, -brē) A region of N Africa on the Mediterranean coast between Egypt and the Atlantic.

Barbary Coast The Mediterranean coastal area of Barbary.

bar·be·cue (bär′bĭ-kyōō′) ►*n.* **1.** A grill, pit, or outdoor fireplace for roasting meat. **2.** Meat roasted over an open fire. **3.** A social gathering at which food is cooked over an open fire. ►*v.* **-cued, -cu·ing** To roast (meat or seafood) over an open fire. [Of Taino orig.]

barbed wire ►*n.* Twisted strands of fence wire with barbs at regular intervals.

bar·bel (bär′bəl) ►*n.* One of the whiskerlike feelers of certain fishes, such as catfishes. [< Med.Lat. *barbula*, little beard.]

bar·bell (bär′bĕl′) ►*n.* A bar with weights at each end, lifted for sport or exercise.

bar·ber (bär′bər) ►*n.* One whose business is to cut hair, usu. of men and boys, and shave or trim beards. ►*v.* To cut the hair or beard (of). [< Lat. *barba*, beard.]

bar·ber·ry (bär′bĕr′ē) ►*n.* Any of various often spiny shrubs having small reddish or blackish berries. [< Med.Lat. *berberis*.]

bar·ber·shop (bär′bər-shŏp′) ►*n.* The place of business of a barber. ►*adj.* Relating to the performance of sentimental songs for unaccompanied, usu. male voices in four-part harmony: *a barbershop quartet.*

bar·bi·tal (bär′bĭ-tôl′, -tăl′) ►*n.* A barbiturate formerly used as a sedative. [< BARBITURIC ACID.]

bar·bi·tu·rate (bär-bĭch′ər-ĭt, -ə-rāt′, -ə-wĭt) ►*n.* Any of a group of barbituric acid derivatives used as sedatives or hypnotics. [BARBITUR(IC ACID) + -ATE².]

bar·bi·tu·ric acid (bär′bĭ-tŏŏr′ĭk, -tyŏŏr′-) ►*n.*

An organic acid, $C_4H_4O_3N_2$, used in the manufacture of barbiturates.

Bar·bu·da (bär-bōō′də) An island of Antigua and Barbuda in the West Indies N of Antigua. **—Bar·bu′dan** *adj. & n.*

barb·wire (bärb′wīr′) ►*n.* Barbed wire.

Bar·ce·lo·na (bär′sə-lō′nə) A city of NE Spain on the Mediterranean Sea.

bar·code (bär′kōd′) ►*n.* A series of vertical bars of varying widths printed on consumer product packages and used esp. for inventory control.

bard (bärd) ►*n.* **1.** One of an ancient Celtic order of singing narrative poets. **2.** A poet, esp. an exalted national poet. [< Ir.Gael. *bárd* and < Welsh *bardd.*] **—bard′ic** *adj.*

bare (bâr) ►*adj.* **bar·er, bar·est 1.** Lacking the usual or appropriate covering or clothing; naked. **2.** Exposed to view. **3.** Lacking the usual furnishings, equipment, or decoration. **4.** Having no addition or qualification: *the bare facts.* **5.** Just sufficient: *the bare necessities.* ►*v.* **bared, bar·ing** To make bare; reveal. [< OE *bær.*] **—bare′ness** *n.*

bare·back (bâr′băk′) ►*adj.* Using no saddle: *a bareback rider.* **—bare′back′** *adv.*

bare·faced (bâr′fāst′) ►*adj.* **1.** Having no covering or beard on the face. **2.** Shameless; brazen: *a barefaced lie.* **—bare′fac′ed·ly** (-fā′sĭd-lē, -fāst′lē) *adv.*

bare·foot (bâr′fŏŏt′) also **bare·foot·ed** (-fŏŏt′ĭd) ►*adj.* Wearing nothing on the feet. **—bare′foot** *adv.*

bare·hand·ed (bâr′hăn′dĭd) ►*adj.* Having no covering on the hands. **—bare′hand′ed** *adv.*

bare·head·ed (bâr′hĕd′ĭd) ►*adj.* Having no covering on the head. **—bare′head′ed** *adv.*

bare·leg·ged (bâr′lĕg′ĭd, -lĕgd′) ►*adj.* Having the legs uncovered. **—bare′leg′ged** *adv.*

bare·ly (bâr′lē) ►*adv.* **1.** By a very little; hardly. **2.** Sparsely; sparely: *a barely furnished room.*

Ba·rents Sea (bär′ənts, bä′rənts) A shallow section of the Arctic Ocean N of Norway and NW Russia.

barf (bärf) ►*v. Slang* To vomit. [Prob. imit.] **—barf** *n.*

bar·fly (bär′flī′) ►*n. Slang* One who frequents drinking establishments.

bar·gain (bär′gĭn) ►*n.* **1.** An agreement between parties fixing obligations that each promises to carry out. See Synonyms at **agreement. 2a.** An agreement establishing the terms of a sale or exchange of goods or services. **b.** Property acquired or services rendered as a result of such an agreement. **3.** Something offered or acquired at a price advantageous to the buyer. ►*v.* **1.** To negotiate the terms of a sale, exchange, or other agreement. **2.** To arrive at an agreement. **3.** To exchange; trade. **—***phrasal verb:* **bargain for** To count on; expect. **—***idiom:* **into (or in) the bargain** More than what is expected. [< OFr. *bargaignier*, haggle.] **—bar′gain·er** *n.*

barge (bärj) ►*n.* **1.** A long, large, usu. flat-bottomed boat for transporting freight. **2.** A large open pleasure boat used for parties. **3.** A powerboat reserved for the use of an admiral. ►*v.* **barged, barg·ing 1.** To carry by barge. **2.** To move about clumsily. **3.** To intrude. [< Lat. *barca*, boat.]

bar graph ►*n.* A graph consisting of parallel, usu. vertical bars or rectangles with lengths proportional to specified quantities.

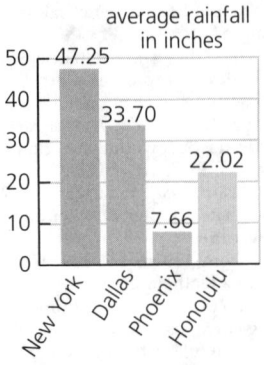

bar graph
average annual rainfall in several cities

bar·ite (bâr′īt, băr′-) ►*n.* A crystalline mineral used in paint and as the chief source of barium compounds. [Gk. *barus*, heavy + –ITE¹.]

bar·i·tone (băr′ĭ-tōn′) ►*n.* **1.** A male singer or voice with a range higher than a bass and lower than a tenor. **2.** A wind instrument with a similar range. [< Gk. *barutonos*, deep-sounding.]

bar·i·um (bâr′ē-əm, băr′-) ►*n. Symbol* **Ba 1.** A soft, silvery-white metal used to deoxidize copper and in various alloys. At. no. 56. See table at **element. 2.** A radiopaque solution containing barium, used to visualize the gastrointestinal tract on x-rays. [< Gk. *barus*, heavy.]

bark¹ (bärk) ►*n.* **1.** The harsh sound made by a dog. **2.** A sound, such as a cough, similar to a dog's bark. ►*v.* **1.** To utter a bark. **2.** To speak sharply; snap. **—***idiom:* **bark up the wrong tree** To misdirect one's efforts. [< OE *beorcan*, to bark.]

bark² (bärk) ►*n.* The tough outer covering of the stems and roots of trees and other woody plants. ►*v.* **1.** To remove bark from. **2.** To scrape; skin: *barked my shin.* [< ON *börkr.*]

bark³ also **barque** (bärk) ►*n.* **1.** A sailing ship with from three to five masts. **2.** A boat that is propelled by oars or sails. [< Lat. *barca*, boat.]

bar·keep·er (bär′kē′pər) or **bar·keep** (-kēp′) ►*n.* **1.** One who owns or runs a bar. **2.** A bartender.

bark·er (bär′kər) ►*n.* **1.** One that barks. **2.** One who stands at the entrance to a show and solicits customers with a loud sales spiel.

bar·ley (bär′lē) ►*n.* A cereal grass that bears grain used as food, livestock feed, and for malt production. [< OE *bærlic.*]

bar·maid (bär′mād′) ►*n.* A woman who serves drinks in a bar.

bar mitz·vah or **bar miz·vah** (bär mĭts′və) ►*n.* **1.** A Jewish male of at least 13 years of age, considered an adult and responsible for observing religious law. **2.** The ceremony that confirms a boy as a bar mitzvah. [Heb. *bar miṣwâ.*]

barn (bärn) ►*n.* A large farm building used for storing farm products and sheltering livestock. [< OE *berærn.*]

bar·na·cle (bär′nə-kəl) ►*n.* A small, hard-shelled crustacean that attaches itself to submerged surfaces. [< Med.Lat. *bernaca.*]

Bar·nard (bär′nərd, bär-närd′), **Christiaan Neethling** 1923–2001. South African surgeon.

barn owl ►*n.* An owl with a white, heart-shaped face, often nesting in barns.

barn·storm (bärn′stôrm′) ►*v.* **1.** To travel about making political speeches, giving lectures, or presenting plays. **2.** To tour in order to exhibit a special skill, such as stunt flying. —**barn′storm′er** *n.*

Bar·num (bär′nəm), **P(hineas) T(aylor)** 1810–91. Amer. circus impresario.

barn·yard (bärn′yärd′) ►*n.* The area surrounding a barn, often enclosed by a fence. ►*adj.* Coarse or indecent: *barnyard jokes.*

bar·o·graph (băr′ə-grăf′) ►*n.* A recording barometer. [< Gk. *baros,* weight.] —**bar′o·graph′ic** *adj.*

ba·rom·e·ter (bə-rŏm′ĭ-tər) ►*n.* **1.** An instrument for measuring atmospheric pressure, used esp. in weather forecasting. **2.** An indicator of change. [< Gk. *baros,* weight.] —**bar′o·met′ric** (băr′ə-mĕt′rĭk), **bar′o·met′ri·cal** *adj.* —**ba·rom′e·try** *n.*

bar·on (băr′ən) ►*n.* **1a.** A British or Japanese nobleman of the lowest rank. **b.** A nobleman of continental Europe, ranked variously in different countries. **2.** One having great power in a specified field. [< OFr.] —**bar′on·age** *n.* —**ba·ro′ni·al** (bə-rō′nē-əl) *adj.* —**bar′o·ny** *n.*

bar·on·ess (băr′ə-nĭs) ►*n.* **1.** The wife or widow of a baron. **2.** A woman holding a baronial title.

bar·on·et (băr′ə-nĭt, băr′ə-nĕt′) ►*n.* A man holding a British hereditary title reserved for commoners. —**bar′on·et·cy** *n.*

bar·on·et·ess (băr′ə-nĭ-tĭs, băr′ə-nĕt′ĭs) ►*n.* A woman holding a British hereditary title reserved for commoners.

ba·roque (bə-rōk′) ►*adj.* **1.** also **Baroque a.** Of an artistic style current in Europe from the early 1600s to mid-1700s, marked by bold forms, dramatic effect, and elaborate ornamentation. **b.** Of a musical style current in Europe from about 1600 to 1750, marked by expressive dissonance and elaborate ornamentation. **2a.** Highly intricate or ornate. **b.** Grotesque; bizarre. **3.** Irregular in shape: *baroque pearls.* [< Ital. *barocco.*] —**ba·roque′ly** *adv.* —**ba·roque′** *n.*

barque (bärk) ►*n.* Var. of **bark³.**

Bar·qui·si·me·to (bär′kē-sē-mĕ′tō) A city of NW Venezuela WSW of Caracas.

bar·rack (băr′ək) ►*v.* To house (e.g., soldiers) in quarters. ►*n.* often **bar·racks** (băr′əks) A building or group of buildings used to house soldiers. [< Sp. *barracas,* soldiers' tents.]

bar·ra·cu·da (băr′ə-kōō′də) ►*n., pl.* **-da** or **-das** A narrow-bodied, chiefly tropical marine fish with very sharp fanglike teeth. [< Sp. *barraco,* bucktooth.]

bar·rage (bə-räzh′) ►*n.* **1.** A concentrated discharge or bombardment of artillery, missiles, or firearms. **2.** An overwhelming, concentrated outpouring, as of words or requests: *a barrage of criticism.* ►*v.* **-raged, -rag·ing** To direct a barrage at. [Fr. *(tir de) barrage,* barrier (fire).]
     Syns: bombard, pelt, pepper **v.**

Bar·ran·quil·la (bä′rän-kē′yä) A city of N Colombia on the Magdalena R. near the Caribbean Sea.

bar·ra·try (băr′ə-trē) ►*n., pl.* **-tries 1.** The act or practice of bringing groundless lawsuits. **2.** An unlawful breach of duty on the part of a

ship's master or crew resulting in injury to the ship's owner. **3.** Sale or purchase of positions in church or state. [< OFr. *barater,* to cheat.]

barre also **bar** (bär) ►*n.* **1.** In ballet, a horizontal rail that is used as a support in exercises. **2.** *Mus.* A technique in which a finger is laid across a fingerboard to stop several strings at once. [Fr.]

bar·rel (băr′əl) ►*n.* **1.** A large cask usu. made of curved wooden staves bound with hoops and having a flat top and bottom. **2.** See table at **measurement. 3a.** The long tube of a firearm. **b.** A cylindrical machine part. **4.** *Informal* A large quantity: *a barrel of fun.* ►*v.* **-reled, -reling** or **-relled, -rel·ling 1.** To put or pack in a barrel. **2.** To move at a high speed. —*idiom:* **over a barrel** In a difficult or frustrating position. [< OFr. *baril.*]

barrel organ ►*n.* A mechanical musical instrument on which a tune is played by a revolving cylinder turned by a hand crank.

barrel roll ►*n.* A flight maneuver in which an aircraft makes a complete rotation on its longitudinal axis.

bar·ren (băr′ən) ►*adj.* **1a.** Not producing or incapable of producing offspring. Used of female animals. **b.** *Often Offensive* Not producing or incapable of producing offspring. Used of women. **2.** Not producing or incapable of producing fruit: *barren trees.* **3.** Lacking vegetation: *barren tundra.* **4.** Unproductive of results. See Synonyms at **futile. 5.** Devoid; lacking: *writing barren of insight.* ►*n.* often **barrens** A tract of unproductive land. [< OFr. *brahaigne.*] —**bar′ren·ness** *n.*

bar·rette (bə-rĕt′) ►*n.* A hair clasp. [Fr.]

bar·ri·cade (băr′ĭ-kād′, băr′ĭ-kād′) ►*n.* A makeshift barrier set up across a route of access. ►*v.* **-cad·ed, -cad·ing** To block or confine with a barricade. [< OProv. *barrica,* barrel.]

bar·ri·er (băr′ē-ər) ►*n.* **1.** A structure, such as a fence, built to bar passage. **2.** Something immaterial that impedes. **3.** A boundary or limit. [< VLat. **barra,* bar.]

barrier island ►*n.* A long narrow island running parallel to the mainland.

barrier reef ►*n.* A long narrow ridge of coral or rock parallel to a coastline and separated from it by a lagoon.

bar·ring (bär′ĭng) ►*prep.* Apart from the occurrence of; excepting.

bar·ri·o (bä′rē-ō′) ►*n., pl.* **-os 1.** A chiefly Spanish-speaking neighborhood in a US city. **2.** An urban district in a Spanish-speaking country. [< Ar. *barr,* open area.]

bar·ris·ter (băr′ĭ-stər) ►*n. Chiefly Brit.* A lawyer who is authorized to argue cases at any court in a jurisdiction. [Prob. < BAR.]

bar·room (bär′rōōm′, -rŏŏm′) ►*n.* A place where alcoholic beverages are sold at a bar.

bar·row¹ (băr′ō) ►*n.* **1.** A flat rectangular tray or cart with handles at each end. **2.** A wheelbarrow. [< OE *bearwe.*]

bar·row² (băr′ō) ►*n.* A large mound of earth or stones placed over a burial site. [< OE *beorg.*]

Barrow, Point The northernmost point of AK, on the Arctic Ocean.

Bar·ry·more (băr′ĭ-môr′) Family of Amer. actors, including **Lionel** (1878–1954), **Ethel** (1879–1959), and **John** (1882–1942).

bar·tend·er (bär′tĕn′dər) ►*n.* A person who

serves alcoholic drinks at a bar.

bar·ter (bär′tər) ►*v.* To trade (goods or services) without using money. [Prob. < OFr. *barater.*] —**bar′ter** *n.* —**bar′ter·er** *n.*

Bar·thol·di (bär-thŏl′dē, -tôl-dē′), **Frédéric Auguste** 1834–1904. French sculptor of the Statue of Liberty.

Bar·thol·o·mew (bär-thŏl′ə-myōo′), Saint. fl. 1st cent. AD. One of the 12 Apostles.

Bart·lett (bärt′lĭt), **John** 1820–1905. Amer. publisher and editor.

Bar·tók (bär′tŏk′, -tôk′), **Béla** 1881–1945. Hungarian pianist and composer.

Bar·ton (bär′tn), **Clara** 1821–1912. Amer. founder of the American Red Cross (1881).

Bar·uch (bâr′ək, bə-rōok′) ►*n.* See table at **Bible.**

bar·y·on (băr′ē-ŏn′) ►*n.* Any of a class of subatomic particles that are both hadrons and fermions, are composed of three quarks, participate in strong interactions, and are generally more massive than mesons and leptons. [Gk. *barus,* heavy + -ON[1].]

Ba·rysh·ni·kov (bə-rĭsh′nĭ-kôf′), **Mikhail Nikolayevich** b. 1948. Soviet-born Amer. ballet dancer and choreographer.

bas·al (bā′səl, -zəl) ►*adj.* **1.** Of, located at, or forming a base. **2.** Of primary importance; basic. —**bas′al·ly** *adv.*

basal metabolism ►*n.* The minimum amount of energy required to maintain vital functions in an organism at complete rest.

ba·salt (bə-sôlt′, bā′sôlt′) ►*n.* A hard, dense, dark igneous rock. [< Gk. *basanitēs,* touchstone.] —**ba·sal′tic** *adj.*

base¹ (bās) ►*n.* **1.** The lowest or bottom part: *the base of a lamp.* **2.** A foundation. **3.** The fundamental principle of a system or theory; basis. **4.** A chief constituent: *a paint with an oil base.* **5a.** *Games* A starting point, safety area, or goal. **b.** *Baseball* Any one of the four corners of an infield marked by a bag or plate. **6a.** A center of organization, supply, or activity; headquarters. **b.** The portion of a social organization, esp. a political party, consisting of its most dedicated members. **7a.** A fortified center of operations. **b.** A supply center for a large force of military personnel. **8.** A facial cosmetic used to even out the complexion or provide a surface for other makeup. **9.** *Math.* **a.** The number that is raised to various powers to generate the principal counting units of a number system. The base of the decimal system, for example, is 10. **b.** The side or face of a geometric figure to which an altitude is or is thought to be drawn. **10.** *Chem.* **a.** Any of a large class of compounds, including the hydroxides and oxides of metals, that have a bitter taste, turn litmus blue, and react with acids to form salts. **b.** A substance that can act as a proton acceptor. **11.** One of the nitrogen-containing purines (adenine and guanine) or pyrimidines (cytosine, thymine, and uracil) that attaches to the sugar component of DNA or RNA. ►*adj.* Forming, serving as, or being a base. ►*v.* **based, bas·ing** **1.** To form or assign a base for: *based the company in Portland.* **2.** To find a basis for; establish. —*idiom:* **off base** Badly mistaken. [< Gk. *basis.*]

base² (bās) ►*adj.* **bas·er, bas·est** **1.** Mean-spirited; contemptible. **2.** Of, containing, or being a metal that is of little value: *base coins.* **3.** *Archaic* Of low birth, rank, or position. [< Med.Lat. *bassus,* low.] —**base′ly** *adv.* —**base′ness** *n.*

base·ball (bās′bôl′) ►*n.* **1.** A game that is played with a bat and ball by two teams of nine players, each team playing alternately in the field and at bat, the players at bat having to run a course of four bases laid out in a diamond pattern in order to score. **2.** The hard ball used in this game.

base·board (bās′bôrd′) ►*n.* A molding concealing the joint between a wall and the floor.

base·born (bās′bôrn′) ►*adj.* **1.** Ignoble; contemptible. **2a.** *Offensive* Born to parents who have never been married to each other. **b.** Of humble birth.

base hit ►*n.* *Baseball* A hit by which the batter reaches base safely.

Ba·sel (bä′zəl) A city of N Switzerland on the Rhine R.

base·less (bās′lĭs) ►*adj.* Having no basis or foundation in fact; unfounded. *Syns: groundless, idle, unfounded, unwarranted adj.*

base·line or **base line** (bās′līn′) ►*n.* **1a.** A line serving as a basis, as for measurement or comparison. **b.** Something used as a basis for comparison: *took x-rays as a baseline for observing later arthritis.* **2.** *Baseball* An area within which a base runner must stay when running between bases. **3.** *Sports* The boundary line at either end of a court, as in basketball or tennis.

base·man (bās′mən) ►*n.* *Baseball* A player assigned to first, second, or third base.

base·ment (bās′mənt) ►*n.* **1.** The substructure or foundation of a building. **2.** The lowest story of a building, usu. below ground. **3.** *Slang* The lowest level, as in competitive standings.

ba·sen·ji (bə-sĕn′jē) ►*n.* A dog lacking a bark and having a reddish-brown coat. [Of Bantu orig.]

base on balls ►*n.* *Baseball* An advance of a batter to first base after taking four pitches that are balls.

ba·ses (bā′sēz′) ►*n.* Pl. of **basis.**

bash (băsh) ►*v.* **1.** To strike with a heavy crushing blow. **2.** *Informal* To criticize (another) harshly. ►*n.* **1.** *Informal* A heavy crushing blow. **2.** *Slang* A party. [?] —**bash′er** *n.*

bash·ful (băsh′fəl) ►*adj.* Shy and self-conscious. [< ME *basshen,* be discomfited.] —**bash′ful·ly** *adv.* —**bash′ful·ness** *n.*

ba·sic (bā′sĭk) ►*adj.* **1.** Of or forming a base; fundamental. **2.** Serving as a starting point: *a basic course.* **3.** *Chem.* **a.** Of, producing, or resulting from a base. **b.** Containing a base, esp. in excess of acid. **c.** Alkaline. ►*n.* A fundamental element or entity: *math basics.* —**ba′si·cal·ly** *adv.* —**ba·sic′i·ty** (-sĭs′ĭ-tē) *n.*

BA·SIC or **Ba·sic** (bā′sĭk) ►*n.* A simple programming language. [B(eginner's) A(ll-purpose) S(ymbolic) I(nstruction) C(ode).]

bas·il (băz′əl, băz′əl) ►*n.* An aromatic annual herb with leaves used as a seasoning. [< Gk. *basilikos,* royal.]

ba·sil·i·ca (bə-sĭl′ĭ-kə) ►*n.* **1a.** A public building of ancient Rome, used as a courtroom or assembly hall. **b.** A Christian church building having a nave with a semicircular apse. **2.** *Rom. Cath. Ch.* A church accorded certain privileges by the pope. [< Gk. *basilikē (stoa),* royal (portico).]

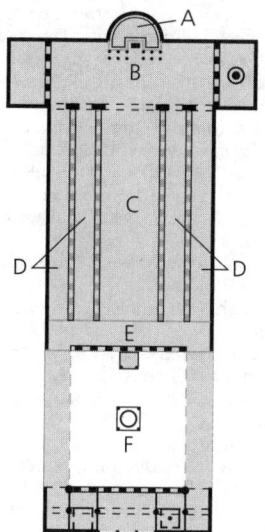

basilica
plan of the 4th-century AD St. Peter's Basilica,
Rome, Italy
A. apse
B. transept
C. nave
D. aisles
E. narthex
F. atrium

bas·i·lisk (băs′ə-lĭsk′, băz′-) ►*n.* **1.** A legendary serpent with lethal breath and glance. **2.** Any of various crested tropical American lizards that can run on their hind legs. [< Gk. *basiliskos.*]

ba·sin (bā′sĭn) ►*n.* **1.** An open, shallow, usu. round container used esp. for holding liquids. **2.** A washbowl; sink. **3a.** An artificially enclosed area of a river or harbor. **b.** A small enclosed or partly enclosed body of water. **4.** A region drained by a single river system: *the Amazon River basin.* **5.** A bowl-shaped depression in the surface of the land or ocean floor. [< OFr. *bacin.*] —**ba′sin·al** *adj.*

ba·sis (bā′sĭs) ►*n., pl.* **-ses** (-sēz′) **1.** A foundation upon which something rests. **2.** The fundamental or chief constituent. **3.** A fundamental principle. **4.** An underlying circumstance or condition: *workers paid on a daily basis.* [< Gk.]

bask (băsk) ►*v.* **1.** To expose oneself to pleasant warmth. **2.** To take great satisfaction: *basked in the teacher's praise.* [ME *basken.*]

bas·ket (băs′kĭt) ►*n.* **1.** A container made of woven material. **2.** A usu. open gondola or a hot-air balloon. **3.** *Basketball* A metal hoop from which an open-bottomed net is suspended, serving as a goal. [< VLat. **baskauta.*]

bas·ket·ball (băs′kĭt-bôl′) ►*n.* **1.** A game played between two teams of five players each, the object being to throw an inflated ball through an elevated basket on the opponent's side of the rectangular court. **2.** The ball for this game.

bas·ket·ry (băs′kĭ-trē) ►*n.* **1.** The craft of making baskets. **2.** Baskets collectively.

bas mitz·vah (bäs mĭts′və) ►*n.* Var. of **bat mitzvah.**

Basque (băsk) ►*n.* **1.** A member of a people of

unknown origin inhabiting the W Pyrenees and the Bay of Biscay in France and Spain. **2.** The language of the Basques, of no known linguistic affiliation. —**Basque** *adj.*

Bas·ra (bäs′rə, bŭs′-) A city of SE Iraq on the Shatt al Arab.

bas-re·lief (bä′rĭ-lēf′) ►*n.* See **low relief.** [< Ital. *bassorilievo.*]

bass¹ (băs) ►*n., pl.* **bass** or **-es** Any of various North American freshwater fishes. [< OE *bærs.*]

bass² (bās) ►*n.* **1.** A low-pitched tone. **2.** The tones in the lowest register of an instrument. **3a.** The lowest singing voice of a man. **b.** A singer or voice having this range. **c.** An instrument, esp. a double bass or bass guitar, having this range. [ME *bas,* lowest musical part < Med. Lat. *bassus,* low.] —**bass** *adj.*

bass clef (bās) ►*n. Mus.* A symbol indicating that the fourth line from the bottom of a staff represents the pitch of F below middle C.

Basse·terre (băs-târ′, bäs-) The capital of St. Kitts and Nevis, in the Leeward Is. of the West Indies.

Basse-Terre (băs-târ′, bäs-) The capital of the French overseas department of Guadeloupe, on **Basse-Terre Island** in the Leeward Is. of the West Indies.

basset hound (băs′ĭt) ►*n.* A short-haired dog with a long body, short legs, and drooping ears. [Fr. *basset,* very short.]

bas·si·net (băs′ə-nĕt′) ►*n.* An oblong basketlike bed for an infant. [Fr., small basin.]

bass·ist (bā′sĭst) ►*n.* One who plays a bass instrument, esp. a double bass or bass guitar.

bas·so (băs′ō, bä′sō) ►*n., pl.* **-sos** or **-si** (-sē) A bass singer, esp. an operatic bass. [Ital. < Med. Lat. *bassus,* low.]

bas·soon (bə-sōōn′, bă-) ►*n.* A low-pitched double-reed woodwind instrument having a long wooden body. [< Ital. *basso,* bass.] —**bas·soon′ist** *n.*

Bass Strait (băs) A channel between Tasmania and SE Australia connecting the Indian Ocean with the Tasman Sea.

bass viol (bās) ►*n.* See **double bass.**

bass·wood (băs′wŏŏd′) ►*n.* **1.** See **linden. 2.** The soft wood of a linden. [< BAST.]

bast (băst) ►*n.* Fibrous plant material used to make cordage and textiles. [< OE *bæst.*]

bas·tard (băs′tərd) ►*n.* **1.** *Offensive* A person born to parents who have never been married to each other. **2.** *Slang* A mean or disagreeable person. ►*adj.* **1.** *Offensive* Born to parents who have never been married to each other. **2.** Not genuine; spurious. [< OFr.] —**bas′tard·ly** *adj.* —**bas′tard·y** *n.*

bas·tard·ize (băs′tər-dīz′) ►*v.* **-ized, -iz·ing** To lower in quality or character; debase. —**bas′tard·i·za′tion** *n.*

baste¹ (bāst) ►*v.* **bast·ed, bast·ing** To sew temporarily with large running stitches. [< OFr. *bastir.*]

baste² (bāst) ►*v.* **bast·ed, bast·ing** To moisten (e.g., meat) periodically with a liquid while cooking. [ME *basten.*] —**bast′er** *n.*

baste³ (bāst) ►*v.* **bast·ed, bast·ing 1.** To beat vigorously; thrash. **2.** To scold; berate. [Prob. of Scand. orig.]

Bas·tille Day (bă-stēl′) ►*n.* July 14, observed in France to commemorate the storming of the

Bastille prison by the citizens of Paris in 1789.

bas·tion (băs′chən, -tē-ən) ►*n.* **1.** A projecting part of a fortification. **2.** A bulwark; stronghold. [< OFr. *bastille*, fortress.]

bat¹ (băt) ►*n.* **1.** A stout wooden stick; cudgel. **2.** A blow, as with a stick. **3.** *Sports* **a.** A rounded, tapered, usu. wooden club used to hit the ball in baseball. **b.** A flat-sided club used in cricket. **c.** A racket, as in table tennis. ►*v.* **bat·ted, bat·ting 1.** To hit with or as if with a bat. **2.** *Sports* **a.** To be the batter or batsman in baseball or cricket. **b.** To have (a certain batting average). **3.** *Informal* To discuss: *bat an idea around.* —*idioms:* **at bat** Taking one's turn at hitting a pitched or bowled ball in baseball or cricket. **go to bat for** To support or defend. **right off the bat** Immediately. [ME.]

bat² (băt) ►*n.* Any of various nocturnal flying mammals having membranous wings. [Of Scand. orig.]

bat³ (băt) ►*v.* **bat·ted, bat·ting** To flutter (e.g., one's eyelashes). [Prob. < *bate*, flap one's wings.]

bat⁴ (băt) ►*n.* *Slang* A binge; spree. [Prob. < *batter*, spree.]

Ba·taan (bə-tăn′, -tän′) A peninsula of W Luzon, Philippines, between Manila Bay and the South China Sea.

batch (băch) ►*n.* **1.** An amount produced at one time. **2.** A group of persons or things. **3.** *Comp.* A set of data to be processed in a single program run. [< OE *bacan*, bake.] —**batch** *v.*

bate (băt) ►*v.* **bat·ed, bat·ing** To lessen the force of; moderate. [< ME *abaten*, abate.]

ba·teau (bă-tō′) ►*n.,* pl. **-teaux** (tōz′) A flat-bottomed boat. [< OFr. *batel*, boat < OE *bāt*.]

Bates (bāts), **Katharine Lee** 1859–1929. Amer. educator and writer.

bath (băth) ►*n.,* pl. **baths** (băthz, băths) **1a.** The act of soaking or cleansing the body, as in water or steam. **b.** The water used for bathing. **2a.** A bathtub. **b.** A bathroom. **3.** A building equipped for bathing. **4.** often **baths** A spa. **5.** A liquid in which something is dipped or soaked in processing. [< OE *bæth*.]

bathe (bāth) ►*v.* **bathed, bath·ing 1a.** To take a bath. **b.** To give a bath. **2.** To go swimming. **3.** To immerse in liquid; wet. **4.** To suffuse, as with light. [< OE *bathian*.] —**bath′er** *n.*

bath·house (băth′hous′) ►*n.* **1.** A building with facilities for bathing. **2.** A building with dressing rooms for swimmers.

bath·ing suit (bā′thĭng) ►*n.* A swimsuit.

ba·thos (bā′thŏs′, -thôs′) ►*n.* **1.** An unintended, ludicrously abrupt transition in style from the exalted to the commonplace. **2.** Grossly sentimental pathos. [Gk., depth.] —**ba·thet′ic** (bə-thĕt′ĭk) *adj.*

bath·robe (băth′rōb′) ►*n.* A robe worn before and after bathing and for lounging.

bath·room (băth′rōōm′, -rōōm′) ►*n.* A room with a sink and toilet and usu. a bathtub or shower.

bath salts ►*pl.n.* Perfumed crystals for softening the water in a bathtub.

Bath·she·ba (băth-shē′bə, băth′shə-) In the Bible, the wife of David and mother of Solomon.

bath·tub (băth′tŭb′) ►*n.* A tub for bathing, esp. one located in a bathroom.

bath·y·scaphe (băth′ĭ-skăf′, -skāf′) also **bath·**

y·scaph (-skăf′) ►*n.* A free-diving deep-sea research vessel with a crewed observation capsule. [< Gk. *bathus*, deep + *skaphos*, hull.]

bath·y·sphere (băth′ĭ-sfîr′) ►*n.* A crewed spherical deep-diving chamber lowered by cable, used to study the oceans and deep-sea life. [Gk. *bathus*, deep + SPHERE.]

ba·tik (bə-tēk′, băt′ĭk) ►*n.* **1.** A method of dyeing fabric by placing removable wax on areas not intended to be dyed. **2.** Fabric so dyed. [Malay *batek*.]

ba·tiste (bə-tēst′, bă-) ►*n.* A fine, plain-woven fabric. [< OFr.]

bat mitz·vah (bät mĭts′və) or **bas mitz·vah** (bäs) ►*n.* **1.** A Jewish girl of 12 or 13 years of age, considered an adult and responsible for observing religious law. **2.** The ceremony that confirms a girl as a bat mitzvah. [Heb. *bat miṣwâ.*]

ba·ton (bə-tŏn′, băt′n) ►*n.* **1.** *Mus.* A slender rod used by a conductor to direct a musical group. **2.** A hollow metal rod with heavy rubber tips twirled by a drum major or majorette. **3.** The hollow cylinder passed to each member of a relay team. [< VLat. *bastō,* stick.]

Bat·on Rouge (băt′n rōōzh′) The capital of LA, in the SE-central part.

bats·man (băts′mən) ►*n.* The player at bat in cricket and baseball.

bat·tal·ion (bə-tăl′yən) ►*n.* **1.** An army unit typically consisting of a headquarters and two or more companies or batteries. **2.** A large body of organized troops. [< VLat. *battalia,* battle.]

bat·ten (băt′n) ►*n.* A flexible wooden strip used esp. in flattening a sail or securing a hatch. ►*v.* To furnish or secure with battens. —*idiom:* **batten down the hatches** To prepare for an imminent disaster or emergency. [< OFr. *bataunt,* clapper.]

bat·ter¹ (băt′ər) ►*v.* **1.** To hit repeatedly with heavy blows. See Synonyms at **beat**. **2.** To damage. **3.** To inflict continuing physical injuries on, as within a family or romantic relationship. **4.** To verbally attack or harass. [< Lat. *battuere.*]

bat·ter² (băt′ər) ►*n.* The player at bat in baseball and cricket.

bat·ter³ (băt′ər) ►*n.* A mixture, as of flour, milk, and eggs, used in cooking. [ME *bater.*]

bat·ter·ing ram (băt′ər-ĭng) ►*n.* **1.** A heavy beam used in ancient warfare to batter down walls and gates. **2.** A heavy metal bar used esp. by authorities to break down walls and doors.

bat·ter·y (băt′ə-rē) ►*n.,* pl. **-ies 1.** *Elect.* A device containing an electric cell or series of electric cells storing chemical energy that can be converted into electrical power, usu. by direct current. **2a.** The act of battering. **b.** The unlawful beating of a person. **3a.** An emplacement for artillery. **b.** A set of heavy guns, as on a warship. **4a.** An array: *a battery of tests.* **b.** An impressive body or group. **5.** The percussion section of an orchestra. [< OFr. *batre,* to batter.]

bat·ting (băt′ĭng) ►*n.* Fiber wadded into rolls or sheets, as for lining quilts.

batting average ►*n.* *Baseball* The ratio of a batter's hits to the number of times at bat, excluding walks, sacrifices, times hit by a pitch, or times interfered with by the catcher.

bat·tle (băt′l) ►*n.* **1a.** An encounter between opposing forces. **b.** Armed fighting; combat.

2a. A protracted struggle. **b.** An intense competition. ►*v.* **-tled, -tling 1.** To engage in or as if in battle. **2.** To fight against. [< LLat. *battuālia,* fighting and fencing exercises.] —**bat′tler** *n.*

bat·tle-ax or **bat·tle-axe** (băt′l-ăks′) ►*n.* A broad heavy ax formerly used as a weapon.

battle cry ►*n.* **1.** A rallying cry uttered in combat. **2.** A militant slogan.

bat·tle·field (băt′l-fēld′) ►*n.* **1.** An area where a battle is fought. **2.** A sphere of conflict.

bat·tle·front (băt′l-frŭnt′) ►*n.* The area where opponents meet in battle.

bat·tle·ground (băt′l-ground′) ►*n.* A battlefield.

bat·tle·ment (băt′l-mənt) ►*n.* A parapet built on top of a wall, with notched indentations for defense. [< OFr. *batillement,* turret.]

battle royal ►*n., pl.* **battles royal 1.** An all-out fight. **2.** A battle with many combatants.

bat·tle·ship (băt′l-shĭp′) ►*n.* Any of the largest, most heavily armed and armored class of warships.

bat·ty (băt′ē) ►*adj.* **-ti·er, -ti·est** *Slang* Crazy.

bau·ble (bô′bəl) ►*n.* A trinket. [< OFr. *babel,* plaything.]

baud (bôd) ►*n. Comp.* A unit of data transfer speed equal to one change in a carrier signal per second. [After Jean Maurice Emile *Baudot* (1845–1903).]

Baude·laire (bōd-lâr′), **Charles Pierre** 1821–67. French writer, translator, and critic.

baux·ite (bôk′sīt′) ►*n.* The principal ore of aluminum, composed mainly of hydrous aluminum oxides and aluminum hydroxides. [After Les *Baux,* French commune.]

Ba·var·i·a (bə-vâr′ē-ə) A region of S Germany. —**Ba·var′i·an** *adj. & n.*

bawd·y (bô′dē) ►*adj.* **-i·er, -i·est** Humorously coarse, lewd, or risqué. —**bawd′i·ly** *adv.* —**bawd′i·ness** *n.*

bawl (bôl) ►*v.* **1.** To sob loudly; wail. **2.** To cry out loudly; bellow. See Synonyms at **yell.** —*phrasal verb:* **bawl out** *Informal* To scold loudly or harshly. [Of Scand. orig.]

bay¹ (bā) ►*n.* A body of water partially enclosed by land but with a wide outlet to the sea. [< OFr. *baie.*]

bay² (bā) ►*n.* **1.** A part of a building marked off by vertical elements, such as columns. **2a.** A bay window. **b.** An opening or recess in a wall. **3.** A section or compartment set off for a specific purpose: *a cargo bay.* [< OFr. *baee,* an opening.]

bay³ (bā) ►*adj.* Reddish-brown. ►*n.* **1.** A reddish brown. **2.** A reddish-brown animal, esp. a horse. [< Lat. *badius.*]

bay⁴ (bā) ►*n.* A deep prolonged bark, as of a hound. —*idioms:* **at bay** Held at a safe distance: *kept trouble at bay.* **to bay** Cornered by and facing pursuers: *bring quarry to bay.* [< OFr. *abaiier,* to bark.] —**bay** *v.*

bay⁵ (bā) ►*n.* **1.** See **laurel** (sense 1). **2.** A tree or shrub with aromatic foliage similar to the laurel. [< Lat. *bāca,* berry.]

bay·ber·ry (bā′bĕr′ē) ►*n.* **1.** A shrub with aromatic foliage and bearing small, round, waxy fruits **2.** The fruit of this shrub.

bay leaf ►*n.* The dried aromatic leaf of the laurel or bay, used as a seasoning.

bay·o·net (bā′ə-nĕt′, bā′ə-nĭt, -nĕt′) ►*n.* A blade adapted to fit the muzzle of a rifle. ►*v.*

-net·ed, -net·ing or **-net·ted, -net·ting** To stab with a bayonet. [After *Bayonne,* France.]

bay·ou (bī′o͞o, bī′ō) ►*n.* **1.** A body of water, such as a creek, that is a tributary of a larger body of water. **2.** A sluggish stream that meanders through marshes or plantation fields. [Poss. < Choctaw *bayuk.*]

bay window ►*n.* A large window or series of windows projecting from a building and forming an alcove within.

ba·zaar also **ba·zar** (bə-zär′) ►*n.* **1.** A market, esp. in the Middle East. **2.** A fair or sale esp. for charity. [< Pers. *bāzār.*]

ba·zoo·ka (bə-zo͞o′kə) ►*n.* A shoulder-held, tube-shaped weapon for firing armor-piercing rockets at short range. [< *bazooka,* a crude wind instrument.]

BB¹ (bē′bē) ►*n.* A small size of lead pellet used in air rifles.

BB² ►*abbr.* base on balls

bbl. ►*abbr.* barrel

BBS ►*abbr. Comp.* bulletin board system

BC ►*abbr.* **1.** also **BC** before Christ **2.** British Columbia

BCE or **BCE** ►*abbr.* before the Common Era

B cell ►*n.* A lymphocyte that matures in the bone marrow in mammals and is involved in the formation of antibodies. [*b(ursa-dependent) cell.*]

be (bē) ►*v. 1st and 3rd pers. sing. p. indic.* **was** (wŭz, wŏz; wəz *when unstressed*), *2nd pers. sing. and pl. and 1st and 3rd pers. pl. p. indic.* **were** (wûr), *p. subjunctive* **were**, *p.part.* **been** (bĭn), *pr.part.* **be·ing** (bē′ĭng), *1st pers. sing. pr. indic.* **am** (ăm), *2nd pers. sing. and pl. and 1st and 3rd pers. pl. pr. indic.* **are** (är), *3rd pers. sing. pr. indic.* **is** (ĭz), *pr. subjunctive* **be 1.** To exist; have life or reality: *I think, therefore I am.* **2a.** To occupy a specified position: *The food is on the table.* **b.** To remain undisturbed or untouched: *Let the dog be.* **3.** To take place; occur: *The test was yesterday.* **4.** To go or come: *Have you ever been to Japan?* **5.** Used as a copula linking a subject and a predicate nominative, adjective, or pronoun, as: **a.** To equal in identity: *Firefighters are brave workers.* **b.** To signify; symbolize: *A is excellent, C is passing.* **c.** To belong to a specified class or group: *The human being is a primate.* **d.** To have or show a specified quality or characteristic: *She is smart.* **6.** To belong; befall: *Woe is me.* **7.** *Informal* Used in combination with *all* or *like* to introduce quotations. —*aux.* **1.** Used with the past participle of a transitive verb to form the passive voice: *The show is held annually.* **2.** Used with the present participle of a verb to express a continuing action: *We are working to improve morale.* **3.** Used with the infinitive of a verb to express intention, obligation, or future action: *She was to call today.* **4.** Used with the past participle of certain intransitive verbs to form the perfect tense: *Those days are gone.* [< OE *bēon.*]

be– ►*pref.* **1.** To make; cause to become: *benumb.* **2a.** To cover with: *befog.* **b.** On; over: *bedaub.* **3.** Used as an intensive: *belabor.* **4.** About: *bewail.* **5.** To remove: *behead.* [< OE.]

beach (bēch) ►*n.* The shore of a body of water, esp. when sandy or pebbly. ►*v.* To haul or run ashore. [Perh. < OE *bece,* stream.]

Beach, Amy Marcy Cheney 1867–1944. Amer. pianist and composer.

beach buggy ►*n.* See **dune buggy.**

beach·comb·er (bēch′kō′mər) ►*n.* **1.** One who scavenges along beaches. **2.** A seaside vacationer.

beach·head (bēch′hĕd′) ►*n.* **1.** A position on an enemy shoreline captured by troops in advance of an invading force. **2.** A first achievement that opens the way; foothold.

bea·con (bē′kən) ►*n.* **1.** A lighthouse. **2.** A radio transmitter that emits a guidance signal for aircraft. **3.** A source of guidance. **4.** A signal fire. [< OE *bēacen.*]

bead (bēd) ►*n.* **1a.** A small piece of material pierced for stringing. **b. beads** A necklace made of beads. **c. beads** A rosary. **2.** A small round object, as: **a.** A drop of moisture: *beads of sweat.* **b.** A knoblike forward sight on a firearm. ►*v.* To decorate with or collect into beads. —*idiom:* **draw (or get) a bead on** To take careful aim at. [< OE *gebed,* prayer.]

bea·dle (bēd′l) ►*n.* A former minor parish official in an English church. [< OE *bydel.*]

bead·y (bē′dē) ►*adj.* **-i·er, -i·est 1.** Small, round, and shiny: *beady eyes.* **2.** Decorated with beads.

bea·gle (bē′gəl) ►*n.* A small hound with drooping ears and a smooth white, black, and tan coat. [ME *begle.*]

beak (bēk) ►*n.* **1.** The horny projecting mandibles of a bird; bill. **2.** A similar structure, as the spout on a pitcher. **3.** *Informal* The human nose. [< Lat. *beccus,* of Celt. orig.]

beak
from top to bottom: black skimmer, pileated woodpecker, and American goldfinch

beak·er (bē′kər) ►*n.* **1.** A wide glass cylinder with a pouring lip, used as a laboratory container. **2.** A large, wide-mouthed drinking cup. [< Med.Lat. *bicārius.*]

beam (bēm) ►*n.* **1.** A horizontal bar or support, esp. one used in construction. **2a.** The maximum breadth of a ship. **b.** The side of a ship. **3a.** A ray of light. **b.** A concentrated stream of particles or waves: *a beam of protons.* ►*v.* **1.** To radiate; shine. **2.** To emit or transmit (e.g., a signal). **3.** To smile expansively. [< OE *bēam.*]

bean (bēn) ►*n.* **1a.** Any of various twining plants with edible pods and seeds. **b.** A seed or pod of a bean plant. **2.** Any of various plants related to or suggestive of beans, including the soybean and coffee bean. **3.** *Slang* A person's head. **4. beans** *Slang* A small amount: *I don't know beans about investing.* ►*v. Slang* To hit

on the head. —*idiom:* **spill the beans** To disclose a secret. [< OE *bēan.*]

bean·bag (bēn′băg′) ►*n.* **1.** A small bag filled with dried beans and thrown in games. **2.** An article, such as a chair, that is constructed as a bag filled with small pellets.

bean ball ►*n. Baseball* A pitch aimed at the batter's head.

bean curd ►*n.* Tofu.

bean·ie (bē′nē) ►*n.* A small brimless cap.

bean·o (bē′nō) ►*n., pl.* **-os** A form of bingo, esp. one using beans as markers.

bean sprouts ►*pl.n.* The tender, edible seedlings of certain bean plants.

bear¹ (bâr) ►*v.* **bore** (bôr), **borne** (bôrn) or **born** (bôrn), **bear·ing 1a.** To carry (something) on one's person from one place to another. **b.** To move from one place to another while containing or supporting (something); transport: *a train bearing grain.* **2.** To carry or hold in the mind over time; harbor: *bear a grudge.* **3.** To have as a visible characteristic or attribute: *a letter bearing her name.* **4.** To conduct (oneself): *bore herself with dignity.* **5a.** To hold up; support: *This wall bears the weight of the roof.* **b.** To be accountable for; assume: *bearing heavy responsibilities.* **6.** To endure: *couldn't bear the pain.* **7.** To warrant: *bears investigation.* **8.** To have relevance; apply: *We studied how psychology bears on politics.* **9.** *p.part.* **born** To give birth to. **10.** To yield: *bear flowers.* See Synonyms at **produce. 11.** To offer; render: *bear witness.* **12.** To proceed in a specified direction: *bear left.* —*phrasal verbs:* **bear down 1.** To exert muscular pressure downward, as in birthing a baby. **2.** To advance in a threatening manner: *The ship bore down on us.* **3.** To apply maximum effort and concentration. **bear out** To prove right; confirm. —*idioms:* **bear a resemblance** To be, appear, or function like. **bear in mind** To remember: *Bear in mind that it will be cold.* [< OE *beran.*] —**bear′a·ble** *adj.* —**bear′a·bly** *adv.*

bear² (bâr) ►*n.* **1.** Any of various large, usu. omnivorous mammals having a shaggy coat and short tail. **2.** A large, clumsy, or ill-mannered person. **3.** One that sells securities or commodities in expectation of falling prices. **4.** Something that is difficult or unpleasant: *The final exam was a bear.* [< OE *bera.*] —**bear′-ish** *adj.*

beard (bîrd) ►*n.* **1.** A growth of hair on the chin, cheeks, and throat of a person, esp. a man. **2.** A hairy or hairlike growth, as on certain animals and plants. ►*v.* To confront boldly. [< OE.] —**beard′ed** *adj.*

bear·er (bâr′ər) ►*n.* **1.** One that carries or supports. **2.** One that holds a check or note for payment.

bear hug ►*n.* A rough, tight hug.

bear·ing (bâr′ĭng) ►*n.* **1.** Deportment; demeanor. **2.** A device that supports, guides, and reduces the friction of motion between fixed and moving machine parts. **3.** Something that supports weight. **4.** Direction, esp. angular direction measured using geographical or celestial reference lines. **5.** often **bearings** Awareness of one's position relative to one's surroundings. **6.** Relevant relationship: *That has no bearing on our work.* **7.** A heraldic emblem.

béar·naise sauce (bâr-nāz′, bā′är-, -ər-) ►*n.* A

sauce of butter and egg yolks that is flavored with herbs. [Fr. *béarnaise*, of Béarn, former region of France.]

bear·skin (bâr′skĭn′) ►*n.* **1.** Something, such as a rug, made from the skin of a bear. **2.** A tall military hat made of black fur.

beast (bēst) ►*n.* **1.** An animal, esp. a large four-footed mammal. **2.** A brutal person. [< Lat. *bēstia.*]

beast·ly (bēst′lē) ►*adj.* **-li·er, -li·est 1.** Of or like a beast; bestial. **2.** Very disagreeable; nasty: *beastly behavior.* **—beast′li·ness** *n.*

beat (bēt) ►*v.* **beat, beat·en** (bēt′n) or **beat, beat·ing 1a.** To strike repeatedly; pound. **b.** To subject to repeated physical abuse; batter. **2.** To flap, esp. wings. **3.** To sound by striking: *beat a drum.* **4a.** To shape by blows; forge. **b.** To make by trampling: *beat a path.* **5.** To mix rapidly: *beat eggs.* **6.** To pulsate; throb. **7.** To defeat. **8.** To strike against repeatedly and with force; pound: *waves beating against the shore.* **9.** *Informal* To be better than: *Riding beats walking.* **10.** *Slang* To baffle: *It beats me.* **11.** *Informal* **a.** To circumvent: *beat the traffic.* **b.** To arrive or finish before (another). ►*n.* **1.** A stroke or blow. **2.** A pulsation; throb. **3.** A steady succession of units of rhythm. **4.** An area regularly covered, as by a reporter or police officer. ►*adj. Informal* Worn-out; fatigued. **—phrasal verb: beat off** To drive away. **—idioms: beat around (**or **about) the bush** To fail to confront a subject directly. **beat it** *Slang* To leave hurriedly. [< OE *bēatan.*] **—beat′er** *n.*
Syns: batter, hammer, pound, pummel, thrash v.

be·a·tif·ic (bē′ə-tĭf′ĭk) ►*adj.* Showing exalted joy or bliss: *a beatific smile.* [< Lat. *beātus,* blessed.] **—be′a·tif′i·cal·ly** *adv.*

be·at·i·fy (bē-ăt′ə-fī′) ►*v.* **-fied, -fy·ing 1.** *Rom. Cath. Ch.* To proclaim (a deceased person) to be worthy of religious veneration. **2.** To exalt; glorify. **—be·at′i·fi·ca′tion** *n.*

be·at·i·tude (bē-ăt′ĭ-tōōd′, -tyōōd′) ►*n.* Supreme blessedness.

beat·nik (bēt′nĭk) ►*n.* A member of a group or movement esp. of the 1950s and early 1960s stressing nonconformity to social and cultural mores. [*beat (generation),* unconventional group of the 1950s and 1960s + –NIK.]

Be·a·trix (bā′ə-trĭks′, bē′-) b. 1938. Queen of the Netherlands (assumed the throne 1980).

beat-up (bēt′ŭp′) ►*adj. Slang* Damaged or worn through neglect or heavy use.

beau (bō) ►*n., pl.* **beaus** or **beaux** (bōz) **1.** A suitor. **2.** A dandy; fop. [Fr., handsome.]

Beau·fort Sea (bō′fərt) A part of the Arctic Ocean N of NE AK and NW Canada.

beau geste (bō zhĕst′) ►*n., pl.* **beaux gestes** or **beau gestes** (bō zhĕst′) **1.** A gracious gesture. **2.** A gesture noble in form but meaningless in substance. [Fr.]

Beau·har·nais (bō-är-nā′), **Josephine de** 1763–1814. Empress of the French (1804–09) as the wife of Napoleon I.

beau i·de·al (bō′ ī-dē′əl) ►*n., pl.* **beau ideals** An ideal type or model. [Fr. *beau idéal.*]

beau monde (bō mŏnd′, mônd′) ►*n., pl.* **beaux mondes** (bō mônd′) or **beau mondes** (bō mŏndz′) Fashionable society. [Fr.]

beau·te·ous (byōō′tē-əs) ►*adj.* Beautiful. **—beau′te·ous·ly** *adv.*

beau·ti·cian (byōō-tĭsh′ən) ►*n.* One skilled in giving cosmetic treatments.

beau·ti·ful (byōō′tə-fəl) ►*adj.* Having beauty. **—beau′ti·ful·ly** *adv.*

beau·ti·fy (byōō′tə-fī′) ►*v.* **-fied, -fy·ing** To make or become beautiful. **—beau′ti·fi·ca′tion** *n.* **—beau′ti·fi′er** *n.*

beau·ty (byōō′tē) ►*n., pl.* **-ties 1.** A quality that pleases the senses or mind, marked by such properties as harmony of form or artistic excellence. **2.** One that is beautiful. **3.** An outstanding example: *That catch was a beauty.* [< Lat. *bellus,* pretty.]

beauty mark ►*n.* A mole or birthmark.

beauty parlor ►*n.* A beauty salon.

beauty salon ►*n.* An establishment providing personal services such as hair styling.

Beau·voir (bō-vwär′), **Simone de** 1908–86. French writer, existentialist, and feminist.

Simone de Beauvoir

beaux (bōz) ►*n.* Pl. of **beau.**

beaux-arts (bō-zär′, -zärt′) ►*pl.n.* The fine arts. [Fr.]

bea·ver (bē′vər) ►*n.* A large aquatic rodent having thick brown fur, webbed hind feet, a broad flat tail, and sharp incisors used for felling trees and building dams. [< OE *beofor.*]

bea·ver·board (bē′vər-bôrd′) ►*n.* A wallboard of compressed wood pulp.

be·bop (bē′bŏp′) ►*n. Mus.* Bop. [Imitation of a two-beat phrase in this music.]

be·calm (bĭ-käm′) ►*v.* **1.** To render (e.g., a ship) motionless for lack of wind. **2.** To make calm; soothe.

be·cause (bĭ-kôz′, -kŭz′) ►*conj.* For the reason that; since. [ME *bi cause.*]

beck (bĕk) ►*n.* A summons. **—idiom: at (someone's) beck and call** Ready to comply with any wish or command. [ME *bek* < *bekenen,* BECKON.]

Beck·ett (bĕk′ĭt), **Samuel** 1906–89. Irish-born writer.

beck·on (bĕk′ən) ►*v.* **1.** To summon by nodding or waving. **2.** To be inviting or enticing (to); attract. [< OE *bēcnan.*]

be·cloud (bĭ-kloud′) ►*v.* To darken with or as if with clouds; obscure.

be·come (bĭ-kŭm′) ►*v.* **-came** (-kām′), **-come, -com·ing 1.** To grow or come to be. **2.** To be suitable to: *That tie does not become him.* **—phrasal verb: become of** To be the fate of: *What will become of us?* [< OE *becuman.*]

be·com·ing (bĭ-kŭm′ĭng) ►*adj.* **1.** Appropriate or suitable. **2.** Pleasing or attractive: *That skirt is* becoming on you. —**be·com′ing·ly** adv.

bed (běd) ►n. **1.** A place for sleeping, esp. a piece of furniture that frames or supports a mattress. **2.** A small plot of cultivated land: *a flower bed.* **3.** A place where one sleeps; lodging: *found bed and board at an inn.* **4.** The bottom of a body of water, such as a stream. **5.** A supporting or underlying part; foundation. **6.** The part of a truck, trailer, or freight car designed to carry loads. **7.** *Geol.* **a.** A large layer of rock or earth extending horizontally; stratum. **b.** A deposit, as of ore. ►v. **bed·ded, bed·ding 1.** To furnish with a bed or sleeping quarters. **2.** To put, send, or go to bed. **3.** To plant in a prepared plot of soil. **4.** To lay flat or arrange in layers. **5.** To embed. —*idiom:* **get into bed with** *Slang* To become closely involved with another person or group, as in an intrigue: *The corrupt police chief was in bed with the thieves.* [< OE.]

be·daub (bǐ-dôb′) ►v. **1.** To smear; soil. **2.** To ornament in a crass fashion.

be·daz·zle (bǐ-dăz′əl) ►v. **-zled, -zling 1.** To dazzle so completely as to confuse or blind. **2.** To enchant. —**be·daz′zle·ment** n.

bed·bug (běd′bŭg′) ►n. A wingless, bloodsucking insect that infests dwellings and bedding.

bed·clothes (běd′klōz′, -klōthz′) ►pl.n. Coverings ordinarily used on a bed.

bed·ding (běd′ĭng) ►n. **1.** Bedclothes. **2.** Material, esp. straw, on which animals sleep. **3.** A foundation.

Bede (běd) 673?–735. Anglo-Saxon theologian and historian.

be·deck (bǐ-děk′) ►v. To adorn in a showy fashion.

be·dev·il (bǐ-děv′əl) ►v. **-iled, -il·ing** or **-illed, -il·ling 1.** To torment mercilessly. **2.** To worry, annoy, or frustrate. **3.** To bewitch. **4.** To spoil; ruin. —**be·dev′il·ment** n.

be·dew (bǐ-dōō′, -dyōō′) ►v. To wet with dew.

bed·fel·low (běd′fěl′ō) ►n. **1.** One with whom a bed is shared. **2.** One that is closely associated or allied with another.

bed·lam (běd′ləm) ►n. **1.** A place of noisy uproar and confusion. **2.** *Archaic* An insane asylum. [ME *Bedlem*, Hospital of Saint Mary of *Bethlehem*, London.]

Bed·ou·in also **Bed·u·in** (běd′ōō-ĭn, běd′wĭn) ►n., pl. **-in** or **-ins** An Arab of any of the nomadic tribes of the Arabian, Syrian, Nubian, or Sahara Deserts. [< Ar. *badawī*.]

bed·pan (běd′păn′) ►n. A receptacle used as a toilet by a bedridden person.

bed·post (běd′pōst′) ►n. A vertical post at the corner of a bed.

be·drag·gled (bǐ-drăg′əld) ►adj. **1.** Wet, drenched, or messy. **2.** Dilapidated: *a street of bedraggled tenements.*

bed·rid·den (běd′rĭd′n) ►adj. Confined to bed, esp. because of illness or infirmity. [< OE *bedrida*, bedridden person.]

bed·rock (běd′rŏk′) ►n. **1.** The solid rock that underlies the loose surface material of the earth. **2a.** Fundamental principles; foundation. **b.** The lowest point: *finances that were at bedrock.*

bed·roll (běd′rōl′) ►n. A portable roll of bedding used esp. for sleeping outdoors.

bed·room (běd′rōōm′, -rŏŏm′) ►n. A room in which to sleep. ►adj. **1.** Inhabited by commuters: *bedroom suburbs.* **2.** Sexually suggestive: *a*

bedroom comedy; bedroom eyes.

bed·side (běd′sīd′) ►n. The side of a bed or the space alongside it. —**bed′side′** adj.

bed·sore (běd′sôr′) ►n. A pressure-induced ulceration of the skin occurring during long confinement to bed.

bed·spread (běd′sprěd′) ►n. A usu. decorative covering for a bed.

bed·stead (běd′stěd′) ►n. The frame supporting a bed.

bedstead

bed·time (běd′tīm′) ►n. The time at which one goes to bed.

Bed·u·in (běd′ōō-ĭn, běd′wĭn) ►n. Var. of **Bedouin**.

bee (bē) ►n. **1.** Any of numerous winged, hairy-bodied, usu. stinging insects that gather nectar and pollen from which some species produce honey. **2.** A social gathering where people work together or compete: *a quilting bee.* —*idiom:* **a bee in (one's) bonnet** A persistent notion. [< OE *bēo*.]

beech (bēch) ►n. A deciduous tree having smooth gray bark, edible nuts, and strong heavy wood. [< OE *bēce*.]

beech·nut (bēch′nŭt′) ►n. The small, three-angled nut of a beech tree.

beef (bēf) ►n., pl. **beeves** (bēvz) or **beef 1a.** A full-grown steer, bull, ox, or cow, esp. one intended for use as meat. **b.** The flesh of a slaughtered steer, bull, ox, or cow. **2.** *Informal* Human muscle; brawn. **3.** pl. **beefs** *Slang* A complaint. ►v. To complain. —*phrasal verb:* **beef up** *Informal* To build up; reinforce: *We must beef up the police force.* [< Lat. *bōs*.]

beef·a·lo (bē′fə-lō′) ►n., pl. **-lo** or **-los** or **-loes** A hybrid that results from a cross between the North American bison (buffalo) and beef cattle, yielding leaner beef. [BEEF + (BUFF)ALO.]

beef·eat·er (bēf′ē′tər) ►n. A yeoman of the British monarch's royal guard.

beef·y (bē′fē) ►adj. **-i·er, -i·est 1.** Muscular in build; brawny. **2.** Filled with beef. —**beef′i·ness** n.

bee·hive (bē′hīv′) ►n. **1.** A hive for bees. **2.** A woman's hairstyle in which the hair is arranged in a tall, rounded peak on top of the head.

bee·keep·er (bē′kē′pər) ►n. One who keeps bees, esp. for commercial or agricultural purposes. —**bee′keep·ing** n.

bee·line (bē′līn′) ►n. A direct, straight course.

Be·el·ze·bub (bē-ĕl′zə-bŭb′) ►n. The Devil. [Prob. < Heb. *ba'al zəbûl*, lord prince.]

been (bĭn) ►v. P.part. of **be**.

beep (bēp) ►n. A sound or signal, as from a horn or electronic device. ►v. **1.** To make or cause to make a beep. **2.** To activate the beeper of (a person) by telephoning its number.

beep·er (bē′pər) ►n. **1.** One that beeps. **2.** A pager that beeps or vibrates to alert the person carrying it that someone is trying to make contact by telephone.

beer (bîr) ►*n.* **1.** An alcoholic beverage brewed from malt and flavored with hops. **2.** A beverage made from extracts of roots and plants. [< OE *bēor*.] —**beer′y** *adj.*

bees·wax (bēz′wăks′) ►*n.* **1.** The wax secreted by honeybees for making honeycombs. **2.** *Informal* A matter of personal concern: *It's none of your beeswax where I'm going.*

beet (bēt) ►*n.* **1.** A cultivated plant with a fleshy, usu. dark-red edible root. **2.** The sugar beet. [< Lat. *bēta.*]

Bee·tho·ven (bā′tō′vən), **Ludwig van** 1770–1827. German composer.

bee·tle[1] (bēt′l) ►*n.* Any of numerous insects with horny forewings that protect the hind wings when at rest. [< OE *bitela* < *bītan*, bite.]

bee·tle[2] (bēt′l) ►*adj.* Jutting; overhanging: *beetle brows.* ►*v.* **-tled, -tling** To jut. [< ME *bitel-brouwed*, grim-browed.]

beeves (bēvz) ►*n.* Pl. of **beef.**

be·fall (bĭ-fôl′) ►*v.* **-fell** (-fĕl′), **-fall·en** (-fô′lən), **-fall·ing** **1.** To come to pass; happen. **2.** To happen to. See Synonyms at **happen.** [< OE *befallen*, fall.]

be·fit (bĭ-fĭt′) ►*v.* **-fit·ted, -fit·ting** To be suitable to or appropriate for.

be·fog (bĭ-fôg′, -fŏg′) ►*v.* **-fogged, -fog·ging** **1.** To fog. **2.** To confuse; muddle.

be·fore (bĭ-fôr′) ►*adv.* **1.** Earlier in time; previously: *She called me the day before.* **2.** In front; ahead: *He was before me in line.* ►*prep.* **1.** Prior to. **2.** In front of. **3.** In store for; awaiting: *The young woman's whole career lies before her.* **4.** Into or in the presence of: *He asked that the visitor be brought before him.* **5.** Under the consideration of: *the case before the court.* **6.** In a position superior to: *She comes before him in rank.* ►*conj.* **1.** In advance of the time when: *See me before you leave.* **2.** Rather than: *I will move before I agree to pay more rent.* [< OE *beforan.*]

before Christ ►*adv.* In a specified year of the pre-Christian area.

be·fore·hand (bĭ-fôr′hănd′) ►*adv. & adj.* In advance; early.

be·foul (bĭ-foul′) ►*v.* **1.** To make dirty; soil. **2.** To speak badly of.

be·friend (bĭ-frĕnd′) ►*v.* To act as a friend to.

be·fud·dle (bĭ-fŭd′l) ►*v.* **-dled, -dling** **1.** To confuse or muddle; perplex. **2.** To stupefy with alcohol.
Syns: addle, discombobulate, fuddle, muddle **v.**

beg (bĕg) ►*v.* **begged, beg·ging** **1.** To ask for (e.g., food or money) from strangers for one's personal needs. See Synonyms at **cadge.** **2.** To entreat. **3.** To evade; dodge: *begged the question.* —*phrasal verb:* **beg off** To ask to be excused from something. —*idiom:* **beg to differ** To disagree in a polite manner. [ME *beggen.*]

be·get (bĭ-gĕt′) ►*v.* **-got** (-gŏt′), **-got·ten** (-gŏt′n) or **-got, -get·ting** **1.** To produce (offspring) by sexual reproduction. Used esp. of a man. **2.** To cause; produce. [< OE *begetan.*]

beg·gar (bĕg′ər) ►*n.* **1.** One who solicits money for a living. **2.** A pauper. ►*v.* **1.** To impoverish. **2.** To exceed the limits of: *beauty that beggars description.* [< OFr. *begart.*] —**beg′gar·ly** *adj.* —**beg′gar·y** *n.*

be·gin (bĭ-gĭn′) ►*v.* **-gan** (-găn′), **-gun** (-gŭn′), **-gin·ning** **1.** To commence or start. **2.** To come

into being: *when life began.* **3.** To say as the first in a series of remarks: *"I've been thinking," she began.* **4.** To have as a first stage or job: *The book began as a diary. The principal began as a math teacher.* [< OE *beginnan.*] —**be·gin′ner** *n.*

Be·gin (bā′gĭn), **Menachem** 1913–92. Russian-born Israeli politician.

be·gin·ning (bĭ-gĭn′ĭng) ►*n.* **1.** The process of being or being brought into being; start. **2.** The time when something begins or is begun. **3.** The place where something begins or is begun. **4.** The source; origin. **5.** The first part. **6.** often **beginnings** An early or rudimentary phase: *the beginnings of human life on this planet.*
Syns: birth, dawn, genesis, rise **Ant:** end **n.**

be·gone (bĭ-gôn′, -gŏn′) ►*interj.* Used chiefly to express dismissal.

be·go·nia (bĭ-gōn′yə) ►*n.* Any of various tropical plants cultivated for their brightly colored leaves. [After Michel *Bégon* (1638–1710).]

be·grime (bĭ-grīm′) ►*v.* **-grimed, -grim·ing** To smear or soil with or as if with dirt.

be·grudge (bĭ-grŭj′) ►*v.* **-grudged, -grudg·ing** **1.** To envy. **2.** To give with reluctance. —**be·grudg′ing·ly** *adv.*

be·guile (bĭ-gīl′) ►*v.* **-guiled, -guil·ing** **1.** To deceive or cheat by guile or charm. **2.** To distract; divert. **3.** To pass (time) pleasantly. **4.** To amuse or delight. See Synonyms at **charm.** —**be·guile′ment** *n.* —**be·guil′ing·ly** *adv.*

be·gum (bā′gəm, bē′-) ►*n.* A Muslim woman of rank. [Urdu *begam.*]

be·half (bĭ-hăf′, -häf′) ►*n.* Interest, support, or benefit. —*idiom:* **on behalf of** For the benefit of or as the agent of. [< OE *be healfe*, on (his) side.]

be·have (bĭ-hāv′) ►*v.* **-haved, -hav·ing** **1a.** To conduct oneself in a specified way. **b.** To conduct oneself in a proper way. **2.** To act, react, function, or perform in a particular way: *This fabric behaves well even in humid weather.* [ME *behaven* < *haven*, have.]

be·hav·ior (bĭ-hāv′yər) ►*n.* **1.** The manner in which one behaves; deportment. **2.** The actions or reactions of persons or things under given circumstances. —**be·hav′ior·al** *adj.*

behavioral science ►*n.* A scientific discipline, such as sociology, anthropology, or psychology, that deals with the study of human behavior.

be·hav·ior·ism (bĭ-hāv′yə-rĭz′əm) ►*n.* A school of psychology that studies only the observable and quantifiable aspects of behavior, excluding all subjective phenomena. —**be·hav′ior·ist** *n.* —**be·hav′ior·is′tic** *adj.*

be·head (bĭ-hĕd′) ►*v.* To decapitate.

be·he·moth (bĭ-hē′məth, bē′ə-məth) ►*n.* **1.** Something enormous in size or power. **2.** A huge animal described in the Bible. [< Heb. *bəhēmā*, beast.]

be·hest (bĭ-hĕst′) ►*n.* **1.** A command. **2.** An urgent request. [< OE *behǣs*, vow.]

be·hind (bĭ-hīnd′) ►*adv.* **1.** In, to, or toward the rear. **2.** In a place or condition that has been passed or left: *left my gloves behind.* **3.** In arrears; late. **4.** In or into an inferior position: *fell behind in class.* **5.** Slow: *My watch is running behind.* ►*prep.* **1.** At the back or in the rear of. **2.** On the farther or other side of. **3.** In a former place, time, or situation. **4.** Later than: *behind schedule.* **5.** Below, as in rank or ability: *behind us in technology.* **6a.** Concealed by: *hatred hid-*

den behind a smile. **b.** Underlying: *the truth behind the rumor.* **7.** In support of: *senators who got behind the bill.* ►*n. Informal* The buttocks. [< OE *behindan.*]

be·hind·hand (bǐ-hīnd′hănd′) ►*adj.* Being late or slow, esp. in paying a debt.

be·hold (bǐ-hōld′) ►*v.* **-held** (-hĕld′), **-hold·ing 1.** To look upon; gaze at. **2.** Used in the imperative to direct attention. [< OE *behaldan.*] **—be·hold′er** *n.*

be·hold·en (bǐ-hōl′dən) ►*adj.* Obliged or indebted, as from gratitude. [ME *biholden.*]

be·hoove (bǐ-hōōv′) ►*v.* **-hooved, -hoov·ing** To be necessary or proper for: *It behooves you at least to try.* [< OE *behōfian.*]

beige (bāzh) ►*n.* A light grayish or yellowish brown. [< OFr. *bege,* undyed woolen fabric.] **—beige** *adj.*

Bei·jing (bā′jǐng′) also **Pe·king** (pē′kǐng′, pā′-) The capital of China, in the NE part.

be·ing (bē′ǐng) ►*n.* **1.** The state or quality of existing. See Synonyms at **existence. 2a.** A person. **b.** An individual form of life; organism. **3.** One's essential nature.

Bei·rut (bā-rōōt′) The capital of Lebanon, in the W part on the Mediterranean.

be·la·bor (bǐ-lā′bər) ►*v.* **1.** To talk or write about at length or excessively; harp on: *Don't belabor the point.* **2.** To attack verbally. **3.** To attack with blows.

Bel·a·rus (bĕl′ə-rōōs′, byĕl′-) A country of E Europe E of Poland. Cap. Minsk.

be·lat·ed (bǐ-lā′tǐd) ►*adj.* Done or sent too late; delayed. **—be·lat′ed·ly** *adv.*

be·lay (bǐ-lā′) ►*v.* **1.** *Naut.* To secure or make fast (e.g., a rope). **2.** To secure (a mountain climber) at the end of a rope. **3.** To stop: *Belay there!* [< OE *belecgan,* surround.] **—be·lay′** *n.*

be·lay·ing pin (bǐ-lā′ǐng) ►*n.* A pin fitted in the rail of a boat for securing rigging lines.

belaying pin

belch (bĕlch) ►*v.* **1.** To expel gas noisily from the stomach through the mouth. **2.** To gush forth violently. [ME *belchen.*] **—belch** *n.*

bel·dam or **bel·dame** (bĕl′dəm, -dăm) ►*n.* An old woman. [ME, grandmother.]

be·lea·guer (bǐ-lē′gər) ►*v.* **1.** To harass; beset. **2.** To surround with troops. [Prob. Du. *belegeren.*]

Bel·fast (bĕl′făst′, bĕl-făst′) The capital of Northern Ireland, in the E part on an inlet of the Irish Sea.

bel·fry (bĕl′frē) ►*n., pl.* **-fries 1.** A bell tower, esp. one attached to a building. **2.** The part of a tower or steeple in which bells are hung. [< OFr. *berfrei,* siege tower.]

Bel·gium (bĕl′jəm) A country of NW Europe on the North Sea. Cap. Brussels. **—Bel′gian** *adj. & n.*

Bel·grade (bĕl′grăd′, -gräd′) The capital of Serbia in the N-central part at the confluence of the Danube and Sava Rivers.

be·lie (bǐ-lī′) ►*v.* **-lied, -ly·ing 1.** To misrepresent or disguise. **2.** To show to be false.

be·lief (bǐ-lēf′) ►*n.* **1.** Trust or confidence: *belief in democracy.* **2.** Conviction that something is true: *belief in ghosts.* **3.** Something believed or accepted as true, esp. a tenet or body of tenets. [< OE *gelēafa.*]

Syns: credence, credit, faith **Ant:** *disbelief* **n.**

be·liev·a·ble (bǐ-lē′və-bəl) ►*adj.* Capable of eliciting belief or trust. See Synonyms at **plausible. —be·liev′a·bil′i·ty** *n.*

be·lieve (bǐ-lēv′) ►*v.* **-lieved, -liev·ing 1.** To accept as true or real. **2.** To credit with veracity: *I believe you.* **3.** To have confidence (in); trust: *I believe in you. I believe the ruby to be genuine.* **4.** To expect or suppose; think. **5.** To have firm faith. [< OE *belēfan.*] **—be·liev′er** *n.*

be·lit·tle (bǐ-lǐt′l) ►*v.* **-tled, -tling** To speak of as small or unimportant; disparage. **—be·lit′tle·ment** *n.* **—be·lit′tler** *n.*

Be·lize (bə-lēz′) **1.** A country of Central America on the Caribbean Sea. Cap. Belmopan. **2.** also **Belize City** The former capital of Belize, in the E part on the Caribbean Sea at the mouth of the **Belize River.**

bell (bĕl) ►*n.* **1.** A hollow metal instrument, usu. cup-shaped with a flared opening, that emits a metallic tone when struck. **2.** Something shaped like a bell. **3.** *Naut.* **a.** A stroke on a bell to mark the hour. **b.** The time thus marked. ►*v.* To put a bell on: *bell the cat.* [< OE *belle.*]

Bell, Alexander Graham 1847–1922. British-born Amer. inventor; received 1st patent for the telephone (1876).

Alexander Graham Bell

bel·la·don·na (bĕl′ə-dŏn′ə) ►*n.* **1.** A poisonous plant with purplish-brown flowers and glossy black berries. **2.** A medicinal drug derived from this plant. [Ital.]

bell-bot·tom (bĕl′bŏt′əm) ►*adj.* Having legs

that flare at the bottom: *bell-bottom pants.*

bell·boy (bĕl′boi′) ►*n.* A male bellhop.

bell curve ►*n.* The typically symmetrical curve of a variable distribution of data around a mean, resembling the profile of a bell.

belle (bĕl) ►*n.* An attractive and admired girl or woman. [< Lat. *bella,* beautiful.]

belles-let·tres (bĕl-lĕt′rə) ►*pl.n.* *(takes sing. v.)* Literature regarded for its artistic value rather than for its content. [Fr.]

bell·flow·er (bĕl′flou′ər) ►*n.* Any of various plants with bell-shaped bluish flowers.

bell·hop (bĕl′hŏp′) ►*n.* A hotel porter.

bel·li·cose (bĕl′ĭ-kōs′) ►*adj.* Warlike or hostile in manner; belligerent. [< Lat. *bellicus,* of war.] —**bel′li·cos′i·ty** (-kŏs′ĭ-tē) *n.*

bel·lig·er·ent (bə-lĭj′ər-ənt) ►*adj.* **1.** Eager to fight; aggressively hostile. **2.** Engaged in warfare. ►*n.* One that is engaged in war. [< Lat. *belligerāre,* wage war.] —**bel·lig′er·ence, bel·lig′er·en·cy** *n.* —**bel·lig′er·ent·ly** *adv.*

Bel·li·ni (bə-lē′nē) Family of Venetian painters, including **Jacopo** (1400?–70?) and his two sons, **Gentile** (1429?–1507) and **Giovanni** (1430?–1516).

bell jar ►*n.* A bell-shaped glass vessel used esp. to establish a controlled atmosphere in scientific experiments.

bel·low (bĕl′ō) ►*v.* **1.** To roar in the manner of a bull. **2.** To shout in a deep voice. See Synonyms at **yell.** [ME *belwen.*] —**bel′low** *n.*

Bellow, Saul 1915–2005. Canadian-born Amer. writer.

bel·lows (bĕl′ōz, -əz) ►*pl.n.* *(takes sing. or pl. v.)* An apparatus for directing a strong current of air, as for increasing the draft to a fire. [< OE *belg,* bag.]

bell pepper ►*n.* A pepper plant cultivated for its edible, bell-shaped fruit.

bell·weth·er (bĕl′wĕth′ər) ►*n.* One that is a leader or indicator of future trends. [ME *bellewether,* belled wether, leader of a flock.]

bel·ly (bĕl′ē) ►*n., pl.* **-lies 1.** See **abdomen** (sense 1). **2.** The underside of the body of an animal. **3.** *Informal* The stomach. **4.** A part that protrudes: *the belly of a sail.* ►*v.* **-lied, -ly·ing** To protrude. See Synonyms at **bulge.** [< OE *belg,* bag.]

bel·ly·ache (bĕl′ē-āk′) ►*n.* **1.** Pain in the abdomen. **2.** *Slang* A whining complaint. ►*v. Slang* To complain in a whining manner.

bel·ly·but·ton (bĕl′ē-bŭt′n) ►*n. Informal* The navel.

belly dance ►*n.* A dance in which the performer makes sinuous movements of the belly. —**bel′-ly-dance′** *v.* —**belly dancer** *n.*

belly flop ►*n. Informal* A dive in which the front of the body hits flat against the surface of the water.

bel·ly·ful (bĕl′ē-fool′) ►*n. Informal* An undesirable or unendurable amount.

belly laugh ►*n.* A deep laugh.

bel·ly-up (bĕl′ē-ŭp′) ►*adj. Informal* Bankrupt.

Bel·mo·pan (bĕl′mō-păn′) The capital of Belize, in the central part.

be·long (bĭ-lông′, -lŏng′) ►*v.* **1.** To be owned by someone. **2.** To have a proper or suitable place: *That book belongs on the top shelf.* **3.** To be a member of a group. **4.** To be a part of or in natural association with something: *These blades belong to the food processor.* [ME *bilongen.*]

be·long·ing (bĭ-lông′ĭng, -lŏng′-) ►*n.* **1.** Acceptance as a natural member or part: *a sense of belonging.* **2.** often **belongings** Personal possessions.

be·lov·ed (bĭ-lŭv′ĭd, -lŭvd′) ►*adj.* Dearly loved. —**be·lov′ed** *n.*

be·low (bĭ-lō′) ►*adv.* **1.** In or to a lower place or level; beneath. **2.** Later in a text: *See below.* **3.** On the ground: *The fields below looked barren.* **4.** Below zero in temperature: *40 degrees below.* ►*prep.* **1.** Underneath; beneath. **2.** In a lower rank; subordinate to: *He is below two supervisors at work.* **3.** Unsuitable to the rank or dignity of: *behavior that is below me.* [ME *bilooghe.*]

belt (bĕlt) ►*n.* **1.** A flexible band worn around the waist, used to support clothing, secure tools or weapons, or serve as decoration. **2.** A seat belt. **3.** A continuous moving band used to transfer motion or to convey materials from one wheel or shaft to another. **4.** A band of tough reinforcing material beneath the tread of a tire. **5.** A geographic region that is distinctive in a specific way. **6.** *Slang* A powerful blow; wallop. **7.** *Slang* A drink of hard liquor. ►*v.* **1.** To encircle; gird. **2.** To attach with a belt. **3.** *Slang* To strike forcefully; punch. **4.** *Slang* To sing loudly. **5.** *Slang* To swig (liquor). —*idioms:* **below the belt** Against the rules; unfairly. **tighten (one's) belt** To exercise frugality. **under (one's) belt** In one's possession or experience: *My sister has three years of Chinese under her belt.* [< Lat. *balteus.*]

belt-tight·en·ing (bĕlt′-tīt′n-ĭng) ►*n.* A reduction in spending; frugality.

belt·way (bĕlt′wā′) ►*n.* **1.** A highway that skirts an urban area. **2. Beltway** The political establishment of Washington DC.

be·lu·ga (bə-loo′gə) ►*n.* **1.** A small toothed whale chiefly of the Arctic Ocean having a rounded forehead and a white body. **2.** A large white sturgeon whose roe is used for caviar. [< Russ. *belyĭ,* white.]

bel·ve·dere (bĕl′vĭ-dîr′) ►*n.* A structure, such as a cupola or summerhouse, situated so as to command a view. [Ital., beautiful view.]

be·moan (bĭ-mōn′) ►*v.* **1.** To mourn over; lament. **2.** To express regret for or disapproval of; deplore.

be·muse (bĭ-myooz′) ►*v.* **-mused, -mus·ing 1.** To cause to be bewildered. **2.** To absorb; preoccupy. —**be·muse′ment** *n.*

bench (bĕnch) ►*n.* **1.** A long seat, often without a back, for two or more persons. **2.** *Law* **a.** The judge's seat in a court. **b.** The office or position of a judge. **c.** often **Bench** The judge or judges composing a court. **3.** A worktable. **4.** *Sports* **a.** The place where team players sit when not playing. **b.** The reserve players on a team. ►*v.* **1.** To seat on a bench. **2.** *Sports* To remove (a player) from a game. [< OE *benc.*]

bench·mark (bĕnch′märk′) ►*n.* **1.** A standard by which something can be judged. **2.** often **bench mark** A surveyor's mark made on a stationary object and used as a reference point.

bench·warm·er (bĕnch′wôr′mər) ►*n. Sports* A substitute player.

bench warrant ►*n.* A warrant issued by a judge or court ordering the apprehension of an offender who has failed to appear in court.

bend (bĕnd) ►*v.* **bent** (bĕnt), **bend·ing 1.** To curve or cause to curve: *bent the wire; flowers* *that bent in the breeze.* **2.** To incline the body; stoop: *bent over to pick up the ball.* **3.** To turn or deflect. **4a.** To render submissive; subdue. **b.** To yield; submit. **5.** To misrepresent; distort: *bend the truth.* **6.** To make an exception to: *bend the rules.* **7.** *Naut.* To fasten. ▸*n.* **1.** The act of bending or the state of being bent. **2.** Something that is bent or that has a curve: *a bend in the river.* **3. bends** *(takes sing. or pl. v.)* Decompression sickness. [< OE *bendan.*]

bend·er (bĕn′dər) ▸*n.* **1.** One that bends. **2.** *Slang* A drinking spree.

be·neath (bĭ-nēth′) ▸*adv.* **1.** In a lower place; below. **2.** Underneath. ▸*prep.* **1.** Lower than; under. **2.** Unworthy of: *It was beneath me to beg.* **3.** Concealed by: *The earth lay beneath the snow.* [< OE *beneothan.*]

Ben·e·dict XVI (bĕn′ĭ-dĭkt′) b. 1927. Pope (2005–2013).

Benedict XVI
photographed in 2009

ben·e·dic·tion (bĕn′ĭ-dĭk′shən) ▸*n.* **1.** A blessing. **2.** An invocation of divine blessing, usu. at the end of a church service. [< Lat. *benedīcere*, bless.]

Benedict of Nur·si·a (nûr′shē-ə, -shə), Saint. AD 480?–547? Italian founder of the Benedictine order (c. 529). —**Ben′e·dic′tine** *adj. & n.*

ben·e·fac·tion (bĕn′ə-făk′shən, bĕn′ə-făk′-) ▸*n.* **1.** The act of conferring a benefit. **2.** A charitable gift or deed. [< Lat. *benefacere*, do a service.]

ben·e·fac·tor (bĕn′ə-făk′tər) ▸*n.* One that gives aid, esp. financial aid.

ben·e·fac·tress (bĕn′ə-făk′trĭs) ▸*n.* A woman who gives aid, esp. financial aid.

ben·e·fice (bĕn′ə-fĭs) ▸*n.* A church office endowed with fixed assets that provide a living. [< Lat. *beneficium*, benefit.]

be·nef·i·cence (bə-nĕf′ĭ-səns) ▸*n.* **1.** The quality of being kind or charitable. **2.** A charitable act or gift. [< Lat. *beneficus*, charitable.] —**be·nef′i·cent** *adj.*

ben·e·fi·cial (bĕn′ə-fĭsh′əl) ▸*adj.* Producing a favorable result; advantageous. —**ben′e·fi′cial·ly** *adv.*

ben·e·fi·ci·ar·y (bĕn′ə-fĭsh′ē-ĕr′ē, -fĭsh′ə-rē) ▸*n., pl.* **-ies** One that receives a benefit, as funds or property from an insurance policy. —**ben′e·fi′ci·ar′y** *adj.*

ben·e·fit (bĕn′ə-fĭt) ▸*n.* **1a.** Something that enhances well-being: *the benefits of exercise.* **b.** A help; aid: *navigating with the benefit of a map.* **2a.** A payment made to qualifying persons by a government agency or insurance company. **b.** A form of compensation, such as paid vacation time, provided to an employee in addition

to wages or salary as part of an employment arrangement. **3.** A fund-raising public entertainment. ▸*v.* **1.** To be helpful or advantageous to. **2.** To derive benefit; profit. [< Lat. *benefactum*, good deed.]

Be·nét (bĭ-nā′), **Stephen Vincent** 1898–1943. Amer. poet.

be·nev·o·lence (bə-nĕv′ə-ləns) ▸*n.* **1.** An inclination to perform kind or charitable acts. **2.** A kindly or charitable act.

be·nev·o·lent (bə-nĕv′ə-lənt) ▸*adj.* **1.** Having or showing benevolence. **2.** Organized for charitable purposes. [< Lat. *benevolēns*, well-wishing.] —**be·nev′o·lent·ly** *adv.*
Syns: *charitable, eleemosynary, philanthropic* *adj.*

Ben·gal (bĕn-gôl′, bĕng-) A region of E India and Bangladesh on the **Bay of Bengal,** an arm of the Indian Ocean between India and Myanmar. —**Ben′ga·lese′** (bĕn′gə-lēz′, -lēs′, bĕng′-) *adj. & n.*

Ben·ga·li (bĕn-gô′lē, bĕng-) ▸*n.* **1.** A native or inhabitant of Bengal. **2.** The modern Indic language of Bangladesh and W Bengal. —**Ben·ga′li** *adj.*

Ben·ga·lu·ru (bĕng′gə-lə-rōō′) A city of S-central India W of Chennai, formerly known as Bangalore.

Ben Gur·i·on (bĕn gŏŏr′ē-ən), **David** 1886–1973. Polish-born Israeli prime minister (1948–53 and 1955–63).

be·night·ed (bĭ-nī′tĭd) ▸*adj.* **1.** Ignorant; unenlightened. **2.** Overtaken by night or darkness. —**be·night′ed·ness** *n.*

be·nign (bĭ-nīn′) ▸*adj.* **1.** Gentle or kind. **2.** Favorable. **3a.** Having little or no detrimental effect. **b.** Not malignant or disease causing. [< Lat. *benignus.*] —**be·nign′ly** *adv.*

be·nig·nant (bĭ-nĭg′nənt) ▸*adj.* Kind and gracious. —**be·nig′nant·ly** *adv.*

Be·nin (bə-nĭn′, bĕ-nēn′) **1.** A former kingdom of W Africa, now part of Nigeria. **2.** A country of W Africa. Cap. Porto-Novo.

Benin, Bight of A wide indentation of the Gulf of Guinea in W Africa.

bent (bĕnt) ▸*v.* P.t. and p.part. of **bend.** ▸*adj.* **1.** Not being straight or even; crooked. **2.** Determined to take a course of action. ▸*n.* A tendency, disposition, or inclination.

be·numb (bĭ-nŭm′) ▸*v.* **1.** To numb, esp. by cold. **2.** To make senseless or inactive, as from shock or boredom.

ben·zene (bĕn′zēn′, bĕn-zēn′) ▸*n.* A clear flammable liquid derived from petroleum and used in other chemical products.

ben·zine (bĕn′zēn′, bĕn-zēn′) ▸*n.* See **naphtha.**

benzo– or **benz–** ▸*pref.* Benzene; benzoic acid: *benzoate.* [< BENZOIN.]

ben·zo·ate (bĕn′zō-āt′) ▸*n.* A salt, ester, or anion of benzoic acid.

ben·zo·ic acid (bĕn-zō′ĭk) ▸*n.* A crystalline acid, $C_7H_6O_2$, used as a food preservative and germicide and in the manufacture of dyes.

ben·zo·in (bĕn′zō-ĭn, -zoin′) ▸*n.* A balsamic resin obtained from certain tropical Asian trees and used in perfumery and medicine. [< Ar. *lubān jāwī*, frankincense of Java.]

ben·zol (bĕn′zôl′, -zōl′, -zol′) ▸*n.* See **benzene.**

be·queath (bĭ-kwēth′, -kwēth′) ▸*v.* **1.** *Law* To

leave or give (property) by will. **2.** To hand down. [< OE *becwethan.*] —**be·queath′al, be·queath′ment** *n.*

be·quest (bǐ-kwĕst′) ►*n.* **1.** The act of giving or leaving personal property by a will. **2.** Something bequeathed; legacy. [ME *biquest.*]

be·rate (bǐ-rāt′) ►*v.* **-rat·ed, -rat·ing** To scold angrily and at length. [BE- + RATE².]

Ber·ber (bûr′bər) ►*n.* **1.** A member of a North African people living in settled or nomadic tribes from Morocco to Egypt. **2.** Any of their Afro-Asiatic languages.

ber·ceuse (bĕr-sœz′) ►*n., pl.* **-ceuses** (-sœz′) *Mus.* **1.** A lullaby. **2.** A soothing composition similar to a lullaby. [Fr.]

be·reave (bǐ-rēv′) ►*v.* **-reaved** or **-reft** (-rĕft′), **-reav·ing** To take a loved one from, esp. by death. [< OE *berēafian.*] —**be·reave′ment** *n.*

be·reaved (bǐ-rēvd′) ►*adj.* Suffering the loss of a loved one. ►*n. (takes pl. v.)* People who are bereaved.

be·reft (bǐ-rĕft′) ►*v.* P.t. and p.part. of **bereave.** ►*adj.* **1.** Lacking or deprived of something: *bereft of dignity.* **2.** Bereaved.

be·ret (bə-rā′) ►*n.* A round, brimless cloth cap. [< LLat. *birrus,* hooded cloak.]

Berg·man (bûrg′mən), **Ingmar** 1918–2007. Swedish film director.

Bergman, Ingrid 1915–82. Swedish actress.

ber·i·ber·i (bĕr′ē-bĕr′ē) ►*n.* A thiamine-deficiency disease causing nerve damage, cardiovascular abnormalities, and edema. [Sinhalese.]

Ber·ing Sea (bîr′ĭng, bâr′-) A northward extension of the Pacific between Siberia and AK, connected with the Arctic Ocean by the **Bering Strait.**

ber·ke·li·um (bər-kē′lē-əm, bûrk′lē-əm) ►*n. Symbol* **Bk** A synthetic radioactive element. At. no. 97. See table at **element.** [After BERKELEY, California.]

Ber·lin (bər-lǐn′) The capital of Germany, in the NE part; formerly divided into **East Berlin** and **West Berlin** (1945–90).

Berlin, Irving 1888–1989. Russian-born Amer. songwriter.

berm (bûrm) ►*n.* **1.** A raised bank or path, as along a roadway or canal. **2.** A protective mound or bank of earth. [< MDu. *bærm.*]

Ber·mu·da (bər-myōō′də) A self-governing British colony comprising about 300 islands in the Atlantic SE of Cape Hatteras. Cap. Hamilton, on **Bermuda Island.** —**Ber·mu′di·an, Ber·mu′dan** *adj. & n.*

Bermuda shorts ►*pl.n.* Short pants that end slightly above the knee.

Bern or **Berne** (bûrn, bĕrn) The capital of Switzerland, in the W-central part.

Ber·noul·li (bər-nōō′lē) Family of Swiss mathematicians and scientists, including **Jakob** or **Jacques** (1654–1705), his brother **Johann** or **Jean** (1667–1748), and Johann's son **Daniel** (1700–82).

Bernoulli effect ►*n.* The phenomenon of internal pressure reduction with increased stream velocity in a fluid. [After Daniel BERNOULLI.]

Bern·stein (bûrn′stīn′, -stēn′), **Leonard** 1918–90. Amer. conductor and composer.

ber·ry (bĕr′ē) ►*n., pl.* **-ries 1.** *Bot.* A fruit derived from a single ovary and having the whole wall fleshy, such as the grape or tomato. **2.** A small,

juicy, many-seeded fruit, such as a blackberry. ►*v.* **-ried, -ry·ing 1.** To hunt for or gather berries. **2.** To bear berries. [< OE *berie.*]

ber·serk (bər-sûrk′, -zûrk′) ►*adj.* **1.** Destructively violent. **2.** Crazed; deranged: *berserk with grief.* [< ON *berserkr,* warrior.] —**ber·serk′** *adv.*

berth (bûrth) ►*n.* **1.** Sufficient space for a ship to maneuver. **2.** A space for a ship to dock or anchor. **3.** A job, esp. on a ship. **4a.** A built-in bed, as on a ship or train. **b.** A place to sleep or stay; accommodations. **5.** A space where a vehicle can be parked, as for loading. ►*v.* To bring (a ship) to a berth. —*idiom:* **a wide berth** Ample space or distance to avoid any trouble. [ME *birth.*]

ber·yl (bĕr′əl) ►*n.* A hard glassy mineral that is the chief source of beryllium and is used as a gem. [Of Indic orig.] —**ber′yl·line** (-ə-lǐn, -lǐn′) *adj.*

be·ryl·li·um (bə-rǐl′ē-əm) ►*n. Symbol* **Be** A high-melting, lightweight, corrosion-resistant, rigid, steel-gray metallic element used as a moderator in nuclear reactors and in sturdy light alloys. At. no. 4. See table at **element.** [< BERYL.]

be·seech (bǐ-sēch′) ►*v.* **-sought** (-sôt′) or **-seeched, -seech·ing** To request urgently; implore. [< OE *sēcan,* seek.]

be·set (bǐ-sĕt′) ►*v.* **-set, -set·ting 1.** To attack from all sides. **2.** To trouble persistently; harass. **3.** To surround. **4.** To stud, as with jewels. [< OE *besettan.*]

be·side (bǐ-sīd′) ►*prep.* **1.** Next to. **2.** In comparison with. **3.** In addition to. **4.** Except for. **5.** Not relevant to: *beside the point.* —*idiom:* **beside (oneself)** Extremely agitated or excited. [< OE *be sīdan.*]

be·sides (bǐ-sīdz′) ►*adv.* **1.** In addition; also. **2.** Moreover; furthermore. **3.** Otherwise; else. ►*prep.* **1.** In addition to. See Usage Note at **together. 2.** Except for.

be·siege (bǐ-sēj′) ►*v.* **-sieged, -sieg·ing 1.** To surround with hostile forces. **2.** To crowd around; hem in. **3.** To harass or importune, as with requests. —**be·sieg′er** *n.*

be·smear (bǐ-smîr′) ►*v.* To smear.

be·smirch (bǐ-smûrch′) ►*v.* **1.** To stain; sully. **2.** To make dirty; soil. —**be·smirch′er** *n.*

be·sot (bǐ-sŏt′) ►*v.* **-sot·ted, -sot·ting** To muddle or stupefy, as with liquor or infatuation.

be·spat·ter (bǐ-spăt′ər) ►*v.* To spatter with or as if with mud.

be·speak (bǐ-spēk′) ►*v.* **-spoke** (-spōk′), **-spoken** (-spō′kən) or **-spoke, -speak·ing 1.** To be or give a sign of; indicate. See Synonyms at **indicate. 2a.** To engage, hire, or order in advance. **b.** To request. **3.** To foretell.

be·sprin·kle (bǐ-sprǐng′kəl) ►*v.* **-kled, -kling** To sprinkle.

Bes·sa·ra·bi·a (bĕs′ə-rā′bē-ə) A region of Moldova and W Ukraine. —**Bes′sa·ra′bi·an** *adj. & n.*

Bes·se·mer process (bĕs′ə-mər) ►*n.* A method for making steel by blasting compressed air through molten iron to burn out excess carbon and impurities. [After Sir Henry *Bessemer* (1813–98).]

best (bĕst) ►*adj.* Superl. of **good. 1.** Surpassing all others in quality. **2.** Most satisfactory or desirable: *the best solution.* **3.** Greatest; most:

the best part of an hour. ►*adv.* Superl. of **well².** **1.** Most creditably or advantageously. **2.** To the greatest degree or extent; most. ►*n.* **1.** One that surpasses all others. **2.** The best part, moment, or value: *Let's get the best out of life.* **3.** The optimum condition or quality: *look your best.* **4.** One's best clothing. **5.** The best effort one can make. **6.** One's regards: *Give them my best.* ►*v.* To surpass; beat. —*idioms:* **at best 1.** Interpreted most favorably: *no more than 40 people at best.* **2.** Under the most favorable conditions: *runs 20 miles per hour at best.* **for the best** For the ultimate good. **get the best of** To outdo or outwit. [< OE *betst.*]

bes·tial (běs′chəl, bēs′-) ►*adj.* **1.** Beastlike. **2.** Marked by brutality or depravity. [< Lat. *bēstia,* beast.] —**bes′ti·al′i·ty** (-chē-ăl′ĭ-tē) *n.* —**bes′tial·ly** *adv.*

bes·ti·ar·y (běs′chē-ĕr′ē, bēs′-) ►*n., pl.* **-ies** A medieval collection of stories providing descriptions of real and imaginary animals along with moral interpretation of their behavior. [< Lat. *bēstia,* beast.]

be·stir (bĭ-stûr′) ►*v.* **-stirred, -stir·ring** To cause to become active; rouse.

best man ►*n.* A bridegroom's chief attendant.

be·stow (bĭ-stō′) ►*v.* To present as a gift or honor; confer. —**be·stow′al** *n.*

be·strew (bĭ-strōō′) ►*v.* **-strewed, -strewed** or **-strewn** (-strōōn′), **-strew·ing 1.** To strew. **2.** To lie scattered about.

be·stride (bĭ-strīd′) ►*v.* **-strode** (-strōd′), **-strid·den** (-strĭd′n), **-strid·ing 1.** To sit or stand astride; straddle. **2.** To dominate by position; tower over.

best·sell·er (běst′sěl′ər) ►*n.* A product, such as a book, that is sold in very large numbers.

bet (bět) ►*n.* **1.** A wager. **2.** The amount or object that is risked in a wager; stake. **3.** One on which a stake is or can be placed. **4.** A considered plan or option: *Your best bet is to make reservations.* ►*v.* **bet** or **bet·ted, bet·ting 1.** To stake (something) in a bet. **2.** To make a bet (with). —*idiom:* **you bet** *Informal* Of course. [?]

be·ta (bā′tə, bē′-) ►*n.* The 2nd letter of the Greek alphabet. [Gk. *bēta* < Phoenician **bēt,* house.]

be·ta-block·er (bā′tə-blŏk′ər, bē′-) ►*n.* A drug that blocks the receptors at sympathetic nerve endings and is used to treat angina, hypertension, and migraine headaches.

beta carotene ►*n.* An isomer of carotene that is efficiently converted to vitamin A by the body.

be·take (bĭ-tāk′) ►*v.* **-took** (-tōōk′), **-tak·en** (-tā′kən), **-tak·ing** To cause (oneself) to go.

beta particle ►*n.* An electron or positron, esp. one emitted at high energy in the decay of certain radioactive nuclei.

beta ray ►*n.* A rapidly moving beta particle or a narrow beam of such particles.

beta sheet ►*n.* A secondary structure that occurs in many proteins and consists of two or more parallel, adjacent polypeptide chains arranged in such a way that hydrogen bonds can form between the chains.

beta test ►*n.* The final testing of software or hardware before it is commercially released. —**be′ta-test′** *v.*

be·ta·tron (bā′tə-trŏn′, bē′-) ►*n.* A magnetic induction electron accelerator that accelerates

electrons to energies of several hundred million electron volts.

beta version ►*n.* The version of software used in a beta test.

beta wave ►*n.* A pattern of electrical waves occurring in electroencephalograms of the brain at a frequency of 13 to 30 cycles per second, usu. when a person is awake and alert.

be·tel (bēt′l) ►*n.* An evergreen vine having heart-shaped or ovate leaves used to wrap betel nuts. [< Tamil *veṟṟilai.*]

Be·tel·geuse (bēt′l-jōōz′, bět′l-jœz′) ►*n.* A bright-red variable star in the constellation Orion. [Prob. < Ar. *yad al-jawzā',* hand of Orion.]

betel nut ►*n.* The seed of the betel palm, chewed with betel leaves as a mild stimulant.

betel palm ►*n.* A tropical Asian palm with large pinnate leaves, cultivated for its seeds.

bête noire (bět nwär′) ►*n.* One that is an object of intense dislike or aversion. [Fr.]

be·think (bĭ-thĭngk′) ►*v.* **-thought** (-thôt′), **-think·ing** To remind (oneself).

Beth·le·hem (běth′lĭ-hěm′, -lē-əm) A town in the West Bank S of Jerusalem; traditional birthplace of Jesus.

Be·thune (bə-thōōn′, -thyōōn′), **Mary McLeod** 1875–1955. Amer. educator.

be·tide (bĭ-tīd′) ►*v.* **-tid·ed, -tid·ing** To happen (to); befall. See Synonyms at **happen.** [< *tīdan,* happen.]

be·times (bĭ-tīmz′) ►*adv.* **1.** Once in a while; on occasion. **2.** Quickly; soon.

be·to·ken (bĭ-tō′kən) ►*v.* To give a sign or portent of. See Synonyms at **indicate.**

be·took (bĭ-tōōk′) ►*v.* P.t. of **betake.**

be·tray (bĭ-trā′) ►*v.* **1.** To commit treason against; be a traitor to. **2.** To be false or disloyal to. **3.** To make known unintentionally. **4.** To reveal unintentionally: *Her hollow laugh betrayed her contempt for him.* **5.** To lead astray; deceive. [< Lat. *trādere,* hand over.] —**be·tray′-al** *n.* —**be·tray′er** *n.*

be·troth (bĭ-trōth′, -trôth′) ►*v.* To become engaged; promise to marry. —**be·troth′al** *n.*

be·trothed (bĭ-trōthd′, -trôtht′) ►*n.* The person to whom one is engaged to be married. ►*adj.* Engaged to be married.

bet·ter (bět′ər) ►*adj.* Comp. of **good. 1.** Greater in excellence or higher in quality. **2.** More appropriate, useful, or desirable: *found a better way to go.* **3.** More skilled: *I'm better at math than spelling.* **4.** Greater or larger: *the better part of an hour.* **5.** Healthier than before. ►*adv.* Comp. of **well². 1.** In a more excellent way. **2.** To a greater extent or degree: *better suited to the job.* **3.** To greater advantage; preferably: *a deed better left undone.* **4.** More: *better than a year.* ►*n.* One that is greater in excellence, skill, or quality. ►*v.* **1.** To make or become better; improve. **2.** To surpass or exceed: *practiced so she could better her competitor.* —*idioms:* **better off** In a better or more prosperous condition. **for the better** Resulting in improvement. **had better** Ought to. **think better of** To change one's mind about. [< OE *betera.*]

bet·ter·ment (bět′ər-mənt) ►*n.* An improvement, often financially or educationally.

bet·tor also **bet·ter** (bět′ər) ►*n.* One that bets.

be·tween (bĭ-twēn′) ►*prep.* **1.** In or through the position or interval separating: *between* the trees; between 11 and 12 o'clock. **2.** Associating in a reciprocal relationship: *an agreement between workers and management.* **3a.** By the combined effort or effect of: *Between them they succeeded.* **b.** In the combined ownership of: *They had only a few dollars between them.* **4.** From one or another of: *choose between us.* **5.** As measured against. Often used to express a reciprocal relationship: *choose between French and Spanish.* ►*adv.* In an intermediate space, position, or time. —*idiom:* **between you and me** In the strictest confidence. [< OE *betwēonum.*]

Usage: With exactly two entities, the only choice possible is *between: the choice between good and evil.* With more than two or an unspecified number of entities, use *between* if the entities are distinct and *among* if they are a mass or collection. In *The balloon landed between the houses,* the houses are points defining the area where the balloon touched down (the balloon hit no house). In *The balloon landed among the houses,* the area of landing is the general location of the houses (i.e., it is uncertain whether any house was hit).

be·twixt (bĭ-twĭkst′) ►*adv. & prep.* Between. —*idiom:* **betwixt and between** In an intermediate position. [< OE *betwix.*]

BeV ►*abbr.* billion electron volts

bev·el (bĕv′əl) ►*n.* **1.** The angle or inclination of a line or surface that meets another at any angle but 90°. **2.** A tool used to measure or draw angles or to fix a surface at an angle. ►*v.* **-eled, -el·ing** or **-elled, -el·ling 1.** To cut at a bevel. **2.** To be inclined; slant. [Poss. < OFr.]

bev·er·age (bĕv′ər-ij, bĕv′rĭj) ►*n.* Any one of various liquids for drinking, usu. excluding water. [< Lat. *bibere,* to drink.]

bev·y (bĕv′ē) ►*n., pl.* **-ies 1.** A group of animals or birds, esp. larks or quail. **2.** A group or assemblage. [< AN *bevee.*]

be·wail (bĭ-wāl′) ►*v.* To express sorrow (about); lament.

be·ware (bĭ-wâr′) ►*v.* **-wared, -war·ing** To be on guard (against); be cautious (of). [ME *ben war.*]

be·wil·der (bĭ-wĭl′dər) ►*v.* To confuse or befuddle, esp. by being complicated or varied. See Synonyms at **perplex.** [< obsolete *wilder,* disorient.] —**be·wil′der·ment** *n.*

be·witch (bĭ-wĭch′) ►*v.* **1.** To place under one's power by magic; cast a spell over. **2.** To captivate completely; fascinate. See Synonyms at **charm.** —**be·witch′ing·ly** *adv.* —**be·witch′ment** *n.*

bey (bā) ►*n.* **1.** A provincial governor in the Ottoman Empire. **2.** A ruler of the former kingdom of Tunis. [Turk.]

be·yond (bē-ŏnd′, bĭ-yŏnd′) ►*prep.* **1.** On the far side of; past. **2.** Later than; after. **3.** Past the understanding, reach, or scope of. **4.** To a degree or amount greater than: *happy beyond his wildest dreams.* **5.** In addition to. [< OE *begeondan.*]

bez·el (bĕz′əl) ►*n.* **1.** A slanting edge on a cutting tool. **2.** The faceted portion of a cut gem. [Perh. < Lat. *bis,* twice.]

bf ►*abbr.* boldface

BF ►*abbr.* **1.** board foot **2.** boyfriend **3.** also **B/F** *Accounting* brought forward

Bh The symbol for **bohrium.**

BHT (bē′ăch-tē′) ►*n.* A crystalline phenolic antioxidant, $C_{15}H_{24}O$, that is used to preserve fats and oils, esp. in foods. [*b(utylated) h(ydroxy)- t(oluene), tolu,* a resin.]

Bhu·tan (bōō-tăn′, -tän′) A country of South Asia in the E Himalayas. Cap. Thimphu. —**Bhu′tan·ese′** *adj. & n.*

Bhut·to (bōō′tō), **Benazir** 1953–2007. Pakistani prime minister (1988–90 and 1993–96).

bi– or **bin–** ►*pref.* **1.** Two; twice: *bipolar.* **2.** Occurring at intervals of two: *bicentennial.* **3.** Occurring twice during: *biweekly.* [Lat. *bis, bi-,* twice, and *bīnī,* two by two.]

Usage: *Bimonthly* and *biweekly* mean "once every two months" and "once every two weeks." For "twice a month" and "twice a week," *semimonthly* and *semiweekly* should be used. Expressions such as *every two months* or *twice a month* are often preferable in order to avoid misinterpretation.

BIA ►*abbr.* Bureau of Indian Affairs

bi·an·nu·al (bī-ăn′yōō-əl) ►*adj.* **1.** Occurring twice each year; semiannual. **2.** Occurring every two years; biennial. —**bi·an′nu·al·ly** *adv.*

bi·as (bī′əs) ►*n.* **1.** A line going diagonally across the grain of fabric. **2.** A preference or inclination that inhibits impartiality; prejudice. ►*adj.* Slanting or diagonal; oblique. ►*v.* **-ased, -as·ing** or **-assed, -as·sing** To influence in an unfair direction; prejudice. [Fr. *biais,* slant.]

Syns: *jaundice, prejudice* **v.**

bi·ath·lon (bī-ăth′lən, -lŏn′) ►*n.* An athletic competition combining cross-country skiing and rifle shooting. [BI– + Gk. *athlon,* contest.]

bib (bĭb) ►*n.* **1.** A small piece of cloth or plastic secured under the chin and and worn esp. by children to protect clothing while eating. **2.** The part of an apron or pair of overalls worn over the chest. ►*v.* **bibbed, bib·bing** To indulge in drinking. [Prob. < ME *bibben,* drink heartily.]

Bib. ►*abbr.* Bible

bi·be·lot (bē′bə-lō′, bē-blō′) ►*n.* A small decorative object. [< OFr. *beubelet.*]

Bi·ble (bī′bəl) ►*n.* **1a.** The sacred book of Christianity, which includes the Old Testament and the New Testament. **b.** The sacred book of Judaism, consisting of the Torah, the Prophets, and the Writings. See table on page 84. **2.** often **bible** A book considered authoritative in its field: *the bible of Chinese cooking.* [< Gk. *biblion,* book.] —**Bib′li·cal** (bĭb′lĭ-kəl) *adj.* —**Bib′li·cal·ly** *adv.*

biblio– ►*pref.* Book: *bibliophile.* [< Gk. *biblion,* book.]

bib·li·og·ra·phy (bĭb′lē-ŏg′rə-fē) ►*n., pl.* **-phies 1.** A list of the works of a specific author or publisher. **2.** A list of writings relating to a given subject or used by an author to prepare a particular work. —**bib′li·og′ra·pher** *n.* —**bib′li·o·graph′i·cal** (-ə-grăf′ĭ-kəl), **bib′li·o·graph′ic** *adj.*

bib·li·o·phile (bĭb′lē-ə-fīl′) ►*n.* A lover or collector of books.

bib·u·lous (bĭb′yə-ləs) ►*adj.* **1.** Given to convivial, often excessive alcoholic drinking. **2.** Very absorbent, as paper or soil. [< Lat. *bibere,* to drink.] —**bib′u·lous·ly** *adv.*

bi·cam·er·al (bī-kăm′ər-əl) ►*adj.* Composed

BOOKS OF THE BIBLE

Books of the Hebrew Scriptures appear as listed in the translation by the Jewish Publication Society of America. Books of the Christian Bible appear as listed in the Jerusalem Bible, a 1966 translation of the 1956 French Roman Catholic version. The Old Testament books shown in italic are considered apocryphal in many Christian churches, but they are accepted as canonical in the Roman Catholic Church, the Eastern Orthodox Church, and the Armenian and the Ethiopian Oriental Orthodox Church. The Christian Old Testament parallels the Hebrew Scriptures with the exception of these books.

Hebrew Scriptures	Christian Bible	

The Torah	Old Testament	New Testament
Genesis	Genesis	Matthew
Exodus	Exodus	Mark
Leviticus	Leviticus	Luke
Numbers	Numbers	John
Deuteronomy	Deuteronomy	Acts of the Apostles
	Joshua	Romans
The Prophets	Judges	I Corinthians
	Ruth	II Corinthians
Joshua	I Samuel	Galatians
Judges	II Samuel	Ephesians
I Samuel	I Kings	Philippians
II Samuel	II Kings	Colossians
I Kings	I Chronicles	I Thessalonians
II Kings	II Chronicles	II Thessalonians
Isaiah	Ezra	I Timothy
Jeremiah	Nehemiah	II Timothy
Ezekiel	*Tobit*	Titus
Hosea	*Judith*	Philemon
Joel	Esther	Hebrews
Amos	*I Maccabees*	James
Obadiah	*II Maccabees*	I Peter
Jonah	Job	II Peter
Micah	Psalms	I John
Nahum	Proverbs	II John
Habakkuk	Ecclesiastes	III John
Zephaniah	Song of Songs	Jude
Haggai	(Song of Solomon)	Revelation
Zechariah	*Wisdom of Solomon*	
Malachi	*Ecclesiasticus*	
	Isaiah	
The Writings	Jeremiah	
	Lamentations	
Psalms	*Baruch*	
Proverbs	Ezekiel	
Job	Daniel	
Song of Songs	Hosea	
Ruth	Joel	
Lamentations	Amos	
Ecclesiastes	Obadiah	
Esther	Jonah	
Daniel	Micah	
Ezra	Nahum	
Nehemiah	Habakkuk	
I Chronicles	Zephaniah	
II Chronicles	Haggai	
	Zechariah	
	Malachi	

of two legislative branches. [BI– + Lat. *camera,* chamber.] —**bi·cam′er·al·ism** *n.*

bi·car·bon·ate (bī-kär′bə-nāt′, -nĭt) ►*n.* The anion HCO₃⁻ or a compound, such as sodium bicarbonate, containing it.

bicarbonate of soda ►*n.* See **baking soda.**

bi·cen·ten·a·ry (bī′sĕn-tĕn′ə-rē, bī-sĕn′tə-nĕr′ē) ►*n., pl.* **-ries** A bicentennial. —**bi′cen·ten′a·ry** *adj.*

bi·cen·ten·ni·al (bī′sĕn-tĕn′ē-əl) ►*n.* A 200th anniversary or its celebration; bicentenary. —**bi′cen·ten′ni·al** *adj.*

bi·ceps (bī′sĕps′) ►*n., pl.* **-ceps** or **-ceps·es** (-sĕp′sĭz) A muscle with two points of origin, esp. the large muscle at the front of the upper arm. [< Lat., two-headed.]

bick·er (bĭk′ər) ►*v.* To engage in a petty quarrel; squabble. ►*n.* A petty quarrel; squabble. [ME *bikeren*, to attack.]

bi·con·cave (bī′kŏn-kāv′, bī-kŏn′kāv′) ►*adj.* Concave on both sides or surfaces. **—bi′con·cav′i·ty** (-kăv′ĭ-tē) *n.*

bi·con·vex (bī′kŏn-vĕks′, bī-kŏn′vĕks′) ►*adj.* Convex on both sides or surfaces. **—bi′con·vex′i·ty** (-vĕk′sĭ-tē) *n.*

bi·cus·pid (bī-kŭs′pĭd) ►*adj.* Having two points or cusps. ►*n.* A bicuspid tooth, esp. a premolar. [BI- + Lat. *cuspis*, point.]

bi·cy·cle (bī′sĭk′əl, -sĭ-kəl) ►*n.* A vehicle consisting of a metal frame mounted on two wire-spoked wheels and having a seat, handlebars for steering, brakes, and pedals. ►*v.* **-cled, -cling** To ride or travel on a bicycle. [Fr.] **—bi′cy·cler, bi′cy·clist** *n.*

bid (bĭd) ►*v.* **bade** (băd, bād) or **bid, bid·den** (bĭd′n) or **bid, bid·ding 1.** To greet. **2.** To command; direct. **3.** *p.t. and p.part.* **bid a.** To offer to pay or accept a specified price. **b.** To offer as a price. **c.** To state one's intention to take (tricks of a certain number or suit) in card games. ►*n.* **1a.** An offer of a price. **b.** The amount offered. **2.** An invitation, esp. one offering membership in a group. **3a.** The act of bidding in card games. **b.** The number of tricks declared. **c.** A player's turn to bid. **4.** An earnest effort to gain something. [< OE *biddan*, to command, and *bēodan*, to offer.] **—bid′der** *n.*

bid·da·ble (bĭd′ə-bəl) ►*adj.* **1.** Strong enough to be bid. Used of a hand of cards. **2.** Obedient; docile.

bid·dy (bĭd′ē) ►*n., pl.* **-dies** A hen. [?]

bide (bīd) ►*v.* **bid·ed** or **bode** (bōd), **bid·ed, bid·ing 1.** To remain; stay. **2.** To wait; tarry. **3.** *p.t.* **bided** To await. [< OE *bīdan*.]

Bi·den (bī′dən), **Joseph Robinette, Jr.** "Joe." b. 1942. US vice president (assumed office 2009).

bi·det (bē-dā′) ►*n.* A bathroom fixture that is straddled for washing the genital and anal areas. [Fr.]

bi·en·ni·al (bī-ĕn′ē-əl) ►*adj.* **1.** Lasting or living for two years. **2.** Happening every second year. **3.** *Bot.* Having a life cycle that normally takes two growing seasons. [< Lat. *biennium*, two-year period.] **—bi·en′ni·al** *n.* **—bi·en′ni·al·ly** *adv.*

bier (bîr) ►*n.* A stand on which a corpse or a coffin is placed before burial. [< OE *bēr*.]

Bierce (bîrs), **Ambrose Gwinett** 1842–1914? Amer. writer.

bi·fo·cal (bī-fō′kəl, bī′fō′-) ►*adj.* **1.** Having two different focal lengths. **2.** Having one section that corrects for distant vision and another that corrects for near vision, as an eyeglass lens. ►*pl.n.* **bi·fo·cals** Eyeglasses with bifocal lenses.

bi·fur·cate (bī′fər-kāt′, bī-fûr′-) ►*v.* **-cat·ed, -cat·ing** To divide into two parts or branches. [< Lat. *furca*, fork.] **—bi′fur·ca′tion** *n.*

big (bĭg) ►*adj.* **big·ger, big·gest 1a.** Of considerable size, number, extent, or strength. See Synonyms at **large. b.** Having great strength or force: *a big wind.* **c.** Of great significance; momentous: *a big decision.* **2.** Grown-up; adult. **3.** Older. Used esp. of a sibling: *my big sister.* **4.** Bountiful; generous: *a big heart.* **5.** Pregnant: *big with child.* **6.** *Informal* Widely liked; popular: *Boots are really big now.* **7.** *Informal* Self-important; cocky. ►*adv.* **1.** In a self-important

or boastful way. **2.** *Informal* With great success. **—idiom: big on** Enthusiastic about; partial to. [ME, perh. of Scand. orig.] **—big′gish** *adj.* **—big′ness** *n.*

big·a·my (bĭg′ə-mē) ►*n., pl.* **-mies** *Law* The criminal offense of marrying one person while still legally married to another. [< LLat. *bigamus*, bigamous.] **—big′a·mist** *n.* **—big′a·mous** *adj.*

Big Bang theory ►*n.* A scientific theory describing the origin of all space, time, matter, and energy approx. 13.7 billion years ago from the violent expansion of a singular point of extremely high density and temperature.

big brother also **Big Brother** ►*n.* An omnipresent, seemingly benevolent figure representing the oppressive control over individuals exerted by an authoritarian government.

Big Dipper ►*n.* A cluster of seven stars in the constellation Ursa Major forming a dipper-shaped configuration.

Big·foot (bĭg′fŏŏt′) ►*n.* A very large, hairy, humanlike creature purported to inhabit the Pacific Northwest and Canada; Sasquatch.

big game ►*n.* Large animals or fish hunted or caught for sport. **—big′-game′** *adj.*

big·heart·ed (bĭg′här′tĭd) ►*adj.* Generous; kind. **—big′heart′ed·ly** *adv.*

big·horn sheep (bĭg′hôrn′) ►*n.* A wild sheep of the mountains of W North America, the male of which has massive, curved horns.

bight (bīt) ►*n.* **1.** A loop in a rope. **2a.** A bend or curve, esp. in a shoreline. **b.** A wide bay formed by a bight. [< OE *byht*, bend.]

big·mouth (bĭg′mouth′) ►*n.* *Slang* A loud-mouthed or gossipy person.

big-name (bĭg′nām′) ►*adj.* *Informal* Widely acclaimed; famous. **—big name** *n.*

big·ot (bĭg′ət) ►*n.* One who is intolerant esp. in matters of religion, race, or politics. [OFr.] **—big′ot·ed** *adj.* **—big′ot·ry** *n.*

big shot ►*n.* *Slang* An important or influential person. **—big′shot′, big′-shot′** *adj.*

Big Sur (sûr) A coastal region of central CA.

big-tick·et (bĭg′tĭk′ĭt) ►*adj.* *Informal* Having a high cost: *big-ticket items.*

big time ►*n.* *Informal* The most prestigious level of attainment in a competitive field or profession. **—big′-time′** *adj.*

big top ►*n.* **1.** The main tent of a circus. **2.** The circus.

big·wig (bĭg′wĭg′) ►*n.* *Slang* A very important person.

bike (bīk) ►*n.* **1.** A bicycle. **2.** A motorcycle or motorbike. **—bike** *v.*

bik·er (bī′kər) ►*n.* **1.** One who rides a bicycle or motorbike. **2.** A motorcyclist.

bi·ki·ni (bĭ-kē′nē) ►*n.* **1.** A woman's brief, close-fitting two-piece bathing suit. **2.** A man's brief bathing trunks. [After BIKINI.]

Bikini An atoll of the Marshall Is. in the W-central Pacific.

bi·lat·er·al (bī-lăt′ər-əl) ►*adj.* **1.** Having two sides; two-sided. **2.** Affecting or undertaken by two sides equally. **—bi·lat′er·al·ly** *adv.*

Bil·ba·o (bĭl-bä′ō, -bou′) A city of N Spain near the Bay of Biscay.

bile (bīl) ►*n.* **1.** A bitter greenish-yellow fluid that is secreted by the liver and aids in the digestion of fats. **2.** Ill temper; irascibility. [< Lat. *bīlis*.] **—bil′i·ar′y** (bĭl′ē-ĕr′ē) *adj.*

bilge (bĭlj) ►*n.* **1.** The lowest inner part of a ship's hull. **2.** Bilge water. **3.** *Slang* Nonsense. [Prob. < BULGE.]

bilge water ►*n.* **1.** Water that collects and stagnates in a ship's bilge. **2.** *Slang* Nonsense.

bi·lin·gual (bī-lĭng′gwəl) ►*adj.* Expressed in or able to speak two languages. [< BI- + Lat. *lingua,* tongue.] —**bi·lin′gual·ism** *n.* —**bi·lin′gual·ly** *adv.*

bil·ious (bĭl′yəs) ►*adj.* **1.** Of or containing bile. **2.** Characterized by or experiencing gastric distress caused by a disorder of the liver or gallbladder. **3.** Peevish or ill-humored. —**bil′ious·ly** *adv.* —**bil′ious·ness** *n.*

bilk (bĭlk) ►*v.* To defraud, cheat, or swindle. [Perh. < BALK.] —**bilk′er** *n.*

bill¹ (bĭl) ►*n.* **1.** A statement of charges for goods or services. **2.** A list of particulars, such as a theater program or menu. **3.** The entertainment offered by a theater. **4.** A public notice, such as an advertising poster. **5.** A piece of legal paper money. **6.** A bill of exchange. **7a.** A draft of a law presented for approval to a legislative body. **b.** The law enacted from such a draft. ►*v.* **1.** To present a statement of costs or charges to. **2.** To enter on a bill. **3.** To advertise by public notice. [< Med.Lat. *bulla,* seal on a document.] —**bill′a·ble** *adj.*

bill² (bĭl) ►*n.* **1.** The horny part of the jaws of a bird; beak. **2.** A beaklike mouth part, as of a turtle. **3.** The visor of a cap. ►*v.* To touch beaks together. [< OE *bile.*]

bill·board (bĭl′bôrd′) ►*n.* A large panel for the display of advertisements.

bil·let (bĭl′ĭt) ►*n.* **1a.** Lodging for troops. **b.** A written order directing that such lodging be provided. **2.** A position of employment; job. ►*v.* To assign quarters to. [< OFr. *billette,* official register.]

bil·let-doux (bĭl′ā-dōō′) ►*n., pl.* **bil·lets-doux** (bĭl′ā-dōōz′) A love letter. [Fr.]

bill·fold (bĭl′fōld′) ►*n.* A wallet.

bil·liards (bĭl′yərdz) ►*pl.n. (takes sing. v.)* Any of various games played on a cloth-covered table, in which a cue is used to hit balls against one another or the raised sides of the table. [< Fr. *billard,* cue.]

bill·ing (bĭl′ĭng) ►*n.* The relative importance of performers as indicated by their listing on programs or advertisements: *top billing.*

bil·lings·gate (bĭl′ĭngz-gāt′, -gĭt) ►*n.* Foul, abusive language. [After *Billingsgate,* a former fish market in London.]

bil·lion (bĭl′yən) ►*n.* **1.** The cardinal number equal to 10⁹. **2.** *Chiefly Brit.* The cardinal number equal to 10¹². [Fr., a million million.] —**bil′lion** *adj. & pron.*

bil·lion·aire (bĭl′yə-nâr′) ►*n.* One whose wealth equals at least a billion dollars, pounds, or the equivalent in other currency. [BILLION + (MILLION)AIRE.]

bil·lionth (bĭl′yənth) ►*n.* **1.** The ordinal number matching the number billion in a series. **2.** One of a billion equal parts. —**bil′lionth** *adj. & adv.*

bill of exchange ►*n.* A written order directing that a specified sum of money be paid to a specified person.

bill of fare ►*n.* **1.** A menu. **2.** A list of events in a presentation; program.

bill of goods ►*n.* **1.** A consignment of items

for sale. **2.** *Informal* A dishonest or misleading promise or offer.

bill of lading ►*n.* A document listing and acknowledging receipt of goods for transport.

bill of rights ►*n.* **1.** A formal summary of the rights of a group of people: *a consumer bill of rights.* **2. Bill of Rights** The first ten amendments to the US Constitution.

bill of sale ►*n.* A document that attests a transfer of personal property.

bil·low (bĭl′ō) ►*n.* **1.** A large wave of water. **2.** A great swell or surge, as of smoke or windblown fabric. ►*v.* **1.** To surge or roll in billows. **2.** To swell or cause to swell in billows. [< ON *bylgja.*] —**bil′low·y** *adj.*

bil·ly club (bĭl′ē) ►*n.* A short wooden club, esp. a police officer's. [Perh. < BULLY.]

billy goat ►*n. Informal* A male goat.

bi·me·tal·lic (bī′mə-tăl′ĭk) ►*adj.* **1.** Consisting of two metals. **2.** Of, based on, or using the principles of bimetallism.

bi·met·al·lism (bī-mĕt′l-ĭz′əm) ►*n.* The use of both gold and silver in a fixed ratio of value as a monetary standard.

Bim·i·nis (bĭm′ə-nēz) A group of small islands of the W Bahamas located in the Straits of Florida.

bi·mod·al (bī-mōd′l) ►*adj.* Having two distinct modes or forms. —**bi′mo·dal′i·ty** (-dăl′ĭ-tē) *n.*

bi·month·ly (bī-mŭnth′lē) ►*adj.* **1.** Happening every two months. **2.** Happening twice a month; semimonthly. ►*n., pl.* **-lies** A bimonthly publication. See Usage Note at **bi-**. —**bi·month′ly** *adv.*

bin (bĭn) ►*n.* A container or enclosed space for storage. [< OE *binne.*]

bin- ►*pref.* Var. of **bi-**.

bi·na·ry (bī′nə-rē) ►*adj.* **1.** Having two distinct parts or components. **2.** Of a number system having 2 as its base. ►*n., pl.* **-ries** A number system having 2 as its base. [< Lat. *bīnī,* two by two.]

binary digit ►*n.* Either of the digits 0 or 1, used in the binary number system.

binary star ►*n.* A system consisting of two stars orbiting about a common center of mass and often appearing as a single object.

bin·au·ral (bī-nôr′əl, bĭn-ôr′-) ►*adj.* **1.** Of or hearing with two ears. **2.** Relating to sound transmission from two sources, which may vary acoustically to give a stereophonic effect. —**bin·au′ral·ly** *adv.*

bind (bīnd) ►*v.* **bound** (bound), **bind·ing 1.** To tie or encircle with or as with a rope or cord. **2.** To bandage. **3.** To hold or restrain. **4a.** To compel or constrain. **b.** To place under legal obligation. **5a.** To cohere or cause to cohere in a mass. **b.** To constipate. **6.** To enclose and fasten (e.g., a book) between covers. **7.** To reinforce or ornament with an edge or border. **8.** To be uncomfortably tight or restricting. ►*n.* **1.** Something that binds. **2.** *Informal* A difficult or restrictive situation. [< OE *bindan.*] —**bind′er** *n.*

bind·er·y (bīn′də-rē) ►*n., pl.* **-ies** A place where books are bound.

bin·di (bĭn′dē) ►*n., pl.* **-dis** An ornamental dot traditionally worn by Hindu women in the middle of the forehead or between the eyebrows. [Hindi *bindī.*]

bindi

bind·ing (bīn′dĭng) ►*n.* Something that binds, as: **a.** The cover that holds together the pages of a book. **b.** A strip sewn along an edge. **c.** Fastenings on a ski for securing the boot. ►*adj.* **1.** Serving to bind. **2.** Requiring adherence to an obligation or commitment: *binding arbitration.*

binge (bĭnj) ►*n.* A period of uncontrolled self-indulgence, esp. in food or drink. ►*v.* **binged, bing·ing** or **binge·ing** To be or go on a binge. [< dial. *binge,* to soak.]

bin·go (bĭng′gō) ►*n.* A game of chance in which players place markers on a grid of numbered squares according to numbers drawn by a caller. ►*interj.* Used to express the occurrence, completion, or correctness of a guess. [?]

bin La·den (bĭn lä′dən), **Osama** 1957–2011. Saudi Arabian–born leader of al-Qaeda.

bin·na·cle (bĭn′ə-kəl) ►*n. Naut.* A case near the helm that supports a ship's compass. [< Lat. *habitāculum,* little house.]

bin·oc·u·lar (bə-nŏk′yə-lər, bī-) ►*adj.* Of or involving both eyes at the same time: *binocular vision.* ►*n.* often **binoculars** A binocular optical device, such as field glasses.

bi·no·mi·al (bī-nō′mē-əl) ►*adj.* Consisting of two names or terms. ►*n.* **1.** *Math.* A polynomial with two terms. **2.** A taxonomic plant or animal name consisting of two terms. [< BI– + Lat. *nōmen,* name.] —**bi·no′mi·al·ly** *adv.*

bi·o (bī′ō) ►*n., pl.* **-os** *Informal* A biography.

bio– ►*pref.* Life; living organism: *biochemistry.* [< Gk. *bios,* life.]

bi·o·chem·is·try (bī′ō-kĕm′ĭ-strē) ►*n.* The study of the chemical substances and vital processes occurring in living organisms. —**bi′·o·chem′i·cal** (-ĭ-kəl) *adj. & n.* —**bi′o·chem′i·cal·ly** *adv.* —**bi′o·chem′ist** *n.*

bi·o·con·ver·sion (bī′ō-kən-vûr′zhən, -shən) ►*n.* The conversion of organic materials into usable products or energy by biological means.

bi·o·de·grad·a·ble (bī′ō-dĭ-grā′də-bəl) ►*adj.* Capable of being decomposed by natural biological processes. —**bi′o·de·grad′a·bil′i·ty** *n.* —**bi′o·deg′ra·da′tion** (-dĕg′rə-dā′shən) *n.* —**bi′o·de·grade′** *v.*

bi·o·die·sel (bī′ō-dē′zəl, -səl) ►*n.* A biofuel made by processing vegetable oils and other fats for use in a diesel engine.

bi·o·di·ver·si·ty (bī′ō-dĭ-vûr′sĭ-tē) ►*n.* The number and variety of organisms found in a specified geographic region or environment.

bi·o·feed·back (bī′ō-fēd′băk′) ►*n.* The technique of using monitoring devices to learn about an involuntary bodily function, such as blood pressure, in order to gain some voluntary control over that function.

bi·o·fuel (bī′ō-fyōō′əl) ►*n.* A fuel, such as biogas or biodiesel, that is produced from renewable resources, esp. plant biomass, vegetable oils, or municipal and industrial wastes. —**bi′o·fueled′** (-fyōōld′) *adj.*

bi·o·gas (bī′ō-găs′) ►*n.* A mixture of methane and carbon dioxide produced by bacterial degradation of organic matter and used as a fuel.

bi·o·gen·ic (bī′ō-jĕn′ĭk) ►*adj.* **1.** Produced by living organisms or biological processes. **2.** Necessary for the maintenance of life.

bi·o·ge·og·ra·phy (bī′ō-jē-ŏg′rə-fē) ►*n.* The study of the geographic distribution of organisms.

bi·og·ra·phy (bī-ŏg′rə-fē) ►*n., pl.* **-phies 1.** An account of a person's life written or produced by someone else. **2.** Biographies collectively, esp. when regarded as a literary form. —**bi·og′ra·pher** *n.* —**bi′o·graph′i·cal** (bī′ə-grăf′ĭ-kəl), **bi′o·graph′ic** *adj.*

bi·o·log·i·cal (bī′ə-lŏj′ĭ-kəl) also **bi·o·log·ic** ►*adj.* **1.** Of or relating to biology. **2.** Related by blood: *the child's biological parents.* **3.** Being male or female in terms of chromosomes. —**bi′o·log′i·cal·ly** *adv.*

biological clock ►*n.* **1.** A mechanism in organisms that controls the periodic occurrence of functions or activities, such as sleep cycles or photosynthesis. **2.** The capacity to conceive a child or the period of time during which conception is still possible, esp. for a woman nearing the end of her reproductive years.

biological warfare ►*n.* Warfare in which biological weapons are used.

biological weapon ►*n.* A pathogen, such as a bacterium or virus, that has been prepared for release with the intention of causing widespread illness or death.

bi·ol·o·gy (bī-ŏl′ə-jē) ►*n.* **1.** The science of life and of living organisms. **2.** The life processes of a particular group or category of living organisms. —**bi·ol′o·gist** *n.*

bi·o·mass (bī′ō-măs′) ►*n.* **1.** The total mass of living matter within a given unit of environmental area. **2.** Plant material or agricultural waste used as a fuel.

bi·ome (bī′ōm′) ►*n.* A major regional biotic community, such as a grassland or desert.

bi·o·me·chan·ics (bī′ō-mĭ-kăn′ĭks) ►*n. (takes sing. v.)* The study of the mechanics of a living body, esp. of the forces exerted on the skeletal structure. —**bi′o·me·chan′i·cal** *adj.*

bi·on·ic (bī-ŏn′ĭk) ►*adj.* Having anatomical structures that are replaced esp. by electronic components. [BI(O)– + (ELECTR)ONIC.]

bi·o·phys·ics (bī′ō-fĭz′ĭks) ►*n. (takes sing. v.)* The physics of biological processes. —**bi′o·phys′i·cal** *adj.* —**bi′o·phys′i·cist** *n.*

bi·o·pros·pect·ing (bī′ō-prŏs′pĕk-tĭng) ►*n.* The attempt to discover in living organisms biochemicals or genetic sequences that have medical, agricultural, or industrial value. —**bi′o·pros′pec·tor** *n.*

bi·op·sy (bī′ŏp′sē) ►*n., pl.* **-sies** The removal and examination of a sample of tissue from a living body for medical diagnosis.

bi·o·re·me·di·a·tion (bī′ō-rĭ-mē′dē-ā′shən) ►*n.* The use of biological agents to decontaminate polluted soil or water.

bi·o·rhythm (bī′ō-rĭ*th*′əm) ►*n.* An innate, cyclical biological process or function.

–biosis ►*suff.* A way of living: *symbiosis.* [< Gk. *biōsis* < *bios,* life.]

bi·o·sphere (bī′ə-sfîr′) ►*n.* The part of the earth and its atmosphere in which living organisms exist.

bi·o·ta (bī-ō′tə) ►*n.* The combined flora and fauna of a region. [< Gk. *biotē,* way of life < *bios,* life.]

bi·o·tech (bī′ō-tĕk′) ►*n.* Biotechnology.

bi·o·tech·nol·o·gy (bī′ō-tĕk-nŏl′ə-jē) ►*n.* **1.** The use of microorganisms or biological substances to perform industrial or manufacturing processes. **2.** See **ergonomics.** —**bi′o·tech′·no·log′i·cal** (-nə-lŏj′ĭ-kəl) *adj.*

bi·ot·ic (bī-ŏt′ĭk) ►*adj.* **1.** Of life or living organisms. **2.** Produced by living organisms. [Gk. *biōtikos* < *bios,* life.]

bi·o·tin (bī′ə-tĭn) ►*n.* A crystalline vitamin of the vitamin B complex, found esp. in liver, egg yolk, milk, and yeast. [< Gk. *biōtos,* life < *bios.*]

bi·par·ti·san (bī-pär′tĭ-zən, -sən) ►*adj.* Of, consisting of, or supported by members of two parties, esp. two major political parties. —**bi·par′ti·san·ship′** *n.*

bi·par·tite (bī-pär′tīt′) ►*adj.* **1.** Having or consisting of two parts. **2a.** Having two corresponding parts, one for each party: *a bipartite contract.* **b.** Having two participants: *a bipartite agreement.*

bi·ped (bī′pĕd′) ►*n.* An animal with two feet.

bi·ped·al (bī-pĕd′l) ►*adj.* Having or walking on two feet.

bi·plane (bī′plān′) ►*n.* An airplane having two pairs of wings fixed at different levels, esp. one above and one below the fuselage.

bi·po·lar (bī-pō′lər) ►*adj.* **1.** Of or having two poles. **2.** Having two opposing sides or systems. **3.** Having bipolar disorder. —**bi′po·lar′i·ty** (-lăr′ĭ-tē) *n.*

bipolar disorder ►*n.* A mood disorder characterized by periods of depression alternating with mania or hypomania.

bi·ra·cial (bī-rā′shəl) ►*adj.* **1.** Of or consisting of members of two races. **2.** Having parents of two different races. —**bi·ra′cial·ism** *n.*

birch (bûrch) ►*n.* **1a.** A deciduous tree having bark that peels in thin papery layers. **b.** The hard wood of a birch. **2.** A birch rod used for whipping. ►*v.* To whip with a birch. [< OE *birce.*]

bird (bûrd) ►*n.* **1.** A warm-blooded, egg-laying, feathered vertebrate with forelimbs modified to form wings. **2.** *Slang* A person: *a sly old bird.* —**idiom: for the birds** Objectionable or worthless. [< OE *brid.*]

Bird, Larry Joe b. 1956. Amer. basketball player and coach.

bird·bath (bûrd′băth′, -bäth′) ►*n.* A water basin for birds to drink from and bathe in.

bird·er (bûr′dər) ►*n.* **1.** A bird watcher. **2a.** A breeder of birds. **b.** A hunter of birds.

bird·house (bûrd′hous′) ►*n.* A box made as a nesting place for birds.

bird·ie (bûr′dē) ►*n.* **1.** One stroke under par for a hole in golf. **2.** See **shuttlecock.** —**bird′ie** *v.*

bird·lime (bûrd′līm′) ►*n.* A sticky substance that is smeared on branches to capture small birds.

bird of paradise ►*n., pl.* **birds of paradise 1.** Any of various Australasian birds usu. having brilliant plumage and long tail feathers in the male. **2.** An African plant having showy orange and blue flowers.

bird's-eye (bûrdz′ī′) ►*adj.* **1.** Marked with a spot or spots resembling a bird's eye. **2.** Derived from or as if from an altitude or distance; comprehensive: *a bird's-eye view.*

bird·shot (bûrd′shŏt′) ►*n.* Small lead shot for shotgun shells.

bird watcher ►*n.* One who observes and identifies birds in their natural surroundings. —**bird watching** *n.*

bi·ret·ta (bə-rĕt′ə) ►*n.* A stiff square cap worn esp. by the Roman Catholic clergy. [< LLat. *birrus,* hooded cloak.]

birr (bîr) ►*n., pl.* **birr** or **birrs** See table at **currency.** [Amharic *bərr,* be white.]

birth (bûrth) ►*n.* **1a.** The fact of being born. **b.** The act of bearing young. **2.** Origin or ancestry: *of Iraqi birth.* **3.** A beginning or commencement. See Synonyms at **beginning.** ►*v.* **1.** To deliver (a baby). **2.** *Regional* To bear (a child). [ME.]

birth canal ►*n.* The passage from the uterus through the cervix and vagina.

birth control ►*n.* Prevention of conception through the use of contraceptive techniques.

birth·day (bûrth′dā′) ►*n.* The day or anniversary of one's birth.

birth defect ►*n.* A physiological abnormality present at the time of birth, esp. as a result of faulty development, heredity, or injury.

birth family ►*n.* A family consisting of one's biological parents and siblings as opposed to adoptive ones.

birth·mark (bûrth′märk′) ►*n.* A mole or blemish present on the skin from birth.

birth parent ►*n.* A biolo⅛gical parent.

birth·place (bûrth′plās′) ►*n.* The place where someone is born or something originates.

birth·rate (bûrth′rāt′) ►*n.* The ratio of live births to total population in a specified community or area over a specified period.

birth·right (bûrth′rīt′) ►*n.* A right, possession, or privilege that is one's due by birth.

birth·stone (bûrth′stōn′) ►*n.* A gemstone associated with the month of a person's birth.

Bis·cay (bĭs′kā), **Bay of** An arm of the Atlantic indenting the W coast of Europe from NW France to NW Spain.

Bis·cayne Bay (bĭs-kān′, bĭs′kān′) An inlet of the Atlantic in SE FL.

bis·cuit (bĭs′kĭt) ►*n.* **1.** A small cake of bread leavened with baking powder or soda. **2.** *Chiefly Brit.* **a.** A thin crisp cracker. **b.** A cookie. **3.** A pale brown. [< Med.Lat. *bis coctus,* twice cooked.]

bi·sect (bī′sĕkt′, bī-sĕkt′) ►*v.* **1.** To cut or divide into two parts, esp. two equal parts. **2.** To split; fork. —**bi·sec′tion** *n.* —**bi·sec′tor** *n.*

bi·sex·u·al (bī-sĕk′shoo-əl) ►*adj.* **1.** Relating to both sexes. **2.** Having both male and female organs. **3.** Having a sexual orientation to persons of either sex. —**bi·sex′u·al** *n.* —**bi′sex·u·al′i·ty** (-ăl′ĭ-tē) *n.* —**bi·sex′u·al·ly** *adv.*

Bish·kek (bĭsh′kĕk, bēsh′-) Formerly **Frunze.**

The capital of Kyrgyzstan, in the N-central part.

bish·op (bĭsh′əp) ►*n.* **1.** A high-ranking Christian cleric, usu. in charge of a diocese. **2.** *Games* A chess piece that can move diagonally across any number of free spaces. [< Gk. *episkopos,* overseer < *skopos,* watcher.]

bish·op·ric (bĭsh′ə-prĭk) ►*n.* The office, rank, or diocese of a bishop. [< OE *bisceoprīce,* diocese of a bishop.]

Bis·marck (bĭz′märk′) The capital of ND, in the S-central part.

Bismarck, Prince Otto Eduard Leopold von. 1815–98. Creator and first chancellor of the German Empire (1871–90). —**Bis·marck′i·an** *adj.*

Bismarck Archipelago A group of volcanic islands and islets of Papua New Guinea in the SW Pacific.

bis·muth (bĭz′məth) ►*n. Symbol* **Bi** A white, crystalline, brittle metallic element used in low-melting alloys. At. no. 83. See table at **element.** [< obsolete Ger. *Wismuth.*]

bi·son (bī′sən, -zən) ►*n.* **1.** A bovine mammal of W North America, having a shaggy mane and massive head with short curved horns; buffalo. **2.** A similar mammal native to central and E Europe. [Lat. *bisōn.*]

bisque (bĭsk) ►*n.* A cream soup. [Fr.]

Bis·sau (bĭ-sou′) The capital of Guinea-Bissau, on an estuary of the Atlantic.

bis·tro (bē′strō, bĭs′trō) ►*n., pl.* **-tros 1.** A small informal restaurant. **2.** A small bar, tavern, or nightclub. [Fr.]

bit¹ (bĭt) ►*n.* **1.** A small portion, degree, or amount. **2.** A moment. **3.** An entertainment routine; act. **4.** A particular kind of action or behavior: *got tired of the macho bit.* **5.** *Informal* An amount equal to ⅛ of a dollar. —*idioms:* **a bit** Somewhat: *a bit warm.* **bit by bit** Gradually. [< OE *bita.*]

bit² (bĭt) ►*n.* **1.** The sharp part of a tool, such as the cutting edge of an ax. **2.** A pointed and threaded tool for drilling and boring that is secured in a brace, bitstock, or drill press. **3.** The metal mouthpiece of a horse's bridle. [< OE, a biting.]

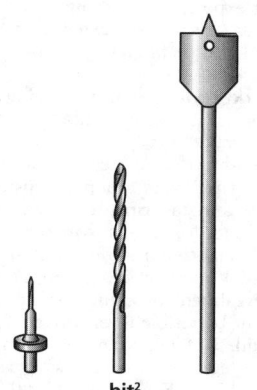

bit²
left to right: pilot, twist, and spade bits

bit³ (bĭt) ►*n. Comp.* A binary digit, having either the value 0 or 1, used to store or represent data. [B(INARY) + (DIG)IT.]

bitch (bĭch) ►*n.* **1.** A female canine animal, esp.

a dog. **2.** *Offensive Slang* A mean or overbearing woman. **3.** *Slang* A complaint. **4.** *Slang* Something very unpleasant or difficult. ►*v. Slang* To complain. [< OE *bicce.*] —**bitch′y** *adj.*

bite (bīt) ►*v.* **bit** (bĭt), **bit·ten** (bĭt′n) or **bit, bit·ing 1.** To cut, grip, or tear with or as if with the teeth. **2.** To pierce the skin of with or as if with fangs. **3.** To cut into with or as if with a sharp instrument. **4.** To corrode. **5.** To take or swallow bait. ►*n.* **1.** The act of biting. **2.** A skin wound or puncture produced by biting. **3a.** A stinging or smarting sensation. **b.** An incisive, penetrating quality. **4a.** A mouthful. **b.** *Informal* A light meal or snack. **5.** The act of taking bait. **6.** The angle at which the upper and lower teeth meet; occlusion. —*idioms:* **bite the bullet** *Slang* To face a painful situation bravely and stoically. **bite the dust** *Slang* To fall dead, esp. in combat. [< OE *bītan.*] —**bit′er** *n.*

bite·wing (bīt′wĭng′) ►*n.* A dental x-ray film with a central projection on which the teeth can close.

bit·ing (bī′tĭng) ►*adj.* **1.** Causing a stinging sensation. **2.** Incisive; penetrating.

bit·map (bĭt′măp′) ►*n. Comp.* A set of bits representing a graphic image, with each bit or group of bits corresponding to a pixel in the image. —**bit′mapped′** *adj.*

bit·ter (bĭt′ər) ►*adj.* **-er, -est 1.** Having or being a taste that is sharp and unpleasant. **2.** Causing sharp pain to the body or great discomfort to the mind: *a bitter wind; bitter sorrow.* **3.** Proceeding from or exhibiting strong animosity: *bitter foes.* **4.** Having or marked by resentment or disappointment: *bitter feelings.* ►*adv.* In an intense or harsh way; bitterly: *a bitter cold night.* [< OE.] —**bit′ter·ly** *adv.* —**bit′ter·ness** *n.*
  Syns: *acerbic, acrid adj.*

bit·tern (bĭt′ərn) ►*n.* A wading bird having mottled brownish plumage and a deep booming cry. [< OFr. *butor.*]

bit·ters (bĭt′ərs) ►*pl.n.* A bitter, usu. alcoholic liquid made with herbs or roots and used in cocktails or as a tonic.

bit·ter·sweet (bĭt′ər-swēt′) ►*adj.* **1.** Bitter and sweet at the same time. **2.** Producing or expressing a mixture of pain and pleasure. ►*n.* **1.** A woody vine having small, round, yellow-orange fruits that split open to expose red seeds. **2.** See **bittersweet nightshade.**

bittersweet nightshade ►*n.* A poisonous climbing or trailing plant having violet flowers and red berries.

bit·ty (bĭt′ē) ►*adj.* **-ti·er, -ti·est** *Informal* Tiny.

bi·tu·men (bĭ-tōo′mən, -tyōo′-, bī-) ►*n.* Any of various flammable mixtures of hydrocarbons and other substances that are constituents of asphalt and tar. [< Lat.]

bi·tu·mi·nous (bĭ-tōo′mə-nəs, -tyōo′-, bī-) ►*adj.* Like or containing bitumen.

bituminous coal ►*n.* Coal containing a high percentage of volatile matter that burns with a smoky yellow flame; soft coal.

bi·va·lent (bī-vā′lənt) ►*adj. Chem.* Divalent.

bi·valve (bī′vălv′) ►*n.* A mollusk, such as an oyster or clam, that has a shell consisting of two hinged valves. —**bi′valve′** *adj.*

biv·ou·ac (bĭv′ōo-ăk′, bĭv′wăk′) ►*n.* A temporary camp in an unsheltered area. ►*v.* **-acked, -ack·ing** To camp in a bivouac. [Fr.]

bi·week·ly (bī-wēk′lē) ►*adj.* **1.** Happening

every two weeks. **2.** Happening twice a week; semiweekly. ►*n., pl.* **-lies** A publication issued every two weeks. See Usage Note at **bi–**. —**bi·week′ly** *adv.*

bi·year·ly (bī-yîr′lē) ►*adj.* **1.** Happening every two years; biennial. **2.** Happening twice a year; semiannual. —**bi·year′ly** *adv.*

bi·zarre (bǐ-zär′) ►*adj.* Strange or unusual, esp. in a striking or shocking way. [< Sp. *bizarro*, brave.] —**bi·zarre′ly** *adv.*

bl. ►*abbr.* barrel

blab (blăb) ►*v.* **blabbed, blab·bing 1.** To reveal (secret matters) esp. through careless talk. **2.** To chatter indiscreetly. [ME *blabben*.] —**blab** *n.*

blab·ber (blăb′ər) ►*v.* To chatter; blab. [ME *blaberen*.] —**blab′ber** *n.* —**blab′ber·er** *n.*

blab·ber·mouth (blăb′ər-mouth′) ►*n. Informal* A gossip or chatterbox.

black (blăk) ►*adj.* **-er, -est 1.** Being of the color black. **2.** Without light: *a black, moonless night.* **3.** also **Black** *a.* Of or belonging to a racial group having brown to black skin, esp. one of African origin. **b.** African-American. **4.** Soiled, as from soot; dirty. **5.** Evil; wicked: *black deeds.* **6.** Depressing; gloomy. **7.** Angry; sullen. **8.** Marked by morbid or grimly satiric humor: *a black comedy.* ►*n.* **1.** The achromatic color of maximum darkness; the color of objects that absorb nearly all light of all visible wavelengths. **2.** Absence of light; darkness. **3.** Something colored black, esp. clothing worn for mourning. **4.** also **Black** *a.* A member of a racial group having brown to black skin. **b.** An African American. **5.** The condition of turning a profit: *in the black.* ►*v.* To make or become black. —*phrasal verb:* **black out 1.** To lose consciousness or memory temporarily. **2.** To produce or cause a blackout. [< OE *blæc.*] —**black′ish** *adj.* —**black′ly** *adv.* —**black′ness** *n.*

black-and-blue (blăk′ən-blōō′) ►*adj.* Discolored from bruising.

black and white ►*n.* **1.** Writing or print. **2.** A visual medium, such as photography, using black and white, and sometimes values of gray. —**black′-and-white′** *adj.*

black·ball (blăk′bôl′) ►*n.* **1.** A negative vote, esp. one that blocks the admission of an applicant to an organization. **2.** A small black ball used as a negative ballot. ►*v.* **1.** To vote against (e.g., an applicant). **2.** To ostracize.

black bear ►*n.* A North American bear usu. having a black or dark brown coat.

black belt ►*n.* **1.** The rank of expert in a martial art such as judo or karate. **2.** The black sash that symbolizes this rank. **3.** One who has attained this rank.

black·ber·ry (blăk′běr′ē) ►*n.* **1.** A shrub having usu. prickly, canelike stems and black or purplish edible fruit. **2.** The fruit of this shrub.

black·bird (blăk′bûrd′) ►*n.* Any of various birds, such as the grackle or cowbird, having predominantly black plumage.

black·board (blăk′bôrd′) ►*n.* A smooth, dark-colored panel for writing on with chalk.

black·bod·y (blăk′bŏd′ē) ►*n.* A theoretically perfect absorber of all incident radiation.

black box ►*n.* **1.** See **event recorder. 2.** A large room with black walls used as a theater.

Black Death ►*n.* An outbreak of virulent plague, esp. its bubonic form, that killed large numbers

of people in Europe and Asia in the 1300s. [From the dark skin lesions or the general despair it caused.]

black·en (blăk′ən) ►*v.* **1.** To make or become black. **2.** To defame. —**black′en·er** *n.*

black eye ►*n.* **1.** Bruised discoloration of the skin around the eye. **2.** A blow to one's reputation.

black-eyed Su·san (blăk′īd′ sōō′zən) ►*n.* A plant having daisylike flowers with orange-yellow rays and dark brown centers.

black·face (blăk′fās′) ►*n.* Makeup for a conventionalized comic travesty of black people, esp. in a minstrel show.

Black·foot (blăk′fŏŏt′) ►*n., pl.* **-foot** or **-feet 1.** A member of a Native American confederacy of three tribes inhabiting the N Great Plains. **2.** Their Algonquian language.

Black Forest A mountainous region of SW Germany between the Rhine and Neckar Rivers.

black·guard (blăg′ərd, -ärd′) ►*n.* A thoroughly unprincipled person; scoundrel.

Black Hawk 1767–1838. Sauk leader in the Black Hawk War (1832).

black·head (blăk′hěd′) ►*n.* A hair follicle that is clogged with fatty secretions, appearing black at the surface.

Black Hills A group of mountains of SW SD .and NE WY.

black hole ►*n.* An area of space-time with a gravitational field so intense that nothing can escape, not even light.

black·jack (blăk′jăk′) ►*n.* **1.** A small leather-covered bludgeon with a short flexible shaft. **2.** A card game in which the object is to accumulate cards with a higher count than that of the dealer but not exceeding 21.

black light ►*n.* Invisible ultraviolet or infrared radiation.

black·list (blăk′lĭst′) ►*n.* A list of disapproved persons or organizations. ►*v.* To place on a blacklist.

black lung ►*n.* A lung disease caused by the long-term inhalation of coal dust.

black magic ►*n.* Magic practiced for evil purposes or in league with evil spirits.

black·mail (blăk′māl′) ►*n.* **1.** Extortion by the threat of exposing something criminal or discreditable. **2.** Something extorted by blackmail. [BLACK + Sc. *mail*, rent.] —**black′mail′** *v.* —**black′mail′er** *n.*

black market ►*n.* The illegal buying or selling of goods or currency. —**black′-mar′ket·er, black′-mar′ket·eer′** *n.*

Black Muslim ►*n.* A member of the Nation of Islam, a religious group espousing Islamic principles and favoring social and economic independence for African Americans.

black·out (blăk′out′) ►*n.* **1.** Lack of illumination caused by an electrical power failure. **2.** The concealment or extinguishment of lights that might be visible to enemy aircraft during an air raid. **3.** A temporary loss of memory or consciousness. **4a.** A suppression, as of news, by censorship. **b.** Restriction of local telecasting of a sports event.

black pepper ►*n.* A pungent spice made from ground peppercorns.

Black Power ►*n.* A movement among African Americans to achieve equality through black political and cultural institutions.

Black Sea An inland sea between Europe and Asia, connected with the Aegean by the Bosporus, the Sea of Marmara, and the Dardanelles.

black sheep ►*n.* One who is considered disreputable or disgraceful by his or her relatives or associates.

black·smith (blăk′smĭth′) ►*n.* One who forges and shapes iron with an anvil and hammer.

black·snake (blăk′snāk′) ►*n.* Any of various dark-colored, chiefly nonvenomous snakes.

black·top (blăk′tŏp′) ►*n.* A bituminous material, such as asphalt, used to pave roads.

Black·well (blăk′wĕl, -wəl), **Elizabeth** 1821–1910. British-born Amer. physician.

Elizabeth Blackwell

black widow ►*n.* A black spider, the female of which has red markings and produces extremely toxic venom.

blad·der (blăd′ər) ►*n.* An organ in the form of a distensible sac, such as the urinary bladder in mammals or the swim bladder in fish, that serves as a receptacle for fluid or gas. [< OE *blǣdre.*]

blade (blād) ►*n.* **1.** The flat-edged cutting part of a sharpened weapon or tool. **2.** A flat thin part or structure similar to a blade: *the blade of an oar; a blade of grass.* **3.** A dashing youth. ►*v.* **blad·ed, blad·ing** To skate on in-line skates. [< OE *blæd.*] —**blad′ed** *adj.*

blain (blān) ►*n.* A skin swelling or sore. [< OE *blegen.*]

Blair (blâr), **Anthony Charles Lynton** "Tony." b. 1953. British prime minister (1997–2007).

Blake (blāk), **William** 1757–1827. British poet and artist.

blame (blām) ►*v.* **blamed, blam·ing 1.** To hold responsible. **2.** To find fault with; censure. ►*n.* **1.** Responsibility for a fault or error; culpability. **2.** Censure, as for a fault; condemnation. [< LLat. *blasphēmāre,* reproach; see BLASPHEME.] —**blam′a·ble, blame′a·ble** *adj.* —**blam′a·bly** *adv.* —**blame′less** *adj.*

blame·wor·thy (blām′wûr′thē) ►*adj.* Deserving blame. —**blame′wor′thi·ness** *n.*

blanch (blănch) ►*v.* **1.** To make or become pale or white. **2.** To scald (food) briefly, as before freezing. [< OFr. *blanchir.*]

blanc·mange (blə-mänj′, -mänzh′) ►*n.* A flavored, sweet milk pudding. [< OFr. *blanc mangier,* white food.]

bland (blănd) ►*adj.* **-er, -est 1.** Characterized by a moderate, unperturbed, or tranquil quality. **2.** Not irritating; soothing: *a bland diet.* **3.** Lacking a distinctive character; dull and insipid. [Lat. *blandus,* flattering.] —**bland′ly** *adv.* —**bland′ness** *n.*

blan·dish (blăn′dĭsh) ►*v.* To coax by flattery or wheedling; cajole. [< Lat. *blandus,* flattering.] —**blan′dish·ment** *n.*

blank (blăngk) ►*adj.* **-er, -est 1a.** Devoid of writing, images, or marks. **b.** Containing no information: *a blank diskette.* **c.** Not completed or filled in. **2.** Not having received final processing: *a blank key.* **3a.** Lacking thoughts or impressions: *a blank mind.* **b.** Lacking expression; vacant: *a blank stare* **4.** Absolute; complete: *a blank refusal.* ►*n.* **1.** An empty space or place; void. **2.** A space to be filled in on a document. **3.** An unfinished manufactured article ready for final processing: *a key blank.* **4.** A gun cartridge with a powder charge but no bullet. ►*v.* **1.** To remove, as from view; obliterate. **2.** To become abstracted: *My mind blanked out for a few seconds.* [< OFr. *blanc,* white.] —**blank′ly** *adv.* —**blank′ness** *n.*

blank check ►*n.* **1.** A signed check without the amount filled in. **2.** Total freedom of action.

blan·ket (blăng′kĭt) ►*n.* **1.** A piece of woven material used as a covering. **2.** A layer that covers or encloses. ►*adj.* Applying to all conditions, instances, or members: *a blanket insurance policy.* ►*v.* To cover with or as if with a blanket. [< OFr., unbleached soft cloth < *blanc,* white.]

blank verse ►*n.* Unrhymed verse with a regular meter, esp. iambic pentameter.

blare (blâr) ►*v.* **blared, blar·ing** To sound loudly and stridently. [ME *bleren.*] —**blare** *n.*

blar·ney (blär′nē) ►*n.* Smooth, flattering talk. [After the *Blarney* Stone in Ireland.]

bla·sé (blä-zā′) ►*adj.* Uninterested or bored, esp. because of past experience. [Fr.]

blas·pheme (blăs-fēm′, blăs′fēm′) ►*v.* **-phemed, -phem·ing** To speak of (God or a sacred entity) in an irreverent, impious manner. [< Gk. *blasphēmein.*] —**blas·phem′er** *n.* —**blas′phe·mous** *adj.* —**blas′phe·mous·ly** *adv.* —**blas′phe·my** *n.*

blast (blăst) ►*n.* **1.** A strong gust of wind. **2.** A forcible stream of air, gas, or steam from an opening. **3.** A sudden loud sound, as of a whistle or trumpet. **4.** An explosion, as of dynamite or a bomb. **5.** A powerful hit, blow, or shot. **6.** A violent verbal assault. **7.** *Slang* A highly exciting or pleasurable experience. ►*v.* **1.** To explode. **2.** To sound loudly; blare. **3.** To hit with great force. **4.** To have a harmful or destructive effect (on). **5.** To criticize vigorously. **6.** To shoot. —***phrasal verb:* blast off** To take off, as a rocket or space vehicle. —*idiom:* **full blast** At full speed, volume, or capacity. [< OE *blǣst.*] —**blast′er** *n.*

Syns: blight, dash, wither, wreck **v.**

blast furnace ►*n.* A furnace in which combustion is intensified by a blast of air.

blast·off (blăst′ôf′, -ŏf′) ►*n.* The launch, esp. of a rocket.

bla·tant (blāt′nt) ►*adj.* **1.** Offensively conspicuous or undisguised: *a blatant lie.* **2.** Unpleasantly loud and noisy. [< Lat. *blatīre,* blab.] —**bla′tan·cy** *n.* —**bla′tant·ly** *adv.*

blath·er (blăth′ər) ►*v.* To talk nonsensically. [ON *bladhra.*] —**blath′er** *n.* —**blath′er·er** *n.*

blaze¹ (blāz) ►*n.* **1a.** A brilliant burst of fire; flame. **b.** A destructive fire. **2.** A bright, direct, or steady light: *the blaze of the desert sun.* **3.** A brilliant, striking display: *a blaze of color.* **4.** A sudden outburst, as of emotion. **5. blazes** Used as an intensive: *Where in blazes are my keys?* ▸*v.* **blazed, blaz·ing 1.** To burn or shine brightly. **2.** To show strong emotion. **3.** To shoot rapidly and continuously. [< OE *blæse.*]

blaze² (blāz) ▸*n.* **1.** A white or light-colored spot on the face of an animal. **2.** A mark cut or painted on a tree to indicate a trail. ▸*v.* **blazed, blaz·ing 1.** To indicate (a trail) by marking trees with blazes. **2.** To pioneer in a endeavor: *blazed the way in space exploration.* [Of Gmc. orig.]

blaz·er (blā′zər) ▸*n.* A lightweight, informal sport jacket.

bla·zon (blā′zən) ▸*v.* **1.** To adorn or embellish with or as if with a coat of arms. **2.** To display ostentatiously. ▸*n.* A coat of arms. [< OFr. *blason*, shield.] **—bla′zon·ry** *n.*

bldg. ▸*abbr.* building

bleach (blēch) ▸*v.* To make or become white or colorless. ▸*n.* A chemical agent used for bleaching. [< OE *blǣcan.*]

bleach·ers (blē′chərz) ▸*pl.n.* An often unroofed outdoor grandstand for seating spectators.

bleak (blēk) ▸*adj.* **-er, -est 1.** Dreary and somber; depressing: *a bleak prognosis.* **2.** Cold; raw: *bleak winds.* **3.** Exposed to the elements; barren. [< ON *bleikr*, pale.] **—bleak′ly** *adv.* **—bleak′ness** *n.*

blear (blîr) ▸*v.* **1.** To blur or redden the eyes. **2.** To blur; dim. ▸*adj.* Indistinct; blurry. [ME *bleren.*] **—blear′i·ly** *adv.* **—blear′y** *adj.*

bleat (blēt) ▸*n.* **1.** The characteristic cry of a goat or sheep. **2.** A sound similar to this cry. [< OE *blǣtan.*] **—bleat** *v.*

bleed (blēd) ▸*v.* **bled** (blĕd), **bleed·ing 1a.** To emit or lose blood. **b.** To extract blood from. **2.** To feel sympathetic grief or anguish: *My heart bleeds for you.* **3.** To exude or extract a fluid such as sap (from). **4.** To extort money from. **5.** To run together, as dyes on wet cloth or paper. **6.** To draw or drain liquid or gaseous contents from: *bleed the pipes.* [< OE *blēdan.*]

bleed·er (blē′dər) ▸*n.* One that bleeds freely, esp. a hemophiliac.

bleed·ing heart (blē′dĭng) ▸*n.* **1.** A garden plant having arching clusters of pink heart-shaped flowers. **2.** One who is excessively sympathetic toward others.

bleep (blēp) ▸*n.* A high-pitched electronic sound. ▸*v.* **1.** To emit a bleep. **2.** To edit out (spoken material) from a broadcast or recording, esp. by replacing with bleeps. [Imit.]

blem·ish (blĕm′ĭsh) ▸*n.* A flaw or defect. ▸*v.* To mar, spoil, or impair by a flaw. [< OFr. *blemir*, make pale.]

blench (blĕnch) ▸*v.* To draw back, as from fear; flinch. [< OE *blencan*, deceive.]

blend (blĕnd) ▸*v.* **blend·ed** or **blent** (blĕnt), **blend·ing 1.** To make or form a uniform mixture. **2.** To combine (varieties or grades) to obtain a new mixture: *blend whiskeys.* **3.** To become merged into one; unite. **4.** To create a harmonious effect or result: *colors that blend well.* ▸*n.* **1.** Something blended: *a blend of coffee and chicory.* **2.** *Ling.* A word produced by combining parts of other words, as *smog* from *smoke* and *fog.* [Prob. < ON *blanda.*]

blend·er (blĕn′dər) ▸*n.* One that blends, esp. an

appliance for mixing or liquefying foods.

bless (blĕs) ▸*v.* **blessed** or **blest** (blĕst), **bless·ing 1.** To make holy by religious rite; sanctify. **2.** To make the sign of the cross over. **3.** To invoke divine favor upon. **4.** To honor as holy; glorify: *Bless the Lord.* **5.** To confer well-being or prosperity upon. **6.** To endow, as with talent. [< OE *blētsian*, consecrate.]

bless·ed (blĕs′ĭd) ▸*adj.* **1.** Worthy of worship; holy. **2.** Bringing happiness or pleasure. **3.** Used as an intensive: *I don't have a blessed dime.* **—bless′ed·ly** *adv.* **—bless′ed·ness** *n.*

bless·ing (blĕs′ĭng) ▸*n.* **1.** The act or ceremony of one who blesses. **2.** A short prayer said at a meal; grace. **3.** Something promoting or contributing to happiness, well-being, or prosperity; boon. **4.** Approbation; approval: *This plan has my blessing.*

blew¹ (blōō) ▸*v.* P.t. of **blow¹.**

blew² (blōō) ▸*v.* P.t. of **blow³.**

blight (blīt) ▸*n.* **1.** A plant disease caused esp. by a bacterium, fungus, or virus. **2.** An adverse environmental condition, such as air pollution. **3.** Something that impairs growth or withers hopes. ▸*v.* **1.** To affect with blight. **2.** To ruin. See Synonyms at **blast. 3.** To frustrate. [?]

blimp (blĭmp) ▸*n.* A nonrigid, buoyant airship. [?]

blind (blīnd) ▸*adj.* **-er, -est 1a.** Sightless. **b.** Greatly impaired in vision. **2.** Of or for sightless persons. **3.** Performed by instruments and without the use of sight: *blind navigation.* **4.** Unable or unwilling to perceive or understand: *blind to a child's faults.* **5.** Not based on reason or evidence: *blind faith.* **6.** Hidden or screened from sight: *a blind seam; a blind intersection.* ▸*n.* **1.** Something, such as a window shade, that shuts out light. **2.** A shelter for concealed observation, as by hunters. **3.** A subterfuge. ▸*adv.* **1.** Without seeing; blindly. **2.** Used as an intensive: *Thieves robbed us blind.* ▸*v.* **1.** To deprive of sight. **2.** To dazzle. **3.** To deprive of perception, insight, or reason: *Prejudice blinded them.* [< OE.] **—blind′ly** *adv.* **—blind′ness** *n.*

blind date ▸*n.* **1.** A social engagement between two persons who have not previously met. **2.** One participating in such a date.

blind·ers (blīn′dərz) ▸*pl.n.* A pair of leather flaps attached to a horse's bridle to curtail side vision.

blind·fold (blīnd′fōld′) ▸*v.* **1.** To cover the eyes of with or as if with a bandage to prevent seeing. **2.** To mislead or delude. [< OE *geblindfellian*, strike blind.] **—blind′fold′** *n.* **—blind′fold·ed** *adj.*

blind side ▸*n.* **1.** The side on which one's peripheral vision is obstructed. **2.** The side away from which one is directing one's attention.

blind·side (blīnd′sīd′) ▸*v.* **1.** To hit or attack on the blind side. **2.** To take unawares, esp. with harmful results.

blind spot ▸*n.* **1.** The small, optically insensitive region of the eye where the optic nerve enters the retina. **2.** A subject about which one is ignorant or prejudiced.

blink (blĭngk) ▸*v.* **1.** To close and open one or both eyes rapidly. **2.** To flash on and off. **3.** To look with feigned ignorance: *blink at corruption.* **4.** To back down from a confrontation: *refused to blink.* ▸*n.* **1.** A brief closing of the eyes. **2.** A flash of light; twinkle. **—idiom: on**

the blink Out of working order. [ME *blinken*, move suddenly.]

blink·er (blǐng′kər) ►*n.* **1.** One that blinks, esp. a light that conveys a signal. **2. blinkers** See **blinders.**

blintz (blǐnts) ►*n.* A thin, rolled pancake usu. filled with cottage cheese and often served with sour cream. [Yiddish *blintse.*]

blip (blǐp) ►*n.* **1.** A spot of light on a radar or sonar screen. **2.** A high-pitched electronic sound; bleep. **3.** A temporary or insignificant anomaly. ►*v.* **blipped, blip·ping** To bleep. [Imit.]

bliss (blǐs) ►*n.* **1.** Extreme happiness; ecstasy. **2.** Religious ecstasy; spiritual joy. [< OE.] —**bliss′ful** *adj.* —**bliss′ful·ly** *adv.*

blis·ter (blǐs′tər) ►*n.* **1.** A local swelling of the skin that contains watery fluid and is caused by burning or irritation. **2.** Something resembling a blister, such as a raised plastic bubble. [Prob. < OFr. *blestre.*] —**blis′ter** *v.* —**blis′ter·y** *adj.*

blis·ter·ing (blǐs′tər-ĭng) ►*adj.* **1.** Intensely hot. **2.** Harsh; severe: *blistering criticism.* **3.** Very rapid: *a blistering pace.*

blister pack ►*n.* A form of packaging in which the product is sealed into a plastic blister.

blithe (blīth, blǐth) ►*adj.* **blith·er, blith·est** Carefree and lighthearted. [< OE *blīthe.*] —**blithe′ly** *adv.* —**blithe′ness** *n.*

blith·er (blǐth′ər) ►*v.* To blather. [Alteration of BLATHER.]

blithe·some (blīth′səm, blǐth′-) ►*adj.* Cheerful; merry. —**blithe′some·ly** *adv.*

blitz (blǐts) ►*n.* **1a.** A blitzkrieg. **b.** A heavy aerial bombardment. **2.** An intense campaign: *a media blitz.* **3.** *Football* A rushing of the quarterback by the defensive team, esp. in a passing situation. [< BLITZKRIEG.] —**blitz** *v.*

blitz·krieg (blǐts′krēg′) ►*n.* A swift, sudden military offensive, usu. by combined air and land forces. [Ger., lightning war.]

bliz·zard (blǐz′ərd) ►*n.* A very heavy snowstorm with high winds. [?]

bloat (blōt) ►*v.* To make or become swollen or inflated, as with gas. [< ON *blautr*, soft.]

blob (blŏb) ►*n.* **1.** A soft formless mass: *a blob of wax.* **2.** A splotch of color. [< ME *blober*, bubble.]

bloc (blŏk) ►*n.* A group of nations, parties, or persons united to act in common. [< OFr., BLOCK.]

block (blŏk) ►*n.* **1.** A solid piece of a hard substance having one or more flat sides. **2.** A stand from which articles are displayed at an auction. **3.** A pulley or a system of pulleys set in a casing. **4.** A set of like items sold or handled as a unit. **5a.** A section of a city or town bounded on each side by consecutive streets. **b.** A segment of a street bounded by consecutive cross streets. **6.** Something that obstructs; obstacle; hindrance. **7.** *Sports* An act of bodily obstruction. **8.** *Med.* Interruption, esp. obstruction, of a neural, digestive, or other physiological function. **9.** *Psychol.* Sudden cessation of speech or a thought process without an immediate observable cause. **10.** *Slang* The human head. ►*v.* **1a.** To stop or impede the passage of: *block traffic.* **b.** To shut out from view: *a curtain blocking the stage.* **2.** To shape or form with or on a block: *block a hat.* **3.** To indicate broadly; sketch: *block out a plan of action.* **4.** *Sports* To obstruct by

physical interference. **5.** *Med.* To interrupt the proper functioning of (a physiological process). **6.** *Psychol.* To fail to remember. —*idiom:* **on the block** Up for sale. [< MDu. *blok.*] —**block′age** *n.* —**block′er** *n.*

Syns: *hide, obscure, obstruct, screen, shroud* **v.**

block·ade (blŏ-kād′) ►*n.* **1.** The military act of isolating a nation, city, or harbor to prevent traffic and commerce. **2.** The forces used in a blockade. ►*v.* **-ad·ed, -ad·ing** To set up a blockade against.

block and tackle ►*n.* An apparatus of pulleys and ropes used for hauling and hoisting.

block·bust·er (blŏk′bŭs′tər) ►*n.* **1.** Something, such as a film, that achieves enormous success. **2.** A large, powerful bomb used esp. in air raids on cities.

block·bust·ing (blŏk′bŭs′tĭng) ►*n. Informal* The practice of persuading homeowners to sell quickly, usu. at a loss, by appealing to the fear that encroaching minority groups will cause property values to decline.

block·head (blŏk′hĕd′) ►*n.* One regarded as stupid.

block·house (blŏk′hous′) ►*n.* A small, sturdy fortification.

blockhouse
Fort Edgecomb
Edgecomb, Maine

blog (blŏg) ►*n.* A website that displays postings by one or more individuals in chronological order and usu. has links to comments on specific postings. ►*v.* **blogged, blog·ging** To write entries in, add material to, or maintain such a website. [< WEBLOG.] —**blog′ger** *n.*

blog·o·sphere (blŏg′ə-sfîr′) ►*n.* The set of all blogs on the Internet along with those who compile them and comment upon them.

blog·roll (blŏg′rōl′) ►*n.* A list of links provided on a blog to other websites.

bloke (blōk) ►*n. Chiefly Brit.* A man. [?]

blond also **blonde** (blŏnd) ►*adj.* **blond·er, blond·est 1.** Having light or fair hair and skin. **2.** Of a flaxen or golden color: *blond hair.* ►*n.* **1.** A blond person. **2.** A light yellowish brown. [< OFr.] —**blond′ish** *adj.* —**blond′ness** *n.*

blood (blŭd) ►*n.* **1a.** The fluid that is circulated by the heart in vertebrates, carrying oxygen and nutrients to and waste materials away from all body tissues. **b.** A similar fluid in an invertebrate. **2.** A vital force; lifeblood. **3.** Bloodshed; murder. **4.** Temperament or disposition: *hot blood; sporting blood.* **5.** Kinship: *related by blood.* **6.** National or racial ancestry. **7.** Membership; personnel: *new blood in the organization.* **8.** A dandy. —*idioms:*

bad blood Long-standing animosity. **in cold blood** Deliberately and dispassionately. [< OE *blōd*.] —**blood′less** *adj.*

blood bank ►*n.* A place where whole blood or plasma is stored for use in transfusion.

blood·bath (blŭd′băth′, -bäth′) ►*n.* A massacre.

blood count ►*n.* A test in which the cells in a blood sample are classified and counted.

blood·cur·dling (blŭd′kûrd′lĭng) ►*adj.* Causing great horror; terrifying.

blood·ed (blŭd′ĭd) ►*adj.* **1.** Having blood or a temperament of a specified kind: *a cold-blooded reptile.* **2.** Thoroughbred: *blooded horses.*

blood group ►*n.* Any of several genetically determined classes of human blood that are based on the presence or absence of certain antigens.

blood·hound (blŭd′hound′) ►*n.* A hound with drooping ears, sagging jowls, and a keen sense of smell, used in tracking.

blood·let·ting (blŭd′lĕt′ĭng) ►*n.* **1.** Bloodshed. **2.** The practice of phlebotomy for therapeutic purposes.

blood·line (blŭd′līn′) ►*n.* Direct line of descent; pedigree.

blood poisoning ►*n.* **1.** See **septicemia. 2.** See **toxemia.**

blood pressure ►*n.* The pressure exerted by the blood against the walls of the blood vessels, esp. the arteries.

blood sausage also **blood pudding** ►*n.* A sausage made of pig's blood and pork fat.

blood·shed (blŭd′shĕd′) ►*n.* Injury or killing, esp. of humans.

blood·shot (blŭd′shŏt′) ►*adj.* Red and inflamed from congested blood vessels: *bloodshot eyes.*

blood·stain (blŭd′stān′) ►*n.* A discoloration caused by blood. —**blood′stained′** *adj.*

blood·stream (blŭd′strēm′) ►*n.* The blood flowing through a circulatory system.

blood·suck·er (blŭd′sŭk′ər) ►*n.* **1.** An animal, such as a leech, that sucks blood. **2.** One who exploits others. —**blood′suck′ing** *adj.*

blood·thirst·y (blŭd′thûr′stē) ►*adj.* Eager for bloodshed. —**blood′thirst′i·ly** *adv.* —**blood′thirst′i·ness** *n.*

blood vessel ►*n.* An elastic tubular channel, such as an artery, vein, or capillary, through which blood circulates.

blood·y (blŭd′ē) ►*adj.* **-i·er, -i·est 1.** Of, emitting, or stained with blood. **2.** Causing or marked by bloodshed: *a bloody fight.* **3.** *Chiefly Brit. Slang* Used as an intensive: *a bloody fool.* ►*v.* **-ied, -y·ing** To stain with or as if with blood. —**blood′i·ly** *adv.* —**blood′i·ness** *n.*

bloody mary also **Bloody Mary** ►*n.* A drink made with vodka and tomato juice.

bloom (blōōm) ►*n.* **1.** The flower of a plant. **2a.** The condition or time of flowering: *a rose in bloom.* **b.** A time of vigor, freshness, and beauty; prime. **3.** A fresh, rosy complexion. **4.** A powdery coating on some fruits or leaves. **5.** A dense growth of plankton. ►*v.* **1.** To bear flowers. **2.** To shine with health and vigor; glow. **3.** To grow or flourish. [< ON *blōm*.]
   Syns: blossom, efflorescence, florescence, flower, flush, prime **n.**

bloom·ers (blōō′mərz) ►*pl.n.* Women's or girls' wide loose pants or underpants gathered at the knee. [< Amelia Jenks *Bloomer* (1818–94), Amer. social reformer.]

bloop·er (blōō′pər) ►*n.* **1.** *Informal* An embarrassing mistake; faux pas. **2.** *Baseball* A short, weakly hit fly ball.

blos·som (blŏs′əm) ►*n.* **1.** A flower or cluster of flowers. **2.** The condition or time of flowering: *peach trees in blossom.* **3.** A period or condition of maximum development. See Synonyms at **bloom.** ►*v.* **1.** To flower; bloom. **2.** To develop; flourish. [< OE *blōstm.*]

blot (blŏt) ►*n.* **1.** A spot or stain: *a blot of ink.* **2.** A moral blemish; disgrace. See Synonyms at **stain.** ►*v.* **blot·ted, blot·ting 1.** To dry with absorbent material. **2.** To make obscure; hide. **3.** To obliterate; cancel. **4.** To spot or stain. **5.** To bring moral disgrace to. [ME.]

blotch (blŏch) ►*n.* **1.** A spot or blot; splotch. **2.** A discoloration on the skin; blemish. [Prob. blend of BLOT and BOTCH.] —**blotch** *v.* —**blotch′i·ness** *n.* —**blotch′y** *adj.*

blot·ter (blŏt′ər) ►*n.* **1.** A piece of blotting paper. **2.** A book containing daily records of occurrences: *a police blotter.*

blot·ting paper (blŏt′ĭng) ►*n.* Absorbent paper used to dry a surface by soaking up excess ink.

blouse (blous, blouz) ►*n.* **1.** A loosely fitting shirt. **2.** The jacket of a military uniform. ►*v.* **bloused, blous·ing** To hang loosely. [Fr.]

blow¹ (blō) ►*v.* **blew** (blōō), **blown** (blōn), **blow·ing 1.** To be in a state of motion, as air or wind. **2a.** To be carried by the wind: *Her hat blew away.* **b.** To cause to move by means of a current of air. **3.** To drive a current of air upon, in, or through. **4a.** To expel a current of air, as from the mouth or a bellows. **b.** To clear by forcing air through: *blow one's nose.* **5.** To sound by expelling a current of air: *blow a trumpet.* **6.** To pant. **7a.** To burst suddenly: *The tire blew.* **b.** To cause to explode. **8.** To melt (a fuse). **9.** To spout. Used of a whale. **10.** To shape (e.g., glass) by forcing air through at the end of a pipe. **11.** *Slang* To spend (money) freely. **12.** *Slang* To handle ineptly. See Synonyms at **botch. 13.** *Slang* To depart. ►*n.* **1.** The act of blowing. **2a.** A blast of air or wind. **b.** A storm. —*phrasal verbs:* **blow out 1.** To extinguish or be extinguished by blowing. **2.** To fail, as an electrical apparatus. **blow over 1.** To subside; wane. **2.** To be forgotten. **blow up 1.** To come into being: *A storm blew up.* **2.** To fill with air; inflate. **3.** To enlarge (a photographic image or print). **4.** To explode. **5.** To lose one's temper. —*idioms:* **blow off steam** To give release to one's anger or other pent-up emotion. **blow (one's) mind** *Slang* To amaze or shock. **blow (one's) top** *Informal* To lose one's temper. [< OE *blāwan.*] —**blow′er** *n.*

blow² (blō) ►*n.* **1.** A sudden hard stroke or hit, as with the fist. **2.** An unexpected shock or calamity. **3.** A sudden attack. [ME *blaw.*]

blow³ (blō) ►*v.* **blew** (blōō), **blown** (blōn), **blow·ing** To bloom or cause to bloom. [< OE *blōwan*, to bloom.]

blow-by-blow (blō′-bī-blō′) ►*adj.* Describing in great detail.

blow-dry (blō′drī′) ►*v.* To dry or style (hair) with a hand-held dryer. —**blow dryer** *n.*

blow·fly (blō′flī′) ►*n.* A fly that deposits its eggs in carrion or open sores.

blow·gun (blō′gŭn′) ►*n.* A long narrow pipe

through which darts may be blown.

blow·hard (blō′härd′) ►*n. Informal* A boaster or braggart.

blow·hole (blō′hōl′) ►*n.* An opening on the head of a whale or dolphin through which it breathes.

blow·out (blō′out′) ►*n.* **1.** A sudden bursting, as of an automobile tire. **2.** A sudden escape of a confined gas or liquid, as from a well. **3.** *Informal* **a.** A large boisterous party. **b.** An overwhelming victory or defeat. **c.** A sale with deep discounts.

blow·torch (blō′tôrch′) ►*n.* A portable burner that mixes gas and oxygen to produce a flame hot enough to melt soft metals.

blow·up (blō′ŭp′) ►*n.* **1.** An explosion. **2.** A violent outburst of temper. **3.** A photographic enlargement.

blow·y (blō′ē) ►*adj.* **-i·er, -i·est** Windy.

blow·zy also **blow·sy** (blou′zē) ►*adj.* **-zi·er, -zi·est** also **-si·er, -si·est** Disheveled and frowzy. [< obsolete *blowze,* beggar girl.]

blub·ber¹ (blŭb′ər) ►*v.* To sob noisily. ►*n.* A loud sobbing. [< ME *bluber,* bubbles, foam.]

blub·ber² (blŭb′ər) ►*n.* **1.** The fat of whales, seals, and other marine mammals, from which an oil is obtained. **2.** Excessive body fat. [ME *bluber,* foam.] —**blub′ber·y** *adj.*

bludg·eon (blŭj′ən) ►*n.* A short heavy club, usu. of wood, that is thicker or loaded at one end. ►*v.* **1.** To hit with or as with a bludgeon. **2.** To threaten or bully. [?]

blue (blōō) ►*n.* **1.** Any of a group of colors whose hue is that of a clear daytime sky, lying between green and indigo on the visible spectrum. **2a.** The sky. **b.** The sea. ►*adj.* **blu·er, blu·est 1.** Of the color blue. **2.** Having a gray or purplish color, as from cold or bruising. **3.** Downhearted or low; gloomy. See Synonyms at **depressed. 4.** Puritanical; strict: *blue laws.* **5.** Indecent; risqué: *a blue joke.* ►*v.* **blued, blu·ing** To make or become blue. —*idiom:* **out of the blue 1.** From an unforeseen source. **2.** At a completely unexpected time. [< OFr. *bleu,* of Gmc. orig.] —**blue′ness** *n.* —**blu′ish, blue′ish** *adj.*

blue baby ►*n.* An infant born with bluish skin from inadequate oxygenation of its blood.

blue·bell (blōō′bĕl′) ►*n.* Any of several plants having blue bell-shaped flowers.

blue·ber·ry (blōō′bĕr′ē) ►*n.* **1.** Any of numerous plants having edible blue-black berries. **2.** The fruit of a blueberry.

blue·bird (blōō′bûrd′) ►*n.* A North American songbird having blue plumage and usu. a rust-colored breast in the male.

blue blood ►*n.* **1.** Noble or aristocratic descent. **2.** A member of the aristocracy. [Prob. < the visible veins of fair-skinned aristocrats.] —**blue′-blood′ed** *adj.*

blue·bon·net (blōō′bŏn′ĭt) ►*n.* A variety of lupine having light blue flowers.

blue·bot·tle (blōō′bŏt′l) ►*n.* Any of several flies that have a bright metallic-blue body.

blue cheese ►*n.* A semisoft tangy cheese streaked with a greenish-blue mold.

blue chip ►*n.* **1.** A stock highly valued for its long record of steady earnings. **2.** A valuable property. —**blue′-chip′** *adj.*

blue-col·lar (blōō′kŏl′ər) ►*adj.* Relating to wage earners whose jobs involve manual labor.

blue·fish (blōō′fĭsh′) ►*n.* A food and game fish of temperate and tropical waters.

blue·gill (blōō′gĭl′) ►*n.* An edible sunfish of North American lakes and streams.

blue·grass (blōō′grăs′) ►*n.* **1.** A usu. bluish lawn and pasture grass. **2.** A type of lively country music originating in the S US, typically played on banjos, guitars, and fiddles.

blue heron ►*n.* Any of several herons with blue or blue-gray plumage.

blue·ing (blōō′ĭng) ►*n.* Var. of **bluing.**

blue jay ►*n.* A North American bird having a crested head, predominantly blue plumage, and a harsh noisy cry.

blue jeans ►*pl.n.* Pants made of blue denim.

blue law ►*n.* A law restricting Sunday activities.

blue moon ►*n. Informal* A relatively long period of time: *once in a blue moon.*

Blue Nile A river of NE Africa flowing about 1,610 km (1,000 mi) from NW Ethiopia to Sudan. At Khartoum it merges with the White Nile to form the Nile R. proper.

blue·nose (blōō′nōz′) ►*n.* A puritanical person.

blue-pen·cil (blōō′pĕn′səl) ►*v.* To edit with or as if with a blue pencil.

blue·print (blōō′prĭnt′) ►*n.* **1.** A print of an architectural plan or other design, esp. one rendered as white lines on a blue background. **2.** A detailed plan of action. See Synonyms at **plan. —blue′print′** *v.*

blue ribbon ►*n.* The first prize in a competition. —**blue′-rib′bon** *adj.*

Blue Ridge Mountains also **Blue Ridge** A range of the Appalachian Mts. extending from S PA to N GA.

blues (blōōz) ►*pl.n. (takes sing. or pl. v.)* **1.** A state of depression or melancholy. **2.** A style of music evolved from southern African-American secular songs and usu. marked by a syncopated 4/4 rhythm, flatted thirds and sevenths, and a 12-bar structure. [< *blue devils,* depression.] —**blues′man** *n.* —**blues′y** *adj.*

blue·stock·ing (blōō′stŏk′ĭng) ►*n.* A woman with strong scholarly or literary interests. [After the *Blue Stocking* Society, a literary club of 18th-century London.]

blu·ets (blōō′ĭts) ►*pl.n. (takes sing. or pl. v.)* A low-growing plant having bluish flowers with yellow centers. [< ME *bleu,* BLUE.]

blue whale ►*n.* A very large baleen whale having a bluish-gray back and grooves on the throat.

bluff¹ (blŭf) ►*v.* To mislead or intimidate, esp. by a false display of confidence. ►*n.* **1.** The act or practice of bluffing. **2.** One that bluffs. [< LGer. *bluffen.*] —**bluff′er** *n.*

bluff² (blŭf) ►*n.* A steep headland, riverbank, or cliff. ►*adj.* **-er, -est** Rough and blunt but not unkind in manner. [Poss. < obsolete Du. *blaf.*] —**bluff′ly** *adv.* —**bluff′ness** *n.*

blu·ing also **blue·ing** (blōō′ĭng) ►*n.* **1.** A coloring agent used to counteract the yellowing of laundered fabrics. **2.** A treatment applied to steel to protect against corrosion.

blun·der (blŭn′dər) ►*n.* A mistake typically caused by ignorance or carelessness. ►*v.* **1.** To make a mistake. **2.** To move clumsily or blindly. [Poss. of Scand. orig.] —**blun′der·er** *n.* —**blun′der·ing·ly** *adv.*

Syns: bumble, flounder, lumber, lurch, stumble v.

blun·der·buss (blŭn′dər-bŭs′) ►*n.* A short musket with a wide muzzle for scattering shot at close range. [< Du. *donderbus*.]

blunt (blŭnt) ►*adj.* **-er, -est 1.** Having a dull edge or end. **2.** Abrupt and frank in speech and manner; brusque. ►*v.* **1.** To make or become blunt. **2.** To make less effective; weaken. [ME.] —**blunt′ly** *adv.* —**blunt′ness** *n.*

blur (blûr) ►*v.* **blurred, blur·ring 1.** To make or become indistinct. **2.** To smear or stain. **3.** To lessen the perception of; dim. ►*n.* **1.** A smear or smudge. **2.** Something indistinct to sight or mind. [Prob. akin to ME *bleren*, blear.] —**blur′ry** *adj.*

blurb (blûrb) ►*n.* A brief publicity notice, as on a book jacket. [Coined by Gelett Burgess (1866–1951).]

blurt (blûrt) ►*v.* To say suddenly and impulsively: *blurt a confession.* [Prob. imit.]

blush (blŭsh) ►*v.* **1.** To become red in the face, esp. from modesty, embarrassment, or shame; flush. **2.** To become red or rosy. **3.** To feel embarrassed or ashamed. ►*n.* Facial makeup used esp. on the cheeks to give a red or rosy tint. [< OE *blyscan*.] —**blush′er** *n.*

blus·ter (blŭs′tər) ►*v.* **1.** To blow in loud violent gusts, as wind in a storm. **2.** To speak in a noisy, arrogant, or bullying manner. [< MLGer. *blüsteren*.] —**blus′ter** *n.* —**blus′ter·er** *n.* —**blus′ter·y** *adj.*

Blvd. ►*abbr.* boulevard

BM ►*abbr.* **1.** basal metabolism **2.** board measure **3.** bowel movement

BMI ►*abbr.* body mass index

bo·a (bō′ə) ►*n.* **1.** Any of various large, nonvenomous tropical snakes, including the anaconda and boa constrictor, that coil around and suffocate their prey. **2.** A long fluffy scarf made of fur or feathers. [< Lat. *boa*, a snake.]

boa constrictor ►*n.* A large boa of tropical America having brown markings.

Bo·ad·i·ce·a (bō′ăd-ĭ-sē′ə) See **Boudicca.**

boar (bôr) ►*n.* **1.** A wild pig. **2.** An uncastrated male pig. [< OE *bār*.]

board (bôrd) ►*n.* **1.** A flat length of sawed lumber; plank. **2.** A flat piece of wood or similar material adapted for a special use, esp.: **a.** A flat piece of rigid material designed to display information, such as a bulletin board. **b.** A flat piece of material designed or equipped to be ridden as a sport, such as a snowboard or surfboard. **3.** A flat surface on which a game is played. **4. boards** A theater stage. **5a.** A table, esp. one set for serving food. **b.** Food or meals considered as a whole: *board and lodging.* **6.** An organized body of administrators. **7.** A circuit board. ►*v.* **1.** To cover or close with boards: *board up a broken window.* **2.** To provide with or receive food and lodging for a charge. **3.** To enter or go aboard (a ship, train, or plane). —*idiom:* **on board 1.** Aboard. **2.** On the job. [< OE *bord*.] —**board′er** *n.*

board foot ►*n., pl.* **board feet** A unit of cubic measure for lumber, equal to one foot square by one inch thick.

board·ing house also **board·ing·house** (bôr′dĭng-hous′) ►*n.* A house where paying guests are provided with meals and lodging.

boarding school ►*n.* A school where pupils are provided with meals and lodging.

board·walk (bôrd′wôk′) ►*n.* A promenade, esp. of planks, along a beach.

boast (bōst) ►*v.* **1.** To talk in a bragging way. **2.** To speak about with excessive pride. **3.** To have (a desirable feature). ►*n.* **1.** An instance of bragging. **2.** A source of pride. [< ME *bost*, a brag.] —**boast′er** *n.* —**boast′ful** *adj.* —**boast′ful·ly** *adv.* —**boast′ful·ness** *n.*

boat (bōt) ►*n.* **1a.** A relatively small, usu. open water craft. **b.** A ship or submarine. **2.** A dish shaped like a boat: *a sauce boat.* ►*v.* To travel or transport by boat. —*idiom:* **in the same boat** In the same situation. [< OE *bāt*.] —**boat′ing** *n.* —**boat′man** *n.*

boat·er (bō′tər) ►*n.* **1.** One who boats. **2.** A stiff straw hat with a flat crown.

boat·swain also **bos′n** or **bos′n** or **bo·sun** (bō′sən) ►*n.* A warrant officer or petty officer in charge of a ship's rigging, anchors, cables, and deck crew.

bob¹ (bŏb) ►*v.* **bobbed, bob·bing** To move or cause to move up and down. ►*n.* **1.** A quick jerky movement. **2.** A fishing float. [ME *bobben*.]

bob² (bŏb) ►*n.* **1.** A small, knoblike pendent object. **2.** A woman's or child's short haircut. **3.** The docked tail of a horse. ►*v.* **bobbed, bob·bing** To cut short: *bobbed her hair.* [ME *bobbe*.]

bob³ (bŏb) ►*n., pl.* **bob** *Chiefly Brit.* A shilling. [?]

bob·bin (bŏb′ĭn) ►*n.* A spool for thread, as on a sewing machine. [Fr. *bobine*.]

bob·ble (bŏb′əl) ►*v.* **-bled, -bling 1.** To bob up and down. **2.** To fumble (e.g., a ball) momentarily. [< BOB¹.] —**bob′ble** *n.*

bob·by (bŏb′ē) ►*n., pl.* **-bies** *Chiefly Brit.* A police officer. [< *Bobby*, nickname for *Robert* < Sir *Robert* Peel (1788–1850), British politician who established the modern London police force.]

bobby pin ►*n.* A small metal hair clip with the ends pressed tightly together. [< BOB².]

bobby socks also **bobby sox** ►*pl.n. Informal* Ankle socks. [Poss. < BOB².]

bob·cat (bŏb′kăt′) ►*n.* A wildcat of North America, having spotted reddish-brown fur, tufted ears, and a short tail.

bob·o·link (bŏb′ə-lĭngk′) ►*n.* An American songbird, the male of which has black, white, and yellow plumage. [Imit. of its song.]

bob·sled (bŏb′slĕd′) ►*n.* A long racing sled with a steering mechanism controlling the front runners. —**bob′sled′** *v.*

bob·tail (bŏb′tāl′) ►*n.* **1.** A short tail or one that has been cut short. **2.** An animal, esp. a horse, having a bobtail. —**bob′tailed′** *adj.*

bob·white (bŏb-wīt′, -hwīt′) ►*n.* A small North American quail. [Imit. of its call.]

Boc·cac·cio (bō-kä′chē-ō′, -chō′), **Giovanni** 1313–75. Italian writer.

bock beer (bŏk) ►*n.* A dark beer traditionally consumed in the springtime. [< Ger. *Einbeckisch Bier*, beer from Einbeck, Germany.]

bod (bŏd) ►*n. Slang* The human body.

bode¹ (bōd) ►*v.* **bod·ed, bod·ing** To be an omen of. [< OE *bodian*, announce.]

bode² (bōd) ►*v.* P.t. of **bide.**

bo·de·ga (bō-dā′gə) ►*n.* A small grocery store specializing in Caribbean and Latin American products. [< Lat. *apothēca*, storehouse.]

bod·ice (bŏd′ĭs) ►*n.* The fitted upper part of a dress. [< *bodies*, pl. of BODY.]

bod·i·less (bŏd′ē-lĭs) ►*adj.* Having no body, form, or substance: *bodiless fears.*

bod·i·ly (bŏd′l-ē) ►*adj.* **1.** Of or belonging to the body. **2.** Physical: *bodily welfare.* ►*adv.* **1.** In person. **2.** As a complete physical entity: *lifted bodily from his chair.*

  Syns: *corporal, corporeal, fleshly, physical, somatic* **adj.**

bod·kin (bŏd′kĭn) ►*n.* **1.** An awl for piercing fabric or leather. **2.** A blunt needle for pulling ribbon through loops or a hem. **3.** A dagger. [ME *boidekin.*]

bod·y (bŏd′ē) ►*n., pl.* **-ies 1a.** The entire material or physical structure of an organism, esp. of a human or animal. **b.** A corpse or carcass. **2.** The trunk or torso. **3a.** A person. **b.** A group of individuals regarded as an entity: *a governing body.* **4.** A collection of related things: *a body of information.* **5.** The main or central part, as of a vehicle, document, or musical instrument. **6.** A well-defined object, mass, or collection of material: *a body of water.* **7.** Consistency of substance, as in paint, textiles, or wine. [< OE *bodig.*] **—bod′ied** *adj.*

body bag ►*n.* A zippered bag for transporting a human corpse.

bod·y·board (bŏd′ē-bôrd′) ►*n.* A short surfboard with one straight end, usu. ridden lying down. **—bod′y·board′** *v.* **—bod′y·board′er** *n.*

bod·y·build·ing (bŏd′ē-bĭl′dĭng) ►*n.* The process of developing the musculature of the body through diet and physical exercise, esp. for competitive exhibition. **—bod′y·build′er** *n.*

body count ►*n.* A count of individual bodies, as those killed in combat operations.

body English ►*n.* Bodily movement in a usu. unconscious attempt to influence the movement of a propelled object, such as a ball.

bod·y·guard (bŏd′ē-gärd′) ►*n.* A person or group of persons, usu. armed, responsible for protecting another or others.

body language ►*n.* The gestures, postures, and facial expressions that indicate a person's physical or emotional state.

body politic ►*n.* The people of a politically organized nation considered as a group.

body shop ►*n.* A garage where the bodies of automotive vehicles are repaired.

body stocking ►*n.* A tight-fitting, usu. one-piece garment that covers the torso and sometimes the arms and legs.

bod·y·suit (bŏd′ē-sōōt′) ►*n.* A tight-fitting one-piece garment for the torso.

bod·y·surf (bŏd′ē-sûrf′) ►*v.* To ride waves to shore without a surfboard.

bod·y·work (bŏd′ē-wûrk′) ►*n.* **1.** The body of a motor vehicle. **2.** The manufacturing or repairing of motor vehicle bodies. **3.** The use of techniques such as massage, yoga, or exercise to promote physical and emotional well-being.

Boer (bôr, bōōr) ►*n.* A Dutch colonist or descendant of a Dutch colonist in South Africa. [Afr. < MDu. *gheboer,* peasant.]

bof·fo (bŏf′ō) ►*adj. Slang* Extremely successful; great. [Prob. < B(OX) OFF(ICE).]

bog (bôg, bŏg) ►*n.* A wetland, esp. one with acidic, peaty soil. ►*v.* **bogged, bog·ging** To hinder or be hindered: *bogged me down with*

details; bogged down in the mud. [< Ir.Gael. *bog,* soft.] **—bog′gy** *adj.*

Bo·gart (bō′gärt), **Humphrey DeForest** 1899–1957. Amer. actor.

bo·gey (bō′gē) ►*n.* also **bo·gy** or **bo·gie** *pl.* **-geys** also **-gies 1.** (*also* bōōg′ē, bōō′gē) An evil or mischievous spirit; hobgoblin. **2.** One golf stroke over par on a hole. **3.** *Slang* An unidentified flying aircraft. ►*v.* **-geyed, -gey·ing** To shoot (a hole in golf) one stroke over par. [Poss. < Sc. *bogill.*]

bo·gey·man or **bo·gy·man** also **boog·ey·man** (bōōg′ē-mǎn′, bō′gē-, bōō′gē-) ►*n.* A terrifying specter; hobgoblin.

bog·gle (bŏg′əl) ►*v.* **-gled, -gling** To overwhelm or be overwhelmed with astonishment. [Poss. < Sc. *bogill,* goblin.]

Bo·go·tá (bō′gə-tä′) The capital of Colombia, in the central part on a plain in the E Andes.

bo·gus (bō′gəs) ►*adj.* **1.** Counterfeit or fake. **2.** *Slang* Disappointing or unfair. [< *bogus,* counterfeit money device.]

Bo·hai Sea also **Bo·hai Gulf** (bō′hī′) An inlet of the Yellow Sea on the NE coast of China.

Bo·he·mi·a (bō-hē′mē-ə) A historical region and former kingdom of the present-day W Czech Republic. **—Bo·he′mi·an** *adj. & n.*

bo·he·mi·an (bō-hē′mē-ən) ►*n.* A person with artistic interests who disregards conventional standards of behavior. **—bo·he′mi·an** *adj.* **—bo·he′mi·an·ism** *n.*

Bohr (bôr), **Niels Henrik David** 1885–1962. Danish physicist.

bohr·i·um (bôr′ē-əm) ►*n. Symbol* **Bh** A synthetic radioactive element. At. no. 107. See table at **element.** [After Niels Henrik David BOHR.]

boil¹ (boil) ►*v.* **1a.** To vaporize (a liquid) by applying heat. **b.** To bring to or reach the boiling point. **2.** To cook or clean by boiling. **3.** To be in a state of agitation; seethe: *a river boiling over the rocks.* **4.** To be greatly excited, as by rage. ►*n.* The condition or act of boiling. **—phrasal verbs: boil down 1.** To reduce in bulk or size by boiling. **2.** To summarize. **boil over** To lose one's temper. [< Lat. *bullīre.*]

boil² (boil) ►*n.* A painful, pus-filled inflammation of the skin usu. caused by bacterial infection. [< OE *bӯle.*]

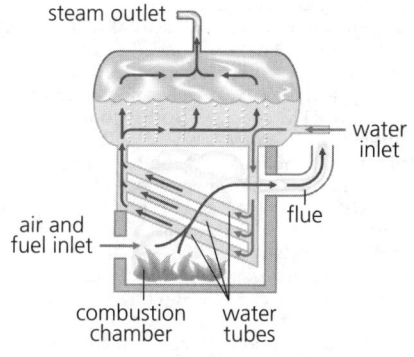

boiler
water-tube boiler

boil·er (boi′lər) ►*n.* **1.** An enclosed vessel in which water is heated and circulated, as either

hot water or steam, for heating or power. **2.** A container for boiling liquids.

boil·ing point (boi′lĭng) ►*n.* **1.** The temperature at which a liquid boils at a fixed pressure, esp. under standard atmospheric conditions. **2.** *Informal* The point at which one loses one's temper.

Boi·se (boi′sē, -zē) The capital of ID, in the SW part of the state.

bois·ter·ous (boi′stər-əs, -strəs) ►*adj.* **1.** Loud, noisy, and unrestrained. **2.** Rough and stormy. [< ME *boistous*, rude.] —**bois′ter·ous·ly** *adv.* —**bois′ter·ous·ness** *n.*

bok choy (bŏk′ choi′) ►*n.* A cabbagelike Chinese vegetable. [Cantonese *baak⁶ coi³.*]

bo·la (bō′lə) also **bo·las** (-ləs) ►*n.* A rope with round weights attached, used esp. in South America to catch cattle or game by entangling their legs. [< Sp. *bola*, ball.]

bold (bōld) ►*adj.* **-er, -est 1a.** Fearless and daring; courageous. **b.** Requiring or exhibiting courage and bravery. **2.** Unduly forward and brazen. **3.** Strikingly different or unconventional: *a bold new proposal.* **4.** Clear and distinct to the eye. **5.** *Print.* Boldface. [< OE *bald.*] —**bold′ly** *adv.* —**bold′ness** *n.*

bold·face (bōld′fās′) ►*n.* *Print.* Type with thick, heavy lines. —**bold′face′, bold′faced′** *adj.*

bole (bōl) ►*n.* A tree trunk. [< ON *bolr.*]

bo·le·ro (bō-lâr′ō, bə-) ►*n., pl.* **-ros 1.** A very short jacket worn open in the front. **2a.** A Spanish dance in triple meter. **b.** The music for this dance. [Sp. < *bola*, ball.]

Bol·eyn (bŏŏl′ĭn, bŏŏ-lĭn′), **Anne** 1507?–36. Queen of England (1533–36) as the second wife of Henry VIII; beheaded.

bo·li·var (bō-lē′vär, bŏl′ə-vər) ►*n., pl.* **-vars** or **-va·res** (bō-lē′vä-rĕs′) See table at **currency.** [After Simón Bolívar.]

Bo·li·var (bō-lē′vär), **Simón** 1783–1830. South American revolutionary leader.

Bo·liv·i·a (bə-lĭv′ē-ə, bō-) A landlocked country of W-central South America. Caps. Sucre and La Paz. —**Bo·liv′i·an** *adj. & n.*

bo·li·vi·a·no (bə-lĭv′ē-ä′nō, bō-) ►*n., pl.* **-nos** See table at **currency.** [Sp., Bolivian.]

boll (bōl) ►*n.* The seedpod esp. of cotton and flax. [< MDu., round object.]

boll weevil ►*n.* A small, grayish, long-snouted beetle that lays its eggs in cotton buds and bolls, causing great damage.

bo·lo·gna (bə-lō′nē, -nə, -nyə) also **ba·lo·ney** or **bo·lo·ney** (-nē) ►*n.* A large sausage of finely ground meat. [After Bologna.]

Bo·lo·gna (bə-lōn′yə) A city of N-central Italy NNE of Florence. —**Bo·lo′gnan, Bo′lo·gnese′** (bō′lə-nēz′, -lən-yēz′) *adj. & n.*

Bol·she·vik (bōl′shə-vĭk′, bŏl′-) ►*n., pl.* **-viks** or **-vi·ki** (-vē′kē) **1.** A member of the radical Marxist party that seized power in Russia (1917–22). **2.** A Communist. [< Russ. *bol'shoĭ*, large.] —**Bol′she·vik′** *adj.* —**Bol′she·vism** *n.* —**Bol′she·vist** *adj. & n.*

bol·ster (bōl′stər) ►*n.* A long narrow pillow or cushion. ►*v.* **1.** To support with or as if with a bolster. **2.** To buoy up; hearten: *bolstered their morale.* [< OE.]

bolt¹ (bōlt) ►*n.* **1.** A sliding bar used to fasten a door or gate. **2.** A metal bar in a lock that is extended or withdrawn by turning the key. **3.** A threaded pin with a head at one end,

used with a mated nut to hold things together. **4.** A flash of lightning; thunderbolt. **5.** A sudden movement toward or away; dash. **6.** A large roll of cloth. ►*v.* **1.** To secure or lock with or as if with a bolt. **2.** To eat hurriedly; gulp. **3.** To desert (a political party). **4.** To move or spring suddenly. **5.** To run away. [< OE, heavy arrow.]

bolt² (bōlt) ►*v.* To sift (e.g., flour) through a sieve. [< MHGer. *biutel*, bag, purse.]

bo·lus (bō′ləs) ►*n., pl.* **-lus·es 1.** A small round mass. **2.** A large dose of a substance taken as a medicine. [< Gk. *bōlos*, lump of earth.]

bomb (bŏm) ►*n.* **1a.** An explosive weapon detonated esp. by impact or a timing mechanism. **b.** A nuclear weapon. Used with *the.* **2.** A weapon detonated to release smoke or gas. **3.** A container that ejects a spray, foam, or gas under pressure. **4.** *Slang* A dismal failure. ►*v.* **1.** To attack or damage with bombs. **2.** *Slang* To fail miserably. [< Ital. *bomba.*]

bom·bard (bŏm-bärd′) ►*v.* **1.** To attack with bombs, shells, or missiles. **2.** To assail persistently; harass or beset. See Synonyms at **barrage. 3.** To irradiate (an atom). [Prob. < Lat. *bombus*, a booming.] —**bom·bard′ment** *n.*

bom·bar·dier (bŏm′bər-dîr′) ►*n.* A member of a combat aircraft crew who operates bombing equipment. [< OFr. *bombarde*, bombard.]

bom·bast (bŏm′băst′) ►*n.* Grandiose or violent expression, esp. in speech or writing. [< OFr. *bombace*, cotton padding.] —**bom·bas′tic** *adj.*

Bom·bay (bŏm-bā′) See **Mumbai.**

bom·ba·zine (bŏm′bə-zēn′) ►*n.* A fine twilled fabric often dyed black. [< Gk. *bombux*, silkworm.]

bombed (bŏmd) ►*adj.* *Slang* Drunk.

bomb·er (bŏm′ər) ►*n.* **1.** A combat aircraft designed to drop bombs. **2.** One who bombs.

bomb·shell (bŏm′shĕl′) ►*n.* **1.** An explosive bomb. **2.** A shocking surprise.

bomb·sight (bŏm′sīt′) ►*n.* A device in a combat aircraft that assists in timing the release of bombs.

bo·na fide (bō′nə fīd′, fī′dē, bŏn′ə) ►*adj.* **1.** Made or carried out in good faith; sincere: *a bona fide offer.* **2.** Authentic; genuine: *a bona fide Rembrandt.* See Synonyms at **authentic.** [Lat. *bonā fidē*, in good faith.]

bo·nan·za (bə-năn′zə) ►*n.* **1.** A rich mine or vein of ore. **2.** A source of great wealth or prosperity. [Sp.]

Bo·na·parte (bō′nə-pärt′) Corsican family, all brothers of Napoleon I, including **Joseph** (1768–1844), king of Naples (1806–08) and Spain (1808–13); **Lucien** (1775–1840); **Louis** (1778–1846), king of Holland (1806–10); and **Jérôme** (1784–1860), king of Westphalia (1807–13).

bon·bon (bŏn′bŏn′) ►*n.* A coated candy with a creamy center. [Fr. < Lat. *bonus*, good.]

bond (bŏnd) ►*n.* **1.** Something that binds, ties, or fastens things together. **2.** often **bonds** Confinement in prison; captivity. **3.** A uniting force or tie; link: *the familial bond.* **4.** A binding agreement; covenant. **5.** A promise or obligation by which one is bound. **6.** A union or cohesion between two or more parts. **7.** A chemical bond. **8.** A certificate of debt issued by a government or corporation guaranteeing payment of the borrowed sum with interest by a specified future date. **9a.** A sum of money paid as bail or surety. **b.** A bail bondsman. ►*v.* **1.** To join securely, as with glue. **2.** To form a close nurturing relationship. **3.** To mortgage or place a guaranteed bond on. **4.** To furnish bond or surety for. [< ON *band.*]

bond·age (bŏn′dĭj) ►*n.* The condition of a slave or serf; servitude. [Ult. < ON *būa,* live.]

bond·man (bŏnd′mən) ►*n.* A male bondservant.

bond paper ►*n.* High-quality white paper containing rag pulp.

bond·ser·vant (bŏnd′sûr′vənt) ►*n.* **1.** A person obligated to serve without wages. **2.** A slave or serf. [< ME *bonde,* serf.]

bonds·man (bŏndz′mən) ►*n.* **1.** One who provides bond or surety for another. **2.** A male bondservant.

bond·wom·an (bŏnd′wŏŏm′ən) ►*n.* A woman bondservant.

bone (bōn) ►*n.* **1a.** The dense, semirigid, porous, calcified tissue forming the skeleton of most vertebrates. **b.** A skeletal structure made of this material. **2.** An animal material, such as whalebone, resembling bone. **3.** Something that is made of bone or similar material. ►*v.* **boned, bon·ing** To remove the bones from. **—phrasal verb: bone up** *Informal* To study intensely, usu. at the last minute: *boned up on the chemical elements.* **—idioms: bone of contention** The subject of dispute. **bone to pick** Grounds for a complaint or dispute. [< OE *bān.*] **—bone′less** *adj.* **—bon′i·ness** *n.* **—bon′y, bon′ey** *adj.*

bone-dry (bōn′drī′) ►*adj.* Completely dry.

bone meal ►*n.* Crushed and coarsely ground bones used as fertilizer and animal feed.

bon·fire (bŏn′fīr′) ►*n.* A large outdoor fire. [ME *bonnefire,* "bone fire".]

bong (bŏng, bông) ►*n.* A deep ringing sound, as of a bell. [Imit.] **—bong** *v.*

bon·go¹ (bŏng′gō, bông′-) ►*n., pl.* **-gos** A large antelope of central Africa, having a reddish-brown body with white stripes. [Prob. of Bantu orig.]

bon·go² (bŏng′gō, bông′-) ►*n., pl.* **-gos** or **-goes** One of a pair of connected tuned drums played with the hands. [Am.Sp. *bongó.*]

bon·ho·mie (bŏn′ə-mē′) ►*n.* A pleasant and affable disposition; geniality. [Fr.]

bo·ni·to (bə-nē′tō) ►*n., pl.* **-to** or **-tos** A food fish that resembles a small tuna. [Sp.]

bon mot (bôn mō′) ►*n., pl.* **bons mots** (bôn mō′, mōz′) A witticism. [Fr.]

Bonn (bŏn, bôn) The former capital of West Germany, in the W-central part of Germany on the Rhine R.

bon·net (bŏn′ĭt) ►*n.* **1.** A hat held in place by ribbons tied under the chin, esp. one worn by women or children. **2.** *Chiefly Brit.* The hood of an automobile. [< OFr. *bonet.*]

bon·ny also **bon·nie** (bŏn′ē) ►*adj.* **-ni·er, -ni·est** *Scots* **1.** Physically attractive or appealing; pretty. **2.** Excellent. [Prob. ult. < Fr. *bon,* good.]

bo·no·bo (bə-nō′bō) ►*n., pl.* **-bos** A species of chimpanzee of W-central Africa having black hair and a relatively slender build. [Of Central African orig.]

bon·sai (bŏn-sī′, bŏn′sī′, -zī′) ►*n., pl.* **-sai** A dwarfed, ornamentally shaped tree grown in a small pot. [J., potted plant.]

bo·nus (bō′nəs) ►*n., pl.* **-es** Something given or paid in addition to what is usual or expected. [< Lat., good.]

bon vi·vant (bôn′ vē-vän′) ►*n., pl.* **bons vi·vants** (bôn′ vē-vän′) One with refined taste, esp. one who enjoys superb food and drink. [Fr.]

bon voy·age (bôn′ vwä-yäzh′) ►*interj.* Used to bid farewell to one beginning a journey. [Fr.]

boo (bōō) ►*n., pl.* **boos** A sound uttered to show contempt, scorn, or disapproval or to frighten or startle. **—boo** *interj.* & *v.*

boob (bōōb) ►*n. Slang* A stupid or foolish person; dolt. [Short for BOOBY.]

boo·by (bōō′bē) ►*n., pl.* **-bies 1.** A stupid person. **2.** A seabird of tropical and subtropical waters. [Prob. < Lat. *balbus,* stammering.]

booby prize ►*n.* An award for the worst score in a game or contest.

booby trap ►*n.* **1.** A concealed, often explosive device triggered when a harmless-looking object is touched. **2.** A situation that catches one off-guard; pitfall. **—boo′by-trap′** *v.*

boo·dle (bōōd′l) ►*n. Slang* **1a.** Money, esp. counterfeit money. **b.** Money accepted as a bribe. **2.** Stolen goods; swag. [< MDu. *bōdel,* estate.]

boog·ey·man (bŏŏg′ē-măn′, bō′gē-, bōō′gē-) ►*n. Slang* Var. of **bogeyman.**

boog·ie (bŏŏg′ē, bōō′gē) ►*v.* **-ied, -y·ing** *Slang* **1.** To dance to rock music. **2.** To move or depart quickly. [< BOOGIE-WOOGIE.]

boog·ie-woog·ie (bŏŏg′ē-wŏŏg′ē, bōō′gē-wŏŏ′gē) ►*n.* A style of blues piano playing marked by a quick tempo and a repeating bass line. [Poss. < Black W African E. *bogi(-bogi),* to dance.]

book (bŏŏk) ►*n.* **1.** A set of written, printed, or blank pages fastened along one side and encased between protective covers. **2a.** A printed or written literary work. **b.** A main division of a larger printed or written work. **3.** A volume in which financial transactions are recorded. **4. Book** The Bible. **5.** A packet of similar items bound together: *a book of matches.* **6.** A record of bets placed on a race. ►*v.* **1.** To reserve or schedule, as by listing in a book. **2.** To record charges against on a police blotter. **—idiom: like a book** Thoroughly; completely. [< OE *bōc.*]

book·case (bŏŏk′kās′) ►*n.* A piece of furniture with shelves for holding books.

book·end (bŏŏk′ĕnd′) ►*n.* A prop used to keep a row of books upright.

book·ie (bŏŏk′ē) ►*n.* See **bookmaker** (sense 2).

book·ing (bŏŏk′ĭng) ►*n.* **1.** A scheduled engagement, as for a performance. **2.** A reservation, as for an airplane flight or a hotel.

book·ish (bŏŏk′ĭsh) ►*adj.* **1.** Fond of books; studious. **2.** Pedantic; dull.

book·keep·ing (bŏŏk′kē′pĭng) ►*n.* The recording of the accounts and transactions of a business. **—book′keep′er** *n.*

book·let (bŏŏk′lĭt) ►*n.* A small bound book.

book·mak·er (bŏŏk′mā′kər) ►*n.* **1.** One who prints or publishes books. **2.** One who accepts and pays off bets, as on a horserace; bookie. **—book′mak′ing** *n.*

book·mark (bŏŏk′märk′) ►*n.* **1.** An object placed between book pages to mark one's place.

2. *Comp.* A link allowing a user to return easily to a previously visited site.

book·plate (bŏok′plāt′) ►*n.* A label bearing the owner's name pasted inside a book.

book value ►*n.* The theoretical value of an asset, esp. as recorded in account books and distinguished from market value.

book·worm (bŏok′wûrm′) ►*n.* **1.** One who spends much time reading or studying. **2.** Any of various insects, esp. silverfish, that infest books and feed on the bindings.

Bool·e·an (bŏo′lē-ən) ►*adj.* Of or relating to an algebraic system used in symbolic logic and in logic circuits in computer science. [After George *Boole* (1815–64).]

boom¹ (bŏom) ►*v.* **1.** To make a deep resonant sound. **2.** To grow or progress rapidly; flourish. ►*n.* **1.** A booming sound. **2.** A sudden increase, as in growth, wealth, or popularity. [ME *bomben*.]

boom² (bŏom) ►*n.* **1.** A spar extending from a mast to hold the bottom of a sail. **2.** A pole extending upward at an angle from the mast of a derrick to support or guide objects being lifted. **3a.** A chain of floating logs enclosing other, free-floating logs. **b.** A floating barrier used to contain an oil spill. **4.** A long movable arm used to maneuver a microphone. [< MDu., tree, pole.]

boom box ►*n. Slang* A portable audio system.

boo·mer·ang (bŏo′mə-răng′) ►*n.* **1.** A flat, curved, usu. wooden missile configured so that when hurled it returns to the thrower. **2.** A statement or course of action that backfires. ►*v.* To have an opposite effect; backfire. [Dharuk (Australian) *bumariny*.]

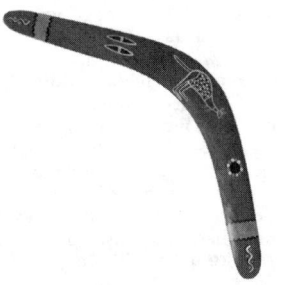

boomerang

boon¹ (bŏon) ►*n.* Something beneficial; blessing. [< ON *bōn*, prayer.]

boon² (bŏon) ►*adj.* Convivial; jolly: *a boon companion to all.* [< Lat. *bonus*, good.]

boon·docks (bŏon′dŏks′) ►*pl.n. Slang* **1.** A jungle. **2.** Rural country; hinterland. [< Tagalog *bundok*, mountain.]

boon·dog·gle (bŏon′dô′gəl, -dŏg′əl) ►*n. Informal* An unnecessary or wasteful project or activity. [< *boondoggle*, plaited leather cord.] **—boon′dog′gle** *v.*

Boone (bŏon), **Daniel** 1734–1820. Amer. frontier settler and folk hero.

boor (bŏor) ►*n.* A crude person with rude, clumsy manners. [< MDu. *gheboer*, peasant.] **—boor′ish** *adj.* **—boor′ish·ly** *adv.*
    Syns: *barbarian, churl, vulgarian* **n.**

boost (bŏost) ►*v.* **1.** To lift by or as if by pushing up from behind or below. **2.** To increase; raise.

3. To promote vigorously; aid. ►*n.* **1.** A push upward or ahead. **2.** An increase. [Poss. < dial. *boostering*, active.]

boost·er (bŏo′stər) ►*n.* **1.** A device for increasing power or effectiveness. **2.** A promoter. **3.** A rocket that provides the main thrust for the launch of a missile or space vehicle. **4.** A booster shot.

boost·er·ism (bŏo′stə-rĭz′əm) ►*n.* The supportive activities of boosters.

booster shot ►*n.* A supplementary dose of a vaccine to sustain the immune response.

boot¹ (bŏot) ►*n.* **1.** Footgear covering the foot and part of the leg. **2.** A protective covering or sheath. **3.** *Chiefly Brit.* An automobile trunk. **4a.** A kick. **b.** *Slang* A dismissal, esp. from a job. **5.** A marine or navy recruit. **6.** The starting or restarting of a computer. ►*v.* **1.** To put boots on. **2.** To kick. **3.** *Slang* To discharge; dismiss. See Synonyms at **dismiss. 4.** To start (a computer) by loading an operating system from a disk. [< OFr. *bote*.]

boot² (bŏot) ►*v.* To be of help; avail. ►*n. Regional* An extra or unexpected gift or benefit. **—idiom: to boot** In addition. [< OE *bōt*, help.]

boot·black (bŏot′blăk′) ►*n.* One who polishes shoes for a living.

boot camp ►*n.* A training camp for military recruits.

boo·tee also **boo·tie** (bŏo′tē) ►*n.* A soft, usu. knitted shoe for a baby.

booth (bŏoth) ►*n., pl.* **booths** (bŏothz, bŏoths) **1.** A small enclosed compartment; box: *a ticket booth.* **2.** A dining area in a restaurant having seats whose high backs serve as partitions. **3.** A small stall for the sale of goods. [ME *bothe*.]

Booth Family of reformers, including **William** (1829–1912) and his wife, **Catherine Mumford Booth** (1829–90), founders of the Salvation Army (1878).

Booth, John Wilkes 1838–65. Amer. assassin of Abraham Lincoln.

Boo·thi·a Peninsula (bŏo′thē-ə) The northernmost tip of the North American mainland, in central Nunavut, Canada.

boot·leg (bŏot′lĕg′) ►*v.* **-legged, -leg·ging** To make, sell, or transport illegally, as liquor or compact discs. **—boot′leg′** *n. & adj.* **—boot′-leg′ger** *n.*

boot·less (bŏot′lĭs) ►*adj.* Useless. See Synonyms at **futile. —boot′less·ness** *n.*

boot·lick (bŏot′lĭk′) ►*v.* To behave in a servile manner. See Synonyms at **fawn¹. —boot′-lick′er** *n.*

boot·strap (bŏot′străp′) ►*n.* A loop sewn at the top rear of a boot to help in pulling it on. **—idiom: by one's (own) bootstraps** By one's own effort.

boo·ty (bŏo′tē) ►*n., pl.* **-ties 1.** Plunder taken from an enemy in war. **2.** Seized or stolen goods. [Prob. < MLGer. *būte*, exchange.]

booze (bŏoz) *Slang* ►*n.* **a.** Hard liquor. **b.** An alcoholic beverage. ►*v.* **boozed, booz·ing** To drink alcoholic beverages excessively. [< MDu. *būsen*, drink to excess.] **—booz′er** *n.* **—booz′y** *adj.*

bop¹ (bŏp) *Informal* ►*v.* **bopped, bop·ping** To hit or strike. ►*n.* A blow; punch. [Imit.]

bop² (bŏp) ►*n.* A style of jazz marked by rhythmic and harmonic complexity and improvised solo performances. ►*v.* **bopped, bop·ping 1.**

To dance to bop. **2.** *Slang* To go: *bopped off to the movies.* [Short for BEBOP.] —**bop′per** *n.* —**bop′py** *adj.*

bo·rate (bôr′āt′) ►*n.* A salt, ester, or anion of boric acid.

bo·rax (bôr′ăks′, -əks) ►*n.* A sodium borate used as a cleaning compound. [< MPers. *būrak.*]

Bor·deaux¹ (bôr-dō′) A city of SW France SW of Paris.

Bor·deaux² (bôr-dō′) ►*n., pl.* **Bor·deaux** (bôr-dō′, -dōz′) A wine from the Bordeaux region.

bor·del·lo (bôr-děl′ō) ►*n., pl.* **-los** A house of prostitution. [< OFr. *borde*, wooden hut.]

bor·der (bôr′dər) ►*n.* **1.** A part that forms the outer edge of something. **2.** A political or geographic boundary. ►*v.* **1.** To share a border with; be next to. **2.** To put a border on. **3.** To be almost like; approach: *an act that borders on heroism.* [< OFr. *border*, to border.]

bor·der·land (bôr′dər-lănd′) ►*n.* **1.** Land on or near a border. **2.** An indeterminate area.

bor·der·line (bôr′dər-līn′) ►*n.* **1.** A boundary. **2.** An indefinite area between two qualities or conditions. ►*adj.* **1.** Verging on a given condition: *borderline poverty.* **2.** Uncertain; dubious: *borderline qualifications.*

bore¹ (bôr) ►*v.* **bored, bor·ing 1.** To make a hole in or through with or as if with a drill. **2.** To form (e.g., a tunnel) by drilling, digging, or burrowing. ►*n.* **1.** A hole or passage made by or as if by drilling. **2.** The interior diameter of a hole, tube, or cylinder. **3.** The caliber of a firearm. **4.** A drilling tool. [< OE *borian.*] —**bor′er** *n.*

bore² (bôr) ►*v.* **bored, bor·ing** To make weary by being dull, repetitive, or tedious. ►*n.* One that bores. [?]

bore³ (bôr) ►*v.* P.t. of **bear¹.**

bo·re·al (bôr′ē-əl) ►*adj.* Northern. [< Lat. *Boreās*, the north wind.]

bore·dom (bôr′dəm) ►*n.* The condition of being bored; ennui.

Bor·ges (bôr′hĕs), **Jorge Luis** 1899–1986. Argentinian writer. —**Bor·ges′i·an** (-hä′sē-ən, -hĕs′ē-) *adj.*

Bor·gia (bôr′jə, -zhə) Italian family, including **Cesare** (1475?–1507), a religious and political leader, and **Lucrezia** (1489–1519), a patron of the arts.

bo·ric acid (bôr′ĭk) ►*n.* A white or colorless crystalline compound, H_3BO_3, used esp. as an antiseptic and preservative.

bor·ing (bôr′ĭng) ►*adj.* Uninteresting and tiresome; dull.

born (bôrn) ►*v.* P.part. of **bear¹.** ►*adj.* **1.** Brought into life by birth. **2.** Having a natural talent: *a born artist.* **3.** Resulting or coming from: *wisdom born of experience.*

borne (bôrn) ►*v.* P.part. of **bear¹.**

Bor·ne·o (bôr′nē-ō′) An island of the W Pacific in the Malay Archipelago between the Sulu and Java Seas. —**Bor′ne·an** *adj.*

Bo·ro·din (bôr′ə-dēn′), **Aleksandr Porfire·vich** 1833–87. Russian composer and chemist.

bo·ron (bôr′ŏn′) ►*n.* *Symbol* **B** A nonmetallic element that is amorphous and brown or crystalline and black, used in flares, nuclear reactor control elements, abrasives, and hard metallic alloys. At. no. 5. See table at **element.** [BOR(AX) + (CARB)ON.]

bor·ough (bûr′ō) ►*n.* **1.** A self-governing incor-

porated town in some US states. **2.** One of the five administrative units of New York City. **3.** A civil division of Alaska that is equivalent to a county. **4.** *Chiefly Brit.* **a.** A town having a municipal corporation. **b.** A town that sends a representative to Parliament. [< OE *burg*, fortified town.]

bor·row (bŏr′ō, bôr′ō) ►*v.* **1.** To obtain or receive (something) on loan with the intent to return it. **2.** To adopt or use as one's own. [< OE *borgian.*] —**bor′row·er** *n.*

bor·row·ing (bŏr′ō-ĭng, bôr′-) ►*n.* Something borrowed, esp. a word borrowed from one language for use in another.

borscht or **borsht** (bôrsht) ►*n.* A beet soup, usu. served with sour cream. [< Russ. *borshch.*]

bor·zoi (bôr′zoi′) ►*n.* A tall slender dog having a narrow pointed head and silky coat. [< Russ. *borzoĭ*, swift.]

Bosch (bŏsh, bôsh), **Hieronymus** 1450?–1516. Dutch painter.

Bose (bōs), **Satyendra Nath** 1894–1974. Indian physicist.

bosh (bŏsh) ►*n.* *Informal* Nonsense. [< Turk. *boş*, empty.] —**bosh** *interj.*

bo's'n or **bos'n** (bō′sən) ►*n.* Vars. of **boatswain.**

Bos·ni·a (bŏz′nē-ə) The N part of Bosnia and Herzegovina. —**Bos′ni·an** *adj. & n.*

Bosnia and Herzegovina or **Bos·ni·a-Her·ze·go·vi·na** (bŏz′nē-ə-hĕrt′sə-gō′vē-nə, -gō-vē′-, -hûrt′-) A country of the NW Balkan Peninsula W of Serbia. Cap. Sarajevo.

Bos·ni·ak (bŏz′nē-ăk′) ►*n.* A Bosnian descendant of those Slavs who converted to Islam under the Ottoman empire. —**Bos′ni·ak′** *adj.*

Bos·ni·an (bŏz′nē-ən) ►*adj.* Of or relating to Bosnia, the Bosniaks, their language, or their culture. ►*n.* **1.** The Slavic language of the Bosniaks. **2.** A Bosniak.

bos·om (bŏoz′əm, bōō′zəm) ►*n.* **1a.** The human chest. **b.** A woman's breast or breasts. **2.** The part of a garment covering the chest. **3.** The heart or center: *the bosom of our family.* ►*adj.* Intimate: *a bosom friend.* [< OE *bōsm.*]

bo·son (bō′sŏn) ►*n.* Any of a class of particles that have integral spins and do not obey the exclusion principle, so that any number of identical particles may occupy the same quantum state. [After Satyendra Nath BOSE.]

Bos·po·rus (bŏs′pər-əs) A narrow strait separating European and Asian Turkey and joining the Black Sea with the Sea of Marmara.

boss¹ (bôs, bŏs) ►*n.* **1.** An employer or supervisor. **2.** A politician who controls a political party or machine. ►*v.* To give orders to. [Du. *baas*, master.] —**boss′y** *adj.*

boss² (bôs, bŏs) ►*n.* A knoblike ornament. ►*v.* To emboss. [< OFr. *boce.*]

Bos·ton (bô′stən, bŏs′tən) The capital of MA, in the E part on an arm of Massachusetts Bay. —**Bos·to′ni·an** (bô-stō′nē-ən, bŏs-) *adj. & n.*

bo·sun (bō′sən) ►*n.* Var. of **boatswain.**

Bos·well (bŏz′wĕl′, -wəl), **James** 1740–95. British lawyer, diarist, and writer.

bot (bŏt) ►*n.* A software program that imitates human behavior, as by querying search engines.

bot·a·ny (bŏt′n-ē) ►*n.* The science or study of plants. [< Gk. *botanē*, plants.] —**bo·tan′i·cal**

(bə-tăn′ĭ-kəl), **bo·tan′ic** adj. —**bot′a·nist** n.

botch (bŏch) ►v. **1.** To ruin through clumsiness. **2.** To repair clumsily. [ME *bocchen*, mend.] —**botch** n. —**botch′er** n. —**botch′i·ly** adv. —**botch′y** adj.
   Syns: *blow, bungle, butcher, fumble, muff* **v.**

both (bōth) ►adj. One and the other; of or being two in conjunction: *Both guests are here.* ►pron. The one and the other: *Both were tall.* ►conj. Used with *and* to indicate that each of two things in a coordinated phrase or clause is included: *Both on and off.* [< OE *bā thā,* both those.]

both·er (bŏth′ər) ►v. **1.** To disturb, annoy, or anger, esp. by minor irritations. See Synonyms at **annoy. 2.** To trouble or concern oneself. ►n. A cause or state of disturbance. ►interj. Used to express annoyance. [Poss. of Celt. orig.] —**both′er·some** (-səm) adj.

Both·ni·a (bŏth′nē-ə), **Gulf of** An arm of the Baltic Sea between Sweden and Finland.

Bot·swa·na (bŏt-swä′nə) A landlocked country of S-central Africa. Cap. Gaborone.

Bot·ti·cel·li (bŏt′ĭ-chĕl′ē), **Sandro** 1444?–1510. Italian painter.

bot·tle (bŏt′l) ►n. **1.** A receptacle having a narrow neck, usu. no handles, and a mouth that can be plugged, corked, or capped. **2.** *Informal* Intoxicating liquor. ►v. **-tled, -tling 1.** To place in a bottle. **2.** To restrain: *bottled up my emotions.* [< LLat. *buttis,* cask.] —**bot′tle·ful′** n. —**bot′tler** n.

bottle gourd ►n. **1.** A vine with white flowers, widely cultivated for its smooth, hard-shelled fruits. **2.** The dried, hollowed-out shell of one of these fruits, often used as a container, drinking utensil, or musical instrument.

bot·tle·neck (bŏt′l-nĕk′) ►n. **1.** A narrow or obstructed section, as of a highway or pipeline, where movement is slowed down. **2.** A hindrance to progress or production.

bot·tom (bŏt′əm) ►n. **1.** The deepest or lowest part: *the bottom of a well; the bottom of the page.* **2.** The underside. **3.** The supporting part; base. **4.** The last or least favorable position: *bottom of the list; bottom of the hierarchy.* **5.** The basic underlying quality; essence. **6.** The solid surface under a body of water. **7.** often **bottoms** Low-lying land adjacent to a river. **8.** *Informal* The buttocks. —*idiom:* **at bottom** Basically. [< OE *botm.*] —**bot′tom·less** adj.

bot·tom·land (bŏt′əm-lănd′) ►n. See **bottom** (sense 7).

bottom line ►n. **1.** The line in a financial statement that shows net income or loss. **2.** Financial matters, esp. profit or loss. **3.** The final result or statement; upshot. **4.** The main or essential point.

bot·u·lism (bŏch′ə-lĭz′əm) ►n. A severe, sometimes fatal food poisoning caused by bacteria that grow in improperly canned foods. [< Lat. *botulus,* sausage.]

Bou·dic·ca (boo-dĭk′ə) also **Bo·ad·i·ce·a** (bō′-ăd-ĭ-sē′ə) 1st cent. AD. Queen of ancient Britain.

bou·doir (boo′dwär′, -dwôr′) ►n. A private room, esp. one belonging to a woman. [< OFr. *bouder,* sulk.]

bouf·fant (boo-fänt′) ►adj. Puffed-out; full: *bouffant sleeves.* ►n. A puffed-out hairstyle. [< OFr. *bouffer,* puff up.]

bou·gain·vil·le·a (boo′gən-vĭl′ē-ə, -vĭl′yə) ►n. A woody tropical shrub or vine with variously colored petallike bracts attached to the flowers. [After Louis Antoine de *Bougainville* (1729–1811).]

bough (bou) ►n. A tree branch, esp. a large or main branch. [< OE *bōh.*]

bought (bôt) ►v. P.t. and p.part. of **buy.**

bouil·la·baisse (boo′yə-bās′, bool′yə-bās′) ►n. A stew of fish and shellfish. [< Prov. *bouiabaisso.*]

bouil·lon (bool′yŏn′, -yən) ►n. A clear thin meat broth. [< OFr. *boulir,* BOIL¹.]

Boul. ►abbr. boulevard

Bou·lan·ger (boo-län-zhā′), **Nadia Juliette** 1887–1979. French composer, conductor, and music teacher.

boul·der (bōl′dər) ►n. A large rock. [ME *bulder.*]

boul·e·vard (bool′ə-värd′, boo′lə-) ►n. **1.** A broad city street, often tree-lined and landscaped. **2.** *Regional* See **median** (sense 2). [< MDu. *bolwer,* BULWARK.]

bounce (bouns) ►v. **bounced, bounc·ing 1.** To rebound or cause to rebound after having struck an object or surface. **2.** To move jerkily; bump: *The car bounced over the potholes.* **3.** To bound; spring. **4.** To be sent back by a bank as valueless: *a check that bounced.* **5.** To be sent back by a mail server as undeliverable: *The e-mail bounced because of a mistyped address.* **6.** To expel or dismiss. ►n. **1.** A bound or rebound. **2.** A spring or leap. **3.** The capacity to rebound. **4.** Spirit; liveliness. —*phrasal verb:* **bounce back** To recover quickly: *bounced back to good health.* [Prob. < ME *bounsen,* beat.] —**bounc′i·ly** adv. —**bounc′y** adj.

bounc·er (boun′sər) ►n. *Slang* A person employed to expel disorderly persons from a public place, esp. a bar.

bounc·ing (boun′sĭng) ►adj. Vigorous; healthy: *a bouncing baby.*

bound¹ (bound) ►v. **1.** To leap or spring. **2.** To move by leaping. **3.** To bounce or rebound. ►n. **1.** A leap; jump. **2.** A rebound; bounce. [< OFr. *bondir,* resound.]

bound² (bound) ►n. **1.** often **bounds** A boundary; limit. **2. bounds** The territory on or within a boundary. ►v. **1.** To limit or confine. **2.** To constitute the limit of. **3.** To demarcate. —*idiom:* **out of bounds 1.** Outside the boundary of a playing field. **2.** Exceeding acceptable rules or standards: *their behavior was out of bounds.* [< Med.Lat. *bodina.*]

bound³ (bound) ►v. P.t. and p.part. of **bind.** ►adj. **1.** Confined by bonds. **2.** Being under legal or moral obligation. **3.** Having a binding. **4.** Certain: *We're bound to be late.*

bound⁴ (bound) ►adj. Heading in a specified direction: *bound for home; south-bound.* [< ON *būinn,* p.part. of *būa,* get ready.]

bound·a·ry (boun′də-rē, -drē) ►n., pl. **-ries** Something that indicates a border or limit.

bound·er (boun′dər) ►n. *Chiefly Brit.* A cad.

bound·less (bound′lĭs) ►adj. Being without limits. —**bound′less·ly** adv. —**bound′less·ness** n.

boun·te·ous (boun′tē-əs) ►adj. Plentiful: *bounteous harvests.* —**boun′te·ous·ly** adv.

boun·ti·ful (boun′tə-fəl) ►adj. **1.** Marked by or producing abundance: *a bountiful land.* **2.** Giving generously. —**boun′ti·ful·ly** *adv.*

boun·ty (boun′tē) ►*n., pl.* **-ties 1.** Liberality in giving: *a patron's bounty.* **2.** Something given liberally. **3.** A reward or inducement, esp. one given by a government for performing a service, such as capturing a fugitive. [< Lat. *bonitās,* goodness.]

bou·quet (bō-kā′, boō-) ►*n.* **1.** A cluster of flowers. **2.** A pleasant fragrance, esp. of a wine. See Synonyms at **fragrance.** [< OFr. *bosquet,* thicket.]

bour·bon (bûr′bən) ►*n.* A whiskey distilled from a fermented mash of corn, malt, and rye. [After *Bourbon* County, Kentucky.]

Bour·bon (boōr′bən, boō-bôn′) French royal family descended from Louis I, Duke of Bourbon (1270?–1342), whose members have ruled in France, Spain, and Italy.

bour·geois (boōr-zhwä′, boōr′zhwä′) ►*n., pl.* **-geois 1.** One belonging to the middle class. **2.** In Marxist theory, a capitalist. ►*adj.* Of or typical of the middle class, esp. in holding conventional attitudes and materialistic values. [< OFr. *burgeis,* citizen of a town.]

bour·geoi·sie (boōr′zhwä-zē′) ►*n.* **1.** The middle class. **2.** In Marxist theory, the social group opposed to the proletariat. [Fr.]

Bourke-White (bûrk′wīt′, -hwīt′), **Margaret** 1906–71. Amer. photographer and writer.

bout (bout) ►*n.* **1.** A contest; match: *a wrestling bout.* **2.** A period of time spent in a particular way; spell: *a bout of the flu.* [< ME *bought,* a turn < *bowen,* BOW².]

bou·tique (boō-tēk′) ►*n.* A small retail shop that specializes in gifts, fashionable items, or food. [< Lat. *apothēca,* storehouse.]

bou·ton·niere (boō′tə-nîr′, -tən-yâr′) ►*n.* A flower worn in a buttonhole. [< OFr., buttonhole < *bouton,* BUTTON.]

bo·vine (bō′vīn′, -vēn′) ►*adj.* **1.** Of or resembling an ox, cow, or buffalo. **2.** Dull and stolid. [< Lat. *bōs,* cow.] —**bo′vine′** *n.*

bow¹ (bou) ►*n.* The front section of a ship or boat. [Poss. of LGer. orig.]

bow² (bou) ►*v.* **1.** To bend the body, head, or knee in order to express greeting, consent, courtesy, or veneration. **2.** To acquiesce; submit. ►*n.* An act of bowing, as in respect. —*phrasal verb:* **bow out** To remove oneself; withdraw. [< OE *būgan.*]

bow³ (bō) ►*n.* **1.** A curve or arch. **2.** A weapon consisting of a curved, flexible strip of material, strung taut from end to end and used to launch arrows. **3.** *Mus.* A rod strung with horsehair, used in playing the violin and related instruments. **4.** A knot usu. having two loops and two ends, as a bowknot. **5.** A rainbow. ►*v.* **1.** To bend into a bow. **2.** *Mus.* To play (a stringed instrument) with a bow. [< OE *boga.*]

bowd·ler·ize (bōd′lə-rīz′, boud′-) ►*v.* **-ized, -iz·ing** To expurgate (e.g., a book) prudishly. [After Thomas *Bowdler* (1754–1825).] —**bowd′ler·i·za′tion** *n.*

bow·el (bou′əl, boul) ►*n.* **1a.** often **bowels** The intestine. **b.** A division of the intestine: *the large bowel.* **2. bowels** The interior of something: *in the bowels of the ship.* [< Lat. *botulus,* sausage.]

bow·er (bou′ər) ►*n.* A shaded, leafy recess. [< OE *būr,* dwelling.]

bow·ie knife (bō′ē, boō′ē) ►*n.* A long, single-edged steel hunting knife. [After James *Bowie* (1796–1836).]

bow·knot (bō′nŏt′) ►*n.* A knot with large decorative loops.

bowl¹ (bōl) ►*n.* **1a.** A rounded hollow vessel for food or fluids. **b.** The contents of such a vessel. **2.** A curved hollow part, as of a spoon or pipe. **3.** A bowl-shaped structure or edifice, such as a stadium. [< OE *bolla.*]

bowl² (bōl) ►*n.* **1.** A large solid ball rolled in certain games. **2.** A roll of the ball in bowling. ►*v.* **1.** To play the game of bowling. **2.** To roll a ball in bowling. **3.** To achieve (a score) in bowling. —*phrasal verb:* **bowl over 1.** To astound. **2.** To knock over. [< Lat. *bulla,* round object.]

bow·leg·ged (bō′lĕg′ĭd, -lĕgd′) ►*adj.* Having legs that curve outward at the knees.

bowl·er¹ (bō′lər) ►*n.* One who bowls.

bowl·er² (bō′lər) ►*n.* A derby hat. [Poss. < BOWL².]

bow·line (bō′lĭn, -līn′) ►*n.* A knot forming a loop that does not slip. [< MLGer. *bōline.*]

bowl·ing (bō′lĭng) ►*n.* **1a.** A game played by rolling a heavy ball down a wooden alley in order to knock down a triangular group of ten pins. **b.** A similar game, such as duckpins. **2.** A game played on a bowling green by rolling a wooden ball as close as possible to a target ball.

bowling alley ►*n.* **1.** A level wooden lane used in bowling. **2.** A place containing such lanes.

bowling green ►*n.* A level grassy area for bowling.

bow·man (bō′mən) ►*n.* An archer.

bow·sprit (bou′sprĭt′, bō′-) ►*n.* A spar extending forward from the bow of a sailing ship. [< MLGer. *bōchsprēt.*]

bow·string (bō′strĭng′) ►*n.* The cord attached to both ends of an archer's bow.

bow tie (bō) ►*n.* A small necktie tied in a bow.

box¹ (bŏks) ►*n.* **1a.** A container, usu. rectangular and often with a lid. **b.** The amount or quantity a box can hold. **2.** A square or rectangle. **3.** A separated seating compartment, as in a theater. **4.** A booth: *a sentry box.* ►*v.* **1.** To place in or as if in a box. **2.** To restrict to a narrow scope or position: *boxed in by new rules.* [< OE, ult. < Gk. *puxis.*] —**box′ful′** *n.* —**box′y** *adj.*

box² (bŏks) ►*n.* A slap or blow with the hand or fist. ►*v.* **1.** To hit with the hand or fist. **2.** To take part in a boxing match. [ME.]

box³ (bŏks) ►*n., pl.* **box** or **box·es 1.** An evergreen shrub or tree widely cultivated as a hedge plant. **2.** The hard yellowish wood of this shrub or tree. [< OE, ult. < Gk. *puxos.*]

box·car (bŏks′kär′) ►*n.* A fully enclosed railroad car used to transport freight.

box·er¹ (bŏk′sər) ►*n. Sports* One who boxes, esp. professionally.

box·er² (bŏk′sər) ►*n.* A medium-sized, short-haired dog having a short, square-jawed muzzle. [Ger. < E., BOXER¹.]

box·ers (bŏk′sərz) ►*pl.n.* Men's undershorts.

box·ing (bŏk′sĭng) ►*n.* The sport of fighting with the fists.

box office ►*n.* A booth, as in a theater, where tickets are sold. —**box′-of′fice** *adj.*

box seat ►*n.* A seat in a box, esp. in a theater or stadium.

box spring ►*n.* A cloth-covered frame containing rows of coil springs used to support a mattress.

box·wood (bŏks′wŏŏd′) ►*n.* See **box³**.

boy (boi) ►*n.* A male child or youth. ►*interj.* Used to express mild elation or disgust. [ME *boi.*] —**boy′hood′** *n.* —**boy′ish** *adj.* —**boy′ish·ly** *adv.* —**boy′ish·ness** *n.*

boy·cott (boi′kŏt′) ►*v.* To abstain from using, buying, dealing with, or participating in as a protest. [After Charles C. *Boycott* (1832–1897).] —**boy′cott′** *n.*

boy·friend (boi′frĕnd′) ►*n.* **1.** A favored male companion or sweetheart. **2.** A male friend.

Boyle (boil), **Robert** 1627–91. Irish-born British physicist and chemist.

Boy Scout ►*n.* A member of a worldwide organization of young men and boys, founded for character development, citizenship training, and outdoor skills.

boy·sen·ber·ry (boi′zən-bĕr′ē) ►*n.* **1.** A prickly bramble derived from a W North American blackberry. **2.** The edible dark red fruit of this plant. [After Rudolph *Boysen* (d. 1950).]

BP ►*abbr.* **1.** basis point **2.** before present (in radiocarbon dating, before 1950) **3.** blood pressure **4.** boiling point

bpd ►*abbr.* barrels per day

Br. ►*abbr.* **1.** Britain **2.** British

bra (brä) ►*n.* A brassiere.

brace (brās) ►*n.* **1.** A clamp. **2.** A device, such as a beam in a building, that steadies or supports a weight. **3. braces** *Chiefly Brit.* Suspenders. **4.** An orthopedic appliance used to support a bodily part. **5.** often **braces** A dental appliance of bands and wires that is fixed to the teeth to correct irregular alignment. **6.** A cranklike handle for securing and turning a bit. **7.** A symbol, { or }, used to enclose written or printed lines that are considered a unit. **8.** *pl.* **brace** A pair of like things: *a brace of pheasants.* ►*v.* **braced, brac·ing 1.** To support, strengthen, or hold steady. **2.** To prepare for a struggle, impact, or danger. **3.** To fill with energy; stimulate. [< Gk. *brakhīon,* upper arm.]

brace·let (brās′lĭt) ►*n.* An ornamental band or chain worn around the wrist or arm. [< Gk. *brakhīon,* upper arm.]

bra·chi·o·sau·rus (brā′kē-ə-sôr′əs, brăk′ē-) or **bra·chi·o·saur** (brā′kē-ə-sôr′, brăk′ē-) ►*n.* A massive herbivorous dinosaur having forelegs longer than the hind legs. [Gk. *brakhīon,* upper arm + *sauros,* lizard.]

brack·en (brăk′ən) ►*n.* A widespread weedy fern having large triangular fronds and tough stems, often forming dense thickets. [ME *braken.*]

brack·et (brăk′ĭt) ►*n.* **1.** An L-shaped fixture, one arm of which is fastened to a vertical surface, the other projecting to support a shelf or other weight. **2.** A shelf supported by brackets. **3.** A square bracket. **4.** A classification or grouping, esp. by income. [Poss. < Fr. *braguette,* codpiece.] —**brack′et** *v.*

brack·ish (brăk′ĭsh) ►*adj.* Being or containing water that is somewhat salty. [< Du. *brak.*]

bract (brăkt) ►*n.* A leaflike plant part located just below a flower, flower stalk, or flower cluster. [< Lat. *bractea,* gold leaf.]

brad (brăd) ►*n.* A thin wire nail with a small head. [< ON *broddr,* spike.] —**brad** *v.*

Brad·bur·y (brăd′bĕr′ē, -bə-rē), **Ray Douglas** 1920–2012. Amer. writer.

Ray Bradbury
photographed in 2007

Brad·ford¹ (brăd′fərd), **William** 1590–1657. English colonist in America.

Brad·ford² (brăd′fərd), **William** 1663–1752. English-born Amer. colonial printer.

Bra·dy (brā′dē), **Mathew B.** 1823–96. Amer. pioneer photographer.

brag (brăg) ►*v.* **bragged, brag·ging** To talk or assert boastfully. [ME *braggen.*] —**brag** *n.* —**brag′ger** *n.*

brag·ga·do·ci·o (brăg′ə-dō′shē-ō′) ►*n.,* *pl.* **-os 1a.** Empty or pretentious bragging. **b.** A swaggering, cocky manner. **2.** A braggart. [After *Braggadocchio,* in *The Faerie Queene* by Spenser.]

brag·gart (brăg′ərt) ►*n.* One given to empty boasting; bragger. [< Fr. *braguer,* to brag, poss. < ME *braggen.*]

Brahe (brä, brä′hē), **Tycho** 1546–1601. Danish astronomer.

Brah·ma (brä′mə) ►*n.* **1.** *Hinduism* The creator god, conceived chiefly as a member of the triad including Vishnu and Shiva. **2.** Var. of **Brahman** (sense 2).

Brah·man (brä′mən) also **Brah·min** (-mĭn) ►*n.* **1.** A member of the highest of the four major castes of traditional Indian society, responsible for officiating at religious rites and studying and teaching the Vedas. **2.** also **Brah·ma** (-mə) A breed of domestic cattle bred from stock originating in India, having a hump between the shoulders. [Skt. *brahma,* brahman-.]

Brah·man·ism (brä′mə-nĭz′əm) also **Brah·min·ism** (-mĭ-) ►*n.* *Hinduism* **1.** The religion of ancient India as reflected in the Vedas. **2.** The social and religious system of Hindus, esp. of Brahmins, based on a caste structure. —**Brah′man·ist** *n.*

Brah·ma·pu·tra (brä′mə-pōō′trə) A river of S Asia rising in SW Tibet and flowing about 2,900 km (1,800 mi) to join the Ganges R.

Brah·min (brä′mĭn) ►*n.* **1.** Var. of **Brahman. 2.** A member of a cultural and social elite: *a Boston Brahmin.* [< Skt. *brāhmaṇa-,* of Brahmins.] —**Brah·min′ic** (-mĭn′ĭk) *adj.*

Brahms (brämz), **Johannes** 1833–97. German composer. —**Brahms′i·an** *adj.*

braid (brād) ►*v.* **1.** To interweave strands or lengths of. **2.** To make by weaving strands together. **3.** To decorate or edge with an interwoven trim. ►*n.* **1.** A braided segment or length, as of hair. **2.** Ornamental cord or ribbon, used esp. for decorating or edging fabrics. [< OE *bregdan*, weave.] —**braid′er** *n.*

Braille or **braille** (brāl) ►*n.* A system of writing and printing for visually impaired people, in which raised dots represent letters and numerals. [After Louis BRAILLE.]

Braille
Braille alphabet and numerals

Braille, Louis 1809–52. French inventor of a writing system for the blind (1829).

brain (brān) ►*n.* **1a.** The portion of the vertebrate central nervous system, enclosed within the cranium and composed of gray matter and white matter, that is the primary center for the regulation and control of bodily activities, the receiving and interpreting of sensory impulses, and the exercising of thought and emotion. **b.** A functionally similar portion of the invertebrate nervous system. **2.** often **brains** Intellectual power; intelligence. **3.** A highly intelligent person. ►*v. Slang* **1.** To smash in the skull of. **2.** To hit on the head. —*idioms:* **beat (one's) brains (out)** *Informal* To try energetically. **on the brain** Obsessively in mind. **pick (someone's) brain** To explore another's ideas through questioning. [< OE *brægen.*] —**brain′i·ness** *n.* —**brain′less** *adj.* —**brain′less·ness** *n.* —**brain′y** *adj.*

brain·child (brān′chīld′) ►*n.* An original idea, plan, or creation.

brain death ►*n.* Irreversible brain damage and loss of brain function, as evidenced by cessation of activity of the central nervous system. —**brain′-dead′** (brān′děd′) *adj.*

brain·pow·er (brān′pou′ər) ►*n.* Intellectual capacity.

brain·storm (brān′stôrm′) ►*n.* A sudden clever plan or idea. ►*v.* To try to solve a problem by proposing and considering possible ideas or solutions. —**brain′storm′ing** *n.*

brain·wash·ing (brān′wŏsh′ĭng, -wô′shĭng) ►*n.* Intensive, forcible indoctrination aimed at replacing a person's basic convictions with an alternate set of fixed beliefs. —**brain′wash′** *v.*

brain wave ►*n.* A rhythmic fluctuation of electric potential between parts of the brain, as seen on an electroencephalogram.

braise (brāz) ►*v.* **braised, brais·ing** To brown in fat and then simmer in a covered container. [< OFr. *brese*, hot coals.]

brake¹ (brāk) ►*n.* A device for slowing or stopping motion, as of a vehicle, esp. by contact friction. ►*v.* **braked, brak·ing** **1.** To reduce the speed of with or as if with a brake. **2.** To operate or apply a brake. [Prob. < MLGer., curb.]

brake² (brāk) ►*n.* Any of several ferns, esp. bracken. [< ME.]

brake³ (brāk) ►*n.* A densely overgrown area; thicket. [< MLGer.]

brake·man (brāk′mən) ►*n.* A railroad employee who assists the conductor and checks on the operation of a train's brakes.

bram·ble (brăm′bəl) ►*n.* A prickly plant or shrub, esp. the blackberry or raspberry. [< OE *bræmbel.*] —**bram′bly** *adj.*

bran (brăn) ►*n.* The outer husks of cereal grain removed during the process of milling and used for dietary fiber. [< OFr.]

branch (brănch) ►*n.* **1a.** A secondary woody stem growing from the trunk, main stem, or limb of a tree or shrub. **b.** A similar structure or part. **2.** Something that resembles a branch of a tree, as the tine of a deer's antlers. **3.** A limited part of a larger or more complex unit or system. **4.** A division of a family or tribe. **5.** A tributary of a river. ►*v.* **1.** To divide or spread out in branches. **2.** To enlarge one's scope: *branch out into new fields.* [< LLat. *branca*, paw.] —**branched** *adj.*

Syns: *arm, fork, offshoot* **n.**

brand (brănd) ►*n.* **1a.** A trademark or distinctive name identifying a product or manufacturer. **b.** A product line so identified. **c.** A distinctive kind. **2.** A mark indicating ownership, burned on the hide of an animal. **3.** A mark burned into the flesh of criminals or slaves. **4.** A mark of disgrace. See Synonyms at **stain. 5.** A branding iron. **6.** A piece of burning wood. ►*v.* **1.** To mark with or as if with a brand. **2.** To stigmatize. [< OE, torch.]

Bran·deis (brăn′dīs′, -dīz′), **Louis Dembitz** 1856–1941. Amer. jurist; US Supreme Court justice (1916–39).

brand·ing iron (brăn′dĭng) ►*n.* An iron that is heated and used for branding.

bran·dish (brăn′dĭsh) ►*v.* To wave or flourish (e.g., a weapon) in a menacing, defiant, or excited way. See Synonyms at **flourish.** [< OFr. *brandir* < *brand*, sword.]

brand name ►*n.* A distinctive name identifying a product, a service, or an organization. —**brand′-name′** *adj.*

brand-new (brănd′nōō′, -nyōō′) ►*adj.* Fresh and unused; completely new.

Bran·do (brăn′dō), **Marlon** 1924–2004. Amer. actor.

bran·dy (brăn′dē) ►*n., pl.* **-dies** An alcoholic liquor distilled from wine or fermented fruit juice. [< Du. *brandewijn.*] —**bran′dy** *v.*

brant (brănt) ►*n., pl.* **brant** or **brants** A small wild goose having a black neck and head. [Poss. < ME *brende*, brindled.]

Brant, Joseph 1742–1807. Mohawk leader.

brash (brăsh) ►*adj.* **-er, -est 1.** Hasty and

unthinking; rash. **2.** Bold; impudent. [Poss. imit.] **—brash′ly** *adv.* **—brash′ness** *n.*

Bra·sí·lia (brə-zĭl′yə) The capital of Brazil, in the central plateau NW of Rio de Janeiro.

brass (brăs) ►*n.* **1a.** A yellowish alloy of copper and zinc. **b.** Objects made of brass. **2.** often **brasses** *Mus.* The brass instruments of an orchestra or band. **3.** *Informal* Bold self-assurance; effrontery. **4.** *Slang* High-ranking military officers. [< OE *bræs.*] **—brass′y** *adj.*

bras·se·rie (brăs′ə-rē′) ►*n.* A bar serving food as well as alcoholic beverages. [< OFr. *bracier,* to brew.]

brass hat ►*n. Slang* One of high rank or position, esp. a high-ranking military officer.

bras·siere (brə-zîr′) ►*n.* A woman's undergarment that supports the breasts. [OFr. *bras,* arm; see BRACE.]

brass tacks ►*pl.n. Informal* Essential facts; basics: *getting down to brass tacks.*

brat (brăt) ►*n.* **1.** An ill-mannered child. **2.** *Informal* A child of a career military person. [Poss. < OE *bratt,* coarse garment.] **—brat′ty** *adj.*

Bra·ti·sla·va (brăt′ĭ-slä′və, brä′tĭ-) The capital of Slovakia, in the SW part on the Danube R.

Braun (brôn, broun), **Wernher Magnus Maximilian von** 1912–77. German-born Amer. rocket engineer.

bra·va·do (brə-vä′dō) ►*n., pl.* **-dos** or **-does** A show of bravery or defiance, esp. in order to mask weakness. [< Sp. *bravada.*]

brave (brāv) ►*adj.* **brav·er, brav·est 1.** Possessing or displaying courage; valiant. **2.** Making a fine display; splendid. ►*n.* A Native American warrior. ►*v.* **braved, brav·ing** To undergo or face courageously. See Synonyms at **defy.** [< OFr. *bravo.*] **—brave′ly** *adv.* **—brave′ness** *n.*

brav·er·y (brā′və-rē, brāv′rē) ►*n.* Courage.

bra·vo (brä′vō, brä-vō′) ►*interj.* Used to express approval, esp. of a performance. ►*n., pl.* **-vos** A cry of "bravo." [Ital.]

bra·vu·ra (brə-vŏŏr′ə, -vyŏŏr′ə) ►*adj.* Displaying brilliant technique or style, esp. in musical performance. [Ital.]

brawl (brôl) ►*n.* A noisy quarrel or fight. [< ME *braullen,* to quarrel.] **—brawl** *v.* **—brawl′er** *n.*
    Syns: *donnybrook, fracas, fray, free-for-all, melee, scrap, scrape, scuffle n.*

brawn (brôn) ►*n.* **1.** Solid and well-developed muscles. **2.** Muscular strength. [< OFr. *braon,* meat, of Gmc. orig.]

brawn·y (brô′nē) ►*adj.* **-i·er, -i·est** Well-muscled; strong. See Synonyms at **muscular.**

bray (brā) ►*v.* To utter the loud harsh cry of a donkey. [< OFr. *braire.*] **—bray** *n.*

braze (brāz) ►*v.* **brazed, braz·ing** To solder together using a solder with a high melting point. [Prob. < OFr. *braser,* to burn.] **—braz′er** *n.*

bra·zen (brā′zən) ►*adj.* **1.** Rudely bold; insolent. **2.** Having a loud harsh sound. **3.** Made of or resembling brass. ►*v.* To face with bold self-assurance: *brazened out the crisis.* [< OE *bræsen,* made of brass.] **—bra′zen·ly** *adv.* **—bra′zen·ness** *n.*

bra·zier¹ (brā′zhər) ►*n.* One who works in brass. [ME *brasier* < *bras,* BRASS.]

bra·zier² (brā′zhər) ►*n.* A metal pan for holding burning coals or charcoal. [< OFr. *brese,* embers.]

Bra·zil (brə-zĭl′) A country of central and E South America. Cap. Brasília. **—Bra·zil′i·an** *adj. & n.*

Brazil nut ►*n.* The hard-shelled edible seed of a South American tree.

Braz·za·ville (brăz′ə-vĭl′) The capital of the Republic of the Congo, in the S part on the Congo R.

breach (brēch) ►*n.* **1.** An opening, tear, or rupture, esp. in a solid structure. **2.** A violation or infraction, as of a law or obligation. **3.** A disruption of friendly relations. **4.** A leap of a whale from the water. [< OE *brēc.*] **—breach** *v.*

bread (brĕd) ►*n.* **1.** A staple food made chiefly from moistened, usu. leavened flour or meal kneaded and baked. **2.** Food in general, regarded as necessary to sustain life. **3.** *Slang* Money. ►*v.* To coat with bread crumbs before cooking. [< OE *brēad.*]

bread·bas·ket (brĕd′băs′kĭt) ►*n.* An abundant grain-producing region.

bread·board (brĕd′bôrd′) ►*n.* **1.** A slicing board. **2.** An experimental model, esp. of an electronic circuit.

bread·fruit (brĕd′frŏŏt′) ►*n.* **1.** A tropical timber tree having large round yellowish starchy fruits. **2.** The edible fruit of this tree.

bread·stuff (brĕd′stŭf′) ►*n.* **1.** Bread in any form. **2.** Flour or grain used in making bread.

breadth (brĕdth) ►*n.* **1.** The measure or dimension from side to side; width. **2a.** Wide range or scope. **b.** Tolerance; broadmindedness: *a jurist of great breadth and wisdom.* [< ME *brede,* broad.]

bread·win·ner (brĕd′wĭn′ər) ►*n.* One whose earnings are the primary source of support for one's dependents.

break (brāk) ►*v.* **broke** (brōk), **bro·ken** (brō′kən), **break·ing 1a.** To separate into or reduce to pieces by sudden force. **b.** To crack without separating into pieces. **2.** To make or become unusable or inoperative. **3.** To give way; collapse. **4.** To force or make a way into, through, or out of. **5.** To pierce the surface of. **6.** To disrupt the uniformity or continuity of: *break ranks.* **7.** To make or become known or noticed, esp. suddenly: *break a story.* **8.** To begin or emerge suddenly: *break into bloom.* **9.** To produce (a sweat) copiously on the skin. **10.** To change suddenly: *broke to the left.* **11.** To surpass or outdo: *broke the record.* **12.** To subdue or exert control over: *break a habit; break a mustang.* **13.** To ruin, as in spirit or health. **14.** To reduce in rank. **15.** To lessen in force or effect: *break a fall.* **16.** To fail to conform (to); violate: *break a law.* ►*n.* **1.** The act or an occurrence of breaking. **2.** The result of breaking, as a crack or separation. **3.** An emergence. **4.** A pause or rest. **5.** A sudden or marked change. **6.** A violation: *a security break.* **7.** A stroke of luck. **8.** *Informal* An instance of favorable treatment: *A corporate tax break.* **—phrasal verbs: break down** To undergo a breakdown. **break in 1.** To train. **2.** To enter forcibly or illegally. **3.** To interrupt. **break off 1.** To separate or become separated. **2.** To stop suddenly. **break out 1.** To develop suddenly. **2.** To erupt. **3.** To escape, as from prison. **—idioms: break bread** To eat together. **break even** To have neither losses or gains. **break new ground** To advance beyond previous achievements. [< OE *brecan.*] —**break′a·ble** *adj.* & *n.*

break·age (brā′kĭj) ►*n.* **1.** The act of breaking. **2.** A quantity broken. **3.** Loss as a result of breaking.

break·down (brāk′doun′) ►*n.* **1a.** The act or process of failing to function. **b.** The condition resulting from this. **2.** A collapse in physical or mental health. **3.** An analysis, outline, or summary consisting of itemized data. **4.** Disintegration or decomposition into parts or elements.

break·er (brā′kər) ►*n.* **1.** One that breaks. **2.** *Elect.* A circuit breaker. **3.** A wave that breaks into foam, esp. against a shoreline.

break·fast (brĕk′fəst) ►*n.* The first meal of the day. [ME *brekfast.*] —**break′fast** *v.*

break·front (brāk′frŭnt′) ►*n.* A cabinet or bookcase having a central section projecting farther forward than the end sections.

break·neck (brāk′nĕk′) ►*adj.* **1.** Dangerously fast. **2.** Hazardous: *a breakneck curve.*

break·out (brāk′out′) ►*n.* A forceful emergence from a restrictive condition.

break·through (brāk′thrōō′) ►*n.* **1.** An act of overcoming or penetrating an obstacle or restriction. **2.** A major success that permits further progress, as in technology.

break·up (brāk′ŭp′) ►*n.* **1.** A division, dispersal, or disintegration. **2.** The discontinuance of a relationship.

break·wa·ter (brāk′wô′tər, -wŏt′ər) ►*n.* A barrier that protects a harbor or shore from the impact of waves.

bream (brēm, brĭm) ►*n., pl.* **bream** or **breams** A freshwater fish having a flattened body and silvery scales. [< OFr. *breme.*]

breast (brĕst) ►*n.* **1.** The mammary gland, esp. of the human female. **2.** The upper front of the human body from the neck to the abdomen. **3.** The seat of affection and emotion. ►*v.* To meet or confront boldly. [< OE *brēost.*]

breast·bone (brĕst′bōn′) ►*n.* See **sternum.**

breastfeed (brĕst′fēd′) ►*v.* To suckle.

breast·plate (brĕst′plāt′) ►*n.* A piece of armor that covers the breast.

breast·stroke (brĕst′strōk′) ►*n.* A swimming stroke in which the arms are extended forward and drawn toward the sides and then back, and the legs do a frog kick.

breast·work (brĕst′wûrk′) ►*n.* A temporary, quickly constructed fortification, usu. breast-high.

breath (brĕth) ►*n.* **1.** The act or process of breathing; respiration. **2.** The air inhaled and exhaled in respiration. **3.** The ability to breathe. **4.** A slight breeze. **5.** A whisper. —*idiom:* **out of breath** Breathing with difficulty; gasping. [< OE *brǣth.*] —**breath′less** *adj.* —**breath′less·ly** *adv.* —**breath′y** *adj.*

breathe (brēth) ►*v.* **breathed, breath·ing** **1.** To inhale and exhale air. **2.** To be alive; live. **3.** To utter quietly; whisper. —*idiom:* **breathe down (someone's) neck** To threaten or annoy by proximity. [ME *brethen.*] —**breath′a·ble** *adj.*

breath·er (brē′thər) ►*n.* **1.** One that breathes. **2.** *Informal* A short rest period.

breath·tak·ing (brĕth′tā′kĭng) ►*adj.* Inspiring awe. —**breath′tak′ing·ly** *adv.*

Brecht (brĕkt, brĕкнt), **Bertolt** 1898–1956. German poet and playwright. —**Brecht′i·an** *adj.*

breech (brēch) ►*n.* **1.** The buttocks. **2.** **breeches** (brĭch′ĭz) **a.** Knee-length trousers. **b.** *Informal* Trousers. **3.** The part of a firearm behind the barrel. [< OE *brēc*, trousers.]

breech·cloth (brēch′klôth′) ►*n.* A loincloth.

breed (brēd) ►*v.* **bred** (brĕd), **breed·ing** **1a.** To produce (offspring). **b.** To reproduce. **2.** To bring about; engender: *acts that breed suspicion.* **3.** To raise or mate animals. **4.** To rear or train; bring up. ►*n.* **1.** A genetic strain, esp. one developed and maintained by controlled propagation. **2.** A kind; sort. [< OE *brēdan.*]

breed·er (brē′dər) ►*n.* **1.** One who breeds animals or plants. **2.** A source or cause.

breeder reactor ►*n.* A nuclear reactor that produces as well as consumes fissionable material.

breed·ing (brē′dĭng) ►*n.* **1.** One's line of descent; ancestry. **2.** Training in the proper forms of social and personal conduct. **3.** The propagation of animals or plants.

breeze (brēz) ►*n.* **1.** A light gentle wind. **2.** *Informal* Something, such as a task, that is easy to do. ►*v.* **breezed, breez·ing** *Informal* To progress swiftly and effortlessly. [Perh. < OSpan. *briza*, northeast wind.] —**breez′i·ly** *adv.* —**breez′i·ness** *n.* —**breez′y** *adj.*
Syns: *cinch, pushover, snap* **n.**

breeze·way (brēz′wā′) ►*n.* A roofed, open-sided passageway connecting two structures, such as a house and garage.

Bre·men (brĕm′ən) A city of NW Germany SW of Hamburg.

breth·ren (brĕth′rən) ►*n.* Pl. of **brother** (sense 2).

Bret·on (brĕt′n) ►*n.* **1.** A native or inhabitant of Brittany. **2.** The Celtic language of Brittany. —**Bret′on** *adj.*

breve (brĕv, brēv) ►*n.* **1.** A symbol (˘) placed over a vowel to show that it has a short sound. **2.** *Mus.* A note equivalent to two whole notes. [< Lat. *brevis*, short.]

bre·vi·ar·y (brē′vē-ĕr′ē, brĕv′ē-) ►*n., pl.* **-ies** A book containing the hymns, offices, and prayers for the canonical hours. [< Lat. *breviārium*, summary < *brevis*, short.]

brev·i·ty (brĕv′ĭ-tē) ►*n.* **1.** Briefness of duration. **2.** Concise expression; terseness. [< Lat. *brevis*, short.]

brew (brōō) ►*v.* **1.** To make (ale or beer) from malt and hops by infusion, boiling, and fermentation. **2.** To make (a beverage) by boiling or steeping. **3.** To be imminent: *Trouble's brewing.* [< OE *brēowan.*] —**brew** *n.* —**brew′er** *n.* —**brew′er·y** *n.*

Brezh·nev (brĕzh′nĕf), **Leonid Ilyich** 1906–82. Soviet political leader.

Bri·an Bo·ru (brī′ən bə-rōō′) 926–1014. Irish king (1002–14).

bri·ar[1] also **bri·er** (brī′ər) ►*n.* **1.** A Mediterranean shrub whose woody roots are used to make tobacco pipes. **2.** A pipe made from this root. [< OFr. *bruyere*, heath.]

bri·ar[2] (brī′ər) ►*n.* Var. of **brier**[1].

bribe (brīb) ►*n.* Something, such as money or a favor, offered or given to induce or influence a person to act dishonestly. ►*v.* **bribed, brib·ing** To give, offer, or promise a bribe (to). [< OFr., alms.] —**brib′a·ble** *adj.* —**brib′er·y** *n.*

bric-a-brac (brĭk′ə-brăk′) ►*n.* Small objects usu.

displayed as ornaments. [Fr. *bric-à-brac.*]

brick (brĭk) ►*n., pl.* **bricks** or **brick 1.** A molded rectangular block of clay baked until hard and used as a building or paving material. **2.** An object shaped like a brick: *a brick of cheese.* ►*v.* To construct, line, or pave with bricks. [< MDu. *bricke.*]

brick-and-mor·tar (brĭk′ənd-môr′tər) ►*adj.* Serving consumers in a physical facility rather than providing remote, esp. online, services.

brick·bat (brĭk′băt′) ►*n.* **1.** A piece of brick, esp. when thrown. **2.** A critical remark.

brick·lay·er (brĭk′lā′ər) ►*n.* One who builds with bricks. —**brick′lay′ing** *n.*

bri·dal (brīd′l) ►*adj.* Of a bride or a wedding.

bride (brīd) ►*n.* A woman recently married or about to be married. [< OE *brȳd.*]

bride·groom (brīd′grōōm′, -grŏŏm′) ►*n.* A man recently married or about to be married. [< OE *brȳdguma* : *brȳd,* bride; see BRIDE + *guma,* man.]

brides·maid (brīdz′mād′) ►*n.* A woman who attends the bride at a wedding.

bridge¹ (brĭj) ►*n.* **1.** A structure spanning and providing passage over an obstacle. **2.** The upper bony ridge of the human nose. **3.** A fixed or removable replacement for missing natural teeth. **4.** *Mus.* A thin, upright piece of wood in some stringed instruments that supports the strings above the sounding board. **5.** A platform or enclosed area above the main deck of a ship from which the ship is controlled. ►*v.* **bridged, bridg·ing 1.** To build a bridge over. **2.** To cross by or as if by a bridge. [< OE *brycg.*] —**bridge′a·ble** *adj.*

bridge² (brĭj) ►*n.* Any of several card games usu. for four people, derived from whist. [Poss. < Russ. *birich,* a call.]

bridge·head (brĭj′hĕd′) ►*n.* A forward position seized by advancing troops in enemy territory as a foothold for further advance.

Bridge·town (brĭj′toun′) The capital of Barbados, in the West Indies.

bridge·work (brĭj′wûrk′) ►*n.* A dental bridge or bridges used to replace missing teeth.

bri·dle (brīd′l) ►*n.* **1.** The harness fitted about a horse's head, used to restrain or guide. **2.** A curb or check. ►*v.* **-dled, -dling 1.** To put a bridle on. **2.** To control or restrain with or as if with a bridle. **3.** To show anger: *bridled at the remark.* [< OE *brīdel.*]

brief (brēf) ►*adj.* **-er, -est 1.** Short in duration or extent. **2.** Succinct; concise. ►*n.* **1.** A short or condensed statement, esp. of a legal case or argument. **2. briefs** Short, tight-fitting underpants. ►*v.* To give a briefing to. [< Lat. *brevis,* short.] —**brief′ly** *adv.* —**brief′ness** *n.*

brief·case (brēf′kās′) ►*n.* A portable, often flat case, used esp. for carrying papers.

brief·ing (brē′fĭng) ►*n.* **1.** The act of giving or receiving preparatory instructions or information. **2.** The information itself.

bri·er¹ also **bri·ar** (brī′ər) ►*n.* Any of several prickly plants, such as certain rosebushes. [< OE *brēr.*] —**bri′er·y** *adj.*

bri·er² (brī′ər) ►*n.* Var. of **briar¹.**

brig (brĭg) ►*n.* **1.** A two-masted square-rigged sailing vessel. **2.** A prison on board a US Navy or Coast Guard vessel.

bri·gade (brĭ-gād′) ►*n.* **1.** A military unit consisting of a variable number of combat battalions or regiments. **2.** A group organized for a specific task: *a fire brigade.* [< OItal. *briga,* strife.]

brig·a·dier general (brĭg′ə-dîr′) ►*n., pl.* **brigadier generals** A rank, as in the US Army, above colonel and below major general.

brig·and (brĭg′ənd) ►*n.* A bandit, esp. one of an outlaw band. [< OItal. *brigare,* to fight.] —**brig′and·age** (-ən-dĭj) *n.*

brig·an·tine (brĭg′ən-tēn′) ►*n.* A two-masted square-rigged sailing vessel having a fore-and-aft mainsail. [< OItal. *brigante,* skirmisher.]

Brig Gen ►*abbr.* brigadier general

bright (brīt) ►*adj.* **-er, -est 1.** Emitting or reflecting light; shining. **2.** Brilliant in color; vivid. **3.** Full of promise and hope: *a bright future.* **4.** Happy; cheerful: *a bright smile.* **5.** Clever; intelligent. [< OE *beorht.*] —**bright′ly** *adv.* —**bright′ness** *n.*

bright·en (brīt′n) ►*v.* To make or become bright or brighter. —**bright′en·er** *n.*

bril·liant (brĭl′yənt) ►*adj.* **1.** Full of light; shining brightly. **2.** Bright and vivid in color. **3.** Displaying great talent or intelligence: *a brilliant mind.* ►*n.* A precious gem, esp. a diamond, cut with numerous facets. [< Fr. *briller,* shine.] —**bril′liance, bril′lian·cy** *n.* —**bril′liant·ly** *adv.*

bril·lian·tine (brĭl′yən-tēn′) ►*n.* An oily, perfumed hairdressing. [Fr. *brillantine.*]

brim (brĭm) ►*n.* **1.** The rim or uppermost edge of a cup or other vessel. **2.** A projecting rim, as on a hat. ►*v.* **brimmed, brim·ming 1.** To be full to the brim. **2.** To overflow. [ME *brimme.*] —**brim′ful′** *adj.*

brim·stone (brĭm′stōn′) ►*n.* Sulfur. [< OE *brynstān.*]

brin·dled (brĭn′dld) ►*adj.* Tawny or grayish with streaks or spots of a darker color. [< ME *brended,* burned.]

brine (brīn) ►*n.* Water saturated with salt. [< OE *brīne.*] —**brin′i·ness** *n.* —**brin′y** *adj.*

bring (brĭng) ►*v.* **brought** (brôt), **bring·ing 1.** To take with oneself to a place. **2.** To lead or force into a specified state or condition: *bring water to a boil; brought the meeting to a close.* **3.** To persuade; induce: *brought the culprit to confess.* **4.** To cause; produce: *bring destruction to the city.* **5.** To be sold for: *books that brought a dollar apiece.* —*phrasal verbs:* **bring about** To cause to happen. **bring down** To cause to fall or collapse. **bring forth** To produce. **bring off** To accomplish successfully. **bring on** To result in; cause. **bring out 1.** To reveal or expose. **2.** To produce or publish. **bring to** To cause to recover consciousness. **bring up 1.** To rear as a parent. **2.** To mention. [< OE *bringan.*]

Usage: *Bring* is used to denote motion toward the place of speaking or the place from which the action is regarded: *Bring it over here.* Take is used to denote motion away from such a place: *Take it over there.* When the relevant point of focus is not the place of speaking itself, the difference obviously depends on the context.

brink (brĭngk) ►*n.* **1.** The upper edge of a steep place. **2.** The verge of something. [ME.]

brink·man·ship (brĭngk′mən-shĭp′) also **brinks·man·ship** (brĭngks′-) ►*n.* A policy aimed at pushing a dangerous situation to the limit so that an opponent will concede.

bri·o (brē′ō) ►*n.* Vigor; vivacity. [Ital.]

bri·oche (brē-ôsh′, -ōsh′) ►*n.* A soft roll made from leavened dough enriched with butter and eggs. [< OFr. *brier,* knead.]

bri·quette also **bri·quet** (brĭ-kĕt′) ►*n.* A block of compressed charcoal, coal dust, or sawdust, used for fuel and kindling. [Fr., small brick < MDu. *bricke.*]

bris (brĭs) ►*n., pl.* **bris·es** *Judaism* The rite of male circumcision. [Ashkenazi Heb. *brīs,* covenant (of circumcision).]

brisk (brĭsk) ►*adj.* **-er, -est 1.** Marked by speed, liveliness, and vigor; energetic. **2.** Stimulating and invigorating. [Prob. of Scand. orig.] —**brisk′ly** *adv.* —**brisk′ness** *n.*

bris·ket (brĭs′kĭt) ►*n.* **1.** The chest of an animal. **2.** The ribs and meat taken from the brisket. [ME *brusket.*]

brisket

bris·ling (brĭz′lĭng, brĭs′-) ►*n.* See **sprat** (sense 1). [Norw. < LGer. *bretling.*]

bris·tle (brĭs′əl) ►*n.* A stiff coarse hair. ►*v.* **-tled, -tling 1.** To stand or erect stiffly on end like bristles. **2.** To raise the bristles stiffly. **3.** To react in an angry or offended manner. **4.** To abound with or as if with bristles: *The path bristled with thorns.* [< OE *byrst.*] —**bris′tly** *adj.*

Bris·tol Channel (brĭs′təl) An inlet of the Atlantic stretching W from the Severn R. and separating Wales from SW England.

Brit (brĭt) ►*n. Informal* A British person.

Brit. ►*abbr.* **1.** Britain **2.** British

Brit·ain (brĭt′n) **1.** The island of Great Britain. **2.** The United Kingdom.

Bri·tan·nic (brĭ-tăn′ĭk) ►*adj.* British.

britch·es (brĭch′ĭz) ►*pl.n.* Breeches.

Brit·i·cism (brĭt′ĭ-sĭz′əm) ►*n.* A word, phrase, or idiom peculiar to British English.

Brit·ish (brĭt′ĭsh) ►*adj.* **1.** Of or relating to Great Britain. **2.** Of or relating to the ancient Britons. ►*n.* **1.** The people of Great Britain. **2.** British English. **3.** The Celtic language of the ancient Britons.

British Columbia A province of W Canada bordering on the Pacific Ocean. Cap. Victoria.

British English ►*n.* The English language as used in England.

British Isles A group of islands off the NW coast of Europe comprising Great Britain, Ireland, and adjacent smaller islands.

British thermal unit ►*n.* The energy required to raise the temperature of one pound of water from 60° to 61°F at a pressure of one atmosphere.

British Virgin Islands A British colony in the E Caribbean E of Puerto Rico and the US Virgin Is. Cap. Road Town.

British West Indies The islands of the West Indies presently or formerly under British control, including Jamaica, the British Virgin Islands, and the Bahamas.

Brit·on (brĭt′n) ►*n.* **1.** A native or inhabitant of Great Britain. **2.** One of a Celtic people inhabiting ancient Britain at the time of the Roman invasion.

Brit·ta·ny (brĭt′n-ē) A historical region and former province of NW France on a peninsula between the English Channel and the Bay of Biscay.

Brit·ten (brĭt′n), **(Edward) Benjamin** 1913–76. British composer.

brit·tle (brĭt′l) ►*adj.* **-tler, -tlest** Likely to break, snap, or crack; fragile. [ME *britel.*]

broach (brōch) ►*v.* **1.** To bring up (a subject) for discussion or debate. **2.** To pierce in order to draw off liquid. [Prob. < OFr. *broche,* a spit.] *Syns: introduce, moot, raise* **v.**

broad (brôd) ►*adj.* **-er, -est 1.** Wide in extent from side to side. **2.** Large in expanse; spacious. **3.** Full; open: *broad daylight.* **4.** Covering a wide scope; general. **5.** Liberal; tolerant. See Synonyms at **broad-minded. 6.** Plain and clear; obvious: *gave us a broad hint to leave.* [< OE *brād.*] —**broad′ly** *adv.* —**broad′ness** *n.*

broad·band (brôd′bănd′) ►*adj.* **1.** Of or having a wide band of electromagnetic frequencies. **2.** Of or relating to the use of multiple channels to transmit multiple pieces of data simultaneously.

broad bean ►*n.* **1.** An annual Old World plant in the pea family. **2.** The edible seed or thick green pod of this plant.

broad·cast (brôd′kăst′) ►*v.* **-cast** or **-cast·ed, -cast·ing 1.** To transmit an audio or visual signal or program to many recipients at once. **2.** To make known over a wide area. See Synonyms at **announce. 3.** To sow (seed) widely, esp. by hand. ►*n.* **1.** The act of broadcasting a program or signal. **2.** A radio or television program. —**broad′cast·er** *n.*

broad·cloth (brôd′klôth′, -klŏth′) ►*n.* A fine-textured cloth, esp. of wool, with a lustrous finish.

broad·en (brôd′n) ►*v.* To make or become broad or broader. —**broad′en·er** *n.*

broad jump ►*n. Sports* See **long jump.**

broad·loom (brôd′lōōm′) ►*adj.* Woven on a wide loom: *a broadloom carpet.*

broad·mind·ed (brôd′mīn′dĭd) ►*adj.* Having or marked by tolerant or liberal views. —**broad′-mind′ed·ness** *n.* *Syns: broad, liberal, open-minded, tolerant* **Ant:** *narrow-minded* **adj.**

broad·side (brôd′sīd′) ►*n.* **1.** The side of a ship above the water line. **2.** The simultaneous discharge of all the guns on one side of a warship. **3.** A forceful verbal attack. ►*adv.* Turned sideways relative to a given object. ►*v.* **-sid·ed, -sid·ing** To collide with full on the side.

broad-spec·trum (brôd′spĕk′trəm) ►*adj.* Widely applicable or effective: *a broad-spectrum antibiotic.*

broad·sword (brôd′sôrd′) ►*n.* A sword with a wide, usu. two-edged blade.

broad·tail (brôd′tāl′) ►*n.* The flat, glossy, wavy pelt of a prematurely born karakul sheep.

Broad·way (brôd′wā′) **1.** The principal N-S thoroughfare on Manhattan Is. **2.** The principal theater district of New York City, on the W Side of midtown Manhattan.

bro·cade (brō-kād′) ►*n.* A heavy fabric interwoven with a rich, raised design. [< Ital. *brocco*, twisted thread.] —**bro·cade′** *v.*

broc·co·li (brŏk′ə-lē) ►*n.* A plant with densely clustered green flower buds and stalks, eaten as a vegetable. [< Ital. *brocco*, sprout.]

bro·chette (brō-shĕt′) ►*n.* A skewer. [< OFr., small spit.]

bro·chure (brō-sho͝or′) ►*n.* A pamphlet, often containing promotional material. [< Fr. *brocher*, to stitch < OFr. *broche*, needle.]

bro·gan (brō′gən) ►*n.* A heavy ankle-high shoe. [Ir.Gael. *brōgan*, small brogue.]

brogue[1] (brōg) ►*n.* A strong oxford shoe. [< OIr. *brōc*, shoe.]

brogue[2] (brōg) ►*n.* A strong dialectal accent, esp. an Irish or Scottish accent. [Prob. < the brogues worn by peasants.]

broil (broil) ►*v.* **1.** To cook by direct radiant heat. **2.** To expose or be exposed to great heat. [< OFr. *bruler*.] —**broil** *n.*

broil·er (broi′lər) ►*n.* **1.** One that broils, esp. a small oven or the part of a stove used for broiling food. **2.** A tender young chicken suitable for broiling.

broke (brōk) ►*v.* P.t. of **break.** ►*adj. Informal* Lacking funds.

bro·ken (brō′kən) ►*v.* P.part. of **break.** ►*adj.* **1.** Shattered; fractured. **2.** Having been violated: *a broken promise.* **3.** Not continuous. **4.** Spoken imperfectly: *broken English.* **5.** Subdued totally; tamed or humbled. **6.** Not functioning; out of order. —**bro′ken·ly** *adv.*

bro·ken-down (brō′kən-doun′) ►*adj.* **1.** Out of working order. **2.** In poor condition.

bro·ken·heart·ed (brō′kən-här′tĭd) ►*adj.* Grievously sad.

bro·ker (brō′kər) ►*n.* One that acts as an agent and negotiates contracts, purchases, or sales in return for a fee or commission. ►*v.* To arrange or manage: *broker an agreement.* [< AN *brocour.*]

bro·ker·age (brō′kər-ĭj) ►*n.* **1.** The business of a broker. **2.** A fee or commission paid to a broker.

bro·me·li·ad (brō-mē′lē-ăd′) ►*n.* Any of various mostly epiphytic tropical American plants usu. having long, stiff leaves and colorful flowers. [After Olaf *Bromelius* (1639–1705).]

bro·mide (brō′mīd′) ►*n.* **1a.** A chemical compound of bromine with another element, such as silver. **b.** Potassium bromide. **2.** A platitude. See Synonyms at **cliché.** —**bro·mid′ic** (-mĭd′ĭk) *adj.*

bro·mine (brō′mēn) ►*n. Symbol* **Br** A heavy, volatile, corrosive, reddish-brown, nonmetallic liquid element used in fumigants, dyes, and photographic chemicals. At. no. 35. See table at **element.** [< Gk. *brōmos*, stench.]

bron·chi·al (brŏng′kē-əl) ►*adj.* Of or relating to either bronchus or their extensions.

bron·chi·tis (brŏn-kī′tĭs, brŏng-) ►*n.* Inflammation of the mucous membrane of the bronchial tubes. —**bron·chit′ic** (-kĭt′ĭk) *adj.*

bron·cho·pul·mo·nar·y (brŏng′kō-pŏol′mə-nĕr′ē, -pŭl′-) ►*adj.* Relating to the bronchi and the lungs.

bron·chus (brŏng′kəs) ►*n., pl.* **-chi** (-kī′, -kē′) Either of two main branches of the trachea, leading directly to the lungs. [< Gk. *bronkhos*, windpipe.]

bron·co (brŏng′kō) ►*n., pl.* **-cos** An untamed horse of W North America. [< Sp., wild.]

bron·co·bust·er (brŏng′kō-bŭs′tər) ►*n.* One who breaks untamed horses to the saddle.

Bron·të (brŏn′tē) Family of British writers, including **Charlotte** (1816–55), **Emily** (1818–48), and **Anne** (1820–49).

bron·to·sau·rus (brŏn′tə-sôr′əs) or **bron·to·saur** (brŏn′tə-sôr′) ►*n.* An apatosaurus. [Gk. *brontē*, thunder + *sauros*, lizard.]

Bronx (brŏngks) A borough of New York City in SE NY on the mainland N of Manhattan.

bronze (brŏnz) ►*n.* **1.** Any of various alloys consisting chiefly of copper and tin. **2.** A work of art made of bronze. **3.** A yellowish to olive brown. ►*v.* **bronzed, bronz·ing** To give the color or appearance of bronze to. [< Ital. *bronzo.*] —**bronze** *adj.*

Bronze Age ►*n.* A period of human culture between the Stone Age and the Iron Age, marked by weapons and tools made of bronze.

brooch (brōch, bro͞och) ►*n.* A piece of jewelry designed to be pinned to clothing. [ME *broche*; see BROACH.]

brood (bro͞od) ►*n.* The young of certain animals, esp. a group of young birds hatched at one time. ►*v.* **1.** To protect developing eggs or young. **2.** To think deeply or worry anxiously. [< OE *brōd.*] —**brood′er** *n.* —**brood′ing·ly** *adv.*

Syns: *dwell, fret, mope, worry* **v.**

brood·mare (bro͞od′mâr′) ►*n.* A mare used for breeding.

brook[1] (bro͝ok) ►*n.* A small stream; creek. [< OE *brōc.*]

brook[2] (bro͝ok) ►*v.* To put up with; tolerate. [< OE *brūcan*, to use.]

Brook·lyn (bro͝ok′lĭn) A borough of New York City in SE NY on W Long I.

brook trout ►*n.* A freshwater game fish of E North America.

broom (bro͞om, bro͝om) ►*n.* **1.** A bunch of twigs, straw, or bristles bound together, attached to a handle, and used for sweeping. **2.** Any of various European shrubs having compound leaves and usu. bright yellow flowers. [< OE *brōm.*]

bros. ►*abbr.* brothers

broth (brôth, brŏth) ►*n.* **1.** The water in which meat, fish, or vegetables have been boiled; stock. **2.** A thin clear soup made with stock. [< OE.]

broth·el (brŏth′əl, brô′thəl) ►*n.* A building where prostitutes work. [< ME, prostitute.]

broth·er (brŭth′ər) ►*n.* **1.** A male having one or both parents in common with another person. **2.** *pl.* **-ers** or **breth·ren** (brĕth′rən) One sharing a common ancestry or allegiance with another, esp.: **a.** A kinsman. **b.** A close male friend. **c.** A fellow African-American male. **3.** A member of a Christian men's religious order who is not a priest. [< OE *brōthor.*] —**broth′er·li·ness** *n.* —**broth′er·ly** *adj.*

broth·er·hood (brŭth′ər-ho͝od′) ►*n.* **1.** The state or relationship of being brothers. **2.** Fellowship. **3.** An association of men united for common purposes. **4.** All the members of a profession or trade.

broth·er-in-law (brŭth′ər-ĭn-lô′) ►*n., pl.* **broth·**

ers-in-law (-ərz-) **1.** The brother of one's spouse. **2.** The husband of one's sibling. **3.** The husband of the sibling of one's spouse.

brougham (brōōm, brōō′əm, brōm) ►*n.* **1.** A closed four-wheeled carriage with an open driver's seat in front. **2.** An automobile with an open driver's seat. [After Henry P. *Brougham* (1778–1868).]

brought (brôt) ►*v.* P.t. and p.part. of **bring.**

brou·ha·ha (brōō′hä-hä′) ►*n.* An uproar. [Fr.]

brow (brou) ►*n.* **1a.** The ridge over the eyes. **b.** The eyebrow. **c.** The forehead. **2.** The projecting upper edge of a steep place. [< OE *brū.*]

brow·beat (brou′bēt′) ►*v.* To intimidate with an overbearing manner; bully.

brown (broun) ►*n.* Any of a group of dull or dark colors between red and yellow in hue. ►*v.* **1.** To make or become brown. **2.** To cook until brown. [< OE *brūn.*] —**brown** *adj.* —**brown′ish** *adj.* —**brown′ness** *n.*

Brown, (James) Gordon b. 1951. British prime minister (2007–2010).

Brown, John 1800–59. Amer. abolitionist.

brown bear ►*n.* Any of several large bears of W North America and N Eurasia, such as the grizzly and Kodiak bears.

brown dwarf ►*n.* A starlike celestial body that does not emit light because it is too small to sustain internal nuclear fusion.

brown·field (broun′fēld′) ►*n.* An abandoned, usu. contaminated commercial property that has potential for redevelopment.

brown·ie (brou′nē) ►*n.* **1. Brownie** A junior member of the Girl Scouts. **2.** A bar of moist, usu. chocolate cake often with nuts. **3.** A small helpful elf in folklore.

Brown·ing (brou′nǐng), **Elizabeth Barrett** 1806–61. British poet.

Elizabeth Barrett Browning

Browning, Robert 1812–89. British poet.

brown·out (broun′out′) ►*n.* A reduction or cutback in electric power.

brown rice ►*n.* Whole grain rice that retains the germ and outer layers.

brown sauce ►*n.* A sauce made from butter and flour browned together and stock.

brown·stone (broun′stōn′) ►*n.* **1.** A reddish-brown sandstone. **2.** A house built or faced with brownstone.

brown sugar ►*n.* Granulated sugar containing residual or added molasses.

browse (brouz) ►*v.* **browsed, brows·ing 1.** To inspect leisurely or casually. **2.** To look for information on the Internet. **3.** To feed on leaves, young shoots, and other vegetation;

graze. [< OFr. *brost,* twig.] —**browse** *n.*

brows·er (brou′zər) ►*n.* **1.** One that browses. **2.** A computer program that accesses and displays data from the Internet or other networks.

bru·in (brōō′ǐn) ►*n.* A bear. [< MDu., brown.]

bruise (brōōz) ►*v.* **bruised, bruis·ing 1a.** To injure (body tissue) without breaking the skin. **b.** To suffer such injury. **2.** To damage (plant tissue), as by abrasion. **3.** To pound; crush. **4.** To hurt or offend. ►*n.* **1.** A bruised area, often marked by discoloration. **2.** A hurt, as to one's feelings. [< OE *brȳsan* and ONFr. *bruisier,* crush.]

bruis·er (brōō′zər) ►*n. Informal* **1.** A usu. large or powerfully built person who is aggressive or readily gets into fights. **2.** A boxer.

bruit (brōōt) ►*v.* To spread news of; repeat. [< OFr., noise.]

brunch (brǔnch) ►*n.* A meal in the late morning or early afternoon that combines breakfast and lunch.

Bru·nei (brōō-nī′) A sultanate of N Borneo on the South China Sea. Cap. Bandar Seri Begawan.

Bru·nel·le·schi (brōō′nə-lĕs′kē), **Filippo** 1377–1446. Italian architect.

bru·net (brōō-nĕt′) ►*adj.* **1.** Of a dark complexion or coloring. **2.** Having dark or brown hair or eyes. ►*n.* A person with dark or brown hair. [< OFr. *brun,* brown.]

bru·nette (brōō-nĕt′) ►*n.* A girl or woman with dark or brown hair. [Fr. < *brunet,* BRUNET.] —**bru·nette′** *adj.*

brunt (brǔnt) ►*n.* The main impact or force, as of an attack or blow. [ME.]

bru·schet·ta (brōō-skĕt′ə, -shĕt′-) ►*n.* Broiled slices of bread brushed with olive oil and layered with any of various toppings. [Ital.]

brush[1] (brǔsh) ►*n.* **1.** A device consisting of bristles fastened into a handle, used in scrubbing, polishing, grooming the hair, or painting. **2.** A light touch in passing; graze. **3.** A contact with something undesirable or dangerous: *a brush with death.* **4.** A sliding connection completing an electrical circuit between a fixed and a moving conductor. ►*v.* **1.** To use a brush (on). **2.** To apply or remove with or as if with motions of a brush. **3.** To dismiss abruptly: *brushed the matter aside.* **4.** To touch lightly in passing; graze. —*phrasal verb:* **brush up 1.** To refresh one's memory. **2.** To renew a skill. [< OFr. *brosse,* brushwood.]

   Syns: *glance, graze, shave, skim* **v.**

brush[2] (brǔsh) ►*n.* **1.** A dense growth of shrubs. **2.** Cut or broken branches. [< OFr. *brosse.*] —**brush′y** *adj.*

brush·off (brǔsh′ôf′, -ŏf′) ►*n.* An abrupt dismissal or snub.

brusque (brǔsk) ►*adj.* Rudely abrupt in manner or speech. [< Ital. *brusco,* coarse.] —**brusque′ly** *adv.* —**brusque′ness** *n.*

Brus·sels (brǔs′əlz) The capital of Belgium, in the central part.

Brussels sprouts ►*pl.n. (takes sing. or pl. v.)* The edible buds that grow on the stem of a plant related to cabbage.

bru·tal (brōōt′l) ►*adj.* **1.** Extremely ruthless or cruel. **2.** Crude or unfeeling. **3.** Harsh; unrelenting: *a brutal winter.* —**bru·tal′i·ty** (-tal′ĭtē) *n.* —**bru′tal·ly** *adv.*

bru·tal·ize (brōōt′l-īz′) ►*v.* **-ized, -iz·ing 1.** To make brutal. **2.** To treat in a brutal manner. —**bru′tal·i·za′tion** *n.*

brute (broot) ►*n.* **1.** An animal; beast. **2.** A brutal person. ►*adj.* **1.** Of or relating to beasts. **2a.** Entirely physical: *brute force.* **b.** Lacking reason or intelligence: *a brute impulse.* [< Lat. *brūtus,* stupid.] —**brut′ish** *adj.* —**brut′ish·ly** *adv.* —**brut′ish·ness** *n.*

Bru·tus (broo′təs), **Marcus Junius** 85?–42 BC. Roman politician and general.

Bryan (brī′ən), **William Jennings** 1860–1925. Amer. lawyer and politician.

Bry·ant (brī′ənt), **William Cullen** 1794–1878. Amer. poet, critic, and editor.

BS ►*abbr.* Bachelor of Science

BTU or **Btu** ►*abbr.* British thermal unit

BTW ►*abbr.* by the way

bu. ►*abbr.* bushel

bub·ba (bŭb′ə) ►*n. Slang* **1.** *Regional* Brother. **2.** A white working-class man of the S US, often seen as uneducated.

bub·ble (bŭb′əl) ►*n.* **1.** A thin, usu. spherical or hemispherical film of liquid filled with air or gas. **2.** A globular body of air or gas formed within a liquid. **3.** An illusion. **4.** An unsustainable rise in prices due to speculation. ►*v.* -**bled,** -**bling** To form or give off bubbles. [< ME *bubelen,* to bubble.] —**bub′bly** *adj.*

bub·ble·gum also **bubble gum** (bŭb′əl-gŭm′) ►*n.* Chewing gum that can be blown into bubbles.

bubble tea ►*n.* Sweetened iced tea with small black balls of boiled tapioca mixed into it. [Trans. of Mandarin *pàomò hóngchá* : *pàomò,* froth (since it was orig. made by shaking tea, milk, and tapioca balls together to make froth) + *hóngchá,* black tea.]

bu·bo (boo′bō, byoo′-) ►*n., pl.* -**boes** A tender swelling of a lymph node, characteristic of certain infectious diseases, such as bubonic plague and syphilis. [< Gk. *boubōn.*]

bu·bon·ic plague (boo-bŏn′ĭk, byoo-) ►*n.* An infectious disease caused by a bacterium, transmitted primarily by the bites of fleas from infected rats, and marked by buboes.

buc·ca·neer (bŭk′ə-nîr′) ►*n.* A pirate. [< Fr. *boucaner,* cure meat.]

Bu·chan·an (byoo-kăn′ən, bə-), **James** 1791–1868. The 15th US president (1857–61).

James Buchanan

Bu·cha·rest (boo′kə-rĕst′, byoo′-) The capital of Romania, in the SE part on a tributary of the Danube R.

buck¹ (bŭk) ►*n.* **1.** The adult male of some animals, such as the deer or rabbit. **2.** A robust or high-spirited young man. ►*v.* **1a.** To leap upward arching the back. Used esp. of horses. **b.** To throw (a rider or burden) by bucking. **2.** To butt (against). **3.** To make sudden jerky movements; jolt. **4.** To resist stubbornly. **5.** *Informal* To strive with determination: *bucking for a promotion.* ►*adj.* Of the lowest rank: *a buck private.* —**phrasal verb: buck up** To raise (one's) spirits; hearten. [< OE *buc,* male deer, and *bucca,* male goat.] —**buck′er** *n.*

buck² (bŭk) ►*n. Informal* A dollar. [< BUCK-SKIN.]

Buck, Pearl Sydenstricker 1892–1973. Amer. writer.

buck·board (bŭk′bôrd′) ►*n.* A four-wheeled open carriage with the seat attached to a flexible board. [Obsolete *buck,* body of a wagon + BOARD.]

buck·et (bŭk′ĭt) ►*n.* **1a.** A cylindrical vessel used for holding or carrying liquids or solids; pail. **b.** The amount that a bucket can hold. **2.** A receptacle, such as the scoop of a power shovel, used to gather and convey material. [< OFr. *buket.*]

bucket seat ►*n.* A single, usu. low seat with a contoured back, as in some cars.

buck·eye (bŭk′ī′) ►*n.* A North American tree or shrub having erect flower clusters and large, shiny brown seeds.

buck·le (bŭk′əl) ►*n.* **1.** A clasp, esp. a frame with a movable tongue, for fastening two ends, as of straps or a belt. **2.** An ornament that resembles a buckle. **3.** A bend or bulge. ►*v.* -**led,** -**ling 1.** To fasten or become fastened with a buckle. **2.** To bend, warp, or crumple under pressure or heat. **3.** To give way; collapse. **4.** To give in; succumb. —**phrasal verbs: buckle down** To begin working hard. **buckle up** To use a safety belt, esp. in an automobile. [< Lat. *buccula,* cheek strap.]

buck·ler (bŭk′lər) ►*n.* A small round shield. [< OFr. *boucle,* boss on a shield.]

buck·min·ster·ful·ler·ene (bŭk′mĭn-stər-fool′ə-rēn′) ►*n.* A spherical carbon molecule, C_{60}, whose structure is reminiscent of a geodesic dome. It was the first fullerene to be discovered. [After Richard Buckminster FULLER, noted for designing geodesic domes.]

buck·ram (bŭk′rəm) ►*n.* A coarse cotton fabric heavily stiffened with glue, used for lining garments and in bookbinding. [Ult. < *Bukhara,* Central Asia.]

buck·saw (bŭk′sô′) ►*n.* A woodcutting saw, usu. in an H-shaped frame. [< *buck,* sawhorse.]

buck·shot (bŭk′shŏt′) ►*n.* Large-diameter lead shot for shotguns, used esp. in hunting big game.

buck·skin (bŭk′skĭn′) ►*n.* **1.** A soft, grayish-yellow leather made from deerskin or sheepskin. **2. buckskins** Clothing made from buckskin.

buck·tooth (bŭk′tooth′) ►*n.* A prominent, projecting upper front tooth. —**buck′toothed′** (-tootht′) *adj.*

buck·wheat (bŭk′wēt′, -hwēt′) ►*n.* **1.** A plant having small, seedlike, triangular seeds. **2.** The edible seeds of this plant, often ground into flour. [Prob. < MDu. *boecweite* : *boek,* beech + *weite,* wheat.]

buck·y·ball (bŭk′ē-bôl′) ►*n.* Buckminsterfullerene. [< *Bucky,* nickname of R. Buckminster FULLER + BALL[1].]

bu·col·ic (byōō-kŏl′ĭk) ►*adj.* Rustic; pastoral. [< Gk. *boukolos,* cowherd < *bous,* cow.]

bud (bŭd) ►*n.* **1.** A small, projecting plant structure containing an undeveloped shoot, leaf, or flower. **2.** An asexual reproductive structure, as in yeast or a hydra, that resembles a bud. **3.** One that is not yet fully developed. ►*v.* **bud·ded, bud·ding 1.** To put forth or cause to put forth buds. **2.** To develop from or as if from a bud. [ME.]

Bu·da·pest (bōō′də-pĕst′, -pĕsht′) The capital of Hungary, in the N-central part on the Danube R.

Bud·dha (bōō′də, bŏŏd′ə) See Siddhartha **Gautama.**

Bud·dhism (bōō′dĭz′əm, bŏŏd′ĭz′-) ►*n.* A religion founded on the teachings of Siddhartha Gautama, esp. that enlightenment obtained through right conduct and meditation releases one from suffering. —**Bud′dhist** *adj. & n.*

bud·ding (bŭd′ĭng) ►*adj.* Being in an early developmental stage: *a budding artist.*

bud·dy (bŭd′ē) ►*n., pl.* **-dies** *Informal* A good friend. [Prob. < BROTHER.]

buddy system ►*n.* An arrangement in which persons are paired, as for mutual safety or assistance.

budge (bŭj) ►*v.* **budged, budg·ing 1.** To move or cause to move slightly. **2.** To alter a position or attitude. [OFr. *bouger.*]

budg·er·i·gar (bŭj′ə-rē-gär′, bŭj′ə-rē′-) ►*n.* A small parakeet having green, yellow, or blue plumage. [Kamilaroi (Australian) *gijirrigaa.*]

budg·et (bŭj′ĭt) ►*n.* **1.** An itemized summary of probable expenditures and income for a given period. **2.** The sum of money allocated for a particular purpose or period of time. ►*v.* **1.** To make a budget. **2.** To plan in advance the expenditure of. **3.** To enter or account for in a budget. [< OFr. *bougette,* small leather bag.] —**budg′et·ar′y** (-ĭ-tĕr′ē) *adj.*

budg·ie (bŭj′ē) ►*n.* *Informal* A budgerigar.

Bue·nos Ai·res (bwā′nəs âr′ēz, bwĕ′nōs ī′rĕs) The capital of Argentina, in the E part on the Río de la Plata.

buff[1] (bŭf) ►*n.* **1.** A soft, thick, undyed leather made chiefly from the skins of buffalo, elk, or oxen. **2.** A yellowish tan. **3.** A piece of soft material used for polishing. ►*adj.* Of the color buff. ►*v.* To polish or shine with a buff. [< LLat. *būfalus,* buffalo.]

buff[2] (bŭf) ►*n.* *Informal* One who is enthusiastic and knowledgeable about a particular subject.

buf·fa·lo (bŭf′ə-lō′) ►*n., pl.* **-lo** or **-loes** or **-los 1.** Any of several oxlike Old World mammals, such as the water buffalo. **2.** The North American bison. ►*v.* To intimidate or bewilder. [< Gk. *boubalos.*]

Buffalo A city of W NY at the E end of Lake Erie.

Buffalo Bill See William Frederick **Cody.**

buff·er[1] (bŭf′ər) ►*n.* One that shines or polishes, esp. a soft cloth or a machine with a soft rotating head.

buff·er[2] (bŭf′ər) ►*n.* **1.** Something that lessens, absorbs, or protects against the shock of an impact. **2.** Something that separates potentially antagonistic entities. **3.** *Chem.* A substance that

minimizes change in the acidity of a solution when an acid or base is added to the solution. **4.** *Comp.* A device or area used to store data temporarily. [Perh. < *buff,* blow, buffet.] —**buf′fer** *v.*

buffer zone ►*n.* A neutral area between hostile forces that serves to prevent conflict.

buf·fet[1] (bə-fā′, bŏŏ-) ►*n.* **1.** A large sideboard. **2.** A counter, as in a restaurant, for serving refreshments. **3.** A meal at which guests serve themselves from dishes on a table. [Fr.]

buf·fet[2] (bŭf′ĭt) ►*n.* A blow or cuff with or as if with the hand. ►*v.* To hit or strike against, esp. repeatedly. [< OFr. *bufet,* light blow.]

buf·foon (bə-fōōn′) ►*n.* A clown; jester. [< OItal. *buffa,* jest.] —**buf·foon′er·y** *n.*

bug (bŭg) ►*n.* **1.** An insect, esp. one with piercing mouthparts such as a bedbug. **2.** A small invertebrate with many legs, such as a spider. **3.** A disease-producing microorganism; germ. **4.** A mechanical, electrical, or other defect, as in a system, design, or computer code. **5.** An enthusiast; buff. **6.** An electronic listening device, such as a wiretap, used in surveillance. ►*v.* **bugged, bug·ging 1.** To annoy; pester. **2.** To equip (e.g., a room) with a bug. **3.** To bulge out. Used of the eyes. [?] —**bug′ger** *n.*

bug·a·boo (bŭg′ə-bōō′) ►*n., pl.* **-boos 1.** An object of obsessive, usu. exaggerated fear or anxiety. **2.** A difficult or persistent problem. [Perh. of Celt. orig.]

bug·bear (bŭg′bâr′) ►*n.* A bugaboo. [ME *bugge,* hobgoblin + BEAR[2].]

bug-eyed (bŭg′īd′) ►*adj.* Agog.

bug·gy[1] (bŭg′ē) ►*n., pl.* **-gies** A small, light, usu. four-wheeled carriage. [?]

bug·gy[2] (bŭg′ē) ►*adj.* **-gi·er, -gi·est 1.** Infested with bugs. **2.** *Comp.* Having many software bugs. **3.** *Slang* Crazy.

bu·gle (byōō′gəl) ►*n.* A trumpetlike musical instrument lacking keys or valves. [< Lat. *būculus,* steer < *bōs,* ox.] —**bu′gle** *v.* —**bu′-gler** *n.*

build (bĭld) ►*v.* **built** (bĭlt), **build·ing 1.** To make by combining parts; construct. **2.** To fashion; create. **3.** To add gradually to: *build support; build up strength.* **4.** To establish a basis for. ►*n.* Physical makeup; physique. —*phrasal verb:* **build up** To develop, increase, or accumulate in stages or by degrees. [< OE *byldan.*] —**build′er** *n.*

build·ing (bĭl′dĭng) ►*n.* **1.** A structure, esp. one built for human habitation; edifice. **2.** The act or art of constructing.

build·up (bĭld′ŭp′) ►*n.* **1.** The act of amassing or increasing. **2.** Widely favorable publicity, esp. by a systematic campaign.

built-in (bĭlt′ĭn′) ►*adj.* **1.** Constructed as part of a larger unit; not detachable. **2.** Forming a permanent element or quality; inherent.

Bu·jum·bu·ra (bōō′jəm-bŏŏr′ə) The capital of Burundi, in the W part on Lake Tanganyika.

bulb (bŭlb) ►*n.* **1.** *Bot.* **a.** A short, modified underground stem, such as that of the onion or tulip, that contains stored food for the shoot within. **b.** A plant that grows from a bulb. **2.** A rounded projection or part. **3.** A light bulb. [< Gk. *bolbos,* bulbous plant.] —**bul′bous** *adj.*

Bul·finch (bŏŏl′fĭnch′), **Thomas** 1796–1867. Amer. writer.

Bul·gar (bŭl′gär′, bŏŏl′-) ►*n.* See **Bulgarian**

(sense 1). [< Turkic *bulghar*, of mixed origin.]

Bul·gar·i·a (bŭl-gâr′ē-ə, bool-) A country of SE Europe on the Black Sea. Cap. Sofia.

Bul·gar·i·an (bŭl-gâr′ē-ən, bool-) ►*n.* **1.** A native or inhabitant of Bulgaria. **2.** The Slavic language of the Bulgarians. —**Bul·gar′i·an** *adj.*

bulge (bŭlj) ►*n.* A protruding part; swelling. ►*v.* **bulged, bulg·ing** To swell or cause to swell outward. [< Lat. *bulga*, bag, of Celt. orig.] —**bulg′i·ness** *n.* —**bulg′y** *adj.*
   Syns: *belly, jut, project, protrude* **v.**

bul·gur also **bul·ghur** (bool-goor′, bŭl′gər) ►*n.* Cracked wheat grains, often used in Middle Eastern dishes. [Ottoman Turk. *bulghūr*.]

bu·li·mi·a (boo-lē′mē-ə, -lĭm′ē-, byoo-) ►*n.* An eating disorder esp. of young women that is marked by episodic binge eating and subsequent feelings of guilt and by measures to prevent weight gain, such as self-induced vomiting. [Gk. *boulimia*, ravenous hunger : *bous*, ox + *limos*, hunger.] —**bu·li′mic** *adj. & n.*

bulk (bŭlk) ►*n.* **1.** Size, mass, or volume, esp. when very large. **2.** The major portion of something. **3.** See **fiber** (sense 6). ►*v.* To be or appear massive in size or importance; loom. ►*adj.* Large in mass, quantity, or volume: *a bulk mailing.* —**idiom: in bulk 1.** Unpacked; loose. **2.** In large numbers or amounts. [ME < ON *bulki*, cargo.] —**bulk′i·ness** *n.* —**bulk′y** *adj.*

bulk·head (bŭlk′hĕd′) ►*n.* **1a.** One of the upright partitions dividing a ship into compartments. **b.** A partition in an aircraft or spacecraft. **2.** A retaining wall in a mine or canal or along a waterfront. [Perh. < *bulk*, stall, partition.]

bull¹ (bool) ►*n.* **1a.** An adult male bovine mammal. **b.** The uncastrated adult male of domestic cattle. **c.** The male of certain other animals, such as alligators, elephants, or moose. **2.** One who buys commodities or securities in anticipation of a rise in prices. **3.** *Slang* A police officer. **4.** *Slang* Empty talk; nonsense. ►*adj.* **1.** Male. **2.** Large and strong. **3.** Marked by rising prices: *a bull market.* [< OE *bula*.] —**bull′ish** *adj.* —**bull′ish·ly** *adv.* —**bull′ish·ness** *n.*

bull² (bool) ►*n.* An official document issued by the pope. [< Lat. *bulla*, seal.]

bull·dog (bool′dôg′, -dŏg′) ►*n.* A short-haired dog having a large head, strong square jaws, and a stocky body. ►*adj.* Stubborn. ►*v.* **-dogged, -dog·ging** To throw (a calf or steer) by seizing its horns and twisting its neck.

bull·doze (bool′dōz′) ►*v.* **-dozed, -doz·ing 1.** To clear, dig up, or move with a bulldozer. **2.** To bully. [Poss. < obsolete *bulldose*, severe beating.]

bull·doz·er (bool′dō′zər) ►*n.* A heavy, driver-operated machine for clearing and grading land, usu. having continuous treads and a broad hydraulic blade in front.

bul·let (bool′ĭt) ►*n.* **1.** A usu. metal projectile that is expelled from a firearm. **2.** *Print.* A heavy dot (·) used for highlighting. [< Lat. *bulla*, ball.] —**bul′let·proof** *adj.*

bul·le·tin (bool′ĭ-tn, -tĭn) ►*n.* **1.** A printed or broadcast statement on a matter of public interest. **2.** A periodical, esp. one published by an organization or society. [Prob. < Ital. *bolletta*, bill.]

bulletin board ►*n.* **1.** A board, usu. mounted on a wall, on which notices are posted. **2.** *Comp.* A system for sending or reading electronic messages of general interest.

bull·fight (bool′fīt′) ►*n.* A public spectacle, esp. in Spain, Portugal, and parts of Latin America, in which a fighting bull is engaged and usu. killed. —**bull′fight′er** *n.*

bull·finch (bool′fĭnch′) ►*n.* A European bird having a short thick bill and a red breast.

bull·frog (bool′frôg′, -frŏg′) ►*n.* A large frog having a deep resonant croak.

bull·head (bool′hĕd′) ►*n.* A North American freshwater catfish.

bull·head·ed (bool′hĕd′ĭd) ►*adj.* Very stubborn; headstrong. —**bull′head′ed·ly** *adv.*

bull·horn (bool′hôrn′) ►*n.* An electric megaphone used esp. to amplify the voice.

bul·lion (bool′yən) ►*n.* Gold or silver bars, ingots, or plates. [< OFr. *billon*, ingot, and *bouillon*, bubble.]

bul·lock (bool′ək) ►*n.* A steer or young bull. [OE *bulloc*, dim. of *bula*, bull.]

Bul·lock's oriole (bool′əks) ►*n.* A North American songbird having black and orange plumage with large white wing patches in the male and yellowish brown plumage in the female. [After William *Bullock* (fl. 19th cent.).]

bull·pen (bool′pĕn′) ►*n.* *Baseball* An area where relief pitchers warm up.

bull session ►*n.* An informal group discussion.

bull's-eye (boolz′ī′) ►*n.* **1.** The small central circle on a target. **2.** A shot that hits this circle. **3.** A direct hit.

bull·whip (bool′wĭp′, -hwĭp′) ►*n.* A long braided rawhide whip with a knotted end.

bul·ly (bool′ē) ►*n., pl.* **-lies** One who is habitually cruel to smaller or weaker people. ►*v.* **-lied, -ly·ing** To behave like a bully (toward). ►*adj.* Excellent; splendid. ►*interj.* Used to express approval. [Poss. < MDu. *broeder*, brother.]

bul·rush (bool′rŭsh′) ►*n.* Any of various grasslike marsh plants. [ME *bulrish*.]

bul·wark (bool′wərk, -wôrk′, bŭl′-) ►*n.* **1.** A wall or embankment raised as a defensive fortification. **2.** Something serving as a defense or safeguard. [< MHGer. *bolwerc* : *bole*, plank + OHGer. *werc*, work.]

bum (bŭm) ►*n.* **1.** A tramp; vagrant. **2.** One who seeks to live off others. ►*v.* **bummed, bumming 1.** To live or acquire by begging and scavenging. See Synonyms at **cadge. 2.** To loaf. ►*adj.* **1.** Inferior; worthless. **2.** Disabled; malfunctioning. **3.** Unfavorable or unfair. [Poss. < Ger. *Bummler*, loafer.]

bum·ble (bŭm′bəl) ►*v.* **-bled, -bling** To speak, behave, or proceed in a faltering or clumsy manner. See Synonyms at **blunder.** [Poss. blend of BUNGLE and STUMBLE.] —**bum′bler** *n.*

bum·ble·bee (bŭm′bəl-bē′) ►*n.* Any of various large, hairy, social bees that nest underground. [< ME *bomblen*, to buzz.]

bump (bŭmp) ►*v.* **1.** To strike or collide (with). **2.** To knock: *bumped my knee on the table.* **3.** To jolt; jerk. **4.** To displace; oust. **5.** To raise; boost. ►*n.* **1.** A blow, collision, or jolt. **2.** A slight swelling or lump. **3.** A rise or increase: *a bump in gas prices.* —**phrasal verbs: bump into** To meet by chance. **bump off** *Slang* To murder. [Imit.] —**bump′i·ness** *n.* —**bump′y** *adj.*

bump·er¹ (bŭm′pər) ►*n.* A horizontal bar

attached to either end of a motor vehicle to absorb the impact in a collision.

bump·er² (bŭm′pər) ►*n.* A drinking vessel filled to the brim. ►*adj.* Unusually abundant or full: *a bumper crop.* [Perh. < BUMP.]

bump·kin (bŭmp′kĭn, bŭm′-) ►*n.* An awkward, unsophisticated person. [Perh. < MDu. *bomme,* barrel.]

bump·tious (bŭmp′shəs) ►*adj.* Crudely or loudly assertive; pushy. [Poss. alteration of BUMP.] —**bump′tious·ly** *adv.*

bun (bŭn) ►*n.* **1.** A small bread roll, often sweetened. **2.** A roll of hair worn at the back of the head. [ME *bunne.*]

bunch (bŭnch) ►*n.* A group, cluster, or clump. [ME *bonche.*] —**bunch** *v.* —**bunch′y** *adj.*

Bunche (bŭnch), **Ralph Johnson** 1904–71. Amer. diplomat.

bun·co (bŭng′kō) ►*n., pl.* **-cos** *Informal* A confidence game; swindle. [Poss. < Sp. *banca,* a card game.] —**bun′co** *v.*

bun·dle (bŭn′dl) ►*n.* **1.** A group of objects held together, as by tying or wrapping; package. **2.** *Informal* A large sum of money. ►*v.* **-dled, -dling 1.** To tie, wrap, or gather together. **2.** To dress warmly. [Prob. < MDu. *bondel.*]

bundt cake (bŭnt, bōōnt) ►*n.* A ring-shaped cake with fluted sides. [Originally a trademark.]

bung (bŭng) ►*n.* A stopper for a bunghole. [< LLat. *puncta,* hole.] —**bung** *v.*

bun·ga·low (bŭng′gə-lō′) ►*n.* A small house or cottage usu. of one story. [< Hindi *baṅglā,* Bengali.]

bun·gee cord (bŭn′jē′) ►*n.* An elasticized rubber cord used to fasten, bear weight, or absorb shock. [< *bunjie,* rubber.]

bungee jumping ►*n.* The sport of jumping from a great height while attached to a secured bungee cord.

bung·hole (bŭng′hōl′) ►*n.* The hole in a cask, keg, or barrel through which liquid is poured in or drained out.

bun·gle (bŭng′gəl) ►*v.* **-gled, -gling** To work, manage, or act ineptly or inefficiently. See Synonyms at **botch.** [Perh. of Scand. orig.] —**bun′gle** *n.* —**bun′gler** *n.*

bun·ion (bŭn′yən) ►*n.* A painful, inflamed swelling around a joint, esp. at the first joint of the big toe. [Perh. < OFr. *bugne,* a swelling.]

bunk¹ (bŭngk) ►*n.* **1.** A narrow built-in bed. **2.** A bunk bed. **3.** A place for sleeping. [Perh. < BUNKER.] —**bunk** *v.*

bunk² (bŭngk) ►*n.* Empty talk; nonsense. [After Buncombe County, North Carolina.]

bunk bed ►*n.* A double-decker bed.

bun·ker (bŭng′kər) ►*n.* **1.** A bin or tank esp. for fuel storage, as on a ship. **2.** An underground fortification, often with a reinforced observation post. **3.** See **sand trap.** [Sc. *bonker,* chest.]

bunk·house (bŭngk′hous′) ►*n.* Sleeping quarters on a ranch or in a camp.

bun·ny (bŭn′ē) ►*n., pl.* **-nies** A rabbit, esp. a young one. [dial. *bun,* rabbit's tail.]

Bun·sen burner (bŭn′sən) ►*n.* A small, adjustable gas-burning laboratory burner. [After R.W. *Bunsen* (1811–99).]

bunt (bŭnt) ►*v.* **1.** *Baseball* **a.** To bat (a pitched ball) by tapping it lightly so that the ball rolls slowly in front of the infielders. **b.** To cause

(a base runner) to advance or (a run) to score by bunting. **2.** To butt with the head. [dial., to push.] —**bunt** *n.* —**bunt′er** *n.*

bunt·ing¹ (bŭn′tĭng) ►*n.* **1.** A light cloth used for making flags. **2.** Flags collectively. **3.** Long colored strips of cloth or material used esp. for festive decoration. [Perh. < Ger. *bunt,* colored.]

bunt·ing² (bŭn′tĭng) ►*n.* Any of various birds having short, cone-shaped bills. [ME.]

Bun·yan (bŭn′yən), **John** 1628–88. English preacher and writer.

buoy (bōō′ē, boi) ►*n.* **1.** A float moored in water to mark a location, warn of danger, or indicate a navigational channel. **2.** A life buoy. ►*v.* **1.** To keep afloat or aloft. **2.** To hearten or inspire. [< OFr. *boue.*]

buoy·an·cy (boi′ən-sē, bōō′yən-) ►*n.* **1a.** The tendency to float in a liquid or to rise in a gas. **b.** The upward force a fluid exerts on an object less dense than itself. **2.** Ability to recover quickly from setbacks. **3.** Cheerfulness. —**buoy′ant** *adj.*

bur¹ also **burr** (bûr) ►*n.* **1.** A rough, prickly husk surrounding the seeds or fruits of certain plants. **2.** A rotary cutting tool designed to be attached to a drill. [ME.]

bur² (bûr) ►*n. & v.* Var. of **burr².**

bur·den (bûr′dn) ►*n.* **1.** Something that is carried. **2.** Something that is emotionally difficult to bear. **3.** A responsibility or duty. **4.** A principal or recurring idea; theme. ►*v.* **1.** To weigh down; oppress. **2.** To load or overload. [< OE *byrthen.*] —**bur′den·some** *adj.*

Syns: *affliction, cross, trial, tribulation* **n.**

bur·dock (bûr′dŏk′) ►*n.* A weedy plant having purplish flowers surrounded by prickly bracts. [BUR¹ + DOCK⁴.]

bu·reau (byŏŏr′ō) ►*n., pl.* **-reaus** or **-reaux** (-ōz) **1.** A chest of drawers. **2a.** A government department or a subdivision of a department. **b.** An office or business that performs a specific duty. [< OFr. *burel,* woolen cloth.]

bu·reauc·ra·cy (byŏŏ-rŏk′rə-sē) ►*n., pl.* **-cies 1a.** Administration of a government chiefly through bureaus and departments staffed with nonelected officials. **b.** The departments and their officials as a group. **2.** The administrative structure of a complex organization. **3.** An unwieldy administrative system. —**bu′reau·crat′** (byŏŏr′ə-krăt′) *n.* —**bu′reau·crat′ic** *adj.*

bu·rette also **bu·ret** (byŏŏ-rĕt′) ►*n.* A glass tube with fine gradations and a stopcock at the bottom, used esp. for accurate fluid dispensing. [< OFr. *buire,* vase.]

burg (bûrg) ►*n. Informal* A city or town. [< OE.]

bur·geon (bûr′jən) ►*v.* **1a.** To put forth new buds, leaves, or greenery; sprout. **b.** To begin to grow or blossom. **2.** To grow and flourish. [< OFr. *burjon,* bud.]

burg·er (bûr′gər) ►*n.* **1.** A hamburger. **2.** A sandwich with a nonbeef patty as a filling: *a crab burger.* [< HAMBURGER.]

Burger, Warren Earl 1907–95. Amer. jurist; chief justice of the US Supreme Court (1969–86).

Bur·gess (bûr′jĭs), **Anthony** John Burgess Wilson. 1917–93. British writer and critic.

burgh (bûrg) ►*n.* A chartered town or borough in Scotland. [Sc.]

burgh·er (bûr′gər) ►*n.* A solid middle-class citizen. [< OHGer. *burgāri.*]

bur·glar (bûr′glər) ►*n.* One who commits burglary; housebreaker. [< AN *burgler* and Med. Lat. *burgulator.*] —**bur′glar·ize** *v.*

bur·gla·ry (bûr′glə-rē) ►*n., pl.* **-ries** The act or an instance of·entering another's premises without authorization in order to commit a crime.

bur·gle (bûr′gəl) ►*v.* **-gled, -gling** To commit burglary (on). [< BURGLAR.]

bur·go·mas·ter (bûr′gə-măs′tər) ►*n.* The principal magistrate of some European cities. [Du. *burgemeester.*]

Bur·goyne (bûr-goin′, bûr′goin′), **John** 1722–92. British general and playwright.

Bur·gun·dy[1] (bûr′gən-dē) also **Bour·gogne** (boor-gôn′yə) A historical region and former province of E France. —**Bur·gun′di·an** (bər-gŭn′dē-ən) *adj. & n.*

Bur·gun·dy[2] (bûr′gən-dē) ►*n., pl.* **-dies 1.** Any of various red or white wines produced in Burgundy, France. **2. burgundy** A dark purplish red.

bur·i·al (bĕr′ē-əl) ►*n.* The act or process of burying. [< OE *byrgels.*]

bur·ka (boor′kə) ►*n.* Variant of **burqa.**

Burke (bûrk), **Edmund** 1729–97. Irish-born British politician and writer.

Bur·ki·na Fa·so (bər-kē′nə fä′sō) Formerly **Upper Volta.** A landlocked country of W Africa on the headwaters of the Volta R. Cap. Ouagadougou.

burl (bûrl) ►*n.* A large rounded outgrowth on a tree. [< OFr. *bourle,* tuft of wool.]

bur·lap (bûr′lăp′) ►*n.* A coarse cloth made of jute, flax, or hemp. [?]

bur·lesque (bər-lĕsk′) ►*n.* **1.** A ludicrous or mocking imitation. **2.** Vaudeville entertainment characterized by ribald comedy and display of nudity. ►*v.* **-lesqued, -lesqu·ing** To imitate mockingly. [< Ital. *burla,* joke.]

bur·ly (bûr′lē) ►*adj.* **-li·er, -li·est** Heavy and strong. See Synonyms at **muscular.** [< OE **borlic,* excellent.] —**bur′li·ness** *n.*

Bur·ma (bûr′mə) See **Myanmar.**

Bur·mese (bər-mēz′, -mēs′) ►*n., pl.* **Bur·mese 1a.** A native or inhabitant of Myanmar. **b.** A person of Burmese ancestry. **2.** The Sino-Tibetan language of Myanmar. —**Bur·mese′** *adj.*

burn (bûrn) ►*v.* **burned** or **burnt** (bûrnt), **burn·ing 1a.** To undergo or cause to undergo combustion. **b.** To damage, destroy, or be damaged or destroyed by fire, heat, radiation, electricity, or a caustic agent. **2.** To consume or use as a fuel: *a furnace that burns coal.* **3.** To execute, esp. by electrocution. **4.** To make or produce by fire or heat: *burn a hole in the rug.* **5.** To impart a sensation of intense heat to: *The chili burned my mouth.* **6.** To make or become very angry. **7.** To emit heat or light by or as if by fire. **8.** To feel or look hot. **9.** To record data on. ►*n.* **1.** An injury produced by fire, heat, radiation, electricity, or a caustic agent. **2.** A sunburn or windburn. **3.** A sensation of intense heat, pain, or irritation. —*phrasal verbs:* **burn out 1.** To stop burning from lack of fuel. **2.** To wear out or fail, esp. because of heat. **3.** To become exhausted from long-term stress. **burn up** To make or become very angry. —*idioms:* **burn (one's) bridges** To eliminate the possibility of return or retreat.

to burn In great amounts: *They had money to burn.* [< OE *beornan* and *bærnan.*]

burned-out (bûrnd′out′) or **burnt-out** (bûrnt′-) ►*adj.* Worn out or exhausted, esp. as a result of long-term stress.

burn·er (bûr′nər) ►*n.* **1.** One that burns, esp.: **a.** A device, as in a furnace, that is lighted to produce a flame. **b.** A device on a stovetop that produces heat. **2.** A unit, such as a furnace, in which fuel is burned.

bur·nish (bûr′nĭsh) ►*v.* To polish by or as if by rubbing. ►*n.* A glossy finish; luster. [< OFr. *burnir.*]

bur·nous also **bur·noose** (bər-nōōs′) ►*n.* A hooded cloak worn esp. by Arabs. [< Ar. *burnus.*]

burn·out (bûrn′out′) ►*n.* **1.** A failure in a device caused by excessive heat or friction. **2.** Termination of rocket or jet-engine operation due to fuel exhaustion or shutoff. **3a.** Exhaustion, esp. from long-term stress. **b.** One who is burned out.

Burns (bûrnz), **Robert** 1759–96. Scottish poet. —**Burns′i·an** *adj.*

Burn·side (bûrn′sīd′), **Ambrose Everett** 1824–81. Amer. general and politician.

burnt (bûrnt) ►*v.* P.t. and p.part. of **burn.**

burp (bûrp) ►*n.* A belch. ►*v.* **1.** To belch. **2.** To cause (a baby) to belch. [Imit.]

bur·qa or **bur·ka** (boor′kə) ►*n.* A loose outer garment worn by Muslim women that covers the head and face and sometimes the entire body. [Ult. < Ar. *burqu‘.*]

burqa

burr[1] (bûr) ►*n.* **1.** A rough edge remaining esp. on metal after it has been cast or cut. **2.** Var. of **bur**[1]. ►*v.* **1.** To form a burr on. **2.** To remove burrs from. [Var. of BUR[1].]

burr[2] also **bur** (bûr) ►*n.* **1.** A trilling of the letter *r,* as in Scottish speech. **2.** A buzzing or whirring sound. [Imit.] —**burr** *v.*

Burr, Aaron 1756–1836. Amer. politician; US vice president (1801–05).

bur·ri·to (boo-rē′tō, bə-) ►*n., pl.* **-tos** A flour tortilla wrapped around a filling, as of beef, beans, or cheese. [Am.Sp.]

bur·ro (bûr′ō, boor′ō, bŭr′ō) ►*n., pl.* **-ros** A small donkey, esp. one used as a pack animal. [< LLat. *burrīcus,* small horse.]

bur·row (bûr′ō, bŭr′ō) ►*n.* A hole or tunnel dug in the ground by an animal for habitation or refuge. ►*v.* **1.** To dig a burrow. **2.** To move or progress by or as if by tunneling. [ME *borow.*]

bur·sa (bûr′sə) ►*n., pl.* **-sae** (-sē) or **-sas** A saclike body cavity, esp. one located between moving structures. [< Gk., wineskin.]

bur·sar (bûr′sər, -sär′) ►*n.* A treasurer, as at a college. [< LLat. *bursa,* PURSE.] **—bur′sa·ry** *n.*

bur·si·tis (bər-sī′tĭs) ►*n.* Inflammation of a bursa, esp. in the shoulder, elbow, or knee.

burst (bûrst) ►*v.* **burst, burst·ing 1a.** To come open or fly apart suddenly, esp. from internal pressure. **b.** To break, shatter, or explode. **2.** To be full to the breaking point. **3.** To emerge or arrive suddenly: *burst out of the door.* **4.** To give sudden utterance or expression: *burst out laughing.* ►*n.* **1.** A sudden outbreak or explosion. **2.** The result of bursting. **3.** An abrupt increase: *a burst of speed.* **4.** A period of intense activity: *cleaning in bursts.* [< OE *berstan.*]

Bu·run·di (bo͞o-ro͞on′dē, -ro͞on′-) A country of E-central Africa with a coastline on Lake Tanganyika. Cap. Bujumbura. **—Bu·run′di·an** *adj. & n.*

bur·y (bĕr′ē) ►*v.* **-ied, -y·ing 1.** To place (a corpse) in a grave, a tomb, or the sea. **2a.** To place in the ground; cover. **b.** To conceal; hide. **3.** To absorb: *I'm buried in work.* **4.** To abandon: *buried their quarrel.* **—idiom: bury the hatchet** To stop fighting. [< OE *byrgan.*]

bus (bŭs) ►*n., pl.* **bus·es** or **bus·ses 1.** A long motor vehicle for carrying passengers. **2.** A circuit that connects a computer's major components. ►*v.* **bused, bus·ing** or **bussed, bus·sing 1.** To transport or travel in a bus. **2.** To clear (dishes) in a restaurant. [< OMNIBUS.]

bus·boy (bŭs′boi′) ►*n.* A restaurant employee who clears dishes and sets tables.

bus·by (bŭz′bē) ►*n., pl.* **-bies** A full-dress fur hat worn in certain regiments of the British army. [Poss. < *Busby.*]

bush (bo͝osh) ►*n.* **1.** A low shrub with many branches. **2a.** Land covered with dense vegetation or undergrowth. **b.** Land remote from settlement. **3.** A shaggy mass, as of hair. ►*v.* To grow or branch out like a bush. ►*adj. Slang* Bush-league. [< OE *busc* and OFr. *bois,* wood.] **—bush′i·ness** *n.* **—bush′y** *adj.*

Bush, George Herbert Walker b. 1924. The 41st US president (1989–93).

George H. W. Bush George W. Bush

Bush, George Walker b. 1946. The 43rd US president (2001–09).

bushed (bo͝osht) ►*adj. Informal* Exhausted.

bush·el (bo͝osh′əl) ►*n.* **1.** See table at **measurement. 2.** A container with the capacity of a bushel. **3.** *Informal* A large amount. [< OFr. *boissiel,* of Celt. orig.]

bush·ing (bo͝osh′ĭng) ►*n.* A cylindrical metal lining used to constrain, guide, or reduce friction. [Poss. < Du. *bus,* box.]

bush-league (bo͝osh′lēg′) ►*adj. Slang* Second-rate.

Bush·man (bo͝osh′mən) ►*n.* See **San.**

bush·mas·ter (bo͝osh′măs′tər) ►*n.* A large venomous snake of tropical America.

bush·whack (bo͝osh′wăk′, -hwăk′) ►*v.* **1.** To force one's way through dense growth. **2.** To ambush. See Synonyms at **ambush.**

busi·ness (bĭz′nĭs) ►*n.* **1.** The activity of buying and selling products or services. **2.** The amount or volume of this activity: *business had fallen off.* **3a.** The variety of this activity in which a person is engaged: *the food business.* **b.** A specific occupation: *the best designer in the business.* **4.** A commercial enterprise or establishment. **5.** Patronage: *took my business elsewhere.* **6.** One's concern or interest. **7.** Serious work: *got down to business.* **8.** An affair or matter. **9.** An incidental action performed by an actor on the stage, as to fill a pause. **10.** *Informal* Verbal criticism; scolding: *gave me the business for being late.* **11.** *Informal* Urination or defecation: *The dog did its business on the lawn.*

business card ►*n.* A small card printed with a person's name and business affiliation.

busi·ness·like (bĭz′nĭs-līk′) ►*adj.* **1.** Methodical and systematic. **2.** Unemotional.

busi·ness·man (bĭz′nĭs-măn′) ►*n.* A man engaged in business. See Usage Note at **man.**

busi·ness·per·son (bĭz′nĭs-pûr′sən) ►*n.* One engaged in business.

busi·ness·wom·an (bĭz′nĭs-wo͝om′ən) ►*n.* A woman engaged in business. See Usage Note at **man.**

bus·ing or **bus·sing** (bŭs′ĭng) ►*n.* The transportation of children by bus to schools outside their neighborhoods, esp. to achieve racial integration.

busk (bŭsk) ►*v.* To play music or perform entertainment in public, esp. while soliciting money. [Perh. ult. < Italian *buscare,* to prowl.] **—busk′er** *n.*

bus·kin (bŭs′kĭn) ►*n.* **1.** A laced half boot worn by actors of Greek and Roman tragedies. **2.** Tragedy. [Poss. < obsolete Fr. *broisequin.*]

bus·man's holiday (bŭs′mənz) ►*n. Informal* A vacation during which one engages in activity similar to one's usual work.

buss (bŭs) ►*v.* To kiss. ►*n.* A kiss. [Poss. < obsolete *bass.*]

bus·ses (bŭs′ĭz) ►*n.* Pl. of **bus.**

bust[1] (bŭst) ►*n.* **1.** A sculpture representing a person's head, shoulders, and upper chest. **2.** A woman's breasts. [< Ital. *busto.*]

bust[2] (bŭst) ►*v.* **1.** *Informal* **a.** To burst or break. **b.** To render or become inoperable. **2.** To break up: *bust the gang.* **3.** To break (a horse). **4.** To bankrupt. **5.** *Informal* **a.** To arrest. **b.** To make a raid on. **6.** *Slang* To reduce in rank; demote. **7.** *Slang* To hit; punch. ►*n.* **1.** A failure; flop. **2.** A widespread financial depression. **3.** *Slang* A punch. **4.** *Informal* A raid or arrest. [< BURST.]

bust·ed (bŭs′tĭd) ►*adj.* **1.** *Slang* **a.** Broken. **b.** Inoperable: *a busted car.* **2.** Bankrupt or out of funds. **3.** *Slang* Arrested: *a busted robber.*

bus·tle[1] (bŭs′əl) ►*v.* **-tled, -tling** To move

energetically and busily. ►*n.* A commotion; stir. [Poss. < *busk*, prepare oneself.]

bus·tle² (bŭs′əl) ►*n.* A frame or pad formerly worn under a woman's skirt to add fullness.

bus·y (bĭz′ē) ►*adj.* **-i·er, -i·est 1.** Engaged in work or activity. **2.** Full of activity: *a busy morning.* **3.** Meddlesome; prying. **4.** Being in use, as a telephone line. **5.** Cluttered with detail: *a busy design.* ►*v.* **-ied, -y·ing** To make busy. [< OE *bisig.*] —**bus′i·ly** *adv.* —**bus′y·ness** *n.*

bus·y·bod·y (bĭz′ē-bŏd′ē) ►*n.* A meddlesome person.

bus·y·work (bĭz′ē-wûrk′) ►*n.* Activity that takes up time but does not necessarily yield productive results.

but (bŭt; bət *when unstressed*) ►*conj.* **1.** On the contrary: *His eyes were not brown but blue.* See Usage Notes at **and, not. 2.** Contrary to expectation; yet: *He is tired but happy.* **3.** Except; save. **4.** Except that: *would have come but I had to work.* **5.** *Informal* Without the result that: *It never rains but it pours.* **6.** *Informal* That. Often used after a negative: *no doubt but we'll win.* **7.** That . . . not. Used after a negative or question: *There never is a tax law but someone opposes it.* **8.** *Informal* Than: *no sooner arrived but they had to go.* ►*prep.* Except: *No one but us.* ►*adv.* Merely; only: *lasted but a moment.* ►*n.* An exception or objection: *no ifs, ands, or buts.* [< OE *būtan.*]

bu·ta·di·ene (byoo′tə-dī′ēn′, -dī-ēn′) ►*n.* A highly flammable hydrocarbon, C_4H_6, obtained from petroleum and used in making synthetic rubber. [BUTA(NE) + DI– + –ENE.]

bu·tane (byoo′tān′) ►*n.* Either of two isomers of a gaseous hydrocarbon, C_4H_{10}, produced from petroleum and used as a household fuel. [BUT(YL) + –ANE.]

butch·er (bŏŏch′ər) ►*n.* **1a.** One who slaughters and dresses animals for food. **b.** One who sells meats. **2.** A cruel or wanton killer. ►*v.* **1.** To slaughter or prepare (animals). **2.** To kill brutally or indiscriminately. **3.** To botch; bungle: *butchered the language.* See Synonyms at **botch.** [< OFr. *bouchier* < *bouc*, he-goat.] —**butch′er·er** *n.* —**butch′er·y** *n.*

bu·te·o (byoo′tē-ō′) ►*n., pl.* **-os** Any of various broad-winged, soaring hawks. [Lat. *būteō.*]

but·ler (bŭt′lər) ►*n.* The head servant in a household, usu. in charge of food service. [< OFr. *bouteillier*, bottle bearer.]

Butler, Samuel 1835–1902. British writer.

butt¹ (bŭt) ►*v.* To hit with the head or horns. ►*n.* A push or blow with the head or horns. —*phrasal verbs:* **butt in 1.** To meddle in other people's affairs. **2.** To interrupt. **3.** To move into a line out of turn. **butt out** *Slang* To disengage from a matter involving another person. [< OFr. *bouter*, strike, of Gmc. orig.]

butt² (bŭt) ►*v.* To join or be joined end to end; abut. [< AN *butter.*] —**butt** *n.*

butt³ (bŭt) ►*n.* An object of ridicule: *the butt of their jokes.* [< OFr. *but*, target.]

butt⁴ (bŭt) ►*n.* **1.** The larger or thicker end: *the butt of a rifle.* **2a.** An unburned end, as of a cigarette. **b.** *Informal* A cigarette. **3.** A short or broken remnant; stub. **4.** *Informal* The buttocks. ►*adv.* *Slang* Very. Used as an intensive: *butt ugly.* [< OFr. *but*, end.]

butt⁵ (bŭt) ►*n.* A large cask. [< LLat. *buttis.*]

butte (byoot) ►*n.* A flat-topped hill that rises

abruptly from the surrounding area. [< OFr. *butt*, mound behind targets.]

butte
West Mitten Butte, Monument Valley
Navajo Tribal Park, Arizona

but·ter (bŭt′ər) ►*n.* **1.** A soft yellowish fatty food churned from milk or cream. **2.** Any of various substances similar to butter. ►*v.* To put butter on or in. —*phrasal verb:* **butter up** To flatter. [< Gk. *bouturon : bous*, cow + *turos*, cheese.] —**but′ter·y** *adj.*

butter bean ►*n.* *Regional* A lima bean.

but·ter·cup (bŭt′ər-kŭp′) ►*n.* Any of numerous plants with usu. glossy yellow flowers.

but·ter·fat (bŭt′ər-făt′) ►*n.* The natural fat of milk from which butter is made.

but·ter·fin·gers (bŭt′ər-fĭng′gərz) ►*pl.n.* *(takes sing. v.)* One who tends to drop things. —**but′ter·fin′gered** *adj.*

but·ter·fish (bŭt′ər-fĭsh′) ►*n.* Any of various fishes having oily edible flesh.

but·ter·fly (bŭt′ər-flī′) ►*n.* **1.** Any of an order of insects having slender bodies and four broad, usu. colorful wings. **2.** One interested principally in frivolous pleasure: *a social butterfly.* **3.** A swimming stroke in which both arms are drawn upward and forward with a simultaneous kick. **4. butterflies** A feeling of unease caused esp. by fearful anticipation. ►*v.* **-flied, -fly·ing, -flies** To cut and spread open flat. [< OE *butorflēoge.*]

but·ter·milk (bŭt′ər-mĭlk′) ►*n.* The sour liquid remaining after butterfat is removed from whole milk or cream by churning.

but·ter·nut (bŭt′ər-nŭt′) ►*n.* **1.** An E North American walnut having light brown wood and a nut enclosed in an egg-shaped husk. **2.** The edible, oily nut of this tree. **3.** A brownish dye obtained from the husks of the butternut. [From the nut's oiliness.]

butternut squash ►*n.* A winter squash with a smooth tan rind and edible orange flesh.

but·ter·scotch (bŭt′ər-skŏch′) ►*n.* **1.** A syrup, candy, or flavoring made by melting butter and brown sugar. **2.** A golden brown.

but·tock (bŭt′ək) ►*n.* **1.** Either of the two rounded prominences posterior to the hips. **2. buttocks** The rear pelvic area of the body. [< OE *buttuc*, strip of land.]

but·ton (bŭt′n) ►*n.* **1.** An often disk-shaped fastener on a garment, designed to fit through a buttonhole or loop. **2.** An object resembling a button, such as a push-button switch or a round flat pin. **3.** *Comp.* A defined area within an interface that one clicks to select a command. ►*v.* To fasten or be fastened with buttons. [< OFr. *bouter*, thrust.]

but·ton-down (bŭt′n-doun′) ►*adj.* **1.** Having buttons extending down the front from the collar to the waist: *a button-down shirt.* **2.** Fastened down by buttons: *a button-down collar.* **3.** Conservative; conventional. —**button-down** *n.*

but·ton·hole (bŭt′n-hōl′) ►*n.* A small slit in a garment or cloth for fastening a button. ►*v.* **-holed, -hol·ing** To hold or detain (a person) in conversation.

but·tress (bŭt′rĭs) ►*n.* **1.** A structure, usu. brick or stone, built against a wall for support. **2.** Something that serves to support or reinforce. ►*v.* To support with or as if with a buttress: *buttress a wall; buttress an argument.* [< OFr. *bouter,* strike against.]

bu·tyl (byoot′l) ►*n.* A hydrocarbon unit, C_4H_9. [< Lat. *butyrum,* BUTTER + –YL.]

bux·om (bŭk′səm) ►*adj.* **1.** Healthily plump. **2.** Full-bosomed. [ME, obedient.]

buy (bī) ►*v.* **bought** (bôt), **buy·ing 1.** To acquire in exchange for money; purchase. **2.** To be capable of purchasing: *the best that money can buy.* **3.** To acquire by sacrifice, exchange, or trade: *buy love with favors.* **4.** To bribe. **5.** *Slang* To accept; believe: *didn't buy my lame excuse.* ►*n.* **1.** Something bought. **2.** *Informal* A bargain. —*phrasal verbs:* **buy into 1.** To acquire a stake or interest in. **2.** To believe in wholeheartedly or uncritically. **buy off** To bribe. **buy out** To purchase the entire stock, business rights, or interests of. **buy up** To purchase all that is available of. [< OE *bycgan.*] —**buy′er** *n.*

buy·back (bī′băk′) ►*n.* The repurchase of stock by the issuing company.

buy·out (bī′out′) ►*n.* **1.** The purchase of the entire holdings of an owner. **2.** The purchase of a company or business.

buzz (bŭz) ►*v.* **1.** To make a low droning or vibrating sound like that of a bee. **2.** To talk excitedly in low tones. **3.** To move busily; bustle. **4.** To signal with a buzzer. **5.** *Informal* To fly low over: *buzzed the control tower.* **6.** To telephone: *Buzz me later.* ►*n.* **1.** A vibrating, humming, or droning sound. **2.** A low murmur. **3.** A telephone call. **4.** *Slang* Pleasant intoxication or overstimulation. **5.** *Slang* Excited interest or attention. —*phrasal verb:* **buzz off** *Informal* To go away. [ME *bussen.*]

buz·zard (bŭz′ərd) ►*n.* **1.** Any of various North American vultures. **2.** *Chiefly Brit.* A broad-winged hawk. [< Lat. *būteō.*]

buzz·er (bŭz′ər) ►*n.* An electric signaling device that makes a buzzing sound.

buzz saw ►*n.* See **circular saw.**

buzz·word (bŭz′wûrd′) ►*n.* **1.** A word or phrase connected with a specialized field that is used esp. to impress laypersons. **2.** A stylish or trendy word or phrase.

b/w or **BW** ►*abbr.* black and white

BWI ►*abbr.* British West Indies

by¹ (bī) ►*prep.* **1.** Next to. **2.** With the use of; through. **3.** Up to and beyond; past. **4.** At or to: *stopped by the bakery; came by the house.* **5.** During: *sleeping by day.* **6.** Not later than: *by 5:30 PM.* **7a.** In the amount of: *recieved e-mails by the thousands.* **b.** To the extent of: *shorter by two inches.* **8a.** According to: *played by the rules.* **b.** With respect to: *siblings by blood.* **9.** In the name of: *swore by the Bible.* **10.** Through the agency or action of: *killed by a bullet.* **11.** In succession to; after: *one by one.* **12a.** Used

in multiplication and division: *4 by 6 is 24.* **b.** Used with measurements: *a room 12 by 18 feet.* **c.** Used with compass directions: *south by east.* ►*adv.* **1.** On hand; nearby: *Stand by.* **2.** Aside; away: *Put it by for later.* **3.** Up to, alongside, and past: *raced by.* **4.** At or to one's home or current location: *Stop by later today.* **5.** Into the past: *as years go by.* —*idiom:* **by and by** In a while. [< OE *bī.*]

by² (bī) ►*n.* Var. of **bye¹.**

by– ►*pref.* **1.** By: *bygone.* **2.** Secondary: *byway.* [ME.]

by-and-by (bī′ən-bī′) ►*n.* Some future time or occasion.

by and large ►*adv.* For the most part.

by-catch (bī′kăch′, -kĕch′) ►*n.* The unwanted portion of a fishing catch.

bye¹ also **by** (bī) ►*n.* **1.** A side issue. **2.** *Sports* The position of one who draws no opponent for a round in a tournament and so advances to the next round. —*idiom:* **by the bye** By the way; incidentally. [< BY¹.]

bye² (bī) ►*interj.* Used to express farewell. [< GOODBYE.]

bye-bye (bī′bī′, bī-bī′) ►*interj.* Used to express farewell. [Reduplication of BYE².]

by·gone (bī′gôn′, -gŏn′) ►*adj.* Gone by; past: *bygone days.* ►*n.* One, esp. a grievance, that is past: *Let bygones be bygones.*

by·law (bī′lô′) ►*n.* **1.** A law or rule governing the internal affairs of an organization. **2.** A secondary law. [ME *bilawe,* local regulations : ON *bȳr,* settlement + ON **lagu,* law.]

by·line also **by-line** (bī′līn′) ►*n.* A line at the head of a newspaper or magazine article carrying the writer's name. —**by′lin′er** *n.*

by·pass also **by-pass** (bī′păs′) ►*n.* **1.** A highway that passes around an obstructed or congested area. **2.** A means of circumvention. **3.** *Elect.* See **shunt** (sense 3). **4.** *Med.* **a.** An alternative passage created surgically to divert the flow of blood or other bodily fluid. **b.** A surgical procedure to create a bypass. ►*v.* **1.** To avoid (an obstacle) by using a bypass. **2.** To ignore: *bypass the rules.*

by-play (bī′plā′) ►*n.* Theatrical action or speech taking place on stage while the main action proceeds.

by·prod·uct or **by-prod·uct** (bī′prŏd′əkt) ►*n.* **1.** Something produced in the making of something else. **2.** A side effect.

By·ron (bī′rən), **George Gordon** Sixth Baron Byron. 1788–1824. British poet. —**By·ron′ic** (bī-rŏn′ĭk) *adj.*

by·stand·er (bī′stăn′dər) ►*n.* One who is present at an event without participating.

byte (bīt) ►*n.* **1.** A unit of data equal to eight bits. **2.** A set of bits constituting the smallest unit of addressable memory in a given computer. [< BIT³ and BITE.]

by·way (bī′wā′) ►*n.* **1.** A side road. **2.** A secondary or arcane field of study.

by·word also **by-word** (bī′wûrd′) ►*n.* **1a.** A proverb. **b.** An often-used word or phrase. **2.** One that represents a type, class, or quality: *Einstein is a byword for genius.*

Byz·an·tine (bĭz′ən-tēn′, -tīn′, bĭ-zăn′tĭn) ►*adj.* **1.** Relating to Byzantium or the Byzantine Empire. **2.** Of the richly decorative artistic or architectural style developed in the Byzantine Empire. **3.** Of the Eastern Orthodox Church or the rites performed in it. **4.** often **byzantine a.** Marked by intrigue; devious. **b.** Highly complex; intricate: *a byzantine tax law.* ►*n.* A native or inhabitant of Byzantium or the Byzantine Empire.

Byzantine Empire The E part of the later Roman Empire, dating from around AD 395.

By·zan·ti·um (bĭ-zăn′shē-əm, -tē-əm) **1.** The Byzantine Empire. **2.** An ancient city of Thrace on the site of present-day Istanbul, Turkey.

C

c¹ or **C** (sē) ►*n., pl.* **c's** or **C's** also **cs** or **Cs 1.** The 3rd letter of the English alphabet. **2.** The third best in quality or rank. **3.** *Mus.* The 1st tone in the scale of C major.

c² The symbol for the speed of light in a vacuum.

c³ ►*abbr.* **1.** *Phys.* candle **2.** carat **3.** also **C** constant **4.** cubic

C¹ also **c** The symbol for the Roman numeral 100.

C² ►*abbr.* **1.** cell phone number **2.** Celsius **3.** centigrade **4.** cold **5.** consonant **6.** coulomb

c. ►*abbr.* **1.** cent **2.** centavo **3.** centime **4.** circa **5.** copyright **6.** cup

C. ►*abbr.* **1.** cape **2.** or **c.** century **3.** chancellor

ca ►*abbr.* circa

CA ►*abbr.* **1.** California **2.** current account

cab (kăb) ►*n.* **1.** A taxicab. **2.** The enclosed compartment for the operator or driver of a heavy vehicle or machine. [< CABRIOLET.]

ca·bal (kə-băl′, -bäl′) ►*n.* **1.** A conspiratorial group. **2.** A secret plot. [< Med.Lat. *cabala,* KABBALAH.]

cab·a·la (kăb′ə-lə, kə-bä′-) ►*n.* Var. of **kabbalah.**

ca·ban·a also **ca·ba·ña** (kə-băn′ə, -băn′yə) ►*n.* **1.** A shelter on a beach or at a pool used as a bathhouse. **2.** A cabin or hut. [< LLat. *capanna,* hut.]

cab·a·ret (kăb′ə-rā′) ►*n.* **1.** A restaurant or nightclub providing live entertainment. **2.** The floor show in a cabaret. [< ONFr. *camberette,* taproom.]

cab·bage (kăb′ĭj) ►*n.* A vegetable of the mustard family, having a large round head of tightly overlapping green to purplish leaves. [< ONFr. *caboche,* head.] —**cab′bag·y** *adj.*

cab·by or **cab·bie** (kăb′ē) ►*n., pl.* **-bies** A cab driver.

cab·in (kăb′ĭn) ►*n.* **1.** A small, roughly built house. **2.** A room in a ship used as living quarters. **3.** The enclosed space in an aircraft or spacecraft for the crew, passengers, or cargo. [< LLat. *capanna,* hut.]

cab·i·net (kăb′ə-nĭt) ►*n.* **1.** An upright case or cupboard with shelves, drawers, or compartments for the safekeeping or display of objects. **2.** The box that houses a computer's main components. **3.** often **Cabinet** A body of persons appointed by a head of state or a prime minister to head the executive departments of the government and to act as official advisers. **4.** *Regional* See **milk shake.** [< ONFr. *cabine,* gambling-room.]

cab·i·net·mak·er (kăb′ə-nĭt-mā′kər) ►*n.* An artisan who makes wooden furniture.

cab·i·net·work (kăb′ə-nĭt-wûrk′) ►*n.* Finished furniture made by a cabinetmaker.

cabin fever ►*n.* Uneasiness resulting from confinement to a limited space or routine.

ca·ble (kā′bəl) ►*n.* **1.** A strong, large-diameter steel or fiber rope. **2a.** *Elect.* A bound or sheathed group of mutually insulated conductors. **b.** A sheathed bundle of optical fibers. **3a.** Cable television. **b.** A similar service providing Internet access. **4.** A cablegram. ►*v.* **-bled, -bling** To send a cablegram (to). [< LLat. *capulum,* lasso.]

cable box ►*n.* An electronic tuning device that allows channels transmitted by cable to be selected for viewing on a television.

cable car ►*n.* A vehicle that is moved along a route by an endless cable.

ca·ble·gram (kā′bəl-grăm′) ►*n.* A telegram sent by submarine cable.

cable television ►*n.* A subscription television service that uses cables to carry signals between local antennas and the subscriber's location.

cab·o·chon (kăb′ə-shŏn′) ►*n.* A highly polished, convex-cut, unfaceted gem. [< ONFr.]

ca·boo·dle (kə-bood′l) ►*n. Informal* The lot, group, or bunch: *donated the whole caboodle.* [Alteration of BOODLE.]

ca·boose (kə-boos′) ►*n.* The last car on a freight train, having kitchen and sleeping facilities for the train crew. [Poss. < obsolete Du. *cabūse,* ship's galley.]

Ca·bri·ni (kə-brē′nē), Saint **Frances Xavier** 1850–1917. Italian-born Amer. religious leader.

Saint Frances Xavier Cabrini

cab·ri·o·let (kăb′rē-ə-lā′) ►*n.* **1.** A two-wheeled, one-horse carriage with a folding top. **2.** A convertible coupe. [Fr.]

ca·ca·o (kə-kā′ō, -kä′ō) ►*n., pl.* **-os 1.** An evergreen tropical American tree having ribbed, reddish-brown fruits. **2.** The seed of this plant, used in making chocolate, cocoa, and cocoa butter. [< Nahuatl *cacahuatl,* cacao bean.]

cac·cia·to·re (kăch′ə-tôr′ē) ►*n.* Prepared with tomatoes, onions, mushrooms, herbs, and sometimes wine: *chicken cacciatore.* [Ital., hunter.]

ca·cha·ca (kə-shä′sə) ►*n.* A white Brazilian rum made from sugar cane. [Brazilian Port. *cachaça.*]

cache (kăsh) ►*n.* **1.** An amount of goods or valuables, esp. when hidden or kept in a place that is hard to reach. **2.** Such a place used for storing goods or valuables. **3.** A fast storage buffer in a computer's central processing unit. ►*v.* **cached, cach·ing** To hide or store in a cache. [< O.Fr. *cacher*, hide, ult. < Lat. *cōgere*, to force; see COGENT.]

ca·chet (kă-shā′) ►*n.* **1.** A mark or quality of distinction, individuality, or authenticity. **2.** Great prestige or appeal. **3.** A seal on a document. [< O.Fr. *cacher*, press; see CACHE.]

cack·le (kăk′əl) ►*v.* **-led, -ling 1.** To make the shrill cry characteristic of a hen after laying an egg. **2.** To laugh or talk in a shrill manner. ►*n.* **1.** The act or sound of cackling. **2.** Shrill laughter. [Prob. < MLGer. *kākeln.*] —**cack′-ler** *n.*

ca·coph·o·ny (kə-kŏf′ə-nē) ►*n., pl.* **-nies** Jarring, discordant sound. [< Gk. *kakophōnos*, dissonant.] —**ca·coph′o·nous** *adj.*

cac·tus (kăk′təs) ►*n., pl.* **-ti** (-tī′) or **-tus·es** Any of various fleshy-stemmed, spiny, usu. leafless plants native to arid regions of the New World. [< Gk. *kaktos*, thistle.]

cad (kăd) ►*n.* A man of unprincipled behavior, esp. toward women. [< CADDIE.] —**cad′dish** *adj.* —**cad′dish·ly** *adv.* —**cad′dish·ness** *n.*

CAD ►*abbr.* **1.** computer-aided design **2.** coronary artery disease

ca·dav·er (kə-dăv′ər) ►*n.* A dead body, esp. one intended for dissection. [< Lat. *cadere*, to fall, die.]

ca·dav·er·ous (kə-dăv′ər-əs) ►*adj.* **1.** Suggestive of death; corpselike. **2.** Pale and gaunt.

cad·die also **cad·dy** (kăd′ē) ►*n., pl.* **-dies 1.** One hired to attend a golfer, esp. by carrying the clubs. **2.** A device for moving, carrying, or holding an item or collection of items, such as a small cart or rack. ►*v.* **-died, -dy·ing** To serve as a caddie. [< Fr. *cadet*, CADET.]

Cad·do·an (kăd′ō-ən) ►*n.* A family of North American Indian languages formerly spoken in the E Great Plains from the Dakotas to Oklahoma, Texas, and Louisiana and now in North Dakota and Oklahoma.

cad·dy (kăd′ē) ►*n., pl.* **-dies 1.** A small container, esp. for tea. **2.** A case for loading a CD-ROM into a disk drive. [< Malay *kati*, a unit of weight.]

ca·dence (kād′ns) ►*n.* **1.** Balanced, rhythmic flow, as of poetry. **2.** The beat of movement, as in marching. **3.** Vocal inflection or modulation. **4.** *Mus.* A progression of chords moving to a harmonic close or sense of resolution. [< Lat. *cadere*, to fall.]

ca·den·cy (kād′n-sē) ►*n., pl.* **-cies** Cadence.

ca·den·za (kə-děn′zə) ►*n.* *Mus.* **1.** An ornamental melodic flourish, as in an aria. **2.** An extended virtuosic section for the soloist usu. near the end of a concerto movement. [< OItal., CADENCE.]

ca·det (kə-dět′) ►*n.* **1.** A student at a military school who is training to be an officer. **2.** A younger son or brother. [< LLat. *capitellum*, dim. of Lat. *caput*, head.]

cadge (kăj) ►*v.* **cadged, cadg·ing** To beg or get by begging. [< ME *cadgear*, peddler.]

Syns: beg, bum, mooch, panhandle, scrounge v.

Cá·diz (kə-dĭz′, kä′dĭz) A city of SW Spain NW of Gibraltar on the **Gulf of Cádiz,** an inlet of the Atlantic.

cad·mi·um (kăd′mē-əm) ►*n.* *Symbol* **Cd** A soft, bluish-white metallic element used in low-friction alloys, solders, and nickel-cadmium storage batteries. At. no. 48. See table at **element.** [After *Cadmus*, founder of Thebes < Gk. *Kadmos.*] —**cad′mic** (-mĭk) *adj.*

cad·re (kä′drā, -drə, kăd′rē, kä′dər) ►*n.* **1.** A nucleus of trained personnel around which a larger organization can be built. **2a.** A tightly knit group, esp. of political activists. **b.** A member of such a group. [< Lat. *quadrum*, a square.]

ca·du·ce·us (kə-do͞o′sē-əs, -shəs, -dyo͞o′-) ►*n., pl.* **-ce·i** (-sē-ī′) **1.** *Gk. Myth.* A winged staff with two serpents twined around it, carried by Hermes. **2.** This staff used as the symbol of the medical profession. [< Gk. *karukeion.*]

cae·cum (sē′kəm) ►*n.* Var. of **cecum.**

Caed·mon (kăd′mən) d. c. 680. Anglo-Saxon poet, considered the earliest English poet.

cae·sar also **Cae·sar** (sē′zər) ►*n.* **1.** Used as a title for Roman emperors. **2.** A dictator or autocrat.

Caesar, Julius Gaius Julius Caesar. 100–44 BC. Roman political and military leader and historian. —**Cae·sar′e·an, Cae·sar′i·an** (sĭ-zâr′ē-ən) *adj.*

cae·sar·e·an or **cae·sar·i·an** (sĭ-zâr′ē-ən) ►*adj. & n.* Vars. of **cesarean.**

cae·si·um (sē′zē-əm) ►*n.* Var. of **cesium.**

cae·su·ra also **ce·su·ra** (sĭ-zho͝or′ə, -zo͞or′ə) ►*n., pl.* **-su·ras** or **-su·rae** (-zho͝or′ē, -zo͞or′ē) A pause in a line of verse dictated by sense or speech rhythm rather than by metrics. [Lat. *caesūra*, a cutting.]

CAFE ►*abbr.* corporate average fuel economy

ca·fé also **ca·fe** (kă-fā′, kə-) ►*n.* A coffeehouse, restaurant, or bar. [Fr. < Ital. *caffè*, COFFEE.]

ca·fé au lait (kă-fā′ ō lā′) ►*n.* **1.** Coffee with hot milk. **2.** A light yellowish brown. [Fr.]

caf·e·te·ri·a (kăf′ĭ-tîr′ē-ə) ►*n.* **1.** A restaurant in which customers are served at a counter and carry their meals on trays to tables. **2.** A dining area, as at a school, where meals may be purchased or brought from home. [Sp. *cafetería*, coffee shop < *café*, COFFEE.]

caf·feine also **caf·fein** (kă-fēn′, kăf′ēn′) ►*n.* A bitter white alkaloid often derived from tea or coffee and used chiefly as a mild stimulant. [Ger. *Kaffein* < Fr. *café*, COFFEE.] —**caf′fein·at′ed** (kăf′ə-nā′tĭd) *adj.*

caf·fe lat·te (kăf′ā lä′tā) ►*n.* Espresso coffee with steamed milk. [Ital. *caffè (e) latte*, coffee (with) milk.]

caf·tan or **kaf·tan** (kăf′tăn′, -tən, kăf-tăn′) ►*n.* A full-length sleeved garment worn chiefly in the E Mediterranean countries. [< Turk. *qaftān.*]

cage (kāj) ►*n.* **1.** A barred or grated enclosure for confining birds or animals. **2.** A similar enclosure or structure. **3a.** *Baseball* A wire backstop used in batting practice. **b.** A goal, as in hockey or soccer, made of a net attached to a frame. ►*v.* **caged, cag·ing** To put in or as if in a cage. See Synonyms at **enclose**. [< Lat. *cavea*.]

ca·gey also **ca·gy** (kā′jē) ►*adj.* **-gi·er, -gi·est 1.** Wary; careful. **2.** Crafty; shrewd: *a cagey lawyer.* [?] —**ca′gi·ly** *adv.* —**ca′gi·ness** *n.*

ca·hoots (kə-hōōts′) ►*pl.n.* Informal Secret partnership: *in cahoots with organized crime.* [Perh. < OFr. *cahute*, cabin.]

cai·man also **cay·man** (kā′mən) ►*n., pl.* **-mans** Any of various tropical American reptiles resembling and closely related to the alligators. [< Carib *acayuman*.]

Cain (kān) In the Bible, the eldest son of Adam and Eve; murdered Abel.

cai·pir·in·ha (kī′pə-rē′nyə) ►*n.* A Brazilian cocktail typically made of cachaca, crushed limes, and sugar. [Brazilian Port. < dim. of *caipira*, hick.]

cairn (kârn) ►*n.* A mound of stones erected as a memorial or marker. [< Sc.Gael. *carn*.]

cairn

Cai·ro (kī′rō) The capital of Egypt, in the NE part on the Nile R.

cais·son (kā′sŏn′, -sən) ►*n.* **1.** A watertight structure within which construction work is carried on under water. **2.** See **camel** (sense 2). **3a.** A horse-drawn vehicle formerly used to carry artillery ammunition. **b.** A large ammunition box. [< OFr., large box.]

caisson disease ►*n.* See **decompression sickness**.

cai·tiff (kā′tĭf) ►*n.* A despicable coward. [< Lat. *captīvus*; see CAPTURE.] —**cai′tiff** *adj.*

ca·jole (kə-jōl′) ►*v.* **-joled, -jol·ing** To persuade, elicit, or obtain by flattery, gentle pleading, or insincere language. [Fr. *cajoler*.] —**ca·jol′er** *n.*

Ca·jun (kā′jən) ►*n.* A member of a group of people in S Louisiana descended from French colonists exiled from Acadia in the 1700s. [Alteration of ACADIAN.] —**Ca′jun** *adj.*

cake (kāk) ►*n.* **1.** A sweet baked food typically made of flour, liquid, and eggs. **2.** A flat mass of baked or fried batter. **3.** A flat mass of chopped food; patty. **4.** A shaped mass, as of soap or ice. **5.** A coat or crust: *a cake of grime in the oven.* ►*v.* **caked, cak·ing** To coat; encrust: *hands caked with mud.* [< ON *kaka*.]

cal ►*abbr.* calorie (small calorie)

Cal ►*abbr.* calorie (large calorie)

cal·a·bash (kăl′ə-băsh′) ►*n.* **1.** See **bottle gourd. 2.** A tropical American tree bearing hard-shelled, gourdlike fruits. **3.** The fruit of a calabash, often dried and hollowed for use as a utensil. [< Sp. *calabaza*, gourd.]

cal·a·boose (kăl′ə-bōōs′) ►*n. Regional* A jail. [< Sp. *calabozo*, dungeon.]

Ca·lais (kă-lā′, kăl′ā) A city of N France on the Strait of Dover opposite Dover, England.

ca·la·ma·ri (kä′lə-mä′rē, kăl′ə-mä′rē) ►*n.* Squid

that is prepared as food. [Ital.]

cal·a·mine (kăl′ə-mīn′, -mĭn) ►*n.* A pink powder of zinc oxide with a small amount of ferric oxide, used in skin lotions. [< Med.Lat. *calamīna*.]

ca·lam·i·ty (kə-lăm′ĭ-tē) ►*n., pl.* **-ties 1.** A disaster. **2.** Dire distress. [< Lat. *calamitās*.] —**ca·lam′i·tous** *adj.*

cal·car·e·ous (kăl-kâr′ē-əs) ►*adj.* Composed of or containing calcium carbonate, calcium, or limestone. [< Lat. *calx, calc-*, lime.]

cal·ces (kăl′sēz) ►*n.* Pl. of **calx**.

calci– or **calc–** ►*pref.* Calcium: *calciferous.* [< Lat. *calx, calc-*, lime.]

cal·cif·er·ous (kăl-sĭf′ər-əs) ►*adj.* Of or containing calcium or calcium carbonate.

cal·ci·fy (kăl′sə-fī′) ►*v.* **-fied, -fy·ing 1.** To make or become calcareous. **2.** To make or become inflexible. —**cal′ci·fi·ca′tion** *n.*

cal·ci·mine (kăl′sə-mīn′) ►*n.* Whitewash, or whitewash with zinc oxide or other pigments, formerly used as a coating for plaster walls and ceilings. [Orig. a trademark.]

cal·cine (kăl-sīn′, kăl′sīn′) ►*v.* **-cined, -cin·ing 1.** To heat (a substance) to a high temperature but below the melting or fusing point, causing loss of moisture, reduction, or oxidation. **2.** To convert to granular solids by drying at very high temperatures. [< LLat. *calcīna*, CALX.] —**cal′ci·na′tion** (-sə-nā′shən) *n.*

cal·cite (kăl′sīt′) ►*n.* A common crystalline form of natural calcium carbonate. —**cal·cit′ic** (-sĭt′ĭk) *adj.*

cal·ci·um (kăl′sē-əm) ►*n. Symbol* **Ca** A silvery metallic element that occurs in bone, shells, limestone, and gypsum and forms compounds used to make plaster, quicklime, cement, and metallurgic and electronic materials. At. no. 20. See table at **element**.

calcium carbonate ►*n.* A colorless or white crystalline compound, $CaCO_3$, occurring naturally as chalk, limestone, and marble, and used in commercial chalk, medicines, and dentifrices.

calcium chloride ►*n.* A white deliquescent solid, $CaCl_2$, used chiefly as a drying agent, antifreeze, and preservative and for controlling dust and ice on roads.

calcium hydroxide ►*n.* A soft white powder, $Ca(OH)_2$, used in making mortar, cements, calcium salts, paints, and petrochemicals.

calcium oxide ►*n.* A white, caustic, lumpy powder, CaO, used as a refractory, as a flux, in making steel, paper, and glass, and in waste treatment and insecticides.

cal·cu·late (kăl′kyə-lāt′) ►*v.* **-lat·ed, -lat·ing 1.** To compute mathematically. **2.** To estimate; evaluate: *calculated our chance of winning.* **3.** To make for a deliberate purpose; design: *a choice calculated to please.* **4.** *Regional* **a.** To suppose; guess. **b.** To depend; rely. [< Lat. *calculus*, small stone for counting.] —**cal′cu·la·ble** *adj.*

cal·cu·lat·ed (kăl′kyə-lā′tĭd) ►*adj.* Undertaken after careful forethought: *a calculated risk.* —**cal′cu·lat′ed·ly** *adv.*

cal·cu·lat·ing (kăl′kyə-lā′tĭng) ►*adj.* **1.** Shrewd; crafty. **2.** Coldly scheming.

cal·cu·la·tion (kăl′kyə-lā′shən) ►*n.* **1a.** The act, process, or result of calculating. **b.** A probable estimate. **2.** Careful, often cunning forethought.

THREE PRINCIPAL CALENDARS

In use throughout most of the modern world, the **Gregorian calendar** was first introduced in 1582 by Pope Gregory XIII. The **Jewish calendar** is used to mark the dates of annual religious events and is the official calendar of the Jewish religious community. The **Islamic calendar** is used to mark religious festivals and is the official calendar in many Muslim countries. It is reckoned from the year of the Hegira in AD 622.

Gregorian	Jewish	Islamic
The solar year of the Gregorian calendar consists of 365 days. Every fourth year is a leap year of 366 days except for centennial years not evenly divisible by 400.	The Jewish year consists of twelve months defined by lunar cycles, with some years having a thirteenth month so that seasonal festivals stay aligned with the solar year. For religious purposes Nisan is the first month, but the New Year is celebrated in Tishri.	The Islamic calendar is based on the lunar year and contains 354 or 355 days. The number of days in each month varies throughout the year with the lunar cycle.

Months	Number of Days	Months		Number of Days	Months	Number of Days
January	31	Nisan	(Mar.–Apr.)	30	Muharram	29 or 30
February	28	Iyar	(Apr.–May)	29	Safar	29 or 30
in leap year	29	Sivan	(May–Jun.)	30	Rabi I	29 or 30
March	31	Tammuz	(Jun.–Jul.)	29	Rabi II	29 or 30
April	30	Av	(Jul.–Aug.)	30	Jumada I	29 or 30
May	31	Elul	(Aug.–Sept.)	29	Jumada II	29 or 30
June	30	Tishri	(Sept.–Oct.)	30	Rajab	29 or 30
July	31	Heshvan	(Oct.–Nov.)	29 or 30	Sha'ban	29 or 30
August	31	Kislev	(Nov.–Dec.)	29 or 30	Ramadan	29 or 30
September	30	Tevet	(Dec.–Jan.)	30	Shawwal	29 or 30
October	31	Shevat	(Jan.–Feb.)	30	Dhu'l-Qa'dah	29 or 30
November	30	Adar	(Feb.–Mar.)	29 or 30	Dhu'l-Hijjah	29 or 30
December	31	Adar Sheni in leap year only		29		

cal·cu·la·tor (kăl′kyə-lā′tər) ►*n.* **1.** One who calculates. **2.** An electronic or mechanical device for the performance of mathematical computations.

cal·cu·lus (kăl′kyə-ləs) ►*n., pl.* **-li** (-lī′) or **-lus·es** **1.** *Med.* An abnormal mineral concretion in the body, as in the gallbladder or kidney; stone. **2.** *Dentistry* Tartar. **3.** *Math.* The mathematics of limits, instantaneous rates of change, and finding areas and volumes. [Lat., pebble.]

Cal·cut·ta (kăl-kŭt′ə) See **Kolkata.**

Cal·der (kôl′dər, kŏl′-), **Alexander** 1898–1976. Amer. sculptor.

cal·de·ra (kăl-dâr′ə, -dîr′ə, kôl-) ►*n.* A large crater formed by volcanic processes. [Sp. < LLat. *caldāria*, cauldron.]

cal·en·dar (kăl′ən-dər) ►*n.* **1.** Any of various systems of reckoning the length and divisions of a year. **2.** A table showing the months, weeks, and days of a year. **3.** A chronological list. ►*v.* To enter in a calendar. [< Lat. *kalendārium*, moneylender's account book.] —**ca·len′dri·cal** (kə-lĕn′drĭ-kəl), **ca·len′dric** *adj.*

cal·en·der (kăl′ən-dər) ►*n.* A machine in which paper or cloth is made smooth and glossy by being pressed through rollers. [< Gk. *kulindros*, roller.] —**cal′en·der** *v.*

cal·ends (kăl′əndz, kā′ləndz) ►*n., pl.* **-ends** The first day of the month in the ancient Roman calendar. [< Lat. *kalendae.*]

calf[1] (kăf) ►*n., pl.* **calves** (kăvz) **1a.** A young cow or bull. **b.** The young of certain other mam-

mals, such as the elephant or whale. **2.** Calfskin. **3.** A large floating chunk of ice split off from a glacier, iceberg, or floe. [< OE *cealf.*]

calf[2] (kăf) ►*n., pl.* **calves** (kăvz) The fleshy muscular back of the human leg between the knee and ankle. [< ON *kálfi.*]

calf·skin (kăf′skĭn′) ►*n.* Fine leather made from the hide of a calf.

Cal·ga·ry (kăl′gə-rē) A city of S Alberta, Canada, S of Edmonton.

Cal·houn (kăl-hōōn′), **John Caldwell** 1782–1850. Vice president of the US (1825–32).

cal·i·ber (kăl′ə-bər) ►*n.* **1a.** The diameter of the inside of a round cylinder, esp. the bore of a firearm. **b.** The diameter of a bullet or projectile. **2.** Degree of worth; quality. [Fr. *calibre.*]

cal·i·brate (kăl′ə-brāt′) ►*v.* **-brat·ed, -brat·ing** **1.** To check or adjust the graduations of (a quantitative measuring instrument). **2.** To determine the caliber of. **3.** To make corrections in; adjust. —**cal′i·bra′tion** *n.*

cal·i·bre (kăl′ə-bər) ►*n. Chiefly Brit.* Var. of **caliber.**

cal·i·co (kăl′ĭ-kō′) ►*n., pl.* **-coes** or **-cos** **1.** A tightly woven cotton cloth having a repeating, often floral design. **2.** A cat having a white coat mottled with red and black. [< *Calicut*, India.] —**cal′i·co** *adj.*

Cal·i·for·nia (kăl′ĭ-fôr′nyə, -fôr′nē-ə) A state of the W US on the Pacific. Cap. Sacramento. —**Cal′i·for′nian** *adj. & n.*

California, Gulf of An arm of the Pacific in

NW Mexico separating Baja California from the mainland.

California condor ►*n.* A very large, nearly extinct vulture of S California.

California poppy ►*n.* A plant of W North America having showy, often orange or yellow flowers.

cal·i·for·ni·um (kăl′ə-fôr′nē-əm) ►*n. Symbol* **Cf** A synthetic radioactive element. At. no. 98. See table at **element**. [< CALIFORNIA.]

Ca·lig·u·la (kə-lĭg′yə-lə) AD 12–41. Emperor of Rome (37–41).

cal·i·per also **cal·li·per** (kăl′ə-pər) ►*n.* **1.** often **calipers** An instrument consisting of two curved hinged legs, used to measure thickness and distances. **2.** A vernier caliper. [Alteration of CALIBER.]

ca·liph also **ca·lif** (kā′lĭf, kăl′ĭf) ►*n.* A leader of an Islamic polity, regarded as a successor of Muhammad. [< Ar. ḫalīfa.] —**ca′liph·ate′** (-fāt′, -fĭt) *n.*

cal·is·then·ics (kăl′ĭs-thĕn′ĭks) ►*n. (takes pl. v.)* Gymnastic exercises designed to develop muscular tone and promote physical well-being. [Gk. *kallos,* beauty + *sthenos,* strength.] —**cal′is·then′ic** *adj.*

calk (kôk) ►*v.* Var. of **caulk**.

call (kôl) ►*v.* **called, call·ing** **1.** To cry or utter loudly or clearly: *call out her name.* **2.** To summon: *call him to the podium.* **3.** To telephone: *call my uncle in Peoria.* **4.** To name; designate: *Don't call me a liar.* **5.** To consider; estimate: *Would you call him an expert?* **6.** To pay a brief visit: *call at the neighbors' house.* **7.** To demand payment of (a loan or bond issue). **8.** *Sports* **a.** To stop or postpone (a game), as for bad weather. **b.** To declare an umpire or referee: *call a runner out.* **9.** To indicate accurately in advance: *call the outcome of an election.* **10.** To challenge: *call her on her grandiose claims; call him on his bad behavior.* ►*n.* **1.** A loud cry; shout. **2.** The characteristic cry of an animal. **3.** A telephone communication. **4.** Demand; occasion: *There's no call for haste.* **5.** A short visit. **6.** A summons or invitation. **7.** A strong urge or prompting. **8.** *Sports* A decision made by an umpire or referee. **9.** A demand for payment, as of a debt. —*phrasal verbs:* **call down** To reprimand. **call for 1.** To stop for: *I'll call for you on my way home.* **2.** To warrant. **call forth** To evoke. **call in 1.** To take out of circulation: *calling in silver dollars.* **2.** To summon for assistance or consultation. **call off 1.** To cancel or postpone. **2.** To restrain: *Call off your dogs!* **call out** To cause to assemble; summon. **call up 1.** To summon to military service. **2.** To bring to mind. **call upon 1.** To order; require: *I call upon you to tell the truth.* **2.** To make a demand or appeal on. —*idioms:* **call it a day** *Informal* To stop one's work for the day; quit. **call it quits** *Informal* To leave off; quit. **call the shots** *Informal* To be in charge. **call to mind** To remind of. **on call 1.** Available when summoned. **2.** Payable on demand. **within call** Accessible. [< ON *kalla.*] —**call′er** *n.*

Syns: assemble, convene, convoke, muster, summon v.

cal·la lily (kăl′ə) ►*n.* Any of several ornamental plants cultivated for their showy, usu. white, yellow, pink, or purple spathes. [Perh. < Gk. *kallos,* beauty.]

caller ID ►*n.* A telephone service that displays an incoming caller's name and telephone number.

cal·lig·ra·phy (kə-lĭg′rə-fē) ►*n.* The art of fine handwriting. [< Gk. *kallos,* beautiful + –GRA-PHY.] —**cal·lig′ra·pher, cal·lig′ra·phist** *n.* —**cal′li·graph′ic** (kăl′ĭ-grăf′ĭk) *adj.*

calligraphy

call-in (kôl′ĭn′) ►*adj.* Inviting listeners or viewers to participate in a program by means of broadcasted phone calls.

call·ing (kô′lĭng) ►*n.* **1.** An inner urge; strong impulse. **2.** An occupation; vocation.

calling card ►*n.* **1.** An engraved card bearing one's full name. **2.** A phone card.

cal·li·o·pe (kə-lī′ə-pē′, kăl′ē-ōp′) ►*n.* A musical instrument fitted with steam whistles, played from a keyboard. [< *Calliope,* muse of epic poetry.]

cal·li·per (kăl′ə-pər) ►*n.* Var. of **caliper**.

call letters ►*pl.n.* The identifying code letters or numbers of a radio or television station.

call loan ►*n.* A loan repayable on demand at any time.

call number ►*n.* A number used in libraries to classify a book and indicate its location on the shelves.

cal·los·i·ty (kə-lŏs′ĭ-tē) ►*n., pl.* **-ties 1.** The condition of being calloused. **2.** Hardheartedness; insensitivity. **3.** See **callus**.

cal·lous (kăl′əs) ►*adj.* **1.** Having calluses; toughened. **2.** Emotionally hardened; unfeeling: *a callous indifference to suffering.* ►*v.* To make or become callous. [< Lat. *callum,* callus.] —**cal′-lous·ly** *adv.* —**cal′lous·ness** *n.*

cal·low (kăl′ō) ►*adj.* Lacking experience; immature: *a callow youth.* [< OE *calu,* bald.]

call-up (kôl′ŭp′) ►*n.* The summoning of reserve military personnel to active service.

cal·lus (kăl′əs) ►*n., pl.* **-lus·es** A localized thickening and enlargement of the horny layer of the skin. [Lat.] —**cal′lus** *v.*

call waiting ►*n.* A telephone service that alerts someone using the phone to an incoming call and allows switching between calls.

calm (käm) ►*adj.* **-er, -est 1.** Nearly or completely motionless; undisturbed: *calm seas.* **2.** Not excited or agitated; composed: *a calm voice.* ►*n.* **1.** An absence of motion; stillness. **2.** Serenity; peace. ►*v.* To make or become calm. [< LLat. *cauma,* heat of the day.] —**calm′ly** *adv.* —**calm′ness** *n.*

calm·a·tive (kä′mə-tĭv, kăl′mə-) ►*adj.* Having sedative properties. ►*n.* A sedative.

cal·o·mel (kăl′ə-mĕl′, -məl) ►*n.* A usu. white tasteless compound, Hg_2Cl_2, used as a purgative and insecticide. [NLat. *kalomelas*.]

ca·lor·ic (kə-lôr′ĭk, -lŏr′-) ►*adj.* **1.** Of or relating to heat. **2.** Of or relating to calories.

cal·o·rie (kăl′ə-rē) ►*n.* **1.** A unit of heat equal to the amount of heat required to raise the temperature of 1 gram of water by 1°C at 1 atmosphere pressure; small calorie. **2a.** A unit of heat equal to the amount of heat required to raise the temperature of 1 kilogram of water by 1°C at 1 atmosphere pressure; large calorie. **b.** A unit of energy-producing potential equal to this amount of heat that is contained in food. [< Lat. *calor*, heat.]

cal·o·rif·ic (kăl′ə-rĭf′ĭk) ►*adj.* Of or generating heat or calories.

cal·o·rim·e·ter (kăl′ə-rĭm′ĭ-tər) ►*n.* An apparatus for measuring the heat generated by a chemical reaction or change of state.

cal·u·met (kăl′yə-mĕt′, kăl′yə-mĕt′) ►*n.* A long-stemmed ceremonial tobacco pipe used by certain Native American peoples. [< Fr. dial., straw.]

ca·lum·ni·ate (kə-lŭm′nē-āt′) ►*v.* **-at·ed, -at·ing** To slander or malign. —**ca·lum′ni·a′tion** *n.* —**ca·lum′ni·a′tor** *n.*

cal·um·ny (kăl′əm-nē) ►*n., pl.* **-nies** **1.** A false statement maliciously made to injure another's reputation. **2.** The utterance of maliciously false statements; slander. [< Lat. *calumnia*.] —**ca·lum′ni·ous** (kə-lŭm′nē-əs) *adj.*

Cal·va·ry (kăl′və-rē) also **Gol·go·tha** (gŏl′gə-thə, gŏl-gŏth′ə) A hill outside ancient Jerusalem where Jesus was crucified.

calve (kăv) ►*v.* **calved, calv·ing** **1.** To give birth to a calf. **2.** To break at an edge. Used of a glacier.

calves (kăvz) ►*n.* Pl. of **calf.**

Cal·vin (kăl′vĭn), **John** 1509–64. French-born Swiss theologian. —**Cal′vin·ism′** *n.* —**Cal′vin·ist** *adj. & n.*

calx (kălks) ►*n., pl.* **-es** or **cal·ces** (kăl′sēz′) **1.** The residue left after a mineral or metal has been calcined. **2.** Calcium oxide. [< Gk. *khalix*, pebble.]

Ca·lyp·so or **ca·lyp·so** (kə-lĭp′sō) ►*n., pl.* **-sos** also **-soes** A type of West Indian music with improvised lyrics on topical or broadly humorous subjects. [?] —**Ca·lyp·so′ni·an** (kə-lĭp-sō′nē-ən, kăl′ĭp-) *n.*

ca·lyx (kā′lĭks, kăl′ĭks) ►*n., pl.* **-es** or **ca·ly·ces** (kā′lĭ-sēz′, kăl′ĭ-) The outermost part of a flower, consisting of the sepals. [< Gk. *kalux*.]

cal·zo·ne (kăl-zō′nē, -zōn′) ►*n.* A baked turnover filled with vegetables, meat, or cheese. [Ital., pant leg, calzone.]

cam (kăm) ►*n.* A wheel that has a projecting part and is mounted on a rotating shaft to produce variable or reciprocating motion in another part. [Du. *kam*, cog, comb.]

ca·ma·ra·der·ie (kä′mə-rä′də-rē, kăm′ə-răd′ə-) ►*n.* Spirited goodwill among friends. [Fr.]

cam·ber (kăm′bər) ►*n.* **1.** A slightly arched surface, as of a road. **2.** A setting of automobile wheels in which they are closer together at the bottom than at the top. [< Lat. *camur*, curved.] —**cam′ber** *v.*

cam·bi·um (kăm′bē-əm) ►*n.* A layer of soft growing tissue in a plant body that develops into new bark and new wood and produces the annual rings. [< Med.Lat., exchange.]

Cam·bo·di·a (kăm-bō′dē-ə) A country of SE Asia on the Gulf of Thailand. Cap. Phnom Penh. —**Cam·bo′di·an** *adj. & n.*

Cam·bri·an (kăm′brē-ən, kăm′-) *Geol.* ►*adj.* Of or being the oldest period of the Paleozoic Era, marked by the development of most modern animal phyla. ►*n.* The Cambrian Period.

cam·bric (kām′brĭk) ►*n.* A fine white linen or cotton fabric. [< *Cambrai*, France.]

Cam·bridge (kām′brĭj) **1.** A city of E-central England NNE of London. **2.** A city of E MA on the Charles R. opposite Boston.

cam·cord·er (kăm′kôr′dər) ►*n.* A lightweight, hand-held video camera.

came (kām) ►*v.* P.t. of **come.**

cam·el (kăm′əl) ►*n.* **1.** A humped, long-necked ruminant mammal domesticated in Old World desert regions as a beast of burden. **2.** A hollow, watertight device used to raise sunken objects. [< Gk. *kamēlos*.]

cam·el·hair (kăm′əl-hâr′) also **cam·el's hair** (kăm′əlz) ►*n.* **1.** The soft fine hair of the camel or a substitute for it. **2.** A soft, heavy, usu. light tan cloth, made chiefly of camelhair.

ca·mel·lia (kə-mēl′yə) ►*n.* Any of a genus of evergreen Asian shrubs having showy, usu. red, white, or pink roselike flowers. [After Georg Josef *Kamel* (1661–1706).]

Cam·e·lot (kăm′ə-lŏt′) ►*n.* **1.** The legendary site of King Arthur's court. **2.** A place or time of idealized beauty and enlightenment.

cam·e·o (kăm′ē-ō′) ►*n., pl.* **-os** **1.** A gem or medallion with a design cut in raised relief, usu. of a contrasting color. **2.** A brief appearance of a prominent actor or celebrity, as in a single scene. [Ital.]

cam·er·a (kăm′ər-ə, kăm′rə) ►*n.* A usu. portable device containing a photosensitive surface that records images through a lens. [LLat., room.]

cam·er·a·man (kăm′ər-ə-măn′, kăm′rə-) ►*n.* A man who operates a movie or television camera. See Usage Note at **man.**

Cam·er·on (kăm′ər-ən, kăm′rən), **David William Donald** b. 1966. British prime minister (appointed 2010).

Cam·e·roon (kăm′ə-rōōn′) also **Came·roun** (kăm-rōōn′) A country of W-central Africa on the Gulf of Guinea. Cap. Yaoundé.

cam·i·sole (kăm′ĭ-sōl′) ►*n.* A woman's sleeveless undergarment or shirt with narrow straps. [< LLat. *camisa*, shirt.]

cam·o·mile (kăm′ə-mīl′, -mēl′) ►*n.* Var. of **chamomile.**

cam·ou·flage (kăm′ə-fläzh′, -fläj′) ►*n.* A means of concealment or a disguise that creates the effect of being part of the natural surroundings. ►*v.* **-flaged, -flag·ing** **1.** To conceal by camouflage. **2.** To mask. See Synonyms at **disguise.** [< Ital. *camuffare*, to disguise.] —**cam′ou·flag′er** *n.*

camp¹ (kămp) ►*n.* **1a.** A place of temporary residence or shelter, as for soldiers or travelers. **b.** The shelters, such as tents or cabins, at such a place. **2.** A usu. rural place offering organized recreation or instruction. **3.** A prison camp or concentration camp. **4.** A group sharing a common cause or opinion. ►*v.* To set up or live in a camp. [< Lat. *campus*, field.]

camp² (kămp) ►*n.* Deliberate affectation or exaggeration of style, esp. of popular or outdated style, for ironic effect. ►*adj.* Showing or characterized by camp. ►*v.* To act in a camp manner. [?] **—camp′y** *adj.*

cam·paign (kăm-pān′) ►*n.* **1.** A series of military operations undertaken to achieve a large-scale objective during a war. **2.** An organized operation to accomplish a purpose: *an ad campaign; a political campaign.* ►*v.* To engage in a campaign. [< LLat. *campānia,* battlefield.] **—cam·paign′er** *n.*

cam·pa·ni·le (kăm′pə-nē′lē) ►*n.* An often freestanding bell tower. [< LLat. *campāna,* bell.]

campanile
Campanile di Giotto, Florence, Italy

camp·er (kăm′pər) ►*n.* **1.** One who camps or attends a camp. **2.** A motor vehicle equipped, as with a rear compartment or attached trailer, for sleeping and housekeeping, used for recreational travel.

camp·fire (kămp′fīr′) ►*n.* An outdoor fire in a camp, used for cooking or warmth.

camp·ground (kămp′ground′) ►*n.* An area for camping, esp. one containing individual campsites.

cam·phor (kăm′fər) ►*n.* A natural aromatic compound used in the manufacture of film and plastics and as a topical medicine. [< Ar. *kāfūr.*] **—cam′phor·at′ed** (-fə-rā′tĭd) *adj.*

camp meeting ►*n.* An evangelistic gathering held in a tent or outdoors.

camp·site (kămp′sīt′) ►*n.* An area suitable or used for camping.

cam·pus (kăm′pəs) ►*n., pl.* **-pus·es** The grounds of a school, college, university, or hospital. [Lat., field.]

cam·shaft (kăm′shăft′) ►*n.* An engine shaft fitted with a cam or cams.

Ca·mus (kä-mōō′, -mü′), **Albert** 1913–60. Algerian-born French writer and philosopher.

can¹ (kăn; kən *when unstressed*) ►*aux.v. P.t.* **could** (kŏŏd) **1.** Used to indicate: **a.** Physical or mental ability: *I can carry both suitcases.* **b.** Possession of a power, right, or privilege: *The President can veto bills.* **c.** Possession of a capability or skill: *I can tune a piano.* **2.** Used to indicate: **a.** Possibility or probability: *I wonder if I could be sick.* **b.** That which is permitted, as by conscience or feelings: *I can hardly blame you for laughing.* **3.** *Informal* Used to request or grant permission. [< OE *cunnan,* know how.]

Usage: Technically, *may* is used to express permission and *can* to express the capacity to do something. Although *can* has a long history of use by educated speakers to express permission, observance of the distinction is often advisable in the interests of clarity.

can² (kăn) ►*n.* **1.** A usu. cylindrical metal container. **2a.** An airtight storage container, usu. made of tin-coated iron and used esp. for foods. **b.** The contents of a can: *ate a can of beans.* **3.** *Slang* A jail. **4.** *Slang* A toilet. ►*v.* **canned, can·ning 1.** To seal in a can or jar; preserve. **2.** *Slang* To dismiss; fire. See Synonyms at **dismiss. 3.** *Slang* To put a stop to: *Can the chatter.* [< OE *canne,* water container.] **—can′ner** *n.*

Ca·naan (kā′nən) An ancient region made up of Palestine or the part of it between the Jordan R. and the Mediterranean. **—Ca′naan·ite′** *adj. & n.*

Can·a·da (kăn′ə-də) A country of N North America. Cap. Ottawa. **—Ca·na′di·an** (kə-nā′dē-ən) *adj. & n.*

Canada Day ►*n.* July 1, observed in Canada in commemoration of the formation of the Dominion in 1867.

Canada goose or **Canadian goose** ►*n.* A large wild goose of North America, having grayish plumage, a black neck and head, and a white throat patch.

Canadian French ►*n.* The French language as used in Canada.

ca·naille (kə-nī′, -nāl′) ►*n.* The common people. [< Ital. *canaglia* < Lat. *canis,* dog.]

ca·nal (kə-năl′) ►*n.* **1.** An artificial waterway used for travel, shipping, or irrigation. **2.** *Anat.* A tube or duct. [< Lat. *canālis,* channel.] **—can′al·i·za′tion** (kăn′ə-lĭ-zā′shən) *n.* **—can′al·ize′** *v.*

can·a·pé (kăn′ə-pā′, -pē) ►*n.* A cracker or small piece of bread topped with cheese, meat, or a spread. [Fr., couch, canapé.]

ca·nard (kə-närd′) ►*n.* An unfounded or false, deliberately misleading story. [Fr.]

ca·nar·y (kə-nâr′ē) ►*n., pl.* **-ies 1.** A small, greenish to yellow finch often kept as a pet. **2.** A sweet white wine. **3.** A light to vivid yellow. [After the CANARY ISLANDS.]

Canary Islands A group of Spanish islands in the Atlantic off the NW coast of Africa.

ca·nas·ta (kə-năs′tə) ►*n.* A card game related to rummy and requiring two decks of cards. [Sp. < *canasto,* basket.]

Can·ber·ra (kăn′bər-ə, -bĕr′ə) The capital of Australia, in the SE part.

can·can (kăn′kăn′) ►*n.* An exuberant dance marked by high kicking. [Fr.]

can·cel (kăn′səl) ►*v.* **-celed, -cel·ing** also **-celled, -cel·ling 1.** To annul or invalidate. **2a.** To cross out with lines or other markings. **b.** To mark or perforate (e.g., a postage stamp or check) to insure against further use. **3.** To counteract; offset. **4.** *Math.* **a.** To remove (a common factor) from the numerator and denominator of a fractional expression. **b.** To remove (a common factor or term) from both sides of an equation or inequality. [< Lat. *cancellus,* lattice.] **—can′cel·a·ble** *adj.* **—can′cel·er** *n.* **—can′cel·la′tion** *n.*

can·cer (kăn′sər) ►*n.* **1a.** A malignant tumor that tends to invade surrounding tissue and spread to new body sites. **b.** The condition characterized by such growths. **2.** A pernicious, spreading evil. [< Lat.] **—can′cer·ous** (-sər-əs) *adj.*

Can·cer (kăn′sər) ►*n.* **1.** A constellation in the Northern Hemisphere. **2.** The 4th sign of the zodiac. [< Lat.]

can·del·a (kăn-dĕl′ə) ►*n.* A unit of luminous intensity equal to ¹⁄₆₀ of the luminous intensity per square cm of a blackbody radiating at the temperature of 2,046°K. [Lat. *candēla*, candle.]

can·de·la·bra (kăn′dl-ä′brə, -ăb′rə, -ä′brə) ►*n.* A candelabrum. [Lat. *candēlābra*, pl. of *candēlābrum*.]

can·de·la·brum (kăn′dl-ä′brəm, -ăb′rəm, -ä′brəm) ►*n., pl.* **-bra** (-brə) or **-brums** A large decorative candlestick having several arms or branches. [Lat. *candēlābrum*.]

can·des·cence (kăn-dĕs′əns) ►*n.* The state of being white hot; incandescence. [< Lat. *candēre*, shine.] —**can·des′cent** *adj.*

can·did (kăn′dĭd) ►*adj.* **1.** Direct and frank; straightforward: *my candid opinion.* **2.** Not posed or rehearsed: *a candid snapshot.* [Lat. *candidus*, white, pure < *candēre*, shine.] —**can′did·ly** *adv.* —**can′did·ness** *n.*

can·di·date (kăn′dĭ-dāt′, -dĭt) ►*n.* One that seeks or is nominated for an office, position, or honor. [Lat. *candidātus*, clothed in white.] —**can′di·da·cy** (-də-sē), **can′di·da·ture′** *n.*

can·dle (kăn′dl) ►*n.* A solid, usu. cylindrical mass of tallow, wax, or other fatty substance with an embedded wick that is burned to provide light. ►*v.* **-dled, -dling** To examine (an egg) in front of a bright light. [< Lat. *candēla* < *candēre*, shine.] —**can′dler** *n.*

can·dle·light (kăn′dl-līt′) ►*n.* Illumination from a candle or candles.

can·dle·pin (kăn′dl-pĭn′) ►*n.* **1.** A slender bowling pin used with a smaller ball in a variation of the game of tenpins. **2. candlepins** *(takes sing. v.)* A bowling game played with such pins.

can·dle·pow·er (kăn′dl-pou′ər) ►*n.* Luminous intensity expressed in candelas.

can·dle·stick (kăn′dl-stĭk′) ►*n.* A holder with a cup or spike for a candle.

can·dor (kăn′dər) ►*n.* Frankness or sincerity of expression. [< Lat. < *candēre*, shine.]

C & W ►*abbr.* country and western

can·dy (kăn′dē) ►*n., pl.* **-dies** A sweet confection made with sugar and often with fruits or nuts. ►*v.* **-died, -dy·ing** To cook, preserve, saturate, or coat with sugar or syrup. [Ult. < Ar. *qand*, cane sugar.]

candy cane ►*n.* A usu. striped stick of peppermint candy with the top curved to resemble a walking cane.

candy striper ►*n.* A usu. young volunteer worker in a hospital.

can·dy·tuft (kăn′dē-tŭft′) ►*n.* Any of several plants with white, pink, red, or purple flowers. [Obsolete *Candy*, Crete + TUFT.]

cane (kān) ►*n.* **1a.** A slender, strong but often flexible stem, as of certain bamboos or reeds. **b.** A plant with such a stem. **c.** Interwoven strips of such stems, esp. rattan. **3.** Sugar cane. **3.** A walking stick or similar rod. ►*v.* **caned, can·ing 1.** To make or repair with cane. **2.** To hit or beat with a rod. [< Gk. *kanna*, reed.]

cane·brake (kān′brāk′) ►*n.* A dense thicket of cane.

cane sugar ►*n.* Sucrose obtained from sugar cane.

ca·nine (kā′nīn) ►*adj.* **1.** Of or belonging to the family of carnivorous mammals that includes dogs, jackals, foxes, and wolves. **2.** Of or being one of the pointed conical teeth between the incisors and bicuspids. ►*n.* **1.** A canine animal, esp. a dog. **2.** A canine tooth; cuspid. [< Lat. *canis*, dog.]

Ca·nis Major (kā′nĭs, kăn′ĭs) ►*n.* A constellation in the Southern Hemisphere containing the star Sirius.

Canis Minor ►*n.* A constellation in the Southern Hemisphere.

can·is·ter (kăn′ĭ-stər) ►*n.* A usu. cylindrical metal, glass, or plastic container. [< Gk. *kanastron*, reed basket.]

can·ker (kăng′kər) ►*n.* Ulceration of the mouth and lips. [< Lat. *cancer*.] —**can′ker·ous** *adj.*

canker sore ►*n.* A small painful ulcer or sore, usu. of the mouth.

can·na (kăn′ə) ►*n.* Any of various tropical plants having large, showy red or yellow flowers. [Lat. *canna*, CANE.]

can·na·bis (kăn′ə-bĭs) ►*n.* **1.** A tall Asian plant having palmate leaves and tough bast fibers. **2.** A mildly euphoriant, intoxicating hallucinogenic drug, such as hashish or marijuana, prepared from this plant. [< Gk. *kannabis*.]

canned (kănd) ►*adj.* **1.** Preserved and sealed in an airtight can or jar. **2.** *Informal* Recorded or taped: *canned laughter.*

can·ner·y (kăn′ə-rē) ►*n., pl.* **-ies** A factory where fish or other foods are canned.

can·ni·bal (kăn′ə-bəl) ►*n.* **1.** A person who eats the flesh of other humans. **2.** An animal that feeds on others of its own kind. [< Carib *karibna*, Carib (allegedly cannibalistic).] —**can′ni·bal·ism** *n.* —**can′ni·bal·is′tic** *adj.*

can·ni·bal·ize (kăn′ə-bə-līz′) ►*v.* **-ized, -iz·ing 1.** To practice cannibalism on. **2.** To remove serviceable parts from (e.g., damaged vehicles) for use in the repair of other equipment of the same kind. —**can′ni·bal·i·za′tion** *n.*

can·no·li (kə-nō′lē, kä-) ►*n.* A fried pastry roll with a sweet creamy filling. [Ital.]

can·non (kăn′ən) ►*n., pl.* **-non** or **-nons** A large mounted weapon, such as a gun or howitzer, that fires heavy projectiles. [< OItal. *cannone*.] —**can′non·eer′** *n.*

Cannon, Annie Jump 1863–1941. Amer. astronomer.

Annie Jump Cannon
photographed c. 1922

can·non·ade (kăn′ə-nād′) ►*n.* An extended discharge of artillery. —**can′non·ade′** *v.*

can·non·ball (kăn′ən-bôl′) ►*n.* **1.** A round projectile fired from a cannon. **2.** A jump into water made with the arms grasping the upraised knees. **—can′non·ball′** *v.*

can·not (kăn′ŏt, kə-nŏt′, kă-) ►*aux.v.* The negative form of **can**[1].

can·nu·la (kăn′yə-lə) ►*n., pl.* **-las** or **-lae** (-lē′) A flexible tube inserted into a body cavity or vessel to drain fluid or administer a medication. [Lat., small tube < *canna*, reed.]

can·ny (kăn′ē) ►*adj.* **-ni·er, -ni·est** **1.** Careful and shrewd. **2.** Thrifty; frugal. [< CAN[1].] **—can′ni·ly** *adv.* **—can′ni·ness** *n.*

ca·noe (kə-nōō′) ►*n.* A light slender boat that has pointed ends and is propelled by paddles. ►*v.* **-noed, -noe·ing** To travel by canoe. [< Sp. *canoa*, of Cariban orig.] **—ca·noe′ist** *n.*

ca·no·la (kə-nō′lə) ►*n.* A variety of the rape plant that yields an oil high in monounsaturated fatty acids. [*Can(ada) o(il,) l(ow) a(cid).*]

can·on[1] (kăn′ən) ►*n.* **1.** A code of laws established by a church council. **2.** A standard list of works considered authentic or exemplary. **3.** The books of the Bible officially accepted by a Christian church. **4.** *Mus.* A composition in which the melody is repeated by successive overlapping voices. [< Gk. *kanōn*, rule.] **—ca·non′i·cal** (kə-nŏn′ĭ-kəl) *adj.*

can·on[2] (kăn′ən) ►*n.* A member of the clergy serving in a cathedral or collegiate church. [< LLat. *canōnicus* < *canōn*, CANON[1].]

canonical hours ►*pl.n.* **1.** The times of day at which canon law prescribes certain prayers to be said. **2.** The prayers said at these times.

can·on·ize (kăn′ə-nīz′) ►*v.* **-ized, -iz·ing** **1.** To declare (a deceased person) a saint. **2.** To exalt; glorify. **—can′on·i·za′tion** *n.*

canon law ►*n.* The body of official rules governing a church or other religious denomination.

can·o·py (kăn′ə-pē) ►*n., pl.* **-pies** **1.** A usu. cloth covering suspended over a throne or bed or held aloft on poles, as over a monarch. **2.** *Archit.* An ornamental rooflike structure. **3.** An awning over a walkway or door. **4.** *Ecol.* The uppermost layer in a forest, formed by the crowns of the trees. **5.** A transparent enclosure over an aircraft cockpit. [< Gk. *kōnōpeion*, bed with mosquito netting.] **—can′o·py** *v.*

canopy

canst (kănst) ►*aux.v.* *Archaic* 2nd pers. sing. pr.t. of **can**[1].

cant[1] (kănt) ►*n.* **1.** Angular deviation from a vertical or horizontal plane or surface. **2.** A slanted or oblique surface. **3.** A thrust or motion that tilts something. ►*v.* To slant or tilt. [< Lat. *canthus*, rim of a wheel.]

cant[2] (kănt) ►*n.* **1.** Insincere speech full of platitudes or pious expressions. **2.** The special vocabulary peculiar to the members of a group. **3.** Whining or singsong speech, such as that of

beggars. ►*v.* **1.** To speak sententiously. **2.** To whine or plead. [< Lat. *cantāre*, sing.]

can't (kănt) Cannot.

can·ta·bi·le (kän-tä′bĭ-lā′) ►*adv. Mus.* In a smooth, lyrical, flowing style. [< Lat. *cantāre*, sing.] **—can·ta′bi·le′** *adj. & n.*

can·ta·loupe also **can·ta·loup** (kăn′tl-ōp′) ►*n.* A melon with a rough tan rind and orange flesh. [Fr. *cantaloup*.]

can·tan·ker·ous (kăn-tăng′kər-əs) ►*adj.* Ill-tempered and quarrelsome. [Perh. < ME *contek*, dissension.] **—can·tan′ker·ous·ly** *adv.* **—can·tan′ker·ous·ness** *n.*

can·ta·ta (kən-tä′tə) ►*n. Mus.* An often sacred composition comprising recitatives, arias, and choruses. [Ital.]

can·teen (kăn-tēn′) ►*n.* **1a.** A snack bar or small cafeteria. **b.** A store for on-base military personnel. **2.** An institutional recreation hall or social club. **3.** A temporary or mobile eating place, esp. one set up in an emergency. **4.** A flask for carrying drinking water. [< Ital. *cantina*, wine cellar.]

can·ter (kăn′tər) ►*n.* A smooth gait, esp. of a horse, slower than a gallop but faster than a trot. [< *Canterbury gallop*.] **—can′ter** *v.*

Can·ter·bur·y (kăn′tər-bĕr′ē, -brē, -tə-) A city of SE England ESE of London; site of Canterbury Cathedral.

can·thus (kăn′thəs) ►*n., pl.* **-thi** (-thī′) The angle formed by the meeting of the upper and lower eyelids. [< Gk. *kanthos.*]

can·ti·cle (kăn′tĭ-kəl) ►*n.* A liturgical chant. [< Lat. *canticulum*, dim. of *cantus*, song.]

can·ti·le·ver (kăn′tl-ē′vər, -ĕv′ər) ►*n.* A structure, such as a beam, that projects out horizontally beyond the point at which it is supported. [Poss. CANT[1] + LEVER.] **—can′ti·le′ver** *v.*

can·ti·na (kăn-tē′nə) ►*n. Regional* A bar that serves liquor. [< Ital., wine cellar.]

can·tle (kăn′tl) ►*n.* The raised rear part of a saddle. [< Med.Lat. *cantellus.*]

can·to (kăn′tō) ►*n., pl.* **-tos** One of the principal divisions of a long poem. [< Lat. *cantus*, song.]

can·ton (kăn′tən, -tŏn′) ►*n.* **1.** A small territorial division of a country, esp. one of the states of Switzerland. **2.** A usu. rectangular area in the upper corner of a flag, next to the staff. [< OItal. *cantone*, corner.] **—can′ton·al** *adj.*

Can·ton (kăn′tŏn, kăn′tŏn′) See **Guangzhou.**

can·ton·ment (kăn-tōn′mənt, -tŏn′-) ►*n.* **1.** Temporary quarters for troops. **2.** Assignment of troops to temporary quarters.

can·tor (kăn′tər) ►*n.* **1.** The Jewish religious official who leads the musical part of a service. **2.** A precentor. [Lat., singer < *canere*, sing.] **—can·to′ri·al** (kăn-tôr′ē-əl, -tŏr′-) *adj.*

Ca·nute (kə-nōōt′, -nyōōt′) 994?–1035. King of England (1016–35), Denmark (1018–35), and Norway (1028–35).

can·vas (kăn′vəs) ►*n.* **1.** A heavy, closely woven fabric of cotton, hemp, or flax, used for tents and sails. **2.** A piece of such fabric on which a painting is executed. **3.** Sails. **4.** The floor of a boxing or wrestling ring. [< Lat. *cannabis*, hemp.]

can·vas·back (kăn′vəs-băk′) ►*n.* A North American duck having a reddish-brown head and neck and a whitish back in the male.

can·vass (kăn′vəs) ►*v.* **1.** To scrutinize. **2a.** To go through (a region) in order to solicit votes or orders. **b.** To conduct a survey. ►*n.* **1.** An examination or discussion. **2.** A solicitation of votes, sales, orders, or opinions. [< obsolete *canvas*, to toss in a canvas sheet as punishment.] **—can′vass·er** *n.*

can·yon (kăn′yən) ►*n.* A narrow chasm with steep cliff walls. [Sp. *cañon.*]

cap (kăp) ►*n.* **1.** A usu. soft and close-fitting head covering, with or without a visor. **2.** A protective cover or seal, esp. one that closes off an end or tip: *a bottle cap.* **3.** An upper limit; ceiling. **4.** The top part of a mushroom. **5a.** A percussion cap. **b.** A small explosive charge enclosed in paper for use in a toy gun. ►*v.* **capped, cap·ping 1.** To cover or seal with a cap. **2.** To lie on top of: *hills capped with snow.* **3.** To set an upper limit on. **—idiom: cap in hand** Respectfully or humbly. [< LLat. *cappa.*]

cap. ►*abbr.* **1.** capacity **2.** capital

ca·pa·ble (kā′pə-bəl) ►*adj.* **1.** Having ability; competent. **2.** Having the potential or inclination: *capable of violence.* [LLat. *capābilis.*] **—ca′pa·bil′i·ty** *n.* **—ca′pa·bly** *adv.*

ca·pa·cious (kə-pā′shəs) ►*adj.* Able to hold a large amount; roomy. See Synonyms at **spacious.** [< Lat. *capāx, capāc-.*] **—ca·pa′cious·ly** *adv.* **—ca·pa′cious·ness** *n.*

ca·pac·i·tance (kə-păs′ĭ-təns) ►*n.* **1.** The ratio of charge to potential on an isolated conductor. **2.** The ratio of the electric charge on one of a pair of conductors to the potential difference between them. **3.** The property of a circuit element that permits it to store charge.

ca·pac·i·tate (kə-păs′ĭ-tāt′) ►*v.* **-tat·ed, -tat·ing** To render fit; enable.

ca·pac·i·tor (kə-păs′ĭ-tər) ►*n.* An electric circuit element used to store charge temporarily, consisting in general of two metallic plates separated by a dielectric.

ca·pac·i·ty (kə-păs′ĭ-tē) ►*n., pl.* **-ties 1.** The ability to receive, hold, or absorb. **2.** The maximum amount that can be contained. **3.** The maximum or optimum amount that can be produced. **4.** The ability to learn or retain knowledge. **5.** The quality of being suitable for or receptive to specified treatment: *the capacity of elastic to be stretched.* **6.** Position; role: *in your capacity as sales manager.* **7.** *Elect.* Capacitance. ►*adj.* As large or numerous as possible: *a capacity crowd.* [< Lat. *capāx, capāc-,* spacious.]

ca·par·i·son (kə-păr′ĭ-sən) ►*n.* An ornamental covering for a horse. [< Sp. *caparazón.*] **—ca·par′i·son** *v.*

cape¹ (kāp) ►*n.* A sleeveless garment often tied at the throat and worn hanging over the shoulders. [< LLat. *cappa.*]

cape² (kāp) ►*n.* A headland projecting into a body of water. [< Lat. *caput,* head.]

Cape Bret·on Island (brĕt′n) An island forming the NE part of Nova Scotia, Canada.

Cape buffalo ►*n.* A large African buffalo having massive downward-curving horns.

Ča·pek (chä′pĕk′), **Karel** 1890–1938. Czech writer.

ca·per¹ (kā′pər) ►*n.* **1.** A playful leap or hop. **2.** A wild escapade. **3.** *Slang* An illegal enterprise, esp. one involving theft. ►*v.* To leap or frisk about. [Alteration of CAPRIOLE.]

ca·per² (kā′pər) ►*n.* The pickled flower bud of a Mediterranean shrub, used as a pungent condiment. [< Gk. *kapparis.*]

Ca·pet (kā′pĭt, kăp′ĭt, kă-pā′) A dynasty of French kings (987–1328), including **Hugh Capet** (940?–996).

Cape Town or **Cape·town** (kāp′toun′) The legislative capital of South Africa, in the extreme SW.

Cape Verde (vûrd) An island country of the Atlantic W of Senegal. Cap. Praia.

cap·il·lar·i·ty (kăp′ə-lăr′ĭ-tē) ►*n.* Capillary action.

cap·il·lar·y (kăp′ə-lĕr′ē) ►*adj.* **1.** Resembling a hair; fine and slender. **2.** Having a very small internal diameter: *a capillary tube.* **3.** Of the capillaries. **4.** Of capillarity. ►*n., pl.* **-ies 1.** One of the tiny blood vessels connecting the arteries and veins. **2.** A tube with a very small internal diameter. [< LLat. *capillus,* hair.]

capillary action ►*n.* The interaction between contacting surfaces of a liquid and a solid that distorts the liquid surface from a planar shape.

capillary attraction ►*n.* The force that causes a liquid to be raised against a vertical surface, as water is in a clean glass tube.

cap·i·tal¹ (kăp′ĭ-tl) ►*n.* **1.** A town or city that is the official seat of government in a political entity. **2.** Wealth, esp. in the form of money or property. **3.** Accumulated assets or advantages. **4.** The net worth of a business. **5.** Capital stock. **6.** Capitalists considered as a group or class. **7.** A capital letter. ►*adj.* **1.** First and foremost; principal. **2.** First-rate; excellent: *a capital idea.* **3.** Of or being a political capital. **4.** Extremely serious: *a capital blunder.* **5.** Involving or punishable by death: *a capital offense.* **6.** Of or relating to financial assets, esp. those that add to the net worth of a business. **7.** Of or being a capital letter. [< Lat. *caput, capit-,* head.]

Usage: The term for a town or city that serves as a seat of government is *capital.* The term for the building in which a legislative assembly meets is *capitol.*

cap·i·tal² (kăp′ĭ-tl) ►*n. Archit.* The top part of a pillar or column. [< LLat. *capitellum.*]

capital gain ►*n.* The amount by which the sale of a capital asset exceeds the original cost.

cap·i·tal·ism (kăp′ĭ-tl-ĭz′əm) ►*n.* An economic system in which the means of production and distribution are privately or corporately owned and development occurs through the accumulation and reinvestment of profits gained in a free market.

cap·i·tal·ist (kăp′ĭ-tl-ĭst) ►*n.* **1.** A supporter of capitalism. **2.** An investor of capital in business. **3.** A person of great wealth. **—cap′i·tal·is′tic** *adj.*

cap·i·tal·ize (kăp′ĭ-tl-īz′) ►*v.* **-ized, -iz·ing 1.** To convert into capital. **2.** To supply with capital. **3a.** To print in capital letters. **b.** To begin (a word) with a capital letter. **4.** To turn something to one's advantage: *capitalize on another's error.* **—cap′i·tal·i·za′tion** *n.*

capital letter ►*n.* A letter written or printed in a size larger than and often in a form differing from its corresponding lowercase letter; uppercase letter.

cap·i·tal·ly (kăp′ĭ-tl-ē) ►*adv.* Excellently.

capital punishment ►*n.* The death penalty.

cap·i·ta·tion (kăp′ĭ-tā′shən) ►*n.* **1.** A poll tax. **2.** A payment or fee of a fixed amount per person. [< Lat. *caput, capit-,* head.]

cap·i·tol (kăp′ĭ-tl) ►*n.* **1.** The building in which a legislature meets. See Usage Note at **capital¹**. **2. Capitol** The building in Washington DC where the US Congress meets. [< Lat. *Capitōlium*, Jupiter's temple in Rome.]

ca·pit·u·late (kə-pĭch′ə-lāt′) ►*v.* **-lat·ed, -lat·ing 1.** To surrender under specified conditions. **2.** To give up all resistance; acquiesce. [Med. Lat. *capitulāre*, draw up in chapters.] —**ca·pit′u·la′tion** *n.*

cap·let (kăp′lĭt) ►*n.* A coated oval medicine tablet. [(CAP(SULE) + (TAB)LET.]

ca·po¹ (kä′pō) ►*n., pl.* **-pos** A small movable bar placed across the fingerboard of a guitar to raise the pitch of all the strings uniformly. [< Ital. *capo*, head.]

ca·po² (kä′pō, kăp′ō) ►*n., pl.* **-pos** The head of a branch of an organized crime syndicate. [Ital.]

ca·pon (kā′pŏn′, -pən) ►*n.* A castrated rooster raised for food. [< Lat. *cāpō.*]

Ca·pone (kə-pōn′), **Alphonse** "Al." Also called "Scarface." 1899–1947. Amer. gangster.

Ca·po·te (kə-pō′tē), **Truman** 1924–84. Amer. writer.

Cap·pa·do·cia (kăp′ə-dō′shə, -shē-ə) An ancient region of Asia Minor in present-day E-central Turkey. —**Cap′pa·do′cian** *adj.*

cap·puc·ci·no (kăp′ə-chē′nō, kä′pə-) ►*n., pl.* **-nos** Espresso coffee with steamed milk or cream. [Ital., Capuchin.]

Cap·ra (kăp′rə), **Frank** 1897–1991. Italian-born Amer. filmmaker.

Ca·pri (kə-prē′, kä′prē) An island of S Italy on the S edge of the Bay of Naples.

ca·pric·cio (kə-prē′chō, -chē-ō′) ►*n., pl.* **-cios** *Mus.* An instrumental work with an improvisatory style and a free form. [Ital., CAPRICE.]

ca·price (kə-prēs′) ►*n.* **1a.** An impulsive change of mind. **b.** An inclination to change one's mind impulsively. **2.** *Mus.* A capriccio. [< Ital. *caporiccio*, a start.]

ca·pri·cious (kə-prĭsh′əs, -prē′shəs) ►*adj.* Impulsive and unpredictable. —**ca·pri′cious·ly** *adv.* —**ca·pri′cious·ness** *n.*

Cap·ri·corn (kăp′rĭ-kôrn′) ►*n.* **1.** A constellation in the Southern Hemisphere. **2.** The 10th sign of the zodiac.

cap·ri·ole (kăp′rē-ōl′) ►*n.* An upward leap made by a trained horse without going forward. [< Lat. *capreolus*, small goat.]

cap·si·cum (kăp′sĭ-kəm) ►*n.* Any of a genus of tropical American pepper plants having pungent fruit used as a condiment. [Poss. < Lat. *capsa*, box.]

cap·sid (kăp′sĭd) ►*n.* The protein shell of a virus particle. [< Lat. *capsa*, box.]

cap·size (kăp′sīz′, kăp-sīz′) ►*v.* **-sized, -siz·ing** To overturn or cause to overturn. Used of a boat.

cap·stan (kăp′stən, -stăn′) ►*n.* **1.** *Naut.* A vertical spool-shaped revolving cylinder for hoisting weights by winding in a cable. **2.** A small cylindrical shaft used to drive magnetic tape at a constant speed in a tape recorder. [< Lat. *capistrum*, halter.]

cap·stone (kăp′stōn′) ►*n.* **1.** The top stone of a structure or wall. **2.** The crowning achievement; acme.

cap·su·late (kăp′sə-lāt′, -lĭt, -syōō-) also **cap·su·lat·ed** (-lā′tĭd) ►*adj.* Enclosed in or formed into a capsule. —**cap′su·la′tion** *n.*

cap·sule (kăp′səl, -sōōl) ►*n.* **1.** A small soluble container, usu. of gelatin, that encloses a dose of oral medicine or vitamins. **2.** A fibrous, membranous, or fatty sheath that encloses a bodily organ or part. **3.** A seed case that dries and splits open. **4.** A pressurized compartment of an aircraft or spacecraft. ►*adj.* **1.** Condensed; brief. **2.** Very small; compact. [< Lat. *capsula*, dim. of *capsa*, box.] —**cap′su·lar** *adj.*

cap·sul·ize (kăp′sə-līz′, -syōō-) ►*v.* **-ized, -iz·ing** To condense or summarize.

Capt. also **Capt** or **CAPT** ►*abbr.* captain

cap·tain (kăp′tən) ►*n.* **1.** One who commands, leads, or guides. **2.** The officer in command of a ship, aircraft, or spacecraft. **3.** The designated leader of a team in sports. **4a.** A rank, as in the US Army, above first lieutenant and below major. **b.** A rank, as in the US Navy, above commander and below commodore. **5.** A leading figure: *a captain of industry.* ►*v.* To command or direct. [< LLat. *capitāneus*, chief < Lat. *caput*, head.] —**cap′tain·cy** *n.* —**cap′tain·ship′** *n.*

cap·tion (kăp′shən) ►*n.* **1.** A short legend or description accompanying an illustration. **2.** A series of words superimposed on the bottom of television or motion picture frames. **3.** A title, as of a document or article. ►*v.* To furnish a caption for. [< Lat. *captiō*, arrest.]

cap·tious (kăp′shəs) ►*adj.* **1.** Inclined to find fault; critical. **2.** Intended to entrap or confuse. [< Lat. *capere*, seize.] —**cap′tious·ly** *adv.*

cap·ti·vate (kăp′tə-vāt′) ►*v.* **-vat·ed, -vat·ing** To attract and hold the interest of, as by charm or beauty. See Synonyms at **charm**. —**cap′ti·va′tion** *n.* —**cap′ti·va′tor** *n.*

cap·tive (kăp′tĭv) ►*n.* **1.** A prisoner. **2.** One who is held in the grip of a strong emotion. ►*adj.* **1.** Held as prisoner. **2.** Kept under restraint or control: *captive birds; a captive nation.* **3.** Restrained by circumstances that prevent free choice: *a captive audience.* **4.** Enraptured. —**cap·tiv′i·ty** *n.*

cap·tor (kăp′tər, -tôr′) ►*n.* One who captures.

cap·ture (kăp′chər) ►*v.* **-tured, -tur·ing 1.** To take captive; seize. **2.** To gain possession or control of. **3.** To attract and hold: *capture the imagination.* **4.** To preserve in lasting form. ►*n.* **1.** The act of capturing; seizure. **2.** One that is seized, caught, or won. [< Lat. *capere*, seize.]

cap·u·chin (kăp′yə-chĭn, -shĭn, kə-pyōō′-) ►*n.* **1. Capuchin** A monk belonging to an independent order of Franciscans. **2.** Any of several long-tailed tropical American monkeys. [< Ital. *cappuccino*, pointed cowl, Capuchin.]

car (kär) ►*n.* **1.** An automobile. **2.** A conveyance with wheels that runs along tracks. **3.** A boxlike enclosure for passengers on a conveyance: *an elevator car.* [< Lat. *carrus*, cart.]

car. ►*abbr.* carat

car·a·bi·ner (kăr′ə-bē′nər) ►*n.* An oblong metal ring with a hinged gate, used to secure ropes. [< Ger. *Karabiner(haken)*, (hook) for a carbine.]

Ca·ra·cas (kə-rä′kəs) The capital of Venezuela, in the N part near the Caribbean coast.

ca·rafe (kə-răf′) ►*n.* A glass or metal bottle, often with a flared lip, used for serving water or wine. [< Sp. *garrafa.*]

car·a·mel (kăr′ə-məl, -mĕl′, kär′məl) ►*n.* **1.** A smooth chewy candy made with sugar, butter, cream or milk, and flavoring. **2.** Burnt sugar, used for coloring and sweetening foods. [< Gk. *kalamos*, cane.]

car·a·pace (kăr′ə-pās′) ►*n. Zool.* A hard outer covering, such as the upper shell of a turtle. [< Sp. *carapacho*.]

car·at (kăr′ət) ►*n.* **1.** A unit of weight for precious stones, equal to 200 mg. **2.** Var. of **karat.** [< Gk. *keration*, small weight.]

Ca·ra·vag·gio (kăr′ə-vä′jō), **Michelangelo Merisi da** 1573–1610. Italian painter.

car·a·van (kăr′ə-văn′) ►*n.* **1.** A company of travelers journeying together, esp. across a desert. **2.** A single file of vehicles or pack animals. **3.** A van. [< Pers. *kārvān*.]

car·a·van·sa·ry (kăr′ə-văn′sə-rē) also **car·a·van·se·rai** (-rī′) ►*n., pl.* **-ries** also **-rais** An inn built around a large court for accommodating caravans in central or W Asia. [Pers. *kārvān*, caravan + *sarāy*, camp.]

car·a·vel or **car·a·velle** (kăr′ə-věl′) ►*n.* A small, light sailing ship used by the Spanish and Portuguese in the 1400s and 1500s. [< OPort. *caravela*.]

car·a·way (kăr′ə-wā′) ►*n.* A plant with aromatic seedlike fruits used in cooking and flavoring. [< OFr. *carvi, caroi*.]

car·bide (kär′bīd′) ►*n.* A binary compound of carbon.

car·bine (kär′bēn′, -bīn′) ►*n.* A lightweight rifle with a short barrel. [Fr. *carabine*.]

carbo– or **carb–** ►*pref.* Carbon: *carbohydrate.* [Fr. < *carbone*, CARBON.]

car·bo·hy·drate (kär′bō-hī′drāt′) ►*n.* Any of a group of photosynthetically produced organic compounds that includes sugars, starches, celluloses, and gums and serves as a major energy source in the diet.

car·bol·ic acid (kär-bŏl′ĭk) ►*n.* See **phenol.** [CARB(O)– + Lat. *oleum*, oil + –IC.]

car·bon (kär′bən) ►*n.* **1.** *Symbol* **C** A naturally abundant nonmetallic element that occurs in many inorganic and in all organic compounds and is capable of chemical self-bonding to form an enormous number of chemically, biologically, and commercially important molecules. At. no. 6. See table at **element. 2a.** A sheet of carbon paper. **b.** A carbon copy. [< Lat. *carbō*, charcoal.] —**car′bon·ize** *v.* —**car′bon·ous** *adj.*

car·bon-14 (kär′bən-fôr-tēn′) ►*n.* A naturally radioactive carbon isotope with atomic mass 14 and half-life 5,730 years, used in radiocarbon dating.

car·bo·na·ceous (kär′bə-nā′shəs) ►*adj.* Of, consisting of, or yielding carbon.

car·bon·ate (kär′bə-nāt′) ►*v.* **-at·ed, -at·ing** To charge (e.g., a beverage) with carbon dioxide gas. ►*n.* (-nāt′, -nĭt) The anionic divalent group CO₃, derived from carbonic acid. —**car′bon·a′tion** *n.*

car·bon·at·ed water (kär′bə-nā′tĭd) ►*n.* Effervescent water charged under pressure with carbon dioxide gas, used as a beverage or mixer.

carbon black ►*n.* A finely divided form of carbon derived from the incomplete combustion of hydrocarbons and used principally in rubber, inks, paints, and polishes.

carbon copy ►*n.* **1.** A copy of a document made by using carbon paper or a photocopier. **2.** A copy of an electronic document sent to people in addition to the addressed recipient. **3.** One that closely resembles another.

carbon dating ►*n.* See **radiocarbon dating.**

carbon dioxide ►*n.* A colorless, odorless, incombustible gas, CO₂, formed during respiration, combustion, and organic decomposition.

car·bon·ic acid (kär-bŏn′ĭk) ►*n.* A weak, unstable acid, H₂CO₃, present in solutions of carbon dioxide in water.

Car·bon·if·er·ous (kär′bə-nĭf′ər-əs) ►*adj.* **1.** *Geol.* Of or being a division of the Paleozoic Era comprising the Mississippian and Pennsylvanian Periods and marked by the deposition of plant remains that later hardened into coal. **2. carboniferous** Producing or containing carbon or coal. ►*n.* The Carboniferous Period.

carbon monoxide ►*n.* A colorless, odorless, highly poisonous gas, CO, formed by the incomplete combustion of carbon.

carbon paper ►*n.* Thin paper coated with a dark waxy pigment, placed between blank sheets so that writing on the top sheet is copied onto the bottom sheet.

carbon tet·ra·chlo·ride (tĕt′rə-klôr′īd′) ►*n.* A poisonous, nonflammable, colorless liquid, CCl₄, used as a solvent.

Car·bo·run·dum (kär′bə-rŭn′dəm) A trademark for a silicon carbide abrasive.

car·boy (kär′boi′) ►*n.* A large bottle, usu. encased in a protective covering and used to hold corrosive liquids. [Pers. *qarābah*.]

car·bun·cle (kär′bŭng′kəl) ►*n.* **1.** A painful, localized, pus-producing bacterial infection of the skin. **2.** A deep-red garnet. **3.** A mythical gemstone. [< Lat. *carbunculus*, dim. of *carbō*, coal.] —**car·bun′cu·lar** (-kyə-lər) *adj.*

car·bu·ret (kär′bə-rāt′, -rĕt′, -byə-) ►*v.* **-ret·ed, -ret·ing** or **-ret·ted, -ret·ting** To mix (air or a gas) with volatile hydrocarbons so as to increase available fuel energy. [< Fr. *carbure*, carbide.] —**car·bu·re′tion** *n.*

car·bu·re·tor (kär′bə-rā′tər, -byə-) ►*n.* A device used in internal-combustion engines to produce an explosive mixture of vaporized fuel and air. [< CARBURET.]

car·bu·rize (kär′bə-rīz′, -byə-) ►*v.* **-rized, -riz·ing** **1.** To treat, combine, or impregnate with carbon. **2.** To carburet. [CARBUR(ET) + –IZE.] —**car′bu·ri·za′tion** *n.*

car·cass (kär′kəs) ►*n.* A dead body, esp. of an animal. [< AN *carcais*.]

car·cin·o·gen (kär-sĭn′ə-jən, kär′sə-nə-jĕn′) ►*n.* A cancer-causing substance or agent. [Gk. *karkinos*, cancer + –GEN.] —**car′ci·no·gen′e·sis** *n.* —**car′ci·no·gen′ic** *adj.*

car·ci·no·ma (kär′sə-nō′mə) ►*n., pl.* **-mas** or **-ma·ta** (-mə-tə) A malignant tumor that is derived from epithelial tissue. [< Gk. *karkinos*, cancer.]

car coat ►*n.* A three-quarter-length overcoat.

card¹ (kärd) ►*n.* **1.** A flat, usu. rectangular piece of stiff paper, cardboard, or plastic, esp.: **a.** One of a set of playing cards. **b.** A greeting card. **c.** A post card. **d.** One bearing the image and statistics of an athlete. **e.** A business card. **f.** A credit card. **2. cards** *(takes sing. or pl. v.)* A game using playing cards. **3.** A circuit board. **4.** A program, esp. for a sports event. **5.** *Informal* An eccentrically amusing person. ►*v.* **1.** To furnish with or attach to a card. **2.** To list (something) on a card; catalog. **3.** To check the identification of, esp. in order to verify legal age. —*idioms:*

card up (one's) sleeve A secret resource or a plan that is held in reserve. **in the cards** Likely or certain to happen. **put (or lay) (one's) cards on the table** To reveal frankly and clearly, as one's motives. [< Gk. *khartēs*, leaf of papyrus.]

card² (kärd) ►*n.* A wire-toothed brush used to disentangle textile fibers. [< Lat. *carduus*, thistle.] —**card** *v.* —**card′er** *n.*

car·da·mom (kär′də-məm) or **car·da·mon** (-mən) ►*n.* A spice derived from the aromatic seed capsules of a tropical Asian plant. [< Gk. *kardamōmon.*]

card·board (kärd′bôrd′) ►*n.* A thick stiff material made of pressed paper pulp or pasted sheets of paper. ►*adj.* **1.** Made of cardboard. **2.** Flimsy; insubstantial.

card-car·ry·ing (kärd′kăr′ē-ĭng) ►*adj.* **1.** Being an enrolled member of an organization, esp. the Communist Party. **2.** Avidly devoted to a group or cause.

card catalog ►*n.* An alphabetical listing, esp. of books in a library, made with a separate card for each item.

car·di·ac (kär′dē-ăk′) ►*adj.* Of or near the heart. [< Gk. *kardia*, heart.]

cardiac arrest ►*n.* Sudden cessation of heartbeat and cardiac function, resulting in the loss of effective circulation.

cardiac massage ►*n.* A resuscitative procedure employing rhythmic compression of the chest and heart, as after cardiac arrest.

Car·diff (kär′dĭf) The capital of Wales, in the SE part on the Bristol Channel.

car·di·gan (kär′dĭ-gən) ►*n.* A sweater or knitted jacket that opens down the full length of the front. [After the 7th Earl of *Cardigan* (1797–1868).]

car·di·nal (kär′dn-əl, kärd′nəl) ►*adj.* **1.** Of foremost importance; paramount. **2.** Dark to deep or vivid red. ►*n.* **1.** *Rom. Cath. Ch.* A high church official, ranking just below the pope. **2.** A North American bird having a crested head, a short thick bill, and bright red plumage in the male. [< Lat. *cardō, cardin-*, hinge.]

car·di·nal·ate (kär′dn-ə-lĭt, -lāt′, kärd′nə-) ►*n. Rom. Cath. Ch.* The position, rank, dignity, or term of a cardinal.

cardinal number ►*n.* A number, such as 3 or 11 or 412, used in counting to indicate quantity but not order.

cardinal point ►*n.* One of the four principal directions on a compass: north, south, east, or west.

cardio– or **cardi–** ►*pref.* Heart: *cardiovascular.* [< Gk. *kardia*, heart.]

car·di·o·gram (kär′dē-ə-grăm′) ►*n.* **1.** The curve traced by a cardiograph, used in the diagnosis of heart disorders. **2.** See **electrocardiogram.**

car·di·o·graph (kär′dē-ə-grăf′) ►*n.* **1.** An instrument used to record graphically the mechanical movements of the heart. **2.** See **electrocardiograph.** —**car′di·og′ra·phy** (-ŏg′rə-fē) *n.*

car·di·ol·o·gy (kär′dē-ŏl′ə-jē) ►*n.* The study of the structure, functioning, and disorders of the heart. —**car′di·ol′o·gist** *n.*

car·di·o·pul·mo·nar·y (kär′dē-ō-pŏŏl′mə-nĕr′ē, -pŭl′-) ►*adj.* Of or involving the heart and lungs.

cardiopulmonary resuscitation ►*n.* A procedure used after cardiac arrest in which cardiac massage, artificial respiration, and drugs are used to restore circulation.

car·di·o·vas·cu·lar (kär′dē-ō-văs′kyə-lər) ►*adj.* Involving the heart and the blood vessels.

card·sharp (kärd′shärp′) ►*n.* An expert in cheating at cards. —**card′sharp′ing** *n.*

care (kâr) ►*n.* **1.** A burdened state of mind; worry. **2.** An object or source of attention or solicitude. **3.** Interest, regard, or liking. **4.** Close attention: *painted the trim with care.* **5.** Upkeep; maintenance: *hair care products.* **6.** Charge or supervision. **7.** Assistance or treatment: *emergency care.* ►*v.* **1. cared, car·ing** To be concerned or interested. **2.** To provide assistance or supervision. **3.** To object or mind. **4.** To wish or have a wish. **5.** To have a liking or attachment: *didn't care for the movie.* [< OE *cearu*.]
Syns: charge, custody, supervision, trust n.

CARE ►*abbr.* Cooperative for American Relief Everywhere

ca·reen (kə-rēn′) ►*v.* **1.** To lurch or swerve while in motion. **2.** To move forward rapidly, esp. with minimal control; career. **3.** To cause (a ship) to lean to one side; tilt. [< Fr. *(en) carène, (on the) keel* < Lat. *carīna.*] —**ca·reen′er** *n.*

ca·reer (kə-rîr′) ►*n.* **1.** A chosen pursuit; profession or occupation. **2.** The general progress in one's working or professional life. ►*v.* To move forward at high speed. [< OFr. *carriere*, racecourse.]

care·free (kâr′frē′) ►*adj.* Free of worries and responsibilities.

care·ful (kâr′fəl) ►*adj.* **1.** Attentive to potential danger, error, or harm; cautious. **2.** Thorough and painstaking; conscientious. —**care′ful·ly** *adv.* —**care′ful·ness** *n.*
Syns: alert, attentive, heedful, mindful, vigilant, watchful Ant: careless adj.

care·giv·er (kâr′gĭv′ər) ►*n.* **1.** One, such as a nurse or social worker, who assists in the treatment of an illness or disability. **2.** One who attends to the needs of a child or dependent adult. —**care′giv′ing** *adj. & n.*

care·less (kâr′lĭs) ►*adj.* **1.** Inattentive; negligent. **2.** Marked by or resulting from lack of thought. **3.** Inconsiderate: *a careless remark.* **4.** Free from cares; cheerful. —**care′less·ly** *adv.* —**care′less·ness** *n.*

ca·ress (kə-rĕs′) ►*n.* A gentle touch of fondness. ►*v.* To touch or stroke fondly. [< Ital. *carezza.*]
Syns: cuddle, fondle, pet, stroke v.

car·et (kăr′ĭt) ►*n.* A proofreading symbol (^) used to indicate where something is to be inserted in a line of printed or written matter. [Lat., there is lacking.]

care·tak·er (kâr′tā′kər) ►*n.* One employed to look after or take charge of goods, property, or a person; custodian.

care·worn (kâr′wôrn′) ►*adj.* Showing the effects of worry or care.

car·fare (kär′fâr′) ►*n.* The fare charged a passenger, as on a streetcar or bus.

car·go (kär′gō) ►*n., pl.* **-goes** or **-gos** The freight carried by a ship, aircraft, or other vehicle. [Sp. < *cargar*, to load.]

Car·ib (kär′ĭb) ►*n., pl.* **-ib** or **-ibs 1.** A member of a group of American Indian peoples of N South America, the Lesser Antilles, and the E coast of Central America. **2.** Any of the languages of the Carib.

Car·i·ban (kăr′ə-bən, kə-rē′bən) ►*n.* A language family comprising the Carib languages.

Car·ib·be·an Sea (kăr′ə-bē′ən, kə-rĭb′ē-ən) An arm of the W Atlantic bounded by the coasts of Central and South America and the West Indies. —**Car′ib·be′an** *adj.*

car·i·bou (kăr′ə-bōō′) ►*n., pl.* **-bou** or **-bous** A large deer of arctic regions, having branched antlers. Eurasian subspecies are usu. called reindeer. [Micmac *g̃alipu.*]

car·i·ca·ture (kăr′ĭ-kə-chŏŏr′, -chər) ►*n.* **1.** A representation, esp. pictorial, in which the subject's distinctive features or peculiarities are exaggerated for comic or grotesque effect. **2.** A mockery; farce. ►*v.* **-tured, -tur·ing** To represent or imitate in a caricature. [< Ital. *caricare,* exaggerate.] —**car′i·ca·tur′ist** *n.*

car·ies (kâr′ēz) ►*n.* Decay of a bone or tooth. [Lat. *cariēs.*]

car·il·lon (kăr′ə-lŏn′, -lən) ►*n.* A stationary set of bells hung in a tower and usu. played from a keyboard. [Fr. < LLat. *quaterniō,* set of four.] —**car′il·lon′** *v.*

car·ing (kâr′ĭng) ►*adj.* Feeling and exhibiting concern and empathy for others.

car·jack or **car-jack** (kär′jăk′) ►*v.* To take or attempt to take (a vehicle) from its users by use of force. [CAR + (HI)JACK.] —**car′jack′er** *n.*

car·load (kär′lōd′) ►*n.* The quantity that a car, esp. a railroad car, can hold.

Car·mel (kär′məl), **Mount** A ridge of NW Israel extending SE from Haifa for about 24 km (15 mi).

Car·mi·chael (kär′mī-kəl), **Hoagland Howard** "Hoagy." 1899–1981. Amer. songwriter.

car·min·a·tive (kär-mĭn′ə-tĭv, kär′mə-nā′-) ►*adj.* Inducing expulsion of intestinal gas. ►*n.* A carminative drug or agent. [< Lat. *carmināre,* to card wool.]

car·mine (kär′mĭn, -mīn′) ►*n.* A strong to vivid red. [< Med.Lat. *carminium.*] —**car′mine** *adj.*

car·nage (kär′nĭj) ►*n.* Massive slaughter or bloodshed. [< Lat. *carō, carn-,* flesh.]

car·nal (kär′nəl) ►*adj.* **1.** Relating to the physical and esp. sexual appetites. **2.** Not spiritual; worldly or earthly: *the carnal world.* [< Lat. *carō, carn-,* flesh.] —**car·nal′i·ty** (-năl′ĭ-tē) *n.*

car·na·tion (kär-nā′shən) ►*n.* A plant cultivated for its fragrant flowers with fringed petals. [Prob. < OFr., flesh-colored.]

car·nau·ba (kär-nô′bə, -nou′-, -nōō′-) ►*n.* **1.** A Brazilian palm tree. **2.** A hard wax obtained from its leaves, used esp. in polishes and floor waxes. [< Tupí *carnaúba.*]

Car·ne·gie (kär′nə-gē, kär-nā′gē, -nĕg′ē), **Andrew** 1835–1919. Scottish-born Amer. industrialist and philanthropist.

car·nel·ian (kär-nĕl′yən) ►*n.* A reddish variety of clear chalcedony. [< OFr. *corneline.*]

car·ni·val (kär′nə-vəl) ►*n.* **1.** A festival marked by merrymaking and feasting just before Lent. **2.** A traveling amusement show. **3.** A festival or revel: *the winter carnival.* [Ital. *carnevale.*]

car·ni·vore (kär′nə-vôr′) ►*n.* A flesh-eating animal, esp. one of a group including dogs, cats, and bears.

car·niv·o·rous (kär-nĭv′ər-əs) ►*adj.* **1.** Relating to carnivores. **2.** Flesh-eating or predatory. [< Lat. *carnivorus.*] —**car·niv′o·rous·ly** *adv.*

car·ny also **car·ney** (kär′nē) ►*n., pl.* **-nies** also **-neys** *Informal* **1.** A carnival. **2.** One who works with a carnival.

car·ob (kăr′əb) ►*n.* **1.** A Mediterranean evergreen tree having large leathery pods. **2.** A chocolatelike powder made from the seeds and pods of the carob. [< Ar. *ḫarrūba,* carob pod.]

car·ol (kăr′əl) ►*n.* A song of praise or joy, esp. for Christmas. [< OFr.] —**car′ol** *v.* —**car′ol·er** *n.*

Car·o·li·nas (kăr′ə-lī′nəz) The colonies (after 1729) or states of NC and SC.

Car·o·line Islands (kăr′ə-līn′, -lĭn) An archipelago of the W Pacific E of the Philippines.

car·om (kăr′əm) ►*n.* **1.** A collision followed by a rebound. **2.** A shot in billiards in which the cue ball successively strikes two other balls. ►*v.* **1.** To collide with and rebound. **2.** To make a carom in billiards. [< Sp. *carambola,* billiards shot.]

car·o·tene (kăr′ə-tēn′) ►*n.* An orange-yellow pigment found in plants such as carrots and squash and converted to vitamin A in the liver. [< Lat. *carōta,* CARROT.]

ca·rot·id (kə-rŏt′ĭd) ►*n.* Either of the two major arteries, one on each side of the neck, that carry blood to the head. [< Gk. *karōtides,* carotid arteries.]

ca·rouse (kə-rouz′) ►*n.* Boisterous, drunken merrymaking. ►*v.* **-roused, -rous·ing** To drink alcohol excessively, esp. in boisterous merrymaking. [Ger. *garaus,* all out, drink up.] —**ca·rous′al** *n.* —**ca·rous′er** *n.*

car·ou·sel or **car·rou·sel** (kăr′ə-sĕl′, -zĕl′) ►*n.* **1.** A merry-go-round. **2.** A circular conveyor on which objects are displayed or rotated. [Fr. *carrousel.*]

carp[1] (kärp) ►*v.* To find fault and complain fretfully. See Synonyms at **quibble.** [< ON *karpa,* boast.] —**carp′er** *n.*

carp[2] (kärp) ►*n., pl.* **carp** or **carps** An edible freshwater fish, often bred commercially. [< Med.Lat. *carpa,* of Gmc. orig.]

-carp ►*suff.* Fruit; fruitlike structure: *mesocarp.* [< Gk. *karpos,* fruit.]

car·pal (kär′pəl) ►*adj.* Of or near the carpus. ►*n.* A bone of the carpus.

carpal tunnel syndrome ►*n.* A condition marked by pain and numbing in the hand, caused by compression of a nerve in the wrist.

Car·pa·thi·an Mountains (kär-pā′thē-ən) A mountain system of central Europe in the Czech Republic, Slovakia, Poland, Ukraine, and Romania.

car·pel (kär′pəl) ►*n.* One of the structural units of a pistil, representing a modified ovule-bearing leaf. [< Gk. *karpos,* fruit.]

car·pen·ter (kär′pən-tər) ►*n.* A skilled worker who makes, finishes, and repairs wooden objects and structures. [< Lat. *carpentārius (artifex),* (maker) of a carriage.]

car·pen·try (kär′pən-trē) ►*n.* The work or trade of a carpenter.

car·pet (kär′pĭt) ►*n.* A heavy, usu. woven or piled covering for a floor. ►*v.* To cover with or as if with a carpet. —*idiom:* **on the carpet** Subject to reprimand by one in authority. [< OItal. *carpita* < Lat. *carpere,* pluck.]

car·pet·bag (kär′pĭt-băg′) ►*n.* A traveling bag made of carpet fabric.

car·pet·bag·ger (kär′pĭt-băg′ər) ►*n.* A Northerner who went to the South after the Civil War for political or financial advantage. —**car′pet·bag′ger·y** *n.*

carpet beetle ►*n.* Any of various small beetles having larvae that are destructive to fabrics.

car·pet-bomb (kär′pĭt-bŏm′) ►*v.* To bomb in a close pattern over a large target area.

car pool ►*n.* **1.** An arrangement whereby several participants travel together in one vehicle and share the costs. **2.** A group participating in a car pool. —**car′-pool′** *v.*

car·port (kär′pôrt′) ►*n.* An open-sided shelter for an automobile formed by a roof projecting from a building.

car·pus (kär′pəs) ►*n., pl.* **-pi** (-pī′) The wrist or its bones. [Gk. *karpos.*]

car·ra·geen also **car·ra·gheen** (kăr′ə-gēn′) ►*n.* See **Irish moss.** [After *Carragheen,* Ireland.]

car·ra·geen·an also **car·ra·geen·in** (kăr′ə-gē′nən) ►*n.* A colloid derived esp. from Irish moss and used as a thickener, stabilizer, and emulsifier.

car·rel also **car·rell** (kăr′əl) ►*n.* A partially partitioned nook near the stacks in a library, used for private study. [ME *carole,* ring, round dance ring; see CAROL.]

car·riage (kăr′ĭj) ►*n.* **1.** A wheeled vehicle, esp. a four-wheeled horse-drawn passenger vehicle. **2.** A baby carriage. **3.** A wheeled support or frame. **4.** A machine part for holding or shifting another part. **5a.** The act of transporting or carrying. **b.** (kăr′ē-ĭj) The charge for transporting. **6.** Posture; bearing. See Synonyms at **posture.** [< ONFr. *carier,* CARRY.]

car·ri·er (kăr′ē-ər) ►*n.* **1.** One that carries or conveys. **2.** One that transports passengers or goods. **3.** *Med.* An immune organism that transmits a pathogen to others. **4.** *Genet.* An individual that carries one gene for a particular recessive trait. **5.** An aircraft carrier. **6.** A telecommunications company.

carrier pigeon ►*n.* A homing pigeon, esp. one trained to carry messages.

carrier wave ►*n.* An electromagnetic wave that can be modulated to transmit sound or images.

car·ri·on (kăr′ē-ən) ►*n.* Dead and decaying flesh. [< Lat. *carō,* flesh.]

Car·roll (kăr′əl), **Lewis** See Charles Lutwidge **Dodgson.**

car·rot (kăr′ət) ►*n.* **1.** A plant widely cultivated for its edible taproot. **2.** Its fleshy orange root, eaten as a vegetable. **3.** A reward or inducement. [< Gk. *karōton.*]

car·rot-and-stick (kăr′ət-ən-stĭk′) ►*adj.* Combining a promised reward with a threatened penalty.

car·rou·sel (kăr′ə-sĕl′, -zĕl′) ►*n.* Var. of **carousel.**

car·ry (kăr′ē) ►*v.* **-ried, -ry·ing 1.** To hold while moving; bear: *carrying a briefcase.* **2.** To convey or transport: *carry messages; carry freight.* **3.** To have on one's person: *carry cash.* **4.** To support the weight of. **5.** To be pregnant with (offspring). **6.** To hold (e.g., the head or body) in a certain way. **7.** To conduct (oneself) in a certain way. **8.** To have as a consequence: *The job carries a heavy workload.* **9.** To support (one that is weaker). **10.** To offer for sale or keep in stock. **11.** To win most of the votes in. **12.** To win support or acceptance for. **13.** To print or broadcast. ►*n., pl.* **-ries 1.** An act of carrying.

2. The range of a gun or projectile. —*phrasal verbs:* **carry away** To move or excite greatly. **carry off 1.** To cause the death of. **2.** To handle (e.g., a situation) successfully. **carry on 1.** To conduct; maintain. **2.** To engage in: *carry on a love affair.* **3.** To continue without halting: *carry on in the face of disaster.* **carry out 1.** To put into practice. **2.** To follow or obey. **carry over** To continue at or retain for a later time. **carry through 1.** To accomplish; complete. **2.** To enable to endure; sustain. [< ONFr. *carre,* cart; see CAR.]

car·ry·all (kăr′ē-ôl′) ►*n.* A large receptacle, such as a bag, basket, or pocketbook.

car·ry-on (kăr′ē-ŏn′) ►*adj.* Small enough to be carried aboard an airplane by a passenger: *carry-on luggage.* —**car′ry-on′** *n.*

car·ry-out (kăr′ē-out′) ►*adj.* Takeout. —**car′ry-out′** *n.*

car·sick (kär′sĭk′) ►*adj.* Nauseated by vehicular travel. —**car′sick′ness** *n.*

Car·son (kär′sən), **Christopher** "Kit." 1809–68. Amer. frontier settler.

Carson, Rachel Louise 1907–64. Amer. environmentalist and writer.

Carson City The capital of NV, in the W part near the CA border.

cart (kärt) ►*n.* **1.** A small wheeled vehicle that is typically pushed by hand: *a shopping cart.* **2.** A two-wheeled vehicle drawn by an animal. **3.** A light motorized vehicle: *a golf cart.* ►*v.* **1.** To convey in a cart or truck: *cart away garbage.* **2.** To convey laboriously or remove unceremoniously. [< OE *cræt* and ON *kartr,* wagon.] —**cart′er** *n.*

cart·age (kär′tĭj) ►*n.* **1.** Transportation by cart or truck. **2.** The cost of cartage.

Car·ta·ge·na (kär′tä-hĕ′nä) **1.** A city of NW Colombia on the Caribbean. **2.** A city of SE Spain on the Mediterranean.

carte blanche (kärt blänsh′, blänch′, blänch′) ►*n.* Unrestricted authority. [Fr.]

car·tel (kär-tĕl′) ►*n.* A monopolistic combination of independent business organizations. [< Ital. *cartello,* placard.]

Car·ter (kär′tər), **James Earl, Jr.** "Jimmy." b. 1924. The 39th US president (1977–81).

Jimmy Carter

Car·te·sian coordinate (kär-tē′zhən) ►*n.* A member of the set of numbers that locates a point in a Cartesian coordinate system.

Cartesian coordinate system ►*n.* A coordinate system in which the coordinates of a point are its distances from a set of perpendicular lines that intersect at an origin, such as two lines in a plane or three in space. [After René Descartes.]

Car·thage (kär′thĭj) An ancient city and state of N Africa on the Bay of Tunis NE of modern Tunis. **—Car′tha·gin′i·an** (-thə-jĭn′ē-ən) *adj. & n.*

car·ti·lage (kär′tl-ĭj) ►*n.* A white fibrous connective tissue found in various parts of the body, such as the joints and larynx. [< Lat. *cartilāgō.*] **—car′ti·lag′i·nous** (-ăj′ə-nəs) *adj.*

cartilaginous fish ►*n.* Any of various fishes that have a skeleton consisting mainly of cartilage rather than bone, such as a shark, skate, or ray.

car·tog·ra·phy (kär-tŏg′rə-fē) ►*n.* The making of maps or charts. [Fr. *cartographie* < *carte,* CHART.] **—car·tog′ra·pher** *n.* **—car′to·graph′ic** (-tə-grăf′ĭk) *adj.*

car·ton (kär′tn) ►*n.* **1.** A container made from cardboard or coated paper. **2.** The contents of a carton. [< Ital. *cartone,* pasteboard.]

car·toon (kär-tōōn′) ►*n.* **1.** A humorous or satirical drawing, often with a caption. **2.** A preliminary full-scale sketch, as for a fresco. **3.** An animated movie or television program. **4.** An animated character in a movie or television program. **5.** A comic strip. [< Ital. *cartone,* pasteboard.] **—car·toon′** *v.* **—car·toon′ist** *n.*

car·tridge (kär′trĭj) ►*n.* **1a.** A cylindrical, usu. metal casing containing the primer and powder of small arms ammunition. **b.** Such a casing fitted with a bullet. **2.** A small modular unit that is designed to be inserted into a larger piece of equipment: *an ink cartridge.* **3.** A magnetic tape cassette. [< Ital. *cartoccio,* small paper horn.]

cart·wheel (kärt′wēl′, -hwēl′) ►*n.* A handspring in which the body turns over sideways with the arms and legs extended. **—cart′wheel′** *v.*

Ca·ru·so (kə-rōō′sō, -zō), **Enrico** 1873–1921. Italian operatic tenor.

carve (kärv) ►*v.* **carved, carv·ing** **1.** To divide into pieces by cutting; slice. **2.** To disjoint, slice, and serve (meat or poultry). **3.** To make or form by or as if by cutting. [< OE *ceorfan.*] **—carv′er** *n.*

Car·ver (kär′vər), **George Washington** 1864?–1943. Amer. botanist, chemist, and educator.

carv·ing (kär′vĭng) ►*n.* **1.** The cutting of material such as stone or wood to form a figure or design. **2.** A figure or design so formed.

car·y·at·id (kăr′ē-ăt′ĭd) ►*n., pl.* **-ids** or **-i·des** (-ĭ-dēz′) *Archit.* A supporting column sculptured in the form of a woman. [< Gk. *Karuatides,* maidens of Caryae, Greece.]

ca·sa·ba (kə-sä′bə) ►*n.* A melon having a yellow rind and sweet whitish flesh. [After *Kasaba* (Turgutlu), Turkey.]

Cas·a·blan·ca (kăs′ə-blăng′kə, kä′sə-bläng′kə) A city of NW Morocco on the Atlantic SSW of Tangier.

Ca·sals (kə-sälz′, -sälz′), **Pablo** 1876–1973. Spanish cellist.

Cas·a·no·va de Sein·galt (kăs′ə-nō′və də săn-gält′), **Giovanni Jacopo** 1725–98. Italian adventurer and writer.

cas·cade (kăs-kād′) ►*n.* **1.** A waterfall or series of small waterfalls. **2.** A fall of material, such as lace. **3.** A succession of stages, processes, opera-

tions, or units. ►*v.* **-cad·ed, -cad·ing** To fall in a cascade. [< Ital. *cascare,* fall.]

Cascade Range A mountain chain extending from British Columbia, Canada, to N CA.

case¹ (kās) ►*n.* **1.** An instance of something; example. **2a.** An occurrence of a disease or disorder. **b.** A person or group being treated or studied, as by a physician, attorney, or social worker. **3.** A set of circumstances or state of affairs. **4.** A question or problem; matter. **5.** *Law* An action or suit or just grounds for an action. **6.** A persuasive argument, demonstration, or justification. **7.** *Ling.* An inflectional pattern or form of nouns, pronouns, and adjectives to express syntactic functions in a sentence. **—idioms:** **in any case** Regardless of what has occurred or will occur. **in case** If it happens that; if. **in case of** If there should happen to be. [< Lat. *cāsus* < *cadere,* fall.]

case² (kās) ►*n.* **1.** A container or receptacle. **2.** A decorative or protective covering. **3.** A set or pair: *a case of pistols.* **4.** The frame of a window, door, or stairway. **5.** A shallow tray with compartments for storing printing type. **6.** The form of a written or printed letter that distinguishes it as being lowercase or uppercase. ►*v.* **cased, cas·ing** **1.** To put into or cover with a case. **2.** *Informal* To examine (e.g., a place) carefully, as in planning a crime. [< Lat. *capsa.*]

case history ►*n.* A historical record of facts pertaining to a case.

ca·sein (kā′sēn′, -sē-ĭn) ►*n.* A white, tasteless, milk protein, used to make plastics, adhesives, paints, and foods. [< Lat. *cāseus,* cheese.]

case·load (kās′lōd′) ►*n.* The number of cases handled in a given period, as by an attorney or social services agency.

case·ment (kās′mənt) ►*n.* **1.** A window sash that opens outward using hinges. **2.** A window with casements. [ME, hollow molding.]

case study ►*n.* A detailed analysis of a person or group, esp. as a model of medical, psychiatric, or social phenomena.

case·work (kās′wûrk′) ►*n.* Social work dealing with the needs of a particular case. **—case′-work′er** *n.*

cash (kăsh) ►*n.* **1.** Money in the form of bills or coins; currency. **2.** Liquid assets, such as bank deposits. **3.** Payment for goods or services in currency. ►*v.* To exchange for or convert into ready money. [Poss. obsolete Fr. *casse,* money box.]

Cash, John "Johnny." 1932–2003. Amer. country and western singer and songwriter.

cash·ew (kăsh′ōō, kə-shōō′) ►*n.* **1.** A tropical American tree bearing edible nutlike seeds. **2.** The kidney-shaped nut or seed of the cashew. [< Tupí *acajú.*]

cash·ier¹ (kă-shîr′) ►*n.* **1.** The officer of a bank or business concern in charge of paying and receiving money. **2.** A store employee who handles cash transactions with customers. [< Fr. *caisse,* money box.]

cash·ier² (kă-shîr′) ►*v.* To dismiss from a position of responsibility, esp. for disciplinary reasons. [< LLat. *cassāre,* quash.]

cash·ier's check (kă-shîrz′) ►*n.* A check drawn by a bank on its own funds and signed by the bank's cashier.

cash machine ►*n.* See **ATM.**

cash·mere (kăzh′mîr′, kăsh′-) ►*n.* **1.** Fine wool

from an Asian goat. **2.** A soft fabric made from cashmere. [< KASHMIR.]

cash register ►*n.* A machine that tabulates the amount of sales transactions and makes a permanent and cumulative record of them.

cas·ing (kā′sĭng) ►*n.* An outer cover; case.

ca·si·no (kə-sē′nō) ►*n., pl.* **-nos** A public room or building for gambling and other entertainment. [Ital. < Lat. *cāsa*, house.]

cask (kăsk) ►*n.* **1.** A sturdy cylindrical container for storing liquids. **2.** The amount a cask holds. [ME *caske.*]

cas·ket (kăs′kĭt) ►*n.* **1.** A coffin. **2.** A small case or chest, as for jewels. [ME.]

Cas·pi·an Sea (kăs′pē-ən) A saline lake between SE Europe and W Asia.

casque (kăsk) ►*n.* A helmet. [< Sp. *casco.*] —**casqued** (kăskt) *adj.*

Cas·san·dra (kə-săn′drə) ►*n.* **1.** *Gk. Myth.* A Trojan prophetess fated by Apollo never to be believed. **2.** One that utters unheeded prophecies. [< Gk. *Kassandra.*]

Cas·satt (kə-săt′), **Mary Stevenson** 1844?– 1926. Amer. painter.

Mary Cassatt
photographed c. 1914

cas·sa·va (kə-sä′və) ►*n.* A tropical American plant grown for its tuberous starchy root, a staple food and the source of tapioca. [Ult. < Taino *casavi*, cassava flour.]

cas·se·role (kăs′ə-rōl′) ►*n.* **1.** A dish, usu. of earthenware, glass, or cast iron, in which food is baked and served. **2.** Food baked and served in a casserole. [Fr., saucepan.]

cas·sette (kə-sĕt′, kă-) ►*n.* A cartridge for holding and winding magnetic tape, photographic film, or typewriter ribbon. [< OFr., small box.]

cassette deck ►*n.* A tape deck designed for recording or playing audiocassettes.

cas·sia (kăsh′ə) ►*n.* **1.** Any of various chiefly tropical trees or shrubs having usu. yellow flowers and long pods. **2.** A tropical Asian evergreen tree having cinnamonlike bark. [< Gk. *kassia*, of Semitic orig.]

Cas·si·o·pe·ia (kăs′ē-ə-pē′ə) ►*n.* A W-shaped constellation in the Northern Hemisphere.

cas·sock (kăs′ək) ►*n.* An ankle-length garment worn by the clergy. [< Pers. *kazhāgand*, padded garment.]

cas·so·war·y (kăs′ə-wĕr′ē) ►*n., pl.* **-ies** A large flightless bird of Australia and New Guinea with brightly colored wattles. [Malay *kesuari.*]

cast (kăst) ►*v.* **cast, cast·ing** **1.** To throw or fling. **2.** To shed or discard; molt. **3.** To deposit or indicate (a ballot or vote). **4.** To turn or direct: *cast a glance at me.* **5a.** To choose actors for. **b.** To assign a role to. **6.** To form (e.g., liquid metal) by molding. **7.** To add up (a column of figures); compute. ►*n.* **1.** A throw. **2.** A throw of dice. **3.** Something, such as molted skin, that is shed or thrown off. **4.** A mold. **5.** A rigid dressing, usu. made of gauze and plaster of Paris, used to immobilize an injured body part. **6.** Outward appearance; look. **7.** The actors in a play, movie, or other theatrical presentation. **8.** A slight trace of color; tinge. [< ON *kasta.*]

cas·ta·nets (kăs′tə-nĕts′) ►*pl.n.* A percussion instrument consisting of a pair of ivory or hardwood shells clapped together with the fingers. [< Lat. *castanea*, CHESTNUT.]

cast·a·way (kăst′ə-wā′) ►*adj.* **1.** Cast adrift or ashore; shipwrecked. **2.** Thrown away; discarded. —**cast′a·way′** *n.*

caste (kăst) ►*n.* **1.** Any of the hereditary social classes of traditional Hindu society, stratified according to Hindu ritual purity. **2a.** A social class separated from others by distinctions of hereditary rank, profession, or wealth. **b.** Social position or status. [< Lat. *castus*, race.]

cast·er (kăs′tər) ►*n.* **1.** One that casts. **2.** also **castor** A small wheel on a swivel, attached to the underside of a heavy object to make it easier to move. **3.** also **castor** A small bottle or cruet for condiments.

cas·ti·gate (kăs′tĭ-gāt′) ►*v.* **-gat·ed, -gat·ing** To punish or rebuke severely. [Lat. *castīgāre.*] —**cas′ti·ga′tion** *n.*

Cas·tile (kăs-tēl′) A region and former kingdom of central and N Spain.

Cas·til·ian (kă-stĭl′yən) ►*n.* **1.** A native or inhabitant of Castille. **2.** The Spanish dialect of Castille. —**Cas·til′ian** *adj.*

cast·ing (kăs′tĭng) ►*n.* **1.** Something cast in a mold. **2.** Something cast off or out.

cast iron ►*n.* A hard, brittle nonmalleable iron-carbon alloy containing 2 to 4.5% carbon and 0.5 to 3% silicon. —**cast′-i′ron** *adj.*

cast-i·ron plant (kăst′ī′ərn) ►*n.* See **aspidistra.**

cas·tle (kăs′əl) ►*n.* **1.** A large fortified building or group of buildings. **2.** A large imposing building. **3.** *Games* See **rook²**. [< Lat. *castellum.*]

cast·off (kăst′ôf′, -ŏf′) ►*n.* One that has been discarded. —**cast′off** *adj.*

cas·tor (kăs′tər) ►*n.* Var. of **caster** (senses 3, 5).

Castor ►*n.* A double star in Gemini.

castor oil ►*n.* An oil extracted from the seeds of a tropical plant and used as a laxative and industrially as a lubricant. [Prob. < *castor*, an oily secretion of beavers.]

cas·trate (kăs′trāt′) ►*v.* **-trat·ed, -trat·ing** To remove the testicles or ovaries of. [Lat. *castrāre.*] —**cas′trat·er, cas′tra·tor** *n.* —**cas·tra′tion** *n.*

Cas·tries (kăs′trēz′, -trēs′) The capital of St. Lucia, in the Windward Is. of the British West Indies.

Cas·tro (kăs′trō), **Fidel** b. 1927. Cuban revolutionary and political leader. In 2006, he passed de facto control of the Cuban government to his brother **Raul Castro** (b. 1931).

Fidel Castro
photographed in 2005

ca·su·al (kăzh′ōō-əl) ▸*adj.* **1a.** Informal or relaxed. **b.** Unpremeditated; offhand: *a casual remark.* **c.** Suited for informal wear or use: *casual clothing.* **2.** Not thorough; superficial. **3.** Nonchalant. **4.** Occurring by chance. **5.** Irregular; occasional. [< Lat. *cāsus,* CASE[1].] —**ca′su·al·ly** *adv.* —**ca′su·al·ness** *n.*

ca·su·al·ty (kăzh′ōō-əl-tē) ▸*n., pl.* **-ties 1.** A disastrous accident. **2.** One injured or killed in an accident. **3.** One injured, killed, captured, or missing in military action.

ca·su·ist·ry (kăzh′ōō-ĭ-strē) ▸*n.* Specious or overly subtle reasoning intended to rationalize or mislead. [< Lat. *cāsus,* CASE[1].] —**ca′su·ist** *n.*

cat (kăt) ▸*n.* **1a.** A small carnivorous mammal domesticated as a catcher of vermin and as a pet. **b.** An animal related to the cat, such as the lion, tiger, or leopard. **2.** *Slang* A person, esp. a man. [< OE *catt.*]

CAT ▸*abbr.* computerized axial tomography

ca·tab·o·lism (kə-tăb′ə-lĭz′əm) ▸*n.* Metabolic activity in which complex substances are broken down into simpler substances. [Gk. *kata-,* down + (META)BOLISM.] —**cat′a·bol′ic** (kăt′-ə-bŏl′ĭk) *adj.*

cat·a·clysm (kăt′ə-klĭz′əm) ▸*n.* A violent and sudden, usu. destructive upheaval. [< Gk. *katakluzein,* inundate.] —**cat′a·clys′mic, cat′a·clys′mal** *adj.* —**cat′a·clys′mi·cal·ly** *adv.*

cat·a·comb (kăt′ə-kōm′) ▸*n.* often **catacombs** An underground chamber or tunnel with recesses for graves. [< LLat. *catacumba.*]

cat·a·falque (kăt′ə-fălk′, -fôlk′) ▸*n.* A decorated platform on which a coffin rests in state during a funeral. [< Ital. *catafalco.*]

Cat·a·lan (kăt′l-ăn′) ▸*n.* **1.** A native or inhabitant of Catalonia. **2.** The Romance language of Catalonia. —**Cat′a·lan′** *adj.*

cat·a·lep·sy (kăt′l-ĕp′sē) ▸*n., pl.* **-sies** *Med.* A condition characterized by muscular rigidity and lack of response to external stimuli. [< Gk. *katalambanein,* seize upon.] —**cat′a·lep′tic** *adj.*

cat·a·log or **cat·a·logue** (kăt′l-ôg′, -ŏg′) ▸*n.* **1.** An itemized, often descriptive list. **2.** A publication containing a catalog. **3.** A card catalog. ▸*v.* **-loged, -log·ing** or **-logued, -logu·ing** **1.** To list in or make a catalog. **2.** To categorize (esp. a book). [< Gk. *katalegein,* count off.] —**cat′a·log′er, cat′a·logu′er** *n.*

Cat·a·lo·nia (kăt′l-ōn′yə) A region of NE Spain bordering on France and the Mediterranean. —**Cat′a·lo′nian** *adj. & n.*

ca·tal·pa (kə-tăl′pə, -tôl′-) ▸*n.* A North American tree having large heart-shaped leaves, showy white flower clusters, and long slender pods. [Creek *katałpa.*]

ca·tal·y·sis (kə-tăl′ĭ-sĭs) ▸*n., pl.* **-ses** (-sēz′) The action of a catalyst, esp. an increase in the rate of a chemical reaction. [< Gk. *kataluein,* dissolve.] —**cat′a·lyt′ic** (kăt′l-ĭt′ĭk) *adj.*

cat·a·lyst (kăt′l-ĭst) ▸*n.* **1.** *Chem.* A substance that modifies and increases the rate of a reaction without being consumed in the process. **2.** An agent of change.

catalytic converter ▸*n.* A device for reducing carbon monoxide and hydrocarbon pollutants in automobile exhaust.

cat·a·lyze (kăt′l-īz′) ▸*v.* **-lyzed, -lyz·ing 1.** To modify the rate of (a chemical reaction) by catalysis. **2.** To bring about change in; transform. —**cat′a·lyz′er** *n.*

cat·a·ma·ran (kăt′ə-mə-răn′) ▸*n.* A boat, esp. a light sailboat, with two parallel hulls or floats. [Tamil *kaṭṭumaram.*]

cat·a·mount (kăt′ə-mount′) ▸*n.* See **cougar.** [< *cat of the mountain.*]

cat·a·pult (kăt′ə-pŭlt′, -pŏolt′) ▸*n.* **1.** An ancient military machine for hurling large missiles. **2.** A mechanism for launching aircraft from the deck of a carrier. [< Gk. *katapaltēs.*] —**cat′a·pult′** *v.*

cat·a·ract (kăt′ə-răkt′) ▸*n.* **1.** A large waterfall. **2.** A downpour. **3.** Opacity of the lens or capsule of the eye, causing partial or total blindness. [< Gk. *katarraktēs.*]

ca·tarrh (kə-tär′) ▸*n.* Inflammation of mucous membranes, esp. of the nose and throat. [< Gk. *katarrous* : *kata-,* down + *rhein,* flow.] —**ca·tarrh′al** *adj.*

ca·tas·tro·phe (kə-tăs′trə-fē) ▸*n.* A great, often sudden calamity; disaster. [< Gk. *katastrephein,* overturn.] —**cat′a·stroph′ic** (kăt′ə-strŏf′ĭk) *adj.* —**cat′a·stroph′i·cal·ly** *adv.*

cat·a·to·ni·a (kăt′ə-tō′nē-ə) ▸*n.* An abnormal condition most often associated with schizophrenia and variously marked by stupor, mania, and either rigidity or extreme flexibility of the limbs. [< Gk. *katatonos,* stretching tight.] —**cat′a·ton′ic** (-tŏn′ĭk) *adj. & n.*

Ca·taw·ba (kə-tô′bə) ▸*n., pl.* **-ba** or **-bas 1.** A member of a Native American people now located in W South Carolina. **2.** The Siouan language of the Catawba.

cat·bird (kăt′bûrd′) ▸*n.* A dark gray North American songbird with a mewing call.

cat·call (kăt′kôl′) ▸*n.* A shrill whistle or call of derision or disapproval. —**cat′call′** *v.*

catch (kăch, kĕch) ▸*v.* **caught** (kôt), **catch·ing** **1a.** To get (something moving) and hold; grab: *caught the ball.* **b.** To take hold of or apprehend suddenly; grasp: *caught me by the arm.* **c.** To stop (oneself) from doing: *caught myself before replying.* **2a.** To capture, esp. after a chase: *catch that thief.* **b.** To snare or trap: *catch a fish.* **c.** To hold or contain: *a pond that catches runoff.* **3.** To discover or become aware of unexpectedly or accidentally. **4a.** To get to in time: *catch a plane.* **b.** To intercept or overtake. **5.** To become or cause to become held, entangled, or fastened. **6.** To hold up; delay. **7.** To become affected by or contract, as by contagion: *catch a cold; caught* *their enthusiasm.* **8.** To apprehend or grasp mentally. **9.** To perceive, esp. suddenly. **10.** To go to see: *caught the late show.* ►*n.* **1a.** The act of catching. **b.** A game of throwing and catching a ball. **2a.** Something caught or noticed. **b.** *Informal* One worth catching. **3.** Something that catches, esp. a device for fastening or for checking motion. **4.** An unsuspected drawback. —*phrasal verbs:* **catch on 1.** To understand or perceive. **2.** To become popular. **catch up 1.** To come up from behind; overtake. **2.** To bring up to date: *caught up on my reading.* —*idioms:* **catch fire 1.** To ignite. **2.** To gain sudden popularity. **catch (one's) breath** To pause or rest briefly. [< Lat. *captāre*, chase.] **Syns:** *enmesh, ensnare, entangle, entrap, snare, tangle, trap* **v.**

Catch-22 ►*n.* A situation in which a desired outcome is impossible to attain because of a set of inherently contradictory rules or conditions. [After the novel *Catch-22*, by Joseph Heller.]

catch·all (kăch′ôl′, kĕch′-) ►*n.* A receptacle or storage area for odds and ends.

catch·er (kăch′ər, kĕch′-) ►*n.* One that catches, esp. the baseball player positioned behind home plate.

catch·ing (kăch′ĭng, kĕch′-) ►*adj.* **1.** Infectious. **2.** Attractive; alluring.

catch·up (kăch′əp, kĕch′-) ►*n.* Var. of **ketch-up.**

catch·word (kăch′wûrd′, kĕch′-) ►*n.* A well-known word or phrase, esp. one that exemplifies a notion, class, or quality.

catch·y (kăch′ē, kĕch′ē) ►*adj.* **-i·er, -i·est 1.** Attractive; appealing: *a catchy idea for a story.* **2.** Easily remembered: *a catchy tune.* **3.** Tricky; deceptive. —**catch′i·ness** *n.*

cat·e·chism (kăt′ĭ-kĭz′əm) ►*n.* A text summarizing the basic principles of a Christian denomination in question-and-answer form. [< LGk. *katēkhismos.*] —**cat′e·chist** *n.* —**cat′-e·chize′** *v.*

cat·e·chu·men (kăt′ĭ-kyōō′mən) ►*n.* One who is being taught the principles of Christianity. [< Gk. *katēkhein*, instruct.]

cat·e·gor·i·cal (kăt′ĭ-gôr′ĭ-kəl, -gŏr′-) also **cat·e·gor·ic** (-ĭk) ►*adj.* **1.** Being without exception or qualification; absolute. **2.** Of or included in a category. —**cat′e·gor′i·cal·ly** *adv.*

cat·e·go·rize (kăt′ĭ-gə-rīz′) ►*v.* **-rized, -riz·ing** To put into categories. —**cat′e·go·riz′a·ble** *adj.* —**cat′e·go·ri·za′tion** *n.*

cat·e·go·ry (kăt′ĭ-gôr′ē) ►*n., pl.* **-ries** A specifically defined division in a system of classification; class. [< Gk. *katēgoria*, accusation.]

ca·ter (kā′tər) ►*v.* **1.** To provide food service (for). **2.** To be attentive or solicitous: *catered to our every need.* [< Norman Fr. *acatour*, buyer.] —**ca′ter·er** *n.*

cat·er-cor·nered (kăt′ər-kôr′nərd, kăt′ē-) also **cat·ty-cor·nered** (kăt′ē-kôr′nərd) or **cat·ty-cor·ner** (-nər) ►*adj.* Diagonal. ►*adv.* Diagonally. [< *cater*, four at dice < Lat. *quattuor.*]

cat·er·pil·lar (kăt′ər-pĭl′ər, kăt′ə-) ►*n.* The wormlike larva of a butterfly or moth. [Prob. < ONFr. *catepelose.*]

cat·er·waul (kăt′ər-wôl′) ►*v.* To make a discordant sound or shriek. [ME *caterwawlen.*] —**cat′er·waul′** *n.*

cat·fish (kăt′fĭsh′) ►*n.* Any of numerous scale-less fishes with whiskerlike feelers near the mouth.

cat·gut (kăt′gŭt′) ►*n.* A tough cord made from the dried intestines of certain animals.

ca·thar·sis (kə-thär′sĭs) ►*n., pl.* **-ses** (-sēz) **1.** *Med.* Purgation, esp. for the digestive system. **2.** A purging of the emotions as a result of experiencing esp. a dramatic work of art. [< Gk. *kathairein*, purge.]

ca·thar·tic (kə-thär′tĭk) ►*adj.* Inducing catharsis; purgative. ►*n.* A purgative.

ca·the·dral (kə-thē′drəl) ►*n.* The principal church of a bishop's diocese. [< Gk. *kathedra*, seat : *kat-*, down + *hedra*, seat.]

Cath·er (kăth′ər), **Willa Sibert** 1873–1947. Amer. writer.

Cath·e·rine II (kăth′ər-ĭn, kăth′rĭn) "the Great." 1729–96. Empress of Russia (1762–96).

Catherine de Mé·di·cis (də mĕd′ĭ-chē′, də mä-dē-sēs′) 1519–89. Queen of France as wife of Henry II and regent during the minority (1560–63) of her son Charles IX.

Catherine of Aragon 1485–1536. The first wife of Henry VIII.

cath·e·ter (kăth′ĭ-tər) ►*n.* A hollow flexible tube for insertion into a bodily channel to allow the passage of fluids or to distend a passageway. [< Gk. *kathienai*, send down.]

cath·ode (kăth′ōd′) ►*n.* **1.** A negatively charged electrode. **2.** The positively charged terminal of a primary cell or storage battery. [Gk. *kathodos*, a way down.] —**ca·thod′ic** (kă-thŏd′ĭk) *adj.*

cath·ode-ray tube (kăth′ōd-rā′) ►*n.* A vacuum tube in which a hot cathode emits electrons that are accelerated and focused on a phosphorescent screen.

cath·o·lic (kăth′ə-lĭk, kăth′lĭk) ►*adj.* **1.** Universal; general. **2. Catholic** Of or involving the Roman Catholic Church or Catholics. ►*n.* **Catholic** A member of the Roman Catholic Church. [< Gk. *katholikos*, universal.] —**ca·thol′i·cal·ly** (kə-thŏl′ĭk-lē) *adv.*

Ca·thol·i·cism (kə-thŏl′ĭ-sĭz′əm) ►*n.* The faith, doctrine, system, and practice of the Roman Catholic Church.

Cat·i·line (kăt′l-īn′) 108?–62 BC. Roman politician and conspirator.

cat·i·on (kăt′ī′ən) ►*n.* An ion or group of ions having a positive charge and characteristically moving toward a negative electrode in electrolysis. [Gk. *kation*, (thing) going down.] —**cat′i·on′ic** (-ŏn′ĭk) *adj.*

cat·kin (kăt′kĭn) ►*n.* A dense, often drooping cluster of scalelike flowers found in willows, birches, and oaks. [< obsolete Du. *katteken*, kitten.]

cat·nap (kăt′năp′) ►*n.* A short nap; light sleep. —**cat′nap′** *v.*

cat·nip (kăt′nĭp′) ►*n.* An aromatic plant to which cats are strongly attracted.

Ca·to¹ (kā′tō), **Marcus Porcius** "the Elder." 234–149 BC. Roman politician and general.

Ca·to² (kā′tō), **Marcus Porcius** "the Younger." 95–46 BC. Roman politician and great-grandson of Cato the Elder.

cat-o′-nine-tails (kăt′ə-nīn′tālz′) ►*n., pl.* **cat-o′-nine-tails** A flogging whip consisting of nine knotted cords fastened to a handle.

CAT scanner (kăt) ►*n.* A device that produces cross-sectional views of a body part using computerized axial tomography. —**CAT scan** *n.*

cat's cradle (kăts) ►*n.* A game in which an intricately looped string is transferred from the hands of one player to another.

cat's-eye (kăts′ī′) ►*n.* A semiprecious gem displaying a band of reflected light that shifts position as the gem is turned.

Cats·kill Mountains (kăt′skĭl′) An upland region in SE NY.

cat's-paw also **cats·paw** (kăts′pô′) ►*n.* A person used by another as a dupe or tool.

cat·sup (kăt′səp, kăch′əp, kĕch′-) ►*n.* Var. of **ketchup.**

cat·tail (kăt′tāl′) ►*n.* A tall-stemmed marsh plant having long straplike leaves and a dense brown cylindrical head.

cat·tle (kăt′l) ►*pl.n.* Bovine mammals such as cows, steers, bulls, and oxen, often raised for meat and dairy products. [< Med.Lat. *capitāle,* property.] —**cat′tle·man** *n.*

cat·ty (kăt′ē) ►*adj.* **-ti·er, -ti·est** Slyly malicious. —**cat′ti·ly** *adv.* —**cat′ti·ness** *n.*

cat·ty-cor·nered (kăt′ē-kôr′nərd) ►*adj. & adv.* Var. of **cater-cornered.**

Ca·tul·lus (kə-tŭl′əs), **Gaius Valerius** 84?–54? BC. Roman lyric poet.

cat·walk (kăt′wôk′) ►*n.* A narrow, often elevated walkway, as on the sides of a bridge.

Cau·ca·sian (kô-kā′zhən) ►*adj.* **1.** Of or being a human racial classification traditionally distinguished by light to brown skin color and including peoples indigenous to Europe, N Africa, W Asia, and India. **2.** Of the Caucasus. ►*n.* **1.** *Anthro.* A member of the Caucasian racial classification. **2.** A native or inhabitant of the Caucasus.

Cau·ca·soid (kô′kə-soid′) ►*adj.* Of or relating to the Caucasian racial classification. No longer in scientific use. See Usage Note at **Negroid.** —**Cau′ca·soid′** *n.*

Cau·ca·sus (kô′kə-səs) also **Cau·ca·sia** (kô-kā′-zhə, -shə) A region between the Black and Caspian Seas that includes Georgia, Azerbaijan, Armenia, and part of Russia.

Caucasus Mountains A range extending from the NW to the SE in the Caucasus.

cau·cus (kô′kəs) ►*n., pl.* **-cus·es** or **-cus·ses 1.** A meeting of the local members of a political party esp. to select delegates to a convention. **2.** A group within a legislative body seeking to represent a specific interest or policy. [After the *Caucus* Club of Boston.] —**cau′cus** *v.*

cau·dal (kôd′l) ►*adj.* Of, at, or near the tail or hind parts; posterior. [< Lat. *cauda,* tail.]

cau·dil·lo (kô-dēl′yō, -dē′yō) ►*n., pl.* **-los** A leader or chief, esp. a military dictator. [Sp. < LLat. *capitellum,* small head.]

caught (kôt) ►*v.* P.t. and p.part. of **catch.**

caul (kôl) ►*n.* A portion of the amnion, esp. when it covers the head of a fetus at birth. [< OE *cawl,* basket.]

caul·dron (kôl′drən) ►*n.* **1.** A large kettle or vat. **2.** A situation of seething unrest. [< LLat. *caldāria,* cooking pot.]

cau·li·flow·er (kô′lĭ-flou′ər, kŏl′ĭ-) ►*n.* A plant related to the cabbage and broccoli, having a large edible whitish head of undeveloped flowers. [Prob. < Lat. *caulis,* stem + *flōs,* flower.]

cauliflower ear ►*n.* An ear swollen and deformed by repeated blows.

caulk also **calk** (kôk) ►*v.* **1.** To make (e.g., pipes) watertight or airtight by sealing. **2.** To make (a

boat) watertight by packing seams with oakum or tar. ►*n.* Caulking. [< ONFr. *cauquer,* to press.] —**caulk′er** *n.*

caulk·ing (kô′kĭng) ►*n.* A usu. impermeable substance used to caulk or seal.

caus·al (kô′zəl) ►*adj.* Of, constituting, or expressing a cause. —**cau·sal′i·ty** (-zăl′ĭ-tē) *n.* —**caus′al·ly** *adv.*

cau·sa·tion (kô-zā′shən) ►*n.* **1.** The act or process of causing. **2.** A causal agency.

cause (kôz) ►*n.* **1.** The one, such as a person, event, or condition, responsible for an action or result. **2.** A reason; motive. **3.** A goal or principle. **4a.** A lawsuit. **b.** A ground for legal action. ►*v.* **caused, caus·ing** To be the cause of; bring about. [< Lat. *causa,* reason.] —**cause′less** *adj.*

cause cé·lè·bre (kôz′ sə-lĕb′, sā-lĕb′rə) ►*n., pl.* **causes cé·lè·bres** (kôz′ sə-lĕb′, kôz′ sā-lĕb′rə) **1.** An issue arousing widespread controversy or heated debate. **2.** A celebrated legal case. [Fr.]

cause·way (kôz′wā′) ►*n.* A raised roadway across water or marshland. [ME *caucewei.*]

caus·tic (kô′stĭk) ►*adj.* **1.** Capable of burning, corroding, or dissolving by chemical action. **2.** Sarcastic; biting. ►*n.* A caustic substance. [< Gk. *kaustikos.*]

cau·ter·ize (kô′tə-rīz′) ►*v.* **-ized, -iz·ing** To burn or sear so as to stop bleeding and prevent infection. [< Gk. *kautērion,* branding iron.] —**cau′ter·i·za′tion** *n.*

cau·tion (kô′shən) ►*n.* **1.** Careful forethought to avoid danger or harm. **2.** A warning or admonition. ►*v.* To warn. [< Lat. *cavēre, caut-,* take care.] —**cau′tion·ar′y** *adj.*

cau·tious (kô′shəs) ►*adj.* Showing or practicing caution; careful. —**cau′tious·ly** *adv.* —**cau′tious·ness** *n.*

cav·al·cade (kăv′əl-kād, kăv′əl-kād′) ►*n.* **1.** A procession of riders or horse-drawn carriages. **2.** A ceremonial procession. [< Med.Lat. *caballicāre,* ride on horseback.]

cav·a·lier (kăv′ə-lîr′) ►*n.* **1.** A gallant gentleman. **2.** A mounted soldier; knight. **3. Cavalier** A supporter of Charles I of England. ►*adj.* **1.** Haughty; disdainful. **2.** Carefree and nonchalant; jaunty. [< Med.Lat. *caballārius,* horseman.] —**cav′a·lier′ly** *adv.*

cav·al·ry (kăv′əl-rē) ►*n., pl.* **-ries** Troops trained to fight on horseback or in light armored vehicles. [< Ital. *cavalleria < cavaliere,* CAVALIER.] —**cav′al·ry·man** *n.*

cave (kāv) ►*n.* A hollow or natural passage under or into the earth with an opening to the surface. ►*v.* **caved, cav·ing 1.** To fall in; collapse. **2.** To capitulate; yield: *caved in to their demands.* **3.** To explore caves. [< Lat. *cava.*] —**cav′er** *n.*

ca·ve·at (kăv′ē-ăt′, kä′vē-ät′) ►*n.* A warning or caution. [< Lat., let him beware.]

cave-in (kāv′ĭn′) ►*n.* A collapse, as of a tunnel or structure.

cave·man (kāv′măn′) ►*n.* **1.** A prehistoric human who lived in caves. **2.** *Informal* A man who is crude, esp. toward women.

cav·ern (kăv′ərn) ►*n.* A large cave. [< Lat. *caverna.*] —**cav′ern·ous** *adj.*

cav·i·ar also **cav·i·are** (kăv′ē-är′, kä′vē-) ►*n.* The roe of a large fish, esp. a sturgeon, salted and eaten as a delicacy. [< Turk. *havyar* < Pers. *khāvyār;* akin to MPers. *khāyak,* egg.]

cav·il (kăv′əl) ►v. **-iled, -il·ing** also **-illed, -il·ling** To find fault unnecessarily. See Synonyms at **quibble.** [< Lat. *cavillārī*, jeer.] —**cav′il** n. —**cav′il·er** n.

cav·i·ty (kăv′ĭ-tē) ►n., pl. **-ties 1.** A hollow or hole. **2.** A pitted area in a tooth caused by decay. [< Lat. *cavus*, hollow.]

ca·vort (kə-vôrt′) ►v. To leap about; caper. [Poss. alteration of *curvet*, a leap.]

caw (kô) ►n. The hoarse raucous sound of a crow or similar bird. [Imit.] —**caw** v.

cay (kē, kā) ►n. A small low island of coral or sand; key. [< Sp. *cayo*.]

Cay·enne (kī-ĕn′, kā-) The capital of French Guiana, in the NE at the mouth of the **Cayenne River.**

cayenne pepper ►n. A condiment made from the fruit of a pungent variety of capsicum pepper. [< Tupí *quiínia*.]

cay·man (kā′mən) ►n. Var. of **caiman.**

Cay·man Islands (kā-măn′, kā′mən) A British-administered group of three islands in the Caribbean Sea NW of Jamaica. Cap. Georgetown.

Ca·yu·ga (kə-yōō′gə, kī-) ►n., pl. **-ga** or **-gas 1.** A member of a Native American people formerly of W-central New York, now living in Ontario, W New York, Wisconsin, and Oklahoma. **2.** Their Iroquoian language.

cay·use (kī-yōōs′, kī′yōōs′) ►n. A horse, esp. an Indian pony of the Pacific Northwest.

Cayuse ►n., pl. **-use** or **-us·es 1.** A member of a Native American people of NE Oregon and SE Washington. **2.** Their language.

CB (sē-bē′) ►abbr. citizens band

CBD ►abbr. central business district

CBO ►abbr. **1.** community-based organization **2.** Congressional Budget Office

CBW ►abbr. chemical and biological warfare

cc ►abbr. **1.** carbon copy **2.** cubic centimeter

CC ►abbr. closed captioned

CCC ►abbr. **1.** Civilian Conservation Corps **2.** Commodity Credit Corporation

cckw. or **ccw.** ►abbr. counterclockwise

CCTV ►abbr. closed-circuit television

CCU ►abbr. **1.** cardiac care unit **2.** coronary care unit **3.** critical care unit

cd ►abbr. **1.** candela **2.** cord

CD ►abbr. **1.** certificate of deposit **2.** civil defense **3.** compact disc

CDC ►abbr. Centers for Disease Control and Prevention

CDO ►abbr. collateralized debt obligation

CDR ►abbr. commander

CD-ROM (sē′dē′rŏm′) ►n. A compact disc that functions as read-only memory.

CDT ►abbr. Central Daylight Time

CE or **CE** ►abbr. Common Era

cease (sēs) ►v. **ceased, ceas·ing** To bring or come to an end. See Synonyms at **stop.** [< Lat. *cessāre*.]

cease-fire (sēs′fīr′) ►n. **1.** An order to stop firing. **2.** Suspension of hostilities; truce.

cease·less (sēs′lĭs) ►adj. Never ending. —**cease′less·ly** adv.

Ceau·ses·cu (chou-shĕs′kōō), **Nicolae** 1918–89. Romanian dictator (1965–89).

Ce·cil·ia (sĭ-sēl′yə), Saint. 3rd cent. AD. Christian martyr.

ce·cum also **cae·cum** (sē′kəm) ►n., pl. **-ca** (-kə) The pouch at the beginning of the large intestine. [< Lat. *(intestīnum) caecum*, blind (intestine).] —**ce′cal** adj. —**ce′cal·ly** adv.

ce·dar (sē′dər) ►n. Any of a genus of evergreen trees having large erect cones and aromatic, usu. reddish wood. [< Gk. *kedros*.]

cede (sēd) ►v. **ced·ed, ced·ing 1.** To surrender possession of, esp. by treaty. **2.** To yield or grant. [< Lat. *cēdere*.]

ce·di (sā′dē) ►n., pl. **-dis** See table at **currency.** [Poss. < Akan (African) *sedi*, cowry.]

ce·dil·la (sĭ-dĭl′ə) ►n. A mark (¸) placed beneath the letter c, as in *façade*, to indicate that the letter is to be pronounced (s). [Obsolete Sp., dim. of *ceda*, the letter z.]

cei·ba (sā′bə) ►n. The kapok tree. [Sp.]

ceil·ing (sē′lĭng) ►n. **1.** The upper interior surface of a room. **2.** An upper limit: *wage and price ceilings.* **3.** The highest altitude under particular weather conditions from which the ground is visible. [ME *celing.*]

Cel·e·bes (sĕl′ə-bēz′, sə-lē′bēz′) See **Sulawesi.**

Celebes Sea A section of the W Pacific between Sulawesi and the S Philippines.

cel·e·brate (sĕl′ə-brāt′) ►v. **-brat·ed, -brat·ing 1.** To observe (a day or event) with ceremonies of respect, festivity, or rejoicing. **2.** To perform (a religious ceremony). **3.** To extol or praise. [< Lat. *celeber*, famous.] —**cel′e·brant** n. —**cel′e·bra′tion** n. —**cel′e·bra′tor** n. —**cel′e·bra·to′ry** (sĕl′ə-brə-tôr′ē, sə-lĕb′rə-) adj.

cel·e·brat·ed (sĕl′ə-brā′tĭd) ►adj. Known and praised widely. See Synonyms at **famous.**

ce·leb·ri·ty (sə-lĕb′rĭ-tē) ►n., pl. **-ties 1.** One who is widely known and of popular interest. **2.** Renown; fame. [< Lat. *celeber*, famous.]

Syns: luminary, name, notable, personage n.

ce·ler·i·ty (sə-lĕr′ĭ-tē) ►n. Swiftness; speed. See Synonyms at **haste.** [< Lat. *celer*, swift.]

cel·er·y (sĕl′ə-rē) ►n. A plant having edible roots, leafstalks, leaves, and seedlike fruits. [< Gk. *selinon.*]

ce·les·ta (sə-lĕs′tə) also **ce·leste** (-lĕst′) ►n. A keyboard instrument with metal plates struck by hammers. [< Fr. *céleste*, CELESTIAL.]

ce·les·tial (sə-lĕs′chəl) ►adj. **1.** Of or relating to the sky or the universe. **2.** Of or suggestive of heaven; heavenly. [< Lat. *caelestis.*]

celestial equator ►n. A great circle on the celestial sphere in the same plane as the earth's equator.

celestial navigation ►n. Navigation based on the positions of celestial bodies.

celestial sphere ►n. An imaginary sphere of infinite extent with the earth at its center.

cel·i·bate (sĕl′ə-bĭt) ►adj. **1.** Abstaining from sexual relations. **2.** Remaining unmarried, esp. for religious reasons. [< Lat. *caelebs.*] —**cel′i·ba·cy** (-bə-sē) n. —**cel′i·bate** n.

cell (sĕl) ►n. **1.** A narrow confining room, as in a prison. **2.** A small enclosed space, as in a honeycomb. **3.** A rectangular box on a spreadsheet where a column and a row intersect. **4.** *Biol.* The smallest structural unit of an organism that is capable of independent functioning, consisting of cytoplasm, usu. one nucleus, and various other organelles, all surrounded by a semipermeable membrane. **5.** The smallest organizational unit of a clandestine group or movement. **6.** *Elect.* **a.** A single unit for electrolysis or conversion of chemical into electric energy, usu. consisting of a container with electrodes and an electrolyte. **b.** A unit that converts radiant energy into electric energy. **7a.** A geographic area or zone surrounding a transmitter in a cellular telephone system. **b.** A cell phone. [< Lat. *cella,* chamber.]

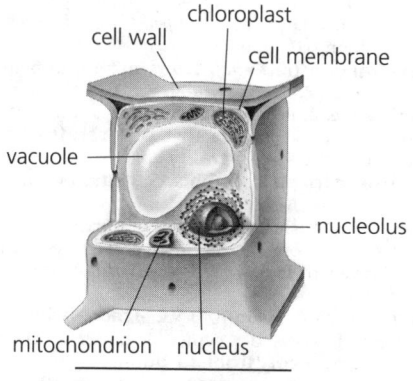

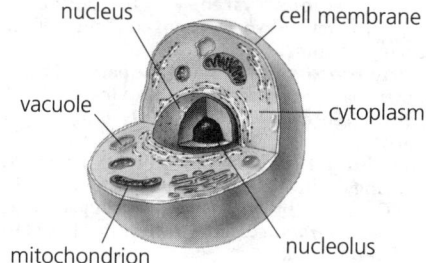

cell
top: plant cell
bottom: animal cell

cel·lar (sĕl′ər) ►*n.* **1.** An underground room usu. beneath a building. **2.** A stock of wines. [< LLat. *cellārium,* pantry.]

cell·block (sĕl′blŏk′) ►*n.* A group of cells that make up a section of a prison.

Cel·li·ni (chə-lē′nē, chĕ-), **Benvenuto** 1500–71. Italian writer and sculptor.

cell·mate (sĕl′māt′) ►*n.* One with whom a cell is shared, esp. in a prison.

cel·lo (chĕl′ō) ►*n., pl.* **-los** *Mus.* An instrument of the violin family, pitched lower than the viola but higher than the double bass. [< VIOLON-CELLO.] **—cel′list** *n.*

cel·lo·phane (sĕl′ə-fān′) ►*n.* **1.** A thin, flexible, transparent cellulose material used as a moistureproof wrapping. **2.** Plastic wrap. [Orig. a trademark.]

cell phone or **cell·phone** (sĕl′fōn′) ►*n.* A portable telephone that sends and receives radio signals through a network of short-range transmitters, with a central station that connects to regular telephone lines.

cel·lu·lar (sĕl′yə-lər) ►*adj.* **1.** Of or resembling a cell. **2.** Consisting of cells. **3.** Of or relating to a cellular telephone.

cellular telephone ►*n.* See **cell phone.**

cel·lu·lite (sĕl′yə-līt′, -lēt′) ►*n.* A fatty deposit causing dimpled skin, as around the thighs.

[Fr. : *cellule,* cell + NLat. -*ītis,* -itis.]

cel·lu·loid (sĕl′yə-loid′) ►*n.* A colorless flammable material made from nitrocellulose and camphor, used to make photographic film. [Orig. a trademark.]

cel·lu·lose (sĕl′yə-lōs′, -lōz′) ►*n.* A natural polysaccharide, $(C_6H_{10}O_5)_n$, the main constituent of the cell wall in most plants, used in the manufacture of paper, textiles, and explosives. [Fr.] **—cel′lu·lo′sic** *adj.*

cellulose acetate ►*n.* A cellulose resin used in lacquers and photographic film.

Cel·si·us (sĕl′sē-əs, -shəs) ►*adj.* Of or according to a temperature scale that registers the freezing point of water as 0° and the boiling point as 100° under normal atmospheric pressure. See table at **measurement.** [After Anders *Celsius* (1701–1744).]

Celt (kĕlt, sĕlt) ►*n.* **1.** One of an ancient people of central and W Europe, esp. a Briton or Gaul. **2.** A speaker of a Celtic language.

Celt·ic (kĕl′tĭk, sĕl′-) ►*n.* A subfamily of the Indo-European language family that includes Welsh, Irish Gaelic, Scottish Gaelic, Breton, and Gaulish. ►*adj.* Of or relating to the Celts or their languages.

ce·ment (sĭ-mĕnt′) ►*n.* **1.** A building material made by grinding calcined limestone and clay to a fine powder, which can be mixed with water and poured to set as a solid mass or used as an ingredient in making mortar or concrete. **2.** A substance that hardens to act as an adhesive; glue. **3.** Var. of **cementum.** ►*v.* **1.** To bind with or as if with cement. **2.** To cover or coat with cement. [< Lat. *caementum,* rough-cut stone.]

cement mixer ►*n.* A revolving container, often mounted on a truck, in which cement, sand, gravel, and water are combined into concrete.

ce·men·tum (sĭ-mĕn′təm) also **ce·ment** (-mĕnt′) ►*n.* A bonelike substance covering the root of a tooth. [< Lat. *caementum,* rough stone.]

cem·e·ter·y (sĕm′ĭ-tĕr′ē) ►*n., pl.* **-ies** A place for burying the dead; graveyard. [< Gk. *koimētērion.*]

–cene ►*suff.* Recent: *Oligocene, Pleistocene.* [< Gk. *kainos,* new.]

cen·o·taph (sĕn′ə-tăf′) ►*n.* A monument to commemorate a dead person whose remains lie elsewhere. [< Gk. *kenotaphion.*]

Ce·no·zo·ic (sĕn′ə-zō′ĭk, sē′nə-) ►*adj.* Of or being the most recent geologic era, including the Tertiary and Quaternary Periods and marked by the formation of modern continents and the diversification of mammals, birds, and plants. ►*n.* The Cenozoic Era. [Gk. *kainos,* new + –ZOIC.]

cen·ser (sĕn′sər) ►*n.* A vessel in which incense is burned, esp. during religious services. [< OFr. *encens,* INCENSE[2].]

cen·sor (sĕn′sər) ►*n.* **1.** One authorized to examine books, films, or other material and remove or suppress what is considered objectionable. **2.** A Roman official responsible for supervising the census. ►*v.* To examine and expurgate. [< Lat. *cēnsēre,* assess.] **—cen·so′ri·al** (sĕn-sôr′ē-əl) *adj.*

cen·so·ri·ous (sĕn-sôr′ē-əs) ►*adj.* Tending to censure; critical. **—cen·so′ri·ous·ly** *adv.*

cen·sor·ship (sĕn′sər-shĭp′) ►*n.* **1.** The act or

process of censoring. **2.** The office of a Roman censor.

cen·sure (sĕn′shər) ►*n.* **1.** An expression of disapproval, blame, or criticism. **2.** An official rebuke. ►*v.* **-sured, -sur·ing** To criticize severely, esp. in an official capacity. —**cen′sur·a·ble** *adj.*

cen·sus (sĕn′səs) ►*n.* A periodic official population count. [< Lat. *cēnsēre*, assess.]

cent (sĕnt) ►*n.* A monetary unit equal to ¹⁄₁₀₀ of various currencies, including the US dollar and the euro. [< Lat. *centum*, hundred.]

cent. ►*abbr.* **1.** centigrade **2.** *Lat.* centum (hundred) **3.** century

cen·taur (sĕn′tôr′) ►*n. Gk. Myth.* One of a race of monsters having the head, arms, and trunk of a man and the body and legs of a horse. [< Gk. *Kentauros.*]

cen·ta·vo (sĕn-tä′vō) ►*n., pl.* **-vos** A unit of currency equal to ¹⁄₁₀₀ of the primary unit in many Central and South American countries and formerly in Portugal. [Sp., hundredth.]

cen·te·nar·i·an (sĕn′tə-nâr′ē-ən) ►*n.* One that is 100 years or older. —**cen′te·nar′i·an** *adj.*

cen·ten·a·ry (sĕn-tĕn′ə-rē, sĕn′tə-nĕr′ē) ►*n., pl.* **-ries 1.** A 100-year period. **2.** A centennial. [< Lat. *centēnārius*, of a hundred.] —**cen·ten′a·ry** *adj.*

cen·ten·ni·al (sĕn-tĕn′ē-əl) ►*n.* A 100th anniversary. [Lat. *centum*, hundred + (BI)ENNIAL.] —**cen·ten′ni·al** *adj.*

cen·ter (sĕn′tər) ►*n.* **1.** A point equidistant from the sides or outer boundaries of something; middle. **2a.** A point equidistant from the vertices of a regular polygon. **b.** A point equidistant from all points on the circumference of a circle or on the surface of a sphere. **3.** A point around which something revolves; axis. **4.** A place of concentrated activity, service, or influence: *a medical center.* **5.** One occupying a middle position. **6.** A political group with views midway between the right and the left. **7.** *Sports* A player who holds a middle position. ►*v.* **1.** To place in, on, or at the center. **2.** To have a center; focus. [< Gk. *kentron.*]

cen·ter·board (sĕn′tər-bôrd′) ►*n.* A movable keel in a sailboat that can be pivoted upward, as in shallow water.

center field ►*n. Baseball* The middle third of the outfield, behind second base. —**center fielder** *n.*

cen·ter·fold (sĕn′tər-fōld′) ►*n.* A magazine center spread, esp. an oversize feature that folds out.

center of mass ►*n., pl.* **centers of mass** The point in a system at which its mass may be considered to be concentrated.

cen·ter·piece (sĕn′tər-pēs′) ►*n.* **1.** A decorative arrangement placed at the center of a table. **2.** The most important feature.

cen·tes·i·mal (sĕn-tĕs′ə-məl) ►*adj.* Relating to or divided into hundredths. [< Lat. *centēsimus.*]

centi– ►*pref.* **1.** One hundredth (10⁻²): *centiliter.* **2.** One hundred: *centipede.* [< Lat. *centum*, hundred.]

cen·ti·grade (sĕn′tĭ-grād′) ►*adj.* Celsius.

cen·ti·gram (sĕn′tĭ-grăm′) ►*n.* See table at measurement.

cen·ti·li·ter (sĕn′tə-lē′tər) ►*n.* See table at **measurement.**

cen·time (sän′tēm′, säɴ-tēm′) ►*n.* A unit of

currency equal to ¹⁄₁₀₀ of the primary unit in many countries where French is spoken as an official language, and formerly in France and Belgium. [Fr.]

cen·ti·me·ter (sĕn′tə-mē′tər) ►*n.* See table at **measurement.**

cen·ti·pede (sĕn′tə-pēd′) ►*n.* A segmented arthropod with a long body, many legs, and venomous claws. [Lat. *centipeda* : CENTI– + *pēs-, ped-*, foot; see –PED.]

cen·tral (sĕn′trəl) ►*adj.* **1.** At, in, near, or being the center. **2.** Key; essential. ►*n.* **1.** A telephone exchange. **2.** A coordinating office at the center of a group of related activities. —**cen·tral′i·ty** (-trăl′ĭ-tē) *n.* —**cen′tral·ly** *adv.*

Central African Republic A country of central Africa. Cap. Bangui.

Central America A region of S North America extending from the S border of Mexico to the N border of Colombia. —**Central American** *adj. & n.*

cen·tral·ize (sĕn′trə-līz′) ►*v.* **-ized, -iz·ing** To bring or come to a center or under a central authority. —**cen′tral·i·za′tion** *n.*

central nervous system ►*n.* The portion of the vertebrate nervous system consisting of the brain and spinal cord.

central processing unit ►*n.* The part of a computer that interprets and executes instructions.

cen·tre (sĕn′tər) ►*n. & v. Chiefly Brit.* Var. of **center.**

cen·trif·u·gal (sĕn-trĭf′yə-gəl, -trĭf′ə-) ►*adj.* **1.** Moving or directed away from a center or axis. **2.** Operated by means of centrifugal force. [< Lat. *centrum*, center + *fugere*, flee.] —**cen·trif′u·gal·ly** *adv.*

centrifugal force ►*n.* The apparent force, equal and opposite to the centripetal force, drawing a rotating body away from the center of rotation, caused by the inertia of the body.

cen·tri·fuge (sĕn′trə-fyōoj′) ►*n.* A compartment spun about a central axis to separate contained materials of different densities or to simulate gravity with centrifugal force. [< Fr., CENTRIFUGAL.] —**cen′tri·fuge′** *v.*

cen·trip·e·tal (sĕn-trĭp′ĭ-tl) ►*adj.* **1.** Moving or directed toward a center or axis. **2.** Operated by means of centripetal force. [< Lat. *centrum*, center + *petere*, seek.] —**cen·trip′e·tal·ly** *adv.*

centripetal force ►*n.* The component of force acting on a body in curvilinear motion that is directed toward the center of curvature or axis of rotation.

cen·trism (sĕn′trĭz′əm) ►*n.* The philosophy of taking a moderate political position. —**cen′trist** *adj. & n.*

centro– or **centr–** or **centri–** ►*pref.* Center: *centrism.* [< Lat. *centrum*, CENTER.]

cen·tu·ri·on (sĕn-tŏor′ē-ən, -tyŏor′-) ►*n.* The commander of a century in the ancient Roman army. [< Lat. *centuriō.*]

cen·tu·ry (sĕn′chə-rē) ►*n., pl.* **-ries 1.** A period of 100 years. **2.** A unit of the ancient Roman army orig. consisting of 100 men. [Lat. *centuria*, a group of a hundred.]

CEO ►*abbr.* chief executive officer

ce·phal·ic (sə-făl′ĭk) ►*adj.* Of or relating to the head. [< Gk. *kephalē*, head.]

ceph·a·lo·pod (sĕf′ə-lə-pŏd′) ►*n.* Any of various marine mollusks, such as the octopus or squid, having a large head, many arms or tentacles, and usu. an ink sac for protection or defense. [Gk. *kephalē,* head + –POD.]

ce·ram·ic (sə-răm′ĭk) ►*n.* **1.** Any of various hard, brittle, heat-resistant and corrosion-resistant materials made by firing clay or other nonmetallic minerals. **2a.** An object made of ceramic. **b. ceramics** *(takes sing. v.)* The art of making objects of ceramic, esp. from fired clay. [< Gk. *keramos,* clay.] —**ce·ram′ic** *adj.*

ce·re·al (sîr′ē-əl) ►*n.* **1.** A grass such as wheat, oats, or corn, whose starchy grains are used as food. **2.** A food prepared from such grains. [< Lat. *Cerēs,* Ceres.]

cer·e·bel·lum (sĕr′ə-bĕl′əm) ►*n., pl.* **-lums** or **-bel·la** (-bĕl′ə) The structure of the brain responsible for control of voluntary muscular movement. [< Lat., dim. of *cerebrum,* brain.] —**cer′e·bel′lar** *adj.*

cer·e·bral (sĕr′ə-brəl, sə-rē′-) ►*adj.* **1.** Of the brain or cerebrum. **2.** Intellectual rather than emotional. —**cer·e′bral·ly** *adv.*

cerebral cortex ►*n.* The outer layer of gray matter that covers the two parts of the cerebrum, largely responsible for higher nervous functions.

cerebral palsy ►*n.* A disorder usu. caused by brain damage at or before birth and marked by poor muscular coordination.

cer·e·brum (sĕr′ə-brəm, sə-rē′-) ►*n., pl.* **-brums** or **-bra** (-brə) The large rounded structure of the brain occupying most of the cranial cavity and divided into two cerebral hemispheres. [Lat., brain.]

cere·cloth (sîr′klôth′, -klŏth′) ►*n.* Cloth coated with wax, formerly used for wrapping the dead. [< Lat. *cēra,* wax.]

cer·e·ment (sĕr′ə-mənt, sîr′mənt) ►*n.* **1.** Cerecloth. **2.** often **cerements** A burial garment. [Fr. *cirement* < OFr. *cirer,* cover with wax.]

cer·e·mo·ni·al (sĕr′ə-mō′nē-əl) ►*adj.* Of or characterized by ceremony. ►*n.* **1.** A set of ceremonies for a specific occasion; ritual. **2.** A ceremony. —**cer′e·mo′ni·al·ly** *adv.*

cer·e·mo·ni·ous (sĕr′ə-mō′nē-əs) ►*adj.* **1.** Strictly observant of ceremony or etiquette; punctilious. **2.** Characterized by ceremony; formal. —**cer′e·mo′ni·ous·ly** *adv.*

cer·e·mo·ny (sĕr′ə-mō′nē) ►*n., pl.* **-nies 1.** A formal act performed as prescribed by ritual, custom, or etiquette. **2.** A conventional social gesture or courtesy: *the ceremony of shaking hands.* **3.** Strict observance of formalities or etiquette. [< Lat. *caerimōnia,* religious rite.]

Ce·res (sîr′ēz) ►*n.* **1.** *Rom. Myth.* The goddess of agriculture. **2.** The closest dwarf planet to the sun, with an orbit between Mars and Jupiter.

ce·re·us (sîr′ē-əs) ►*n.* Any of a genus of cactus that includes the saguaro and several night-blooming species. [< Lat. *cēreus,* candle.]

ce·rise (sə-rēs′, -rēz′) ►*n.* A purplish red. [< OFr., CHERRY.]

ce·ri·um (sîr′ē-əm) ►*n.* *Symbol* **Ce** A lustrous, iron-gray, malleable metallic element, used in metallurgy and glassmaking. At. no. 58. See table at **element.** [< the dwarf planet *Ceres.*]

cer·tain (sûr′tn) ►*adj.* **1.** Definite; fixed. **2.** Sure to happen: *certain success.* **3.** Established beyond doubt. **4.** Having no doubt; confident. **5.** Not identified but assumed to be known: *a certain teacher.* **6.** Limited: *to a certain degree.* ►*pron.* An indefinite number; some. [< Lat.

cernere, cert-, determine.] —**cer′tain·ly** *adv.*
Syns: *inescapable, inevitable, sure, unavoidable adj.*

cer·tain·ty (sûr′tn-tē) ►*n., pl.* **-ties 1.** The fact, quality, or state of being certain, esp.: **a.** Inevitability: *the certainty of death.* **b.** The quality of being established as true: *the certainty that the earth orbits the sun.* **2.** Something that is clearly established.

cer·tif·i·cate (sər-tĭf′ĭ-kĭt) ►*n.* **1.** A document establishing authenticity: *a certificate of birth.* **2.** A document certifying completion of requirements, as of a course of study. **3.** A document certifying ownership. [< LLat. *certificāre,* CERTIFY.]

cer·ti·fi·ca·tion (sûr′tə-fĭ-kā′shən) ►*n.* **1a.** The act of certifying. **b.** The state of being certified. **2.** A certified statement.

cer·ti·fied check (sûr′tə-fīd′) ►*n.* A check guaranteed by a bank to be covered by sufficient funds on deposit.

certified public accountant ►*n.* An accountant certified by a state examining board as having met the state's legal requirements.

cer·ti·fy (sûr′tə-fī′) ►*v.* **1. -fied, -fy·ing** To confirm formally as true, accurate, or genuine. **2.** To acknowledge on (a check) that the maker has sufficient funds on deposit for payment. **3.** To issue a certificate to. **4.** To declare that it is medically necessary to commit (someone) to a psychiatric facility. [< Lat. *certus,* CERTAIN.] —**cer′ti·fi′a·ble** *adj.* —**cer′ti·fi′a·bly** *adv.* —**cer′ti·fi′er** *n.*

cer·ti·tude (sûr′tĭ-tōōd′, -tyōōd′) ►*n.* The state of being completely confident in something. [< Lat. *certus,* CERTAIN.]

ce·ru·le·an (sə-rōō′lē-ən) ►*adj.* Azure; sky-blue. [< Lat. *caeruleus,* dark blue.]

ce·ru·men (sə-rōō′mən) ►*n.* See **earwax.** [< Lat. *cēra,* wax.] —**ce·ru′mi·nous** *adj.*

Cer·van·tes Sa·a·ve·dra (sər-văn′tēz sä′ə-vā′-drə), **Miguel de** 1547–1616. Spanish writer.

cer·vi·cal (sûr′vĭ-kəl) ►*adj.* Of or relating to a neck or cervix.

cer·vix (sûr′vĭks) ►*n., pl.* **-vix·es** or **-vi·ces** (-vĭ-sēz′, sər-vī′sēz) **1.** The neck. **2.** A neck-shaped anatomical structure, such as the outer end of the uterus. [Lat. *cervīx.*]

ce·sar·e·an also **cae·sar·e·an** or **cae·sar·i·an** or **ce·sar·i·an** (sĭ-zâr′ē-ən) ►*n.* A cesarean section. —**ce·sar′e·an** *adj.*

cesarean section ►*n.* A surgical incision through the abdominal wall and uterus to deliver a fetus. [< the tradition that Julius CAESAR was so delivered.]

ce·si·um also **cae·si·um** (sē′zē-əm) ►*n.* *Symbol* **Cs** A soft, silvery-white metallic element with a positive electric charge, used in photoelectric cells. At. no. 55. See table at **element.** [< Lat. *caesius,* bluish gray.]

ces·sa·tion (sĕ-sā′shən) ►*n.* A ceasing; halt. [< Lat. *cessāre,* cease.]

ces·sion (sĕsh′ən) ►*n.* A ceding or surrendering, as of territory to another country by treaty. [< Lat. *cēdere, cess-,* yield.]

cess·pool (sĕs′pōōl′) ►*n.* A covered hole or pit for receiving drainage, waste, or sewage. [< ME *suspiral,* vent.]

ce·su·ra (sĭ-zhōōr′ə, -zōōr′ə) ►*n.* Var. of **cae·sura.**

ce·ta·cean (sĭ-tā′shən) ►*n.* Any of a group of

aquatic, chiefly marine mammals that includes the whales, dolphins, and porpoises. [< Lat. *cētus*, whale.] —**ce·ta′cean, ce·ta′ceous** *adj.*

Cey·lon (sĭ-lŏn′, sā-) See **Sri Lanka.** —**Cey′lo·nese′** (-nĕz′, -nēs′) *adj. & n.*

Cé·zanne (sā-zăn′, -zän′), **Paul** 1839–1906. French postimpressionist artist.

CF ▸*abbr.* **1.** carried forward **2.** center field **3.** cost and freight **4.** cystic fibrosis

cf. ▸*abbr. Lat.* confer (compare)

CFC ▸*abbr.* chlorofluorocarbon

CFS ▸*abbr.* chronic fatigue syndrome

cg ▸*abbr.* centigram

CG ▸*abbr.* **1.** coast guard **2.** computer graphics

CGI ▸*abbr.* computer-generated imagery

ch ▸*abbr.* chain (measurement)

ch. ▸*abbr.* **1.** chapter **2.** check (bank order)

Ch. ▸*abbr.* **1.** chaplain **2.** church

Cha·blis (shă-blē′, shä-, shăb′lē) ▸*n.* A very dry white Burgundy wine. [After *Chablis*, France.]

cha-cha (chä′chä) ▸*n.* A rhythmic ballroom dance that originated in Latin America. [Am. Sp. *chachachá*.] —**cha′-cha** *v.*

Chad (chăd) A country of N-central Africa. Cap. N'Djamena. —**Chad′i·an** *adj. & n.*

Chad, Lake A lake of N-central Africa in Chad, Cameroon, Niger, and Nigeria.

Chad·ic (chăd′ĭk) ▸*n.* A branch of the Afro-Asiatic language family, spoken in west-central Africa.

cha·dor (chä-dôr′) ▸*n.* A long, loose cloak worn by many Muslim women, covering most of the body while leaving the face uncovered or partly covered. [< Skt. *chattram*, screen.]

chafe (chāf) ▸*v.* **chafed, chaf·ing 1.** To make or become worn or sore by rubbing. **2.** To annoy; vex. **3.** To warm by rubbing, as with the hands. [< Lat. *calefacere*, make warm.]

chaff[1] (chăf) ▸*n.* **1.** Grain husks, as of wheat, removed during threshing. **2.** Trivial or worthless matter. [< OE *ceaf*.]

chaff[2] (chăf) ▸*v.* To tease good-naturedly. [Poss. < CHAFE.] —**chaff** *n.*

chaf·finch (chăf′ĭnch) ▸*n.* A small European songbird. [< OE *ceaffinc*.]

chaf·ing dish (chā′fĭng) ▸*n.* A pan mounted above a heating device, used to cook food or keep it warm at the table.

Cha·gall (shə-gäl′), **Marc** 1887–1985. Russian-born artist.

cha·grin (shə-grĭn′) ▸*n.* A feeling of embarrassment, humiliation, or annoyance. ▸*v.* To cause to feel chagrin. See Synonyms at **embarrass.** [Fr.]

chai (chī) ▸*n.* A beverage made from spiced black tea, milk, and sugar or honey. [Hindi *chāy*, ult. < Chin. (Mandarin) *chá*, tea.]

chain (chān) ▸*n.* **1.** A connected, flexible series of usu. metal links. **2. chains a.** Bonds, fetters, or shackles. **b.** Bondage. **3.** A series of related things. **4.** A number of commercial establishments under common ownership. **5.** A range of mountains. **6a.** An instrument used in surveying, consisting of 100 linked pieces of iron or steel. **b.** A unit of length equal to 100 links, or 66 ft (20.1 m). ▸*v.* **1.** To bind or make fast with a chain. **2.** To fetter. [< Lat. *catēna*.]

chain gang ▸*n.* A group of convicts chained together, esp. for outdoor labor.

chain mail ▸*n.* Flexible armor made of joined metal links.

chain reaction ▸*n.* **1.** A series of events in which each induces or influences the next. **2.** *Phys.* A multistage nuclear reaction, esp. a self-sustaining series of fissions in which the release of neutrons from the splitting of one atom triggers the splitting of others. **3.** *Chem.* A series of reactions in which a product of one reaction is a reactant in another reaction. —**chain′-re·act′** *v.*

chain·saw (chān′sô′) ▸*n.* A portable power saw with teeth linked to form a loop of chain.

chain-smoke (chān′smōk′) ▸*v.* To smoke (e.g., cigarettes) in close succession. —**chain smoker** *n.*

chain store ▸*n.* One of a number of retail stores operating under the same brand name and selling similar merchandise.

chair (châr) ▸*n.* **1.** A seat with a back, designed to accommodate one person. **2a.** A seat of office, authority, or dignity, such as that of a bishop, chairperson, or professor. **b.** One who holds such a chair. **3.** *Slang* The electric chair. **4.** A sedan chair. ▸*v.* To preside over as chairperson. [< Gk. *kathedra*; see CATHEDRAL.]

chair·lift (châr′lĭft′) ▸*n.* A series of seats suspended from a cable, used to mechanically transport people up or down a mountain slope.

chair·man (châr′mən) ▸*n.* The presiding officer of a meeting, committee, or board. See Usage Note at **man.** —**chair′man·ship′** *n.*

chair·per·son (châr′pûr′sən) ▸*n.* A chairman or chairwoman. See Usage Note at **man.**

chair·wom·an (châr′wŏŏm′ən) ▸*n.* A woman presiding officer of a meeting, committee, or board. See Usage Note at **man.**

chaise (shāz) ▸*n.* **1.** A two-wheeled, horse-drawn carriage with a collapsible hood. **2.** A post chaise. [< OFr. *chaiere*, CHAIR.]

chaise longue (lông′) ▸*n., pl.* **chaise longues** (lông′) A reclining chair with a lengthened seat to support the outstretched legs. [Fr.]

chal·ced·o·ny (kăl-sĕd′n-ē) ▸*n., pl.* **-nies** A translucent milky or grayish quartz. [< Gk. *khalkēdōn*, a mystical stone.]

Chal·de·a or **Chal·dae·a** (kăl-dē′ə) An ancient region of S Mesopotamia. —**Chal·de′an** *adj. & n.*

cha·let (shă-lā′, shăl′ā) ▸*n.* A wooden dwelling with a low-pitched roof and wide eaves, common in Alpine regions. [Fr.]

chal·ice (chăl′ĭs) ▸*n.* **1.** A cup or goblet. **2.** A cup for the consecrated wine of the Eucharist. [< Lat. *calix*.]

chalk (chôk) ▸*n.* **1.** A soft compact calcite, $CaCO_3$, derived chiefly from fossil seashells. **2.** A piece of chalk or similar material used for marking on a surface. ▸*v.* To mark, draw, or write with chalk. —*phrasal verb:* **chalk up 1.** To earn or score. **2.** To credit: *Chalk it up to experience.* [< Lat. *calx*, limestone.] —**chalk′y** *adj.*

chalk·board (chôk′bôrd′) ▸*n.* A blackboard.

chal·lenge (chăl′ənj) ▸*n.* **1.** A call to engage in a contest, fight, or competition. **2.** An act of defiance: *a challenge to the king's authority.* **3.** An undertaking that tests one's abilities. **4.** A formal objection, esp. to the qualifications of a juror or voter. ▸*v.* **-lenged, -leng·ing 1a.** To call to engage in a contest. **b.** To invite with defiance; dare. **2.** To call into question; dispute.

3. To order to halt and be identified. **4.** To take formal objection to (a juror or voter). **5.** To summon to action or effort; stimulate. [< Lat. *calumnia*, accusation.] —**chal′leng·er** *n.*

chal·lenged (chăl′ənjd) ►*adj.* **1.** Having a disability or impairment. **2.** Deficient or lacking: *ethically challenged.*

chal·leng·ing (chăl′ən-jĭng) ►*adj.* Calling for full use of one's abilities or resources.

cham·ber (chām′bər) ►*n.* **1.** A room, esp. a bedroom. **2. chambers** A judge's office. **3.** A hall, esp. for the meetings of a legislative or other assembly. **4.** A legislative, judicial, or deliberative body. **5.** An enclosed space; a compartment or cavity. **6.** A compartment in a firearm that holds the cartridge. [< LLat. *camera*.] —**cham′bered** *adj.*

cham·ber·lain (chām′bər-lĭn) ►*n.* **1a.** A chief steward. **b.** A high-ranking official in a royal court. **2.** A treasurer. [< OFr. *chamberlenc*.]

Chamberlain, (Arthur) Neville 1869–1940. British prime minister (1937–40).

Chamberlain, Wilton Norman "Wilt." 1936–99. Amer. basketball player.

cham·ber·maid (chām′bər-mād′) ►*n.* A maid who cleans bedrooms, as in a hotel.

chamber music ►*n.* Music, as for a trio or quartet, appropriate for performance in a small concert hall.

chamber of commerce ►*n.* An association of businesses for the promotion of commercial interests in the community.

cham·bray (shăm′brā′) ►*n.* A fine, lightweight fabric woven with white threads across a colored warp. [After *Cambrai*, France.]

cha·me·leon (kə-mēl′yən, -mē′lē-ən) ►*n.* **1.** Any of various tropical Old World lizards capable of changing color. **2.** See **anole**. **3.** A changeable person. [< Gk. *khamaileōn* : *khamai*, on the ground + *leōn*, lion.]

chameleon

cham·fer (chăm′fər) ►*v.* **1.** To cut off the edge or corner of; bevel. **2.** To cut a groove in; flute. [Poss. < OFr. *chanfreindre*, to bevel.] —**cham′fer** *n.*

cham·ois (shăm′ē) ►*n.*, *pl.* **cham·ois** (shăm′ēz) **1.** A goat antelope of mountainous regions of Europe. **2.** also **cham·my** or **sham·my** (shăm′ē) *pl.* **-mies a.** A soft leather made from the hide of a chamois or other animal. **b.** A piece of such leather used esp. as a polishing cloth. [< LLat. *camōx*.]

cham·o·mile or **cam·o·mile** (kăm′ə-mīl′, -mēl′) ►*n.* An aromatic plant having daisylike white flower heads that are used for herbal tea and in flavorings. [< Gk. *khamaimēlon* : *khamai*, on the ground + *mēlon*, apple.]

champ¹ (chămp) ►*v.* To chew upon noisily. —*idiom:* **champ at the bit** To show impatience at being delayed. [Prob. imit.]

champ² (chămp) ►*n. Informal* A champion.

cham·pagne (shăm-pān′) ►*n.* A sparkling white wine orig. produced in Champagne.

Cham·pagne (shăm-pān′, shän-pän′yə) A region and former province of NE France.

cham·pi·on (chăm′pē-ən) ►*n.* **1.** One that holds first place or wins first prize in a contest. **2.** An ardent defender or supporter of a cause or another person. ►*v.* To fight for, defend, or support as a champion. [< Med.Lat. *campiō* < Lat. *campus*, field.]

cham·pi·on·ship (chăm′pē-ən-shĭp′) ►*n.* **1.** The position or title of a winner. **2.** Defense or support. **3.** A competition held to determine a champion.

chance (chăns) ►*n.* **1a.** The unknown and unpredictable element in happenings that seems to have no assignable cause. **b.** This element viewed as a cause of events; luck. **2.** often **chances** The likelihood of something happening; probability. **3.** An opportunity. **4.** A risk or hazard: *take a chance.* ►*v.* **chanced, chanc·ing** **1.** To come about by chance. See Synonyms at **happen**. **2.** To risk; hazard. —*phrasal verb:* **chance on** To find accidentally; happen upon. [< OFr. < Lat. *cadere*, befall.]

chan·cel (chăn′səl) ►*n.* The space around the altar of a church for the clergy and often the choir. [< OFr. < LLat. *cancellus*, latticework.]

chan·cel·ler·y or **chan·cel·lor·y** (chăn′sə-lə-rē, -slə-rē) ►*n.*, *pl.* **-ies 1.** The rank or position of a chancellor. **2.** The office or department of a chancellor. **3.** The office of an embassy or consulate.

chan·cel·lor (chăn′sə-lər, -slər) ►*n.* **1.** The chief minister of state in some countries. **2.** The head of a university. **3.** *Law* The presiding judge of a court of equity. [< LLat. *cancellārius*, doorkeeper.] —**chan′cel·lor·ship′** *n.*

chan·cer·y (chăn′sə-rē) ►*n.*, *pl.* **-ies 1.** *Law* **a.** A court with jurisdiction in equity. **b.** An office of archives. **2.** The office of a chancellor. [< ME *chancelrie*, chancellery.]

chan·cre (shăng′kər) ►*n.* A dull red, hard, insensitive lesion that is the first sign of syphilis. [< Lat. *cancer*, crab, tumor.] —**chan′crous** (-krəs) *adj.*

chanc·y (chăn′sē) ►*adj.* **-i·er, -i·est** Uncertain as to outcome; risky.

chan·de·lier (shăn′də-lîr′) ►*n.* A branched lighting fixture holding bulbs or candles, usu. suspended from a ceiling. [< Lat. *candēlābrum*, candelabrum.]

chan·dler (chănd′lər) ►*n.* **1.** One that makes or sells candles. **2.** A dealer in nautical supplies. [< Lat. *candēla*, CANDLE.] —**chan′dler·y** (chănd′lə-rē) *n.*

Chan·dra·se·khar (shän′drə-sā′kär, chŭn′drə-shä′kər), **Subrahmanyan** 1910–95. Indianborn Amer. astrophysicist.

change (chānj) ►*v.* **changed, chang·ing 1.** To be or cause to be different; alter: *change the rules.* **2.** To interchange: *change places.* **3.** To exchange for or replace with another: *changed his name.*

4. To transfer from (one vehicle) to another: *change planes.* **5.** To give or receive an equivalent sum of money in lower denominations or in foreign currency. **6.** To put fresh clothes or coverings on: *change the bed.* ►*n.* **1.** The act or result of changing. **2.** A fresh set of clothing. **3a.** Money of smaller denomination changed for money of higher denomination. **b.** The balance of money returned when an amount given is more than what is due. **c.** Coins. [< Lat. *cambiāre,* exchange.] —**change′a·bil′i·ty** *n.* —**change′a·ble** *adj.*

change·ling (chānj′lĭng) ►*n.* A child secretly exchanged for another.

change of life ►*n.* Menopause.

change·o·ver (chānj′ō′vər) ►*n.* A conversion, as from one system to another.

Chang·jiang (chäng′jyäng′) See **Yangtze.**

chan·nel (chăn′əl) ►*n.* **1.** The bed of a stream or river. **2.** The deeper part of a river or harbor, esp. a navigable passage. **3.** A strait. **4.** A trench, furrow, or groove. **5.** A tubular passage. **6.** often **channels** Official routes of communication. **7.** A specified frequency band for the transmission and reception of electromagnetic signals. **8.** A continuous program of audio or video content distributed by a television, radio, or Internet broadcaster. ►*v.* **-neled, -nel·ing** also **-nelled, -nel·ling** **1.** To make or form channels in. **2.** To direct along a channel or path. **3.** To act as a medium through which a spirit communicates. [< Lat. *canālis.*] —**chan′-nel·i·za′tion** *n.* —**chan′nel·ize′** *v.*

Channel Islands A group of islands in the English Channel off the coast of Normandy, France, governed as British crown dependencies.

chan·nel-surf (chăn′əl-sûrf′) ►*v.* To watch different television channels in rapid succession. —**channel surfer** *n.*

chan·son (shän-sôn′) ►*n.* A song, esp. a French one. [< OFr. < Lat. *cantāre,* sing.]

chant (chănt) ►*n.* **1a.** A series of syllables sung on the same note or a limited range of notes. **b.** A canticle sung thus. **2.** A monotonous rhythmic call or shout. ►*v.* **1.** To sing (a chant). **2.** To celebrate in song. **3.** To utter (e.g., a slogan) in the manner of a chant. [< Lat. *cantus,* song.] —**chant′er** *n.*

chan·teuse (shän-tœz′) ►*n.* A woman singer, esp. in a nightclub. [Fr. < *chanter,* sing.]

chan·tey (shăn′tē, chăn′-) ►*n., pl.* **-teys** A song sung by sailors to the rhythm of their work. [Prob. < OFr. *chanter,* sing.]

chan·ti·cleer (chăn′tĭ-klîr′, shăn′-) ►*n.* A rooster. [< OFr. *chantecler.*]

Cha·nu·kah (кнä′nə-kə, hä′-) ►*n.* Var. of **Hanukkah.**

cha·os (kā′ŏs′) ►*n.* **1.** Great disorder or confusion. **2. Chaos** In some systems of belief, the disordered state that preceded the ordered universe. [< Gk. *khaos,* unformed matter.] —**cha·ot′ic** *adj.* —**cha·ot′i·cal·ly** *adv.*

chap[1] (chăp) ►*v.* **chapped, chap·ping** To split or roughen (the skin), esp. from cold. [ME *chappen.*]

chap[2] (chăp) ►*n.* Informal A man or boy; fellow. [< CHAPMAN.]

chap·ar·ral (shăp′ə-răl′) ►*n.* A dense thicket of shrubs esp. in a region that is relatively arid. [Sp.]

cha·pa·ti (chə-pä′tē) ►*n., pl.* **-ti** A flat, unleavened, disk-shaped bread of N India. [Hindi *capātī.*]

chap·el (chăp′əl) ►*n.* **1.** A place of worship that is smaller than and subordinate to a church, esp. in a prison, college, or hospital. **2.** A place of worship for those not belonging to an established church. **3.** The services held at a chapel. [< OFr. *chapele.*]

chap·er·one or **chap·er·on** (shăp′ə-rōn′) ►*n.* **1.** An older person who attends and supervises a social gathering for young people. **2.** A person, esp. an older or married woman, who accompanies a young unmarried woman in public. ►*v.* **-oned, -on·ing** To act as chaperone to or for. [< OFr., hood.]

chap·lain (chăp′lĭn) ►*n.* A member of the clergy attached to a chapel, legislative assembly, or military unit. [< Med.Lat. *capellānus* < *capella,* chapel.] —**chap′lain·cy, chap′lain·ship′** *n.*

chap·let (chăp′lĭt) ►*n.* **1.** A wreath for the head. **2.** *Rom. Cath. Ch.* A string of beads resembling a rosary, used to count repeated prayers. [< OFr. *chapelet,* small hat.]

Chap·lin (chăp′lĭn), Sir **Charles Spencer** "Charlie." 1889–1977. British-born actor, director, and producer.

chap·man (chăp′mən) ►*n. Chiefly Brit.* A peddler. [< OE *cēapman.*]

chaps (chăps, shăps) ►*pl.n.* Heavy leather trousers without a seat, worn by horseback riders to protect their legs. [< Am.Sp. *chaparreras.*]

chap·ter (chăp′tər) ►*n.* **1.** A main division of a book. **2.** A local branch of a club or fraternity. **3.** An assembly of members, as of a religious order. [< Lat. *capitulum.*]

char[1] (chär) ►*v.* **charred, char·ring** **1.** To scorch or become scorched. **2.** To reduce or be reduced to carbon or charcoal by incomplete combustion. [< CHARCOAL.]

char[2] (chär) ►*n., pl.* **char** or **chars** Any of several fishes related to the trout and salmon. [?]

char[3] (chär) *Chiefly Brit.* ►*n.* A charwoman. ►*v.* **charred, char·ring** To work as a charwoman. [< OE *cierr,* a turn, job.]

char·ac·ter (kăr′ək-tər) ►*n.* **1a.** The qualities that distinguish one person or group from another. **b.** A distinguishing feature or attribute. **2a.** Moral strength; integrity. **b.** Reputation. **3.** *Biol.* A structure, function, or attribute determined by heredity or environment. **4.** An eccentric person. **5.** A person portrayed in literature, drama, or art. **6.** A symbol in a writing system. **7.** *Comp.* **a.** A symbol, such as a letter or number, that expresses information. **b.** The code that represents such a symbol. [< Gk. *kharaktēr.*]

char·ac·ter·is·tic (kăr′ək-tə-rĭs′tĭk) ►*adj.* Distinctive; typical. ►*n.* A distinguishing attribute. —**char′ac·ter·is′ti·cal·ly** *adv.*

char·ac·ter·ize (kăr′ək-tə-rīz′) ►*v.* **-ized, -iz·ing** **1.** To describe the qualities of. **2.** To be a distinctive feature or mark of. —**char′ac·ter·iz′er** *n.* —**char′ac·ter·i·za′tion** *n.*

cha·rade (shə-rād′) ►*n.* **1. charades** *(takes sing. or pl. v.)* A game in which words or phrases are represented in pantomime until guessed by the other players. **2.** A pretense; sham. [Fr.]

char·broil (chär′broil′) ►*v.* To broil over charcoal: *charbroil a steak.*

char·coal (chär′kōl′) ►*n.* **1.** A black, porous material consisting mostly of carbon, produced from wood by pyrolysis and used as a fuel, filter, and adsorbent. **2.** A drawing pencil made from charcoal. **3.** A dark gray. [ME *charcol*.]

chard (chärd) ►*n.* Swiss chard. [< Fr. *carde*.]

charge (chärj) ►*v.* **charged, charg·ing 1.** To impose a duty or responsibility on. **2.** To instruct authoritatively; command. **3.** To set as a price. **4.** To demand payment from. **5.** To purchase on credit. **6a.** To load or fill. **b.** To saturate: *an atmosphere charged with tension.* **7.** To accuse or blame. **8.** To attack violently. **9.** *Elect.* **a.** To cause formation of a net electric charge on or in (a conductor). **b.** To energize (a storage battery). ►*n.* **1.** Price; cost. **2a.** A burden; load. **b.** The quantity that a container or apparatus can hold. **3.** A quantity of explosive to be set off at one time. **4.** A duty or responsibility. **5.** One entrusted to another's care. **6a.** Supervision; management. **b.** Care; custody: *a child in my charge.* See Synonyms at **care. 7.** A command or injunction. **8.** An accusation or indictment. **9.** A rushing, forceful attack. **10.** A debt in an account. **11.** *Phys.* **a.** The intrinsic property of matter responsible for all electric phenomena, occurring in two forms designated *negative* and *positive.* **b.** A measure of this property. **12.** *Informal* A feeling of pleasant excitement; thrill. [< LLat. *carricāre*, to load.]

charge account ►*n.* A standing agreement by which a customer may purchase goods or services on credit.

charge card ►*n.* See **credit card.**

char·gé d'af·faires (shär-zhā' də-fâr', dä-) ►*n., pl.* **char·gés d'affaires** (-zhā', -zhäz') A diplomat who temporarily substitutes for an absent ambassador or minister. [Fr.]

charg·er (chär'jər) ►*n.* **1.** One that charges, such as a device that charges storage batteries. **2.** A horse trained for battle.

char·i·ot (chăr'ē-ət) ►*n.* An ancient horse-drawn two-wheeled vehicle used in war, races, and processions. [< Lat. *carrus*, vehicle.] —**char'i·o·teer'** *n.*

cha·ris·ma (kə-rĭz'mə) ►*n.* A personal quality attributed to those who arouse fervent popular devotion and enthusiasm. [Gk. *kharisma*, divine favor.]

char·is·mat·ic (kăr'ĭz-măt'ĭk) ►*adj.* **1.** Of or relating to charisma. **2.** Of or being a type of Christianity that emphasizes personal religious experience and divinely inspired powers. ►*n.* A member of a Christian charismatic group.

char·i·ta·ble (chăr'ĭ-tə-bəl) ►*adj.* **1.** Generous to the needy. **2.** Of or for charity. See Synonyms at **benevolent. 3.** Lenient or forbearing in judging others: *a charitable interpretation of their remarks.* —**char'i·ta·bly** *adv.*

char·i·ty (chăr'ĭ-tē) ►*n., pl.* **-ties 1.** Help or relief given to the poor. **2.** An organization or fund that helps the needy. **3.** Benevolence toward others. **4.** Forbearance in judging others. **5.** often **Charity** *Christianity* Love directed first toward God but also toward oneself and one's neighbors. [< Lat. *cāritās*, affection.]

char·la·tan (shär'lə-tən) ►*n.* One who makes fraudulent claims to skill or knowledge. [< Ital. *ciarlatano*.] —**char'la·tan·ism** *n.*

Char·le·magne (shär'lə-mān') Also called Charles I or "Charles the Great." 742?–814. King of the Franks (768–814); emperor of the West (800–814).

Charles (chärlz) Prince of Wales. b. 1948. Prince of Wales (invested 1969).

Charles I 1600–49. King of England, Scotland, and Ireland (1625–49).

Charles II 1630–85. King of England, Scotland, and Ireland (1660–85).

Charles V 1500–58. Holy Roman emperor (1519–58) and king of Spain as Charles I (1516–56).

Charles IX 1550–74. King of France (1560–74).

Charles, Ray Raymond Charles Robinson. 1930–2004. Amer. musician and composer.

Charles Mar·tel (mär-tĕl') 688?–741. Frankish ruler (715–741).

Charles·ton[1] (chärl'stən) **1.** A city of SE SC NE of Savannah. **2.** The capital of WV, in the W-central part.

Charles·ton[2] (chärl'stən) ►*n.* A fast popular dance of the 1920s. [After CHARLESTON[1], South Carolina.]

char·ley horse (chär'lē) ►*n. Informal* A muscle cramp, esp. in the leg. [?]

Char·lotte (shär'lət) A city of S NC.

Charlotte A·ma·lie (ə-mäl'yə) The capital of the US Virgin Islands, on St. Thomas I. in the West Indies E of Puerto Rico.

Char·lotte·town (shär'lət-toun') The capital of Prince Edward I., Canada, on the S coast.

charm (chärm) ►*n.* **1.** The quality of pleasing or delighting. **2.** A small ornament worn, esp. on a bracelet. **3.** An item worn for its supposed magical benefit; amulet. **4.** An action or formula thought to have magical power. ►*v.* **1.** To attract or delight greatly. **2.** To cast or seem to cast a spell on; bewitch. [< Lat. *carmen*, incantation.] —**charm'er** *n.* —**charm'less** *adj.*

   Syns: *beguile, bewitch, captivate, enchant, entrance, fascinate* **v.**

char·nel house (chär'nəl) ►*n.* **1.** A repository for the bones or bodies of the dead. **2.** A scene of great carnage or loss of life. [< Lat. *carnālis*, of flesh.]

Char·on (kâr'ən) ►*n. Gk. Myth.* The ferryman of Hades.

chart (chärt) ►*n.* **1.** A map. **2.** A sheet presenting information in the form of graphs or tables. ►*v.* **1.** To make a chart of. **2.** To plan. [< Lat. *charta*, papyrus paper; see CARD[1].]

char·ter (chär'tər) ►*n.* **1.** A document issued by a government authority, creating a corporation and defining its privileges and purposes. **2.** A document outlining the organization of a corporate body. **3.** An authorization from an organization to establish a local chapter. **4a.** A contract to lease a vessel. **b.** The hiring of an aircraft, vessel, or other vehicle. ►*v.* **1.** To grant a charter to. **2.** To hire or lease by charter. [< Lat. *chartula*, piece of papyrus.]

charter member ►*n.* An original member of an organization.

charter school ►*n.* An independent public school, often with a distinct curriculum and educational philosophy.

char·treuse (shär-trōoz') ►*n.* A strong greenish yellow to yellowish green. [< *Chartreuse*, trademark for a type of liqueur.]

char·wom·an (chär'wŏom'ən) ►*n.* A cleaning woman.

char·y (châr'ē) ►*adj.* **-i·er, -i·est 1.** Very cautious. **2.** Not giving freely; sparing. [< OE *cearig*, sorrowful.] —**char'i·ly** *adv.*

chase¹ (chās) ►*v.* **chased, chas·ing 1.** To follow rapidly in order to catch; pursue. **2.** To hunt. **3.** To put to flight: *chased the dog away.* ►*n.* **1.** The act of chasing. **2.** The hunting of game. [< Lat. *captāre.*]

chase² (chās) ►*n.* **1.** A groove cut in an object; slot. **2.** A trench or channel for drainpipes or wiring. ►*v.* **chased, chas·ing** To decorate (metal) by engraving or embossing. [Prob. < Lat. *capsa,* box.]

chas·er (chā′sər) ►*n.* **1.** One that chases. **2.** *Informal* A drink, as of beer or water, taken after hard liquor.

chasm (kăz′əm) ►*n.* **1.** A deep opening in the earth; gorge. **2.** A great disparity, as of opinion or interests. [< Gk. *khasma.*]

Chas·sid (кнä′sĭd, кнô′-, hä′-) ►*n.* Var. of **Hasid.** —**Chas·si′dic** *adj.* —**Chas·si′dism** *n.*

chas·sis (chăs′ē) ►*n., pl.* **chas·sis** (-ēz) **1.** The rectangular steel frame that holds the body and motor of an automotive vehicle. **2.** The landing gear of an aircraft. **3.** The framework to which the components of a radio, television, or other electronic device are attached. [< OFr., frame < Lat. *capsa,* box.]

chaste (chāst) ►*adj.* **chast·er, chast·est 1a.** Virginal. **b.** Adhering to standards of sexual morality. **c.** Abstaining from sexual relations. **2.** Not involving or suggestive of sexual desire or indecency: *a chaste kiss.* **3.** Simple in design or style; austere. [< Lat. *castus.*] —**chaste′ly** *adv.* —**chaste′ness** *n.* —**chas′ti·ty** (chăs′tĭ-tē) *n.*

chas·ten (chā′sən) ►*v.* **1.** To correct by punishment or reproof. **2.** To restrain; subdue. [< Lat. *castigāre.*] —**chas′ten·er** *n.*

chas·tise (chăs-tīz′, chăs′tīz′) ►*v.* **-tised, -tis·ing 1.** To punish, as by beating. **2.** To criticize severely. [< ME *chastien,* CHASTEN.] —**chas·tise′ment** *n.* —**chas·tis′er** *n.*

chas·u·ble (chăz′ə-bəl, chăzh′-, chăs′-) ►*n.* A long sleeveless vestment worn over the alb by a priest at Mass. [< LLat. *casubla,* hooded garment, dim. of *casa,* house.]

chat (chăt) ►*v.* **chat·ted, chat·ting 1.** To converse in an easy manner. **2.** To converse in real time over a computer network. ►*n.* **1.** An informal conversation. **2.** Any of several birds with a chattering call. [< ME *chattern,* chatter.] —**chat′ti·ness** *n.* —**chat′ty** *adj.*

cha·teau also **châ·teau** (shă-tō′) ►*n., pl.* **-teaus** or **-teaux** (-tōz′) A castle or manor house, esp. in France. [< OFr. *chastel,* CASTLE.]

Châ·teau·bri·and (shă-tō′brē-äN′, shă-), Vicomte **François René de** 1768–1848. French diplomat and writer.

chat·room (chăt′rōōm′, -rōōm′) ►*n.* A site on a computer network where online conversations are held in real time.

chat·tel (chăt′l) ►*n.* **1.** *Law* An article of personal, movable property. **2.** A slave. [< Med.Lat. *capitāle,* property.]

chat·ter (chăt′ər) ►*v.* **1.** To talk rapidly and incessantly on trivial subjects. **2.** To utter inarticulate speechlike sounds. **3.** To click quickly and repeatedly, as the teeth from cold. ►*v.* **1.** Idle, trivial talk. **2.** Communication between people suspected of involvement in terrorism or espionage, as monitored by a government agency. [ME *chateren.*]

chat·ter·box (chăt′ər-bŏks′) ►*n.* An extremely talkative person.

Chau·cer (chô′sər), **Geoffrey** 1340?–1400. English poet. —**Chau·cer′i·an** (-sîr′ē-ən) *adj. & n.*

chauf·feur (shō′fər, shō-fûr′) ►*n.* One employed to drive an automobile. [Fr., stoker.] —**chauf′feur** *v.*

chau·vin·ism (shō′və-nĭz′əm) ►*n.* **1.** Fanatical patriotism. **2.** Prejudiced belief in the superiority of one's own group. [Fr. *chauvinisme,* after Nicolas *Chauvin,* legendary French soldier.] —**chau′vin·ist** *n.* —**chau′vin·is′tic** *adj.*

Chá·vez (chä′věz′, shä′-), **César Estrada** 1927–93. Amer. labor organizer.

César Chávez

cheap (chēp) ►*adj.* **-er, -est 1a.** Inexpensive: *cheap airline tickets.* **b.** Charging low prices: *a cheap restaurant.* **2.** Achieved with little effort: *cheap laughs.* **3.** Of poor quality **4.** Vulgar or contemptible: *a cheap thug.* **5.** Stingy: *a cheap tipper.* ►*adv.* **-er, -est** Inexpensively: *got the new car cheap.* [< OE *cēap,* trade < Lat. *caupō,* shopkeeper.] —**cheap′ly** *adv.* —**cheap′ness** *n.*

cheap·en (chē′pən) ►*v.* **1.** To make or become cheap. **2.** To debase or degrade.

cheap shot ►*n.* An unfair verbal attack on a vulnerable target.

cheap·skate (chēp′skāt′) ►*n.* *Slang* A miser.

cheat (chēt) ►*v.* **1.** To deceive by trickery; swindle. **2.** To act dishonestly. **3.** To elude; escape: *cheat death.* **4.** To be sexually unfaithful. ►*n.* **1.** A fraud or swindle. **2.** One that cheats. [ME *cheten,* confiscate.] —**cheat′er** *n.*

Chech·en (chěch′ən) ►*n.* **1.** A native or inhabitant of Chechnya. **2.** The Caucasian language of the Chechens.

Chech·nya (chěch′nē-ə, chěch-nyä′) A region of SW Russia in the N Caucasus bordering on Georgia.

check (chěk) ►*n.* **1a.** An inspection or test. **b.** A mark to show verification. **2.** A curb or restraint. **3a.** A slip for identification: *a baggage check.* **b.** A bill at a restaurant or bar. **4.** An abrupt stop or halt. **5.** *Sports* The act of checking in ice hockey. **6.** A written order to a bank to pay an amount from funds on deposit. **7a.** A pattern of small squares. **b.** A fabric patterned with squares. **8.** *Games* A move in chess that directly attacks an opponent's king. ►*v.* **1a.** To inspect, as to determine accuracy or quality: *check the brakes.* **b.** To verify. **c.** To put a check mark on. **2a.** To arrest the motion of abruptly. **b.** To curb; restrain. **c.** *Sports* To block or impede (an opposing player with the puck) in ice hockey by using one's body or one's stick. **3.** To deposit for temporary safekeeping: *check one's coat.* **—phrasal verbs: check in** To register, as at a hotel. **check out 1.** To settle one's bill and leave, as from a hotel. **2.** To withdraw (an item) after recording the withdrawal: *check out books.* **3.** To pay for purchases, as at a supermarket. [< Ar. *šāh*, check in chess < Pers., king.]

check·book (chĕk'boۨok') ►*n.* A book containing blank checks issued by a bank.

check·er (chĕk'ər) ►*n.* **1a.** One that checks. **b.** One who receives items for temporary safekeeping: *a baggage checker.* **2.** *Games* **a. checkers** *(takes sing. v.)* A game played on a checkerboard by two players, each using 12 pieces. **b.** One of the round flat pieces used in this game. ►*v.* To mark with a checked or squared pattern. [< OFr. *eschequier,* chessboard.]

check·er·board (chĕk'ər-bôrd') ►*n.* A board on which chess and checkers are played, divided into 64 squares of two alternating colors.

check·ered (chĕk'ərd) ►*adj.* **1.** Divided into squares. **2.** Having light and dark patches. **3.** Marked by shameful events or actions: *a checkered career.*

check·ing account (chĕk'ĭng) ►*n.* A bank account in which checks may be written against amounts on deposit.

check·mate (chĕk'māt') ►*v.* **-mat·ed, -mat·ing 1.** To attack (a chess opponent's king) in such a manner that no escape or defense is possible, thus ending the game. **2.** To defeat completely. [< Ar. *šāh māt,* the king is dead < Pers.] **—check'mate'** *n.*

check·out (chĕk'out') ►*n.* **1.** The act, time, or place of checking out, as at a hotel, library, or supermarket. **2.** A test, as of a machine, for proper functioning. **3.** An investigation.

check·point (chĕk'point') ►*n.* A point where a check is performed: *checkpoints along the border.*

check·rein (chĕk'rān') ►*n.* A short rein that extends from a horse's bit to the saddle to keep the horse from lowering its head.

check·room (chĕk'ro͞om', -ro͝om') ►*n.* A place where items, such as hats or packages, can be stored temporarily.

check·up (chĕk'ŭp') ►*n.* **1.** An examination or inspection. **2.** A physical examination.

Ched·dar also **ched·dar** (chĕd'ər) ►*n.* Any of several types of smooth hard cheese varying in flavor from mild to extra sharp. [After *Cheddar,* England.]

cheek (chĕk) ►*n.* **1.** The fleshy part of either side of the face below the eye and between the nose and ear. **2.** Either of the buttocks. **3.** Impertinence. [< OE *cēace.*]

cheek·bone (chĕk'bōn') ►*n.* A small bone forming the prominence of the cheek.

cheek·y (chē'kē) ►*adj.* **-i·er, -i·est** Impertinent. **—cheek'i·ly** *adv.* **—cheek'i·ness** *n.*

cheep (chēp) ►*n.* A faint shrill sound like that of a young bird. ►*v.* To chirp. [Imit.]

cheer (chîr) ►*n.* **1.** A shout of encouragement or congratulation. **2.** Gaiety or joy. **3.** A source of happiness or comfort. ►*v.* **1.** To encourage with cheers. See Synonyms at **encourage. 2.** To salute or acclaim with cheers. **3.** To shout cheers. **4.** To make or become happier. [< OFr.

chiere, face.] **—cheer'y** *adj.* **—cheer'less** *adj.* **—cheer'i·ly** *adv.* **—cheer'i·ness** *n.*

cheer·ful (chîr'fəl) ►*adj.* **1.** In good spirits: *a cheerful worker.* **2.** Promoting cheer: *a cheerful color.* **—cheer'ful·ly** *adv.* **—cheer'ful·ness** *n.*

cheer·lead·er (chîr'lē'dər) ►*n.* One who leads the cheering of spectators, as at a sports contest.

cheers (chîrz) ►*interj.* Used as a toast.

cheese (chēz) ►*n.* A solid food prepared from the pressed curd of milk. [< Lat. *cāseus.*]

cheese·burg·er (chēz'bûr'gər) ►*n.* A hamburger topped with melted cheese.

cheese·cake (chēz'kāk') ►*n.* **1.** A cake made of cottage or cream cheese, eggs, milk, and sugar. **2.** *Informal* Photographs of minimally attired women.

cheese·cloth (chēz'klôth', -klŏth') ►*n.* A coarse, loosely woven cotton gauze.

cheese·steak (chēz'stāk') ►*n.* A sandwich consisting of a long roll filled with thinly sliced grilled beef, cheese, and often grilled onions.

chees·y (chē'zē) ►*adj.* **-i·er, -i·est 1.** Containing or resembling cheese. **2.** *Informal* Of poor quality; shoddy: *cheesy special effects.* **—chees'i·ness** *n.*

chee·tah (chē'tə) ►*n.* A long-legged, swift-running spotted wild cat of Africa and SW Asia. [< Skt. *citrakāyaḥ,* leopard.]

Chee·ver (chē'vər), **John** 1912–82. Amer. writer.

chef (shĕf) ►*n.* A cook, esp. a chief cook. [Fr., CHIEF.]

chef-d'oeu·vre (shā-dœ'vrə, -dûrv') ►*n., pl.* **chefs-d'oeuvre** (shā-) A masterpiece. [Fr.]

chef's salad (shĕfs) ►*n.* A tossed green salad usu. with raw vegetables, hard-boiled eggs, and julienne strips of cheese and meat.

Che·khov (chĕk'ôf, -ŏf'), **Anton Pavlovich** 1860–1904. Russian writer. **—Che·kho'vi·an** (chĕ-kō'vē-ən) *adj.*

chem·i·cal (kĕm'ĭ-kəl) ►*adj.* **1.** Of or relating to chemistry. **2.** Involving or produced by chemicals. ►*n.* A substance produced by or used in a chemical process. [< Med.Lat. *alchimicus.*] **—chem'i·cal·ly** *adv.*

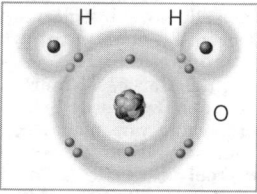

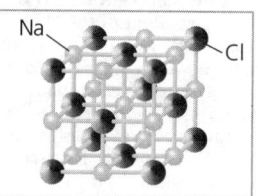

chemical bond
top: covalent bonding in a water molecule
bottom: ionic bonding in sodium chloride

chemical bond ►*n.* Any of several forces, esp. the ionic bond, covalent bond, and metallic bond, by which atoms or ions are bound in a molecule or crystal.

chemical dependency ▸*n.* A physical and psychological habituation to a mood- or mind-altering drug, such as alcohol or cocaine.

chemical engineering ▸*n.* The technology of large-scale chemical production. —**chemical engineer** *n.*

chemical warfare ▸*n.* Warfare involving chemical weapons.

chemical weapon ▸*n.* A toxic chemical that has been prepared for release on the battlefield or within a civilian population with the intent of causing widespread illness or death.

chem·i·lu·mi·nes·cence (kĕm′ə-lōō′mə-nĕs′-əns) ▸*n.* Emission of light as a result of a chemical reaction. —**chem′i·lu′mi·nes′cent** *adj.*

che·mise (shə-mēz′) ▸*n.* **1.** A woman's loose, shirtlike undergarment. **2.** A dress that hangs straight from the shoulders. [< LLat. *camisia*, shirt.]

chem·ist (kĕm′ĭst) ▸*n.* **1.** A scientist specializing in chemistry. **2.** *Chiefly Brit.* A pharmacist.

chem·is·try (kĕm′ĭ-strē) ▸*n., pl.* **-tries 1.** The science of the composition, structure, properties, and reactions of matter, esp. of atomic and molecular systems. **2.** The composition, structure, properties, and reactions of a substance. **3.** The interrelation of elements in a complex entity: *the team's chemistry.* **4.** Mutual attraction; rapport: *chemistry between the actors.*

che·mo (kē′mō, kĕm′ō) ▸*n. Informal* Chemotherapy.

chemo– or **chemi–** or **chem–** ▸*pref.* Chemicals; chemical: *chemurgy.* [< CHEMICAL.]

che·mo·re·cep·tion (kē′mō-rĭ-sĕp′shən, kĕm′-ō-) ▸*n.* The response of a sense organ to a chemical stimulus. —**che′mo·re·cep′tive** *adj.* —**che′mo·re·cep′tor** *n.*

che·mo·syn·the·sis (kē′mō-sĭn′thĭ-sĭs, kĕm′-ō-) ▸*n.* Synthesis of organic compounds using energy obtained by chemical oxidation of simple inorganic compounds. —**che′mo·syn·thet′ic** *adj.*

che·mo·ther·a·py (kē′mō-thĕr′ə-pē, kĕm′ō-) ▸*n.* **1.** The treatment of cancer by means of specific chemical agents. **2.** The treatment of infectious diseases by means of specific chemical agents. —**che′mo·ther′a·peu′tic** *adj.* —**che′mo·ther′a·pist** *n.*

chem·ur·gy (kĕm′ər-jē, kĭ-mûr′-) ▸*n.* The development of new industrial chemical products from organic raw materials, esp. from those of agricultural origin. —**che·mur′gic, che·mur′gi·cal** *adj.*

Che·ney (chā′nē, chē′-), **Richard Bruce** "Dick." b. 1941. Vice president of the US (2001–09).

che·nille (shə-nēl′) ▸*n.* **1.** A soft tufted cord of silk, cotton, or worsted. **2.** Fabric made of this cord. [< Lat. *canīcula*, caterpillar.]

Chen·nai (chə-nī′) A city of SE India on the Bay of Bengal, formerly known as Madras.

Che·ops (kē′ŏps) Orig. **Khu·fu** (kōō′fōō′) 2609–2584 BC. Second king of the IV Dynasty of Egypt.

cheque (chĕk) ▸*n. Chiefly Brit.* Var. of **check.**

cheq·uer (chĕk′ər) ▸*n. Chiefly Brit.* Var. of **checker.**

cher·ish (chĕr′ĭsh) ▸*v.* To treat with affection; hold dear. [< Lat. *cārus*, dear.]

Cher·o·kee (chĕr′ə-kē′, chĕr′ə-kē′) ▸*n., pl.* **-kee** or **-kees 1.** A member of a Native American people formerly of the S Appalachians, now living in NE Oklahoma and W North Carolina. **2.** The Iroquoian language of the Cherokee.

che·root (shə-rōōt′) ▸*n.* A cigar with square-cut ends. [< Tamil *curuṭṭu.*]

cher·ry (chĕr′ē) ▸*n., pl.* **-ries 1.** Any of several trees or shrubs having pink or white flowers and small juicy drupes. **2.** The yellow, red, or blackish fruit of any of these plants. **3.** The wood of a cherry tree. **4.** A strong red to purplish red. [< Gk. *kerasia, kerasos,* cherry tree.]

cherry tomato ▸*n.* A variety of tomato having small red to yellow fruits.

chert (chûrt) ▸*n.* A variety of silica containing microcrystalline quartz. [?]

cher·ub (chĕr′əb) ▸*n.* **1.** *pl.* **cher·u·bim** (chĕr′-ə-bĭm′, -yə-bĭm′) An angel of the 2nd rank in medieval theology. **2.** *pl.* **cher·ubs** A small angel, portrayed as a winged child with a chubby, rosy face. [< Heb. *kərûb.*] —**che·ru′bic** (chə-rōō′bĭk) *adj.*

cher·vil (chûr′vəl) ▸*n.* A Eurasian herb with parsleylike leaves used as a seasoning or garnish. [< Gk. *khairephullon.*]

Ches·a·peake Bay (chĕs′ə-pēk′) An inlet of the Atlantic separating the Delmarva Peninsula from mainland MD and VA.

chess (chĕs) ▸*n.* A board game for two players, each beginning with 16 pieces, with the objective of checkmating the opposing king. [< OFr. *eschec,* CHECK.]

chess·board (chĕs′bôrd′) ▸*n.* A board with 64 squares, used in playing chess.

chess·man (chĕs′măn′, -mən) ▸*n.* One of the pieces used in chess.

chest (chĕst) ▸*n.* **1.** The part of the body between the neck and the abdomen. **2a.** A sturdy box with a lid, used for storage. **b.** A small closet or cabinet: *a medicine chest.* **3.** A bureau; dresser. [< Gk. *kistē,* box.]

Ches·ter·ton (chĕs′tər-tən), **Gilbert Keith** 1874–1936. British writer and critic.

chest·nut (chĕs′nŭt′, -nət) ▸*n.* **1.** Any of several deciduous trees having nuts enclosed in a prickly husk. **2.** The often edible nut of these trees. **3.** The wood of a chestnut tree. **4.** A deep reddish brown. **5.** A stale joke or story. [< Gk. *kastanea.*]

chev·a·lier (shĕv′ə-lîr′) ▸*n.* **1.** A member of certain orders of knighthood or merit. **2.** A French nobleman of the lowest rank. [< LLat. *caballārius,* horseman.]

Chev·i·ot (shĕv′ē-ət, chĕv′-) ▸*n.* **1.** A hornless sheep with short thick wool. **2.** also **cheviot** A woolen fabric with a coarse twill weave. [< the *Cheviot* Hills, England.]

chev·ron (shĕv′rən) ▸*n.* A badge or insignia consisting of stripes meeting at an angle, worn on the sleeve of a military or police uniform to indicate rank, merit, or length of service. [< OFr. *chevron,* rafter.]

chew (chōō) ▸*v.* **1.** To grind and crush with the teeth. **2.** To ponder: *chew a problem over.* ▸*n.* **1.** The act of chewing. **2.** Something chewed, esp. tobacco. —*phrasal verb:* **chew out** *Slang* To scold. —*idiom:* **chew the fat** *Slang* To talk in a leisurely way. [< OE *cēowan.*] —**chew′a·ble** *adj.* —**chew′er** *n.*

chew·ing gum (chōō′ĭng) ▸*n.* A sweetened,

flavored preparation for chewing, formerly made of chicle.

chew·y (chōō'ē) ►*adj.* **-i·er, -i·est** Needing much chewing. —**chew'i·ness** *n.*

Chey·enne[1] (shī-ĕn', -ăn') ►*n., pl.* **-enne** or **-ennes 1.** A member of a Native American people of the W Great Plains, now living in Montana and Oklahoma. **2.** The Algonquian language of the Cheyenne.

Chey·enne[2] (shī-ăn', -ĕn') The capital of WY, in the SE part.

chi[1] (kī) ►*n.* The 22nd letter of the Greek alphabet. [Gk. *khi.*]

chi[2] or **qi** (chē) ►*n.* The vital force believed in Taoism and other Chinese thought to be inherent in all things. [Mandarin *qì.*]

Chiang Kai-shek (chăng' kī'shĕk', jyäng') 1887–1975. Chinese military and political leader.

chi·a·ro·scu·ro (kē-är'ə-skoor'ō, -skyoor'ō) ►*n.* The technique of using light and shade in pictorial representation. [Ital., light and dark.] —**chi·a'ro·scu'rist** *n.*

chic (shēk) ►*adj.* **chic·er, chic·est** Stylish. See Synonyms at **fashionable.** [Fr.] —**chic** *n.* —**chic'ly** *adv.* —**chic'ness** *n.*

Chi·ca·go (shī-kä'gō, -kô'-) A city of NE IL on Lake Michigan. —**Chi·ca'go·an** *n.*

Chi·ca·na (chĭ-kä'nə, shĭ-) ►*n.* A Mexican-American woman or girl. See Usage Note at **Chicano.** [< Am.Sp. *Mexicana.*]

chi·can·er·y (shĭ-kā'nə-rē, chĭ-) ►*n., pl.* **-ies 1.** Deception by trickery or sophistry. **2.** A trick; subterfuge. [< OFr. *chicaner,* to quibble.]

Chi·ca·no (chĭ-kä'nō, shĭ-) ►*n., pl.* **-nos** A Mexican American. [< Am.Sp. *Mexicano.*] —**Chi·ca'no** *adj.*
Usage: Chicano is used only of Mexican Americans, not of Mexicans living in Mexico. While *Chicano* is a term of pride for many, it is not necessarily espoused by all Mexican Americans, and outsiders may be better off using the term *Mexican American* instead. See Usage Note at **Hispanic.**

chi·chi (shē'shē) ►*adj.* **-chi·er, -chi·est** Ostentatiously stylish. [Fr.]

chick (chĭk) ►*n.* **1.** A young chicken. **2.** Any young bird. **3.** *Often Offensive* A young woman.

chick·a·dee (chĭk'ə-dē') ►*n.* A small, gray, dark-crowned North American bird. [Imit. of its call.]

Chick·a·saw (chĭk'ə-sô') ►*n., pl.* **-saw** or **-saws 1.** A member of a Native American people formerly of NE Mississippi and NW Alabama, now living in Oklahoma. **2.** The Muskogean language of the Chickasaw.

chick·en (chĭk'ən) ►*n.* **1.** The common domestic fowl or its young. **2.** The flesh of this fowl. **3.** *Slang* A coward. ►*adj. Slang* Afraid; cowardly. ►*v. Slang* To act in a cowardly manner: *chickened out at the last moment.* [< OE *cīcen.*]

chicken feed ►*n. Slang* A trifling amount of money.

chick·en-fried (chĭk'ən-frīd') ►*adj.* Coated with batter and seasoned flour and fried.

chick·en-liv·ered (chĭk'ən-lĭv'ərd) ►*adj.* Cowardly; timid.

chick·en·pox or **chicken pox** (chĭk'ən-pŏks') ►*n.* A contagious viral disease, primarily of children, marked by skin eruptions and fever.

chicken wire ►*n.* A light-gauge galvanized wire fencing usu. of hexagonal mesh.

chick·pea (chĭk'pē') ►*n.* **1.** An Old World plant cultivated for its edible pealike seeds. **2.** A seed of this plant. [< Lat. *cicer.*]

chick·weed (chĭk'wēd') ►*n.* A low weedy plant with small white flowers.

chic·le (chĭk'əl, chē'klĕ) ►*n.* The coagulated milky juice of a tropical American tree, formerly used to make chewing gum. [< Nahuatl *chictli.*]

chic·o·ry (chĭk'ə-rē) ►*n., pl.* **-ries 1.** A plant having blue daisylike flowers and leaves used as salad. **2.** The roasted ground roots of this plant, used as a coffee admixture or substitute. [< Gk. *kikhora.*]

chide (chīd) ►*v.* **chid·ed** or **chid** (chĭd), **chid·ed** or **chid** or **chid·den** (chĭd'n), **chid·ing** To scold mildly; reprimand. [< OE *cīdan.*]

chief (chēf) ►*n.* One who is highest in rank or authority. ►*adj.* **1.** Highest in rank or authority. **2.** Most important. [< OFr. *chef* < Lat. *caput,* head.] —**chief'ly** *adj. & adv.*

chief justice also **Chief Justice** ►*n.* The presiding judge of a high court having several judges, esp. the US Supreme Court.

chief master sergeant ►*n.* The highest noncommissioned rank in the US Air Force.

chief of staff ►*n., pl.* **chiefs of staff 1.** often **Chief of Staff** The ranking officer of the US Army, Navy, or Air Force, responsible to the secretary of his or her branch and to the President. **2.** The senior military staff officer at the division level or higher.

chief of state ►*n., pl.* **chiefs of state** The formal head of a nation, distinct from the head of the government.

chief petty officer ►*n.* A rank, as in the US Navy, below senior chief petty officer.

chief·tain (chēf'tən) ►*n.* The leader esp. of a clan or tribe. [< LLat. *capitāneus.*]

chif·fon (shĭ-fŏn', shĭf'ŏn') ►*n.* A fabric of sheer silk, cotton, or rayon. [< Fr. *chiffe,* old rag.]

chif·fo·nier (shĭf'ə-nîr') ►*n.* A narrow, high chest of drawers. [< Fr. *chiffon,* rag; see CHIFFON.]

chig·ger (chĭg'ər) ►*n.* **1.** A parasitic mite larva whose bite causes severe itching. **2.** See **chigoe** (sense 1). [Alteration of CHIGOE.]

chi·gnon (shēn-yŏn', shēn'yŏn') ►*n.* A roll of hair worn esp. at the nape of the neck. [< OFr. *chaignon,* chain.]

chig·oe (chĭg'ō, chē'gō) ►*n.* **1.** A small tropical flea, the fertilized female of which burrows under the skin and causes intense irritation and sores. **2.** See **chigger** (sense 1). [Poss. < Galibi (Carib) *chico,* or of African orig.]

Chi·hua·hua[1] (chē-wä'wä) A city of N Mexico.

Chi·hua·hua[2] (chĭ-wä'wä, -wə) ►*n.* A very small dog having pointed ears and a short smooth coat. [< CHIHUAHUA[1].]

chil·blain (chĭl'blān') ►*n.* An inflammation of the hands, feet, or ears, due to exposure to moist cold. [CHIL(L) + *blain,* a pain.]

child (chīld) ►*n., pl.* **chil·dren** (chĭl'drən) **1.** A person between birth and puberty. **2.** An immature person. **3.** A son or daughter; offspring. [< OE *cild.*] —**child'hood'** *n.* —**child'less** *adj.* —**child'like'** *adj.*

Child, Julia McWilliams 1912–2004. Amer. cookery expert.

child·bear·ing (chīld'bâr'ĭng) ►*n.* Pregnancy and childbirth. —**child'bear'ing** *adj.*

child·birth (chīld'bûrth') ►*n.* The act of giving birth.

child·care (chīld'kâr') ►*n.* The provision of care for a child by someone other than a parent or guardian.

child·ish (chīl'dĭsh) ►*adj.* **1.** Of or suitable for a child. **2.** Immature in behavior. —**child'ish·ly** *adv.* —**child'ish·ness** *n.*

child·proof (chīld'pro͞of') ►*adj.* Designed to resist tampering by young children.

chil·dren (chīl'drən) ►*n.* Pl. of **child.**

child's play (chīldz) ►*n.* **1.** Something very easy to do. **2.** A trivial matter.

Chil·e (chīl'ē, chē'lĕ) A country of SW South America with a long Pacific coastline. Cap. Santiago. —**Chil'e·an** *adj. & n.*

chil·i (chĭl'ē) also **chil·e** or **chil·li** ►*n., pl.* **-ies** also **-es** or **-lis 1.** The pungent pod of several varieties of capsicum pepper, used esp. as a flavoring in cooking. **2.** A spicy stew of meat or beans (or both) and usu. tomatoes. [< Nahuatl *chilli.*]

chili con car·ne (kŏn kär'nē) ►*n.* Chili made with beef or other meat. [Sp.]

chil·i·dog (chĭl'ē-dôg', -dŏg') ►*n.* A hot dog covered with chili.

chili sauce ►*n.* A spiced sauce made with chilies and tomatoes.

chill (chĭl) ►*n.* **1.** A moderate but penetrating cold. **2.** A cold or clammy sensation, as from fever or fear, often accompanied by shivering and pallor. **3.** A dampening of enthusiasm or spirit. ►*adj.* Chilly. ►*v.* **1.** To make or become cold. **2.** To dispirit. **3.** *Slang* To calm down or relax. Often used with *out.* [< OE *cele.*]

chill·y (chĭl'ē) ►*adj.* **-i·er, -i·est 1.** Cold enough to cause shivering. See Synonyms at **cold. 2.** Seized with cold; shivering. **3.** Cool; unfriendly. —**chill'i·ness** *n.*

chime (chīm) ►*n.* **1.** often **chimes** A set of tuned bells used as a musical instrument. **2.** The sound produced by or as if by a bell or bells. ►*v.* **chimed, chim·ing 1.** To sound with a harmonious ring when struck. **2.** To agree; harmonize. **3.** To signal by chiming. —*phrasal verb:* **chime in** To interrupt, as in a conversation. [< Lat. *cymbalum,* CYMBAL.]

chi·me·ra (kī-mîr'ə, kĭ-) ►*n.* **1.** An impossible or foolish fantasy. **2.** *Biol.* An organism, organ, or part consisting of two or more tissues of different genetic composition. [< Gk. *khimaira.*]

Chi·me·ra (kī-mîr'ə, kĭ-) ►*n. Gk. Myth.* A fire-breathing she-monster usu. represented as a composite of a lion, goat, and serpent.

chi·mer·i·cal (kī-mĕr'ĭ-kəl, -mîr'-, kĭ-) ►*adj.* Imaginary; unreal. —**chi·mer'i·cal·ly** *adv.*

chim·ney (chĭm'nē) ►*n., pl.* **-neys 1.** A usu. vertical passage through which smoke and gases escape from a fire or furnace. **2.** A glass tube for enclosing the flame of a lamp. [< LLat. *camīnāta,* fireplace.]

chim·ney·piece (chĭm'nē-pēs') ►*n.* **1.** The mantel of a fireplace. **2.** A decoration over a fireplace.

chimney pot ►*n.* A short pipe placed on the top of a chimney to improve the draft.

chimney sweep ►*n.* A worker employed to clean soot from chimneys.

chimney swift ►*n.* A small swallowlike New World bird that often nests in chimneys.

chimp (chĭmp) ►*n. Informal* A chimpanzee.

chim·pan·zee (chĭm'păn-zē', chĭm-păn'zē) ►*n.* Either of two highly intelligent African apes having black hair and a bare face, including the common chimpanzee and the bonobo. [< Vili (African) *ci-mpenzi.*]

chin (chĭn) ►*n.* The central forward portion of the lower jaw. ►*v.* **chinned, chin·ning** To pull (oneself) up with the arms while grasping an overhead horizontal bar until the chin is level with the bar. [< OE *cin.*]

Chin. ►*abbr.* Chinese

chi·na (chī'nə) ►*n.* **1.** High-quality porcelain or other ceramic ware. **2.** Porcelain or earthenware used for the table. [< *China ware.*]

China A country of E Asia. Cap. Beijing.

China, Republic of See **Taiwan.**

chinch bug (chĭnch) ►*n.* **1.** A small black and white insect that is destructive to grains and grasses. **2.** A bedbug. [< Lat. *cīmex,* bug.]

chin·chil·la (chĭn-chĭl'ə) ►*n.* **1a.** A squirrellike South American rodent having soft, pale-gray fur. **b.** The fur of this animal. **2.** A thick wool cloth used for overcoats. [Sp.]

chine (chīn) ►*n.* **1a.** The backbone or spine, esp. of an animal. **b.** A cut of meat containing part of the backbone. **2.** A ridge or crest. [< OFr. *eschine,* of Gmc. orig.]

Chi·nese (chī-nēz', -nēs') ►*adj.* Of or relating to China or its peoples, cultures, or languages and dialects. ►*n., pl.* **-nese 1a.** A native or inhabitant of China. **b.** A person of Chinese ancestry. **c.** See **Han. 2a.** A branch of the Sino-Tibetan language family that consists of the various languages and dialects spoken by the Chinese people. **b.** Any of these languages and dialects.

Chinese cabbage ►*n.* **1.** Napa cabbage. **2.** Bok choy.

Chinese checkers ►*pl.n. (takes sing. or pl. v.)* A game played with marbles on a board shaped like a six-pointed star.

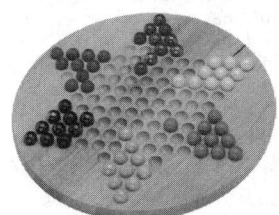

Chinese checkers

Chinese lantern ►*n.* A decorative collapsible lantern of thin, brightly colored paper.

Chinese puzzle ►*n.* **1.** A very intricate puzzle of pieces that lock together. **2.** Something very difficult or complex.

chink¹ (chĭngk) ►*n.* A narrow opening, such as a crack or fissure. ►*v.* To fill cracks or chinks in. [Prob. < OE *cine,* crack.]

chink² (chĭngk) ►*n.* A slight clinking sound. ►*v.* To make a chink. [Imit.]

chi·no (chē'nō, shē'-) ►*n., pl.* **-nos 1.** A coarse twilled cotton fabric. **2.** often **chinos** Trousers made of chino. [Am.Sp., yellowish.]

chi·nook (shĭ-no͝ok', chĭ-) ►*n.* **1.** A moist warm marine wind in the Pacific NW. **2.** A warm dry wind of the E Rocky Mountains. [< *Chinook wind*.]

Chinook ▸*n., pl.* **-nook** or **-nooks 1.** A member of any of various Chinookan-speaking peoples of the Columbia R. valley in Washington and Oregon. **2.** Any of their Chinookan languages.

Chi·nook·an (shĭ-nōōk′ən, chĭ-) ▸*n.* A Native American language family of Washington and Oregon. —**Chi·nook′an** *adj.*

Chinook Jargon ▸*n.* A pidgin language combining words from Native American languages, French, and English, formerly used as a lingua franca in the Pacific Northwest.

Chinook salmon ▸*n.* A large salmon of N Pacific waters having black spots on its back.

chin·qua·pin (chĭng′kə-pĭn′) ▸*n.* **1.** A chestnut of E North America, growing as a shrub or small tree. **2.** Any of various evergreen trees of the Pacific Northwest and E and SE Asia. **3.** The nut of a chinquapin. [Of Algonquian orig.]

chintz (chĭnts) ▸*n.* A printed and glazed cotton fabric, usu. of bright colors. [< Hindi *cīṇṭ*, calico cloth.]

chintz·y (chĭnt′sē) ▸*adj.* **-i·er, -i·est 1.** Gaudy or cheap; trashy. **2.** Stingy; miserly.

chin-up (chĭn′ŭp′) ▸*n.* The act of chinning oneself, practiced esp. as a fitness exercise.

chip (chĭp) ▸*n.* **1.** A small broken or cut off piece, as of wood, stone, or glass. **2.** A crack or flaw caused by the removal of such a piece. **3a.** A coinlike disk used as a counter, as in poker. **b. chips** *Slang* Money. **4.** A small, thin piece of semiconductor bearing numerous circuits integrated into its substrate. Most of a computer's circuitry is built from chips mounted on circuit boards. **5a.** often **chips** A thin, usu. fried slice of food: *a potato chip.* **b.** A very small piece of food or candy: *chocolate chips.* **c. chips** *Chiefly Brit.* French fries. **6.** *Sports* A chip shot. ▸*v.* **chipped, chip·ping** To break, chop, or cut a small piece from. —*phrasal verb:* **chip in** To contribute. —*idioms:* **chip off the old block** A child who closely resembles his or her parent. **chip on (one's) shoulder** A habitually hostile attitude. [< Lat. *cippus*, beam.] —**chip′per** *n.*

Chip·e·wy·an (chĭp′ə-wī′ən) ▸*n., pl.* **-an** or **-ans 1.** A member of a Native American people of N-central Canada. **2.** The Athabaskan language of the Chipewyan.

chip·munk (chĭp′mŭngk′) ▸*n.* Any of several small terrestrial rodents having a striped back. [Perh. < Ojibwa *ajidamoonʔ*, red squirrel.]

chipped beef (chĭpt) ▸*n.* Dried beef smoked and sliced very thin.

chip·per (chĭp′ər) ▸*adj.* In lively spirits; cheerful. [Perh. < dial. *kipper*, lively.]

Chip·pe·wa (chĭp′ə-wô′, -wä′, -wā′) ▸*n., pl.* **-wa** or **-was** See **Ojibwa.**

chip shot ▸*n.* A short lofted golf stroke, used in approaching the green.

Chi·rac (shē-räk′), **Jacques René** b. 1932. French president (1995–2007) and prime minister (1974–76 and 1986–88).

chiro– ▸*pref.* Hand: *chiropractic.* [< Gk. *kheir.*]

chi·ro·man·cy (kī′rə-măn′sē) ▸*n.* Palmistry. [CHIRO– + Gk. *manteia*, divination.]

chi·rop·o·dy (kĭ-rŏp′ə-dē, shĭ-) ▸*n.* See **podia-try.** —**chi·rop′o·dist** *n.*

chi·ro·prac·tic (kī′rə-prăk′tĭk) ▸*n.* A system of therapy typically involving manipulation of the spinal column and other bodily structures.

[CHIRO– + Gk. *praktikos*, effective.] —**chi′ro·prac′tor** *n.*

chirp (chûrp) ▸*n.* A short, high-pitched sound, as of a small bird or insect. [Imit.] —**chirp** *v.*

chis·el (chĭz′əl) ▸*n.* A metal tool with a sharp beveled edge, used to cut and shape stone, wood, or metal. ▸*v.* **-eled, -el·ing** or **-elled, -el·ling 1.** To shape or cut with a chisel. **2.** *Informal* To swindle or obtain by swindling; cheat. [< OFr. *cisiel.*] —**chis′el·er** *n.*

Chis·holm (chĭz′əm), **Shirley Anita Saint Hill** 1924–2005. Amer. politician.

Chi·şi·năŭ (kĭsh′ə-nou′) The capital of Moldova, in the S part near the Romanian border NW of Odessa, formerly known as Kishinev.

chit¹ (chĭt) ▸*n.* **1.** A statement of an amount owed for food and drink. **2.** A voucher redeemable for food and drink. [< Hindi *ciṭṭhī*, note.]

chit² (chĭt) ▸*n.* **1.** A child. **2.** A saucy girl or young woman. [ME, young animal.]

chit·chat (chĭt′chăt′) ▸*n.* Casual conversation. [Reduplication of CHAT.] —**chit′chat′** *v.*

chi·tin (kīt′n) ▸*n.* A tough protective substance that is the principal component of crustacean shells and insect exoskeletons. [< Gk. *khitōn*, chiton.] —**chi′tin·ous** *adj.*

chi·ton (kīt′n, kī′tŏn′) ▸*n.* **1.** Any of a class of marine mollusks that live on rocks and have shells with eight overlapping calcareous plates. **2.** A tunic worn by men and women in ancient Greece. [Gk. *khitōn.*]

chit·ter·lings also **chit·lins** or **chit·lings** (chĭt′-lĭnz) ▸*pl.n.* The small intestines of pigs, cooked as food. [< ME *chiterling.*]

chiv·al·ry (shĭv′əl-rē) ▸*n., pl.* **-ries 1.** The medieval system of knighthood. **2a.** Qualities, such as bravery, honor, and gallantry toward women, idealized by knighthood. **b.** A gallant or courteous act. [< OFr. *chevalier*, knight; see CHEVA-LIER.] —**chiv′al·rous, chi·val′ric** *adj.*

chive (chīv) ▸*n.* often **chives** A plant with grasslike onion-flavored leaves used as seasoning. [< Lat. *cēpa*, onion.]

chla·myd·i·a (klə-mĭd′ē-ə) ▸*n., pl.* **-i·ae** (-ē-ē′) **1.** Any of various bacteria causing diseases in humans and other animals. **2.** A sexually transmitted disease caused by one of these bacteria. [NLat., genus name < Gk. *khlamus*, hood.]

chloral hydrate (klôr′əl) ▸*n.* A colorless crystalline compound, $C_2H_3Cl_3O_2$, used as a sedative and hypnotic drug and in the manufacture of DDT. [CHLOR(O)– + AL(COHOL) + HYDR(O)– + –ATE².]

chlo·rate (klôr′āt′) ▸*n.* The inorganic group ClO_3 or a compound containing it.

chlor·dane (klôr′dān) also **chlor·dan** (-dăn′) ▸*n.* A colorless, odorless, viscous liquid, $C_{10}H_6Cl_8$, used as an insecticide. [CHLOR(O)– + *(in)d(ene)* + –ANE.]

chlo·rel·la (klə-rĕl′ə) ▸*n.* Any of a genus of unicellular green algae. [< Gk. *khlōros*, green.]

chlo·ric acid (klôr′ĭk) ▸*n.* A strongly oxidizing unstable acid, $HClO_3$, found only in solution.

chlo·ride (klôr′īd′) ▸*n.* A binary compound of chlorine. —**chlo·rid′ic** (klə-rĭd′ĭk) *adj.*

chlo·ri·nate (klôr′ə-nāt′) ▸*v.* **-nat·ed, -nat·ing** To treat or combine with chlorine or a chlorine compound. —**chlo′ri·na′tion** *n.*

chlo·rine (klôr′ēn′, -ĭn) ▸*n. Symbol* **Cl** A highly reactive, poisonous greenish-yellow gaseous element used to purify water, as a disinfectant and bleaching agent, and in the manufacture of many compounds. At. no. 17. See table at **element.**

chlo·ro– or **chlor–** ►*pref.* **1.** Green: *chlorophyll.* **2.** Chlorine: *chloroform.* [< Gk. *khlōros,* green.]

chlo·ro·fluor·o·car·bon (klôr′ō-floͮor′ō-kär′- bən, -flôr′-) ►*n.* Any of various gaseous compounds of carbon, hydrogen, chlorine, and fluorine, once used widely as aerosol propellants and refrigerants, now believed to cause depletion of the atmospheric ozone layer.

chlo·ro·form (klôr′ə-fôrm′) ►*n.* A clear colorless liquid, CHCl₃, used in refrigerants, propellants, and resins, as a solvent, and sometimes as an anesthetic. ►*v.* To anesthetize or kill with chloroform. [CHLORO– + *formyl.*]

chlo·ro·phyll (klôr′ə-fĭl) ►*n.* Any of a group of green pigments essential in photosynthesis. [CHLORO– + Gk. *phullon,* leaf.]

chlo·ro·plast (klôr′ə-plăst′) ►*n.* A chlorophyll-containing plastid found in algal and green plant cells. [CHLORO– + Gk. *plastos,* molded.]

chock (chŏk) ►*n.* A block or wedge placed under something else, such as a wheel, to keep it from moving. ►*v.* To secure by a chock. [Poss. < ONFr. *choque,* log.]

chock-a-block or **chock·a·block** (chŏk′ə-blŏk′) ►*adj.* Squeezed together; jammed.

chock-full or **chock·full** (chŏk′foͮol′) ►*adj.* As full as possible.

choc·o·late (chô′kə-lĭt, chôk′lĭt, chŏk′-) ►*n.* **1.** Fermented, roasted, and ground cacao seeds, often sweetened. **2.** A candy or beverage made from chocolate. [< Nahuatl *xocolatl.*] —**choc′o·late** *adj.*

Choc·taw (chŏk′tô) ►*n., pl.* **-taw** or **-taws** **1.** A member of a Native American people formerly of S Mississippi and SW Alabama, now living in Mississippi, Alabama, and Oklahoma. **2.** The Muskogean language of the Choctaw.

choice (chois) ►*n.* **1.** The act of choosing; selection: *made a choice.* **2.** The power, right, or liberty to choose: *had no choice in the matter.* **3.** One that is chosen: *declared him to be the voters' choice.* **4.** A number or variety from which to choose. ►*adj.* **choic·er, choic·est 1.** Of very fine quality: *choice plums.* **2.** Selected with care: *choice phrases.* [< OFr. *choisir,* choose.]

choir (kwīr) ►*n.* **1.** An organized company of singers, esp. one singing in a church. **2.** The part of a church used by a choir. **3.** A group of similar orchestral instruments: *a bell choir.* [< Lat. *chorus,* choral dance; see CHORUS.]

choke (chōk) ►*v.* **choked, chok·ing 1a.** To have difficulty in breathing, swallowing, or speaking. **b.** To cause to choke, as by constricting or obstructing the windpipe. **2.** To check or repress forcibly: *choke back a sob.* **3.** To block up or obstruct; clog: *leaves that choke the gutters.* **4.** To reduce the air intake of (a carburetor), thereby enriching the fuel mixture. **5.** To fail to perform effectively because of nervousness. ►*n.* A device used in choking a carburetor. —*phrasal verb:* **choke up** To be unable to speak because of strong emotion. [< OE *āceōcian.*]

choke collar ►*n.* A chain collar that tightens like a noose when the leash is pulled, used esp. in canine obedience training.

chok·er (chō′kər) ►*n.* **1.** One that chokes. **2.** A tight-fitting necklace.

chol·er (kŏl′ər, kō′lər) ►*n.* Anger; irritability. [<

Gk. *kholera,* jaundice < *kholē,* bile.]

chol·er·a (kŏl′ər-ə) ►*n.* An infectious, often fatal disease characterized by profuse watery diarrhea, vomiting, muscle cramps, and severe dehydration. [< Lat.; see CHOLER.] —**chol′e·ra′ic** (-ə-rā′ĭk) *adj.*

chol·er·ic (kŏl′ə-rĭk, kə-lĕr′ĭk) ►*adj.* Easily angered; bad-tempered; irritable.

cho·les·ter·ol (kə-lĕs′tə-rôl′, -rōl′) ►*n.* A white crystalline substance, C₂₇H₄₅OH, found in animal tissues and various foods, that is synthesized by the liver and transported in the blood as different types of lipoproteins, including HDL cholesterol and LDL cholesterol. [Gk. *kholē,* bile + *stereos,* solid + –OL.]

chol·la (choi′ə) ►*n.* Any of a genus of spiny, shrubby or treelike cacti having cylindrical, often detachable stem segments. [Am.Sp.]

chomp (chŏmp) ►*v.* To chew or bite noisily or repeatedly. [Var. of CHAMP¹.]

choose (chooz) ►*v.* **chose** (chōz), **cho·sen** (chō′zən), **choos·ing 1.** To decide on and pick out; select: *chose a new dress.* **2.** To determine or decide: *chose not to attend the lecture.* [< OE *cēosan.*] —**choos′er** *n.*

choos·y also **choos·ey** (chooʹzē) ►*adj.* **-i·er, -i·est** Highly selective. —**choos′i·ness** *n.*

chop (chŏp) ►*v.* **chopped, chop·ping 1a.** To cut by striking with a heavy sharp tool. **b.** To cut into small pieces. **2.** *Sports* To hit with a short, swift downward stroke. ►*n.* **1a.** A swift, short, cutting blow or stroke. **b.** *Sports* A short downward stroke. **2.** A cut of meat, usu. taken from the rib, shoulder, or loin and containing a bone. **3.** A short irregular motion of waves. [ME *choppen.*]

chop·house (chŏp′hous′) ►*n.* A restaurant that specializes in steaks and chops.

Cho·pin (shō′pǎn′, shō-pǎn′), **Frédéric François** 1810–49. Polish-born French composer and pianist.

chop·per (chŏp′ər) ►*n. Informal* **1.** A helicopter. **2. choppers** Teeth or dentures. **3.** A usu. customized motorcycle.

chop·ping block (chŏp′ĭng) ►*n.* A wooden block on which food or wood is chopped.

chop·py (chŏp′ē) ►*adj.* **-pi·er, -pi·est 1.** Having many small waves. **2.** Marked by abrupt starts and stops. —**chop′pi·ly** *adv.*

chops (chŏps) ►*pl.n.* The jaws, cheeks, or jowls. [< CHOP.]

chop shop ►*n. Slang* A place where stolen cars are disassembled for parts that are then sold.

chop·stick (chŏp′stĭk′) ►*n.* One of a pair of slender sticks used as an eating utensil chiefly in Asian countries. [< Pidgin E. *chop,* quick, of Chin. orig.]

chop su·ey (soo′ē) ►*n.* A Chinese-American dish consisting of small pieces of meat or chicken cooked with bean sprouts and other vegetables and served with rice. [Cantonese *zaap⁶ seoi³,* mixed pieces.]

cho·ral (kôr′əl) ►*adj. Mus.* Of or for a chorus or choir. —**cho′ral·ly** *adv.*

cho·rale also **cho·ral** (kə-răl′, -räl′) ►*n.* **1.** A harmonized hymn. **2.** A chorus or choir. [Ger. *Choral(gesang),* choral (song).]

chord¹ (kôrd) *Mus.* ►*n.* A combination of three or more pitches sounded simultaneously. ►*v.* To play chords on: *chord a guitar.* [< OFr. *acorde,* agreement; see ACCORD.]

chord¹
E major chord in opening bar of Edvard Grieg's
Morgenstemning

chord² (kôrd) ►*n.* **1.** A line segment that joins two points on a curve. **2.** *Anat.* Var. of **cord** (sense 3). **3.** An emotional feeling or response: *a sympathetic chord.* [Alteration of CORD.]

chore (chôr) ►*n.* **1. chores** Daily or routine domestic tasks. **2.** An unpleasant task. [Var. of CHAR³.]

cho·re·a (kô-rē′ə, kō-, kə-) ►*n.* Any of various disorders of the nervous system marked by uncontrollable movements, esp. of the arms, legs, and face. [< Gk. *khoreia,* choral dance.]

cho·re·o·graph (kôr′ē-ə-grăf′) ►*v.* **-graphed, -graph·ing** **1.** To create the choreography of. **2.** To prearrange or coordinate the details of. —**cho′re·og′ra·pher** *n.*

cho·re·og·ra·phy (kôr′ē-ŏg′rə-fē) ►*n.* The art of creating and arranging dances or ballets. [Gk. *khoreia,* choral dance + –GRAPHY.]

cho·ris·ter (kôr′ĭ-stər, kŏr′-) ►*n.* A singer in a choir. [< Med.Lat. *chorista.*]

cho·ri·zo (chə-rē′zō, -sō) ►*n.* A spicy pork sausage seasoned esp. with garlic. [Sp.]

cho·roid (kôr′oid′) or **cho·ri·oid** (kôr′ē-oid′) ►*n.* The vascular coat of the eye between the sclera and retina. [< Gk. *khoroeidēs,* like an afterbirth.]

chor·tle (chôr′tl) ►*n.* A snorting, joyful laugh or chuckle. [Blend of CHUCKLE and SNORT.] —**chor′tle** *v.* —**chor′tler** *n.*

cho·rus (kôr′əs) ►*n., pl.* **-rus·es** **1a.** A body of singers who perform choral compositions. **b.** A body of singers and dancers who support the leading performers in operas, musical comedies, and revues. **2a.** A composition written for a large number of singers. **b.** A refrain in a song, esp. one sung by the entire group of performers or by the audience. **3.** A group of persons who speak or recite together, esp. in a play. **4.** A simultaneous utterance by many voices. [Lat., choral dance < Gk. *khoros.*] —**cho′rus** *v.*

chose (chōz) ►*v.* P.t. of **choose.**

cho·sen (chō′zən) ►*v.* P.part. of **choose.** ►*adj.* Selected from or preferred above others.

Chou En-lai (jō′ ĕn-lī′) See **Zhou Enlai.**

chow (chou) *Slang* ►*n.* Food. ►*v.* To eat: *chowed down on pizza.* [Poss. < Cantonese *zaap⁶,* mixture, food.]

chow chow ►*n.* A heavy-set dog having a usu. reddish-brown coat and a blue-black tongue. [< *chow-chow,* pickles exported from China (since chow chows originated in China), ult. < Cantonese *zaap⁶,* mixture.]

chow·der (chou′dər) ►*n.* A thick soup, usu. containing seafood and often having a milk base. [< LLat. *caldāria,* stew pot.]

chow mein (chou′ mān′) ►*n.* A Chinese-American dish consisting of various stewed vegetables and meat served over fried noodles. [Mandarin *chǎo miàn.*]

chrism (krĭz′əm) ►*n.* *Eccles.* Consecrated oil and balsam, used for anointing, esp. in baptism and confirmation. [< Gk. *khrisma,* an anointing.] —**chris′mal** *adj.*

Christ (krīst) ►*n.* **1.** The Messiah, as foretold by the prophets of the Hebrew Scriptures. **2.** Jesus as considered in Christianity to be the Messiah. [< Gk. *khristos,* anointed.] —**Christ′like** *adj.*

chris·ten (krĭs′ən) ►*v.* **1a.** To baptize into a Christian church. **b.** To give a name to at baptism. **2.** To name and dedicate ceremonially: *christen a ship.* [< OE *cristnian.*] —**chris′ten·ing** *n.*

Chris·ten·dom (krĭs′ən-dəm) ►*n.* **1.** Christians collectively. **2.** The regions where Christianity is the dominant religion.

Chris·tian (krĭs′chən) ►*adj.* **1.** Professing belief in Christianity. **2.** Of or derived from Jesus's teachings. **3.** Of Christianity or its adherents. ►*n.* An adherent of Christianity. —**Chris′tian·ize′** *v.*

Christian era ►*n.* The period beginning with the birth of Jesus.

Chris·ti·an·i·ty (krĭs′chē-ăn′ĭ-tē, krĭs′tē-) ►*n.* **1.** A religion based on the worship of Jesus as the son of God, second person of the Trinity, and redeemer of humanity. **2.** Christendom. **3.** The state or fact of being a Christian.

Christian name ►*n.* **1.** *Christianity* A name given at baptism. **2.** A given name.

Usage: Because it presupposes that an entire society is Christian, the term *Christian name* when used generically can be taken as offensive in diverse societies. Writers seeking a way to avoid this problem can use *first name* or *given name* instead.

Christian Science ►*n.* The church and the religious system founded by Mary Baker Eddy, emphasizing healing through spiritual means. —**Christian Scientist** *n.*

Chris·tie (krĭs′tē), Dame **Agatha Mary Clarissa** 1890–1976. British writer.

Dame Agatha Christie
photographed in the mid-1950s

Christ·mas (krĭs′məs) ►*n.* **1.** A Christian feast commemorating the birth of Jesus. **2.** December 25, the day of this feast, observed as a public holiday in many countries. [< OE *Crīstes mæsse,* Christ's festival.]

Christ·mas·tide (krĭs′məs-tīd′) ►*n.* The season of Christmas.

Christmas tree ►*n.* An evergreen or artificial tree decorated during the Christmas season.

Chris·to·pher (krĭs′tə-fər), Saint. fl. 3rd cent. AD. Legendary Christian martyr.

chro·mat·ic (krō-măt′ĭk) ►*adj.* **1.** Relating to colors or color. **2.** *Mus.* Proceeding by half tones. [< Gk. *khrōma*, color.] —**chro·mat′i·cal·ly** *adv.* —**chro·mat′i·cism** *n.*

chrome (krōm) ►*n.* **1.** Chromium or a chromium alloy. **2.** Something plated with chrome. [< Gk. *khrōma*, color.]

chro·mi·um (krō′mē-əm) ►*n. Symbol* **Cr** A lustrous, hard, steel-gray metallic element used to harden steel alloys, to produce stainless steels, and in corrosion-resistant platings. At. no. 24. See table at **element.** [< Fr. *chrome*, CHROME.]

chromo– or **chrom–** ►*pref.* Color: *chromosome.* [< Gk. *khrōma*, color.]

chro·mo·some (krō′mə-sōm′) ►*n.* A cellular structure that consists of a linear strand of DNA bonded to various proteins and that carries the genes determining heredity. —**chro′mo·so′mal** *adj.*

chron·ic (krŏn′ĭk) ►*adj.* **1.** Of long duration or repeated recurrence: *chronic money problems; chronic colitis.* **2.** Firmly established by habit: *a chronic liar.* [< Gk. *khronos*, time.] —**chron′i·cal·ly** *adv.*
    Syns: confirmed, habitual, inveterate *adj.*

chronic fatigue syndrome ►*n.* A syndrome marked by debilitating fatigue and flulike symptoms.

chron·i·cle (krŏn′ĭ-kəl) ►*n.* **1.** A chronological account of historical events. **2. Chronicles** *(takes sing. v.)* See table at **Bible.** ►*v.* **-cled, -cling** To record in or in the form of a chronicle. [< Gk. *khronika*, annals.]

chrono– or **chron–** ►*pref.* Time: *chronometer.* [< Gk. *khronos*, time.]

chron·o·log·i·cal (krŏn′ə-lŏj′ĭ-kəl, krō′nə-) also **chron·o·log·ic** (-lŏj′ĭk) ►*adj.* **1.** Arranged in order of time of occurrence. **2.** Relating to or in accordance with chronology. —**chron′o·log′i·cal·ly** *adv.*

chro·nol·o·gy (krə-nŏl′ə-jē) ►*n., pl.* **-gies 1.** The determination of dates and sequence of events. **2.** The arrangement of events in time. **3.** A chronological list or table. —**chro·nol′o·gist** *n.*

chro·nom·e·ter (krə-nŏm′ĭ-tər) ►*n.* An exceptionally precise timepiece.

chrys·a·lis (krĭs′ə-lĭs) ►*n.* A pupa, esp. of a butterfly, enclosed in a firm case or cocoon. [< Gk. *khrusallis*.]

chry·san·the·mum (krĭ-săn′thə-məm, -zăn′-) ►*n.* Any of a genus of plants cultivated for their showy flower heads. [< Gk. *khrusanthemon*, gold flower.]

chub (chŭb) ►*n., pl.* **chub** or **chubs 1.** Any of various freshwater fishes related to the carps and minnows. **2.** Any of several North American food fishes. [ME *chubbe.*]

chub·by (chŭb′ē) ►*adj.* **-bi·er, -bi·est** Rounded and plump. [Prob. < CHUB.] —**chub′bi·ly** *adv.*

chuck¹ (chŭk) ►*v.* **1.** To pat or squeeze playfully, esp. under the chin. **2.** *Informal* **a.** To throw or toss. **b.** To throw out; discard. [Perh. < OFr. *choc*, SHOCK¹.] —**chuck** *n.*

chuck² (chŭk) ►*n.* **1.** A cut of beef extending from the neck to the ribs. **2.** A clamp that holds a tool or the material being worked, as in a drill or lathe. [dial. *chuck*, lump.]

chuck·le (chŭk′əl) ►*v.* **-led, -ling** To laugh quietly. ►*n.* A quiet laugh of mild amusement. [Poss. < ME *chukken*, to cluck.]

chuck wagon ►*n.* A wagon equipped with food and cooking utensils, as on a ranch.

chug¹ (chŭg) ►*n.* A brief dull explosive sound made by or as if by a laboring engine. ►*v.* **chugged, chug·ging 1.** To make chugs. **2.** To move at a steady speed. [Imit.]

chug² (chŭg) ►*v. Slang* To chugalug.

chug·a·lug (chŭg′ə-lŭg′) ►*v.* **-lugged, -lug·ging** *Slang* To swallow (a liquid) without pausing. [Imit.]

chuk·ka (chŭk′ə) ►*n.* An ankle-length, usu. suede leather boot. [< CHUKKER.]

chuk·ker also **chuk·kar** (chŭk′ər) ►*n.* A period of play, lasting 7½ minutes, in a polo match. [< Skt. *cakram*, circle.]

chum¹ (chŭm) ►*n.* An intimate friend. ►*v.* **chummed, chum·ming** To spend time with a friend. [Perh. < *chamber fellow*, roommate.]

chum² (chŭm) ►*n.* Bait, esp. oily fish, ground up and scattered on the water. [?]

Chu·mash (chōō′măsh) ►*n., pl.* **-mash** or **-mash·es** A member of a Hokan-speaking Native American people of S California.

chum·my (chŭm′ē) ►*adj.* **-mi·er, -mi·est** Intimate; friendly. —**chum′mi·ly** *adv.*

chump (chŭmp) ►*n.* **1.** A gullible person; dupe. **2.** A foolish person; dolt. [Poss. blend of CHUNK and LUMP¹ or STUMP.]

chunk (chŭngk) ►*n.* **1.** A thick mass or piece. **2.** *Informal* A substantial amount. [Poss. < CHUCK².]

chunk·y (chŭng′kē) ►*adj.* **-i·er, -i·est 1.** Short and thick; stocky. **2.** Containing small thick pieces: *chunky soup.* —**chunk′i·ness** *n.*

church (chûrch) ►*n.* **1.** A building for public, esp. Christian worship. **2.** often **Church a.** All Christians regarded as a spiritual body. **b.** A specified Christian denomination. **3.** A congregation. **4.** A religious service: *was late for church.* **5.** Ecclesiastical power: *the separation of church and state.* [< Gk. *kuriakos*, of the lord.]

church·go·er (chûrch′gō′ər) ►*n.* One who attends church. —**church′go′ing** *adj. & n.*

Sir Winston Churchill
photographed in 1953

Chur·chill (chûr′chĭl′, chûrch′hĭl′), Sir **Winston Leonard Spencer** 1874–1965. British prime minister (1940–45 and 1951–55) and writer. —**Chur·chill′i·an** (chûr-chĭl′ē-ən) adj.

church key ►n. A can or bottle opener having a usu. triangular head.

church·man (chûrch′mən) ►n. **1.** A man who is a cleric. **2.** A man who is a member of a church.

Church of Christ, Scientist ►n. See **Christian Science.**

Church of England ►n. The Anglican church as established in England and headed by the Archbishop of Canterbury.

Church of Jesus Christ of Latter-day Saints ►n. See **Mormon Church.**

church·war·den (chûrch′wôr′dn) ►n. A lay officer who handles the secular affairs of an Anglican church.

church·wom·an (chûrch′wŏŏm′ən) ►n. **1.** A woman who is a cleric. **2.** A woman who is a member of a church. See Usage Note at **man.**

church·yard (chûrch′yärd′) ►n. A yard adjacent to a church, esp. a cemetery.

churl (chûrl) ►n. A rude, surly person. See Synonyms at **boor.** [< OE *ceorl,* peasant.] —**churl′ish** adj. —**churl′ish·ness** n.

churn (chûrn) ►n. A vessel or device in which cream or milk is agitated to make butter. ►v. **1a.** To agitate or stir (milk or cream) to make butter. **b.** To make (butter) by churning. **2.** To shake or stir vigorously. See Synonyms at **agitate.** —*phrasal verb:* **churn out** To produce in an abundant and automatic manner: *churns out four novels a year.* [< OE *cyrn.*]

chute (shŏŏt) ►n. **1.** An inclined trough or passage through or down which things may pass. **2.** A waterfall or rapid. **3.** A parachute. [< Fr. *cheoir,* to fall.]

chut·ney (chŭt′nē) ►n. A pungent relish made of fruits, spices, and herbs. [Hindi and Urdu *caṭnī.*]

chutz·pah (KHŏŏt′spə, hŏŏt′-) ►n. Utter nerve; gall. [< Mishnaic Heb. *ḥuṣpâ.*]

Ci ►*abbr.* curie

CIA ►*abbr.* Central Intelligence Agency

ciao (chou) ►*interj.* Used to express greeting or farewell. [Ital.]

ci·bo·ri·um (sĭ-bôr′ē-əm) ►n., pl. **-bo·ri·a** (-bôr′ē-ə) **1.** A vaulted canopy over an altar. **2.** A covered receptacle for the consecrated wafers of the Eucharist. [< Gk. *kibōrion,* drinking cup.]

ci·ca·da (sĭ-kā′də, -kä′-) ►n., pl. **-das** or **-dae** (-dē′) An insect with a broad head, membranous wings, and in the male a pair of organs that produce a shrill drone. [< Lat. *cicāda.*]

cic·a·trix (sĭk′ə-trĭks′, sĭ-kā′trĭks) ►n., pl. **-tri·ces** (-trī′sēz, -trī-sēz′) A scar. [< Lat. *cicātrīx.*] —**cic′a·tri′cial** (-trĭsh′əl) adj.

Cic·e·ro (sĭs′ə-rō′), **Marcus Tullius** 106–43 BC. Roman political leader and orator. —**Cic′e·ro′ni·an** adj.

Cid (sĭd), **the** Rodrigo Díaz de Vivar. 1043?–99. Spanish soldier and hero.

–cide ►*suff.* **1.** Killer: *pesticide.* **2.** Act of killing: *genocide.* [< Lat. *caedere,* kill.]

ci·der (sī′dər) ►n. **1.** The unfermented juice pressed esp. from fruit, esp. apples, used as a beverage or to make other products, such as vinegar. **2.** An alcoholic beverage made by fermenting juice pressed from fruit, esp. apples. [< Semitic; akin to Heb. *šēkār,* intoxicating drink.]

ci·gar (sĭ-gär′) ►n. A compact roll of tobacco leaves prepared for smoking. [Sp. *cigarro.*]

cig·a·rette also **cig·a·ret** (sĭg′ə-rĕt′, sĭg′ə-rĕt′) ►n. A small roll of finely cut tobacco for smoking, usu. enclosed in a wrapper of thin paper. [Fr., dim. of *cigare,* CIGAR.]

ci·lan·tro (sĭ-lăn′trō) ►n. The leaves and stems of the coriander plant, used in salads and as a flavoring. [Sp. < Lat. *coriandrum,* CORIANDER.]

cil·i·a (sĭl′ē-ə) ►n. Pl. of **cilium.**

cil·i·ate (sĭl′ē-ĭt, -āt′) ►adj. or **cil·i·at·ed** (-ā′tĭd) Having cilia. ►n. Any of a class of protozoans characterized by numerous cilia.

cil·i·um (sĭl′ē-əm) ►n., pl. **-i·a** (-ē-ə) **1.** A microscopic hairlike process extending from a cell or unicellular organism and capable of rhythmical motion. **2.** An eyelash. [Lat., eyelid.] —**cil′i·ar′y** (-ĕr′ē)

cinch (sĭnch) ►n. **1a.** A girth for a pack or saddle. **b.** An encircling cord, band, or belt. **2.** Something easy to accomplish. See Synonyms at **breeze. 3.** A sure thing; certainty. [< Lat. *cingere,* gird.] —**cinch** v.

cin·cho·na (sĭng-kō′nə, sĭn-chō′-) ►n. **1.** Any of a genus of South American trees whose bark yields quinine and other medicinal alkaloids. **2.** The dried bark of a cinchona. [Supposedly after Francisca H. de Ribera (1576–1639), Countess of *Chinchón.*]

Cin·cin·na·ti (sĭn′sə-năt′ē, -năt′ə) A city of SW OH on the Ohio R.

Cin·cin·na·tus (sĭn′sə-năt′əs, -nä′təs), **Lucius Quinctius** 519?–438 BC. Roman statesman.

cinc·ture (sĭngk′chər) ►n. A belt or sash; girdle. [< Lat. *cingere,* gird.] —**cinc′ture** v.

cin·der (sĭn′dər) ►n. **1a.** A small piece of burned substance that is not reduced to ashes but cannot be burned further. **b.** A piece of charred substance that can burn further but without flame. **2. cinders** Ashes. **3. cinders** Geol. See **scoria** (sense 1). **4.** See **scoria** (sense 3). [< OE *sinder,* dross.] —**cin′der·y** adj.

cinder block ►n. A usu. hollow building block made with concrete and coal cinders.

cin·e·ma (sĭn′ə-mə) ►n. **1.** A movie theater. **2.** Movies collectively, esp. when considered as an art form. [Fr. *cinéma* < *cinématographe,* motion-picture projector.] —**cin′e·mat′ic** (-măt′ĭk) adj. —**cin′e·mat′i·cal·ly** adv.

cin·e·ma·tog·ra·phy (sĭn′ə-mə-tŏg′rə-fē) ►n. The art or technique of movie photography. —**cin′e·ma·tog′ra·pher** n.

ci·né·ma vé·ri·té (sē′nä-mä′ vā′rē-tā′) ►n. Documentary filmmaking that stresses unbiased realism. [Fr.]

cin·e·rar·i·a (sĭn′ə-râr′ē-ə) ►n. Any of several tropical plants cultivated as house plants for their showy, daisylike flowers. [< Lat. *cinerārius,* of ashes.]

cin·e·rar·i·um (sĭn′ə-râr′ē-əm) ►n., pl. **-i·a** (-ē-ə) A place for keeping the ashes of a cremated body. [< Lat. *cinis, ciner-,* ashes.] —**cin′er·ar′y** (sĭn′ə-rĕr′ē) adj.

cin·na·bar (sĭn′ə-bär′) ►n. **1.** A heavy reddish compound, HgS, that is the principal ore of mercury. **2.** A vivid red; vermilion. [< Gk. *kinnabari.*]

cin·na·mon (sĭn′ə-mən) ►n. **1.** The aromatic

reddish or yellowish-brown inner bark of certain tropical Asian trees, dried and often ground for use as a spice. **2.** A light reddish brown. [< Gk. *kinnamōmon.*] —**cin′na·mon** *adj.*

CIO ►*abbr.* chief information officer

ciop·pi·no (chə-pē′nō) ►*n., pl.* -**nos** A stew of fish and shellfish, tomatoes, and white wine. [Ital.]

ci·pher (sī′fər) ►*n.* **1.** The mathematical symbol (0) denoting absence of quantity; zero. **2.** An Arabic numeral or figure. **3.** A nonentity. **4a.** A cryptographic system in which units of text, usu. letters, are substituted according to a predetermined code. **b.** The key to such a system. **c.** A message in cipher. ►*v.* **1.** To compute arithmetically. **2.** To put in secret writing; encode. [< Ar. *ṣifr.*]

ci·pher·text (sī′fər-tĕkst′) ►*n.* A text in encrypted form, as opposed to plaintext.

cir·ca (sûr′kə) ►*prep.* About: *born circa 1750.* [Lat. *circā.*]

cir·ca·di·an (sər-kā′dē-ən, -kăd′ē-, sûr′kə-dī′ən, -dē′-) ►*adj. Biol.* Exhibiting approx. 24-hour periodicity. [< Lat. *circā*, around + *diēs*, day.]

cir·cle (sûr′kəl) ►*n.* **1a.** A plane curve everywhere equidistant from a given fixed point, the center. **b.** A planar region bounded by a circle. **c.** Something shaped like a plane curve. **2.** A group of people sharing an interest or activity. **3.** A sphere of influence or interest. ►*v.* -**cled, -cling 1.** To make a circle around: *The hedge circles the fountain.* **2.** To move in a circle around: *The ship circles the island.* [< Gk. *kirkos.*]

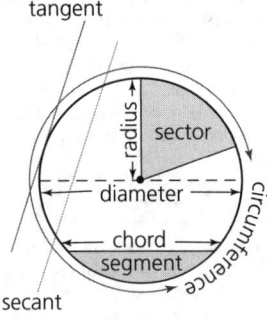

circle

cir·clet (sûr′klĭt) ►*n.* A small circle.

cir·cuit (sûr′kĭt) ►*n.* **1a.** A closed, usu. circular line around an area. See Synonyms at **circumference. b.** The region enclosed by such a line. **2.** A closed path or route. **3a.** A closed path followed by an electric current. **b.** A configuration of electrically or electromagnetically connected components or devices. **4a.** A regular or accustomed course from place to place, as that of a salesperson. **b.** The area covered by such a course, esp. by the judge or judges of a court. ►*v.* To make a circuit (of). [< Lat. *circumīre*, go around.]

circuit board ►*n. Comp.* An insulated board on which conductive pathways are constructed and components such as chips are mounted.

circuit breaker ►*n.* An automatic switch that interrupts an overloaded electric circuit.

circuit court ►*n.* A court serving a particular geographic area, esp. in multiple locations.

cir·cu·i·tous (sər-kyoo′ĭ-təs) ►*adj.* **1.** Being or taking a roundabout course. **2.** Marked by indirect, evasive, or complex language: *a circuitous argument.* —**cir·cu′i·tous·ly** *adv.* —**cir·cu′i·ty, cir·cu′i·tous·ness** *n.*

cir·cuit·ry (sûr′kĭ-trē) ►*n., pl.* -**ries 1.** The design of or a detailed plan for an electric circuit. **2.** Electric circuits collectively.

cir·cu·lar (sûr′kyə-lər) ►*adj.* **1.** Of or relating to a circle. **2a.** Shaped like a circle; round. **b.** Moving in or forming a circle. **3.** Circuitous. **4.** Self-referential: *circular reasoning.* ►*n.* A printed advertisement or notice for mass distribution. —**cir′cu·lar′i·ty** (-lăr′ĭ-tē) *n.* —**cir′cu·lar·ly** *adv.*

circular saw ►*n.* A power saw consisting of a toothed disk rotated at high speed.

cir·cu·late ►*v.* -**lat·ed, -lat·ing 1.** To move in or flow through a circle or circuit. **2.** To move around, as from person to person or place to place. **3.** To move about or flow freely, as air. **4.** To disseminate. —**cir′cu·la′tive** *adj.* —**cir′cu·la′tor** *n.* —**cir′cu·la·to′ry** (-lə-tôr′ē) *adj.*

cir·cu·la·tion (sûr′kyə-lā′shən) ►*n.* **1.** Movement in a circuit, esp. the movement of blood through the body as a result of the heart's pumping action. **2.** The passing of something, such as money, from place to place or person to person. **3a.** The distribution of printed material, esp. newspapers or magazines. **b.** The number of copies sold or distributed.

circulatory system ►*n.* The heart, blood vessels, and lymphatic system of the body.

circum– ►*pref.* Around; about: *circumlunar.* [Lat. < *circum*, around.]

cir·cum·cise (sûr′kəm-sīz′) ►*v.* -**cised, -cis·ing 1.** To remove the prepuce of (a male). **2.** To remove all or part of the clitoris, prepuce, or labia of (a female). [< Lat. *circumcīdere, circumcīs-*, cut around.] —**cir′cum·ci′sion** (-sĭzh′ən) *n.*

cir·cum·fer·ence (sər-kŭm′fər-əns) ►*n.* **1.** The boundary line of a circle. **2a.** The boundary line of an area or object. **b.** The length of such a line. **3.** The margin or area surrounding something. [< Lat. *circumferre*, carry around : CIRCUM– + *ferre*, carry.] —**cir·cum′fer·en′tial** (-fə-rĕn′shəl) *adj.*

   Syns: *circuit, compass, perimeter, periphery* **n.**

cir·cum·flex (sûr′kəm-flĕks′) ►*n.* Any of several marks, esp. (^), used over a vowel to indicate quality of pronunciation. [< Lat. *circumflectere*, bend around.]

cir·cum·lo·cu·tion (sûr′kəm-lō-kyoo′shən) ►*n.* **1.** The use of wordy and indirect language, esp. in being vague or evasive. **2.** A roundabout or evasive expression.

cir·cum·lu·nar (sûr′kəm-loo′nər) ►*adj.* Revolving about or surrounding the moon.

cir·cum·nav·i·gate (sûr′kəm-năv′ĭ-gāt′) ►*v.* -**gat·ed, -gat·ing** To go or proceed completely around: *circumnavigating the earth.* —**cir′cum·nav′i·ga′tion** *n.*

cir·cum·po·lar (sûr′kəm-pō′lər) ►*adj.* Located or found in one of the polar regions.

cir·cum·scribe (sûr′kəm-skrīb′) ►*v.* -**scribed, -scrib·ing 1.** To draw a line around. **2a.** To delineate: *The hedge circumscribes the property.* **b.** To limit narrowly: *Their plans were circumscribed by lack of money.* **3.** To enclose (a polygon or polyhedron) within a configuration of lines, curves, or surfaces so that every vertex of the enclosed object touches the enclosing configuration. [< Lat. *circumscrībere*, write around.] **—cir′cum·scrip′tion** (-skrĭp′shən) *n.*

cir·cum·so·lar (sûr′kəm-sō′lər) ►*adj.* Revolving around or surrounding the sun.

cir·cum·spect (sûr′kəm-spĕkt′) ►*adj.* Heedful of potential consequences; prudent. [< Lat. *circumspicere*, take heed : CIRCUM– + *specere*, look.] **—cir′cum·spec′tion** *n.* **—cir′cum·spect′ly** *adv.*

cir·cum·stance (sûr′kəm-stăns′) ►*n.* **1.** A condition or fact attending an event and having some bearing on it. **2.** The sum of determining factors beyond willful control. **3. circumstances** Financial status or means. **4.** Formal display; ceremony: *pomp and circumstance.* **—idioms: under no circumstances** Never. **under (or in) the circumstances** Given these conditions. [< Lat. *circumstāre*, stand around : CIRCUM– + *stāre*, stand.]

cir·cum·stan·tial (sûr′kəm-stăn′shəl) ►*adj.* **1.** Of or dependent on circumstances. **2.** Of minor import; incidental. **3.** Complete and particular. **—cir′cum·stan′tial·ly** *adv.*

circumstantial evidence ►*n.* Evidence not bearing directly on the fact in dispute but on various attendant circumstances from which the judge or jury might infer the occurrence of the fact in dispute.

cir·cum·stan·ti·ate (sûr′kəm-stăn′shē-āt′) ►*v.* **-at·ed, -at·ing** To give detailed proof or description of. **—cir′cum·stan′ti·a′tion** *n.*

cir·cum·ter·res·tri·al (sûr′kəm-tə-rĕs′trē-əl) ►*adj.* Revolving around or surrounding the earth.

cir·cum·vent (sûr′kəm-vĕnt′) ►*v.* **1.** To entrap or overcome by ingenuity. **2.** To avoid or get around: *circumvent a regulation.* [< Lat. *circumvenīre* : CIRCUM– + *venīre*, go.] **—cir′cum·ven′tion** *n.* **—cir′cum·ven′tive** *adj.*

cir·cus (sûr′kəs) ►*n.* **1a.** A public entertainment consisting typically of a variety of performances by acrobats, clowns, and trained animals. **b.** A traveling company that performs such entertainments. **2.** *Informal* A humorous or rowdy time or event. [< Lat., CIRCLE.]

cirque (sûrk) ►*n.* A steep hollow at the upper end of a mountain valley, esp. one forming the head of a glacier. [< Lat. *circus*, CIRCLE.]

cir·rho·sis (sĭ-rō′sĭs) ►*n.* A chronic, sometimes fatal liver disease caused esp. by alcohol abuse or hepatitis. [< Gk. *kirros*, tawny.] **—cir·rhot′ic** (-rŏt′ĭk) *adj.*

cir·ro·cu·mu·lus (sîr′ō-kyōōm′yə-ləs) ►*n.* A high-altitude cloud composed of a series of small, regularly arranged cloudlets in the form of ripples or grains.

cir·ro·strat·us (sîr′ō-străt′əs, -strā′təs) ►*n.* A high-altitude, thin, hazy cloud or cloud cover, often producing a halo effect.

cir·rus (sîr′əs) ►*n., pl.* **cir·ri** (sîr′ī′) A high-altitude cloud composed of thin, usu. white fleecy bands or patches. [Lat., curl of hair.]

cis·tern (sĭs′tərn) ►*n.* A receptacle for holding water, esp. a tank for catching and storing rainwater. [< Lat. *cisterna.*]

cit. ►*abbr.* **1.** citation **2.** cited

cit·a·del (sĭt′ə-dəl, -dĕl′) ►*n.* **1.** A fortress in a commanding position in or near a city. **2.** A stronghold. [< Ital. *cittadella*, small city.]

cite (sīt) ►*v.* **cit·ed, cit·ing 1a.** To quote (a book, e.g.) as an authority in making an argument. **b.** To invoke an existing legal precedent. Sometimes used with *to: The lower court cited to the Supreme Court decision.* **2.** To mention as support, illustration, or proof. **3.** To commend officially for meritorious action, esp. in military service. **4.** To summon before a court of law. [< Lat. *citāre.*] **—ci·ta′tion** *n.*

cit·i·fy (sĭt′ĭ-fī′) ►*v.* **-fied, -fy·ing 1.** To make urban. **2.** To impart the styles and manners of a city to. **—cit′i·fi·ca′tion** *n.* **—cit′i·fied′** *adj.*

cit·i·zen (sĭt′ĭ-zən) ►*n.* **1.** A person owing loyalty to and entitled by birth or naturalization to the protection of a state or nation. **2.** A resident of a city or town. [< AN *citesein.*]

cit·i·zen·ry (sĭt′ĭ-zən-rē) ►*n., pl.* **-ries** Citizens collectively.

cit·i·zens band (sĭt′ĭ-zənz) ►*n.* A radio-frequency band officially allocated for private use by individuals.

cit·i·zen·ship (sĭt′ĭ-zən-shĭp′) ►*n.* The status of a citizen with its duties, rights, and privileges.

cit·rate (sĭt′rāt′) ►*n.* A salt or ester of citric acid.

cit·ric acid (sĭt′rĭk) ►*n.* A colorless acid derived from citrus and pineapple juices and used in flavorings and metal polishes.

ci·trine (sĭ-trēn′, sĭt′rēn′) ►*n.* **1.** A pale yellow quartz resembling topaz. **2.** A light olive color. [< Lat. *citrus*, citron.] **—ci·trine′** *adj.*

cit·ron (sĭt′rən) ►*n.* **1.** A thorny evergreen shrub with large, lemonlike fruits. **2.** Its fruit, whose rind is often candied and used in confections. [< Lat. *citreum*, citrus.]

cit·ro·nel·la (sĭt′rə-nĕl′ə) ►*n.* A pale yellow aromatic oil obtained from a tropical Asian grass and used in perfumery, insect repellents, and flavorings. [< Fr. *citronnelle.*]

cit·rus (sĭt′rəs) ►*n., pl.* **-rus** or **-rus·es** Any of various shrubs or trees such as the grapefruit, lemon, or orange, bearing juicy edible fruits with an aromatic rind. [Lat., citron tree.]

cit·y (sĭt′ē) ►*n., pl.* **-ies 1.** A town of significant size and importance. **2.** An incorporated US municipality with definite boundaries and legal powers that are set forth in a state charter. **3.** The inhabitants of a city as a group. [< Lat. *cīvitās.*]

city council ►*n.* The governing body of a city.

city desk ►*n.* The newspaper department that handles local news.

city hall ►*n.* **1.** The building housing the administrative offices of a municipal government. **2.** A municipal government.

city manager ►*n.* An administrator appointed by a city council to manage municipal affairs.

cit·y-state (sĭt′ē-stāt′) ►*n.* A sovereign state consisting of an independent city and its surrounding territory.

civ·et (sĭv′ĭt) ►*n.* **1.** A catlike mammal of Africa and Asia that secretes a musky fluid. **2.** This fluid, used in perfumery. [< Ar. *zabād*, civet perfume.]

civ·ic (sĭv′ĭk) ►*adj.* Of a city, a citizen, or citizenship. [< Lat. *cīvis*, citizen.]

civ·ics (sĭv′ĭks) ►*n. (takes sing. v.)* The study of civic affairs and the rights and duties of citizens.

civ·ies (sĭv′ēz) ►*pl.n. Slang* Var. of **civvies.**

civ·il (sĭv′əl) ►*adj.* **1.** Of or relating to a citizen or citizens. **2.** Of ordinary community life as distinguished from the military or the ecclesiastical. **3.** Civilized. **4.** Not rude; polite: *uttred a civil reply*. [< Lat. *cīvis*, citizen.] —**civ′il·ly** *adv.*

civil defense ▸*n.* Emergency measures to be taken by organized civilian volunteers for protection of life and property in the event of natural disaster or enemy attack.

civil disobedience ▸*n.* Refusal to obey a law as a result of moral objections, esp. through passive resistance.

civil engineer ▸*n.* An engineer trained in the design and construction of public works, as bridges or dams. —**civil engineering** *n.*

ci·vil·ian (sĭ-vĭl′yən) ▸*n.* A person following the pursuits of civil or nonmilitary life. —**ci·vil′ian** *adj.*

ci·vil·i·ty (sĭ-vĭl′ĭ-tē) ▸*n.*, *pl.* **-ties 1.** Politeness; courtesy. **2.** A courteous act.

civ·i·li·za·tion (sĭv′ə-lĭ-zā′shən) ▸*n.* **1.** An advanced state of cultural and material development in human society, marked by political and social complexity and progress in the arts and sciences. **2.** The culture that is developed by a particular society or epoch. **3.** Cultural refinement. **4.** Modern society with its conveniences.

civ·i·lize (sĭv′ə-līz′) ▸*v.* **-lized, -liz·ing 1.** To raise (a society) to an advanced stage of development. **2.** To educate in manners; sophisticate. —**civ′i·liz′er** *n.*

civil law ▸*n.* **1.** The body of laws governing the behavior of individuals and corporations. **2.** The law determining private rights and liabilities.

civil liberties ▸*pl.n.* Fundamental individual rights, such as freedom of speech and religion, esp. as protected by constitutional guarantees.

civil rights ▸*pl.n.* The rights belonging to an individual by virtue of citizenship, esp. the rights to due process, equal protection of the laws, and freedom from discrimination. —**civil rights, civ′il-rights′** *adj.*

civil service ▸*n.* Those branches of public service that are not legislative, judicial, or military. —**civil servant** *n.*

civil union ▸*n.* A legally sanctioned relationship between two people, esp. of the same sex, having many of the rights and responsibilities of marriage.

civil war ▸*n.* **1.** A war between factions or regions of the same country. **2.** **Civil War** The war in the US between the Union and the Confederacy from 1861 to 1865.

civ·vies also **civ·ies** (sĭv′ēz) ▸*pl.n. Slang* Civilian clothes.

CJ ▸*abbr.* Chief Justice

cl ▸*abbr.* centiliter

clab·ber (klăb′ər) ▸*n.* Sour, curdled milk. ▸*v.* To curdle. [< Ir.Gael. *bainne clabair*.]

clack (klăk) ▸*v.* To make or cause to make a sharp sound, as by the collision of hard surfaces. ▸*n.* A clacking sound. [< ON *klaka*.]

clad¹ (klăd) ▸*v.* **clad, clad·ding** To cover (a metal) with a bonded metal coating. [Poss. < CLAD².]

clad² (klăd) ▸*v.* P.t. and p.part. of **clothe.**

clad·dagh (klä′də) ▸*n.* A ring formed of two hands clasping a crowned heart. [After *Claddagh*, suburb of Galway.]

claddagh

clade (klād) ▸*n.* A grouping of organisms on the basis of their presumed evolutionary history, consisting of a common ancestor and all of its descendants. [< Gk. *klados*, branch.]

claim (klām) ▸*v.* **1.** To ask for as one's due: *claim a reward*. **2.** To take in a violent manner as if by right: *a storm that claimed two lives*. **3.** To state to be true; assert: *claimed he had won*. **4.** To call for: *problems that claim her attention*. ▸*n.* **1.** A demand for something as one's due. **2.** A title or right. **3.** Something claimed formally or legally. **4.** A statement of something as a fact. —*idiom:* **lay claim to** To assert one's right to. [< Lat. *clāmāre*, to call.] —**claim′a·ble** *adj.*

claim·ant (klā′mənt) ▸*n.* One making a claim.

clair·voy·ance (klâr-voi′əns) ▸*n.* The supposed power to see objects or events that cannot be perceived by the senses. [Fr. : *clair,* CLEAR + Lat. *vidēre*, see.] —**clair·voy′ant** *adj. & n.*

clam (klăm) ▸*n.* **1.** Any of a class of bivalve mollusks, many of which are edible. **2.** *Slang* A dollar. ▸*v.* **clammed, clam·ming** To hunt for clams. —*phrasal verb:* **clam up** *Informal* To refuse to talk. [< *clam*, clamp.] —**clam′mer** *n.*

clam·bake (klăm′bāk′) ▸*n.* A picnic where clams, corn, and other foods are baked in layers on hot stones covered with seaweed.

clam·ber (klăm′bər, klăm′ər) ▸*v.* To climb with difficulty, esp. on all fours; scramble. [ME *clambren*.] —**clam′ber·er** *n.*

clam·my (klăm′ē) ▸*adj.* **-mi·er, -mi·est 1.** Disagreeably moist, sticky, and usu. cold: *a clammy handshake*. **2.** Damp and unpleasant: *clammy weather*. [ME, sticky.] —**clam′mi·ness** *n.*

clam·or (klăm′ər) ▸*n.* **1.** A loud outcry; hubbub. See Synonyms at **noise. 2.** A vehement outcry or protest. [< Lat. *clāmor*, shout.] —**clam′or** *v.* —**clam′or·ous** *adj.*

clamp (klămp) ▸*n.* Any of various devices used to join, grip, support, or compress mechanical or structural parts. ▸*v.* To fasten or grip with or as if with a clamp. —*phrasal verb:* **clamp down** To become more repressive. [< MDu. *klampe*.]

clamp·down (klămp′doun′) ▸*n.* An imposing of restrictions or controls.

clan (klăn) ▸*n.* **1.** A traditional social unit in the Scottish highlands, consisting of a number of families claiming a common ancestor. **2.** A division of a tribe tracing descent from a common ancestor. **3.** A large group of relatives or associates. [< OIr. *cland*, offspring.] —**clan′nish** *adj.* —**clans′man** *n.* —**clans′wom′an** *n.*

clan·des·tine (klăn-dĕs′tĭn) ▸*adj.* Kept or done in secret. [Lat. *clandestīnus*.]

clang (klăng) ▸*n.* A loud, resonant, metallic sound. [Prob. < Lat. *clangere*, to ring.] —**clang** *v.*

clan·gor (klăng′ər, klăng′gər) ▸*n.* **1.** A repeated clanging. **2.** A din. [Lat. < *clangere*, to clang.] —**clan′gor** *v.*

clank (klăngk) ►*n.* A sharp, hard metallic sound. [Prob. imit.] —**clank** *v.*

clap (klăp) ►*v.* **clapped, clap·ping 1.** To strike the palms of the hands together with a sudden explosive sound, as in applauding. **2.** To come together suddenly with a sharp sound. **3.** To strike lightly with the open hand, as in greeting. **4.** To put or send suddenly: *clapped the thief in jail.* ►*n.* **1.** The act or sound of clapping the hands. **2.** A loud or explosive sound: *a clap of thunder.* **3.** A slap. [< OE *clæppan,* throb, and ON *klappa,* clap.]

clap·board (klăb′ərd, klăp′bôrd′) ►*n.* A long narrow board with one edge thicker than the other, overlapped horizontally to cover the outer walls of frame structures. [< Du. *klaphout,* split board.]

clap·per (klăp′ər) ►*n.* One that claps, esp. the hammerlike tongue of a bell.

clap·trap (klăp′trăp′) ►*n.* Pretentious, insincere, or empty language.

claque (klăk) ►*n.* A group of persons hired to applaud at a performance. [Fr.]

clar·et (klăr′ĭt) ►*n.* A dry red table wine. [< OFr. (*vin*) *claret,* (light-colored) wine.]

clar·i·fy (klăr′ə-fī′) ►*v.* **-fied, -fy·ing** To make or become clear. [< LLat. *clārificāre.*] —**clar′i·fi·ca′tion** *n.*

clar·i·net (klăr′ə-nĕt′) ►*n.* A woodwind instrument having a straight cylindrical tube with a flaring bell and a single-reed mouthpiece. [< Lat. *clārus,* clear.] —**clar′i·net′ist** *n.*

clar·i·on (klăr′ē-ən) ►*adj.* Loud and clear. [< Lat. *clārus,* clear.]

clar·i·ty (klăr′ĭ-tē) ►*n.* The quality or condition of being clear. [< Lat. *clārus,* clear.]

Clark (klärk), **William** 1770–1838. Amer. explorer.

clash (klăsh) ►*v.* **1.** To collide or strike together with a loud harsh noise. **2.** To conflict; disagree. **3.** To have an inharmonious effect when juxtaposed: *colors that clash.* ►*n.* **1.** A loud metallic noise. **2.** A usu. hostile conflict. **3.** An incongruity or unpleasant juxtaposition. [Imit.]

clasp (klăsp) ►*n.* **1.** A fastening, such as a hook, used to hold two objects or parts together. **2a.** An embrace. **b.** A grip of the hand. ►*v.* **1.** To fasten with or as if with a clasp. **2.** To hold in a tight embrace. **3.** To grip firmly in or with the hand. [ME *claspe.*]

class (klăs) ►*n.* **1.** A group whose members have certain attributes in common; category. **2.** A division based on quality or grade. **3.** A social or economic stratum whose members share similar characteristics. **4.** *Informal* Elegance of style or manner. **5a.** A group of students or alumni who have the same year of graduation. **b.** A group of students who meet to study the same subject. **c.** The set of lessons taught to such a group: *found the class difficult.* **d.** The time during which such a group meets. **6.** *Biol.* A taxonomic category ranking below a phylum and above an order. ►*v.* To classify. [< Lat. *classis,* class of citizens.]

class action ►*n.* A lawsuit brought by one or more plaintiffs on behalf of a large group of others who have a common legal claim.

clas·sic (klăs′ĭk) ►*adj.* **1.** Adhering to established standards and principles. **2.** Being a lasting example of excellence: *a classic sports car.* **3.** Relating to ancient Greek and Roman literature and art; classical. ►*n.* **1.** A work gen. considered to be of lasting excellence. **2.** **classics** The languages and literature of ancient Greece and Rome. **3.** *Informal* An outstanding example of its kind: *His excuse was a classic.* **4.** A traditional event, as in sports.

clas·si·cal (klăs′ĭ-kəl) ►*adj.* **1a.** Of or relating to the ancient Greeks and Romans, esp. their art, literature, or culture. **b.** Conforming to the artistic models of ancient Greece and Rome. **2.** *Mus.* **a.** Of European music during the late 1700s and early 1800s. **b.** Of concert music, such as symphony and opera, as opposed to popular or folk music. **3.** Relating to historically codified principles or techniques: *classical physics; classical ballet.* —**clas′si·cal·ly** *adv.*

clas·si·cism (klăs′ĭ-sĭz′əm) ►*n.* **1.** Aesthetic attitudes and principles manifested in the art, architecture, and literature of ancient Greece and Rome and characterized by emphasis on form, simplicity, proportion, and restraint. **2.** Adherence to such attitudes and principles.

clas·si·cist (klăs′ĭ-sĭst) ►*n.* **1.** A classical scholar. **2.** An adherent of classicism.

clas·si·fied (klăs′ə-fīd′) ►*adj.* **1.** Arranged in classes or categories. **2.** Available to authorized persons only; secret.

classified advertisement ►*n.* An advertisement, usu. brief and composed only of text, listed in a newspaper or magazine or on a website.

clas·si·fy (klăs′ə-fī′) ►*v.* **-fied, -fy·ing 1.** To arrange or organize according to class or category. **2.** To designate (e.g., a document) as confidential, secret, or top secret. —**clas′si·fi·ca′tion** *n.* —**clas′si·fi′er** *n.*

class·less (klăs′lĭs) ►*adj.* Lacking social or economic distinctions of class.

class·mate (klăs′māt′) ►*n.* A member of the same class at school.

class·room (klăs′rōōm′, -rŏŏm′) ►*n.* A room in which academic classes meet.

class·y (klăs′ē) ►*adj.* **-i·er, -i·est** *Informal* Highly stylish; elegant. —**class′i·ness** *n.*

clat·ter (klăt′ər) ►*v.* To make or cause to make a noisy, rattling sound. ►*n.* A noisy, rattling sound. [ME *clateren.*]

Clau·di·us I (klô′dē-əs) 10 BC–AD 54. Emperor of Rome (AD 41–54).

clause (klôz) ►*n.* **1.** *Gram.* A group of words containing a subject and a predicate and forming part of a compound or complex sentence. **2.** A distinct article, stipulation, or provision in a document. [< Lat. *claudere, claus-,* to close.] —**claus′al** *adj.*

claus·tro·pho·bi·a (klô′strə-fō′bē-ə) ►*n.* An abnormal fear of narrow or enclosed spaces. [< Lat. *claustrum,* enclosed place.] —**claus′tro·phobe′** *n.* —**claus′tro·pho′bic** *adj.*

clav·i·chord (klăv′ĭ-kôrd′) ►*n.* *Mus.* An early keyboard instrument. [< Lat. *clāvis,* key + *chorda,* string.] —**clav′i·chord′ist** *n.*

clav·i·cle (klăv′ĭ-kəl) ►*n.* Either of two slender bones that connect the sternum and the scapula; collarbone. [< Lat. *clāvīcula,* dim. of *clāvis,* key.]

cla·vier (klə-vîr′, klä′vē-ər, klăv′ē-) ►*n.* *Mus.* A stringed keyboard instrument, such as a harpsichord. [Ult. < Lat. *clāvis,* key.]

claw (klô) ►*n.* **1.** A sharp curved nail on the toe of a mammal, reptile, or bird. **2.** A pincerlike part, as of a lobster. **3.** Something resembling a claw. ▸*v.* To scratch or dig with or as if with claws. [< OE *clawu*.]

clay (klā) ▸*n.* A fine-grained, firm earthy material that is pliable when wet and hardens when heated, used in making bricks, tiles, and pottery. [< OE *clæg*.] —**clay′ey** (klā′ē) *adj.*

Clay¹, Cassius Marcellus 1810–1903. Amer. abolitionist.

Clay², Cassius Marcellus See Muhammad **Ali.**

Clay, Henry 1777–1852. Amer. politician.

clay pigeon ▸*n.* A clay disk thrown as a flying target for skeet and trapshooting.

clean (klēn) ▸*adj.* **-er, -est 1.** Free from dirt or impurities. **2.** Free from infection. **3.** Producing relatively little pollution: *clean fuels.* **4.** Even; regular: *a clean, straight line.* **5.** Thorough; complete: *a clean getaway.* **6.** Morally pure; virtuous. **7.** *Informal* Refraining from using addictive or illicit substances. **8.** Obeying the rules; honest or fair. ▸*adv.* **-er, -est** In a clean manner. ▸*v.* To make or become clean. —*phrasal verbs:* **clean out** *Informal* **1.** To deprive completely, as of money. **2.** To drive or force out. **clean up** *Slang* To make a large profit. —*idiom:* **clean house** *Slang* To eliminate or discard what is undesirable. [< OE *clǣne.*] —**clean′a·ble** *adj.* —**clean′er** *n.* —**clean′ness** *n.*

clean-cut (klēn′kŭt′) ▸*adj.* **1.** Clearly defined. **2.** Neat and trim in appearance.

clean·ly (klĕn′lē) ▸*adv.* (klēn′lē) In a clean manner. ▸*adj.* **-li·er, -li·est** Habitually neat and clean. —**clean′li·ness** (klĕn′lē-nĭs) *n.*

clean room ▸*n.* A room kept virtually free of contaminants, used for laboratory work and in the production of precision parts.

cleanse (klĕnz) ▸*v.* **cleansed, cleans·ing** To free from dirt, defilement, or guilt. [< OE *clǣnsian.*] —**cleans′er** *n.*

clean·up (klēn′ŭp′) ▸*n.* **1.** A thorough cleaning or ordering. **2.** *Slang* A very large profit. **3.** *Baseball* The 4th position in the batting order. —**clean′up′** *adj.*

clear (klîr) ▸*adj.* **-er, -est 1.** Free from anything that dims, obscures, or darkens: *a clear day; clear daylight.* **2.** Easily seen through; transparent: *clear water.* **3.** Free from impediment; open: *a clear path to victory.* **4.** Evident: *a clear case of cheating.* See Synonyms at **apparent. 5.** Easily perceptible; distinct. **6.** Discerning or perceiving easily: *a clear mind.* **7.** Free from doubt or confusion. **8.** Free from qualification or limitation: *a clear winner.* **9.** Free from burden, obligation, or guilt. **10.** Freed from contact or connection: *clear of the danger; clear of the reef.* ▸*adv.* **1.** Distinctly; clearly: *spoke loud and clear.* **2.** Out of the way: *stood clear of the doors.* **3.** *Informal* Completely; entirely: *slept clear through the night.* ▸*v.* **1.** To make or become light, clear, or bright. **2.** To rid of impurities or blemishes. **3.** To make plain or intelligible: *He cleared up our questions.* **4.** To rid of obstructions: *cleared the road of debris.* **5.** To remove the occupants of: *clear the theater.* **6.** To free from blame. **7.** To pass without making contact. **8.** To gain as net profit. **9.** To pass through a clearinghouse, as a check. **10.** To authorize. —*phrasal verb:* **clear out** *Informal* To leave a place, usu. quickly. [< Lat. *clārus.*] —**clear′ly** *adv.*

Syns: *limpid, pellucid, transparent* **Ant:** *opaque adj.*

clear·ance (klîr′əns) ▸*n.* **1.** The act or process of clearing. **2.** The amount by which a moving object clears something. **3.** Permission to proceed.

clear-cut (klîr′kŭt′) ▸*adj.* **1.** Distinctly defined or outlined. **2.** Not ambiguous; obvious. See Synonyms at **apparent.** ▸*v.* To log (an area) by removing all the trees at one time.

clear·ing (klîr′ĭng) ▸*n.* An open space, esp. a tract of woodland clear of trees.

clear·ing-house (klîr′ĭng-hous′) ▸*n.* An office where banks exchange checks and drafts and settle accounts.

cleat (klēt) ▸*n.* **1.** One of a set of projections on the sole of a shoe, used to prevent slipping. **2.** A piece of metal or wood having projecting arms or ends on which a rope can be wound or secured. [ME *clete.*]

cleav·age (klē′vĭj) ▸*n.* **1.** The act of splitting or cleaving. **2.** A fissure or division.

cleave¹ (klēv) ▸*v.* **cleft** (klĕft) or **cleaved** or **clove** (klōv), **cleft** or **cleaved** or **clo·ven** (klō′vən), **cleav·ing** To split; divide. [< OE *clēofan.*]

cleave² (klēv) ▸*v.* **cleaved, cleav·ing** To adhere, cling, or stick fast. [< OE *cleofian.*]

cleav·er (klē′vər) ▸*n.* A heavy, broad-bladed knife or hatchet used esp. by butchers.

clef (klĕf) ▸*n. Mus.* A symbol indicating the pitch represented by one line of a staff, from which the others can be determined. [Fr., key < Lat. *clāvis.*]

cleft (klĕft) ▸*v.* P.t. and p.part. of **cleave¹.** ▸*adj.* Divided; split. ▸*n.* A crevice.

cleft lip ▸*n.* A congenital cleft or pair of clefts in the upper lip.

cleft palate ▸*n.* A congenital fissure in the roof of the mouth.

clem·a·tis (klĕm′ə-tĭs, klĭ-măt′ĭs) ▸*n.* A climbing plant having showy, variously colored flowers. [< Gk. *klēma*, twig.]

Cle·men·ceau (klĕm′ən-sō′), **Georges** 1841–1929. French prime minister (1906–09 and 1917–20).

clem·en·cy (klĕm′ən-sē) ▸*n., pl.* **-cies 1.** Leniency; mercy. **2.** Mildness, as of weather.

Clem·ens (klĕm′ənz), **Samuel Langhorne** Pen name Mark Twain. 1835–1910. Amer. author.

clem·ent (klĕm′ənt) ▸*adj.* **1.** Lenient or merciful. **2.** Mild; pleasant: *clement weather.* [< Lat. *clēmēns.*] —**clem′ent·ly** *adv.*

Cle·men·te (klə-mĕn′tā), **Roberto Walker** 1934–72. Puerto Rican–born Amer. baseball player.

clench (klĕnch) ▸*v.* **1.** To close tightly: *clench one's teeth; clenched my fists in anger.* **2.** To grasp or grip tightly. ▸*n.* **1.** A tight grip or grasp. **2.** A device that clenches. [< OE *beclencan.*]

Cle·o·pa·tra (klē′ə-păt′rə) 69–30 BC. Egyptian queen (51–49 and 48–30).

clere·sto·ry (klîr′stôr′ē) ▸*n., pl.* **-ries** A windowed wall above the roofed section of a building. [ME *clerestorie.*]

cler·gy (klûr′jē) ▸*n., pl.* **-gies** The body of people ordained or recognized by a religious community as ritual or spiritual leaders. [< LLat. *clēricus,* CLERK.]

cler·gy·man (klûr′jē-mən) ▸*n.* A man who is a member of the clergy.

cler·gy·wom·an (klûr′jē-woom′ən) ▸*n.* A woman who is a member of the clergy.

cler·ic (klĕr′ĭk) ►*n.* A member of the clergy. [< LLat. *clēricus,* CLERK.]

cler·i·cal (klĕr′ĭ-kəl) ►*adj.* **1.** Of or relating to clerks or office work. **2.** Of the clergy.

cler·i·cal·ism (klĕr′ĭ-kə-lĭz′əm) ►*n.* A policy of supporting the power and influence of the clergy in political or secular matters.

clerk (klûrk) ►*n.* **1.** One who works in an office performing such tasks as keeping records and filing. **2.** One who performs the business of a court or legislative body. **3.** A salesclerk. ►*v.* To work or serve as a clerk: *clerked in a store; clerks for a judge.* [< Gk. *klērikos,* of the clergy.] **—clerk′ship′** *n.*

Cleve·land (klēv′lənd) A city of NE OH on Lake Erie.

Cleveland, (Stephen) Grover 1837–1908. The 22nd and 24th US president (1885–89 and 1893–97).

Grover Cleveland

clev·er (klĕv′ər) ►*adj.* **-er, -est 1.** Mentally quick and original. **2.** Dexterous. **3.** Ingenious. **4.** Cunning. [ME *cliver,* of LGer. orig.] **—clev′er·ly** *adv.* **—clev′er·ness** *n.*

clev·is (klĕv′ĭs) ►*n.* A U-shaped metal fastener. [Poss. of Scand. orig.]

clew (kloo) ►*n.* **1.** A ball of yarn or thread. **2.** *Naut.* The lower corner of a sail. [< OE *cliwen.*]

cli·ché (klē-shā′) ►*n.* A trite or overused expression or idea. [< Fr. *clicher,* to stereotype.]
Syns: *bromide, platitude, truism* **n.**

cli·chéd (klē-shād′) ►*adj.* Trite; hackneyed.

click (klĭk) ►*n.* **1.** A brief sharp sound. **2.** An act of clicking. ►*v.* **1.** To make or cause to make a click. **2.** *Comp.* To press down and release a button on a pointing device, as to select an icon. **3.** *Slang* **a.** To function well together. **b.** To be a great success. [Imit.]

click·er (klĭk′ər) ►*n.* One that clicks, as: **a.** A remote control. **b.** A computer mouse.

cli·ent (klī′ənt) ►*n.* **1.** One for whom professional services are rendered. **2.** A customer. **3.** A computer or program that can download files, run applications, or request services from a file server. [< Lat. *cliēns,* dependent.]

cli·en·tele (klī′ən-tĕl′, klē′än-) ►*n.* Clients or customers collectively. [< Lat. *clientēla,* clientship < *cliēns,* CLIENT.]

cliff (klĭf) ►*n.* A high, steep, or overhanging face of rock. [< OE *clif.*] **—cliff′y** *adj.*

cliff dweller ►*n.* A member of an ancient native people of the SW US who built dwellings in the sides of cliffs. **—cliff dwelling** *n.*

cliff·hang·er (klĭf′hăng′ər) ►*n.* **1.** A melodra-

matic serial in which each episode ends in suspense. **2.** A close, suspenseful contest.

cli·mac·ter·ic (klī-măk′tər-ĭk, klī′măk-tĕr′ĭk) ►*n.* **1.** See **menopause. 2.** A critical period. [< Gk. *klimaktēr,* crisis < *klimax;* see CLIMAX.]

cli·mac·tic (klī-măk′tĭk) ►*adj.* Of or constituting a climax. **—cli·mac′ti·cal·ly** *adv.*

cli·mate (klī′mĭt) ►*n.* **1.** The prevailing weather conditions in a particular region. **2.** A region having certain weather conditions: *lives in a cold climate.* **3.** A general atmosphere or attitude: *a climate of unrest.* [< Gk. *klima,* region.] **—cli·mat′ic** (-măt′ĭk) *adj.* **—cli·mat′i·cal·ly** *adv.*

cli·ma·tol·o·gy (klī′mə-tŏl′ə-jē) ►*n.* The meteorological study of climate. **—cli′ma·to·log′i·cal** *adj.* **—cli′ma·tol′o·gist** *n.*

cli·max (klī′măks′) ►*n.* **1.** The point of greatest intensity, force, or effect in an ascending series. **2.** See **orgasm.** ►*v.* To bring to or reach a climax. [< Gk. *klimax,* ladder.]

climax community ►*n. Ecol.* A community of organisms, esp. plants, that has reached a stable, self-perpetuating balance.

climb (klīm) ►*v.* **1a.** To move up or ascend, esp. by using the hands and feet. **b.** To move in a specified direction: *climbed down the ladder.* **2.** To grow upward. **3.** To rise: *prices climbed in June.* ►*n.* **1.** An act of climbing. **2.** A place to be climbed. [< OE *climban.*] **—climb′er** *n.*

clime (klīm) ►*n.* Climate.

clinch (klĭnch) ►*v.* **1.** To secure (a nail, e.g.) by bending a protruding point down. **2.** To settle conclusively. **3.** *Sports* To embrace so as to immobilize an opponent's arms. ►*n.* An act or instance of clinching. [Var. of CLENCH.]

clinch·er (klĭn′chər) ►*n.* One that clinches, esp. a decisive point, fact, or remark.

cling (klĭng) ►*v.* **clung** (klŭng), **cling·ing 1.** To hold fast or adhere to something or someone. **2.** To remain emotionally attached. [< OE *clingan.*] **—cling′y** *adj.*

cling·stone (klĭng′stōn′) ►*n.* A fruit, esp. a peach, having flesh that adheres closely to the stone. **—cling′stone′** *adj.*

clin·ic (klĭn′ĭk) ►*n.* **1.** A facility, often associated with a hospital, that deals mainly with outpatients. **2.** A medical establishment run by several specialists working in cooperation. **3.** A center that offers special counseling or instruction. **4.** A training session in which medical students observe the examination and treatment of patients, as at the bedside. [< Gk. *klinikos,* clinical < *klinē,* couch, bed.]

clin·i·cal (klĭn′ĭ-kəl) ►*adj.* **1.** Of or connected with a clinic. **2.** Of or based on direct observation of patients. **3.** Objective; analytical. **—clin′i·cal·ly** *adv.*

clinical psychologist ►*n.* A person who is trained and licensed to diagnose and treat people with psychological disorders.

cli·ni·cian (klĭ-nĭsh′ən) ►*n.* A health professional who is directly involved in patient care.

clink¹ (klĭngk) ►*v.* To make or cause to make a light sharp ringing sound. [< MDu. *klinken.*] **—clink** *n.*

clink² (klĭngk) ►*n. Slang* A prison or jail. [After *Clink,* a London prison.]

clink·er (klĭng′kər) ►*n.* **1.** A fused lump of incombustible residue that remains after coal has burned. **2.** A mistake; blunder. [Obsolete Du. *klinckaerd.*]

Clin·ton (klĭn'tən), **Hillary Rodham** b. 1947. Amer. public official; US first lady (1993–2001), senator (2001–09), and secretary of state (appointed 2009).
Clinton, William Jefferson "Bill." b. 1946. The 42nd US president (1993–2001).

Bill Clinton
photographed in 1994

clip¹ (klĭp) ▸*v.* **clipped, clip·ping 1.** To cut off or out with or as if with shears. **2.** To shorten; trim: *clip a hedge.* **3.** *Informal* To hit with a sharp blow. **4.** *Football* To block (an opponent) illegally. ▸*n.* **1.** Something clipped off, esp. a short extract from a movie or television program. **2.** *Informal* A brisk pace. [< ON *klippa.*]
clip² (klĭp) ▸*n.* **1.** A clasp or fastener. **2.** A container for holding cartridges. ▸*v.* **clipped, clip·ping** To hold tightly; fasten. [< OE *clyppan,* to embrace.]
clip art ▸*n.* Ready-made graphic art used in decorating documents.
clip·board (klĭp'bôrd') ▸*n.* **1.** A small writing board with a spring clip at the top for holding papers or a pad. **2.** An area in a computer's memory where cut or copied text and graphics can be stored temporarily.
clip·per (klĭp'ər) ▸*n.* **1.** often **clippers** A tool for cutting, clipping, or shearing. **2.** A tall, fast sailing ship.
clip·ping (klĭp'ĭng) ▸*n.* Something cut out, esp. an item from a newspaper.
clique (klēk, klĭk) ▸*n.* A small, exclusive group of people. [Fr.] —**cliqu'ey, cliqu'y** *adj.*
clit·o·ris (klĭt'ər-ĭs, klĭ-tôr'-, klĭ'tər-) ▸*n.* A small erectile organ at the upper part of the vulva. [< Gk. *kleitoris.*] —**clit'o·ral** *adj.*
clo·a·ca (klō-ā'kə) ▸*n., pl.* **-cae** (-sē') **1.** The cavity into which the intestinal, genital, and urinary tracts open in most nonplacental vertebrates. **2.** A similar cavity in certain invertebrates. [Lat. *cloāca,* sewer.]
cloak (klōk) ▸*n.* **1.** A loose outer garment, such as a cape. **2.** Something that covers or conceals: *a cloak of secrecy.* ▸*v.* **1.** To cover with a cloak. **2.** To conceal. See Synonyms at **disguise.** [< Med. Lat. *clocca,* bell.]
cloak-and-dag·ger (klōk'ən-dăg'ər) ▸*adj.* Marked by melodramatic intrigue and spying.
clob·ber (klŏb'ər) ▸*v. Slang* **1.** To hit or pound with great force. **2.** To defeat decisively. [?]
cloche (klōsh) ▸*n.* A close-fitting woman's hat with a bell-like shape. [< OFr., bell.]
clock (klŏk) ▸*n.* An instrument for measuring or indicating time. ▸*v.* **1.** To time, as with a stopwatch. **2.** To measure the speed of. [< Med. Lat. *clocca,* bell.] —**clock'er** *n.*
clock·wise (klŏk'wīz') ▸*adv. & adj.* In the same direction as the rotating hands of a clock.
clock·work (klŏk'wûrk') ▸*n.* A mechanism of geared wheels driven by a wound spring, as in a mechanical clock. —**idiom: like clockwork** With machinelike precision.
clod (klŏd) ▸*n.* **1.** A lump or chunk, esp. of earth or clay. **2.** A dull, stupid person; dolt. [ME < OE *clot.*] —**clod'dish** *adj.* —**clod'dish·ly** *adv.*
clod·hop·per (klŏd'hŏp'ər) ▸*n.* **1.** A rube or bumpkin. **2.** A big heavy shoe.
clog (klŏg, klôg) ▸*n.* **1.** An obstruction or hindrance. **2.** A heavy, usu. wooden-soled shoe. ▸*v.* **clogged, clog·ging 1.** To make or become obstructed. **2.** To hamper or impede. [ME *clogge,* block attached to an animal's leg.]
cloi·son·né (kloi'zə-nā', klə-wä'zə-) ▸*n.* Decorative work in which a surface is covered by different colors of enamel separated by thin strips of metal. [< OFr. *cloison,* partition.] —**cloi·son·né'** *adj.*
clois·ter (kloi'stər) ▸*n.* **1.** A covered walk with an open colonnade on one side, running along the walls of buildings that face a quadrangle. **2.** A monastery or convent. ▸*v.* To seclude in or as if in a cloister. [< Lat. *claustrum,* enclosed place.] —**clois'tral** *adj.*
clone (klōn) ▸*n.* **1.** One or more organisms descended asexually from and genetically identical to a single common ancestor. **2.** A replica of a DNA sequence, such as a gene, produced by genetic engineering. **3.** One that closely resembles another, as in appearance or function. ▸*v.* **cloned, clon·ing 1.** To make multiple identical copies of (a DNA sequence). **2.** To reproduce asexually. **3.** To propagate (an organism) as a clone. [Gk. *klōn,* twig.] —**clon'al** *adj.*
clop (klŏp) ▸*n.* A sharp hollow sound, as of a horse's hoof striking pavement. [Imit.] —**clop** *v.*
close (klōs) ▸*adj.* **clos·er, clos·est 1.** Being near in space, time, or relation. **2.** Bound by mutual interests or affections; intimate. **3.** Compact: *a close weave.* **4.** Being near a surface, as of the skin: *a close haircut.* **5.** Being on the brink of: *close to tears.* **6.** Decided by a narrow margin; almost even: *a close election.* **7.** Faithful to the original: *a close copy.* **8.** Rigorous; thorough: *close attention.* **9.** Confined in space; crowded. **10.** Fitting tightly. **11.** Lacking fresh air; stuffy. **12.** Confined to specific persons; restricted. **13.** Hidden; secluded. **14.** Secretive; reticent. **15.** Stingy; miserly. ▸*v.* (klōz) **closed, clos·ing 1a.** To shut or become shut. **b.** To shut in; enclose. **2.** To fill or stop up. **3.** To make unavailable: *closed the area to visitors.* **4.** To bring or come to an end; finish. **5.** To complete negotiations on: *close a deal.* **6.** To cease operation: *The shop closes at six.* **7.** To engage at close quarters: *close with the enemy.* ▸*n.* (klōz) A conclusion; finish. ▸*adv.* (klōs) **clos·er, clos·est** In a close manner. —**phrasal verb: close out** To dispose of (a line of merchandise) at reduced prices. [< Lat. *claudere, claus-,* to close.] —**close'ly** *adv.* —**close'ness** *n.*
   Syns: *immediate, near, proximate* **Ant:** *far adj.*
closed-cap·tioned (klōzd'kăp'shənd) ▸*adj.*

Broadcast with captions that are only visible if the viewer opts to enable them.

closed circuit (klōzd) ►*n.* **1.** An electric circuit providing an uninterrupted, endless path for the flow of current. **2.** Television that is transmitted to a limited number of receivers. **—closed′-cir′cuit** *adj.*

closed-mind·ed (klōzd′mīn′dĭd) or **close-mind·ed** (klōs′-, klōz′-) ►*adj.* Intolerant of the beliefs and opinions of others. **—closed′-mind′ed·ness** *n.*

closed shop ►*n.* See **union shop.**

close-fist·ed (klōs′fĭs′tĭd) ►*adj.* Stingy.

close-mouthed (klōs′mou*th*d′, -moutht′) ►*adj.* Giving little information; tightlipped.

close·out (klōz′out′) ►*n.* A sale in which all remaining stock is disposed of, usu. at greatly reduced prices.

clos·et (klŏz′ĭt, klô′zĭt) ►*n.* **1.** A small room for storing supplies or clothing. **2.** A small private room. **3.** A state of secrecy or cautious privacy. ►*v.* To enclose in a private room, as for discussion. ►*adj.* Private; secret: *a closet liberal.* [< Lat. *clausum,* enclosure.]

clos·et·ed (klŏz′ĭ-tĭd, klô′zĭ-) ►*adj.* Being in a state of secrecy or cautious privacy.

close-up (klōs′ŭp′) ►*n.* **1.** A photograph or film shot in which the subject is tightly framed and shown at a relatively large scale. **2.** An intimate view or description. **—close′-up′** *adj.*

clos·ing (klō′zĭng) ►*n.* **1.** A concluding part. **2.** A meeting for concluding esp. a real estate transaction.

clo·sure (klō′zhər) ►*n.* **1.** The act of closing or the state of being closed. **2.** Something that closes or shuts. **3.** A feeling of finality or resolution. **4.** See **cloture.**

clot (klŏt) ►*n.* A thick or solid mass or lump formed from liquid. ►*v.* **clot·ted, clot·ting** To form or cause to form into a clot. [< OE *clott.*]

cloth (klôth, klŏth) ►*n., pl.* **cloths** (klô*th*z, klŏ*th*z, klôths, klŏths) **1.** Fabric formed by weaving, knitting, or pressing natural or synthetic fibers. **2.** A piece of fabric used for a specific purpose, as a tablecloth. **3.** The characteristic attire of a profession, esp. that of the clergy. [< OE *clāth.*]

clothe (klō*th*) ►*v.* **clothed** or **clad** (klăd), **cloth·ing 1.** To put clothes on; dress. **2.** To cover as if with clothing. [< OE *clāthian.*]

clothes (klōz, klō*th*z) ►*pl.n.* Articles of dress; wearing apparel; garments.

clothes·horse (klōz′hôrs′, klō*th*z′-) ►*n.* **1.** A frame on which clothes are hung to dry. **2.** One excessively concerned with dress.

clothes·line (klōz′līn′, klō*th*z′-) ►*n.* A cord, rope, or wire on which clothes are hung to dry.

clothes·pin (klōz′pĭn′, klō*th*z′-) ►*n.* A clip for fastening clothes to a clothesline.

cloth·ier (klō*th*′yər, klō′*th*ē-ər) ►*n.* One that makes or sells clothing or cloth.

cloth·ing (klō′*th*ĭng) ►*n.* Clothes collectively.

clo·ture (klō′chər) ►*n.* A parliamentary procedure by which debate is ended and an immediate vote is taken. [< OFr. *closture,* closure.]

cloud (kloud) ►*n.* **1a.** A visible body of fine water droplets or ice particles suspended in the earth's atmosphere. **b.** A similar mass, as of dust, suspended in the atmosphere or in outer space. **2.** A swarm. **3.** Something that darkens or fills with gloom. ►*v.* **1.** To cover with or as if with clouds. **2.** To become overcast. **3.** To make

or become gloomy or troubled. [< OE *clūd,* hill.] **—cloud′less** *adj.*

cloud·burst (kloud′bûrst′) ►*n.* A sudden heavy rainstorm; downpour.

cloud chamber ►*n.* A device in which the path of charged subatomic particles can be detected by the formation of chains of droplets on ions generated by their passage.

cloud nine ►*n. Informal* A state of elation or great happiness.

cloud·y (klou′dē) ►*adj.* **-i·er, -i·est 1.** Full of or covered with clouds. **2.** Of or like clouds. **3.** Not transparent. **4.** Obscure or vague. **—cloud′i·ly** *adv.* **—cloud′i·ness** *n.*

clout (klout) ►*n.* **1a.** Influence; pull. **b.** Power; muscle. **2.** A blow, esp. with the fist. ►*v.* To hit, esp. with the fist. [Prob. < OE *clūt,* cloth patch.]

clove¹ (klōv) ►*n.* The aromatic dried flower buds of a tropical evergreen tree, used as a spice. [< OFr. *clou (de girofle),* nail (of the clove tree) < Lat. *clāvus.*]

clove² (klōv) ►*n.* A small section of a separable bulb, as that of garlic. [< OE *clufu.*]

clove³ (klōv) ►*v.* P.t. of **cleave¹.**

clo·ven (klō′vən) ►*v.* P.part. of **cleave¹.** ►*adj.* Split; divided: *a cloven hoof.*

clo·ver (klō′vər) ►*n.* Any of various herbaceous plants having compound leaves with three leaflets and small flowers. [< OE *clāfre.*]

clo·ver·leaf (klō′vər-lēf′) ►*n.* A highway interchange whose curving entrance and exit ramps resemble a four-leaf clover.

cloverleaf

Clo·vis I (klō′vĭs) AD 466?–511. King of the Franks (481–511).

clown (kloun) ►*n.* **1.** A buffoon who entertains by jokes, antics, and tricks, as in a circus. **2.** A coarse, rude person. ►*v.* To behave like a clown. [Of Scand. or LGer. orig.] **—clown′ish** *adj.*

cloy (kloi) ►*v.* To surfeit, esp. with something too rich or sweet. [< ME *acloien.*] **—cloy′ing·ly** *adv.* **—cloy′ing·ness** *n.*

club (klŭb) ►*n.* **1.** A heavy stick, usu. thicker at one end, suitable for use as a weapon. **2.** Something resembling such a stick. **3.** *Sports* A stick used in some games to drive a ball. **4.** *Games* Any of a suit of playing cards marked with a black figure shaped like a clover leaf. **5.** A group of people organized for a common purpose. **6.** The facilities used for the meetings of a club. **7.** A nightclub. ►*v.* **clubbed, club·bing 1.** To strike or beat with or as if with a

club. 2. To contribute or combine for common purpose. [< ON *klubba.*]

club car ►*n.* A railroad passenger car equipped with a buffet or bar and other comforts.

club·foot (klŭb'fŏŏt') ►*n.* **1.** A congenital deformity of the foot, usu. marked by a curled shape of the ankle, heel, and toes. **2.** A foot so deformed. —**club'foot'ed** *adj.*

club·house (klŭb'hous') ►*n.* **1.** A building occupied by a club. **2.** The locker room of an athletic team.

club sandwich ►*n.* A sandwich, usu. of three slices of bread with a filling of various meats, tomato, lettuce, and dressing.

club soda ►*n.* Carbonated water containing dissolved salts, used esp. as a mixer.

cluck (klŭk) ►*n.* **1.** The characteristic sound made by a hen when brooding or calling its chicks. **2.** *Informal* A stupid or foolish person. [< OE *cloccian.*] —**cluck** *v.*

clue (klōō) ►*n.* Something that guides or directs in the solution of a problem or mystery. ►*v.* **clued, clue·ing** or **clu·ing** To give guiding information to. [< CLEW.]

clue·less (klōō'lĭs) ►*adj.* Lacking understanding or knowledge.

clump (klŭmp) ►*n.* **1.** A clustered mass or thick grouping; lump. **2.** A heavy dull sound. ►*v.* **1.** To form clumps (of). **2.** To walk with a heavy dull sound. [Prob. < MLGer. *klumpe.*]

clum·sy (klŭm'zē) ►*adj.* **-si·er, -si·est 1.** Lacking physical coordination, skill, or grace; awkward. **2.** Gauche; inept: *a clumsy excuse.* [< ME *clomsen,* be numb with cold.] —**clum'si·ly** *adv.* —**clum'si·ness** *n.*

clung (klŭng) ►*v.* P.t. and p.part. of **cling.**

clunk (klŭngk) ►*n.* A dull heavy sound. [Imit.] —**clunk** *v.*

clunk·y (klŭng'kē) ►*adj.* **-i·er, -i·est** Clumsy in form or manner; awkward.

clus·ter (klŭs'tər) ►*n.* A group of things gathered or occurring closely together; bunch. ►*v.* To form a cluster or clusters. [< OE *clyster.*]

clutch¹ (klŭch) ►*v.* **1.** To grasp or attempt to grasp and hold tightly. **2.** To work a motor vehicle's clutch. ►*n.* **1.** A tight grasp. **2.** often **clutches** Control or power. **3.** A device for engaging and disengaging two working parts of a shaft or of a shaft and a driving mechanism. **4.** A tense, critical situation. [< OE *clyccan.*]

clutch² (klŭch) ►*n.* **1.** A set of eggs incubated at one time. **2.** A brood of chickens. **3.** A cluster. [< dial. *cletch,* hatch < ON *klekja.*]

clut·ter (klŭt'ər) ►*n.* A confused or disordered state or collection. [< ME *cloteren,* to clot.] —**clut'ter** *v.*

Clyde (klīd) A river of SW Scotland flowing about 171 km (106 mi) NW to the **Firth of Clyde,** an estuary of the Atlantic Ocean.

Clydes·dale (klīdz'dāl') ►*n.* A large powerful draft horse having long white hair on the lower legs. [After the CLYDE Valley.]

cm ►*abbr.* centimeter

CMA ►*abbr.* certified medical assistant

Cmdr. ►*abbr.* commander

Cn The symbol for **copernicium.**

CNG ►*abbr.* compressed natural gas

cni·dar·i·an (nī-dâr'ē-ən) ►*n.* Any of a phylum of chiefly marine invertebrates having a radially symmetrical body and saclike internal cavity and including the jellyfishes and corals. [< Gk. *knidē,* sea nettle.]

CO ►*abbr.* **1.** cash order **2.** Colorado **3.** commanding officer **4.** conscientious objector

Co. ►*abbr.* **1.** company **2.** county

c/o ►*abbr.* care of

co– ►*pref.* **1.** Together; joint; jointly: *coeducation.* **2a.** Partner or associate in an activity: *coauthor.* **b.** Subordinate or assistant: *copilot.* **3.** To the same extent or degree: *coextensive.* **4.** Complement of an angle: *cotangent.* [< Lat.]

coach (kōch) ►*n.* **1a.** A bus. **b.** A railroad passenger car. **2.** A large, closed, four-wheeled carriage with an elevated exterior seat for the driver. **3.** An economical passenger class on an airplane or train. **4.** One who trains or directs athletes or athletic teams. **5.** One who gives private instruction. ►*v.* To train or instruct; teach. [< Hung. *kocsi.*]

coach·man (kōch'mən) ►*n.* A man who drives a horse-drawn coach.

co·ad·ju·tor (kō'ə-jōō'tər, kō-ăj'ə-tər) ►*n.* **1.** An assistant or coworker. **2.** An assistant to a bishop. [< Lat. *coadiūtor.*]

co·ag·u·lant (kō-ăg'yə-lənt) ►*n.* An agent that causes coagulation. —**co·ag'u·lant** *adj.*

co·ag·u·late (kō-ăg'yə-lāt') ►*v.* **-lat·ed, -lat·ing** To form a soft semisolid or solid mass. [< Lat. *coāgulum,* rennet : co– + *agere,* drive.] —**co·ag'u·la'tion** *n.*

coal (kōl) ►*n.* **1.** A natural dark brown to black carbon-containing material formed from fossilized plants and used as a fuel. **2.** An ember. [< OE *col.*]

co·a·lesce (kō'ə-lĕs') ►*v.* **-lesced, -lesc·ing** To grow or come together so as to form one whole; fuse; unite. [Lat. *coalēscere.*] —**co'a·les'cence** *n.* —**co'a·les'cent** *adj.*

coal gas ►*n.* A gaseous mixture distilled from coal and used as a fuel.

co·a·li·tion (kō'ə-lĭsh'ən) ►*n.* An alliance or union, esp. a temporary one. [< Lat. *coalēscere,* grow together.]

coal oil ►*n.* **1.** A flammable hydrocarbon oil distilled from coal. **2.** See **kerosene.**

coal tar ►*n.* A viscous black liquid distilled from coal, used for waterproofing and insulating and in dyes, drugs, and paints.

coarse (kôrs) ►*adj.* **coars·er, coars·est 1a.** Lacking refinement. **b.** Vulgar or indecent. **2.** Consisting of large particles: *coarse sand.* **3.** Rough, esp. to the touch: *a coarse tweed.* [ME *cors.*] —**coarse'ly** *adv.* —**coarse'ness** *n.*

coars·en (kôr'sən) ►*v.* To make or become coarse.

coast (kōst) ►*n.* **1.** Land next to the sea: *a map of cities along the coast.* **2.** The water near this land: *fish of the Atlantic coast.* ►*v.* **1.** To slide or roll down an incline through the effect of gravity. **2.** To move without expending energy: *stopped pedaling and coasted to a halt.* **3.** To get by without care or effort: *coasted through high school.* [< Lat. *costa,* side.] —**coast'al** (kō'stəl) *adj.*

coast·er (kō'stər) ►*n.* **1.** One that coasts. **2.** A disk or small mat used to protect a table top or other surface beneath.

coast guard also **Coast Guard** ►*n.* The branch of a nation's armed forces that is responsible for coastal defense, rescue operations, and law enforcement at sea.

coast·line (kōst'līn') ►*n.* The shape or outline of a coast.

coat (kōt) ►*n.* **1.** A sleeved outer garment extending from the shoulders to the waist or below. **2.** A natural or outer covering, such as the fur of an animal. **3.** A layer of material covering something else. ►*v.* To provide or cover with a coat or layer. [< OFr. *cote.*] —**coat'ed** *adj.* —**coat'ing** *n.*

co·a·ti (kō-ä'tē) ►*n.* An omnivorous mammal of tropical America having a long snout and a ringed tail. [< Tupí *coati.*]

co·a·ti·mun·di (kō-ä'tē-mŭn'dē) ►*n.* A coati. [Poss. Tupí *coati* + *mundé,* animal trap.]

coat of arms ►*n., pl.* **coats of arms** An emblem in the form of a shield with markings indicating ancestry and distinction.

coat of mail ►*n., pl.* **coats of mail** An armored coat made of chain mail.

coat·tail (kōt'tāl') ►*n.* The lower back part of a coat. —*idiom:* **on (someone's) coattails** With the help or on the success of another.

co·au·thor or **co-au·thor** (kō-ô'thər) ►*n.* A joint author. —**co·au'thor** *v.*

coax (kōks) ►*v.* **1.** To persuade by pleading or flattery. **2.** To obtain by persistent persuasion. [Obsolete *cokes,* to fool.]

co·ax·i·al (kō-ăk'sē-əl) ►*adj.* Having or mounted on a common axis.

coaxial cable ►*n.* A cable consisting of a conducting outer metal tube insulated from a central conducting core, used for transmission of electronic signals.

cob (kŏb) ►*n.* **1.** A corncob. **2.** A male swan. **3.** A thickset, short-legged horse. [Prob. < obsolete *cob,* round object.]

co·balt (kō'bôlt') ►*n.* Symbol **Co** A hard, brittle metallic element used for magnetic alloys, high-temperature alloys, and for blue glass and ceramic pigments. At. no. 27. See table at **element.** [< MHGer. *kobolt,* goblin.]

cobalt blue ►*n.* A vivid blue to greenish blue.

Cobb (kŏb), **Tyrus Raymond** "Ty." 1886–1961. Amer. baseball player and manager.

cob·ble (kŏb'əl) ►*v.* **-bled, -bling** **1.** To make or mend (boots or shoes). **2.** To put together clumsily. [Prob. < COBBLER[1].]

cob·bler¹ (kŏb'lər) ►*n.* One who mends or makes boots and shoes. [ME *cobeler.*]

cob·bler² (kŏb'lər) ►*n.* A deep-dish fruit pie with a thick top crust. [?]

cob·ble·stone (kŏb'əl-stōn') ►*n.* A naturally rounded paving stone. [ME *cobelston.*]

CO·BOL or **Co·bol** (kō'bôl') ►*n.* A programming language, used esp. for business applications, that has some syntactic features that resemble English. [*Co(mmon) B(usiness-) O(riented) L(anguage).*]

co·bra (kō'brə) ►*n.* A venomous snake of Asia and Africa capable of expanding the skin of the neck to form a flattened hood. [< Lat. *colubra,* snake.]

cob·web (kŏb'wĕb') ►*n.* **1.** The web spun by a spider to catch its prey. **2.** A single thread of such a web. [ME *coppeweb.*]

co·ca (kō'kə) ►*n.* **1.** An Andean evergreen shrub whose leaves contain cocaine. **2.** Dried coca leaves chewed for a stimulating effect and used for extraction of cocaine. [< Quechua *kúka.*]

co·caine (kō-kān', kō'kān') ►*n.* A stimulant alkaloid extracted from coca leaves, sometimes used as a local anesthetic and widely as an illegal drug. [Fr. *cocaïne* < Sp. *coca,* cocaine plant.]

coc·cus (kŏk'əs) ►*n., pl.* **coc·ci** (kŏk'sī, kŏk'ī) A bacterium having a spherical or spheroidal shape. [< Gk. *kokkos,* grain.]

–coccus ►*suff.* A microorganism of spheroidal shape: *streptococcus.* [< COCCUS.]

coc·cyx (kŏk'sĭks) ►*n., pl.* **coc·cy·ges** (kŏk-sī'-jēz, kŏk'sĭ-jēz') A small bone at the base of the spinal column. [< Gk. *kokkux,* cuckoo.]

coch·i·neal (kŏch'ə-nēl', kŏch'ə-nēl, kō'chə-, kō'chə-) ►*n.* A brilliant red dye made of the dried bodies of a tropical American insect. [< Lat. *coccinus,* scarlet < Gk. *kokkos,* a kind of berry.]

Co·chise (kō-chēs', -chēz') d. 1874. Apache leader.

coch·le·a (kŏk'lē-ə, kō'klē-ə) ►*n., pl.* **-le·ae** (-lē-ē', -lē-ī') also **-le·as** A spiral tube of the inner ear that contains nerve endings essential for hearing. [< Gk. *kokhlias,* snail.] —**coch'-le·ar** *adj.*

cock¹ (kŏk) ►*n.* **1a.** An adult male chicken; rooster. **b.** An adult male of various other birds. **2.** A faucet or valve. ►*v.* **1.** To set the hammer of (a firearm) in position for firing. **2.** To tilt, raise, or draw back: *cock an eyebrow.* [< OE *cocc.*]

cock² (kŏk) ►*n.* A cone-shaped pile of straw or hay. [ME *cok.*]

cock·ade (kŏ-kād') ►*n.* An ornament, such as a rosette, usu. worn on the hat as a badge. [< OFr. *coquarde,* cocky.]

cock·a·poo (kŏk'ə-pōō') ►*n.* A hybrid dog that is a cross between a cocker spaniel and a poodle.

cock·a·tiel also **cock·a·teel** (kŏk'ə-tēl') ►*n.* A small crested Australian parrot having gray and yellow plumage. [Du. *kaketielje,* ult. < Malay *kakatua,* cockatoo.]

cock·a·too (kŏk'ə-tōō') ►*n., pl.* **-toos** A large parrot of Australia and adjacent areas, having a long crest. [< Malay *kakatua.*]

cock·a·trice (kŏk'ə-trĭs, -trīs') ►*n. Myth.* A serpent having the power to kill by its glance. [< Med.Lat. *cocātrix.*]

cocked hat (kŏkt) ►*n.* A two- or three-cornered hat.

cock·er·el (kŏk'ər-əl) ►*n.* A young rooster. [ME *cokerel,* dim. of *cok,* COCK[1].]

cock·er spaniel (kŏk'ər) ►*n.* A dog having long drooping ears and a variously colored silky coat. [Used in hunting woodcock.]

cock·eyed (kŏk'īd') ►*adj. Informal* **1.** Foolish; ridiculous: *a cockeyed idea.* **2.** Askew; crooked.

cock·fight (kŏk'fīt') ►*n.* A fight between gamecocks, often fitted with metal spurs, held as a spectacle. —**cock'fight'ing** *n.*

cock·le¹ (kŏk'əl) ►*n.* **1.** Any of various bivalve mollusks having rounded or heart-shaped ribbed shells. **2.** *Naut.* A cockleshell. [< Gk. *konkhulion,* small mussel.]

cock·le² (kŏk'əl) ►*n.* Any of several weedy plants growing esp. in grain fields. [< OE *coccel.*]

cock·le·shell (kŏk'əl-shĕl') ►*n.* **1.** The shell of a cockle. **2.** A small light boat.

cock·ney (kŏk'nē) ►*n., pl.* **-neys** **1.** often **Cockney** A native of the East End of London. **2.** The dialect or accent of cockneys. [ME *cokenei,* pampered child : *cok,* COCK[1] + *ei,* egg (< OE *ǣg.*)]

cock·pit (kŏk'pĭt') ►*n.* **1.** The space set apart in

the fuselage of an aircraft for the pilot and crew.
2. A pit or enclosed area for cockfights. **3.** An
area in a small vessel toward the stern, from
which it is steered.

cock·roach (kŏk'rōch') ►*n.* Any of various
oval, flat-bodied insects common as household
pests. [< Sp. *cucaracha.*]

cocks·comb (kŏks'kōm') ►*n.* **1.** The comb of
a rooster. **2.** The cap of a jester, decorated to
resemble a rooster's comb.

cock·sure (kŏk'shoor') ►*adj.* **1.** Completely
sure; certain. **2.** Cocky.

cock·tail (kŏk'tāl') ►*n.* **1.** A mixed alcoholic
drink. **2.** An appetizer, usu. seafood or fruit. **3.**
A combination of drugs used as part of a treatment regimen. [?]

cock·y (kŏk'ē) ►*adj.* **-i·er, -i·est** Overly self-
assertive or self-confident. —**cock'i·ly** *adv.*
—**cock'i·ness** *n.*

co·coa (kō'kō) ►*n.* **1.** A powder made from
processed cacao seeds. **2.** A beverage made by
mixing this powder with sugar in hot water or
milk. [Alteration of CACAO.]

co·co·nut also **co·coa·nut** (kō'kə-nŭt', -nət)
►*n.* **1.** The fruit of the coconut palm, consisting
of a fibrous husk surrounding a large seed. **2.**
The hard-shelled seed of the coconut, having
edible white flesh and a hollow center filled
with watery fluid. [Port. *côco,* skull, coconut
+ NUT.]

coconut palm ►*n.* A tropical feather-leaved
palm cultivated for its large edible seeds.

co·coon (kə-kōon') ►*n.* **1.** A protective case of
silk or fibrous material spun by the larvae of
moths and other insects. **2.** A private, comfortable retreat; refuge. [< Prov. *coucoun,* little
shell.] —**co·coon'** *v.*

cod (kŏd) ►*n., pl.* **cod** or **cods 1.** An important
food fish of N Atlantic waters. **2.** A fish in the
cod family, such as the haddock. [ME.]

Cod, Cape A hook-shaped peninsula of SE MA.

COD ►*abbr.* **1.** cash on delivery **2.** collect on
delivery

co·da (kō'də) ►*n. Mus.* The final passage of a
movement or work. [< Lat. *cauda,* tail.]

cod·dle (kŏd'l) ►*v.* **-dled, -dling 1.** To cook in
water just below the boiling point. **2.** To treat
indulgently; baby. [< *caudle,* a medicinal drink.]
—**cod'dler** *n.*

code (kōd) ►*n.* **1a.** A system of signals used in
transmitting messages. **b.** A system of symbols
or words given arbitrary meanings, used for
transmitting brief or secret messages. **2.** A
system of symbols and rules used to represent
instructions to a computer. **3.** The genetic
code. **4.** A systematic, comprehensive collection of laws or rules. ►*v.* **cod·ed, cod·ing 1.**
To arrange or convert into a code. **2.** To write
or revise a computer program. **3.** To contain
genetic information linked to a particular trait.
[< Lat. *cōdex,* book.]

co·deine (kō'dēn', -dē-ĭn) ►*n.* An alkaloid narcotic derived from opium or morphine and
used as an analgesic and cough suppressant. [<
Gk. *kōdeia,* poppy head.]

co·de·pen·dent (kō'dĭ-pĕn'dənt) ►*adj.* **1.**
Mutually dependent. **2.** Of a relationship in
which one person is psychologically dependent on someone addicted to a self-destructive
behavior. —**co'de·pen'dence, co'de·pen'-
den·cy** *n.* —**co'de·pen'dent** *n.*

co·dex (kō'dĕks') ►*n., pl.* **co·di·ces** (kō'dĭ-
sēz', kŏd'ĭ-) A manuscript volume, esp. of an
ancient text. [Lat. *cōdex.*]

cod·fish (kŏd'fĭsh') ►*n.* See **cod.**

codg·er (kŏj'ər) ►*n. Derogatory* A somewhat
eccentric man, esp. an old one. [Poss. < obsolete
cadger, peddler.]

cod·i·cil (kŏd'ə-sĭl) ►*n.* A supplement or appendix to a will. [< Lat. *cōdex,* volume.]

cod·i·fy (kŏd'ĭ-fī', kō'də-) ►*v.* **-fied, -fy·ing** To
arrange or systematize. —**cod'i·fi·ca'tion** *n.*

cod-liv·er oil (kŏd'lĭv'ər) ►*n.* Oil obtained from
the liver esp. of a cod and used as a source of
vitamins A and D.

Co·dy (kō'dē), **William Frederick** "Buffalo
Bill." 1846–1917. Amer. frontier scout.

co·ed (kō'ĕd') *Informal* ►*adj.* Coeducational.

co·ed·u·ca·tion (kō-ĕj'ə-kā'shən) ►*n.* The education of both men and women at the same
institution. —**co·ed'u·ca'tion·al** *adj.*

co·ef·fi·cient (kō'ə-fĭsh'ənt) ►*n.* **1.** A number
or symbol multiplied with a variable in an algebraic term, as 4 in the term $4x$. **2.** A numerical
measure of a physical or chemical property that
is constant for a specified system.

coe·len·ter·ate (sĭ-lĕn'tə-rāt', -tər-ĭt) ►*n.* Any
of various aquatic invertebrates such as the cnidarians, having a radially symmetrical, saclike
body. [Gk. *koilos,* hollow + *enteron,* intestine.]

coe·lom (sē'ləm) ►*n.* The body cavity of most
multicellular animals other than cnidarians.
[Ger. *Koelom* < Gk. *koilōma,* cavity < *koilos,*
hollow.]

co·e·qual (kō-ē'kwəl) ►*adj.* Equal with one
another, as in rank or size. ►*n.* An equal. —**co'-
e·qual'i·ty** (-kwŏl'ĭ-tē) *n.*

co·erce (kō-ûrs') ►*v.* **-erced, -erc·ing 1.** To
pressure, intimidate, or force (someone) into
doing something. **2.** To bring about by force.
[Lat. *coercēre,* confine.] —**co·erc'er** *n.* —**co·
erc'i·ble** *adj.* —**co·er'cion** (kō-ûr'zhən,
-shən) *n.* —**co·er'cive** *adj.*

co·e·val (kō-ē'vəl) ►*adj.* Of, originating, or
existing during the same period or time. [<
LLat. *coaevus* < *aevum,* age.] —**co·e'val** *n.*
—**co·e'val·ly** *adv.*

co·ev·o·lu·tion (kō'ĕv-ə-lōo'shən, -ē-və-) ►*n.*
The evolution of two or more species, each
adapting to changes in the other. —**co'ev·o·
lu'tion·ar·y** *adj.* —**co'e·volve'** (-ĭ-vŏlv') *v.*

co·ex·ist (kō'ĭg-zĭst') ►*v.* **1.** To exist together, at
the same time, or in the same place. **2.** To live
in peace with another or others despite differences. —**co'ex·is'tence** *n.*

co·ex·ten·sive (kō'ĭk-stĕn'sĭv) ►*adj.* Having the
same limits, boundaries, or scope.

cof·fee (kô'fē, kŏf'ē) ►*n.* **1.** A stimulating, dark
brown aromatic beverage prepared from the
roasted ground beanlike seeds of a tropical
tree. **2.** The whole or ground seeds themselves.
[< Ar. *qahwa.*]

cof·fee·cake (kô'fē-kāk', kŏf'ē-) ►*n.* A cake
or sweetened bread, often containing nuts or
raisins.

cof·fee·house also **coffee house** (kô'fē-hous',
kŏf'ē-) ►*n.* A restaurant serving coffee and
refreshments and often having musical entertainment.

coffee klatch or **coffee klatsch** (klăch, kläch)
►*n.* A casual gathering for coffee and conversation. [Ger. *Kaffeeklatsch* < *Klatsch,* gossip.]

cof·fee·mak·er (kô′fē-mā′kər, kŏf′ē-) ►*n.* An apparatus used to brew coffee.

cof·fee·pot (kô′fē-pŏt′, kŏf′ē-) ►*n.* A pot for brewing or serving coffee.

coffee shop ►*n.* A small restaurant in which coffee and light meals are served.

coffee table ►*n.* A long low table, often placed before a sofa.

cof·fer (kô′fər, kŏf′ər) ►*n.* **1.** A strongbox. **2.** often **coffers** Financial resources; funds. [< Lat. *cophinus*, basket; see COFFIN.]

cof·fer·dam (kô′fər-dăm′, kŏf′ər-) ►*n.* A temporary watertight enclosure that is pumped dry to expose the bottom of a body of water so that construction, as of piers, can occur.

cof·fin (kô′fĭn, kŏf′ĭn) ►*n.* A box in which a corpse is buried. [< Gk. *kophinos*, basket.]

cog (kŏg, kôg) ►*n.* **1.** One of the teeth on the rim of a wheel or gear. **2.** A subordinate member of an organization. [ME *cogge*.]

co·gen·er·a·tion (kō-jĕn′ə-rā′shən) ►*n.* The generation of both electricity and useful heat from a single power source.

co·gent (kō′jənt) ►*adj.* Forcefully convincing: *a cogent argument.* [< Lat. *cōgere*, to force : CO– + *agere*, drive.] —**co′gen·cy** (-jən-sē) *n.* —**co′gent·ly** *adv.*

cog·i·tate (kŏj′ĭ-tāt′) ►*v.* -**tat·ed**, -**tat·ing** To think carefully (about); ponder. [Lat. *cōgitāre* : CO– + *agitāre*, consider; see AGITATE.] —**cog′i·ta′tion** *n.*

co·gnac (kōn′yăk′, kŏn′-, kôn′-) ►*n.* A fine French brandy. [After *Cognac*, France.]

cog·nate (kŏg′nāt′) ►*adj.* **1.** Having a common ancestor or origin, esp. culturally or linguistically akin. **2.** Analogous in nature. [Lat. *cognātus.*] —**cog′nate′** *n.*

cog·ni·tion (kŏg-nĭsh′ən) ►*n.* The mental process of knowing. [< Lat. *cognōscere*, learn.] —**cog′ni·tive** *adj.*

cog·ni·zance (kŏg′nĭ-zəns) ►*n.* **1.** Conscious knowledge or recognition; awareness. **2.** Observance; notice. [< Lat. *cognōscere*, know.] —**cog′ni·zant** *adj.*

cog·no·men (kŏg-nō′mən) ►*n., pl.* -**no·mens** or -**nom·i·na** (-nŏm′ə-nə) **1.** A surname. **2.** A nickname. [Lat. *cognōmen.*]

co·gno·scen·te (kŏn′yə-shĕn′tē, kŏg′nə-) ►*n., pl.* -**ti** (-tē) A connoisseur. [Obsolete Italian < Lat. *cognōscere*, know.]

cog·wheel (kŏg′wēl′, -hwēl′, kôg′-) ►*n.* A toothed gear wheel within a mechanism.

co·hab·it (kō-hăb′ĭt) ►*v.* To live together in a sexual relationship, esp. when unmarried. [LLat. *cohabitāre*, live together.] —**co·hab′i·ta′tion** *n.*

co·here (kō-hîr′) ►*v.* -**hered**, -**her·ing** **1.** To stick or hold together. **2.** To be logically connected: *a wild story that failed to cohere.* [Lat. *cohaerēre, cohaes-.*]

co·her·ent (kō-hîr′ənt, -hĕr′-) ►*adj.* **1.** Sticking together; cohering. **2.** Marked by an orderly and logically consistent relation of parts: *a coherent essay.* —**co·her′ence, co·her′en·cy** *n.* —**co·her′ent·ly** *adv.*

co·he·sion (kō-hē′zhən) ►*n.* **1.** The process or condition of cohering. **2.** *Phys.* The attraction by which the elements of a body are held together. —**co·he′sive** (-sĭv, -zĭv) *adj.* —**co·he′sive·ly** *adv.* —**co·he′sive·ness** *n.*

co·hort (kō′hôrt′) ►*n.* **1.** A group or band of people. **2.** A companion or associate. **3.** A group of soldiers, esp. in ancient Rome. [< Lat. *cohors*, an army division.]

co·host or **co-host** (kō′hōst′) ►*n.* A joint host, as of a social event. —**co′host′** *v.*

coif (koif) ►*n.* **1.** (*also* kwäf) A coiffure. **2.** A tight-fitting cap. ►*v.* (*also* kwäf) To style or dress (the hair). [< LLat. *cofea*, helmet.]

coif·fure (kwä-fyŏor′) ►*n.* A hairstyle. [Fr. < *coiffer*, arrange hair.]

coil (koil) ►*n.* **1.** A series of connected spirals or concentric rings formed by gathering or winding. **2.** A spiral or ring. **3.** *Elect.* A wound spiral of insulated wire. [< Lat. *colligere*, gather together.] —**coil** *v.*

coin (koin) ►*n.* **1.** A piece of metal authorized by a government for use as money. **2.** Metal money collectively. ►*v.* **1.** To make coins from metal. **2.** To invent (a new word or phrase). [< Lat. *cuneus*, wedge, stamp.] —**coin′er** *n.*

coin·age (koi′nĭj) ►*n.* **1.** The process of making coins. **2.** Metal currency. **3.** A new word or phrase.

co·in·cide (kō′ĭn-sīd′) ►*v.* -**cid·ed**, -**cid·ing** **1.** To occupy the same position in space. **2.** To happen at the same time. **3.** To correspond exactly. [Med.Lat. *coincidere*, occur together.]

co·in·ci·dence (kō-ĭn′sĭ-dəns, -dĕns′) ►*n.* **1.** The act or state of coinciding. **2.** A sequence of events that although accidental seems to have been planned or arranged. —**co·in′ci·den′tal, co·in′ci·dent** *adj.* —**co·in′ci·den′tal·ly** *adv.*

coit·us (koi′təs, kō′ĭ-təs, kō-ē′-) ►*n.* Sexual intercourse. [Lat.] —**co′i·tal** *adj.*

coke¹ (kōk) ►*n.* The solid residue of coal after removal of volatile material, used as fuel. [Poss. < ME *colk*, core.]

coke² (kōk) ►*n. Slang* Cocaine.

Col. or **Col** or **COL** ►*abbr.* colonel

col–¹ ►*pref.* Var. of com–.

col–² ►*pref.* Var. of colo–.

co·la¹ (kō′lə) ►*n.* A carbonated soft drink containing an extract of the kola nut.

co·la² (kō′lə) ►*n.* Pl. of colon².

co·la³ (kō′lə) ►*n.* See kola.

COLA ►*abbr.* cost-of-living adjustment

col·an·der (kŏl′ən-dər, kŭl′-) ►*n.* A bowl-shaped kitchen utensil with perforations for draining off liquids. [< OProv. *colador*, strainer < Lat. *cōlāre*, strain.]

cold (kōld) ►*adj.* -**er**, -**est** **1a.** Having a low temperature. **b.** Having a lower temperature than normal: *cold oatmeal.* **2a.** Feeling uncomfortably chilled. **b.** Unconscious: *knocked cold.* **3.** Lacking emotion; objective. **4.** Not friendly; aloof. **5.** No longer fresh: *a cold scent.* ►*adv.* Totally; thoroughly: *cold sober.* ►*n.* **1.** Relative lack of warmth. **2.** The sensation of lacking warmth. **3.** A viral infection of the mucous membranes of the upper respiratory passages. —*idiom:* **out in the cold** Neglected; ignored. [< OE *ceald.*] —**cold′ly** *adv.* —**cold′ness** *n.*
   Syns: arctic, chilly, cool, frigid, frosty, gelid, glacial, icy **Ant:** hot **adj.**

cold-blood·ed (kōld′blŭd′ĭd) ►*adj.* **1.** Ectothermic. **2.** Lacking feeling or emotion: *a cold-blooded killer.* —**cold′-blood′ed·ly** *adv.* —**cold′-blood′ed·ness** *n.*

cold cream ►*n.* An emulsion for softening and cleansing the skin.

cold cuts ►*pl.n.* Slices of cold cooked meat.

cold duck ►*n.* A beverage made of sparkling Burgundy and champagne. [Translation of Ger. *Kalte Ente.*]

cold feet ►*pl.n. Slang* Failure of nerve.

cold frame ►*n.* An unheated outdoor structure consisting of a usu. wooden frame and glass top, used for protecting young plants.

cold-heart·ed (kōld′här′tĭd) ►*adj.* Lacking sympathy or feeling. —**cold′-heart′ed·ly** *adv.* —**cold′-heart′ed·ness** *n.*

cold shoulder ►*n. Informal* Deliberate coldness or disregard. —**cold′shoul′der** *v.*

cold sore ►*n.* A small blister occurring on or near the lips, caused by a herpes virus.

cold turkey ►*n. Slang* Immediate, complete withdrawal esp. from an addictive drug.

cold war ►*n.* A state of political tension and military rivalry between nations that stops short of full-scale war. —**cold warrior** *n.*

Cole (kōl), **Nat "King"** 1919–65. Amer. singer and pianist.

Nat "King" Cole
photographed in the 1950s

Cole·ridge (kōl′rĭj, kō′lə-rĭj), **Samuel Taylor** 1772–1834. British poet and critic.

cole·slaw also **cole slaw** (kōl′slô′) ►*n.* A salad of shredded raw cabbage. [Du. *koolsla.*]

Co·lette (kŏ-lĕt′, kô-), **(Sidonie Gabrielle Claudine)** 1873–1954. French novelist.

co·le·us (kō′lē-əs) ►*n.* A plant of the mint family, cultivated for its showy leaves. [< Gk. *koleos,* sheath.]

col·ic (kŏl′ĭk) ►*n.* **1.** Severe abdominal pain. **2.** A condition of unknown cause seen in infants, marked by continuous inconsolable crying. [< Gk. *kōlikos,* having colic < *kolon,* colon.] —**col′-ick·y** (kŏl′ĭ-kē) *adj.*

col·i·se·um (kŏl′ĭ-sē′əm) ►*n.* A large public amphitheater. [< Lat. *Colossēum,* an amphitheater in Rome < *colossus,* COLOSSUS.]

co·li·tis (kə-lī′tĭs) ►*n.* Inflammation of the colon.

col·lab·o·rate (kə-lăb′ə-rāt′) ►*v.* **-rat·ed, -rat·ing 1.** To work together, esp. in a joint intellectual effort. **2.** To cooperate treasonably. [LLat. *collabōrāre.*] —**col·lab′o·ra′tion** *n.* —**col·lab′o·ra′tive** *adj.* —**col·lab′o·ra′tor** *n.*

col·lage (kō-läzh′, kə-) ►*n.* An artistic composition of materials and objects pasted over a surface. [Fr. < *coller,* to glue.]

col·la·gen (kŏl′ə-jən) ►*n.* The fibrous protein constituent of bone, cartilage, and connective tissue. [Gk. *kolla,* glue + –GEN.]

col·lapse (kə-lăps′) ►*v.* **-lapsed, -laps·ing 1.** To fall down or inward suddenly; cave in. **2.** To break down suddenly in strength or health and thereby cease to function. **3.** To fold compactly. [Lat. *collābī, collāps-,* fall together.] —**col·lapse′** *n.* —**col·laps′i·ble** *adj.*

col·lar (kŏl′ər) ►*n.* **1.** The part of a garment that encircles the neck. **2.** A restraining or identifying band around the neck of an animal. **3.** An encircling structure, device, or marking. **4.** *Slang* An arrest. ►*v. Slang* To seize or detain. [< Lat. *collum,* neck.] —**col′lared** *adj.*

col·lar·bone (kŏl′ər-bōn′) ►*n.* See **clavicle**.

col·lard (kŏl′ərd) ►*n.* An edible plant in the mustard family, having large smooth spreading leaves. [Var. of *colewort,* a kind of cabbage.]

col·late (kə-lāt′, kŏl′āt′, kō′lāt′) ►*v.* **-lat·ed, -lat·ing 1.** To examine and compare (texts) carefully. **2.** To assemble pages in proper sequence. [< Lat. *collātus,* p.part. of *cōnferre,* bring together.]

col·lat·er·al (kə-lăt′ər-əl) ►*adj.* **1.** Situated or running side by side. **2.** Serving to corroborate. **3.** Incidental to one's primary concern: *collateral damage.* **4.** Relating to the use of an asset as security for a loan. **5.** Having an ancestor in common but descended from a different line. ►*n.* An asset used as security for a loan. [< Med. Lat. *collāterālis.*]

col·la·tion (kə-lā′shən, kŏ-, kō-) ►*n.* **1.** The act or process of collating. **2.** A light meal.

col·league (kŏl′ēg′) ►*n.* A fellow member of a profession; associate. [< Lat. *collēga.*]

col·lect ►*v.* **1.** To bring or come together in a group; gather. **2.** To accumulate: *collect signatures.* **3.** To obtain payment of: *collect taxes.* **4.** To recover control of: *collect one's emotions.* ►*adv. & adj.* With payment to be made by the receiver: *called collect.* [< Lat. *colligere, collēct-.*] —**col·lect′i·ble, col·lect′a·ble** *adj. & n.* —**col·lec′tion** *n.* —**col·lec′tor** *n.*

col·lect·ed (kə-lĕk′tĭd) ►*adj.* **1.** Brought together from various sources: *the collected works of Shakespeare.* **2.** Self-possessed; composed.

col·lec·tive (kə-lĕk′tĭv) ►*adj.* **1.** Assembled into a whole. **2.** Of or made by a number of people acting as a group: *a collective decision.* ►*n.* An undertaking or business controlled by the workers involved. —**col·lec′tive·ly** *adv.* —**col·lec′tiv·i·ty** *n.* —**col·lec′tiv·ize′** *v.* —**col·lec′tiv·i·za′tion** *n.*

collective bargaining ►*n.* Negotiation between representatives of workers and an employer.

collective noun ►*n.* A noun denoting a group of persons or things regarded as a unit.

Usage: A collective noun takes a singular verb when it refers to the collection considered as a whole, as in *The family was united on this question.* It takes a plural verb when it refers to the members of the group as individuals, as in *My family are always fighting among themselves.* Common collective nouns include *committee, company, enemy, group, family, public,* and *team.*

col·lec·tiv·ism (kə-lĕk′tə-vĭz′əm) ►*n.* Ownership and control of the means of production and distribution by the people collectively. —**col·lec′tiv·ist** *n.*

col·leen (kŏ-lēn′, kŏl′ēn′) ►*n.* An Irish girl. [Ir. Gael. *cailín.*]

col·lege (kŏl′ĭj) ►*n.* **1.** An institution of higher

learning that grants the bachelor's degree. **2.** An undergraduate division or school of a university. **3.** A junior college. **4.** A technical or professional school. **5.** The building or buildings occupied by any such school. [< Lat. *collēgium,* association < *collēga,* colleague.] —**col·le′giate** (kə-lē′jĭt, -jē-ĭt) *adj.*

col·le·gi·al (kə-lē′jē-əl, -jəl) ▸*adj.* Having power and authority vested equally among colleagues.

col·le·gian (kə-lē′jən, -jē-ən) ▸*n.* A college student or recent college graduate.

col·lide (kə-līd′) ▸*v.* **-lid·ed, -lid·ing 1.** To come together with violent, direct impact. **2.** To clash; conflict. [Lat. *collīdere,* strike together.] —**col·li′sion** (-lĭzh′ən) *n.*

col·lie (kŏl′ē) ▸*n.* A large, long-haired dog orig. used to herd sheep. [Sc.]

col·lier (kŏl′yər) ▸*n.* **1.** A coal miner. **2.** A coal ship. [< OE *col,* coal.]

col·lier·y (kŏl′yə-rē) ▸*n., pl.* **-ies** A coal mine and its outbuildings.

col·lin·e·ar (kə-lĭn′ē-ər, kŏ-) ▸*adj.* **1.** Lying on the same line. **2.** Containing a common line; coaxial.

col·lo·cate (kŏl′ə-kāt′) ▸*v.* **-cat·ed, -cat·ing 1.** To place together, esp. side by side. **2.** *Ling.* To occur in a collocation. Used of words. [Lat. *collocāre.*]

col·lo·ca·tion (kŏl′ō-kā′shən) ▸*n.* **1.** The act of collocating or the state of being collocated. **2.** An arrangement of words or other elements, esp. those that commonly co-occur, as *dead serious.*

col·lo·di·on (kə-lō′dē-ən) ▸*n.* A highly flammable, syrupy solution used in topical medications. [< Gk. *kollōdēs,* gluelike.]

col·loid (kŏl′oid′) ▸*n.* A suspension of finely divided particles in a continuous medium from which the particles do not settle out rapidly and cannot be readily filtered. [< Gk. *kolla,* glue.] —**col·loi′dal** (kə-loid′l, kŏ-) *adj.*

col·lo·qui·al (kə-lō′kwē-əl) ▸*adj.* Characteristic of or appropriate to informal speech. [< COL-LOQUY.] —**col·lo′qui·al·ism** *n.* —**col·lo′qui·al·ly** *adv.*

col·lo·qui·um (kə-lō′kwē-əm) ▸*n., pl.* **-qui·ums** or **-qui·a** (-kwē-ə) **1.** An informal conference. **2.** An academic seminar. [< Lat. *colloquī,* talk together.]

col·lo·quy (kŏl′ə-kwē) ▸*n., pl.* **-quies** A conversation, esp. a formal one. [Lat. *colloquium,* COLLOQUIUM.]

col·lude (kə-lōōd′) ▸*v.* **-lud·ed, -lud·ing** To act together, often in secret, to achieve an illegal or improper purpose. [Lat. *collūdere.*] —**col·lu′sion** *n.* —**col·lu′sive** *adj.*

colo– or **col–** ▸*pref.* Colon: colostomy. [< COLON².]

co·logne (kə-lōn′) ▸*n.* A scented liquid made of alcohol and fragrant oils. [< Fr. *(eau de) Cologne,* (water of) Cologne.]

Co·lom·bi·a (kə-lŭm′bē-ə) A country of NW South America with coastlines on the Pacific Ocean and the Caribbean Sea. Cap. Bogotá. —**Co·lom′bi·an** *adj. & n.*

Co·lom·bo (kə-lŭm′bō) The capital of Sri Lanka, on the W coast on the Indian Ocean.

co·lon¹ (kō′lən) ▸*n., pl.* **-lons** A punctuation mark (:) used to introduce a quotation, explanation, example, or series. [< Gk. *kōlon,* metrical unit.]

co·lon² (kō′lən) ▸*n., pl.* **-lons** or **-la** (-lə) The section of the large intestine extending from the cecum to the rectum. [< Gk. *kolon.*] —**co·lon′ic** (kə-lŏn′ĭk) *adj.*

co·lon³ (kō-lōn′) ▸*n., pl.* **-lons** or **-lo·nes** (-lō′nās′) See table at **currency.** [Sp. *colón,* after Cristóbal Colón, Christopher Columbus.]

colo·nel (kûr′nəl) ▸*n.* A rank, as in the US Army, above lieutenant colonel and below brigadier general. [< OItal. *colonello* < dim. of *colonna,* COLUMN.] —**colo′nel·cy** *n.*

co·lo·ni·al (kə-lō′nē-əl) ▸*adj.* **1.** Relating to a colony or colonies. **2.** often **Colonial** Relating to the 13 British colonies that became the United States of America. ▸*n.* A native or inhabitant of a colony. —**co·lo′ni·al·ly** *adv.*

co·lo·ni·al·ism (kə-lō′nē-ə-lĭz′əm) ▸*n.* The exertion of control by one country over others, esp. by establishing settlements or exploiting resources. —**co·lo′ni·al·ist** *n.*

col·o·nist (kŏl′ə-nĭst) ▸*n.* An inhabitant or original settler of a colony.

col·o·nize (kŏl′ə-nīz′) ▸*v.* **-nized, -niz·ing** To establish a colony (in). —**col′o·ni·za′tion** *n.* —**col′o·niz′er** *n.*

col·on·nade (kŏl′ə-nād′) ▸*n. Archit.* A series of regularly spaced columns. [< Ital. *colonna,* COLUMN.] —**col′on·nad′ed** *adj.*

col·o·ny (kŏl′ə-nē) ▸*n., pl.* **-nies 1.** A group of emigrants who settle in a distant territory but remain subject to their parent country. **2.** A region controlled by a distant country. **3.** A group of people with the same interests concentrated in a particular area. **4.** A group of the same kind of organisms living together. [< Lat. *colōnus,* settler.]

col·o·phon (kŏl′ə-fŏn′, -fən) ▸*n.* **1.** An inscription placed usu. at the end of a book, giving facts about its publication. **2.** A publisher's emblem, placed usu. on the spine or title page of a book. [< Gk. *kolophōn,* finishing touch.]

col·or (kŭl′ər) ▸*n.* **1a.** The visible aspect of things caused by differing qualities of the light reflected or emitted by them. **b.** A gradation or variation of this aspect; hue. **2.** A dye, pigment, or paint that imparts a hue. **3.** Skin tone. **4. colors a.** A flag or banner, as of a country or military unit. **b.** Character or nature: *showed their true colors.* **5.** Vivid, picturesque detail. ▸*v.* **1.** To impart color to. **2.** To give a distinctive character to; influence. **3.** To blush. [< Lat.]

Col·o·ra·do (kŏl′ə-răd′ō, -rä′dō) A state of the W-central US. Cap. Denver. —**Col′o·ra′dan** *adj. & n.*

Colorado River 1. A river of the SW US rising in the Rocky Mts. and flowing about 2,350 km (1,450 mi) to the Gulf of California in NW Mexico. **2.** A river rising in NW TX and flowing about 1,450 km (900 mi) SE to the Gulf of Mexico.

col·or·ant (kŭl′ər-ənt) ▸*n.* Something, esp. a dye, that colors something else.

col·or·a·tion (kŭl′ə-rā′shən) ▸*n.* Arrangement of colors.

col·or·a·tu·ra (kŭl′ər-ə-tŏŏr′ə, -tyŏŏr′ə) ▸*n.* Ornamental trills and runs in vocal music. [< LLat. *colōrātūra,* coloring.]

col·or·blind or **col·or-blind** (kŭl′ər-blīnd′) ▸*adj.* **1.** Partially or totally unable to distinguish certain colors. **2.** Not subject to racial prejudices. —**col′or·blind′ness** *n.*

col·or·code (kŭl′ər-kōd′) ►v. To color, as wires or papers, for easy identification.

col·ored (kŭl′ərd) ►adj. **1.** Having color. **2.** *Often Offensive* Of or belonging to a racial group not categorized as white. **3.** Distorted or biased, as by incorrect information.

Usage: Although the use of *colored* to refer to persons of non-European origin is now generally considered offensive, the terms *person of color* and *people of color* are increasingly popular in American English and are generally regarded as not only acceptable but respectful.

col·or·ful (kŭl′ər-fəl) ►adj. **1.** Full of color. **2.** Vividly distinctive. —**col′or·ful·ly** adv.

color guard ►n. A ceremonial escort for the flag, esp. of a country.

col·or·ing (kŭl′ər-ĭng) ►n. **1.** A substance used to color something. **2.** Appearance with regard to color. **3.** False or misleading appearance.

col·or·less (kŭl′ər-lĭs) ►adj. **1.** Lacking color. **2.** Drab; lifeless. See Synonyms at **dull.** —**col′or·less·ly** adv. —**col′or·less·ness** n.

color line ►n. A barrier, created by custom, law, or economic differences, separating nonwhite persons from whites.

co·los·sal (kə-lŏs′əl) ►adj. Immense in size, extent, or degree. —**co·los′sal·ly** adv.

Co·los·sians (kə-lŏsh′ənz) ►pl.n. (takes sing. v.) See table at **Bible.**

co·los·sus (kə-lŏs′əs) ►n., pl. **-los·si** (-lŏs′ī′) or **-sus·es 1.** A huge statue. **2.** Something of enormous size or importance. [< Gk. *kolossos.*]

co·los·to·my (kə-lŏs′tə-mē) ►n., pl. **-mies** Surgical construction of an artificial excretory opening from the colon. [COLO– + Gk. *stoma,* opening.]

co·los·trum (kə-lŏs′trəm) ►n. The thin yellowish fluid secreted by the mammary glands at the time of parturition. [Lat.]

col·our (kŭl′ər) ►n. & v. *Chiefly Brit.* Var. of **color.**

colt (kōlt) ►n. A young male horse. [< OE.] —**colt′ish** adj. —**colt′ish·ness** n.

Co·lum·bi·a (kə-lŭm′bē-ə) The capital of SC, in the central part.

Columbia River A river rising in SE British Columbia, Canada, and flowing about 2,000 km (1,240 mi) along the WA-OR border to the Pacific.

col·um·bine (kŏl′əm-bīn′) ►n. Any of various plants having showy flowers with five spurred petals. [< Lat. *columba,* dove.]

Co·lum·bus (kə-lŭm′bəs) The capital of OH, in the central part.

Columbus, Christopher 1451–1506. Italian explorer in the service of Spain whose voyage to the West Indies (1492) began a new era of European colonization in the Americas.

Columbus Day ►n. A holiday observed in the US on the 2nd Monday in October to commemorate Christopher Columbus's landfall in America (October 12, 1492).

col·umn (kŏl′əm) ►n. **1.** A vertical member used as a support in building construction or standing alone as a monument. **2.** Something resembling a pillar in form or function. **3a.** One of two or more vertical sections of text. **b.** An arrangement of numbers in a single vertical line. **4.** A feature article that appears regularly in a publication. **5.** A formation in rows or ranks, as of troops. [< Lat. *columna.*] —**co-**

lum′nar (kə-lŭm′nər) adj. —**col′umned** adj.

col·um·nist (kŏl′əm-nĭst, -ə-mĭst) ►n. A writer of a column in a publication.

Com. ►abbr. **1.** commander **2.** commodore

com– or **col–** or **con–** ►pref. Together; jointly: *commingle.* [< Lat.]

co·ma (kō′mə) ►n. A deep prolonged unconsciousness, usu. the result of injury, disease, or poison. [Gk. *kōma,* deep sleep.]

Co·man·che (kə-măn′chē) ►n., pl. **-che** or **-ches 1.** A member of a Native American people formerly of the S Great Plains, now living in Oklahoma. **2.** The Uto-Aztecan language of the Comanche.

co·ma·tose (kō′mə-tōs′, kŏm′ə-) ►adj. **1.** Of or affected with coma. **2.** Lethargic; torpid.

comb (kōm) ►n. **1.** A thin toothed strip, as of plastic, used to arrange the hair. **2.** Something resembling a comb in shape or use. **3.** The fleshy crest on the crown of the head of domestic fowl and other birds. **4.** A honeycomb. ►v. **1a.** To arrange with or as if with a comb. **b.** To move through with a raking action: *The wind combed the wheat fields.* **2.** To card (wool or other fiber). **3.** To search thoroughly. [< OE.]

comb

com·bat (kəm-băt′, kŏm′băt′) ►v. **-bat·ed, -bat·ing** or **-bat·ted, -bat·ting 1.** To fight against. **2.** To act in order to eliminate or curtail: *efforts to combat crime.* ►n. (kŏm′băt′) **1.** Fighting, esp. armed battle. **2.** Contention or strife: *rhetorical combat.* [< LLat. *combattere,* beat together.] —**com·bat′ant** n.

com·bat·ive (kəm-băt′ĭv) ►adj. Eager or disposed to fight; belligerent. —**com·bat′ive·ly** adv. —**com·bat′ive·ness** n.

comb·er (kō′mər) ►n. **1.** One that combs. **2.** A long cresting wave.

com·bi·na·tion (kŏm′bə-nā′shən) ►n. **1.** The act of combining or the state of being combined. **2.** A sequence of numbers or letters used to open certain locks.

com·bine (kəm-bīn′) ►v. **-bined, -bin·ing 1.** To make or become united. **2.** To join (two or more substances) to make a single substance. ►n. (kŏm′bīn′) **1.** A harvesting machine that cuts, threshes, and cleans grain. **2.** An association of people united for political or commercial interests. [< LLat. *combīnāre.*]

com·bo (kŏm′bō) ►n., pl. **-bos 1.** A small jazz band. **2.** *Informal* A combination: *a sandwich/salad combo.* [< COMBINATION.]

com·bust (kəm-bŭst′) ►v. **1a.** To catch fire. **b.**

To burn. **2.** To become suddenly angry. [Back-formation < COMBUSTION.]

com·bus·ti·ble (kəm-bŭs′tə-bəl) ►*adj.* Capable of igniting and burning. ►*n.* A combustible substance. —**com·bus′ti·bil′i·ty** *n.* —**com·bus′ti·bly** *adv.*

com·bus·tion (kəm-bŭs′chən) ►*n.* **1.** The process of burning. **2.** A chemical change, esp. oxidation, accompanied by heat and light. [< Lat. *combūrere, combust-,* burn up.] —**com·bus′tive** (-tĭv) *adj.*

Comdr. ►*abbr.* commander

Comdt. ►*abbr.* commandant

come (kŭm) ►*v.* **came** (kām), **come, com·ing 1.** To advance; approach. **2.** To make progress. **3.** To arrive. **4.** To move into view. **5.** To occur: *Happiness came to her late in life.* **6.** To arrive at a particular result or condition. **7.** To issue forth; originate. **8.** To become: *The knot came loose.* **9.** To be obtainable. —*phrasal verbs:* **come about** To happen. **come across 1.** To meet by chance. **2.** *Slang* To give an impression: *come across as honest.* **come around 1.** To recover. **2.** To change one's opinion. **come by** To acquire. **come into** To inherit. **come off 1.** To happen. **2.** To be successful. **come out 1.** To become known. **2.** To be issued. **come through** To do what is required. **come to** To recover consciousness. —*idioms:* **come clean** To confess all. **come to grips with** To confront squarely and resolutely. **come to light** To be clearly revealed or disclosed. **come up with** To produce or discover. [< OE *cuman.*]

come·back (kŭm′băk′) ►*n.* **1.** A return to former status or prosperity. **2.** A retort.

co·me·di·an (kə-mē′dē-ən) ►*n.* **1.** An entertainer who tells jokes or performs various other comic acts. **2.** A writer of comedy.

co·me·di·enne (kə-mē′dē-ĕn′) ►*n.* A female entertainer who tells jokes or performs various other comic acts. [Fr. *comédienne.*]

come·down (kŭm′doun′) ►*n.* **1.** A decline in status or level. **2.** A cause or feeling of disappointment or depression.

com·e·dy (kŏm′ĭ-dē) ►*n., pl.* **-dies 1.** A dramatic work that is humorous and usu. has a happy ending. **2.** The genre made up of such works. **3.** A literary work having humorous themes or characters. **4.** Popular entertainment composed of jokes and satire. [< Gk. *kōmōidia.*]

come·ly (kŭm′lē) ►*adj.* **-li·er, -li·est** Pleasing in appearance; attractive. [< OE *cȳmlic.*] —**come′li·ness** *n.*

come-on (kŭm′ŏn′, -ôn′) ►*n.* Something offered to allure or attract; inducement.

com·er (kŭm′ər) ►*n.* **1.** One that comes. **2.** One showing promise of attaining success.

co·mes·ti·ble (kə-mĕs′tə-bəl) ►*adj.* Edible. [< Lat. *comedere, comēs-,* eat up : COM– + *edere,* eat.] —**co·mes′ti·ble** *n.*

com·et (kŏm′ĭt) ►*n.* A celestial body consisting of a dense nucleus of frozen gases and dust, which develops a luminous halo and tail when its orbit approaches the sun. [< Gk. *(astēr) komētēs,* long-haired (star).]

come·up·pance (kŭm′ŭp′əns) ►*n.* A punishment that one deserves.

com·fit (kŭm′fĭt, kŏm′-) ►*n.* A confection; candy. [< Lat. *cōnficere,* prepare.]

com·fort (kŭm′fərt) ►*v.* To soothe in time of affliction or distress. ►*n.* **1.** A condition of

pleasurable ease or well-being. **2.** Solace. **3a.** Something that provides convenience. See Synonyms at **amenity. b.** One that brings consolation: *a friend who was a comfort to me.* [< LLat. *cōnfortāre,* strengthen.] —**com′fort·ing** *adj.*
Syns: console, solace v.

com·fort·a·ble (kŭm′fər-tə-bəl, kŭmf′tə-bəl, kŭmf′tər-) ►*adj.* **1.** Providing comfort. **2.** At ease. **3.** Sufficient; adequate: *comfortable earnings.* —**com′fort·a·bly** *adv.*

com·fort·er (kŭm′fər-tər) ►*n.* **1.** One that comforts. **2.** A quilted bedcover.

com·frey (kŭm′frē) ►*n.* Any of a genus of Eurasian herbs used in herbal medicine. [< Lat. *cōnfervēre,* boil together.]

com·fy (kŭm′fē) ►*adj.* **-fi·er, -fi·est** *Informal* Comfortable.

com·ic (kŏm′ĭk) ►*adj.* **1.** Of or relating to comedy. **2.** Amusing; humorous. ►*n.* **1.** A comedian. **2. comics** Comic strips. [< Gk. *kōmos,* revel.]

com·i·cal (kŏm′ĭ-kəl) ►*adj.* Causing amusement; funny. —**com′i·cal·i·ty** (-kăl′ĭ-tē), **com′i·cal·ness** *n.* —**com′i·cal·ly** *adv.*

comic book ►*n.* A book of comic strips.

comic relief ►*n.* A humorous incident introduced into a serious literary work to relieve tension or heighten emotional impact.

comic strip ►*n.* A narrative series of cartoons.

com·ing (kŭm′ĭng) ►*adj.* **1.** Approaching; next. **2.** Showing promise of success. ►*n.* Arrival; advent.

com·i·ty (kŏm′ĭ-tē) ►*n., pl.* **-ties** Civility; courtesy. [< Lat. *cōmis,* friendly.]

com·ma (kŏm′ə) ►*n.* A punctuation mark (,) indicating a separation of ideas or elements within a sentence. [< Gk. *komma,* short clause.]

com·mand (kə-mănd′) ►*v.* **1.** To give orders to. **2.** To have authority (over). **3.** To receive as due; exact: *command respect.* **4.** To dominate by position; overlook. ►*n.* **1.** The act of commanding. **2.** An order given with authority. **3.** *Comp.* A signal that initiates an operation defined by an instruction. **4.** Ability to control. **5.** A military unit or region under the control of one officer. [< LLat. *commandāre,* entrust to.]

com·man·dant (kŏm′ən-dănt′, -dänt′) ►*n.* The commanding officer of a military organization.

com·man·deer (kŏm′ən-dîr′) ►*v.* **1.** To seize for military use; confiscate. **2.** To take by force. See Synonyms at **appropriate.** [Afr. *kommandeer* < Fr. *commander,* command.]

com·mand·er (kə-măn′dər) ►*n.* **1.** One who commands. **2.** A rank, as in the US Navy, above lieutenant commander and below captain.

commander in chief ►*n., pl.* **commanders in chief** The supreme commander of all the armed forces of a nation.

com·mand·ing (kə-măn′dĭng) ►*adj.* **1.** Having command; controlling. **2.** Dominating: *a commanding view; a commanding lead.*

com·mand·ment (kə-mănd′mənt) ►*n.* **1.** A command. **2.** One of the Ten Commandments.

com·man·do (kə-măn′dō) ►*n., pl.* **-dos** or **-does** A member of a small military unit specially trained to make quick raids. [Afr. *kommando,* ult. < LLat. *commandāre,* to command.]

com·mem·o·rate (kə-mĕm′ə-rāt′) ►*v.* **-rat·ed, -rat·ing 1.** To honor the memory of. **2.** To serve as a memorial to. [Lat. *commemorāre,* remind.] —**com·mem′o·ra′tion** *n.* —**com·mem′o·ra·tive** (-ər-ə-tǐv, -ə-rā′-) *adj. & n.*

com·mence (kə-mĕns′) ►*v.* **-menced, -menc·ing** To make or have a beginning; start. [< VLat. **cominitiāre.*]

com·mence·ment (kə-mĕns′mənt) ►*n.* **1.** A beginning; start. **2.** A graduation ceremony.

com·mend (kə-mĕnd′) ►*v.* **1.** To represent as worthy or qualified; recommend. **2.** To praise. **3.** To put in the care of another; entrust. [< Lat. *commendāre.*] —**com·mend′a·ble** *adj.* —**com·mend′a·bly** *adv.*

com·men·da·tion (kŏm′ən-dā′shən) ►*n.* **1.** The act of commending. **2.** An official award or citation.

com·men·da·to·ry (kə-mĕn′də-tôr′ē) ►*adj.* Serving to commend.

com·men·sal·ism (kə-mĕn′sə-lǐz′əm) ►*n.* A symbiotic relationship between two organisms of different species in which one derives some benefit while the other is unaffected.

com·men·su·ra·ble (kə-mĕn′sər-ə-bəl, -shər-) ►*adj.* Measurable by a common standard. [LLat. *commēnsūrābilis.*] —**com·men′su·ra·bly** *adv.*

com·men·su·rate (kə-mĕn′sər-ĭt, -shər-) ►*adj.* **1.** Of the same size, extent, or duration. **2.** Corresponding in scale; proportionate. [LLat. *commēnsūrātus.*] —**com·men′su·rate·ly** *adv.* —**com·men′su·ra′tion** *n.*

com·ment (kŏm′ĕnt) ►*n.* **1.** An explanation, illustration, or criticism. **2.** A statement of opinion. [< LLat. *commentum,* interpretation < Lat. *comminīscī,* devise.] —**com′ment** *v.*

com·men·tar·y (kŏm′ən-tĕr′ē) ►*n., pl.* **-ies** **1.** Explanation or interpretation in the form of a series of comments or observations. **2.** An ongoing series of spoken remarks, esp. during a broadcast of an event: *commentary for a football game.*

com·men·tate (kŏm′ən-tāt′) ►*v.* **-tat·ed, -tat·ing** To serve as commentator.

com·men·ta·tor (kŏm′ən-tā′tər) ►*n.* A broadcaster or writer who reports and analyzes events in the news.

com·merce (kŏm′ərs) ►*n.* The buying and selling of goods, esp. on a large scale. [< Lat. *commercium* : COM– + *merx,* merchandise.]

com·mer·cial (kə-mûr′shəl) ►*adj.* **1.** Of or engaged in commerce. **2.** Having profit as a chief aim. **3.** Supported by advertising. ►*n.* A paid media advertisement. —**com·mer′cial·ism** *n.* —**com·mer′cial·ist** *n.* —**com·mer′cial·is′tic** *adj.* —**com·mer′cial·ly** *adv.*

commercial bank ►*n.* A bank whose principal functions are to receive demand deposits and to make short-term loans.

com·mer·cial·ize (kə-mûr′shə-līz′) ►*v.* **-ized, -iz·ing** To apply methods of business to for profit. —**com·mer′cial·i·za′tion** *n.*

com·min·gle (kə-mǐng′gəl) ►*v.* **-gled, -gling** To blend together; mix.

com·mis·er·ate (kə-mǐz′ə-rāt′) ►*v.* **-at·ed, -at·ing** To feel or express sympathy (for). [Lat. *commiserārī.*] —**com·mis′er·a′tion** *n.* —**com·mis′er·a′tive** *adj.* —**com·mis′er·a′tor** *n.*

com·mis·sar (kŏm′ĭ-sär′) ►*n.* A Communist Party official in charge of indoctrination and enforcement of party loyalty. [Russ. *komissar.*]

com·mis·sar·i·at (kŏm′ĭ-sâr′ē-ĭt) ►*n.* An army department in charge of providing food and supplies. [< Med.Lat. *commissārius,* agent; see COMMISSARY.]

com·mis·sar·y (kŏm′ĭ-sĕr′ē) ►*n., pl.* **-ies** **1.** A store where food and equipment are sold, esp. on a military post. **2.** A cafeteria, esp. in a film studio. [< Med.Lat. *commissārius,* agent < Lat. *committere,* entrust.]

com·mis·sion (kə-mǐsh′ən) ►*n.* **1a.** Authorization to carry out a task. **b.** The authority so granted. **c.** The task so authorized. **d.** A document conferring such authorization. **2.** A group authorized to perform certain duties or functions. **3.** A committing; perpetrating: *the commission of a crime.* **4.** An allowance to a sales representative or agent for services rendered. **5.** A document conferring the rank of a military officer. ►*v.* **1.** To grant a commission to. See Synonyms at **authorize. 2a.** To place an order for: *commission a portrait.* **b.** To authorize (someone) to do something: *commission an architect to design a building.* —*idioms:* **in commission** In use or in usable condition. **out of commission** Not in use or in working condition. [< Lat. *committere,* entrust.]

com·mis·sioned officer (kə-mǐsh′ənd) ►*n.* A military officer who holds a commission and ranks above an enlisted person, noncommissioned officer, or warrant officer.

com·mis·sion·er (kə-mǐsh′ə-nər) ►*n.* **1.** A member of a commission. **2.** A government official in charge of a department. **3.** An administrative head of a professional sport.

com·mit (kə-mǐt′) ►*v.* **-mit·ted, -mit·ting** **1.** To do, perform, or perpetrate: *commit murder.* **2.** To consign; entrust. **3.** To place in confinement or custody. **4.** To pledge or obligate (oneself): *is committed to following orders.* [< Lat. *committere,* entrust.] —**com·mit′ment** *n.* —**com·mit′ta·ble** *adj.* —**com·mit′tal** *n.*

com·mit·tee (kə-mǐt′ē) ►*n.* A group of people officially delegated to perform a function, such as investigating, considering, reporting, or acting on a matter. [< AN *comité,* trustee < *cometre,* COMMIT.] —**com·mit′tee·man** *n.* —**com·mit′tee·wom′an** *n.*

com·mode (kə-mōd′) ►*n.* **1.** A low cabinet or chest of drawers. **2.** A movable stand containing a washbowl. **3.** A toilet. [Fr., convenient; see COMMODIOUS.]

com·mo·di·ous (kə-mō′dē-əs) ►*adj.* Spacious; roomy. See Synonyms at **spacious.** [< Lat. *commodus,* convenient.] —**com·mo′di·ous·ly** *adv.* —**com·mo′di·ous·ness** *n.*

com·mod·i·ty (kə-mŏd′ĭ-tē) ►*n., pl.* **-ties** **1.** Something useful that can be turned to commercial advantage. **2.** A product or service that is indistinguishable from its competitors' offerings and whose sales are therefore driven primarily by price. [< Lat. *commodus,* convenient.]

com·mo·dore (kŏm′ə-dôr′) ►*n.* **1.** A naval rank above captain and below rear admiral. **2.** The senior captain of a naval squadron or merchant fleet. [Prob. < Du. *komandeur,* commander < Fr. *commandeur.*]

com·mon (kŏm′ən) ►*adj.* **-er, -est** **1.** Belonging equally to all; joint. See Synonyms at **general. 2.** Of or relating to the whole community; public: *the common good.* **3.** Widespread; prevalent. **4.** Frequent or habitual; usual. **5.** Most widely known; ordinary. **6.** Without noteworthy characteristics; average. **7.** Unrefined; coarse. ►*n.* **1.** often **Commons** See **House of Commons. 2.** A tract of land belonging to a whole community. —*idiom:* **in common** Equally with or by all. [< Lat. *commūnis.*] —**com′mon·ly** *adv.* —**com′mon·ness** *n.*

com·mon·al·ty (kŏm′ə-nəl-tē) ►*n., pl.* **-ties** The common people, as distinct from the upper classes. [< LLat. *commūnālis*, of the community.]

common denominator ►*n.* **1.** A quantity into which all the denominators of a set of fractions may be divided without a remainder. **2.** A commonly shared trait.

com·mon·er (kŏm′ə-nər) ►*n.* A person without noble rank.

Common Era ►*n.* The period beginning with the traditional birth year of Jesus, designated as year 1.

common fraction ►*n.* A fraction whose numerator and denominator are both integers.

common ground ►*n.* A foundation for mutual understanding.

common law ►*n.* Law established by court decisions rather than by legislative statutes. —**com′mon-law′** *adj.*

common logarithm ►*n.* A logarithm to the base 10.

common market ►*n.* An economic association of nations.

common multiple ►*n.* A quantity into which each of two or more quantities may be divided with zero remainder.

com·mon·place (kŏm′ən-plās′) ►*adj.* **1.** Ordinary; common. **2.** Uninteresting; unremarkable. ►*n.* **1.** A trite or obvious saying. **2.** Something that is ordinary or common.

common sense ►*n.* Sound judgment not based on specialized knowledge.

common stock ►*n.* Capital stock that is secondary to preferred stock in the distribution of dividends and often of assets.

common time ►*n. Mus.* A meter with four quarter notes to the measure.

com·mon·weal (kŏm′ən-wēl′) ►*n.* **1.** The public good. **2.** *Archaic* A commonwealth.

com·mon·wealth (kŏm′ən-wĕlth′) ►*n.* **1.** The people of a nation or state. **2.** A nation or state governed by the people; republic.

Commonwealth of Independent States A federation of self-governing states in E Europe and Asia, including most of the former republics of the Soviet Union.

Commonwealth of Nations An association comprising the United Kingdom, its dependencies, and many former British colonies.

com·mo·tion (kə-mō′shən) ►*n.* Violent or turbulent motion; agitation; tumult. [< Lat. *commovēre, commōt-*, disturb.]

com·mu·nal (kə-myōō′nəl, kŏm′yə-) ►*adj.* **1.** Of or relating to a commune or community. **2.** Public. —**com·mu′nal·ly** *adv.*

com·mune¹ (kə-myōōn′) ►*v.* **-muned, -muning 1.** To experience heightened receptivity: *hikers communing with nature.* **2.** To receive the Eucharist. [< OFr. *communier.*]

com·mune² (kŏm′yōōn′, kə-myōōn′) ►*n.* **1.** A small, often rural community whose members share work and income and often own property collectively. **2.** The smallest local political division of various European coun-

tries. [< Lat. *commūnis*, common.]

com·mu·ni·ca·ble (kə-myōō′nĭ-kə-bəl) ►*adj.* **1.** Capable of being transmitted or communicated. **2.** Talkative. —**com·mu′ni·ca·bil′i·ty** *n.* —**com·mu′ni·ca·bly** *adv.*

com·mu·ni·cant (kə-myōō′nĭ-kənt) ►*n.* **1.** A person who receives Communion. **2.** One who communicates.

com·mu·ni·cate (kə-myōō′nĭ-kāt′) ►*v.* **-cated, -cating 1.** To make known; impart. **2.** To spread, as a disease. **3.** To receive Communion. [Lat. *commūnicāre.*] —**com·mu′ni·ca′tive** (-kā′tĭv, -kə-tĭv) *adj.* —**com·mu′ni·ca′tive·ly** *adv.* —**com·mu′ni·ca′tor** *n.*

com·mu·ni·ca·tion (kə-myōō′nĭ-kā′shən) ►*n.* **1.** The act of communicating. **2.** The exchange of thoughts, messages, or information. **3.** Something communicated; message. **4. communications a.** A system for communicating. **b.** The art and technology of communicating. —**com·mu′ni·ca′tion·al** *adj.*

com·mun·ion (kə-myōōn′yən) ►*n.* **1.** A sharing of thoughts or feelings. **2.** Religious or spiritual fellowship. **3.** A Christian denomination. **4. Communion a.** The Eucharist. **b.** The consecrated elements of the Eucharist. [< Lat. *commūniō*, mutual participation.]

com·mu·ni·qué (kə-myōō′nĭ-kā′, -myōō′nĭ-kā′) ►*n.* An official announcement. [Fr. < p.part. of *communiquer*, announce.]

com·mu·nism (kŏm′yə-nĭz′əm) ►*n.* **1.** An economic system characterized by collective ownership of property and by the organization of labor for common advantage. **2. Communism a.** A system of government in which the state plans and controls the economy and a single, often authoritarian party holds power. **b.** The Marxist-Leninist version of Communist doctrine. [< Fr. *commun*, COMMON.] —**com′mu·nist** *n.* —**com′mu·nis′tic** *adj.* —**com′mu·nis′ti·cal·ly** *adv.*

com·mu·ni·ty (kə-myōō′nĭ-tē) ►*n., pl.* **-ties 1a.** A group of people living in the same locality and under the same government. **b.** The locality in which such a group lives. **2.** A group of people having common interests. **3.** Similarity: *a community of interests.* **4.** A group of plants and animals living with one another in a specific region. [< Lat. *commūnitās.*]

community college ►*n.* A junior college without residential facilities that is often funded by the government.

community property ►*n.* In certain jurisdictions, joint ownership of property acquired during a marriage except property acquired by gift or will.

com·mu·nize (kŏm′yə-nīz′) ►*v.* **-nized, -nizing 1.** To subject to public ownership or control. **2.** To convert to Communist principles or control. —**com′mu·ni·za′tion** *n.*

com·mu·ta·tion (kŏm′yə-tā′shən) ►*n.* **1.** A substitution or exchange. **2.** The travel of a commuter. **3.** *Law* Reduction of a penalty.

com·mu·ta·tive (kŏm′yə-tā′tĭv, kə-myōō′tə-tĭv) ►*adj.* **1.** Of or involving substitution, interchange, or exchange. **2.** Logically or mathematically independent of order. —**com·mu′ta·tiv′i·ty** (kə-myōō′tə-tĭv′ĭ-tē) *n.*

com·mu·ta·tor (kŏm′yə-tā′tər) ►*n.* A device in a direct current motor or generator that reverses current direction.

com·mute (kə-myōōt′) ►v. **-mut·ed, -mut·ing**
1. To travel as a commuter. **2.** To substitute;
interchange. **3.** To change (a penalty or payment) to a less severe one. ►n. A trip made by
a commuter. [< Lat. *commūtāre*, transform.]
com·mut·er (kə-myōō′tər) ►n. One who travels regularly from one place to another, esp.
between home and work.
Com·o·ros (kŏm′ə-rōz′) An island country in
the **Comoro Islands** of the Indian Ocean
between Mozambique and Madagascar. Cap.
Moroni.
com·pact¹ (kəm-păkt′, kŏm-, kŏm′păkt′) ►adj.
1. Closely and firmly packed together. **2.** Occupying little space. **3.** Concise. ►v. (kəm-păkt′)
To press or join together. ►n. (kŏm′păkt′) **1.**
A small cosmetic case. **2.** A small automobile.
[< Lat. *compingere, compāct-*, join together.]
—**com·pact′ly** adv. —**com·pact′ness** n.
com·pact² (kŏm′păkt′) ►n. An agreement or
covenant. See Synonyms at **agreement**. [<
Lat. *compacīscī, compact-*, make an agreement.]
com·pact disc (kŏm′păkt′) or **compact disk**
►n. A small optical disc on which data or music
is digitally encoded.
com·pac·tor or **com·pact·er** (kəm-păk′tər,
kŏm′păk′-) ►n. An apparatus that compresses
refuse for disposal.
com·pa·dre (kəm-pä′drā) ►n. Regional A close
friend; companion. [Sp., godfather, friend.]
com·pan·ion (kəm-păn′yən) ►n. **1a.** An associate; comrade. **b.** A domestic partner. **2.** A
person employed to live or travel with another.
3. One of a pair or set of things. [< VLat.
compāniō.] —**com·pan′ion·ship′** n.
com·pan·ion·a·ble (kəm-păn′yə-nə-bəl) ►adj.
Sociable; friendly. See Synonyms at **social**.
—**com·pan′ion·a·bly** adv.
com·pan·ion·way (kəm-păn′yən-wā′) ►n. A
staircase leading below deck on a ship. [Prob. <
OFr. *compagne*, storeroom.]
com·pa·ny (kŭm′pə-nē) ►n., pl. **-nies 1.** A
group of persons. **2.** One's companions or
associates. **3.** A guest or guests. **4.** Companionship; fellowship. **5.** A business enterprise; firm.
6. A troupe of dramatic or musical performers.
7. Military A subdivision of a regiment or battalion. **8.** A ship's crew and officers. [< OFr.
compaignie < VLat. *compāniō*, companion.]
com·pa·ra·ble (kŏm′pər-ə-bəl, -prə-bəl) ►adj.
1. Admitting of comparison. **2.** Similar or
equivalent. —**com′pa·ra·bil′i·ty** n. —**com′-
pa·ra·bly** adv.
com·par·a·tive (kəm-păr′ə-tĭv) ►adj. **1.** Of,
based on, or involving comparison. **2.** Relative: *a comparative newcomer*. **3.** Gram. Of or
being the intermediate degree of comparison
of adjectives or adverbs. ►n. Gram. **1.** The
comparative degree. **2.** An adjective or adverb
expressing the comparative degree. —**com·
par′a·tive·ly** adv.
com·pare (kəm-pâr′) ►v. **-pared, -par·ing 1.**
To describe as similar, equal, or analogous.
2. To examine in order to note the similarities or differences of. ►n. Comparison: *rich
beyond compare*. —*idiom:* **compare notes** To
exchange ideas or opinions. [< Lat. *comparāre*,
match up.]
com·par·i·son (kəm-păr′ĭ-sən) ►n. **1.** The act of
comparing. **2.** Similarity. **3.** Gram. The modification or inflection of an adjective or adverb to

denote the positive, comparative, or superlative
degree. [< Lat. *comparātiō.*]
com·part·ment (kəm-pärt′mənt) ►n. One of
the parts or spaces into which an area is
subdivided. [< LLat. *compartīrī*, share with.]
—**com′part·men′tal** (kŏm′pärt-mĕn′tl) adj.
com·part·men·tal·ize (kŏm′pärt-mĕn′tl-īz′,
kəm-pärt′-) ►v. **-ized, -iz·ing** To separate
into distinct areas or categories. —**com′part·
men′tal·i·za′tion** (-ĭ-zā′shən) n.
com·pass (kŭm′pəs, kŏm′-) ►n. **1.** A device
used to determine geographic direction, usu.
consisting of a magnetic needle that is free to
pivot until aligned with the earth's magnetic
field. **2.** A hinged V-shaped device for drawing
circles or circular arcs. **3.** An enclosing line
or boundary; circumference. See Synonyms at
circumference. **4.** A restricted space or area.
5. Range or scope. See Synonyms at **range**. ►v.
1. To make a circuit of; circle. **2.** To surround;
encircle. **3.** To accomplish. **4.** To scheme; plot.
[< VLat. **compassāre*, pace off.]
com·pas·sion (kəm-păsh′ən) ►n. Deep awareness of the suffering of another. [< LLat.
compatī, compass-, suffer with.]
com·pas·sion·ate (kəm-păsh′ə-nĭt) ►adj. Feeling or showing compassion. —**com·pas′sion·
ate·ly** adv.
com·pat·i·ble (kəm-păt′ə-bəl) ►adj. **1.** Capable
of existing or functioning well with another
or others. **2.** Med. Capable of being grafted
or transplanted without rejection. [< LLat.
compatī, sympathize with.] —**com·pat′i·bil′i·
ty** n. —**com·pat′i·bly** adv.
com·pa·tri·ot (kəm-pā′trē-ət, -ŏt′) ►n. A person from one's own country.
com·peer (kŏm′pîr′, kəm-pîr′) ►n. A person of
equal status; peer.
com·pel (kəm-pĕl′) ►v. **-pelled, -pel·ling**
To force; constrain. [< Lat. *compellere*, force
together.]
com·pel·ling (kəm-pĕl′ĭng) ►adj. **1.** Urgently
requiring attention. **2.** Drivingly forceful.
com·pen·di·um (kəm-pĕn′dē-əm) ►n., pl. **-di·
ums** or **-di·a** (-dē-ə) **1.** A short detailed summary. **2.** A list or collection of items. [Lat., a
shortening < *compendere*, weigh together.]
com·pen·sate (kŏm′pən-sāt′) ►v. **-sat·ed, -sat·
ing 1.** To make up for; offset. **2.** To make payment to; reimburse. [Lat. *compēnsāre*, weigh
together.] —**com′pen·sa′tion** n. —**com·
pen′sa·to′ry** (kəm-pĕn′sə-tôr′ē) adj.
com·pete (kəm-pēt′) ►v. **-pet·ed, -pet·ing** To
strive against another or others. [LLat. *competere*, to strive together.]
com·pe·tence (kŏm′pĭ-təns) also **com·pe·ten·
cy** (-tən-sē) ►n. **1.** The ability to do something
well or efficiently. **2.** A specific range of skill,
knowledge, or ability.
com·pe·tent (kŏm′pĭ-tənt) ►adj. **1.** Properly
or well qualified. **2.** Adequate for the purpose.
3. Legally qualified to perform an act. [< Lat.
competere, be suitable.] —**com′pe·tent·ly** adv.
com·pe·ti·tion (kŏm′pĭ-tĭsh′ən) ►n. **1.** The act
of competing. **2.** A contest. **3.** A competitor:
The competition has cornered the market. —**com·
pet′i·tive** (kəm-pĕt′ĭ-tĭv) adj. —**com·pet′i·
tive·ly** adv. —**com·pet′i·tive·ness** n.
com·pet·i·tor (kəm-pĕt′ĭ-tər) ►n. One that
competes, as in sports or business; rival.
com·pile (kəm-pīl′) ►v. **-piled, -pil·ing 1.** To

gather into a single book. **2.** To compose from materials gathered from several sources. **3.** *Comp.* To translate (a program) into machine language. [< OFr. *compiler.*] —**com·pi·la′tion** (kŏm′pə-lā′shən) *n.* —**com·pil′er** *n.*

com·pla·cence (kəm-plā′səns) also **com·pla·cen·cy** (-sən-sē) ►*n.* **1.** Contented self-satisfaction. **2.** Lack of concern. [< Lat. *complacēre*, to please.] —**com·pla′cent** *adj.* —**com·pla′cent·ly** *adv.*

com·plain (kəm-plān′) ►*v.* **1.** To express feelings of pain, dissatisfaction, or resentment. **2.** To make a formal accusation or bring a formal charge. [< VLat. *complangere*, to lament.] —**com·plain′er** *n.*

com·plain·ant (kəm-plā′nənt) ►*n.* **1.** A plaintiff. **2.** A prosecuting witness in a criminal case. **3.** One who files a formal accusation or brings a formal charge.

com·plaint (kəm-plānt′) ►*n.* **1.** An expression of pain, dissatisfaction, or resentment. **2.** A cause or reason for complaining; grievance. **3.** A bodily disorder or disease. **4.** A formal charge or accusation. [< OFr. *complainte.*]

com·plai·sance (kəm-plā′səns, -zəns) ►*n.* Willing compliance; amiability. [< OFr. *complaire*, to please.] —**com·plai′sant** *adj.* —**com·plai′sant·ly** *adv.*

com·ple·ment (kŏm′plə-mənt) ►*n.* **1.** Something that completes or makes up a whole. **2.** The quantity or number needed to make up a whole. **3.** An angle related to another so that the sum of their measures is 90°. **4.** *Gram.* A word or group of words that completes a predicate construction. **5.** *Immunol.* Any of several blood proteins that combine with antibodies to destroy antigens. ►*v.* (-mĕnt′) To serve as a complement to. [< Lat. *complēmentum* < *complēre*, fill out.]

Usage: Complement means "something that completes or brings to perfection": *The antique silver was a complement to the beautifully set table.* Compliment means "an expression of courtesy or praise": *They gave us a compliment on our beautiful table.*

com·ple·men·ta·ry (kŏm′plə-mĕn′tə-rē, -trē) ►*adj.* **1.** Forming or serving as a complement. **2.** Supplying mutual needs or offsetting mutual lacks. —**com′ple·men′ta·ri·ly** *adv.*

com·plete (kəm-plēt′) ►*adj.* -**plet·er**, -**plet·est 1.** Having all necessary or normal parts. **2.** Ended; concluded. **3.** Thorough; total: *a complete coward.* ►*v.* -**plet·ed**, -**plet·ing 1.** To end. **2.** To make whole. [< Lat. *complēre*, *complēt-*, fill out.] —**com·plete′ly** *adv.* —**com·plete′ness** *n.* —**com·ple′tion** *n.*

com·ple·tive (kəm-plē′tĭv) ►*n.* A word in a phrase or a morpheme in a word that conveys completeness, such as *up* in *drink up.*

com·plex (kəm-plĕks′, kŏm′plĕks′) ►*adj.* **1.** Consisting of two or more interconnected parts. **2.** Intricate; complicated. **3.** *Gram.* **a.** Containing at least one bound form. Used of a word. **b.** Consisting of an independent clause and at least one other clause. Used of a sentence. ►*n.* (kŏm′plĕks′) **1.** A whole composed of interconnected parts. **2.** A building or group of buildings used for a single purpose. **3.** In psychology, a group of repressed ideas and impulses that compel patterns of feelings and behavior. No longer in scientific use. [< Lat.

complectī, *complex-*, entwine.] —**com·plex′i·ty** *n.* —**com·plex′ly** *adv.*

Syns: complicated, intricate, involved, tangled *adj.*

complex fraction ►*n.* A fraction in which the numerator or the denominator or both contain fractions.

com·plex·ion (kəm-plĕk′shən) ►*n.* **1.** The natural color, texture, and appearance of the skin. **2.** General character or appearance. [< LLat. *complexiō*, balance of the humors.]

complex number ►*n.* A number of the form $a + bi$, where a and b are real numbers and $i^2 = -1$.

com·pli·ance (kəm-plī′əns) also **com·pli·an·cy** (-ən-sē) ►*n.* **1.** The act of complying with a wish, request, or demand. **2.** A disposition or tendency to yield to others. —**com·pli′ant** *adj.* —**com·pli′ant·ly** *adv.*

com·pli·cate (kŏm′plĭ-kāt′) ►*v.* -**cat·ed**, -**cat·ing** To make or become complex, intricate, or perplexing. [Lat. *complicāre*, fold together.] —**com′pli·ca′tion** *n.*

com·pli·cat·ed (kŏm′plĭ-kā′tĭd) ►*adj.* **1.** Containing intricately combined parts. See Synonyms at **complex. 2.** Hard to understand or analyze.

com·plic·i·ty (kəm-plĭs′ĭ-tē) ►*n., pl.* -**ties** Involvement as an accomplice, as in a crime. [< LLat. *complex, complic-*, accomplice.]

com·pli·ment (kŏm′plə-mənt) ►*n.* **1.** An expression of praise or admiration. See Usage Note at **complement. 2. compliments** Good wishes; regards. ►*v.* To pay a compliment to. [< Lat. *complēre*, fill up.]

com·pli·men·ta·ry (kŏm′plə-mĕn′tə-rē, -trē) ►*adj.* **1.** Expressing a compliment. **2.** Given free as a courtesy. —**com′pli·men′ta·ri·ly** *adv.*

com·ply (kəm-plī′) ►*v.* -**plied**, -**ply·ing** To act in accordance with another's command or wish. [< Lat. *complēre*, fill up.]

com·po·nent (kəm-pō′nənt) ►*n.* An element of a system. ►*adj.* Being or functioning as a constituent. [< Lat. *compōnere*, put together.] —**com′po·nen′tial** (kŏm′pə-nĕn′shəl) *adj.*

com·port (kəm-pôrt′) ►*v.* **1.** To conduct (oneself) in a particular manner. **2.** To agree; harmonize. [< Lat. *comportāre*, bring together.] —**com·port′ment** *n.*

com·pose (kəm-pōz′) ►*v.* -**posed**, -**pos·ing 1.** To make up; constitute: *the many ethnic groups that compose our nation.* See Usage Note at **comprise. 2.** To make by putting together parts or elements. **3.** To create (a literary or musical piece). **4.** To make calm or tranquil. **5.** To settle; adjust. **6.** *Print.* To arrange or set (type). [< Lat. *compōnere*, put together.] —**com·pos′er** *n.*

com·posed (kəm-pōzd′) ►*adj.* Serenely self-possessed; calm: *remained composed even when heckled.* —**com·pos′ed·ly** (-pō′zĭd-lē) *adv.*

com·pos·ite (kəm-pōz′ĭt) ►*adj.* **1a.** Made up of distinct components or elements. **b.** Made by combining two or more existing things, such as photographs. **2.** *Math.* Having factors. **3.** Relating to a family of flowering plants, such as the daisy, whose flower heads consist of many small flowers. ►*n.* **1.** A composite structure or entity. **2.** A composite plant. ►*v.* -**it·ed**, -**it·ing** To make by combining two or more images. [< Lat. *compōnere*, *composit-*, put together.] —**com·pos′ite·ly** *adv.*

com·po·si·tion (kŏm′pə-zĭsh′ən) ►*n.* **1.** The act of composing. **2.** General makeup: *the changing composition of the electorate.* **3.** The arrangement of artistic parts so as to form a unified whole. **4a.** A work of music, literature, or art. **b.** A short essay. **5.** Typesetting. —**com′po·si′tion·al** *adj.*

com·pos·i·tor (kəm-pŏz′ĭ-tər) ►*n.* A typesetter.

com·post (kŏm′pōst′) ►*n.* A mixture of decayed organic matter used as fertilizer. ►*v.* **1.** To convert (organic matter) to compost. **2.** To fertilize with compost. [< Lat. *compositum*, mixture.]

com·po·sure (kəm-pō′zhər) ►*n.* Calmness and self-possession; equanimity.

com·pote (kŏm′pōt) ►*n.* **1.** Fruit stewed or cooked in syrup. **2.** A long-stemmed dish used for holding fruit, nuts, or candy. [< OFr. *composte*, mixture.]

com·pound¹ (kŏm-pound′, kŏm′pound′) ►*v.* **1.** To combine; mix. **2.** To produce by combining. **3.** To compute (interest) on the principal and accrued interest. **4.** To make worse. ►*adj.* (kŏm′pound′, kŏm-pound′) Consisting of two or more parts. ►*n.* (kŏm′pound′) **1.** A combination of two or more elements or parts. **2.** A word, such as *loudspeaker* or *self-portrait*, that consists of two or more elements that are independent words. **3.** A substance consisting of two or more different elements in definite proportions, having properties unlike those of its constituent elements. [< Lat. *compōnere*, put together.] —**com·pound′a·ble** *adj.* —**com·pound′er** *n.*

com·pound² (kŏm′pound′) ►*n.* A building or buildings set off and enclosed by a barrier. [Alteration of Malay *kampong*, village.]

compound eye ►*n.* The eye of most insects and some crustaceans, composed of many visual units that each form a portion of an image.

compound fraction ►*n.* See **complex fraction.**

compound interest ►*n.* Interest computed on accumulated unpaid interest as well as on the original principal.

compound leaf ►*n.* A leaf whose blade is divided into two or more distinct leaflets.

compound number ►*n.* A quantity expressed in two or more different units, such as 3 feet 4 inches.

compound sentence ►*n.* A sentence of two or more independent clauses.

com·pre·hend (kŏm′prĭ-hĕnd′) ►*v.* **1.** To understand the meaning or importance of. **2.** To take in; include. [< Lat. *comprehendere.*] —**com′pre·hen′si·ble** *adj.* —**com′pre·hen′si·bly** *adv.* —**com′pre·hen′sion** *n.*

com·pre·hen·sive (kŏm′prĭ-hĕn′sĭv) ►*adj.* Having a large scope. —**com′pre·hen′sive·ly** *adv.* —**com′pre·hen′sive·ness** *n.*

com·press (kəm-prĕs′) ►*v.* **1.** To press together; compact. **2.** To make smaller or shorter; condense. ►*n.* (kŏm′prĕs′) A soft pad applied to a part of the body to control bleeding or reduce pain. [< LLat. *compressāre.*] —**com·press′i·bil′i·ty** *n.* —**com·press′i·ble** *adj.* —**com·pres′sion** *n.*

com·pres·sor (kəm-prĕs′ər) ►*n.* One that compresses, esp. a machine used to compress gases.

com·prise (kəm-prīz′) ►*v.* **-prised, -pris·ing 1.** To be composed of. **2.** To compose or make up.

[< Lat. *comprehendere.*] —**com·pris′a·ble** *adj.*

Usage: The traditional rule states that the whole *comprises* the parts and the parts *compose* the whole. In strict usage: *The Union comprises 50 states. Fifty states compose* (or *make up*) *the Union.* Even though careful writers often maintain this distinction, *comprise* is increasingly used in place of *compose*, especially in the passive, as in *The Union is comprised of 50 states.*

com·pro·mise (kŏm′prə-mīz′) ►*n.* **1.** A settlement of differences in which each side makes concessions. **2.** Something that combines qualities of different things. **3.** A weakening of one's principles: *a compromise of morality.* **4.** Impairment, as by injury or disease. ►*v.* **-mised, -mis·ing 1.** To settle by concessions. **2a.** To expose to danger, suspicion, or disrepute: **b.** To reduce in quality, value, or degree. **3.** To impair, as by disease or injury. [< Lat. *comprōmissum*, mutual promise.] —**com′pro·mis′er** *n.*

comp time (kŏmp) ►*n. Informal* Time off given to an employee in place of overtime pay. [< *compensatory time.*]

comp·trol·ler (kŏmp-trō′lər, kŏmp′trō′-, kən-trō′-) ►*n.* Var. of **controller** (sense 2).

com·pul·sion (kəm-pŭl′shən) ►*n.* **1.** The act of compelling. **2.** The state of being compelled. **3.** An irresistible impulse to act. [< Lat. *compellere, compuls-,* compel.] —**com·pul′sive** *adj.* —**com·pul′sive·ly** *adv.* —**com·pul′sive·ness** *n.*

com·pul·so·ry (kəm-pŭl′sə-rē) ►*adj.* **1.** Obligatory; required. **2.** Coercive. —**com·pul′so·ri·ly** *adv.*

com·punc·tion (kəm-pŭngk′shən) ►*n.* A strong uneasiness caused by guilt. See Synonyms at **penitence.** [< LLat. *compungere, compūnct-,* to sting.]

com·pute (kəm-pyōōt′) ►*v.* **-put·ed, -put·ing 1.** To determine by mathematics, esp. by numerical methods. **2.** To determine by use of a computer. [Lat. *computāre.*] —**com·put′a·ble** *adj.* —**com′pu·ta′tion** (kŏm′pyōō-tā′shən) *n.* —**com′pu·ta′tion·al** *adj.*

com·put·er (kəm-pyōō′tər) ►*n.* **1.** A device that computes, esp. a programmable electronic machine that performs mathematical or logical operations or that assembles, stores, or processes information. **2.** One who computes.

com·put·er·ize (kəm-pyōō′tə-rīz′) ►*v.* **-ized, -iz·ing 1.** To furnish with a computer or computer system. **2.** To enter, process, or store (information) in a computer or computer system. —**com·put′er·i·za′tion** *n.*

com·rade (kŏm′răd′, -rəd) ►*n.* A friend, associate, or companion. [< OFr. *camarade*, roommate.] —**com′rade·ship′** *n.*

con¹ (kŏn) ►*adv.* Against. ►*n.* An argument or opinion against something. [< CONTRA–.]

con² (kŏn) ►*v.* **conned, con·ning 1.** To study, peruse, or examine carefully. **2.** To memorize. [< OE *cunnan*, know.]

con³ (kŏn) *Slang* ►*v.* **conned, con·ning** To swindle or dupe. ►*n.* A swindle. ►*adj.* Of or involving a swindle. [< CONFIDENCE.]

con⁴ (kŏn) ►*n. Slang* A convict.

con– ►*pref.* Var. of **com–.**

Con·a·kry (kŏn′ə-krē) The capital of Guinea, in the SW part on the Atlantic.

con·cat·e·nate (kŏn-kăt′n-āt′, kən-) ►*v.* **-nat·**

ed, -nat·ing To connect or link in a series. [LLat. *concatēnāre* < Lat. *catēna*, chain.] —**con·cat′e·nate** (-nĭt, -nāt′) *adj.* —**con·cat′e·na′tion** *n.*

con·cave (kŏn-kāv′, kŏn′kāv′) ►*adj.* Curved like the inner surface of a sphere. [< Lat. *concavus*, vaulted.] —**con·cave′ly** *adv.* —**con·cav′i·ty** (-kăv′ĭ-tē) *n.*

con·ceal (kən-sēl′) ►*v.* To keep from being seen, found, or discovered; hide. [< Lat. *concēlāre.*] —**con·ceal′a·ble** *adj.* —**con·ceal′er** *n.* —**con·ceal′ment** *n.*

con·cede (kən-sēd′) ►*v.* **-ced·ed, -ced·ing 1.** To acknowledge, often reluctantly, as being true. **2a.** To admit (defeat). **b.** To admit defeat in: *concede an election.* **3a.** To surrender (something owned or disputed, such as land): *conceded the region when signing the treaty.* **b.** To grant (e.g., a privilege). **4.** To make a concession; yield. [< Lat. *concēdere.*] —**con·ced′er** *n.*

con·ceit (kən-sēt′) ►*n.* **1.** An unduly high opinion of one's own abilities or worth. **2.** A fanciful poetic image, esp. an elaborate comparison. [< LLat. *conceptus,* CONCEPT.]

Syns: *egoism, egotism, narcissism, vanity* **Ant:** *humility* **n.**

con·ceit·ed (kən-sē′tĭd) ►*adj.* Vain. —**con·ceit′ed·ly** *adv.* —**con·ceit′ed·ness** *n.*

con·ceive (kən-sēv′) ►*v.* **-ceived, -ceiv·ing 1.** To become pregnant (with). **2.** To form in the mind; devise. **3.** To think; imagine. [< Lat. *concipere.*] —**con·ceiv′a·ble** *adj.* —**con·ceiv′a·bly** *adv.* —**con·ceiv′er** *n.*

con·cen·trate (kŏn′sən-trāt′) ►*v.* **-trat·ed, -trat·ing 1.** To direct or draw toward a common center; focus. **2.** To direct one's thoughts or attention. **3.** To make (a solution) less dilute. ►*n.* A product of concentration: *orange juice concentrate.* [< Lat. *com-,* com- + *centrum,* center.] —**con′cen·tra′tive** *adj.* —**con′cen·tra′tor** *n.*

con·cen·tra·tion (kŏn′sən-trā′shən) ►*n.* **1.** The act of concentrating or state of being concentrated. **2.** Something concentrated. **3.** *Chem.* The amount of one substance in a unit amount of another substance.

concentration camp ►*n.* A camp where persons are confined, usu. without hearings and typically under harsh conditions, often as a result of their membership in a group the government has identified as suspect.

con·cen·tric (kən-sĕn′trĭk) also **con·cen·tri·cal** (-trĭ-kəl) ►*adj.* Having a common center. [< Lat. *com-,* com- + *centrum,* center.] —**con·cen′tri·cal·ly** *adv.* —**con′cen·tric′i·ty** (kŏn′sĕn-trĭs′ĭ-tē) *n.*

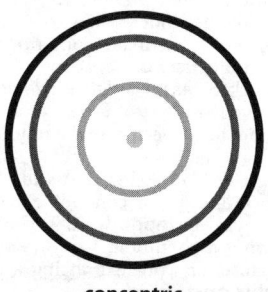

concentric

Con·cep·ción (kŏn′sĕp-syôn′) A city of W-central Chile near the Pacific coast SSW of Santiago.

con·cept (kŏn′sĕpt′) ►*n.* **1.** A general understanding of something. **2.** A plan or original idea. **3.** A unifying theme, esp. for a product or service. ►*adj.* Having an experimental design, esp. to demonstrate new features: *a concept car.* [< Lat. *concipere, concept-,* conceive.] —**con·cep′tu·al** (kən-sĕp′chōō-əl) *adj.* —**con·cep′tu·al·ly** *adv.*

con·cep·tion (kən-sĕp′shən) ►*n.* **1.** Formation of a viable zygote by the union of the male sperm and the female ovum; fertilization. **2a.** The ability to form or understand mental concepts. **b.** A concept, thought, or belief. **c.** The formation of an idea or plan. [< Lat. *concipere, concept-,* conceive.]

con·cep·tu·al·ize (kən-sĕp′chōō-ə-līz′) ►*v.* **-ized, -iz·ing** To form concepts (of). —**con·cep′tu·al·i·za′tion** *n.*

con·cern (kən-sûrn′) ►*v.* **1.** To have to do with; relate to. **2.** To engage the attention of; involve. **3.** To cause anxiety or uneasiness in. ►*n.* **1.** A matter that relates to or affects one. **2.** Serious interest in. **3.** A troubled state of mind. **4.** A business establishment. [< LLat. *concernere,* mingle together.]

con·cerned (kən-sûrnd′) ►*adj.* **1.** Interested. **2.** Anxious; troubled.

con·cern·ing (kən-sûr′nĭng) ►*prep.* In reference to.

con·cert (kŏn′sûrt′, -sərt) ►*n.* **1.** A musical performance. **2.** Agreement in purpose, feeling, or action. ►*v.* (kən-sûrt′) To plan by mutual agreement. —*idiom:* **in concert** All together; in agreement. [< Ital. *concerto.*]

con·cert·ed (kən-sûr′tĭd) ►*adj.* Planned or accomplished together: *a concerted effort to solve the problem.* —**con·cert′ed·ly** *adv.*

con·cer·ti·na (kŏn′sər-tē′nə) ►*n.* A small hexagonal accordion with buttons for keys.

con·cert·mas·ter (kŏn′sərt-măs′tər) ►*n.* The first violinist in a symphony orchestra.

con·cer·to (kən-chĕr′tō) ►*n., pl.* **-tos** or **-ti** (-tē) A composition for an orchestra and one or more solo instruments. [Ital.]

con·ces·sion (kən-sĕsh′ən) ►*n.* **1.** The act of conceding. **2.** Something conceded. **3.** Land granted by a government for a specific purpose. **4a.** The privilege of maintaining a subsidiary business in a certain place. **b.** The business itself. [< Lat. *concēdere, concess-,* concede.]

con·ces·sion·aire (kən-sĕsh′ə-nâr′) ►*n.* The holder or operator of a concession. [Fr.]

conch (kŏngk, kŏnch) ►*n., pl.* **conchs** (kŏngks) or **conch·es** (kŏn′chĭz) A tropical marine mollusk having a large spiral shell and edible flesh. [< Gk. *konkhē,* mussel.]

con·cierge (kôn-syârzh′) ►*n.* A staff member of a hotel or apartment complex who assists guests or residents. [< Lat. *cōnservus,* fellow slave.]

con·cil·i·ate (kən-sĭl′ē-āt′) ►*v.* **-at·ed, -at·ing 1.** To overcome the distrust of; appease. **2.** To make compatible; reconcile. [Lat. *conciliāre* < *concilium,* meeting.] —**con·cil′i·a′tion** *n.* —**con·cil′i·a′tor** *n.* —**con·cil′i·a·to′ry** (-ə-tôr′ē) *adj.*

con·cise (kən-sīs′) ►*adj.* Expressing much in few words; clear and succinct. [Lat. *concīsus,* p.part.

of *concīdere*, cut up.] —**con·cise′ly** *adv.* —**con·cise′ness** *n.* —**con·ci′sion** (-sĭzh′ən) *n.*

con·clave (kŏn′klāv′, kŏng′-) ►*n.* A secret meeting, esp. one in which the cardinals of the Catholic Church meet to elect a pope. [< Lat. *conclāve*, lockable room.]

con·clude (kən-klōōd′) ►*v.* **-clud·ed, -clud·ing** **1.** To bring or come to an end; close. **2.** To come to an agreement or settlement of. **3.** To arrive at (a logical conclusion) by reasoning. [< Lat. *conclūdere*.]

con·clu·sion (kən-klōō′zhən) ►*n.* **1.** The close or finish: *the conclusion of the movie.* **2.** A result; outcome. **3.** A judgment or decision reached after deliberation. See Synonyms at **decision.** **4.** A final arrangement.

con·clu·sive (kən-klōō′sĭv) ►*adj.* Serving to put an end to doubt. See Synonyms at **decisive.** —**con·clu′sive·ly** *adv.*

con·coct (kən-kŏkt′) ►*v.* **1.** To prepare by mixing ingredients. **2.** To devise. [Lat. *concoquere, concoct-*, cook up.] —**con·coct′er, con·coc′tor** *n.* —**con·coc′tion** *n.*

con·com·i·tant (kən-kŏm′ĭ-tənt) ►*adj.* Occurring or existing concurrently. ►*n.* One that is concomitant with another. [< Lat. *concomitārī*, accompany.] —**con·com′i·tant·ly** *adv.* —**con·com′i·tance** *n.*

con·cord (kŏn′kôrd′, kŏng′-) ►*n.* Agreement of interests or feelings; accord. [< Lat. *concors, concord-*, agreeing : COM- + *cor*, heart.]

Con·cord (kŏng′kərd) **1.** A town of E MA WNW of Boston; site of an early battle of the Revolutionary War. **2.** The capital of NH, in the S-central part.

con·cor·dance (kən-kôr′dns) ►*n.* **1.** Agreement; concord. **2.** An index of the words in a text or texts, showing every context in which they occur.

con·cor·dant (kən-kôr′dnt) ►*adj.* Harmonious; agreeing. —**con·cor′dant·ly** *adv.*

con·cor·dat (kən-kôr′dăt′) ►*n.* A formal agreement. [< Med.Lat. *concordātum*.]

con·course (kŏn′kôrs′, kŏng′-) ►*n.* **1.** A large open space for the gathering or passage of crowds. **2.** A broad thoroughfare. [< Lat. *concursus*.]

con·cres·cence (kən-krĕs′əns) ►*n.* *Biol.* The growing together of related parts. [< Lat. *concrēscere*, grow together.] —**con·cres′cent** *adj.*

con·crete (kŏn-krēt′, kŏng-, kŏn′krēt′, kŏng′-) ►*adj.* **1.** Relating to an actual, specific thing or instance; particular: *concrete evidence.* **2.** Existing in reality or in real experience. **3.** Formed by the coalescence of separate particles or parts into one mass; solid. **4.** Made of concrete. ►*n.* (kŏn′krēt′, kŏng′-, kŏn-krēt′, kŏng-) **1.** A construction material consisting of sand, gravel, broken stone, or slag in a mortar or cement matrix. **2.** A mass formed by the coalescence of particles. ►*v.* (kŏn′krēt′, kŏng′-, kŏn-krēt′, kŏng-) **-cret·ed, -cret·ing** **1.** To build, treat, or cover with concrete. **2.** To form into a mass by coalescence or cohesion of particles. [< Lat. *concrētus*, p.part. of *concrēscere*, grow together.] —**con·crete′ly** *adv.* —**con·crete′ness** *n.*

con·cre·tion (kən-krē′shən) ►*n.* **1.** The act or process of concreting into a mass; coalescence. **2.** A solid, hard mass.

con·cu·bine (kŏng′kyə-bīn′, kŏn′-) ►*n.* *Law* **1.** A woman who cohabits with a man without being legally married to him. **2.** A woman contracted to a man as a secondary wife, often having few legal rights and low social status. [< Lat. *concubīna*.]

con·cu·pis·cence (kŏn-kyōō′pĭ-səns) ►*n.* Sexual desire; lust. [< Lat. *concupere*, desire strongly.] —**con·cu′pis·cent** *adj.*

con·cur (kən-kûr′) ►*v.* **-curred, -cur·ring** **1.** To agree. **2.** To act together. **3.** To occur at the same time. **4.** To grant or concede. [< Lat. *concurrere*, coincide.] —**con·cur′rence** *n.* —**con·cur′rent** *adj.* —**con·cur′rent·ly** *adv.*

con·cus·sion (kən-kŭsh′ən) ►*n.* **1.** A violent jarring. **2.** An injury to an organ, esp. the brain, produced by a violent blow. [< Lat. *concutere, concuss-*, strike together.] —**con·cus′sive** (-kŭs′ĭv) *adj.*

con·demn (kən-dĕm′) ►*v.* **1.** To express disapproval of: *condemned the waste of food.* **2.** To pronounce judgment against; sentence. **3.** To declare unfit for use. **4.** *Law* To appropriate (property) for public use. [< Lat. *condemnāre*.] —**con·dem′na·ble** (-dĕm′nə-bəl) *adj.* —**con′dem·na′tion** (kŏn′dĕm-nā′shən) *n.* —**con·dem′na·to·ry** (-nə-tôr′ē) *adj.*

con·dense (kən-dĕns′) ►*v.* **-densed, -dens·ing** **1.** To make or become more compact. **2.** To abridge. **3.** To cause (a gas or vapor) to change to a liquid. [< Lat. *condēnsāre*, thicken.] —**con·dens′a·bil′i·ty** *n.* —**con·dens′a·ble, con·dens′i·ble** *adj.* —**con′den·sa′tion** (kŏn′dĕn-sā′shən) *n.*

con·dens·er (kən-dĕn′sər) ►*n.* **1.** One that condenses, esp. an apparatus that condenses vapor. **2.** See **capacitor.**

con·de·scend (kŏn′dĭ-sĕnd′) ►*v.* **1.** To do something that one regards as beneath one's social rank or dignity. See Synonyms at **stoop¹. 2.** To behave in a patronizing or superior manner toward someone. [< LLat. *condēscendere*.] —**con′de·scend′ing** *adj.* —**con′de·scend′ing·ly** *adv.* —**con′de·scen′sion** *n.*

con·dign (kən-dīn′) ►*adj.* Deserved; adequate: *condign censure.* [< Lat. *condignus*.]

con·di·ment (kŏn′də-mənt) ►*n.* A substance, such as a relish, vinegar, ketchup, or a spice, that is used to complement food. [< Lat. *condīmentum*.]

con·di·tion (kən-dĭsh′ən) ►*n.* **1a.** A mode or state of being: *a car in excellent condition.* **b. conditions** The existing circumstances: *Economic conditions have improved.* **2.** A state of health: *the patient's condition.* **3.** A disease or ailment: *a heart condition.* **4.** A prerequisite. **5.** A qualification: *made a promise with one condition.* **6.** *Gram.* The dependent clause of a conditional sentence. ►*v.* **1.** To make conditional. **2a.** To shape or influence. **b.** To adapt. **c.** To render fit for work or use: *conditioned the old car.* **d.** To improve the physical fitness of. **e.** To cause to respond in a specific manner to a specific stimulus. [< Lat. *condiciō*, stipulation.]

con·di·tion·al (kən-dĭsh′ə-nəl) ►*adj.* **1.** Imposing, depending on, or containing a condition. See Synonyms at **dependent. 2.** *Gram.* Stating or implying a condition. ►*n.* *Gram.* A mood, tense, clause, or word expressing a condition. —**con·di′tion·al·ly** *adv.*

con·di·tioned (kən-dĭsh′ənd) ►*adj.* **1.** Subject to conditions. **2.** Physically fit: *a conditioned athlete.* **3.** Prepared for a specific action. **4.** *Psychol.* Exhibiting or trained to exhibit a specific response.

con·do (kŏn′dō′) ►*n., pl.* **-dos** *Informal* A condominium.

con·dole (kən-dōl′) ►*v.* **-doled, -dol·ing** To express sympathy or sorrow. [LLat. *condolēre,* grieve with.] —**con·do′lence** *n.*

con·dom (kŏn′dəm, kŭn′-) ►*n.* A usu. latex sheath used to cover the penis during sex to prevent conception or disease. [?]

con·do·min·i·um (kŏn′də-mĭn′ē-əm) ►*n., pl.* **-min·i·ums** also **-min·i·a** (-mĭn′ē-ə) **1a.** An apartment complex in which individuals own their apartments and share joint ownership in common elements with other unit owners. **b.** A unit in such a complex. **2.** Joint sovereignty, esp. joint rule over a territory. [COM– + Lat. *dominium,* property.]

con·done (kən-dōn′) ►*v.* To overlook, forgive, or disregard (an offense) without protest or censure. [Lat. *condōnāre,* give, permit.] —**con·don′a·ble** *adj.*

con·dor (kŏn′dôr′, -dər) ►*n.* Either of two large vultures of the Andes or mountains of California. [< Quechua *kuntur.*]

Con·dor·cet (kôn-dôr-sĕ′) Marie Jean Antoine Nicolas Caritat. 1743–94. French mathematician and philosopher.

con·duce (kən-dōōs′, -dyōōs′) ►*v.* **-duced, -duc·ing** To lead to a specific result. [Lat. *condūcere.*] —**con·du′cive** *adj.* —**con·du′cive·ness** *n.*

con·duct (kən-dŭkt′) ►*v.* **1.** To direct the course of; control. **2.** To lead or guide. **3.** To direct the performance of a musical group. **4.** To serve as a medium for conveying; transmit. **5.** To behave (oneself) in a specified way. ►*n.* (kŏn′dŭkt′) **1.** The way one acts; behavior. **2.** Management. [< Lat. *condūcere.*] —**con·duct′i·ble** *adj.*

con·duc·tance (kən-dŭk′təns) ►*n.* A measure of the ability of a material to conduct electric charge.

con·duc·tion (kən-dŭk′shən) ►*n.* Transmission through a medium or passage, esp. the transmission of electric charge or heat. —**con·duc′tive** *adj.* —**con′duc·tiv′i·ty** (kŏn′dŭk-tĭv′ĭ-tē) *n.*

con·duc·tor (kən-dŭk′tər) ►*n.* **1.** One who conducts, esp.: **a.** One in charge of a bus, train, or streetcar. **b.** One who directs a musical group. **2.** A substance that conducts heat, light, sound, or esp. an electric charge.

con·duit (kŏn′dōō-ĭt, -dĭt) ►*n.* **1.** A pipe or channel for conveying fluids. **2.** A tube or duct for enclosing electric wires or cable. **3.** A means of passing or transmitting: *a conduit of information.* [< OFr. < Lat. *condūcere, conduct-,* lead to.]

cone (kōn) ►*n.* **1.** *Math.* **a.** The surface generated by a straight line passing through a fixed point or vertex and moving along a fixed curve, usu. a circle. **b.** The figure that is formed by such a surface, bound by its vertex and an intersecting plane. **2.** *Bot.* A scaly, rounded or cylindrical seed-bearing structure, as of a pine. **3.** *Physiol.* A photoreceptor in the retina. [< Gk. *kōnos.*]

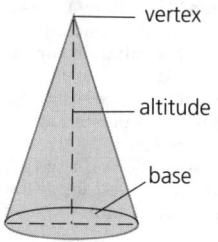

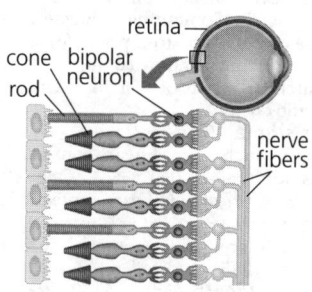

cone
top: right circular cone
bottom: cones and rods of a human eye

cone·flow·er (kōn′flou′ər) ►*n.* Any of various North American plants having flowers with a dark cone-shaped center surrounded by colorful rays.

Con·es·to·ga wagon (kŏn′ĭ-stō′gə) ►*n.* A heavy covered wagon with broad wheels, used by American pioneers. [After *Conestoga,* Pennsylvania.]

co·ney also **co·ny** (kō′nē, kŭn′ē) ►*n., pl.* **-neys** also **-nies 1.** A rabbit, esp. of an Old World species. **2.** The fur of a rabbit. **3.** See **pika. 4.** See **hyrax.** [< Lat. *cunĭculus.*]

Co·ney Island (kō′nē) A resort district of Brooklyn, NY, on the Atlantic Ocean.

con·fab·u·late (kən-făb′yə-lāt′) ►*v.* **-lat·ed, -lat·ing** To talk casually; chat. [Lat. *cōnfābulārī.*] —**con·fab′u·la′tion** *n.*

con·fec·tion (kən-fĕk′shən) ►*n.* A sweet preparation, such as candy. [< Lat. *cōnficere, cōnfect-,* put together.] —**con·fec′tion·er** *n.*

con·fec·tion·er·y (kən-fĕk′shə-nĕr′ē) ►*n., pl.* **-ies 1.** Candies and other confections collectively. **2.** A confectioner's shop.

con·fed·er·a·cy (kən-fĕd′ər-ə-sē) ►*n., pl.* **-cies 1.** A political union of persons, parties, or states; league. **2. Confederacy** The 11 Southern states that seceded from the US in 1860 and 1861.

con·fed·er·ate (kən-fĕd′ər-ĭt) ►*n.* **1.** An associate; ally. **2.** An accomplice. **3. Confederate** A supporter of the American Confederacy. ►*v.* (-ə-rāt′) **-at·ed, -at·ing** To form into or become part of a confederacy. [< LLat. *cōnfoederāre,* unite.] —**con·fed′er·ate** (-ĭt) *adj.* —**con·fed′er·ate·ly** *adv.*

con·fed·er·a·tion (kən-fĕd′ə-rā′shən) ►*n.* **1a.** The act of confederating. **b.** The state of being confederated. **2.** A confederacy.

con·fer (kən-fûr′) ►*v.* **-ferred, -fer·ring 1.** To bestow (e.g., an honor). **2.** To hold a meeting. [Lat. *cōnferre : com-,* com- + *ferre,* bring.]

—**con·fer·ee'** (kŏn'fə-rē') *n.* —**con·fer'ral** *n.*

con·fer·ence (kŏn'fər-əns, -frəns) ►*n.* **1.** A meeting for consultation or discussion. **2.** *Sports* An association of teams.

conference call ►*n.* A telephone call that connects three or more persons at once.

con·fess (kən-fĕs') ►*v.* **1.** To disclose (something damaging about oneself); admit. **2.** To tell one's sins to a priest for absolution. [< Lat. *cōnfitērī, cōnfess-,* admit to.] —**con·fess'ed·ly** (-ĭd-lē) *adv.*

con·fes·sion (kən-fĕsh'ən) ►*n.* **1.** The act of confessing. **2.** Something confessed, esp. disclosure of one's sins to a priest for absolution. **3.** A statement acknowledging one's guilt. **4.** A church or group of worshipers adhering to a specific creed.

con·fes·sion·al (kən-fĕsh'ə-nəl) ►*n.* A small booth in which a priest hears confessions.

con·fes·sor (kən-fĕs'ər) ►*n.* **1.** One who confesses. **2.** A priest who hears confessions.

con·fet·ti (kən-fĕt'ē) ►*pl.n. (takes sing. v.)* Small pieces of colored paper scattered during festive occasions. [Ital., candies.]

con·fi·dant (kŏn'fĭ-dănt', -dänt', kŏn'fĭ-dănt', -dänt') ►*n.* One to whom secrets or private matters are disclosed.

con·fide (kən-fīd') ►*v.* **-fid·ed, -fid·ing 1.** To tell (something) in confidence. **2.** To put into another's keeping. [< Lat. *cōnfīdere.*]

con·fi·dence (kŏn'fĭ-dəns) ►*n.* **1a.** A conviction that an outcome will be favorable. **b.** Belief in the certainty of something. **2.** Belief in oneself; self-confidence. **3.** Trust or faith in a person or thing. **4.** A trusting relationship. **5a.** Something confided. **b.** A feeling of assurance that a confidant will keep a secret. —**con'fi·dent** *adj.* —**con'fi·dent·ly** *adv.*

confidence game ►*n.* A fraud perpetrated after the victim's confidence has been won.

confidence man ►*n.* A man who swindles his victims by using a confidence game.

con·fi·den·tial (kŏn'fĭ-dĕn'shəl) ►*adj.* **1.** Told in confidence; secret. **2.** Entrusted with the confidence of another. —**con'fi·den'ti·al·i·ty** (-shē-ăl'ĭ-tē) *n.* —**con'fi·den'tial·ly** *adv.*

con·fig·u·ra·tion (kən-fĭg'yə-rā'shən) ►*n.* Arrangement of parts or elements. —**con·fig'·u·ra'tive, con·fig'u·ra'tion·al** *adj.*

con·fig·ure (kən-fĭg'yər) ►*v.* **-ured, -ur·ing** To design, arrange, or shape for specific applications or uses. [< Lat. *cōnfigūrāre,* give form to.]

con·fine (kən-fīn') ►*v.* **-fined, -fin·ing 1.** To keep within bounds; restrict. **2.** To imprison. [< Lat. *cōnfīnis,* adjoining : *com-,* com- + *fīnis,* border.] —**con·fin'a·ble, con·fine'a·ble** *adj.* —**con·fine'ment** *n.* —**con·fin'er** *n.*

con·fines (kŏn'fīnz') ►*pl.n.* **1.** The limits of a space or area. **2.** Restraining elements: *escape the confines of bureaucracy.* [OFr. *confins,* ult. < Latin *com-,* com- + Latin *fīnis,* border.]

con·firm (kən-fûrm') ►*v.* **1.** To establish the validity or existence of; verify. **2.** To make firmer; strengthen. **3.** To ratify. **4.** To administer the religious rite of confirmation to. [< Lat. *cōnfirmāre.*] —**con·firm'a·ble** *adj.* —**con·firm'a·to'ry** (-fûr'mə-tôr'ē) *adj.*

con·fir·ma·tion (kŏn'fər-mā'shən) ►*n.* **1.** The act of confirming. **2.** A verification. **3a.** A Christian rite admitting a baptized person to full membership in a church. **b.** A ceremony in Judaism that marks the end of a young person's religious training.

con·firmed (kən-fûrmd') ►*adj.* **1.** Firmly settled in habit. See Synonyms at **chronic. 2.** Ratified; verified. **3.** Having received confirmation. —**con·firm'ed·ly** (-fûr'mĭd-lē) *adv.*

con·fis·cate (kŏn'fĭ-skāt') ►*v.* **-cat·ed, -cat·ing 1.** To seize (private property) for the public treasury. **2.** To seize by authority. See Synonyms at **appropriate.** [Lat. *confiscāre < fiscus,* treasury.] —**con'fis·ca'tion** *n.* —**con'fis·ca'tor** *n.* —**con·fis'ca·to'ry** (kən-fĭs'kə-tôr'ē) *adj.*

con·fla·gra·tion (kŏn'flə-grā'shən) ►*n.* A large destructive fire. [< Lat. *cōnflagrāre,* burn up.]

conflate (kən-flāt') ►*v.* **-flat·ed, -flat·ing** To bring together; meld or fuse: *conflated several historical figures into a single legendary hero.* —**con·fla'tion** *n.*

con·flict (kŏn'flĭkt') ►*n.* **1.** Prolonged fighting. **2.** Disharmony between persons or ideas. **3.** *Psychol.* A struggle between mutually exclusive impulses or desires. ►*v.* (kən-flĭkt') To be in opposition; differ. [< Lat. *cōnflīgere, cōnflīct-,* strike together.] —**con·flic'tive** *adj.*

con·flu·ence (kŏn'flōō-əns) ►*n.* **1a.** A flowing together of two or more streams. **b.** The point where such streams meet. **2.** A gathering together. [< Lat. *cōnfluere,* flow together.] —**con'flu·ent** *adj.*

con·form (kən-fôrm') ►*v.* **1.** To correspond; be similar. **2.** To act or be in agreement; comply. See Synonyms at **adapt. 3.** To act in accordance with traditional customs or prevailing standards. [< Lat. *cōnfōrmāre,* shape after.] —**con·form'a·bil'i·ty** *n.* —**con·form'a·ble** *adj.* —**con·form'a·bly** *adv.* —**con·form'er** *n.*

con·for·mance (kən-fôr'məns) ►*n.* Conformity.

con·for·ma·tion (kŏn'fər-mā'shən) ►*n.* **1.** The structure or shape of an item or entity. **2.** A symmetrical arrangement of parts.

con·form·ist (kən-fôr'mĭst) ►*n.* A person who uncritically conforms to the customs or styles of a group. —**con·form'ist** *adj.*

con·form·i·ty (kən-fôr'mĭ-tē) ►*n., pl.* **-ties 1.** Similarity; agreement. **2.** Behavior conforming to current customs or styles.

con·found (kən-found', kŏn-) ►*v.* **1.** To confuse or perplex. See Synonyms at **perplex. 2.** To mix up. **3.** To make (something bad) worse. [< Lat. *cōnfundere,* confuse.] —**con·found'er** *n.*

con·found·ed (kən-foun'dĭd, kŏn-) ►*adj.* **1.** Confused; befuddled. **2.** Used as an intensive: *a confounded fool.* —**con·found'ed·ly** *adv.*

con·fra·ter·ni·ty (kŏn'frə-tûr'nĭ-tē) ►*n., pl.* **-ties** An association of persons united in a common purpose or profession.

con·frere (kŏn'frâr') ►*n.* A colleague. [< Med. Lat. *cōnfrāter* : COM- + Lat. *frāter,* brother.]

con·front (kən-frŭnt') ►*v.* **1.** To bring or come face to face with, esp. with hostility. **2.** To meet; encounter. [< Med.Lat. *cōnfrontāre.*] —**con'·fron·ta'tion** (kŏn'frŭn-tā'shən) *n.* —**con'·fron·ta'tion·al** *adj.*

Con·fu·cius (kən-fyōō'shəs) c. 551–479 BC. Chinese philosopher. —**Con·fu'cian** *adj. & n.* —**Con·fu'cian·ism** *n.* —**Con·fu'cian·ist** *n.*

con·fuse (kən-fyōōz') ►*v.* **-fused, -fus·ing 1.** To cause to be unable to think clearly; bewilder. See Synonyms at **perplex. 2.** To mistake (one thing for another). **3.** To make more difficult to understand. [< Lat. *cōnfundere, cōnfūs-*, mix together.] —**con·fu′sion** *n.*

con·fused (kən-fyōōzd′) ►*adj.* **1.** Unclear in mind; addled. **2a.** Lacking logical order or sense: *a confused set of instructions.* **b.** Chaotic; jumbled. —**con·fus′ed·ly** (-fyōō′zĭd-lē) *adv.*

con·fute (kən-fyōōt′) ►*v.* **-fut·ed, -fut·ing** To prove to be wrong or false; refute decisively. [Lat. *cōnfūtāre.*] —**con·fut′a·ble** *adj.* —**con′fu·ta′tion** (kŏn′fyōō-tā′shən) *n.*

con game ►*n. Slang* A confidence game.

con·geal (kən-jēl′) ►*v.* **1.** To solidify or coagulate. **2.** To come together so as to form a whole. [< Lat. *congelāre* : COM- + *gelāre*, freeze.] —**con·geal′a·ble** *adj.* —**con·geal′ment** *n.*

con·gen·ial (kən-jēn′yəl) ►*adj.* **1.** Having the same tastes or temperament. **2.** Friendly. **3.** Suited to one's needs or nature; agreeable. [Prob. < CON- + Lat. *genius*, spirit.] —**con·ge′ni·al′i·ty** (-jē′nē-ăl′ĭ-tē), **con·gen′ial·ness** *n.* —**con·gen′ial·ly** *adv.*

con·gen·i·tal (kən-jĕn′ĭ-tl) ►*adj.* **1.** Existing at or before birth. **2.** Constitutional; inherent. [< Lat. *congenitus*, born with.] —**con·gen′i·tal·ly** *adv.*

con·ger (kŏng′gər) ►*n.* A large scaleless marine eel. [< Gk. *gongros.*]

con·ge·ries (kən-jîr′ēz′, kŏn′jə-rēz′) ►*n. (takes sing. v.)* A collection; aggregation. [Lat. *congeriēs* < *congerere*, heap together.]

con·gest (kən-jĕst′) ►*v.* **1.** To overfill; clog. **2.** To cause the accumulation of excessive blood or fluid in (a vessel or organ). [Lat. *congerere, congest-*, heap together.] —**con·ges′tion** *n.* —**con·ges′tive** *adj.*

con·glom·er·ate (kən-glŏm′ə-rāt′) ►*v.* **-at·ed, -at·ing** To form or cause to form into a mass. ►*n.* (-ər-ĭt) **1.** A corporation made up of several companies in diverse fields. **2.** A heterogeneous mass; cluster. **3.** *Geol.* A rock consisting of fragments cemented together. [Lat. *conglomerāre* < *glomus*, ball.] —**con·glom′er·ate** (-ĭt) *adj.* —**con·glom′er·a′tion** *n.*

Con·go (kŏng′gō) **1.** Officially **Democratic Republic of the Congo** Formerly (1971–97) **Za·ire** (zī′îr, zä-îr′) A country of central Africa astride the equator. Cap. Kinshasa. **2.** Officially **Republic of the Congo** A country of W-central Africa with a short coastline on the Atlantic Ocean. Cap. Brazzaville. —**Con′go·lese′** (-lēz′, -lēs′) *adj. & n.*

Congo River A river of central Africa flowing about 4,700 km (2,920 mi) through Dem. Rep. of the Congo to the Atlantic.

con·grat·u·late (kən-grăch′ə-lāt′, -grăj′-, kəng-) ►*v.* **-lat·ed, -lat·ing** To extend congratulations to. [Lat. *congrātulārī.*] —**con·grat′u·la′tor** *n.* —**con·grat′u·la·to′ry** (-lə-tôr′ē) *adj.*

con·grat·u·la·tion (kən-grăch′ə-lā′shən, -grăj′-, kəng-) ►*n.* **1.** The act of expressing joy or acknowledgment, as for the achievement or good fortune of another. **2.** **congratulations** An expression of such joy or acknowledgment.

con·gre·gate (kŏng′grĭ-gāt′) ►*v.* **-gat·ed, -gat·ing** To bring or come together in a group. [< Lat. *congregāre.*] —**con′gre·ga′tor** *n.*

con·gre·ga·tion (kŏng′grĭ-gā′shən) ►*n.* **1.** The act of assembling. **2.** An assemblage; gathering. **3.** The members of a specific religious group who regularly worship together.

con·gre·ga·tion·al (kŏng′grĭ-gā′shə-nəl) ►*adj.* **1.** Of or relating to a congregation. **2.** **Congregational** Of or relating to a Protestant denomination in which each member church is self-governing. —**con′gre·ga′tion·al·ism** *n.* —**con′gre·ga′tion·al·ist** *n.*

con·gress (kŏng′grĭs) ►*n.* **1.** A formal assembly to discuss problems. **2.** The national legislative body of a nation, esp. a republic. **3.** **Congress** The US legislature, consisting of the Senate and the House of Representatives. [< Lat. *congredī, congress-*, convene.] —**con·gres′sion·al** (kən-grĕsh′ə-nəl, kəng-) *adj.* —**con·gres′sion·al·ly** *adv.* —**con′gress·man** *n.* —**con′gress·per′son** *n.* —**con′gress·wom′an** *n.*

con·gru·ent (kŏng′grōō-ənt, kən-grōō′-) ►*adj.* **1.** Corresponding; congruous. **2.** *Math.* Coinciding exactly when superimposed. [< Lat. *congruere*, agree.] —**con′gru·ence, con′gru·en·cy** *n.* —**con′gru·ent·ly** *adv.*

con·gru·ous (kŏng′grōō-əs) ►*adj.* **1.** Corresponding in character or kind. **2.** *Math.* Congruent. [< Lat. *congruere*, agree.] —**con·gru′i·ty** (kən-grōō′ĭ-tē, kŏn-) *n.* —**con′gru·ous·ly** *adv.* —**con′gru·ous·ness** *n.*

con·ic (kŏn′ĭk) or **con·i·cal** (-ĭ-kəl) ►*adj.* Of or shaped like a cone.

conic section ►*n.* The intersection of a cone and a plane, which generates one of a group of curves, including the circle, ellipse, hyperbola, and parabola.

con·i·fer (kŏn′ə-fər, kō′nə-) ►*n.* A cone-bearing tree such as a pine or fir. [< Lat. *cōnifer*, cone-bearing : *cōnus*, CONE + -FER.] —**co·nif′er·ous** (kō-nĭf′ər-əs, kə-) *adj.*

conj. ►*abbr.* **1.** conjugation **2.** conjunction

con·jec·tur·al (kən-jĕk′chər-əl) ►*adj.* Based on or involving conjecture. See Synonyms at **supposed.** —**con·jec′tur·al·ly** *adv.*

con·jec·ture (kən-jĕk′chər) ►*n.* Judgment based on inconclusive or incomplete evidence; guesswork. ►*v.* **-tured, -tur·ing** To guess. [< Lat. *conicere, coniect-*, infer.] —**con·jec′tur·a·ble** *adj.* —**con·jec′tur·er** *n.*

con·join (kən-join′) ►*v.* To join together; unite. [< Lat. *coniungere* : COM- + *iungere*, join.] —**con·join′er** *n.* —**con·joint′** *adj.* —**con·joint′ly** *adv.*

con·joined twin (kən-joind′) ►*n.* Either of a pair of identical twins born with their bodies joined at some point.

con·ju·gal (kŏn′jə-gəl) ►*adj.* Of or relating to marriage or the marital relationship. [< Lat. *coniūnx, coniug-*, spouse < *coniungere*, CONJOIN.] —**con′ju·gal′i·ty** *n.* —**con′ju·gal·ly** *adv.*

con·ju·gate (kŏn′jə-gāt′) ►*v.* **-gat·ed, -gat·ing** To inflect (a verb). ►*adj.* (-gĭt, -gāt′) Joined together, esp. in pairs. [Lat. *coniugāre*, join together : COM- + *iugum*, yoke.] —**con′ju·gate′ly** *adv.* —**con′ju·ga′tive** *adj.*

con·ju·ga·tion (kŏn′jə-gā′shən) ►*n.* **1a.** The inflection of a verb. **b.** A presentation of the inflected forms of a verb. **2.** *Biol.* A process in which two one-celled organisms temporarily unite to transfer nuclear material. —**con′ju·ga′tion·al** *adj.* —**con′ju·ga′tion·al·ly** *adv.*

con·junct (kən-jŭngkt′, kŏn′jŭngkt′) ►*adj.* Joined together; united. [< Lat. *coniungere, coniūnct-*, CONJOIN.] —**con·junct′ly** *adv.*

con·junc·tion (kən-jŭngk′shən) ►*n.* **1.** The act of joining or state of being joined. **2.** A joint or simultaneous occurrence. **3.** *Gram.* A word such as *and*, *but*, or *because* that connects other words, phrases, clauses, or sentences. —**con·junc′tion·al** *adj.* —**con·junc′tion·al·ly** *adv.*

con·junc·ti·va (kŏn′jŭngk-tī′və) ►*n.*, *pl.* **-vas** or **-vae** (-vē) The mucous membrane that lines the inner surface of the eyelid and the exposed surface of the eyeball. [< Med.Lat. *(membrāna) coniūnctīva*, connective (membrane).] —**con′·junc·ti′val** *adj.*

con·junc·tive (kən-jŭngk′tĭv) ►*adj.* **1.** Connective. **2.** Joined together; combined. **3.** *Gram.* Used as a conjunction. ►*n.* A conjunction. —**con·junc′tive·ly** *adv.*

con·junc·ti·vi·tis (kən-jŭngk′tə-vī′tĭs) ►*n.* Inflammation of the conjunctiva.

con·junc·ture (kən-jŭngk′chər) ►*n.* A critical set of circumstances; crisis.

con·jure (kŏn′jər, kən-jŏŏr′) ►*v.* **-jured, -jur·ing 1.** To summon (a spirit) by magical power. **2.** To evoke: *a song that conjured up old memories.* **3.** To perform magic tricks. [< Lat. *coniūrāre*, swear together.] —**con′ju·ra′tion** *n.* —**con′jur·er, con′jur·or** *n.*

conk (kŏngk) ►*v. Slang* To hit, esp. on the head. —*phrasal verb:* **conk out 1.** To stop functioning; fail. **2.** To fall asleep, esp. suddenly. [Ult. < *conk*, the head, perh. var. of CONCH.]

con man ►*n. Slang* A confidence man.

con·nect (kə-nĕkt′) ►*v.* **1.** To join or become joined together. **2.** To associate or consider as related. **3.** To join to or by means of a communications circuit. **4.** To make a connection. —*idiom:* **connect the dots 1.** To draw lines connecting numbered dots so as to produce a design. **2.** To draw inferences connecting pieces of information to reveal something previously unknown. [< Lat. *cōnectere*, tie together.] —**con·nec′tor, con·nect′er** *n.*

Con·nect·i·cut (kə-nĕt′ĭ-kət) A state of the NE US. Cap. Hartford.

con·nec·tion (kə-nĕk′shən) ►*n.* **1.** Union; junction. **2.** A link. **3.** An association or relation. **4.** The logical ordering of words or ideas; coherence. **5.** Reference to something else; context. **6.** A person, esp. one of influence, with whom one is associated. **7.** A scheduled run providing service between means of transportation. **8.** A line of communication between two or more points in a telecommunications system. —*idiom:* **in connection with** In relation to.

con·nec·tive (kə-nĕk′tĭv) ►*adj.* Serving or tending to connect. ►*n. Gram.* A connecting word, such as a conjunction. —**con·nec′tive·ly** *adv.* —**con′nec·tiv′i·ty** *n.*

connective tissue ►*n.* Tissue, such as cartilage and bone, that forms the supporting and connecting structures of the body.

con·nip·tion (kə-nĭp′shən) ►*n. Informal* A fit of violent emotion. [Mock Latin (perh. influenced by SNIP).]

con·nive (kə-nīv′) ►*v.* **-nived, -niv·ing 1.** To cooperate secretly in an illegal action. **2.** To scheme; plot. **3.** To feign ignorance of a wrong, thus implying consent. [Lat. *cōnīvēre*, close one's eyes.] —**con·niv′ance** *n.* —**con·niv′er** *n.* —**con·niv′er·y** *n.*

con·nois·seur (kŏn′ə-sûr′, -sŏŏr′) ►*n.* A person of discriminating taste. [Obsolete Fr., ult. < Lat. *cognōscere*, learn.]

con·note (kə-nōt′) ►*v.* **-not·ed, -not·ing 1.** To

suggest or imply in addition to literal meaning: *Spring connotes flowers and new life.* **2.** To have as a related condition: *For a political leader, hesitation is apt to connote weakness.* [Med.Lat. *connotāre*, to mark along with.] —**con′no·ta′tion** (kŏn′ə-tā′shən) *n.* —**con′no·ta′tive** *adj.*

con·nu·bi·al (kə-nŏŏ′bē-əl, -nyŏŏ′-) ►*adj.* Relating to marriage or the married state; conjugal. [< Lat. *cōnūbium*, marriage.] —**con·nu′bi·al·ly** *adv.*

con·quer ►*v.* **1.** To defeat or subdue by military force. **2.** To overcome; surmount: *conquered my fear of heights.* [< Lat. *conquīrere*, procure.] —**con′quer·a·ble** *adj.* —**con′quer·or, con′quer·er** *n.*

con·quest (kŏn′kwĕst′, kŏng′-) ►*n.* **1.** The act or process of conquering. **2.** Something acquired by conquering. [< VLat. **conquaesīta < *conquaerere*, CONQUER.]

con·quis·ta·dor (kŏn-kwĭs′tə-dôr′, kŏng-kē′stə-) ►*n.*, *pl.* **-dors** or **-dor·es** (-dôr′ās, -ēz) One of the 16th-cent. Spanish conquerors of Mexico, Central America, or Peru. [Sp. < *conquistar*, CONQUER.]

Con·rad (kŏn′răd′), **Joseph** 1857–1924. Polish-born British novelist.

con·san·guin·e·ous (kŏn′săn-gwĭn′ē-əs, -săng-) also **con·san·guine** (kŏn-săng′gwĭn, kən-) ►*adj.* Having a common ancestor. [< Lat. *cōnsanguineus* : COM– + *sanguis*, blood.] —**con′san·guin′e·ous·ly** *adv.* —**con′san·guin′i·ty** *n.*

con·science (kŏn′shəns) ►*n.* **1.** The awareness of a moral or ethical aspect to one's conduct. **2.** Conformity to one's own sense of right conduct. —*idioms:* **in (all good) conscience** By any reasonable standard. **on (one's) conscience** Causing one to feel guilty or uneasy. [< Lat. *cōnscīre*, be conscious of.]

con·sci·en·tious (kŏn′shē-ĕn′shəs) ►*adj.* **1.** Guided by one's conscience; principled. **2.** Thorough and careful. —**con′sci·en′tious·ly** *adv.* —**con′sci·en′tious·ness** *n.*

conscientious objector ►*n.* One who refuses to participate in military service on the basis of moral or religious beliefs.

con·scious (kŏn′shəs) ►*adj.* **1a.** Characterized by or having an awareness of one's environment and one's own existence. **b.** Not asleep; awake. **2.** Capable of thought, will, or perception. **3.** Subjectively known: *conscious remorse.* **4.** Deliberate: *a conscious insult.* **5.** Sensitive to something: *conscious of being stared at.* [< Lat. *cōnscius*.] —**con′scious·ly** *adv.*

con·scious·ness (kŏn′shəs-nĭs) ►*n.* **1.** A sense of one's personal or collective identity. **2.** Special awareness of or sensitivity to a particular issue or situation.

con·script (kŏn′skrĭpt′) ►*n.* One compulsorily enrolled for service, esp. in the armed forces. [< Lat. *cōnscrībere, cōnscrīpt-*, enroll.] —**con·script′** (kən-skrĭpt′) *v.* —**con·scrip′tion** *n.*

con·se·crate (kŏn′sĭ-krāt′) ►*v.* **-crat·ed, -crat·ing 1.** To declare or set apart as sacred. **2.** *Christianity* **a.** To sanctify (bread and wine) for Eucharistic use. **b.** To initiate (a priest) into the order of bishops. **3.** To dedicate to a service or goal. [< Lat. *cōnsecrāre*.] —**con′se·cra′tion** *n.* —**con′se·cra′tive** *adj.* —**con′se·cra′tor** *n.*

con·sec·u·tive (kən-sĕk′yə-tĭv) ►*adj.* Following one after another without interruption.

[< Lat. *cōnsequī, cōnsecūt-*, follow closely.]
—**con·sec'u·tive·ly** *adv.* —**con·sec'u·tive·
ness** *n.*

con·sen·su·al (kən-sĕn'shoō-əl) ►*adj.* **1.** *Law*
Entered into by mutual consent. **2.** Involving
the willing participation of both or all parties.
—**con·sen'su·al·ly** *adv.*

con·sen·sus (kən-sĕn'səs) ►*n.* **1.** An opinion
or position reached by a group as a whole or
by majority will. **2.** General agreement. [Lat.
cōnsēnsus < cōnsentīre, agree.]

con·sent (kən-sĕnt') ►*v.* To give assent; agree.
►*n.* Acceptance; agreement. See Synonyms at
permission. [< Lat. *cōnsentīre*.]

con·se·quence (kŏn'sĭ-kwĕns', -kwəns) ►*n.* **1.**
Something that follows from an action or
condition. **2.** Significance; importance: *an issue
of consequence.*

con·se·quent (kŏn'sĭ-kwĕnt', -kwənt) ►*adj.*
Following as an effect, result, or conclusion.
[< Lat. *cōnsequī*, follow closely.] —**con'se·
quent'ly** *adv.*

con·se·quen·tial (kŏn'sĭ-kwĕn'shəl) ►*adj.* **1.**
Having important consequences. **2.** Important; influential. —**con'se·quen'ti·al'i·ty** *n.*
—**con'se·quen'tial·ly** *adv.*

con·ser·va·tion (kŏn'sûr-vā'shən) ►*n.* **1.** The
act or process of conserving. **2.** The preservation or restoration of resources: *land conservation.* —**con'ser·va'tion·al** *adj.* —**con'ser·
va'tion·ist** *n.*

con·ser·va·tism (kən-sûr'və-tĭz'əm) ►*n.* **1.** The
inclination, esp. in politics, to maintain the
existing or traditional order. **2.** Caution or
moderation, as in behavior or outlook.

con·ser·va·tive (kən-sûr'və-tĭv) ►*adj.* **1.** Favoring traditional views and values; tending to
oppose change. **2.** Traditional in style. **3.** Moderate; cautious: *a conservative estimate.* **4.** Of a
branch of Judaism that allows certain authorized modifications in the law. ►*n.* A conservative person. —**con·ser'va·tive·ly** *adv.* —**con·
ser'va·tive·ness** *n.*

con·ser·va·tor (kən-sûr'və-tər, kŏn'sər-vā'tər)
►*n.* **1.** A person in charge of maintaining or
restoring valuable items. **2.** A guardian. **3.** *Law*
One placed in charge of the property or personal affairs of an incompetent person.

con·ser·va·to·ry (kən-sûr'və-tôr'ē) ►*n., pl.*
-ries 1. A greenhouse, esp. one in which plants
are displayed. **2.** A school of music or drama.

con·serve (kən-sûrv') ►*v.* **-served, -serv·ing**
1a. To protect from loss or depletion; preserve.
b. To use carefully or sparingly: *conserve energy.*
2. To preserve (fruits). ►*n.* (kŏn'sûrv') A jam
made of stewed fruits. [< Lat. *cōnservāre*.]
—**con·serv'a·ble** *adj.*

con·sid·er (kən-sĭd'ər) ►*v.* **1.** To think carefully
about. **2.** To regard as. **3.** To take into account.
[< Lat. *cōnsīderāre < sīdus, sīder-*, star.]

con·sid·er·a·ble (kən-sĭd'ər-ə-bəl) ►*adj.* **1.**
Large in amount, extent, or degree. **2.** Worthy
of consideration. —**con·sid'er·a·bly** *adv.*

con·sid·er·ate (kən-sĭd'ər-ĭt) ►*adj.* Having
regard for the needs or feelings of others;
thoughtful. —**con·sid'er·ate·ly** *adv.* —**con·
sid'er·ate·ness** *n.*

con·sid·er·a·tion (kən-sĭd'ə-rā'shən) ►*n.* **1.**
Careful thought. **2.** A factor to be considered
in making a decision. **3.** Thoughtful concern
for others. **4.** Recompense.

con·sid·ered (kən-sĭd'ərd) ►*adj.* Reached after
careful thought; deliberate.

con·sid·er·ing (kən-sĭd'ər-ĭng) ►*prep.* In view
of; taking into consideration. ►*adv. Informal*
All things considered: *We had a good trip,
considering.*

con·sign (kən-sīn') ►*v.* **1.** To give over to the
care of another; entrust. **2.** To set apart, as for
a special use or purpose. **3.** To deliver (merchandise) for sale. [< Lat. *cōnsignāre*, certify.]
—**con·sign'a·ble** *adj.* —**con·sig'nor, con·
sign'er** *n.*

con·sign·ment (kən-sīn'mənt) ►*n.* **1.** The act of
consigning. **2.** Something consigned. —*idiom:*
on consignment With the provision that
payment is expected only on completed sales.

con·sist (kən-sĭst') ►*v.* **1.** To be made up or
composed. **2.** To reside: *Its beauty consists in
its simplicity.* [Lat. *cōnsistere* : COM– + *sistere*,
cause to stand.]

con·sis·ten·cy (kən-sĭs'tən-sē) ►*n., pl.* **-cies
1.** Agreement or coherence among things or
parts. **2.** Uniformity of successive results or
events. **3.** Degree or texture of firmness. —**con·
sis'tent** *adj.* —**con·sis'tent·ly** *adv.*

con·sis·to·ry (kən-sĭs'tə-rē) ►*n., pl.* **-ries 1.**
Rom. Cath. Ch. An assembly of cardinals presided over by the pope. **2.** A council.

con·so·la·tion (kŏn'sə-lā'shən) ►*n.* **1a.** The
act or an instance of consoling. **b.** The state
of being consoled. **2.** One that consoles; a
comfort.

consolation prize ►*n.* A prize given to a competitor who loses.

con·sole¹ (kən-sōl') ►*v.* **-soled, -sol·ing** To
allay the sorrow or grief of. See Synonyms
at **comfort.** [< Lat. *cōnsōlārī*.] —**con·sol'a·
ble** *adj.* —**con'so·la'tion** *n.* —**con·so'la·to'·
ry** (-sō'lə-tôr'ē, -sŏl'ə-) *adj.* —**con·sol'er** *n.*
—**con·sol'ing·ly** *adv.*

con·sole² (kŏn'sōl') ►*n.* **1a.** A central control
panel for a mechanical or electronic system. **b.**
A computer system designed to play a specific
format of video game. **2.** The part of an organ
containing the keyboard, stops, and pedals. **3.**
A freestanding cabinet for a radio, television
set, or phonograph. [Fr.]

con·sol·i·date (kən-sŏl'ĭ-dāt') ►*v.* **-dat·
ed, -dat·ing 1.** To unite into one system or
whole; combine. **2.** To make strong or secure;
strengthen. [Lat. *cōnsolidāre < solidus*, solid.]
—**con·sol'i·da'tion** *n.* —**con·sol'i·da'tor** *n.*

con·som·mé (kŏn'sə-mā', kŏn'sə-mā') ►*n.* A
clear soup made of meat or vegetable stock. [Fr.,
p.part. of *consommer*, use up.]

con·so·nance (kŏn'sə-nəns) ►*n.* **1.** Agreement;
harmony. **2.** The repetition of consonants esp.
at the ends of words, as in *blank* and *think.*

con·so·nant (kŏn'sə-nənt) ►*adj.* **1.** In agreement or accord. **2.** Harmonious in sound.
►*n.* **1.** A speech sound produced by partial or
complete obstruction of the air stream. **2.** A
letter or character representing a consonant.
[< Lat. *cōnsonāre*, agree.] —**con'so·nan'tal**
adj. —**con'so·nan'tal·ly** *adv.* —**con'so·nant·
ly** *adv.*

con·sort (kŏn'sôrt') ►*n.* A husband or wife,
esp. of a monarch. ►*v.* (kən-sôrt') **1.** To keep
company; associate. **2.** To be in agreement. [<
Lat. *cōnsors*, partner.]

con·sor·ti·um (kən-sôr'tē-əm, -shē-əm) ►*n.,*

pl. **-ti·a** (-tē-ə, -shē-ə) **1.** An association of businesses, financial institutions, or investors engaging in a joint venture. **2.** A cooperative arrangement among institutions. [Lat. *cōnsortium,* partnership.]

con·spic·u·ous (kən-spĭk′yōō-əs) ►*adj.* **1.** Obvious: *a conspicuous mistake.* **2.** Attracting attention; noticeable. [< Lat. *cōnspicere,* observe : COM– + *specere,* look.] —**con·spic′u·ous·ly** *adv.* —**con·spic′u·ous·ness** *n.*

con·spir·a·cy (kən-spîr′ə-sē) ►*n., pl.* **-cies** A plot, esp. an illegal one. [< Lat. *cōnspīrātiō.*]

con·spire (kən-spīr′) ►*v.* **-spired, -spir·ing 1.** To plan together secretly to commit an illegal act. **2.** To join or act together; combine. [< Lat. *cōnspīrāre.*] —**con·spir′a·tor** (-spîr′ə-tər) *n.* —**con·spir′a·tor′i·al** *adj.* —**con·spir′a·tor′i·al·ly** *adv.*

con·sta·ble (kŏn′stə-bəl, kŭn′-) ►*n.* **1.** A peace officer with less authority than a sheriff. **2.** *Chiefly Brit.* A police officer. [< LLat. *comes stabulī,* officer of the stable : *comes,* officer + Lat. *stabulum,* stable.]

con·stab·u·lar·y (kən-stăb′yə-lĕr′ē) ►*n., pl.* **-ies 1.** The body of constables of a district or city. **2.** An armed police force organized like a military unit.

con·stant (kŏn′stənt) ►*adj.* **1.** Continually occurring; persistent. **2.** Unchanging; invariable. **3.** Steadfast; faithful. ►*n.* **1.** Something unchanging. **2.** A condition, factor, or quantity that is invariant in specified circumstances. [< Lat. *cōnstāre,* stand firm : COM– + *stāre,* stand.] —**con′stan·cy** *n.* —**con′stant·ly** *adv.*

Con·stan·tine I (kŏn′stən-tēn′, -tīn′) "the Great." AD 285?–337. Emperor of Rome (306–337).

Con·stan·ti·no·ple (kŏn′stăn-tə-nō′pəl) See **Istanbul.**

con·stel·la·tion (kŏn′stə-lā′shən) ►*n.* **1.** A formation of stars perceived as a figure or design. **2.** Any of the 12 groupings of the stars of the Zodiac, regarded by astrologers as a factor in the determination of one's character or fate. **3.** A gathering or assemblage. [< LLat. *cōnstēllātiō* : COM– + *stēlla,* star.]

con·ster·na·tion (kŏn′stər-nā′shən) ►*n.* Great agitation or dismay. [< Lat. *cōnsternāre,* to dismay.]

con·sti·pa·tion (kŏn′stə-pā′shən) ►*n.* Difficult, incomplete, or infrequent evacuation of the bowels. [< Lat. *cōnstīpāre,* crowd together.] —**con′sti·pate′** *v.*

con·stit·u·en·cy (kən-stĭch′ōō-ən-sē) ►*n., pl.* **-cies 1a.** The voters represented by an elected legislator or official. **b.** The district so represented. **2.** A group of supporters.

con·stit·u·ent (kən-stĭch′ōō-ənt) ►*adj.* **1.** Serving as part of a whole; component. **2.** Authorized to make or amend a constitution: *a constituent assembly.* ►*n.* **1.** A component. See Synonyms at **element. 2.** A resident of a district represented by an elected official. [< Lat. *cōnstituere,* set up; see CONSTITUTE.] —**con·stit′u·ent·ly** *adv.*

con·sti·tute (kŏn′stĭ-tōōt′, -tyōōt′) ►*v.* **-tut·ed, -tut·ing 1a.** To be the parts of; compose. **b.** To amount to. **2.** To set up; establish. **3.** To appoint to an office; designate. [Lat. *cōnstituere,* set up : COM– + *statuere,* set up.]

con·sti·tu·tion (kŏn′stĭ-tōō′shən, -tyōō′-) ►*n.*

1. The act or process of composing or establishing. **2a.** The composition of something. **b.** The physical makeup of a person. **3a.** The system of laws and principles that prescribes the functions and limits of a government. **b.** The written document describing such a system.

con·sti·tu·tion·al (kŏn′stĭ-tōō′shə-nəl, -tyōō′-) ►*adj.* **1.** Of or relating to a constitution. **2.** Consistent with, sanctioned by, or operating under a constitution. **3.** Basic; inherent: *a constitutional inability to lie.* ►*n.* A walk taken regularly for one's health. —**con′sti·tu′tion·al′i·ty** *n.* —**con′sti·tu′tion·al·ly** *adv.*

con·sti·tu·tive (kŏn′stĭ-tōō′tĭv, -tyōō′-) ►*adj.* Inherent; essential.

con·strain (kən-strān′) ►*v.* **1a.** To confine. **b.** To restrain. **2.** To compel; oblige. [< Lat. *cōnstringere,* compress.] —**con·strain′a·ble** *adj.* —**con·strain′er** *n.*

con·straint (kən-strānt′) ►*n.* **1.** Force used to compel another; coercion. **2.** Restraint; confinement. **3.** Something that restricts; check. **4.** Reticence; awkwardness.

con·strict (kən-strĭkt′) ►*v.* **1.** To make smaller or narrower; compress. **2.** To restrict; cramp: *lives constricted by poverty.* [Lat. *cōnstringere, cōnstrict-.*] —**con·stric′tion** *n.* —**con·stric′tive** *adj.*

con·stric·tor (kən-strĭk′tər) ►*n.* **1.** One that constricts, as a muscle that contracts a part of the body. **2.** A snake, such as the boa, that coils around and asphyxiates its prey.

con·struct (kən-strŭkt′) ►*v.* To form by assembling or combining parts; build. ►*n.* (kŏn′strŭkt′) **1.** Something formed from parts. **2.** A schematic idea. [Lat. *cōnstruere, cōnstrŭct-.*] —**con·struct′i·ble** *adj.* —**con·struc′tor, con·struct′er** *n.*

con·struc·tion (kən-strŭk′shən) ►*n.* **1.** The act, process, or business of building. **2.** A structure. **3.** An interpretation: *put a favorable construction on his reply.* **4.** *Gram.* An arrangement of words that forms a phrase, clause, or sentence.

construction paper ►*n.* A heavy paper in a variety of colors, used in artwork.

con·struc·tive (kən-strŭk′tĭv) ►*adj.* **1.** Serving to improve; helpful. **2.** Structural. —**con·struc′tive·ly** *adv.* —**con·struc′tive·ness** *n.*

con·strue (kən-strōō′) ►*v.* **-strued, -stru·ing 1.** To interpret. See Synonyms at **explain. 2.** To translate. [< Lat. *cōnstruere,* build.]

con·sul (kŏn′səl) ►*n.* **1.** An official appointed by a government to reside in a foreign country and represent its interests there. **2.** Either of the two chief magistrates of the Roman Republic. [< Lat. *cōnsul.*] —**con′su·lar** *adj.* —**con′sul·ship′** *n.*

con·su·late (kŏn′sə-lĭt) ►*n.* The residence or official premises of a consul.

con·sult (kən-sŭlt′) ►*v.* **1.** To seek advice or information of. **2.** To exchange views. **3.** To work or serve in an advisory capacity. ►*n.* A consultation, esp. between physicians. [< Lat. *cōnsulere, cōnsult-,* take counsel.] —**con·sul′tant** *n.* —**con′sul·ta′tion** *n.* —**con′sul·ta′tive** *adj.*

con·sul·tan·cy (kən-sŭl′tn-sē) ►*n., pl.* **-cies** A business offering expert advice in a field.

con·sume (kən-sōōm′) ►*v.* **-sumed, -sum·ing 1.** To eat or drink up. See Synonyms at **eat. 2.** To expend; use up. **3.** To purchase (goods or services) for use or ownership. **4.** To waste; squander. **5.** To destroy totally; ravage. **6.** To absorb; engross: *consumed with jealousy.* See Synonyms at **engross.** [< Lat. *cōnsūmere.*] —**con·sum′a·ble** *adj. & n.*

con·sum·er (kən-sōō′mər) ►*n.* One that consumes, esp. a buyer of goods or services.

con·sum·er·ism (kən-sōō′mə-rĭz′əm) ►*n.* **1.** A movement seeking to protect and inform consumers by requiring honest packaging and advertising, product guarantees, and improved standards. **2.** Materialism. —**con·sum′er·ist** *n.*

consumer price index ►*n.* An index of the change in the cost of basic goods and services in comparison with a fixed base period.

con·sum·mate (kŏn′sə-māt′) ►*v.* -**mat·ed,** -**mat·ing 1.** To bring to completion; conclude. **2.** To complete (a marriage) with the first act of sexual intercourse. ►*adj.* (kən-sŭm′ĭt, kŏn′sə-mət) **1.** Complete; lacking nothing. See Synonyms at **perfect. 2.** Supremely accomplished. [< Lat. *cōnsummāre* : COM– + *summa,* SUM.] —**con·sum′mate·ly** *adv.* —**con′sum·ma′tion** *n.* —**con′sum·ma′tor** *n.*

con·sump·tion (kən-sŭmp′shən) ►*n.* **1a.** The act or process of consuming. **b.** An amount consumed. **2.** *Econ.* The using up of goods and services esp. by consumer purchasing. **3.** *Med.* **a.** A wasting away of body tissue. **b.** Pulmonary tuberculosis. [< Lat. *cōnsūmere, cōnsūmpt-,* consume.]

con·sump·tive (kən-sŭmp′tĭv) ►*adj.* **1.** Wasteful. **2.** Of or afflicted with consumption. ►*n.* A person afflicted with consumption. —**con·sump′tive·ly** *adv.*

cont. ►*abbr.* **1.** contents **2.** continent **3.** continued **4.** contraction

con·tact (kŏn′tăkt′) ►*n.* **1.** A coming together or touching, as of objects or surfaces. **2.** Interaction; communication. **3.** Association; relationship. **4.** A useful person; connection. **5.** A connection between two electric conductors. **6.** A contact lens. ►*v.* (kŏn′tăkt′, kən-tăkt′) **1.** To get in touch with: *contacted my friend by e-mail.* **2.** To come into contact with. [< Lat. *contingere, contāct-,* to touch.]

contact lens ►*n.* A thin corrective lens fitted directly over the cornea.

con·ta·gion (kən-tā′jən) ►*n.* **1a.** Disease transmission by direct or indirect contact. **b.** A disease so transmitted. **2.** The tendency to spread, as of a doctrine, influence, or emotional state. [< Lat. *contāgiō.*]

con·ta·gious (kən-tā′jəs) ►*adj.* **1.** Transmissible by direct or indirect contact; communicable. **2.** Carrying or capable of transmitting disease. **3.** Tending to spread: *a contagious smile.* —**con·ta′gious·ly** *adv.* —**con·ta′gious·ness** *n.*

con·tain (kən-tān′) ►*v.* **1.** To have within; hold. **2.** To have as a constituent part; include. **3.** To hold back; restrain. [< Lat. *continēre.*] —**con·tain′a·ble** *adj.*

con·tain·er (kən-tā′nər) ►*n.* A receptacle.

con·tain·er·ize ►*v.* -**ized, -iz·ing** To package (cargo) in large standardized containers for efficient shipping and handling. —**con·tain′er·i·za′tion** *n.*

con·tain·ment (kən-tān′mənt) ►*n.* **1.** A policy of checking the expansion of a hostile power or ideology. **2.** A system designed to prevent the accidental release of radioactive materials from a reactor.

con·tam·i·nate (kən-tăm′ə-nāt′) ►*v.* -**nated, -nat·ing 1.** To make impure or unclean by contact or mixture. **2.** To permeate with radioactivity. [< Lat. *contāmināre.*] —**con·tam′i·nant** *n.* —**con·tam′i·na′tion** *n.* —**con·tam′i·na′tive** *adj.* —**con·tam′i·na′tor** *n.*
    Syns: foul, poison, pollute, taint **v.**

contd. ►*abbr.* continued

con·temn (kən-tĕm′) ►*v.* To view with contempt. See Synonyms at **despise.** [< Lat. *contemnere.*]

con·tem·plate (kŏn′təm-plāt′) ►*v.* -**plat·ed, -plat·ing 1.** To consider or ponder thoughtfully. **2.** To intend or anticipate. [Lat. *contemplārī.*] —**con′tem·pla′tion** *n.* —**con·tem′pla·tive** (kən-tĕm′plə-tĭv) *adj.* —**con·tem′pla·tive·ly** *adv.* —**con′tem·pla′tor** *n.*

con·tem·po·ra·ne·ous (kən-tĕm′pə-rā′nē-əs) ►*adj.* Existing or happening during the same period of time. [< Lat. *contemporāneus* : COM– + *tempus, tempor-,* time.] —**con·tem′po·ra·ne′i·ty** (-pər-ə-nē′ĭ-tē, -nā′-) *n.* —**con·tem′po·ra′ne·ous·ly** *adv.*

con·tem·po·rar·y (kən-tĕm′pə-rĕr′ē) ►*adj.* **1.** Contemporaneous. **2.** Current; modern. ►*n., pl.* -**ies 1.** One of the same time or age. **2.** A person of the present age. —**con·tem′po·rar′i·ly** (-râr′ə-lē) *adv.*

con·tempt (kən-tĕmpt′) ►*n.* **1.** Disparaging or haughty disdain. **2.** The state of being despised or dishonored. **3.** Open disrespect or willful disobedience of the authority of a court of law. [< Lat. *contemptus,* p.part. of *contemnere,* despise.]

con·tempt·i·ble (kən-tĕmp′tə-bəl) ►*adj.* Deserving of contempt; despicable. —**con·tempt′i·bil′i·ty** *n.* —**con·tempt′i·bly** *adv.*

con·temp·tu·ous (kən-tĕmp′chōō-əs) ►*adj.* Manifesting or feeling contempt; scornful. —**con·temp′tu·ous·ly** *adv.* —**con·temp′tu·ous·ness** *n.*

con·tend (kən-tĕnd′) ►*v.* **1.** To strive in opposition; struggle. **2.** To compete. **3.** To maintain or assert. [< Lat. *contendere.*] —**con·tend′er** *n.*

con·tent¹ (kŏn′tĕnt′) ►*n.* **1.** often **contents** Something contained in a receptacle. **2.** often **contents** The subject matter of a written work. **3a.** The substance of a written work, esp. as contrasted with its form. **b.** Information, such as text, video, and sound. **4.** The proportion of a specified substance. [< Lat. *continēre, content-,* contain.]

con·tent² (kən-tĕnt′) ►*adj.* Satisfied; happy. ►*v.* To make satisfied. ►*n.* Contentment; satisfaction. [< Lat. *contentus,* p.part. of *continēre,* to contain.]

con·tent·ed (kən-tĕn′tĭd) ►*adj.* Satisfied; happy. —**con·tent′ed·ly** *adv.*

con·ten·tion (kən-tĕn′shən) ►*n.* **1.** Controversy; dispute. **2.** Rivalry: *in contention for first place.* [< Lat. *contendere, content-,* contend.]

con·ten·tious (kən-tĕn′shəs) ►*adj.* Quarrelsome. See Synonyms at **argumentative.** —**con·ten′tious·ly** *adv.* —**con·ten′tious·ness** *n.*

con·tent·ment (kən-tĕnt′mənt) ►*n.* The state of being contented.

con·ter·mi·nous (kən-tûr′mə-nəs) also **co·ter·mi·nous** (kō-) ►*adj.* Having a boundary

in common; contiguous. [< Lat. *conterminus.*]
—**con·ter′mi·nous·ly** *adv.*

con·test (kŏn′tĕst′) ►*n.* **1.** A struggle between rivals. **2.** A competition. ►*v.* (kən-tĕst′, kŏn′-tĕst′) **1.** To compete for. **2.** To dispute: *contest a will.* [< Lat. *contestārī,* call to witness.] —**con·test′a·ble** *adj.* —**con·test′er** *n.*

con·tes·tant (kən-tĕs′tənt, kŏn′tĕs′tənt) ►*n.* A competitor, as in a contest or game.

con·text (kŏn′tĕkst′) ►*n.* **1.** The part of a text or statement that surrounds a particular word or passage and determines its meaning. **2.** The circumstances in which an event occurs. [< Lat. *contexere,* join together : COM– + *texere,* weave.] —**con·tex′tu·al** (kən-tĕks′chōō-əl) *adj.* —**con·tex′tu·al·ly** *adv.*

con·tig·u·ous (kən-tĭg′yōō-əs) ►*adj.* **1.** Touching. **2.** Neighboring; adjacent. [< Lat. *contingere, contig-,* touch.] —**con·ti·gu′i·ty** (kŏn′-tĭ-gyōō′ĭ-tē) —**con·tig′u·ous·ly** *adv.* —**con·tig′u·ous·ness** *n.*

con·ti·nence (kŏn′tə-nəns) ►*n.* **1.** Voluntary control over bladder and bowel functions. **2.** Self-restraint, esp. abstinence from sexual intercourse. [< Lat. *continēre,* contain.] —**con′ti·nent** *adj.*

con·ti·nent (kŏn′tə-nənt) ►*n.* **1.** One of the principal land masses of the earth. **2. the Continent** The mainland of Europe. [Lat. *(terra) continēns,* continuous (land).]

con·ti·nen·tal (kŏn′tə-nĕn′tl) ►*adj.* **1.** Of or relating to a continent. **2.** often **Continental** European. **3. Continental** Of the American colonies during the Revolutionary War. ►*n.* **1.** often **Continental** A European. **2. Continental** An American Revolutionary War soldier. —**con′ti·nen′tal·ly** *adv.*

continental divide ►*n.* A watershed that separates continental river systems flowing in opposite directions.

Continental Divide A series of mountain ridges extending from AK to Mexico that forms the watershed of North America.

continental shelf ►*n.* A submerged, relatively shallow border of a continent.

con·tin·gen·cy (kən-tĭn′jən-sē) ►*n., pl.* **-cies** An event that may occur; possibility. —**con·tin′gen·cy** *adj.*

con·tin·gent (kən-tĭn′jənt) ►*adj.* **1.** Liable to occur but not certain; possible. **2.** Conditional. See Synonyms at **dependent.** ►*n.* A representative group. [< Lat. *contingere,* touch.] —**con·tin′gent·ly** *adv.*

contingent worker ►*n.* A temporary or part-time worker.

con·tin·u·al (kən-tĭn′yōō-əl) ►*adj.* **1.** Recurring frequently. **2.** Not interrupted; constant. —**con·tin′u·al·ly** *adv.*

con·tin·u·ance (kən-tĭn′yōō-əns) ►*n.* **1.** The act or fact of continuing. **2.** Duration. **3.** A continuation or sequel. **4.** *Law* Postponement or adjournment to a future date.

con·tin·u·a·tion (kən-tĭn′yōō-ā′shən) ►*n.* **1.** The act of persisting. **2.** An extension. **3.** A resumption after an interruption.

con·tin·ue (kən-tĭn′yōō) ►*v.* **-ued, -u·ing** **1.** To persist. **2.** To endure; last. **3.** To remain in a state, capacity, or place. **4.** To go on after an interruption; resume. **5.** To extend. **6.** To retain. **7.** *Law* To postpone or adjourn. [< Lat. *continuāre.*] —**con·tin′u·er** *n.*

con·ti·nu·i·ty (kŏn′tə-nōō′ĭ-tē, -nyōō′-) ►*n., pl.* **-ties** **1.** The state of being continuous. **2.** An uninterrupted succession.

con·tin·u·ous (kən-tĭn′yōō-əs) ►*adj.* Uninterrupted in time, sequence, substance, or extent. —**con·tin′u·ous·ly** *adv.* —**con·tin′u·ous·ness** *n.*

con·tin·u·um (kən-tĭn′yōō-əm) ►*n., pl.* **-tin·u·a** (-tĭn′yōō-ə) or **-tin·u·ums** A continuous extent or whole, no part of which can be distinguished from neighboring parts except by arbitrary division. [< Lat. *continuus,* continuous.]

con·tort (kən-tôrt′) ►*v.* **1.** To twist or wrench out of shape. **2.** To cause to deviate from what is normal, proper, or accurate. [Lat. *contorquēre, contort-,* twist together.] —**con·tor′tion** *n.* —**con·tor′tive** *adj.*

con·tor·tion·ist (kən-tôr′shə-nĭst) ►*n.* An acrobat capable of twisting into extraordinary positions. —**con·tor′tion·is′tic** *adj.*

con·tour (kŏn′tŏŏr′) ►*n.* The outline of a figure or body. See Synonyms at **outline.** ►*v.* To make or shape the outline of. ►*adj.* Following the outline or form of something. [< Ital. *contornare,* draw in outline.]

contour map ►*n.* A map showing elevations and topography by means of spaced lines.

contra– ►*pref.* Against; opposite; contrasting: *contraindicate.* [< Lat. *contrā,* against.]

con·tra·band (kŏn′trə-bănd′) ►*n.* **1a.** Goods prohibited in trade. **b.** Banned goods, as in a prison or school. **2a.** Smuggling. **b.** Smuggled goods. [Ital. *contrabbando* : CONTRA– + *bando,* proclamation.] —**con′tra·band′ist** *n.*

con·tra·bass (kŏn′trə-bās′) ►*n.* See **double bass.** [Ital. *contrabbasso* : *contra-,* against (< Lat. *contrā,* CONTRA–) + *basso,* bass (< LLat. *bassus,* low).]

con·tra·cep·tion (kŏn′trə-sĕp′shən) ►*n.* Prevention of conception, as by use of a device, drug, or chemical agent. —**con′tra·cep′tive** *adj. & n.*

con·tract (kŏn′trăkt′) ►*n.* An enforceable agreement between parties. ►*v.* (kən-trăkt′, kŏn′-trăkt′) **1.** To enter into or establish by contract. **2.** To catch (a disease). **3.** To shrink by drawing together. **4.** To shorten (a word or words) by omitting some of the letters or sounds. [< Lat. *contrahere, contract-,* draw together.] —**con·tract′i·bil′i·ty** *n.* —**con·tract′i·ble** *adj.* —**con·trac′tion** *n.*

con·trac·tile (kən-trăk′təl, -tīl′) ►*adj.* Capable of contracting, as muscle tissue.

con·trac·tor (kŏn′trăk′tər) ►*n.* One that agrees to perform services at a specified price, esp. for construction work.

con·trac·tu·al (kən-trăk′chōō-əl) ►*adj.* Of or like a contract. —**con·trac′tu·al·ly** *adv.*

con·tra·dict (kŏn′trə-dĭkt′) ►*v.* **1.** To assert to be untrue, esp. by saying the opposite. See Synonyms at **deny.** **2.** To assert the opposite of a statement or idea put forward by (someone). **3.** To be contrary to or inconsistent with. [Lat. *contrādīcere,* speak against.] —**con′tra·dict′a·ble** *adj.* —**con′tra·dict′er, con′tra·dic′tor** *n.* —**con′tra·dic′tion** *n.* —**con′tra·dic′to·ry** *adj.*

con·tra·dis·tinc·tion (kŏn′trə-dĭ-stĭngk′-shən) ►*n.* Distinction by contrasting qualities. —**con′tra·dis·tinc′tive** *adj.* —**con′tra·dis·tinc′tive·ly** *adv.*

con·trail (kŏn′trāl′) ►*n.* A visible trail of condensed water vapor or ice crystals formed in the wake of an aircraft at high altitudes. [*con(densation) trail.*]

con·tra·in·di·cate (kŏn′trə-ĭn′dĭ-kāt′) ►*v.* To indicate the inadvisability of. —**con′tra·in′di·ca′tion** *n.* —**con′tra·in·dic′a·tive** (-ĭn-dĭk′-ə-tĭv) *adj.*

con·tral·to (kən-trăl′tō) ►*n., pl.* -**tos 1.** The lowest female voice or voice part. **2.** A woman having a contralto voice. [Ital.]

con·trap·tion (kən-trăp′shən) ►*n.* A mechanical device; gadget. [Perh. blend of CONTRIVE and TRAP.]

con·tra·pun·tal (kŏn′trə-pŭn′tl) ►*adj. Mus.* Of or using counterpoint. [< Obsolete Ital. *contrapunto,* counterpoint.] —**con′tra·pun′tal·ly** *adv.*

con·trar·i·an (kən-trâr′ē-ən) ►*n.* One who takes a contrary view or action, esp. an investor whose decisions contradict prevailing wisdom.

con·trar·i·wise (kŏn′trĕr′ē-wīz′, kən-trâr′-) ►*adv.* **1.** From a contrasting point of view. **2.** In the opposite way.

con·trar·y (kŏn′trĕr′ē) ►*adj.* **1.** Opposed; counter: *contrary opinions.* **2.** Opposite, as in character or direction. **3.** Adverse; unfavorable. **4.** (*also* kən-trâr′ē) Willful or perverse. ►*n.; pl.* -**ies** Something that is opposite or contrary. ►*adv.* Contrariwise; counter. [< Lat. *contrārius* < *contrā,* against.] —**con′trar′i·ly** (kŏn′trĕr′ə-lē, kən-trâr′-) *adv.* —**con′tra·ri′e·ty** (-trə-rī′ĭ-tē) *n.* —**con′trar′i·ness** *n.*

con·trast (kən-trăst′, kŏn′trăst′) ►*v.* **1.** To set in opposition in order to show differences. **2.** To show differences when compared. ►*n.* (kŏn′trăst′) **1.** The act of contrasting or the state of being contrasted. **2.** A difference between things compared. **3.** One thing that is strikingly different from another. **4.** The use of opposing elements for effect in a work of art. **5.** The difference in brightness between the light and dark areas of an image. [< Med.Lat. *contrāstāre* : CONTRA- + Lat. *stāre,* stand.] —**con·trast′a·ble** *adj.* —**con·trast′ing·ly** *adv.*

con·tra·vene (kŏn′trə-vēn′) ►*v.* -**vened, -vening 1.** To act or be in violation of; violate: *contravened a direct order.* **2.** To be inconsistent with; be contrary to. [< LLat. *contrāvenīre,* oppose : CONTRA- + Lat. *venīre,* come.] —**con′tra·ven′tion** (-vĕn′shən) *n.*

con·tre·temps (kŏn′trə-tän′, kôN′trə-tän′) ►*n., pl.* -**temps** (-tänz′, -tänz′) **1.** An inopportune or embarrassing occurrence. **2.** An argument; dispute. [Fr.]

con·trib·ute (kən-trĭb′yo͞ot) ►*v.* -**ut·ed, -ut·ing 1.** To give or supply a share (to); participate (in). **2.** To help bring about a result. [Lat. *contribuere,* bring together.] —**con′tri·bu′tion** (kŏn′trĭ-byo͞o′shən) *n.* —**con·trib′u·tive** *adj.* —**con·trib′u·tor** *n.* —**con·trib′u·to′ry** (-tôr′ē) *adj.*

con·trite (kən-trīt′, kŏn′trīt′) ►*adj.* Repentant; penitent. [< Lat. *contrītus,* p.part. of *conterere,* grind up.] —**con·trite′ly** *adv.*

con·tri·tion (kən-trĭsh′ən) ►*n.* Remorse for wrongdoing. See Synonyms at **penitence.**

con·triv·ance (kən-trī′vəns) ►*n.* **1.** A clever plan; scheme. **2.** A mechanical device.

con·trive (kən-trīv′) ►*v.* -**trived, -triv·ing 1.** To plan with ingenuity; devise. **2.** To invent or

fabricate. **3.** To bring about or manage. [< Med. Lat. *contropāre,* compare.] —**con·triv′er** *n.*

con·trived (kən-trīvd′) ►*adj.* Not spontaneous; labored: *a contrived plot.* —**con·triv′ed·ly** (-trī′vĭd-lē, -trīvd′lē) *adv.*

con·trol (kən-trōl′) ►*v.* -**trolled, -trol·ling 1.** To exercise authority or influence over; direct. **2.** To hold in restraint; check. **3.** To verify or regulate by systematic comparison. ►*n.* **1.** Power to manage, direct, or dominate. **2.** often **controls** A set of instruments used to operate a machine. **3.** A restraint; curb. **4.** A standard of comparison for verifying experimental results. [< Med.Lat. *contrārotulāre,* to check by duplicate register < Lat. *rotulus,* roll.] —**con·trol′la·bil′i·ty** *n.* —**con·trol′la·ble** *adj.*

control key ►*n.* A key on a computer keyboard pressed in combination with other keys to activate a command.

con·trolled substance (kən-trōld′) ►*n.* A drug or chemical substance whose possession and use are prohibited or regulated by law.

con·trol·ler (kən-trō′lər) ►*n.* **1.** One that controls, esp. a regulating mechanism in a vehicle or machine. **2.** *also* **comp·trol·ler** (kŏmp-trō′-lər, kŏmp′trō′-, kən-trō′-) An executive or official who supervises financial affairs.

control stick ►*n.* A lever used to control the motion of an aircraft by changing the angle of the elevators and ailerons.

control tower ►*n.* An observation tower at an airfield from which air traffic is controlled by radio.

con·tro·ver·sy (kŏn′trə-vûr′sē) ►*n., pl.* -**sies** A dispute, esp. a public one, between sides holding opposing views. [< Lat. *contrōversus,* disputed.] —**con′tro·ver′sial** (-shəl, -sē-əl) *adj.* —**con′tro·ver′sial·ly** *adv.*

con·tro·vert (kŏn′trə-vûrt′, kŏn′trə-vûrt′) ►*v.* To argue against; contradict. —**con′tro·vert′i·ble** *adj.*

con·tu·ma·cious (kŏn′tə-mā′shəs, -tyə-) ►*adj.* Obstinately disobedient or rebellious; insubordinate. [< Lat. *contumāx,* insolent.] —**con′tu·ma′cious·ly** *adv.*

con·tu·me·ly (kŏn′to͞o-mə-lē, -tyo͞o-, -təm-lē) ►*n., pl.* -**lies** Insulting treatment; insolence. [< Lat. *contumēlia.*]

con·tuse (kən-to͞oz′, -tyo͞oz′) ►*v.* -**tused, -tus·ing** To injure without breaking the skin; bruise. [< Lat. *contundere, contūs-,* beat up.] —**con·tu′sion** *n.*

co·nun·drum (kə-nŭn′drəm) ►*n.* **1.** A riddle. **2.** A dilemma. [?]

con·ur·ba·tion (kŏn′ər-bā′shən) ►*n.* A predominantly urban region including adjacent towns. [CON- + Lat. *urbs,* city + -ATION.]

con·va·lesce (kŏn′və-lĕs′) ►*v.* -**lesced, -lesc·ing** To recuperate from an illness or injury. [Lat. *convalēscere* < *valēre,* be strong.] —**con′va·les′cence** *n.* —**con′va·les′cent** *adj. & n.*

con·vect (kən-vĕkt′) ►*v.* To transfer by or undergo convection. [< CONVECTION.]

con·vec·tion (kən-vĕk′shən) ►*n.* Heat transfer in a gas or liquid by the circulation of currents from one region to another. [< LLat. *convehere, convect-,* carry together.] —**con·vec′tion·al** *adj.* —**con·vec′tive** *adj.*

convection oven ►*n.* An oven that shortens cooking time by circulating hot air uniformly around the food.

con·vene (kən-vēn′) ►v. -vened, -ven·ing To assemble or cause to assemble formally. See Synonyms at **call**. [< Lat. *convenīre* : COM– + *venīre*, come.] —**con·ven′a·ble** *adj.* —**con·ven′er** *n.*

con·ven·ience (kən-vēn′yəns) ►n. 1. Suitability to one's purposes. 2. Personal comfort or advantage. 3. Something that increases comfort or saves work. See Synonyms at **amenity**.

con·ven·ient (kən-vēn′yənt) ►adj. 1. Suited to one's comfort or needs. 2. Easy to reach; accessible. [< Lat. *convenīre*, be suitable.] —**con·ven′ient·ly** *adv.*

con·vent (kŏn′vənt, -vĕnt′) ►n. A monastic community or house, esp. of nuns. [< Lat. *convenīre*, assemble; see CONVENE.] —**con·ven′tu·al** (kən-vĕn′chōō-əl) *adj.*

con·ven·ti·cle (kən-vĕn′tĭ-kəl) ►n. A religious meeting, esp. a secret one. [< Lat. *conventiculum*, dim. of *conventus*, assembly; see CONVENT.]

con·ven·tion (kən-vĕn′shən) ►n. 1a. A formal meeting or assembly, as of a political party. b. The delegates attending such an assembly. 2. An international agreement or compact. 3. General usage or custom. 4. An accepted or prescribed practice. [< Lat. *convenīre*, *convent-*, CONVENE.]

con·ven·tion·al (kən-vĕn′shə-nəl) ►adj. 1. Following accepted practice; customary. 2. Unimaginative or commonplace; ordinary. 3. Using means other than nuclear weapons or energy. —**con·ven′tion·al′i·ty** *n.* —**con·ven′tion·al·ly** *adv.*

con·ven·tion·al·ize (kən-vĕn′shə-nə-līz′) ►v. -ized, -iz·ing To make conventional. —**con·ven′tion·al·i·za′tion** *n.*

con·verge (kən-vûrj′) ►v. -verged, -verg·ing To tend or move toward a common point or result. [LLat. *convergere*, incline together.] —**con·ver′gence** *n.* —**con·ver′gent** *adj.*

con·ver·sant (kən-vûr′sənt, kŏn′vər-) ►adj. Familiar, as by study or experience. —**con·ver′sant·ly** *adv.*

con·ver·sa·tion (kŏn′vər-sā′shən) ►n. The exchange of thoughts and feelings by means of speech or sign language. —**con′ver·sa′tion·al** *adj.* —**con′ver·sa′tion·al·ly** *adv.*

con·ver·sa·tion·al·ist (kŏn′vər-sā′shə-nə-lĭst) ►n. One given to conversation.

conversation piece ►n. An unusual object that arouses comment or interest.

con·verse[1] (kən-vûrs′) ►v. -versed, -vers·ing To engage in conversation. ►n. (kŏn′vûrs′) Conversation. [< Lat. *conversārī*, associate with.]

con·verse[2] (kən-vûrs′, kŏn′vûrs′) ►adj. Reversed in position, order, or action. ►n. (kŏn′vûrs′) The reverse or opposite of something. [Lat. *conversus*, p.part. of *convertere*, turn around.] —**con·verse′ly** *adv.*

con·ver·sion (kən-vûr′zhən, -shən) ►n. 1. The act of converting or the state of being converted. 2. A change in which one adopts a new religion or belief. 3. *Law* The unlawful appropriation of another's property. 4. *Football* A score made on a try for a point or points after a touchdown. 5. The expression of a quantity in alternative units, as of length or weight.

con·vert (kən-vûrt′) ►v. 1. To change into another form, substance, or state: *convert water into ice.* 2. To adapt to a new or different purpose: *convert a forest into farmland.* 3. To persuade or be persuaded to adopt a particular religion or belief. 4. To exchange for something of equal value. 5. To express in alternative units: *convert feet into meters.* 6. *Law* To appropriate (another's property) without right to one's own use. 7. *Football* To make a conversion. ►n. (kŏn′vûrt′) One who has been converted, as to a religion. [< Lat. *convertere*, turn around.] —**con·vert′er, con·ver′tor** *n.*

Syns: metamorphose, transfigure, transform, transmogrify, transmute v.

con·vert·i·ble (kən-vûr′tə-bəl) ►adj. Capable of being converted. ►n. 1. Something that can be converted. 2. An automobile with a top that can be folded back or removed.

con·vex (kŏn′vĕks′, kən-vĕks′) ►adj. Curved outward, as the exterior of a sphere. [Lat. *convexus.*] —**con·vex′i·ty** *n.* —**con′vex′ly** *adv.*

con·vey (kən-vā′) ►v. 1. To carry; transport. 2. To transmit. 3. To communicate; impart. 4. *Law* To transfer ownership of or title to. [< Med.Lat. *conviāre*, to escort.] —**con·vey′a·ble** *adj.* —**con·vey′or, con·vey′er** *n.*

con·vey·ance (kən-vā′əns) ►n. 1. The act of conveying. 2. A vehicle. 3. A document effecting the transfer of title to property.

conveyor belt ►n. A continuous moving belt used to transport materials or objects.

con·vict (kən-vĭkt′) ►v. *Law* To find or prove guilty of an offense or crime. ►n. (kŏn′vĭkt′) A person found guilty of a crime, esp. one serving a prison sentence. [< Lat. *convincere*, *convict-*, prove wrong.]

con·vic·tion (kən-vĭk′shən) ►n. 1. *Law* The act of convicting or the state of being convicted. 2. A strong opinion or belief.

con·vince (kən-vĭns′) ►v. -vinced, -vinc·ing To bring to belief by argument or evidence; persuade. [Lat. *convincere*, prove wrong.] —**con·vinc′ing** *adj.* —**con·vinc′ing·ly** *adv.*

con·viv·i·al (kən-vĭv′ē-əl) ►adj. 1. Enjoying good company. See Synonyms at **social**. 2. Merry; festive. [< Lat. *convīvium*, banquet : COM– + *vīvere*, live.] —**con·viv′i·al′i·ty** (-ăl′ĭ-tē) *n.* —**con·viv′i·al·ly** *adv.*

con·vo·ca·tion (kŏn′və-kā′shən) ►n. 1. The act of convoking. 2. A formal assembly.

con·voke (kən-vōk′) ►v. -voked, -vok·ing To cause to assemble; convene. See Synonyms at **call**. [< Lat. *convocāre*, call together.]

con·vo·lut·ed (kŏn′və-lōō′tĭd) ►adj. 1. Having numerous overlapping coils or folds. 2. Intricate; complex. [< Lat. *convolūtus*, p.part. of *convolvere*, roll together.]

con·vo·lu·tion (kŏn′və-lōō′shən) ►n. 1. A form or part that is folded or coiled. 2. One of the convex folds of the surface of the brain.

con·voy (kŏn′voi′) ►n. 1. An accompanying and protecting force, as of ships. 2. A group traveling together for safety. ►v. (kŏn′voi′, kən-voi′) To accompany, esp. for protection. [< OFr. *convoier*, CONVEY.]

con·vulse (kən-vŭls′) ►v. -vulsed, -vuls·ing 1. To disturb violently. See Synonyms at **agitate**. 2. To throw into convulsions. [Lat. *convellere*, *convuls-*, pull violently.] —**con·vul′sive** *adj.* —**con·vul′sive·ly** *adv.*

con·vul·sion (kən-vŭl′shən) ►n. 1. An intense, paroxysmal, involuntary muscular contraction.

2. An uncontrolled fit, as of laughter; paroxysm. **3.** Violent turmoil.

co·ny (kō′nē, kŭn′ē) ►*n.* Var. of **coney.**

coo (ko͞o) ►*v.* **1.** To utter the murmuring sound of a dove or pigeon. **2.** To talk in fond or amorous murmurs. [Imit.] —**coo** *n.*

cook (ko͝ok) ►*v.* **1.** To prepare (food) for eating by applying heat. **2.** To prepare or treat by heating. **3.** *Slang* To alter or falsify; doctor. ►*n.* One who prepares food for eating. —*phrasal verb:* **cook up** *Informal* To concoct: *cook up an excuse.* [< Lat. *coquere.*]

Cook, Mount The highest mountain, 3,754 m (12,316 ft), of New Zealand, on South I. in the Southern Alps.

cook·book (ko͝ok′bo͝ok′) ►*n.* A book with recipes and advice about food preparation.

cook·er·y (ko͝ok′ə-rē) ►*n., pl.* **-ies** The art or practice of preparing food.

cook·ie also **cook·y** (ko͝ok′ē) ►*n., pl.* **-ies 1.** A small cake, usu. flat and crisp, made from sweetened dough. **2.** Information stored on a Web user's computer, used by websites to identify previous visitors to that site. [Du. *koekje,* dim. of *koek,* cake.]

Cook Islands An island group of the S Pacific E of Samoa.

cook·out (ko͝ok′out′) ►*n.* A meal cooked and served outdoors.

Cook Strait A narrow channel separating North I. and South I. in New Zealand.

cook·top (ko͝ok′tŏp′) ►*n.* A flat cooking surface, as on a stove, usu. consisting of glass-covered electric heating elements.

cool (ko͞ol) ►*adj.* **-er, -est 1.** Moderately cold. See Synonyms at **cold. 2.** Giving or suggesting relief from heat. **3.** Marked by calm self-control. **4.** Marked by indifference, disdain, or dislike. **5.** *Slang* **a.** Reflecting the latest trends or fashions. **b.** Excellent; first-rate. ►*v.* **1.** To make or become less warm. **2.** To make or become less intense or ardent. ►*n.* **1.** A cool place, part, or time. **2.** *Slang* Composure; poise. —*idiom:* **cool it** *Slang* To calm down; relax. [< OE *cōl.*] —**cool′ly** *adv.* —**cool′ness** *n.*

cool·ant (ko͞o′lənt) ►*n.* Something that cools, esp. a fluid that draws off heat by circulating through an engine or by bathing a part.

cool·er (ko͞o′lər) ►*n.* **1.** A device or container that cools or keeps something cool. **2.** A tall cold drink. **3.** *Slang* A jail.

Calvin Coolidge

Coo·lidge (ko͞o′lĭj), **(John) Calvin** 1872–1933. The 30th US president (1923–29).

coon (ko͞on) ►*n. Informal* A raccoon. [Short for RACCOON.]

coon·skin (ko͞on′skĭn′) ►*n.* **1.** The pelt of a raccoon. **2.** An article made of coonskin.

coop (ko͞op) ►*n.* A cage, esp. one for poultry. ►*v.* To confine in or as if in a coop. [ME *coupe.*]

co-op (kō′ŏp′, kō-ŏp′) ►*n.* A cooperative.

coop·er (ko͞o′pər) ►*n.* One who makes wooden barrels and tubs. [< MDu. *kuper* < *kupe,* basket, tub.] —**coop′er·age** *n.*

Cooper, James Fenimore 1789–1851. Amer. novelist.

co·op·er·ate (kō-ŏp′ə-rāt′) ►*v.* **-at·ed, -at·ing** To work together for a common end. [LLat. *cooperārī,* work together.] —**co·op′er·a′tion** *n.* —**co·op′er·a′tor** *n.*

co·op·er·a·tive (kō-ŏp′ər-ə-tĭv, -ə-rā′tĭv, -ŏp′rə-rā′tĭv) ►*adj.* **1.** Willing to cooperate. **2.** Engaged in joint economic activity. ►*n.* **1.** An enterprise owned and operated by those who use its services. **2a.** A building in which residents buy shares of stock in a building corporation and are given a lease to a specific apartment. **b.** An apartment in such a building. —**co·op′er·a·tive·ly** *adv.* —**co·op′er·a·tive·ness** *n.*

co-opt (kō-ŏpt′, kō′ŏpt′) ►*v.* **1.** To elect or appoint as a fellow member or colleague. **2.** To appropriate. **3.** To take over through assimilation into an established group or culture. [Lat. *cooptāre.*] —**co′-op·ta′tion** *n.*

co·or·di·nate (kō-ôr′dn-āt′, -ĭt) ►*n.* **1.** One that is equal in rank or degree. **2.** *Math.* Any of a set of numbers that determines the position of a point in a space of a given dimension. ►*adj.* (-ĭt, -āt′) **1.** Of equal rank or degree. **2.** Of or involving coordination. **3.** Of or based on coordinates. ►*v.* (-āt′) **-nat·ed, -nat·ing 1.** To place in the same order, class, or rank. **2.** To harmonize in a common action or effort. **3.** To be coordinate. [CO– + ORDINATE.] —**co·or′di·nate·ly** (-ĭt-lē) *adv.* —**co·or′di·na′tive** *adj.* —**co·or′di·na′tor** *n.*

co·or·di·nat·ed universal time (kō-ôr′dn-ā′tĭd) ►*n.* An international time standard that is calculated by atomic clock and that serves as the basis for standard time around the world.

co·or·di·na·tion (kō-ôr′dn-ā′shən) ►*n.* **1.** The act of coordinating or the state of being coordinated. **2.** Harmonious functioning of muscles in the execution of movements. [< CO– + Lat. *ōrdinātus,* put in order.]

coot (ko͞ot) ►*n.* A gray waterbird with a black head and white bill. [ME *coote.*]

coo·tie (ko͞o′tē) ►*n. Slang* A body louse. [Poss. < Malay *kutu.*]

cop¹ (kŏp) *Slang* ►*n.* A police officer. [Short for *copper* < COP².]

cop² (kŏp) *Slang* ►*v.* **copped, cop·ping 1.** To get hold of. **2.** To steal. —*phrasal verb:* **cop out** To avoid fulfilling a commitment or responsibility. —*idioms:* **cop a feel** To fondle someone in a surreptitious way. **cop a plea** To plead guilty to a lesser charge to avoid a more serious charge. [Prob. var. of earlier *cap,* perh. < Lat. *capere,* catch.]

co·pa·cet·ic or **co·pa·set·ic** (kō′pə-sĕt′ĭk) ►*adj.* Very satisfactory or acceptable. [?]

co·pay·ment (kō′pā′mənt) ►*n.* A specified sum of money that patients covered by a health care plan pay for a given type of service.

COPD ►*abbr.* chronic obstructive pulmonary disease

cope[1] (kōp) ►*v.* **coped, cop·ing** To contend with difficulties, esp. successfully. [< OFr. *couper*, strike < LLat. *colpus*, a blow < Gk. *kolaphos*.]

cope[2] (kōp) ►*n.* **1.** A long ecclesiastical capelike vestment. **2.** A coping. [< LLat. *cappa*, cloak.]

Co·pen·ha·gen (kō′pən-hā′gən, -hä′-) The capital of Denmark, in the E part.

co·per·ni·ci·um (kō′pər-nē′sē-əm, -shē-) ►*n.* Symbol **Cn** A synthetic radioactive element. At. no. 112. See table at **element.** [After Nicolaus COPERNICUS.]

Co·per·ni·cus (kō-pûr′nə-kəs, kə-), **Nicolaus** 1473–1543. Polish astronomer.

Nicolaus Copernicus

cop·i·er (kŏp′ē-ər) ►*n.* One that copies, esp. an office machine that makes copies.

co·pi·lot (kō′pī′lət) ►*n.* The second or relief pilot of an aircraft.

cop·ing (kō′pĭng) ►*n.* The top layer of a wall, usu. slanted to shed water. [< COPE[2].]

co·pi·ous (kō′pē-əs) ►*adj.* **1.** Yielding or containing plenty; ample. See Synonyms at **plentiful.** **2.** Large in quantity; abundant: *copious rainfall.* [< Lat. *cōpia*, abundance.] —**co′pi·ous·ly** *adv.* —**co′pi·ous·ness** *n.*

Cop·land (kōp′lənd), **Aaron** 1900–90. Amer. composer.

Cop·ley (kŏp′lē), **John Singleton** 1738–1815. Amer. painter.

cop-out (kŏp′out′) ►*n.* Slang A failure to fulfill a commitment or responsibility.

cop·per (kŏp′ər) ►*n.* **1.** Symbol **Cu** A ductile, malleable, reddish-brown metallic element that is an excellent conductor of heat and electricity and is used for electrical wiring, water piping, and corrosion-resistant parts. At. no. 29. See table at **element.** **2.** A copper object or coin. **3.** A reddish brown. [< Lat. *Cyprium (aes)*, (metal) of Cyprus.] —**cop′per·y** *adj.*

cop·per·head (kŏp′ər-hĕd′) ►*n.* A venomous reddish-brown snake of the E US.

co·pra (kō′prə, kŏp′rə) ►*n.* Dried coconut meat from which coconut oil is extracted. [< Malayalam *koppara*.]

copse (kŏps) ►*n.* A thicket of small trees. [< OFr. *copeiz < couper*, cut; see COPE[1].]

Copt (kŏpt) ►*n.* **1.** A member or descendant of the people of pre-Islamic Egypt. **2.** A member of the Christian church of Egypt. —**Cop′tic** *adj.*

cop·ter (kŏp′tər) ►*n.* Informal A helicopter.

cop·u·la (kŏp′yə-lə) ►*n.* A verb, such as a form of *be* or *seem*, that identifies the predicate of a sentence with the subject. [Lat. *cōpula*, link.] —**cop′u·lar** *adj.* —**cop′u·la′tive** *adj. & n.* —**cop′u·la′tive·ly** *adv.*

cop·u·late (kŏp′yə-lāt′) ►*v.* **-lat·ed, -lat·ing** To engage in sexual intercourse. [< Lat. *cōpula*, link.] —**cop′u·la′tion** *n.* —**cop′u·la·to′ry** (-lə-tôr′ē) *adj.*

cop·y (kŏp′ē) ►*n., pl.* **-ies 1a.** An imitation or reproduction of an original; duplicate. **b.** *Comp.* A file that has the same data as another file. **2.** One specimen of a printed text or picture. **3.** Material, such as a manuscript, that is to be set in type. **4.** Suitable source material for journalism. ►*v.* **-ied, -y·ing 1.** To make a copy or copies (of). **2.** To follow as a model or pattern; imitate. **3.** To include as an additional recipient of a written communication. **4.** To hear clearly over radio communication. [< Lat. *cōpia*, profusion.] —**cop′y·a·ble** *adj.*

cop·y·book (kŏp′ē-bo͝ok′) ►*n.* A book of models of penmanship for imitation.

cop·y·cat (kŏp′ē-kăt′) ►*n.* Informal An imitator. —**cop′y·cat′** *adj.*

copy desk ►*n.* The desk in a news office where copy is edited and prepared for typesetting.

cop·y·ed·it or **cop·y-ed·it** (kŏp′ē-ĕd′ĭt) ►*v.* To correct and prepare (a manuscript) for typesetting. —**cop′y·ed′i·tor** *n.*

copy protection ►*n.* Prevention of unauthorized copying of copyrighted material on electronic media, usu. by making it impossible to access the content of any of the copies. —**cop′y-pro·tect′ed** *adj.*

cop·y·right (kŏp′ē-rīt′) ►*n.* The legal right to exclusive publication, production, sale, or distribution of a literary or artistic work. ►*adj.* also **cop·y·right·ed** (-rī′tĭd) Protected by copyright. ►*v.* To secure a copyright for.

cop·y·writ·er (kŏp′ē-rī′tər) ►*n.* One who writes copy, esp. for advertising.

co·quette (kō-kĕt′) ►*n.* A flirtatious woman. [Fr. < OFr. *coc*, cock.] —**co·quet′tish** *adj.* —**co·quet′tish·ness** *n.*

cor·a·cle (kôr′ə-kəl, kŏr′-) ►*n.* A boat made of waterproof material stretched over a wicker or wooden frame. [Welsh *corwgl*.]

cor·al (kôr′əl, kŏr′-) ►*n.* **1a.** Any of a class of marine polyps that secrete a rocklike skeleton. **b.** Such skeletons collectively, often forming reefs or islands in warm seas. **c.** The secretions of certain corals used in jewelry. **2.** A strong pink to red or reddish orange. [< Gk. *korallion*.] —**cor′al** *adj.*

Coral Sea An arm of the SW Pacific bounded by Vanuatu, NE Australia, and SE New Guinea.

coral snake ►*n.* A venomous snake characteristically having red, yellow, and black banded markings.

cor·bel (kôr′bəl, -bĕl′) ►*n.* A usu. stone bracket projecting from the face of a wall and used to support a cornice or arch. [< OFr., dim. of *corp*, raven < Lat. *corvus*.] —**cor′bel** *v.*

cord (kôrd) ►*n.* **1.** A string of twisted strands or fibers. **2.** An insulated, flexible electric wire fitted with a plug. **3.** also **chord** *Anat.* A long ropelike structure: *a spinal cord.* **4a.** A raised rib on the surface of cloth. **b.** A fabric with such ribs. **5.** A unit of quantity for cut fuel wood, equal to a stack measuring 4 × 4 × 8 ft = 128 cu ft (3.62 cu m). ►*v.* **1.** To fasten or bind with a cord. **2.** To pile (wood) in cords. [< Gk. *khordē*.] —**cord′er** *n.*

cord·age (kôr′dĭj) ►*n.* Cords or ropes, esp. the ropes in the rigging of a ship.

cor·dial (kôr′jəl) ►*adj.* **1.** Warm and sincere; friendly. **2.** Polite and respectful. ►*n.* **1.** A liqueur. **2.** A stimulant; tonic. [< Lat. *cor, cord-,* heart.] —**cor·dial′i·ty** (-jăl′ĭ-tē, -jē-ăl′-) *n.* —**cor′dial·ly** *adv.*

cor·dil·le·ra (kôr′dl-yâr′ə, kôr-dĭl′ər-ə) ►*n.* A mountain chain. [Sp. < *cuerda*, CORD.] —**cor′dil·le′ran** (-yâr′ən) *adj.*

cord·ite (kôr′dīt′) ►*n.* A smokeless explosive powder consisting chiefly of nitrocellulose, nitroglycerin, and petrolatum.

cord·less (kôrd′lĭs) ►*adj.* Having no cord; battery operated: *a cordless drill.*

cor·do·ba (kôr′də-bə, -və) ►*n.* See table at **currency.** [After Francisco Fernández de *Córdoba* (1475?–1526).]

Cór·do·ba (kôr′də-bə, -thō-vä) A city of S Spain ENE of Seville. —**Cor′do·van** (-vən) *adj. & n.*

cor·don (kôr′dn) ►*n.* **1.** A line of people, military posts, or ships stationed around an area to enclose or guard it. **2.** A border stretched around an area to indicate that access is restricted. **3.** A ribbon worn as an ornament, badge of honor, or decoration. ►*v.* To form a cordon around: *Troops cordoned off the riot zone.* [< OFr. < *corde*, CORD.]

cor·do·van (kôr′də-vən) ►*n.* A soft fine-grained leather. [After *Córdova* (Córdoba), Spain.]

cor·du·roy (kôr′də-roi′) ►*n.* **1.** A durable ribbed fabric, usu. made of cotton. **2. corduroys** Corduroy trousers. [Prob. CORD + obsolete *duroy*, coarse woolen fabric.]

core (kôr) ►*n.* **1.** The central or innermost part. **2.** The hard or fibrous central part of certain fruits, such as the apple, containing the seeds. **3.** The most important part. See Synonyms at **substance. 4.** The part of a nuclear reactor where fission occurs. ►*v.* **cored, cor·ing** To remove the core of. [ME.]

co·re·lig·ion·ist (kō′rĭ-lĭj′ə-nĭst) ►*n.* One having the same religion as another.

co·re·spon·dent (kō′rĭ-spŏn′dənt) ►*n.* A person charged as an adulterer with the defendant in a divorce suit.

co·ri·an·der (kôr′ē-ăn′dər) ►*n.* **1.** An aromatic Eurasian herb having seedlike fruit used as a seasoning. **2.** See **cilantro.** [< Gk. *koriandron*.]

Cor·inth (kôr′ĭnth, kŏr′-) A city of ancient Greece in the NE Peloponnesus on the Gulf of Corinth.

Corinth, Gulf of An inlet of the Ionian Sea between the Peloponnesus and central Greece.

Corinth, Isthmus of A narrow isthmus connecting central Greece with the Peloponnesus.

Co·rin·thi·an (kə-rĭn′thē-ən) ►*adj.* Of or relating to ancient Corinth. ►*n.* **1.** A native or inhabitant of Corinth. **2. Corinthians** (*takes sing. v.*) See table at **Bible.**

Corinthian order ►*n. Archit.* A classical order marked by slender fluted columns with ornate capitals.

cork (kôrk) ►*n.* **1.** The lightweight, porous, outer bark of a Mediterranean tree, used for stoppers, insulation, and floats. **2.** Something made of cork, esp. a bottle stopper. **3.** *Bot.* The outermost layer of bark in woody plants.

[< Sp. *alcorque*, cork-soled shoe.] —**cork** *v.* —**cork′y** *adj.*

Cork A city of S Ireland near the head of **Cork Harbor,** an inlet of the Atlantic.

cork·er (kôr′kər) ►*n. Slang* One that is remarkable or astounding.

cork·screw (kôrk′skrōō′) ►*n.* A device for drawing corks from bottles. ►*adj.* Spiral in shape: *a corkscrew turn.*

corm (kôrm) ►*n.* A rounded food-storing underground stem similar to a bulb. [< Gk. *kormos*, a trimmed tree trunk.]

cor·mo·rant (kôr′mər-ənt, kôr′mə-rănt′) ►*n.* A diving bird having dark plumage, webbed feet, and a hooked bill. [< OFr. : *corp*, raven; see CORBEL + *marenc, marine (< Lat. *mare*, sea).]

corn[1] (kôrn) ►*n.* **1a.** A tall, widely cultivated cereal plant bearing grains or kernels on large ears. **b.** The edible grains or kernels of this plant. **2.** A single grain of various cereal plants. **3.** *Slang* Something trite or overly sentimental. ►*v.* To preserve in brine. [< OE, grain.]

corn[2] (kôrn) ►*n.* A horny thickening of the skin, usu. on or near a toe, resulting from pressure or friction. [< Lat. *cornū*, horn.]

corn·ball (kôrn′bôl′) ►*adj. Slang* Mawkish; corny: *cornball humor.*

corn bread or **corn·bread** (kôrn′brĕd′) ►*n.* Bread made from cornmeal.

corn·cob (kôrn′kŏb′) ►*n.* The woody core of an ear of corn.

corn·crib (kôrn′krĭb′) ►*n.* A structure for storing and drying ears of corn.

corn dog ►*n.* A baked or fried frankfurter encased in corn bread.

cor·ne·a (kôr′nē-ə) ►*n.* The tough transparent membrane of the eyeball, covering the iris and the pupil. [Med.Lat. *cornea* (*tēla*), horny (tissue).] —**cor′ne·al** *adj.*

corned beef (kôrnd) ►*n.* Beef that is seasoned with spices and cured in brine. [< CORN[1], to preserve with granulated salt or brine.]

Cor·neille (kôr-nā′), **Pierre** 1606–84. French playwright.

cor·ner (kôr′nər) ►*n.* **1a.** The position at which two lines, surfaces, or edges meet and form an angle. **b.** The area enclosed or bounded by such an angle. **2.** The place where two roads or streets meet. **3.** A remote or secret place. **4.** A speculative monopoly of a stock or commodity created by controlling the available supply so as to raise its price. ►*v.* **1.** To place or drive into a corner. **2.** To form a corner in (a stock or commodity). **3.** To turn, as at a corner. [< AN < Lat. *cornū*, horn.]

corner kick ►*n.* In soccer, a direct free kick given to the offense when the defense has driven the ball out of bounds beyond the goal line.

cor·ner·stone (kôr′nər-stōn′) ►*n.* **1.** A stone at the corner of a building uniting two intersecting walls, esp. one laid with a special ceremony. **2.** A fundamental basis.

cor·net (kôr-nĕt′) ►*n.* A three-valved brass wind instrument resembling a trumpet. [< OFr. < Lat. *cornū*, horn.] —**cor·net′ist** *n.*

corn·flow·er (kôrn′flou′ər) ►*n.* An annual plant having showy blue, purple, pink, or white flowers; bachelor's button.

cor·nice (kôr′nĭs) ►*n.* **1.** A horizontal molded projection that crowns or completes a building or wall. **2.** The top part of an entablature. [< Ital.]

Cor·nish (kôr′nĭsh) ►*adj.* Of or relating to Cornwall or the Cornish language. ►*n.* **1.** The extinct Celtic language of Cornwall. **2.** English domestic chickens usu. prepared by roasting.

corn·meal (kôrn′mēl′) ►*n.* Coarse meal made from corn.

corn·pone or **corn pone** (kôrn′pōn′) ►*n. Regional* See **johnnycake.** [CORN¹ + Virginia Algonquian *poan,* cornbread.]

corn·row (kôrn′rō′) ►*n.* A portion of hair braided close to the scalp to form a row with others. —**corn′row′** *v.*

corn·stalk (kôrn′stôk′) ►*n.* The stalk or stem of a corn plant.

corn·starch (kôrn′stärch′) ►*n.* Starch prepared from corn grains, used industrially and as a thickener in cooking.

corn syrup ►*n.* A syrup prepared from cornstarch, used esp. as a sweetener.

cor·nu·co·pi·a (kôr′nə-kō′pē-ə, -nyə-) ►*n.* **1.** A cone-shaped container overflowing with fruit, flowers, and grain; horn of plenty. **2.** An abundance. [< Lat. *cornū cōpiae,* horn of plenty.]

Corn·wall (kôrn′wôl′) A region of extreme SW England on a peninsula bounded by the Atlantic Ocean and English Channel.

Corn·wal·lis (kôrn-wŏl′ĭs, -wô′lĭs), **Charles** 1st Marquis Cornwallis. 1738–1805. British military and political leader.

corn·y (kôr′nē) ►*adj.* **-i·er, -i·est** Trite, dated, or mawkish. —**corn′i·ness** *n.*

co·rol·la (kə-rŏl′ə, -rō′lə) ►*n.* The petals of a flower considered as a unit. [Lat. *corōlla,* dim. of *corōna,* CROWN.]

cor·ol·lar·y (kôr′ə-lĕr′ē, kŏr′-) ►*n., pl.* **-ies 1.** A proposition that follows from one already proven. **2.** A natural consequence or effect; result. [< Lat. *corōllārium,* gratuity < *corōlla,* garland; see COROLLA.]

co·ro·na (kə-rō′nə) ►*n., pl.* **-nas** or **-nae** (-nē) **1.** A ring of diffracted light visible esp. around the sun or moon during hazy conditions. **2.** The luminous outer atmosphere of the sun. [Lat. *corōna,* CROWN.]

Co·ro·na·do (kôr′ə-nä′dō), **Francisco Vásquez de** 1510–54. Spanish explorer.

cor·o·nar·y (kôr′ə-něr′ē, kŏr′-) ►*adj.* **1.** Of or relating to the coronary arteries or coronary veins. **2.** Relating to the heart. ►*n., pl.* **-ies** A coronary thrombosis. [< Lat. *corōna,* CROWN.]

coronary artery ►*n.* Either of two arteries that originate in the aorta and supply blood to the muscular tissue of the heart.

coronary artery bypass graft ►*n. Abbr.* **CABG** An operation in which an obstructed coronary artery is repaired by grafting a vein between the aorta and a part of the artery below the level of the obstruction.

coronary thrombosis ►*n.* Obstruction of a coronary artery by a blood clot, often leading to destruction of heart muscle.

coronary vein ►*n.* Any one of the veins that drains blood from the muscular tissue of the heart.

cor·o·na·tion (kôr′ə-nā′shən, kŏr′-) ►*n.* The act or ceremony of crowning a sovereign. [< Lat. *corōna,* CROWN.]

cor·o·ner (kôr′ə-nər, kŏr′-) ►*n.* A public officer who investigates any death thought to be of other than natural causes. [< AN *corouner,* officer of the crown.]

cor·o·net (kôr′ə-nĕt′, kŏr′-) ►*n.* **1.** A small crown worn by nobles below the rank of sovereign. **2.** A jeweled headband. [< OFr. *coronette,* dim. of *corone,* CROWN.]

Co·rot (kô-rō′, kə-), **Jean Baptiste Camille** 1796–1875. French painter.

corp. ►*abbr.* corporation

cor·po·ra (kôr′pər-ə) ►*n.* Pl. of **corpus.**

cor·po·ral¹ (kôr′pər-əl, kôr′prəl) ►*adj.* Of the body. See Synonyms at **bodily.** [< Lat. *corpus, corpor-,* body.] —**cor′po·ral·ly** *adv.*

cor·po·ral² (kôr′pər-əl, kôr′prəl) ►*n.* The lowest noncommissioned rank, as in the US Army or Marine Corps. [< OItal. *caporale* < *capo,* head.]

cor·po·rate (kôr′pər-ĭt, kôr′prĭt) ►*adj.* **1.** Formed into a corporation; incorporated. **2.** Of a corporation. **3.** United or combined into one body; collective. [< Lat. *corpus, corpor-,* body.] —**cor′po·rate·ly** *adv.*

cor·po·ra·tion (kôr′pə-rā′shən) ►*n.* **1.** An entity that is comprised of a body of persons but is legally sanctioned to operate as a single person, allowing it to enter into contracts and engage in transactions under its own identity. **2.** Such a body created for purposes of government.

cor·po·re·al (kôr-pôr′ē-əl) ►*adj.* **1a.** Of the body. See Synonyms at **bodily. b.** Manifesting in bodily form. **2.** Of a material nature; tangible: *corporeal property.* [< Lat. *corporeus* < *corpus,* body.] —**cor·po′re·al′i·ty** (-ăl′ĭ-tē) *n.* —**cor·po′re·al·ly** *adv.*

corps (kôr) ►*n., pl.* **corps** (kôrz) **1.** A specialized branch or department of the armed forces. **2.** A body of persons under common direction: *the press corps.* [< OFr. < Lat. *corpus,* body.]

corpse (kôrps) ►*n.* A dead body, esp. of a human. [< Lat. *corpus,* body.]

corps·man (kôr′mən, kôrz′mən) ►*n.* An enlisted person in the armed forces trained in first aid.

cor·pu·lence (kôr′pyə-ləns) ►*n.* Excessive fatness; obesity. [< Lat. *corpulentia* < *corpus,* body.] —**cor′pu·lent** *adj.*

cor·pus (kôr′pəs) ►*n., pl.* **-po·ra** (-pər-ə) **1.** A large collection of specialized writings. **2.** *Anat.* The main part of a bodily structure or organ. [< Lat., body.]

cor·pus·cle (kôr′pə-səl, -pŭs′əl) ►*n.* **1.** An unattached or free-moving body cell, such as a blood or lymph cell. **2.** A minute globular particle. [Lat. *corpusculum,* dim. of *corpus,* body.] —**cor·pus′cu·lar** (kôr-pŭs′kyə-lər) *adj.*

corpus de·lic·ti (dĭ-lĭk′tī′) ►*n.* **1.** *Law* The corroborating evidence showing that a crime has been committed. **2.** A corpse. [NLat., body of crime.]

cor·ral (kə-răl′) ►*n.* An enclosure for confining livestock. ►*v.* **-ralled, -ral·ling 1.** To drive into and hold in a corral. **2.** To seize or procure. [Sp. < Lat. *currere,* run.]

cor·rect (kə-rĕkt′) ►*v.* **1a.** To make or put right. **b.** To remove errors from. **c.** To mark the errors in. **2.** To punish for the purpose of improving. **3.** To remedy or counteract (e.g., an undesirable behavior). ►*adj.* **1.** True; accurate. **2.** Conforming to standards; proper. [< Lat. *corrigere, corrēct-,* make right.] —**cor·rect′a·ble, cor·rect′i·ble** *adj.* —**cor·rec′tive** *adj. & n.* —**cor·rect′ly** *adv.* —**cor·rect′ness** *n.*

cor·rec·tion (kə-rĕk′shən) ►*n.* **1.** The act or process of correcting. **2.** Something offered or substituted for a mistake or fault. **3.** Punishment intended to improve. **4.** A quantity added or subtracted in order to correct. —**cor·rec′tion·al** *adj.*

Cor·reg·gio (kə-rĕj′ō, -ē-ō′), **Antonio Allegri da** 1494?–1534. Italian Renaissance painter.

Cor·reg·i·dor (kə-rĕg′ĭ-dôr′) An island off the N Philippines at the entrance to Manila Bay.

cor·re·la·tion (kôr′ə-lā′shən) ►*n.* A relationship or connection between two things based on co-occurrence: *a correlation between poverty and crime.* [Med.Lat. *correlātiō*.] —**cor′re·late′** *v. & adj.* —**cor′re·la′tion·al** *adj.*

cor·rel·a·tive (kə-rĕl′ə-tĭv) ►*adj.* **1.** Related; corresponding. **2.** *Gram.* Reciprocally related, as the conjunctions *neither* and *nor.* ►*n.* **1.** Either of two correlative entities. **2.** *Gram.* A correlative word or expression. —**cor·rel′a·tive·ly** *adv.*

cor·re·spond (kôr′ĭ-spŏnd′, kŏr′-) ►*v.* **1.** To be in agreement, harmony, or conformity. **2.** To be similar, parallel, or equivalent, as in nature or function. **3.** To communicate by letter or e-mail. [< Med.Lat. *correspondēre.*] —**cor′re·spond′ing·ly** *adv.*

cor·re·spon·dence (kôr′ĭ-spŏn′dəns, kŏr′-) ►*n.* **1.** The act, fact, or state of agreeing or conforming. **2.** Similarity or analogy. **3a.** Communication by the exchange of letters, e-mails, or other forms of written messages. **b.** The messages sent or received.

cor·re·spon·dent (kôr′ĭ-spŏn′dənt, kŏr′-) ►*n.* **1.** One who communicates by letter or e-mail. **2.** One employed by the media to supply news, esp. from a distant place. **3.** Something that corresponds; correlative. ►*adj.* Corresponding.

cor·ri·dor (kôr′ĭ-dər, kŏr′-) ►*n.* **1.** A narrow hallway or passageway, often with rooms opening onto it. **2a.** A tract of land used for a specific purpose. **b.** A route designated for a specific purpose. **3.** A thickly populated strip of land connecting urban areas. [Fr. < Lat. *currere*, run.]

cor·ri·gen·dum (kôr′ə-jĕn′dəm, kŏr′-) ►*n., pl.* **-da** (-də) **1.** An error to be corrected. **2.** **corrigenda** A list of errors in a book along with their corrections. [Lat. < *corrigere*, to correct.]

cor·rob·o·rate (kə-rŏb′ə-rāt′) ►*v.* **-rat·ed, -rat·ing** To strengthen or support (other evidence). [Lat. *corrōborāre* : COM- + *rōborāre*, strengthen (< *rōbur*, strength).] —**cor·rob′o·ra′tion** *n.* —**cor·rob′o·ra′tive** (-ə-rā′tĭv, -ər-ə-tĭv) *adj.* —**cor·rob′o·ra′tor** *n.*

cor·rode (kə-rōd′) ►*v.* **-rod·ed, -rod·ing** To wear away gradually, esp. by chemical action. [< Lat. *corrōdere*, gnaw away.] —**cor·rod′i·ble, cor·ro·si·ble** (-rō′sə-bəl) *adj.* —**cor·ro′sion** *n.* —**cor·ro′sive** *adj. & n.* —**cor·ro′sive·ness** *n.*

cor·ru·gate (kôr′ə-gāt′, kŏr′-) ►*v.* **-gat·ed, -gat·ing** To shape into folds or parallel and alternating ridges and grooves. [Lat. *corrūgāre*, wrinkle up.] —**cor′ru·ga′tion** *n.*

cor·rupt (kə-rŭpt′) ►*adj.* **1.** Marked by immorality; depraved. **2.** Venal or dishonest: *a corrupt mayor.* **3.** Containing errors, esp. ones that prevent proper use: *a corrupt computer file.* **4.** *Archaic* Tainted; putrid. ►*v.* **1.** To make or become corrupt. **2.** To damage (data) in a file or on a disk. [< Lat. *corrumpere, corrupt-*, destroy.]

—**cor·rupt′er, cor·rup′tor** *n.* —**cor·rupt′i·ble** *adj.* —**cor·rup′tion** *n.* —**cor·rupt′ly** *adv.*
    Syns: *debase, debauch, deprave, pervert, vitiate* **v.**

cor·sage (kôr-säzh′, -säj′) ►*n.* A small bouquet worn on the wrist or at the shoulder or waist. [< OFr., torso.]

cor·sair (kôr′sâr′) ►*n.* **1.** A pirate. **2.** A swift pirate ship. [< Med.Lat. *cursārius.*]

cor·set (kôr′sĭt) ►*n.* A close-fitting undergarment, often reinforced with stays, worn esp. to shape the waist and hips. [< OFr.]

Cor·si·ca (kôr′sĭ-kə) An island of France in the Mediterranean Sea north of Sardinia. —**Cor′si·can** *adj. & n.*

cor·tege (kôr-tĕzh′) ►*n.* **1.** A train of attendants. **2.** A ceremonial procession, esp. for a funeral. [< OItal. *corte*, COURT.]

Cor·tés (kôr-tĕz′, -tĕs′), **Hernando** or **Hernán** 1485–1547. Spanish explorer and conquistador.

cor·tex (kôr′tĕks′) ►*n., pl.* **-ti·ces** (-tĭ-sēz′) or **-tex·es 1a.** The outer layer of a bodily organ. **b.** The layer of gray matter covering most of the brain. **2.** The region of tissue in a root or stem surrounding the vascular tissue. [Lat., bark.] —**cor′ti·cal** *adj.*

cor·ti·co·ste·roid (kôr′tĭ-kō-stěr′oid′,-stîr′-) ►*n.* Any of the steroid hormones produced by the adrenal cortex or their synthetic equivalents.

cor·ti·sone (kôr′tĭ-sōn′, -zōn′) ►*n.* A corticosteroid active in carbohydrate metabolism and used esp. to treat rheumatoid arthritis. [Alteration of *corticosterone*, a type of hormone.]

co·run·dum (kə-rŭn′dəm) ►*n.* An extremely hard mineral, aluminum oxide, occurring in gem varieties and in a common form used chiefly in abrasives. [Tamil *kuruntam*.]

cor·us·cate (kôr′ə-skāt′, kŏr′-) ►*v.* **-cat·ed, -cat·ing** To sparkle and glitter. [Lat. *coruscāre.*] —**cor′us·ca′tion** *n.*

cor·vette (kôr-vĕt′) ►*n.* **1.** A fast, lightly armed warship, smaller than a destroyer. **2.** An obsolete sailing warship, smaller than a frigate. [Fr., a kind of warship.]

cor·ymb (kôr′ĭmb, -ĭm, kŏr′-) ►*n.* A usu. flat-topped flower cluster. [< Gk. *korumbos*, head.]

co·ry·za (kə-rī′zə) ►*n.* See **cold** (sense 3). [< Gk. *koruza*, catarrh.]

cos ►*abbr.* cosine

Cos·by (kŏz′bē, kôz′-), **William Henry, Jr.** "Bill." b. 1937. Amer. comedian and actor.

co·se·cant (kō-sē′kănt′, -kənt) ►*n.* The reciprocal of the sine of an angle in a right triangle.

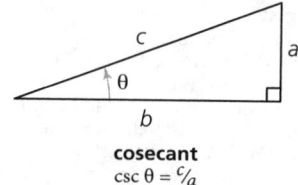

cosecant
$\csc\theta = {}^c\!/_a$

co·sign (kō-sīn′) ►*v.* **1.** To sign (a document) jointly. **2.** To endorse (another's signature), as for a loan. —**co·sign′er** *n.*

co·sig·na·to·ry (kō-sĭg′nə-tôr′ē) ►*adj.* Signed jointly. ►*n., pl.* **-ries** A cosigner.

co·sine (kō′sīn′) ►*n.* In a right triangle, the

ratio of the side adjacent to an acute angle to the hypotenuse.

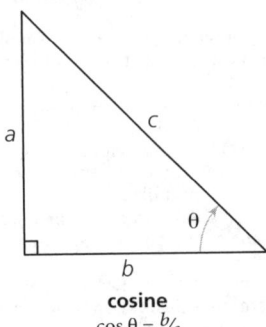

cosine
$$\cos \theta = {}^{b}\!/_{c}$$

cos·met·ic (kŏz-mĕt′ĭk) ►*adj.* **1.** Serving to beautify the body. **2.** Serving to improve the appearance of a bodily feature. **3.** Lacking significance; superficial. ►*n.* A cosmetic preparation. [< Gk. *kosmētikos*, skilled in arranging.] **—cos·met′i·cal·ly** *adv.*

cos·me·tol·o·gy (kŏz′mĭ-tŏl′ə-jē) ►*n.* The study or art of cosmetics and their use. [Fr. *cosmétologie*.] **—cos′me·tol′o·gist** *n.*

cos·mic (kŏz′mĭk) ►*adj.* **1.** Relating to the universe, esp. as distinct from Earth. **2.** Limitless; vast. **—cos′mi·cal·ly** *adv.*

cosmic ray ►*n.* A very rapidly moving particle of extraterrestrial origin, esp. one that collides with the earth's atmosphere. Most cosmic rays are protons, or alpha particles, but some are light atomic nuclei or high-energy electrons.

cosmo– or **cosm–** ►*pref.* Universe; world: *cosmology.* [< Gk. *kosmos*, universe.]

cos·mog·o·ny (kŏz-mŏg′ə-nē) ►*n.* **1.** The astrophysical study of the origin and evolution of the universe. **2.** A philosophical, religious, or mythical explanation of the origin of the universe. [Gk. *kosmogonia*, creation of the world.] **—cos·mog′o·nist** *n.*

cos·mog·ra·phy (kŏz-mŏg′rə-fē) ►*n., pl.* **-phies 1.** The mapping of the universe as a whole system. **2.** A description of the world or universe. **—cos·mog′ra·pher** *n.*

cos·mol·o·gy (kŏz-mŏl′ə-jē) ►*n., pl.* **-gies 1.** The study of the physical universe as a totality of phenomena in time and space. **2.** The astrophysical study of the history, structure, and constituent dynamics of the universe. **3.** A philosophical, religious, or mythical explanation of the nature and structure of the universe. **—cos′mo·log′i·cal** (-mə-lŏj′ĭ-kəl) *adj.* **—cos·mol′o·gist** *n.*

cos·mo·naut (kŏz′mə-nôt′) ►*n.* A Russian or Soviet astronaut. [Russ. *kosmonavt.*]

cos·mo·pol·i·tan (kŏz′mə-pŏl′ĭ-tn) ►*adj.* **1.** Common to the whole world. **2.** Of the entire world or from many different parts of the world. **3.** At home in all parts of the world or in many spheres of interest. ►*n.* **1.** A cosmopolitan person. **2.** A cocktail made of vodka, orange liqueur, cranberry juice, and lime juice.

cos·mop·o·lite (kŏz-mŏp′ə-līt′) ►*n.* A cosmopolitan person. [Gk. *kosmopolitēs*, citizen of the world.]

cos·mos (kŏz′məs, -mŏs′, -mōs′) ►*n.* **1.** The universe regarded as an orderly, harmonious whole. **2.** An ordered, harmonious whole. **3.** A garden annual with daisylike flowers. [Gk. *kosmos.*]

Cos·sack (kŏs′ăk) ►*n.* A member of a people of S European Russia. Many Cossacks served as cavalrymen in the armies of the czars. [< Turk. *kazak*, adventurer.] **—Cos′sack′** *adj.*

cost (kôst) ►*n.* **1.** An amount paid or required in payment for a purchase. **2.** A loss, sacrifice, or penalty. **3. costs** *Law* Charges incurred in bringing litigation. ►*v.* **cost, cost·ing** To require a specified payment, expenditure, effort, or loss. [< Lat. *cōnstāre*, be fixed; see CONSTANT.]

co·star also **co-star** (kō′stär′) ►*n.* A starring actor or actress given equal status with another or others in a play or film. **—co′star′** *v.*

Cos·ta Ri·ca (kŏs′tə rē′kə, kô′stə, kō′-) A country of Central America between Panama and Nicaragua. Cap. San José. **—Cos′ta Ri′can** (-kən) *adj. & n.*

cost·ly (kôst′lē) ►*adj.* **-li·er, -li·est 1.** Of high price or value; expensive. **2.** Entailing great loss or sacrifice. **—cost′li·ness** *n.*

cost of living ►*n.* **1.** The average cost of the necessities of life, such as food, shelter, and clothing. **2.** The cost of necessities as defined by an accepted standard.

cost-of-liv·ing adjustment (kôst′əv-lĭv′ĭng) ►*n.* An adjustment made in wages that corresponds with a change in the cost of living.

cost-of-living index ►*n.* See **consumer price index.**

cost-plus (kôst′plŭs′) ►*n.* The cost of production plus a fixed rate of profit.

cos·tume (kŏs′tōōm′, -tyōōm′) ►*n.* **1.** A style of dress characteristic of a particular country or period. **2.** A set of clothes for a particular occasion or season. **3.** An outfit worn by one playing a part. [< Ital., style.] **—cos′tum·er** *n.*

costume jewelry ►*n.* Jewelry made from inexpensive metals and imitation or semiprecious stones.

cot[1] (kŏt) ►*n.* A narrow bed, esp. a collapsible one. [< Skt. *khaṭvā.*]

cot[2] ►*abbr.* cotangent

co·tan·gent (kō-tăn′jənt, kō′tăn′-) ►*n.* The reciprocal of the tangent of an angle.

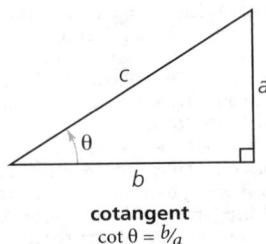

cotangent
$$\cot \theta = {}^{b}\!/_{a}$$

cote (kōt) ►*n.* A small shed or shelter for sheep or birds. [< OE.]

Côte d'I·voire (dĕ-vwär′) also **Ivory Coast** A country of W Africa on the Gulf of Guinea. Caps. Abidjan and Yamoussoukro. **—I·vo′ri·an** (ī-vôr′ē-ən) *adj. & n.*

co·ter·ie (kō′tə-rē, kō′tə-rē′) ►*n.* A close circle of friends or associates. [Fr.]

co·ter·mi·nous (kō-tûr′mə-nəs) ►*adj.* Var. of **conterminous.**

co·til·lion (kō-tĭl′yən, kə-) ▸*n.* **1.** A formal debutante ball. **2.** A lively group dance. [< OFr. *cotillon,* petticoat.]

cot·tage (kŏt′ĭj) ▸*n.* **1.** A small house, esp. in the country. **2.** A small vacation house. [< AN *cotage,* of Gmc. orig.] —**cot′tag·er** *n.*

cottage cheese ▸*n.* A soft mild white cheese made of strained curds of skim milk.

cot·ter (kŏt′ər) ▸*n.* A bolt or pin inserted through a slot to hold parts together. [?]

cotter pin ▸*n.* A split cotter inserted through a hole or holes and bent at the ends to fasten two or more parts together.

cot·ton (kŏt′n) ▸*n.* **1a.** A shrubby plant grown for the soft, white, downy fibers surrounding its oil-rich seeds. **b.** The fiber of this plant, used esp. in making textiles. **2.** Thread or cloth made from cotton fiber. ▸*v. Informal* To take a liking; become friendly. [< Ar. *qutn.*]

cotton candy ▸*n.* A candy of threaded sugar, often tinted and twirled onto a stick.

cotton gin ▸*n.* A machine that separates the seeds and seed hulls from cotton fibers.

cot·ton·mouth (kŏt′n-mouth′) ▸*n.* See **water moccasin.**

cot·ton·seed (kŏt′n-sēd′) ▸*n.* The seed of the cotton plant, used as a source of oil and meal.

cot·ton·tail (kŏt′n-tāl′) ▸*n.* A New World rabbit having a tail often with a white underside.

cot·ton·wood (kŏt′n-wood′) ▸*n.* A North American poplar having triangular leaves and seeds with a tuft of cottony hairs.

cot·y·le·don (kŏt′l-ēd′n) ▸*n.* An embryonic plant leaf, the first to appear from a sprouting seed. [< Gk. *kotulēdōn,* a kind of plant.] —**cot′·y·le′do·nous** *adj.*

couch (kouch) ▸*n.* A sofa. ▸*v.* To word in a certain manner; phrase. [< OFr. *couchier,* lie down.]

cou·gar (koo′gər) ▸*n.* A large wild cat of mountainous regions of the Americas, having an unmarked tawny body and a long tail. [Ult. < Tupí *suasuarana.*]

cough (kôf, kŏf) ▸*v.* **1.** To expel air from the lungs suddenly and noisily, often to clear the respiratory passages. **2.** To expel by coughing. [ME *coughen.*] —**cough** *n.*

could (kood) ▸*aux.v.* P.t. of **can¹. 1.** Used to indicate ability, possibility, or permission in the past. **2.** Used to indicate condition or politeness: *If we could help, we would.*

could·n't (kood′nt) Could not.

cou·lee (koo′lē) ▸*n.* A deep ravine, esp. in the W US. [< Fr. *couler,* flow.]

cou·lomb (koo′lŏm′, -lŏm′) ▸*n.* A unit of electric charge equal to approx. 6×10^{18} times the charge of a proton. [After Charles A. de Coulomb (1736–1806).]

coun·cil (koun′səl) ▸*n.* **1.** An assembly of persons called together for deliberation or discussion. **2.** An administrative, legislative, or advisory body. [< Lat. *concilium.*] —**coun′cil·man** *n.* —**coun′cil·wom′an** *n.*

Usage: Council and *councilor* refer principally to a deliberative assembly or its membership. *Counsel* and *counselor* pertain chiefly to advice and guidance, or to a person who provides advice and guidance.

coun·cil·or also **coun·cil·lor** (koun′sə-lər, -slər) ▸*n.* A member of a council. See Usage Note at **council.**

coun·sel (koun′səl) ▸*n.* **1.** The act of exchanging opinions and ideas; consultation. **2.** Advice or guidance. See Synonyms at **advice. 3.** Private thoughts or opinions: *keep one's own counsel.* **4.** A lawyer or group of lawyers. ▸*v.* **-seled, -sel·ing** or **-selled, -sel·ling 1.** To give counsel (to). **2.** To recommend: *counseled caution.* See Usage Note at **council.** [< Lat. *cōnsilium.*]

coun·sel·or also **coun·sel·lor** (koun′sə-lər, -slər) ▸*n.* **1.** An adviser. **2.** An attorney, esp. a trial lawyer. **3.** One who supervises at a summer camp. See Usage Note at **council.** —**coun′se·lor·ship′** *n.*

count¹ (kount) ▸*v.* **1.** To name or list one by one in order to determine a total. **2.** To recite numerals in ascending order. **3.** To include in a reckoning: *ten dogs, counting the puppies.* **4.** To believe or consider to be. **5.** To merit consideration. **6.** To have a specified importance or value: *counts for two points.* ▸*n.* **1.** The act of counting. **2.** A number reached by counting. **3.** *Law* Any of the charges or causes of action in an indictment or complaint. —*phrasal verb:* **count on** To rely on; depend on. [< Lat. *computāre,* calculate.] —**count′a·ble** *adj.*

count² (kount) ▸*n.* A nobleman in some European countries. [< LLat. *comes,* occupant of a state office.]

count·down (kount′doun′) ▸*n.* The counting backward to indicate the time remaining before an event or operation, such as the launching of a missile or space vehicle.

coun·te·nance (koun′tə-nəns) ▸*n.* **1.** Appearance, esp. the expression of the face. **2.** The face. **3.** Support or approval. ▸*v.* **-nanced, -nanc·ing** To approve or sanction. [< OFr. *contenance.*] —**coun′te·nanc·er** *n.*

coun·ter¹ (koun′tər) ▸*adj.* Contrary; opposing. ▸*n.* One that is counter; opposite. ▸*v.* To move or act in opposition (to). ▸*adv.* In a contrary manner or direction. [< COUNTER–.]

count·er² (koun′tər) ▸*n.* **1.** A flat surface on which money is counted, business is transacted, or food is prepared or served. **2.** A piece, as of wood or ivory, used for keeping a count or a place in games. [< Med.Lat. *computātōrium,* countinghouse.]

count·er³ (koun′tər) ▸*n.* One that counts, esp. a device that automatically counts occurrences or repetitions of phenomena or events.

counter– ▸*pref.* **1.** Contrary; opposing: *counteract.* **2.** Reciprocation: *countersign.* [< Lat. *contrā,* against.]

coun·ter·act (koun′tər-ăkt′) ▸*v.* To oppose and lessen the effects of by contrary action; check. —**coun′ter·ac′tion** *n.*

coun·ter·at·tack (koun′tər-ə-tăk′) ▸*n.* A return attack. —**coun′ter·at·tack′** *v.*

coun·ter·bal·ance (koun′tər-băl′əns) ▸*n.* **1.** A force or influence equally counteracting another. **2.** A weight that acts to balance another. —**coun′ter·bal′ance** *v.*

coun·ter·charge (koun′tər-chärj′) ▸*n.* A charge in opposition to another charge. —**coun′ter·charge′** *v.*

coun·ter·claim (koun′tər-klām′) ▸*n. Law* A claim pled against a plaintiff by a defendant. —**coun′ter·claim′** *v.* —**coun′ter·claim′ant** *n.*

coun·ter·clock·wise (koun′tər-klŏk′wīz′)

▸*adv. & adj.* In a direction opposite to the rotating hands of a clock.

coun·ter·cul·ture (koun′tər-kŭl′chər) ▸*n.* A culture, esp. of young people, with antiestablishment values or lifestyles.

coun·ter·es·pi·o·nage (koun′tər-ĕs′pē-ə-näzh′, -nĭj) ▸*n.* Espionage undertaken to detect and counteract enemy espionage.

coun·ter·feit (koun′tər-fĭt′) ▸*v.* **1.** To make a copy of, usu. with intent to defraud. **2.** To pretend; feign. ▸*adj.* **1.** Made in imitation of what is genuine, usu. with intent to defraud. **2.** Simulated; feigned. ▸*n.* A fraudulent imitation. [< OFr. *contrefait*, made in imitation.] —**coun′ter·feit′er** *n.*

coun·ter·in·sur·gen·cy (koun′tər-ĭn-sûr′jən-sē) ▸*n.* Political and military action undertaken to suppress insurgency. —**coun′ter·in·sur′gent** *n.*

coun·ter·in·tel·li·gence (koun′tər-ĭn-tĕl′ə-jəns) ▸*n.* The branch of an intelligence service charged with keeping sensitive information from an enemy and preventing subversion and sabotage.

coun·ter·in·tu·i·tive (koun′tər-ĭn-tōō′ĭ-tĭv, -tyōō′-) ▸*adj.* Contrary to what intuition and common sense would indicate. —**coun′ter·in·tu′i·tive·ly** *adv.*

coun·ter·mand (koun′tər-mănd′) ▸*v.* **1.** To reverse (an order). **2.** To recall by a contrary order. [< OFr. *contremander*.]

coun·ter·meas·ure (koun′tər-mĕzh′ər) ▸*n.* A measure or action taken to counter or offset another one.

coun·ter·of·fen·sive (koun′tər-ə-fĕn′sĭv) ▸*n.* A large-scale counterattack by an armed force, intended to stop an enemy offensive.

coun·ter·pane (koun′tər-pān′) ▸*n.* A cover for a bed; bedspread. [< OFr. *coultepointe* < Med. Lat. *culcita pūncta*, stitched quilt.]

coun·ter·part (koun′tər-pärt′) ▸*n.* One that closely resembles another, as in function, characteristics, or relation.

coun·ter·plot (koun′tər-plŏt′) ▸*n.* **1.** A plot or scheme intended to subvert another plot. **2.** See **subplot.** ▸*v.* To plot against; thwart with a counterplot.

coun·ter·point (koun′tər-point′) ▸*n.* **1.** *Mus.* The technique of combining two or more melodic lines in a harmonic relationship while retaining their linear individuality. **2.** A contrasting but parallel element or theme.

coun·ter·poise (koun′tər-poiz′) ▸*n.* **1.** A counterbalancing weight. **2.** A force or influence that balances or counteracts another. **3.** The state of being balanced or in equilibrium. —**coun′ter·poise′** *v.*

coun·ter·pro·duc·tive (koun′tər-prə-dŭk′tĭv) ▸*adj.* Tending to hinder rather than serve one's purpose.

coun·ter·rev·o·lu·tion (koun′tər-rĕv′ə-lōō′-shən) ▸*n.* **1.** A movement arising in opposition to a previous revolution. **2.** A movement to oppose revolutionary tendencies and developments. —**coun′ter·rev′o·lu′tion·ar′y** *adj. & n.*

coun·ter·sign (koun′tər-sīn′) ▸*v.* To sign (a previously signed document) to vouch for its authenticity. ▸*n.* **1.** A second or confirming signature. **2.** A password.

coun·ter·sig·na·ture (koun′tər-sĭg′nə-chər)

▸*n.* See **countersign** (sense 1).

coun·ter·sink (koun′tər-sĭngk′) ▸*n.* **1.** A hole with the top part enlarged so that the head of a screw or bolt will lie flush with or below the surface. **2.** A tool for making such a hole. ▸*v.* **1.** To make a countersink on or in. **2.** To set into a countersink.

coun·ter·spy (koun′tər-spī′) ▸*n.* A spy working in opposition to enemy espionage.

coun·ter·ten·or (koun′tər-tĕn′ər) ▸*n.* A male singer with a range above a tenor's.

coun·ter·weight (koun′tər-wāt′) ▸*n.* A weight used as a counterbalance.

count·ess (koun′tĭs) ▸*n.* **1.** A woman holding the title of count or earl. **2.** The wife or widow of a count or earl.

count·ing·house also **count·ing house** (koun′tĭng-hous′) ▸*n.* An office in which a business firm carries on operations such as accounting and correspondence.

count·less (kount′lĭs) ▸*adj.* Innumerable. See Synonyms at **incalculable.**

coun·tri·fied also **coun·try·fied** (kŭn′trĭ-fīd′) ▸*adj.* **1.** Characteristic of country life; rural. **2.** Lacking sophistication.

coun·try (kŭn′trē) ▸*n., pl.* **-tries 1a.** A nation or state. **b.** The territory or people of a nation or state. **2.** The land of a person's birth or citizenship. **3.** A large tract of land distinguishable by features of topography, biology, or culture. **4.** A rural area. **5.** *Informal* Country music. [< VLat. *(terra) contrāta,* (land) opposite.]

country and western ▸*n.* See **country music.**

country club ▸*n.* A suburban club for social and sports activities.

coun·try-dance (kŭn′trē-dăns′) ▸*n.* A folk dance of English origin in which two lines of dancers face each other.

coun·try·man (kŭn′trē-mən) ▸*n.* **1.** A person from one's own country; compatriot. **2.** A rustic.

country mile ▸*n.* *Informal* A great distance.

country music ▸*n.* Popular music based on folk styles of the rural American South and West.

coun·try·side (kŭn′trē-sīd′) ▸*n.* **1.** A rural region. **2.** The inhabitants of a rural region.

coun·try·wom·an (kŭn′trē-wŏŏm′ən) ▸*n.* **1.** A woman from one's own country; compatriot. **2.** A rustic woman.

coun·ty (koun′tē) ▸*n., pl.* **-ties** An administrative subdivision of a state or territory. [< Med. Lat. *comitātus,* territory of a count.]

coup (kōō) ▸*n., pl.* **coups** (kōōz) **1.** A brilliantly executed stratagem. **2.** A coup d'état. [Fr., a stroke; see COPE¹.]

coup de grâce (kōō′ də gräs′) ▸*n., pl.* **coups de grâce 1.** A deathblow delivered to end the misery of a mortally wounded victim. **2.** A finishing or decisive stroke. [Fr.]

coup d'é·tat (dā-tä′) ▸*n., pl.* **coups d'état** The sudden overthrow of a government by a usu. small group of influential persons. [Fr.]

cou·pé (kōō-pā′) or **coupe** (kōōp) ▸*n.* A closed two-door automobile. [Fr. *coupé.*]

cou·ple (kŭp′əl) ▸*n.* **1.** Two items of the same kind; pair. **2.** Something that joins two things; link. **3.** *(takes sing. or pl. v.)* **a.** Two people united, as by marriage. **b.** Two people together. **4.** *Informal* A few; several: *a couple of days.* ▸*v.* **-pled, -pling 1.** To link together. **2.** To form pairs. [< Lat. *cōpula*, bond, pair.] —**cou′-pler** *n.*

   Usage: When used to refer to two people who function socially as a unit, as in *a married couple,* the word *couple* may take either a singular or a plural verb, depending on whether the members are considered individually or collectively.

cou·plet (kŭp′lĭt) ►*n.* Two successive lines of verse, usu. rhyming and having the same meter. [< OFr., dim. of *couple,* COUPLE.]

cou·pling (kŭp′lĭng) ►*n.* **1.** The act of forming couples. **2.** A device that links or connects.

cou·pon (kōō′pŏn′, kyōō′-) ►*n.* **1.** A certificate that entitles the bearer to certain benefits, such as a cash refund. **2a.** A periodic interest payment due to the holder of a bond. **b.** One of a set of small certificates that may be detached from a bond certificate and redeemed for such an interest payment. [Fr.]

cour·age (kûr′ĭj, kŭr′-) ►*n.* The quality of mind that enables one to face danger with self-possession, confidence, and resolution; bravery. [< OFr. *corage* < Lat. *cor,* heart.] —**cou·ra′geous** (kə-rā′jəs) *adj.* —**cou·ra′geous·ly** *adv.*

cou·ri·er (kōōr′ē-ər, kûr′-, kŭr′-) ►*n.* A messenger, esp. one on urgent or official business. [< OItal. *corriere,* runner.]

course (kôrs) ►*n.* **1.** Development in a particular way; progress. **2.** The route or path taken by something that moves. **3a.** The designated route of a race. **b.** See **golf course. 4.** A mode of action or behavior. **5.** Regular development. **6a.** A body of prescribed studies constituting a curriculum. **b.** A unit of such a curriculum. **7.** A part of a meal served as a unit at one time. ►*v.* **coursed, cours·ing 1.** To move swiftly (through or over); traverse. **2.** To hunt (game) with hounds. —*idioms:* **in due course** At the proper or right time. **of course** Naturally or obviously. **off course** Away from the planned or intended course. **on course** Following the planned or intended course. **run (or take) its course** To follow its natural progression. [< Lat. *cursus* < p.part. of *currere,* run.]

cours·er (kôr′sər) ►*n.* A swift horse.

court (kôrt) ►*n.* **1.** A courtyard. **2.** A short street. **3a.** A royal mansion or palace. **b.** The retinue of a sovereign. **c.** A sovereign's governing body, including ministers and advisers. **4a.** A judge or panel of judges. **b.** The place where such cases are heard. **c.** The regular session of a judicial assembly. **5.** An open, level area marked with appropriate lines, upon which a game, such as tennis or basketball, is played. ►*v.* **1.** To attempt to gain; seek. **2.** To behave so as to invite: *court disaster.* **3.** To woo. **4.** To attempt to gain the favor of by attention or flattery. —*idiom:* **pay court to 1.** To flatter in an attempt to obtain something. **2.** To woo. [< Lat. *cohors.*]

cour·te·ous (kûr′tē-əs) ►*adj.* Graciously considerate of others. —**cour′te·ous·ly** *adv.* —**cour′-te·ous·ness** *n.*

cour·te·san (kôr′tĭ-zən) ►*n.* A woman prostitute, esp. one whose clients are men of rank or wealth. [< OItal. *cortigiana* < *corte,* COURT.]

cour·te·sy (kûr′tĭ-sē) ►*n., pl.* **-sies 1a.** Polite behavior. **b.** A polite gesture or remark. **2.** Generosity, esp. as a sponsor. [< OFr. *courtesie.*]

court·house (kôrt′hous′) ►*n.* A building housing judicial courts.

court·i·er (kôr′tē-ər, -tyər) ►*n.* An attendant at a sovereign's court.

court·ly (kôrt′lē) ►*adj.* **-li·er, -li·est** Elegant in manners. —**court′li·ness** *n.*

court-mar·tial (kôrt′mär′shəl) ►*n., pl.* **courts-mar·tial** (kôrts′-) **1.** A military or naval court of officers appointed by a commander to try persons for offenses under military law. **2.** A trial by court-martial. —**court′-mar′tial** *v.*

court order ►*n.* An order issued by a court directing a party or participant in a case to take a certain action.

court·room (kôrt′rōōm′, -rŏŏm′) ►*n.* A room for court proceedings.

court·ship (kôrt′shĭp′) ►*n.* The act or period of courting or wooing.

court·yard (kôrt′yärd′) ►*n.* An open space surrounded by walls or buildings.

cous·cous (kōōs′kōōs′) ►*n.* **1.** A pasta of North African origin made of crushed and steamed semolina. **2.** A North African dish consisting of this pasta steamed with a meat and vegetable stew. [< Ar. *kuskus.*]

cous·in (kŭz′ĭn) ►*n.* **1.** A child of one's aunt or uncle. **2.** A relative descended from a common ancestor. **3.** A member of a kindred group. [< Lat. *cōnsōbrīnus* : COM– + *sōbrīnus,* maternal cousin.]

cou·ture (kōō-tōōr′) ►*n.* The business of designing, making, and selling highly fashionable clothing for women. [Fr., sewing < Lat. *cōnsuere,* sew together : COM– + *suere,* sew.]

cou·tu·rier (kōō-tōōr′ē-ər, -ē-ā′) ►*n.* One who designs for or owns an establishment engaged in couture. [Fr.]

co·va·lent bond (kō-vā′lənt) ►*n.* A chemical bond formed by the sharing of one or more electrons between atoms.

cove (kōv) ►*n.* A small sheltered bay of a sea, river, or lake. [< OE *cofa,* cave.]

cov·en (kŭv′ən, kō′vən) ►*n.* An assembly of 13 witches. [Perh. < ME *covent,* CONVENT.]

cov·e·nant (kŭv′ə-nənt) ►*n.* A formal binding agreement; contract. See Synonyms at **agreement.** ►*v.* To enter into a covenant (with). [< OFr. *convenir,* agree.] —**cov′e·nant·er** *n.*

cov·er (kŭv′ər) ►*v.* **1.** To place something upon, over, or in front of so as to protect, shut in, or conceal. **2a.** To spread over the surface of: *Dust covered the table.* **b.** To extend over: *a farm covering 100 acres.* **3.** To hide or conceal: *covered up their mistakes.* **4.** To travel or pass over. **5a.** To protect by insurance. **b.** To take measures to protect (oneself) from being held responsible for something. **c.** To be enough to pay for or make up for. **6a.** To deal with. **b.** To report the details of (an event or situation). **7.** To hold within the range and aim of a weapon, such as a firearm. **8.** To act as a substitute during someone's absence. ►*n.* **1.** Something that covers. **2.** Something that provides shelter. **3.** Something that screens, conceals, or disguises. **4.** A table setting for one person. [< Lat. *cooperīre,* cover completely.]

cov·er·age (kŭv′ər-ĭj) ►*n.* **1.** The extent or degree to which something is observed, analyzed, and reported. **2.** The protection given by an insurance policy. **3.** The percentage of persons reached by a medium of communication.

cov·er·alls (kŭv′ər-ôlz′) ►*pl.n.* A loose-fitting one-piece garment worn to protect clothes.

cover charge ►*n.* A fixed amount paid when arriving or added to the bill at a nightclub, esp. for entertainment.

cover crop ►*n.* A crop, such as clover, planted to prevent soil erosion and provide humus or nitrogen when plowed under.

covered wagon (kŭv′ərd) ►*n.* A large wagon with an arched canvas top, used esp. by American pioneers for prairie travel.

cov·er·ing (kŭv′ər-ĭng) ►*n.* Something that covers, so as to protect or conceal.

cov·er·let (kŭv′ər-lĭt) ►*n.* A bedspread.

cover letter ►*n.* A letter sent with other documents as an introduction or summary.

cov·ert (kō′vərt, kō-vûrt′, kŭv′ərt) ►*adj.* **1.** Concealed, hidden, or secret. **2.** Sheltered. ►*n.* **1.** A covered shelter or hiding place. **2.** Thick underbrush affording cover for game. [< OFr., covered.] —**cov′ert·ly** *adv.*

cov·er-up or **cov·er·up** (kŭv′ər-ŭp′) ►*n.* An effort or strategy designed to conceal something, such as a crime or scandal.

cov·et (kŭv′ĭt) ►*v.* **1.** To desire (that which is rightfully another's). **2.** To wish for longingly. See Synonyms at **desire.** [< OFr. *coveitier.*]

cov·et·ous (kŭv′ĭ-təs) ►*adj.* Excessively desirous of another's possessions. —**cov′et·ous·ness** *n.*

cov·ey (kŭv′ē) ►*n., pl.* **-eys** A small flock or group, esp. of birds. [< OFr. *covee,* brood.]

cow¹ (kou) ►*n.* **1.** The mature female of cattle. **2.** The mature female of other large animals, such as whales or elephants. **3.** A domesticated bovine. [< OE *cū.*]

cow² (kou) ►*v.* To frighten or subdue with threats or a show of force. [Prob. of Scand. orig.]

cow·ard (kou′ərd) ►*n.* One who shows ignoble fear in the face of danger or pain. [< OFr. *coue,* tail.] —**cow′ard·ly** *adv.*

Coward, Sir **Noel Pierce.** 1899–1973. British actor, playwright, and composer.

cow·ard·ice (kou′ər-dĭs) ►*n.* Lack of courage or resoluteness.

cow·bird (kou′bûrd′) ►*n.* A blackbird that lays its eggs in other birds' nests and often accompanies herds of grazing cattle.

cow·boy (kou′boi′) ►*n.* A hired man, esp. in the American West, who tends cattle, typically on horseback.

cow·catch·er (kou′kăch′ər, -kĕch′-) ►*n.* The metal frame affixed to the front of a locomotive to clear the track of obstructions.

cow·er (kou′ər) ►*v.* To cringe in fear. [ME *couren,* of Scand. orig.]

cow·girl (kou′gûrl′) ►*n.* A hired woman, esp. in the American West, who tends cattle, typically on horseback.

cow·hand (kou′hănd′) ►*n.* A cowboy or cowgirl.

cow·herd (kou′hûrd′) ►*n.* One who herds or tends cattle.

cow·hide (kou′hīd′) ►*n.* **1.** The hide of a cow. **2.** The leather made from this hide.

cowl (koul) ►*n.* **1.** The hood or hooded robe worn esp. by a monk. **2.** A cowl neck. [< Lat. *cucullus,* hood.]

cow·lick (kou′lĭk′) ►*n.* A projecting tuft of hair on the head that will not lie flat.

cowl·ing (kou′lĭng) ►*n.* A removable metal covering esp. for an aircraft engine.

cowl neck ►*n.* A wide, low, loosely draped collar, as on a sweater or blouse. —**cowl′-necked′** (-nĕkt′) *adj.*

cowl neck

co·work·er (kō′wûr′kər) ►*n.* A colleague.

cow·poke (kou′pōk′) ►*n.* A cowhand.

cow·pox (kou′pŏks′) ►*n.* A skin disease of cattle caused by a virus that is isolated and used to vaccinate humans against smallpox.

cow·punch·er (kou′pŭn′chər) ►*n.* A cowhand.

cow·rie or **cow·ry** (kou′rē) ►*n., pl.* **-ries** Any of various tropical marine gastropods having glossy, often brightly marked shells. [< Skt. *kapardikā,* small shell.]

cow·slip (kou′slĭp′) ►*n.* **1.** A Eurasian primrose having fragrant yellow flowers. **2.** See **marsh marigold.** [< OE *cūslyppe* : *cū,* cow + *slypa,* slime.]

cox·comb (kŏks′kōm′) ►*n.* A conceited dandy; fop. [ME *cokkes comb,* cock's comb.]

cox·swain (kŏk′sən, -swān′) ►*n.* **1.** One who steers a ship's boat. **2.** One who directs the crew of a racing shell. [ME *cokswayne.*]

coy (koi) ►*adj.* **-er, -est 1.** Affectedly or flirtatiously shy or modest. **2.** Unwilling to divulge information: *He was coy about his age.* [< Lat. *quiētus,* quiet.] —**coy′ly** *adv.* —**coy′ness** *n.*

coy·o·te (kī-ō′tē, kī′ōt′) ►*n.* A small wolflike carnivorous mammal of N and Central America. [< Nahuatl *cóyotl.*]

coz·en (kŭz′ən) ►*v.* **1.** To deceive; cheat. **2.** To persuade by cajoling or wheedling. [Perh. < ME *cosin,* trickery.]

co·zy (kō′zē) ►*adj.* **-zi·er, -zi·est** Snug, comfortable, and warm. ►*v.* **-zied, -zy·ing** *Informal* **1.** To make oneself snug and comfortable: *cozy up with the Sunday paper.* **2.** *Informal* To ingratiate oneself: *cozy up to the boss.* ►*n., pl.* **-zies 1.** A padded insulating cover for a teapot. **2.** A hollow cylindrical holder used to keep a beverage cold while being held. [Prob. of Scand. orig.] —**co′zi·ly** *adv.* —**co′zi·ness** *n.*

CP ►*abbr.* **1.** or **cp** candlepower **2.** cerebral palsy **3.** command post **4.** Communist Party

cp. ►*abbr.* compare

CPA ►*abbr.* certified public accountant

CPI ►*abbr.* consumer price index

CPO ►*abbr.* chief petty officer

CPR ►*abbr.* cardiopulmonary resuscitation

cps ►*abbr.* **1.** characters per second **2.** cycles per second

CPT ►*abbr.* captain

CPU ►*abbr.* central processing unit

crab¹ (krăb) ►*n.* **1.** Any of various chiefly marine crustaceans having a broad flattened carapace and pincers on the front legs. **2.** A horseshoe crab. **3.** A crab louse. [< OE *crabba.*]

crab² (krăb) ►*n.* A quarrelsome, ill-tempered person. [ME *crabbe.*] —**crab** *v.*

crab·ap·ple (krăb′ăp′əl) ►*n.* **1.** A tree with white, pink, or reddish flowers. **2.** The small tart applelike fruit of such a tree.

crab·bed (krăb′ĭd) ►*adj.* **1.** Irritable; ill-tempered. **2.** Difficult to read, as handwriting. [ME < *crabbe,* CRAB¹.] —**crab′bed·ly** *adv.* —**crab′-bed·ness** *n.*

crab·by (krăb′ē) ►*adj.* **-bi·er, -bi·est** Grouchy; ill-tempered. —**crab′bi·ly** *adv.* —**crab′bi·ness** *n.*

crab·grass (krăb′grăs′) ►*n.* A coarse spreading grass usu. considered a weed in lawns.

crab louse ►*n.* A body louse that infests the pubic region and causes severe itching.

crack (krăk) ►*v.* **1a.** To break without complete separation of parts. **b.** To break with a sharp snapping sound. **2.** To have a mental or physical breakdown. **3.** To change sharply in pitch or timbre, as the voice from emotion. **4.** To strike. **5.** To break open or into. **6.** To discover the solution to, esp. after great effort. **7.** *Informal* To tell (a joke). **8.** To reduce (petroleum) to simpler compounds. ►*n.* **1.** A sharp snapping sound. **2a.** A partial split or break; fissure. **b.** A narrow opening. **3.** A sharp resounding blow. **4.** A cracking of the voice. **5.** A try; chance: *gave him a crack at it.* **6.** A witty or sarcastic remark. **7.** *Slang* Chemically purified cocaine prepared for smoking. ►*adj.* Superior; first rate. —*phrasal verbs:* **crack down** *Informal* To become more severe or strict. **crack up** *Informal* **1.** To have a mental or physical breakdown. **2.** To laugh or cause to laugh boisterously. [< OE *cracian.*]

crack·down (krăk′doun′) ►*n.* An act or instance of cracking down.

cracked (krăkt) ►*adj.* **1.** Broken without dividing into parts: *a cracked mirror.* **2.** *Informal* Crazy.

crack·er (krăk′ər) ►*n.* **1.** A thin crisp wafer or biscuit. **2.** A firecracker.

crack·er·jack (krăk′ər-jăk′) ►*adj. Slang* Of excellent quality. —**crack′er·jack′** *n.*

crack·le (krăk′əl) ►*v.* **-led, -ling 1.** To make or cause to make slight sharp snapping noises. **2.** To develop a network of fine cracks. [< CRACK.] —**crack′le** *n.* —**crack′ly** *adj.*

crack·pot (krăk′pŏt′) ►*n.* An eccentric or harebrained person.

crack·up (krăk′ŭp′) ►*n. Informal* **1.** A crash or collision, as of an automobile. **2.** A mental or physical breakdown.

–cracy ►*suff.* Government; rule: *technocracy.* [< Gk. *-kratia* < *kratos,* power.]

cra·dle (krād′l) ►*n.* **1.** A low bed for an infant, often with rockers. **2.** A place of origin. **3.** A supporting framework. ►*v.* **-dled, -dling** To hold gently in or as if in a cradle. [< OE *cradel.*]

cra·dle·board (krād′l-bôrd′) ►*n.* A board or frame used by certain Native Americans as a portable cradle or to carry an infant on the back.

cradleboard

craft (krăft) ►*n.* **1.** Skill in doing or making something, as in the arts. See Synonyms at **skill. 2.** Skill in evasion or deception; guile. **3a.** A trade, esp. one requiring skilled artistry. **b.** The membership of such a trade; guild. **4.** *pl.* **craft** A boat, ship, or aircraft. ►*v.* To make or devise, esp. with great care. [< OE *cræft.*] —**crafts′man** *n.* —**crafts′man·ship′** *n.* —**crafts′per·son** *n.* —**crafts′wom′an** *n.*

craft·y (krăf′tē) ►*adj.* **-i·er, -i·est** Marked by underhandedness, deviousness, or deception. —**craft′i·ly** *adv.* —**craft′i·ness** *n.*

crag (krăg) ►*n.* A steep, rugged mass of rock. [ME, of Celt. orig.] —**crag′gy** *adj.*

cram (krăm) ►*v.* **crammed, cram·ming 1.** To squeeze into an insufficient space; stuff. **2.** To fill too tightly. **3.** To gorge with food. **4.** *Informal* To study intensively just before an examination. [< OE *crammian.*]

cramp¹ (krămp) ►*n.* **1.** A sudden painful involuntary muscular contraction. **2.** A temporary partial paralysis of habitually or excessively used muscles. **3. cramps** Sharp persistent abdominal pains. ►*v.* To be affected with or as if with a cramp. [< OFr. *crampe,* of Gmc. orig.]

cramp² (krămp) ►*n.* Something that confines or restricts. ►*v.* To restrict; hamper. [Prob. MDu. *crampe,* hook.]

cram·pon (krăm′pŏn′, -pən) ►*n.* A spiked metal framework attached to a boot to prevent slipping on ice. [< OFr., of Gmc. orig.]

cran·ber·ry (krăn′bĕr′ē) ►*n.* **1.** A mat-forming, evergreen shrub of E North America, cultivated in artificial bogs for its edible fruit. **2.** The tart red fruit of a cranberry. [< LGer. *Kraanbere.*]

crane (krān) ►*n.* **1.** A large wading bird having a long neck, long legs, and a long bill. **2.** A machine for hoisting heavy objects. ►*v.* **craned, cran·ing** To stretch (one's neck) for a better view. [< OE *cran.*]

Crane, Stephen 1871–1900. Amer. writer.

cra·ni·um (krā′nē-əm) ►*n., pl.* **-ni·ums** or **-ni·a** (-nē-ə) **1.** The skull of a vertebrate. **2.** The portion of the skull enclosing the brain. [< Gk. *kranion.*] —**cra′ni·al** *adj.*

crank (krăngk) ►*n.* **1.** A device for transmitting rotary motion, consisting of a handle attached at right angles to a shaft. **2.** *Informal* **a.** A grouchy person. **b.** An eccentric person. ►*v.* To start or operate by turning a crank. —*phrasal*

verb: crank out To produce rapidly and mechanically. [< OE *cranc.]

crank·case (krăngk′kās′) ►*n.* The metal case enclosing a crankshaft.

crank·shaft (krăngk′shăft′) ►*n.* A shaft that turns or is turned by a crank.

crank·y (krăng′kē) ►*adj.* **-i·er, -i·est 1.** Ill-tempered; peevish. **2.** Eccentric; odd. **3.** Working or operating unpredictably.

cran·ny (krăn′ē) ►*n., pl.* **-nies** A small opening, as in a wall; crevice. [Perh. < OFr. *cran,* notch.]

crap (krăp) ►*n. Slang* **1.** Nonsense; bunk. **2.** Worthless or shoddy material or work. **3.** Junk; clutter. **4.** Insolent talk or behavior. [< ME *crappe,* chaff.]

crape (krāp) ►*n.* **1.** See **crepe** (sense 1). **2.** A black band worn as a sign of mourning. [Alteration of Fr. *crêpe;* see CREPE.]

crap·pie (krŏp′ē) ►*n., pl.* **-pies** Either of two edible North American sunfishes. [Canadian Fr. *crapet.*]

craps (krăps) ►*pl.n. (takes sing. or pl. v.)* A gambling game played with two dice. [Louisiana Fr.]

crap·shoot (krăp′shoōt′) ►*n. Slang* An enterprise whose outcome is determined by chance.

crap·shoot·er (krăp′shoō′tər) ►*n.* One who plays craps.

crash (krăsh) ►*v.* **1.** To fall or collide violently or noisily. **2.** To make a sudden loud noise. **3.** To fail suddenly, as a market or computer. **4.** To cause to collide or fail. **5.** *Informal* To join or enter uninvited: *crash a party.* **6.** *Slang* **a.** To lodge overnight: *crashed at a friend's house.* **b.** To fall asleep from exhaustion. ►*n.* **1.** A wreck or collision. **2.** A sudden loud noise. **3.** A sudden economic or business failure. **4.** *Comp.* A sudden failure of hardware or software. ►*adj. Informal* All-out: *a crash diet.* [ME *crasshen.*]

crash-land (krăsh′lănd′) ►*v.* To land and usu. damage an aircraft or spacecraft under emergency conditions. —**crash landing** *n.*

crass (krăs) ►*adj.* **-er, -est** Crude and undiscriminating; coarse. [Lat. *crassus,* dense.] —**crass′ly** *adv.* —**crass′ness** *n.*

–crat ►*suff.* A participant in or supporter of a specified form of government: *technocrat.* [< Gk. *-kratēs,* ruler < *kratos,* power.]

crate (krāt) ►*n.* A large, sturdy shipping box. ►*v.* **crat·ed, crat·ing** To pack into a crate. [Lat. *crātis,* wickerwork.]

cra·ter (krā′tər) ►*n.* **1.** A bowl-shaped depression at the mouth of a volcano. **2.** A depression or pit made by an explosion or impact. [< Gk. *kratēr,* mixing vessel.] —**cra′ter** *v.*

crater
meteor crater

cra·ton (krā′tŏn′) ►*n.* A large portion of a continental plate that has been relatively undisturbed since the Precambrian Era.

cra·vat (krə-văt′) ►*n.* A necktie. [Fr. *cravate.*]

crave (krāv) ►*v.* **craved, crav·ing 1.** To want intensely. See Synonyms at **desire. 2.** To beg earnestly for; implore. [< OE *crafian,* beg.]

cra·ven (krā′vən) ►*adj.* Cowardly. [ME *cravant.*] —**cra′ven·ly** *adv.* —**cra′ven·ness** *n.*

crav·ing (krā′vĭng) ►*n.* A consuming desire.

craw (krô) ►*n.* The crop of a bird or stomach of an animal. [ME *crawe.*]

craw·dad (krô′dăd′) ►*n. Regional* See **crayfish.** [Prob. alteration of *crawfish,* crayfish.]

crawl (krôl) ►*v.* **1.** To move slowly on hands and knees or by dragging the body along the ground. **2.** To advance slowly or feebly. **3.** To be or feel as if covered with moving things. ►*n.* **1.** A very slow pace. **2.** A rapid swimming stroke with alternating overarm movements. [< ON *krafla.*] —**crawl′er** *n.* —**crawl′y** *adj.*

cray·fish (krā′fĭsh′) also **craw·fish** (krô′-) ►*n., pl.* **-fish** or **-fish·es** A small lobsterlike freshwater crustacean. [< OFr. *crevice,* of Gmc. orig.]

cray·on (krā′ŏn′, -ən) ►*n.* A stick of colored wax, charcoal, or chalk, used for drawing. [Fr. < Lat. *crēta,* chalk.] —**cray′on′** *v.*

craze (krāz) ►*v.* **crazed, craz·ing** To become or cause to become mentally deranged or obsessed. ►*n.* A fad. [ME *crasen,* shatter.]

cra·zy (krā′zē) ►*adj.* **-zi·er, -zi·est 1.** Mentally deranged. **2.** *Informal* **a.** Possessed by enthusiasm or excitement: *The crowd at the game went crazy.* **b.** Intensely involved or preoccupied: *crazy about cars.* **c.** Foolish or impractical: *crazy schemes.* —**cra′zi·ly** *adv.* —**cra′zi·ness** *n.*

Crazy Horse 1849?–77. Lakota leader.

crazy quilt ►*n.* A patchwork quilt with irregular pieces of cloth arranged haphazardly.

creak (krēk) ►*v.* To make a grating or squeaking sound. ►*n.* A grating or squeaking sound. [ME *creken.*] —**creak′i·ly** *adv.* —**creak′y** *adj.*

cream (krēm) ►*n.* **1.** The yellowish fatty part of milk. **2.** A substance resembling cream. **3.** A yellowish white. **4.** The choicest part. ►*v.* **1.** To beat into a creamy consistency. **2.** To prepare in a cream sauce. **3.** *Slang* To defeat overwhelmingly. [< OFr. *craime.*] —**cream′i·ness** *n.* —**cream′y** *adj.*

cream cheese ►*n.* A soft white cheese made of cream and milk.

cream·er (krē′mər) ►*n.* **1.** A small pitcher for cream. **2.** A substitute for cream.

cream·er·y (krē′mə-rē) ►*n., pl.* **-ies** An establishment where dairy products are prepared or sold.

cream puff ►*n.* **1.** A light pastry with a creamy filling. **2.** *Slang* A weakling.

cream sauce ►*n.* A white sauce made by mixing flour and butter with milk or cream.

crease (krēs) ►*n.* A line made by pressing, folding, or wrinkling. [Perh. < ME *creste,* ridge; see CREST.] —**crease** *v.* —**crease′less** *adj.* —**crease′proof′** *adj.*

cre·ate (krē-āt′) ►*v.* **-at·ed, -at·ing 1.** To cause to exist; bring into being. See **establish. 2.** To produce through artistic or imaginative effort. [< Lat. *creāre.*]

cre·a·tion (krē-ā′shən) ►*n.* **1.** The act of creating. **2.** Something created. **3.** The world and all things in it. **4. Creation** In various religions, the divine act by which the world was created.

cre·a·tion·ism (krē-ā′shə-nĭz′əm) ►*n.* Belief

that the universe, living things, or humans were divinely or supernaturally created. **—cre·a′tion·ist** n.

cre·a·tive (krē-ā′tĭv) ►adj. Characterized by originality; imaginative. **—cre·a′tive·ly** adv. **—cre′a·tiv′i·ty, cre·a′tive·ness** n.

cre·a·tor (krē-ā′tər) ►n. One that creates.

crea·ture (krē′chər) ►n. **1.** A living being, esp. an animal. **2.** A human.

crèche (krĕsh) ►n. A representation of the Nativity. [< OFr. cresche, crib, of Gmc. orig.]

cre·dence (krēd′ns) ►n. **1.** Acceptance as true; belief. See Synonyms at **belief**. **2.** Credibility; plausibility. [< Lat. crēdere, believe.]

cre·den·tial (krĭ-dĕn′shəl) ►n. **1.** Something that entitles one to confidence or authority. **2. credentials** Evidence concerning one's authority. [< Med.Lat. crēdentia, trust, authority; see CREDENCE.]

cre·den·za (krĭ-dĕn′zə) ►n. A buffet or sideboard, esp. one without legs. [Ital. < Med.Lat. crēdentia, trust; see CREDENCE.]

cred·i·ble (krĕd′ə-bəl) ►adj. **1.** Believable. See Synonyms at **plausible**. **2.** Trustworthy; reliable. [< Lat. crēdere, believe.] **—cred′i·bil′i·ty** n. **—cred′i·bly** adv.

cred·it (krĕd′ĭt) ►n. **1.** An arrangement for deferred payment of a loan or purchase. **2.** Accounting Deduction of a payment made by a debtor from an amount due. **3.** The amount remaining in a person's account. **4.** Reputation for solvency and integrity. **5.** Certification of completion of a course of study. **6.** often **credits** An acknowledgment of work done, as in a motion picture. **7.** The quality of being trustworthy. **8.** A source of honor: a credit to her family. **9.** Approval; praise. **10.** Confidence in the truth of something. See Synonyms at **belief**. ►v. **1.** To give credit to. **2.** To believe in; trust. **3.** To ascribe to; attribute. [< Lat. crēditum, a loan < crēdere, believe.]

cred·it·a·ble (krĕd′ĭ-tə-bəl) ►adj. Deserving of commendation. **—cred′it·a·bly** adv.

credit card ►n. A card authorizing the holder to buy goods or services on credit.

cred·i·tor (krĕd′ĭ-tər) ►n. One to whom money is owed.

credit union ►n. A cooperative organization that makes low-interest loans to its members.

cre·do (krē′dō, krā′-) ►n., pl. **-dos** A creed. [< Lat. crēdō, I believe < crēdere, believe.]

cred·u·lous (krĕj′ə-ləs) ►adj. Disposed to believe too readily; gullible. [< Lat. crēdulus < crēdere, believe.] **—cre·du′li·ty** (krĭ-dōō′lĭ-tē, -dyōō′-) n. **—cred′u·lous·ly** adv. **—cred′u·lous·ness** n.

Cree (krē) ►n., pl. **Cree** or **Crees 1.** A member of a Native American people formerly of central Canada, now living from E Canada to Alberta. **2.** The Algonquian language of the Cree.

creed (krēd) ►n. **1.** A formal statement of religious belief. **2.** A system of belief, principles, or opinions. [< OE crēda < Lat. crēdō, I believe; see CREDO.]

creek (krēk, krĭk) ►n. A small stream, often a tributary to a river. **—idiom: up the creek** Informal In a difficult position. [Prob. < ON kriki, bend.]

Creek (krēk) ►n., pl. **Creek** or **Creeks 1.** A member of a Native American people formerly of Alabama, Georgia, and NW Florida, now

chiefly in Oklahoma. **2.** The Muskogean language of the Creek.

creel (krēl) ►n. A wicker basket used to carry fish. [< Lat. crātīcula, fine wattle.]

creep (krēp) ►v. **crept** (krĕpt), **creep·ing 1.** To move with the body close to the ground. **2.** To move stealthily or slowly. **3.** Bot. To grow along a surface, as a vine. **4.** To have a tingling sensation. ►n. **1.** The act of creeping. **2.** Slang An annoying or repulsive person. **3. creeps** Informal A sensation of fear or repugnance. [< OE crēopan.]

creep·er (krē′pər) ►n. A plant that spreads by means of stems that creep.

creep·y (krē′pē) ►adj. **-i·er, -i·est** Informal **1.** Inducing a sensation of uneasiness or fear, as of things crawling on one's skin. **2.** Annoyingly unpleasant. **—creep′i·ness** n.

cre·mate (krē′māt′, krĭ-māt′) ►v. **-mat·ed, -mat·ing** To incinerate (a corpse). [Lat. cremāre.] **—cre·ma′tion** n.

cre·ma·to·ri·um (krē′mə-tôr′ē-əm) ►n., pl. **-to·ri·ums** or **-to·ri·a** (-tôr′ē-ə) A furnace or establishment for the incineration of corpses.

cre·ma·to·ry (krē′mə-tôr′ē, krĕm′ə-) ►n., pl. **-ries** A crematorium.

cren·e·lat·ed also **cren·el·lat·ed** (krĕn′ə-lā′tĭd) ►adj. Having battlements. [< OFr. crenel, notch.] **—cren′e·la′tion** n.

Cre·ole (krē′ōl′) ►n. **1.** A person of European descent born in the West Indies or Latin America. **2a.** A person descended from the original French settlers of Louisiana. **b.** The French dialect of these people. **3.** often **creole** A person of mixed African and European, esp. French or Spanish descent. **4. creole** A pidgin that has developed and become the native language of its users. ►adj. **creole** Cooked with a spicy sauce containing tomatoes, onions, and peppers. [< Port. crioulo, of the household.]

cre·o·sote (krē′ə-sōt′) ►n. An oily liquid obtained from coal tar and used as a wood preservative and disinfectant. [Ger. Kreosot.]

crepe also **crêpe** (krāp) ►n. **1.** A thin crinkled fabric of silk, cotton, wool, or other fiber. **2.** See **crape** (sense 2). **3.** Crepe paper. **4.** (also krĕp) A thin small pancake. [< OFr. crespe, curly < Lat. crīspus.]

crepe paper ►n. Crinkled tissue paper, used for decorations.

crept (krĕpt) ►v. P.t. and p.part. of **creep**.

cre·pus·cu·lar (krĭ-pŭs′kyə-lər) ►adj. **1.** Of or like twilight. **2.** Zool. Active at dusk or dawn or both. [< Lat. crepusculum, twilight.]

cres·cen·do (krə-shĕn′dō) ►n., pl. **-dos 1.** Mus. A gradual increase in the volume of sound. **2.** A steady increase in intensity or force. [Ital. < Lat. crēscere, increase.] **—cres·cen′do** adj. & adv.

cres·cent (krĕs′ənt) ►n. **1.** The figure of the moon in its first or last quarter, with concave and convex edges terminating in points. **2.** Something shaped like a crescent. ►adj. Crescent-shaped. [< AN cressaunt < Lat. crēscere, increase.]

cress (krĕs) ►n. Any of several plants with pungent leaves, often used in salads. [< OE cærse, cresse.]

crest (krĕst) ►n. **1.** A tuft or similar projection on the head of a bird or other animal. **2.** Her. A device placed above the shield on a coat of arms. **3.** The top, as of a hill or wave. ►v. **1.** To form into a crest. **2.** To reach the crest (of). [< Lat. *crista*.]

crest·fall·en (krĕst′fô′lən) ►*adj.* Dispirited; dejected.

Cre·ta·ceous (krĭ-tā′shəs) *Geol.* ►*adj.* Of or being the 3rd and last period of the Mesozoic Era, marked by the development of flowering plants and the extinction of the dinosaurs. ►*n.* The Cretaceous Period. [< Lat. *crēta*, chalk.]

Crete (krēt) An island of SE Greece in the E Mediterranean Sea. —**Cre′tan** *adj. & n.*

cre·tin (krēt′n) ►*n.* A person afflicted with cretinism. [< VLat. **christiānus*, Christian.]

cre·tin·ism (krēt′n-ĭz′əm) ►*n.* A thyroid deficiency resulting in dwarfed stature and mental retardation.

cre·vasse (krĭ-văs′) ►*n.* **1.** A deep fissure, as in a glacier. **2.** A breach in a levee. [< OFr. *crevace*, CREVICE.]

crev·ice (krĕv′ĭs) ►*n.* A narrow crack. [< OFr. *crevace* < Lat. *crepāre*, to crack.]

crew¹ (kroo) ►*n.* **1.** A group of people working together. **2.** The personnel operating a boat, ship, or aircraft. **3.** A team of rowers. [ME *creue*, military reinforcement.]

crew² (kroo) ►*v. Chiefly Brit.* P.t. of **crow²**.

crew·cut or **crew cut** (kroo′kŭt′) ►*n.* A closely cropped haircut.

crewed (krood) ►*adj.* Operated by an onboard crew: *a crewed space flight.*

crew·el (kroo′əl) ►*n.* Loosely twisted worsted yarn used for embroidery. [ME *crule*.]

crew neck ►*n.* A round, close-fitting neckline.

crib (krĭb) ►*n.* **1.** A child's bed with high sides. **2.** A small building for storing corn. **3.** A rack or trough for fodder. **4a.** Plagiarism. **b.** See **pony** (sense 2). **5.** *Slang* One's home. ►*v.* **cribbed, crib·bing 1.** To confine in or as if in a crib. **2.** To plagiarize. [< OE *cribb*, manger.] —**crib′ber** *n.*

crib·bage (krĭb′ĭj) ►*n.* A card game scored by inserting pegs into holes on a board. [< CRIB.]

crib death ►*n.* See **sudden infant death syndrome**.

crick¹ (krĭk) ►*n.* A painful cramp, as in the neck. [ME *crike*.]

crick² (krĭk) ►*n. Regional* A creek.

Crick, Francis Harry Compton 1916–2004. British molecular biologist.

crick·et¹ (krĭk′ĭt) ►*n.* A leaping insect, the male of which produces a shrill chirping sound. [< OFr. *criquet* < *criquer*, to click.]

crick·et² (krĭk′ĭt) ►*n.* A game played with bats, a ball, and wickets by two teams of 11 players each. [Poss. < OFr. *criquet*, target stick in a bowling game.] —**crick′et·er, crick′et·eer′** (-ĭ-tîr′) *n.*

cri·er (krī′ər) ►*n.* **1.** One who cries or weeps. **2.** One who shouts out public announcements.

crime (krīm) ►*n.* **1.** An act committed or omitted in violation of a law. **2.** An unjust or senseless act. [< Lat. *crīmen*.]

Cri·me·a (krī-mē′ə, krī-) A region and peninsula of S Ukraine on the Black Sea and Sea of Azov. —**Cri·me′an** *adj.*

crim·i·nal (krĭm′ə-nəl) ►*adj.* **1.** Of or involving crime. **2.** Guilty of crime. ►*n.* One who has committed a crime. —**crim′i·nal′i·ty** (-năl′ĭ-tē) *n.* —**crim′i·nal·ly** *adv.*

crim·i·nal·ize (krĭm′ə-nə-līz′) ►*v.* **-ized, -iz·** ing To make criminal; outlaw. —**crim′i·nal·i·za′tion** *n.*

crim·i·nol·o·gy (krĭm′ə-nŏl′ə-jē) ►*n.* The scientific study of crime and criminals. —**crim′i·no·log′i·cal** (-nə-lŏj′ĭ-kəl) *adj.* —**crim′i·nol′o·gist** *n.*

crimp (krĭmp) ►*v.* **1.** To press or pinch into small folds or ridges. **2.** To curl (hair). **3.** To have a hampering or obstructive effect on. ►*n.* **1.** The act of crimping. **2.** An obstructing agent or force. [Du. or LGer. *krimpen*.] —**crimp′er** *n.*

crim·son (krĭm′zən) ►*n.* A vivid purplish red. [< Ar. *qirmizī*.] —**crim′son** *adj. & v.*

cringe (krĭnj) ►*v.* **cringed, cring·ing** To shrink back, as in fear. [ME *crengen*.] —**cringe** *n.*

crin·kle (krĭng′kəl) ►*v.* **-kled, -kling** To form wrinkles or ripples. [< ME *crinkled*, wrinkled.] —**crin′kle** *n.* —**crin′kly** *adj.*

crin·o·line (krĭn′ə-lĭn) ►*n.* **1.** A stiff fabric used to line garments. **2.** A petticoat made of this fabric. [Fr. < Ital. *crinolino*.]

crip·ple (krĭp′əl) ►*n.* One that is partially disabled or lame. ►*v.* **-pled, -pling** To disable or damage. [< OE *crypel*.]
   Usage: The noun *cripple* and the adjective *crippled* are generally acceptable when applied to an animal, but are considered offensive when applied to a disabled person.

cri·sis (krī′sĭs) ►*n., pl.* **-ses** (-sēz) **1.** A crucial point or situation. **2.** An emotionally stressful event or traumatic change in a person's life. [< Gk. *krisis* < *krinein*, to separate.]

crisp (krĭsp) ►*adj.* **-er, -est 1.** Firm but easily broken; brittle. **2.** Firm and fresh: *crisp celery.* **3.** Bracing; invigorating. **4.** Clear and concise: *a crisp reply.* ►*n.* A dessert of fruit baked with a sweet crumbly topping. [< OE *curly* < Lat. *crīspus*.] —**crisp** *v.* —**crisp′ly** *adv.* —**crisp′ness** *n.* —**crisp′y** *adj.*

criss·cross (krĭs′krôs′, -krŏs′) ►*v.* **1.** To mark with crossing lines. **2.** To move back and forth through or over. ►*n.* A pattern of crossing lines. [< ME *Crist crosse*, mark of a cross.] —**criss′cross′** *adj. & adv.*

cri·te·ri·on (krī-tîr′ē-ən) ►*n., pl.* **-te·ri·a** (-tîr′ē-ə) or **-te·ri·ons** A standard or test on which a judgment can be based. [Gk. *kritērion*.]
   Usage: Like *phenomenon*, *criterion* is a singular noun. The plural is generally *criteria*, although *criterions* is sometimes also used.

crit·ic (krĭt′ĭk) ►*n.* **1.** One who analyzes, interprets, or evaluates artistic works. **2.** A faultfinder. [< Gk. *kritikos*, able to discern < *krinein*, to separate.]

crit·i·cal (krĭt′ĭ-kəl) ►*adj.* **1.** Judging severely and finding fault: *critical of the government.* **2.** Reflecting careful analysis and judgment: *critical appreciation.* **3.** Of or relating to critics or criticism. **4.** Crucial: *a critical point in the campaign.* See Synonyms at **decisive. 5.** Extremely important or essential. See Synonyms at **indispensable. 6.** Of or forming a crisis: *a critical food shortage.* —**crit′i·cal·ly** *adv.*

crit·i·cism (krĭt′ĭ-sĭz′əm) ►*n.* **1.** The act of criticizing, esp. adversely. **2.** A critical comment or judgment. **3.** The practice of analyzing, interpreting, or evaluating artistic works. **4.** A critical essay; critique.

crit·i·cize (krĭt′ĭ-sīz′) ►*v.* **-cized, -ciz·ing 1.** To find fault with. **2.** To judge the merits and faults of; evaluate. —**crit′i·ciz′er** *n.*

cri·tique (krĭ-tēk′) ►*n.* A critical review or commentary. [Fr.] —**cri·tique′** *v.*

crit·ter (krĭt′ər) ►*n. Informal* A creature, esp. a domestic animal. [< CREATURE.]

croak (krōk) ►*n.* A low hoarse sound, as that of a frog. ►*v.* **1.** To utter a croak. **2.** *Slang* To die. [< ME *croken*, to croak.]

Cro·at (krō′ăt′, -ät′, krōt) ►*n.* **1.** A native or inhabitant of Croatia. **2.** Serbo-Croatian as used by the Croats.

Cro·a·tia (krō-ā′shə) A country of SE Europe along the NE Adriatic coast. Cap. Zagreb.

Cro·a·tian (krō-ā′shən) ►*n.* **1.** See **Croat. 2.** The Slavic language of the Croats. —**Cro·a′tian** *adj.*

Cro·ce (krō′chĕ), **Benedetto** 1866–1952. Italian philosopher, historian, and critic.

cro·chet (krō-shā′) ►*v.* -**cheted** (-shād′), -**chet·ing** (-shā′ĭng) To make by looping thread with a hooked needle: *crochet a scarf.* [< OFr., hook.]

crock (krŏk) ►*n.* An earthenware vessel. [< OE *crocc.*]

crock·er·y (krŏk′ə-rē) ►*n.* Earthenware.

Crock·ett (krŏk′ĭt), **David** "Davy." 1786–1836. Amer. pioneer and politician.

croc·o·dile (krŏk′ə-dīl′) ►*n.* A large tropical aquatic reptile with armorlike skin and long tapering jaws. [< Gk. *krokodilos.*] —**croc′o·dil′i·an** (krŏk′ə-dĭl′ē-ən, -dīl′yən) *adj. & n.*

crocodile tears ►*pl.n.* An insincere display of grief.

cro·cus (krō′kəs) ►*n., pl.* -**cus·es** or -**ci** (-sī, -kī) A variously colored spring or fall flower grown from corms. [< Gk. *krokos.*]

Croe·sus (krē′səs) d. c. 546 BC. Last king of Lydia (560–546).

Crohn's disease (krōnz) ►*n.* A form of ileitis marked by abdominal pain, ulceration, and fibrous tissue buildup. [After Burrill Bernard *Crohn* (1884–1983).]

crois·sant (krwä-sän′, krə-sänt′) ►*n.* A rich, crescent-shaped roll. [< OFr. *creissant,* CRESCENT.]

Cro·Mag·non (krō-măg′nən, -măn′yən) ►*n.* An early form of modern human of Europe in the late Pleistocene. [After *Cro-Magnon* cave, France.] —**Cro-Mag′non** *adj.*

Crom·well (krŏm′wĕl, -wəl, krŭm′-), **Oliver** 1599–1658. English military, political, and religious leader. —**Crom·well′i·an** *adj.*

crone (krōn) ►*n.* **1.** *Derogatory* An old woman, esp. one considered ugly. **2.** A woman venerated for experience and wisdom. [< VLat. *carōnia,* CARRION.]

cro·ny (krō′nē) ►*n., pl.* -**nies** A close friend or companion. [Perh. < Gk. *khronios,* long-lasting < *khronos,* time.]

cro·ny·ism (krō′nē-ĭz′əm) ►*n.* Favoritism shown to old friends without regard for their qualifications.

crook (krŏok) ►*n.* **1.** A bent or curved implement, such as a staff. **2.** A curve or bend. **3.** *Informal* One who makes a living by crime or deceit. ►*v.* To curve or bend. [< ON *krókr.*]

crook·ed (krŏok′ĭd) ►*adj.* **1.** Having bends or curves. **2.** Askew: *Your necktie is crooked.* **3.** *Informal* Dishonest; fraudulent. —**crook′ed·ly** *adv.* —**crook′ed·ness** *n.*

croon (krŏon) ►*v.* To hum or sing softly. [< MDu. *krōnen,* to lament.] —**croon** *n.* —**croon′er** *n.*

crop (krŏp) ►*n.* **1a.** A particular kind of agricultural produce. **b.** The total yield of such produce. **2.** A group of things or people arriving together: *the new crop of college graduates.* **3.** A short haircut. **4a.** A short riding whip. **b.** The stock of a whip. **5.** *Zool.* A pouchlike enlargement of a bird's gullet in which food is digested or stored. ►*v.* **cropped, crop·ping 1.** To cut or bite off the tops of. **2.** To cut very short. **3.** To trim. —*phrasal verb:* **crop up** To appear unexpectedly. [< OE *cropp,* ear of grain.]

crop-dust·ing (krŏp′dŭs′tĭng) ►*n.* The process of spraying crops, as with insecticides, from an aircraft. —**crop′-dust′** *v.*

crop-dusting

cro·quet (krō-kā′) ►*n.* An outdoor game in which players drive wooden balls through wickets using mallets. [< ONFr., crook.]

cro·quette (krō-kĕt′) ►*n.* A small cake of minced food usu. fried in deep fat. [Fr.]

cro·sier or **cro·zier** (krō′zhər) ►*n.* A crooked staff, esp. of a bishop. [< OFr. *crosse.*]

cross (krôs, krŏs) ►*n.* **1.** An upright post with a transverse piece near the top. **2a.** often **Cross** The cross upon which Jesus was crucified. **b.** Any of various modifications of the cross design. **3.** A trial or affliction. See Synonyms at **burden. 4.** A pattern formed by the intersection of two lines. **5.** One that combines the qualities of two other things. **6.** *Biol.* **a.** A hybrid plant or animal. **b.** A hybridization. ►*v.* **1.** To go or extend across. **2.** To intersect. **3.** To draw a line across. **4.** To place crosswise. **5.** To encounter in passing. **6.** To thwart or obstruct. **7.** *Biol.* To breed by hybridizing. ►*adj.* **1.** Lying crosswise. **2.** Contrary or opposing. **3.** Showing ill humor; annoyed. **4.** Hybrid. [< Lat. *crux.*] —**cross′er** *n.* —**cross′ly** *adv.* —**cross′ness** *n.*

cross·bar (krôs′bär′, krŏs′-) ►*n.* A horizontal bar or line.

cross·bones (krôs′bōnz′, krŏs′-) ►*pl.n.* Two bones placed crosswise, usu. under a skull.

cross·bow (krôs′bō′, krŏs′-) ►*n.* A weapon consisting of a bow fixed crosswise on a wooden stock with a trigger mechanism.

cross·breed (krôs′brēd′, krŏs′-) ►*v.* To hybridize. ►*n.* A hybrid.

cross-coun·try (krôs′kŭn′trē, krŏs′-) ►*adj.* **1.** Moving across open country rather than roads. **2.** From one side of a country to the opposite side. —**cross′-coun′try** *adv.*

cross-country skiing ►*n.* The sport of skiing over the countryside rather than downhill.

cross-cul·tur·al (krôs′kŭl′chər-əl, krŏs′-) ►*adj.* Involving two or more different cultures. —**cross′-cul′tur·al·ly** *adv.*

cross·cur·rent (krôs′kûr′ənt, -kŭr′-, krŏs′-) ►*n.* **1.** A current flowing across another. **2.** A conflicting tendency.

cross·cut (krôs′kŭt′, krŏs′-) ►v. To cut or run crosswise. ►adj. **1.** Used for cutting crosswise. **2.** Cut across the grain.

cross-dress (krôs′drĕs′, krŏs′-) ►v. To dress in clothing usu. worn by the opposite sex. **—cross′-dress′er** n.

cross-ex·am·ine (krôs′ĭg-zăm′ĭn, krŏs′-) ►v. To question (a person) closely, esp. with regard to answers or information given previously. **—cross′-ex·am′i·na′tion** n.

cross-eye (krôs′ī′, krŏs′-) ►n. An imbalance of the eye muscles in which one or both of the eyes deviate inward toward the nose. **—cross′-eyed′** adj.

cross·fire (krôs′fīr′, krŏs′-) ►n. **1.** Lines of gunfire crossing each other. **2.** Rapid, heated discussion.

cross·hatch (krôs′hăch′, krŏs′-) ►v. To shade with intersecting sets of parallel lines.

cross·ing (krô′sĭng, krŏs′ĭng) ►n. **1.** An intersection, as of roads. **2.** A place at which something, as a river, may be crossed.

cross·piece (krôs′pēs′, krŏs′-) ►n. A transverse or horizontal piece, as of a structure.

cross-pol·li·nate (krôs′pŏl′ə-nāt′, krŏs′-) ►v. To fertilize (a flower) with pollen from a flower of another plant of the same kind. **—cross′-pol′li·na′tion** n.

cross-pur·pose (krôs′pûr′pəs, krŏs′-) ►n. A conflicting or contrary purpose. **—idiom: at cross-purposes** Pursuing conflicting goals, esp. unintentionally.

cross-ques·tion (krôs′kwĕs′chən, krŏs′-) ►v. To cross-examine.

cross-ref·er·ence (krôs′rĕf′ər-əns, -rĕf′rəns, krŏs′rĕf′ər-əns, -rĕf′rəns) ►n. A reference from one part of a book or file to another part containing related information. **—cross′re·fer′** v.

cross·road (krôs′rōd′, krŏs′-) ►n. **1.** A road that intersects another. **2. crossroads** (takes sing. v.) A place where two or more roads meet. **3.** A crucial point.

cross section ►n. **1a.** A section formed by a plane cutting through an object, usu. at right angles to an axis. **b.** A piece so cut or a graphic representation of it. **2.** A sample meant to be representative of the whole.

cross-train (krôs′trān′, krŏs′-) ►v. **1.** To train in different tasks or skills. **2.** To train in different sports, esp. by alternating regimens.

cross·walk (krôs′wôk′, krŏs′-) ►n. A street crossing marked for pedestrians.

cross·wise (krôs′wīz′, krŏs′-) also **cross·ways** (-wāz′) ►adv. So as to be in a cross direction; across. **—cross′wise′** adj.

cross·word (krôs′wûrd′, krŏs′-) ►n. A puzzle consisting of numbered squares to be filled with words in answer to clues.

crotch (krŏch) ►n. The angle formed by the junction of two parts, as branches or legs. [Poss. < CRUTCH and OFr. croche, crook.] **—crotched** (krŏcht) adj.

crotch·et·y (krŏch′ĭ-tē) ►adj. Stubbornly perverse or peevish. [< ME crochet, hook (< OFr.; see CROCHET), -Y¹.]

crouch (krouch) ►v. To stoop, esp. with the knees bent. [Prob. < ONFr. *crouchir, be bent.] **—crouch** n.

croup (krōōp) ►n. Inflammation of the larynx, esp. in children, marked by labored breathing and a hoarse cough. [< dial. croup, croak.] **—croup′ous, croup′y** adj.

crou·pi·er (krōō′pē-ər, -pē-ā′) ►n. An attendant at a gaming table. [Fr.]

crou·ton (krōō′tŏn′, krōō-tŏn′) ►n. A small piece of toasted bread. [Fr. croûton, dim. of croûte, crust.]

crow¹ (krō) ►n. A large, glossy black bird with a raucous call. **—idiom: as the crow flies** In a straight line. [< OE crāwe.]

crow² (krō) ►v. **1.** To utter the shrill cry of a rooster. **2.** To exult loudly; boast. [< OE crāwan.] **—crow** n.

Crow ►n., pl. **Crow** or **Crows 1.** A member of a Native American people of the N Great Plains, now chiefly in SE Montana. **2.** The Siouan language of the Crow.

crow·bar (krō′bär′) ►n. A metal bar with the working end shaped like a forked chisel, used as a lever.

crowd (kroud) ►n. **1.** A large number of persons gathered together. **2.** A particular group: the over-30 crowd. ►v. **1.** To gather closely together; throng. **2.** To advance by pressing or shoving. **3.** To press or force tightly together. [< OE crūdan, hasten.]

Syns: crush, flock, horde, mob, throng **n.**

crown (kroun) ►n. **1.** An ornamental circlet worn on the head as a symbol of sovereignty. **2.** often **Crown** The power of a monarch. **3.** Something resembling a crown in shape. **4.** A former British coin. **5.** The top part of something, as the head. **6.** The part of a tooth above the gum line. ►v. **1.** To put a crown on. **2.** To invest with regal power. **3.** To confer honor upon. **4.** To be the highest or most notable part of. **5.** Games To make (a piece in checkers that has reached the last row) into a king by placing another piece upon it. [< Gk. korōnē, wreath.]

crown prince ►n. The male heir apparent to a throne.

crown princess ►n. **1.** The female heir apparent to a throne. **2.** The wife of a crown prince.

crow's-feet (krōz′fēt′) ►pl.n. Wrinkles at the outer corner of the eye.

crow's-nest (krōz′nĕst′) ►n. A small lookout platform near the top of a ship's mast.

cro·zier (krō′zhər) ►n. Var. of **crosier.**

CRT ►abbr. cathode-ray tube

cru·cial (krōō′shəl) ►adj. **1.** Extremely significant or important. **2.** Vital to the resolution of a crisis. See Synonyms at **decisive.** [< Lat. crux, cruc-, cross.] **—cru′cial·ly** adv.

cru·ci·ble (krōō′sə-bəl) ►n. **1.** A vessel used for melting materials at high temperatures. **2.** A severe test. See Synonyms at **trial.** [< Med. Lat. crūcibulum.]

cru·ci·fix (krōō′sə-fĭks′) ►n. A figure of Jesus on the cross. [< Lat. crucifigere, crucifix-, crucify.]

cru·ci·fix·ion (krōō′sə-fĭk′shən) ►n. **1.** Execution on a cross. **2. Crucifixion** The crucifying of Jesus. **3.** A representation of Jesus on the cross.

cru·ci·form (krōō′sə-fôrm′) ►adj. Shaped like a cross. [< Lat. crux, cruc-, cross.]

cru·ci·fy (krōō′sə-fī′) ►v. **-fied, -fy·ing 1.** To put to death by nailing or binding to a cross. **2.** To torture; torment. [< Lat. crucifigere.]

crude (krōōd) ►adj. **crud·er, crud·est 1.** In an unrefined or natural state; raw. **2.** Lacking tact, refinement, or taste. **3.** Roughly made.

►*n.* Unrefined petroleum. [< Lat. *crūdus.*] —**crude′ly** *adv.* —**cru′di·ty, crude′ness** *n.*

cru·el (krōo′əl) ►*adj.* **-el·er, -el·est** or **-el·ler, -el·lest** Inflicting pain, esp. maliciously or carelessly. [< Lat. *crūdēlis.*] —**cru′el·ly** *adv.* —**cru′el·ty** *n.*

cru·et (krōo′ĭt) ►*n.* A small bottle for vinegar or oil. [< OFr. *crue,* flask.]

cruise (krōoz) ►*v.* **cruised, cruis·ing 1.** To sail or travel about, as for pleasure. **2.** To travel at a steady or efficient speed. [Du. *kruisen,* to cross.] —**cruise** *n.*

cruise missile ►*n.* A winged guided missile capable of flying at low altitudes.

cruis·er (krōo′zər) ►*n.* **1.** A fast warship of medium tonnage. **2.** A cabin cruiser. **3.** See **squad car.**

crul·ler (krŭl′ər) ►*n.* A usu. oblong, twisted cake of deep-fried dough. [< MDu. *crulle,* curly.]

crumb (krŭm) ►*n.* **1.** A very small piece broken from bread or pastry. **2.** A fragment or scrap. [< OE *cruma.*]

crum·ble (krŭm′bəl) ►*v.* **-bled, -bling 1.** To break into small pieces. **2.** To disintegrate. [< OE **crymelen,* break into crumbs.] —**crum′-bly** *adj.*

crum·my also **crumb·y** (krŭm′ē) ►*adj.* **-mi·er, -mi·est** also **-i·er, -i·est** *Slang* **1.** Miserable. **2.** Shabby; cheap. [< CRUMB.]

crum·pet (krŭm′pĭt) ►*n.* A small flat round of bread, baked on a griddle. [Poss. < ME *crompid (cake),* curled (cake).]

crum·ple (krŭm′pəl) ►*v.* **-pled, -pling 1.** To crush together into wrinkles; rumple. **2.** To fall apart; collapse. [ME *crumplen,* prob. < *crumpen,* curl up.] —**crum′ply** *adj.*

crunch (krŭnch) ►*v.* **1.** To chew with a crackling noise. **2.** *Slang* To perform operations on (numbers or data). ►*n.* **1.** A partial sit-up. **2.** A critical situation, esp. one resulting from a shortage of time or resources. [Prob. imit.] —**crunch** *n.* —**crunch′y** *adj.*

cru·sade (krōo-sād′) ►*n.* **1.** often **Crusade** Any of the Christian military expeditions undertaken in the 11th, 12th, and 13th cent. to reclaim the Holy Land from the Muslims. **2.** A vigorous concerted movement for a cause or against an abuse. ►*v.* **-sad·ed, -sad·ing** To engage in a crusade. [< Lat. *crux,* cross.] —**cru·sad′er** *n.*

crush (krŭsh) ►*v.* **1.** To press or squeeze so as to break or injure. **2.** To break, pound, or grind into small fragments or powder. **3.** To put down; subdue. **4.** To shove or crowd. ►*n.* **1.** The act of crushing. **2.** A throng. See Synonyms at **crowd. 3.** *Informal* A temporary infatuation. [< OFr. *croissir.*] —**crush′er** *n.*
Syns: mash, smash, squash v.

crust (krŭst) ►*n.* **1.** The usu. hard outer surface of bread. **2.** A stale piece of bread. **3.** A pastry shell, as of a pie. **4.** A hard covering or surface. **5.** *Geol.* The exterior layer of the earth. ►*v.* To cover with or harden into a crust. [< Lat. *crūsta,* shell.] —**crust′y** *adj.*

crus·ta·cean (krŭ-stā′shən) ►*n.* Any of various chiefly aquatic arthropods, including lobsters, crabs, and shrimps, having a segmented body, a hard outer shell, and often gills. [< Lat. *crūsta,* shell.]

crutch (krŭch) ►*n.* **1.** A staff or support used as an aid in walking, usu. designed to rest under the armpit or along the forearm. **2.** Something

on which one depends, often excessively: *used alcohol as a crutch.* [< OE *crycc.*]

crux (krŭks, krŏoks) ►*n.* **1.** A central or critical point. **2.** A puzzling problem. [< Lat., cross.]

cry (krī) ►*v.* **cried** (krīd), **cry·ing 1.** To weep, as from grief or other powerful emotion. **2.** To call loudly; shout. **3.** To utter a characteristic sound or call, as does an animal. **4.** To demand or require remedy: *grievances crying out for redress.* ►*n., pl.* **cries** (krīz) **1.** A loud shout, exclamation, or utterance. **2.** A fit of weeping. **3.** The characteristic call of an animal. —*idioms:* **cry over spilled milk** To regret in vain what cannot be undone. **cry wolf** To raise a false alarm. [< Lat. *quirītāre,* cry out.]

cry·ba·by (krī′bā′bē) ►*n.* One who cries or complains frequently with little cause.

cryo– ►*pref.* Cold; freezing: *cryogenics.* [< Gk. *kruos,* icy cold.]

cry·o·gen (krī′ə-jən) ►*n.* A liquid used to obtain very low temperatures; refrigerant. —**cry′o·gen′ic** *adj.*

cry·o·gen·ics (krī′ə-jĕn′ĭks) ►*n. (takes sing. or pl. v.)* The production of low temperatures or the study of low-temperature phenomena.

cry·o·sur·ger·y (krī′ō-sûr′jə-rē) ►*n.* Destruction of abnormal tissue by exposure to extreme cold.

crypt (krĭpt) ►*n.* **1.** An underground vault, esp. one under a church used as a burial place. **2.** A small pit or glandular cavity in the body. [< Gk. *kruptē.*]

cryp·tic (krĭp′tĭk) ►*adj.* **1.** Having an ambiguous or hidden meaning. See Synonyms at **mysterious. 2.** Using code. [< Gk. *kruptikos.*] —**cryp′-ti·cal·ly** *adv.*

crypto– or **crypt–** ►*pref.* Hidden; secret: *cryptogram.* [< Gk. *kruptos,* hidden.]

cryp·to·gram (krĭp′tə-grăm′) ►*n.* A piece of writing in code or cipher.

cryp·tog·ra·phy (krĭp-tŏg′rə-fē) ►*n.* The process or skill of using or deciphering secret writings. —**cryp·tog′ra·pher** *n.*

crys·tal (krĭs′təl) ►*n.* **1.** A homogenous solid formed by a repeating, three-dimensional pattern of atoms, ions, or molecules and having fixed distances between constituent parts. **2.** A high-quality clear glass. **3.** A clear protective cover for a watch or clock face. [< Gk. *krustallos.*] —**crys′tal·line** *adj.*

crys·tal·lize (krĭs′tə-līz′) ►*v.* **-lized, -liz·ing 1.** To form or cause to form a crystalline structure. **2.** To take on a definite, precise, and usu. permanent form: *a plan that slowly crystallized.* —**crys′tal·li·za′tion** (-lĭ-zā′shən) *n.*

crys·tal·log·ra·phy (krĭs′tə-lŏg′rə-fē) ►*n.* The science of crystal structure and phenomena. —**crys′tal·log′ra·pher** *n.*

CSA ►*abbr.* Confederate States of America

csc ►*abbr.* cosecant

C-sec·tion (sē′sĕk′shən) ►*n.* A cesarean section.

CST ►*abbr.* Central Standard Time

CT ►*abbr.* **1.** Central Time **2.** computerized tomography **3.** Connecticut

ct. ►*abbr.* **1.** cent **2.** certificate **3. Ct.** court

cu. ►*abbr.* cubic

cub (kŭb) ►*n.* **1.** The young of certain carnivorous animals, such as the bear. **2.** A youth or novice. [?]

Cu·ba (kyōo′bə) An island country in the West

Indies S of FL. Cap. Havana. —**Cu′ban** *adj. & n.*

cub·by·hole (kŭb′ē-hōl′) ►*n.* A small or cramped space. [< *cub*, pen, hutch.]

cube (kyo͞ob) ►*n.* **1.** *Math.* A regular solid having six congruent square faces. **2a.** Something shaped like a cube: *a cube of sugar.* **b.** A cubicle, used for work or study. **3.** *Math.* The third power of a number or quantity. ►*v.* **cubed, cub·ing 1.** *Math.* To raise (a quantity or number) to the third power. **2.** To form or cut into cubes; dice. [< Gk. *kubos.*]

cu·bic (kyo͞o′bĭk) ►*adj.* **1.** Having the shape of a cube. **2a.** Having three dimensions. **b.** Having a volume equal to a cube whose edge is of a stated length: *a cubic foot.* **3.** *Math.* Of the third power, order, or degree.

cu·bi·cal (kyo͞o′bĭ-kəl) ►*adj.* **1.** Cubic. **2.** Of or relating to volume. —**cu′bi·cal·ly** *adv.*

cu·bi·cle (kyo͞o′bĭ-kəl) ►*n.* A small compartment, as for work or sleeping. [< Lat. *cubiculum* < *cubāre*, lie down.]

cub·ism (kyo͞o′bĭz′əm) ►*n.* A 20th-cent. school of painting and sculpture characterized by abstract, often geometric structures. —**cub′ist** *n.* —**cu·bis′tic** *adj.*

cu·bit (kyo͞o′bĭt) ►*n.* An ancient unit of linear measure, approx. 17 to 22 in. (43 to 56 cm). [< Lat. *cubitum.*]

cuck·old (kŭk′əld, ko͞ok′-) ►*n.* A man whose wife is unfaithful. ►*v.* To make a cuckold of. [< AN *cucuald* < *cucu*, cuckoo.]

cuck·oo (ko͞o′ko͞o, ko͞ok′o͞o) ►*n., pl.* -**oos 1.** A grayish bird of Eurasia and Africa that lays its eggs in the nests of other birds. **2.** Its two-note call. ►*adj. Slang* Foolish or crazy. [ME *cuccu*, of imit. orig.]

cu·cum·ber (kyo͞o′kŭm′bər) ►*n.* **1.** A vine bearing an edible cylindrical fruit with a green rind and crisp white flesh. **2.** The fruit itself. [< Lat. *cucumis, cucumer-.*]

cud (kŭd) ►*n.* Food regurgitated from the first stomach to the mouth of a ruminant and chewed again. [< OE *cudu.*]

cud·dle (kŭd′l) ►*v.* -**dled, -dling 1.** To hug tenderly. See Synonyms at **caress. 2.** To nestle; snuggle. [?] —**cud′dly** *adj.*

cudg·el (kŭj′əl) ►*n.* A short heavy club. [< OE *cycgel.*] —**cudg′el** *v.*

cue¹ (kyo͞o) ►*n.* A long tapered rod used to strike the cue ball in billiards and pool. [Var. of QUEUE.] —**cue** *v.*

cue² (kyo͞o) ►*n.* **1.** A word or signal, as in a play, used esp. to prompt another actor's speech or entrance. **2.** A reminder or hint. ►*v.* **cued, cu·ing 1.** To give a cue to. **2.** To position (an audio or video recording) in readiness for playing. [Perh. < *q* < Lat. *quandō*, when.]

cue ball ►*n.* The white ball propelled with the cue in billiards and pool.

cuff¹ (kŭf) ►*n.* **1.** A fold or band at the bottom of a sleeve. **2.** The turned-up fold at the bottom of a trouser leg. **3.** A handcuff. **4.** A bracelet made of a curved, open-ended band that fits the wrist firmly without a clasp. ►*v.* To put handcuffs on. —*idiom:* **off the cuff** Extemporaneously. [ME *cuffe*, mitten.]

cuff² (kŭf) ►*v.* To strike with the open hand; slap. [?] —**cuff** *n.*

cuff·link (kŭf′lĭngk′) ►*n.* A paired or jointed fastening for a shirt cuff.

cui·sine (kwĭ-zēn′) ►*n.* **1.** A manner or style of preparing food: *Cuban cuisine.* **2.** Food; fare. [< Lat. *coquīna*, cookery.]

cul-de-sac (kŭl′dĭ-săk′, ko͞ol′-) ►*n., pl.* **culs-de-sac** (kŭlz′-, ko͞olz′-) or **cul-de-sacs 1.** A dead-end street. **2.** An impasse. [Fr.]

cu·li·nar·y (kŭl′ə-nĕr′ē, kyo͞o′lə-) ►*adj.* Of or relating to cooking or cookery. [< Lat. *culīna*, kitchen.]

cull (kŭl) ►*v.* **1.** To pick out from others; select. **2.** To gather; collect. **3.** To remove rejected members or parts from (a herd, e.g.). [< Lat. *colligere*, collect.] —**cull′er** *n.*

cul·mi·nate (kŭl′mə-nāt′) ►*v.* -**nat·ed, -nat·ing 1.** To reach the highest point or degree. **2.** To end. [< Lat. *culmen*, peak.] —**cul′mi·na′tion** *n.*

cu·lottes (ko͞o-lŏts′, kyo͞o-, ko͞o′lŏts′, kyo͞o′-) ►*pl.n.* A woman's full trousers cut to resemble a skirt. [Fr., dim. of *cul*, rump.]

cul·pa·ble (kŭl′pə-bəl) ►*adj.* Deserving of blame; blameworthy. [< Lat. *culpa*, fault.] —**cul′pa·bil′i·ty** *n.* —**cul′pa·bly** *adv.*

cul·prit (kŭl′prĭt) ►*n.* One charged with or guilty of a crime. [< *cul. prit* : abbr. of AN *culpable*, guilty + **prit*, ready.]

cult (kŭlt) ►*n.* **1.** A religion or sect considered extremist or false. **2.** A system of religious worship and ritual. **3a.** Obsessive devotion to a person or principle. **b.** The object of such devotion. [Lat. *cultus*, worship.] —**cult′ism** *n.* —**cult′ist** *n.*

cul·ti·var (kŭl′tə-vär′, -vâr′) ►*n.* A plant variety created or selected intentionally and maintained through cultivation.

cul·ti·vate (kŭl′tə-vāt′) ►*v.* -**vat·ed, -vat·ing 1.** To improve and prepare (land) for raising crops. **2.** To grow or tend (a plant or crop). **3.** To foster. See Synonyms at **nurture. 4.** To form and refine, as by education. **5.** To seek the acquaintance or good will of: *cultivate a friendship.* [Med.Lat. *cultivāre* < Lat. *colere, cult-*, till.] —**cul′ti·va′tion** *n.* —**cul′ti·va′tor** *n.*

cul·ture (kŭl′chər) ►*n.* **1.** The arts, beliefs, customs, institutions, and other products of human work and thought considered as a unit, esp. with regard to a particular time or social group. **2.** Mental refinement and sophisticated taste resulting from the appreciation of the arts and sciences: *a woman of great culture.* **3.** The set of predominating attitudes and behavior that characterize a group: *corporate culture.* **4.** The breeding of animals or growing of plants, esp. to improve stock. **5.** *Biol.* The growth of microorganisms, tissue cells, or other living matter in a specially prepared nutrient medium. ►*v.* -**tured, -tur·ing** To grow (microorganisms or other living matter) in a specially prepared nutrient medium. [< Lat. *cultūra* < *colere*, cultivate.] —**cul′tur·al** *adj.* —**cul′tur·al·ly** *adv.* —**cul′tured** *adj.*

cul·vert (kŭl′vərt) ►*n.* A drain crossing under a road or embankment. [?]

cum·ber (kŭm′bər) ►*v.* **1.** To weigh down: *cumbered with duties.* **2.** To litter; clutter up: *Weeds cumbered the garden paths.* [< OFr. *combrer*, annoy < *combre*, hindrance.] —**cum′brous** *adj.*

Cum·ber·land Gap (kŭm′bər-lənd) A natural passage through the Cumberland Mountains near the junction of KY, VA, and TN.

Cumberland Mountains A range of the Appalachian Mts., extending from W VA to E TN and abutted on the W by the **Cumberland Plateau.**

cum·ber·some (kŭm′bər-səm) ►*adj.* **1.** Difficult to handle; unwieldy: *cumbersome luggage.* **2.** Difficult to deal with: *cumbersome instructions.*

cum·in (kŭm′ĭn, ko͞o′mĭn, kyo͞o′-) ►*n.* A plant having aromatic seedlike fruit used for seasoning. [< Gk. *kuminon.*]

cum·mer·bund (kŭm′ər-bŭnd′) ►*n.* A broad pleated sash worn with a tuxedo. [Hindi *kamarband.*]

Cum·mings (kŭm′ĭngz), **Edward Estlin** e.e. cummings. 1894–1962. Amer. poet.

cu·mu·la·tive (kyo͞om′yə-lā′tĭv, -yə-lə-tĭv) ►*adj.* **1.** Increasing or enlarging by successive addition. **2.** Relating to interest that is added to the next payment if not paid when due. [< Lat. *cumulāre,* heap up.]

cu·mu·lo·nim·bus (kyo͞om′yə-lō-nĭm′bəs) ►*n., pl.* **-bus·es** or **-bi** (-bī) An extremely dense cumulus extending to great heights, usu. producing heavy rains or thunderstorms. [CUMUL(US) + NIMBUS.]

cu·mu·lus (kyo͞om′yə-ləs) ►*n., pl.* **-li** (-lī′) A dense, white, fluffy flat-based cloud with a multiple rounded top and a well-defined outline. [Lat., heap.]

cu·ne·i·form (kyo͞o′nē-ə-fôrm′, kyo͞o-nē′-) ►*adj.* Wedge-shaped, as the characters used in ancient Mesopotamian writing. ►*n.* Cuneiform writing. [< Lat. *cuneus,* wedge.]

cun·ning (kŭn′ĭng) ►*adj.* **1.** Shrewdly deceptive. **2.** Exhibiting ingenuity. ►*n.* **1.** Skill in deception. **2.** Skill in execution or performance. [< OE *cunnan,* know.] **—cun′ning·ly** *adv.*

cup (kŭp) ►*n.* **1a.** A small open container used for drinking. **b.** Such a container and its contents. **2.** See table at **measurement. 3.** A cuplike object, such as a trophy. ►*v.* **cupped, cup·ping** To shape like a cup: *cup one's hand.* [< LLat. *cuppa,* drinking vessel.]

cup·board (kŭb′ərd) ►*n.* A closet or cabinet used esp. for storing food and cookware.

cup·cake (kŭp′kāk′) ►*n.* A small, cup-shaped cake.

Cu·pid (kyo͞o′pĭd) ►*n.* **1.** *Rom. Myth.* The god of love; the son of Venus. **2. cupid** A representation of Cupid as a boy having wings and a bow and arrow. [< Lat. *cupere,* to desire.]

cu·pid·i·ty (kyo͞o-pĭd′ĭ-tē) ►*n.* Excessive desire, esp. for wealth. [< Lat. *cupere,* to desire.]

cu·po·la (kyo͞o′pə-lə) ►*n.* A small, usu. domed structure surmounting a roof. [Ital.]

cur (kûr) ►*n.* **1.** A mongrel dog. **2.** A base person. [ME *curre.*]

Cu·ra·çao (ko͞or′ə-sou′, kyo͞or′-, ko͞or′ə-sou′, kyo͞or′-) An island territory of the Netherlands in the S Caribbean Sea off the NW coast of Venezuela.

cu·ra·re (ko͞o-rä′rē, kyo͞o-) ►*n.* Any of several plant extracts used as an arrow poison or as a drug to relax skeletal muscles during anesthesia. [Of Cariban and Tupian orig.]

cu·rate (kyo͞or′ĭt) ►*n.* **1.** A cleric who has charge of a parish. **2.** A cleric who assists a rector or vicar. [< Med.Lat. *cūrātus* < Lat. *cūra,* care.]

cu·ra·tive (kyo͞or′ə-tĭv) ►*adj.* Serving or tending to cure. **—cur′a·tive** *n.*

cu·ra·tor (kyo͞o-rā′tər, kyo͞or′ə-tər) ►*n.* One in charge of a collection, as at a museum or library. [< Lat. *cūrātor,* overseer < *cūra,* care.] **—cu′ra·to′ri·al** (kyo͞or′ə-tôr′ē-əl) *adj.* **—cu′ra′tor·ship′** *n.*

curb (kûrb) ►*n.* **1.** A concrete or stone edging along a street. **2.** Something that checks or restrains. **3.** A chain or strap used with a bit to restrain a horse. ►*v.* **1.** To check, restrain, or control. **2.** To lead (a dog) off the sidewalk into the gutter so that it can excrete waste. [< Lat. *curvus,* curved.]

curb·stone (kûrb′stōn′) ►*n.* A stone or row of stones that constitutes a curb.

curd (kûrd) ►*n.* The coagulated part of sour milk, used to make cheese. [ME, var. of *crud.*]

cur·dle (kûr′dl) ►*v.* **-dled, -dling 1.** To change into curd. **2.** To become congealed or lumpy: *The sauce curdled in the pan.* **3.** To become spoiled: *Warm feelings curdled into distrust.*

cure (kyo͞or) ►*n.* **1.** Restoration of health: *likeliness of cure.* **2.** A drug or course of medical treatment used to restore health. ►*v.* **cured, cur·ing 1.** To cause to be free of a disease or medical disorder. **2.** To preserve (e.g., meat), as by salting, smoking, or aging. **3.** To remedy (something): *cure the desire to eat sweets.* [< Lat. *cūra,* care.] **—cur′a·ble** *adj.* **—cur′er** *n.*

cure-all (kyo͞or′ôl′) ►*n.* Something that cures all diseases or evils; panacea.

cu·ret·tage (kyo͞or′ĭ-täzh′) ►*n.* The removal of tissue from a body cavity by scraping. [Fr. < *curette,* surgical scoop < Lat. *cūra,* care.]

cur·few (kûr′fyo͞o) ►*n.* **1.** A regulation or rule requiring certain or all people to leave the streets or be at home at a prescribed hour. **2.** The signal, as a bell, announcing the hour of a curfew. [< OFr. *cuevrefeu* : *covrir,* COVER + *feu,* fire.]

cu·ri·a or **Cu·ri·a** (ko͞or′ē-ə, kyo͞or′-) ►*n., pl.* **-ri·ae** (-ē-ē′) **1.** The central administration governing the Catholic Church. **2.** The ensemble of central administrative and governmental services in imperial Rome. [Lat. *cūria,* council.] **—cu′ri·al** *adj.*

cu·rie (kyo͞or′ē, kyo͞o-rē′) ►*n.* A former unit of radioactivity, equal to the amount of a radioactive isotope that decays at the rate of 3.7×10^{10} disintegrations per second. [After Marie CURIE.]

Cu·rie (kyo͞or′ē, kyo͞o-rē′), **Marie Skłodowska** 1867–1934. Polish-born French chemist.

Marie Curie

Curie, Pierre 1859–1906. French physicist.

cu·ri·o (kyŏŏr′ē-ō′) ►*n., pl.* **-os** A curious or unusual object of art. [Short for CURIOSITY.]

cu·ri·ous (kyŏŏr′ē-əs) ►*adj.* **1.** Eager to learn. **2.** Unduly inquisitive; prying. **3.** Arousing interest because of novelty or strangeness: *A curious fact.* [< Lat. *cūriōsus* < *cūra*, care.] —**cu′ri·ous·ly** *adv.* —**cu′ri·os′i·ty** (-ŏs′ĭ-tē) *n.*

cu·ri·um (kyŏŏr′ē-əm) ►*n. Symbol* **Cm** A silvery metallic synthetic radioactive element. At. no. 96. See table at **element.** [After Marie CURIE and Pierre CURIE.]

curl (kûrl) ►*v.* **1.** To form or twist into ringlets or coils. **2.** To assume or form into a coiled or spiral shape. ►*n.* **1.** A ringlet of hair. **2.** Something with a spiral or coiled shape. [< ME *crulle*, curly.] —**curl′y** *adj.* —**curl′er** *n.*

cur·lew (kûrl′yŏŏ, kûr′lŏŏ) ►*n.* A brownish, long-legged shorebird with a slender, downward-curving bill. [< OFr. *courlieu.*]

curl·i·cue (kûr′lĭ-kyŏŏ′) ►*n.* A fancy twist or curl. [CURLY + *cue*, tail.]

curl·ing (kûr′lĭng) ►*n.* A game in which two four-person teams slide stones toward the center of a circle at either end of a length of ice.

cur·mudg·eon (kər-mŭj′ən) ►*n.* A cantankerous person. [?]

cur·rant (kûr′ənt, kûr′-) ►*n.* **1.** Any of various shrubs having edible, usu. red or blackish berries. **2.** The fruit of any of these plants. **3.** A small seedless raisin. [< ME *(raysons of) coraunte*, (raisins of) Corinth.]

cur·ren·cy (kûr′ən-sē, kûr′-) ►*n., pl.* **-cies 1.** Money in any form when in actual use as a medium of exchange. **2.** General acceptance or use: *the currency of a slang term.* **3.** The state of being current.

cur·rent (kûr′ənt, kûr′-) ►*adj.* **1.** Belonging to the present time. **2.** Being in progress now: *current negotiations.* ►*n.* **1.** A steady onward movement. See Synonyms at **flow. 2.** The part of a body of liquid or gas that is in flow. **3a.** A flow of electric charge. **b.** The amount of charge flowing past a specified circuit point per unit time. [< Lat. *currere*, run.] —**cur′rent·ly** *adv.*

cur·ric·u·lum (kə-rĭk′yə-ləm) ►*n., pl.* **-la** (-lə) or **-lums** The courses of study offered by an educational institution. [Lat., course.] —**cur·ric′u·lar** *adj.*

curriculum vi·tae (vī′tē, vē′tī) ►*n., pl.* **curricula vitae** A summary of one's education, professional history, and job qualifications. [Lat. *curriculum vītae*, the race of life.]

cur·ry¹ (kûr′ē, kûr′ē) ►*v.* **-ried, -ry·ing 1.** To groom (a horse) with a currycomb. **2.** To prepare (tanned hides) for use. —*idiom:* **curry favor** To seek favor by flattery. [< VLat. **conrēdāre* : COM– + **-rēdāre*, make ready.]

cur·ry² (kûr′ē, kûr′ē) ►*n., pl.* **-ries 1.** A pungent seasoning typically made with ground spices, including cumin, coriander, and turmeric. **2.** A sauce or dish seasoned with curry. ►*v.* **-ried, -ry·ing** To season (food) with curry. [Tamil *kaṟi.*]

cur·ry·comb (kûr′ē-kōm′, kûr′-) ►*n.* A comb with metal teeth, used for grooming horses.

curse (kûrs) ►*n.* **1a.** An appeal for evil or misfortune to befall a person or thing. **b.** Evil or misfortune resulting from or as if from a curse. **2.** A source or cause of evil. **3.** A profane word or phrase. ►*v.* **cursed** or **curst** (kûrst), **curs·ing 1.** To invoke evil upon. **2.** To swear (at). **3.** To bring a curse upon. [< OE *curs.*]

curs·ed (kûr′sĭd, kûrst) also **curst** (kûrst) ►*adj.* Detestable; damned.

cur·sive (kûr′sĭv) ►*adj.* Having the successive letters joined: *cursive writing.* [< Med.Lat. *(scrīpta) cursīva*, running (script).]

cur·sor (kûr′sər) ►*n. Comp.* A movable indicator on a display, marking a position where typed characters will appear or where an option can be selected. [< Lat., runner.]

cur·so·ry (kûr′sə-rē) ►*adj.* Performed with haste and scant attention to detail. [< Lat. *currere*, *curs-*, run.] —**cur′so·ri·ly** *adv.*

curt (kûrt) ►*adj.* **-er, -est 1.** Rudely brief or abrupt. **2.** Terse; condensed. [< Lat. *curtus*, cut short.] —**curt′ly** *adv.* —**curt′ness** *n.*

cur·tail (kər-tāl′) ►*v.* To cut short. See Synonyms at **shorten.** [< OFr. *courtauld*, docked + *tailler*, cut; see TAILOR.] —**cur·tail′ment** *n.*

cur·tain (kûr′tn) ►*n.* **1.** Material that hangs in a window or other opening as a decoration, shade, or screen. **2.** Something resembling a screen: *a curtain of fire.* **3.** The drape in a theater that separates the stage from the auditorium. **4. curtains** *Slang* The end or ruin of something: *If he doesn't shape up, it's curtains.* [< LLat. *cōrtīna* < Lat. *cōrs, cōrt-*, COURT.] —**cur′tain** *v.*

curt·sy or **curt·sey** (kûrt′sē) ►*n., pl.* **-sies** or **-seys** A gesture of respect made chiefly by women by bending the knees with one foot forward. [Var. of COURTESY.] —**curt′sy** *v.*

cur·va·ceous (kûr-vā′shəs) ►*adj.* Having a full or voluptuous figure.

cur·va·ture (kûr′və-chŏŏr′, -chər) ►*n.* The act of curving or the state of being curved.

curve (kûrv) ►*n.* **1a.** A line that deviates from straightness in a smooth, continuous fashion. **b.** A surface that deviates from planarity in such a fashion. **2.** Something that has the shape of a curve. ►*v.* **curved, curv·ing** To move in, form, or cause to form a curve. [< Lat. *curvus.*] —**curv′y** *adj.*

cush·ion (kŏŏsh′ən) ►*n.* **1.** A soft pad or pillow for resting, reclining, or kneeling. **2.** Something that absorbs or softens an impact. **3.** Something that mitigates an adverse effect: *extra funds as a cushion against inflation.* ►*v.* **1.** To absorb the shock of. **2.** To protect from impacts or disturbing effects. [< Lat. *coxa*, hip.]

Cush·it·ic (kŏŏ-shĭt′ĭk) ►*n.* A branch of the Afro-Asiatic language family spoken in Somalia, Ethiopia, and N Kenya.

cush·y (kŏŏsh′ē) ►*adj.* **-i·er, -i·est** *Informal* Making few demands; comfortable: *a cushy job with no responsibilities.* [?]

cusp (kŭsp) ►*n.* **1.** A point or pointed end, as of a tooth or crescent. **2.** A triangular fold or flap of a heart valve. —*idiom:* **on the cusp** On the threshold of a development or action: *an actor on the cusp of becoming a star.* [Lat. *cuspis.*]

cus·pid (kŭs′pĭd) ►*n.* See **canine** (sense 2). [< Lat. *cuspis, cuspid-*, point.]

cus·pi·dor (kŭs′pĭ-dôr′) ►*n.* A spittoon. [Port. < *cuspir*, to spit.]

cuss (kŭs) *Informal* ►*v.* To curse (at). ►*n.* **1.** A curse. **2.** A stubborn or perverse person. [Alteration of CURSE.]

cus·tard (kŭs′tərd) ►*n.* A dish of milk, eggs, flavoring, and sugar, cooked until set. [< Lat. *crūsta*, crust.]

CURRENCY TABLE: LISTED BY BASIC UNIT

Unit	Country
afghani	Afghanistan
ariary	Madagascar
baht	Thailand
balboa	Panama
birr	Ethiopia
bolivar	Venezuela
boliviano	Bolivia
cedi	Ghana
colon	Costa Rica
	El Salvador
cordoba	Nicaragua
dalasi	Gambia
denar	Macedonia
dinar	Algeria
	Bahrain
	Iraq
	Jordan
	Kuwait
	Libya
	Serbia
	Sudan
	Tunisia
dirham	Morocco
	United Arab Emirates
dobra	São Tomé and Príncipe
dollar	Antigua and Barbuda
	Australia
	Bahamas
	Barbados
	Belize
	Brunei
	Canada
	Dominica
	East Timor
	Ecuador
	Fiji
	Grenada
	Guyana
	Jamaica
	Kiribati
	Liberia
	Marshall Islands
	Micronesia
	Namibia
	Nauru
	New Zealand
	Palau
	Saint Kitts and Nevis
	Saint Lucia
	Saint Vincent and the Grenadines
	Singapore
	Solomon Islands
	Suriname
	Trinidad and Tobago
	Tuvalu
	United States
	Zimbabwe
dong	Vietnam
dram	Armenia
escudo	Cape Verde
euro	Andorra
	Austria
	Belgium
	Cyprus
	Estonia
	Finland
	France
	Germany
	Greece
	Ireland
	Italy
	Kosovo
	Luxembourg
	Malta
	Monaco
	Montenegro
	Netherlands
	Portugal
	San Marino
	Slovakia
	Slovenia
	Spain
	Vatican City
forint	Hungary
franc	Benin
	Burkina Faso
	Burundi
	Cameroon
	Central African Republic
	Chad
	Comoros
	Congo (Rep. of)
	Congo (Dem. Rep. of)
	Côte d'Ivoire
	Djibouti
	Equatorial Guinea
	Gabon
	Guinea
	Guinea-Bissau
	Liechtenstein
	Mali
	Niger
	Rwanda
	Senegal
	Switzerland
	Togo
gourde	Haiti
guarani	Paraguay
hryvnia	Ukraine
kina	Papua New Guinea
kip	Laos
koruna	Czech Republic
krona	Iceland
	Sweden
krone	Denmark
	Norway
kuna	Croatia
kwacha	Malawi
	Zambia
kwanza	Angola
kyat	Myanmar
lari	Georgia
lats	Latvia
lek	Albania
lempira	Honduras
leone	Sierra Leone
leu	Moldova
	Romania
lev	Bulgaria
lilangeni	Swaziland
lira	Turkey
litas	Lithuania
livre	Lebanon
loti	Lesotho
manat	Azerbaijan
	Turkmenistan
marka	Bosnia and Herzegovina
metical	Mozambique
naira	Nigeria
nakfa	Eritrea
ngultrum	Bhutan
ouguiya	Mauritania
pa'anga	Tonga
peso	Argentina
	Chile
	Colombia
	Cuba
	Dominican Republic
	Mexico
	Uruguay
piso	Philippines
pound	Egypt
	Lebanon
	Syria
	United Kingdom
pula	Botswana
quetzal	Guatemala
rand	South Africa
real	Brazil
rial	Iran
	Oman
	Yemen
riel	Cambodia
ringgit	Malaysia
riyal	Qatar
	Saudi Arabia
rubel	Belarus
ruble	Russia
rufiyaa	Maldives
rupee	India
	Mauritius
	Nepal
	Pakistan
	Seychelles
	Sri Lanka
rupiah	Indonesia
sheqel	Israel
shilin	Somalia
shilling	Kenya
	Tanzania
	Uganda
sol	Peru
som	Kyrgyzstan
	Uzbekistan
somoni	Tajikistan
taka	Bangladesh
tala	Samoa
tenge	Kazakhstan
tögrög	Mongolia
vatu	Vanuatu
won	North Korea
	South Korea
yen	Japan
yuan	China
	Taiwan
zloty	Poland

Cus·ter (kŭs′tər), **George Armstrong** 1839–76. Amer. soldier.

cus·to·di·al (kŭ-stō′dē-əl) ►*adj.* **1.** Relating to a custodian: *custodial duties at the high school.* **2.** Relating to custody: *custodial parent.*

cus·to·di·an (kŭ-stō′dē-ən) ►*n.* **1.** One that has charge of something; caretaker. **2.** A janitor. —**cus·to′di·an·ship′** *n.*

cus·to·dy (kŭs′tə-dē) ►*n., pl.* **-dies 1.** The control and care of a person or property, esp. when granted by a court. See Synonyms at **care. 2.** The state of being held under guard, esp. by the police. [< Lat. *custōs, custōd-,* guard.]

cus·tom (kŭs′təm) ►*n.* **1.** A practice followed by people of a particular group or region. **2.** A person's habitual practice: *her custom of reading before sleep.* **3. customs a.** Duties or taxes on imported goods. **b.** *(takes sing. v.)* The governmental agency authorized to collect these duties. ►*adj.* Made to order: *a custom suit.* [< Lat. *cōnsuētūdo.*]

cus·tom·ar·y (kŭs′tə-mĕr′ē) ►*adj.* **1.** Commonly practiced or used; usual. See Synonyms at **usual. 2.** Established by custom. —**cus′tom·ar′i·ly** (-mâr′ə-lē) *adv.*

cus·tom·er (kŭs′tə-mər) ►*n.* **1.** One that buys goods or services. **2.** An individual with whom one must deal: *That teacher is a tough customer.*

cus·tom·house (kŭs′təm-hous′) ►*n.* A building or office where customs are collected and ships are cleared for entering or leaving the country.

cus·tom·ize (kŭs′tə-mīz′) ►*v.* **-ized, -iz·ing** To make or alter to individual specifications. —**cus′tom·i·za′tion** *n.*

cus·tom-made (kŭs′təm-mād′) ►*adj.* Made according to the specifications of the buyer.

customs union ►*n.* An international association organized to eliminate customs restrictions between member nations and to set a tariff policy toward nonmembers.

cut (kŭt) ►*v.* **cut, cut·ting 1.** To penetrate with a sharp edge. **2.** To separate into parts with a sharp-edged instrument; sever: *cut cloth.* **3.** To sever the edges or ends of; shorten: *cut hair.* **4.** To mow; harvest: *cut grass.* **5.** To have (a new tooth) grow through the gums. **6.** To form or shape by incising: *a doll cut from paper.* **7.** To separate from a main body; detach: *cut a limb from a tree.* **8.** To remove or delete: *cut six players from the team.* **9.** To reduce the size, amount, or duration of: *cut the budget.* **10.** *Comp.* To remove (a segment) from a file for storage in a buffer. **11.** To dilute: *cut whiskey with water.* **12.** To hurt keenly. **13.** To fail to attend purposely: *cut a class.* **14.** To stop: *cut the noise.* **15.** To stop filming (a movie scene). **16.** To make a recording of. **17.** To make out and issue: *cut a check to cover expenses.* ►*n.* **1.** The act or result of cutting. **2.** A part that has been cut from a main body: *a cut of beef.* **3.** A passage made by digging or eroding. **4.** The reduction or elimination of something: *a cut in a speech.* **5.** The style in which a garment is cut. **6.** A portion of profits or earnings; a share. **7.** An insult. **8.** A film at a given stage in its editing: *The director approved the final cut.* —*phrasal verbs:* **cut back 1.** To prune. **2.** To reduce or decrease. **cut down 1.** To kill. **2.** To reduce consumption or use. **cut in 1.** To enter a line out of turn. **2.** To interrupt. **cut off 1.** To isolate. **2.** To discontinue. **cut out 1.** To be suited: *not cut out to be*

a hero. **2.** To stop. **cut up** *Informal* To behave in a playful way. —*idioms:* **cut and run** To leave an unsettled situation or abandon a risky enterprise. **cut corners** To do something in the easiest or cheapest way. [ME *cutten.*]

cut-and-dried (kŭt′n-drīd′) ►*adj.* In accordance with a standard formula; routine.

cu·ta·ne·ous (kyōō-tā′nē-əs) ►*adj.* Relating to the skin. [< Lat. *cutis,* skin.]

cut·back (kŭt′băk′) ►*n.* A decrease; curtailment: *cutbacks in federal funding.*

cute (kyōōt) ►*adj.* **cut·er, cut·est 1.** Attractive: *wore a cute outfit.* **2.** Clever or witty, esp. impertinently or evasively: *Don't get cute with me.* [Short for ACUTE.] —**cute′ly** *adv.* —**cute′ness** *n.*

cute·sy (kyōōt′sē) ►*adj.* **-si·er, -si·est** *Informal* Deliberately or affectedly cute.

cu·ti·cle (kyōō′tĭ-kəl) ►*n.* **1.** The outermost layer of the skin of vertebrates; epidermis. **2.** The strip of hardened skin at the base of a fingernail or toenail. [< *cutis,* skin.]

cut·lass (kŭt′ləs) ►*n.* A short heavy sword with a curved blade. [< Lat. *cultellus,* dim. of *culter,* knife.]

cut·ler·y (kŭt′lə-rē) ►*n.* Cutting instruments and tools, esp. tableware. [< OFr. *coutel,* knife; see CUTLASS.]

cut·let (kŭt′lĭt) ►*n.* **1.** A thin slice of meat cut from the leg or ribs. **2.** A patty of chopped meat or fish, usu. coated with bread crumbs and fried. [Fr. *côtelette* < OFr. *costelette* < Lat. *costa.*]

cut·off (kŭt′ôf′, -ŏf′) ►*n.* **1.** A designated limit or end. **2.** A shortcut or bypass. **3.** A device that cuts off a flow of fluid.

cut-rate (kŭt′rāt′) ►*adj.* Reduced in price.

cut·ter (kŭt′ər) ►*n.* **1.** A person or device that cuts. **2.** A ship's boat used for transporting stores or passengers. **3.** A small, lightly armed Coast Guard boat.

cut·throat (kŭt′thrōt′) ►*n.* **1.** A murderer. **2.** A ruthless person. ►*adj.* **1.** Cruel; murderous. **2.** Relentless in competition.

cut·ting (kŭt′ĭng) ►*n.* A part cut off from a main body, esp. a shoot removed from a plant for rooting or grafting. ►*adj.* **1.** Capable of or designed for incising, shearing, or severing. **2.** Injuring the feelings of others.

cut·tle·bone (kŭt′l-bōn′) ►*n.* The chalky internal shell of a cuttlefish, used as a dietary supplement for cage birds or as a mold for metal casting.

cut·tle·fish (kŭt′l-fĭsh′) ►*n.* A ten-armed, squidlike marine mollusk that has a chalky internal shell. [< OE *cudele.*]

cut·up (kŭt′ŭp′) ►*n.* *Informal* A prankster.

CV ►*abbr.* **1.** cardiovascular **2.** curriculum vitae

cwt ►*abbr.* hundredweight

–cy ►*suff.* **1.** Condition; quality: *bankruptcy.* **2.** Rank; office: *baronetcy.* **3.** Action; practice: *conspiracy.* [< Lat. *-cia, -tia* and Gk. *-kia, -tia.*]

cy·an (sī′ăn′, -ən) ►*n.* A greenish blue color. [Gk. *kuanos,* dark blue.]

cy·a·nide (sī′ə-nīd′) ►*n.* Any of various compounds containing a CN group, esp. potassium cyanide and sodium cyanide.

cyano– or **cyan–** ►*pref.* **1.** Blue: *cyanosis.* **2.** Cyanide: *cyanogen.* [< Gk. *kuanos,* dark blue.]

cy·an·o·gen (sī-ăn′ə-jən) ►*n.* A colorless, flammable, highly poisonous gas, used as a rocket propellant.

cy·a·no·sis (sī′ə-nō′sĭs) ►*n.* A bluish discoloration of the skin and mucous membranes resulting from inadequate oxygenation of the blood. —**cy′a·not′ic** (-nŏt′ĭk) *adj.*

cyber– ►*pref.* **1.** Computer: *cyberpunk.* **2.** Computer network: *cyberspace.*

cy·ber·net·ics (sī′bər-nĕt′ĭks) ►*n.* (*takes sing. v.*) The theoretical study of control processes in biological, mechanical, and electronic systems, esp. the comparison of these processes in biological and artificial systems. [< Gk. *kubernētēs,* governor.] —**cy′ber·net′ic** *adj.*

cy·ber·punk (sī′bər-pŭnk′) ►*n.* Fast-paced science fiction involving futuristic computer-based societies.

cy·ber·space (sī′bər-spās′) ►*n.* The electronic medium of computer networks, in which online communication takes place.

cy·cla·men (sī′klə-mən, sĭk′lə-) ►*n.* A houseplant with showy, variously colored flowers. [< Gk. *kuklaminos.*]

cy·cle (sī′kəl) ►*n.* **1.** An interval of time during which a regularly repeated event occurs. **2a.** A single occurrence of a periodically repeated phenomenon. **b.** A periodically repeated sequence of events. **3.** The orbit of a celestial body. **4.** A group of literary or musical works that concern a central theme or hero. **5.** A bicycle or motorcycle. ►*v.* **-cled, -cling 1.** To occur in or pass through a cycle. **2.** To ride a bicycle or motorcycle. [< Gk. *kuklos,* circle.] —**cy′cler** *n.* —**cy′clic** (sī′klĭk, sĭk′lĭk), **cy′cli·cal** *adj.*

cy·clist (sī′klĭst) ►*n.* One who rides a vehicle such as a bicycle or motorcycle.

cyclo– or **cycl–** ►*pref.* Circle: *cyclometer.* [< Gk. *kuklos.*]

cy·clom·e·ter (sī-klŏm′ĭ-tər) ►*n.* **1.** An instrument that records the revolutions of a wheel to indicate distance traveled. **2.** An instrument that measures circular arcs.

cy·clone (sī′klōn′) ►*n.* **1.** An atmospheric system characterized by the rapid inward circulation of air masses about a low-pressure center. **2.** A violent rotating windstorm, esp. a tornado. [< Gk. *kuklōn* < *kuklos,* circle.] —**cy·clon′ic** (-klŏn′ĭk) *adj.*

Cy·clops (sī′klŏps) ►*n., pl.* **Cy·clo·pes** (sī-klō′-pēz′) *Gk. Myth.* **1.** Any of three one-eyed Titans who forged thunderbolts for Zeus. **2.** Any of a race of one-eyed giants reputedly descended from these Titans.

cy·clo·tron (sī′klə-trŏn′) ►*n.* A circular particle accelerator that accelerates charged subatomic particles in a spiral path by an alternating electric field in a constant magnetic field.

cyg·net (sĭg′nĭt) ►*n.* A young swan. [< Gk. *kuknos,* swan.]

Cyg·nus (sĭg′nəs) ►*n.* A constellation in the Northern Hemisphere. [Lat. < Gk. *kuknos,* swan.]

cyl·in·der (sĭl′ən-dər) ►*n.* **1.** *Math.* **a.** The surface generated by a straight line intersecting and moving along a closed plane curve while remaining parallel to a fixed straight line that is not on or parallel to the plane of the closed curve. **b.** A solid bounded by two parallel planes and such a surface having a closed curve, esp. a circle. **2.** A cylindrical object. **3.** The chamber in which a piston moves. **4.** The rotating chamber of a revolver that holds the cartridges. **5.** The rotating chamber of a revolver that holds the cartridges. [< Gk. *kulindros.*] —**cy·lin′dri·cal** *adj.* —**cy·lin′dri·cal·ly** *adv.*

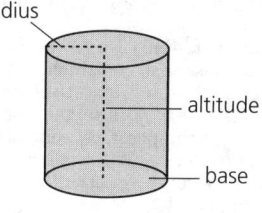

cylinder
To calculate the volume of a right circular cylinder, multiply the area of the base by the altitude.

cym·bal (sĭm′bəl) ►*n. Mus.* A percussion instrument that makes a loud clashing tone when hit with a drumstick or when used in pairs. [< Gk. *kumbalon.*]

cyn·ic (sĭn′ĭk) ►*n.* A person who believes all people are motivated only by self-interest. [< Gk. *kunikos,* like a dog < *kuōn,* dog.] —**cyn′i·cal** *adj.* —**cyn′i·cal·ly** *adv.* —**cyn′i·cism** *n.*

cy·no·sure (sī′nə-shŏŏr′, sĭn′ə-) ►*n.* A focal point of attention and admiration. [< Gk. *kunosoura,* Ursa Minor.]

cy·press (sī′prĭs) ►*n.* An evergreen tree or shrub having scalelike leaves and woody cones. [< Gk. *kuparissos.*]

Cy·prus (sī′prəs) An island country in the E Mediterranean S of Turkey. Cap. Nicosia. —**Cyp′ri·an** (sĭp′rē-ən), **Cyp′ri·ot** (-ət, -ŏt′) *adj. & n.*

Cy·ra·no de Ber·ge·rac (sîr′ə-nō də bûr′zhə-răk′, bĕr′-), **Savinien de** 1619–55. French satirist and duelist.

Cyr·il (sîr′əl), Saint. 827–869. Christian missionary and theologian.

Cy·ril·lic (sə-rĭl′ĭk) ►*adj.* Relating to an alphabet based esp. on that of Byzantine Greek and used for some Slavic languages, such as Russian.

Cyrus II (sī′rəs) "the Great." 600?–529? BC. King of Persia (550–529) and founder of the Persian Empire.

cyst (sĭst) ►*n. Med.* An abnormal membranous sac in the body containing usu. a liquid substance. [< Gk. *kustis,* bladder.]

cys·tic fibrosis (sĭs′tĭk) ►*n.* A hereditary disease of the exocrine glands, affecting mainly the pancreas, respiratory system, and sweat glands, marked by production of viscous mucus and resulting in chronic respiratory infections and impaired pancreatic function.

cys·to·scope (sĭs′tə-skōp′) ►*n.* A tubular instrument used to examine the urinary bladder. [Gk. *kustis,* bladder + –SCOPE.]

–cyte ►*suff.* Cell: *leukocyte.* [< Gk. *kutos,* hollow vessel.]

cyto– or **cyt–** ►*pref.* Cell: *cytoplasm.* [< Gk. *kutos,* hollow vessel.]

cy·to·kine (sī′tə-kīn′) ►*n.* Any of several regulatory proteins, such as the interleukins and lymphokines, that are released by cells of the immune system and act as intercellular mediators in the generation of an immune response. [CYTO– + Greek *kīnein,* to move.]

cy·tol·o·gy (sī-tŏl′ə-jē) ►*n.* The branch of biology that deals with the formation, structure, and function of cells. —**cy'to·log'ic** (-tə-lŏj'-ĭk), **cy'to·log'i·cal** *adj.* —**cy·tol'o·gist** *n.*

cy·to·plasm (sī'tə-plăz'əm) ►*n.* The protoplasm enclosed by the plasma membrane of a cell, excluding the nucleus or cellular DNA. —**cy'-to·plas'mic** *adj.*

cy·to·sine (sī'tə-sēn') ►*n.* A pyrimidine base that is an essential constituent of RNA and DNA. [CYT(O)– + (RIB)OS(E) + –INE².]

czar (zär, tsär) ►*n.* **1.** also **tsar** or **tzar** (zär, tsär) A king or emperor, esp. one of the former emperors of Russia. **2.** An official having special authority: *an energy czar.* [Russ. *tsar'* < Lat. *Caesar*, emperor.]

cza·ri·na (zä-rē'nə, tsä-) ►*n.* The wife of a Russian czar. [Alteration of Russ. *tsaritsa*, feminine of *tsar'*, czar.]

czar·ism (zär'ĭz'əm, tsär'-) ►*n.* The system of government in Russia under the czars. —**czar'-ist** *adj. & n.*

Czech (chĕk) ►*n.* **1.** A native or inhabitant of the Czech Republic. **2.** The Slavic language of the Czechs. —**Czech** *adj.*

Czech·o·slo·va·ki·a (chĕk'ə-slə-vä'kē-ə, -ō-slō-) A former country of central Europe; divided in 1993 into the Czech Republic and Slovakia. —**Czech'o·slo'vak, Czech'o·slo·va'ki·an** *adj. & n.*

Czech Republic A country of central Europe. Cap. Prague.

D

d or **D** (dē) ►*n., pl.* **d's** or **D's** also **ds** or **Ds 1.** The 4th letter of the English alphabet. **2.** *Mus.* The 2nd tone of the C major scale. **3. D** The lowest passing grade given to a student.

D¹ also **d** The symbol for the Roman numeral 500.

D² ►*abbr.* **1.** day **2.** *Sports* defense **3.** Democrat **4.** divorced **5.** down

d. ►*abbr.* **1.** date **2.** daughter **3.** died **4.** *Chiefly Brit.* penny ($\frac{1}{12}$ of a shilling)

DA ►*abbr.* **1.** district attorney **2.** Doctor of Arts

dab (dăb) ►*v.* **dabbed, dab·bing 1.** To apply or remove with short poking strokes: *dabbed paint on worn spots; dabbed tears from his eyes.* **2.** To pat lightly: *dabbed a napkin to her lips.* ►*n.* **1.** A small amount. **2.** A quick light pat. [ME *dabben.*]

dab·ble (dăb'əl) ►*v.* **-bled, -bling 1.** To splash or spatter with or as if with a liquid. **2.** To undertake something superficially or without serious intent. [Poss. < Du. *dabbelen.*] —**dab'-bler** *n.*

da ca·po (dä kä'pō) ►*adv. Mus.* From the beginning; used as a direction to repeat a passage. [Ital.]

Dac·ca (dăk'ə, dä'kə) See **Dhaka.**

dace (dās) ►*n., pl.* **dace** or **dac·es** A small freshwater fish related to the carps and minnows. [< LLat. *darsus.*]

da·cha (dä'chə) ►*n.* A Russian country house. [Russ.]

dachs·hund (däks'ho͝ont', däk'sənt, -sənd) ►*n.* A small dog having a long body, drooping ears, and very short legs. [Ger. : OHGer. *dahs*, badger + OHGer. *hunt*, dog.]

Da·cron (dā'krŏn', dăk'rŏn') A trademark for a synthetic polyester fabric or fiber.

dac·tyl (dăk'təl) ►*n.* **1.** A metrical foot consisting of one long or accented syllable followed by two short or unaccented ones. **2.** A finger or toe. [< Gk. *daktulos*, finger, dactyl.] —**dac·tyl'ic** (-tĭl'ĭk) *adj. & n.*

dad (dăd) ►*n. Informal* A father. [Of baby-talk orig.]

Da·da (dä'dä) ►*n.* A European artistic and literary movement (1916–23) that flouted conventional values in works marked by nonsense and incongruity. [Fr.] —**Da'da·ism** *n.* —**Da'da·ist** *adj. & n.*

dad·dy (dăd'ē) ►*n., pl.* **-dies** *Informal* A father.

daddy long·legs (lông'lĕgz', lŏng'-) ►*n., pl.* **daddy longlegs** A spiderlike arachnid with a small rounded body and long slender legs.

da·do (dā'dō) ►*n., pl.* **-does 1.** The section of a pedestal between the base and cornice or cap. **2.** The lower portion of an interior wall, decorated differently from the upper section, as with panels. [Ital. < Lat. *dare, dat-*, give.]

daf·fo·dil (dăf'ə-dĭl) ►*n.* A bulbous plant having showy, usu. yellow flowers with a trumpet-shaped central crown. [Alteration of ME *affodil*, ASPHODEL.]

daf·fy (dăf'ē) ►*adj.* **-fi·er, -fi·est** *Informal* **1.** Silly; zany. **2.** Crazy. [< ME *daffe*, fool.] —**daf'-fi·ly** *adv.* —**daf'fi·ness** *n.*

daft (dăft) ►*adj.* **-er, -est 1.** Crazy; deranged. **2.** Foolish; stupid. [< OE *gedæfte*, meek.] —**daft'-ly** *adv.* —**daft'ness** *n.*

dag·ger (dăg'ər) ►*n.* **1.** A short pointed weapon with sharp edges. **2.** Something that agonizes or torments. **3.** *Print.* See **obelisk** (sense 2). [ME *daggere.*]

da·guerre·o·type (də-gâr'ē-ə-tīp') ►*n.* A photograph made by an early process with the image developed on a light-sensitive silver-coated metallic plate. [After Louis J.M. *Daguerre* (1789–1851).]

dahl (däl) ►*n.* A spicy South Asian stew made with lentils. [< Skt. *dalaḥ*, piece split off.]

Dahl (däl), **Roald** 1916–90. British writer.

dahl·ia (dăl'yə, däl'-, dāl'-) ►*n.* A New World plant cultivated for its showy, variously colored flowers. [After Anders *Dahl* (1751–87).]

dai·kon (dī'kŏn', -kən) ►*n.* A large white radish with a long root, eaten in E Asia. [J.]

dai·ly (dā'lē) ►*adj.* **1.** Happening or done every day. **2.** Happening or done during the day. ►*adv.* **1.** Every day. **2.** Once a day. ►*n., pl.* **-lies 1.** A newspaper published every day or weekday. **2. dailies** Unedited movie film, usu. viewed after a day's shooting. [< OE *dæglic.*]

daily double ►*n.* A bet won by choosing both winners of two specified races on one day, as in horse racing.

dain·ty (dān'tē) ►*adj.* **-ti·er, -ti·est 1.** Delicately beautiful; exquisite. **2.** Fastidious; finicky: *They were too dainty to eat the local food.* **3.** Frail in health. ►*n., pl.* **-ties** A delicacy. [< Lat. *dignitās*, excellence.] —**dain'ti·ly** *adv.* —**dain'ti·ness** *n.*

daiq·ui·ri (dăk′ə-rē) ►*n., pl.* **-ris** An iced cocktail of rum, lime or lemon juice, and sugar. [After *Daiquirí*, Cuba.]

dair·y (dâr′ē) ►*n., pl.* **-ies 1.** An establishment for processing or selling milk and milk products. **2.** A dairy farm. **3.** Food containing milk or milk products. [< ME *daie*, dairymaid + AN *-erie*, place.] —**dair′y** *adj.* —**dair′y·maid′** *n.* —**dair′y·man** *n.* —**dair′y·wom′an** *n.*

dair·y·ing (dâr′ē-ĭng) ►*n.* The business of operating a dairy or a dairy farm.

da·is (dā′ĭs, dī′-) ►*n.* A raised platform, as in a lecture hall, for honored guests. [< LLat. *discus*, table; see DISK.]

dai·sy (dā′zē) ►*n., pl.* **-sies** A plant having flower heads with a yellow center and white or pinkish rays. [< OE *dæges ēage*, day's eye.]

Da·kar (də-kär′, dăk′är′) The capital of Senegal, in the W part.

Da·ko·ta (də-kō′tə) ►*n., pl.* **-ta** or **-tas 1.** See Santee. **2.** The Siouan language of the Santee. —**Da·ko′tan** *adj. & n.*

Da·lai Lama (dä′lī) ►*n.* The traditional head of the dominant sect of Buddhism in Tibet and Mongolia, held to be compassion incarnate. [Tibetan, ocean monk.]

da·la·si (dä-lä′sē) ►*n., pl.* **-si** See table at **currency.** [Mende.]

dale (dāl) ►*n.* A valley. [< OE *dæl.*]

Da·lí (dä-lē′, dä′lē), **Salvador** 1904–89. Spanish surrealist artist. —**Da′li·esque′** *adj.*

Da·lit (dä′lĭt) ►*n.* A member of the lowest class in traditional Indian society, falling outside the Hindu caste categories and subject to extensive social restrictions. [Hindi *dalit*, crushed, oppressed.]

Dal·las (dăl′əs) A city of NE TX E of Fort Worth.

dal·ly (dăl′ē) ►*v.* **-lied, -ly·ing 1.** To play amorously. See Synonyms at **flirt. 2.** To dawdle or linger: *Don't dally or we'll miss the train.* [< OFr. *dalier*.] —**dal′li·ance** *n.* —**dal′li·er** *n.*

Dal·ma·ti·a (dăl-mā′shə) A historical region of SE Europe on the Adriatic Sea.

Dal·ma·tian (dăl-mā′shən) ►*n.* **1.** A native or inhabitant of Dalmatia. **2.** also **dalmatian** A dog with a short white coat covered with black spots. ►*adj.* Relating to Dalmatia.

dam¹ (dăm) ►*n.* **1.** A barrier built across a waterway to control the flow of water. **2.** A barrier against the passage of liquid, as a rubber sheet used to isolate a tooth from the rest of the mouth. ►*v.* **dammed, dam·ming 1.** To build a dam across. **2.** To hold back; check. [ME.]

dam² (dăm) ►*n.* A female parent of an animal, esp. a domesticated mammal such as a horse. [ME *dame*, lady; see DAME.]

dam·age (dăm′ĭj) ►*n.* **1.** Harm or injury to property or person. **2. damages** *Law* Money ordered to be paid as compensation for injury or loss. ►*v.* **-aged, -ag·ing** To cause damage to. [< Lat. *damnum*, loss.] —**dam′age·a·ble** *adj.* —**dam′ag·ing·ly** *adv.*

Da·mas·cus (də-măs′kəs) The capital of Syria, in the SW part. —**Dam′a·scene′** (dăm′ə-sēn′) *adj. & n.*

dam·ask (dăm′əsk) ►*n.* **1.** A rich patterned fabric of cotton, linen, silk, or wool. **2.** A fine, twilled table linen. [ME, Damascus.]

damask rose ►*n.* A rose with fragrant red or pink flowers used as a source of attar.

dame (dām) ►*n.* **1.** A married woman. **2.** *Often Offensive Slang* A woman. **3.** *Chiefly Brit.* **a.** A woman holding a nonhereditary title. **b.** The wife of a knight. [< Lat. *domina*, lady.]

damn (dăm) ►*v.* **1.** To criticize severely. **2.** To bring to ruin. **3.** To condemn to everlasting punishment. **4.** To swear at. ►*interj.* Used to express anger, contempt, or disappointment. ►*n. Informal* The least bit: *not worth a damn.* ►*adv. & adj.* Damned. [< Lat. *damnum*, damage.] —**dam·na′tion** (-nā′shən) *n.*

dam·na·ble (dăm′nə-bəl) ►*adj.* Deserving condemnation; odious. —**dam′na·bly** *adv.*

damned (dămd) ►*adj.* **-er, -est 1.** In certain religions, condemned to eternal punishment. **2.** *Informal* Dreadful; awful. **3.** Used as an intensive: *a damned fool.* ►*adv.* **-er, -est** Used as an intensive: *a damned poor excuse.* ►*n.* People who are damned considered as a group.

Dam·o·cles (dăm′ə-klēz′) fl. 4th cent. BC. Greek courtier who according to legend was forced to sit under a sword suspended by a single hair.

damp (dămp) ►*adj.* **-er, -est 1.** Slightly wet; moist. **2.** Humid: *damp air.* ►*n.* **1.** Moisture; humidity. **2.** Foul or poisonous gas in coal mines. ►*v.* **1.** To moisten. **2.** To restrain or check: *news that damped our enthusiasm.* **3.** To extinguish or suppress (a fire) by reducing or cutting off air. [ME, poison gas.] —**damp′ish** *adj.* —**damp′ly** *adv.* —**damp′ness** *n.*

damp·en (dăm′pən) ►*v.* **1.** To make or become damp. **2.** To deaden or depress: *dampen one's spirits.* **3.** To soundproof. —**damp′en·er** *n.*

damp·er (dăm′pər) ►*n.* **1.** One that deadens or depresses: *Rain put a damper on our plans.* **2.** An adjustable plate, as in a flue, for controlling the draft.

dam·sel (dăm′zəl) ►*n.* A young woman or girl. [< VLat. *dominicella* < Lat. *domina*, lady.]

dam·sel·fly (dăm′zəl-flī′) ►*n.* Any of various dragonflies having wings that are held together at rest.

dam·son (dăm′zən, -sən) ►*n.* A Eurasian plum tree bearing oval, bluish-black fruit. [< Lat. *Damascēnum*, of Damascus.]

Da·na (dā′nə), **Richard Henry** 1815–82. Amer. lawyer and writer.

Da Nang or **Da·nang** (də-năng′, dä′năng′) A city of central Vietnam on the South China Sea.

dance (dăns) ►*v.* **danced, danc·ing 1.** To move rhythmically usu. to music. **2.** To leap or skip about. **3.** To bob up and down: *The leaves danced in the wind.* **4.** *Zool.* To perform a specialized set of movements to communicate with other members of the same species. ►*n.* **1.** A series of motions and steps, usu. performed to music. **2.** The art of dancing: *studied dance in college.* **3.** A party at which people dance. **4.** *Zool.* An act of communication by dancing: *a peacock's courtship dance.* [< OFr. *danser*.] —**dance′a·ble** *adj.* —**danc′er** *n.*

dance·hall (dăns′hôl′) ►*n.* **1.** or **dance hall** A building or part of a building with facilities for dancing. **2.** A style of reggae music that incorporates hip-hop and rhythm and blues elements.

D and C ►*n.* Dilation and curettage.

dan·de·li·on (dăn′dl-ī′ən) ►*n.* A weedy plant having many-rayed yellow flower heads, sometimes used in salads and to make wine. [<

OFr. *dent de lion* : Lat. *dēns, dent-*, tooth + Lat. *leō*, lion.]

dan·der¹ (dăn′dər) ▸*n. Informal* Temper: *got my dander up.* [?]

dan·der² (dăn′dər) ▸*n.* Scurf from the coat or feathers of various animals, often of an allergenic nature. [Alteration of DANDRUFF.]

dan·dle (dăn′dl) ▸*v.* **-dled, -dling 1.** To move (a small child) up and down on one's knees in a playful way. **2.** To pamper. [?]

dan·druff (dăn′drəf) ▸*n.* Small flakes of scaly, dry skin shed from the scalp. [*dand-*, of unknown orig. + dial. *hurf*, scurf.]

dan·dy (dăn′dē) ▸*n., pl.* **-dies 1.** A man who affects extreme elegance in clothes; fop. **2.** *Informal* Something very good or agreeable. ▸*adj.* **-di·er, -di·est 1.** Foppish. **2.** *Informal* Fine; good. [Perh. < *jack-a-dandy*, fop.] —**dan′di·fy′** *v.* —**dan′dy·ism** *n.*

Dane (dān) ▸*n.* A native or inhabitant of Denmark.

dan·ger (dān′jər) ▸*n.* **1.** Exposure or vulnerability to harm or risk. **2.** A source of risk or peril. [< VLat. **dominiārium*, power < Lat. *dominus*, lord.]

dan·ger·ous (dān′jər-əs) ▸*adj.* **1.** Full of danger. **2.** Able or likely to do harm. —**dan′ger·ous·ly** *adv.* —**dan′ger·ous·ness** *n.*

dan·gle (dăng′gəl) ▸*v.* **-gled, -gling** To hang or cause to hang loosely and swing to and fro. [Poss. of Scand. orig.] —**dan′gler** *n.*

dan·gling (dăng′glĭng) ▸*adj.* Of or being a modifier, esp. a participle or participial phrase, that grammatically modifies the subject of its sentence but semantically modifies another element or an unstated referent, as *approaching Dallas* in the sentence *Approaching Dallas, the skyline came into view.*

Dan·iel (dăn′yəl) ▸*n. Bible* **1.** A Hebrew prophet of the 6th cent. BC. **2.** See table at **Bible.**

da·ni·o (dā′nē-ō′) ▸*n., pl.* **-os** A small, brightly colored freshwater fish popular as an aquarium fish. [NLat., genus name.]

Dan·ish (dā′nĭsh) ▸*adj.* Of Denmark, the Danes, or the Danish language. ▸*n.* **1.** The Germanic language of the Danes. **2.** *pl.* **-ish** or **-ish·es** A Danish pastry.

Danish pastry ▸*n.* A sweet buttery pastry made with raised dough.

dank (dăngk) ▸*adj.* **-er, -est** Disagreeably damp or humid: *a dank cave.* [ME.] —**dank′ly** *adv.* —**dank′ness** *n.*

Dan·te A·li·ghie·ri (dän′tā ä′lē-gyĕ′rē, dăn′tē) 1265–1321. Italian poet. —**Dan′te·an** *adj. & n.* —**Dan·tesque′** (dän-tĕsk′, dăn-) *adj.*

Dan·ube (dăn′yoob) A river of S-central Europe rising in SW Germany and flowing about 2,850 km (1,770 mi) to the Black Sea. —**Dan·u′bi·an** *adj.*

Dan·zig (dăn′sĭg, dän′tsĭk) See **Gdańsk.**

Dao (dou) ▸*n.* Var. of **Tao.**

Dao·ism (dou′ĭz′əm) ▸*n.* Var. of **Taoism.** —**Dao′ist** *n.*

dap·per (dăp′ər) ▸*adj.* **1a.** Neatly dressed; trim. **b.** Stylish. **2.** Lively and alert. [ME *daper*, elegant.] —**dap′per·ly** *adv.* —**dap′per·ness** *n.*

dap·ple (dăp′əl) ▸*v.* **-pled, -pling** To mark or mottle with spots. ▸*n.* A mottled or spotted marking, as on a horse's coat. ▸*adj.* Dappled. [< DAPPLED.]

dap·pled (dăp′əld) ▸*adj.* Spotted; mottled.

[Prob. < ON *depill*, small pool, splash.]

DAR ▸*abbr.* Daughters of the American Revolution

Dar·da·nelles (där′dn-ĕlz′) Formerly **Hellespont.** A strait connecting the Aegean Sea with the Sea of Marmara.

dare (dâr) ▸*v.* **dared, dar·ing 1.** To have the courage required for. **2.** To challenge (someone) to do something requiring boldness: *dared me to dive off the high board.* **3.** To confront boldly: *dared the mountain's dizzying heights.* See Synonyms at **defy.** ▸*n.* A challenge. [< OE *durran.*] —**dar′er** *n.*

Dare, Virginia 1587–87? The first child of English parents born in America.

dare·dev·il (dâr′dĕv′əl) ▸*n.* One who is recklessly bold. ▸*adj.* Recklessly bold. See Synonyms at **adventurous.**

dare·say (dâr′sā′) ▸*v.* To think very likely. Used in the 1st person sing. present tense: *I daresay you're wrong.*

Dar es Sa·laam (där′ ĕs sə-läm′) The largest city and former capital of Tanzania, in the E part.

dar·ing (dâr′ĭng) ▸*adj.* Bold and venturesome. See Synonyms at **adventurous.** ▸*n.* Audacious bravery. —**dar′ing·ly** *adv.*

Da·ri·us I (də-rī′əs) "the Great." 550?–486 BC. King of Persia (521–486).

dark (därk) ▸*adj.* **-er, -est 1.** Lacking light or brightness. **2.** Of a shade of color tending toward black. **3.** Gloomy; dismal. **4.** Sullen or threatening: *a dark scowl.* **5.** Unknown or concealed; mysterious: *a dark secret.* **6.** Lacking enlightenment: *a dark era.* **7.** Evil; sinister. ▸*n.* **1.** Absence of light. **2.** Night; nightfall. —*idiom:* **in the dark 1.** In secret. **2.** In ignorance; uninformed. [< OE *deorc.*] —**dark′ish** *adj.* —**dark′ly** *adv.* —**dark′ness** *n.*

Dark Ages ▸*pl.n.* The early part of the Middle Ages from about A.D. 476 to A.D. 1000.

dark·en (där′kən) ▸*v.* **1.** To make or become dark or darker. **2.** To make somber or gloomy. **3.** To tarnish: *darkened their good name.*

dark horse ▸*n.* An unexpectedly successful entrant in a race or contest.

dark matter ▸*n.* Matter that emits little or no detectable radiation, thought to be part of the universe's missing mass.

dark·room (därk′room′, -room′) ▸*n.* A room in which photographic materials are processed in complete darkness or with a safelight.

dar·ling (där′lĭng) ▸*n.* **1.** A dearly beloved person. **2.** A favorite. ▸*adj.* **1.** Much loved. **2.** *Informal* Charming or adorable: *a darling hat.* [< OE *dēorling.*]

darm·stadt·i·um (därm′shtät′ē-əm) ▸*n. Symbol* **Ds** A synthetic radioactive element. At. no. 110. See table at **element.** [After *Darmstadt*, Germany.]

darn¹ (därn) ▸*v.* To mend by weaving thread across a hole. ▸*n.* A hole repaired by darning. [Fr. dial. *darner.*] —**darn′er** *n.*

darn² (därn) ▸*v., interj., n., adv., & adj.* Damn. [Alteration of DAMN.]

darned (därnd) ▸*adj. & adv.* Damned.

darn·ing needle (där′nĭng) ▸*n.* **1.** A long, large-eyed needle used in darning. **2.** *Regional* A dragonfly.

Dar·row (dăr′ō), **Clarence Seward** 1857–1938. Amer. lawyer.

dart (därt) ▸*n.* **1.** A slender pointed missile

thrown by hand or shot from a blowgun. **2. darts** *(takes sing. or pl. v.)* A game in which darts are thrown at a target. **3.** A sudden rapid movement. **4.** A tapered tuck sewn in a garment. ►*v.* To move suddenly and rapidly: *darted across the street.* [< OFr., of Gmc. orig.]

dart·er (där′tər) ►*n.* **1.** A small, often brilliantly colored freshwater fish. **2.** One that moves suddenly and rapidly.

Dar·win (där′wĭn), **Charles Robert** 1809–82. British naturalist. —**Dar·win′i·an** *adj. & n.*

Charles Darwin
photographed c. 1878

Dar·win·ism (där′wĭ-nĭz′əm) ►*n.* A theory of biological evolution developed by Charles Darwin and others, stating that all species of organisms have developed from other species, primarily through natural selection. —**Dar′win·ist** *n.* —**Dar′win·is′tic** *adj.*

dash (dăsh) ►*v.* **1.** To move with haste; rush: *dashed inside.* **2.** To break or smash to pieces. **3.** To hurl or thrust violently. **4.** To splash; spatter. **5.** To perform or complete hastily: *dash off a letter; dashed down a glass of milk.* **6.** To destroy or wreck. See Synonyms at **blast**. ►*n.* **1.** A swift blow or stroke. **2a.** A splash. **b.** A small amount of an added ingredient. **3.** A sudden movement; rush. **4.** *Sports* A relatively short footrace run at top speed. **5.** Verve. See Synonyms at **vigor**. **6.** A punctuation mark (—) used to indicate a break or omission. **7.** A long sound or symbol used esp. in Morse code. **8.** A dashboard. [ME *dashen*.] —**dash′er** *n.*

dash·board (dăsh′bôrd′) ►*n.* **1.** A panel under the windshield of a vehicle, containing indicator dials and controls. **2.** A user interface on a computer display that presents constantly updated information.

da·shi·ki (də-shē′kē) ►*n., pl.* **-kis** A loose brightly colored African garment. [Yoruba *dàṣíkí*.]

dash·ing (dăsh′ĭng) ►*adj.* **1.** Bold and gallant; spirited. **2.** Stylish. —**dash′ing·ly** *adv.*

das·tard (dăs′tərd) ►*n.* A sneaking, malicious coward. [ME.] —**das′tard·li·ness** *n.* —**das′tard·ly** *adj.*

dat. ►*abbr.* dative

da·ta (dā′tə, dăt′ə, dä′tə) ►*pl.n. (takes sing. or pl. v.)* **1.** Facts that can be used to gain knowledge or make decisions; information. **2.** Statistics or other information represented in a form suitable for processing by computer. **3.** Pl. of **datum** (sense 1). [Lat., pl. of *datum*, something

given < p.part. of *dare*, give.]
   Usage: Although *data* came from a Latin plural form and is sometimes used with a plural verb in English, most people usu. think of *data* as a singular mass entity like *information* and use *data* with a singular verb.

da·ta·base (dā′tə-bās′, dăt′ə-) ►*n.* A collection of data arranged for ease of search and retrieval.

data processing ►*n.* The storing or processing of data by a computer. —**data processor** *n.*

date¹ (dāt) ►*n.* **1a.** Time stated in terms of the day, month, and year. **b.** A statement of calendar time, as on a document. **2.** A specified day of a month. **3.** A particular time at which something happened or is expected to happen. **4.** The time or historical period to which something belongs: *fossils from an earlier date.* **5a.** An appointment to go out socially, esp. out of romantic interest. **b.** A companion on such an outing. **6.** An engagement for a performance. ►*v.* **dat·ed, dat·ing 1.** To mark or supply with a date: *date a letter.* **2.** To determine the date of. **3.** To betray the age of: *Pictures of old cars date the book.* **4.** To have origin in a particular time in the past: *This statue dates from 500 BC.* **5.** To go on a date or dates (with). —*idiom:* **to date** Up to the present time. [< Lat. *data (Romae)*, issued (at Rome) (on a certain day) < *dare*, give.] —**dat′a·ble, date′a·ble** *adj.*

date² (dāt) ►*n.* The sweet edible oblong fruit of the date palm. [< Gk. *daktulos*, date.]

dat·ed (dā′tĭd) ►*adj.* **1.** Marked with a date. **2.** Old-fashioned. —**dat′ed·ness** *n.*

date·line (dāt′līn′) ►*n.* A phrase in a news story that gives its date and place of origin.

date palm ►*n.* A palm tree native to W Asia and N Africa, having featherlike leaves and clusters of dates.

date rape ►*n.* Rape committed by a person who has been socializing or on a date with the victim.

da·tive (dā′tĭv) ►*adj.* Of or being the grammatical case that marks the indirect object. ►*n.* The dative case. [< Lat. *(cāsus) datīvus*, (case) of giving < *dare*, give.]

da·tum (dā′təm, dăt′əm, dä′təm) ►*n.* **1.** *pl.* **-ta** (-tə) A fact or proposition used to draw a conclusion or make a decision. See Usage Note at **data**. **2.** *pl.* **-tums** A point, line, or surface used as a reference, as in surveying. [Lat., something given, neuter p.part. of *dare*, give.]

daub (dôb) ►*v.* **1.** To cover or smear with a soft sticky substance. **2.** To apply with quick or crude strokes, as paint or glue. [< Lat. *dēalbāre*, to whitewash.] —**daub** *n.* —**daub′er** *n.*

daugh·ter (dô′tər) ►*n.* **1.** One's female child. **2.** A woman considered as if in a relationship of child to parent: *a daughter of the nation.* [< OE *dohtor*.] —**daugh′ter·ly** *adj.*

daugh·ter-in-law (dô′tər-ĭn-lô′) ►*n., pl.* **daugh·ters-in-law** (-tərz-) The wife of one's child.

daunt (dônt, dänt) ►*v.* To intimidate or discourage. [< Lat. *domitāre*, to tame.]

daunt·less (dônt′lĭs, dänt′-) ►*adj.* Fearless. —**daunt′less·ly** *adv.*

dau·phin (dô′fĭn) ►*n.* **1.** The eldest son of the king of France from 1349 to 1830. **2.** Used as a title for such a nobleman. [< OFr. < *dalfin*, dolphin.]

dau·phine (dô-fēn′) ►*n.* The wife of a dauphin. [Fr.]

dav·en·port (dăv′ən-pôrt′) ►*n.* A large sofa. [After the A.H. *Davenport* Company, a furniture manufacturer.]

Da·vid (dā′vĭd) d. c. 962 BC. The 2nd king of Judah and Israel.

Da·vid (dä-vēd′), **Jacques Louis** 1748–1825. French painter.

da Vin·ci (də vĭn′chē, dä), **Leonardo** See **Leonardo da Vinci.**

Da·vis (dā′vĭs), **Bette** 1908–89. Amer. actress.

Davis, Jefferson 1808–89. Amer. soldier and president of the Confederacy (1861–65).

dav·it (dăv′ĭt, dā′vĭt) ►*n.* A small crane that projects over the side of a ship, used to hoist boats, anchors, and cargo. [< Norman Fr. *daviot,* dim. of *Davi,* David.]

Da·vy (dā′vē), Sir **Humphry** 1778–1829. British chemist.

daw·dle (dôd′l) ►*v.* **-dled, -dling 1.** To take more time than necessary. **2.** To waste time; idle. [Perh. alteration of dial. *daddle.*] —**daw′dler** *n.*

dawn (dôn) ►*n.* **1.** The time each morning at which daylight begins. **2.** A first appearance. See Synonyms at **beginning.** ►*v.* **1.** To begin to become light in the morning. **2.** To begin to appear or develop. **3.** To become apparent: *The truth dawned on us.* [< OE *dagung.*]

day (dā) ►*n.* **1.** The period of light between dawn and nightfall. **2a.** The 24-hour period during which the earth completes one rotation on its axis. **b.** The analogous period of a celestial body. **3.** One of the numbered 24-hour periods into which a week, month, or year is divided. **4.** The portion of a day that is devoted to work or school: *an eight-hour day.* **5.** A period of activity or prominence: *a writer who has had her day.* **6.** often **days** A period of time: *a book about the days of the Roman Empire.* —*idiom:* **day in, day out** All the time; continuously. [< OE *dæg.*]

Da·yan (dä-yän′), **Moshe** 1915–81. Israeli military leader.

day bed ►*n.* A couch convertible into a bed.

day·book (dā′bo͝ok′) ►*n.* **1.** A book in which daily entries are recorded. **2.** A diary.

day·break (dā′brāk′) ►*n.* Dawn.

day·care or **day care** (dā′kâr′) ►*n.* Provision of daytime supervision and recreation, esp. for preschool children.

day·dream (dā′drēm′) ►*n.* A dreamlike musing or fantasy while awake. ►*v.* To have daydreams.

Day-Glo (dā′glō′) A trademark for fluorescent coloring agents and materials.

day labor ►*n.* Labor hired and paid by the day. —**day laborer** *n.*

day·light (dā′līt′) ►*n.* **1.** The light of day. **2a.** Dawn. **b.** Daytime. **3. daylights** *Slang* One's wits: *scared the daylights out of me.* —*idiom:* **see daylight** To make enough progress that completion seems possible.

day·light-sav·ing time (dā′līt-sā′vĭng) ►*n.* Time during which clocks are set one hour or more ahead of standard time to provide more daylight at the end of the working day.

day·lil·y or **day lily** (dā′lĭl′ē) ►*n.* A perennial plant with large, colorful flowers, which remain open for only one day.

Day of Atonement ►*n.* See **Yom Kippur.**

day school ►*n.* A private school for pupils living at home.

day student ►*n.* A nonresident student at a residential school or college.

day·time (dā′tīm′) ►*n.* The time between sunrise and sunset. —**day′time′** *adj.*

day-to-day (dā′tə-dā′) ►*adj.* **1.** Occurring on a daily or routine basis. **2.** Subsisting one day at a time.

day trade ►*n.* A trade of a security that is bought and sold on the same day. —**day trader** *n.* —**day trading** *n.*

day-trip·per (dā′trĭp′ər) ►*n.* One who takes a one-day trip without staying overnight.

daze (dāz) ►*v.* **dazed, daz·ing 1.** To stun, as with a blow or shock. **2.** To dazzle. ►*n.* A stunned or bewildered condition. [ME *dasen,* of Scand. orig.]

daz·zle (dăz′əl) ►*v.* **-zled, -zling 1.** To dim the vision of, esp. to blind with intense light. **2.** To amaze or bewilder with spectacular display. [Frequentative of DAZE.] —**daz′zle** *n.* —**daz′zler** *n.* —**daz′zling·ly** *adv.*

dB ►*abbr.* decibel

DC ►*abbr.* **1.** da capo **2.** direct current **3.** District of Columbia **4.** Doctor of Chiropractic

DCM ►*abbr.* Distinguished Conduct Medal

DD ►*abbr.* **1.** dishonorable discharge **2.** *Lat.* Divinitatis Doctor (Doctor of Divinity)

D-day (dē′dā′) ►*n.* The unnamed day on which an operation or offensive is to be launched. [*D* (abbr. of DAY) + DAY.]

DDS ►*abbr.* **1.** Doctor of Dental Science **2.** Doctor of Dental Surgery

DDT (dē′dē-tē′) ►*n.* An insecticide banned since 1972 from US agricultural use for its persistent toxicity in the environment. [*d(ichloro)-d(iphenyl)t(richloroethane).*]

DE ►*abbr.* Delaware

de– ►*pref.* **1.** Reverse: *deactivate.* **2.** Remove: *defog.* **3.** Out of: *deplane.* **4.** Reduce: *degrade.* [ME *de-* < Lat. *dē,* from.]

dea·con (dē′kən) ►*n.* **1.** A cleric ranking just below a priest in the Anglican, Eastern Orthodox, and Roman Catholic churches. **2.** A lay assistant to a Protestant minister. [< Gk. *diakonos,* attendant.] —**dea′con·ry** *n.*

dea·con·ess (dē′kə-nĭs) ►*n.* A laywoman serving as assistant to a Protestant minister.

de·ac·ti·vate (dē-ăk′tə-vāt′) ►*v.* To render inactive or ineffective. —**de·ac′ti·va′tion** *n.*

dead (dĕd) ►*adj.* **-er, -est 1.** No longer alive. **2.** Lacking feeling; unresponsive: *They were dead to our pleas for help.* **3.** Weary and worn-out. **4a.** Inanimate. **b.** Lifeless; barren: *dead soil.* **5a.** No longer in existence or use. **b.** No longer relevant. **c.** Dormant: *a dead volcano.* **6.** Not circulating; stagnant: *dead air.* **7.** Dull; quiet: *There's nothing to do in this dead town.* **8.** Having grown cold. **9.** Not running or working: *The motor is dead.* **10a.** Sudden; abrupt: *a dead stop.* **b.** Complete: *dead silence.* **c.** Exact: *dead center.* **11a.** Lacking connection to a source of electric current. **b.** Discharged: *a dead battery.* ►*n.* **1.** *(takes pl. v.)* People who have died. **2.** A period of greatest intensity: *the dead of winter.* ►*adv.* **1.** Absolutely; altogether: *dead sure.* **2.** Directly; exactly. **3.** Suddenly: *stop dead.* [< OE *dēad.*] —**dead′ness** *n.*

dead·beat (dĕd′bēt′) ►*n.* *Informal* **1.** One who

does not pay one's debts. **2.** A lazy person; loafer.

dead bolt ►*n.* A bolt on a lock that is moved by turning the key or knob without activation of a spring.

dead·en (dĕd′n) ►*v.* **1.** To make less intense, sensitive, or strong: *deaden the pain; deaden curiosity.* **2.** To make soundproof. **3.** To make or become less vigorous, lively, or colorful.

dead end ►*n.* **1.** An end of a street or passage that affords no exit. **2.** A situation or subject that allows for no progress or development.

dead-end (dĕd′ĕnd′) ►*adj.* **1.** Having no exit. **2.** Permitting no opportunity for advancement: *a dead-end job.* —**dead′-end′** *v.*

dead·eye (dĕd′ī′) ►*n. Slang* An expert shooter.

dead hand ►*n.* **1.** The oppressive influence of past events. **2.** Mortmain. [ME *dede hond.*]

dead heat ►*n.* A race in which two or more contestants finish at the same time.

dead letter ►*n.* An unclaimed or undelivered letter.

dead·line (dĕd′līn′) ►*n.* A time limit, as for completion of a task.

dead·lock (dĕd′lŏk′) ►*n.* **1.** A standstill resulting from the opposition of two unrelenting forces. **2.** A tied score. —**dead′lock′** *v.*

dead·ly (dĕd′lē) ►*adj.* **-li·er, -li·est 1.** Causing or capable of causing death. **2.** Suggestive of death: *a deadly pallor.* **3.** Wanting to kill; implacable: *deadly enemies.* **4.** Destructive in effect: *gave the film a deadly review.* **5.** Dull: *a deadly lecture.* ►*adv.* To an extreme: *deadly serious.* —**dead′li·ness** *n.*

deadly nightshade ►*n.* See **belladonna** (sense 1).

deadly sin ►*n. Christianity* One of the seven sins—anger, covetousness, envy, gluttony, lust, pride, and sloth—believed to endanger one's salvation.

dead·pan (dĕd′păn′) ►*adj. & adv.* Impassively matter-of-fact, esp. with an expressionless face. —**dead′pan′** *v.*

dead reckoning ►*n.* **1.** Navigation without astronomical observations, as by applying to a previously determined position the course and distance traveled since. **2.** Calculation based on inference. [Poss. < *ded.*, abbr. of *deduced.*]

Dead Sea A landlocked salt lake at the mouth of the Jordan River. It is the lowest point on earth at about 420 m (1,380 ft) below sea level.

dead weight ►*n.* **1.** The unrelieved weight of a heavy motionless mass. **2.** An oppressive burden or difficulty.

dead·wood (dĕd′wŏŏd′) ►*n.* **1.** Dead tree branches or wood. **2.** One that is burdensome or superfluous.

deaf (dĕf) ►*adj.* **-er, -est 1.** Partially or completely unable to hear. **2.** Unwilling to listen: *was deaf to our pleas.* ►*n.* (takes pl. v.) **1.** Deaf people collectively. **2. Deaf** The community of deaf people who use American Sign Language as a primary means of communication. [< OE *dēaf.*] —**deaf′en** *v.* —**deaf′ly** *adv.* —**deaf′ness** *n.*

deaf-mute (dĕf′myōōt′) ►*n. Offensive* A person who can neither hear nor speak. See Usage Note at **mute.** —**deaf-mute′** *adj.*

deal¹ (dēl) ►*v.* **dealt** (dĕlt), **deal·ing 1.** To distribute or apportion. **2.** To sell. **3.** To administer; deliver: *deal a blow.* **4.** To distribute (play-

ing cards) among players. **5.** To be occupied or concerned: *a book that deals with ecology.* **6.** To behave in a specified way toward another or others: *deal honestly with clients.* **7.** To take action: *deal with a complaint.* **8.** To do business; trade: *deal in gems.* **9.** To cope: *I can't deal with all of this stress!* ►*n.* **1.** The act of dealing. **2a.** The cards dealt in a card game; hand. **b.** The right or turn of a player to deal. **3.** An indefinite quantity or degree: *a great deal of luck.* **4.** An agreement, esp. one that is mutually beneficial. See Synonyms at **agreement. 5.** *Informal* A good buy; bargain. **6.** *Informal* The situation or background information regarding something: *What's the deal with the new boss?* [< OE *dǣlan.*]

deal² (dēl) ►*n.* Fir or pine wood, esp. cut to standard size. [< MLGer. *dele*, plank.]

deal·er (dē′lər) ►*n.* **1.** A person who buys and sells. **2.** *Games* The person who deals the cards.

deal·er·ship (dē′lər-shĭp′) ►*n.* A franchise to sell specified items in a certain area.

deal·ing (dē′lĭng) ►*n.* **1. dealings** Transactions or relations with others, usu. in business. **2.** Conduct in relation to others.

dean (dēn) ►*n.* **1.** An administrative officer in a high school, college, or university. **2.** The senior member of a body or group. [< LLat. *decānus*, chief of ten.]

dear (dîr) ►*adj.* **-er, -est 1.** Loved and cherished. **2.** Highly esteemed or regarded. Used in direct address: *Dear Mr. Dawson.* **3.** High-priced. ►*n.* **1.** A greatly loved person; darling. **2.** An endearing person. ►*interj.* Used as a polite exclamation of surprise or distress: *Oh, dear.* [< OE *dēore.*] —**dear′ly** *adv.* —**dear′ness** *n.*

dearth (dûrth) ►*n.* A scarce supply; lack. [< OE **dēorthu*, costliness < *dēore*, costly.]

death (dĕth) ►*n.* **1.** The act of dying or state of being dead; termination of life. **2.** The cause or manner of dying: *Drugs were the death of him.* **3.** Termination; extinction. —*idiom:* **to death** To an extreme degree: *worried to death.* [< OE *dēath.*]

death·bed (dĕth′bĕd′) ►*n.* The bed on which a person dies.

death·blow (dĕth′blō′) ►*n.* **1.** A stroke or blow that causes death. **2.** A destructive event: *a deathblow to our hopes.*

death·less (dĕth′lĭs) ►*adj.* Undying; immortal. —**death′less·ness** *n.*

death·ly (dĕth′lē) ►*adj.* **1.** Of, resembling, or characteristic of death. **2.** Causing death; fatal. ►*adv.* Extremely; very: *deathly pale.*

death penalty ►*n.* **1.** A sentence or punishment of death by execution. **2.** The practice of allowing punishment by death for people convicted of certain crimes.

death rate ►*n.* The ratio of total deaths to total population in a specified community over a specified period of time.

death rattle ►*n.* A gurgling or rattling sound sometimes made in the throat of a dying person.

death row (rō) ►*n.* The part of a prison for housing inmates who have received the death penalty.

death's-head (dĕths′hĕd′) ►*n.* The human skull as a symbol of mortality or death.

death squad ►*n.* A clandestine, usu. military,

group employed to carry out political assassinations.

death·trap (dĕth′trăp′) ▸*n.* An unsafe building or other structure.

Death Valley An arid desert basin of E CA and W NV.

death·watch (dĕth′wŏch′) ▸*n.* **1.** A vigil kept beside a dying or dead person. **2.** One who guards a condemned person before execution.

deb (dĕb) ▸*n. Informal* A debutante.

de·ba·cle (dĭ-bä′kəl, -băk′əl, dĕb′ə-kəl) ▸*n.* A sudden disastrous downfall, defeat, or failure. [< OFr. *desbacler,* unbar.]

de·bar (dē-bär′) ▸*v.* **-barred, -bar·ring 1.** To exclude or shut out; bar. **2.** To forbid or prevent. [< OFr. *desbarer,* unbar.] —**de·bar′ment** *n.*

de·bark (dĭ-bärk′) ▸*v.* **1.** To unload, as from a ship or airplane. **2.** To disembark. [Fr. *débarquer* : DE– + *barque,* ship.] —**de′bar·ka′tion** (dē′bär-kā′shən) *n.*

de·base (dĭ-bās′) ▸*v.* **-based, -bas·ing** To lower in character, quality, or value; degrade. See Synonyms at **corrupt.** —**de·base′ment** *n.* —**de·bas′er** *n.*

  Syns: *degrade, abase, demean* **v.**

de·bate (dĭ-bāt′) ▸*v.* **-bat·ed, -bat·ing 1.** To consider; deliberate. **2.** To discuss opposing points. **3.** To discuss or argue formally. ▸*n.* **1.** A discussion involving opposing points; argument. **2.** Deliberation; consideration. **3.** A formal contest of argumentation in which two opposing teams defend and attack a given proposition. [< OFr. *debatre.*] —**de·bat′a·ble** *adj.* —**de·bat′er** *n.*

de·bauch (dĭ-bôch′) ▸*v.* **1.** To corrupt morally. **2.** To reduce the value or quality of; debase. See Synonyms at **corrupt.** [< OFr. *desbauchier,* roughhew timber, lead astray.] —**de·bauch′er** *n.* —**de·bauch′er·y** *n.*

de·ben·ture (dĭ-bĕn′chər) ▸*n.* **1.** A voucher acknowledging a debt. **2.** An unsecured bond issued by a civil or governmental agency. [< Lat. *dēbentur,* they are due.]

de·bil·i·tate (dĭ-bĭl′ĭ-tāt′) ▸*v.* **-tat·ed, -tat·ing** To sap the strength of; enervate. [< Lat. *dēbilis,* weak.] —**de·bil′i·ta′tion** *n.* —**de·bil′i·ta′tive** *adj.*

de·bil·i·ty (dĭ-bĭl′ĭ-tē) ▸*n., pl.* **-ties** Feebleness.

deb·it (dĕb′ĭt) ▸*n.* **1.** An item of debt as recorded in an account. **2.** The sum of such entries. ▸*v.* **1.** To enter a debit in an account. **2.** To charge with a debit. [< Lat. *dēbitum,* DEBT.]

debit card ▸*n.* A bankcard used in charging electronic transactions against funds on deposit.

deb·o·nair also **deb·o·naire** (dĕb′ə-nâr′) ▸*adj.* **1.** Sophisticated; urbane. **2.** Carefree; jaunty. [< OFr. *de bon aire,* of good disposition.] —**deb′o·nair′ly** *adv.*

De·bre·cen (dĕb′rĭt-sĕn′, -rĕ-tsĕn′) A city of E Hungary E of Budapest.

de·brief (dē-brēf′) ▸*v.* To interview (a person, usu. a government agent) at the end of an assignment, as to obtain intelligence. —**de·brief′ing** *n.*

de·bris also **dé·bris** (də-brē′, dā-, dā′brē′) ▸*n.* The scattered remains of something broken or destroyed; rubble or wreckage. [< OFr. *debrisier,* break to pieces.]

Debs (dĕbz), **Eugene Victor** 1855–1926. Amer. labor organizer and socialist leader.

debt (dĕt) ▸*n.* **1.** Something owed, as money, goods, or services. **2.** The condition of owing. **3.** Financial instruments, such as bonds, mortgages, and loans, that represent a claim to payment and rights of creditorship. [< Lat. *dēbitum* < p.part. of *dēbēre,* owe.] —**debt′or** *n.*

de·bug (dē-bŭg′) ▸*v.* **-bugged, -bug·ging 1.** To remove a hidden electronic surveillance device from. **2.** To search for and eliminate malfunctioning elements or errors in (e.g., computer software). **3.** To remove insects from, as with a pesticide. —**de·bug′ger** *n.*

de·bunk (dē-bŭngk′) ▸*v.* To expose or ridicule the falseness or exaggerated claims of. —**de·bunk′er** *n.*

De·bus·sy (dĕb′yoō-sē′), **Claude Achille** 1862–1918. French composer.

de·but also **dé·but** (dā-byoō′, dā′byoō′) ▸*n.* **1.** A first public appearance. **2.** The formal presentation of a young woman to society. **3.** The beginning of something. ▸*v.* **-buted** (-byoōd′), **-but·ing** (-byoō′ĭng) To make a debut. [Fr. *début* < *débuter,* begin.]

deb·u·tante (dĕb′yoō-tänt′, dā′byoō-) ▸*n.* A young woman making a formal debut into society. [Fr. *débutante* < *débuter,* begin.]

deca– or **dec–** also **deka–** or **dek–** ▸*pref.* Ten: *decagram.* [< Gk. *deka,* ten.]

dec·ade (dĕk′ād′, dĕ-kād′) ▸*n.* A period of ten years. [< Gk. *dekas,* group of ten.]

dec·a·dence (dĕk′ə-dəns, dĭ-kād′ns) ▸*n.* A process, condition, or period of deterioration; decay. [< VLat. **dēcadere,* DECAY.] —**dec′a·dent** *adj. & n.* —**dec′a·dent·ly** *adv.*

de·caf (dē′kăf′) ▸*n. Informal* Decaffeinated coffee. —**de′caf′** *adj.*

de·caf·fein·at·ed (dē-kăf′ə-nā′tĭd, -kăf′ē-ə-) ▸*adj.* Having the caffeine removed. —**de·caf′fein·ate′** *v.* —**de·caf′fein·a′tion** *n.*

dec·a·gon (dĕk′ə-gŏn′) ▸*n.* A polygon having ten sides. —**de·cag′o·nal** (dĭ-kăg′ə-nəl) *adj.* —**de·cag′o·nal·ly** *adv.*

dec·a·gram or **dek·a·gram** (dĕk′ə-grăm′) ▸*n.* See table at **measurement.**

dec·a·he·dron (dĕk′ə-hē′drən) ▸*n., pl.* **-drons** or **-dra** (-drə) A polyhedron having ten faces. —**dec′a·he′dral** *adj.*

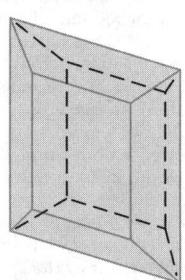

decahedron

de·cal (dē′kăl′) ▸*n.* **1.** A design transferred by decalcomania. **2.** A decorative sticker.

de·cal·ci·fy (dē-kăl′sə-fī′) ▸*v.* **-fied, -fy·ing** To remove calcium or calcium compounds from. —**de·cal′ci·fi·ca′tion** *n.* —**de·cal′ci·fi′er** *n.*

de·cal·co·ma·ni·a (dē-kăl′kə-mā′nē-ə, -mān′-yə) ▸*n.* The process of transferring designs printed on specially prepared paper to materials such as glass or metal. [< Fr. *décalquer*, transfer by tracing.]

dec·a·li·ter or **dek·a·li·ter** (děk′ə-lē′tər) ►*n.* See table at **measurement.**

Dec·a·logue or **Dec·a·log** (děk′ə-lôg′, -lŏg′) ►*n. Bible* The Ten Commandments. [< Gk. *dekalogos.*]

dec·a·me·ter or **dek·a·me·ter** (děk′ə-mē′tər) ►*n.* See table at **measurement.**

de·camp (dǐ-kămp′) ►*v.* **1.** To depart secretly or suddenly. **2.** To depart from a camp or camping ground. [< OFr. *descamper.*] —**de·camp′ment** *n.*

de·cant (dǐ-kănt′) ►*v.* **1.** To pour off (e.g., wine) without disturbing the sediment. **2.** To pour (a liquid) from one container into another. [< Med.Lat. *dēcanthāre* : DE– + Lat. *canthus*, rim.] —**de′can·ta′tion** (dē′kǎn-tā′shən) *n.*

de·cant·er (dǐ-kǎn′tər) ►*n.* A vessel used for decanting, esp. a bottle for serving wine.

de·cap·i·tate (dǐ-kǎp′ǐ-tāt′) ►*v.* **-tat·ed, -tat·ing** To cut off the head of. [LLat. *dēcapitāre* < Lat. *caput, capit-*, head.] —**de·cap′i·ta′tion** *n.* —**de·cap′i·ta′tor** *n.*

dec·a·syl·la·ble (děk′ə-sǐl′ə-bəl) ►*n.* A line of verse having ten syllables. —**dec′a·syl·lab′ic** (-sə-lăb′ǐk) *adj.*

de·cath·lon (dǐ-kăth′lən, -lŏn′) ►*n.* An athletic contest in which each contestant participates in ten track and field events. [DECA– + Gk. *athlon*, contest.] —**de·cath′lete** *n.*

de·cay (dǐ-kā′) ►*v.* **1.** To decompose; rot. **2.** *Phys.* To disintegrate in a process of radioactive decay or particle decay. **3.** To decline or decrease in quality or quantity. **4.** To fall into ruin. ►*n.* **1.** Decomposition. **2.** *Phys.* **a.** See **radioactive decay. b.** See **particle decay. 3.** A gradual deterioration: *urban decay.* **4.** A falling into ruin. [< VLat. **dēcadere*, fall away.] *Syns: decompose, molder, putrefy, rot, spoil* **v.**

de·cease (dǐ-sēs′) ►*v.* **-ceased, -ceas·ing** To die. ►*n.* Death. [< Lat. *dēcēdere*, go away, die.]

de·ceased (dǐ-sēst′) ►*adj.* No longer living; dead. ►*n., pl.* **deceased** A dead person.

de·ce·dent (dǐ-sēd′nt) ►*n. Law* A dead person. [< Lat. *dēcēdere*, go away, die.]

de·ceit (dǐ-sēt′) ►*n.* **1.** Misrepresentation; deception. **2.** A stratagem; trick. [< OFr. *deceite* < p.part. of *deceveir*, DECEIVE.] —**de·ceit′ful** *adj.* —**de·ceit′ful·ly** *adv.* —**de·ceit′ful·ness** *n.*

de·ceive (dǐ-sēv′) ►*v.* **-ceived, -ceiv·ing** To cause to believe what is not true; mislead. [< Lat. *dēcipere.*] —**de·ceiv′er** *n.* —**de·ceiv′ing·ly** *adv.*

de·cel·er·ate (dē-sěl′ə-rāt′) ►*v.* **-at·ed, -at·ing** To decrease in speed. [DE– + (AC)CELERATE.] —**de·cel′er·a′tion** *n.*

De·cem·ber (dǐ-sěm′bər) ►*n.* The 12th month of the Gregorian calendar. See table at **calendar.** [< Lat., the tenth month.]

de·cen·ni·al (dǐ-sěn′ē-əl) ►*adj.* **1.** Of or lasting for ten years. **2.** Occurring every ten years. ►*n.* A tenth anniversary. [< Lat. *decennium*, decade.] —**de·cen′ni·al·ly** *adv.*

de·cent (dē′sənt) ►*adj.* **1a.** Conforming to standards of propriety; moral: *leads a decent life.* **b.** Kind or obliging: *very decent of them to reconsider.* **2.** Adequate; satisfactory: *a decent night's sleep.* **3a.** Suitable; fitting: *had nothing*

decent to wear to a formal dinner. **b.** *Informal* Properly or modestly dressed. [< Lat. *decēre*, be fitting.] —**de′cen·cy** *n.* —**de′cent·ly** *adv.* —**de′cent·ness** *n.*

de·cen·tral·ize (dē-sěn′trə-līz′) ►*v.* **-ized, -iz·ing 1.** To distribute the functions of (a central authority) among local authorities. **2.** To cause to withdraw or disperse from an area of concentration: *decentralize a university complex.* —**de·cen′tral·i·za′tion** *n.*

de·cep·tion (dǐ-sěp′shən) ►*n.* **1.** The use of deceit. **2.** The fact or state of being deceived. [< Lat. *dēcipere, dēcept-*, deceive.]

de·cep·tive (dǐ-sěp′tǐv) ►*adj.* Intended or tending to deceive. —**de·cep′tive·ly** *adv.* —**de·cep′tive·ness** *n.*

deci– ►*pref.* One tenth (10^{-1}): decigram. [< Lat. *decimus*, tenth.]

de·ci·bel (děs′ə-bəl, -běl′) ►*n.* A unit used to express relative difference in power, usu. between acoustic or electric signals, equal to ten times the common logarithm of the ratio of the two levels. [DECI– + *bel*, after Alexander Graham BELL.]

de·cide (dǐ-sīd′) ►*v.* **-cid·ed, -cid·ing 1.** To reach a conclusion or form an opinion about (something) by reasoning or consideration. **2.** To settle conclusively all uncertainty about: *decide a case.* **3.** To influence or determine the outcome of: *a few votes decided the election.* **4.** To make up one's mind. [< Lat. *dēcīdere*, cut off.] —**de·cid′a·ble** *adj.* —**de·cid′er** *n.*

de·cid·ed (dǐ-sī′dǐd) ►*adj.* **1.** Without doubt or question; definite: *a decided success.* **2.** Resolute. —**de·cid′ed·ly** *adv.* —**de·cid′ed·ness** *n.*

de·cid·u·ous (dǐ-sǐj′ōō-əs) ►*adj.* **1.** Falling off at a specific season or stage of growth. **2.** Shedding foliage at the end of the growing season. **3.** Of or relating to the primary teeth. [< Lat. *dēciduus* < *dēcidere*, fall off.] —**de·cid′u·ous·ly** *adv.* —**de·cid′u·ous·ness** *n.*

dec·i·gram (děs′ǐ-grăm′) ►*n.* See table at **measurement.**

de·cil·lion (dǐ-sǐl′yən) ►*n.* **1.** The cardinal number equal to 10^{33}. **2.** *Chiefly Brit.* The cardinal number equal to 10^{60}. [Lat. *decem*, ten + (M)ILLION.] —**de·cil′lion** *adj.* —**de·cil′lionth** *adj. & n.*

dec·i·mal (děs′ə-məl) ►*n.* **1.** A linear array of integers that represents a fraction, every decimal place indicating a multiple of a negative power of 10. For example, the decimal 0.1 = $\frac{1}{10}$, 0.12 = $\frac{12}{100}$, 0.003 = $\frac{3}{1000}$. **2.** A number written using the base 10. ►*adj.* **1.** Expressed or expressible as a decimal. **2a.** Based on 10. **b.** Numbered or ordered by groups of 10. [< Lat. *decima*, tenth part.] —**dec′i·mal·ly** *adv.*

decimal place ►*n.* The position of a digit to the right of a decimal point, usu. identified by successive ascending ordinal numbers with the digit immediately to the right of the decimal point being first.

decimal point ►*n.* A dot that is written in a decimal number to indicate where the place values change from positive to negative powers of 10.

dec·i·mate (děs′ə-māt′) ►*v.* **-mat·ed, -mat·ing 1.** To destroy or kill a large part of. **2.** *Informal* **a.** To inflict great damage on: *Deer decimated the new garden.* **b.** To reduce markedly in amount: *hospital bills that decimated our sav-*

ings. [Lat. *decimāre* < *decimus*, tenth.] —**dec′i·ma′tion** *n.*

  Usage: *Decimate* orig. referred to killing every tenth person, but commonly can be extended to include killing any large proportion of a group. Use of *decimate* to refer to large-scale destruction other than killing is less acceptable.

dec·i·me·ter (děs′ə-mē′tər) ►*n.* See table at **measurement.**

de·ci·pher (dǐ-sī′fər) ►*v.* **1.** To read or interpret (e.g., illegible matter). **2.** To decode. —**de·ci′pher·a·ble** *adj.* —**de·ci′pher·ment** *n.*

de·ci·sion (dǐ-sǐzh′ən) ►*n.* **1.** A conclusion or judgment reached after consideration. **2.** Firmness of character or action; determination: *a woman of decision.* **3a.** A victory in boxing won on points when no knockout has occurred. **b.** A win or loss accorded to a pitcher in baseball. [< Lat. *dēcīdere, dēcīs-,* decide.]
  Syns: *conclusion, determination **n.***

de·ci·sive (dǐ-sī′sǐv) ►*adj.* **1.** Conclusive: *the decisive battle in the war.* **2.** Determined; resolute: *a decisive leader.* —**de·ci′sive·ly** *adv.*
  Syns: *conclusive, critical, crucial, definitive, determinative **Ant:** indecisive **adj.***

deck¹ (děk) ►*n.* **1.** A platform extending horizontally from one side of a ship to the other. **2.** A similar platform or surface, esp. a roofless floored area adjoining a house. **3.** A pack of playing cards. —*idiom:* **on deck** Waiting to take one's turn. [MDu. *dec,* covering.]

deck² (děk) ►*v.* **1.** To clothe with finery; adorn. Often used with *out: all decked out for the party.* **2.** To decorate. [< MDu. *decken,* to cover.]

deck chair ►*n.* A folding chair, usu. with arms and a leg rest.

deck chair

de·claim (dǐ-klām′) ►*v.* **1.** To deliver a formal recitation. **2.** To speak loudly and vehemently. [< Lat. *dēclāmāre,* cry out.] —**de·claim′er** *n.* —**dec·la·ma′tion** (děk′lə-mā′shən) *n.* —**de·clam′a·to·ry** (dǐ-klăm′ə-tôr′ē) *adj.*

de·clare (dǐ-klâr′) ►*v.* **-clared, -clar·ing** **1.** To make known formally, officially, or authoritatively. See Synonyms at **announce. 2.** To reveal or show: *His smile declared his agreement.* **3.** To make a full statement of (e.g., dutiable goods). **4.** To proclaim one's support or opinion. [< Lat. *dēclārāre.*] —**dec′la·ra′tion** (děk′lə-rā′shən) *n.* —**de·clar′a·tive** *adj.* —**de·clar′er** *n.*

de·clas·si·fy (dē-klăs′ə-fī′) ►*v.* To remove official security classification from (a document). —**de·clas′si·fi·ca′tion** *n.*

de·clen·sion (dǐ-klěn′shən) ►*n.* **1.** *Ling.* **a.** The inflection of nouns, pronouns, and adjectives for case, number, and gender. **b.** A class of words with the same inflections. **2.** A descent. **3.** A decline or deterioration. [< Lat. *dēclīnātiō* < *dēclīnāre,* decline.] —**de·clen′sion·al** *adj.*

de·cline (dǐ-klīn′) ►*v.* **-clined, -clin·ing** **1.** To express polite refusal. **2.** To slope downward: *The roof declines at an angle.* **3.** To deteriorate gradually; fail: *Her health has been declining for years.* **4.** *Gram.* To inflect (a noun, pronoun, or adjective). ►*n.* **1.** The process or result of declining. **2.** A downward slope. **3.** A deterioration of health: *The patient's slow decline.* [< Lat. *dēclīnāre,* turn aside : DE– + *-clīnāre,* lean.] —**de·clin′a·ble** *adj.* —**dec′li·na′tion** (děk′lə-nā′shən) *n.* —**dec′li·na′tion·al** *adj.* —**de·clin′er** *n.*

de·cliv·i·ty (dǐ-klǐv′ĭ-tē) ►*n., pl.* **-ties** A downward slope. [< Lat. *dēclīvis,* sloping down : DE– + *clīvus,* slope.]

de·code (dē-kōd′) ►*v.* To convert from code into plaintext. —**de·cod′er** *n.*

dé·colle·tage (dā′kôl-täzh′) ►*n.* A low neckline, esp. on a dress. [Fr. < *décolleter,* lower a neckline.]

dé·colle·té (dā′kôl-tā′) ►*adj.* Cut low at the neckline. [Fr.]

de·col·o·nize (dē-kŏl′ə-nīz′) ►*v.* To free (a colony) from dependent status. —**de·col′o·ni·za′tion** *n.*

de·com·mis·sion (dē′kə-mĭsh′ən) ►*v.* To withdraw (e.g., a ship) from active service.

de·com·pose (dē′kəm-pōz′) ►*v.* **1.** To separate into components or basic elements. **2.** To rot or cause to rot. See Synonyms at **decay.** —**de′com·pos′a·ble** *adj.* —**de′com·pos′er** *n.* —**de′com·po·si′tion** (dē-kŏm′pə-zĭsh′ən) *n.*

de·com·press (dē′kəm-prěs′) ►*v.* **1.** To relieve of pressure. **2.** To adjust to normal atmospheric pressure after exposure to increased pressure. **3.** *Informal* To relax. —**de′com·pres′sion** *n.*

decompression sickness ►*n.* A disorder seen esp. in deep-sea divers, caused by nitrogen bubbles in body tissues following a sudden drop in surrounding pressure when ascending from a dive, and marked by severe pain and paralysis.

de·con·gest (dē′kən-jěst′) ►*v.* To relieve the congestion of (e.g., sinuses). —**de′con·ges′tion** *n.* —**de′con·ges′tive** *adj.*

de·con·ges·tant (dē′kən-jěs′tənt) ►*n.* A medication that decreases congestion.

de·con·tam·i·nate (dē′kən-tăm′ə-nāt′) ►*v.* **1.** To eliminate contamination in. **2.** To make safe by eliminating poisonous or harmful substances, such as radioactive material. —**de′con·tam′i·nant** *n.* —**de′con·tam′i·na′tion** *n.*

de·con·trol (dē′kən-trōl′) ►*v.* To stop control of, esp. by the government.

dé·cor or **de·cor** (dā′kôr′, dā-kôr′) ►*n.* **1.** Decoration. **2.** A decorative style or scheme, as of a room. [Fr.]

dec·o·rate (děk′ə-rāt′) ►*v.* **-rat·ed, -rat·ing** **1.** To provide or adorn with something ornamental. **2.** To confer a medal or other honor on. [< Lat. *decorāre* < *decus,* ornament.] —**dec′o·ra′tion** *n.* —**dec′o·ra·tive** *adj.* —**dec′o·ra·tive·ly** *adv.*

dec·o·ra·tor (děk′ə-rā′tər) ►*n.* One who decorates, esp. an interior decorator.

dec·o·rous (dĕk′ər-əs, dĭ-kôr′əs) ►*adj.* Marked by decorum; proper. [< Lat. *decor*, seemliness.] —**dec′o·rous·ly** *adv.* —**dec′o·rous·ness** *n.*

de·co·rum (dĭ-kôr′əm) ►*n.* Appropriateness of behavior or conduct; propriety. [Lat. *decōrum*.]

de·cou·page also **dé·cou·page** (dā′kōō-päzh′) ►*n.* The technique of decorating a surface with cutouts, as of paper. [Fr. *découpage* < *découper*, cut up.]

de·coy (dē′koi′, dĭ-koi′) ►*n.* **1.** A living or artificial animal used to entice game. **2.** A means used to mislead or lead into danger. ►*v.* (dĭ-koi′) To lure or entrap by or as if by a decoy. [Poss. < Du. *de kooi*, the cage.] —**de·coy′er** *n.*

de·crease (dĭ-krēs′) ►*v.* **-creased, -creas·ing** To diminish gradually; reduce. ►*n.* (dē′krēs′) **1.** The act or process of decreasing. **2.** The amount by which something decreases. [< Lat. *dēcrēscere* : DE– + *crēscere*, grow.]

de·cree (dĭ-krē′) ►*n.* **1.** An authoritative order having the force of law. **2.** *Law* The judgment of a court of equity or of a court. ►*v.* **-creed, -cree·ing** To ordain, establish, or decide by decree. [< Lat. *dēcrētum* < p.part. of *dēcernere*, decide.]

dec·re·ment (dĕk′rə-mənt) ►*n.* **1.** A gradual decrease. **2.** The amount lost by gradual diminution or waste. [Lat. *dēcrēmentum* < *dēcrēscere*, DECREASE.] —**dec′re·ment′al** *adj.*

de·crep·it (dĭ-krĕp′ĭt) ►*adj.* Weakened, worn out, or broken down by old age, illness, or hard use. [< Lat. *dēcrepitus*.] —**de·crep′it·ly** *adv.* —**de·crep′i·tude′** *n.*

de·cre·scen·do (dā′krə-shĕn′dō, dē′-) ►*n., pl.* **-dos** *Mus.* A gradual decrease in force or loudness. [Ital.] —**de′cre·scen′do** *adv. & adj.*

de·crim·i·nal·ize (dē-krĭm′ə-nə-līz′) ►*v.* **-ized, -iz·ing** To reduce or abolish criminal penalties for. —**de·crim′i·nal·i·za′tion** *n.*

de·cry (dĭ-krī′) ►*v.* **-cried, -cry·ing** To condemn openly. [< OFr. *descrier*.] —**de·cri′er** *n.*

de·crypt (dē-krĭpt′) ►*v.* **1.** To decipher. **2.** To decode. [DE– + *-crypt* (as in CRYPTOGRAM).] —**de·crypt′** *n.* —**de·cryp′tion** *n.*

ded·i·cate (dĕd′ĭ-kāt′) ►*v.* **-cat·ed, -cat·ing** **1.** To set apart for a special use: *dedicated their money to research.* **2.** To commit (oneself) to a course of action. **3.** To inscribe (e.g., a book) to another. **4.** To open to public use: *dedicate a new library.* [< Lat. *dēdicāre*.] —**ded′i·ca′tion** *n.* —**ded′i·ca′tive, ded′i·ca·to′ry** (-kə-tôr′ē) *adj.*

de·duce (dĭ-dōōs′, -dyōōs′) ►*v.* **-duced, -duc·ing** **1.** To reach (a conclusion) by reasoning. **2.** To infer from a general principle; reason deductively: *deduced from physical laws that the plane would fly.* [< Lat. *dēdūcere*, lead away.] —**de·duc′i·ble** *adj.*

de·duct (dĭ-dŭkt′) ►*v.* **1.** To take away or subtract. **2.** To derive by deduction; deduce. [< Lat. *dēdūcere, dēduct-*.]

de·duct·i·ble (dĭ-dŭk′tə-bəl) ►*adj.* That can be deducted, esp. for income taxes. ►*n.* **1.** Something, such as an expense, that can be deducted. **2.** The specified amount in an insurance policy that must be paid by the insured before the insurer will pay on a claim. —**de·duct′i·bil′i·ty** *n.*

de·duc·tion (dĭ-dŭk′shən) ►*n.* **1.** The act of deducting; subtraction. **2.** An amount that is or may be deducted: *tax deductions.* **3.** *Logic* **a.**

The process of reasoning in which a conclusion follows necessarily from the stated premises. **b.** A conclusion reached by this process. —**de·duc′tive** *adj.* —**de·duc′tive·ly** *adv.*

deed (dēd) ►*n.* **1.** Something that is carried out; act or action. **2.** Action or performance in general: *Deeds, not words, matter most.* **3.** *Law* A document conveying an interest in real property. ►*v.* To transfer by means of a deed. [< OE *dǣd.*]

deem (dēm) ►*v.* To regard as; consider: *deemed the results unsatisfactory.* [< OE *dēman.*]

deep (dēp) ►*adj.* **-er, -est 1a.** Extending far downward below a surface: *a deep hole in the ice.* **b.** Extending far inward from an outer surface: *a deep cut.* **c.** Extending far from front to rear or side to side. **d.** Far distant down or in: *deep in the woods.* **2.** Extending a specific distance in a given direction: *snow four feet deep.* **3.** Far distant in time or space: *deep in the past.* **4.** Difficult to understand. **5.** Of a grave or extreme nature: *deep trouble* **6.** Very absorbed or involved: *deep in thought.* **7.** Profound in quality or feeling: *a deep trance.* **8.** Of an intense shade of color: *a deep red.* **9.** Low in pitch; resonant: *a deep voice.* ►*adv.* To a great depth; deeply. ►*n.* **1.** often **deeps** A deep place in land or in a body of water. **2.** The most intense or extreme part: *the deep of night.* **3.** The ocean. —*idiom:* **in deep water** In difficulty. [< OE *dēop.*] —**deep′ly** *adv.* —**deep′ness** *n.*

deep·en (dē′pən) ►*v.* To make or become deep or deeper.

deep-fry (dēp′frī′) ►*v.* To fry by immersing in a deep pan of fat or oil. —**deep′-fried′** *adj.*

deep-root·ed (dēp′rōō′tĭd, -rŏōt′ĭd) ►*adj.* Firmly implanted; well-established.

deep-sea (dēp′sē′) ►*adj.* Of or occurring in deep parts of the sea.

deep-seat·ed (dēp′sē′tĭd) ►*adj.* **1.** Deeply rooted; ingrained. **2.** Being so far below the surface as to be unsusceptible to superficial examination: *a deep-seated infection.*

deep-set (dēp′sĕt′) ►*adj.* **1.** Deeply set or placed. **2.** Deep-seated: *deep-set hatred.*

deep-six (dēp′sĭks′) ►*v. Slang* **1.** To toss overboard. **2.** To get rid of.

deep space ►*n.* The regions beyond the gravitational influence of Earth, encompassing interplanetary, interstellar, and intergalactic space.

deep venous thrombosis ►*n.* A condition in which one or more clots form in a vein deep inside the body, esp. in the leg or pelvis, and can potentially be carried to the lungs.

deer (dîr) ►*n., pl.* **deer** Any of various hoofed mammals, including the elk, moose, and caribou, most of whose males grow and shed antlers each year. [< OE *dēor*, beast.]

deer fly ►*n.* Any of various bloodsucking flies that are smaller than the related horseflies.

deer·skin (dîr′skĭn′) ►*n.* Leather made from the hide of a deer.

de-es·ca·late (dē-ĕs′kə-lāt′) ►*v.* To decrease the scope or intensity of. —**de-es′ca·la′tion** *n.*

de·face (dĭ-fās′) ►*v.* **-faced, -fac·ing** To mar or spoil the appearance or surface of. —**de·face′-ment** *n.* —**de·fac′er** *n.*

de fac·to (dĭ făk′tō, dā) ►*adj.* Existing in actuality, esp. when not established by law. [Lat. *dē factō*, according to the fact.] —**de facto** *adv.*

de·fal·cate (dĭ-făl′kāt′, -fôl′-, dĕf′əl-) ►*v.* **-cat·**

ed, -cat·ing To embezzle. [Med.Lat. *dēfalcāre*, mow < Lat. *falx*, sickle.] —**de·fal′ca′tor** *n.*

de·fame (dĭ-fām′) ►*v.* **-famed, -fam·ing** To damage the reputation or good name of by slander or libel. [< Lat. *diffāmāre*.] —**def′a·ma′tion** (dĕf′ə-mā′shən) *n.* —**de·fam′a·to′·ry** (dĭ-făm′ə-tôr′ē) *adj.*

de·fault (dĭ-fôlt′) ►*n.* **1.** Failure to perform a task or fulfill an obligation, esp. failure to fulfill to meet a financial obligation: *in default on a loan.* **2.** Failure to participate in a contest: *won by default.* **3.** *Comp.* A particular value for a variable assigned automatically by an operating system. ►*v.* **1a.** To fail to do what is required. **b.** To fail to pay money when it is due. **2.** To lose by not appearing, completing, or participating. [< OFr. *defaute* < *defaillir*, fail.]

de·feat (dĭ-fēt′) ►*v.* **1.** To win victory over; beat. **2.** To prevent the success of; thwart: *defeat one's own purposes.* **3.** To dishearten: *The last setback defeated him, and he gave up.* ►*n.* The act of defeating or state of being defeated. [< OFr. *desfait*, p.part. of *desfaire*, destroy.]

de·feat·ism (dĭ-fē′tĭz′əm) ►*n.* Acceptance of or resignation to the prospect of defeat. —**de·feat′ist** *adj. & n.*

def·e·cate (dĕf′ĭ-kāt′) ►*v.* **-cat·ed, -cat·ing** **1.** To void feces from the bowels. **2.** To remove impurities from (a liquid), esp. in sugar refining. [< *faex, faec-*, dregs.] —**def′e·ca′tion** *n.*

de·fect (dē′fĕkt′, dĭ-fĕkt′) ►*n.* An imperfection; shortcoming. ►*v.* (dĭ-fĕkt′) To disown allegiance to a country, position, or group and adopt or join another. [< Lat. *dēfectus* < p.part. of *dēficere*, be wanting.] —**de·fec′tion** *n.* —**de·fec′tor** *n.*

de·fec·tive (dĭ-fĕk′tĭv) ►*adj.* Having a defect: *a defective motor.* —**de·fec′tive·ly** *adv.* —**de·fec′tive·ness** *n.*

de·fence (dĭ-fĕns′) ►*n. & v.* Chiefly *Brit.* Var. of **defense.**

de·fend (dĭ-fĕnd′) ►*v.* **1.** To protect from danger or harm. **2.** To support or maintain; justify: *defended a friend's decision.* **3.** To compete in an attempt to retain (a championship or title). **4.** *Law* **a.** To represent (a defendant) in a civil or criminal action. **b.** To contest (an action or claim). [< Lat. *dēfendere*, ward off.] —**de·fend′a·ble** *adj.* —**de·fend′er** *n.*

de·fen·dant (dĭ-fĕn′dənt) ►*n.* *Law* The party against which an action is brought.

de·fense (dĭ-fĕns′) ►*n.* **1.** The act of defending. **2.** A means or method of defending or protecting. **3.** An argument in support or justification. **4.** *Law* **a.** The act of defending a case. **b.** A fact or law that provides exoneration of a defendant in a lawsuit or prosecution. **c.** The defendant and his or her legal counsel. **5.** (*often* dē′fĕns′) *Sports* The players on a team attempting to stop the opposition from scoring. [< Lat. *dēfēnsa* < *dēfendere*, ward off.] —**de·fense′less** *adj.* —**de·fense′less·ly** *adv.*

defense mechanism ►*n.* **1.** A physiological reaction of an organism used in self-protection. **2.** A usu. unconscious mental process, including denial and rationalization, that protects the ego from shame, anxiety, or other painful thoughts or feelings.

de·fen·si·ble (dĭ-fĕn′sə-bəl) ►*adj.* Capable of

being defended or justified. —**de·fen′si·bil′i·ty** *n.* —**de·fen′si·bly** *adv.*

de·fen·sive (dĭ-fĕn′sĭv) ►*adj.* **1.** Of, intended for, or relating to defense. **2.** *Psychol.* Constantly protecting oneself from perceived threats to the ego. ►*n.* An attitude or position of defense. —*idiom:* **on the defensive** Prepared to withstand attack. —**de·fen′sive·ly** *adv.* —**de·fen′sive·ness** *n.*

de·fer¹ (dĭ-fûr′) ►*v.* **-ferred, -fer·ring 1.** To put off; postpone. **2.** To postpone the induction of (one eligible for the military draft). [ME *differ·ren*; see DIFFER.] —**de·fer′ra·ble** *adj.*
  Syns: postpone, shelve, suspend v.

de·fer² (dĭ-fûr′) ►*v.* **-ferred, -fer·ring** To submit to the opinion, wishes, or decision of another. [< Lat. *dēferre*, refer to : DE– + *ferre*, carry.] —**de·fer′rer** *n.*

def·er·ence (dĕf′ər-əns, dĕf′rəns) ►*n.* Submission or courteous respect given to another, often in recognition of authority. —**def′er·en′tial** *adj.* —**def′er·en′tial·ly** *adv.*

de·fer·ment (dĭ-fûr′mənt) ►*n.* **1.** The act or an instance of delaying. **2.** Official postponement of compulsory military service.

de·fer·ral (dĭ-fûr′əl) ►*n.* Deferment.

de·fi·ant (dĭ-fī′ənt) ►*adj.* Marked by bold resistance to authority or an opposing force. —**de·fi′ance** *n.* —**de·fi′ant·ly** *adv.*

deficiency disease ►*n.* A disease, such as scurvy, caused by a dietary deficiency of specific nutrients.

de·fi·cient (dĭ-fĭsh′ənt) ►*adj.* **1.** Lacking an essential quality or element. **2.** Inadequate; insufficient. [< Lat. *dēficere*, be wanting.] —**de·fi′cien·cy** *n.* —**de·fi′cient·ly** *adv.*

def·i·cit (dĕf′ĭ-sĭt) ►*n.* **1.** Inadequacy or insufficiency: *a deficit in grain production.* **2.** The amount by which a sum of money falls short of the required amount: *budget deficits.* **3.** A deficiency in mental or physical functioning: *cognitive deficits.* [< Lat. *dēficit*, it is lacking.]

deficit spending ►*n.* The spending of public funds obtained by borrowing rather than taxation.

de·fi·er (dĭ-fī′ər) ►*n.* One that defies: *a defier of tradition.*

de·file¹ (dĭ-fīl′) ►*v.* **-filed, -fil·ing 1.** To make filthy or dirty. **2.** To debase the pureness or excellence of: *a landscape defiled by urban sprawl.* **3.** To profane or sully (e.g., a good name). **4.** To make unfit for ceremonial use. [< OE *fȳlan*, befoul, and OFr. *defouler*, trample.] —**de·file′ment** *n.* —**de·fil′er** *n.*

de·file² (dĭ-fīl′) ►*v.* **-filed, -fil·ing** To march in single file or in columns. ►*n.* **1.** A narrow gorge or pass that restricts lateral movement, as of troops. **2.** A march in a line. [Fr. *défiler* < OFr. *filer*, spin thread.]

de·fine (dĭ-fīn′) ►*v.* **-fined, -fin·ing 1.** To state the precise meaning of (e.g., a word). **2.** To describe the basic qualities of: *define the goals of the committee.* **3.** To make clear the outline of: *hills that were defined against the sky.* **4.** To specify distinctly; distinguish: *define the weapons to be used.* [< Lat. *dēfinīre* < *finis*, boundary.] —**de·fin′a·ble** *adj.* —**de·fin′a·bly** *adv.* —**de·fin′er** *n.*

def·i·nite (dĕf′ə-nĭt) ►*adj.* **1a.** Clearly defined; precise. See Synonyms at **explicit. b.** Forthright and unambiguous: *The doctor was very* *definite about your medication.* **2.** Clearly developed or decided: *no definite idea of where to live.* [< Lat. *dēfinīre,* DEFINE.] —**def′i·nite·ly** *adv.*

definite article ►*n.* A determiner that particularizes a noun. In English, *the* is the definite article.

def·i·ni·tion (dĕf′ə-nĭsh′ən) ►*n.* **1.** A statement of the meaning of a word, phrase, or term, as in a dictionary entry. **2.** The act of making clear and distinct. **3.** The level of detail in a recording, production, or digital encoding of an image or sound. **4.** The state of being clearly outlined or determined: *With the snow, the trees lost their definition against the horizon.*

de·fin·i·tive (dĭ-fĭn′ĭ-tĭv) ►*adj.* **1.** Serving to define or identify as distinct from others. **2.** Being a final settlement. See Synonyms at **decisive. 3.** Authoritative and complete: *a definitive biography.* —**de·fin′i·tive·ly** *adv.*

de·flate (dĭ-flāt′) ►*v.* **-flat·ed, -flat·ing 1a.** To release contained air or gas from. **b.** To collapse by such a release. **2.** To reduce or lessen the size or importance of: *Losing the contest deflated my ego.* **3.** *Econ.* To reduce the amount or availability of (currency or credit), effecting a decline in prices. [DE– + (IN)FLATE.] —**de·fla′tion** *n.* —**de·fla′tion·ar·y** *adj.* —**de·fla′tor** *n.*

de·flect (dĭ-flĕkt′) ►*v.* To turn aside or cause to turn aside. [Lat. *dēflectere.*] —**de·flect′a·ble** *adj.* —**de·flec′tion** *n.* —**de·flec′tive** *adj.* —**de·flec′tor** *n.*

De·foe (dĭ-fō′), **Daniel** 1660–1731. English writer.

de·fog (dē-fôg′, -fŏg′) ►*v.* **-fogged, -fog·ging** To remove fog from. —**de·fog′ger** *n.*

de·fo·li·ant (dē-fō′lē-ənt) ►*n.* A chemical sprayed or dusted on plants to cause the leaves to fall off.

de·fo·li·ate (dē-fō′lē-āt′) ►*v.* **-at·ed, -at·ing** To deprive of leaves, esp. by the use of chemicals. —**de·fo′li·ate** (-ĭt) *adj.* —**de·fo′li·a′tion** *n.* —**de·fo′li·a′tor** *n.*

de·for·est (dē-fôr′ĭst, -fŏr′-) ►*v.* To clear away trees from. —**de·for′es·ta′tion** *n.*

de·form (dĭ-fôrm′) ►*v.* **1.** To spoil the beauty or appearance of; disfigure. **2.** To become disfigured. **3.** *Phys.* To alter the shape of by pressure or stress. —**de·form′a·ble** *adj.* —**de′for·ma′tion** (dē′fôr-mā′shən, dĕf′ər-) *n.*

de·for·mi·ty (dĭ-fôr′mĭ-tē) ►*n., pl.* **-ties 1.** The state of being deformed. **2.** A bodily malformation or disfigurement.

de·fraud (dĭ-frôd′) ►*v.* To swindle. —**de′fraud·a′tion** *n.* —**de·fraud′er** *n.*

de·fray (dĭ-frā′) ►*v.* To undertake the payment of; pay. [< OFr. *desfrayer.*] —**de·fray′a·ble** *adj.* —**de·fray′al** *n.*

de·frock (dē-frŏk′) ►*v.* **1.** To strip of priestly privileges. **2.** To deprive of the right to practice a profession.

de·frost (dē-frôst′, -frŏst′) ►*v.* **1.** To remove ice or frost from. **2.** To thaw or cause to thaw. —**de·frost′er** *n.*

deft (dĕft) ►*adj.* **-er, -est** Skillful; adroit: *a deft maneuver.* [< ME *dafte,* DAFT.] —**deft′ly** *adv.* —**deft′ness** *n.*

de·funct (dĭ-fŭngkt′) ►*adj.* No longer in operation: *a defunct business.* [Lat. *dēfūnctus,* p.part. of *dēfungī,* finish.]

de·fuse (dē-fyōōz′) ►*v.* **-fused, -fus·ing 1.** To remove the fuse from (an explosive). **2.** To make less dangerous or hostile.

de·fy (dĭ-fī′) ►*v.* **-fied, -fy·ing 1.** To oppose or resist with boldness. **2.** To resist or withstand. **3.** To dare (someone) to do something. [< VLat. **disfīdāre.*]
    Syns: *brave, dare, face* **v.**

deg. ►*abbr.* degree

De·gas (də-gä′), **(Hilaire Germain) Edgar** 1834–1917. French artist.

de Gaulle (də gōl′, gôl′), **Charles André Joseph Marie** 1890–1970. French general and politician.

de·gauss (dē-gous′) ►*v.* **1.** To neutralize the magnetic field of. **2.** To erase information from (e.g., a magnetic disk). [DE– + *gauss,* unit of electromagnetism.]

de·gen·er·ate (dĭ-jĕn′ər-ĭt) ►*adj.* Having declined, as in function, from a former state. ►*n.* A depraved or corrupt person. ►*v.* (-ə-rāt′) **-at·ed, -at·ing 1.** To fall below a normal or desirable state. **2.** To decline in quality. [< Lat. *dēgenerāre,* deteriorate.] —**de·gen′er·ate·ly** *adv.* —**de·gen′er·a·cy** *n.* —**de·gen′er·a′tion** *n.* —**de·gen′er·a·tive** *adj.*

de·grad·a·ble (dĭ-grā′də-bəl) ►*adj.* Capable of being chemically degraded: *degradable plastic.* —**de·grad′a·bil′i·ty** *n.*

de·grade (dĭ-grād′) ►*v.* **-grad·ed, -grad·ing 1.** To lower in quality or value. **2.** To lower in dignity; dishonor or disgrace. See Synonyms at **debase. 3.** To reduce in rank or status; demote. [< LLat. *dēgradāre.*] —**deg′ra·da′tion** (dĕg′rə-dā′shən) *n.*

de·gree (dĭ-grē′) ►*n.* **1.** One of a series of steps in a process or course; stage. **2.** Relative social or official rank or position. **3.** Relative amount or intensity. **4.** The extent or measure of a state of being or action. **5.** A unit division of a temperature scale. **6.** *Math.* A unit of angular measure equal in magnitude to $\frac{1}{360}$ of a complete revolution. **7.** A unit of latitude or longitude, equal to $\frac{1}{360}$ of a great circle. **8.** *Math.* The greatest sum of the exponents of the variables in a term of a polynomial or polynomial equation. **9.** An academic distinction given to someone who has completed a course of study or as an honor. **10.** *Law* A classification of a crime or injury according to its seriousness. **11.** *Gram.* One of the forms used in the comparison of adjectives and adverbs. **12.** *Mus.* One of the seven notes of a diatonic scale. —*idiom:* **to a degree** In a limited way. [< VLat. **dēgradus;* DE– + Lat. *gradus,* step.]

de·gree-day (dĭ-grē′dā′) ►*n.* A unit of measurement equal to a difference of one degree between the mean outdoor temperature on a certain day and a reference temperature, used in estimating the energy needs for heating or cooling a building.

de·hisce (dē-hĭs′) ►*v.* **-hisced, -hisc·ing 1.** *Bot.* To open at definite places, discharging seeds or other contents, as the ripe capsules or pods of some plants. **2.** *Med.* To rupture or break open. [< Lat. *hīscere,* split.] —**de·hisc′ent** *adj.* —**de·hisc′ence** *n.*

de·hu·man·ize (dē-hyōō′mə-nīz′) ►*v.* **1.** To deprive of human qualities such as individuality or compassion. **2.** To render mechanical and routine. —**de·hu′man·i·za′tion** *n.*

de·hu·mid·i·fy (dē′hyōō-mĭd′ə-fī′) ►*v.* To

remove atmospheric moisture from. —**de′hu·mid′i·fi·ca′tion** *n.* —**de′hu·mid′i·fi′er** *n.*

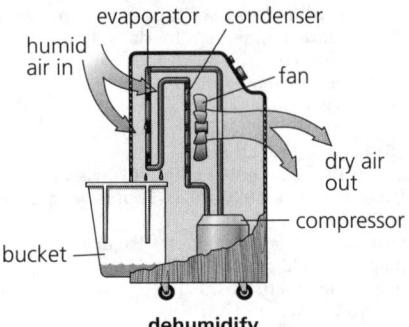

dehumidify
dehumidifying unit

de·hy·drate (dē-hī′drāt′) ►*v.* **1.** To remove water from. **2.** To deplete the bodily fluids of. See Synonyms at **dry.** —**de′hy·dra′tion** *n.* —**de·hy′dra′tor** *n.*

de·hy·dro·gen·ate (dē′hī-drŏj′ə-nāt′, dē-hī′drə-jə-) ►*v.* To remove hydrogen from. —**de·hy′dro·gen·a′tion** *n.*

de·ice (dē-īs′) ►*v.* **-iced, -ic·ing** To make or keep free of ice. —**de·ic′er** *n.*

de·i·fy (dē′ə-fī′, dā′-) ►*v.* **-fied, -fy·ing 1.** To make a god of. **2.** To worship; exalt. [< LLat. *deificāre.*] —**de′i·fi·ca′tion** *n.*

deign (dān) ►*v.* To do something that one considers beneath one's dignity; condescend. See Synonyms at **stoop¹.** [< Lat. *dignārī,* regard as worthy.]

de·in·sti·tu·tion·al·ize (dē-ĭn′stĭ-tōō′shə-nə-līz′, -tyōō′-) ►*v.* **1.** To remove the status of an institution from. **2.** To release (e.g., a mental health patient) from an institution for placement and care in the community. —**de·in′sti·tu′tion·al·i·za′tion** *n.*

de·ism (dē′ĭz′əm) ►*n.* A religious belief that the universe is created by God but operates rationally without miracles or supernatural revelation. [< Lat. *deus,* god.] —**de′ist** *n.* —**de·is′tic** *adj.* —**de·is′ti·cal·ly** *adv.*

de·i·ty (dē′ĭ-tē, dā′-) ►*n., pl.* **-ties 1.** A god or goddess. **2.** Divinity. [< Lat. *deus.*]

dé·jà vu (dā′zhä vü′) ►*n.* An impression of having seen or experienced something before. [Fr., already seen.]

de·ject (dĭ-jĕkt′) ►*v.* To lower the spirits of; dishearten. [< Lat. *dēicere, dēiect-,* cast down.] —**de·jec′tion** *n.*

de·ject·ed (dĭ-jĕk′tĭd) ►*adj.* Being in low spirits; depressed. See Synonyms at **depressed.** —**de·ject′ed·ly** *adv.*

de ju·re (dē jōōr′ē, dā yōōr′ā) ►*adv. & adj.* According to law; by right. [Lat. *dē iūre.*]

dek– or **deka–** ►*pref.* Vars. of **deca–.**

de Koo·ning (dĭ kōō′nĭng), **Willem** 1904–97. Dutch-born Amer. painter.

De·la·croix (də-lä-krwä′), **(Ferdinand Victor) Eugène** 1798–1863. French romantic painter.

Del·a·ware¹ (dĕl′ə-wâr′) ►*n., pl.* **-ware** or **-wares 1.** A member of a group of Native American peoples formerly of the Delaware and lower Hudson river valleys, now chiefly in Oklahoma. **2.** The Algonquian language of the Delaware.

Del·a·ware² (dĕl′ə-wâr′) A state of the E US on the Atlantic Ocean. Cap. Dover.

Delaware River A river rising in SE NY and flowing about 580 km (360 mi) to the **Delaware Bay** in N DE.

De La Warr (dĕl′ə wâr′, wər), Baron Thomas West. 1577–1618. English-born Amer. colonial administrator.

de·lay (dĭ-lā′) ►*v.* **1.** To postpone; defer. **2.** To cause to be later than expected. **3.** To act or move slowly. ►*n.* **1.** The act of delaying or condition of being delayed; postponement: *responded without delay.* **2.** The period of time one is delayed. [< OFr. *deslaier.*] —**de·lay′er** *n.*

de·lec·ta·ble (dĭ-lĕk′tə-bəl) ►*adj.* **1.** Pleasing to the taste. See Synonyms at **delicious. 2.** Delightful. [< Lat. *dēlectāre,* to please.] —**de·lec′ta·bil′i·ty** *n.* —**de·lec′ta·bly** *adv.*

de·lec·ta·tion (dē′lĕk-tā′shən) ►*n.* Delight; pleasure. [< Lat. *dēlectāre,* to please.]

del·e·gate (dĕl′ĭ-gāt′, -gĭt) ►*n.* **1.** A person authorized to act as representative for another. **2.** A representative to a convention. ►*v.* (-gāt′) **-gat·ed, -gat·ing 1.** To authorize and send (another person) as one's representative. **2.** To commit or entrust to another. [< Lat. *dēlēgāre,* to dispatch.]

del·e·ga·tion (dĕl′ĭ-gā′shən) ►*n.* **1.** The act of delegating. **2.** A body of delegates.

de·lete (dĭ-lēt′) ►*v.* **-let·ed, -let·ing 1.** To remove by striking out or canceling. **2.** To remove (a file, e.g.) from a hard drive or other storage medium. [Lat. *dēlēre.*] —**de·le′tion** *n.*

del·e·te·ri·ous (dĕl′ĭ-tîr′ē-əs) ►*adj.* Harmful; injurious. [< Gk. *dēlētēr,* destroyer.] —**del′e·te′ri·ous·ly** *adv.* —**del′e·te′ri·ous·ness** *n.*

delft (dĕlft) ►*n.* A style of glazed earthenware, usu. blue and white. [< *Delft,* a city of the Netherlands.]

Del·hi (dĕl′ē) A city of N-central India.

del·i (dĕl′ē) ►*n., pl.* **-is** *Informal* A delicatessen.

de·lib·er·ate (dĭ-lĭb′ər-ĭt) ►*adj.* **1.** Done with full consciousness of the effects; intentional. **2.** Marked by careful consideration: *a deliberate decision.* **3.** Unhurried and careful: *moved at a deliberate pace.* ►*v.* (-ə-rāt′) **-at·ed, -at·ing** To consider or discuss a matter carefully. [< Lat. *dēlīberāre,* consider.] —**de·lib′er·ate·ly** *adv.*

de·lib·er·a·tion (dĭ-lĭb′ə-rā′shən) ►*n.* **1.** The act or process of deliberating. **2. deliberations** Careful discussion and consideration. —**de·lib′er·a′tive** *adj.* —**de·lib′er·a′tive·ly** *adv.*

del·i·ca·cy (dĕl′ĭ-kə-sē) ►*n., pl.* **-cies 1.** The quality of being delicate. **2.** A choice food. **3.** Fineness of appearance or construction; elegance: *brushwork of great delicacy.* **4.** The need for tact in handling: *a topic of some delicacy.*

del·i·cate (dĕl′ĭ-kĭt) ►*adj.* **1.** Pleasing to the senses, esp. in a subtle way: *a delicate flavor.* **2a.** Easily broken or damaged. **b.** Exquisitely fine or dainty: *delicate china.* See Synonyms at **exquisite. c.** Frail in constitution. **3.** Marked by sensitivity of discrimination: *delicate perception.* **4a.** Having or showing great consideration or care. **b.** Requiring careful or tactful treatment: *a delicate situation.* **5.** Fine or soft in touch or skill. [< Lat. *dēlicātus,* pleasing.] —**del′i·cate·ly** *adv.* —**del′i·cate·ness** *n.*

del·i·ca·tes·sen (dĕl′ĭ-kə-tĕs′ən) ►*n.* A shop that sells prepared foods that are ready for serving. [Ger. *Delikatessen*, delicacies.]

de·li·cious (dĭ-lĭsh′əs) ►*adj.* Highly pleasing to the senses, esp. of taste or smell. [< Lat. *dēlicia*, pleasure.] **—de·li′cious·ly** *adv.* **—de·li′cious·ness** *n.*

　　Syns: delectable, luscious, scrumptious, yummy adj.

de·light (dĭ-līt′) ►*n.* **1.** Great pleasure; joy: *Her face beamed with delight.* **2.** Something that gives great pleasure or enjoyment: *The vacation was a delight.* ►*v.* **1.** To take great pleasure or joy. **2.** To please greatly. See Synonyms at **please.** [< Lat. *dēlectāre*, to please.] **—de·light′ed·ly** *adv.* **—de·light′ed·ness** *n.*

de·light·ful (dĭ-līt′fəl) ►*adj.* Greatly pleasing. **—de·light′ful·ly** *adv.*

De·li·lah (də-lī′lə) In the Bible, Samson's lover who betrayed him by having his hair shorn, thus depriving him of his strength.

de·lim·it (dĭ-lĭm′ĭt) ►*v.* To establish the limits of. [< Lat. *līmes*, boundary line.] **—de·lim′i·ta′tion** *n.* **—de·lim′it·er** *n.*

de·lin·e·ate (dĭ-lĭn′ē-āt′) ►*v.* **-at·ed, -at·ing 1a.** To draw or depict. **b.** To describe or characterize in words. **2.** To show the outline or border of: *delineated the crime scene with yellow tape.* **3.** To show or contain a distinguishing characteristic of; distinguish. [Lat. *dēlīneāre.*] **—de·lin′e·a′tion** *n.* **—de·lin′e·a′tive** *adj.* **—de·lin′e·a′tor** *n.*

de·lin·quent (dĭ-lĭng′kwənt, -lĭn′-) ►*adj.* **1.** Failing to do what is required. **2.** Overdue in payment: *a delinquent account.* ►*n.* **1.** A juvenile delinquent. **2.** A person who fails to do what is required. [< Lat. *dēlinquere*, offend.] **—de·lin′quen·cy** *n.* **—de·lin′quent·ly** *adv.*

del·i·quesce (dĕl′ĭ-kwĕs′) ►*v.* **-quesced, -quesc·ing 1.** *Chem.* To dissolve and become liquid by absorbing moisture from the air. **2.** To melt away. [Lat. *dēliquēscere < liquēre*, be liquid.] **—del′i·ques′cence** *n.* **—del′i·ques′cent** *adj.*

de·lir·i·um (dĭ-lîr′ē-əm) ►*n., pl.* **-i·ums** or **-i·a** (-ē-ə) **1.** A temporary state of mental confusion resulting from high fever, intoxication, or other causes, marked by anxiety, disorientation, hallucinations, delusions, and incoherent speech. **2.** Uncontrolled excitement or emotion. [Lat. *dēlīrium : dē-*, out of + *līra*, furrow.] **—de·lir′i·ous** *adj.* **—de·lir′i·ous·ly** *adv.* **—de·lir′i·ous·ness** *n.*

delirium tre·mens (trē′mənz) ►*n.* An acute episode of delirium caused by withdrawal from alcohol following habitual excessive drinking. [NLat., trembling delirium.]

de·liv·er (dĭ-lĭv′ər) ►*v.* **1.** To take to the proper place or recipient. **2.** To utter: *deliver a lecture.* **3a.** To give birth to. **b.** To assist in the birth of: *The midwife delivered the baby.* **4.** To give forth or produce. **5.** To set free: *deliver a slave from captivity.* **6.** To produce what is expected; make good: *She delivered on her promise.* [< LLat. *dēlīberāre*, set free.] **—de·liv′er·a·ble** *adj.* **—de·liv′er·ance** *n.* **—de·liv′er·er** *n.*

de·liv·er·y (dĭ-lĭv′ə-rē, -lĭv′rē) ►*n., pl.* **-ies 1a.** The act of delivering. **b.** Something delivered. **2.** The act or manner of throwing or discharging. **3.** The act of giving birth. **4.** The act or manner of speaking or singing.

dell (dĕl) ►*n.* A small wooded valley. [< OE.]

Del·mon·i·co steak (dĕl-mŏn′ĭ-kō′) ►*n.* A small, often boned steak from the front section of the short loin of beef. [After Lorenzo Delmonico (1813–81).]

Del·phi (dĕl′fī′) An ancient town of central Greece near Mount Parnassus.

del·phin·i·um (dĕl-fĭn′ē-əm) ►*n.* A tall cultivated plant having showy, variously colored spurred flowers. [< Gk. *delphinion*, larkspur, dim. of *delphis*, dolphin.]

del·ta (dĕl′tə) ►*n.* **1.** The 4th letter of the Greek alphabet. **2.** A usu. triangular deposit at the mouth of a river. [Gk. < Phoenician *dalt*, door.]

del·toid (dĕl′toid′) ►*n.* A thick triangular muscle covering the shoulder joint, used to raise the arm from the side. [< Gk. *deltoeidēs*, triangular : *delta*, DELTA + -OID.]

de·lude (dĭ-lōōd′) ►*v.* **-lud·ed, -lud·ing** To cause to hold a false belief; deceive. [< Lat. *dēlūdere.*] **—de·lud′er** *n.*

del·uge (dĕl′yōōj) ►*n.* **1.** A great flood; downpour. **2.** Something that overwhelms: *a deluge of mail.* **3. Deluge** The Flood. ►*v.* **-uged, -ug·ing** To overrun with or as if with water; inundate. [< Lat. *dīluvium < dīluere*, wash away : DIS- + *-luere*, wash.]

de·lu·sion (dĭ-lōō′zhən) ►*n.* **1.** The act of deluding or state of being deluded. **2.** A false belief or opinion. **3.** *Psychiat.* A false belief or perception that is a manifestation of mental illness: *delusions of persecution.* **—de·lu′sion·al, de·lu′sive** *adj.* **—de·lu′sive·ly** *adv.*

de·luxe (dĭ-lŭks′) ►*adj.* Particularly luxurious or elaborate for its kind. [Fr., of luxury.]

delve (dĕlv) ►*v.* **delved, delv·ing 1.** To search deeply and laboriously: *delved through court records.* **2.** To undertake a task undeterred by difficulty: *delved into finding a job.* **3.** To explain something, esp. in detail: *The article delves into city politics.* [< OE *delfan*, dig.]

dem. ►*abbr.* demonstrative

Dem. ►*abbr.* **1.** Democrat **2.** Democratic

de·mag·net·ize (dē-măg′nĭ-tīz′) ►*v.* To remove magnetic properties from. **—de·mag′net·i·za′tion** *n.*

dem·a·gogue or **dem·a·gog** (dĕm′ə-gôg′, -gŏg′) ►*n.* A leader who obtains power by appealing to the emotions and prejudices of the populace. [Gk. *dēmagōgos*, popular leader : *dēmos*, people + *agein*, to lead.] **—dem′a·gog′ic** (-gŏj′ĭk, -gŏg′-), **dem′a·gog′i·cal** *adj.* **—dem′a·gogu′er·y** *n.* **—dem′a·gog′y** (-gŏj′ē, -gô′jē, -gŏg′ē) *n.*

de·mand (dĭ-mănd′) ►*v.* **1.** To ask for insistently: *demanded to speak to the manager.* **2.** To claim as just or due: *demand repayment of the loan.* **3.** To require; call for: *a gem that demands a fine setting.* ►*n.* **1.** An urgent request. **2.** Something demanded. **3.** An essential requirement or need. **4.** The state of being sought after: *in great demand as a speaker.* **5.** *Econ.* The desire for goods or services in an economy, measured as the amount people are ready to buy at a given price. [< Lat. *dēmandāre*, entrust.] **—de·mand′a·ble** *adj.* **—de·mand′er** *n.*

de·mand·ing (dĭ-măn′dĭng) ►*adj.* **1.** Requiring much effort or attention. **2.** Requiring others to work hard or meet high expectations: *a demanding teacher* **—de·mand′ing·ly** *adv.*

de·mar·cate (dĭ-mär′kāt′, dē′mär-kāt′) ►*v.* **-cat·ed, -cat·ing** To set the boundaries of;

delimit. —**de·mar′ca′tor** *n.*

de·mar·ca·tion (dē′mär-kā′shən) ►*n.* **1.** The setting or marking of boundaries or limits. **2.** A separation: *a line of demarcation.* [Sp. *demarcación.*]

de·mean¹ (dĭ-mēn′) ►*v.* To behave (oneself) in a particular manner: *demeaned themselves well in class.* [< OFr. *mener,* to conduct.]

de·mean² (dĭ-mēn′) ►*v.* To lower in status or character; degrade or humble. See Synonyms at **debase.**

de·mean·or (dĭ-mē′nər) ►*n.* The way a person behaves. [< OFr. *demener,* govern.]

de·ment·ed (dĭ-měn′tĭd) ►*adj.* **1.** Suffering from dementia. **2.** *Slang* Crazy. [< Lat. *dēmēns, dēment-,* senseless : DE– + *mēns,* mind.]

de·men·tia (dĭ-měn′shə) ►*n.* Deterioration of intellectual faculties resulting from an organic disease of the brain. [Lat. *dēmentia.*]

de·mer·it (dĭ-měr′ĭt) ►*n.* **1.** A mark made against one's record for a fault or misconduct. **2.** A quality deserving of censure; fault. [< Lat. *dēmeritum,* neuter p.part. of *dēmerēre,* deserve.]

de·mesne (dĭ-mān′, -mēn′) ►*n.* **1.** The grounds of a mansion or country house. **2.** An extensive piece of landed property; an estate. **3.** A district; territory. [< OFr. *demaine,* DOMAIN.]

De·me·ter (dĭ-mē′tər) ►*n. Gk. Myth.* The goddess of the harvest.

dem·i-glace (děm′ē-glăs′) ►*n.* A rich, reduced brown sauce usu. seasoned with wine and used as a base for other sauces. [Fr. : *demi-,* half + *glace,* glaze.]

dem·i·god (děm′ē-gŏd′) ►*n.* **1.** *Myth.* **a.** A male being, the offspring of a deity and a mortal. **b.** A minor god. **2.** A person who is highly revered. [*demi-,* partly + GOD.]

dem·i·john (děm′ē-jŏn′) ►*n.* A large bottle usu. encased in wickerwork. [Prob. < Fr. *dame-Jeanne,* lady Jane.]

de·mil·i·ta·rize (dē-mĭl′ĭ-tə-rīz′) ►*v.* To remove or forbid military troops (in an area). —**de·mil′i·ta·ri·za′tion** *n.*

De Mille (də mĭl′), **Agnes George** 1905–93. Amer. choreographer.

De Mille, Cecil Blount 1881–1959. Amer. filmmaker.

dem·i·mon·daine (děm′ē-mŏn-dān′, -mŏn′dān′) ►*n.* A woman belonging to the demimonde.

dem·i·monde (děm′ē-mŏnd′) ►*n.* **1a.** A class of women supported by wealthy lovers and considered promiscuous or otherwise unrespectable. **b.** Women prostitutes collectively. **2.** A group whose respectability is dubious: *the literary demimonde of hacks.* [Fr.]

de·min·er·al·ize (dē-mĭn′ər-ə-līz′) ►*v.* To remove minerals or mineral salts from (a liquid). —**de·min′er·al·i′zer** *n.*

de·mise (dĭ-mīz′) ►*n.* **1.** Death. **2.** The end; termination. [< OFr. *dimis,* transfer of property < *demettre,* release.]

dem·i·tasse (děm′ē-tăs′, -täs′) ►*n.* **1.** A small cup of strong coffee. **2.** The small cup used to serve this drink. [Fr.]

dem·o (děm′ō) ►*n., pl.* **-os** *Informal* **1.** A demonstration, as of a product. **2.** A product used for demonstration and often sold later at a discount. **3.** A brief recording that illustrates the abilities of a musician. —**dem′o** *v.*

de·mo·bil·ize (dē-mō′bə-līz′) ►*v.* To discharge from military service or use. —**de·mo′bil·i·za′tion** *n.*

de·moc·ra·cy (dĭ-mŏk′rə-sē) ►*n., pl.* **-cies 1.** Government by the people, exercised either directly or through elected representatives. **2.** A political unit that has such a government. **3.** Majority rule. **4.** The principles of social equality and respect for the individual within a community. [< Gk. *dēmokratia.*]

dem·o·crat (děm′ə-krăt′) ►*n.* **1.** An advocate of democracy. **2. Democrat** A member of the Democratic Party.

dem·o·crat·ic (děm′ə-krăt′ĭk) ►*adj.* **1.** Characterized by or advocating democracy. **2.** Of or for the people in general; popular: *a democratic movement.* **3.** Believing in or practicing social equality. **4. Democratic** Of or relating to the Democratic Party. —**dem′o·crat′i·cal·ly** *adv.*

Democratic Party ►*n.* One of the two major US political parties.

de·moc·ra·tize (dĭ-mŏk′rə-tīz′) ►*v.* **-tized, -tiz·ing** To make democratic. —**de·moc′ra·ti·za′tion** *n.*

De·moc·ri·tus (dĭ-mŏk′rĭ-təs) 460?–370? BC. Greek philosopher.

de·mod·u·late (dē-mŏj′ə-lāt′, -mŏd′yə-) ►*v.* **-lat·ed, -lat·ing** To extract (information) from a modulated carrier wave. —**de·mod′u·la′tion** *n.* —**de·mod′u·la′tor** *n.*

dem·o·graph·ics (děm′ə-grăf′ĭks, dē′mə-) ►*n.* *(takes pl. v.)* The characteristics of human population segments.

de·mog·ra·phy (dĭ-mŏg′rə-fē) ►*n.* The statistical study of human populations. [Gk. *dēmos,* people + –GRAPHY.] —**de·mog′ra·pher** *n.* —**dem′o·graph′ic** (děm′ə-grăf′ĭk, dē′mə-) *adj.* —**dem′o·graph′i·cal·ly** *adv.*

de·mol·ish (dĭ-mŏl′ĭsh) ►*v.* **1.** To tear down completely; raze. **2.** To put an end to: *a loss that demolished our hopes.* [< Lat. *dēmōlīrī.*]

dem·o·li·tion (děm′ə-lĭsh′ən, dē′mə-) ►*n.* The act or process of destroying, esp. by explosives. —**dem′o·li′tion·ist** *n.*

de·mon (dē′mən) ►*n.* **1.** An evil supernatural being; devil. **2.** A persistently tormenting person, force, or passion. **3.** One who is extremely zealous or diligent: *a real demon at math.* [< Gk. *daimōn,* divine power.] —**de·mon′ic** (dĭ-mŏn′ĭk) *adj.* —**de·mon′i·cal·ly** *adv.*

de·mon·e·tize (dē-mŏn′ĭ-tīz′, -mŭn′-) ►*v.* To divest (currency) of monetary value. —**de·mon′e·ti·za′tion** *n.*

de·mo·ni·ac (dĭ-mō′nē-ăk′) *also* **de·mo·ni·a·cal** (dē′mə-nī′ə-kəl) ►*adj.* **1.** Possessed by or as if by a demon. **2.** Devilish; fiendish. —**de·mo′ni·a·cal·ly** *adv.*

de·mon·ize (dē′mə-nīz′) ►*v.* **-ized, -iz·ing 1.** To turn into or as if into a demon. **2.** To possess by or as by a demon. **3.** To represent as evil. —**de′mon·i·za′tion** *n.*

de·mon·ol·o·gy (dē′mə-nŏl′ə-jē) ►*n.* The study of demons. —**de′mon·ol′o·gist** *n.*

de·mon·stra·ble (dĭ-mŏn′strə-bəl) ►*adj.* Capable of being shown or proved. —**de·mon′stra·bil′i·ty** *n.* —**de·mon′stra·bly** *adv.*

dem·on·strate (děm′ən-strāt′) ►*v.* **-strat·ed, -strat·ing 1.** To show clearly and deliberately. **2.** To show to be true by reasoning or evidence. **3.** To explain and illustrate. **4.** To show the use of (a product) to a prospective buyer. **5.**

To participate in a public display of opinion: *demonstrate against the war.* [Lat. *dēmōnstrāre* : *dē-*, completely + *mōnstrum*, portent (< *monēre*, warn).] **—dem'on·stra'tion** *n.* **—dem'on·stra'tor** *n.*

de·mon·stra·tive (dĭ-mŏn'strə-tĭv) ►*adj.* **1.** Serving to manifest or prove. **2.** Given to the open expression of emotion. **3.** *Gram.* Specifying the person or thing referred to: *the demonstrative pronouns* these *and* that. ►*n. Gram.* A demonstrative pronoun or adjective. **—de·mon'stra·tive·ly** *adv.*

de·mor·al·ize (dĭ-môr'ə-līz', -mŏr'-) ►*v.* **-ized, -iz·ing** **1.** To undermine the confidence or morale of; dishearten. **2.** To corrupt. **—de·mor'al·i·za'tion** *n.* **—de·mor'al·iz'er** *n.*

De·mos·the·nes (dĭ-mŏs'thə-nēz') 384–322 BC. Greek orator.

de·mote (dĭ-mōt') ►*v.* **-mot·ed, -mot·ing** To reduce in grade, rank, or status. [DE– + (PRO)MOTE.] **—de·mo'tion** *n.*

de·mot·ic (dĭ-mŏt'ĭk) ►*adj.* **1.** Of or relating to the common people; popular. **2.** Of or written in a simplified ancient Egyptian hieratic script. **3. Demotic** Relating to a form of modern Greek based on colloquial use. [< Gk. *dēmotēs*, commoner.]

de·mul·cent (dĭ-mŭl'sənt) ►*adj.* Serving to soothe or soften. ►*n.* A soothing, usu. jellylike or oily substance, used esp. to relieve pain in mucous membranes. [< Lat. *dēmulcēre*, soften.]

de·mur (dĭ-mûr') ►*v.* **-murred, -mur·ring** To voice opposition; object. [< Lat. *dēmorārī*, to delay.]

de·mure (dĭ-myŏor') ►*adj.* **-mur·er, -mur·est** **1.** Modest in manner; reserved: *a demure guest.* **2.** Characterized by or suggestive of reserve or modesty: *a demure outfit.* [ME.] **—de·mure'ly** *adv.* **—de·mure'ness** *n.*

de·mys·ti·fy (dē-mĭs'tə-fī') ►*v.* To make less mysterious; clarify.

de·my·thol·o·gize (dē'mĭ-thŏl'ə-jīz') ►*v.* To remove the mysterious or mythological aspects from. **—de'my·thol'o·gi·za'tion** *n.*

den (dĕn) ►*n.* **1.** The shelter or retreat of a wild animal; lair. **2.** A hidden or squalid dwelling place: *a den of thieves.* **3.** A usu. secluded room for relaxation or leisure. [< OE *denn.*]

De·na·li (də-nä'lē) See Mount McKinley.

den·ar (dĕn'är) ►*n., pl.* **-a·ri** (-är-ē) See table at **currency.** [Macedonian.]

de·na·ture (dē-nā'chər) ►*v.* **-tured, -tur·ing** **1.** To change the nature of. **2.** To render unfit to eat or drink without destroying usefulness in other capacities, esp. to add methanol to. **—de·na'tur·ant** *n.*

den·drite (dĕn'drīt') ►*n.* A branched protoplasmic extension of a nerve cell that conducts impulses toward the cell body.

dendro– or **dendri–** or **dendr–** ►*pref.* Tree; treelike: *dendrite.* [< Gk. *dendron*, tree.]

den·gue (dĕng'gē, -gā) ►*n.* An acute viral tropical disease transmitted by mosquitoes and marked by fever, rash, and muscle pain. [< Swahili *ki-dinga.*]

Deng Xiao·ping (dŭng' shou'pĭng') 1904–97. Chinese political leader.

de·ni·a·ble (dĭ-nī'ə-bəl) ►*adj.* Possible to declare untrue: *deniable charges.* **—de·ni'a·bil'i·ty** *n.* **—de·ni'a·bly** *adv.*

de·ni·al (dĭ-nī'əl) ►*n.* **1.** A refusal to comply with a request. **2.** A refusal to grant the truth of a statement; contradiction. **3.** A disavowal; repudiation. **4.** A refusal to accept a doctrine or belief: *denied the existence of a supernatural being.* **5.** *Psych.* A defense mechanism marked by refusal to acknowledge painful realities, thoughts, or feelings.

den·ier (dən-yā', dĕn'yər) ►*n.* A unit of fineness for rayon, nylon, and silk fibers. [< OFr. *dener*, a coin < Lat. *dēnārius.*]

den·i·grate (dĕn'ĭ-grāt') ►*v.* **-grat·ed, -grat·ing** **1.** To attack the reputation of; defame. **2.** To disparage. [Lat. *dēnigrāre* < *niger*, black.] **—den'i·gra'tion** *n.* **—den'i·gra'tor** *n.*

den·im (dĕn'ĭm) ►*n.* A coarse cotton cloth used for jeans, overalls, and work uniforms. [Fr. *(serge) de Nîmes*, (serge) of Nîmes.]

den·i·zen (dĕn'ĭ-zən) ►*n.* **1.** An inhabitant; resident. **2.** One that frequents a particular place. [< LLat. *dēintus*, from within.]

Den·mark (dĕn'märk') A country of N Europe on Jutland and adjacent islands. Cap. Copenhagen.

de·nom·i·na·tion (dĭ-nŏm'ə-nā'shən) ►*n.* **1.** An organized group of religious congregations. **2.** A unit of specified value in a system of currency or weights. **3.** A name or designation, esp. for a class or group. [< Lat. *dēnōmināre*, designate < *nōmen*, name.] **—de·nom'i·na'tion·al** *adj.* **—de·nom'i·na'tion·al·ly** *adv.*

de·nom·i·na·tor (dĭ-nŏm'ə-nā'tər) ►*n.* **1.** *Math.* The expression written below the line in a fraction that indicates the number of parts into which one whole is divided. **2.** A common trait or characteristic.

de·note (dĭ-nōt') ►*v.* **-not·ed, -not·ing** **1.** To mark; indicate. **2.** To signify: *A flashing yellow light denotes caution.* [< Lat. *dēnotāre.*] **—de'no·ta'tion** *n.* **—de·no'ta·tive** *adj.*

de·noue·ment also **dé·noue·ment** (dā'noo-män') ►*n.* **1.** The resolution of a dramatic or narrative plot. **2.** The outcome of a sequence of events. [< OFr. *desnouement*, an untying.]

de·nounce (dĭ-nouns') ►*v.* **-nounced, -nounc·ing** **1.** To condemn openly as being wrong or reprehensible. **2.** To accuse publicly. [< Lat. *dēnūntiāre.*] **—de·nounce'ment** *n.* **—de·nounc'er** *n.*

dense (dĕns) ►*adj.* **dens·er, dens·est** **1.** Having relatively high density. **2.** Crowded together. **3.** Hard to penetrate; thick: *a dense jungle.* **4.** Slow to apprehend. **5.** Hard to understand because of complexity or obscurity: *a dense novel.* [Lat. *dēnsus.*] **—dense'ly** *adv.* **—dense'ness** *n.*

den·si·ty (dĕn'sĭ-tē) ►*n., pl.* **-ties 1a.** The quantity of something per unit measure, esp. per unit length, area, or volume. **b.** The mass per unit volume of a substance under specified conditions of pressure and temperature. **2.** Thickness of consistency; impenetrability. **3.** Complexity of structure or content.

dent (dĕnt) ►*n.* **1.** A depression in a surface made by pressure or a blow. **2.** *Informal* Meaningful progress; headway. ►*v.* To make a dent in. [< OE *dynt*, a blow.]

den·tal (dĕn'tl) ►*adj.* **1.** Of or relating to the teeth. **2.** *Ling.* Articulated with the tip of the tongue near or against the upper front teeth. ►*n. Ling.* A dental consonant.

dental floss ►*n.* A thread used to clean between the teeth.

dental hygienist ►*n.* One who assists a dentist.

denti– or **dent–** ►*pref.* Tooth: *dentition.* [< Lat. *dēns, dent-,* tooth.]

den·ti·frice (děn′tə-frĭs′) ►*n.* A substance, such as a paste, for cleaning the teeth. [< Lat. *dentifricium* : DENTI– + *fricāre,* rub.]

den·tin (děn′tĭn) or **den·tine** (-tēn′) ►*n.* The calcified part of a tooth, beneath the enamel. —**den′tin·al** (děn′tə-nəl, děn-tē′-) *adj.*

den·tist (děn′tĭst) ►*n.* A person trained and licensed in the diagnosis, prevention, and treatment of diseases of the teeth and gums. [Fr. *dentiste* < Lat. *dēns, dent-,* tooth.] —**den′tist·ry** *n.*

den·ti·tion (děn-tĭsh′ən) ►*n.* **1.** The type, number, and arrangement of a set of teeth. **2.** The process of growing new teeth; teething.

den·ture (děn′chər) ►*n.* A set of artificial teeth.

de·nude (dĭ-no͞od′, -nyo͞od′) ►*v.* -**nud·ed,** -**nud·ing** To strip of covering; make bare. [Lat. *dēnūdāre.*] —**de′nu·da′tion** (dē′no͞o-dā′shən, -nyo͞o-, děn′yo͞o-) *n.*

de·nun·ci·a·tion (dĭ-nŭn′sē-ā′shən, -shē-) ►*n.* The act of denouncing, esp. a public condemnation. —**de·nun′ci·a′tive, de·nun′ci·a·to′ry** (-ə-tôr′ē) *adj.*

Den·ver (děn′vər) The capital of CO, in the N-central part.

de·ny (dĭ-nī′) ►*v.* -**nied,** -**ny·ing** **1.** To declare untrue. **2.** To refuse to believe; reject: *denies the existence of evil spirits.* **3a.** To decline to grant: *deny a request.* **b.** To restrain (oneself) esp. from indulgence in pleasures. [< Lat. *dēnegāre.*] *Syns: contradict, gainsay Ant: affirm v.*

de·o·dor·ant (dē-ō′dər-ənt) ►*n.* A substance used to counteract undesirable odors.

de·o·dor·ize (dē-ō′də-rīz′) ►*v.* -**ized,** -**iz·ing** To mask or neutralize the odor of. —**de·o′dor·i·za′tion** *n.* —**de·o′dor·iz′er** *n.*

de·ox·y·ri·bo·nu·cle·ic acid (dē-ŏk′sē-rī′bō-no͞o-klē′ĭk, -klā′-, -nyo͞o-) ►*n.* DNA.

de·part (dĭ-pärt′) ►*v.* **1.** To go away; leave. **2.** To die. **3.** To vary; deviate: *depart from custom.* See Synonyms at **swerve.** [< OFr. *departir,* divide, split.]

de·part·ment (dĭ-pärt′mənt) ►*n.* **1.** A distinct, usu. specialized division of an organization, business, government, or institution. **2.** *Informal* An area of particular knowledge or responsibility: *washing the dishes is my department.* [Fr. *département.*] —**de′part·men′tal** (dē′-pärt-měn′tl) *adj.* —**de′part·men′tal·ly** *adv.*

de·part·men·tal·ize (dē′pärt-měn′tl-īz′) ►*v.* -**ized,** -**iz·ing** To organize into departments. —**de′part·men′tal·i·za′tion** *n.*

department store ►*n.* A large retail store offering a variety of merchandise.

de·par·ture (dĭ-pär′chər) ►*n.* **1.** The act of leaving. **2.** A starting out, as on a trip. **3.** A divergence, as from a set procedure: *ordered curry as a departure from his usual diet.*

de·pend (dĭ-pěnd′) ►*v.* **1.** To rely, esp. for support: *depend on one's parents.* **2.** To place trust: *depends on her reliability.* **3.** To be determined or contingent: *a grade that depends on the final exam.* **4.** To have a dependence. [< Lat. *dēpendēre,* hang from.]

de·pend·a·ble (dĭ-pěn′də-bəl) ►*adj.* Trustworthy. See Synonyms at **reliable.** —**de·pend′a·bil′i·ty** *n.* —**de·pend′a·bly** *adv.*

de·pen·dence also **de·pen·dance** (dĭ-pěn′dəns) ►*n.* **1.** The state of being dependent, as for support. **2.** Trust; reliance. **3.** The condition of being determined or influenced by something else. **4.** A compulsive or chronic need; addiction: *an alcohol dependence.*

de·pen·den·cy also **de·pen·dan·cy** (dĭ-pěn′dən-sē) ►*n., pl.* -**cies** **1.** Dependence. **2.** A minor territory under the jurisdiction of a government.

de·pen·dent (dĭ-pěn′dənt) ►*adj.* **1.** Contingent on another: *Plants are dependent on sunlight.* **2.** Relying on the aid of another for financial support: *dependent children.* **3.** Compulsively using a drug or substance or engaging in a behavior and unable to stop without significant symptoms of withdrawal: *dependent on nicotine.* ►*n.* also **de·pen·dant** One who relies on another for financial support. —**de·pen′dent·ly** *adv. Syns: conditional, contingent, subject Ant: independent adj.*

de·pict (dĭ-pĭkt′) ►*v.* **1.** To represent in a picture. **2.** To describe in words. [< Lat. *dēpingere, dēpict-.*] —**de·pic′tion** *n.*

de·pil·a·to·ry (dĭ-pĭl′ə-tôr′ē) ►*n., pl.* -**ries** A substance used to remove unwanted hair from the body. [< Lat. *dēpilāre,* remove hair.] —**de·pil′a·to′ry** *adj.*

de·plane (dē-plān′) ►*v.* -**planed,** -**plan·ing** To disembark from an airplane.

de·plete (dĭ-plēt′) ►*v.* -**plet·ed,** -**plet·ing** To use up or exhaust: *depleted all of the supplies.* [Lat. *dēplēre,* to empty : DE– + *plēre,* fill.] —**de·ple′tion** *n.*

de·plore (dĭ-plôr′) ►*v.* -**plored,** -**plor·ing** To strongly disapprove; condemn. [< Lat. *dēplōrāre.*] —**de·plor′a·ble** *adj.* —**de·plor′a·bly** *adv.*

de·ploy (dĭ-ploi′) ►*v.* **1.** To position (troops) in readiness for combat. **2.** To distribute (persons or forces) systematically or strategically. **3.** To put into use or action. [< Lat. *displicāre,* scatter.] —**de·ploy′a·ble** *adj.* —**de·ploy′ment** *n.*

de·po·nent (dĭ-pō′nənt) ►*n.* One who gives testimony by affidavit or deposition. [< Lat. *dēpōnere,* put down.]

de·pop·u·late (dē-pŏp′yə-lāt′) ►*v.* To reduce sharply the population of. —**de·pop′u·la′tion** *n.*

de·port (dĭ-pôrt′) ►*v.* **1.** To expel from a country. **2.** To conduct (oneself) in a given manner. [< Lat. *dēportāre,* carry away.] —**de′por·ta′tion** (dē′pôr-tā′shən) *n.* —**de′por·tee′** *n.*

de·port·ment (dĭ-pôrt′mənt) ►*n.* Personal conduct; behavior.

de·pose (dĭ-pōz′) ►*v.* -**posed,** -**pos·ing** **1.** To remove from office or power. **2.** *Law* **a.** To give a deposition; testify. **b.** To take a deposition from. [< OFr. *deposer.*]

de·pos·it (dĭ-pŏz′ĭt) ►*v.* **1.** To put or set down. **2.** To lay down by a natural process: *glaciers that deposited their debris.* **3.** To place for safekeeping, as money in a bank. **4.** To give as partial payment or security. ►*n.* **1.** Something entrusted for safekeeping, as money in a bank. **2.** The condition of being deposited: *funds on deposit with a broker.* **3.** A partial or initial payment of a cost or debt. **4.** Something deposited, esp. by a natural process. [Lat. *dēpōnere, dēposit-,* put aside.] —**de·pos′i·tor** *n.*

dep·o·si·tion (děp′ə-zĭsh′ən) ►*n.* **1.** The act

of deposing, as from high office. **2.** The act of depositing, esp. the laying down of matter by a natural process. **3.** A deposit. **4.** *Law* Sworn testimony recorded for later use in court. —**dep′·o·si′tion·al** *adj.*

de·pos·i·to·ry (dĭ-pŏz′ĭ-tôr′ē) ►*n., pl.* **-ries** A place where something is deposited, as for safekeeping.

de·pot (dē′pō, dĕp′ō) ►*n.* **1.** A railroad or bus station. **2.** A warehouse or storehouse. **3.** A storage installation for military equipment and supplies. [< Lat. *dēpositum*, something deposited.]

de·prave (dĭ-prāv′) ►*v.* **-praved, -prav·ing** To debase, esp. morally. See Synonyms at **corrupt**. [< Lat. *dēprāvāre*.] —**de·praved′** *adj.* —**de·prav′i·ty** (-prăv′ĭ-tē) *n.*

dep·re·cate (dĕp′rĭ-kāt′) ►*v.* **-cat·ed, -cat·ing 1.** To express disapproval of. **2.** To belittle; depreciate. [Lat. *dēprecārī*, ward off by prayer.] —**dep′re·ca′tion** *n.* —**dep′re·ca′tor** *n.* —**dep′re·ca·to′ry** (-kə-tôr′ē) *adj.*

de·pre·ci·ate (dĭ-prē′shē-āt′) ►*v.* **-at·ed, -at·ing 1.** To diminish in price or value. **2.** To belittle. [< Lat. *dēpretiāre* < *pretium*, price.] —**de·pre′ci·a′tion** *n.* —**de·pre′ci·a′tor** *n.* —**de·pre′cia·to′ry** (-shə-tôr′ē), **de·pre′cia·tive** *adj.*

dep·re·da·tion (dĕp′rĭ-dā′shən) ►*n.* **1.** A predatory attack; raid. **2.** Damage or destruction. [< LLat. *dēpraedārī*, to plunder.]

de·press (dĭ-prĕs′) ►*v.* **1.** To lower in spirits; deject. **2.** To cause to drop; lower: *a drought that depressed the water level.* **3.** To press down: *depressed the space bar.* **4.** To lessen the activity or force of; weaken: *Inflation will depress the economy.* [< Lat. *dēprimere, dēpress-*.] —**de·pres′sive** *adj.* —**de·pres′sive·ly** *adv.* —**de·pres′sor** *n.*

de·pres·sant (dĭ-prĕs′ənt) ►*adj.* Slowing vital physiological activities. ►*n.* An agent, esp. a drug, that decreases the rate of vital physiological activities.

de·pressed (dĭ-prĕst′) ►*adj.* **1.** Low in spirits; dejected. **2.** Suffering from psychiatric depression. **3.** Lower in amount, degree, or position. **4.** Suffering from socioeconomic hardship. **5.** Sunk below the surrounding region.
  Syns: *blue, dejected, disconsolate, dispirited, downcast, downhearted* **adj.**

de·pres·sion (dĭ-prĕsh′ən) ►*n.* **1.** The act of depressing or condition of being depressed. **2.** A sunken area; hollow. **3.** The condition of feeling sad or despondent. **4.** A mood disorder marked usu. by anhedonia, extreme sadness, sleep problems, and loss of appetite. **5.** A period of drastic decline in an economy. **6.** A region of low barometric pressure. **7.** A reduction in amount, vigor, or activity.

de·prive (dĭ-prīv′) ►*v.* **-prived, -priv·ing 1.** To take something away from. **2.** To keep from possessing or enjoying: *Poverty deprived her of a happy childhood.* [< Med.Lat. *dēprīvāre*.] —**dep′ri·va′tion** (dĕp′rə-vā′shən) *n.*

de·pro·gram (dē-prō′grăm′, -grəm) ►*v.* To counteract the effect of an indoctrination, esp. a cult indoctrination. —**de·pro′gram′mer** *n.*

dept. ►*abbr.* **1.** department **2.** deputy

depth (dĕpth) ►*n.* **1.** The quality of being deep. **2.** The extent or dimension downward, backward, or inward: *dove to a depth of 30*

feet. **3.** often **depths** A deep part or place. **4.** The severest or worst part: *the depth of an economic depression.* **5.** Intellectual complexity; profundity: *a novel of great depth.* **6.** The range of one's competence: *out of my depth.* **7.** Thoroughness: *the depth of her research.* [ME *depthe* < *dep,* DEEP.]

depth charge ►*n.* A charge designed for detonation under water, used esp. against submarines.

dep·u·ta·tion (dĕp′yə-tā′shən) ►*n.* **1.** A person or group appointed to represent others. **2.** The act of deputing.

de·pute (dĭ-pyōōt′) ►*v.* **-put·ed, -put·ing** To appoint or authorize as a representative. [< LLat. *dēputāre*, allot.]

dep·u·tize (dĕp′yə-tīz′) ►*v.* **-tized, -tiz·ing** To appoint as a deputy.

dep·u·ty (dĕp′yə-tē) ►*n., pl.* **-ties 1.** A person empowered to act for another. **2.** An assistant exercising full authority in the absence of a superior. **3.** A legislative representative in certain countries. [< OFr. *depute < deputer*, DEPUTE.]

De Quin·cey (dĭ kwĭn′sē, -zē), **Thomas** 1785–1859. British writer.

de·rail (dē-rāl′) ►*v.* **1.** To run or cause to run off the rails. **2.** To come or bring to a sudden halt: *a campaign derailed by lack of funds.* —**de·rail′ment** *n.*

de·rail·leur (dĭ-rā′lər) ►*n.* A device for shifting gears on a bicycle by moving the chain between sprocket wheels of different sizes. [< Fr. *dérailler*, derail.]

de·range (dĭ-rānj′) ►*v.* **-ranged, -rang·ing 1.** To disarrange or disturb the order or functioning of: *an asteroid impact large enough to derange the climate.* **2.** To cause to be psychotic or otherwise severely mentally unsound. [< OFr. *desrengier.*] —**de·range′ment** *n.*

der·by (dûr′bē; *British* där′bē) ►*n., pl.* **-bies 1.** An annual horse race, esp. for three-year-olds. **2.** A race that is open to all contestants. **3.** A stiff felt hat with a round crown and narrow brim. [After the 12th Earl of *Derby* (1752–1834).]

der·e·lict (dĕr′ə-lĭkt′) ►*adj.* **1.** Deserted by an owner or keeper; abandoned: *derelict railroad tracks.* **2.** Run-down; dilapidated: *a derelict building.* **3.** Neglectful of duty or obligation; remiss. See Synonyms at **negligent**. ►*n.* A homeless or jobless person; vagrant. [< Lat. *dērelinquere, dērelict-,* abandon.]

der·e·lic·tion (dĕr′ə-lĭk′shən) ►*n.* **1.** Willful neglect, as of duty. **2.** The act of abandoning.

de·ride (dĭ-rīd′) ►*v.* **-rid·ed, -rid·ing** To speak of or treat dismissively or contemptuously. [Lat. *dērīdēre.*] —**de·ri′sion** (-rĭzh′ən) *n.* —**de·ri′sive** (-rī′sĭv) *adj.* —**de·ri′sive·ly** *adv.*

de ri·gueur (də rē-gœr′) ►*adj.* Socially obligatory. [Fr., of rigor, strictness.]

der·i·va·tion (dĕr′ə-vā′shən) ►*n.* **1.** The act or process of deriving. **2.** The origin or source of something. **3.** The historical origin and development of a word; etymology. —**der′i·va′tion·al** *adj.*

de·riv·a·tive (dĭ-rĭv′ə-tĭv) ►*adj.* **1.** Resulting from derivation: *a derivative word.* **2.** Unoriginal. ►*n.* **1.** Something derived. **2.** A word formed from another by derivation. **3.** *Math.* The slope of the tangent line to the graph of a function at a given point. **—de·riv'a·tive·ly** *adv.*

de·rive (dĭ-rīv') ►*v.* **-rived, -riv·ing 1a.** To obtain from a source: *confidence derived from years of experience.* **b.** To originate. See Synonyms at **stem¹**. **2.** To deduce or infer: *derive a conclusion from facts.* **3.** To generate (a linguistic structure) from another structure: *That word derives from Old English.* **4.** To produce or obtain (a compound) from another substance by chemical reaction. [< Lat. *dērīvāre.*] **—de·riv'a·ble** *adj.*

der·ma·ti·tis (dûr'mə-tī'tĭs) ►*n.* Inflammation of the skin.

der·ma·tol·o·gy (dûr'mə-tŏl'ə-jē) ►*n.* The branch of medicine that relates to the skin. **—der'ma·tol'o·gist** *n.*

der·mis (dûr'mĭs) ►*n.* The layer of the skin below the epidermis, containing nerve endings, sweat glands, and blood and lymph vessels. [NLat. < EPIDERMIS.] **—der'mal** *adj.*

der·o·gate (dĕr'ə-gāt') ►*v.* **-gat·ed, -gat·ing 1.** To take away; detract: *behavior that derogates from your reputation.* **2.** To disparage; belittle. **3.** To deviate from a standard: *derogate from the agreement during a crisis.* [< Lat. *dērogāre.*] **—der'o·ga'tion** *n.*

de·rog·a·to·ry (dĭ-rŏg'ə-tôr'ē) ►*adj.* **1.** Disparaging; belittling: *a derogatory comment.* **2.** Tending to detract or diminish. **—de·rog'a·to'ri·ly** *adv.*

der·rick (dĕr'ĭk) ►*n.* **1.** A machine for hoisting and moving heavy objects. **2.** A tall framework over a drilled hole, esp. an oil well, used to support boring equipment or to move pipe. [Obsolete *derick,* hangman, gallows.]

der·ri·ère also **der·ri·ere** (dĕr'ē-âr') ►*n.* The buttocks. [< OFr. *deriere,* in back of.]

der·ring-do (dĕr'ĭng-dōō') ►*n.* Daring or reckless action. [< ME *durring don,* daring to do.]

der·rin·ger (dĕr'ĭn-jər) ►*n.* A small, short-barreled pistol. [After Henry *Deringer* (1786–1868).]

der·vish (dûr'vĭsh) ►*n.* A member of any of various Muslim ascetic orders, some of which perform whirling dances in ecstatic devotion. [< Pers. *darvēsh,* mendicant.]

de·sal·i·nate (dē-săl'ə-nāt') ►*v.* **-nat·ed, -nat·ing** To desalinize. **—de·sal'i·na'tion** *n.* **—de·sal'i·na'tor** *n.*

de·sal·i·nize (dē-săl'ə-nīz') ►*v.* **-nized, -niz·ing** To remove salts and other chemicals from (e.g., seawater). **—de·sal'i·ni·za'tion** *n.*

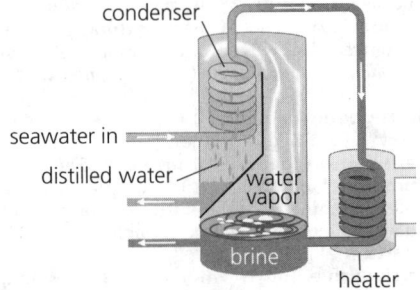

desalinize
schematic diagram of a distillation process to desalinize seawater

des·cant (dĕs'kănt') ►*n.* **1.** *Mus.* An ornamental melody sung or played above a theme. **2.** A discourse on a theme. [< Med.Lat. *discantus,* refrain.] **—des'cant'** *v.*

Des·cartes (dā-kärt'), **René** 1596–1650. French mathematician, philosopher, and scientist.

de·scend (dĭ-sĕnd') ►*v.* **1.** To move from a higher to a lower place; come or go down. **2.** To slope, extend, or incline downward. **3.** To come from an ancestor: *He descends from Greek immigrants.* **4.** To pass by inheritance. **5.** To lower oneself; stoop: *The parents had descended to the level of their children.* **6.** To arrive or attack in an overwhelming manner: *tourists descending on the village.* **7.** To progress downward as in rank or scale: *listed in descending order of importance.* [< Lat. *dēscendere.*]

de·scen·dant (dĭ-sĕn'dənt) ►*n.* **1.** One descended from specified ancestors. **2.** Something derived from an earlier form. ►*adj.* Var. of **descendent.**

de·scen·dent also **de·scen·dant** (dĭ-sĕn'dənt) ►*adj.* **1.** Moving downward. **2.** Proceeding by descent from an ancestor.

de·scent (dĭ-sĕnt') ►*n.* **1.** The act or an instance of descending. **2.** A downward incline. **3.** Hereditary derivation; lineage. **4.** *Law* Transmission of property to a hereditary heir by an intestate owner. **5.** A decline, as in status: *a career that went into descent when she got sick.* **6.** A sudden attack: *the descent of the pirates on the ship.* [< OFr.]

de·scribe (dĭ-skrīb') ►*v.* **-scribed, -scrib·ing 1.** To give an account of in speech or writing. **2.** To represent pictorially. **3.** To trace the outline of: *describe a circle with a compass.* [< Lat. *dēscrībere,* write down.] **—de·scrib'a·ble** *adj.*
  Syns: *narrate, recite, recount, relate, report* **v.**

de·scrip·tion (dĭ-skrĭp'shən) ►*n.* **1.** The act of describing. **2.** A statement, written account, or picture describing something. **3.** A kind or sort: *cars of every description.* **—de·scrip'tive** *adj.* **—de·scrip'tive·ly** *adv.*

de·scry (dĭ-skrī') ►*v.* **-scried, -scry·ing 1.** To catch sight of. **2.** To discover by careful observation: *descried hope in their words.* [< OFr. *descrier,* call, cry out.]

des·e·crate (dĕs'ĭ-krāt') ►*v.* **-crat·ed, -crat·ing** To violate the sacredness of; profane. [DE- + (CON)SECRATE.] **—des'e·crat'er, des'e·cra'tor** *n.* **—des'e·cra'tion** *n.*

de·seg·re·gate (dē-sĕg'rĭ-gāt') ►*v.* To abolish segregation in, esp. by force of law. **—de·seg're·ga'tion** *n.* **—de·seg're·ga'tion·ist** *n.*

de·sen·si·tize (dē-sĕn'sĭ-tīz') ►*v.* **1.** To make less sensitive or insensitive. **2.** To make (a person) nonreactive or insensitive to an antigen, as in treatment for allergy. **—de·sen'si·ti·za'tion** *n.*

des·ert¹ (dĕz'ərt) ►*n.* **1.** A dry, often sandy region of little rainfall and sparse vegetation. **2.** An empty or forsaken place; wasteland: *a cultural desert.* [< LLat. *dēsertum.*]

de·sert² (dĭ-zûrt') ►*n.* often **deserts** Something deserved, esp. a punishment. [< OFr. *deserte* < p.part. of *deservir,* DESERVE.]

de·sert³ (dĭ-zûrt') ►*v.* **1.** To forsake or leave alone. **2.** To abandon one's duty or post, esp. in the armed forces. [< Lat. *dēserere, dēsert-,* abandon.] **—de·sert'er** *n.* **—de·ser'tion** *n.*

de·sert·i·fi·ca·tion (dĭ-zûr'tə-fĭ-kā'shən) ►*n.*

The transformation of arable or habitable land to desert.

de·serve (dǐ-zûrv′) ►*v.* **-served, -serv·ing** To be worthy of; merit. See Synonyms at **earn.** [< Lat. *dēservīre,* serve zealously.]

de·served (dǐ-zûrvd′) ►*adj.* Merited or earned. **—de·serv′ed·ly** (-zûr′vĭd-lē) *adv.*

de·serv·ing (dǐ-zûr′vǐng) ►*adj.* Worthy, as of reward or praise. **—de·serv′ing·ly** *adv.*

des·ic·cant (děs′ĭ-kənt) ►*n.* A substance used as a drying agent.

des·ic·cate (děs′ĭ-kāt′) ►*v.* **-cat·ed, -cat·ing** **1.** To dry or dry out thoroughly. **2.** To preserve (foods) by removing the moisture. See Synonyms at **dry.** [Lat. *dēsiccāre* < *siccus,* dry.] **—des′ic·ca′tion** *n.* **—des′ic·ca′tive** *adj.*

de·sid·er·a·tum (dǐ-sĭd′ə-rä′təm, -rä′-) ►*n., pl.* **-ta** (-tə) Something necessary or desirable. [< Lat. *dēsīderāre,* to desire.]

de·sign (dǐ-zīn′) ►*v.* **1.** To conceive; invent: *design an excuse for not attending.* **2.** To make a graphic or schematic representation of something: *design a new car model.* **3.** To formulate a plan for; devise. **4.** To have as a goal or purpose; intend. ►*n.* **1.** A drawing or sketch, esp. a detailed plan for construction or manufacture. **2.** The purposeful arrangement of parts or details. **3.** The art or practice of making designs. **4.** An ornamental pattern. See Synonyms at **figure. 5.** A plan or project. See Synonyms at **plan. 6.** A reasoned purpose; intent: *It was her design to open her own shop.* **7.** often **designs** A secretive plot or scheme. [< Lat. *dēsignāre,* designate.] **—de·sign′er** *n.*

des·ig·nate (děz′ĭg-nāt′) ►*v.* **-nat·ed, -nat·ing 1.** To indicate or specify: *a fence that designates a property boundary.* **2.** To give a name to. **3.** To select and set aside for a duty, office, or purpose. See Synonyms at **allocate, appoint.** ►*adj.* (-nĭt) Appointed but not yet installed in office: *the commissioner designate.* [Lat. *dēsignāre.*] **—des′ig·na′tion** *n.* **—des′-ig·na′tive** *adj.*

des·ig·nat·ed driver (děz′ĭg-nā′tĭd) ►*n.* One who agrees to remain sober, as at a party, in order to drive others home safely.

designated hitter ►*n.* Baseball A player designated to bat instead of the pitcher.

de·sign·ing (dǐ-zī′nǐng) ►*adj.* **1.** Conniving. **2.** Showing or exercising forethought.

de·sir·a·ble (dǐ-zīr′ə-bəl) ►*adj.* **1.** Worth having or doing: *a desirable job; a desirable outcome.* **2.** Arousing desire. **—de·sir′a·bil′i·ty, de·sir′a·ble·ness** *n.* **—de·sir′a·bly** *adv.*

de·sire (dǐ-zīr′) ►*v.* **-sired, -sir·ing 1.** To wish or long for; want: *desires to travel.* **2.** To want to have sex with (another person). ►*n.* **1.** A wish or longing for something. **2a.** Sexual appetite; passion. **b.** An object of such feeling or passion. [< Lat. *dēsīderāre.*] **—de·sir′er** *n.*

Syns: covet, crave, want, wish **v.**

de·sir·ous (dǐ-zīr′əs) ►*adj.* Wanting; desiring. **—de·sir′ous·ly** *adv.*

de·sist (dǐ-sĭst′, -zĭst′) ►*v.* To cease doing something. See Synonyms at **stop.** [< Lat. *dēsistere* < *sistere,* stop.]

desk (děsk) ►*n.* **1.** A piece of furniture typically having a flat top for writing. **2.** A counter or booth at which specified services are performed: *an information desk.* **3.** A specialized department of a large organization: *a newspaper*

city desk. [< OItal. *desco,* table.]

desk·top (děsk′tŏp′) ►*n.* **1.** The top of a desk. **2.** *Comp.* The area of a display screen where images, windows, and other graphical items appear. ►*adj.* Designed for use on a desk.

desktop publishing ►*n.* The design and production of publications using personal computers with graphics capability.

Des Moines (dǐ moin′) The capital of IA, in the S-central part.

des·o·late (děs′ə-lĭt, děz′-) ►*adj.* **1.** Devoid of inhabitants; deserted: *desolate streets.* **2.** Barren; lifeless: *the rocky, desolate surface of the moon.* **3.** Feeling, showing, causing, or expressing sadness or loneliness. ►*v.* (-lāt′) **-lat·ed, -lat·ing** To make desolate. [< Lat. *dēsōlātus,* p.part. of *dēsōlāre,* abandon.] **—des′o·late·ly** *adv.* **—des′o·la′tion** *n.*

de·spair (dǐ-spâr′) ►*v.* To lose all hope. ►*n.* **1.** Complete loss of hope. **2.** One that causes despair: *unruly students that are their teachers' despair.* [< Lat. *dēspērāre,* lose hope.]

des·per·a·do (děs′pə-rä′dō, -rä′-) ►*n., pl.* **-does** or **-dos** A bold or desperate outlaw. [Sp. < p.part. of *desesperar,* DESPAIR.]

des·per·ate (děs′pər-ĭt) ►*adj.* **1.** Having lost all hope; despairing. **2.** Reckless or violent because of despair: *a desperate criminal.* **3.** Undertaken out of extreme urgency or as a last resort: *a desperate attempt to get help.* **4.** Nearly hopeless; critical: *a desperate situation.* **5.** Extreme; great: *a desperate urge.* [< Lat. *dēspērātus,* p.part. of *dēspērāre,* lose hope.] **—des′per·ate·ly** *adv.* **—des′per·a′tion** (děs′pə-rā′shən) *n.*

de·spic·a·ble (dǐ-spĭk′ə-bəl, děs′pĭ-kə-) ►*adj.* Deserving of contempt or scorn; vile. [< Lat. *dēspicārī,* despise.] **—de·spic′a·ble·ness** *n.* **—de·spic′a·bly** *adv.*

de·spise (dǐ-spīz′) ►*v.* **-spised, -spis·ing 1.** To regard with scorn. **2.** To dislike intensely: *despised the frigid weather.* [< Lat. *dēspicere* : *dē-,* down + *specere,* look.] **—de·spis′er** *n.*

Syns: contemn, disdain, scorn **Ant** *esteem* **v.**

de·spite (dǐ-spīt′) ►*prep.* In spite of. [< OFr. *despit,* spite < Lat. *dēspicere,* DESPISE.]

de·spoil (dǐ-spoil′) ►*v.* **1.** To sack; plunder. **2.** To deprive of something valuable. [< Lat. *dēspoliāre.*] **—de·spoil′ment** *n.* **—de·spo′li·a′tion** (-spō′lē-ā′shən) *n.*

de·spond (dǐ-spŏnd′) ►*v.* To become discouraged. ►*n.* Despondency. [Lat. *dēspondēre,* give up.] **—de·spond′ing·ly** *adv.*

de·spon·den·cy (dǐ-spŏn′dən-sē) ►*n.* Loss of hope; dejection. **—de·spon′dent** *adj.* **—de·spon′dent·ly** *adv.*

des·pot (děs′pət) ►*n.* A ruler with absolute power; tyrant. [< Gk. *despotēs.*] **—des·pot′-ic** (dǐ-spŏt′ĭk) *adj.* **—des·pot′i·cal·ly** *adv.* **—des′pot·ism′** *n.*

des·sert (dǐ-zûrt′) ►*n.* A usu. sweet dish served at the end of a meal. [Fr. < OFr. *desservir,* clear the table.]

de·sta·bi·lize (dē-stā′bə-līz′) ►*v.* **-lized, -liz·ing 1.** To upset the stability of. **2.** To undermine the power of (a government) by subversive acts. **—de·sta′bi·li·za′tion** *n.*

des·ti·na·tion (děs′tə-nā′shən) ►*n.* **1.** The place to which one is going or directed. **2.** An ultimate purpose or goal.

des·tine (děs′tĭn) ►*v.* **-tined, -tin·ing 1.** To cause to have a certain outcome: *a film destined* *to be a classic.* **2.** To assign for a specific use or purpose: *money destined to pay for college.* **3.** To direct toward a given destination: *a flight destined for Tokyo* [< Lat. *dēstināre,* determine.]

des·ti·ny (dĕs′tə-nē) ►*n., pl.* **-nies 1.** One's inevitable fate. **2.** A predetermined course of events. **3.** The power thought to predetermine events: *Destiny brought them together.* [< OFr. *destiner,* DESTINE.]

des·ti·tute (dĕs′tĭ-tōōt′, -tyōōt′) ►*adj.* **1.** Utterly lacking; devoid: *destitute of any experience.* **2.** Lacking means of subsistence; impoverished. [< Lat. *dēstitūtus,* p.part. of *dēstituere,* abandon : DE- + *statuere,* to set.] —**des′ti·tu′tion** *n.*

de·stroy (dĭ-stroi′) ►*v.* **1.** To completely ruin the structure of: *The fire destroyed the library.* **2.** To put an end to: *Corruption destroyed his campaign.* **3.** To put (an animal) to death: *destroy a rabid dog.* **4.** To cause extreme emotional trauma to: *the divorce destroyed him.* [< Lat. *dēstruere.*]

de·stroy·er (dĭ-stroi′ər) ►*n.* **1.** One that destroys. **2.** A small fast warship.

de·struct (dĭ-strŭkt′, dē′strŭkt′) ►*n.* The intentional, usu. remote-controlled destruction of a space vehicle, rocket, or missile after launching. —**de·struct′** *v.*

de·struc·ti·ble (dĭ-strŭk′tə-bəl) ►*adj.* Easily destroyed. —**de·struc′ti·bil′i·ty** *n.*

de·struc·tion (dĭ-strŭk′shən) ►*n.* **1.** The act of destroying or condition of having been destroyed. **2.** The cause or means of destroying: *weapons that could cause the planet's destruction.* [< Lat. *dēstrūctiō < dēstruere,* destroy.] —**de·struc′tive** *adj.* —**de·struc′tive·ly** *adv.* —**de·struc′tive·ness** *n.*

des·ue·tude (dĕs′wĭ-tōōd′, -tyōōd′) ►*n.* A state of disuse. [< Lat. *dēsuētūdō.*]

des·ul·to·ry (dĕs′əl-tôr′ē, dĕz′-) ►*adj.* **1.** Without purpose or intent; aimless: *desultory discussion.* **2.** Occurring randomly or sporadically. [< Lat. *dēsultor,* a leaper.] —**des′ul·to′ri·ly** *adv.*

de·tach (dĭ-tăch′) ►*v.* **1.** To separate; disconnect. **2.** To send (troops, e.g.) on a special mission. [< OFr. *destachier.*] —**de·tach′a·bil′i·ty** *n.* —**de·tach′a·ble** *adj.*

de·tached (dĭ-tăcht′) ►*adj.* **1.** Separated; disconnected. **2.** Free from emotional involvement; cool; aloof.

de·tach·ment (dĭ-tăch′mənt) ►*n.* **1.** The act or process of disconnecting; separation. **2.** Indifference to the concerns of others; aloofness: *a chilly detachment from his family.* **3.** Impartiality; disinterest: *maintained her professional detachment.* **4a.** The dispatch of troops or ships from a larger body for special duty. **b.** A small permanent unit organized for special duties.

de·tail (dĭ-tāl′, dē′tāl′) ►*n.* **1.** An individual part. **2.** Itemized or minute treatment of particulars: *attention to detail.* **3.** An inconsequential item or aspect. **4a.** A group of military personnel selected to do a specified task. **b.** The duty assigned: *garbage detail.* ►*v.* (dĭ-tāl′) **1.** To report or relate minutely: *detailed the charges against the defendant.* **2.** To name or state explicitly. **3.** To provide with decorative detail. **4.** To clean (a vehicle) meticulously. [< OFr., piece cut off.]

de·tain (dĭ-tān′) ►*v.* **1.** To keep from proceeding; delay. **2.** To keep in custody or confinement. [< Lat. *dētinēre,* hold back.] —**de·tain′-**

ment *n.* —**de·tain·ee′** (dē′tā-nē′, dĭ-tā′-) *n.*

de·tect (dĭ-tĕkt′) ►*v.* To discover or ascertain the existence, presence, or fact of. [< Lat. *dētegere, dētēct-,* uncover.] —**de·tect′a·ble, de·tect′i·ble** *adj.* —**de·tec′tion** *n.* —**de·tect′er** *n.*

de·tec·tive (dĭ-tĕk′tĭv) ►*n.* A person, usu. a member of a police force, who investigates crimes and obtains evidence.

de·tec·tor (dĭ-tĕk′tər) ►*n.* One that detects, esp. a mechanical or electrical device that identifies and records a stimulus.

dé·tente (dā-tänt′, -tänt′) ►*n.* A relaxing of tension between rivals, esp. nations or blocs. [Fr., a releasing.]

de·ten·tion (dĭ-tĕn′shən) ►*n.* **1.** The act of detaining or condition of being detained. **2.** A forced or punitive confinement. **3.** A form of punishment by which a student is made to stay after regular school hours. [< Lat. *dētinēre,* detain.]

de·ter (dĭ-tûr′) ►*v.* **-terred, -ter·ring 1.** To prevent or discourage from acting, as by means of fear or doubt: *alarms to deter burglars.* **2.** To prevent or discourage (an action or circumstance): *precautions to deter vandalism; protocols to deter infection.* [Lat. *dēterrēre,* frighten away.] —**de·ter′ment** *n.*

de·ter·gent (dĭ-tûr′jənt) ►*n.* A cleansing substance made from chemical compounds rather than fats and lye. ►*adj.* Having cleansing power. [< Lat. *dētergēre,* wipe off.]

de·te·ri·o·rate (dĭ-tîr′ē-ə-rāt′) ►*v.* **-rat·ed, -rat·ing 1.** To grow worse; degenerate. **2.** To weaken; decay: *deteriorating roadways.* [< Lat. *dēterior,* worse.] —**de·te′ri·o·ra′tion** *n.*

de·ter·mi·nant (dĭ-tûr′mə-nənt) ►*adj.* Determinative. ►*n.* An influencing or determining factor.

de·ter·mi·nate (dĭ-tûr′mə-nĭt) ►*adj.* **1.** Precisely limited or defined; definite: *a determinate distance.* **2.** Conclusively settled; final.

de·ter·mi·na·tion (dĭ-tûr′mə-nā′shən) ►*n.* **1a.** The act of arriving at a decision. See Synonyms at **decision. b.** The decision reached. **2.** Firmness of purpose; resolve. **3.** The ascertaining or fixing of the quantity, quality, position, or character of something: *determination of the ship's longitude.* **4.** The bringing about of a result or outcome.

de·ter·mi·na·tive (dĭ-tûr′mə-nā′tĭv, -nə-) ►*adj.* Able or serving to determine: *a determinative factor.* See Synonyms at **decisive.** ►*n.* A determining factor. —**de·ter′mi·na′tive·ly** *adv.*

de·ter·mine (dĭ-tûr′mĭn) ►*v.* **-mined, -min·ing 1.** To decide, establish, or ascertain definitely: *The judge determined that he was innocent.* See Synonyms at **discover. 2.** To cause to come to a conclusion or resolution; influence. **3.** To decide or settle (a dispute, e.g.) conclusively. **4.** To be the cause of: *Genes determine eye color.* [< Lat. *dētermināre,* to limit < *terminus,* boundary.] —**de·ter′min·a·ble** *adj.* —**de·ter′min·a·bly** *adv.*

de·ter·mined (dĭ-tûr′mĭnd) ►*adj.* Showing determination. —**de·ter′mined·ly** *adv.*

de·ter·min·er (dĭ-tûr′mə-nər) ►*n.* A word belonging to a group of noun modifiers that includes articles, demonstratives, and possessive adjectives, and, in English, occupying the first position in a noun phrase.

de·ter·min·ism (dĭ-tûr′mə-nĭz′əm) ►*n.* The

philosophical doctrine that every state of affairs, including every human event, act, and decision, is the inevitable consequence of antecedent states of affairs. —de·ter′min·ist *n.* —de·ter′min·is′tic *adj.*

de·ter·rent (dĭ-tûr′ənt, -tŭr′-) ►*adj.* Tending to deter. ►*n.* Something that deters. —de·ter′rence *n.*

de·test (dĭ-tĕst′) ►*v.* To dislike intensely; abhor. [< Lat. *dētestārī,* to curse.] —de·test′a·ble *adj.* —de·test′a·bly *adv.* —de·tes·ta′tion (dē′-tĕ-stā′shən) *n.*

de·throne (dē-thrōn′) ►*v.* -throned, -throning 1. To remove from the throne; depose. 2. To remove from a prominent position. —de·throne′ment *n.*

det·o·nate (dĕt′n-āt′) ►*v.* -nat·ed, -nat·ing To explode or cause to explode. [Lat. *dētonāre,* thunder down.] —det′o·na′tion *n.* —det′o·na′tor *n.*

de·tour (dē′tŏŏr′, dĭ-tŏŏr′) ►*n.* 1. A roundabout way, esp. a road used temporarily instead of a main route. 2. A deviation from a course of action: *took a detour from college to work abroad.* ►*v.* To go or cause to go by a detour. [< OFr. *destorner,* turn away.]

de·tox (dē-tŏks′) *Informal* ►*v.* To detoxify. ►*n.* (dē′tŏks′) 1. A place where patients are detoxified. 2. A course of treatment in which patients are detoxified.

de·tox·i·fy (dē-tŏk′sə-fī′) ►*v.* -fied, -fy·ing 1. To remove poison or the effects of poison from. 2. To treat (an individual) for alcohol or drug dependence, usu. under medical supervision. —de·tox′i·fi·ca′tion *n.*

de·tract (dĭ-trăkt′) ►*v.* To take away (from); divert: *He could detract little from their argument.* [< Lat. *dētrahere, dētract-.*] —de·trac′tion *n.* —de·trac′tor *n.*

de·train (dē-trān′) ►*v.* To leave or cause to leave a railroad train.

det·ri·ment (dĕt′rə-mənt) ►*n.* 1. Damage, harm, or loss. 2. Something that causes damage, harm, or loss. See Synonyms at **disadvantage.** [< Lat. *dētrīmentum.*] —det′ri·men′tal *adj.* —det′ri·men′tal·ly *adv.*

de·tri·tus (dĭ-trī′təs) ►*n., pl.* -tus 1. Loose fragments or grains worn away from rock. 2. Debris. [< Lat. *dētrītus.*]

De·troit (dĭ-troit′) A city of SE MI opposite Windsor, Ontario.

deuce[1] (dōōs, dyōōs) ►*n.* 1. A playing card or side of a die having two pips. 2. A tied score in tennis in which each player or side has 40 points, or 5 or more games. [< Lat. *duōs,* two.]

deuce[2] (dōōs, dyōōs) ►*n.* *Informal* 1. The devil. Used as a mild oath. 2. An outstanding example, esp. of something difficult or bad: *a deuce of a family fight.* [Prob. < LGer. *duus,* a throw of two in dice games.]

deu·te·ri·um (dōō-tîr′ē-əm, dyōō-) ►*n.* A naturally occurring isotope of hydrogen with one proton and one neutron in the nucleus. [< Gk. *deuteros,* second.]

Deu·ter·on·o·my (dōō′tə-rŏn′ə-mē, dyōō′-) ►*n.* See table at **Bible.** [< Gk. *deuteronomion,* a second law.]

deutsche mark (doich′ märk′) ►*n.* The primary unit of currency in Germany before the adoption of the euro. [Ger., German mark.]

De Va·le·ra (dĕv′ə-lĕr′ə, -lîr′ə), **Eamon** 1882–

1975. Amer.-born Irish political leader; president of the Republic of Ireland (1959–73).

de·val·ue (dē-văl′yōō) also **de·val·u·ate** (-văl′yōō-āt′) ►*v.* -ued, -u·ing also -at·ed, -at·ing 1. To lessen the value of. 2. To lower the exchange value of (a currency). —de·val′u·a′tion *n.*

dev·as·tate (dĕv′ə-stāt′) ►*v.* -tat·ed, -tat·ing 1. To lay waste; destroy. 2. To overwhelm; stun: *was devastated when he lost his job.* [< Lat. *vāstus.*] —dev′as·ta′tion *n.* —dev′as·ta′tor *n.*

de·vel·op (dĭ-vĕl′əp) ►*v.* 1. To bring, grow, or evolve from latency to or toward fulfillment: *a teacher who develops the abilities of each student.* 2. To progress from earlier to later stages of a life cycle: *Caterpillars develop into butterflies.* 3. To expand or enlarge: *developed a business into a national corporation.* 4. To add detail to; elaborate: *had a good idea but developed it without imagination.* 5. To come gradually into existence or activity: *Our friendship developed over time.* 6. To make available and effective: *developed the site for housing.* 7. To process (a photosensitive medium such as exposed film) to produce a photographic image. [< OFr. *desveloper.*] —de·vel′op·er *n.* —de·vel′op·ment *n.* —de·vel′op·men′tal *adj.* —de·vel′op·men′tal·ly *adv.*

de·vi·ant (dē′vē-ənt) ►*adj.* Differing from a norm or accepted societal standards. —de′vi·ance *n.* —de′vi·ant *n.*

de·vi·ate (dē′vē-āt′) ►*v.* -at·ed, -at·ing To turn away or differ from an established course or way. See Synonyms at **swerve.** ►*n.* (-ĭt) A deviant. [LLat. *dēviāre.*] —de′vi·a′tion *n.*

de·vice (dĭ-vīs′) ►*n.* 1. Something designed for a particular purpose, esp. a machine. 2. A literary contrivance, such as parallelism or personification, used to achieve a particular effect. 3. A decorative design, figure, or pattern, as one used in embroidery. See Synonyms at **figure.** 4. A graphic symbol or motto, esp. in heraldry. —*idiom:* **leave to (one's) own devices** 1. To allow (someone) to do as he or she pleases: *left me to my own devices in the afternoon.* 2. To force (someone) to cope or manage without assistance. [< OFr. *deviser,* devise.]

dev·il (dĕv′əl) ►*n.* 1. often **Devil** In some religions, the major spirit of evil and foe of God. Used with *the.* 2. A subordinate evil spirit; demon. 3. A wicked or malevolent person. 4. A person: *a handsome devil; the poor devil.* 5. A mischievous or daring person. 6. An outstanding example, esp. of something difficult or negative: *has a devil of a temper.* ►*v.* -iled, -il·ing or -illed, -il·ling 1. To season (food) heavily. 2. To annoy, torment, or harass. [< Gk. *diabolos,* slanderer.]

dev·il·ish (dĕv′ə-lĭsh) ►*adj.* 1. Of or like a devil; fiendish. 2. Mischievous. 3. Excessive; extreme: *devilish heat.* ►*adv.* Extremely; very. —dev′il·ish·ly *adv.*

dev·il·try (dĕv′əl-trē) or **dev·il·ry** (-əl-rē) ►*n., pl.* -tries or -ries 1. Reckless mischief. 2. Wickedness. 3. Witchcraft. [Alteration of *devilry.*]

de·vi·ous (dē′vē-əs) ►*adj.* 1. Not straightforward; deceitful. 2. Deviating from the straight or direct course: *a devious route.* [< Lat. *dēvius,* out-of-the-way.] —de′vi·ous·ly *adv.* —de′vi·ous·ness *n.*

de·vise (dǐ-vīz′) ►v. **-vised, -vis·ing 1.** To plan or arrange in the mind; design or contrive: *devised a new system for handling mail orders.* **2.** *Law* To transmit (real property) by will. ►n. *Law* **1.** The act of transmitting real property by will. **2.** A will or clause in a will devising real property. [< Lat. *dīvidere, dīvīs-*, divide.] —**de·vis′a·ble** *adj.* —**de·vis′er** *n.*

de·vi·tal·ize (dē-vīt′l-īz′) ►v. To diminish or destroy the strength or vitality of.

de·void (dǐ-void′) ►adj. Completely lacking: *devoid of wit.* [< OFr. *desvoidier*, remove.]

de·volve (dǐ-vŏlv′) ►v. **-volved, -volv·ing** To pass on or be passed on to another: *the estate devolved to a unlikely heir.* [< Lat. *dēvolvere*, roll down.] —**dev′o·lu′tion** (dĕv′ə-lōō′shən) *n.*

De·vo·ni·an (dǐ-vō′nē-ən) *Geol.* ►adj. Of or being the 4th period of the Paleozoic Era, marked by the appearance of amphibians and insects and the first forests. ►n. The Devonian Period. [After *Devon*, England.]

de·vote (dǐ-vōt′) ►v. **-vot·ed, -vot·ing 1.** To give or apply (one's time, attention, or self) entirely. **2.** To set apart for a specific purpose. [Lat. *dēvovēre, dēvōt-*, to vow.]

de·vot·ed (dǐ-vō′tǐd) ►adj. Feeling or displaying strong affection or attachment; ardent. —**de·vot′ed·ly** *adv.*

dev·o·tee (dĕv′ə-tē′, -tā′) ►n. An enthusiast.

de·vo·tion (dǐ-vō′shən) ►n. **1.** Ardent attachment or affection. **2.** The act of devoting or being devoted: *the devotion of resources to research.* **3.** Religious ardor. **4.** often **devotions** Prayers, esp. when private. —**de·vo′tion·al** *adj.*

de·vour (dǐ-vour′) ►v. **1.** To eat up greedily. See Synonyms at **eat. 2.** To destroy, consume, or waste. **3.** To take in eagerly: *devour a novel.* **4.** To preoccupy or obsess: *devoured by jealousy.* [< Lat. *dēvorāre*, swallow up.]

de·vout (dǐ-vout′) ►adj. **-er, -est 1.** Deeply religious; pious. **2.** Fervent or earnest: *devout wishes for their success.* [< Lat. *dēvōtus*, devoted.] —**de·vout′ly** *adv.* —**de·vout′ness** *n.*

dew (dōō, dyōō) ►n. **1.** Water droplets condensed from the air, usu. at night, onto cool surfaces. **2.** Something moist, fresh, pure, or renewing. [< OE *dēaw.*] —**dew′i·ly** *adv.* —**dew′i·ness** *n.* —**dew′y** *adj.*

DEW ►abbr. distant early warning

dew·ber·ry (dōō′bĕr′ē, dyōō′-) ►n. **1.** A trailing prickly shrub having fruits that resemble blackberries. **2.** The fruit of this plant.

dew·claw (dōō′klô′, dyōō′-) ►n. A vestigial digit on the feet of certain mammals. [?]

dew·drop (dōō′drŏp′, dyōō′-) ►n. A drop of dew.

Dew·ey (dōō′ē, dyōō′ē), **John** 1859–1952. Amer. philosopher and educator.

Dewey, Thomas Edmund 1902–71. Amer. politician.

dew·lap (dōō′lăp′, dyōō′-) ►n. A fold of loose skin hanging from the neck of a person or certain animals. [ME *dewlappe.*]

dew point ►n. The temperature at which air becomes saturated and produces dew.

dex·ter·i·ty (dĕk-stĕr′ĭ-tē) ►n. **1.** Skill in the use of the hands or body; adroitness. **2.** Mental skill or cleverness.

dex·ter·ous (dĕk′stər-əs, -strəs) also **dex·trous** (-strəs) ►adj. **1.** Skillful in the use of the hands or mind. **2.** Done with dexterity. [< Lat. *dexter*, skillful.] —**dex′ter·ous·ly** *adv.*

dex·trin (dĕk′strĭn) ►n. A polysaccharide obtained from starch, used mainly as an adhesive. [< Lat. *dexter*, right.]

dex·trose (dĕk′strōs′) ►n. A colorless sugar, $C_6H_{12}O_6·H_2O$, found in animal and plant tissue and also made synthetically from starch. [*dexter*, right + −OSE².]

DFC ►abbr. Distinguished Flying Cross

dg ►abbr. decigram

DH ►abbr. **1.** designated hitter **2.** Doctor of Humanities

Dha·ka or **Dac·ca** (dăk′ə, dä′kə) The capital of Bangladesh, in the E-central part.

dhar·ma (där′mə, dûr′-) ►n. *Hinduism & Buddhism* **1.** The principle or law that orders the universe. **2.** Individual conduct in conformity with this principle. [Skt.]

Dhu'l-Hij·jah (dōōl-hĭj′ä) ►n. The 12th month of the Islamic calendar. See table at **calendar.** [Ar. *ḏū-l-ḥijja.*]

Dhu'l-Qa'·dah (dōōl-kä′dä) ►n. The 11th month of the Islamic calendar. See table at **calendar.** [Ar. *ḏū-l-qaʻda.*]

di– ►pref. **1.** Two; twice; double: *digraph.* **2.** Containing two atoms, radicals, or groups: *dioxide.* [Gk.]

dia. ►abbr. diameter

di·a·be·tes (dī′ə-bē′tǐs, -tēz) ►n. Diabetes mellitus. [< Gk. *diabētēs*, siphon, diabetes : *dia-*, through + *bainein*, go.] —**di′a·bet′ic** (-bĕt′ĭk) *adj. & n.*

diabetes mel·li·tus (mə-lī′təs, mĕl′ĭ-) ►n. A chronic metabolic disease caused by insulin deficiency, either hereditary or acquired, that results in excess sugar in the blood. [NLat., honey-sweet diabetes.]

di·a·bol·i·cal (dī′ə-bŏl′ĭ-kəl) also **di·a·bol·ic** (-ĭk) ►adj. Fiendish; wicked. [< Lat. *diabolus*, DEVIL.] —**di′a·bol′i·cal·ly** *adv.*

di·a·crit·ic (dī′ə-krĭt′ĭk) ►adj. **1.** Diacritical. **2.** *Med.* Diagnostic or distinctive. ►n. A mark that is added to a letter to indicate a special phonetic value or to distinguish otherwise identical words. [Gk. *diakritikos*, distinguishing.]

´	acute
`	grave
~	tilde
^	circumflex
–	macron
˘	breve
¨	dieresis
¸	cedilla

diacritic
common diacritics

di·a·crit·i·cal (dī′ə-krĭt′ĭ-kəl) ►*adj.* **1.** Marking a distinction; distinguishing. **2.** Able to distinguish. **3.** Serving as a diacritic. —**di′a·crit′i·cal·ly** *adv.*

Dí·a de la Ra·za (dē′ä dĕ lä rä′sä) ►*n.* October 12, celebrated in many Spanish-speaking areas to commemorate Christopher Columbus's first encounter with indigenous peoples of the Americas.

di·a·dem (dī′ə-dĕm′, -dəm) ►*n.* **1.** A crown or headband. **2.** Royal power or dignity. [< Gk. *diadēma.*]

di·aer·e·sis (dī-ĕr′ĭ-sĭs) ►*n.* Var. of **dieresis.**

di·ag·no·sis (dī′əg-nō′sĭs) ►*n., pl.* -**ses** (-sēz) Identification, esp. of a disease, by examination and analysis. [Gk. *diagnōsis,* discernment.] —**di′ag·nose′** *v.* —**di′ag·nos′tic** (-nŏs′tĭk) *adj.* —**di′ag·nos′ti·cal·ly** *adv.* —**di′ag·nos·ti′cian** (-stĭsh′ən) *n.*

di·ag·o·nal (dī-ăg′ə-nəl) ►*adj.* **1.** *Math.* Joining two nonadjacent vertices. **2.** Having a slanted or oblique direction. ►*n. Math.* A diagonal line or plane. [< Gk. *diagōnios,* from angle to angle.] —**di·ag′o·nal·ly** *adv.*

di·a·gram (dī′ə-grăm′) ►*n.* A schematic plan or drawing designed to explain how something works or to clarify the relationship between the parts of a whole. ►*v.* -**grammed, -gramming** or -**gramed, -gram·ing** To represent by a diagram. [< Gk. *diagramma* : *dia-,* across + *graphein,* write.] —**di′a·gram·mat′ic** (-grə-măt′ĭk), **di′a·gram·mat′i·cal** *adj.*

di·al (dī′əl) ►*n.* **1.** A graduated surface or face on which a measurement, such as speed, is indicated by a moving needle or pointer. **2.** A sundial. **3.** A rotatable disk, as of a telephone, radio, or television, for making calls or changing channels. ►*v.* -**aled, -al·ing** or -**alled, -al·ling** **1.** To indicate or select by means of a dial. **2.** To call on a telephone. [< Med.Lat. *diālis,* daily.]

di·a·lect (dī′ə-lĕkt′) ►*n.* A regional or social variety of a language distinguished by pronunciation, grammar, or vocabulary. [< Gk. *dialektos,* speech.] —**di′a·lec′tal** *adj.*

di·a·lec·tic (dī′ə-lĕk′tĭk) ►*n.* **1.** The art or practice of arriving at the truth by the exchange of logical arguments. **2. dialectics** (*takes sing. v.*) A method of argument that weighs contradictory facts or ideas with a view to resolving real or apparent contradictions. [< Gk. *dialektikē (tekhnē),* (art) of debate.] —**di′a·lec′ti·cal, di′a·lec′tic** *adj.*

dialog box ►*n.* A window that appears on a computer screen, presenting information or requesting input.

di·a·logue or **di·a·log** (dī′ə-lôg′, -lŏg′) ►*n.* **1.** A conversation between two or more people. **2.** Conversation between characters in a drama or narrative. **3.** An exchange of ideas or opinions. [< Gk. *dialogos.*]

dial-up (dī′əl-ŭp′, dīl′-) ►*adj.* Relating to a network connection, usu. to the Internet, made by dialing a phone number.

di·al·y·sis (dī-ăl′ĭ-sĭs) ►*n., pl.* -**ses** (-sēz′) The separation of smaller molecules from larger molecules or of dissolved substances from colloidal particles in a solution by selective diffusion through a semipermeable membrane. [Gk. *dialusis,* separating.]

di·a·mag·net·ic (dī′ə-măg-nĕt′ĭk) ►*adj.* Of or relating to a substance that generates a magnetic field in the direction opposite to an externally applied magnetic field and is thereby repelled by it. [Gk. *dia,* through + MAGNETIC.] —**di′a·mag′ne·tism** *n.*

di·am·e·ter (dī-ăm′ĭ-tər) ►*n.* **1a.** A straight line segment passing through the center of a figure, esp. of a circle or sphere. **b.** The length of such a segment. **2.** Thickness or width. [< Gk. *diametros.*]

di·a·met·ri·cal (dī′ə-mĕt′rĭ-kəl) also **di·a·met·ric** (-rĭk) ►*adj.* **1.** Of or along a diameter. **2.** Exactly opposite; contrary. —**di′a·met′ri·cal·ly** *adv.*

di·a·mond (dī′ə-mənd, dī′mənd) ►*n.* **1.** An extremely hard, highly refractive crystalline form of carbon, usu. colorless, used as a gemstone when pure and chiefly in abrasives and cutting tools otherwise. **2.** A rhombus or lozenge. **3.** Any of a suit of playing cards marked with a red, diamond-shaped symbol. **4.** *Baseball* **a.** An infield. **b.** The whole playing field. [< Lat. *adamās,* ADAMANT.]

di·a·mond·back rattlesnake (dī′ə-məndbăk′, dī′mənd-) ►*n.* A large venomous rattlesnake of SW North America.

Di·an·a (dī-ăn′ə) ►*n. Rom. Myth.* The goddess of chastity, hunting, and the moon.

di·a·pa·son (dī′ə-pā′zən, -sən) ►*n. Mus.* **1.** The entire range of an instrument or voice. **2.** Either of the two principal stops on a pipe organ that form the tonal basis for the entire scale of the instrument. [< Gk. *(dia) pasōn (khordōn),* (through) all (the notes).]

di·a·per (dī′ə-pər, dī′pər) ►*n.* A piece of absorbent material, such as paper or cloth, that is typically placed between the legs and fastened at the waist to contain excretions. ►*v.* To put a diaper on. [< OFr. *diaspre,* a patterned fabric.]

di·aph·a·nous (dī-ăf′ə-nəs) ►*adj.* **1.** Sufficiently thin or airy as to be translucent. **2.** Delicate: *diaphanous butterfly wings.* [< Gk. *diaphainein,* be transparent.] —**di·aph′a·nous·ly** *adv.*

di·a·pho·re·sis (dī′ə-fə-rē′sĭs, dī-ăf′ə-) ►*n.* Copious perspiration, esp. when medically induced. [< Gk. *diaphorēsis* : *dia-,* through + *pherein,* carry.]

di·a·phragm (dī′ə-frăm′) ►*n.* **1.** A muscular membranous partition separating the abdominal and thoracic cavities and functioning in respiration. **2.** A similar membranous part that divides or separates. **3.** A thin disk, esp. in a microphone or telephone receiver, that vibrates in response to sound waves to produce electric signals, or vice versa. **4.** A contraceptive device consisting of a flexible disk that covers the uterine cervix. **5.** A disk used to restrict the amount of light that passes through a lens or optical system. [< Gk. *diaphragma,* partition.] —**di′a·phrag·mat′ic** (-frăg-măt′ĭk) *adj.*

di·ar·rhe·a (dī′ə-rē′ə) ►*n.* Excessively frequent watery bowel movements, usu. indicating gastrointestinal disorder. [< Gk. *diarrhoia* : *dia-,* through + *rhein,* flow.]

di·a·ry (dī′ə-rē) ►*n., pl.* -**ries** **1.** A daily record, esp. of personal experiences or measurable phenomena; journal: *kept a diary of blood sugar levels.* **2.** A book or computer file that is used for keeping such a record. [Lat. *diārium.*] —**di′a·rist** *n.*

di·as·to·le (dī-ăs′tə-lē) ►*n.* The normal rhythmically occurring relaxation and dilatation of the heart chambers, esp. the ventricles, during which they fill with blood. [Gk. *diastolē*, dilation.] —**di·as·tol·ic** (dī'ə-stŏl'ĭk) *adj.*

diastolic pressure ►*n.* The lowest arterial blood pressure reached when the ventricles are relaxed.

di·a·ther·my (dī'ə-thûr'mē) ►*n.* The therapeutic generation of local heat in body tissues by high-frequency electromagnetic currents. [Gk. *dia*, through + *thermē*, heat.] —**di·a·ther'mic** *adj.*

di·a·tom (dī'ə-tŏm') ►*n.* Any of numerous one-celled photosynthetic organisms that have a silica cell wall made up of two interlocking parts and are a major component of phytoplankton. [< Gk. *diatomos*, cut in half.] —**di·a·to·ma'ceous** (dī'ə-tə-mā'shəs, dī-ăt'ə-) *adj.*

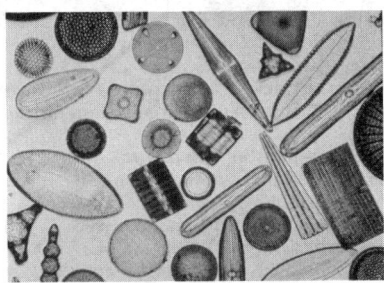

diatom

di·a·tom·ic (dī'ə-tŏm'ĭk) ►*adj.* Made up of two atoms.

di·a·ton·ic (dī'ə-tŏn'ĭk) ►*adj. Mus.* Of or using the seven tones of a standard scale. [< Gk. *diatonikos*.] —**di·a·ton'i·cal·ly** *adv.* —**di·a·ton'i·cism** (-ĭ-sĭz'əm) *n.*

di·a·tribe (dī'ə-trīb') ►*n.* A bitter, abusive denunciation. [< Gk. *diatribē*, lecture.]

di·az·e·pam (dī-ăz'ə-păm') ►*n.* A drug used to treat anxiety and as a sedative, skeletal muscle relaxant, and anticonvulsant. [*diaz(o)* + *ep(oxide)* + AM(MONIA).]

dib·ble (dĭb'əl) ►*n.* A pointed implement used to make holes in soil, esp. for planting bulbs. [ME *dibbel.*] —**dib'ble** *v.*

dibs (dĭbz) ►*pl.n. Slang* A claim; rights: *I have dibs on that last piece of pie.* [< *dibstones*, counters used in a game.]

dice (dīs) ►*n.* **1.** Pl. of **die²** (sense 2). **2.** *pl.* **dice** also **dic·es** A small cube, as of food. ►*v.* **diced, dic·ing** **1.** To play or gamble with dice. **2.** To cut into small cubes. [Pl. of DIE².]

dic·er (dī'sər) ►*n.* A device used for dicing food.

dic·ey (dī'sē) ►*adj.* **-i·er, -i·est** Involving or full of danger or risk. [< DICE.]

di·chot·o·my (dī-kŏt'ə-mē) ►*n., pl.* **-mies** A division into two contrasting things or parts. [< Gk. *dikhotomos*, cut in two.] —**di·chot'o·mous** *adj.*

dick (dĭk) ►*n. Slang* A detective.

dick·ens (dĭk'ənz) ►*n. Informal* **1.** A reprimand: *gave me the dickens for being late.* **2.** Used as an intensive: *What in the dickens is that?* [Perh. < the name *Dickens.*]

Dickens, Charles John Huffam 1812–70. British writer. —**Dick·en'si·an** (dĭ-kĕn'zē-ən) *adj.*

Charles Dickens   **Emily Dickinson**

dick·er (dĭk'ər) ►*v.* To bargain; barter. [Poss. < ME *diker*, quantity of ten.]

dick·ey also **dick·ie** or **dick·y** (dĭk'ē) ►*n., pl.* **-eys** also **-ies 1a.** A woman's blouse front worn under a jacket or low-necked garment. **b.** A man's detachable shirt front. **2.** A small bird. [< *Dick*, nickname for *Richard.*]

Dick·in·son (dĭk'ĭn-sən), **Emily Elizabeth** 1830–86. Amer. poet.

di·cot·y·le·don (dī'kŏt'l-ēd'n) also **di·cot** (dī'kŏt') ►*n.* Any of various plants having two embryonic seed leaves and foliage with a netlike pattern of veins. —**di'cot·y·le·don·ous** *adj.*

dic·tate (dĭk'tāt', dĭk-tāt') ►*v.* **-tat·ed, -tat·ing** **1.** To say or read aloud for transcription. **2.** To prescribe or command with authority. ►*n.* (dĭk'tāt') **1.** A directive. **2.** A guiding principle. [Lat. *dictāre* < *dīcere*, say.] —**dic·ta'tion** *n.*

dic·ta·tor (dĭk'tā'tər, dĭk-tā'-) ►*n.* **1.** A ruler having absolute power, esp. a tyrant. **2.** One who dictates: *These initials are those of the dictator of the letter.* —**dic·ta'tor·ship** *n.*

dic·ta·to·ri·al (dĭk'tə-tôr'ē-əl) ►*adj.* **1.** Domineering. **2.** Relating to or characteristic of a dictator or dictatorship. —**dic'ta·to'ri·al·ly** *adv.*

Syns: autocratic, authoritarian, imperious, tyrannical *adj.*

dic·tion (dĭk'shən) ►*n.* **1.** Choice and use of words in speech or writing. **2.** Clarity and distinctness of pronunciation. [< Lat. *dictiō-*, rhetorical delivery < *dīcere*, say.]

dic·tion·ar·y (dĭk'shə-nĕr'ē) ►*n., pl.* **-ies** A reference book containing an alphabetical list of words, with information given for each word, usu. including meaning, pronunciation, and etymology, or equivalent translations into another language.

dic·tum (dĭk'təm) ►*n., pl.* **-ta** (-tə) or **-tums** **1.** An authoritative, often formal pronouncement. **2.** *Law* A side remark made in a judicial opinion that is not necessary for the decision in the case and therefore is not to be regarded as establishing the law of the case or setting legal precedent. [Lat. < p.part. of *dīcere*, say.]

did (dĭd) ►*v.* P.t. of **do¹.**

di·dac·tic (dī-dăk'tĭk) also **di·dac·ti·cal** (-tĭ-kəl) ►*adj.* **1.** Intended to instruct. **2.** Morally instructive. [< Gk. *didaskein, didak-*, teach.] —**di·dac'ti·cal·ly** *adv.*

did·dle¹ (dĭd'l) ►*v.* **-dled, -dling** *Slang* To cheat or swindle. [?] —**did'dler** *n.*

did·dle² (dĭd'l) ►*v.* **1.** To toy or fiddle: *diddling with the controls.* **2.** To waste time: *diddled around all day.* [Prob. alteration of dial. *didder*, tremble, ult. of imit. orig.]

Di·de·rot (dē′də-rō′, dē-drō′), **Denis** 1713–84. French philosopher and writer.

did·n't (dĭd′nt) Did not.

Did·rik·son (dĭd′rĭk-sən), **Mildred Ella** See Mildred Ella Didrikson **Zaharias**.

didst (dĭdst) ►v. *Archaic* 2nd pers. sing. p.t. of **do**¹.

die¹ (dī) ►v. **died, dy·ing** (dī′ĭng) **1.** To cease living; become dead; expire. **2.** To cease existing, esp. by degrees. **3.** *Informal* To desire greatly. **4.** To lose force or vitality; cease operation. —*phrasal verb:* **die out** To become extinct: *customs that died out centuries ago.* [Prob. < ON *deyja*.]

die² (dī) ►n. **1.** *pl.* **dies** A device used for cutting out, forming, punching, or stamping materials. **2.** *pl.* **dice** (dīs) A small cube marked on each side with from one to six dots, usu. used in pairs in gambling and in various other games. —*idiom:* **no dice** No. Used as a refusal to a request. [< OFr. *de*, gaming die < Lat. *dare*, give.]

die-hard also **die·hard** (dī′härd′) ►adj. Stubbornly resisting change or clinging to a cause. —**die′-hard′** *n.*

di·e·lec·tric (dī′ĭ-lĕk′trĭk) ►n. A nonconductor of electricity. [Gk. *dia*, through + ELECTRIC.] —**di′e·lec′tric** *adj.*

di·er·e·sis or **di·aer·e·sis** (dī-ĕr′ĭ-sĭs) ►n., *pl.* **-ses** (-sēz′) A mark (¨) placed over the second of two adjacent vowels to indicate that they are to be pronounced as separate sounds rather than a diphthong, as in *naïve*. [< Gk. *diairesis*, separation.]

die·sel (dē′zəl, -səl) ►n. A vehicle powered by a diesel engine.

diesel engine ►n. An internal-combustion engine that uses the heat of highly compressed air to ignite a spray of fuel introduced after the start of the compression stroke. [After Rudolf *Diesel* (1858–1913).]

di·et¹ (dī′ĭt) ►n. **1.** One's usual food and drink. **2.** A regulated selection of foods, esp. as for medical reasons or cosmetic weight loss. ►v. To eat and drink according to a regulated or prescribed system. [< Gk. *diaita*, way of living.] —**di′e·tar′y** *adj.* —**di′et·er** *n.*

di·et² (dī′ĭt) ►n. A legislative assembly. [< Med. Lat. *diēta*, ult. < Gk. *diaita*; see DIET¹.]

di·e·tet·ic (dī′ĭ-tĕt′ĭk) ►adj. Specially prepared or processed for restrictive diets.

di·e·tet·ics (dī′ĭ-tĕt′ĭks) ►n. *(takes sing. v.)* The study of nutrition as it relates to health.

di·e·ti·tian or **di·e·ti·cian** (dī′ĭ-tĭsh′ən) ►n. A person specializing in dietetics.

dif·fer (dĭf′ər) ►v. **1.** To be unlike. **2.** To be of a different opinion; disagree. [< Lat. *differre* : *dis-*, apart + *ferre*, carry.]

dif·fer·ence (dĭf′ər-əns, dĭf′rəns) ►n. **1.** The fact, condition, or degree of being unlike. **2.** A disagreement or controversy. **3.** *Math.* **a.** The amount by which one quantity is greater or less than another. **b.** A remainder.

dif·fer·ent (dĭf′ər-ənt, dĭf′rənt) ►adj. **1.** Unlike or dissimilar. **2.** Distinct or separate. **3.** Differing from all others; unusual: *a different point of view.* —**dif′fer·ent·ly** *adv.*

dif·fer·en·tial (dĭf′ə-rĕn′shəl) ►adj. **1.** Of, showing, or constituting a difference. **2.** *Math.* Of or relating to differentiation. ►n. **1.** A difference between comparable things, as in wage rate or in price. **2.** A differential gear.

differential gear ►n. An arrangement of gears that permits one turning shaft to drive two others at different speeds.

dif·fer·en·ti·ate (dĭf′ə-rĕn′shē-āt′) ►v. **-at·ed, -at·ing 1.** To constitute or perceive a distinction. **2.** To make or become different, distinct, or specialized. —**dif′fer·en′ti·a′tion** *n.*

dif·fi·cult (dĭf′ĭ-kŭlt′, -kəlt) ►adj. **1.** Not easy to do, accomplish, or comprehend: *a difficult task; a difficult puzzle.* **2.** Not easy to please, satisfy, or manage: *a difficult child.* [< DIFFICULTY.] —**dif′fi·cult′ly** *adv.*

dif·fi·cul·ty (dĭf′ĭ-kŭl′tē, -kəl-) ►n., *pl.* **-ties 1.** The condition or quality of being difficult. **2.** often **difficulties** A troublesome or embarrassing state of affairs: *facing financial difficulties.* [< Lat. *difficultās*.]
Syns: hardship, rigor, vicissitude **n.**

dif·fi·dent (dĭf′ĭ-dənt, -dĕnt′) ►adj. Lacking self-confidence; timid. [< Lat. *diffīdere*, to mistrust.] —**dif′fi·dence** *n.*

dif·frac·tion (dĭ-frăk′shən) ►n. Change in the directions and intensities of a group of waves after passing by an obstacle or through an aperture. [< Lat. *diffringere, diffrāct-*, shatter.]

dif·fuse (dĭ-fyōoz′) ►v. **-fused, -fus·ing** To pour or spread out and disperse. ►adj. (dĭ-fyōos′) **1.** Widely spread or scattered. **2.** Verbose. See Synonyms at **wordy**. [< Lat. *diffundere, diffūs-*, spread.] —**dif·fuse′ly** (-fyōos′lē) *adv.* —**dif·fu′sion** *n.*

dig (dĭg) ►v. **dug** (dŭg), **dig·ging 1.** To break up, turn over, or remove (e.g., earth or sand) with a tool or the hands. **2.** To make (an excavation) by or as if by digging. **3.** To learn or discover. **4.** To thrust against; poke or prod: *dug me in the ribs.* **5.** *Slang* To understand, take notice of, or enjoy. ►n. **1.** A poke or thrust. **2.** A sarcastic remark; gibe. **3.** An archaeological excavation. —*phrasal verb:* **dig in 1.** To begin to work intensively. **2.** To begin to eat heartily. [ME *diggen*.] —**dig′ger** *n.*

di·ge·net·ic (dī′jə-nĕt′ĭk) ►adj. Having two or more hosts through the course of the life cycle, as in some parasites.

dig·er·a·ti (dĭj′ə-rä′tē) ►pl.n. People knowledgeable about digital technologies. [DIG(ITAL) + (LIT)ERATI.]

di·gest (dī-jĕst′, dĭ-) ►v. **1.** To convert (food) into a form that can easily be absorbed and assimilated by the body. **2.** To absorb mentally. **3.** To organize into a systematic arrangement. ►n. (dī′jĕst′) A collection of written material in condensed form. [< Lat. *digerere, dīgest-*, to separate.] —**di·gest′i·ble** *adj.* —**di·ges′tion** *n.* —**di·ges′tive** *adj.*

di·ges·tif (dē′zhĕs-tēf′) ►n. An alcoholic drink taken after a meal, often thought to aid digestion. [Fr., digestive.]

digestive system ►n. The digestive tract and digestive glands regarded as an integrated system responsible for the ingestion, digestion, and absorption of food.

digestive tract ►n. The mucous membrane-lined tube of the digestive system that extends from the mouth to the anus and includes the pharynx, esophagus, stomach, and intestines.

dig·i·cam (dĭg′ĭ-kăm′) ►n. *Informal* A digital camera.

dig·it (dĭj′ĭt) ►n. **1.** A finger or toe. **2.** One of the ten Arabic number symbols, 0 through 9. **3.** *Slang* A telephone number: *put her digits in my cell phone.* [< Lat. *digitus*, finger, toe.]

dig·i·tal (dĭj′ĭ-tl) ▸*adj.* **1.** Of or relating to a digit, esp. a finger. **2.** *Electronics* **a.** Relating to a device that can generate, record, process, receive, transmit, or display data that is represented in discrete numerical form. **b.** Relating to a service that provides information expressed in discrete numerical form: *digital cable.* **3.** Relating to a profession or activity that is performed using digital devices: *a digital librarian; digital photography.* **4.** Expressed as or giving a readout in digits: *a digital clock.* **5.** Characterized by widespread use of computers: *living in the digital age.* —**dig′i·tal·ly** *adv.*

dig·i·tal·is (dĭj′ĭ-tăl′ĭs) ▸*n.* A drug prepared from the seeds and dried leaves of the foxglove, used in medicine as a cardiac stimulant. [Lat. *digitālis*, finger-shaped.]

dig·ni·fy (dĭg′nə-fī′) ▸*v.* **-fied, -fy·ing** To give distinction or honor to. [< LLat. *dignificāre.*]

dig·ni·tar·y (dĭg′nĭ-tĕr′ē) ▸*n., pl.* **-ies** A person of high rank or position.

dig·ni·ty (dĭg′nĭ-tē) ▸*n., pl.* **-ties** **1.** The quality or state of being worthy of esteem or respect. **2.** Nobility of character, manner, or language. **3.** A high office or rank. [< Lat. *dignitās* < *dignus*, worthy.]

di·graph (dī′grăf′) ▸*n.* A pair of letters representing a single speech sound.

di·gress (dī-grĕs′, dĭ-) ▸*v.* To stray temporarily, esp. from the main subject in writing or speaking. See Synonyms at **swerve.** [Lat. *dīgredī, dīgress-.*] —**di·gres′sion** *n.* —**di·gres′sive** *adj.*

Di·jon (dē-zhôN′) A city of E France N of Lyon.

dike (dīk) ▸*n.* **1.** A wall or embankment of earth and rock built to prevent floods. **2.** A ditch or channel. [< OE *dīc*, trench, and ON *dīki*, ditch.]

di·lap·i·dat·ed (dĭ-lăp′ĭ-dā′tĭd) ▸*adj.* In a state of disrepair, deterioration, or ruin. [< Lat. *dīlapidāre*, demolish.] —**di·lap′i·da′tion** *n.*

dil·a·ta·tion (dĭl′ə-tā′shən, dī-) ▸*n.* Dilation.

di·late (dī-lāt′, dī′lāt′) ▸*v.* **-lat·ed, -lat·ing** To make or become wider or larger; expand. [< Lat. *dīlātāre*, expand.] —**di·lat′a·ble** *adj.* —**di·la′tion** *n.* —**di·la′tor** *n.*

dilation and curettage also **dilatation and curettage** ▸*n.* A surgical procedure in which the lining of the uterus is scraped with a curette, performed for the diagnosis and treatment of various uterine conditions.

dil·a·to·ry (dĭl′ə-tôr′ē) ▸*adj.* Tending to delay. [< Lat. *dīlātus*, p.part. of *differre*, to delay.] —**dil′a·to′ri·ly** *adv.*

di·lem·ma (dĭ-lĕm′ə) ▸*n.* A situation that requires a choice between options, usu. equally unfavorable or unsatisfactory. [< Gk. *dilēmma*, ambiguous proposition.]

dil·et·tante (dĭl′ĭ-tänt′, dĭl′ĭ-tänt′, -tănt′) ▸*n., pl.* **-tantes** also **-tan·ti** (-tän′tē) One who dabbles in an art or a field of knowledge. [< Lat. *dēlectāre*, delight.] —**dil′et·tan′tism** *n.*

Dil·i (dĭl′ē) The capital of East Timor, on the N coast of Timor.

dil·i·gent (dĭl′ə-jənt) ▸*adj.* Marked by persevering, painstaking effort. [< Lat. *dīligere*, to love.] —**dil′i·gence** *n.* —**dil′i·gent·ly** *adv.*

dill (dĭl) ▸*n.* An herb having aromatic leaves and

seeds used as seasoning. [< OE *dile.*]

dil·ly (dĭl′ē) ▸*n., pl.* **-lies** *Slang* One that is remarkable, as in size. [< DELIGHTFUL.]

dil·ly-dal·ly (dĭl′ē-dăl′ē) ▸*v.* **-lied, -lying** To waste time, esp. in indecision; dawdle or vacillate. [< DALLY.]

dil·u·ent (dĭl′yōō-ənt) ▸*n. Chem.* An inert substance used to dilute. [< Lat. *dīluere*, DILUTE.]

di·lute (dī-lōōt′, dĭ-) ▸*v.* **-lut·ed, -lut·ing** To make thinner or weaker, as by adding a liquid such as water. ▸*adj.* Weakened; diluted. [Lat. *dīluere* : *dis-*, away + *-luere*, wash.] —**di·lu′tion** *n.*

dim (dĭm) ▸*adj.* **dim·mer, dim·mest** **1.** Faintly lighted: *a dim room.* **2.** Lacking luster; dull: *dim, faded colors.* **3.** Obscure or indistinct; faint. **4.** Lacking sharpness or clarity; vague. **5.** Negative, unfavorable, or disapproving. ▸*v.* **dimmed, dim·ming** **1.** To make or become dim. **2.** To put on low beam: *dimmed the headlights.* ▸*n.* Low beam. [< OE.] —**dim′ly** *adv.* —**dim′ness** *n.*

dim. ▸*abbr.* **1.** dimension **2.** diminished **3.** diminutive

Di·Mag·gio (də-mä′zhē-ō, -măj′ē-ō), **Joseph Paul** 1914–99. Amer. baseball player.

dime (dīm) ▸*n.* A US or Canadian coin that is worth ten cents. [< Lat. *decima (pars)*, tenth (part).]

di·men·sion (dĭ-mĕn′shən, dī-) ▸*n.* **1.** A measure of spatial extent, esp. width, height, or length. **2.** often **dimensions** Extent or magnitude; scope. **3.** *Math.* One of the least number of independent coordinates required to specify uniquely a point in space. **4.** *Phys.* A physical property, such as mass, length, or time, that is regarded as a fundamental measure. [< Lat. *dīmēnsiō.*] —**di·men′sion·al** *adj.* —**di·men′sion·al′i·ty** (-shə-năl′ĭ-tē) *n.* —**di·men′sion·al·ly** *adv.*

dime store ▸*n.* See **five-and-ten.**

di·min·ish (dĭ-mĭn′ĭsh) ▸*v.* **1.** To make or become smaller or less. **2.** To taper. [ME *diminishen.*] —**di·min′ish·a·ble** *adj.* —**di·min′ish·ment** *n.*

di·min·u·en·do (dĭ-mĭn′yōō-ĕn′dō) ▸*n., adv., & adj. Mus.* Decrescendo. [Ital.]

dim·i·nu·tion (dĭm′ə-nōō′shən, -nyōō′-) ▸*n.* The act, process, or result of reducing. [Lat. *dīminūtiō < dīminuere*, diminish.]

di·min·u·tive (dĭ-mĭn′yə-tĭv) ▸*adj.* **1.** Extremely small. See Synonyms at **small. 2.** Of or being a suffix that indicates smallness or affection, as *-let* in *booklet.* ▸*n.* A diminutive suffix, word, or name.

dim·mer (dĭm′ər) ▸*n.* A device used to vary the brightness of an electric light.

di·mor·phism (dī-môr′fĭz′əm) ▸*n. Biol.* The existence among animals of the same species of two distinct forms that differ in one or more characteristics, such as coloration, size, or shape.

dim·ple (dĭm′pəl) ▸*n.* **1.** A small natural indentation in the flesh on a part of the human body, esp. in the cheek or chin. **2.** A slight depression in a surface. ▸*v.* **-pled, -pling** To form dimples, as by smiling. [ME *dimpel.*]

dim sum (dĭm′ sōōm′) ▸*n.* Small portions of a variety of traditional Chinese foods, including steamed or fried dumplings, served in succession. [< Cantonese *dim² sam¹.*]

dim·wit (dĭm'wĭt') ►*n. Slang* A stupid person. —**dim'wit'ted** *adj.*

din (dĭn) ►*n.* A jumble of loud, usu. discordant sounds. See Synonyms at **noise.** ►*v.* **dinned, din·ning** To stun with deafening noise. [< OE *dyne.*]

di·nar (dĭ-när', dē'när') ►*n.* See table at **currency.** [Ar. *dīnār.*]

Di·nar·ic Alps (dĭ-năr'ĭk) A range of the Balkan Peninsula extending about 644 km (400 mi) along the E coast of the Adriatic Sea.

dine (dīn) ►*v.* **dined, din·ing 1.** To have dinner: *dined at 6:00.* **2.** To entertain at dinner: *wined and dined.* [< OFr. *diner.*]

din·er (dī'nər) ►*n.* **1.** One that dines. **2.** A railroad dining car. **3.** A restaurant shaped like a dining car.

Di·ne·sen (dē'nĭ-sən, dĭn'ĭ-), **Isak** Baroness Karen Blixen. 1885–1962. Danish writer.

di·nette (dī-nĕt') ►*n.* A nook or alcove used for informal meals.

ding¹ (dĭng) ►*v.* To ring or cause to ring; clang. ►*n.* A ringing sound. [Imit.]

ding² (dĭng) ►*n. Informal* A small dent or nick, as in the body of a car. [< *ding,* to strike.] —**ding** *v.*

din·ghy (dĭng'ē) ►*n., pl.* **-ghies** A small open boat. [Hindi *ḍīṅgī.*]

din·go (dĭng'gō) ►*n., pl.* **-goes** A wild dog of Asia and Australia, having a reddish-brown or yellow coat. [Dharuk (Australian) *ḍiṅgu.*]

din·gy (dĭn'jē) ►*adj.* **-gi·er, -gi·est 1.** Darkened with smoke or grime. **2.** Shabby, drab, or squalid. [Poss. < ME *dinge, dung.*] —**din'gi·ly** *adv.* —**din'gi·ness** *n.*

din·ky (dĭng'kē) ►*adj.* **-ki·er, -ki·est** *Informal* Of small size or consequence; insignificant. [Prob. < Sc. *dink,* neat.]

din·ner (dĭn'ər) ►*n.* **1.** The main meal of the day. **2.** A formal banquet. [< OFr. *disner,* dine, morning meal.]

dinner jacket ►*n.* See **tuxedo.**

di·no·saur (dī'nə-sôr') ►*n.* Any of various extinct, often gigantic, carnivorous or herbivorous reptiles of the Mesozoic Era. [Gk. *deinos,* monstrous + *sauros,* lizard.]

dint (dĭnt) ►*n.* **1.** Force or effort: *succeeded by dint of hard work.* **2.** A dent. [ME, DENT.]

di·o·cese (dī'ə-sĭs, -sēs', -sēz') ►*n.* The district or churches under the jurisdiction of a bishop; bishopric. [< Gk. *dioikēsis,* administration.] —**di·oc'e·san** (dī-ŏs'ə-sən) *adj.*

Di·o·cle·tian (dī'ə-klē'shən) AD 245?–313? Emperor of Rome (284–305).

di·ode (dī'ōd') ►*n.* A two-terminal semiconductor device, esp. one that restricts current flow chiefly to one direction.

Di·og·e·nes (dī-ŏj'ə-nēz') d. c. 320 BC. Greek philosopher.

Di·o·nys·i·an (dī'ə-nĭsh'ən, -nĭzh'ən, -nĭs'ē-ən) ►*adj.* **1.** *Gk. Myth.* Of or relating to Dionysus. **2.** often **dionysian** Of an orgiastic or irrational nature.

Di·o·ny·sus (dī'ə-nī'səs, -nē'-) ►*n. Gk. & Rom. Myth.* The god of wine, drama, and of an orgiastic religion celebrating the power and fertility of nature. [< Gk. *Dionusos.*]

di·o·ram·a (dī'ə-răm'ə, -rä'mə) ►*n.* A three-dimensional scene with modeled figures against a painted background. [Gk. *dia,* through + (PAN)ORAMA.]

di·ox·ide (dī-ŏk'sīd) ►*n.* A compound with two oxygen atoms per molecule.

di·ox·in (dī-ŏk'sĭn) ►*n.* Any of several carcinogenic, mutagenic, or teratogenic hydrocarbons that can occur as impurities in or byproducts of various environmental pollutants. [DI– + *ox(o)*-, oxygen + –IN.]

dip (dĭp) ►*v.* **dipped, dip·ping 1.** To plunge briefly into a liquid. **2.** To scoop up (liquid): *dip water out of a bucket.* **3.** To lower and raise (a flag) in salute. **4.** To drop or sink suddenly. **5.** To slope downward. **6.** To dabble: *dip into medieval history.* ►*n.* **1.** A brief plunge or immersion, esp. a quick swim. **2.** A liquid into which something is dipped. **3.** A savory creamy mixture into which crackers or other foods may be dipped. **4.** An amount taken up by dipping. **5.** A downward slope. **6.** A decline. **7.** A hollow or depression. **8.** *Slang* A foolish person. **9.** Finely shredded tobacco usu. placed between the lower lip and gum. [< OE *dyppan.*]

diph·the·ri·a (dĭf-thîr'ē-ə, dĭp-) ►*n.* An acute infectious bacterial disease marked by high fever, weakness, and the formation of a false membrane in the throat and other respiratory passages, causing difficulty in breathing. [< Gk. *diphthera,* piece of leather.] —**diph'the·rit'ic** (-thə-rĭt'ĭk), **diph·ther'ic** (-thĕr'ĭk), **diph·the'ri·al** *adj.*

diph·thong (dĭf'thông', -thŏng', dĭp'-) ►*n.* A complex speech sound that begins with one vowel and gradually changes to another vowel within the same syllable, as (oi) in *boil.* [< Gk. *diphthongos.*]

dip·loid (dĭp'loid') ►*adj.* Having two sets of chromosomes. [< Gk. *diploos,* double.] —**dip'loid'** *n.*

di·plo·ma (dĭ-plō'mə) ►*n.* **1.** A document issued by an educational institution, such as a university, testifying that the recipient has earned a degree or successfully completed a course of study. **2.** A certificate conferring a privilege or honor. [< Gk. *diplōma,* folded document < *diploos,* double.]

di·plo·ma·cy (dĭ-plō'mə-sē) ►*n.* **1.** The art or practice of conducting international relations. **2.** Tact and skill in dealing with people. [Ult. < Gk. *diplōma,* document.]

dip·lo·mat (dĭp'lə-măt') ►*n.* One skilled in or working in diplomacy.

dip·lo·mat·ic (dĭp'lə-măt'ĭk) ►*adj.* **1.** Of or involving diplomacy or diplomats. **2.** Tactful. —**dip'lo·mat'i·cal·ly** *adv.*

di·pole (dī'pōl') ►*n.* **1.** *Phys.* A pair of separated electric charges or magnetic poles, of equal magnitude but of opposite sign or polarity. **2.** *Electron.* An antenna, usu. fed from the center, consisting of two equal rods extending outward in a straight line. —**di·po'lar** *adj.*

dip·per (dĭp'ər) ►*n.* **1.** One that dips, esp. a container for taking up water. **2.** A small bird that dives into swift streams and feeds along the bottom.

dip·so·ma·ni·a (dĭp'sə-mā'nē-ə, -mān'yə) ►*n.* An insatiable craving for alcoholic beverages. [Gk. *dipsa,* thirst + –MANIA.] —**dip'so·ma'ni·ac'** *adj. & n.*

dip·stick (dĭp'stĭk') ►*n.* A graduated rod for measuring the depth of liquid.

dire (dīr) ►*adj.* **dir·er, dir·est 1.** Warning of

disaster. **2.** Urgent; desperate: *in dire poverty.* [Lat. *dīrus*, terrible.] —**dire′ful** *adj.* —**dire′ful·ly** *adv.* —**dire′ly** *adv.*

di·rect (dĭ-rĕkt′, dī-) ►*v.* **1a.** To manage or conduct the affairs of; to be in charge of. **b.** To supervise (an activity or process). **2.** To oversee or give interpretive dramatic guidance and instructions to the actors in a play or film. **3a.** To cause to move in a certain direction: *directed the light upward.* **b.** To concentrate or focus on a particular object or activity. See Synonyms at **aim.** ►*adj.* **1.** Proceeding in a straight course or line. **2.** Straightforward: *a direct response.* **3.** Having no intervening persons, conditions, or agencies; immediate: *direct contact.* **4.** By action of voters, rather than through elected delegates. **5.** Being of unbroken descent; lineal. **6.** Consisting of the exact words of the writer or speaker: *a direct quotation.* **7.** Absolute; total: *direct opposites.* **8.** *Math.* Varying in the same manner as another quantity, esp. increasing if another quantity increases or decreasing if it decreases. ►*adv.* Straight; directly. [< Lat. *dīrigere, dīrect-.*] —**di·rect′-ness** *n.*

direct current ►*n.* An electric current flowing in one direction only.

direct deposit ►*n.* The electronic transfer of a payment from the payer's account to that of the payee.

di·rec·tion (dĭ-rĕk′shən, dī-) ►*n.* **1.** The management or guidance of a group or operation. **2a.** An order or command. **b. directions** Instructions in how to do something or reach a destination. **3a.** The course along which a person or thing must move to reach a destination: *a northwesterly direction.* **b.** The point toward which a person or thing faces or is oriented: *opposite directions.* **4.** A tendency toward a particular end or goal. —**di·rec′tion·al** *adj.* —**di·rec′tion·al′i·ty** *n.*

di·rec·tive (dĭ-rĕk′tĭv, dī-) ►*n.* An order or instruction, esp. from a central authority.

di·rect·ly (dĭ-rĕkt′lē, dī-) ►*adv.* **1.** In a direct line or manner. **2.** Without anyone or anything intervening: *directly responsible.* **3.** Exactly: *directly opposite.* **4.** Instantly.

direct mail ►*n.* Advertising matter sent by mail without being requested to residences and workplaces. —**di·rect′-mail′** *adj.*

direct object ►*n.* The word or phrase in a sentence referring to the receiver of the action of a transitive verb. For example, in *call him, him* is the direct object.

di·rec·tor (dĭ-rĕk′tər, dī-) ►*n.* **1.** A manager. **2.** One of a group chosen to govern the affairs of an institution or corporation. **3.** One who supervises or guides the performers in a play, film, or musical performance. —**di·rec′to·ri·al** (-tôr′ē-əl) *adj.* —**di·rec′tor·ship′** *n.*

di·rec·tor·ate (dĭ-rĕk′tər-ĭt, dī-) ►*n.* **1.** The office or position of a director. **2.** A board of directors.

di·rec·to·ry (dĭ-rĕk′tə-rē, dī-) ►*n., pl.* **-ries 1.** An alphabetical or classified listing of names, addresses, and usu. telephone numbers. **2.** *Comp.* An organizational unit for files contained in a storage device.

dirge (dûrj) ►*n.* **1.** A funeral song. **2.** A slow, mournful piece of music. [< Med.Lat. *dīrige Domine*, direct, O Lord.]

dir·ham (dîr′həm) ►*n.* See table at **currency.** [Ar. < Gk. *drakhmē*, drachma.]

dir·i·gi·ble (dĭr′ə-jə-bəl, də-rĭj′ə-bəl) ►*n.* An airship. [< Lat. *dīrigere*, to direct.]

dirk (dûrk) ►*n.* A dagger. [Sc. *durk.*]

dirn·dl (dûrn′dl) ►*n.* A full skirt with a gathered waistband. [< Ger. *Dirndlkleid.*]

dirt (dûrt) ►*n.* **1.** Earth or soil. **2.** A filthy or soiling substance, such as mud. **3.** One that is contemptible or vile. **4a.** Obscene language. **b.** Malicious or scandalous gossip. [< ON *drit*, filth.]

dirt bike ►*n.* A lightweight motorcycle designed for use on rough surfaces.

dirt bike

dirt-cheap (dûrt′chēp′) ►*adv. & adj.* Very inexpensive.

dirt·y (dûr′tē) ►*adj.* **-i·er, -i·est 1.** Soiled or grimy; unclean. **2.** Obscene or indecent. **3.** Dishonorable or unfair: *a dirty fighter.* **4.** Expressing hostility: *a dirty look.* **5.** Dull in color. **6a.** Relating to a bomb having the potential to contaminate an area with low-level radiation. **b.** Relating to a nuclear weapon that produces a very great amount of long-lived radioactive fallout. **7.** Stormy: *dirty weather.* ►*v.* **-ied, -y·ing** To make or become soiled. —**dirt′i·ly** *adv.* —**dirt′i·ness** *n.*

dis (dĭs) ►*v.* **dissed, dis·sing** *Informal* To show disrespect to. [*dis(respect).*]

dis– ►*pref.* **1.** Not: *dissimilar.* **2a.** Absence of: *disinterest.* **b.** Opposite of: *disfavor.* **3.** Undo: *disarrange.* **4a.** Deprive of: *disfranchise.* **b.** Remove: *disbar.* [< Lat. *dis*, apart.]

dis·a·bil·i·ty (dĭs′ə-bĭl′ĭ-tē) ►*n.* **1.** The condition of being disabled; incapacity. **2.** A disadvantage or deficiency, esp. a physical or mental impairment that prevents or restricts normal achievement. See Usage Note at **handi-capped.**

dis·a·ble (dĭs-ā′bəl) ►*v.* **-bled, -bling** To deprive of capability or effectiveness, esp. to impair the physical abilities of.

dis·a·bled (dĭs-ā′bəld) ►*adj.* **1.** Inoperative: *a disabled vehicle.* **2.** Impaired, as in physical functioning: *a disabled veteran.* ►*n.* (takes *pl. v.*) Physically or mentally impaired people as a group: *the disabled.* See Usage Note at **handicapped.**

dis·a·buse (dĭs′ə-byōōz′) ►*v.* **-bused, -bus·ing** To free from a falsehood or misconception. [Fr. *désabuser.*]

di·sac·cha·ride (dī-săk′ə-rīd′) ►*n.* Any of a class of carbohydrates, including lactose and sucrose, that are composed of two monosaccharides.

dis·ad·van·tage (dĭs′əd-văn′tĭj) ►*n.* **1.** An

unfavorable condition or circumstance. **2.** Damage, harm, or loss. —**dis·ad′van·ta′geous** (dĭs-ăd′vən-tā′jəs) *adj.*
   Syns: *detriment, drawback, handicap* **n.**

dis·ad·van·taged (dĭs′əd-văn′tĭjd) ►*adj.* **1.** Socially or economically deprived. **2.** Being at a disadvantage. ►*n. (takes pl. v.)* Deprived people collectively: *the disadvantaged.*

dis·af·fect (dĭs′ə-fĕkt′) ►*v.* To cause to lose affection or loyalty. —**dis′af·fect′ed** *adj.* —**dis′af·fec′tion** *n.*

dis·a·gree (dĭs′ə-grē′) ►*v.* **1a.** To have a differing opinion. **b.** To dispute; quarrel. **2.** To fail to correspond: *Our figures disagree.* **3.** To cause adverse effects: *Caffeine disagrees with me.* —**dis′a·gree′ment** *n.*

dis·a·gree·a·ble (dĭs′ə-grē′ə-bəl) ►*adj.* **1.** Unpleasant, distasteful, or offensive. **2.** Bad-tempered. —**dis′a·gree′a·ble·ness** *n.* —**dis′a·gree′a·bly** *adv.*

dis·al·low (dĭs′ə-lou′) ►*v.* To refuse to allow; reject. —**dis′al·low′ance** *n.*

dis·ap·pear (dĭs′ə-pîr′) ►*v.* **1.** To pass out of sight. **2.** To be missing: *Her purse disappeared.* **3.** To cease to exist: *When did dinosaurs disappear?* —**dis′ap·pear′ance** *n.*
   Syns: *evanesce, evaporate, fade, vanish* **Ant:** *appear* **v.**

dis·ap·point (dĭs′ə-point′) ►*v.* To fail to satisfy the hope, desire, or expectation of: *was disappointed by the movie.* [< OFr. *desapointier,* remove from office.] —**dis′ap·point′ing·ly** *adv.* —**dis′ap·point′ment** *n.*

dis·ap·pro·ba·tion (dĭs-ăp′rə-bā′shən) ►*n.* Moral disapproval; condemnation.

dis·ap·prov·al (dĭs′ə-prōō′vəl) ►*n.* The act of disapproving; condemnation or censure.

dis·ap·prove (dĭs′ə-prōōv′) ►*v.* **1.** To have an unfavorable opinion (of). **2.** To refuse to approve. —**dis′ap·prov′ing·ly** *adv.*

dis·arm (dĭs-ärm′) ►*v.* **1a.** To divest or deprive of weapons. **b.** To render helpless or harmless. **2.** To overcome the hostility of. **3.** To reduce one's arms or armed forces.

dis·ar·ma·ment (dĭs-är′mə-mənt) ►*n.* A reduction of armed forces and armaments.

dis·ar·range (dĭs′ə-rānj′) ►*v.* To upset the order of. —**dis′ar·range′ment** *n.*

dis·ar·ray (dĭs′ə-rā′) ►*n.* **1.** A state of disorder; confusion. **2.** Disordered dress. ►*v.* To throw into confusion; upset.

dis·as·sem·ble (dĭs′ə-sĕm′bəl) ►*v.* To take or come apart.

dis·as·so·ci·ate (dĭs′ə-sō′shē-āt′, -sē-) ►*v.* To remove from association. —**dis′as·so′ci·a′tion** *n.*

dis·as·ter (dĭ-zăs′tər, -săs′-) ►*n.* Great destruction, distress, or misfortune. [< Ital. *disastro* : DIS– + *astro,* star (< Gk. *astron*).] —**dis·as′trous** *adj.* —**dis·as′trous·ly** *adv.*

dis·a·vow (dĭs′ə-vou′) ►*v.* **1.** To disclaim knowledge of, responsibility for, or association with. **2.** To assert to be wrong or of little value. —**dis′a·vow′al** *n.*

dis·band (dĭs-bănd′) ►*v.* To dissolve or become dissolved. —**dis·band′ment** *n.*

dis·bar (dĭs-bär′) ►*v.* **-barred, -bar·ring** To prohibit (an attorney) from the practice of law. —**dis·bar′ment** *n.*

dis·be·lieve (dĭs′bĭ-lēv′) ►*v.* To refuse to accept. —**dis′be·lief′** *n.*

dis·burse (dĭs-bûrs′) ►*v.* **-bursed, -burs·ing** To pay out, as from a fund; expend. [< OFr. *desborser* < LLat. *bursa,* PURSE.] —**dis·burse′ment, dis·bur′sal** *n.*

disc (dĭsk) ►*n.* Var. of disk.

dis·card (dĭ-skärd′) ►*v.* **1.** To throw away; reject. **2.** *Games* To throw out (a playing card) from one's hand. ►*n.* (dĭs′kärd′) **1.** The act of discarding. **2.** One that is discarded or rejected.

dis·cern (dĭ-sûrn′) ►*v.* **1.** To detect or perceive with the eyes or intellect. **2.** To perceive the distinctions of; discriminate. [< Lat. *discernere.*] —**dis·cern′i·ble** *adj.* —**dis·cern′i·bly** *adv.* —**dis·cern′ment** *n.*

dis·cern·ing (dĭ-sûr′nĭng) ►*adj.* Insightful or perceptive.

dis·charge (dĭs-chärj′) ►*v.* **-charged, -charg·ing** **1a.** To release or dismiss: *discharge a patient; discharge a soldier.* **b.** To let go; empty out: *a train discharging commuters.* **c.** To pour forth; emit: *a vent discharging steam.* **d.** To shoot: *discharge a pistol.* **2.** To remove from office or employment. See Synonyms at **dismiss. 3.** To perform the obligations or demands of (a duty). **4.** To comply with the terms of (e.g., a debt or promise). **5.** *Elect.* To cause or undergo electrical discharge. ►*n.* (dĭs′chärj′, dĭs-chärj′) **1.** The act of removing a load or burden. **2.** The act of shooting a projectile or weapon. **3a.** A pouring forth; emission: *a discharge of pus.* **b.** The amount or rate of emission or ejection. **c.** Something that is discharged: *a watery discharge.* **4.** A relieving from an obligation. **5a.** Dismissal or release from employment, service, care, or confinement. **b.** An official document certifying such release, esp. from military service. **6.** *Elect.* **a.** Release of stored energy in a capacitor by the flow of current between its terminals. **b.** Conversion of chemical energy to electric energy in a storage battery. **c.** A flow of electricity in a dielectric, esp. in a rarefied gas. [< LLat. *discarricāre,* unload.]

dis·ci·ple (dĭ-sī′pəl) ►*n.* **1.** One who embraces and assists in spreading the teachings of another. **2.** often **Disciple** One of the original followers of Jesus. [< Lat. *discipulus,* pupil < *discere,* learn.]

dis·ci·pli·nar·i·an (dĭs′ə-plə-nâr′ē-ən) ►*n.* One that enforces or believes in strict discipline.

dis·ci·pli·nar·y (dĭs′ə-plə-nĕr′ē) ►*adj.* Of or used for discipline.

dis·ci·pline (dĭs′ə-plĭn) ►*n.* **1.** Training expected to produce a specific character or pattern of behavior, esp. training that produces moral or mental improvement. **2.** Controlled behavior resulting from such training. **3.** A state of order that is based on submission to rules and authority. **4.** Punishment intended to correct or train. **5.** A set of rules or methods. **6.** A branch of knowledge or teaching. ►*v.* **-plined, -plin·ing** **1.** To train by instruction and practice. **2.** To punish. [< Lat. *disciplīna* < *discipulus,* DISCIPLE.]

dis·ci·plined (dĭs′ə-plĭnd) ►*adj.* Possessing or indicative of discipline: *a disciplined mind.*

disc jockey also **disk jockey** ►*n.* **1.** An announcer who presents popular recorded music, esp. on the radio. **2.** A turntablist.

dis·claim (dĭs-klām′) ►*v.* **1.** To deny or renounce any claim to or connection with. **2.** To decline to accept responsibility for.

dis·claim·er (dĭs-klā′mər) ►*n.* A repudiation or denial fo responsibility, connection, or liability.

dis·close (dĭ-sklōz′) ►*v.* **1.** To expose to view. **2.** To reveal (something secret). —**dis·clo′sure** (-sklō′zhər) *n.*

dis·co (dĭs′kō) ►*n., pl.* **-cos 1.** A discotheque. **2.** Popular dance music, popularized in the late 1970s, marked by strong repetitive bass rhythms. —**dis′co** *adj.*

dis·col·or (dĭs-kŭl′ər) ►*v.* To make or become a different color, as by staining or fading. —**dis·col′or·a′tion** *n.*

dis·com·bob·u·late (dĭs′kəm-bŏb′yə-lāt′) ►*v.* **-lat·ed, -lat·ing** To throw into a state of confusion. See Synonyms at **befuddle.** [Perh. < DISCOMPOSE.]

dis·com·fit (dĭs-kŭm′fĭt) ►*v.* To make uneasy or perplexed; disconcert. See Synonyms at **embarrass.** [< OFr. *desconfit,* p.part. of *desconfire,* to defeat.] —**dis·com′fi·ture** *n.*

dis·com·fort (dĭs-kŭm′fərt) ►*n.* **1.** Mental or bodily distress. **2.** Something that disturbs comfort. ►*v.* To make uncomfortable.

dis·com·mode (dĭs′kə-mōd′) ►*v.* **-mod·ed, -mod·ing** To inconvenience; disturb. [< DIS– + Lat. *commodus,* convenient.]

dis·com·pose (dĭs′kəm-pōz′) ►*v.* **1.** To disturb the composure of; perturb. **2.** To put into disorder. —**dis′com·po′sure** *n.*

dis·con·cert (dĭs′kən-sûrt′) ►*v.* **1.** To cause to lose composure; confuse. See Synonyms at **embarrass. 2.** To throw into disorder; disarrange. —**dis′con·cert′ing·ly** *adv.*

dis·con·nect (dĭs′kə-nĕkt′) ►*v.* **1.** To sever the connection of or between. **2.** To shut off the current to. —**dis′con·nec′tion** *n.*

dis·con·nect·ed (dĭs′kə-nĕk′tĭd) ►*adj.* **1.** Not connected. **2.** Marked by unrelated parts; incoherent. —**dis′con·nect′ed·ly** *adv.*

dis·con·so·late (dĭs-kŏn′sə-lĭt) ►*adj.* **1.** Hopelessly sad; extremely dejected. See Synonyms at **depressed. 2.** Gloomy; dismal. [< Med.Lat. *discōnsōlātus.*] —**dis·con′so·late·ly** *adv.*

dis·con·tent (dĭs′kən-tĕnt′) ►*n.* Absence of contentment; dissatisfaction. ►*adj.* Discontented. ►*v.* To make discontented. —**dis′con·tent′ment** *n.*

dis·con·tent·ed (dĭs′kən-tĕn′tĭd) ►*adj.* Restlessly unhappy; malcontent. —**dis′con·tent′ed·ly** *adv.* —**dis′con·tent′ed·ness** *n.*

dis·con·tin·ue (dĭs′kən-tĭn′yōō) ►*v.* To stop doing, making, or providing (something): *discontinued ferry service; discontinued the sports car.* See Synonyms at **stop.** —**dis′con·tin′u·ance, dis′con·tin′u·a′tion** *n.*

dis·con·tin·u·ous (dĭs′kən-tĭn′yōō-əs) ►*adj.* Marked by breaks or interruptions. —**dis·con·ti·nu·i·ty** (dĭs-kŏn′tə-nōō′ĭ-tē, -nyōō′-) *n.* —**dis′con·tin′u·ous·ly** *adv.*

dis·cord (dĭs′kôrd′) ►*n.* **1.** Lack of agreement; dissension. **2.** A harsh mingling of sounds. **3.** *Mus.* An inharmonious combination of simultaneously sounded tones; dissonance. [< Lat. *discordia* : DIS– + *cor,* heart.] —**dis·cor′dant** *adj.* —**dis·cor′dant·ly** *adv.*

dis·co·theque (dĭs′kə-tĕk′, dĭs′kə-tĕk′) ►*n.* A nightclub, usu. with showy lighting, featuring dancing to music. [Fr. *discothèque.*]

dis·count (dĭs′kount′, dĭs-kount′) ►*v.* **1a.** To offer for sale at a reduced price. **b.** To reduce in quantity or value: *discounting all merchandise.*

2. To deduct or subtract from a cost or price: *discounted 30 dollars off the price of the coat.* **3a.** To determine the present value of (a future payment or series of payments). **b.** To price (a debt security) at a reduction to its face value. **4.** To disregard as being untrustworthy or exaggerated. **5.** To anticipate and make allowance for. ►*n.* (dĭs′kount′) **1.** A reduction from the full amount of a price or value. **2.** The amount by which the face value of a debt security exceeds its market price. [< OFr. *desconter.*]

dis·coun·te·nance (dĭs-koun′tə-nəns) ►*v.* **1.** To view with disfavor. **2.** To disconcert.

dis·cour·age (dĭ-skûr′ĭj, -skûr′-) ►*v.* **-aged, -ag·ing 1.** To deprive of confidence, hope, or spirit: *Making so little progress after so much effort discouraged us.* **2.** To deter (someone) from doing something: *My advisor discouraged me from applying to big universities.* **3.** To try to prevent, as by raising objections: *The agency discouraged all travel to the areas hardest hit by the disease.* —**dis·cour′age·ment** *n.* —**dis·cour′ag·ing·ly** *adv.*

Syns: *dishearten, dismay, dispirit* **Ant:** *encourage v.*

dis·course (dĭs′kôrs′) ►*n.* **1.** Verbal exchange; conversation. **2.** A formal discussion of a subject, either written or spoken. ►*v.* (dĭ-skôrs′) **-coursed, -cours·ing** To speak or write formally and at length. [< Med.Lat. *discursus.*]

dis·cour·te·ous (dĭs-kûr′tē-əs) ►*adj.* Lacking courtesy; not polite. —**dis·cour′te·ous·ly** *adv.* —**dis·cour′te·sy** *n.*

dis·cov·er (dĭ-skŭv′ər) ►*v.* **1.** To notice or learn, esp. by making an effort. **2.** To be the first to find, learn of, or observe. [< LLat. *discooperīre,* uncover.] —**dis·cov′er·a·ble** *adj.* —**dis·cov′er·er** *n.*

Syns: *ascertain, determine, learn v.*

dis·cov·er·y (dĭ-skŭv′ə-rē) ►*n., pl.* **-ies 1.** The act or an instance of discovering. **2.** Something discovered.

dis·cred·it (dĭs-krĕd′ĭt) ►*v.* **1.** To disgrace; dishonor. **2.** To cast doubt on. **3.** To refuse to believe. ►*n.* **1.** Damage to one's reputation. **2.** Lack or loss of trust or belief. —**dis·cred′it·a·ble** *adj.*

dis·creet (dĭ-skrēt′) ►*adj.* Having or showing prudence and self-restraint in speech and behavior. [< Med.Lat. *discrētus* < Lat. *discernere,* discern.] —**dis·creet′ly** *adv.* —**dis·creet′ness** *n.*

dis·crep·an·cy (dĭ-skrĕp′ən-sē) ►*n., pl.* **-cies** Lack of agreement, as between facts or claims; difference.

dis·crep·ant (dĭ-skrĕp′ənt) ►*adj.* Marked by discrepancy. [< Lat. *discrepāre,* disagree.]

dis·crete (dĭ-skrēt′) ►*adj.* **1.** Individually distinct; separate: *Computers treat time as a series of discrete moments rathern than a continuous flow.* **2.** Consisting of unconnected distinct parts: *society viewed as a discrete whole of individual agents.* See Synonyms at **distinct.** [< Lat. *discrētus,* p.part. of *discernere,* to separate.]

dis·cre·tion (dĭ-skrĕsh′ən) ►*n.* **1.** The quality of being discreet. **2.** Freedom of action or judgment: *The choice was left to our discretion.* —**dis·cre′tion·ar·y** *adj.*

dis·crim·i·nate (dĭ-skrĭm′ə-nāt′) ►*v.* **-nat·ed, -nat·ing 1.** To make a clear distinction; differentiate. **2.** To make distinctions on the basis of preference or prejudice. [Lat. *discrīmināre.*] —**dis·crim′i·na′tion** *n.* —**dis·crim′i·na·tive, dis·crim′i·na·to′ry** *adj.*

dis·crim·i·nat·ing (dĭ-skrĭm′ə-nā′tĭng) ►*adj.* Able to recognize or draw fine distinctions or judgments.

dis·cur·sive (dĭ-skûr′sĭv) ►*adj.* Covering a wide field of subjects; digressive. [< Lat. *discursus,* running about.] —**dis·cur′sive·ly** *adv.* —**dis·cur′sive·ness** *n.*

dis·cus (dĭs′kəs) ►*n.* A disk, typically wooden, plastic, or rubber, that is thrown for distance in athletic competitions. [Lat., DISK.]

dis·cuss (dĭ-skŭs′) ►*v.* **1.** To speak with others about; talk over. **2.** To examine (a subject) in speech or writing: *an essay that discusses pollution.* [< Lat. *discutere,* break up.] —**dis·cus′sion** *n.*

dis·cus·sant (dĭ-skŭs′ənt) ►*n.* A participant in a formal discussion.

dis·dain (dĭs-dān′) ►*v.* **1.** To regard or treat with contempt. See Synonyms at **despise. 2.** To reject (doing something) as beneath oneself. ►*n.* Haughty contempt. [< Lat. *dēdignārī.*] —**dis·dain′ful** *adj.* —**dis·dain′ful·ly** *adv.*

dis·ease (dĭ-zēz′) ►*n.* A condition of an organism that impairs physiological functioning, resulting from causes such as infection, genetic defect, or environmental stress. [< OFr. *disese,* misery.] —**dis·eased′** *adj.*

dis·em·bark (dĭs′ĕm-bärk′) ►*v.* **1.** To exit or cause to exit from a conveyance, esp. a ship or aircraft. **2.** To put, go, or cause to go ashore from a ship. —**dis·em′bar·ka′tion** *n.*

dis·em·bod·y (dĭs′ĕm-bŏd′ē) ►*v.* **1.** To free (the spirit) from the body. **2.** To divest of material form or existence. —**dis′em·bod′i·ment** *n.*

dis·em·bow·el (dĭs′ĕm-bou′əl) ►*v.* **-eled, -el·ing** or **-elled, -el·ling** To remove the entrails from. —**dis′em·bow′el·ment** *n.*

dis·en·chant (dĭs′ĕn-chănt′) ►*v.* To free from false belief. —**dis′en·chant′ment** *n.*

dis·en·cum·ber (dĭs′ĕn-kŭm′bər) ►*v.* To relieve of burdens or hardships.

dis·en·fran·chise (dĭs′ĕn-frăn′chīz′) ►*v.* To disfranchise. —**dis′en·fran′chise′ment** (-chīz′-mənt, -chĭz-) *n.*

dis·en·gage (dĭs′ĕn-gāj′) ►*v.* To release from something that holds fast, connects, or obliges. See Synonyms at **extricate.** —**dis′en·gage′-ment** *n.*

dis·en·tan·gle (dĭs′ĕn-tăng′gəl) ►*v.* To free from entanglement. See Synonyms at **extri-cate.** —**dis′en·tan′gle·ment** *n.*

dis·es·tab·lish (dĭs′ĭ-stăb′lĭsh) ►*v.* To revoke the established status of, esp. of a national church. —**dis′es·tab′lish·ment** *n.*

dis·fa·vor (dĭs-fā′vər) ►*n.* **1.** Disapproval. **2.** The condition of being regarded with disapproval. —**dis·fa′vor** *v.*

dis·fig·ure (dĭs-fĭg′yər) ►*v.* **-ured, -ur·ing** To spoil the appearance or shape of; mar. —**dis·fig′ure·ment** *n.*

dis·fran·chise (dĭs-frăn′chīz′) ►*v.* To deprive of a privilege, immunity, or right of citizenship, esp. the right to vote. —**dis·fran′chise′-ment** *n.*

dis·gorge (dĭs-gôrj′) ►*v.* **-gorged, -gorg·ing 1.** To vomit. **2.** To discharge violently; spew. [< OFr. *desgorger.*] —**dis·gorge′ment** *n.*

dis·grace (dĭs-grās′) ►*n.* **1.** Loss of honor, respect, or reputation; shame. **2.** The condition of being strongly disapproved. **3.** One that brings disfavor. ►*v.* **-graced, -grac·ing** To bring shame or dishonor on. [< Ital. *disgrazia.*] —**dis·grace′ful** *adj.* —**dis·grace′ful·ly** *adv.*

dis·grun·tle (dĭs-grŭn′tl) ►*v.* **-tled, -tling** To make discontented. [DIS– + *gruntle,* grumble.] —**dis·grun′tle·ment** *n.*

dis·guise (dĭs-gīz′) ►*v.* **-guised, -guis·ing 1.** To modify the manner or appearance of in order to prevent recognition. **2.** To conceal or obscure by false show; misrepresent. ►*n.* **1.** Clothes or accessories worn to conceal one's true identity. **2.** A pretense or misrepresentation. [< OFr. *desguiser.*]

    Syns: camouflage, cloak, dissemble, dissimulate, mask **v.**

dis·gust (dĭs-gŭst′) ►*v.* To make (someone) feel sick, repelled, averse, or offended. ►*n.* A feeling of profound aversion, repugnance, or offensiveness. [< OFr. *desgouster,* lose one's appetite.] —**dis·gust′ed** *adj.* —**dis·gust′ed·ly** *adv.*

    Syns: nauseate, repel, revolt, sicken **v.**

dis·gust·ing (dĭs-gŭs′tĭng) ►*adj.* Arousing disgust; repugnant. See Synonyms at **offensive.** —**dis·gust′ing·ly** *adv.*

dish (dĭsh) ►*n.* **1.** A flat or shallow container for holding, cooking, or serving food. **2.** A particular variety or preparation of food. **3.** Something shaped like a dish. ►*v.* To serve in or as if in a dish. —*phrasal verb:* **dish out** To dispense freely. [< OE *disc* < Lat. *discus,* DISK.]

dis·ha·bille (dĭs′ə-bēl′, -bē′) ►*n.* The state of being partially, casually, or sloppily dressed. [Fr. *déshabillé* < p.part. of *déshabiller,* to undress.]

dish antenna ►*n.* A parabolic antenna.

dis·har·mo·ny (dĭs-här′mə-nē) ►*n.* Lack of harmony. —**dis′har·mo′ni·ous** (-mō′nē-əs) *adj.*

dish·cloth (dĭsh′klôth′, -klŏth′) ►*n.* A cloth for washing dishes.

dis·heart·en (dĭs-här′tn) ►*v.* To cause to lose hope or enthusiasm; dispirit. See Synonyms at **discourage.** —**dis·heart′en·ing·ly** *adv.*

di·shev·el (dĭ-shĕv′əl) ►*v.* **-eled, -el·ing** or **-elled, -el·ling** To put into disarray or disorder, esp. hair or clothing. [< OFr. *descheveler,* disarrange one's hair.] —**di·shev′el·ment** *n.*

dis·hon·est (dĭs-ŏn′ĭst) ►*adj.* **1.** Disposed to lie, cheat, defraud, or deceive; untrustworthy. **2.** Resulting from or marked by fraud. —**dis·hon′est·ly** *adv.* —**dis·hon′es·ty** *n.*

dis·hon·or (dĭs-ŏn′ər) ►*n.* **1.** Loss of honor, respect, or reputation. **2.** A cause of loss of honor. **3.** Failure to pay a note, bill, or other commercial obligation. ►*v.* **1.** To bring shame or disgrace upon. **2.** To fail or refuse to pay. —**dis·hon′or·a·ble** *adj.* —**dis·hon′or·a·bly** *adv.*

dishonorable discharge ►*n.* Expulsion from the armed services resulting from a court-martial conviction of a serious violation of the military code, such as desertion, rape, or murder.

dish·rag (dĭsh′răg′) ►*n.* A dishcloth.

dish·wash·er (dĭsh′wŏsh′ər, -wô′shər) ►*n.* One, esp. a machine, that washes dishes.

dis·il·lu·sion (dĭs′ĭ-lōō′zhən) ►*v.* To free or deprive of illusion. —**dis′il·lu′sion·ment** *n.*

dis·in·cline (dĭs′ĭn-klīn′) ►*v.* To make or be reluctant. —**dis·in′cli·na′tion** (-klə-nā′shən) *n.*

dis·in·fect (dĭs′ĭn-fĕkt′) ►*v.* To rid of disease-carrying microorganisms. —**dis′in·fec′tant** *adj.* & *n.* —**dis′in·fec′tion** *n.*

dis·in·gen·u·ous (dĭs′ĭn-jĕn′yōō-əs) ►*adj.* Not straightforward or candid. —**dis′in·gen′u·ous·ly** *adv.* —**dis′in·gen′u·ous·ness** *n.*

dis·in·her·it (dĭs′ĭn-hĕr′ĭt) ►*v.* To exclude from inheriting or the right to inherit.

dis·in·te·grate (dĭs-ĭn′tĭ-grāt′) ►*v.* **1.** To separate into pieces; fragment. **2.** To decay or undergo a transformation, as an atomic nucleus. —**dis·in′te·gra′tion** *n.* —**dis·in′te·gra′tive** *adj.* —**dis·in′te·gra′tor** *n.*

dis·in·ter (dĭs′ĭn-tûr′) ►*v.* To remove from a grave or tomb. —**dis′in·ter′ment** *n.*

dis·in·ter·est·ed (dĭs-ĭn′trĭ-stĭd, -ĭn′tə-rĕs′tĭd) ►*adj.* **1.** Free of bias and self-interest; impartial. **2.** *Informal* Not interested; indifferent. —**dis·in′ter·est** *n.* —**dis·in′ter·est·ed·ly** *adv.*
Usage: Many maintain that *disinterested* can legitimately be used only in its sense of "unbiased or impartial." The use meaning "uninterested" is often considered a mistake.

dis·join (dĭs-join′) ►*v.* To separate.

dis·joint (dĭs-joint′) ►*v.* **1.** To take or come apart at the joints. **2.** To separate or disconnect; disjoin.

dis·joint·ed (dĭs-join′tĭd) ►*adj.* **1.** Separated at the joints. **2.** Lacking order or coherence. —**dis·joint′ed·ly** *adv.* —**dis·joint′ed·ness** *n.*

disk also **disc** (dĭsk) ►*n.* **1.** A thin, flat, circular object or plate. **2.** The central part of a composite flower, such as the daisy. **3.** *Anat.* A broad cartilaginous plate lying between adjacent vertebrae. **4.** *Comp.* **a.** An optical disc, esp. a compact disc. **b.** A magnetic disk, esp. a hard disk. **5.** often **disc** A phonograph record. [< Gk. *diskos*, quoit.]

disk drive ►*n. Comp.* A device that reads data stored on a disk and writes data onto it for storage.

dis·like (dĭs-līk′) ►*v.* To regard with distaste or aversion. ►*n.* An attitude or feeling of distaste or aversion.

dis·lo·cate (dĭs′lō-kāt′, dĭs-lō′kāt′) ►*v.* **1.** To move out of the normal position, esp. to displace (a bone) from a socket or joint. **2.** To disrupt. —**dis′lo·ca′tion** *n.*

dis·lodge (dĭs-lŏj′) ►*v.* To force out of a position previously occupied. —**dis·lodge′ment, dis·lodg′ment** *n.*

dis·loy·al (dĭs-loi′əl) ►*adj.* Lacking loyalty. —**dis·loy′al·ly** *adv.* —**dis·loy′al·ty** *n.*

dis·mal (dĭz′məl) ►*adj.* Causing or showing gloom or depression; dreary. [< Med.Lat. *diēs malī*, evil days.] —**dis′mal·ly** *adv.*

dis·man·tle (dĭs-măn′tl) ►*v.* **-tled, -tling** **1.** To take apart; tear down; disassemble. **2.** To strip of furnishings or equipment. [< OFr. *desmanteler*, demolish fortifications.] —**dis·man′tle·ment** *n.*

dis·may (dĭs-mā′) ►*v.* **1.** To cause to lose enthusiasm or resolution; disillusion. See Synonyms at **discourage. 2.** To upset or distress. ►*n.* A sudden and complete loss of courage in the face of trouble or danger. [< AN *desmaiier : DE- + VLat. *exmagāre, deprive of power (EX– + Gmc. *magan, be able).]

dis·mem·ber (dĭs-mĕm′bər) ►*v.* **1.** To cut, tear, or pull off the limbs of. **2.** To divide into pieces. —**dis·mem′ber·ment** *n.*

dis·miss (dĭs-mĭs′) ►*v.* **1.** To discharge, as from employment or service. **2.** To direct or allow to leave: *dismiss students.* **3a.** To rid one's mind of; dispel. **b.** To reject or repudiate. **4.** *Law* To adjudicate (a cause of action) as insufficient to proceed further in court. [< Lat. *dīmittere, dīmiss-*, send away.] —**dis·miss′i·ble** *adj.* —**dis·miss′al** *n.*
Syns: *boot, can, discharge, fire, sack* **v.**

dis·mis·sive (dĭs-mĭs′ĭv) ►*adj.* **1.** Serving to dismiss. **2.** Showing indifference or disregard.

dis·mount (dĭs-mount′) ►*v.* **1.** To get off or down, as from a horse or vehicle. **2.** To unseat or throw off, as from a horse. **3.** To remove from a support, setting, or mounting. **4.** To disassemble (e.g., a mechanism). —**dis·mount′** *n.* —**dis·mount′a·ble** *adj.*

Dis·ney (dĭz′nē), **Walter Elias** "Walt." 1901–66. Amer. animator and film producer.

dis·o·be·di·ence (dĭs′ə-bē′dē-əns) ►*n.* Refusal or failure to obey. —**dis′o·be′di·ent** *adj.* —**dis′o·be′di·ent·ly** *adv.*

dis·o·bey (dĭs′ə-bā′) ►*v.* To fail to obey.

dis·o·blige (dĭs′ə-blīj′) ►*v.* **1.** To refuse or fail to comply with the wishes of. **2.** To inconvenience. **3.** To offend.

dis·or·der (dĭs-ôr′dər) ►*n.* **1.** A lack of order; confusion. **2.** A public disturbance. **3.** An ailment. ►*v.* To throw into disarray.

dis·or·der·ly (dĭs-ôr′dər-lē) ►*adj.* **1.** Not neat or tidy. **2.** Undisciplined; unruly. **3.** *Law* Disturbing the public peace. —**dis·or′der·li·ness** *n.*

dis·or·gan·ize (dĭs-ôr′gə-nīz′) ►*v.* To destroy the systematic arrangement of. —**dis·or′gan·i·za′tion** *n.*

dis·o·ri·ent (dĭs-ôr′ē-ĕnt′) ►*v.* To cause to lose orientation. —**dis·o′ri·en·ta′tion** *n.*

dis·own (dĭs-ōn′) ►*v.* To refuse to acknowledge or accept as one's own; repudiate.

dis·par·age (dĭ-spăr′ĭj) ►*v.* **-aged, -ag·ing** To speak of in a slighting way; belittle. [< OFr. *desparager*, degrade.] —**dis·par′age·ment** *n.* —**dis·par′ag·ing·ly** *adv.*

dis·pa·rate (dĭs′pər-ĭt, dĭ-spăr′ĭt) ►*adj.* Entirely distinct or different. [Lat. *disparātus*, p.part. of *disparāre*, to separate.] —**dis′pa·rate·ly** *adv.* —**dis·par′i·ty** (dĭ-spăr′ĭ-tē) *n.*

dis·pas·sion·ate (dĭs-păsh′ə-nĭt) ►*adj.* Not influenced by emotion or bias. —**dis·pas′sion** *n.* —**dis·pas′sion·ate·ly** *adv.*

dis·patch (dĭ-spăch′) ►*v.* **1.** To send to a specific destination. See Synonyms at **send. 2.** To perform promptly. **3.** To kill. ►*n.* **1.** The act of dispatching. **2.** Speed in performance or movement. See Synonyms at **haste. 3.** An important message. **4.** (*also* dĭs′păch′) A news item sent to a news organization, as by a correspondent. [Sp. *despachar* or Ital. *dispacciare*.] —**dis·patch′er** *n.*

dis·pel (dĭ-spĕl′) ►*v.* **-pelled, -pel·ling** To rid of by or as if by scattering: *dispel doubts.* [< Lat. *dispellere*, drive away.]

dis·pens·a·ble (dĭ-spĕn′sə-bəl) ►*adj.* Capable of being dispensed with.

dis·pen·sa·ry (dĭ-spĕn′sə-rē) ►*n., pl.* **-ries** A place where medical supplies, preparations, and treatments are dispensed.

dis·pen·sa·tion (dĭs′pən-sā′shən) ►*n.* **1a.** The act of dispensing. **b.** Something dispensed. **2.** A system for ordering or administering affairs. **3.** An official exemption or release from an obligation or rule. **4.** A religious system considered to have been divinely appointed.

dis·pense (dǐ-spěns′) ►*v.* **-pensed, -pens·ing 1a.** To deal out in portions; distribute: *a machine that dispenses candy.* **b.** To prepare and give out (medicines). **2.** To carry out or administer (e.g., laws). —*phrasal verb:* **dispense with 1.** To manage without; forgo. **2.** To get rid of. [< Lat. *dispēnsāre* < *dispendere*, weigh out.] —**dis·pens′er** *n.*

dis·perse (dǐ-spûrs′) ►*v.* **-persed, -pers·ing 1.** To break up and scatter. **2.** To disseminate or distribute. [< Lat. *dispergere.*] —**dis·pers′i·ble** *adj.* —**dis·per′sion** (-spûr′zhən, -shən), **dis·per′sal** *n.*

dis·pir·it (dǐ-spǐr′ǐt) ►*v.* To lower the spirits of; dishearten. See Synonyms at **discourage.** [DI(S)– + SPIRIT.]

dis·pir·it·ed (dǐ-spǐr′ǐ-tǐd) ►*adj.* Affected or marked by low spirits; dejected. See Synonyms at **depressed.** —**dis·pir′it·ed·ly** *adv.*

dis·place (dǐs-plās′) ►*v.* **1.** To move from the usual place or position, esp. to force to leave a place of residence: *refugees who were displaced by the war.* **2.** To take the place of; supplant. **3.** To discharge from a job, office, or position.

dis·place·ment (dǐs-plās′mənt) ►*n.* **1.** The act of displacing. **2a.** The weight or volume of a fluid displaced by a floating body. **b.** The distance from an initial position to a subsequent position assumed by a body.

displacement ton ►*n.* A unit for measuring the displacement of a ship afloat, equivalent to one long ton.

dis·play (dǐ-splā′) ►*v.* **1.** To present or hold up to view. **2.** To show (images or information) on a screen. ►*n.* **1a.** The act of displaying. **b.** Something displayed, esp. an elaborate public exhibition. **2.** *Comp.* A device that accepts video signals from a computer and gives information in a visual form, as on a screen. —*idiom:* **on display** In public view. [< Lat. *displicāre*, scatter.]

dis·please (dǐs-plēz′) ►*v.* To cause annoyance or vexation (to). —**dis·pleas′ing·ly** *adv.* —**dis·pleas′ure** (-plězh′ər) *n.*

dis·port (dǐ-spôrt′) ►*v.* To play; frolic. [< OFr. *desporter*, divert.]

dis·pos·a·ble (dǐ-spō′zə-bəl) ►*adj.* **1.** Designed to be disposed of after use: *disposable razors.* **2a.** Remaining after taxes have been deducted: *disposable income.* **b.** Free for use; available: *all disposable means.* ►*n.* An article that can be disposed of after one use. —**dis·pos′a·bil′i·ty** *n.*

dis·pos·al (dǐ-spō′zəl) ►*n.* **1.** A particular order, distribution, or placement. **2.** A method of attending to or settling matters. **3.** Transference by gift or sale. **4.** The act of throwing out or away. **5.** A device installed below a sink that grinds and flushes garbage away. **6.** The power to use something: *funds at our disposal.*

dis·pose (dǐ-spōz′) ►*v.* **-posed, -pos·ing 1.** To put into a certain frame of mind: *past experiences that disposed me to avoid taking risks.* **2.** To place in a particular order; arrange. **3.** To settle a matter. —*phrasal verb:* **dispose of** To get rid of. [< Lat. *dispōnere.*] —**dis·pos′er** *n.*

dis·po·si·tion (dǐs′pə-zǐsh′ən) ►*n.* **1.** Temperament. **2.** A tendency or inclination. **3.** Arrangement, positioning, or distribution. **4.** An act of disposing of something.

dis·pos·sess (dǐs′pə-zěs′) ►*v.* To deprive of possession of (e.g., land or property). —**dis′pos·ses′sion** *n.*

dis·praise (dǐs-prāz′) ►*v.* To disparage. ►*n.* Disapproval; reproach.

dis·pro·por·tion (dǐs′prə-pôr′shən) ►*n.* Absence of proper proportion or harmony. —**dis′pro·por′tion·al, dis′pro·por′tion·ate** (-nǐt) *adj.* —**dis′pro·por′tion·al·ly, dis′pro·por′tion·ate·ly** *adv.*

dis·prove (dǐs-prōōv′) ►*v.* To prove to be false. —**dis·prov′al** *n.*

dis·pu·ta·tion (dǐs′pyə-tā′shən) ►*n.* **1.** An argument or debate. **2.** An oral defense of a thesis done as an academic exercise.

dis·pu·ta·tious (dǐs′pyə-tā′shəs) ►*adj.* Inclined to dispute. See Synonyms at **argumentative.** —**dis′pu·ta′tious·ly** *adv.*

dis·pute (dǐ-spyōōt′) ►*v.* **-put·ed, -put·ing 1.** To argue (about); debate: *an issue that was disputed at the convention.* **2.** To question the truth or validity of; doubt. **3a.** To strive to gain or win: *The two countries disputed the region.* **b.** To strive against: *disputed the advance of the marauders.* ►*n.* **1.** An argument; debate. **2.** A quarrel. [< Lat. *disputāre*, examine.] —**dis·put′a·ble** *adj.* —**dis·put′a·bly** *adv.* —**dis·pu′tant, dis·put′er** *n.*

dis·qual·i·fy (dǐs-kwŏl′ə-fī′) ►*v.* To declare or render unqualified or ineligible. —**dis·qual′i·fi·ca′tion** *n.*

dis·qui·et (dǐs-kwī′ǐt) ►*v.* To trouble; bother. ►*n.* Disquietude.

dis·qui·e·tude (dǐs-kwī′ǐ-tōōd′, -tyōōd′) ►*n.* A condition of worried unease; anxiety.

dis·qui·si·tion (dǐs′kwǐ-zǐsh′ən) ►*n.* A formal discourse or treatise. [< Lat. *disquīrere, disquīsīt-*, investigate.]

Dis·rae·li (dǐz-rā′lē), **Benjamin** First Earl of Beaconsfield. 1804–81. British prime minister (1868 and 1874–80) and novelist.

dis·re·gard (dǐs′rǐ-gärd′) ►*v.* To pay no attention to; ignore. ►*n.* Lack of thoughtful attention or due regard.

dis·re·pair (dǐs′rǐ-pâr′) ►*n.* The condition of being in need of repair.

dis·rep·u·ta·ble (dǐs-rěp′yə-tə-bəl) ►*adj.* Lacking respectability, as in character or behavior. —**dis·rep′u·ta·bly** *adv.*

dis·re·pute (dǐs′rǐ-pyōōt′) ►*n.* Damage to or loss of reputation; disgrace.

dis·re·spect (dǐs′rǐ-spěkt′) ►*n.* Lack of respect; rudeness. —**dis′re·spect′** *v.* —**dis′re·spect′ful** *adj.* —**dis′re·spect′ful·ly** *adv.*

dis·robe (dǐs-rōb′) ►*v.* To undress.

dis·rupt (dǐs-rǔpt′) ►*v.* **1.** To throw into confusion. **2.** To break apart or impair the functionality of: *radiation that disrupts DNA.* [Lat. *disrumpere, disrupt-*, break apart.] —**dis·rupt′er, dis·rup′tor** *n.* —**dis·rup′tion** *n.* —**dis·rup′tive** *adj.*

dis·sat·is·fac·tion (dǐs-sǎt′ǐs-fǎk′shən) ►*n.* **1.** Discontent. **2.** A cause of discontent. —**dis·sat′is·fac′to·ry** (-tə-rē) *adj.*

dis·sat·is·fy (dǐs-sǎt′ǐs-fī′) ►*v.* To fail to satisfy.

dis·sect (dǐ-sěkt′, dī-, dī′sěkt′) ►*v.* **1.** To cut apart or separate (tissue), esp. for anatomical study. **2.** To analyze or criticize in minute detail. See Synonyms at **analyze.** [Lat. *dissecāre, dissect-*, cut apart.] —**dis·sec′tion** *n.*

dis·sem·ble (dĭ-sĕm′bəl) ►v. **-bled, -bling** To disguise or conceal one's real nature, motives, or feelings behind a false appearance. See Synonyms at **disguise.** [< OFr. *dessembler*, be different.] —**dis·sem′bler** n.

dis·sem·i·nate (dĭ-sĕm′ə-nāt′) ►v. **-nat·ed, -nat·ing** To spread or become spread; diffuse. [Lat. *dissēmināre.*] —**dis·sem′i·na′tion** n. —**dis·sem′i·na′tor** n.

dis·sen·sion (dĭ-sĕn′shən) ►n. Difference of opinion. [< Lat. *dissentīre,* to dissent.]

dis·sent (dĭ-sĕnt′) ►v. To disagree with a prevailing position. ►n. **1.** Difference of opinion. **2.** The refusal to conform to the authority of an established church. [< Lat. *dissentīre.*] —**dis·sent′er** n. —**dis·sent′ing** adj.

dis·ser·ta·tion (dĭs′ər-tā′shən) ►n. A treatise, esp. one written as a doctoral thesis. [< Lat. *dissertāre,* to deal with.]

dis·ser·vice (dĭs-sûr′vĭs) ►n. A harmful action, esp. one undertaken unknowingly or with good intentions.

dis·si·dent (dĭs′ĭ-dənt) ►adj. Disagreeing, as in opinion or belief. ►n. One who disagrees; dissenter. [< *dissidēre,* disagree : *dis-,* apart + *sedēre,* sit.] —**dis′si·dence** n.

dis·sim·i·lar (dĭ-sĭm′ə-lər) ►adj. Different or distinct; unlike. —**dis·sim′i·lar′i·ty** (-lăr′ĭ-tē) n. —**dis·sim′i·lar·ly** adv.

dis·si·mil·i·tude (dĭs′ə-mĭl′ĭ-tŏŏd′, -tyŏŏd′) ►n. Lack of resemblance.

dis·sim·u·late (dĭ-sĭm′yə-lāt′) ►v. **-lat·ed, -lat·ing** To disguise under a feigned appearance; dissemble. See Synonyms at **disguise.** [< Lat. *dissimulāre.*] —**dis·sim′u·la′tion** n. —**dis·sim′u·la′tor** n.

dis·si·pate (dĭs′ə-pāt′) ►v. **-pat·ed, -pat·ing** **1.** To break up and drive away. **2.** To vanish or disappear. **3.** To spend wastefully; squander. See Synonyms at **waste.** **4.** To indulge in the intemperate pursuit of pleasure. [< Lat. *dissipāre.*] —**dis′si·pat′ed** adj. —**dis′si·pa′tion** n.

dis·so·ci·ate (dĭ-sō′shē-āt′, -sē-) ►v. **-at·ed, -at·ing** To separate or cause to separate. [Lat. *dissociāre.*] —**dis·so′ci·a′tion** n. —**dis·so′ci·a′tive** adj.

dis·so·lute (dĭs′ə-lŏŏt′) ►adj. Lacking in moral restraint; wanton. [< Lat. *dissolūtus,* p.part. of *dissolvere,* dissolve.] —**dis′so·lute′ly** adv.

dis·so·lu·tion (dĭs′ə-lŏŏ′shən) ►n. **1.** Decomposition into fragments; disintegration. **2.** Sensual indulgence; debauchery. **3.** Termination or extinction by dispersion. **4.** Death. **5.** Termination of a legal bond or relationship. **6.** Formal dismissal of an assembly. **7.** Reduction to a liquid form.

dis·solve (dĭ-zŏlv′) ►v. **-solved, -solv·ing 1a.** To enter or cause to pass into solution: *dissolve salt in water.* **b.** To make or become liquid; melt. **c.** To make or become less defined; blur: *The snow dissolved into puddles.* **2a.** To vanish or cause to vanish: *The sun dissolved the fog.* **b.** To break or become broken into component parts: *The company dissolved into three separate businesses.* **c.** To terminate: *dissolve a marriage.* **d.** To dismiss: *dissolve parliament.* **3.** To collapse emotionally: *dissolve into helpless laughter.* [< Lat. *dissolvere.*] —**dis·solv′a·ble** adj. —**dis·solv′er** n.

dis·so·nance (dĭs′ə-nəns) ►n. **1.** A harsh, dis-

agreeable combination of sounds; discord. **2.** *Mus.* A combination of harsh tones considered to suggest unrelieved tension. [< Lat. *dissonāre,* be dissonant.] —**dis′so·nant** adj. —**dis′so·nant·ly** adv.

dis·suade (dĭ-swād′) ►v. **-suad·ed, -suad·ing** To prevent (someone) from a purpose or course of action by persuasion: *dissuaded him from dropping out of school.* [Lat. *dissuādēre* : DIS– + *suādēre,* advise.] —**dis·sua′sion** n. —**dis·sua′sive** adj.

dist. ►abbr. **1.** distance **2.** district

dis·taff (dĭs′tăf′) ►n. **1.** A staff that holds on its cleft end the flax, wool, or tow in spinning. **2.** Women collectively. ►adj. **1.** Of or relating to females. **2.** Relating to or being the maternal branch of a family. [< OE *distæf.*]

dis·tal (dĭs′təl) ►adj. **1.** Anatomically located far from the point of attachment, as a bone. **2.** Situated farthest from the middle front of the jaw, as a tooth. [< DISTANT.]

dis·tance (dĭs′təns) ►n. **1.** Separation in space or time. **2.** The interval separating any two specified points in space or instants in time. **3.** *Math.* The length of a line segment joining two points. **4a.** The extent of space between points on a measured course. **b.** The length of a race. **5.** A point or area that is far away. **6.** The whole way: *went the distance.* **7.** Emotional reserve; aloofness. ►v. **-tanced, -tanc·ing 1.** To place at or as if at a distance. **2.** To outrun or outstrip.

dis·tant (dĭs′tənt) ►adj. **1a.** Separate or apart in space or time. **b.** Far removed; remote. **2.** Coming from, located at, or going to a distance. **3.** Far apart in relationship: *a distant cousin.* **4.** Aloof or chilly. [< Lat. *dīstāre,* be remote : *dī-, dis-,* apart + *stāre,* stand.] —**dis′tant·ly** adv.

dis·taste (dĭs-tāst′) ►n. Dislike. —**dis·taste′ful** adj. —**dis·taste′ful·ly** adv.

Dist. Atty. ►abbr. district attorney

dis·tem·per (dĭs-tĕm′pər) ►n. An infectious, often fatal viral disease occurring in dogs, cats, and certain other mammals.

dis·tend (dĭ-stĕnd′) ►v. To swell or cause to swell. [< Lat. *distendere.*] —**dis·ten′si·ble** adj. —**dis·ten′tion, dis·ten′sion** n.

dis·till also **dis·til** (dĭ-stĭl′) ►v. **-tilled, -till·ing 1.** To subject to or derive from distillation. **2.** To separate from. **3.** To exude in drops. [< Lat. *dēstillāre,* drip down.] —**dis·till′er** n. —**dis·till′er·y** n.

dis·til·late (dĭs′tə-lāt′, -lĭt, dĭ-stĭl′ĭt) ►n. A liquid condensed from vapor in distillation.

dis·til·la·tion (dĭs′tə-lā′shən) ►n. The evaporation of a liquid and subsequent condensation and collection of the vapors as a means of purification or of extraction of volatile components.

dis·tinct (dĭ-stĭngkt′) ►adj. **1.** Distinguishable from all others. **2.** Easily perceived by the senses. **3.** Clearly defined; unquestionable. [< Lat. *dīstīnctus,* p.part. of *dīstinguere,* distinguish.] —**dis·tinct′ly** adv. —**dis·tinct′ness** n. **Syns:** *discrete, separate, several* **adj.**

dis·tinc·tion (dĭ-stĭngk′shən) ►n. **1a.** The act of distinguishing; differentiation. **b.** A difference. **2.** A distinguishing factor or characteristic. **3a.** Excellence or eminence. **b.** Honor: *graduated with distinction.*

dis·tinc·tive (dĭ-stĭngk′tĭv) ►adj. Serving to distinguish or set apart from others. —**dis·tinc′-**

tive·ly *adv.* —**dis·tinc′tive·ness** *n.*

dis·tin·guish (dĭ-stĭng′gwĭsh) ►*v.* **1a.** To recognize or describe as being distinct. **b.** To perceive distinctly; discern. **2.** To judge wisely: *distinguish right from wrong.* **3.** To set apart. **4.** To make eminent. [< Lat. *dīstinguere.*] —**dis·tin′guish·a·ble** *adj.* —**dis·tin′guish·a·bly** *adv.*

dis·tin·guished (dĭ-stĭng′gwĭsht) ►*adj.* **1.** Characterized by excellence or distinction; eminent: *distinguished scientists.* **2.** Dignified in conduct or appearance: *a distinguished gentleman.*

dis·tort (dĭ-stôrt′) ►*v.* **1.** To twist out of a proper or natural shape or position. **2.** To give a false or misleading account of; misrepresent. **3.** *Electron.* To disrupt (a signal or waveform) in a way that adversely affects its quality. [Lat. *distorquēre, distort-.*] —**dis·tor′tion** *n.*

dis·tract (dĭ-străkt′) ►*v.* **1.** To sidetrack; divert. **2.** To upset emotionally; unsettle. [ME *distracten* < Lat. *distrahere, distract-*, pull away.] —**dis·tract′ing·ly** *adv.* —**dis·trac′tion** *n.*

dis·traught (dĭ-strôt′) ►*adj.* Deeply agitated, as from worry or grief. [< ME *distract*, p.part. of *distracten*, DISTRACT.]

dis·tress (dĭ-strĕs′) ►*v.* **1.** To cause anxiety or suffering to. See Synonyms at **trouble. 2.** To mar or treat (e.g., an object or fabric) to give the appearance of an antique. ►*n.* **1.** Pain or suffering of mind or body. **2a.** The condition of being in need of immediate assistance: *a motorist in distress.* **b.** Suffering caused by poverty. [< Lat. *dīstrictus*, p.part. of *dīstringere*, draw tight.] —**dis·tress′ful** *adj.* —**dis·tress′ing·ly** *adv.*

dis·trib·ute (dĭ-strĭb′yo͞ot) ►*v.* -**ut·ed,** -**ut·ing 1.** To divide and give out in portions. **2.** To market, esp. as a wholesaler. **3.** To deliver or hand out. **4.** To spread or diffuse over an area. **5.** To classify. [< Lat. *distribuere.*] —**dis′tri·bu′tion** *n.* —**dis·trib′u·tive** *adj.*

dis·trib·u·tor (dĭ-strĭb′yə-tər) ►*n.* **1.** One that distributes, esp. a device that applies electric current to the spark plugs of an engine. **2.** One that markets goods, esp. a wholesaler.

dis·trict (dĭs′trĭkt) ►*n.* **1.** A division of an area, as for administrative purposes. **2.** A region having a distinguishing feature. ►*v.* To divide into districts. [< Med.Lat. *dīstrictus* < Lat. *dīstringere*, hinder.]

district attorney ►*n.* A public officer who prosecutes cases on behalf of a state, usu. within a defined locale.

District of Columbia A federal district of the E US on the Potomac R. between VA and MD; coextensive with the city of Washington.

dis·trust (dĭs-trŭst′) ►*n.* Lack of trust or confidence; suspicion. ►*v.* To have no confidence in. —**dis·trust′ful** *adj.* —**dis·trust′ful·ly** *adv.* —**dis·trust′ful·ness** *n.*

dis·turb (dĭ-stûrb′) ►*v.* **1.** To destroy the tranquility, order, or settled state of. **2.** To trouble emotionally or mentally. **3.** To intrude on or interfere with; interrupt. [< Lat. *disturbāre.*] —**dis·tur′bance** *n.* —**dis·turb′ing·ly** *adv.*

dis·turbed (dĭ-stûrbd′) ►*adj.* **1.** Unsettled or broken up: *disturbed soil.* **2.** Being or resulting from being emotionally or mentally troubled.

dis·u·nite (dĭs′yo͞o-nīt′) ►*v.* -**nit·ed,** -**nit·ing** To separate; divide.

dis·u·ni·ty (dĭs-yo͞o′nĭ-tē) ►*n., pl.* -**ties** Lack of unity; dissension.

dis·use (dĭs-yo͞os′) ►*n.* The state of not being used or no longer being in use.

ditch (dĭch) ►*n.* A trench dug in the ground. ►*v.* **1.** To dig or make a ditch. **2.** To drive (a vehicle) into a ditch. **3.** *Slang* **a.** To get rid of; discard: *ditched the old sofa.* **b.** To skip (class or school). [< OE *dīc.*]

dith·er (dĭth′ər) ►*n.* Indecisive agitation. [< ME *dideren*, tremble.] —**dith′er** *v.*

dit·to (dĭt′ō) ►*n., pl.* -**tos 1.** The same as stated above or before. **2.** A duplicate or copy. **3.** A pair of small marks (") used to indicate that the word, phrase, or figure given above is to be repeated. [Ital. dial., said.]

dit·ty (dĭt′ē) ►*n., pl.* -**ties** A simple song. [< Lat. *dictātum* < p.part. of *dictāre*, DICTATE.]

di·u·ret·ic (dī′ə-rĕt′ĭk) ►*adj.* Tending to increase the discharge of urine. [< Gk. *diourētikos* < *diourein*, pass urine.] —**di′u·ret′ic** *n.*

di·ur·nal (dī-ûr′nəl) ►*adj.* **1.** Of or occurring in a 24-hour period; daily. **2.** Occurring or active during the daytime. [< Lat. *diurnus.*] —**di·ur′nal·ly** *adv.*

div. ►*abbr.* **1.** dividend **2.** divorced

di·va (dē′və) ►*n., pl.* -**vas** or -**ve** (-vā) **1.** An operatic prima donna. **2.** A very successful female singer of nonoperatic music. [< Lat. *dīva*, goddess.]

di·va·gate (dī′və-gāt′, dĭv′ə-) ►*v.* -**gat·ed,** -**gat·ing** To wander or drift about. [LLat. *dīvagārī* < Lat. *vagus*, wandering.] —**di′va·ga′tion** *n.*

di·va·lent (dī-vā′lənt) ►*adj. Chem.* Having a valence of 2.

di·van (dĭ-vän′, -văn′) ►*n.* A long backless sofa; couch. [< Pers. *dīvān*, place of assembly.]

dive (dīv) ►*v.* **dived** or **dove** (dōv), **dived, div·ing 1.** To plunge, esp. headfirst, into water. **2.** To go toward the bottom of a body of water: *dive for pearls.* **3.** To fall or drop sharply and rapidly; plummet. **4.** To lunge, leap, or dash. ►*n.* **1.** The act or an instance of diving. **2.** A quick pronounced drop. **3.** A rapid or abrupt decrease: *Stock prices took a dive.* **4.** *Slang* A disreputable or run-down bar or nightclub. [< OE *dȳfan*, dip, and *dūfan*, sink.] —**div′er** *n.*

dive-bomb (dīv′bŏm′) ►*v.* To bomb from an airplane at the end of a steep dive toward the target. —**dive′-bomb′er** *n.*

di·verge (dĭ-vûrj′, dī-) ►*v.* -**verged,** -**verg·ing 1.** To extend in different directions from a common point. **2.** To differ, as in opinion: *Opinions diverged on how to deal with the crisis.* **3.** To deviate from a norm. See Synonyms at **swerve.** [Lat. *dīvergere*, bend apart.] —**di·ver′gence** *n.* —**di·ver′gent** *adj.* —**di·ver′gent·ly** *adv.*

di·vers (dī′vərz) ►*adj.* Various. [ME, DIVERSE.]

di·verse (dĭ-vûrs′, dī-, dī′vûrs′) ►*adj.* **1.** Differing one from another. **2a.** Made up of distinct characteristics or elements: *a city with a rich and diverse past.* **b.** Relating to people from different ethnicities and social backgrounds: *a diverse workforce.* [< Lat. *dīversus*, p.part. of *dīvertere*, divert.] —**di·verse′ly** *adv.* —**di·verse′ness** *n.*

di·ver·si·fy (dĭ-vûr′sə-fī′, dī-) ►*v.* -**fied,** -**fy·ing 1.** To give variety to; vary. **2.** To spread out activities or investments, esp. in business. —**di·ver′si·fi·ca′tion** *n.*

di·ver·sion (dĭ-vûr′zhən, -shən, dī-) ►*n.* **1.** The act or instance of diverting or turning aside. **2.** That which diverts. —**di·ver′sion·ar·y** *adj.*

di·ver·si·ty (dĭ-vûr′sĭ-tē, dī-) ►*n., pl.* **-ties 1a.** The quality or condition of being diverse. **b.** The condition of having or including people from different ethnicities and social backgrounds: *diversity on campus.* **2.** A variety or assortment: *a panel that sought out a diversity of opinions.*

di·vert (dĭ-vûrt′, dī-) ►*v.* **1.** To turn aside from a course or direction. **2.** To distract. **3.** To amuse or entertain. [< Lat. *dīvertere.*]

di·ver·ti·men·to (dĭ-vĕr′tə-mĕn′tō) ►*n., pl.* **-tos** also **-ti** (-tē) A chiefly 18th-cent. form of instrumental chamber music having several short movements. [Ital.]

di·vest (dĭ-vĕst′, dī-) ►*v.* **1.** To strip, as of clothes. **2.** To deprive, as of rights; dispossess. [< OFr. *desvestir.*] **—di·vest′ment** *n.*

di·ves·ti·ture (dĭ-vĕs′tĭ-chər, -chŏŏr′, dī-) ►*n.* **1.** An act of divesting. **2.** The sale, liquidation, or spinoff of a corporate division or subsidiary.

di·vide (dĭ-vīd′) ►*v.* **-vid·ed, -vid·ing 1.** To separate or become separated into parts, sections, or groups. **2.** To form a border or barrier between. **3.** To classify. **4.** To set at odds; disunite. **5.** To distribute among a number; apportion. **6.** *Math.* **a.** To subject to the process of division. **b.** To be an exact divisor of. **7.** To branch out, as a river. ►*n.* A watershed. [< Lat. *dīvidere.*]

div·i·dend (dĭv′ĭ-dĕnd′) ►*n.* **1.** *Math.* A quantity to be divided. **2.** A share of profits received by a stockholder. **3.** A bonus. [< Lat. *dīvidere,* divide.]

di·vid·er (dĭ-vī′dər) ►*n.* **1.** One that divides, esp. a partition. **2.** A compasslike device used for dividing lines and transferring measurements.

div·i·na·tion (dĭv′ə-nā′shən) ►*n.* **1.** The art or act of foretelling future events or revealing occult knowledge by means of augury or alleged supernatural agency. **2.** An inspired guess or presentiment.

di·vine (dĭ-vīn′) ►*adj.* **-vin·er, -vin·est 1a.** Being a deity. **b.** Of or relating to a deity. **2.** Superhuman; godlike. **3.** Supremely good; magnificent. ►*n.* **1.** A cleric. **2.** A theologian. ►*v.* **-vined, -vin·ing 1.** To foretell, esp. by divination. See Synonyms at **foretell. 2.** To guess, infer, or conjecture. [< Lat. *dīvīnus,* foreseeing, divine.] **—di·vine′ly** *adv.* **—di·vin′er** *n.*

diving board ►*n.* A flexible board from which a dive may be executed.

di·vin·ing rod (dĭ-vī′nĭng) ►*n.* A forked rod believed to indicate underground water or minerals by bending downward when held over a source.

di·vin·i·ty (dĭ-vĭn′ĭ-tē) ►*n., pl.* **-ties 1.** The state or quality of being divine. **2. the Divinity** God. **3.** Theology.

di·vis·i·ble (dĭ-vĭz′ə-bəl) ►*adj.* Capable of being divided. **—di·vis′i·bil′i·ty** *n.*

di·vi·sion (dĭ-vĭzh′ən) ►*n.* **1.** The act or process of dividing or the state of being divided. **2.** *Math.* The operation of determining how many times one quantity is contained in another. **3.** Something that serves to divide or separate. **4.** One of the parts, sections, or groups into which something is divided. **5.** A self-contained military unit smaller than a corps. **6.** Disagreement; disunion. [< Lat. *dīvidere, dīvīs-,* divide.] **—di·vi′sion·al** *adj.*

di·vi·sive (dĭ-vī′sĭv) ►*adj.* Creating dissension or discord. **—di·vi′sive·ly** *adv.* **—di·vi′sive·ness** *n.*

di·vi·sor (dĭ-vī′zər) ►*n.* The quantity by which another, the dividend, is divided.

di·vorce (dĭ-vôrs′) ►*n.* **1a.** The legal dissolution of a marriage. **b.** An official document establishing such a dissolution. **2.** A complete severance. ►*v.* **-vorced, -vorc·ing 1.** To dissolve the marriage bond between. **2.** To separate or disunite. [< Lat. *dīvortium* < *dīvertere,* divert.]

di·vor·cé (dĭ-vôr-sā′, -sē′) ►*n.* A divorced man. [Fr.]

di·vor·cée (dĭ-vôr-sā′, -sē′) ►*n.* A divorced woman. [Fr.]

div·ot (dĭv′ət) ►*n.* A piece of turf torn up by a golf club in striking a ball. [Sc., a turf.]

di·vulge (dĭ-vŭlj′) ►*v.* **-vulged, -vulg·ing** To make known (something secret). [< Lat. *dīvulgāre,* publish.] **—di·vul′gence** *n.*

div·vy (dĭv′ē) ►*v.* **-vied, -vy·ing** *Slang* To divide: *divvied up the loot.* [< DIVIDEND.]

Dix (dĭks), **Dorothea Lynde** 1802–87. Amer. reformer and educator.

Dorothea Dix
1868 portrait

Dix·ie (dĭk′sē) A region of the SE US, usu. comprising the states that joined the Confederacy.

Dix·ie·land (dĭk′sē-lănd′) ►*n.* An instrumental jazz style usu. performed by combos and featuring improvisation.

DIY ►*abbr.* do-it-yourself

di·zy·got·ic (dī′zī-gŏt′ĭk) ►*adj.* Derived from two separately fertilized eggs. Used esp. of fraternal twins.

diz·zy (dĭz′ē) ►*adj.* **-zi·er, -zi·est 1.** Having a whirling sensation. **2.** Bewildered or confused. **3.** *Slang* Scatterbrained or silly. [< OE *dysig,* foolish.] **—diz′zi·ly** *adv.* **—diz′zi·ness** *n.* **—diz′zy** *v.*

DJ ►*abbr.* **1.** disc jockey **2.** district judge **3.** *Lat.* Doctor Juris (Doctor of Law)

Dja·kar·ta (jə-kär′tə) See **Jakarta.**

Dji·bou·ti (jĭ-bōō′tē) **1.** A country of E Africa on the Gulf of Aden. **2.** The capital of Djibouti, in the SE part on an inlet of the Gulf of Aden.

DMD ►*abbr. Lat.* Dentariae Medicinae Doctor (Doctor of Dental Medicine)

DMV ►*abbr.* Department of Motor Vehicles

DMZ ►*abbr.* demilitarized zone

DNA (dē′ĕn-ā′) ►*n.* A nucleic acid that carries the genetic information in cells and some viruses, consisting of two long chains of nucleotides twisted into a double helix and joined by hydrogen bonds. [D(EOXYRIBO)N(UCLEIC) A(CID).]

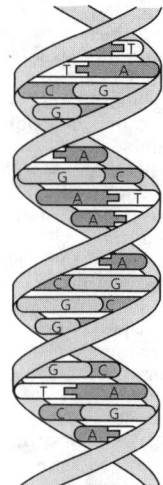

DNA
A. adenine
T. thymine
C. cytosine
G. guanine

Dnie·per (nē′pər) A river rising in W Russia and flowing about 2,285 km (1,420 mi) through Belarus and Ukraine to the Black Sea.

Dnies·ter (nē′stər) A river rising in W Ukraine and flowing about 1,365 km (850 mi) to the Black Sea near Odessa.

DNR ▸*abbr.* **1.** Department of Natural Resources **2.** do not resuscitate

do¹ (dōō) ▸*v.* **did** (dĭd), **done** (dŭn), **do·ing, does** (dŭz) **1.** To perform or execute: *do a somersault.* **2.** To fulfill; complete: *do one's duty.* **3.** To produce: *do a comedy show.* **4.** To bring about; effect: *do no harm.* **5.** To render: *do justice to both sides.* **6.** To put forth; exert: *Do the best you can.* **7.** To prepare, as by cleaning or washing: *did the dishes after dinner.* **8.** To work at: *What do you do?* **9.** *Informal* **a.** To travel (a specified distance): *did 100 miles before sunset.* **b.** To go (a specified rate): *did 80 mph on the highway.* **10a.** To meet the needs of sufficiently; suit. **b.** To be adequate: *That'll do.* **11.** To set or style (the hair). **12.** *Informal* To serve (a prison term). **13.** *Slang* To cheat; swindle: *did her out of an inheritance.* **14.** To behave; act: *Do as I say.* **15.** To get along; fare: *doing well.* **16.** Used as a substitute for an antecedent verb: *worked as hard as everyone else did.* —*aux.* **1.** Used in questions, negative statements, and inverted phrases: *Do you understand? I did not sleep well. Little did we know.* **2.** Used for emphasis: *I do want to be sure.* ▸*n., pl.* **do's** or **dos 1.** A statement of what should be done: *a list of the do's and don'ts.* **2.** *Informal* A party. **3.** *Informal* A hairdo. —*phrasal verbs:* **do by** To behave toward: *did well by his aged parents.* **do in** *Slang* **1.** To tire completely; exhaust. **2.** To kill. **do up** To adorn or dress lavishly. —*idiom:* **do away with** To make an end of; eliminate. [< OE *dōn.*]

do² (dō) ▸*n. Mus.* The 1st tone of the diatonic scale. [Ital.]

DOA ▸*abbr.* dead on arrival

do·a·ble (dōō′ə-bəl) ▸*adj.* Possible to do.

DOB ▸*abbr.* date of birth

Do·ber·man pin·scher (dō′bər-mən pĭn′shər) ▸*n.* A fairly large dog originating in Germany and having a smooth short-haired coat. [Ger. *Dobermann* (after Ludwig *Dobermann*) + *Pinscher,* terrier.]

do·bra (dō′brə) ▸*n.* See table at **currency.** [Port.]

doc·ile (dŏs′əl, -īl′) ▸*adj.* Easily managed or taught; tractable. [Lat. *docilis* < *docēre,* teach.] —**do·cil′i·ty** (dŏ-sĭl′ĭ-tē, dō-) *n.*

dock¹ (dŏk) ▸*n.* **1.** A pier or wharf. **2.** often **docks** A group of piers on a commercial waterfront. **3.** The area of water between two piers or alongside a pier that receives a ship. **4.** A loading platform for trucks or trains. ▸*v.* **1.** To maneuver into or next to a dock. **2.** To couple (two or more spacecraft) in space. [< MDu. *doc.*]

dock² (dŏk) ▸*v.* **1.** To clip short or cut off (e.g., an animal's tail). **2.** To withhold or deduct a part from (one's salary or wages). [ME *dokken.*]

dock³ (dŏk) ▸*n.* An enclosed place where the defendant stands or sits in a court of law. [Obsolete Flem. *docke,* cage.]

dock⁴ (dŏk) ▸*n.* See **sorrel¹.** [< OE *docce.*]

dock·age (dŏk′ĭj) ▸*n.* **1.** A charge for docking privileges. **2.** Facilities for docking vessels.

dock·et (dŏk′ĭt) ▸*n.* **1a.** A calendar of the cases awaiting action in a court. **b.** A brief entry of the court proceedings in a legal case. **c.** The book containing such entries. **2.** A list of things to be done; agenda. **3.** A label affixed to a package listing contents or directions. ▸*v.* To enter in a court calendar. [ME *doggett,* summary, digest.]

dock·hand (dŏk′hănd′) ▸*n.* A dockworker.

dock·work·er (dŏk′wûr′kər) ▸*n.* A worker who loads and unloads ships.

dock·yard (dŏk′yärd′) ▸*n.* A shipyard.

doc·tor (dŏk′tər) ▸*n.* **1.** A person who has trained at a school of medicine, chiropractic, optometry, podiatry, dentistry, or veterinary medicine and is licensed to practice. **2.** One holding the highest academic degree awarded by a college or university. ▸*v.* **1.** *Informal* To give medical treatment to. **2.** To repair, esp. in a makeshift manner. **3.** To falsify or change: *doctored the evidence.* **4.** To add ingredients to, esp. to improve or conceal taste or appearance. [< Lat., teacher < *docēre,* teach.] —**doc′tor·al** *adj.*

doc·tor·ate (dŏk′tər-ĭt) ▸*n.* The degree or status of an academic doctor.

doc·tri·naire (dŏk′trə-nâr′) ▸*adj.* Marked by inflexible attachment to a doctrine or theory without regard to its practicality. [Fr.] —**doc′-tri·nair′ism** *n.*

doc·trine (dŏk′trĭn) ▸*n.* **1.** A body of principles presented for acceptance or belief, as by a religious, political, or philosophic group. **2.** A statement of official government policy, esp. in foreign affairs. [< Lat. *doctrīna,* teaching.] —**doc′tri·nal** (dŏk′trə-nəl, dŏk-trī′-) *adj.*

doc·u·dra·ma (dŏk′yə-drä′mə, -drăm′ə) ▸*n.* A television or movie dramatization based on fact. [DOCU(MENTARY) + DRAMA.]

doc·u·ment (dŏk′yə-mənt) ▸*n.* **1.** A paper that provides evidence or information. **2.** Something (e.g., a photograph) that contains information. **3.** *Comp.* A computer file containing data for use by an application such as a word processor. ►*v.* (-měnt′) To support (a claim) with evidence. [< Lat. *documentum,* example < *docēre,* teach.] —**doc′u·men·ta′tion** *n.*

doc·u·men·ta·ry (dŏk′yə-měn′tə-rē) ►*n., pl.* **-ries** A work, such as a film or television program, presenting factual information, as by means of interviews or new footage. ►*adj.* **1.** Of or based on documents. **2.** Of or being a documentary.

dod·der (dŏd′ər) ►*v.* To shake or tremble, as from old age. [ME *daderen.*]

do·dec·a·gon (dō-děk′ə-gŏn′) ►*n.* A polygon having 12 sides. [Gk. *dōdeka,* twelve + –GON.]

do·dec·a·he·dron (dō′děk-ə-hē′drən) ►*n., pl.* **-drons** or **-dra** (-drə) A polyhedron having 12 faces. [Gk. *dōdeka,* twelve + –HEDRON.]

dodge (dŏj) ►*v.* **dodged, dodg·ing 1.** To avoid by moving quickly aside. **2.** To evade by cunning or deceit. **3.** To move aside by twisting suddenly. ►*n.* **1.** The act of dodging. **2.** A cunning act intended to evade or trick. [?] —**dodg′er** *n.*

Dodg·son (dŏj′sən), **Charles Lutwidge** Lewis Carroll. 1832–98. British writer.

do·do (dō′dō) ►*n., pl.* **-does** or **-dos 1.** A large flightless bird extinct since the 1600s. **2.** *Informal* **a.** One who is hopelessly passé. **b.** A stupid person. [Port. *dodó.*]

Do·do·ma (dō′də-mä′, -dō-) The official capital of Tanzania, in the central part.

doe (dō) ►*n., pl.* **doe** or **does** The adult female of some animals, such as the deer. [< OE *dā.*]

do·er (dōō′ər) ►*n.* One who does something, esp. an active, energetic person.

does (dŭz) ►*v.* 3rd pers. sing. pr.t. of **do**[1].

doe·skin (dō′skĭn′) ►*n.* **1.** Soft leather made from the skin of a doe, lamb, or goat. **2.** A fine, soft, smooth woolen fabric.

does·n't (dŭz′ənt) Does not.

doff (dôf, dŏf) ►*v.* **1.** To take off: *doff one's clothes.* **2.** To tip or lift (one's hat) in salutation. [< ME *don off,* do off.]

dog (dôg, dŏg) ►*n.* **1.** A domesticated canine mammal of various breeds that are kept as pets or used for hunting, herding, drawing sleds, or other tasks. **2.** Any of various other canines, such as the dingo. **3.** A male canine animal. **4.** *Informal* A person: *a lucky dog.* **5.** A contemptible person. **6.** An inferior product or creation. **7. dogs** *Slang* The feet. **8.** *Slang* A hot dog. ►*v.* **dogged, dog·ging** To track or trail persistently. —*idiom:* **go to the dogs** To go to ruin. [< OE *docga.*]

dog·catch·er (dôg′kăch′ər, dŏg′-) ►*n.* An official charged with impounding stray dogs.

doge (dōj) ►*n.* The elected chief magistrate of the former republics of Venice and Genoa. [Ital. dial. < Lat. *dux,* leader.]

dog-ear (dôg′îr′, dŏg′-) ►*n.* A turned-down corner of a page in a book. —**dog′-ear′** *v.* —**dog′-eared′** *adj.*

dog-eat-dog (dôg′ět-dôg′, dŏg′ět-dŏg′) ►*adj.* Ruthlessly acquisitive or competitive.

dog·fight (dôg′fĭt′, dŏg′-) ►*n.* **1.** A fight between dogs. **2.** An aerial battle between fighter planes.

dog·fish (dôg′fĭsh′, dŏg′-) ►*n.* Any of various small sharks.

dog·ged (dô′gĭd, dŏg′ĭd) ►*adj.* Stubbornly

persevering; tenacious. —**dog′ged·ly** *adv.* —**dog′ged·ness** *n.*

dog·ger·el (dô′gər-əl, dŏg′ər-) ►*n.* Clumsy verse, often irregular in form and humorous in effect. [< ME, worthless.]

dog·gy or **dog·gie** (dô′gē, dŏg′ē) ►*n., pl.* **-gies** A dog, esp. a small one.

dog·house (dôg′hous′, dŏg′-) ►*n.* A shelter for a dog. —*idiom:* **in the doghouse** *Slang* In disfavor or trouble.

do·gie also **do·gy** (dō′gē) ►*n., pl.* **-gies** *Regional* A stray or motherless calf. [?]

dog·leg (dôg′lěg′, dŏg′-) ►*n.* A sharp bend or turn. —**dog′leg′** *v.*

dog·ma (dôg′mə, dŏg′-) ►*n., pl.* **-mas** or **-ma·ta** (-mə-tə) **1.** A doctrine or body of doctrines set forth as authoritative by a religion. **2.** A doctrine or principle considered to be authoritative. [< Gk., opinion < *dokein,* seem.]

dog·mat·ic (dôg-măt′ĭk, dŏg-) ►*adj.* Marked by an authoritative, arrogant assertion of unproved principles. —**dog·mat′i·cal·ly** *adv.* —**dog′ma·tism′** *n.* —**dog′ma·tist** *n.*

do-good·er (dōō′gŏŏd′ər) ►*n.* A naive idealist who supports philanthropic or humanitarian causes.

dog paddle ►*n.* A swimming stroke in which the body is prone, the head is held out of the water and the limbs remain submerged while paddling alternately.

dog tag ►*n.* **1.** An identification disk attached to a dog's collar. **2.** A metal identification tag worn around the neck by members of the armed forces.

dog·trot (dôg′trŏt′, dŏg′-) ►*n.* A steady trot like that of a dog. —**dog′trot′** *v.*

dog·wood (dôg′wŏŏd′, dŏg′-) ►*n.* A tree with small greenish flowers surrounded by four large white or pink petallike bracts.

Do·ha (dō′hə, -hä) The capital of Qatar, on the Persian Gulf.

doi·ly (doi′lē) ►*n., pl.* **-lies** A small ornamental mat, usu. of lace or linen. [After *Doily* or *Doyly,* 18th-century London draper.]

do·ings (dōō′ĭngz) ►*pl.n.* Ongoing activities.

do-it-your·self (dōō′ĭt-yər-sělf′) ►*adj.* Relating to work done by an amateur or as a hobby. —**do′-it-your·self′er** *n.*

dol·drums (dōl′drəmz′, dôl′-, dŏl′-) ►*pl.n.* (takes sing. or pl. v.) **1a.** A period of stagnation or slump. **b.** A period of depression or unhappy listlessness. **2.** An ocean region near the equator, marked by calms. [< obsolete *doldrum,* dullard.]

dole (dōl) ►*n.* **1.** Government welfare or relief. **2.** Charitable dispensation of goods, esp. money, food, or clothing. **3.** A share of such goods. ►*v.* **doled, dol·ing** To distribute, esp. sparingly. [< OE *dāl,* portion.]

dole·ful (dōl′fəl) ►*adj.* Filled with grief; mournful. [< Lat. *dolus,* grief.] —**dole′ful·ly** *adv.* —**dole′ful·ness** *n.*

doll (dŏl) ►*n.* **1.** A figure in the shape of a human, esp. such a figure used as a toy. **2.** *Slang* **a.** An attractive person. **b.** A woman. **c.** A helpful person. [< *Doll,* nickname for *Dorothy.*]

dol·lar (dŏl′ər) ►*n.* See table at **currency.** [< LGer. *Daler,* a silver coin.]

dol·lop (dŏl′əp) ►*n.* A lump or portion, as of ice cream. [Perh. of Scand. orig.]

dol·ly (dŏl′ē) ►*n., pl.* **-lies 1.** *Informal* A doll. **2.**

A low wheeled platform used for transporting heavy loads. **3.** A wheeled apparatus used to transport a movie or television camera.

dol·men (dōl′mən, dŏl′-) ►*n.* See **portal tomb.** [Fr. < Breton.]

dol·o·mite (dō′lə-mīt′, dŏl′ə-) ►*n.* A magnesia-rich sedimentary rock resembling limestone. [After Déodat de *Dolomieu* (1750–1801).] —**dol′o·mit′ic** (-mĭt′ĭk) *adj.*

do·lor (dō′lər) ►*n.* Sorrow; grief. [< Lat., pain.] —**do′lor·ous** *adj.* —**do′lor·ous·ly** *adv.*

dol·phin (dŏl′fĭn) ►*n.* **1.** Any of a family of small whales having a curved dorsal fin, a beaklike snout, and a streamlined body. **2.** A dolphinfish. [< Gk. *delphis.*]

dol·phin·fish (dŏl′fĭn-fĭsh′, dôl′-) ►*n.* Either of two marine game fishes having iridescent coloring.

dolt (dōlt) ►*n.* A stupid person. [ME *dulte* < *dul,* dull.] —**dolt′ish** *adj.*

–dom ►*suff.* **1.** State; condition: *stardom.* **2a.** Domain; position; rank: *dukedom.* **b.** A group having a specified position, office, or character: *officialdom.* [< OE *-dōm.*]

do·main (dō-mān′) ►*n.* **1.** A territory over which control is exercised. **2.** A sphere of activity, concern, or function. See Synonyms at **field. 3.** A group of networked computers having a common communications address. [< Lat. *dominium,* property < *dominus,* lord.]

dome (dōm) ►*n.* **1.** A roof or vault of gen. hemispherical shape. **2.** A geodesic dome. **3.** Something resembling a dome. [< Lat. *domus* and Gk. *dōma,* house.] —**domed** *adj.*

dome
c. 685–691 AD Dome of the Rock, Jerusalem

do·mes·tic (də-měs′tĭk) ►*adj.* **1.** Of or relating to the family or household. **2.** Fond of home life and household affairs. **3.** Tame or domesticated. **4.** Of or relating to a country's internal affairs. **5.** Produced in or indigenous to a particular country. ►*n.* A household servant. [< Lat. *domesticus* < *domus,* house.] —**do·mes′ti·cal·ly** *adv.* —**do′mes·tic′i·ty** (dō′mě-stĭs′ĭ-tē) *n.*

do·mes·ti·cate (də-měs′tĭ-kāt′) ►*v.* -**cat·ed,** -**cat·ing** To adapt or make fit for domestic use or life; tame. —**do·mes′ti·ca′tion** *n.*

domestic partner ►*n.* A person other than a spouse with whom one lives and is romantically involved.

dom·i·cile (dŏm′ĭ-sīl′, -səl, dō′mĭ-) ►*n.* A legal residence; home. [< Lat. *domicilium* < *domus,* house.] —**dom′i·cile′** *v.*

dom·i·nant (dŏm′ə-nənt) ►*adj.* **1.** Exercising the most influence or control. **2.** Most abundant or conspicuous; predominant. **3.** *Genet.* Producing the same phenotypic effect whether inherited with an identical or dissimilar gene. —**dom′i·nance** *n.* —**dom′i·nant·ly** *adv.*

dom·i·nate (dŏm′ə-nāt′) ►*v.* -**nat·ed,** -**nat·ing 1.** To control, govern, or rule. **2.** To occupy a position more elevated or superior to others. [Lat. *dominārī* < *dominus,* lord.] —**dom′i·na′-tion** *n.* —**dom′i·na′tor** *n.*

dom·i·neer (dŏm′ə-nîr′) ►*v.* To rule over arrogantly; tyrannize. [Du. *domineren,* ult. < Lat. *dominārī,* DOMINATE.]

Dom·i·nic (dŏm′ə-nĭk), Saint. 1170?–1221. Spanish-born priest who founded the Dominican order of friars (1216). —**Do·min′i·can** *adj. & n.*

Dom·i·ni·ca (dŏm′ə-nē′kə, də-mĭn′ĭ-kə) An island country of the E Caribbean between Guadeloupe and Martinique. Cap. Roseau. —**Dom′i·ni′can** *adj. & n.*

Do·min·i·can Republic (də-mĭn′ĭ-kən) A country of the West Indies on the E part of the island of Hispaniola. Cap. Santo Domingo. —**Do·min′i·can** *adj. & n.*

do·min·ion (də-mĭn′yən) ►*n.* **1.** Control or exercise of control; sovereignty. **2.** A sphere of influence or control; realm. [< Lat. *dominium,* property; see DOMAIN.]

dom·i·no¹ (dŏm′ə-nō′) ►*n., pl.* -**noes** or -**nos 1.** A small rectangular block marked by zero to twelve dots. **2. dominoes** or **dominos** *(takes sing. or pl. v.)* A game played with dominoes. [Fr., prob. < *domino,* mask; see DOMINO².]

dom·i·no² (dŏm′ə-nō′) ►*n., pl.* -**noes** or -**nos** A masquerade costume consisting of a hooded robe and an eye mask. [Fr., prob. < Lat. *(benedīcāmus) dominō,* (let us praise) the Lord; see DOMAIN.]

Dom·i·no (dŏm′ə-nō′), **Fats** Antoine Domino. b. 1928. Amer. singer, pianist, and songwriter.

domino effect ►*n.* An effect produced when one event sets off a chain of similar events.

Do·mi·tian (də-mĭsh′ən) AD 51–96. Emperor of Rome (81–96) who completed the conquest of Britain.

don¹ (dŏn) ►*n.* **1. Don** A Spanish courtesy title for a man. **2.** *Chiefly Brit.* A teacher at a college of Oxford or Cambridge. **3.** The leader of an organized-crime family. [< Lat. *dominus,* lord.]

don² (dŏn) ►*v.* **donned, don·ning** To put on (clothing). [< ME *do on,* put on.]

Do·ña (dō′nyä) ►*n.* A Spanish courtesy title for a woman. [< Lat. *domina,* feminine of *dominus,* lord.]

do·nate (dō′nāt′, dō-nāt′) ►*v.* -**nat·ed,** -**nat·ing 1.** To give to a fund or cause; contribute. **2.** To provide (blood, or a body part) for transfusion or transplant. [< Lat. *dōnāre* < *dōnum,* gift.] —**do·na′tion** *n.* —**do′na·tor** *n.*

Don·a·tel·lo (dŏn′ə-tĕl′ō, dō′nä-tĕl′lō) 1386?–1466. Italian sculptor.

done (dŭn) ►*v.* P.part. of **do¹.** ►*adj.* **1.** Completely accomplished or finished. **2.** Cooked adequately. **3.** Socially acceptable.

dong (dông, dŏng) ►*n.* See table at **currency.** [Vietnamese < Chin. (Mandarin) *tóng,* copper.]

don·key (dŏng′kē, dŭng′-, dông′-) ►*n., pl.* -**keys** The domesticated ass, having long ears and a loud bray. [?]

Donne (dŭn), **John** 1572–1631. English metaphysical poet.

don·ny·brook (dŏn′ē-brŏŏk′) ►*n.* A free-for-all. See Synonyms at **brawl.** [After *Donnybrook* fair, Ireland.]

do·nor (dō′nər) ►*n.* One that contributes, gives, or donates. [< Lat. *dōnātor* < *dōnāre*, give.]

Don River A river of W Russia flowing about 1,960 km (1,220 mi) into the Sea of Azov.

don't (dōnt) Do not.

do·nut (dō′nŭt′, -nət) ►*n.* Var. of **doughnut.**

doo·dad (dōō′dăd′) ►*n. Informal* An unnamed or nameless gadget or trinket. [?]

doo·dle (dōōd′l) ►*v.* **-dled, -dling** To scribble or draw aimlessly, esp. when preoccupied. [E. dial., fritter away time.] —**doo′dle** *n.*

doo·dle·bug (dōōd′l-bŭg′) ►*n.* An antlion. [Perh. < LGer. *dudel,* fool, simpleton.]

doom (dōōm) ►*n.* **1.** Inevitable destruction or ruin. **2.** Judgment, esp. involving condemnation to a severe penalty. ►*v.* To condemn to ruination or death. [< OE *dōm,* judgment.]

doom·say·er (dōōm′sā′ər) ►*n.* One who predicts calamity at every opportunity.

dooms·day (dōōmz′dā′) ►*n.* **1.** Judgment Day. **2.** An anticipated or feared catastrophic event. [< OE *dōmes dæg.*]

door (dôr) ►*n.* **1.** A movable panel used to close off an entrance. **2.** An entrance to a room, building, or passage. [< OE *duru.*]

do-or-die (dōō′ər-dī′) ►*adj.* Requiring supreme effort to avoid dire consequences.

door·jamb (dôr′jăm′) ►*n.* Either of the two vertical pieces framing a doorway.

door·knob (dôr′nŏb′) ►*n.* A knob-shaped handle for opening and closing a door.

door·man (dôr′măn′, -mən) ►*n.* An attendant at the entrance of a building.

door·mat (dôr′măt′) ►*n.* **1.** A mat placed before a doorway for wiping the shoes. **2.** *Slang* One who submits meekly to mistreatment by others.

door prize ►*n.* A prize awarded by lottery to a ticketholder at a function.

door·step (dôr′stĕp′) ►*n.* A step leading to a door.

door·yard (dôr′yärd′) ►*n.* The yard in front of the door of a house.

doo·zy or **doo·zie** (dōō′zē) ►*n., pl.* **-zies** *Slang* Something extraordinary or bizarre. [Poss. blend of DAISY and *Duesenberg,* a luxury car.]

do·pa (dō′pə) ►*n.* An amino acid formed in the liver and converted to dopamine in the brain. [*d(ihydr)o(xy)p(henyl)a(lanine).*]

do·pa·mine (dō′pə-mēn′) ►*n.* A neurotransmitter formed in the brain, essential to the normal functioning of the central nervous system. [DOP(A) + *amine,* a nitrogen compound.]

dope (dōp) ►*n.* **1.** *Informal* **a.** A narcotic. **b.** An illicit drug, esp. marijuana. **2.** A narcotic preparation used to stimulate a racehorse. **3.** *Informal* A stupid person. **4.** *Informal* Factual information. ►*v.* **doped, dop·ing** *Informal* **1.** To add or administer a narcotic to. **2.** To administer a performance-enhancing substance to (an athlete). [Du. *doop,* sauce.] —**dop′er** *n.*

dop·ey also **dop·y** (dō′pē) ►*adj.* **-i·er, -i·est** *Slang* **1.** Dazed or lethargic, as if drugged. **2.** Stupid; foolish.

Dop·pler effect (dŏp′lər) ►*n. Phys.* A change in the observed frequency of a wave, as of sound or light, when the source and observer are either approaching or moving apart. [After Christian Johann *Doppler* (1803–53).]

Dor·ic (dôr′ĭk, dŏr′-) ►*n.* A dialect of ancient Greek. —**Dor′ic** *adj.*

Doric order ►*n. Archit.* A classical order marked by heavy fluted columns with plain, saucer-shaped capitals and no base.

dork (dôrk) ►*n. Slang* A stupid, inept, or foolish person. [?] —**dork′y** *adj.*

dorm (dôrm) ►*n. Informal* A dormitory.

dor·mant (dôr′mənt) ►*adj.* **1.** In a state resembling sleep. **2.** Latent. **3.** Temporarily inactive: *a dormant volcano.* See Synonyms at **inactive.** **4.** *Biol.* In a condition of suspended growth or development. [< Lat. *dormīre,* to sleep.] —**dor′man·cy** *n.*

dor·mer (dôr′mər) ►*n.* A small structure projecting outward from a sloping roof, often having one or more windows. [Obsolete Fr. *dormeor,* sleeping room < *dormir,* to sleep; see DORMANT.]

dor·mi·to·ry (dôr′mĭ-tôr′ē) ►*n., pl.* **-ries 1.** A residence hall, as at a school. **2.** A room providing sleeping quarters for several people. [< Lat. *dormīre,* to sleep.]

dor·mouse (dôr′mous′) ►*n.* A small squirrel-like Old World rodent. [ME.]

dor·sal (dôr′səl) ►*adj.* Of, toward, on, or near the back. [< Lat. *dorsum,* back.] —**dor′sal·ly** *adv.*

do·ry (dôr′ē) ►*n., pl.* **-ries** A small flat-bottomed boat with high sides. [?]

dose (dōs) ►*n.* A specified quantity of a therapeutic agent to be taken at one time or at stated intervals. ►*v.* **dosed, dos·ing** To give a dose to. [< Gk. *dosis* < *didonai,* give.] —**dos′age** *n.*

do·sim·e·ter (dō-sĭm′ĭ-tər) ►*n.* An instrument that measures x-rays or radiation absorbed over time.

Dos Pas·sos (dōs păs′ōs), **John Roderigo** 1896–1970. Amer. writer.

dos·si·er (dŏs′ē-ā′, dô′sē-ā′) ►*n.* A file containing detailed information about a particular person or subject. [< OFr., bundle of papers labeled on the back < *dos,* back.]

dost (dŭst) ►*v. Archaic* 2nd pers. sing. pr.t. of **do**[1].

Dos·to·yev·sky or **Dos·to·ev·ski** (dŏs′tə-yĕf′-skē, -toi-, dŭs-), **Feodor Mikhailovich** 1821–81. Russian writer. —**Dos′to·yev′ski·an** *adj.*

dot (dŏt) ►*n.* **1.** A tiny round mark made by or as if by a pointed instrument; spot. **2.** A short sound or symbol used esp. in Morse code. **3.** *Mus.* A mark after a note indicating an increase in time value by half. **4.** A period that separates strings of characters, as in e-mail addresses or URLs. ►*v.* **dot·ted, dot·ting 1.** To mark with a dot. **2.** To cover with or as if with dots. [< OE *dott,* head of a boil.]

dot·age (dō′tĭj) ►*n.* A deterioration of the mind with age; senility.

dot·ard (dō′tərd) ►*n.* A senile person. [< ME *doten,* dote.]

dot-com (dŏt′kŏm′) ►*adj.* Of or relating to business conducted on the Internet: *dot-com advertising.* ►*n.* A dot-com company. [Pronunciation of *.com,* used in company Internet addresses.]

dote (dōt) ►*v.* **dot·ed, dot·ing** To show excessive love or fondness. [ME *doten.*]

doth (dŭth) ►*v. Archaic* 3rd pers. sing. pr.t. of **do**[1].

dot·ty (dŏt′ē) ►*adj.* **-ti·er, -ti·est** Eccentric; daft; absurd. [< ME *doten,* dote.]

dou·ble (dŭb′əl) ►*adj.* **1.** Twice as much in size, strength, number, or amount. **2.** Composed of two parts: *double doors.* **3.** Twofold; dual: *a double meaning.* **4.** Designed for two: *a double bed.* ▸*n.* **1.** Something increased twofold: *asked the bartender for a double.* **2.** A duplicate; counterpart: *mistook me for my double.* **3.** An actor's understudy or stand-in. **4. doubles** *Sports* A game, such as tennis or handball, having two players on each side. **5.** *Baseball* A hit enabling the batter to reach second base. **6.** *Games* A bid doubling one's opponent's bid in bridge. ▸*v.* **-bled, -bling 1.** To make or become twice as great. **2.** To be twice as much as. **3.** To fold in two. **4.** To reverse one's direction: *doubled back on our tracks.* **5.** To serve in an additional capacity. **6.** *Baseball* To make a double. **7.** *Games* To challenge with a double in bridge. ▸*adv.* **1.** To twice the amount or extent; doubly. **2.** Two together; in pairs. **3.** In two: *bent double.* —*phrasal verb:* **double up 1.** To bend suddenly, as in pain or laughter. **2.** To share accommodations meant for one person. [< Lat. *duplus.*] —**dou′bly** *adv.*

double agent ▸*n.* A spy working simultaneously for two opposed governments.

double bass (bās) ▸*n.* The largest and lowest-pitched member of the violin family.

double blind ▸*n.* A testing procedure designed to avoid biased results by ensuring that at the time of the test neither the administrators nor the subjects know which subjects are receiving a test treatment and which belong to a control group. —**dou′ble-blind′** *adj.*

dou·ble-breast·ed (dŭb′əl-brĕs′tĭd) ▸*adj.* Fastened by lapping one edge of the front over the other: *a double-breasted jacket.*

dou·ble-click (dŭb′əl-klĭk′) ▸*v.* To press a button, as on a mouse, twice in rapid succession to activate a command.

dou·ble-cross (dŭb′əl-krôs′, -krŏs′) ▸*v.* To betray by acting in contradiction to a prior agreement. —**dou′ble-cross′** *n.*

Dou·ble·day (dŭb′əl-dā′), **Abner** 1819–93. Amer. army officer traditionally considered the inventor of baseball.

dou·ble-deal·ing (dŭb′əl-dē′lĭng) ▸*n.* Duplicity; treachery. —**dou′ble-deal′er** *n.*

dou·ble-deck·er (dŭb′əl-dĕk′ər) ▸*n.* Something, as a vehicle or sandwich, that has two decks or layers. —**dou′ble-deck′er** *adj.*

double digits ▸*pl.n.* The range of numbers or percentages between 10 and 99: *inflation in the double digits.* —**dou′ble-dig′it** *adj.*

dou·ble-en·ten·dre (dŭb′əl-än-tän′drə, dōō-blän-tän′drə) ▸*n.* A word or phrase having a double meaning, esp. when one meaning is risqué. [Obsolete Fr.]

dou·ble-head·er (dŭb′əl-hĕd′ər) ▸*n.* Two games or events held in succession on the same program, esp. in baseball.

double helix ▸*n.* The coiled structure of double-stranded DNA in which strands form a spiral configuration.

double jeopardy ▸*n.* The prosecution of a person a second time for the same offense, prohibited by the Fifth Amendment to the US Constitution.

dou·ble-joint·ed (dŭb′əl-join′tĭd) ▸*adj.* Having unusually flexible joints, esp. of the limbs or fingers.

double negative ▸*n. Gram.* A construction that employs two negatives, esp. to express a single negation.

Usage: A double negative is considered unacceptable in formal writing when it is used to convey or reinforce a negative meaning, as in *He didn't say nothing.*

double play ▸*n. Baseball* A play in which two players are put out.

dou·ble·speak (dŭb′əl-spēk′) ▸*n.* See **double talk** (sense 2).

double star ▸*n.* See **binary star.**

dou·blet (dŭb′lĭt) ▸*n.* **1.** A close-fitting jacket formerly worn by European men. **2.** One of a pair of similar things. [< OFr.]

double take ▸*n.* A delayed reaction to an unusual remark or circumstance.

double talk ▸*n.* **1.** Meaningless speech that consists of nonsense syllables mixed with intelligible words; gibberish. **2.** Deliberately ambiguous or evasive language.

dou·bloon (dŭ-blōōn′) ▸*n.* An obsolete Spanish gold coin. [Sp. *doblón.*]

doubt (dout) ▸*v.* **1.** To be uncertain or skeptical about. **2.** To distrust. ▸*n.* **1.** A lack of certainty or conviction. **2.** A lack of trust. [< Lat. *dubitāre,* waver.] —**doubt′er** *n.*

doubt·ful (dout′fəl) ▸*adj.* **1.** Subject to or causing doubt. **2.** Experiencing or showing doubt. **3.** Of uncertain outcome. —**doubt′ful·ly** *adv.* —**doubt′ful·ness** *n.*

doubt·less (dout′lĭs) ▸*adv.* **1.** Certainly. **2.** Presumably; probably. ▸*adj.* Certain; assured. —**doubt′less·ly** *adv.*

douche (dōōsh) ▸*n.* **1.** A stream of fluid or air applied to a body part or cavity. **2.** An instrument for applying a douche. [Fr., shower.] —**douche** *v.*

dough (dō) ▸*n.* **1.** A soft thick mixture of flour and other ingredients that is kneaded, shaped, and baked, esp. as bread or pastry. **2.** *Slang* Money. [< OE *dāg.*] —**dough′y** *adj.*

dough·boy (dō′boi′) ▸*n.* An American infantryman in World War I.

dough·nut also **do·nut** (dō′nŭt′, -nət) ▸*n.* A small ring-shaped cake made of rich light dough and fried in deep fat.

dough·ty (dou′tē) ▸*adj.* **-ti·er, -ti·est** Stouthearted; brave. [< OE *dohtig.*]

Doug·las (dŭg′ləs), **Stephen Arnold** 1813–1861. Amer. politician.

Douglas fir ▸*n.* A tall evergreen timber tree of NW North America. [After David *Douglas* (1798–1834).]

Doug·lass (dŭg′ləs), **Frederick** 1817–95. Amer. abolitionist.

Frederick Douglass

dour (dŏŏr, dour) ►*adj.* **-er, -est 1.** Stern; forbidding. **2.** Silently ill-humored; gloomy. [Prob. < Lat. *dūrus*, hard.] —**dour′ness** *n.*

Dou·ro (dôr′ōō, dō′rōō) A river rising in N-central Spain and flowing about 800 km (495 mi) through Portugal to the Atlantic.

douse¹ (dous) ►*v.* **doused, dous·ing 1.** To wet thoroughly; drench. **2.** To put out; extinguish. [< obsolete *douse*, strike.] —**dous′er** *n.*

douse² (douz) ►*v.* Var. of **dowse.**

dove¹ (dŭv) ►*n.* **1.** A pigeon or related bird, esp. an undomesticated species. **2.** A person who advocates peace and negotiation instead of war. [< OE *dūfe.*] —**dov′ish** *adj.*

dove² (dōv) ►*v.* P.t. of **dive.**

Do·ver (dō′vər) **1.** A town of SE England on the Strait of Dover opposite Calais, France. **2.** The capital of DE, in the central part.

Dover, Strait of A narrow channel at the E end of the English Channel between SE England and N France.

dove·tail (dŭv′tāl′) ►*n.* A fan-shaped tenon that forms a tight interlocking joint when fitted into a corresponding mortise. ►*v.* **1.** To join by means of dovetails. **2.** To combine or interlock into a unified whole.

dow·a·ger (dou′ə-jər) ►*n.* **1.** A widow with a title derived from her husband. **2.** An elderly woman of high social station. [< OFr. *douage*, dowry, ult. < Lat. *dōs*, dowry.]

dow·dy (dou′dē) ►*adj.* **-di·er, -di·est** Lacking stylishness; shabby. [< ME *doude*, unattractive woman.] —**dow′di·ness** *n.*

dow·el (dou′əl) ►*n.* A usu. round pin that fits into a corresponding hole to fasten or align two adjacent pieces. [ME *doule*, part of a wheel.] —**dow′el** *v.*

dow·er (dou′ər) ►*n.* **1.** The part of a deceased man's real estate allotted by law to his widow for her lifetime. **2.** See **dowry.** ►*v.* To give a dower to; endow. [< Med.Lat. *dōtārium*; see DOWRY.]

down¹ (doun) ►*adv.* **1a.** From a higher to a lower place: *hiked down from the peak.* **b.** Toward or on the floor or ground: *tripped and fell down.* **c.** In or to a seated or reclining position: *sat down.* **d.** In writing: *jotted notes down.* **e.** As an initial payment: *paid $100 down.* **f.** Into a secured position: *tied down.* **2a.** Southward: *flew down to Florida.* **b.** Away from a center of activity: *down on the farm.* **c.** To a specific location: *tracking a fugitive down.* **3a.** Toward a lower point on a scale: *turn down the volume.* **b.** From earlier times: *passed down a tradition.* **4.** To a concentrated form: *pared the lecture down.* **5.** Into a quiescent or inactive state: *calmed himself down; shut down the factory.* ►*adj.* **1a.** Moving or directed downward: *a down elevator.* **b.** Low or lower: *Stock prices are down.* **2.** Sick: *down with a cold.* **3.** Malfunctioning or not operating, esp. temporarily: *The computer is down.* **4.** Low in spirits; depressed: *feeling down today.* **5.** Learned or known perfectly: *had algebra down.* **6.** *Sports & Games* Trailing an opponent: *down 20 points.* ►*prep.* **1.** In a descending direction along, upon, into, or through. **2.** Along the course of: *walked down the street.* ►*n.* **1.** A downward movement; descent. **2.** *Football* Any of a series of four plays during which a team must advance at least ten yards to retain possession of the ball. ►*v.* **1.** To bring, put, strike, or throw down. **2.** To swal-

low hastily: *downed a glass of water.* [< OE *dūne*, downwards < *dūn*, hill.]

down² (doun) ►*n.* **1.** Fine, soft, fluffy feathers. **2.** Something similar to down. [< ON *dūnn.*] —**down′y** *adj.*

down³ (doun) ►*n.* often **downs** A rolling, grassy, upland expanse. [< OE *dūn.*]

down-and-out (doun′ənd-out′, -ən-) ►*adj.* Lacking funds, resources, or prospects.

down·beat (doun′bēt′) ►*n.* **1.** The first beat of a measure of music. **2.** The downward stroke of a conductor to indicate the first beat of a measure. ►*adj.* Cheerless; pessimistic.

down·cast (doun′kăst′) ►*adj.* **1.** Directed downward: *a downcast glance.* **2.** Low in spirits; depressed. See Synonyms at **depressed.**

down·er (dou′nər) ►*n.* *Slang* **1.** A depressant or sedative drug, such as a barbiturate or tranquilizer. **2.** One that depresses, such as an experience or person.

down·fall (doun′fôl′) ►*n.* **1.** A sudden loss, as of wealth or reputation; ruin. **2.** A downpour. —**down′fall′en** *adj.*

down·grade (doun′grād′) ►*v.* **1.** To lower the status or salary of. **2.** To minimize the importance or value of. ►*n.* A descending slope, as in a road.

down·heart·ed (doun′här′tĭd) ►*adj.* Low in spirit; depressed. See Synonyms at **depressed.**

down·hill (doun′hĭl′) ►*adv.* **1.** Down the slope of a hill. **2.** Toward a worse condition: *Her health went downhill.* ►*adj.* **1.** Relating to downward slopes: *downhill skiing.* **2.** Marked by deterioration. **3.** Involving progressively fewer difficulties: *The worst is over—it's all downhill from here.*

down-home (doun′hōm′) ►*adj.* Of or reminiscent of a simple life, esp. that associated with the rural S US.

down·load (doun′lōd′) ►*v.* To transfer (data or programs) from a server or host computer to one's own computer or device. —**down′-load′** *n.*

down payment ►*n.* A partial payment made at the time of purchase.

down·play (doun′plā′) ►*v.* To minimize the significance of.

down·pour (doun′pôr′) ►*n.* A heavy rainfall.

down·range (doun′rānj′) ►*adv. & adj.* In a direction away from the launch site and along the flight line of a missile test range.

down·right (doun′rīt′) ►*adj.* **1.** Thoroughgoing; unequivocal: *a downright lie.* **2.** Forthright; candid. ►*adv.* Thoroughly.

down·size (doun′sīz′) ►*v.* To reduce in size, as a corporation.

down·stage (doun′stāj′) ►*adv.* Toward or at the front of a stage. —**down′stage′** *adj.*

down·stairs (doun′stârz′) ►*adv.* **1.** Down the stairs. **2.** To or on a lower floor. —**down′-stairs′** *adj.* —**down′stairs′** *n.*

down·stream (doun′strēm′) ►*adj.* Being or moving away from the source of a stream; in the direction of the current. —**down′-stream′** *adv.*

down·swing (doun′swĭng′) ►*n.* **1.** A swing downward, as of a golf club. **2.** A decline, as of a business.

Down syndrome (doun) or **Down's syn·drome** (dounz) ►*n.* A congenital disorder marked by mild to moderate mental retardation and short stature. [After John L.H. *Down* (1828–96).]

down·time (doun′tīm′) ▸*n.* **1.** A period when something is not in operation. **2.** A period when one is not working or active.

down-to-earth (doun′tōō-ûrth′) ▸*adj.* **1.** Realistic; sensible. **2.** Not pretentious or affected.

down·town (doun′toun′) ▸*n.* The business center of a city or town. ▸*adv.* (doun′toun′) To, toward, or in the business center of a city or town. —**down′town′** *adj.*

down·trod·den (doun′trŏd′n) ▸*adj.* Oppressed; tyrannized.

down·turn (doun′tûrn′) ▸*n.* A tendency downward, esp. in economic activity.

down·ward (doun′wərd) ▸*adv. & adj.* **1.** From a higher to a lower place, point, or level. **2.** From a prior source or earlier time. —**down′ward·ly** *adv.* —**down′wards** *adv.*

down·wind (doun′wĭnd′) ▸*adv.* In the direction in which the wind blows. —**down′wind′** *adj.*

dow·ry (dou′rē) ▸*n., pl.* **-ries** Money or property brought by a bride to her husband at marriage. [< Med.Lat. *dōtārium,* dower < Lat. *dōs,* dowry.]

dowse also **douse** (douz) ▸*v.* **dowsed, dows·ing** also **doused, dous·ing** To use a divining rod to search for underground water or minerals. [?]

dows·er (dou′zər) ▸*n.* **1.** A person who dowses. **2.** A divining rod.

dox·ol·o·gy (dŏk-sŏl′ə-jē) ▸*n., pl.* **-gies** An expression of praise to God, esp. a short hymn sung as part of a Christian liturgy. [< Gk. *doxologia,* praise.] —**dox′o·log′i·cal** (dŏk′-sə-lŏj′ĭ-kəl) *adj.*

Doyle (doil), Sir **Arthur Conan** 1859–1930. British writer.

doze (dōz) ▸*v.* **dozed, doz·ing** To sleep lightly; nap. [Prob. of Scand. orig.] —**doze** *n.*

doz·en (dŭz′ən) ▸*n.* **1.** *pl.* **dozen** A set of twelve. **2. dozens** Many: *dozens of errands to run.* ▸*adj.* Twelve. [< Lat. *duodecim,* twelve.] —**doz′enth** *adj.*

DP ▸*abbr.* **1.** data processing **2.** double play

DPT ▸*abbr.* diphtheria, pertussis, tetanus (vaccine)

DPW ▸*abbr.* Department of Public Works

dr. ▸*abbr.* dram

Dr. ▸*abbr.* **1.** doctor **2.** drive

drab[1] (drăb) ▸*adj.* **drab·ber, drab·best 1.** Of a dull light brown or khaki color. **2.** Dull or commonplace; dreary. See Synonyms at **dull.** [< OFr. *drap,* cloth < LLat. *drappus.*] —**drab** *n.* —**drab′ly** *adv.* —**drab′ness** *n.*

drab[2] (drăb) ▸*n.* A negligible amount. [Prob. alteration of *drib.*]

drach·ma (drăk′mə) ▸*n., pl.* **-mas** or **-mae** (-mē) **1.** The primary unit of currency in Greece before the adoption of the euro. **2.** An ancient Greek silver coin. [< Gk. *drakhmē.*]

Dra·co (drā′kō) 7th cent. BC. Athenian lawgiver and politician.

dra·co·ni·an (drā-kō′nē-ən, drə-) ▸*adj.* Exceedingly harsh; very severe. [After DRACO.]

draft (drăft) ▸*n.* **1.** A current of air. **2.** A device that controls air circulation. **3a.** The act of pulling loads; traction. **b.** The load pulled or drawn. **4.** *Naut.* The depth of a vessel's keel below the water line. **5.** A document for transferring

money. **6a.** A gulp, swallow, or inhalation. **b.** The amount taken in by such an act. **7.** The drawing, or the amount drawn, of a liquid, as from a keg. **8a.** The selection of individuals from a group, as for military duty. **b.** Compulsory enrollment in the armed forces; conscription. **9.** *Sports* A system in which new players are distributed among professional teams. **10.** A preliminary outline of a plan, document, or picture. ▸*v.* **1.** To take, as for compulsory military service. **2.** To select from a group for placement on a sports team. **3.** To draw up a preliminary version of. ▸*adj.* **1.** Suited for drawing heavy loads. **2.** Drawn from a cask or tap. [ME *draught,* a drawing.]

draft·ee (drăf-tē′) ▸*n.* One who is drafted, esp. for military service.

draft·ing (drăf′tĭng) ▸*n.* The drawing of mechanical and architectural structures to scale.

drafts·man (drăfts′mən) ▸*n.* A man who draws plans or designs, as of structures to be built. —**drafts′man·ship′** *n.*

drafts·wom·an (drăfts′wŏŏm′ən) ▸*n.* A woman who draws plans or designs, as of structures to be built.

draft·y (drăf′tē) ▸*adj.* **-i·er, -i·est** Having or exposed to drafts of air. —**draft′i·ness** *n.*

drag (drăg) ▸*v.* **dragged, drag·ging 1.** To pull along with effort, esp. by force; haul. See Synonyms at **pull.** **2.** To pull along the ground. **3.** *Comp.* **a.** To move (e.g., a mouse) while pressing one of its buttons. **b.** To move (e.g., an icon) on a screen using a pointing device. **4.** To search or sweep the bottom of (a body of water), as with a grappling hook. **5.** To prolong tediously: *dragged the story out.* **6.** To proceed slowly or laboriously. **7.** To draw on a cigarette, pipe, or cigar. ▸*n.* **1.** The act of dragging. **2.** Something, as a harrow, dragged along the ground. **3.** Something that retards motion or progress. **4.** The degree of resistance involved in dragging or hauling. **5.** *Slang* Something obnoxiously tiresome. **6.** A puff on a cigarette, pipe, or cigar. **7.** *Slang* A street or road: *the main drag.* **8.** The clothing characteristic of one sex when worn by a member of the opposite sex. [Prob. < ON *draga.*] —**drag′ger** *n.*

drag·net (drăg′nĕt′) ▸*n.* **1.** A system of procedures for apprehending criminal suspects. **2.** A net for trawling.

drag·o·man (drăg′ə-mən) ▸*n., pl.* **-mans** or **-men** An interpreter of Arabic, Turkish, or Persian. [< Ar. *tarjumān.*]

drag·on (drăg′ən) ▸*n.* A mythical monster usu. represented as a gigantic winged reptile with lion's claws. [< Gk. *drakōn,* large serpent.]

drag·on·fly (drăg′ən-flī′) ▸*n.* Any of an order of large slender insects with two pairs of net-veined wings.

dra·goon (drə-gōōn′, dră-) ▸*n.* Formerly, a heavily armed trooper. ▸*v.* To subjugate or compel by violent measures; coerce. [< OFr. *dragon,* DRAGON.]

drag race ▸*n.* A race between two cars to determine which can accelerate faster from a standstill. —**drag racer** *n.* —**drag racing** *n.*

drag·ster (drăg′stər) ▸*n.* **1.** An automobile built or modified for drag racing. **2.** A person who races such an automobile.

drain (drān) ▸*v.* **1.** To draw or flow off by a

gradual process: *drained water from the sink; gasoline drained from the can with the hole.* **2.** To make or become empty or dry. **3.** To deplete gradually, esp. to the point of exhaustion. ►*n.* **1.** A pipe or channel by which liquid is drawn off. **2.** The act or process of draining. **3a.** A gradual loss; consumption or depletion. **b.** Something that causes a gradual loss. [< OE *drēahnian.*] —**drain′er** *n.*

drain·age (drā′nĭj) ►*n.* **1.** The action or a method of draining. **2.** A system of drains. **3.** Something drained off.

drain·pipe (drān′pīp′) ►*n.* A pipe for carrying off water or sewage.

drake (drāk) ►*n.* A male duck. [ME.]

dram¹ (drăm) ►*n.* See table at **measurement.** [< Lat. *drachma,* DRACHMA.]

dram² (drăm) ►*n.* See table at **currency.** [Armenian.]

dra·ma (drä′mə, drăm′ə) ►*n.* **1.** A prose or verse composition, esp. one for performance by actors; a play. **2.** Plays of a given type or period. **3.** The art of writing or producing dramatic works. **4.** A situation that involves conflicts or suspense and builds to a climax. **5.** The quality or condition of being dramatic. [< Gk.] —**dra·mat′ic** *adj.* —**dra·mat′i·cal·ly** *adv.*

dra·mat·ics (drə-măt′ĭks) ►*n.* *(takes sing. or pl. v.)* **1.** The art or practice of acting and stagecraft. **2.** Dramatic or stagy behavior.

dram·a·tist (drăm′ə-tĭst, drä′mə-) ►*n.* One who writes plays; playwright.

dram·a·tize (drăm′ə-tīz′, drä′mə-) ►*v.* **-tized, -tiz·ing** **1.** To adapt (a literary work) for dramatic presentation, as in a theater. **2.** To present or view in a dramatic or melodramatic way. —**dram′a·ti·za′tion** *n.*

drank (drăngk) ►*v.* P.t. of **drink.**

dr. ap. ►*abbr.* apothecaries' dram

drape (drāp) ►*v.* **draped, drap·ing** **1.** To cover, hang, or decorate with cloth in loose folds. **2.** To arrange in loose folds: *draping the banner from the balcony.* **3.** To hang or rest limply: *draped my legs over the chair.* ►*n.* **1.** A drapery; curtain. **2.** A cloth arranged over a patient's body during a medical procedure. **3.** The way cloth falls or hangs. [< LLat. *drappus,* cloth.]

drap·er·y (drā′pə-rē) ►*n.,* *pl.* **-ies** **1.** Cloth gracefully arranged in loose folds. **2.** Heavy fabric hanging straight in loose folds, used as a curtain. **3.** Cloth; fabric.

dras·tic (drăs′tĭk) ►*adj.* Extreme in effect; severe or radical: *drastic measures.* [Gk. *drastikos,* active < *dran,* do.] —**dras′ti·cal·ly** *adv.*

draught (drăft) ►*n., v., & adj.* Chiefly Brit. Var. of **draft.**

draughts (drăfts, dräfts) ►*n.* *(takes sing. or pl. v.)* Chiefly Brit. The game of checkers. [< ME *draught,* a move at chess.]

dr. avdp. ►*abbr.* avoirdupois dram

Dra·vid·i·an (drə-vĭd′ē-ən) ►*n.* **1.** A large family of languages spoken esp. in S India and N Sri Lanka that includes Tamil, Telugu, and Malayalam. **2.** A speaker of a Dravidian language. —**Dra·vid′i·an** *adj.*

draw (drô) ►*v.* **drew** (dro͞o), **drawn** (drôn), **draw·ing** **1a.** To cause to move in a given direction by applying continuous force; drag. See Synonyms at **pull. b.** To cause to move in a given direction or to a given position, as by leading: *drew us into the room.* **2.** To cause to

flow forth: *a blow that drew blood.* **3.** To suck or take in (e.g., air); inhale. **4.** To take or pull out: *drew a gun from beneath the counter.* **5.** To extract for one's own use: *draw strength from one's friends.* **6.** To eviscerate; disembowel. **7.** To attract; entice: *a casino that draws undesirable elements.* **8.** To select or take in: *draw clients from all levels of society.* **9.** To bring about deliberately; provoke: *drew enemy fire.* **10.** To elicit: *drew jeers from the audience.* **11.** To earn; gain: *draw interest.* **12.** To withdraw (money). **13.** To receive on a regular basis: *draw a pension.* **14.** To take or receive by chance: *draw lots.* **15.** *Games* To take (cards) from a dealer or stack. **16.** To end or leave (a contest) tied. **17.** To pull back the string of (a bow). **18a.** To inscribe (a line or lines) with a marking implement. **b.** To make a likeness of on a surface; depict with lines. **19.** To formulate or devise from evidence at hand: *draw a comparison.* **20.** To compose in legal format: *draw a deed.* ►*n.* **1.** An act or result of drawing. **2.** Something drawn, esp. a lot or card. **3.** An inhalation, as on a pipe or cigar. **4.** Something that attracts interest, customers, or spectators. **5.** A contest ending with neither side winning. —*phrasal verbs:* **draw out** To prolong; protract. **draw up** To compose or write in a set form. —*idioms:* **draw a blank** To fail to find or remember something. **draw straws** To decide by a lottery with straws of unequal lengths. [< OE *dragan.*]

draw·back (drô′băk′) ►*n.* A disadvantage. See Synonyms at **disadvantage.**

draw·bridge (drô′brĭj′) ►*n.* A bridge that can be raised or drawn aside to permit passage beneath it.

draw·down (drô′doun′) ►*n.* **1.** The act, process, or result of reducing or depleting: *the drawdown of oil supplies* **2.** A reduction of military personnel in a deployment.

draw·er (drô′ər) ►*n.* **1.** One that draws, esp. one that draws an order for the payment of money. **2.** *(also* drôr) A sliding boxlike compartment in furniture. **3.** **drawers** (drôrz) Underpants.

draw·ing (drô′ĭng) ►*n.* **1.** The art of representing objects or forms on a surface by means of lines. **2.** A work so produced.

drawing room ►*n.* **1.** A large room in which guests are entertained. **2.** A large private room on a railroad sleeping car. [< *withdrawing room.*]

drawl (drôl) ►*v.* To speak with lengthened or drawn-out vowels. [Poss. < LGer. *drauelen,* loiter.] —**drawl** *n.*

drawn (drôn) ►*v.* P.part. of **draw.** ►*adj.* Haggard, as from fatigue or ill health: *a drawn face.*

draw·string (drô′strĭng′) ►*n.* A cord or ribbon run through a hem or casing and pulled to tighten or close an opening.

dray (drā) ►*n.* A low heavy cart without sides. [ME *draie,* cart < OE *dragan,* draw.]

dread (drĕd) ►*v.* **1.** To be in terror of. **2.** To anticipate with alarm, distaste, or reluctance: *dreaded the long drive.* ►*n.* **1.** Profound fear; terror. **2.** Fearful or anxious anticipation. ►*adj.* **1.** Causing terror or fear: *a dread disease.* **2.** Inspiring awe. [< OE *adrǣdan.*]

dread·ful (drĕd′fəl) ►*adj.* **1.** Inspiring dread; terrible. **2.** Extremely unpleasant; distasteful or shocking. —**dread′ful·ly** *adv.* —**dread′ful·ness** *n.*

dread·locks (drĕd′lŏks′) ►*pl.n.* Long ropelike locks or thin braids of twisted or styled hair radiating from the scalp.

dread·nought (drĕd′nôt′) ►*n.* **1.** A heavily armed battleship. **2.** An acoustic guitar with a larger body than typical.

dream (drēm) ►*n.* **1.** A series of images, ideas, emotions, and sensations occurring during sleep. **2.** A daydream; reverie. **3.** An ambition; aspiration: *the dream of owning their own business.* **4.** A wild fancy or unrealistic hope. **5.** One that is extremely gratifying: *Your new boyfriend is a dream.* ►*v.* **dreamed** or **dreamt** (drĕmt), **dream·ing 1.** To experience a dream in sleep: *dreamed of meeting an old friend.* **2.** To daydream. **3.** To aspire. **4.** To conceive of; imagine: *I never dreamed it would snow so much!* **5.** To have as an aspiration or hope: *dreams of becoming a pilot.* **6.** To pass (time) idly or in reverie. —*phrasal verb:* **dream up** To invent; concoct. [< OE *drēam,* joy.] —**dream′er** *n.* —**dream′i·ly** *adv.* —**dream′y** *adj.*

dream·land (drēm′lănd′) ►*n.* **1.** An ideal or imaginary land. **2.** A state of sleep.

drear (drîr) ►*adj.* Dreary.

drea·ry (drîr′ē) ►*adj.* **-ri·er, -ri·est 1.** Dismal; bleak. **2.** Boring; dull: *dreary tasks.* [< OE *drēor,* blood, gore.] —**drea′ri·ly** *adv.* —**drea′ri·ness** *n.*

dredge¹ (drĕj) ►*n.* **1.** A machine used to deepen harbors and waterways. **2.** *Naut.* A boat or barge equipped with a dredge. **3.** A net fixed to a frame, used for gathering shellfish. ►*v.* **dredged, dredg·ing 1.** To deepen or bring up with a dredge: *dredged up the silt.* **2.** To come up with; unearth: *dredged up old memories.* [ME *dredge-* < OE *dragan,* draw.] —**dredg′er** *n.*

dredge² (drĕj) ►*v.* **dredged, dredg·ing** To coat (food) by sprinkling, as with flour. [< Gk. *tragēmata,* sweetmeats.]

dregs (drĕgz) ►*pl.n.* **1.** The sediment in a liquid, such as wine or coffee. **2.** The least desirable portion: *the dregs of humanity.* [< ON *dregg.*]

drei·del also **drei·dl** (drād′l) ►*n.* A small spinning top used in games played at Hanukkah. [Yiddish *dreydl* < *dreyen,* to turn.]

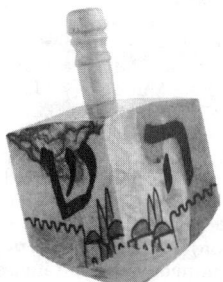

dreidel

Drei·ser (drī′sər, -zər), **Theodore Herman Albert** 1871–1945. Amer. writer and editor.

drench (drĕnch) ►*v.* To wet thoroughly; soak. [< OE *drencan,* give to drink.]

Dres·den (drĕz′dən) A city of E-central Germany on the Elbe R. ESE of Leipzig.

dress (drĕs) ►*v.* **1.** To put clothes on; clothe. **2.** To decorate or adorn: *dress a Christmas tree.* **3.** To arrange a display in: *dress a store window.*

4. To garnish: *dressed the entree with parsley.* **5.** To apply bandages and other treatments to (a wound). **6.** To clean (fish or fowl) for cooking or sale. **7.** To wear formal clothes: *dress for dinner.* ►*n.* **1.** Clothing; apparel. **2.** A style of clothing: *dancers in peasant dress.* **3.** A one-piece outer garment for women or girls. ►*adj.* Suitable for formal occasions: *dress shoes.* —*phrasal verbs:* **dress down 1.** To scold; reprimand. **2.** To wear informal clothes. **dress up 1.** To wear a style of clothing or costume, esp. formal attire: *dressed up for Halloween.* **2.** To improve the outward appearance of: *The new pillows dressed up the room.* [< OFr. *drecier,* arrange < Lat. *dīrigere,* DIRECT.]

dres·sage (drə-säzh′, drĕ-) ►*n.* The guiding of a horse through a series of complex maneuvers by slight movements of the rider's hands, legs, and weight.

dress·er¹ (drĕs′ər) ►*n.* One that dresses or assists in dressing.

dress·er² (drĕs′ər) ►*n.* A chest of drawers used for holding clothes and personal items. [< OFr. *dreceur,* table for preparing food < *drecier,* arrange; see DRESS.]

dress·ing (drĕs′ĭng) ►*n.* **1.** Therapeutic material applied to a wound. **2.** A sauce, as for salads. **3.** A stuffing, as for poultry.

dressing gown ►*n.* A robe worn for lounging.

dressing table ►*n.* A low table with a mirror at which one sits while applying makeup.

dress·mak·er (drĕs′mā′kər) ►*n.* One that makes women's clothing, esp. dresses. —**dress′mak′-ing** *n.*

dress·y (drĕs′ē) ►*adj.* **-i·er, -i·est 1.** Requiring or characterized by formal dress: *a dressy occasion.* **2.** Formal or elegant in style: *dressy shoes.* —**dress′i·ness** *n.*

drew (drōo) ►*v.* P.t. of **draw.**

drib·ble (drĭb′əl) ►*v.* **-bled, -bling 1.** To flow or fall in drops or an unsteady stream; trickle. **2.** To let saliva drip from the mouth; drool. **3.** *Sports* To move (a ball) by repeated light bounces or kicks, as in basketball or soccer. [Frequentative of obsolete *drib,* alteration of DRIP.] —**drib′ble** *n.* —**drib′bler** *n.*

drib·let (drĭb′lĭt) ►*n.* **1.** A tiny, falling drop of liquid. **2.** A small amount or portion. [< alteration of DRIP.]

dried (drīd) ►*v.* P.t. and p.part. of **dry.**

dri·er¹ also **dry·er** (drī′ər) ►*n.* **1.** A substance added to paint, varnish, or ink to speed drying. **2.** One that dries.

dri·er² (drī′ər) ►*adj.* Comp. of **dry.**

dri·est (drī′ĭst) ►*adj.* Superl. of **dry.**

drift (drĭft) ►*v.* **1.** To be carried along by currents of air or water. **2.** To move unhurriedly and smoothly: *drifting among the party guests.* **3.** To move from place to place, esp. without purpose or regular employment. **4.** To wander; stray. **5.** To pile up in banks by the force of a current: *snow drifting to four feet.* ►*n.* **1.** The act or condition of drifting. **2.** Something that drifts. **3.** A bank or pile, as of sand or snow, heaped up by currents of air or water. **4.** A general trend, as of opinion. **5.** The main idea; gist: *caught the drift of the conversation.* [< ME, act of driving.] —**drift′y** *adj.*

drift·er (drĭf′tər) ►*n.* A person who moves aimlessly from place to place or job to job.

drift net ►*n.* A large fishing net buoyed up by

floats that is carried along with the current or tide.

drift·wood (drĭft′wŏŏd′) ►*n.* Wood floating in or washed up by the water.

drill¹ (drĭl) ►*n.* **1.** An implement for boring holes in hard materials. **2.** A task or exercise for teaching a skill or procedure. ►*v.* **1.** To make a hole with a drill. **2.** To instruct thoroughly by repetition. [< MDu. *drillen*, to bore.] —**drill′er** *n.*

drill² (drĭl) ►*n.* **1.** A shallow trench or furrow in which seeds are planted. **2.** A row of planted seeds. **3.** An implement for planting seeds. [?] —**drill** *v.*

drill³ (drĭl) ►*n.* Durable cotton or linen twill. [< Lat. *trilīx*, triple-twilled.]

drill instructor ►*n.* A noncommissioned officer who instructs recruits in military drill and discipline.

drill·mas·ter (drĭl′măs′tər) ►*n.* **1.** A drill instructor. **2.** An instructor given to extremely rigorous training.

drill press ►*n.* A powered vertical drilling machine in which the drill is pressed to the work automatically or by a hand lever.

drink (drĭngk) ►*v.* **drank** (drăngk), **drunk** (drŭngk), **drink·ing 1a.** To take into the mouth and swallow (a liquid). **b.** To swallow the liquid contents of (a vessel): *drank a cup of tea.* **2.** To soak up; absorb: *spongy earth that drank in the rain.* **3.** To take in eagerly through the senses or intellect: *drank in every word.* **4.** To give or make a toast to: *We'll drink to your health.* **5.** To imbibe alcoholic liquors, esp. to excess. ►*n.* **1.** An amount of liquid swallowed: *took a drink from the fountain.* **2.** Excessive indulgence in alcohol. [< OE *drincan.*] —**drink′a·bil′i·ty** *n.* —**drink′a·ble** *adj.* —**drink′er** *n.*

drip (drĭp) ►*v.* **dripped, drip·ping 1.** To fall or let fall in drops. **2.** To shed drops: *a raincoat dripping on the floor.* **3.** To ooze as if with liquid: *a speech dripping with sarcasm.* ►*n.* **1.** The process of forming and falling in drops. **2.** Liquid that falls in drops. **3.** The sound made by dripping liquid. **4.** *Slang* A tiresome person. [ME *drippen.*]

drip·pings (drĭp′ĭngz) ►*pl.n.* The fat and juices exuded from roasting meat, used in making gravy.

drive (drīv) ►*v.* **drove** (drōv), **driv·en** (drĭv′ən), **driv·ing 1.** To push, propel, or urge onward forcibly. **2.** To repulse forcefully; put to flight: *drive out thoughts of failure.* **3a.** To guide, control, or direct (a vehicle). **b.** To operate or be transported in a vehicle. **4.** To supply power to and cause to function: *Steam drives the engine.* **5.** To motivate deeply: *Her goals drive her to be the best dancer she can be.* **6.** To force into a particular act or state: *Traffic drives me crazy.* **7.** To force to go through or penetrate: *drive a nail.* **8.** To carry through vigorously to a conclusion: *drive a hard bargain.* **9.** To throw or strike (e.g., a ball), hard or rapidly. **10.** To rush or advance violently: *The wind drove into my face.* ►*n.* **1.** A trip or journey in a vehicle. **2.** A road, esp. a driveway, for vehicles. **3.** The apparatus for transmitting motion or power to or in a machine. **4.** *Comp.* A device that reads data from and often writes data onto a storage medium, such as an optical disc or flash memory. **5.** A strong organized effort to

accomplish a purpose. **6.** Energy; initiative: *a student with a lot of drive.* **7.** *Psychol.* An instinct related to self-preservation or reproduction. **8.** The act of propelling a ball forcefully. **9.** The act of driving cattle. —*phrasal verb:* **drive at** To mean to do or say: *I don't know what you're driving at.* [< OE *drīfan.*] —**driv′a·bil′i·ty** *n.* —**driv′a·ble** *adj.*

drive-by (drīv′bī′) ►*adj.* Performed from a moving vehicle: *a drive-by shooting.* —**drive′-by′** *n.*

drive-in (drīv′ĭn′) ►*n.* An establishment, esp. an outdoor movie theater, that permits customers to remain in their motor vehicles while being accommodated. —**drive′-in′** *adj.*

driv·el (drĭv′əl) ►*v.* **-eled, -el·ing** or **-elled, -el·ling 1.** To slobber; drool. **2.** To talk stupidly or childishly. [< OE *dreflian.*] —**driv′el** *n.* —**driv′el·er** *n.*

driv·er (drī′vər) ►*n.* **1.** One that drives. **2.** A tool, such as a screwdriver, used to impart forceful pressure on another object. **3.** A golf club used for long shots from the tee. **4.** Software that enables a computer to communicate with a specific hardware device.

drive shaft ►*n.* A rotating shaft that transmits mechanical power from an engine to a point of application.

drive·train (drīv′trān′) ►*n.* The components of an automotive vehicle that connect the transmission with the driving axles and include the universal joint and drive shaft.

drive·way (drīv′wā′) ►*n.* A private road, as to a house or garage.

driz·zle (drĭz′əl) ►*v.* **-zled, -zling 1.** To rain gently in fine mistlike drops. **2.** To let fall in fine drops: *drizzled sauce over the meat.* [< ME *drisning,* fall of dew.] —**driz′zle** *n.* —**driz′zly** *adj.*

drogue (drōg) ►*n.* A parachute used to slow a fast-moving object, such as a spacecraft during reentry. [Poss. < DRAG.]

droll (drōl) ►*adj.* **-er, -est** Amusingly odd or whimsically comical. [Fr. *drôle.*] —**droll′er·y, droll′ness** *n.* —**drol′ly** *adv.*

–drome ►*suff.* **1.** Racecourse: *hippodrome.* **2.** Field; arena: *airdrome.* [< Gk. *dromos,* racecourse.]

drom·e·dar·y (drŏm′ĭ-dĕr′ē, drŭm′-) ►*n., pl.* **-ies** The one-humped domesticated camel of desert regions of N Africa and W Asia, widely used as a beast of burden. [< LLat. *dromedārius* < Gk. *dromas,* running.]

drone¹ (drōn) ►*n.* **1.** A male bee, esp. a honeybee. **2.** An idle person who lives off others. **3.** A pilotless, remote-controlled aircraft. **4.** A person who does tedious or menial work; drudge. [< OE *drān.*]

drone² (drōn) ►*v.* **droned, dron·ing 1.** To make a continuous low dull humming sound. **2.** To speak in a monotonous tone. [Prob. < DRONE¹.] —**drone** *n.*

drool (drŏŏl) ►*v.* **1.** To let saliva run from the mouth; drivel. **2.** *Informal* To make an extravagant show of desire: *drooled over the new car.* [Perh. alteration of DRIVEL.] —**drool** *n.*

droop (drŏŏp) ►*v.* **1.** To bend or hang downward. **2.** To sag in dejection or exhaustion. [< ON *drūpa.*] —**droop** *n.* —**droop′i·ly, droop′ing·ly** *adv.* —**droop′y** *adj.*

drop (drŏp) ►*n.* **1.** A quantity of liquid heavy enough to fall in a spherical mass. **2.** Something resembling a drop. **3.** The act of falling. **4.** A swift decline or decrease, as in quality. **5.** The vertical distance from a higher to a lower level: *The cliff has a drop of 50 feet.* **6.** A sheer incline, such as a cliff. **7.** Personnel and equipment landed by parachute. **8.** A place where something, such as mail, is brought and distributed. **9.** A trace or hint: *not a drop of pity.* ►*v.* **dropped, drop·ping 1.** To fall or let fall in drops. **2.** To fall or let fall from a higher to a lower place. **3.** To become less, as in amount or intensity: *The temperature dropped below zero.* **4.** To descend. **5.** To sink into a state of exhaustion. **6.** To pass into a specified condition: *dropped into a doze.* **7.** To say or offer casually: *drop a hint.* **8.** To write at leisure: *drop me a note.* **9.** To cease consideration or treatment of: *drop the subject.* **10.** To stop participating in; quit: *drop a course.* **11.** To leave out (e.g., a letter) in speaking or writing. **12.** To leave or set down; unload: *dropped the mail on the desk.* **13.** *Slang* To take by mouth, as a drug: *drop LSD.* —*phrasal verbs:* **drop by** To visit briefly. **drop off** To fall asleep. **drop out 1.** To leave school without graduating. **2.** To withdraw from society. [< OE *dropa.*]

drop·let (drŏp′lĭt) ►*n.* A tiny drop.

drop-off (drŏp′ôf′, -ŏf′) ►*n.* **1.** An abrupt downward slope. **2.** A noticeable decrease: *a drop-off in attendance.*

drop·out (drŏp′out′) ►*n.* One who drops out, as from school.

drop·per (drŏp′ər) ►*n.* One that drops, esp. a small tube with a suction bulb at one end for drawing in a liquid and releasing it in drops.

dro·soph·i·la (drō-sŏf′ə-lə, drə-) ►*n.* A fruit fly used extensively in genetic research. [< Gk. *drosos,* dew + NLat. -*philus,* -phile.]

dross (drŏs, drôs) ►*n.* **1.** A waste product formed on the surface of molten metal, caused by oxidation. **2.** Worthless or trivial matter. [< OE *drōs,* dregs.] —**dross′y** *adj.*

drought (drout) also **drouth** (drouth) ►*n.* **1.** A long period of low rainfall. **2.** A prolonged dearth or shortage. [< OE *drūgoth.*]

drove[1] (drōv) ►*v.* P.t. of **drive.**

drove[2] (drōv) ►*n.* A flock, herd, or large group being driven or moving in a body. [< OE *drāf* < *drīfan,* drive.]

drown (droun) ►*v.* **1.** To die or kill by suffocating in water or another liquid. **2.** To cover with or as if with a liquid. **3.** To mask (a sound) with a louder sound: *shouts drowned out by the passing train.* **4.** To deaden one's awareness of; blot out: *he drowned his troubles in drink.* [ME *drounen.*]

drowse (drouz) ►*v.* **drowsed, drows·ing** To be half-asleep; doze. [Perh. < OE *drūsian,* be sluggish.] —**drowse** *n.*

drows·y (drou′zē) ►*adj.* **-i·er, -i·est 1.** Sleepy. **2.** Causing sleepiness; soporific. —**drows′i·ly** *adv.* —**drows′i·ness** *n.*

dr. t. ►*abbr.* troy dram

drub (drŭb) ►*v.* **drubbed, drub·bing 1.** To thrash with a stick. **2.** To instill forcefully: *drubbed the lesson into my head.* **3.** To defeat thoroughly. **4.** To berate harshly. [Perh. Ar. *ḍaraba,* to beat.] —**drub′ber** *n.*

drudge (drŭj) ►*n.* A person who does tedious, menial, or unpleasant work. ►*v.* **drudged, drudg·ing** To do the work of a drudge. [< ME *druggen,* to labor.] —**drudg′er·y** *n.*

drug (drŭg) ►*n.* **1.** A substance used in the diagnosis, treatment, or prevention of a disease. **2.** A narcotic or hallucinogen. ►*v.* **drugged, drug·ging 1.** To administer a drug to, esp. to treat pain or induce anesthesia. **2.** To give a drug to, esp. surreptitiously, in order to induce stupor. **3.** To poison or mix (food or drink) with a drug. [< OFr. *drogue.*]

drug·gist (drŭg′ĭst) ►*n.* A pharmacist.

drug·store also **drug store** (drŭg′stôr′) ►*n.* A store where prescriptions are filled and drugs and other articles are sold.

dru·id also **Dru·id** (drōō′ĭd) ►*n.* A member of an order of priests in ancient Gaul and Britain who appear in legend as prophets and sorcerers. [< Lat. *druidēs,* druids, of Celt. orig.] —**dru·id′ic, dru·id′i·cal** *adj.* —**dru′id·ism** *n.*

drum (drŭm) ►*n.* **1.** A percussion instrument consisting of a hollow cylinder with a membrane stretched tightly over one or both ends, played by beating with the hands or sticks. **2.** Something like a drum in shape or structure, esp. a barrellike metal container. ►*v.* **drummed, drum·ming 1.** To play a drum. **2.** To thump or tap rhythmically or continually: *nervously drummed on the desk.* **3.** To instill by constant repetition: *drummed the answers into my head.* **4.** To expel or dismiss in disgrace: *was drummed out of the army.* —*phrasal verb:* **drum up 1.** To bring about by continuous effort: *drum up new business.* **2.** To devise: *drum up an alibi.* [ME *drom* < MDu. *tromme.*] —**drum′mer** *n.*

drum·beat (drŭm′bēt′) ►*n.* **1.** The sound produced by beating a drum. **2.** Vehement advocacy of a cause: *the drumbeat of media criticism.*

drum·lin (drŭm′lĭn) ►*n.* An elongated hill or ridge of glacial drift. [< Ir.Gael. *druim,* ridge.]

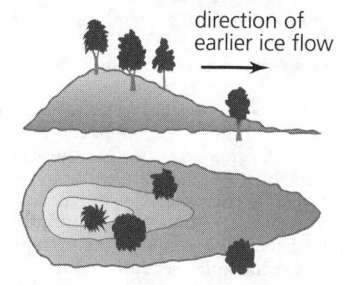

direction of earlier ice flow

drumlin

drum major ►*n.* A person who leads a marching band, often twirling a baton.

drum ma·jor·ette (mā′jə-rĕt′) ►*n.* A girl or woman who leads a marching band, often twirling a baton.

drum·stick (drŭm′stĭk′) ►*n.* **1.** A stick for beating a drum. **2.** The lower part of the leg of a fowl, esp. when cooked.

drunk (drŭngk) ►*v.* P.part. of **drink.** ►*adj.* **1.** Intoxicated with alcohol; inebriated. **2.** Overcome by emotion: *drunk with power.* ►*n.* **1.** A drunkard. **2.** A bout of drinking.

drunk·ard (drŭng′kərd) ►*n.* One who is habitually drunk.

drunk·en (drŭng′kən) ►*adj.* **1.** Intoxicated: *a drunken guest.* **2.** Habitually drunk. **3.** Of or occurring during intoxication: *a drunken brawl.* —**drunk′en·ly** *adv.* —**drunk′en·ness** *n.*

drupe (dro̅o̅p) ▸*n.* A fleshy fruit, as a peach or plum, with a single hard stone that encloses a seed. [< Gk. *drupa*, olive.]

drupe·let (dro̅o̅p′lĭt) ▸*n.* A small drupe, such as one of the many subdivisions of a raspberry.

dry (drī) ▸*adj.* **dri·er, dri·est** or **dry·er, dry·est 1.** Free or freed from liquid or moisture: *a dry towel.* **2.** Marked by little or no rain: *a dry climate.* **3.** Not under water: *dry land.* **4.** Lacking a mucous or watery discharge: *a dry cough.* **5.** Needing moisture or drink: *a dry mouth.* **6.** Of solid rather than liquid commodities: *dry weight.* **7.** Not sweet: *a dry wine.* **8.** Matter-of-fact; impersonal: *rattled off facts in a dry, mechanical tone.* **9.** Wearisome; dull: *a dry lecture.* **10.** Humorous or sarcastic in a shrewd way: *dry wit.* **11.** Prohibiting the sale of alcoholic beverages: *a dry county.* ▸*v.* **dried, dry·ing 1.** To make or become dry. **2.** To preserve (food) by extracting the moisture. [< OE *drȳge*.] **—dry′ly, dri′ly** *adv.* **—dry′ness** *n.*
Syns: dehydrate, desiccate, parch **Ant:** *moisten v.*

dry·ad (drī′əd, -ăd′) ▸*n. Gk. Myth.* A wood nymph. [< Gk. *Druas, Druad-.*]

dry cell ▸*n.* An electric cell having an electrolyte in the form of moist paste.

dry-clean (drī′klēn′) ▸*v.* To clean (fabrics) with chemical solvents that have little or no water. **—dry cleaner** *n.* **—dry cleaning** *n.*

Dry·den (drīd′n), **John** 1631–1700. English writer.

dry dock ▸*n.* A large basinlike dock from which the water can be emptied, used for building or repairing ships.

dry·er (drī′ər) ▸*n.* **1.** An appliance that removes moisture. **2.** Var. of **drier**¹.

dry farming ▸*n.* Farming practiced in arid areas without irrigation. **—dry′-farm′** *v.*

dry goods ▸*pl.n.* Textiles, clothing, and related articles of trade.

dry ice ▸*n.* Solid carbon dioxide used primarily as a coolant.

dry measure ▸*n.* A system of units for measuring dry commodities such as grains.

dry rot ▸*n.* A fungal disease that causes timber to become brittle and crumble into powder.

dry run ▸*n.* A trial exercise or rehearsal, as a military exercise without live ammunition.

drywall (drī′wôl′) ▸*n.* A building material consisting of rectangular sections, used esp. in the construction of interior walls and ceilings. ▸*v.* To construct using drywall.

Ds The symbol for **darmstadtium.**

DSC ▸*abbr.* Distinguished Service Cross

DSL ▸*abbr.* digital subscriber line

DSM ▸*abbr.* Distinguished Service Medal

DSO ▸*abbr.* Distinguished Service Order

DSP ▸*abbr. Lat. decessit sine prole* (died without issue)

DST ▸*abbr.* daylight-saving time

DTP ▸*abbr.* diphtheria, tetanus, pertussis (vaccine)

DTs or **DT's** (dē′tēz′) ▸*n.* (*takes sing. or pl. v.*) Delirium tremens.

du·al (do̅o̅′əl, dyo̅o̅′-) ▸*adj.* **1.** Composed of two parts; double. **2.** Having a double character or purpose. [Lat. *duālis* < *duo*, two.] **—du·al′i·ty** (-ăl′ĭ-tē) *n.* **—du′al·ly** *adv.*

du·al·ism (do̅o̅′ə-lĭz′əm, dyo̅o̅′-) ▸*n.* **1.** The condition of being dual. **2.** *Philos.* The view that the world consists of two fundamental entities, such as mind and matter. **—du′al·is′tic** *adj.*

dub¹ (dŭb) ▸*v.* **dubbed, dub·bing 1.** To confer knighthood on. **2.** To give a name to playfully; nickname. [< OE *dubbian.*]

dub² (dŭb) ▸*v.* **dubbed, dub·bing 1a.** To transfer (recorded material) onto a new recording medium. **b.** To copy (an audiotape, e.g.). **2.** To insert a new sound track into (a film). **3.** To add (sound) into a film or tape. [< DOUBLE.] **—dub** *n.* **—dub′ber** *n.*

Du·bai (do̅o̅-bī′) A sheikdom and city of E United Arab Emirates on the Persian Gulf.

du·bi·e·ty (do̅o̅-bī′ĭ-tē, dyo̅o̅-) ▸*n., pl.* **-ties 1.** A feeling or matter of doubt. **2.** The condition of being doubtful or uncertain. [LLat. *dubietās* < Lat. *dubius*, doubtful.]

du·bi·ous (do̅o̅′bē-əs, dyo̅o̅′-) ▸*adj.* **1.** Fraught with uncertainty; undecided. **2.** Arousing doubt; questionable: *a dubious distinction.* [< Lat. *dubius.*] **—du′bi·ous·ly** *adv.*

Dub·lin (dŭb′lĭn) The capital of Ireland, in the E part on the Irish Sea. **—Dub′lin·er** *n.*

dub·ni·um (do̅o̅b′nē-əm) ▸*n. Symbol* **Db** A short-lived, synthetic radioactive element. At. no. 105. See table at **element.**

Du Bois (do̅o̅ bois′), **W(illiam) E(dward) B(urghardt)** 1868–1963. Amer. writer and civil rights leader.

du·cal (do̅o̅′kəl, dyo̅o̅′-) ▸*adj.* Of or relating to a duke or dukedom.

duc·at (dŭk′ət) ▸*n.* Any of various gold coins formerly used in Europe. [< Med.Lat. *ducātus*, DUCHY.]

duch·ess (dŭch′ĭs) ▸*n.* **1.** A woman holding title to a duchy. **2.** The wife or widow of a duke. [< Med.Lat. *ducissa* < Lat. *dux*, leader.]

duch·y (dŭch′ē) ▸*n., pl.* **-ies** The territory ruled by a duke or duchess; dukedom. [< Med.Lat. *ducātus* < Lat. *dux*, leader.]

duck¹ (dŭk) ▸*n.* A waterbird having a broad flat bill, short legs, and webbed feet. [< OE *dūce.*]

duck² (dŭk) ▸*v.* **1.** To lower quickly, esp. to avoid something. **2.** To evade; dodge: *duck responsibility.* **3.** To push suddenly under water. [ME *douken*, dive.] **—duck** *n.*

duck³ (dŭk) ▸*n.* **1.** A durable, closely woven cotton fabric. **2. ducks** Clothing made of duck, esp. white trousers. [< MDu. *doec*, cloth.]

duck·bill (dŭk′bĭl′) ▸*n.* See **platypus.**

duck·board (dŭk′bôrd′) ▸*n.* A board or boardwalk laid across wet ground or flooring.

duck·ling (dŭk′lĭng) ▸*n.* A young duck.

duck·pin (dŭk′pĭn′) ▸*n.* **1.** A bowling pin shorter and squatter than a tenpin. **2. duckpins** (*takes sing. v.*) A bowling game played with such pins.

duck·weed (dŭk′wēd′) ▸*n.* A small, stemless, free-floating aquatic flowering plant.

duck·y (dŭk′ē) ▸*adj.* **-i·er, -i·est** *Slang* Excellent; fine.

duct (dŭkt) ▸*n.* **1.** A channel for conveying a substance, esp. a liquid or gas. **2.** *Anat.* A tubular bodily passage, esp. one for carrying glandular secretions. **3.** A tube or pipe for enclosing electrical cables or wires. [Lat. *ductus*, act of leading < *dūcere*, to lead.] **—duct′ed** *adj.* **—duct′less** *adj.*

duc·tile (dŭk′təl, -tīl′) ▸*adj.* **1.** Easily drawn into wire or hammered thin: *ductile metals.* **2.** Easily molded or shaped; malleable. **3.** Capable of being readily influenced; tractable: *a ductile young mind.* [< Lat. *ductilis* < *dūcere*, to lead.] —**duc·til/i·ty** (-tĭl/ĭ-tē), **duc/ti·li·bil/i·ty** *n.*

dud (dŭd) ►*n.* **1.** A bomb, shell, or explosive that fails to detonate. **2.** *Informal* One that is disappointingly ineffective or unsuccessful. **3. duds** *Informal* Clothing or personal belongings. [ME *dudde,* cloak.]

dude (dōōd, dyōōd) ►*n.* **1.** *Informal* An Easterner or city person vacationing on a ranch in the West. **2.** *Informal* A man who is very fancy in dress and demeanor. **3.** *Slang* **a.** A man; fellow. **b.** A person of either sex. [?]

dude ranch ►*n.* A resort patterned after a Western ranch, featuring outdoor activities.

dudg·eon (dŭj/ən) ►*n.* A sullen, angry, or indignant humor. [?]

due (dōō, dyōō) ►*adj.* **1.** Payable immediately or on demand. **2.** Owed as a debt: *the amount still due.* **3.** Meeting special requirements; sufficient: *due cause to honor them.* **4.** Appropriate: *due respect.* **5.** Anticipated or expected: *a long due promotion; due for some rain.* **6.** Capable of being attributed. See Usage Note at **due to.** ►*n.* **1.** Something owed or deserved. **2. dues** A membership fee. ►*adv.* Straight; directly: *due west.* [< OFr. *deu* < Lat. *dēbēre,* owe.]

du·el (dōō/əl, dyōō/-) ►*n.* **1.** A prearranged formal combat between two persons, usu. fought to settle a point of honor. **2.** A struggle for domination between two persons or groups. ►*v.* -**eled, -el·ing** or -**elled, -el·ling 1.** To fight in a duel. **2.** To oppose forcefully. [< Lat. *duellum,* war.] —**du/el·er, du/el·ist** *n.*

due process ►*n.* An established course for judicial proceedings designed to safeguard the legal rights of the individual.

du·et (dōō-ĕt/, dyōō-) ►*n.* **1.** *Mus.* A composition for two voices or instruments. **2.** A group of two musicians. [Ital. *duetto,* dim. of *duo* < Lat. *duō,* two.]

due to ►*prep.* Because of.
    Usage: According to some critics, it is incorrect to say *The concert was canceled due to the rain,* where *due to* is a compound preposition, as opposed to the acceptable *The cancellation of the concert was due to the rain,* where *due* functions as an adjective modifying *cancellation.*

duff·er (dŭf/ər) ►*n. Informal* **1.** An incompetent or dull-witted person. **2.** A casual or mediocre player of a sport, esp. golf. [?]

duf·fle bag (dŭf/əl) or **duf·fel bag** ►*n.* A large cylindrical cloth bag for carrying personal belongings.

dug¹ (dŭg) ►*n.* A breast or teat. [?]

dug² (dŭg) ►*v.* P.t. and p.part. of **dig.**

dug·out (dŭg/out/) ►*n.* **1.** A boat or canoe made of a hollowed-out log. **2.** A pit dug into the ground or on a hillside and used as a shelter. **3.** *Baseball* A sunken shelter at the side of a field where players stay while not on the field.

duh (dŭ) ►*interj.* Used to express disdain, esp. for something deemed obvious. [Imit. of utterance attributed to stupid people.]

DUI ►*abbr.* driving under the influence (of drugs or alcohol)

du jour (də zhōōr/, dōō) ►*adj.* **1.** Offered on a given day: *the soup du jour.* **2.** Current: *the trend du jour.* [Fr., of the day.]

duke (dōōk, dyōōk) ►*n.* **1.** A nobleman with the highest hereditary rank, esp. in Great Britain.

2. A sovereign prince who rules an independent duchy. **3. dukes** *Slang* The fists: *Put up your dukes!* ►*v.* **duked, duk·ing** To fight, esp. with fists: *duking it out.* [< Lat. *dux,* leader.] —**duke/dom** *n.*

dul·cet (dŭl/sĭt) ►*adj.* **1.** Pleasing to the ear; melodious. **2.** Soothing; agreeable. [< OFr. *doucet* < Lat. *dulcis.*]

dul·ci·mer (dŭl/sə-mər) ►*n. Mus.* **1.** A zither-like instrument played by striking with padded hammers. **2.** A long, narrow, usu. four-stringed fretted instrument played by plucking or strumming. [< OFr. *doulcemer.*]

dull (dŭl) ►*adj.* -**er, -est 1.** Uninteresting; boring. **2.** Not having a sharp edge; blunt. **3.** Not brisk or rapid; sluggish: *Business has been dull.* **4.** Lacking alertness; insensitive: *half-asleep and dull to the loud noise.* **5.** Not intensely or keenly felt: *a dull ache.* **6.** Intellectually obtuse; stupid. **7.** Not bright or vivid: *a dull finish on the furniture.* **8.** Muffled; indistinct: *a dull thud.* ►*v.* To make or become dull. [ME *dul.*] —**dull/ness, dul/ness** *n.* —**dul/ly** *adv.*
    Syns: *colorless, drab, humdrum, lackluster, pedestrian, stodgy, uninspired* **Ant** *lively* **adj.**

dull·ard (dŭl/ərd) ►*n.* A stupid person; dolt.

du·ly (dōō/lē, dyōō/-) ►*adv.* **1.** In a proper manner: *a duly appointed official.* **2.** At the expected time.

Du·mas (dōō-mä/, dyōō-, dü-), **Alexandre** "Dumas père." 1802–70. French writer.

dumb (dŭm) ►*adj.* -**er, -est 1.** Stupid; silly. **2.** Unintentional: *dumb luck.* **3a.** Lacking the power of speech. Used of animals and objects. **b.** *Offensive* Incapable of using speech; mute. Used of humans. **4.** Temporarily speechless, as with shock or fear: *I was dumb with disbelief.* [< OE.] —**dumb/ly** *adv.* —**dumb/ness** *n.*

dumb·bell (dŭm/bĕl/) ►*n.* **1.** A weight consisting of a short bar with a metal ball or disk at each end lifted for muscular exercise. **2.** *Slang* A stupid person.

dumb·found also **dum·found** (dŭm/found/) ►*v.* To fill with astonishment and perplexity; confound. [DUMB + (CON)FOUND.]

dum·my (dŭm/ē) ►*n., pl.* -**mies 1.** An imitation of a real object used as a substitute. **2a.** A mannequin used in displaying clothes. **b.** A figure of a person or animal manipulated by a ventriloquist. **3.** A stupid person. **4.** A person secretly in the service of another. **5.** *Games* The partner in bridge who exposes his or her hand to be played by the declarer. ►*adj.* **1.** Simulating or replacing something but lacking its function: *a dummy pocket.* **2.** Serving as a front for another: *a dummy corporation.* [< DUMB.]

dump (dŭmp) ►*v.* **1.** To release in a large mass. **2.** To empty (material) out of a container or vehicle. **3.** *Informal* To get rid of; discard: *dump an old friend.* **4.** To place (e.g., goods or stock) on the market in large quantities at a low price. **5.** *Comp.* To transfer (data) from one place to another, as from a memory to a printout, without processing. **6.** *Slang* To criticize another severely: *was always dumping on me.* ►*n.* **1.** A place where refuse is dumped. **2.** A storage place; depot. **3.** *Comp.* An instance or the result of dumping stored data. **4.** *Slang* A poorly maintained or disreputable place. [ME *dumpen.*] —**dump/er** *n.*

dump·ling (dŭmp/lĭng) ►*n.* **1.** A piece of dough,

sometimes filled, cooked in liquid such as soup.
2. Sweetened dough wrapped around fruit and served as a dessert. [Perh. < *dump*, lump.]

dumps (dŭmps) ►*pl.n.* A melancholy state of mind; depression. [Prob. < Du. *domp*, haze.]

dump truck ►*n.* A truck having a bed that tilts backward to dump loose material.

dump·y¹ (dŭm′pē) ►*adj.* **-i·er, -i·est** Short and stout; squat. [Prob. < *dump*, lump.] —**dump′i·ness** *n.*

dum·py² (dŭm′pē) ►*adj.* **-i·er, -i·est** Resembling a dump; shabby; disreputable.

dun¹ (dŭn) ►*v.* **dunned, dun·ning** To importune (a debtor) for payment. [?] —**dun** *n.*

dun² (dŭn) ►*n.* **1.** A neutral brownish gray. **2.** A horse of this color. [< OE *dunn*.]

Dun·bar (dŭn′bär), **Paul Laurence** 1872–1906. Amer. writer.

Dun·can (dŭng′kən), **Isadora** 1877–1927. Amer. dancer.

dunce (dŭns) ►*n.* A stupid person. [After John *Duns* Scotus (1265?–1308).]

dun·der·head (dŭn′dər-hĕd′) ►*n.* A dunce. [Perh. Du. *donder*, thunder + HEAD.]

dune (dōōn, dyōōn) ►*n.* A hill or ridge of wind-blown sand. [< MDu. *dūne*.]

dune buggy ►*n.* A recreational vehicle having oversize tires designed for use on sand.

dung (dŭng) ►*n.* Animal excrement; manure. [< OE.]

dun·ga·ree (dŭng′gə-rē′) ►*n.* **1.** A sturdy, often blue denim fabric. **2. dungarees** Trousers or overalls made of denim. [Hindi *dungrī*.]

dun·geon (dŭn′jən) ►*n.* A dark, often underground prison cell. [Poss. < Med.Lat. *domniō*, lord's tower < Lat. *dominus*, lord.]

dunk (dŭngk) ►*v.* **1.** To plunge into liquid; immerse. **2.** To dip (food) into a liquid food, such as sauce, before eating it. **3.** *Basketball* To slam (a ball) through the basket. **4.** To submerge oneself briefly in water. [Penn.Du. *dunke*.] —**dunk** *n.*

du·o (dōō′ō, dyōō′ō) ►*n., pl.* **-os 1.** *Mus.* A duet. **2.** A pair. [Ital. < Lat. *duō*, two.]

du·o·dec·i·mal (dōō′ə-dĕs′ə-məl, dyōō′-) ►*adj.* Of or based on the number 12. [< Lat. *duodecim*, twelve.]

du·o·de·num (dōō′ə-dē′nəm, dyōō′-, dōō-ŏd′-n-əm, dyōō-) ►*n., pl.* **du·o·de·na** (-nə) or **du·o·de·nums** The beginning portion of the small intestine. [< Med.Lat. *intestīnum duodēnum digitōrum*, (intestine) of twelve (fingers' length).] —**du·o·de′nal** *adj.*

dupe (dōōp, dyōōp) ►*n.* A person who is easily deceived or is used to carry out the designs of another. ►*v.* **duped, dup·ing** To deceive. [< OFr.] —**dup′a·ble** *adj.* —**dup′er** *n.*

du·ple (dōō′pəl, dyōō′-) ►*adj.* **1.** Double. **2.** *Mus.* Consisting of two or a multiple of two beats to the measure. [Lat. *duplus*.]

du·plex (dōō′plĕks′, dyōō′-) ►*adj.* Twofold; double. ►*n.* A house divided into two living units, usu. with separate entrances. [Lat.]

du·pli·cate (dōō′plĭ-kĭt, dyōō′-) ►*adj.* **1.** Identically copied from an original. **2.** Existing in two corresponding parts; double. ►*n.* An identical copy; facsimile. ►*v.* (-kāt′) **-cat·ed, -cat·ing 1.** To make an exact copy of. **2.** To make or perform again; repeat. [< Lat. *duplicāre*, to double.] —**du′pli·ca′tion** *n.* —**du′pli·ca′tor** *n.*

du·plic·i·ty (dōō-plĭs′ĭ-tē, dyōō-) ►*n., pl.* **-ties**

Deliberate deceptiveness in behavior or speech. [< Lat. *duplex, duplic-*, twofold.] —**du·plic′i·tous** *adj.* —**du·plic′i·tous·ness** *n.*

du·ra·ble (dŏor′ə-bəl, dyŏor′-) ►*adj.* **1.** Capable of withstanding wear and tear. **2.** Lasting; stable: *a durable friendship*. [< Lat. *dūrāre*, to last.] —**du′ra·bil′i·ty, du′ra·ble·ness** *n.* —**du′ra·bly** *adv.*

du·ra ma·ter (dŏor′ə mā′tər, mä′-, dyŏor′ə) ►*n.* The tough fibrous membrane covering the brain and spinal cord. [< Med.Lat. *dūra mater*, hard mother.]

du·rance (dŏor′əns, dyŏor′-) ►*n.* Imprisonment. [< Lat. *dūrāre*, to last.]

du·ra·tion (dŏo-rā′shən, dyŏo-) ►*n.* **1.** Continuance in time. **2.** A period of existence or persistence: *sat through the duration of the show*. [< Lat. *dūrāre*, to last.]

du·ress (dŏo-rĕs′, dyŏo-) ►*n.* **1.** Constraint by threat; coercion: *confessed under duress*. **2.** *Law* Illegal coercion or confinement. **3.** Constraint or difficulty caused by misfortune: *under extreme duress after losing her job*. [< Lat. *dūritia*, hardness.]

dur·ing (dŏor′ĭng, dyŏor′-) ►*prep.* **1.** Throughout the course of. **2.** At some time in: *born during a storm*. [ME < *duren*, to last < Lat. *dūrāre*.]

du·rum (dŏor′əm, dyŏor′-, dûr′-) ►*n.* A type of wheat having hard grains, used chiefly in making pasta. [< Lat. *dūrus*, hard.]

Du·shan·be (dōō-shäm′bə) The capital of Tajikistan, in the W part.

dusk (dŭsk) ►*n.* The darker stage of twilight. [< OE *dox*.]

dusk·y (dŭs′kē) ►*adj.* **-i·er, -i·est 1.** Marked by dim light; shadowy. **2.** Rather dark in color: *dusky blue*. —**dusk′i·ness** *n.*

dust (dŭst) ►*n.* **1.** Fine, dry particles of matter. **2.** The earthy remains of a corpse. **3.** The surface of the ground. **4.** Something of no worth. **5.** Confusion; commotion: *Let's wait for the dust to settle*. ►*v.* **1.** To remove dust from by wiping or brushing. **2.** To sprinkle with a powdery substance: *dust crops with fertilizer*. —***phrasal verb:* dust off** To restore to use: *dusted off my party dress*. [< OE *dūst*.] —**dust′y** *adj.*

dust bowl ►*n.* A region reduced to aridity by drought and dust storms.

dust devil ►*n.* A small whirlwind that swirls dust and debris.

dust·er (dŭs′tər) ►*n.* **1.** One that dusts. **2.** A cloth or brush used to remove dust. **3.** A smock worn to protect clothing from dust. **4.** A woman's loose housecoat. **5.** A device for scattering a powdery substance. ►

dust·ing (dŭs′tĭng) ►*n.* **1.** A light sprinkling. **2.** *Slang* A beating or defeat: *gave the other team a good dusting*.

dust·pan (dŭst′păn′) ►*n.* A short-handled pan into which dust is swept.

dust storm ►*n.* A severe windstorm that sweeps clouds of dust across an arid region.

Dutch (dŭch) ►*adj.* **1.** Of or relating to the Netherlands or its people or language. **2.** *Archaic* German. **3.** Of or relating to the Pennsylvania Dutch. ►*n.* **1.** The people of the Netherlands. **2.** The Germanic language of the Netherlands. **3.** *Slang* Anger or temper. —***idioms:* go Dutch** To pay one's own expenses on a date. **in Dutch** In trouble. —**Dutch′man** *n.* —**Dutch′wom′an** *n.*

Dutch door ►*n.* A door divided horizontally so that either part can be left open or closed.

Dutch elm disease ►*n.* A fungal disease of elm trees resulting in eventual death.

Dutch oven ►*n.* A large heavy pot, usu. of cast iron, used for slow cooking.

Dutch treat ►*n.* An outing, as for dinner or a movie, in which all persons pay their own expenses.

du·te·ous (do͞o′tē-əs, dyo͞o′-) ►*adj.* Obedient; dutiful. **—du′te·ous·ly** *adv.*

du·ti·a·ble (do͞o′tē-ə-bəl, dyo͞o′-) ►*adj.* Subject to import tax.

du·ti·ful (do͞o′tĭ-fəl, dyo͞o′-) ►*adj.* **1.** Careful to fulfill obligations. **2.** Expressing or filled with a sense of obligation. **—du′ti·ful·ly** *adv.*

du·ty (do͞o′tē, dyo͞o′-) ►*n., pl.* **-ties 1.** An act or course of action required of one: *the duties of a critical care nurse.* **2.** Moral or legal obligation. **3.** Active military service: *a tour of duty.* **4.** Function or work; service: *jury duty.* See Synonyms at **function. 5.** A tax charged by a government, esp. on imports. [< AN *duete* < *due,* var. of OFr. *deu,* DUE.]

DVD (dē′vē-dē′) ►*n.* A high-density optical disc for storing large amounts of data esp. for high-resolution audio-visual material. [*d*(*igital*) *v*(*ideo*)*d*(*isc*) and *d*(*igital*) *v*(*ersatile*) *d*(*isc*).]

DVM ►*abbr.* Doctor of Veterinary Medicine

Dvoř·ák (dvôr′zhäk, -zhäk), **Anton** 1841–1904. Czech composer.

DVR ►*abbr.* digital video recorder

dwarf (dwôrf) ►*n., pl.* **dwarfs** or **dwarves** (dwôrvz) **1.** An abnormally small, often atypically proportioned person, animal, or plant. **2.** A small creature appearing in fairy tales. ►*v.* **1.** To check the growth of; stunt. **2.** To cause to appear small by comparison. [< OE *dweorh.*] **—dwarf′ish** *adj.* **—dwarf′ish·ness** *n.*

dwarf planet ►*n.* A celestial body that orbits the sun, is large enough to have a nearly round shape, does not clear the neighborhood around its orbit, and is not a satellite of a planet.

dwell (dwĕl) ►*v.* **dwelt** (dwĕlt) or **dwelled, dwell·ing 1.** To live as a resident; reside. **2.** To exist in a given place or state: *dwell in joy.* **3a.** To fasten one's attention, esp. moodily or persistently: *dwelling on what went wrong.* See Synonyms at **brood. b.** To speak or write at length: *dwelt on balancing the budget.* [< OE *dwellan,* mislead, delay.] **—dwell′er** *n.*

dwell·ing (dwĕl′ĭng) ►*n.* A place to live in.

DWI ►*abbr.* driving while intoxicated

dwin·dle (dwĭn′dl) ►*v.* **-dled, -dling** To make or become gradually less until little remains. [< OE *dwīnan,* shrink.]

dyb·buk (dĭb′o͝ok, dē-bo͞ok′) ►*n., pl.* **-buks** or **dyb·buk·im** (dĭ-bo͞ok′ĭm, dē′bo͞o-kēm′) In Jewish folklore, the soul of a dead person that enters and takes control of the body of a living person. [< Heb. *dibbūq.*]

dye (dī) ►*n.* **1.** A substance used to color materials. **2.** A color imparted by dyeing. ►*v.* **dyed, dye·ing 1.** To color (a material) with a dye. **2.** To take on or impart color. [< OE *dēag, dēah.*] **—dy′er** *n.*

dy·ing (dī′ĭng) ►*adj.* **1.** About to die. **2.** Drawing to an end; declining: *shadows seen in the dying light.* **3.** Done or uttered just before death.

dy·nam·ic (dī-năm′ĭk) ►*adj.* also **dy·nam·i·cal** (-ĭ-kəl) **1.** Of or relating to energy or to objects in motion. **2.** Marked by continuous change or activity: *a dynamic housing market.* **3.** Marked by intensity and vigor; forceful. **4.** Relating to variation of intensity, as in musical sound. ►*n.* **1.** An interactive system, esp. one involving conflicting forces. **2.** A force, esp. political, social, or psychological: *the main dynamic behind the revolution.* [< Gk. *dunamis,* power.] **—dy·nam′i·cal·ly** *adv.*

dy·nam·ics (dī-năm′ĭks) ►*n.* **1a.** *(takes sing. v.)* The branch of mechanics concerned with the effects of forces on the motion of a body or system, esp. of forces not originating in the system. **b.** *(takes pl. v.)* The physical forces that characterize a system: *the dynamics of ocean waves.* **2.** *(takes pl. v.)* The social, intellectual, or moral forces that produce activity and change in a given sphere: *the dynamics of international trade.*

dy·na·mite (dī′nə-mīt′) ►*n.* **1.** A powerful explosive composed of nitroglycerin or ammonium nitrate dispersed in an absorbent medium. **2.** *Slang* Something exceptionally exciting or dangerous. ►*v.* **-mit·ed, -mit·ing** To blow up or destroy with dynamite. ►*adj. Slang* Outstanding; superb. [Swed. *dynamit.*]

dy·na·mo (dī′nə-mō′) ►*n., pl.* **-mos 1.** A generator, esp. one for producing direct current. **2.** An energetic and forceful person. [< *dynamo-electric machine.*]

dy·na·mom·e·ter (dī′nə-mŏm′ĭ-tər) ►*n.* An instrument used to measure mechanical power. [Fr. *dynamomètre.*] **—dy′na·mom′e·try** *n.*

dy·nas·ty (dī′nə-stē) ►*n., pl.* **-ties 1.** A succession of rulers from the same family or line. **2.** A group that maintains power for several generations: *a political dynasty controlling the city.* [< Gk. *dunasteia,* lordship.] **—dy·nas′tic** (dī-năs′tĭk) *adj.*

dys– ►*pref.* Abnormal; impaired; difficult; bad: *dysplasia.* [< Gk. *dus-.*]

dys·en·ter·y (dĭs′ən-tĕr′ē) ►*n.* An inflammatory disorder of the lower intestinal tract, resulting in severe diarrhea often with blood and mucus. [< Gk. *dusenteria.*] **—dys′en·ter′ic** *adj.*

dys·func·tion (dĭs-fŭngk′shən) ►*n.* **1.** Abnormal or impaired functioning, esp. of a bodily system or organ. **2.** Failure to achieve or sustain a behavioral norm or expected condition, as in a social relationship. **—dys·func′tion·al** *adj.*

dys·lex·i·a (dĭs-lĕk′sē-ə) ►*n.* A learning disorder marked by impairment of the ability to recognize and understand written words. [DYS– + Gk. *lexis,* speech.] **—dys·lex′ic** *adj. & n.*

dys·pep·sia (dĭs-pĕp′shə, -sē-ə) ►*n.* Indigestion. [< Gk. *duspepsia.*] **—dys·pep′tic** *adj. & n.*

dys·pla·sia (dĭs-plā′zhə, -zhē-ə) ►*n.* Abnormal development of tissues, organs, or cells. **—dys·plas′tic** (-plăs′tĭk) *adj.*

dys·pro·si·um (dĭs-prō′zē-əm, -zhē-əm) ►*n. Symbol* **Dy** A soft, silvery rare-earth element used in nuclear reactors and laser materials. At. no. 66. See table at **element.** [< Gk. *dusprositos,* difficult to approach (from its rarity in nature).]

dys·tro·phy (dĭs′trə-fē) ►*n.* **1.** A degenerative disorder caused by inadequate nutrition. **2.** Any of several disorders, esp. muscular dystrophy, in which the muscles weaken and atrophy. **—dys·troph′ic** *adj.*

dz. ►*abbr.* dozen

E

e¹ or **E** (ē) ►*n., pl.* **e's** or **E's** also **es** or **Es 1.** The 5th letter of the English alphabet. **2.** *Mus.* The 3rd tone of the C major scale. **3. E** A failing grade.

e² ►*abbr.* electron

E ►*abbr.* **1.** east **2.** *Baseball* error

e– ►*pref.* Computer or computer network: *e-commerce.* [< ELECTRONIC.]

ea. ►*abbr.* each

each (ēch) ►*adj.* Being one of two or more considered individually; every. See Usage Note at **every.** ►*pron.* Every one of a group considered individually; each one. ►*adv.* For or to each one; apiece. [< OE *ǣlc.*]

each other ►*pron.* Each the other. Used to indicate a reciprocal relationship or action: *The children like each other.*

ea·ger (ē′gər) ►*adj.* **-er, -est** Having or showing keen interest or impatient expectancy. [< Lat. *ācer,* sharp.] —**ea′ger·ly** *adv.* —**ea′ger·ness** *n.*

ea·gle (ē′gəl) ►*n.* **1.** A large bird of prey with a powerful hooked bill and strong soaring flight. **2.** A golf score of two under par on a hole. [< Lat. *aquila.*]

ea·glet (ē′glĭt) ►*n.* A young eagle.

ear¹ (îr) ►*n.* **1.** *Anat.* **a.** The vertebrate organ of hearing, responsible for maintaining equilibrium and sensing sound. **b.** The visible outer part of this organ. **2.** The sense of hearing. **3.** Aural sensitivity, esp. to differences in musical pitch. **4.** Sympathetic attention. **5.** Something resembling the vertebrate ear. —*idioms:* **all ears** Acutely attentive. **up to (one's) ears** Deeply involved. [< OE *ēare.*] —**eared** *adj.* —**ear′less** *adj.*

ear² (îr) ►*n.* The seed-bearing spike of a cereal plant, such as corn. [< OE *ēar.*]

ear·ache (îr′āk′) ►*n.* Pain in the ear.

ear·bud (îr′bŭd′) ►*n.* A small headphone that fits inside the ear.

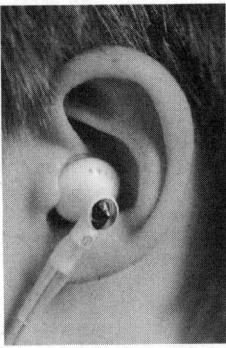

earbud

ear canal ►*n.* The narrow, tubelike passage through which sound enters the ear.

ear·drum (îr′drŭm′) ►*n.* The thin membrane that separates the middle ear from the external ear.

ear·flap (îr′flăp′) ►*n.* A flap attached to a cap used to cover the ears.

ear·ful (îr′fool′) ►*n.* **1.** An excessive amount of something heard, such as gossip. **2.** A reprimand.

Ear·hart (âr′härt′), **Amelia** 1897?–1937. Amer. aviator.

Amelia Earhart
photographed in 1932

earl (ûrl) ►*n.* A British nobleman next in rank above a viscount and below a marquis. [< OE *eorl,* nobleman.] —**earl′dom** *n.*

ear·lobe (îr′lōb′) ►*n.* The soft pendulous lower part of the external ear.

ear·ly (ûr′lē) ►*adj.* **-li·er, -li·est 1.** Of or occurring near the beginning of a series, period of time, or course of events. **2.** Belonging to a previous or remote period of time: *early mammals.* **3.** Occurring or developing before the expected time. **4.** Occurring in the near future: *predicted an early end to the negotiations.* ►*adv.* **-lier, -liest 1.** Near the beginning of a given series, period of time, or course of events. **2.** At or during a remote or initial period. **3.** Before the expected or usual time: *arrived early.* [< OE *ǣrlīce.*] —**ear′li·ness** *n.*

ear·mark (îr′märk′) ►*n.* **1.** An identifying feature or characteristic. **2.** A brand on the ear of a domestic animal. **3.** A provision in a legislative bill that allots money in a specific locale and is sponsored by a representative from that area. ►*v.* **1.** To set aside for a particular purpose. See Synonyms at **allocate. 2.** To brand with an earmark. **3.** To specify (funds) to be spent in a legislative earmark.

ear·muff (îr′mŭf′) ►*n.* Either of a pair of ear coverings worn to protect against the cold.

earn (ûrn) ►*v.* **1.** To gain esp. for the performance of service or labor. **2.** To acquire or deserve as a result of effort or action. **3.** To yield as return or profit. [< OE *earnian.*] —**earn′er** *n.*

> *Syns: deserve, merit, rate, win* **v.**

earned run (ûrnd) ►*n.* *Baseball* A run scored when no errors have been made to allow runners to advance, charged as the pitcher's responsibility.

ear·nest (ûr′nĭst) ►*adj.* Showing sincerity or seriousness. —*idiom:* **in earnest** With a purposeful or sincere intent. [< OE *eornoste.*] —**ear′nest·ly** *adv.*

earnest money ►*n.* Money paid as partial payment of a purchase price in order to establish a binding contract of sale.

earn·ings (ûr′nĭngz) ►*pl.n.* **1.** Salary or wages. **2.** Profits from business or investments.

ear·phone (îr′fōn′) ►*n.* A small speaker that is worn in or over the ear, esp. as one of a pair.

ear·piece (îr′pēs′) ►*n.* **1a.** A part, as of a telephone receiver, that fits in or is held next to the ear. **b.** An earphone, esp. when not part of a pair. **2.** Either of the two parts of an eyeglasses frame that extend over the ear.

ear·plug (îr′plŭg′) ►*n.* A soft plug fitted into the ear canal to keep out water or sound.

ear·ring (îr′rĭng, îr′ĭng) ►*n.* An ornament worn on the ear, esp. the earlobe.

ear·shot (îr′shŏt′) ►*n.* The range within which sound can be heard.

ear·split·ting (îr′splĭt′ĭng) ►*adj.* Loud and shrill enough to hurt the ears: *an earsplitting shriek.*

earth (ûrth) ►*n.* **1a.** The land surface of the world. **b.** Soil, esp. productive soil. **2.** often **Earth** The 3rd planet from the sun, at a mean distance of approx. 149.6 million km (92.96 million mi) and with an average radius of 6,378 km (3,963 mi). **3.** The realm of mortal existence. **4.** Worldly pursuits. —*idioms:* **down to earth** Sensible; realistic. **on earth** Among all the possibilities: *Why on earth did you go?* [< OE *eorthe.*]

earth·en (ûr′thən, -thən) ►*adj.* Made of earth or clay.

earth·en·ware (ûr′thən-wâr′, -thən-) ►*n.* Pottery made from a porous clay fired at low temperatures.

earth·ling (ûrth′lĭng) ►*n.* One that inhabits the planet Earth.

earth·ly (ûrth′lē) ►*adj.* **1.** Of or characteristic of this earth; terrestrial. **2.** Not heavenly or divine; worldly. **3.** Conceivable; possible: *no earthly reason.* —**earth′li·ness** *n.*

earth·mov·er (ûrth′mōō′vər) ►*n.* A machine, such as a bulldozer, used for digging or pushing earth. —**earth′mov′ing** *adj.*

earth·quake (ûrth′kwāk′) ►*n.* A sudden movement of the earth's crust caused by the release of stress accumulated along geologic faults or by volcanic activity.

earth science ►*n.* Any of several geologic sciences concerned with the origin, structure, and physical phenomena of the earth.

earth·shak·ing (ûrth′shā′kĭng) ►*adj.* Of great consequence or importance.

earth·ward (ûrth′wərd) ►*adv. & adj.* To or toward the earth. —**earth′wards** *adv.*

earth·work (ûrth′wûrk′) ►*n.* An earthen embankment, esp. one used as a fortification.

earth·worm (ûrth′wûrm′) ►*n.* Any of various annelid worms that burrow into the soil.

earth·y (ûr′thē) ►*adj.* **-i·er, -i·est** **1.** Of, consisting of, or resembling earth. **2.** Crude; indecent. **3.** Hearty or uninhibited. —**earth′i·ly** *adv.* —**earth′i·ness** *n.*

ear·wax (îr′wăks′) ►*n.* The waxlike secretion of certain glands lining the canal of the external ear.

ear·wig (îr′wĭg′) ►*n.* An elongate insect having a pair of usu. pincerlike appendages protruding from the rear of the abdomen. [< OE *ēarwicga* : *ēar,* EAR[1] + *wicga,* insect.]

ease (ēz) ►*n.* **1a.** Freedom from pain, worry, or agitation. **b.** Freedom from constraint or embarrassment; naturalness. **2a.** Freedom from difficulty, hardship, or effort. **b.** Dexterity in performance; facility. **3.** Freedom from financial difficulty. ►*v.* **eased, eas·ing** **1.** To free from pain, worry, or agitation. **2.** To lessen the discomfort or pain of. **3.** To give respite from. **4.** To slacken; loosen. **5.** To reduce the difficulty of. **6.** To maneuver slowly and carefully. [< OFr. *aise,* perh. < Lat. *adiacēns,* ADJACENT.]

ea·sel (ē′zəl) ►*n.* An upright frame for supporting an artist's canvas. [< MDu. *esel,* ass.]

ease·ment (ēz′mənt) ►*n.* **1.** The act of easing or the condition of being eased. **2.** *Law* A right to make limited use of another's land, such as a right of way.

east (ēst) ►*n.* **1a.** The compass point 90° clockwise from north. **b.** The direction of the earth's axial rotation; the general direction of sunrise. **2.** often **East** Asia. **3.** often **East** The eastern part of a region or country. ►*adj.* **1.** To, toward, of, or in the east. **2.** Coming from the east: *an east wind.* ►*adv.* In, from, or toward the east. [< OE *ēast.*] —**east′ward, east′ward·ly** *adj. & adv.* —**east′wards** *adv.*

East Asia A region of Asia consisting of China, Japan, Korea, and nearby countries. —**East Asian** *adj. & n.*

East China Sea An arm of the W Pacific bounded by China, South Korea, Taiwan, and the Ryukyu and Kyushu Islands.

Eas·ter (ē′stər) ►*n.* A Christian feast commemorating the Resurrection of Jesus, observed on a Sunday in March or April. [< OE *ēastre.*]

Easter Island An island of Chile in the S Pacific about 3,700 km (2,300 mi) W of the mainland, famous for its colossal heads carved from volcanic rock.

east·er·ly (ē′stər-lē) ►*adj.* **1.** Situated toward the east. **2.** From the east: *easterly winds.* —**east′er·ly** *adv.*

east·ern (ē′stərn) ►*adj.* **1.** Of, in, or toward the east. **2.** From the east: *eastern breezes.* **3.** often **Eastern** Of or characteristic of eastern regions or the East. **4. Eastern a.** Of those Christian churches centered in Asia, North Africa, and Eastern Europe. **b.** Of the Eastern Orthodox Church. [< OE *ēasterne.*]

east·ern·er also **East·ern·er** (ē′stər-nər) ►*n.* A native or inhabitant of the east, esp. the E US.

Eastern Hemisphere The half of the earth comprising Europe, Africa, Asia, and Australia.

Eastern Orthodox Church ►*n.* Any of the Christian churches in communion with the patriarch of Constantinople.

East Germany A former country of N Europe on the Baltic Sea (1949–90). —**East German** *adj. & n.*

East Indies **1.** The islands comprising Indonesia. **2.** A general term formerly used for India and SE Asia. —**East Indian** *adj.*

East Timor A country of the W Pacific Ocean made up of the E part of Timor, a small enclave in the W part, and two offshore islands. Cap. Dili.

eas·y (ē′zē) ►*adj.* **-i·er, -i·est** **1a.** Capable of being accomplished without difficulty. **b.** Likely to happen by accident or without intention. **2.** Requiring or exhibiting little effort or endeavor. **3.** Free from worry, anxiety, trouble, or pain. **4.** Causing little hardship or distress. **5.** Socially at ease. **6a.** Relaxed in attitude; easygoing. **b.** Not strict or severe; lenient. **7.** Readily exploited, imposed on, or tricked. **8.** Not hurried or forced; moderate. ►*adv.* Without strain or difficulty; in a relaxed manner. [< OFr. *aaisier*, to put at ease < *aise*, EASE.] —**eas′i·ly** *adv.* —**eas′i·ness** *n.*

easy chair ►*n.* A large comfortable chair.

eas·y·go·ing (ē′zē-gō′ĭng) ►*adj.* **1.** Living without worry or concern; relaxed. **2.** Not rigorous, demanding, or stressful. **3.** Unhurried.

eat (ēt) ►*v.* **ate** (āt), **eat·en** (ēt′n), **eat·ing 1.** To consume (food). **2.** To consume or ravage as if by eating. **3.** To erode or corrode. **4.** *Slang* To absorb the cost of. **5.** *Informal* To bother or annoy. —*idioms:* **eat crow** To be forced to accept a humiliating defeat. **eat (one's) words** To retract an assertion. **eat out of (someone's) hand** To be manipulated by another. [< OE *etan.*] —**eat′a·ble** *adj. & n.* —**eat′er** *n.*
Syns: *consume, devour, ingest* **v.**

eat·er·y (ē′tə-rē) ►*n.*, *pl.* **-ies** A restaurant.

eat·ing disorder (ē′tĭng) ►*n.* A psychiatric disorder, such as anorexia nervosa, characterized by disturbances in eating behavior.

eau de toi·lette (ō′ də twä-lĕt′) ►*n.*, *pl.* **eaux de toilette** (ō′, ōz′) A scented liquid with a high alcohol content used in bathing or applied as a skin freshener. [Fr. : *eau*, water + *de*, of + *toilette*, toilette.]

eaves (ēvz) ►*pl.n.* The projecting overhang at the lower edge of a roof. [< OE *efes.*]

eaves·drop (ēvz′drŏp′) ►*v.* **-dropped, -drop·ping** To listen secretly to private conversations. [< ME *evesdrop*, place where water falls from the eaves.]

E·ban (ē′bən), **Abba** 1915–2002. South African–born Israeli politician.

ebb (ĕb) ►*n.* **1.** The period of a tide between high tide and a following low tide. **2.** A period of decline or diminution. ►*v.* **1.** To fall back from the flood stage. **2.** To decline or diminish. See Synonyms at **recede.** [< OE *ebba.*]

EBITDA ►*abbr.* earnings before interest, taxes, depreciation, and amortization

EbN ►*abbr.* east by north

eb·on·ite (ĕb′ə-nīt′) ►*n.* A hard rubber used as an electrical insulating material.

eb·on·y (ĕb′ə-nē) ►*n.*, *pl.* **-ies 1.** The hard dark wood of a tropical Asian tree. **2.** The color black. ►*adj.* Of or like ebony; black. [< Gk. *ebeninos*, of ebony, of Egypt. orig.]

Eb·ro (ē′brō, ĕ′vrō) A river rising in N Spain and flowing about 925 km (575 mi) to the Mediterranean.

EbS ►*abbr.* east by south

e·bul·lient (ĭ-bŏŏl′yənt, ĭ-bŭl′-) ►*adj.* **1.** Zestfully enthusiastic. **2.** Boiling or seeming to boil; bubbling. [< Lat. *ēbullīre*, to bubble up.] —**e·bul′lience** *n.* —**e·bul′lient·ly** *adv.*

eb·ul·li·tion (ĕb′ə-lĭsh′ən) ►*n.* **1.** The state or process of boiling. **2.** A sudden outpouring, as of emotion.

ec·cen·tric (ĭk-sĕn′trĭk, ĕk-) ►*adj.* **1.** Departing from a conventional pattern. **2.** Deviating from a circular path, as in an elliptical orbit. **3.** Not situated at or in the geometric center. ►*n.* **1.** One that deviates from conventional patterns. **2.** *Phys.* A disk or wheel having its axis of revolution displaced from its center so that it is capable of imparting reciprocating motion.

[< Gk. *ekkentros*, not having the same center.] —**ec·cen′tri·cal·ly** *adv.* —**ec′cen·tric′i·ty** *n.*

Ec·cle·si·as·tes (ĭ-klē′zē-ăs′tēz′) ►*n. (takes sing. v.)* See table at **Bible.**

ec·cle·si·as·tic (ĭ-klē′zē-ăs′tĭk) ►*adj.* Ecclesiastical. ►*n.* A minister or priest; cleric. [< Gk. *ekklēsiastēs*, member of the assembly.]

ec·cle·si·as·ti·cal (ĭ-klē′zē-ăs′tĭ-kəl) ►*adj.* Of or relating to a church, esp. as an institution. —**ec·cle′si·as′ti·cal·ly** *adv.*

Ec·cle·si·as·ti·cus (ĭ-klē′zē-ăs′tĭ-kəs) ►*n.* See table at **Bible.**

ec·dy·sis (ĕk′dĭ-sĭs) ►*n.*, *pl.* **-ses** (-sēz′) The shedding of an outer layer, as by insects, crustaceans, and snakes; molting. [Gk. *ekdusis*, a stripping off < *ekduein*, to take off.]

ECG ►*abbr.* **1.** electrocardiogram **2.** electrocardiograph

ech·e·lon (ĕsh′ə-lŏn′) ►*n.* **1.** A steplike formation, as of troops or aircraft. **2.** A subdivision of a military force. **3.** A level of authority in a hierarchy; rank. [< OFr. *eschelon*, rung of a ladder.]

ech·i·na·ce·a (ĕk′ə-nā′sē-ə, -nā′shə) ►*n.* Any of several usu. pinkish-purple coneflower plants used in herbal medicine. [Ult. < Lat. *echīnus*, sea urchin (from its rough leaves).]

e·chi·no·derm (ĭ-kī′nə-dûrm′) ►*n.* Any of various gen. spiny marine invertebrates having an internal calcareous skeleton, including starfishes and sea urchins. [< Gk. *ekhinos*, sea urchin.]

ech·o (ĕk′ō) ►*n.*, *pl.* **-oes 1a.** Repetition of a sound by reflection of sound waves from a surface. **b.** The sound that is produced in this manner. **2.** A remnant or vestige. **3.** One who imitates another. **4.** A consequence or repercussion. ►*v.* **-oed, -o·ing 1.** To repeat or be repeated by or as if by an echo; imitate: *followers echoing the cries of their leader.* **2.** To resound; reverberate. [< Gk. *ēkhō.*] —**ech′o·er** *n.* —**e·cho′ic** *adj.*
Syns: *reflect, resound, reverberate* **v.**

Echo ►*n.* Gk. Myth. A nymph whose unrequited love for Narcissus caused her to pine away until only her voice remained.

echo chamber ►*n.* A room with acoustically reflective walls used in broadcasting and recording.

ech·o·gram (ĕk′ō-grăm′) ►*n.* A sonogram.

ech·o·lo·ca·tion (ĕk′ō-lō-kā′shən) ►*n.* **1.** *Zool.* A sensory system, as in bats or dolphins, in which usu. high-pitched sounds are emitted and their echoes interpreted to determine the location of objects. **2.** *Electron.* Ranging by acoustical echo analysis. —**ech′o·lo·cate′** *v.*

é·clair (ā-klâr′, ā′klâr′) ►*n.* An elongated pastry filled with custard or whipped cream and usu. iced with chocolate. [< OFr. *esclair*, lightning.]

é·clat (ā-klä′, ā′klä′) ►*n.* **1.** Great brilliance, as of achievement. **2.** Great acclamation. [< OFr. *esclater*, burst out.]

e·clec·tic (ĭ-klĕk′tĭk) ►*adj.* Selecting or employing individual elements from a variety of sources, systems, or styles. [< Gk. *eklegein*, select.] —**e·clec′tic** *n.* —**e·clec′ti·cal·ly** *adv.* —**e·clec′ti·cism′** *n.*

e·clipse (ĭ-klĭps′) ►*n.* **1a.** The partial or complete obscuring of one celestial body by another. **b.** The period of time during which such an obscuration occurs. **2.** A fall into obscurity or disuse; decline. ►*v.* **e·clipsed, e·clips·ing 1.** To cause an eclipse of. **2.** To surpass; outshine. [< Gk. *ekleipsis* < *ekleipein*, fail to appear.]

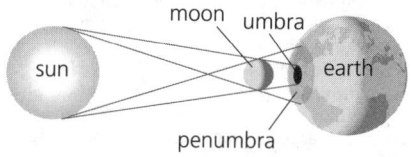

eclipse
solar eclipse

e·clip·tic (ĭ-klĭp′tĭk) ►*n.* **1.** The plane defined by the earth's orbit projected onto the celestial sphere, along which the sun appears to move as viewed from the earth. **2.** The plane defined by the earth's solar orbit, with the sun at its center, that extends throughout the solar system. [< Med.Lat. *(línea) eclíptica*, (line) of eclipses.]

ec·logue (ĕk′lôg′, -lŏg′) ►*n.* A pastoral poem. [< Gk. *eklogē*, selection.]

e·col·o·gy (ĭ-kŏl′ə-jē) ►*n.* The science of the relationships between organisms and their environments. [Ger. *Ökologie* : Gk. *oikos*, house + –LOGY.] —**ec′o·log′i·cal** (ĕk′ə-lŏj′ĭ-kəl, ē′kə-), **ec′o·log′ic** *adj.* —**ec′o·log′i·cal·ly** *adv.* —**e·col′o·gist** *n.*

e-com·merce (ē′kŏm′ərs) ►*n.* Commerce transacted electronically, as over the Internet.

e·con·o·met·rics (ĭ-kŏn′ə-mĕt′rĭks) ►*n.* (takes *sing. v.*) Application of mathematical and statistical techniques to economics.

ec·o·nom·ic (ĕk′ə-nŏm′ĭk, ē′kə-) ►*adj.* **1.** Of or relating to the production, development, and management of material wealth, as of a country. **2.** Of or relating to the necessities of life. **3.** Efficient; economical.

ec·o·nom·i·cal (ĕk′ə-nŏm′ĭ-kəl, ē′kə-) ►*adj.* **1.** Designed to make effective use of money or effort invested: *an economical heating system.* **2.** Prudent and thrifty; not wasteful. **3.** Sparing in the amount of items involved to achieve a desired result: *an economical writing style.* —**ec′o·nom′i·cal·ly** *adv.*

ec·o·nom·ics (ĕk′ə-nŏm′ĭks, ē′kə-) ►*n.* **1.** (takes *sing. v.*) The science that deals with the production, distribution, and consumption of goods and services. **2.** (takes *sing. or pl. v.*) Economic matters. —**e·con′o·mist** (ĭ-kŏn′ə-mĭst) *n.*

e·con·o·mize (ĭ-kŏn′ə-mīz′) ►*v.* **-mized, -miz·ing** To practice economy, as by avoiding waste.

e·con·o·my (ĭ-kŏn′ə-mē) ►*n., pl.* **-mies 1a.** Careful, thrifty management of resources. **b.** An example of such management. **2.** The system of economic activity in a country or region. **3.** Efficient or sparing use. [< Gk. *oikonomia*, management of a household.]

e·co·sys·tem (ē′kō-sĭs′təm, ĕk′ō-) ►*n.* An ecological community together with its environment, functioning as a unit.

e·co·tour·ism (ē′kō-tŏŏr′ĭz′əm, ĕk′ō-) ►*n.* Travel to areas of ecological interest, usu. with a guide. [ECO(LOGY) + TOURISM.]

ec·ru (ĕk′rōō, ā′krōō) ►*n.* A light tan color. [< OFr. *escru*, raw, unbleached.]

ec·sta·sy (ĕk′stə-sē) ►*n., pl.* **-sies** Intense joy or delight; rapture. [< Gk. *ekstasis*, astonishment : *ex-*, out of + *histanai*, to place.] —**ec·stat·ic** (ĕk-stăt′ĭk) *adj.* —**ec·stat′i·cal·ly** *adv.*

–ectomy ►*suff.* Surgical removal: *tonsillectomy.* [Gk. *ek-*, out + NLat. *-tomia*, a cutting.]

ec·top·ic pregnancy (ĕk-tŏp′ĭk) ►*n.* Implantation and subsequent development of a fertilized ovum outside the uterus, as in a fallopian tube. [< Gk. *ektopos*, out of place.]

ec·to·therm (ĕk′tə-thûrm′) ►*n.* An organism that depends on external sources for its body heat. [Gk. *ektos*, outside + *thermos*, heat.] —**ec′to·ther′mic, ec′to·ther′mal, ec′to·ther′mous** *adj.*

Ec·ua·dor (ĕk′wə-dôr′) A country of NW South America on the Pacific Ocean. Cap. Quito. —**Ec′ua·dor′i·an** *adj. & n.*

ec·u·men·i·cal (ĕk′yə-mĕn′ĭ-kəl) also **ec·u·men·ic** (-mĕn′ĭk) ►*adj.* **1.** Of worldwide scope or applicability; universal. **2.** Of or relating to ecumenism. [< Gk. *(hē) oikoumenē (gē)*, (the) inhabited (world) < *oikein*, inhabit.] —**ec′u·men′i·cal·ly** *adv.*

ec·u·me·nism (ĕk′yə-mə-nĭz′əm) ►*n.* A movement promoting unity among Christian churches or denominations. —**ec′u·men′ist** *n.*

ec·ze·ma (ĕk′sə-mə, ĕg′zə-, ĭg-zē′-) ►*n.* A noncontagious skin inflammation marked by redness, itching, and lesions. [< Gk. *ekzema*, boil over.]

ed. ►*abbr.* **1.** edition **2.** editor

–ed¹ ►*suff.* Used to form the past tense of regular verbs: *waited.* [< OE *-ade, -ede, -ode.*]

–ed² ►*suff.* Used to form the past participle of regular verbs: *linked.* [< OE *-ad, -ed, -od.*]

–ed³ ►*suff.* Having; characterized by; resembling: *longhaired.* [< OE *-ed, -od.*]

E·dam (ē′dəm, ē′dăm′) ►*n.* A mild yellow Dutch cheese, usu. covered with red wax. [After *Edam*, the Netherlands.]

ed·a·ma·me (ĕd′ə-mä′mā) ►*pl.n.* Fresh green soybeans, typically prepared by boiling in salted water. [J. : *eda*, twig + *mame*, bean.]

ed·dy (ĕd′ē) ►*n., pl.* **-dies** A current, as of water or air, moving contrary to the direction of the main current, esp. in a circular motion. [ME *ydy.*] —**ed′dy** *v.*

Eddy, Mary (Morse) Baker 1821–1910. Amer. religious leader who founded Christian Science (1879).

e·del·weiss (ā′dəl-vīs′, -wīs′) ►*n.* An alpine plant having downy leaves and small whitish flowers. [Ger.]

edelweiss

e·de·ma (ĭ-dē′mə) ►*n. Med.* An excessive amount of watery fluid in cells, tissues, or serous cavities. [< Gk. *oidēma,* a swelling.] —**e·dem′a·tous** (ĭ-dĕm′ə-təs) *adj.*

E·den (ēd′n) ►*n.* **1.** *Bible* The garden of God and first home of Adam and Eve. **2.** A state of innocence or bliss. [< Heb. *ʿēden,* delight.] —**E·den′ic** (ē-dĕn′ĭk) *adj.*

Eden, Sir **(Robert) Anthony.** 1st Earl of Avon. 1897–1977. British prime minister (1955–57).

edge (ĕj) ►*n.* **1a.** A thin sharpened side, as of the blade of a cutting instrument. **b.** A penetrating, incisive quality. **c.** A slight but noticeable sharpness or harshness. **d.** Keenness; zest. **2a.** The line of intersection of two surfaces. **b.** A rim or brink. **3.** An advantage. ►*v.* **edged, edg·ing** **1.** To give an edge to. **2.** To advance or push gradually. —*idiom:* **on edge** Highly tense or nervous; irritable. [< OE *ecg.*] —**edg′er** *n.*

edge·wise (ĕj′wīz′) also **edge·ways** (-wāz′) ►*adv.* With the edge foremost.

edg·ing (ĕj′ĭng) ►*n.* Something that forms an edge or border.

edg·y (ĕj′ē) ►*adj.* **-i·er, -i·est** **1.** Nervous or irritable. **2.** Having a sharp or biting edge. —**edg′i·ly** *adv.* —**edg′i·ness** *n.*

ed·i·ble (ĕd′ə-bəl) ►*adj.* Fit to be eaten. [< Lat. *edere,* eat.] —**ed′i·bil′i·ty, ed′i·ble·ness** *n.* —**ed′i·ble** *n.*

e·dict (ē′dĭkt′) ►*n.* A proclamation issued by an authority. [Lat. *ēdictum* < p.part. of *ēdīcere,* declare.]

ed·i·fice (ĕd′ə-fĭs) ►*n.* A building, esp. one of imposing size. [< Lat. *aedificium.*]

ed·i·fy (ĕd′ə-fī′) ►*v.* **-fied, -fy·ing** To instruct, esp. to encourage moral or spiritual improvement. [< Lat. *aedificāre,* build.] —**ed′i·fi·ca′tion** *n.* —**ed′i·fi′er** *n.*

Ed·in·burgh (ĕd′n-bûr′ə, -bûr′ə, -brə) The capital of Scotland, in the E part on an inlet of the North Sea.

Ed·i·son (ĕd′ĭ-sən), **Thomas Alva** 1847–1931. Amer. inventor.

ed·it (ĕd′ĭt) ►*v.* **1.** To prepare (e.g., a manuscript) for publication, as by correcting or revising. **2.** To supervise the publication of. **3.** To assemble the components of (e.g., a film or soundtrack), as by cutting and splicing. [< Lat. *ēdere, ēdit-,* publish : EX– + *dare,* give.] —**ed′it** *n.* —**ed′i·tor** *n.* —**ed′i·tor·ship′** *n.*

e·di·tion (ĭ-dĭsh′ən) ►*n.* **1.** The entire number of copies of a publication issued at one time. **2.** The form in which a book is published: *a paperback edition.* **3.** One that resembles an original; version.

ed·i·to·ri·al (ĕd′ĭ-tôr′ē-əl) ►*n.* **1.** An article in a publication expressing the opinion of its editors or publishers. **2.** A commentary on television or radio expressing the opinion of the station or network. ►*adj.* **1.** Of or relating to editing. **2.** Of or like an editorial. —**ed′i·to′ri·al·ly** *adv.*

ed·i·to·ri·al·ize (ĕd′ĭ-tôr′ē-ə-līz′) ►*v.* **-ized, -iz·ing** **1.** To express an opinion in or as if in an editorial. **2.** To present an opinion in the guise of an objective report.

Ed·mon·ton (ĕd′mən-tən) The capital of Alberta, Canada, in the central part of the province.

EDP ►*abbr.* electronic data processing

EDT ►*abbr.* Eastern Daylight Time

ed·u·ca·ble (ĕj′ə-kə-bəl) ►*adj.* Capable of being educated. —**ed′u·ca·bil′i·ty** *n.*

ed·u·cate (ĕj′ə-kāt′) ►*v.* **-cat·ed, -cat·ing** **1.** To develop the mental, moral, or social capabilities of, esp. by schooling or instruction. **2.** To provide with knowledge in a particular area. **3.** To provide with information. [< Lat. *ēducāre.*] —**ed′u·ca′tor** *n.*

ed·u·cat·ed (ĕj′ə-kā′tĭd) ►*adj.* **1.** Having an education, esp. one above the average. **2.** Showing evidence of schooling, training, or experience. **3.** Based on experience or knowledge: *an educated guess.*

ed·u·ca·tion (ĕj′ə-kā′shən) ►*n.* **1.** The act or process of educating or being educated. **2.** The knowledge or skill obtained. **3.** The field of study concerned with teaching and learning. —**ed′u·ca′tion·al** *adj.*

e·duce (ĭ-do͞os′, ĭ-dyo͞os′) ►*v.* **e·duced, e·duc·ing** **1.** To draw out; elicit. **2.** To deduce. [< Lat. *ēdūcere.*]

ed·u·tain·ment (ĕj′o͞o-tān′mənt, ĕj′ə-) ►*n.* Educational entertainment, esp. through media such as television or computer software. [EDU(CATION) + (ENTER)TAINMENT.]

Ed·ward¹ (ĕd′wərd) “the Confessor.” 1003?–66. King of the English (1042–66).

Edward² Prince of Wales. “the Black Prince.” 1330–76. English soldier during the Hundred Years’ War.

Edward I 1239–1307. King of England (1272–1307).

Edward II 1284–1327. King of England (1307–27).

Edward III 1312–77. King of England (1327–77).

Edward IV 1442–83. King of England (1461–70 and 1471–83).

Edward V 1470–83. King of England (1483); murdered.

Edward VI 1537–53. King of England and Ireland (1547–53).

Edward VII 1841–1910. King of Great Britain and Ireland (1901–10).

Edward VIII Duke of Windsor. 1894–1972. King of Great Britain and Ireland (1936); abdicated.

Ed·wards (ĕd′wərdz), **Jonathan** 1703–58. Amer. theologian and philosopher.

EE ►*abbr.* **1.** electrical engineer **2.** electrical engineering

–ee¹ ►*suff.* **1.** One that receives or benefits from a specified action: *addressee.* **2.** One that performs a specified action: *standee.* [< Lat. *-ātus,* –ATE¹.]

–ee² ►*suff.* **1.** One resembling: *goatee.* **2.** A particular, esp. a diminutive kind of: *bootee.* [Var. of –Y¹.]

EEC ►*abbr.* European Economic Community

EEE ►*abbr.* Eastern equine encephalitis

EEG ►*abbr.* **1.** electroencephalogram **2.** electroencephalograph

eel (ēl) ►*n., pl.* **eel** or **eels** Any of various long snakelike marine or freshwater fishes. [< OE *ǣl.*]

EEOC ►*abbr.* Equal Employment Opportunity Commission

–eer ►*suff.* One concerned with or engaged in: *auctioneer.* [< Lat. *-ārius,* –ARY.]

ee·rie or **ee·ry** (îr′ē) ►*adj.* **-ri·er, -ri·est** Inspiring inexplicable fear or uneasiness. See Synonyms at **weird.** [< OE *earg,* timid.] —**ee′ri·ly** *adv.* —**ee′ri·ness** *n.*

ef·face (ĭ-fās′) ►*v.* **-faced, -fac·ing** **1.** To wipe out; erase. **2.** To make indistinct. **3.** To conduct (oneself) inconspicuously. **4.** *Med.* To cause to become shorter, softer, and thinner during labor: *The cervix was effaced as the contractions continued.* [< OFr. *esfacier.*] **—ef·face′ment** *n.*

ef·fect (ĭ-fĕkt′) ►*n.* **1.** Something brought about by a cause or agent; result. **2.** The power to achieve a result; influence. **3.** Advantage; avail. **4.** The condition of being in full force. **5.** Something that produces a specific impression. **6.** The basic or general meaning: *words to that effect.* **7. effects** Movable belongings. ►*v.* To bring about; make happen; cause or accomplish. See Usage Note at **affect¹.** *—idiom:* **in effect** In essence; to all purposes. [< Lat. *effectus,* p.part. of *efficere,* accomplish.]

ef·fec·tive (ĭ-fĕk′tĭv) ►*adj.* **1.** Having an intended or expected effect. **2.** Producing a strong impression or response; striking. **3.** Operative; in effect. **—ef·fec′tive·ly** *adv.*

ef·fec·tor (ĭ-fĕk′tər) ►*n.* A muscle, gland, or organ capable of responding to a stimulus, esp. a nerve impulse.

ef·fec·tu·al (ĭ-fĕk′chōō-əl) ►*adj.* Producing or sufficient to produce a desired effect; fully adequate. **—ef·fec′tu·al·ly** *adv.*

ef·fec·tu·ate (ĭ-fĕk′chōō-āt′) ►*v.* **-at·ed, -at·ing** To bring about; effect. [< Lat. *effectus,* EFFECT.] **—ef·fec′tu·a′tion** *n.*

ef·fem·i·nate (ĭ-fĕm′ə-nĭt) ►*adj.* Having or showing qualities or characteristics more often associated with females than males. [< Lat. *effēmināre,* make feminine.] **—ef·fem′i·na·cy** *n.* **—ef·fem′i·nate·ly** *adv.*

ef·fer·ent (ĕf′ər-ənt) ►*adj.* **1.** Directed away from a central organ or section. **2.** Carrying impulses from the central nervous system to an effector. ►*n.* An efferent organ or body part, such as a blood vessel. [< Lat. *efferre,* carry away : EX- + *ferre,* carry.]

ef·fer·vesce (ĕf′ər-vĕs′) ►*v.* **-vesced, -vesc·ing** **1.** To emit small bubbles of gas, as a carbonated liquid. **2.** To escape from a liquid as bubbles; bubble up. **3.** To show high spirits or excitement. [Lat. *effervēscere,* boil over.] **—ef′fer·ves′cence** *n.* **—ef′fer·ves′cent** *adj.*

ef·fete (ĭ-fēt′) ►*adj.* **1a.** Characterized by extreme refinement or self-indulgence. **b.** Pretentious or snobbish. **2.** Depleted of vitality or effectiveness. [Lat. *effētus,* worn out, exhausted.] **—ef·fete′ly** *adv.* **—ef·fete′ness** *n.*

ef·fi·ca·cious (ĕf′ĭ-kā′shəs) ►*adj.* Producing a desired effect; effective. [< Lat. *efficāx.*] **—ef′fi·ca′cious·ly** *adv.* **—ef′fi·ca′cious·ness** *n.* **—ef′fi·ca·cy** (ĕf′ĭ-kə-sē) *n.*

ef·fi·cient (ĭ-fĭsh′ənt) ►*adj.* **1.** Acting or producing effectively with a minimum of waste, expense, or effort. **2.** Causing less waste or requiring less effort than comparable devices or methods. Used in combination: *energy-efficient wind turbines.* [< Lat. *efficere,* bring about.] **—ef·fi′cien·cy** *n.* **—ef·fi′cient·ly** *adv.*

ef·fi·gy (ĕf′ə-jē) ►*n., pl.* **-gies** A likeness or image, esp. a crude figure or dummy representing a hated person or group. [< Lat. *effigiēs,* likeness.]

effigy mound ►*n.* A large earthen mound in the form of an animal, esp. one built by any of various Native American peoples of the Ohio and upper Mississippi Valleys.

ef·flo·resce (ĕf′lə-rĕs′) ►*v.* **-resced, -resc·ing** To blossom; bloom. [Lat. *efflōrēscere* < *flōs, flōr-,* flower.]

ef·flo·res·cence (ĕf′lə-rĕs′əns) ►*n.* **1.** *Bot.* A state or time of flowering. **2a.** A gradual process of unfolding or developing. **b.** The point or time of greatest vigor; culmination. See Synonyms at **bloom. —ef′flo·res′cent** *adj.*

ef·flu·ent (ĕf′lōō-ənt) ►*adj.* Flowing out or forth. ►*n.* Something that flows out or forth, esp. a discharge of liquid waste. [< Lat. *effluere,* flow out.] **—ef′flu·ence** *n.*

ef·flu·vi·um (ĭ-flōō′vē-əm) ►*n., pl.* **-vi·a** (-vē-ə) or **-vi·ums** A usu. invisible emanation, often foul or harmful. [Lat. < *effluere,* flow out.] **—ef·flu′vi·al** *adj.*

ef·fort (ĕf′ərt) ►*n.* **1.** The use of physical or mental energy to do something; exertion. **2.** An earnest attempt. **3.** Something done through exertion; achievement. [< Med.Lat. *exfortiāre,* to force < Lat. *fortis,* strong.] **—ef′fort·less** *adj.*

ef·front·er·y (ĭ-frŭn′tə-rē) ►*n., pl.* **-ies** Brazen boldness; presumptuousness. [Poss. < LLat. *effrōns,* shameless.]

ef·ful·gent (ĭ-fŏŏl′jənt, ĭ-fŭl′-) ►*adj.* Shining brilliantly; resplendent. [< Lat. *effulgēre,* shine out.] **—ef·ful′gence** *n.*

ef·fuse (ĭ-fyōōs′) ►*adj. Bot.* Spreading out loosely. ►*v.* (ĭ-fyōōz′) **-fused, -fus·ing** **1.** To pour out (a liquid). **2.** To radiate; diffuse. [< Lat. *effundere, effūs-,* pour out.]

ef·fu·sion (ĭ-fyōō′zhən) ►*n.* **1.** Pouring forth; effusing. **2.** An unrestrained outpouring of feeling. **3.** *Med.* The abnormal seeping of fluid into a body cavity or tissue. **—ef·fu′sive** *adj.* **—ef·fu′sive·ly** *adv.* **—ef·fu′sive·ness** *n.*

eft (ĕft) ►*n.* A newt in its juvenile terrestrial stage. [< OE *efeta.*]

e.g. ►*abbr. Lat.* exempli gratia (for example)

e·gal·i·tar·i·an (ĭ-găl′ĭ-târ′ē-ən-) ►*adj.* Affirming political, economic, and social equality for all. [< Fr. *égalité,* equality.] **—e·gal′i·tar′i·an** *n.* **—e·gal′i·tar′i·an·ism** *n.*

egg¹ (ĕg) ►*n.* **1a.** A female reproductive cell; ovum. **b.** The round or oval reproductive body of various animals, such as birds, reptiles, fishes, and insects, containing the embryo and covered with a shell or membrane. **2.** A hen's egg used as food. [< ON, bird's egg.]

egg² (ĕg) ►*v.* To encourage or incite to action: *egged them on.* [< ON *eggja.*]

egg·beat·er (ĕg′bē′tər) ►*n.* A kitchen utensil with rotating blades for beating or mixing.

egg drop soup ►*n.* A Chinese soup into which beaten egg is drizzled immediately before serving and cooked into soft strands.

egg·head (ĕg′hĕd′) ►*n. Informal* An intellectual; highbrow.

egg·nog (ĕg′nŏg′) ►*n.* A drink consisting of milk, sugar, eggs, and flavorings often mixed with a liquor such as rum or brandy. [EGG¹ + *nog,* ale.]

egg·plant (ĕg′plănt′) ►*n.* **1.** A plant cultivated for its large, usu. ovoid fruit that are chiefly purple. **2.** The fruit of this plant.

egg roll ►*n.* A usu. deep-fried cylindrical casing of thin egg dough, filled with minced vegetables and often meat.

egg·shell (ĕg′shĕl′) ►*n.* **1.** The thin, brittle, exterior covering of an egg. **2.** A yellowish white. **—egg′shell′** *adj.*

e·gis (ē′jĭs) ►*n.* Var. of **aegis.**

eg·lan·tine (ĕg′lən-tīn′, -tēn′) ►*n.* See **sweet-brier.** [< VLat. **aculentum* < Lat. *acūleus*, spine < *acus*, needle.]

e·go (ē′gō) ►*n., pl.* **e·gos 1.** The self, esp. as distinct from all others. **2.** In psychoanalysis, the part of the psyche that is conscious, controls thought and behavior, and is most in touch with external reality. **3.** An exaggerated sense of self-importance; conceit. [Lat., I.]

e·go·cen·tric (ē′gō-sĕn′trĭk) ►*adj.* Interested only in one's own needs or affairs; self-centered. —**e′go·cen′tric** *n.* —**e′go·cen·tric′i·ty** (-trĭs′ĭ-tē) *n.* —**e′go·cen′trism** *n.*

e·go·ism (ē′gō-ĭz′əm) ►*n.* **1.** The belief that self-interest is the just and proper motive for all human conduct. **2.** Egotism; conceit. See Synonyms at **conceit.** —**e′go·ist** *n.* —**e′go·is′tic, e′go·is′ti·cal** *adj.* —**e′go·is′ti·cal·ly** *adv.*

e·go·ma·ni·a (ē′gō-mā′nē-ə, -mān′yə) ►*n.* Obsessive preoccupation with the self. —**e′go·ma′ni·ac′** *n.* —**e′go·ma·ni′a·cal** (-mə-nī′ə-kəl) *adj.* —**e′go·ma·ni′a·cal·ly** *adv.*

e·go·tism (ē′gə-tĭz′əm) ►*n.* An inflated sense of one's own importance; conceit. See Synonyms at **conceit.** —**e′go·tist** *n.* —**e′go·tis′tic, e′go·tis′ti·cal** *adj.* —**e′go·tis′ti·cal·ly** *adv.*

ego trip ►*n. Slang* An act, experience, or course of behavior that gratifies the ego.

e·gre·gious (ĭ-grē′jəs, -jē-əs) ►*adj.* Conspicuously bad or offensive. [< Lat. *ēgregius*, outstanding.] —**e·gre′gious·ly** *adv.*

e·gress (ē′grĕs′) ►*n.* **1.** An act of or opening for going out. **2.** The right to leave or go out: *denied the refugees egress.* **3.** A path or opening for going out. [Lat. *ēgressus* < *ēgredī*, go out.]

e·gret (ē′grĭt, ĕg′rĭt) ►*n.* Any of several usu. white herons having long, showy, drooping plumes. [< OFr., ult. < OProv. *aigron*, heron.]

E·gypt (ē′jĭpt) A country of NE Africa on the Mediterranean Sea. Cap. Cairo.

E·gyp·tian (ĭ-jĭp′shən) ►*n.* **1.** A native or inhabitant of Egypt. **2.** The extinct Afro-Asiatic language of the ancient Egyptians. —**E·gyp′tian** *adj.*

EHF ►*abbr.* extremely high frequency

ei·der (ī′dər) ►*n.* A large sea duck of northern regions, having soft, commercially valuable down. [< ON *ædhr.*]

ei·der·down also **eider down** (ī′dər-doun′) ►*n.* The down of the eider.

eight (āt) ►*n.* **1.** The cardinal number equal to 7 + 1. **2.** The 8th in a set or sequence. [< OE *eahta.*] —**eight** *adj. & pron.*

eight ball ►*n. Games* A black pool ball that bears the number 8. —*idiom:* **behind the eight ball** *Slang* In an unfavorable position.

eight·een (ā-tēn′) ►*n.* **1.** The cardinal number equal to 17 + 1. **2.** The 18th in a set or sequence. —**eight·een′** *adj. & pron.*

eight·eenth (ā-tēnth′) ►*n.* **1.** The ordinal number matching the number 18 in a series. **2.** One of 18 equal parts. —**eight·eenth′** *adv. & adj.*

eighth (ātth, āth) ►*n.* **1.** The ordinal number matching the number 8 in a series. **2.** One of eight equal parts. —**eighth** *adv. & adj.*

eight·i·eth (ā′tē-ĭth) ►*n.* **1.** The ordinal number matching the number 80 in a series. **2.** One of 80 equal parts. —**eight′i·eth** *adv. & adj.*

eight·y (ā′tē) ►*n., pl.* **-ies** The cardinal number equal to 8 × 10. —**eight′y** *adj. & pron.*

Eind·ho·ven (īnt′hō′vən) A city of S Netherlands SE of Rotterdam.

Ein·stein (īn′stīn′), **Albert** 1879–1955. German-born Amer. theoretical physicist.

ein·stei·ni·um (īn-stī′nē-əm) ►*n. Symbol* **Es** A synthetic radioactive element first produced in a thermonuclear explosion. At. no. 99. See table at **element.** [After Albert EINSTEIN.]

Eir·e (âr′ə, ī′rə) See **Ireland** (sense 2).

Ei·sen·how·er (ī′zən-hou′ər), **Dwight David** 1890–1969. 34th US president (1953–61).

Dwight Eisenhower
photographed c. 1959

ei·ther (ē′thər, ī′thər) ►*pron.* One or the other of two. ►*conj.* Used before the first of two or more coordinates or clauses linked by *or: Either we go now or we remain here forever.* ►*adj.* **1.** Any one of two; one or the other: *Wear either coat.* **2.** One and the other; each: *rings on either hand.* ►*adv.* Likewise; also: *If you don't order a dessert, I won't either.* [< OE *ǣghwæther.*]

e·jac·u·late (ĭ-jăk′yə-lāt′) ►*v.* **-lat·ed, -lat·ing 1.** To eject abruptly, esp. to discharge (semen) in orgasm. **2.** To utter suddenly and passionately; exclaim. ►*n.* (-lĭt) Fluid discharged in an ejaculation, esp. semen. [Lat. *ēiaculārī.*] —**e·jac′u·la′tion** *n.* —**e·jac′u·la′tor** *n.* —**e·jac′u·la·to′ry** (-lə-tôr′ē) *adj.*

e·ject (ĭ-jĕkt′) ►*v.* To throw out forcefully; expel. [< Lat. *ēicere, ēiect-.*] —**e·jec′tion** *n.* —**e·jec′tor** *n.*

ejection seat ►*n.* A seat designed to eject the occupant clear of an aircraft during an in-flight emergency.

eke (ēk) ►*v.* **eked, ek·ing 1.** To make or supplement with effort: *eked out an income by working two jobs.* **2.** To make (a supply) last by practicing strict economy: *rationed food to eke out supplies.* [< OE *ēcan*, increase.]

EKG ►*abbr.* electrocardiogram

el. ►*abbr.* elevation

e·lab·o·rate (ĭ-lăb′ər-ĭt) ►*adj.* **1.** Planned or executed with attention to details. **2.** Intricate and rich in detail: *an elaborate pattern.* ►*v.* (-ə-rāt′) **-rat·ed, -rat·ing 1.** To work out carefully; develop thoroughly. **2.** To express at greater length or in greater detail. [Lat. *ēlabōrātus*, p.part. of *ēlabōrāre*, work out.] —**e·lab′o·rate·ly** *adv.* —**e·lab′o·ra′tion** *n.* —**e·lab′o·ra′tor** *n.*

El Al·a·mein (ĕl ăl′ə-mān′, ä′lə-) A town of N Egypt on the Mediterranean Sea; site of a British victory over Germany (1942).

E·lam (ē′lǝm) An ancient country of SW Asia in present-day SW Iran.

é·lan (ā-läɴ′, ā-län′) ►*n.* **1.** Enthusiastic vigor and liveliness. **2.** Distinctive style or flair. [< OFr. *eslancer,* hurl.]

e·land (ē′lǝnd) ►*n., pl.* **eland** also **e·lands** Either of two large African antelopes having spirally twisted horns. [Ult. of Balt. orig.]

el·a·pid (ĕl′ǝ-pĭd) ►*n.* Any of a family of venomous snakes having hollow, fixed fangs, including cobras, mambas, and coral snakes. [< Med. Gk. *elaps,* fish.]

e·lapse (ĭ-lăps′) ►*v.* **e·lapsed, e·laps·ing** To slip by, as time; pass. [Lat. *ēlābī, ēlāps-.*]

e·las·tic (ĭ-lăs′tĭk) ►*adj.* **1.** Easily resuming original shape after being stretched or expanded; flexible. **2.** Quick to recover, as from disappointment. **3.** Capable of adapting to change or a variety of circumstances. ►*n.* **1.** A flexible, stretchable fabric. **2.** A rubber band. [< LGk. *elastos,* beaten, ductile.] —**e·las′ti·cal·ly** *adv.* —**e·las·tic′i·ty** (ĭ-lă-stĭs′ĭ-tē, ē′lă-) *n.*

e·late (ĭ-lāt′) ►*v.* **e·lat·ed, e·lat·ing** To fill with great joy or happiness; delight. [< Lat. *ēlātus,* p.part. of *efferre,* carry away.] —**e·la′tion** *n.*

El·ba (ĕl′bǝ) An island of Italy in the Tyrrhenian Sea between Corsica and the mainland.

El·be (ĕl′bǝ, ĕlb) A river of the Czech Republic and Germany flowing about 1,165 km (725 mi) to the North Sea.

El·bert (ĕl′bǝrt), **Mount** A peak, 4,402.1 m (14,433 ft), in the Sawatch Range of central CO.

el·bow (ĕl′bō′) ►*n.* **1a.** The joint or bend of the arm between the forearm and the upper arm. **b.** The bony outer projection of this joint. **2.** Something, esp. a length of pipe, bent like an elbow. ►*v.* **1.** To push or jostle with the elbow. **2.** To make one's way by elbowing. [< OE *elnboga.*]

elbow grease ►*n. Informal* Strenuous effort.

el·bow·room (ĕl′bō-rōōm′, -rŏŏm′) ►*n.* Adequate room to move or work in. See Synonyms at **room.**

El·brus (ĕl-brōōs′), **Mount** A peak, 5,643 m (18,513 ft), in the Caucasus Mts. of SW Russia; highest mountain of Europe.

El·burz Mountains (ĕl-bŏŏrz′) A range of N Iran rising to 5,774.9 m (18,934 ft).

eld·er¹ (ĕl′dǝr) ►*adj.* **1.** Older. **2.** Elderly. ►*n.* **1.** An older person. **2.** An older, influential member of a family, tribe, or community. **3.** A governing officer of a church. [< OE *eldra.*]

Usage: Elder and *eldest* generally apply to persons, unlike *older* and *oldest,* which also apply to things. *Elder* and *eldest* are used principally with reference to seniority: *elder sister; elder statesman; John the Elder.*

el·der² (ĕl′dǝr) ►*n.* See **elderberry** (sense 1). [< OE *ellærn.*]

el·der·ber·ry (ĕl′dǝr-bĕr′ē) ►*n.* **1.** A shrub or small tree having small white flowers and small red or purplish-black berrylike fruit. **2.** The fruit of this plant, used to make wine or preserves.

eld·er·ly (ĕl′dǝr-lē) ►*adj.* **1.** Approaching old age. **2.** Of or characteristic of older persons. ►*n., pl.* **elderly** *(takes pl. v.)* Older people collectively. Used with *the.*

eld·est (ĕl′dĭst) ►*adj.* Greatest in age or seniority. See Usage Note at **elder¹.**

El Do·ra·do (dǝ-rä′dō) ►*n.* A place of fabulous wealth. [Sp., legendary South American land.]

El·ea·nor of Aquitaine (ĕl′ǝ-nǝr, -nôr′) 1122?– 1204. Queen of France (1137–52) and England (1152–1204).

e·lect (ĭ-lĕkt′) ►*v.* **1.** To select by vote for an office or for membership. **2.** To pick out; select. ►*adj.* **1.** Chosen deliberately; singled out. **2.** Elected but not yet installed: *the governor-elect.* ►*n.* **1.** One that is chosen or selected. **2.** *(takes pl. v.)* An exclusive group of people. [< Lat. *ēligere, ēlēct-.*] —**e·lec′tion** *n.*

e·lec·tion·eer (ĭ-lĕk′shǝ-nîr′) ►*v.* To work actively for a candidate or political party.

e·lec·tive (ĭ-lĕk′tĭv) ►*adj.* **1.** Filled or obtained by election. **2.** Having the power to elect. **3.** Optional. ►*n.* An optional academic course or subject.

e·lec·tor (ĭ-lĕk′tǝr) ►*n.* **1.** A qualified voter. **2.** A member of the Electoral College. —**e·lec′tor·al** *adj.*

Electoral College ►*n.* A body of electors chosen to elect the president and vice president of the US.

e·lec·tor·ate (ĭ-lĕk′tǝr-ĭt) ►*n.* A body of qualified voters.

E·lec·tra (ĭ-lĕk′trǝ) ►*n. Gk. Myth.* Daughter of Agamemnon who with her brother Orestes avenged their father's murder by killing their mother Clytemnestra.

e·lec·tric (ĭ-lĕk′trĭk) ►*adj.* **1.** Of or operated by electricity. **2.** Amplified by an electronic device: *an electric guitar.* **3.** Emotionally exciting; thrilling. —**e·lec′tri·cal·ly** *adv.*

electric chair ►*n.* **1.** A device used in the electrocution of a person sentenced to death. **2.** The sentence of death by electrocution.

electric eel ►*n.* A long, cylindrical freshwater fish of South America, having organs that produce a powerful electric discharge.

e·lec·tri·cian (ĭ-lĕk-trĭsh′ǝn, ē′lĕk-) ►*n.* One whose occupation is the installation, maintenance, repair, or operation of electric equipment and circuitry.

e·lec·tric·i·ty (ĭ-lĕk-trĭs′ĭ-tē, ē′lĕk-) ►*n.* **1.** The physical phenomena arising from the attraction of particles with opposite charges and the repulsion of particles with the same charge. **2.** Electric current used or regarded as a source of power. **3.** Intense emotional excitement.

e·lec·tri·fy (ĭ-lĕk′trǝ-fī′) ►*v.* **-fied, -fy·ing 1.** To produce electric charge on or in. **2.** To wire or equip for the use of electric power. **3.** To thrill, startle greatly, or shock. —**e·lec′tri·fi·ca′tion** *n.*

electro- or **electr-** ►*pref.* **1.** Electric; electricity: *electrochemistry.* **2.** Electron: *electrode.* [< Gk. *ēlektron,* amber.]

e·lec·tro·car·di·o·gram (ĭ-lĕk′trō-kär′dē-ǝ-grăm′) ►*n.* **1.** A graphic record of heart muscle activity recorded by an electrocardiograph. **2.** The procedure performed to produce such a record.

e·lec·tro·car·di·o·graph (ĭ-lĕk′trō-kär′dē-ǝ-grăf′) ►*n.* An instrument that measures electrical potentials associated with heart muscle activity. —**e·lec′tro·car′di·o·graph′ic** *adj.* —**e·lec′tro·car′di·og′ra·phy** (-kär′dē-ŏg′rǝ-fē) *n.*

e·lec·tro·chem·is·try (ĭ-lĕk′trō-kĕm′ĭ-strē) ►*n.* The science of the interaction of electric and chemical phenomena. —**e·lec′tro·chem′i·cal·ly** *adv.* —**e·lec′tro·chem′ist** *n.*

e·lec·tro·con·vul·sive therapy (ĭ-lĕk′trō-kən-vŭl′sĭv) ►*n.* Administration of electric current to the brain to induce seizure activity, used esp. to treat acute depression.

e·lec·tro·cute (ĭ-lĕk′trə-kyōōt′) ►*v.* **-cut·ed, -cut·ing** **1.** To kill with electricity. **2.** To execute (a person sentenced to death) by electricity. [ELECTRO– + (EXE)CUTE.] —**e·lec′tro·cu′tion** *n.*

e·lec·trode (ĭ-lĕk′trōd′) ►*n.* A solid electric conductor through which an electric current enters or leaves an electrolytic cell or other medium.

e·lec·tro·en·ceph·a·lo·gram (ĭ-lĕk′trō-ĕn-sĕf′ə-lə-grăm′) ►*n.* **1.** A graphic record of the electrical activity of the brain as recorded by an electroencephalograph. **2.** The procedure performed to produce such a record.

e·lec·tro·en·ceph·a·lo·graph (ĭ-lĕk′trō-ĕn-sĕf′ə-lə-grăf′) ►*n.* An instrument that measures electrical potentials on the scalp and generates a record of the electrical activity of the brain. —**e·lec′tro·en·ceph′a·lo·graph′ic** *adj.* —**e·lec′tro·en·ceph′a·log′ra·phy** (-lŏg′rə-fē) *n.*

e·lec·trol·o·gist (ĭ-lĕk-trŏl′ə-jĭst, ē′lĕk-) ►*n.* One who removes body hair by means of an electric current.

e·lec·trol·y·sis (ĭ-lĕk-trŏl′ĭ-sĭs, ē′lĕk-) ►*n.* **1.** Chemical change, esp. decomposition, produced in an electrolyte by an electric current. **2.** Destruction of living tissue, esp. of hair roots, by an electric current.

e·lec·tro·lyte (ĭ-lĕk′trə-līt′) ►*n.* **1.** A chemical compound that ionizes when dissolved or molten to produce an electrically conductive medium. **2.** *Physiol.* Any of various ions required by cells to regulate the electric charge and flow of water molecules across the cell membrane.

e·lec·tro·lyt·ic (ĭ-lĕk′trə-lĭt′ĭk) ►*adj.* **1.** Of or relating to electrolysis. **2.** Of electrolytes. —**e·lec′tro·lyt′i·cal·ly** *adv.*

e·lec·tro·mag·net (ĭ-lĕk′trō-măg′nĭt) ►*n.* A magnet consisting of a coil of insulated wire wrapped around a steel or iron core that is magnetized only when current flows through the wire.

electromagnetic radiation ►*n.* Energy having both the form of electromagnetic waves and the form of a stream of photons and traveling at the speed of light in a vacuum. The entire range of frequencies and wavelengths of electromagnetic radiation makes up the electromagnetic spectrum.

electromagnetic spectrum ►*n.* The entire range of electromagnetic radiation, which includes, in order of increasing frequency and decreasing wavelength, radio waves, microwaves, infrared radiation, visible light, ultraviolet radiation, x-rays, and gamma rays.

e·lec·tro·mag·net·ism (ĭ-lĕk′trō-măg′nĭ-tĭz′-əm) ►*n.* **1.** The physics of electricity and magnetism. **2.** An interaction between electricity and magnetism, as when an electric current or a changing electric field generates a magnetic field, or when a changing magnetic field generates an electric field. —**e·lec′tro·mag·net′ic** *adj.*

e·lec·tro·mo·tive (ĭ-lĕk′trō-mō′tĭv) ►*adj.* Of or producing electric current.

electromotive force ►*n.* The energy per unit charge that is converted reversibly from chemical, mechanical, or other forms of energy into electrical energy in a battery or dynamo.

e·lec·tron (ĭ-lĕk′trŏn′) ►*n.* A stable elementary particle having a unit negative electric charge and a rest mass of approx. 9.11×10^{-28} grams.

e·lec·tron·ic (ĭ-lĕk-trŏn′ĭk, ē′lĕk-) ►*adj.* **1.** Of or involving electrons or electronics. **2.** Implemented on or controlled by a computer. —**e·lec·tron′i·cal·ly** *adv.*

e·lec·tron·ics (ĭ-lĕk-trŏn′ĭks, ē′lĕk-) ►*n.* **1.** *(takes sing. v.)* The science and technology of electronic phenomena. **2.** *(takes pl. v.)* Electronic devices and systems.

electron microscope ►*n.* A microscope that uses electrons rather than visible light to produce magnified images.

electron tube ►*n.* A sealed enclosure in which electrons can be made sufficiently mobile to act as the principal carriers of current between at least one pair of electrodes.

electron volt ►*n.* A unit of energy equal to the energy acquired by an electron falling through a potential difference of one volt.

e·lec·tro·pho·re·sis (ĭ-lĕk′trō-fə-rē′sĭs) ►*n.* **1.** The migration of charged colloidal particles through a medium under the influence of an applied electric field. **2.** A method of separating substances, esp. proteins, based on the rate of movement of each component in a colloidal suspension while under the influence of an electric field.

e·lec·tro·plate (ĭ-lĕk′trə-plāt′) ►*v.* **-plat·ed, -plat·ing** To coat or cover electrolytically with a thin layer of metal.

e·lec·tro·shock (ĭ-lĕk′trō-shŏk′) ►*n.* See **electroconvulsive therapy.**

e·lec·tro·stat·ic (ĭ-lĕk′trō-stăt′ĭk) ►*adj.* **1.** Of or relating to electric charges at rest. **2.** Of electrostatics. —**e·lec′tro·stat′i·cal·ly** *adv.*

e·lec·tro·stat·ics (ĭ-lĕk′trō-stăt′ĭks) ►*n.* *(takes sing. v.)* The physics of electrostatic phenomena.

el·ee·mos·y·nar·y (ĕl′ə-mŏs′ə-nĕr′ē, ĕl′ē-ə-) ►*adj.* Of or dependent on charity. See Synonyms at **benevolent.** [< LLat. *eleēmosyna,* ALMS.]

el·e·gance (ĕl′ĭ-gəns) ►*n.* **1.** Refinement and grace in movement, appearance, or manners. **2.** Tasteful opulence in form, decoration, or presentation. **3.** Scientific exactness and precision.

el·e·gant (ĕl′ĭ-gənt) ►*adj.* Marked by refined, tasteful beauty of manner, form, or style. See Synonyms at **exquisite.** [< Lat. *ēligere,* select.] —**el′e·gant·ly** *adv.*

el·e·gi·ac (ĕl′ə-jī′ək, ĭ-lē′jē-ăk′) ►*adj.* **1.** Of or relating to an elegy. **2.** Expressing sorrow; mournful. —**el′e·gi′ac** *n.* —**el′e·gi′a·cal** *adj.* —**el′e·gi′a·cal·ly** *adv.*

el·e·gy (ĕl′ə-jē) ►*n., pl.* **-gies** A mournful poem or song, esp. one lamenting a dead person. [< Gk. *elegos,* song.] —**el′e·gist** *n.* —**el′e·gize′** *v.*

el·e·ment (ĕl′ə-mənt) ►*n.* **1.** A substance composed of atoms having an identical number of protons in each nucleus and not reducible to a simpler substance. Elements 113 through 118 have been produced in the laboratory but have not yet been officially named. See the Periodic Table of elements on pages 276–277. **2.** A fundamental or essential part of a whole. **3.** *Math.* **a.** A member of a set. **b.** A point, line, or plane. **c.** A part of a geometric configuration, as an angle in a triangle. **4. elements** The forces that constitute the weather, esp. inclement weather. **5.** An environment naturally suited to or associated with an individual. [< Lat. *elementum*, fundamental constituent.]

　　Syns: component, constituent, factor, ingredient n.

el·e·men·tal (ĕl'ə-mĕn'tl) ►*adj.* **1.** Of or being an element. **2.** Fundamental or essential. **3.** Of or resembling a force of nature in power or effect. —**el'e·men'tal** *n.* —**el'e·men'tal·ly** *adv.*

el·e·men·ta·ry (ĕl'ə-mĕn'tə-rē, -trē) ►*adj.* **1.** Of or constituting the essential or fundamental part. **2.** Of or involving the fundamental or simplest aspects of a subject. **3.** Of or relating to an elementary school or elementary education. **4.** Of, relating to, or being an elementary particle. —**el'e·men·ta'ri·ly** (-tĕr'ə-lē) *adv.*

elementary particle ►*n.* Any of the smallest, discrete particles that compose matter and energy and that are not made up of other particles.

elementary school ►*n.* A school attended for the first six to eight years of a child's formal education.

el·e·phant (ĕl'ə-fənt) ►*n.* A very large herbivorous mammal of Africa and Asia with a long flexible trunk and long tusks. [< Gk. *elephas*.]

el·e·phan·ti·a·sis (ĕl'ə-fən-tī'ə-sĭs) ►*n.* Enlargement and hardening of tissues, esp. of the lower body, resulting from lymphatic obstruction and usu. caused by parasitic worms. [< Gk.]

el·e·phan·tine (ĕl'ə-făn'tēn', -tīn', ĕl'ə-fən-) ►*adj.* **1.** Of or relating to an elephant. **2a.** Enormous in size or strength. **b.** Ponderously clumsy.

elev. ►*abbr.* elevation

el·e·vate (ĕl'ə-vāt') ►*v.* **-vat·ed, -vat·ing** **1.** To raise to a higher position; lift. **2.** To promote to a higher rank. **3.** To raise to a higher moral, cultural, or intellectual level. **4.** To lift the spirits of; elate. [< Lat. *ēlevāre*.]

el·e·va·tion (ĕl'ə-vā'shən) ►*n.* **1.** The act of elevating or condition of being elevated. **2.** The height to which something is elevated above a point of reference, esp. mean sea level. **3.** An elevated place or position.

　　Syns: altitude, height n.

el·e·va·tor (ĕl'ə-vā'tər) ►*n.* **1.** A platform or enclosure raised and lowered in a vertical shaft to transport people or freight. **2.** A movable control surface on an aircraft, used to move the aircraft up or down. **3.** A granary with devices for hoisting and discharging grain.

e·lev·en (ĭ-lĕv'ən) ►*n.* **1.** The cardinal number equal to 10 + 1. **2.** The 11th in a set or sequence. [< OE *endleofan*.] —**e·lev'en** *adj. & pron.*

e·lev·enth (ĭ-lĕv'ənth) ►*n.* **1.** The ordinal number matching the number 11 in a series. **2.** One of 11 equal parts. —**e·lev'enth** *adv. & adj.*

elf (ĕlf) ►*n., pl.* **elves** (ĕlvz) A small, often mischievous fairy. [< OE *ælf.*] —**elf'in** *adj.* —**elf'ish** *adj.*

ELF ►*abbr.* extremely low frequency

El·gar (ĕl'gär', -gər), Sir **Edward** 1857–1934. British composer.

El Grec·o (grĕk'ō) See El **Greco.**

e·lic·it (ĭ-lĭs'ĭt) ►*v.* To call forth, draw out, or evoke. [Lat. *ēlicere*.] —**e·lic'i·ta'tion** *n.*

e·lide (ĭ-līd') ►*v.* **e·lid·ed, e·lid·ing** **1.** To omit or slur over (a syllable or word) in pronunciation. **2.** To eliminate or leave out of consideration. [Lat. *ēlīdere*, strike out.]

el·i·gi·ble (ĕl'ĭ-jə-bəl) ►*adj.* **1.** Qualified to be chosen. **2.** Worthy of choice, esp. for marriage. [< Lat. *ēligere*, select.] —**el'i·gi·bil'i·ty** *n.* —**el'i·gi·bly** *adv.*

E·li·jah (ĭ-lī'jə) 9th cent. BC. Hebrew prophet.

e·lim·i·nate (ĭ-lĭm'ə-nāt') ►*v.* **-nat·ed, -nat·ing** **1.** To get rid of; remove. **2.** To leave out or omit; reject. **3.** *Physiol.* To excrete (bodily wastes). [Lat. *ēlīmināre*, banish.] —**e·lim'i·na'tion** *n.* —**e·lim'i·na'tive, e·lim'i·na·to'ry** (-nə-tôr'ē) *adj.* —**e·lim'i·na'tor** *n.*

　　Syns: eradicate, extirpate v.

El·i·ot (ĕl'ē-ət), **George** Pen name of Mary Ann Evans. 1819–80. British writer.

Eliot, T(homas) S(tearns) 1888–1965. Amer.-born British writer.

E·li·sha (ĭ-lī'shə) 9th cent. BC. Hebrew prophet.

e·lite or **é·lite** (ĭ-lēt', ā-lēt') ►*n., pl.* **elite** or **e·lites** A group or class of persons considered to be superior to others because of their intelligence, social standing, or wealth. [< OFr. *eslire*, ELECT.] —**e·lite'** *adj.*

e·lit·ism or **é·lit·ism** (ĭ-lē'tĭz'əm, ā-lē'-) ►*n.* **1.** The belief that certain persons or members of certain classes or groups deserve favored treatment. **2a.** Behavior arising from or indicative of such a belief. **b.** Control, rule, or domination by such a group or class. —**e·lit'ist** *adj. & n.*

e·lix·ir (ĭ-lĭk'sər) ►*n.* **1.** A sweetened aromatic solution of alcohol and water containing medicine. **2.** A substance believed to cure all ills. [< Ar. *al-'iksīr*.]

Elizabeth I 1533–1603. Queen of England and Ireland (1558–1603).

Elizabeth II b. 1926. Queen of Great Britain and Northern Ireland (assumed the throne 1952).

Elizabeth II
photographed in 2009

PERIODIC TABLE OF THE ELEMENTS

The periodic table arranges the chemical elements in two ways. The first is by **atomic number**, starting with hydrogen (atomic number = 1) in the upper left-hand corner and continuing in ascending order from left to right. The second is by the number of electrons in the outermost **shell**. Elements having the same number of electrons in the outermost shell are grouped in the same column. Since the number of electrons in the outermost shell in large part determines the chemical nature of an element, elements in the same column have similar chemical properties.

This arrangement of the elements was devised by **Dmitri Mendeleev** in 1869, before

KEY

	1 — atomic number
1 H Hydrogen 1.00794	H — symbol
	Hydrogen 1.00794 — atomic weight (or mass number of most stable isotope if in parentheses)

	1	2	3	4	5	6	7	8	9
1	1 H Hydrogen 1.00794								
2	3 Li Lithium 6.941	4 Be Beryllium 9.0122							
3	11 Na Sodium 22.9898	12 Mg Magnesium 24.305							
4	19 K Potassium 39.098	20 Ca Calcium 40.08	21 Sc Scandium 44.956	22 Ti Titanium 47.87	23 V Vanadium 50.942	24 Cr Chromium 51.996	25 Mn Manganese 54.938	26 Fe Iron 55.845	27 Co Cobalt 58.9332
5	37 Rb Rubidium 85.47	38 Sr Strontium 87.62	39 Y Yttrium 88.906	40 Zr Zirconium 91.22	41 Nb Niobium 92.906	42 Mo Molybdenum 95.96	43 Tc Technetium (98)	44 Ru Ruthenium 101.07	45 Rh Rhodium 102.905
6	55 Cs Cesium 132.905	56 Ba Barium 137.33	57–71* Lanthanides	72 Hf Hafnium 178.49	73 Ta Tantalum 180.948	74 W Tungsten 183.84	75 Re Rhenium 186.2	76 Os Osmium 190.2	77 Ir Iridium 192.22
7	87 Fr Francium (223)	88 Ra Radium (226)	89–103** Actinides	104 Rf Rutherfordium (261)	105 Db Dubnium (262)	106 Sg Seaborgium (266)	107 Bh Bohrium (264)	108 Hs Hassium (277)	109 Mt Meitnerium (268)

*LANTHANIDES	57 La Lanthanum 138.91	58 Ce Cerium 140.12	59 Pr Praseodymium 140.908	60 Nd Neodymium 144.24	61 Pm Promethium (145)	62 Sm Samarium 150.36	63 Eu Europium 151.96
**ACTINIDES	89 Ac Actinium (227)	90 Th Thorium 232.038	91 Pa Protactinium 231.036	92 U Uranium 238.03	93 Np Neptunium (237)	94 Pu Plutonium (244)	95 Am Americium (243)

E·liz·a·be·than (ĭ-lĭz′ə-bē′thən, -bĕth′ən) ►*adj.* Of or characteristic of Elizabeth I of England or her reign. —**E·liz′a·be′than** *n.*

elk (ĕlk) ►*n., pl.* **elk** or **elks** A large North American deer having long, branching antlers in the male; wapiti. [Prob. < OE *eolh.*]

ell¹ (ĕl) ►*n.* A wing of a building at right angles to the main structure. [Poss. from L.]

ell² (ĕl) ►*n.* An English linear measure equal to 45 in. (114 cm). [< OE *eln*, the length from elbow to finger tips.]

El·ling·ton (ĕl′ĭng-tən), **Edward Kennedy** "Duke." 1899–1974. Amer. jazz composer and musician.

el·lipse (ĭ-lĭps′) ►*n.* A plane curve that is the locus of points for which the sum of the distances from each point to two fixed points is equal. [< Gk. *elleipsis.*]

PERIODIC TABLE OF THE ELEMENTS, continued

many of the elements now known were discovered. To maintain the overall logic of the table, Mendeleev allowed space for undiscovered elements whose existence he predicted, and this space has since been filled in. Elements 113 through 118 have been isolated experimentally but not yet officially named.

The **lanthanide** series (elements 57–71) and the **actinide** series (elements 89–103) are composed of elements whose chemical properties are similar to those of elements in column 3. They are placed below the main body of the table to make it easier to read.

10	11	12	13	14	15	16	17	18
								2 **He** Helium 4.0026
			5 **B** Boron 10.811	6 **C** Carbon 12.011	7 **N** Nitrogen 14.0067	8 **O** Oxygen 15.9994	9 **F** Fluorine 18.9984	10 **Ne** Neon 20.18
			13 **Al** Aluminum 26.9815	14 **Si** Silicon 28.086	15 **P** Phosphorus 30.9738	16 **S** Sulfur 32.066	17 **Cl** Chlorine 35.453	18 **Ar** Argon 39.948
28 **Ni** Nickel 58.69	29 **Cu** Copper 63.546	30 **Zn** Zinc 65.38	31 **Ga** Gallium 69.72	32 **Ge** Germanium 72.64	33 **As** Arsenic 74.9216	34 **Se** Selenium 78.96	35 **Br** Bromine 79.904	36 **Kr** Krypton 83.80
46 **Pd** Palladium 106.4	47 **Ag** Silver 107.868	48 **Cd** Cadmium 112.41	49 **In** Indium 114.82	50 **Sn** Tin 118.71	51 **Sb** Antimony 121.76	52 **Te** Tellurium 127.60	53 **I** Iodine 126.9045	54 **Xe** Xenon 131.29
78 **Pt** Platinum 195.08	79 **Au** Gold 196.967	80 **Hg** Mercury 200.59	81 **Tl** Thallium 204.38	82 **Pb** Lead 207.2	83 **Bi** Bismuth 208.98	84 **Po** Polonium (209)	85 **At** Astatine (210)	86 **Rn** Radon (222)
110 **Ds** Darmstadtium (281)	111 **Rg** Roentgenium (280)	112 **Cn** Copernicium (285)	113 (284)	114 (289)	115 (288)	116 (293)	117 (293)	118 (294)

64 **Gd** Gadolinium 157.25	65 **Tb** Terbium 158.925	66 **Dy** Dysprosium 162.50	67 **Ho** Holmium 164.930	68 **Er** Erbium 167.26	69 **Tm** Thulium 168.934	70 **Yb** Ytterbium 173.05	71 **Lu** Lutetium 174.97
96 **Cm** Curium (247)	97 **Bk** Berkelium (247)	98 **Cf** Californium (251)	99 **Es** Einsteinium (252)	100 **Fm** Fermium (257)	101 **Md** Mendelevium (258)	102 **No** Nobelium (259)	103 **Lr** Lawrencium (262)

el·lip·sis (ĭ-lĭp′sĭs) ►*n., pl.* **-ses** (-sēz) **1.** The omission of a word or phrase that is not necessary for understanding. **2.** A mark or series of marks, often three periods (. . .), used to indicate an omission. [< Gk. *elleipsis.*]

el·lip·soid (ĭ-lĭp′soid′) ►*n.* A geometric surface whose plane sections are ellipses or circles. —**el′lip·soid′, el′lip·soi′dal** (-soid′l) *adj.*

el·lip·tic (ĭ-lĭp′tĭk) or **el·lip·ti·cal** (-tĭ-kəl) ►*adj.* **1.** Of or shaped like an ellipse. **2.** Containing an

ellipsis. **3.** Obscure or incomplete. [< Gk. *elleiptikos* < *elleipsis*, ellipsis.] —**el·lip′ti·cal·ly** *adv.*

El·li·son (ĕl′ĭ-sən), **Ralph Waldo** 1914–94. Amer. novelist.

elm (ĕlm) ►*n.* Any of various deciduous trees having arching or curving branches, serrate leaves, and small winged fruit. [< OE.]

El Ni·ño (nēn′yō) ►*n.* A periodic climatic event characterized by warming of surface waters and reduced upwelling of cold, nutrient-rich water off the W coast of South America that affects global weather patterns. [Sp., the (Christ) child (< its onset being around Christmas).]

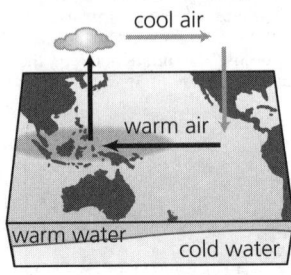

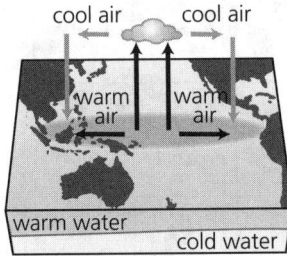

El Niño
top: normal water conditions
bottom: El Niño conditions

e·lo·cu·tion (ĕl′ə-kyōō′shən) ►*n.* The art of public speaking, emphasizing gesture and vocal delivery. [< Lat. *ēloquī*, speak out.] —**el′o·cu′-tion·ar′y** *adj.* —**el′o·cu′tion·ist** *n.*

e·lon·gate (ĭ-lông′gāt′, ĭ-lŏng′-) ►*v.* **-gat·ed, -gat·ing** To make or grow longer. [LLat. *ēlongāre.*] —**e·lon′ga′tion** *n.*

e·lope (ĭ-lōp′) ►*v.* **e·loped, e·lop·ing** To run away with a lover, esp. to get married. [Poss. AN *aloper*, to run away from one's husband with a lover.] —**e·lope′ment** *n.*

el·o·quent (ĕl′ə-kwənt) ►*adj.* Capable of or characterized by eloquence: *an eloquent speaker; an eloquent sermon.* [< Lat. *ēloquī*, speak out.] —**el′o·quence** *n.* —**el′o·quent·ly** *adv.*

El Pas·o (păs′ō) A city of extreme W TX on the Rio Grande.

El Sal·va·dor (săl′və-dôr′) A country of Central America bordering on the Pacific Ocean. Cap. San Salvador. —**El Sal′va·dor′i·an** *adj. & n.*

else (ĕls) ►*adj.* **1.** Other; different: *Ask somebody else.* **2.** Additional; more: *Would you like anything else?* ►*adv.* **1.** In a different time, place, or manner: *Where else would you like to go?* **2.** If not; otherwise: *Be careful, or else you may err.* —*idiom:* **or else 1.** Used to indicate an alternative: *Eat the leftovers or else buy more food.* **2.** Used to indicate negative consequences that will result if an action is not followed: *Pay the bill, or else the electricity will be shut off.* **3.** Used after a command or demand to make a threat: *Be there on time, or else!* [< OE *elles.*]
Usage: When a pronoun is followed by *else,* the possessive form is generally written thus: *someone else's* (not *someone's else*). Both *who else's* and *whose else* are in use, but not *whose else's.*

else·where (ĕls′wâr′, -hwâr′) ►*adv.* In or to another place.

e·lu·ci·date (ĭ-lōō′sĭ-dāt′) ►*v.* **-dat·ed, -dat·ing** To make clear or plain, esp. by explanation; clarify. See Synonyms at **explain.** [LLat. *ēlūcidāre* < Lat. *lūcidus*, bright.] —**e·lu′ci·da′-tion** *n.*

e·lude (ĭ-lōōd′) ►*v.* **e·lud·ed, e·lud·ing 1.** To evade or escape from, as by daring or skill. **2.** To escape the understanding or grasp of. [Lat. *ēlūdere.*]

E·lul (ĕl′ōōl, ĕ-lōōl′) ►*n.* The 6th month of the Jewish calendar. See table at **calendar.** [Heb. *'Ĕlûl* < Akkadian.]

e·lu·sive (ĭ-lōō′sĭv, -zĭv) ►*adj.* **1.** Tending to elude. **2.** Difficult to define or describe. —**e·lu′sive·ly** *adv.* —**e·lu′sive·ness** *n.*

e·lute (ĭ-lōōt′) ►*v.* **e·lut·ed, e·lut·ing** To extract (one material) from another. [< Lat. *ēluere, ēlūt-,* wash out : *ē-, ex-,* ex- + *-luere,* wash.] —**e·lu′tion** *n.*

el·ver (ĕl′vər) ►*n.* See **glass eel.** [< *eelfare,* the migration of young eels.]

elves (ĕlvz) ►*n.* Pl. of **elf.**

E·ly·si·um (ĭ-lĭz′ē-əm, ĭ-lĭzh′-) ►*n.* A place or condition of ideal happiness. —**E·ly′sian** (-lĭzh′ən) *adj.*

em (ĕm) ►*n. Print.* The width of a square piece of type, used as a unit of measure.

em–¹ ►*pref.* Var. of **en–¹.**

em–² ►*pref.* Var. of **en–².**

'em (əm) ►*pron. Informal* Them. [< OE *heom.*]

e·ma·ci·ate (ĭ-mā′shē-āt′) ►*v.* **-at·ed, -at·ing** To make or become extremely thin, esp. from starvation. [Lat. *ēmaciāre,* make thin.] —**e·ma′ci·a′tion** *n.*

e-mail or **e·mail** (ē′māl′) ►*n.* A message or messages sent and received electronically over a computer network. [*e(lectronic) mail.*] —**e′-mail′** *v.*

em·a·lan·ge·ni (ĕm′ə-läng-gĕn′ē) ►*n.* Pl. of **lilangeni.**

em·a·nate (ĕm′ə-nāt′) ►*v.* **-nat·ed, -nat·ing** To come or send forth from a source; issue; stem: *light that emanated from a lamp.* [Lat. *ēmānāre,* flow out.] —**em′a·na′tion** *n.*

e·man·ci·pate (ĭ-măn′sə-pāt′) ►*v.* **-pat·ed, -pat·ing** To free from bondage, oppression, or restraint; liberate. [Lat. *ēmancipāre.*] —**e·man′-ci·pa′tion** *n.* —**e·man′ci·pa′tor** *n.*

e·mas·cu·late (ĭ-măs′kyə-lāt′) ►*v.* **-lat·ed, -lat·ing 1.** To castrate. **2.** To make weak. [Lat. *ēmasculāre.*] —**e·mas′cu·la′tion** *n.* —**e·mas′-cu·la·to·ry** (-lə-tôr′ē) *adj.* —**e·mas′cu·la′tor** *n.*

em·balm (ĕm-bäm′) ►*v.* To treat (a corpse) with preservatives in order to prevent decay. [< OFr. *embasmer* < *basme,* BALM.] —**em·balm′er** *n.* —**em·balm′ment** *n.*

em·bank·ment (ĕm-băngk′mənt) ►*n.* A mound of earth or stone built to hold back water or to support a roadway.

em·bar·ca·de·ro (ĕm-bär′kə-dâr′ō) ►*n., pl.* **-ros** *Regional* A pier, wharf, or landing place esp. on a river. [Sp.]

em·bar·go (ĕm-bär′gō) ►*n., pl.* **-goes 1.** A government order prohibiting the movement of merchant ships into or out of its ports. **2.** A prohibition by a government on certain or all trade with a foreign nation. ►*v.* To impose an embargo on. [Sp. < *embargar,* impede.]

em·bark (ĕm-bärk′) ►*v.* **1.** To board or cause to board a vessel or aircraft, esp. at the start of a journey. **2.** To set out; commence. [Fr. *embar-quer*.] —**em·bar·ka·tion** *n.*

em·bar·rass (ĕm-bărʹəs) ►*v.* **1.** To cause to feel self-conscious or ill at ease; disconcert. **2.** To hinder with obstacles or difficulties; impede. [< Ital. *imbarazzo*, obstacle.] —**em·barʹrass·ing·ly** *adv.* —**em·barʹrass·ment** *n.*
 Syns: abash, chagrin, discomfit, disconcert, faze **v.**

em·bas·sy (ĕmʹbə-sē) ►*n., pl.* **-sies 1.** A building containing the offices of an ambassador and staff. **2.** The position or function of an ambassador. **3.** A mission headed by an ambassador. [< Med.Lat. *ambactiāta* < Lat. *ambactus*, servant.]

em·bat·tled (ĕm-bătʹld) ►*adj.* Beset with attackers, criticism, or controversy.

em·bed (ĕm-bĕdʹ) ►*v.* **-bed·ded, -bed·ding 1.** To fix or become fixed firmly in a surrounding mass. **2.** To assign (a journalist) to travel with a military unit during an armed conflict.

em·bel·lish (ĕm-bĕlʹĭsh) ►*v.* **1.** To make beautiful, as by ornamentation; decorate. **2.** To add fictitious details to. [< OFr. *embellir* < *bel*, beautiful.] —**em·belʹlish·ment** *n.*

em·ber (ĕmʹbər) ►*n.* **1.** A piece of live coal or wood from a fire. **2. embers** The smoldering coal or ash of a dying fire. [< OE *ǣmerge*.]

em·bez·zle (ĕm-bĕzʹəl) ►*v.* **-zled, -zling** To take (money that one has been entrusted) for personal use. [< AN *enbesiler*.] —**em·bezʹzle·ment** *n.* —**em·bezʹzler** *n.*

em·bit·ter (ĕm-bĭtʹər) ►*v.* **1.** To make bitter. **2.** To arouse bitter feelings in. —**em·bit·ter·ment** *n.*

em·bla·zon (ĕm-blāʹzən) ►*v.* **1.** To adorn (a surface) with a prominent marking, such as a heraldic symbol. **2.** To inscribe (a heraldic symbol, e.g.) on a surface. **3.** To make resplendent with brilliant colors. —**em·bla·zonʹer** *n.* —**em·blaʹzon·ment** *n.*

em·blem (ĕmʹbləm) ►*n.* **1.** A distinctive badge, design, or device. **2.** An object or representation that functions as a symbol. [< Gk. *emblēma*, embossed design.] —**emʹblem·atʹic, emʹblem·atʹi·cal** *adj.* —**emʹblem·atʹi·cal·ly** *adv.*

em·bod·y (ĕm-bŏdʹē) ►*v.* **-bod·ied, -bod·y·ing 1.** To give a bodily form to. **2.** To represent in bodily or material form. **3.** To make part of a system or whole; incorporate. —**em·bodʹi·ment** *n.*

em·bold·en (ĕm-bōlʹdən) ►*v.* To foster boldness or courage in. See Synonyms at **encourage.**

em·bo·lism (ĕmʹbə-lĭzʹəm) ►*n.* **1.** Obstruction or occlusion of a blood vessel by an embolus. **2.** An embolus. [< Gk. *embolismos*, insertion.]

em·bo·lus (ĕmʹbə-ləs) ►*n., pl.* **-li** (-līʹ) A mass in the bloodstream that lodges so as to block a blood vessel. [< Gk. *embolos*, stopper.]

em·boss (ĕm-bôsʹ, -bŏsʹ) ►*v.* **1.** To mold or carve in relief: *emboss a design on a coin.* **2.** To decorate with a raised design. [< OFr. *embocer* < *boce*, knob.]

em·bou·chure (ämʹbŏŏ-shŏŏrʹ) ►*n.* **1.** The mouthpiece of a woodwind or brass instrument. **2.** The manner in which the lips and tongue are applied to such a mouthpiece. [< OFr. *emboucher*, put in the mouth < *bouche*, mouth.]

em·brace (ĕm-brāsʹ) ►*v.* **-braced, -brac·ing 1.** To clasp or hold close with the arms. **2.** To surround; enclose. **3.** To include as part of something broader. **4.** To take up willingly or eagerly: *embrace a cause.* ►*n.* An act of embracing. [< OFr. *embracer* < *brace*, the two arms.] —**em·braceʹa·ble** *adj.* —**em·braceʹment** *n.*

em·bra·sure (ĕm-brāʹzhər) ►*n.* **1.** An opening in a thick wall for a door or window. **2.** A flared opening for a gun in a wall or parapet. [Fr.]

em·bro·cate (ĕmʹbrə-kātʹ) ►*v.* **-cat·ed, -cat·ing** To moisten and rub (a part of the body) with a liniment or lotion. [< Gk. *embrekhein*.] —**emʹbro·caʹtion** *n.*

em·broi·der (ĕm-broiʹdər) ►*v.* **1.** To ornament with needlework: *embroider a pillowcase.* **2.** To add embellishments or fanciful details to. [ME *embrouderen*.] —**em·broiʹder·er** *n.*

em·broi·der·y (ĕm-broiʹdə-rē) ►*n., pl.* **-ies 1.** The act or art of embroidering. **2.** Something that has been embroidered.

em·broil (ĕm-broilʹ) ►*v.* **1.** To involve in argument, contention, or hostile actions. **2.** To throw into confusion or disorder; entangle. [Fr. *embrouiller*.] —**em·broilʹment** *n.*

em·bry·o (ĕmʹbrē-ōʹ) ►*n., pl.* **-os 1a.** An organism in its early stages of development, esp. before it has reached a distinctively recognizable form. **b.** In humans, the product of conception from implantation through the eighth week of development. **2.** A rudimentary or beginning stage. [< Gk. *embruon*.] —**emʹbry·onʹic** (-ŏnʹĭk) *adj.* —**emʹbry·onʹi·cal·ly** *adv.*

em·bry·ol·o·gy (ĕmʹbrē-ŏlʹə-jē) ►*n.* The branch of biology that deals with the formation, early growth, and development of living organisms. —**emʹbry·o·logʹic** (-ə-lŏjʹĭk), **emʹbry·o·logʹi·cal** *adj.* —**emʹbry·ol·o·gist** *n.*

em·cee (ĕmʹsēʹ) ►*n.* A master of ceremonies. ►*v.* **-ceed, -cee·ing** To act as master of ceremonies (of). [Pronunciation of *M.C.*, abbr. of *master of ceremonies*.]

e·mend (ĭ-mĕndʹ) ►*v.* To improve (a text) by critical editing. [< Lat. *ēmendāre*.] —**e·menʹda·tion** *n.*

em·er·ald (ĕmʹər-əld, ĕmʹrəld) ►*n.* **1.** A brilliant, transparent green beryl, used as a gemstone. **2.** A strong yellowish green. [< Gk. *smaragdos*.]

e·merge (ĭ-mûrjʹ) ►*v.* **e·merged, e·merg·ing 1.** To move out or away from a surrounding fluid, covering, or shelter. **2.** To come into view. **3.** To come into existence. [Lat. *ēmergere*.] —**e·merʹgence** *n.* —**e·merʹgent** *adj.*

e·mer·gen·cy (ĭ-mûrʹjən-sē) ►*n., pl.* **-cies** A serious, unexpected situation or occurrence that demands immediate action. ►*adj.* For use during emergencies: *emergency food rations.*

e·mer·i·tus (ĭ-mĕrʹĭ-təs) ►*adj.* Retired but retaining an honorary title. [Lat. *emeritus*, p.part. of *ēmerēre*, earn by service.]

Em·er·son (ĕmʹər-sən), **Ralph Waldo** 1803–82. Amer. writer and philosopher. —**Emʹer·soʹni·an** (-sōʹnē-ən) *adj.*

em·er·y (ĕmʹə-rē, ĕmʹrē) ►*n.* A fine-grained impure corundum used for grinding and polishing. [< LLat. *smericulum* < Gk. *smiris*.]

e·met·ic (ĭ-mĕtʹĭk) ►*adj.* Causing vomiting. [< Gk. *emein*, to vomit.] —**e·metʹic** *n.*

EMF ►*abbr.* electromotive force

–emia or **–hemia** also **–aemia** or **–haemia** ►*suff.* Blood: *leukemia.* [< Gk. *haima*, blood.]

em·i·grate (ĕm′ĭ-grāt′) ►*v.* **-grat·ed, -grat· ing** To leave one country or region to settle in another. See Usage Note at **migrate.** [Lat. *ēmigrāre.*] —**em′i·grant** (-grənt) *n.* —**em′i· gra′tion** *n.*

é·mi·gré (ĕm′ĭ-grā′) ►*n.* One who has left a native country, esp. for political reasons. [Fr.]

em·i·nence (ĕm′ə-nəns) ►*n.* **1.** A position of great distinction or superiority. **2.** A rise of ground; hill. **3.** A person of high station or great achievements.

em·i·nent (ĕm′ə-nənt) ►*adj.* **1.** Well-known and respected, esp. for achievement in a particular field. See Synonyms at **famous. 2.** Outstanding; remarkable. **3.** Standing out above others; prominent: *an eminent peak.* [< Lat. *ēminēre,* stand out.] —**em′i·nent·ly** *adv.*

eminent domain ►*n.* A government's power to take private property for public use without the owner's consent, provided just compensation is given.

e·mir (ĭ-mîr′, ā-mîr′) ►*n.* A prince, chieftain, or governor, esp. in the Middle East. [< Ar. *ʾamīr,* commander.]

em·i·rate (ĕm′ə-rĭt, -rāt′) ►*n.* **1.** The office of an emir. **2.** The nation or territory ruled by an emir.

em·is·sar·y (ĕm′ĭ-sĕr′ē) ►*n., pl.* **-ies** An agent sent on a mission to represent another. [Lat. *ēmissārius.*]

e·mit (ĭ-mĭt′) ►*v.* **e·mit·ted, e·mit·ting 1.** To release or send out matter or energy. **2.** To utter; express. **3.** To put (currency) into circulation. [Lat. *ēmittere.*] —**e·mis′sion** (ĭ-mĭsh′ən) *n.* —**e·mit′ter** *n.*

e·mo (ē′mō) ►*n.* Rock music that is characterized by confessional lyrics about emotional topics.

e·mol·lient (ĭ-mŏl′yənt) ►*adj.* Softening and soothing, esp. to the skin. [< Lat. *ēmollīre,* soften.] —**e·mol′lient** *n.*

e·mol·u·ment (ĭ-mŏl′yə-mənt) ►*n.* Payment for an office or employment; compensation. [< Lat. *ēmolumentum.*]

e·mote (ĭ-mōt′) ►*v.* **e·mot·ed, e·mot·ing** To express emotion, esp. in an excessive or theatrical manner. [< EMOTION.]

e·mo·ti·con (ĭ-mō′tĭ-kŏn′) ►*n.* A series of keyed characters used, as in instant messages, to indicate an emotion or attitude, as [:-)] to indicate intended humor. [EMOT(ION) + ICON.]

e·mo·tion (ĭ-mō′shən) ►*n.* **1.** A strong feeling, as of joy, sorrow, or hate. **2.** A state of mental agitation or disturbance. [< VLat. **exmovēre, exmōt-,* excite.]

e·mo·tion·al (ĭ-mō′shə-nəl) ►*adj.* **1.** Of or exhibiting emotion. **2.** Readily affected with emotion. **3.** Arousing the emotions: *an emotional appeal.* —**e·mo′tion·al·ism** *n.* —**e·mo′· tion·a·lize′** *v.* —**e·mo′tion·al·ly** *adv.*

e·mo·tive (ĭ-mō′tĭv) ►*adj.* **1.** Of or relating to emotion. **2.** Expressing or exciting emotion: *an emotive trial lawyer.* —**e·mo′tive·ly** *adv.*

em·pa·na·da (ĕm′pə-nä′də) ►*n.* A turnover with a flaky crust and a savory or sweet filling. [Sp.< *pan,* bread.]

em·pan·el (ĕm-păn′əl) ►*v.* Var. of **impanel.**

em·pa·thy (ĕm′pə-thē) ►*n.* The ability to identify with or understand another's situation or feelings. [EN-² + –PATHY.] —**em′pa·thet′ic, em·path′ic** (-păth′ĭk) *adj.* —**em′pa·thize′** *v.*

em·per·or (ĕm′pər-ər) ►*n.* The male ruler of an empire. [< Lat. *imperātor.*]

em·pha·sis (ĕm′fə-sĭs) ►*n., pl.* **-ses** (-sēz′) **1.** Special forcefulness of expression that gives importance to something singled out. **2.** Special attention or effort directed toward something. **3.** Stress given to a syllable, word, or words. [Gk. < *emphainein,* to exhibit.] —**em′· pha·size′** *v.* —**em·phat′ic** (-făt′ĭk) *adj.* —**em· phat′i·cal·ly** *adv.*

Syns: *accent, stress* **n.**

em·phy·se·ma (ĕm′fĭ-sē′mə, -zē′-) ►*n.* A disease of the lungs marked by an abnormal increase in the size of the air spaces, resulting in labored breathing and an increased susceptibility to infection. [Gk. *emphusēma,* inflation.] —**em′phy·se′mic** *adj. & n.*

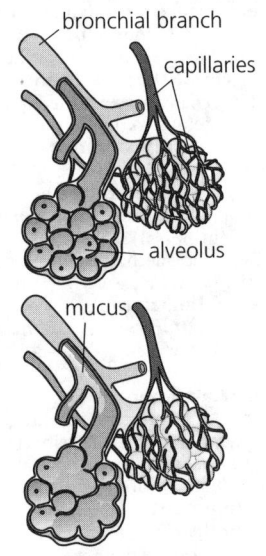

emphysema
top: normal bronchial branch and alveoli
bottom: diseased bronchial branch with mucus, enlarged air sacs in the alveoli, and fewer capillaries

em·pire (ĕm′pīr′) ►*n.* **1.** A political unit having an extensive territory or comprising a number of territories or nations and ruled by a single supreme authority. **2.** An extensive enterprise under a central authority: *a publishing empire.* **3.** Imperial sovereignty, domination, or control. [< Lat. *imperium.*]

em·pir·i·cal (ĕm-pîr′ĭ-kəl) ►*adj.* **1.** Based on observation or experiment. **2.** Guided by practical experience and not theory. [< Gk. *empeirikos,* experienced.] —**em·pir′i·cal·ly** *adv.*

em·pir·i·cism (ĕm-pîr′ĭ-sĭz′əm) ►*n.* **1.** The view that experience, esp. of the senses, is the only source of knowledge. **2.** Employment of empirical methods, as in science. —**em·pir′i·cist** *n.*

em·place·ment (ĕm-plās′mənt) ►*n.* **1.** A prepared position for a military weapon. **2.** The act of putting (something) into a certain position. **3.** Position; location. [Fr.]

em·ploy (ĕm-ploi′) ►*v.* **1.** To provide work to (someone) for pay. **2.** To put to use or service. ►*n.* Employment. [< Lat. *implicāre,* involve.]

—**em·ploy·a·bil·i·ty** *n.* —**em·ploy·a·ble** *adj.* —**em·ploy·er** *n.*

em·ploy·ee also **em·ploy·e** (ĕm-ploi/ē, ĭm-, ĕm/ploi-ē/) ►*n.* A person who works for another in return for compensation.

em·ploy·ment (ĕm-ploi/mənt) ►*n.* **1a.** The act of employing. **b.** The state of being employed. **2.** The work in which one is engaged; occupation.

em·po·ri·um (ĕm-pôr/ē-əm) ►*n., pl.* **-po·ri·ums** or **-po·ri·a** (-pôr/ē-ə) **1.** A marketplace. **2.** A large retail store carrying a variety of goods. [< Gk. *emporion.*]

em·pow·er (ĕm-pou/ər) ►*v.* **1.** · To invest esp. with legal power. See Synonyms at **authorize**. **2.** To equip or supply with an ability; enable. —**em·pow·er·ment** *n.*

em·press (ĕm/prĭs) ►*n.* **1.** The woman ruler of an empire. **2.** The wife or widow of an emperor. [< OFr. *emperesse.*]

emp·ty (ĕmp/tē) ►*adj.* **-ti·er, -ti·est 1.** Containing nothing. **2.** Having no occupants or inhabitants; vacant. **3.** Lacking purpose or substance; meaningless. See Synonyms at **vain**. ►*v.* **-tied, -ty·ing 1.** To make or become empty. **2.** To pour or discharge: *The river empties into a bay.* ►*n., pl.* **-ties** *Informal* An empty container. [< OE *æmetta*, leisure.] —**emp/ti·ly** *adv.* —**emp/ti·ness** *n.*

emp·ty-hand·ed (ĕmp/tē-hăn/dĭd) ►*adj.* **1.** Bearing nothing. **2.** Having received or gained nothing.

em·py·re·an (ĕm/pī-rē/ən, ĕm-pîr/ē-ən) ►*n.* **1.** The highest reaches of heaven. **2.** The sky. [< Gk. *empurios*, fiery < *pur*, fire.] —**em/py·re/an** *adj.*

EMT ►*abbr.* emergency medical technician

e·mu (ē/myo͞o) ►*n.* A large, flightless Australian bird that has shaggy brown plumage and is raised for its meat, oil, and leather. [Port. *ema*, flightless bird of South America.]

em·u·late (ĕm/yə-lāt/) ►*v.* **-lat·ed, -lat·ing 1.** To strive to equal or excel, esp. through imitation. **2.** *Comp.* To imitate the function of (another system). [Lat. *aemulārī.*] —**em/u·la/tion** *n.* —**em/u·la/tive** *adj.* —**em/u·la/tor** *n.*

e·mul·si·fy (ĭ-mŭl/sə-fī/) ►*v.* **-fied, -fy·ing** To make into an emulsion. —**e·mul/si·fi·ca/tion** *n.* —**e·mul/si·fi/er** *n.*

e·mul·sion (ĭ-mŭl/shən) ►*n.* **1.** A suspension of small globules of one liquid in a second liquid with which the first will not mix. **2.** A photosensitive coating, usu. of silver halide grains in a thin gelatin layer, on photographic film, paper, or glass. [< Lat. *ēmulgēre, ēmuls-*, milk out.] —**e·mul/sive** *adj.*

en (ĕn) ►*n. Print.* A space equal to half the width of an em.

en-1 or **em-** or **in-** ►*pref.* **1a.** To put into or onto: *encapsulate.* **b.** To go into or onto: *entrain.* **2.** To cover or provide with: *enrobe.* **3.** To cause to be: *endear.* **4.** Thoroughly. Used often as an intensive: *entangle.* [< Lat. *in*, in.]

en-2 or **em-** ►*pref.* In; into; within: *endemic.* [< Gk.]

–en1 ►*suff.* **1a.** To cause to be: *cheapen.* **b.** To become: *redden.* **2a.** To cause to have: *hearten.* **b.** To come to have: *lengthen.* [< OE *-nian.*]

–en2 ►*suff.* Made of; resembling: *earthen.* [< OE.]

en·a·ble (ĕ-nā/bəl) ►*v.* **-bled, -bling 1.** To supply with the means, knowledge, or opportunity;

make able. **2.** To give legal power, capacity, or sanction to. **3.** To make (e.g., a device) operational. —**en·a/bler** *n.*

en·act (ĕn-ăkt/) ►*v.* **1.** To make (a bill) into law. **2.** To act out, as on a stage. —**en·act/ment** *n.* —**en·ac/tor** *n.*

e·nam·el (ĭ-năm/əl) ►*n.* **1.** A vitreous, usu. opaque protective coating on metal, glass, or ceramic ware. **2.** A paint that dries to a hard glossy finish. **3.** The hard substance covering the exposed portion of a tooth. ►*v.* **-eled, -el·ing** or **-elled, -el·ling** To coat or decorate with enamel. [< AN *enamailler*, to put on enamel.] —**e·nam/el·ware** *n.*

en·am·or (ĭ-năm/ər) ►*v.* To inspire with love; captivate. [< OFr. *enamourer < amour*, love; see AMOUR.]

en·am·our (ĭ-năm/ər) ►*v. Chiefly Brit.* Var. of **enamor**.

en bloc (än blôk/, ĕn blŏk/) ►*adv.* As a unit; all together. [Fr.]

enc. ►*abbr.* **1.** enclosed **2.** enclosure

en·camp (ĕn-kămp/) ►*v.* To set up or live in a camp. —**en·camp/ment** *n.*

en·cap·su·late (ĕn-kăp/sə-lāt/) ►*v.* **-lat·ed, -lat·ing 1.** To encase in or as if in a capsule. **2.** To express in a brief summary. —**en·cap/su·la/tion** *n.*

en·case (ĕn-kās/) ►*v.* **-cased, -cas·ing** To enclose in or as if in a case. —**en·case/ment** *n.*

–ence ►*suff.* **1.** State or condition: *dependence.* **2.** Action: *emergence.* [< Lat. *-entia.*]

en·ceph·a·li·tis (ĕn-sĕf/ə-lī/tĭs) ►*n.* Inflammation of the brain. —**en·ceph/a·lit/ic** (-lĭt/ĭk) *adj.*

encephalo– or **encephal–** ►*pref.* Brain: *encephalitis.* [< Gk. *enkephalos*, in the head.]

en·ceph·a·lo·gram (ĕn-sĕf/ə-lə-grăm/, -ə-lō-) ►*n.* An x-ray picture of the brain. —**en·ceph/a·log/ra·phy** (ĕn-sĕf/ə-lŏg/rə-fē) *n.*

en·chain (ĕn-chān/) ►*v.* To bind with or as if with chains. —**en·chain/ment** *n.*

en·chant (ĕn-chănt/) ►*v.* **1.** To cast a spell over; bewitch. **2.** To attract and delight; entrance. See Synonyms at **charm**. [< Lat. *incantāre*, cast a spell.] —**en·chant/er** *n.* —**en·chant/ment** *n.* —**en·chant/ress** *n.*

en·chi·la·da (ĕn/chə-lä/də) ►*n.* A rolled tortilla with a meat or cheese filling, served with a sauce spiced with chili. [Am.Sp.]

en·ci·pher (ĕn-sī/fər) ►*v.* To put (a message) into cipher. —**en·ci/pher·ment** *n.*

en·cir·cle (ĕn-sûr/kəl) ►*v.* **-cled, -cling 1.** To form a circle around. **2.** To move or go around; make a circuit of: *The moon encircles the earth.* —**en·cir/cle·ment** *n.*

encl. ►*abbr.* **1.** enclosed **2.** enclosure

en·clave (ĕn/klāv/, ŏn/-) ►*n.* A distinctly bounded area enclosed within a larger unit, esp. a country or part of a country lying wholly within the boundaries of another. [< VLat. **inclāvāre*, enclose.]

en·close (ĕn-klōz/) ►*v.* **-closed, -clos·ing 1.** To surround on all sides; close in. **2.** To include in the same envelope or package: *enclose a check with the order.* [< Lat. *inclūdere, inclūs-.*] —**en·clo/sure** (-klō/zhər) *n.*

Syns: *cage, fence, hem, pen, wall* **v.**

en·code (ĕn-kōd/) ►*v.* **-cod·ed, -cod·ing 1.** To put (a message or other information) into code.

2. To format (electronic data) according to a standard format. —**en·cod′er** *n.*

en·co·mi·um (ĕn-kō′mē-əm) ►*n., pl.* -**mi·ums** or -**mi·a** (-mē-ə) Lofty praise; tribute. [< Gk. *enkōmios,* of the victory procession.]

en·com·pass (ĕn-kŭm′pəs) ►*v.* **1.** To form a circle or ring around; encircle. **2.** To enclose; envelop. **3.** To have as part of something larger; include. —**en·com′pass·ment** *n.*

en·core (ŏn′kôr′) ►*n.* **1.** A demand by an audience for an additional performance. **2.** An additional performance in response to such a demand. ►*interj.* Used to demand an encore. [Fr., again.]

en·coun·ter (ĕn-koun′tər) ►*n.* **1.** A meeting, esp. one that is unexpected or brief. **2.** A hostile confrontation; clash. ►*v.* **1.** To meet, esp. unexpectedly. **2.** To confront in battle. **3.** To experience or undergo. [< LLat. *incontrāre,* meet with.]

en·cour·age (ĕn-kûr′ĭj, -kŭr′-) ►*v.* -**aged, -ag·ing** **1.** To inspire with hope, courage, or confidence. **2.** To give support to; foster. [< OFr. *encoragier* < *corage,* COURAGE.] —**en·cour′age·ment** *n.* —**en·cour′ag·ing·ly** *adv.*
　　Syns: *cheer, embolden, hearten, inspire* **Ant:** *discourage* **v.**

en·croach (ĕn-krōch′) ►*v.* To take another's possessions or rights gradually or stealthily. [< OFr. *encrochier,* seize.] —**en·croach′er** *n.* —**en·croach′ment** *n.*

en·crust (ĕn-krŭst′) ►*v.* **1.** To cover with or as if with a crust. **2.** To decorate by inlaying or overlaying with a contrasting material. —**en′·crust·a′tion** *n.*

en·crypt (ĕn-krĭpt′) ►*v.* **1.** To put into code or cipher. **2.** *Comp.* To alter (data) using a mathematical algorithm so as to be unintelligible to unauthorized parties. [EN-² + *-crypt* (as in CRYPTOGRAM).] —**en·cryp′tion** *n.*

en·cum·ber (ĕn-kŭm′bər) ►*v.* **1.** To weigh down; burden. **2.** To hinder or impede. See Synonyms at **hinder. 3.** To burden with legal or financial obligations. [< OFr. *encombrer,* block up.] —**en·cum′brance** *n.*

-ency ►*suff.* Condition or quality: *complacency.* [ME, var. of *-ence,* -ence.]

en·cyc·li·cal (ĕn-sĭk′lĭ-kəl) ►*n. Rom. Cath. Ch.* A papal letter addressed to the bishops. [< Gk. *enkuklios,* circular.]

en·cy·clo·pe·di·a (ĕn-sī′klə-pē′dē-ə) ►*n.* A comprehensive reference work containing articles on a wide range of subjects or on numerous aspects of a particular field. [< Gk. *enkuklios paideia,* general education.] —**en·cy′clo·pe′dic** *adj.*

en·cyst (ĕn-sĭst′) ►*v.* To enclose or become enclosed in a cyst. —**en·cyst′ment, en′cys·ta′tion** *n.*

end (ĕnd) ►*n.* **1.** Either extremity of something that has length. **2.** The outside or extreme edge or physical limit; boundary. **3.** The point in time when something ceases or is completed; conclusion. **4.** A result; outcome. **5.** Something toward which one strives; goal. **6.** Death. **7.** The ultimate extent; the very limit. **8.** A remainder; remnant. **9.** A share of a responsibility or obligation. **10.** *Football* Either of the players in the outermost position on the line of scrimmage. ►*v.* **1.** To bring or come to a conclusion. **2.** To form the concluding part of. **3.** To destroy.

—*idioms:* **in the end** Eventually; ultimately. **no end** A great deal. [< OE *ende.*]

en·dan·ger (ĕn-dān′jər) ►*v.* **1.** To expose to harm or danger; imperil. **2.** To threaten with extinction. —**en·dan′gered** *adj.* —**en·dan′ger·ment** *n.*
　　Syns: *hazard, imperil, jeopardize, risk* **v.**

endangered species ►*n.* A species present in such small numbers that it is at risk of extinction.

en·dear (ĕn-dîr′) ►*v.* To make beloved.

en·dear·ment (ĕn-dîr′mənt) ►*n.* An expression of affection.

en·deav·or (ĕn-dĕv′ər) ►*n.* A concerted effort toward an end; earnest attempt. ►*v.* To attempt through concerted effort: *endeavored to improve my grades.* [< ME *(putten) in dever,* (put oneself) under obligation.]

en·dem·ic (ĕn-dĕm′ĭk) ►*adj.* Prevalent in or limited to a particular locality, region, or people. [< Gk. *endēmos,* among the people.] —**en·dem′i·cal·ly** *adv.*

en·dive (ĕn′dīv′, ŏn′dēv′) ►*n.* **1.** A plant with bitter ruffled leaves, grown as a salad green. **2.** A variety of chicory with a narrow, pointed cluster of leaves used in salads. [Ult. < Gk. *entubon.*]

end·less (ĕnd′lĭs) ►*adj.* **1.** Being or seeming to be without an end or limit; boundless. **2.** Formed with the ends joined; continuous. —**end′less·ly** *adv.* —**end′less·ness** *n.*

end·most (ĕnd′mōst′) ►*adj.* Being at or closest to the end; last.

endo- or **end-** ►*pref.* Inside; within: *endogenous.* [< Gk. *endon,* within.]

en·do·crine (ĕn′də-krĭn, -krēn′) ►*adj.* **1.** Secreting internally. **2.** Of or relating to endocrine glands or the hormones secreted by them. [Fr. : ENDO- + Gk. *krinein,* to separate.]

endocrine gland ►*n.* A gland, such as the thyroid, adrenal, or pituitary, producing hormones that are secreted directly into the bloodstream.

en·do·cri·nol·o·gy (ĕn′də-krə-nŏl′ə-jē) ►*n.* The branch of medicine that deals with the diagnosis and treatment of diseases and disorders of the endocrine glands. —**en′do·cri′no·log′ic** (-krĭn′ə-lŏj′ĭk), **en′do·crin′o·log′i·cal** *adj.* —**en′do·cri·nol′o·gist** *n.*

en·do·don·tics (ĕn′dō-dŏn′tĭks) ►*n. (takes sing. v.)* The branch of dentistry that deals with the diagnosis and treatment of diseases and disorders of the tooth root, dental pulp, and surrounding tissue. [ENDO- + (ORTHO)DONTICS.] —**en′do·don′tic** *adj.* —**en′do·don′tist** *n.*

en·dog·e·nous (ĕn-dŏj′ə-nəs) ►*adj. Biol.* Originating within an organism or part. —**en·dog′e·nous·ly** *adv.*

en·do·me·tri·o·sis (ĕn′dō-mē′trē-ō′sĭs) ►*n.* A usu. painful condition marked by the abnormal occurrence of endometrial tissue outside the uterus.

en·do·me·tri·um (ĕn′dō-mē′trē-əm) ►*n., pl.* -**tri·a** (-trē-ə) The glandular mucous membrane that lines the uterus. [NLat. : ENDO- + Gk. *mētra,* uterus.] —**en′do·me′tri·al** *adj.*

en·dor·phin (ĕn-dôr′fĭn) ►*n.* Any of a group of peptide hormones that bind to opiate receptors and are found mainly in the brain. [ENDO(GENOUS) + (MO)RPHIN(E).]

en·dorse (ĕn-dôrs′) ►*v.* -**dorsed, -dors·ing** **1.** To give approval of or support to, esp. by public statement; sanction. **2.** To write one's signature on the back of (a check) to obtain the amount payable. [< Med.Lat. *indorsāre* < Lat. *dorsum*, back.] **—en·dorse′ment** *n.* **—en·dors′er, en·dor′sor** *n.*

en·do·scope (ĕn′də-skōp′) ►*n.* An instrument for viewing the interior of a body canal or a hollow organ such as the colon or stomach. **—en′do·scop′ic** (-skŏp′ĭk) *adj.* **—en·dos′co·py** (ĕn-dŏs′kə-pē) *n.*

en·do·therm (ĕn′də-thûrm′) ►*n.* An organism that generates heat to maintain its body temperature, typically above the temperature of its surroundings. [ENDO– + Gk. *thermos*, heat.]

en·do·vas·cu·lar (ĕn′dō-văs′kyə-lər) ►*adj.* **1.** Intravascular. **2.** Relating to a surgical procedure in which a catheter is inserted through the skin into a blood vessel in order to diagnose and treat vascular disease.

en·dow (ĕn-dou′) ►*v.* **1.** To provide with property, income, or a source of income. **2.** To equip or supply with a talent or quality. [< AN *endouer* : EN–¹ + Lat. *dōtāre*, provide a dowry (< *dōs*, dowry).] **—en·dow′ment** *n.*

end-stage (ĕnd′stāj′) ►*adj.* Relating to the final phase of a terminal disease.

en·due (ĕn-dōō′, -dyōō′) ►*v.* **-dued, -du·ing** To provide with a quality or trait. [< Lat. *indūcere*, INDUCT, and *induere*, put on.]

en·dure (ĕn-dōōr′, -dyōōr′) ►*v.* **-dured, -dur·ing** **1.** To carry on through, despite hardships; undergo. **2.** To continue in existence; last. **3.** To suffer patiently without yielding. [< Lat. *indūrāre*, make hard.] **—en·dur′a·ble** *adj.* **—en·dur′ance** *n.*

end·wise (ĕnd′wīz′) also **end·ways** (-wāz′) ►*adv.* **1.** On end; upright. **2.** With the end foremost.

end zone ►*n. Football* The area at either end of the playing field between the goal line and the end line.

ENE ►*abbr.* east-northeast

–ene ►*suff.* An unsaturated organic compound, esp. one containing a double bond between carbon atoms: *ethylene*. [< Gk. *-ēnē*, feminine adj. suff.]

en·e·ma (ĕn′ə-mə) ►*n.* The injection of liquid into the rectum for cleansing or other therapeutic purposes. [< Gk. < *enienai*, send in.]

en·e·my (ĕn′ə-mē) ►*n., pl.* **-mies 1a.** One who feels hatred toward, intends injury to, or opposes the interests of another; foe. **b.** One who opposes or is hostile to an idea or cause. **2.** A hostile power or force, such as a nation. **3.** A group of foes or hostile forces. See Usage Note at **collective noun.** ►*adj.* Of, relating to, or being a hostile power or force. [< Lat. *inimīcus.*]
    Syns: *foe, opponent* **n.**

en·er·get·ic (ĕn′ər-jĕt′ĭk) ►*adj.* **1.** Possessing, exerting, or displaying energy. **2.** Of or relating to energy. [Gk. *energētikos* < *energos*, active; see ENERGY.] **—en′er·get′i·cal·ly** *adv.*

en·er·gize (ĕn′ər-jīz′) ►*v.* **-gized, -giz·ing 1.** To give energy to; invigorate. **2.** To supply with an electric current. **—en′er·giz′er** *n.*

en·er·gy (ĕn′ər-jē) ►*n., pl.* **-gies 1.** The capacity for work or vigorous activity. **2.** Exertion of vigor or power. **3.** Usable heat or power. **4.** *Phys.* The capacity of a physical system to

do work. [< Gk. *energos*, active : EN–² + *ergon*, work.]

en·er·vate (ĕn′ər-vāt′) ►*v.* **-vat·ed, -vat·ing** To weaken or destroy the strength or vitality of. [Lat. *ēnervāre*.] **—en′er·va′tion** *n.* **—en′er·va′tive** *adj.*

en·fee·ble (ĕn-fē′bəl) ►*v.* **-bled, -bling** To make feeble. **—en·fee′ble·ment** *n.*

en·fi·lade (ĕn′fə-lād′, -läd′) ►*n.* Gunfire directed along the length of a target, as a column of troops. [< OFr. *enfiler*, to thread.]

en·fold (ĕn-fōld′) ►*v.* **1.** To cover with or as if with folds; envelop. **2.** To embrace.

en·force (ĕn-fôrs′) ►*v.* **-forced, -forc·ing** To compel observance of or obedience to. **—en·force′a·bil′i·ty** *n.* **—en·force′a·ble** *adj.* **—en·force′ment** *n.* **—en·forc′er** *n.*

en·fran·chise (ĕn-frăn′chīz′) ►*v.* **-chised, -chis·ing 1.** To endow with the rights of citizenship, esp. the right to vote. **2.** To free, as from bondage. **3.** To bestow a franchise on. **—en·fran′chise′ment** *n.*

Eng. ►*abbr.* **1.** England **2.** English

en·gage (ĕn-gāj′) ►*v.* **-gaged, -gag·ing 1.** To hire; employ. **2.** To reserve. **3.** To pledge, esp. to marry. **4.** To attract and hold: *a project that engaged her interest.* **5.** To participate: *engage in conversation.* **6.** To enter into conflict with: *engage the enemy.* **7.** To interlock or cause to interlock; mesh. **8.** To assume an obligation; agree. [< OFr. *engagier*, pledge something as security.]

en·gaged (ĕn-gājd′) ►*adj.* **1.** Employed, occupied, or busy. **2.** Pledged to marry; betrothed. **3.** Involved in conflict or battle. **4.** Being in gear; meshed.

en·gage·ment (ĕn-gāj′mənt) ►*n.* **1.** The act of engaging or the state of being engaged. **2.** Betrothal. **3.** A promise or agreement to be at a particular place at a particular time. **4.** Employment, esp. for a specified time. **5.** A hostile encounter; battle.

en·gag·ing (ĕn-gā′jĭng) ►*adj.* Charming; attractive. **—en·gag′ing·ly** *adv.*

en garde (äN gärd′) ►*interj.* Used to warn a fencer to assume the position preparatory to a match. [Fr.]

Eng·els (ĕng′əlz, -əls), **Friedrich** 1820–95. German social theorist and writer.

en·gen·der (ĕn-jĕn′dər) ►*v.* **1.** To give rise to. **2.** To propagate. [< Lat. *ingenerāre.*]

en·gine (ĕn′jĭn) ►*n.* **1.** A machine that converts energy into mechanical force or motion. **2.** A mechanical appliance, instrument, or tool. **3.** A locomotive. [< Lat. *ingenium*, skill.]

engine block ►*n.* The cast metal block containing the cylinders of an internal-combustion engine.

en·gi·neer (ĕn′jə-nîr′) ►*n.* **1.** One trained or professionally engaged in a branch of engineering. **2.** One who operates an engine. ►*v.* **1.** To plan, construct, or manage as an engineer. **2.** To alter or produce by methods of genetic engineering. **3.** To plan, manage, and bring about by contrivance. [< Med.Lat. *ingeniātor*, contriver.]

en·gi·neer·ing (ĕn′jə-nîr′ĭng) ►*n.* The application of scientific principles to practical ends, as the design, manufacture, and operation of systems, structures, and machines.

Eng·land (ĭng′glənd) A division of the United

Kingdom, in S Great Britain. Cap. London.

Eng·lish (ĭng′glĭsh) ▸*adj.* **1.** Of or characteristic of England or its people or culture. **2.** Of the English language. ▸*n.* **1.** The people of England. **2.** The Germanic language of England, the US, and other countries. **3.** A course in the study of English language, literature, or composition. **4.** often **english** *Sports & Games* The spin given to a ball by striking it on one side or releasing it with a sharp twist. —**Eng′lish·man** *n.* —**Eng′lish·wom′an** *n.*

English Channel An arm of the Atlantic between France and England, opening to the North Sea through the Str. of Dover.

English horn ▸*n.* A double-reed woodwind instrument similar to but larger than the oboe and pitched lower by a fifth.

English setter ▸*n.* A medium-sized dog developed in England having a long silky white coat usu. with black or brownish markings.

en·gorge (ĕn-gôrj′) ▸*v.* **-gorged, -gorg·ing** **1.** To devour greedily. **2.** To fill to excess, as with fluid. [< OFr. *engorgier* < *gorge,* throat; see GORGE.] —**en·gorge′ment** *n.*

en·graft (ĕn-grăft′) ▸*v.* To graft (a scion) onto or into another plant.

en·grave (ĕn-grāv′) ▸*v.* **-graved, -grav·ing** **1.** To carve, cut, or etch into a material. **2a.** To cut into a block or surface used for printing. **b.** To print from a block or plate made by such a process. **3.** To impress deeply as if by carving or etching. —**en·grav′er** *n.*

en·grav·ing (ĕn-grā′vĭng) ▸*n.* **1.** The art or technique of one that engraves. **2.** A design or text engraved on a surface. **3.** An engraved surface for printing. **4.** A print made from an engraved plate or block.

en·gross (ĕn-grōs′) ▸*v.* To occupy exclusively; absorb: *a novel that engrosses every reader.* [< OFr. *en gros,* in large quantity.]

    Syns: absorb, consume, preoccupy v.

en·gulf (ĕn-gŭlf′) ▸*v.* To swallow up or overwhelm by or as if by overflowing and enclosing.

en·hance (ĕn-hăns′) ▸*v.* **-hanced, -hanc·ing** To improve or augment, esp. in effectiveness or attractiveness. [< LLat. *inaltāre,* heighten.] —**en·hance′ment** *n.* —**en·hanc′er** *n.*

e·nig·ma (ĭ-nĭg′mə) ▸*n.* **1.** One that is puzzling, ambiguous, or inexplicable. **2.** A perplexing speech or text. [< Gk. *ainigma.*] —**en′ig·mat′-ic** (ĕn′ĭg-măt′ĭk), **en′ig·mat′i·cal** *adj.*

en·join (ĕn-join′) ▸*v.* **1a.** To direct (a person) to do something. **b.** To require or impose (e.g., an action or behavior) with authority and emphasis. **2.** To forbid. [< Lat. *iniungere* < *iungere,* join.] —**en·join′ment** *n.*

en·joy (ĕn-joi′) ▸*v.* **1.** To receive pleasure or satisfaction from. **2.** To have the use or benefit of: *enjoys good health.* [< OFr. *enjoir.*] —**en·joy′a·ble** *adj.* —**en·joy′ment** *n.*

en·large (ĕn-lärj′) ▸*v.* **-larged, -larg·ing** **1.** To make or become larger. **2.** To make larger in scope or effect; expand. **3.** To speak or write at greater length or in greater detail; elaborate. —**en·large′ment** *n.* —**en·larg′er** *n.*

en·light·en (ĕn-līt′n) ▸*v.* **1.** To give spiritual or intellectual insight to. **2.** To inform or instruct. —**en·light′en·ment** *n.*

en·list (ĕn-lĭst′) ▸*v.* **1.** To engage (a person) for service in the armed forces. **2.** To engage the support or cooperation of. **3.** To enter the armed forces. —**en·list′ment** *n.*

en·liv·en (ĕn-lī′vən) ▸*v.* To make lively or spirited; animate. —**en·liv′en·ment** *n.*

en masse (ŏn măs′) ▸*adv.* In one group or body; all together. [Fr.]

en·mesh (ĕn-mĕsh′) ▸*v.* To entangle, involve, or catch in or as if in a mesh. See Synonyms at **catch.**

en·mi·ty (ĕn′mĭ-tē) ▸*n., pl.* **-ties** Deep-seated, often mutual hatred. [< Lat. *inimīcus,* enemy.]

en·no·ble (ĕn-nō′bəl) ▸*v.* **-bled, -bling** **1.** To make noble. **2.** To confer nobility upon. —**en·no′ble·ment** *n.*

en·nui (ŏn-wē′, ŏn′wē) ▸*n.* Listlessness and dissatisfaction resulting from lack of interest; boredom. [< OFr. *enui* < *ennuier,* ANNOY.]

e·nol·o·gy also **oe·nol·o·gy** (ē-nŏl′ə-jē) ▸*n.* The study of wine and winemaking. [Gk. *oinos,* wine + –LOGY.] —**e·nol′o·gist** *n.*

e·nor·mi·ty (ĭ-nôr′mĭ-tē) ▸*n., pl.* **-ties** **1.** Excessive wickedness or outrageousness. **2.** A monstrous offense or evil; outrage. **3.** *Informal* Great size; immensity.

e·nor·mous (ĭ-nôr′məs) ▸*adj.* **1.** Very great in size, extent, or amount. **2.** Very great in scope or amount. [< Lat. *ēnormis.*] —**e·nor′mous·ly** *adv.* —**e·nor′mous·ness** *n.*

e·nough (ĭ-nŭf′) ▸*adj.* Sufficient to meet a need or satisfy a desire; adequate. See Synonyms at **sufficient.** ▸*pron.* An adequate quantity. ▸*adv.* **1.** To a satisfactory amount or degree. **2.** Very; quite: *glad enough to leave.* **3.** Tolerably; rather: *She sang well enough.* ▸*interj.* Used to express impatience or exasperation. [< OE *genōg.*]

en·rage (ĕn-rāj′) ▸*v.* **-raged, -rag·ing** To put into a rage; infuriate.

en·rap·ture (ĕn-răp′chər) ▸*v.* **-tured, -tur·ing** To fill with rapture or delight.

en·rich (ĕn-rĭch′) ▸*v.* **1.** To make rich or richer. **2.** To make fuller, more meaningful, or more rewarding. **3.** To add nutrients to. **4.** To add to the beauty or character of; adorn. **5.** *Phys.* To increase the amount of one or more radioactive isotopes in (a material, esp. a nuclear fuel). —**en·rich′ment** *n.*

en·roll also **en·rol** (ĕn-rōl′) ▸*v.* **-rolled, -roll·ing** To enter or register in a roll, list, or record. —**en·roll′ment, en·rol′ment** *n.*

en route (ŏn rōōt′, ĕn) ▸*adv. & adj.* On or along the way. [Fr.]

ENS or **Ens.** ▸*abbr.* ensign

en·sconce (ĕn-skŏns′) ▸*v.* **-sconced, -sconc·ing** **1.** To settle securely or comfortably. **2.** To place or conceal in a secure place. [EN-¹ + *sconce,* small fort.]

en·sem·ble (ŏn-sŏm′bəl) ▸*n.* **1.** A unit or group of complementary parts that contribute to a single effect. **2.** A coordinated outfit or costume. **3.** A group of musicians, singers, dancers, or actors who perform together. **4.** *Mus.* A work for two or more vocalists or instrumentalists. [< LLat. *īnsimul,* at the same time.]

en·shrine (ĕn-shrīn′) ▸*v.* **-shrined, -shrin·ing** **1.** To enclose in or as if in a shrine. **2.** To cherish as sacred. —**en·shrine′ment** *n.*

en·shroud (ĕn-shroud′) ▸*v.* To cover with or as if with a shroud.

en·sign (ĕn′sən, -sīn′) ▸*n.* **1.** A standard or banner, as of a military unit. **2.** (ĕn′sən) The lowest commissioned rank in the US Navy or Coast

Guard. **3.** A badge of office or power; emblem. [< Lat. *insignia,* INSIGNIA.]

en·slave (ĕn-slāv′) ►*v.* **-slaved, -slav·ing** To make into or as if into a slave. **—en·slave′-ment** *n.* **—en·slav′er** *n.*

en·snare (ĕn-snâr′) ►*v.* **-snared, -snar·ing** To catch in or as if in a snare; trap. See Synonyms at **catch. —en·snare′ment** *n.* **—en·snar′er** *n.*

en·sue (ĕn-sōō′) ►*v.* **-sued, -su·ing** To take place afterward or as a result. [< Lat. *insequī,* follow.]

en·sure (ĕn-shŏor′) ►*v.* **-sured, -sur·ing** To make sure or certain; insure.

–ent ►*suff.* **1a.** Doing, or causing a specified action: *absorbent.* **b.** Being in a specified state or condition: *different.* **2.** One that performs, does, or causes a specified action: *president.* [< Lat. *-ēns, -ent-,* pr. part. suff.]

en·tab·la·ture (ĕn-tăb′lə-chŏor′) ►*n.* The horizontal upper section of a classical building, resting on the columns. [Obsolete Fr. < Ital. *intavolatura.*]

en·tail (ĕn-tāl′, ĭn-) ►*v.* **1.** To have, impose, or require as a necessary accompaniment or consequence. **2.** To limit the inheritance of (property) to a specified succession of heirs. [ME *entaillen,* limit inheritance to specific heirs.] **—en·tail′ment** *n.*

en·tan·gle (ĕn-tăng′gəl) ►*v.* **-gled, -gling 1.** To twist together into a confusing mass; snarl. **2.** To involve in a complicated situation or in circumstances from which it is difficult to disengage. See Synonyms at **catch. —en·tan′gle·ment** *n.*

en·tente (ŏn-tŏnt′) ►*n.* **1.** An agreement between two or more governments or powers for cooperative action or policy. **2.** The parties to such an agreement. [Fr.]

en·ter (ĕn′tər) ►*v.* **1.** To come or go into. **2.** To penetrate; pierce. **3.** To insert. **4.** To become or cause to become a participant, member, or part of; join or enroll. **5.** To embark on; begin. **6.** To write or put in. **7.** To place formally on record; submit. **8.** To go to or occupy in order to claim possession of (land). **—phrasal verbs: enter into 1.** To participate in. **2.** To become party to (a contract). **enter on** or **upon** To set out on; begin. [< Lat. *intrāre.*]

en·ter·ic (ĕn-tĕr′ĭk) also **en·ter·al** (ĕn′tər-əl) ►*adj.* Of or being within the intestine. [< Gk. *enteron,* intestine.]

en·ter·i·tis (ĕn′tə-rī′tĭs) ►*n.* Inflammation of the intestine. [< Gk. *enteron,* intestine.]

en·ter·prise (ĕn′tər-prīz′) ►*n.* **1.** An undertaking, esp. one of some scope, complication, and risk. **2.** A business organization. **3.** Industrious, systematic activity, esp. when directed toward profit. **4.** Willingness to undertake new ventures; initiative. [ME < OFr. *entreprise* < OFr. *entreprendre,* undertake.]

en·ter·pris·ing (ĕn′tər-prī′zĭng) ►*adj.* Willing and eager to undertake new projects.

en·ter·tain (ĕn′tər-tān′) ►*v.* **1.** To hold the attention of with something amusing or diverting. **2.** To extend hospitality to. **3.** To consider; contemplate. [< OFr. *entretenir.*] **—en′ter·tain′er** *n.* **—en′ter·tain′ment** *n.*

en·thrall (ĕn-thrôl′) ►*v.* **1.** To hold spellbound. **2.** To enslave. **—en·thrall′ment** *n.*

en·throne (ĕn-thrōn′) ►*v.* **-throned, -thron·ing 1.** To seat on a throne. **2.** To raise to a lofty position; exalt. **—en·throne′ment** *n.*

en·thuse (ĕn-thōōz′) ►*v.* **-thused, -thus·ing** *Informal* **1.** To make or act enthusiastic. **2.** To utter with enthusiasm.

en·thu·si·asm (ĕn-thōō′zē-ăz′əm) ►*n.* **1.** Great excitement for or interest in a subject or cause. **2.** A source or cause of great excitement or interest. [< Gk. *enthousiasmos.*] **—en·thu′si·ast′** *n.* **—en·thu′si·as′tic** *adj.* **—en·thu′si·as′ti·cal·ly** *adv.*

en·tice (ĕn-tīs′) ►*v.* **-ticed, -tic·ing** To attract by arousing hope or desire; lure. [< OFr. *enticier,* instigate.] **—en·tice′ment** *n.* **—en·tic′er** *n.* **—en·tic′ing·ly** *adv.*

en·tire (ĕn-tīr′) ►*adj.* **1a.** Having no part excluded or left out. See Synonyms at **whole. b.** Constituting the full amount, extent, or duration. **2.** Complete: *gave us his entire attention.* [< Lat. *integer.*] **—en·tire′ly** *adv.*

en·tire·ty (ĕn-tī′rĭ-tē, -tīr′tē) ►*n., pl.* **-ties 1.** Wholeness. **2.** The entire amount or extent.

en·ti·tle (ĕn-tīt′l) ►*v.* **-tled, -tling 1.** To give a name to. **2.** To furnish with a right or claim to something. [< Med.Lat. *intitulāre* < Lat. *titulus,* title.] **—en·ti′tle·ment** *n.*

entitlement program ►*n.* A government program that guarantees benefits to all members of a particular group.

en·ti·ty (ĕn′tĭ-tē) ►*n., pl.* **-ties 1.** Something that exists as a particular and discrete unit. **2.** The fact of existence; being. [< Lat. *ēns, ent-,* pr.part. of *esse,* be.]

en·tomb (ĕn-tōōm′) ►*v.* **1.** To place in or as if in a tomb or grave. **2.** To serve as a tomb for. **—en·tomb′ment** *n.*

en·to·mol·o·gy (ĕn′tə-mŏl′ə-jē) ►*n.* The scientific study of insects. [< Gk. *entomon,* insect.] **—en′to·mo·log′i·cal** (-mə-lŏj′ĭ-kəl) *adj.* **—en′to·mol′o·gist** *n.*

en·tou·rage (ŏn′tōō-räzh′) ►*n.* A group of attendants or associates; retinue. [< OFr. *entour,* surroundings.]

en·tr'acte (ŏn′trăkt′, äN-träkt′) ►*n.* **1.** The interval between two acts of a theatrical performance. **2.** Another performance, as of music or dance, provided between two acts of a theatrical performance. [Fr.]

en·trails (ĕn′trālz′, -trəlz) ►*pl.n.* The internal organs, esp. the intestines. [< Med.Lat. *intrālia* < Lat. *interāneus,* internal.]

en·trance[1] (ĕn′trəns) ►*n.* **1.** The act or an instance of entering. **2.** A means or point by which to enter. **3.** Permission or power to enter; admission. [< OFr. *entraunce* < *entrer,* ENTER.]

en·trance[2] (ĕn-trăns′) ►*v.* **-tranced, -tranc·ing 1.** To put into a trance. **2.** To fill with delight or enchantment. See Synonyms at **charm. —en·trance′ment** *n.* **—en·tranc′ing·ly** *adv.*

en·trant (ĕn′trənt) ►*n.* One that enters a competition.

en·trap (ĕn-trăp′) ►*v.* **-trapped, -trap·ping 1.** To catch in or as if in a trap. **2.** To lure into danger or a compromising situation. See Synonyms at **catch. —en·trap′ment** *n.*

en·treat (ĕn-trēt′) ►*v.* To make an earnest request of; plead. [< AN *entreter.*] **—en·treat′-ing·ly** *adv.* **—en·treat′ment** *n.*

en·treat·y (ĕn-trē′tē) ►*n., pl.* **-ies** An earnest request; plea.

en·trée or **en·tree** (ŏn′trā, ŏn-trā′) ►*n.* **1.** The main dish of a meal. **2.** The power or liberty to enter. [< OFr., entry.]

en·trench (ĕn-trĕnch′) ►*v.* **1.** To dig or provide with a trench. **2.** To fix (e.g., an idea or custom) firmly. **3.** To encroach or trespass. **—en·trench′ment** *n.*

en·tre·pre·neur (ŏn′trə-prə-nûr′, -nŏŏr′) ►*n.* A person who organizes, operates, and assumes the risk for a business venture. [< OFr. *entreprendre*, undertake.] **—en′tre·pre·neur′i·al** *adj.* **—en′tre·pre·neur′ism** *n.* **—en′tre·pre·neur′ship′** *n.*

en·tro·py (ĕn′trə-pē) ►*n., pl.* **-pies** **1.** For a closed thermodynamic system, a measure of the amount of thermal energy not available to do work. **2.** A measure of the disorder or randomness of a system. [Ger. *Entropie*.] **—en·tro′pic** (ĕn-trō′pĭk, -trŏp′ĭk) *adj.*

en·trust (ĕn-trŭst′) ►*v.* **1.** To give over (something) to another for care, protection, or performance. **2.** To give as a trust to (someone).

en·try (ĕn′trē) ►*n., pl.* **-tries** **1.** The act or an instance of entering. **2.** A means by which to enter. **3a.** The inclusion of an item, as in a record. **b.** An item entered in this way. **4.** An entry word, as in a dictionary; headword. **5.** One entered in a competition.

en·twine (ĕn-twīn′) ►*v.* **-twined, -twin·ing** To twine around or together.

e·nu·mer·ate (ĭ-nŏŏ′mə-rāt′, ĭ-nyŏŏ′-) ►*v.* **-at·ed, -at·ing** **1.** To name one by one; list. **2.** To determine the number of; count. [Lat. *ēnumerāre*, count out.] **—e·nu′mer·a′tion** *n.* **—e·nu′mer·a′tive** (-mə-rā′tĭv, -mər-ə-) *adj.* **—e·nu′mer·a′tor** *n.*

e·nun·ci·ate (ĭ-nŭn′sē-āt′) ►*v.* **-at·ed, -at·ing** **1.** To pronounce, esp. with clarity; articulate. **2.** To set forth precisely or systematically. **3.** To announce; proclaim. [Lat. *ēnūntiāre*.] **—e·nun′ci·a′tion** *n.* **—e·nun′ci·a′tor** *n.*

en·vel·op (ĕn-vĕl′əp) ►*v.* **-oped, -op·ing** To wrap, enclose, or cover. [< OFr. *envoloper*, wrap up.] **—en·vel′op·er** *n.* **—en·vel′op·ment** *n.*

en·ve·lope (ĕn′və-lōp′, ŏn′-) ►*n.* **1.** A flat, folded paper container, esp. for a letter. **2.** Something that envelops or encloses. **3.** The bag containing the gas in a balloon or airship. [< OFr. *envoloper*, wrap up.]

en·ven·om (ĕn-vĕn′əm) ►*v.* **1.** To make poisonous or noxious. **2.** To embitter.

en·vi·a·ble (ĕn′vē-ə-bəl) ►*adj.* So desirable as to arouse envy. **—en′vi·a·bly** *adv.*

en·vi·ous (ĕn′vē-əs) ►*adj.* Feeling, expressing, or characterized by envy. **—en′vi·ous·ly** *adv.* **—en′vi·ous·ness** *n.*

en·vi·ron·ment (ĕn-vī′rən-mənt, -vī′ərn-) ►*n.* **1.** The totality of the natural world. **2.** An ecosystem. **3.** The social and physical aspects of one's surroundings: *a hostile work environment.* **—en·vi′ron·men′tal** *adj.* **—en·vi′ron·men′tal·ly** *adv.*

en·vi·ron·men·tal·ism (ĕn-vī′rən-mĕn′tl-ĭz′əm, -vī′ərn-) ►*n.* Advocacy for or work toward protecting the natural environment from destruction or pollution. **—en·vi′ron·men′tal·ist** *n.*

en·vi·rons (ĕn-vī′rənz, -vī′ərnz) ►*pl.n.* A surrounding area, esp. of a city. [< OFr. *environ*, around.]

en·vis·age (ĕn-vĭz′ĭj) ►*v.* **-aged, -ag·ing** To conceive an image or picture of, esp. as a future possibility. [Fr. *envisager*.]

en·vi·sion (ĕn-vĭzh′ən) ►*v.* To picture in the mind; imagine.

en·voy[1] (ĕn′voi′, ŏn′-) ►*n.* **1.** A representative of a government who is sent on a special diplomatic mission. **2.** A messenger; agent. [< OFr. *envoier*, send < LLat. *inviāre*, be on the way.]

en·voy[2] also **en·voi** (ĕn′voi′, ŏn′-) ►*n.* A short closing stanza in certain verse forms dedicating the poem to a patron or summarizing its main ideas. [< OFr. *envoier*, send; see ENVOY[1].]

en·vy (ĕn′vē) ►*n., pl.* **-vies** **1.** Discontent and resentment aroused by desire for the possessions or qualities of another. **2.** The object of such feeling. ►*v.* **-vied, -vy·ing** To feel envy toward. [< Lat. *invidia* < *invidēre*, look at with envy : *in-*, in, on + *vidēre*, see.] **—en′vi·er** *n.*

en·zyme (ĕn′zīm) ►*n.* Any of numerous proteins that are produced by living organisms and function as biochemical catalysts. [< Med. Gk. *enzumos*, leavened.] **—en′zy·mat′ic** (-zə-măt′ĭk) *adj.*

eo– ►*pref.* Most primitive; earliest: *Eocene.* [< Gk. *ēōs*, dawn.]

E·o·cene (ē′ə-sēn′) *Geol.* ►*adj.* Of or being the 2nd epoch of the Tertiary Period, marked by the rise of mammals. ►*n.* The Eocene Epoch.

EOE ►*abbr.* equal opportunity employer

e·o·li·an (ē-ō′lē-ən, ē-ōl′yən) ►*adj.* Relating to, caused by, or carried by the wind. [< *Aeolus*, god of the winds in classical myth.]

EOM ►*abbr.* **1.** end of message **2.** end of month

e·on also **ae·on** (ē′ŏn′, ē′ən) ►*n.* **1.** An indefinitely long period of time; age. **2.** The longest division of geologic time, containing two or more eras. [< Gk. *aiōn.*]

E·os (ē′ŏs′) ►*n. Gk. Myth.* The goddess of the dawn.

–eous ►*suff.* Characterized by; resembling: *beauteous.* [< Lat. *-ōsus* and Lat. *-eus.*]

EPA ►*abbr.* Environmental Protection Agency

ep·au·let also **ep·au·lette** (ĕp′ə-lĕt′, ĕp′ə-lĕt′) ►*n.* A shoulder ornament, esp. a fringed strap on a uniform. [< OFr. *espaule*, shoulder < LLat. *spatula.*]

é·pée also **e·pee** (ā-pā′, ĕp′ā) ►*n.* A fencing sword with a bowl-shaped guard and a long narrow blade that has no cutting edge. [Fr. < Lat. *spatha*, sword.]

e·phed·rine (ĭ-fĕd′rĭn, ĕf′ĭ-drēn′) ►*n.* A white odorless alkaloid, $C_{10}H_{15}NO$, used in the treatment of allergies and asthma. [< Lat. *ephedra*, horsetail : Gk. *epi*, upon + *hedra*, seat.]

e·phem·er·al (ĭ-fĕm′ər-əl) ►*adj.* Lasting for a brief time; fleeting; evanescent. [< Gk. *ephēmeros.*] **—e·phem′er·al·ly** *adv.*

E·phe·sian (ĭ-fē′zhən) ►*n.* **1.** A native or inhabitant of ancient Ephesus. **2. Ephesians** *(takes sing. v.)* See table at **Bible.** [< Gk. *Ephesioi*, inhabitants of Ephesus.] **—E·phe′sian** *adj.*

Eph·e·sus (ĕf′ĭ-səs) An ancient Greek city of Asia Minor in present-day W Turkey.

epi– or **ep–** ►*pref.* **1.** On; upon: *epiphyte.* **2.** Over; above: *epicenter.* **3.** Around; covering: *epithelium.* [< Gk. *epi.*]

ep·ic (ĕp′ĭk) ►*n.* **1.** A long narrative poem celebrating the feats of a traditional hero. **2.** A literary or dramatic work that suggests the characteristics of epic poetry. ►*adj.* **1.** Of or resembling an epic; heroic; grand. **2.** Of great size or duration. [< Gk. *epos*, song.]

ep·i·cene (ĕp′ĭ-sēn′) ►*adj.* **1.** Having the characteristics of both sexes. **2.** Effeminate. ►*n.* One that is epicene. [< Gk. *epikoinos*.]

ep·i·cen·ter (ĕp′ĭ-sĕn′tər) ►*n.* The point on the earth's surface directly above the focus of an earthquake.

ep·i·cure (ĕp′ĭ-kyŏŏr′) ►*n.* A person with refined taste, esp. in food. [< Epicurus.]

ep·i·cu·re·an (ĕp′ĭ-kyŏŏ-rē′ən, -kyŏŏr′ē-) ►*adj.* **1.** Devoted to the pursuit of pleasure. **2.** Suited to the tastes of an epicure. —**ep′i·cu·re′an** *n.*

Ep·i·cu·rus (ĕp′ĭ-kyŏŏr′əs) 341?–270 BC. Greek philosopher.

ep·i·dem·ic (ĕp′ĭ-dĕm′ĭk) ►*adj.* Spreading rapidly among many individuals in an area. ►*n.* **1.** A widespread outbreak of a contagious disease. **2.** A rapid spread or development. [< Gk. *epidēmos*, prevalent.]

ep·i·der·mis (ĕp′ĭ-dûr′mĭs) ►*n.* The outer, protective layer of the skin. —**ep′i·der′mal** *adj.*

ep·i·du·ral (ĕp′ĭ-dŏŏr′əl, -dyŏŏr′-) ►*n.* An injection, esp. of an anesthetic, into the space over the dura mater of the spine.

ep·i·glot·tis (ĕp′ĭ-glŏt′ĭs) ►*n.* The elastic flap of cartilage located at the root of the tongue that prevents food from entering the windpipe during swallowing.

ep·i·gram (ĕp′ĭ-grăm′) ►*n.* A short witty poem or remark. [< Gk. *epigramma*, inscription < *epigraphein*, write on; see EPIGRAPH.] —**ep′i·gram·mat′ic** *adj.*

ep·i·graph (ĕp′ĭ-grăf′) ►*n.* **1.** An inscription, as on a statue or building. **2.** A motto or quotation, as at the beginning of a book, setting forth a theme. [< Gk. *epigraphein*, write on : EPI– + *graphein*, write.] —**ep′i·graph′ic** *adj.*

e·pig·ra·phy (ĭ-pĭg′rə-fē) ►*n.* The study esp. of ancient inscriptions. —**e·pig′ra·pher** *n.*

ep·i·lep·sy (ĕp′ə-lĕp′sē) ►*n.* Any of various neurological disorders marked by sudden recurring attacks of motor or sensory dysfunction, often with convulsions or loss of consciousness. [< Gk. *epilēpsis*, a taking hold.] —**ep′i·lep′tic** *adj. & n.*

ep·i·logue (ĕp′ə-lôg′, -lŏg′) ►*n.* **1.** A short poem or speech spoken directly to the audience at the end of a play. **2.** A short section at the end of a literary work, often discussing the future of its characters. [< Gk. *epilogos*.]

ep·i·neph·rine also **ep·i·neph·rin** (ĕp′ə-nĕf′rĭn) ►*n.* An adrenal hormone that constricts blood vessels and raises blood pressure, used also as a drug in synthetic form as a heart stimulant or bronchial relaxant; adrenaline. [EPI– + NEPHR(O)– + –INE².]

e·piph·a·ny (ĭ-pĭf′ə-nē) ►*n., pl.* -nies **1. Epiphany** A Christian feast observed on January 6 celebrating the visit of the Magi to Jesus. **2.** A revelatory manifestation esp. of a divine being. [< Gk. *epiphaneia*, manifestation.]

ep·i·phyte (ĕp′ə-fīt′) ►*n.* A plant, such as Spanish moss or a tropical orchid, that grows on another plant or object that provides support but not nutrients. —**ep′i·phyt′ic** (-fĭt′ĭk) *adj.*

e·pis·co·pa·cy (ĭ-pĭs′kə-pə-sē) ►*n., pl.* -cies **1.** See **episcopate** (sense 3). **2.** A system of church government headed by bishops.

e·pis·co·pal (ĭ-pĭs′kə-pəl) ►*adj.* **1.** Of or relating to a bishop. **2.** Governed by bishops. **3. Episcopal** Of the Episcopal Church. [< Gk. *episkopos*,

overseer : EPI– + *skopos*, watcher.]

Episcopal Church ►*n.* The church in the US that is in communion with the Church of England.

E·pis·co·pa·lian (ĭ-pĭs′kə-pā′lē-ən, -pāl′yən) ►*adj.* Of or belonging to the Episcopal Church. —**E·pis′co·pa′lian** *n.*

e·pis·co·pate (ĭ-pĭs′kə-pĭt, -pāt′) ►*n.* **1.** The position, term, or office of a bishop. **2.** The jurisdiction of a bishop; diocese. **3.** Bishops collectively.

e·pis·i·ot·o·my (ĭ-pĭz′ē-ŏt′ə-mē, ĭ-pē′zē-) ►*n., pl.* -mies Surgical incision of the perineum during childbirth to ease delivery. [Gk. *epision*, pubic region + –TOMY.]

ep·i·sode (ĕp′ĭ-sōd′) ►*n.* **1.** An incident in the course of an experience. **2.** An incident that forms a unit in a narrative or dramatic work. **3.** A separate part of a serialized work such as a television series. [< Gk. *epeisodion*, parenthetic narrative.] —**ep′i·sod′ic** (-sŏd′ĭk) *adj.*

e·pis·te·mol·o·gy (ĭ-pĭs′tə-mŏl′ə-jē) ►*n.* The branch of philosophy that examines the nature and theory of knowledge. [< Gk. *epistēmē*, knowledge < *epistasthai*, understand : EPI– + *histanai*, *stē*-, place, determine.] —**e·pis′te·mo·log′i·cal** *adj.* —**e·pis′te·mol′o·gist** *n.*

e·pis·tle (ĭ-pĭs′əl) ►*n.* **1.** A letter, esp. a formal one. **2. Epistle** *Bible* One of the letters included as a book in the New Testament. [< Gk. *epistolē*.] —**e·pis′to·lar′y** (-tə-lĕr′ē) *adj.*

ep·i·taph (ĕp′ĭ-tăf′) ►*n.* An inscription, as on a tombstone, in memory of a deceased person. [< Gk. *epitaphion*, funeral oration.]

ep·i·the·li·um (ĕp′ə-thē′lē-əm) ►*n., pl.* -li·a (-lē-ə) or -li·ums A thin membranous tissue that covers most internal and external surfaces of the body and its organs. [< EPI– + Gk. *thēlē*, nipple.] —**ep′i·the′li·al** *adj.*

ep·i·thet (ĕp′ə-thĕt′) ►*n.* A term, often abusive or contemptuous, used to characterize a person or thing. [< Gk. *epithetos*, added.]

e·pit·o·me (ĭ-pĭt′ə-mē) ►*n.* A typical or perfect example of its kind. [< Gk. *epitomē*, an abridgment.]

e·pit·o·mize (ĭ-pĭt′ə-mīz′) ►*v.* -mized, -mizing To be a typical example of; embody.

ep·och (ĕp′ək, ē′pŏk′) ►*n.* **1.** A particular period of history, esp. one that is noteworthy; era. **2.** A unit of geologic time that is a division of a period. [< Gk. *epokhē*, point in time.] —**ep′och·al** *adj.*

ep·o·nym (ĕp′ə-nĭm′) ►*n.* **1.** A word or name derived from a proper noun. **2.** One whose name is the source of another name or word. [< Gk. *epōnumos*, named after.] —**e·pon′y·mous** (ĭ-pŏn′ə-məs) *adj.*

ep·ox·y (ĭ-pŏk′sē) ►*n., pl.* -ies Any of various usu. thermosetting resins used esp. in surface coatings and adhesives. [EP(I)– + OXY(GEN).] —**ep·ox′y** *v.*

ep·si·lon (ĕp′sə-lŏn′, -lən) ►*n.* The 5th letter of the Greek alphabet. [Gk. *e psilon*, simple e.]

Ep·som salts (ĕp′səm) ►*pl.n.* (*takes sing. v.*) Hydrated magnesium sulfate, used as a cathartic and to reduce inflammation. [After Epsom, England.]

eq. ►*abbr.* **1.** equal **2.** equation **3.** equivalent

eq·ua·ble (ĕk′wə-bəl, ē′kwə-) ►*adj.* **1.** Unvarying; steady. **2.** Even-tempered. [< Lat. *aequāre*, make even.] —**eq′ua·bil′i·ty** *n.* —**eq′ua·bly** *adv.*

e·qual (ē′kwəl) ►*adj.* **1.** Having the same capability, quantity, effect, measure, or value as another. **2.** *Math.* Being identical to in value. **3.** Having the same privileges, status, or rights. **4.** Having the requisite qualities for a task or situation. ►*n.* One that is equal to another. ►*v.* **e·qualed, e·qual·ing** or **e·qualled, e·qual·ling 1.** To be equal to, esp. in value. **2.** To do, make, or produce something equal to: *equaled the world record.* [< Lat. *aequus.*] —**e·qual′i·ty** (ĭ-kwŏl′ĭ-tē) *n.* —**e′qual·ly** *adv.*

e·qual·ize (ē′kwə-līz′) ►*v.* **-ized, -iz·ing** To make equal, uniform, or balanced. —**e′qual·i·za′tion** *n.* —**e′qual·iz′er** *n.*

equal sign ►*n.* The symbol (=) used to indicate mathematical equality.

e·qua·nim·i·ty (ē′kwə-nĭm′ĭ-tē, ĕk′wə-) ►*n.* Calmness; composure. [< Lat. *aequanimis,* even-tempered.]

e·quate (ĭ-kwāt′) ►*v.* **e·quat·ed, e·quat·ing 1.** To make, treat, or regard as equal or equivalent. **2.** To be or seem to be equal; correspond. [< Lat. *aequāre* < *aequus,* even.]

e·qua·tion (ĭ-kwā′zhən, -shən) ►*n.* **1.** The act or process of equating or the condition of being equated. **2.** A statement, as in mathematics, that two expressions are equal.

e·qua·tor (ĭ-kwā′tər) ►*n.* **1.** The imaginary great circle around the earth's surface, equidistant from the poles and perpendicular to the earth's axis of rotation, that divides the earth into the Northern Hemisphere and the Southern Hemisphere. **2.** A similar great circle on a celestial body. [< Med.Lat. *aequātor* (*diēī et noctis*), equalizer (of day and night).] —**e′qua·to′ri·al** (ē′kwə-tôr′ē-əl, ĕk′wə-) *adj.*

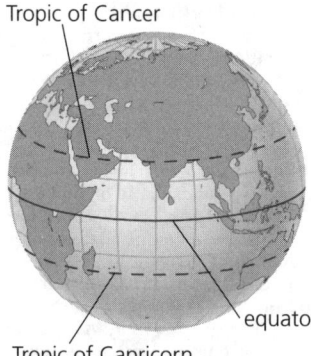

Tropic of Cancer

equator

Tropic of Capricorn

equator

Equatorial Guinea A country of W-central Africa including islands in the Gulf of Guinea. Cap. Malabo.

eq·uer·ry (ĕk′wə-rē) ►*n., pl.* **-ries 1.** An attendant to the British royal household. **2.** An officer who is in charge of the horses in a royal or noble household. [< OFr. *escuier,* SQUIRE.]

e·ques·tri·an (ĭ-kwĕs′trē-ən) ►*adj.* **1.** Of or relating to horseback riding. **2.** Depicted or represented on horseback. ►*n.* One who rides a horse or performs on horseback. [< Lat. *equester* < *eques,* horseman.]

equi– ►*pref.* Equal; equally: *equiangular.* [< Lat. *aequus,* equal.]

e·qui·an·gu·lar (ē′kwē-ăng′gyə-lər, ĕk′wē-) ►*adj.* Having all angles equal.

e·qui·dis·tant (ē′kwĭ-dĭs′tənt, ĕk′wĭ-) ►*adj.* Equally distant. —**e′qui·dis′tance** *n.*

e·qui·lat·er·al (ē′kwə-lăt′ər-əl, ĕk′wə-) ►*adj.* Having all sides equal. —**e′qui·lat′er·al** *n.*

e·qui·lib·ri·um (ē′kwə-lĭb′rē-əm, ĕk′wə-) ►*n.* **1.** A condition of balance between opposed forces, influences, or actions. **2.** Mental or emotional balance. [Lat. *aequilibrium.*]

e·quine (ē′kwīn′, ĕk′wīn′) ►*adj.* **1.** Of or like a horse. **2.** Of the taxonomic family which includes the horses, asses, and zebras. [< Lat. *equus,* horse.] —**e′quine′** *n.*

e·qui·noc·tial (ē′kwə-nŏk′shəl, ĕk′wə-) ►*adj.* Relating to an equinox.

e·qui·nox (ē′kwə-nŏks′, ĕk′wə-) ►*n.* Either of the two times during a year, occurring in the spring and autumn, when the sun crosses the celestial equator and when the length of day and night are approx. equal. [< Lat. *aequinoctium* : EQUI– + *nox,* night.]

e·quip (ĭ-kwĭp′) ►*v.* **e·quipped, e·quip·ping** To supply with the necessary materials for an undertaking. [< OFr. *esquiper.*]

e·quip·ment (ĭ-kwĭp′mənt) ►*n.* **1.** The act of equipping or the state of being equipped. **2.** The things with which one is equipped.
   Syns: *apparatus, gear, materiel, outfit, paraphernalia* **n.**

e·qui·poise (ē′kwə-poiz′, ĕk′wə-) ►*n.* **1.** Equality in distribution, as of weight. **2.** A counterbalance.

eq·ui·ta·ble (ĕk′wĭ-tə-bəl) ►*adj.* Just and fair; impartial. [< OFr. *equite,* EQUITY.] —**eq′ui·ta·ble·ness** *n.* —**eq′ui·ta·bly** *adv.*

eq·ui·ta·tion (ĕk′wĭ-tā′shən) ►*n.* The art and practice of riding a horse. [< Lat. *equitāre,* ride horseback.]

eq·ui·ty (ĕk′wĭ-tē) ►*n., pl.* **-ties 1.** The state or quality of being just and fair. **2.** Something that is equitable. **3.** *Law* Justice achieved in accordance with the unique facts of the case. **4.** The residual value of a business or property beyond any debt or liability. **5. equities** Corporate stock. [< Lat. *aequitās.*]

e·quiv·a·lent (ĭ-kwĭv′ə-lənt) ►*adj.* **1.** Equal. **2.** Similar or identical in function or effect. [< LLat. *aequivalēre,* have equal force.] —**e·quiv′a·lence, e·quiv′a·len·cy** *n.* —**e·quiv′a·lent** *n.* —**e·quiv′a·lent·ly** *adv.*

e·quiv·o·cal (ĭ-kwĭv′ə-kəl) ►*adj.* **1.** Ambiguous. **2.** Questionable or inconclusive. [< LLat. *aequivocus.*] —**e·quiv′o·cal·ly** *adv.*

e·quiv·o·cate (ĭ-kwĭv′ə-kāt′) ►*v.* **-cat·ed, -cat·ing** To use ambiguous language; hedge. [< Med.Lat. *aequivocāre.*] —**e·quiv′o·ca′tion** *n.* —**e·quiv′o·ca′tor** *n.*

ER ►*abbr.* emergency room

–er¹ ►*suff.* **1.** One that performs a specified action: *swimmer.* **2.** One associated or involved with: *banker.* **3.** A native or resident of: *New Yorker.* **4.** One that is: *foreigner.* [< OE *-ere* and < Lat. *-ārius, -ary.*]

–er² ►*suff.* Used to form the comparative degree of adjectives and adverbs: *darker; faster.* [< OE *-re, -ra.*]

e·ra (ir′ə, ĕr′ə) ►*n.* **1.** A period of time using a specific date in history as a basis. **2.** A period of time characterized by a particular circumstance, event, or person. **3.** The longest division of geologic time, made up of one or more periods. [< Lat. *aera*, counters.]

ERA ►*abbr.* **1.** earned run average **2.** Equal Rights Amendment

e·rad·i·cate (ĭ-răd′ĭ-kāt′) ►*v.* **-cat·ed, -cat·ing 1.** To tear up by the roots. **2.** To get rid of; eliminate. See Synonyms at **eliminate.** [< Lat. *ērādīcāre* : EX– + *rādix*, root.] —**e·rad′i·ca·ble** *adj.* —**e·rad′i·ca′tion** *n.* —**e·rad′i·ca′tor** *n.*

e·rase (ĭ-rās′) ►*v.* **e·rased, e·ras·ing 1.** To remove (e.g., something written) by or as if by rubbing. **2.** To delete (recorded material or data) from a storage medium: *erased the files.* **3.** To delete recorded material from (a storage medium): *erased the hard drive.* **4.** To remove all traces of. [Lat. *ērādere, ērās-*, scratch out.] —**e·ras′a·ble** *adj.* —**e·ras′er** *n.* —**e·ra′sure** *n.*

E·ras·mus (ĭ-răz′məs), **Desiderius** 1466?–1536. Dutch scholar and theologian.

er·bi·um (ûr′bē-əm) ►*n. Symbol* **Er** A soft, malleable, silvery rare-earth element. At. no. 68. See table at **element.** [After *Ytterby*, Sweden.]

ere (âr) ►*prep.* Previous to; before. ►*conj.* Rather than; before. [< OE *ær.*]

e·rect (ĭ-rĕkt′) ►*adj.* **1.** Being in a vertical, upright position. **2.** *Physiol.* Stiff; rigid. ►*v.* **1.** To build or construct. **2.** To raise upright. **3.** To set up; establish. [< Lat. *ērēctus*, p.part. of *ērigere*, set up.] —**e·rect′ly** *adv.* —**e·rect′ness** *n.* —**e·rec′tor** *n.*

e·rec·tile (ĭ-rĕk′təl, -tīl′) ►*adj.* **1.** Capable of being raised to an upright position. **2.** Of or relating to vascular tissue that is capable of filling with blood and becoming rigid.

e·rec·tion (ĭ-rĕk′shən) ►*n.* **1.** The act of erecting or the state of being erected. **2.** *Physiol.* The condition of erectile tissue, esp. of the penis, when filled with blood.

ere·long (âr-lông′, -lŏng′) ►*adv.* Before long.

er·e·mite (âr′ə-mīt′) ►*n.* A hermit, esp. a religious recluse. [< Gk. *erēmitēs*, HERMIT.]

erg (ûrg) ►*n.* A unit of energy or work equal to 10^{-7} joule. [< Gk. *ergon*, work.]

er·go (ûr′gō, âr′-) ►*conj. & adv.* Consequently; therefore. [Lat. *ergō.*]

er·go·nom·ics (ûr′gə-nŏm′ĭks) ►*n. (takes sing. v.)* The applied science of equipment design intended to reduce operator fatigue and discomfort. [Gk. *ergon*, work + (ECO)NOMICS.] —**er′go·nom′ic, er′go·no·met′ric** *adj.*

er·got (ûr′gət, -gŏt′) ►*n.* **1.** A fungus that infects rye and other cereal plants. **2.** The plant disease caused by such a fungus. [< OFr. *argot*, cock's spur.]

Er·ic·son (ĕr′ĭk-sən), **Leif** fl. c. 1000. Norwegian navigator.

Er·ic the Red (ĕr′ĭk) fl. 10th cent. Norwegian navigator.

E·rie¹ (îr′ē) ►*n., pl.* **E·rie** or **E·ries 1.** A member of a Native American people formerly inhabiting the S shore of Lake Erie. **2.** The Iroquoian language of the Erie.

Erie, Lake One of the Great Lakes, bounded by S Ontario, W NY, NW PA, N OH, and SE MI.

Erie Canal An artificial waterway extending about 580 km (360 mi) across central NY from Albany to Buffalo.

Er·in (ĕr′ĭn) A poetic name for Ireland.

Er·i·tre·a (ĕr′ĭ-trē′ə) A country N of Ethiopia bordering on the Red Sea. Cap. Asmara. —**Er′i·tre′an** *adj. & n.*

er·mine (ûr′mĭn) ►*n.* **1.** A weasel having dark brown fur that in winter changes to white. **2.** The white fur of this animal. [< OFr.]

Ernst (ĕrnst), **Max** 1891–1976. German-born artist.

e·rode (ĭ-rōd′) ►*v.* **e·rod·ed, e·rod·ing 1.** To wear away or destroy gradually by or as if by abrasion. **2.** To eat into or away; corrode. [Lat. *ērōdere*, eat away.] —**e·rod′i·ble** *adj.*

e·rog·e·nous (ĭ-rŏj′ə-nəs) ►*adj.* **1.** Responsive to sexual stimulation. **2.** Arousing sexual desire. [< Gk. *erōs*, sexual love.]

Er·os (ĕr′ŏs′, îr′-) ►*n. Gk. Myth.* The god of love, son of Aphrodite.

e·ro·sion (ĭ-rō′zhən) ►*n.* The process of eroding or the condition of being eroded. —**e·ro′sive** *adj.*

e·rot·ic (ĭ-rŏt′ĭk) ►*adj.* Of, relating to, or tending to arouse sexual desire. [< Gk. *erōs, erōt-*, sexual love.] —**e·rot′i·cal·ly** *adv.* —**e·rot′i·cism** *n.*

e·rot·i·ca (ĭ-rŏt′ĭ-kə) ►*pl.n. (takes sing. or pl. v.)* Literature or art intended to arouse sexual desire. [Gk. *erōtika* < *erōtikos*, EROTIC.]

err (ûr, ĕr) ►*v.* **1.** To make an error or mistake. **2.** To do wrong. [< Lat. *errāre*, wander.]

er·rand (ĕr′ənd) ►*n.* **1.** A short trip taken to perform a specified task. **2.** The purpose or object of an errand. [< OE *ærend.*]

er·rant (ĕr′ənt) ►*adj.* **1.** Roving, esp. in search of adventure. **2.** Straying from the intended course. **3.** Failing to follow moral standards. [< AN *erraunt.*] —**er′rant·ly** *adv.* —**er′rant·ry** *n.*

er·rat·ic (ĭ-răt′ĭk) ►*adj.* **1.** Lacking consistency or uniformity; irregular. **2.** Unconventional; eccentric. [< Lat. *errāticus*, wandering.] —**er·rat′i·cal·ly** *adv.*

er·ra·tum (ĭ-rä′təm, ĭ-rā′-) ►*n., pl.* **-ta** (-tə) An error in a printed text. [Lat. *errātum.*]

er·ro·ne·ous (ĭ-rō′nē-əs) ►*adj.* Incorrect or mistaken. [< Lat. *errō, errōn-*, vagabond.] —**er·ro′ne·ous·ly** *adv.*

er·ror (ĕr′ər) ►*n.* **1.** An unintentional deviation from what is correct, right, or true. **2.** The condition of being incorrect or wrong. **3.** *Baseball* A defensive misplay. [< Lat.] —**er′ror·less** *adj.*

er·satz (ĕr′zäts′, ĕr-zäts′) ►*adj.* Being an imitation or substitute. [Ger., replacement < OHGer. *irsezzan*, replace : *ir-*, out + *sezzan*, set.]

Erse (ûrs) *Archaic* ►*n.* **1.** The Gaelic language of Ireland; Irish. **2.** The Scottish Gaelic language. [< OE *Iras*, the Irish.] —**Erse** *adj.*

erst·while (ûrst′wīl′, -hwīl′) ►*adv.* In the past. ►*adj.* Former. [< OE *ærest.*]

e·ruct (ĭ-rŭkt′) ►*v.* To belch. [Lat. *ērūctāre.*] —**e·ruc·ta′tion** *n.*

er·u·dite (ĕr′yə-dīt′, ĕr′ə-) ►*adj.* Marked by great learning. See Synonyms at **learned.** [< Lat. *ērudītus*, p.part. of *ērudīre*, instruct, polish.] —**er′u·dite′ly** *adv.*

er·u·di·tion (ĕr′yə-dĭsh′ən, ĕr′ə-) ►*n.* Deep, extensive learning.

e·rupt (ĭ-rŭpt′) ►*v.* **1.** To break out violently from restraint or limits: *erupt in anger.* **2.** To become violently active, as a volcano. **3.** To appear on the skin. Used of a rash or blemish. **4.** To break through the gums. Used of teeth. [Lat. *ērumpere, ērupt-*.] —**e·rup′tion** *n.* —**e·rup′tive** *adj.*

–ery or **–ry** ►*suff.* **1.** A place for: *bakery.* **2.** A state or condition of: *slavery.* **3.** Act; practice:

bribery. **4.** Characteristics or qualities of: *snobbery.* [< OFr. *-erie.*]

er·y·sip·e·las (ĕr'ĭ-sĭp'ə-ləs, îr'-) ►*n.* An acute disease of the skin caused by a streptococcus and marked by spreading inflammation and fever. [< Gk. *erusipelas* : *erusi-*, red + *-pelas*, skin.]

e·ryth·ro·cyte (ĭ-rĭth'rə-sīt') ►*n.* See **red blood cell.** [Gk. *eruthros*, red + –CYTE.] **—e·ryth'ro·cyt'ic** (-sĭt'ĭk) *adj.*

e·ryth·ro·my·cin (ĭ-rĭth'rə-mī'sĭn) ►*n.* An antibiotic obtained from a strain of bacteria, effective against gram-positive and some gram-negative bacteria. [Gk. *eruthros*, red + –MYCIN.]

–es[1] ►*suff.* Var. of **–s[1].**

–es[2] ►*suff.* Var. of **–s[2].**

E·sau (ē'sô) In the Bible, the elder son of Isaac and Rebecca.

es·ca·late (ĕs'kə-lāt') ►*v.* **-lat·ed, -lat·ing** To increase or intensify. [< ESCALATOR.] **—es'ca·la'tion** *n.*

es·ca·la·tor (ĕs'kə-lā'tər) ►*n.* A moving stairway consisting of steps attached to a continuously circulating belt. [Orig. a trademark.]

es·ca·pade (ĕs'kə-pād') ►*n.* A reckless adventure. [< VLat. **excappāre*, ESCAPE.]

es·cape (ĭ-skāp') ►*v.* **-caped, -cap·ing** **1.** To break out (of). **2.** To avoid capture, danger, or harm. **3.** To succeed in avoiding. **4.** To fail to come to mind: *Her name escapes me.* **5.** To leak or issue (from). ►*n.* **1.** The act or a means of escaping. **2.** Comp. A key used esp. to interrupt a command or exit a program. [< VLat. **excappāre* < Med.Lat. *cappa*, cloak.] **—es·cap'er** *n.*

es·cap·ee (ĭ-skā'pē', ĕs'kā-) ►*n.* One that has escaped, esp. an escaped prisoner.

escape velocity ►*n.* The velocity needed for a body to overcome the gravitational pull of another body, such as the earth.

es·cap·ism (ĭ-skā'pĭz'əm) ►*n.* The avoidance of reality through daydreaming, fantasy, or entertainment. **—es·cap'ist** *adj. & n.*

es·ca·role (ĕs'kə-rōl') ►*n.* A salad plant having relatively broad, mildly bitter leaves. [< LLat. *ēscāriola*, chicory < Lat. *ēsca*, food < *edere*, eat.]

es·carp·ment (ĭ-skärp'mənt) ►*n.* **1.** A steep slope or long cliff. **2.** A steep slope in front of a fortification. [< Ital. *scarpa*, slope.]

–escence ►*suff.* State; process: *luminescence.* [< Lat. *-ēscentia.*]

–escent ►*suff.* **1.** Beginning to be; becoming: *obsolescent.* **2.** Characterized by; resembling: *evanescent.* [< Lat. *-ēscēns.*]

Esch·er (ĕsh'ər, ĕs'ĸĦər), **M(aurits) C(ornelis)** 1898–1972. Dutch artist.

es·chew (ĕs-chōō') ►*v.* To avoid or shun. [< OFr. *eschivir*, of Gmc. orig.]

es·cort (ĕs'kôrt') ►*n.* **1.** One that accompanies another to guide, protect, or show honor. **2.** One who accompanies another, esp. socially. ►*v.* (ĭ-skôrt', ĕs'kôrt') To accompany as an escort. [< Ital. *scorta* < *scorgere*, to guide.]

es·cri·toire (ĕs'krĭ-twär') ►*n.* A writing table. [< Med.Lat. *scrīptōrium*, a study.]

es·crow (ĕs'krō, ĕ-skrō') ►*n.* Money, property, a deed, or a bond put into the custody of a third party until fulfillment of certain conditions. [< AN *escrowe*, SCROLL.]

es·cu·do (ĭ-skōō'dō) ►*n., pl.* **-dos** See table at

currency. [< Lat. *scūtum*, shield.]

es·cutch·eon (ĭ-skŭch'ən) ►*n.* A shield or shield-shaped emblem bearing a coat of arms. [< Lat. *scūtum*, shield.]

ESE ►*abbr.* east-southeast

–ese ►*suff.* **1.** Of, characteristic of, or originating in a specified place: *Vietnamese.* **2.** Native or inhabitant of: *Taiwanese.* **3a.** Language or dialect of: *Chinese.* **b.** Literary style or diction of: *journalese.* [< Lat. *-ēnsis*, originating in.]

Es·ki·mo (ĕs'kə-mō') ►*n., pl.* **-mo** or **-mos 1.** A member of a group of peoples inhabiting the Arctic coast of North America and parts of Greenland and NE Siberia. **2.** Any of the languages of the Eskimo. **—Es'ki·mo', Es'ki·mo'an** *adj.*

   Usage: Outside of the United States, esp. in Canada, *Eskimo* is often considered to be derogatory. Canadians prefer the term *Inuit* for the native people of the Arctic. However, *Eskimo* applies to a broader range of peoples than Inuit and is widely used in Alaska.

ESL ►*abbr.* English as a second language

e·soph·a·gus (ĭ-sŏf'ə-gəs) ►*n., pl.* **-gi** (-jī', -gī') The muscular tube by which food passes from the pharynx to the stomach. [< Gk. *oisophagos.*] **—e·soph'a·ge'al** (-jē'əl) *adj.*

es·o·ter·ic (ĕs'ə-tĕr'ĭk) ►*adj.* **1.** Intended for or understood by only a few. See Synonyms at **mysterious. 2.** Not known by or suitable for the public; private. [< Gk. *esōterō*, further in.]

ESP (ē'ĕs-pē') ►*n.* The supposed ability to perceive by means other than the physical senses. [*e(xtra)s(ensory) p(erception).*]

esp. ►*abbr.* especially

es·pa·drille (ĕs'pə-drĭl') ►*n.* A shoe usu. having a fabric upper and a rope or rubber sole. [< Prov. *espardilho.*]

es·pal·ier (ĭ-spăl'yər, -yā') ►*n.* A tree or shrub trained to grow in a flat plane against a wall, often in a symmetrical pattern. [< Ital. *spalliera*, shoulder support.] **—es·pal'ier** *v.*

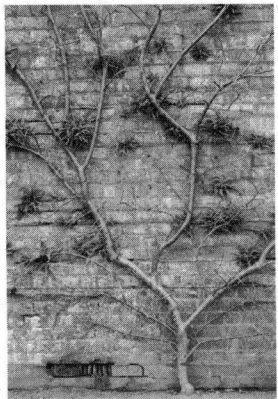

espalier

es·pe·cial (ĭ-spĕsh'əl) ►*adj.* Of special importance or significance; particular; exceptional. [< Lat. *speciālis*, of a kind < *speciēs*, kind.] **—es·pe'cial·ly** *adv.*

Es·pe·ran·to (ĕs'pə-rän'tō, -răn'-) ►*n.* An artificial international language based on many European languages. [After Dr. *Esperanto*, pseudonym of L.L. Zamenhof (1859–1917).]

es·pi·o·nage (ĕs′pē-ə-näzh′, -nĭj) ►*n.* The act or practice of spying. [< OItal. *spione,* of Gmc. orig.]

es·pla·nade (ĕs′plə-näd′, -nād′) ►*n.* A flat, open stretch of pavement or grass used as a promenade. [< Lat. *explānāre,* make plain.]

es·pous·al (ĭ-spou′zəl, -səl) ►*n.* **1a.** A betrothal. **b.** A wedding ceremony. **2.** Adoption of an idea or cause.

es·pouse (ĭ-spouz′) ►*v.* **-poused, -pous·ing 1.** To adhere to or advocate: *espouse a cause.* **2.** To marry. [< Lat. *spondēre,* betroth.]

es·pres·so (ĭ-sprĕs′ō, ĕ-sprĕs′ō) ►*n., pl.* **-sos** A strong coffee brewed by forcing hot water through darkly roasted, finely ground coffee beans. [< Ital., p.part. of *esprimere,* press out.]

es·prit (ĕ-sprē′) ►*n.* Liveliness of mind or spirit; wittiness or sprightliness. [< Lat. *spīritus,* SPIRIT.]

esprit de corps (də kôr′) ►*n.* A common spirit of enthusiasm and devotion among members of a group. [Fr.]

es·py (ĭ-spī′) ►*v.* **-pied, -py·ing** To catch sight of; glimpse. [< OFr. *espier,* to watch, of Gmc. orig.]

Esq. ►*abbr.* esquire (title)

–esque ►*suff.* In the manner of; resembling: *picturesque.* [< VLat. *-iscus,* of Gmc. orig.]

es·quire (ĕs′kwīr′, ĭ-skwīr′) ►*n.* **1.** A member of the English gentry ranking directly below a knight. **2. Esquire** Used as an honorific, usu. in its abbreviated form *Esq.,* esp. after the name of an attorney or a consular officer. **3.** A candidate for knighthood serving a knight as attendant. [< LLat. *scūtārius,* shield bearer.]

–ess ►*suff.* Female: *lioness.* [< Gk. *-issa.*]

Usage: When used in occupational terms like *sculptress, waitress,* and *stewardess,* the feminine suffix *–ess* is often considered sexist and demeaning, although in a few words, such as *goddess* and *lioness,* the *–ess* suffix is still entirely acceptable. See Usage Note at **man.**

es·say (ĕs′ā′) ►*n.* **1.** A short literary composition on a single subject, usu. presenting the personal view of the author. **2.** (*also* ĕ-sā′) An attempt or endeavor, esp. a tentative one. ►*v.* (ĕ-sā′, ĕs′ā′) To make an attempt at; try. [< LLat. *exagium,* a weighing : EX– + Lat. *agere,* drive.] **—es·say′er** *n.*

es·say·ist (ĕs′ā′ĭst) ►*n.* A writer of essays.

es·sence (ĕs′əns) ►*n.* **1.** The intrinsic or indispensable properties that identify something. **2.** A concentrated extract of a substance that retains its fundamental properties. **3.** A perfume or scent. [< Lat. *essentia* < *esse,* be.]

es·sen·tial (ĭ-sĕn′shəl) ►*adj.* **1.** Constituting or being part of the essence of something; inherent. **2.** Basic or indispensable; necessary. See Synonyms at **indispensable.** ►*n.* Something essential. **—es·sen′ti·al′i·ty, es·sen′tial·ness** *n.* **—es·sen′tial·ly** *adv.*

EST ►*abbr.* Eastern Standard Time

est. ►*abbr.* **1.** established **2.** estate **3.** estimate

–est[1] ►*suff.* Used to form the superlative degree of adjectives and adverbs: *earliest.* [< OE.]

–est[2] or **–st** ►*suff.* Used to form the archaic 2nd person sing. of English verbs: *comest.* [< OE.]

es·tab·lish (ĭ-stăb′lĭsh) ►*v.* **1.** To found or create; set up. **2.** To place or settle in a secure position or condition. **3.** To cause to be recognized and accepted. **4.** To prove the truth of. [< Lat. *stabilīre* < *stabilis,* firm.] **—es·tab′lish·er** *n.*

Syns: *create, found, institute, organize* **v.**

es·tab·lish·ment (ĭ-stăb′lĭsh-mənt) ►*n.* **1.** The act of establishing or the condition of being established. **2.** A place of residence or business with its members, staff, and possessions. **3.** often **the Establishment** An exclusive or powerful group who control or strongly influence a government, society, or field of activity.

es·tate (ĭ-stāt′) ►*n.* **1.** A landed property, usu. of considerable size. **2.** All of one's property and possessions, esp. those left at death. **3.** A stage, condition, or status of life. [< OFr. *estat,* STATE.]

es·teem (ĭ-stēm′) ►*v.* **1.** To regard with respect; prize. **2.** To regard as; consider. ►*n.* Favorable regard; respect. [< Lat. *aestimāre,* appraise.]

es·ter (ĕs′tər) ►*n.* Any of a class of organic compounds usu. resulting from the reaction of an oxygen-containing acid and an alcohol. [Ger. < *Essigäther* : *Essig,* vinegar (< Lat. *acētum*) + *Äther,* ETHER.]

Es·ther (ĕs′tər) ►*n.* **1.** In the Bible, the Jewish queen of Persia who saved her people from massacre. **2.** See table at **Bible.**

es·thete (ĕs′thēt) ►*n.* Var. of **aesthete. —es·thet′ic** (-thĕt′ĭk) *adj.*

es·ti·ma·ble (ĕs′tə-mə-bəl) ►*adj.* **1.** Deserving of esteem; admirable. **2.** Possible to estimate. **—es′ti·ma·bly** *adv.*

es·ti·mate (ĕs′tə-māt′) ►*v.* **-mat·ed, -mat·ing 1.** To calculate approximately the amount, extent, magnitude, position, or value of. **2.** To evaluate. ►*n.* (-mĭt) **1.** A rough calculation. **2.** A preliminary statement of the cost of work to be done. **3.** An opinion. [Lat. *aestimāre.*] **—es′ti·ma′tion** *n.* **—es′ti·ma′tor** *n.*

es·ti·vate also **aes·ti·vate** (ĕs′tə-vāt′) ►*v.* **-vat·ed, -vat·ing 1.** To spend the summer, as at a special place. **2.** *Zool.* To pass the summer in a dormant or torpid state. [< Lat. *aestās,* summer.] **—es′ti·va′tion** *n.*

Es·to·ni·a (ĕ-stō′nē-ə) A country of NE Europe on the Baltic Sea. Cap. Tallinn.

Es·to·ni·an (ĕ-stō′nē-ən) ►*n.* **1.** A native or inhabitant of Estonia. **2.** The Finno-Ugric language of Estonia. **—Es·to′ni·an** *adj.*

es·trange (ĭ-strānj′) ►*v.* **-tranged, -trang·ing** To make hostile, unsympathetic, or indifferent; alienate. [< Lat. *extrāneāre,* treat as a stranger.] **—es·trange′ment** *n.*

es·tro·gen (ĕs′trə-jən) ►*n.* Any of several hormones produced chiefly by the ovaries that regulate certain female reproductive functions and maintain female secondary sex characteristics. [ESTR(US) + –GEN.] **—es′tro·gen′ic** (-jĕn′ĭk) *adj.* **—es′tro·gen′i·cal·ly** *adv.*

es·trus (ĕs′trəs) ►*n.* The state of sexual excitement in most female mammals that immediately precedes ovulation; heat. [< Gk. *oistros,* gadfly, frenzy.] **—es′trous** *adj.*

es·tu·ar·y (ĕs′chōō-ĕr′ē) ►*n., pl.* **-ies 1.** The wide lower course of a river where its current is met by the tides. **2.** An inland arm of the sea that meets the mouth of a river. [< Lat. *aestus,* heat, tide, surge.]

ET ►*abbr.* **1.** Eastern Time **2.** extraterrestrial

–et ►*suff.* **1.** Small: *eaglet.* **2.** Something worn on: *anklet.* [< VLat. *-ittum.*]

e·ta (āʹtə, ēʹtə) ►*n.* The 7th letter of the Greek alphabet. [Gk. *ēta.*]

ETA ►*abbr.* estimated time of arrival

e-tail·er (ēʹtāʹlər) ►*n.* One that sells goods electronically, as over the Internet. [E– + (RE)-TAILER.]

et al. ►*abbr. Lat.* et alii (and others)

etc. ►*abbr.* et cetera

et cet·er·a (ĕt sĕtʹər-ə, sĕtʹrə) And other things of the same class; and so forth. [Lat. *et cētera,* and the rest.]

etch (ĕch) ►*v.* **1.** To make (a pattern) on a surface with acid. **2.** To impress or delineate clearly: *images etched in my memory.* [< OHGer. *ezzen,* eat.] —**etchʹer** *n.*

etch·ing (ĕchʹĭng) ►*n.* **1.** The art or technique of preparing etched plates, esp. metal plates. **2.** A design etched on a plate. **3.** An impression made from an etched plate.

ETD ►*abbr.* estimated time of departure

e·ter·nal (ĭ-tûrʹnəl) ►*adj.* **1.** Being without beginning or end. **2.** Seemingly endless; interminable. [< Lat. *aeternus.*] —**e·terʹnal·ly** *adv.*

e·ter·ni·ty (ĭ-tûrʹnĭ-tē) ►*n., pl.* -**ties 1.** Continuance without beginning or end. **2.** The state or quality of being eternal. **3.** Immortality. **4.** A very long or seemingly endless time. [< Lat. *aeternus,* eternal.]

–eth¹ or **–th** ►*suff.* Used to form the archaic 3rd person sing. of English verbs: *leadeth.* [< OE.]

–eth² ►*suff.* Var. of **-th².**

eth·ane (ĕthʹānʹ) ►*n.* A colorless, odorless gas, C_2H_6, that occurs in natural gas and is used as a fuel and refrigerant. [ETH(YL) + –ANE.]

eth·a·nol (ĕthʹə-nôlʹ, -nōlʹ, -nŏlʹ) ►*n.* See **alcohol** (sense 2). [ETHAN(E) + –OL.]

Eth·el·bert (ĕthʹəl-bûrtʹ) 552?–616. Anglo-Saxon king who codified English law (604).

e·ther (ēʹthər) ►*n.* **1.** Any of a class of organic compounds in which two hydrocarbon groups are linked by an oxygen atom. **2.** A highly flammable liquid, $C_4H_{10}O$, used as a reagent, solvent, and anesthetic. **3.** The regions of space beyond the earth's atmosphere; the clear sky. **4.** An all-pervading, infinitely elastic, massless medium formerly postulated as the medium of propagation of electromagnetic waves. [< Gk. *aithēr,* the upper air.]

e·the·re·al (ĭ-thîrʹē-əl) ►*adj.* **1.** Extremely light or delicate. **2.** Heavenly. [< Gk. *aitherios.*] —**e·theʹre·al·ly** *adv.* —**e·theʹre·al·ness** *n.*

eth·ic (ĕthʹĭk) ►*n.* **1.** A principle or system of right or good conduct. **2. ethics** *(takes sing. v.)* The study of the nature of morals and of moral choices. **3. ethics** *(takes sing. or pl. v.)* The standards governing the conduct of the members of a profession. [< Gk. *ēthos,* character.]

eth·i·cal (ĕthʹĭ-kəl) ►*adj.* **1.** Of or dealing with ethics. **2.** Being in accordance with the accepted principles that govern the conduct of a group, esp. of a profession. —**ethʹi·cal·ly** *adv.*

E·thi·o·pi·a (ēʹthē-ōʹpē-ə) Formerly **Ab·ys·sin·i·a** (ăbʹĭ-sĭnʹē-ə). A country of NE Africa. Cap. Addis Ababa. —**Eʹthi·oʹpi·an** *adj. & n.*

eth·nic (ĕthʹnĭk) ►*adj.* Of or relating to sizable groups of people sharing a common and distinctive racial, national, religious, linguistic, or cultural heritage. —**ethʹni·cal·ly** *adv.*

ethnic cleansing ►*n.* The systematic elimination of an ethnic group from a region or society, as by expulsion or genocide.

eth·nic·i·ty (ĕth-nĭsʹĭ-tē) ►*n.* Ethnic character, background, or affiliation.

ethno– ►*pref.* Race; people: *ethnology.* [< Gk. *ethnos.*]

eth·no·cen·trism (ĕthʹnō-sĕnʹtrĭzʹəm) ►*n.* Belief in the superiority of one's own ethnic group. —**ethʹno·cenʹtric** *adj.*

eth·nog·ra·phy (ĕth-nŏgʹrə-fē) ►*n.* The branch of anthropology that deals with the scientific description of specific human cultures. —**eth·nogʹra·pher** *n.* —**ethʹno·graphʹic** (ĕthʹnə-grăfʹĭk), **ethʹno·graphʹi·cal** *adj.*

eth·nol·o·gy (ĕth-nŏlʹə-jē) ►*n.* **1.** The science that analyzes and compares human cultures, as in social structure, language, religion, and technology. **2.** The branch of anthropology that deals with the origin, distribution, and characteristics of ethnic groups. —**ethʹno·logʹic** (ĕthʹnə-lŏjʹĭk), **ethʹno·logʹi·cal** *adj.* —**ethʹno·logʹi·cal·ly** *adv.* —**eth·nolʹo·gist** *n.*

e·thol·o·gy (ĭ-thŏlʹə-jē, ē-thŏlʹ-) ►*n.* **1.** The scientific study of animal behavior. **2.** The study of human ethos. [Gk. *ēthos,* character + –LOGY.] —**ethʹo·logʹi·cal** (ĕthʹə-lŏjʹĭ-kəl) *adj.* —**e·tholʹo·gist** *n.*

e·thos (ēʹthŏsʹ) ►*n.* The character or values peculiar to a specific person, people, culture, or movement. [Gk. *ēthos,* character.]

eth·yl (ĕthʹəl) ►*adj.* Relating to or being a hydrocarbon unit, C_2H_5. [ETH(ER) + –YL.]

ethyl alcohol ►*n.* See **alcohol** (sense 2).

eth·yl·ene (ĕthʹə-lēnʹ) ►*n.* A colorless flammable gas, C_2H_4, derived from natural gas and petroleum.

ethylene glycol ►*n.* A colorless viscous alcohol used as an antifreeze.

e·ti·ol·o·gy (ēʹtē-ŏlʹə-jē) ►*n., pl.* -**gies 1.** The study of causes, origins, or reasons. **2.** The cause or origin of a disease or disorder as determined by medical diagnosis. [< Gk. *aitiologia < aitia,* a cause.] —**eʹti·o·logʹic** (-ə-lŏjʹĭk), **eʹti·o·logʹi·cal** *adj.* —**eʹti·olʹo·gist** *n.*

et·i·quette (ĕtʹĭ-kĕtʹ, -kĭt) ►*n.* The practices and forms prescribed by social convention or by authority. [< OFr. *estiquet,* label.]

Et·na (ĕtʹnə), **Mount** An active volcano, about 3,345 m (10,975 ft) high, of E Sicily.

E·tru·ri·a (ĭ-trŏŏrʹē-ə) An ancient country of W-central Italy in modern Tuscany and parts of Umbria. —**E·truʹri·an** *adj. & n.*

E·trus·can (ĭ-trŭsʹkən) ►*n.* **1.** A native or inhabitant of ancient Etruria. **2.** The extinct language of the Etruscans, of unknown affiliation. —**E·trusʹcan** *adj.*

–ette ►*suff.* **1.** Small; diminutive: *kitchenette.* **2.** Female: *suffragette.* **3.** An imitation or inferior kind of cloth: *leatherette.* [< OFr., feminine of *-et,* –ET.]

e·tude (āʹtōōdʹ, -tyōōdʹ) ►*n. Mus.* A composition written to develop or display a specific point of technique. [< OFr. *estudie,* a study.]

et·y·mol·o·gy (ĕtʹə-mŏlʹə-jē) ►*n., pl.* -**gies 1.** The origin and development of a word. **2.** The branch of linguistics that deals with etymologies. [< Gk. *etumon,* true sense of a word.] —**etʹy·mo·logʹi·cal** (-mə-lŏjʹĭ-kəl) *adj.* —**etʹy·molʹo·gist** *n.*

EU ►*abbr.* European Union

eu– ►*pref.* Good; well; true: *euphony.* [< Gk.]

eu·ca·lyp·tus (yōōʹkə-lĭpʹtəs) ►*n., pl.* -**tus·es** or **-ti** (-tīʹ) An Australian tree having aromatic leaves and used as source of oil, gum, and wood. [EU– + Gk. *kaluptos,* covered.]

Eu·cha·rist (yōō′kər-ĭst) ►*n.* The Christian sacrament instituted at the Last Supper, in which bread and wine are consecrated and consumed in remembrance of Jesus's death; Communion. [< Gk. *eukharistia,* gratitude.] —**Eu′cha·ris′tic** *adj.*

eu·chre (yōō′kər) ►*n.* A card game played usu. with the highest 32 cards. ►*v.* **-chred, -chring** To deceive or cheat. [?]

Eu·clid (yōō′klĭd) 3rd cent. BC. Greek mathematician.

Eu·clid·e·an (yōō-klĭd′ē-ən) ►*adj.* Of or relating to Euclid's geometric principles.

eu·di·cot·y·le·don (yōō′dī-kŏt′l-ēd′n) or **eu·di·cot** (yōō-dī′kŏt′) ►*n.* A flowering plant with two cotyledons in the seed, pollen grains with three pores, and usu. flower parts in multiples of four or five.

eu·gen·ics (yōō-jĕn′ĭks) ►*n. (takes sing. v.)* The study or practice of trying to improve a human population by encouraging the reproduction of people thought to have desirable hereditary traits and by discouraging the reproduction of people thought to have undesirable hereditary traits. —**eu·gen′ic** *adj.*

eu·kar·y·ote (yōō-kăr′ē-ōt, -ē-ət) ►*n.* An organism whose cells contain a distinct membrane-bound nucleus. [EU– + Gk. *karuon,* nut, kernel.] —**eu·kar′y·ot′ic** (-ŏt′ĭk) *adj.*

eu·lo·gize (yōō′lə-jīz′) ►*v.* **-gized, -giz·ing** To praise highly in speech or writing. —**eu′lo·giz′er** *n.*

eu·lo·gy (yōō′lə-jē) ►*n., pl.* **-gies** A spoken or written tribute, esp. one praising someone who has died. [< Gk. *eulogia,* praise.] —**eu′lo·gist** *n.* —**eu′lo·gis′tic** *adj.*

eu·nuch (yōō′nək) ►*n.* A castrated man, traditionally a harem attendant in certain Asian courts. [< Gk. *eunoukhos.*]

eu·phe·mism (yōō′fə-mĭz′əm) ►*n.* The substitution of an inoffensive term for one considered blunt or offensive. [< Gk. *euphēmia,* use of auspicious words.] —**eu′phe·mist** *n.* —**eu′phe·mis′tic** *adj.* —**eu′phe·mize′** *v.*

eu·pho·ny (yōō′fə-nē) ►*n., pl.* **-nies** Agreeable sound, esp. of words pleasing to the ear. —**eu·pho′ni·ous** (-fō′nē-əs) *adj.*

eu·pho·ri·a (yōō-fôr′ē-ə) ►*n.* A feeling of great happiness or well-being. [Gk. < *euphoros,* healthy : EU– + *pherein,* carry.] —**eu·phor′ic** (-fôr′ĭk, -fŏr′-) *adj.*

eu·pho·ri·ant (yōō-fôr′ē-ənt) ►*n.* A drug that induces euphoria. —**eu·pho′ri·ant** *adj.*

Eu·phra·tes (yōō-frā′tēz) A river of SW Asia flowing about 2,800 km (1,740 mi) from central Turkey to Iraq, where it joins the Tigris R. to form the Shatt al Arab.

Eur·a·sia (yōō-rā′zhə) The landmass comprising the continents of Europe and Asia.

Eur·a·sian (yōō-rā′zhən) ►*adj.* **1.** Of or relating to Eurasia. **2.** Of mixed European and Asian descent. ►*n.* **1.** A person of mixed European and Asian descent. **2.** A native or inhabitant of Eurasia.

eu·re·ka (yōō-rē′kə) ►*interj.* Used to express triumph upon finding or discovering something. [Gk. *heurēka,* I have found (it).]

Eu·rip·i·des (yōō-rĭp′ĭ-dēz′) 480?–406 BC. Greek dramatist. —**Eu·rip′i·de′an** *adj.*

eu·ro or **Eu·ro** (yōŏr′ō) ►*n., pl.* **-ros** The basic unit of currency among participating European Union countries. See table at **currency.**

Eu·ro-A·mer·i·can (yōŏr′ō-ə-mĕr′ĭ-kən) ►*n.* A US citizen or resident of European ancestry. ►*adj.* **1.** Relating to Euro-Americans. **2.** Relating to Europe and America.

Eu·ro·cen·tric (yōŏr′ō-sĕn′trĭk) ►*adj.* Centered or focused on Europe or European peoples. —**Eu′ro·cen′trism** *n.* —**Eu′ro·cen′trist** *adj. & n.*

Eu·ro·cur·ren·cy (yōŏr′ō-kûr′ən-sē) ►*n., pl.* **-cies** Currency held and traded in a bank outside the currency's country of origin.

Eu·ro·dol·lar (yōŏr′ō-dŏl′ər) ►*n.* A US dollar on deposit in a foreign bank.

Eu·ro·pa (yōō-rō′pə) ►*n. Gk. Myth.* A Phoenician princess abducted to Crete by Zeus, who had assumed the form of a white bull.

Eu·rope (yōŏr′əp) The sixth-largest continent, consisting of the section of Eurasia that extends W from the Dardanelles, Black Sea, and Ural Mountains.

Eu·ro·pe·an (yōŏr′ə-pē′ən) ►*n.* **1.** A native or inhabitant of Europe. **2.** A person of European descent. ►*adj.* Of Europe or its peoples, languages, or cultures.

European Union An economic and political union established in 1993 orig. by several countries in W Europe, with many other European countries joining since then.

eu·ro·pi·um (yōō-rō′pē-əm) ►*n. Symbol* **Eu** A silvery-white, soft rare-earth element used in lasers and nuclear research. At. no. 63. See table at **element.** [< EUROPE.]

Eu·ryd·i·ce (yōō-rĭd′ĭ-sē) ►*n. Gk. Myth.* The wife of Orpheus.

eu·sta·chian tube or **Eu·sta·chian tube** (yōō-stā′shən, -shē-ən, -kē-ən) ►*n.* A narrow tube that connects the middle ear with the pharynx and serves to equalize air pressure on either side of the eardrum. [After Bartolomeo *Eustachio* (1520–74).]

eu·tha·na·sia (yōō′thə-nā′zhə, -zhē-ə) ►*n.* The act of ending the life of a person or animal having a terminal illness that causes suffering perceived as incompatible with an acceptable quality of life, as by lethal injection or suspending medical treatment. [Gk.] —**eu′than·ize′** *v.*

eu·then·ics (yōō-thĕn′ĭks) ►*n. (takes sing. v.)* The study of the improvement of human functioning and well-being by improvement of living conditions. [< Gk. *euthenein,* to flourish.] —**eu·then′ist** *n.*

eV ►*abbr.* electron volt

EVA ►*abbr.* extravehicular activity

e·vac·u·ate (ĭ-văk′yōō-āt′) ►*v.* **-at·ed, -at·ing 1.** To withdraw, esp. from a threatened area. **2a.** To remove the contents of. **b.** To remove (e.g., fluid) from a closed space. **3.** To excrete waste matter from (the bowel). [< Lat. *ēvacuāre.*] —**e·vac′u·a′tion** *n.*

e·vac·u·ee (ĭ-văk′yōō-ē′) ►*n.* A person evacuated from a dangerous or threatened area.

e·vade (ĭ-vād′) ►*v.* **e·vad·ed, e·vad·ing 1.** To escape or avoid: *evade legal responsibility.* **2.** To be beyond the memory or understanding of: *Your point evades me.* [< Lat. *ēvādere.*] —**e·vad′er** *n.*

e·val·u·ate (ĭ-văl′yōō-āt′) ►*v.* **-at·ed, -at·ing** To ascertain the effectiveness, significance, or value of; assess. [< OFr. *evaluer.*] —**e·val′u·a′tion** *n.* —**e·val′u·a·tor** *n.*

ev·a·nesce (ĕv′ə-nĕs′) ►*v.* -**nesced**, -**nesc·ing** To dissipate gradually; fade away like vapor. See Synonyms at **disappear.** [Lat. *ēvānēscere,* vanish < *vānus,* empty.] —**ev′a·nes′cence** *n.* —**ev′a·nes′cent** *adj.*

e·van·gel·i·cal (ē′văn-jĕl′ĭ-kəl, ĕv′ən-) also **e·van·gel·ic** (-jĕl′ĭk) ►*adj.* **1.** Of or in accordance with the Christian gospel or Gospels. **2. Evangelical** Relating to a Christian church that stresses the inerrancy of the Bible, salvation only through conversion, and public witness to faith. [< Gk. *evangelos,* bringing good news.] —**E′van·gel′i·cal** *n.* —**e′van·gel′i·cal·ism** *n.*

e·van·gel·ism (ĭ-văn′jə-lĭz′əm) ►*n.* Zealous preaching of the gospel, as through missionary work. —**e·van′gel·is′tic** *adj.*

e·van·gel·ist (ĭ-văn′jə-lĭst) ►*n.* **1.** often **Evangelist** Any one of the authors of the New Testament Gospels. **2.** One who practices evangelism, esp. a Protestant preacher or missionary.

e·van·gel·ize (ĭ-văn′jə-līz′) ►*v.* -**ized**, -**iz·ing** **1.** To preach the gospel (to). **2.** To convert to Christianity.

e·vap·o·rate (ĭ-văp′ə-rāt′) ►*v.* -**rat·ed**, -**rat·ing** **1.** To change into a vapor. **2.** To vanish: *Our fears evaporated.* See Synonyms at **disappear.** [< Lat. *ēvapōrāre.*] —**e·vap′o·ra′tion** *n.* —**e·vap′o·ra′tive** *adj.* —**e·vap′o·ra′tor** *n.*

e·va·sion (ĭ-vā′zhən) ►*n.* **1.** The act of evading. **2.** A means of evading. [< LLat. *ēvāsiō.*]

e·va·sive (ĭ-vā′sĭv) ►*adj.* **1.** Inclined or intended to evade. **2.** Intentionally vague or ambiguous. —**e·va′sive·ly** *adv.* —**e·va′sive·ness** *n.*

eve (ēv) ►*n.* **1.** The evening or day preceding a holiday. **2.** The period immediately preceding a certain event: *the eve of war.* **3.** Evening. [ME, var. of EVEN².]

Eve In the Bible, the first woman and the wife of Adam.

e·ven¹ (ē′vən) ►*adj.* **1a.** Flat: *an even floor.* **b.** Smooth. **c.** Level; parallel: *The picture is even with the window.* **2a.** Uniform, steady, or regular: *an even rhythm of breathing.* **b.** Placid; calm: *an even temperament.* **3.** *Math.* Exactly divisible by 2. **4.** Exact: *an even pound.* **5.** As likely as not: *an even chance of winning.* **6a.** Having nothing due on either side: *If we split the lunch bill, we'll be even.* **b.** Having gotten full revenge: *got even with his betrayer.* **7.** *Sports* Having an equal score. ►*adv.* **1.** To a greater degree: *an even worse condition.* **2.** Indeed; moreover: *unhappy, even weeping.* **3.** At that very time: *Even as we watched, the building collapsed.* **4.** So much as: *couldn't even do a single pushup.* **5.** In spite of: *Even with his head start, I beat him.* ►*v.* To make or become even. [< OE *efen.*] —**e′ven·ly** *adv.* —**e′ven·ness** *n.*

e·ven² (ē′vən) ►*n.* Archaic Evening. [< OE *ǣfen.*]

e·ven·hand·ed (ē′vən-hăn′dĭd) ►*adj.* Showing no partiality; fair. —**e′ven·hand′ed·ly** *adv.* —**e′ven·hand′ed·ness** *n.*

eve·ning (ēv′nĭng) ►*n.* The period of decreasing daylight between afternoon and night. [< OE *ǣfnung.*]

evening star ►*n.* A planet, esp. Venus or Mercury, that is prominent in the west shortly after sunset.

e·vent (ĭ-vĕnt′) ►*n.* **1.** An occurrence or incident. **2.** A social gathering or activity: *an event for charity.* **3.** A contest or an item in a sports program. [Lat. *ēventus* < p.part. of *ēvenīre,* happen : EX– + *venīre,* come.]

e·vent·ful (ĭ-vĕnt′fəl) ►*adj.* **1.** Full of events. **2.** Important; momentous: *an eventful decision.* —**e·vent′ful·ly** *adv.* —**e·vent′ful·ness** *n.*

e·ven·tide (ē′vən-tīd′) ►*n.* Evening. [< OE *ǣfentīd.*]

event recorder ►*n.* A crash-resistant, water-resistant, and fire-resistant device that records data about an aircraft or other vehicle's operation.

e·ven·tu·al (ĭ-vĕn′chōō-əl) ►*adj.* Occurring at an unspecified time in the future: *her eventual success.* [Fr. *éventuel.*] —**e·ven′tu·al·ly** *adv.*

e·ven·tu·al·i·ty (ĭ-vĕn′chōō-ăl′ĭ-tē) ►*n.,* pl. -**ties** Something that may occur; possibility.

e·ven·tu·ate (ĭ-vĕn′chōō-āt′) ►*v.* -**at·ed**, -**at·ing** To result ultimately; culminate.

ev·er (ĕv′ər) ►*adv.* **1.** At all times; always: *ever hoping to strike it rich.* **2.** At any time: *Have you ever been to India?* **3.** In any way; at all: *How did they ever manage?* **4.** To a great extent or degree: *Was she ever mad!* [< OE *ǣfre.*]

Ev·er·est (ĕv′ər-ĭst, ĕv′rĭst), **Mount** The world's highest mountain, 8,848 m (29,029 ft), in the central Himalayas on the border of Tibet and Nepal.

ev·er·glade (ĕv′ər-glād′) ►*n.* A tract of marshland, usu. under water and covered in places with tall grass.

Ev·er·glades (ĕv′ər-glādz′) A subtropical wetland area of S FL including **Everglades National Park.**

ev·er·green (ĕv′ər-grēn′) ►*adj.* Having foliage that persists and remains green throughout the year. ►*n.* An evergreen tree, shrub, or plant.

ev·er·last·ing (ĕv′ər-lăs′tĭng) ►*adj.* Lasting forever; eternal. —**ev′er·last′ing·ly** *adv.*

ev·er·more (ĕv′ər-môr′) ►*adv.* Forever; always.

eve·ry (ĕv′rē) ►*adj.* **1a.** Each without exception: *every student in the class.* **b.** Being all possible: *had every chance of winning.* **2.** Being each of a specified series: *every third seat.* **3.** Being the highest degree or expression of: *had every hope of succeeding.* —*idioms:* **every bit** Informal In all ways; equally. **every so often** Occasionally. [< OE *ǣfre ǣlc,* ever each.]

Usage: Every is representative of a large class of English words and expressions that are singular in form but felt to be plural in sense. The class includes, for example, noun phrases introduced by *every, any,* and certain uses of *some.* These expressions invariably take a singular verb: *Every car has been tested.*

eve·ry·bod·y (ĕv′rē-bŏd′ē, -bŭd′ē) ►*pron.* Every person; everyone.

eve·ry·day (ĕv′rē-dā′) ►*adj.* **1.** Appropriate for ordinary occasions. **2.** Commonplace; ordinary: *everyday worries.*

eve·ry·one (ĕv′rē-wŭn′) ►*pron.* Every person; everybody.

eve·ry·thing (ĕv′rē-thĭng′) ►*pron.* **1.** All things or all relevant matters. **2.** The most important consideration: *In business, timing is everything.*

eve·ry·where (ĕv′rē-wâr′, -hwâr′) ►*adv.* In every place; in all places.

e·vict (ĭ-vĭkt′) ►*v.* **1.** To expel (a tenant) by legal process. **2.** To eject. [< Lat. *ēvincere, ēvict-,* vanquish.] —**e·vic′tion** *n.* —**e·vic′tor** *n.*

ev·i·dence (ĕv′ĭ-dəns) ►*n.* **1.** The data on which a conclusion or judgment can be established. **2.** Something indicative; an outward sign: *The house showed evidence of neglect.* **3.** *Law* The means by which an allegation may be proven, such as oral testimony, documents, or physical objects. ►*v.* **-denced, -denc·ing** To indicate clearly. —*idiom:* **in evidence** Plainly visible; conspicuous.

ev·i·dent (ĕv′ĭ-dənt) ►*adj.* Easily seen or understood; obvious. See Synonyms at **apparent.** [< Lat. *ēvidēns* : *ē-, ex-,* ex- + *vidēre,* see.] —**ev′i·dent′ly** *adv.*

ev·i·den·tial (ĕv′ĭ-dĕn′shəl) ►*adj.* Of, providing, or constituting legal evidence.

e·vil (ē′vəl) ►*adj.* **-er, -est 1.** Morally bad or wrong; wicked. **2.** Harmful or injurious: *evil effects of smoking cigarettes.* ►*n.* **1.** The quality of being morally bad or wrong; wickedness. **2.** Something that causes harm, misfortune, suffering, or destruction. [< OE *yfel.*] —**e′vil·ly** *adv.* —**e′vil·ness** *n.*

e·vil·do·er (ē′vəl-dōō′ər) ►*n.* One that performs evil acts. —**e′vil·do′ing** *n.*

evil eye ►*n.* A look believed to have the power to cause injury to others, esp. by magic or supernatural means.

e·vince (ĭ-vĭns′) ►*v.* **e·vinced, e·vinc·ing** To show or demonstrate clearly; manifest. [Lat. *ēvincere,* prove.] —**e·vinc′i·ble** *adj.*

e·vis·cer·ate (ĭ-vĭs′ə-rāt′) ►*v.* **-at·ed, -at·ing 1.** To remove the entrails of. **2.** To take away a vital or essential part of. **3.** *Med.* To protrude through a wound or incision. [Lat. *ēviscerāre* < *viscera,* VISCERA.] —**e·vis′cer·a′tion** *n.*

ev·i·ta·ble (ĕv′ĭ-tə-bəl) ►*adj.* Avoidable. [< Lat. *ēvītāre,* shun.]

e·voke (ĭ-vōk′) ►*v.* **e·voked, e·vok·ing** To summon or call forth; elicit: *evoke memories.* [Lat. *ēvocāre.*] —**ev′o·ca·ble** (ĕv′ə-kə-bəl, ĭ-vō′kə-) *adj.* —**ev′o·ca′tion** *n.* —**e·voc′a·tive** (ĭ-vŏk′ə-tĭv) *adj.* —**e·voc′a·tive·ly** *adv.*

ev·o·lu·tion (ĕv′ə-lōō′shən, ē′və-) ►*n.* **1.** A gradual process in which something changes into a different and usu. more complex form. **2.** *Biol.* **a.** Change in the genetic composition of a population during successive generations, often resulting in the development of new species. **b.** The historical development of a related group of organisms; phylogeny. [< Lat. *ēvolvere, ēvolūt-,* unroll.] —**ev′o·lu′tion·ar′y** *adj.*

e·volve (ĭ-vŏlv′) ►*v.* **e·volved, e·volv·ing 1.** To develop or work out; achieve gradually: *evolve a plan.* **2.** *Biol.* To develop or arise through evolutionary processes. [Lat. *ēvolvere,* unroll.] —**e·volve′ment** *n.*

e·vul·sion (ĭ-vŭl′shən) ►*n.* A forcible extraction. [< Lat. *ēvellere, ēvuls-,* pull out.]

ewe (yōō) ►*n.* A female sheep. [< OE *eōwu.*]

ew·er (yōō′ər) ►*n.* A pitcher, esp. one with a flaring spout. [< VLat. **aquāria* < Lat. *aqua,* water.]

ex¹ (ĕks) ►*prep.* Not including; without: *a stock price ex dividend.* [Lat.]

ex² (ĕks) ►*n. Slang* A former spouse or partner. [< EX-.]

ex. ►*abbr.* example

ex– ►*pref.* **1.** Outside; out of; away from: *exurbia.* **2.** Former: *ex-president.* [< Lat. *ex,* out of.]

ex·a·byte (ĕk′sə-bīt′) ►*n. Abbr.* **EB 1.** A unit of computer memory or data storage capacity equal to 1,024 petabytes (2^{60} bytes). **2.** One quintillion (10^{18}) bytes. [*exa-,* one quintillion (alteration of HEXA–, since one quintillion equals 1000^6) + BYTE.]

ex·ac·er·bate (ĭg-zăs′ər-bāt′) ►*v.* **-bat·ed, -bat·ing** To increase the severity of; aggravate: *exacerbate tensions; exacerbate pain.* [Lat. *exacerbāre* < *acerbus,* harsh.] —**ex·ac′er·ba′tion** *n.*

ex·act (ĭg-zăkt′) ►*adj.* **1.** Strictly and completely in accord with fact: *an exact replica; your exact words.* **2.** Characterized by accurate measurements: *an exact figure.* ►*v.* **1.** To force the payment or yielding of; extort. **2.** To inflict: *exact revenge.* [Lat. *exāctus,* p.part. of *exigere,* demand : EX– + *agere,* weigh.] —**ex·act′ly** *adv.* —**ex·act′ness** *n.*

ex·act·ing (ĭg-zăk′tĭng) ►*adj.* **1.** Making rigorous demands. **2.** Requiring great care or effort. —**ex·act′ing·ly** *adv.*

ex·ac·ti·tude (ĭg-zăk′tĭ-tōōd, -tyōōd′) ►*n.* The state or quality of being exact.

ex·ag·ger·ate (ĭg-zăj′ə-rāt′) ►*v.* **-at·ed, -at·ing** To consider, represent, or cause to appear as larger, more important, or more extreme than is actually the case; overstate. [Lat. *exaggerāre.*] —**ex·ag′ger·a′tion** *n.* —**ex·ag′ger·a·to′ry** (-ə-tôr′ē) *adj.* —**ex·ag′ger·a′tor** *n.*

Syns: inflate, magnify, overstate **Ant:** minimize *v.*

ex·alt (ĭg-zôlt′) ►*v.* **1.** To raise in rank or status; elevate. **2.** To glorify, praise, or honor. **3.** To inspire; heighten: *art that exalts the imagination.* [< Lat. *exaltāre* < *altus,* high.] —**ex′al·ta′tion** (ĕg′zôl-tā′shən) *n.*

ex·am (ĭg-zăm′) ►*n.* An examination; test.

ex·am·i·na·tion (ĭg-zăm′ə-nā′shən) ►*n.* **1.** The act of examining or the state of being examined. **2.** A set of questions or exercises testing knowledge or skill. —**ex·am′i·na′tion·al** *adj.*

ex·am·ine (ĭg-zăm′ĭn) ►*v.* **-ined, -in·ing 1.** To inspect or analyze (a person, thing, or situation) in detail. **2.** To determine the qualifications or skills of (someone) by means of questions or tests. **3.** To question formally to elicit facts; interrogate. **4.** To check the health or condition of: *examine a patient.* [< Lat. *exāmināre* < *exigere,* weigh out; see EXACT.] —**ex·am′in·ee′** *n.* —**ex·am′in·er** *n.*

ex·am·ple (ĭg-zăm′pəl) ►*n.* **1.** One that is representative of a group as a whole. **2.** One serving as a pattern of a specific kind: *set a good example.* **3.** A punishment given as a deterrent: *His suspension was an example to all rule breakers.* **4.** A problem used to illustrate a principle. [< Lat. *exemplum.*]

ex·as·per·ate (ĭg-zăs′pə-rāt′) ►*v.* **-at·ed, -at·ing** To make very angry or impatient; provoke. [Lat. *exasperāre* < *asper,* rough.] —**ex·as′per·at′ing·ly** *adv.* —**ex·as′per·a′tion** *n.*

ex·ca·vate (ĕk′skə-vāt′) ►*v.* **-vat·ed, -vat·ing 1.** To dig or hollow out. **2.** To remove by digging or scooping out. **3.** To uncover by digging: *excavate an archaeological site.* [Lat. *excavāre.*] —**ex′ca·va′tion** *n.* —**ex′ca·va′tor** *n.*

ex·ceed (ĭk-sēd′) ►*v.* **1.** To be greater than; surpass. **2.** To go to or be beyond the limits of: *exceeded their authority.* [< Lat. *excēdere.*]

ex·ceed·ing (ĭk-sē′dĭng) ►*adj.* Extreme; extraordinary. —**ex·ceed′ing·ly** *adv.*

ex·cel (ĭk-sĕl′) ►*v.* **-celled, -cel·ling** To be superior to; surpass; outdo. [< Lat. *excellere*.]

ex·cel·lence (ĕk′sə-ləns) ►*n.* **1.** The quality or condition of excelling. **2.** Something in which one excels. **3. Excellence** Excellency.

Ex·cel·len·cy (ĕk′sə-lən-sē) ►*n., pl.* **-cies** Used with *His, Her,* or *Your* as a title for certain high officials.

ex·cel·lent (ĕk′sə-lənt) ►*adj.* Of the highest or finest quality; exceptionally good; superb. —**ex′cel·lent·ly** *adv.*

ex·cel·si·or (ĭk-sĕl′sē-ər) ►*n.* Wood shavings used esp. for packing. [Orig. a trademark.]

ex·cept (ĭk-sĕpt′) ►*prep.* Other than; but: *everyone except me.* ►*conj.* **1.** If it were not for the fact that; only: *I would go to the park, except that it's raining.* **2.** Otherwise than: *They didn't open their mouths except to complain.* ►*v.* To leave out; exclude. [< Lat. *exceptus,* p.part. of *excipere,* take out.]

ex·cept·ing (ĭk-sĕp′tĭng) ►*prep.* With the exception of; except.

ex·cep·tion (ĭk-sĕp′shən) ►*n.* **1.** The act of excepting; exclusion. **2.** One that is excepted. **3.** An objection or criticism: *opinions that are open to exception.*

ex·cep·tion·a·ble (ĭk-sĕp′shə-nə-bəl) ►*adj.* Open to objection. —**ex·cep′tion·a·bly** *adv.*

ex·cep·tion·al (ĭk-sĕp′shə-nəl) ►*adj.* **1.** Being an exception; uncommon. **2.** Deviating widely from a norm, as of physical or mental ability: *special education for exceptional children.* —**ex·cep′tion·al·ly** *adv.*

ex·cerpt (ĕk′sûrt′) ►*n.* A passage or segment taken from a longer work, such as a speech, book, or film. [< Lat. *excerpere, excerpt-,* pick out.] —**ex·cerpt′** *v.*

ex·cess (ĭk-sĕs′, ĕk′sĕs′) ►*n.* **1.** An amount or quantity beyond what is required; surplus. **2.** Intemperance; overindulgence: *drank to excess.* ►*adj.* Being more than what is required. See Synonyms at **superfluous.** [< Lat. *excessus,* p.part. of *excēdere,* exceed.] —**ex·ces′sive** *adj.* —**ex·ces′sive·ly** *adv.* —**ex·ces′sive·ness** *n.*

ex·change (ĭks-chānj′) ►*v.* **-changed, -chang·ing** **1.** To give something in return for something received; trade. **2.** To turn in for replacement: *exchange the gift.* ►*n.* **1.** The act or an instance of exchanging. **2.** A place where things are exchanged, esp. a center where securities are traded. **3.** A central system that establishes connections between individual telephones. **4.** A dialogue: *a heated exchange between the two partners.* [< VLat. **excambiāre.*] —**ex·change′a·ble** *adj.*

exchange rate ►*n.* The ratio at which the unit of currency of one country may be exchanged for the unit of currency of another country.

ex·cheq·uer (ĕks′chĕk′ər, ĭks-chĕk′ər) ►*n.* A treasury, as of a nation or organization. [< OFr. *eschequier,* counting table.]

ex·cip·i·ent (ĭk-sĭp′ē-ənt) ►*n.* An inert substance used as a diluent or vehicle for a drug. [< Lat. *excipere,* take out.]

ex·cise[1] (ĕk′sīz′) ►*n.* **1.** A tax on the production, sale, or consumption of a commodity within a country. **2.** A fee levied for certain privileges, such as owning a car. [MDu. *excijs.*]

ex·cise[2] (ĕk-sīz′) ►*v.* **-cised, -cis·ing** To remove by or as if by cutting. [Lat. *excīdere, excīs-,* cut out.] —**ex·ci′sion** (-sĭzh′ən) *n.*

ex·cit·a·ble (ĭk-sī′tə-bəl) ►*adj.* Easily excited.

—**ex·cit′a·bil′i·ty** *n.* —**ex·cit′a·bly** *adv.*

ex·ci·tant (ĭk-sīt′nt) ►*n.* An agent or stimulus that excites; stimulant. —**ex·ci′tant** *adj.*

ex·cite (ĭk-sīt′) ►*v.* **-cit·ed, -cit·ing** **1a.** To arouse strong feeling in; provoke: *The band excited the crowd.* **b.** To arouse sexually. **2.** To call forth; elicit: *excited my curiosity.* **3.** *Physiol.* To produce increased activity or response in a body part: *The drug excited his heart.* **4.** *Phys.* To raise (e.g., an atom) to a higher energy level. [< Lat. *excitāre.*] —**ex′ci·ta′tion** (ĕk′sī-tā′-shən) *n.* —**ex·cit′ed·ly** *adv.* —**ex·cite′ment** *n.* —**ex·cit′ing·ly** *adv.*

ex·claim (ĭk-sklām′) ►*v.* To cry out or speak suddenly or vehemently. [< Lat. *exclāmāre.*]

ex·cla·ma·tion (ĕk′sklə-mā′shən) ►*n.* **1.** A sudden forceful utterance. **2.** *Gram.* An interjection. —**ex·clam′a·to′ry** (ĭk-sklăm′ə-tôr′ē) *adj.*

exclamation point ►*n.* A punctuation mark (!) used after an exclamation.

ex·clude (ĭk-sklood′) ►*v.* **-clud·ed, -clud·ing** **1.** To prevent from entering; keep out; bar. **2.** To put out; expel. [< Lat. *exclūdere,* shut out.] —**ex·clu′sion** *n.*

exclusion principle ►*n.* The principle that two particles of a given type, such as electrons, protons, or neutrons, cannot simultaneously occupy a particular quantum state.

ex·clu·sive (ĭk-skloo′sĭv) ►*adj.* **1.** Not divided or shared with others: *exclusive rights.* **2.** Excluding or tending to exclude: *an exclusive club.* **3.** Catering to a wealthy clientele; expensive: *exclusive shops.* **4.** Not accompanied by others; sole: *his exclusive function.* ►*n.* **1.** A news item initially released to only one publication or broadcaster. **2.** An exclusive right. —**ex·clu′sive·ly** *adv.* —**ex·clu′sive·ness, ex′clu·siv′i·ty** (ĕk′skloo-sĭv′ĭ-tē) *n.*

ex·com·mu·ni·cate (ĕks′kə-myoo′nĭ-kāt′) ►*v.* **-cat·ed, -cat·ing** To deprive of the right of church membership by ecclesiastical authority. ►*n.* (-kĭt) A person who has been excommunicated. [< LLat. *excommūnicāre.*] —**ex′com·mu′ni·ca′tion** *n.* —**ex′com·mu′ni·ca′tor** *n.*

ex·co·ri·ate (ĭk-skôr′ē-āt′) ►*v.* **-at·ed, -at·ing** **1.** To censure strongly; denounce. **2.** To criticize harshly. **3.** To tear or wear off the skin of. [< Lat. *excoriāre < corium,* skin.] —**ex·co′ri·a′tion** *n.*

ex·cre·ment (ĕk′skrə-mənt) ►*n.* Bodily waste, esp. fecal matter. [Lat. *excrēmentum < excernere,* excrete.] —**ex′cre·men′tal** *adj.*

ex·cres·cence (ĭk-skrĕs′əns) ►*n.* An outgrowth or enlargement, esp. an abnormal one. [< Lat. *excrēscere,* grow out.] —**ex·cres′cent** *adj.*

ex·crete (ĭk-skrēt′) ►*v.* **-cret·ed, -cret·ing** To separate and discharge (waste matter) from the blood, tissues, or organs. [Lat. *excernere, excrēt-.*] —**ex·cre′tion** *n.* —**ex′cre·to′ry** (ĕk′skrĭ-tôr′ē) *adj.*

ex·cru·ci·at·ing (ĭk-skroo′shē-ā′tĭng) ►*adj.* **1.** Intensely painful or distressing. **2.** Very intense and extreme: *wrote with excruciating precision.* [< Lat. *excruciāre,* crucify, torture.] —**ex·cru′ci·at′ing·ly** *adv.*

ex·cul·pate (ĕk′skəl-pāt′, ĭk-skŭl′-) ►*v.* **-pat·ed, -pat·ing** To clear of guilt or blame. [Med. Lat. *exculpāre.*] —**ex′cul·pa′tion** *n.* —**ex·cul′pa·to′ry** (ĭk-skŭl′pə-tôr′ē) *adj.*

ex·cur·sion (ĭk-skûr′zhən) ►*n.* **1.** A short pleasure trip; outing. **2.** A roundtrip on a vehicle or boat at a special low fare. **3.** A digression from a main topic. [Lat. *excursiō.*]

ex·cur·sive (ĭk-skûr′sĭv) ►*adj.* Marked by digression; rambling. —**ex·cur′sive·ly** *adv.*

ex·cuse (ĭk-skyōōz′) ►*v.* **-cused, -cus·ing 1.** To make allowance for; overlook: *Excuse the interruption.* **2.** To grant pardon to; forgive. **3.** To apologize for (oneself) for an act that could cause offense: *She excused herself for being late.* **4.** To justify: *Stress at work doesn't excuse bad manners.* **5.** To free, as from an obligation; exempt: *She was excused from jury duty because she knew the plaintiff.* **6.** To give permission to leave: *The children asked to be excused after dinner.* ►*n.* (ĭk-skyōōs′) **1.** An explanation offered to obtain forgiveness. **2.** A reason for being excused. **3.** *Informal* An inferior example: *a poor excuse for a car.* [< Lat. *excūsāre.*] —**ex·cus′a·ble** *adj.* —**ex·cus′er** *n.*

ex·e·cra·ble (ĕk′sĭ-krə-bəl) ►*adj.* **1.** Detestable or hateful. **2.** Extremely inferior. —**ex′e·cra·bly** *adv.*

ex·e·crate (ĕk′sĭ-krāt′) ►*v.* **-crat·ed, -crat·ing 1.** To protest vehemently against; denounce. **2.** To loathe; abhor. [Lat. *execrārī.*] —**ex′e·cra′tion** *n.* —**ex′e·cra′tor** *n.*

ex·e·cute (ĕk′sĭ-kyōōt′) ►*v.* **-cut·ed, -cut·ing 1.** To carry out; perform. **2.** To make valid or legal, as by signing: *execute a deed.* **3.** To carry out what is required by: *execute a will.* **4.** To put to death, esp. by a lawful sentence. **5.** *Comp.* To run (a program or instruction). [< Med. Lat. *execūtāre.*] —**ex′e·cut′a·ble** *adj.* —**ex′e·cut′er** *n.* —**ex′e·cu′tion** *n.*

ex·e·cu·tion·er (ĕk′sĭ-kyōō′shə-nər) ►*n.* One who executes a condemned person.

ex·ec·u·tive (ĭg-zĕk′yə-tĭv) ►*n.* **1.** A person or group having administrative or managerial authority in an organization. **2.** The branch of government charged with putting a country's laws into effect. ►*adj.* **1.** Relating to or capable of carrying out or executing: *executive powers.* **2.** Of or relating to the executive branch of government.

ex·ec·u·tor (ĭg-zĕk′yə-tər, ĕk′sĭ-kyōō′tər) ►*n.* **1.** *Law* A person designated to execute the terms of a will. **2.** A person who carries out or performs something.

ex·e·ge·sis (ĕk′sə-jē′sĭs) ►*n., pl.* **-ses** (-sēz) Critical interpretation or explanation of a text. [Gk. *exēgēsis,* interpretation.] —**ex′e·get′ic** (-jĕt′ĭk), **ex′e·get′i·cal** *adj.*

ex·em·plar (ĭg-zĕm′plär′, -plər) ►*n.* **1.** One that is worthy of imitation; model. **2.** One that is typical; example. [< LLat. *exemplārium* < Lat. *exemplum,* example.] —**ex·em′pla·ry** *adj.*

ex·em·pli·fy (ĭg-zĕm′plə-fī′) ►*v.* **-fied, -fy·ing 1.** To illustrate by example. **2.** To serve as an example of. [< Lat. *exemplum,* example.] —**ex·em′pli·fi·ca′tion** *n.*

ex·empt (ĭg-zĕmpt′) ►*v.* To free from an obligation, duty, or liability to which others are subject. ►*adj.* **1.** Freed from an obligation, duty, or liability to which others are subject; excused. **2.** Not subject to certain federal workplace laws or protections, esp. those requiring overtime compensation. [< Lat. *eximere, exēpt-,* take out.] —**ex·empt′i·ble** *adj.* —**ex·emp′tion** *n.*

ex·er·cise (ĕk′sər-sīz′) ►*n.* **1a.** Physical activity, esp. to develop or maintain fitness. **b.** A specific activity performed to develop or maintain fitness or a skill: *sit-ups and other exercises; a piano exercise.* **2.** The active use or application of something: *the exercise of good judgment.* **3.** An activity having a specified aspect: *an undertaking that was an exercise in futility.* **4.** A military maneuver or training activity. **5. exercises** A public program that includes speeches, awards, and other ceremonial activities. ►*v.* **-cised, -cis·ing 1.** To engage in exercise. **2.** To put into operation; employ: *exercise restraint.* **3.** To put through exercises. See Synonyms at **practice.** [< Lat. *exercēre, exercit-,* to exercise.] —**ex′er·cis′er** *n.*

ex·ert (ĭg-zûrt′) ►*v.* **1.** To bring to bear: *exert influence.* **2.** To put (oneself) to strenuous effort. [Lat. *exserere, exsert-,* put forth.] —**ex·er′tion** *n.*

ex·hale (ĕks-hāl′, ĕk-sāl′) ►*v.* **-haled, -hal·ing 1.** To breathe out. **2.** To emit (e.g., smoke). [< Lat. *exhālāre.*] —**ex′ha·la′tion** (ĕks′hə-lā′-shən, ĕk′sə-) *n.*

ex·haust (ĭg-zôst′) ►*v.* **1.** To wear out completely; tire. **2.** To use up completely; consume: *a project that exhausted our funds.* **3.** To treat or cover thoroughly: *exhaust all possibilities.* **4.** To let out or draw off (a liquid or gas). ►*n.* **1a.** The escape or release of vaporous waste material, as from an engine. **b.** Vapors or gases so released. **2.** A duct or pipe through which waste material is emitted. [Lat. *exhaurīre, exhaust-.*] —**ex·haust′i·bil′i·ty** *n.* —**ex·haust′i·ble** *adj.* —**ex·haus′tion** *n.*

ex·haus·tive (ĭg-zô′stĭv) ►*adj.* Comprehensive; thorough: *an exhaustive study.* —**ex·haus′tive·ly** *adv.*

ex·hib·it (ĭg-zĭb′ĭt) ►*v.* To show or display, esp. to public view. ►*n.* **1.** The act of exhibiting. **2.** Something exhibited. **3.** *Law* Something marked for identification with the purpose of being introduced as evidence in court. [< Lat. *exhibēre, exhibit-.*] —**ex·hib′i·tor** *n.* —**ex′hi·bi′tion** (ĕk′sə-bĭsh′ən) *n.*

ex·hi·bi·tion·ism (ĕk′sə-bĭsh′ə-nĭz′əm) ►*n.* The practice of deliberately behaving in a certain way so as to attract attention. —**ex′hi·bi′tion·ist** *n.* —**ex′hi·bi′tion·is′tic** *adj.*

ex·hil·a·rate (ĭg-zĭl′ə-rāt′) ►*v.* **-rat·ed, -rat·ing 1.** To make joyous and energetic; elate. **2.** To invigorate or stimulate. [Lat. *exhilarāre* < *hilaris,* cheerful.] —**ex·hil′a·ra′tion** *n.*

ex·hort (ĭg-zôrt′) ►*v.* To urge by strong argument, admonition, advice, or appeal. [< Lat. *exhortārī.*] —**ex′hor·ta′tion** *n.* —**ex·hor′ta·tive** *adj.* —**ex·hort′er** *n.*

ex·hume (ĭg-zōōm′, -zyōōm′, ĕks-hyōōm′) ►*v.* **-humed, -hum·ing 1.** To remove from a grave. **2.** To bring to light, esp. after a period of obscurity. [< Med.Lat. *exhumāre* : EX– + Lat. *humus,* ground.] —**ex′hu·ma′tion** *n.*

ex·i·gence (ĕk′sə-jəns) ►*n.* Exigency.

ex·i·gen·cy (ĕk′sə-jən-sē, ĭg-zĭj′ən-) ►*n., pl.* **-cies 1.** A pressing or urgent situation. **2.** An urgent requirement. [< Lat. *exigere,* to demand; see EXACT.] —**ex′i·gent** *adj.*

ex·ig·u·ous (ĭg-zĭg′yōō-əs, ĭk-sĭg′-) ►*adj.* Scanty; meager. [< Lat. *exigere,* measure; see EXACT.] —**ex′i·gu′i·ty** (ĕk′sĭ-gyōō′ĭ-tē) *n.*

ex·ile (ĕg′zīl′, ĕk′sīl′) ►*n.* **1.** Enforced removal or self-imposed absence from one's native country. **2.** One who chooses or is sent into exile. ►*v.* **-iled, -il·ing** To send into exile; banish. [< Lat. *exilium.*]

ex·ist (ĭg-zĭst′) ►*v.* **1.** To have actual being; be real: *doesn't believe that ghosts exist.* **2.** To have life; live. **3.** To occur: *Poverty exists in most cities.* [Lat. *exsistere,* be manifest : *ex-,* ex- + *sistere,* stand.]

ex·is·tence (ĭg-zĭs′təns) ►*n.* **1.** The fact or state of existing. **2.** Presence; occurrence. —**ex·is′tent** *adj.*
Syns: **actuality, being** **n.**

ex·is·ten·tial (ĕg′zĭ-stĕn′shəl, ĕk′sĭ-) ►*adj.* **1.** Of or relating to existence. **2.** Based on experience; empirical. **3.** Of or relating to existentialism. —**ex′is·ten′tial·ly** *adv.*

ex·is·ten·tial·ism (ĕg′zĭ-stĕn′shə-lĭz′əm, ĕk′sĭ-) ►*n.* A philosophy that emphasizes the uniqueness and isolation of the individual in a hostile or indifferent universe and stresses freedom of choice and responsibility for the consequences of one's acts. —**ex′is·ten′tial·ist** *adj. & n.*

ex·it (ĕg′zĭt, ĕk′sĭt) ►*n.* **1.** The act of going out. **2.** A passage or way out. **3.** The departure of a performer from the stage. [< Lat. *exīre,* go out.] —**ex′it** *v.*

exo– ►*pref.* Outside; external: *exoskeleton.* [< Gk. *exō,* outside of.]

ex·o·bi·ol·o·gy (ĕk′sō-bī-ŏl′ə-jē) ►*n.* The scientific search for extraterrestrial life. —**ex′o·bi·ol′o·gist** *n.*

ex·o·crine (ĕk′sə-krĭn, -krēn, -krīn′) ►*adj.* Having or secreting through a duct: *an exocrine gland.* [EXO– + Gk. *krinein,* to separate.]

ex·o·dus (ĕk′sə-dəs) ►*n.* **1.** A departure or emigration of a large number of people. **2. Exodus a.** The departure of the Israelites from Egypt. **b.** See table at **Bible.** [< Gk. *exodos.*]

ex of·fi·ci·o (ĕks′ ə-fĭsh′ē-ō′) ►*adv. & adj.* By virtue of office or position. [Lat. *ex officiō.*]

ex·og·e·nous (ĕk-sŏj′ə-nəs) ►*adj.* **1.** Originating outside a cell, tissue, or organism: *an exogenous disease.* **2.** Originating externally: *an exogenous model of economic growth.* —**ex·og′e·nous·ly** *adv.*

ex·on·er·ate (ĭg-zŏn′ə-rāt′) ►*v.* **-at·ed, -at·ing** To free from blame or responsibility. [< Lat. *exonerāre,* to free from a burden.] —**ex·on′er·a′tion** *n.* —**ex·on′er·a′tive** *adj.* —**ex·on′er·a′tor** *n.*

ex·o·plan·et (ĕk′sō-plăn′ĭt) ►*n.* An extrasolar planet.

ex·or·bi·tant (ĭg-zôr′bĭ-tənt) ►*adj.* Exceeding what is reasonable or customary, esp. in cost. [< LLat. *exorbitāre,* deviate.] —**ex·or′bi·tance** *n.* —**ex·or′bi·tant·ly** *adv.*

ex·or·cise (ĕk′sôr-sīz′, -sər-) ►*v.* **-cised, -cis·ing** **1.** To expel (an evil spirit) by or as if by incantation or prayer. **2.** To free from evil spirits. **3.** To eliminate (a negative feeling or experience): *sought to exorcise the apathy among the students.* [< Gk. *exorkizein* < *horkos,* oath.] —**ex′or·cism** *n.* —**ex′or·cist** *n.*

ex·o·skel·e·ton (ĕk′sō-skĕl′ĭ-tn) ►*n.* A hard outer structure, such as the shell of an insect or crustacean, that provides protection or support for an organism. —**ex′o·skel′e·tal** (-ĭ-tl) *adj.*

ex·o·sphere (ĕk′sō-sfîr′) ►*n.* The outermost region of a planet's atmosphere.

ex·o·ther·mic (ĕk′sō-thûr′mĭk) also **ex·o·ther·mal** (-məl) ►*adj.* Releasing heat: *an exothermic reaction.* —**ex′o·ther′mi·cal·ly** *adv.*

ex·ot·ic (ĭg-zŏt′ĭk) ►*adj.* **1.** From another part of the world. See Synonyms at **foreign. 2.** Intriguingly unusual, different, or beautiful. **3.** Of or involving striptease: *an exotic dancer.* [< Gk. *exōtikos* < *exō,* outside.] —**ex·ot′ic·n.** —**ex·ot′i·cal·ly** *adv.*

exp ►*abbr.* **1.** exponent **2.** exponential

exp. ►*abbr.* **1.** expenses **2.** experiment **3.** expiration **4.** export **5.** express

ex·pand (ĭk-spănd′) ►*v.* **1.** To increase or become increased in size, quantity, or scope. **2.** To express in detail; enlarge on: *expanded his remarks.* **3.** To spread out; unfold: *The chair expands to form a day bed.* [< Lat. *expandere.*] —**ex·pand′a·ble** *adj.*

ex·panse (ĭk-spăns′) ►*n.* **1.** A wide, open extent, as of land, sea, or sky. **2.** The distance or amount of expansion. [Lat. *expānsum* < p.part. of *expandere,* spread out.]

ex·pan·sion (ĭk-spăn′shən) ►*n.* **1.** The act or process of expanding or the state of being expanded. **2.** A product of expanding: *a book that is an expansion of a magazine article.*

ex·pan·sion·ism (ĭk-spăn′shə-nĭz′əm) ►*n.* A nation's practice or policy of territorial or economic expansion. —**ex·pan′sion·ar′y** *adj.* —**ex·pan′sion·ist** *adj. & n.*

ex·pan·sive (ĭk-spăn′sĭv) ►*adj.* **1.** Capable of expanding or tending to expand. **2.** Broad; comprehensive: *expansive police powers.* **3.** Talkative or effusive: *Wine made the host expansive.* **4.** Grand in scale: *an expansive lifestyle.* —**ex·pan′sive·ly** *adv.*

ex par·te (ĕks pär′tē) ►*adv. & adj.* Relating to an action taken in a legal proceeding by one party without the participation of the opposing party. [Lat.]

ex·pa·ti·ate (ĭk-spā′shē-āt′) ►*v.* **-at·ed, -at·ing** To speak or write at length; elaborate. [Lat. *expatiārī* < *spatium,* space.] —**ex·pa′ti·a′tion** *n.*

ex·pa·tri·ate (ĕk-spā′trē-āt′) ►*v.* **-at·ed, -at·ing 1.** To exile; banish. **2.** To leave one's country to reside in another. [Med.Lat. *expatriāre* : EX– + Lat. *patria,* native land (< *pater,* father).] —**ex·pa′tri·ate** (-ĭt, -āt′) *adj. & n.* —**ex·pa′tri·a′tion** *n.*

ex·pect (ĭk-spĕkt′) ►*v.* **1.** To look forward to the occurrence or appearance of: *expects a phone call.* **2.** To consider reasonable or due: *We expect an apology.* **3.** To be pregnant. Used in progressive tenses: *She is expecting.* **4.** To require: *We expect you to be on time.* **5.** *Informal* To presume or suppose. [Lat. *exspectāre* : EX– + *spectāre,* look at (< *specere,* see).]

ex·pec·tan·cy (ĭk-spĕk′tən-sē) ►*n., pl.* **-cies 1.** Expectation. **2.** Something expected, esp. an amount calculated on statistical probability: *life expectancy.*

ex·pec·tant (ĭk-spĕk′tənt) ►*adj.* **1.** Having expectation: *an expectant look.* **2.** Pregnant. —**ex·pec′tant·ly** *adv.*

ex·pec·ta·tion (ĕk′spĕk-tā′shən) ►*n.* **1.** The act or condition of expecting. **2.** Eager anticipation. **3. expectations** Prospects, esp. of success or gain.

ex·pec·to·rant (ĭk-spĕk′tər-ənt) ►*adj.* Promoting secretion or expulsion of mucus or other matter from the respiratory system. —**ex·pec′to·rant** *n.*

ex·pec·to·rate (ĭk-spĕk′tə-rāt′) ►*v.* **-rat·ed,**

-rat·ing To eject from the mouth; spit. [Lat. *expectorāre*, drive from the chest.] —**ex·pec′-to·ra′tion** *n.*

ex·pe·di·ence (ĭk-spē′dē-əns) ▸*n.* Expediency.

ex·pe·di·en·cy (ĭk-spē′dē-ən-sē) ▸*n., pl.* **-cies** **1.** Appropriateness to the purpose at hand. **2.** Adherence to self-serving means.

ex·pe·di·ent (ĭk-spē′dē-ənt) ▸*adj.* **1.** Appropriate to a particular purpose. **2.** Convenient but based on a concern for self-interest rather than principle: *changed his position when it was politically expedient.* ▸*n.* Something expedient. [< Lat. *expedīre*, make ready; see EXPEDITE.] —**ex·pe′di·ent·ly** *adv.*

ex·pe·dite (ĕk′spĭ-dīt′) ▸*v.* **-dit·ed, -dit·ing** To speed up the progress of or execute quickly. [Lat. *expedīre*, make ready : EX– + *pēs, ped-,* foot.] —**ex′pe·dit′er, ex′pe·di′tor** *n.*

ex·pe·di·tion (ĕk′spĭ-dĭsh′ən) ▸*n.* **1a.** A journey undertaken with a definite objective. **b.** The group making such a journey. **2.** Speed in performance. See Synonyms at **haste.**

ex·pe·di·tion·ar·y (ĕk′spĭ-dĭsh′ə-nĕr′ē) ▸*adj.* **1.** Relating to an expedition. **2.** Designed for military operations abroad: *the French expeditionary force in Indochina.*

ex·pe·di·tious (ĕk′spĭ-dĭsh′əs) ▸*adj.* Acting or done with speed and efficiency. —**ex′pe·di′-tious·ly** *adv.*

ex·pel (ĭk-spĕl′) ▸*v.* **-pelled, -pel·ling** **1.** To force or drive out; eject forcefully. **2.** To dismiss officially. **3.** To discharge from or as if from a receptacle: *expelled a sigh of relief.* [< Lat. *expellere.*] —**ex·pel′la·ble** *adj.* —**ex·pel′ler** *n.*

ex·pend (ĭk-spĕnd′) ▸*v.* **1.** To spend. **2.** To use up; consume: *expended a lot of effort.* [< Lat. *expendere,* pay out.]

ex·pend·a·ble (ĭk-spĕn′də-bəl) ▸*adj.* **1.** Subject to use or consumption. **2.** Nonessential; dispensable.

ex·pen·di·ture (ĭk-spĕn′dĭ-chər) ▸*n.* **1.** The act or process of expending. **2.** Something expended, esp. money.

ex·pense (ĭk-spĕns′) ▸*n.* **1a.** Something spent to accomplish a purpose. **b.** A loss for the sake of something gained; sacrifice: *speed at the expense of accuracy.* **2. expenses a.** Charges incurred by an employee in the performance of work. **b.** Money allotted for payment of such charges. **3.** Something requiring the expenditure of money. [< Lat. *expēnsus,* paid out.]

ex·pen·sive (ĭk-spĕn′sĭv) ▸*adj.* Having a high price; costly. —**ex·pen′sive·ly** *adv.* —**ex·pen′sive·ness** *n.*

ex·pe·ri·ence (ĭk-spîr′ē-əns) ▸*n.* **1.** The apprehension of an object, thought, or emotion through the senses or mind. **2a.** Activity or practice through which knowledge or skill is gained: *experience with roof repair.* **b.** Knowledge or skill so derived. **3a.** An event or a series of events undergone or lived through. **b.** The totality or effect of such events. ▸*v.* **-enced, -enc·ing** To participate in personally; undergo: *experience a great adventure.* [< Lat. *experīrī,* try.]

ex·pe·ri·enced (ĭk-spîr′ē-ənst) ▸*adj.* Skilled or knowledgeable through experience.

ex·pe·ri·en·tial (ĭk-spîr′ē-ĕn′shəl) ▸*adj.* Relating to or derived from experience. —**ex·pe′ri·en′tial·ly** *adv.*

ex·per·i·ment (ĭk-spĕr′ə-mənt) ▸*n.* **1.** A test made to demonstrate a known truth, examine the validity of a hypothesis, or determine the nature of something. **2.** An innovative act: *The new dress code is an experiment.* ▸*v.* (-mĕnt′) **1.** To conduct an experiment. **2.** To try something new: *experiment with new methods of teaching.* [< Lat. *experīmentum.*] —**ex·per′i·men′tal** *adj.* —**ex·per′i·men′tal·ly** *adv.* —**ex·per′i·men·ta′tion** *n.*

ex·pert (ĕk′spûrt′) ▸*n.* A person with a high degree of skill in or knowledge of a certain subject or field. ▸*adj.* (ĕk′spûrt, ĭk-spûrt′) Highly skilled or knowledgeable. [< Lat. *expertus,* p.part. of *experīrī,* try.] —**ex′pert′ly** *adv.*

ex·per·tise (ĕk′spûr-tēz′) ▸*n.* Skill or knowledge in a particular area. See Synonyms at **skill.** [Fr. < *expert,* experienced.]

ex·pi·ate (ĕk′spē-āt′) ▸*v.* **-at·ed, -at·ing** To atone or make amends (for). [Lat. *expiāre.*] —**ex′pi·a′tion** *n.* —**ex′pi·a′tor** *n.* —**ex′pi·a·to′ry** (-ə-tôr′ē) *adj.*

ex·pire (ĭk-spīr′) ▸*v.* **-pired, -pir·ing** **1.** To come to an end; terminate. **2.** To die. **3.** To exhale. [< Lat. *exspīrāre,* breathe out.] —**ex′pi·ra′tion** (ĕk′spə-rā′shən) *n.*

ex·pi·ry (ĭk-spîr′ē) ▸*n., pl.* **-ries** **1.** An expiration, esp. of a contract. **2.** Death.

ex·plain (ĭk-splān′) ▸*v.* **1.** To make plain or comprehensible. **2.** To define; expound: *explained our plan.* **3.** To offer reasons for; justify: *explain an error.* [< Lat. *explānāre,* make plain.] —**ex·plain′a·ble** *adj.* —**ex′pla·na′tion** (ĕk′splə-nā′shən) *n.* —**ex·plan′a·to′ri·ly** *adv.* —**ex·plan′a·to′ry** (-splăn′ə-tôr′ē) *adj.*

Syns: *construe, elucidate, explicate, interpret* **v.**

ex·ple·tive (ĕk′splĭ-tĭv) ▸*n.* An exclamation or oath, esp. one that is profane. [< Lat. *explēre, explēt-,* fill out.]

ex·pli·ca·ble (ĭk-splĭk′ə-bəl, ĕk′splĭ-kə-) ▸*adj.* Possible to explain. —**ex′plic·a·bly** *adv.*

ex·pli·cate (ĕk′splĭ-kāt′) ▸*v.* **-cat·ed, -cat·ing** To explain, esp. in detail. See Synonyms at **explain.** [Lat. *explicāre,* unfold.] —**ex′pli·ca′tion** *n.* —**ex′pli·ca′tive** *adj.* —**ex′pli·ca′tor** *n.*

ex·plic·it (ĭk-splĭs′ĭt) ▸*adj.* **1.** Fully and clearly expressed, defined, or formulated. **2.** Describing or portraying nudity or sexual activity in graphic detail. [Lat. *explicitus,* p.part. of *explicāre,* unfold.] —**ex·plic′it·ly** *adv.* —**ex·plic′it·ness** *n.*

Syns: *definite, express, specific* **Ant:** *ambiguous* **adj.**

ex·plode (ĭk-splōd′) ▸*v.* **-plod·ed, -plod·ing** **1.** To cause or undergo an explosion. **2.** To burst or cause to burst by explosion. **3.** To shatter with a loud noise: *The vase exploded into tiny pieces when it hit the floor.* **4.** To make an emotional outburst: *exploded in rage.* **5.** To increase suddenly, sharply, and without control: *the population level exploded.* [Lat. *explōdere,* drive out by clapping.] —**ex·plod′a·ble** *adj.*

ex·ploit (ĕk′sploit′, ĭk-sploit′) ▸*n.* An act or deed, esp. a heroic or brilliant one. See Synonyms at **feat.** ▸*v.* (ĭk-sploit′, ĕk′sploit′) **1.** To utilize fully or advantageously. **2.** To make use of selfishly or unethically. See Synonyms at **manipulate.** [< Lat. *explicitum.*] —**ex·ploit′a·ble** *adj.* —**ex·ploi·ta′tion** *n.* —**ex·ploit′a′tive** *adj.* —**ex·ploit′er** *n.*

ex·plore (ĭk-splôr′) ▸*v.* **-plored, -plor·ing** **1.**

To investigate systematically: *explore every possibility.* **2.** To search or travel into for the purpose of discovery. **3.** *Med.* To investigate (a body part or cavity) for diagnostic purposes, esp. by surgery. [Lat. *explōrāre.*] —**ex′plo·ra′tion** (ĕk′splə-rā′shən) *n.* —**ex·plor′a·to′ry** (-tôr′ē) *adj.* —**ex·plor′er** *n.*

ex·plo·sion (ĭk-splō′zhən) ►*n.* **1a.** A sudden violent release of mechanical, chemical, or nuclear energy. **b.** The loud sound accompanying such a release. **2.** A sudden, often vehement outburst, esp. of emotion. **3.** A sudden sharp increase: *a population explosion.* [Lat. *explōsiō.*]

ex·plo·sive (ĭk-splō′sĭv) ►*adj.* **1.** Of or causing an explosion. **2.** Tending to explode. **3.** Highly unstable; volatile. ►*n.* A substance, esp. a prepared chemical, that explodes or causes explosion. —**ex·plo′sive·ly** *adv.* —**ex·plo′sive·ness** *n.*

ex·po·nent (ĭk-spō′nənt, ĕk′spō′nənt) ►*n.* **1.** One that expounds, interprets, or advocates. **2.** A number or symbol, as 3 in $(x + y)^3$, placed to the right and above another number, symbol, or expression, denoting the power to which it is to be raised. [< Lat. *expōnere,* set forth.] —**ex′po·nen′tial** (ĕk′spə-nĕn′shəl) *adj.* —**ex′po·nen′tial·ly** *adv.*

ex·port (ĭk-spôrt′, ĕk′spôrt′) ►*v.* **1.** To send or transport abroad, esp. for trade or sale. **2.** *Comp.* To send (data) from one program to another. ►*n.* (ĕk′spôrt′) Exportation. [< Lat. *exportāre,* carry out.] —**ex·port′a·ble** *adj.* —**ex·port′er** *n.*

ex·por·ta·tion (ĕk′spôr-tā′shən) ►*n.* **1.** The act of exporting. **2.** Something exported; export.

ex·pose (ĭk-spōz′) ►*v.* -**posed, -pos·ing 1a.** To subject or allow to be subjected to an action or influence. **b.** To subject (a photographic film or plate) to the action of light. **2.** To make visible or known; reveal. **3.** To lay bare; uncover. **4.** To engage in indecent exposure of (oneself). [< Lat. *expōnere,* to set out.] —**ex·pos′er** *n.*

ex·po·sé (ĕk′spō-zā′) ►*n.* A public revelation of something discreditable. [Fr.]

ex·po·si·tion (ĕk′spə-zĭsh′ən) ►*n.* **1.** The systematic explanation of a subject. **2.** A discourse that conveys information about or explains a subject. **3.** A public exhibition of broad scope. —**ex·pos′i·to′ry** (-tôr′ē) *adj.*

ex post fac·to (ĕks′ pōst făk′tō) ►*adj.* Formulated, enacted, or operating retroactively. [Lat. *ex postfactō,* from what is done afterwards.]

ex·pos·tu·late (ĭk-spŏs′chə-lāt′) ►*v.* -**lat·ed, -lat·ing** To reason earnestly with someone, esp. to dissuade or correct. [Lat. *expostulāre,* demand strongly.] —**ex·pos′tu·la′tion** *n.* —**ex·pos′tu·la′tor** *n.* —**ex·pos′tu·la·to′ry** (-lə-tôr′ē) *adj.*

ex·po·sure (ĭk-spō′zhər) ►*n.* **1.** The act or an instance of exposing. **2.** The condition of being exposed, esp. to severe weather: *hospitalized for exposure after falling through the ice.* **3.** A position in relation to points of the compass. **4a.** The act or time of exposing a photographic film or plate. **b.** A film or plate so exposed.

ex·pound (ĭk-spound′) ►*v.* To explain in detail; elucidate. [< Lat. *expōnere,* set forth.] —**ex·pound′er** *n.*

ex·press (ĭk-sprĕs′) ►*v.* **1a.** To set forth in words; state: *express an opinion.* **b.** To communicate, as by a gesture; show: *express anger with* a frown. **2.** To convey or suggest a representation of; depict. **3.** To press out, as juice from an orange. **4.** To send by rapid transport. ►*adj.* **1.** Definitely and clearly stated: *their express wish.* See Synonyms at **explicit. 2a.** Rapid and having few or no stops or interruptions: *express delivery; an express bus.* **b.** Relating to or appropriate for rapid travel: *express lanes.* ►*adv.* By express transportation. ►*n.* **1.** A rapid, efficient system for the delivery of goods and mail. **2.** A means of transport, such as a train, that travels rapidly, usu. nonstop. [< Med.Lat. *expressāre.*] —**ex·press′i·ble** *adj.* —**ex·press′ly** *adv.*

ex·pres·sion (ĭk-sprĕsh′ən) ►*n.* **1.** The act of expressing in words, art, music, or movement: *an expression of rural values.* **2.** Something that expresses: *The award is an expression of our gratitude.* **3.** *Math.* A symbol or combination of symbols representing a quantity or a relationship between quantities. **4.** A particular word or phrase: *an old Yankee expression.* **5.** A facial aspect or a look that conveys a special feeling. **6.** The act of squeezing out: *expression of juice from the grapes.* **7.** The act of expressing a gene.

ex·pres·sion·ism (ĭk-sprĕsh′ə-nĭz′əm) ►*n.* An artistic style during the early 1900s marked by expression of the artist's psychological perceptions. —**ex·pres′sion·ist** *n.* —**ex·pres′sion·is′tic** *adj.*

ex·pres·sive (ĭk-sprĕs′ĭv) ►*adj.* **1.** Expressing or serving to express or indicate. **2.** Communicating meaning or feeling effectively: *an expressive glance.* —**ex·pres′sive·ly** *adv.* —**ex·pres′sive·ness** *n.*

ex·press·way (ĭk-sprĕs′wā′) ►*n.* A major divided highway designed for high-speed travel.

ex·pro·pri·ate (ĕk-sprō′prē-āt′) ►*v.* -**at·ed, -at·ing** To take (a property) for public use. [< Med. Lat. *expropriāre* < Lat. *proprius,* one's own.] —**ex·pro′pri·a′tion** *n.* —**ex·pro′pri·a′tor** *n.*

ex·pul·sion (ĭk-spŭl′shən) ►*n.* The act of expelling or the state of being expelled.

ex·punge (ĭk-spŭnj′) ►*v.* -**punged, -pung·ing** To erase or strike out. [Lat. *expungere.*]

ex·pur·gate (ĕk′spər-gāt′) ►*v.* -**gat·ed, -gat·ing** To remove obscene or objectionable material from. [Lat. *expūrgāre,* purify.] —**ex′pur·ga′tion** *n.* —**ex′pur·ga′tor** *n.*

ex·qui·site (ĕk′skwĭ-zĭt, ĭk-skwĭz′ĭt) ►*adj.* **1.** Beautifully made or designed. **2.** Excellent or outstanding, esp. by appealing to refined taste. **3.** Extremely subtle or precise: *exquisite detail.* **4.** Intense; keen: *exquisite delight.* [< Lat. *exquīsītus,* p.part. of *exquīrere,* search out.] —**ex′qui·site·ly** *adv.* —**ex′qui·site·ness** *n.* **Syns:** *delicate, elegant, fine* **adj.**

ex·tant (ĕk′stənt, ĕk-stănt′) ►*adj.* Still in existence; not destroyed, lost, or extinct. [< Lat. *exstāre,* stand out : EX– + *stāre,* stand.]

ex·tem·po·ra·ne·ous (ĭk-stĕm′pə-rā′nē-əs) ►*adj.* Carried out or performed with little or no preparation; impromptu. [< Lat. *ex tempore,* extempore.] —**ex·tem′po·ra′ne·ous·ly** *adv.*

ex·tem·po·rar·y (ĭk-stĕm′pə-rĕr′ē) ►*adj.* Extemporaneous. [< EXTEMPORE.]

ex·tem·po·re (ĭk-stĕm′pə-rē) ►*adj.* Extemporaneous. ►*adv.* Extemporaneously. [Lat. *ex tempore,* out of the time.]

ex·tem·po·rize (ĭk-stĕm′pə-rīz′) ►*v.* -**rized, -riz·ing** To do or perform (something) extemporaneously. —**ex·tem′po·ri·za′tion** *n.*

ex·tend (ĭk-stĕnd′) ►*v.* **1.** To stretch, spread, or enlarge to greater length, area, scope, or period of time; expand. **2.** To exert vigorously or to full capacity: *The climbers really extended themselves to reach the summit.* **3.** To make available: *extend credit.* **4.** To present; offer: *extend one's greetings.* [< Lat. *extendere.*] —**ex·tend′i·bil·i·ty, ex·ten′si·bil′i·ty** *n.* —**ex·tend′i·ble, ex·ten′si·ble** *adj.*

ex·ten·sion (ĭk-stĕn′shən) ►*n.* **1.** The act of extending or condition of being extended. **2.** An extended or added part. [< Lat. *extēnsiō.*]

ex·ten·sive (ĭk-stĕn′sĭv) ►*adj.* Large in extent, range, or amount. —**ex·ten′sive·ly** *adv.* —**ex·ten′sive·ness** *n.*

ex·ten·sor (ĭk-stĕn′sər) ►*n.* A muscle that extends or straightens a limb or body part. [NLat. < Lat. *extendere,* stretch out.]

ex·tent (ĭk-stĕnt′) ►*n.* **1.** The area or distance over which a thing extends; size. **2.** The range or degree to which a thing extends; scope: *prosecuted to the full extent of the law.* [< Lat. *extendere,* extend.]

ex·ten·u·ate (ĭk-stĕn′yōō-āt′) ►*v.* **-at·ed, -at·ing** To lessen the seriousness of, esp. by providing partial excuses. [Lat. *extenuāre,* make thin.] —**ex·ten′u·a′tion** *n.* —**ex·ten′u·a′tor** *n.*

ex·te·ri·or (ĭk-stîr′ē-ər) ►*adj.* **1.** Outer; external. **2.** Suitable for use outside: *an exterior paint.* ►*n.* **1.** An outer or outward part, surface, or aspect. **2.** An outward appearance: *a friendly exterior.* [Lat., comp. of *exter,* outward.]

ex·ter·mi·nate (ĭk-stûr′mə-nāt′) ►*v.* **-nat·ed, -nat·ing** To destroy completely; wipe out. [Lat. *extermināre,* drive out.] —**ex·ter′mi·na′tion** *n.* —**ex·ter′mi·na′tor** *n.*

ex·ter·nal (ĭk-stûr′nəl) ►*adj.* **1.** Of, on, or for the outside or outer part. **2.** Acting or coming from the outside: *external pressure.* **3.** For outward show; superficial. **4.** Relating to foreign countries: *the minister of external affairs.* **5.** Suitable for application to the outside: *external paint.* ►*n.* **externals** Outward appearances. [< Lat. *externus.*] —**ex·ter′nal·ly** *adv.*

external ear ►*n.* The outer portion of the ear including the auricle and the passage leading to the eardrum.

ex·tinct (ĭk-stĭngkt′) ►*adj.* **1.** No longer existing or living. **2.** No longer active or in use: *an extinct volcano; extinct customs.* [< Lat. *exstinctus,* p.part. of *exstinguere,* EXTINGUISH.] —**ex·tinc′tion** *n.*

ex·tin·guish (ĭk-stĭng′gwĭsh) ►*v.* **1.** To put out (e.g., a fire); quench. **2.** To put an end to; destroy. [Lat. *exstinguere.*] —**ex·tin′guish·a·ble** *adj.* —**ex·tin′guish·er** *n.*

ex·tir·pate (ĕk′stər-pāt′) ►*v.* **-pat·ed, -pat·ing** **1.** To destroy totally; exterminate. See Synonyms at **eliminate. 2.** To uproot or cut out. [Lat. *exstirpāre,* root out.] —**ex′tir·pa′tion** *n.* —**ex′tir·pa′tive** *adj.* —**ex′tir·pa′tor** *n.*

ex·tol also **ex·toll** (ĭk-stōl′) ►*v.* **-tolled, -tol·ling** To praise highly. [< Lat. *extollere,* lift up.] —**ex·tol′ler** *n.* —**ex·tol′ment** *n.*

ex·tort (ĭk-stôrt′) ►*v.* To obtain from by coercion or intimidation. [Lat. *extorquēre, extort-,* wring out.] —**ex·tor′tion** *n.* —**ex·tor′tion·ate** (-ĭt) *adj.* —**ex·tor′tion·ist** *n.*

ex·tra (ĕk′strə) ►*adj.* **1.** More than what is usual, expected, or necessary. See Synonyms at **superfluous. 2.** Subject to an additional

charge: *Coffee doesn't come with lunch; it's extra.* ►*n.* **1.** Something that is extra. **2.** Something for which there is an additional charge: *Leather seats are an extra for that car model.* **3.** A special edition of a newspaper. **4.** A performer hired to play a minor part, as in a crowd scene in a film. ►*adv.* Especially; unusually. [Prob. < EXTRAORDINARY.]

extra– ►*pref.* Outside; beyond: *extraterrestrial.* [< Lat. *extrā,* outside.]

ex·tract (ĭk-stråkt′) ►*v.* **1.** To draw or pull out forcibly. **2.** To obtain despite resistance: *extract a promise.* **3.** To obtain in a concentrated form by chemical or mechanical action. **4.** To remove for separate consideration or publication; excerpt. **5.** *Math.* To determine (the root of a number). ►*n.* (ĕk′stråkt′) **1.** A literary excerpt. **2.** A substance prepared by extracting; essence; concentrate. [< Lat. *extrahere, extract-,* draw out.] —**ex·tract′a·ble, ex·tract′i·ble** *adj.* —**ex·trac′tor** *n.*

ex·trac·tion (ĭk-stråk′shən) ►*n.* **1.** The act of extracting or the condition of being extracted. **2.** Something obtained by extracting; extract. **3.** Origin; lineage: *of French extraction.*

ex·tra·cur·ric·u·lar (ĕk′strə-kə-rĭk′yə-lər) ►*adj.* Being outside the regular curriculum of a school: *extracurricular activities like sports and drama.*

ex·tra·dite (ĕk′strə-dīt′) ►*v.* **-dit·ed, -dit·ing** To give up or deliver (e.g., a fugitive) to the legal jurisdiction of another government or authority. [< Fr. *extradition,* extradition : EX– + Lat. *trāditiō,* handing over; see TRADITION.] —**ex′tra·dit′a·ble** *adj.* —**ex′tra·di′tion** (ĕk′strə-dĭsh′ən) *n.*

ex·tra·ga·lac·tic (ĕk′strə-gə-låk′tĭk) ►*adj.* Located or originating beyond the Milky Way.

ex·tra·le·gal (ĕk′strə-lē′gəl) ►*adj.* Not permitted or governed by law. —**ex′tra·le′gal·ly** *adv.*

ex·tra·mar·i·tal (ĕk′strə-măr′ĭ-tl) ►*adj.* Adulterous: *an extramarital affair.*

ex·tra·mu·ral (ĕk′strə-myōōr′əl) ►*adj.* Occurring or situated outside of the walls or boundaries, as of a community or school. [< EXTRA– + Lat. *mūrus,* wall.]

ex·tra·ne·ous (ĭk-strā′nē-əs) ►*adj.* **1.** Not essential. See Synonyms at **irrelevant. 2.** Coming from the outside. [< Lat. *extrāneus < extrā,* outside.] —**ex·tra′ne·ous·ly** *adv.* —**ex·tra′ne·ous·ness** *n.*

ex·traor·di·nar·y (ĭk-strôr′dn-ĕr′ē, ĕk′strə-ôr′-) ►*adj.* Beyond what is ordinary or usual; remarkable. —**ex·traor′di·nar′i·ly** *adv.*

ex·trap·o·late (ĭk-stråp′ə-lāt′) ►*v.* **-lat·ed, -lat·ing** To infer (unknown information) from known information. [EXTRA– + (INTER)POLATE.] —**ex·trap′o·la′tion** *n.*

ex·tra·sen·so·ry (ĕk′strə-sĕn′sə-rē) ►*adj.* Being outside the normal range of sense perception.

ex·tra·so·lar (ĕk′strə-sō′lər) ►*adj.* Being or originating outside the solar system: *an extrasolar planet.*

ex·tra·ter·res·tri·al (ĕk′strə-tə-rĕs′trē-əl) ►*adj.* From or occurring outside Earth or its atmosphere. —**ex′tra·ter·res′tri·al** *n.*

ex·tra·ter·ri·to·ri·al (ĕk′strə-tĕr′ĭ-tôr′ē-əl) ►*adj.* Located outside the territorial boundaries of a nation or state.

ex·tra·ter·ri·to·ri·al·i·ty (ĕk′strə-tĕr′ĭ-tôr′-

ē-ăl′ĭ-tē) ►*n.* **1.** Exemption from local legal jurisdiction, such as that granted to foreign diplomats. **2.** The operation of the law of a state or county outside of its physical boundaries.

ex·trav·a·gance (ĭk-străv′ə-gəns) ►*n.* **1.** The quality of being extravagant. **2.** Immoderate expense or display: *His extravagance led to financial ruin.* **3.** Something extravagant. See Synonyms at **luxury.**

ex·trav·a·gant (ĭk-străv′ə-gənt) ►*adj.* **1.** Lavish or imprudent in spending money. **2.** Exceeding reasonable bounds; excessive: *extravagant demands.* **3.** Unreasonably expensive: *extravagant fees.* [< Med.Lat. *extrāvagārī,* wander.] —**ex·trav′a·gant·ly** *adv.*

ex·trav·a·gan·za (ĭk-străv′ə-găn′zə) ►*n.* An elaborate, spectacular entertainment or display. [Ital. *estravaganza.*]

ex·treme (ĭk-strēm′) ►*adj.* **1.** Most remote; outermost or farthest. **2.** Very great; intense: *extreme pain.* **3.** Extending far beyond the norm. **4.** Drastic; severe. ►*n.* **1.** The greatest or utmost degree. **2.** Either of the two things at opposite ends of a scale, series, or range. **3.** An extreme condition. **4.** A drastic expedient: *resorted to extremes in a crisis.* [< Lat. *extrēmus.*] —**ex·treme′ly** *adv.* —**ex·treme′ness** *n.*

ex·trem·ist (ĭk-strē′mĭst) ►*n.* One who advocates or resorts to measures beyond the norm, esp. in politics. —**ex·trem′ism** *n.*

ex·trem·i·ty (ĭk-strĕm′ĭ-tē) ►*n., pl.* **-ties 1.** The outermost or farthest point or part: *the peninsula's extremity.* **2.** The utmost degree: *the extremity of despair.* **3.** Grave danger, necessity, or distress. **4.** *Anat.* **a.** A bodily limb. **b. extremities** The hands and feet: *frostbite affects the extremities first.*

ex·tre·mo·phile (ĭk-strē′mə-fīl′) ►*n.* An organism that requires extreme conditions of temperature, pressure, or chemical concentration in order to thrive.

ex·tri·cate (ĕk′strĭ-kāt′) ►*v.* **-cat·ed, -cat·ing** To release from an entanglement or difficulty. [Lat. *extricāre.*] —**ex′tri·ca·ble** (-kə-bəl) *adj.* —**ex′tri·ca′tion** *n.*

Syns: disengage, disentangle, untangle **v.**

ex·trin·sic (ĭk-strĭn′sĭk, -zĭk) ►*adj.* **1.** Not essential or inherent. **2.** Originating from the outside; external. [Lat. *extrīnsecus,* from outside.] —**ex·trin′si·cal·ly** *adv.*

ex·tro·vert also **ex·tra·vert** (ĕk′strə-vûrt′) ►*n.* One whose interest and behavior are primarily directed toward others as opposed to self; outgoing. [< EXTRA– + Lat. *vertere,* turn.] —**ex′tro·ver′sion** *n.*

ex·trude (ĭk-strōōd′) ►*v.* **-trud·ed, -trud·ing** **1.** To thrust out. **2.** To shape (e.g., a plastic) by forcing through a die. [Lat. *extrūdere.*] —**ex·tru′sion** *n.* —**ex·tru′sive** *adj.*

ex·u·ber·ant (ĭg-zōō′bər-ənt) ►*adj.* **1.** Full of unrestrained enthusiasm or joy. **2.** Abundant; plentiful. See Synonyms at **profuse.** [< Lat. *exūberāre,* be exuberant.] —**ex·u′ber·ance** *n.* —**ex·u′ber·ant·ly** *adv.*

ex·ude (ĭg-zōōd′, ĭk-sōōd′) ►*v.* **-ud·ed, -ud·ing** **1.** To discharge (e.g., a liquid or gas) gradually. **2.** To exhibit in abundance: *exude confidence.* [Lat. *exsūdāre.*] —**ex′u·date′** (ĕks′yŏō-dāt′) *n.* —**ex′u·da′tion** *n.*

ex·ult (ĭg-zŭlt′) ►*v.* To rejoice greatly, as in triumph. [Lat. *exsultāre,* leap up.] —**ex·ul′-**

tant *adj.* —**ex·ul′tant·ly** *adv.* —**ex·ul·ta′tion** (ĕk′səl-tā′shən, ĕg′zəl-) *n.*

ex·urb (ĕk′sûrb′) ►*n.* A semirural region lying just beyond the suburbs of a city. [EX– + (SUB)URB.] —**ex·ur′ban** *adj.* —**ex·ur′ban·ite′** *n.*

ex·ur·bi·a (ĕk-sûr′bē-ə, ĕg-zûr′-) ►*n.* A typically exurban area.

–ey ►*suff.* Var. of **–y**[1].

Eyck (īk), **Jan van** 1390?–1441. And his brother **Hubert** (d. 1426). Flemish painters.

eye (ī) ►*n.* **1.** The organ in animals that allows vision. **2.** The faculty of seeing; vision. **3.** The ability to perceive or discern. **4.** A point of view; opinion: *To my eye, the wallpaper is attractive.* **5.** Attention: *The billboard got my eye.* **6.** Something suggestive of an eye: *the eye of a needle; the eye of a potato.* ►*v.* **eyed, eye·ing** or **ey·ing** To look at. —*idiom:* **eye to eye** In agreement. [< OE *ēage.*]

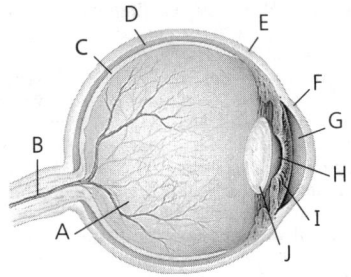

eye
cross section of a human eye
A. vitreous humor
B. optic nerve
C. retina
D. choroid
E. sclera
F. cornea
G. aqueous humor
H. pupil
I. iris
J. lens

eye·ball (ī′bôl′) ►*n.* The ball-shaped part of the eye enclosed by the socket and eyelids. ►*v.* To measure or estimate roughly by sight.

eye·brow (ī′brou′) ►*n.* The hairs covering the bony ridge over the eye.

eye·drop·per (ī′drŏp′ər) ►*n.* A dropper for applying liquid medicines, esp. to the eye.

eye·ful (ī′fŏŏl′) ►*n.* **1.** A good or thorough look. **2.** A pleasing sight.

eye·glass (ī′glăs′) ►*n.* **1a. eyeglasses** Glasses for the eyes. **b.** A monocle. **2.** See **eyepiece.**

eye·lash (ī′lăsh′) ►*n.* Any of the short hairs fringing the edge of the eyelid.

eye·let (ī′lĭt) ►*n.* **1.** A small hole for a lace, cord, or hook to fit through. **2.** A metal ring designed to reinforce such a hole. [< OFr. *oillet,* dim. of *oil,* eye < Lat. *oculus.*]

eye·lid (ī′lĭd′) ►*n.* Either of two folds of skin and muscle that can be closed over an eye.

eye opener ►*n. Informal* A startling or shocking revelation.

eye·piece (ī′pēs′) ►*n.* The lens or lens group closest to the eye in an optical instrument.

eye shadow ►*n.* A cosmetic applied esp. to the eyelids to enhance the eyes.

eye·sight (ī′sīt′) ►*n.* The faculty or range of sight; vision.

eye·sore (ī′sôr′) ►*n.* An ugly sight.

eye·strain (ī′strān′) ►*n.* Pain and fatigue in one or more of the eye muscles.

eye·tooth (ī′tōoth′) ►*n.* A canine tooth of the upper jaw.

eye·wall (ī′wôl′) ►*n.* The mass of clouds that whirls around the eye of a hurricane, where the destructive force of the storm is most intense.

eye·wash (ī′wŏsh′, ī′wôsh′) ►*n.* A solution applied as a cleanser for the eyes.

eye·wit·ness (ī′wĭt′nĭs) ►*n.* One who has personally seen someone or something and can bear witness to the fact.

ey·rie (âr′ē, îr′ē) ►*n.* Var. of **aerie.**

E·ze·ki·el (ĭ-zē′kē-əl) ►*n.* **1.** A Hebrew prophet of the 6th cent. BC. **2.** See table at **Bible.**

e-zine (ē′zēn′) ►*n.* A magazine that is published electronically, esp. on the Internet.

Ez·ra (ĕz′rə) ►*n.* **1.** 5th cent. BC Hebrew priest and scribe. **2.** See table at **Bible.**

F

f¹ or **F** (ĕf) ►*n.*, *pl.* **f's** or **F's** also **fs** or **Fs 1.** The 6th letter of the English alphabet. **2.** F A failing grade. **3.** *Mus.* The 4th tone of the C major scale.

f² ►*abbr.* **1.** feminine **2.** focal length **3.** function

F ►*abbr.* **1.** Fahrenheit **2.** fail **3.** farad **4.** fax machine number **5.** female

F. ►*abbr.* **1.** also **f.** folio **2.** French

f/ ►*abbr.* f-stop

fa (fä) ►*n. Mus.* The 4th tone of the diatonic scale.

FAA ►*abbr.* Federal Aviation Administration

fa·ble (fā′bəl) ►*n.* **1.** A fictitious story making a moral point and often using animals as characters. **2.** A story about legendary persons and exploits. **3.** A falsehood; lie. ►*v.* **-bled, -bling** To recount as if true. [< Lat. *fābula.*] —**fab′u·list** (făb′yə-lĭst) *n.*

fa·bled (fā′bəld) ►*adj.* **1.** Made known or famous by fables; legendary. **2.** Fictitious.

fab·ric (făb′rĭk) ►*n.* **1.** A cloth produced esp. by knitting or weaving fibers. **2.** A complex underlying structure; framework: *the fabric of society.* [< Lat. *fabrica,* workshop.]

fab·ri·cate (făb′rĭ-kāt′) ►*v.* **-cat·ed, -cat·ing 1.** To make; create. **2.** To construct or build. **3.** To make up in order to deceive: *fabricated an excuse.* —**fab′ri·ca′tion** *n.*

fab·u·lous (făb′yə-ləs) ►*adj.* **1.** Extremely pleasing or successful: *a fabulous vacation.* **2.** Barely credible; astonishing. **3a.** Of the nature of a fable; legendary. **b.** Told of or celebrated in fables. [< Lat. *fābula,* fable.] —**fab′u·lous·ly** *adv.* —**fab′u·lous·ness** *n.*

fa·çade also **fa·cade** (fə-säd′) ►*n.* **1.** The face of a building, esp. the principal face. **2.** An artificial or deceptive appearance: *put on a façade of sincerity.* [< Ital. *facciata.*]

face (fās) ►*n.* **1.** The surface of the front of the head. **2.** A facial expression; countenance. **3.** A grimace. **4.** Outward appearance; aspect. **5.** Value or standing; prestige: *lose face.* **6.** Effrontery; impudence. **7.** The front or most significant surface of an object: *the face of a clock.* **8.** A planar surface of a geometric solid. ►*v.* **faced, fac·ing 1.** To turn or be turned in the direction of. **2.** To front on: *a window that faces the south.* **3a.** To confront. See Synonyms at **defy. b.** To encounter: *face problems later on.* **4.** To furnish with a surface or cover of a different material. **5.** To trim the edge of (cloth), esp. with contrasting material. —*phrasal verbs:* **face down** To overcome by a stare or a resolute manner. **face off** *Sports* To start play with a face-off. **face up** To confront with resolution. —*idioms:* **face the music** To accept unpleasant consequences. **face to face 1.** In each other's presence. **2.** Directly confronting: *face to face with death.* **in the face of 1.** Despite the opposition of. **2.** In view of. **on the face of it** From appearances alone. **to (one's) face** In one's presence. [< Lat. *faciēs.*] —**face′less** *adj.*

face card ►*n. Games* A king, queen, or jack of a deck of playing cards.

face·less (fās′lĭs) ►*adj.* **1.** Having no face. **2.** Without character; anonymous.

face-lift also **face·lift** (fās′lĭft′) ►*n.* **1.** Plastic surgery to tighten facial tissues. **2.** A renovation, as of a building. —**face′-lift′** *v.*

face-off (fās′ôf′, -ŏf′) ►*n.* **1.** A method of starting play, as in ice hockey or lacrosse, by releasing the puck or ball between two opposing players. **2.** A confrontation.

fac·et (făs′ĭt) ►*n.* **1.** One of the flat surfaces cut on a gemstone. **2.** One of numerous aspects of a subject. [< OFr. *facette,* dim. of *face,* FACE.] —**fac′et·ed** *adj.*

fa·ce·tious (fə-sē′shəs) ►*adj.* Playfully jocular; humorous. [< Lat. *facētus,* witty.] —**fa·ce′tious·ly** *adv.* —**fa·ce′tious·ness** *n.*

face value ►*n.* **1.** The value printed on the face, as of a bill or bond. **2.** Apparent significance or value.

fa·cial (fā′shəl) ►*adj.* Of the face. ►*n.* A cosmetic treatment for the face.

fac·ile (făs′əl) ►*adj.* **1.** Working, acting, or done with ease and fluency: *a facile writer; facile prose.* **2.** Excessively simple; superficial: *a facile solution to a complex problem.* [< Lat. *facilis.*] —**fac′ile·ly** *adv.* —**fac′ile·ness** *n.*

fa·cil·i·tate (fə-sĭl′ĭ-tāt′) ►*v.* **-tat·ed, -tat·ing** To make easy or easier; assist. [< Ital. *facilitare.*] —**fa·cil′i·ta′tion** *n.* —**fa·cil′i·ta′tor** *n.*

fa·cil·i·ty (fə-sĭl′ĭ-tē) ►*n., pl.* **-ties 1.** Ease in moving, acting, or doing, resulting from skill or aptitude. **2. often facilities a.** A venue and accompanying equipment, designed to serve a function: *urgent care facilities.* **b.** Something that facilitates an action or process: *transportation facilities.* **3. facilities** A restroom.

fac·ing (fā′sĭng) ►*n.* **1.** A piece of material sewn to the edge of a garment as lining or decoration. **2.** A layer applied to a surface for protection or decoration.

fac·sim·i·le (făk-sĭm′ə-lē) ►*n.* **1.** An exact copy or reproduction. **2.** See **fax.** [< Lat. *fac simile,* make similar.]

fact (făkt) ►*n.* **1.** Knowledge or information based on real occurrences. **2.** Something having real, demonstrable existence. **3.** Something believed to be true or real: *a report laced with mistaken facts.* **4.** Something done, esp. a crime: *an accessory before the fact.* [Lat. *factum,* deed < p.part. of *facere,* do.]

fact-find·ing (făkt′fīn′dĭng) ►*n.* Discovery or determination of facts. —**fact′-find′ing** *adj.*

fac·tion[1] (făk′shən) ►*n.* **1.** A cohesive, usu. contentious minority within a larger group. **2.** Internal dissension or discord. [< Lat. *factiō* < p.part. of *facere,* do.] —**fac′tion·al** *adj.* —**fac′tion·al·ism** *n.*

fac·tion[2] (făk′shən) ►*n.* A genre or work of literature or film that mixes fact and fiction. [Blend of FACT and FICTION.]

–faction ►*suff.* Production; making: *petrifaction.* [< Lat. *-factiō.*]

fac·tious (făk′shəs) ►*adj.* Given to, characterized by, or promoting internal dissension. —**fac′tious·ly** *adv.*

fac·ti·tious (făk-tĭsh′əs) ►*adj.* **1.** Produced artificially. **2.** False; sham. [< Lat. *factīcius* < *factus* < *facere,* make.]

fact of life ►*n.* **1.** Something unavoidable that must be dealt with. **2.** **facts of life** The basic physiological functions involved in sex and reproduction.

fac·toid (făk′toid) ►*n.* **1.** A piece of unverified or inaccurate information accepted as true because of frequent repetition. **2.** A brief, somewhat interesting fact.

fac·tor (făk′tər) ►*n.* **1.** One that actively contributes to a result or process. See Synonyms at **element**. **2.** One who acts for someone else; agent. **3.** *Math.* **a.** One of two or more quantities that divides a given quantity without a remainder: *2 and 3 are factors of 6.* **b.** A quantity by which something is multiplied or divided: *increased by a factor of 10.* **4.** *Biol.* A substance, such as a vitamin, that functions in a specific biochemical reaction or bodily process, such as blood coagulation. ►*v. Math.* **1.** To determine the factors of. **2.** To figure: *factor in inflation.* [< Lat., maker.]

fac·to·ry (făk′tə-rē) ►*n., pl.* **-ries** A building or group of buildings in which goods are manufactured; plant.

fac·to·tum (făk-tō′təm) ►*n.* An employee or assistant with a wide range of duties. [< Lat. *fac tōtum,* do everything.]

fac·tu·al (făk′chōō-əl) ►*adj.* Based on or containing facts. —**fac′tu·al·i·ty** (-ăl′ĭ-tē) *n.* —**fac′tu·al·ly** *adv.*

fac·ul·ty (făk′əl-tē) ►*n., pl.* **-ties 1.** An inherent power or ability. **2a.** The teachers in a college, university, or school. **b.** A division of learning at a college or university. [< Lat. *facultās* < *facilis,* easy.]

fad (făd) ►*n.* A briefly popular fashion; craze. [?] —**fad′dist** *n.* —**fad′dish** *adj.*

fade (fād) ►*v.* **fad·ed, fad·ing 1.** To lose or cause to lose brightness or loudness. **2.** To lose strength or freshness; wither. **3.** To disappear gradually; vanish. See Synonyms at **disappear**. [< OFr. *fader.*]

fade-in (fād′ĭn′) ►*n.* A gradual appearance or increase in intensity of an image, light, or sound, as in a cinematic work.

fade-out (fād′out′) or **fade·out** ►*n.* A gradual,

complete reduction in intensity of an image, light, or sound, as in a cinematic work.

fa·er·ie (fā′ə-rē, fâr′ē) ►*n.* **1.** A fairy. **2.** Fairyland. [ME *faierie,* FAIRY.]

Faer·oe Islands (fâr′ō) See **Faroe Islands**.

fag[1] (făg) ►*n.* A drudge. ►*v.* **fagged, fag·ging** To exhaust or work to exhaustion; fatigue. [< *fag,* droop.]

fag[2] (făg) ►*n. Slang* A cigarette. [< FAG END.]

fag end ►*n.* **1.** The frayed end of a length of cloth or rope. **2.** The last and least useful part. [ME *fag.*]

fag·ot also **fag·got** (făg′ət) ►*n.* A bundle of twigs or sticks. [< OProv.] —**fag′ot** *v.*

Fahr. ►*abbr.* Fahrenheit

Fahr·en·heit (făr′ən-hīt′, fä′rən-) ►*adj.* Of or according to a temperature scale that registers the freezing point of water as 32° and the boiling point as 212° at one atmosphere of pressure. See table at **measurement**. [After Gabriel Daniel *Fahrenheit* (1686–1736).]

fa·ience also **fa·ïence** (fī-äns′, -äNS′, fä-) ►*n.* Earthenware decorated with colorful opaque glazes. [After *Faenza,* Italy.]

fail (fāl) ►*v.* **1.** To be deficient or unsuccessful. **2.** To give or receive an unacceptable academic grade. **3.** To decline, weaken, or cease to function. **4.** To disappoint or forsake. **5.** To omit or neglect: *failed to appear.* **6.** To become bankrupt. —*idiom:* **without fail** Absolutely. [ME *failen* < VLat. **fallīre,* deceive.]

fail·ing (fā′lĭng) ►*n.* A minor fault; shortcoming. ►*prep.* In the absence of: *Failing new evidence, the case will be lost.*

fail-safe (fāl′sāf′) ►*adj.* **1.** Compensating automatically for a failure, as of a mechanical system. **2.** Certain not to fail.

fail·ure (fāl′yər) ►*n.* **1.** The act, condition, or fact of failing. **2.** One that fails. **3.** The act or fact of becoming bankrupt.

fain (fān) *Archaic* ►*adv.* Happily; gladly. ►*adj.* **1.** Willing; glad. **2.** Obliged or required. [< OE *fægen,* glad.]

faint (fānt) ►*adj.* **-er, -est 1.** Lacking strength or vigor; feeble. **2a.** Lacking brightness; dim. **b.** Indistinct. **3.** Dizzy and weak. ►*n.* An abrupt, usu. brief loss of consciousness; blackout. ►*v.* To fall into a faint. [< OFr., p.part. of *feindre,* feign.] —**faint′ly** *adv.* —**faint′ness** *n.*

faint-hearted (fānt′här′tĭd) ►*adj.* Lacking conviction or courage; timid. —**faint′-heart′ed·ly** *adv.* —**faint′-heart′ed·ness** *n.*

fair[1] (fâr) ►*adj.* **-er, -est 1.** Beautiful; lovely. **2.** Light in color: *fair hair.* **3.** Clear and sunny. **4.** Just; equitable. **5.** Consistent with rules; permissible. **6.** *Baseball* Passing or landing between the foul lines: *a fair ball.* **7.** Moderately good; average. ►*adv.* In a fair manner; properly. —*idiom:* **fair and square** Just and honest. [ME < OE *fæger.*] —**fair′ness** *n.*

fair[2] (fâr) ►*n.* **1.** A gathering for buying and selling goods; market. **2.** An exhibition, as of farm products or handicrafts, usu. judged competitively. **3.** An exhibition to inform people about a product or business opportunity. [< Lat. *fēriae,* holidays.]

Fair·banks (fâr′băngks′) A city of central AK NNE of Anchorage.

fair·ground (fâr′ground′) ►*n.* A piece of land where fairs are held.

fair·ly (fâr′lē) ►*adv.* **1.** In a fair or just manner;

equitably. **2.** Moderately; rather. **3.** Actually; fully.

fair·mind·ed (fâr′mīn′dĭd) ►*adj.* Just and impartial. —**fair′-mind′ed·ness** *n.*

fair shake ►*n. Informal* A fair chance, as at achieving success.

fair-trade (fâr′trād′) ►*adj.* Of or being trade that respects workers' rights and minimizes environmental damage.

fair·way (fâr′wā′) ►*n.* The mowed part of a golf course from the tee to the green.

fair-weath·er (fâr′wĕth′ər) ►*adj.* Dependable only in good times: *fair-weather friends.*

fair·y (fâr′ē) ►*n., pl.* **-ies** An imaginary being in human form depicted as possessing magical powers. [< OFr. *faerie* < VLat. *Fāta,* goddess of fate.]

fairy tale ►*n.* **1.** A fanciful tale of legendary deeds and creatures, usu. intended for children. **2.** A fanciful story or explanation. —**fair′-y-tale′** *adj.*

fait ac·com·pli (fā′tä-kôɴ-plē′, fĕt′ä-) ►*n., pl.* **faits ac·com·plis** (fā′tä-kôɴ-plē′, -plēz′, fĕt′-ä-) An accomplished deed or fact. [Fr.]

faith (fāth) ►*n.* **1.** Belief in God or in a set of religious doctrines. **2.** A religion. **3.** Confident belief or trust in a person, idea, or thing. See Synonyms at **belief. 4.** Loyalty; allegiance. [< Lat. *fidēs.*] —**faith′less** *adj.*

faith·ful (fāth′fəl) ►*adj.* **1.** Adhering firmly and devotedly; loyal. **2.** Worthy of trust; reliable. **3.** Accurate; true. ►*n., pl.* **-ful** or **-fuls 1.** The practicing members of a religious faith. **2.** The adherents of a cause: *the party faithful.* —**faith′ful·ly** *adv.* —**faith′ful·ness** *n.*

fa·ji·ta (fə-hē′tə) ►*n.* often **fajitas** A dish of grilled strips of marinated meat served in a tortilla, usu. with spicy condiments. [Am.Sp.]

fake (fāk) ►*adj.* Not genuine; fraudulent. ►*n.* One that is not authentic or genuine; a counterfeit, impostor, or sham. ►*v.* **faked, fak·ing 1.** To contrive and present as genuine; counterfeit. **2.** To pretend; feign. **3.** *Sports* To deceive one's opponent with a brief feint or sudden change in direction. [?] —**fak′er** *n.* —**fak′er·y** *n.*

fa·kir (fə-kîr′, fä-, fă-) ►*n.* A Muslim or Hindu religious mendicant, esp. one who performs feats of magic or endurance. [Ar. *faqīr.*]

fa·la·fel (fə-lä′fəl) ►*n.* **1.** A mixture of ground spiced chickpeas. **2.** A fried ball made from such a mixture. [Ar. *falāfil,* pl. of *filfil,* pepper.]

fal·con (făl′kən, fôl′-, fô′kən) ►*n.* Any of various swift hawklike birds of prey with long pointed wings. [< LLat. *falcō.*]

fal·con·ry (făl′kən-rē, fôl′-, fô′kən-) ►*n.* **1.** Hunting of game with falcons. **2.** The art of training falcons for hunting. —**fal′con·er** *n.*

Falk·land Islands (fôk′lənd, fôlk′-) A British territory consisting of a group of islands in the S Atlantic E of the Strait of Magellan.

fall (fôl) ►*v.* **fell** (fĕl), **fall·en** (fô′lən), **fall·ing 1.** To drop freely under the influence of gravity. **2.** To move oneself to a lower position. **3.** To be killed or severely wounded. **4.** To hang down: *Her hair fell in ringlets.* **5.** To come as if by descending: *Night fell on the town.* **6.** To occur at a specified time or place. **7.** To assume an expression of disappointment: *His face fell.* **8.** To be conquered or overthrown. **9.** To decline in status or importance. **10.** To slope downward. **11.** To lessen in amount or degree.

12. To give in to temptation. **13.** To pass into a particular state or condition: *We fell silent.* **14.** To come to rest by chance: *My gaze fell on the letter.* **15.** To be allotted: *The task fell to me.* **16.** To be within the range of something. ►*n.* **1.** The act or an instance of falling. **2.** Something that has fallen: *a fall of hail.* **3a.** An amount that has fallen: *a light fall of rain.* **b.** The distance that something falls. **4.** Autumn. **5. falls** *(takes sing. or pl. v.)* A waterfall. **6.** An overthrow or collapse: *the fall of a government.* **7.** A decline or reduction. **8.** A moral lapse. —*phrasal verbs:* **fall back** To retreat. **fall behind** To fail to keep up with. **fall for 1.** To become infatuated with. **2.** To be deceived or swindled by. **fall in** To take one's place in a military formation. **fall off** To become less; decrease. **fall on** To attack suddenly. **fall out 1.** To quarrel. **2.** To leave a military formation. **fall through** To fail or miscarry. **fall to** To begin energetically. —*idioms:* **fall back on** To rely on. **fall flat** To fail miserably. **fall in with 1.** To agree with. **2.** To associate with. **fall short** To fail to reach or attain. **fall through the cracks** To pass unnoticed. [< OE *feallan.*]

fal·la·cious (fə-lā′shəs) ►*adj.* **1.** Containing or based on a fallacy. **2.** Tending to mislead; deceptive. —**fal·la′cious·ly** *adv.*

fal·la·cy (făl′ə-sē) ►*n., pl.* **-cies 1.** A false idea or notion. **2.** Incorrectness of reasoning or belief. [< Lat. *fallācia,* deceit.]

fall·back (fôl′băk′) ►*n.* A last resort or retreat.

fall guy ►*n. Slang* A scapegoat.

fal·li·ble (făl′ə-bəl) ►*adj.* Capable of making an error. [< Lat. *fallere,* deceive.] —**fal′li·bil′i·ty** *n.* —**fal′li·bly** *adv.*

fall·ing-out (fô′lĭng-out′) ►*n., pl.* **fall·ings-out** or **fall·ing-outs** A quarrel.

fall·ing star (fô′lĭng) ►*n.* See **meteor.**

fal·lo·pi·an tube also **Fal·lo·pi·an tube** (fə-lō′pē-ən) ►*n.* Either of a pair of slender ducts through which ova pass from the ovaries to the uterus in the female reproductive system of humans and higher mammals. [After Gabriele *Fallopio* (1523–62).]

fall·out (fôl′out′) ►*n.* **1a.** The slow descent of minute particles of radioactive debris in the atmosphere after a nuclear explosion. **b.** These particles. **2.** An incidental result or side effect: *political fallout.*

fal·low (făl′ō) ►*adj.* **1.** Plowed but left unseeded during a growing season. **2.** Inactive. [< OE *fealh,* fallow land.]

false (fôls) ►*adj.* **fals·er, fals·est 1.** Contrary to fact or truth. **2.** Unfaithful or disloyal. **3.** Not real; artificial. **4.** *Mus.* Of incorrect pitch. [< Lat. *falsus,* p.part. of *fallere,* deceive.] —**fal′si·ty** (fôl′sĭ-tē) *adv.* —**false′ly** *adv.* —**false′ness** *n.*

false alarm ►*n.* **1.** An emergency alarm set off unnecessarily. **2.** A groundless warning.

false arrest ►*n.* Unlawful physical restraint of a person, esp. under asserted legal authority.

false-heart·ed (fôls′här′tĭd) ►*adj.* Deceitful.

false·hood (fôls′hŏŏd′) ►*n.* **1.** An untrue statement. **2.** The practice of lying. **3.** Lack of conformity to truth or fact; inaccuracy.

fal·set·to (fôl-sĕt′ō) ►*n., pl.* **-tos** A voice in an upper register beyond its normal range. [Ital.] —**fal·set′to** *adv.*

fal·si·fy (fôl′sə-fī′) ►*v.* **-fied, -fy·ing 1.** To state untruthfully. **2.** To alter (e.g., a document) so as to deceive. **3.** To counterfeit; forge. **4.** To show to be false. [< LLat. *falsificāre*.] —**fal′si·fi·ca′·tion** *n.* —**fal′si·fi′er** *n.*

fal·ter (fôl′tər) ►*v.* **1.** To weaken or be unsteady in purpose or action; waver. **2.** To stammer. **3.** To stumble. ►*n.* Unsteadiness in speech or action. [ME *falteren*, stagger.] —**fal′ter·er** *n.* —**fal′ter·ing·ly** *adv.*

fame (fām) ►*n.* Great reputation and recognition; renown. [< Lat. *fāma*.] —**famed** *adj.*

fa·mil·iar (fə-mĭl′yər) ►*adj.* **1.** Often encountered; common. **2.** Having knowledge of something. **3.** Intimate. **4.** Unduly forward; bold. ►*n.* **1.** A close friend or associate. **2.** An attendant spirit, often in animal form. [< Lat. *familiāris*, of the family.] —**fa·mil′iar·ly** *adv.*

fa·mil·iar·i·ty (fə-mĭl′yăr′ĭ-tē, -mĭl′ē-ăr′-) ►*n.,* *pl.* -**ties 1.** Considerable acquaintance with or knowledge of something. **2.** Close friendship; intimacy. **3.** An excessively familiar act; impropriety.

fa·mil·iar·ize (fə-mĭl′yə-rīz′) ►*v.* -**ized, -iz·ing** To make acquainted with. —**fa·mil′iar·i·za′tion** *n.*

fam·i·ly (făm′ə-lē, făm′lē) ►*n.,* *pl.* -**lies 1.** Parents and their children. **2.** The members of one household. **3.** A group of persons related by blood or marriage. See Usage Note at **collective noun. 4.** A group of like things; class. **5.** *Biol.* The category ranking below an order and above a genus in the hierarchy of taxonomic classification. **6.** *Ling.* A group of languages descended from the same parent language. [< Lat. *familia*, household.] —**fa·mil′ial** (fə-mĭl′yəl) *adj.*

family leave ►*n.* A usu. unpaid absence from work granted for taking care of a family member, such as a baby or sick parent.

family name ►*n.* See **surname.**

family planning ►*n.* The regulation of the number and spacing of children in a family through birth-control techniques.

family tree ►*n.* A genealogical diagram of a family's ancestry.

fam·ine (făm′ĭn) ►*n.* **1.** A drastic, wide-reaching food shortage. **2.** A drastic lack; dearth. [< OFr. < Lat. *famēs*, hunger.]

fam·ish (făm′ĭsh) ►*v.* To starve. [< VLat. *affamāre*, be hungry.] —**fam′ished** *adj.*

fa·mous (fā′məs) ►*adj.* **1.** Well or widely known. **2.** First-rate; excellent. [< Lat. *fāmōsus* < *fāma*, fame.] —**fa′mous·ly** *adv.*
Syns: celebrated, eminent, illustrious, notable, noted, preeminent, renowned **Ant:** obscure

fan¹ (făn) ►*n.* **1.** An electrical device that rotates rigid vanes in order to move air, as for cooling. **2.** A hand-held, usu. wedge-shaped device that is waved to create a cool breeze. **3.** Something resembling an open hand-held fan. ►*v.* **fanned, fan·ning 1.** To direct a current of air upon, esp. in order to cool. **2.** To stir up: *fanned resentment.* **3.** To spread: *fanned out on their search.* [< Lat. *vannus*.]

fan² (făn) ►*n. Informal* An ardent devotee; enthusiast. [Short for FANATIC.]

fa·nat·ic (fə-năt′ĭk) ►*n.* One having extreme, unreasoning enthusiasm, as for a cause. ►*adj.* Fanatical. [< Lat. *fānum*, temple.] —**fa·nat′·i·cal** *adj.* —**fa·nat′i·cal·ly** *adv.* —**fa·nat′i·cism** *n.*

fan·ci·er (făn′sē-ər) ►*n.* One who has a special enthusiasm or interest, as for raising a specific plant or animal.

fan·ci·ful (făn′sĭ-fəl) ►*adj.* **1.** Created in the fancy; imaginary: *a fanciful story.* **2.** Tending to indulge in fancy. **3.** Quaint or whimsical in design. —**fan′ci·ful·ly** *adv.*

fan·cy (făn′sē) ►*adj.* -**ci·er, -ci·est 1a.** Highly decorated; elaborate: *a fancy hat.* **b.** Complex or intricate: *fancy footwork.* **2.** Stylish and expensive: *a fancy restaurant.* **3.** Of superior grade: *fancy preserves.* ►*n., pl.* -**cies 1.** Imagination, esp. of a whimsical or fantastic nature. **2.** A notion or whim. **3.** A capricious liking or inclination. ►*v.* -**cied, -cy·ing 1.** To imagine. **2.** To be fond of. **3.** To suppose; guess. [< ME *fantsy*, FANTASY.] —**fan′ci·ly** *adv.* —**fan′ci·ness** *n.*

fancy dress ►*n.* A masquerade costume.

fan·cy-free (făn′sē-frē′) ►*adj.* **1.** Having no restrictions; carefree. **2.** Not in love; unattached.

fan·cy·work (făn′sē-wûrk′) ►*n.* Decorative needlework, such as embroidery.

fan·dan·go (făn-dăng′gō) ►*n., pl.* -**gos** A lively Spanish or Latin-American dance. [Sp.]

fan·fare (făn′fâr′) ►*n.* **1.** A flourish of trumpets. **2.** A spectacular public display. [Fr.]

fang (făng) ►*n.* A long pointed tooth, esp.: **a.** A hollow, poison-injecting tooth of a venomous snake. **b.** A canine tooth of a carnivorous animal. [< OE, what is taken.] —**fanged** *adj.*

fan·light (făn′līt′) ►*n.* A semicircular or semielliptical window, often with leading arranged like the ribs of a fan.

fanlight

fan·ny (făn′ē) ►*n., pl.* -**nies** *Slang* The buttocks.

fan·tail (făn′tāl′) ►*n.* **1.** A fanlike tail or end. **2.** The stern overhang of a ship.

fan·ta·sia (făn-tā′zhə, -zhē-ə, făn′tə-zē′ə) ►*n. Mus.* A freeform composition. [Ital.]

fan·ta·size (făn′tə-sīz′) ►*v.* -**sized, -siz·ing 1.** To indulge in fantasies. **2.** To imagine.

fan·tas·tic (făn-tăs′tĭk) also **fan·tas·ti·cal** (-tĭ-kəl) ►*adj.* **1.** Strange in conception or appearance. **2.** Unreal or illusory. **3.** Superb. [< Gk. *phantastikos*, creating mental images.] —**fan·tas′ti·cal·ly** *adv.*

fan·ta·sy (făn′tə-sē, -zē) ►*n., pl.* -**sies 1.** The creative imagination. **2.** A product of the fancy; illusion. **3.** A delusion. **4.** Fiction marked by highly fanciful or supernatural elements. **5.** A daydream. **6.** *Mus.* See **fantasia.** [< Gk. *phantasia*, appearance.] —**fan′ta·sy** *v.*

fan·zine (făn′zēn) ►*n.* An amateur-produced

fan magazine. [FAN² + (MAGA)ZINE.]

FAQ (făk) ►*n.* A list of frequently asked questions and their answers. [*f(requently) a(sked) q(uestions).*]

far (fär) ►*adv.* **far·ther** (fär′thər), **far·thest** (fär′thĭst) or **fur·ther** (fûr′thər), **fur·thest** (fûr′thĭst) **1.** To, from, or at considerable distance. **2.** To or at a specific distance, degree, or position. **3.** To a considerable degree; much: *felt far better.* ►*adj.* **farther, farthest** or **further, furthest 1.** Distant in space or time: *a far country.* **2.** More distant or remote: *the far corner.* —*idioms:* **as far as** To the extent that. **by far** To the most extreme degree. **far and away** By a great margin. **far and wide** Everywhere. **far cry 1.** Very different: *bland food that is a far cry from gourmet fare.* **2.** A long way. **far from** Not at all: *far from satisfied.* **so far** Up to now. [< OE *feor*, distant.]

far·ad (făr′əd, -ăd′) ►*n.* The unit of capacitance equal to that of a capacitor having an opposite charge of 1 coulomb on each plate and a potential difference of 1 volt. [After Michael *Faraday* (1791–1867).]

far·a·way (fär′ə-wā′) ►*adj.* **1.** Very distant; remote. **2.** Abstracted; dreamy.

farce (färs) ►*n.* **1.** A humorous play having a highly improbable plot and exaggerated characters. **2.** A ludicrous, empty show; mockery. [< Lat. *farcīre*, to stuff.] —**far′ci·cal** *adj.* —**far′ci·cal·ly** *adv.*

fare (fâr) ►*v.* **fared, far·ing 1.** To get along. **2.** To travel; go. ►*n.* **1.** A transportation charge. **2.** A passenger transported for a fee. **3.** Food and drink. [< OE *faran*.] —**far′er** *n.*

Far East The region encompassing East Asia, Southeast Asia, and sometimes South Asia. —**Far Eastern** *adj.*

fare·well (fâr-wĕl′) ►*interj.* Used to express goodbye. ►*n.* **1.** A goodbye. **2.** The act of leave-taking.

far-fetched (fär′fĕcht′) ►*adj.* Implausible.

far-flung (fär′flŭng′) ►*adj.* **1.** Remote; distant. **2.** Widely distributed; wide-ranging.

fa·ri·na (fə-rē′nə) ►*n.* Fine meal, as of cereal grain, often used as a cooked cereal or in puddings. [< Lat. *farīna.*]

far·i·na·ceous (făr′ə-nā′shəs) ►*adj.* **1.** Made from or containing starch. **2.** Mealy or powdery in texture.

farm (färm) ►*n.* **1.** A tract of land on which crops or animals are raised. **2.** An area of water used for raising aquatic animals: *a trout farm.* **3a.** A place where a group of similar devices or storage containers are set up: *a server farm; a tank farm.* **b.** A facility for the collection of a particular type of energy: *a wind farm.* ►*v.* **1.** To raise crops or livestock. **2.** To use (land) for this purpose. —*phrasal verb:* **farm out** To send out (work) to be done elsewhere. [< OFr. *ferme*, leased land.] —**farm′er** *n.* —**farm′ing** *n.*

farm hand ►*n.* A hired farm laborer.

farm·house (färm′hous′) ►*n.* A dwelling on a farm.

farm·land (färm′lănd′, -lənd) ►*n.* An expanse of land suitable or used for farming.

farm·stead (färm′stĕd′) ►*n.* A farm, including its land and buildings.

farm·yard (färm′yärd′) ►*n.* An area surrounded by or adjacent to farm buildings.

far·o (fâr′ō) ►*n.* A card game in which the players bet on the top card of the dealer's pack. [Alteration of PHARAOH.]

Far·oe Islands or **Faer·oe Islands** (fâr′ō) A Danish territory consisting of a group of islands in the N Atlantic between Iceland and the Shetland Is. —**Far′o·ese′** *adj. & n.*

far-off (fär′ôf′, -ŏf′) ►*adj.* Remote in space or time; distant.

far-out (fär′out′) ►*adj. Slang* Extremely unconventional.

far·ra·go (fə-rä′gō, -rā′-) ►*n., pl.* **-goes** An assortment or medley; conglomeration. [Lat. *farrāgō.*]

far-reach·ing (fär′rē′chĭng) ►*adj.* Having a wide range, influence, or effect.

far·ri·er (făr′ē-ər) ►*n.* One who shoes horses. [Obsolete Fr. *ferrier*, ult. < Lat. *ferrum*, iron.]

far·row (făr′ō) ►*n.* A litter of pigs. ►*v.* To give birth to a farrow. [< OE *fearh*, pig.]

far·see·ing (fär′sē′ĭng) ►*adj.* Foresighted.

far·sight·ed or **far-sight·ed** (fär′sī′tĭd) ►*adj.* **1.** Able to see distant objects better than objects at close range. **2.** Prudent; foresighted. —**far′sight′ed·ness** *n.*

far·ther (fär′thər) ►*adv.* Comp. of **far. 1.** To or at a more distant point. **2.** To or at a more advanced point or stage. **3.** To a greater extent or degree. ►*adj.* Comp. of **far.** More distant; remoter. [ME, var. of *further*, FURTHER.]

far·ther·most (fär′thər-mōst′) ►*adj.* Most distant; farthest.

far·thest (fär′thĭst) ►*adj.* Superl. of **far.** Most remote or distant. ►*adv.* Superl. of **far. 1.** To or at the most distant or remote point. **2.** To or at the most advanced point or stage. **3.** By the greatest extent or degree. [ME *farthest.*]

far·thing (fär′thĭng) ►*n.* **1.** A coin formerly used in Great Britain worth one fourth of a penny. **2.** Something of little value. [< OE *fēorthung.*]

far·thin·gale (fär′thĭn-gāl′, -thĭng-) ►*n.* A support, such as a hoop, worn beneath a skirt by European women in the 1500s and 1600s. [< OSpan. *verdugado.*]

fas·ci·cle (făs′ĭ-kəl) ►*n.* **1.** A small bundle. **2.** One of the parts of a book published in separate sections. [Lat. *fasciculus.*] —**fas′ci·cled** *adj.*

fas·ci·nate (făs′ə-nāt′) ►*v.* **-nat·ed, -nat·ing** To hold an intense interest or attraction for. See Synonyms at **charm.** [< Lat. *fascinum*, evil spell.] —**fas′ci·na′tion** *n.* —**fas′ci·na′tor** *n.*

fas·cism (făsh′ĭz′əm) ►*n.* **1.** often **Fascism a.** Totalitarianism marked by right-wing dictatorship and bellicose nationalism. **b.** A political philosophy or movement advocating such a system of government. **2.** Oppressive, dictatorial control. [< Ital. *fascio*, group.] —**fas′cist** *adj. & n.* —**fas·cis′tic** (fə-shĭs′tĭk) *adj.*

fash·ion (făsh′ən) ►*n.* **1.** The prevailing style or custom, as in dress. **2.** Something, such as a garment, that is in the current mode. **3.** Manner; way. **4.** Kind; sort. ►*v.* **1.** To give shape or form to; make. **2.** To adapt, as to a purpose or an occasion. —*idiom:* **after a fashion** To a limited extent. [< Lat. *factiō*, a making.] —**fash′ion·er** *n.*

fash·ion·a·ble (făsh′ə-nə-bəl) ►*adj.* **1.** In the current style; stylish. **2.** Associated with persons of fashion. —**fash′ion·a·ble·ness** *n.* —**fash′ion·a·bly** *adv.*

Syns: *chic, in, sharp, smart, stylish, swanky, trendy* **adj.**

fast¹ (făst) ►*adj.* **-er, -est 1.** Acting or moving quickly; swift. **2.** Accomplished in little time. **3.** Indicating a time ahead of the actual time: *The clock is fast.* **4.** Adapted to or suitable for speed: *a fast running track.* **5.** Flouting moral standards; wild. **6.** Resistant: *fast colors.* **7.** Firmly fixed or fastened. **8.** Firm in loyalty: *fast friends.* ►*adv.* **1.** Securely; tightly. **2.** Deeply: *fast asleep.* **3.** Rapidly; quickly. **4.** In quick succession: *New ideas followed fast.* **5.** In a dissipated, immoderate way: *living fast.* [< OE *fæst,* firm, fixed.]

fast² (făst) ►*v.* To abstain from food, esp. as a religious discipline. ►*n.* The act or a period of abstention from food. [< OE *fæstan.*]

fast·back (făst′băk′) ►*n.* An automobile having a curving downward slope from roof to rear.

fas·ten (făs′ən) ►*v.* **1.** To attach or become attached to something else; join; connect. **2.** To make fast or secure; close. **3.** To fix or direct steadily: *fastened his gaze on the clock.* [< OE *fæstnian.*] **—fas′ten·er** *n.* **—fas′ten·ing** *n.*
Syns: *anchor, fix, moor, secure* **v.**

fast food ►*n.* Inexpensive food, such as hamburgers, prepared and served quickly. **—fast′-food′** *adj.*

fast-for·ward (făst-fôr′wərd) ►*n.* A control on an audio or video player that rapidly advances the recording. **—fast-for′ward** *v.*

fas·tid·i·ous (fă-stĭd′ē-əs, fə-) ►*adj.* **1.** Attentive to detail. **2.** Difficult to please; exacting. **3.** Excessively scrupulous, esp. in matters of propriety. [< Lat. *fastīdium,* squeamishness.] **—fas·tid′i·ous·ness** *n.*

fast·ness (făst′nĭs) ►*n.* **1.** Rapidity; swiftness. **2.** Firmness; security. **3.** A secure or fortified place.

fast-talk (făst′tôk′) ►*v.* To persuade, mislead, or get with smooth talk. **—fast′-talk′er** *n.*

fast track ►*n.* A course leading to rapid advancement or change. **—fast′-track′** *adj.* **—fast track′er** *n.*

fat (făt) ►*n.* **1a.** Any of various soft solid or semisolid organic compounds occurring widely in animal and plant tissue and often serving the purpose of energy storage. **b.** Organic tissue containing such substances. **c.** A solidified animal or vegetable oil. **2.** Obesity; corpulence. **3.** Unnecessary excess. ►*adj.* **fat·ter, fat·test 1.** Having much flesh. **2.** Full of fat or oil; greasy. **3.** Fertile or productive; rich. **4.** Having an abundance; well-stocked: *a fat larder.* **5a.** Lucrative or rewarding: *a fat promotion.* **b.** Prosperous; wealthy: *grew fat on profits.* **6.** Thick; large: *a fat book.* **—idiom: fat chance** *Slang* Little or no chance. [< OE *fætt,* fatted.] **—fat′ness** *n.* **—fat′ty** *adj.*

fa·tal (fāt′l) ►*adj.* **1.** Causing or capable of causing death. **2.** Causing destruction. **3.** Of decisive importance; fateful. [< Lat. *fātālis* < *fātum,* FATE.] **—fa′tal·ly** *adv.*

fa·tal·ism (fāt′l-ĭz′əm) ►*n.* The doctrine that all events are determined by fate and are therefore unalterable. **—fa′tal·ist** *n.* **—fa′tal·is′tic** *adj.* **—fa′tal·is′ti·cal·ly** *adv.*

fa·tal·i·ty (fā-tăl′ĭ-tē, fə-) ►*n., pl.* **-ties 1.** A death resulting from an accident or disaster. **2.** The quality of being determined by fate.

fat·back (făt′băk′) ►*n.* Salt-cured fat from the upper part of a side of pork.

fat cat ►*n. Slang* A wealthy and privileged person.

fate (fāt) ►*n.* **1.** The supposed force, principle, or power that predetermines events. **2a.** The inevitable events predestined by this force. **b.** A final result or consequence; outcome: *What was the fate of your project?* **3.** An unfavorable outcome in life; doom or death. **4. Fates** *Gk. & Rom. Myth.* The three goddesses, Clotho, Lachesis, and Atropos, who control human destiny. [< Lat. *fātum* < p.part. of *fārī,* speak.]

fat·ed (fā′tĭd) ►*adj.* **1.** Predetermined. **2.** Doomed.

fate·ful (fāt′fəl) ►*adj.* **1.** Being of great consequence; momentous. **2.** Controlled by or as if by fate. **3.** Bringing death or disaster; fatal. **4.** Ominously prophetic; portentous. **—fate′ful·ly** *adv.* **—fate′ful·ness** *n.*

fath or **fath.** ►*abbr.* fathom

fat·head (făt′hĕd′) ►*n. Slang* A stupid person. **—fat′head′ed** *adj.*

fa·ther (fä′thər) ►*n.* **1.** A man who begets or raises a child. **2.** A male ancestor. **3.** A man who creates or originates something: *the founding fathers of the nation.* **4.** One of the leading men, as of a city: *the town fathers.* **5. Father** God. **6.** A title used for a male priest in some Christian churches. ►*v.* To beget; sire. [< OE *fæder.*] **—fa′ther·hood′** *n.* **—fa′ther·li·ness** *n.* **—fa′ther·ly** *adj.*

father figure ►*n.* An older man who elicits the emotions usu. reserved for a father.

fa·ther-in-law (fä′thər-ĭn-lô′) ►*n., pl.* **fa·thers-in-law** (-ərz-) The father of one's spouse.

fa·ther·land (fä′thər-lănd′) ►*n.* One's native or ancestral land.

fa·ther·less (fä′thər-lĭs) ►*adj.* **1.** Having no living father. **2.** Having no known father. **—fa′ther·less·ness** *n.*

fath·om (făth′əm) ►*n., pl.* **-om** or **-oms** A unit of length equal to 6 ft (1.83 m), used principally in the measurement of marine depths. ►*v.* **1.** To determine the depth of; sound. **2.** To comprehend. [< OE *fæthm,* outstretched arms.] **—fath′om·a·ble** *adj.*

fath·om·less (făth′əm-lĭs) ►*adj.* **1.** Too deep to be fathomed or measured. **2.** Too obscure or complicated to be understood.

fa·tigue (fə-tēg′) ►*n.* **1.** Physical or mental weariness resulting from exertion. **2.** The weakening of a material, such as metal or wood, resulting from prolonged stress. **3. fatigues** Clothing worn by military personnel for labor or field duty. ►*v.* **-tigued, -tigu·ing** To tire or weaken. [< Lat. *fatīgāre,* to fatigue.] **—fat′i·ga·ble** (făt′ĭ-gə-bəl) *adj.*

fat·ten (făt′n) ►*v.* To make or become plump or fat. **—fat′ten·er** *n.*

fatty acid ►*n.* Any of a large group of organic acids, esp. those found in animal and vegetable fats and oils, having the general formula $C_nH_{2n+1}COOH$.

fa·tu·i·ty (fə-tōō′ĭ-tē, -tyōō′-) ►*n.* Smug stupidity; utter foolishness.

fat·u·ous (făch′ōō-əs) ►*adj.* Smugly and unconsciously foolish. [< Lat. *fatuus.*] **—fat′u·ous·ly** *adv.* **—fat′u·ous·ness** *n.*

fat·wa (făt′wä′) ►*n.* A ruling issued by an Islamic legal scholar. [Ar. *fatwā.*]

fau·cet (fô′sĭt) ►*n.* A device for regulating the

flow of a liquid, as from a pipe. [< OFr. *fausser*, break in.]

Faulk·ner (fôk′nər), **William** 1897–1962. Amer. writer. —**Faulk·ner′i·an** (-nîr′ē-ən) *adj.*

fault (fôlt) ►*n.* **1.** A character weakness, esp. a minor one. **2.** A mistake; error. **3.** Responsibility for a mistake or offense. **4.** *Geol.* A fracture in the continuity of a rock formation caused by a shifting or dislodging of the earth's crust, in which adjacent surfaces are differentially displaced parallel to the plane of fracture. **5.** *Sports* A bad service, as in tennis. ►*v.* **1.** To find error or defect in; criticize or blame. **2.** To commit a mistake or an error. **3.** *Geol.* To produce a fault in; fracture. —*idioms:* **at fault** Guilty. **find fault** To criticize. **to a fault** To an excessive degree. [< Lat. *fallere*, to deceive, fail.] —**fault′i·ly** *adv.* —**fault′i·ness** *n.* —**fault′y** *adj.*

fault·find·ing (fôlt′fīn′dĭng) ►*n.* Petty or nagging criticism; carping. ►*adj.* Disposed to find fault; critical. —**fault′find′er** *n.*

fault·less (fôlt′lĭs) ►*adj.* Being without fault. See Synonyms at **perfect.** —**fault′less·ly** *adv.* —**fault′less·ness** *n.*

faun (fôn) ►*n. Rom. Myth.* Any of numerous rural deities represented as part man and part goat. [< Lat. *Faunus*, Roman god of nature.]

fau·na (fô′nə) ►*n., pl.* **-nas** or **-nae** (-nē′) Animals, esp. of a region or period. [< Lat. *Fauna*, Roman goddess of nature.] —**fau′nal** *adj.*

Faust (foust) also **Faus·tus** (fou′stəs, fô′-) ►*n.* A magician and alchemist in German legend who sells his soul to the devil for pleasure and knowledge. —**Faust′i·an** (fou′stē-ən) *adj.*

fau·vism (fō′vĭz′əm) ►*n.* An early 20th-cent. movement in painting marked by the use of bold, often distorted forms and vivid colors. [Fr. *fauvisme* < *fauve*, wild animal.] —**fau′vist** *adj.*

faux (fō) ►*adj.* Artificial; fake: *faux pearls.* [Fr.]

faux pas (fō pä′) ►*n., pl.* **faux pas** (fō päz′) A social blunder. [Fr.]

fa·va bean (fä′və) ►*n.* See **broad bean.** [Ital. *fava* < Lat. *faba*, broad bean.]

fa·vor (fā′vər) ►*n.* **1.** A gracious, friendly, or obliging act that is freely granted. **2a.** Friendly regard; approval or support. **b.** A state of being held in such regard. **3.** Unfair partiality; favoritism. **4a.** A privilege or concession. **b. favors** Permission to engage in sexual activity, esp. as granted by a woman. **5.** A small gift given to each guest at a party. **6.** Advantage; benefit: *an error in our favor.* ►*v.* **1.** To perform a service for; oblige. See Synonyms at **oblige. 2.** To treat or regard with approval or support. **3.** To be advantageous to: *a climate that favors conifers.* **4.** To be gentle with: *favored my wounded leg.* **5.** *Regional* To resemble: *She favors her father.* —*idiom:* **in favor of 1.** In support of. **2.** To the advantage of. [< Lat.]

fa·vor·a·ble (fā′vər-ə-bəl, fāv′rə-) ►*adj.* **1.** Advantageous; helpful: *favorable winds.* **2.** Encouraging; propitious: *a favorable diagnosis.* **3.** Manifesting approval; commendatory: *a favorable report.* **4.** Winning approval; pleasing: *a favorable impression.* **5.** Granting what has been requested. —**fa′vor·a·ble·ness** *n.* —**fa′vor·a·bly** *adv.*

fa·vor·ite (fā′vər-ĭt, fāv′rĭt) ►*n.* **1a.** One enjoying special favor or regard. **b.** One trusted or preferred above others, esp. by a superior. **2.** A competitor regarded as most likely to win. [< OItal. *favorito,* p.part. of *favorire,* to favor.] —**fa′vor·ite** *adj.*

favorite son ►*n.* A man favored for nomination as a presidential candidate by his own state delegates at a national political convention.

fa·vor·it·ism (fā′vər-ĭ-tĭz′əm, fāv′rĭ-) ►*n.* A display of partiality toward a favored person or group.

Fawkes (fôks), **Guy** 1570–1606. English Gunpowder Plot conspirator.

fawn[1] (fôn) ►*v.* **1.** To exhibit affection or attempt to please, as a dog does. **2.** To seek favor or attention by obsequiousness. [< OE *fagnian,* rejoice < *fægen,* glad.] —**fawn′er** *n.* —**fawn′ing·ly** *adv.*

 Syns: bootlick, kowtow, slaver, toady, truckle v.

fawn[2] (fôn) ►*n.* **1.** A young deer. **2.** A grayish yellow brown. [< OFr. *faon,* young animal < Lat. *fētus,* offspring.]

fax (făks) ►*n.* **1.** A fax machine. **2.** A document transmitted or received by a fax machine. ►*v.* To transmit (a document) by electronic means. [Alteration of FACSIMILE.]

fax machine ►*n.* A device that sends and receives copies of documents over telephone lines.

fay (fā) ►*n.* A fairy or elf. [< OFr. *fae;* see FAIRY.]

faze (fāz) ►*v.* **fazed, faz·ing** To disconcert. See Synonyms at **embarrass.** [< OE *fēsian,* drive away.]

FBI ►*abbr.* Federal Bureau of Investigation

FCC ►*abbr.* Federal Communications Commission

F clef ►*n.* See **bass clef.**

FDA ►*abbr.* Food and Drug Administration

FDIC ►*abbr.* Federal Deposit Insurance Corporation

fe·al·ty (fē′əl-tē) ►*n., pl.* **-ties 1.** The fidelity owed by a vassal to his feudal lord. **2.** Faithfulness; allegiance. See Synonyms at **fidelity.** [< Lat. *fidēlitās,* faithfulness.]

fear (fîr) ►*n.* **1a.** An unpleasant feeling of agitation caused by the presence or perception of danger. **b.** A state marked by this feeling. **2.** A feeling of anxiety or apprehension. **3.** A reason for dread or apprehension. **4.** Reverence or awe, as toward a deity. ►*v.* **1.** To be afraid of. **2.** To be apprehensive about. **3.** To expect: *I fear you are wrong.* **4.** To be in awe of. [< OE *fǣr,* danger.] —**fear′er** *n.* —**fear′less** *adj.* —**fear′less·ly** *adv.* —**fear′less·ness** *n.*

fear·ful (fîr′fəl) ►*adj.* **1a.** Experiencing fear; frightened. **b.** Timid; nervous. **2.** Indicating anxiety or terror. **3.** Causing or capable of causing fear; frightening: *a fearful howl.* **4.** Extreme, as in degree or extent. —**fear′ful·ly** *adv.* —**fear′ful·ness** *n.*

fear·some (fîr′səm) ►*adj.* **1.** Causing or capable of causing fear. **2.** Fearful; timid. —**fear′some·ly** *adv.* —**fear′some·ness** *n.*

fea·si·ble (fē′zə-bəl) ►*adj.* **1.** Capable of being accomplished or brought about. **2.** Capable of being used successfully. [< OFr. *faire, fais-,* do.] —**fea′si·bil′i·ty** *n.* —**fea′si·bly** *adv.*

feast (fēst) ►*n.* **1.** A large elaborate meal; banquet. **2.** A religious festival. ►*v.* **1.** To entertain or feed sumptuously. **2.** To eat heartily. **3.** To experience something with gratification or delight. —*idiom:* **feast (one's) eyes on** To be delighted by the sight of. [< Lat. *fēstum.*] —**feast'er** *n.*

feat (fēt) ►*n.* A notable act or deed, esp. of courage. [< Lat. *factum.*]
    Syns: *achievement, exploit, masterstroke* **n.**

feath·er (fĕth'ər) ►*n.* **1.** One of the light, flat, hollow-shafted growths forming the plumage of birds. **2.** Character, kind, or nature: *friends of a different feather.* ►*v.* **1.** To cover, dress, or decorate with or as if with feathers. **2.** To fit (an arrow) with a feather. **3.** To turn (an oar blade) almost horizontal as it is carried back after each stroke. **4.** To alter the pitch of (a propeller) so that the chords of the blades are parallel with the line of flight. —*idioms:* **feather in (one's) cap** An act or deed to one's credit. **feather (one's) nest** To grow wealthy esp. by abusing a position of trust. [< OE *fether.*] —**feath'er·y** *adj.*

feather bed ►*n.* A mattress stuffed with feathers.

feath·er·bed·ding (fĕth'ər-bĕd'ĭng) ►*n.* The hiring of more workers than necessary or the limiting of worker productivity in order to allow employment of more persons. —**feath'·er·bed'** *v.*

feath·er·brain (fĕth'ər-brān') ►*n.* A flighty or empty-headed person. —**feath'er·brained'** *adj.*

feath·er·edge (fĕth'ər-ĕj') ►*n.* A thin fragile edge, esp. of a tapered board.

feath·er·stitch (fĕth'ər-stĭch') ►*n.* An embroidery stitch that produces a decorative zigzag line. —**feath'er·stitch'** *v.*

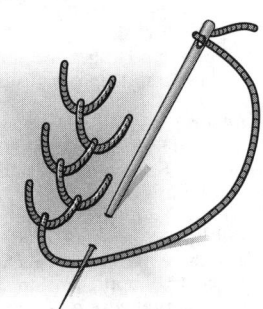

featherstitch

feath·er·weight (fĕth'ər-wāt') ►*n.* A boxer weighing from 119 to 126 lbs., between a bantamweight and a lightweight.

fea·ture (fē'chər) ►*n.* **1a.** Any of the distinct parts of the face, as the eyes or mouth. **b.** often **features** The overall appearance of the face. **2.** A prominent or distinctive quality or characteristic. **3a.** The main film presentation at a theater. **b.** A full-length movie. **4.** A prominent article or story in a newspaper or periodical. **5.** An item offered as an inducement. ►*v.* -**tured,** -**tur·ing 1.** To include as a prominent part or characteristic. **2.** To publicize or make prominent. [< Lat. *factūra,* a making.]

feb·rile (fĕb'rəl, fē'brəl) ►*adj.* Relating to or having a fever. [< Lat. *febris,* fever.]

Feb·ru·ar·y (fĕb'rōō-ĕr'ē, fĕb'yōō-) ►*n.,* pl. -**ies** The 2nd month of the Gregorian calendar. See table at **calendar.** [< Lat. *Februārius.*]

fe·ces (fē'sēz) ►*pl.n.* Waste eliminated from the bowels; excrement. [< Lat. *faex, faec-,* dregs.] —**fe'cal** (fēkəl) *adj.*

feck·less (fĕk'lĭs) ►*adj.* **1.** Careless; irresponsible. **2.** Feeble or ineffective. [Sc. *feck,* effect + –LESS.] —**feck'less·ly** *adv.* —**feck'less·ness** *n.*

fe·cund (fē'kənd, fĕk'ənd) ►*adj.* Capable of producing offspring or vegetation; fruitful. See Synonyms at **fertile.** [< Lat. *fēcundus.*] —**fe·cun'di·ty** (fĭ-kŭn'dĭ-tē) *n.*

fed (fĕd) ►*v.* P.t. and p.part. of **feed.**

fed. ►*abbr.* **1.** federal **2.** federation

fed·er·al (fĕd'ər-əl, fĕd'rəl) ►*adj.* **1.** Relating to or being a form of government in which a union of states recognizes a central authority while retaining certain powers of government. **2. Federal** Of or loyal to the Union cause during the American Civil War. **3.** often **Federal** Of or being the central government of the US. ►*n.* **1. Federal** A Union soldier or supporter during the American Civil War. **2.** often **Federal** A federal agent or official. [< Lat. *foedus, foeder-,* league.] —**fed'er·al·ly** *adv.*

fed·er·al·ism (fĕd'ər-ə-lĭz'əm, fĕd'rə-) ►*n.* **1.** A system of federal government. **2.** Advocacy of such a system of government. **3. Federalism** The doctrine of the Federalist Party.

fed·er·al·ist (fĕd'ər-ə-lĭst, fĕd'rə-) ►*n.* **1.** An advocate of federalism. **2. Federalist** A member of a US political party of the 1790s advocating a strong federal government. —**fed'er·al·ist** *adj.*

fed·er·al·ize (fĕd'ər-ə-līz', fĕd'rə-) ►*v.* -**ized,** -**iz·ing 1.** To unite in a federal union. **2.** To put under federal control. —**fed'er·al·i·za'tion** *n.*

fed·er·ate (fĕd'ə-rāt') ►*v.* -**at·ed,** -**at·ing** To join or unite in a league, federal union, or similar association. [Lat. *foederāre.*] —**fed'er·a'tion** *n.*

fe·do·ra (fĭ-dôr'ə) ►*n.* A soft felt hat with a fairly low crown creased lengthwise and a flexible brim. [After *Fédora,* a play by Victorien Sardou (1831–1908).]

fed up ►*adj.* Unable or unwilling to put up with something any longer.

fee (fē) ►*n.* **1.** A fixed sum charged for a privilege. **2.** A charge for professional services. **3.** *Law* An inherited or heritable estate in land. **4.** In feudal law, an estate granted by a lord to a vassal on condition of homage and service. [< OFr. *fie, fief,* of Gmc. orig.]

fee·ble (fē'bəl) ►*adj.* -**bler,** -**blest 1.** Lacking strength; weak. **2.** Lacking vigor, force, or effectiveness. [< Lat. *flēbilis,* lamentable.] —**fee'ble·ness** *n.* —**fee'bly** *adv.*

fee·ble-mind·ed (fē'bəl-mīn'dĭd) ►*adj.* **1.** Deficient in intelligence. No longer in scientific use. **2.** Exhibiting a lack of intelligent consideration: *feeble-minded excuses.* —**fee'ble-mind'ed·ly** *adv.* —**fee'ble-mind'ed·ness** *n.*

feed (fēd) ►*v.* **fed** (fĕd), **feed·ing 1a.** To give food to; nourish. **b.** To eat. **2.** To supply with something essential for growth, maintenance, or operation. **3.** To transmit (media content) by means of a communications network or satellite. **4.** To support or promote; encourage. ►*n.* **1.** Food for animals, esp. livestock. **2a.** Material supplied, as to a machine. **b.** The act of supplying such material. **3.** The transmission or conveyance of published content, as by satellite, on the Internet, or by broadcast over a network of stations. [< OE *fēdan*.] —**feed′er** *n.*

feed·back (fēd′băk′) ►*n.* **1a.** The return of a portion of the output of a process or system to the input. **b.** The portion of the output so returned. **2.** Sound created when a transducer picks up sound from a speaker connected to an amplifier and regenerates it back through the amplifier. **3.** An evaluative response.

feed·lot (fēd′lŏt′) ►*n.* A place where livestock are fattened for market.

feed·stuff (fēd′stŭf′) ►*n.* Food for livestock; fodder.

feel (fēl) ►*v.* **felt** (fĕlt), **feel·ing** **1.** To perceive through the sense of touch. **2a.** To touch. **b.** To examine by touching. **3a.** To experience as an emotion: *felt a great curiosity.* **b.** To be aware of; sense: *felt the anger in the room* **4.** To believe; think. **5.** To have compassion or sympathy: *felt for the grieving family.* **6.** To produce a sensory or emotional impression: *a fabric that feels soft; a defeat that feels like victory.* ►*n.* **1.** The sense of touch. **2.** The quality of something perceived by or as if by touch. **3.** Overall effect; atmosphere. **4.** Intuitive awareness or natural ability. —*idiom:* **feel like** *Informal* To have an inclination for. [< OE *fēlan.*]

feel·er (fē′lər) ►*n.* **1.** Something, such as a hint or question, designed to elicit the attitudes or intentions of others. **2.** *Zool.* A sensory organ, such as an antenna.

feel·ing (fē′lĭng) ►*n.* **1a.** The sense of touch. **b.** A sensation experienced through touch. **c.** A physical sensation. **2.** An emotional state or disposition; an emotion. **3. feelings** Susceptibility to emotional response; sensibilities. **4.** Opinion based on sentiment. **5.** A general impression: *a feeling that something was wrong.* **6.** Intuitive awareness or aptitude: *has a feeling for language.* ►*adj.* **1.** Sensitive. **2.** Sympathetic. —**feel′ing·ly** *adv.*

feet (fēt) ►*n.* Pl. of **foot.**

feign (fān) ►*v.* **1.** To give a false appearance (of). **2.** To represent falsely; pretend to. [< Lat. *fingere*, to shape, form.]

feint (fānt) ►*n.* A feigned attack designed to draw defensive action away from an intended target. [< OFr. *feinte.*] —**feint** *v.*

feist·y (fī′stē) ►*adj.* **-i·er, -i·est** **1.** Plucky or spunky. **2.** Touchy; quarrelsome. [< dial. *feist*, a small dog.] —**feist′i·ness** *n.*

fe·la·fel (fə-lä′fəl) ►*n.* Var. of **falafel.**

feld·spar (fĕld′spär′, fĕl′-) ►*n.* Any of a group of abundant rock-forming minerals consisting of silicates of aluminum with potassium, sodium, calcium, and, rarely, barium. [< obsolete Ger. *Feldspath.*]

fe·lic·i·tate (fĭ-lĭs′ĭ-tāt′) ►*v.* **-tat·ed, -tat·ing** To congratulate. —**fe·lic′i·ta′tion** *n.*

fe·lic·i·tous (fĭ-lĭs′ĭ-təs) ►*adj.* **1.** Admirably suited; apt. **2.** Exhibiting an agreeable manner or style. —**fe·lic′i·tous·ness** *n.*

fe·lic·i·ty (fĭ-lĭs′ĭ-tē) ►*n., pl.* **-ties** **1.** Great happiness; bliss. **2.** A cause of happiness. **3.** An appropriate and pleasing manner or style. [< Lat. *fēlīx, fēlīc-*, fortunate.]

fe·line (fē′līn′) ►*adj.* **1.** Of or belonging to cats or related animals, as lions and tigers. **2.** Suggestive of a cat, as in suppleness or stealthiness. ►*n.* A feline animal. [< Lat. *fēlēs*, cat.] —**fe·lin′i·ty** (fĭ-lĭn′ĭ-tē) *n.*

fell¹ (fĕl) ►*v.* **1.** To cut or knock down. **2.** To kill. [< OE *fyllan.*] —**fell′a·ble** *adj.*

fell² (fĕl) ►*adj.* **1.** Cruel; fierce. **2.** Deadly; lethal. **3.** Dire; sinister. [< OFr. *fel.*]

fell³ (fĕl) ►*n.* The hide of an animal; pelt. [< OE *fell.*]

fell⁴ (fĕl) ►*v.* P.t. of **fall.**

fel·lah (fĕl′ə, fə-lä′) ►*n., pl.* **fel·la·hin** or **-heen** (fĕl′ə-hēn′, fə-lä-hēn′) A peasant or agricultural laborer in an Arab country. [< Ar. *fallāh.*]

Fel·li·ni (fə-lē′nē, fĕl-), **Federico** 1920–93. Italian filmmaker.

fel·low (fĕl′ō) ►*n.* **1.** A man or boy. **2.** *Informal* A boyfriend. **3.** A comrade or associate. **4.** One of a pair; mate. **5.** A member of a learned society. **6.** A graduate student receiving financial aid for further study. ►*adj.* Being of the same kind, group, occupation, or locality: *fellow workers.* [< ON *fēlagi*, business partner : *fē*, property + *lag*, a laying down.]

fel·low·ship (fĕl′ō-shĭp′) ►*n.* **1.** Congenial companionship on a basis of equality. **2.** The financial grant made to a fellow in a college or university.

fellow traveler ►*n.* One who sympathizes with the tenets of an organized group, such as the Communist Party, without being a member.

fel·on (fĕl′ən) ►*n.* One who has committed a felony. [< Med.Lat. *fellō*, villain.]

fel·o·ny (fĕl′ə-nē) ►*n., pl.* **-nies** *Law* A serious crime, such as murder, rape, or burglary. —**fe·lo′ni·ous** (fə-lō′nē-əs) *adj.*

felt¹ (fĕlt) ►*n.* **1.** A fabric of matted, compressed fibers, as of wool. **2.** A material resembling this fabric. [< OE.] —**felt** *adj.*

felt² (fĕlt) ►*v.* P.t. and p.part. of **feel.**

fem. ►*abbr.* **1.** female **2.** feminine

FEMA ►*abbr.* Federal Emergency Management Agency

fe·male (fē′māl′) ►*adj.* **1a.** Relating to or being the sex that produces ova or bears young. **b.** Consisting of members of this sex. **2.** *Bot.* **a.** Of or being an organ, such as a pistil or ovary, that produces seeds after fertilization. **b.** Bearing pistils but not stamens. **3.** Designed to receive or fit around a complementary male part, as a slot or receptacle: *a female pipe fitting.* ►*n.* A member of the female sex. [< Lat. *fēmella*, dim. of *fēmina*, woman.] —**fe·male′ness** *n.*

fem·i·nine (fĕm′ə-nĭn) ►*adj.* **1.** Of or relating to women or girls. **2.** Marked by qualities gen. attributed to a woman. **3.** *Gram.* Of or being the gender of words referring to things classified as female. ►*n. Gram.* **1.** The feminine gender. **2.** A word belonging to this gender. [< Lat. *fēminīnus.*] —**fem′i·nine·ly** *adv.* —**fem′i·nine·ness** *n.* —**fem′i·nin′i·ty** *n.*

fem·i·nism (fĕm′ə-nĭz′əm) ►*n.* **1.** Belief in women's social, political, and economic rights, esp. with regard to equality of the sexes. **2.** The movement advocating these rights. —**fem′i·nist** *n.*

femme fa·tale (fĕm′ fə-tăl′, -täl′) ►*n., pl.* **femmes fa·tales** (fĕm′ fə-tăl′, -tälz′, -täl′, -tälz′) An alluring and seductive woman, esp. one who leads men into compromising situations. [Fr.]

fe·mur (fē′mər) ►*n., pl.* **fe·murs** or **fem·o·ra** (fĕm′ər-ə) A bone of the lower or hind limb in vertebrates, situated between the pelvis and knee in humans. [Lat., thigh.] —**fem′-or·al** *adj.*

fen (fĕn) ►*n.* An area of low marshy land. [< OE *fenn.*] —**fen′ny** *adj.*

fence (fĕns) ►*n.* **1.** An enclosure, barrier, or boundary, usu. made of posts or stakes joined together by boards, wire, or rails. **2a.** One who receives and sells stolen goods. **b.** A place where stolen goods are received and sold. ►*v.* **fenced, fenc·ing 1.** To enclose with or as if with a fence. See Synonyms at **enclose. 2a.** To act as a conduit for stolen goods. **b.** To sell (stolen goods) to a fence. **3.** To practice the art or sport of fencing. —*idiom:* **on the fence** *Informal* Undecided; neutral. [ME *fens* < *defens,* DEFENSE.] —**fenc′er** *n.*

fenc·ing (fĕn′sĭng) ►*n.* **1.** The art or sport of using a foil, épée, or saber. **2.** Material for fences.

fend (fĕnd) ►*v.* **1.** To ward off; repel. **2.** To manage; get by: *You'll have to fend for yourself.* [ME *fenden* < *defenden,* DEFEND.]

fend·er (fĕn′dər) ►*n.* **1.** A guard over a wheel of a vehicle. **2.** A screen or metal framework placed in front of a fireplace.

fen·es·tra·tion (fĕn′ĭ-strā′shən) ►*n.* The design and placement of windows in a building. [< Lat. *fenestra,* window.]

feng shui (fŭng′ shwā′) ►*n.* The traditional Chinese practice of positioning objects, esp. buildings and graves, so as to harmonize with the flow of chi. [Mandarin *fēng shuǐ,* wind (and) water.]

Fe·ni·an (fē′nē-ən) ►*n.* **1.** One of a legendary group of heroic Irish warriors of the 2nd and 3rd cent. A.D. **2.** A member of a secret revolutionary organization in the US and Ireland in the mid-19th cent. dedicated to the overthrow of British rule in Ireland. —**Fe′ni·an** *adj.* —**Fe′ni·an·ism** *n.*

fen·nel (fĕn′əl) ►*n.* **1.** A plant having aromatic seeds used as flavoring. **2.** The seeds or edible stalks of this plant. [< Lat. *faeniculum.*]

–fer ►*suff.* One that bears: *conifer.* [< Lat. *ferre,* carry.]

fe·ral (fîr′əl, fĕr′-) ►*adj.* **1.** Existing in a wild or untamed state. **2.** Having returned to wildness from domestication. **3.** Of or suggestive of a wild animal; savage. [< Lat. *ferus,* wild.]

fer-de-lance (fĕr′dl-äns′, -äns′) ►*n., pl.* **fer-de-lance** A venomous tropical American pit viper having brown and grayish markings. [Fr., spearhead.]

Fer·di·nand V (fûr′dn-ănd′) 1452–1516. Spanish king of Aragon, Castile and Léon, Sicily, and Naples.

fer·ment (fûr′mĕnt′) ►*n.* **1.** Something, such as yeast, that causes fermentation. **2.** A state of agitation or unrest. ►*v.* (fər-mĕnt′) **1.** To undergo or cause to undergo fermentation. **2.** To produce by or as if by fermentation. **3.** To be turbulent; seethe. [< Lat. *fermentum.*] —**fer·ment′a·bil′i·ty** *n.* —**fer·ment′a·ble** *adj.*

fer·men·ta·tion (fûr′mən-tā′shən, -mĕn-) ►*n.* **1.** A chemical reaction that splits complex organic compounds into relatively simple substances, esp. the conversion of sugar to carbon dioxide and alcohol by yeast. **2.** Unrest; agitation. —**fer·men′ta·tive** (fər-mĕn′tə-tĭv) *adj.*

Fer·mi (fĕr′mē), **Enrico** 1901–54. Italian-born Amer. physicist.

fer·mi·on (fûr′mē-ŏn′, fĕr′-) ►*n.* Any of a class of particles having a spin that is half an odd integer and obeying the exclusion principle, by which no more than one identical particle may occupy the same state in quantum physics. [After Enrico FERMI.]

fer·mi·um (fûr′mē-əm, fĕr′-) ►*n. Symbol* **Fm** A synthetic metallic element. At. no. 100. See table at **element.** [After Enrico FERMI.]

fern (fûrn) ►*n.* Any of numerous flowerless plants reproducing by spores and usu. having fronds. [< OE *fearn.*] —**fern′y** *adj.*

fe·ro·cious (fə-rō′shəs) ►*adj.* **1.** Extremely savage; fierce. **2.** Powerfully destructive: *a ferocious gale.* **3.** Intense; extreme: *ferocious heat.* [< Lat. *ferōx, ferōc-,* fierce.] —**fe·ro′cious·ly** *adv.* —**fe·ro′cious·ness, fe·roc′i·ty** (fə-rŏs′ĭ-tē) *n.*

–ferous ►*suff.* Bearing; producing; containing: *carboniferous.* [–FER + –OUS.]

fer·ret (fĕr′ĭt) ►*n.* **1.** A domesticated weasel with an elongated flexible body, often kept as a pet and sometimes trained to hunt rats or rabbits. **2.** A North American weasel with black masklike markings. ►*v.* **1.** To hunt with ferrets. **2.** To drive out, as from a hiding place; expel. **3.** To uncover and bring to light by searching: *ferret out the solution.* [< VLat. **fūrittus* < Lat. *fūr,* thief.]

fer·ric (fĕr′ĭk) ►*adj.* Of or containing iron, esp. with a valence of 3.

ferric oxide ►*n.* A dark red compound, Fe_2O_3, occurring naturally as rust.

Fer·ris wheel ►*n.* A large upright rotating wheel having suspended seats that remain in a horizontal position as the wheel revolves. [After George W.G. *Ferris* (1859–96).]

ferro– or **ferr–** ►*pref.* Iron: *ferromagnetic.* [< Lat. *ferrum,* iron.]

fer·ro·mag·net·ic (fĕr′ō-măg-nĕt′ĭk) ►*adj.* Of or characteristic of substances such as iron or nickel and various alloys that exhibit magnetic properties. —**fer′ro·mag′net** (-măg′nĭt) *n.* —**fer′ro·mag′net·ism** *n.*

fer·ro·man·ga·nese (fĕr′ō-măng′gə-nēz′, -nēs′) ►*n.* An alloy of iron, manganese, and carbon, used as a deoxidizer in steel production.

fer·ro·type (fĕr′ə-tīp′) ►*n.* A positive photograph made directly on an iron plate varnished with a thin sensitized film.

fer·rous (fĕr′əs) ►*adj.* Of or containing iron, esp. with a valence of 2.

ferrous oxide ►*n.* A black powder, FeO, used in the manufacture of steel and glass.

fer·rule (fĕr′əl) ►*n.* A metal ring or cap placed around a pole or shaft for reinforcement. [< Lat. *viriola,* little bracelet.]

fer·ry (fĕr′ē) ►*v.* **-ried, -ry·ing 1.** To transport by boat across a body of water. **2.** To cross by a ferry. **3.** To transport from one point to another. ►*n., pl.* **-ries 1.** A ferryboat. **2.** A place where a ferryboat embarks. [< OE *ferian.*]

fer·ry·boat (fĕr′ē-bōt′) ►*n.* A boat used to ferry passengers, vehicles, or goods.

fer·tile (fûr′tl) ►*adj.* **1.** *Biol.* Capable of initiating, sustaining, or supporting reproduction. **2.** Rich in material needed to sustain plant growth: *fertile soil.* **3.** Highly or continuously productive; prolific: *a fertile imagination.* [< Lat. *fertilis* < *ferre,* to bear.] —**fer′tile·ly** *adv.* —**fer·til′i·ty** (fər-tĭl′ĭ-tē), **fer′tile·ness** *n.*

Syns: fecund, fruitful, productive, prolific **Ant:** *infertile* **adj.**

Fertile Crescent A region of the Middle East extending from the Nile Valley to the Tigris and Euphrates Rivers.

fer·til·ize (fûr′tl-īz′) ►*v.* **-ized, -iz·ing 1.** To initiate biological reproduction, esp. to provide with pollen or sperm. **2.** To make fertile, as by spreading fertilizer. —**fer′til·iz′a·ble** *adj.* —**fer′til·i·za′tion** *n.*

fer·til·iz·er (fûr′tl-ī′zər) ►*n.* Any of many natural and synthetic materials, including manure and chemical compounds, added to soil to increase its capacity to support plant growth.

fer·ule (fĕr′əl) ►*n.* A cane or flat stick used in punishing children. [< Lat. *ferula*, rod.]

fer·vent (fûr′vənt) ►*adj.* **1.** Greatly emotional or zealous; ardent. **2.** Extremely hot; glowing. [< Lat. *fervēre*, to boil.] —**fer′ven·cy** *n.* —**fer′vent·ly** *adv.*

fer·vid (fûr′vĭd) ►*adj.* **1.** Passionate; zealous. **2.** Extremely hot. [Lat. *fervidus*.] —**fer′vid·ly** *adv.*

fer·vor (fûr′vər) ►*n.* **1.** Great warmth and intensity of emotion. **2.** Intense heat. [< Lat.]

fes·cue (fĕs′kyoō) ►*n.* Any of various grasses often cultivated as pasturage. [< Lat. *festūca*, straw.]

fes·tal (fĕs′təl) ►*adj.* Of a feast or festival; festive. [< Lat. *fēstum*, feast.]

fes·ter (fĕs′tər) ►*v.* **1.** To generate pus. **2.** To undergo decay; rot. **3.** To be or become a source of increasing irritation. [< Lat. *fistula*, fistula.] —**fes′ter** *n.*

fes·ti·val (fĕs′tə-vəl) ►*n.* **1.** A feast or celebration, esp. a religious one. **2.** A programmed series of cultural performances, exhibitions, or competitions: *a film festival.* **3.** Revelry; conviviality.

fes·tive (fĕs′tĭv) ►*adj.* **1.** Relating to or appropriate for a feast or festival. **2.** Merry; joyous. [Lat. *fēstīvus*.] —**fes′tive·ly** *adv.*

fes·tiv·i·ty (fĕ-stĭv′ĭ-tē) ►*n., pl.* **-ties 1.** A joyous feast or celebration. **2.** The merriment of a festival or celebration. **3. festivities** The activities of a festival.

fes·toon (fĕ-stoōn′) ►*n.* **1.** A garland, as of leaves or flowers, between two looped points. **2.** A representation of such a garland, as in painting. ►*v.* **1.** To decorate with or as if with festoons. **2.** To form festoons. [< Ital. *festone*.]

fet·a (fĕt′ə, fä′tə) ►*n.* A white semisoft cheese made usu. from goat's or sheep's milk. [Mod. Gk. *(turi) pheta*, (cheese) slice.]

fe·tal (fēt′l) ►*adj.* Of or relating to a fetus.

fetal alcohol syndrome ►*n.* A group of abnormalities occurring in an infant born to an alcoholic mother, including growth retardation and developmental disabilities.

fetal position ►*n.* A position of the body at rest in which the spine is curved, the head is bowed, and the limbs are drawn in toward the chest. [From its resemblance to the position of a fetus in the womb.]

fetch (fĕch) ►*v.* **1.** To go after and bring back; retrieve. **2.** To cause to come; bring forth. **3.** To bring as a price. [< OE *feccean*.] —**fetch′er** *n.*

fetch·ing (fĕch′ĭng) ►*adj.* Attractive; charming. —**fetch′ing·ly** *adv.*

fete also **fête** (fāt, fĕt) ►*n.* **1.** A festival or feast. **2.** An elaborate, usu. outdoor party. ►*v.* **fet·ed,**

fet·ing also **fêt·ed, fêt·ing 1.** To celebrate or honor with a feast or elaborate entertainment. **2.** To pay honor to. [< OFr. *feste*, FEAST.]

fet·id (fĕt′ĭd, fē′tĭd) ►*adj.* Having an offensive odor. [< Lat. *fētidus*.] —**fet′id·ly** *adv.* —**fet′id·ness** *n.*

fet·ish (fĕt′ĭsh, fē′tĭsh) ►*n.* **1.** An object believed to have spiritual powers. **2.** An object of excessive attention or reverence. **3.** An obsessive attachment; fixation. **4.** Something, such as a material object or nonsexual part of the body, by which a person habitually becomes sexually aroused. [< Lat. *factīcius*, artificial.] —**fet′ish·ism** *n.* —**fet′ish·ist** *n.* —**fet′ish·is′tic** *adj.*

fet·lock (fĕt′lŏk′) ►*n.* A projection on the lower part of the leg of a horse or related animal, above and behind the hoof. [ME *fitlok*.]

fet·ter (fĕt′ər) ►*n.* **1.** A chain or shackle for the ankles. **2.** often **fetters** Something that restricts or restrains. ►*v.* **1.** To shackle. **2.** To restrict or restrain: *thinking that is fettered by prejudice.* See Synonyms at **hobble.** [< OE *feter*.]

fet·tle (fĕt′l) ►*n.* Condition; emotional state: *in fine fettle.* [< ME *fetlen*, make ready.]

fet·tuc·ci·ne (fĕt′ə-chē′nē) ►*n.* Pasta in narrow flat strips. [Ital., pl. dim. of *fettucia*, ribbon.]

fe·tus (fē′təs) ►*n., pl.* **-tus·es 1.** The unborn young of a viviparous vertebrate. **2.** In humans, the unborn young from the end of the eighth week after conception to birth, as distinguished from the earlier embryo. [< Lat. *fētus*, offspring.]

feud (fyoōd) ►*n.* A bitter, often prolonged quarrel or state of enmity. [< OFr. *faide*, of Gmc. orig.] —**feud** *v.*

feu·dal (fyoōd′l) ►*adj.* Of or characteristic of feudalism. [< Med.Lat. *feudum*, feudal estate.]

feu·dal·ism (fyoōd′l-ĭz′əm) ►*n.* A political and economic system, as in medieval Europe, by which a landowner grants land to a vassal in exchange for homage and military service. —**feu′dal·ist** *n.* —**feu′dal·is′tic** *adj.* —**feu′dal·i·za′tion** *n.* —**feu′dal·ize′** *v.*

fe·ver (fē′vər) ►*n.* **1.** Abnormally high body temperature. **2.** A disease marked by such temperature. **3.** Heightened activity or excitement. **4.** A usu. short-lived enthusiasm or craze. [< Lat. *febris*.] —**fe′ver·ish** *adj.* —**fe′ver·ish·ly** *adv.* —**fe′ver·ish·ness** *n.*

fever blister ►*n.* See **cold sore.**

few (fyoō) ►*adj.* **-er, -est** Amounting to or consisting of a small number. ►*n. (takes pl. v.)* **1.** An indefinitely small number: *A few of the cars are new.* **2.** An exclusive or limited number: *the fortunate few.* ►*pron. (takes pl. v.)* A small number: *Few of them are left.* [< OE *fēawe*.]

Usage: **Fewer** is used with expressions denoting things that can be counted (*fewer than four players*), while *less* is used with mass terms denoting things of measurable extent (*less paper*). However, *less* is idiomatic in *less than* used before a plural noun that denotes a measure of time, amount, or distance, as in *less than 50 miles*, and is sometimes used with plural nouns in the expressions *no less than* and *or less.*

fey (fā) ►*adj.* **1.** Overrefined, exaggerated, or affected. **2.** Otherworldly, magical, or fairylike. [< OE *fǣge*, fated to die.] —**fey′ness** *n.*

fez (fĕz) ►*n., pl.* **fez·zes** A man's felt cap shaped like a flat-topped cone, usu. red with a black tassel hanging from the crown. [< *Fez*, city of N-central Morocco.]

FHA ►*abbr.* Federal Housing Administration

fi·an·cé (fē'än-sā', fē-än'sā') ►*n.* A man to whom one is engaged. [Fr. < p.part. of *fiancer*, betroth, ult. < Lat. *fīdere*, trust.]

fi·an·cée (fē'än-sā', fē-än'sā') ►*n.* A woman to whom one is engaged.

fi·as·co (fē-ǎs'kō, -ä'skō) ►*n., pl.* **-coes** or **-cos** A complete failure. [< Ital., bottle.]

fi·at (fē'ət, -ǎt', -ät') ►*n.* An arbitrary order or decree. [< Lat., let it be done < *fierī*, become, be done.]

fib (fĭb) ►*n.* An insignificant or childish lie. ►*v.* **fibbed, fib·bing** To tell a fib. [Perh. < alteration of FABLE.] —**fib'ber** *n.*

fi·ber (fī'bər) ►*n.* **1.** A slender threadlike structure. **2.** *Bot.* An elongated, thick-walled cell strengthening and supporting plant tissue. **3.** *Anat.* Any of various elongated cells, esp. a muscle or nerve fiber. **4.** A filament, as of cotton or nylon, capable of being spun into yarn. **5a.** An element of a person's character. **b.** Strength of character; fortitude. **6.** Indigestible plant matter, consisting esp. of cellulose, that stimulates intestinal peristalsis. [< Lat. *fibra*.] —**fi'brous** (fī'brəs) *adj.*

fi·ber·board (fī'bər-bôrd') ►*n.* A building material composed of wood chips or plant fibers bonded together and compressed into rigid sheets.

fi·ber·glass (fī'bər-glăs') ►*n.* A material consisting of glass fibers, often in a matrix of resin.

fiber optics ►*n.* *(takes sing. v.)* **1.** The technology of light transmission through very fine, flexible glass or plastic fibers. **2.** A cable or network of cables containing optical fibers. —**fi'ber·op'tic** *adj.*

fi·bril (fī'brəl, fĭb'rəl) ►*n.* A small slender fiber or filament. [NLat. *fibrilla* < Lat. *fibra*, fiber.]

fib·ril·la·tion (fĭb'rə-lā'shən, fī'brə-) ►*n.* Rapid uncoordinated twitching movements in the atria or ventricles of the heart. —**fib'ril·late'** *v.*

fi·brin (fī'brĭn) ►*n.* An insoluble whitish protein formed from fibrinogen during blood coagulation.

fi·brin·o·gen (fī-brĭn'ə-jən) ►*n.* A protein in the blood plasma that is converted to fibrin and is essential for blood coagulation.

fibro– or **fibr–** ►*pref.* Fiber, esp. fibrous tissue: *fibroma*. [< Lat. *fibra*, fiber.]

fi·broid (fī'broid') ►*adj.* Composed of or resembling fibrous tissue. ►*n.* A fibroma occurring esp. in the uterine wall.

fi·bro·ma (fī-brō'mə) ►*n., pl.* **-mas** or **-ma·ta** (-mə-tə) A benign, usu. enclosed tumor of primarily fibrous tissue.

fi·bro·my·al·gia (fī'brō-mī-ăl'jə) ►*n.* A syndrome marked by chronic, widespread pain in the muscles and soft tissues with defined points of tenderness and often multiple other symptoms, such as fatigue, sleep disturbance, anxiety, and bowel dysfunction.

fi·bro·sis (fī-brō'sĭs) ►*n.* *Med.* The formation of excessive fibrous tissue. —**fi·brot'ic** (-brŏt'ĭk) *adj.*

fib·u·la (fĭb'yə-lə) ►*n., pl.* **-lae** (-lē') or **-las** The outer and narrower of two bones of the human lower leg or of the hind leg of an animal. [Lat. *fibula*, clasp < *fīgere*, fasten.]

–fic ►*suff.* Causing; making: *honorific*. [Lat. *-ficus* < *facere*, make.]

FICA ►*abbr.* Federal Insurance Contributions Act

–fication ►*suff.* Production; making: *certification*. [< Lat. *-ficāre*, make < *facere*.]

fich·u (fĭsh'oo, fē-shoo') ►*n.* A woman's triangular scarf, worn over the shoulders and crossed or tied in a loose knot at the breast. [Fr. < p.part. of *ficher*, FIX.]

fick·le (fĭk'əl) ►*adj.* Erratic or changeable, esp. in affections; capricious. [< OE *ficol*, deceitful.] —**fick'le·ness** *n.* —**fick'ly** *adv.*

fic·tion (fĭk'shən) ►*n.* **1a.** A work, as of literature or drama, whose content is produced by the imagination and is not necessarily based on fact. **b.** The category comprising works of this kind. **2.** An imaginative creation or pretense. **3.** A lie. [< Lat. *fictiō* < *fingere*, to form.] —**fic'tion·al** *adj.* —**fic'tion·al·i·za'tion** *n.* —**fic'tion·al·ize'** *v.* —**fic'tion·al·ly** *adv.*

fic·ti·tious (fĭk-tĭsh'əs) ►*adj.* **1.** Concocted or fabricated: *a fictitious name.* **2.** Relating to the imaginary contents of a work of fiction. [< Lat. *fictīcius*.] —**fic·ti'tious·ly** *adv.* —**fic·ti'tious·ness** *n.*

fic·tive (fĭk'tĭv) ►*adj.* **1.** Relating to or being fiction; fictional. **2.** Not genuine; sham.

fid·dle (fĭd'l) ►*n.* A violin. ►*v.* **-dled, -dling 1.** To play a violin. **2.** To play idly; tinker: *fiddled with the knobs.* **3.** To meddle; tamper. [< OE *fithele*.] —**fid'dler** *n.*

fiddler crab ►*n.* A burrowing crab with one of the front claws much larger in the male.

fid·dle·sticks (fĭd'l-stĭks') ►*interj.* Used to express mild annoyance or impatience.

fi·del·i·ty (fĭ-dĕl'ĭ-tē, fī-) ►*n., pl.* **-ties 1.** Faithfulness to obligations or duties. **2.** Exact correspondence with fact; accuracy. **3.** The degree to which an electronic system reproduces the sound or image of its input signal. [< Lat. *fidēlis*, faithful.]
*Syns: allegiance, fealty, loyalty **n.***

fidg·et (fĭj'ĭt) ►*v.* To move nervously or restlessly. ►*n.* often **fidgets** Restlessness manifested by nervous movements. [< obsolete *fidge*, move about restlessly.] —**fidg'et·y** *adj.*

fi·du·ci·ar·y (fĭ-doo'shē-ĕr'ē, -shə-rē, -dyoo'-) ►*adj.* **1.** Of or relating to the faithful discharge of one's duties toward another. **2.** Held in trust. ►*n., pl.* **-ies** One having a duty to act in another's interest. [< Lat. *fidūcia*, a trust.]

fie (fī) ►*interj.* Used to express distaste or disapproval.

fief (fēf) ►*n.* **1.** See **fee** (sense 4). **2.** A fiefdom. [< OFr., FEE.]

fief·dom (fēf'dəm) ►*n.* **1.** The estate of a feudal lord. **2.** An organization or department over which one person or group exercises control.

field (fēld) ►*n.* **1a.** A broad, level, open expanse of land. **b.** A meadow. **c.** A cultivated expanse of land. **d.** A portion of land or a geologic formation containing a specified natural resource. **2.** A battleground. **3.** A background area, as on a flag. **4.** A setting of practical activity outside an office, school, or laboratory: *a product tested in the field.* **5.** *Sports* **a.** An area in which an athletic event takes place. **b.** All the contestants in an event. **6.** An area of human activity. **7.** *Phys.* A region of space characterized by a physical property, such as gravitational force, having a determinable value at every point in the region. **8.** *Comp.* **a.** An element of a database record in which one piece of information is stored. **b.** A space, as on an online form or request for information, that accepts the input of text. ►*v.* **1.** *Sports* **a.** To retrieve (a ball) and perform the required maneuver, esp. in baseball. **b.** To place in the field to play. **2.** To give an unrehearsed response to (a question). **3.** To enter (data) into a field. [< OE *feld.*] —**field′er** *n.*

    Syns: *bailiwick, domain, province, realm, sphere, territory* **n.**

field day ►*n.* **1.** A day set aside for sports or athletic competition. **2.** *Informal* A time of great pleasure, activity, or opportunity.

field event ►*n.* A throwing or jumping event of a track-and-field meet.

field glass ►*n.* often **field glasses** A portable binocular telescope.

field goal ►*n.* **1.** *Football* A score worth three points made from scrimmage on one of four downs by kicking the ball over the crossbar and between the goal posts. **2.** *Basketball* A score made by throwing the ball through the basket during regularly timed play.

field hockey ►*n.* A game played on turf in which two teams of players, using curved sticks, try to drive a ball into each other's goal.

Field·ing (fēl′dĭng), **Henry** 1707–54. British writer.

field marshal ►*n.* An officer in some European armies, usu. ranking just below the commander in chief.

field mouse ►*n.* Any of various small mice or voles inhabiting meadows and fields.

field of force ►*n.* A region of space throughout which the force produced by a single agent, such as an electric current, is operative.

field-test (fēld′tĕst′) ►*v.* To test (e.g., a product) in actual operation or use.

field trial ►*n.* **1.** A test of young, untried hunting dogs for their competence in pointing and retrieving. **2.** A trial of a new product in actual use.

field trip ►*n.* A group excursion for firsthand observation, as to a museum.

field·work (fēld′wûrk′) ►*n.* Work done or observations made in the field as opposed to laboratory work. —**field′work′er** *n.*

fiend (fēnd) ►*n.* **1.** An evil spirit; devil. **2.** An evil or wicked person. **3.** *Informal* **a.** An addict. **b.** One obsessed with an activity. [< OE *fēond.*] —**fiend′ish** *adj.* —**fiend′ish·ly** *adv.*

fierce (fîrs) ►*adj.* **fierc·er, fierc·est 1.** Having a violent nature; ferocious: *a fierce beast.* **2.** Severe or violent: *a fierce storm.* **3.** Intense or ardent: *fierce loyalty.* [< Lat. *ferus.*] —**fierce′ly** *adv.* —**fierce′ness** *n.*

fier·y (fîr′ē, fī′ə-rē) ►*adj.* **-i·er, -i·est 1.** Consisting of, containing, or like fire. **2a.** Easily excited: *a fiery temper.* **b.** Charged with emotion: *a fiery speech.* [< ME *fier,* FIRE.] —**fier′i·ly** *adv.* —**fier′i·ness** *n.*

fi·es·ta (fē-ĕs′tə) ►*n.* **1.** A festival or religious holiday, esp. in Spanish-speaking regions. **2.** A party. [Sp. < VLat. *fēsta,* FEAST.]

fife (fīf) ►*n.* A small, high-pitched flute used to accompany drums in a military or marching band. [< VLat. *pīpa.*] —**fif′er** *n.*

fif·teen (fĭf-tēn′) ►*n.* **1.** The cardinal number equal to 14 + 1. **2.** The 15th in a set or sequence.

[< OE *fīftēne.*] —**fif·teen′** *adj. & pron.*

fif·teenth (fĭf-tēnth′) ►*n.* **1.** The ordinal number matching the number 15 in a series. **2.** One of 15 equal parts. —**fif·teenth′** *adv. & adj.*

fifth (fĭfth) ►*n.* **1.** The ordinal number matching the number 5 in a series. **2.** One of five equal parts. **3.** One fifth of a gallon or four fifths of a quart of liquor. **4.** *Mus.* A tone five degrees above or below a given tone in a diatonic scale. [< OE *fīfta.*] —**fifth** *adv. & adj.*

fifth column ►*n.* A secret organization working within a country to further an enemy's aims.

fifth wheel ►*n.* An extra and unnecessary person or thing.

fif·ti·eth (fĭf′tē-ĭth) ►*n.* **1.** The ordinal number matching the number 50 in a series. **2.** One of 50 equal parts. —**fif′ti·eth** *adv. & adj.*

fif·ty (fĭf′tē) ►*n., pl.* **-ties** The cardinal number equal to 5 × 10. [< OE *fīftig.*] —**fif′ty** *adj. & pron.*

fif·ty-fif·ty (fĭf′tē-fĭf′tē) ►*adj.* **1.** Divided in two equal portions. **2.** Being equally likely and unlikely. —**fif′ty-fif′ty** *adv.*

fig (fĭg) ►*n.* **1a.** Any of various Mediterranean trees or shrubs widely cultivated for their edible fruit. **b.** The sweet, pear-shaped fruit of this plant. **2.** A trivial amount: *not worth a fig.* [< Lat. *ficus.*]

fight (fīt) ►*v.* **fought** (fôt), **fight·ing 1.** To attempt to harm or subdue an adversary by blows or with weapons. **2.** To quarrel; argue. **3.** To strive vigorously and resolutely: *fight for justice.* **4.** To contend with physically or in battle. **5.** To wage or carry on (a battle). **6.** To struggle against: *fight temptation.* **7.** To compete against, as in a boxing ring. **8.** To try to extinguish (an uncontrolled fire). ►*n.* **1.** A confrontation in which each opponent attempts to harm or subdue the other. **2.** A quarrel or conflict. **3.** A competition between two athletes, as in a boxing ring. **4.** A struggle for an objective. **5.** The inclination to fight; pugnacity. —*phrasal verb:* **fight off** To defend against or drive back. [< OE *feohtan.*]

fight·er (fī′tər) ►*n.* **1.** One who fights. **2.** A fast, maneuverable combat aircraft. **3.** A pugnacious or determined person.

fig·ment (fĭg′mənt) ►*n.* Something invented or made up. [< Lat. *figmentum.*]

fig·u·ra·tive (fĭg′yər-ə-tĭv) ►*adj.* **1.** Based on figures of speech; metaphorical. **2.** Represented by a figure or resemblance; symbolic. **3.** Depicting recognizable objects, esp. human figures. —**fig′u·ra·tive·ly** *adv.*

fig·ure (fĭg′yər) ►*n.* **1a.** A written or printed symbol, esp. a number. **b. figures** Mathematical calculations. **c.** An amount represented in numbers. **2.** A geometric form consisting of points, lines, or planes. **3.** The outline, form, or silhouette of a thing, esp. a human. **4.** A person, esp. a well-known one. **5.** Impression or appearance made. **6.** A diagram, design, or pattern. **7.** A distinct group of steps or movements in a dance or in ice skating. ►*v.* **-ured, -ur·ing 1.** To calculate with numbers; compute. **2.** To make a likeness of; depict. **3.** To adorn with a design or figures. **4.** To conclude, believe, or predict. **5.** To be pertinent or involved. **6.** *Informal* To seem reasonable or expected: *It figures.* —*phrasal verbs:* **figure on** *Informal* **1.** To count on. **2.** To expect: *figured on an hour's*

delay. **figure out** To discover, decide, or solve. [< Lat. *figūra.*] —**fig′ur·er** *n.*
  Syns: *design, device, motif, pattern* **n.**

fig·ure·head (fĭg′yər-hĕd′) ►*n.* **1.** A carved figure on the prow of a ship. **2.** A person with nominal leadership but no actual authority.

figurehead

figure of speech ►*n.* An expression that uses words in a nonliteral way or that changes normal word order to heighten rhetorical effect.

figure skating ►*n.* Ice-skating in which the skater performs a program of spins, jumps, and dancelike maneuvers. —**figure skater** *n.*

fig·u·rine (fĭg′yə-rēn′) ►*n.* A small sculptured figure; statuette. [< Ital. *figurina.*]

Fi·ji (fē′jē) A country of the SW Pacific comprising about 320 islands. Cap. Suva.

fil·a·ment (fĭl′ə-mənt) ►*n.* **1.** A fine thin thread or fiber. **2.** A slender, threadlike structure. **3.** A fine wire heated electrically to incandescence in an electric lamp. [< Lat. *filum,* thread.] —**fil′a·men′tous** (-mĕn′təs), **fil′a·men′ta·ry** (-mĕn′tə-rē, -mĕn′trē) *adj.*

fi·lar·i·a (fə-lâr′ē-ə) ►*n., pl.* **-i·ae** (-ē-ē′) Any of various slender parasitic nematode worms often transmitted as larvae by mosquitoes. [NLat. < Lat. *filum,* thread.] —**fi·lar′i·al, fi·lar′i·an** *adj.*

fil·bert (fĭl′bərt) ►*n.* A hazelnut. [< AN *philber,* after Saint *Philibert* (d. 684).]

filch (fĭlch) ►*v.* To steal in a furtive manner. [ME *filchen.*] —**filch′er** *n.*

file¹ (fīl) ►*n.* **1.** A container, such as a cabinet or folder, for keeping papers in order. **2.** A collection of papers or published materials kept in convenient order. **3.** *Comp.* A collection of related data or program records stored as a unit. **4.** A line of persons, animals, or things positioned one behind the other. ►*v.* **filed, fil·ing** **1.** To put or keep in useful order. **2.** To enter (a legal document) on record. **3.** To make an application: *filed for an extension on his taxes.* **4.** To march or walk in a line. —*idiom:* **on file** In or as if in a file for easy reference. [< Lat. *filum,* thread.]

file² (fīl) ►*n.* A hardened steel tool with sharp parallel ridges for cutting into esp. metallic surfaces. ►*v.* **filed, fil·ing** To smooth or grind with or as if with a file. [< OE *fīl.*]

file server ►*n.* A computer on which users of a network can store data.

fi·let (fĭ-lā′, fĭl′ā′) ►*n.* Var. of **fillet** (sense 3). ►*v.* Var. of **fillet** (sense 3).

fi·let mi·gnon (fĭ-lā′ mēn-yôN′, fĭl′ā) ►*n., pl.* **fi·lets mi·gnons** (fĭ-lā′ mēn-yôN′, fĭl′ā) A small, round, choice cut of beef from the loin. [Fr.]

fil·i·al (fĭl′ē-əl) ►*adj.* Of or befitting a son or daughter: *filial respect.* [< Lat. *filius,* son.] —**fil′i·al·ly** *adv.*

fil·i·bus·ter (fĭl′ə-bŭs′tər) ►*n.* The use of prolonged speechmaking to obstruct or delay legislative action. ►*v.* To delay or obstruct (a legislative measure) by prolonged speechmaking. [< Sp. *filibustero,* freebooter.]

fil·i·gree (fĭl′ĭ-grē′) ►*n.* **1.** Ornamental work made from gold, silver, or other fine twisted wire. **2.** Intricate, delicate, or fanciful ornamentation. [< Ital. *filigrana* : Lat. *filum,* thread + Lat. *grānum,* grain.] —**fil′i·gree′** *v.*

fil·ing (fī′lĭng) ►*n.* A particle removed by a file.

Fil·i·pi·no (fĭl′ə-pē′nō) ►*n., pl.* **-nos 1.** A native or inhabitant of the Philippines. **2.** The official language of the Philippines, based on Tagalog. —**Fil′i·pi′no** *adj.*

fill (fĭl) ►*v.* **1.** To make or become full. **2.** To put something into (e.g., a container) to a particular level: *filled the glass only partway.* **3.** To build up the level of (low-lying land) with material such as earth or gravel. **4.** To stop or plug up. **5.** To occupy completely; pervade. **6.** To satisfy or meet; fulfill. See Synonyms at **satisfy. 7.** To supply as required: *fill a prescription.* **8.** To place a person in: *fill a job vacancy.* ►*n.* **1.** An amount needed to make full, complete, or satisfied: *eat one's fill.* **2.** Material for filling. —*phrasal verb:* **fill in 1.** To provide with missing information. **2.** To take another's place. —*idiom:* **fill the bill** *Informal* To serve a particular purpose. [< OE *fyllan.*]

fill·er (fĭl′ər) ►*n.* **1.** Something added to augment weight or size or to fill space. **2.** A material used to fill in flaws in a surface. **3.** A short item to fill space in a publication or radio or television program.

fil·let (fĭl′ĭt) ►*n.* **1.** A narrow strip of ribbon or similar material. **2.** *also* **fi·let** (fĭ-lā′, fĭl′ā′) A boneless piece of meat or fish. ►*v.* **1.** To bind or decorate with or as if with a fillet. **2.** *also* **fi·let** (fĭ-lā′, fĭl′ā′) To make into fillets. [< OFr., dim. of *fil,* thread < Lat. *filum.*]

fill·ing (fĭl′ĭng) ►*n.* **1.** Something used to fill a space, cavity, or container: *a gold filling in a tooth.* **2.** An edible mixture used to fill pastries, sandwiches, or cakes: *pie filling.*

filling station ►*n.* See **gas station.**

fil·lip (fĭl′əp) ►*n.* **1.** A snap of the fingers. **2.** Something that excites. [Imit.] —**fil′lip** *v.*

Fill·more (fĭl′môr′), **Millard** 1800–74. The 13th US president (1850–53).

Millard Fillmore

fil·ly (fĭl′ē) ►*n., pl.* **-lies** A young female horse. [< ON *fylja.*]

film (fĭlm) ►*n.* **1.** A thin skin or membrane. **2.** A thin covering or coating. **3.** A thin transparent sheet, as of plastic, used in packaging. **4.** A thin sheet or strip of material coated with a photosensitive emulsion and used to make photographic negatives or transparencies. **5a.** A movie. **b.** Movies collectively. ►*v.* **1.** To cover with or as if with a film. **2.** To make a movie (of). [< OE *filmen,* thin coating.] —**film′i·ly** *adv.* —**film′i·ness** *n.* —**film′y** *adj.*

film·mak·ing (fĭlm′mā′kĭng) ►*n.* The making of movies. —**film′mak′er** *n.*

film noir (nwär) ►*n.* A movie marked by low-key lighting, a bleak urban setting, and corrupt, cynical characters. [Fr., black film.]

film·strip (fĭlm′strĭp′) ►*n.* A length of film containing graphic matter prepared for still projection one frame at a time.

fil·ter (fĭl′tər) ►*n.* **1.** A porous material through which a liquid or gas is passed in order to separate the fluid from suspended particulate matter. **2.** Any of various devices used to reject signals, vibrations, or radiations of certain frequencies while passing others. **3.** *Comp.* A program that blocks e-mail or restricts website access under certain conditions. ►*v.* **1.** To pass through a filter. **2.** To remove by passing through a filter. **3.** *Comp.* To use a filter, as on a browser or an e-mail program. [< Med.Lat. *filtrum,* of Gmc. orig.] —**fil′ter·a·bil′i·ty** *n.* —**fil′ter·a·ble, fil′tra·ble** *adj.*

filth (fĭlth) ►*n.* **1.** Foul or dirty matter. **2.** Corruption; vileness. **3.** Something considered obscene or immoral. [< OE *fȳlth.*] —**filth′i·ly** *adv.* —**filth′i·ness** *n.* —**filth′y** *adj.*

fil·trate (fĭl′trāt′) ►*v.* **-trat·ed, -trat·ing** To put or go through a filter. ►*n.* Material that has passed through a filter. [< Med.Lat. *filtrum,* FILTER.] —**fil·tra′tion** *n.*

fin (fĭn) ►*n.* **1.** A membranous appendage extending from the body of a fish or other aquatic animal that is used for propelling, steering, or balancing the body in the water. **2.** Something, such as an airfoil, that resembles a fin. **3.** A wide, rubber covering for the foot that is used in swimming. [< OE *finn.*] —**fin′ny** *adj.*

fi·na·gle (fə-nā′gəl) ►*v.* **-gled, -gling** *Informal* To obtain or achieve by cleverness, persuasiveness, or deceit. [Prob. < dial. *fainaigue,* cheat.] —**fi·na′gler** *n.*

fi·nal (fī′nəl) ►*adj.* **1.** Forming or occurring at the end; last. **2.** Of or constituting the end result of a succession or process; ultimate. **3.** Definitive; unalterable. ►*n.* **1.** The last of a series of contests. **2.** The last examination of an academic course. [< Lat. *finis,* end.] —**fi·nal′i·ty** (fī-năl′ĭ-tē, fə-) *n.* —**fi′nal·ly** *adv.*

fi·nal·e (fə-năl′ē, -nä′lē) ►*n.* The concluding part, esp. of a musical composition. [Ital.]

fi·nal·ist (fī′nə-lĭst) ►*n.* A contestant in the final session of a competition.

fi·nal·ize (fī′nə-līz′) ►*v.* **-ized, -iz·ing** To put into final form. —**fi′nal·i·za′tion** *n.*

   Usage: Although *finalize* has been criticized for its association with the language of bureaucracy, it is becoming more acceptable in general use. Rough synonyms can be found in *complete, conclude, make final,* and *put into final form.*

fi·nance (fə-năns′, fī-, fī′năns′) ►*n.* **1.** The management of money, banking, investments, and credit. **2. finances** Monetary resources; funds. ►*v.* **-nanced, -nanc·ing** **1.** To provide or raise the funds or capital for. **2.** To furnish credit to. [< OFr. *finer,* pay ransom.] —**fi·nan′cial** *adj.* —**fi·nan′cial·ly** *adv.*

fin·an·cier (fĭn′ən-sîr′, fə-năn′-, fī′nən-) ►*n.* One who invests or raises large sums of money. [Fr.]

finch (fĭnch) ►*n.* Any of various small birds having a short stout bill. [< OE *finc.*]

find (fīnd) ►*v.* **found** (found), **find·ing** **1.** To come upon, often by accident. **2.** To come upon after a search. **3.** To discover through observation, experience, or study. **4.** To perceive to be: *found the movie dull.* **5.** To recover; regain: *found her voice.* **6.** To arrive at; attain: *found happiness at last.* **7.** To decide and make a declaration about: *find a verdict of guilty.* **8.** To perceive (oneself) to be in a specific place or condition: *found myself alone in the house.* ►*n.* **1.** The act of finding. **2.** An unexpectedly valuable discovery. —*phrasal verb:* **find out** **1.** To ascertain, as through examination or inquiry. **2.** To detect the true character of; expose. [< OE *findan.*] —**find′a·ble** *adj.* —**find′er** *n.*

fin-de-siè·cle (făN′də-sē-ĕk′lə) ►*adj.* Of or characteristic of the last part of the 1800s, esp. its artistic climate of effete sophistication. [Fr.]

find·ing (fīn′dĭng) ►*n.* **1.** A conclusion reached after examination or investigation. **2.** A document containing an authoritative conclusion.

fine[1] (fīn) ►*adj.* **fin·er, fin·est** **1.** Of superior quality, skill, or appearance: *a fine day.* **2.** Very small in size, weight, or thickness: *fine type.* **3.** Very sharp: *a blade with a fine edge.* **4.** Carefully or delicately made or done: *fine china.* See Synonyms at **exquisite.** **5.** Consisting of very small particles: *fine dust.* **6.** Subtle or precise: *a fine difference.* **7.** Marked by refinement or elegance. **8.** Satisfactory; acceptable: *It'll be fine if you're five minutes late.* **9.** Being in good condition or health. **10.** Used as an intensive: *a fine mess.* ►*adv. Informal* Very well: *doing fine.* [< Lat. *finis,* end.] —**fine′ly** *adv.* —**fine′ness** *n.*

fine[2] (fīn) ►*n.* A sum of money imposed as a penalty for an offense. ►*v.* **fined, fin·ing** To impose a fine on: *fined him for littering.* —*idiom:* **in fine** **1.** In conclusion. **2.** In brief. [< Lat. *finis,* end.]

fi·ne[3] (fē′nä) ►*n. Mus.* The end. [Ital. < Lat. *finis,* end.]

fine art (fīn) ►*n.* **1.** Art intended primarily for beauty rather than utility. **2.** often **fine arts** Any of the art forms, such as sculpture, painting, and music, used to create this art.

fine print ►*n.* The portion of a document that contains qualifications or restrictions in small type or obscure language.

fin·er·y (fī′nə-rē) ►*n., pl.* **-ies** Elaborate adornment, esp. fine clothing.

fi·nesse (fə-nĕs′) ►*n.* **1.** Refinement and delicacy of performance, execution, or artisanship. **2.** Subtlety; tact. ►*v.* **-nessed, -ness·ing** To handle with subtle or evasive strategy: *finesse an embarrassing question.* [Fr. < *fin,* FINE[1].]

fine-tune (fīn′to͞on′, -tyo͞on′) ►*v.* To make

small adjustments in for optimal performance or effectiveness.

fin·ger (fĭng′gər) ►*n.* **1.** One of the five digits of the hand, esp. one other than the thumb. **2.** The part of a glove that fits a finger. **3.** Something that resembles a finger. ►*v.* **1.** To touch with the fingers; handle. **2.** *Mus.* To play (an instrument) by using the fingers in a particular order or way. **3.** *Slang* **a.** To inform on. **b.** To designate, esp. as an intended victim. [< OE.]

fin·ger·board (fĭng′gər-bôrd′) ►*n.* A strip of wood on the neck of a stringed instrument against which the strings are pressed in playing.

finger bowl ►*n.* A small bowl that holds water for rinsing the fingers at the table.

fin·ger·ing (fĭng′gər-ĭng) ►*n.* The technique used in playing a musical instrument with the fingers.

Finger Lakes A group of elongated glacial lakes in W-central NY.

fin·ger·ling (fĭng′gər-lĭng) ►*n.* A young or small fish.

fin·ger·nail (fĭng′gər-nāl′) ►*n.* The nail on a finger.

fin·ger·print (fĭng′gər-prĭnt′) ►*n.* **1.** An impression formed by the curves in the ridges on a fingertip, used esp. as a means of identification. **2.** A distinctive mark. —**fin′ger·print′** *v.*

fin·ger·tip (fĭng′gər-tĭp′) ►*n.* The extreme end of a finger. —*idiom:* **at (one's) fingertips** Readily available.

fin·i·al (fĭn′ē-əl) ►*n.* An ornamental projection or terminating part, as on a gable. [ME.]

fin·ick·y (fĭn′ĭ-kē) ►*adj.* **-i·er, -i·est** Difficult to please; fussy. [Prob. ult. < FINE¹.] —**fin′ick·i·ness** *n.*

fin·is (fĭn′ĭs, fī′nĭs, fē-nē′) ►*n.* The end. [ME < Lat. *fīnis.*]

fin·ish (fĭn′ĭsh) ►*v.* **1.** To reach the end (of). **2.** To bring to an end; terminate. **3.** To consume all of; use up. **4.** To give (a surface) a desired texture. **5.** To destroy; kill. ►*n.* **1.** The final part; the conclusion. **2.** Surface texture. **3.** Completeness or refinement of execution; polish. [< Lat. *fīnīre,* to complete.] —**fin′ish·er** *n.*

fi·nite (fī′nīt′) ►*adj.* **1.** Having bounds; limited. **2.** *Math.* Being neither infinite nor infinitesimal. **3.** *Gram.* Limited by person, number, tense, and mood. Used of a verb. [< Lat. *fīnītus.*] —**fi′nite·ly** *adv.* —**fi′nite′ness** *n.*

fink (fĭngk) *Slang* ►*n.* **1.** A contemptible person. **2.** An informer. ►*v.* **1.** To inform against another person. **2.** To let another down. [?]

Fin·land (fĭn′lənd) A country of N Europe on the Gulf of Bothnia and the Gulf of Finland. Cap. Helsinki.

Finland, Gulf of An arm of the Baltic Sea bordered by Finland, Russia, and Estonia.

Finn (fĭn) ►*n.* A native or inhabitant of Finland.

Fin·nic (fĭn′ĭk) ►*n.* A branch of Finno-Ugric that includes Finnish, Estonian, and Sami.

Finn·ish (fĭn′ĭsh) ►*adj.* Of or relating to Finland or its people or language. ►*n.* The Finno-Ugric language of the Finns.

Fin·no-U·gric (fĭn′ō-ōō′grĭk, -yōō′-) also **Fin·no-U·gri·an** (-ōō′grē-ən, -yōō′-) ►*n.* A subfamily of the Uralic language family that includes Finnish, Hungarian, and other languages of E and NE Europe. —**Finno-Ugric** *adj.*

fir (fûr) ►*n.* **1.** Any of a genus of evergreen trees having flattened needles and erect cones. **2.** The wood of a fir. [ME *firre.*]

fire (fīr) ►*n.* **1.** A rapid chemical reaction that releases heat and light by oxidation and is accompanied by flame. **2.** A destructive burning: *insured against fire.* **3.** Enthusiasm; ardor. **4.** Brilliance; sparkle: *the fire of a cut gem.* **5.** The discharge of firearms. **6.** Intense, repeated attack or criticism. ►*v.* **fired, fir·ing 1.** To ignite. **2.** To bake in a kiln. **3.** To arouse the emotions of: *demonstrators who were fired up by the orator.* **4.** To detonate or discharge (a weapon). **5.** To throw with force; hurl: *A cannon that fires harpoons.* **6.** To discharge from a position; dismiss. See Synonyms at **dismiss.** —*idiom:* **on fire 1.** Ignited; ablaze. **2.** Ardent; impassioned. [< OE *fȳr.*] —**fir′er** *n.*

fire ant ►*n.* Any of various ants of the S US and tropical America that inflict a painful sting.

fire·arm (fīr′ärm′) ►*n.* A weapon, esp. a pistol or rifle, that uses explosive charges to hurl projectiles.

fire·ball (fīr′bôl′) ►*n.* **1.** A brilliantly burning sphere. **2.** A highly luminous, intensely hot spherical cloud generated by a nuclear explosion.

fire·bomb (fīr′bŏm′) ►*n.* A bomb designed to start a fire. —**fire′bomb′** *v.*

fire·brand (fīr′brănd′) ►*n.* **1.** A piece of burning wood. **2.** One who stirs up trouble; agitator.

fire·break (fīr′brāk′) ►*n.* A strip of cleared or plowed land used to stop the spread of a fire.

fire·brick (fīr′brĭk′) ►*n.* A refractory brick, usu. of fire clay, used for lining furnaces, chimneys, or fireplaces.

fire·bug (fīr′bŭg′) ►*n. Informal* An arsonist.

fire clay (fīr′klā′) ►*n.* A type of heat-resistant clay used esp. to make firebricks.

fire·crack·er (fīr′krăk′ər) ►*n.* A small explosive charge and a fuse in a heavy paper casing, exploded for entertainment.

fire·damp (fīr′dămp′) ►*n.* A combustible gas, chiefly methane, that occurs in coal mines and forms an explosive mixture with air.

fire engine ►*n.* A large truck that carries firefighters and often ladders or pumping equipment to a fire.

fire escape ►*n.* An outside stairway for exiting a building in the event of fire.

fire extinguisher ►*n.* A portable apparatus containing chemicals that can be discharged in a rapid stream to extinguish a small fire.

fire·fight (fīr′fīt′) ►*n.* An exchange of gunfire, as between infantry units.

fire·fight·er (fīr′fī′tər) ►*n.* A member of a fire department who fights fires. See Usage Note at **man.** —**fire′fight′ing** *adj. & n.*

fire·fly (fīr′flī′) ►*n.* Any of various nocturnal beetles having luminescent chemicals in the tip of the abdomen that produce a flashing light.

fire·house (fīr′hous′) ►*n.* See **fire station.**

fire hydrant ►*n.* An upright pipe with a nozzle or spout for drawing water from a water main.

fire irons ►*pl.n.* Implements, such as tongs and a poker, used to tend a fireplace.

fire·man (fīr′mən) ►*n.* **1.** A firefighter. See Usage Note at **man. 2.** A man who tends fires; stoker.

fire·place (fīr′plās′) ►*n.* An open recess for holding a fire at the base of a chimney.

fire·plug (fīr′plŭg′) ►*n.* See **fire hydrant.**

fire·pow·er (fīr′pou′ər) ►*n.* The capacity, as of a military unit, for delivering fire.

fire·proof (fīr′pro͞of′) ►*adj.* Impervious to damage by fire. ►*v.* To make fireproof.

fire·side (fīr′sīd′) ►*n.* The area immediately surrounding a fireplace.

fire station ►*n.* A building for fire equipment and firefighters.

fire tower ►*n.* A tower in which a lookout for fires is posted.

fire·trap (fīr′trăp′) ►*n.* A building that can catch fire easily or is difficult to escape from in the event of fire.

fire·wall (fīr′wôl) ►*n.* **1.** A fireproof wall used as a barrier to prevent the spread of fire. **2.** *Comp.* A program or device that prevents unauthorized users from accessing a network.

fire·wa·ter (fīr′wô′tər, -wŏt′ər) ►*n.* *Slang* Strong liquor, esp. whiskey. [Translation of Ojibwa *ishkodewaaboo,* whiskey.]

fire·wood (fīr′wo͝od′) ►*n.* Wood used as fuel.

fire·works (fīr′wûrks′) ►*pl.n.* **1.** Explosives and combustibles that are set off to generate colored lights, smoke, and noise for amusement. **2.** A spectacular display, as of musical virtuosity.

fir·ing line (fīr′ĭng) ►*n.* **1.** The line of positions from which fire is directed at a target. **2.** The forefront of an activity; vanguard.

firing pin ►*n.* The part of the bolt of a firearm that strikes the primer and detonates the charge of a projectile.

firm¹ (fûrm) ►*adj.* **-er, -est 1.** Resistant to externally applied pressure. **2.** Marked by the tone and resiliency of healthy tissue: *firm muscles.* **3.** Indicating determination or resolution: *a firm voice.* **4.** Constant; steadfast: *a firm ally.* **5.** Fixed and definite: *a firm offer.* **6.** Strong and sure: *a firm grasp.* ►*v.* To make or become firm. ►*adv.* **-er, -est** Resolutely: *stand firm.* [< Lat. *firmus.*] —**firm′ly** *adv.* —**firm′ness** *n.*

firm² (fûrm) ►*n.* **1.** A business enterprise. **2.** An unincorporated business, particularly a partnership. [< Med.Lat. *firmāre,* ratify by signature, ult. < Lat. *firmus,* firm.]

fir·ma·ment (fûr′mə-mənt) ►*n.* The vault or expanse of the heavens; sky. [< Lat. *firmāmentum,* support.]

firm·ware (fûrm′wâr′) ►*n.* Software stored in a computer's ROM.

first (fûrst) ►*n.* **1.** The ordinal number matching the number 1 in a series. **2.** The one coming, occurring, or ranking before all others. **3.** The beginning; outset: *from the first.* **4.** The lowest forward gear in a motor vehicle. **5.** The winning position in a contest. ►*adj.* **1.** Coming before all others in order or location. **2.** Prior to all others in time; earliest. **3.** Ranking above all others; foremost. **4.** Belonging to the household of the chief executive of a country, state, or city: *the first daughters.* ►*adv.* **1.** Before or above all others in time, order, rank, or importance. **2.** For the first time. **3.** Rather; preferably: *would die first.* **4.** To begin with. [< OE *fyrst.*]

first aid ►*n.* Emergency treatment given to an injured or sick person or animal, esp. by someone who does not have medical training.

first base ►*n. Baseball* The first base reached by a runner moving counterclockwise from home plate. —**first baseman** *n.*

first-born (fûrst′bôrn′) ►*adj.* First in order of birth. —**first′born′** *n.*

first class ►*n.* **1.** The first, highest, or best group in a system of classification. **2.** The most expensive class of accommodations, as on an airplane or ship. —**first′-class′** *adj. & adv.*

first cousin ►*n.* See **cousin** (sense 1).

first-de·gree burn (fûrst′dĭ-grē′) ►*n.* A mild burn that produces redness of the skin but no blistering.

first-gen·er·a·tion (fûrst′jĕn′ə-rā′shən) ►*adj.* **1.** Relating to an immigrant to another country. **2.** Relating to one whose parents are immigrants. **3.** Relating to the first available version of something: *a first-generation electric car.*

first·hand (fûrst′hănd′) ►*adj.* Received from the original source. —**first′hand′** *adv.*

first-in, first-out (fûrst′ĭn′ fûrst′out′) ►*n.* A method of inventory accounting in which the oldest remaining items are assumed to have been the first sold.

first lady ►*n.* The wife or hostess of the chief executive of a country, state, or city.

first·ly (fûrst′lē) ►*adv.* To begin with.

first mate ►*n.* An officer on a merchant ship ranking immediately below the captain.

first person ►*n.* The form of a verb or pronoun designating the speaker or writer of the sentence in which it appears.

first-rate (fûrst′rāt′) ►*adj.* Foremost in quality, rank, or importance.

first sergeant ►*n.* A rank in the US Army and Marine Corps equivalent in rank to master sergeant.

first strike ►*n.* A preemptive attack against an enemy, esp. one using nuclear weapons. —**first′-strike′** *adj.*

first string ►*n.* A group of players that play regularly or start games for a sports team.

firth (fûrth) ►*n. Scots* A long narrow inlet of the sea. [< ON *fjördhr.*]

fis·cal (fĭs′kəl) ►*adj.* **1.** Of or relating to government expenditures, revenues, and debt. **2.** Of or relating to finance or finances. [< Lat. *fiscus,* treasury.] —**fis′cal·ly** *adv.*

fiscal year ►*n.* A 12-month period for which an organization plans the use of its funds.

fish (fĭsh) ►*n., pl.* **fish** or **fish·es 1.** Any of numerous cold-blooded aquatic vertebrates having fins, gills, and a streamlined body. **2.** The edible flesh of a fish. ►*v.* **1.** To catch or try to catch fish. **2.** To grope: *fished in both pockets for a coin.* **3.** To seek something indirectly: *fish for compliments.* [< OE *fisc.*] —**fish′er** *n.* —**fish′ing** *n.*

fish·bowl (fĭsh′bōl′) ►*n.* **1.** A transparent bowl in which live fish are kept. **2.** *Informal* A place lacking in privacy.

fish·er·man (fĭsh′ər-mən) ►*n.* **1.** One who fishes as an occupation or for sport. **2.** A commercial fishing vessel.

fish·er·y (fĭsh′ə-rē) ►*n., pl.* **-ies 1.** The industry of catching, processing, or selling fish. **2.** A fishing ground. **3.** A fish hatchery.

fish·eye (fĭsh′ī′) ►*adj.* Of or being a camera lens that covers an angle of about 180°.

fish hawk ►*n.* See **osprey.**

fish·hook (fĭsh′ho͝ok′) ►*n.* A barbed metal hook for catching fish.

fishing rod ►*n.* A rod used with a line for catching fish.

fish ladder ►*n.* A steplike series of artificial pools by which fish can pass around a dam.

fish ladder

fish·meal (fĭsh′mēl′) ►*n.* Ground dried fish used as animal feed and fertilizer.

fish·net (fĭsh′nĕt′) ►*n.* **1.** Netting used to catch fish. **2.** A mesh fabric resembling such netting, often used to make stockings.

fish story ►*n. Informal* An implausible, boastful story.

fish·wife (fĭsh′wīf′) ►*n.* **1.** A woman who sells fish. **2.** A woman regarded as coarse and shrewish.

fish·y (fĭsh′ē) ►*adj.* **-i·er, -i·est 1.** Resembling or suggestive of fish. **2.** *Informal* Inspiring doubt or suspicion. —**fish′i·ly** *adv.* —**fish′i·ness** *n.*

fis·sile (fĭs′əl, -īl′) ►*adj.* **1.** Possible to split. **2.** *Phys.* Fissionable, esp. by neutrons of all energies. [< Lat. *findere, fiss-*, split.] —**fis·sil′i·ty** (fĭ-sĭl′ĭ-tē) *n.*

fis·sion (fĭsh′ən) ►*n.* **1.** The act or process of splitting into parts. **2.** A nuclear reaction in which an atomic nucleus splits into fragments, generating about 100 million electron volts of energy. **3.** *Biol.* An asexual reproductive process in which a unicellular organism divides into two or more independently maturing cells. [< Lat. *findere, fiss-*, split.] —**fis′sion·a·ble** *adj.*

fis·sure (fĭsh′ər) ►*n.* A long narrow opening. [< Lat. *fissūra* < *findere*, split.] —**fis′sure** *v.*

fist (fĭst) ►*n.* The hand closed tightly with the fingers bent against the palm. [< OE *fȳst*.]

fist·fight (fĭst′fīt′) ►*n.* A fight with the bare fists.

fist·ful (fĭst′fool′) ►*n., pl.* **-fuls** The amount a clenched fist can hold.

fist·i·cuffs (fĭs′tĭ-kŭfs′) ►*pl.n.* **1.** A fistfight. **2.** The activity of fighting with the fists.

fis·tu·la (fĭs′chə-lə) ►*n., pl.* **-las** or **-lae** (-lē′) An abnormal duct or passage that connects a hollow organ to the body surface or to another hollow organ. [< Lat.]

fit¹ (fĭt) ►*v.* **fit·ted** or **fit, fit·ted, fit·ting 1.** to be the proper size and shape (for): *These shoes fit me.* **2.** To be appropriate to; suit. **3.** To make suitable. See Synonyms at **adapt. 4.** To equip; outfit: *fit out a ship.* **5.** To provide a place or time for: *The doctor can fit you in today.* ►*adj.* **fit·ter, fit·test 1.** Suited, adapted, or acceptable for a given circumstance or purpose. **2.** Appropriate; proper. **3.** Physically healthy. ►*n.* The manner in which something fits: *a tight fit.* [ME *fitten*, be suitable.] —**fit′ly** *adv.* —**fit′ter** *n.*

fit² (fĭt) ►*n.* **1.** *Med.* **a.** A seizure or convulsion, esp. one caused by epilepsy. **b.** The sudden appearance of a symptom such as coughing or sneezing. **2.** A sudden outburst: *a fit of jealousy.* **3.** A sudden period of vigorous activity. [ME, hardship.]

fit·ful (fĭt′fəl) ►*adj.* Intermittent; irregular. —**fit′ful·ly** *adv.* —**fit′ful·ness** *n.*

fit·ness (fĭt′nĭs) ►*n.* **1.** The state of being physically fit, esp. as the result of exercise and proper nutrition. **2.** *Biol.* The ability to survive or to produce offspring in a particular environment.

fit·ting (fĭt′ĭng) ►*adj.* Suitable; appropriate. ►*n.* **1.** The act of trying on clothes for fit. **2.** A small detachable part for a machine. —**fit′ting·ly** *adv.* —**fit′ting·ness** *n.*

Fitz·ger·ald (fĭts-jĕr′əld), **Ella Jane** 1917–96. Amer. jazz singer.

Fitzgerald, F(rancis) Scott (Key) 1896–1940. Amer. writer.

F. Scott Fitzgerald
photographed in the 1920s

five (fīv) ►*n.* **1.** The cardinal number equal to 4 + 1. **2.** The 5th in a set or sequence. [< OE *fīf*.] —**five** *adj. & pron.*

five-and-ten (fīv′ən-tĕn′) ►*n.* A retail store selling a wide variety of inexpensive articles. [Short for *five-and-ten-cent store*.]

fix (fĭks) ►*v.* **1.** To correct or set right; adjust. **2.** To restore to proper condition; repair. **3.** To make ready; prepare: *fixed lunch.* **4.** To spay or castrate (an animal). **5.** To influence the outcome of by improper or unlawful means: *fixed the boxing match.* **6a.** To place securely. See Synonyms at **fasten. b.** To secure to another; attach. **7a.** To put into a stable or unalterable form. **b.** To make (a chemical substance) non-volatile or solid. **c.** To convert (nitrogen or carbon) into biologically assimilable compounds. **d.** To prevent discoloration of (a photographic image) by coating with a chemical preservative. **8.** To direct steadily: *fixed her eyes on the road.* **9.** To establish definitely; specify: *fix a time to meet.* **10.** To assign; attribute: *fix blame.* **11.** *Informal* To get even with. ►*n.* **1.** The act of adjusting, correcting, or repairing. **2.** A solution: *a quick fix.* **3.** The position, as of a ship or aircraft, determined by observation or equipment. **4.** An instance of prearranging an improper or illegal outcome, esp. by means of bribery. **5.** A predicament. **6.** *Slang* A dose of a narcotic. [< Lat. *figere, fix-*, fasten.] —**fix′a· ble** *adj.* —**fix′er** *n.*

fix·ate (fĭk′sāt′) ►*v.* -**at·ed, -at·ing 1.** To cause (a person or the eyes) to look at or pay attention to something steadily. **2.** To command the attention of exclusively or repeatedly; preoccupy obsessively. **3.** *Psychol.* To cause to become emotionally attached in an immature or pathological manner. —**fix·a′tion** *n.*

fix·a·tive (fĭk′sə-tĭv) ►*n.* A substance that fixes or preserves. —**fix′a·tive** *adj.*

fixed (fĭkst) ►*adj.* **1.** Stationary: *a fixed dwelling.* **2.** Determined; established: *a fixed price.* **3.** Invariable; constant: *lives on a fixed income.* **4.** *Chem.* **a.** Nonvolatile. **b.** In a stable, combined form. **5.** Firmly, often dogmatically held: *fixed notions.* **6.** Illegally prearranged: *a fixed election.* —**fix′ed·ly** (fĭk′sĭd-lē) *adv.* —**fix′ed·ness** *n.*

fix·ings (fĭk′sĭngz) ►*pl.n. Informal* Accessories; trimmings: *turkey with all the fixings.*

fix·i·ty (fĭk′sĭ-tē) ►*n.* The quality or condition of being fixed; stability.

fix·ture (fĭks′chər) ►*n.* **1.** Something attached as a permanent apparatus or appliance: *plumbing fixtures.* **2.** One long associated with a place or setting. [< LLat. *fīxūra.*]

fizz (fĭz) ►*n.* **1.** A hissing or bubbling sound. **2.** Effervescence. [Imit.] —**fizz** *v.* —**fizz′y** *adj.*

fiz·zle (fĭz′əl) ►*v.* -**zled, -zling 1.** To make a hissing or sputtering sound. **2.** *Informal* To fail or end weakly, esp. after a hopeful beginning. ►*n. Informal* A failure. [Prob. < obsolete *fist*, break wind.]

fjord (fyôrd) ►*n.* A long, narrow, deep inlet of the sea between steep slopes. [< ON *fjördhr.*]

FL ►*abbr.* **1.** Florida **2.** focal length

fl. ►*abbr.* **1.** *Lat.* floruit (flourished) **2.** fluid

flab (flăb) ►*n.* Soft, fatty body tissue.

flab·ber·gast (flăb′ər-găst′) ►*v.* To overwhelm with astonishment; astound. [?]

flab·by (flăb′ē) ►*adj.* -**bi·er, -bi·est 1.** Soft and hanging loosely or in folds: *a flabby belly.* **2.** Having a body characterized by fleshiness or softness: *He is flabby around the waist.* **3.** Lacking force; feeble. [< *flappy*, tending to flap < FLAP.] —**flab′bi·ly** *adv.* —**flab′bi·ness** *n.*

flac·cid (flăs′ĭd, flăk′sĭd) ►*adj.* Lacking firmness, resilience, or muscle tone. [< Lat. *flaccus.*] —**flac·cid′i·ty** *n.* —**flac′cid·ly** *adv.*

flack[1] (flăk) ►*n.* A press agent. [Perh. after Gene *Flack*, a 20th-cent. movie press agent.]

flack[2] (flăk) ►*n.* Var. of **flak.**

flac·on (flăk′ən, -ŏn′) ►*n.* A small stoppered bottle. [< OFr., FLAGON.]

flag[1] (flăg) ►*n.* **1.** A piece of cloth of distinctive color and design, used as a symbol, signal, or emblem. **2.** A marker; tab. ►*v.* **flagged, flag·ging 1.** To mark with a flag. **2.** To signal with or as if with a flag: *flagged the car to stop.* [?] —**flag′ger** *n.*

flag[2] (flăg) ►*n.* A plant, as an iris, that has long bladelike leaves. [ME *flagge*, reed.]

flag[3] (flăg) ►*v.* **flagged, flag·ging** To lose strength; weaken: *The conversation flagged.* [Poss. of Scand. orig.]

flag[4] (flăg) ►*n.* A flagstone. [< ON *flaga*, slab of stone.]

flag·el·late (flăj′ə-lāt′) ►*v.* -**lat·ed, -lat·ing 1.** To whip or flog; scourge. **2.** To reproach or punish severely: *flagellated himself for being*

so late. [< Lat. *flagellum*, FLAIL.] —**flag′el· la′tion** *n.*

fla·gel·lum (flə-jĕl′əm) ►*n., pl.* -**gel·la** (-jĕl′ə) **1.** A whiplike extension of certain cells or unicellular organisms that functions as an organ in locomotion. **2.** A whip. [Lat., FLAIL.]

flag·on (flăg′ən) ►*n.* A large vessel with a handle and spout, used for holding wine or liquors. [< LLat. *flascō*, bottle; see FLASK.]

flag·pole (flăg′pōl′) ►*n.* A pole on which a flag is raised.

fla·grant (flā′grənt) ►*adj.* Conspicuously bad, offensive, or reprehensible. [< Lat. *flagrāre*, burn.] —**fla′gran·cy, fla′grance** *n.* —**fla′- grant·ly** *adv.*

flag·ship (flăg′shĭp′) ►*n.* **1.** A ship that carries a fleet or squadron commander and bears the commander's flag. **2.** The chief one of a group: *the flagship of a newspaper chain.*

flag·staff (flăg′stăf′) ►*n.* See **flagpole.**

flag·stone (flăg′stōn′) ►*n.* A flat, evenly layered paving stone.

flag-wav·ing (flăg′wā′vĭng) ►*n.* Excessive or fanatical patriotism. —**flag′-wav′er** *n.*

flail (flāl) ►*n.* A manual threshing device with a long wooden handle and a short, free-swinging stick on the end. ►*v.* **1.** To beat with or as if with a flail. **2.** To wave or swing vigorously; thrash: *flailed my arms to get attention.* [< LLat. *flagellum* < Lat. *flagrum*, whip.]

flair (flâr) ►*n.* **1.** A talent or aptitude. **2.** Instinctive discernment; keenness: *a flair for fashion.* **3.** Distinctive elegance or style: *served us with flair.* [< OFr., fragrance < Lat. *frāgrāre*, emit an odor.]

flak also **flack** (flăk) ►*n.* **1a.** Antiaircraft artillery. **b.** The bursting shells fired from such artillery. **2.** *Informal* **a.** Excessive criticism. **b.** Dissension; opposition. [Ger.]

flake (flāk) ►*n.* **1.** A flat thin piece or layer; chip. **2.** A crystal of snow. **3.** *Slang* A somewhat eccentric person; oddball. ►*v.* **flaked, flak· ing** To break into or come off in flakes. [ME.] —**flak′er** *n.* —**flak′i·ly** *adv.* —**flak′i·ness** *n.* —**flak′y, flak′ey** *adj.*

flam·bé (fläm-bā′, fläN-) ►*adj.* Served flaming in ignited liquor. [Fr., p.part. of *flamber*, to flame.] —**flam·bé′** *v.*

flam·boy·ant (flăm-boi′ənt) ►*adj.* **1.** Marked by elaborate, ostentatious, or audacious display or behavior. See Synonyms at **showy. 2.** Richly or brightly colored; resplendent. [< OFr. *flamboyer*, to blaze.] —**flam·boy′ance, flam· boy′an·cy** *n.* —**flam·boy′ant·ly** *adv.*

flame (flām) ►*n.* **1.** The zone of burning gases and fine suspended matter associated with rapid combustion. **2.** A violent or intense passion. **3.** *Informal* A sweetheart. **4.** An insulting or malicious remark, as on a computer network. ►*v.* **flamed, flam·ing 1.** To burn brightly; blaze. **2.** To color suddenly: *cheeks that flamed with embarrassment.* **3.** *Informal* To insult or criticize provokingly, as on a computer network. [< Lat. *flamma.*] —**flam′er** *n.*

fla·men·co (flə-mĕng′kō) ►*n., pl.* -**cos 1.** A dance style of the Andalusian Romani, with forceful, often improvised rhythms. **2.** The guitar music that usu. accompanies such a dance. [Sp., Flemish < MDu. *Vlāming.*]

flame·out (flām′out′) ►*n.* **1.** Failure of a jet aircraft engine, esp. in flight. **2.** Sudden failure or disgrace, esp. of a highly successful person.

flame·throw·er (flām′thrō′ər) ►*n.* A weapon that projects a steady stream of ignited fuel.

fla·min·go (flə-mǐng′gō) ►*n., pl.* **-gos** or **-goes** A large wading bird with pinkish plumage, long legs, and a long flexible neck. [Prob. < OProv. *flamenc.*]

flamingo

flam·ma·ble (flăm′ə-bəl) ►*adj.* Easily ignited and capable of burning rapidly. [< Lat. *flammāre*, set fire to.] **—flam′ma·bil′i·ty** *n.* **—flam′ma·ble** *n.*

Usage: Because some people mistakenly believe that *inflammable* means "not flammable," use *flammable* to avoid confusion.

flan (flăn, flän, flän) ►*n.* **1.** A custard baked in a caramel-lined mold. **2.** A tart with a filling of custard, fruit, or cheese. [< LLat. *fladō*, flat cake, of Gmc. orig.]

Flan·ders (flăn′dərz) A historical region of NW Europe including parts of N France, W Belgium, and SW Netherlands.

flange (flănj) ►*n.* A protruding rim or edge, as on a wheel, used to strengthen an object or hold it in place. [Perh. ult. < Fr. *flanc*, side.] **—flange** *v.*

flank (flăngk) ►*n.* **1.** The section of flesh between the last rib and the hip; side. **2.** A cut of meat from an animal's flank. **3.** A lateral part or side: *the flank of a mountain.* **4.** The right or left side of a military formation. ►*v.* **1.** To protect or guard the flank of. **2.** To menace or attack the flank of. **3.** To place or be placed at the side of: *Guards flanked the entrance.* [< OFr. *flanc.*]

flan·nel (flăn′əl) ►*n.* **1.** A soft woven cloth of wool or a blend of wool and cotton or synthetics. **2. flannels** Clothing made of this cloth. [ME.]

flap (flăp) ►*n.* **1.** A projecting or hanging piece usu. attached to something on one side and often intended to protect or cover: *an envelope flap.* **2.** Either of the folded ends of a book jacket that fit inside the front and back covers. **3.** The act of waving or fluttering. **4.** A commotion or disturbance. ►*v.* **flapped, flap·ping** **1.** To wave (e.g., wings or arms) up and down. **2.** To wave loosely; flutter. [ME *flappe*, a slap.]

flap·jack (flăp′jăk′) ►*n.* See **pancake.**

flap·per (flăp′ər) ►*n.* **1.** A broad, flexible part, such as a flipper. **2.** A young woman in the 1920s whose dress and behavior showed disdain for conventional norms.

flare (flâr) ►*v.* **flared, flar·ing** **1.** To flame up with a bright, wavering light. **2.** To burst into

intense, sudden flame. **3.** To erupt or intensify suddenly. **4.** To expand or open outward in shape, as a skirt. ►*n.* **1.** A brief, wavering blaze of light. **2.** A device that produces a bright light for signaling or illumination. **3.** An outbreak, as of emotion. **4.** An expanding outward. [?]

flare-up (flâr′ŭp′) ►*n.* **1.** A sudden outburst, as of flame or anger. **2.** A recurrence, esp. of a disease or condition: *a flare-up of arthritis.*

flash (flăsh) ►*v.* **1.** To burst forth into or as if into flame. **2.** To give off light or be lighted in sudden or intermittent bursts. **3.** To appear or cause to appear suddenly. **4.** To move rapidly. **5.** To communicate (information) at great speed. **6.** To display ostentatiously; flaunt. ►*n.* **1.** A sudden, brief, intense display of light. **2.** A sudden perception. **3.** A split second; instant. **4.** A brief news dispatch or transmission. **5a.** Instantaneous illumination for photography. **b.** A device used to produce such illumination. [ME *flashen*, to splash.]

flash·back (flăsh′băk′) ►*n.* **1.** A literary or cinematic device in which an earlier event is inserted into the normal chronological order of a narrative. **2.** *Psychiat.* A recurring, intensely vivid mental image of a past traumatic experience: *flashbacks of the war.* **3.** An unexpected recurrence of the effects of a hallucinogenic drug long after its original use. **4.** A vivid memory that arises spontaneously or is provoked by an experience.

flash·bulb or **flash bulb** (flăsh′bŭlb′) ►*n.* A glass bulb filled with finely shredded metal foil that is ignited by electricity to produce a bright flash for taking photographs.

flash flood ►*n.* A sudden flood of great volume, usu. caused by heavy rain.

flash-for·ward (flăsh′fôr′wərd) ►*n.* A literary or cinematic device in which the chronological sequence of events is interrupted by the interjection of a future event.

flash·gun (flăsh′gŭn′) ►*n.* A dry-cell powered photographic apparatus that holds and electrically triggers a flashbulb.

flash·ing (flăsh′ĭng) ►*n.* Sheet metal used to reinforce and weatherproof the joints and angles of a roof.

flash·light (flăsh′līt′) ►*n.* A small portable lamp usu. powered by batteries.

flash point ►*n.* **1.** The lowest temperature at which the vapor of a combustible liquid or solid can be made to ignite. **2.** The point at which eruption into which violence or other significant action occurs: *a crisis that brought community tension to the flash point.*

flash·y (flăsh′ē) ►*adj.* **-i·er, -i·est** **1.** Cheap and showy. See Synonyms at **garish.** **2.** Having a momentary or superficial brilliance. **—flash′i·ly** *adv.* **—flash′i·ness** *n.*

flask (flăsk) ►*n.* **1.** A flat, relatively thin container that is used for holding liquor. **2.** A vial or round long-necked vessel for laboratory use. **3.** A case for carrying gunpowder. [< LLat. *flascō*, of Gmc. orig.]

flat¹ (flăt) ►*adj.* **flat·ter, flat·test** **1.** Having a horizontal surface without a slope, tilt, or curvature. **2.** Stretched out or lying at full length along the ground; prone. **3.** Free of qualification; absolute: *a flat refusal.* **4.** Fixed; unvarying: *a flat rate.* **5.** Lacking interest or excitement; dull. **6a.** Lacking in flavor. **b.** Having lost effervescence. **7.** Deflated, as a tire. **8.** *Mus.* **a.** Being below the correct pitch. **b.** Being one half step lower than the corresponding natural key: *the key of B flat* ►*adv.* **1.** Level with the ground; horizontally. **2.** On or up against a flat surface; at full length. **3a.** Directly; completely: *flat broke.* **b.** Exactly; precisely: *arrived in six minutes flat.* **4.** *Mus.* Below the intended pitch. ►*n.* **1.** A flat surface or part. **2.** often **flats** A stretch of level ground. **3.** A shallow frame or box for seeds or seedlings. **4.** A deflated tire. **5.** A shoe with a flat heel. **6.** *Mus.* **a.** A sign (♭) used to indicate that a note is to be lowered by a half step. **b.** A note that is lowered a half step. ►*v.* **flat·ted, flat·ting 1.** To make flat; flatten. **2.** *Mus.* **a.** To lower (a note) a semitone. **b.** To sing or play below the proper pitch. [< ON *flatr.*] —**flat′ly** *adv.* —**flat′ness** *n.*

flat² (flăt) ►*n.* An apartment on one floor of a building. [< OE *flet,* floor, dwelling.]

flat·bed (flăt′bĕd′) ►*n.* An open truck bed or trailer with no sides.

flat·boat (flăt′bōt′) ►*n.* A boat with a flat bottom used for transporting freight on inland waterways.

flat·car (flăt′kär′) ►*n.* A railroad freight car without sides or roof.

flat·fish (flăt′fĭsh′) ►*n.* A chiefly marine fish, including flounder or sole, having a laterally compressed body with both eyes on the upper side.

flat·foot (flăt′fŏŏt′) ►*n.* **1.** *pl.* **-feet** (-fēt′) A condition in which the arch of the foot is flattened so that the entire sole makes contact with the ground. **2.** *pl.* **-foots** *Slang* A police officer. —**flat′-foot′ed** *adj.*

Flat·head (flăt′hĕd′) ►*n., pl.* **-head** or **-heads 1.** A member of a Native American people of W Montana and N Idaho. **2.** The Salishan language of the Flathead.

flat·i·ron (flăt′ī′ərn) ►*n.* An iron for pressing clothes.

flat·line (flăt′līn′) ►*v.* **-lined, -lin·ing 1.** To show a horizontal line indicating the absence of any electrical activity in an electrocardiogram or an electroencephalogram. **2.** *Informal* To die. **3.** To be in an unchanging condition: *Participation in civic activities has flatlined in recent years.* ►*adj.* Being or relating to an electrocardiogram or an electroencephalogram that shows no electrical activity.

flat-pan·el (flăt′păn′əl) ►*adj.* Of or relating to a thin monitor or television. —**flat panel** *n.*

flat·ten (flăt′n) ►*v.* **1.** To make or become flat or flatter. **2.** To knock down. —**flat′ten·er** *n.*

flat·ter (flăt′ər) ►*v.* **1.** To compliment excessively and often insincerely, esp. to win favor. **2.** To please or gratify the vanity of. **3.** To portray favorably: *a photograph that flatters its subject.* [< OFr. *flater,* of Gmc. orig.] —**flat′ter·er** *n.* —**flat′ter·ing·ly** *adv.* —**flat′ter·y** *n.*

flat·top (flăt′tŏp′) ►*n.* **1.** An aircraft carrier. **2.** A short haircut in which the hair is brushed straight up and cropped flat across the top.

flat·u·lent (flăch′ə-lənt) ►*adj.* **1.** Afflicted with or caused by excessive gas in the digestive tract. **2.** Pompous; bloated. [< Lat. *flātus,* a blowing, snorting.] —**flat′u·lence** *n.*

flat·ware (flăt′wâr′) ►*n.* **1.** Tableware that is fairly flat and fashioned usu. of a single piece,

as plates. **2.** Table utensils such as knives, forks, and spoons.

flat·worm (flăt′wûrm′) ►*n.* A soft, flat-bodied worm, as the tapeworm.

Flau·bert (flō-bâr′), **Gustave** 1821–80. French writer.

flaunt (flônt) ►*v.* To exhibit ostentatiously or shamelessly; show off. [?] —**flaunt′er** *n.*
   Usage: Some use *flaunt* to mean "to flout or show contempt for." This usage is still widely seen as erroneous and is best avoided.

flau·tist (flô′tĭst, flou′-) ►*n.* A flutist. [Ital. *flautista* < *flauto,* flute.]

fla·vor (flā′vər) ►*n.* **1.** Distinctive taste; savor. **2.** A distinctive yet intangible quality: *the show's vulgar flavor.* **3.** A flavoring. ►*v.* To give flavor to. [< VLat. **flātor,* aroma.] —**fla′vor·ful** *adj.* —**fla′vor·less** *adj.*

fla·vor·ing (flā′vər-ĭng) ►*n.* A substance, as an extract or spice, that imparts flavor.

flaw (flô) ►*n.* An imperfection or blemish; defect. ►*v.* To make or become defective. [ME *flaue,* splinter.]

flaw·less (flô′lĭs) ►*adj.* Being entirely without flaw or imperfection. See Synonyms at **perfect.** —**flaw′less·ly** *adv.* —**flaw′less·ness** *n.*

flax (flăks) ►*n.* **1.** A plant having blue flowers, seeds that yield oil, and slender, fibrous stems. **2.** The fine, light-colored textile fiber obtained from flax. [< OE *fleax.*]

flax·en (flăk′sən) ►*adj.* **1.** Made of or resembling flax. **2.** Having the pale yellowish color of flax fiber.

flay (flā) ►*v.* **1.** To strip off the skin of. **2.** To scold or criticize harshly. **3.** To whip or lash. [< OE *flēan.*] —**flay′er** *n.*

fl. dr. ►*abbr.* fluid dram

flea (flē) ►*n.* A small, wingless, bloodsucking insect that is a parasite of mammals and birds. [< OE *flēah.*]

flea collar ►*n.* A pet collar containing a substance that repels or kills fleas.

flea market ►*n.* A market, usu. held outdoors, where antiques, used household goods, and curios are sold.

fleck (flĕk) ►*n.* **1.** A tiny mark or spot. **2.** A small bit or flake: *a fleck of dandruff.* ►*v.* To spot or streak. [Prob. < ME *flekked,* spotted.]

fledg·ling or **fledge·ling** (flĕj′lĭng) ►*n.* **1.** A young bird that has recently acquired flight feathers. **2.** An inexperienced person. [Prob. < OE **flycge,* featherbed.] —**fledg′ling** *adj.*

flee (flē) ►*v.* **fled** (flĕd), **flee·ing 1.** To run away, as from trouble or danger. **2.** To pass swiftly away; vanish. [< OE *flēon.*] —**fle′er** *n.*

fleece (flēs) ►*n.* **1.** The coat of wool of a sheep or similar animal. **2.** A soft, warm, usu. synthetic fabric with a deep pile, used primarily for clothing and blankets. ►*v.* **fleeced, fleec·ing 1.** To defraud of money or property; swindle. **2.** To shear the fleece from. [< OE *flēos.*] —**fleec′er** *n.* —**fleec′i·ly** *adv.* —**fleec′y** *adj.*

fleet¹ (flēt) ►*n.* **1.** A number of warships operating under one command. **2.** A group of vessels or vehicles, such as taxicabs, owned or operated as a unit. [< OE *flēot* < *flēotan,* float.]

fleet² (flēt) ►*adj.* **-er, -est 1.** Moving swiftly; nimble. **2.** Fleeting; evanescent. ►*v.* To move or pass swiftly. [Prob. < ON *fljótr.*] —**fleet′ly** *adv.* —**fleet′ness** *n.*

fleet·ing (flē′tĭng) ►*adj.* Passing quickly;

ephemeral. **—fleet′ing·ly** *adv.*

Flem·ing (flĕm′ĭng) ►*n.* **1.** A native or inhabitant of Flanders. **2.** A Belgian who speaks Flemish.

Fleming, Sir **Alexander.** 1881–1955. British bacteriologist.

Flem·ish (flĕm′ĭsh) ►*adj.* Of Flanders or the Flemings. ►*n.* **1.** The Germanic language of the Flemings. **2.** The Flemings.

flesh (flĕsh) ►*n.* **1.** The soft tissue of the body, consisting mainly of skeletal muscle and fat. **2.** Such tissue of an animal, used as food. **3.** The pulpy, usu. edible part of a fruit or vegetable. **4.** The body as opposed to the mind or soul. ►*v.* To give substance or detail to; fill out: *fleshed out the novel with a subplot.* **—idiom: in the flesh 1.** Alive. **2.** In person; present. [< OE *flǽsc.*]

flesh·ly (flĕsh′lē) ►*adj.* **-li·er, -li·est 1.** Relating to the body. See Synonyms at **bodily. 2.** Relating to bodily and esp. sexual pleasure; sensual. **—flesh′li·ness** *n.*

flesh·y (flĕsh′ē) ►*adj.* **-i·er, -i·est 1.** Relating to or resembling flesh. **2.** Having abundant flesh. **3.** Having a juicy or pulpy texture: *ripe, fleshy peaches.* **4.** Fleshly; carnal. **—flesh′i·ness** *n.*

Fletch·er (flĕch′ər), **John** 1579–1625. English playwright.

fleur-de-lis (flûr′də-lē′, floŏr′-) ►*n., pl.* **fleurs-de-lis** (flûr′də-lēz′, floŏr′-) A decorative motif consisting of a stylized three-petaled iris flower. [< OFr. *flor de lis,* flower of the lily.]

flew (floō) ►*v.* P.t. of **fly¹.**

flex (flĕks) ►*v.* **1.** To bend (something pliant or elastic). **2.** To contract (e.g., a muscle). **3.** To exhibit or show off the strength of. [Lat. *flectere, flex-,* bend.]

flex·i·ble (flĕk′sə-bəl) ►*adj.* **1.** Capable of being bent or flexed; pliable. **2.** Responsive to change; adaptable: *a flexible administrator.* **3.** Capable of being adjusted to meet varied needs: *a job with flexible hours.* **—flex′i·bil′i·ty, flex′i·ble·ness** *n.* **—flex′i·bly** *adv.*

flex·or (flĕk′sər) ►*n.* A muscle that when contracted acts to bend a joint or limb in the body. [< Lat. *flectere, flex-,* bend.]

flex·time (flĕks′tīm′) ►*n.* An arrangement by which employees may set their own work schedules. [FLEX(IBLE) + TIME.]

flex·ure (flĕk′shər) ►*n.* A curve, turn, or fold.

flick¹ (flĭk) ►*n.* **1.** A light quick blow, jerk, or touch: *a flick of the wrist.* **2.** A light splash, dash, or daub. ►*v.* **1.** To touch or hit with a light quick blow. **2.** To cause to move with a sudden movement, jerk, or light blow: *flicked the lint off the coat; flick a switch.* [Imit.]

flick² (flĭk) ►*n. Slang* A movie. [< FLICKER¹.]

flick·er¹ (flĭk′ər) ►*v.* **1.** To move waveringly; flutter: *shadows flickering on the wall.* **2a.** To burn unsteadily or fitfully: *The candle flickered before sputtering out.* **b.** To be displayed with fluctuating brightness: *The movie flickered on the screen.* **3.** To appear briefly: *A smile flickered on her face.* ►*n.* **1.** A brief movement; tremor. **2.** An inconstant or wavering light. **3.** A brief feeling or sensation: *a flicker of doubt.* [< OE *flicerian,* flutter.]

flick·er² (flĭk′ər) ►*n.* A large woodpecker that has a long tail and large feet and often forages on the ground. [Perh. < FLICK¹.]

flied (flīd) ►*v.* P.t. and p.part. of **fly¹** (sense 6).

fli·er also **fly·er** (flī′ər) ►*n.* **1.** One that flies,

esp. a pilot. **2.** A passenger in an aircraft. **3.** A circular for mass distribution.

flight¹ (flīt) ►*n.* **1.** The act or process of flying. **2.** A swift passage or movement: *barely noticed the flight of time.* **3.** A scheduled airline trip. **4.** A group, esp. of birds or aircraft, flying together. **5.** An exuberant or transcendent effort or display: *a flight of the imagination.* **6.** A series of stairs rising from one landing to another. [< OE *flyht.*]

flight² (flīt) ►*n.* An act of running away. [< OE **flyht.*]

flight deck ►*n.* **1.** The upper deck of an aircraft carrier, used as a runway. **2.** An elevated compartment in certain aircraft, used by the pilot, copilot, and flight engineer.

flight engineer ►*n.* The crew member responsible for the mechanical performance of an aircraft in flight.

flight·less (flīt′lĭs) ►*adj.* Incapable of flying, as certain birds.

flight recorder ►*n.* An event recorder on an aircraft.

flight·y (flī′tē) ►*adj.* **-i·er, -i·est 1.** Impulsive, esp. in an irresponsible way. **2.** Easily excited; skittish. **—flight′i·ly** *adv.* **—flight′i·ness** *n.*

flim·flam (flĭm′flăm′) ►*n. Informal* **1.** Nonsense; humbug. **2.** A deception; swindle. [Prob. of Scand. orig.] **—flim′flam′** *v.* **—flim′flam′-mer** *n.* **—flim′flam′mer·y** *n.*

flim·sy (flĭm′zē) ►*adj.* **-si·er, -si·est 1.** Light, thin, and insubstantial. **2.** Lacking strength; easily damaged: *a flimsy table.* **3.** Lacking plausibility; unconvincing. [?] **—flim′si·ly** *adv.* **—flim′si·ness** *n.*

flinch (flĭnch) ►*v.* **1.** To start or wince involuntarily, as from pain. **2.** To recoil, as from something unpleasant. [Obsolete Fr. *flenchir,* of Gmc. orig.] **—flinch** *n.* **—flinch′er** *n.*

fling (flĭng) ►*v.* **flung** (flŭng), **fling·ing 1.** To throw or move quickly and forcefully. **2.** To throw (oneself) into an activity with abandon and energy. **3.** To cast aside; discard. ►*n.* **1.** The act of flinging. **2.** A brief period of indulging one's impulses. **3.** *Informal* A usu. brief attempt or effort. **4.** A brief, casual romantic or sexual relationship. [ME *flingen,* of Scand. orig.]

flint (flĭnt) ►*n.* **1.** A very hard, fine-grained quartz that sparks when struck with steel. **2.** A small solid cylinder of a spark-producing alloy, used in lighters to ignite the fuel. [< OE.] **—flint′y** *adj.*

Flint A city of SE-central MI NNW of Detroit.

flint·lock (flĭnt′lŏk′) ►*n.* **1.** An obsolete gunlock in which a flint ignites the charge. **2.** A firearm having a flintlock.

flip (flĭp) ►*v.* **flipped, flip·ping 1a.** To throw or toss with a light brisk motion. **b.** To toss in the air, imparting a spin: *to flip a coin.* **2a.** To turn over, esp. with a quick motion. **b.** To turn through; leaf: *flipped the pages of the report.* **3.** To flick. **4.** To move or operate (e.g., a lever or switch) with a quick motion. **5.** To turn a somersault. **6.** To turn over from one side to another or end over end: *The canoe flipped over.* **7a.** *Slang* To go crazy. **b.** To react strongly and esp. enthusiastically. ►*n.* The act of flipping, esp.: **a.** A flick. **b.** A short quick movement. **c.** A somersault. ►*adj.* **flip·per, flip·pest** *Informal* Impertinent: *a flip answer.* [Perh. imit.]

flip-flop (flĭp′flŏp′) ►*n.* **1.** A reversal, as of a

stand or position. **2.** A backless, often foam rubber sandal. **3.** A backward somersault or handspring. **—flip′-flop′** *v.*

flip·pant (flĭp′ənt) ▸*adj.* Marked by disrespectful casualness or levity: *flippant remarks.* [Prob. < FLIP.] **—flip′pan·cy** *n.* **—flip′pant·ly** *adv.*

flip·per (flĭp′ər) ▸*n.* **1.** A wide flat limb, as of a seal, adapted for swimming. **2.** See **fin** (sense 3). **3.** One who flips: *a flipper of hamburgers.*

flirt (flûrt) ▸*v.* **1.** To act as if one is sexually attracted to another person, usu. playfully. **2.** To deal triflingly with danger: *flirt with danger.* ▸*n.* One given to flirting. [?] **—flir·ta′tion** *n.* **—flir·ta′tious** *adj.* **—flir·ta′tious·ly** *adv.*

> **Syns:** *dally, toy, trifle* **v.**

flit (flĭt) ▸*v.* **flit·ted, flit·ting** To move quickly and nimbly. [< ON *flytja,* carry about.] **—flit′-ter** *n.*

flit·ter (flĭt′ər) ▸*v.* To flutter. [Frequentative of FLIT.]

float (flōt) ▸*v.* **1a.** To remain or cause to remain suspended in or on a fluid without sinking. **b.** To be or cause to be suspended in space. **2.** To move from place to place, esp. at random. **3.** To move easily or lightly: *The couple floated on the dance floor.* **4.** To release (a security) for sale. **5.** To offer for consideration; suggest: *floated an idea.* **6.** To rise or fall freely in response to the market: *allowed the dollar to float.* **7.** To arrange for (a loan). ▸*n.* **1.** Something that floats, such as a raft. **2.** A buoyant object that holds a net or fishing line afloat. **3.** A decorated exhibit on a mobile platform in a parade. **4.** A soft drink with ice cream floating in it. [< OE *floti-an.*]

float·er (flō′tər) ▸*n.* **1.** One that floats. **2.** One who wanders; drifter. **3.** An employee reassigned from job to job or shift to shift within an operation. **4.** An insurance policy that protects movable property.

flock¹ (flŏk) ▸*n.* **1.** A group of animals that live, travel, or feed together. **2.** A group of people, esp. under the leadership of one person. See Synonyms at **crowd. 3.** A large number; host. ▸*v.* To congregate or travel in a flock or crowd. [< OE *floc.*]

flock² (flŏk) ▸*n.* **1.** A tuft, as of fiber or hair. **2.** Pulverized fibers applied to paper or cloth to produce a texture or pattern. [< Lat. *floccus,* tuft of wool.] **—flock** *v.*

floe (flō) ▸*n.* A large flat mass of floating ice. [Prob. < ON *flō,* layer.]

flog (flŏg, flôg) ▸*v.* **flogged, flog·ging** To beat severely with a whip or rod. [Perh. < Lat. *flagellāre,* FLAGELLATE.] **—flog′ger** *n.*

flood (flŭd) ▸*n.* **1.** An overflowing of water onto normally dry land. **2.** A large amount or number, esp. when moving from one place to another: *a flood of applications.* See Synonyms at **flow. 3.** A floodlight. **4. Flood** The universal deluge recorded in the Bible. ▸*v.* **1.** To cover with or as if with a flood; inundate. **2.** To pour forth; overflow: *The river floods every spring.* [< OE *flōd.*]

flood·gate (flŭd′gāt′) ▸*n.* **1.** A gate that controls the flow of a body of water. **2.** Something that restrains a flood or outpouring.

flood·light (flŭd′līt′) ▸*n.* **1.** Artificial light in an intensely bright and broad beam. **2.** A unit that produces such a beam. ▸*v.* To illuminate with a floodlight.

flood·plain (flŭd′plān′) ▸*n.* A plain bordering a river and subject to flooding.

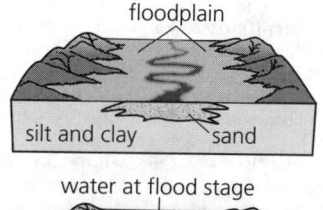

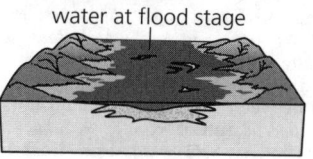

floodplain
top: a river at normal level
bottom: a river at flood stage

floor (flôr) ▸*n.* **1.** The surface of a room on which one stands. **2.** A story or level of a building. **3a.** The part of a legislative chamber where members are seated and from which they speak. **b.** The right to address an assembly. **c.** The body of assembly members. **4.** The part of a room or building where the principal business or work takes place. **5.** The ground or lowermost surface, as of a forest or ocean. **6.** A lower limit or base: *a pricing floor.* ▸*v.* **1.** To provide with a floor. **2.** To knock down. **3.** To stun; overwhelm: *The idea floored me.* [< OE *flōr.*]

floor leader ▸*n.* The member of a legislature chosen by fellow party members to be in charge of party activities on the floor.

floor plan ▸*n.* A scale diagram of a room or building.

floor show ▸*n.* The entertainment presented in a nightclub.

floor·walk·er (flôr′wô′kər) ▸*n.* An employee of a large store who supervises sales personnel and assists customers.

floo·zy *also* **floo·zie** (flōō′zē) ▸*n., pl.* **-zies** *Slang* A woman who is tawdry or sexually promiscuous. [?]

flop (flŏp) ▸*v.* **flopped, flop·ping 1.** To fall or lie down heavily: *flop onto the sofa.* **2.** To move about loosely or limply. **3.** *Informal* To fail utterly: *The play flopped.* ▸*n.* **1.** The act or sound of flopping. **2.** *Informal* An utter failure. [Alteration of FLAP.]

flop·house (flŏp′hous′) ▸*n.* A cheap, rundown hotel or boardinghouse.

flop·py (flŏp′ē) ▸*adj.* **-pi·er, -pi·est** Tending to flop; loose and flexible. **—flop′pi·ly** *adv.*

flo·ra (flôr′ə) ▸*n., pl.* **flo·ras** *or* **flo·rae** (flôr′ē′) Plants collectively, esp. the plants of a particular region or time. [< Lat. *flōs, flōr-,* flower.]

flo·ral (flôr′əl) ▸*adj.* Of or relating to flowers. **—flo′ral·ly** *adv.*

Flor·ence (flôr′əns) A city of central Italy E of Pisa.

flo·res·cence (flô-rĕs′əns, flə-) ▸*n.* A condition or period of flowering or vigor. See Synonyms at **bloom.** [< Lat. *flōrēscere,* begin to bloom.] **—flo·res′cent** *adj.*

flor·id (flôr′ĭd) ▸*adj.* **1.** Flushed with rosy color; ruddy. **2.** Very ornate; flowery. [< Lat. *flōridus* < *flōs,* flower.] **—flo·rid′i·ty** (flə-rĭd′ĭ-tē, flô-),

flor'id·ness n. —**flor'id·ly** adv.

Flor·i·da (flôr′ĭ-də) A state of the SE US. Cap. Tallahassee. —**Flo·rid′i·an** (flə-rĭd′ē-ən), **Flor′i·dan** (-ĭd-n) adj. & n.

Florida, Straits of A sea passage between Cuba and S Florida, linking the Gulf of Mexico with the Atlantic.

flor·in (flôr′ĭn) ►n. **1.** A guilder. **2.** A former British coin worth two shillings. [< OItal. fiore, flower.]

flo·rist (flôr′ĭst) ►n. One who raises or sells flowers and plants. [< Lat. flōs, flōr-, flower.]

floss (flôs, flŏs) ►n. **1.** Dental floss. **2.** Short or waste silk fibers. **3.** A soft, loosely twisted thread. **4.** A silky fibrous substance. ►v. To clean between (teeth) with dental floss. [Perh. < Lat. floccus, tuft of wool.]

floss·y (flô′sē, flŏs′ē) ►adj. -**i·er, -i·est 1.** Superficially stylish; slick. **2.** Made of or resembling floss. —**floss′i·ness** n.

flo·ta·tion (flō-tā′shən) ►n. The act or condition of floating.

flo·til·la (flō-tĭl′ə) ►n. **1.** A small fleet. **2.** A fleet of small craft. [< ON floti, fleet.]

flot·sam (flŏt′səm) ►n. Wreckage or cargo that remains afloat after a ship has sunk. [< OFr. floter, float, of Gmc. orig.]

flounce[1] (flouns) ►n. A strip of usu. gathered material attached by one edge, as to a skirt or curtain. [< OFr. fronce, pleat.]

flounce[2] (flouns) ►v. **flounced, flounc·ing 1.** To move in a lively or bouncy manner. **2.** To move with exaggerated or affected motions: flounced out of the room. [Poss. of Scand. orig.]

floun·der[1] (floun′dər) ►v. **1.** To move clumsily or with little progress. See Synonyms at **blunder. 2.** To act or proceed in confusion; struggle. See Usage Note at **founder.** [Poss. alteration of FOUNDER.]

floun·der[2] (floun′dər) ►n., pl. -**der** or -**ders** Any of various marine flatfishes, including important food fishes. [< AN floundre.]

flour (flou′ər, flour) ►n. A fine powdery foodstuff obtained by grinding grain, esp. wheat. ►v. To coat with flour. [ME.] —**flour′y** adj.

flour·ish (flûr′ĭsh, flŭr′-) ►v. **1.** To grow well or luxuriantly; thrive. **2.** To do or fare well; succeed. **3.** To make bold, sweeping movements: The banner flourished in the wind. ►n. **1.** A dramatic movement or gesture. **2.** An embellishment or ornamentation, esp. in handwriting. [< VLat. *flōrīre < Lat. flōs, flower.]

Syns: brandish, wave **v.**

flout (flout) ►v. To ignore or disregard (e.g., a rule) in an open or defiant way. See Usage Note at **flaunt.** [Poss. < ME flouten, play the flute.] —**flout′er** n.

flow (flō) ►v. **1.** To move or run freely in or as if in a stream. **2.** To circulate, as the blood in the body. **3.** To proceed steadily and easily. **4.** To appear smooth, harmonious, or graceful. **5.** To hang loosely and gracefully. **6.** To rise. Used of the tide. **7.** To arise. See Synonyms at **stem**[1]. **8.** To be abundant; teem. ►n. **1.** The smooth motion characteristic of fluids. **2.** A stream or current. **3a.** A continuous output: a flow of ideas. **b.** A continuous movement or circulation: the flow of traffic. **4.** The amount that flows in a given period of time. **5.** The rising of the tide. [< OE flōwan.]

Syns: current, flood, rush, stream, tide **n.**

flow chart ►n. A schematic representation of a sequence of operations.

flow·er (flou′ər) ►n. **1.** The reproductive structure of a seed-bearing plant, having specialized male and/or female organs and usu. colorful petals. **2.** A plant cultivated for its blossoms. **3.** The period of highest development; peak. See Synonyms at **bloom. 4.** The time of having developed flowers: The roses were in full flower. **5.** The highest example or best representative: the flower of our generation. ►v. **1.** To produce flowers; blossom. **2.** To develop fully; mature: Her artistic talents flowered early. [< OFr. flor < Lat. flōs.]

flow·er·ing plant (flou′ər-ĭng) ►n. A plant that produces flowers and fruit.

flow·er·pot (flou′ər-pŏt′) ►n. A pot in which plants are grown.

flow·er·y (flou′ə-rē) ►adj. -**i·er, -i·est 1.** Relating to or suggestive of flowers: a flowery perfume. **2.** Full of ornate or grandiloquent expressions: a flowery speech.

flown (flōn) ►v. P.part. of **fly**[1].

fl. oz. ►abbr. fluid ounce

flu (flōō) ►n. Informal Influenza.

flub (flŭb) ►v. **flubbed, flub·bing** Informal To botch or bungle. [?]

fluc·tu·ate (flŭk′chōō-āt′) ►v. -**at·ed, -at·ing** To vary irregularly, esp. in amount: School enrollment fluctuates from year to year. [< Lat. flūctus, a flowing < fluere, flow.] —**fluc′tu·ant** (-ənt) adj. —**fluc′tu·a′tion** n.

flue (flōō) ►n. A pipe, tube, or channel for conveying hot air, gas, steam, or smoke, as in a chimney. [?]

flu·ent (flōō′ənt) ►adj. **1.** Having facility in the use of a language. **2.** Flowing effortlessly; polished: a fluent performance of the aria. **3.** Flowing or capable of flowing; fluid. [< Lat. fluere, to flow.] —**flu′en·cy** n. —**flu′ent·ly** adv.

fluff (flŭf) ►n. **1.** Light down or fuzz. **2.** Something having a light, soft, or frothy consistency or appearance: a fluff of meringue. **3.** Something of little consequence. **4.** Informal An error or lapse of memory, esp. by an actor or announcer. ►v. **1.** To make light and puffy by shaking or patting into a soft loose mass: fluff a pillow. **2.** Informal To misread or forget: fluff a line of dialogue. [?] —**fluff′i·ness** n. —**fluff′y** adj.

flu·id (flōō′ĭd) ►n. A substance, such as a liquid or a gas, whose molecules move freely past one another and that tends to assume the shape of its container. ►adj. **1.** Characteristic of a fluid. **2.** Smooth and graceful: The fluid motion of a swan. **3.** Readily changing; variable: a fluid situation. **4.** Convertible into cash: fluid assets. [< Lat. fluere, flow.] —**flu·id′i·ty** n. —**flu′id·ly** adv.

fluid ounce ►n. See table at **measurement.**

fluke[1] (flōōk) ►n. **1.** Any of various parasitic flatworms, including the trematodes, some of which infect humans. **2.** A flatfish, esp. a species of flounder. [< OE flōc.]

fluke[2] (flōōk) ►n. **1.** The triangular blade at the end of an arm of an anchor. **2.** A barb or barbed head, as on an arrow or harpoon. **3.** Either of the two flattened divisions of a whale's tail. [Poss. < FLUKE[1].]

fluke[3] (flōōk) ►n. A chance occurrence: That May snowstorm was a fluke. [?] —**fluk′y** adj.

flume (flōōm) ►n. **1.** A narrow gorge, usu. with a

stream flowing through it. **2.** An open artificial channel or chute for carrying a stream of water, as for conveying logs. [< Lat. *flūmen*, river.]

flum·mox (flŭm′əks) ►*v. Informal* To confuse; perplex. [Prob. of dialectal orig.]

flung (flŭng) ►*v.* P.t. and p.part. of **fling.**

flunk (flŭngk) ►*v. Informal* **1.** To fail, esp. in a course or examination. **2.** To give a failing grade to. [?]

flun·ky also **flun·key** (flŭng′kē) ►*n., pl.* **-kies** also **-keys 1.** A person of slavish or fawning obedience; lackey. **2.** One who does menial or trivial work; drudge. [Sc.]

fluo·resce (floo-rĕs′, flô-) ►*v.* **-resced, -resc·ing** To undergo, produce, or show fluorescence.

fluo·res·cence (floo-rĕs′əns, flô-) ►*n.* **1.** The emission of electromagnetic radiation, esp. of visible light, stimulated in a substance by the absorption of incident radiation and lasting as long as the stimulating radiation is continued. **2.** The radiation so emitted. —**fluo·res′cent** *adj.*

fluor·i·date (floor′ĭ-dāt′, flôr′-) ►*v.* **-dat·ed, -dat·ing** To add a fluorine compound to (e.g., a water supply) for the purpose of reducing tooth decay. —**fluor′i·da′tion** *n.*

fluor·ide (floor′īd′, flôr′-) ►*n.* Univalent fluorine or a binary compound of fluorine.

fluor·ine (floor′ēn′, -ĭn, flôr′-) ►*n. Symbol* **F** A pale-yellow, corrosive, poisonous gaseous element. At. no. 9. See table at **element.** [NLat. *fluor*, mineral used as a flux + −INE².]

fluoro– or **fluor–** ►*pref.* **1.** Fluorine: *fluorocarbon.* **2.** Fluorescence: *fluoroscope.* [< FLUOR-INE.]

fluor·o·car·bon (floor′ō-kär′bən, flôr′-) ►*n.* A compound in which fluorine replaces hydrogen, used as aerosol propellants, refrigerants, lubricants, and in making plastics and resins.

fluor·o·scope (floor′ə-skōp′, flôr′-) ►*n.* A device with a fluorescent screen on which the internal structures of an opaque object can be viewed as shadows formed by the transmission of x-rays. —**fluor′o·scope′** *v.* —**fluor′o·scop′ic** (-skŏp′ĭk) *adj.* —**fluo·ros′co·py** (floo-rŏs′kə-pē) *n.*

flur·ry (flûr′ē, flŭr′ē) ►*n., pl.* **-ries 1.** A brief light snowfall. **2.** A sudden gust of wind. **3.** A sudden burst of activity; stir: *a flurry of preparations.* [Poss. < *flurr*, scatter.] —**flur′ry** *v.*

flush¹ (flŭsh) ►*v.* **1.** To redden or cause to redden; blush. **2.** To glow, esp. with a reddish color. **3.** To flow suddenly and abundantly; flood. **4.** To wash out or clean by a rapid brief flow of water. **5.** To excite or elate: *The team was flushed with the triumph of victory.* ►*n.* **1.** A brief copious flow or rush, as of water. **2.** A reddish tinge; blush. **3.** A rush of strong feeling: *a flush of pride.* **4.** A state of freshness, vigor, or growth. See Synonyms at **bloom.** ►*adj.* **-er, -est 1.** Having a healthy reddish color; blushing. **2.** Prosperous; affluent. **3.** Abundant; plentiful: *flush times.* **4a.** Having surfaces in the same plane; even. **b.** Arranged with adjacent sides, surfaces, or edges close together. **5.** Direct or straightforward. ►*adv.* **1.** So as to be even, in one plane, or aligned with a margin. **2.** Squarely or solidly: *a hit flush on the face.* [Poss. < FLUSH³.] —**flush′ness** *n.*

flush² (flŭsh) ►*n.* A hand in certain card games in which all the cards are of the same suit

but not in numerical sequence. [< Lat. *flūxus*, FLUX.]

flush³ (flŭsh) ►*v.* **1.** To frighten (e.g., a game bird) from cover. **2.** To drive or force into the open. [ME *flusshen*.]

flus·ter (flŭs′tər) ►*v.* To make or become anxious or upset. ►*n.* A state of agitation or excitement. [< ME *flostring*, agitation, prob. of Scand. orig.]

flute (floot) ►*n.* **1.** A high-pitched tubular woodwind instrument. **2a.** *Archit.* A long, usu. rounded, incised groove, as on the shaft of a column. **b.** A similar groove, as in cloth or furniture. **3.** A tall narrow wineglass, often used for champagne. [< OProv. *flauto.*] —**flut′ed** *adj.* —**flut′ing** *n.*

flut·ist (floo′tĭst) ►*n.* One who plays the flute.

flut·ter (flŭt′ər) ►*v.* **1.** To wave or flap lightly, rapidly, and irregularly. **2.** To fly by a quick light flapping of the wings. **3.** To vibrate or beat rapidly or erratically. **4.** To move quickly in a nervous, restless, or excited fashion. ►*n.* **1.** The act of fluttering. **2.** A condition of nervous excitement or agitation. [< OE *floterian.*] —**flut′ter·y** *adj.*

flu·vi·al (floo′vē-əl) ►*adj.* Of, inhabiting, or produced by a river or stream. [< Lat. *fluvius*, river.]

flux (flŭks) ►*n.* **1a.** A flow or flowing of a liquid. **b.** The flowing in of the tide. **2.** Constant or frequent change; fluctuation. **3.** *Chem.* A substance applied to facilitate flowing, as of solder or plastics. **4.** *Phys.* **a.** The rate of flow of fluid, particles, or energy through a given surface. **b.** The strength of a magnetic field across a given surface. ►*v.* **1.** To melt; fuse. **2.** To apply a flux to. **3.** To flow; stream. [< Lat. *flūxus* < *fluere*, flow.]

fly¹ (flī) ►*v.* **flew** (floo), **flown** (flōn), **fly·ing 1.** To engage in flight, esp.: **a.** To move through the air by means of wings or winglike parts. **b.** To travel by air. **c.** To operate an aircraft or spacecraft. **2.** To rise, float, or cause to float in the air. **3a.** To move with great speed; rush: *The children flew down the hall.* **b.** To try to escape; flee. **4.** To pass by swiftly: *the years have flown.* **5.** *Informal* To gain acceptance: *That idea won't fly.* **6.** p.t. and p.part. **flied** (flīd) *Baseball* To hit a baseball in a high arc. ►*n., pl.* **flies 1.** The opening on the front of a pair of pants. **2.** A piece of material used as a supplementary covering over a tent or over the entrance of a tent. **3.** A baseball batted in a high arc. **4. flies** The area directly over the stage of a theater, containing overhead lights, curtains, and equipment. —*idioms:* **fly high** To be elated. **fly off the handle** *Informal* To become suddenly enraged. [< OE *flēogan.*] —**fly′a·ble** *adj.*

fly² (flī) ►*n., pl.* **flies 1a.** Any of various two-winged insects, such as a housefly, horsefly, or fruit fly. **b.** Any of various other flying insects, such as a mayfly. **2.** A fishing lure simulating a fly. [< OE *flēoge.*]

fly·blown (flī′blōn′) ►*adj.* **1.** Contaminated with the eggs or larvae of blowflies. **2.** Dirty; squalid. **3.** Tainted; corrupt.

fly·by also **fly-by** (flī′bī′) ►*n., pl.* **-bys** A flight, as of a spacecraft, passing close to a specified target or position.

fly-by-night (flī′bī-nīt′) ►*adj.* **1.** Unreliable, esp. in business. **2.** Temporary.

fly·catch·er (flī′kăch′ər, -kĕch′-) ►*n.* Any of various birds that feed on insects, usu. catching them in flight.

fly·er (flī′ər) ►*n.* Var. of **flier.**

fly-fish (flī′fĭsh′) ►*v.* To fish using artificial flies for bait and usu. a fly rod for casting. —**fly′-fish′er** *n.*

fly·ing buttress (flī′ĭng) ►*n.* An arched masonry support serving to bear thrust away from a main structure to an outer pier or buttress.

flying fish ►*n.* A marine fish having enlarged winglike fins that sustain it in brief gliding flights over the water.

flying saucer ►*n.* An unidentified flying object of presumed extraterrestrial origin, typically described as a luminous moving disk.

flying squirrel ►*n.* A nocturnal squirrel having membranes between the legs that allow it to glide between trees.

fly·leaf (flī′lēf′) ►*n.* A blank page at the beginning or end of a book.

fly·pa·per (flī′pā′pər) ►*n.* Paper coated with a sticky substance used to catch flies.

fly rod ►*n.* A long flexible fishing rod used in fly-fishing.

fly·speck (flī′spĕk′) ►*n.* **1.** A stain made by the excrement of a fly. **2.** A minute spot.

fly·way (flī′wā′) ►*n.* A seasonal route followed by birds migrating to and from their breeding areas.

fly·weight (flī′wāt′) ►*n.* A boxer weighing 112 lbs. or less, lighter than a bantamweight.

fly·wheel (flī′wēl′, -hwēl′) ►*n.* A heavy-rimmed rotating wheel used to keep a shaft of a machine turning at a steady speed.

FM ►*abbr.* frequency modulation

FNMA ►*abbr.* Federal National Mortgage Association

f-num·ber (ĕf′nŭm′bər) ►*n.* The ratio of the focal length of a lens or lens system to the effective diameter of its aperture. [F(OCAL LENGTH) + NUMBER.]

foal (fōl) ►*n.* The young offspring of a horse, esp. one under a year old. ►*v.* To give birth to a foal. [< OE *fola.*]

foam (fōm) ►*n.* **1.** A dispersion of a gas in a liquid or solid medium, such as shaving cream. **2.** A light, semirigid or porous material used as a building material, or for insulation or shock absorption, as in packaging. ►*v.* To produce or cause to produce foam. [< OE *fām.*] —**foam′i·ness** *n.* —**foam′y** *adj.*

foam rubber ►*n.* A light, firm, spongy rubber used in upholstery and for insulation.

fob¹ (fŏb) ►*n.* **1.** A short chain on a pocket watch. **2.** An ornament attached to a watch chain. [Prob. of Gmc. orig.]

fob² (fŏb) ►*v.* **fobbed, fob·bing** *Archaic* To cheat or deceive (another). —*phrasal verb:* **fob off** To dispose of (something) by fraud or deception: *fobbed off the zircon as a diamond.* [ME *fobben.*]

fo·cac·ci·a (fə-kä′chē-ə, -chə, fō-) ►*n.* A flat Italian bread flavored with olive oil. [Ital., hearth-cake < Lat. *focus,* hearth.]

focal length ►*n.* The distance of a lens or mirror to its focal point.

focal point ►*n.* See **focus** (sense 2a).

fo·c′s′le (fōk′səl) ►*n.* Var. of **forecastle.**

fo·cus (fō′kəs) ►*n., pl.* **-cus·es** or **-ci** (-sī′, -kī′) **1a.** The distinctness or clarity of an image rendered by an optical system. **b.** Adjustment for distinctness or clarity. **2a.** A point at which rays of light or other radiation converge or from which they appear to diverge, as after refraction or reflection in an optical system. **b.** See **focal length. 3.** A center of interest or activity. ►*v.* **-cused, -cus·ing** or **-cussed, -cus·sing 1.** To converge or cause to converge at a focus. **2a.** To produce a clear image (of). **b.** To adjust (e.g., a lens) to produce a clear image. **3.** To concentrate (on). [Lat., hearth.] —**fo′cal** *adj.* —**fo′cal·ly** *adv.*

fod·der (fŏd′ər) ►*n.* **1.** Feed for livestock, esp. coarsely chopped hay or straw. **2.** Raw material, as for artistic creation. [< OE *fōdor.*]

foe (fō) ►*n.* **1.** A personal enemy or opponent. See Synonyms at **enemy. 2.** An enemy in war. [< OE *gefā < fāh,* hostile.]

foe·tid (fē′tĭd) ►*adj.* Var. of **fetid.**

foe·tus (fē′təs) ►*n.* Var. of **fetus.** —**foe′tal** *adj.*

fog (fôg, fŏg) ►*n.* **1.** Condensed water vapor lying close to the ground in cloudlike masses and limiting visibility. **2.** A mist or film clouding a surface. **3.** A state of confusion. ►*v.* **fogged, fog·ging** To cover or be obscured with fog. [Perh. of Scand. orig.] —**fog′gi·ly** *adv.* —**fog′gi·ness** *n.* —**fog′gy** *adj.*

fog·horn (fôg′hôrn′, fŏg′-) ►*n.* A horn used to warn ships of danger in fog or darkness.

fo·gy also **fo·gey** (fō′gē) ►*n., pl.* **-gies** also **-geys** A person of old-fashioned habits and attitudes. [Sc. *fogey.*] —**fo′gy·ish** *adj.*

foi·ble (foi′bəl) ►*n.* A minor weakness or failing of character. [< OFr. *feble,* weak; see FEEBLE.]

foil¹ (foil) ►*v.* To prevent from being successful; thwart. [ME *foilen,* trample.]

foil² (foil) ►*n.* **1.** Metal that has been formed into a thin, flexible sheet. **2.** One that by contrast enhances the distinctive characteristics of another: *an emcee who served as the comedian's foil.* **3a.** An airfoil. **b.** A hydrofoil. [< Lat. *folium,* leaf.]

foil³ (foil) ►*n.* A fencing sword having a usu. circular guard and a thin flexible blade with a blunt point to prevent injury. [?]

foist (foist) ►*v.* **1.** To pass off as genuine, valuable, or worthy. **2.** To impose something unwanted upon another by coercion or trickery: *foisted the work onto those who stayed late.* [< MDu. *vuist,* fist.]

fold¹ (fōld) ►*v.* **1.** To bend over or double up so that one part lies on another part. **2.** To bring from an extended to a closed position: *The hawk folded its wings.* **3.** To place together and intertwine: *fold one's arms.* **4.** To envelop or clasp; enfold: *folded his children to his breast.* **5.** To blend in (a cooking ingredient) by slowly and gently turning one part over another. **6.** To discontinue operating; close: *folded the company.* ►*n.* **1.** The act or an instance of folding. **2.** A line or mark made by folding; crease. **3.** *Geol.* A bend in a stratum of rock. [< OE *fealdan.*]

fold² (fōld) ►*n.* **1.** A fenced enclosure for domestic animals, esp. sheep. **2.** A flock of sheep. **3.** A group of people or institutions bound together by common beliefs and aims. [< OE *fald.*]

–fold ►*suff.* **1.** Divided into a specified number of parts: *fourfold.* **2.** Multiplied by a specified number: *twofold.* [< OE *-feald.*]

fold·er (fōl′dər) ►*n.* **1.** Something that folds, such as a booklet made of folded sheets of paper. **2.** A flexible cover folded in the center, used to hold loose paper. **3.** An organizational unit for files that reside on a storage device.

fol·de·rol (fŏl′də-rŏl′) ►*n.* **1.** Nonsense. **2.** A trinket. [From a refrain in some old songs.]

fold·out (fōld′out′) ►*n.* **1.** *Print.* A folded insert or section, as of a cover, whose full size exceeds that of the regular page. **2.** A piece or part that folds out, as of furniture. —**fold′out′** *adj.*

fo·li·age (fō′lē-ĭj, fō′lĭj) ►*n.* Plant leaves, esp. tree leaves, considered as a group. [< OFr. *foille,* leaf; see FOIL².]

fo·lic acid (fō′lĭk, fŏl′ĭk) ►*n.* A compound of the vitamin B complex, found in foods such as dark leafy vegetables, fruits, and yeast. [< Lat. *folium,* leaf.]

fo·li·o (fō′lē-ō′) ►*n., pl.* **-os 1a.** A large sheet of paper folded once in the middle. **b.** A book of the largest common size, consisting of such folded sheets. **2.** A page number in a book. [< Lat. *folium,* leaf.]

folk (fōk) ►*n., pl.* **folk** or **folks 1.** The common people of a society or region, esp. as the representatives of a distinctive culture. **2. folks** *Informal* People in general: *Folks here are pretty friendly.* **3.** often **folks** People of a specified group or kind: *rich folks.* **4. folks** *Informal* One's parents. ►*adj.* Of or originating among the common people: *a folk hero.* [< OE *folc.*]

folk·lore (fōk′lôr′) ►*n.* The traditional beliefs, legends, and practices of a people, passed down orally. —**folk′lor′ist** *n.*

folk magic ►*n.* The practice of using charms, spells, or rituals to control events or influence others.

folk music ►*n.* Music originating among the common people of a nation or region.

folk-rock (fōk′rŏk′) ►*n.* Music combining elements of rock 'n' roll and folk music.

folk·sing·er (fōk′sĭng′ər) ►*n.* A singer of folksongs.

folk·song (fōk′sông′, -sŏng′) ►*n.* A song belonging to the folk music of a people or area, often existing in several versions.

folk·sy (fōk′sē) ►*adj.* **-si·er, -si·est** *Informal* Simple; unpretentious. —**folk′si·ness** *n.*

folk·way (fōk′wā′) ►*n.* A practice, custom, or belief shared by the members of a group as part of their common culture.

fol·li·cle (fŏl′ĭ-kəl) ►*n.* **1.** A small body cavity or sac, such as one in the skin from which hair grows. **2.** A cavity in an ovary containing a mature ovum. [Lat. *folliculus,* little bag.]

fol·low (fŏl′ō) ►*v.* **1.** To come or go after; proceed behind. **2.** To pursue: *would follow his enemy anywhere.* **3.** To move along the course of: *follow a path.* **4.** To comply with; obey: *follow the rules.* **5.** To accept the leadership of: *follow a spiritual leader.* **6.** To come after or bring about after in order, time, or position: *Night follows day.* **7.** To take as a model; imitate: *followed my example.* **8.** To adhere to: *follow a diet.* **9.** To be attentive to: *follow a sermon.* **10.** To grasp the meaning or logic of; understand: *follow an argument.* [< OE *folgian.*]

fol·low·er (fŏl′ō-ər) ►*n.* **1.** One who follows. **2.** One who accepts the guidance, command, or leadership of another. **3.** One who has a strong interest in or pays close attention to something.

fol·low·ing (fŏl′ō-ĭng) ►*adj.* **1.** Coming next in time or order. **2.** Now to be enumerated: *The*

following men will report for duty. ►*n.* A group or gathering of followers. ►*prep.* Subsequent to; after: *Following lunch, brandy was served.*

fol·low-up or **fol·low·up** (fŏl′ō-ŭp′) ►*n.* The act or an instance of following up, as to review or to further an end.

fol·ly (fŏl′ē) ►*n., pl.* **-lies 1.** A lack of good sense, understanding, or foresight. **2a.** An act or instance of foolishness. **b.** A costly undertaking having an absurd or ruinous outcome. **3. follies** *(takes sing. or pl. v.)* An elaborate theatrical revue consisting of music, dance, and skits. [< OFr. *folie* < LLat. *follis,* FOOL.]

fo·ment (fō-mĕnt′) ►*v.* **1.** To promote the growth of; incite. **2.** To treat (e.g., the skin) with heat and moisture. [< Lat. *fōmentum,* a poultice.] —**fo′men·ta′tion** *n.*

fond (fŏnd) ►*adj.* **-er, -est 1.** Having a strong liking, inclination, or affection: *fond of ballet.* **2.** Affectionate; tender: *a fond embrace* **3.** Deeply felt; dear: *my fondest hopes.* [Prob. < ME *fonne,* a fool.] —**fond′ly** *adv.* —**fond′ness** *n.*

Fon·da (fŏn′də), **Henry** 1905–82. Amer. actor.

fon·dle (fŏn′dl) ►*v.* **-dled, -dling** To handle or stroke lovingly. See Synonyms at **caress.** [< obsolete *fond,* show affection for.]

fon·due also **fon·du** (fŏn-dōō′, -dyōō′) ►*n.* **1.** A hot dish made of melted cheese and wine and eaten with bread. **2.** A hot dish made of a melted sauce, such as chocolate, in which pieces of food are dipped. [Fr. < *fondre,* melt.]

font¹ (fŏnt) ►*n.* **1.** A basin for holding baptismal or holy water. **2.** An abundant source. [< Lat. *fōns,* fountain.]

font² (fŏnt) ►*n. Print.* A complete set of type of one size and face. [< Lat. *fundere,* pour out.]

food (fōōd) ►*n.* **1.** Material, usu. of plant or animal origin, that contains essential body nutrients, taken in and assimilated by an organism to maintain life and growth; nourishment. **2.** A specified kind of nourishment: *plant food.* **3.** Nourishment eaten in solid form. **4.** Something that stimulates or encourages: *food for thought.* [< OE *fōda.*]

food chain ►*n.* A succession of organisms, each kind serving as a source of nourishment as it consumes a lower member and in turn is preyed upon by a higher member.

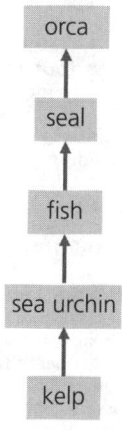

food chain
marine food chain diagram

food poisoning ►*n.* An acute, often severe gastrointestinal disorder that is caused by eating food contaminated with bacteria or natural toxins.

food stamp ►*n.* A stamp or coupon issued by the government to persons with low incomes and redeemable for food at stores.

food·stuff (fōōd′stŭf′) ►*n.* A substance that can be used or prepared for use as food.

food web ►*n.* A complex of interrelated food chains.

fool (fōōl) ►*n.* **1.** One who is deficient in judgment, sense, or understanding. **2.** One who has been tricked or made to feel ridiculous; dupe: *They made a fool of me by pretending I had won.* **3.** A jester. ►*v.* **1.** To deceive or trick; dupe. **2.** *Informal* To speak or act in jest; joke. **3.** To toy, tinker, or meddle: *shouldn't fool with matches.* —*phrasal verb:* **fool around** *Informal* **1.** To waste time; idle. **2.** To engage in frivolous activity; play. [< Lat. *follis,* bellows.]

fool·er·y (fōō′lə-rē) ►*n., pl.* **-ies** **1.** Foolish behavior or speech. **2.** A jest.

fool·har·dy (fōōl′här′dē) ►*adj.* **-di·er, -di·est** Unwisely bold, daring, or venturesome; rash. [< OFr. *fol hardi.*] —**fool′har′di·ly** *adv.* —**fool′har′di·ness** *n.*

fool·ish (fōō′lĭsh) ►*adj.* **1.** Lacking good sense or judgment; silly. **2.** Resulting from stupidity or misinformation; unwise: *a foolish decision.* **3.** Absurd or ridiculous: *a foolish grin.* —**fool′ish·ly** *adv.* —**fool′ish·ness** *n.*
   Syns: *absurd, ludicrous, preposterous, ridiculous, silly* **adj.**

fool·proof (fōōl′prōōf′) ►*adj.* **1.** Designed to be impervious to incompetence, error, or misuse. **2.** Effective; infallible: *a foolproof scheme.*

fools·cap (fōōlz′kăp′) ►*n. Chiefly Brit.* A sheet of writing paper approx. 13 by 16 in. [From the watermark orig. used for this paper.]

fool's gold (fōōlz) ►*n.* See **pyrite.**

foot (fōōt) ►*n., pl.* **feet** (fēt) **1.** The lower extremity of the leg that is in direct contact with the ground in standing or walking. **2.** An invertebrate structure used for locomotion. **3.** Something suggestive of a foot in position or function: *the foot of a mountain; the foot of a bed.* **4.** A unit of poetic meter consisting of stressed and unstressed syllables in various set combinations. **5.** See table at **measurement.** ►*v.* **1.** To walk: *had to foot it home.* **2.** To add up; total: *footed up the bill.* **3.** To pay: *footed the travel expenses.* —*idioms:* **foot in the door** *Slang* An initial opportunity for advancement. **get (one's) feet wet** To begin a new activity, such as a job. **on foot** Walking rather than riding. **on (one's) feet 1.** Standing up. **2.** Fully recovered, as after an illness. [< OE *fōt.*]

foot·age (fōōt′ĭj) ►*n.* **1.** Length, extent, or amount based on measurement in feet. **2.** Recorded film or video, esp. of a certain subject.

foot·ball (fōōt′bôl′) ►*n.* **1a.** A game played by two teams of 11 players each on a 100-yard-long field with goal lines and goal posts at either end, the object being to gain possession of a ball and advance it between the opponent's goalposts or across its goal line. **b.** The inflated oval ball used in this game. **2.** *Chiefly Brit.* **a.** rugby or soccer. **b.** The ball used in rugby or soccer.

foot·board (fōōt′bôrd′) ►*n.* **1.** An upright board across the foot of a bedstead. **2.** A board or small raised platform on which to support or rest the feet.

foot·bridge (fōōt′brĭj′) ►*n.* A bridge designed for pedestrians.

foot·ed (fōōt′ĭd) ►*adj.* Having feet or a specified kind or number of feet: *a footed sofa; web-footed; four-footed.*

foot·fall (fōōt′fôl′) ►*n.* See **footstep** (sense 1).

foot·hill (fōōt′hĭl′) ►*n.* A hill near the base of a mountain or mountain range.

foot·hold (fōōt′hōld′) ►*n.* **1.** A place providing support for the foot in climbing or standing. **2.** A firm or secure position that provides a base for further advancement.

foot·ing (fōōt′ĭng) ►*n.* **1.** Secure placement of the feet in standing or moving. **2.** A basis or foundation: *Business began on a good footing.* **3a.** Position in relation to others. **b.** Terms of social interaction: *neighbors on a friendly footing.*

foot·lights (fōōt′līts′) ►*pl.n.* **1.** Lights placed in a row along the front of a stage floor. **2.** The theater as a profession.

foot·lock·er (fōōt′lŏk′ər) ►*n.* A trunk for storing personal belongings, esp. one kept at the foot of a bed, as in a barracks.

foot·loose (fōōt′lōōs′) ►*adj.* Having no attachments; free to do as one pleases.

foot·man (fōōt′mən) ►*n.* A man employed as a servant.

foot·note (fōōt′nōt′) ►*n.* A note of comment or reference at the bottom of a page of a book. —**foot′note′** *v.*

foot·path (fōōt′păth′, -päth′) ►*n.* A narrow path for persons on foot.

foot·print (fōōt′prĭnt′) ►*n.* An outline or indentation left by a foot on a surface.

foot·race (fōōt′rās′) ►*n.* A race run by contestants on foot.

foot·rest (fōōt′rĕst′) ►*n.* A support on which to rest the feet.

foot soldier ►*n.* A soldier trained to fight on foot; infantry trooper.

foot·sore (fōōt′sôr′) ►*adj.* Having sore or tired feet. —**foot′sore′ness** *n.*

foot·step (fōōt′stĕp′) ►*n.* **1a.** A step with the foot. **b.** The sound of a foot stepping. **2.** The distance covered by a step. **3.** A footprint.

foot·stool (fōōt′stōōl′) ►*n.* A low stool for supporting the feet.

foot·wear (fōōt′wâr′) ►*n.* Attire, such as shoes or slippers, for the feet.

foot·work (fōōt′wûrk′) ►*n.* The manner in which the feet are used or maneuvered, as in boxing, figure skating, or dancing.

fop (fŏp) ►*n.* A man preoccupied with clothes and manners; dandy. [ME, fool.] —**fop′per·y** *n.* —**fop′pish** *adj.* —**fop′pish·ly** *adv.*

for (fôr; fər *when unstressed*) ►*prep.* **1a.** Used to indicate the object or purpose of an action or activity: *plans to run for senator.* **b.** Used to indicate a destination: *headed for town.* **2a.** On behalf of: *spoke for us all.* **b.** In favor of: *I'm for the proposal.* **c.** In place of: *a substitute for eggs.* **3a.** As equivalent or equal to: *word for word.* **b.** Used to indicate correlation: *two steps back for one step forward.* **4.** Used to indicate amount, extent, or duration: *walked for miles.* **5.** As being: *mistook me for the boss.* **6.** As a result of: *jumped for joy.* **7.** Used to indicate appropriateness or suitability: *not for us to decide.* **8.** Notwithstanding; despite: *For all the problems, it was worth it.* **9.** Considering the nature of: *was spry for his age.* **10.** In honor of: *named for her.* ►*conj.* Because; since. ►*adv.* Because of this; for this reason: *She did it for love.* [< OE.]

fo·ra (fôr′ə) ►*n.* Pl. of **forum.**

for·age (fôr′ĭj, fŏr′-) ►*n.* **1.** Food for domestic animals; fodder. **2.** A search for food or provisions. ►*v.* **-aged, -ag·ing** To search, as for food. [< OFr. *fourrage* < *feurre,* fodder.] —**for′ag·er** *n.*

For·a·ker (fôr′ə-kər, fŏr′-), **Mount** A peak, 5,307 m (17,400 ft), in the Alaska Range of S-central AK

for·ay (fôr′ā′, fŏr′ā′) ►*n.* **1.** A sudden raid or military advance. **2.** A first venture or attempt. [< ME *forraien,* to plunder.] —**for′ay′** *v.*

forb (fôrb) ►*n.* A broad-leaved herb other than a grass. [< Gk. *phorbē,* fodder.]

for·bear¹ (fôr-bâr′) ►*v.* **-bore** (-bôr′), **-borne** (-bôrn′), **-bear·ing** **1.** To keep oneself from doing something; hold back. See Synonyms at **refrain¹. 2.** To be tolerant or patient. [< OE *forberan,* endure.] —**for·bear′ance** *n.*

for·bear² (fôr′bâr′) ►*n.* Var. of **forebear.**

for·bid (fər-bĭd′, fôr-) ►*v.* **-bade** (-băd′, -bād′) or **-bad** (-băd′), **-bid·den** (-bĭd′n) or **-bid, -bid·ding** **1.** To command (someone) not to do something: *I forbid you to go.* **2.** To command against doing (something): *forbid smoking on trains.* **3.** To preclude. [< OE *forbēodan.*] —**for·bid′dance** *n.*

Syns: ban, prohibit, proscribe Ant: *permit* v.

for·bid·ding (fər-bĭd′ĭng, fôr-) ►*adj.* **1.** Tending to threaten or menace: *forbidding rapids.* **2.** Unpleasant; disagreeable.

force (fôrs) ►*n.* **1a.** Energy, strength, or active power. **b.** The exertion of such power. **2a.** Physical power or violence. **b.** Intellectual power or vigor. **c.** Moral strength. **3.** A body of persons organized for a certain purpose, esp. for the use of military power. **4.** *Phys.* A vector quantity that tends to produce an acceleration of a body in the direction of its application. ►*v.* **forced, forc·ing** **1.** To compel to perform an action. **2a.** To gain by force or coercion. **b.** To move (something) against resistance. **c.** To inflict or impose. **3.** To produce with effort: *force a laugh.* **4.** To move, break down, open, or clear by force: *forced our way.* **5.** *Bot.* To cause to grow or mature artificially. —*idiom:* **in force** **1.** In full strength. **2.** In effect; operative: *a rule now in force.* [< Lat. *fortis,* strong.] —**force′ful** *adj.* —**force′ful·ly** *adv.* —**force′ful·ness** *n.*

force-feed (fôrs′fēd′) ►*v.* To compel to ingest food, esp. by mechanical means.

force field ►*n.* See **field of force.**

for·ceps (fôr′səps, -sĕps) ►*n., pl.* **-ceps** An instrument used for grasping, manipulating, or extracting, esp. in surgery. [Lat.]

forc·i·ble (fôr′sə-bəl) ►*adj.* **1.** Effected through force. **2.** Characterized by force; powerful. —**forc′i·bly** *adv.*

ford (fôrd) ►*n.* A shallow place in a body of water where one can walk, ride, or drive across. [< OE.] —**ford** *v.* —**ford′a·ble** *adj.*

Ford, Gerald Rudolph 1913–2006. The 38th US president (1974–77).

Gerald Ford

Ford, Henry 1863–1947. Amer. automobile manufacturer.

fore (fôr) ►*adj. & adv.* At, in, near, or toward the front; forward. ►*n.* The front part. ►*interj.* Used by a golfer to warn others that a ball is headed their way. [< OE, beforehand.]

fore– ►*pref.* **1.** Before; earlier: *forebode.* **2.** In front of; front: *foreground.* [< OE.]

fore-and-aft (fôr′ən-ăft′) ►*adj.* **1.** From the bow of a ship to the stern; lengthwise. **2.** In or at the front and back.

fore·arm¹ (fôr-ärm′) ►*v.* To arm or prepare in advance of a conflict.

fore·arm² (fôr′ärm′) ►*n.* The part of the arm between the wrist and elbow.

fore·bear also **for·bear** (fôr′bâr′) ►*n.* A person from whom one is descended. See Synonyms at **ancestor.** [ME : FORE– + *been,* BE.]

fore·bode (fôr-bōd′) ►*v.* **1.** To indicate the likelihood of; portend: *financial woes that portended bankruptcy.* **2.** To have a premonition of (a future misfortune). —**fore·bod′ing** *n.*

fore·cast (fôr′kăst′) ►*v.* **-cast** or **-cast·ed, -cast·ing** **1.** To estimate or predict in advance: *forecast tomorrow's weather.* **2.** To foreshadow: *price increases that foreshadow inflation.* ►*n.* A prediction. [ME *forecasten,* plan beforehand.] —**fore′cast′er** *n.*

fore·cas·tle (fōk′səl, fôr′kăs′əl) also **fo′c′s′le** (fōk′səl) ►*n.* **1.** The section of the upper deck of a ship located forward of the foremast. **2.** The crew's quarters at the bow of a merchant ship. [ME *forecastel.*]

fore·close (fôr-klōz′) ►*v.* **-closed, -clos·ing** **1.** To take legal possession of property from an owner who has defaulted esp. on a mortgage or taxes: *The bank foreclosed on the house.* **2.** To preclude; bar. [< OFr. *forclore,* exclude.] —**fore·clo′sure** *n.*

fore·court (fôr′kôrt′) ►*n.* **1.** A courtyard in front of a building. **2.** The part of a court nearest the net or wall, as in tennis or handball.

fore·fa·ther (fôr′fä′thər) ►*n.* **1.** An ancestor. **2.** A founder or originator.

fore·fin·ger (fôr′fĭng′gər) ►*n.* See **index finger.**

fore·foot (fôr′fŏŏt′) ►*n.* Either of the front feet of an animal.

fore·front (fôr′frŭnt′) ►*n.* **1.** The foremost part or area. **2.** The most important position.

fore·go¹ (fôr-gō′) ►*v.* To precede, as in time or place. —**fore·go′er** *n.*

fore·go² (fôr-gō′) ►*v.* Var. of **forgo.**

fore·go·ing (fôr-gō'ĭng, fôr'gō'ĭng) ►*adj.* Just before or past; previous.

fore·gone ►*adj.* (fôr'gôn', -gŏn') So certain as to be known in advance: *a foregone conclusion.* [< FOREGO¹.]

fore·ground (fôr'ground') ►*n.* **1.** The part of a scene or picture nearest to the viewer. **2.** The forefront; vanguard.

fore·hand (fôr'hănd') ►*adj.* Made with the palm of the dominant hand facing forward: *a forehand tennis stroke.* ►*n.* A forehand stroke. —**fore'hand'** *adv.*

fore·head (fôr'hĕd', -ĭd, fôr'-) ►*n.* The part of the face between the eyebrows and the normal hairline. [< OE *forhēafod.*]

for·eign (fôr'ĭn, fŏr'-) ►*adj.* **1.** Located away from one's native country. **2.** Characteristic of or from a place or country other than one's own: *a foreign custom.* **3.** Conducted or involved with other nations: *foreign trade.* **4.** Situated in an abnormal place in the body: *a foreign object in the eye.* **5.** Not natural; alien: *Jealousy is foreign to her nature.* **6.** Irrelevant. [< LLat. *forānus,* outsider < Lat. *forās,* outside.] —**for'eign·ness** *n.*

Syns: *alien, exotic, strange* **adj.**

for·eign·er (fôr'ə-nər, fŏr'-) ►*n.* One who is from a foreign country or place.

foreign minister ►*n.* A cabinet minister in charge of a nation's foreign affairs.

foreign office ►*n.* The governmental department in charge of foreign affairs in certain countries.

fore·knowl·edge (fôr-nŏl'ĭj) ►*n.* Knowledge of something before its occurrence.

fore·leg (fôr'lĕg') ►*n.* Either of the front legs of an animal.

fore·limb (fôr'lĭm') ►*n.* A front part, such as a leg, wing, or flipper.

fore·lock (fôr'lŏk') ►*n.* A lock of hair that grows from or falls on the forehead.

fore·man (fôr'mən) ►*n.* **1.** A man in charge of a group of workers, as at a factory or ranch. **2.** A man who chairs and speaks for a jury.

fore·mast (fôr'məst, -măst') ►*n.* The forward mast on a sailing vessel.

fore·most (fôr'mōst') ►*adj. & adv.* First in position or rank. [< ME *formest* < OE *forma,* first.]

fore·noon (fôr'nōōn') ►*n.* The period between sunrise and noon; morning.

fo·ren·sic (fə-rĕn'sĭk, -zĭk) ►*adj.* **1.** Of or used in legal proceedings or formal debate. **2.** Relating to the use of science or technology in the investigation and establishment of legal evidence: *a forensic laboratory.* [< Lat. *forēnsis,* of the forum.] —**fo·ren'si·cal·ly** *adv.*

fo·ren·sics (fə-rĕn'sĭks, -zĭks) ►*n.* (takes sing. v.) **1.** The art or study of formal debate. **2.** The use of science and technology to investigate and establish facts in courts of law.

fore·or·dain (fôr'ôr-dān') ►*v.* To determine or appoint beforehand; predestine.

fore·part (fôr'pärt') ►*n.* The part at the front or beginning.

fore·quar·ter (fôr'kwôr'tər) ►*n.* **1.** The front section of a side of meat. **2.** The foreleg and shoulder of an animal.

fore·run·ner (fôr'rŭn'ər) ►*n.* **1.** A predecessor. **2.** One that comes before and indicates the approach of another.

fore·sail (fôr'səl, -sāl') ►*n.* The principal square

sail hung to the foremast of a square-rigged sailing vessel.

fore·see (fôr-sē') ►*v.* To imagine or know as a probable occurrence; anticipate or predict: *foresaw economic decline.* —**fore·see'a·ble** *adj.*

fore·shad·ow (fôr-shăd'ō) ►*v.* To present an indication or hint of beforehand.

fore·shore (fôr'shôr') ►*n.* The part of a shore that is covered at high tide.

fore·short·en (fôr-shôr'tn) ►*v.* **1.** To shorten the lines of (a figure or design) in a drawing or painting so as to produce an illusion of depth or distance. **2.** To reduce the length of.

fore·sight (fôr'sīt') ►*n.* **1.** The ability or action of imagining or anticipating what might happen in the future. Care in providing for the future: *Saving money shows a lot of foresight.* —**fore'sight'ed** *adj.* —**fore'sight'ed·ly** *adv.*

fore·skin (fôr'skĭn') ►*n.* The loose fold of skin that covers the glans of the penis.

for·est (fôr'ĭst, fŏr'-) ►*n.* A dense growth of trees, plants, and underbrush covering a large area. [< Med.Lat. *forestis (silva),* outside (forest) < Lat. *forīs,* outside.] —**for'es·ta'tion** *n.*

fore·stall (fôr-stôl') ►*v.* To delay, hinder, or prevent by taking measures beforehand. [< OE *foresteall,* an ambush.]

for·est·ry (fôr'ĭ-strē, fŏr'-) ►*n.* The science and art of cultivating, maintaining, and developing forests.

fore·taste (fôr'tāst') ►*n.* An advance realization, token, or warning. —**fore·taste'** *v.*

fore·tell (fôr-tĕl') ►*v.* To tell of or indicate beforehand; predict. —**fore·tell'er** *n.*

Syns: *augur, divine, prophesy* **v.**

fore·thought (fôr'thôt') ►*n.* Deliberation, consideration, or planning for the future.

fore·to·ken (fôr-tō'kən) ►*v.* To give warning of beforehand; presage. —**fore'to'ken** *n.*

for·ev·er (fôr-ĕv'ər, fər-) ►*adv.* **1.** For all time; eternally. **2.** At all times; incessantly.

for·ev·er·more (fôr-ĕv'ər-môr', fər-) ►*adv.* Forever.

fore·warn (fôr-wôrn') ►*v.* To warn in advance.

fore·wing (fôr'wĭng') ►*n.* Either of a pair of front wings of a four-winged insect.

fore·wom·an (fôr'wōōm'ən) ►*n.* **1.** A woman who serves as the leader of a work crew, as in a factory. **2.** A woman who chairs and speaks for a jury.

fore·word (fôr'wərd) ►*n.* A preface, as for a book, esp. by a person other than the author.

for·feit (fôr'fĭt) ►*n.* **1.** Something that is given up on account of an offense, error, or failure to fulfill an agreement. **2.** The act of giving something up in this way. ►*v.* To lose (something) as a forfeit. [< OFr. *forfaire,* act outside the law.]

for·fei·ture (fôr'fĭ-chōōr', -chər) ►*n.* **1.** The act of forfeiting. **2.** A loss of property as a result of failing to comply with a legal requirement.

for·gath·er (fôr-găth'ər) ►*v.* To gather together; assemble.

forge¹ (fôrj) ►*n.* A furnace or hearth where metals are heated and wrought; smithy. ►*v.* **forged, forg·ing 1.** To form (e.g., metal) by heating in a forge and beating or hammering into shape. **2.** To give form or shape to; devise: *forge a treaty.* **3.** To fashion or reproduce fraudulently; counterfeit: *forge a signature.* [< Lat. *fabrica.*] —**forg'er** *n.* —**for'ger·y** *n.*

forge² (fôrj) ►*v.* **forged, forg·ing 1.** To advance

gradually but steadily. **2.** To advance with an abrupt increase in speed: *forged into first place.* [Poss. < FORGE¹.]

for·get (fər-gĕt′, fôr-) ►*v.* **-got** (-gŏt′), **-got·ten** (-gŏt′n) or **-got, -get·ting 1.** To be unable to remember (something). **2.** To treat with inattention; neglect: *forget one's family.* **3.** To fail to become aware at the proper moment: *forget a date.* —*idiom:* **forget oneself** To lose one's temper or self-restraint. [< OE *forgietan.*] —**for·get′ful** *adj.* —**for·get′ful·ly** *adv.* —**for·get′ful·ness** *n.* —**for·get′ta·ble** *adj.*

for·get-me-not (fər-gĕt′mē-nŏt′, fôr-) ►*n.* A herbaceous plant with small blue flowers.

for·give (fər-gĭv′, fôr-) ►*v.* **-gave** (-gāv′), **-giv·en** (-gĭv′ən), **-giv·ing 1.** To give up resentment against or stop wanting to punish (someone) for an offense or fault; pardon. **2.** To relent in being angry or in wishing to exact punishment for (e.g., an offense). **3.** To absolve from payment of (e.g., a debt.) [< OE *forgiefan.*] —**for·giv′a·ble** *adj.* —**for·give′ness** *n.*

for·go also **fore·go** (fôr-gō′) ►*v.* **-went** (-wĕnt′), **-gone** (-gôn′, -gŏn′), **-go·ing** To give up; relinquish. [< OE *forgān.*]

fo·rint (fôr′ĭnt′) ►*n.* See table at **currency.** [Hung. < Ital. *fiorino,* FLORIN.]

fork (fôrk) ►*n.* **1.** A utensil with two or more prongs, used for eating or serving food. **2.** An implement with two or more prongs, esp. a farm or garden tool used for digging. **3a.** A separation into two or more branches. **b.** The place of such a separation: *a fork in the road.* **c.** One of the branches: *took the right fork.* See Synonyms at **branch.** ►*v.* **1.** To raise, carry, or pierce with a fork. **2.** To divide into branches. **3.** *Informal* To pay: *forked over $50.* [< Lat. *furca.*] —**fork′ful′** *n.*

forked (fôrkt, fôr′kĭd) ►*adj.* Having or shaped like a fork: *a forked river; forked lightning.*

fork·lift (fôrk′lĭft′) ►*n.* An industrial vehicle with a power-operated pronged platform that can be raised and lowered for lifting and carrying loads.

for·lorn (fər-lôrn′, fôr-) ►*adj.* **1.** Deserted or abandoned. **2.** Wretched in appearance or condition. **3.** Bereft or deprived. **4.** Nearly hopeless; desperate. [< OE *forlēosan,* abandon.] —**for·lorn′ly** *adv.* —**for·lorn′ness** *n.*

form (fôrm) ►*n.* **1a.** The shape and structure of an object: *the form of a snowflake.* **b.** The body, esp. of a person; figure. **2.** The way in which a thing manifests itself: *an element found in the form of a gas.* **3.** A kind, type, or variety: *A cat is a form of mammal.* **4.** Conduct as determined by decorum or custom: *Arriving late is considered bad form.* **5.** A document with blanks for the insertion of requested information. **6.** Fitness with regard to health or training. **7.** A meaningful unit of language. ►*v.* **1a.** To shape or become shaped. **b.** To develop in the mind: *form an opinion.* **2a.** To arrange oneself in: *The acrobats formed a pyramid.* **b.** To develop by instruction or precept: *formed the recruits into good soldiers.* **3.** To develop or acquire: *form a habit.* **4.** To constitute or compose, esp. out of separate elements: *the bones that form the skeleton.* **5.** To come into being by taking form; arise: *Clouds formed in the sky.* **6.** To enter into (a relationship): *form a friendship.* [< Lat. *fôrma,* perh. < Gk. *morphē.*]

–form ►*suff.* Having the form of: *cruciform.*

for·mal (fôr′məl) ►*adj.* **1a.** Of or involving outward form or structure. **b.** Being or relating to essential form or constitution: *a formal principle.* **2.** Following accepted forms or conventions: *a formal education.* **3.** Marked by strict observation of forms; methodical: *formal in their business transactions.* **4.** Stiff or reserved: *a formal manner.* **5.** Done for the sake of procedure only: *a formal requirement.* ►*n.* Something, such as a gown or social affair, that is formal in nature. —**for′mal·ly** *adv.*

for·mal·de·hyde (fôr-măl′də-hīd′) ►*n.* A gaseous compound, HCHO, used in aqueous solution as a preservative and disinfectant. [*form(ic acid),* HCOOH + ALDEHYDE.]

for·mal·ism (fôr′mə-lĭz′əm) ►*n.* Rigorous or excessive adherence to recognized forms, as in religion or art. —**for′mal·ist** *adj. & n.* —**for′mal·is′tic** *adj.*

for·mal·i·ty (fôr-măl′ĭ-tē) ►*n., pl.* **-ties 1.** The quality or condition of being formal. **2.** Rigorous or ceremonious adherence to rules. **3.** An established rule or custom, esp. one followed merely for the sake of procedure or decorum.

for·mal·ize (fôr′mə-līz′) ►*v.* **-ized, -iz·ing 1.** To make formal. **2.** To give formal endorsement to. —**for′mal·i·za′tion** *n.*

for·mat (fôr′măt′) ►*n.* **1.** A plan for the organization and arrangement of something. **2.** The layout of a publication. **3.** *Comp.* The arrangement of data for storage or display. ►*v.* **-mat·ted, -mat·ting 1.** To plan or arrange in a specified form. **2.** *Comp.* **a.** To divide (a disk) into marked sectors to allow for the storage of data. **b.** To determine the arrangement of (data) for storage or display. [< Lat. *fôrma,* FORM.]

for·ma·tion (fôr-mā′shən) ►*n.* **1.** The act or process of forming. **2.** Something formed: *cloud formations.* **3.** The manner in which something is formed; structure: *the distinctive formation of the human eye.* **4.** A specified arrangement, as of troops. —**for·ma′tion·al** *adj.*

formation
the Blue Angels of the US Navy

for·ma·tive (fôr′mə-tĭv) ►*adj.* **1.** Forming or capable of forming. **2.** Of or relating to formation or growth: *his formative years.*

for·mer (fôr′mər) ►*adj.* **1.** Relating to or taking place in the past: *in former times.* **2.** Being the first of two mentioned. **3.** Having been so in the past: *a former ambassador.* ►*n.* The first of two persons or things mentioned. [< OE *forma,* first.]

for·mer·ly (fôr′mər-lē) ►*adv.* At an earlier or former time; once.

form·fit·ting (fôrm′fĭt′ĭng) ►*adj.* Snugly fitting the body's contours: *formfitting jeans.*

For·mi·ca (fôr-mī′kə) A trademark for laminated sheeting of synthetic resin typically used as a surface on tables and counters.

for·mi·da·ble (fôr′mĭ-də-bəl, fôr-mĭd′ə-) ►*adj.* **1.** Arousing fear, dread, or alarm. **2.** Inspiring admiration or wonder: *formidable intelligence.* **3.** Difficult to undertake or defeat: *a formidable opponent.* [< Lat. *formīdō*, fear.] —**for′mi·da·bil′i·ty** *n.* —**for′mi·da·bly** *adv.*

form letter ►*n.* A letter in a standardized format sent to multiple recipients.

For·mo·sa (fôr-mō′sə) See **Taiwan.**

for·mu·la (fôr′myə-lə) ►*n.,* *pl.* **-las** or **-lae** (-lē′) **1.** A set of words, symbols, or rules for use in a ceremony or procedure. **2.** *Chem.* A set of symbols that show the composition and structure of a compound. **3.** A recipe. **4.** A liquid food for infants, containing most of the nutrients of human milk. **5.** *Math.* A statement, esp. an equation, of a fact, rule, principle, or other logical relation. [Lat. *fōrmula* < *fōrma*, FORM.] —**for′mu·la′ic** (-lā′ĭk) *adj.*

for·mu·late (fôr′myə-lāt′) ►*v.* **-lat·ed, -lat·ing 1.** To state as a formula. **2.** To express in systematic terms or concepts. **3.** To devise or invent: *formulate strategy.* **4.** To prepare according to a specified formula. —**for′mu·la′tion** *n.* —**for′mu·la′tor** *n.*

for·ni·ca·tion (fôr′nĭ-kā′shən) ►*n.* Sexual intercourse between partners who are not married. [< Lat. *fornix*, brothel.] —**for′ni·cate′** *v.* —**for′ni·ca′tor** *n.*

for·sake (fôr-sāk′, fər-) ►*v.* **-sook** (-sŏŏk′), **-sak·en** (-sā′kən), **-sak·ing 1.** To give up; renounce. **2.** To leave altogether; abandon: *forsook her career to stay home.* [< OE *forsacan.*]

for·sooth (fôr-sŏŏth′, fər-) ►*adv.* In truth; indeed. [< OE *forsōth.*]

For·ster (fôr′stər), **E(dward) M(organ)** 1879–1970. British writer.

for·swear (fôr-swâr′) ►*v.* **-swore** (fôr-swôr′), **-sworn** (fôr-swôrn′), **-swear·ing 1.** To renounce seriously or under oath. **2.** To commit perjury. [< OE *forswerian.*]

for·syth·i·a (fôr-sĭth′ē-ə) ►*n.* A widely cultivated shrub with early-blooming yellow flowers. [After William *Forsyth* (1737–1804).]

fort (fôrt) ►*n.* A fortified place, esp. an army post. [< Lat. *fortis*, strong.]

Fort-de-France (fôr-də-fräns′) The capital of Martinique, on the W coast.

for·te¹ (fôr′tā′, fôrt) ►*n.* Something in which one excels. [< OFr. *fort*, strong.]

Usage: The word *forte* is traditionally pronounced with one syllable, like the French word from which it is derived. But many people, including three-quarters of the Usage Panel, pronounce English *forte* with two syllables, as (fôr′tā′). Some people consider this a mistake, because the two-syllable pronunciation originates with the music term derived from Italian *forte,* but both one- and two-syllable pronunciations are widespread and must be considered acceptable.

for·te² (fôr′tā′) ►*adv. & adj. Mus.* In a loud, forceful manner. [Ital.] —**for′te′** *n.*

forth (fôrth) ►*adv.* **1.** Forward or onward. **2.** Out into view. [< OE.]

forth·com·ing (fôrth-kŭm′ĭng) ►*adj.* **1.** About to appear or take place. **2.** Available when required or as promised: *Federal forms were not forthcoming.* **3.** Willing to help; cooperative.

forth·right (fôrth′rīt′) ►*adj.* Direct and without evasion; straightforward. —**forth′right′ly** *adv.* —**forth′right′ness** *n.*

forth·with (fôrth-wĭth′, -wĭth′) ►*adv.* At once; immediately.

for·ti·eth (fôr′tē-ĭth) ►*n.* **1.** The ordinal number matching the number 40 in a series. **2.** One of 40 equal parts. —**for′ti·eth** *adv. & adj.*

for·ti·fy (fôr′tə-fī′) ►*v.* **-fied, -fy·ing 1.** To strengthen and secure (a position) militarily. **2.** To strengthen physically; invigorate. **3.** To strengthen spiritually or mentally; encourage: *Family support fortified us during our crisis.* **4.** To enrich (food), as by adding vitamins. [< Lat. *fortis*, strong.] —**for′ti·fi·ca′tion** *n.*

for·tis·si·mo (fôr-tĭs′ə-mō′) ►*adv. & adj. Mus.* In a very loud manner. [Ital.] —**for·tis′si·mo′** *n.*

for·ti·tude (fôr′tĭ-tōōd′, -tyōōd′) ►*n.* Strength of mind that allows one to endure pain or adversity with courage. [< Lat. *fortis*, strong.]

fort·night (fôrt′nīt′) ►*n.* A period of 14 days; two weeks. [ME *fourtenight* : OE *fēowertēne*, FOURTEEN + OE *niht*, NIGHT.] —**fort′night′ly** *adv. & adj.*

for·tress (fôr′trĭs) ►*n.* A fortified place, esp. one that includes a town. [< Med.Lat. *fortalitia* < Lat. *fortis*, strong.]

for·tu·i·tous (fôr-tōō′ĭ-təs, -tyōō′-) ►*adj.* **1.** Happening by accident or chance; unplanned. **2.** Resulting in good fortune; lucky. [< Lat. *forte*, by chance.] —**for·tu′i·tous·ly** *adv.* —**for·tu′i·tous·ness** *n.*

for·tu·i·ty (fôr-tōō′ĭ-tē, -tyōō′-) ►*n., pl.* **-ties 1.** A chance occurrence or event. **2.** The quality or condition of being fortuitous.

for·tu·nate (fôr′chə-nĭt) ►*adj.* Occurring by or having good fortune. —**for′tu·nate·ly** *adv.*

    Syns: happy, lucky adj.

for·tune (fôr′chən) ►*n.* **1.** Good or bad luck. **2. fortunes** The turns of luck in one's lifetime. **3.** A large sum of money: *The car cost a fortune.* **4.** Fate; destiny: *told my fortune with tarot cards.* [< Lat. *fortūna.*]

for·tune-tell·er (fôr′chən-tĕl′ər) ►*n.* One who professes to predict future events. —**for′tune·tell′ing** *adj. & n.*

Fort Worth A city of NE TX W of Dallas.

for·ty (fôr′tē) ►*n., pl.* **-ties** The cardinal number equal to 4 × 10. [< OE *fēowertig.*] —**for′ty** *adj. & pron.*

for·ty-five (fôr′tē-fīv′) ►*n.* **1.** A .45-caliber pistol. **2.** A phonograph record designed to be played at 45 revolutions per minute.

for·ty-nin·er (fôr′tē-nī′nər) ►*n.* One who took part in the 1849 California gold rush.

forty winks ►*pl.n. Informal* A short nap.

fo·rum (fôr′əm) ►*n., pl.* **-rums** also **fo·ra** (fôr′ə) **1.** The public square or marketplace of an ancient Roman city. **2.** A public place or medium for open discussion. **3.** A court of law; tribunal. [< Lat.]

for·ward (fôr′wərd) ►*adj.* **1.** At, near, belonging to, or located in the front: *the forward section of the aircraft.* **2.** Going, tending, or moving toward the front. **3.** Presumptuous or bold. **4.** Being ahead of current economic, political, or technological trends; progressive. **5.** Exceptionally advanced; precocious. ►*adv.* also **for·wards** (-wərdz) **1.** Toward or tending to the front; frontward: *step forward.* **2.** In or toward the future: *looking forward to seeing you.* **3.** Earlier or later: *moved the appointment forward.* ►*n.* Sports A player at the front of the offense, as in hockey. ►*v.* **1.** To send on to a subsequent destination or address. See Synonyms at **send. 2.** To help advance; promote. See Synonyms at **advance.** [< OE *fōreweard.*] —**for′ward·ly** *adv.* —**for′ward·ness** *n.*

for·wards (fôr′wərdz) ►*adv.* Variant of **forward.**

for·went (fôr-wĕnt′) ►*v.* P.t. of **forgo.**

Fos·se (fŏs′ē), **Robert Louis** "Bob." 1927–87. Amer. choreographer and director.

fos·sil (fŏs′əl) ►*n.* **1.** A remnant or trace of an organism of a past geologic age, such as a skeleton or leaf imprint, embedded in the earth's crust. **2.** One that is outdated. [< Lat. *fossilis,* dug up < *fodere,* dig.]

fossil fuel ►*n.* A hydrocarbon-based fuel, such as coal or natural gas, derived from living matter of a previous geologic time.

fos·sil·ize (fŏs′ə-līz′) ►*v.* **-ized, -iz·ing 1.** To convert into or become a fossil. **2.** To make or become outmoded or inflexible with time; antiquate. —**fos′sil·i·za′tion** *n.*

fos·ter (fô′stər, fŏs′tər) ►*v.* **1.** To bring up; nurture: *foster offspring.* See Synonyms at **nurture. 2.** To promote the development of. See Synonyms at **advance.** ►*adj.* Giving or receiving parental care although not related legally or by blood: *foster parents.* [< OE *fōstor,* food.]

Fos·ter (fô′stər), **Stephen Collins** 1826–64. Amer. songwriter.

Fou·cault (foo-kō′), **(Jean Bernard) Léon** 1819–68. French physicist and inventor.

fought (fôt) ►*v.* P.t. and p.part. of **fight.**

foul (foul) ►*adj.* **-er, -est 1.** Offensive to the senses; revolting: *a foul flavor.* **2.** Having an offensive odor. **3.** Rotten or putrid: *foul meat.* **4a.** Dirty; filthy. **b.** Full of impurities; polluted: *foul air.* **5.** Morally detestable; wicked. **6.** Vulgar; obscene: *foul language.* **7.** Bad or unfavorable; unpleasant: *foul weather.* **8.** Unfair; dishonorable: *win by foul means.* **9a.** Sports Contrary to the rules of a game or sport. **b.** Designating lines that limit the playing area. ►*n.* **1.** Sports An infraction of the rules. **2.** Baseball A foul ball. ►*adv.* In a foul manner. ►*v.* **1.** To make or become foul; pollute. **2.** To bring into dishonor. **3.** To clog or obstruct. **4.** Sports To commit a foul (against). —*phrasal verb:* **foul up** To blunder or cause to blunder because of mistakes or poor judgment. [< OE *fūl.*] —**foul′ly** *adv.* —**foul′ness** *n.*

fou·lard (foo-lärd′) ►*n.* A lightweight twill or plain-woven fabric of silk, usu. having a printed design, esp. used for neckties. [Fr.]

foul ball ►*n.* Baseball A batted ball that touches the ground outside of fair territory.

foul·mouthed (foul′mouthd′, -moutht′) ►*adj.* Using abusive or obscene language.

foul play ►*n.* Inappropriate, unethical, or unlawful conduct, esp. that which is criminal.

foul shot ►*n.* Basketball An unobstructed shot awarded to a fouled player and scored as one point if successful.

foul-up (foul′ŭp′) ►*n.* **1.** A condition of confusion caused by mistakes or poor judgment. **2.** A mechanical failure.

found¹ (found) ►*v.* **1.** To establish or set up (e.g., a college). **2.** To establish the foundation

or basis of. See Synonyms at **establish.** [< Lat. *fundāre.*] —**found′er** *n.*

found² (found) ►*v.* **1.** To melt (metal) and pour into a mold. **2.** To make (objects) by founding. [< Lat. *fundere.*] —**found′er** *n.*

found³ (found) ►*v.* P.t. and p.part. of **find.**

foun·da·tion (foun-dā′shən) ►*n.* **1.** The act of founding, esp. the establishment of an institution. **2.** The basis on which a thing stands; underlying support; base. **3a.** An endowment. **b.** An endowed institution. **4.** A cosmetic used as a base for facial makeup. —**foun·da′tion·al** *adj.*

foun·der (foun′dər) ►*v.* **1.** To sink or cause to sink below the water. **2.** To fail utterly; collapse. **3.** To go lame, as a horse. [< OFr. *fondrer,* sink to the ground.]

    Usage: Founder means "to fail utterly, collapse." *Flounder* means "to proceed in confusion." If John is foundering in a course, he had better drop it. If he is floundering, he may yet pull through.

found·ling (found′lĭng) ►*n.* An abandoned child of unknown parentage. [ME.]

foun·dry (foun′drē) ►*n., pl.* **-dries** A place where metal is melted and molded.

fount¹ (fount) ►*n.* **1.** A fountain. **2.** One that initiates or dispenses; a source. [< Lat. *fōns, font-.*]

fount² (fount) ►*n. Chiefly Brit.* Var. of **font².**

foun·tain (foun′tən) ►*n.* **1a.** An artificially created stream of water. **b.** A structure or device from which such a stream issues. **2.** A spring of water from the earth, esp. a stream's source. **3.** A soda fountain. **4.** A point of origin. [< LLat. *fontāna* < Lat. *fōns, font-.*]

foun·tain·head (foun′tən-hĕd′) ►*n.* **1.** A spring that is the source of a stream. **2.** A chief and copious source or origin.

fountain pen ►*n.* A pen having a refillable or replaceable ink reservoir that feeds ink to the nib.

four (fôr) ►*n.* **1.** The cardinal number equal to 3 + 1. **2.** The 4th in a set or sequence. [< OE *fēower.*] —**four** *adj. & pron.*

4-H Club ►*n.* A youth organization sponsored by the Department of Agriculture and teaching agriculture and home economics. [From its goals of improving head, heart, hands, and health.]

Fou·rier (foor′ē-ā′, foo-ryā′), **Baron Jean Baptiste Joseph.** 1768–1830. French mathematician and physicist.

four-in-hand (fôr′ĭn-hănd′) ►*n.* **1.** A team of four horses controlled by one driver. **2.** A necktie tied in a slipknot with long ends left hanging one in front of the other.

four-leaf clover (fôr′lēf′) ►*n.* A clover leaf having four leaflets instead of three, considered an omen of good luck.

four-o'clock (fôr′ə-klŏk′) ►*n.* A plant cultivated for its trumpet-shaped, variously colored flowers that open late in the afternoon.

401(k) ►*n.* A retirement plan in which a portion of one's wages are invested in a tax-deferred account.

four-post·er (fôr′pō′stər) ►*n.* A bed having tall corner posts orig. intended to support curtains or a canopy.

four·score (fôr′skôr′) ►*adj.* Four times twenty; eighty.

four·some (fôr′səm) ►*n.* **1.** A group of four

persons or things. **2.** An activity involving four people, such as a golf match.

four·square (fôr′skwâr′) ►*adj.* **1.** Square. **2.** Marked by firm, unwavering conviction or expression; forthright. —**four′square′** *adv.*

four·teen (fôr-tēn′) ►*n.* **1.** The cardinal number equal to 13 + 1. **2.** The 14th in a set or sequence. [< OE *fēowertēne.*] —**four·teen′** *adj. & pron.*

four·teenth (fôr-tēnth′) ►*n.* **1.** The ordinal number matching the number 14 in a series. **2.** One of 14 equal parts. —**four·teenth′** *adv. & adj.*

fourth (fôrth) ►*n.* **1.** The ordinal number matching the number 4 in a series. **2.** One of four equal parts. **3.** *Mus.* A tone four degrees above or below a given tone in a diatonic scale. [< OE *fēorth.*] —**fourth** *adv. & adj.*

fourth dimension ►*n.* Time regarded as a coordinate dimension and required, along with three spatial dimensions, to specify completely the location of any event.

fourth estate ►*n.* Journalists considered as a group.

Fourth of July ►*n.* See **Independence Day.**

four-wheel drive (fôr′wēl′, -hwēl′) ►*n.* An automotive drive system in which mechanical power is transmitted from the drive shaft to all four wheels.

fowl (foul) ►*n., pl.* **fowl** or **fowls** A bird, esp. one that is raised domestically or hunted as game. ►*v.* To hunt, trap, or shoot wildfowl. [< OE *fugol.*]

fox (fŏks) ►*n., pl.* **-es** also **fox 1a.** Any of various canine mammals that are similar to but smaller than wolves and have a pointed snout and a long bushy tail. **b.** The fur of a fox. **2.** A crafty or sly person. **3.** *Slang* A sexually attractive person. ►*v.* To trick or fool by ingenuity or cunning; outwit. [< OE.] —**fox′i·ly** *adv.* —**fox′i·ness** *n.* —**fox′y** *adj.*

Fox ►*n., pl.* **Fox** or **-es 1.** A member of a Native American people formerly of the upper Midwest, now in central Iowa and Oklahoma. **2.** The Algonquian language of the Fox.

Fox, George 1624–91. English founder of the Quakers (1647–48).

fox·fire (fŏks′fīr′) ►*n.* A phosphorescent glow, esp. that of fungi on rotting wood.

fox·glove (fŏks′glŭv′) ►*n.* A plant having a long cluster of large, tubular, pinkish-purple flowers and leaves that are the source of the drug digitalis.

fox·hole (fŏks′hōl′) ►*n.* A pit dug by a soldier for protection against enemy fire.

fox terrier ►*n.* A small terrier orig. developed in England for driving foxes from their burrows.

fox trot ►*n.* A ballroom dance in 4/4 time, encompassing a variety of slow and fast steps. —**fox′trot′** (fŏks′trŏt′) *v.*

foy·er (foi′ər, foi′ā′) ►*n.* **1.** A lobby, as of a theater or hotel. **2.** An entrance hall; vestibule. [< VLat. **focārium,* fireplace < Lat. *focus,* hearth.]

fps ►*abbr.* **1.** feet per second **2.** foot-pound-second **3.** frames per second

fr. ►*abbr.* **1.** franc **2.** from

Fr. ►*abbr.* **1.** father (title) **2.** French **3.** Frau **4.** friar

fra·cas (frā′kəs, frăk′əs) ►*n.* A rowdy fight. See Synonyms at **brawl.** [< Ital. *fracasso.*]

frac·tal (frăk′təl) ►*n.* An object whose parts, at infinitely many levels of magnification, appear

geometrically similar to the whole. [< Lat. *frangere, frāct-,* break.]

frac·tion (frăk′shən) ►*n.* **1.** *Math.* A quotient of two quantities shown as a numerator over a denominator. **2.** A disconnected piece; fragment. **3.** A small part; bit. [< Lat. *frangere, frāct-,* break.] —**frac′tion·al** *adj.* —**frac′tion·al·ly** *adv.*

frac·tious (frăk′shəs) ►*adj.* **1.** Inclined to make trouble; unruly. **2.** Having a peevish nature; cranky. [< FRACTION, discord.] —**frac′tious·ly** *adv.* —**frac′tious·ness** *n.*

frac·ture (frăk′chər) ►*n.* **1.** The act or process of breaking or the condition of being broken. **2.** A break, rupture, or crack, esp. in bone or cartilage. ►*v.* **-tured, -tur·ing** To break or cause to break; crack. [< Lat. *frangere, frāct-,* break.]

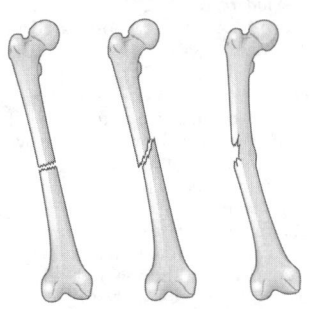

fracture
various types of fractures

frag·ile (frăj′əl, -īl′) ►*adj.* **1.** Easily broken or damaged; delicate. **2.** Tenuous or flimsy: *a fragile claim to fame.* [< Lat. *fragilis < frangere,* break.] —**frag′ile·ly** *adv.* —**fra·gil′i·ty** (frə-jĭl′ĭ-tē), frag′ile·ness** *n.*

frag·ment (frăg′mənt) ►*n.* **1.** A small part broken off. **2.** Something incomplete. ►*v.* (-mĕnt′) To break into fragments. [< Lat. *fragmentum < frangere,* break.] —**frag′men·ta′tion** *n.*

frag·men·tar·y (frăg′mən-tĕr′ē) ►*adj.* Consisting of small, disconnected parts. —**frag′men·tar′i·ly** (-târ′ə-lē) *adv.*

fra·grance (frā′grəns) ►*n.* **1.** A sweet or pleasant odor. **2.** A substance (e.g., perfume or cologne) designed to emit a pleasant odor. [< Lat. *frāgrāre,* emit an odor.] —**fra′grant** *adj.* —**fra′grant·ly** *adv.*

Syns: aroma, bouquet, perfume, redolence, scent n.

frail (frāl) ►*adj.* **-er, -est 1.** Physically weak. **2.** Easily broken. **3.** Not substantial; slight. [< Lat. *fragilis,* FRAGILE.] —**frail′ly** *adv.*

frail·ty (frāl′tē) ►*n., pl.* **-ties 1.** The condition or quality of being frail. **2.** A fault, esp. a moral weakness.

frame (frām) ►*n.* **1a.** A structure that gives shape or support. **b.** The human body; physique. **c.** An open structure or rim: *a window frame.* **2a.** A general structure or system: *the frame of government.* **b.** A general state or condition: *frame of mind.* **3a.** One of the set of still images that constitute a film or video. **b.** A rectangular area in which text or graphics can be shown, esp. one of several such areas on a web page displaying different documents simultaneously. **4.** A round of play in some games, such as bowling. ► ►*v.* **framed, fram·**

ing **1a.** To enclose in a frame. **b.** To put together the structural parts of. **2.** To conceive or design. **3.** To establish the context for and terminology regarding (a topic of debate), esp. so as to exclude an unwanted point of view. **4.** To put into words; formulate. **5.** To rig evidence or events so as to incriminate (a person) falsely. [< OE *framian*, to further.] —**fram′er** *n.*

frame-up (frām′ŭp′) ►*n.* *Informal* A fraudulent scheme, esp. one that involves falsified charges or evidence to incriminate an innocent person.

frame·work (frām′wûrk′) ►*n.* **1.** A structure for supporting or enclosing something. **2.** A fundamental system or design.

franc (frăngk) ►*n.* **1.** See table at **currency.** **2.** The primary unit of currency in Belgium, France, Luxembourg, and Monaco before the adoption of the euro. [< OFr.]

France (frăns) A country of W Europe on the Atlantic, the Mediterranean, and the English Channel. Cap. Paris.

fran·chise (frăn′chīz′) ►*n.* **1.** A privilege or right granted by law, esp. the right to vote. **2.** Authorization granted to someone to sell a company's goods or services. **3.** The territory or limits within which a privilege or right may be exercised. ►*v.* **-chised, -chis·ing** To grant a franchise to. [< OFr. *franchise*, freedom, exemption.] —**fran′chis·ee′** *n.* —**fran′chis′-er, fran′chi′sor** *n.*

Fran·cis (frăn′sĭs) b. 1936. Pope (elected 2013).

Fran·cis II 1768–1835. Last Holy Roman emperor (1792–1806); emperor of Austria (1804–35) as Francis I.

Francis Fer·di·nand (fûr′dn-ănd′) See **Franz Ferdinand.**

Francis Jo·seph I (jō′zəf, -səf, yō′zĕf) See **Franz Josef I.**

Francis of As·si·si (ə-sē′zē, -sē, ə-sĭs′ē), Saint. 1182?–1226. Italian friar; founder of the Franciscan order (1209). —**Fran·cis′can** *adj. & n.*

fran·ci·um (frăn′sē-əm) ►*n.* *Symbol* **Fr** An extremely unstable synthetic radioactive element. At. no. 87. See table at **element.** [After FRANCE.]

Fran·co (frăng′kō, fräng′-), **Francisco** 1892–1975. Spanish general and dictator.

Franco– ►*pref.* French: *Francophone.* [< LLat. *Francus*, a Frank.]

Fran·co·phone (frăng′kə-fōn′) ►*n.* A French-speaking person, esp. in a region of linguistic diversity. ►*adj.* French-speaking.

fran·gi·ble (frăn′jə-bəl) ►*adj.* Easily broken; breakable. [< Lat. *frangere*, break.] —**fran′gi·bil′i·ty** *n.*

frank¹ (frăngk) ►*adj.* **-er, -est** Open and sincere in expression; straightforward. ►*v.* **1.** To put an official mark on (a piece of mail) so that it can be sent free of charge. **2.** To send (mail) free of charge. ►*n.* **1.** A mark or signature on a piece of mail to indicate the right to send it free. **2.** The right to send mail free. [< OFr. *franc*, free.] —**frank′ly** *adv.* —**frank′ness** *n.*

frank² (frăngk) ►*n.* *Informal* A frankfurter.

Frank ►*n.* A member of a Germanic people who conquered Gaul about A.D. 500. —**Frank′-ish** *adj.*

Frank (frăngk, frängk), **Anne** 1929–45. German Jewish diarist.

Frank·en·stein (frăng′kən-stīn′) ►*n.* **1.** A creation that destroys its creator. **2.** A monster

having the appearance of a man. [After *Frankenstein*, the creator of the artificial monster in *Frankenstein* by Mary Wollstonecraft Shelley.]

Frank·fort (frăngk′fərt) The capital of KY, in the N-central part.

Frank·furt (frănk′fərt, frängk′foŏrt′) A city of W-central Germany NW of Munich.

frank·furt·er (frănk′fər-tər) ►*n.* A smoked sausage of beef or beef and pork made in long reddish links. [After *Frankfurt*, Germany.]

Frankfurter, Felix 1882–1965. Austrian-born Amer. jurist; US Supreme Court justice (1939–62).

frank·in·cense (frăng′kĭn-sĕns′) ►*n.* An aromatic gum resin used as incense and in perfumes. [< OFr. *franc encens*, pure incense.]

Frank·lin (frăngk′lĭn), **Aretha** b. 1942. Amer. singer.

Frank·lin (frăngk′lĭn), **Benjamin** 1706–90. Amer. public official, writer, scientist, and printer.

Benjamin Franklin
c. 1785 portrait

fran·tic (frăn′tĭk) ►*adj.* **1.** Highly excited with strong emotion; frenzied: *frantic with worry.* **2.** Marked by rapid and disordered activity: *a frantic last-minute search.* [< OFr. *frenetique*, FRENETIC.] —**fran′ti·cal·ly, fran′tic·ly** *adv.*

Franz Fer·di·nand (frănz fûr′dn-ănd′, frănts, fränts) also **Francis Ferdinand** 1863–1914. Austrian archduke whose assassination precipitated World War I.

Franz Jo·sef I (fränts yō′zĕf) also **Fran·cis Jo·seph I** (frăn′sĭs jō′zəf, -səf, yō′zĕf) 1830–1916. Emperor of Austria (1848–1916); king of Hungary (1867–1916).

frappe (frăp) ►*n.* *Regional* See **milk shake.** [Alteration of FRAPPÉ.]

frap·pé (fră-pā′, frăp) ►*n.* **1.** A frozen mixture similar to sherbet. **2.** A beverage poured over shaved ice. [< Fr., chilled.]

Fra·ser River (frā′zər) A river of British Columbia, Canada, flowing about 1,370 km (850 mi) from the Rocky Mts. to the Pacific Ocean at Vancouver.

fra·ter·nal (frə-tûr′nəl) ►*adj.* **1a.** Of brothers. **b.** Brotherly. **2.** Of or constituting a fraternity. **3.** *Biol.* Of or being a twin developed from separately fertilized ova. [< Lat. *fräter*, brother.] —**fra·ter′nal·ism** *n.* —**fra·ter′nal·ly** *adv.*

fra·ter·ni·ty (frə-tûr′nĭ-tē) ►*n., pl.* **-ties 1.** A group of people associated or joined by similar backgrounds, occupations, or interests. **2.** A social organization at a college or university, traditionally consisting of male students. **3.** Brotherhood.

frat·er·nize (frăt′ər-nīz′) ►*v.* **-nized, -niz·ing 1.** To associate with others in a brotherly or congenial way. **2.** To associate with an enemy or opposing group. **—frat′er·ni·za′tion** *n.* **—frat′er·niz′er** *n.*

frat·ri·cide (frăt′rĭ-sīd′) ►*n.* **1.** The killing of one's brother or sister. **2.** One who has killed a sibling. **3.** The accidental killing of an ally caused by a discharge of a military weapon. [Lat. *frāter*, brother + –CIDE.] **—frat′ri·cid′-al** *adj.*

Frau (frou) ►*n., pl.* **Frau·en** (frou′ən) A German courtesy title for a woman. [Ger.]

fraud (frôd) ►*n.* **1.** A deliberate deception for unfair or unlawful gain; swindle. **2a.** One that defrauds; cheat. **b.** One who assumes a false pose; impostor. [< Lat. *fraus, fraud-*.]

fraud·u·lent (frô′jə-lənt) ►*adj.* Constituting or gained by fraud. [< Lat. *fraudulentus.*] **—fraud′u·lence** *n.* **—fraud′u·lent·ly** *adv.*

fraught (frôt) ►*adj.* **1.** Filled with a specified element; charged: *work fraught with danger.* **2.** Distressful; upsetting. [ME < *fraughten*, to load.]

Fräu·lein (froi′līn′, frou′-) ►*n., pl.* **-lein** A German courtesy title for a girl or young woman. [Ger., dim. of *Frau*, Frau.]

fray¹ (frā) ►*n.* **1.** A fight or scuffle. See Synonyms at **brawl. 2.** A heated dispute. **3.** A military engagement; battle. [< ME *affrai*, AFFRAY.]

fray² (frā) ►*v.* **1.** To strain; chafe: *fray the nerves.* **2.** To wear away, unravel, or tatter by rubbing. [< Lat. *fricāre*, rub.]

fraz·zle (frăz′əl) ►*v.* **-zled, -zling** *Informal* **1.** To fray. **2.** To exhaust physically or emotionally. [Perh. blend of FRAY² and dial. *fazzle*, unravel.] **—fraz′zle** *n.*

freak (frēk) ►*n.* **1.** A person, thing, or event that is abnormal or markedly unusual. **2.** A whim; vagary. **3.** *Slang* **a.** A drug addict. **b.** A fan or enthusiast. Highly unusual or irregular: *a freak storm.* ►*v. Slang* **1.** To experience or cause to experience hallucinations or feelings of paranoia, esp. as induced by a drug. Often used with *out.* **2.** To make or become agitated or excited: *a find that freaked me out.* [?] **—freak′i·ly** *adv.* **—freak′ish** *adj.* **—freak′y** *adj.*

freak-out (frēk′out′) ►*n. Slang* An act or an instance of freaking out.

freck·le (frĕk′əl) ►*n.* A brownish spot on the skin, often darkening with exposure to the sun. ►*v.* **-led, -ling** To dot or become dotted with freckles or spots. [< ME *fraknes*, freckles.] **—freck′ly** *adj.*

Fred·er·ick I (frĕd′rĭk, -ər-ĭk) "Frederick Barbarossa." 1123?–90. Holy Roman emperor (1152–90); king of Germany (1152–90) and Italy (1155–90).

Frederick II¹ 1194–1250. Holy Roman emperor (1212–50); king of Sicily (1198–1250) as Frederick I.

Frederick II² "the Great." 1712–86. King of Prussia (1740–86).

Fred·er·ic·ton (frĕd′rĭk-tən) The capital of New Brunswick, Canada, in the S-central part.

free (frē) ►*adj.* **fre·er, fre·est 1a.** Not imprisoned or confined. **b.** Not under obligation or necessity: *is free to leave.* **2a.** Having political independence: *a free nation.* **b.** Governed by consent and possessing civil liberties. **3a.** Not affected by a given condition or circumstance: *free of disease.* **b.** Exempt: *free of all taxes.* **4.** Not literal or exact: *a free translation.* **5.** Costing nothing; gratuitous. **6a.** Unobstructed: *a free lane on the highway.* **b.** Not occupied or used: *a free locker.* **7a.** Liberal or lavish. **b.** Guileless; frank: *is free with his opinions.* **8.** *Chem.* Not fixed in position; capable of relatively unrestricted motion: *a free electron.* ►*adv.* **1.** In a free manner. **2.** Without charge. ►*v.* **freed, free·ing 1.** To set at liberty. **2.** To rid of; release. **3.** To disengage or untangle. [< OE *frēo.*] **—free′ly** *adv.*

free·base or **free-base** (frē′bās′) ►*v.* **-based, -bas·ing** To prepare or use purified cocaine by burning it and inhaling the fumes.

free·bie also **free·bee** (frē′bē) ►*n. Slang* Something that is given or received free. [< FREE.]

free·board (frē′bôrd′) ►*n.* The distance between the water line and the uppermost full deck of a ship.

free·boot·er (frē′bōō′tər) ►*n.* A pirate or plunderer. [< Du. *vrijbuit*, plunder.]

free·born (frē′bôrn′) ►*adj.* **1.** Born as a free person. **2.** Of or befitting a person born free.

freed·man (frēd′mən) ►*n.* A man who has been freed from slavery.

free·dom (frē′dəm) ►*n.* **1.** The condition of being free. **2a.** Political independence. **b.** Possession of civil rights. **3.** Unrestricted use or access. **4.** The capacity to act by choice rather than by determination. **5.** Ease of movement. [< OE *frēodōm.*]

freedom of speech ►*n.* The right to express any opinion in public without government censorship or restraint.

freed·wom·an (frēd′wŏŏm′ən) ►*n.* A woman who has been freed from slavery.

free enterprise ►*n.* The freedom of private businesses to operate competitively for profit with minimal government regulation.

free fall ►*n.* **1.** The fall of a body toward the earth without a drag-producing device such as a parachute. **2.** Rapid uncontrolled decline.

free-for-all (frē′fər-ôl′) ►*n.* **1.** A fight or competition in which everyone present takes part. See Synonyms at **brawl. 2.** A disorderly situation with little regard for authority.

free·form (frē′fôrm′) ►*adj.* Having a usu. flowing asymmetrical shape or outline: *freeform sculpture.* **—free′form′** *adv.*

free·hand (frē′hănd′) ►*adj.* Drawn by hand without mechanical aids. **—free′hand′** *adv.*

free hand ►*n.* Freedom to do as one sees fit.

free·hand·ed (frē′hăn′dĭd) ►*adj.* Openhanded; generous. See Synonyms at **liberal. —free′-hand′ed·ly** *adv.* **—free′hand′ed·ness** *n.*

free·hold (frē′hōld′) ►*n.* **1.** A form of estate in which possession is held, usu. in fee, for the life of a specific person. **2.** The tenure by which such an estate is held. **—free′hold′er** *n.*

free kick ►*n.* An unobstructed kick of a stationary ball, as in soccer.

free·lance (frē′lăns′) ►*v.* **-lanced, -lanc·ing, -lanc·es** To work as a freelancer. ►*n.* A freelancer. **—free′lance′** *adv. & adj.*

free·lanc·er (frē′lăn′sər) ►*n.* A person who sells services to employers without a long-term commitment to any of them.

free·load (frē′lōd′) ►*v.* To take advantage of

the generosity or hospitality of others. —**free′-load′er** *n.*

free love ►*n.* The practice of sexual relations without romantic commitment between or among partners.

free lunch ►*n. Slang* Something acquired without due effort or cost.

free·man (frē′mən) ►*n.* **1.** A person not in slavery. **2.** One who possesses the rights or privileges of a citizen.

Free·ma·son (frē′mā′sən) ►*n.* A member of the Free and Accepted Masons, an international fraternal charitable organization with secret rites and signs. —**Free′ma′son·ry** *n.*

free on board ►*adj. & adv.* Without charge to the buyer for delivery on board a carrier at a specified location.

free port ►*n.* A port where imported goods can be processed free of customs duties before reexport.

free radical ►*n.* An unstable, highly reactive atom or group of atoms that can damage cells in animal tissue.

free-range (frē′rānj′) ►*adj.* Of or produced by animals, esp. poultry, that range freely for food rather than being confined.

free ride or **free·rid·ing** (frē′rī′dĭng) ►*n.* **1.** The act of taking credit or deriving other benefit from the efforts or contributions of others. **2.** The sport of mountain biking, snowboarding, or skiing that combines multiple styles and terrains. —**free′-ride′** *adj. & v.*

free speech ►*n.* **1.** See **freedom of speech. 2.** Speech protected from government restraint by legal means.

free·stand·ing (frē′stăn′dĭng) ►*adj.* Standing without support or attachment.

free·stone (frē′stōn′) ►*n.* **1.** A stone, such as limestone, soft enough to be cut easily without shattering. **2.** A fruit, esp. a peach, that has a stone not adhering to the pulp.

free·style (frē′stīl′) ►*n.* **1a.** A rapid swimming stroke consisting of alternating overarm strokes and a flutter kick; the crawl. **b.** A swimming event in which any stroke is permissible. **2.** A competition, as in skiing, in which any maneuver is allowed and competitors are judged on their artistic expression and technical skill. —**free′style′** *adv. & adj.*

free·think·er (frē′thĭng′kər) ►*n.* One who rejects authority and dogma, esp. in religious thinking. —**free′think′ing** *adj. & n.*

free throw ►*n.* See **foul shot.**

Free·town (frē′toun′) The capital of Sierra Leone, in the W part on the Atlantic.

free trade ►*n.* Trade between nations without protective customs tariffs.

free verse ►*n.* Verse composed of lines having no fixed metrical pattern.

free·ware (frē′wâr′) ►*n.* Free software, usu. available over the Internet.

free·way (frē′wā′) ►*n.* **1.** See **expressway. 2.** A highway without tolls.

free·wheel·ing (frē′wē′lĭng, -hwē′-) ►*adj.* **1.** Free of restraints or rules, as in organization or procedure. **2.** Heedless; carefree.

free·will (frē′wĭl′) ►*adj.* Voluntary.

free will ►*n.* **1.** The ability or discretion to choose. **2.** The power to make choices that are neither determined by natural causality nor predestined by fate.

freeze (frēz) ►*v.* **froze** (frōz), **fro·zen** (frō′zən), **freez·ing 1a.** To pass or cause to pass from liquid to solid by loss of heat. **b.** To acquire a surface of ice. **2.** To be at that degree of temperature at which ice forms. **3.** To damage or be damaged by cold or frost. **4.** To be uncomfortably cold. **5.** To make or become inoperative by or as if by frost or ice. **6.** To become unable to act or react, as from fear or shyness. **7.** To become icily silent. **8.** To make or become rigid and inflexible. **9.** To preserve by subjecting to freezing temperatures. **10a.** To fix (prices or wages) at a current level. **b.** To prohibit further manufacture or use of. **c.** To prevent or restrict the exchange, liquidation, or granting of by law. **11.** To anesthetize by chilling. ►*n.* **1.** The act of freezing or the condition of being frozen. **2.** A cold spell; frost. [< OE *frēosan.*]

freeze-dry (frēz′drī′) ►*v.* To preserve by rapid freezing and drying in a high vacuum.

freez·er (frē′zər) ►*n.* An insulated compartment, cabinet, or room for the rapid freezing and storing of perishable food.

freez·ing point (frē′zĭng) ►*n.* The temperature at which a liquid of specified composition solidifies under a fixed pressure.

freight (frāt) ►*n.* **1.** Goods carried by a vessel or vehicle; cargo. **2.** A burden; load. **3a.** Commercial transportation of goods. **b.** The charge for transporting goods. **4.** A railway train carrying goods only. ►*v.* **1.** To convey commercially as cargo. **2.** To load with cargo. [< MDu. or MLGer. *vrecht.*]

freight·er (frā′tər) ►*n.* A vehicle, esp. a ship, used for carrying freight.

fre·na (frē′nə) ►*n.* Pl. of **frenum.**

French (frĕnch) ►*adj.* Of or relating to France or its people or language. ►*n.* **1.** The Romance language of France, Quebec, and various other areas. **2.** The people of France. —**French′man** *n.* —**French′wom′an** *n.*

French Canadian ►*n.* A Canadian of French descent. —**French′-Ca·na′di·an** *adj.*

French curve ►*n.* A flat drafting tool with curved edges and scroll-shaped cutouts used to draw curves esp. in engineering.

French door ►*n.* A door with glass panes extending for most of its length.

french fry ►*n.* A deep-fried potato strip.

french-fry (frĕnch′frī′) ►*v.* To deep-fry.

French Guiana A French overseas department of NE South America on the Atlantic. Cap. Cayenne.

French horn ►*n.* A valved brass wind instrument with a long narrow coiled tube that ends in a flaring bell.

French leave ►*n.* An unannounced or abrupt departure.

French Polynesia A French overseas territory in the S-central Pacific, including the Society, Marquesas, and Austral Islands and the Tuamotu archipelago. Cap. Papeete, on Tahiti.

French toast ►*n.* Sliced bread soaked in a batter of milk and egg and lightly fried.

fre·net·ic (frə-nĕt′ĭk) ►*adj.* Wildly excited or active; frantic; frenzied. [< Gk. *phrenitis,* inflammation of the brain < *phrēn,* mind.] —**fre·net′i·cal·ly** *adv.*

fre·num (frē′nəm) ►*n., pl.* **fre·nums** or **fre·na** (frē′nə) *Anat.* The band of tissue that connects the tongue to the floor of the mouth. [Lat.

frēnum, bridle < *frendere,* to grind.]

fren·zy (frĕn′zē) ►*n., pl.* **-zies 1.** Violent mental agitation or wild excitement. **2.** Temporary madness. **3.** A mania; craze. [< Lat. *phrenēsis* < *phrenēticus,* FRENETIC.] —**fren′zied** *adj.*

fre·quen·cy (frē′kwən-sē) ►*n., pl.* **-cies 1.** The property of occurring at frequent intervals. **2.** *Math. & Phys.* The number of times a specified phenomenon occurs within a specified interval, as the number of complete cycles of a periodic process occurring per unit time. [< Lat. *frequentia,* multitude.]

frequency modulation ►*n.* The encoding of a carrier wave by variation of its frequency in accordance with an input signal.

fre·quent (frē′kwənt) ►*adj.* **1.** Occurring or appearing often or at close intervals. **2.** Habitual or regular. ►*v.* (*also* frē-kwĕnt′) To visit (a place) often. [< Lat. *frequēns.*] —**fre·quent′er** *n.* —**fre′quent·ly** *adv.*

fres·co (frĕs′kō) ►*n., pl.* **-coes** or **-cos 1.** The art of painting on fresh plaster with pigments dissolved in water. **2.** A painting executed in this way. [Ital., fresh.]

fresh (frĕsh) ►*adj.* **-er, -est 1a.** New to one's experience; not encountered before. **b.** Unusual or different. **2a.** Recently made, produced, or harvested; not stale or spoiled. **b.** Not preserved, as by canning or freezing. **3.** Not salty: *fresh water.* **4a.** Not yet used or soiled; clean: *a fresh sheet of paper.* **b.** Free from impurity or pollution: *fresh air.* **c.** Not dull or faded: *a fresh memory.* **5.** Untried; inexperienced: *fresh recruits.* **6a.** Revived; refreshed. **b.** Having the unspoiled appearance of youth: *a fresh complexion.* **7.** *Informal* Impudent. ►*adv.* Recently; newly: *fresh out of milk.* [< OFr. *freis,* of Gmc. orig.] —**fresh′ly** *adv.* —**fresh′ness** *n.*

fresh·en (frĕsh′ən) ►*v.* **1.** To make or become fresh. **2.** To add to or strengthen (a drink). —**fresh′en·er** *n.*

fresh·et (frĕsh′ĭt) ►*n.* A sudden overflow of a stream due to a heavy rain or a thaw.

fresh·man (frĕsh′mən) ►*n.* **1.** A first-year student of a US high school or college. **2.** A beginner; novice. —**fresh′man** *adj.*

fresh·wa·ter (frĕsh′wô′tər, -wŏt′ər) ►*adj.* Of, living in, or consisting of water that is not salty.

fret[1] (frĕt) ►*v.* **fret·ted, fret·ting 1.** To be vexed or cause to be vexed; worry. See Synonyms at **brood. 2a.** To gnaw or wear away. **b.** To produce a hole or worn spot in; corrode. **3.** To rub or chafe. ►*n.* Irritation of mind. [< OE *fretan,* devour.] —**fret′ful** *adj.* —**fret′ful·ly** *adv.*

fret[2]
on the neck of an electric guitar

fret[2] (frĕt) ►*n. Mus.* One of the ridges set across the fingerboard of certain stringed instruments. [?]

fret[3] (frĕt) ►*n.* A design of repeated symmetrical figures within a band or border. [< OFr. *frete.*]

fret·work (frĕt′wûrk′) ►*n.* **1.** Ornamental work consisting of three-dimensional frets. **2.** Fretwork represented two dimensionally.

Freud (froid), **Sigmund** 1856–1939. Austrian physician and founder of psychoanalysis. —**Freud′i·an** *adj.*

Frey (frā) also **Freyr** (frâr) ►*n. Myth.* The Norse god of peace and prosperity.

Frey·a also **Frey·ja** (frā′ə) ►*n. Myth.* The Norse goddess of love and beauty.

fri·a·ble (frī′ə-bəl) ►*adj.* Readily crumbled; brittle. [< Lat. *friāre,* crumble.]

fri·ar (frī′ər) ►*n.* A member of a usu. mendicant Roman Catholic order. [< Lat. *frāter,* brother.]

fric·as·see (frĭk′ə-sē′, frĭk′ə-sē′) ►*n.* Poultry or meat cut up and stewed in gravy. [< OFr. *fricasser,* fry.] —**fric′as·see′** *v.*

fric·a·tive (frĭk′ə-tĭv) ►*n.* A consonant, such as *f* or *s* in English, produced by the forcing of breath through a constricted passage. [< Lat. *fricāre,* rub.] —**fric′a·tive** *adj.*

fric·tion (frĭk′shən) ►*n.* **1.** The rubbing of one object or surface against another. **2.** Conflict, as between persons having dissimilar ideas or interests; clash. **3.** *Phys.* A force that resists the relative motion or tendency to such motion of two bodies or substances in contact. [< Lat. *fricāre, frict-,* rub.] —**fric′tion·al** *adj.* —**fric′tion·al·ly** *adv.*

friction tape ►*n.* A sturdy, moisture-resistant adhesive tape used chiefly to insulate electrical conductors.

Fri·day (frī′dē, -dā′) ►*n.* The 6th day of the week. [< OE *Frīgedæg.*]

fridge (frĭj) ►*n. Informal* A refrigerator.

Frie·dan (frē-dăn′), **Betty Naomi** 1921–2006. Amer. feminist.

friend (frĕnd) ►*n.* **1.** A person whom one knows, likes, and trusts. **2.** One who supports, sympathizes with, or patronizes a group, cause, or movement. **3. Friend** A member of the Society of Friends; Quaker. ►*v.* **friend·ed, friend·ing, friends** *Informal* To add (someone) as a friend on a social networking website. [< OE *frēond.*] —**friend′ship** *n.*

friend·ly (frĕnd′lē) ►*adj.* **-li·er, -li·est 1a.** Characteristic of or behaving as a friend. **b.** Outgoing and pleasant in social relations. **c.** Favorably disposed; not antagonistic. **2.** Easy for one to use or understand: *a reader-friendly type design.* —**friend′li·ly** *adv.* —**friend′li·ness** *n.*

fri·er (frī′ər) ►*n.* Var. of **fryer.**

frieze (frēz) ►*n.* **1.** The part of an entablature between the architrave and cornice. **2.** A decorative horizontal band, as along the upper part of a wall in a room. [< Med.Lat. *frisium,* embroidery.]

frig·ate (frĭg′ĭt) ►*n.* **1.** A warship that is smaller than a destroyer and used primarily for escort duty. **2.** A high-speed, medium-sized sailing war vessel of the 1600s, 1700s, and 1800s. [< Ital. *fregata.*]

fright (frīt) ►*n.* **1.** Sudden intense fear. **2.** *Informal* Something extremely unsightly or alarming. [< OE *fyrhto.*]

fright·en (frīt′n) ►*v.* **1.** To make or become

suddenly afraid; alarm. **2.** To drive or force by arousing fear. —**fright′en·ing·ly** *adv.*

fright·ful (frīt′fəl) ►*adj.* **1.** Causing disgust or shock; horrifying. **2.** Causing fright; terrifying. **3.** *Informal* **a.** Excessive; extreme: *a frightful liar.* **b.** Disagreeable; distressing. —**fright′ful·ly** *adv.* —**fright′ful·ness** *n.*

frig·id (frĭj′ĭd) ►*adj.* **1.** Extremely cold. See Synonyms at **cold. 2.** Lacking warmth or feeling; cold in manner. **3.** Showing little or no enthusiasm. **4.** *Often Offensive* Lacking sexual desire or unwilling to engage in sexual activity. Used esp. of women. [< Lat. *frīgus,* the cold.] —**fri·gid′i·ty** (frĭ-jĭd′ĭ-tē), **frig′id·ness** *n.* —**frig′id·ly** *adv.*

frill (frĭl) ►*n.* **1.** A ruffled, gathered, or pleated border or projection. **2.** *Informal* Something desirable but not essential. See Synonyms at **luxury.** [?] —**frill** *v.* —**frill′y** *adj.*

fringe (frĭnj) ►*n.* **1.** A decorative border or edging of hanging threads, cords, or strips. **2.** Something like a fringe. **3.** A marginal or secondary part. **4.** Those members of a group or political party holding extreme views. **5.** A fringe benefit. [< LLat. *fimbria.*] —**fringe** *v.* —**fring′y** *adj.*

fringe benefit ►*n.* An employment benefit given in addition to wages or salary.

frip·per·y (frĭp′ə-rē) ►*n., pl.* **-ies 1.** Gaudy or showy ornaments or dress. **2.** Something trivial or nonessential. [< OFr. *frepe,* rag.]

Fri·sian Islands (frīzh′ən, frē′zhən) A chain of islands in the North Sea off the coast of the Netherlands, Germany, and Denmark. —**Fri′sian** *adj. & n.*

frisk (frĭsk) ►*v.* **1.** To search (a person) for something concealed, esp. a weapon, by passing the hands quickly over clothes or through pockets. **2.** To move about briskly and playfully; frolic. [< OFr. *frisque,* lively, of Gmc. orig.] —**frisk** *n.* —**frisk′er** *n.*

frisk·y (frĭs′kē) ►*adj.* **-i·er, -i·est** Energetic and playful. —**frisk′i·ness** *n.*

frit·ta·ta (frĭ-tä′tə) ►*n.* An open-faced omelet with other ingredients mixed into the eggs before cooking. [Ital. < *friggere,* to fry.]

frit·ter[1] (frĭt′ər) ►*v.* To reduce or squander little by little. See Synonyms at **waste.** [Prob. < *fritter,* fragment.]

frit·ter[2] (frĭt′ər) ►*n.* A small fried cake made of batter and often fruit, vegetables, or fish. [< LLat. *frīctūra* < Lat. *frīgere,* fry.]

friv·o·lous (frĭv′ə-ləs) ►*adj.* **1.** Unworthy of serious attention; trivial. **2.** Inappropriately silly. [Prob. < Lat. *frīvolus.*] —**friv′o·lous·ly** *adv.* —**friv′o·lous·ness, fri·vol′i·ty** (frĭ-vŏl′ĭ-tē) *n.*

frizz (frĭz) ►*v.* To form or be formed into small tight curls. ►*n.* A small tight curl. [< OFr. *friser.*] —**friz′zly, friz′zy** *adj.*

friz·zle[1] (frĭz′əl) ►*v.* **-zled, -zling 1.** To fry until crisp and curled. **2.** To fry or sear with a sizzling noise. [Poss. blend of FRY[1] and SIZZLE.]

friz·zle[2] (frĭz′əl) ►*v.* **-zled, -zling** To form or cause to be formed into small tight curls. ►*n.* A small tight curl. [?]

fro (frō) ►*adv.* Away; back: *moving to and fro.* [ME, prob. < ON *frā.*]

frock (frŏk) ►*n.* **1.** A woman's dress. **2.** A long loose outer garment; smock. **3.** A robe worn by monks and other clerics; habit. [< OFr. *froc,* habit, of Gmc. orig.]

frock coat ►*n.* A man's dress coat or suit coat with knee-length skirts.

frog (frôg, frŏg) ►*n.* **1a.** Any of numerous tailless aquatic or terrestrial amphibians characteristically having a large head, long hind legs used for leaping, and a tadpole stage as larvae. **b.** Any of various usu. aquatic members of this group that have smooth skin and long hind legs, as distinguished from the toads. **2.** An ornamental looped braid or cord with a button or knot for fastening the front of a garment. **3.** *Informal* Hoarseness or phlegm in the throat. [< OE *frogga.*]

frog kick ►*n.* A swimming kick in which the knees are drawn up close to the hips and the feet are thrust outward and backward and then drawn together.

frog·man (frôg′măn′, -mən, frŏg′-) ►*n.* A swimmer equipped to execute underwater maneuvers, esp. military maneuvers.

frol·ic (frŏl′ĭk) ►*n.* Playful behavior or merriment. ►*v.* **-icked, -ick·ing** To behave playfully; romp. [< MDu. *vrolijc,* merry.] —**frol′ick·er** *n.* —**frol′ic·some** *adj.*

from (frŭm, frŏm; frəm *when unstressed*) ►*prep.* **1.** Used to indicate: **a.** A place or time as a starting point: *from six o'clock on.* **b.** A specified point as the first of two limits: *from a to z.* **c.** A source, cause, agent, or instrument: *a note from me.* **d.** Separation, removal, or exclusion: *freed from bondage.* **e.** Differentiation: *know right from wrong.* **2.** Because of: *faint from hunger.* [< OE.]

frond (frŏnd) ►*n.* The leaf esp. of a fern or palm. [Lat. *frōns, frond-,* foliage.]

front (frŭnt) ►*n.* **1.** The forward part or surface. **2.** The area, location, or position directly ahead. **3.** A position of leadership or superiority. **4.** Demeanor or bearing, esp. in the presence of danger or difficulty. **5.** A false appearance or manner: *a good front.* **6.** Land bordering a lake, river, or street. **7.** The most forward line of a combat force. **8.** The interface between air masses of different temperatures or densities. **9.** A field of activity: *the economic front.* **10a.** A united movement. **b.** A nominal leader lacking real authority. **c.** An apparently respectable person or business used as a cover for secret or illegal activities. ►*adj.* Of, aimed at, or located in the front. ►*v.* **1.** To look out on; face. **2.** To confront. **3.** To provide or serve as a front for. [< Lat. *frōns, front-.*]

front·age (frŭn′tĭj) ►*n.* **1a.** The front part of a piece of property. **b.** The land between a building and the street. **2.** Land adjacent to something, as a street or body of water.

fron·tal (frŭn′tl) ►*adj.* **1.** Of, directed toward, or situated at the front. **2.** *Anat.* Of or in the region of the forehead. **3.** Of a meteorological front. —**fron′tal·ly** *adv.*

fron·tier (frŭn-tîr′, frŏn-) ►*n.* **1.** An international border or the area along it. **2.** A region just beyond or beside a settled area. **3.** An undeveloped area for discovery or research. [< OFr. < *front,* FRONT.] —**fron·tiers′man** *n.* —**fron·tiers′wom·an** *n.*

fron·tis·piece (frŭn′tĭ-spēs′) ►*n.* An illustration that faces or immediately precedes the title page of a book. [< LLat. *frontispicium,* façade :

Lat. *frōns*, front + Lat. *specere*, look at.]

front·line also **front line** (frŭnt′līn′) ►*n.* **1.** A front or boundary, esp. between military or political positions. **2.** *Football* A team's linemen. ►*adj.* or **front-line 1.** Located or used at a military front. **2.** Being in the forefront; leading. **3.** *Sports* Of the frontline. **4.** Performing the most basic tasks or interacting daily with customers, patients, or clients.

front money ►*n.* Money paid in advance.

front office ►*n.* The executive or policymaking officers of an organization.

front-run·ner (frŭnt′rŭn′ər) ►*n.* One in a leading position in a competition.

frost (frôst, frŏst) ►*n.* A deposit of minute ice crystals formed when water vapor condenses at a temperature below freezing. ►*v.* **1.** To cover or become covered with frost. **2.** To damage or kill by frost. **3.** To cover (glass or metal) with frosting. **4.** To decorate with icing. [< OE.]

Frost, Robert Lee 1874–1963. Amer. poet.

frost·bite (frôst′bīt′, frŏst′-) ►*n.* Destruction of body tissue resulting from prolonged exposure to freezing or subfreezing temperatures. —**frost′bite′** *v.*

frost·ing (frô′stĭng, frŏs′tĭng) ►*n.* **1.** Icing, as on a cake. **2.** A roughened or speckled surface imparted to glass or metal.

frost line ►*n.* **1.** The depth to which frost penetrates the earth. **2.** The altitude below which frost does not occur.

frost·y (frô′stē, frŏs′tē) ►*adj.* **-i·er, -i·est 1.** Producing or marked by frost; freezing. See Synonyms at **cold. 2.** Covered with frost. **3.** Cold in manner. **4.** Lacking enthusiasm: *received a frosty review.* —**frost′i·ly** *adv.* —**frost′i·ness** *n.*

froth (frôth, frŏth) ►*n.* **1.** A mass of bubbles in or on a liquid; foam. **2.** Salivary foam released as a result of disease or exhaustion. **3.** Something unsubstantial or trivial. ►*v.* (*also* frôth, frŏth) **1.** To cover with foam. **2.** To cause to foam. **3.** To exude or expel foam. [< ON *frodha.*] —**froth′i·ly** *adv.* —**froth′i·ness** *n.* —**froth′y** *adj.*

frou·frou also **frou-frou** (frōō′frōō) ►*n.* **1.** Fussy or showy dress or ornamentation. **2.** A rustling sound, as of silk. [Fr.]

fro·ward (frō′wərd, -ərd) ►*adj.* Stubbornly contrary and disobedient. [ME < *fro,* FRO.] —**fro′-ward·ly** *adv.* —**fro′ward·ness** *n.*

frown (froun) ►*v.* **1.** To wrinkle the brow, as in thought or displeasure. **2.** To regard something with disapproval or distaste. ►*n.* A wrinkling of the brow; scowl. [< OFr. *frogne,* a grimace, of Celt. orig.]

Syns: glower, lower, scowl

frow·zy also **frow·sy** (frou′zē) ►*adj.* **-zi·er, -zi·est** also **-si·er, -si·est** Unkempt; slovenly. [?] —**frow′zi·ness** *n.*

froze (frōz) ►*v.* P.t. of **freeze.**

fro·zen (frō′zən) ►*v.* P.part. of **freeze.** ►*adj.* **1.** Made into, covered with, or surrounded by ice. **2.** Very cold. **3.** Preserved by freezing. **4.** Rendered immobile. **5.** Expressive of cold unfriendliness or disdain. **6a.** Kept at a fixed level: *frozen rents.* **b.** Impossible to withdraw, sell, or liquidate: *frozen assets.*

fruc·ti·fy (frŭk′tə-fī′) ►*v.* **-fied, -fy·ing** To be or make fruitful or productive. [< Lat. *frūctificāre* < *frūctus,* FRUIT.] —**fruc′ti·fi·ca′tion** *n.*

fruc·tose (frŭk′tōs′, frōōk′-) ►*n.* A sweet sugar,

$C_6H_{12}O_6$, occurring in many fruits and honey. [Lat. *frūctus,* FRUIT + -OSE².]

fru·gal (frōō′gəl) ►*adj.* **1.** Practicing or marked by economy. **2.** Costing little; inexpensive. [< Lat. *frūx, frūg-,* produce, value.] —**fru·gal′i·ty** (frōō-gǎl′ĭ-tē), **fru′gal·ness** *n.* —**fru′gal·ly** *adv.*

fruit (frōōt) ►*n., pl.* **fruit** or **fruits 1.** The ripened, seed-bearing part of a plant, esp. when fleshy and edible. **2.** The fertile, often spore-bearing structure of a plant that does not bear seeds. **3.** A plant crop or product. **4.** Result; outcome. ►*v.* To produce fruit. [< Lat. *frūctus* < *fruī,* enjoy.]

fruit·cake (frōōt′kāk′) ►*n.* **1.** A heavy spiced cake containing nuts and candied or dried fruits. **2.** *Slang* An eccentric person.

fruit fly ►*n.* Any of various small flies that feed on ripening or fermenting fruits and vegetables.

fruit·ful (frōōt′fəl) ►*adj.* **1.** Producing fruit. **2.** Producing useful or desired results; productive. See Synonyms at **fertile.** —**fruit′ful·ly** *adv.* —**fruit′ful·ness** *n.*

fru·i·tion (frōō-ĭsh′ən) ►*n.* **1.** Realization of something desired or worked for. **2.** The condition of bearing fruit.

fruit·less (frōōt′lĭs) ►*adj.* **1.** Producing no fruit. **2.** Not leading to success; unproductive. See Synonyms at **futile.** —**fruit′less·ly** *adv.* —**fruit′less·ness** *n.*

fruit·y (frōō′tē) ►*adj.* **-i·er, -i·est 1.** Tasting or smelling of fruit. **2.** Excessively sentimental or sweet. **3.** *Slang* Eccentric. —**fruit′i·ness** *n.*

frump (frŭmp) ►*n.* A dull, plain, or unfashionable person. [Poss. < MDu. *verrompelen,* to wrinkle.] —**frump′i·ly** *adv.* —**frump′i·ness** *n.* —**frump′y** *adj.*

frump·ish (frŭm′pĭsh) ►*adj.* **1.** Dull or plain. **2.** Prim and sedate. —**frump′ish·ly** *adv.* —**frump′ish·ness** *n.*

frus·trate (frŭs′trāt′) ►*v.* **-trat·ed, -trat·ing 1a.** To prevent from accomplishing a purpose or fulfilling a desire; thwart. **b.** To cause discouragement or lack of fulfillment in. **2.** To prevent from coming to fruition. [< Lat. *frūstrārī* < *frūstrā,* in vain.] —**frus·tra′tion** *n.*

fry¹ (frī) ►*v.* **fried** (frīd), **fry·ing 1.** To cook over direct heat in hot oil or fat. **2.** To destroy (electronic circuitry) with excessive heat or current. ►*n., pl.* **fries** (frīz) **1.** A french fry. **2.** A social gathering at which fried food is served. [< Lat. *frīgere.*]

fry² (frī) ►*n., pl.* **fry 1.** *pl.* **fry** A recently hatched fish. **2.** *pl.* **fry** or **fries** An individual, esp. a young or insignificant person. [Prob. < AN *frie.*]

fry·er also **fri·er** (frī′ər) ►*n.* **1.** One that fries, as a deep utensil usu. equipped with a basket and used for frying foods. **2.** A young chicken suitable for frying.

fry·ing pan (frī′ĭng) ►*n.* A shallow, long-handled pan used for frying food.

f-stop (ĕf′stŏp′) ►*n.* A camera lens aperture setting that corresponds to an f-number. [F(OCAL LENGTH) + STOP.]

FT ►*abbr.* **1.** free throw **2.** full-time

ft. ►*abbr.* **1.** or **ft** foot **2. Ft.** fort

FTC ►*abbr.* Federal Trade Commission

fth. ►*abbr.* fathom

FTP (ĕf′tē-pē′) ►*n.* A protocol governing file transfers over a computer network. ►*v.* **FTPed,**

FTPing To transfer (a file) using FTP. [*F(ile) T(ransfer) P(rotocol).*]

fuch·sia (fyōō′shə) ►*n.* **1.** A widely cultivated plant with showy drooping purplish, reddish, or white flowers. **2.** A vivid purplish red. [After Leonhard *Fuchs* (1501–66).] —**fuch′sia** *adj.*

fud·dle (fŭd′l) ►*v.* **-dled, -dling 1.** To put into a state of confusion. See Synonyms at **befuddle. 2.** To make drunk; intoxicate. [?] —**fud′dle** *n.*

fud·dy-dud·dy (fŭd′ē-dŭd′ē) ►*n., pl.* **-dies** An old-fashioned, fussy person. [?]

fudge (fŭj) ►*n.* **1.** A soft rich candy made of sugar, milk, and butter. **2.** Nonsense; humbug. ►*v.* **fudged, fudg·ing 1.** To fake or falsify: *fudged the data.* **2.** To evade; dodge. [?]

fu·el (fyōō′əl) ►*n.* Something consumed to produce energy, esp.: **a.** A material such as wood or oil burned to produce heat or power. **b.** Fissionable material used in a nuclear reactor. **c.** Nutritive material metabolized by a living organism; food. ►*v.* **-eled, -el·ing** also **-elled, -el·ling** To provide with or take in fuel. [< VLat. **focālia* < Lat. *focus,* hearth.] —**fu′el·er** *n.*

fuel cell ►*n.* A device in which a fuel and an oxidant react and the energy released is converted into electricity.

fuel oil ►*n.* A liquid petroleum product that is used to generate heat or power.

fuel rod ►*n.* A protective metal tube containing pellets of fuel for a nuclear reactor.

Fuen·tes (fōō-ĕn′täs′, fwĕn′tĕs), **Carlos** 1928–2012. Mexican writer.

Carlos Fuentes
photographed in 2008

fu·gi·tive (fyōō′jĭ-tĭv) ►*adj.* **1.** Running away or fleeing, as from the law. **2.** Lasting only a short time; fleeting: *fugitive hours.* ►*n.* One who flees. [< Lat. *fugere,* flee.]

fugue (fyōōg) ►*n.* **1.** *Mus.* A polyphonic composition in which one or more themes stated successively are developed contrapuntally. **2.** *Psychiat.* A dissociative state, usu. caused by trauma, marked by sudden travel or wandering away from home and an inability to remember one's past. [< Lat. *fuga,* flight.] —**fu′gal** (fyōō′gəl) *adj.* —**fu′gal·ly** *adv.*

füh·rer also **fueh·rer** (fyōōr′ər) ►*n.* A leader, esp. one exercising the powers of a tyrant. [Ger.]

Fu·ji (fōō′jē), **Mount** The highest peak in Japan, a snowcapped volcano rising to 3,776 m (12,388 ft) in central Honshu WSW of Tokyo.

-ful ►*suff.* **1.** Full of: *playful.* **2.** Marked by; resembling: *masterful.* **3.** Tending, given, or able to: *useful.* **4.** A quantity that fills: *armful.* [< OE.]

ful·crum (fōōl′krəm, fŭl′-) ►*n., pl.* **-crums** or **-cra** (-krə) The point or support on which a lever pivots. [Lat., bedpost.]

ful·fill also **ful·fil** (fōōl-fĭl′) ►*v.* **-filled, -fill·ing 1.** To bring into actuality; effect: *fulfilled their promises.* **2.** To carry out. **3.** To measure up to; satisfy. See Synonyms at **satisfy.** [< OE *fullfyllan.*] —**ful·fill′ment, ful·fil′ment** *n.*

full¹ (fōōl) ►*adj.* **-er, -est 1.** Containing all that is normal or possible. **2.** Complete in every particular. **3.** Of maximum or highest degree. **4.** Having a great deal or many: *full of errors.* **5.** Totally qualified or accepted: *a full member.* **6a.** Rounded in shape. **b.** Of generous dimensions; wide. **7.** Satiated, esp. with food or drink. **8.** Having depth and body. ►*adv.* **1.** To a complete extent; entirely: *knowing full well.* **2.** Exactly; directly: *full in the path of the truck.* ►*n.* The maximum or complete size or amount. [< OE.] —**full′ness, ful′ness** *n.*

full² (fōōl) ►*v.* To increase the density and usu. the thickness of (cloth) by shrinking and beating or pressing. [< VLat. **fullāre.*]

full·back (fōōl′băk′) ►*n.* **1.** *Football* An offensive player who lines up behind the quarterback and carries the ball, usu. more ruggedly built than a halfback. **2.** A defensive player who plays near the goalie, as in soccer.

full-blood·ed (fōōl′blŭd′ĭd) ►*adj.* **1.** Of unmixed ancestry; purebred. **2.** Vigorous; vital. —**full′-blood′ed·ness** *n.*

full-blown (fōōl′blōn′) ►*adj.* **1.** Having blossomed or opened completely. **2.** Fully developed or matured. **3.** Having or displaying all the characteristics necessary for completeness.

full-bod·ied (fōōl′bŏd′ēd) ►*adj.* Having richness of flavor or aroma.

full dress ►*n.* Attire appropriate for formal or ceremonial events.

Ful·ler (fōōl′ər), **R(ichard) Buckminster** 1895–1983. Amer. architect and inventor.

Fuller, (Sarah) Margaret 1810–50. Amer. writer and critic.

ful·ler·ene (fōōl′ə-rēn′) ►*n.* Any of various often spherical molecules that consist only of an even number of carbon atoms arranged in hexagonal and pentagonal groups. [< (BUCK-MINSTER)FULLERENE.]

full-fledged (fōōl′flĕjd′) ►*adj.* **1.** Having reached full development; mature. **2.** Having full status or rank: *a full-fledged lawyer.*

full moon ►*n.* The phase of the moon at which the moon, as viewed from Earth, appears to be fully illuminated by the sun.

full-scale (fōōl′skāl′) ►*adj.* **1.** Of actual or full size. **2.** Employing all resources.

ful·ly (fōōl′ē) ►*adv.* **1.** Totally or completely. **2.** At least.

ful·mi·nate (fōōl′mə-nāt′, fŭl′-) ►*v.* **-nat·ed, -nat·ing 1.** To issue a severe denunciation. **2.** To explode. [< Lat. *fulmen, fulmin-,* lightning.] —**ful′mi·na′tion** *n.*

ful·some (fōōl′səm) ►*adj.* Excessively flattering or insincerely earnest. See Synonyms at **unctuous.** [ME *fulsom,* abundant, disgusting.] —**ful′some·ly** *adv.* —**ful′some·ness** *n.*

Ful·ton (fōōl′tən), **Robert** 1765–1815. Amer. engineer and inventor.

fum·ble (fŭm′bəl) ►*v.* **-bled, -bling 1.** To touch

or handle nervously or idly. **2.** To grope awkwardly to find something: *fumble for a key.* **3.** To proceed awkwardly and uncertainly; blunder. **4.** *Sports* To mishandle or drop a ball that is in play. **5.** To bungle. See Synonyms at **botch.** ►*n.* **1.** The act or an instance of fumbling. **2.** *Sports* A ball that has been fumbled. [ME *fomelen,* grope.] —**fum′bler** *n.*

fume (fyo͞om) ►*n.* **1.** Vapor, gas, or smoke, esp. if irritating, harmful, or strong. **2.** A strong or acrid odor. ►*v.* **fumed, fum·ing 1.** To subject to or treat with fumes. **2.** To give off in or as if in fumes. **3.** To feel or show resentment or anger. [< Lat. *fūmus.*]

fu·mi·gate (fyo͞o′mĭ-gāt′) ►*v.* **-gat·ed, -gat·ing** To treat with fumes in order to exterminate pests. [Lat. *fūmigāre,* to smoke : *fūmus,* smoke + *agere,* make.] —**fu′mi·ga′tion** *n.* —**fu′mi·ga′tor** *n.*

fun (fŭn) ►*n.* **1.** Enjoyment; amusement. **2.** A source of enjoyment, amusement, or pleasure. —*idiom:* **for fun** As a joke; playfully. [Poss. < ME *fonne,* a fool.]

func·tion (fŭngk′shən) ►*n.* **1.** The action or purpose for which a person or thing is suited or employed, esp.: **a.** A person's role or occupation. **b.** *Comp.* A procedure within an application. **2.** An official ceremony or a formal social occasion. **3.** Something closely related to another thing and dependent on it for its existence or value. **4.** *Math.* A rule of correspondence between two sets such that there is exactly one element in the second set assigned to each element in the first set. ►*v.* To have or perform a function; serve. [< Lat. *fungī, fūnct-,* perform.]
    Syns: duty, office, role **n.**

func·tion·al (fŭngk′shə-nəl) ►*adj.* **1.** Of or relating to a function. **2.** Designed for or adapted to a particular purpose. **3.** Capable of performing; operative. **4.** *Med.* Involving physiological function rather than anatomical structure. —**func′tion·al·ly** *adv.*

func·tion·al·i·ty (fŭngk′shə-năl′ĭ-tē) ►*n.* **1.** The quality of being functional. **2.** A useful function in a computer program. **3.** The capacity of a computer program to provide a useful function.

func·tion·ar·y (fŭngk′shə-nĕr′ē) ►*n., pl.* **-ies** One who holds an office or performs a particular function; official.

function key ►*n.* One of a set of keys on a computer keyboard that execute a function.

function word ►*n.* A word, such as a preposition or article, that indicates a grammatical relationship.

fund (fŭnd) ►*n.* **1.** A source of supply; stock. **2a.** A sum of money or other resources set aside for a specific purpose. **b. funds** Available money. **3.** An organization established to administer and manage a sum of money. ►*v.* To provide funds for. [Lat. *fundus,* piece of land.]

fun·da·men·tal (fŭn′də-mĕn′tl) ►*adj.* **1.** Basic; elementary: *fundamental laws of nature.* **2.** Of central importance; essential. **3.** Involving all aspects; radical: *fundamental change.* [< Lat. *fundāmentum,* foundation < *fundus,* bottom.] —**fun′da·men′tal·ly** *adv.*

fun·da·men·tal·ism (fŭn′də-mĕn′tl-ĭz′əm) ►*n.* **1.** A usu. religious movement marked by rigid adherence to basic principles. **2.** often **Funda-**

mentalism A Protestant movement holding the Bible to be the sole authority. —**fun′da·men′tal·ist** *adj. & n.*

fund·rais·er (fŭnd′rā′zər) ►*n.* **1.** One that raises funds. **2.** A social function held for raising funds.

Fun·dy (fŭn′dē), **Bay of** An inlet of the Atlantic in SE Canada between New Brunswick and Nova Scotia.

fu·ner·al (fyo͞o′nər-əl) ►*n.* **1.** The ceremonies held in connection with the burial or cremation of the dead. **2.** The procession accompanying a body to the grave. [< Lat. *fūnus.*] —**fu′ner·ar′y** (-nə-rĕr′ē) *adj.*

funeral director ►*n.* One whose business is to arrange burials or cremations.

funeral home ►*n.* An establishment in which the dead are prepared for burial or cremation.

fu·ne·re·al (fyo͞o-nîr′ē-əl) ►*adj.* Appropriate for or suggestive of a funeral; mournful. [< Lat. *fūnus, fūner-,* funeral.] —**fu·ne′re·al·ly** *adv.*

fun·gi·cide (fŭn′jĭ-sīd′, fŭng′gĭ-) ►*n.* A substance that destroys fungi. —**fun′gi·cid′al** *adj.*

fun·gus (fŭng′gəs) ►*n., pl.* **fun·gi** (fŭn′jī, fŭng′gī) or **-gus·es** Any of numerous spore-producing organisms lacking chlorophyll, including mushrooms, yeasts, smuts, rusts, and many molds. [Lat.] —**fun′gal, fun′gous** *adj.*

fu·nic·u·lar (fyo͞o-nĭk′yə-lər, fə-) ►*n.* A cable railway on a steep incline, esp. one with simultaneously ascending and descending cars counterbalancing one another. [< Lat. *funiculus,* thin rope.]

funicular

funk¹ (fŭngk) ►*n.* A strong, usu. unpleasant smell; reek. [Prob. < Fr. dial. *funquer,* to smoke.]

funk² (fŭngk) ►*n.* A type of popular music combining elements of jazz, blues, and soul. [Back-formation < FUNKY.]

funk³ (fŭngk) ►*n.* **1.** A state of cowardly fright. **2.** A state of severe depression. [Poss. < obsolete Flem. *fonck,* agitation.]

funk·y (fŭng′kē) ►*adj.* **-i·er, -i·est 1.** Having a strong offensive odor. **2.** *Mus.* Having a style reminiscent of simple blues; bluesy. **3.** *Slang* Eccentric in style or manner: *funky clothes.* —**funk′i·ness** *n.*

fun·nel (fŭn′əl) ►*n.* **1.** A conical utensil with a narrow tube at the bottom, used to channel the flow of a substance into a container. **2.** A flue or stack, esp. the smokestack of a ship. ►*v.* **-neled, -nel·ing** or **-nelled, -nel·ling** To move through or as if through a funnel. [< LLat. *fundibulum.*]

fun·ny (fŭn′ē) ►*adj.* **-ni·er, -ni·est 1.** Causing laughter or amusement. **2a.** Difficult to account for: *a funny feeling.* **b.** Suspiciously odd. **3.** *Informal* Somewhat ill, painful, or abnormal: *I* felt funny after eating those clams. ►*n., pl.* **-nies** *Informal* **1.** A joke. **2. funnies** Comic strips. —**fun′ni·ly** *adv.* —**fun′ni·ness** *n.*

funny bone ►*n. Informal* **1.** A point on the elbow where pressure against the underlying nerve produces a sharp tingling sensation. **2.** A sense of humor.

fur (fûr) ►*n.* **1.** The thick coat of soft hair covering the skin of various mammals. **2.** The dressed pelt of such a mammal, used esp. for clothing. **3.** A furlike coating. [Prob. < OFr. *fuerre*, lining.] —**furred** *adj.*

fur. ►*abbr.* furlong

fur·be·low (fûr′bə-lō′) ►*n.* **1.** A ruffle on a garment. **2.** A piece of showy ornamentation. [Prob. < Prov. *farbello*, fringe.]

fur·bish (fûr′bĭsh) ►*v.* **1.** To brighten by cleaning or rubbing; polish. **2.** To renovate. [< OFr. *fourbir*, of Gmc. orig.]

fu·ri·ous (fyŏŏr′ē-əs) ►*adj.* **1.** Extremely angry; raging. See Synonyms at **angry. 2.** Full of intensity; energetic or fierce. [< Lat. *furia*, fury.] —**fu′ri·ous·ly** *adv.*

furl (fûrl) ►*v.* To roll up and secure (a flag or sail) to something else. [< OFr. *ferlier*, tie firmly.]

fur·long (fûr′lông′, -lŏng′) ►*n.* See table at **measurement.** [< OE *furlang.*]

fur·lough (fûr′lō) ►*n.* **1.** A leave of absence or vacation, esp. of a member of the armed forces. **2.** A usu. temporary layoff from work. [< MDu. *verlof.*] —**fur′lough** *v.*

fur·nace (fûr′nĭs) ►*n.* An enclosure in which heat is generated by the combustion of a suitable fuel. [< Lat. *fornāx.*]

fur·nish (fûr′nĭsh) ►*v.* **1.** To equip, esp. with furniture. **2.** To supply; give. [< OFr. *fournir*, of Gmc. orig.] —**fur′nish·er** *n.*

fur·nish·ings (fûr′nĭ-shĭngz) ►*pl.n.* **1.** The furniture and other movable articles in a home or building. **2.** Clothes and accessories.

fur·ni·ture (fûr′nĭ-chər) ►*n.* The movable articles in a room or establishment that equip it for living or working. [OFr. *fourniture* < *fournir*, furnish.]

fu·ror (fyŏŏr′ôr′, -ər) ►*n.* **1.** A public uproar. **2.** Violent anger; frenzy. **3.** Intense excitement. [< Lat. < *furere*, to rage.]

fur·ri·er (fûr′ē-ər) ►*n.* One who designs, sells, or repairs furs. [Alteration (influenced by CLOTHIER) < AN *furrere.*]

fur·ring (fûr′ĭng) ►*n.* Strips of wood or metal attached to a wall or other surface to provide a level substratum, as for paneling.

fur·row (fûr′ō, fûr′ō) ►*n.* **1.** A long shallow trench made in the ground by a plow or other tool. **2.** A deep wrinkle in the skin. [< OE *furh.*] —**fur′row** *v.*

fur·ry (fûr′ē, fûr′ē) ►*adj.* **-ri·er, -ri·est 1.** Consisting of or similar to fur. **2.** Covered with fur or a furlike substance.

fur seal ►*n.* A seal having external ears and thick fur.

fur·ther (fûr′thər) ►*adj.* Comp. of **far. 1.** More distant in degree, time, or space. **2.** Additional. ►*adv.* Comp. of **far. 1.** To a greater extent; more. **2.** In addition; furthermore. **3.** At or to a more distant or advanced point. ►*v.* To help the progress of. See Synonyms at **advance.** [< OE *furthor.*] —**fur′ther·ance** *n.*

fur·ther·more (fûr′thər-môr′) ►*adv.* In addition; moreover.

fur·ther·most (fûr′thər-mōst′) ►*adj.* Most distant or remote.

fur·thest (fûr′thĭst) ►*adj.* Superl. of **far.** Most distant in degree, time, or space. ►*adv.* Superl. of **far. 1.** To the greatest extent or degree. **2.** At or to the most distant point in space or time. [ME.]

fur·tive (fûr′tĭv) ►*adj.* Marked by stealth; surreptitious. [< Lat. *furtum*, theft < *fūr*, thief.] —**fur′tive·ly** *adv.* —**fur′tive·ness** *n.*

fu·ry (fyŏŏr′ē) ►*n., pl.* **-ries 1.** Violent anger; rage. **2.** Violent or frenzied action. **3. Fury** *Gk. & Rom. Myth.* Any of the spirits who pursue and torment the doers of unavenged crimes. [< Lat. *furia* < *furere*, to rage.]

furze (fûrz) ►*n.* See **gorse.** [< OE *fyrs.*]

fuse¹ also **fuze** (fyŏŏz) ►*n.* **1.** A cord of readily combustible material that is lighted at one end to carry a flame along its length to detonate an explosive at the other end. **2.** often **fuze** A mechanical or electrical mechanism used to detonate an explosive device. [< Lat. *fūsus*, spindle.] —**fuse** *v.*

fuse² (fyŏŏz) ►*v.* **fused, fus·ing 1.** To join (different pieces or elements) together physically, esp. by melting or heating. **2.** To liquefy or reduce to a plastic state by heating; melt. ►*n.* A safety device for an electric circuit that melts when current exceeds a specific amperage, thus opening the circuit. [< Lat. *fundere*, *fūs-*, melt.] —**fus′i·ble** *adj.*

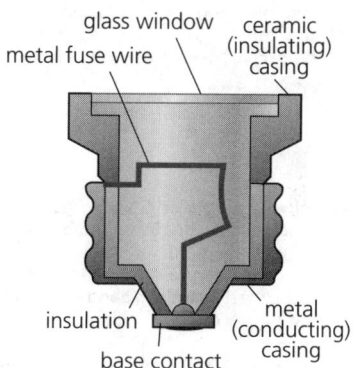

glass window   ceramic (insulating) casing

metal fuse wire

insulation   metal (conducting) casing

base contact

fuse²
electric plug fuse

fu·see also **fu·zee** (fyŏŏ-zē′) ►*n.* **1.** A usu. cone-shaped pulley with a spiral groove, used in a cord- or chain-winding clock to maintain even travel in the timekeeping mechanism. **2a.** A colored flare used as a warning signal for trucks and trains. **b.** A match with a large head capable of burning in a wind. [< Lat. *fūsus*, spindle.]

fu·se·lage (fyŏŏ′sə-läzh′, -zə-) ►*n.* The central body of an aircraft, to which the wings and tail assembly are attached. [Fr. < *fuselé*, spindle-shaped.]

fu·sil·lade (fyŏŏ′sə-läd′, -lād′, -zə-) ►*n.* **1.** A simultaneous or rapid discharge from many firearms. **2.** A barrage. [Fr. < *fusiller*, shoot.]

fu·sion (fyŏŏ′zhən) ►*n.* **1.** The act or procedure of liquefying or melting by heat. **2.** The liquid or melted state that is induced by heat. **3.** The merging of different elements into a union.

4. *Phys.* A nuclear reaction in which nuclei release energy when combining to form more massive nuclei.

fuss (fŭs) ►*n.* **1.** Useless or nervous activity; commotion. **2.** Needless concern or worry. **3.** An angry or fretful protest. **4.** A display of affectionate excitement and attention: *made a fuss over the baby.* ►*v.* **1.** To trouble or worry over trifles. **2.** To be excessively careful or solicitous. **3.** To be in a state of nervous activity: *fussed with his collar.* **4.** To fret or complain. [?]

fuss·budg·et (fŭs′bŭj′ĭt) ►*n.* A person who fusses over trifles.

fuss·y (fŭs′ē) ►*adj.* **-i·er, -i·est 1.** Easily upset; given to bouts of ill temper. **2.** Meticulous; fastidious. **3.** Requiring great attention to sometimes trivial details. **4.** Requiring attention to small details. —**fuss′i·ly** *adv.* —**fuss′i·ness** *n.*

fus·tian (fŭs′chən) ►*n.* **1.** A coarse sturdy cloth. **2.** Pompous language. [< Med.Lat. *fustāneum.*] —**fus′tian** *adj.*

fus·ty (fŭs′tē) ►*adj.* **-ti·er, -ti·est 1.** Smelling of mildew or decay; musty. **2.** Old-fashioned; antique. [< OFr. *fust,* wine cask.] —**fus′ti·ly** *adv.* —**fus′ti·ness** *n.*

fut. ►*abbr.* future

fu·tile (fyōōt′l, fyōō′tīl′) ►*adj.* Having no useful result; ineffectual. [Lat. *fūtilis.*] —**fu′tile·ly** *adv.* —**fu·til′i·ty** (fyōō-tĭl′ĭ-tē) *n.*
Syns: *barren, bootless, fruitless, ineffectual, unavailing, useless, vain* **Ant:** *useful* **adj.**

fu·ton (fōō′tŏn) ►*n.* A pad usu. of tufted cotton batting used on a floor or on a raised frame as a bed. [J., of Chin. orig.]

fu·ture (fyōō′chər) ►*n.* **1.** The indefinite time yet to come. **2.** Something that will happen in the time to come. **3.** Chance of success or advancement: *a position with no future.* **4.**

futures A financial instrument that obligates the holder to buy or sell an asset at a set price on a specified date. **5.** *Gram.* The form of a verb used in speaking of action in the future. ►*adj.* That is to be or to come. [< Lat. *futūrus,* about to be.]

fu·tur·is·tic (fyōō′chə-rĭs′tĭk) ►*adj.* **1.** Of or relating to the future. **2.** Expressing a vision of life and society in the future. —**fu′tur·is′ti·cal·ly** *adv.*

fu·tu·ri·ty (fyōō-tōōr′ĭ-tē, -tyōōr′-, -chōōr′-) ►*n., pl.* **-ties 1.** The future. **2.** The quality or condition of being in or of the future. **3.** A future event or possibility.

fu·tur·ol·o·gy (fyōō′chə-rŏl′ə-jē) ►*n.* The study or forecasting of potential developments, as in science, technology, and society.

fuze (fyōōz) ►*n. & v.* Var. of **fuse**¹.

fu·zee (fyōō-zē′) ►*n.* Var. of **fusee**.

fuzz¹ (fŭz) ►*n.* A mass or coating of fine light fibers, hairs, or particles; down. ►*v.* To make blurred or indistinct. [Perh. < FUZZY.]

fuzz² (fŭz) ►*n. Slang* The police. [?]

fuzz·y (fŭz′ē) ►*adj.* **-i·er, -i·est 1.** Covered with fuzz. **2.** Of or resembling fuzz. **3.** Not clear; indistinct. [Perh. < LGer. *fussig,* spongy.] —**fuzz′i·ly** *adv.* —**fuzz′i·ness** *n.*

fwd ►*abbr.* forward

FY ►*abbr.* fiscal year

-fy or **-ify** ►*suff.* Cause to become; make: *calcify.* [< Lat. *-ficāre < -ficus,* –FIC.]

FYI ►*abbr.* for your information

G

g¹ or **G** (jē) ►*n., pl.* **g's** or **G's** also **gs** or **Gs 1.** The 7th letter of the English alphabet. **2.** *Mus.* The 5th tone in the C major scale. **3.** A unit of acceleration equal to the acceleration caused by gravity at the earth's surface, about 9.8 m (32 ft) per second per second.

g² ►*abbr.* gram

G¹ (jē) A trademark for a movie rating granting admission to persons of all ages.

G² ►*abbr.* **1.** goal **2.** gravitational constant

GA ►*abbr.* **1.** General Assembly **2.** Georgia **3.** goals against (goals scored by opponents)

gab (găb) ►*v.* **gabbed, gab·bing** *Slang* To talk idly or incessantly; chatter. [< ON *gabba,* scoff.] —**gab** *n.* —**gab′ber** *n.*

gab·ar·dine (găb′ər-dēn′, găb′ər-dēn′) ►*n.* A sturdy fabric of cotton, wool, or rayon twill. [< OFr. *galvardine,* a long cloak.]

gab·ble (găb′əl) ►*v.* **-bled, -bling 1.** To speak rapidly or incoherently; jabber. **2.** To make low muttering or quacking sounds, as a goose or duck. [Poss. < GAB.] —**gab′ble** *n.*

gab·by (găb′ē) ►*adj.* **-bi·er, -bi·est** *Slang* Talkative; garrulous. —**gab′bi·ness** *n.*

ga·ble (gā′bəl) ►*n.* A usu. triangular end section of wall between the two slopes of a pitched roof. [OFr.] —**ga′bled** *adj.*

Gable, (William) Clark 1901–60. Amer. actor.

Ga·bon (gă-bōN′) A country of W-central Africa on the Atlantic Ocean. Cap. Libreville.

Ga·bo·ro·ne (gä′bə-rō′nē) The capital of Botswana, in the SE part.

gad (găd) ►*v.* **gad·ded, gad·ding** To move about restlessly, as in search of pleasure. [ME *gadden,* to hurry.] —**gad′der** *n.*

gad·a·bout (găd′ə-bout′) ►*n.* One who roams about in search of pleasure or amusement.

gad·fly (găd′flī′) ►*n.* **1.** A persistent, irritating critic. **2.** One that provokes or goads. **3.** Any of various flies that bite or annoy livestock. [*goad,* a gad + FLY².]

gadg·et (găj′ĭt) ►*n.* A small specialized mechanical or electronic device. [?] —**gadg′et·ry** *n.*

gad·o·lin·i·um (găd′l-ĭn′ē-əm) ►*n. Symbol* **Gd** A silvery-white, malleable rare-earth element. At. no. 64. See table at **element**. [After Johan Gadolin (1760–1852).]

Gae·a (jē′ə) also **Gai·a** (gā′ə) ►*n. Gk. Myth.* The goddess of the earth, who bore and married Uranus and became the mother of the Titans and the Cyclops.

Gael (gāl) ►*n.* A Gaelic-speaking Celt of Scotland, Ireland, or the Isle of Man.

Gael·ic (gā′lĭk) ►*n.* Any of the Celtic languages of Ireland, Scotland, or the Isle of Man. —**Gael′ic** *adj.*

gaff (găf) ►*n.* **1.** A large iron hook attached to a pole and used to land large fish. **2.** A spar used to extend the upper edge of a fore-and-aft sail. [< OProv. *gaf.*] —**gaff** *v.*

gaffe (găf) ►*n.* **1.** A clumsy social error. **2.** A blatant mistake. [Fr.]

gaf·fer (găf′ər) ►*n.* **1.** An electrician in charge of lighting on a movie or television set. **2.** *Chiefly Brit.* An old man. [Poss. < GODFATHER.]

gag (găg) ►*n.* **1.** Something forced into or put over the mouth to prevent speaking or crying out. **2.** An obstacle to free speech. **3.** A device placed in the mouth to keep it open, as in dentistry. **4a.** A practical joke. **b.** A comic remark. ►*v.* **gagged, gag·ging 1.** To prevent from speaking by using a gag. **2.** To restrain from exercising free speech: *gagged the media.* **3.** To choke or retch. **4.** To make jokes. [< ME *gaggen,* suffocate.]

ga·ga (gä′gä′) ►*adj. Informal* **1.** Silly; crazy. **2.** Completely absorbed or infatuated. [< Fr., old fool.]

Ga·ga·rin (gə-gär′ĭn), **Yuri Alekseyevich** 1934–68. Soviet cosmonaut; first person in space (1961).

gage[1] (gāj) ►*n.* **1.** Something deposited or given as security; pledge. **2.** Something, such as a glove, that is offered or thrown down as a challenge to fight. [< OFr.]

gage[2] (gāj) ►*n. & v.* Var. of **gauge.**

Gage, Thomas 1721?–87. British general and colonial administrator.

gag·gle (găg′əl) ►*n.* **1.** A flock of geese. **2.** A group. [ME *gagel* < *gagelen,* cackle.]

gag law ►*n.* A law that limits speech, such as that of public officials.

gag order ►*n.* A court order forbidding parties in a legal action, lawyers, witnesses, and jurors from speaking to the media about a case they are involved with.

gag rule ►*n.* A rule, as in a legislative body, limiting discussion or debate on an issue.

Gai·a (gā′ə) ►*n. Gk. Myth.* Var. of **Gaea.**

gai·e·ty (gā′ĭ-tē) ►*n., pl.* **-ties 1.** Joyful exuberance or merriment; vivacity. **2.** Merry activity; festivity. [< OFr. *gai,* cheerful.]

gai·ly (gā′lē) ►*adv.* **1.** In a joyful, cheerful, or happy manner. **2.** Colorfully; showily.

gain (gān) ►*v.* **1.** To come into possession of; acquire: *gain vital information.* **2.** To win: *gained victory.* **3.** To obtain through effort or merit: *gained recognition.* **4.** To earn: *gain a living.* **5.** To increase by: *gained 15 pounds.* **6.** To increase; grow: *gained in wisdom.* **7.** To close a gap; get closer: *runners who gained on the leader.* ►*n.* Something gained or acquired; profit; advantage; increase. [< OFr. *gaaignier,* of Gmc. orig.]

gain·er (gā′nər) ►*n.* **1.** One that gains. **2.** *Sports* A dive in which the diver leaves the board facing forward, does a back somersault, and enters the water feet first.

gain·ful (gān′fəl) ►*adj.* Providing a gain or profit. —**gain′ful·ly** *adv.*

gain·say (gān-sā′, gān′sā′) ►*v.* **-said** (-săd′, -sĕd′), **-say·ing 1.** To declare false. See Synonyms at **deny. 2.** To oppose (someone), esp. by contradiction. [ME *gainsayen,* speak against.]

gait (gāt) ►*n.* **1.** A way of moving on foot: *a clumsy gait.* **2.** Any of the ways a horse can move by lifting the feet in different order or rhythm. **3.** A rate or pace. [< ON *gata,* path.]

gai·ter (gā′tər) ►*n.* **1.** A cloth or leather covering for the legs extending from the instep to the ankle or knee. **2.** An ankle-high shoe with elastic sides. **3.** An overshoe with a cloth top. **4.** A tubular collar fitting closely around the neck, often worn by skiers. [Fr. *guêtre.*]

gal (găl) ►*n. Informal* A woman or girl. [Alteration of GIRL.]

gal. ►*abbr.* gallon

ga·la (gā′lə, găl′ə, gä′lə) ►*n.* A festive occasion, esp. a lavish social event. [< OFr. *galer,* make merry.] —**ga′la** *adj.*

ga·lac·tose (gə-lăk′tōs′) ►*n.* A simple sugar, $C_6H_{12}O_6$, commonly occurring in whey. [Gk. *gala, galakt-,* milk + -OSE[2].]

Gal·a·had (găl′ə-hăd′) ►*n.* **1.** In Arthurian legend, the purest Knight of the Round Table. **2.** A model of nobleness and purity.

Ga·lá·pa·gos Islands (gə-lä′pə-gəs, -lăp′ə-) A group of volcanic islands in the Pacific W of Ecuador, to which they belong.

Ga·la·tians (gə-lā′shənz) ►*pl.n. (takes sing. v.)* See table at **Bible.**

gal·ax·y (găl′ək-sē) ►*n., pl.* **-ies 1a.** Any of numerous large-scale aggregates of stars, gas, and dust, containing an average of 100 billion solar masses and ranging in diameter from 1,500 to 300,000 light-years. **b.** often **Galaxy** The Milky Way. **2.** An assembly of brilliant, glamorous, or distinguished persons or things. [< Gk. *galaxias,* milky.] —**ga·lac′tic** (gə-lăk′-tĭk) *adj.*

gale (gāl) ►*n.* **1.** A very strong wind. **2.** A storm at sea. **3.** A forceful outburst, as of laughter. [?]

Ga·len (gā′lən) AD 130?–200? Greek anatomist, physician, and philosopher.

ga·le·na (gə-lē′nə) ►*n.* A soft gray mineral, the principal ore of lead. [Lat. *galēna,* lead ore.]

Ga·li·cia (gə-lĭsh′ə, -ē-ə) ►*n.* **1.** A historical region of central Europe in SE Poland and W Ukraine. **2.** A region and ancient kingdom of NW Spain on the Atlantic S of the Bay of Biscay. —**Ga·li′cian** *adj. & n.*

Gal·i·lee (găl′ə-lē′) A region of N Israel on the **Sea of Galilee,** a large freshwater lake. —**Gal′i·le′an** *adj. & n.*

Ga·li·le·o Ga·li·lei (găl′ə-lē′ō găl′ə-lā′, -lā′ō) 1564–1642. Italian astronomer and mathematician. —**Gal′i·le′an** *adj.*

gall[1] (gôl) ►*n.* **1.** Outrageous insolence; effrontery. **2a.** Bitterness of feeling; rancor. **b.** Something bitter to endure. **3.** See **bile** (sense 1). [< OE *gealla.*]

gall[2] (gôl) ►*n.* **1.** A skin sore caused by rubbing. **2.** Exasperation. ►*v.* **1.** To exasperate. **2.** To make or become sore by rubbing. [< OE *gealla.*]

gall[3] (gôl) ►*n.* An abnormal swelling of plant tissue caused by insects, microorganisms, or external injury. [< Lat. *galla.*]

gal·lant (găl′ənt) ►*adj.* **1.** Smartly stylish; dashing. **2.** Courageous; valiant. **3.** Nobly or selflessly resolute. **4a.** Courteously attentive; chivalrous. **b.** Flirtatious. ►*n.* (gə-länt′, -lănt′, găl′ənt) **1.** A fashionable young man. **2a.** A man courteously attentive to women. **b.** A male lover, esp. one who is courteously attentive. [< OFr. *galer,* make merry, of Gmc. orig.] —**gal′lant·ly** *adv.* —**gal′lant·ry** *n.*

gall·blad·der also **gall bladder** (gôl′blăd′ər) ►*n.* A small muscular sac under the right lobe of the liver, in which bile secreted by the liver is stored.

gal·le·on (gălʹē-ən, gălʹyən) ►*n.* A large three-masted sailing ship used from the 15th to 17th cent. for trade or warfare. [Sp. *galeón* < OFr. *galie,* GALLEY.]

gal·ler·y (gălʹə-rē) ►*n., pl.* **-ies 1.** A long interior or exterior balcony. **2a.** A long enclosed passage, esp. a corridor between two parts of a building. **b.** An underground tunnel. **3a.** A rear or side balcony in a theater or auditorium. **b.** The seats in such a section. **c.** The cheapest seats in a theater. **d.** The audience occupying these seats. **4.** The general public. **5a.** A building, room, or website for the exhibition of artistic work. **b.** An establishment that displays and sells works of art. **6.** A collection; assortment. [Ult. < Lat. *Galilea,* Galilee.]

gal·ley (gălʹē) ►*n., pl.* **-leys 1a.** A large medieval ship propelled by sails and oars, used for trade or warfare in the Mediterranean. **b.** An ancient Mediterranean ship propelled by oars. **2.** The kitchen of an airliner or ship. **3.** *Print.* **a.** A long tray for holding composed type. **b.** A printer's proof taken from such type. [< Med.Gk. *galea.*]

Gal·lic (gălʹĭk) ►*adj.* Relating to Gaul or France.

Gal·li·cism (gălʹĭ-sĭzʹəm) ►*n.* A French phrase appearing in another language.

gal·li·um (gălʹē-əm) ►*n. Symbol* **Ga** A rare metallic element, liquid near room temperature, used in semiconductors. At. no. 31. See table at **element.** [< Lat. *gallus,* cock.]

gal·li·vant (gălʹə-vănt′) ►*v.* **1.** To roam about in search of pleasure or amusement. **2.** To flirt. [Perh. alteration of GALLANT.]

gal·lon (gălʹən) ►*n.* See table at **measurement.** [< ONFr. *galon,* a liquid measure.]

gal·lop (gălʹəp) ►*n.* **1.** A gait of a horse, faster than a canter, in which all four feet are off the ground at the same time during each stride. **2.** A rapid pace. [< OFr. *galoper,* to gallop, of Gmc. orig.] —**galʹlop** *v.*

gal·lows (gălʹōz) ►*n., pl.* **gallows** or **-lows·es** A framework from which a noose is suspended, used for execution by hanging. [< OE *galga.*]

gallows humor ►*n.* Humorous treatment of a grave or dire situation.

gall·stone (gôlʹstōn′) ►*n.* A small hard mass formed in the gallbladder or in a bile duct.

ga·lore (gə-lôrʹ) ►*adj.* In great numbers; in abundance: *opportunities galore.* [Ir.Gael. *go leór,* enough.]

ga·losh (gə-lŏshʹ) ►*n.* A waterproof overshoe. [< OFr. *galoche,* wooden-soled shoe.]

galosh

Gal·va·ni (găl-väʹnē, gäl-), **Luigi** 1737–98. Italian physiologist and physician.

gal·van·ic (găl-vănʹĭk) ►*adj.* **1.** Of or relating to direct-current electricity, esp. when produced chemically. **2.** Having the effect of an electric shock: *a galvanic revelation.* [After Luigi GAL-VANI.] —**galʹvan·ism** *n.*

gal·va·nize (gălʹvə-nīz′) ►*v.* **-nized, -niz·ing 1.** To stimulate or shock with an electric current. **2.** To arouse to awareness or action; spur. **3.** To coat (iron or steel) with rust-resistant zinc. —**galʹva·ni·zaʹtion** *n.*

gal·va·nom·e·ter (găl′və-nŏmʹĭ-tər) ►*n.* An instrument used to detect or measure small electric currents by means of mechanical effects produced by a coil in a magnetic field. —**galʹ-va·no·metʹric** (-nō-mĕtʹrĭk) *adj.*

Gal·ves·ton (gălʹvĭ-stən) A city of SE TX on **Galveston Bay,** an arm of the Gulf of Mexico.

Gal·way (gôlʹwā′) A city of W-central Ireland on **Galway Bay,** an inlet of the Atlantic.

Gam·bi·a (gămʹbē-ə) A country of W Africa on the Atlantic. Cap. Banjul. —**Gamʹbi·an** *adj. & n.*

Gambia River A river of W Africa flowing about 1,130 km (700 mi) from N Guinea through SE Senegal and Gambia to the Atlantic.

gam·bit (gămʹbĭt) ►*n.* **1.** An opening in chess in which the player risks one or more minor pieces, usu. a pawn, in order to gain a favorable position. **2.** A maneuver, stratagem, or opening remark, esp. one intended to bring about a desired result. [< Ital. *gambetto,* a tripping up < *gamba,* leg.]

gam·ble (gămʹbəl) ►*v.* **-bled, -bling 1a.** To bet on an uncertain outcome, as of a contest. **b.** To play a game of chance for stakes. **2.** To take a risk in the hope of gaining an advantage. **3.** To expose to hazard: *gamble one's life.* ►*n.* **1.** A wager. **2.** A risk: *took a gamble that stock prices would rise.* [Perh. < OE *gamenian,* to play.] —**gamʹbler** *n.*

gam·bol (gămʹbəl) ►*v.* **-boled, -bol·ing** or **-bolled, -bol·ling** To leap about playfully; frolic. [< OItal. *gamba,* leg.] —**gamʹbol** *n.*

gam·brel roof (gămʹbrəl) ►*n.* A ridged roof with two slopes on each side, the lower slope having the steeper pitch. [< ONFr. *gamberel,* hock of an animal < *gambe,* leg.]

game¹ (gām) ►*n.* **1.** An activity providing entertainment or amusement; pastime. **2a.** A competitive activity or sport: *the game of chess.* **b.** A single instance of such an activity. **3.** The total number of points required to win a game. **4.** A particular style or manner of playing a game: *improved my tennis game with practice.* **5.** *Informal* A business or occupation: *the insurance game.* **6.** *Informal* A calculated strategy: *saw through their game.* **7.** Wild animals, birds, or fish hunted for food or sport. **8.** An object of attack or pursuit: *fair game.* ►*v.* **gamed, gam·ing 1.** To gamble. **2.** To manipulate dishonestly for personal gain; rig: *gamed the system to get a huge payoff.* ►*adj.* **gam·er, gam·est 1.** Unyielding in spirit; resolute. **2.** Ready and willing. [< OE *gamen.*] —**gameʹly** *adv.*

game² (gām) ►*adj.* **gam·er, gam·est** Crippled; lame: *a game leg.* [?]

game·cock (gāmʹkŏk′) ►*n.* A rooster trained for cockfighting.

game·keep·er (gāmʹkē′pər) ►*n.* One employed to protect and maintain wildlife, as on a private estate.

gam·er (gāʹmər) ►*n.* One who plays a game, esp. a role-playing or computer game.

game show ►*n.* A television show in which

contestants compete for prizes by playing games of knowledge or chance.

games·man·ship (gāmz′mən-shĭp′) ►*n.* The use of dubious tactics to further one's aims, better one's position, or gain an advantage.

gam·ete (găm′ēt′, gə-mēt′) ►*n.* A reproductive cell, esp. a mature sperm or egg capable of participating in fertilization. [< Gk. *gametēs*, husband.] —**ga·met′ic** (-mĕt′ĭk) *adj.*

gam·in (găm′ĭn) ►*n.* A boy who lives on or roams the streets. [Fr.]

ga·mine (gă-mēn′, găm′ēn) ►*n.* **1.** An often homeless girl who roams about the streets; urchin. **2.** A petite, charming girl or woman, esp. one with a playful demeanor.

gam·ma (găm′ə) ►*n.* The 3rd letter of the Greek alphabet. [Gk.]

gamma globulin ►*n.* A protein fraction of blood serum containing antibodies that protect against bacterial and viral infections.

gamma ray ►*n.* **1.** A photon of electromagnetic radiation emitted by radioactive decay and having very high energy, greater than about 100,000 electron volts. **2.** A narrow beam of such photons.

gam·mon (găm′ən) ►*n.* A victory in backgammon reached before the loser has removed a single piece. [Prob. < ME *gamen*, game.]

–gamous ►*suff.* Having a specified number of marriages: *monogamous.* [< Gk. *gamos*, marriage.]

gam·ut (găm′ət) ►*n.* A complete range or extent. [< Med.Lat. *gamma ut*, low G.]

gam·y also **gam·ey** (gā′mē) ►*adj.* **-i·er, -i·est 1.** Having the flavor or odor of game, esp. slightly spoiled game. **2.** Spirited; plucky. **3a.** Corrupt; tainted. **b.** Sexually suggestive; racy.

–gamy ►*suff.* Marriage: *polygamy.* [< Gk. *gamos*, marriage.]

gan·der (găn′dər) ►*n.* **1.** A male goose. **2.** *Informal* A look or glance: *Take a gander at this picture.* [< OE *gandra.*]

Gan·dhi (gän′dē, gŭn′-), **Indira Priyadarshini** 1917–84. Indian prime minister (1966–77 and 1980–84).

Gandhi, Mohandas Karamchand "Mahatma." 1869–1948. Indian nationalist and spiritual leader.

Mahatma Gandhi

gang (găng) ►*n.* **1.** A group of criminals or hoodlums who band together for mutual protection and profit. **2.** A group of adolescents who band together, esp. a group of delinquents.

3. *Informal* A group of people who associate regularly on a social basis. **4.** A work crew. **5.** A matched set, as of tools. ►*v.* To band together as a group or gang. —*phrasal verb:* **gang up** To join together esp. in opposition or attack. [< OE, journey, and ON *gangr*, group.]

Gan·ges (găn′jēz′) A river of N India and Bangladesh rising in the Himalayas and flowing about 2,510 km (1,560 mi) to the Bay of Bengal.

gan·gling (găng′glĭng) ►*adj.* Awkwardly tall or long-limbed. [Poss. < dial. *gang*, go.]

gan·gli·on (găng′glē-ən) ►*n., pl.* **-gli·a** (-glē-ə) or **-gli·ons 1.** A group of nerve cells forming a nerve center, esp. one located outside the brain or spinal cord. **2.** A benign cyst occurring in a tendon sheath or joint capsule. [Gk., cystlike tumor.] —**gan′gli·on′ic** (-ŏn′ĭk) *adj.*

gan·gly (găng′glē) ►*adj.* **-gli·er, -gli·est** Gangling. [Alteration of GANGLING.]

gang·plank (găng′plăngk′) ►*n.* A board or ramp used as a removable footway between a ship and a pier. [< GANG, a going.]

gan·grene (găng′grēn′, găng-grēn′) ►*n.* Death and decay of body tissue, often a limb, caused by insufficient blood supply following injury or disease. [< Gk. *gangraina.*] —**gan′grene** *v.* —**gan′gre·nous** (găng′grə-nəs) *adj.*

gang·ster (găng′stər) ►*n.* **1.** A member of an organized group of criminals; racketeer. **2.** A member of a gang of delinquents. —**gang′ster·dom** *n.* —**gang′ster·ism** *n.*

gang·way (găng′wā′) ►*n.* **1.** A passage along a ship's upper deck. **2.** See **gangplank.** ►*interj.* Used to clear a passage through a crowded area. [< GANG, a going.]

gan·ja (gän′jə) ►*n.* Marijuana. [< Skt. *gañjaḥ*, hemp.]

gan·net (găn′ĭt) ►*n.* A large seabird of the N Atlantic, having white plumage with black wingtips. [< OE *ganot.*]

gant·let (gônt′lĭt, gänt′-) ►*n.* **1.** Var. of **gauntlet**[1]. **2.** Var. of **gauntlet**[2].

gan·try (găn′trē) ►*n., pl.* **-tries 1.** A bridgelike mount for a traveling crane. **2.** A massive vertical frame used in assembling or servicing a rocket. [< Lat. *canthērius*, wooden frame.]

gaol (jāl) ►*n. & v. Chiefly Brit.* Var. of **jail.**

gap (găp) ►*n.* **1.** An opening, as in a wall; breach. **2.** A pass through mountains. **3.** A space between objects or points. **4.** An interruption of continuity. **5.** A wide difference; disparity: *the gap between rich and poor.* [< ON, chasm.]

gape (gāp, găp) ►*v.* **gaped, gap·ing 1.** To open the mouth wide; yawn. **2.** To stare wonderingly or stupidly, often with the mouth open. **3.** To be or become open or wide. ►*n.* **1.** An act of gaping. **2.** A large opening. [< ON *gapa.*]

gar (gär) ►*n.* Any of several fishes having an elongated body and a long narrow jaws with sharp teeth. [Short for *garfish* < OE *gār*, spear.]

GAR ►*abbr.* Grand Army of the Republic

ga·rage (gə-räzh′, -räj′) ►*n.* **1.** A structure for housing a motor vehicle. **2.** A commercial establishment where cars are repaired, serviced, or parked. [Fr. < *garer*, to shelter.] —**ga·rage′** *v.*

garage sale ►*n.* A sale of used household items or clothing held at one's home.

ga·ram ma·sa·la (gä-räm′ mä-sä′lä) ►*n.* Any of various blends of dry-roasted, ground spices, such as black pepper, cardamom, cinnamon, coriander seed, cumin, and cloves, used in South Asian cuisine. [Hindi and Urdu *garam masālā* : *garm*, *garam*, hot + *masālā*, spices.]

garb (gärb) ►*n.* **1.** A distinctive style of clothing; dress. **2.** An outward appearance; guise. [< Ital. *garbo*, grace.] —**garb** *v.*

gar·bage (gär′bĭj) ►*n.* **1a.** Food wastes, as from a kitchen. **b.** Refuse; trash. **2.** Worthless matter. [ME, offal from fowls.]

gar·ban·zo (gär-bän′zō) ►*n., pl.* **-zos** See **chick-pea.** [Sp. < OSpan. *arvanço.*]

gar·ble (gär′bəl) ►*v.* **-bled, -bling** To mix up or distort (e.g., a message) to such an extent as to make misleading or unintelligible. [Ult. < Lat. *crībrum*, sieve.] —**gar′bler** *n.*

Gar·bo (gär′bō), **Greta** 1905–90. Swedish-born Amer. actress.

Gar·cí·a Lor·ca (gär-sē′ə lôr′kä, gär-thē′ä), **Federico** 1898–1936. Spanish writer.

Gar·cí·a Már·quez (gär-sē′ə mär′kəs, -kĕs), **Gabriel** b. 1928. Colombian-born writer.

gar·den (gär′dn) ►*n.* **1.** A plot of land used for growing flowers, vegetables, herbs, or fruit. **2.** often **gardens** Grounds laid out with ornamental plants and trees and used for public recreation or display. **3.** A yard or lawn. **4.** A fertile, well-cultivated region. ►*v.* To plant or tend a garden. ►*adj.* Of, suitable to, or used in a garden: *garden plants.* [< ONFr. *gardin*, of Gmc. orig.] —**gar′den·er** *n.*

gar·de·nia (gär-dēn′yə) ►*n.* **1.** A shrub having glossy evergreen leaves. **2.** The large fragrant white flower of this plant. [After Alexander *Garden* (1730?–91).]

gar·den-va·ri·e·ty (gär′dn-və-rī′ĭ-tē) ►*adj.* Common; unremarkable.

Gar·field (gär′fēld′), **James Abram** 1831–81. The 20th US president (1881).

James Garfield
1881 portrait

gar·gan·tu·an (gär-găn′chōō-ən) ►*adj.* **1.** Of immense size; gigantic. **2.** Of exceedingly great scope or nature: *a gargantuan effort.* [After the hero of *Gargantua and Pantagruel* by Rabelais.]

gar·gle (gär′gəl) ►*v.* **-gled, -gling** **1.** To force exhaled air through a liquid held in the back of the mouth in order to cleanse or medicate the mouth or throat. **2.** To produce the sound of gargling when speaking or singing. ►*n.* **1.** A medicated solution for gargling. **2.** A gargling sound. [< OFr. *gargouiller.*]

gar·goyle (gär′goil′) ►*n.* A roof spout that is usu. in the form of a grotesque or fantastic

creature. [< OFr. *gargouille*, throat.]

gar·ish (gâr′ĭsh, găr′-) ►*adj.* Overly bright or ornamented, esp. in a vulgar or tasteless way; gaudy: *a garish tie.* [?] —**gar′ish·ly** *adv.* —**gar′ish·ness** *n.*

Syns: *flashy, gaudy, loud, tawdry* **adj.**

gar·land (gär′lənd) ►*n.* A wreath or festoon, esp. of plaited flowers or leaves. ►*v.* To ornament with a garland. [< OFr. *garlande.*]

Garland, Judy Frances Gumm. 1922–69. Amer. actress and singer.

gar·lic (gär′lĭk) ►*n.* An onionlike plant having a bulb whose cloves have a strong distinctive odor and flavor and are widely used as a seasoning. [< OE *gārlēac.*] —**gar′lick·y** *adj.*

gar·ment (gär′mənt) ►*n.* An article of clothing. [< OFr. *garnement* < *garnir*, equip.]

gar·ner (gär′nər) ►*v.* To amass; acquire. [< Lat. *grānārium*, GRANARY.]

gar·net (gär′nĭt) ►*n.* **1.** Any of several common, usu. crystallized silicate minerals, colored red, brown, black, green, yellow, or white and used as gemstones and abrasives. **2.** A dark red. [< OFr. *grenat*, pomegranate-colored.]

gar·nish (gär′nĭsh) ►*v.* **1.** To embellish; adorn. **2.** To decorate (food or drink) with small colorful or savory items. **3.** *Law* **a.** To seize (property such as wages) by garnishment. **b.** To serve (someone) with papers announcing the garnishment of that person's property in order to satisfy a debt. ►*n.* An ornamentation, esp. one added to a food or drink. [< OFr. *garnir*, equip.]

gar·nish·ee (gär′nĭ-shē′) ►*n.* A party who is in possession of money or property of a debtor and has been notified by a legal body that that money or property must be available to satisfy a monetary judgment to the party owed by the debtor.

gar·nish·ment (gär′nĭsh-mənt) ►*n.* A legal proceeding in which a plaintiff seeks the satisfaction of a debt by obtaining a judgment that directs a third party in possession of the property of the defendant to make it available to satisfy the judgment.

gar·ret (găr′ĭt) ►*n.* An attic room or rooms, typically under a pitched roof. [< OFr. *garite*, watchtower < *garir*, defend.]

gar·ri·son (găr′ĭ-sən) ►*n.* A permanent military post or the troops stationed there. ►*v.* To assign (troops) to a military post. [< OFr. *garison* < *garir*, defend.]

Garrison, William Lloyd 1805–79. Amer. abolitionist leader.

gar·rote or **gar·rotte** (gə-rŏt′, -rōt′) ►*n.* **1a.** A method of execution by strangulation with an iron collar. **b.** The collar used for this. **2a.** Strangulation, esp. in order to rob. **b.** A cord or wire used for strangling. [Sp. *garrote*, instrument of torture.] —**gar·rote′** *v.*

gar·ru·lous (găr′ə-ləs, găr′yə-) ►*adj.* Tiresomely talkative; rambling. [< Lat. *garrulus.*] —**gar′ru·lous·ly** *adv.* —**gar′ru·lous·ness** *n.*

gar·ter (gär′tər) ►*n.* An elastic band or suspender worn to hold up hose. [< ONFr. *gartier* < *garet*, bend of the knee.] —**gar′ter** *v.*

garter snake ►*n.* A nonvenomous North American snake with longitudinal stripes.

Gar·vey (gär′vē), **Marcus (Moziah) Aurelius** 1887–1940. Jamaican black nationalist active in the US.

gas (găs) ▸*n., pl.* **gas·es** or **gas·ses 1a.** The state of matter distinguished from the solid and liquid states by relatively low density and viscosity, the ability to diffuse readily, and the spontaneous tendency to become distributed uniformly throughout any container. **b.** A substance in this state. **2.** A gaseous fuel, such as natural gas. **3.** Gasoline. **4.** A gaseous asphyxiant, irritant, or poison. **5.** A gaseous anesthetic. **6.** Flatulence. **7.** *Slang* Idle or boastful talk. **8.** *Slang* One that provides great fun or entertainment. ▸*v.* **gassed, gas·sing 1.** To treat chemically with gas. **2.** To overcome or kill with poisonous fumes. —*phrasal verb:* **gas up** To supply a vehicle with gasoline. [Du. < Gk. *khaos*, chaos.] —**gas'e·ous** (găs'ē-əs, găsh'əs) *adj.*

gas chamber ▸*n.* An enclosed space where a poisonous gas is emitted to kill the person inside, often as a form of execution.

Gas·co·ny (găs'kə-nē) A historical region of SW France. —**Gas'con** *adj. & n.*

gash (găsh) ▸*v.* To make a long deep cut in. ▸*n.* A long deep cut. [< ONFr. *garser*, to slit.]

gas·ket (găs'kĭt) ▸*n.* Any of a variety of seals or packings used between matched machine parts or around pipe joints to prevent the escape of a gas or fluid. [Perh. < Fr. *garcette*, small cord.]

gas·light (găs'līt') ▸*n.* **1.** Light produced by burning illuminating gas. **2.** A gas lamp.

gas mask ▸*n.* A respirator that contains a chemical air filter and is worn over the face as protection against toxic gases.

gas·o·hol (găs'ə-hôl') ▸*n.* A blend of ethyl alcohol and unleaded gasoline used as a fuel. [GAS(OLINE) + (ALC)OHOL.]

gas·o·line (găs'ə-lēn') ▸*n.* A volatile mixture of flammable liquid hydrocarbons derived chiefly from crude petroleum and used principally as a fuel for internal-combustion engines.

gasp (găsp) ▸*v.* **1.** To draw in the breath sharply, as from shock. **2.** To breathe convulsively or laboriously. ▸*n.* A short convulsive intake or catching of the breath. [< ON *geispa*, to yawn.] —**gasp** *n.*

gas station ▸*n.* A retail establishment where motor vehicles are refueled.

gas·sy (găs'ē) ▸*adj.* **-si·er, -si·est** Containing, full of, or resembling gas. —**gas'si·ness** *n.*

gas·tric (găs'trĭk) ▸*adj.* Of or associated with the stomach.

gastric juice ▸*n.* The watery, acidic digestive fluid secreted by glands in the stomach.

gas·tri·tis (gă-strī'tĭs) ▸*n.* Chronic or acute inflammation of the stomach.

gastro– or **gastr–** ▸*pref.* Stomach: *gastritis.* [Gk. < *gastēr*, belly.]

gas·tro·en·ter·i·tis (găs'trō-ĕn'tə-rī'tĭs) ▸*n.* Inflammation of the mucous membrane of the stomach and intestines.

gas·tro·in·tes·ti·nal (găs'trō-ĭn-tĕs'tə-nəl) ▸*adj.* Of the stomach and intestines.

gas·trol·o·gy (gă-strŏl'ə-jē) ▸*n.* The medical study of the stomach and its diseases. —**gas'-tro·log'i·cal** (găs'trə-lŏj'ĭ-kəl), **gas'tro·log'ic** *adj.* —**gas·trol'o·gist** *n.*

gas·tron·o·my (gă-strŏn'ə-mē) ▸*n., pl.* **-mies 1.** The art of good eating. **2.** Cooking, as of a particular region. [< Gk. *gastronomia*.] —**gas'tro·nome'** (găs'trə-nōm') *n.* —**gas'tro·nom'ic** (găs'trə-nŏm'ĭk) *adj.*

gas·tro·pod (găs'trə-pŏd') ▸*n.* Any of a class of mollusks, such as the snail or slug, having a single, usu. coiled shell or no shell at all and a muscular foot for locomotion.

gas·works (găs'wûrks') ▸*pl.n.* (*takes sing. v.*) A factory where gas for heating and lighting is produced.

gate (gāt) ▸*n.* **1a.** A structure that can be swung, drawn, or lowered to block an entrance or passageway. **b.** A gateway. **2.** A passageway, as in an airport terminal, through which passengers arrive or depart. **3.** The total paid attendance at a public event. **4.** A device for controlling the passage of water or gas through a dam or conduit. **5.** *Electron.* A circuit with one output that is energized only by certain combinations of two or more inputs. [< OE *geat.*]

gate·crash·er (gāt'krăsh'ər) ▸*n. Slang* One who gains admittance, as to a party or concert, without being invited or without paying. —**gate'crash'** *v.*

gat·ed community (gā'tĭd) ▸*n.* A private neighborhood with entry permitted only to residents and guests.

Gates (gāts), **Horatio** 1728?–1806. Amer. Revolutionary general.

Gates, William Henry "Bill." b. 1955. Amer. computer software designer and business executive.

gate·way (gāt'wā') ▸*n.* **1.** An opening, as in a wall or fence, that may be closed by a gate. **2.** A means of access.

gath·er (găth'ər) ▸*v.* **1a.** To bring or come together. **b.** To draw (someone or something) closer to oneself. **c.** To draw (e.g., cloth) into small folds or puckers. **2.** To harvest or pick. **3.** To conclude; infer: *I gather you're ready.* **4.** To summon up: *gathered up my courage.* **5.** To accumulate gradually: *The bookshelf gathered dust.* **6.** To gain by a process of gradual increase: *gather speed.* ▸*n.* **1.** An act of gathering. **2.** A small fold or pucker in cloth. [< OE *gadrian.*] —**gath'er·er** *n.* —**gath'er·ing** *n.*

ga·tor or **ga·ter** (gā'tər) ▸*n. Informal* An alligator.

gauche (gōsh) ▸*adj.* Lacking social polish; tactless. [< OFr., awkward.] —**gauche'ly** *adv.* —**gauche'ness** *n.*

gau·cho (gou'chō) ▸*n., pl.* **-chos** A cowboy of the South American pampas. [Am.Sp.]

gaud·y (gô'dē) ▸*adj.* **-i·er, -i·est** Showy in a tasteless or vulgar way. See Synonyms at **garish.** [Ult. < Lat. *gaudēre*, make merry.] —**gaud'i·ly** *adv.* —**gaud'i·ness** *n.*

gauge also **gage** (gāj) ▸*n.* **1.** A standard dimension, quality, or capacity, as: **a.** The distance between the two rails of a railroad. **b.** The distance between two wheels on an axle. **c.** The diameter of a shotgun barrel. **d.** Thickness or diameter, as of sheet metal or wire. **2.** A standard or scale of measurement. **3.** An instrument for measuring the dimensions, capacity, or amount of something. **4.** A means of estimating or evaluating. ▸*v.* **gauged, gaug·ing** also **gaged, gag·ing 1.** To measure the dimensions, capacity, proportions, or amount of (something). **2.** To evaluate. [< ONFr., measuring rod.]

Gau·guin (gō-găN'), **(Eugène Henri) Paul** 1848–1903. French artist.

Gaul¹ (gôl) ▸*n.* A Celt of ancient Gaul.

Gaul² (gôl) An ancient region of W Europe

corresponding roughly to modern-day France and Belgium.

Gaul·ish (gô′lĭsh) ►*n.* The extinct Celtic language of Gaul.

gaunt (gônt) ►*adj.* **-er, -est 1.** Thin or emaciated. **2.** Bleak; desolate. [ME.] **—gaunt′ly** *adv.* **—gaunt′ness** *n.*

gaunt·let¹ also **gant·let** (gônt′lĭt, gänt′-) ►*n.* **1.** A protective glove. **2.** A challenge to fight or compete. [< OFr. *gant,* glove.]

gaunt·let² also **gant·let** (gônt′lĭt, gänt′-) ►*n.* **1.** A form of punishment in which two lines of persons facing each other and armed with sticks or clubs beat the person forced to run between them. **2.** A series of difficult or trying experiences. [< Swed. *gatlopp.*]

Gau·ta·ma (gô′tə-mə, gou′-), **Siddhartha** Known as "the Buddha." 563?–483? BC. Indian mystic and founder of Buddhism.

gauze (gôz) ►*n.* A thin transparent fabric with a loose open weave. [Fr. *gaze.*] **—gauz′i·ly** *adv.* **—gauz′i·ness** *n.* **—gauz′y** *adj.*

gave (gāv) ►*v.* P.t. of **give.**

gav·el (găv′əl) ►*n.* A small mallet, esp. one that a judge raps to signal for order or that an auctioneer raps to mark the end of a transaction. [?] **—gav′el** *v.*

ga·votte (gə-vŏt′) ►*n.* **1.** A French peasant dance in duple meter. **2.** The music for this dance. [< Prov. *gavoto.*]

gawk (gôk) ►*v.* To stare or gape stupidly. [Perh. < obsolete *gaw,* gape.] **—gawk′er** *n.* **—gawk′y** *adj.*

gay (gā) ►*adj.* **-er, -est 1.** Of or having a sexual orientation to persons of the same sex. **2.** Cheerful and lighthearted; merry. **3.** Bright or lively, esp. in color. ►*n.* A person whose sexual orientation is to persons of the same sex. [< OFr. *gai.*] **—gay′ness** *n.*

    Usage: Many writers reserve *gay* for males, but since the word is also used to refer to both sexes, the phrase *gay and lesbian* is often useful to avoid ambiguity.

Gay, John 1685–1732. English writer.

Ga·za (gä′zə, găz′ə) A city of SW Asia in the **Gaza Strip,** a narrow coastal area along the Mediterranean Sea adjoining Israel and Egypt.

gaze (gāz) ►*v.* **gazed, gaz·ing** To look steadily, intently, and with fixed attention. ►*n.* A steady, fixed look. [ME *gasen.*] **—gaz′er** *n.*

ga·ze·bo (gə-zā′bō, -zē′-) ►*n., pl.* **-bos** or **-boes** A small, usu. open-sided roofed structure in a garden or park. [?]

gazebo

ga·zelle (gə-zĕl′) ►*n.* Any of various small swift antelopes of Africa and Asia. [< Ar. *ǧazāl.*]

ga·zette (gə-zĕt′) ►*n.* **1.** A newspaper. **2.** An official journal. [< Ital. *gazzetta.*]

gaz·et·teer (găz′ĭ-tîr′) ►*n.* A geographic dictionary or index.

gaz·pa·cho (gə-spä′chō, gəz-pä′-) ►*n.* A chilled soup of chopped tomatoes, cucumbers, onions, peppers, and herbs. [Sp.]

GB ►*abbr.* **1.** gigabyte **2.** Great Britain

G clef ►*n.* See **treble clef.** [From its locating the note G above middle C.]

Gdańsk (gə-dänsk′, -dănsk′, -dīnsk′) also **Danzig** (dăn′sĭg, dän′tsĭk) A city of N Poland on the Baltic Sea.

GDP ►*abbr.* gross domestic product

gear (gîr) ►*n.* **1a.** A toothed machine part, such as a wheel or cylinder, that meshes with another toothed part to transmit motion or to change speed or direction. **b.** A transmission configuration for a specific ratio of engine to axle torque in a motor vehicle. **2.** Equipment, such as tools or clothing, used for a particular activity. See Synonyms at **equipment. 3.** Personal belongings. ►*v.* **1a.** To equip with or connect by gears. **b.** To put into gear. **2.** To adjust or adapt. [< ON *gervi,* equipment.]

gear·box (gîr′bŏks′) ►*n.* **1.** See **transmission** (sense 3). **2.** A casing for a system of gears.

gear·shift (gîr′shĭft′) ►*n.* A mechanism for changing from one gear to another.

geck·o (gĕk′ō) ►*n., pl.* **-os** or **-oes** Any of various chiefly nocturnal tropical and subtropical lizards characteristically having toe pads covered with numerous tiny bristles that adhere to vertical surfaces. [Javanese *ge'kok.*]

gee (jē) ►*interj.* Used as an exclamation, as of surprise. [Alteration of JESUS.]

geek (gēk) ►*n. Slang* **1a.** An inept or clumsy person. **b.** One accomplished in scientific or technical pursuits but regarded as socially inept. **2.** A carnival performer featuring bizarre acts. [Perh. < LGer. *gek,* fool.] **—geek′y** *adj.*

geese (gēs) ►*n.* Pl. of **goose.**

gee·zer (gē′zər) ►*n.* An eccentric old man. [Prob. < dial. *guiser,* masquerader.]

Geh·rig (gĕr′ĭg), **Henry Louis** "Lou." 1903–41. Amer. baseball player.

Gehr·y (gâr′ē, gär′ē), **Frank** b. 1929. Canadian-born Amer. architect.

Gei·ger counter (gī′gər) ►*n.* An instrument that detects and measures the intensity of radiation, such as particles from radioactive material. [After H.W. *Geiger* (1882–1945).]

Gei·sel (gī′zəl), **Theodor Seuss** Dr. Seuss (soōs) 1904–91. Amer. writer and illustrator.

gei·sha (gā′shə, gē′-) ►*n., pl.* **-sha** or **-shas** A Japanese woman who is trained to entertain gatherings of men with conversation, dancing, and singing. [J.]

gel (jĕl) ►*n.* A jellylike mixture formed when the particles of a colloid become relatively large. [< GELATIN.] **—gel** *v.*

gel·a·tin also **gel·a·tine** (jĕl′ə-tn) ►*n.* **1.** A transparent brittle protein formed by boiling the specially prepared skin, bones, and connective tissue of animals and used in foods, drugs, and photographic film. **2.** A jelly made with gelatin. [< Ital. *gelata,* jelly < Lat. *gelāre,* freeze.] **—ge·lat′i·nous** (jə-lăt′n-əs) *adj.*

geld (gĕld) ►*v.* **geld·ed** or **gelt** (gĕlt), **geld·ing** To castrate (e.g., a horse). [< ON *gelda.*] **—geld′ing** *n.*

gel·id (jĕl′ĭd) ►*adj.* Very cold. See Synonyms at

cold. [Lat. *gelidus* < *gelū*, frost.] —**ge·lid′i·ty** (jə-lĭd′ĭ-tē), **gel′id·ness** *n.*

gel·ig·nite (jĕl′ĭg-nīt′) ►*n.* An explosive mixture composed of nitroglycerine, guncotton, wood pulp, and potassium nitrate. [GEL(ATIN) + Lat. *ignis*, fire + –ITE¹.]

gem (jĕm) ►*n.* **1.** A pearl or mineral that has been cut and polished for use as an ornament. **2.** Something valued highly. [< Lat. *gemma.*] —**gem′my** *adj.*

Gem·i·ni (jĕm′ə-nī′, -nē′) ►*pl.n.* *(takes sing. v.)* **1.** A constellation in the Northern Hemisphere containing the stars Castor and Pollux. **2.** The 3rd sign of the zodiac. [< Lat. *Geminī*, twins.]

gem·ol·o·gy or **gem·mol·o·gy** (jĕ-mŏl′ə-jē) ►*n.* The study of precious or semiprecious stones. —**gem′o·log′i·cal** (jĕm′ə-lŏj′ĭ-kəl) *adj.* —**gem·ol′o·gist** *n.*

gem·stone (jĕm′stōn′) ►*n.* A precious or semiprecious stone that may be used as a jewel when cut and polished.

Gen. or **GEN** ►*abbr.* general

–gen or **–gene** ►*suff.* Producer: *androgen.* [< Gk. *-genēs*, born.]

gen·darme (zhän′därm′, zhäN′därm′) ►*n.* A member of the French national police. [< OFr. *gens d'armes*, men-at-arms.]

gen·der (jĕn′dər) ►*n.* **1.** Either of the two groups into which organisms are classified based on their reproductive organs and functions; sex. **2.** Females or males considered as a group: *Discrimination in the workplace based on gender is illegal.* **3.** One's identity as female or male or as neither entirely female nor entirely male. **4.** *Gram.* A category used in the classification of nouns, pronouns, adjectives, and, in some languages, verbs that determines agreement with modifiers, referents, or grammatical forms. [< Lat. *genus, gener-*, kind.] —**gen′der·less** *adj.*

gene (jēn) ►*n.* A hereditary unit that occupies a specific location on a chromosome and is transcribed into an RNA molecule that may function directly or be translated into an amino acid chain. [< Gk. *genos*, race.]

ge·ne·al·o·gy (jē′nē-ŏl′ə-jē, -ăl′-, jĕn′ē-) ►*n., pl.* **-gies 1.** A record of ancestral descent; family tree. **2.** Direct descent from an ancestor. **3.** The study of ancestry. [< Gk. *genea*, family.] —**ge′ne·a·log′i·cal** (-ə-lŏj′ĭ-kəl) *adj.* —**ge′ne·al′o·gist** *n.*

gene pool ►*n.* The collective genetic information contained within a population of sexually reproducing organisms.

gen·er·a (jĕn′ər-ə) ►*n.* Pl. of **genus.**

gen·er·al (jĕn′ər-əl) ►*adj.* **1.** Applicable to or affecting the whole or every member of a category. **2.** Widespread; prevalent. **3.** Of or affecting the entire body: *general malaise; general anesthetic.* **4.** Being usually the case. **5.** Not limited in scope or category: *a general rule; general merchandise.* **6.** Broad but not thorough: *a general grasp of the subject.* **7.** Highest or superior in rank: *the general manager.* ►*n.* A rank, as in the US Army, above lieutenant general. —*idiom:* **in general** For the most part. [< Lat. *genus, gener-*, kind.] —**gen′er·al·ly** *adv.*
*Syns: common, universal **Ant** particular **adj.***

general anesthetic ►*n.* An anesthetic that causes loss of sensation in the entire body and induces unconsciousness.

general assembly ►*n.* **1.** A legislative body. **2. General Assembly** The main deliberative body of the United Nations, in which each member nation has one vote.

gen·er·al·is·si·mo (jĕn′ər-ə-lĭs′ə-mō′) ►*n., pl.* **-mos** The commander in chief of all the armed forces in certain countries. [Ital.]

gen·er·al·i·ty (jĕn′ə-răl′ĭ-tē) ►*n., pl.* **-ties 1.** The state of being general. **2.** An observation or principle having general application; generalization. **3.** A vague statement or idea.

gen·er·al·ize (jĕn′ər-ə-līz′) ►*v.* **-ized, -iz·ing 1.** To render general rather than specific. **2.** To draw inferences or a general conclusion (from). **3.** To deal in generalities; speak or write vaguely. —**gen′er·al·i·za′tion** *n.*

General of the Air Force ►*n.* The highest rank in the US Air Force.

General of the Army ►*n.* The highest rank in the US Army.

general practitioner ►*n.* A physician who does not specialize in a particular area but treats a variety of medical problems.

general relativity ►*n.* The geometric theory of gravitation developed by Albert Einstein, extending the theory of special relativity to accelerated frames of reference and introducing the principle that gravity is a consequence of matter causing a curvature in space-time.

gen·er·al·ship (jĕn′ər-əl-shĭp′) ►*n.* **1.** The rank, office, or tenure of a general. **2.** Skill in the conduct of war. **3.** Leadership.

gen·er·ate (jĕn′ə-rāt′) ►*v.* **-at·ed, -at·ing 1.** To bring into being; produce. **2.** To produce (a program) by instructing a computer to follow given parameters with a skeleton program. [Lat. *generāre.*] —**gen′er·a·tive** (-ər-ə-tĭv, -ə-rā′-) *adj.*

gen·er·a·tion (jĕn′ə-rā′shən) ►*n.* **1.** The people born and living about the same time, considered as a group. **2.** The average interval of time between the birth of parents and the birth of their offspring. **3.** All of the offspring that are at the same stage of descent from a common ancestor. **4a.** A period of sequential technological development and innovation. **b.** A class of objects derived from a preceding class. **5.** The act of generating. —**gen·er·a′tion·al** *adj.*

Generation X ►*n.* The generation following the post–World War II baby boom, esp. in the US and Canada. [< title of a novel by Douglas Coupland (b. 1961).]

Generation Y ►*n.* The generation following Generation X.

gen·er·a·tor (jĕn′ə-rā′tər) ►*n.* One that generates, esp. a machine that converts mechanical energy into electrical energy.

ge·ner·ic (jə-nĕr′ĭk) ►*adj.* **1.** Relating to or descriptive of an entire group. **2.** *Biol.* Of or relating to a genus. **3.** Not having a trademark or brand name. ►*n.* A product or substance sold under a generic name. [< Lat. *genus, gener-*, kind.] —**ge·ner′i·cal·ly** *adv.*

gen·er·ous (jĕn′ər-əs) ►*adj.* **1.** Liberal in giving or sharing. See Synonyms at **liberal. 2.** Magnanimous. **3.** Abundant; ample. [< Lat. *generōsus*, of noble birth.] —**gen′er·os′i·ty** (-ə-rŏs′ĭ-tē) *n.* —**gen′er·ous·ly** *adv.*

gen·e·sis (jĕn′ĭ-sĭs) ►*n., pl.* **-ses** (-sēz′) **1.** The origin of something. See Synonyms at **beginning. 2. Genesis** See table at **Bible.** [< Gk.]

–gen·e·sis ►*suff.* Origin; production: *morphogenesis.* [< Gk.]

Ge·net (zhə-nā′), **Jean** 1910–86. French writer.

gene therapy ►*n.* Treatment of esp. genetic disorders by introducing engineered genes into a subject's cells.

ge·net·ic (jə-nĕt′ĭk) ►*adj.* **1a.** Of or relating to genetics. **b.** Affecting or affected by genes. **2.** Of or influenced by the origin or development of something. [< Gk. *genetikos,* genitive < *genesis,* origin.] **—ge·net′i·cal·ly** *adv.*

genetic code ►*n.* The set of DNA and RNA sequences that determine the amino acid sequences used in the synthesis of an organism's proteins. It is the biochemical basis of heredity.

genetic engineering ►*n.* Scientific alteration of the structure of genetic material in a living organism. **—genetic engineer** *n.*

ge·net·ics (jə-nĕt′ĭks) ►*n. (takes sing. v.)* The branch of biology that deals with heredity, esp. the mechanisms of hereditary transmission and the variation of inherited characteristics. **—ge·net′i·cist** *n.*

Ge·ne·va (jə-nē′və) A city of SW Switzerland on the Rhone R. and **Lake Geneva.**

Gen·ghis Khan (jĕng′gĭs kän′, gĕng′-) also **Jen·ghiz Khan** (jĕn′gĭz kän′, jĕng′-) 1162?–1227. Mongol conqueror.

gen·ial (jēn′yəl) ►*adj.* Having a pleasant or friendly disposition or manner. [< Lat. *genius,* spirit.] **—ge′ni·al′i·ty** (jē′nē-ăl′ĭ-tē), **gen′ial·ness** *n.* **—gen′ial·ly** *adv.*

–genic ►*suff.* **1.** Producing; generating: *allergenic.* **2.** Produced or generated by: *psychogenic.* **3.** Suitable for production or reproduction by a specified medium: *photogenic.* [–GEN + –IC.]

ge·nie (jē′nē) ►*n.* A supernatural creature who does one's bidding when summoned. [< Lat. *genius,* guardian spirit.]

gen·i·tal (jĕn′ĭ-tl) ►*adj.* **1.** Of or relating to biological reproduction. **2.** Of the genitals. **3.** Of the third and final stage of psychosexual development in psychoanalytic theory. [< Lat. *genitālis.*] **—gen′i·tal·ly** *adv.*

gen·i·ta·li·a (jĕn′ĭ-tā′lē-ə) ►*pl.n.* The genitals.

gen·i·tals (jĕn′ĭ-tlz) ►*pl.n.* The reproductive organs, esp. the external sex organs and associated structures in humans and other mammals. [< Lat. *genitālis,* GENITAL.]

gen·i·tive (jĕn′ĭ-tĭv) ►*adj.* Of or designating a grammatical case that expresses possession, measurement, or source. ►*n.* **1.** The genitive case. See Usage Note at **of. 2.** A word or form in the genitive case. [< Lat. *(cāsus) genetīvus,* (case) of origin.]

gen·i·to·u·ri·nar·y (jĕn′ĭ-tō-yŏŏr′ə-nĕr′ē) ►*adj.* Of or relating to the genital and urinary organs or their functions.

gen·ius (jēn′yəs) ►*n., pl.* **-ius·es 1a.** Extraordinary intellectual and creative power. **b.** A person of extraordinary intellect and talent. **2.** A strong natural talent or aptitude. **3.** The distinctive character of a place, person, or era. [Lat., guardian spirit.]

Gen·o·a (jĕn′ō-ə) A city of NW Italy on the Ligurian Sea. **—Gen′o·ese′** (-ēz′, -ēs′), **Gen′o·vese′** (-vēz′, -vēs′) *adj. & n.*

gen·o·cide (jĕn′ə-sīd′) ►*n.* The systematic, planned extermination of a national, racial, political, or ethnic group. [Gk. *genos,* race +

–CIDE.] **—gen′o·cid′al** (-sīd′l) *adj.* **—gen′o·cid′al·ly** *adv.*

ge·nome (jē′nōm′) ►*n.* **1.** The genetic material contained in a haploid set of chromosomes in eukaryotes, in a single chromosome in bacteria, or in the DNA or RNA of viruses. **2.** An organism's genetic material. [GEN(E) + Gk. *-ōma,* n. suff.] **—ge·nom′ic** (-nŏm′ĭk) *adj.*

ge·no·mics (jə-nō′mĭks) ►*n. (takes sing. v.)* The study of the genome of a cell or organism.

gen·o·type (jĕn′ə-tīp′, jē′nə-) ►*n.* **1.** The genetic makeup of an organism or group of organisms. **2.** The combination of alleles located on homologous chromosomes that determines a specific characteristic or trait. [Gk. *genos,* race + TYPE.] **—gen′o·typ′ic** (-tĭp′ĭk), **gen′o·typ′i·cal** *adj.*

–genous ►*suff.* **1.** Producing; generating: *erogenous.* **2.** Produced by or in a specified manner: *endogenous.* [–GEN + –OUS.]

gen·re (zhän′rə) ►*n.* **1a.** An established class or category of artistic composition, as in literature or film. **b.** A realistic style of painting that depicts everyday life. **2.** A type or class. [< OFr., a kind < Lat. *genus, gener-.*]

gent (jĕnt) ►*n. Informal* A gentleman.

gen·teel (jĕn-tēl′) ►*adj.* **1.** Refined or polite, often in an affected way. **2.** Typical or characteristic of the upper class. **3.** Elegantly stylish or fashionable. [< OFr. *gentil;* see GENTLE.] **—gen·teel′ly** *adv.* **—gen·teel′ness** *n.*

gen·tian (jĕn′shən) ►*n.* Any of numerous plants having showy, usu. blue flowers. [< Lat. *gentiāna.*]

gen·tile or **Gen·tile** (jĕn′tīl′) ►*n.* **1.** One who is not a Jew. **2.** *Archaic* A pagan or heathen. [< LLat. *gentīlis,* pagan; see GENTLE.]

gen·til·i·ty (jĕn-tĭl′ĭ-tē) ►*n.* **1.** The quality of being well-mannered. **2.** The condition of being born to the gentry.

gen·tle (jĕn′tl) ►*adj.* **-tler, -tlest 1.** Considerate or kindly. **2.** Not harsh or severe; soft; mild. **3.** Easily managed or handled; docile. **4.** Not steep or sudden; gradual. **5.** Of good family; wellborn. [< Lat. *gentīlis,* of the same clan < *gēns, gent-,* clan.] **—gen′tle** *v.* **—gen′tle·ness** *n.* **—gen′tly** *adv.*

gen·tle·man (jĕn′tl-mən) ►*n.* **1.** A man of superior social position. **2.** A polite or well-mannered man. **3.** A man of independent means who does not need to work for a living. **4.** A man. **—gen′tle·man·ly** *adj.*

gen·tle·wom·an (jĕn′tl-wŏŏm′ən) ►*n.* **1.** A woman of superior social position. **2.** A polite or well-mannered woman.

gen·too penguin (jĕn′tōō′) ►*n.* A penguin of Antarctic and subantarctic regions, having a white patch or band above the eye and a reddish-orange bill. [Perh. < Sp. *Juanito,* dim. of *Juan,* John.]

gen·tri·fi·ca·tion (jĕn′trə-fĭ-kā′shən) ►*n.* The restoration and upgrading of deteriorated urban property by the middle classes, often resulting in displacement of lower-income people. **—gen′tri·fy′** *v.*

gen·try (jĕn′trē) ►*n., pl.* **-tries 1.** People of good family or high social position. **2.** The class of English landowners ranking just below the nobility. [< OFr. *genterise,* nobility < OFr. *gentil,* noble; see GENTLE.]

gen·u·flect (jĕn′yə-flĕkt′) ►*v.* To bend the knee

or touch one knee to the floor or ground, as in worship. [LLat. *genūflectere.*] —**gen′u·flec′tion** *n.*

gen·u·ine (jĕn′yōō-ĭn) ▸*adj.* **1.** Actually possessing the alleged or apparent attribute or character. **2.** Not spurious or counterfeit. See Synonyms at **authentic.** [Lat. *genuīnus,* natural.] —**gen′u·ine·ly** *adv.* —**gen′u·ine·ness** *n.*

ge·nus (jē′nəs) ▸*n., pl.* **gen·er·a** (jĕn′ər-ə) **1.** *Biol.* The category ranking below a family and above a species in the hierarchy of taxonomic classification. **2.** A class, group, or kind with common attributes. [Lat., a kind.]

–geny ▸*suff.* Production; origin: *ontogeny.* [< Gk. -*genēs,* born.]

geo– ▸*pref.* **1.** Earth: *geocentric.* **2.** Geography: *geopolitics.* [< Gk. *gē,* earth.]

ge·o·cach·ing (jē′ō-kăsh′ĭng) ▸*n.* A pastime in which one searches for hidden objects that are found by using exact GPS coordinates.

ge·o·cen·tric (jē′ō-sĕn′trĭk) ▸*adj.* **1.** Of or measured from the center of the earth. **2.** Having the earth as a center. —**ge′o·cen′tri·cal·ly** *adv.*

ge·o·chro·nol·o·gy (jē′ō-krə-nŏl′ə-jē) ▸*n.* The chronology of the earth's history as determined by geologic events. —**ge′o·chron′o·log′ic** (-krŏn′ə-lŏj′ĭk), **ge′o·chron′o·log′i·cal** *adj.* —**ge′o·chro·nol′o·gist** *n.*

ge·ode (jē′ōd′) ▸*n.* A hollow, usu. spheroidal rock with crystals lining the inside wall. [< Gk. *geōdēs,* earthlike : GEO– + –OID.]

ge·o·des·ic (jē′ə-dĕs′ĭk, -dē′sĭk) ▸*adj.* **1.** Of geodesy or a geodesic. **2.** Having a structure consisting of straight elements joined so as to form interlocking polygons whose vertices lie on an imaginary sphere. ▸*n.* The shortest path between two points on any mathematically defined surface.

ge·od·e·sy (jē-ŏd′ĭ-sē) ▸*n.* The geologic science of the size and shape of the earth. [< Gk. *geōdaisia.*] —**ge′o·des′ist** *n.*

ge·og·ra·phy (jē-ŏg′rə-fē) ▸*n., pl.* **-phies 1.** The science dealing with the earth's natural features, climate, resources, and population. **2.** The physical characteristics, esp. the surface features, of an area. **3.** A book on geography. —**ge·og′ra·pher** *n.* —**ge′o·graph′ic** (jē′ə-grăf′ĭk) *adj.* —**ge′o·graph′i·cal·ly** *adv.*

ge·ol·o·gy (jē-ŏl′ə-jē) ▸*n., pl.* **-gies 1.** The science of the origin, history, and structure of the earth. **2.** The structure of a specific region of the earth's crust. —**ge′o·log′ic** (jē′ə-lŏj′ĭk), **ge′o·log′i·cal** *adj.* —**ge′o·log′i·cal·ly** *adv.* —**ge·ol′o·gist** *n.*

ge·o·mag·net·ism (jē′ō-măg′nĭ-tĭz′əm) ▸*n.* The magnetism of the earth. —**ge′o·mag·net′ic** *adj.* —**ge′o·mag·net′i·cal·ly** *adv.*

geometric progression ▸*n. Math.* A sequence, such as 1, 3, 9, 27, 81, in which each term is multiplied by the same factor to obtain the next term.

ge·om·e·try (jē-ŏm′ĭ-trē) ▸*n., pl.* **-tries 1.** The mathematics of the properties, measurement, and relationships of points, lines, angles, surfaces, and solids. **2.** Configuration; arrangement. **3.** A surface shape. [< Gk. *geōmetrein,* measure land.] —**ge′o·met′ric** (jē′ə-mĕt′rĭk) *adj.* —**ge′o·met′ri·cal·ly** *adv.* —**ge·om′e·**

tri·cian (jē-ŏm′ĭ-trĭsh′ən, jē′ə-mĭ-), **ge·om′e·ter** *n.*

ge·o·phys·ics (jē′ō-fĭz′ĭks) ▸*n.* (*takes sing. v.*) The physics of geologic phenomena. —**ge′o·phys′i·cal** *adj.* —**ge′o·phys′i·cal·ly** *adv.* —**ge′o·phys′i·cist** (-ĭ-sĭst) *n.*

ge·o·pol·i·tics (jē′ō-pŏl′ĭ-tĭks) ▸*n.* (*takes sing. v.*) The study of the relationship between politics and geography. —**ge′o·po·lit′i·cal** (-pə-lĭt′ĭ-kəl) *adj.* —**ge′o·po·lit′i·cal·ly** *adv.*

George (jôrj), Saint. d. c. AD 303. Christian martyr and patron saint of England.

George III 1738–1820. King of Great Britain and Ireland (1760–1820).

George IV 1762–1830. King of Great Britain and Ireland (1820–30).

George V 1865–1936. King of Great Britain and Northern Ireland and emperor of India (1910–36).

George VI 1895–1952. King of Great Britain and Northern Ireland (1936–52) and emperor of India (1936–47).

George·town (jôrj′toun′) **1.** The capital of the Cayman Is., on Grand Cayman in the West Indies W of Jamaica. **2.** The capital of Guyana, in the N part on the Atlantic coast.

Geor·gia (jôr′jə) **1.** A country of the Caucasus on the Black Sea S of Russia. Cap. Tbilisi. **2.** A state of the SE US. Cap. Atlanta. —**Geor′gian** *adj. & n.*

Georgia, Strait of A channel that separates Vancouver I. from mainland British Columbia and N WA State.

ge·o·sta·tion·ar·y (jē′ō-stā′shə-nĕr′ē) ▸*adj.* Of or being a satellite that travels above the earth's equator at an angular speed matching that of the earth's rotation, thus remaining stationary as observed from any location on the earth's surface.

ge·o·syn·chro·nous (jē′ō-sĭng′krə-nəs, -sĭn′-) ▸*adj.* Geostationary. —**ge′o·syn′chro·nous·ly** *adv.*

ge·o·ther·mal (jē′ō-thûr′məl) also **ge·o·ther·mic** (-mĭk) ▸*adj.* Of or relating to the internal heat of the earth. —**ge′o·ther′mal·ly** *adv.*

Ger. ▸*abbr.* German

ge·ra·ni·um (jə-rā′nē-əm) ▸*n.* **1.** Any of various plants widely cultivated for their rounded, often variegated leaves and showy clusters of red, pink, or white irregular flowers. **2.** Any of various plants having palmately divided leaves and pink or purplish regular flowers. [< Gk. *geranos,* crane.]

ger·bil (jûr′bəl) ▸*n.* **1.** A small mouselike rodent of arid regions of Africa and Asia. **2.** A related Mongolian rodent, commonly domesticated and kept as a pet. [< NLat. *Gerbillus,* dim. of *gerbō,* JERBOA.]

ger·i·at·rics (jĕr′ē-ăt′rĭks) ▸*n.* (*takes sing. v.*) The branch of medicine that deals with the diagnosis and treatment of diseases and problems specific to old age. [< Gk. *gēras,* old age.] —**ger′i·at′ric** *adj. & n.*

germ (jûrm) ▸*n.* **1.** *Biol.* A small mass of protoplasm or cells from which a new organism or one of its parts may develop. **2.** The earliest form of an organism; a seed, bud, or spore. **3.** A microorganism, esp. a pathogen. **4.** Something that may serve as the basis of further growth or development. [< Lat. *germen,* bud.]

Ger·man (jûr′mən) ▸*adj.* Of or relating to

Germany or its people or language. ►*n.* **1.** A native or inhabitant of Germany. **2.** The Germanic language of Germany, Austria, and part of Switzerland.

ger·mane (jər-mān′) ►*adj.* Related to a matter at hand; relevant. [< Lat. *germānus,* having the same parents.] —**ger·mane′ly** *adv.* —**ger·mane′ness** *n.*

Ger·man·ic (jər-măn′ĭk) ►*adj.* **1.** Of or relating to Germany. **2.** Teutonic. **3.** Of or relating to the Germanic languages. ►*n.* A branch of the Indo-European language family that includes English and German.

ger·ma·ni·um (jər-mā′nē-əm) ►*n. Symbol* **Ge** A brittle, crystalline, gray-white element, widely used as a semiconductor and as an alloying agent and catalyst. At. no. 32. See table at **element.** [< Lat. *Germānia,* Germany.]

German measles ►*n. (takes sing. or pl. v.)* See **rubella.**

German shepherd ►*n.* A large dog having a dense brownish or black coat and often trained to assist police.

Ger·ma·ny (jûr′mə-nē) A country of N-central Europe bordered on the N by the Baltic and North Seas; formerly divided into **East Germany** and **West Germany** (1949–90). Cap. Berlin.

germ cell ►*n.* An ovum or a sperm cell or one of its developmental precursors.

ger·mi·cide (jûr′mĭ-sīd′) ►*n.* An agent that kills germs; disinfectant. —**ger′mi·cid′al** (-sīd′-l) *adj.*

ger·mi·nal (jûr′mə-nəl) ►*adj.* **1.** Of or relating to a germ cell. **2.** Of or relating to the earliest stage of development. [< Lat. *germen, germin-,* sprout, bud.] —**ger′mi·nal·ly** *adv.*

ger·mi·nate (jûr′mə-nāt′) ►*v.* **-nat·ed, -nat·ing** To begin or cause to sprout or grow. [< Lat. *germen, germin-,* seed.] —**ger′mi·na′tion** *n.* —**ger′mi·na′tive** *adj.*

Ge·ron·i·mo (jə-rŏn′ə-mō′) 1829–1909. Apache leader.

Geronimo
photographed in 1904

ger·on·toc·ra·cy (jĕr′ən-tŏk′rə-sē) ►*n., pl.* **-cies** Government based on rule by elders. —**ge·ron′to·crat′** (jə-rŏn′tə-krăt′) *n.*

ger·on·tol·o·gy (jĕr′ən-tŏl′ə-jē) ►*n.* The study of the biological, psychological, and sociological phenomena associated with old age and aging. [< Gk. *gerōn, geront-,* old man.] —**ge·ron′to·log′i·cal** (jə-rŏn′tə-lŏj′ĭ-kəl), **ge·ron′-**

to·log′ic *adj.* —**ger′on·tol′o·gist** *n.*

Ger·ry (gĕr′ē), **Elbridge** 1744–1814. Vice president of the US (1813–14).

ger·ry·man·der (jĕr′ē-măn′dər, gĕr′-) ►*v.* To divide (a geographic area) into voting districts in a way that gives one party an unfair advantage in elections. [After Elbridge GERRY + (SALA)MANDER.] —**ger′ry·man′der** *n.*

Gersh·win (gûrsh′wĭn), **George** 1898–1937. Amer. composer.

ger·und (jĕr′ənd) ►*n.* **1.** In English, a verbal noun ending in *-ing,* as *singing* in *We admired the choir's singing.* **2.** In Latin, a noun derived from a verb and having all case forms except the nominative. **3.** A similar verbal noun in another language. [< Lat. *gerendum,* gerundive of *gerere,* carry on.] —**ge·run′di·al** (jə-rŭn′-dē-əl) *adj.*

ge·run·dive (jə-rŭn′dĭv) ►*n.* A Latin verbal adjective that expresses the notion of fitness or obligation or is used as a future passive participle. [< LLat. *gerundium,* GERUND.]

ge·stalt or **Ge·stalt** (gə-shtält′, -shtôlt′, -stält′, -stôlt′) ►*n.* A configuration or pattern of elements so unified as a whole that its properties cannot be derived from a simple summation of its parts. [Ger., shape, form.]

Gestalt psychology ►*n.* The school in psychology holding that psychological, physiological, and behavioral phenomena are irreducible experiential configurations.

Ge·sta·po (gə-stä′pō, -shtä′-) ►*n.* The German internal security police during the Nazi regime. [Ger. *Ge(heime) Sta(ats)po(lizei),* secret state police.]

ges·ta·tion (jĕ-stā′shən) ►*n.* The period of development in the uterus from conception until birth; pregnancy. [< Lat. *gestāre,* bear.] —**ges′tate′** *v.* —**ges·ta′tion·al** *adj.*

ges·tic·u·late (jĕ-stĭk′yə-lāt′) ►*v.* **-lat·ed, -lat·ing** To make gestures, esp. while speaking. [< Lat. *gesticulus,* dim. of *gestus,* GESTURE.] —**ges·tic′u·la′tive** *adj.* —**ges·tic′u·la′tor** *n.*

ges·tic·u·la·tion (jĕ-stĭk′yə-lā′shən) ►*n.* **1.** The action of gesticulating. **2.** An emphatic gesture.

ges·ture (jĕs′chər) ►*n.* **1.** A motion of the limbs or body made to express thought or to emphasize speech. **2.** An act or remark made as a sign of intention or attitude. [< Lat. *gestus* < p.part. of *gerere,* behave.] —**ges′ture** *v.*

ge·sund·heit (gə-zŏont′hīt′) ►*interj.* Used to wish good health to a person who has just sneezed. [Ger., health.]

get (gĕt) ►*v.* **got** (gŏt), **got·ten** (gŏt′n) or **got, get·ting** **1.** To receive: *got a present from a friend.* **2a.** To go after and bring. **b.** To buy. **3a.** To obtain or acquire: *get knowledge from a book.* **b.** To earn. **4.** To capture. **5.** To reach or catch: *get the bus.* **6.** To contract; catch: *get the flu.* **7.** To understand: *They don't get your point.* **8.** To become aware of by one of the senses: *get a whiff of perfume.* **9.** To cause to be in a specific condition: *got the shirt clean.* **10a.** To cause to move or go: *Get me out of here!* **b.** To go or come: *We'll get to the hotel at noon.* **11.** To prevail upon: *Get him to come early.* **12a.** To puzzle or annoy: *His cold manner gets me.* **b.** To take revenge on: *I'll get you for that.* **c.** *Informal* To hit or strike: *The bullet got him in the arm.* **13.** To begin: *Let's get working on this.* **14.** To become or be: *Get well* soon. **15.** Used in the present perfect: **a.** To have or possess: *I've got lots of friends.* **b.** To have as an obligation: *You've got to see this.* ►*n.* Progeny; offspring. —*phrasal verbs:* **get across** To make or be understandable. **get along 1.** To be on friendly terms. **2.** To manage with reasonable success. **get around 1.** To evade or circumvent. **2.** To become known; circulate. **get away** To escape. **get by** To manage; survive. **get into** To be interested or involved in: *got into computers.* **get off 1.** To write and send. **2.** To escape from punishment. **get on 1.** To be on friendly terms. **2.** To make progress; continue. **get out 1.** To leave or escape. **2.** To become public: *The secret got out.* **get over** To recover from. **get through** To finish or complete. **get to 1.** To start to deal with: *finally got to the housework.* **2.** To annoy. **get up 1.** To arise, as from bed. **2.** To create or organize. **3.** To find within oneself: *got up the courage to speak.* —*idioms:* **get around to** To find the time for. **get away with** To escape the consequences of. **get even** To obtain revenge. **get somewhere** *Informal* To make progress. [< ON *geta*.]

get·a·way (gĕt′ə-wā′) ►*n.* **1.** An act of escaping. **2.** The start, as of a race.

get-to·geth·er (gĕt′tə-gĕth′ər) ►*n. Informal* A casual social gathering.

Get·tys·burg (gĕt′ēz-bûrg′) A town of S PA; site of a Union victory in the Civil War (July 1–3, 1863).

get-up (gĕt′ŭp′) ►*n.* An outfit or costume.

gew·gaw (gyōō′gô′, gōō′-) ►*n.* A trinket; bauble. [ME *giuegaue.*]

gey·ser (gī′zər) ►*n.* A natural hot spring that intermittently ejects a column of water and steam into the air. [< ON *geysa*, gush.]

Gha·na (gä′nə, găn′ə) A country of W Africa on the N shore of the Gulf of Guinea. Cap. Accra. —**Gha′na·ian** (gä′nə-yən, gə-nā′ən), **Gha′ni·an** (gä′nē-ən) *adj.* & *n.*

ghast·ly (găst′lē) ►*adj.* **-li·er, -li·est 1.** Causing shock or revulsion; terrifying. **2.** Resembling ghosts. **3.** Extremely unpleasant. [< ME *gasten*, terrify; see AGHAST.] —**ghast′li·ness** *n.*

gher·kin (gûr′kĭn) ►*n.* A small cucumber, esp. one used for pickling. [< Du. *agurk.*]

ghet·to (gĕt′ō) ►*n., pl.* **-tos** or **-toes 1.** A usu. poor section of a city inhabited primarily by people of the same race, religion, or social background, often because of discrimination. **2.** An often walled quarter in a European city to which Jews were restricted beginning in the Middle Ages. [Ital.]

ghet·to·ize (gĕt′ō-īz′) ►*v.* **-ized, -iz·ing** To set apart in or as if in a ghetto. —**ghet′to·i·za′tion** *n.*

ghost (gōst) ►*n.* **1.** The spirit of a dead person, esp. one believed to haunt living persons. **2.** A faint trace. **3.** A faint false image produced along with the correct television or photographic image. **4.** *Informal* A ghostwriter. ►*v. Informal* To ghostwrite. [< OE *gāst*, spirit.] —**ghost′ly** *adj.*

ghost town ►*n.* A once thriving town, esp. a boomtown of the American West, that has been completely abandoned.

ghost·writ·er (gōst′rī′tər) ►*n.* One who writes for and gives credit of authorship to another. —**ghost′write′** *v.*

ghoul (gōōl) ►*n.* **1.** One who delights in the revolting, morbid, or loathsome. **2.** A grave robber. **3.** An evil spirit in Muslim folklore believed to plunder graves and feed on corpses. [Ar. *ġūl.*] —**ghoul′ish** *adj.* —**ghoul′ish·ly** *adv.*

GHQ ►*abbr.* general headquarters

gi or **gi.** ►*abbr.* gill (liquid measure)

GI[1] (jē′ī′) ►*n.* An enlisted person in or a veteran of the US armed forces. [Abbr. of *government issue.*] —**GI** *adj.*

GI[2] ►*abbr.* **1.** gastrointestinal **2.** general issue **3.** Government Issue

gi·ant (jī′ənt) ►*n.* **1.** A person of great size, power, or importance. **2.** *Myth.* A human-like being of enormous strength and stature. ►*adj.* Of exceptionally great size, magnitude, or power: *a giant wave.* [< Gk. *gigas.*]

gi·ant·ess (jī′ən-tĭs) ►*n.* A female giant.

gib·ber·ish (jĭb′ər-ĭsh) ►*n.* **1.** Unintelligible or nonsensical talk or writing. **2.** Unnecessarily pretentious or vague language. [Prob. *gibber*, speak nonsense + –ISH.] —**gib′ber** *v.*

gib·bet (jĭb′ĭt) ►*n.* A gallows. ►*v.* **-bet·ed, -bet·ing** or **-bet·ted, -bet·ting 1.** To execute by hanging on a gibbet. **2.** To expose to public ridicule. [< OFr. *gibe*, staff.]

gib·bon (gĭb′ən) ►*n.* Any of several small arboreal apes of SE Asia, having a slender body, long arms, and no tail. [Fr.]

Gibbon, Edward 1737–94. British historian.

gib·bous (gĭb′əs) ►*adj.* More than half but less than fully illuminated: *the gibbous moon.* [< Lat. *gibbus*, hump.] —**gib′bous·ly** *adv.*

gibe also **jibe** (jīb) ►*v.* **gibed, gib·ing** also **jibed, jib·ing** To make taunting, heckling, or jeering remarks. [Poss. < OFr. *giber*, handle roughly.] —**gibe** *n.* —**gib′er** *n.* —**gib′ing·ly** *adv.*

gib·lets (jĭb′lĭts) ►*pl.n.* The edible heart, liver, or gizzard of a fowl. [< OFr. *gibelet*, game stew.]

Gi·bral·tar (jə-brôl′tər) A British colony centered on the **Rock of Gibraltar,** a peninsula on the S-central coast of Spain in the **Strait of Gibraltar,** connecting the Mediterranean and the Atlantic between Spain and N Africa.

Gib·ran (jə-brän′), **(Gibran) Kahlil** 1883–1931. Amer. mystic poet and painter born in the Ottoman Empire.

Gib·son (gĭb′sən), **Althea** 1927–2003. Amer. tennis player.

Althea Gibson
photographed in 1957

gid·dy (gĭd′ē) ►*adj.* **-di·er, -di·est 1a.** Dizzy. **b.** Causing dizziness: *a giddy climb.* **2.** Frivolous; flighty: *giddy with excitement.* ►*v.* **-died, -dy·ing** To become or make giddy. [< OE *gidig.*] —**gid′di·ly** *adv.* —**gid′di·ness** *n.*

gift (gĭft) ►*n.* **1.** Something bestowed voluntarily and without compensation. **2.** The act, right, or power of giving. **3.** A talent or aptitude: *has a gift for singing.* ►*v.* **1.** To present something as a gift to (someone). **2.** To give (something) as a gift. [< ON.]

gift·ed (gĭf′tĭd) ►*adj.* **1.** Endowed with great natural ability, intelligence, or talent: *a gifted pianist.* **2.** Revealing special talent. —**gift′ed·ly** *adv.*

gig¹ (gĭg) ►*n.* **1.** A light, two-wheeled horse-drawn carriage. **2.** A long, light ship's boat. [< obsolete *gig,* spinning top.]

gig² (gĭg) ►*n.* A pronged spear for fishing. [< *fishgig,* spear for fishing.] —**gig** *v.*

gig³ (gĭg) ►*n. Slang* A demerit given in the military. [?] —**gig** *v.*

gig⁴ (gĭg) ►*n. Slang* A job, esp. a booking for musicians. [?]

gig⁵ (gĭg, jĭg) ►*n. Informal* A gigabyte.

giga– ►*pref.* **1.** One billion (10^9): *gigahertz.* **2.** 1,073,741,824 (2^{30}): *gigabyte.* [< Gk. *gigas,* giant.]

gig·a·bit (gĭg′ə-bĭt′, jĭg′-) ►*n. Comp.* **1.** One billion bits. **2.** 1,073,741,824 (2^{30}) bits.

gig·a·byte (gĭg′ə-bīt′, jĭg′-) ►*n.* **1.** A unit of computer memory or data storage capacity equal to 1,024 megabytes (2^{30} bytes). **2.** One billion bytes.

gig·a·hertz (gĭg′ə-hûrtz′, jĭg′-) ►*n.* One billion cycles per second.

gi·gan·tic (jī-găn′tĭk) ►*adj.* Extremely large or extensive; huge. [< Gk. *gigas, gigant-,* giant.] —**gi·gan′ti·cal·ly** *adv.*

gig·gle (gĭg′əl) ►*v.* **-gled, -gling** To laugh with repeated short, spasmodic sounds. [Imit.] —**gig′gle** *n.* —**gig′gler** *n.* —**gig′gly** *adj.*

gig·o·lo (jĭg′ə-lō′, zhĭg′-) ►*n., pl.* **-los 1.** A man supported financially by a usu. older woman in return for sexual favors. **2.** A professional male escort. [Fr.]

Gi·la monster (hē′lə) ►*n.* A large stocky venomous lizard of SW US and W Mexico. [After the Gila River.]

Gila River A river rising in the mountains of W NM and flowing about 1,050 km (650 mi) across S AZ to the Colorado R.

Gil·bert (gĭl′bərt), Sir **William Schwenck** 1836–1911. British playwright and lyricist.

gild (gĭld) ►*v.* **gild·ed** or **gilt** (gĭlt), **gild·ing 1.** To cover with or as if with a thin layer of gold. **2.** To give an often deceptively attractive appearance to. [< OE *gyldan.*]

Gil·e·ad (gĭl′ē-əd) A mountainous region of ancient Palestine E of the Jordan R.

gill¹ (gĭl) ►*n.* The respiratory organ of most aquatic animals that obtain oxygen from water. [ME *gile.*] —**gilled** *adj.*

gill² (jĭl) ►*n.* **1.** See table at **measurement. 2.** A unit of volume or capacity equal to ¼ of a British Imperial pint (142 ml). [< LLat. *gillō,* vessel.]

gil·ly·flow·er (jĭl′ē-flou′ər) ►*n.* A carnation or other plant with fragrant flowers. [< Gk. *karuophullon,* clove.]

gilt (gĭlt) ►*v.* P.t. and p.part. of **gild.** ►*adj.* Gilded.

►*n.* A thin layer of gold or goldlike material applied in gilding.

gilt-edged (gĭlt′ějd′) ►*adj.* **1.** Having gilded edges, as book pages. **2.** Of the highest quality or value: *gilt-edged securities.*

gim·bal (gĭm′bəl, jĭm′-) ►*n.* **1.** A rigid frame or ring in which an object is supported by pivots. Two such rings mounted on axes at right angles to each other can allow an object such as a ship's compass to remain suspended in a horizontal plane between them regardless of any motion of its support. **2.** often **gimbals** A device consisting of gimbals. [< Lat. *gemellus,* twin.]

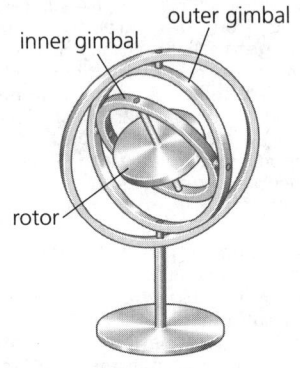

gimbal
a gyroscope with two gimbals

gim·crack (jĭm′krăk′) ►*n.* A cheap showy object of little or no use. [Poss. < ME *gibecrake,* ornament.] —**gim′crack′er·y** *n.*

gim·let (gĭm′lĭt) ►*n.* **1.** A small hand tool for boring holes. **2.** A cocktail of vodka or gin and sweetened lime juice. [< AN *guimbelet.*]

gim·mick (gĭm′ĭk) ►*n.* **1.** A device employed to cheat, deceive, or trick. **2a.** A stratagem used esp. to promote a project. **b.** A significant feature that is obscured or misrepresented; catch. [?] —**gim′mick·ry** *n.* —**gim′mick·y** *adj.*

gimp (gĭmp) ►*n. Slang* A limp or limping gait. [?] —**gimp** *v.* —**gimp′y** *adj.*

gin¹ (jĭn) ►*n.* A strong, colorless alcoholic liquor distilled from grain spirits and flavored usu. with juniper berries. [< VLat. **iiniperus,* JUNIPER.] —**gin′ny** *adj.*

gin² (jĭn) ►*n.* **1.** A snare or trap for game. **2.** A cotton gin. ►*v.* **ginned, gin·ning** To remove the seeds from (cotton) with a cotton gin. [< OFr. < *engin,* skill; see ENGINE.]

gin³ (jĭn) ►*n.* Gin rummy.

gin·ger (jĭn′jər) ►*n.* The pungent aromatic rhizome of a plant from SE Asia, used fresh or ground as a spice. [< Gk. *zingiberis.*]

ginger ale ►*n.* A carbonated soft drink flavored with ginger.

gin·ger·bread (jĭn′jər-brěd′) ►*n.* **1.** A dark molasses cake flavored with ginger. **2.** Elaborate ornamentation, esp. in architecture.

gin·ger·ly (jĭn′jər-lē) ►*adv.* With great care; cautiously. [Poss. < OFr. *gensor,* gentler.] —**gin′ger·li·ness** *n.* —**gin′ger·ly** *adj.*

gin·ger·snap (jĭn′jər-snăp′) ►*n.* A flat brittle cookie spiced with ginger and sweetened with molasses.

ging·ham (gĭng′əm) ►*n.* A yarn-dyed cotton

fabric usu. woven in checks, plaids, or stripes. [< Malay *genggang, ginggang.*]

gin·gi·va (jĭn′jə-və, jĭn-jī′-) ►*n.*, *pl.* **-vae** (-vē′) See **gum²**. [< Lat. *gingīva.*]

gin·gi·vi·tis (jĭn′jə-vī′tĭs) ►*n.* Inflammation of the gums.

gink·go also **ging·ko** (gĭng′kō) ►*n.*, *pl.* **-goes** also **-koes** A Chinese tree having fan-shaped leaves used in herbal medicine. [Obsolete J. *ginkyō,* ginkgo (literally, silver apricot).]

gin rummy ►*n.* A variety of rummy in which a player may win by matching all his or her cards or may end the game by melding.

Gins·berg (gĭnz′bərg), **(Irwin) Allen** 1926–97. Amer. poet.

gin·seng (jĭn′sĕng′) ►*n.* A plant of E Asia or North America, having forked roots used in herbal medicine. [Mandarin *rén shēn.*]

Giot·to (jŏt′ō, jô′tō) 1267?–1337. Florentine painter.

Gip·sy (jĭp′sē) ►*n.* Var. of **Gypsy**.

gi·raffe (jə-răf′) ►*n.*, *pl.* **-raffes** or **-raffe** An African ruminant with a long neck and legs, a tan coat with orange-brown blotches, and short horns. [< Ar. dial. *zirāfa.*]

gird (gûrd) ►*v.* **gird·ed** or **girt** (gûrt), **gird·ing** **1.** To encircle or fasten with a belt or band. **2.** To surround. **3.** To prepare (oneself) for action. [< OE *gyrdan.*]

gird·er (gûr′dər) ►*n.* A strong beam used as a main horizontal support in building.

gir·dle (gûr′dl) ►*n.* **1.** A belt or sash worn around the waist. **2.** An elasticized, flexible undergarment worn over the waist and hips to give the body a more slender appearance. ►*v.* **-dled, -dling** To encircle with or as if with a belt. [< OE *gyrdel.*] —**gird′ler** n.

girl (gûrl) ►*n.* A female child or youth. [ME *girle.*] —**girl′hood′** n. —**girl′ish** adj. —**girl′-ish·ly** adv. —**girl′ish·ness** n.

girl·friend (gûrl′frĕnd′) ►*n.* **1.** A favored female companion or sweetheart. **2.** A female friend.

Girl Scout ►*n.* A member of an organization of young women and girls founded for character development and citizenship training.

girth (gûrth) ►*n.* **1.** The distance around something; circumference. **2.** A strap encircling an animal's body in order to secure a load or saddle. [< ON *gjördh,* girdle.]

Gis·card d'Es·taing (zhĭ-skär′ dĕs-tăng′, -tăɴ′), **Valéry** b. 1926. French president (1974–81).

gist (jĭst) ►*n.* The central idea; essence. See Synonyms at **substance**. [< AN, it lies.]

give (gĭv) ►*v.* **gave** (gāv), **giv·en** (gĭv′ən), **giv·ing** **1.** To make a present of: *We gave her flowers.* **2.** To place in the hands of; pass: *Give me the scissors.* **3.** To deliver in exchange or recompense; pay: *give five dollars for the book.* **4.** To administer: *gave him some medicine.* **5a.** To convey: *Give her my best wishes.* **b.** To inflict, esp. as punishment: *She gave me a bloody nose.* **6.** To grant or bestow: *give permission.* **7.** To furnish or contribute: *gave time to help others.* **8.** To emit or utter: *gave a groan.* **9.** To submit for consideration or opinion: *give me your opinion.* **10.** To offer as entertainment: *give a party.* **11.** To cause to catch: *The draft gave me a cold.* **12.** To yield or produce: *Cows give milk.* **13.** To permit one to have or take: *Give me an hour to get ready.* ►*n.* Resilience; springiness. —*phrasal verbs:* **give away 1.** To make a gift of. **2.** To

present (a bride) to the bridegroom at a wedding ceremony. **3.** To expose or betray. **give back** To return. **give in** To surrender; yield. **give off** To send forth; emit: *The radiator gave off heat.* **give out 1.** To distribute. **2.** To break down. **3.** To become used up. **give up 1.** To surrender. **2.** To stop: *gave up smoking.* **3.** To part with; relinquish. —*idiom:* **give way 1.** To yield the right of way. **2.** To collapse. [< OE *giefan* and ON *gefa.*] —**giv′er** n.

give-and-take (gĭv′ən-tāk′) ►*n.* **1.** The practice of compromise. **2.** Lively exchange of ideas or conversation.

give·a·way (gĭv′ə-wā′) ►*n.* **1.** An inadvertent revealing of something that is meant to be concealed. **2.** Something given away at no charge.

giv·en (gĭv′ən) ►*v.* P.part. of **give**. ►*adj.* **1.** Specified; fixed: *meet at a given time.* **2.** Granted as a supposition; acknowledged or assumed. **3.** Having a tendency; inclined: *given to lavish spending.* —**giv′en** n.

given name ►*n.* A name given at birth or at baptism as distinguished from a surname.

Gi·za (gē′zə) A city of N Egypt on the Nile R. near Cairo; site of the Great Pyramids and the Sphinx.

giz·zard (gĭz′ərd) ►*n.* A digestive organ in birds, often containing ingested grit. [< Lat. *gigēria,* cooked entrails of poultry.]

Gk. ►*abbr.* Greek

gla·cial (glā′shəl) ►*adj.* **1.** Relating to or produced by a glacier. **2.** Very slow, like a glacier's movement: *a glacial pace.* **3.** Marked or dominated by the existence of glaciers: *a glacial epoch.* **4.** Extremely cold. See Synonyms at **cold**. [< Lat. *glaciālis,* icy < *glaciēs,* ice.] —**gla′cial·ly** adv.

gla·ci·ate (glā′shē-āt′, -sē-) ►*v.* **-at·ed, -at·ing** **1.** To subject to glacial action. **2.** To freeze. [< Lat. *glaciēs,* ice.] —**gla′ci·a′tion** n.

gla·cier (glā′shər) ►*n.* A huge mass of ice slowly flowing over a landmass, formed from compacted snow. [< Lat. *glaciēs,* ice.]

glad (glăd) ►*adj.* **glad·der, glad·dest 1.** Experiencing, showing, or giving joy and pleasure. **2.** Very willing: *glad to help.* [< OE *glæd.*] —**glad′ly** adv. —**glad′ness** n.

glad·den (glăd′n) ►*v.* To make glad. See Synonyms at **please**.

glade (glād) ►*n.* An open space in a forest. [ME, perh. < *glad,* shining; see GLAD.]

glad hand ►*n.* *Informal* A hearty but often insincere greeting. —**glad′-hand′** v.

glad·i·a·tor (glăd′ē-ā′tər) ►*n.* A man trained to entertain the public by engaging in mortal combat in ancient Roman arenas. [< Lat. *gladius,* sword.] —**glad′i·a·to′ri·al** (-ə-tôr′-ē-əl) adj.

glad·i·o·lus (glăd′ē-ō′ləs) ►*n.*, *pl.* **-li** (-lī, -lē) or **-lus·es** Any of a genus of plants having sword-shaped leaves and showy, variously colored flowers. [< Lat., wild iris, dim. of *gladius,* sword.]

glad·some (glăd′səm) ►*adj.* Causing or showing gladness or joy. —**glad′some·ly** adv.

Glad·stone (glăd′stōn′, -stən), **William Ewart** 1809–98. British prime minister (1868–74, 1880–85, 1886, and 1892–94).

glam·or·ize also **glam·our·ize** (glăm′ə-rīz′) ►*v.* **-ized, -iz·ing** To make glamorous. —**glam′or·i·za′tion** n. —**glam′or·iz′er** n.

glam·our also **glam·or** (glăm′ər) ►*n.* Exciting or mysterious attractiveness usu. associated with striking physical beauty, luxury, or celebrity. [Sc., magic spell, alteration of GRAMMAR.] —**glam′or·ous** *adj.* —**glam′or·ous·ly** *adv.*

glance (glăns) ►*v.* **glanced, glanc·ing 1a.** To direct the gaze briefly: *glanced in the mirror.* **b.** To read quickly: *glanced at the menu.* **2a.** To strike (a surface) and be deflected: *The arrow glanced the target but didn't stick. A pebble glanced off the windshield.* See Synonyms at **brush**¹. **b.** To be reflected, esp. in flashes: *sunlight glanced off the water.* ►*n.* **1.** A brief or cursory look. **2.** A gleam. [ME *glauncen* < OFr. *glacer*, to slide.]

glanc·ing (glăn′sĭng) ►*adj.* **1.** Oblique in direction; deflected. **2.** Not straightforward; indirect. —**glanc′ing·ly** *adv.*

gland (glănd) ►*n.* An organ or group of cells that secretes a substance, such as a hormone, that is used or excreted by the body. [< Lat. *glāns, gland-*, acorn.] —**glan′du·lar** (glăn′jə-lər) *adj.* —**glan′du·lar·ly** *adv.*

glans (glănz) ►*n., pl.* **glan·des** (glăn′dēz) The tip of the penis or clitoris. [Lat. *glāns*, acorn.]

glare (glâr) ►*v.* **glared, glar·ing 1.** To stare fixedly and angrily. **2.** To shine intensely and blindingly. **3.** To stand out obtrusively: *a headline that glared from the page.* ►*n.* **1.** A fierce or angry stare. **2.** An intense, blinding light: *the glare of the spotlights.* **3.** Overwhelming attention or intrusiveness: *the glare of publicity.* [ME *glaren*, glitter.]

glar·ing (glâr′ĭng) ►*adj.* **1.** Shining intensely: *the glaring sun.* **2.** Conspicuous; obvious: *a glaring error.* **3.** Staring with anger or hostility. —**glar′ing·ly** *adv.*

Glas·gow (glăs′kō, -gō, glăz′-) A city of SW Scotland on the Clyde R.

glas·nost (glăs′nəst, -nôst) ►*n.* An official policy of the former Soviet government emphasizing candid discussion of social problems. [Russ. *glasnost′*, public information.]

glass (glăs) ►*n.* **1.** Any of a large class of materials that solidify from the molten state without crystallization, are gen. transparent or translucent, and are considered to be supercooled liquids rather than true solids. **2.** Something usu. made of glass, esp.: **a.** A drinking vessel. **b.** A mirror. **c.** A window or windowpane. **3. glasses** A pair of lenses mounted in a light frame, used to correct faulty vision or protect the eyes. **4.** The quantity contained by a drinking vessel; glassful. [< OE *glæs*.] —**glass′i·ly** *adv.* —**glass′i·ness** *n.* —**glass′y** *adj.*

glass ceiling ►*n.* An unofficial discriminatory barrier that keeps women and minorities from positions of power, as in a corporation.

glass eel ►*n.* An eel in its transparent, post-larval stage.

glau·co·ma (glou-kō′mə, glô-) ►*n.* An eye disease marked by abnormally high intraocular fluid pressure, optic disk damage, and gradual vision loss. [< Gk. *glaukōma*, cataract.]

glau·cous (glô′kəs) ►*adj.* Of a pale grayish green. [Lat. *glaucus* < Gk. *glaukos*.]

glaze (glāz) ►*n.* **1.** A thin, smooth, shiny coating, as on ceramics. **2.** A thin glassy coating of ice. **3.** A coating, as of syrup, applied to food. ►*v.* **glazed, glaz·ing 1.** To furnish with glass: *glaze a window.* **2.** To apply a glaze to: *glaze a doughnut.* **3.** To become glassy: *His eyes glazed over from boredom.* [ME *glasen* < *glas*, GLASS.]

gla·zier (glā′zhər) ►*n.* One that cuts and fits glass, as for windows. —**gla′zier·y** *n.*

gleam (glēm) ►*n.* **1.** A brief flash of light. **2.** A steady but subdued shining; glow. **3.** A brief or dim indication: *a gleam of intelligence.* ►*v.* **1.** To flash or glow. **2.** To be reflected as a gleam: *The sun gleamed on the water.* **3.** To be manifested briefly or faintly. [< OE *glǣm*.]

glean (glēn) ►*v.* **1.** To gather grain left behind by reapers. **2.** To collect bit by bit. [< LLat. *glennāre*.] —**glean′er** *n.* —**glean′ings** *pl.n.*

glee (glē) ►*n.* **1.** Jubilant delight; joy. **2.** An unaccompanied choral song. [< OE *glēo*.] —**glee′ful** *adj.* —**glee′ful·ly** *adv.*

glee club ►*n.* A group of singers who perform usu. short pieces of choral music.

glen (glĕn) ►*n.* A valley. [< OIr. *glenn*.]

Glenn (glĕn), **John Herschel, Jr.** b. 1921. Amer. astronaut and politician.

gli·a·din (glī′ə-dĭn) ►*n.* Any of several proteins that are a component of wheat gluten and can cause celiac disease by inducing a destructive immune response in the small intestine of susceptible individuals. [Ult. < Med.Gr. *glia*, glue.]

glib (glĭb) ►*adj.* **glib·ber, glib·best 1.** Performed with a natural, offhand ease: *glib conversation.* **2.** Characterized by fluency of speech or writing that often suggests insincerity, superficiality, or a lack of concern. [Poss. of LGer. orig.] —**glib′ly** *adv.* —**glib′ness** *n.*

glide (glīd) ►*v.* **glid·ed, glid·ing 1.** To move smoothly and effortlessly. **2.** To fly without propulsion. ►*n.* **1.** The act of gliding. **2.** *Ling.* **a.** The sound made by passing from the position of one speech sound to another. **b.** See **semivowel.** [< OE *glīdan*.]

glid·er (glī′dər) ►*n.* **1.** A light engineless aircraft designed to glide after being towed aloft. **2.** A swinging couch suspended from a vertical frame.

glider

glim·mer (glĭm′ər) ►*n.* **1.** A dim or unsteady flicker or flash of light. **2.** A faint suggestion or indication. ►*v.* **1.** To give off a dim, intermittent light. **2.** To be reflected in dim, intermittent flashes: *Starlight glimmered on the pond.* **3.** To appear faintly. [< ME *glimeren*, to glitter.]

glimpse (glĭmps) ►*n.* A brief, incomplete look. ►*v.* **glimpsed, glimps·ing** To get a glimpse of. [< ME *glimsen*, to glance.]

glint (glĭnt) ►*n.* A brief flash of light; sparkle. [ME *glent*.] —**glint** *v.*

glis·san·do (glĭ-sän′dō) ►*n., pl.* **-di** (-dē) or **-dos** A rapid slide through a series of consecutive musical tones. [< Fr. *glissade*, a sliding.]

glis·ten (glĭs′ən) ►*v.* **1.** To shine with reflected

light. **2.** To be reflected with a sparkling luster. [< OE *glisnian*.] —**glis′ten** *n.*

glitch (glĭch) ►*n.* **1.** A minor malfunction; snag: *a computer glitch.* **2.** A false electronic signal caused by a brief power surge. [Yiddish *glitsh*, a slip.]

glit·ter (glĭt′ər) ►*n.* **1.** A sparkling or glistening light. **2.** Showy, often superficial attractiveness. **3.** Small pieces of reflective decorative material. ►*v.* **1.** To sparkle brilliantly; glisten. **2.** To be reflected as a sparkling or glistening light: *The sun glittered on the snow.* [< ON *glitra*, to sparkle.] —**glit′ter·y** *adj.*

glitz (glĭts) ►*n. Informal* Ostentatious showiness; flashiness. [Prob. < Ger. *glitzern*, to glitter.] —**glitz′i·ness** *n.* —**glitz′y** *adj.*

gloam·ing (glō′mĭng) ►*n.* Twilight; dusk. [< OE *glōm.*]

gloat (glōt) ►*v.* To feel or express great, often malicious, pleasure or self-satisfaction. [Perh. of Scand. orig.] —**gloat′er** *n.*

glob (glŏb) ►*n.* **1.** A globule. **2.** A soft lump or mass. [< Lat. *globus*, globular mass.]

glob·al (glō′bəl) ►*adj.* **1.** Involving the entire earth; worldwide. **2.** Comprehensive; total. **3.** *Comp.* Relating to an entire program, file, or document. —**glob′al·i·za′tion** *n.* —**glob′al·ize′** *v.* —**glob′al·ly** *adv.*

Global Positioning System ►*n.* A system for determining one's position on the earth by comparing radio signals received from different satellites.

global warming ►*n.* An increase in the average temperature of the earth's atmosphere, esp. one sufficient to cause climatic change.

globe (glōb) ►*n.* **1.** A spherical body, esp. a model of the earth as a hollow ball. **2.** The earth. **3.** A spherical or bowllike object. [< Lat. *globus.*]

globe·trot (glōb′trŏt′) ►*v.* To travel widely, esp. for sightseeing. —**globe′trot′ter** *n.*

glob·u·lar (glŏb′yə-lər) ►*adj.* **1.** Spherical. **2.** Consisting of globules. —**glob′u·lar·ly** *adv.*

glob·ule (glŏb′yo͞ol) ►*n.* A small spherical mass, as of liquid. [< Lat. *globulus.*]

glob·u·lin (glŏb′yə-lĭn) ►*n.* A protein found extensively in blood plasma, muscle, milk, and plant seeds.

glock·en·spiel (glŏk′ən-spēl′, -shpēl′) ►*n.* A percussion instrument with a series of metal bars played with two light hammers. [Ger.]

gloom (glo͞om) ►*n.* **1.** Partial or total darkness. **2.** A state of melancholy or depression. [Prob. < ME *gloumen*, become dark.]

gloom·y (glo͞o′mē) ►*adj.* **-i·er, -i·est 1.** Partially or totally dark: *a damp, gloomy day.* **2.** Showing or filled with gloom: *gloomy faces.* **3.** Causing gloom; depressing: *gloomy news.* —**gloom′i·ly** *adv.* —**gloom′i·ness** *n.*

glo·ri·fy (glôr′ə-fī′) ►*v.* **-fied, -fy·ing 1.** To give honor or high praise to; exalt. **2.** To exaggerate the glory or excellence of. **3.** To worship; extol. [< Lat. *glōrificāre.*] —**glo′ri·fi·ca′tion** *n.* —**glo′ri·fi′er** *n.*

glo·ri·ous (glôr′ē-əs) ►*adj.* **1.** Having or deserving glory; famous. **2.** Splendid; magnificent: *a glorious sunset.* —**glo′ri·ous·ly** *adv.*

glo·ry (glôr′ē) ►*n., pl.* **-ries 1.** Great honor or distinction; renown. **2.** A highly praiseworthy asset. **3.** Adoration and praise offered in worship. **4.** Majestic beauty: *The sun set in a blaze of*

glory. **5.** A height of achievement, enjoyment, or prosperity. ►*v.* **-ried, -ry·ing** To rejoice triumphantly; exult. [< Lat. *glōria.*]

gloss¹ (glôs, glŏs) ►*n.* **1.** A surface shininess or luster. **2.** A kind of paint that dries to a shiny finish. **3.** A cosmetic that adds shine or luster. **4.** A superficially attractive appearance. ►*v.* **1.** To make attractive or acceptable esp. by superficial treatment: *glossed over the candidate's faults.* **2.** To apply a gloss to: *glossed her lips.* [Perh. of Scand. orig.]

gloss² (glôs, glŏs) ►*n.* **1.** A brief explanatory note or translation of a difficult or technical expression. **2.** A translation or commentary accompanying a text. ►*v.* To provide (e.g., a text) with a gloss. [< LLat. *glōssa*, foreign word < Gk., language.] —**gloss′er** *n.*

glos·sa·ry (glô′sə-rē, glŏs′ə-) ►*n., pl.* **-ries** A list of difficult or specialized words with their definitions. [< Lat. *glōssārium.*]

gloss·y (glô′sē, glŏs′ē) ►*adj.* **-i·er, -i·est 1.** Having a smooth shiny surface: *glossy satin.* **2.** Superficially attractive; showy. ►*n., pl.* **-ies** A photographic print on smooth shiny paper. —**gloss′i·ly** *adv.* —**gloss′i·ness** *n.*

glot·tal stop (glŏt′l) ►*n.* A speech sound produced by a momentary complete closure of the glottis, followed by an explosive release.

glot·tis (glŏt′ĭs) ►*n., pl.* **-tis·es** or **glot·ti·des** (glŏt′ĭ-dēz′) The opening between the vocal cords at the upper part of the larynx. [Gk. *glōttis* < *glōtta*, tongue.]

glove (glŭv) ►*n.* **1.** A fitted covering for the hand with a separate sheath for each finger and the thumb. **2.** *Sports* An oversized padded leather covering for the hand, esp. one used in baseball or boxing. [< OE *glōf.*] —**glove** *v.*

glow (glō) ►*v.* **1.** To shine brightly and steadily, esp. without a flame: *The embers glowed.* **2.** To have a bright ruddy color: *Their cheeks glowed from the cold.* **3.** To be exuberant or radiant: *glowing with pride.* ►*n.* **1.** A light produced by a heated body. **2.** Brilliance or warmth of color. **3.** A warm feeling. [< OE *glōwan.*] —**glow′ing** *adj.*

glow·er (glou′ər) ►*v.* To look or stare angrily or sullenly. See Synonyms at **frown.** [ME *gloren.*] —**glow′er** *n.* —**glow′er·ing·ly** *adv.*

glow·worm (glō′wûrm′) ►*n.* Any of various luminous female beetles or beetle larvae.

glox·in·i·a (glŏk-sĭn′ē-ə) ►*n.* A tropical South American plant grown as a houseplant for its showy, variously colored flowers. [After Benjamin Peter *Gloxin*, 18th-cent. botanist.]

gloze (glōz) ►*v.* **glozed, gloz·ing** To minimize; gloss: *glozed over the errors.* [< OFr. *gloser* < *glose*, GLOSS².]

glu·ca·gon (glo͞o′kə-gŏn′) ►*n.* A pancreatic hormone that raises blood sugar levels. [Prob. GLUC(OSE) + Gk. *agōn*, pr.part. of *agein*, lead, drive.]

glu·cose (glo͞o′kōs′) ►*n.* **1.** A monosaccharide sugar, $C_6H_{12}O_6$, that occurs widely in most plant and animal tissue and is the major energy source of the body. **2.** A syrupy mixture of dextrose and maltose with water, used in confectionery and alcoholic fermentation. [< Gk. *gleukos*, sweet wine.]

glue (glo͞o) ►*n.* **1.** A strong liquid adhesive, esp. one made from animal parts. **2.** An adhesive force or factor. ►*v.* **glued, glu·ing 1.** To stick or fasten with or as if with glue. **2.** To fasten on something attentively: *Our eyes were glued to the TV.* [< Lat. *glūten*.] —**glu′ey** *adj.*

glum (glŭm) ▸*adj.* **glum·mer, glum·mest** Moody and melancholy; dejected. [Prob. akin to ME *gloumen*, darken.] —**glum′ly** *adv.* —**glum′ness** *n.*

glu·on (glōō′ŏn) ▸*n.* A massless, neutral vector boson that mediates strong interactions between quarks, binding them together within hadrons. [GLU(E) + −ON[1].]

glut (glŭt) ▸*v.* **glut·ted, glut·ting 1.** To fill beyond capacity, esp. with food; satiate. **2.** To flood (a market) so that supply exceeds demand. ▸*n.* An oversupply. [< Lat. *gluttīre*, eat greedily.]

glu·ten (glōōt′n) ▸*n.* A tough, sticky mixture of plant proteins found in cereal grains such as wheat, rye, and barley, sometimes used as a food additive. [< Lat. *glūten*, glue.] —**glu′ten·ous** *adj.*

glu·te·us (glōō′tē-əs, glōō-tē′-) ▸*n., pl.* **-te·i** (-tē-ī′, -tē′ī′) Any of three large muscles of the buttocks. [< Gk. *gloutos*, buttock.] —**glu′te·al** *adj.*

glu·ti·nous (glōōt′n-əs) ▸*adj.* Gluey; sticky. [< Lat. *glūten*, glue.] —**glu′ti·nous·ly** *adv.*

glut·ton (glŭt′n) ▸*n.* One who eats or consumes immoderate amounts. [< Lat. *gluttō*.] —**glut′ton·ous** *adj.* —**glut′ton·y** *n.*

glyc·er·in also **glyc·er·ine** (glĭs′ər-ĭn) ▸*n.* Glycerol. [< Gk. *glukeros*, sweet.]

glyc·er·ol (glĭs′ə-rôl′) ▸*n.* A syrupy liquid from fats and oils used as a solvent, antifreeze, and sweetener and in making dynamite, soaps, and lubricants. [GLYCER(IN) + −OL.]

gly·co·gen (glī′kə-jən) ▸*n.* A polysaccharide, $(C_6H_{10}O_5)_n$, that is the main form of carbohydrate storage in animals and occurs primarily in the liver. [Gk. *glukus*, sweet + −GEN.] —**gly′co·gen′ic** (-jĕn′ĭk) *adj.*

gly·co·gen·e·sis (glī′kə-jĕn′ĭ-sĭs) ▸*n.* The synthesis of glycogen. [Gr. *glukus*, sweet + GEN-ESIS.] —**gly′co·ge·net′ic** (-jə-nĕt′ĭk) *adj.*

gly·co·side (glī′kə-sīd′) ▸*n.* An organic compound that yields a sugar and one or more nonsugar substances when hydrolyzed, occurring abundantly in plants. [*glycose*, a monosaccharide (variant of GLUCOSE) + −IDE.]

glyph (glĭf) ▸*n.* **1.** *Archit.* A vertical groove. **2.** A symbol, as a figure on a sign, that imparts information nonverbally. [Gk. *gluphē*, carving.]

gm. ▸*abbr.* gram

GMO ▸*abbr.* genetically modified organism

GMT ▸*abbr.* Greenwich mean time

gnarl (närl) ▸*n.* A protruding knot on a tree. [< ME *knarre*, knot in wood.] —**gnarled** *adj.*

gnash (năsh) ▸*v.* To grind (the teeth) together. [< ME *gnasten*.]

gnat (năt) ▸*n.* Any of various small flies, esp. those that form swarms. [< OE *gnæt*.]

gnaw (nô) ▸*v.* **1.** To bite or chew on with the teeth. **2.** To erode or diminish gradually as if by gnawing. **3.** To cause persistent worry or pain. [< OE *gnagan*.] —**gnaw′er** *n.*

gneiss (nīs) ▸*n.* A banded, granitelike metamorphic rock. [Ger. *Gneis*.]

GNMA ▸*abbr.* Government National Mortgage Association

gnoc·chi (nyô′kē) ▸*pl.n.* Dumplings made of flour or potatoes. [Ital.]

gnome (nōm) ▸*n.* One of a fabled race of dwarflike creatures who live underground and guard treasure hoards. [< NLat. *gnomus*.]

Gnos·tic (nŏs′tĭk) ▸*adj.* **1. gnostic** Of or relating to intellectual or spiritual knowledge. **2.** Of Gnosticism. [< Gk. *gnōsis*, knowledge.] —**Gnos′tic** *n.*

Gnos·ti·cism (nŏs′tĭ-sĭz′əm) ▸*n.* The doctrines of various esoteric sects in the ancient Near East, teaching that the soul can transcend material existence.

GNP ▸*abbr.* gross national product

gnu (nōō, nyōō) ▸*n.* A large bearded African antelope with curved horns. [< Xhosa *i-ngu*.]

go¹ (gō) ▸*v.* **went** (wĕnt), **gone** (gôn, gŏn), **go·ing, goes** (gōz) **1.** To move or travel. **2.** To move away; depart. **3.** To extend in a certain direction: *The road goes west.* **4.** To function properly: *The car won't go.* **5.** Used to indicate future intent or expectation: *I am going to do it.* **6a.** To continue in a certain condition or continue an activity: *go barefoot all day.* **b.** To become: *go mad.* **7.** To belong: *Where do the plates go?* **8.** To be allotted. **9.** To serve: *It goes to show how it is.* **10.** To elapse, as time. **11.** To be used up. **12.** To be discarded or abolished: *The foolish policy has to go.* **13.** To fail: *Her eyes are going.* **14.** To come apart or break up. **15.** To die. **16.** To get along; fare. **17.** To be suitable; harmonize: *The shirt and tie don't go.* **18.** To participate up to: *go halves on a dessert.* **19.** *Informal* To say. ▸*n., pl.* **goes 1.** An attempt; try: *had a go at it.* **2.** *Informal* Energy; vitality: *had lots of go.* —*phrasal verbs:* **go about** To undertake: *went about my chores.* **go along** To cooperate. **go down 1.** To fall or sink. **2.** To be accepted: *His proposal went down well.* **3.** To be remembered. **go for 1.** To choose or accept: *I went for the cheaper option.* **2.** To try to attain: *She is going for the world record.* **3.** *Informal* To have a liking for: *I really go for jazz.* **go off 1.** To be fired; explode. **2.** To make a noise: *The siren went off at noon.* **go on 1.** To happen. **2.** To continue: *Life goes on.* **3.** To proceed. **go out 1.** To be extinguished. **2.** To socialize outside the home. **3.** To be romantically involved. **4.** To feel sympathy or pity. **go over 1.** To gain acceptance. **2.** To examine. **go through 1.** To examine carefully. **2.** To experience; undergo. **go under** To fail or be ruined. —*idioms:* **go back on** To fail to honor. **go in for** To have an interest in. **go places** *Informal* To be successful. **go steady** To date someone exclusively. **go to pieces** To lose one's self-control. **on the go** Constantly busy. **to go 1.** To be taken out, as restaurant food. **2.** Remaining: *I've got two exams down and two to go.* [< OE *gān*.]

go² (gō) ▸*n.* A board game of Chinese origin. [J., of Chin. orig.]

goad (gōd) ▸*n.* **1.** A long pointed stick for prodding animals. **2.** A means of prodding; stimulus. ▸*v.* To prod or urge. [< OE *gād*.]

go-a·head (gō′ə-hĕd′) ▸*n.* *Informal* Permission to proceed.

goal (gōl) ▸*n.* **1.** A desired purpose; objective. **2.** *Sports* **a.** A structure or area into which players endeavor to propel a ball or puck in order to score points. **b.** The score that is awarded for this. **c.** The finish line of a race. [ME *gol*, boundary.]

goal·ie (gō′lē) ►*n.* See **goalkeeper.**

goal·keep·er (gōl′kē′pər) ►*n.* A player who is assigned to protect the goal in various sports such as soccer.

goal kick ►*n.* A free kick in soccer awarded to a defensive team when the ball has been driven out of bounds over the goal line by an opponent.

goal line ►*n.* **1.** *Sports* A line located at either end of a playing area, on which a goal or goal post is positioned. **2.** *Football* A line at either end of the playing field over which the ball must be moved to score a touchdown.

goat (gōt) ►*n.* **1.** Any of a genus of horned, bearded mammals widely domesticated for wool, milk, and meat. **2.** A lecherous man. [< OE *gāt.*] —**goat′ish** *adj.*

goat antelope ►*n.* Any of various ruminants resembling both goats and antelopes.

goat·ee (gō-tē′) ►*n.* A small chin beard.

goatee

goat·skin (gōt′skĭn′) ►*n.* **1.** The skin of a goat, used for leather. **2.** A container, as for wine, made from goatskin.

gob[1] (gŏb) ►*n.* **1.** A small mass or lump. **2.** often **gobs** *Informal* A large quantity. [Prob. < OFr. *gobe,* mouthful.]

gob[2] (gŏb) ►*n.* *Slang* A sailor. [?]

gob·ble[1] (gŏb′əl) ►*v.* **-bled, -bling 1.** To devour greedily. **2.** To take greedily; grab: *gobble up scarce resources.* [< ME *gobben,* drink greedily; see GOB[1].]

gob·ble[2] (gŏb′əl) ►*n.* The guttural chortling sound of a male turkey. [Imit.] —**gob′ble** *v.*

gob·ble·dy·gook also **gob·ble·de·gook** (gŏb′əl-dē-gŏŏk′) ►*n.* Unclear, wordy jargon. [Imit. of the gobbling of a turkey.]

go-be·tween (gō′bĭ-twēn′) ►*n.* An intermediary between two sides.

Go·bi (gō′bē) A desert of SE Mongolia and N China.

gob·let (gŏb′lĭt) ►*n.* A drinking glass with a stem and base. [< OFr. *gobelet,* small cup.]

gob·lin (gŏb′lĭn) ►*n.* A grotesque elfin creature thought to work mischief or evil. [< Norman Fr. **gobelin,* a famous ghost.]

god (gŏd) ►*n.* **1. God** A being conceived as the perfect, omnipotent, omniscient originator and ruler of the universe, the principal object of faith and worship in monotheistic religions. **2.** A being of supernatural powers, believed in and worshiped by a people. **3.** One that is worshiped or idealized. [< OE.] —**god′hood**′ *n.* —**god′like**′ *adj.*

god·child (gŏd′chīld′) ►*n.* A person for whom another serves as sponsor at baptism.

God·dard (gŏd′ərd), **Robert Hutchings** 1882–1945. Amer. rocketry pioneer.

god·daugh·ter (gŏd′dô′tər) ►*n.* A female godchild.

god·dess (gŏd′ĭs) ►*n.* **1.** A female deity. **2.** A woman of great beauty or grace.

god·fa·ther (gŏd′fä′thər) ►*n.* **1.** A man who sponsors a person at baptism. **2.** *Slang* The leader of an organized crime family.

god·for·sak·en (gŏd′fər-sā′kən) ►*adj.* **1.** Located in a dismal or remote area. **2.** Desolate; forlorn.

god·head (gŏd′hĕd′) ►*n.* Divinity; godhood. [ME *godhede* < OE *godhād.*]

god·less (gŏd′lĭs) ►*adj.* **1.** Recognizing or worshiping no god. **2.** Impious or immoral. **3.** Having no god. —**god′less·ly** *adv.*

god·ly (gŏd′lē) ►*adj.* **-li·er, -li·est 1.** Pious. **2.** Divine. —**god′li·ness** *n.*

god·moth·er (gŏd′mŭth′ər) ►*n.* A woman who sponsors a person at baptism.

god·par·ent (gŏd′pâr′ənt, -păr′-) ►*n.* A godfather or godmother.

god·send (gŏd′sĕnd′) ►*n.* Something wanted or needed that comes unexpectedly.

god·son (gŏd′sŭn′) ►*n.* A male godchild.

Go·du·nov (gŏŏd′n-ôf′), **Boris Fyodorovich** 1551?–1605. Czar of Russia (1598–1605).

goes (gōz) ►*v.* 3rd pers. sing. pr.t. of **go**[1].

Goe·the (gœ′tə), **Johann Wolfgang von** 1749–1832. German writer and scientist.

go-get·ter (gō′gĕt′ər, -gĕt′-) ►*n. Informal* An enterprising person.

gog·gle (gŏg′əl) ►*v.* **-gled, -gling** To stare with wide and bulging eyes. ►*n.* **goggles** Tight-fitting, often tinted eyeglasses worn to protect the eyes, as from wind, water, glare, or flying debris. [ME *gogelen,* squint.] —**gog′gly** *adj.*

go-go (gō′gō′) ►*adj. Informal* Of or relating to discotheques or to the energetic music and dancing performed at discotheques. [< Fr. *à gogo,* galore.]

Go·gol (gô′gəl, gō′gôl), **Nikolai Vasilievich** 1809–52. Russian writer.

go·ing (gō′ĭng) ►*n.* **1.** Departure. **2.** The condition underfoot as it affects walking or riding. **3.** *Informal* Progress toward a goal. ►*adj.* **1.** Working; running. **2.** Current; prevailing: *The going rates are high.* —*idiom:* **going on** Approaching: *The child is six, going on seven years of age.*

goi·ter (goi′tər) ►*n.* A noncancerous enlargement of the thyroid gland, visible as a swelling at the front of the neck. [< Lat. *guttur,* throat.] —**goi′trous** (-trəs) *adj.*

Go·lan Heights (gō′län′) An upland region between NE Israel and SW Syria NE of the Sea of Galilee.

gold (gōld) ►*n.* **1a.** *Symbol* **Au** A soft, yellow, corrosion-resistant, highly malleable and ductile metallic element used as an international monetary standard, in jewelry, for decoration, and as a plated coating on a wide variety of electrical and mechanical components. At. no. 79. See table at **element. b.** Coinage made of gold. **2.** Money; riches. **3.** A moderate to vivid yellow. [< OE.] —**gold** *adj.*

gold·brick (gōld′brĭk′) ►*n. Slang* One who avoids work; shirker. —**gold′brick**′ *v.*

Gold Coast A section of coastal W Africa along the Gulf of Guinea roughly corresponding to present-day Ghana.

gold·en (gōl′dən) ►*adj.* **1.** Made of or containing gold. **2.** Having the color of gold. **3.** Suggestive of gold, as in richness or splendor: *an actor with a golden voice.* **4.** Precious: *golden memories.* **5.** Marked by prosperity: *a golden era.* **6.** Excellent.

golden eagle ►*n.* A large eagle with a brownish-yellow head and neck.

Golden Gate A strait in W CA joining the Pacific and San Francisco Bay.

golden mean ►*n.* The course between extremes.

gold·en·rod (gōl′dən-rŏd′) ►*n.* Any of a genus of North American plants having clusters of small usu. yellow flower heads.

gold·finch (gōld′fĭnch′) ►*n.* **1.** A small American finch having yellow plumage with a black forehead, wings, and tail. **2.** A small Eurasian or African finch having brownish plumage with black-and-yellow wings and a red patch across the face.

gold·fish (gōld′fĭsh′) ►*n.* A typically reddish freshwater Asian carp bred in many ornamental forms as an aquarium fish.

Gold·ing (gōl′dĭng), Sir **William Gerald** 1911–93. British writer.

gold leaf ►*n.* Gold beaten into extremely thin sheets, used for gilding.

Gold·man (gōld′mən), **Emma** 1869–1940. Lithuanian-born Amer. anarchist.

gold rush ►*n.* A rush of migrants to an area where gold has been discovered.

gold·smith (gōld′smĭth′) ►*n.* An artisan who makes or deals in articles of gold.

Goldsmith, Oliver 1730?–74. Irish-born British writer.

gold standard ►*n.* **1.** A monetary standard under which the basic unit of currency is equal in value to a specified amount of gold. **2.** A model of excellence; paragon.

go·lem (gō′ləm) ►*n.* In Jewish folklore, an artificially created human supernaturally endowed with life. [Heb. *gōlem,* fool.]

golf (gŏlf, gôlf) ►*n.* A game played on a 9- or 18-hole course, the object being to hit a small ball with the use of various clubs into each hole with as few strokes as possible. [ME.] —**golf** *v.* —**golf′er** *n.*

golf course ►*n.* A large tract of land laid out for golf.

Gol·go·tha (gŏl′gə-thə, gŏl-gŏth′ə) See **Calvary.**

Go·li·ath (gə-lī′əth) In the Bible, a giant warrior who was slain by David.

Go·mor·rah (gə-môr′ə, -mŏr′ə) An ancient city of Palestine near Sodom.

–gon ►*suff.* A figure having a specified kind or number of angles: *polygon.* [< Gk. *gōniā,* angle.]

go·nad (gō′năd′) ►*n.* An organ in animals that produces gametes, esp. a testis or ovary. [< Gk. *gonos,* procreation.] —**go·nad′al, go·nad′ic** *adj.*

gon·do·la (gŏn′dl-ə, gŏn-dō′lə) ►*n.* **1.** A lightweight narrow barge used on the canals of Venice. **2.** An open shallow freight car with low sides. **3.** A compartment suspended from a balloon or dirigible. **4.** An enclosed pas-senger cabin that moves along an overhead cable. [Ital.]

gon·do·lier (gŏn′dl-îr′) ►*n.* The person who propels a Venetian gondola.

gone (gôn, gŏn) ►*v.* P.part. of **go**¹. ►*adj.* **1.** Missing or lost. **2a.** Used up; exhausted. **b.** Past; bygone. **c.** Dying or dead. **3.** Ruined; lost. **4.** Carried away; absorbed. **5.** *Slang* Infatuated.

gon·er (gô′nər, gŏn′ər) ►*n. Slang* One that is ruined or doomed.

gong (gông, gŏng) ►*n.* A metal disk struck to produce a loud sonorous tone. [Malay *gōng.*]

gon·or·rhe·a (gŏn′ə-rē′ə) ►*n.* A sexually transmitted disease of the genital and urinary tracts, often marked by a purulent discharge and painful or difficult urination. [< Gk. *gonorrhoia.*]

goo (gōo) ►*n. Informal* A sticky, wet, viscous substance. [Perh. < *burgoo,* thick oatmeal gruel.] —**goo′ey** *adj.*

goo·ber (gōo′bər) ►*n. Regional* A peanut. [Of Bantu orig.]

good (gŏod) ►*adj.* **bet·ter** (bĕt′ər), **best** (bĕst) **1.** Being positive or desirable in nature. **2a.** Having desirable qualities. **b.** Suitable; appropriate. **3a.** Not spoiled. **b.** In excellent condition; sound. **4.** Superior to the average: *a good student.* **5a.** Of high quality: *good books.* **b.** Discriminating: *good taste.* **6a.** Virtuous; upright. **b.** Benevolent; kind. **c.** Loyal; staunch. **d.** Well-behaved; obedient. **7.** Beneficial; salutary: *a good night's rest.* **8.** Competent; skilled. **9.** Complete; thorough. **10a.** Reliable; sure. **b.** Valid or true. **c.** Genuine; real. **11.** In effect; operative. **12.** Full: *a good mile away.* **13a.** Pleasant; enjoyable. **b.** Favorable. ►*n.* **1.** Something good. **2.** Welfare; benefit. **3.** Goodness; virtue. **4. goods a.** Commodities; wares. **b.** Portable personal property. —*idioms:* **as good as** Nearly; almost. **for good** Permanently. **good and** *Informal* Very; thoroughly. [< OE *gōd.*]

Usage: **Good** is properly used as an adjective with linking verbs such as *be, seem,* or *appear: The future looks good.* It should not be used as an adverb with other verbs: *The car runs well* (not *good*).

Good·all (gŏod′ôl), **Jane** b. 1934. British zoologist.

Jane Goodall
photographed in 2004

good·bye or **good-bye** also **good-by** (goŏod-bī′) ►*interj.* Used to express farewell. [< *God be with you.*] —**good-bye′** *n.*

Good Friday ►*n.* The Friday before Easter, observed by Christians in commemoration of the crucifixion of Jesus.

good·heart·ed (goŏod′här′tĭd) ►*adj.* Kind and generous. —**good′heart′ed·ly** *adv.* —**good′-heart′ed·ness** *n.*

Good Hope, Cape of A promontory on the SW coast of South Africa S of Cape Town.

good-hu·mored (goŏod′hyoō′mərd) ►*adj.* Cheerful; amiable. —**good′-hu′mored·ly** *adv.*

good-look·ing (goŏod′loŏok′ĭng) ►*adj.* Of a pleasing appearance; attractive.

good·ly (goŏod′lē) ►*adj.* **-li·er, -li·est 1.** Quite large; considerable. **2.** Of pleasing appearance; comely. —**good′li·ness** *n.*

Good·man (goŏod′mən), **Benjamin David** "Benny." 1909–86. Amer. clarinetist.

good-na·tured (goŏod′nā′chərd) ►*adj.* Having an easygoing, cheerful disposition. —**good′-na′tured·ly** *adv.*

good·ness (goŏod′nĭs) ►*n.* **1.** The state or quality of being good. **2.** The beneficial part. ►*interj.* Used to express mild surprise.

Good Samaritan ►*n.* A person who unselfishly helps others, esp. strangers. [From the parable of the good Samaritan in the New Testament.]

good·will also **good will** (goŏod′wĭl′) ►*n.* **1.** An attitude of kindness or friendliness; benevolence. **2.** Cheerful willingness. **3.** A good relationship, as between nations. **4.** The positive reputation of a business, considered as part of its market value.

good·y (goŏod′ē) ►*n., pl.* **-ies** *Informal* Something attractive or delectable, esp. something sweet to eat. —**good′y** *interj.*

good·y-good·y (goŏod′ē-goŏod′ē) ►*adj.* Affectedly sweet, good, or virtuous. —**good′y-good′y** *n.*

goof (goŏof) *Slang* ►*n.* **1.** An incompetent, foolish, or stupid person. **2.** A careless mistake; slip. ►*v.* **1.** To blunder. **2.** To waste or kill time: *goofed off all day.* [Poss. < dial. *goff*, fool.] —**goof′i·ly** *adv.* —**goof′i·ness** *n.* —**goof′y** *adj.*

goof·ball (goŏof′bôl′) ►*n. Slang* **1.** A foolish or goofy person. **2.** A barbiturate or tranquilizer in pill form. —**goof′ball** *adj.*

goo·gol (goŏo′gôl′) ►*n.* The number 10 raised to the power 100 (10^{100}). [A coinage.]

gook (goŏok, goŏok) ►*n.* Var. of **guck.**

goon (goŏon) ►*n. Slang* **1.** A thug hired to intimidate or harm opponents. **2.** A stupid or oafish person. [Prob. < *gooney*, albatross.]

goose (goŏos) ►*n., pl.* **geese** (gēs) **1a.** Any of various waterbirds related to the ducks and swans. **b.** The female of such a bird. **c.** The flesh of such a bird used as food. **2.** *Informal* A silly person. [< OE *gōs.*]

goose·ber·ry (goŏos′běr′ē, -bə-rē, goŏoz′-) ►*n.* **1.** A spiny shrub having edible greenish berries. **2.** The fruit of this plant. [< Fr. *groseille.*]

goose bumps or **goose·bumps** (goŏos′bŭmps) ►*pl.n.* Momentary roughness of the skin in response to cold or fear.

goose flesh ►*n.* See **goose bumps.**

goose·neck (goŏos′něk′) ►*n.* A slender curved object or part, such as the flexible shaft of a type of desk lamp. —**goose′necked′** *adj.*

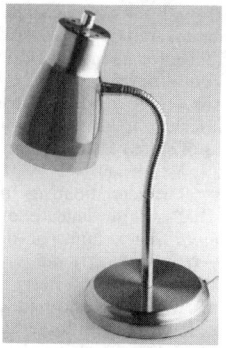
gooseneck
gooseneck desk lamp

goose step ►*n.* A military parade step executed by swinging the legs from the hips with the knees locked. —**goose′-step′** *v.*

GOP ►*abbr.* Grand Old Party (Republican Party)

go·pher (gō′fər) ►*n.* Any of various burrowing North American rodents having external cheek pouches. [?]

Gor·ba·chev (gôr′bə-chôf′, -chŏf′), **Mikhail Sergeyevich** b. 1931. Soviet politician.

gore¹ (gôr) ►*v.* **gored, gor·ing** To pierce or stab with a horn or tusk. [< OE *gār*, spear.]

gore² (gôr) ►*n.* A triangular or tapering piece of cloth, as in a skirt or sail. [< OE *gāra*, triangular land.] —**gore** *v.* —**gored** *adj.*

gore³ (gôr) ►*n.* Blood, esp. from a wound. [< OE *gor*, filth.]

Gore, Albert, Jr. "Al." b. 1948. US vice president (1993–2001).

gorge (gôrj) ►*n.* **1.** A deep narrow passage with steep sides. **2.** The throat; gullet. **3.** Something swallowed. ►*v.* **gorged, gorg·ing 1.** To stuff (oneself) with food; glut. **2.** To eat greedily. [< LLat. *gurga*, throat.]

gor·geous (gôr′jəs) ►*adj.* **1.** Dazzlingly beautiful or magnificent: *a gorgeous gown.* **2.** *Informal* Wonderful; delightful. [< OFr. *gorgias*, elegant.] —**gor′geous·ly** *adv.* —**gor′geous·ness** *n.*

go·ril·la (gə-rĭl′ə) ►*n.* A large African ape having a stocky body and coarse dark hair. [< Gk. *Gorillai*, a tribe of hairy women described by an ancient voyager in Africa.]

Gor·ky also **Gor·ki** (gôr′kē), **Maksim** 1868–1936. Russian writer.

gor·mand·ize (gôr′mən-dīz′) ►*v.* **-ized, -iz·ing** To eat gluttonously. [< OFr. *gormandise*, gluttony.] —**gor′mand·iz′er** *n.*

gorse (gôrs) ►*n.* A spiny evergreen European shrub having fragrant yellow flowers. [< OE *gorst*, bramble.]

go·ry (gôr′ē) ►*adj.* **-ri·er, -ri·est 1.** Covered with gore; bloody. **2.** Full of bloodshed and violence. —**gor′i·ly** *adv.* —**gor′i·ness** *n.*

gosh (gŏsh) ►*interj.* Used to express mild surprise. [Alteration of GOD.]

gos·hawk (gŏs′hôk′) ►*n.* A large hawk having broad rounded wings and a long tail. [< OE *gōshafoc.*]

gos·ling (gŏz′lĭng) ►*n.* A young goose. [< ON *gæslingr.*]

gos·pel (gŏs′pəl) ►*n.* **1.** often **Gospel** The proclamation of the redemption preached by Jesus and the Apostles. **2a.** often **Gospel** *Bible* One of the first four books of the New Testament. **b.** A similar narrative. **3.** Gospel music. **4.** Something accepted as unquestionably true. [< OE *gōdspel*, good news.]

gospel music ►*n.* A kind of Christian music based on American folk music, typically blending elements of spirituals, blues, and jazz.

gos·sa·mer (gŏs′ə-mər) ►*n.* **1.** A fine film of cobwebs often seen floating in the air. **2.** Something that is light, delicate, or sheer, such as fabric. ►*adj.* Sheer, light, or delicate. [ME *gossomer*.] **—gos′sa·mer·y** *adj.*

gos·sip (gŏs′əp) ►*n.* **1.** Rumor or talk of a personal, sensational, or intimate nature. **2.** A person who habitually indulges in gossip. **3.** Trivial, chatty talk or writing. [< OE *godsibb*, godparent.] **—gos′sip** *v.* **—gos′sip·er** *n.* **—gos′sip·y** *adj.*

got (gŏt) ►*v.* P.t. and p.part. of **get.**

Gö·te·borg (yœ′tə-bôr′ē) A city of SW Sweden on the Kattegat.

Goth (gŏth) ►*n.* A member of a Germanic people who invaded the Roman Empire in the early centuries of the Christian era.

Goth·ic (gŏth′ĭk) ►*adj.* **1a.** Of the Goths or their language. **b.** Germanic. **2.** Medieval. **3.** Of an architectural style prevalent in W Europe from the 12th through the 15th cent., marked esp. by pointed arches and strong vertical elements. **4.** often **gothic** Of a style of fiction that emphasizes the grotesque and mysterious: *a gothic novel.* ►*n.* The extinct Germanic language of the Goths.

Got·land (gŏt′lənd, gôt′lŭnd) A region of SE Sweden comprising several islands in the Baltic Sea, including **Gotland Island.**

got·ten (gŏt′n) ►*v.* P.part. of **get.**

Gou·da (gōō′də, gou′-) ►*n.* A mild, close-textured, pale yellow cheese. [After *Gouda*, city in Netherlands.]

gouge (gouj) ►*n.* **1.** A chisel with a rounded troughlike blade. **2.** A groove or hole scooped out with or as if with such a chisel. **3.** *Informal* A large amount, as of money, extracted or extorted. ►*v.* **gouged, goug·ing 1.** To cut or scoop out with or as if with a gouge. **2.** *Informal* To extort from. **3.** *Slang* To swindle. [< LLat. *gubia*, of Celt. orig.] **—goug′er** *n.*

gou·lash (gōō′läsh′, -läsh′) ►*n.* A meat and vegetable stew seasoned esp. with paprika. [Hung. *gulyás (hús)*, herdsman's (meat).]

Gou·nod (gōō′nō, gōō-nō′), **Charles François** 1818–93. French composer.

gourd (gôrd, gōōrd) ►*n.* **1.** A trailing or climbing plant bearing fruits with a hard rind. **2a.** The fruit of such a plant. **b.** The dried and hollowed-out shell of one of these fruits, often used as a container or for decoration. [< Lat. *cucurbita*.]

gourde (gōōrd) ►*n.* See table at **currency.** [Haitian < Fr. *gourd*, dull.]

gour·mand (gōōr-mänd′, gōōr′mənd) ►*n.* **1.** A lover of good food. **2.** A person who often eats too much. [< OFr. *gormant*, glutton.]

gour·met (gōōr-mā′, gōōr′mā′) ►*n.* A connoisseur of fine food and drink. [< OFr. *groumet*, wine merchant's servant < ME *grom*, a groom.]

gout (gout) ►*n.* **1.** A disease of uric-acid metabolism occurring esp. in males, that is characterized by arthritis and painful inflammation of the joints. **2.** A large blob or clot. [< Lat. *gutta*,

drop.] **—gout′i·ness** *n.* **—gout′y** *adj.*

Gov. ►*abbr.* governor

gov·ern (gŭv′ərn) ►*v.* **1.** To make and administer public policy and affairs. **2.** To regulate. **3.** To control; restrain. **4.** To decide or determine. [Ult. < Gk. *kubernan*.] **—gov′ern·a·ble** *adj.* **—gov′er·nance** *n.*

gov·er·ness (gŭv′ər-nĭs) ►*n.* A woman employed to educate and train the children of a private household.

gov·ern·ment (gŭv′ərn-mənt) ►*n.* **1.** The act or process of governing, esp. the administration of public policy. **2.** The means by which a governing agent or agency uses authority. **3.** A governing body or organization. **4.** Political science. **—gov′ern·men′tal** (-mĕn′tl) *adj.* **—gov′ern·men′tal·ly** *adv.*

   Usage: In American usage, *government* always takes a singular verb. In British usage, in the sense of a governing group of officials *government* is usu. construed as a plural collective and therefore takes a plural verb. See Usage Note at **collective noun.**

gov·er·nor (gŭv′ər-nər) ►*n.* **1.** A person who governs, esp. the chief executive of a state in the US. **2.** The manager or administrative head of an organization or institution. **3.** A commandant. **4.** A device on an engine that regulates speed, pressure, or temperature. **—gov′er·nor·ship′** *n.*

govt. ►*abbr.* government

gown (goun) ►*n.* **1.** A long, loose, flowing garment, as a robe or nightgown. **2.** A woman's formal dress. **3.** A distinctive outer robe worn on ceremonial occasions, as by scholars or clerics. **4.** The faculty and student body of a university: *town and gown.* [< LLat. *gunna*, leather garment.]

Go·ya y Lu·ci·en·tes (goi′ə ē lōō-syĕn′tēs), **Francisco José de** 1746–1828. Spanish artist.

GP ►*abbr.* **1.** games played **2.** general practitioner

GPA ►*abbr.* grade point average

GPO ►*abbr.* **1.** general post office **2.** Government Printing Office

GPS ►*abbr.* Global Positioning System

GQ ►*abbr.* general quarters

gr. ►*abbr.* **1.** grain (measurement) **2.** gram **3.** gross

Gr. ►*abbr.* Greek

grab (grăb) ►*v.* **grabbed, grab·bing 1.** To take or grasp suddenly. **2.** To capture or restrain; arrest. **3.** To obtain unscrupulously or illegally. **4.** To take hurriedly. [< MDu. or MLGer. *grabben*.] **—grab** *n.* **—grab′ber** *n.* **—grab′by** *adj.*

grab bag ►*n.* **1.** A container filled with articles, such as party gifts, to be drawn unseen. **2.** *Slang* A miscellaneous collection.

Grac·chus (grăk′əs), **Tiberius Sempronius** c. 163–133 BC. Roman social reformer; known with his brother **Gaius Sempronius Gracchus** (c. 153–121 BC) as "the Gracchi."

grace (grās) ►*n.* **1.** Seemingly effortless beauty of movement, form, or proportion. **2.** A pleasing characteristic or quality. **3.** A sense of fitness or propriety. **4a.** Good will. **b.** Mercy; clemency. **5.** A temporary immunity or exemption; reprieve. **6. Graces** *Gk. & Rom. Myth.* Three sister goddesses who dispense charm and beauty. **7.** *Christianity* **a.** Divine favor bestowed freely on people, as in granting redemption from sin. **b.** The state of having received such favor. **8.** A short prayer said at mealtime. **9. Grace** Used with *His, Her,* or *Your* as a title for a duke, duchess, or archbishop. ►*v.* **graced, grac·ing 1.** To honor or favor. **2.** To give beauty, elegance, or charm to. —*idiom:* **in the good (or bad) graces of** In (or out of) favor with. [< Lat. *grātia*.] —**grace′ful** *adj.* —**grace′ful·ly** *adv.* —**grace′ful·ness** *n.* —**grace′less** *adj.* —**grace′less·ly** *adv.* —**grace′less·ness** *n.*

grace note ►*n. Mus.* A note added as an embellishment and not counted in rhythm.

grace period ►*n.* A period after a due date or deadline during which an obligation may still be fulfilled without penalty.

gra·cious (grā′shəs) ►*adj.* **1.** Marked by kindness and warm courtesy. **2.** Tactful. **3.** Merciful or compassionate. **4.** Marked by elegance and good taste. [< Lat. *grātiōsus*.] —**gra′cious·ly** *adv.* —**gra′cious·ness** *n.*

grack·le (grăk′əl) ►*n.* Any of several American blackbirds with iridescent blackish plumage. [< Lat. *grāculus,* jackdaw.]

grad (grăd) ►*n. Informal* A graduate.

gra·da·tion (grā-dā′shən) ►*n.* **1.** A series of gradual, successive stages. **2.** A degree or stage in such a progression. See Synonyms at **nuance. 3.** The act of arranging in grades. [< Lat. *gradus,* step.] —**gra·da′tion·al** *adj.*

grade (grăd) ►*n.* **1.** A stage or degree in a process. **2.** A position in a scale. **3.** An accepted standard. **4.** A level of study at an elementary, middle, or secondary school. **5.** The students at such a level. **6.** A mark indicating a student's level of accomplishment. **7.** A military, naval, or civil service rank. **8.** The degree of inclination of a slope. **9.** A slope or gradual inclination, esp. of a road or railroad track. ►*v.* **graded, grad·ing 1.** To arrange in degrees; rank; sort. **2a.** To evaluate. **b.** To give a grade to. **3.** To level or smooth (a surface) to a desired gradient. [< Lat. *gradus,* step.] —**grad′er** *n.*

grade school ►*n.* See **elementary school.** —**grade′-school′er** *n.*

gra·di·ent (grā′dē-ənt) ►*n.* A rate of inclination; slope. [Perh. < GRADE.]

grad·u·al (grăj′ōō-əl) ►*adj.* Occurring in small stages or advancing by regular or continuous degrees. [< Lat. *gradus,* step.] —**grad′u·al·ism** *n.* —**grad′u·al·ly** *adv.* —**grad′u·al·ness** *n.*

grad·u·ate (grăj′ōō-āt′) ►*v.* **-at·ed, -at·ing 1.** To grant or be granted an academic degree or diploma. **2.** To arrange into categories, steps, or grades. **3.** To divide into marked intervals, esp. for use in measurement. ►*n.* (-ĭt) A person who has received an academic degree or diploma. ►*adj.* (-ĭt) **1.** Possessing an academic degree or diploma. **2.** Of studies beyond a bachelor's degree. [< Med.Lat. *graduāri,* take a degree.]

grad·u·a·tion (grăj′ōō-ā′shən) ►*n.* **1.** Conferral or receipt of an academic degree or diploma marking completion of studies. **2.** A commencement ceremony. **3.** An interval on a graduated scale.

graf·fi·ti (grə-fē′tē) ►*n.* (takes sing. or pl. v.) Drawings or inscriptions made on a wall or other surface, usu. so as to be seen by the public. [Ital., pl. of *graffito;* see GRAFFITO.]

graf·fi·to (grə-fē′tō) ►*n.* Sing. of **graffiti.**

[Ital. < *graffiare,* scribble, ult. < Gk. *graphein,* write.]

graft¹ (grăft) ►*v.* **1.** To unite (a shoot, bud, or plant) with a growing plant by insertion or placing in close contact. **2.** To transplant or implant (tissue) into a bodily part. ►*n.* **1a.** A detached shoot or bud that is grafted onto a growing plant. **b.** The point of union of such plant parts. **2.** Material, esp. tissue or an organ, grafted onto a bodily part. [< OFr. *graffe,* stylus < Lat. *graphium* < Gk. *graphein,* write.] —**graft′er** *n.*

graft¹

graft² (grăft) ►*n.* **1.** Illegal use of one's position for profit or advantages. **2.** Money or advantage obtained by such means. [?] —**graft** *v.* —**graft′er** *n.*

Graham (grăm, grā′əm), **Martha** 1894–1991. Amer. dancer and choreographer.

Martha Graham
photographed c. 1943

graham flour ►*n.* Whole-wheat flour. [After Sylvester *Graham* (1794–1851).]

grail (grāl) ►*n.* **1. Grail** A legendary cup or plate used by Jesus at the Last Supper. **2.** often **Grail** The object of a prolonged endeavor. [< Med. Lat. *gradālis,* flat dish.]

grain (grān) ►*n.* **1a.** A small, one-seeded fruit of a cereal grass. **b.** The fruits of cereal grasses collectively, esp. after harvesting. **2.** Cereal grasses collectively. **3.** A particle. **4.** See table at **measurement. 5.** The arrangement, direction, or pattern of the fibrous tissue in wood. **6.** Texture: *A stone with fine grain.* **7.** Basic temperament; disposition. —*idiom:* **with a grain of salt** With reservations;

skeptically. [< Lat. *grānum.*] —**grain′i·ness** *n.*
—**grain′y** *adj.*

grain alcohol ▸*n.* See **alcohol** (sense 2).

grain elevator ▸*n.* A tall building used for storing grain.

gram (grăm) ▸*n.* See table at **measurement.** [< Gk. *gramma,* small weight.]

–gram ▸*suff.* Something written or drawn; a record: *cardiogram.* [< Gk. *gramma,* letter.]

gram·mar (grăm′ər) ▸*n.* **1.** The study of how words and their component parts combine to form sentences. **2.** The system of inflections, syntax, and word formation of a language. **3a.** A normative or prescriptive set of rules setting forth the current standard of usage. **b.** Writing or speech judged with regard to such rules. **4.** A book containing the inflectional, syntactic, and semantic rules for a specific language. [< Lat. *grammatica* < Gk. *gramma,* letter.] —**gram·mar′i·an** (grə-mâr′ē-ən) *n.* —**gram·mat′i·cal** (grə-măt′ĭ-kəl) *adj.* —**gram·mat′i·cal·ly** *adv.*

grammar school ▸*n.* **1.** See **elementary school. 2.** A school for the study of classical languages.

gram-neg·a·tive or **Gram-neg·a·tive** (grăm′-nĕg′ə-tĭv) ▸*adj.* Not retaining the violet stain used in the Gram stain method.

gram·o·phone (grăm′ə-fōn′) ▸*n.* A phonograph. [Orig. a trademark.]

gram-pos·i·tive or **Gram-pos·i·tive** (grăm′-pŏz′ĭ-tĭv) ▸*adj.* Retaining the violet stain used in the Gram stain method.

gram·pus (grăm′pəs) ▸*n.* A large dolphin with a short beak. [< Med.Lat. *craspiscis,* fat fish.]

Gram stain (grăm) also **Gram's stain** (grămz) ▸*n.* A staining technique used to classify bacteria based on the ability or inability to retain a violet stain. [After H.C.J. *Gram* (1853–1938).]

Gra·na·da (grə-nä′də) A city of S Spain SE of Córdoba.

gran·a·ry (grăn′ə-rē, grā′nə-) ▸*n., pl.* **-ries 1.** A building for storing threshed grain. **2.** A region yielding much grain. [Lat. *grānārium* < *grānum,* grain.]

grand (grănd) ▸*adj.* **-er, -est 1.** Large and impressive in size, scope, or extent. **2a.** Wonderful; very pleasing. **b.** Rich and sumptuous. **3a.** Most important; principal: *the grand ballroom.* **b.** Having higher rank than others of the same category: *a grand admiral.* **4.** Solemn or stately. **5.** Including or covering all units or aspects: *the grand total.* ▸*n.* **1.** A grand piano. **2.** *Slang* A thousand dollars. [< Lat. *grandis.*] —**grand′ly** *adv.* —**grand′ness** *n.*

gran·dam (grăn′dăm′, -dəm) also **gran·dame** (-dăm′, -däm, -dəm) ▸*n.* **1.** A grandmother. **2.** An old woman. [< OFr. *dame-grande,* great lady.]

Grand Canyon A gorge of the Colorado R. in NW AZ, up to 1,830 m (6,000 ft) deep, 25 km (15 mi) wide, and more than 445 km (275 mi) long.

grand·child (grănd′chīld′, grăn′-) ▸*n.* A child of one's son or daughter.

grand·daugh·ter (grăn′dô′tər) ▸*n.* A daughter of one's child.

gran·deur (grăn′jər, -jŏor′) ▸*n.* The quality of being grand; magnificence. [< OFr. < *grand,* GRAND.]

grand·fa·ther (grănd′fä′thər, grăn′-) ▸*n.* **1.** The father of one's mother or father. **2.** A forefather;

ancestor. ▸*v.* To exempt (one already existing) from new regulations.

gran·dil·o·quence (grăn-dĭl′ə-kwəns) ▸*n.* Pompous or bombastic speech or expression. [< Lat. *grandiloquus,* speaking loftily.] —**gran·dil′o·quent** *adj.* —**gran·dil′o·quent·ly** *adv.*

gran·di·ose (grăn′dē-ōs′, grăn′dē-ōs′) ▸*adj.* **1.** Great in scope or intent; grand. **2.** Affectedly grand; pompous. [< Ital. *grandioso* < Lat. *grandis,* great.] —**gran·di·os′i·ty** (-ŏs′ĭ-tē) *n.*

grand jury ▸*n.* A jury convened to evaluate criminal accusations and to determine whether the evidence warrants indictment.

grand·ma (grănd′mä′, grăn′-, grăm′mä′, grăm′ə) ▸*n. Informal* A grandmother.

grand mal (grăn′ măl′, măl′, grănd′) ▸*n.* A severe form of epilepsy marked by generalized seizures and loss of consciousness. [Fr.]

grand·moth·er (grănd′mŭth′ər, grăn′-) ▸*n.* **1.** The mother of one's father or mother. **2.** A female ancestor.

grand·pa (grănd′pä′, grăn′-, grăm′pä′, grăm′-pə) ▸*n. Informal* A grandfather.

grand·par·ent (grănd′pâr′ənt, -păr′-, grăn′-) ▸*n.* A parent of one's mother or father.

grand piano ▸*n.* A piano having the strings strung in a horizontal harp-shaped frame.

grand slam ▸*n.* **1.** *Baseball* A home run hit with three runners on base. **2.** The set of all the major competitions in a sport, esp. when won in a single season. **3.** The winning of all the tricks during a hand in bridge.

grand·son (grănd′sŭn′, grăn′-) ▸*n.* A son of one's child.

grand·stand (grănd′stănd′, grăn′-) ▸*n.* A roofed stand for spectators at a stadium or racetrack. ▸*v.* To act ostentatiously to impress an audience. —**grand′stand′er** *n.*

grand unified theory ▸*n. Phys.* A theory in which the known elementary physical forces are viewed as low-energy manifestations of a single unified interaction.

grange (grānj) ▸*n.* **1. Grange** A US farmers' association founded in 1867. **2.** *Chiefly Brit.* A farm with its outbuildings. [< VLat. **grānica,* granary < Lat. *grānum,* GRAIN.]

gran·ite (grăn′ĭt) ▸*n.* A common, coarse-grained, hard igneous rock consisting chiefly of quartz, feldspar, and mica, often used in construction. [< Ital. *granito,* grainy < *grano,* GRAIN.] —**gra·nit′ic** (grə-nĭt′ĭk, grə-) *adj.*

gran·ny or **gran·nie** (grăn′ē) ▸*n., pl.* **-nies** *Informal* A grandmother. [< GRANDMOTHER.]

gra·no·la (grə-nō′lə) ▸*n.* Rolled oats baked with ingredients such as dried fruit, brown sugar, and nuts, used esp. as a breakfast cereal. [Orig. a trademark.]

grant (grănt) ▸*v.* **1.** To consent to the fulfillment of: *granted a request.* **2.** To confer formally: *granted him permission to sit down.* **3.** To transfer (property) by a deed. **4.** To concede; acknowledge: *She granted that her story sounded implausible.* ▸*n.* **1.** The act of granting. **2a.** Something granted, esp. a giving of funds for a specific purpose. **b.** A document outlining the terms of a grant. **3a.** A transfer of property by deed. **b.** The property so transferred. **c.** The deed of transfer. [< VLat. **crēdentāre,* assure < Lat. *crēdere,* believe.] —**grant′er, gran′tor** *n.*

Grant, Ulysses Simpson 1822–85. The 18th US president (1869–77) and a Civil War general.

Ulysses S. Grant
1869 portrait

gran·u·lar (grăn′yə-lər) ►*adj.* **1.** Composed of granules or grains. **2.** Having a grainy texture. —**gran′u·lar′i·ty** (-lăr′ĭ-tē) *n.*

gran·u·late (grăn′yə-lāt′) ►*v.* **-lat·ed, -lat·ing** **1.** To form into grains or granules. **2.** To make rough and grainy. —**gran′u·la′tion** *n.* —**gran′u·la′tive** *adj.*

gran·ule (grăn′yōōl) ►*n.* A small grain or particle. [LLat. *grānulum* < Lat. *grānum*, GRAIN.]

grape (grāp) ►*n.* **1.** Any of a genus of woody vines bearing clusters of edible fruit. **2.** The fleshy, smooth-skinned, purple, red, or green fruit of a grape. **3.** Grapeshot. [< OFr., bunch of grapes.]

grape·fruit (grāp′frōōt′) ►*n.* **1.** A semitropical citrus tree cultivated for its edible fruit. **2.** The large round fruit of this tree, having a yellow rind and juicy acid pulp.

grape·shot (grāp′shŏt′) ►*n.* Artillery ammunition consisting of clusters of small iron balls, formerly used against personnel.

grape sugar ►*n.* Dextrose from grapes.

grape·vine (grāp′vīn′) ►*n.* **1.** A vine on which grapes grow. **2.** The informal transmission of information or rumor from person to person.

graph (grăf) ►*n.* **1.** A diagram in which the coordinates of plotted points illustrate the relationship between two sets of numbers. **2.** A drawing or diagram used to display quantitative relationships. ►*v.* **1.** To represent by a graph. **2.** To plot (a function) on a graph. [< *graphic formula*.]

–graph ►*suff.* **1.** Something written or drawn: *monograph.* **2.** An instrument for writing, drawing, or recording: *seismograph.* [< Gk. *graphein*, write.]

–grapher ►*suff.* One who writes about a specified subject or in a specified manner: *stenographer.*

graph·ic (grăf′ĭk) ►*adj.* also **graph·i·cal** (-ĭ-kəl) **1.** Relating to written or pictorial representation. **2.** Relating to a graph. **3.** Described or depicted in vivid detail. See Synonyms at **vivid**. **4.** Of the graphic arts. ►*n.* **1.** A work of graphic art. **2.** A graphic image or display, esp. one generated by a computer. [< Gk. *graphein*, to write.] —**graph′i·cal·ly** *adv.*

graphical user interface ►*n.* GUI.

graphic arts ►*pl.n.* The arts, such as painting, drawing, and engraving, that involve representing, writing, or printing on two-dimensional surfaces.

graph·ics (grăf′ĭks) ►*n.* **1.** *(takes sing. or pl. v.)*

The pictorial representation and manipulation of data, as used in computer-aided design, typesetting, and the graphic arts. **2.** *(takes sing. v.)* The making of drawings, as in engineering or architecture.

graph·ite (grăf′īt′) ►*n.* A soft, steel-gray to black form of carbon used in lead pencils, lubricants, paints, and coatings. [Gk. *graphein*, write + –ITE[1].] —**gra·phit′ic** (gră-fĭt′ĭk) *adj.*

gra·phol·o·gy (gră-fŏl′ə-jē) ►*n.* The study of handwriting. —**graph′o·log′i·cal** (grăf′ə-lŏj′-ĭ-kəl) *adj.* —**gra·phol′o·gist** *n.*

–graphy ►*suff.* **1.** Writing or representation produced in a specified manner or by a specified process: *photography.* **2.** Writing about a specified subject: *oceanography.* [< Gk. *graphein*, write.]

grap·nel (grăp′nəl) ►*n.* **1.** A small anchor with three or more flukes. **2.** See **grapple** (sense 1a). [Prob. < OFr. *grapin*, hook.]

grap·ple (grăp′əl) ►*n.* **1a.** An iron shaft with claws at one end, esp. one that was formerly used for drawing and holding an enemy ship alongside. **b.** See **grapnel** (sense 1). **2.** The act of grappling. ►*v.* **-pled, -pling** **1.** To seize and hold fast. **2.** To grip or grasp firmly, as in wrestling. **3.** To struggle: *grapple with one's conscience.* [< OFr. *grapil*, small hook.] —**grap′pler** *n.*

grappling iron ►*n.* See **grapple** (sense 1a).

grasp (grăsp) ►*v.* **1.** To seize or attempt to seize firmly. **2.** To comprehend. ►*n.* **1.** A firm hold or grip. **2.** The ability or power to seize. **3.** Understanding; comprehension. [ME *graspen*.]

grasp·ing (grăs′pĭng) ►*adj.* Greedy; avaricious. —**grasp′ing·ly** *adv.*

grass (grăs) ►*n.* **1a.** Any of various plants with narrow leaves, jointed stems, and spikes or clusters of minute flowers. **b.** Such plants collectively. **2.** Ground, such as a lawn, covered with grass. **3.** *Slang* Marijuana. [< OE *græs.*] —**grass′y** *adj.*

grass·hop·per (grăs′hŏp′ər) ►*n.* Any of various insects having long powerful hind legs adapted for jumping.

grass·land (grăs′lănd′) ►*n.* An area, such as a prairie, of grass or grasslike vegetation.

grass·roots (grăs′rōōts′, -rŏŏts′) ►*pl.n.* *(takes sing. or pl. v.)* **1.** The lowest or most basic level of an organization or movement. **2.** The people at this level. —**grass′roots′** *adj.*

grate[1] (grāt) ►*v.* **grat·ed, grat·ing** **1.** To shred or pulverize by rubbing against a rough surface. **2.** To make or cause to make a harsh rasping sound. **3.** To irritate persistently. ►*n.* A harsh rasping sound. [< OFr. *grater*, scrape.] —**grat′er** *n.*

grate[2] (grāt) ►*n.* **1.** A framework of parallel or latticed bars over an opening. **2.** A framework of metal bars to hold fuel or food in a stove or fireplace. [< Lat. *crātis*, wickerwork.] —**grat′ed** *adj.*

grate·ful (grāt′fəl) ►*adj.* **1.** Appreciative; thankful. **2.** Expressing gratitude. **3.** Pleasing; agreeable. [< Lat. *grātus*, pleasing.] —**grate′ful·ly** *adv.* —**grate′ful·ness** *n.*

grat·i·fy (grăt′ə-fī′) ►*v.* **-fied, -fy·ing** **1.** To please or satisfy. See Synonyms at **please**. **2.** To give what is desired to; indulge. [< Lat. *grātificārī*, to favor.] —**grat′i·fi·ca′tion** *n.* —**grat′i·fi′er** *n.* —**grat′i·fy′ing** *adj.*

grat·ing (grā′tĭng) ►*n.* A grill or network of bars; grate.

grat·is (grăt′ĭs, grä′tĭs, grā′-) ►*adv. & adj.* Without charge. [< Lat. *grātīs.*]

grat·i·tude (grăt′ĭ-tōōd′, -tyōōd′) ►*n.* Thankfulness. [< Lat. *grātus*, pleasing.]

gra·tu·i·tous (grə-tōō′ĭ-təs, -tyōō′-) ►*adj.* **1.** Given without return; unearned. **2.** Unnecessary or unwarranted: *gratuitous criticism.* [< Lat. *grātuītus.*] —**gra·tu′i·tous·ly** *adv.* —**gra·tu′i·tous·ness** *n.*

gra·tu·i·ty (grə-tōō′ĭ-tē, -tyōō′-) ►*n.*, *pl.* **-ties** A tip for service. [< Med.Lat. *grātuītās.*]

grave[1] (grāv) ►*n.* **1.** An excavation for a burial. **2.** A place of burial. [< OE *græf.*]

grave[2] (grāv) ►*adj.* **grav·er, grav·est 1.** Requiring serious thought; momentous. **2.** Fraught with danger or harm. **3.** Dignified in conduct or character. **4.** (*also* gräv) Written with the mark (` ), as the è in *Sèvres.* ►*n.* (*also* gräv) The mark ( `) indicating a grave vowel. [< Lat. *gravis*, heavy.] —**grave′ly** *adv.* —**grave′ness** *n.*

grave[3] (grāv) ►*v.* **graved, grav·en** (grā′vən) or **graved, grav·ing** To engrave. [< OE *grafan.*] —**grav′er** *n.*

grav·el (grăv′əl) ►*n.* A loose mixture of rock fragments or pebbles. [< OFr. *gravele*, dim. of *grave*, pebbly shore.] —**grav′el·ly** *adj.*

grave·stone (grāv′stōn′) ►*n.* A tombstone.

grave·yard (grāv′yärd′) ►*n.* A cemetery.

graveyard shift A work shift that runs during the early morning hours, as from midnight to 8 A.M.

grav·id (grăv′ĭd) ►*adj.* Carrying developing young or eggs: *a gravid sea turtle.* [Lat. *gravidus.*] —**gra·vid′i·ty** (grə-vĭd′ĭ-tē) *n.*

grav·i·met·ric (grăv′ə-mĕt′rĭk) also **grav·i·met·ri·cal** (-rĭ-kəl) ►*adj.* **1.** Of measurement by weight. **2.** Of measurement of variations in a gravitational field. [< Lat. *gravis*, heavy + -METER.] —**grav′i·met′ri·cal·ly** *adv.*

grav·i·tate (grăv′ĭ-tāt′) ►*v.* **-tat·ed, -tat·ing 1.** To move in response to the force of gravity. **2.** To be attracted. —**grav′i·tat′er** *n.*

grav·i·ta·tion (grăv′ĭ-tā′shən) ►*n.* **1a.** The fundamental force of attraction between bodies that have mass. **b.** The act of gravitating. **2.** A movement toward a source of attraction. —**grav′i·ta′tion·al** *adj.* —**grav′i·ta′tion·al·ly** *adv.* —**grav′i·ta′tive** *adj.*

grav·i·ton (grăv′ĭ-tŏn′) ►*n.* A massless particle hypothesized to be the quantum of gravitational interaction.

grav·i·ty (grăv′ĭ-tē) ►*n.* **1.** *Phys.* **a.** The value of the gravitational force between any two bodies, directly proportional to the product of their masses and inversely proportional to the square of the distance between them. **b.** See **gravitation** (sense 1). **2.** Grave consequence; seriousness. **3.** Solemnity or dignity of manner. [< Lat. *gravis*, heavy.]

gra·vure (grə-vyōōr′) ►*n.* **1.** A method of printing with etched plates or cylinders. **2.** Photogravure. [< OFr. *graver*, engrave.]

gra·vy (grā′vē) ►*n.*, *pl.* **-vies 1.** The juices that drip from cooking meat. **2.** A sauce made from these juices. **3.** *Slang* Money or profit gained easily. [< OFr. *grave.*]

gray also **grey** (grā) ►*adj.* **-er, -est 1.** Of the color gray. **2.** Having gray hair. **3.** Intermediate in character or position. ►*n.* A neutral color between black and white. [< OE *græg.*] —**gray′ish** *adj.* —**gray′ness** *n.*

Gray, Thomas 1716–71. British poet.

gray·beard (grā′bîrd′) ►*n.* An old man.

gray matter ►*n.* **1.** The brownish-gray nerve tissue of the brain and spinal cord. **2.** *Informal* Brains; intellect.

gray whale ►*n.* A baleen whale of N Pacific waters having grayish-black coloring with white blotches.

gray wolf ►*n.* A large, usu. gray wolf of N North America and Eurasia.

graze[1] (grāz) ►*v.* **grazed, graz·ing 1.** To feed on growing grasses and herbage. **2.** *Informal* To eat frequent snacks. [< OE *grasian* < *græs*, grass.] —**graz′er** *n.*

graze[2] (grāz) ►*v.* **grazed, graz·ing** To touch or scrape lightly in passing. See Synonyms at **brush**[1]. [Perh. < GRAZE[1].] —**graze** *n.*

grease (grēs) ►*n.* **1.** Melted animal fat. **2.** A thick oil or viscous lubricant. ►*v.* (grēs, grēz) **greased, greas·ing 1.** To coat, smear, lubricate, or soil with grease. **2.** To facilitate the progress of, as with money or bribes. [< Lat. *crassus*, fat.] —**grease′less** *adj.*

grease·paint (grēs′pānt′) ►*n.* Theatrical make-up.

grease·wood (grēs′wŏod′) ►*n.* A spiny shrub of W North America, having white stems and greenish flowers.

greas·y (grē′sē, -zē) ►*adj.* **-i·er, -i·est 1.** Coated or soiled with grease. **2.** Containing grease, esp. too much grease. —**greas′i·ly** *adv.* —**greas′i·ness** *n.*

great (grāt) ►*adj.* **-er, -est 1.** Very large in size, quantity, or number. See Synonyms at **large. 2.** Remarkable in magnitude or extent: *a great crisis.* **3.** Of outstanding importance: *a great work of art.* **4.** Powerful; influential: *a great nation.* **5.** Eminent; distinguished: *a great philosopher.* **6.** *Informal* Very good: *great at algebra.* **7.** Being one generation removed from the relative specified: *a great-granddaughter.* ►*n.* One that is great: *the greats of the opera world.* [< OE *grēat*, thick.] —**great′ly** *adv.* —**great′ness** *n.*

great ape ►*n.* Any of a family of apes which includes the chimpanzees, gorillas, orangutans, and humans.

Great Barrier Reef The world's largest coral reef, about 2,010 km (1,250 mi) long, off the NE coast of Australia.

Great Basin A desert region of the W US comprising most of NV and parts of UT, CA, ID, WY, and OR.

Great Bear Lake A lake of central Northwest Terrs., Canada.

Great Britain An island off the W coast of Europe comprising England, Scotland, and Wales, which together constitute most of the United Kingdom.

great circle ►*n.* A circle described by the intersection of the surface of a sphere with a plane passing through its center.

great·coat (grāt′kōt′) ►*n.* A heavy overcoat.

Great Dane ►*n.* A tall muscular dog having a short smooth coat and narrow head.

great·er (grā′tər) ►*adj.* Of or being a city considered together with its suburbs.

Greater Antilles An island group of the N West Indies including Cuba, Jamaica, Hispaniola, and Puerto Rico.

great horned owl ►*n.* A large owl having prominent ear tufts and brownish plumage.

Great Lakes 1. A group of five freshwater lakes of central North America between the US and Canada, including Lakes Superior, Michigan, Huron, Erie, and Ontario. **2.** A group of several large lakes in and around the Great Rift Valley in E Africa.

Great Plains A vast grassland region of central North America extending from the Canadian provinces of Alberta, Saskatchewan, and Manitoba S to TX.

Great Rift Valley A system of geologic depressions of SW Asia and E Africa extending from the Jordan R. valley to Mozambique.

Great Salt Lake A saline lake of NW UT.

Great Slave Lake A lake of S Northwest Terrs., Canada.

Great Smoky Mountains A range of the Appalachian Mts. on the NC–TN border.

great white shark ►*n.* A large shark of temperate and tropical waters that feeds on fish and marine mammals.

grebe (grēb) ►*n.* Any of various diving birds having a pointed bill and lobed fleshy membranes along each toe. [Fr. *grèbe.*]

Gre·cian (grē′shən) ►*adj.* Greek. ►*n.* A native or inhabitant of Greece.

Grec·o (grĕk′ō), **El** 1541–1614. Greek-born Spanish painter.

Grec·o-Ro·man (grĕk′ō-rō′mən, grē′kō-) ►*adj.* Relating to both Greece and Rome.

Greece (grēs) A country of SE Europe on the S Balkan Peninsula and including numerous islands in the Mediterranean Sea. Cap. Athens.

greed (grēd) ►*n.* An excessive desire for more than one needs or deserves. [< GREEDY.]

greed·y (grē′dē) ►*adj.* **-i·er, -i·est** Wishing to possess more than one needs or deserves. [< OE *grǣdig.*] **—greed′i·ly** *adv.* **—greed′i·ness** *n.*

Greek (grēk) ►*n.* **1.** A native or inhabitant of Greece. **2.** The Indo-European language of the Greeks. **3.** *Informal* Something unintelligible: *Quantum mechanics is Greek to me.* **—Greek** *adj.*

Greek Orthodox Church ►*n.* The state church of Greece, an autonomous part of the Eastern Orthodox Church.

Gree·ley (grē′lē), **Horace** 1811–72. Amer. journalist and politician.

green (grēn) ►*n.* **1.** Any of a group of colors whose hue is that of growing grass, lying between yellow and blue on the visible spectrum. **2. greens** Leafy plants or plant parts used as food or for decoration. **3.** A grassy lawn or plot: *a putting green.* ►*adj.* **-er, -est 1.** Of the color green. **2.** Covered with green growth or foliage. **3.** Not mature or ripe. **4.** Inexperienced. **5.** Beneficial to the environment or minimizing impact on the environment. ►*v.* To make or become green. [< OE *grēne.*] **—green′ish** *adj.* **—green′ness** *n.*

green·back (grēn′bǎk′) ►*n.* A note of US currency.

green bean ►*n.* See **string bean.**

green card ►*n.* An official document issued by the US government to aliens, allowing them to work legally in the US.

Greene (grēn), **(Henry) Graham** 1904–91. British writer.

green·er·y (grē′nə-rē) ►*n., pl.* **-ies** Green foliage; verdure.

green-eyed (grēn′īd′) ►*adj.* Jealous.

green·horn (grēn′hôrn′) ►*n.* An inexperienced or immature person, esp. one who is easily deceived. [ME *greene horn*, horn of a freshly slaughtered animal.]

green·house (grēn′hous′) ►*n.* A structure, usu. of glass, in which temperature and humidity can be controlled for the cultivation of plants.

greenhouse effect ►*n.* A phenomenon in which a planet's atmospheric gases such as carbon dioxide, water vapor, and methane allow incoming sunlight to pass through but retain much of the heat radiated back from the planet's surface.

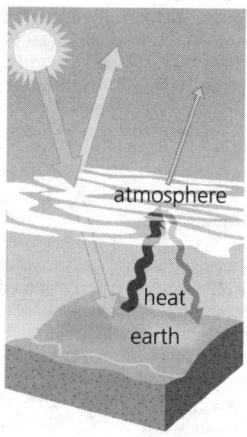

greenhouse effect
Energy radiated by the sun converts to heat when it reaches the earth. Some heat is reflected back through the atmosphere, while some is absorbed by atmospheric gases and radiated back to the earth.

greenhouse gas ►*n.* An atmospheric gas that contributes to the greenhouse effect.

Green·land (grēn′lənd, -lǎnd′) A large island in the N Atlantic off NE Canada, constituting a self-governing territory of Denmark. **—Green·land′ic** *adj.*

green light ►*n.* **1.** The green-colored light that signals traffic to proceed. **2.** *Informal* Permission to proceed.

green·sward (grēn′swôrd′) ►*n.* Ground that is green with grass; turf.

green tea ►*n.* Tea made from leaves that are not fermented before being dried.

green thumb ►*n.* An unusual ability to make plants grow well.

Green·wich (grĕn′ĭch) A borough of Greater London in SE England; on the Prime Meridian.

Greenwich Mean Time ►*n.* **1.** See **coordinated universal time. 2.** See **universal time.**

greet (grēt) ►*v.* **1.** To welcome or salute in a friendly and respectful way. **2.** To receive with a specified reaction. **3.** To be perceived by: *A din greeted our ears.* [< OE *grētan.*] **—greet′er** *n.*

greet·ing (grē′tĭng) ►*n.* A word or gesture of welcome or salutation.

greeting card ►*n.* A folded, decorated card bearing a message, as of greeting or congratulation.

gre·gar·i·ous (grĭ-gâr′ē-əs) ▸*adj.* **1.** Seeking and enjoying the company of others; sociable. See Synonyms at **social. 2.** Tending to move in or form a group. [< Lat. *gregārius* < *grex, greg-,* flock.] —**gre·gar′i·ous·ly** *adv.* —**gre·gar′i·ous·ness** *n.*

Gre·go·ri·an calendar (grĭ-gôr′ē-ən) ▸*n.* The calendar in use throughout most of the world, sponsored by Pope Gregory XIII in 1582. See table at **calendar.**

Gregorian chant ▸*n. Rom. Cath. Ch.* An unaccompanied, monophonic liturgical chant. [After Saint GREGORY I.]

Greg·o·ry I (grĕg′ə-rē), Saint. "the Great." 540?–604. Pope (590–604).

Gregory VII, Saint. 1020?–85. Pope (1073–85).

Gregory XIII 1502–85. Pope (1572–85).

grem·lin (grĕm′lĭn) ▸*n.* An imaginary gnome-like creature to whom mechanical problems are attributed. [Perh. < Ir.Gael. *gruamín.*]

Gre·na·da (grə-nā′də) A country in the Windward Is. of the West Indies comprising the island of **Grenada** and the S Grenadines. Cap. St. George's.

gre·nade (grə-nād′) ▸*n.* A small bomb detonated by a fuse and thrown by hand or fired from a launcher. [< OFr. *(pome) grenate,* POME-GRANATE.]

gren·a·dier (grĕn′ə-dîr′) ▸*n.* A soldier belonging to an elite unit formerly armed with grenades. [Fr. < *grenade,* GRENADE.]

gren·a·dine (grĕn′ə-dēn′, grĕn′ə-dēn′) ▸*n.* A thick sweet syrup made from pomegranates. [< OFr. *grenate,* POMEGRANATE.]

Gren·a·dines (grĕn′ə-dēnz′) An archipelago in the Windward Is. of the E Caribbean, divided between Grenada and the country of St. Vincent and the Grenadines.

Gretz·ky (grĕt′skē), **Wayne** b. 1961. Canadian hockey player.

grew (grōō) ▸*v.* P.t. of **grow.**

grey (grā) ▸*adj. & n.* Var. of **gray.**

Grey, Lady **Jane.** 1537–54. Queen of England for nine days (1553).

Grey, Zane 1875–1939. Amer. writer.

grey·hound (grā′hound′) ▸*n.* A slender, swift-running dog having a narrow head and long legs. [< OE *grīghund.*]

grid (grĭd) ▸*n.* **1.** A framework of crisscrossed or parallel bars. **2.** A pattern of regularly spaced horizontal and vertical lines, as on a map, used as a reference for locating points. **3a.** An interconnected system for the distribution of electricity or electromagnetic signals over a wide area. **b.** A conducting plate in a storage battery. [< GRIDIRON.]

grid·dle (grĭd′l) ▸*n.* A flat pan or metal surface used for frying. [< Lat. *crātīcula* < *crātis,* lattice work.]

grid·dle·cake (grĭd′l kāk′) ▸*n.* See **pancake.**

grid·i·ron (grĭd′ī′ərn) ▸*n.* **1.** A football field. **2.** A flat metal grid or grate used for broiling. [< ME *gridere,* alteration of *gridel,* GRIDDLE.]

grid·lock (grĭd′lŏk′) ▸*n.* **1.** A traffic jam in which no vehicular movement is possible. **2.** A situation in which progress is stalled by competing interests. —**grid′lock′** *v.* —**grid′locked′** *adj.*

grief (grēf) ▸*n.* **1.** Deep mental anguish, as that arising from bereavement. **2.** A source of sorrow or anguish. **3.** Annoyance or frustration. **4.** *Informal* Criticism or rude talk: *gave me grief for being late.* [< OFr. < *grever,* GRIEVE.]

Grieg (grēg, grĭg), **Edvard Hagerup** 1843–1907. Norwegian composer.

griev·ance (grē′vəns) ▸*n.* **1.** A circumstance regarded as just cause for protest. **2.** A complaint based on such a circumstance.

grieve (grēv) ▸*v.* **grieved, griev·ing 1.** To cause sorrow to; distress. **2.** To feel or express grief. [< Lat. *gravāre,* to burden.] *Syns: lament, mourn, sorrow Ant: rejoice v.*

griev·ous (grē′vəs) ▸*adj.* Causing grief, pain, or anguish. —**griev′ous·ly** *adv.* —**griev′ous·ness** *n.*

grif·fin also **grif·fon** or **gryph·on** (grĭf′ən) ▸*n.* A fabulous beast with the head and wings of an eagle and the body of a lion. [< Lat. *grȳphus* < Gk. *grups.*]

Grif·fith (grĭf′ĭth), **D(avid Lewelyn) W(ark)** 1875–1948. Amer. filmmaker.

grill (grĭl) ▸*v.* **1.** To broil on a gridiron. **2.** *Informal* To question relentlessly; cross-examine. ▸*n.* **1.** A cooking surface of parallel metal bars. **2.** A restaurant where grilled foods are served. **3.** Var. of **grille.** [< Lat. *crātīcula,* GRIDDLE.]

grille also **grill** (grĭl) ▸*n.* A usu. metal grating used as a screen or barrier. [< OFr. *greille,* gridiron; see GRIDDLE.]

grim (grĭm) ▸*adj.* **grim·mer, grim·mest 1.** Dismal; gloomy. **2.** Stern or forbidding. **3.** Repellent or horrifying. **4.** Unrelenting or uncompromising. [< OE, fierce.] —**grim′ly** *adv.* —**grim′ness** *n.*

grim·ace (grĭm′ĭs, grĭ-mās′) ▸*n.* A contortion of the face expressive of pain, contempt, or disgust. [< OFr. *grimache.*] —**grim′ace** *v.*

grime (grīm) ▸*n.* Black dirt or soot clinging to or ingrained in a surface. [ME *grim.*] —**grim′i·ness** *n.* —**grim′y** *adj.*

Grimm (grĭm), **Jakob Ludwig Karl** (1785–1863) and **Wilhelm Karl** (1786–1859). German philologists and folklorists.

grin (grĭn) ▸*v.* **grinned, grin·ning** To smile broadly, showing the teeth. [< OE *grennian,* to grimace.] —**grin** *n.* —**grin′ner** *n.*

grind (grīnd) ▸*v.* **ground** (ground), **grind·ing 1a.** To crush or pulverize by friction. **b.** To shape, sharpen, or refine with friction: *grind a lens.* **2a.** To rub together harshly; gnash: *grind the teeth.* **b.** To move with noisy friction: *grind to a halt.* **3.** To oppress or weaken gradually. **4.** To operate or produce by turning a crank. **5.** To produce mechanically or without inspiration: *grinding out novels.* **6.** *Informal* To devote oneself to study or work. ▸*n.* **1.** A specific degree of pulverization. **2.** *Informal* A laborious task, routine, or study. **3.** *Informal* A student thought to work or study excessively. [< OE *grindan.*] —**grind′ing·ly** *adv.*

grind·er (grīn′dər) ▸*n.* **1.** One that grinds, esp.: **a.** One who sharpens cutting edges. **b.** A mechanical device that grinds. **2.** A submarine sandwich.

grind·stone (grīnd′stōn′) ▸*n.* **1.** A revolving stone disk used for grinding, polishing, or sharpening tools. **2.** A millstone. —*idiom:* **put (one's) nose to the grindstone** *Informal* To work in earnest.

grip (grĭp) ▸*n.* **1.** A tight hold; firm grasp. **2.** A manner of grasping and holding. **3.** Mastery; command: *a good grip on the subject.* **4.** Mental or emotional composure: *lost his grip after he was fired.* **5.** A part designed to be grasped; handle. **6.** A suitcase. **7.** A stagehand or member of a film crew who helps move scenery or adjust lighting and props. ►*v.* **gripped, grip·ping 1.** To secure and maintain a tight hold on. **2.** To hold the interest or attention of. [< OE *gripe.*] —**grip′per** *n.* —**grip′ping·ly** *adv.*

gripe (grīp) ►*v.* **griped, grip·ing 1.** *Informal* To complain naggingly or petulantly; grumble. **2.** To cause or have sharp pains in the bowels. **3.** *Informal* To irritate; annoy: *Your meddling really gripes me.* ►*n.* **1.** *Informal* A complaint. **2. gripes** Sharp pains in the bowels. [< OE *grīpan.*] —**grip′er** *n.*

grippe also **grip** (grĭp) ►*n.* See **influenza** (sense 1). [Fr. < OFr. *gripper,* seize.] —**grip′py** *adj.*

gris·ly (grĭz′lē) ►*adj.* **-li·er, -li·est** Horrifying; gruesome: *a grisly murder.* [< OE *grislīc.*] —**gris′li·ness** *n.*

grist (grĭst) ►*n.* Grain to be ground or already ground. —*idiom:* **grist for (one's) mill** Something that can be used to advantage. [< OE *grīst.*]

gris·tle (grĭs′əl) ►*n.* Cartilage, esp. in meat. [< OE.] —**gris′tly** *adj.*

grit (grĭt) ►*n.* **1.** Tiny rough granules, as of sand or stone. **2.** *Informal* Indomitable spirit. ►*v.* **grit·ted, grit·ting** To clamp (the teeth) together. [< OE *grēot.*] —**grit′ti·ly** *adv.* —**grit′ti·ness** *n.* —**grit′ty** *adj.*

grits (grĭts) ►*pl.n.* *(takes sing. or pl. v.)* **1.** A coarse meal made of ground hominy. **2.** A mush made from this meal. [< OE *grytta,* coarse meal.]

griz·zled (grĭz′əld) ►*adj.* Grizzly.

griz·zly (grĭz′lē) ►*adj.* **-zli·er, -zli·est** Grayish or flecked with gray. ►*n., pl.* **-zlies** A grizzly bear. [< OFr. *grisel,* gray < *gris.*]

grizzly bear ►*n.* A North American brown bear usu. having a grizzled coat.

grizzly bear

groan (grōn) ►*v.* To voice a deep inarticulate sound, as of pain, grief, or displeasure. [< OE *grānian.*] —**groan** *n.*

groats (grōts) ►*pl.n.* *(takes sing. or pl. v.)* Hulled, usu. crushed grain, esp. oats. [< OE *grotan.*]

gro·cer (grō′sər) ►*n.* One that sells foodstuffs and household supplies. [< Med.Lat. *grossārius,* wholesale dealer.]

gro·cer·y (grō′sə-rē) ►*n., pl.* **-ies 1.** A store selling foodstuffs and household supplies. **2. groceries** Goods sold by a grocer.

grog (grŏg) ►*n.* An alcoholic liquor, esp. rum diluted with water. [After Old *Grog,* Admiral Edward Vernon (1684–1757).]

grog·gy (grŏg′ē) ►*adj.* **-gi·er, -gi·est** Unsteady and dazed; shaky. —**grog′gi·ly** *adv.* —**grog′gi·ness** *n.*

groin (groin) ►*n.* **1.** *Anat.* The area around the

crease where the thighs meet the trunk. **2.** *Archit.* The curved edge at the junction of two intersecting vaults. [< ME *grinde.*]

grom·met (grŏm′ĭt) ►*n.* A reinforced eyelet, as in cloth or leather, through which a fastener may be passed. [Prob. < OFr. *gormette,* chain joining the ends of a bit.]

groom (groom, groom) ►*n.* **1.** One employed to take care of horses. **2.** A man recently married or about to be married. ►*v.* **1.** To make neat and trim. **2.** To clean and brush (an animal). **3.** To prepare, as for a specific position or purpose. [ME *grom.*] —**groom′er** *n.*

groove (groov) ►*n.* **1.** A long narrow furrow or channel. **2.** *Slang* A settled routine. **3.** *Slang* A pleasurable experience. ►*v.* **grooved, groov·ing 1.** To cut a groove or grooves. **2.** *Slang* To enjoy oneself. [Prob. < MDu. *groeve,* ditch.]

groov·y (groo′vē) ►*adj.* **-i·er, -i·est** *Slang* Delightful; wonderful. —**groov′i·ness** *n.*

grope (grōp) ►*v.* **groped, grop·ing 1.** To reach about uncertainly; feel one's way. **2.** To search blindly or uncertainly: *grope for an answer.* **3.** *Informal* To fondle (someone) for sexual pleasure. ►*n.* The act of groping. [< OE *grāpian.*] —**grop′er** *n.* —**grop′ing·ly** *adv.*

Gro·pi·us (grō′pē-əs), **Walter Adolph** 1883–1969. German-born Amer. architect.

gros·beak (grōs′bēk′) ►*n.* Any of various finches having a thick conical bill. [< Fr. *grosbec.*]

gross (grōs) ►*adj.* **-er, -est 1.** Exclusive of deductions; total: *gross profits.* **2.** Utter: *gross incompetence.* **3.** Glaringly obvious: *gross injustice.* **4a.** Coarse; crude. **b.** Disgusting. **5.** Overweight; corpulent. **6.** Not fine or detailed: *gross motor skills.* ►*n.* **1.** *pl.* **gross·es** The entire body or amount, as of income. **2.** *pl.* **gross** A group of 144 items; 12 dozen. ►*v.* To earn as a total before deductions. —*phrasal verb:* **gross out** *Slang* To fill with disgust. [< LLat. *grossus,* thick.] —**gross′ly** *adv.* —**gross′ness** *n.*

gross national product ►*n.* The total market value of all the goods and services produced by a nation during a specified period.

gro·tesque (grō-tĕsk′) ►*adj.* **1.** Marked by ludicrous, repulsive, or incongruous distortion, as of appearance. **2.** Outlandish or bizarre. [< Ital. *grottesco,* of a grotto.] —**gro·tesque′** *n.* —**gro·tesque′ly** *adv.* —**gro·tesque′ness** *n.* —**gro·tes′que·ry** *n.*

Gro·ti·us (grō′shē-əs, -shəs), **Hugo** 1583–1645. Dutch jurist and politician.

grot·to (grŏt′ō) ►*n., pl.* **-toes** or **-tos** A small natural or artificial cave. [< Ital. *grotta* < Lat. *crypta,* CRYPT.]

grouch (grouch) ►*n.* A habitually complaining or irritable person. ►*v.* To grumble or sulk. [< ME *grucchen,* complain; see GRUDGE.] —**grouch′i·ly** *adv.* —**grouch′i·ness** *n.* —**grouch′y** *adj.*

ground¹ (ground) ►*n.* **1.** The solid surface of the earth. **2.** Soil; earth. **3.** often **grounds** An area of land designated for a particular purpose. **4. grounds** The land surrounding a building. **5.** A position contested in or as if in battle. **6.** A background. **7.** often **grounds** The foundation or basis for an argument, action, or belief: *grounds for suspicion.* **8. grounds** The sediment at the bottom of a liquid. **9.** *Elect.* **a.** A large conducting body, such as the earth, used as an arbitrary zero of potential. **b.** A conducting object, such as a wire, connected to such a position of zero potential. ►*v.* **1.** To place on or cause to touch the ground. **2.** To provide a basis for; justify. **3.** To supply with basic information. **4a.** To prevent (an aircraft or pilot) from flying. **b.** *Informal* To restrict (someone) to a certain place as a punishment. **5.** *Elect.* To connect (an electric circuit) to a ground. **6.** To run (a vessel) aground. **7.** *Baseball* To hit (a ball) on the ground. [< OE *grund.*]

ground² (ground) ►*v.* P.t. and p.part. of **grind.**

ground·break·ing (ground′brā′kĭng) ►*n.* The act or ceremony of breaking ground to begin a construction project. ►*adj.* Highly original; new: *a groundbreaking technology.*

ground floor ►*n.* **1.** The floor of a building at or nearest ground level. **2.** *Informal* The beginning of a venture.

ground·hog (ground′hôg′, -hŏg′) ►*n.* See **woodchuck.**

ground·less (ground′lĭs) ►*adj.* Having no ground or foundation; unsubstantiated. See Synonyms at **baseless.** —**ground′less·ly** *adv.*

ground rule ►*n.* **1.** *Sports* A rule governing the playing of a game on a particular field, course, or court. **2.** A basic rule.

ground squirrel ►*n.* Any of several terrestrial squirrels usu. living in burrows and hibernating during the winter.

ground·swell (ground′swĕl′) ►*n.* **1.** A broad gathering of force, as of public opinion. **2.** A deep swell of the ocean.

ground·wa·ter also **ground water** (ground′-wô′tər, -wŏt′ər) ►*n.* Subterranean water that supplies wells and springs.

ground·work (ground′wûrk′) ►*n.* A foundation; basis.

ground zero ►*n.* **1.** The site of a violently destructive event, such as the detonation of a nuclear weapon. **2.** The center of rapid or intense development or change.

group (gro͞op) ►*n.* A number of persons or objects gathered, located, or classified together. See Usage Note at **collective noun.** ►*v.* To place in or form a group. [< Ital. *gruppo*, prob. of Gmc. orig.]

grou·per (gro͞o′pər) ►*n.*, *pl.* **-er** or **-pers** Any of various large food and game fishes which inhabit warm seas. [Port. *garupa.*]

group·ie (gro͞o′pē) ►*n.* *Slang* A fan who follows rock musicians or other performers around on tours.

grouse¹ (grous) ►*n.*, *pl.* **grouse** or **grous·es** A plump chickenlike game bird having mottled brown or grayish plumage. [?]

grouse² (grous) ►*v.* **groused, grous·ing** *Informal* To complain. [Perh. < OFr. *grouchier*, grumble.] —**grouse** *n.* —**grous′er** *n.*

grout (grout) ►*n.* A thin mortar used to fill cracks and crevices, as between tiles. ►*v.* To fill or finish with grout. [< OE *grūt*, coarse meal.] —**grout′er** *n.*

grove (grōv) ►*n.* A small stand of trees lacking dense undergrowth. [< OE *grāf.*]

grov·el (grŏv′əl, grŭv′-) ►*v.* **-eled, -el·ing** also **-elled, -el·ling 1.** To behave in a servile or obsequious manner. **2.** To prostrate oneself, as in humility. [< ON *ā grūfu*, lying face down.] —**grov′el·er** *n.* —**grov′el·ing·ly** *adv.*

grow (grō) ►*v.* **grew** (gro͞o), **grown** (grōn), **grow·ing 1a.** To increase or cause to increase in size by a natural process. **b.** To cultivate;

raise: *grow vegetables.* **2.** To expand or intensify. **3.** To develop and reach maturity. **4.** To originate; stem: *love that grew from friendship.* **5.** To become: *grow angry; grow closer.* —**phrasal verbs: grow on** To become gradually more pleasurable or acceptable to. **grow up** To become an adult. [< OE *grōwan.*] —**grow′-er** *n.*

growl (groul) ►*n.* A low, guttural, menacing sound, as of a dog. [Prob. < OFr. *grouler*, of Gmc. orig.] —**growl** *v.* —**growl′er** *n.* —**growl′y** *adj.*

grown (grōn) ►*v.* P.part. of **grow.** ►*adj.* Adult; mature.

grown·up also **grown-up** (grōn′ŭp′) ►*n.* An adult.

grown-up (grōn′ŭp′) ►*adj.* Of or intended for adults; mature.

growth (grōth) ►*n.* **1.** The process of growing or developing. **2.** Evolution. **3.** An increase, as in size or number. **4.** Something that has grown: *a new growth of grass.* **5.** *Med.* An abnormal mass of tissue in or on a living organism.

growth ring ►*n.* **1.** A growth layer in secondary xylem seen in a cross section. **2.** A layer of hard material deposited in a single period of growth of an animal, as in the plates of a turtle's shell.

Groz·ny (grôz′nē) The capital of Chechnya in SW Russia.

grub (grŭb) ►*v.* **grubbed, grub·bing 1.** To dig up by or as if by the roots. **2.** To clear of roots and stumps. **3a.** To search laboriously; rummage. **b.** To toil arduously; drudge. **4.** *Slang* To obtain by begging: *grub a cigarette.* ►*n.* **1.** The thick wormlike larva of certain insects. **2.** *Slang* Food. [ME *grubben.*] —**grub′ber** *n.*

grub·by (grŭb′ē) ►*adj.* **-bi·er, -bi·est** Dirty; grimy. —**grub′bi·ly** *adv.* —**grub′bi·ness** *n.*

grub·stake (grŭb′stāk′) ►*n.* Supplies or funds advanced to a mining prospector or a person starting a business in return for a share of the profits. —**grub′stake′** *v.*

grudge (grŭj) ►*v.* **grudged, grudg·ing** To be reluctant to give or admit. ►*n.* A lasting feeling of resentment. [< OFr. *grouchier*, grumble.] —**grudg′er** *n.* —**grudg′ing·ly** *adv.*

gru·el (gro͞o′əl) ►*n.* A thin watery porridge. [< OFr., of Gmc. orig.]

gru·el·ing also **gru·el·ling** (gro͞o′ə-lĭng, gro͞o′-lĭng) ►*adj.* Physically or mentally demanding. —**gru′el·ing·ly** *adv.*

grue·some (gro͞o′səm) ►*adj.* Causing horror and repugnance; frightful and shocking. [Obsolete *grue*, to shudder + –SOME¹.] —**grue′some·ly** *adv.* —**grue′some·ness** *n.*

gruff (grŭf) ►*adj.* **-er, -est 1.** Brief and unfriendly: *a gruff reply.* **2.** Hoarse; harsh. [< MDu. *grof.*] —**gruff′ly** *adv.* —**gruff′ness** *n.*

grum·ble (grŭm′bəl) ►*v.* **-bled, -bling** To mutter discontentedly. [< MDu. *grommelen.*] —**grum′ble** *n.* —**grum′bler** *n.*

grump (grŭmp) ►*n.* **1.** A cranky, complaining person. **2. grumps** A fit of ill temper. [?] —**grump** *v.* —**grump′i·ly** *adv.* —**grump′i·ness** *n.* —**grump′y** *adj.*

grunge (grŭnj) ►*n.* **1.** *Informal* Filth; dirt. **2.** Rock music that incorporates elements of punk rock and heavy metal, often expressing a bleak or nihilistic outlook. [Back-formation < GRUNGY.]

grun·gy (grŭn′jē) ►*adj.* **-gi·er, -gi·est** *Informal*

In a dirty or run-down condition. [?]

grunt (grŭnt) ►*v.* To utter (with) a deep guttural sound, as a hog does. ►*n.* **1.** A deep guttural sound. **2.** Any of various tropical fishes that produce grunting sounds. **3.** *Slang* An infantryman in the US military. **4.** *Slang* A menial; drudge. [< OE *grunnettan.*] —**grunt′er** *n.*

gr. wt. ►*abbr.* gross weight

gryph·on (grĭf′ən) ►*n.* Var. of **griffin.**

GU ►*abbr.* **1.** genitourinary **2.** Guam

gua·ca·mo·le (gwä′kə-mō′lē) ►*n.* A thick paste of mashed and seasoned avocado, served as a dip. [< Nahuatl *ahuacamolli.*]

Gua·da·la·ja·ra (gwŏd′l-ə-hä′rə) A city of W-central Mexico WNW of Mexico City.

Gua·dal·ca·nal (gwŏd′l-kə-năl′) A volcanic island of the W Pacific, the largest of the Solomon Is.

Gua·de·loupe (gwŏd′l-ōōp′, gwŏd′l-ōōp′) An overseas department of France in the Leeward Is. of the West Indies. Cap. Basse-Terre.

Guam (gwäm) An unincorp. territory of the US, the largest of the Mariana Is. in the W Pacific. Cap. Agana. —**Gua·ma′ni·an** (gwä-mä′nē-ən) *adj. & n.*

gua·na·ba·na (gwə-nä′bə-nə) ►*n.* See **soursop.** [Am.Sp. *guanábana.*]

Guang·zhou (gwäng′jō′) also **Kwang·chow** (kwäng′chō′) Formerly **Canton.** A city of S China on a delta near the South China Sea.

gua·nine (gwä′nēn′) ►*n.* A purine base, $C_5H_5ON_5$, that is an essential constituent of both RNA and DNA. [< GUANO.]

gua·no (gwä′nō) ►*n., pl.* **-nos** The dung of seabirds or bats, used as fertilizer. [< Quechua *huanu,* dung.]

Guan·tá·na·mo (gwän-tä′nə-mō′) A city of SE Cuba N of **Guantánamo Bay,** an inlet of the Caribbean Sea.

guar (gwär) ►*n.* An annual plant cultivated in semiarid regions for its seeds. [Hindi *guār.*]

gua·ra·ni (gwä′rə-nē′) ►*n., pl.* **-ni** or **-nis** See table at **currency.** [Sp. *guaraní,* Guarani.]

Guaraní ►*n., pl.* **-ní** or **-nis 1.** A member of a South American Indian people of Paraguay, N Argentina, and S Brazil. **2.** The language of the Guaraní.

guar·an·tee (găr′ən-tē′) ►*n.* **1.** Something assuring a particular outcome or condition. **2a.** A usu. written assurance as to the quality or durability of a product or service. **b.** A pledge that something will be performed in a specified manner. **3.** A guaranty. **4.** A guarantor. ►*v.* **-teed, -tee·ing 1.** To assume responsibility for the debt or default of. **2.** To assume responsibility for the quality or performance of. **3.** To undertake to accomplish or ensure: *guarantees free speech.* **4.** To make certain: *The rain guarantees a good crop this year.* **5.** To furnish security for. **6.** To declare with conviction. [< OFr. *garant,* a warrant.]

guar·an·tor (găr′ən-tôr′, găr′ən-tər) ►*n.* One that gives a promise, assurance, or pledge.

guar·an·ty (găr′ən-tē) ►*n., pl.* **-ties 1.** A promise to be answerable for the debt or obligation of another in the event of nonpayment or nonperformance. **2a.** Something given as security for the execution or completion of something else. **b.** The act of providing such security. **3.** A guarantee. [< OFr. *garant,* a warrant.]

guard (gärd) ►*v.* **1a.** To protect from harm; watch over: *guarded the president.* **b.** To supervise the entry and exit through: *guarded the door.* **c.** To watch over to prevent escape: *guarded the prisoner.* **d.** To keep from risk or curtailment: *guarded her privacy.* **2.** *Sports* To keep (an opposing player) from scoring. **3.** To serve as a guard. ►*n.* **1.** One who protects or keeps watch. **2.** One who supervises prisoners. **3.** An honor guard. **4.** *Football* One of the two offensive linemen on either side of the center. **5.** *Basketball* Either of the two players positioned in the backcourt. **6.** A device or attachment that prevents injury, damage, or loss. —*idiom:* **on (or off) (one's) guard** Being (or not being) alert and watchful. [< OFr. *guarder.*] —**guard′er** *n.*

guard·ed (gär′dĭd) ►*adj.* **1.** Protected; supervised. **2.** Cautious; restrained: *guarded optimism.* —**guard′ed·ly** *adv.*

guard·house (gärd′hous′) ►*n.* **1.** A building that accommodates a military guard. **2.** A military jail.

guard·i·an (gär′dē-ən) ►*n.* **1.** One that guards or protects. **2.** One legally responsible for the person or property of an incompetent or minor. —**guard′i·an·ship′** *n.*

guards·man (gärdz′mən) ►*n.* A member of the National Guard.

guar gum ►*n.* A paste made from the seeds of the guar, used as an ingredient in foods and pharmaceuticals.

Guar·ne·ri (gwär-nĕr′ē, -nyĕr′ē) Family of Italian violin makers, including **Andrea** (1626?–98) and **Giuseppe** (1687?–1745).

Gua·te·ma·la (gwä′tə-mä′lə) **1.** A country of N Central America. Cap. Guatemala. **2.** Also **Guatemala City** The capital of Guatemala, in the S-central part. —**Gua′te·ma′lan** *adj. & n.*

gua·va (gwä′və) ►*n.* The edible fruit of a tropical American tree, usu. having greenish skin and sweet white or pink flesh. [Sp. *guayaba.*]

gu·ber·na·to·ri·al (gōō′bər-nə-tôr′ē-əl, gyōō′-) ►*adj.* Of or relating to a governor. [< Lat. *gubernātor,* governor.]

guck (gŭk, gŏŏk) also **gook** (gŏŏk, gōōk) ►*n.* *Slang* A thick messy substance, such as sludge. [Poss. G(OO) + (M)UCK.]

Guern·sey[1] (gûrn′zē) An island in the Channel Is. between England and France, governed as a British dependency.

Guern·sey[2] (gûrn′zē) ►*n., pl.* **-seys** A breed of brown and white dairy cattle orig. developed on the island of Guernsey.

guer·ril·la or **gue·ril·la** (gə-rĭl′ə) ►*n.* A member of an irregular military force operating in small bands in occupied territory to harass and undermine the enemy. ►*adj.* **1.** Of or relating to guerrillas or their tactics. **2.** Using unconventional and usu. inexpensive means to generate public interest. [Sp., raiding party < *guerra,* war.]

guess (gĕs) ►*v.* **1.** To predict (a result or event) without sufficient information. **2.** To estimate correctly. **3.** To suppose; think: *I guess he was wrong.* ►*n.* **1.** An act of guessing. **2.** A conjecture arrived at by guessing. [ME *gessen.*] —**guess′er** *n.*

guess·work (gĕs′wûrk′) ►*n.* The process or result of making guesses.

guest (gĕst) ►*n.* **1.** One who receives hospitality at the home or table of another. **2.** One who pays for meals or accommodations at a restaurant or hotel. **3.** A visiting performer or contestant, as on a television program. [< ON *gestr.*]

guest worker ▸*n.* A foreigner who is permitted to work in a country on a temporary basis.

Gue·va·ra (gə-vär′ə), **Ernesto "Che."** 1928–67. Argentine-born Cuban revolutionary leader.

guff (gŭf) ▸*n. Slang* **1.** Nonsense; baloney. **2.** Back talk. [Perh. imit.]

guf·faw (gə-fô′) ▸*n.* A boisterous burst of laughter. [Prob. imit.] —**guf·faw′** *v.*

GUI (gōō′ē) ▸*n. Comp.* An interface in which a pointing device, such as a mouse, is used to manipulate graphical images on a monitor. [*g(raphical) u(ser) i(nterface).*]

Gui·an·a (gē-ăn′ə, -ä′nə, gī-) A region of NE South America including SE Venezuela, part of N Brazil, and French Guiana, Suriname, and Guyana.

guid·ance (gīd′ns) ▸*n.* **1.** The act or process of guiding. **2.** Counseling; advice. **3.** Any of various processes for guiding the path of a vehicle, esp. a missile.

guide (gīd) ▸*n.* **1.** One who shows the way by leading, directing, or advising, esp. one employed to conduct others, as on a tour or expedition. **2.** Something, such as a pamphlet, that offers basic information or instruction. **3.** Something that serves to direct. **4.** A device, such as a ruler, that serves as an indicator or regulates motion. ▸*v.* **guid·ed, guid·ing 1.** To serve as a guide for. **2.** To direct the course of; steer. **3.** To exert control or influence over. [< OProv. *guidar*, to guide, of Gmc. orig.] —**guid′er** *n.*
Syns: lead, pilot, shepherd, steer, usher **v.**

guide·book (gīd′bŏŏk′) ▸*n.* A handbook of information, esp. for travelers or tourists.

guid·ed missile (gī′dĭd) ▸*n.* A self-propelled missile that can be guided while in flight.

guide dog ▸*n.* A dog trained to guide a blind or visually impaired person.

guide·line (gīd′līn′) ▸*n.* A statement or rule of policy or procedure.

guide·post (gīd′pōst′) ▸*n.* A post with a sign giving directions for travelers.

gui·don (gī′dŏn′, gīd′n) ▸*n.* A small flag carried by a military unit. [< OItal. *guidone* < *guidare*, GUIDE.]

guild (gĭld) ▸*n.* An association of persons of the same trade, formed to protect common interests and maintain standards. [< ON *gildi*, payment.]

guil·der (gĭl′dər) ▸*n.* The primary unit of currency in the Netherlands before the adoption of the euro. [< MDu. *gulden*, golden.]

guile (gīl) ▸*n.* Treacherous cunning; skillful deceit. [< OFr.] —**guile′ful** *adj.* —**guile′ful·ly** *adv.* —**guile′less** *adj.* —**guile′less·ly** *adv.* —**guile′less·ness** *n.*

guil·lo·tine (gĭl′ə-tēn′, gē′ə-) ▸*n.* A device consisting of a heavy blade held aloft between upright guides and dropped to behead a person condemned to die. ▸*v.* **-tined, -tin·ing** To behead with a guillotine. [After J.I. *Guillotin* (1738–1814).]

guilt (gĭlt) ▸*n.* **1a.** The fact of being responsible for the commission of an offense. **b.** *Law* The fact of having been found to have violated a criminal law. **2a.** Remorseful awareness of hav-

ing done something wrong. **b.** Self-reproach, as for inadequacy. [< OE *gylt*, crime.] —**guilt′less** *adj.* —**guilt′less·ly** *adv.*

guilt·y (gĭl′tē) ▸*adj.* **-i·er, -i·est 1.** Responsible for a crime or wrongdoing. **2.** Suffering from or prompted by a sense of guilt. —**guilt′i·ly** *adv.* —**guilt′i·ness** *n.*

guin·ea (gĭn′ē) ▸*n.* A former English gold coin worth one pound and one shilling. [After the *Guinea* coast of Africa.]

Guinea A country of W Africa on the Atlantic. Cap. Conakry. —**Guin′e·an** *adj. & n.*

Guinea, Gulf of A broad inlet of the Atlantic formed by the great bend in the W-central coast of Africa.

Guin·ea-Bis·sau (gĭn′ē-bĭ-sou′) A country of W Africa on the Atlantic. Cap. Bissau.

guinea fowl ▸*n.* A domesticated African bird having blackish plumage flecked with small white spots. [After the *Guinea* coast of Africa.]

guinea pig ▸*n.* **1.** A small, stocky, short-eared rodent having no visible tail, often kept as a pet or used in biomedical research. **2.** *Informal* A person used for experimentation or research. [Poss. alteration of GUIANA.]

Guin·e·vere (gwĭn′ə-vîr′) also **Guen·e·vere** (gwĕn′-) ▸*n.* The wife of King Arthur and lover of Lancelot in Arthurian legend.

guise (gīz) ▸*n.* **1.** Outward appearance; aspect. **2.** False appearance. [< OFr., manner.]

gui·tar (gĭ-tär′) ▸*n.* A musical instrument having a large flat-backed sound box, a long fretted neck, and usu. six strings. [< Gk. *kithara*, lyre.] —**gui·tar′ist** *n.*

Gu·ja·ra·ti (gōō′jə-rä′tē) ▸*n.* An Indic language spoken in W India.

gu·lag also **Gu·lag** (gōō′läg) ▸*n.* A network of forced labor camps in the former Soviet Union, esp. for political dissidents. [Russ.]

gulch (gŭlch) ▸*n.* A small ravine. [Perh. < ME *gulchen*, spew.]

gulf (gŭlf) ▸*n.* **1.** A large area of a sea or ocean partially enclosed by land. **2.** A deep, wide chasm; abyss. **3.** A wide gap, as in understanding. [< Gk. *kolpos.*]

Gulf Stream ▸*n.* A generally N-flowing warm ocean current of the N Atlantic off E North America.

gulf·weed (gŭlf′wēd′) ▸*n.* A brownish, tropical Atlantic seaweed often forming dense floating masses.

gull¹ (gŭl) ▸*n.* Any of various chiefly coastal seabirds having long wings, webbed feet, and usu. gray and white plumage. [ME *gulle*, poss. of Celt. orig.]

gull² (gŭl) ▸*n.* A person who is easily tricked; dupe. ▸*v.* To deceive or cheat. [Prob. < *gull*, to swallow.]

Gul·lah (gŭl′ə) ▸*n.* **1.** One of a group of people of African ancestry inhabiting coastal areas of South Carolina, Georgia, and N Florida. **2.** The English-based creole of the Gullahs.

gul·let (gŭl′ĭt) ▸*n.* **1.** The esophagus. **2.** The throat. [< OFr. *goulet* < Lat. *gula.*]

gul·li·ble (gŭl′ə-bəl) ▸*adj.* Easily deceived or duped. —**gul′li·bil′i·ty** *n.* —**gul′li·bly** *adv.*

gul·ly (gŭl′ē) ▸*n., pl.* **-lies** A deep ditch cut in the earth by running water. [< GULLET.]

gulp (gŭlp) ▸*v.* **1.** To swallow greedily or rapidly in large amounts. **2.** To swallow air audibly, as in nervousness. ►*n.* **1.** The act of gulping. **2.** A large mouthful. [ME *gulpen.*]

gum¹ (gŭm) ►*n.* **1.** Any of various viscous plant substances that dry into water-soluble, non-crystalline, brittle solids. **2.** A sticky or adhesive substance. **3.** Any of various trees yielding gum. **4.** Chewing gum. ►*v.* **gummed, gum·ming 1.** To cover, seal, or fix in place with gum. **2.** To become sticky or clogged. —*phrasal verb:* **gum up** To ruin or bungle. [< Gk. *kommi.*] —**gum′mi·ness** *n.* —**gum′my** *adj.*

gum² (gŭm) ►*n.* The firm connective tissue that surrounds the bases of the teeth. ►*v.* **gummed, gum·ming** To chew (food) with toothless gums. [< OE *gōma,* palate.]

gum arabic ►*n.* A gum that is exuded by various African trees and is used as a thickener and emulsifier in food, pharmaceutical, and industrial products.

gum·bo (gŭm′bō) ►*n., pl.* **-bos 1a.** See **okra** (sense 1). **b.** *Regional* See **okra** (sense 3). **2.** A soup or stew thickened with okra pods. [Louisiana Fr. *gombo.*]

gum·drop (gŭm′drŏp′) ►*n.* A small candy made of sweetened gum arabic or gelatin.

gump·tion (gŭmp′shən) ►*n. Informal* Boldness of enterprise; initiative. [Sc.]

gum·shoe (gŭm′shōō′) ►*n.* **1.** A rubber overshoe. **2.** *Slang* A detective.

gun (gŭn) ►*n.* **1.** A weapon consisting of a metal tube from which a projectile is fired. **2.** A portable firearm. **3.** A device that discharges something under pressure or at great speed: *a grease gun.* ►*v.* **gunned, gun·ning 1.** To shoot (a person): *gun down a robber.* **2.** To open the throttle of: *gunned the engine.* —*phrasal verb:* **gun for 1.** To intend harm to (someone). **2.** To go after in earnest. —*idiom:* **under the gun** Under great pressure or threat. [< shortening of ME *Gunilda,* woman's name applied to a siege engine < ON *gunnr,* war.]

gun·boat (gŭn′bōt′) ►*n.* A small armed vessel.

gun·cot·ton (gŭn′kŏt′n) ►*n.* See **nitrocellulose.**

gun·fight (gŭn′fīt′) ►*n.* A duel or battle with firearms. —**gun′fight′er** *n.*

gun·fire (gŭn′fīr′) ►*n.* The firing of guns.

gung ho (gŭng′ hō′) ►*adj. Slang* Extremely enthusiastic and dedicated. [Orig. a US Marine battalion motto < Mandarin *gōnghé,* slogan of the Chinese Industrial Cooperative Society < *gōng(yè)hé(zuòshè),* Chinese Industrial Cooperative Society.]

gun·lock (gŭn′lŏk′) ►*n.* A device for igniting the charge of a firearm.

gun·man (gŭn′mən) ►*n.* A man, esp. a criminal, armed with a gun.

gun·met·al (gŭn′mĕt′l) ►*n.* **1.** An alloy of copper with tin. **2.** Metal used for guns. **3.** A dark gray.

gun·nel (gŭn′əl) ►*n.* Var. of **gunwale.**

gun·ner (gŭn′ər) ►*n.* A member of the armed forces who operates a gun.

gun·ner·y (gŭn′ə-rē) ►*n.* The science of constructing and operating guns.

gunnery sergeant ►*n.* A rank in the US Marine Corps above staff sergeant.

gun·ny (gŭn′ē) ►*n.* A coarse heavy fabric made of jute or hemp. [< Skt. *goṇī,* sack.]

gun·ny·sack (gŭn′ē-săk′) ►*n.* A sack made of burlap or gunny.

gun·play (gŭn′plā′) ►*n.* A shooting of guns with intent to inflict harm.

gun·pow·der (gŭn′pou′dər) ►*n.* An explosive powder that is used to propel projectiles from guns.

gun·shot (gŭn′shŏt′) ►*n.* **1.** The shooting of a gun. **2.** The range of a gun: *within gunshot.* **3.** Shot fired from a gun.

gun-shy (gŭn′shī′) ►*adj.* **1.** Afraid of loud noise, esp. gunfire. **2.** Extremely wary.

gun·smith (gŭn′smĭth′) ►*n.* One who makes or repairs firearms.

gun·wale also **gun·nel** (gŭn′əl) ►*n.* The upper edge of the side of a ship or boat.

gup·py (gŭp′ē) ►*n., pl.* **-pies** A small, brightly colored freshwater fish. [After R.J. Lechmere *Guppy* (1836–1916).]

gur·gle (gûr′gəl) ►*v.* **-gled, -gling 1.** To flow in a broken, irregular current with a bubbling sound. **2.** To make a sound similar to this. [< Lat. *gurguliō,* gullet.] —**gur′gle** *n.* —**gur′gling·ly** *adv.*

gur·ney (gûr′nē) ►*n., pl.* **-neys** A metal stretcher with wheeled legs that is used for transporting patients. [Prob. after J. Theodore *Gurney.*]

gu·ru (gŏŏr′ōō, gŏŏ-rōō′) ►*n., pl.* **-rus 1.** In Hinduism and Tibetan Buddhism, a personal spiritual teacher. **2.** Any of the ten spiritual leaders who developed Sikhism. **3a.** A trusted counselor and adviser. **b.** A popular or influential leader or advocate: *the guru of high finance.* [< Skt. *guru-,* venerable.]

gush (gŭsh) ►*v.* **1.** To flow forth suddenly in great volume. **2.** To make an excessive display of sentiment or enthusiasm. ►*n.* **1.** A copious outflow. **2.** Excessively demonstrative language or behavior. [ME *gushen.*] —**gush′i·ly** *adv.* —**gush′i·ness** *n.* —**gush′y** *adj.*

gush·er (gŭsh′ər) ►*n.* One that gushes, esp. a gas or oil well.

gus·set (gŭs′ĭt) ►*n.* A triangular insert for added strength or expansion in a garment. [< OFr. *gousset.*]

gus·sy (gŭs′ē) ►*v.* **-sied, -sy·ing** *Slang* To dress or adorn elaborately. [Poss. < Australian slang *gussie,* effeminate man.]

gust (gŭst) ►*n.* **1.** A strong abrupt rush of wind. **2.** A sudden burst, as of rain. **3.** An outburst of emotion. ►*v.* To blow in gusts. [< ON *gustr.*] —**gust′i·ly** *adv.* —**gust′y** *adj.*

gus·ta·to·ry (gŭs′tə-tôr′ē) ►*adj.* Of or relating to the sense of taste. [< Lat. *gustāre,* to taste.] —**gus′ta·to′ri·ly** *adv.*

Gus·tav I Va·sa (gŏŏs′tăv′; vä′sä) 1496–1560. King of Sweden (1523–60).

Gustav II Ad·olf (äd′ôlf) 1594–1632. King of Sweden (1611–32).

gus·to (gŭs′tō) ►*n.* Vigorous enjoyment: *ate the roast turkey with gusto.* See Synonyms at **zest.** [Ital.]

gut (gŭt) ►*n.* **1.** The digestive tract or a portion thereof, esp. the intestine or stomach. **2. guts** The bowels; entrails. **3.** *Slang* **a.** One's innermost being. **b. guts** The inner or essential parts. **4. guts** *Slang* **a.** Courage; fortitude. **b.** Nerve; audacity. **5.** A tough cord made from animal intestines. ►*v.* **gut·ted, gut·ting 1.** To disembowel. **2.** To remove the essence or substance of. **3.** To destroy the interior of: *Fire gutted the house.* ►*adj. Slang* Deeply felt: *a gut response.* [< OE *guttas,* entrails.]

Gu·ten·berg (gōōt′n-bûrg′), **Johann** 1400?–68? German printer.

Johann Gutenberg

Guth·rie (gŭth′rē), **Woodrow Wilson** "Woody." 1912–67. Amer. folk singer and composer.

gut·less (gŭt′lĭs) ►*adj. Slang* Lacking courage or drive. —**gut′less·ness** *n.*

guts·y (gŭt′sē) ►*adj.* **-i·er, -i·est** *Slang* Courageous; plucky. —**guts′i·ly** *adv.* —**guts′i·ness** *n.*

gut·ta-per·cha (gŭt′ə-pûr′chə) ►*n.* A rubbery substance obtained from certain tropical trees, used as an electrical insulator and in golf balls. [Malay *getah perca*.]

gut·ter (gŭt′ər) ►*n.* **1.** A channel for draining off water along the edge of a street or roof. **2.** A trough on either side of a bowling alley. **3.** A squalid state of human existence. ►*v.* **1.** To flow in channels. **2.** To burn low and unsteadily; flicker: *The candle guttered and died.* [< Lat. *gutta*, a drop.]

gut·ter·snipe (gŭt′ər-snīp′) ►*n.* A street urchin.

gut·tur·al (gŭt′ər-əl) ►*adj.* **1.** Of or produced in the throat. **2.** Harsh; throaty. **3.** *Ling.* Velar. [< Lat. *guttur*, throat.] —**gut′tur·al·ly** *adv.*

guy[1] (gī) ►*n.* A rope, cord, or cable used to steady, guide, or secure something. [< OFr. *guier*, to guide and < LGer. *gie*, a guide.] —**guy** *v.*

guy[2] (gī) ►*n. Informal* **1.** A man; fellow. **2. guys** Persons of either sex. [After *Guy* FAWKES.]

Guy·a·na (gī-ăn′ə, -ä′nə) A country of NE South America on the Atlantic. Cap. Georgetown. —**Guy′a·nese′** (-nēz′, -nēs′) *adj. & n.*

guz·zle (gŭz′əl) ►*v.* **-zled, -zling** To drink greedily. [?] —**guz′zler** *n.*

gym (jĭm) ►*n.* **1.** A gymnasium. **2.** A school course in physical education.

gym·na·si·um (jĭm-nā′zē-əm) ►*n., pl.* **-si·ums** or **-si·a** (-zē-ə) **1.** A room or building equipped for indoor sports. **2.** (gĭm-nä′zē-ōōm′) A college-preparatory school in some European countries. [< Gk. *gumnasion*, school < *gumnos*, nude.]

gym·nas·tics (jĭm-năs′tĭks) ►*n.* (takes pl. v.) Physical exercises that develop and display strength, balance, and agility, esp. those performed on or with specialized apparatus. [< Gk. *gumnastēs*, athletic trainer.] —**gym′nast′** *n.* —**gym·nas′tic** *adj.* —**gym·nas′ti·cal·ly** *adv.*

gym·no·sperm (jĭm′nə-spûrm′) ►*n.* A vascular plant, such as a conifer, whose seeds are not enclosed within an ovary. [< Gk. *gumnospermos*, having naked seeds.] —**gym′no·sper′mous** *adj.* —**gym′no·sper′my** *n.*

gy·ne·col·o·gy (gī′nĭ-kŏl′ə-jē, jĭn′ĭ-, jī′nĭ-) ►*n.* The branch of medicine dealing with the health of women and esp. of the female reproductive system. [Gk. *gunē, gunaik-*, woman + –LOGY.] —**gy′ne·co·log′i·cal** (-kə-lŏj′ĭ-kəl), **gy′ne·co·log′ic** *adj.* —**gy′ne·col′o·gist** *n.*

gyp (jĭp) *Offensive Slang* ►*v.* **gypped, gyp·ping** To cheat or swindle. ►*n.* A fraud or swindle. [Prob. < GYPSY.] —**gyp′per** *n.*

gyp·sum (jĭp′səm) ►*n.* A white mineral form of calcium sulfate, used to manufacture plaster of Paris, various plaster products, and fertilizers. [< Gk. *gupsos*.]

Gyp·sy (jĭp′sē) ►*n., pl.* **-sies 1a.** A Romani. **b.** The Romani language. **2.** A member of any of various traditionally itinerant groups unrelated to the Romani. **3. gypsy** One inclined to a nomadic way of life.

gypsy moth ►*n.* A moth having caterpillars that are destructive to trees, esp. in the NE US.

gy·rate (jī′rāt′) ►*v.* **-rat·ed, -rat·ing 1.** To revolve around a fixed point or axis. **2.** To revolve in a circle or spiral. [< Lat. *gȳrus*, circle.] —**gy·ra′tion** *n.* —**gy′ra·tor** *n.*

gyr·fal·con (jûr′făl′kən, -fôl′-, -fô′-) ►*n.* A large Arctic falcon with color phases from black to gray to white. [< OFr. *girfaut*.]

gy·ro[1] (jī′rō) ►*n., pl.* **-ros** A gyroscope.

gy·ro[2] (yē′rō, jī′-, jē′-) ►*n., pl.* **-ros** A sandwich made usu. of sliced roasted lamb, onion, and tomato on pita bread. [< Mod.Gk. *guros*, a turning.]

gy·ro·com·pass (jī′rō-kŭm′pəs, -kŏm′-) ►*n.* A compass with a motorized gyroscope that maintains a true north-south orientation.

gy·ro·scope (jī′rə-skōp′) ►*n.* A device consisting of a spinning mass, usu. a disk or wheel, mounted on a base so that its axis can turn freely in one or more directions and thereby maintain its orientation regardless of any movement of the base. [Gk. *guros*, circle + –SCOPE.] —**gy′ro·scop′ic** (-skŏp′ĭk) *adj.* —**gy′ro·scop′i·cal·ly** *adv.*

H

h[1] or **H** (āch) ►*n., pl.* **h's** or **H's** also **hs** or **Hs** The 8th letter of the English alphabet.

h[2] ►*abbr.* **1.** height **2.** hour

H ►*abbr.* **1.** *Baseball* hit **2.** home telephone number **3.** hot **4.** humidity

ha[1] also **hah** (hä) ►*interj.* Used to express surprise, laughter, or triumph.

ha[2] ►*abbr.* hectare

Ha·bak·kuk (hăb′ə-kŭk′, -kōōk′, hə-băk′ək) ►*n.* **1.** A Hebrew prophet of the late 7th cent. BC. **2.** See table at **Bible.**

ha·be·as corpus (hā′bē-əs) ►*n.* A writ that a person may seek from a court to obtain immediate release from an unlawful confinement. [< Med.Lat. *habeās corpus*, you must have the body.]

hab·er·dash·er (hăb′ər-dăsh′ər) ►*n.* A dealer in men's attire. [< AN *haberdassher*.]

hab·er·dash·er·y (hăb′ər-dăsh′ə-rē) ►*n., pl.* **-ies 1.** A haberdasher's shop. **2.** The goods sold by a haberdasher.

ha·bil·i·ments (hə-bĭl′ə-mənts) ►*pl.n.* Clothing, esp. the clothing associated with a special occasion or office. [< OFr. *habiller*, clothe.]

hab·it (hăb′ĭt) ►*n.* **1.** A pattern of behavior acquired through repetition. **2.** Customary practice. **3.** An addiction. **4.** Characteristic appearance or manner of growth, as of a plant. **5.** A distinctive costume, esp. of a religious order. [< Lat. *habitus*, p.part. of *habēre*, have.]

hab·it·a·ble (hăb′ĭ-tə-bəl) ►*adj.* Suitable to live in. [< Lat. *habitāre*, inhabit.] **—hab′it·a·bil′i·ty** *n.* **—hab′it·a·bly** *adv.*

hab·i·tat (hăb′ĭ-tăt′) ►*n.* **1.** The area or environment in which an organism or population normally lives or occurs. **2.** The place in which a person or thing is likely to be found. [< Lat., it dwells.]

hab·i·ta·tion (hăb′ĭ-tā′shən) ►*n.* **1.** The act of inhabiting or the state of being inhabited. **2a.** A natural environment or locality. **b.** A place of residence. [< Lat. *habitāre*, dwell.]

hab·it-form·ing (hăb′ĭt-fôr′mĭng) ►*adj.* Tending to become a habit, esp. as a result of physiological dependence.

ha·bit·u·al (hə-bĭch′ō͞o-əl) ►*adj.* **1a.** Done by habit: *habitual lying.* **b.** Being so by habit: *a habitual liar.* See Synonyms at **chronic. 2.** Customary; usual. See Synonyms at **usual. —ha·bit′u·al·ly** *adv.* **—ha·bit′u·al·ness** *n.*

ha·bit·u·ate (hə-bĭch′ō͞o-āt′) ►*v.* **-at·ed, -at·ing** To accustom by repetition or exposure. [< Lat. *habitus*, HABIT.] **—ha·bit′u·a′tion** *n.*

ha·bit·u·é (hə-bĭch′ō͞o-ā′, hə-bĭch′ō͞o-ā′) ►*n.* One who frequents a particular place, as a café or bar. [Fr.]

Habs·burg also **Haps·burg** (hăps′bûrg′) Austrian royal family that produced many rulers of the Holy Roman Empire.

ha·ci·en·da (hä′sē-ĕn′də) ►*n.* **1.** A large estate in a Spanish-speaking region. **2.** The main house of such an estate. [Sp.]

hack¹ (hăk) ►*v.* **1.** To cut or chop with heavy, irregular blows. **2.** To cough roughly or harshly. **3.** *Slang* To cope with successfully; manage. **4.** *Informal* **a.** To alter (a computer program): *hacked her text editor to read HTML.* **b.** To access (a computer file or network) illegally: *hacked into a government network.* ►*n.* **1.** A cut made by hacking. **2.** A tool used for hacking. **3.** A rough, dry cough. [< OE *-haccian*.]

hack² (hăk) ►*n.* **1.** A hackney. **2.** A worn-out horse for hire. **3a.** A hireling. **b.** A writer hired to produce routine writing. **4.** *Informal* **a.** A taxicab. **b.** A taxicab driver. ►*v.* To employ or work as a hack. ►*adj.* **1.** By or for a hack. **2.** Hackneyed. [< HACKNEY.]

hack·a·more (hăk′ə-môr′) ►*n.* A halter used in breaking horses to a bridle. [< Sp. *jáquima*, halter < Ar. *šakīma*, bit.]

hack·er (hăk′ər) ►*n.* **1a.** A computer buff. **b.** One who illegally gains access to another's electronic system. **2.** An enthusiastic amateur at a sport. [< *hacker*, inept golf player, or < *hack*, clever trick.]

hack·le (hăk′əl) ►*n.* **1.** Any of the long slender feathers on the neck of a bird. **2. hackles** The erectile hairs along the back of the neck of an animal, esp. a dog. **—idiom: get (one's) hackles up** To be extremely insulted or irritated. [ME *hakell.*]

hack·ney (hăk′nē) ►*n., pl.* **-neys 1.** A horse suited for routine riding or driving. **2.** A coach or carriage for hire. ►*v.* To make banal and trite. [ME *hakenei.*]

hack·neyed (hăk′nēd) ►*adj.* Banal; trite.

hack·saw (hăk′sô′) ►*n.* A tough, fine-toothed saw stretched in a frame, used for cutting metal. [< ME *hagge-saw.*] **—hack′saw′** *v.*

had (hăd) ►*v.* P.t. and p.part. of **have.**

had·dock (hăd′ək) ►*n., pl.* **-dock** or **-docks** A N Atlantic food fish related to the cod. [ME *haddok.*]

Ha·des (hā′dēz) ►*n.* **1.** *Gk. Myth.* **a.** The god of the netherworld. **b.** The abode of the dead; netherworld **2.** also **hades** Hell. [Gk. *Haidēs.*]

had·n't (hăd′nt) Had not.

Ha·dri·an (hā′drē-ən) AD 76–138. Emperor of Rome (117–138).

had·ron (hăd′rŏn′) ►*n.* Any of a class of subatomic particles that are composed of two or three quarks and participate in strong interactions. [Gk. *hadros*, thick + –ON¹.]

had·ro·saur (hăd′rə-sôr′) ►*n.* Any of various herbivorous dinosaurs that had a broad, toothless beak. [Gk. *hadros*, thick + *sauros*, lizard.]

hadst (hădst) ►*v. Archaic* 2nd pers. sing. p.t. of **have.**

–haemia ►*suff.* Var. of **–emia.**

haf·ni·um (hăf′nē-əm) ►*n. Symbol* **Hf** A brilliant silvery metallic element used in nuclear reactor control rods and in tungsten filament alloys. At. no. 72. See table at **element.** [After *Hafnia*, Medieval Latin name for Copenhagen, Denmark.]

haft (hăft) ►*n.* A handle or hilt, esp. of a tool or weapon. [< OE *hæft.*]

hag (hăg) ►*n.* **1.** *Offensive* An old woman considered to be ugly or frightening. **2.** A witch; sorceress. [Perh. < OE *hægtesse*, witch.] **—hag′gish** *adj.*

Hag·ga·i (hăg′ē-ī′, hăg′ī′) ►*n.* **1.** A Hebrew prophet of the 6th cent. BC. **2.** See table at **Bible.**

hag·gard (hăg′ərd) ►*adj.* Appearing worn and gaunt. [< OFr. *hagard*, wild hawk.] **—hag′gard·ly** *adv.* **—hag′gard·ness** *n.*

hag·gle (hăg′əl) ►*v.* **-gled, -gling** To argue in an attempt to bargain. [< ON *höggva*, cut.] **—hag′gle** *n.* **—hag′gler** *n.*

hag·i·og·ra·phy (hăg′ē-ŏg′rə-fē, hā′jē-) ►*n., pl.* **-phies 1.** A biography of a saint. **2.** A worshipful or idealizing biography. [Gk. *hagios*, holy + –GRAPHY.] **—hag′i·og′raph·er** *n.* **—hag′i·o·graph′ic** (-ə-grăf′ĭk), **hag′i·o·graph′i·cal** *adj.*

Hague (hāg), **The** The de facto capital of the Netherlands, in the W part near the North Sea.

hah (hä) ►*interj.* Var. of **ha¹.**

Hai·da (hī′də) ►*n., pl.* **-da** or **-das 1.** A member of a Native American people inhabiting W British Columbia, Canada, and S Alaska. **2.** The language of the Haida.

Hai·fa (hī′fə) A city of NW Israel on the Mediterranean Sea.

hai·ku (hī′kōō) ►*n., pl.* **-ku** also **-kus** An unrhymed Japanese poem having three lines of five, seven, and five syllables. [J.]

hail¹ (hāl) ►*n.* **1.** Precipitation in the form of ice pellets, usu. associated with thunderstorms. **2.** Something with the force of a shower of hail: *a hail of criticism.* ►*v.* **1.** To precipitate hail. **2.** To pour down or forth. [< OE *hægel.*]

hail² (hāl) ►*v.* **1a.** To salute or greet. **b.** To greet or acclaim enthusiastically. **2.** To signal or call out to: *hail a cabdriver.* ►*n.* **1.** The act of hailing. **2.** Hailing distance. ►*interj.* Used to express a greeting or tribute. —*phrasal verb:* **hail from** To come or originate from. [< ON *(ves) heill,* (be) healthy.] —**hail′er** *n.*

Hai·le Se·las·sie I (hī′lē sə-lăs′ē, -lä′sē) Title of Ras Tafari Makonnen. 1892–1975. Emperor of Ethiopia (1930–74).

hail·stone (hāl′stōn′) ►*n.* A pellet of hail.

hail·storm (hāl′stôrm′) ►*n.* A storm with hail.

hair (hâr) ►*n.* **1a.** A fine threadlike outgrowth, esp. from the skin of a mammal. **b.** A covering of such outgrowths, as on the human head. **2a.** A minute distance or narrow margin: *won by a hair.* **b.** A precise degree: *calibrated to a hair.* [< OE *hær.*] —**hair′less** *adj.*

hair·breadth (hâr′brĕdth′) ►*adj.* Extremely close: *a hairbreadth escape.*

hair·brush (hâr′brŭsh′) ►*n.* A brush for the hair.

hair·cloth (hâr′klôth′, -klŏth′) ►*n.* A wiry fabric woven esp. from horsehair and used for upholstering.

hair·cut (hâr′kŭt′) ►*n.* **1.** The act or an instance of cutting the hair. **2.** A style in which hair is cut. —**hair′cut′ter** *n.*

hair·do (hâr′dōō′) ►*n., pl.* **-dos** A hairstyle.

hair·dress·er (hâr′drĕs′ər) ►*n.* One who cuts or styles hair. —**hair′dress·ing** *n.*

hair·line (hâr′līn′) ►*n.* **1.** The outline of the growth of hair on the head, esp. across the front. **2.** A very slender line.

hair·net (hâr′nĕt′) ►*n.* A mesh for holding the hair in place.

hair·piece (hâr′pēs′) ►*n.* A covering or bunch of human or artificial hair used to conceal baldness or give shape to a hairstyle.

hair·pin (hâr′pĭn′) ►*n.* **1.** A thin U-shaped pin used to secure a hairdo or headdress. **2.** A sharp U-shaped turn in a road.

hairpin

hair-rais·ing (hâr′rā′zĭng) ►*adj.* Causing excitement, terror, or thrills.

hair·split·ting (hâr′splĭt′ĭng) ►*n.* The making of unreasonably fine distinctions. —**hair′split′-ter** *n.* —**hair′split′ting** *adj.*

hair spray ►*n.* A sticky, quick-drying liquid sprayed on the hair to keep it in place.

hair·spring (hâr′sprĭng′) ►*n.* A fine coiled spring that regulates the movement of the balance wheel in a watch or clock.

hair·style (hâr′stīl′) ►*n.* A manner of arranging hair. —**hair′styl′ing** *n.* —**hair′styl′ist** *n.*

hair trigger ►*n.* A gun trigger adjusted to respond to a very slight pressure.

hair-trig·ger (hâr′trĭg′ər) ►*adj.* Responding to the slightest provocation or stimulation: *a hair-trigger temper.*

hair weave ►*n.* A hairpiece attached to the wearer's own hair, as by interweaving or fusing, or to portions of the scalp, as by gluing. —**hair′weav′ing** (hâr′wē′vĭng) *n.*

hair·y (hâr′ē) ►*adj.* **-i·er, -i·est 1.** Covered with hair. **2.** Of or like hair. **3.** *Slang* Fraught with difficulties; hazardous: *a hairy escape.* —**hair′i·ness** *n.*

Hai·ti (hā′tē) A country of the West Indies comprising the W part of the island of Hispaniola and two offshore islands. Cap. Port-au-Prince. —**Hai′tian** *adj. & n.*

haj (hăj) ►*n., pl.* **-es** *Islam* A pilgrimage to Mecca. [Ar. *ḥajj.*]

haj·i (hăj′ē) ►*n., pl.* **-is** *Islam* One who has made a pilgrimage to Mecca. [Pers. *ḥājī.*]

hake (hāk) ►*n., pl.* **hake** or **hakes** Any of various marine food fishes related to the cod. [ME.]

hal– ►*pref.* Var. of **halo–**.

ha·lal (hə-läl′) ►*adj. Islam* **1.** Of or being meat from animals slaughtered in the manner prescribed by the shari'a: *a halal butcher.* **2.** In accordance with or permitted under the shari'a. [Ar. *ḥalāl.*]

hal·berd (hăl′bərd, hôl′-) ►*n.* A weapon of the 1400s and 1500s having an axlike blade and a steel spike mounted on the end of a long shaft. [< MHGer. *helmbarte.*]

hal·cy·on (hăl′sē-ən) ►*adj.* **1.** Calm and peaceful. **2.** Prosperous; golden: *halcyon years.* [< Gk. *alkuōn, halkuōn,* mythical bird.]

hale¹ (hāl) ►*adj.* **hal·er, hal·est** Free from infirmity or illness; sound. [< OE *hāl.*] —**hale′-ness** *n.*

hale² (hāl) ►*v.* **haled, hal·ing** To compel to go. [< OFr. *haler,* HAUL.]

Hale, Nathan 1755–76. Amer. Revolutionary soldier.

half (hăf) ►*n., pl.* **halves** (hăvz) **1a.** One of two equal parts that constitute a whole. **b.** One part approx. equal to the remaining part. **2.** *Sports* **a.** One of two playing periods into which a game is divided. **b.** A halfback. ►*adj.* **1a.** Being one of two equal parts. **b.** Being approx. a half. **2.** Partial or incomplete: *a half smile.* ►*adv.* **1.** To the extent of exactly or nearly a half: *The tank is half empty.* **2.** Not completely; partly: *only half right.* —*idioms:* **by half 1.** By a considerable extent. **2.** By an excessive amount: *too clever by half.* **by halves** In a reluctant manner; unenthusiastically. **not half** Not at all: *not half bad.* [< OE *healf.*]

half·back (hăf′băk′) ►*n. Sports* **1.** In football, an offensive player who lines up behind the quarterback and carries the ball. **2.** One of several players who are stationed behind the forwards in certain sports like soccer.

half-baked (hăf′bākt′) ▸*adj.* **1.** Only partly baked. **2.** *Informal* Insufficiently thought out: *a half-baked scheme.* **3.** *Informal* Lacking common sense.

half boot ▸*n.* A low boot extending just above the ankle.

half-breed (hăf′brēd′) ▸*n. Offensive* A person of mixed racial descent.

half brother ▸*n.* A brother to whom one is biologically related through one parent only.

half·cocked (hăf′kŏkt′) ▸*adj. Informal* Inadequately or poorly prepared: *a halfcocked plan.* —**half′cocked′** *adv.*

half-dol·lar (hăf′dŏl′ər) ▸*n.* A US coin worth 50 cents.

half·heart·ed (hăf′här′tĭd) ▸*adj.* Exhibiting or feeling little interest or enthusiasm. —**half′-heart′ed·ly** *adv.* —**half′heart′ed·ness** *n.*

half-life (hăf′līf′) ▸*n.* **1.** *Phys.* The time required for half the nuclei in a sample of a specific isotopic species to undergo radioactive decay. **2.** *Biol.* The time required for half the quantity of a drug or other substance to be metabolized or eliminated.

half-mast (hăf′măst′) ▸*n.* The position about halfway up a mast or pole at which a flag is flown as a symbol of mourning or as a signal of distress.

half-moon (hăf′mōon′) ▸*n.* **1.** The moon when only half its disk is illuminated. **2.** Something shaped like a crescent.

half nelson ▸*n.* A wrestling hold in which one arm is passed under the opponent's arm from behind to the back of the neck.

half note ▸*n. Mus.* A note having half the value of a whole note.

half·pipe or **half pipe** (hăf′pīp′, häf′-) ▸*n.* A smooth-surfaced structure shaped like a trough and used for stunts in snowboarding and other sports.

half sister ▸*n.* A sister to whom one is biologically related through one parent only.

half-slip (hăf′slĭp′) ▸*n.* A woman's skirtlike undergarment that hangs from the waist.

half-staff (hăf′stăf′) ▸*n.* See **half-mast.**

half step ▸*n.* See **semitone.**

half·time (hăf′tīm′) ▸*n.* The intermission between halves in a game, such as basketball or football.

half-track (hăf′trăk′) ▸*n.* A lightly armored military motor vehicle with continuous tracks in the rear for power and conventional wheels in front for steering.

half-truth (hăf′trōoth′) ▸*n.* A statement, esp. one intended to deceive, that is only partially true.

half·way (hăf′wā′) ▸*adj.* **1.** Midway between two points or conditions. **2.** Partial: *halfway measures.* —**half′way′** *adv.*

half-wit (hăf′wĭt′) ▸*n.* A foolish or stupid person. —**half′-wit′ted** *adj.* —**half′-wit′ted·ly** *adv.* —**half′-wit′ted·ness** *n.*

hal·i·but (hăl′ə-bət, hŏl′-) ▸*n., pl.* **-but** or **-buts** Any of several large edible flatfishes of N Atlantic or Pacific waters. [ME.]

hal·ide (hăl′īd′, hā′līd′) ▸*n.* A compound of a halogen, esp. a binary compound of a halogen.

Hal·i·fax (hăl′ə-făks′) The capital of Nova Scotia, Canada, in the S-central part on the Atlantic.

hal·ite (hăl′īt′, hā′līt′) ▸*n.* Sodium chloride, esp. in natural mineral form.

hal·i·to·sis (hăl′ĭ-tō′sĭs) ▸*n.* See **bad breath.** [< Lat. *hālitus,* breath.]

hall (hôl) ▸*n.* **1.** A corridor or passageway in a building. **2.** A large entrance room; lobby. **3a.** A building for public gatherings or entertainments. **b.** The large room in which such events are held. **4.** A building used by a social or religious organization. **5a.** A college or university building. **b.** A large room in such a building. **6.** The main house on a landed estate. **7.** The castle or house of a medieval monarch or noble. [< OE *heall.*]

hal·le·lu·jah (hăl′ə-lōo′yə) ▸*interj.* Used to express praise or joy. [Heb. *halləlû-yāh.*]

hall·mark (hôl′märk′) ▸*n.* **1.** A mark indicating quality or excellence. **2.** A conspicuous feature or characteristic. [After Goldsmith's *Hall,* London.]

Hall of Fame ▸*n.* **1.** A group of persons judged outstanding, as in a sport. **2.** A building housing memorials to illustrious persons.

hal·loo (hə-lōo′) ▸*interj.* Used to catch someone's attention. [< obsolete *holla,* stop!] —**hal·loo′** *n.*

hal·low (hăl′ō) ▸*v.* **1.** To make or set apart as holy. **2.** To respect or honor greatly; revere. [< OE *hālgian.*]

Hal·low·een also **Hal·low·e'en** (hăl′ə-wĕn′, hŏl′-) ▸*n.* October 31, celebrated by children wearing costumes and asking for treats and playing pranks. [< *All Hallow Even.*]

hal·lu·ci·na·tion (hə-lōo′sə-nā′shən) ▸*n.* **1a.** False perception of visual, auditory, and other experiences. **b.** The objects or events so perceived. **2.** A false or mistaken idea. [< Lat. *ālūcinārī,* to dream.] —**hal·lu′ci·nate** *v.* —**hal·lu′ci·na′tion·al, hal·lu′ci·na′tive, hal·lu′ci·na·to′ry** (hə-lōo′sə-nə-tôr′ē) *adj.*

hal·lu·ci·no·gen (hə-lōo′sə-nə-jən) ▸*n.* A substance that induces hallucination. —**hal·lu′ci·no·gen′ic** (-jĕn′ĭk) *adj.*

hall·way (hôl′wā′) ▸*n.* **1.** A corridor in a building. **2.** An entrance hall.

ha·lo (hā′lō) ▸*n., pl.* **-los** or **-loes 1.** A luminous ring of light surrounding the heads or bodies of sacred figures in religious paintings. **2.** A circular band of colored light around a light source, as around the sun or moon. [< Gk. *halōs.*] —**ha′lo** *v.*

halo
solar halo

halo– or **hal–** ►*pref.* **1.** Salt: *halite.* **2.** Halogen: *halocarbon.* [< Gk. *hals.*]

hal·o·car·bon (hăl′ə-kär′bən) ►*n.* An organic compound, such as a fluorocarbon, that contains one or more halogens.

hal·o·gen (hăl′ə-jən) ►*n.* Any of a group of five chemically related nonmetallic elements including fluorine, chlorine, bromine, iodine, and astatine. —**ha·log′e·nous** (hă-lŏj′ə-nəs) *adj.*

Hals (hälz, häls), **Frans** 1580?–1666. Dutch painter.

halt (hôlt) ►*n.* A suspension of movement or progress, esp. a temporary one: *The car rolled to a halt.* ►*v.* **1.** To cause to stop. See Synonyms at **stop. 2.** To stop; pause. [< OHGer. *haltan,* hold back.]

hal·ter (hôl′tər) ►*n.* **1.** A device made of rope or leather straps that fits around the head or neck of an animal, used to lead or secure it. **2.** A noose used for execution by hanging. **3.** A garment for women that ties behind the neck and across the back. ►*v.* **1.** To put a halter on. **2.** To control with or as if with a halter. [< OE *hælftre.*]

halt·ing (hôl′tĭng) ►*adj.* **1.** Hesitant or wavering: *a halting voice.* **2.** Limping; lame. —**halt′-ing·ly** *adv.*

hal·vah (häl-vä′, häl′vä) ►*n.* A confection of honey and crushed sesame seeds. [< Ar. *ḥalwā.*]

halve (hăv) ►*v.* **halved, halv·ing 1.** To divide into two equal parts. **2.** To lessen or reduce by half: *halved the recipe.* **3.** *Informal* To share equally. [ME *halven* < *half,* HALF.]

halves (hăvz) ►*n.* Pl. of **half.**

hal·yard (hăl′yərd) ►*n.* A rope used to raise or lower a sail, flag, or yard. [< ME *halier* < *halen,* pull; see HALE².]

ham (hăm) ►*n.* **1.** The thigh of an animal, esp. a hog. **2.** A cut of meat from the ham. **3.** The back of the knee or thigh. **4.** A performer who exaggerates. **5.** A licensed amateur radio operator. ►*v.* **hammed, ham·ming** To exaggerate or overact. [< OE *hamm.*]

ham·a·dry·ad (hăm′ə-drī′əd) ►*n., pl.* **-ads** or **-a·des** (-ə-dēz′) *Gk. & Rom. Myth.* A wood nymph. [< Gk. *Hamadruas.*]

ha·man·tasch (hä′mən-täsh′) ►*n., pl.* **-tasch·en** (-tä′shən) A triangular pastry with a usu. sweet filling, traditionally served in Jewish communities around Purim. [Yiddish *homentash.*]

Ham·burg (hăm′bûrg′) A city of N Germany on the Elbe R. NE of Bremen.

ham·burg·er (hăm′bûr′gər) also **ham·burg** (-bûrg′) ►*n.* **1a.** Ground meat, usu. beef. **b.** A cooked patty of such meat. **2.** A sandwich made with a patty of ground meat usu. in a roll or bun. [After HAMBURG.]

Ha·mil·car Bar·ca (hə-mĭl′kär′ bär′kə, hăm′əl-) 270?–228? BC. Carthaginian general and father of Hannibal.

Ham·il·ton (hăm′əl-tən) The capital of Bermuda, on Bermuda I.

Hamilton, Alexander 1755?–1804. Amer. politician; killed in a duel with Aaron Burr. —**Ham′il·to′ni·an** (-tō′nē-ən) *adj. & n.*

Hamilton, Edith 1867–1963. German-born Amer. classicist.

Ham·ite (hăm′īt′) ►*n.* A member of a group of peoples of N and NE Africa, including the Berbers, the Tuaregs, and the ancient Egyptians. No longer in technical use. —**Ha·mit′ic** (hă-mĭt′ĭk) *adj.*

ham·let (hăm′lĭt) ►*n.* A small village. [< OFr. *ham,* village.]

ham·mer (hăm′ər) ►*n.* **1.** A hand tool used for striking, consisting of a handle with a perpendicularly attached head. **2.** A tool or device similar in function or action, as: **a.** The part of a gunlock that hits the primer or firing pin or explodes the percussion cap. **b.** One of the padded wooden pieces of a piano that strikes the strings. **c.** A part of an apparatus that strikes a gong or bell, as in a clock. **3.** See **malleus. 4.** *Sports* A metal ball having a long handle from which it is thrown for distance. ►*v.* **1.** To hit, esp. repeatedly; pound. See Synonyms at **beat. 2.** To beat into a shape with a hammer or similar tool. **3.** To accomplish or produce with difficulty or effort: *hammered out an agreement.* **4.** *Informal* To keep at something continuously: *hammered away at the problem.* [< OE *hamor.*] —**ham′mer·er** *n.*

ham·mered (hăm′ərd) ►*adj.* *Slang* Drunk.

ham·mer·head (hăm′ər-hĕd′) ►*n.* **1.** The head of a hammer. **2.** A large predatory shark having eyes set in wide fleshy extensions at the sides of the head.

ham·mer·lock (hăm′ər-lŏk′) ►*n.* A wrestling hold in which the opponent's arm is pulled behind the back and twisted upward.

Ham·mer·stein (hăm′ər-stīn′, -stēn′), **Oscar, II** 1895–1960. Amer. lyricist.

ham·mock (hăm′ək) ►*n.* A hanging bed of canvas or heavy netting suspended between two supports. [< Taíno *hamaca.*]

Ham·mu·ra·bi (hăm′ə-rä′bē, hä′mōō-) d. 1750 BC. Babylonian king (1792–1750).

ham·per¹ (hăm′pər) ►*v.* To prevent the free movement, action, or progress of: *Fog hampered the rescue effort.* See Synonyms at **hinder.** [ME *hamperen.*]

ham·per² (hăm′pər) ►*n.* A large basket, usu. with a cover. [< OFr. *hanepier,* case for holding goblets.]

ham·ster (hăm′stər) ►*n.* A small rodent with large cheek pouches and a short tail, often kept as a pet or used in laboratory research. [Poss. < OHGer. *hamustro,* of Slav. orig.]

ham·string (hăm′strĭng′) ►*n.* **1.** Any of the tendons at the rear hollow of the human knee. **2.** or **hamstrings** The muscles constituting the back of the upper leg. **3.** The large tendon in the back of the hock of a quadruped. ►*v.* **1.** To cripple by cutting the hamstring. **2.** To hinder the efficiency of.

Han (hän) ►*n., pl.* **Han** or **Hans** A member of the largest ethnic group of China.

Han·cock (hăn′kŏk′), **John** 1737–93. Amer. politician and Revolutionary leader.

hand (hănd) ►*n.* **1.** The terminal part of the human arm, consisting of the wrist, palm, four fingers, and thumb. **2.** A unit of length equal to 4 in. (10.2 cm), used esp. to specify the height of a horse. **3.** Something suggesting the shape or function of the human hand, esp.: **a.** A rotating pointer on the face of a clock. **b.** A pointer on a gauge or dial. **4.** See **index** (sense 3). **5.** Lateral direction: *at my right hand.* **6.** Handwriting; penmanship. **7.** A round of applause. **8.** Assistance; help: *lend a hand.* **9a.**

The cards held by or dealt to a player in a card game. **b.** A full round of play: *a hand of poker.* **10a.** A manual laborer: *a factory hand.* **b.** A member of a group or crew. **11.** A participant: *an old hand at diplomacy.* **12.** often **hands a.** Possession or keeping. **b.** Control; care: *His fate is in your hands.* **13a.** Involvement or participation. **b.** An influence or effect: *had a hand in all the decisions.* **14.** A pledge to wed. ►*v.* **1.** To give or pass with or as if with the hands: *Hand me your keys.* **2.** To aid, direct, or conduct with the hands. —*phrasal verbs:* **hand down 1.** To bequeath as an inheritance. **2.** To deliver (a verdict). **hand in** To turn in; submit. **hand out** To distribute. **hand over** To relinquish to another. —*idioms:* **at hand 1.** Close by; near. **2.** Soon; imminent. **by hand** Performed manually. **hand in glove** In close association. **hand in hand** In cooperation. **hand it to** To give credit to. **hand over fist** At a tremendous rate. **hands down** Easily: *won hands down.* **in hand** Under control. **off (one's) hands** No longer in one's care or within one's responsibility. **on hand** Available. **on (one's) hands** In one's care or possession, often as an imposition. **out of hand** Out of control. **show** (or **tip**) **(one's) hand** To reveal one's intentions. **to hand 1.** Nearby. **2.** In one's possession. [< OE.]

hand·bag (hănd′băg′) ►*n.* **1.** A woman's purse. **2.** A piece of small hand luggage.

hand·ball (hănd′bôl′) ►*n.* **1.** A game played by two or more players who hit a ball against a wall with their hands. **2.** The small rubber ball used in this game.

hand·bill (hănd′bĭl′) ►*n.* A printed sheet or pamphlet distributed by hand.

hand·book (hănd′boŏk′) ►*n.* A manual or reference book providing information or instruction about a subject or place.

hand·car (hănd′kär′) ►*n.* A small open railroad car propelled by a hand pump or a small motor.

hand·cart (hănd′kärt′) ►*n.* A small, usu. two-wheeled cart pulled or pushed by hand.

hand·clasp (hănd′klăsp′) ►*n.* The act of clasping the hand of another, esp. in friendship.

hand·cuff (hănd′kŭf′) ►*n.* often **handcuffs** A restraining device consisting of a pair of strong connected hoops that can be tightened and locked about the wrists. ►*v.* **1.** To restrain with or as if with handcuffs. **2.** To render ineffective. See Synonyms at **hobble.**

hand·ed (hăn′dĭd) ►*adj.* **1.** Of or relating to dexterity or preference with respect to a hand or hands: *one-handed; left-handed.* **2.** Relating to a specified number of people: *a four-handed card game.*

Han·del (hăn′dl), **George Frideric** 1685–1759. German-born British composer.

hand·ful (hănd′foŏl′) ►*n., pl.* **-fuls 1.** The amount that a hand can hold. **2.** A small, undefined number or quantity: *a handful of people.* **3.** *Informal* One that is difficult to control or manage: *Our toddler is a handful.*

hand·gun (hănd′gŭn′) ►*n.* A firearm that can be used with one hand.

hand·held also **hand-held** (hănd′hĕld′) ►*adj.* Compact enough to be used or operated while being held in the hand: *bought a handheld video camera.* ►*n.* A digital device, such as a com-

puter, PDA, or cell phone, that is small enough to be held and operated in one hand.

hand·i·cap (hăn′dē-kăp′) ►*n.* **1a.** A race or contest in which advantages or compensations are given to different contestants to equalize the chances of winning. **b.** An advantage or penalty so given. **2.** A physical or mental disability. See Usage Note at **handicapped. 3.** A disadvantage or inconvenience. See Synonyms at **disadvantage.** ►*v.* **-capped, -cap·ping 1.** To assign a handicap to (a contestant). **2.** To hinder; impede. [< obsolete *hand in cap,* a game in which forfeits were held in a cap.]

hand·i·capped (hăn′dē-kăpt′) ►*adj.* Physically or mentally disabled. ►*n.* Physically or mentally disabled people as a group: *the handicapped.*

Usage: Although *handicapped* is widely used in both law and everyday speech to refer to people having physical or mental disabilities, those described by the word tend to prefer the expressions *disabled* or *people with disabilities.*

hand·i·craft (hăn′dē-krăft′) also **hand·craft** (hănd′krăft′) ►*n.* **1.** Skill and facility with the hands. **2.** An occupation requiring such skill. **3.** An object crafted by skilled hands.

hand·i·work (hăn′dē-wûrk′) ►*n.* **1.** Work performed by hand. **2.** The product of a person's efforts and actions.

hand·ker·chief (hăng′kər-chĭf, -chēf′) ►*n., pl.* **-chiefs** also **-chieves** (-chĭvz, -chēvz′) A small square of cloth used esp. for wiping the nose or mouth.

han·dle (hăn′dl) ►*v.* **-dled, -dling 1.** To touch, lift, or hold with the hands. **2.** To operate with the hands: *can handle a drill.* **3.** To have responsibility for; manage: *handles legal matters.* **4.** To cope with or dispose of. **5.** To act or function in a given way: *a car that handles well in the snow.* ►*n.* **1.** A part held or operated with the hand: *a suitcase handle; a faucet handle.* **2.** A means of understanding or control: *has a handle on the situation.* **3.** An opportunity. **4.** *Slang* A person's name. [< OE *handlian.*]

han·dle·bar (hăn′dl-bär′) ►*n.* often **handlebars** A cylindrical, straight or curved steering bar, as on a bicycle.

han·dler (hănd′lər) ►*n.* **1.** One that handles or directs something or someone: *the candidate's campaign handlers.* **2.** One who trains or exhibits an animal, such as a dog.

hand·made (hănd′mād′) ►*adj.* Made or prepared by hand rather than by machine.

hand·maid (hănd′mād′) also **hand·maid·en** (hănd′mād′n) ►*n.* A woman attendant or servant.

hand-me-down (hănd′mē-doun′) ►*adj.* **1.** Handed down to one person after being used and discarded by another. **2.** Of inferior quality; shabby. ►*n.* Something handed down from one person to another.

hand·off (hănd′ôf′, -ŏf′) ►*n.* **1.** *Football* A play in which one player hands the ball to another. **2.** The act or an instance of passing something or the control of it to another.

hand·out (hănd′out′) ►*n.* **1.** Food, clothing, or money given to the needy. **2.** A folder or leaflet circulated free of charge. **3.** A sheet or sheets of paper with information, given to those attending a lecture or meeting.

hand·pick (hănd′pĭk′) ►v. **1.** To gather or pick by hand. **2.** To select personally. —**hand′- picked′** adj.

hand·rail (hănd′rāl′) ►n. A narrow railing that is grasped with the hand for support.

hand·set (hănd′sĕt′) ►n. The handle of a telephone, containing the receiver and transmitter and often a dial or push buttons.

hand·shake (hănd′shāk′) ►n. The grasping of hands by two people, as in greeting.

hands-off (hăndz′ôf′, -ŏf′) ►adj. Marked by nonintervention: *a hands-off foreign policy.*

hand·some (hăn′səm) ►adj. -som·er, -som·est **1.** Pleasing in form or appearance, esp. having strong or distinguished features. **2.** Large in amount or measure; generous or considerable: *a handsome reward.* [ME *handsom,* handy.] —**hand′some·ly** adv. —**hand′some·ness** n.

hands-on (hăndz′ŏn′, -ôn′) ►adj. Involving active participation.

hand·spring (hănd′sprĭng′) ►n. A gymnastic feat in which the body is flipped completely forward or backward from an upright position, landing first on the hands and then on the feet.

hand·stand (hănd′stănd′) ►n. The act of balancing on the hands with one's feet in the air.

hand-to-hand (hănd′tə-hănd′) ►adj. Being at close quarters: *hand-to-hand combat.* —**hand to hand** adv.

hand-to-mouth (hănd′tə-mouth′) ►adj. Having or providing only the bare essentials.

hand·work (hănd′wûrk′) ►n. Work done by hand rather than by machine.

hand·writ·ing (hănd′rī′tĭng) ►n. **1.** Writing done with the hand. **2.** The writing characteristic of a particular person.

hand·y (hăn′dē) ►adj. -i·er, -i·est **1.** Easy to use or handle: *a handy tool.* **2.** Readily accessible: *found a handy spot for the hammer.* **3.** Skillful in using one's hands. —**hand′i·ly** adv. —**hand′i·ness** n.

Handy, W(illiam) C(hristopher) 1873–1958. Amer. musician and composer.

hand·y·man (hăn′dē-măn′) ►n. A man who does odd jobs or various small tasks.

hand·y·wom·an (hăn′dē-wŏŏm′ən) ►n. A woman who does odd jobs or various small tasks.

hang (hăng) ►v. **hung** (hŭng), **hang·ing 1.** To fasten from above with no support from below; suspend. **2.** To suspend or fasten so as to allow movement at the point of suspension: *hang a door.* **3.** *p.t.* and *p.part.* **hanged** (hăngd) To execute by hanging: *They hanged the prisoner at dawn.* **4.** To furnish by suspending objects about: *hang a room with curtains.* **5.** To hold or incline downward; droop: *hang one's head.* **6.** To attach to a wall, esp. to display: *hang a painting.* **7.** To deadlock (a jury) by failing to render a unanimous verdict. **8.** To depend: *It all hangs on one vote.* ►n. **1.** The way in which something hangs. **2.** Particular meaning or significance. **3.** *Informal* The proper method for doing or using something. —*phrasal verbs:* **hang around** To loiter. **hang back** To hesitate. **hang on 1.** To cling to something. **2.** To persevere. **hang out** *Slang* **1.** To spend one's free time in a certain place. **2.** To pass time idly. **hang up 1.** To end a telephone conversation by replacing the receiver. **2.** To delay or impede; hinder. —*idioms:* **give** (or **care**) **a hang** To

be concerned. **let it all hang out** *Slang* **1.** To be relaxed. **2.** To be completely candid. [< OE *hangian* and *hōn.*]

Usage: Hanged, as a past tense and a past participle of *hang,* is used only in the sense of "to put to death by hanging."

han·gar (hăng′ər, hăng′gər) ►n. A shelter for housing or repairing aircraft. [< OFr. *hangard,* shelter.]

hang·dog (hăng′dôg′, -dŏg′) ►adj. **1.** Shamefaced or guilty. **2.** Downcast; intimidated.

hang·er (hăng′ər) ►n. **1.** One who hangs something. **2.** A contrivance to which something hangs or by which something is hung.

hang·er-on (hăng′ər-ŏn′, -ôn′) ►n., pl. **hang·ers-on** (hăng′ərz-) A sycophant.

hang glider ►n. **1.** A kitelike device from which a harnessed rider hangs while gliding from a height. **2.** The rider of such a device. —**hang′-glide′** v.

hang glider

hang·ing (hăng′ĭng) ►n. **1.** A method of execution whereby the person is dropped and suspended from a rope around the neck. **2.** Something, such as a tapestry, that is hung.

hang·man (hăng′mən) ►n. One employed to execute condemned prisoners by hanging.

hang·nail (hăng′nāl′) ►n. A small, partly detached piece of dead skin at the side or the base of a fingernail. [< OE *angnægel.*]

hang·out (hăng′out′) ►n. *Slang* A place where one frequently spends one's spare time.

hang·o·ver (hăng′ō′vər) ►n. **1.** A temporary, unpleasant physical condition following the heavy use of alcohol. **2.** A vestige; holdover.

hang-up (hăng′ŭp′) ►n. *Informal* **1.** A psychological or emotional difficulty or inhibition. **2.** An obstacle.

Hang·zhou (hăng′jō′) also **Hang·chow** or **Hang·chou** (hăng′chou′, hăng′jō′) A city of E China at the head of **Hangzhou Bay,** an inlet of the East China Sea.

hank (hăngk) ►n. A coil or loop. [< ON *hönk.*]

han·ker (hăng′kər) ►v. To have a strong, often restless desire. [Perh. < Du. dial. *hankeren.*] —**hank′er·er** n. —**hank′er·ing** n.

han·kie also **han·ky** (hăng′kē) ►n., pl. -kies *Informal* A handkerchief.

han·ky-pan·ky (hăng′kē-păng′kē) ►n. *Slang* Devious or mischievous activity. [< alteration of HOCUS-POCUS.]

Han·ni·bal (hăn′ə-bəl) 247–183? BC. Carthaginian general.

Ha·noi (hă-noi′, hə-) The capital of Vietnam, in the N part on the Red R.

Han·o·ver or **Han·no·ver** (hăn′ō′vər, hä-nō′-) **1.** A former kingdom and province of NW

Germany. **2.** A city of NW Germany SE of Bremen.

Hans·ber·ry (hănz′bĕr-ē), **Lorraine Vivian** 1930–65. Amer. playwright.

han·som (hăn′səm) ►*n.* A two-wheeled covered carriage with the driver's seat at the rear. [After J.A. *Hansom* (1803–82).]

Ha·nuk·kah or **Ha·nu·kah** also **Cha·nu·kah** (кнä′nə-kə, hä′-) ►*n. Judaism* An eight-day festival commemorating the victory of the Maccabees over Antiochus Epiphanes. [Heb. *ḥănukkâ,* dedication.]

hap (hăp) ►*n.* **1.** Fortune; chance. **2.** An occurrence. [< ON *happ.*]

hap·haz·ard (hăp-hăz′ərd) ►*adj.* Dependent upon or marked by mere chance. —**hap·haz′-ard·ly** *adv.* —**hap·haz′ard·ness** *n.*

hap·less (hăp′lĭs) ►*adj.* Luckless. See Synonyms at **unfortunate.** —**hap′less·ly** *adv.*

hap·loid (hăp′loid′) ►*adj.* **1.** Having the same number of chromosomes as a germ cell or half as many as a somatic cell. **2.** Having a single set of chromosomes. [Gk. *haplous,* single + –OID.]

hap·lo·type (hăp′lə-tīp′) ►*n.* A set of alleles of different genes that are closely linked on one chromosome and are usu. inherited as a unit. [Greek *haplous,* single + TYPE.]

hap·ly (hăp′lē) ►*adv.* By chance or accident.

hap·pen (hăp′ən) ►*v.* **1a.** To come to pass. **b.** To be the fate: *What will happen to the business when the owner retires?* **2.** To come upon something by chance: *happened upon an interesting fact.* **3.** To come or go casually: *happened by around dinnertime.* **4.** To have the fortune (to be or do something): *happened to know the answer.* [ME *happenen* < *hap,* HAP.]
   Syns: *befall, betide, chance, occur* **v.**

hap·pen·ing (hăp′ə-nĭng) ►*n.* An occurrence.

hap·pen·stance (hăp′ən-stăns′) ►*n.* A chance circumstance.

hap·py (hăp′ē) ►*adj.* **-pi·er, -pi·est 1.** Enjoying, showing, or marked by pleasure. **2.** Cheerful; willing: *happy to help.* **3.** Lucky; fortunate. See Synonyms at **fortunate. 4.** Well adapted; felicitous: *a happy turn of phrase.* [ME < *hap,* luck; see HAP.] —**hap′pi·ly** *adv.* —**hap′pi·ness** *n.*

hap·py-go-luck·y (hăp′ē-gō-lŭk′ē) ►*adj.* Taking things easily; carefree.

happy hour ►*n.* A period of time during which a bar features drinks at reduced prices.

Haps·burg (hăps′bûrg′) See **Habsburg.**

ha·ra-ki·ri (här′ĭ-kîr′ē, hä′rē-) ►*n., pl.* **-ris** See **seppuku.** [J.]

ha·rangue (hə-răng′) ►*n.* **1.** A long pompous speech. **2.** A tirade. [< OItal. *aringare,* speak in public.] —**ha·rangue** *v.* —**ha·rangu′er** *n.*

Ha·ra·re (hə-rär′ā) The capital of Zimbabwe, in the NE part.

ha·rass (hə-răs′, hăr′əs,) ►*v.* **1.** To subject (another) to hostile or prejudicial remarks or actions. **2.** To irritate or torment persistently. **3.** To exhaust (an enemy) by repeated attacks. [Poss. < OFr. *harer,* set a dog on.] —**ha·rass′er** *n.* —**ha·rass′ment** *n.*

har·bin·ger (här′bĭn-jər) ►*n.* One that indicates or foreshadows what is to come; forerunner. [< OFr. *herbergeor,* one sent to arrange lodgings.]

har·bor (här′bər) ►*n.* **1.** A sheltered part of a body of water deep enough to provide anchorage for ships. **2.** A place of shelter; refuge. ►*v.*

1. To give shelter to. **2.** To provide a place or habitat for. **3.** To hold or nourish: *harbor a grudge.* [ME *herberwe.*]

hard (härd) ►*adj.* **-er, -est 1.** Resistant to pressure; not readily penetrated. **2.** Difficult to do, understand, or endure. **3.** Intense in force or degree: *a hard blow.* **4a.** Stern or strict. **b.** Lacking compassion; callous. **5.** Oppressive or unjust. **6a.** Harsh or severe. **b.** Bitter; resentful: *hard feelings.* **7.** Bad; adverse: *hard luck.* **8.** Diligent; assiduous: *a group of hard workers.* **9a.** Real and unassailable: *hard evidence.* **b.** Definite; firm. **c.** Based on quantifiable data: *the hard sciences.* **10.** Backed by bullion rather than by credit. Used of currency. **11.** Written or printed rather than electronic: *a hard copy.* **12a.** Having high alcoholic content. **b.** Fermented: *hard cider.* **13.** Containing salts that interfere with the lathering of soap. Used of water. **14.** *Ling.* Velar, as the *c* in *cape.* **15.** Dangerously addictive: *a hard drug.* —***idioms:*** **hard and fast** Fixed and invariable. **hard of hearing** Having a partial loss of hearing. **hard put** Undergoing great difficulty. **hard up** *Informal* In need; poor. [< OE *heard.*] —**hard** *adv.* —**hard′ness** *n.*

hard·back (härd′băk′) ►*adj. & n.* Hardcover.

hard·ball (härd′bôl′) ►*n.* **1.** Baseball. **2.** *Informal* The use of any means, however ruthless, to attain an objective.

hard-bit·ten (härd′bĭt′n) ►*adj.* Toughened by experience.

hard-boiled (härd′boild′) ►*adj.* **1.** Cooked to a solid consistency by boiling. Used of eggs. **2.** Callous or unfeeling; tough.

hard cider ►*n.* See **cider** (sense 2).

hard coal ►*n.* See **anthracite.**

hard copy ►*n.* A printed copy, as of the output of a computer.

hard·core (härd′kôr′) ►*adj.* also **hard-core** (härd′kôr′) **1.** Intensely loyal; die-hard. **2.** Stubbornly resistant to change: *pockets of hardcore poverty.* **3.** Extremely explicit: *hardcore pornography.* ►*n.* A form of exceptionally harsh punk rock.

hard·cov·er (härd′kŭv′ər) ►*adj.* Bound in cloth, cardboard, or leather rather than paper. Used of books. —**hard′cov′er** *n.*

hard disk ►*n.* A rigid magnetic disk fixed permanently within a drive unit and used for storing computer data.

hard drive ►*n.* A disk drive that reads data stored on hard disks.

hard·en (här′dn) ►*v.* **1.** To make hard or harder. **2.** To enable to withstand hardship. **3.** To make unsympathetic or callous.
   Syns: *acclimate, acclimatize, season, toughen* **Ant:** *soften* **v.**

hard·hat or **hard-hat** (härd′hăt′) ►*n.* **1.** A protective helmet worn esp. by construction workers. **2.** *Informal* A construction worker. —**hard′hat′** *adj.*

hard·head·ed (härd′hĕd′ĭd) ►*adj.* **1.** Stubborn; willful. **2.** Pragmatic. —**hard′head′ed·ly** *adv.* —**hard′head′ed·ness** *n.*

hard·heart·ed (härd′här′tĭd) ►*adj.* Lacking in feeling or compassion; cold. —**hard′heart′ed·ly** *adv.* —**hard′heart′ed·ness** *n.*

har·di·hood (här′dē-hood′) ►*n.* **1.** Boldness and daring. **2.** Impudence or insolence.

Har·ding (här′dĭng), **Warren Gamaliel** 1865–

1923. The 29th US president (1921–23); died in office.

Warren Harding

hard line ►*n.* An uncompromising position or stance. —**hard′-line′** *adj.* —**hard′-lin′er** *n.*

hard·ly (härd′lē) ►*adv.* **1.** Barely; just. **2.** Probably or almost surely not. **3.** With great difficulty or effort: *I could hardly get up the stairs.* [< OE *heardlīce,* boldly.]
Usage: The use of *hardly, rarely,* and *scarcely* with a negative, as in *I couldn't hardly see him,* is avoided in Standard English.

hard-nosed (härd′nōzd′) ►*adj.* Hardheaded.

hard palate ►*n.* The relatively hard, bony anterior portion of the palate.

hard·pan (härd′păn′) ►*n.* A layer of hard subsoil or clay.

hard-pressed (härd′prĕst′) ►*adj.* Experiencing great difficulty.

hard rock ►*n.* A style of rock music characterized by a harsh, amplified sound and loud, distorted electric guitars.

hard sell ►*n. Informal* Aggressive, high-pressure selling or promotion.

hard·ship (härd′shĭp′) ►*n.* **1.** Extreme privation; suffering. **2.** A thing that causes extreme suffering or difficulty. See Synonyms at **difficulty.**

hard·tack (härd′tăk′) ►*n.* A hard biscuit or bread made with only flour and water. [HARD + *tack,* food.]

hard·top (härd′tŏp′) ►*n.* An automobile designed to look like a convertible but having a rigidly fixed, hard top.

hard·ware (härd′wâr′) ►*n.* **1.** Metal goods and utensils. **2a.** A computer and the associated physical equipment directly involved in data processing or communications. **b.** Machines and other physical equipment directly involved in performing an industrial, technological, or military function.

hard·wire (härd′wīr′) ►*v.* **1.** *Comp.* To implement (a capability) through permanently connected electronic circuitry not subject to change by programming. **2.** To provide with a response or capability by genetic inheritance: *Humans are hardwired for speech.*

hard·wood (härd′wŏŏd′) ►*n.* **1.** The wood of a broad-leaved tree as distinguished from that of a conifer. **2.** Such a tree.

har·dy (här′dē) ►*adj.* **-di·er, -di·est 1.** Able to withstand adverse conditions; robust. **2.** Cou-

rageous; intrepid. **3.** *Archaic* Brazenly daring; audacious. [< OFr. *hardi,* hardened, of Gmc. orig.] —**har′di·ly** *adv.* —**har′di·ness** *n.*

Hardy, Thomas 1840–1928. British writer.

hare (hâr) ►*n.* A mammal similar to a rabbit but having longer ears and legs. [< OE *hara.*]

hare·brained (hâr′brānd′) ►*adj.* Having or showing little sense; foolish.

hare·lip (hâr′lĭp′) ►*n. Often Offensive* Cleft lip. —**hare′lipped′** *adj.*

har·em (hâr′əm, hăr′-) ►*n.* **1.** A house or rooms reserved for the women of a Muslim household. **2.** The women occupying a harem. [< Ar. *ḥarīm,* forbidden place.]

hark (härk) ►*v.* To listen attentively. —*idiom:* **hark back** To return to a previous point, as in a narrative. [ME *herken.*]

Har·lem (här′ləm) A section of New York City in N Manhattan. —**Har′lem·ite′** *n.*

har·le·quin (här′lĭ-kwĭn, -kĭn) ►*n.* **1. Harlequin** A conventional buffoon of comic theater, traditionally presented in a mask and particolored tights. **2.** A clown; buffoon. [< OFr. *Herlequin,* a demon.]

har·lot (här′lət) ►*n.* A woman prostitute. [< OFr. *arlot,* vagabond.] —**har′lot·ry** (-lə-trē) *n.*

harm (härm) ►*n.* **1.** Physical or psychological injury or damage. **2.** Wrong; evil. ►*v.* To do harm to. [< OE *hearm.*] —**harm′ful** *adj.* —**harm′ful·ly** *adv.* —**harm′less** *adj.* —**harm′less·ly** *adv.*

har·mon·ic (här-mŏn′ĭk) ►*adj.* **1.** Of or relating to musical harmony or harmonics. **2.** Pleasing to the ear. ►*n.* **1.** A tone produced on a stringed instrument by lightly touching a vibrating string at a given fraction of its length so that both segments vibrate. **2. harmonics** *(takes sing. v.)* The theory or study of the physical properties of musical sound. **3.** *Phys.* A periodic wave whose frequency is an integral multiple of a fundamental frequency. —**har·mon′i·cal·ly** *adv.*

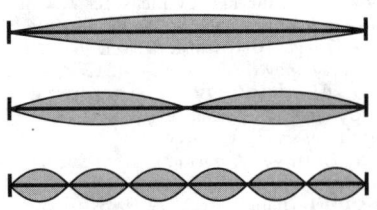

harmonic
Visual representation of harmonics in the periodic motion of a vibrating guitar string. First (or fundamental) harmonic *(top),* second harmonic *(center),* and sixth harmonic *(bottom).*

har·mon·i·ca (här-mŏn′ĭ-kə) ►*n.* A small rectangular musical instrument played by exhaling or inhaling through a row of reeds. [< Ital. *armonico,* harmonious.]

har·mo·ni·ous (här-mō′nē-əs) ►*adj.* **1.** Exhibiting accord in feeling or action. **2.** Having elements pleasingly combined. **3.** Marked by harmony of sound; melodious. —**har·mo′ni·ous·ly** *adv.* —**har·mo′ni·ous·ness** *n.*

har·mo·ni·um (här-mō′nē-əm) ►*n.* An organ-like keyboard instrument with metal reeds. [Fr. < *harmonie,* HARMONY.]

har·mo·nize (här′mə-nīz′) ►*v.* **-nized, -niz-**

ing 1. To bring or come into harmony. **2a.** To provide harmony for (a melody). **b.** To sing or play in harmony. —**har′mo·ni·za′tion** *n.* —**har′mo·niz′er** *n.*

har·mo·ny (här′mə-nē) ►*n., pl.* -**nies 1.** Agreement in feeling or opinion; accord. **2.** A pleasing combination of elements in a whole. **3.** Combination and progression of chords in musical structure. [< Gk. *harmonia,* articulation < *harmos,* joint.]

har·ness (här′nĭs) ►*n.* **1.** The gear or tackle with which a draft animal pulls a vehicle or implement. **2.** Something resembling such gear. ►*v.* **1.** To put a harness on. **2.** To control and direct the force of. [< OFr. *harneis,* of Gmc. orig.] —**har′ness·er** *n.*

Har·old II (hăr′əld) 1022?–66. King of England (1066) and the last of the Anglo-Saxon monarchs.

harp (härp) ►*n.* A musical instrument consisting of an upright frame with strings of graded length played by plucking. ►*v.* To play a harp. —*phrasal verb:* **harp on** To dwell on tediously. [< OE *hearpe.*] —**harp′ist** *n.*

Har·per (här′pər), **Stephen Joseph** b. 1959. Canadian prime minister (took office 2006).

har·poon (här-po͞on′) ►*n.* A spearlike weapon with a barbed head used in hunting whales and large fish. [< OFr. *harpon.*] —**har·poon′** *v.* —**har·poon′er** *n.*

harp·si·chord (härp′sĭ-kôrd′) ►*n.* A keyboard instrument whose strings are plucked by means of quills or plectrums. [< Ital. *arpicordo.*] —**harp′si·chord′ist** *n.*

Har·py (här′pē) ►*n., pl.* -**pies 1.** *Gk. Myth.* A monster with the head and trunk of a woman and the tail, wings, and talons of a bird. **2.** **harpy** A woman regard as shrewish.

har·que·bus (här′kə-bəs, -kwə-) ►*n.* A heavy, portable matchlock gun invented during the 1400s. [< MDu. *hakebus.*]

har·ri·dan (hăr′ĭ-dn) ►*n.* A woman regarded as critical and scolding. [Poss. < Fr. *haridelle,* old nag.]

har·ri·er¹ (hăr′ē-ər) ►*n.* **1.** One that harries. **2.** A slender, narrow-winged hawk.

har·ri·er² (hăr′ē-ər) ►*n.* **1.** A small hound orig. used in hunting hares and rabbits. **2.** A cross-country runner. [Poss. < OFr. *errier,* wanderer.]

Har·ris·burg (hăr′ĭs-bûrg′) The capital of PA, in the SE-central part.

Har·ri·son (hăr′ĭ-sən), **Benjamin** 1833–1901. The 23rd US president (1889–93).

Benjamin Harrison   **William Henry Harrison**

Harrison, William Henry 1773–1841. The 9th US president (1841); died in office.

har·row (hăr′ō) ►*n.* A farm implement consisting of a heavy frame with teeth or upright disks, used to break up and even off plowed ground. ►*v.* **1.** To break up and level (soil) with a harrow. **2.** To inflict great distress or torment on. [ME *harwe.*]

har·row·ing (hăr′ō-ĭng) ►*adj.* Extremely distressing; agonizing.

har·ry (hăr′ē) ►*v.* -**ried, -ry·ing 1.** To disturb, distress, or exhaust, as by repeated attacks. **2.** To raid; pillage. [< OE *hergian.*]

harsh (härsh) ►*adj.* -**er, -est 1.** Disagreeable to the senses, esp. to the hearing. **2.** Extremely severe or exacting; stern. [ME *harsk.*] —**harsh′ly** *adv.* —**harsh′ness** *n.*

hart (härt) ►*n., pl.* **harts** or **hart** A male deer, esp. a male red deer. [< OE *heorot.*]

Harte (härt), **(Francis) Bret** 1836–1902. Amer. writer.

Hart·ford (härt′fərd) The capital of CT, in the N-central part on the Connecticut R.

har·um-scar·um (hâr′əm-skâr′əm, hăr′əm-skăr′əm) ►*adj.* Reckless. ►*adv.* With abandon; recklessly. [< *hare,* frighten + SCARE.]

har·vest (här′vĭst) ►*n.* **1.** The gathering in of a crop. **2a.** The crop that ripens or is gathered in a season. **b.** The time or season of such gathering. **3.** The result or consequence of an activity. ►*v.* To gather or collect (a crop or other renewable resource). [< OE *hærfest.*] —**har′vest·er** *n.*

harvest moon ►*n.* The full moon that occurs nearest the autumnal equinox.

Har·vey (här′vē), **William** 1578–1657. English physician and anatomist.

has (hăz) ►*v.* 3rd pers. sing. pr.t. of **have.**

has-been (hăz′bĭn′) ►*n. Informal* One that is no longer famous, successful, or useful.

hash¹ (hăsh) ►*n.* **1.** A dish of chopped meat and potatoes, usu. browned. **2.** A jumble; hodgepodge. ►*v.* **1.** To chop into pieces; mince. **2.** *Informal* To discuss carefully; review: *hash over future plans.* [< OFr. *hachier,* chop up < *hache,* ax.]

hash² (hăsh) ►*n. Slang* Hashish.

hash·ish (hăsh′ēsh′, hă-shēsh′) ►*n.* Resin prepared from the female flowers of marijuana plants. [Ar. *ḥašīš,* hemp.]

hash mark ►*n.* A service stripe on the sleeve of an enlisted person's uniform. [Alteration of HATCH³.]

Ha·sid or **Has·sid** also **Chas·sid** (кнä′sĭd, hä′-) ►*n., pl.* -**si·dim** (кнä-sē′dĭm, кнô-, hä-) A member of a Jewish mystic movement founded in 18th-cent. E Europe that emphasized piety over Talmudic learning. [< Heb. *ḥāsîd,* pious.] —**Ha·si′dic** *adj.* —**Ha·si′dism** *n.*

has·n't (hăz′ənt) Has not.

hasp (hăsp) ►*n.* A metal fastener that fits over a staple and is secured by a pin, bolt, or padlock. [< OE *hæpse.*] —**hasp** *v.*

has·si·um (hä′sē-əm) ►*n. Symbol* **Hs** A synthetic radioactive element. At. no. 108. See table at **element.** [< Med.Lat. *Hassia,* Hesse (German state where the element was first synthesized).]

has·sle (hăs′əl) *Informal* ►*n.* **1.** An argument or fight. **2.** Trouble; bother. ►*v.* -**sled, -sling 1.** To argue or fight. **2.** To bother or harass. [?]

has·sock (hăs′ək) ►*n.* A thick cushion used as a footstool or for kneeling. [< OE *hassuc,* clump of grass.]

hast (hăst) ►*v. Archaic* 2nd pers. sing. pr.t. of **have.**

haste (hāst) ►*n.* **1.** Rapidity of action or motion. **2.** Rash or headlong action; precipitateness. —*idiom:* **make haste** To move or act swiftly; hurry. [< OFr.]
   Syns: *celerity, dispatch, expedition, hurry, speed* **Ant:** *deliberation* **n.**

has·ten (hā′sən) ►*v.* **1.** To move or cause to move swiftly. **2.** To speed up: *a drug to hasten clotting.*

hast·y (hā′stē) ►*adj.* **-i·er, -i·est** **1.** Hurried, esp. by pressing circumstances. **2.** Done or made too quickly to be accurate or wise; rash: *a hasty decision.* See Synonyms at **impetuous.** —**hast′i·ly** *adv.* —**hast′i·ness** *n.*

hat (hăt) ►*n.* A covering for the head, esp. one with a shaped crown and brim. —*idioms:* **at the drop of a hat** At the slightest pretext or provocation. **hat in hand** Humbly. **pass the hat** To take up a collection of money. **take (one's) hat off to** To admire or congratulate. [< OE *hæt.*]

hatch[1] (hăch) ►*n.* **1.** An opening, as in the deck of a ship or in an aircraft. **2.** The cover for such an opening. **3.** A hatchway. [< OE *hæc,* small door.]

hatch[2] (hăch) ►*v.* **1.** To emerge from an egg. **2.** To produce (young) from an egg. **3.** To cause (an egg) to produce young. **4.** To devise or originate, esp. in secret: *hatch a plot.* [ME *hacchen.*] —**hatch′er** *n.*

hatch[3] (hăch) ►*v.* To shade by drawing fine parallel or crossed lines on. [< OFr. *hachier,* cut up; see HASH[1].] —**hatch** *n.*

hatch·back (hăch′băk′) ►*n.* An automobile having a sloping back with a hatch that opens upward.

hatchback

hatch·er·y (hăch′ə-rē) ►*n., pl.* **-ies** A place where eggs, esp. of fish or poultry, are hatched.

hatch·et (hăch′ĭt) ►*n.* A small, short-handled ax. [< OFr. *hachete,* dim. of *hache,* ax.]

hatchet man ►*n. Slang* **1.** A man hired to commit murder. **2.** One who is assigned to carry out a disagreeable task.

hatch·ling (hăch′lĭng) ►*n.* A newly hatched animal.

hatch·way (hăch′wā′) ►*n.* **1.** A hatch leading to a hold, compartment, or cellar. **2.** A ladder or stairway within a hatchway.

hate (hāt) ►*v.* **hat·ed, hat·ing** **1.** To feel hostility or animosity toward; detest. **2.** To feel dis-like or distaste for. ►*n.* Hatred. [< OE *hatian.*] —**hate′ful** *adj.* —**hate′ful·ly** *adv.* —**hate′-ful·ness** *n.* —**hat′er** *n.*

hate crime ►*n.* A crime motivated by prejudice against a social group.

hath (hăth) ►*v. Archaic* 3rd pers. sing. pr.t. of **have.**

ha·tha yoga (hŭ′tə, hä′thə) ►*n.* A system of yoga exercises emphasizing specific postures and controlled breathing. [Skt. *haṭhayogaḥ,* force yoga.]

ha·tred (hā′trĭd) ►*n.* Intense animosity or hostility. [ME.]

Hat·ter·as (hăt′ər-əs), **Cape** A promontory of E NC at the SE tip of **Hatteras Island.**

hau·berk (hô′bərk) ►*n.* A tunic of chain mail. [< OFr. *hauberc,* of Gmc. orig.]

haugh·ty (hô′tē) ►*adj.* **-ti·er, -ti·est** Scornfully and condescendingly proud. [< Lat. *altus,* high.] —**haugh′ti·ly** *adv.* —**haugh′ti·ness** *n.*

haul (hôl) ►*v.* **1.** To pull or drag forcibly. See Synonyms at **pull. 2.** To transport, as with a truck or cart. ►*n.* **1.** The act of hauling. **2.** A distance, esp. over which something is hauled. **3.** Something hauled. **4.** An amount collected or acquired: *a haul of fish.* [< OFr. *haler,* of Gmc. orig.] —**haul′er** *n.*

haul·age (hô′lĭj) ►*n.* **1.** The act or process of hauling. **2.** A charge made for hauling.

haunch (hônch, hŏnch) ►*n.* **1.** The hip, buttock, and upper thigh. **2.** The loin and leg of an animal, esp. as used for food. [< OFr. *hanche,* of Gmc. orig.]

haunt (hônt, hŏnt) ►*v.* **1.** To inhabit, visit, or appear to in the form of a ghost or spirit. **2.** To frequent. **3.** To come to the mind of continually: *the memories that haunted me.* **4.** To be continually present in; pervade: *the melancholy that haunts the composer's music.* ►*n.* A place much frequented. [< OFr. *hanter,* to frequent.] —**haunt′er** *n.* —**haunt′ing·ly** *adv.*

Hau·sa (hou′sə, -zə) ►*n., pl.* **-sa** or **-sas** **1.** A member of a people of N Nigeria and S Niger. **2.** Their Chadic language.

haute couture (ōt) ►*n.* **1.** The leading designers of exclusive fashions for women. **2a.** The creation of exclusive fashions for women. **b.** The fashions created. [Fr.]

haute cuisine ►*n.* Elaborate or skillfully prepared food. [Fr.]

hau·teur (hō-tûr′, ō-tœr′) ►*n.* Haughtiness; arrogance. [Fr. < OFr. *haut,* HAUGHTY.]

Ha·van·a (hə-văn′ə) The capital of Cuba, in the NW part on the Gulf of Mexico. —**Ha·van′an** *adj. & n.*

Ha·var·ti (hə-vär′tē) ►*n.* A mild, pale yellow cheese of Danish origin. [After *Havarti,* experimental farm in Denmark.]

have (hăv) ►*v.* **had** (hăd), **hav·ing, has** (hăz) **1.** To possess; own. **2.** To possess as a characteristic or part: *He has a lot of energy. The car has bad brakes.* **3.** To stand in relation to: *had few friends.* **4.** To hold in the mind; know or entertain: *have doubts.* **5.** To exhibit: *have compassion.* **6.** To partake of: *have some peas.* **7a.** To suffer from: *has a bad cold.* **b.** To experience: *had a great summer.* **8.** To cause to: *had him run an errand.* **9.** To beget or give birth to: *have a baby.* **10.** To be obliged: *had to go.* —*aux.* Used with a past participle to form the present perfect, past perfect, and future perfect tenses:

I have written you. I had given up smoking for a year. I will have left when you get there. ▸*n.* One who has wealth. —*phrasal verbs:* **have at** To attack. **have on** To wear. —*idioms:* **had better (or best)** To be wise or obliged to; should or must: *You had better do what the teacher tells you to do. You had best bring a raincoat in this rainy weather.* **have done with** To stop; cease. **have had it** To be exhausted or disgusted. **have it in for** To intend to harm. **have it out** To settle, esp. by an argument. **have to do with** To be concerned or associated with. [< OE *habban.*]

Ha·vel (hä′vəl), **Václav** 1936–2011. Czech writer and politician.

haven (hā′vən) ▸*n.* **1.** A harbor; port. **2.** A place of refuge or rest. [< OE *hæfen.*]

have-not (hăv′nŏt′) ▸*n.* One having little or no material wealth.

have·n't (hăv′ənt) Have not.

hav·er·sack (hăv′ər-săk′) ▸*n.* A bag carried over one shoulder to transport supplies. [< obsolete Ger. *Habersack*, oat sack.]

hav·oc (hăv′ək) ▸*n.* **1.** Widespread destruction; devastation. **2.** Disorder or chaos. [< OFr. *havot*, plundering.]

haw (hô) ▸*n.* **1.** The fruit of a hawthorn. **2.** A hawthorn or similar tree. [< OE *haga.*]

Ha·wai·i (hə-wä′ē, -wī′ē) **1.** A state of the US in the central Pacific, including all of the Hawaiian Is. except Midway. Cap. Honolulu. **2.** The largest of the Hawaiian Is., at the SE end of the chain.

Ha·wai·ian (hə-wä′yən) ▸*n.* **1.** A native or inhabitant of Hawaii or the Hawaiian Islands. **2a.** A Native Hawaiian. **b.** The Polynesian language of Hawaii. —**Ha·wai′ian** *adj.*

Hawaiian Islands A group of islands in the central Pacific roughly coextensive with HI.

ha·wa·la (hə-wä′lə) ▸*n.* An informal system for transferring money, esp. across borders, through a network of trusted agents. [Ar. *ḥawāla*, bill of exchange.]

hawk¹ (hôk) ▸*n.* **1.** Any of various birds of prey characteristically having a short hooked bill and strong claws adapted for seizing. **2.** One who favors an aggressive or warlike foreign policy. [< OE *hafoc.*] —**hawk′ish** *adj.* —**hawk′ish·ly** *adv.* —**hawk′ish·ness** *n.*

hawk² (hôk) ▸*v.* To peddle goods aggressively, esp. by calling out. [Prob. < MLGer. *hōken*, peddle.] —**hawk′er** *n.*

hawk³ (hôk) ▸*v.* To clear the throat by or as if by coughing up phlegm. [Imit.] —**hawk** *n.*

hawk-eyed (hôk′īd′) ▸*adj.* Having very keen eyesight.

haw·ser (hô′zər) ▸*n.* A cable or rope used in mooring or towing a ship. [< OFr. *haucier*, to hoist < VLat. *altiāre.*]

haw·thorn (hô′thôrn′) ▸*n.* A usu. thorny tree or shrub having white or pinkish flowers and reddish fruits. [< OE *hagathorn.*]

Haw·thorne (hô′thôrn′), **Nathaniel** 1804–64. Amer. writer.

hay (hā) ▸*n.* Grass or other plants cut and dried for fodder. ▸*v.* To mow and cure grass and herbage for hay. [< OE *hīeg.*]

Haydn (hīd′n), **Franz Joseph** 1732–1809. Austrian composer.

Hayes (hāz), **Rutherford Birchard** 1822–93. The 19th US president (1877–81).

Rutherford Hayes

hay fever ▸*n.* An allergic condition affecting the mucous membranes of the upper respiratory tract and the eyes, usu. caused by an abnormal sensitivity to airborne pollen.

hay·fork (hā′fôrk′) ▸*n.* **1.** A pitchfork. **2.** A machine-operated fork for moving hay.

hay·loft (hā′lôft′, -lŏft′) ▸*n.* A loft for storing hay.

hay·seed (hā′sēd′) ▸*n.* **1.** Chaff that falls from hay. **2.** *Informal* An unsophisticated person from a rural area; a bumpkin.

hay·stack (hā′stăk′) ▸*n.* A large stack of hay, esp. as left in a field to dry.

hay·wire (hā′wīr′) ▸*adj. Informal* **1.** Not functioning properly; broken. **2.** Crazy.

haz·ard (hăz′ərd) ▸*n.* **1.** A chance; accident. **2.** A possible source of danger. **3.** An obstacle on a golf course. ▸*v.* **1.** To venture: *hazard a guess.* **2.** To expose to danger or risk. See Synonyms at **endanger.** [Poss. < Ar. *az-zahr*, gaming die.] —**haz′ard·ous** *adj.* —**haz′ard·ous·ly** *adv.*

hazardous waste ▸*n.* Waste material, such as nuclear waste or an industrial byproduct, that is potentially harmful to humans or other organisms.

haze¹ (hāz) ▸*n.* **1.** Atmospheric moisture, dust, smoke, and vapor that diminishes visibility. **2.** A vague or confused state of mind. [Prob. < HAZY.]

haze² (hāz) ▸*v.* **hazed, haz·ing** To persecute or harass with meaningless, difficult, or humiliating tasks. [Perh. < OFr. *haser*, annoy.] —**haz′er** *n.*

ha·zel (hā′zəl) ▸*n.* **1.** A shrub or small tree bearing edible nuts enclosed in a leafy husk. **2.** A light or yellowish brown. [< OE *hæsel.*] —**ha′zel** *adj.*

ha·zel·nut (hā′zəl-nŭt′) ▸*n.* The nut of a hazel.

haz·y (hā′zē) ▸*adj.* **-i·er, -i·est** **1.** Marked by the presence of haze. **2.** Not clearly defined; unclear or vague. [?] —**haz′i·ly** *adv.* —**haz′i·ness** *n.*

Hb ▸*abbr.* hemoglobin

H-bomb (āch′bŏm′) ▸*n.* A hydrogen bomb.

hcf ▸*abbr.* highest common factor

HD ▸*abbr.* high definition

HDL cholesterol (āch′dē-ĕl′) ▸*n.* A lipoprotein with high concentrations of protein and low concentrations of lipids that transports cholesterol in the blood and is associated at low levels with an increased risk of heart disease. [*h(igh-) d(ensity) l(ipoprotein).*]

HDPE ▸*abbr.* high-density polyethylene

hdqrs. ▸*abbr.* headquarters

HDTV ▸*abbr.* high-definition television

he (hē) ▸*pron.* **1.** Used to refer to the male previously mentioned or implied. See Usage Note at

I. 2. Used to refer to a person whose gender is unspecified or unknown. ►*n.* A male person or animal: *Is the cat a he?* [< OE *hē.*]

Usage: Use of *he* as a gender-neutral pronoun, as in *A novelist should write about what he knows best,* is often considered sexist. The easiest way to avoid such constructions is to change to the plural, so that *they* is the pronoun, or to use forms such as *he/she* or *he or she,* although these can be cumbersome in sustained use.

head (hĕd) ►*n.* **1.** The uppermost or forwardmost part of the body, containing the brain and in vertebrates the eyes, ears, nose, mouth, and jaws. **2.** The intellect or mind; intelligence. **3.** Mental ability or aptitude. **4.** often **heads** *(takes sing. v.)* The side of a coin having the principal design. **5a.** An individual: *charged five dollars a head.* **b.** *pl.* **head** A single animal: *20 head of cattle.* **6.** A leader, chief, or director. **7.** The foremost or leading position. **8.** The pressure exerted by a liquid or gas: *a head of steam.* **9.** The foam that rises to the top in pouring an effervescent liquid, such as beer. **10.** A turning point: *bring matters to a head.* **11.** A projecting or striking part. **12.** The rounded proximal end of a long bone. **13.** A rounded compact mass, as of leaves or buds: *a head of cabbage.* **14.** The uppermost part; the top. **15.** The end considered the most important: *the head of the table.* **16.** A toilet, esp. on a ship. **17.** A headline or heading. ►*adj.* **1.** Foremost in rank or importance. **2.** Placed at the top or the front. ►*v.* **1.** To be in charge of; lead. **2.** To be in the first or foremost position of. **3.** To aim or proceed in a certain direction. **4.** To provide with a head: *head each column with a number.* **—phrasal verb: head off** To intercept. **—idioms: head over heels 1.** Rolling, as in a somersault. **2.** Completely; hopelessly: *head over heels in love.* **off (or out of) (one's) head** Crazy. [< OE *hēafod.*] **—head′less** *adj.*

head·ache (hĕd′āk′) ►*n.* **1.** A pain in the head. **2.** *Informal* An annoying problem. **—head′ach′y** *adj.*

head·band (hĕd′bănd′) ►*n.* A band worn around the head.

head·board (hĕd′bôrd′) ►*n.* A board or panel that forms the head, as of a bed.

head·dress (hĕd′drĕs′) ►*n.* A covering or an ornament for the head.

head·first (hĕd′fûrst′) ►*adv.* **1.** With the head leading; headlong. **2.** Impetuously; brashly. **—head′first′** *adj.*

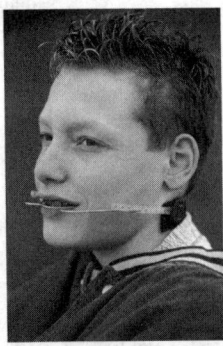

headgear

head·gear (hĕd′gîr′) ►*n.* **1.** A covering, such as a hat or helmet, for the head. **2.** An orthodontic brace held in place by a strap around the head or neck.

head·hunt·ing (hĕd′hŭn′tĭng) ►*n.* **1.** The custom of cutting off and preserving the heads of enemies as trophies. **2.** *Informal* The business of recruiting personnel, esp. executive personnel, as for a corporation. **—head′hunt′er** *n.*

head·ing (hĕd′ĭng) ►*n.* **1.** The title, subtitle, or topic that stands at the top or beginning, as of a text. **2.** The direction in which a ship or an aircraft is pointing or moving.

head·land (hĕd′lənd, -lănd′) ►*n.* A usu. high point of land extending out into a body of water.

head·light (hĕd′līt′) ►*n.* **1.** A light with a reflector mounted on the front of a vehicle. **2.** A lamp mounted on a miner's or spelunker's hardhat.

head·line (hĕd′līn′) ►*n.* The title or heading of a news article, usu. set in large type. ►*v.* **-lined, -lin·ing 1.** To supply (a page or passage) with a headline. **2.** To receive prominent billing at: *headline a variety show.* **—head′lin′er** *n.*

head·lock (hĕd′lŏk′) ►*n.* A wrestling hold in which the head of one wrestler is encircled and locked by the arm and body of the other.

head·long (hĕd′lông′, -lŏng′) ►*adv.* **1.** Headfirst. **2.** In an impetuous manner: *rushed headlong into an agreement.* See Synonyms at **impetuous.** [ME *(bi) hedlong.*] **—head′long′** *adj.*

head·man (hĕd′mən, -măn′) ►*n.* The chief man esp. of a tribal or traditional village.

head·mas·ter (hĕd′măs′tər) ►*n.* A man who is a principal, usu. of a private school.

head·mis·tress (hĕd′mĭs′trĭs) ►*n.* A woman who is a principal, usu. of a private school.

head of state ►*n.* See **chief of state.**

head-on (hĕd′ŏn′, -ôn′) ►*adj.* **1.** Facing forward; frontal. **2.** With the front end foremost: *a head-on collision.* **—head′-on′** *adv.*

head·phone (hĕd′fōn′) ►*n.* A small speaker worn over or in the ear.

head·piece (hĕd′pēs′) ►*n.* A protective covering for the head.

head·pin (hĕd′pĭn′) ►*n.* The front pin in an arrangement of bowling pins.

head·quar·ters (hĕd′kwôr′tərz) ►*pl.n.* *(takes sing. or pl. v.)* **1.** The offices of a commander, as of a military unit. **2.** A center of operations or administration.

Usage: The noun *headquarters* can be used with either a singular or a plural verb. The plural is more common: *The corporation's headquarters are in Boston.* But when referring to authority rather than physical location, many people prefer the singular: *Division headquarters has approved the new benefits package.*

head·rest (hĕd′rĕst′) ►*n.* A support for the head.

head·room (hĕd′rōōm′, -rŏŏm′) ►*n.* Space above one's head, as in a vehicle or tunnel; clearance.

head·set (hĕd′sĕt′) ►*n.* A pair of headphones, often with microphone attached.

head shop ►*n.* *Slang* A shop that sells paraphernalia for use with illegal drugs.

head·stand (hĕd′stănd′) ►*n.* A position in which one supports oneself vertically on one's head with the hands braced for support on the floor.

head start ►*n.* An early start that confers an advantage.

head·stone (hĕd′stōn′) ►*n.* **1.** A memorial stone set at the head of a grave. **2.** See **keystone** (sense 1).

head·strong (hĕd′strông′, -strŏng′) ►*adj.* Determined to have one's own way; willful.

head·wait·er (hĕd′wā′tər) ►*n.* A person in charge of the waiters and waitresses in a restaurant.

head·wa·ters (hĕd′wô′tərz, -wŏt′ərz) ►*pl.n.* The waters from which a river rises.

head·way (hĕd′wā′) ►*n.* **1.** Forward movement, esp. of a ship. **2.** Progress toward a goal. **3.** Overhead clearance; headroom.

head·wind (hĕd′wĭnd′) ►*n.* A wind blowing against the course of an aircraft or ship.

head·y (hĕd′ē) ►*adj.* **-i·er, -i·est 1.** Intoxicating: *a heady liqueur.* **2.** Exhilarating: *the heady thrill of victory.* —**head′i·ly** *adv.* —**head′i·ness** *n.*

heal (hēl) ►*v.* **1.** To restore to or regain health or soundness. **2.** To experience relief from emotional distress. **3.** To set right; repair: *healed the rift between us.* [< OE *hǣlan.*] —**heal′a·ble** *adj.* —**heal′er** *n.*

health (hĕlth) ►*n.* **1.** The overall condition of an organism at a given time. **2.** Soundness, esp. of body or mind. **3.** A condition of well-being. [< OE *hǣlth.*] —**health′ful** *adj.* —**health′ful·ly** *adv.* —**health′ful·ness** *n.*

health care or **health·care** (hĕlth′kâr′) ►*n.* The prevention and treatment of illness through the delivery of medical services. —**health care, health-care** *adj.*

health care proxy ►*n.* A legal document in which the signer designates another person to make decisions about the signer's medical care if the signer becomes incapable of doing so.

health food ►*n.* A food believed to be beneficial to one's health. —**health′-food′** *adj.*

health maintenance organization ►*n.* An HMO.

health·y (hĕl′thē) ►*adj.* **-i·er, -i·est 1.** Possessing good health. **2.** Conducive to good health; healthful. **3.** Indicative of sound thinking or mind: *a healthy attitude.* **4.** Sizable; considerable: *a healthy portion.* ►*adv.* So as to promote one's health; in a healthy way: *eating healthy.* —**health′i·ly** *adv.* —**health′i·ness** *n.*

Hea·ney (hē′nē), **Seamus Justin** b. 1939. Irish poet.

heap (hēp) ►*n.* **1.** A group of things placed or thrown, one on top of the other. **2.** often **heaps** *Informal* A great amount; a lot. ►*v.* **1.** To put or throw in a pile: *heaped the clothes on the bed.* **2.** To fill completely or to overflowing: *heap a plate with vegetables.* **3.** To bestow in abundance: *heaped praise on them.* [< OE *hēap.*]
Syns: *mound, pile, stack* n.

hear (hîr) ►*v.* **heard** (hûrd), **hear·ing 1.** To perceive by the ear. **2.** To learn by hearing. **3a.** To listen to attentively. **b.** To listen to in an official capacity. [< OE *hīeran.*] —**hear′er** *n.*

hear·ing (hîr′ĭng) ►*n.* **1.** The sense by which sound is perceived. **2.** Range of audibility; earshot. **3.** An opportunity to be heard. **4a.** A legal proceeding in which evidence is taken and arguments are given as the basis for a decision to be issued. **b.** A session, as of a grand jury, at which testimony is taken from witnesses.

hearing aid ►*n.* A small electronic amplifying device that is worn to aid poor hearing.

hear·ing-im·paired (hîr′ĭng-ĭm-pârd′) ►*adj.* **1.** Hard of hearing. **2.** Completely incapable of hearing; deaf. —**hear′ing-im·paired′** *n.*

hear·ken (här′kən) ►*v.* To listen attentively; give heed. [< OE *hercnian.*]

hear·say (hîr′sā′) ►*n.* **1.** Unverified information that is heard from another. **2.** *Law* Evidence, such as testimony regarding statements made by someone other than the witness, that may be inadmissible because it cannot be verified.

hearse (hûrs) ►*n.* A vehicle for conveying a coffin to a church or cemetery. [ME *herse,* frame for holding candles < Lat. *hirpex,* harrow.]

Hearst (hûrst), **William Randolph** 1863–1951. Amer. newspaper and magazine publisher.

heart (härt) ►*n.* **1.** The chambered, muscular organ that pumps blood received from the veins into the arteries, maintaining the flow of blood through the circulatory system. **2.** The vital center and source of one's being, feelings, and emotions. **3a.** Sympathy or generosity; compassion. **b.** Love; affection. **4.** Resolution; fortitude: *lose heart.* **5.** The most important or essential part: *get to the heart of the matter.* **6.** Any of a suit of playing cards marked with a red, heart-shaped figure. —*idioms:* **by heart** By memory. **heart and soul** Completely; entirely. **take to heart** To take seriously and be affected by. **with all (one's) heart 1.** With great willingness or pleasure. **2.** With deepest feeling. [< OE *heorte.*]

heart·ache (härt′āk′) ►*n.* Emotional anguish; sorrow.

heart attack ►*n.* Interruption of blood supply to the heart, usu. caused by an occlusion of a coronary artery and resulting in necrosis of a region of the heart muscle.

heart·beat (härt′bēt′) ►*n.* **1.** A single complete pulsation of the heart. **2.** An instant: *accepted the offer in a heartbeat.*

heart·break (härt′brāk′) ►*n.* Overwhelming grief or disappointment, esp. in love. —**heart′break′er** *n.* —**heart′break′ing** *adj.* —**heart′break′ing·ly** *adv.*

heart·bro·ken (härt′brō′kən) ►*adj.* Suffering from heartbreak. —**heart′bro′ken·ly** *adv.*

heart·burn (härt′bûrn′) ►*n.* A burning sensation, usu. in the middle of the chest, caused by acidic stomach fluids.

heart·en (här′tn) ►*v.* To give strength, courage, or hope to. See Synonyms at **encourage.**

heart·felt (härt′fĕlt′) ►*adj.* Deeply or sincerely felt; earnest.

hearth (härth) ►*n.* **1.** The floor of a fireplace, usu. extending into a room. **2.** Family life; the home. **3.** The lowest part of a blast furnace, from which the molten metal flows. [< OE *heorth.*]

hearth·stone (härth′stōn′) ►*n.* Stone used in the construction of a hearth.

heart·land (härt′lănd′) ►*n.* A central region, esp. one that is vital to a nation.

heart·less (härt′lĭs) ►*adj.* Devoid of compassion or feeling; pitiless. —**heart′less·ly** *adv.* —**heart′less·ness** *n.*

heart-rend·ing (härt′rĕn′dĭng) ►*adj.* Causing anguish or arousing deep sympathy.

heart·sick (härt′sĭk′) ►*adj.* Profoundly disappointed; despondent. —**heart′sick′ness** *n.*

heart·strings (härt′strĭngz′) ►*pl.n.* The deepest feelings or affections.

heart·throb (härt′thrŏb′) ►*n.* **1.** A heartbeat. **2.** One who is the object of popular romantic infatuation or desire. Usu. used of men.

heart-to-heart (härt′tə-härt′) ►*adj.* Candid; frank. ►*n.* An intimate conversation.

heart·wood (härt′wŏŏd′) ►*n.* The older, nonliving central wood of a tree or woody plant.

heart·y (här′tē) ►*adj.* **-i·er, -i·est 1.** Expressed warmly and exuberantly. **2.** Complete or thorough. **3.** Vigorous; robust. **4.** Nourishing; satisfying: *a hearty stew.* ►*n., pl.* **-ies** A good fellow; comrade. —**heart′i·ly** *adv.* —**heart′i·ness** *n.*

heat (hēt) ►*n.* **1.** *Phys.* A form of energy associated with the motion of atoms or molecules and transferred from bodies at a higher temperature to those at a lower temperature. **2.** The sensation of such energy as warmth or hotness. **3.** A degree of warmth or hotness: *low heat.* **4.** The warming of a room or building, as by a furnace. **5.** Intensity, as of emotion. **6.** Estrus. **7.** *Sports* **a.** One round of several in a competition. **b.** A preliminary contest held to determine finalists. **8.** *Informal* Pressure; stress. **9.** *Slang* An intensification of police activity in pursuing criminals. **10.** *Slang* Adverse comments or criticism. **11.** *Slang* A firearm, esp. a pistol. ►*v.* **1.** To make or become warm or hot. **2.** To excite the feelings of; inflame. [< OE *hætu.*]

heat·ed (hē′tĭd) ►*adj.* Angry; vehement: *a heated argument.* —**heat′ed·ly** *adv.*

heat·er (hē′tər) ►*n.* **1.** An apparatus that heats or provides heat. **2.** *Slang* A pistol.

heat exhaustion ►*n.* A condition caused by exposure to heat, marked by subsequent dehydration resulting in weakness, dizziness, nausea, and sometimes collapse.

heath (hēth) ►*n.* **1.** Any of various usu. low-growing shrubs having small evergreen leaves and small, colorful flowers. **2.** A tract of uncultivated open land covered with low shrubs; moor. [< OE *hǣth.*]

Heath, Sir **Edward Richard George.** 1916–2005. British prime minister (1970–74).

hea·then (hē′thən) ►*n., pl.* **-thens** or **-then 1.** *Offensive* One who adheres to a religion other than Judaism, Christianity, or Islam. **2.** *Informal* One regarded as irreligious, uncivilized, or unenlightened. [< OE *hǣthen.*] —**hea′then, hea′then·ish** *adj.* —**hea′then·dom** *n.*

heath·er (hĕth′ər) ►*n.* **1.** A low shrub growing in dense masses and having small evergreen leaves and pinkish-purple flowers. **2.** See **heath** (sense 1). [< ME *hather.*]

heat lightning ►*n.* Intermittent flashes of light near the horizon without thunder.

heat rash ►*n.* An inflammatory skin condition caused by obstruction of the sweat gland ducts and marked by itching or prickling.

heat stroke ►*n.* A condition caused by prolonged exposure to excessive heat and marked by cessation of sweating, headache, fever, hot dry skin, and in serious cases, collapse and coma.

heave (hēv) ►*v.* **heaved, heav·ing 1.** To raise or lift, esp. with great effort. **2.** To throw, esp. with great effort. **3.** To utter with effort or pain: *heaved a sigh.* **4.** To vomit. **5.** *p.t.* and *p.part.* **hove** *Naut.* **a.** To raise or haul by means of a rope or cable. **b.** To position or be positioned in a certain way: *the ship hove alongside.* **6.** To rise up or swell. ►*n.* **1.** The effort of heaving. **2.** A throw. **3.** An upward movement. **4.** An act of gagging or vomiting. [< OE *hebban.*]

heav·en (hĕv′ən) ►*n.* **1.** often **heavens** The sky or universe; firmament. **2.** often **Heaven** *Christianity* The abode of God, the angels, and the souls of those who are granted salvation. **3.** Any of the places in or beyond the sky conceived of as domains of divine beings in various religions. **4.** A state or place of great happiness. [< OE *heofon.*] —**heav′en·li·ness** *n.* —**heav′en·ly** *adj.*

heav·y (hĕv′ē) ►*adj.* **-i·er, -i·est 1.** Having relatively great weight. **2.** Having relatively high density. **3.** Large, as in number, quantity, or yield: *a heavy turnout.* **4.** Of great intensity: *heavy fighting.* **5a.** Having great power or force: *a heavy punch.* **b.** Violent; rough: *heavy seas.* **6a.** Equipped with massive armaments and weapons: *heavy infantry.* **b.** Large enough to fire powerful shells: *heavy guns.* **7.** Indulging or participating to a great degree: *a heavy drinker.* **8a.** Dense; thick: *a heavy fog; a heavy coat.* **b.** Too rich to digest easily: *a heavy dessert.* **9a.** Weighed down; burdened: *trees heavy with plums.* **b.** Marked by weariness: *heavy lids.* **10.** Not easily borne; oppressive: *heavy taxes.* **11.** Of or involving large-scale production: *heavy industry.* **12.** *Phys.* Of an isotope with an atomic mass greater than the average mass of that element. **13.** *Slang* Of great significance or profundity. ►*n., pl.* **-ies 1.** *Slang* A villain in a story or play. **2.** *Slang* A mobster. **3.** *Slang* One that is important or influential. [< OE *hefig.*] —**heav′i·ness** *n.* —**heav′y, heav′i·ly** *adv.*

heav·y-dut·y (hĕv′ē-dŏŏ′tē, -dyŏŏ′-) ►*adj.* Made to withstand hard use or wear.

heav·y-hand·ed (hĕv′ē-hăn′dĭd) ►*adj.* **1.** Clumsy; awkward. **2.** Tactless; indiscreet. **3.** Oppressive; harsh. —**heav′y-hand′ed·ly** *adv.* —**heav′y-hand′ed·ness** *n.*

heav·y-heart·ed (hĕv′ē-här′tĭd) ►*adj.* Melancholy; depressed; sad. —**heav′y-heart′ed·ly** *adv.* —**heav′y-heart′ed·ness** *n.*

heavy metal ►*n.* **1.** A metal with a specific gravity greater than about 5.0. **2.** Very loud, brash rock music.

heav·y·set (hĕv′ē-sĕt′) ►*adj.* Having a stout or compact build.

heavy water ►*n.* An isotopic variety of water containing deuterium in place of ordinary hydrogen.

heav·y·weight (hĕv′ē-wāt′) ►*n.* **1.** One of above average weight. **2.** A contestant in the heaviest weight class of a sport, esp. a boxer weighing more than 200 pounds. **3.** *Informal* A person of great importance.

He·bra·ic (hĭ-brā′ĭk) ►*adj.* Of or relating to the Hebrews or their language or culture.

He·bra·ist (hē′brā′ĭst) ►*n.* A Hebrew scholar.

He·brew (hē′brŏŏ) ►*n.* **1a.** A member of an ancient Semitic people claiming descent from Abraham, Isaac, and Jacob; Israelite. **b.** A descendant of this people; Jew. **2a.** The Semitic language of the ancient Hebrews. **b.** Any of the various later forms of this language, esp. that spoken in modern Israel. **3. Hebrews** *(takes sing. v.)* See table at **Bible.** —**He′brew** *adj.*

Hebrew Scriptures ►*pl.n.* The Torah, the Prophets, and the Writings. See table at **Bible.**

Heb·ri·des (hĕb′rĭ-dēz′) An island group of W and NW Scotland in the Atlantic, divided into the **Inner Hebrides,** closer to the Scottish mainland, and the **Outer Hebrides,** to the NW. —**Heb′ri·de′an** *adj. & n.*

heck (hĕk) ▸*interj.* Used as a mild oath. [Alteration of HELL.]

heck·le (hĕk′əl) ▸*v.* **-led, -ling** To interrupt (esp. a speaker or performer) with taunts or insults. [ME *hekelen,* to comb flax.] —**heck′-ler** *n.*

hec·tare (hĕk′târ′) ▸*n.* See table at **measurement.**

hec·tic (hĕk′tĭk) ▸*adj.* Marked by intense activity, confusion, or haste. [< Gk. *hektikos,* habitual.] —**hec′ti·cal·ly** *adv.*

hecto– or **hect–** ▸*pref.* One hundred (10²): *hectare.* [< Gk. *hekaton,* hundred.]

hec·to·gram (hĕk′tə-grăm′) ▸*n.* See table at **measurement.**

hec·to·li·ter (hĕk′tə-lē′tər) ▸*n.* See table at **measurement.**

hec·to·me·ter (hĕk′tə-mē′tər, hĕk-tŏm′ĭ-tər) ▸*n.* See table at **measurement.**

hec·tor (hĕk′tər) ▸*v.* To intimidate in a blustering way. [< HECTOR.]

Hector ▸*n.* *Gk. Myth.* A Trojan prince killed by Achilles in Homer's *Iliad.*

he'd (hēd) **1.** He had. **2.** He would.

hedge (hĕj) ▸*n.* **1.** A row of closely planted shrubs forming a boundary. **2.** Protection, esp. against financial loss. **3.** An intentionally ambiguous statement. ▸*v.* **hedged, hedg·ing 1.** To enclose or bound with or as if with hedges. **2.** To limit the financial risk of (e.g., a bet) by a counterbalancing transaction. **3.** To avoid making a clear, direct response. [< OE *hecg.*] —**hedg′er** *n.*

hedge·hog (hĕj′hôg′, -hŏg′) ▸*n.* Any of several small insectivorous Old World mammals having the back covered with dense spines.

he·don·ism (hēd′n-ĭz′əm) ▸*n.* **1.** Pursuit of or devotion to pleasure. **2.** The ethical doctrine that only what is pleasant is intrinsically good. [< Gk. *hēdonē,* pleasure.] —**he′don·ist** *n.* —**he′don·is′tic** *adj.* —**he′don·is′ti·cal·ly** *adv.*

–hedral ▸*suff.* Having a specified kind or number of surfaces: *tetrahedral.* [< –HEDRON.]

–hedron ▸*suff.* A crystal or geometric figure having a specified kind or number of surfaces: *polyhedron.* [< Gk. *hedra,* face.]

hee·bie-jee·bies (hē′bē-jē′bēz) ▸*pl.n. Slang* A feeling of uneasiness; jitters. [Coined by Billy De Beck (1890–1942).]

heed (hēd) ▸*v.* To pay attention (to). ▸*n.* Close attention; notice. [< OE *hēdan.*] —**heed′less** *adj.* —**heed′less·ly** *adv.* —**heed′less·ness** *n.*

heed·ful (hēd′fəl) ▸*adj.* Attentive; mindful. See Synonyms at **careful.** —**heed′ful·ly** *adv.*

heel¹ (hēl) ▸*n.* **1a.** The rounded posterior portion of the human foot under and behind the ankle. **b.** The corresponding part of the hind foot of other vertebrates. **2.** The part, as of a sock or shoe, that covers or supports the heel. **3.** One of the crusty ends of a loaf of bread. **4.** A lower, rearward surface. **5.** *Informal* A dishonorable person. ▸*v.* **1.** To furnish with a heel. **2.** To follow at one's heels. —*idioms:* **down at the heels** Shabby; poor. **on (or upon) the heels of 1.** Directly behind. **2.**

Immediately following. **take to (one's) heels** To flee. [< OE *hēla.*]

heel² (hēl) ▸*v.* To tilt or cause to tilt (e.g., a boat) to one side. [< OE *hieldan.*] —**heel** *n.*

heft (hĕft) ▸*n.* Weight; heaviness. ▸*v.* **1.** To judge the weight of by lifting. **2.** To hoist; heave. [ME < *heven,* HEAVE.]

heft·y (hĕf′tē) ▸*adj.* **-i·er, -i·est 1.** Heavy. **2.** Rugged and powerful. **3.** *Informal* Large; substantial. —**heft′i·ness** *n.*

He·gel (hā′gəl), **Georg Wilhelm Friedrich** 1770–1831. German philosopher.

he·gem·o·ny (hĭ-jĕm′ə-nē, hĕj′ə-mō′nē) ▸*n., pl.* **-nies** The dominance of one state or social group over others. [< Gk. *hēgemōn,* leader.] —**heg′e·mon′ic** (hĕj′ə-mŏn′ĭk) *adj.* —**he·gem′o·nism** *n.* —**he·gem′o·nist** *adj. & n.*

he·gi·ra (hĭ-jī′rə, hĕj′ər-ə) ▸*n.* **1.** A flight to escape danger. **2.** also **Hegira** The flight of Muhammad from Mecca to Medina in 622. [< Ar. *hijra,* emigration.]

Hei·deg·ger (hī′dĕg′ər, -dĭ-gər), **Martin** 1889–1976. German philosopher.

heif·er (hĕf′ər) ▸*n.* A young cow, esp. one that has not calved. [< OE *hēahfore.*]

height (hīt) ▸*n.* **1a.** The distance from the base of something to the top. **b.** Elevation above a given level; altitude. See Synonyms at **elevation. 2a.** The condition of being high or tall. **b.** Stature, esp. of the human body. **3.** An eminence, such as a hill. **4.** The highest or uppermost point. **5a.** The most advanced degree; zenith. **b.** The point of highest intensity; climax. [< OE *hēahthu.*]

height·en (hīt′n) ▸*v.* **1.** To rise or increase in quantity or degree; intensify. **2.** To make or become high or higher.

Heim·lich maneuver (hīm′lĭk′, -lĭĸн′) ▸*n.* An emergency technique to eject a lodged object from the trachea of a choking person in which an upward thrust is applied below the rib cage to force air up from the lungs. [After Henry J. *Heimlich* (b. 1920).]

Hei·ne (hī′nə), **Heinrich** 1797–1856. German writer.

hei·nous (hā′nəs) ▸*adj.* Wicked; abominable. [< OFr. *haine,* hatred.] —**hei′nous·ly** *adv.* —**hei′nous·ness** *n.*

heir (âr) ▸*n.* A person who inherits or is entitled to inherit the estate, rank, title, or office of another. [< Lat. *hērēs.*]

heir apparent ▸*n., pl.* **heirs apparent** An heir who will inherit as a matter of course provided he or she survives an ancestor.

heir·ess (âr′ĭs) ▸*n.* A woman who is an heir, esp. to great wealth. See Usage Note at **–ess.**

heir·loom (âr′lōōm′) ▸*n.* **1.** A valued possession that is passed down in a family through succeeding generations. **2.** *Law* An article of personal property included in an inherited estate. **3.** A usu. old-fashioned variety of a vegetable or fruit that is not widely grown. [ME *heirlome.*]

heir presumptive ▸*n., pl.* **heirs presumptive** An heir whose claim can be defeated by the birth of a closer relative before the death of the ancestor.

heist (hīst) *Slang* ▸*v.* To steal; rob. ▸*n.* A robbery; burglary. [Alteration of HOIST.]

held (hĕld) ▸*v.* P.t. and p.part. of **hold¹.**

Hel·en (hĕl′ən) ▸*n.* *Gk. Myth.* The wife of Menelaus whose abduction by Paris caused the Trojan War.

Hel·e·na (hĕl′ə-nə) The capital of Montana, in the W-central part.

hel·i·cal (hĕl′ĭ-kəl, hē′lĭ-) ►*adj.* Shaped like a helix; spiral. —**hel′i·cal·ly** *adv.*

hel·i·cop·ter (hĕl′ĭ-kŏp′tər) ►*n.* An aircraft that derives its lift from blades that rotate about an approx. vertical central axis. [Fr. *hélicoptère.*] —**hel′i·cop′ter** *v.*

helio– or **heli–** ►*pref.* Sun: *heliocentric.* [< Gk. *hēlios,* sun.]

he·li·o·cen·tric (hē′lē-ō-sĕn′trĭk) also **he·li·o·cen·tri·cal** (-trĭ-kəl) ►*adj.* Centered on the sun: *a heliocentric orbit.* —**he′li·o·cen·tric′i·ty** (-sĕn-trĭs′ĭ-tē) *n.*

he·li·o·trope (hē′lē-ə-trōp′) ►*n.* **1.** Any of several plants having small, highly fragrant purplish flowers. **2.** Any of various plants that turn toward the sun. [< Gk. *hēliotropion.*]

hel·i·port (hĕl′ə-pôrt′) ►*n.* A place for helicopters to land and take off.

he·li·um (hē′lē-əm) ►*n. Symbol* **He** A colorless, odorless inert gaseous element used in lasers and as a refrigerant and a lifting gas for balloons. At. no. 2. See table at **element.** [< Gk. *hēlios,* sun.]

he·lix (hē′lĭks) ►*n., pl.* **-lix·es** or **hel·i·ces** (hĕl′ĭ-sēz′, hē′lĭ-) **1.** A three-dimensional curve that lies on a cylinder or cone, so that its angle to a plane perpendicular to the axis is constant. **2.** A spiral form. [< Gk.]

hell (hĕl) ►*n.* **1.** often **Hell** *Christianity* The abode of condemned souls and devils. **2.** In various religions, the abode of the dead; underworld. **3a.** A situation or place of evil, misery, or destruction. **b.** Torment; anguish. **4.** *Informal* One that causes trouble, agony, or annoyance. **5.** A sharp scolding: *gave me hell.* ►*interj.* Used to express anger, disgust, or impatience. —*idiom:* **for the hell of it** For no particular reason. [< OE *helle.*]

he'll (hĕl) He will.

hell-bent (hĕl′bĕnt′) ►*adj.* Recklessly determined to do something.

hel·le·bore (hĕl′ə-bôr′) ►*n.* Any of various usu. poisonous plants of Eurasia and North America. [< Gk. *helleboros.*]

Hel·lene (hĕl′ēn′) ►*n.* A Greek.

Hel·len·ic (hĕ-lĕn′ĭk) ►*adj.* Of or relating to the ancient Hellenes or their language; Greek. ►*n.* The branch of Indo-European that consists only of Greek.

Hel·len·ism (hĕl′ə-nĭz′əm) ►*n.* **1.** An idiom or custom of the Greeks. **2.** The civilization of ancient Greece. **3.** Admiration for Greek culture. —**Hel′le·ni·za′tion** *n.* —**Hel′le·nize′** *v.* —**Hel′le·niz′er** *n.*

Hel·le·nist (hĕl′ə-nĭst) ►*n.* **1.** In ancient times, a non-Greek who adopted Greek language and culture. **2.** A student of Greek literature, language, or civilization.

Hel·le·nis·tic (hĕl′ə-nĭs′tĭk) ►*adj.* **1.** Relating to the Hellenists. **2.** Of or relating to Greek history and culture from the death of Alexander the Great to the accession of Augustus.

Hel·les·pont (hĕl′ĭ-spŏnt′) See **Dardanelles.**

hell·gram·mite (hĕl′grə-mīt′) ►*n.* A large brownish aquatic insect larva, often used as fishing bait. [?]

hell·hole (hĕl′hōl′) ►*n.* A place of extreme wretchedness or squalor.

hel·lion (hĕl′yən) ►*n. Informal* A mischievous, troublesome person. [Prob. alteration of dial. *hallion,* worthless person.]

hell·ish (hĕl′ĭsh) ►*adj.* **1.** Of, resembling, or worthy of hell; fiendish. **2.** Highly unpleasant. —**hell′ish·ly** *adv.* —**hell′ish·ness** *n.*

hel·lo (hĕ-lō′, hə-) ►*interj.* Used as a greeting or to express surprise. ►*n., pl.* **-los** A calling or greeting of "hello." [< obsolete *holla,* stop!]

helm (hĕlm) ►*n.* **1.** The steering gear of a ship, esp. the tiller or wheel. **2.** A position of leadership or control. [< OE *helma.*]

hel·met (hĕl′mĭt) ►*n.* A rigid protective head covering, as of metal or plastic. [< OFr.]

hel·minth (hĕl′mĭnth′) ►*n.* A parasitic worm, esp. a roundworm or tapeworm. [< Gk. *helmins, helminth-.*]

helms·man (hĕlmz′mən) ►*n.* A man who steers a ship.

helms·wom·an (hĕlmz′woŏm′ən) ►*n.* A woman who steers a ship.

Hé·lo·ise (ĕl′ō-wēz′, ā-lō-ēz′) 1098?–1164. French scholar and religious figure; secretly married Peter Abelard.

help (hĕlp) ►*v.* **1a.** To assist; aid. **b.** To give material or financial aid (to). **c.** To wait on, as in a store. **2a.** To improve; advance: *did nothing to help the situation.* **b.** To ease; relieve: *medication to help your cold.* **3.** To refrain from: *couldn't help laughing.* ►*n.* **1.** Aid or assistance. **2.** Relief; remedy. **3.** One that helps. **4.** Domestic servants considered as a group. —*idiom:* **help (oneself) to** To serve or provide oneself with. [< OE *helpan.*] —**help′er** *n.*

help·ful (hĕlp′fəl) ►*adj.* Providing help; useful. —**help′ful·ly** *adv.* —**help′ful·ness** *n.*

help·ing (hĕl′pĭng) ►*n.* A single portion of food.

help·less (hĕlp′lĭs) ►*adj.* **1.** Unable to manage by oneself; incompetent. **2.** Lacking support or protection: *They were left helpless in the storm.* **3.** Involuntary: *helpless laughter.* —**help′less·ly** *adv.* —**help′less·ness** *n.*

help·mate (hĕlp′māt′) ►*n.* A helper and companion, esp. a spouse. [Alteration of HELPMEET.]

help·meet (hĕlp′mēt′) ►*n.* A helpmate. [< misunderstanding of *an help meet,* a suitable helper.]

Hel·sin·ki (hĕl′sĭng′kē, hĕl-sĭng′-) The capital of Finland, in the S part on the Gulf of Finland.

hel·ter-skel·ter (hĕl′tər-skĕl′tər) ►*adv.* **1.** In disorderly haste; confused. **2.** Haphazardly. ►*adj.* **1.** Hurried and confused. **2.** Haphazard. ►*n.* Turmoil; confusion. [?]

hem[1] (hĕm) ►*n.* A smooth edge on a piece of cloth made by folding an edge under and stitching it down. ►*v.* **hemmed, hem·ming** **1.** To fold back and stitch down the edge of. **2.** To surround and shut in. See Synonyms at **enclose.** [< OE.] —**hem′mer** *n.*

hem[2] (hĕm) ►*n.* A short cough or clearing of the throat, as to gain attention, warn another, or hide embarrassment. —*idiom:* **hem and haw** To be hesitant and indecisive. [< ME *heminge,* coughing.]

he-man (hē′măn′) ►*n. Informal* A man considered strong and virile.

he·ma·tite (hē′mə-tīt′) ►*n.* A blackish-red to brick-red mineral, the chief ore of iron. [< Gk.

(lithos) haimatitēs, bloodlike (stone).]

hemato– or **hemat–** ►*pref.* Blood: *hematology.* [< Gk. *haima, haimat-,* blood.]

he·ma·tol·o·gy (hē′mə-tŏl′ə-jē) ►*n.* The branch of medicine dealing with diagnosis and treatment of diseases of the blood and bone marrow. —**he′ma·to·log′ic** (-tə-lŏj′ĭk), **he′-ma·to·log′i·cal** *adj.* —**he′ma·tol′o·gist** *n.*

he·ma·to·ma (hē′mə-tō′mə) ►*n.* A localized swelling filled with blood.

heme (hēm) ►*n.* The deep red, nonprotein, ferrous component of hemoglobin. [Ult. < Gk. *haima,* blood.]

–hemia ►*suff.* Var. of **–emia.**

Hem·ing·way (hĕm′ĭng-wā′), **Ernest Miller** 1899–1961. Amer. writer.

Ernest Hemingway
photographed in 1960

hem·i·sphere (hĕm′ĭ-sfîr′) ►*n.* **1a.** A half of a sphere bounded by a great circle. **b.** A half of a symmetrical, approx. spherical object as divided by a plane of symmetry. **2.** Either the northern or southern half of the earth as divided by the equator or the eastern or western half as divided by a meridian. **3.** *Anat.* **a.** Either of the lateral halves of the cerebrum. **b.** Either of the lateral halves of the cerebellum. [< Gk. *hēmisphairion.*] —**hem′i·spher′ic** (-sfîr′ĭk, -sfĕr′-), **hem′i·spher′i·cal** *adj.*

hem·line (hĕm′līn′) ►*n.* The bottom edge of a skirt, dress, or coat.

hem·lock (hĕm′lŏk′) ►*n.* **1a.** Any of a genus of coniferous evergreen trees having small cones and short flat leaves. **b.** The wood of a hemlock. **2a.** The poison hemlock. **b.** A poison obtained from the poison hemlock. [< OE *hymlice,* poisonous hemlock.]

hemo– ►*pref.* Blood: *hemodialysis.* [< Gk. *haima,* blood.]

he·mo·di·al·y·sis (hē′mō-dī-ăl′ĭ-sĭs) ►*n., pl.* **-ses** (-sēz′) A procedure for removing metabolic waste products or toxic substances from the bloodstream by dialysis.

he·mo·glo·bin (hē′mə-glō′bĭn) ►*n.* The iron-containing respiratory pigment in red blood cells. [Short for *hematinoglobulin.*]

he·mo·phil·i·a (hē′mə-fĭl′ē-ə, -fēl′yə) ►*n.* Any of several hereditary disorders occurring almost exclusively in males, in which the blood fails to clot normally because of a defective clotting factor. —**he′mo·phil′i·ac′** *n.*

hem·or·rhage (hĕm′ər-ĭj) ►*n.* **1.** Copious or excessive bleeding. **2.** A copious loss of some-

thing valuable: *a hemorrhage of corporate earnings.* [< Gk. *haimorrhagia.*] —**hem′or·rhage** *v.* —**hem′or·rhag′ic** (hĕm′ə-răj′ĭk) *adj.*

hem·or·rhoid (hĕm′ə-roid′) ►*n.* **1.** An itching or painful mass of dilated veins in swollen anal tissue. **2. hemorrhoids** The pathological condition in which hemorrhoids occur. [< Gk. *haimorrhoïs* : HEMO– + *rhein,* to flow.] —**hem′-or·rhoi′dal** *adj.*

he·mo·stat (hē′mə-stăt′) ►*n.* **1.** An agent used to stop bleeding. **2.** A surgical clamp used to constrict a blood vessel. —**he′mo·stat′ic** *adj.*

hemp (hĕmp) ►*n.* **1.** Cannabis. **2.** The tough coarse fiber of the cannabis plant, used esp. to make cordage. [< OE *hænep.*]

hem·stitch (hĕm′stĭch′) ►*n.* A decorative stitch used esp. on hems. —**hem′stitch′** *v.*

hen (hĕn) ►*n.* A female bird, esp. the adult female chicken. [< OE.]

hence (hĕns) ►*adv.* **1.** For this reason; therefore. **2.** From this time; from now. **3.** Away from here. [< OE *heonan,* from here.]

hence·forth (hĕns′fôrth′) ►*adv.* From this time forth; from now on.

hence·for·ward (hĕns-fôr′wərd) ►*adv.* Henceforth.

hench·man (hĕnch′mən) ►*n.* **1.** A loyal follower or subordinate. **2.** A person who supports a political figure for selfish interests. [ME *hengsman,* squire.]

hen·na (hĕn′ə) ►*n.* **1a.** A tree or shrub having fragrant white or reddish flowers. **b.** A reddish-orange cosmetic dye prepared from the leaves of this plant. **2.** A reddish brown. ►*v.* To dye with henna. [Ar. *ḥinnā.*] —**hen′na** *adj.*

hen·peck (hĕn′pĕk′) ►*v. Informal* To dominate or harass with persistent nagging.

hen·ry (hĕn′rē) ►*n., pl.* **-ries** or **-rys** The unit of inductance at which an induced electromotive force of one volt is produced when the current is varied at the rate of one ampere per second. [After Joseph *Henry* (1791–1878).]

Henry III 1207–72. King of England (1216–72).

Henry IV[1] 1050–1106. Holy Roman emperor and king of Germany (1056–1106).

Henry IV[2] "Henry Bolingbroke." 1366?–1413. King of England (1399–1413).

Henry IV[3] "Henry of Navarre." 1553–1610. King of France (1589–1610).

Henry V 1387–1422. King of England (1413–22).

Henry VI 1421–71. King of England (1422–61 and 1470–71).

Henry VII "Henry Tudor." 1457–1509. King of England (1485–1509).

Henry VIII 1491–1547. King of England (1509–47).

Henry, Patrick 1736–99. Amer. Revolutionary leader and orator.

hep (hĕp) ►*adj. Slang* Var. of **hip**[2].

HEPA ►*abbr.* **1.** high-efficiency particulate air **2.** high-efficiency particulate arresting

hep·a·rin (hĕp′ər-ĭn) ►*n.* A polysaccharide, found esp. in lung and liver tissue, that slows blood clotting, used as a drug in the treatment of thrombosis. [< Gk. *hēpar,* liver.]

he·pat·ic (hĭ-păt′ĭk) ►*adj.* **1.** Of or relating to the liver. **2.** Acting on or occurring in the liver. [< Gk. *hēpar, hēpat-,* liver.]

he·pat·i·ca (hĭ-păt′ĭ-kə) ►*n.* A woodland plant having three-lobed leaves and white or lavender flowers. [< Med.Lat. *hēpatica*, liverwort.]

hep·a·ti·tis (hĕp'ə-tī'tĭs) ►*n.* Inflammation of the liver, caused by infectious or toxic agents and characterized by jaundice, fever, liver enlargement, and abdominal pain. [Gk. *hēpar, hēpat-*, liver + –ITIS.]

Hep·burn (hĕp'bûrn'), **Audrey** Audrey Kathleen Ruston. 1929–93. Belgian-born Amer. actress.

Hepburn, Katharine Houghton 1907–2003. Amer. actress.

He·phaes·tus (hĭ-fĕs'təs) ►*n. Gk. Myth.* The god of fire and metalworking.

hepta– or **hept–** ►*pref.* Seven: *heptagon.* [Gk. < *hepta*, seven.]

hep·ta·gon (hĕp'tə-gŏn') ►*n.* A polygon having seven sides. —**hep·tag'o·nal** (-tăg'ə-nəl) *adj.*

her (hər, ər; hûr *when stressed*) ►*adj.* The possessive form of **she.** Used as a modifier before a noun: *her mother; her goals.* ►*pron.* The objective case of **she. 1.** Used as a direct or indirect object: *I know her; They gave her a ride.* **2.** Used as the object of a preposition: *The call is for her.* See Usage Note at **I. 3.** Used after a linking verb such as *is: It's her.* [< OE *hire.*]

He·ra (hîr'ə) ►*n. Gk. Myth.* The goddess of women, marriage, and childbirth; the wife and sister of Zeus.

her·ald (hĕr'əld) ►*n.* **1.** One who carries important news; messenger. **2.** One that gives a sign or indication of something to come. **3.** An official formerly charged with making royal proclamations. ►*v.* To proclaim; announce. [< AN, of Gmc. orig.]

he·ral·dic (hə-răl'dĭk) ►*adj.* Of or relating to heraldry. —**he·ral'di·cal·ly** *adv.*

her·ald·ry (hĕr'əl-drē) ►*n., pl.* **-ries 1.** The study or art of devising and describing coats of arms, tracing genealogies, and ruling on questions of rank or protocol. **2.** Pomp and ceremony; pageantry. —**her'ald·ist** *n.*

He·rat (hĕ-rät') A city of NW Afghanistan W of Kabul.

herb (ûrb, hûrb) ►*n.* **1.** A plant that does not have a woody stem and usu. dies back at the end of each growing season. **2.** Any of various often aromatic plants used in medicine or as seasoning. [< Lat. *herba.*]

her·ba·ceous (hûr-bā'shəs, ûr-) ►*adj.* **1.** Relating to an herb as distinguished from a woody plant. **2.** Green and leaflike.

herb·age (ûr'bĭj, hûr'-) ►*n.* **1.** Herbaceous plant growth, esp. as used for pasturage. **2.** The fleshy, often edible parts of plants.

herb·al (ûr'bəl, hûr'-) ►*adj.* Relating to or containing herbs. ►*n.* A book about plants and herbs, esp. those useful to humans.

herb·al·ism (ûr'bə-lĭz'əm, hûr'-) ►*n.* Herbal medicine. —**herb'al·ist** *n.*

herbal medicine ►*n.* **1.** The study or use of medicinal herbs to prevent or treat disease. **2.** A medicinal preparation made from plants.

her·bar·i·um (hûr-bâr'ē-əm, ûr-) ►*n., pl.* **-i·ums** or **-i·a** (-ē-ə) **1.** A collection of dried plants mounted and labeled for scientific study. **2.** A place where such a collection is kept. [LLat. *herbārium.*]

Her·bert (hûr'bərt), **George** 1593–1633. Welsh-born English poet.

her·bi·cide (hûr'bĭ-sīd', ûr'-) ►*n.* A substance used to destroy or inhibit plants, esp. weeds.

—**her'bi·cid'al** (-sīd'l) *adj.*

her·bi·vore (hûr'bə-vôr', ûr'-) ►*n.* An animal that feeds chiefly on plants. [< NLat. *herbivorus*, plant-eating.] —**her·biv'o·rous** (-bĭv'ər-əs) *adj.* —**her·biv'o·rous·ly** *adv.*

Her·cu·les (hûr'kyə-lēz') ►*n. Gk. & Rom. Myth.* A hero of extraordinary strength. —**Her'cu·le'an** (hûr'kyə-lē'ən, hûr-kyōō'lē-ən) *adj.*

herd (hûrd) ►*n.* **1.** A group of animals, esp. large herbivorous mammals, kept or living together. **2.** A large number of people; crowd. ►*v.* **1.** To come together in a herd. **2.** To gather, keep, or drive in or as if in a herd. [< OE *heord.*] —**herd'er** *n.* —**herds'man** *n.*

here (hîr) ►*adv.* **1.** At or in this place: *Stop here for a rest.* **2.** At this time; now: *We'll adjourn the meeting here.* **3.** At or on this point or item: *Here I must disagree.* **4.** To this place: *Come here.* See Usage Note at **there.** ►*interj.* Used esp. to respond to a roll call, attract attention, or command an animal. —*idiom:* **neither here nor there** Irrelevant. [< OE *hēr.*]

here·a·bout (hîr'ə-bout') also **here·a·bouts** (-bouts') ►*adv.* In this vicinity.

here·af·ter (hîr-ăf'tər) ►*adv.* **1.** From here or now on. **2.** In a future time or state. ►*n.* The afterlife.

here·by (hîr-bī', hîr'bī') ►*adv.* By this act, decree, or document.

he·red·i·tar·y (hə-rĕd'ĭ-tĕr'ē) ►*adj.* **1.** Genetically transmitted or transmissible. **2.** *Law* **a.** Passing down by inheritance. **b.** Having title or possession through inheritance. —**he·red'i·tar'i·ly** (-târ'ə-lē) *adv.*

he·red·i·ty (hə-rĕd'ĭ-tē) ►*n., pl.* **-ties 1.** The genetic transmission of characteristics from parent to offspring. **2.** The set of characteristics transmitted genetically to an individual organism. [< Lat. *hērēs, hērēd-*, heir.]

here·in (hîr-ĭn') ►*adv.* In or into this.

here·of (hîr-ŭv', -ŏv') ►*adv.* Of this.

here·on (hîr-ŏn', -ôn') ►*adv.* On this.

her·e·sy (hĕr'ĭ-sē) ►*n., pl.* **-sies 1a.** An opinion or doctrine at variance with religious orthodoxy. **b.** Adherence to such opinion or doctrine. **2a.** A controversial opinion or doctrine. **b.** Adherence to such opinion or doctrine. [< Gk. *hairesis*, faction.]

her·e·tic (hĕr'ĭ-tĭk) ►*n.* A person who holds unorthodox opinions. [< Gk. *hairetikos*, factious.] —**he·ret'i·cal** (hə-rĕt'ĭ-kəl) *adj.*

here·to (hîr-tōō') ►*adv.* To this document or matter.

here·to·fore (hîr'tə-fôr') ►*adv.* Before this; previously. [ME.]

here·un·to (hîr-ŭn'tōō) ►*adv.* Hereto.

here·up·on (hîr'ə-pŏn', -pôn') ►*adv.* **1.** Immediately after this. **2.** At or on this.

here·with (hîr-wĭth', -wĭth') ►*adv.* **1.** Along with this. **2.** By this means; hereby.

her·i·ta·ble (hĕr'ĭ-tə-bəl) ►*adj.* Capable of being inherited; hereditary. [< OFr.] —**her'i·ta·bil'i·ty** *n.* —**her'i·ta·bly** *adv.*

her·i·tage (hĕr'ĭ-tĭj) ►*n.* **1.** Property that is or can be inherited. **2.** Something passed down from preceding generations; tradition. **3.** A domesticated animal or a crop of a traditional breed, usu. not widely produced for commercial purposes. [< OFr. < *heriter*, inherit.]
Syns: inheritance, legacy, tradition n.

her·maph·ro·dite (hər-măf'rə-dīt') ►*n.* **1.** A

person having the reproductive organs and many of the secondary sex characteristics of both sexes. **2.** A plant or animal having both female and male reproductive organs. [< Gk. *Hermaphroditos*, Hermaphroditus, son of Hermes and Aphrodite.] —**her·maph′ro·dit′ic** (-dĭt′ĭk) *adj.*

Her·mes (hûr′mēz) ►*n. Gk. Myth.* The messenger of the gods and patron deity of commerce, invention, and theft.

her·met·ic (hər-mĕt′ĭk) also **her·met·i·cal** (-ĭ-kəl) ►*adj.* **1.** Completely sealed, esp. against the escape or entry of air. **2.** Impervious to outside interference or influence. [< Med.Lat. *Hermēs Trismegistus*, legendary alchemist.] —**her·met′i·cal·ly** *adv.*

her·mit (hûr′mĭt) ►*n.* One who lives a solitary existence; recluse. [< Gk. *erēmitēs* < *erēmos*, solitary.] —**her·mit′ic** *adj.*

her·mit·age (hûr′mĭ-tĭj) ►*n.* **1.** The habitation of a hermit. **2.** A monastery or abbey. **3.** A hideaway or retreat.

hermit crab ►*n.* A crab that protects its soft, unarmored abdomen by occupying and carrying the empty shell of a snail or other mollusk.

her·ni·a (hûr′nē-ə) ►*n., pl.* **-ni·as** or **-ni·ae** (-nē-ē′) The protrusion of an organ or other bodily structure through the wall that normally contains it; rupture. [< Lat.] —**her′ni·al** *adj.*

he·ro (hîr′ō) ►*n., pl.* **-roes 1.** In mythology and legend, a man celebrated for his bold exploits. **2.** A person noted for feats of courage or nobility of purpose. **3.** A person noted for special achievement in a particular field. **4.** The principal character in a literary work. **5.** A submarine sandwich. [< Gk. *hērōs.*]

Her·od (hĕr′əd) "the Great." 73?–4 BC. King of Judea (40–4).

Herod An·ti·pas (ăn′tĭ-păs′, -pəs) d. c. AD 40. Ruler of a portion of Judea (4 BC –AD 40).

He·rod·o·tus (hĭ-rŏd′ə-təs) 5th cent. BC. Greek historian.

he·ro·ic (hĭ-rō′ĭk) also **he·ro·i·cal** (-ĭ-kəl) ►*adj.* **1.** Of or like the heroes of literature, legend, or myth. **2.** Displaying qualities characteristic of a hero; courageous. **3.** Impressive in size or scope; grand: *heroic undertakings.* ►*n.* **hero·ics 1.** Heroic acts; heroism. **2.** Melodramatic behavior or language. —**he·ro′i·cal·ly** *adv.*

heroic couplet ►*n.* A verse unit of two rhymed lines in iambic pentameter.

her·o·in (hĕr′ō-ĭn) ►*n.* A white, odorless compound that is derived from morphine and is a highly addictive illegal narcotic. [Ger., orig. a trademark.]

her·o·ine (hĕr′ō-ĭn) ►*n.* **1.** A woman noted for courage and daring action. **2.** A woman noted for special achievement in a particular field. **3.** The principal female character in a literary work. [< Gk. *hērōinē.*]

her·o·ism (hĕr′ō-ĭz′əm) ►*n.* **1.** Heroic conduct or behavior. **2.** Heroic qualities; courage.

her·on (hĕr′ən) ►*n.* Any of various wading birds having a long neck, long legs, and a long pointed bill. [< OFr., of Gmc. orig.]

her·pes (hûr′pēz) ►*n.* A viral infection causing eruption of small vesicles on the skin or mucous membranes. [< Gk. *herpēs.*] —**her·pet′ic** (hər-pĕt′ĭk) *adj.*

herpes sim·plex (sĭm′plĕks′) ►*n.* Either of two recurrent viral infections, one marked

by blisters usu. on the mouth and face and the other by blisters on the genitals. [NLat., simple herpes.]

her·pe·tol·o·gy (hûr′pĭ-tŏl′ə-jē) ►*n.* The branch of zoology that deals with reptiles and amphibians. [< Gk. *herpeton*, reptile.] —**her′pe·to·log′ic** (-tə-lŏj′ĭk), **her′pe·to·log′i·cal** *adj.* —**her′pe·tol′o·gist** *n.*

Herr (hĕr) ►*n., pl.* **Her·ren** (hĕr′ən) A German courtesy title for a man. [Ger.]

her·ring (hĕr′ĭng) ►*n., pl.* **-ring** or **-rings** A silvery fish of the Atlantic and Pacific waters that is commercially important. [< OE *hǣring.*]

her·ring·bone (hĕr′ĭng-bōn′) ►*n.* **1.** A pattern consisting of rows of short, slanted parallel lines with the direction of the slant alternating row by row. **2.** A twilled fabric woven in this pattern.

herringbone

herring gull ►*n.* A common seagull having gray and white plumage with black wingtips.

hers (hûrz) ►*pron. (takes sing. or pl. v.)* Used to indicate the one or ones belonging to her: *I found my keys, but not hers.* [ME *hires.*]

Her·schel (hûr′shəl) Family of British astronomers, including Sir **William Herschel** (1738–1822), **Caroline Herschel** (1750–1848), and Sir **John Frederick William Herschel** (1792–1871).

her·self (hûr-sĕlf′) ►*pron.* **1.** That one identical with her: **a.** Used reflexively as the direct or indirect object of a verb or as the object of a preposition: *She hurt herself.* **b.** Used for emphasis: *She herself saw it.* **2.** Her normal or healthy condition: *She's feeling herself again.*

hertz (hûrts) ►*n., pl.* **hertz** A unit of frequency equal to one cycle per second. [After H.R. *Hertz* (1857–94).]

Her·ze·go·vi·na (hĕrt′sə-gō′vē-nə, -gō-vē′-, hûrt′-) The S region of Bosnia and Herzegovina.

Her·zl (hĕrt′səl), **Theodor** 1860–1904. Hungarian-born Austrian founder of Zionism.

he's (hēz) **1.** He is. **2.** He has.

Hesh·van also **Hesh·wan** (кнĕsh′vən, -vän) ►*n.* The 8th month of the Jewish calendar. See table at **calendar.** [Heb. *ḥešwān.*]

He·si·od (hē′sē-əd, hĕs′ē-) fl. 8th cent. BC. Greek poet.

hes·i·tant (hĕz′ĭ-tənt) ►*adj.* Inclined or tending to hesitate. —**hes′i·tan·cy** *n.* —**hes′i·tant·ly** *adv.*

hes·i·tate (hĕz′ĭ-tāt′) ▸*v.* **-tat·ed, -tat·ing 1.** To be slow to act, speak, or decide; waver. **2.** To be reluctant: *hesitant to drive in the storm.* **3.** To speak haltingly; falter. [Lat. *haesitāre.*] —**hes′i·tat′ing·ly** *adv.* —**hes′i·ta′tion** *n.*

Hes·se (hĕs′ə), **Hermann** 1877–1962. German-born Swiss writer.

Hes·ti·a (hĕs′tē-ə) ▸*n.* Gk. Myth. The goddess of the hearth.

hetero– or **heter–** ▸*pref.* Other; different: *heterochromatic.* [Gk. < *heteros,* other.]

het·er·o·dox (hĕt′ər-ə-dŏks′) ▸*adj.* **1.** Not in agreement with accepted beliefs, esp. in theology. **2.** Holding unorthodox opinions. [Gk. *heterodoxos.*] —**het′er·o·dox′y** *n.*

het·er·o·ge·ne·ous (hĕt′ər-ə-jē′nē-əs, -jēn′yəs) ▸*adj.* also **het·er·og·e·nous** (hĕt′ə-rŏj′ə-nəs) Consisting of dissimilar elements or parts; not homogeneous. [< Gk. *heterogenēs.*] —**het′er·o′ge·ne′i·ty** *n.* —**het′er·o·ge′ne·ous·ly** *adv.*

het·er·o·sex·u·al (hĕt′ə-rō-sĕk′shōō-əl) ▸*adj.* Sexually oriented to persons of the opposite sex. ▸*n.* A heterosexual person. —**het′er·o·sex′u·al′i·ty** *n.*

het·er·o·troph (hĕt′ər-ə-trŏf′, -trŏf′) ▸*n.* An organism that depends on complex organic substances for nutrition because it cannot synthesize its own food. [HETERO– + Gk. *trophos,* feeder; see –TROPHY.] —**het′er·o·troph′ic** (-trŏf′ĭk, -trō′fĭk) *adj.* —**het′er·o·troph′i·cal·ly** *adv.* —**het′er·ot′ro·phy** (-ə-rŏt′rə-fē) *n.*

heu·ris·tic (hyŏŏ-rĭs′tĭk) ▸*adj.* Of an educational method in which students learn through investigation and discovery. [< Gk. *heuriskein,* find.] —**heu·ris′tic** *n.* —**heu·ris′ti·cal·ly** *adv.* —**heu·ris′tics** *n.*

hew (hyōō) ▸*v.* **hewed, hewn** (hyōōn) or **hewed, hew·ing 1.** To make or shape with or as if with an ax. **2.** To cut down with an ax. **3.** To adhere or conform strictly: *hew to the line.* [< OE *hēawan.*] —**hew′er** *n.*

hex¹ (hĕks) ▸*n.* **1.** An evil spell; curse. **2.** One that brings bad luck. ▸*v.* To put a hex on. [Penn. Du. < Ger. *Hexe,* witch.] —**hex′er** *n.*

hex² (hĕks) ▸*adj.* Hexagonal. Used of hardware: *a hex wrench.*

hexa– or **hex–** ▸*pref.* Six: *hexagon.* [Gk. < *hex,* six.]

hex·a·dec·i·mal (hĕk′sə-dĕs′ə-məl) ▸*adj.* Of or based on the number 16.

hex·a·gon (hĕk′sə-gŏn′) ▸*n.* A polygon having six sides. —**hex·ag′o·nal** (hĕk-săg′ə-nəl) *adj.* —**hex·ag′o·nal·ly** *adv.*

hex·am·e·ter (hĕk-săm′ĭ-tər) ▸*n.* Verse composed in lines of six metrical feet. —**hex′a·met′ric** (hĕk-sə-mĕt′rĭk), **hex′a·met′ri·cal** (-rĭ-kəl) *adj.*

hey (hā) ▸*interj.* **1.** Used to attract attention or to express surprise, appreciation, wonder, or pleasure. **2.** Used to express greeting.

hey·day (hā′dā′) ▸*n.* The period of greatest popularity, success, or power; prime. [Perh. < ME *hey,* hey.]

HF ▸*abbr.* high frequency

HFC ▸*abbr.* hydrofluorocarbon

hgt. ▸*abbr.* height

HH ▸*abbr.* **1.** His (or Her) Highness **2.** His Holiness

hi (hī) ▸*interj.* Used to express greeting.

HI ▸*abbr.* Hawaii

hi·a·tus (hī-ā′təs) ▸*n., pl.* **-tus·es** or **-tus** A gap or interruption in space, time, or continuity. [Lat. *hiātus* < *hiāre,* gape.] —**hi·a′tal** *adj.*

Hi·a·wa·tha (hī′ə-wŏth′ə, -wô′thə, hē′ə-) fl. 1550. Onondagan leader.

hi·ba·chi (hĭ-bä′chē) ▸*n., pl.* **-chis** A portable charcoal-burning brazier with a grill, used chiefly for cooking. [J.]

hi·ber·nate (hī′bər-nāt′) ▸*v.* **-nat·ed, -nat·ing** To pass the winter in a dormant or torpid state. [< Lat. *hībernus,* of winter.] —**hi′ber·na′tion** *n.* —**hi′ber·na′tor** *n.*

hi·bis·cus (hī-bĭs′kəs) ▸*n.* Any of a genus of chiefly tropical shrubs or trees having large, showy, variously colored flowers. [LLat. < Lat. *hibiscum,* marsh mallow.]

hic·cup also **hic·cough** (hĭk′əp) ▸*n.* **1.** A spasm of the diaphragm resulting in a rapid involuntary inhalation that is stopped by the sudden closure of the glottis and accompanied by a sharp, distinctive sound. **2.** hiccups also hiccoughs An attack of these spasms. ▸*v.* **-cupped, -cup·ping** also **-coughed, -cough·ing** To have the hiccups. [Imit.]

hick (hĭk) ▸*n. Derogatory* A gullible, provincial person; yokel. ▸*adj.* Provincial; unsophisticated. [< *Hick,* a nickname for *Richard.*]

hick·o·ry (hĭk′ə-rē) ▸*n., pl.* **-ries 1.** Any of a genus of North American trees having smooth or shaggy bark, compound leaves, and hard nuts with an edible kernel. **2.** The wood of a hickory. [Of Algonquian orig.]

hi·dal·go (hĭ-dăl′gō) ▸*n., pl.* **-gos** A member of the minor nobility in Spain. [Sp.]

hide¹ (hīd) ▸*v.* **hid** (hĭd), **hid·den** (hĭd′n) or **hid, hid·ing 1.** To put or keep out of sight: *hid the money in a sock.* **2.** To prevent the disclosure of: *hid the facts.* **3.** To cut off from sight; cover up: *Clouds hid the stars.* See Synonyms at **block.** [< OE *hȳdan.*]

hide² (hīd) ▸*n.* The skin of an animal, esp. of a large animal. [< OE *hȳd.*]

hide-and-seek (hīd′n-sēk′) ▸*n.* A children's game in which one player tries to find and catch others who are hiding.

hide·a·way (hīd′ə-wā′) ▸*n.* **1.** A place of concealment; hideout. **2.** A secluded or isolated place.

hide·bound (hīd′bound′) ▸*adj.* **1.** Stubbornly narrow-minded or inflexible. **2.** Having abnormally dry, stiff skin that adheres to the underlying flesh. Used esp. of cattle.

hid·e·ous (hĭd′ē-əs) ▸*adj.* **1.** Repulsive, esp. to the sight. See Synonyms at **ugly. 2.** Terrible: *a hideous disease.* [< OFr. *hide,* fear.] —**hid′e·ous·ly** *adv.* —**hid′e·ous·ness** *n.*

hide·out (hīd′out′) ▸*n.* A place of shelter or concealment.

hie (hī) ▸*v.* **hied, hie·ing** or **hy·ing** (hī′ĭng) To go quickly; hasten. [< OE *hīgian,* exert oneself.]

hi·er·ar·chy (hī′ə-rär′kē, hī′rär′-) ▸*n., pl.* **-chies 1.** A body of persons having authority. **2.** An arrangement of persons or things in a graded series. [< Gk. *hierarkhia,* rule of a high priest.] —**hi′er·ar′chal, hi′er·ar′chic, hi′er·ar′chi·cal** *adj.* —**hi′er·ar′chi·cal·ly** *adv.*

hi·er·at·ic (hī′ə-răt′ĭk, hī-răt′-) ▸*adj.* **1.** Of or relating to sacred persons or offices; sacerdotal. **2.** Of or relating to a simplified style of

Egyptian hieroglyphic script. [Lat. *hierāticus* < Gk. *hieratikos* < Gk. *hiereus*, priest.] —**hi′er·at′i·cal·ly** *adv.*

hi·er·o·glyph (hī′ər-ə-glĭf′, hī′rə-) ►*n.* **1.** A symbol used in hieroglyphic writing. **2.** Something that suggests a hieroglyph.

hi·er·o·glyph·ic (hī′ər-ə-glĭf′ĭk, hī′rə-) ►*adj.* Relating to a system of writing in which pictorial symbols represent meaning or sound or both. ►*n.* **1a.** A hieroglyph. **b.** often **hieroglyphics** (*takes sing. or pl. v.*) Hieroglyphic writing, esp. that of the ancient Egyptians. **2.** Something illegible or undecipherable. [< Gk. *hierogluphikos* : *hieros*, holy + *gluphein*, carve.] —**hi′er·o·glyph′i·cal·ly** *adv.*

hi-fi (hī′fī′) ►*n., pl.* -**fis** *Informal* **1.** High fidelity. **2.** An electronic system for reproducing high-fidelity sound. —**hi′-fi′** *adj.*

hig·gle·dy-pig·gle·dy (hĭg′əl-dē-pĭg′əl-dē) ►*adv.* In utter disorder or confusion. [?]

high (hī) ►*adj.* -**er**, -**est 1a.** Relatively great in elevation. **b.** Extending a specified distance upward. **2a.** At or near a peak or culminating stage. **b.** Advanced in development or complexity. **3.** Relating to sounds produced by relatively fast vibrations; piercing. **4a.** Of great importance: *a high priority on housing.* **b.** Eminent in rank or status: *a high official.* **c.** Serious; grave: *high crimes.* **d.** Constituting a climax: *the high point of a film.* **5.** Lofty or exalted in quality. **6a.** Relatively great, as in quantity or degree. **b.** Favorable: *has a high opinion of him.* **7a.** Indicating excitement or euphoria. **b.** *Slang* Intoxicated by or as if by alcohol or a drug. ►*adv.* -**er**, -**est** At, in, or to a lofty position, level, or degree. ►*n.* **1.** A high level, degree, or point. **2.** The gear configuration of a transmission that maximizes output speed at the expense of power. **3.** A center of high atmospheric pressure. **4.** *Slang* An intoxicated or euphoric condition. —***idioms:* high and dry** Helpless; stranded. **high and low** Everywhere: *searched high and low.* [< OE *hēah.*] —**high′ly** *adv.*

high·ball (hī′bôl′) ►*n.* A cocktail made with liquor added to water or soda, served in a tall glass.

high beam ►*n.* The beam of a vehicle's headlight that provides long-range illumination.

high·born (hī′bôrn′) ►*adj.* Of noble birth.

high·boy (hī′boi′) ►*n.* A tall chest of drawers divided into two sections.

high·bred (hī′brĕd′) ►*adj.* Of superior breed or stock.

high·brow (hī′brou′) ►*n.* One who has or affects a high degree of culture or learning. ►*adj.* also **high′browed′** (-broud′) Highly cultured or intellectual.

high·chair (hī′châr′) ►*n.* A very young child's feeding chair that has long legs.

high-class (hī′klăs′) ►*adj.* Of superior quality; first-class.

high·er-up (hī′ər-ŭp′) ►*n.* *Informal* One who has a superior rank, position, or status.

high·fa·lu·tin or **hi·fa·lu·tin** (hī′fə-lōōt′n) ►*adj. Informal* Pompous; pretentious. [?]

high fashion ►*n.* **1.** See **high style. 2.** See **haute couture.**

high fidelity ►*n.* The electronic reproduction of sound with minimal distortion. —**high′-fi·del′i·ty** *adj.*

high-flown (hī′flōn′) ►*adj.* **1.** Highly preten-

tious or inflated: *high-flown rhetoric.* **2.** Lofty or exalted.

high frequency ►*n.* A radio frequency in the range between 3 and 30 megahertz.

high·hand·ed (hī′hăn′dĭd) ►*adj.* Arrogant; overbearing. —**high′hand′ed·ly** *adv.* —**high′hand′ed·ness** *n.*

high-hat (hī′hăt′) *Informal* ►*v.* -**hat·ted, -hat·ting** To treat condescendingly or superciliously. ►*adj.* Snobbish; haughty.

high jinks or **hi·jinks** (hī′jĭnks′) ►*pl.n.* Playful, often noisy and rowdy activity.

high jump ►*n.* A jump for height made over a horizontal bar in a track-and-field contest. —**high jumper** *n.*

high·land (hī′lənd) ►*n.* **1.** Elevated land. **2. highlands** A mountainous section of a country. —**high′land** *adj.* —**high′land·er** *n.*

high·light (hī′līt′) ►*n.* **1.** An esp. notable detail or event. **2. highlights** Strands of hair that have been lightened. ►*v.* **1.** To make prominent; emphasize. **2.** To be a highlight of: *The duet highlighted the concert.* **3.** To mark (passages of text) with a marker for later reference.

high-mind·ed (hī′mīn′dĭd) ►*adj.* Elevated in ideals or conduct; noble. —**high′-mind′ed·ly** *adv.* —**high′-mind′ed·ness** *n.*

high·ness (hī′nĭs) ►*n.* **1.** The quality or condition of being high. **2. Highness** Used with *His, Her,* or *Your* as a title for a prince or princess.

high-pres·sure (hī′prĕsh′ər) ►*adj.* **1.** Relating to pressures higher than normal. **2.** *Informal* Aggressive and persistent. **3.** Imposing great stress or tension.

high profile ►*n.* An intentionally conspicuous, well-publicized presence or stance. —**high′-pro′file** *adj.*

high relief ►*n.* Sculptural relief in which the modeled forms project from the background by at least half their depth.

high-rise (hī′rīz′) ►*adj.* **1.** Relating to or being a multistoried building that is equipped with elevators. **2.** Related to pants with a waistline resting well above the waist. ►*n.* or **high rise** A high-rise building

high·road or **high road** (hī′rōd′) ►*n.* **1.** A direct or sure path. **2.** The most ethical or diplomatic course. **3.** *Chiefly Brit.* A main road; highway.

high roller ►*n.* **1.** One who spends extravagantly, as for luxuries or entertainment. **2.** One who gambles rashly or for high stakes.

high school ►*n.* A secondary school that usu. includes grades 9 or 10 through 12. —**high′-school′** *adj.* —**high school′er** *n.*

high seas ►*pl.n.* The open ocean waters beyond the territorial limits of a country.

high-sound·ing (hī′soun′dĭng) ►*adj.* Pretentious; pompous.

high-spir·it·ed (hī′spĭr′ĭ-tĭd) ►*adj.* **1.** Having a proud or unbroken spirit. **2.** Vivacious; lively. —**high′-spir′it·ed·ness** *n.*

high-strung (hī′strŭng′) ►*adj.* Tending to be very anxious and easily agitated.

high style ►*n.* The latest in fashion, usu. for an exclusive clientele. —**high′-style′** *adj.*

high·tail (hī′tāl′) ►*v. Slang* To go as fast as possible, esp. in retreat.

high-tech (hī′tĕk′) ►*adj. Informal* Related to or resembling high technology.

high technology ►*n.* Technology involving

highly advanced systems or devices. **—high′-tech·nol′o·gy** *adj.*

high-ten·sion (hī′tĕn′shən) ►*adj.* Having a high voltage.

high-test (hī′tĕst′) ►*adj.* **1.** Relating to highly volatile gasoline. **2.** Meeting exacting standards. **—high′test′** *n.*

high tide ►*n.* **1a.** The tide at its highest level. **b.** The time at which this tide occurs. **2.** A point of culmination; climax.

high-toned (hī′tōnd′) ►*adj.* **1.** Intellectually, morally, or socially superior. **2.** Fashionable or pretentious.

high·way (hī′wā′) ►*n.* A main public road.

high·way·man (hī′wā′mən) ►*n.* A robber who holds up travelers on a road.

high wire ►*n.* A tightrope that is stretched high above the ground. **—high′-wire′** *adj.*

hi·jack also **high·jack** (hī′jăk′) ►*v. Informal* **1.** To steal (goods) from a vehicle in transit. **2.** To seize control of (a moving vehicle) by force, esp. to reach an alternate destination or as an act of terrorism. **—hi′jack′er** *n.*

hike (hīk) ►*v.* **hiked, hik·ing 1.** To go on a long walk for pleasure or exercise. **2.** To increase in amount, esp. abruptly: *store owners who hiked their prices for tourists.* **3.** To pull or raise abruptly: *hiked up her socks.* **4.** *Football* To snap (the ball). ►*n.* **1.** A long walk. **2.** An often abrupt increase or rise: *a price hike.* **3.** *Football* See **snap** (sense 9). [?] **—hik′er** *n.*

hi·lar·i·ous (hī-lâr′ē-əs, -lăr′-, hĭ-) ►*adj.* Boisterously funny. [< Gk. *hilaros*, cheerful.] **—hi·lar′i·ous·ly** *adv.* **—hi·lar′i·ty** *n.*

Hil·de·gard von Bing·en (hĭl′də-gärd′ vŏn bĭng′ən) 1098–1179. German nun, poet, and composer.

Hildegard von Bingen
detail from the 12th-century illuminated
Liber Scivias

hill (hĭl) ►*n.* **1.** A well-defined natural elevation smaller than a mountain. **2.** A small heap, pile, or mound. **—idiom: over the hill** *Informal* Past one's prime. [< OE *hyll.*] **—hill′i·ness** *n.* **—hill′y** *adj.*

Hil·la·ry (hĭl′ə-rē), Sir **Edmund Percival** 1919–2008. New Zealand mountaineer.

hill·bil·ly (hĭl′bĭl′ē) ►*n., pl.* **-lies** *Often Offensive* A person from the backwoods or a remote mountain area.

Hil·lel (hĭl′ĕl, hĭl′āl, hē-lĕl′) fl. 1st cent. BC–1st cent. AD. Palestinian rabbi.

hill·ock (hĭl′ək) ►*n.* A small hill. [ME *hillok.*]

hill·side (hĭl′sīd′) ►*n.* The slope of a hill.

hill·top (hĭl′tŏp′) ►*n.* The crest of a hill.

hilt (hĭlt) ►*n.* The handle of a weapon or tool. **—idiom: to the hilt** To the limit; completely. [< OE.]

Hil·ton (hĭl′tən), **James** 1900–54. British novelist.

him (hĭm) ►*pron.* The objective case of **he. 1.** Used as a direct or indirect object: *They chose him; I gave him a raise.* **2.** Used as the object of a preposition: *This call is for him.* See Usage Note at **I. 3.** *Informal* Used after a linking verb such as *is: It's him.* [< OE.]

Him·a·la·ya Mountains (hĭm′ə-lā′ə, hĭ-mäl′yə) A mountain system of S-central Asia extending about 2,400 km (1,500 mi) through Kashmir, N India, S Tibet, Nepal, and Bhutan.

Him·a·lay·an (hĭm′ə-lā′ən, hĭ-mäl′yən) ►*adj.* Relating to or indigenous to the Himalaya Mountains. ►*n.* A variety of the Persian cat having long white fur with dark markings on the face, ears, feet, and tail.

him·self (hĭm-sĕlf′) ►*pron.* **1.** That one identical with him: **a.** Used reflexively as the direct or indirect object of a verb or the object of a preposition: *He cut himself.* **b.** Used for emphasis: *He himself did it.* **2.** His normal or healthy condition: *He's feeling himself again.*

hind¹ (hīnd) ►*adj.* Located at the back or rear; posterior: *hind legs.* [< OE *bihindan.*]

hind² (hīnd) ►*n.* A female red deer. [< OE.]

Hin·de·mith (hĭn′də-mĭth, -mĭt), **Paul** 1895–1963. German violist and composer.

hin·der (hĭn′dər) ►*v.* **1.** To obstruct or delay the progress of. **2.** To interfere with action or progress. [< OE *hindrian.*] **—hin′der·er** *n.*

Syns: *encumber, hamper, impede, obstruct* **v.**

Hin·di (hĭn′dē) ►*n.* **1.** A group of Indic dialects spoken in N India. **2.** The literary and official language based on these dialects. **—Hin′di** *adj.*

hind·most (hīnd′mōst′) also **hind·er·most** (hīn′dər-) ►*adj.* Farthest to the rear; last.

hind·quar·ter (hīnd′kwôr′tər) ►*n.* **1.** The back portion of a side of meat. **2. hindquarters** The rump of a four-footed animal.

hin·drance (hĭn′drəns) ►*n.* **1.** The act of hindering or condition of being hindered. **2.** One that hinders.

hind·sight (hīnd′sīt′) ►*n.* Understanding of events after their occurrence.

Hin·du (hĭn′dōō) ►*adj.* Relating to Hinduism or the Hindus. ►*n.* An adherent of Hinduism.

Hin·du·ism (hĭn′dōō-ĭz′əm) ►*n.* A diverse body of religion, philosophy, and culture native to India.

Hindu Kush (kōōsh, kŭsh) A mountain range of SW Asia extending W from N Pakistan to NE Afghanistan.

Hin·du·stan (hĭn′dōō-stän′, -stăn′) A historical region of India considered at various times to include only the upper Ganges R. plateau or all of N India.

Hin·du·sta·ni (hĭn′dōō-stä′nē, -stăn′ē) ►*n.* A group of Indic dialects that includes Urdu and Hindi. ►*adj.* Of or relating to Hindustan or the Hindustani language.

hinge (hĭnj) ►*n.* **1.** A jointed device that allows the turning of a part, such as a door, on a frame. **2.** A similar structure, as the valves of a mollusk. ▸*v.* **hinged, hing·ing 1.** To attach by or equip with or as if with a hinge. **2.** To be contingent; depend: *This plan hinges on her approval.* [ME.]

hint (hĭnt) ▸*n.* **1.** A slight indication or intimation. **2.** A barely perceptible amount: *just a hint of color.* ▸*v.* **1.** To make known in an indirect manner. **2.** To give a hint. [Poss. < OE *hentan,* to grasp.] —**hint′er** *n.*

hin·ter·land (hĭn′tər-lănd′) ▸*n.* **1.** The land adjacent to and inland from a coast. **2.** A region remote from urban areas. [Ger.]

hip¹ (hĭp) ▸*n.* **1.** The part of the human body between the waist and the thigh that projects laterally from the pelvis. **2.** The hip joint. [< OE *hype.*]

hip² (hĭp) also **hep** (hĕp) ▸*adj.* **hip·per, hip·pest** also **hep·per, hep·pest** *Slang* **1.** Keenly aware of the latest trends or developments. **2.** Very fashionable or stylish. [?] —**hip′ness** *n.*

hip³ (hĭp) ▸*n.* The fleshy, usu. red fruit of the rose, used for tea. [< OE *hēope.*]

hip·bone (hĭp′bōn′) ▸*n.* Either of two large flat bones each forming one of the halves of the pelvis.

hip-hop (hĭp′hŏp′) ▸*n.* **1.** A style of music usu. based on rap and often including elements of other styles such as funk or rhythm and blues. **2.** A popular urban youth culture, closely associated with hip-hop music and the style of inner-city African Americans. [Prob. HIP² + HOP¹.]

hip joint ▸*n.* The ball-and-socket joint formed by the head of the femur and the hipbone.

hip·pie also **hip·py** (hĭp′ē) ▸*n., pl.* **-pies** *Slang* A member of a counterculture associated with unconventional dress and liberal attitudes toward sexuality and drugs. [< HIP².]

hip·po (hĭp′ō) ▸*n., pl.* **-pos** A hippopotamus.

Hip·poc·ra·tes (hĭ-pŏk′rə-tēz′) 460?–377? BC. Greek physician.

Hip·po·crat·ic oath (hĭp′ə-krăt′ĭk) ▸*n.* An oath of ethical professional behavior sworn by new physicians. [After HIPPOCRATES.]

hip·po·drome (hĭp′ə-drōm′) ▸*n.* **1.** An arena for horse shows. **2.** An open-air stadium for horse and chariot races in ancient Greece and Rome. [< Gk. *hippodromos.*]

hip·po·pot·a·mus (hĭp′ə-pŏt′ə-məs) ▸*n., pl.* **-mus·es** or **-mi** (-mī′) A large African aquatic mammal with thick, dark, almost hairless skin, short legs, and a broad, wide-mouthed muzzle. [< Gk. *hippopotamos.*]

hip roof or **hipped roof** (hĭpt) ▸*n.* A four-sided roof having sloping ends and sides.

hip·ster (hĭp′stər) ▸*n.* *Slang* One who is hip.

hi·ra·ga·na (hĭr′ə-gä′nə) ▸*n.* The cursive variety of kana used in most modern Japanese texts. [J. : *hira,* ordinary, plain + *kana,* kana.]

hire (hīr) ▸*v.* **hired, hir·ing** To engage the services or use of for a fee: *hired a new clerk; hire a car for the day.* ▸*n.* **1.** The act of hiring or the condition of being hired. **2.** Payment for services or the use of something. [< OE *hȳrian.*]

hire·ling (hīr′lĭng) ▸*n.* One who works solely for compensation, esp. at performing tasks considered offensive.

Hi·ro·hi·to (hĭr′ō-hē′tō) 1901–89. Emperor of Japan (1926–89).

Hi·ro·shi·ma (hĭr′ə-shē′mə, hĭ-rō′shə-mə) ▸ a city of SW Honshu, Japan; destroyed by US

forces with the first atomic bomb used in warfare (August 6, 1945).

Hiroshima
aftermath of the atomic bombing

hir·sute (hûr′soōt′, hîr′-, hər-soōt′) ▸*adj.* Hairy. [Lat. *hirsūtus.*] —**hir′sute′ness** *n.*

his (hĭz) ▸*adj.* The possessive form of **he.** Used as a modifier before a noun: *his brother; his ideas.* ▸*pron.* (takes *sing.* or *pl. v.*) Used to indicate the one or ones belonging to him: *If you can't find your hat, take his.* [< OE.]

His·pan·ic (hĭ-spăn′ĭk) ▸*adj.* **1.** Relating to Spain or Spanish-speaking Latin America. **2.** Relating to a Spanish-speaking people or culture. ▸*n.* **1.** A Spanish-speaking person. **2.** A US citizen or resident of Latin-American or Spanish ancestry.

Usage: Though often used interchangeably, *Hispanic* and *Latino* are not identical terms. *Hispanic* is arguably the broader of the two, potentially encompassing all Spanish-speaking peoples in both hemispheres and emphasizing the common denominator of language between otherwise diverse communities. *Latino* refers more exclusively to persons of Latin American origin, and, with its Spanish sound and its ability to show the feminine form *Latina* when used of women, is favored by some as a term of ethnic pride. See Usage Note at **Chicano.**

His·pan·io·la (hĭs′pən-yō′lə) An island of the West Indies E of Cuba, divided between Haiti and the Dominican Republic.

hiss (hĭs) ▸*n.* **1.** A sharp sibilant sound similar to a sustained *s.* **2.** An expression of disapproval or contempt conveyed by a hiss. ▸*v.* **1.** To make a hiss. **2.** To express disapproval by hissing. [ME *hissen,* to hiss.]

his·ta·mine (hĭs′tə-mēn′, -mĭn) ▸*n.* A white crystalline compound in plant and animal tissue that is released by immune cells in allergic reactions, dilates blood vessels, and constricts bronchial smooth muscle. [*hist(idine)* + AMINE.] —**his′ta·min′ic** (-mĭn′ĭk) *adj.*

his·to·com·pat·i·bil·i·ty (hĭs′tō-kəm-păt′ə-bĭl′ĭ-tē) ▸*n., pl.* **-ties** A state or condition in which the absence of immunological interference permits the grafting of tissue or the transfusion of blood without rejection. —**his′to·com·pat′i·ble** *adj.*

his·to·gram (hĭs′tə-grăm′) ▸*n.* A bar graph of a frequency distribution in which the horizontal axis lists each unique value in a set of data, and the height of each bar represents the frequency of that value. [Gk. *histos,* bar + –GRAM.]

his·tol·o·gy (hĭ-stŏl′ə-jē) ▸*n., pl.* **-gies 1.** The study of the microscopic structure of animal and plant tissues. **2.** The microscopic structure of tissue. [< Gk. *histos,* tissue.] —**his′to·log′i·**

cal (hĭs′tə-lŏj′ĭ-kəl), **his′to·log′ic** adj. —**his′-to·log′i·cal·ly** adv. —**his·tol′o·gist** n.

his·to·ri·an (hĭ-stôr′ē-ən, -stŏr′-) ►n. A scholar or writer of history.

his·tor·ic (hĭ-stôr′ĭk, -stŏr′-) ►adj. Having importance in or influence on history.

Usage: Because they have similar meanings, *historic* and *historical* are easy to mix up. Nonetheless, they have different uses. *Historic* refers to what is important in history. *Historical* refers to whatever existed in the past, whether regarded as important or not: *a historical character.*

his·tor·i·cal (hĭ-stôr′ĭ-kəl, -stŏr′-) ►adj. **1.** Relating to history. **2.** Based on or concerned with events in history. **3.** Important or famous in history. See Usage Note at **historic.** —**his·tor′i·cal·ly** adv.

his·to·ri·og·ra·phy (hĭ-stôr′ē-ŏg′rə-fē) ►n. **1.** The principles or methodology of historical research. **2.** The writing of history based on critical analysis of original source materials. **3.** A body of historical literature. —**his·to′ri·og′ra·pher** n. —**his·to′ri·o·graph′ic** (-ē-ə-grăf′ĭk), **his·to′ri·o·graph′i·cal** adj.

his·to·ry (hĭs′tə-rē) ►n., pl. **-ries 1.** A chronological record of events, often including commentary: *a history of the Vikings.* **2.** An established record of a condition or behavior: *an inmate with a history of mental illness.* **3.** The branch of knowledge that records and analyzes past events. **4.** The events of the past: *tools used throughout human history.* **5.** An interesting past: *a house with a history.* [< Gk. *historia* < *historein,* inquire < *histōr,* learned person.]

his·tri·on·ic (hĭs′trē-ŏn′ĭk) also **his·tri·on·i·cal** (-ĭ-kəl) ►adj. **1.** Excessively dramatic; theatrical: *a histrionic response to losing the game.* **2.** Relating to actors or acting. [< Lat. *histriō,* actor.] —**his′tri·on′i·cal·ly** adv.

his·tri·on·ics (hĭs′trē-ŏn′ĭks) ►n. **1.** *(takes sing. or pl. v.)* Behavior that is deliberately dramatic or theatrical. **2.** *(takes pl. v.)* Dramatic arts or performances.

hit (hĭt) ►v. **hit, hit·ting 1.** To come or cause to come into contact with forcefully; strike. **2.** To strike with a missile: *hit me with a snowball.* **3.** To press or push (a key or button). **4.** To propel (e.g., a ball) with a blow. **5.** *Baseball* To execute (a base hit) successfully. **6.** To affect adversely. **7.** *Informal* To discover, esp. by chance: *hit on a solution to the problem.* **8.** *Informal* To attain or reach: *Sales hit a new high.* ►n. **1.** A collision or impact. **2.** A successfully executed shot, blow, or throw. **3.** A successful or popular venture. **4.** *Baseball* A base hit. **5.** *Comp.* **a.** A match of data in a search string against data that one is searching. **b.** A connection made to a website. **6.** *Slang* A dose of a narcotic drug. **7.** *Slang* A murder, esp. for hire. —*phrasal verbs:* **hit on** *Slang* To pay unsolicited romantic attention to. **hit up** *Slang* To approach and ask (someone) for something. —*idioms:* **hit it off** *Informal* To get along well together. **hit the hay** *Slang* To go to bed. **hit the road** *Slang* To set out; leave. **hit the roof** *Slang* To express vehement anger. **hit the spot** To satisfy a specific desire. [< ON *hitta.*] —**hit′ter** n.

hit-and-run (hĭt′n-rŭn′) ►adj. Relating to a vehicular accident in which the driver at fault leaves the scene.

hitch (hĭch) ►v. **1.** To fasten or catch temporar-

ily with or as if with a loop, hook, or noose. **2.** To connect or attach: *hitch an ox to the plow.* **3.** To move or raise by pulling or jerking: *hitch up one's suspenders.* **4.** *Informal* To hitchhike. **5.** To marry: *They got hitched last month.* ►n. **1.** A knot used as a temporary fastening. **2.** A short jerk or tug. **3.** An impediment or delay: *a hitch in our plans.* **4.** A term of military service. [Prob. < ME *hytchen,* move, jerk.] —**hitch′er** n.

Hitch·cock (hĭch′kŏk′), Sir **Alfred Joseph** 1899–1980. British film director.

hitch·hike (hĭch′hīk′) ►v. **-hiked, -hik·ing** To travel by soliciting free rides along a road. —**hitch′hik′er** n.

hith·er (hĭth′ər) ►adv. To or toward this place. ►adj. Located on the near side. [< OE *hider.*]

hith·er·to (hĭth′ər-tōō′, hĭth′ər-tōō′) ►adv. Until this time.

Hit·ler (hĭt′lər), **Adolf** 1889–1945. Austrian-born German Nazi dictator. —**Hit·ler′i·an** (hĭt-lîr′ē-ən) adj.

hit man ►n. *Slang* A hired killer.

hit-or-miss (hĭt′ər-mĭs′) ►adj. Haphazard; random. —**hit or miss** adv.

Hit·tite (hĭt′īt′) ►n. **1.** A member of an ancient people living in Anatolia about 2000–1200 BC. **2.** The Indo-European language of the Hittites.

HIV (āch′ī-vē′) ►n. A retrovirus that causes AIDS. [*h(uman) i(mmunodeficiency) v(irus).*]

hive (hīv) ►n. **1.** A structure for housing domesticated honeybees. **2.** A colony of bees living in a hive. **3.** A place swarming with activity. [< OE *hȳf.*] —**hive** v.

hives (hīvz) ►pl.n. *(takes sing. or pl. v.)* A rash marked by itching welts with multiple causes, including drugs and food. [?]

HM ►abbr. Her (or His) Majesty

HMO (āch′ĕm-ō′) ►n. A health care plan in which costs are contained by limiting services to a specified network of medical personnel and facilities. [H(EALTH) M(AINTENANCE) O(R-GANIZATION).]

Hmong (hmông) ►n., pl. **Hmong** or **Hmongs 1.** A member of a people of S China and SE Asia. **2.** The language of the Hmong.

HMS ►abbr. Her (or His) Majesty's Ship

hoa·gie also **hoa·gy** (hō′gē) ►n., pl. **-gies** *Regional* A submarine sandwich. [Alteration of *hoggy.*]

hoard (hôrd) ►n. **1.** A supply hidden or stored for future use. **2.** A collection or supply, as of memories or information, that one keeps to oneself for future use. ►v. **1.** To accumulate a hoard (of). **2.** To accumulate as much of (something) as one can, as when fearing a shortage. [< OE *hord.*] —**hoard′er** n.

hoar·frost (hôr′frôst′, -frŏst′) ►n. A white coating of ice crystals formed by the sublimation of atmospheric water vapor on a surface. [< OE *hār.*]

hoarse (hôrs) ►adj. **hoars·er, hoars·est 1.** Rough or grating in sound. **2.** Having or characterized by a husky voice. [< OE *hās.*] —**hoarse′ly** adv. —**hoarse′ness** n.

hoar·y (hôr′ē) ►adj. **-i·er, -i·est 1.** Gray or white with or as if with age. **2.** Covered with grayish hair. **3.** Very old; ancient. [< OE *hār.*] —**hoar′i·ness** n.

hoax (hōks) ►n. An act intended to deceive or trick. ►v. To deceive or cheat by using a hoax. [Perh. < HOCUS-POCUS.] —**hoax′er** n.

hob (hŏb) ►*n. Chiefly Brit.* A hobgoblin, sprite, or elf. [< ME *Hob*, nickname for Robert.]

Hobbes (hŏbz), **Thomas** 1588–1679. English philosopher. —**Hobbes′i·an** *adj.*

hob·ble (hŏb′əl) ►*v.* **-bled, -bling 1.** To walk with difficulty; limp. **2.** To impede the movement or progress of. ►*n.* **1.** A hobbling walk or gait. **2.** A device used to join the legs esp. of a horse so as to hamper but not prevent its movement. [ME *hobblen,* of LGer. orig.] —**hob′bler** *n.*

Syns: *fetter, handcuff, hogtie, manacle, shackle* v.

hob·by (hŏb′ē) ►*n., pl.* **-bies** An activity or interest pursued at one's leisure for enjoyment. [< ME *hobi,* small horse.] —**hob′by·ist** *n.*

hob·by·horse (hŏb′ē-hôrs′) ►*n.* **1.** A riding toy made of a long stick with an imitation horse's head on one end. **2.** See **rocking horse. 3.** A favorite or obsessive topic.

hob·gob·lin (hŏb′gŏb′lĭn) ►*n.* **1.** An ugly, mischievous elf or goblin. **2.** An object or source of fear or dread; bugaboo.

hob·nail (hŏb′nāl′) ►*n.* A short nail with a thick head used to protect the soles of shoes or boots. [*hob,* peg + NAIL.] —**hob′nailed′** *adj.*

hob·nob (hŏb′nŏb′) ►*v.* **-nobbed, -nob·bing** To associate familiarly: *hobnobs with the executives.* [< *(drink) hob or nob,* (toast) one another alternately.]

ho·bo (hō′bō) ►*n., pl.* **-boes** or **-bos** A homeless person, esp. a vagrant. [?]

Ho Chi Minh (hō′ chē′ mĭn′) 1890–1969. Vietnamese leader; first president of North Vietnam (1954–69).

Ho Chi Minh City Formerly **Saigon.** A city of S Vietnam near the South China Sea.

Ho-Chunk (hō′chŭngk′) ►*n., pl.* **-Chunk** or **-Chunks 1.** A member of a Native American people of Wisconsin, now also in Nebraska. **2.** The Siouan language of the Ho-Chunk.

hock¹ (hŏk) ►*n.* The joint of the hind leg of a quadruped, such as a horse, corresponding to the human ankle. [< OE *hōh,* heel.]

hock² (hŏk) *Slang* ►*v.* To pawn. ►*n.* **1.** The state of being in pawn. **2.** Debt: *in hock for 500 dollars.* [Prob. < Du. *hok,* prison.]

hock·ey (hŏk′ē) ►*n.* **1.** Ice hockey. **2.** Field hockey. [?]

ho·cus-po·cus (hō′kəs-pō′kəs) ►*n.* **1.** Nonsense words or phrases used when performing magic tricks. **2.** Deception; trickery. [Poss. alteration of Lat. *hoc est corpus (meum),* this is (my) body (a phrase used in the Eucharist).]

hod (hŏd) ►*n.* **1.** A trough carried over the shoulder for transporting bricks or mortar. **2.** A coal scuttle. [Perh. < OFr. *hotte,* pannier.]

hodge·podge (hŏj′pŏj′) ►*n.* A haphazard mixture; jumble. [< OFr. *hochepot,* stew.]

Hodg·kin's disease (hŏj′kĭnz) ►*n.* A malignant, progressive, sometimes fatal disease marked by enlargement of the lymph nodes, spleen, and liver. [After Thomas *Hodgkin* (1798–1866), British physician.]

hoe (hō) ►*n.* A tool with a flat blade attached to a long handle, used for weeding and cultivating. [< OFr. *houe,* of Gmc. orig.] —**hoe** *v.* —**ho′er** *n.*

hoe·down (hō′doun′) ►*n.* A social gathering at which square dancing takes place.

hog (hôg, hŏg) ►*n.* **1a.** An animal of the pig family, such as the boar or warthog. **b.** A domesticated pig, esp. one full-grown. **2a.** A gluttonous person. **b.** One that uses too much of something. **3.** *Slang* A big, heavy motorcycle. ►*v.* **hogged, hog·ging** *Informal* To take more than one's share of. —*idiom:* **high on the hog** In high or lavish style. [< OE *hogg.*]

ho·gan (hō′gän′, -gən) ►*n.* A one-room Navajo structure, traditionally facing east and used as a dwelling or for ceremonial purposes. [Navajo *hooghan.*]

hogan

hogs·head (hôgz′hĕd′, hŏgz′-) ►*n.* **1.** A unit of capacity used in the US, equal to 63 gal. (238 l). **2.** A large barrel or cask with this capacity.

hog·tie also **hog-tie** (hôg′tī′, hŏg′-) ►*v.* **1.** To tie together the feet or legs of. **2.** *Informal* To impede in movement or action. See Synonyms at **hobble.**

hog·wash (hôg′wŏsh′, -wôsh′, hŏg′-) ►*n.* **1.** Worthless, false, or ridiculous language; nonsense. **2.** Garbage fed to hogs; swill.

hog-wild (hôg′wīld′, hŏg′-) ►*adj. Informal* Wildly enthusiastic or unrestrained. —**hog′-wild′** *adv.*

hoi pol·loi (hoi′ pə-loi′) ►*n.* The common people. [Gk., the many.]

hoist (hoist) ►*v.* To raise or haul up. ►*n.* **1.** An apparatus for lifting heavy or cumbersome objects. **2.** The act of hoisting; lift. [< dial. *hoise.*] —**hoist′er** *n.*

Ho·kan (hō′kən) ►*n.* A proposed grouping of a number of Native American language families of W North America.

Hok·kai·do (hŏ-kī′dō, hō′kī-dō′) An island of Japan N of Honshu.

hol– ►*pref.* Var. of **holo–.**

Hol·bein (hōl′bīn, hôl′-) **Hans** (1465?–1524), "the Elder," and **Hans** (1497?–1543), "the Younger." German artists.

hold¹ (hōld) ►*v.* **held** (hĕld), **hold·ing 1a.** To have in one's grasp: *held a package.* **b.** To support; keep up. **2.** To retain the attention of: *a book that held my interest.* **3.** To contain: *This drawer holds socks.* **4.** To have in one's possession. **5a.** To maintain control over. **b.** To maintain occupation of by force. **c.** To maintain in a given condition or situation. **6a.** To restrain; curb: *held her temper.* **b.** To stop or delay: *Hold the presses!* **c.** To keep from use: *held the tickets for him.* **7.** To obligate: *held me to my promise.* **8a.** To assert; affirm. **b.** To regard or consider. **9.** To cause to take place: *hold a yard sale.* **10.** To withstand pressure or stress. **11.** To continue in a direction or condition. **12.** To be valid or true. ►*n.* **1.** The act or means of grasping. **2.** Something that may be grasped, as for support. **3.** Control or power. **4.** A prison cell. —*phrasal verbs:* **hold forth** To talk at great length. **hold out 1.** To continue in supply; last. **2.** To continue to resist. **hold over 1.** To postpone. **2.** To keep in an earlier state. **hold up 1.** To obstruct or delay. **2.** To rob. **3.** To endure. **—idioms: hold the line** To maintain the current position or state. **hold water** To stand up to critical examination. **on hold** In a state of delay. [< OE *healdan*.] **—hold′er** *n.*

hold² (hōld) ►*n.* The interior section of a ship or airplane in which cargo is stored. [< OE *hulu*, hull.]

hold·ing (hōl′dĭng) ►*n.* **1.** Land rented or leased from another. **2.** often **holdings** Legally owned property, as land or stocks.

holding company ►*n.* A company with partial or complete control over other companies.

hold·out (hōld′out′) ►*n.* One that withholds agreement or consent.

hold·o·ver (hōld′ō′vər) ►*n.* One that remains from an earlier time.

hold·up (hōld′ŭp′) ►*n.* **1.** An interruption; delay. **2.** An armed robbery.

hole (hōl) ►*n.* **1.** A cavity in a solid. **2.** An opening or perforation; gap. **3.** An animal's burrow. **4.** An ugly, squalid, or depressing place. **5.** A bad situation; predicament. **6.** *Sports* **a.** The small pit lined with a cup into which a golf ball must be hit. **b.** One of the divisions of a golf course, from tee to cup. [< OE *hol.*]

hol·i·day (hŏl′ĭ-dā′) ►*n.* **1.** A day free from work, esp. one on which ordinary business halts to commemorate or celebrate a particular event. **2.** A holy day. **3.** *Chiefly Brit.* A vacation. [< OE *hālig dæg*, holy day.]

Holiday, Eleanora "Billie." 1915–59. Amer. singer.

ho·li·ness (hō′lē-nĭs) ►*n.* **1.** The quality of being holy; sanctity. **2. Holiness** Used with *His* or *Your* as a title for the head of certain religions, such as the Pope or Dalai Lama.

ho·lism (hō′lĭz′əm) ►*n.* A theory or belief emphasizing the importance of the whole and the interdependence of its parts. **—ho′list** *n.* **—ho·lis′tic** *adj.* **—ho·lis′ti·cal·ly** *adv.*

holistic medicine ►*n.* Medical care emphasizing treatment of a person's complete physical and mental state.

Hol·land (hŏl′ənd) See **Netherlands.**

hol·lan·daise sauce (hŏl′ən-dāz′) ►*n.* A sauce of butter, egg yolks, and lemon juice or vinegar. [< Fr. *Hollandais*, Dutch.]

hol·ler (hŏl′ər) ►*v.* To yell; shout. See Synonyms at **yell.** [< obsolete *hollo*, stop!] **—hol′ler** *n.*

hol·low (hŏl′ō) ►*adj.* **-er, -est 1.** Having a cavity or space within. **2.** Deeply indented or concave; sunken: *hollow cheeks.* **3.** Without substance or character. See Synonyms at **vain. 4.** Devoid of truth; specious. **5.** Having a deep reverberating sound. ►*n.* **1.** A cavity or interior space. **2.** An indented or concave surface or area. **3.** A void. **4.** also **hol·ler** (hŏl′ər) *Regional* A mountain valley. ►*v.* To make hollow. [< OE *holh*, hole.] **—hol′low·ly** *adv.* **—hol′low·ness** *n.*

hol·ly (hŏl′ē) ►*n., pl.* **-lies** A tree or shrub usu. having bright red berries and glossy evergreen leaves with spiny margins. [< OE *holen.*]

Holly, Buddy Charles Hardin Holley. 1936–59. Amer. musician and songwriter.

hol·ly·hock (hŏl′ē-hŏk′) ►*n.* A tall garden plant with showy, variously colored flowers. [ME *holihocke*, marsh mallow.]

Hol·ly·wood (hŏl′ē-wood′) A district of Los Angeles, CA; a film and entertainment center.

Holmes (hōmz, hōlmz), **Oliver Wendell** 1809–94. Amer. physician and writer.

Holmes, Oliver Wendell, Jr. 1841–1935. Amer. jurist; US Supreme Court justice (1902–32).

hol·mi·um (hōl′mē-əm) ►*n. Symbol* **Ho** A relatively soft, malleable, rare-earth element. At. no. 67. See table at **element.** [After *Holmia* (Stockholm), Sweden.]

holo– or **hol–** ►*pref.* Whole; entire; entirely: *holograph.* [< Gk. *holos.*]

hol·o·caust (hŏl′ə-kôst′, hō′lə-) ►*n.* **1.** Great or total destruction, esp. by fire. **2. Holocaust** The genocide of European Jews and others by the Nazis during World War II. [< Gk. *holokaustos*, burnt whole.]

Hol·o·cene (hŏl′ə-sēn′, hō′lə-) *Geol.* ►*adj.* Of or being the more recent epoch of the Quaternary Period, extending to the present. ►*n.* The Holocene Epoch.

hol·o·gram (hŏl′ə-grăm′, hō′lə-) ►*n.* The pattern produced on a photosensitive medium that has been exposed by holography and then photographically developed.

hol·o·graph (hŏl′ə-grăf′, hō′lə-) ►*n.* **1.** A document written in the handwriting of its signer. **2.** See **hologram. —hol′o·graph′ic, hol′o·graph′i·cal** *adj.* **—hol′o·graph′i·cal·ly** *adv.*

ho·log·ra·phy (hō-lŏg′rə-fē) ►*n.* A method of producing a three-dimensional image of an object by recording the pattern of interference formed by a split laser beam and then illuminating the pattern.

Hol·stein (hōl′stīn′, -stēn′) ►*n.* A breed of large black and white dairy cattle.

hol·ster (hōl′stər) ►*n.* **1.** A usu. leather case shaped to hold a pistol. **2.** A belt designed to carry small tools. ►*v.* To put in a holster. [Du.] **—hol′stered** *adj.*

ho·ly (hō′lē) ►*adj.* **-li·er, -li·est 1.** Of or associated with a divine power; sacred. **2.** Worthy of veneration or awe; revered. **3.** Spiritually pure; saintly. [< OE *hālig.*] **—ho′li·ly** *adv.* **—ho′li·ness** *n.*

Holy Ark ►*n. Judaism* The cabinet in a synagogue in which the Torah scrolls are kept.

Holy Communion ►*n.* The Eucharist.

holy day ►*n.* A day for religious observance.

Holy Ghost ►*n.* The Holy Spirit.

Holy Land The biblical region of Palestine.

Holy Roman Empire A loosely federated political entity of central and W Europe (962–1806).

Holy Spirit ►*n.* The third person of the Christian Trinity.

holy war ►*n.* A war declared for a religious or high moral purpose.

hom·age (hŏm′ĭj, ŏm′-) ►*n.* **1.** Special honor or respect shown or expressed publicly. **2.** Something created or done in honor or admiration of someone or something. [< OFr., prob. < Lat. *homō*, person.]

hom·bre (ŏm′brā′, -brē) ►*n. Slang* A man; fellow. [Sp. < Lat. *homō.*]

Hom·burg also **hom·burg** (hŏm′bûrg′) ►*n.* A man's felt hat having a soft dented crown and a shallow, slightly rolled brim. [*Homburg*, Germany.]

home (hōm) ►*n.* **1.** A place where one lives; residence. **2.** A structure or unit for domestic living. **3.** A household. **4.** A place of origin. **5.** The native habitat, as of a plant or animal. **6.** *Baseball* Home plate. **7.** An institution where people are cared for. ▸*adj.* Of or relating to a home, esp. one's household. ▸*adv.* **1.** At or to the direction of home. **2.** On target: *The arrow struck home.* **3.** To the very center: *Your comment hit home.* ▸*v.* **homed, hom·ing 1.** To go or return home. **2.** To be guided to a target automatically, as by radio waves. **3.** To move toward a goal: *home in on the truth.* —*idiom:* **at home** Comfortable and relaxed. [< OE *hām.*]

home base ▸*n.* **1a.** *Games* An objective toward which players progress. **b.** *Baseball* Home plate. **2.** A base of operations.

home·bod·y (hōm′bŏd′ē) ▸*n., pl.* **-ies** One whose interests center on the home.

home·boy (hōm′boi′) ▸*n. Slang* **1.** A male friend from one's neighborhood or hometown. **2.** A fellow male gang member.

home·com·ing (hōm′kŭm′ĭng) ▸*n.* **1.** A return home. **2.** An annual event at schools and colleges for visiting graduates.

home economics ▸*n. (takes sing. or pl. v.)* The science and art of home management.

home front ▸*n.* The civilian population or the civilian activities of a country at war.

home·girl (hōm′gûrl′) ▸*n. Slang* **1.** A female friend from one's neighborhood or hometown. **2.** A fellow female gang member.

home·land (hōm′lănd′) ▸*n.* **1.** One's native land. **2.** A state or region closely identified with a particular people.

home·less (hōm′lĭs) ▸*adj.* Having no home or haven. ▸*n. (takes pl. v.)* People without homes considered as a group.

home·ly (hōm′lē) ▸*adj.* **-li·er, -li·est 1.** Not attractive or good-looking. **2.** Simple or unpretentious; plain: *homely truths.* **3.** Characteristic of the home. —**home′li·ness** *n.*

home·made (hōm′mād′) ▸*adj.* **1.** Made or prepared in the home. **2.** Made by oneself. **3.** Crudely or simply made.

home·mak·er (hōm′mā′kər) ▸*n.* One who manages a household. —**home′mak′ing** *n.*

homeo- ▸*pref.* Similar; constant: *homeostasis.* [< Gk. *homoios.*]

ho·me·op·a·thy (hō′mē-ŏp′ə-thē) ▸*n., pl.* **-thies** A system for treating disease based on the administration of minute doses of a drug that in massive amounts produces symptoms similar to those of the disease itself. —**ho′me·o·path′** (-ə-păth′), **ho′me·op′a·thist** *n.* —**ho′me·o·path′ic** *adj.*

ho·me·o·sta·sis (hō′mē-ō-stā′sĭs) ▸*n.* A state of equilibrium, as in an organism or cell, maintained by self-regulating processes: *The kidneys maintain homeostasis in the body by regulating the amount of salt and water excreted.* —**ho′me·o·stat′ic** (-stăt′ĭk) *adj.*

ho·me·o·therm (hō′mē-ə-thûrm′) ▸*n.* An organism, such as a mammal or bird, having a constant body temperature independent of the temperature of its surroundings.

home·page or **home page** (hōm′pāj′) ▸*n.* **1.** The main page of a website, usu. providing information about the site. **2.** The first webpage that a web browser displays when opened.

home plate ▸*n. Baseball* The base at which a batter stands when hitting and which a runner must finally touch in order to score.

hom·er (hō′mər) ▸*n. Baseball* A home run. ▸*v.* To hit a home run.

Homer fl. c. 750 BC. Greek epic poet.

Homer, Winslow 1836–1910. Amer. painter.

home rule ▸*n.* Self-government in the internal affairs of a dependent country or region.

home run ▸*n. Baseball* A hit that allows the batter to make a complete circuit of the diamond and score a run.

home·school (hōm′skōōl′) ▸*v.* To educate at home rather than in an established school. —**home′school′er** *n.*

home·sick (hōm′sĭk′) ▸*adj.* Longing for one's home. —**home′sick′ness** *n.*

home·spun (hōm′spŭn′) ▸*adj.* **1.** Spun or woven in the home. **2.** Made of a homespun fabric. **3.** Simple; unpretentious. ▸*n.* A plain, coarse cloth made of homespun yarn.

home·stead (hōm′stĕd′) ▸*n.* A house, esp. a farmhouse, with adjoining buildings and land. ▸*v.* To settle and farm land. —**home′stead′er** *n.*

home·stretch (hōm′strĕch′) ▸*n.* **1.** The part of a racetrack from the last turn to the finish line. **2.** The final stage of a task.

home·ward (hōm′wərd) ▸*adv. & adj.* Toward home. —**home′wards** (-wərdz) *adv.*

home·work (hōm′wûrk′) ▸*n.* **1.** Work, such as schoolwork, done at home. **2.** Preparatory or preliminary work.

hom·ey also **hom·y** (hō′mē) ▸*adj.* **-i·er, -i·est** *Informal* Having a feeling of home; comfortable. —**hom′ey·ness** *n.*

hom·i·cide (hŏm′ĭ-sīd′, hō′mĭ-) ▸*n.* **1.** The killing of one person by another, regardless of intention or legality. **2.** A person who kills another. [< Lat. *homō,* person + –CIDE.] —**hom′i·cid′al** *adj.*

hom·i·let·ic (hŏm′ə-lĕt′ĭk) ▸*adj.* **1.** Of or like a homily. **2.** Relating to preaching. [< Gk. *homilētos,* conversation.] —**hom′i·let′i·cal·ly** *adv.* —**hom′i·let′ics** *n.*

hom·i·ly (hŏm′ə-lē) ▸*n., pl.* **-lies 1.** A sermon. **2.** A tedious moralizing lecture. [< Gk. *homilia,* discourse < *homilos,* crowd.] —**hom′i·list** *n.*

hom·ing pigeon (hō′mĭng) ▸*n.* A pigeon trained to return to its home roost.

hom·i·nid (hŏm′ə-nĭd) ▸*n.* A primate of the family Hominidae, which includes orangutans, gorillas, chimpanzees, and modern humans, and their extinct relatives. [< NLat. *Hominidae,* family name < Lat. *homō, homin-,* human.] —**hom′i·nid** *adj.*

hom·i·nin (hŏm′ĭ-nĭn′) ▸*n.* A primate of the tribe Hominini, which includes living humans *(Homo sapiens)* and some of their extinct ancestors. The hominins were formerly referred to as hominids. [< NLat. *Hominīnī,* tribe name < Lat. *homō, homin-,* human.] —**hom′i·nin′** *adj.*

hom·i·ny (hŏm′ə-nē) ▸*n.* Whole or ground kernels of corn from which the hull and germ have been removed, as by boiling in a solution of water and lye. [Of Algonquian orig.]

homo- or **hom-** ▸*pref.* Same; like: *homophone.* [< Gk. *homos.*]

ho·mo·ge·ne·ous (hō′mə-jē′nē-əs, -jēn′yəs) ▸*adj.* **1.** Uniform in structure throughout. **2.** Of the same or similar nature or kind. [< Gk. *homogenēs.*] —**ho′mo·ge·ne′i·ty** (-jə-nē′ĭ-tē, -nā′-) *n.* —**ho′mo·ge′ne·ous·ly** *adv.*

ho·mog·e·nize (hə-mŏj′ə-nīz′, hō-) ▸*v.* **-nized, -niz·ing 1.** To make homogeneous. **2a.** To reduce to particles and disperse throughout a fluid. **b.** To make uniform in consistency, esp. to render (milk) uniform in consistency by emulsifying the fat content. [< HOMOGENEOUS.] —ho·mog'e·ni·za'tion *n.*

ho·mog·e·ny (hō-mŏj'ə-nē, hō-) ►*n.* Similarity of structure between organs related by common descent. [Gk. *homogenia,* community of origin.] —ho·mog'e·nous *adj.*

hom·o·graph (hŏm'ə-grăf', hō'mə-) ►*n.* One of two or more words that have the same spelling but differ in origin and meaning, as *light,* "not dark," and *light,* "not heavy." —hom'o·graph'ic *adj.*

ho·mol·o·gous (hə-mŏl'ə-gəs, hō-) ►*adj.* 1. Corresponding or similar esp. in structure or function. 2. *Biol.* Similar in structure and evolutionary origin but not necessarily in function. 3. *Genet.* Relating to chromosomes that have the same morphology and linear sequence of genes. [< Gk. *homologos,* agreeing.] —hom'o·logue', hom'o·log' (hŏm'ə-lôg', -lŏg', hō'mə-) *n.* —ho·mol'o·gy (-ə-jē) *n.*

hom·o·nym (hŏm'ə-nĭm', hō'mə-) ►*n.* 1. One of two or more words that have the same sound and often the same spelling but differ in meaning, as *bear,* "carry"; *bear* (the animal); and *bare,* "naked." 2. *Biol.* A taxonomic name identical to one previously applied to a different species or genus and therefore unacceptable in its new use. [< Gk. *homōnumon.*] —hom'o·nym'ic, ho·mon'y·mous (hō-mŏn'ə-məs, hə-) *adj.*

ho·mo·pho·bi·a (hō'mə-fō'bē-ə) ►*n.* Fear, hatred, or mistrust of lesbians and gay men. —ho'mo·phobe' *n.* —ho'mo·pho'bic *adj.*

hom·o·phone (hŏm'ə-fōn', hō'mə-) ►*n.* One of two or more words, such as *night* and *knight,* that are pronounced the same but differ in meaning, origin, and sometimes spelling. —ho·moph'o·nous (hō-mŏf'ə-nəs) *adj.*

Ho·mo sa·pi·ens (hō'mō sā'pē-ənz, -ĕnz') ►*n.* The modern species of humans. [NLat. *Homō sapiēns,* wise man.]

ho·mo·sex·u·al (hō'mə-sĕk'shoō-əl, -mō-) ►*adj.* Of or having a sexual orientation to persons of the same sex. ►*n.* A homosexual person; a gay man or lesbian. See Usage Note at **gay.** —ho'mo·sex'u·al'i·ty *n.*

hom·y (hō'mē) ►*adj.* Var. of **homey.**

Hon. ►*abbr.* 1. honorable (title) 2. hon. honorary

hon·cho (hŏn'chō) ►*n., pl.* **-chos** *Slang* One who is in charge; leader. [J. *hanchō,* squad leader.]

Hon·du·ras (hŏn-doŏr'əs, -dyoŏr'-) A country of N Central America. Cap. Tegucigalpa. —Hon·du'ran *adj. & n.*

hone (hōn) ►*n.* A fine-grained whetstone for sharpening a tool. ►*v.* **honed, hon·ing** 1. To sharpen on or as if on a hone. 2. To perfect or make more intense or effective. —*phrasal verb:* **hone in** 1. To move toward a goal. 2. To direct one's attention. [< OE *hān.*]

hon·est (ŏn'ĭst) ►*adj.* 1. Marked by or displaying integrity; upright. 2. Not deceptive or fraudulent; genuine. 3a. True; not false: *honest reporting.* b. Sincere; frank: *an honest critique.* 4. Without affectation; plain: *honest folk.* [< Lat. *honestus* < *honōs,* honor.] —hon'es·ty *adv.*

hon·ey (hŭn'ē) ►*n., pl.* **-eys** 1. A sweet, thick fluid produced by bees from the nectar of flowers. 2. *Informal* Sweetheart. [< OE *hunig.*]

hon·ey·bee or honey bee (hŭn'ē-bē') ►*n.* Any

of several social bees that produce honey.

hon·ey·comb (hŭn'ē-kōm') ►*n.* 1. A structure of hexagonal, thin-walled cells constructed from beeswax by honeybees to hold honey and larvae. 2. Something resembling this structure. ►*v.* To fill with or as if with holes; riddle.

hon·ey·dew melon (hŭn'ē-doō', -dyoō') ►*n.* A melon having a smooth whitish rind and sweet green flesh.

hon·eyed also hon·ied (hŭn'ēd) ►*adj.* Sweet; sugary: *honeyed words.*

hon·ey·moon (hŭn'ē-moōn') ►*n.* 1. A trip taken by a newly married couple. 2. An early harmonious period in a relationship. —hon'ey·moon' *v.* —hon'ey·moon'er *n.*

hon·ey·suck·le (hŭn'ē-sŭk'əl) ►*n.* A shrub or vine having fragrant, usu. paired tubular flowers. [< OE *hunīsūce.*]

Hong Kong (hŏng'kŏng', hông'kông') An administrative region of SE China, on the coast SE of Guangzhou.

Ho·ni·a·ra (hō'nē-är'ə) The capital of the Solomon Is., on the NW coast of Guadalcanal.

honk (hŏngk, hôngk) ►*n.* 1. The raucous, resonant sound of a goose. 2. A similar sound, esp. the blaring sound of an automobile horn. ►*v.* To emit or cause to emit a honk. [Imit.] —honk'er *n.*

hon·ky-tonk (hông'kē-tôngk', hŏng'kē-tŏngk') ►*n. Slang* 1. A cheap, noisy bar or dance hall. 2. A type of ragtime music typically played on a tinny piano. [?] —hon'ky-tonk' *adj. & v.*

Hon·o·lu·lu (hŏn'ə-loō'loō) The capital of HI, on the S coast of Oahu.

hon·or (ŏn'ər) ►*n.* 1. High respect; esteem. 2. Great privilege. 3. A token or gesture of respect or distinction, such as a military decoration. 4. **honors a.** Special recognition for unusual academic achievement. **b.** A program of individual advanced study for exceptional students. 5. **Honor** Used with *His, Her,* or *Your* as a form of address for certain officials, such as judges and mayors. 6. Personal integrity. ►*v.* **1a.** To esteem. **b.** To show respect for. **c.** To confer distinction on. 2. To accept or pay as valid: *honor a check.* [< Lat.] —hon'or·ee' *n.*

hon·or·a·ble (ŏn'ər-ə-bəl) ►*adj.* 1. Deserving honor and respect. 2. Bringing distinction or recognition. 3. Possessing integrity. 4. **Honorable** Used as a title of respect for certain high government officials. —hon'or·a·bly *adv.*

honorable discharge ►*n.* Discharge from the armed forces with a commendable record.

hon·o·rar·i·um (ŏn'ə-râr'ē-əm) ►*n., pl.* **-i·ums** or **-i·a** (-ē-ə) A payment that is given to a professional person for services for which fees are not legally or traditionally required. [Lat. *honōrārium.*]

hon·or·ar·y (ŏn'ə-rĕr'ē) ►*adj.* Held or given as an honor, without fulfillment of the usual requirements.

honor guard ►*n.* A group of people serving as an escort or performing drill exhibitions on ceremonial occasions.

hon·or·if·ic (ŏn'ə-rĭf'ĭk) ►*adj.* Conferring or showing respect or honor. ►*n.* A title or grammatical form conveying respect. —hon'or·if'i·cal·ly *adv.*

hon·our (ŏn'ər) ►*n. & v. Chiefly Brit.* Var. of **honor.**

Hon·shu (hŏn'shoō) The largest island of Japan,

in the central part between the Sea of Japan and the Pacific.

hood¹ (ho͝od) ►*n.* **1.** A loose pliable covering for the head and neck. **2.** Something resembling a hood. **3.** The hinged metal lid over the engine of a motor vehicle. ►*v.* To supply or cover with a hood. [< OE *hōd.*] —**hood′ed** *adj.*

hood² (ho͝od) ►*n. Slang* A hoodlum.

Hood, Mount A volcanic peak, 3,426 m (11,239 ft), in the Cascade Range of NW OR.

–hood ►*suff.* **1a.** Condition; state; quality: *man-hood.* **b.** An instance of a specified state or quality: *falsehood.* **2.** A group sharing a specified state or quality: *sisterhood.* [< OE *-hād.*]

hood·ie (ho͝od′ē) ►*n. Informal* A hooded garment, esp. a hooded sweatshirt.

hoodie

hood·lum (ho͝od′ləm, ho͞od′-) ►*n.* **1.** A gangster; thug. **2.** A tough, often aggressive young man. [?] —**hood′lum·ism** *n.*

hoo·doo (ho͞o′do͞o) ►*n., pl.* **-doos 1.** Magic healing and control, esp. in African-based folk medicine. **2.** Voodoo. **3a.** Bad luck. **b.** One that brings bad luck. [Of West African orig.] —**hoo′doo** *v.*

hood·wink (ho͝od′wĭngk′) ►*v.* To deceive; cheat. —**hood′wink′er** *n.*

hoo·ey (ho͞o′ē) ►*n. Slang* Nonsense. [?]

hoof (ho͝of, ho͞of) ►*n., pl.* **hooves** (ho͝ovz, ho͞ovz) or **hoofs 1.** The horny sheath covering the foot of some mammals. **2.** A hoofed foot, esp. of a horse. ►*v. Slang* **1.** To dance. **2.** To walk. [< OE *hōf.*] —**hoofed** *adj.*

hook (ho͝ok) ►*n.* **1.** A curved or sharply bent device, usu. of metal, used to catch, drag, suspend, or fasten something. **2.** Something shaped like a hook. **3.** *Slang* A means of attracting interest; enticement. **4.** *Sports* **a.** A short swinging blow in boxing delivered with a crooked arm. **b.** A thrown or struck ball that curves. ►*v.* **1.** To catch, suspend, fasten, or connect with or as if with a hook. **2.** *Slang* To steal; snatch. **3.** *Slang* To cause to become addicted. —**phrasal verb: hook up 1.** To assemble or wire (a mechanism). **2.** *Slang* To connect. —**idioms: by hook or (by) crook** By whatever means possible. **off the hook** Freed, as from blame or obligation. [< OE *hōc.*] —**hooked** *adj.*

hook·ah (ho͝ok′ə) ►*n.* A pipe in which the smoke is cooled by passing through a long tube submerged in an urn of water. [< Ar. *ḥuqqa,* the hookah's water urn.]

hook and eye ►*n.* A fastener consisting of a small hook that is inserted in a loop.

hook·er (ho͝ok′ər) ►*n. Slang* A prostitute.

Hooker, Thomas 1586?–1647. English-born Amer. cleric.

hook·up (ho͝ok′ŭp′) ►*n.* **1.** *Elect.* A system of circuits and equipment designed to operate together. **2.** A configuration of parts or devices providing a link between a supply source and a user.

hook·worm (ho͝ok′wûrm′) ►*n.* A parasitic worm having hooked mouthparts that fasten to the intestinal walls of a host.

hook·y (ho͝ok′ē) ►*n. Informal* Truancy: *play hooky.* [Perh. < *hook it,* to make off.]

hoo·li·gan (ho͞o′lĭ-gən) ►*n. Informal* A tough and aggressive or violent youth. [?] —**hoo′li·gan·ism** *n.*

hoop (ho͞op, ho͝op) ►*n.* **1.** A circular band put around a cask or barrel to bind the staves together. **2.** Something resembling a hoop. **3.** A circular earring. **4.** *Basketball* The basket. [ME *hop.*] —**hoop** *v.*

hoop·la (ho͞op′lä′, ho͝op′-) ►*n. Slang* **1.** Great commotion or fuss. **2.** Extravagant publicity. [< Fr. *houp-là,* an interjection.]

hoop skirt ►*n.* A long full skirt belled out with a series of connected hoops.

hoo·ray (ho͞o-rā′, hə-) also **hur·rah** (-rä′, -rô′) or **hur·ray** (-rā′) ►*interj.* Used as an exclamation of approval, elation, or victory. —**hoo·ray′** *n. & v.*

hoose·gow (ho͞os′gou′) ►*n. Slang* A jail. [Sp. *juzgado,* courtroom < *juzgar,* to judge < Latin *jūdicāre,* JUDICATURE.]

hoot (ho͞ot) ►*v.* **1.** To utter the characteristic cry of an owl. **2.** To make a loud, derisive cry. **3.** To drive off with jeering cries. [ME *houten.*] —**hoot** *n.* —**hoot′er** *n.*

hoot·en·an·ny (ho͞ot′n-ăn′ē) ►*n., pl.* **-nies** An informal performance by folk singers. [?]

Hoo·ver (ho͞o′vər), **Herbert Clark** 1874–1964. The 31st US president (1929–33).

Herbert Hoover

Hoover, J(ohn) Edgar 1895–1972. Amer. director of the FBI (1924–72).

hooves (ho͝ovz, ho͞ovz) ►*n.* Pl. of **hoof.**

hop¹ (hŏp) ►*v.* **hopped, hop·ping 1.** To move with light bounding skips or leaps. **2.** To jump on one foot or with both feet at the same time. **3.** To make a quick trip, esp. in an airplane. **4.** To jump aboard. ►*n.* **1.** A light springy jump or leap. **2.** *Informal* A dance or dance party. **3a.**

A short distance. **b.** A short trip, esp. by air. —*idiom:* **hop to it** To begin a task energetically. [< OE *hoppian.*]

hop² (hŏp) ►*n.* **1.** A twining vine having lobed leaves and spikes of green flowers. **2. hops** The dried female inflorescences of this plant, used as a flavoring in brewing beer. ►*v.* **hopped, hop·ping** To flavor with hops. —*phrasal verb:* **hop up** *Slang* **1.** To increase the power of. **2.** To stimulate with or as if with a narcotic. [< MDu. *hoppe.*] —**hop′py** *adj.*

hope (hōp) ►*v.* **hoped, hop·ing** To wish for something that one deems possible. ►*n.* **1a.** Desire accompanied by belief in the possibility of its fulfillment. **b.** An instance of such desire. **2.** A source of or reason for hope. [< OE *hopian.*] —**hope′ful** *adj.* —**hope′ful·ness** *n.*

hope·ful·ly (hōp′fə-lē) ►*adv.* **1.** In a hopeful manner. **2.** It is to be hoped.
Usage: In formal contexts, it is best to avoid using *hopefully* as a sentence adverb, as in *Hopefully, the proposed law will be adopted.* Although this use is widespread, it is traditionally considered to be incorrect.

hope·less (hōp′lĭs) ►*adj.* **1.** Having no hope. **2.** Having no possibility of being solved or improved. —**hope′less·ly** *adv.*

Ho·pi (hō′pē) ►*n., pl.* **-pi** or **-pis 1.** A member of a Pueblo people of NE Arizona. **2.** The Uto-Aztecan language of the Hopi.

Hop·kins (hŏp′kĭnz), **Gerard Manley** 1844–89. British poet.

hop·per (hŏp′ər) ►*n.* **1.** One that hops. **2.** A usu. funnel-shaped container in which materials are held ready for dispensing.

hop·scotch (hŏp′skŏch′) ►*n.* A children's game in which players hop or jump through a pattern of numbered spaces.

ho·ra also **ho·rah** (hôr′ə) ►*n.* A traditional dance of Romania and Israel, usu. performed in a circle.

Hor·ace (hôr′əs, hŏr′-) 65–8 BC. Roman lyric poet. —**Ho·ra′tian** (hə-rā′shən) *adj.*

hor·cha·ta (hôr-chä′tə) ►*n.* A drink made of rice, almonds, or the ground nutlike tubers of a sedge combined with water, sweetened with sugar, and often flavored with cinnamon, usu. served cold. [Sp., ult. < Lat. *hordeum,* barley.]

horde (hôrd) ►*n.* A large group or crowd; swarm. See Synonyms at **crowd.** [Ult. < O. Turkic *ordī,* residence.]

hore·hound (hôr′hound′) ►*n.* An aromatic plant having downy leaves that yield a bitter extract used in flavoring and as a cough remedy. [< OE *hārehūne.*]

ho·ri·zon (hə-rī′zən) ►*n.* **1.** The apparent intersection of the earth and sky as seen by an observer. **2.** The range of one's knowledge, experience, or interest. [< Gk. *horizein,* to limit.]

hor·i·zon·tal (hôr′ĭ-zŏn′tl, hŏr′-) ►*adj.* **1.** Of or near the horizon. **2.** At right angles to a vertical line. ►*n.* Something horizontal. [< Lat. *horizōn, horizont-,* HORIZON.] —**hor′i·zon′tal·ly** *adv.*

hor·mone (hôr′mōn′) ►*n.* **1.** A substance produced by one tissue and conveyed by the bloodstream to another to effect physiological activity, such as growth or metabolism. **2.** A compound that acts like a hormone in the body. [< Gk. *horman,* urge on.] —**hor·mon′al** (-mō′nəl) *adj.* —**hor·mon′al·ly** *adv.*

Hor·muz (hôr′mŭz′, hôr-mōōz′), **Strait of** also **Strait of Ormuz** A waterway linking the Persian Gulf with the Gulf of Oman.

horn (hôrn) ►*n.* **1a.** One of the hard, usu. permanent structures projecting from the head of certain mammals, such as cattle or sheep. **b.** The hard, smooth material forming the outer covering of a horn. **2.** A growth or protuberance similar to a horn. **3.** A container made from a horn: *a powder horn.* **4.** *Mus.* **a.** A brass wind instrument, esp. a French horn. **b.** A trumpet. **c.** A saxophone. **5.** A signaling device that produces a loud, resonant sound: *an automobile horn.* [< OE.] —**horned** *adj.* —**horn′less** *adj.* —**horn′y** *adj.*

Horn, Cape A headland of extreme S Chile in the Tierra del Fuego archipelago.

horned lizard ►*n.* A lizard having short horns on the head and a wide spiny body.

hor·net (hôr′nĭt) ►*n.* Any of various stinging wasps that typically build large papery nests. [< OE *hyrnet.*]

horn of plenty ►*n., pl.* **horns of plenty** See **cornucopia** (sense 1).

horn·pipe (hôrn′pīp′) ►*n.* A spirited British folk dance.

ho·rol·o·gy (hə-rŏl′ə-jē) ►*n.* **1.** The science of measuring time. **2.** The art of making timepieces. [Gk. *hōra,* hour + –LOGY.] —**ho·rol′o·gist** *n.*

hor·o·scope (hôr′ə-skōp′, hŏr′-) ►*n.* **1.** A diagram of the positions of the planets and stars, esp. at the moment of a person's birth, used by astrologers. **2.** An astrological forecast, as of a person's future, based on such a diagram. [< Gk. *hōroskopos :* *hōra,* hour + *skopos,* observer.]

hor·ren·dous (hô-rĕn′dəs, hə-) ►*adj.* Hideous. [< Lat. *horrendus,* gerundive of *horrēre,* tremble.] —**hor·ren′dous·ly** *adv.*

hor·ri·ble (hôr′ə-bəl, hŏr′-) ►*adj.* **1.** Arousing horror; dreadful. **2.** Very unpleasant. [< Lat. *horribilis* < *horrēre,* tremble.] —**hor′ri·ble·ness** *n.* —**hor′ri·bly** *adv.*

hor·rid (hôr′ĭd, hŏr′-) ►*adj.* **1.** Causing horror; dreadful. **2.** Extremely disagreeable; offensive. [< ME *horred,* bristling < Lat. *horrēre,* tremble.] —**hor′rid·ly** *adv.* —**hor′rid·ness** *n.*

hor·rif·ic (hô-rĭf′ĭk, hŏ-) ►*adj.* Terrifying. [Lat. *horrificus* < *horrēre,* tremble.] —**hor·rif′i·cal·ly** *adv.*

hor·ri·fy (hôr′ə-fī′, hŏr′-) ►*v.* **-fied, -fy·ing 1.** To cause to feel horror. **2.** To cause unpleasant surprise to. [Lat. *horrificāre.*] —**hor′ri·fy′ing·ly** *adv.*

hor·ror (hôr′ər, hŏr′-) ►*n.* **1.** An intense feeling of repugnance and fear. **2.** Intense dislike; abhorrence. **3.** A cause of horror. **4.** A genre of fiction or other artistic work evoking suspense and horror, esp. through the depiction of gruesome or supernatural elements. [< Lat. *horror.*]

hors de com·bat (ôr′ də kôn-bä′) ►*adv. & adj.* Out of action; disabled. [Fr.]

hors d'oeuvre (ôr dûrv′) ►*n., pl.* **hors d'oeuvres** (ôr dûrvz′) or **hors d'oeuvre** An appetizer served before a meal. [Fr.]

horse (hôrs) ►*n.* **1.** A large hoofed mammal having a long mane and tail, domesticated for riding and for drawing or carrying loads. **2.** A supporting frame, usu. with four legs. **3.** *Sports* A vaulting horse. **4.** often **horses** Horsepower. ►*v.* **horsed, hors·ing** To provide with a horse.

—*phrasal verb:* **horse around** *Informal* To indulge in horseplay or frivolous activity. —*idioms:* **hold (one's) horses** To restrain oneself. **the horse's mouth** The original source. [< OE *hors.*]

horse·back (hôrs′băk′) ►*adv. & adj.* On the back of a horse.

horse chestnut ►*n.* **1.** A tree having erect clusters of white flowers and shiny brown seeds. **2.** The seed of this tree.

horse·flesh (hôrs′flĕsh′) ►*n.* **1.** The flesh of a horse. **2.** Horses collectively, esp. for riding or racing.

horse·fly (hôrs′flī′) ►*n.* Any of numerous large flies, the females of which suck the blood of various mammals.

horse·hair (hôrs′hâr′) ►*n.* **1.** The hair of a horse, esp. from the mane or tail. **2.** Cloth made of horsehair.

horse·hide (hôrs′hīd′) ►*n.* **1.** The hide of a horse. **2.** Leather made from this hide.

horse·man (hôrs′mən) ►*n.* A man who rides a horse or breeds and raises horses.

horse·man·ship (hôrs′mən-shĭp′) ►*n.* The skill of riding horses.

horse·play (hôrs′plā′) ►*n.* Rowdy play.

horse·pow·er (hôrs′pou′ər) ►*n.* A unit of power equal to 745.7 watts or 33,000 footpounds per minute.

horse·rad·ish (hôrs′răd′ĭsh) ►*n.* **1.** A coarse plant having a thick, whitish, pungent root. **2.** A condiment made of its grated roots.

horse sense ►*n. Informal* Common sense.

horse·shoe (hôrs′shoō′, hôrsh′-) ►*n.* **1.** A flat U-shaped metal plate fitted and nailed to a horse's hoof. **2.** **horseshoes** (*takes sing. v.*) A game in which players toss horseshoes at a stake to encircle it.

horseshoe crab ►*n.* A marine arthropod having a large rounded body and a stiff pointed tail.

horse·tail (hôrs′tāl′) ►*n.* A nonflowering plant having a hollow stem and narrow leaves.

horse·whip (hôrs′wĭp′, -hwĭp′) ►*n.* A whip used to control a horse. —**horse′whip′** *v.*

horse·wom·an (hôrs′woŏm′ən) ►*n.* A woman who rides a horse or breeds and raises horses.

hors·y also **hors·ey** (hôr′sē) ►*adj.* **-i·er, -i·est** **1.** Of or resembling a horse. **2.** Devoted to horses or riding. **3.** Large and clumsy. —**hors′i·ly** *adv.* —**hors′i·ness** *n.*

hor·ta·to·ry (hôr′tə-tôr′ē) ►*adj.* Marked by exhortation. [< Lat. *hortārī,* exhort.]

hor·ti·cul·ture (hôr′tĭ-kŭl′chər) ►*n.* The science or art of cultivating fruits, vegetables, flowers, or ornamental plants. [Lat. *hortus,* garden + (AGRI)CULTURE.] —**hor′ti·cul·tur·al** *adj.* —**hor′ti·cul·tur·al·ly** *adv.* —**hor′ti·cul′tur·ist** *n.*

ho·san·na also **ho·san·nah** (hō-zăn′ə) ►*interj.* Used to express praise or adoration to God. [< Heb. *hôšaʿnāʾ,* deliver us.]

hose (hōz) ►*n.* **1.** *pl.* **hose** Stockings; socks. **2.** *pl.* **hos·es** A flexible tube for conveying liquids or gases. ►*v.* **hosed, hos·ing** To water or wash with a hose. [< OE *hosa.*]

Ho·se·a (hō-zē′ə, -zā′ə) ►*n.* **1.** A Hebrew prophet of the 8th cent. BC. **2.** See table at **Bible.**

ho·sier·y (hō′zhə-rē) ►*n.* Socks and stockings. [< ME, HOSE.]

hos·pice (hŏs′pĭs) ►*n.* **1.** A shelter or lodging for travelers or the needy. **2.** A program that provides care for terminally ill patients. [< Lat. *hospitium,* hospitality < *hospes,* host.]

hos·pi·ta·ble (hŏs′pĭ-tə-bəl, hŏ-spĭt′ə-bəl) ►*adj.* **1.** Cordial and generous to guests. **2.** Favorable to growth and development. [< Lat. *hospes, hospit-,* host.] —**hos′pi·ta·bly** *adv.*

hos·pi·tal (hŏs′pĭ-tl, -pĭt′l) ►*n.* An institution that provides medical, surgical, or psychiatric care and treatment for the sick or the injured. [< Lat. *hospitālis,* of a guest < *hospes,* guest.]

hos·pi·tal·i·ty (hŏs′pĭ-tăl′ĭ-tē) ►*n., pl.* **-ties** Cordial and generous reception of guests.

hos·pi·tal·ize (hŏs′pĭt-l-īz′) ►*v.* **-ized, -iz·ing** To place in a hospital for treatment or observation. —**hos′pi·tal·i·za′tion** *n.*

host¹ (hōst) ►*n.* **1.** One who receives or entertains guests. **2.** One who manages an inn or hotel. **3.** One that furnishes facilities and resources for an event. **4.** The emcee or interviewer on a radio or television program. **5.** *Biol.* The organism on or in which a parasite lives. **6.** *Comp.* **a.** A device providing data or services to a remote computer by means of a network. **b.** A computer that is connected to the Internet or a similar network. ►*v.* **1.** To serve as host to or for. **2.** To provide software that offers data or services over a computer network. [< Lat. *hospes, hospit-.*]

host² (hōst) ►*n.* **1.** An army. **2.** A great number; multitude. [< Lat. *hostis,* enemy.]

host³ also **Host** (hōst) ►*n. Eccles.* The consecrated bread or wafer of the Eucharist. [< Lat. *hostia,* sacrifice.]

hos·tage (hŏs′tĭj) ►*n.* A person held by force as security that specified terms will be met. [< OFr., prob. < *host,* guest; see HOST¹.]

hos·tel (hŏs′təl) ►*n.* **1.** A supervised inexpensive lodging for young travelers. **2.** An inn. [< Med.Lat. *hospitāle,* inn; see HOSPITAL.] —**hos′tel·er** *n.*

hos·tel·ry (hŏs′təl-rē) ►*n., pl.* **-ries** An inn.

host·ess (hō′stĭs) ►*n.* **1.** A woman who receives or entertains guests. **2.** A woman employed to greet and assist patrons, as in a restaurant. See Usage Note at **-ess.**

hos·tile (hŏs′təl, -tīl′) ►*adj.* **1.** Of or characteristic of an enemy. **2.** Feeling or showing enmity: *a hostile remark.* [< Lat. *hostis,* enemy.] —**hos′tile** *n.* —**hos′tile·ly** *adv.*

hos·til·i·ty (hŏ-stĭl′ĭ-tē) ►*n., pl.* **-ties** **1.** Antagonism or enmity. **2a.** A hostile act. **b. hostilities** Overt warfare.

hos·tler (hŏs′lər, ŏs′-) ►*n.* **1.** One who tends horses, esp. at an inn. **2.** One who services a large vehicle or engine, such as a locomotive. [< AN *hostiler* < OFr. *hostel,* HOSTEL.]

hot (hŏt) ►*adj.* **hot·ter, hot·test** **1a.** Having or giving off great heat. **b.** Being at a high temperature. **2.** Warmer than normal or desirable. **3.** Causing a burning sensation, as in the mouth; spicy: *hot peppers.* **4a.** Charged or energized with electricity. **b.** Radioactive. **5.** Marked by intensity of emotion. **6.** *Informal* Arousing intense interest or controversy: *a hot topic.* **7.** *Slang* Recently stolen: *a hot car.* **8.** *Informal* **a.** Most recent; new: *a hot news item.* **b.** Currently popular: *the hottest young talents.* **9.** *Slang* **a.** Performing with great skill. **b.** Unusually lucky. —*idioms:* **hot under the collar** *Informal* Angry. **hot water** Trouble; difficulty. [< OE *hāt.*] —**hot′ly** *adv.* —**hot′ness** *n.*

hot air ▸*n. Slang* Empty, exaggerated talk.

hot·bed (hŏt′bĕd′) ▸*n.* An environment conducive to growth or development, esp. of something undesirable: *a hotbed of intrigue.*

hot-blood·ed (hŏt′blŭd′ĭd) ▸*adj.* Easily excited or aroused. —**hot′-blood′ed·ness** *n.*

hot·box (hŏt′bŏks′) ▸*n.* An axle or journal box, as on a railway car, overheated by friction.

hot button ▸*n. Slang* Something that elicits a strong emotional response. —**hot′-but′-ton** *adj.*

hot·cake (hŏt′kāk′) ▸*n.* See **pancake.** —*idiom:* **go (**or **sell) like hotcakes** To be in great demand.

hot dog or **hot·dog** (hŏt′dôg′, -dŏg′) ▸*n.* **1.** A frankfurter. **2.** *Slang* One who performs showy, often dangerous stunts. —**hot′-dog′** *v.* —**hot′-dog′ger** *n.*

ho·tel (hō-tĕl′) ▸*n.* An establishment that provides lodging and often meals esp. for travelers. [< OFr. *hostel,* HOSTEL.]

hot flash ▸*n.* A sudden brief sensation of heat sometimes experienced during menopause.

hot·foot (hŏt′fŏŏt′) ▸*v. Informal* To go in haste: *hotfoot it out of town.*

hot·head·ed (hŏt′hĕd′ĭd) ▸*adj.* **1.** Easily angered; quick-tempered. **2.** Impetuous; rash. —**hot′head′** *n.* —**hot′head′ed·ly** *adv.* —**hot′head′ed·ness** *n.*

hot·house (hŏt′hous′) ▸*n.* A heated greenhouse. ▸*adj.* **1.** Grown in a hothouse. **2.** Delicate; sensitive.

hot·line or **hot line** (hŏt′līn′) ▸*n.* **1.** A communications line, esp. between heads of government, for use in a crisis. **2.** A telephone line that gives quick and direct access to a source of information or help.

hot·link (hŏt′lĭngk′) ▸*n. Comp.* See **link** (sense 4).

hot plate ▸*n.* An electrically heated plate for cooking food.

hot rod also **hot-rod** (hŏt′rŏd′) ▸*n. Slang* An automobile that is modified for speed and acceleration. —**hot′-rod′** *v.* —**hot rodder, hot′-rod′der** *n.*

hot seat ▸*n.* **1.** *Slang* The electric chair. **2.** *Informal* A position of stress or discomfort.

hot·shot (hŏt′shŏt′) ▸*n. Slang* A person of impressive, often aggressive skill. —**hot′shot′** *adj.*

hot toddy ▸*n.* A drink made of usu. whiskey mixed with hot water, sugar, and spices.

hot tub ▸*n.* A large tub filled with hot water for bathing or soaking.

hot-wire (hŏt′wīr′) ▸*v. Informal* To start the engine of (e.g., a car) without a key, as by short-circuiting the ignition system.

Hou·di·ni (hoo-dē′nē), **Harry** Ehrich Weiss. 1874–1926. Hungarian-born Amer. escape artist.

hound (hound) ▸*n.* **1a.** Any of various hunting dogs usu. having drooping ears and a deep resonant voice. **b.** A dog. **2.** A scoundrel. **3.** An avid enthusiast. ▸*v.* **1.** To pursue relentlessly. **2.** To nag. [< OE *hund.*]

hour (our) ▸*n.* **1.** One of the 24 equal parts of a day. **2.** The time of day. **3a.** A customary time: *the dinner hour.* **b. hours** A specified time: *banking hours.* [< Gk. *hōra,* season, time.]

hour·glass (our′glăs′) ▸*n.* An instrument that is used to measure time by trickling sand from an upper to a lower glass chamber.

hou·ri (hoor′ē, hoo′rē) ▸*n., pl.* **-ris** One of the beautiful virgins of the Koranic paradise. [Pers. *hūrī.*]

hour·ly (our′lē) ▸*adj.* **1.** Occurring every hour. **2.** Frequent; continual. **3.** By the hour as a unit: *hourly pay.* ▸*adv.* **1.** At or during every hour. **2.** Frequently; continually.

house (hous) ▸*n., pl.* **hous·es** (hou′zĭz, -sĭz) **1a.** A structure serving as a dwelling for one or more persons. **b.** A household. **2.** A dwelling for a group of people who live together as a unit: *a sorority house.* **3a.** A building used for a particular purpose: *a movie house.* **b.** The audience or patrons of such a place: *a full house.* **4a.** A commercial firm: *a brokerage house.* **b.** A publishing company. **5.** often **House** A legislative assembly. ▸*v.* (houz) **housed, hous·ing 1.** To provide living quarters for; lodge. **2.** To shelter, keep, or store. —*idiom:* **on the house** At the expense of the establishment; free. [< OE *hūs.*]

house·boat (hous′bōt′) ▸*n.* A barge equipped for use as a dwelling.

house·break (hous′brāk′) ▸*v.* **-broke** (-brōk′), **-bro·ken** (-brō′kən), **-break·ing, -breaks 1.** To train (a dog) to urinate and defecate outdoors and not indoors. **2.** To subdue; tame.

house·break·ing (hous′brā′kĭng) ▸*n.* The unlawful breaking into and entering another's house. —**house′break′er** *n.*

house·fly (hous′flī′) ▸*n.* A common fly that frequents human dwellings and transmits a wide variety of diseases.

house·hold (hous′hōld′) ▸*n.* A domestic unit consisting of the people who live together in a single dwelling. ▸*adj.* **1.** Of or relating to a household. **2.** Commonly known; familiar: *a household name.* [ME.] —**house′hold′er** *n.*

house·keep·er (hous′kē′pər) ▸*n.* One hired to perform or direct domestic tasks.

house·keep·ing (hous′kē′pĭng) ▸*n.* **1.** Performance or management of household tasks. **2.** Routine maintenance; upkeep.

house·moth·er (hous′mŭth′ər) ▸*n.* A woman employed as supervisor of a residence for young people.

House of Commons ▸*n.* The lower house of Parliament in the United Kingdom and Canada.

House of Lords ▸*n.* The upper house of Parliament in the United Kingdom.

house organ ▸*n.* A periodical published by an organization for its employees or clients.

house·plant (hous′plănt′) ▸*n.* A usu. decorative plant suitable for growing indoors.

house·wares (hous′wârz′) ▸*pl.n.* Articles used in a home, esp. in the kitchen.

house·warm·ing (hous′wôr′mĭng) ▸*n.* A celebration of the occupancy of a new home.

house·wife (hous′wīf′) ▸*n.* A married woman who manages her household as her main occupation. —**house′wife′ly** *adj.* —**house′wif′er·y** *n.*

house·work (hous′wûrk′) ▸*n.* The tasks, such as cleaning and cooking, performed in housekeeping.

hous·ing (hou′zĭng) ▸*n.* **1a.** Buildings in which people live. **b.** A dwelling. **2.** Provision of lodging or shelter. **3.** A cover or protective case, esp. for a mechanical part.

Hous·man (hous′mən), **A(lfred) E(dward)** 1859–1936. British poet and scholar.

Hous·ton (hyōō′stən) A city of SE TX NW of Galveston. **—Hous·to′ni·an** (-stō′nē-ən) n.

Houston, Samuel "Sam." 1793–1863. Amer. soldier and politician.

HOV ►*abbr.* high-occupancy vehicle

hove (hōv) ►*v.* P.t. and p.part. of **heave** (sense 5).

hov·el (hŭv′əl, hŏv′-) ►*n.* A small miserable dwelling. [ME, hut.]

hov·er (hŭv′ər, hŏv′-) ►*v.* **1.** To remain floating or suspended in the air. **2.** To linger in a place. **3.** To remain in an uncertain state; waver. [ME *hoveren.*]

hov·er·craft (hŭv′ər-krăft′, hŏv′-) ►*n.* A usu. propeller-driven vehicle for traveling over land or water on a cushion of air.

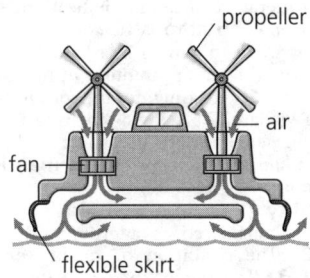

hovercraft
front cutaway

HOV lane (āch′ō-vē′) ►*n.* An expressway lane restricted to vehicles with a set minimum of occupants, usu. two.

how (hou) ►*adv.* **1.** In what manner or way; by what means. **2.** In what state or condition. **3.** To what extent, amount, or degree. **4.** For what reason or purpose; why. **5.** With what meaning: *How should I take that remark?* ►*conj.* **1.** The manner or way in which: *forgot how it was done.* **2.** In whatever way or manner: *Cook it how you please.* **—idioms: how about** Used to make a suggestion or to offer something: *How about a cup of tea?* **how come** *Informal* How is it that; why. [< OE *hū.*]

How·ard (hou′ərd), **Catherine** 1520?–42. Queen of England as the fifth wife of Henry VIII (1540–42).

how·be·it (hou-bē′ĭt) ►*adv.* Nevertheless.

how·dah (hou′də) ►*n.* A covered seat on the back of an elephant or camel. [< Ar. *hawdaj.*]

Howe (hou), **Elias** 1819–67. Amer. inventor.

Howe, Julia Ward 1819–1910. Amer. writer and feminist.

How·ells (hou′əlz), **William Dean** 1837–1920. Amer. writer and editor.

how·ev·er (hou-ĕv′ər) ►*adv.* **1.** In spite of that; nevertheless. **2.** On the other hand; by contrast. **3.** To whatever degree or extent. ►*conj.* In whatever manner or way.

how·it·zer (hou′ĭt-sər) ►*n.* A short cannon that delivers shells at a high trajectory. [< Czech *haufnice.*]

howl (houl) ►*v.* **1.** To utter a long mournful sound. **2.** To cry or wail loudly. See Synonyms at **yell.** **3.** *Slang* To laugh heartily. [ME *houlen.*] **—howl** n.

howl·er (hou′lər) ►*n.* **1.** One that howls. **2.** *Slang* A laughably stupid blunder.

how·so·ev·er (hou′sō-ev′ər) ►*adv.* **1.** To whatever extent. **2.** By whatever means.

hoy·den (hoid′n) ►*n.* A high-spirited, boisterous, or saucy woman. [Prob. < MDu. *heiden,* heathen.] **—hoy′den·ish** adj.

hp ►*abbr.* horsepower

HQ ►*abbr.* headquarters

HR ►*abbr.* **1.** home run **2.** House of Representatives **3.** human resources

hr. ►*abbr.* hour

HRH ►*abbr.* Her (or His) Royal Highness

hryv·nia (hrĭv′nyä) ►*n.* See table at **currency.** [Ukrainian.]

Hs The symbol for **hassium.**

HST ►*abbr.* Hawaii-Aleutian Standard Time

ht ►*abbr.* height

HTML (āch′tē-ĕm-ĕl′) ►*n.* A markup language used to structure and set up hypertext links between documents, esp. on the World Wide Web. [*h(yper)t(ext) m(arkup) l(anguage).*]

HTTP or **http** (āch′tē-tē-pē′) ►*n.* A protocol used to request and transmit files, esp. over the Internet. [*h(yper)t(ext) t(ransfer) p(rotocol).*]

Huang He (hwäng′ hə′) See **Yellow River.**

hua·ra·che (wə-rä′chē, hə-) ►*n.* A flat-heeled sandal with an upper of woven leather strips. [Am.Sp.]

hub (hŭb) ►*n.* **1.** The center part of a wheel, fan, or propeller. **2.** A center of activity or interest. [Prob. < hob, projection.]

Hub·ble (hŭb′əl), **Edwin Powell** 1889–1953. Amer. astronomer.

hub·bub (hŭb′ŭb′) ►*n.* **1.** A loud confusing noise. **2.** A confused situation; tumult. See Synonyms at **noise.** [Prob. of Ir. Gael. orig.]

hub·cap (hŭb′kăp′) ►*n.* A round covering over the hub of an automobile wheel.

hu·bris (hyōō′brĭs) ►*n.* Overbearing pride; arrogance. [Gk.]

huck·le·ber·ry (hŭk′əl-bĕr′ē) ►*n.* **1.** A shrub related to the blueberry. **2.** The fruit of this plant. [Prob. alteration of *hurtleberry,* a kind of berry.]

huck·ster (hŭk′stər) ►*n.* **1.** A peddler or hawker. **2.** An aggressive salesperson or promoter. [ME.] **—huck′ster·ism** n.

HUD ►*abbr.* (Department of) Housing and Urban Development

hud·dle (hŭd′l) ►*n.* **1.** A densely packed group. **2.** *Football* A brief gathering of a team's players behind the line of scrimmage to receive instructions for the next play. **3.** A small private conference. ►*v.* **-dled, -dling 1.** To crowd together. **2.** To curl up or crouch. **3.** *Football* To gather in a huddle. **4.** *Informal* To gather together for consultation. [Poss. of LGer. orig.] **—hud′dler** n.

Hud·son (hŭd′sən), **Henry** d. 1611. English navigator and explorer.

Hud·son Bay (hŭd′sən) An inland sea of E-central Canada connected to the Atlantic by **Hudson Strait.**

Hudson River A river rising in NE NY and flowing about 510 km (315 mi) to Upper New York Bay at New York City.

hue (hyōō) ►*n.* **1.** The property of colors by which they can be perceived as ranging from red through yellow, green, and blue. **2.** A particular gradation of color; shade or tint. **3.**

Color. [< OE *hīw*.]

Hue (hyoo-ā′, hwā) A city of central Vietnam near the South China Sea NW of Da Nang.

hue and cry ▸*n.* A public clamor, as of protest or demand. [< AN *hu e cri.*]

huff (hŭf) ▸*n.* A fit of anger or annoyance; pique. ▸*v.* **1.** To puff; blow. **2.** To bluster. **3.** *Slang* To inhale the fumes of (e.g., a volatile chemical) as a means of becoming intoxicated. [Imit.] —**huff′i·ly** *adv.* —**huff′y** *adj.*

hug (hŭg) ▸*v.* **hugged, hug·ging 1.** To clasp or hold closely; embrace. **2.** To cherish. **3.** To stay close to. ▸*n.* A close embrace. [Prob. of Scand. orig.] —**hug′ger** *n.*

huge (hyooj) ▸*adj.* **hug·er, hug·est** Exceedingly large; tremendous. [< OFr. *ahuge.*] —**huge′-ly** *adv.* —**huge′ness** *n.*

Hughes, (James) Langston 1902–67. Amer. writer.

Langston Hughes

Hu·go (hyoo′gō, ü-gō′), **Victor Marie** 1802–85. French writer.

Hu·gue·not (hyoo′gə-nŏt′) ▸*n.* A French Protestant of the 16th to 18th cent.

huh (hŭ) ▸*interj.* Used to express interrogation, surprise, contempt, or indifference.

Hu Jin·tao (hoo′ jĭn′tou′) b. 1942. Chinese president (2003–2013).

hu·la (hoo′lə) ▸*n.* A Polynesian dance that in traditional form dramatizes a song or chant, esp. through arm movements and hand gestures. [Hawaiian.]

hulk (hŭlk) ▸*n.* **1.** *Naut.* **a.** A heavy, unwieldy ship. **b.** A wrecked hull. **2.** One that is bulky, clumsy, or unwieldy. ▸*v.* To loom as a massive form. [< Med.Lat. *hulcus.*]

hulk·ing (hŭl′kĭng) also **hulk·y** (hŭl′kē) ▸*adj.* Unwieldy or bulky; massive.

hull (hŭl) ▸*n.* **1.** The dry outer covering of a fruit, seed, or nut; husk. **2.** The frame or body of a ship. **3.** The outer casing of a rocket, guided missile, or spaceship. ▸*v.* To remove the hulls of (fruit or seeds). [< OE *hulu.*]

hul·la·ba·loo also **hul·la·bal·loo** (hŭl′ə-bə-loo′) ▸*n., pl.* **-loos** A loud noise or a condition of noisy confusion. See Synonyms at **noise.** [< alteration of *holla*, hello.]

hum (hŭm) ▸*v.* **hummed, hum·ming 1.** To emit a continuous low droning sound. **2.** To be in a state of busy activity. **3.** To sing without opening the lips. [ME *hummen.*] —**hum** *n.* —**hum′ma·ble** *adj.* —**hum′mer** *n.*

hu·man (hyoo′mən) ▸*n.* A member of the primate genus *Homo* and esp. of the species *H. sapiens*, distinguished from other apes by a large brain and the capacity for speech. ▸*adj.* **1.** Of or characteristic of humans. **2.** Made up of humans: *formed a human bridge across the ice.* [< Lat. *hūmānus.*] —**hu′man·hood′** *n.* —**hu′man·ly** *adv.* —**hu′man·ness** *n.*

human being ▸*n.* A human.

hu·mane (hyoo-mān′) ▸*adj.* **1.** Kind or compassionate. **2.** Emphasizing humanistic values and concerns. [ME *humain*, HUMAN.] —**hu·mane′-ly** *adv.* —**hu·mane′ness** *n.*

hu·man·ism (hyoo′mə-nĭz′əm) ▸*n.* **1.** A system of thought that centers on humans and their values, capacities, and worth. **2. Humanism** A Renaissance movement that emphasized human potential to attain excellence and promoted direct study of classical Greek and Roman literature, art, and civilization. —**hu′man·ist** *n.* —**hu′man·is′tic** *adj.*

hu·man·i·tar·i·an (hyoo-măn′ĭ-târ′ē-ən) ▸*n.* One devoted to the promotion of human welfare. ▸*adj.* **1.** Relating to the promotion of human welfare. **2.** Being a situation in which many human lives are in danger of harm or death: *a humanitarian crisis.* —**hu·man′i·tar′i·an·ism** *n.*

hu·man·i·ty (hyoo-măn′ĭ-tē) ▸*n., pl.* **-ties 1.** Humans considered as a group; the human race. **2.** The condition or quality of being human. **3.** The quality of being humane. **4. humanities** Those disciplines, such as philosophy and art, concerned with human thought and culture; the liberal arts.

hu·man·ize (hyoo′mə-nīz′) ▸*v.* **-ized, -iz·ing 1.** To make human or humanlike. **2.** To make humane; civilize. —**hu′man·i·za′tion** *n.* —**hu′man·iz′er** *n.*

hu·man·kind (hyoo′mən-kīnd′) ▸*n.* The human race.

hu·man·oid (hyoo′mə-noid′) ▸*adj.* Having human characteristics or form. ▸*n.* A being having human form.

hum·ble (hŭm′bəl) ▸*adj.* **-bler, -blest 1.** Meek or modest. **2.** Deferentially respectful. **3.** Low in rank or station. ▸*v.* **-bled, -bling 1.** To cause to feel meek; humiliate. **2.** To make lower or lesser; abase. [< Lat. *humilis* < *humus*, ground.] —**hum′bler** *n.* —**hum′bly** *adv.*

Hum·boldt (hŭm′bōlt′), Baron **(Friedrich Heinrich) Alexander von** 1769–1859. German scientist and writer.

hum·bug (hŭm′bŭg′) ▸*n.* **1.** A hoax or fraud. **2.** An impostor. **3.** Nonsense; rubbish. ▸*v.* **-bugged, -bug·ging** To deceive or trick. [?] —**hum′bug′** *interj.* —**hum′bug′ger** *n.* —**hum′bug′ger·y** *n.*

hum·ding·er (hŭm′dĭng′ər) ▸*n. Slang* One that is extraordinary. [?]

hum·drum (hŭm′drŭm′) ▸*adj.* Monotonous; boring. See Synonyms at **dull.** [Poss. < HUM.]

Hume (hyoom), **David** 1711–76. British philosopher and historian.

hu·mer·us (hyoo′mər-əs) ▸*n., pl.* **-mer·i** (-mə-rī′) The long bone of the arm, extending from the shoulder to the elbow. [Lat., upper arm.]

hu·mid (hyoo′mĭd) ▸*adj.* Containing a high amount of water vapor. [Lat. *hūmidus* < *hūmēre*, be moist.] —**hu·mid′i·ty** *n.*

hu·mid·i·fy (hyoō-mĭd′ə-fī′) ►*v.* **-fied, -fy·ing** To make humid. —**hu·mid′i·fi·ca′tion** *n.* —**hu·mid′i·fi′er** *n.*

hu·mi·dor (hyoō′mĭ-dôr′) ►*n.* A container designed for storing cigars at a constant humidity. [HUMID + -OR¹.]

hu·mil·i·ate (hyoō-mĭl′ē-āt′) ►*v.* **-at·ed, -at·ing** To cause (someone) to feel a loss of pride, dignity, or self-respect. [LLat. *humiliāre* < *humilis,* HUMBLE.] —**hu·mil′i·a′tion** *n.*

hu·mil·i·ty (hyoō-mĭl′ĭ-tē) ►*n.* The quality or condition of being humble. [< *humilis,* HUMBLE.]

hum·ming·bird (hŭm′ĭng-bûrd′) ►*n.* Any of a family of very small birds having brilliant iridescent plumage, a long slender bill, and hovering flight.

hum·mock (hŭm′ək) ►*n.* **1.** A low mound or ridge of earth. **2.** A ridge or hill of ice in an ice field. [?] —**hum′mock·y** *adj.*

hum·mus (hoōm′əs, hŭm′-) ►*n.* A thick dip or spread made of mashed chickpeas, tahini, oil, lemon juice, and garlic. [Ar. *ḥummuṣ,* chickpea.]

hu·mor (hyoō′mər) ►*n.* **1.** The quality that makes something laughable or amusing. **2.** The ability to perceive, enjoy, or express what is amusing or comical. **3.** *Physiol.* A body fluid, such as blood, lymph, or bile. **4.** A state of mind; mood: *a bad humor.* **5.** A sudden whim. ►*v.* To comply with the wishes or ideas of; indulge. [< Lat. *ūmor,* fluid.] —**hu′mor·ist** *n.* —**hu′mor·less** *adj.* —**hu′mor·less·ly** *adv.* —**hu′mor·ous** *adj.* —**hu′mor·ous·ly** *adv.*

hump (hŭmp) ►*n.* **1.** A rounded mass, as on the back of a camel. **2.** A low mound. ►*v.* **1.** To bend into a hump; arch. **2.** *Slang* To exert (oneself). **3.** *Slang* To hurry. —*idiom:* **over the hump** Past the worst stage. [Prob. of LGer. orig.]

hump·back (hŭmp′băk′) ►*n.* **1.** See **hunchback** (sense 1). **2.** A humped upper back. **3.** A humpback whale. —**hump′backed′** *adj.*

humpback whale ►*n.* A large baleen whale noted for its communicative songs.

hu·mus (hyoō′məs) ►*n.* A brown or black organic substance consisting of decayed vegetable or animal matter. [Lat., soil.]

Hun (hŭn) ►*n.* **1.** A member of a group of Central Asian nomadic peoples who invaded Europe in the 4th and 5th cent. AD. **2.** often **hun** A barbarous person.

hunch (hŭnch) ►*n.* An intuitive feeling. ►*v.* **1.** To bend or draw up into a hump. **2.** To assume a crouched or cramped posture. [?]

hunch·back (hŭnch′băk′) ►*n.* **1.** One whose back is hunched due to abnormal curvature of the upper spine. **2.** An abnormally humped back. —**hunch′backed′** *adj.*

hun·di (hoōn′dē) ►*n., pl.* **-dis** An informal system for transferring money, esp. in South Asia, through a network of trusted agents. [Hindi & Urdu *huṇḍī,* bill of exchange.]

hun·dred (hŭn′drĭd) ►*n., pl.* **-dred** or **-dreds 1.** The cardinal number equal to 10×10 or 10^2. **2. hundreds** The numbers between 100 and 999: *a crowd numbering in the hundreds.* [< OE.] —**hun′dred** *adj. & pron.*

hun·dredth (hŭn′drĭdth) ►*n.* **1.** The ordinal number matching the number 100 in a series. **2.** One of 100 equal parts. —**hun′dredth** *adj.*

hun·dred·weight (hŭn′drĭd-wāt′) ►*n., pl.* **-weight** or **-weights 1.** A unit of weight equal to 100 lbs. (45.36 kg). **2.** *Chiefly Brit.* A unit of weight equal to 112 lbs. (50.80 kg).

hung (hŭng) ►*v.* P.t. and p.part. of **hang.** See Usage Note at **hang.**

Hun·gar·i·an (hŭng-gâr′ē-ən) ►*n.* **1.** A native or inhabitant of Hungary. **2.** The Finno-Ugric language of the Hungarians. —**Hun·gar′i·an** *adj.*

Hun·ga·ry (hŭng′gə-rē) A country of central Europe E of Austria. Cap. Budapest.

hun·ger (hŭng′gər) ►*n.* **1a.** A strong desire for food. **b.** The discomfort, weakness, or pain caused by a lack of food. **2.** A strong desire or craving. ►*v.* **1.** To have a need or desire for food. **2.** To have a strong desire or craving; yearn. [< OE *hungor.*] —**hun′gri·ly** *adv.* —**hun′gri·ness** *n.* —**hun′gry** *adj.*

hung jury ►*n.* A jury unable to agree on a verdict.

hunk (hŭngk) ►*n.* **1.** *Informal* A large piece. **2.** *Slang* An attractive man. [Perh. < Flem. *hunke,* a piece of food.]

hun·ker (hŭng′kər) ►*v.* **1.** To squat; crouch. **2.** To assume a defensive position: *hunkered down against the unfavorable criticism.* [Perh. of Scand. orig.]

Hunk·pa·pa (hŭngk′pä′pä) ►*n., pl.* **Hunkpapa** or **-pas** A member of a Native American people constituting a subdivision of the Lakota, formerly inhabiting an area from the W Dakotas to SE Montana and now along the border between North and South Dakota.

hun·ky-do·ry (hŭng′kē-dôr′ē) ►*adj. Slang* Perfectly satisfactory; fine. [Prob. < alteration of obsolete *hunk,* goal < Frisian.]

hunt (hŭnt) ►*v.* **1.** To pursue (game) for food or sport. **2.** To search for prey: *hunted the backwoods.* **3.** To pursue so as to capture. **4.** To search (for). ►*n.* **1.** The act or sport of hunting. **2.** A hunting expedition. **3.** The hunting season for a particular animal. **4.** A diligent search. [< OE *huntian.*] —**hunt′er** *n.* —**hunt′ress** *n.*

hunts·man (hŭnts′mən) ►*n.* A man who hunts, esp. one who manages a pack of hounds in the field.

hur·dle (hûr′dl) ►*n.* **1.** *Sports* **a.** A light portable barrier to be jumped over in certain races. **b.** **hurdles** A race in which such barriers must be jumped. **2.** An obstacle to be overcome. ►*v.* **-dled, -dling 1.** To leap over (a barrier). **2.** To overcome; surmount. [< OE *hyrdel.*] —**hur′dler** *n.*

hurdles
left to right: Konstadinos Douvalidis, David Payne, and Mikel Thomas at the 2008 Olympic Games

hur·dy-gur·dy (hûr′dē-gûr′dē, hûr′dē-gûr′dē) ►*n., pl.* **-dies** A musical instrument, such as a barrel organ, played by turning a crank. [Prob. imit.]

hurl (hûrl) ►*v.* **1.** To throw forcefully; fling. **2.** To cause to move with great force. **3.** To utter vehemently: *hurl insults.* **4.** To pitch a baseball. [ME *hurlen.*] —**hurl** *n.* —**hurl′er** *n.*

hur·ly-bur·ly (hûr′lē-bûr′lē) ►*n., pl.* **-lies** Noisy confusion; tumult. [< HURL.]

Hu·ron (hyŏōr′ən, -ŏn′) ►*n., pl.* **-ron** or **-rons** **1.** A member of a Native American confederacy formerly of SE Ontario, now in Quebec and Oklahoma. **2.** The Iroquoian language of the Huron.

Huron, Lake The second largest of the Great Lakes, between SE Ontario, Canada, and E MI.

hur·rah (hŏō-rä′, -rô′, hə-) or **hur·ray** (-rā′) ►*interj., n., & v.* Vars. of **hooray.**

hur·ri·cane (hûr′ī-kān′, hŭr′-) ►*n.* A tropical cyclone usu. involving heavy rains and winds exceeding 74 mph (119 kph). [< Carib *huracan.*]

hur·ry (hûr′ē, hŭr′-) ►*v.* **-ried, -ry·ing 1.** To move or cause to move with speed or haste. **2.** To act or cause to act with undue haste; rush. **3.** To speed the completion of; expedite. ►*n., pl.* **-ries** Haste. See Synonyms at **haste.** [Poss. ME *horien.*] —**hur′ried** *adj.* —**hur′ried·ly** *adv.*

Hur·ston (hûr′stən), **Zora Neale** 1891–1960. Amer. writer and folklorist.

Zora Neale Hurston

hurt (hûrt) ►*v.* **hurt, hurt·ing 1.** To feel or cause to feel pain. **2.** To aggrieve; distress. **3.** To damage or impair. ►*n.* **1.** Something that hurts. **2.** Mental suffering; anguish. **3.** A wrong; harm. [Poss. < OFr. *hurter*, bang into.] —**hurt′ful** *adj.* —**hurt′ful·ly** *adv.*

hur·tle (hûr′tl) ►*v.* **-tled, -tling 1.** To move with or as if with great speed. **2.** To throw forcefully; hurl. [ME *hurtlen*, collide.]

Hus or **Huss** (hŭs, hŏōs), **Jan** or **John** 1372?–1415. Czech religious reformer.

hus·band (hŭz′bənd) ►*n.* A male spouse. ►*v.* To use economically: *husband one's energy.* [< ON *húsbóndi* : *hūs*, house + *būandi*, householder (< *būa*, dwell).]

hus·band·man (hŭz′bənd-mən) ►*n.* A farmer.

hus·band·ry (hŭz′bən-drē) ►*n.* **1.** The act or practice of cultivating crops and breeding and raising livestock. **2.** Careful management of resources; economy.

hush (hŭsh) ►*v.* **1.** To make or become silent.

2. To calm; soothe. **3.** To suppress mention of: *hush up the evidence.* ►*n.* A silence or stillness. [Prob. < ME *husht*, silent.]

hush-hush (hŭsh′hŭsh′) ►*adj. Informal* Secret; confidential.

hush puppy ►*n.* A small round cornmeal fritter fried in deep fat. [?]

husk (hŭsk) ►*n.* **1.** The outer covering of some fruits or seeds, as that of an ear of corn. **2.** A shell or outer covering, esp. when considered worthless. ►*v.* To remove the husk from. [ME.] —**husk′er** *n.*

husk·y[1] (hŭs′kē) ►*adj.* **-i·er, -i·est** Hoarse or throaty. [< HUSK.] —**husk′i·ly** *adv.*

husk·y[2] (hŭs′kē) ►*adj.* **-i·er, -i·est** Strongly built; burly. [Perh. < HUSK.]

hus·ky[3] (hŭs′kē) ►*n., pl.* **-kies** An Arctic sled dog having a dense, variously colored coat. [Prob. < alteration of ESKIMO.]

Huss (hŭs, hŏōs), **John** See Jan **Hus.**

hus·sar (hə-zär′, -sär′) ►*n.* A member of any of various European units of light cavalry. [< OItal. *corsaro,* CORSAIR.]

Hus·sein (hŏō-sān′) King Hussein bin Talal. 1935–99. King of Jordan (1953–99).

Hussein, Saddam 1937–2006. Iraqi military and political leader.

Hus·serl (hŏōs′ərl, -ĕrl), **Edmund** 1859–1938. Austrian philosopher and mathematician.

hus·sy (hŭz′ē, hŭs′ē) ►*n., pl.* **-sies 1.** A brazen or promiscuous woman. **2.** A saucy or impudent girl or young woman. [< ME *houswif,* housewife.]

hust·ings (hŭs′tĭngz) ►*pl.n. (takes sing. or pl. v.)* **1.** A place where political campaign speeches are made. **2.** The activities involved in political campaigning. [< ON *hūsthing,* assembly, court.]

hus·tle (hŭs′əl) ►*v.* **-tled, -tling 1.** To jostle or shove roughly. **2.** To hurry along. **3.** To act aggressively, esp. in business dealings. **4.** *Slang* To sell or get by questionable or aggressive means. ►*n.* Energetic activity; drive. [< MDu. *hustelen.*] —**hus′tler** *n.*

hut (hŭt) ►*n.* A crude or makeshift dwelling; shack. [Fr. *hutte*, of Gmc. orig.]

hutch (hŭch) ►*n.* **1.** A coop for small animals, esp. rabbits. **2.** A cupboard with drawers and usu. open shelves on top. **3.** A hut. [< Med.Lat. *hūtica,* chest.]

Hutch·in·son (hŭch′ĭn-sən), **Anne** 1591–1643. English-born Amer. religious leader.

Hu·tu (hŏō′tŏō′) ►*n., pl.* **-tu, -tus** A member of a Bantu people inhabiting Rwanda and Burundi.

Hux·ley (hŭks′lē), **Aldous Leonard** 1894–1963. British writer.

huz·zah also **huz·za** (hə-zä′) ►*interj.* Used to express joy, encouragement, or triumph. —**huz·zah′** *n.*

hwy ►*abbr.* highway

hy·a·cinth (hī′ə-sĭnth) ►*n.* **1a.** A bulbous plant having narrow leaves and variously colored, usu. fragrant flowers. **b.** A similar or related plant. **2.** A deep purplish blue to vivid violet. [< Gk. *huakinthos.*]

hy·brid (hī′brĭd) ►*n.* **1.** The offspring of genetically dissimilar parents, esp. of different varieties or species. **2a.** Something of mixed origin or composition. **b.** Something having two kinds of components that produce the same or similar results, such as a vehicle powered by both an electric motor and an internal combustion engine. [Lat. *hybrida*.] **—hy′brid** *adj.* **—hy′brid·ism** *n.*

hy·brid·ize (hī′brĭ-dīz′) ►*v.* **-ized, -iz·ing** To produce or cause to produce hybrids; crossbreed. **—hy′brid·i·za′tion** *n.*

hy·dra (hī′drə) ►*n.* A small freshwater cnidarian having a cylindrical body and a mouth surrounded by tentacles. [< Gk. *Hudra*, a many-headed monster.]

hy·dran·gea (hī-drān′jə, -drăn′-) ►*n.* A shrub having large rounded clusters of white, pink, or blue flowers. [Gk. *hudro-*, HYDRO– + *angeion*, vessel.]

hy·drant (hī′drənt) ►*n.* A fire hydrant.

hy·drate (hī′drāt′) ►*n.* A solid compound containing water molecules combined in a definite ratio as an integral part of the crystal. Often used in combination: *pentahydrate.* ►*v.* **-drat·ed, -drat·ing 1.** To rehydrate. **2.** To supply water to (e.g., a person) in order to restore or maintain fluid balance. **3.** To become a hydrate. **—hy·dra′tion** *n.* **—hy′dra′tor** *n.*

hy·drau·lic (hī-drô′lĭk) ►*adj.* **1.** Of, involving, or operated by a fluid, esp. water, under pressure. **2.** Able to set and harden under water, as Portland cement. **3.** Of or relating to hydraulics. [< Gk. *hudraulis*, water organ : *hudro-*, HYDRO– + *aulos*, flute.] **—hy·drau′li·cal·ly** *adv.*

hy·drau·lics (hī-drô′lĭks) ►*n.* *(takes sing. v.)* The physical science and technology of the static and dynamic behavior of fluids.

hydro– or **hydr–** ►*pref.* **1a.** Water: *hydroelectric.* **b.** Fluid: *hydrodynamics.* **2.** Hydrogen: *hydrocarbon.* [< Gk. *hudōr*, water.]

hy·dro·car·bon (hī′drə-kär′bən) ►*n.* An organic compound, such as benzene or methane, that contains only carbon and hydrogen. **—hy′dro·car′bo·na′ceous** (-bə-nā′shəs), **hy′dro·car·bon′ic** (-bŏn′ĭk) *adj.*

hy·dro·ceph·a·lus (hī′drō-sĕf′ə-ləs) also **hy·dro·ceph·a·ly** (-lē) ►*n.* A congenital defect in which accumulation of fluid in the cerebral ventricles causes enlargement of the skull and compression of the brain. [HYDRO– + Gk. *kephalē*, head.] **—hy′dro·ce·phal′ic** (-sə-făl′ĭk), **hy′dro·ceph′a·loid′, hy′dro·ceph′a·lous** *adj.*

hy·dro·chlo·ric acid (hī′drə-klôr′ĭk) ►*n.* A clear, fuming, poisonous aqueous solution of hydrogen chloride, HCl, used in petroleum production, food processing, pickling, and metal cleaning.

hy·dro·cor·ti·sone (hī′drə-kôr′tĭ-sōn′, -zōn′) ►*n.* **1.** A steroid hormone, $C_{21}H_{30}O_5$, produced by the adrenal cortex, that regulates carbohydrate metabolism and maintains blood pressure. **2.** A preparation of this hormone that is used to treat inflammations and adrenal failure.

hy·dro·dy·nam·ics (hī′drō-dī-năm′ĭks) ►*n.* **1.** *(takes sing. v.)* The branch of science that deals with the dynamics of fluids, esp. incompressible fluids, in motion. **2.** *(takes pl. v.)* The dynamics of fluids in motion. **—hy′dro·dy·nam′i·cist** *n.*

hy·dro·e·lec·tric (hī′drō-ĭ-lĕk′trĭk) ►*adj.* Of or relating to electricity generated by conversion of the energy of running water. **—hy′dro·e·lec·tric′i·ty** (-ĭ-lĕk-trĭs′ĭ-tē) *n.*

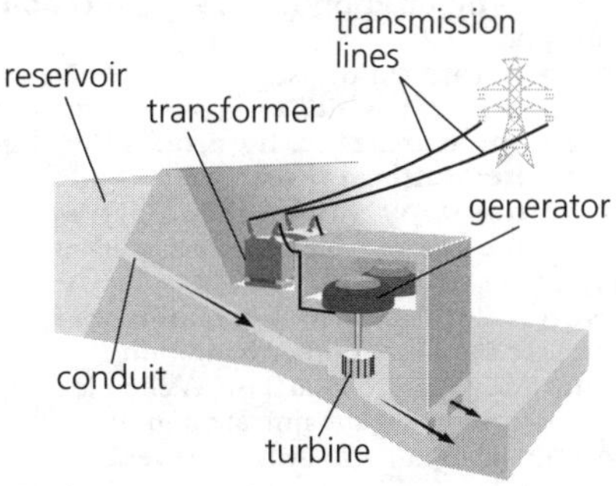

hydroelectric
The mechanical energy of moving water is transferred by a rotating turbine to a generator, where it is converted to electric energy and conveyed along transmission lines.

hy·dro·fluor·o·car·bon (hī′drō-flo͝or′ə-kär′bən -flôr′-) ►*n.* An organic compound that contains carbon, fluorine, and hydrogen, used as refrigerants and in other products in place of chlorofluorocarbons.

hy·dro·foil (hī′drə-foil′) ►*n.* **1.** A winglike structure on the hull of a boat that raises the hull out of the water for efficient high-speed operation. **2.** A boat with hydrofoils.

hy·dro·gen (hī′drə-jən) ►*n.* *Symbol* **H** A colorless, highly flammable gaseous element, the most abundant element in the universe and present in most organic compounds. At. no. 1. See table at **element. —hy·drog′e·nous** (-drŏj′ə-nəs) *adj.*

hy·dro·gen·ate (hī′drə-jə-nāt′, hī-drŏj′ə-) ►*v.* **-at·ed, -at·ing** To combine with hydrogen, esp. to combine (an unsaturated oil) with hydrogen to produce a solid fat.

hydrogen bomb ►*n.* A bomb whose explosive power is caused by the fusion of hydrogen nuclei into helium nuclei.

hydrogen peroxide ►*n.* A colorless, strongly oxidizing liquid, H_2O_2, used esp. as an antiseptic, bleaching agent, oxidizing agent, and laboratory reagent.

hy·drol·y·sis (hī-drŏl′ĭ-sĭs) ►*n.* The reaction of water with another compound to form two or more products, involving ionization of the water molecule and usu. splitting of the other compound. **—hy′dro·lyte′** (-līt′) *n.* **—hy′dro·lyt′ic** (-drə-lĭt′ĭk) *adj.* **—hy′dro·ly·za′tion** (hī′drə-lĭ-zā′shən) *n.* **—hy′dro·lyze′** *v.*

hy·drom·e·ter (hī-drŏm′ĭ-tər) ►*n.* An instrument used to determine the specific gravity of a fluid. **—hy′dro·met′ric** (hī′drə-mĕt′rĭk), **hy′dro·met′ri·cal** *adj.* **—hy·drom′e·try** *n.*

hy·dro·pho·bi·a (hī′drə-fō′bē-ə) ►*n.* **1.** Fear of water. **2.** Rabies. **—hy′dro·pho′bic** *adj.*

hy·dro·plane (hī′drə-plān′) ►*n.* **1.** See **seaplane. 2.** A motorboat designed to skim the water's surface at high speeds. **3.** See **hydrofoil** (sense 2). ►*v.* **-planed, -plan·ing 1.** To drive or ride in a hydroplane. **2a.** To skim along on the surface of the water. **b.** To lose control by skimming along the surface of a wet road. Used of a motor vehicle.

hy·dro·pon·ics (hī′drə-pŏn′ĭks) ►*n.* *(takes sing. v.)* Cultivation of plants in nutrient solution rather than in soil. [HYDRO– + Gk. *ponein*, to work.] —**hy′dro·pon′ic** adj. —**hy′dro·pon′i·cal·ly** adv.

hy·dro·stat·ics (hī′drə-stăt′ĭks) ►n. (takes sing. v.) The physics of fluids at rest and under pressure. —**hy′dro·stat′ic, hy′dro·stat′i·cal** adj. —**hy′dro·stat′i·cal·ly** adv.

hy·dro·ther·a·py (hī′drə-thĕr′ə-pē) ►n., pl. **-pies** The use of water to treat pain and the symptoms of disease.

hy·drous (hī′drəs) ►adj. Containing water, esp. water of crystallization or hydration.

hy·drox·ide (hī-drŏk′sīd′) ►n. A chemical compound containing the univalent group OH.

hy·e·na (hī-ē′nə) ►n. Any of several carnivorous mammals of Africa and Asia feeding chiefly on carrion. [< Gk. huaina, feminine of hus, swine.]

hy·giene (hī′jēn′) ►n. **1.** The science of the promotion and preservation of health. **2.** Conditions and practices that promote or preserve health. [< Gk. hugiēs, healthy.] —**hy′gien′ic** (-jĕn′ĭk) adj. —**hy′gien′i·cal·ly** adv. —**hy·gien′ist** (hī-jē′nĭst, -jĕn′ĭst) n.

hy·grom·e·ter (hī-grŏm′ĭ-tər) ►n. Any of several instruments that measure atmospheric humidity. [Gk. hugros, wet + –METER.] —**hy′gro·met′ric** (hī′grə-mĕt′rĭk) adj. —**hy·grom′e·try** n.

hy·ing (hī′ĭng) ►v. Pr.part. of **hie.**

hy·men (hī′mən) ►n. A membranous fold of tissue closing the external vaginal orifice. [< Gk. humēn, membrane.] —**hy′men·al** adj.

hy·me·ne·al (hī′mə-nē′əl) ►adj. Of a wedding or marriage. [< Gk. humēn, HYMEN.]

hymn (hĭm) ►n. A song of praise or thanksgiving, esp. to God. [< Gk. humnos.]

hym·nal (hĭm′nəl) ►n. A book or collection of church hymns. [< Med.Lat. hymnāle.]

hype¹ (hīp) ►n. Slang **1.** Excessive publicity. **2.** Extravagant claims made esp. in advertising. [< hype, a swindle.] —**hype** v.

hype² (hīp) Slang ►n. A hypodermic injection or syringe. ►v. **hyped, hyp′ing** To stimulate or excite. Often used with up. [< HYPODERMIC.]

hy·per (hī′pər) ►adj. Slang **1.** Excitable; highstrung. **2.** Emotionally stimulated or overexcited. [< HYPERACTIVE.]

hyper– ►pref. **1.** Over; above; beyond: hypersonic. **2.** Excessive; excessively: hypercritical. [< Gk. huper.]

hy·per·ac·tive (hī′pər-ăk′tĭv) ►adj. **1.** Highly or excessively active: a hyperactive thyroid gland. **2.** Having behavior characterized by overactivity. **3.** Having attention deficit disorder. Not in scientific use. —**hy′per·ac′tive·ly** adv. —**hy′per·ac·tiv′i·ty** n.

hy·per·bo·la (hī-pûr′bə-lə) ►n., pl. **-las** or **-lae** (-lē) Math. A plane curve having two branches, formed by the intersection of a plane with both halves of a right circular cone at an angle parallel to the axis of the cone. [< Gk. huperbolē, excess; see HYPERBOLE.]

hy·per·bo·le (hī-pûr′bə-lē) ►n. A figure of speech in which exaggeration is used for emphasis or effect, as in I could sleep for a year. [< Gk. huperbolē, excess : HYPER– + ballein, throw.]

hy·per·bol·ic (hī′pər-bŏl′ĭk) also **hy·per·bol·i·cal** (-ĭ-kəl) ►adj. **1.** Of or employing hyperbole. **2.** Math. Of or shaped like a hyperbola. —**hy′per·bol′i·cal·ly** adv.

hy·per·crit·i·cal (hī′pər-krĭt′ĭ-kəl) ►adj. Excessively critical. —**hy′per·crit′i·cal·ly** adv.

hy·per·gly·ce·mi·a (hī′pər-glī-sē′mē-ə) ►n. An excess of glucose in the blood. [HYPER– + Gk. glukus, sweet + –EMIA.] —**hy′per·gly·ce′mic** adj.

hy·per·link (hī′pər-lĭngk′) Comp. ►n. See **link** (sense 4). ►v. To follow a hypertext link to an electronic document.

hy·per·sen·si·tive (hī′pər-sĕn′sĭ-tĭv) ►adj. Abnormally sensitive. —**hy′per·sen′si·tiv′i·ty** n. —**hy′per·sen′si·tize′** (-tīz′) v.

hy·per·son·ic (hī′pər-sŏn′ĭk) ►adj. Of or relating to speed equal to or exceeding five times the speed of sound. —**hy′per·son′i·cal·ly** adv.

hy·per·ten·sion (hī′pər-tĕn′shən) ►n. **1.** Abnormally high arterial blood pressure. **2.** Arterial disease marked by chronic high blood pressure. —**hy′per·ten′sive** adj. & n.

hy·per·text (hī′pər-tĕkst′) ►n. Digital text that contains hyperlinks to other texts.

hy·per·thy·roid·ism (hī′pər-thī′roi-dĭz′əm) ►n. **1.** Excessive production of thyroid hormones. **2.** Excessive activity of the thyroid gland, characterized by increased basal metabolism.

hy·per·tro·phy (hī-pûr′trə-fē) ►n., pl. **-phies** A nontumorous enlargement of an organ or a tissue. [HYPER– + Gk. trophē, food.] —**hy′per·tro′phic** (-trō′fĭk, -trŏf′ĭk) adj. —**hy·per′tro·phy** v.

hy·per·ven·ti·late (hī′pər-vĕn′tl-āt′) ►v. **-lat·ed, -lat·ing 1.** To breathe so as to effect hyperventilation. **2.** To breathe fast or deeply, as from excitement or anxiety.

hy·per·ven·ti·la·tion (hī′pər-vĕn′tl-ā′shən) ►n. Fast or deep respiration resulting in abnormally low levels of carbon dioxide in the blood.

hy·phen (hī′fən) ►n. A punctuation mark (-) used between the parts of a compound word or between the syllables of a word, esp. when divided at the end of a line of text. [< Gk. huph′ hen, in one.]

hy·phen·ate (hī′fə-nāt′) ►v. **-at·ed, -at·ing** To divide or connect with a hyphen. —**hy′phen·a′tion** n.

hyp·no·sis (hĭp-nō′sĭs) ►n., pl. **-ses** (-sēz) An artificially induced sleeplike state, characterized by heightened suggestibility and receptivity to direction. [Gk. hupnos, sleep + –OSIS.]

hyp·not·ic (hĭp-nŏt′ĭk) ►adj. **1.** Of or relating to hypnosis. **2.** Inducing or tending to induce sleep. ►n. An agent that causes sleep. [< Gk. hupnōtikos, inducing sleep < hupnos, sleep.] —**hyp·not′i·cal·ly** adv.

hyp·no·tism (hĭp′nə-tĭz′əm) ►n. **1.** The theory, practice, or act of inducing hypnosis. **2.** Hypnosis. —**hyp′no·tist** n.

hyp·no·tize (hĭp′nə-tīz′) ►v. **-tized, -tiz·ing 1.** To put into a state of hypnosis. **2.** To fascinate; mesmerize. —**hyp′no·ti·za′tion** n. —**hyp′no·tiz′er** n.

hy·po (hī′pō) ►n., pl. **-pos** Informal A hypodermic syringe or injection.

hypo– or **hyp–** ►pref. **1.** Below; beneath; under: hypodermic. **2.** Lower than normal: hypothermia. [< Gk. hupo, beneath.]

hy·po·al·ler·gen·ic (hī′pō-ăl′ər-jĕn′ĭk) ►adj. Having a decreased tendency to provoke an allergic reaction: hypoallergenic cosmetics.

hy·po·chon·dri·a (hī′pə-kŏn′drē-ə) ►n. The persistent conviction that one is ill, often involving symptoms when illness is neither present nor likely. [< Gk. *hupokhondrion,* abdomen.] —**hy′po·chon′dri·ac′** *adj. & n.*

hy·poc·ri·sy (hĭ-pŏk′rĭ-sē) ►*n., pl.* -**sies** The professing of beliefs or virtues one does not possess. [< Gk. *hupokrisis,* pretense.]

hyp·o·crite (hĭp′ə-krĭt′) ►*n.* A person given to hypocrisy. [< Gk. *hupocritēs,* actor.] —**hyp′o·crit′i·cal** *adj.* —**hyp′o·crit′i·cal·ly** *adv.*

hy·po·der·mic (hī′pə-dûr′mĭk) ►*adj.* **1.** Injected into tissues beneath the skin, as a muscle or vein. **2.** Penetrating the skin to deliver an injection or aspirate a fluid: *a hypodermic needle.* —**hy′po·der′mi·cal·ly** *adv.*

hy·po·gly·ce·mi·a (hī′pō-glī-sē′mē-ə) ►*n.* An abnormally low level of glucose in the blood. [< HYPO– + Gk. *glukus,* sweet + –EMIA.] —**hy′po·gly·ce′mic** *adj.*

hy·po·ma·ni·a (hī′pə-mā′nē-ə, -mān′yə) ►*n.* A mood disorder that is milder than mania and is marked by symptoms of elevated or agitated mood such as increased energy and irritability, esp. as a component of bipolar disorder. —**hy′po·man′ic** (-măn′ĭk) *adj.*

hy·pot·e·nuse (hī-pŏt′n-ōōs′, -yōōs′) ►*n. Math.* The side of a right triangle opposite the right angle. [< Gk. *hupoteinousa.*]

hy·po·thal·a·mus (hī′pō-thăl′ə-məs) ►*n.* The part of the brain that lies below the thalamus and regulates bodily temperature, certain metabolic processes, and other autonomic activities. —**hy′po·tha·lam′ic** (-thə-lăm′ĭk) *adj.*

hy·po·ther·mi·a (hī′pə-thûr′mē-ə) ►*n.* Abnormally low body temperature. —**hy′po·ther′mic** *adj.*

hy·poth·e·sis (hī-pŏth′ĭ-sĭs) ►*n., pl.* -**ses** (-sēz′) A tentative explanation for an observation or phenomenon that can be tested by further investigation. [< Gk. *hupothesis.*] —**hy·poth′e·size** *v.*

hy·po·thet·i·cal (hī′pə-thĕt′ĭ-kəl) also **hy·po·thet·ic** (-thĕt′ĭk) ►*adj.* **1.** Of or based on a hypothesis. **2.** Conditional; contingent. [< Gk. *hupothetikos.*] —**hy′po·thet′i·cal** *n.* —**hy′po·thet′i·cal·ly** *adv.*

hy·po·thy·roid·ism (hī′pō-thī′roi-dĭz′əm) ►*n.* **1.** Insufficient production of thyroid hormones. **2.** Insufficient functioning of the thyroid gland.

hy·rax (hī′răks′) ►*n., pl.* -**rax·es** or -**ra·ces** (-rə-sēz′) An herbivorous mammal of Africa and the Middle East, resembling the woodchuck but more closely related to hoofed mammals. [Gk. *hurax,* shrew mouse.]

hys·sop (hĭs′əp) ►*n.* A woody plant having spikes of small blue flowers and aromatic leaves. [< Gk. *hussōpos.*]

hys·ter·ec·to·my (hĭs′tə-rĕk′tə-mē) ►*n., pl.* -**mies** Surgical removal of the uterus. [Gk. *hustera,* womb + –ECTOMY.]

hys·ter·i·a (hĭ-stĕr′ē-ə, -stîr′-) ►*n.* **1.** Behavior exhibiting excessive or uncontrollable emotion, such as fear or panic. **2.** A group of psychiatric symptoms, including attention-seeking behavior and physical symptoms in the absence of organic pathology. No longer in clinical use. [< Gk. *hustera,* womb.]

hys·ter·ic (hĭ-stĕr′ĭk) ►*n.* **1. hysterics** *(takes sing. or pl. v.)* A fit of uncontrollable laughing or crying. **2.** A person suffering from hysteria. No longer in clinical use. [< Gk. *hustera,* womb.]

hys·ter·i·cal (hĭ-stĕr′ĭ-kəl) ►*adj.* **1.** Laughing or crying for a prolonged period of time. **2.** *Informal* Extremely funny: *a hysterical story.* —**hys·ter′i·cal·ly** *adv.*

Hz ►*abbr.* hertz

I

i¹ or **I** (ī) ►*n., pl.* **i's** or **I's** also **is** or **Is** The 9th letter of the English alphabet.

i² The symbol for **imaginary unit.**

I (ī) ►*pron.* Used to refer to oneself as speaker or writer. ►*n.* The self; the ego. [< OE *ic.*]

Usage: The nominative forms of pronouns should be used in formal speech and writing in such sentences as *John and she* (not *her*) *will be giving the talk.* • *Between you and I,* a construction in which the pronouns occur as the objects of a preposition, is widely regarded as a mistake in formal English; use *between you and me.*

IA or **Ia.** ►*abbr.* Iowa

–ia¹ ►*suff.* **1.** Disease; disorder: *dyslexia.* **2.** Territory; country: *suburbia.* [< Lat. and Gk.]

–ia² ►*suff.* Things derived from or relating to: *marginalia.* [< Lat. and Gk.]

–ial ►*suff.* Of, relating to, or characterized by: *axial.* [< Lat. *-iālis.*]

i·amb (ī′ămb′, ī′ăm′) ►*n., pl.* **i·ambs** A metrical foot consisting of one short or unaccented syllable followed by one long or accented one. [< Gk. *iambos.*] —**i·am′bic** *adj. & n.*

–ian ►*suff.* **1.** Of, relating to, or resembling: *Devonian.* **2.** One relating to, belonging to, or resembling: *tragedian.* [< Lat. *-iānus.*]

–iana ►*suff.* Var. of –ana.

–iatric ►*suff.* Of or relating to a specified kind of medical practice: *pediatric.* [< Gk. *iatros,* physician.]

–iatrics ►*suff.* Medical treatment: *pediatrics.*

–iatry ►*suff.* Medical treatment: *psychiatry.* [< Gk. *iatros,* physician.]

I·be·ri·a (ī-bîr′ē-ə) **1.** An ancient country of Transcaucasia roughly corresponding to E Georgia. **2.** See **Iberian Peninsula.** —**I·be′ri·an** *adj. & n.*

Iberian Peninsula also **Iberia** A peninsula of SW Europe occupied by Spain and Portugal.

i·bex (ī′bĕks′) ►*n., pl.* **ibex** or **i·bex·es** A wild goat native to Eurasia and N Africa and having long curving horns. [Lat.]

ibid. ►*abbr.* ibidem

i·bi·dem (ĭb′ĭ-dĕm′, ĭ-bī′dəm) ►*adv.* In the same place, as in a book cited before. [Lat. *ibīdem.*]

i·bis (ī′bĭs) ►*n., pl.* **ibis** or **i·bis·es** Any of a family of storklike wading birds having a long, downward-curving bill. [< Gk.]

–ible ►*suff.* Var. of –able.

Ibn Sa·ud (ĭb′ən sä-ōōd′) Abdul Aziz bin Abdul Rahman al-Saud. 1880?–1953. Arab leader; founder and first king of Saudi Arabia (1932–53).

I·bo (ē′bō) ►*n.* Var. of **Igbo.**

Ib·sen (ĭb′sən, ĭp′-), **Henrik Johan** 1828–1906. Norwegian playwright.

i·bu·pro·fen (ī′byōō-prō′fən) ►*n.* An anti-inflammatory medication used for its analgesic and antipyretic properties. [< the chemical name *i(so)bu(tyl)phen(yl) pro(pionic acid)*.]

IC ►*abbr.* **1.** integrated circuit **2.** intensive care

–ic ►*suff.* **1.** Of, relating to, or characterized by: *seismic.* **2.** Having a valence higher than corresponding *–ous* compounds: *ferric.* [< Lat. *-icus* and Gk. *-ikos.*]

ICBM ►*abbr.* intercontinental ballistic missile

ice (īs) ►*n.* **1.** Water frozen solid. **2.** A dessert consisting of sweetened and flavored crushed ice. **3.** *Slang* Diamonds. **4.** Extreme unfriendliness or reserve. ►*v.* **iced, ic·ing 1a.** To form ice; freeze. **b.** To coat with ice. **2.** To chill or freeze. **3.** To cover or decorate with icing. **4.** *Slang* To ensure of victory; clinch. —*idiom:* **on ice** In reserve or readiness. [< OE *īs.*]

ICE ►*abbr.* in case of emergency

ice age ►*n.* **1.** A cold period marked by episodes of extensive glaciation. **2. Ice Age** The most recent glacial period.

ice bag ►*n.* See **ice pack** (sense 2).

ice·berg (īs′bûrg′) ►*n.* A massive floating body of ice broken away from a glacier. [< MDu. *ijsbergh.*]

ice·boat (īs′bōt′) ►*n.* **1.** A boatlike vehicle with sharp runners, used for sailing on ice. **2.** See **icebreaker** (sense 1). —**ice′boat′er** *n.* —**ice′boat′ing** *n.*

ice·bound (īs′bound′) ►*adj.* Locked in or covered over by ice.

ice·box (īs′bŏks′) ►*n.* A refrigerator.

ice·break·er (īs′brā′kər) ►*n.* **1.** A ship built for breaking a passage through icebound waters. **2.** Something done or said to relax an unduly formal situation. —**ice′break′ing** *n.*

ice·cap or **ice cap** (īs′kăp′) ►*n.* An extensive perennial cover of ice and snow.

ice cream ►*n.* A sweet frozen food prepared from milk products and flavorings.

ice-fish (īs′fĭsh′) ►*v.* To fish through a hole in the ice covering a body of water. —**ice′-fish′ing** *n.*

ice hockey ►*n.* A game played on ice in which two teams of skaters use curved sticks to drive a puck into each other's goal.

ice·house (īs′hous′) ►*n.* A place where ice is made, stored, or sold.

Ice·land (īs′lənd) An island country in the North Atlantic near the Arctic Circle. Cap. Reykjavík. —**Ice′land·er** *n.*

Ice·land·ic (īs-lăn′dĭk) ►*adj.* Of or relating to Iceland or its people or language. ►*n.* The Germanic language of Iceland.

ice milk ►*n.* A frozen dessert prepared from milk products, containing less butterfat than ice cream.

ice pack ►*n.* **1.** A floating mass of compacted ice fragments. **2.** A sac that is filled with crushed ice and is applied to sore or swollen parts of the body.

ice pick ►*n.* An awl for chipping or breaking ice.

ice skate ►*n.* A boot with a metal blade fitted to the sole, used for skating on ice. —**ice′-skate′** *v.* —**ice skater** *n.*

ice storm ►*n.* A storm in which snow or rain freezes on contact.

ichthyo– or **ichthy–** ►*pref.* Fish: *ichthyology.* [< Gk. *ikhthus,* fish.]

ich·thy·ol·o·gy (ĭk′thē-ŏl′ə-jē) ►*n.* The branch of zoology that deals with fishes. —**ich′thy·o·log′ic** (-ə-lŏj′ĭk), **ich′thy·o·log′i·cal** *adj.* —**ich′thy·ol′o·gist** *n.*

ich·thy·o·saur (ĭk′thē-ə-sôr′) ►*n.* An extinct marine reptile of the Mesozoic Era having a long flexible body with fins and an elongated snout. [ICHTHYO– + Gk. *sauros,* lizard.]

–ician ►*suff.* One who practices; a specialist: *beautician.* [< OFr. *-icien.*]

i·ci·cle (ī′sĭ-kəl) ►*n.* **1.** A tapering spike of ice formed by the freezing of dripping water. **2.** *Informal* An aloof person. [ME *isikel.*]

ic·ing (ī′sĭng) ►*n.* A sweet glaze used on cakes and cookies.

i·con (ī′kŏn′) ►*n.* **1a.** An image or representation. **b.** A representation of a sacred Christian personage, traditionally venerated in the Eastern Church. **2.** *Comp.* A picture on a screen that represents a specific file, directory, window, or program. [< Gk. *eikōn,* likeness.]

i·con·o·clast (ī-kŏn′ə-klăst′) ►*n.* **1.** One who attacks traditional ideas or institutions. **2.** One who destroys sacred images. [< Med.Gk. *eikonoklastēs.*] —**i·con′o·clasm′** *n.* —**i·con′o·clas′tic** *adj.* —**i·con′o·clas′ti·cal·ly** *adv.*

–ics ►*suff.* **1.** Study; knowledge; skill: *graphics.* **2.** Actions, activities, or practices of: *athletics.* **3.** Qualities or operations of: *mechanics.* [< –IC.]

ic·tus (ĭk′təs) ►*n., pl.* **-tus** or **-tus·es** *Med.* A sudden seizure. [Lat., stroke.]

ICU ►*abbr.* intensive care unit

ic·y (ī′sē) ►*adj.* **-i·er, -i·est 1.** Containing or covered with ice. **2.** Bitterly cold; freezing. See Synonyms at **cold. 3.** Chilling in manner: *an icy smile.* —**ic′i·ly** *adv.* —**ic′i·ness** *n.*

id (ĭd) ►*n.* In psychoanalysis, the part of the psyche that is the source of instinctual impulses and demands for satisfaction of primitive needs. [< Lat., it.]

ID[1] (ī′dē′) *Informal* ►*n.* A form of identification, such as a card or passport. ►*v.* **ID'ed, ID'ing** To check the identification of; card.

ID[2] ►*abbr.* **1.** Idaho **2.** identification

id. ►*abbr.* idem

I'd (īd) **1.** I had. **2.** I would.

I·da·ho (ī′də-hō′) A state of the NW US. Cap. Boise. —**I′da·ho′an** *adj. & n.*

–ide ►*suff.* **1.** Chemical compound: *chloride.* **2.** Chemical element with properties similar to another: *lanthanide.* [< (OX)IDE.]

i·de·a (ī-dē′ə) ►*n.* **1.** Something, such as a thought, that is the product of mental activity. **2.** An opinion, conviction, or principle. **3.** A plan, purpose, or goal. **4.** The gist or significance. [< Gk.]

i·de·al (ī-dē′əl, ī-dēl′) ►*n.* **1.** A concept of something as perfect. **2.** A standard of perfection or excellence. **3.** An ultimate or worthy objective; goal. ►*adj.* **1.** Perfect or highly satisfactory. **2.** Existing only in the mind; imaginary. [< LLat. *ideālis* < Lat. *idea.*] —**i·de′al·ly** *adv.*

i·de·al·ism (ī-dē′ə-lĭz′əm) ►*n.* **1.** The practice of envisioning things in an ideal form. **2.** Pursuit of one's ideals. **3.** *Philos.* The theory that things, in themselves or as perceived, consist of ideas. —**i·de′al·ist** *n.* —**i·de′al·is′tic** *adj.* —**i·de′al·is′ti·cal·ly** *adv.*

i·de·al·ize (ī-dē′ə-līz′) ►*v.* **-ized, -iz·ing** To

regard, envision, or represent as ideal. —**i·de′-al·i·za′tion** *n*. —**i·de′al·iz′er** *n*.

i·de·ate (ī′dē-āt′) ►*v*. **-at·ed, -at·ing** To form an idea (of). —**i′de·a′tion** *n*. —**i′de·a′tion·al** *adj*.

i·dem (ī′dĕm′) ►*pron*. Something mentioned previously. [Lat. *īdem* < *id*, it.]

i·den·ti·cal (ī-dĕn′tĭ-kəl) ►*adj*. **1.** Being the same. **2.** Exactly equal and alike. **3.** *Biol*. Of or relating to a twin or twins developed from the same ovum. [< Med.Lat. *identicus*.] —**i·den′ti·cal·ly** *adv*. —**i·den′ti·cal·ness** *n*.

i·den·ti·fi·ca·tion (ī-dĕn′tə-fĭ-kā′shən) ►*n*. **1.** The act of identifying. **2.** The state of being identified. **3.** Proof of identity. **4.** *Psychol*. A person's association with the characteristics or views of another person.

i·den·ti·fy (ī-dĕn′tə-fī′) ►*v*. **-fied, -fy·ing 1a.** To establish or recognize the identity of. **b.** To ascertain as having a certain characteristic or feature. **2.** To equate. **3.** To associate (oneself) closely with a person or group. [Med.Lat. *identificāre*, make the same as.] —**i·den′ti·fi′a·ble** *adj*. —**i·den′ti·fi′a·bly** *adv*.

i·den·ti·ty (ī-dĕn′tĭ-tē) ►*n*., *pl*. **-ties 1a.** The condition of being a certain person or thing. **b.** The set of characteristics by which an individual is recognizable. **c.** The awareness that an individual or group has of being a distinct, persisting entity. **2.** The quality or condition of being the same as something else. **3.** Information used to establish or prove a person's individuality. **4.** *Math*. An equation satisfied by any number that replaces the letter for which the equation is defined. [< LLat. *identitās*.]

identity element ►*n*. *Math*. The element of a set of numbers that when combined with another number in a particular operation leaves that number unchanged.

ideo- ►*pref*. Idea: ideogram. [< Gk. *idea*, idea.]

id·e·o·gram (ĭd′ē-ə-grăm′, ī′dē-) ►*n*. **1.** A character or symbol representing an idea or a thing without expressing the pronunciation of a particular word or words for it. **2.** A graphic symbol, such as &, $, or @. —**id′e·o·gram·mat′ic** (-grə-măt′ĭk) *adj*.

i·de·o·logue (ī′dē-ə-lôg′, -lŏg′, ĭd′ē-) ►*n*. An advocate of a particular ideology. [Fr. *idéologue* < *idéologie*, ideology.]

i·de·ol·o·gy (ī′dē-ŏl′ə-jē, ĭd′ē-) ►*n*., *pl*. **-gies 1.** The body of ideas reflecting the social needs and aspirations of an individual, group, class, or culture. **2.** A systematic set of doctrines or beliefs. —**i′de·o·log′i·cal** (ī′dē-ə-lŏj′ĭ-kəl, ĭd′ē-) *adj*. —**i′de·o·log′i·cal·ly** *adv*. —**i′de·ol′o·gist** *n*.

ides (īdz) ►*pl.n*. (takes sing. or pl. v.) The 15th day of March, May, July, or October or the 13th day of the other months in the ancient Roman calendar. [< Lat. *īdūs*.]

id·i·o·cy (ĭd′ē-ə-sē) ►*n*., *pl*. **-cies 1.** Extreme folly or stupidity. **2.** The condition of profound mental retardation. [< IDIOT.]

id·i·om (ĭd′ē-əm) ►*n*. **1.** An expression having a meaning that cannot be understood from the individual meanings of its elements, as in *hand over fist*. **2.** The specific grammatical, syntactic, and structural character of a given language. **3.** Regional speech or dialect. [< Gk. *idiōma* < *idios*, one's own.] —**id′i·o·mat′ic** (-ə-măt′ĭk) *adj*. —**id′i·o·mat′i·cal·ly** *adv*.

id·i·op·a·thy (ĭd′ē-ŏp′ə-thē) ►*n*. A disease of unknown cause. [Gk. *idios*, one's own + -PATHY.] —**id′i·o·path′ic** (-ə-păth′ĭk) *adj*.

id·i·o·syn·cra·sy (ĭd′ē-ō-sĭng′krə-sē) ►*n*., *pl*. **-sies** A structural or behavioral peculiarity; eccentricity. [Gk. *idiosunkrasia*.] —**id′i·o·syn·crat′ic** (-sĭn-krăt′ĭk) *adj*. —**id′i·o·syn·crat′i·cal·ly** *adv*.

id·i·ot (ĭd′ē-ət) ►*n*. A foolish or stupid person. [< Gk. *idiōtēs*, layman < *idios*, private.] —**id′i·ot′ic** (-ŏt′ĭk) *adj*. —**id′i·ot′i·cal·ly** *adv*.

i·dle (īd′l) ►*adj*. **i·dler, i·dlest 1a.** Not employed or busy. See Synonyms at **inactive. b.** Disinclined to work; lazy. **c.** Not in use or operation: *idle mills*. **2.** Lacking substance or basis. See Synonyms at **baseless, vain.** ►*v*. **i·dled, i·dling 1.** To pass time without being engaged in purposeful activity. **2.** To move slowly or without purpose. **3.** To run or cause to run at a slow speed or out of gear. [< OE *īdel*.] —**i′dle·ness** *n*. —**i′dler** *n*. —**i′dly** *adv*.

i·dol (īd′l) ►*n*. **1.** An image used as an object of worship. **2.** One that is adored. [< Gk. *eidōlon*, image < *eidos*, form.]

i·dol·a·try (ī-dŏl′ə-trē) ►*n*., *pl*. **-tries 1.** Worship of idols. **2.** Excessive devotion. [Ult. < Gk. *eidōlolatria* : *eidōlon*, IDOL + *latreia*, service.] —**i·dol′a·ter** *n*. —**i·dol′a·trous** *adj*. —**i·dol′a·trous·ly** *adv*.

i·dol·ize (īd′l-īz′) ►*v*. **-ized, -iz·ing 1.** To regard with excessive or uncritical admiration or devotion. **2.** To worship as an idol. —**i′dol·i·za′tion** *n*. —**i′dol·iz′er** *n*.

i·dyll also **i·dyl** (īd′l) ►*n*. **1.** A short poem idealizing rural life. **2.** A scene or event of a simple and tranquil nature. **3.** A romantic interlude. [< Gk. *eidullion*, dim. of *eidos*, form.] —**i·dyl′lic** (ī-dĭl′ĭk) *adj*. —**i·dyl′li·cal·ly** *adv*.

IE ►*abbr*. **1.** Indo-European **2.** industrial engineer **3.** industrial engineering

i.e. ►*abbr*. Lat. id est (that is)

-ie ►*suff*. Var. of **-y³**.

IED ►*abbr*. improvised explosive device

if (ĭf) ►*conj*. **1a.** In the event that: *If I were to go, I would be late.* **b.** Granting that: *If that is true, what can we do?* **c.** On the condition that: *She will sing only if she is paid.* **2.** Even though: *a handsome if useless trinket.* **3.** Whether: *Ask if he plans to come.* **4.** Used to introduce an exclamatory clause, indicating a wish: *If only he were here!* ►*n*. A possibility, condition, or stipulation: *no ifs, ands, or buts.* [< OE *gif*.]

Usage: In spoken English there is a growing tendency to use *would have* in place of subjunctive *had* in contrary-to-fact clauses, as in *if you would have kept quiet*. This usage is usu. considered incorrect in formal writing.

if·fy (ĭf′ē) ►*adj*. **-fi·er, -fi·est** *Informal* Doubtful; uncertain: *an iffy proposition.* —**if′fi·ness** *n*.

-ify ►*suff*. Var. of **-fy.**

Ig ►*abbr*. immunoglobulin

Ig·bo (ĭg′bō) also **I·bo** (ē′bō) ►*n*., *pl*. **Igbo** or **-bos** also **Ibo** or **-bos 1.** A member of a people of SE Nigeria. **2.** The language of the Igbo.

ig·loo (ĭg′lōō) ►*n*., *pl*. **-loos** A house made of blocks of snow, such as those built by the Inuit. [Inuit *iglu*, house, igloo.]

Ig·na·tius of Loy·o·la (ĭg-nā′shəs, loi-ō′lə), Saint. 1491–1556. Spanish ecclesiastic who founded the Jesuits.

ig·ne·ous (ĭg′nē-əs) ►*adj*. **1.** Of or relating to

fire. **2.** *Geol.* Formed by solidification from a molten state. [< Lat. *igneus* < *ignis*, fire.]

ig·nis fat·u·us (ĭg′nĭs făch′ōō-əs) ▸*n., pl.* **ig·nes fat·u·i** (ĭg′nēz făch′ōō-ī′) **1.** A phosphorescent light that hovers over swampy ground at night. **2.** Something that misleads or deludes; an illusion. [Med.Lat., foolish fire.]

ig·nite (ĭg-nīt′) ▸*v.* **-nit·ed, -nit·ing 1.** To set fire to or catch fire. **2.** To excite; kindle. [< Lat. *ignis*, fire.]

ig·ni·tion (ĭg-nĭsh′ən) ▸*n.* **1.** An act or instance of igniting. **2.** An electrical system that provides the spark to ignite the fuel mixture in an internal-combustion engine.

ig·no·ble (ĭg-nō′bəl) ▸*adj.* **1.** Not noble in quality or purpose; base or dishonorable. **2.** Not of high social status; common. [< Lat. *ignōbilis.*] —**ig′no·bil′i·ty** *n.* —**ig·no′bly** *adv.*

ig·no·min·y (ĭg′nə-mĭn′ē, -mə-nē) ▸*n., pl.* **-ies 1.** Personal dishonor or humiliation. **2.** Shameful or disgraceful conduct. [< Lat. *ignōminia.*] —**ig′no·min′i·ous** *adj.* —**ig′no·min′i·ous·ly** *adv.*

ig·no·ra·mus (ĭg′nə-rā′məs) ▸*n., pl.* **-mus·es** An ignorant person. [< Lat. *ignōrāmus,* we do not know.]

ig·no·rant (ĭg′nər-ənt) ▸*adj.* **1.** Lacking education or knowledge. **2.** Showing a lack of education or knowledge. **3.** Unaware or uninformed. [< Lat. *ignōrāre,* not know.] —**ig′no·rance** *n.* —**ig′no·rant·ly** *adv.*

ig·nore (ĭg-nôr′) ▸*v.* **-nored, -nor·ing** To choose not to pay attention to; disregard. [< Lat. *ignōrāre,* not know.] —**ig·nor′a·ble** *adj.* —**ig·nor′er** *n.*

i·gua·na (ĭ-gwä′nə) ▸*n.* A usu. large herbivorous lizard usu. of tropical America. [< Arawak *iwana.*]

IL ▸*abbr.* Illinois

il– ▸*pref.* Var. of **in–**¹.

–ile ▸*suff.* Of, relating to, or capable of: *infantile.* [< Lat. *-ilis.*]

il·e·i·tis (ĭl′ē-ī′tĭs) ▸*n.* Inflammation of the ileum. [ILE(UM) + -ITIS.]

il·e·um (ĭl′ē-əm) ▸*n., pl.* **-e·a** (-ē-ə) The terminal portion of the small intestine extending from the jejunum to the cecum. [LLat. *īleum,* groin.] —**il′e·al** *adj.*

il·i·um (ĭl′ē-əm) ▸*n., pl.* **-i·a** (-ē-ə) The uppermost of the three fused bones constituting either half of the pelvis. [LLat. *īlium,* groin, flank.] —**il′i·ac′** (-ăk′) *adj.*

ilk (ĭlk) ▸*n.* Type or kind: *a remark of that ilk.* [< OE *ilca,* same.]

ill (ĭl) ▸*adj.* **worse** (wûrs), **worst** (wûrst) **1.** Not healthy; sick. **2.** Unsound; bad: *ill effects.* **3.** Resulting in suffering; distressing. **4.** Hostile or unfriendly. **5.** Not favorable; unpropitious: *ill omen.* **6.** Not up to standard: *ill treatment.* **7.** *Slang* Excellent; outstanding. ▸*adv.* **worse, worst 1.** In a bad, inadequate, or improper manner. **2.** In an unfavorable way. **3.** Scarcely or with difficulty. ▸*n.* **1.** Evil. **2.** Something that causes suffering. —*idiom:* **ill at ease** Anxious or unsure; uneasy. [< ON *illr,* bad.]

I'll (īl) I will.

ill-ad·vised (ĭl′əd-vīzd′) ▸*adj.* Done without wise counsel or careful deliberation. —**ill′-ad·vis′ed·ly** (-vī′zĭd-lē) *adv.*

ill-bred (ĭl′brĕd′) ▸*adj.* Badly brought up; impolite and crude.

ill-con·sid·ered (ĭl′kən-sĭd′ərd) ▸*adj.* Unwise; foolish.

il·le·gal (ĭ-lē′gəl) ▸*adj.* **1.** Prohibited by law. **2.** *Sports & Games* Prohibited by official rules. **3.** Not performable by a computer. —**il·le·gal′i·ty** (ĭl′ē-găl′ĭtē) *n.* —**il·le′gal·ly** *adv.*

il·leg·i·ble (ĭ-lĕj′ə-bəl) ▸*adj.* Not legible. —**il·leg′i·bil′i·ty** *n.* —**il·leg′i·bly** *adv.*

il·le·git·i·mate (ĭl′ĭ-jĭt′ə-mĭt) ▸*adj.* **1.** Illegal. **2.** *Offensive* Born to parents who have never been married to each other. **3.** Incorrectly deduced; illogical. **4.** Not valid or defensible: *illegitimate reason for being late.* —**il·le·git′i·ma·cy** *n.* —**il·le·git′i·mate·ly** *adv.*

ill-fat·ed (ĭl′fā′tĭd) ▸*adj.* **1.** Destined for misfortune; doomed: *an ill-fated expedition.* **2.** Causing misfortune: *an ill-fated decision.* See Synonyms at **unfortunate.**

ill-fa·vored (ĭl′fā′vərd) ▸*adj.* **1.** Ugly or unattractive. See Synonyms at **ugly. 2.** Objectionable; offensive.

ill-found·ed (ĭl′foun′dĭd) ▸*adj.* Having no factual basis.

ill-got·ten (ĭl′gŏt′n) ▸*adj.* Obtained by dishonest or immoral means: *ill-gotten gains.*

ill humor ▸*n.* An irritable state of mind; surliness. —**ill′-hu′mored** (-mərd) *adj.*

il·lib·er·al (ĭ-lĭb′ər-əl) ▸*adj.* Narrow-minded; bigoted. —**il·lib·er·al′i·ty** (-ə-răl′ĭ-tē), **il·lib′er·al·ness** *n.*

il·lic·it (ĭ-lĭs′ĭt) ▸*adj.* Not permitted by custom or law; improper or unlawful. —**il·lic′it·ly** *adv.*

il·lim·it·a·ble (ĭ-lĭm′ĭ-tə-bəl) ▸*adj.* Impossible to limit; limitless. —**il·lim′it·a·bly** *adv.*

Il·li·nois¹ (ĭl′ə-noi′) ▸*n., pl.* **-nois 1.** A member of a Native American confederacy formerly inhabiting parts of Wisconsin, Illinois, Iowa, and Missouri. **2.** The Algonquian language of the Illinois.

Il·li·nois² (ĭl′ə-noi′) A state of the N-central US. Cap. Springfield. —**Il·li·nois′an** (-noi′ən) *adj. & n.*

il·lit·er·ate (ĭ-lĭt′ər-ĭt) ▸*adj.* **1.** Having little or no formal education, esp. unable to read and write. **2.** Unfamiliar with language and literature. **3.** Ignorant of the fundamentals of a given art or branch of knowledge. ▸*n.* A person who is illiterate. —**il·lit′er·a·cy** *n.*

ill-man·nered (ĭl′măn′ərd) ▸*adj.* Lacking good manners; rude.

ill-na·tured (ĭl′nā′chərd) ▸*adj.* Surly; disagreeable. —**ill′-na′tured·ly** *adv.*

ill·ness (ĭl′nĭs) ▸*n.* Sickness.

il·log·i·cal (ĭ-lŏj′ĭ-kəl) ▸*adj.* Contradicting or disregarding the principles of logic. —**il·log′i·cal′i·ty** (-kăl′ĭ-tē) *n.* —**il·log′i·cal·ly** *adv.*

ill-starred (ĭl′stärd′) ▸*adj.* Ill-fated; unlucky. See Synonyms at **unfortunate.**

ill-tem·pered (ĭl′tĕm′pərd) ▸*adj.* Having a bad temper; irritable. —**ill′-tem′pered·ly** *adv.*

ill-treat (ĭl′trēt′) ▸*v.* To treat unkindly or harshly; maltreat. —**ill′-treat′ment** *n.*

il·lu·mi·nate (ĭ-lōō′mə-nāt′) ▸*v.* **-nat·ed, -nat·ing 1.** To provide or brighten with light. **2a.** To make understandable; clarify. **b.** To enable to understand; enlighten. **3.** To adorn (a page of a book) with designs in brilliant colors. [< Lat. *illūmināre.*] —**il′lu·mi·na′tion** *n.* —**il·lu′mi·na′tor** *n.*

il·lu·mine (ĭ-lōō′mĭn) ▸*v.* **-mined, -min·ing** To give light to; illuminate. [< Lat. *illūmināre.*]

ill·us·age (ĭl′yo͞o′sĭj, -zĭj) ►*n.* Bad treatment; ill-use.

ill-use (ĭl′yo͞oz′) ►*v.* To treat badly or unjustly; maltreat. —**ill′-use′** (ĭl′yo͞os′) *n.*

il·lu·sion (ĭ-lo͞o′zhən) ►*n.* **1a.** An erroneous perception of reality. **b.** An erroneous concept or belief. **2.** Illusionism. [< Lat. *illūdere, illūs-*, to mock.] —**il·lu′sion·al, il·lu′sion·ar′y** (-zhə-nĕr′ē) *adj.*

il·lu·sion·ism (ĭ-lo͞o′zhə-nĭz′əm) ►*n.* The use of techniques such as foreshortening to produce the illusion of reality, esp. in visual art. —**il·lu′sion·ist** *n.* —**il·lu′sion·is′tic** *adj.*

il·lu·sive (ĭ-lo͞o′sĭv) ►*adj.* Illusory. —**il·lu′sive·ly** *adv.* —**il·lu′sive·ness** *n.*

il·lu·so·ry (ĭ-lo͞o′sə-rē, -zə-rē) ►*adj.* Produced by or based on an illusion; deceptive.

il·lus·trate (ĭl′ə-strāt′, ĭ-lŭs′trāt′) ►*v.* **-trat·ed, -trat·ing** **1a.** To clarify, as by use of examples. **b.** To serve as an instructive example of. **2.** To provide (a publication) with explanatory or decorative graphic features. [Lat. *illūstrāre.*] —**il′lus·tra′tor** *n.*

il·lus·tra·tion (ĭl′ə-strā′shən) ►*n.* **1.** The act of illustrating or the state of being illustrated. **2.** An image that is used to decorate or clarify a text. **3.** An example that is used to clarify or explain something.

il·lus·tra·tive (ĭ-lŭs′trə-tĭv, ĭl′ə-strā′tĭv) ►*adj.* Acting or serving as an illustration.

il·lus·tri·ous (ĭ-lŭs′trē-əs) ►*adj.* Highly distinguished; eminent. See Synonyms at **famous.** [< Lat. *illūstris,* shining.] —**il·lus′tri·ous·ly** *adv.* —**il·lus′tri·ous·ness** *n.*

ill will ►*n.* Unfriendly feeling; enmity.

Il·lyr·i·a (ĭ-lĭr′ē-ə) An ancient region of the Balkan Peninsula on the Adriatic coast. —**Il·lyr′i·an** *adj. & n.*

IM ►*v.* **IMed, IMing** **1.** To send (someone) an instant message. **2.** To express in an instant message. ►*n.* An instant message.

im-¹ ►*pref.* Var. of **in-¹.**

im-² ►*pref.* Var. of **in-².**

I'm (īm) I am.

im·age (ĭm′ĭj) ►*n.* **1.** A representation of the form of a person or object, such as a painting, photograph, or sculptured likeness. **2.** *Phys.* An optically formed duplicate of an object, esp. one formed by a lens or mirror. **3.** One that closely resembles another. **4.** An outward impression of character, esp. one projected to the public. **5.** A personification: *the image of good health.* **6.** A mental picture of something not real or present. **7.** A vivid description or representation in words, esp. a metaphor or simile. ►*v.* **-aged, -ag·ing** **1a.** To make a likeness of. **b.** To mirror or reflect. **2.** To picture mentally; imagine. **3.** To describe, esp. vividly. [< Lat. *imāgō, imāgin-.*]

im·age·ry (ĭm′ĭj-rē) ►*n., pl.* **-ries** **1.** Mental images. **2.** The use of vivid or figurative language to represent objects, actions, or ideas. **3.** Representative images.

i·mag·i·na·ble (ĭ-măj′ə-nə-bəl) ►*adj.* Capable of being imagined. —**i·mag′i·na·bly** *adv.* —**i·mag′i·na·ble·ness** *n.*

i·mag·i·nar·y (ĭ-măj′ə-nĕr′ē) ►*adj.* **1.** Having existence only in the imagination. **2.** *Math.* Of or being an imaginary number.

imaginary number ►*n. Math.* A complex number in which the imaginary part is not zero.

imaginary unit ►*n. Symbol* **i** The square root of −1.

i·mag·i·na·tion (ĭ-măj′ə-nā′shən) ►*n.* **1a.** The ability to form mental images of things that are not real or present. **b.** The formation of such images. **2.** Creative power. **3.** Attention, interest, or enthusiasm. —**i·mag′i·na·tive** (ĭ-măj′ə-nə-tĭv, -nā′tĭv) *adj.* —**i·mag′i·na·tive·ly** *adv.*

i·mag·ine (ĭ-măj′ĭn) ►*v.* **-ined, -in·ing** **1.** To form a mental image of. **2.** To think; conjecture. **3.** To fancy. [< Lat. *imāginārī.*]

i·ma·go (ĭ-mā′gō, ĭ-mä′-) ►*n., pl.* **-goes** or **-gi·nes** (-gə-nēz′) An insect in its sexually mature adult stage. [Lat. *imāgō,* image.]

i·mam also **I·mam** (ĭ-mäm′) ►*n. Islam* **1a.** The caliph who is successor to Muhammad as the leader of the Islamic community. **b.** The male prayer leader in a mosque. **2a.** Any of the founders of the four schools of law and theology. **b.** An authoritative scholar who founds a school of law or theology. [Ar. *'imām.*]

im·bal·ance (ĭm-băl′əns) ►*n.* A lack of balance, as in distribution. —**im·bal′anced** *adj.*

im·be·cile (ĭm′bə-sĭl, -səl) ►*n.* **1.** A stupid or silly person. **2.** *Psychol.* A person of moderate to severe mental retardation. No longer in use and now considered offensive. [< Lat. *imbēcillus.*] —**im′be·cil′ic** *adj.* —**im′be·cil′i·ty** *n.*

im·bibe (ĭm-bīb′) ►*v.* **-bibed, -bib·ing** **1.** To drink. **2.** To absorb or take in as if by drinking. [< Lat. *imbibere,* drink in.] —**im·bib′er** *n.*

im·bro·glio (ĭm-brōl′yō) ►*n., pl.* **-glios** **1a.** A difficult or intricate situation. **b.** A confused or complicated disagreement. **2.** A confused heap; tangle. [Ital.]

im·bue (ĭm-byo͞o′) ►*v.* **-bued, -bu·ing** **1.** To inspire or influence thoroughly; pervade. **2.** To stain or dye deeply. [< Lat. *imbuere.*]

Syns: *permeate, pervade, saturate, suffuse* **v.**

IMF ►*abbr.* International Monetary Fund

im·i·tate (ĭm′ĭ-tāt′) ►*v.* **-tat·ed, -tat·ing** **1a.** To use or follow as a model. **b.** To copy the mannerisms or speech of. **2.** To copy exactly; reproduce. **3.** To appear like; resemble. [Lat. *imitārī.*] —**im′i·ta·ble** *adj.* —**im′i·ta′tor** *n.*

im·i·ta·tion (ĭm′ĭ-tā′shən) ►*n.* **1.** The act of imitating. **2.** Something derived or copied from an original, often in an inferior way. —**im′i·ta′tion** *adj.*

im·i·ta·tive (ĭm′ĭ-tā′tĭv) ►*adj.* **1.** Of or involving imitation. **2.** Not original; derivative. **3.** Tending to imitate. **4.** Onomatopoeic. —**im′i·ta′tive·ly** *adv.*

im·mac·u·late (ĭ-măk′yə-lĭt) ►*adj.* **1.** Impeccably clean. **2.** Free from sin. **3.** Free from fault or error: *an immaculate record on the job.* [< Lat. *immaculātus.*] —**im·mac′u·late·ly** *adv.* —**im·mac′u·late·ness** *n.*

im·ma·nent (ĭm′ə-nənt) ►*adj.* **1.** Existing or remaining within; inherent. **2.** Restricted entirely to the mind; subjective. [< LLat. *immanēre,* remain in.] —**im′ma·nence, im′ma·nen·cy** *n.* —**im′ma·nent·ly** *adv.*

im·ma·te·ri·al (ĭm′ə-tîr′ē-əl) ►*adj.* **1.** Of no importance; inconsequential. See Synonyms at **irrelevant. 2.** Having no material body or form. —**im′ma·te′ri·al·ly** *adv.*

im·ma·ture (ĭm′ə-tyo͝or′, -cho͝or′, -to͝or′) ►*adj.* **1.** Not fully grown or developed. **2.** Marked by or suggesting a lack of normal maturity. —**im′-**

ma·ture′ly *adv.* —**im′ma·tur′i·ty** *n.*

im·meas·ur·a·ble (ĭ-mĕzh′ər-ə-bəl) ▸*adj.* Impossible to measure; limitless. See Synonyms at **incalculable.** —**im·meas′ur·a·bil′i·ty** *n.* —**im·meas′ur·a·bly** *adv.*

im·me·di·a·cy (ĭ-mē′dē-ə-sē) ▸*n., pl.* **-cies 1.** Directness. **2.** Urgency.

im·me·di·ate (ĭ-mē′dē-ĭt) ▸*adj.* **1.** Occurring at once; instant. **2.** Of or near the present time: *in the immediate future.* **3.** Close at hand; near: *in the immediate vicinity.* See Synonyms at **close. 4.** Next in line: *an immediate successor.* **5.** Occurring without interposition; direct. [< LLat. *immediātus.*] —**im·me′di·ate·ly** *adv.*

im·me·mo·ri·al (ĭm′ə-môr′ē-əl) ▸*adj.* Reaching beyond the limits of memory, tradition, or history. —**im′me·mo′ri·al·ly** *adv.*

im·mense (ĭ-mĕns′) ▸*adj.* **1.** Extremely large; huge. **2.** Of immeasurable size or extent. **3.** *Informal* Excellent. [< Lat. *immēnsus.*] —**im·mense′ly** *adv.* —**im·men′si·ty** *n.*

im·merse (ĭ-mûrs′) ▸*v.* **-mersed, -mers·ing 1.** To cover completely in a liquid. **2.** To baptize by submerging in water. **3.** To engage deeply; absorb. [< Lat. *immergere.*] —**im·mer′sion** *n.* —**im·mer′sive** *adj.*

im·mesh (ĭm-mĕsh′) ▸*v.* To enmesh.

im·mi·grant (ĭm′ĭ-grənt) ▸*n.* **1.** One who immigrates. **2.** A plant or animal that establishes itself in a new area or habitat.

im·mi·grate (ĭm′ĭ-grāt′) ▸*v.* **-grat·ed, -grat·ing** To enter and settle in a foreign country. See Usage Note at **migrate.** [Lat. *immigrāre.*]

im·mi·gra·tion (ĭm′ĭ-grā′shən) ▸*n.* **1.** The act or process of immigrating. **2.** The place where authorities check the documents of people entering a country.

im·mi·nent (ĭm′ə-nənt) ▸*adj.* About to occur. [< Lat. *imminēre,* hang over.] —**im′mi·nence** *n.* —**im′mi·nent·ly** *adv.*

im·mo·bile (ĭ-mō′bəl, -bēl′, -bīl′) ▸*adj.* **1.** Immovable; fixed. **2.** Not moving; motionless. —**im′mo·bil′i·ty** (-bĭl′ĭ-tē) *n.*

im·mo·bi·lize (ĭ-mō′bə-līz′) ▸*v.* **-lized, -liz·ing 1.** To render immobile. **2.** To fix the position of (a joint or fractured limb), as with a splint or cast. —**im·mo′bi·li·za′tion** *n.*

im·mod·er·ate (ĭ-mŏd′ər-ĭt) ▸*adj.* Extreme; excessive. —**im·mod′er·ate·ly** *adv.* —**im·mod′er·a′tion** *n.*

im·mod·est (ĭ-mŏd′ĭst) ▸*adj.* Not conforming to traditional sexual mores; indecent. —**im·mod′est·ly** *adv.* —**im·mod′es·ty** *n.*

im·mo·late (ĭm′ə-lāt′) ▸*v.* **-lat·ed, -lat·ing 1.** To kill (e.g., an animal) as a religious sacrifice. **2.** To kill, esp. by fire. [Lat. *immolāre,* sprinkle with meal.] —**im′mo·la′tion** *n.* —**im′mo·la′tor** *n.*

im·mor·al (ĭ-môr′əl, -mŏr′-) ▸*adj.* Contrary to established moral principles. —**im′mor·al′i·ty** *n.* —**im·mor′al·ly** *adv.*

im·mor·tal (ĭ-môr′tl) ▸*adj.* **1.** Not subject to death. **2.** Never to be forgotten; everlasting. [< Lat. *immortālis.*] —**im·mor′tal** *n.* —**im′mor·tal′i·ty** *n.* —**im·mor′tal·ize′** *v.*

im·mov·a·ble (ĭ-mōō′və-bəl) ▸*adj.* **1a.** Impossible to move. **b.** Incapable of movement. **2.** Unyielding; steadfast. **3.** Impassive; insensitive. **4.** *Law* Of or relating to things, such as trees and buildings, attached to real property. —**im·mov′a·bil′i·ty** *n.* —**im·mov′a·bly** *adv.*

im·mune (ĭ-myoōn′) ▸*adj.* **1.** Exempt. **2.** Resistant to infection by a specific pathogen. [< Lat. *immūnis.*] —**im·mun′i·ty** *n.*

immune response ▸*n.* An integrated bodily response to an antigen, esp. one mediated by lymphocytes and involving recognition of antigens by specific antibodies or previously sensitized lymphocytes.

immune system ▸*n.* The integrated body system of organs, tissues, cells, and cell products such as antibodies that differentiates self from nonself and neutralizes potentially pathogenic organisms or substances.

im·mu·nize (ĭm′yə-nīz′) ▸*v.* **-nized, -niz·ing** To render immune. —**im′mu·ni·za′tion** *n.*

immuno– ▸*pref.* Immune; immunity: *immunology.* [< IMMUNE.]

im·mu·no·de·fi·cien·cy (ĭm′yə-nō-dĭ-fĭsh′ən-sē, ĭ-myoō′-) ▸*n., pl.* **-cies** An inability to develop a normal immune response. —**im′mu·no·de·fi′cient** *adj.*

im·mu·no·glob·u·lin (ĭm′yə-nō-glŏb′yə-lĭn, ĭ-myoō′-) ▸*n.* Any of a group of proteins that function as antibodies in the body's immune response.

im·mu·nol·o·gy (ĭm′yə-nŏl′ə-jē) ▸*n.* The branch of medicine dealing with the immune system. —**im′mu·no·log′ic** (-nə-lŏj′ĭk), **im′mu·no·log′i·cal** *adj.* —**im′mu·no·log′i·cal·ly** *adv.* —**im′mu·nol′o·gist** *n.*

im·mu·no·sup·pres·sion (ĭm′yə-nō-sə-prĕsh′ən, ĭ-myoō′-) ▸*n.* Suppression of the immune response, as by drugs or radiation. —**im′mu·no·sup·pres′sant** (-prĕs′ənt) *n.* —**im′mu·no·sup·pres′sive** *adj.*

im·mure (ĭ-myoōr′) ▸*v.* **-mured, -mur·ing 1.** To confine within or as if within walls; imprison. **2.** To build into or entomb within a wall. [Med.Lat. *immūrāre* < Lat. *mūrus,* wall.] —**im·mure′ment** *n.*

im·mu·ta·ble (ĭ-myoō′tə-bəl) ▸*adj.* Not susceptible to change. —**im·mu·ta·bil′i·ty** *n.* —**im·mu′ta·bly** *adv.*

imp (ĭmp) ▸*n.* **1.** A mischievous child. **2.** A small demon. [< OE *impa,* young shoot, ult. < Gk. *emphuein,* implant : EN-² + *phuein,* make grow.] —**imp′ish** *adj.* —**imp′ish·ly** *adv.* —**imp′ish·ness** *n.*

im·pact (ĭm′păkt′) ▸*n.* **1a.** A collision. **b.** The force transmitted by a collision. **2.** The effect or impression of one thing on another. ▸*v.* (ĭm-păkt′, ĭm′păkt′) **1.** To pack firmly together. **2.** To strike forcefully. **3.** To affect or change. [< Lat. *impāctus,* p.part. of *impingere,* push against.] —**im·pac′tion** *n.*

im·pact·ed (ĭm-păk′tĭd) ▸*adj.* Wedged inside the gum in a manner prohibiting eruption into a normal position: *an impacted tooth.*

im·pair (ĭm-pâr′) ▸*v.* To diminish in strength, value, or quality; damage. [< VLat. *impēiōrāre,* make worse < Lat. *pēior,* worse.] —**im·pair′ment** *n.*

im·paired (ĭm-pârd′) ▸*adj.* **1.** Diminished; weakened: *structurally impaired.* **2.** Functioning poorly or incompetently: *an impaired driver.* **3.** Having a physical or mental disability: *learning-impaired.* ▸*n.* People who have a physical or mental disability considered as a group: *the visually impaired.*

im·pa·la (ĭm-pä′lə) ▸*n.* An African antelope noted for its leaping ability. [Zulu *im-pala.*]

im·pale (ĭm-pāl′) ►v. **-paled, -pal·ing 1.** To pierce with or as if with a sharp point. **2.** To torture or kill by impaling. [Med.Lat. *impālāre* < Lat. *pālus*, stake.] —**im·pale′ment** n. —**im·pal′er** n.

im·pal·pa·ble (ĭm-păl′pə-bəl) ►adj. **1.** Not perceptible to the touch; intangible. **2.** Difficult for the mind to grasp. —**im·pal′pa·bil′i·ty** n. —**im·pal′pa·bly** adv.

im·pan·el (ĭm-păn′əl) also **em·pan·el** (ĕm-) ►v. **-eled, -el·ing** also **-elled, -el·ling 1.** To include (a person's name) on a list of persons selected for jury duty. **2.** To select (a jury) for trial from such a list. —**im·pan′el·ment** n.

im·part (ĭm-pärt′) ►v. **1.** To grant a share of; bestow. **2.** To make known; disclose. **3.** To pass on: *imparts forward motion.* [< Lat. *impartīre*, share with.]

im·par·tial (ĭm-pär′shəl) ►adj. Not partial or biased; unprejudiced. —**im′par·ti·al′i·ty** (-shē-ăl′ĭ-tē) n. —**im·par′tial·ly** adv.

im·pass·a·ble (ĭm-păs′ə-bəl) ►adj. Impossible to pass or cross. —**im·pass′a·bil′i·ty** n. —**im·pass′a·bly** adv.

im·passe (ĭm′păs′) ►n. **1.** A road or passage having no exit. **2.** A situation allowing for no further progress; stalemate: *reached an impasse in the negotiations.* [Fr.]

im·pas·si·ble (ĭm-păs′ə-bəl) ►adj. **1.** Not subject to suffering or pain. **2.** Unfeeling.

im·pas·sioned (ĭm-păsh′ənd) ►adj. Filled with passion; fervent.

im·pas·sive (ĭm-păs′ĭv) ►adj. **1.** Not susceptible to emotion. **2.** Revealing no emotion; expressionless. —**im·pas′sive·ly** adv. —**im·pas′sive·ness, im′pas·siv′i·ty** n.

im·pa·tiens (ĭm-pā′shənz, -shəns) ►n., pl. **impatiens** Any of various plants of a genus which includes the jewelweed, esp. several species that are widely cultivated for their attractive flowers and foliage. [Lat. *impatiēns*, impatient.]

im·pa·tient (ĭm-pā′shənt) ►adj. **1.** Unable to wait patiently or tolerate delay; restless. **2.** Unable to endure opposition; intolerant. **3.** Restively eager or desirous; anxious. —**im·pa′tience** n. —**im·pa′tient·ly** adv.

im·peach (ĭm-pēch′) ►v. **1.** To bring formal charges against (a public official) for wrongdoing while in office. **2.** To raise doubts about: *impeach a witness's credibility.* [< LLat. *impedicāre*, entangle : IN-² + Lat. *pedica*, fetter.] —**im·peach′a·ble** adj. —**im·peach′er** n. —**im·peach′ment** n.
Usage: The verb *impeach* often occurs in popular usage with the meaning "to remove from office," but this use does not accord with the legal meaning of the word, which is limited to the formal accusation of wrongdoing. In strict usage, an official is impeached (accused), tried, and then convicted or acquitted.

im·pec·ca·ble (ĭm-pĕk′ə-bəl) ►adj. **1.** Having no flaws. See Synonyms at **perfect. 2.** Not capable of sinning or not liable to sin. [Lat. *impeccābilis* : IN-¹ + *peccāre*, to sin.] —**im·pec′ca·bil′i·ty** n. —**im·pec′ca·bly** adv.

im·pe·cu·ni·ous (ĭm′pĭ-kyo͞o′nē-əs) ►adj. Having little or no money. [< IN-¹ + Lat. *pecūnia*, money.] —**im′pe·cu′ni·ous·ly** adv. —**im′pe·cu′ni·ous·ness** n.

im·ped·ance (ĭm-pēd′ns) ►n. Symbol **Z** A measure of the total opposition to current flow in an alternating current circuit.

im·pede (ĭm-pēd′) ►v. **-ped·ed, -ped·ing** To retard or obstruct the progress of. See Synonyms at **hinder.** [Lat. *impedīre*.] —**im·ped′er** n.

im·ped·i·ment (ĭm-pĕd′ə-mənt) ►n. **1.** Something that impedes; hindrance or obstruction. **2.** A physical defect, esp. one that interferes with speech. [< Lat. *impedīmentum* < *impedīre*, IMPEDE.]

im·ped·i·men·ta (ĭm-pĕd′ə-mĕn′tə) ►pl.n. Objects, such as baggage, that impede or encumber. [Lat. *impedīmenta*.]

im·pel (ĭm-pĕl′) ►v. **-pelled, -pel·ling 1.** To urge to action. **2.** To drive forward; propel. [< Lat. *impellere*, drive against.]

im·pel·ler (ĭm-pĕl′ər) ►n. A rotor or rotor blade.

im·pend (ĭm-pĕnd′) ►v. **1.** To be about to occur. **2.** To threaten to happen; menace. [Lat. *impendēre*, hang over.]

im·pen·e·tra·ble (ĭm-pĕn′ĭ-trə-bəl) ►adj. **1.** Impossible to penetrate or enter. **2.** Impossible to understand. —**im·pen′e·tra·bil′i·ty** n. —**im·pen′e·tra·bly** adv.

im·pen·i·tent (ĭm-pĕn′ĭ-tənt) ►adj. Not repentant. —**im·pen′i·tence** n. —**im·pen′i·tent** n. —**im·pen′i·tent·ly** adv.

im·per·a·tive (ĭm-pĕr′ə-tĭv) ►adj. **1.** Necessary or urgent. **2.** Expressing a command or plea. **3.** *Gram.* Of or relating to the mood that expresses a command. [< Lat. *imperāre*, to command.] —**im·per′a·tive** n. —**im·per′a·tive·ly** adv.

im·per·cep·ti·ble (ĭm′pər-sĕp′tə-bəl) ►adj. **1.** Impossible or difficult to perceive. **2.** Insignificantly small or slight. —**im′per·cep′ti·bil′i·ty** n. —**im′per·cep′ti·bly** adv.

im·per·fect (ĭm-pûr′fĭkt) ►adj. **1.** Not perfect. **2.** *Gram.* Of or being a verb tense expressing a past action or condition as incomplete or continuous. ►n. *Gram.* **1.** The imperfect tense. **2.** A verb in the imperfect tense. —**im·per′fect·ly** adv.

im·per·fec·tion (ĭm′pər-fĕk′shən) ►n. **1.** The quality or condition of being imperfect. **2.** A defect; flaw.

im·pe·ri·al (ĭm-pîr′ē-əl) ►adj. **1.** Of or relating to an empire, emperor, or empress. **2.** Ruling over extensive territories or over colonies or dependencies. **3.** Regal; majestic. [< Lat. *imperium*, rule.] —**im·pe′ri·al·ly** adv.

im·pe·ri·al·ism (ĭm-pîr′ē-ə-lĭz′əm) ►n. The extension of a nation's authority by the establishment of economic and political dominance over other nations. —**im·pe′ri·al·ist** adj. & n. —**im·pe′ri·al·is′tic** adj.

im·per·il (ĭm-pĕr′əl) ►v. **-iled, -il·ing** or **-illed, -il·ling** To expose to peril. See Synonyms at **endanger.** —**im·per′il·ment** n.

im·pe·ri·ous (ĭm-pîr′ē-əs) ►adj. **1.** Arrogantly domineering or overbearing. See Synonyms at **dictatorial. 2.** Urgent; pressing. [< Lat. *imperium*, absolute rule.] —**im·pe′ri·ous·ly** adv. —**im·pe′ri·ous·ness** n.

im·per·ish·a·ble (ĭm-pĕr′ĭ-shə-bəl) ►adj. Not perishable. —**im·per′ish·a·bil′i·ty** n. —**im·per′ish·a·bly** adv.

im·per·ma·nent (ĭm-pûr′mə-nənt) ►adj. Not lasting; transient. —**im·per′ma·nence** n. —**im·per′ma·nent·ly** adv.

im·per·me·a·ble (ĭm-pûr′mē-ə-bəl) ►adj.

Impossible to permeate. —**im·per′me·a·bil′i·ty** *n.* —**im·per′me·a·bly** *adv.*

im·per·mis·si·ble (ĭm′pər-mĭs′ə-bəl) ►*adj.* Forbidden. —**im′per·mis′si·bil/i·ty** *n.*

im·per·son·al (ĭm-pûr′sə-nəl) ►*adj.* **1.** Not being a person: *an impersonal force.* **2a.** Showing no emotion: *an impersonal manner.* **b.** Not responsive to or expressive of human personalities: *an impersonal corporation.* —**im·per′-son·al/i·ty** (-sə-năl/ĭ-tē) *n.* —**im·per′son·al·ly** *adv.*

im·per·son·ate (ĭm-pûr′sə-nāt′) ►*v.* **-at·ed, -at·ing** To assume the character or appearance of. —**im·per′son·a′tion** *n.* —**im·per′son·a′tor** *n.*

im·per·ti·nent (ĭm-pûr′tn-ənt) ►*adj.* **1.** Impudent; insolent. **2.** Not pertinent. See Synonyms at **irrelevant.** —**im·per′ti·nence** *n.* —**im·per′ti·nent·ly** *adv.*

im·per·turb·a·ble (ĭm′pər-tûr′bə-bəl) ►*adj.* Unshakably calm and collected. —**im′per·turb′a·bil′i·ty** *n.* —**im′per·turb′a·bly** *adv.*

im·per·vi·ous (ĭm-pûr′vē-əs) ►*adj.* **1.** Incapable of being penetrated, as by water. **2.** Incapable of being affected: *impervious to fear.* —**im·per′vi·ous·ly** *adv.* —**im·per′vi·ous·ness** *n.*

im·pe·ti·go (ĭm′pĭ-tī′gō) ►*n.* A contagious bacterial skin infection marked by pustules. [< Lat. *impetīgō* < *impetere*, to attack.]

im·pet·u·ous (ĭm-pĕch′ōō-əs) ►*adj.* Acting or done quickly with little or inadequate thought. [< Lat. *impetus,* IMPETUS.] —**im·pet′u·os′i·ty** (ĭm-pĕch′ōō-ŏs′ĭ-tē) *n.* —**im·pet′u·ous·ly** *adv.* —**im·pet′u·ous·ness** *n.*

Syns: hasty, headlong, precipitate

im·pe·tus (ĭm′pĭ-təs) ►*n., pl.* **-tus·es 1.** An impelling force; impulse. **2.** The force or energy associated with a moving body. **3.** Something that incites; stimulus. [< Lat. *impetere,* go towards, attack.]

im·pi·e·ty (ĭm-pī′ĭ-tē) ►*n., pl.* **-ties 1.** The quality or state of being impious. **2.** An impious act.

im·pinge (ĭm-pĭnj′) ►*v.* **-pinged, -ping·ing 1a.** To encroach on something, such as a right. **b.** To have an effect upon. **2a.** To collide or strike against something. **b.** To advance over or press upon something. [Lat. *impingere,* fasten on.] —**im·pinge′ment** *n.* —**im·ping′er** *n.*

im·pi·ous (ĭm-pī′əs, ĭm′pē-) ►*adj.* Lacking reverence; not pious. —**im′pi·ous·ly** *adv.*

im·plac·a·ble (ĭm-plăk′ə-bəl, -plā′kə-) ►*adj.* Impossible to reconcile or appease: *implacable foes.* —**im·plac′a·bil′i·ty** *n.* —**im·plac′a·bly** *adv.*

im·plant (ĭm-plănt′) ►*v.* **1.** To set or fix firmly. **2.** To establish securely, as in the mind; instill. **3.** *Med.* To insert or embed (a tissue or device) surgically. **4.** To become attached to the uterine lining. Used of a fertilized egg. ►*n.* Something implanted, esp. a surgically implanted tissue or device. —**im′plan·ta′tion** *n.*

im·plau·si·ble (ĭm-plô′zə-bəl) ►*adj.* Difficult to believe; not plausible. —**im·plau′si·bil′i·ty** *n.* —**im·plau′si·bly** *adv.*

im·ple·ment (ĭm′plə-mənt) ►*n.* A tool or utensil. ►*v.* (-mĕnt′) To put into effect. [< Lat. *implēre,* fill up.] —**im′ple·men·ta′tion** *n.*

im·pli·cate (ĭm′plĭ-kāt′) ►*v.* **-cat·ed, -cat·ing 1.** To involve, esp. incriminatingly. **2.** To imply. [< Lat. *implicāre.*] —**im′pli·ca′tion** *n.*

im·plic·it (ĭm-plĭs′ĭt) ►*adj.* **1.** Implied or understood though not directly expressed. **2.** Contained in the nature of something though not readily apparent. **3.** Having no reservations; unquestioning: *implicit trust.* [Lat. *implicitus* < *implicāre,* implicate.] —**im·plic′it·ly** *adv.* —**im·plic′it·ness** *n.*

im·plode (ĭm-plōd′) ►*v.* **-plod·ed, -plod·ing 1.** To collapse inward violently. **2.** To demolish (a building) by causing to collapse inward. [IN-² + (EX)PLODE.] —**im·plo′sion** (-plō′zhən) *n.*

im·plore (ĭm-plôr′) ►*v.* **-plored, -plor·ing** To appeal to; beseech. [Lat. *implōrāre,* weep for.] —**im·plor′ing·ly** *adv.*

im·ply (ĭm-plī′) ►*v.* **-plied, -ply·ing 1.** To express or indicate indirectly. See Usage Note at **infer. 2.** To involve by logical necessity; entail. [< Lat. *implicāre,* implicate.]

im·po·lite (ĭm′pə-līt′) ►*adj.* Not polite; discourteous. —**im′po·lite′ly** *adv.* —**im′po·lite′ness** *n.*

im·pol·i·tic (ĭm-pŏl′ĭ-tĭk) ►*adj.* Not wise or expedient. —**im·pol′i·tic·ly** *adv.*

im·pon·der·a·ble (ĭm-pŏn′dər-ə-bəl) ►*adj.* That cannot undergo precise evaluation. —**im·pon′der·a·ble** *n.* —**im·pon′der·a·bil′i·ty** *n.* —**im·pon′der·a·bly** *adv.*

im·port (ĭm-pôrt′, ĭm′pôrt′) ►*v.* **1.** To bring in from an outside source, esp. from a foreign country, for sale. **2.** *Comp.* To receive (data) from one program into another. **3.** To signify. ►*n.* (ĭm′pôrt′, -pôrt′) **1.** Something imported. **2.** The occupation of importing goods or materials. **3.** Signification. **4.** Importance; significance. [< Lat. *importāre.*] —**im·port′er** *n.*

im·por·tant (ĭm-pôr′tnt) ►*adj.* **1.** Strongly affecting the course of events. **2.** Having high social rank or influence; prominent. **3.** Having or suggesting an air of authority; authoritative. [< Lat. *importāre,* be significant.] —**im·por′tance** *n.* —**im·por′tant·ly** *adv.*

im·por·ta·tion (ĭm′pôr-tā′shən) ►*n.* The act or business of importing.

im·por·tu·nate (ĭm-pôr′chə-nĭt) ►*adj.* Troublesomely urgent or persistent. —**im·por′tu·nate·ly** *adv.* —**im·por′tu·nate·ness** *n.*

im·por·tune (ĭm′pôr-tōōn′, -tyōōn′, ĭm-pôr′-chən) ►*v.* **-tuned, -tun·ing** To make an earnest request of (someone), esp. insistently or repeatedly. [< Lat. *importūnus,* inopportune.] —**im′por·tune′ly** *adv.* —**im′por·tun′er** *n.*

im·pose (ĭm-pōz′) ►*v.* **-posed, -pos·ing 1.** To establish as compulsory; levy: *impose a tax.* **2.** To apply or make prevail by authority or force: *impose a settlement.* **3.** To force (oneself) on others. **4.** To pass off on others: *imposed a fraud on consumers.* **5.** To take unfair advantage: *imposing on their generosity.* [< Lat. *impōnere,* place upon.] —**im·pos′er** *n.* —**im′po·si′tion** (ĭm′pə-zĭsh′ən) *n.*

im·pos·ing (ĭm-pō′zĭng) ►*adj.* Impressive. —**im·pos′ing·ly** *adv.*

im·pos·si·ble (ĭm-pŏs′ə-bəl) ►*adj.* **1.** Incapable of existing or occurring. **2.** Not capable of being accomplished. **3.** Unacceptable. **4.** Extremely difficult to deal with or tolerate. —**im·pos′si·bil′i·ty** *n.* —**im·pos′si·bly** *adv.*

im·post (ĭm′pōst′) ►*n.* A tax or duty. [< Med. Lat. *impostum* < Lat. *impōnere,* place upon.]

im·pos·tor (ĭm-pŏs′tər) ►*n.* One who deceives under an assumed identity. [< LLat.]

im·pos·ture (ĭm-pŏs′chər) ►*n.* The act or instance of engaging in deception under an assumed identity. [< LLat. *impostūra* < Lat. *impōnere,* IMPOSE.]

im·po·tent (ĭm′pə-tənt) ►*adj.* **1.** Lacking physical strength or vigor. **2.** Lacking in power; helpless. **3.** *Physiol.* Incapable of penile erection. —**im′po·tence** *n.* —**im′po·tent·ly** *adv.*

im·pound (ĭm-pound′) ►*v.* **1.** To confine in or as if in a pound: *impound stray dogs.* **2.** To place (something) in legal custody until a dispute involving it is decided. **3.** To set aside in a fund rather than spend as prescribed. **4.** To accumulate and store (water) in a reservoir. ►*n.* A place where impounded property is stored. —**im·pound′er** *n.* —**im·pound′ment** *n.*

im·pov·er·ish (ĭm-pŏv′ər-ĭsh, -pŏv′rĭsh) ►*v.* **1.** To reduce to poverty. **2.** To deprive of richness or strength. [< OFr. *empovrir* < *povre,* poor.] —**im·pov′er·ish·ment** *n.*

im·prac·ti·ca·ble (ĭm-prăk′tĭ-kə-bəl) ►*adj.* Impossible to do or carry out. —**im·prac′ti·ca·bil′i·ty** *n.* —**im·prac′ti·ca·bly** *adv.*

im·prac·ti·cal (ĭm-prăk′tĭ-kəl) ►*adj.* **1.** Unwise to implement or maintain in practice. **2.** Unable to deal efficiently with practical matters. **3.** Impracticable. —**im·prac′ti·cal′i·ty** (-kăl′ĭ-tē) *n.*

im·pre·ca·tion (ĭm′prĭ-kā′shən) ►*n.* A curse. [< Lat. *imprecārī,* to curse.]

im·pre·cise (ĭm′prĭ-sīs′) ►*adj.* Not precise. —**im′pre·cise′ly** *adv.* —**im′pre·ci′sion** (-sĭzh′ən) *n.*

im·preg·na·ble (ĭm-prĕg′nə-bəl) ►*adj.* **1.** Impossible to capture or enter by force. **2.** Beyond challenge or refutation. [< OFr. *imprenable.*]

im·preg·nate (ĭm-prĕg′nāt) ►*v.* **-nat·ed, -nat·ing** **1.** To make pregnant; inseminate. **2.** To fertilize (an ovum). **3.** To fill throughout; saturate. **4.** To permeate or imbue: *impregnate a speech with optimism.* [Prob. < LLat. *impraegnātus,* pregnant < Lat. *praegnāns.*] —**im′preg·na′tion** *n.* —**im·preg′na′tor** *n.*

im·pre·sa·ri·o (ĭm′prĭ-sär′ē-ō′, -sâr′-) ►*n., pl.* **-os** **1.** One who sponsors or produces entertainment, esp. the director of an opera company. **2.** A manager; producer. [Ital. < *impresa,* undertaking.]

im·press¹ (ĭm-prĕs′) ►*v.* **1.** To affect strongly, often favorably. **2.** To produce a vivid impression of. **3.** To mark or stamp with pressure. **4.** To apply with pressure. ►*n.* (ĭm′prĕs′) **1.** The act of impressing. **2.** A mark or pattern produced by impressing. **3.** A stamp or seal to be impressed. [< Lat. *imprimere, impress-,* imprint.] —**im·press′i·bil′i·ty** *n.* —**im·press′i·ble** *adj.*

im·press² (ĭm-prĕs′) ►*v.* **1.** To compel (a person) to serve in a military force. **2.** To confiscate (property), esp. for military purposes. [IN-² + *press,* force into service.] —**im·press′ment** *n.*

im·pres·sion (ĭm-prĕsh′ən) ►*n.* **1.** An effect, feeling, or image retained after an experience. **2.** A vague notion, remembrance, or belief. **3.** A mark produced on a surface by pressure. **4.** *Print.* **a.** All the copies of a publication printed at one time from the same set of type. **b.** A single copy of such a printing. **5.** A humorous imitation esp. of a famous person.

im·pres·sion·a·ble (ĭm-prĕsh′ə-nə-bəl) ►*adj.* Readily or easily influenced; suggestible.

—**im·pres′sion·a·bil′i·ty** *n.*

im·pres·sion·ism (ĭm-prĕsh′ə-nĭz′əm) ►*n.* A style of painting marked by concentration on the immediate visual impression produced by a scene and by the use of unmixed primary colors and small strokes to simulate actual reflected light. —**im·pres′sion·ist** *n.* —**im·pres′sion·is′tic** *adj.* —**im·pres′sion·is′ti·cal·ly** *adv.*

im·pres·sive (ĭm-prĕs′ĭv) ►*adj.* Making a strong positive impression; inspiring admiration: *an impressive achievement.* —**im·pres′sive·ly** *adv.* —**im·pres′sive·ness** *n.*

im·pri·ma·tur (ĭm′prə-mä′tŏŏr, -mä′tər) ►*n.* **1.** Official approval or license to print or publish, esp. as granted by a censor or an ecclesiastical authority. **2.** Official approval; sanction. [NLat. *imprimātur,* let it be printed.]

im·print (ĭm-prĭnt′) ►*v.* **1.** To produce (a mark or pattern) on a surface. **2.** To impart a strong impression of. **3.** To fix firmly, as in the mind. ►*n.* (ĭm′prĭnt′) **1.** A mark or pattern produced by imprinting. **2.** A distinguishing influence or effect: *the imprint of Islamic rule.* **3.** A publisher's name, printed at the bottom of a title page. [< OFr. *empreinte,* impression.]

im·pris·on (ĭm-prĭz′ən) ►*v.* To put in or as if in prison. [< OFr. *emprisoner.*] —**im·pris′on·a·ble** *adj.* —**im·pris′on·ment** *n.*

im·prob·a·ble (ĭm-prŏb′ə-bəl) ►*adj.* Unlikely to happen or be true. —**im·prob′a·bil′i·ty** *n.* —**im·prob′a·bly** *adv.*

im·promp·tu (ĭm-prŏmp′tŏŏ, -tyŏŏ) ►*adj.* **1.** Prompted by the occasion rather than being planned in advance. **2.** Extemporaneous. [< Lat. *in prŏmptū,* in readiness.]

im·prop·er (ĭm-prŏp′ər) ►*adj.* **1.** Not suited to circumstances or needs; unsuitable. **2.** Not in keeping with conventional mores; indecorous. **3.** Not consistent with fact; incorrect. —**im·prop′er·ly** *adv.*

improper fraction ►*n.* A fraction in which the numerator is larger than or equal to the denominator.

im·pro·pri·e·ty (ĭm′prə-prī′ĭ-tē) ►*n., pl.* **-ties** **1.** The quality of being improper. **2.** An improper act or expression.

im·prove (ĭm-prŏŏv′) ►*v.* **-proved, -prov·ing** **1.** To make or become better. **2.** To increase the productivity or value of (property). [ME *improwen,* to enclose (land) for cultivation.]

im·prove·ment (ĭm-prŏŏv′mənt) ►*n.* **1a.** The act or process of improving. **b.** The state of being improved. **2.** A change or addition that improves.

im·prov·i·dent (ĭm-prŏv′ĭ-dənt) ►*adj.* Not providing for the future; thriftless. —**im·prov′i·dence** *n.* —**im·prov′i·dent·ly** *adv.*

im·pro·vise (ĭm′prə-vīz′) ►*v.* **-vised, -vis·ing** **1.** To invent, compose, or recite without preparation. **2.** To make or provide from available materials: *improvised a hasty dinner.* [< Lat. *imprŏvīsus,* unforeseen : IN-¹ + *prŏvidēre,* foresee; see PROVIDE.] —**im·prov′i·sa′tion** (ĭm-prŏv′ĭ-zā′shən) *n.* —**im′pro·vis′er** *n.*

im·pru·dent (ĭm-prŏŏd′nt) ►*adj.* Unwise or indiscreet; not prudent. —**im·pru′dence** *n.* —**im·pru′dent·ly** *adv.*

im·pu·dent (ĭm′pyə-dənt) ►*adj.* Brashly bold; insolent; impertinent. [< Lat. *impudēns,* immodest.] —**im′pu·dence** *n.* —**im′pu·dent·ly** *adv.*

im·pugn (ĭm-pyo͞on′) ►*v.* To attack as false or questionable; challenge. [< Lat. *impugnāre*, fight against.] —**im·pugn′a·ble** *adj.* —**im·pugn′er** *n.*

im·pulse (ĭm′pŭls′) ►*n.* **1a.** An impelling force. **b.** The motion produced by such a force. **2.** A sudden wish or urge that prompts an unpremeditated act. **3.** A motivating force. **4.** *Physiol.* The electrochemical transmission of a signal along a nerve fiber that produces a response at a target tissue. [Lat. *impulsus* < p.part. of *impellere*, impel.]

im·pul·sive (ĭm-pŭl′sĭv) ►*adj.* **1.** Inclined to act on impulse rather than thought. **2.** Resulting from impulse; spontaneous. **3.** Having power to impel. —**im·pul′sive·ly** *adv.* —**im·pul′sive·ness** *n.*

im·pu·ni·ty (ĭm-pyo͞o′nĭ-tē) ►*n.* Exemption from punishment or penalty. [< Lat. *impūne*, without punishment.]

im·pure (ĭm-pyo͞or′) ►*adj.* **1.** Not clean; contaminated. **2.** Immoral or sinful. **3.** Mixed with another substance; adulterated. —**im·pure′ly** *adv.* —**im·pure′ness** *n.* —**im·pu′ri·ty** *n.*

im·pute (ĭm-pyo͞ot′) ►*v.* **-put·ed, -put·ing 1.** To charge with the fault or responsibility for. **2.** To attribute; credit. [< Lat. *imputāre*, reckon in.] —**im·put′a·ble** *adj.* —**im′pu·ta′tion** *n.*

in¹ (ĭn) ►*prep.* **1.** Within the limits, bounds, or area of. **2.** From the outside to the inside of; into: *threw it in the wastebasket.* **3.** To or at a situation or condition of: *in love.* **4.** Having the activity, occupation, or function of: *a life in politics.* **5.** By means of: *paid in cash.* **6.** With reference to: *six inches in depth.* ►*adv.* **1.** To or toward the inside. **2.** To or toward a place. **3.** Within a place, as of business or residence. ►*adj.* **1.** Located inside; inner. **2.** Incoming. **3.** Holding office; having power. **4.** *Informal* Currently fashionable. See Synonyms at **fashionable.** ►*n.* **1.** One with position, influence, or power. **2.** *Informal* Influence. [< OE.]

in² or **in.** ►*abbr.* inch

IN ►*abbr.* Indiana

in–¹ or **il–** or **im–** or **ir–** ►*pref.* Not: *inarticulate.* [< Lat.]

in–² or **im–** or **ir–** ►*pref.* **1.** In; into; within: *irradiate.* **2.** Var. of **en–¹.** [< Lat. *in* and OE *in.*]

–in ►*suff.* **1.** Neutral chemical compound: *globulin; pepsin.* **2.** A pharmaceutical: *niacin.* **3.** An antibiotic: *penicillin.* **4.** Var. of **–ine²** (sense 1). [Var. of **–INE².**]

in·a·bil·i·ty (ĭn′ə-bĭl′ĭ-tē) ►*n.* Lack of ability or means.

in ab·sen·tia (ĭn ăb-sĕn′shə, -shē-ə) ►*adv.* While or although not present. [Lat. *in absentiā.*]

in·ac·ces·si·ble (ĭn′ăk-sĕs′ə-bəl) ►*adj.* Not accessible; unapproachable. —**in′ac·ces′si·bil′i·ty** *n.* —**in′ac·ces′si·bly** *adv.*

in·ac·cu·rate (ĭn-ăk′yər-ĭt) ►*adj.* Mistaken or incorrect; not accurate. —**in·ac′cu·ra·cy** *n.* —**in·ac′cu·rate·ly** *adv.*

in·ac·tion (ĭn-ăk′shən) ►*n.* Lack or absence of action.

in·ac·ti·vate (ĭn-ăk′tə-vāt′) ►*v.* **-vat·ed, -vat·ing** To render inactive. —**in·ac′ti·va′tion** *n.*

in·ac·tive (ĭn-ăk′tĭv) ►*adj.* **1.** Not active or functioning; idle. **2.** Retired from duty or service. —**in·ac′tive·ly** *adv.* —**in′ac·tiv′i·ty** *n.*
    Syns: idle, inert, dormant, latent adj.

in·ad·e·quate (ĭn-ăd′ĭ-kwĭt) ►*adj.* Not adequate; insufficient. —**in·ad′e·qua·cy** *n.* —**in·ad′e·quate·ly** *adv.*

in·ad·mis·si·ble (ĭn′əd-mĭs′ə-bəl) ►*adj.* Not admissible. —**in′ad·mis′si·bil′i·ty** *n.* —**in′ad·mis′si·bly** *adv.*

in·ad·ver·tent (ĭn′əd-vûr′tnt) ►*adj.* **1.** Marked by carelessness. **2.** Unintentional. **3.** Unwitting. [< Med.Lat. *inadvertentia*, inadvertence.] —**in′ad·ver′tence** *n.* —**in′ad·ver′tent·ly** *adv.*

in·ad·vis·a·ble (ĭn′əd-vī′zə-bəl) ►*adj.* Not recommended; unwise. —**in′ad·vis′a·bil′i·ty** *n.*

in·al·ien·a·ble (ĭn-āl′yə-nə-bəl, -ā′lē-ə-) ►*adj.* That cannot be transferred to another. —**in·al′ien·a·bil′i·ty** *n.* —**in·al′ien·a·bly** *adv.*

in·ane (ĭn-ān′) ►*adj.* **-an·er, -an·est** Lacking sense or substance. [Lat. *inānis.*] —**in·ane′ly** *adv.* —**in·an′i·ty** (ĭ-năn′ĭ-tē) *n.*

in·an·i·mate (ĭn-ăn′ə-mĭt) ►*adj.* Lacking the qualities of active, living organisms; not animate. —**in·an′i·mate·ly** *adv.*

in·a·ni·tion (ĭn′ə-nĭsh′ən) ►*n.* Exhaustion, as from lack of nourishment or vitality. [< Lat. *inānīre*, make empty < *inānis*, empty.]

in·ap·pli·ca·ble (ĭn-ăp′lĭ-kə-bəl, ĭn′ə-plĭk′ə-) ►*adj.* Not applicable. —**in·ap′pli·ca·bil′i·ty** *n.*

in·ap·pre·cia·ble (ĭn′ə-prē′shə-bəl) ►*adj.* Too small to be noticed; negligible. —**in′ap·pre′cia·bly** *adv.*

in·ap·pro·pri·ate (ĭn′ə-prō′prē-ĭt) ►*adj.* Unsuitable or improper; not appropriate. —**in′ap·pro′pri·ate·ly** *adv.* —**in′ap·pro′pri·ate·ness** *n.*

in·apt (ĭn-ăpt′) ►*adj.* Inappropriate. —**in·apt′ly** *adv.* —**in·apt′ness** *n.*

in·ar·tic·u·late (ĭn′är-tĭk′yə-lĭt) ►*adj.* **1.** Uttered without the use of normal words or syllables. **2.** Unable to speak; speechless. **3.** Unable to speak with clarity or eloquence. **4.** Going unexpressed: *inarticulate sorrow.* **5.** *Biol.* Not having joints. —**in′ar·tic′u·late·ly** *adv.*

in·as·much as (ĭn′əz-mŭch′) ►*conj.* Because of the fact that; since.

in·at·ten·tion (ĭn′ə-tĕn′shən) ►*n.* Lack of attention, notice, or regard. —**in′at·ten′tive** *adj.* —**in′at·ten′tive·ly** *adv.* —**in′at·ten′tive·ness** *n.*

in·au·di·ble (ĭn-ô′də-bəl) ►*adj.* Impossible to hear. —**in·au′di·bly** *adv.*

in·au·gu·ral (ĭn-ô′gyər-əl, -gər-) ►*adj.* **1.** Of or relating to an inauguration. **2.** Initial; first. ►*n.* An inaugural speech.

in·au·gu·rate (ĭn-ô′gyə-rāt′, -gə-) ►*v.* **-rat·ed, -rat·ing 1.** To induct into office by a formal ceremony. **2.** To begin, esp. formally. [Lat. *inaugurāre* : IN–² + *augur*, seer.] —**in·au′gu·ra′tor** *n.*

in·au·gu·ra·tion (ĭn-ô′gyə-rā′shən, -gə-) ►*n.* **1.** Formal induction into office. **2.** A formal beginning or introduction.

in·aus·pi·cious (ĭn′ô-spĭsh′əs) ►*adj.* Not favorable; not auspicious. —**in′aus·pi′cious·ly** *adv.* —**in′aus·pi′cious·ness** *n.*

in·board (ĭn′bôrd′) ►*adj.* **1.** Within the hull of a vessel. **2.** Close to the fuselage of an aircraft: *the inboard engines.* —**in′board′** *adv.*

in·born (ĭn′bôrn′) ►*adj.* Existing by heredity rather than being learned through experience.

in·bound (ĭn′bound′) ►*adv. & adj.* Incoming: *a subway traveling inbound; inbound traffic.*

in·bred (ĭn′brĕd′) ►*adj.* **1.** Produced by inbreeding. **2.** Involving a homogenous group of people. **3.** Innate; deep-seated.

in·breed (ĭn′brēd′) ►v. To breed by the continued mating of closely related individuals.

Inc. ►abbr. incorporated

In·ca (ĭng′kə) ►n., pl. **-ca** or **-cas 1.** A member of a Quechuan people who established an empire centered in highland Peru before the Spanish conquest. **2.** A ruler of the Inca empire. —**In′can** adj.

in·cal·cu·la·ble (ĭn-kăl′kyə-lə-bəl) ►adj. **1.** Impossible to calculate, esp. too great to be conceived. **2.** Unforeseeable; unpredictable. —**in·cal′cu·la·bly** adv.

    Syns: countless, immeasurable, inestimable, infinite, innumerable, measureless **Ant:** *calculable* **adj.**

in·can·des·cent (ĭn′kən-dĕs′ənt) ►adj. **1.** Emitting visible light as a result of being heated. **2.** Shining brilliantly; very bright. [< Lat. *incandēscere,* to glow.] —**in′can·des′cence** n. —**in′can·des′cent·ly** adv.

in·can·ta·tion (ĭn′kăn-tā′shən) ►n. **1.** Ritual recitation of verbal charms or spells to produce a magic effect. **2.** A charm or spell used in ritual recitation. [< Lat. *incantāre,* enchant.] —**in′can·ta′tion·al** adj.

in·ca·pa·ble (ĭn-kā′pə-bəl) ►adj. Lacking the necessary ability, capacity, or power to perform adequately. —**in·ca′pa·bil′i·ty, in·ca′pa·ble·ness** n. —**in·ca′pa·bly** adv.

in·ca·pac·i·tate (ĭn′kə-păs′ĭ-tāt′) ►v. **-tat·ed, -tat·ing** To deprive of strength or ability; disable. —**in·ca′pac·i·ta′tion** n.

in·ca·pac·i·ty (ĭn′kə-păs′ĭ-tē) ►n., pl. **-ties 1.** Inadequate capacity, strength, or ability. **2.** A defect or handicap; disability.

in·car·cer·ate (ĭn-kär′sə-rāt′) ►v. **-at·ed, -at·ing 1.** To imprison. **2.** To confine. [Med.Lat. *incarcerāre* < Lat. *carcer,* prison.] —**in·car′cer·a′tion** n.

in·car·nate (ĭn-kär′nĭt) ►adj. **1.** Invested with bodily nature and form. **2.** Personified: *evil incarnate.* ►v. (-nāt′) **-nat·ed, -nat·ing 1.** To give bodily, esp. human, form to. **2.** To personify; embody. [< LLat. *incarnātus,* p.part. of *incarnāre,* make flesh.]

in·car·na·tion (ĭn′kär-nā′shən) ►n. **1.** The act of incarnating or condition of being incarnated. **2. Incarnation** The Christian doctrine that God the Son became man. **3.** One who personifies something.

in·cau·tious (ĭn-kô′shəs) ►adj. Not cautious; rash. —**in·cau′tious·ly** adv.

in·cen·di·ar·y (ĭn-sĕn′dē-ĕr′ē) ►adj. **1a.** Causing or designed to cause fires. **b.** Intentionally started or set. **2.** Tending to arouse conflict; inflammatory. [< Lat. *incendium,* fire.] —**in·cen′di·ar′y** n.

in·cense[1] (ĭn-sĕns′) ►v. **-censed, -cens·ing** To cause to be extremely angry; infuriate. [< Lat. *incendere, incēns-,* set on fire.]

in·cense[2] (ĭn′sĕns′) ►n. **1.** An aromatic substance burned to produce a pleasant odor. **2.** The smoke or odor produced by the burning of incense. [< Lat. *incēnsum.*]

in·cen·tive (ĭn-sĕn′tĭv) ►n. Something, such as a punishment or reward, that induces action. [< LLat. *incentīvus,* inciting.]

in·cep·tion (ĭn-sĕp′shən) ►n. The beginning of something. [< Lat. *incipere, incept-,* take up, begin.] —**in·cep′tive** adj.

in·cer·ti·tude (ĭn-sûr′tĭ-tōōd′, -tyōōd′) ►n. **1.** Uncertainty. **2.** Insecurity or instability.

in·ces·sant (ĭn-sĕs′ənt) ►adj. Continuing without interruption. [< Lat. *incessāns,* unceasing.] —**in·ces′san·cy** n. —**in·ces′sant·ly** adv.

in·cest (ĭn′sĕst′) ►n. **1.** Sexual relations between persons so closely related that their marriage is illegal or forbidden by custom. **2.** The crime of sexual relations with a person defined by statute as too closely related. [< Lat. *incestus,* unchaste.] —**in·ces′tu·ous** (ĭn-sĕs′chōō-əs) adj. —**in·ces′tu·ous·ly** adv.

inch (ĭnch) ►n. **1.** See table at **measurement. 2.** A very small degree or amount: *won't budge an inch.* ►v. To move or cause to move slowly or by small degrees. [< Lat. *uncia,* twelfth part.]

In·cheon also **In·chon** (ĭn′chŏn′) A city of NW South Korea on an inlet of the Yellow Sea SW of Seoul.

in·cho·ate (ĭn-kō′ĭt) ►adj. Being in a beginning or early stage; incipient. [< Lat. *inchoāre,* begin.] —**in·cho′ate·ly** adv.

inch·worm (ĭnch′wûrm′) ►n. A caterpillar that moves by looping the body in alternate contractions and expansions.

in·ci·dence (ĭn′sĭ-dəns) ►n. The rate or extent of occurrence or effect.

in·ci·dent (ĭn′sĭ-dənt) ►n. **1.** A particular occurrence, esp. one of minor importance. **2a.** A usu. violent or disruptive occurrence, esp. one that precipitates a larger crisis. **b.** An occurrence that interrupts normal procedure or functioning; mishap. ►adj. **1.** Tending to arise or occur as a result. **2.** *Phys.* Striking a surface: *incident radiation.* [< Lat. *incidere,* happen.]

in·ci·den·tal (ĭn′sĭ-dĕn′tl) ►adj. **1.** Occurring or likely to occur as a minor consequence. **2.** Of a minor or casual nature: *incidental expenses.* ►n. A minor accompanying item or expense. —**in′ci·den′tal·ly** adv.

in·cin·er·ate (ĭn-sĭn′ə-rāt′) ►v. **-at·ed, -at·ing** To consume by fire; burn to ashes. [Med.Lat. *incinerāre* < Lat. *cinis,* ashes.]

in·cin·er·a·tor (ĭn-sĭn′ə-rā′tər) ►n. An apparatus for burning waste.

in·cip·i·ent (ĭn-sĭp′ē-ənt) ►adj. Beginning to exist or appear. [< Lat. *incipere,* begin.] —**in·cip′i·en·cy, in·cip′i·ence** n. —**in·cip′i·ent·ly** adv.

in·cise (ĭn-sīz′) ►v. **-cised, -cis·ing 1.** To cut into or mark with a sharp instrument. **2.** To engrave (e.g., designs) into a surface; carve. [< Lat. *incīdere, incīs-.*]

in·ci·sion (ĭn-sĭzh′ən) ►n. **1.** The act of incising. **2a.** A cut, esp. a surgical cut into soft tissue. **b.** The scar resulting from such a cut.

in·ci·sive (ĭn-sī′sĭv) ►adj. Penetrating, clear, and sharp: *incisive comments.* —**in·ci′sive·ly** adv. —**in·ci′sive·ness** n.

in·ci·sor (ĭn-sī′zər) ►n. A tooth adapted for cutting or gnawing, located at the apex of the dental arch.

in·cite (ĭn-sīt′) ►v. **-cit·ed, -cit·ing** To provoke to action; stir up: *incite a mob.* [< Lat. *incitāre,* urge forward.] —**in·cite′ment** n. —**in·cit′er** n.

in·ci·vil·i·ty (ĭn′sĭ-vĭl′ĭ-tē) ►n., pl. **-ties** Rudeness.

incl. ►abbr. **1.** including **2.** inclusive

in·clem·ent (ĭn-klĕm′ənt) ►adj. **1.** Stormy: *inclement weather.* **2.** Unmerciful. —**in·clem′-**

en·cy *n.* **—in·clem′ent·ly** *adv.*

in·cli·na·tion (ĭn′klə-nā′shən) ►*n.* **1.** A bend or tilt. **2a.** A slant: *the inclination of the roof.* **b.** The angle between two lines or planes: *the inclination of the comet's orbit with respect to that of Earth.* **c.** An incline; slope. **3a.** A tendency to act in a certain way. **b.** A preference or liking: *his musical inclinations.*

in·cline (ĭn-klīn′) ►*v.* **-clined, -clin·ing 1.** To cause (someone) to have a certain tendency. **2.** To dispose (someone) to have a certain opinion or to take a course of action: *I'm inclined to agree with you.* **3.** To cause to lean, slant, or slope. See Synonyms at **slant. 4.** To bend or lower in a nod or bow. ►*n.* (ĭn′klīn′) An inclined surface; slope. [< Lat. *inclīnāre* : IN-² + *-clīnāre,* lean.] **—in·clin′er** *n.*

in·clined plane (ĭn-klīnd′) ►*n.* A plane set at an angle to the horizontal, esp. a simple machine used in raising or lowering loads.

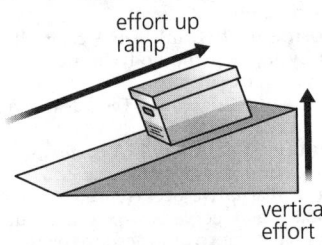

effort up ramp

vertical effort

inclined plane
pushing a load up a gentle slope requires less effort than lifting it

in·clude (ĭn-klood′) ►*v.* **-clud·ed, -clud·ing 1.** To have as a part, element, or member; contain. **2.** To allow into a group or class. [< Lat. *inclūdere.*] **—in·clu′sion** *n.* **—in·clu′sive** *adj.* **—in·clu′sive·ly** *adv.* **—in·clu′sive·ness** *n.*

in·cog·ni·to (ĭn′kŏg-nē′tō, ĭn-kŏg′nĭ-tō′) ►*adv. & adj.* With one's identity disguised or concealed. [Ital. < Lat. *incognitus,* unknown.]

in·co·her·ent (ĭn′kō-hîr′ənt) ►*adj.* **1.** Lacking cohesion; not coherent. **2.** Unable to express one's thoughts in an orderly manner. **—in′co·her′ence** *n.* **—in′co·her′ent·ly** *adv.*

in·com·bus·ti·ble (ĭn′kəm-bŭs′tə-bəl) ►*adj.* Incapable of burning. **—in′com·bus′ti·bil′i·ty** *n.* **—in′com·bus′ti·ble** *n.* **—in′com·bus′ti·bly** *adv.*

in·come (ĭn′kŭm′) ►*n.* The amount of money or its equivalent received in exchange for labor or services, from the sale of goods or property, or as profit from investments.

income tax ►*n.* A tax levied on net income.

in·com·ing (ĭn′kŭm′ĭng) ►*adj.* Coming in or about to come in.

in·com·men·su·rate (ĭn′kə-mĕn′sər-ĭt, -shər-) ►*adj.* **1.** Not commensurate; disproportionate. **2.** Inadequate. **—in′com·men′su·rate·ly** *adv.*

in·com·mode (ĭn′kə-mōd′) ►*v.* **-mod·ed, -mod·ing** To inconvenience; disturb.

in·com·mu·ni·ca·do (ĭn′kə-myoo′nĭ-kä′dō) ►*adv. & adj.* Without the means or right of communicating. [Sp. *incomunicado,* p.part. of *incomunicar,* deny communication to.]

in·com·pa·ra·ble (ĭn-kŏm′pər-ə-bəl) ►*adj.* **1.** Being such that comparison is impossible.

2. Beyond comparison; unsurpassed. **—in·com′pa·ra·bil′i·ty, in·com′pa·ra·ble·ness** *n.* **—in·com′pa·ra·bly** *adv.*

in·com·pat·i·ble (ĭn′kəm-păt′ə-bəl) ►*adj.* **1.** Not compatible; not in harmony or agreement. **2.** Mutually exclusive. **—in′com·pat′i·bil′i·ty** *n.* **—in′com·pat′i·bly** *adv.* **—in′com·pat′i·ble·ness** *n.*

in·com·pe·tent (ĭn-kŏm′pĭ-tənt) ►*adj.* **1a.** Lacking qualities necessary for effective conduct or action: *an incompetent manager.* **b.** Not functioning properly in the body: *an incompetent heart valve.* **2.** *Law* Lacking sufficient mental ability or awareness. **—in·com′pe·tence, in·com′pe·ten·cy** *n.* **—in·com′pe·tent** *n.* **—in·com′pe·tent·ly** *adv.*

in·com·plete (ĭn′kəm-plēt′) ►*adj.* Not complete. **—in′com·plete′ly** *adv.* **—in′com·plete′ness, in′com·ple′tion** *n.*

in·com·pre·hen·si·ble (ĭn′kŏm-prĭ-hĕn′sə-bəl, ĭn-kŏm′-) ►*adj.* **1.** Impossible to understand; unintelligible. **2.** Impossible to fathom. **—in′com·pre·hen′si·bil′i·ty** *n.* **—in′com·pre·hen′si·bly** *adv.* **—in′com·pre·hen′sion** *n.*

in·com·press·i·ble (ĭn′kəm-prĕs′ə-bəl) ►*adj.* **1.** Impossible to compress. **2.** Resistant to compression. **—in′com·press′i·bil′i·ty** *n.*

in·con·ceiv·a·ble (ĭn′kən-sē′və-bəl) ►*adj.* **1.** Impossible to comprehend or grasp fully. **2.** Implausible; incredible. **—in′con·ceiv′a·bil′i·ty** *n.* **—in′con·ceiv′a·bly** *adv.*

in·con·clu·sive (ĭn′kən-kloo′sĭv) ►*adj.* Not conclusive. **—in′con·clu′sive·ly** *adv.* **—in′con·clu′sive·ness** *n.*

in·con·gru·ent (ĭn-kŏng′groo-ənt, ĭn′kŏn-groo′ənt) ►*adj.* Not congruent. **—in·con′gru·ence** *n.* **—in·con′gru·ent·ly** *adv.*

in·con·gru·ous (ĭn-kŏng′groo-əs) ►*adj.* **1.** Lacking in harmony; incompatible. **2.** Not in keeping with what is correct, proper, or logical; inappropriate. **—in′con·gru′i·ty** (ĭn′kŏn-groo′ĭ-tē) *n.* **—in·con′gru·ous·ly** *adv.* **—in·con′gru·ous·ness** *n.*

in·con·se·quen·tial (ĭn-kŏn′sĭ-kwĕn′shəl, ĭn′-kŏn-) ►*adj.* Lacking importance. **—in·con′se·quence** (-kwəns) *n.* **—in·con′se·quen′ti·al′i·ty** (-kwĕn′shē-ăl′ĭ-tē) *n.* **—in·con′se·quen′tial·ly** *adv.*

in·con·sid·er·a·ble (ĭn′kən-sĭd′ər-ə-bəl) ►*adj.* Trivial. **—in′con·sid′er·a·bly** *adv.*

in·con·sid·er·ate (ĭn′kən-sĭd′ər-ĭt) ►*adj.* **1.** Thoughtless of others. **2.** Ill-considered. **—in′con·sid′er·ate·ly** *adv.* **—in′con·sid′er·ate·ness** *n.*

in·con·sis·tent (ĭn′kən-sĭs′tənt) ►*adj.* Displaying a lack of consistency, esp. erratic, contradictory, or incompatible. **—in′con·sis′ten·cy** *n.* **—in′con·sis′tent·ly** *adv.*

in·con·sol·a·ble (ĭn′kən-sō′lə-bəl) ►*adj.* Impossible to console; forlorn. **—in′con·sol′a·bil′i·ty** *n.* **—in′con·sol′a·bly** *adv.*

in·con·spic·u·ous (ĭn′kən-spĭk′yoo-əs) ►*adj.* Not readily noticeable. **—in′con·spic′u·ous·ly** *adv.* **—in′con·spic′u·ous·ness** *n.*

in·con·stant (ĭn-kŏn′stənt) ►*adj.* **1.** Changing, esp. often and erratically. **2.** Fickle. **—in·con′stan·cy** *n.* **—in·con′stant·ly** *adv.*

in·con·test·a·ble (ĭn′kən-tĕs′tə-bəl) ►*adj.* Beyond dispute; unquestionable. **—in′con·test′a·bil′i·ty** *n.* **—in′con·test′a·bly** *adv.*

in·con·ti·nent (ĭn-kŏn′tə-nənt) ▸*adj.* **1.** Not restrained. **2.** Lacking normal voluntary control of excretory functions. —**in·con′ti·nence** *n.* —**in·con′ti·nent·ly** *adv.*

in·con·tro·vert·i·ble (ĭn-kŏn′trə-vûr′tə-bəl, ĭn′kŏn-) ▸*adj.* Impossible to dispute; unquestionable. —**in·con′tro·vert′i·bil′i·ty** *n.* —**in·con′tro·vert′i·bly** *adv.*

in·con·ven·ience (ĭn′kən-vēn′yəns) ▸*n.* **1.** The state or quality of being inconvenient. **2.** Something inconvenient. ▸*v.* **-ienced, -ienc·ing** To cause inconvenience to.

in·con·ven·ient (ĭn′kən-vēn′yənt) ▸*adj.* Not convenient, esp.: **a.** Not accessible. **b.** Not suited to one's purpose or needs. **c.** Inopportune. —**in′con·ven′ient·ly** *adv.*

in·cor·po·rate (ĭn-kôr′pə-rāt′) ▸*v.* **-rat·ed, -rat·ing 1.** To unite or combine (one thing) with something else. **2.** To form or cause to form into a legal corporation. **3.** To give material form to; embody. [< LLat. *incorporāre*, form into a body < *corpus*, body.] —**in·cor′po·ra′tion** *n.* —**in·cor′po·ra·tive** *adj.* —**in·cor′po·ra·tor** *n.*

in·cor·po·re·al (ĭn′kôr-pôr′ē-əl) ▸*adj.* Lacking material form or substance. —**in′cor·po′re·al′i·ty** (-ăl′ĭ-tē) *n.*

in·cor·rect (ĭn′kə-rĕkt′) ▸*adj.* **1.** Not correct; erroneous. **2.** Improper; inappropriate. —**in′cor·rect′ly** *adv.* —**in′cor·rect′ness** *n.*

in·cor·ri·gi·ble (ĭn-kôr′ĭ-jə-bəl, -kŏr′-) ▸*adj.* Incapable of being corrected or reformed. [< Lat. *incorrigibilis.*] —**in·cor′ri·gi·bil′i·ty, in·cor′ri·gi·ble·ness** *n.* —**in·cor′ri·gi·bly** *adv.*

in·cor·rupt·i·ble (ĭn′kə-rŭp′tə-bəl) ▸*adj.* **1.** Incapable of being morally corrupted. **2.** Not subject to decay. —**in′cor·rupt′i·bil′i·ty** *n.* —**in′cor·rupt′i·bly** *adv.*

in·crease (ĭn-krēs′) ▸*v.* **-creased, -creas·ing 1.** To make or become greater or larger. **2.** To multiply; reproduce. ▸*n.* (ĭn′krēs′) **1.** The act of increasing. **2.** The amount or rate by which something is increased. [< Lat. *incrēscere.*] —**in·creas′ing·ly** *adv.*

in·cred·i·ble (ĭn-krĕd′ə-bəl) ▸*adj.* **1.** So implausible as to elicit disbelief. **2.** Astonishing. —**in·cred′i·bil′i·ty, in·cred′i·ble·ness** *n.* —**in·cred′i·bly** *adv.*

in·cred·u·lous (ĭn-krĕj′ə-ləs) ▸*adj.* **1.** Skeptical; disbelieving. **2.** Expressive of disbelief. —**in′cre·du′li·ty** (ĭn′krĭ-dōō′lĭ-tē, -dyōō′-) *n.* —**in·cred′u·lous·ly** *adv.* —**in·cred′u·lous·ness** *n.*

in·cre·ment (ĭn′krə-mənt, ĭng′-) ▸*n.* **1.** The process of increasing. **2.** Something added or gained, esp. one of a series of small additions. [< Lat. *incrēmentum.*] —**in′cre·men′tal** (-mĕn′tl) *adj.* —**in′cre·men′tal·ly** *adv.*

in·crim·i·nate (ĭn-krĭm′ə-nāt′) ▸*v.* **-nat·ed, -nat·ing** To accuse of or implicate in a crime or other wrongful act. [LLat. *incrīmināre.*] —**in·crim′i·na′tion** *n.* —**in·crim′i·na·to·ry** (-nə-tôr′ē) *adj.*

in·cu·bate (ĭn′kyə-bāt′, ĭng′-) ▸*v.* **-bat·ed, -bat·ing 1.** To warm (eggs) esp. with the body to promote hatching. **2.** To maintain at optimal environmental conditions for development. **3.** To form or consider slowly and protectively: *incubated an idea.* [Lat. *incubāre*, lie down on.] —**in′cu·ba′tion** *n.*

in·cu·ba·tor (ĭn′kyə-bā′tər, ĭng′kyə-bā′tər) ▸*n.* **1.** An apparatus in which environmental conditions, such as temperature and humidity, can be controlled, used for incubating or culturing. **2.** An apparatus that is used for maintaining an infant in an environment of controlled temperature, humidity, and oxygen concentration.

in·cu·bus (ĭn′kyə-bəs, ĭng′-) ▸*n., pl.* **-bus·es** or **-bi** (-bī′) An evil spirit believed to violate sleeping women. [< LLat.]

in·cul·cate (ĭn-kŭl′kāt′, ĭn′kŭl-) ▸*v.* **-cat·ed, -cat·ing** To teach or impress by frequent instruction or repetition; instill. [Lat. *inculcāre*, force upon < *calcāre*, trample.] —**in′cul·ca′tion** *n.* —**in·cul′ca·tor** *n.*

in·cul·pa·ble (ĭn-kŭl′pə-bəl) ▸*adj.* Free of guilt; blameless.

in·cul·pate (ĭn-kŭl′pāt′, ĭn′kŭl-) ▸*v.* **-pat·ed, -pat·ing** To incriminate. [Lat. *inculpāre.*] —**in′cul·pa′tion** *n.*

in·cum·bent (ĭn-kŭm′bənt) ▸*adj.* **1.** Imposed as an obligation or duty; obligatory. **2.** Lying, leaning, or resting on something else. **3.** Currently holding a specified office. ▸*n.* A person who holds an office. [< Lat. *incumbere*, lean upon.] —**in·cum′ben·cy** *n.*

in·cu·nab·u·lum (ĭn′kyə-năb′yə-ləm, ĭng′-) ▸*n., pl.* **-la** (-lə) A book printed before 1501. [< Lat. *incūnābula*, cradle.]

in·cur (ĭn-kûr′) ▸*v.* **-curred, -cur·ring 1.** To acquire or come into; sustain: *incurred substantial losses.* **2.** To become liable or subject to as a result of one's actions; bring upon oneself. [< Lat. *incurrere*, run into.]

in·cur·a·ble (ĭn-kyŏŏr′ə-bəl) ▸*adj.* **1.** Impossible to cure. **2.** Inveterate: *an incurable optimist.* —**in·cur′a·bil′i·ty** *n.* —**in·cur′a·ble** *n.* —**in·cur′a·bly** *adv.*

in·cu·ri·ous (ĭn-kyŏŏr′ē-əs) ▸*adj.* Lacking curiosity. —**in·cu′ri·ous·ly** *adv.*

in·cur·sion (ĭn-kûr′zhən, -shən) ▸*n.* A raid or invasion. [< Lat. *incurrere*, run at.]

in·cus (ĭng′kəs) ▸*n., pl.* **in·cu·des** (ĭng-kyōō′dēz) An anvil-shaped bone in the middle ear. [Lat. *incūs*, anvil.]

Ind. ▸*abbr.* **1.** Independent **2.** Indian **3.** Indies

in·debt·ed (ĭn-dĕt′ĭd) ▸*adj.* **1.** Owing money, goods, or services to someone. **2.** Morally or socially obligated to another; beholden. —**in·debt′ed·ness** *n.*

in·de·cent (ĭn-dē′sənt) ▸*adj.* **1.** Offensive to accepted standards of decency or modesty; lewd or vulgar: *an indecent movie.* **2.** Not appropriate or becoming; unseemly: *indecent enthusiasm.* —**in·de′cen·cy** *n.* —**in·de′cent·ly** *adv.*

in·de·ci·pher·a·ble (ĭn′dĭ-sī′fər-ə-bəl) ▸*adj.* Impossible to decipher. —**in′de·ci′pher·a·bil′i·ty** *n.* —**in′de·ci′pher·a·bly** *adv.*

in·de·ci·sion (ĭn′dĭ-sĭzh′ən) ▸*n.* Inability to make up one's mind; irresolution.

in·de·ci·sive (ĭn′dĭ-sī′sĭv) ▸*adj.* **1.** Marked by indecision. **2.** Inconclusive. —**in′de·ci′sive·ly** *adv.* —**in′de·ci′sive·ness** *n.*

in·dec·o·rous (ĭn-dĕk′ər-əs) ▸*adj.* Lacking propriety or good taste. —**in·dec′o·rous·ly** *adv.* —**in·dec′o·rous·ness** *n.*

in·deed (ĭn-dēd′) ▸*adv.* **1.** Without a doubt; certainly. **2.** In fact; in reality. ▸*interj.* Used to express surprise, skepticism, or irony. [ME *in dede*, in fact.]

indef. ►*abbr.* indefinite

in·de·fat·i·ga·ble (ĭn′dĭ-făt′ĭ-gə-bəl) ►*adj.* Having or showing a capacity for persistent effort. See Synonyms at **tireless.** [< Lat. *indēfatīgābilis < dēfatīgāre,* tire out.] —**in′de·fat′i·ga·bil′i·ty, in′de·fat′i·ga·ble·ness** *n.* —**in′de·fat′i·ga·bly** *adv.*

in·de·fen·si·ble (ĭn′dĭ-fĕn′sə-bəl) ►*adj.* **1.** Inexcusable; unpardonable. **2.** Invalid; untenable. **3.** Vulnerable to physical attack. —**in′de·fen′si·bly** *adv.*

in·de·fin·a·ble (ĭn′dĭ-fī′nə-bəl) ►*adj.* Impossible to define, describe, or analyze. —**in′de·fin′a·bil′i·ty** *n.* —**in′de·fin′a·bly** *adv.*

in·def·i·nite (ĭn-dĕf′ə-nĭt) ►*adj.* **1.** Unclear; vague. **2.** Lacking precise limits. **3.** Uncertain; undecided. —**in·def′i·nite·ly** *adv.* —**in·def′i·nite·ness** *n.*

indefinite article ►*n.* An article, such as English *a* or *an,* that does not fix the identity of the noun modified.

in·del·i·ble (ĭn-dĕl′ə-bəl) ►*adj.* **1.** Impossible to remove, erase, or wash away. **2.** Making a mark not easily erased or washed away. [Lat. *indēlēbilis < dēlēre,* wipe out.] —**in·del′i·bil′i·ty** *n.* —**in·del′i·bly** *adv.*

in·del·i·cate (ĭn-dĕl′ĭ-kĭt) ►*adj.* **1.** Slightly improper, offensive, or coarse. **2.** Tactless. —**in·del′i·ca·cy** *n.* —**in·del′i·cate·ly** *adv.*

in·dem·ni·fy (ĭn-dĕm′nə-fī′) ►*v.* **-fied, -fy·ing** **1.** To protect against damage or loss; insure. **2.** To compensate for damage suffered. [< Lat. *indemnis,* uninjured.] —**in·dem′ni·fi·ca′tion** *n.* —**in·dem′ni·fi′er** *n.*

in·dem·ni·ty (ĭn-dĕm′nĭ-tē) ►*n.,* pl. **-ties** **1.** Security against damage or injury. **2.** Compensation for damage, loss, or injury suffered. [< Lat. *indemnis,* uninjured.]

in·dent[1] (ĭn-dĕnt′) ►*v.* **1.** To set (the first line of a paragraph) in from the margin. **2.** To notch or serrate the edge of; make jagged. ►*n.* (ĭn-dĕnt′, ĭn′dĕnt′) An indentation. [< Med. Lat. *indentāre,* to notch < Lat. *dēns, dent-,* tooth.]

in·dent[2] (ĭn-dĕnt′) ►*v.* To impress (e.g., a design); stamp.

in·den·ta·tion (ĭn′dĕn-tā′shən) ►*n.* **1.** The act of indenting or condition of being indented. **2.** The blank space between a margin and the beginning of an indented line. **3.** A notch or jagged cut; recess.

in·den·ture (ĭn-dĕn′chər) ►*n.* **1.** often **indentures** A contract binding one party into the service of another for a specified term. **2a.** A deed executed by more than one party. **b.** An instrument or agreement specifying the terms of a bond or trust. ►*v.* **-tured, -tur·ing** To bind by indenture. [< AN *endenter,* INDENT[1].]

Independence Day ►*n.* July 4, celebrated in the US to commemorate the adoption in 1776 of the Declaration of Independence.

in·de·pen·dent (ĭn′dĭ-pĕn′dənt) ►*adj.* **1.** Not governed by a foreign power. **2.** Free from the influence, guidance, or control of others; self-reliant. **3.** Not contingent. **4.** often **Independent** Not committed to any one political party. **5a.** Financially self-sufficient. **b.** Providing or being sufficient income to enable one to live without working. ►*n.* often **Independent** One that is independent, esp. a person who is not committed to any one party. —**in′de·pen′dence** *n.* —**in′de·pen′dent·ly** *adv.*

independent living ►*n.* A living arrangement that maximizes the independence and self-determination of disabled persons.

in-depth (ĭn′dĕpth′) ►*adj.* Detailed; thorough.

in·de·scrib·a·ble (ĭn′dĭ-skrī′bə-bəl) ►*adj.* Impossible to describe adequately. —**in′de·scrib′a·bly** *adv.*

in·de·struc·ti·ble (ĭn′dĭ-strŭk′tə-bəl) ►*adj.* Impossible to destroy. —**in′de·struc′ti·bil′i·ty** *n.* —**in′de·struc′ti·bly** *adv.*

in·de·ter·mi·nate (ĭn′dĭ-tûr′mə-nĭt) ►*adj.* **1a.** Not precisely determined. **b.** Not precisely fixed. **c.** Lacking clarity or precision. **d.** Not known in advance. **e.** Not leading up to a definite result. **2.** *Bot.* Not terminating in a flower and continuing to grow at the apex. —**in′de·ter′mi·na·cy** *n.* —**in′de·ter′mi·nate·ly** *adv.*

in·dex (ĭn′dĕks′) ►*n.,* pl. **-dex·es** or **-di·ces** (-dĭ-sēz′) **1.** An alphabetized list of names, places, and subjects treated in a printed work. **2.** Something that reveals or indicates; sign. **3.** *Print.* A character (☞) used in printing to call attention to a particular paragraph. **4.** *Math.* A number or symbol, often a subscript or superscript to a mathematical expression, that indicates a specific element of a set or sequence. **5.** A number derived from a formula, used to characterize a set of data: *the cost-of-living index.* ►*v.* **1.** To furnish with or enter in an index. **2.** To indicate or signal. [< Lat., forefinger.] —**in′dex·er** *n.*

index finger ►*n.* The finger next to the thumb.

index of refraction ►*n.* The ratio of the speed of light in a vacuum to the speed of light in a medium under consideration.

In·di·a (ĭn′dē-ə) **1.** A peninsula and subcontinent of South Asia S of the Himalayas, comprising India, Nepal, Bhutan, Pakistan, and Bangladesh. **2.** A country of South Asia. Cap. New Delhi.

In·di·an (ĭn′dē-ən) ►*n.* **1.** A native or inhabitant of India or of the East Indies. **2.** See **Native American.** See Usage Note at **Native American. 3.** Any of the languages of the Native Americans. —**In′di·an** *adj.*

In·di·an·a (ĭn′dē-ăn′ə) A state of the N-central US. Cap. Indianapolis. —**In′di·an′an, In′di·an′i·an** *adj. & n.*

In·di·an·ap·o·lis (ĭn′dē-ə-năp′ə-lĭs) The capital of IN, in the central part.

Indian corn ►*n.* **1.** See **corn**[1] (sense 1). **2.** Dried ears of corn, usu. hung in a cluster for decoration.

Indian Ocean A body of water extending from S Asia to Antarctica and from E Africa to SE Australia.

Indian pipe ►*n.* A waxy white woodland plant with scalelike leaves and a nodding flower.

Indian summer ►*n.* **1.** A period of mild weather occurring in late autumn. **2.** A pleasant or tranquil period occurring near the end of something: *the Indian summer of the administration.*

Indian Territory A former territory of the S-central US, located mainly in present-day OK.

In·dic (ĭn′dĭk) ►*n.* A branch of Indo-European that comprises the languages of the Indian subcontinent and Sri Lanka. —**In′dic** *adj.*

indic. ►*abbr.* indicative

in·di·cate (ĭn′dĭ-kāt′) ►*v.* **-cat·ed, -cat·ing** **1.**

To show the way to or point out. **2.** To serve as a sign or token of; signify. **3.** To suggest the necessity or advisability of. **4.** To state or express briefly. [Lat. *indicāre* < *index, indic-,* forefinger.] —**in′di·ca′tion** *n.* —**in′di·ca′tor** *n.*
Syns: *attest, bespeak, betoken* **v.**

in·dic·a·tive (ĭn-dĭk′ə-tĭv) ►*adj.* **1.** Serving to indicate. **2.** *Gram.* Of, relating to, or being the mood of the verb used in ordinary objective statements. ►*n. Gram.* **1.** The indicative mood. **2.** A verb in the indicative mood. —**in·dic′a·tive·ly** *adv.*

in·di·ces (ĭn′dĭ-sēz′) ►*n.* Pl. of **index.**

in·dict (ĭn-dīt′) ►*v.* **1.** *Law* To charge (a party) by indictment. **2.** To accuse of wrongdoing or criticize severely. [< ME *enditen,* INDITE.] —**in·dict′a·ble** *adj.* —**in′dict·ee′** (ĭn′dī-tē′) *n.* —**in·dict′er, in·dict′or** *n.* —**in·dict′ment** *n.*

In·dies (ĭn′dēz) **1.** See **East Indies. 2.** See **West Indies.**

in·dif·fer·ent (ĭn-dĭf′ər-ənt, -dĭf′rənt) ►*adj.* **1a.** Having no particular interest in or concern for; apathetic. **b.** Having no marked feeling for or against. **2.** Not mattering one way or the other. **3.** Not partial; unbiased. **4.** Neither good nor bad; mediocre. —**in·dif′fer·ence** *n.* —**in·dif′fer·ent·ly** *adv.*

in·dig·e·nous (ĭn-dĭj′ə-nəs) ►*adj.* **1.** Originating, growing, or produced in a certain place. **2a.** Being a member of the original inhabitants of a particular place. **b.** Of, belonging to, or characteristic of such inhabitants. [< Lat. *indigena,* a native.] —**in·dig′e·nous·ly** *adv.*

in·di·gent (ĭn′dĭ-jənt) ►*adj.* Lacking the means of subsistence; impoverished. [< Lat. *indigēre,* be in need of.] —**in′di·gence** *n.* —**in′di·gent** *n.* —**in′di·gent·ly** *adv.*

in·di·gest·i·ble (ĭn′dĭ-jĕs′tə-bəl, -dī-) ►*adj.* Difficult or impossible to digest. —**in′di·gest′i·bil′i·ty** *n.* —**in′di·gest′i·bly** *adv.*

in·di·ges·tion (ĭn′dĭ-jĕs′chən, -dī-) ►*n.* **1.** Inability to properly digest food. **2.** Discomfort or illness resulting from indigestion.

in·dig·nant (ĭn-dĭg′nənt) ►*adj.* Feeling or expressing indignation. See Synonyms at **angry.** [< Lat. *indignus,* unworthy.] —**in·dig′nant·ly** *adv.*

in·dig·na·tion (ĭn′dĭg-nā′shən) ►*n.* Anger aroused by something perceived as unjust or mean. [< Lat. *indignārī,* deem unworthy.]

in·dig·ni·ty (ĭn-dĭg′nĭ-tē) ►*n., pl.* **-ties 1.** Humiliating or degrading treatment. **2.** A source of offense, as to a person's pride or sense of dignity; affront.

in·di·go (ĭn′dĭ-gō′) ►*n., pl.* **-gos** or **-goes 1a.** A plant that yields a blue dye. **b.** The blue dye orig. obtained from this plant, now also produced synthetically. **2.** A dark to purplish blue. [< Gk. *Indikon (pharmakon),* Indian (dye).]

indigo bunting ►*n.* A small bird of the Americas, the male of which has deep blue plumage.

in·di·rect (ĭn′dĭ-rĕkt′, -dī-) ►*adj.* **1.** Diverging from a direct course; roundabout. **2a.** Not proceeding straight to the point. **b.** Not forthright and candid; devious. **3.** Not directly planned for; secondary: *indirect benefits.* —**in′di·rec′tion** *n.* —**in′di·rect′ly** *adv.* —**in′di·rect′ness** *n.*

indirect object ►*n.* An object indirectly affected by the action of a verb, as *me* in *Please sing me a song.*

in·dis·cern·i·ble (ĭn′dĭ-sûr′nə-bəl) ►*adj.* Impossible to perceive; imperceptible. —**in′dis·cern′i·bly** *adv.*

in·dis·creet (ĭn′dĭ-skrēt′) ►*adj.* Lacking discretion; injudicious. —**in′dis·creet′ly** *adv.* —**in′dis·creet′ness** *n.* —**in′dis·cre′tion** (ĭn′dĭ-skrĕsh′ən) *n.*

in·dis·crim·i·nate (ĭn′dĭ-skrĭm′ə-nĭt) ►*adj.* **1.** Not making or based on careful distinctions; unselective. **2.** Random; haphazard. **3.** Confused; chaotic. —**in′dis·crim′i·nate·ly** *adv.*

in·dis·pens·a·ble (ĭn′dĭ-spĕn′sə-bəl) ►*adj.* Absolutely necessary; essential. —**in′dis·pens′a·bil′i·ty, in′dis·pens′a·ble·ness** *n.* —**in′dis·pens′a·bly** *adv.*
Syns: *critical, essential, necessary, requisite* **adj.**

in·dis·posed (ĭn′dĭ-spōzd′) ►*adj.* **1.** Mildly ill. **2.** Averse; disinclined. —**in·dis′po·si′tion** (ĭn′dĭs-pə-zĭsh′ən) *n.*

in·dis·put·a·ble (ĭn′dĭ-spyōo′tə-bəl) ►*adj.* Beyond doubt; undeniable. —**in′dis·put′a·bly** *adv.*

in·dis·sol·u·ble (ĭn′dĭ-sŏl′yə-bəl) ►*adj.* Impossible to dissolve, disintegrate, or undo. —**in′dis·sol′u·bil′i·ty** *n.* —**in′dis·sol′u·bly** *adv.*

in·dis·tinct (ĭn′dĭ-stĭngkt′) ►*adj.* **1.** Not clearly or sharply delineated. **2.** Hazy, vague. —**in′dis·tinct′ly** *adv.* —**in′dis·tinct′ness** *n.*

in·dis·tin·guish·a·ble (ĭn′dĭ-stĭng′gwĭ-shə-bəl) ►*adj.* **1.** Impossible to differentiate or tell apart. **2.** Impossible to discern; imperceptible. —**in′dis·tin′guish·a·bly** *adv.*

in·dite (ĭn-dīt′) ►*v.* **-dit·ed, -dit·ing** To write; compose. [< VLat. **indictāre.*]

in·di·um (ĭn′dē-əm) ►*n.* **Symbol In** A soft, malleable, silvery-white metallic element used as a plating for aircraft bearings and mirrors and in compounds for making liquid crystal displays and transistors. At. no. 49. See table at **element.** [IND(IGO) + –IUM.]

in·di·vid·u·al (ĭn′də-vĭj′ōo-əl) ►*adj.* **1a.** Of or relating to a single human. **b.** By or for one person: *an individual portion.* **2.** Existing singly; separate: *individual words.* **3.** Distinguished by particular attributes; distinctive: *an individual way of dressing.* ►*n.* A human or organism considered by itself. [< Lat. *indīviduus,* indivisible, single.] —**in′di·vid′u·al·ly** *adv.*

in·di·vid·u·al·ism (ĭn′də-vĭj′ōo-ə-lĭz′əm) ►*n.* **1.** Belief in the primary importance of the individual and personal independence. **2.** The doctrine that the interests of the individual should take precedence over those of the state.

in·di·vid·u·al·ist (ĭn′də-vĭj′ōo-ə-lĭst) ►*n.* **1.** A person of independent thought and action. **2.** An advocate of individualism. —**in′di·vid′u·al·is′tic** *adj.*

in·di·vid·u·al·i·ty (ĭn′də-vĭj′ōo-ăl′ĭ-tē) ►*n.* **1.** The aggregate of qualities that distinguish one individual from another. **2.** The quality of being individual.

in·di·vid·u·al·ize (ĭn′də-vĭj′ōo-ə-līz′) ►*v.* **-ized, -iz·ing 1.** To give individuality to. **2.** To consider or treat individually. **3.** To modify to suit a particular individual. —**in′di·vid′u·al·i·za′tion** *n.*

individual retirement account ►*n.* A government-sponsored account that offers tax incentives to people who save money for retirement.

in·di·vis·i·ble (ĭn′də-vĭz′ə-bəl) ►*adj.* Incapable of division. —**in′di·vis′i·bly** *adv.*

In·do·chi·na (ĭn′dō-chī′nə) **1.** A peninsula of SE Asia comprising Vietnam, Laos, Cambodia, Thailand, Myanmar, and the mainland territory of Malaysia. **2.** The former French colonial empire in SE Asia, including much of the E part of the Indochinese peninsula. —**In′do·chi′nese′** (-nēz′, -nēs′) *adj.* & *n.*

in·doc·tri·nate (ĭn-dŏk′trə-nāt′) ►*v.* **-nat·ed, -nat·ing 1.** To instruct in a body of doctrine. **2.** To imbue with a partisan point of view. —**in·doc′tri·na′tion** *n.*

In·do-Eu·ro·pe·an (ĭn′dō-yŏor′ə-pē′ən) ►*n.* **1a.** A family of languages consisting of most of the languages of Europe as well as those of Iran, the Indian subcontinent, and other parts of Asia. **b.** Proto-Indo-European. **2.** A member of any of the peoples speaking an Indo-European language. —**In′do-Eu′ro·pe′an** *adj.*

In·do-I·ra·ni·an (ĭn′dō-ĭ-rā′nē-ən) ►*n.* **1.** A subfamily of the Indo-European language family that comprises the Indic and Iranian branches. **2.** A member of any of the peoples speaking an Indo-Iranian language. —**In′do-I·ra′ni·an** *adj.*

in·do·lent (ĭn′də-lənt) ►*adj.* Disinclined to work; habitually lazy. See Synonyms at **lazy.** [LLat. *indolēns,* painless.] —**in′do·lence** *n.* —**in′do·lent·ly** *adv.*

in·dom·i·ta·ble (ĭn-dŏm′ĭ-tə-bəl) ►*adj.* Impossible to overcome; unconquerable. [LLat. *indomitābilis.*] —**in·dom′i·ta·bly** *adv.*

In·do·ne·sia (ĭn′də-nē′zhə, -dō-) A country of SE Asia in the Malay Archipelago comprising Sumatra, Java, Sulawesi, the Moluccas, parts of Borneo, New Guinea, and Timor, and many smaller islands. Cap. Jakarta, on Java.

In·do·ne·sian (ĭn′də-nē′zhən) ►*n.* **1.** A native or inhabitant of Indonesia. **2.** A subfamily of Austronesian that includes Malay, Tagalog, and the languages of Indonesia. ►*adj.* Of or relating to Indonesia or its people, languages, or cultures.

in·door (ĭn′dôr′) ►*adj.* Of, situated in, or intended for use in the interior of a building.

in·doors (ĭn-dôrz′) ►*adv.* In or into a building.

in·du·bi·ta·ble (ĭn-dōō′bĭ-tə-bəl, -dyōō′-) ►*adj.* Too apparent to be doubted; unquestionable. [LLat. *indubitābilis.*] —**in·du′bi·ta·bly** *adv.*

in·duce (ĭn-dōōs′, -dyōōs′) ►*v.* **-duced, -duc·ing 1.** To persuade or move to action; influence. **2.** To bring about the occurrence of; cause: *a drug used to induce labor.* [< Lat. *indūcere.*] —**in·duc′i·ble** *adj.* —**in·duce′ment** *n.*

in·duct (ĭn-dŭkt′) ►*v.* **1.** To place formally in office; install. **2a.** To admit as a member; initiate. **b.** To take into military service. [< Lat. *indūcere,* lead in.] —**in′duc·tee′** *n.*

in·duc·tance (ĭn-dŭk′təns) ►*n.* A circuit element in which electromotive force is generated by electromagnetic induction.

in·duc·tion (ĭn-dŭk′shən) ►*n.* **1.** The act of inducting or the process of being inducted. **2.** *Elect.* **a.** The generation of electromotive force in a closed circuit by a varying magnetic flux through the circuit. **b.** The charging of an isolated conducting object by momentarily grounding it while a charged body is nearby. **3.** *Logic* The process of deriving general principles from particular facts or instances.

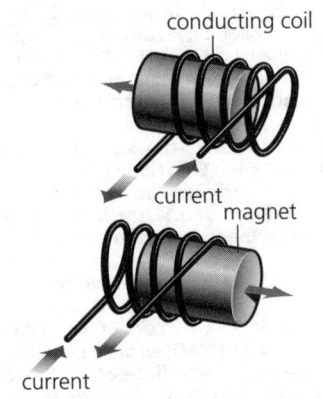

induction
top: current flows from right to left
bottom: current flows from left to right

in·duc·tive (ĭn-dŭk′tĭv) ►*adj.* **1.** Of or using logical induction. **2.** *Elect.* Of or arising from inductance. —**in·duc′tive·ly** *adv.*

in·dulge (ĭn-dŭlj′) ►*v.* **-dulged, -dulg·ing 1a.** To yield to; gratify: *indulge a craving for chocolate.* **b.** To yield to the desires or whims of (someone), often excessively. **2.** To allow (oneself) a special pleasure. [Lat. *indulgēre.*] —**in·dulg′er** *n.*

in·dul·gence (ĭn-dŭl′jəns) ►*n.* **1a.** The act of indulging. **b.** The state of being indulgent; tolerance. **c.** Something indulged in. **2.** *Rom. Cath. Ch.* The remission of punishment still due, esp. in purgatory, for a sin that has been sacramentally absolved.

in·dul·gent (ĭn-dŭl′jənt) ►*adj.* **1.** Showing, characterized by, or given to permissiveness or generosity with regard to others. **2.** Showing, characterized by, or given to self-indulgence. —**in·dul′gent·ly** *adv.*

in·du·rate (ĭn′də-rāt′, -dyə-) ►*v.* **-rat·ed, -rat·ing 1.** To make or become hard; harden. **2.** To inure, as to hardship or ridicule. [Lat. *indūrāre,* harden.] —**in′dur·a′tion** *n.*

In·dus (ĭn′dəs) A river of S Asia rising in SW Tibet and flowing about 2,900 km (1,800 mi) through N India and Pakistan to the Arabian Sea.

in·dus·tri·al (ĭn-dŭs′trē-əl) ►*adj.* **1.** Of or relating to the manufacturing industry. **2.** Having a highly developed manufacturing industry. **3.** Used in the manufacturing industry: *industrial diamonds.* —**in·dus′tri·al·ly** *adv.*

in·dus·tri·al·ist (ĭ-dŭs′trē-ə-lĭst) ►*n.* One who owns or has a financial interest in an industrial enterprise.

in·dus·tri·al·ize (ĭn-dŭs′trē-ə-līz′) ►*v.* **-ized, -iz·ing** To make or become industrial. —**in·dus′tri·al·i·za′tion** *n.*

industrial park ►*n.* An area zoned for industries and businesses.

in·dus·tri·ous (ĭn-dŭs′trē-əs) ►*adj.* Hard-working; diligent. —**in·dus′tri·ous·ly** *adv.*

in·dus·try (ĭn′də-strē) ►*n., pl.* **-tries 1a.** The sector of an economy made up of manufacturing enterprises: *government regulation of industry.* **b.** A sector of an economy: *the advertising industry.* **2.** Hard work; diligence. [< Lat. *industria,* diligence.]

–ine¹ ►*suff.* **1.** Of or relating to: *Benedictine.* **2.** Made of; resembling: *opaline.* [< Lat. *-īnus* and Gk. *-inos.*]

–ine² ►*suff.* **1.** also **-in** A chemical substance, esp.: **a.** Halogen: *bromine.* **b.** Basic compound: *amine.* **c.** Alkaloid: *quinine.* **2.** Amino acid: *glycine.* **3.** A mixture of compounds: *gasoline.* **4.** Commercial material: *glassine.* [< Lat. *-īna.*]

in·e·bri·ate (ĭn-ē′brē-āt′) ►*v.* **-at·ed, -at·ing** To make drunk; intoxicate. ►*n.* (-ĭt) An intoxicated person. [Lat. *inēbriāre* < *ēbrius,* drunk.] —**in·e′bri·a′tion** *n.*

in·ed·i·ble (ĭn-ĕd′ə-bəl) ►*adj.* Not edible. —**in·ed′i·bil′i·ty** *n.* —**in·ed′i·bly** *adv.*

in·ef·fa·ble (ĭn-ĕf′ə-bəl) ►*adj.* **1.** Incapable of being expressed; indescribable. **2.** Not to be uttered; taboo. [< Lat. *ineffābilis.*] —**in·ef′fa·bly** *adv.*

in·ef·face·a·ble (ĭn′ĭ-fā′sə-bəl) ►*adj.* Impossible to efface; indelible.

in·ef·fec·tive (ĭn′ĭ-fĕk′tĭv) ►*adj.* **1.** Not effective; ineffectual. **2.** Incompetent. —**in′ef·fec′tive·ly** *adv.* —**in′ef·fec′tive·ness** *n.*

in·ef·fec·tu·al (ĭn′ĭ-fĕk′chōō-əl) ►*adj.* **1.** Not producing the desired effect. See Synonyms at **futile. 2.** Lacking forcefulness; inadequate. —**in′ef·fec′tu·al·ly** *adv.*

in·ef·fi·cient (ĭn′ĭ-fĭsh′ənt) ►*adj.* Not efficient; wasteful of time, energy, or materials. —**in′ef·fi′cien·cy** *n.* —**in′ef·fi′cient·ly** *adv.*

in·el·e·gant (ĭn-ĕl′ĭ-gənt) ►*adj.* Lacking refinement; not elegant. —**in·el′e·gance** *n.* —**in·el′e·gant·ly** *adv.*

in·el·i·gi·ble (ĭn-ĕl′ĭ-jə-bəl) ►*adj.* Disqualified by law or rule. —**in·el′i·gi·bil′i·ty** *n.* —**in·el′i·gi·bly** *adv.*

in·e·luc·ta·ble (ĭn′ĭ-lŭk′tə-bəl) ►*adj.* Not to be avoided or escaped; inevitable. [Lat. *inēluctābilis.*] —**in′e·luc′ta·bly** *adv.*

in·ept (ĭn-ĕpt′) ►*adj.* **1.** Not apt or fitting; inappropriate. **2a.** Lacking judgment or sense; foolish. **b.** Bungling or clumsy; incompetent. [Lat. *ineptus.*] —**in·ept′ly** *adv.* —**in·ept′ness, in·ep′ti·tude** (-ĕp′tĭ-tōōd′, -tyōōd′) *n.*

in·e·qual·i·ty (ĭn′ĭ-kwŏl′ĭ-tē) ►*n., pl.* **-ties 1.** The condition of being unequal. **2.** Social or economic disparity. **3.** Lack of regularity; unevenness. **4.** A mathematical statement that two quantities are not equal.

in·eq·ui·ta·ble (ĭn-ĕk′wĭ-tə-bəl) ►*adj.* Not equitable; unfair. —**in·eq′ui·ta·bly** *adv.*

in·eq·ui·ty (ĭn-ĕk′wĭ-tē) ►*n., pl.* **-ties 1.** Injustice; unfairness. **2.** An instance of unfairness.

in·er·ran·cy (ĭn-ĕr′ən-sē) ►*n.* Freedom from error or untruths; infallibility.

in·ert (ĭn-ûrt′) ►*adj.* **1a.** Incapable of moving or acting. See Synonyms at **inactive. b.** Sluggish in action or motion; lethargic. **2.** *Chem.* Not readily reactive with other elements. **3.** Having no pharmacological or physiological effect. [Lat. *iners, inert-,* inactive.] —**in·ert′ly** *adv.* —**in·ert′ness** *n.*

in·er·tia (ĭ-nûr′shə) ►*n.* **1.** *Phys.* The tendency of a body to remain at rest or stay in motion unless acted on by an outside force. **2.** Resistance to motion, action, or change. [Lat., idleness.] —**in·er′tial** *adj.*

in·es·cap·a·ble (ĭn′ĭ-skā′pə-bəl) ►*adj.* Impossible to escape; inevitable. See Synonyms at **certain.** —**in′es·cap′a·bly** *adv.*

in·es·ti·ma·ble (ĭn-ĕs′tə-mə-bəl) ►*adj.* **1.** Impossible to estimate or compute. See Synonyms at **incalculable. 2.** Of immeasurable worth; invaluable. —**in·es′ti·ma·bly** *adv.*

in·ev·i·ta·ble (ĭn-ĕv′ĭ-tə-bəl) ►*adj.* **1.** Impossible to avoid or prevent. See Synonyms at **certain. 2.** Predictable. [LLat. *inēvītābilis* : IN-¹ + *ēvītāre,* shun.] —**in·ev′i·ta·bil′i·ty** *n.* —**in·ev′i·ta·bly** *adv.*

in·ex·act (ĭn′ĭg-zăkt′) ►*adj.* Not accurate or precise; not exact. —**in′ex·act′ly** *adv.* —**in′ex·act′ness** *n.*

in·ex·cus·a·ble (ĭn′ĭk-skyōō′zə-bəl) ►*adj.* Impossible to excuse; unpardonable. —**in′ex·cus′a·bly** *adv.*

in·ex·haust·i·ble (ĭn′ĭg-zô′stə-bəl) ►*adj.* **1.** That cannot be used up. **2.** Never wearying; tireless. —**in′ex·haust′i·bil′i·ty** *n.* —**in′ex·haust′i·bly** *adv.*

in·ex·o·ra·ble (ĭn-ĕk′sər-ə-bəl) ►*adj.* **1.** Impossible to alter or resist; inevitable. **2.** Not capable of being persuaded by entreaty; relentless. [Lat. *inexōrābilis.*] —**in·ex′o·ra·bil′i·ty** *n.* —**in·ex′o·ra·bly** *adv.*

in·ex·pen·sive (ĭn′ĭk-spĕn′sĭv) ►*adj.* Not costly; cheap. —**in′ex·pen′sive·ly** *adv.*

in·ex·pe·ri·ence (ĭn′ĭk-spîr′ē-əns) ►*n.* Lack of experience. —**in′ex·pe′ri·enced** *adj.*

in·ex·pert (ĭn-ĕk′spûrt′) ►*adj.* Not expert; unskilled. —**in·ex′pert′ly** *adv.*

in·ex·pli·ca·ble (ĭn-ĕk′splĭ-kə-bəl, ĭn′ĭk-splĭk′ə-bəl) ►*adj.* Impossible to explain or account for. —**in·ex′pli·ca·bly** *adv.*

in·ex·press·i·ble (ĭn′ĭk-sprĕs′ə-bəl) ►*adj.* Impossible to express; indescribable: *inexpressible grief.* —**in′ex·press′i·bly** *adv.*

in·ex·tin·guish·a·ble (ĭn′ĭk-stĭng′gwĭ-shə-bəl) ►*adj.* Difficult or impossible to extinguish.

in ex·tre·mis (ĭn ĕk-strē′mĭs) ►*adv.* At the point of death. [Lat. *in extrēmīs,* at the end.]

in·ex·tri·ca·ble (ĭn-ĕk′strĭ-kə-bəl, ĭn′ĭk-strĭk′ə-bəl) ►*adj.* **1.** Difficult or impossible to disentangle or untie. **2.** Too involved or complicated to solve. —**in·ex′tri·ca·bil′i·ty** *n.* —**in·ex′tri·ca·bly** *adv.*

inf. ►*abbr.* **1.** inferior **2.** infinitive

in·fal·li·ble (ĭn-făl′ə-bəl) ►*adj.* **1.** Incapable of erring. **2.** Incapable of failing; certain: *an infallible antidote.* —**in·fal′li·bil′i·ty** *n.* —**in·fal′li·bly** *adv.*

in·fa·mous (ĭn′fə-məs) ►*adj.* **1.** Having an exceedingly bad reputation; notorious. **2.** Causing or deserving severe public condemnation. —**in′fa·mous·ly** *adv.* —**in′fa·mous·ness** *n.*

in·fa·my (ĭn′fə-mē) ►*n., pl.* **-mies 1.** Very bad reputation; notoriety. **2.** The condition of being infamous. **3.** An infamous act. [< Lat. *īnfāmia.*]

in·fan·cy (ĭn′fən-sē) ►*n., pl.* **-cies 1.** The state or period of being an infant. **2.** An early stage of existence.

in·fant (ĭn′fənt) ►*n.* **1.** A child in the earliest period of life; baby. **2.** *Law* A minor. [< Lat. *īnfāns,* not speaking.] —**in′fant** *adj.*

in·fan·ti·cide (ĭn-făn′tĭ-sīd′) ►*n.* **1.** The killing of an infant. **2.** One who kills an infant.

in·fan·tile (ĭn′fən-tīl′, -tĭl) ►*adj.* **1.** Of or relating to infants or infancy. **2.** Immature; childish.

infantile paralysis ►*n.* See **poliomyelitis.**

in·fan·try (ĭn′fən-trē) ►*n., pl.* **-tries** The branch of an army made up of units trained to fight on foot. [< OItal. *infanteria* < *infante*, youth.] —**in·fan·try·man** *n.*

in·farct (ĭn′färkt′, ĭn-färkt′) ►*n.* An area of tissue that undergoes necrosis as a result of obstruction of the local blood supply. [< Lat. *infarcīre*, cram in.] —**in·farct′ed** *adj.* —**in·farc′tion** *n.*

in·fat·u·ate (ĭn-făch′ōō-āt′) ►*v.* -at·ed, -at·ing To inspire with unreasoning love or attachment. [Lat. *īnfatuāre* < *fatuus*, foolish.] —**in·fat′u·at′ed** *adj.* —**in·fat′u·a′tion** *n.*

in·fea·si·ble (ĭn-fē′zə-bəl) ►*adj.* Not feasible; impracticable.

in·fect (ĭn-fĕkt′) ►*v.* **1.** To contaminate with a pathogenic microorganism. **2.** To communicate a disease to. **3.** To contaminate or corrupt: *a land infected by hate.* [< Lat. *īnficere*, infect-, to stain.] —**in·fec′tion** *n.*

in·fec·tious (ĭn-fĕk′shəs) ►*adj.* **1.** Capable of causing infection. **2.** Caused or transmitted by infection. **3.** Easily or readily communicated, as laughter. —**in·fec′tious·ly** *adv.*

infectious mononucleosis ►*n.* An acute infectious disease caused by Epstein-Barr virus and marked by fever, swollen lymph nodes, sore throat, and lymphocyte abnormalities.

in·fe·lic·i·tous (ĭn′fĭ-lĭs′ĭ-təs) ►*adj.* Inappropriate or ill-chosen, as a remark. —**in′fe·lic′i·tous·ly** *adv.* —**in′fe·lic′i·ty** *n.*

in·fer (ĭn-fûr′) ►*v.* -ferred, -fer·ring **1.** To conclude from evidence or by reasoning. **2.** To involve by logical necessity; entail. [Lat. *īnferre* : IN-² + *ferre*, bring.]
Usage: When we say that someone implies something, we mean that it is conveyed or suggested without being stated outright: *She implied by her smile that we had won the award.* Inference, on the other hand, is the activity performed in deriving conclusions that are not explicit in what is said: *We inferred from her smile that we had won the award.*

in·fer·ence (ĭn′fər-əns) ►*n.* **1.** The act or process of inferring. **2.** Something inferred. **3.** A hint or suggestion.

in·fe·ri·or (ĭn-fîr′ē-ər) ►*adj.* **1.** Low or lower in order, degree, rank, quality, or estimation. **2.** Situated under or beneath. [< Lat. *īnferior* < *īnferus*, low.] —**in·fe′ri·or** *n.* —**in·fe′ri·or′i·ty** (-ôr′ĭ-tē, -ŏr′-) *n.*

in·fer·nal (ĭn-fûr′nəl) ►*adj.* **1.** Of or relating to hell. **2.** Fiendish; diabolical. **3.** Abominable; awful. [< Lat. *īnfernus*, lower.]

in·fer·no (ĭn-fûr′nō) ►*n., pl.* -nos **1.** Hell. **2.** A place of fiery heat or destruction. [Ital. < LLat. *īnfernus*, INFERNAL.]

in·fer·tile (ĭn-fûr′tl) ►*adj.* Not fertile; unproductive or barren. —**in′fer·til′i·ty** (-fər-tĭl′ĭ-tē) *n.*

in·fest (ĭn-fĕst′) ►*v.* To inhabit or overrun in numbers large enough to be harmful or obnoxious. [< Lat. *īnfestus*, hostile.] —**in′fes·ta′tion** *n.*

in·fi·del (ĭn′fĭ-dəl, -dĕl′) ►*n.* **1.** *Often Offensive* An unbeliever with respect to a particular religion, esp. Christianity or Islam. **2.** One with no religious beliefs. [< Lat. *īnfidēlis*, unfaithful.]

in·fi·del·i·ty (ĭn′fĭ-dĕl′ĭ-tē) ►*n., pl.* -ties **1.** Lack of fidelity or loyalty, esp. to a spouse. **2.** Lack of religious belief.

in·field (ĭn′fēld′) ►*n.* *Baseball* **1.** The area of the field within the baselines. **2.** The defensive positions of first base, second base, third base,

and shortstop. —**in′field′er** *n.*

in·fight·ing (ĭn′fī′tĭng) ►*n.* **1.** Contentious rivalry within an organization. **2.** Fighting at close range. —**in′fight′er** *n.*

in·fil·trate (ĭn-fĭl′trāt′, ĭn′fĭl-) ►*v.* -trat·ed, -trat·ing **1.** To pass, enter, or join gradually or surreptitiously. **2.** To pass or cause (a liquid or gas) to pass into. —**in′fil·tra′tion** *n.* —**in′fil·tra′tor** *n.*

in·fi·nite (ĭn′fə-nĭt) ►*adj.* **1.** Having no boundaries or limits; impossible to measure or calculate. See Synonyms at **incalculable. 2.** *Math.* **a.** Being beyond or greater than any arbitrarily large value. **b.** Spatially unlimited: *a line of infinite length.* —**in′fin·ite** *n.* —**in′fi·nite·ly** *adv.*

in·fin·i·tes·i·mal (ĭn′fĭn-ĭ-tĕs′ə-məl) ►*adj.* **1.** Immeasurably or incalculably small. **2.** *Math.* Capable of having values approaching zero as a limit. [< Lat. *īnfinitus*, infinite.] —**in′fin·i·tes′i·mal·ly** *adv.*

in·fin·i·tive (ĭn-fĭn′ĭ-tĭv) ►*n.* A verb form that in English is often preceded by *to* and may be followed by an object or complement, as *be* in *I want to be president.* [< Lat. *īnfinitus*, infinite.]

in·fin·i·tude (ĭn-fĭn′ĭ-tōōd′, -tyōōd′) ►*n.* **1.** The state or quality of being infinite. **2.** An immeasurably large quantity, number, or extent.

in·fin·i·ty (ĭn-fĭn′ĭ-tē) ►*n., pl.* -ties **1.** The quality or condition of being infinite. **2.** Unbounded space, time, or quantity. **3.** An indefinitely large number or amount.

in·firm (ĭn-fûrm′) ►*adj.* **1.** Weak in body or mind, esp. from old age or disease. **2.** Not strong or stable; shaky. —**in·firm′ly** *adv.*

in·fir·ma·ry (ĭn-fûr′mə-rē) ►*n., pl.* -ries A place for the care of the sick or injured.

in·fir·mi·ty (ĭn-fûr′mĭ-tē) ►*n., pl.* -ties **1.** A bodily ailment or weakness. **2.** Frailty; feebleness. **3.** A defect in a person's character.

in·flame (ĭn-flām′) ►*v.* -flamed, -flam·ing **1.** To arouse to strong feeling or action. **2.** To intensify. **3.** To produce or be affected by an inflammation. **4.** To set on fire; kindle.

in·flam·ma·ble (ĭn-flăm′ə-bəl) ►*adj.* **1.** Easily ignited and capable of burning rapidly; flammable. See Usage Note at **flammable. 2.** Quickly aroused to strong emotion. [< Lat. *īnflammāre*, set afire.] —**in·flam′ma·bil′i·ty** *n.* —**in·flam′ma·ble** *n.*

in·flam·ma·tion (ĭn′flə-mā′shən) ►*n.* A localized reaction of tissue to irritation, injury, or infection, characterized by pain, redness, swelling, and sometimes loss of function.

in·flam·ma·to·ry (ĭn-flăm′ə-tôr′ē) ►*adj.* **1.** Arousing strong emotion, esp. anger. **2.** Marked or caused by inflammation.

in·flate (ĭn-flāt′) ►*v.* -flat·ed, -flat·ing **1.** To fill and swell with air or gas: *inflated the balloon with helium.* **2.** To represent as greater or more important than is in fact the case: *inflated the receipts to mislead the investors.* See Synonyms at **exaggerate. 3.** To cause (e.g., wages) to undergo inflation. [< Lat. *īnflāre*, blow in.] —**in·fla′tor, in·flat′er** *n.*

in·fla·tion (ĭn-flā′shən) ►*n.* **1.** The act of inflating or the state of being inflated. **2a.** A persistent increase in prices or a persistent decline in the purchasing power of money. **b.** The rate at which this increase occurs. —**in·fla′tion·ar′y** (-shə-nĕr′ē) *adj.*

in·flect (ĭn-flĕkt′) ►*v.* **1.** To alter (the voice) in tone or pitch; modulate. **2.** *Gram.* To alter (a word) by inflection. **3.** To turn from a course; bend. [< Lat. *înflectere*, bend down.] —**in·flec′tive** *adj.*

in·flec·tion (ĭn-flĕk′shən) ►*n.* **1.** Alteration in pitch or tone of the voice. **2a.** A change in the form of a word in accordance with grammar, syntax, or meaning, as in *near, nearer* or *man, men's.* **b.** The paradigm of a word. **c.** A pattern of forming paradigms, as of nouns or verbs. —**in·flec′tion·al** *adj.* —**in·flec′tion·al·ly** *adv.*

in·flex·i·ble (ĭn-flĕk′sə-bəl) ►*adj.* **1.** Not easily bent; rigid. **2.** Incapable of being changed; unalterable. **3.** Unyielding. —**in·flex′i·bil′i·ty** *n.* —**in·flex′i·bly** *adv.*

in·flict (ĭn-flĭkt′) ►*v.* **1.** To cause (something injurious or harmful), as to a person, group or area: *a storm that inflicted widespread damage.* **2.** To deal or administer (e.g., a blow). [Lat. *înfligere, înflict-.*] —**in·flict′er, in·flic′tor** *n.* —**in·flic′tion** *n.*

in·flo·res·cence (ĭn′flə-rĕs′əns) ►*n.* A cluster of flowers arranged in a characteristic way on a stem. [< LLat. *înflôrēscere,* begin to flower.] —**in′flo·res′cent** *adj.*

in·flow (ĭn′flō′) ►*n.* A flowing in or into.

in·flu·ence (ĭn′flōō-əns) ►*n.* **1.** A power indirectly or intangibly affecting a person or course of events. **2a.** Power to sway or affect based on prestige, wealth, ability, or position. **b.** One exercising such power. ►*v.* **-enced, -enc·ing 1.** To modify: *a report that influenced the election's outcome.* **2.** To affect or sway: *negative ads that are intended to influence voters.* —**idiom: under the influence** Intoxicated, esp. with alcohol. [< Lat. *înfluere,* flow in.] —**in′flu·en′tial** (-ĕn′shəl) *adj.* —**in′flu·en′tial·ly** *adv.*

in·flu·en·za (ĭn′flōō-ĕn′zə) ►*n.* **1.** An acute viral infection marked by inflammation of the respiratory tract and by fever, chills, and pain. **2.** A viral infection of domestic animals marked by fever and respiratory involvement. [< Med.Lat. *înfluentia,* influence; see INFLUENCE.]

in·flux (ĭn′flŭks′) ►*n.* A flowing in. [LLat. *înflūxus* < Lat. *înfluere,* flow in.]

in·fo (ĭn′fō) ►*n. Informal* Information.

in·fold (ĭn-fōld′) ►*v.* **1.** To fold inward. **2.** To enfold.

in·form (ĭn-fôrm′) ►*v.* **1.** To impart information to. **2.** To imbue with a quality. **3.** To give or disclose information. [< Lat. *înfôrmāre,* give form to.]

in·for·mal (ĭn-fôr′məl) ►*adj.* **1.** Not formal or ceremonious; casual. **2.** Not in accord with prescribed regulations. **3.** Suited for everyday use: *informal clothes.* —**in′for·mal′i·ty** (-măl′ĭ-tē) *n.* —**in·for′mal·ly** *adv.*

in·for·mant (ĭn-fôr′mənt) ►*n.* **1.** One that gives information. **2.** An informer.

in·for·ma·tion (ĭn′fər-mā′shən) ►*n.* **1.** Knowledge learned, esp. about a certain subject. **2.** Informing or being informed; communication of knowledge. **3.** *Comp.* Processed, stored, or transmitted data. —**in′for·ma′tion·al** *adj.*

in·for·ma·tive (ĭn-fôr′mə-tĭv) ►*adj.* Providing or disclosing information; instructive. —**in·for′ma·tive·ly** *adv.*

in·formed (ĭn-fôrmd′) ►*adj.* **1.** Possessing or based on reliable information. **2.** Knowledgeable; educated: *the informed consumer.*

in·form·er (ĭn-fôr′mər) ►*n.* An informant, esp.

one who informs against others.

infra– ►*pref.* Inferior to, below, or beneath: *infrasonic.* [< Lat. *înfrā,* beneath.]

in·frac·tion (ĭn-frăk′shən) ►*n.* The act or an instance of infringing; violation. [< Lat. *înfringere, înfrāct-,* infringe.]

in·fra·red (ĭn′frə-rĕd′) ►*adj.* Of or relating to electromagnetic radiation between microwaves and red visible light in the electromagnetic spectrum.

in·fra·son·ic (ĭn′frə-sŏn′ĭk) ►*adj.* Generating or using waves or vibrations with frequencies below that of audible sound.

in·fra·struc·ture (ĭn′frə-strŭk′chər) ►*n.* **1.** An underlying base esp. for an organization or system. **2.** The basic facilities, services, and installations needed for a community or society.

in·fre·quent (ĭn-frē′kwənt) ►*adj.* **1.** Not occurring regularly; rare. **2.** Situated at wide intervals in time or space. —**in·fre′quence, in·fre′quen·cy** *n.* —**in·fre′quent·ly** *adv.*

in·fringe (ĭn-frĭnj′) ►*v.* **-fringed, -fring·ing 1.** To transgress; violate. **2.** To encroach; trespass. [Lat. *înfringere,* break.] —**in·fringe′ment** *n.* —**in·fring′er** *n.*

in·fu·ri·ate (ĭn-fyŏŏr′ē-āt′) ►*v.* **-at·ed, -at·ing** To make furious; enrage. [Med.Lat. *înfuriāre* < Lat. *furia,* rage.] —**in·fu′ri·at′ing·ly** *adv.*

in·fuse (ĭn-fyŏŏz′) ►*v.* **-fused, -fus·ing 1.** To put into as if by pouring. **2.** To fill; imbue. **3.** To steep or soak without boiling. [< Lat. *înfundere, înfūs-,* pour in.] —**in·fus′er** *n.* —**in·fus′i·ble** *adj.* —**in·fu′sion** *n.*

–ing¹ ►*suff.* **1.** Used to form the present participle of verbs: *seeing.* **2.** Used to form adjectives resembling present participles but not derived from verbs: *swashbuckling.* [< OE *-ende.*]

–ing² ►*suff.* **1.** Action, process, or art: *dancing.* **2a.** Something necessary to perform an action or process: *mooring* **b.** The result of an action or process: *drawing.* **c.** Something connected with a specified thing or concept: *siding.* [< OE *-ung.*]

in·gen·ious (ĭn-jēn′yəs) ►*adj.* **1.** Having great inventive skill and imagination: *an ingenious negotiator.* **2.** Marked by originality or inventiveness: *an ingenious solution to the problem.* [< Lat. *ingenium,* talent, skill.] —**in·gen′ious·ly** *adv.* —**in·gen′ious·ness** *n.*

in·gé·nue (ăn′zhə-nōō′) ►*n.* **1.** An artless, innocent girl or young woman. **2.** An actress playing an ingénue. [Fr.]

in·ge·nu·i·ty (ĭn′jə-nōō′ĭ-tē, -nyōō′-) ►*n., pl.* **-ties** Inventive skill or imagination; cleverness. [Lat. *ingenuitās,* frankness.]

in·gen·u·ous (ĭn-jĕn′yōō-əs) ►*adj.* **1.** Unsophisticated; innocent or naive. **2.** Straightforward; candid. [< Lat. *ingenuus,* honest.] —**in·gen′u·ous·ly** *adv.* —**in·gen′u·ous·ness** *n.*

in·gest (ĭn-jĕst′) ►*v.* To take into the body by the mouth for digestion or absorption. See Synonyms at eat. [Lat. *ingerere, ingest-.*] —**in·ges′tion** *n.*

in·glo·ri·ous (ĭn-glôr′ē-əs) ►*adj.* **1.** Ignominious; disgraceful. **2.** Not famous or renowned. —**in·glo′ri·ous·ly** *adv.*

in·got (ĭng′gət) ►*n.* A mass of metal cast in a shape for convenient storage or shipment. [ME, mold for casting metal.]

in·grain (ĭn-grān′) ►*v.* To fix deeply or indelibly, as in the mind. ►*n.* (ĭn′grān′) Yarn or fiber dyed before manufacture. [IN–² + GRAIN, dye (obs.).]

in·grained (ĭn-grānd′) ►*adj.* **1.** Firmly established; deep-seated: *ingrained prejudice.* **2.** Worked deeply into the fiber: *ingrained dirt.*

in·grate (ĭn′grāt′) ►*n.* An ungrateful person. [< Lat. *ingrātus,* ungrateful.]

in·gra·ti·ate (ĭn-grā′shē-āt′) ►*v.* **-at·ed, -at·ing** To bring (oneself) into the favor of another. [< Lat. *in grātiam,* into favor.]

in·grat·i·tude (ĭn-grăt′ĭ-tōōd′, -tyōōd′) ►*n.* Lack of gratitude; ungratefulness.

in·gre·di·ent (ĭn-grē′dē-ənt) ►*n.* **1.** An edible substance used in making a dish or other food. **2.** An element in a mixture or compound; constituent. See Synonyms at **element.** [< Lat. *ingredī,* enter.]

In·gres (ăn′grə), **Jean Auguste Dominique** 1780–1867. French painter.

in·gress (ĭn′grĕs′) ►*n.* **1.** A going in or entering. **2.** A means of entering. [< Lat. *ingredī,* step in.]

in-group (ĭn′grōōp′) ►*n.* A clique.

in·grown (ĭn′grōn′) ►*adj.* **1.** Grown abnormally into the flesh. **2.** Inbred; innate: *ingrown habits.*

in·gui·nal (ĭng′gwə-nəl) ►*adj.* Relating to or located in the groin. [< Lat. *inguen,* groin.]

in·hab·it (ĭn-hăb′ĭt) ►*v.* To live or reside in. [< Lat. *inhabitāre.*] —**in·hab′it·a·bil′i·ty** *n.* —**in·hab′it·a·ble** *adj.*

in·hab·i·tant (ĭn-hăb′ĭ-tənt) ►*n.* A permanent resident.

in·ha·lant (ĭn-hā′lənt) ►*n.* Something inhaled, esp. a medication.

in·ha·la·tor (ĭn′hə-lā′tər) ►*n.* See **inhaler** (sense 2).

in·hale (ĭn-hāl′) ►*v.* **-haled, -hal·ing** To draw into the lungs by breathing. [Lat. *inhālāre.*] —**in′ha·la′tion** (-hə-lā′shən) *n.*

in·hal·er (ĭn-hā′lər) ►*n.* **1.** One that inhales. **2.** A device that produces a vapor to ease breathing.

in·here (ĭn-hîr′) ►*v.* **-hered, -her·ing** To be inherent or innate. [Lat. *inhaerēre.*]

in·her·ent (ĭn-hîr′ənt, -hĕr′-) ►*adj.* Existing as an essential constituent or characteristic; intrinsic. —**in·her′ent·ly** *adv.*

in·her·it (ĭn-hĕr′ĭt) ►*v.* **1.** *Law* **a.** To take (property) by law of descent from an intestate owner. **b.** To receive (property) by will. **2.** To take over from a predecessor. **3.** *Biol.* To receive from one's parents by genetic transmission. **4.** To gain (something) as one's right. [< LLat. *inhērēditāre.*] —**in·her′it·a·bil′i·ty** *n.* —**in·her′it·a·ble** *adj.* —**in·her′i·tor** *n.*

in·her·i·tance (ĭn-hĕr′ĭ-təns) ►*n.* **1.** Something inherited or to be inherited. **2.** Something regarded as a heritage. See Synonyms at **heritage.**

in·hib·it (ĭn-hĭb′ĭt) ►*v.* **1a.** To hold back; restrain. **b.** To cause (a person) to behave in a restrained way. **c.** *Psychol.* To suppress (behavior, an impulse, or a desire) consciously or unconsciously. **2.** To prohibit (an ecclesiastic) from performing clerical duties. [< Lat. *inhibēre.*] —**in·hib′i·tive, in·hib′i·to′ry** (-tôr′ē) *adj.*

in·hi·bi·tion (ĭn′hə-bĭsh′ən, ĭn′ə-) ►*n.* **1.** The act of inhibiting or the state of being inhibited. **2.** *Psychol.* Conscious or unconscious restraint of a behavioral process, desire, or impulse.

in·hib·i·tor also **in·hib·it·er** (ĭn-hĭb′ĭ-tər) ►*n.* One that inhibits, as a substance that retards or stops a chemical reaction.

in·hos·pi·ta·ble (ĭn-hŏs′pĭ-tə-bəl, ĭn′hŏ-spĭt′ə-bəl) ►*adj.* **1.** Displaying no hospitality; unfriendly. **2.** Unfavorable to life or growth; hostile. —**in·hos′pi·ta·bly** *adv.*

in-house (ĭn′hous′) ►*adj.* Conducted or being within an organization or firm.

in·hu·man (ĭn-hyōō′mən) ►*adj.* **1.** Lacking kindness or pity; cruel. **2.** Not suited for human needs. **3.** Not of ordinary human nature, form, or character. —**in·hu′man·ly** *adv.*

in·hu·mane (ĭn′hyōō-mān′) ►*adj.* Lacking pity or compassion. —**in′hu·mane′ly** *adv.*

in·hu·man·i·ty (ĭn′hyōō-măn′ĭ-tē) ►*n., pl.* **-ties** **1.** Lack of pity or compassion. **2.** An inhuman or cruel act.

in·im·i·cal (ĭ-nĭm′ĭ-kəl) ►*adj.* **1.** Injurious or harmful. **2.** Unfriendly; hostile. [< Lat. *inimīcus,* enemy.] —**in·im′i·cal·ly** *adv.*

in·im·i·ta·ble (ĭ-nĭm′ĭ-tə-bəl) ►*adj.* Defying imitation; matchless. —**in·im′i·ta·bly** *adv.*

in·iq·ui·ty (ĭ-nĭk′wĭ-tē) ►*n., pl.* **-ties** **1.** Gross immorality or injustice. **2.** A grossly immoral act; sin. [< Lat. *inīquus,* unjust.] —**in·iq′ui·tous** *adj.*

in·i·tial (ĭ-nĭsh′əl) ►*adj.* Of or occurring at the beginning; first. ►*n.* The first letter of a name or word. ►*v.* **-tialed, -tial·ing** also **-tialled, -tial·ling** To mark or sign with initials, esp. as authorization or approval. [< Lat. *initium,* beginning.] —**in·i′tial·ly** *adv.*

in·i·tial·ism (ĭ-nĭsh′ə-lĭz′əm) ►*n.* An abbreviation that is pronounced as a series of individual letters, such as *IRS* for *Internal Revenue Service.*

in·i·tial·ize (ĭ-nĭsh′ə-līz′) ►*v.* **-ized, -iz·ing** *Comp.* **1.** To set to a starting position or value. **2.** To prepare (e.g., a printer) for use. —**in·i′tial·i·za′tion** *n.*

in·i·ti·ate (ĭ-nĭsh′ē-āt′) ►*v.* **-at·ed, -at·ing** **1.** To begin or originate. **2.** To introduce to a new field, interest, skill, or activity. **3.** To admit into membership, as with ceremonies or ritual. ►*n.* (-ĭt) One who has been initiated. [Lat. *initiāre.*] —**in·i′ti·a′tion** *n.* —**in·i′ti·a·tor** *n.* —**in·i′ti·a·to′ry** (-ə-tôr′ē) *adj.*

in·i·tia·tive (ĭ-nĭsh′ə-tĭv) ►*n.* **1.** The ability to begin or follow through with a plan or task; enterprise. **2.** A first step: *took the initiative in breaking the deadlock.* **3.** The right and procedure by which citizens can propose a law by petition and ensure its submission to the electorate.

in·ject (ĭn-jĕkt′) ►*v.* **1.** To force or drive (a fluid) into. **2.** To introduce (e.g., a drug) into a body part, esp. by means of a syringe. **3.** To introduce into conversation or consideration: *injected a note of humor.* **4.** To place into circulation: *inject money into the economy.* [Lat. *inicere, iniect-,* throw in.] —**in·jec′tion** *n.* —**in·jec′tor** *n.*

in·ju·di·cious (ĭn′jōō-dĭsh′əs) ►*adj.* Showing a lack of judgment or discretion; unwise. —**in′ju·di′cious·ly** *adv.*

in·junc·tion (ĭn-jŭngk′shən) ►*n.* **1.** A command, directive, or order. **2.** *Law* A court order requiring a party to refrain from doing a particular act or to do a particular act. [< Lat. *iniungere,* enjoin.] —**in·junc′tive** *adj.*

in·jure (ĭn′jər) ►*v.* **-jured, -jur·ing** **1a.** To cause physical harm to: *The fall injured his knee.* **b.** To experience injury in (oneself or a body part). **2a.** To cause damage to: *The gossip injured his reputation.* **b.** To commit an injustice or offense against: *people who were injured by the false accusations.* [< Lat. *iniūriārī.*]

in·ju·ri·ous (ĭn-jŏŏr′ē-əs) ►*adj.* Causing injury; harmful. —**in·ju′ri·ous·ly** *adv.*

in·ju·ry (ĭn′jə-rē) ►*n., pl.* **-ries 1.** An act that harms or damages. **2.** A wound or other particular form of hurt, damage, or loss. **3.** Injustice. [< Lat. *iniūria,* injustice.]

in·jus·tice (ĭn-jŭs′tĭs) ►*n.* **1.** Violation of another's rights or of what is right; lack of justice. **2.** An unjust act; wrong.

ink (ĭngk) ►*n.* **1.** A pigmented liquid or paste used esp. for writing or printing. **2.** A dark liquid ejected for protection, as by the squid and octopus. ►*v.* To cover or stain with ink. [< LLat. *encaustum,* purple ink.] —**ink′y** *adj.*

ink·blot (ĭngk′blŏt′) ►*n.* **1.** A blotted pattern of spilled ink. **2.** A pattern resembling an inkblot that is used in Rorschach tests.

inkblot test ►*n.* Rorschach test.

ink·jet printer (ĭngk′jĕt′) ►*n.* A printer that directs electrically charged ink streams onto a page.

in·kling (ĭng′klĭng) ►*n.* **1.** A slight hint or indication. **2.** A vague idea or notion. [Prob. < ME *ningkiling,* suggestion.]

ink·well (ĭngk′wĕl′) ►*n.* A small reservoir for ink.

in·laid (ĭn′lād′) ►*v.* P.t. and p.part. of **inlay.** ►*adj.* Decorated with a pattern set into a surface.

in·land (ĭn′lənd) ►*adj.* **1.** Of or located in the interior part of a country. **2.** *Chiefly Brit.* Operating or applying within a country; domestic. —**in′land** *adv. & n.*

in-law (ĭn′lô′) ►*n.* A relative by marriage.

in·lay (ĭn′lā′, ĭn-lā′) ►*v.* **-laid** (-lād′), **-lay·ing** To set into a surface to form a design. ►*n.* **1.** An inlaid object, design, or decoration. **2.** A solid filling, as of gold, fitted and cemented to a tooth.

in·let (ĭn′lĕt′, -lĭt) ►*n.* **1.** A stream or bay leading inland, as from the ocean; estuary. **2.** A narrow passage of water, as between two islands.

in-line skate (ĭn′līn′) ►*n.* A roller skate whose wheels are arranged in a straight line.

in·mate (ĭn′māt′) ►*n.* An occupant of a communal dwelling, esp. a person confined to an institution such as a prison or hospital.

in me·di·as res (ĭn mē′dē-əs rās′) ►*adv.* In or into the middle of a sequence of events. [Lat. *in mediās rēs.*]

in me·mo·ri·am (ĭn′ mə-môr′ē-əm) ►*prep.* In memory of. [Lat.]

inn (ĭn) ►*n.* **1.** A hotel. **2.** A tavern. [< OE.]

in·nards (ĭn′ərdz) ►*pl.n. Informal* **1.** Internal bodily organs; viscera. **2.** The inner parts, as of a machine. [Alteration of *inwards,* entrails.]

in·nate (ĭ-nāt′, ĭn′āt′) ►*adj.* **1.** Existing naturally rather than being learned through experience. **2.** Possessed as an essential characteristic; inherent. [< Lat. *innātus,* p.part. of *innāscī,* be born in.] —**in·nate′ly** *adv.*

in·ner (ĭn′ər) ►*adj.* **1.** Located farther inside: *an inner room.* **2.** Of or relating to the mind or spirit. **3.** More exclusive, influential, or important: *the inner circles of government.* [< OE *innera.*] —**in′ner·ness** *n.*

inner city ►*n.* The usu. older central part of a city, esp. when characterized by crowded neighborhoods in which low-income groups predominate. —**in′ner-cit′y** *adj.*

inner ear ►*n.* The part of the vertebrate ear that includes the semicircular canals, vestibule, and cochlea.

Inner Mongolia An autonomous region of NE China.

in·ner·most (ĭn′ər-mōst′) ►*adj.* **1.** Situated farthest within. **2.** Most intimate.

inner planet ►*n.* Any of the four planets, Mercury, Venus, Earth, and Mars, whose orbits are closest to the sun.

inner tube ►*n.* A flexible, airtight hollow ring, usu. made of rubber, inserted into the casing of a pneumatic tire for holding compressed air.

in·ning (ĭn′ĭng) ►*n.* A division of a baseball game in which each team has a turn at bat.

inn·keep·er (ĭn′kē′pər) ►*n.* One who owns or manages an inn or hotel.

in·no·cent (ĭn′ə-sənt) ►*adj.* **1.** Uncorrupted by evil, malice, or wrongdoing; sinless. **2.** Not guilty of a specific crime or offense; legally blameless. **3.** Not dangerous or harmful; innocuous. **4a.** Not experienced or worldly; naive. **b.** Without deception or guile; artless. [< Lat. *innocēns, innocent-,* harmless.] —**in′no·cence** *n.* —**in′no·cent** *n.* —**in′no·cent·ly** *adv.*

Innocent III 1161–1216. Pope (1198–1216).

in·noc·u·ous (ĭ-nŏk′yōō-əs) ►*adj.* **1.** Having no adverse effect; harmless. **2.** Not likely to provoke strong emotion; insipid. [< Lat. *innocuus.*] —**in·noc′u·ous·ly** *adv.*

in·nom·i·nate (ĭ-nŏm′ə-nĭt) ►*adj.* **1.** Having no name. **2.** Anonymous. [LLat. *innōminātus.*]

in·no·vate (ĭn′ə-vāt′) ►*v.* **-vat·ed, -vat·ing** To begin or introduce (something new). [< Lat. *innovāre,* renew < *novus,* new.] —**in′no·va′tive** *adj.* —**in′no·va′tor** *n.*

in·no·va·tion (ĭn′ə-vā′shən) ►*n.* **1.** The act of introducing something new. **2.** Something newly introduced. —**in′no·va′tion·al** *adj.*

in·nu·en·do (ĭn′yōō-ĕn′dō) ►*n., pl.* **-does** An indirect or subtle, usu. derogatory insinuation. [< Lat. *innuere,* nod to.]

in·nu·mer·a·ble (ĭ-nōō′mər-ə-bəl, ĭ-nyōō′-) ►*adj.* Too numerous to be counted. See Synonyms at **incalculable.**

in·oc·u·late (ĭ-nŏk′yə-lāt′) ►*v.* **-lat·ed, -lat·ing** To introduce a serum, vaccine, or antigenic substance into, esp. to produce or boost immunity to a specific disease. [< Lat. *inoculāre, inoculāt-,* engraft.] —**in·oc′u·la′tion** *n.*

in·of·fen·sive (ĭn′ə-fĕn′sĭv) ►*adj.* Giving no offense; unobjectionable.

in·op·er·a·ble (ĭn-ŏp′ər-ə-bəl, -ŏp′rə-) ►*adj.* **1.** Not working; inoperative. **2.** Not able to be treated surgically.

in·op·er·a·tive (ĭn-ŏp′ər-ə-tĭv, -ŏp′rə-) ►*adj.* Not working or functioning.

in·op·por·tune (ĭn-ŏp′ər-tōōn′, -tyōōn′) ►*adj.* Inappropriate or ill-timed. —**in·op′por·tune′ly** *adv.*

in·or·di·nate (ĭn-ôr′dn-ĭt) ►*adj.* Exceeding reasonable limits; immoderate. [< Lat. *inōrdinātus.*] —**in·or′di·nate·ly** *adv.*

in·or·gan·ic (ĭn′ôr-găn′ĭk) ►*adj.* **1a.** Involving neither organic life nor the products of organic life. **b.** Not composed of organic matter. **2.** *Chem.* Of or relating to compounds not usu. classified as organic. —**in′or·gan′i·cal·ly** *adv.*

in·pa·tient (ĭn′pā′shənt) ►*n.* A patient who is admitted to a hospital for treatment. ►*adj.* Of or relating to inpatients or their care.

in·put (ĭn′pŏŏt′) ►*n.* **1.** Something put into a system to achieve a result, esp.: **a.** Energy, work, or power used to drive a machine. **b.** Information put into a computer system for processing. **2.** Contribution of information or a comment or viewpoint. —**in′put′** *v.*

in·quest (ĭn′kwĕst′) ►*n.* **1.** *Law* **a.** An investigation conducted into the cause of death of a person when the cause may be criminal. **b.** A judicial inquiry into a specified matter, such as a person's mental condition. **2.** An investigation. [< Lat. *inquīrere, inquīsīt-,* inquire.]

in·quire (ĭn-kwīr′) ►*v.* **-quired, -quir·ing** **1.** To ask or ask about. **2.** To make an inquiry or investigation. [< Lat. *inquīrere.*] —**in·quir′er** *n.* —**in·quir′ing·ly** *adv.*

in·quir·y (ĭn-kwīr′ē, ĭn′kwə-rē) ►*n., pl.* **-ies** **1.** The act or process of inquiring. **2.** A question; query. **3.** A close examination of a matter in a search for information or truth.
Syns: inquisition, investigation, probe **n.**

in·qui·si·tion (ĭn′kwĭ-zĭsh′ən, ĭng′-) ►*n.* **1.** An investigation, such as an inquest. See Synonyms at **inquiry.** **2a. Inquisition** A former Roman Catholic tribunal established to suppress heresy. **b.** A rigorous or severe questioning. [< Lat. *inquīrere, inquīsīt-,* inquire.] —**in·quis′i·tor** (-kwĭz′ĭ-tər) *n.* —**in·quis′i·to′ri·al** (-kwĭz′-ĭ-tôr′ē-əl) *adj.*

in·quis·i·tive (ĭn-kwĭz′ĭ-tĭv) ►*adj.* **1.** Eager for knowledge. **2.** Unduly curious. —**in·quis′i·tive·ly** *adv.* —**in·quis′i·tive·ness** *n.*

in re (ĭn rā′, rē′) ►*prep.* **1.** *Law* In the matter of. Used in cases that lack parties, such as one concerning the probate of a will. **2.** In regard to. [Lat. *in rē.*]

in·road (ĭn′rōd′) ►*n.* **1.** An advance, esp. at another's expense; encroachment. **2.** A hostile invasion; raid. [IN¹ + ROAD, raid (obs.).]

in·rush (ĭn′rŭsh′) ►*n.* A sudden influx.

ins. ►*abbr.* **1.** inches **2.** inspector

in·sa·lu·bri·ous (ĭn′sə-lōō′brē-əs) ►*adj.* Not promoting health; unwholesome.

in·sane (ĭn-sān′) ►*adj.* **1a.** Of, exhibiting, or afflicted with mental derangement. Not used in psychiatric diagnosis. **b.** *Law* Having been determined to be in a condition that meets the legal definition of insanity. **2.** Very foolish; absurd. —**in·sane′ly** *adv.*

in·san·i·ty (ĭn-săn′ĭ-tē) ►*n., pl.* **-ties** **1.** Severe mental illness or derangement. Not used in psychiatric diagnosis. **2.** *Law* Unsoundness of mind sufficient to warrant involuntary hospitalization, render a person unfit to maintain legal relationships such as contracts, or absolve the person from responsibility for a crime. **3.** Extreme foolishness or irrationality.

in·sa·tia·ble (ĭn-sā′shə-bəl, -shē-ə-) ►*adj.* Impossible to satiate or satisfy. —**in·sa′tia·bil′i·ty, in·sa′tia·ble·ness** *n.* —**in·sa′tia·bly** *adv.*

in·scribe (ĭn-skrīb′) ►*v.* **-scribed, -scrib·ing** **1a.** To write, print, carve, or engrave (words or letters) on or in a surface. **b.** To mark or engrave with words or letters. **2.** To enter (a name) on a list. **3.** To dedicate to someone. **4.** *Math.* To draw (one figure) within another figure so that every vertex of the enclosed figure touches the

outer figure. [Lat. *īnscrībere.*] —**in·scrib′er** *n.* —**in·scrip′tion** (-skrĭp′shən) *n.*

in·scru·ta·ble (ĭn-skrōō′tə-bəl) ►*adj.* Difficult to understand or interpret. [< LLat. *īnscrūtābilis.*] —**in·scru′ta·bil′i·ty** *n.* —**in·scru′ta·bly** *adv.*

in·seam (ĭn′sēm′) ►*n.* The inside seam of a pant leg.

in·sect (ĭn′sĕkt′) ►*n.* Any of a class of usu. winged invertebrate animals, such as flies, beetles, and butterflies, having an adult stage marked by three pairs of legs and a three-segmented body. [Lat. *īnsectum* < *īnsecāre,* cut up.]

in·sec·ti·cide (ĭn-sĕk′tĭ-sīd′) ►*n.* A substance used to kill insects. —**in·sec′ti·cid′al** *adj.*

in·sec·ti·vore (ĭn-sĕk′tə-vôr′) ►*n.* An insect-eating organism. —**in′sec·tiv′o·rous** (-tĭv′-ər-əs) *adj.*

in·se·cure (ĭn′sĭ-kyŏŏr′) ►*adj.* **1.** Inadequately guarded or protected; unsafe. **2.** Not firm or fixed; shaky. **3.** Lacking self-confidence. —**in′se·cure′ly** *adv.* —**in′se·cu′ri·ty** *n.*

in·sem·i·nate (ĭn-sĕm′ə-nāt′) ►*v.* **-nat·ed, -nat·ing** To introduce or inject semen into the reproductive tract of (a female). [Lat. *īnsēmināre,* implant < *sēmen,* seed.] —**in·sem′i·na′tion** *n.* —**in·sem′i·na′tor** *n.*

in·sen·sate (ĭn-sĕn′sāt′, -sĭt) ►*adj.* **1a.** Inanimate. **b.** Unconscious. **2.** Lacking sensibility; unfeeling. **3.** Lacking sense; foolish.

in·sen·si·ble (ĭn-sĕn′sə-bəl) ►*adj.* **1.** Imperceptible; inappreciable. **2a.** Unconscious. **b.** Inanimate. **c.** Insensitive; numb. **3a.** Unaware. **b.** Callous; indifferent. —**in·sen′si·bil′i·ty** *n.* —**in·sen′si·bly** *adv.*

in·sen·si·tive (ĭn-sĕn′sĭ-tĭv) ►*adj.* **1.** Not physically sensitive; numb. **2.** Unresponsive to or unaffected by the feelings of others. —**in·sen′si·tive·ly** *adv.* —**in·sen′si·tiv′i·ty** *n.*

in·sen·tient (ĭn-sĕn′shənt) ►*adj.* Devoid of sensation or consciousness. —**in·sen′tience** *n.*

in·sep·a·ra·ble (ĭn-sĕp′ər-ə-bəl, -sĕp′rə-) ►*adj.* **1.** Impossible to separate. **2.** Very closely associated. —**in·sep′a·ra·bil′i·ty** *n.* —**in·sep′a·ra·bly** *adv.*

in·sert (ĭn-sûrt′) ►*v.* **1.** To put, place, or set into: *inserted a key in a lock.* **2.** To interpolate. ►*n.* (ĭn′sûrt′) Something inserted or intended for insertion, as a chart into a text. [Lat. *īnserere.*] —**in·ser′tion** *n.*

in·set (ĭn′sĕt′, ĭn-sĕt′) ►*v.* To set in; insert. —**in′set′** *n.*

in·shore (ĭn′shôr′) ►*adv. & adj.* Close to or coming toward a shore.

in·side (ĭn-sīd′, ĭn′sīd′) ►*n.* **1.** An inner or interior part. **2.** An inner side or surface. **3. insides** *Informal* **a.** The inner organs; entrails. **b.** The inner parts or workings: *the insides of a TV set.* ►*adv.* Into or in the interior; within. ►*prep.* **1.** Within: *inside an hour.* **2.** Into the interior of: *going inside the house.* —*idioms:* **inside of** Within: *inside of an hour.* **inside out 1.** With the inner surface turned out. **2.** *Informal* Thoroughly: *knew the city inside out.* **on the inside** In a position of confidence or influence. —**in·side′** *adv.*

Inside Passage A natural protected waterway extending about 1,600 km (1,000 mi) through coastal British Columbia, Canada, and the panhandle of AK.

in·sid·er (ĭn-sī′dər) ►*n.* **1.** An accepted member of a group. **2.** One who has special knowledge or access to confidential information.

inside track ►*n. Informal* An advantageous position, as in a competition.

in·sid·i·ous (ĭn-sĭd′ē-əs) ►*adj.* **1.** Working or spreading harmfully in a subtle or stealthy manner. **2.** Intended to entrap; treacherous. **3.** Beguiling but harmful. [< Lat. *īnsidēre,* lie in wait < *sedēre,* sit.] —**in·sid′i·ous·ly** *adv.* —**in·sid′i·ous·ness** *n.*

in·sight (ĭn′sīt′) ►*n.* The capacity to discern the true nature of a situation; penetration. —**in′sight′ful** *adj.* —**in′sight′ful·ness** *n.*

in·sig·ni·a (ĭn-sĭg′nē-ə) ►*n., pl.* **-ni·a** or **-ni·as** A distinguishing badge of office, rank, membership, or nationality. [< Lat. *īnsignis,* marked.]

in·sig·nif·i·cant (ĭn′sĭg-nĭf′ĭ-kənt) ►*adj.* **1.** Lacking in importance; trivial. **2.** Small in size, power, value, or amount. **3.** Having little or no meaning. —**in′sig·nif′i·cance** *n.* —**in′sig·nif′i·cant·ly** *adv.*

in·sin·cere (ĭn′sĭn-sîr′) ►*adj.* Not sincere; hypocritical. —**in′sin·cere′ly** *adv.* —**in′sin·cer′i·ty** (-sĕr′ĭ-tē) *n.*

in·sin·u·ate (ĭn-sĭn′yōō-āt′) ►*v.* **-at·ed, -at·ing** **1.** To express (e.g., a thought) in an indirect or insidious way. **2a.** To maneuver or insert (oneself) into a place. **b.** To cause (oneself) to be involved or accepted by subtle and artful means. **3.** To hint. [Lat. *īnsinuāre* < *sinus,* curve.] —**in·sin′u·a′tion** *n.*

in·sip·id (ĭn-sĭp′ĭd) ►*adj.* **1.** Lacking flavor or zest; not tasty. **2.** Lacking excitement or interest; dull. [< LLat. *īnsipidus.*] —**in·sip′id·ly** *adv.*

in·sist (ĭn-sĭst′) ►*v.* **1.** To be resolute in a demand or course. **2.** To assert or demand (something) firmly and persistently. [Lat. *īnsistere,* persist < *sistere,* stand.] —**in·sis′tence, in·sis′ten·cy** *n.* —**in·sis′tent** *adj.* —**in·sis′tent·ly** *adv.*

in si·tu (ĭn sī′tōō, sē′-) ►*adv. & adj.* In the original position. [Lat. *in situ.*]

in·so·far as (ĭn′sō-fär′) ►*conj.* To the extent that.

in·sole (ĭn′sōl′) ►*n.* **1.** The inner sole of a shoe or boot. **2.** An extra strip of material put inside a shoe for comfort or protection.

in·so·lent (ĭn′sə-lənt) ►*adj.* Audaciously rude or disrespectful; impertinent. [< Lat. *īnsolēns.*] —**in′so·lence** *n.* —**in′so·lent·ly** *adv.*

in·sol·u·ble (ĭn-sŏl′yə-bəl) ►*adj.* **1.** Incapable of being dissolved. **2.** Difficult or impossible to solve or explain. —**in·sol′u·bil′i·ty** *n.* —**in·sol′u·bly** *adv.*

in·sol·vent (ĭn-sŏl′vənt) ►*adj.* Unable to pay one's debts. —**in·sol′ven·cy** *n.*

in·som·ni·a (ĭn-sŏm′nē-ə) ►*n.* Chronic inability to sleep. [< Lat. *īnsomnis,* sleepless < *somnus,* sleep.] —**in·som′ni·ac′** (-ăk′) *adj. & n.*

in·so·much as (ĭn′sō-mŭch′) ►*conj.* Inasmuch as; since.

in·sou·ci·ant (ĭn-sōō′sē-ənt) ►*adj.* Blithely unconcerned. [Fr.] —**in·sou′ci·ance** *n.*

in·spect (ĭn-spĕkt′) ►*v.* **1.** To examine carefully and critically, esp. for flaws. **2.** To review or examine officially. [Lat. *īnspicere, īnspect-* < *specere,* look at.] —**in·spec′tion** *n.* —**in·spec′tor** *n.*

inspector general ►*n., pl.* **inspectors general** An officer with general investigative powers within a civil, military, or other organization.

in·spi·ra·tion (ĭn′spə-rā′shən) ►*n.* **1a.** Stimulation of the mind or emotions to a high level of feeling or activity. **b.** The condition of being so stimulated. **2.** One that inspires. **3.** Something that is inspired. **4.** Inhalation. —**in′spi·ra′tion·al** *adj.* —**in′spi·ra′tion·al·ly** *adv.*

in·spire (ĭn-spīr′) ►*v.* **-spired, -spir·ing** **1.** To fill with noble or reverent emotion; exalt. **2.** To stimulate to action; motivate: *was inspired by the prospect of a bonus.* See Synonyms at **encourage.** **3.** To cause to have a particular feeling; affect: *inspired them with disgust.* See Synonyms at **encourage. 4.** To elicit or create in another: *a teacher who inspired respect.* **5.** To inhale. [< Lat. *īnspīrāre.*] —**in·spir′er** *n.*

in·spir·it (ĭn-spĭr′ĭt) ►*v.* To instill courage or life into.

inst. ►*abbr.* **1.** institute **2.** institution

in·sta·bil·i·ty (ĭn′stə-bĭl′ĭ-tē) ►*n., pl.* **-ties** Lack of stability.

in·stall also **in·stal** (ĭn-stôl′) ►*v.* **-stalled, -stall·ing** **1.** To set in position and connect or adjust for use. **2.** To induct into an office, rank, or position. **3.** To put or place. [< Med.Lat. *īnstallāre.*] —**in′stal·la′tion** (-stə-lā′shən) *n.* —**in·stall′er** *n.*

in·stall·ment also **in·stal·ment** (ĭn-stôl′mənt) ►*n.* **1.** One of a number of successive payments of a debt. **2.** A portion of something, such as a publication, issued at intervals.

in·stance (ĭn′stəns) ►*n.* **1.** A case or example. **2.** An occurrence or occasion. **3.** A suggestion or request: *called at the instance of his attorney.* ►*v.* **-stanced, -stanc·ing** To offer as an example; cite. [< Lat. *īnstantia,* presence < *īnstāns,* present; see INSTANT.]

in·stant (ĭn′stənt) ►*n.* **1.** A period of time so short as to be almost imperceptible. **2.** A particular point in time. ►*adj.* **1.** Immediate. **2.** Imperative; urgent: *an instant need.* **3.** Designed, prepared, or processed for quick preparation: *instant coffee.* [< Lat. *īnstāns,* present < *īnstāre,* approach < *stāre,* stand.]

in·stan·ta·ne·ous (ĭn′stən-tā′nē-əs) ►*adj.* **1.** Occurring or completed without perceptible delay: *Relief was instantaneous.* **2.** Present or occurring at a specific instant. —**in′stan·ta′ne·ous·ly** *adv.* —**in′stan·ta′ne·ous·ness** *n.*

in·stant·ly (ĭn′stənt-lē) ►*adv.* At once.

instant message ►*n.* An electronic message transmitted by instant messaging.

instant messaging ►*n.* The transmission of an electronic message over a computer network using software that immediately displays the message on the screen of the recipient.

in·stead (ĭn-stĕd′) ►*adv.* In the place of that previously mentioned. —*idiom:* **instead of** In place of; rather than.

in·step (ĭn′stĕp′) ►*n.* The arched middle part of the human foot between the toes and ankle.

in·sti·gate (ĭn′stĭ-gāt′) ►*v.* **-gat·ed, -gat·ing** **1.** To urge on. **2.** To incite. [Lat. *īnstīgāre.*] —**in′sti·ga′tion** *n.* —**in′sti·ga′tor** *n.*

in·still also **in·stil** (ĭn-stĭl′) ►*v.* **-stilled, -still·ing** **1.** To introduce gradually; implant. **2.** To pour in (e.g., medicine) drop by drop. [< Lat. *īnstillāre,* drip in.] —**in′stil·la′tion** (-stə-lā′shən) *n.* —**in·still′er** *n.*

in·stinct (ĭn′stĭngkt′) ►*n.* **1.** An inner pattern of behavior that is not learned and results in complex animal responses such as building of nests and nursing of young. **2.** A powerful motivation or impulse. **3.** A natural capability or aptitude. [< Lat. *īnstinguere, īnstīnct-*, impel.] —**in·stinc′tive** *adj.* —**in·stinc′tive·ly** *adv.* —**in·stinc′tu·al** (-stĭngk′chōo-əl) *adj.*

in·sti·tute (ĭn′stĭ-tōōt′, -tyōōt′) ►*v.* **-tut·ed, -tut·ing 1.** To establish, organize, or introduce. See Synonyms at **establish. 2.** To initiate; begin. ►*n.* **1.** An organization founded to promote a cause. **2.** An educational institution. **3.** A seminar or workshop. [< Lat. *īnstituere* : IN-² + *statuere,* set up.]

in·sti·tu·tion (ĭn′stĭ-tōō′shən, -tyōō′-) ►*n.* **1.** The act of instituting. **2.** An established custom, practice, or relationship in a society. **3a.** An organization or foundation, esp. one dedicated to education or culture. **b.** The building housing such an organization. **c.** A place for care of the disabled or mentally ill. —**in′sti·tu′tion·al** *adj.* —**in′sti·tu′tion·al·ly** *adv.*

in·sti·tu·tion·al·ize (ĭn′stĭ-tōō′shə-nə-līz′, -tyōō′-) ►*v.* **-ized, -iz·ing 1.** To make into an institution. **2.** To (confine) in an institution. —**in′sti·tu′tion·al·i·za′tion** *n.*

in·struct (ĭn-strŭkt′) ►*v.* **1.** To give orders to; direct. **2.** To teach; educate. [< Lat. *īnstruere, īnstrūct-,* prepare.] —**in·struc′tive** *adj.* —**in·struc′tive·ly** *adv.*

in·struc·tion (ĭn-strŭk′shən) ►*n.* **1.** The act, practice, or profession of instructing. **2a.** Something learned. **b.** A lesson. **3a.** An authoritative direction; order. **b. instructions** Detailed directions on procedure. **4.** *Comp.* A sequence of bits that tells a central processing unit to perform a particular operation. —**in·struc′tion·al** *adj.*

in·struc·tor (ĭn-strŭk′tər) ►*n.* One who instructs, esp. a college teacher ranking below assistant professor. —**in·struc′tor·ship′** *n.*

in·stru·ment (ĭn′strə-mənt) ►*n.* **1.** An implement used to facilitate work. **2.** A device for recording or measuring, esp. one functioning as part of a control system. **3.** A device for playing or producing music. **4.** A means by which something is done; agency. **5.** A legal document. ►*v.* (-mĕnt′) To provide with instruments. [< Lat. *īnstrūmentum,* tool.]

in·stru·men·tal (ĭn′strə-mĕn′tl) ►*adj.* **1.** Serving as a means or agency. **2.** *Mus.* Performed on or written for an instrument as opposed to a voice or voices. —**in′stru·men′tal·ly** *adv.*

in·stru·men·tal·ist (ĭn′strə-mĕn′tl-ĭst) ►*n.* One who plays a musical instrument.

in·stru·men·tal·i·ty (ĭn′strə-mĕn-tăl′ĭ-tē) ►*n., pl.* **-ties 1.** The state or quality of being instrumental. **2.** A means; agency.

in·stru·men·ta·tion (ĭn′strə-mĕn-tā′shən) ►*n.* **1.** The application or use of instruments. **2.** The arrangement of music for instruments.

instrument landing ►*n.* An aircraft landing made by means of instruments and ground-based radio equipment only.

in·sub·or·di·nate (ĭn′sə-bôr′dn-ĭt) ►*adj.* Not submissive to authority. —**in′sub·or′di·nate·ly** *adv.* —**in′sub·or′di·na′tion** *n.*

in·sub·stan·tial (ĭn′səb-stăn′shəl) ►*adj.* **1.** Not firm or solid; flimsy. **2.** Small or negligible, as in importance, size, or amount. **3.** Lacking or appearing to lack substance or reality. —**in′sub·stan′ti·al′i·ty** (-shē-ăl′ĭ-tē) *n.*

in·suf·fer·a·ble (ĭn-sŭf′ər-ə-bəl, -sŭf′rə-) ►*adj.* Impossible to endure; intolerable. —**in·suf′fer·a·bly** *adv.*

in·suf·fi·cient (ĭn′sə-fĭsh′ənt) ►*adj.* Not sufficient; inadequate. —**in′suf·fi′cien·cy** *n.* —**in′suf·fi′cient·ly** *adv.*

in·su·lar (ĭn′sə-lər, ĭns′yə-) ►*adj.* **1.** Of or constituting an island. **2a.** Isolated. **b.** Narrow-minded. [< Lat. *īnsula,* island.] —**in′su·lar′i·ty** *n.*

in·su·late (ĭn′sə-lāt′, ĭns′yə-) ►*v.* **-lat·ed, -lat·ing 1.** To prevent the passage of heat, electricity, or sound into or out of, esp. by covering with a nonconducting material. **2.** To detach. See Synonyms at **isolate.** [< Lat. *īnsula,* island.] —**in′su·la′tion** *n.* —**in′su·la′tor** *n.*

in·su·lin (ĭn′sə-lĭn) ►*n.* **1.** A pancreatic hormone that regulates the metabolism of carbohydrates and fats by controlling blood glucose levels. **2.** A pharmaceutical preparation containing this hormone. [Lat. *insula,* island + -IN.]

insulin shock ►*n.* Acute hypoglycemia usu. resulting from excessive insulin in the blood.

in·sult (ĭn-sŭlt′) ►*v.* To speak to or treat with disrespect or contempt. ►*n.* (ĭn′sŭlt′) An insulting remark or act. [< Lat. *īnsultāre.*]

in·su·per·a·ble (ĭn-sōō′pər-ə-bəl) ►*adj.* Impossible to overcome; insurmountable. —**in·su′per·a·bil′i·ty** *n.* —**in·su′per·a·bly** *adv.*

in·sup·port·a·ble (ĭn′sə-pôr′tə-bəl) ►*adj.* **1.** Not endurable; intolerable. **2.** Unjustifiable. —**in′sup·port′a·bly** *adv.*

in·sur·ance (ĭn-shŏŏr′əns) ►*n.* **1.** The act or business of insuring or state of being insured. **2a.** An agreement that protects someone from incurring future losses, esp. a contract that transfers the risk of a specified loss to another party in exchange for the payment of a premium. **b.** The sum for which something is insured. **3.** A protective measure.

in·sure (ĭn-shŏŏr′) ►*v.* **-sured, -sur·ing 1.** To cover with insurance. **2.** To make sure, certain, or secure. [< OFr. *enseurer,* assure.] —**in·sur′a·ble** *adj.* —**in·sur′er** *n.*

in·sured (ĭn-shŏŏrd′) ►*n.* One that is covered by insurance.

in·sur·gent (ĭn-sûr′jənt) ►*adj.* **1.** Rising in revolt; rebellious. **2.** Rebelling against the leadership of a political party. ►*n.* One who is insurgent. [< Lat. *īnsurgere,* rise up.] —**in·sur′-gence, in·sur′gen·cy** *n.*

in·sur·mount·a·ble (ĭn′sər-moun′tə-bəl) ►*adj.* Impossible to surmount; insuperable. —**in′-sur·mount′a·bil′i·ty** *n.* —**in′sur·mount′a·bly** *adv.*

in·sur·rec·tion (ĭn′sə-rĕk′shən) ►*n.* The act or an instance of open revolt against civil authority or a government. [< Lat. *īnsurgere, īnsurrēct-,* rise up.] —**in′sur·rec′tion·ist** *n.*

int. ►*abbr.* **1.** interest **2.** intermediate **3.** international **4.** intransitive

in·tact (ĭn-tăkt′) ►*adj.* Not impaired in any way. [< Lat. *intāctus,* untouched.] —**in·tact′ness** *n.*

in·ta·glio (ĭn-tăl′yō, -tăl′-) ►*n., pl.* **-glios** A figure or design carved deeply into the surface of hard metal or stone. [Ital. < *intagliare,* engrave.]

in·take (ĭn′tāk′) ►*n.* **1.** An opening by which a fluid enters a container or pipe. **2a.** The act of taking in. **b.** The quantity taken in.

in·tan·gi·ble (ĭn-tăn′jə-bəl) ►*adj.* **1.** Incapable of being perceived by the senses. **2.** Incapable of being realized or defined. ►*n.* **1.** Something intangible. **2.** often **intangibles a.** An asset that cannot be perceived by the senses, such as intellectual property. **b.** Property or assets that cannot be physically possessed, such as bank deposits, stocks, and bonds. —**in·tan′gi·bil′·i·ty, in·tan′gi·ble·ness** *n.* —**in·tan′gi·bly** *adv.*

in·te·ger (ĭn′tĭ-jər) ►*n.* A member of the set of positive whole numbers (1, 2, 3, . . .), negative whole numbers (−1, −2, −3, . . .), and zero (0). [< Lat., whole.]

in·te·gral (ĭn′tĭ-grəl, ĭn-tĕg′rəl) ►*adj.* **1.** Essential or necessary for completeness; constituent. **2.** Whole; entire. **3.** (ĭn′tĭ-grəl) *Math.* Expressed or expressible as or in terms of integers. ►*n.* A complete unit; whole. [< Lat. *integer*, whole.]

in·te·grate (ĭn′tĭ-grāt′) ►*v.* **-grat·ed, -grat·ing 1.** To make into a whole; unify. **2.** To join with something else; unite. **3.** To open to people of all races or ethnic groups without restriction; desegregate. [< Lat. *integer*, whole.] —**in′te·gra′tion** *n.* —**in′te·gra′tion·ist** *adj. & n.* —**in′te·gra′tive** *adj.*

in·te·grat·ed circuit (ĭn′tĭ-grā′tĭd) ►*n.* An electronic circuit whose components are etched or deposited on a single slice of semiconductor material to produce a chip.

in·teg·ri·ty (ĭn-tĕg′rĭ-tē) ►*n.* **1.** Steadfast adherence to a strict moral or ethical code. **2.** Soundness. **3.** Completeness; unity. [< Lat. *integer*, whole.]

in·teg·u·ment (ĭn-tĕg′yŏŏ-mənt) ►*n.* A natural outer covering, such as the skin or a seed coat. [Lat. *integumentum* : IN-² + *tegere*, cover.]

in·tel·lect (ĭn′tl-ĕkt′) ►*n.* **1a.** The ability to learn, reason, and understand. **b.** One's individual ability to think and reason. **2.** A person of great intellectual ability. [< Lat. *intellegere*, *intellēct-*, perceive.]

in·tel·lec·tu·al (ĭn′tl-ĕk′chŏŏ-əl) ►*adj.* **1a.** Of, engaging, or requiring use of the intellect. **b.** Rational. **2a.** Having or showing intellect, esp. to a high degree. **b.** Given to pursuits that require exercise of the intellect. ►*n.* An intellectual person. —**in′tel·lec′tu·al·ly** *adv.*

in·tel·lec·tu·al·ize (ĭn′tl-ĕk′chŏŏ-ə-līz′) ►*v.* **-ized, -iz·ing 1.** To make rational. **2.** *Psychol.* To analyze (an emotional problem) intellectually, esp. so as to avoid a more direct confrontation. —**in′tel·lec′tu·al·i·za′tion** *n.*

intellectual property ►*n.* **1.** Any of various products of the intellect that have commercial value, including copyrighted property such as literary or artistic works, and ideational property, such as patents and business methods. **2.** The set of property rights protecting original work from unlawful infringement.

in·tel·li·gence (ĭn-tĕl′ə-jəns) ►*n.* **1.** The ability to acquire, understand, and use knowledge. **2a.** Secret information gathered about an enemy. **b.** The gathering of such information. **c.** An agency or organization whose purpose is to gather such information.

intelligence quotient ►*n.* A number seen as a measure of a person's intelligence, usu. representing the person's score on a standardized test designed to gauge intelligence as expressed in relation to the scores of others who have taken the same test, with the average score set at 100.

in·tel·li·gent (ĭn-tĕl′ə-jənt) ►*adj.* **1.** Having intelligence: *intelligent life.* **2.** Having a high degree of intelligence. **3.** Showing intelligence:

an *intelligent act.* [< Lat. *intellegere*, perceive.] —**in·tel′li·gent·ly** *adv.*

intelligent design ►*n.* **1.** The belief that physical and biological systems observed in the universe result chiefly from purposeful design by an intelligent being rather than from chance and other undirected natural processes. **2.** The purposeful design perceived in the universe or one of its parts and attributed to such a being.

in·tel·li·gent·si·a (ĭn-tĕl′ə-jĕnt′sē-ə, -gĕnt′-) ►*n.* The intellectual elite of a society. [Russ. *intelligentsiya.*]

in·tel·li·gi·ble (ĭn-tĕl′ĭ-jə-bəl) ►*adj.* Capable of being understood; comprehensible. [< Lat. *intellegere*, perceive.] —**in·tel′li·gi·bil′i·ty** *n.* —**in·tel′li·gi·bly** *adv.*

in·tem·per·ance (ĭn-tĕm′pər-əns, -prəns) ►*n.* Lack of temperance, esp. in the drinking of alcoholic beverages. —**in·tem′per·ate** *adj.* —**in·tem′per·ate·ly** *adv.*

in·tend (ĭn-tĕnd′) ►*v.* **1.** To have in mind; plan. **2.** To design for a specific purpose. **3.** To signify or mean. [< Lat. *intendere.*]

in·tend·ed (ĭn-tĕn′dĭd) ►*adj.* **1.** Deliberate; intentional. **2.** Prospective; future. ►*n. Informal* One engaged to be married.

in·tense (ĭn-tĕns′) ►*adj.* **-tens·er, -tens·est 1.** Displaying a distinctive feature to an extreme degree. **2.** Extreme in degree, strength, or size. **3.** Involving or showing great concentration or strain. **4.** Deeply felt; profound. [< Lat. *intēnsus*, p.part. of *intendere*, intend.] —**in·tense′ly** *adv.* —**in·tense′ness** *n.*

in·ten·si·fy (ĭn-tĕn′sə-fī′) ►*v.* **-fied, -fy·ing** To make or become intense or more intense. —**in·ten′si·fi·ca′tion** *n.*

in·ten·si·ty (ĭn-tĕn′sĭ-tē) ►*n., pl.* **-ties 1.** Exceptionally great concentration, power, or force. **2.** *Phys.* The amount or degree of strength of electricity, light, heat, or sound per unit area or volume.

in·ten·sive (ĭn-tĕn′sĭv) ►*adj.* **1.** Relating to or marked by intensity: *intensive training.* **2.** *Gram.* Adding emphasis. ►*n. Gram.* A word or word element, such as the adverb *awfully*, that adds emphasis but no new meaning. —**in·ten′sive·ly** *adv.*

in·tent (ĭn-tĕnt′) ►*n.* **1.** An aim or purpose. **2.** *Law* The state of mind necessary for an act to constitute a crime. ►*adj.* **1.** Firmly fixed; concentrated. **2.** Engrossed. **3.** Focused on a specific purpose. [< Lat. *intendere*, intend.] —**in·tent′ly** *adv.* —**in·tent′ness** *n.*

in·ten·tion (ĭn-tĕn′shən) ►*n.* **1.** The action or fact of intending. **2.** An aim that guides action.

in·ten·tion·al (ĭn-tĕn′shə-nəl) ►*adj.* Done deliberately; intended. —**in·ten′tion·al′i·ty** (-năl′ĭ-tē) *n.* —**in·ten′tion·al·ly** *adv.*

in·ter (ĭn-tûr′) ►*v.* **-terred, -ter·ring** To place in a grave; bury. [< Med.Lat. *interrāre* < Lat. *terra*, earth.]

inter– ►*pref.* **1.** Between; among: *international.* **2.** Mutual; reciprocal: *interdependent.* [< Lat. *inter*, among.]

in·ter·act (ĭn′tər-ăkt′) ►*v.* To act on each other.

in·ter·ac·tion (ĭn′tər-ăk′shən) ►*n.* **1.** The act or process of interacting. **2.** *Phys.* Any of four ways that elementary particles and bodies can influence each other, classified as strong, weak, electromagnetic, and gravitational.

in·ter·ac·tive (ĭn′tər-ăk′tĭv) ►*adj.* **1.** Acting

on each other. **2.** *Comp.* Of or relating to a program that responds to user activity. **3.** Of a form of television entertainment in which the viewer can affect events on the screen. **—in′ter·ac′tive·ly** *adv.*

in·ter a·li·a (ĭn′tər ā′lē-ə, ä′lē-ə) ►*adv.* Among other things. [Lat.]

in·ter·breed (ĭn′tər-brēd′) ►*v.* **1.** To crossbreed. **2.** To breed or cause to breed within a narrow range; inbreed.

in·ter·ca·lar·y (ĭn-tûr′kə-lĕr′ē, ĭn′tər-kăl′ə-rē) ►*adj.* **1.** Inserted in the calendar, as an extra day or month. **2.** Inserted between other elements or parts; interpolated. [Lat. *intercalārius* < Lat. *calāre*, proclaim.]

in·ter·cede (ĭn′tər-sēd′) ►*v.* **-ced·ed, -ced·ing** **1.** To plead on another's behalf. **2.** To mediate. [Lat. *intercēdere*, intervene.]

in·ter·cel·lu·lar (ĭn′tər-sĕl′yə-lər) ►*adj.* *Biol.* Located among or between cells.

in·ter·cept (ĭn′tər-sĕpt′) ►*v.* **1.** To stop or interrupt the progress of. **2.** *Math.* To include or bound (a part of a space or curve) between two points or lines. [< Lat. *intercipere, intercept-*.] **—in′ter·cept′** *n.* **—in′ter·cep′tion** *n.* **—in′ter·cep′tor** *n.*

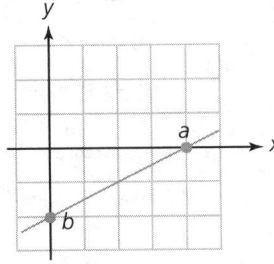

intercept
The intercept form of the equation of a line is
$$\tfrac{x}{a} + \tfrac{y}{b} = 1.$$

in·ter·ces·sion (ĭn′tər-sĕsh′ən) ►*n.* **1.** A prayer or petition to God in behalf of another. **2.** Mediation. [< Lat. *intercēdere*, intervene.] **—in′ter·ces′sion·al** *adj.* **—in′ter·ces′sor** *n.* **—in′ter·ces′so·ry** *adj.*

in·ter·change (ĭn′tər-chānj′) ►*v.* **1.** To switch each into the place of the other. **2.** To exchange. **3.** To alternate. ►*n.* (ĭn′tər-chānj′) **1.** An exchange. **2.** A highway intersection allowing traffic to move freely from one road to another without crossing another line of traffic. **—in′ter·change′a·ble** *adj.* **—in′ter·change′a·bly** *adv.*

in·ter·col·le·giate (ĭn′tər-kə-lē′jĭt, -jē-ĭt) ►*adj.* Involving two or more colleges.

in·ter·com (ĭn′tər-kŏm′) ►*n.* An electronic two-way communication system, as between two rooms. [< INTERCOMMUNICATION.]

in·ter·com·mu·ni·cate (ĭn′tər-kə-myōō′nĭ-kāt′) ►*v.* **1.** To communicate with each other. **2.** To be connected or adjoined, as rooms or passages. **—in′ter·com·mu′ni·ca′tion** *n.* **—in′ter·com·mu′ni·ca′tive** *adj.*

in·ter·con·nect (ĭn′tər-kə-nĕkt′) ►*v.* To connect or be connected with each other. **—in′ter·con·nec′tion** *n.*

in·ter·con·ti·nen·tal (ĭn′tər-kŏn′tə-nĕn′tl)

►*adj.* **1.** Taking place between continents. **2.** Traveling from one continent to another.

in·ter·cos·tal (ĭn′tər-kŏs′təl) ►*adj.* Located or occurring between the ribs. [< INTER- + Lat. *costa*, rib.]

in·ter·course (ĭn′tər-kôrs′) ►*n.* **1.** Social interchange; communication. **2.** Sexual intercourse. [< Lat. *intercurrere, intercurs-*, mingle with.]

in·ter·de·pen·dent (ĭn′tər-dĭ-pĕn′dənt) ►*adj.* Mutually dependent. **—in′ter·de·pen′dence** *n.*

in·ter·dict (ĭn′tər-dĭkt′) ►*v.* **1.** To prohibit or forbid. **2.** To confront and halt the activities or entry of. [< Lat. *interdīcere, interdict-*.] **—in′ter·dict′** *n.* **—in′ter·dic′tion** *n.*

in·ter·dis·ci·pli·nar·y (ĭn′tər-dĭs′ə-plə-nĕr′ē) ►*adj.* Of or involving two or more usu. distinct academic disciplines.

in·ter·est (ĭn′trĭst, -tər-ĭst, -trĕst′) ►*n.* **1a.** A state of curiosity or concern about or attention to something. **b.** Something that evokes this mental state. **2.** often **interests** Advantage or benefit. **3.** A right, claim, or legal share: *an interest in the will.* **4.** A charge for a loan, usu. a percentage of the amount loaned. ►*v.* **1.** To arouse interest in. **2.** To cause to become involved. [< Lat., it is of importance.]

in·ter·est·ed (ĭn′trĭ-stĭd, -tər-ĭ-stĭd, -tə-rĕs′tĭd) ►*adj.* **1.** Having or showing interest. **2.** Possessing a right, claim, or share. See Usage Note at **disinterested.**

interest group ►*n.* A group of persons strongly supporting a particular cause, such as an item of legislation.

in·ter·est·ing (ĭn′trĭ-stĭng, -tər-ĭ-stĭng, -tə-rĕs′-tĭng) ►*adj.* Arousing or holding the attention; absorbing. **—in′ter·est·ing·ly** *adv.*

in·ter·face (ĭn′tər-fās′) ►*n.* **1.** A surface forming a common boundary between adjacent regions. **2.** A point at which independent systems or diverse groups interact. **3.** *Comp.* A system of interaction or communication between a computer and another entity, such as a printer, another computer, a network, or a human operator. **—in′ter·face′** *v.* **—in′ter·fa′cial** (-fā′shəl) *adj.*

in·ter·fere (ĭn′tər-fîr′) ►*v.* **-fered, -fer·ing** **1.** To hinder or impede. **2.** *Sports* To impede illegally the catching of a pass or the playing of a ball or puck. **3.** To intervene or intrude in the affairs of others; meddle. **4.** To inhibit or prevent clear reception of broadcast signals. [< OFr. *entreferer*, meddle.] **—in′ter·fer′ence** *n.* **—in′ter·fer′er** *n.*

in·ter·fe·rom·e·ter (ĭn′tər-fə-rŏm′ĭ-tər) ►*n.* An instrument that uses interference phenomena between waves to make measurements, as of wavelengths or very small distances. **—in′ter·fe·rom′e·try** *n.*

in·ter·fer·on (ĭn′tər-fîr′ŏn′) ►*n.* A cellular protein produced in response to and acting to prevent replication of an infectious viral form within an infected cell. [< INTERFERE.]

in·ter·ga·lac·tic (ĭn′tər-gə-lăk′tĭk) ►*adj.* Between galaxies.

in·ter·im (ĭn′tər-ĭm) ►*n.* A period between two events. ►*adj.* Serving or taking place during an interim. See Synonyms at **temporary.** [< Lat., in the meantime.]

in·te·ri·or (ĭn-tîr′ē-ər) ►*adj.* **1.** Of or located on the inside; inner. **2.** Inland. ►*n.* **1.** The internal portion or area. **2.** One's mental or spiritual life. **3.** The inland part of a geographic area. **4.** A representation of the inside of a building or room. [< Lat., comp. of *inter*, between.]

interior decoration ►*n.* The arrangement, furnishing, and decoration of an architectural interior. —**interior decorator** *n.*

interj. ►*abbr.* interjection

in·ter·ject (ĭn′tər-jĕkt′) ►*v.* To insert between elements; interpose. [< Lat. *intericere.*] —**in′ter·jec′to·ry** *adj.*

in·ter·jec·tion (ĭn′tər-jĕk′shən) ►*n.* **1.** An exclamation. **2.** A part of speech usu. expressing emotion and capable of standing alone grammatically, such as *Ugh!* or *Wow!*

in·ter·lard (ĭn′tər-lärd′) ►*v.* To insert something foreign or different into. [< OFr. *entrelarder*, mix fat into.]

in·ter·leu·kin (ĭn′tər-lōō′kĭn) ►*n.* Any of a group of proteins produced by the immune system that regulate the body's immune response. [INTER– + Gk. *leukos*, white + –IN.]

in·ter·lin·ing (ĭn′tər-lī′nĭng) ►*n.* An extra lining between the outer fabric and regular lining of a garment.

in·ter·lock (ĭn′tər-lŏk′) ►*v.* **1.** To unite or join closely. **2.** To connect together (e.g., parts of a mechanism) so that the operating parts affect one another. ►*n.* A mechanical device that prevents a component from functioning when another component is functioning or situated in a particular way.

in·ter·loc·u·tor (ĭn′tər-lŏk′yə-tər) ►*n.* One who takes part in a conversation or dialogue. [< Lat. *interloquī, interlocūt-*, interrupt.]

in·ter·loc·u·to·ry (ĭn′tər-lŏk′yə-tôr′ē) ►*adj.* Determining a matter during the course of a case and not part of a final decision.

in·ter·lop·er (ĭn′tər-lō′pər) ►*n.* One who interferes; meddler. [INTER– + MDu. *loopen*, run.] —**in′ter·lope′** *v.*

in·ter·lude (ĭn′tər-lōōd′) ►*n.* **1.** An intervening episode, feature, or period of time. **2.** An entertainment between the acts of a play. **3.** *Mus.* A short piece inserted between the parts of a longer composition. [< Med.Lat. *interlūdium*, dramatic entertainment.]

in·ter·mar·ry (ĭn′tər-măr′ē) ►*v.* **1.** To marry a member of another religion, nationality, race, or group. **2.** To be bound together by the marriages of members. **3.** To marry within one's own group. —**in′ter·mar′riage** *n.*

in·ter·me·di·ar·y (ĭn′tər-mē′dē-ĕr′ē) ►*adj.* **1.** In between; intermediate. **2.** Acting as a mediator. ►*n.*, *pl.* **-ies 1.** A mediator; go-between. **2.** An intermediate state or stage.

in·ter·me·di·ate (ĭn′tər-mē′dē-ĭt) ►*adj.* Lying or occurring between two extremes; in between. ►*n.* **1.** One that is intermediate. **2.** An intermediary. [< Lat. *intermedius.*] —**in′ter·me′di·ate·ly** *adv.*

in·ter·ment (ĭn-tûr′mənt) ►*n.* The act or ritual of interring or burying.

in·ter·mez·zo (ĭn′tər-mĕt′sō, -mĕd′zō) ►*n.*, *pl.* **-zos** or **-zi** (-sē, -zē) *Mus.* **1.** A short movement separating the major sections of a lengthy composition or work. **2.** A short independent instrumental composition. [Ital. < Lat. *intermedius*, intermediate.]

in·ter·mi·na·ble (ĭn-tûr′mə-nə-bəl) ►*adj.* Tiresomely long. —**in·ter′mi·na·bly** *adv.*

in·ter·min·gle (ĭn′tər-mĭng′gəl) ►*v.* To mix or become mixed together.

in·ter·mis·sion (ĭn′tər-mĭsh′ən) ►*n.* An interval between periods of activity, as between the acts of a play. See Synonyms at **pause.** [< Lat. *intermittere, intermiss-*, interrupt.]

in·ter·mit·tent (ĭn′tər-mĭt′nt) ►*adj.* Stopping and starting at intervals. [< Lat. *intermittere*, suspend.] —**in′ter·mit′tent·ly** *adv.*

in·tern also **in·terne** (ĭn′tûrn′) ►*n.* A student or a recent graduate, as of a medical school, undergoing supervised practical training. ►*v.* **1.** To train or serve as an intern. **2.** (*also* ĭn-tûrn′) To confine, esp. in wartime. [< Lat. *internus*, internal.] —**in·tern′ment** *n.* —**in′tern·ship′** *n.*

in·ter·nal (ĭn-tûr′nəl) ►*adj.* **1.** Inner; interior. **2.** Intrinsic; inherent. **3.** Located, acting, or effective within the body. **4.** Of or relating to the domestic affairs of a nation, group, or business. [< Lat. *internus.*] —**in·ter′nal·ly** *adv.*

in·ter·nal-com·bus·tion engine (ĭn-tûr′nəl-kəm-bŭs′chən) ►*n.* An engine in which fuel is burned within the engine.

in·ter·nal·ize (ĭn-tûr′nə-līz′) ►*v.* **-ized, -iz·ing** To make internal, personal, or subjective. —**in·ter′nal·i·za′tion** *n.*

internal medicine ►*n.* The branch of medicine dealing with the diagnosis and nonsurgical treatment of diseases in adults.

in·ter·na·tion·al (ĭn′tər-năsh′ə-nəl) ►*adj.* Of or involving two or more nations or nationalities. —**in′ter·na′tion·al·ly** *adv.*

International Date Line ►*n.* An imaginary line through the Pacific Ocean roughly corresponding to 180° longitude, to the east of which, by international agreement, the calendar date is one day earlier than to the west.

in·ter·na·tion·al·ism (ĭn′tər-năsh′ə-nə-līz′əm) ►*n.* A policy of cooperation among nations, esp. in politics and economics. —**in′ter·na′tion·al·ist** *n.*

in·ter·na·tion·al·ize (ĭn′tər-năsh′ə-nə-līz′) ►*v.* **-ized, -iz·ing** To put under international control. —**in′ter·na′tion·al·i·za′tion** *n.*

international law ►*n.* The set of laws that govern relations between countries, as established by custom and agreement.

in·ter·nec·ine (ĭn′tər-nĕs′ēn′, -ĭn, -nē′sīn′) ►*adj.* **1.** Relating to struggle within a nation, organization, or group. **2.** Mutually destructive. [< Lat. *internecāre*, to slaughter.]

in·tern·ee (ĭn′tûr-nē′) ►*n.* One who is interned, esp. in wartime.

In·ter·net also **in·ter·net** (ĭn′tər-nĕt′) ►*n.* A publicly accessible system of networks that connects computers around the world.

in·ter·nist (ĭn-tûr′nĭst) ►*n.* A physician specializing in internal medicine.

in·ter·of·fice (ĭn′tər-ô′fĭs, -ŏf′ĭs) ►*adj.* Transmitted or taking place between offices.

in·ter·per·son·al (ĭn′tər-pûr′sə-nəl) ►*adj.* Relating to or occurring among several people. —**in′ter·per′son·al·ly** *adv.*

in·ter·plan·e·tar·y (ĭn′tər-plăn′ĭ-tĕr′ē) ►*adj.* Existing or occurring between planets.

in·ter·play (ĭn′tər-plā′) ►*n.* Reciprocal action and reaction; interaction. —**in′ter·play′** *v.*

in·ter·po·late (ĭn-tûr′pə-lāt′) ►*v.* **-lat·ed, -lat·ing 1.** To insert or introduce between other elements or parts. **2.** To change (a text) by introducing new or false material. **3.** *Math.* To estimate a value of (a function) between two known values. [Lat. *interpolāre*, touch up.] —**in·ter′po·la′tion** *n.* —**in·ter′po·la′tor** *n.*

in·ter·pose (ĭn′tər-pōz′) ►*v.* **-posed, -pos·ing 1a.** To insert or introduce between parts. **b.** To place (oneself) between. **2.** To introduce or interject into a discourse or conversation. **3.** To intervene. [< Lat. *interpōnere.*] —**in′ter·pos′er** *n.* —**in′ter·po·si′tion** (-pə-zĭsh′ən) *n.*

in·ter·pret (ĭn-tûr′prĭt) ►*v.* **1.** To explain or clarify the meaning of. See Synonyms at **explain. 2.** To understand the significance of; construe. **3.** To present or conceptualize the meaning of by means of art or criticism. **4.** To serve as translator for speakers of different languages. [< Lat. *interpretārī* < *interpres*, negotiator.] —**in·ter′pret·a·ble** *adj.* —**in·ter′pret·er** *n.*

in·ter·pre·ta·tion (ĭn-tûr′prĭ-tā′shən) ►*n.* **1.** An explanation. **2.** A concept of a work of art as expressed by its representation or performance. —**in·ter′pre·ta′tion·al** *adj.*

in·ter·pre·tive (ĭn-tûr′prĭ-tĭv) also **in·ter·pre·ta·tive** (-tā′tĭv) ►*adj.* Marked by interpretation; explanatory. —**in·ter′pre·tive·ly** *adv.*

in·ter·ra·cial (ĭn′tər-rā′shəl) ►*adj.* Of or between different races.

in·ter·reg·num (ĭn′tər-rĕg′nəm) ►*n., pl.* **-nums** or **-na** (-nə) **1.** The interval of time between two successive reigns or governments. **2.** A gap in continuity. [Lat.] —**in′ter·reg′nal** *adj.*

in·ter·re·late (ĭn′tər-rĭ-lāt′) ►*v.* To place in or come into mutual relationship. —**in′ter·re·la′tion** *n.* —**in′ter·re·la′tion·ship′** *n.*

in·ter·ro·gate (ĭn-tĕr′ə-gāt′) ►*v.* **-gat·ed, -gat·ing** To question formally. [< Lat. *interrogāre.*] —**in·ter′ro·ga′tion** *n.* —**in·ter′ro·ga′tion·al** *adj.* —**in·ter′ro·ga′tor** *n.*

in·ter·rog·a·tive (ĭn′tə-rŏg′ə-tĭv) ►*adj.* **1.** Of the nature of a question. **2.** *Gram.* Used to ask a question: *an interrogative pronoun.* —**in′ter·rog′a·tive** *n.* —**in′ter·rog′a·tive·ly** *adv.*

in·ter·rog·a·to·ry (ĭn′tə-rŏg′ə-tôr′ē) ►*adj.* Interrogative. ►*n., pl.* **-ries** *Law* A question that must be answered under oath and is asked by a party in a lawsuit of another party or of a potential witness prior to trial.

in·ter·rupt (ĭn′tə-rŭpt′) ►*v.* **1.** To break the continuity or uniformity of. **2.** To stop (someone engaged in an activity) by saying or doing something. **3.** To cause an activity to stop by saying or doing something. [< Lat. *interrumpere*, break off.] —**in′ter·rupt′er** *n.* —**in′ter·rup′tion** *n.* —**in′ter·rup′tive** *adj.*

in·ter·sect (ĭn′tər-sĕkt′) ►*v.* **1.** To cut across or through. **2.** To form an intersection (with); cross. [Lat. *intersecāre*, *intersect-.*]

in·ter·sec·tion (ĭn′tər-sĕk′shən, ĭn′tər-sĕk′-) ►*n.* **1.** The act or result of intersecting. **2.** A place where things intersect, esp. where roads cross. **3.** *Math.* The point or locus of points common to two or more geometric figures.

in·ter·sperse (ĭn′tər-spûrs′) ►*v.* **-spersed, -spers·ing 1.** To distribute among other things at intervals. **2.** To supply or diversify with things distributed at intervals. [< Lat. *interspergere*, *interspers-.*] —**in′ter·sper′sion** (-spûr′zhən, -shən) *n.*

in·ter·state (ĭn′tər-stāt′) ►*adj.* Involving, between, or connecting two or more states. ►*n.* One of a national system of expressways

connecting major population centers in the US.

in·ter·stel·lar (ĭn′tər-stĕl′ər) ►*adj.* Between the stars.

in·ter·stice (ĭn-tûr′stĭs) ►*n., pl.* **-stic·es** (-stĭ-sēz′, -sĭz) A small or narrow space between things or parts. [< Lat. *interstitium* < *intersistere*, make a break : INTER- + *sistere*, set up.] —**in′ter·sti′tial** (ĭn′tər-stĭsh′əl) *adj.*

in·ter·twine (ĭn′tər-twīn′) ►*v.* To join or become joined by twining together.

in·ter·val (ĭn′tər-vəl) ►*n.* **1.** A space between two objects or points. **2.** A period of time between two events. **3.** *Math.* The set of all numbers that lie between two given numbers, sometimes including either or both of the given numbers. **4.** *Mus.* The difference, usu. expressed in the number of steps, between two pitches. [< Lat. *intervallum.*]

in·ter·vene (ĭn′tər-vēn′) ►*v.* **-vened, -ven·ing 1a.** To come in or between so as to hinder or alter an action: *intervened to prevent a fight.* **b.** To interfere, usu. through force, in the affairs of another nation. **2.** To come or occur between two things, events, or points of time. [Lat. *intervenīre* : INTER- + *venīre*, come.] —**in′ter·ven′tion** (-vĕn′shən) *n.*

in·ter·view (ĭn′tər-vyōō′) ►*n.* **1.** A formal face-to-face meeting, esp. one conducted for the assessment of an applicant. **2.** A conversation between a reporter and one from whom facts or statements are elicited. [< OFr. *entrevoir*, see : INTER- + *voir*, see (< Lat. *vidēre*).] —**in′ter·view′** *v.* —**in′ter·view·ee′** *n.* —**in′ter·view′er** *n.*

in·ter·weave (ĭn′tər-wēv′) ►*v.* **1.** To weave together. **2.** To intertwine.

in·tes·tate (ĭn-tĕs′tāt′, -tĭt) ►*adj.* **1.** Having made no legal will. **2.** Not disposed of by a legal will. [< Lat. *intestātus.*]

in·tes·tine (ĭn-tĕs′tĭn) ►*n.* often **intestines** The portion of the digestive tract extending from the outlet of the stomach to the anus. [< Lat. *intestīnus*, internal.] —**in·tes′ti·nal** *adj.* —**in·tes′ti·nal·ly** *adv.*

in·ti·fa·da (ĭn′tə-fä′də) ►*n.* A grassroots campaign of protest or violent resistance, esp. either of two Palestinian uprisings beginning in 1987 and 2000, protesting Israeli occupation of the Gaza Strip and West Bank. [Ar. *intifāḍa*, shudder, uprising.]

in·ti·mate¹ (ĭn′tə-mĭt) ►*adj.* **1.** Marked by close acquaintance, association, or familiarity. **2.** Essential; innermost. **3.** Comfortably private: *an intimate café.* **4.** Very personal. **5.** Of or involving a sexual relationship. ►*n.* A close friend or confidant. [Lat. *intimātus*, p.part. of *intimāre*, INTIMATE².] —**in′ti·ma·cy** *n.* —**in′ti·mate·ly** *adv.*

in·ti·mate² (ĭn′tə-māt′) ►*v.* **-mat·ed, -mat·ing 1.** To state or express indirectly. **2.** To make evident indirectly. [Lat. *intimāre* < *intimus*, innermost.] —**in′ti·ma′tion** *n.*

in·tim·i·date (ĭn-tĭm′ĭ-dāt′) ►*v.* **-dat·ed, -dat·ing 1.** To make timid; fill with fear. **2.** To coerce or deter, as with threats. [Med.Lat. *intimidāre* < Lat. *timidus*, timid.] —**in·tim′i·dat′ing·ly** *adv.* —**in·tim′i·da′tion** *n.* —**in·tim′i·da′tor** *n.*

intl. ►*abbr.* international

in·to (ĭn′tōō) ►*prep.* **1.** To the inside of. **2a.** To the activity or occupation of: *go into banking.* **b.** To the condition or form of. **c.** So as to be in or within. **d.** *Informal* Interested or involved with: *into vegetarianism.* **3.** To a time or place in the course of: *well into the week.* **4.** Toward: *pointed into the sky.* **5.** Against: *crashed into a tree.*

in·tol·er·a·ble (ĭn-tŏl′ər-ə-bəl) ►*adj.* Unbearable: *intolerable agony.* —**in·tol′er·a·bly** *adv.*

in·tol·er·ant (ĭn-tŏl′ər-ənt) ►*adj.* **1.** Not tolerant of differences in beliefs of others; bigoted. **2.** Unable to endure: *intolerant of certain drugs.* —**in·tol′er·ance** *n.* —**in·tol′er·ant·ly** *adv.*

in·to·na·tion (ĭn′tə-nā′shən, -tō-) ►*n.* **1.** The act of intoning or chanting. **2.** A manner of producing musical tones, esp. with regard to pitch. **3.** *Ling.* The use of changing pitch to convey syntactic information: *a questioning intonation.* **4.** A use of pitch characteristic of a speaker or dialect.

in·tone (ĭn-tōn′) ►*v.* **-toned, -ton·ing** To recite in a singing or chanting voice. [< Med.Lat. *intonāre* < Lat. *tonus,* tone.]

in to·to (ĭn tō′tō) ►*adv.* Totally; altogether. [Lat. *in tōtō.*]

in·tox·i·cate (ĭn-tŏk′sĭ-kāt′) ►*v.* **-cat·ed, -cat·ing** **1.** To make drunk. **2.** To stimulate or excite. [< Med.Lat. *intoxicāre* < Lat. *toxicum,* poison.] —**in·tox′i·cant** (-kənt) *adj. & n.* —**in·tox′i·ca′tion** *n.*

intr. ►*abbr.* intransitive

intra– ►*pref.* Within: *intracellular.* [< Lat. *intrā.*]

in·tra·cel·lu·lar (ĭn′trə-sĕl′yə-lər) ►*adj.* Occurring or situated within a cell or cells.

in·trac·ta·ble (ĭn-trăk′tə-bəl) ►*adj.* Difficult to manage, deal with, or change to an acceptable condition. —**in·trac′ta·bil′i·ty** *n.* —**in·trac′ta·bly** *adv.*

in·tra·mu·ral (ĭn′trə-myŏor′əl) ►*adj.* Existing or carried on within an institution, esp. a school. [< INTRA– + Lat. *mūrus,* wall.]

in·tra·net (ĭn′trə-nĕt′) ►*n.* A restricted-access computer network, as within an organization.

in·tran·si·gent (ĭn-trăn′sə-jənt, -zə-) ►*adj.* Refusing to moderate a position, esp. an extreme one. [< IN–¹ + Lat. *trānsigere,* reach agreement (TRANS– + *agere,* drive).] —**in·tran′si·gence, in·tran′si·gen·cy** *n.* —**in·tran′si·gent** *n.* —**in·tran′si·gent·ly** *adv.*

in·tran·si·tive (ĭn-trăn′sĭ-tĭv, -zĭ-) ►*adj.* Designating a verb that does not require a direct object to complete its meaning. ►*n.* An intransitive verb. —**in·tran′si·tive·ly** *adv.* —**in·tran′si·tive·ness, in·tran′si·tiv′i·ty** *n.*

in·tra·oc·u·lar (ĭn′trə-ŏk′yə-lər) ►*adj.* Within the eyeball.

in·tra·state (ĭn′trə-stāt′) ►*adj.* Existing within the boundaries of a state.

in·tra·u·ter·ine (ĭn′trə-yŏo′tər-ĭn, -tə-rīn′) ►*adj.* Within the uterus.

intrauterine device ►*n.* A birth control device inserted into the uterus to prevent implantation.

in·tra·vas·cu·lar (ĭn′trə-văs′kyə-lər) ►*adj.* Within blood vessels or a blood vessel.

in·tra·ve·nous (ĭn′trə-vē′nəs) ►*adj.* Within or administered into a vein. —**in′tra·ve′nous·ly** *adv.*

in·trep·id (ĭn-trĕp′ĭd) ►*adj.* Resolutely courageous; fearless. [Lat. *intrepidus.*] —**in·trep′id·ness** —**in·trep′id·ly** *adv.*

in·tri·cate (ĭn′trĭ-kĭt) ►*adj.* **1.** Having many complexly arranged elements: *an intricate procedure.* **2.** Difficult to comprehend for having

many interconnected elements. See Synonyms at **complex.** [< Lat. *intrīcāre,* entangle.] —**in′tri·ca·cy** (-kə-sē) *n.* —**in′tri·cate·ly** *adv.*

in·trigue (ĭn′trēg′, ĭn-trēg′) ►*n.* **1.** A secret or underhand scheme; plot. **2.** A secret love affair. ►*v.* (ĭn-trēg′) **-trigued, -trigu·ing** **1.** To arouse the interest or curiosity of. **2.** To engage in or effect by secret scheming or plotting. [< Lat. *intrīcāre,* entangle.] —**in·trigu′er** *n.*

in·trin·sic (ĭn-trĭn′zĭk, -sĭk) ►*adj.* Relating to the essential nature of a thing; inherent. [< LLat. *intrīnsecus,* inward.] —**in·trin′si·cal·ly** *adv.*

in·tro (ĭn′trō′) ►*n., pl.* **-tros** *Informal* An introduction.

intro– ►*pref.* Inward: *introvert.* [Lat. *intrō–.*]

in·tro·duce (ĭn′trə-dōōs′, -dyōōs′) ►*v.* **-duced, -duc·ing** **1a.** To identify and present, esp. to make (strangers) acquainted. **b.** To preface. **2.** To bring forward (e.g., a plan) for consideration. See Synonyms at **broach.** **3.** To inform (someone) of something for the first time. **4.** To originate. **5.** To put into; insert or inject. [< Lat. *intrōdūcere,* bring in.] —**in′tro·duc′tion** (-dŭk′shən) *n.*

in·tro·duc·to·ry (ĭn′trə-dŭk′tə-rē) ►*adj.* Relating to an introduction; initial or preparatory. See Synonyms at **preliminary.**

in·tro·spec·tion (ĭn′trə-spĕk′shən) ►*n.* Contemplation of one's own thoughts and feelings; self-examination. [< Lat. *intrōspicere,* look within : INTRO– + *specere,* look.] —**in′tro·spect′** *v.* —**in′tro·spec′tive** *adj.* —**in′tro·spec′tive·ly** *adv.*

in·tro·vert (ĭn′trə-vûrt′) ►*n.* One whose thoughts and feelings are directed inward. [INTRO– + Lat. *vertere,* turn.] —**in′tro·ver′sion** *n.*

in·trude (ĭn-trōōd′) ►*v.* **-trud·ed, -trud·ing** To put or force in without being wanted or asked; barge in. [< Lat. *intrūdere,* thrust in.] —**in·trud′er** *n.* —**in·tru′sion** *n.* —**in·tru′sive** *adj.* —**in·tru′sive·ly** *adv.*

in·tu·it (ĭn-tōō′ĭt, -tyōō′-) ►*v.* To know by intuition. [< INTUITION.]

in·tu·i·tion (ĭn′tōō-ĭsh′ən, -tyōō-) ►*n.* **1.** The faculty of knowing something without reasoning or proof. **2.** An impression gained by the use of this faculty. [< Lat. *intuērī,* intuit-, contemplate.] —**in′tu·i′tion·al** *adj.* —**in·tu′i·tive** (ĭn-tōō′ĭ-tĭv, -tyōō′-) *adj.* —**in·tu′i·tive·ly** *adv.* —**in·tu′i·tive·ness** *n.*

In·u·it (ĭn′ōō-ĭt, -yōō-) ►*n., pl.* **-it** or **-its** **1.** A member of a group of Eskimoan peoples inhabiting the Arctic from N Alaska eastward to E Greenland. **2.** Any of the Eskimoan languages of the Inuit. —**In·u·it** *adj.*

in·un·date (ĭn′ŭn-dāt′) ►*v.* **-dat·ed, -dat·ing** To cover or overwhelm with or as if with a flood. [Lat. *inundāre* : IN–² + *unda,* wave.] —**in′un·da′tion** *n.*

in·ure (ĭn-yŏor′) ►*v.* **-ured, -ur·ing** To make used to something undesirable; harden. [< ME *in ure,* customary.] —**in·ure′ment** *n.*

in u·ter·o (ĭn yōō′tə-rō) ►*adv. & adj.* In the uterus. [Lat. *in uterō.*]

in·vade (ĭn-vād′) ►*v.* **-vad·ed, -vad·ing** **1.** To enter by force in order to conquer. **2.** To trespass or intrude on; violate. **3.** To overrun or infest. **4.** To enter and permeate, esp. harmfully. [< Lat. *invādere.*] —**in·vad′er** *n.*

in·va·lid¹ (ĭn′və-lĭd) ►*n.* One incapacitated by a

chronic illness or injury. ►*adj.* Incapacitated by illness or injury. [< INVALID².]

in·val·id² (ĭn-văl′ĭd) ►*adj.* **1.** Not legally valid; null. **2.** Falsely based or reasoned; unjustified. [Lat. *invalidus*, weak.] —**in′va·lid′i·ty** (-və-lĭd′ĭ-tē) *n.* —**in·val′id·ly** *adv.*

in·val·i·date (ĭn-văl′ĭ-dāt′) ►*v.* **-dat·ed, -dat·ing** To make invalid; nullify. —**in·val′i·da′tion** *n.* —**in·val′i·da′tor** *n.*

in·val·u·a·ble (ĭn-văl′yo͞o-ə-bəl) ►*adj.* Of inestimable value; priceless. —**in·val′u·a·bly** *adv.*

in·var·i·a·ble (ĭn-vâr′ē-ə-bəl) ►*adj.* Not changing or subject to change; constant. —**in·var′i·a·bil′i·ty, in·var′i·a·ble·ness** *n.* —**in·var′i·a·bly** *adv.*

in·va·sion (ĭn-vā′zhən) ►*n.* **1.** The act of invading, esp. entrance by force. **2.** A large-scale onset of something harmful, such as a disease. **3.** An intrusion or encroachment.

in·va·sive (ĭn-vā′sĭv) ►*adj.* **1.** Of or engaging in armed aggression. **2.** Relating to a disease or condition that tends to spread, esp. into healthy tissue. **3.** Relating to a medical procedure in which a body part is entered. **4.** Not native to and tending to spread widely in a habitat.

in·vec·tive (ĭn-věk′tĭv) ►*n.* Harsh and insulting language used to attack or denounce. [< Lat. *invehī, invect-,* inveigh against.]

in·veigh (ĭn-vā′) ►*v.* To protest or disapprove vehemently. [Lat. *invehī.*]

in·vei·gle (ĭn-vā′gəl, -vē′-) ►*v.* **-gled, -gling 1.** To win over by coaxing, flattery, or artful talk. **2.** To obtain by cajolery. [< OFr. *aveugler,* to blind.] —**in·vei′gle·ment** *n.* —**in·vei′gler** *n.*

in·vent (ĭn-věnt′) ►*v.* **1.** To conceive of or produce first; originate. **2.** To make up; fabricate: *invent a likely excuse.* [Lat. *invenīre, invent-,* find : IN-² + *venīre,* come.] —**in·ven′tor** *n.*

in·ven·tion (ĭn-věn′shən) ►*n.* **1.** The act or process of inventing. **2.** A new device, method, or process developed from study and experimentation. **3.** A mental fabrication, esp. a falsehood. **4.** Skill in inventing.

in·ven·tive (ĭn-věn′tĭv) ►*adj.* **1.** Of or characterized by invention. **2.** Skillful at inventing. —**in·ven′tive·ly** *adv.* —**in·ven′tive·ness** *n.*

in·ven·to·ry (ĭn′vən-tôr′ē) ►*n., pl.* **-ries 1.** A detailed list of things, esp. a periodic survey of all goods and materials in stock. **2.** The process of making such a list. **3.** The items included in such a list. **4.** The supply of goods on hand; stock. —**in′ven·to′ry** *v.*

in·verse (ĭn-vûrs′, ĭn′vûrs′) ►*adj.* Reversed in order, nature, or effect. ►*n.* (ĭn′vûrs′, ĭn-vûrs′) Something opposite, as in sequence, effect, or character; reverse. [< Lat. *inversus,* p.part. of *invertere,* invert.] —**in·verse′ly** *adv.*

in·ver·sion (ĭn-vûr′zhən) ►*n.* **1.** The act of inverting or the state of being inverted. **2.** A reversal of position or order in a sequence. **3.** *Meteorol.* An atmospheric condition in which the air temperature rises with increasing altitude, holding surface air down.

in·vert (ĭn-vûrt′) ►*v.* **1.** To turn inside out or upside down. **2.** To reverse the position, order, or condition of. [Lat. *invertere.*] —**in·vert′er** *n.* —**in·vert′i·ble** *adj.*

in·ver·te·brate (ĭn-vûr′tə-brĭt, -brāt′) ►*adj.* Lacking a backbone or spinal column; not vertebrate. —**in·ver′te·brate** *n.*

in·vest (ĭn-věst′) ►*v.* **1.** To commit (money or

capital) in order to gain a financial return. **2.** To spend or devote (time or effort) for future benefit. **3.** To endow with authority or power. **4.** To install in office; inaugurate. **5.** To surround or envelop. [< Lat. *investīre,* surround.] —**in·ves′tor** *n.*

in·ves·ti·gate (ĭn-věs′tĭ-gāt′) ►*v.* **-gat·ed, -gat·ing** To observe or inquire into in detail; examine systematically. [Lat. *investīgāre* < *vestīgium,* footprint.] —**in·ves′ti·ga′tive** *adj.* —**in·ves′ti·ga′tor** *n.*

in·ves·ti·ga·tion (ĭn-věs′tĭ-gā′shən) ►*n.* **1.** The act or process of investigating. **2.** A careful examination in order to gain information. See Synonyms at **inquiry.**

in·ves·ti·ture (ĭn-věs′tĭ-cho͝or′, -chər) ►*n.* The act or ceremony of conferring the authority of a high office. [< Lat. *investīre,* clothe.]

in·vest·ment (ĭn-věst′mənt) ►*n.* **1.** The act of investing. **2.** An amount invested. **3.** Property acquired for future income. **4.** Investiture.

in·vet·er·ate (ĭn-vět′ər-ĭt) ►*adj.* **1.** Firmly and long established. See Synonyms at **usual. 2.** Persisting in an ingrained habit: *an inveterate liar.* See Synonyms at **chronic.** [< Lat. *inveterārī,* grow old < *vetus,* old.] —**in·vet′er·a·cy** (-ər-ə-sē) *n.* —**in·vet′er·ate·ly** *adv.*

in·vid·i·ous (ĭn-vĭd′ē-əs) ►*adj.* **1.** Tending to rouse ill will or envy. **2.** Discriminatory. [< Lat. *invidia,* envy.] —**in·vid′i·ous·ly** *adv.*

in·vig·or·ate (ĭn-vĭg′ə-rāt′) ►*v.* **-at·ed, -at·ing** To impart vigor or vitality to; animate. —**in·vig′or·at′ing·ly** *adv.* —**in·vig′or·a′tion** *n.* —**in·vig′or·a′tive** *adj.*

in·vin·ci·ble (ĭn-vĭn′sə-bəl) ►*adj.* Unconquerable. [< Lat. *invincibilis* < *vincere,* conquer.] —**in·vin′ci·bil′i·ty** *n.* —**in·vin′ci·bly** *adv.*

in·vi·o·la·ble (ĭn-vī′ə-lə-bəl) ►*adj.* **1.** Secure from violation or profanation. **2.** Impregnable. —**in·vi′o·la·bil′i·ty** *n.* —**in·vi′o·la·bly** *adv.*

in·vi·o·late (ĭn-vī′ə-lĭt) ►*adj.* Not violated or profaned; intact. —**in·vi′o·late·ly** *adv.*

in·vis·i·ble (ĭn-vĭz′ə-bəl) ►*adj.* **1.** Incapable of being seen. **2.** Hidden from view. **3.** Inconspicuous. —**in·vis′i·bil′i·ty** *n.* —**in·vis′i·bly** *adv.*

in·vi·ta·tion (ĭn′vĭ-tā′shən) ►*n.* **1.** The act of inviting. **2.** A request for someone's presence or participation. **3.** An allurement or enticement. —**in′vi·ta′tion·al** *adj. & n.*

in·vite (ĭn-vīt′) ►*v.* **-vit·ed, -vit·ing 1.** To request the presence or participation of. **2.** To request formally. **3.** To welcome: *invite questions.* **4.** To tend to bring on; provoke. **5.** To entice; lure. ►*n.* (ĭn′vīt′) *Informal* An invitation. [< Lat. *invītāre.*]

in·vit·ing (ĭn-vī′tĭng) ►*adj.* Attractive; tempting. —**in·vit′ing·ly** *adv.*

in vi·tro (ĭn vē′trō) ►*adv. & adj.* In an artificial environment outside a living organism. [NLat. *in vitrō,* in glass.]

in vi·vo (vē′vō) ►*adv. & adj.* Within a living organism. [NLat. *in vīvō.*]

in·vo·ca·tion (ĭn′və-kā′shən) ►*n.* **1.** The act of invoking, esp. an appeal to a higher power. **2.** A prayer or other formula used in invoking. [< Lat. *invocāre,* call upon.]

in·voice (ĭn′vois) ►*n.* **1.** A list of goods shipped or services rendered, detailing all costs. **2.** The goods or services so itemized. [< obsolete *invoyes* < Fr. *envoi,* shipment; see ENVOY¹.] —**in′voice** *v.*

in·voke (ĭn-vōk′) ►*v.* **-voked, -vok·ing 1.** To call on (a higher power) for help or inspiration. **2.** To appeal to; petition. **3.** To call for earnestly. **4.** To conjure. **5.** To use or apply: *invoked the veto power.* [< Lat. *invocāre.*] —**in·vok′er** *n.*

in·vol·un·tar·y (ĭn-vŏl′ən-tĕr′ē) ►*adj.* **1.** Performed against one's will. **2.** Not subject to control: *an involuntary twitch.* —**in·vol′un·tar′i·ly** (-târ′ə-lē) *adv.* —**in·vol′un·tar′i·ness** *n.*

in·vo·lu·tion (ĭn′və-loo′shən) ►*n.* **1.** The act of involving or the state of being involved. **2.** Something, such as a long grammatical construction, that is intricate or complex. **3.** *Math.* An operation, such as negation, which, when applied to itself, returns the original number. **4.** *Med.* A decrease in size of an organ, as of the uterus following childbirth. [< Lat. *involvere, involūt-*, enwrap.]

in·volve (ĭn-vŏlv′) ►*v.* **-volved, -volv·ing 1.** To have as a necessary feature or consequence. **2.** To engage or draw in; embroil. **3.** To engross. **4.** To make complex; complicate. [< Lat. *involvere,* enwrap.] —**in·volve′ment** *n.*

in·vul·ner·a·ble (ĭn-vŭl′nər-ə-bəl) ►*adj.* **1.** Immune to attack; impregnable. **2.** Impossible to damage or injure. —**in·vul′ner·a·bil′i·ty** *n.* —**in·vul′ner·a·bly** *adv.*

in·ward (ĭn′wərd) ►*adj.* **1.** Located inside; inner. **2.** Directed or moving toward the interior. **3.** Existing in the mind. ►*adv.* **1.** Toward the inside or center. **2.** Toward the mind or the self. —**in′wards** *adv.*

in·ward·ly (ĭn′wərd-lē) ►*adv.* **1.** On or in the inside; within. **2.** To oneself; privately.

IOC ►*abbr.* International Olympic Committee

i·o·dide (ī′ə-dīd′) ►*n.* Univalent anionic iodine or a binary compound of iodine.

i·o·dine (ī′ə-dīn′, -dĭn, -dēn′) ►*n.* **1.** *Symbol* **I** A lustrous, purple-black, corrosive, poisonous element having radioactive isotopes used as tracers and in thyroid disease diagnosis and therapy, and compounds used as germicides, antiseptics, and dyes. At. no. 53. See table at **element. 2.** An antiseptic preparation containing iodine in solution, used to treat wounds. [< Gk. *ioeidēs*, violet-colored + -INE².]

i·o·dize (ī′ə-dīz′) ►*v.* **-dized, -diz·ing** To treat or combine with iodine or an iodide.

iodo- or **iod-** ►*pref.* Iodine: *iodize.* [< Fr. *iode,* iodine.]

i·on (ī′ən, ī′ŏn′) ►*n.* An atom or group of atoms that has acquired a net electric charge by gaining or losing one or more electrons. [Gk., something that goes.] —**i·on′ic** (-ŏn′ĭk) *adj.*

-ion ►*suff.* **1a.** Action or process: *completion.* **b.** Result of an action or process: *invention.* **2.** State or condition: *dehydration.* [< Lat. *-iō, -iōn-.*]

I·o·nes·co (ē′ə-nĕs′kō, yə-), **Eugène** 1912?–94. Romanian-born French dramatist.

I·o·ni·a (ī-ō′nē-ə) An ancient region of W Asia Minor along the Aegean coast. —**I·o′ni·an** *adj. & n.*

Ionian Islands A chain of islands in W Greece in the Ionian Sea.

Ionian Sea An arm of the Mediterranean between W Greece and S Italy.

ionic bond ►*n.* A chemical bond between two ions with opposite charges.

Ionic order ►*n. Archit.* A classical order that is marked by two opposed volutes in the column capital.

i·on·ize (ī′ə-nīz′) ►*v.* **-ized, -iz·ing** To convert or be converted totally or partially into ions. —**i′on·i·za′tion** *n.*

i·on·o·sphere (ī-ŏn′ə-sfîr′) ►*n.* An electrically conducting region of the earth's atmosphere, extending from altitudes of 70 km (43 mi) to 400 km (250 mi).

i·o·ta (ī-ō′tə) ►*n.* **1.** The 9th letter of the Greek alphabet. **2.** A very small amount; bit. [< Gk. *iōta.*]

IOU (ī′ō-yoo′) ►*n.* A usu. written promise to pay a debt.

-ious ►*suff.* Characterized by or full of: *bilious.* [< Lat. *-ius* and *-iōsus.*]

I·o·wa¹ (ī′ə-wə) ►*n., pl.* **-wa** or **-was 1.** A member of a Native American people formerly of Iowa and SW Minnesota, later in Nebraska, Kansas, and Oklahoma. **2.** The Siouan language of the Iowa.

I·o·wa² (ī′ə-wə) A state of the N-central US. Cap. Des Moines. —**I′o·wan** *adj. & n.*

IPA ►*abbr.* International Phonetic Alphabet

ip·e·cac (ĭp′ĭ-kăk′) ►*n.* A preparation made from the roots of a tropical American shrub, used to induce vomiting. [< Tupí *ipekaaguéne.*]

IPO ►*abbr.* initial public offering

ip·so fac·to (ĭp′sō făk′tō) ►*adv.* By the fact itself; by that very fact. [< Lat. *ipsō factō.*]

IQ ►*abbr.* intelligence quotient

I·qal·u·it (ĭ-kăl′oo-ĭt, ē-kä′loo-ēt) The capital of Nunavut, Canada, on Baffin I.

ir-¹ ►*pref.* Var. of **in-¹**.

ir-² ►*pref.* Var. of **in-²**.

IRA ►*abbr.* **1.** individual retirement account **2.** Irish Republican Army

I·ran (ĭ-răn′, ĭ-rän′) Formerly **Per·sia** (pûr′zhə, -shə). A country of SW Asia. Cap. Tehran.

I·ra·ni·an (ĭ-rä′nē-ən, ĭ-răn′-, ī-rä′-) ►*n.* **1.** A native or inhabitant of Iran. **2.** A branch of the Indo-European language family that includes Persian, Kurdish, and Pashto. —**I·ra′ni·an** *adj.*

I·raq (ĭ-răk′, ĭ-räk′) A country of SW Asia. Cap. Baghdad. —**I·ra′qi** (-răk′ē, -rä′kē) *adj. & n.*

i·ras·ci·ble (ĭ-răs′ə-bəl, ī-răs′-) ►*adj.* Prone to outbursts of temper; easily angered. [< Lat. *īrāscī,* be angry < *īra,* anger.] —**i·ras′ci·bil′i·ty** *n.* —**i·ras′ci·bly** *adv.*

i·rate (ī-rāt′, ī′rāt′) ►*adj.* Extremely angry; enraged. See Synonyms at **angry.** [Lat. *īrātus* < *īra,* anger.] —**i·rate′ly** *adv.*

ire (īr) ►*n.* Anger; wrath. [< Lat. *īra.*]

ire·ful (īr′fəl) ►*adj.* Full of ire. See Synonyms at **angry.** —**ire′ful·ly** *adv.*

Ire·land (īr′lənd) **1.** An island in the N Atlantic W of Great Britain. **2.** also **Eir·e** (âr′ə, ī′rə) A country occupying most of the island of Ireland. Cap. Dublin.

ir·i·des·cent (ĭr′ĭ-dĕs′ənt) ►*adj.* **1.** Producing a display of lustrous, rainbowlike colors: *an iridescent oil slick.* **2.** Appearing brilliant or colorful. [Gk. *iris, irid-,* rainbow + -ESCENT.] —**ir′i·des′cence** *n.*

i·rid·i·um (ĭ-rĭd′ē-əm) ►*n. Symbol* **Ir** A hard, brittle, exceptionally corrosion-resistant whitish-yellow metallic element used as an alloy with platinum. At. no. 77. See **v.** [Gk. *iris, irid-,* rainbow + -IUM.]

i·ris (ī′rĭs) ►*n., pl.* **i·ris·es** or **i·ri·des** (ī′rĭ-dēz′, ĭr′ĭ-) **1.** The pigmented, round, contractile membrane of the eye, situated between the cornea and lens and perforated by the pupil.

2. A plant having narrow sword-shaped leaves and showy, variously colored flowers. [< Gk.]

I·rish (ī′rĭsh) ▸*adj.* Of or relating to Ireland or its people or language. ▸*n.* **1.** The people of Ireland. **2a.** The Gaelic language of Ireland. **b.** English as spoken by the Irish. **3.** *Informal* Fieriness of temper or passion. —**I′rish·man** *n.* —**I′rish·wom′an** *n.*

Irish bull ▸*n.* A statement containing an incongruity or a logical absurdity.

Irish moss ▸*n.* An edible North Atlantic seaweed that yields carrageenan.

Irish Sea An arm of the N Atlantic between Ireland and Great Britain.

Irish setter ▸*n.* A setter having a silky reddishbrown coat with feathered ears, legs, and tail.

irk (ûrk) ▸*v.* To annoy; irritate. See Synonyms at **annoy.** [ME *irken.*]

irk·some (ûrk′səm) ▸*adj.* Annoying; bothersome; tedious. —**irk′some·ly** *adv.* —**irk′-some·ness** *n.*

Ir·kutsk (ĭr-ko͞otsk′) A city of S-central Russia near S Lake Baikal.

i·ron (ī′ərn) ▸*n.* **1.** *Symbol* **Fe** A silvery-white, malleable, magnetic or magnetizable metallic element used alloyed in many structural materials. At. no. 26. See table at **element. 2.** An implement made of iron alloy or a similar metal, esp. a bar heated for use in curling hair. **3.** Great hardness or strength: *a will of iron.* **4.** A golf club with a metal head. **5.** An appliance with a weighted flat bottom, used when heated to press fabric. **6. irons** Fetters; shackles. ▸*adj.* Of or like iron. ▸*v.* To press and smooth with a heated iron. —***phrasal verb:*** **iron out** To discuss and settle; work out. [< OE *īren.*] —**i′ron·er** *n.* —**i′ron·ing** *n.*

Iron Age ▸*n.* The period of human culture succeeding the Bronze Age, marked by the introduction of iron metallurgy and beginning in Europe around the 8th cent. BC.

i·ron·clad (ī′ərn-klăd′) ▸*adj.* **1.** Covered with iron plates for protection. **2.** Rigid; fixed: *an ironclad rule.*

iron curtain or **Iron Curtain** ▸*n.* The military, political, and ideological barrier existing between the Soviet bloc and W Europe from 1945 until 1990.

i·ron·ic (ī-rŏn′ĭk) also **i·ron·i·cal** (-ĭ-kəl) ▸*adj.* **1.** Marked by or constituting irony. **2.** Given to the use of irony. —**i·ron′i·cal·ly** *adv.*

iron lung ▸*n.* A tank that encloses all of the body except the head and forces the lungs to inhale and exhale by changing the air pressure.

i·ron·stone (ī′ərn-stōn′) ▸*n.* **1.** A hard white pottery. **2.** An iron ore.

i·ron·ware (ī′ərn-wâr′) ▸*n.* Iron utensils and other products made of iron.

i·ron·work (ī′ərn-wûrk′) ▸*n.* Work in iron, such as gratings and rails.

i·ron·work·er (ī′ərn-wûr′kər) ▸*n.* **1.** A construction worker who builds steel structures. **2.** One who makes iron articles.

i·ron·works (ī′ərn-wûrks′) ▸*pl.n.* (*takes sing. or pl. v.*) A building or establishment where iron is smelted or iron products are made.

i·ro·ny (ī′rə-nē, ī′ər-) ▸*n.*, *pl.* **-nies 1.** The use of words to convey the opposite of their literal meaning. **2.** Incongruity between what might be expected and what actually occurs. [< Gk. *eirōneia,* feigned ignorance.] —**i′ro·nist** *n.*

Ir·o·quoi·an (ĭr′ə-kwoi′ən) ▸*n.* **1.** A family of Native American languages of E North America. **2.** A member of an Iroquoian-speaking people. —**Ir′o·quoi′an** *adj.*

Ir·o·quois (ĭr′ə-kwoi′) ▸*n.*, *pl.* **-quois** (-kwoi′, -kwoiz′) **1.** A member of a Native American confederacy of New York State composed of the Mohawk, Oneida, Onondaga, Cayuga, Seneca, and later the Tuscarora peoples. **2.** Any of the languages of the Iroquois.

ir·ra·di·ate (ĭ-rā′dē-āt′) ▸*v.* **-at·ed, -at·ing 1.** To expose to or treat with radiation. **2.** To shed light on; illuminate. **3.** To emit in or as if in rays; radiate. [Lat. *irradiāre,* shine on < *radius,* ray.] —**ir·ra′di·a′tion** *n.* —**ir·ra′di·a′tive** *adj.* —**ir·ra′di·a′tor** *n.*

ir·ra·tion·al (ĭ-răsh′ə-nəl) ▸*adj.* **1a.** Not endowed with reason. **b.** Incoherent, as from shock. **c.** Illogical: *an irrational dislike.* **2.** *Math.* Relating to an irrational number. —**ir·ra′tion·al·i·ty** (-ə-năl′ĭ-tē) *n.* —**ir·ra′tion·al·ly** *adv.*

irrational number ▸*n.* A real number that cannot be expressed as a ratio between two integers.

Ir·ra·wad·dy (ĭr′ə-wŏd′ē, -wô′dē) A river of Myanmar flowing about 2,170 km (1,350 mi) to the Bay of Bengal and the Andaman Sea.

ir·rec·on·cil·a·ble (ĭ-rĕk′ən-sī′lə-bəl, ĭ-rĕk′ən-sī′-) ▸*adj.* Impossible to reconcile: *irreconcilable differences.* —**ir·rec′on·cil′a·bil′i·ty** *n.* —**ir·rec′on·cil′a·bly** *adv.*

ir·re·cov·er·a·ble (ĭr′ĭ-kŭv′ər-ə-bəl) ▸*adj.* Impossible to recover; irreparable: *irrecoverable losses.* —**ir′re·cov′er·a·bly** *adv.*

ir·re·deem·a·ble (ĭr′ĭ-dē′mə-bəl) ▸*adj.* **1.** That cannot be bought back or paid off. **2.** Not convertible into coin. **3.** Impossible to redeem or reform. —**ir′re·deem′a·bly** *adv.*

ir·re·den·tist (ĭr′ĭ-dĕn′tĭst) ▸*n.* One who advocates the recovery of territory culturally or historically related to one's nation but now subject to a foreign government. [< Ital. *irredenta,* unredeemed.] —**ir′re·den′tism** *n.*

ir·re·duc·i·ble (ĭr′ĭ-do͞o′sə-bəl, -dyo͞o′-) ▸*adj.* Impossible to reduce to a simpler or smaller form or amount. —**ir′re·duc′i·bil′i·ty** *n.* —**ir′-re·duc′i·bly** *adv.*

ir·ref·u·ta·ble (ĭ-rĕf′yə-tə-bəl, ĭr′ĭ-fyo͞o′-) ▸*adj.* Impossible to refute or disprove. —**ir·ref′u·ta·bil′i·ty** *n.* —**ir·ref′u·ta·bly** *adv.*

irreg. ▸*abbr.* irregular

ir·re·gard·less (ĭr′ĭ-gärd′lĭs) ▸*adv. Nonstandard* Regardless.

Usage: *Irregardless* is a word that many people mistakenly believe to be correct in formal style, when in fact it is used chiefly in nonstandard speech or casual writing.

ir·reg·u·lar (ĭ-rĕg′yə-lər) ▸*adj.* **1.** Contrary to rule, accepted order, or general practice. **2.** Not straight, uniform, or symmetrical. **3.** Of uneven rate, occurrence, or duration. **4.** Deviating from a type; atypical. **5.** Not up to standard or specification; imperfect. **6.** *Gram.* Departing from the usual pattern of inflection. **7.** Not belonging to a permanent, organized military force. ▸*n.* **1.** One that is irregular. **2.** A guerrilla. —**ir·reg′u·lar′i·ty** (-yə-lăr′ĭ-tē) *n.* —**ir·reg′u·lar·ly** *adv.*

ir·rel·e·vant (ĭ-rĕl′ə-vənt) ▸*adj.* Unrelated to the matter at hand. —**ir·rel′e·vance, ir·rel′e·van·cy** *n.* —**ir·rel′e·vant·ly** *adv.*

Syns: *extraneous, immaterial, impertinent*
Ant: *relevant adj.*

ir·re·li·gious (ĭr′ĭ-lĭj′əs) ►*adj.* Hostile or indifferent to religion. —**ir′re·li′gious·ly** *adv.*

ir·re·me·di·a·ble (ĭr′ĭ-mē′dē-ə-bəl) ►*adj.* Impossible to remedy, correct, or repair. —**ir′re·me′di·a·bly** *adv.*

ir·rep·a·ra·ble (ĭ-rĕp′ər-ə-bəl) ►*adj.* Impossible to repair, rectify, or amend. —**ir·rep′a·ra·bil′i·ty** *n.* —**ir·rep′a·ra·bly** *adv.*

ir·re·place·a·ble (ĭr′ĭ-plā′sə-bəl) ►*adj.* Impossible to replace.

ir·re·press·i·ble (ĭr′ĭ-prĕs′ə-bəl) ►*adj.* Impossible to control or hold back. —**ir′re·press′i·bil′i·ty** *n.* —**ir′re·press′i·bly** *adv.*

ir·re·proach·a·ble (ĭr′ĭ-prō′chə-bəl) ►*adj.* Being beyond reproach: *irreproachable conduct.* —**ir′re·proach′a·bly** *adv.*

ir·re·sis·ti·ble (ĭr′ĭ-zĭs′tə-bəl) ►*adj.* **1.** Impossible to resist. **2.** Overwhelming. —**ir′re·sis′ti·bil′i·ty** *n.* —**ir′re·sis′ti·bly** *adv.*

ir·res·o·lute (ĭ-rĕz′ə-lōōt′) ►*adj.* **1.** Unsure of how to act or proceed; undecided. **2.** Lacking in resolution; indecisive. —**ir·res′o·lute′ly** *adv.* —**ir·res′o·lute′ness, ir·res′o·lu′tion** *n.*

ir·re·spec·tive of (ĭr′ĭ-spĕk′tĭv) ►*prep.* Without consideration of; regardless of.

ir·re·spon·si·ble (ĭr′ĭ-spŏn′sə-bəl) ►*adj.* **1.** Marked by a lack of responsibility: *irresponsible accusations.* **2.** Unreliable. —**ir′re·spon′si·bil′i·ty** *n.* —**ir′re·spon′si·bly** *adv.*

ir·re·triev·a·ble (ĭr′ĭ-trē′və-bəl) ►*adj.* Impossible to retrieve or recover. —**ir′re·triev′a·bil′i·ty** *n.* —**ir′re·triev′a·bly** *adv.*

ir·rev·er·ence (ĭ-rĕv′ər-əns) ►*n.* **1.** Lack of reverence or due respect. **2.** A disrespectful act or remark. —**ir·rev′er·ent** *adj.* —**ir·rev′er·ent·ly** *adv.*

ir·re·vers·i·ble (ĭr′ĭ-vûr′sə-bəl) ►*adj.* Impossible to reverse. —**ir′re·vers′i·bil′i·ty** *n.* —**ir′re·vers′i·bly** *adv.*

ir·rev·o·ca·ble (ĭ-rĕv′ə-kə-bəl) ►*adj.* Impossible to retract or revoke. —**ir·rev′o·ca·bil′i·ty, ir·rev′o·ca·ble·ness** *n.* —**ir·rev′o·ca·bly** *adv.*

ir·ri·gate (ĭr′ĭ-gāt′) ►*v.* **-gat·ed, -gat·ing 1.** To supply land or crops with water by means of ditches, pipes, or streams. **2.** *Med.* To wash out with water or a medicated fluid. [Lat. *irrigāre.*] —**ir′ri·ga·ble** (ĭr′ĭ-gə-bəl) *adj.* —**ir′ri·ga′tion** *n.* —**ir′ri·ga′tion·al** *adj.* —**ir′ri·ga′tor** *n.*

ir·ri·ta·ble (ĭr′ĭ-tə-bəl) ►*adj.* **1.** Easily irritated or annoyed. **2.** *Med.* Abnormally sensitive. **3.** Responsive to stimuli. [< Lat. *irrītāre,* irritate.] —**ir′ri·ta·bil′i·ty, ir′ri·ta·ble·ness** *n.* —**ir′ri·ta·bly** *adv.*

ir·ri·tant (ĭr′ĭ-tənt) ►*adj.* Causing irritation, esp. physical irritation. ►*n.* A source of irritation.

ir·ri·tate (ĭr′ĭ-tāt′) ►*v.* **-tat·ed, -tat·ing 1.** To make impatient or angry; annoy. See Synonyms at **annoy. 2.** To chafe or inflame. [Lat. *irrītāre.*] —**ir′ri·ta′tion** *n.* —**ir′ri·ta′tor** *n.*

IRS ►*abbr.* Internal Revenue Service

Ir·tysh or **Ir·tish** (ĭr-tĭsh′) A river of NW China, E Kazakhstan, and central Russia flowing about 4,250 km (2,650 mi) to the Ob R.

Irving, Washington 1783–1859. Amer. writer.

is (ĭz) ►*v.* 3rd pers. sing. pr. indic. of **be.**

Is. ►*abbr.* island

I·saac (ī′zək) In the Bible, the son of Abraham.

Is·a·bel·la I (ĭz′ə-bĕl′ə) "the Catholic." 1451–1504. Queen of Castile and Léon (1474–1504).

Isabella I

I·sa·iah (ī-zā′ə, ī-zī′ə) ►*n.* **1.** A Hebrew prophet of the 8th cent. BC. **2.** See table at **Bible.**

ISBN ►*abbr.* International Standard Book Number

is·che·mi·a (ĭ-skē′mē-ə) ►*n.* A decrease in the blood supply to a bodily organ or part caused by constriction or obstruction of the blood vessels. [< Gk. *iskhaimos,* stopping of the blood.] —**i·sche′mic** *adj.*

–ish ►*suff.* **1.** Of, relating to, or being: *Swedish.* **2a.** Characteristic of: *girlish.* **b.** Having the qualities of: *childish.* **3.** Approximately; somewhat: *greenish.* **4.** Tending toward; preoccupied with: *selfish.* [< OE *-isc.*]

i·sin·glass (ī′zən-glăs′, ī′zĭng-) ►*n.* **1.** A transparent gelatin prepared from the swim bladder esp. of the sturgeon. **2.** Mica in thin, transparent sheets. [< obsolete Du. *huizenblas.*]

I·sis (ī′sĭs) ►*n. Myth.* An ancient Egyptian goddess of fertility and magic who was the sister and wife of Osiris.

Isl. ►*abbr.* island

Is·lam (ĭs-läm′, ĭs′läm′, ĭz′-) ►*n.* **1.** A monotheistic religion marked by the doctrine of absolute submission to God and by reverence for Muhammad as the chief and last prophet of God. **2.** The people or nations that practice Islam; the Muslim world. —**Is·lam′ic** *adj.*

Is·lam·a·bad (ĭs-lä′mə-bäd′) The capital of Pakistan, in the NE.

Islamic calendar ►*n.* The lunar calendar used by Muslims, reckoned from the year of the Hegira in AD 622. See table at **calendar.**

is·land (ī′lənd) ►*n.* **1.** A landmass, esp. one smaller than a continent, surrounded by water. **2.** Something that is completely isolated or surrounded. [< OE *īegland : īeg* + *land,* land.] —**is′land·er** *n.*

isle (īl) ►*n.* An island, esp. a small one. [< Lat. *īnsula.*]

is·let (ī′lĭt) ►*n.* A very small island.

ism (ĭz′əm) ►*n. Informal* A distinctive doctrine, system, or theory. [< –ISM.]

–ism ►*suff.* **1.** Action; process; practice: *terrorism.* **2.** Characteristic behavior or quality: *heroism.* **3a.** State; condition; quality: *pauperism.* **b.** State or condition resulting from an excess of something specified: *strychninism.* **4.** Distinctive or characteristic trait: *Latinism.* **5a.** Doctrine; theory; system of principles: *pacifism.* **b.** An attitude of prejudice against a given group: *racism.* [< Gk. *-ismos,* n. suff.]

is·n't (ĭz′ənt) Is not.

iso– or **is–** ▸*pref.* **1.** Equal; uniform: *isobar*. **2.** Isomeric: *isopropyl*. [< Gk. *isos*, equal.]

i·so·bar (ī′sə-bär′) ▸*n.* A line on a weather map connecting points of equal atmospheric pressure. [ISO– + Gk. *baros*, weight.] —**i′so·bar′ic** (-bär′ĭk, -băr′-) *adj.*

i·so·gon (ī′sə-gŏn′) ▸*n.* A polygon whose angles are equal. —**i′so·gon′ic** *adj.*

i·so·late (ī′sə-lāt′) ▸*v.* **-lat·ed, -lat·ing** **1.** To cause to be alone or apart. **2.** To place in quarantine. [< Lat. *īnsula*, island.] —**i′so·late** (-lĭt, -lāt′) *adj. & n.* —**i′so·la′tion** *n.* —**i′so·la′tor** *n.*

Syns: insulate, seclude, segregate, sequester v.

i·so·la·tion·ism (ī′sə-lā′shə-nĭz′əm) ▸*n.* A national policy of abstaining from political or economic entanglements with other countries. —**i′so·la′tion·ist** *n. & adj.*

i·so·mer (ī′sə-mər) ▸*n.* **1.** *Chem.* A substance having the same molecular formula as another but differing in the way its atoms are connected or arranged. **2.** *Phys.* A nucleus that has the same mass number and atomic number as the nucleus of another atom but has differing radioactive properties and can exist in any of several energy states for a measurable period. —**i′so·mer′ic** (-mĕr′ĭk) *adj.*

i·so·met·ric (ī′sə-mĕt′rĭk) also **i·so·met·ri·cal** (-rĭ-kəl) ▸*adj.* **1.** Exhibiting equality in dimensions or measurements. **2.** *Physiol.* Involving muscular contraction against resistance in which the length of the muscle remains the same. [< Gk. *isometros*, having equal measure.]

i·so·met·rics (ī′sə-mĕt′rĭks) ▸*n. (takes sing. or pl. v.)* Exercise in which isometric contraction is used to strengthen and tone muscles.

i·so·morph (ī′sə-môrf′) ▸*n.* An organism or substance exhibiting isomorphism.

i·so·mor·phism (ī′sə-môr′fĭz′əm) ▸*n.* Similarity of form, as in organisms of different ancestry, or of structure, as in chemical substances. —**i′so·mor′phic** *adj.*

i·so·pro·pyl alcohol (ī′sə-prō′pəl) ▸*n.* A clear, colorless, flammable mobile liquid used in antifreeze compounds, lotions, cosmetics, and as a solvent.

i·sos·ce·les (ī-sŏs′ə-lēz′) ▸*adj.* Having at least two equal sides: *an isosceles triangle*. [< Gk. *isoskelēs* : ISO– + *skelos*, leg.]

i·so·therm (ī′sə-thûrm′) ▸*n.* A line on a weather map linking all points of equal or constant temperature. [< ISO– + Gk. *thermē*, heat.] —**i′so·ther′mal** *adj.*

i·so·tope (ī′sə-tōp′) ▸*n.* One of two or more atoms having the same atomic number but different mass numbers. [ISO– + Gk. *topos*, place.] —**i′so·top′ic** (-tŏp′ĭk) *adj.*

i·so·tro·pic (ī′sə-trō′pĭk, -trŏp′ĭk) ▸*adj.* Invariant with respect to direction; identical in all directions. —**i·sot′ro·py** (ī-sŏt′rə-pē), **i·sot′ro·pism** (-pĭz′əm) *n.*

ISP ▸*abbr.* Internet Service Provider

Is·ra·el[1] (ĭz′rē-əl) ▸*n.* **1a.** In the Bible, Jacob. **b.** The descendants of Jacob. **2.** *Judaism* The Hebrew people, past, present, and future.

Is·ra·el[2] (ĭz′rē-əl) **1.** An ancient kingdom of the Hebrews in SW Asia on the E Mediterranean. **2.** A country of SW Asia on the E Mediterranean. Cap. Jerusalem.

Is·rae·li (ĭz-rā′lē) ▸*adj.* Of or relating to modern-day Israel or its people. ▸*n., pl.* **-lis** A citizen of modern-day Israel.

Is·ra·el·ite (ĭz′rē-ə-līt′) ▸*n.* **1.** A native or inhabitant of ancient Israel. **2.** A Jew.

is·sue (ĭsh′ōō) ▸*n.* **1a.** A point of discussion. **b.** A matter of public concern. **2a.** Something produced, published, or offered, as stamps or coins. **b.** A single copy of a periodical. **c.** Proceeds from estates or fines. **d.** Something proceeding from a specified source. **e.** The final result of an action. **3a.** The act or an instance of flowing, passing, or giving out. **b.** An outlet. **4.** *Med.* A discharge, as of blood. **5.** Offspring; progeny. ▸*v.* **-sued, -su·ing** **1a.** To go or come out. **b.** To come forth or cause to come forth. See Synonyms at **stem**[1]. **c.** To end or result. **2.** To be born or be descended. **3.** To publish or be published. **4.** To circulate, as coins. —*idioms:* **at issue** In dispute. **take issue** To disagree. [< VLat. **exūta* < Lat. *exīre*, go out.] —**is′su·ance** *n.* —**is′su·er** *n.*

–ist ▸*suff.* **1a.** One that performs a specified action: *lobbyist.* **b.** One that produces, operates, or is connected with a specified thing: *novelist.* **2.** A specialist in a specified field: *biologist.* **3.** An adherent or advocate of a specified doctrine, theory, or school of thought: *anarchist.* **4.** One that is characterized by a specified trait or quality: *romanticist.* [< Gk. *-istēs*, agent n. suff.]

Is·tan·bul (ĭs′tăn-bōōl′, -tän-, ĭ-stän′bōōl) Formerly **Con·stan·ti·no·ple** (kŏn′stăn-tə-nō′pəl). The largest city of Turkey, in the NW part on the Bosporus at its entrance into the Sea of Marmara.

Isth. ▸*abbr.* isthmus

isth·mus (ĭs′məs) ▸*n.* **1.** A narrow strip of land connecting two larger masses of land. **2.** *Anat.* **a.** A narrow strip of tissue joining two larger organs or parts of an organ. **b.** A narrow passage connecting two larger cavities. [< Gk. *isthmos.*] —**isth′mi·an** *adj.*

it (ĭt) ▸*pron.* **1.** Used to refer to a nonhuman entity, an animal or human whose sex is unknown or irrelevant, a group of persons, or an abstraction. **2.** Used as the subject of an impersonal verb: *It is snowing.* **3.** Used to refer to a general condition or state of affairs: *She couldn't stand it.* **4.** *Games* Used to designate a player, as in tag, who attempts to find or catch the other players. [< OE *hit.*]

IT ▸*abbr.* information technology

It. or **Ital.** ▸*abbr.* Italian

ital. ▸*abbr.* **1.** italic **2.** italics

I·tal·ian (ĭ-tăl′yən) ▸*adj.* Of or relating to Italy or its people or language. ▸*n.* **1.** A native or inhabitant of Italy. **2.** The Romance language of the Italians and parts of Switzerland.

I·tal·ic (ĭ-tăl′ĭk, ī-tăl′-) ▸*n.* **1.** A branch of Indo-European that includes Latin. **2.** often **italics** Italic print or typeface. ▸*adj.* **1.** Relating to ancient Italy. **2.** Relating to the branch of Indo-European that includes Latin. **3. italic** Of or being a style of printing type with the letters slanting to the right: *This sentence is in italic type.* [< Lat. *Italia*, Italy.]

i·tal·i·cize (ĭ-tăl′ĭ-sīz′, ī-tăl′-) ▸*v.* **-cized, -ciz·ing** To print in italic type. —**i·tal′i·ci·za′tion** *n.*

It·a·ly (ĭt′l-ē) **1.** A peninsula of S Europe projecting into the Mediterranean between the Tyrrhenian and Adriatic Seas. **2.** A country of S Europe comprising the peninsula of Italy, Sardinia, Sicily, and several smaller islands. Cap. Rome.

itch (ĭch) ►*n.* **1.** A skin sensation causing a desire to scratch. **2.** A skin disorder marked by intense irritation and itching. **3.** A restless desire or craving. [< OE *gicce.*] —**itch** *v.* —**itch′i•ness** *n.* —**itch′y** *adj.*

–**ite¹** ►*suff.* **1.** Native or resident of: *urbanite.* **2.** Adherent or follower of: *Trotskyite.* **3.** A part of an organ or body: *dendrite.* **4a.** Rock; mineral: *graphite.* **b.** Fossil: *trilobite.* **5a.** Product: *metabolite.* **b.** A commercial product: *ebonite.* [< Gk. *-itēs.*]

–**ite²** ►*suff.* A salt or ester of an acid named with an adjective ending in *-ous: sulfite.* [Alteration of –ATE².]

i•tem (ī′təm) ►*n.* **1.** A single article or unit in a group, series, or list. **2a.** A bit of information; detail. **b.** A short piece in a newspaper or magazine. **3.** A romantically involved couple. [< Lat., also.]

i•tem•ize (ī′tə-mīz′) ►*v.* **-ized, -iz•ing** **1.** To set down by item; list. **2.** To list deductions from taxable income on a tax return. —**i′tem•i•za′tion** *n.* —**i′tem•iz′er** *n.*

it•er•ate (ĭt′ə-rāt′) ►*v.* **-at•ed, -at•ing** To say or perform again. See Synonyms at **repeat.** [< Lat. *iterum,* again.] —**it′er•a′tion** *n.*

I•thá•ki (ē-thä′kē) also **Ith•a•ca** (ĭth′ə-kə) An island of W Greece in the Ionian Is.

i•tin•er•ant (ī-tĭn′ər-ənt, ĭ-tĭn′-) ►*adj.* Traveling from place to place, esp. to perform work. ►*n.* An itinerant person. [< LLat. *itinerārī,* travel < Lat. *iter, itiner-,* journey.] —**i•tin′er•an•cy, i•tin′er•a•cy** *n.*

i•tin•er•ar•y (ī-tĭn′ə-rĕr′ē, ĭ-tĭn′-) ►*n., pl.* **-ies** **1.** A route or proposed route of a journey. **2.** An account or record of a journey. **3.** A traveler's guidebook. [< Lat. *iter, itiner-,* journey.]

–**itis** ►*suff.* Inflammation or disease of: *laryngitis.* [Gk., n. suff.]

it'll (ĭt′l) It will.

its (ĭts) ►*adj.* The possessive form of **it.** Used as a modifier before a noun: *The dog ate its food.*
   Usage: Its, the possessive form of the pronoun *it,* is correctly written without an apostrophe. The contraction *it's* (for *it is* or *it has*) is always written with an apostrophe.

it's (ĭts) **1.** It is. **2.** It has.

it•self (ĭt-sĕlf′) ►*pron.* **1.** That one identical with it. Used: **a.** Reflexively as the direct or indirect object of a verb or the object of a preposition: *The cat scratched itself.* **b.** For emphasis: *The trouble is in the machine itself.* **2.** Its normal condition or state: *The car is acting itself again since the oil change.*

–**ity** ►*suff.* State; quality: *abnormality.* [< Lat. *-itās.*]

IU ►*abbr.* international unit

IUD ►*abbr.* intrauterine device

–**ium** ►*suff.* Chemical element or group: *iridium.* [Alteration of Lat. *-um,* neuter suff.]

IV ►*abbr.* intravenous

I•van III Va•sil•ie•vich (ī′vən, ē-vän′; və-sĭl′yə-vĭch′) "the Great." 1440–1505. Grand duke of Muscovy (1462–1505).

Ivan IV Vasilievich "the Terrible." 1530–84. The first czar of Russia (1547–84).

–**ive** ►*suff.* Performing or tending toward a specified action: *demonstrative.* [< Lat. *-īvus.*]

I've (īv) I have.

i•vo•ry (ī′və-rē, īv′rē) ►*n., pl.* **-ries** **1.** A hard, smooth, yellowish-white substance that forms the tusks of certain animals, esp. the elephant. **2.** An article made of ivory. **3.** A substance resembling ivory. **4.** A yellowish white. **5.** often **ivories a.** Piano keys. **b.** Dice. [< Lat. *ebur,* of Egypt. orig.] —**i′vo•ry** *adj.*

Ivory Coast See **Côte d'Ivoire.**

ivory tower ►*n.* A place or attitude of retreat, esp. preoccupation with intellectual considerations rather than practical life.

i•vy (ī′vē) ►*n., pl.* **i•vies** Any of a genus of climbing or trailing plants having lobed evergreen leaves. [< OE *ifig.*]

I•wo Ji•ma (ē′wə jē′mə, ē′wō) The largest of the Volcano Is. of Japan, in the NW Pacific E of Taiwan.

I•yar also **Iy•yar** (ē-yär′, ē′yär′) ►*n.* The 2nd month in the Jewish calendar. See table at **calendar.** [Heb. *'iyyār.*]

–**ization** ►*suff.* Action, process, or result of doing or making: *colonization.*

–**ize** ►*suff.* **1a.** To cause to be or become: *dramatize.* **b.** To cause to conform to or resemble: *Hellenize.* **c.** To treat as: *idolize.* **2a.** To treat or affect with: *anesthetize.* **b.** To subject to: *tyrannize.* **3.** To treat according to or practice the method of: *pasteurize.* **4.** To become; become like: *materialize.* **5.** To perform, engage in, or produce: *botanize.* [< Gk. *-izein,* v. suff.]

J

j or **J** (jā) ►*n., pl.* **j's** or **J's** also **js** or **Js** The 10th letter of the English alphabet.

J ►*abbr.* **1.** *Games* jack **2.** or **j** joule

J. ►*abbr.* **1.** Japanese **2.** judge

JA ►*abbr.* **1.** joint account **2.** judge advocate

jab (jăb) ►*v.* **jabbed, jab•bing** **1.** To poke abruptly, esp. with something sharp. **2.** To punch with short straight blows. ►*n.* **1.** A quick stab or blow. **2.** *Informal* A hypodermic injection. [ME *jobben.*]

jab•ber (jăb′ər) ►*v.* To talk rapidly or unintelligibly. [ME *javeren.*] —**jab′ber** *n.*

ja•bot (zhă-bō′, jăb′ō) ►*n.* A cascade of ruffles down the front of a shirt. [Fr., bird's crop.]

jac•a•ran•da (jăk′ə-răn′də) ►*n.* A tropical American tree having purple flowers. [Port. *jacarandá,* of Tupian orig.]

jack (jăk) ►*n.* **1.** often **Jack** *Informal* A man; fellow. **2.** *Games* A playing card showing the figure of a knave and ranking below a queen. **3.** *Games* **a.** **jacks** *(takes sing. or pl. v.)* A game played with a set of small six-pointed metal pieces and a rubber ball, the object being to pick up the pieces in various combinations. **b.** One of the metal pieces so used. **4.** A usu. portable device for raising heavy objects. **5.** A small flag flown at the bow of a ship, usu. to indicate nationality. **6.** The male of certain animals, esp. the ass. **7.** A socket that accepts a plug at one end and attaches to electric circuitry at the other. ►*v.* **1.** To hoist with a jack. **2.** To raise: *jack up prices.* [< the name *Jack.*]

jack·al (jăk′əl, -ôl′) ►*n.* A doglike mammal of Africa, Asia, and SE Europe. [< Skt. *śṛgālaḥ.*]

jack·ass (jăk′ăs′) ►*n.* **1.** A male ass or donkey. **2.** A foolish or stupid person.

jack·boot (jăk′bōōt′) ►*n.* **1.** A stout military boot extending above the knee. **2.** A person who uses bullying tactics.

jack·daw (jăk′dô′) ►*n.* A small crow of Eurasia and N Africa. [JACK + *daw*, jackdaw.]

jack·et (jăk′ĭt) ►*n.* **1.** A short coat usu. extending to the hips. **2.** An outer covering or casing. [< OFr. *jaque*, short jacket.] —**jack′et·ed** *adj.*

jack·ham·mer (jăk′hăm′ər) ►*n.* A handheld pneumatic machine for drilling rock and breaking up pavement. —**jack′ham′mer** *v.*

jack-in-the-box (jăk′ĭn-*thə*-bŏks′) ►*n., pl.* **-box·es** or **jacks-in-the-box** (jăks′-) A toy consisting of a clownlike puppet that springs out of a box when the lid is raised.

jack-in-the-pul·pit (jăk′ĭn-*thə*-pōōl′pĭt, -pŭl′-) ►*n., pl.* **-pits** A plant having a leaflike spathe that curls over an upright spadix.

jack·knife (jăk′nīf′) ►*n.* **1.** A large clasp knife. **2.** A dive in which one bends at the waist, touches the toes, and then straightens out. ►*v.* To fold or double like a jackknife.

jack-of-all-trades (jăk′əv-ôl′trādz′) ►*n., pl.* **jacks-of-all-trades** (jăks′-) One who can do many kinds of work.

jack-o'-lan·tern (jăk′ə-lăn′tərn) ►*n.* A lantern made from a hollowed pumpkin with a carved face.

jack·pot (jăk′pŏt′) ►*n.* A cumulative pool or top prize in various games.

jack·rab·bit (jăk′răb′ĭt) ►*n.* A large, long-eared hare. [JACK(ASS) + RABBIT.]

jack·screw (jăk′skrōō′) ►*n.* A jack operated by a screw.

Jack·son (jăk′sən) The capital of MS, in the W-central part.

Jackson, Andrew "Old Hickory." 1767–1845. The 7th US president (1829–37).

Andrew Jackson

Jackson, Jesse Louis b. 1941. Amer. civil rights leader and politician.

Jackson, Thomas Jonathan "Stonewall." 1824–63. Amer. Confederate general.

Jack·son·ville (jăk′sən-vĭl′) A city of NE FL near the Atlantic and the GA border.

Ja·cob (jā′kəb) In the Bible, the son of Isaac and grandson of Abraham.

Jac·o·be·an (jăk′ə-bē′ən) ►*adj.* Relating to the reign of James I of England or his times. [< Lat. *Iacōbus*, James.] —**Jac′o·be′an** *n.*

Jac·o·bin (jăk′ə-bĭn) ►*n.* **1.** A radical leftist. **2.** A radical republican during the French Revolution. [After the *Jacobin* friars, in whose convent the Jacobins first met.]

Ja·cob's ladder (jā′kəbz) ►*n.* **1.** *Naut.* A rope or chain ladder with rigid rungs. **2.** A plant having usu. blue flowers and compound leaves. [From the ladder seen by Jacob.]

jade (jād) ►*n.* Either of two distinct minerals, nephrite and jadeite, that are gen. pale green and used mainly as gemstones. [< Sp. *(piedra de) ijada*, (stone of the) flank.]

jad·ed (jā′dĭd) ►*adj.* **1.** Worn out; wearied. **2.** Dulled by surfeit; sated. **3.** Cynically callous. —**jad′ed·ly** *adv.*

jade·ite (jā′dīt′) ►*n.* A rare, usu. emerald to light green but sometimes white, auburn, buff, or violet variety of jade.

Jaf·fa (jăf′ə, yä′fə) A former city of W-central Israel on the Mediterranean Sea; part of Tel Aviv–Yafo since 1950.

jag¹ (jăg) ►*n.* A sharp point; barb. [ME *jagge.*]

jag² (jăg) ►*n. Slang* **1.** A bout of drinking or drug use. **2.** A period of overindulgence in an activity; spree: *a shopping jag; a crying jag.* [?]

JAG ►*abbr.* judge advocate general

jag·ged (jăg′ĭd) ►*adj.* Having sharp or ragged projections. —**jag′ged·ly** *adv.* —**jag′ged·ness** *n.*

jag·uar (jăg′wär′, jăg′yōō-är′) ►*n.* A large leopardlike mammal of Mexico, Central America, and South America. [< Guaraní *jaguá*, dog.]

jai a·lai (hī′ lī′, hī′ ə-lī′, hī′ ə-lī′) ►*n.* A fast court game in which players use a long hand-shaped basket to propel the ball against a wall. [< Basque.]

jail (jāl) ►*n.* A place for lawful detention, esp. of those accused but not convicted or those serving short sentences for minor crimes. ►*v.* To detain in a jail. [< OFr. *jaiole.*]

jail·bird (jāl′bûrd′) ►*n. Informal* A prisoner or ex-convict.

jail·break (jāl′brāk′) ►*n.* An escape from jail.

jail·er also **jail·or** (jā′lər) ►*n.* The keeper of a jail.

Ja·kar·ta or **Dja·kar·ta** (jə-kär′tə) The capital of Indonesia, on the NE coast of Java.

ja·la·pe·ño (hä′lə-pān′yō) ►*n., pl.* **-ños** A cultivated variety of capsicum pepper having a pungent green or red fruit used in cooking. [After *Jalapa*, Mexico.]

ja·lop·y (jə-lŏp′ē) ►*n., pl.* **-ies** *Informal* An old dilapidated automobile. [?]

jal·ou·sie (jăl′ə-sē) ►*n.* A blind or shutter having adjustable horizontal slats. [< Fr., jealousy.]

jam¹ (jăm) ►*v.* **jammed, jam·ming 1.** To drive or squeeze into a tight position. **2.** To activate or apply suddenly. **3.** To lock or cause to lock into an unworkable position. **4.** To fill to excess; cram. **5.** To block or clog. **6.** To interfere electronically with the reception of (broadcast signals). **7.** *Mus.* To play improvisations. ►*n.* **1.** The act of jamming or the condition of being jammed. **2.** A crush or congestion. **3.** A predicament. [?] —**jam′mer** *n.*

jam² (jăm) ►*n.* A preserve that is made from

fruit boiled with sugar. [Perh. < JAM¹.]

Ja·mai·ca (jə-mā′kə) An island country in the Caribbean Sea S of Cuba. Cap. Kingston. —**Ja·mai′can** *adj. & n.*

jamb (jăm) ►*n.* One of the vertical posts of a door or window frame. [< LLat. *gamba,* horse's hock.]

jam·ba·lay·a (jŭm′bə-lī′ə) ►*n.* A spicy Creole dish of rice and meat or seafood. [< Prov. *jambalaia.*]

jam·bo·ree (jăm′bə-rē′) ►*n.* **1.** A noisy celebration. **2.** A large assembly, as of Boy Scouts or Girl Scouts. [?]

James (jāmz) ►*n.* See table at **Bible.**

James¹, Saint. "The Great." d. AD 44. One of the 12 Apostles.

James², Saint. "The Just." d. c. AD 62. Traditionally regarded as the brother of Jesus.

James³, Saint. "The Less." fl. 1st cent. AD. One of the 12 Apostles.

James I 1566–1625. King of England (1603–25) and of Scotland as James VI (1567–1625).

James II 1633–1701. King of England, Scotland, and Ireland (1685–88).

James, Henry 1843–1916. Amer. writer and critic.

James, William 1842–1910. Amer. psychologist and philosopher.

James Bay The S arm of Hudson Bay, between NE Ontario and W Quebec, Canada.

James·town (jāmz′toun′) **1.** The capital of St. Helena, in the S Atlantic. **2.** A former village of SE VA; first permanent English settlement in America (1607).

jan·gle (jăng′gəl) ►*v.* **-gled, -gling 1.** To make or cause to make a harsh metallic sound. **2.** To grate on or jar (the nerves). [< OFr. *jangler.*] —**jan′gle** *n.* —**jan′gler** *n.*

jan·i·tor (jăn′ĭ-tər) ►*n.* One employed to maintain and clean a building. [Lat. *iānitor,* doorkeeper.] —**jan′i·to′ri·al** (-tôr′ē-əl) *adj.*

Jan·u·ar·y (jăn′yōō-ĕr′ē) ►*n., pl.* **-ies** The 1st month of the Gregorian calendar. See table at **calendar.** [< Lat. *Iānuārius (mēnsis),* (month) of Janus.]

Ja·nus (jā′nəs) ►*n. Rom. Myth.* The god of gates and doorways, depicted with two faces looking in opposite directions.

ja·pan (jə-păn′) ►*n.* A black enamel used to produce a durable glossy finish. [< JAPAN.] —**ja·pan′** *v.*

Japan A country of Asia on an archipelago off the E coast of the mainland. Cap. Tokyo.

Japan, Sea of An enclosed arm of the W Pacific between Japan and the Asian mainland.

Jap·a·nese (jăp′ə-nēz′, -nēs′) ►*adj.* Of or relating to Japan or its people or language. ►*n., pl.* **-nese 1.** A native or inhabitant of Japan. **2.** The language of the Japanese.

Japanese beetle ►*n.* A metallic-green beetle that is a plant pest in North America.

jape (jāp) ►*v.* **japed, jap·ing** To joke or quip. ►*n.* A joke or quip. [< OFr. *japer,* to chatter.] —**jap′er** *n.* —**jap′er·y** *n.*

jar¹ (jär) ►*n.* A cylindrical glass or earthenware vessel with a wide mouth. [< Ar. *jarra,* earthen vessel.] —**jar′ful′** *n.*

jar² (jär) ►*v.* **jarred, jar·ring 1a.** To cause to vibrate: *The ride over the old road was jarring.* **b.** To cause to vibrate from impact: *The ride on the donkey jarred my bones.* **2.** To disturb or irritate;

grate. **3.** To clash or conflict. ►*n.* A jolt; shock. [Perh. imit.] —**jar′ring·ly** *adv.*

jar·di·nière (jär′dn-îr′, zhär′dn-yâr′) ►*n.* A large decorative stand or pot for plants. [Fr. < OFr. *jardin,* GARDEN.]

jar·gon (jär′gən) ►*n.* **1.** The specialized language of a trade or profession. **2.** Nonsensical or incoherent language. [< OFr.]

Jarls·berg (yärlz′bûrg′) A trademark for a mild, pale yellow, hard Norwegian cheese.

jas·mine (jăz′mĭn) also **jes·sa·mine** (jĕs′ə-mĭn) ►*n.* Any of a genus of vines or shrubs having fragrant white or yellow flowers. [< Pers. *yasmīn.*]

jas·per (jăs′pər) ►*n.* An opaque red, yellow, or brown quartz. [< Gk. *iaspis.*]

ja·to (jā′tō) ►*n., pl.* **-tos** An aircraft takeoff aided by an auxiliary rocket. [*j(et-)a(ssisted) t(ake)o(ff).*]

jaun·dice (jôn′dĭs, jän′-) ►*n.* Yellowish discoloration of the eyes and tissues caused by deposition of bile salts. ►*v.* **-diced, -dic·ing 1.** To affect with jaundice. **2.** To affect with envy, prejudice, or hostility. See Synonyms at **bias.** [< OFr. *jaunice,* yellowness.]

jaunt (jônt, jänt) ►*n.* A short trip or excursion.

jaun·ty (jôn′tē, jän′-) ►*adj.* **-ti·er, -ti·est 1.** Having a buoyant or self-confident air. **2.** Sprightly; spirited. [< OFr. *gentil,* noble; see GENTLE.] —**jaun′ti·ly** *adv.* —**jaun′ti·ness** *n.*

ja·va (jä′və, jăv′ə) ►*n. Informal* Brewed coffee. [< JAVA.]

Java An island of Indonesia separated from Borneo by the **Java Sea,** an arm of the Pacific. —**Jav′a·nese′** *adj. & n.*

jave·lin (jăv′lĭn, jăv′ə-) ►*n.* **1.** A light spear, thrown as a weapon. **2.** A metal or metal-tipped spear, used in contests of distance throwing. [< OFr. *javeline,* of Celt. orig.]

javelin
Marjaana Vare at the 2008 Paralympic Games

jaw (jô) ►*n.* **1.** Either of two bony or cartilaginous structures that in most vertebrates form the framework of the mouth and hold the teeth. **2.** Either of two opposed hinged parts in a mechanical device. **3. jaws** A dangerous situation. **4.** *Slang* **a.** Back talk. **b.** A chat. ►*v. Slang* To talk; converse. [ME *jawe.*] —**jaw′less** *adj.*

jaw·bone (jô′bōn′) ►*n.* A bone of the jaw, esp. of the lower jaw. ►*v.* **-boned, -bon·ing** *Slang* To try to influence through strong persuasion.

jaw·break·er (jô′brā′kər) ►*n.* **1.** A very hard

candy. **2.** *Slang* A word difficult to pronounce.

jay (jā) ►*n.* Any of various usu. brightly colored birds gen. having a loud harsh call. [< LLat. *gāius.*]

Jay, John 1745–1829. Amer. diplomat and first chief justice of the US Supreme Court (1789–95).

jay·walk (jā′wôk′) ►*v.* To cross a street in violation of traffic regulations. [< *jay*, inexperienced person.] —**jay′walk′er** *n.*

jazz (jăz) ►*n.* **1.** A style of American music marked by a strong but flexible rhythmic understructure with solo and ensemble improvisations and a highly sophisticated harmonic idiom. **2.** *Slang* **a.** Animation; enthusiasm. **b.** Nonsense. **c.** Miscellaneous, unspecified things. ►*v. Slang* To exaggerate or lie (to): *Don't jazz me.* —*phrasal verb:* **jazz up** *Slang* To make more interesting; enliven. [?]

jazz·y (jăz′ē) ►*adj.* **-i·er, -i·est 1.** Of or resembling jazz. **2.** *Slang* Showy; flashy. —**jazz′i·ly** *adv.* —**jazz′i·ness** *n.*

JCS ►*abbr.* Joint Chiefs of Staff

jct. ►*abbr.* junction

JD ►*abbr.* **1.** *Lat.* Juris Doctor (Doctor of Law) **2.** Justice Department **3.** juvenile delinquent

jeal·ous (jĕl′əs) ►*adj.* **1.** Envious or resentful of another's good fortune or achievements: *felt jealous when my coworker was promoted.* **2.** Fearful or wary of losing one's position or situation to someone else, esp. in a sexual relationship. **3.** Arising from feelings of envy, apprehension, or bitterness: *jealous thoughts.* **4.** Vigilant in guarding something: *We are jealous of our good name.* [< VLat. *zēlōsus* < LLat. *zēlus,* ZEAL.] —**jeal′ous·ly** *adv.* —**jeal′ous·y** *n.*

jean (jēn) ►*n.* **1.** A heavy cotton. **2. jeans** Pants made of jean or denim. [< OFr. *Genes,* Genoa.]

jeep (jēp) ►*n.* A small durable US Army motor vehicle with four-wheel drive. [probably < *GP* < the manufacturer's designation for this vehicle.]

jeer (jîr) ►*v.* To speak or shout derisively. [?] —**jeer** *n.* —**jeer′er** *n.*

Jef·fer·son (jĕf′ər-sən), **Thomas** 1743–1826. The 3rd US president (1801–09). —**Jef′fer·so′ni·an** *adj. & n.*

Thomas Jefferson

Jefferson City The capital of MO, in the central part on the Missouri R.

Je·hosh·a·phat (jə-hŏsh′ə-făt′, -hŏs′-) 9th cent. BC. King of Judah.

Je·ho·vah (jĭ-hō′və) ►*n.* In the Old Testament, God. [Blend of consonants of YAHWEH and vowels of Heb. *ădônāy,* my lord.]

je·june (jə-jōōn′) ►*adj.* **1.** Not interesting. **2.** Lacking maturity. [< Lat. *iēiūnus,* dry, fasting.]

je·ju·num (jə-jōō′nəm) ►*n., pl.* **-na** (-nə) The section of the small intestine between the duodenum and the ileum. [< Med.Lat. *iēiūnum (intestīnum),* fasting (intestine).]

jell (jĕl) ►*v.* **1.** To make or become firm or gelatinous. **2.** To take shape; crystallize. [Prob. < JELLY.]

jel·ly (jĕl′ē) ►*n., pl.* **-lies 1.** A soft semisolid food typically made by the boiling and setting of fruit juice, sugar, and pectin or gelatin. **2.** Something having the consistency of jelly. ►*v.* **-lied, -ly·ing** To make into or become jelly. [< Lat. *gelāre,* freeze.]

jel·ly·bean (jĕl′ē-bēn′) ►*n.* A small chewy candy.

jel·ly·fish (jĕl′ē-fĭsh′) ►*n.* **1.** A gelatinous, free-swimming marine animal often having a bell-shaped stage as the dominant phase of its life cycle. **2.** *Informal* A weakling.

jel·ly·roll (jĕl′ē-rōl′) ►*n.* A thin sheet of sponge cake layered with jelly and then rolled up.

Jen·ghiz Khan (jĕn′gĭz kän′, jĕng′-) See **Genghis Khan.**

jen·ny (jĕn′ē) ►*n., pl.* **-nies 1.** The female of certain animals, esp. the donkey and wren. **2.** A spinning jenny. [< the name *Jenny.*]

jeop·ard·ize (jĕp′ər-dīz′) ►*v.* **-ized, -iz·ing** To expose to loss or injury. See Synonyms at **endanger.**

jeop·ard·y (jĕp′ər-dē) ►*n., pl.* **-ies** Risk of loss or injury; danger. [< OFr. *jeu parti,* even game.]

jer·bo·a (jər-bō′ə) ►*n.* A small nocturnal leaping rodent of Asia and Africa. [< Ar. *jarbū'.*]

jer·e·mi·ad (jĕr′ə-mī′əd) ►*n.* A bitter lament or righteous prophecy of doom. [Fr. *jérémiade* < *Jérémie,* Jeremiah.]

Jer·e·mi·ah (jĕr′ə-mī′ə) ►*n.* **1.** A Hebrew prophet of the 7th and 6th centuries BC. **2.** See table at **Bible.**

Jer·i·cho (jĕr′ĭ-kō′) An ancient city of Palestine near the NW shore of the Dead Sea.

jerk¹ (jûrk) ►*v.* **1.** To give a sudden quick thrust, pull, or twist to. **2.** To move in sudden abrupt motions. ►*n.* **1.** A sudden yank, twist, or jolt. **2.** A muscle spasm. **3.** *Slang* A foolish, rude, or contemptible person. [?] —**jerk′i·ly** *adv.* —**jerk′i·ness** *n.* —**jerk′y** *adj.*

jerk² (jûrk) ►*v.* To cut (meat) into long strips and sun-dry or cure by smoking. [< JERKY.]

jer·kin (jûr′kĭn) ►*n.* A close-fitting sleeveless jacket. [?]

jerk·y (jûr′kē) ►*n.* Meat cured by jerking. [< Quechua *ch'arki.*]

jer·o·bo·am (jĕr′ə-bō′əm) ►*n.* A wine bottle holding ⅘ gal. (3.03 l). [After *Jeroboam I* king of Israel in the 10th cent. BC.]

jer·ry-build (jĕr′ē-bĭld′) ►*v.* **-built, -build·ing** To build shoddily and cheaply. [< dial. *jerry,* defective.]

jer·sey (jûr′zē) ►*n., pl.* **-seys 1a.** A soft, plain-knitted fabric. **b.** A shirt or other garment made of jersey. **2.** often **Jersey** A breed of fawn-colored dairy cattle. [< JERSEY.]

Jersey The largest of the Channel Is. in the English Channel.

Je·ru·sa·lem (jə-rōō′sə-ləm, -zə-) The capital of Israel, in the E-central part.

jes·sa·mine (jĕs′ə-mĭn) ►*n.* Var. of **jasmine.**

Jes·se (jĕs′ē) In the Bible, King David's father.

jest (jĕst) ►*n.* **1.** A frivolous mood. **2.** A playful remark or act. **3.** An object of ridicule. ►*v.* **1.** To make witty remarks. **2.** To act in a playful manner. [ME *geste,* tale < Lat. *gesta,* deeds.]

jest·er (jĕs′tər) ►*n.* One who jests, esp. a paid fool at medieval courts.

Jes·u·it (jĕzh′ōō-ĭt, jĕz′ōō-, -yōō-) ►*n.* Rom. Cath. Ch. A member of the Society of Jesus, an order founded by Saint Ignatius of Loyola in 1534.

Je·sus (jē′zəs) 4? BC–AD 29? ►*n.* Jewish religious leader and founder of Christianity, regarded by Christians as the Christ and the Son of God.

jet[1] (jĕt) ►*n.* **1.** A dense black coal that takes a high polish and is used for jewelry. **2.** A deep black. [< Gk. *gagatēs,* after *Gagas,* a town of ancient Asia Minor.] —**jet** *adj.*

jet[2] (jĕt) ►*n.* **1a.** A fluid stream forced under pressure out of a small-diameter opening. **b.** An outlet for emitting such a stream. **c.** Something emitted in or as if in such a stream. **2.** A jet-propelled vehicle, esp. an aircraft. ►*v.* **jet·ted, jet·ting 1.** To travel by jet aircraft. **2.** To squirt. [< Lat. *iactāre,* throw out.]

jet engine ►*n.* **1.** An engine that develops thrust by ejecting a jet of gaseous combustion products. **2.** An engine that obtains the oxygen needed from the atmosphere, used esp. to propel aircraft.

jet lag ►*n.* A disruption of bodily rhythms caused by high-speed air travel across time zones. —**jet′-lagged′** *adj.*

jet-pro·pelled (jĕt′prə-pĕld′) ►*adj.* Driven by one or more jet engines. —**jet propulsion** *n.*

jet·sam (jĕt′səm) ►*n.* **1.** Goods that are cast overboard from a ship, esp. in an attempt to lighten the ship. **2.** Discarded odds and ends. [< ME *jetteson,* throwing overboard; see JETTISON.]

jet set ►*n.* An international social set made up of wealthy people who travel from one fashionable place to another. —**jet′-set′** *adj.* —**jet setter** *n.*

jet stream ►*n.* A high-speed, meandering wind current that gen. flows westerly at altitudes of 10 to 15 km (6 to 9 mi).

jet·ti·son (jĕt′ĭ-sən, -zən) ►*v.* **1.** To cast overboard or off. **2.** *Informal* To discard. [< VLat. *iectātiō,* a throwing.]

jet·ty (jĕt′ē) ►*n., pl.* **-ties 1.** A structure that projects into a body of water to influence the current or to protect a harbor. **2.** A wharf. [< OFr. *jetee* < *jeter,* to project.]

Jew (jōō) ►*n.* **1.** An adherent of Judaism. **2.** A member of the people tracing their descent from the ancient Hebrews and sharing an ethnic heritage based on Judaism.

jew·el (jōō′əl) ►*n.* **1a.** A precious stone; gem. **b.** A small natural or artificial gem used as a bearing in a watch. **2.** A costly ornament of precious metal or gems. **3.** One that is treasured or esteemed. ►*v.* **-eled, -el·ing** or **-elled, -el·ling** To adorn or fit with jewels. [< AN *juel.*] —**jew′el·ry** *n.*

jewel box ►*n.* **1.** A usu. lined box for holding jewelry. **2.** A hinged plastic case for holding a compact disc and usu. a printed insert.

jew·el·er also **jew·el·ler** (jōō′ə-lər) ►*n.* One who makes, repairs, or deals in jewelry.

jew·el·weed (jōō′əl-wēd′) ►*n.* Any of several plants having yellowish spurred flowers and five-valved seedpods.

Jew·ish (jōō′ĭsh) ►*adj.* Of or relating to the Jews or their culture or religion. —**Jew′ish·ness** *n.*

Jewish calendar ►*n.* The calendar used to mark the events of the Jewish year, dating the creation of the world at 3761 BC. See table at **calendar.**

Jew·ry (jōō′rē) ►*n.* The Jewish people.

Jew's harp or **jew's harp** (jōōz′) ►*n.* A small musical instrument consisting of a lyre-shaped metal frame held between the teeth and a steel tongue that is plucked to produce a soft twanging sound.

jez·e·bel (jĕz′ə-bĕl′, -bəl) ►*n.* A wicked, scheming woman. [After JEZEBEL.]

Jez·e·bel (jĕz′ə-bĕl′) fl. 9th cent. BC. Phoenician princess and queen of Israel.

jib (jĭb) ►*n.* A triangular sail set forward of the mast of a sailing vessel. [?]

jibe[1] (jĭb) ►*v.* **jibed, jib·ing** To shift a fore-and-aft sail from one side of a vessel to the other while sailing before the wind. [< obsolete Du. *gijben.*]

jibe[2] (jĭb) ►*v.* **jibed, jib·ing** To be in accord; agree. [?]

jibe[3] (jĭb) ►*v. & n.* Var. of **gibe.**

Jid·da (jĭd′ə) A city of W-central Saudi Arabia on the Red Sea.

jif·fy (jĭf′ē) ►*n., pl.* **jif·fies** *Informal* A moment.

jig (jĭg) ►*n.* **1.** Any of various lively dances in triple time. **2.** A fishing lure with one or more hooks. **3.** A device for guiding a tool or for holding work in place. ►*v.* **jigged, jig·ging 1.** To dance a jig. **2.** To bob or jerk rapidly. **3.** To operate a jig. [?]

jig·ger (jĭg′ər) ►*n.* A small measure for liquor, usu. holding 1½ oz.

jig·gle (jĭg′əl) ►*v.* **-gled, -gling** To move or cause to move jerkily up and down or to and fro. [Frequentative of JIG.] —**jig′gle** *n.* —**jig′gly** *adj.*

jig·gy (jĭg′ē) ►*adj.* **-er, -est** *Slang* **1.** Moving excitedly, esp. when dancing: *getting jiggy on the dance floor.* **2.** Engaged in sexual intercourse. **3.** Affiliated or identified: *Politicians trying to get jiggy with younger voters.* [JIG + –Y[1].]

jig·saw (jĭg′sô′) ►*n.* A saw with a narrow vertical blade, used to cut sharp curves.

jigsaw puzzle ►*n.* A puzzle consisting of irregularly shaped pieces that form a picture when fitted together.

ji·had (jĭ-häd′) ►*n.* *Islam* **1.** An individual's striving for spiritual self-perfection. **2.** A Muslim holy war for the propagation or defense of Islam. [Ar. *jihād.*]

jilt (jĭlt) ►*v.* To drop (a lover) suddenly or callously. [Poss. < obsolete *jilt,* harlot.]

Jim Crow (jĭm) ►*n.* The practice of discriminating against and segregating black people. [From the title of a 19th-cent. song.]

jim·my (jĭm′ē) ►*n., pl.* **-mies** A short crowbar with curved ends. ►*v.* **-mied, -my·ing** To pry (something) open with or as if with a jimmy. [Prob. < *Jimmy.*]

jim·son·weed (jĭm′sən-wēd′) ►*n.* A poisonous annual plant having large, trumpet-shaped white or purplish flowers. [< *Jamestown weed.*]

jin·gle (jĭng′gəl) ►*v.* **-gled, -gling** To make or cause to make a tinkling or ringing metallic sound. ►*n.* **1.** A jingling sound. **2.** A catchy, often musical advertising slogan. [ME *ginglen.*] —**jin′gly** *adj.*

jin·go·ism (jĭng′gō-ĭz′əm) ►*n.* Extreme nationalism marked esp. by a belligerent foreign policy. [< the phrase *by jingo,* used in a bellicose British song.] —**jin′go·ist** *n.* —**jin′go·is′tic** *adj.*

jin·ni (jĭn′ē, jĭ-nē′) ►*n., pl.* **jinn** (jĭn) In the Koran and Muslim tradition, a supernatural spirit. [Ar. *jinnī.*]

jin·rik·sha (jĭn-rĭk′shô′) ►*n.* A small, two-wheeled carriage drawn by one or two persons; ricksha. [J. *jinrikisha.*]

jinx (jĭngks) *Informal* ►*n.* **1.** A person or thing believed to bring bad luck. **2.** A period of bad luck. ►*v.* **jinxed, jinx·ing** To bring bad luck to. [Poss. < Gk. *iunx,* a bird used in magic.]

jit·ney (jĭt′nē) ►*n., pl.* **-neys** A small motor vehicle that transports passengers on a route for a low fare. [< earlier *jetton,* a token < Fr. *jeton.*]

jit·ter (jĭt′ər) ►*v.* To be nervous or uneasy; fidget. ►*n.* **jitters** A fit of nervousness. [?] —**jit′ter·i·ness** *n.* —**jit′ter·y** *adj.*

jit·ter·bug (jĭt′ər-bŭg′) ►*n.* A lively dance consisting of two-step patterns embellished with twirls and other maneuvers. —**jit′ter·bug′** *v.*

jive (jīv) ►*n.* **1a.** Jazz or swing music. **b.** The jargon of jazz musicians. **2.** *Slang* Deceptive, nonsensical, or glib talk. [?] —**jive** *v. & adj.*

Jnr. ►*abbr.* junior

Joan of Arc (jŏn), Saint. 1412?–31. French military leader and mystic.

job (jŏb) ►*n.* **1.** A regular activity performed for payment. **2.** A position of employment. **3a.** A task that must be done. **b.** A specified duty or responsibility. **4.** A specific piece of work to be done for a set fee. **5.** *Informal* A criminal act, esp. a robbery. ►*v.* **jobbed, job·bing 1.** To work at odd jobs. **2.** To act as a jobber. **3.** To subcontract. [Perh. < obsolete *jobbe,* piece.] —**job′less** *adj.* —**job′less·ness** *n.*

Job (jŏb) ►*n.* **1.** In the Bible, an upright man tested by God. **2.** See table at **Bible.**

job action (jŏb) ►*n.* An action, such as a strike or slowdown, by workers to increase bargaining power with management.

job·ber (jŏb′ər) ►*n.* **1.** One that buys merchandise from manufacturers and sells it to retailers. **2.** One that works by the contract.

job·hold·er (jŏb′hōl′dər) ►*n.* One who has a regular job.

job lot ►*n.* Miscellaneous merchandise sold in one lot.

Jobs (jŏbz), **Steven Paul** 1955–2011. Amer. computer engineer and business executive.

job-share (jŏb′shâr′) ►*v.* To share one job in alternation with one or more part-time workers.

jock¹ (jŏk) ►*n.* **1.** A jockey. **2.** A disc jockey.

jock² (jŏk) ►*n.* **1.** An athletic supporter. **2.** An athlete. [< JOCKSTRAP.]

jock·ey (jŏk′ē) ►*n., pl.* **-eys** One who rides horses in races, esp. as a profession. ►*v.* **1.** To ride (a horse) as jockey. **2.** To direct or maneuver by cleverness or skill. **3.** To maneuver for a certain position or advantage. [Dim. of Sc. *Jock,* nickname for *John.*]

jock·strap (jŏk′străp′) ►*n.* An elastic support for the male genitals, worn esp. during sports. [*jock,* male genitals + STRAP.]

jo·cose (jō-kōs′) ►*adj.* Given to joking; merry. [Lat. *iocōsus < iocus,* joke.] —**jo·cose′ly** *adv.* —**jo·cose′ness, jo·cos′i·ty** (-kŏs′ĭ-tē) *n.*

joc·u·lar (jŏk′yə-lər) ►*adj.* Given to or marked by joking. [Lat. *ioculāris < iocus,* joke.] —**joc′u·lar′i·ty** (-lăr′ĭ-tē) *n.* —**joc′u·lar·ly** *adv.*

joc·und (jŏk′ənd, jō′kənd) ►*adj.* Lighthearted; merry. [< Lat. *iūcundus.*] —**jo·cun′di·ty** (jō-kŭn′dĭ-tē) *n.* —**joc′und·ly** *adv.*

jodh·purs (jŏd′pərz) ►*pl.n.* Wide-hipped riding pants of heavy cloth, fitting tightly from knee to ankle. [After *Jodhpur,* a city and district of W India.]

Jo·el (jō′əl) ►*n.* See table at **Bible.**

jo·ey (jō′ē) ►*n., pl.* **-eys** *Australian* A young marsupial, esp. a baby kangaroo. [?]

jog¹ (jŏg) ►*v.* **jogged, jog·ging 1.** To jar or move by shoving, bumping, or jerking. **2.** To nudge. **3.** To run or ride at a steady slow trot, esp. for exercise or sport. **4.** To proceed in a leisurely manner. ►*n.* **1.** A slight nudge. **2.** A slow steady trot. [?] —**jog′ger** *n.*

jog² (jŏg) ►*n.* **1.** A protruding or receding part in a surface or line. **2.** An abrupt change in direction. [Var. of JAG¹.] —**jog** *v.*

jog·gle (jŏg′əl) ►*v.* **-gled, -gling** To jar slightly. [Poss. frequentative of JOG¹.] —**jog′gle** *n.*

Jo·han·nes·burg (jō-hăn′ĭs-bûrg′, -hä′nĭs-) A city of NE South Africa.

John¹ (jŏn) 1167?–1216. King of England (1199–1216).

John² (jŏn) ►*n.* See table at **Bible.**

John, Saint. fl. 1st cent. AD. One of the 12 Apostles and the traditionally accepted author of the fourth Gospel.

John XXIII 1881–1963. Pope (1958–63).

John Doe ►*n.* Used as a name in legal proceedings to designate an unknown male or to protect the identity of a known male.

john·ny·cake (jŏn′ē-kāk′) ►*n. Regional* A flat cornmeal bread usu. fried on a griddle. [Perh. < *jonakin.*]

John of Gaunt (gônt, gänt) Duke of Lancaster. 1340–99. English military leader.

John Paul I 1912–78. Pope (1978).

John Paul II 1920–2005. Pope (1978–2005).

John·son (jŏn′sən), **Andrew** 1808–75. The 17th US president (1865–69).

Andrew Johnson   **Lyndon B. Johnson**

Johnson, Lyndon Baines 1908–73. The 36th US president (1963–69).

Johnson, Samuel 1709–84. British writer and lexicographer.

John the Baptist, Saint. fl. 1st cent. AD. Jewish prophet who in the New Testament baptized Jesus.

joie de vi·vre (zhwä′ də vē′vrə) ►*n.* Carefree enjoyment of life. [Fr.]

join (join) ►*v.* **1.** To put or bring together. **2.** To put or bring into close association or relationship. **3.** To connect, as with a straight line. **4.** To meet and merge with. **5.** To become a part or member of. **6.** To come or act together. **7.** To take part; participate. [< Lat. *iungere.*]

join·er (joi′nər) ►*n.* **1.** A carpenter, esp. a cabinetmaker. **2.** *Informal* A person given to joining groups.

joint (joint) ►*n.* **1.** A place or part at which two or more things are joined. **2.** *Anat.* A point of articulation between two or more bones, esp. one that allows motion. **3.** A cut of meat for roasting. **4.** *Slang* A cheap or disreputable gathering place. **5.** *Slang* A marijuana cigarette. ►*adj.* **1.** Shared by or common to two or more. **2.** Formed or marked by cooperation or united action. ►*v.* **1.** To provide with joints. **2.** To separate (meat) at the joints. —*idiom:* **out of joint 1.** Dislocated, as a bone. **2.** *Informal* **a.** Not harmonious. **b.** Out of order; unsatisfactory. **c.** In bad humor. [< OFr., p.part. of *joindre,* JOIN.] —**joint′ly** *adv.*

joist (joist) ►*n.* Any of the parallel horizontal beams set from wall to wall or across girders to support a floor or ceiling. [< OFr. *giste.*]

jo·jo·ba (hə-hō′bə, hō-) ►*n.* A shrub of the SW US and N Mexico having leathery leaves and seeds that yield an oil used in cosmetics and as a lubricant. [Am.Sp.]

joke (jōk) ►*n.* **1.** Something said or done to evoke laughter, esp. an amusing story with a punch line. **2.** A mischievous trick. **3.** A ludicrous incident or situation. **4.** *Informal* A laughingstock. ►*v.* **joked, jok·ing 1.** To tell or play jokes. **2.** To speak in fun; be facetious. [Lat. *iocus.*] —**jok′ing·ly** *adv.*

jok·er (jō′kər) ►*n.* **1a.** One who tells or plays jokes. **b.** *Informal* A person, esp. an annoying one. **2.** A playing card used in certain games as the highest-ranking card or as a wild card. **3.** A clause in a legislative bill or a contract that appears innocuous but renders the bill or contract inoperative.

jol·li·ty (jŏl′ĭ-tē) ►*n.* Merriment; mirth.

jol·ly (jŏl′ē) ►*adj.* **-li·er, -li·est 1.** Full of good humor. **2.** Merry: *a jolly tune.* ►*adv. Chiefly Brit.* Very: *a jolly good cook.* [< OFr. *joli.*] —**jol′li·ly** *adv.* —**jol′li·ness** *n.*

jolt (jōlt) ►*v.* **1.** To shake or jar with or as if with a sudden hard blow. **2.** To move or cause to move jerkily. ►*n.* **1.** A hard jarring or jerking. **2.** A sudden shock, as of surprise. [?] —**jolt′y** *adj.*

Jo·nah (jō′nə) ►*n.* **1.** In the Bible, a prophet swallowed by a great fish and disgorged unharmed. **2.** See table at **Bible.**

Jones (jōnz), **John Paul** 1747–92. British-born Amer. naval officer.

jon·quil (jŏng′kwəl, jŏn′-) ►*n.* An ornamental plant with short-tubed, fragrant yellow flowers. [Sp. *junquilla.*]

Jon·son (jŏn′sən), **Benjamin** "Ben." 1572–1637. English dramatist and poet.

Jop·lin (jŏp′lĭn), **Scott** 1868–1917. Amer. pianist and composer.

Jor·dan (jôr′dn) A country of SW Asia in NW Arabia. Cap. Amman. —**Jor·da′ni·an** (jôr-dā′nē-ən) *adj. & n.*

Jordan, Michael Jeffrey b. 1963. Amer. basketball player.

Jordan River A river of SW Asia rising in Syria and Lebanon and flowing about 360 km (225 mi) through the Sea of Galilee to the Dead Sea.

Jo·seph[1] (jō′zəf, -səf) In the Bible, a son of Jacob and Rachel.

Jo·seph[2] (jō′zəf, -səf) "Chief Joseph." 1840?–1904. Nez Perce leader.

Chief Joseph
1903 photograph

Joseph, Saint. In the New Testament, the husband of Mary, mother of Jesus.

Jo·se·phine (jō′zə-fēn′, -sə-) See Josephine de **Beauharnais.**

Joseph of Ar·i·ma·the·a (ăr′ə-mə-thē′ə) fl. 1st cent. AD. In the New Testament, the disciple who buried Jesus.

Jo·se·phus (jō-sē′fəs), **Flavius** AD 37–100? Jewish general and historian.

josh (jŏsh) ►*v.* To tease good-humoredly. [?] —**josh′er** *n.*

Josh·u·a (jŏsh′ōō-ə) ►*n.* **1.** In the Bible, a Hebrew leader. **2.** See table at **Bible.**

jos·tle (jŏs′əl) ►*v.* **-tled, -tling 1.** To come in rough contact (with); push and shove. **2.** To make one's way by pushing or elbowing. **3.** To vie (with) for advantage or position. [< OFr. *juster,* JOUST.] —**jos′tle** *n.* —**jos′tler** *n.*

jot (jŏt) ►*n.* The smallest bit; iota. ►*v.* **jot·ted, jot·ting** To write down briefly or hastily. [< Gk. *iōta,* iota.] —**jot′ting** *n.*

joule (jōōl, joul) ►*n.* A unit of electrical energy equal to the work done when a current of 1 ampere is passed through a resistance of 1 ohm for 1 second. [After James P. *Joule* (1818–89).]

jounce (jouns) ►*v.* **jounced, jounc·ing** To move with bumps and jolts; bounce. [ME *jouncen.*] —**jounce** *n.* —**jounc′y** *adj.*

jour·nal (jûr′nəl) ►*n.* **1a.** A personal record of experiences and reflections; diary. **b.** An official record of daily proceedings, as of a legislative body. **2.** A newspaper. **3.** A specialized periodical. **4.** The part of a shaft or axle supported by a bearing. [< LLat. *diurnālis,* daily.]

jour·nal·ese (jûr′nə-lēz′, -lēs′) ►*n.* A slick, superficial style of writing often deemed typical of newspapers and magazines.

jour·nal·ism (jûr′nə-lĭz′əm) ►*n.* **1.** The collecting, writing, editing, and presenting of news or news articles. **2.** Material written for publication or broadcast as news. —**jour′nal·ist** *n.* —**jour′nal·is′tic** *adj.*

jour·ney (jûr′nē) ►*n., pl.* **-neys 1a.** Travel from one place to another, esp. over a considerable distance. **b.** A distance to be traveled or the time required for a trip. **2.** A process likened to traveling; passage. ►*v.* To travel. [< VLat. *diurnāta,* day's travel < Lat. *diurnus,* of a day.]

jour·ney·man (jûr′nē-mən) ►*n.* **1.** One who has served an apprenticeship in a trade and works in another's employ. **2.** A competent worker.

joust (joust, jŭst, jōōst) ►*n.* **1.** A combat between two mounted knights using lances. **2.** A personal competition suggestive of combat with lances. ►*v.* To engage in a joust. [< OFr. *juste,* ult. < Lat. *iūxtā,* close together.] —**joust′er** *n.*

Jove (jōv) ►*n. Rom. Myth.* See **Jupiter** (sense 1).

jo·vi·al (jō′vē-əl) ►*adj.* Mirthful; jolly. [< Lat. *Iovis,* Jupiter.] —**jo′vi·al′i·ty** (-ăl′ĭ-tē) *n.* —**jo′vi·al·ly** *adv.*

jowl[1] (joul) ►*n.* **1.** The jaw, esp. the lower jaw. **2.** The cheek. [< OE *ceafl.*]

jowl[2] (joul) ►*n.* The flesh under the lower jaw, esp. when plump or flabby. [< ME *cholle.*]

joy (joi) ►*n.* **1.** Intense or elated happiness. **2.** A source of great pleasure. ►*v.* To rejoice. [< Lat. *gaudia.*] —**joy′less** *adj.* —**joy′less·ly** *adv.* —**joy′less·ness** *n.*

Joyce (jois), **James Augustine Aloysius** 1882–1941. Irish writer. —**Joyc′e·an** *adj.*

joy·ful (joi′fəl) ►*adj.* Feeling, causing, or showing joy. —**joy′ful·ly** *adv.* —**joy′ful·ness** *n.*

joy·ous (joi′əs) ►*adj.* Joyful. —**joy′ous·ly** *adv.* —**joy′ous·ness** *n.*

joy ride ►*n. Slang* An often reckless automobile ride taken for fun and thrills.

joy·stick (joi′stĭk′) ►*n. Slang* **1.** A control stick. **2.** A manual control device, as for a video game.

JP ►*abbr.* justice of the peace

jr. or **Jr.** ►*abbr.* junior

Juan Car·los (wän kär′ləs, -lōs, hwän) b. 1938. Spanish king (assumed the throne 1975).

Juan de Fu·ca (də fōō′kə, fyōō′-), **Strait of** A strait between NW WA and Vancouver I., British Columbia, Canada.

Juba (jōō′bə) The capital of South Sudan, in the S part.

ju·bi·lant (jōō′bə-lənt) ►*adj.* Exultingly joyful. [< Lat. *iūbilāre,* shout for joy.] —**ju′bi·lance** *n.* —**ju′bi·lant·ly** *adv.*

ju·bi·la·tion (jōō′bə-lā′shən) ►*n.* **1.** The act of rejoicing. **2.** A joyful celebration.

ju·bi·lee (jōō′bə-lē′, jōō′bə-lē′) ►*n.* **1.** A special anniversary, esp. a 50th anniversary. **2.** A season or occasion of joyful celebration. **3.** Jubilation; rejoicing. [< Heb. *yōbēl,* ram's horn, the Jewish year of jubilee.]

Ju·dah[1] (jōō′də) In the Bible, a son of Jacob and Leah.

Ju·dah[2] (jōō′də) An ancient kingdom of S Palestine between the Mediterranean and the Dead Sea.

Ju·da·ic (jōō-dā′ĭk) also **Ju·da·i·cal** (-ĭ-kəl) ►*adj.* Of or relating to Jews or Judaism.

Ju·da·ism (jōō′dē-ĭz′əm) ►*n.* The monotheistic religion of the Jews, having its spiritual and ethical principles embodied chiefly in the Hebrew Scriptures and the Talmud.

Ju·das (jōō′dəs) ►*n.* One who betrays another under the guise of friendship. [After JUDAS ISCARIOT.]

Judas Is·car·i·ot (ĭ-skăr′ē-ət) d. c. AD 30. One of the 12 Apostles and the betrayer of Jesus.

Jude (jōōd) ►*n.* See table at **Bible.**

Jude, Saint. fl. 1st cent. AD. One of the 12 Apostles.

Ju·de·a (jōō-dē′ə, -dā′ə) An ancient region of S Palestine comprising present-day S Israel, the S West Bank, and SW Jordan. —**Ju·de′an** *adj. & n.*

judge (jŭj) ►*v.* **judged, judg·ing 1.** To form an opinion (of). **2.** To hear and decide on in a court of law; try. **3.** To determine or declare after deliberation. **4.** *Informal* To think; suppose. ►*n.* **1.** One who makes estimates as to worth, quality, or fitness. **2.** A public official who hears and decides cases brought before a court of law or another official venue. **3.** One appointed to decide the winners of a contest or competition. **4. Judges** (*takes sing. v.*) See table at **Bible.** [< Lat. *iūdex,* a judge.] —**judge′ship′** *n.*

judg·ment also **judge·ment** (jŭj′mənt) ►*n.* **1a.** The act or process of judging. **b.** An opinion formed after due consideration. **2.** The mental ability to form opinions, distinguish relationships, or draw sound conclusions. **3.** *Law* **a.** A judicial decision. **b.** A court decision establishing that an obligation is owed. **4.** A misfortune believed to be sent by God as a punishment.

judg·men·tal (jŭj-mĕn′tl) ►*adj.* **1.** Of or relating to judgment. **2.** Inclined to make judgments, esp. moral or personal ones. —**judg·men′tal·ly** *adv.*

Judgment Day ►*n.* **1.** In Judeo-Christian and Muslim traditions, the day when God judges all humans. **2. judgment day** A day of reckoning.

ju·di·ca·ture (jōō′dĭ-kə-chŏŏr′) ►*n.* **1.** Administration of justice. **2.** A system of courts of law. [< Lat. *iūdicāre,* to judge < *iūdex,* judge.]

ju·di·cial (jōō-dĭsh′əl) ►*adj.* **1a.** Of or proper to courts of law or the administration of justice. **b.** Decreed by or proceeding from a court of justice. **2.** Marked by or expressing judgment. [< Lat. *iūdicium,* judgment < *iūdex,* a judge.]

ju·di·ci·ar·y (jōō-dĭsh′ē-ĕr′ē, -dĭsh′ə-rē) ►*n., pl.* **-ies 1.** The judicial branch of government. **2a.** A system of courts of law. **b.** The judges of these courts.

ju·di·cious (jōō-dĭsh′əs) ►*adj.* Having or exhibiting sound judgment. —**ju·di′cious·ly** *adv.* —**ju·di′cious·ness** *n.*

Ju·dith (jōō′dĭth) ►*n.* See table at **Bible.**

ju·do (jōō′dō) ►*n.* A sport using principles of balance and leverage adapted from jujitsu. [J. *jūdō.*]

jug

jug (jŭg) ►*n.* **1.** An often earthenware or glass vessel with a small mouth, a handle, and usu. a stopper or cap. **2.** *Slang* A jail. [ME *jugge.*]

jug band ►*n.* A musical group that uses unconventional instruments, such as jugs, kazoos, and washboards.

jug·ger·naut (jŭg′ər-nôt′) ►*n.* An overwhelming or unstoppable force. [< Skt. *jagannāthaḥ*, lord of the world : *jagat*, world (< *jigāti*, goes) + *nāthaḥ*, lord (< *nāthate*, helps).]

jug·gle (jŭg′əl) ►*v.* **-gled, -gling** **1.** To toss and catch (two or more objects) so that at least one of them is in the air at all times. **2.** To keep (more than two activities) in progress at one time. **3.** To manipulate in order to deceive: *juggle figures in a ledger.* ►*n.* The act of juggling. [< Lat. *ioculārī*, to jest.] —**jug′gler** *n.*

jug·u·lar (jŭg′yə-lər) ►*adj.* Of or located in the neck or throat. ►*n.* A jugular vein. [< Lat. *iugulum*, collarbone < *iugum*, yoke.]

juice (jōōs) ►*n.* **1a.** A fluid naturally contained in plant or animal tissue. **b.** A bodily secretion. **2.** *Slang* **a.** Electric current. **b.** Fuel for an engine. ►*v.* **juiced, juic·ing** To extract the juice from. [< Lat. *iūs.*]

juic·er (jōō′sər) ►*n.* An appliance used to extract juice from fruits and vegetables.

juic·y (jōō′sē) ►*adj.* **-i·er, -i·est** **1.** Full of juice. **2.** Interesting, racy, or titillating. **3.** Rewarding or gratifying: *a juicy raise.* —**juic′i·ly** *adv.* —**juic′i·ness** *n.*

ju·jit·su also **ju·jut·su** (jōō-jĭt′sōō) ►*n.* An art of weaponless self-defense developed in Japan that uses throws, holds, and blows and derives added power from the attacker's own weight and strength. [J. *jūjitsu.*]

ju·jube (jōō′jōōb′, -jōō-bē′) ►*n.* A fruit-flavored candy or lozenge. [< Gk. *zizuphon*, a fruit tree.]

juke (jōōk) *Regional* ►*n.* A roadside tavern offering music for dancing. ►*v.* **juked, juk·ing** To dance. [Of Western African orig.]

juke·box (jōōk′bŏks′) ►*n.* A money-operated phonograph or compact disc player.

ju·lep (jōō′lĭp) ►*n.* A mint julep. [< Pers. *gulāb*, rosewater.]

Jul·ian (jōōl′yən) AD 331?–363. Emperor of Rome (361–363).

ju·li·enne (jōō′lē-ĕn′, zhü-lyĕn′) ►*adj.* Cut into long thin strips: *julienne potatoes.* [Fr.]

Ju·ly (jōō-lī′) ►*n.* The 7th month of the Gregorian calendar. See table at **calendar.** [< Lat. *Iūlius*, (of Julius (Caesar).]

Ju·ma·da (jōō-mä′dä) ►*n.* Either the 5th or the 6th month of the Islamic calendar. See table at **calendar.** [Ar. *jumādā.*]

jum·ble (jŭm′bəl) ►*v.* **-bled, -bling** **1.** To mix in a confused way. **2.** To confuse. [?] —**jum′ble** *n.*

jum·bo (jŭm′bō) ►*n., pl.* **-bos** An unusually large person, animal, or thing. ►*adj.* Unusually large. [After *Jumbo*, an elephant exhibited by P.T. Barnum.]

jump (jŭmp) ►*v.* **1.** To spring off the ground or from some other base by a muscular effort of the legs and feet. **2.** To move involuntarily, as in surprise. **3.** To react quickly: *jump at a bargain.* **4.** To enter eagerly into an activity. **5.** To form an opinion hastily. **6.** To spring upon in sudden attack. **7.** To rise suddenly and markedly. **8.** To move discontinuously; skip: *jumps*

from one subject to another. **9.** To be displaced suddenly from (e.g., a track). **10.** To move over (an opponent's playing piece) in a board game. **11.** *Slang* To be lively; bustle. ►*n.* **1.** The act of jumping; leap. **2.** *Informal* An initial advantage; head start. **3.** A sudden rise, as in price. **4.** A sudden transition. **5a.** An involuntary nervous movement. **b.** **jumps** A condition of nervousness. —**idiom: jump the gun** To start something too soon. [Perh. < ME *jumpen.*]

jump·er[1] (jŭm′pər) ►*n.* **1.** One that jumps. **2.** *Elect.* A short length of wire used temporarily to complete or bypass a circuit.

jump·er[2] (jŭm′pər) ►*n.* **1.** A sleeveless dress worn over a blouse or sweater. **2.** A loose protective smock or coat. **3. jumpers** A child's overalls. [Prob. < *jump*, short coat.]

jump shot ►*n.* *Basketball* A shot made by a player at the highest point of a jump.

jump suit ►*n.* **1.** A parachutist's uniform. **2.** A one-piece garment consisting of a blouse or shirt with attached slacks or shorts.

jump·y (jŭm′pē) ►*adj.* **-i·er, -i·est** On edge; nervous. —**jump′i·ness** *n.*

jun·co (jŭng′kō) ►*n., pl.* **-cos** or **-coes** A sparrow of N and Central America having predominantly gray plumage. [Sp., reed < Lat. *iuncus.*]

junc·tion (jŭngk′shən) ►*n.* **1.** The act of joining or the condition of being joined. **2.** A place where two things join or meet. [< Lat. *iungere*, *iūnct-*, join.]

junc·ture (jŭngk′chər) ►*n.* **1.** The act of joining or the condition of being joined. **2.** A place where two things are joined; joint. **3.** A point in time, esp. one requiring a decision to be made. [< Lat. *iungere*, *iūnct-*, join.]

June (jōōn) ►*n.* The 6th month of the Gregorian calendar. See table at **calendar.** [< Lat. *Iūnius (mēnsis)*, (month of) Juno.]

Ju·neau (jōō′nō′) The capital of AK, in the SE part.

June beetle or **June bug** ►*n.* A large, chiefly brownish beetle having leaf-feeding adults that emerge in the spring and larvae that damage plant roots.

Jung (yŏŏng), **Carl Gustav** 1875–1961. Swiss psychiatrist. —**Jung′i·an** *adj. & n.*

jun·gle (jŭng′gəl) ►*n.* **1.** Land densely overgrown with tropical vegetation. **2.** A dense thicket or growth. **3.** A bewildering complex or maze. **4.** A place of ruthless competition or struggle for survival. [< Skt. *jaṅgala-*, desert, waste.] —**jun′gly** (-glē) *adj.*

jungle gym ►*n.* A structure of poles and bars for children to climb and play on.

jun·ior (jōōn′yər) ►*adj.* **1.** Younger. Used to distinguish a son from his father when they have the same given name. **2.** Intended for youthful persons: *junior fashions.* **3.** Lower in rank or shorter in length of tenure. **4.** Of the third year of a US high school or college. **5.** Lesser in scale than the usual. ►*n.* **1.** A person who is younger than another. **2.** A person lesser in rank or time of service. **3.** A third-year student in a US high school or college. [< Lat. *iūnior*, younger.]

junior college ►*n.* A school offering a two-year course that is the equivalent of the first two years of a four-year college.

junior high school ►*n.* A school including the 7th, 8th, and sometimes 9th grades.

ju·ni·per (jōō′nə-pər) ►*n.* An evergreen tree or shrub with scalelike leaves and aromatic, bluish-gray, berrylike cones. [< Lat. *iūniperus.*]

junk¹ (jŭngk) ►*n.* **1.** Discarded material that may be reused in some form. **2.** *Informal* **a.** Cheap or shoddy material. **b.** Something worthless or meaningless. **3.** *Slang* Heroin. ►*v.* To throw away or discard as useless. [ME *jonk,* an old rope.] —**junk′y** *adj.*

junk² (jŭngk) ►*n.* A Chinese flat-bottomed sailing ship. [< Javanese *djong.*]

junk bond ►*n.* A corporate bond having a high yield and high risk of default.

jun·ket (jŭng′kĭt) ►*n.* **1.** A trip taken by a public official or businessperson at public or corporate expense. **2.** A party or outing. **3.** A dessert made from flavored milk and rennet. [ME *jonket,* rush basket.] —**jun′ket** *v.* —**jun′ket·er** *n.*

junk food ►*n.* A high-calorie food that is low in nutritional value.

junk·ie also **junk·y** (jŭng′kē) ►*n., pl.* **-ies** *Slang* **1.** A narcotics addict, esp. one using heroin. **2.** One who has an insatiable devotion or interest.

junk mail ►*n.* Third-class mail, such as advertisements, mailed in large quantities.

junk·yard (jŭngk′yärd′) ►*n.* A yard or lot used to store junk.

Ju·no (jōō′nō) ►*n. Rom. Myth.* The principal goddess of the pantheon, wife and sister of Jupiter.

jun·ta (hŏōn′tə, jŭn′-) ►*n.* A group of military officers ruling a country after seizing power. [Sp., meeting, council, ult. < Lat. *iungere, iūnct-,* join.]

Ju·pi·ter (jōō′pĭ-tər) ►*n.* **1.** *Rom. Myth.* The supreme god, brother and husband of Juno. **2.** The largest of the planets and the 5th from the sun, at a mean distance of 779 million km (484 million mi), having a diameter of approx. 143,000 km (89,000 mi).

Ju·ra Mountains (jōōr′ə, zhü-rä′) A range extending about 241 km (150 mi) along the French-Swiss border.

Ju·ras·sic (jōō-răs′ĭk) *Geol.* ►*adj.* Of or being the 2nd period of the Mesozoic Era, marked by the appearance of the earliest birds. ►*n.* The Jurassic Period. [After the *Jura* Mts. along the border between France and Switzerland.] —**Ju·ras′sic** *n.*

ju·rid·i·cal (jōō-rĭd′ĭ-kəl) also **ju·rid·ic** (-ĭk) ►*adj.* Of or relating to the law and its administration. [< Lat. *iūridicus.*] —**ju·rid′i·cal·ly** *adv.*

ju·ris·dic·tion (jōōr′ĭs-dĭk′shən) ►*n.* **1.** The right of a court to hear a particular case. **2a.** Authority or control. **b.** The extent of authority or control: *beyond the school's jurisdiction.* **3.** The territorial range of authority or control. [< Lat. *iūrisdictiō.*] —**ju′ris·dic′tion·al** *adj.*

ju·ris·pru·dence (jōōr′ĭs-prōōd′ns) ►*n.* **1.** The philosophy or science of law. **2.** A division, type, or particular body of law. [LLat. *iūrisprūdentia.*] —**ju′ris·pru·den′tial** (-prōō-dĕn′shəl) *adj.*

ju·rist (jōōr′ĭst) ►*n.* One skilled in the law, esp. a judge or legal scholar. [< Lat. *iūs, iūr-,* law.]

ju·ris·tic (jōō-rĭs′tĭk) also **ju·ris·ti·cal** (-tĭ-kəl) ►*adj.* **1.** Of or relating to a jurist. **2.** Of law or legality. **3.** As legally defined.

ju·ror (jōōr′ər, -ôr′) ►*n.* A member of a jury.

ju·ry (jōōr′ē) ►*n., pl.* **-ries 1.** A body of persons selected to decide a verdict in a legal case, based upon the evidence presented, after being instructed on the applicable law. **2.** A committee to select winners in a competition. [< AN *jurer,* swear < Lat. *iūrāre.*]

just (jŭst) ►*adj.* **1.** Honorable and fair in one's dealings and actions: *a just ruler.* **2.** Consistent with what is morally right: *a just cause.* **3.** Properly due or merited: *just deserts.* **4.** Valid within the law; lawful: *just claims.* **5.** Suitable; fitting. **6.** Based on sound reason; well-founded: *a just appraisal.* ►*adv.* (jəst, jĭst; jŭst *when stressed*) **1.** Exactly: *just enough salt.* **2.** Only a moment ago: *He just arrived.* **3.** By a narrow margin: *just missed being hit.* **4.** At a little distance: *just down the road.* **5.** Merely; only: *just a scratch.* **6.** Simply: *It's just beautiful!* [< Lat. *iūstus.*] —**just′ly** *adv.* —**just′ness** *n.*

jus·tice (jŭs′tĭs) ►*n.* **1.** The quality of being just; fairness. **2.** The principle of moral rightness. **3a.** The attainment of what is just, esp. that which is fair, moral, right, merited, or in accordance with law. **b.** The upholding of what is just, esp. fair treatment and due reward in accordance with honor, standards, or law. **c.** The administration, system, methods, or procedures of law. **4.** Conformity to fact or sound reason. **5.** A judge on the highest court of a government. —*idiom:* **do justice to** To treat adequately, fairly, or with full appreciation. [< Lat. *iūstitia < iūstus,* just.]

justice of the peace ►*n.* An official with judicial power over certain civil and criminal cases and having other limited powers, such as the power to perform marriages.

jus·ti·fi·ca·tion (jŭs′tə-fĭ-kā′shən) ►*n.* **1.** The act of justifying or the condition of being justified. **2.** Something, such as a fact or circumstance, that justifies.

jus·ti·fy (jŭs′tə-fī′) ►*v.* **-fied, -fy·ing 1.** To demonstrate to be just, right, or valid. **2.** To demonstrate sufficient legal reason for (an action taken). **3.** To format (e.g., a paragraph) so that the lines of text begin and end evenly at a straight margin. [< Lat. *iūstificāre,* act justly toward.] —**jus′ti·fi′a·ble** *adj.* —**jus′ti·fi′a·bly** *adv.*

Jus·tin·i·an I (jŭ-stĭn′ē-ən) AD 483–565. Byzantine emperor (527–565).

jut (jŭt) ►*v.* **jut·ted, jut·ting** To extend outward or upward; project. See Synonyms at **bulge.** [< ME *gete,* JETTY.] —**jut** *n.*

jute (jōōt) ►*n.* **1.** Either of two Asian plants yielding a fiber used for sacking and cordage. **2.** The fiber obtained from these plants. [< Skt. *jūṭaḥ,* twisted hair.]

Jute ►*n.* A member of a Germanic people who migrated to Britain in the 5th and 6th cent. A.D.

Jut·land (jŭt′lənd) A peninsula of N Europe comprising mainland Denmark and N Germany.

Ju·ve·nal (jōō′və-nəl) AD 60?–140? Roman satirist.

ju·ve·nile (jōō′və-nīl′, -nəl) ►*adj.* **1.** Not fully grown; young. **2.** Intended for or appropriate to children or young people. **3.** Immature; childish. ►*n.* **1a.** A young person; child. **b.** A young animal that has not reached sexual maturity.

2. An actor who plays children. [< Lat. *iuvenis, young.*] —**ju′ve·nile′ly** *adv.*

juvenile delinquent ►*n.* A juvenile guilty of antisocial or criminal behavior. —**juvenile delinquency** *n.*

jux·ta·pose (jŭk′stə-pōz′) ►*v.* **-posed, -pos· ing** To place side by side. [Fr. *juxtaposer* : Lat. *iūxtā,* next to + Fr. *poser,* to place; see POSE.] —**jux′ta·po·si′tion** (-pə-zĭsh′ən) *n.*

JV ►*abbr.* junior varsity

K

k¹ or **K** (kā) ►*n., pl.* **k's** or **K's** also **ks** or **Ks** The 11th letter of the English alphabet.

k² ►*abbr.* karat

K ►*abbr.* **1.** kelvin **2.** kilobyte **3.** kilometer **4.** kindergarten **5.** *Games* king **6.** strikeout

K2 (kā′tōō′) Also **Mount Godwin Austen** A peak, 8,611 m (28,251 ft), in the Karakoram Range of N Kashmir.

kab·ba·lah or **ca·ba·la** (kăb′ə-lə, kə-bä′lə) ►*n.* **1.** often **Kabbalah** A body of mystical teachings of rabbinical origin, often based on an esoteric interpretation of the Hebrew Scriptures. **2.** A secret doctrine resembling these teachings. [< Heb. *qabbālâ,* tradition.] —**kab′ba·lism** *n.* —**kab′ba·list** *n.* —**kab′ba· list′ic** *adj.*

ka·bob (kə-bŏb′) ►*n.* Var. of **kebab.**

Ka·bu·ki (kə-bōō′kē) ►*n.* A type of popular Japanese drama in which elaborately costumed performers perform stylized movements, danc- es, and songs. [J. : *ka,* singing + *bu,* dancing + *ki,* art.]

Ka·bul (kä′bŏol, kə-bōol′) The capital of Afghanistan, in the E part near the border with Pakistan.

ka·chi·na (kə-chē′nə) or **kat·si·na** (kə-chē′nə, kət-sē′-) ►*n.* **1.** A deified ancestral spirit of the Pueblo peoples. **2.** A carved doll resembling such a spirit. [Hopi *katsina.*]

Ká·dar (kä′där), **János** 1912–89. Hungarian politician.

Kad·dish (kä′dĭsh) ►*n. Judaism* A prayer recited in the daily synagogue services and by mourn- ers after the death of a close relative. [Aram. *qaddīš.*]

Kaf·ka (käf′kə, -kä), **Franz** 1883–1924. Prague- born writer. —**Kaf′ka·esque′** *adj.*

kaf·tan (käf′tăn′, -tən, käf-tăn′) ►*n.* Var. of **caftan.**

Kah·lo (kä′lō), **Frida** 1907–54. Mexican artist.

Kai·ser (kī′zər) ►*n.* Any of the emperors of the Holy Roman Empire (962–1806), of Austria (1806–1918), or of Germany (1871–1918). [< Lat. *Caesar,* Caesar.]

Kai·ser·in (kī′zər-ĭn) ►*n.* The wife of a Kaiser.

kai·zen (kī′zĕn′) ►*n.* A business management philosophy aimed at producing ongoing incre- mental improvements, esp. in quality and effi- ciency. [J. : *kai,* change + *zen,* good.]

kale (kāl) ►*n.* A variety of cabbage having dark green leaves that are eaten as a vegetable. [< Lat. *caulis,* cabbage.]

ka·lei·do·scope (kə-lī′də-skōp′) ►*n.* **1.** A tube- shaped optical instrument that is rotated to produce a succession of symmetrical designs by means of mirrors reflecting the constantly changing patterns made by bits of colored objects at one end of the tube. **2.** A constantly changing set of colors. **3.** A series of changing phases or events. [Gk. *kalos,* beautiful + *eidos,*

form + -SCOPE.] —**ka·lei′do·scop′ic** (-skŏp′- ĭk) *adj.* —**ka·lei′do·scop′i·cal·ly** *adv.*

ka·lim·ba (kə-lĭm′bə) ►*n.* See **mbira.** [Of Bantu orig.]

Ka·li·nin·grad (kə-lē′nĭn-grăd′) A city of extreme W Russia on the Baltic Sea between Poland and Lithuania.

Kam·chat·ka (kăm-chăt′kə) A peninsula of E Russia between the Sea of Okhotsk and the Bering Sea.

kam·eez (kə-mēz′) ►*n.* A long loose tunic, gen. of three-quarter length and slit to the waist at the sides, worn chiefly by women in S Asia. [Punjabi and Hindi and Urdu, qamīz.]

Ka·me·ha·me·ha I (kə-mā′ə-mā′ə) 1758–1819. King of the Hawaiian Is. (1795–1819).

ka·mi·ka·ze (kä′mĭ-kä′zē) ►*n.* **1.** A Japanese pilot trained in World War II to make a suicidal crash attack. **2.** An airplane loaded with explo- sives for such an attack. [J.]

Kam·pa·la (käm-pä′lə) The capital of Uganda, in the S part on Lake Victoria.

ka·na (kä′nə) ►*n., pl.* **kana** or **-nas** Japanese syllabic writing. [J.]

Kan·din·sky or **Kan·din·ski** (kăn-dĭn′skē), **Wassily** 1866–1944. Russian abstract painter.

kan·ga·roo (kăng′gə-rōō′) ►*n., pl.* **-roo** or **-roos** Any of various large herbivorous marsu- pials of Australia and adjacent islands, having short forelimbs, large hind limbs used for leap- ing, and a long tapered tail. [Guugu Yimidhirr (Australian) *gaŋgurru.*]

kangaroo

kangaroo court ►*n.* A mock court, esp. one hastily improvised and gen. marked by dishon- esty or incompetence.

Kan·sas (kăn′zəs) A state of the central US. Cap. Topeka. —**Kan′san** *adj. & n.*

Kansas City 1. A city of NE KS on the Missouri R. adjacent to Kansas City, MO **2.** A city of W MO on the Missouri R. WNW of St. Louis.

Kant (kănt, känt), **Immanuel** 1724–1804. Ger- man philosopher. —**Kant′i·an** *adj. & n.*

ka·o·lin also **ka·o·line** (kā′ə-lĭn) ►*n.* A fine clay used esp. in ceramics and refractories. [< Mandarin *gāo lĭng*, an area in China.]

ka·pok (kā′pŏk′) ►*n.* A silky fiber obtained from the pods of the kapok tree, used for insulation and as padding. [Malay.]

kapok tree ►*n.* A spiny tropical tree cultivated for its leathery pods that contain kapok.

Ka·po·si's sarcoma (kə-pō′sēz, kăp′ə-) ►*n.* A cancer endemic to equatorial Africa that often occurs in people with AIDS and is characterized by bluish-red nodules on the skin. [After Moritz *Kaposi* (1837–1902).]

kap·pa (kăp′ə) ►*n.* The 10th letter of the Greek alphabet. [Gk.]

ka·put also **ka·putt** (kä-pōōt′, -pŏŏt′, kə-) ►*adj.* Incapacitated or destroyed. [Ger. *kaputt* < Fr. *capot*, not having won a trick at cards.]

Ka·ra·chi (kə-rä′chē) A city of S Pakistan on the Arabian Sea.

Ka·ra·ko·ram Range (kăr′ə-kôr′əm, kär′-) A mountain system of N Pakistan and India and SW China.

kar·a·kul (kăr′ə-kəl) ►*n.* **1.** A Central Asian sheep having a wide tail and wool that is curled and glossy in the young but wiry and coarse in the adult. **2.** Fur made from the pelt of a karakul lamb. [After *Kara Kul*, a lake of S Tajikistan.]

kar·a·o·ke (kăr′ē-ō′kē) ►*n.* A music entertainment system providing prerecorded accompaniment to songs that a performer sings live. [J. : *kara*, empty + *oke(sutora)*, ORCHESTRA.]

kar·at also **car·at** (kăr′ət) ►*n.* A unit of measure for the fineness of gold, equal to ¼₄ part; e.g., gold that is 50 percent pure is 12 karat. [Var. of CARAT.]

ka·ra·te (kə-rä′tē) ►*n.* A Japanese martial art in which sharp blows and kicks are administered to an opponent. [J.]

kar·ma (kär′mə) ►*n.* **1.** *Hinduism & Buddhism* **a.** The totality of a person's actions during successive incarnations, regarded as causally influencing the person's destiny. **b.** The law or principle through which such influence is believed to operate. **2.** Fate; destiny. **3.** A distinctive aura or feeling. [Skt. *karma*, a doing.]

karst (kärst) ►*n.* A limestone region marked by fissures, sinkholes, underground streams, and caverns. [Ger.]

kar·y·o·type (kăr′ē-ə-tīp′) ►*n.* The characterization of the chromosomal complement of an individual or a species according to the number, form, and size of the chromosomes. [Gk. *karuon*, nut, kernel + TYPE.]

Kash·mir (kăsh′mîr′, kăsh-mîr′) A region of S Asia in NW India and NE Pakistan. **—Kash·mir′i** *adj. & n.*

ka·ta·ka·na (kä′tä-kä′nä) ►*n.* A relatively angular kana used esp. to write foreign words, onomatopoetic words, and the names of plants and animals in Japanese. [J.]

Kath·man·du also **Kat·man·du** (kăt′măn-dōō′) The capital of Nepal, in the central part in the E Himalayas.

ka·ty·did (kā′tē-dĭd′) ►*n.* A usu. green insect, the male of which produces a shrill sound. [Imit. of its sound.]

Kau·ai (kou′ī′) An island of HI NW of Oahu.

ka·va (kä′və) ►*n.* **1.** A shrub native to the Pacific islands. **2.** A substance derived from the roots

of this plant, used as a sedative. [Tongan.]

kay·ak (kī′ăk′) ►*n.* **1.** An Inuit or Yupik canoe covered with watertight skins except for a single or double opening in the center. **2.** A similar lightweight boat. [Inuit and Yupik *qajaq*.] **—kay′ak′** *v.* **—kay′ak′er** *n.*

kay·o (kā-ō′, kā′ō′) ►*n., pl.* **-os** A knockout in boxing. [< KO < K(NOCK)O(UT).] **—kay′o** *v.*

Ka·zakh (kä′zăk′, kə-zäk′) ►*adj.* Of or relating to Kazakhstan or its people or language. ►*n., pl.* **-zakh** or **-zakhs 1a.** A native or inhabitant of Kazakhstan. **b.** A member of a Turkic people living in Kazakhstan and NW China. **2.** The Turkic language of the Kazakh.

Ka·zakh·stan (kä′zăk-stän′, kə-zäk′-) A country S of Russia and NE of the Caspian Sea. Cap. Astana.

Ka·zan (kə-zăn′, -zän′) A city of W-central Russia on the Volga R. E of Moscow.

ka·zoo (kə-zōō′) ►*n., pl.* **-zoos** A toy musical instrument in which a membrane is vibrated by the performer's voice. [Imit.]

kc ►*abbr.* kilocycle

KC ►*abbr.* **1.** Kansas City **2.** King's Counsel **3.** Knights of Columbus

kcal ►*abbr.* kilocalorie

Keats (kēts), **John** 1795–1821. British poet. **—Keats′i·an** *adj.*

ke·bab or **ke·bob** also **ka·bob** (kə-bŏb′) ►*n.* Shish kebab.

kedge (kĕj) ►*n.* A light anchor used for warping a vessel. ►*v.* **kedged, kedg·ing** To move (a vessel) with a kedge. [Poss. < ME *caggen*, to tie.]

keel (kēl) ►*n.* **1a.** The principal structural member of a boat or ship, running along the center of the hull from bow to stern, to which the frames are attached. **b.** A projecting ridge or fin on the bottom of the hull of a boat or ship that improves directional control. **2.** The principal structural member of an aircraft, resembling a ship's keel in shape and function. **3.** The breastbone of a bird. **4.** A pair of united petals in certain flowers, as those of the pea. ►*v.* To capsize. **—*phrasal verb:* keel over** To collapse or fall, as from death or fainting. [< ON *kjölr.*]

keel·boat (kēl′bōt′) ►*n.* A riverboat with a keel, used for carrying freight.

keel·haul (kēl′hôl′) ►*v.* To punish by dragging under the keel of a ship. [< Du. *kielhalen.*]

keen[1] (kēn) ►*adj.* **-er, -est 1.** Having a fine sharp edge or point. **2.** Intellectually acute. **3.** Acutely sensitive: *a keen ear.* **4.** Sharp; vivid. **5.** Intense; bracing: *a keen wind.* **6.** Pungent; acrid. **7a.** Ardent; enthusiastic. **b.** Eagerly desirous: *keen on going.* **8.** *Slang* Great; splendid. [< OE *cēne*, brave.] **—keen′ly** *adv.* **—keen′ness** *n.*

keen[2] (kēn) ►*n.* A loud wailing or lament for the dead. [< Ir.Gael. *caoineadh.*] **—keen** *v.* **—keen′er** *n.*

keep (kēp) ►*v.* **kept** (kĕpt), **keep·ing 1.** To retain possession of. **2.** To provide (e.g., a family) with maintenance and support. **3.** To put customarily; store. **4.** To raise: *keep chickens.* **5.** To maintain: *keep a diary.* **6.** To manage or have charge of. **7a.** To detain: *was kept after school.* **b.** To prevent: *kept them from entering.* **c.** To refrain from divulging: *keep a secret.* **d.** To save; reserve. **8.** To adhere to: *keep one's word.* **9.** To celebrate; observe. **10.** To remain in a state or condition; stay. **11.** To continue: *keep* *talking.* **12.** To remain fresh or unspoiled. ►*n.* **1.** Care; charge. **2.** A means of support: *earn one's keep.* **3a.** The stronghold of a castle. **b.** A jail. —*phrasal verbs:* **keep down** To prevent from accomplishing or succeeding. **keep up 1.** To maintain in good condition. **2.** To persevere in. **3.** To continue at the same level or pace. —*idiom:* **for keeps 1.** For an indefinitely long period. **2.** Permanently: *We're separating for keeps.* [< OE *cēpan,* observe.] —**keep′er** *n.*

keep·sake (kēp′sāk′) ►*n.* Something that one keeps because of the memories it calls to mind.

keg (kĕg) ►*n.* A small barrel. [< ON *kaggi.*]

Kel·ler (kĕl′ər), **Helen Adams** 1880–1968. Amer. memoirist and lecturer.

Helen Keller

kelp (kĕlp) ►*n.* Any of various brown seaweeds, often growing very large and forming dense beds. [ME *culp.*]

kel·vin (kĕl′vĭn) ►*n., pl.* **kelvin** A unit of the absolute temperature scale, the zero point of which equals −273.15°C. [After 1st Baron KEL-VIN.]

Kelvin, 1st Baron. William Thomson. 1824–1907. British physicist.

Ke·mal At·a·türk (kə-mäl′ ăt′ə-tûrk′) 1881–1938. Turkish national leader.

ken (kĕn) ►*n.* **1.** Perception; understanding. **2.** Range of vision; view. ►*v.* **kenned** or **kent** (kĕnt), **ken·ning** *Scots* To know. [< OE *cennan,* declare.]

Ken·ne·dy (kĕn′ĭ-dē), **John Fitzgerald** 1917–63. The 35th US president (1961–63).

John F. Kennedy
photographed in the early 1960s

Kennedy, Robert Francis 1925–68. Amer. politician.

ken·nel (kĕn′əl) ►*n.* **1.** A shelter for a dog. **2.** An establishment where dogs are bred, trained, or boarded. [< VLat. **canīle* < Lat. *canis,* dog.] —**ken′nel** *v.*

Ken·ny (kĕn′ē), **Elizabeth** 1880?–1952. Australian nurse.

ken·te (kĕn′tā) ►*n.* **1.** A brightly patterned, hand-woven ceremonial cloth of the Ashanti. **2.** A fabric resembling this cloth. [Twi, cloth.]

Ken·tuck·y (kən-tŭk′ē) A state of the E-central US. Cap. Frankfort. —**Ken·tuck′i·an** *adj. & n.*

Ken·ya (kĕn′yə, kēn′-) A country of E-central Africa bordering on the Indian Ocean. Cap. Nairobi. —**Ken′yan** *adj. & n.*

Kenya, Mount An extinct volcano, 5,199 m (17,057 ft), in central Kenya.

Ken·yat·ta (kĕn-yä′tə), **Jomo** 1893?–1978. Kenyan politician; first president of independent Kenya (1964–78).

Ke·ogh plan (kē′ō) ►*n.* A retirement plan for the self-employed. [After E.J. *Keogh* (1907–1989).]

ke·pi (kā′pē, kĕp′ē) ►*n., pl.* **-pis** A French military cap with a flat circular top and a visor. [< Ger. dial. *Käppi* < Ger. *Kappe,* cap.]

Kep·ler (kĕp′lər), **Johannes** 1571–1630. German astronomer and mathematician.

kept (kĕpt) ►*v.* P.t. and p.part. of **keep.**

ker·a·tin (kĕr′ə-tĭn) ►*n.* A tough insoluble protein that is the chief constituent of hair, nails, horns, and hooves. [Gk. *keras, kerat-,* horn + −IN.] —**ke·rat′i·nous** (kə-răt′n-əs) *adj.*

kerb (kûrb) ►*n. Chiefly Brit.* Var. of **curb.**

ker·chief (kûr′chĭf, -chēf′) ►*n., pl.* **-chiefs** also **-chieves** (-chĭvz, -chēvz) **1.** A square scarf, often worn as a head covering. **2.** A handkerchief. [< AN *courchief.*]

kerf (kûrf) ►*n.* A groove or notch that is made by a cutting tool, such as a saw. [< OE *cyrf,* a cutting.]

ker·nel (kûr′nəl) ►*n.* **1.** A grain or seed, as of a cereal grass. **2.** The inner, usu. edible seed of a nut or fruit stone. **3.** The central part; core. [< OE *cyrnel.*]

ker·o·sene (kĕr′ə-sēn′, kĕr′ə-sēn′) ►*n.* A thin oil distilled from petroleum or shale oil, used as a fuel and as a denaturant for alcohol. [Gk. *kēros,* wax + −ENE.]

Ker·ou·ac (kĕr′ŏŏ-ăk′), **Jack** 1922–69. Amer. writer.

kes·trel (kĕs′trəl) ►*n.* A small falcon noted for its habit of hovering. [< OFr. *cresserele.*]

ketch (kĕch) ►*n.* A two-masted fore-and-aft-rigged sailing vessel with a smaller mast aft of the mainmast but forward of the rudder. [ME *cache.*]

ketch·up (kĕch′əp, kăch′-) also **catch·up** (kăch′əp, kĕch′-) or **cat·sup** (kăt′səp, kăch′əp, kĕch′-) ►*n.* A thick, smooth, spicy sauce usu. made from tomatoes. [Malay *kicap,* sauce made from fermented fish.]

ke·tone (kē′tōn′) ►*n.* Any of a class of organic compounds having the group —OH— linked to two hydrocarbon radicals. [Ger. *Keton* < *Aketon,* acetone.]

ket·tle (kĕt′l) ►*n.* A metal pot or container for boiling or stewing. [< ON *ketill* and OE *cetel.*]

ket·tle·drum (kĕt′l-drŭm′) ►*n.* A large hemispherical drum, often made of copper or brass with a parchment head.

kettledrum

key¹ (kē) ►*n., pl.* **keys 1a.** A notched, usu. metal implement that is turned to open or close a lock. **b.** A similar implement or electronic device used for activating something. **c.** A device, such as a pin, inserted to lock together mechanical or structural parts. **d.** A keycard. **2.** A determining factor in achieving something. **3a.** Something that provides understanding of something else. **b.** A set of answers to a test. **c.** A table, gloss, or cipher for decoding or explaining. **d.** *Comp.* A number used by a cryptographic algorithm to encrypt or decrypt data. **4a.** A button or lever that is pressed to operate a machine. **b.** A button that is depressed to cause a character or function to be typed or executed by a typewriter or to be accepted as input by a computer. **c.** *Mus.* A button or lever that is pressed to produce or modulate the sound of an instrument. **5.** *Mus.* A tonal system consisting of seven tones in fixed relationship to a tonic; tonality. **6.** The pitch of a voice or other sound. **7.** A characteristic tone or level of intensity. ►*adj.* Of crucial importance; significant. ►*v.* **1.** To lock with a key. **2.** To be the crucial factor in. **3.** *Mus.* To regulate the pitch of. **4.** To bring into harmony; adjust or adapt. **5.** To supply an explanatory key for. **6a.** To operate (a device) by means of a keyboard. **b.** To enter (data) into a computer by means of a keyboard. —*phrasal verb:* **key up** To make intense, excited, or nervous. [< OE *cǽg*.]

key² (kē) ►*n., pl.* **keys** A low offshore island or reef; cay. [< Sp. *cayo,* cay.]

Key, Francis Scott 1779–1843. Amer. lawyer and poet.

key·board (kē′bôrd′) ►*n.* **1.** A panel of buttons used for typing and performing other functions on a computer or typewriter. **2.** *Mus.* **a.** A row of keys that produce or modulate the sound of an instrument when pressed. **b.** Any of various, often electronic instruments played by means of a set of pianolike keys. ►*v. Comp.* To enter (text or data) by means of a keyboard. —**key′board′er** *n.*

key·card (kē′kärd′) ►*n.* A plastic card with a magnetically coded strip that is scanned to operate a mechanism such as a door.

key·hole (kē′hōl′) ►*n.* The hole in a lock into which a key fits.

Keynes (kānz), **John Maynard** 1st Baron of Tilton. 1883–1946. British economist.

key·note (kē′nōt′) ►*n.* **1.** The tonic of a musical key. **2.** A prime element or theme.

keynote address ►*n.* An opening address, as at a political convention.

key·pad (kē′păd′) ►*n.* An input device consisting of a set of usu. numeric keys arranged in a grid, as on a cell phone.

key·punch (kē′pŭnch′) ►*n.* A keyboard machine used to punch holes in cards or tapes for data-processing systems. ►*v.* To process on a keypunch. —**key′punch′er** *n.*

key signature ►*n. Mus.* The group of sharps or flats placed to the right of the clef on a staff to identify the key.

key·stone (kē′stōn′) ►*n.* **1.** The central wedge-shaped stone of an arch that locks its parts together. **2.** A basic or fundamental element.

key·stroke (kē′strōk′) ►*n.* A stroke of a key, as on a computer keyboard.

Key West A city of extreme S FL on the island of **Key West** in the Gulf of Mexico.

kg ►*abbr.* kilogram

KGB (kā′jē-bē′) ►*n.* The intelligence and internal security agency of the former Soviet Union. [Russ. < *K(omitét) G(osudárstvennoĭ) B(ezopásnosti),* committee for state security.]

Kha·da·fy (kə-dä′fē), **Muammar al-** See Muammar al-**Qaddafi.**

khak·i (kăk′ē, kä′kē) ►*n.* **1.** A light yellow brown. **2a.** A sturdy cloth of this color. **b. khakis** A uniform or garment of this cloth. **c. khakis** Pants made of cotton fabric, usu. of this color. [< Pers. *khāk,* dust.] —**khak′i** *adj.*

khan (kän, kăn) ►*n.* **1.** A ruler, official, or important person in India and some central Asian countries. **2.** A medieval ruler of a Mongol, Tatar, or Turkish tribe. [< Turk. *khān.*]

Khar·toum (kär-tōōm′) The capital of Sudan, in the E-central part at the confluence of the Blue Nile and the White Nile.

Khmer (kmâr) ►*n., pl.* **Khmer** or **Khmers 1.** A member of a people of Cambodia. **2.** The official language of Cambodia.

Khoi·san (koi′sän′) ►*n.* A family of languages of S Africa.

Kho·mei·ni (kō-mā′nē, κнō-), **Ayatollah Ruholla** 1900–89. Iranian Shiite leader and head of state (1979–89).

Khru·shchev (krōōsh′chĕf, -chôf), **Nikita Sergeyevich** 1894–1971. Soviet politician.

Khu·fu (kōō′fōō′) See **Cheops.**

Khy·ber Pass (kī′bər) A mountain pass on the border between E Afghanistan and N Pakistan.

kib·butz (kĭ-bōōts′, -bōōts′) ►*n., pl.* **kib·but·zim** (kĭb′ōŏt-sēm′, -ōōt-) A collective farm or settlement in modern Israel. [Heb. *qibbûṣ,* gathering.]

kib·itz (kĭb′ĭts) ►*v. Informal* **1.** To chat. **2.** To offer unwanted advice. [Yiddish *kibitsen.*] —**kib′itz·er** *n.*

ki·bosh (kī′bŏsh′, kĭ-bŏsh′) ►*n. Informal* A check, end, or stop: *put the kibosh on a plan.* [?]

kick (kĭk) ►*v.* **1.** To strike or strike out with the foot. **2.** *Sports* To score or gain ground by kicking a ball. **3.** To recoil, as a gun when fired. ►*n.* **1.** A vigorous blow or motion with the foot or feet. **2.** A way in which the legs are moved in swimming. **3.** A jolting recoil, as of a gun. **4.** *Slang* Power; force. **5.** *Slang* **a.** A feeling of pleasurable stimulation: *got a kick out of the show.* **b. kicks** Fun: *just for kicks.* **6.** *Slang* Temporary, often obsessive interest. **7a.** The act or an instance of kicking a ball. **b.** A kicked ball. **c.** The distance

spanned by a kicked ball. —*phrasal verbs:*
kick around 1. *Informal* To treat badly; abuse.
2. To move from place to place. **kick in** *Informal*
To contribute (one's share). **kick off 1.** To begin
or resume play with a kickoff. **2.** *Informal* To
begin; start. **kick out** *Slang* To throw out; eject
or expel. —*idioms:* **kick the bucket** *Slang* To
die. **kick the habit** *Slang* To free oneself of an
addiction. [ME *kiken.*]
Kick·a·poo (kĭk′ə-po͞o′) ►*n., pl.* **-poo** or **-poos**
1. A member of a Native American people
formerly of S Wisconsin and N Illinois, now
chiefly in Kansas and Oklahoma. **2.** The Algonquian language of the Kickapoo.
kick·back (kĭk′băk′) ►*n.* **1.** A sharp reaction;
repercussion. **2.** *Slang* A secret payment to one
who has facilitated a profitable deal.
kick·er (kĭk′ər) ►*n.* **1.** One that kicks. **2.** *Infor-*
mal A sudden surprising turn of events.
kick·off or **kick-off** (kĭk′ôf′, -ŏf′) ►*n.* **1.** A place
kick in football or soccer with which play is
begun. **2.** *Informal* A beginning.
kid (kĭd) ►*n.* **1.** A young goat. **2.** Kidskin. **3.**
Informal A child. ►*adj.* **1.** Made of kidskin. **2.**
Informal Younger than oneself: *my kid brother.*
►*v.* **kid·ded, kid·ding 1.** To mock playfully;
tease. **2.** To deceive in fun; fool. [< ON *kidh.*]
—**kid′der** *n.* —**kid′ding·ly** *adv.*
Kidd (kĭd), **William** "Captain Kidd." 1645?–
1701. Scottish pirate.
kid·nap (kĭd′năp′) ►*v.* **-napped, -nap·ping**
or **-naped, -nap·ing** To abduct (a person)
unlawfully. [KID + *nap*, to snatch.] —**kid′nap′-**
per, kid′nap′er *n.*
kid·ney (kĭd′nē) ►*n., pl.* **-neys 1.** Either of a pair
of organs in the vertebrate abdominal cavity
functioning to maintain proper water balance
and to filter the blood of metabolic wastes for
excretion. **2.** Kind; sort. [ME *kidenei.*]
kidney bean ►*n.* **1.** A bean cultivated in many
forms for its edible pods and seeds. **2.** A form
of this bean with dark red seeds.
kiel·ba·sa (kĭl-bä′sə, kēl-) ►*n.* A spicy smoked
Polish sausage. [Pol. *kiełbasa.*]
Kier·ke·gaard (kîr′kĭ-gärd′, -gôr′), **Søren**
Aaby 1813–55. Danish religious philosopher.
Ki·ev (kē′ĕf, -ĕv) The capital of Ukraine, in the
N-central part on the Dnieper R.
Ki·ga·li (kĭ-gä′lē, kē-) The capital of Rwanda, in
the central part.
Ki·ku·yu (kĭ-ko͞o′yo͞o) ►*n., pl.* **-yu** or **-yus 1.** A
member of a people of central and S Kenya. **2.**
The Bantu language of the Kikuyu.
Kil·i·man·ja·ro (kĭl′ə-mən-jär′ō), **Mount** The
highest mountain in Africa, in NE Tanzania
near Kenya's border, rising to 5,895 m (19,341 ft).
kill¹ (kĭl) ►*v.* **1a.** To put to death. **b.** To deprive
of life. **2a.** To put an end to; extinguish. **b.**
To veto: *kill a congressional bill.* **3.** To cause to
cease operating: *killed the motor.* **4.** To use up:
kill time. **5.** To cause extreme discomfort to: *My*
shoes are killing me. **6.** To delete. **7.** *Informal* To
overwhelm, esp. with hilarity. ►*n.* **1.** The act of
killing. **2.** One that is killed, as an animal in
hunting. **3.** An enemy aircraft, vessel, or missile that has been destroyed. —*phrasal verb:*
kill off To destroy in such large numbers as to
render extinct. [ME *killen.*] —**kill′er** *n.*
kill² (kĭl) ►*n. Regional* A creek. [< MDu. *kille.*]
kill·deer (kĭl′dîr′) ►*n., pl.* **-deer** or **-deers** A
New World plover having a distinctive noisy

cry. [Imit. of its call.]
killer whale ►*n.* See **orca.**
kill·ing (kĭl′ĭng) ►*n.* **1.** The act or action of causing death. **2.** A large profit. ►*adj.* **1.** Fatal. **2.**
Thoroughly exhausting. **3.** *Informal* Hilarious.
kill·joy (kĭl′joi′) ►*n.* One who spoils the enthusiasm or fun of others.
kiln (kĭln, kĭl) ►*n.* An oven for hardening, firing,
or drying. [< Lat. *culīna*, stove.]
ki·lo (kē′lō) ►*n., pl.* **-los** A kilogram.
kilo– ►*pref.* **1.** One thousand (10³): *kilowatt.* **2.**
1,024 (2¹⁰): *kilobyte.* [< Gk. *khilioi*, thousand.]
kil·o·bit (kĭl′ə-bĭt′) ►*n. Comp.* **1.** One thousand
bits. **2.** 1,024 (2¹⁰) bits.
kil·o·byte (kĭl′ə-bīt′) ►*n.* **1.** A unit of computer
memory or data storage capacity equal to 1,024
(2¹⁰) bytes. **2.** One thousand bytes.
kil·o·cal·o·rie (kĭl′ə-kăl′ə-rē) ►*n.* See **calorie**
(sense 2a).
kil·o·cy·cle (kĭl′ə-sī′kəl) ►*n.* Kilohertz.
kil·o·gram (kĭl′ə-grăm′) ►*n.* See table at **meas-**
urement.
kil·o·hertz (kĭl′ə-hûrts′) ►*n.* A unit of frequency equal to 1,000 hertz.
kil·o·li·ter (kĭl′ə-lē′tər) ►*n.* See table at **meas-**
urement.
kil·o·me·ter (kĭ-lŏm′ĭ-tər, kĭl′ə-mē′tər) ►*n.* See
table at **measurement.** —**kil′o·met′ric** (kĭl′-
ə-mĕt′rĭk) *adj.*
kil·o·ton (kĭl′ə-tŭn′) ►*n.* **1.** A unit of weight
equal to 1,000 tons. **2.** An explosive force
equivalent to that of 1,000 metric tons of TNT.
kil·o·watt (kĭl′ə-wŏt′) ►*n.* A unit of power
equal to 1,000 watts.
kil·o·watt-hour (kĭl′ə-wŏt-our′) ►*n.* A unit of
electric energy equal to the work done by one
kilowatt acting for one hour.
kilt (kĭlt) ►*n.* A knee-length pleated skirt, usu.
of a tartan wool, traditionally worn by men in
the Scottish highlands. [< ME *kilten*, tuck up,
of Scand. orig.]
kil·ter (kĭl′tər) ►*n.* Good condition; proper
form: *out of kilter.* [?]
kim·chi (kĭm′chē) ►*n., pl.* **-chis** A Korean dish
made of salted, fermented vegetables. [Korean
kimch'i, of Chin. orig.]
Kim Jong Il also **Kim Jong-il** (kĭm′ jŏng′
ĭl′) 1941–2011. North Korean head of state
(1994–2011).
ki·mo·no (kə-mō′nō) ►*n., pl.* **-nos 1.** A long,
wide-sleeved Japanese robe worn with an obi.
2. A loose robe worn chiefly by women. [J.]

kimono

kin (kĭn) ►*n.* **1.** *(takes pl. v.)* One's relatives. **2.** A family member. ►*adj.* Related; akin. [< OE *cyn.*]

–kin ►*suff.* Little one: *napkin.* [ME, prob. < MDu.]

ki·na (kē′nə) ►*n., pl.* **-na** or **-nas** See table at **currency.** [Indigenous word in Papua New Guinea.]

kind¹ (kīnd) ►*adj.* **-er, -est** Having or showing a generous or warm-hearted nature. [< OE *gecynde,* natural.] —**kind′ness** *n.*

kind² (kīnd) ►*n.* **1.** A group of individuals or instances sharing common traits. **2.** A doubtful member of a given category: *a kind of bluish color.* —*idioms:* **in kind 1.** With produce or commodities rather than with money. **2.** In the same manner. **kind of** *Informal* Rather; somewhat: *a dinner that was kind of expensive.* [< OE *gecynd,* race, kind.]

kin·der·gar·ten (kĭn′dər-gär′tn, kĭn′dər-gär′dn) ►*n.* A class for four- to six-year-old children. [Ger.] —**kin′der·gart′ner, kin′der·gar′ten·er** *n.*

kind·heart·ed (kīnd′här′tĭd) ►*adj.* Kind, sympathetic, or generous. —**kind′heart′ed·ly** *adv.*

kin·dle (kĭn′dl) ►*v.* **-dled, -dling 1.** To start (a fire); ignite. **2.** To glow or cause to glow. **3.** To arouse; stir up. [Prob. < ON *kynda.*]

kin·dling (kĭnd′lĭng) ►*n.* Easily ignited material, used to start a fire.

kind·ly (kīnd′lē) ►*adj.* **-li·er, -li·est** Of a sympathetic, helpful, or benevolent nature. ►*adv.* **1.** In a kind manner. **2.** In an accommodating manner: *Would you kindly close the door?* —**kind′li·ness** *n.*

kin·dred (kĭn′drĭd) ►*n.* **1.** A group of related persons. **2.** *(takes pl. v.)* Kinfolk. ►*adj.* Being similar or related. [< OE *cynrēde.*]

kine (kīn) ►*n.* Archaic Pl. of **cow¹.** [< OE *cȳna.*]

kin·e·mat·ics (kĭn′ə-măt′ĭks) ►*n. (takes sing. v.) Phys.* The study of motion without regard to the influence of mass or force. [< Gk. *kinēma, kinēmat-,* motion.] —**kin′e·mat′ic** *adj.* —**kin′e·mat′i·cal·ly** *adv.*

kin·e·scope (kĭn′ĭ-skōp′, kī′nĭ-) ►*n.* **1.** See **picture tube. 2.** A film of a transmitted television program. [Originally a trademark.]

ki·net·ic (kə-nĕt′ĭk, kī-) ►*adj.* Of, relating to, or produced by motion. [Gk. *kinētikos.*] —**ki·net′i·cal·ly** *adv.*

kinetic energy ►*n.* The energy possessed by a body because of its motion.

ki·net·ics (kə-nĕt′ĭks, kī-) ►*n. (takes sing. v.)* **1.** See **dynamics** (sense 1a). **2.** The branch of chemistry concerned with the rates of change of reactants in a chemical reaction.

kin·folk (kĭn′fōk′) also **kins·folk** (kĭnz′fōk′) or **kin·folks** (kĭn′fōks′) ►*pl.n.* One's relatives.

king (kĭng) ►*n.* **1.** A male sovereign. **2.** One that is preeminent in a group, category, or sphere. **3a.** A playing card bearing the figure of a king. **b.** The principal chess piece. **c.** A piece in checkers that has been crowned. **4. Kings** *(takes sing. v.)* See table at **Bible.** [< OE *cyning.*] —**king′ly** *adj. & adv.* —**king′ship′** *n.*

King, Coretta Scott 1927–2006. Amer. civil rights leader.

King, Martin Luther, Jr. 1929–68. Amer. cleric and civil rights leader.

Martin Luther King, Jr.
at the Lincoln Memorial, Washington, DC, during the March on Washington, August 28, 1963

King, (William Lyon) Mackenzie 1874–1950. Canadian prime minister (1921–26, 1926–30, and 1935–48).

king·bolt (kĭng′bōlt′) ►*n.* A vertical bolt that joins the body of a wagon or other vehicle to its front axle and usu. acts as a pivot.

king crab ►*n.* A large edible crab of coastal waters of Alaska, Japan, and Siberia.

king·dom (kĭng′dəm) ►*n.* **1.** A land ruled by a king or queen. **2.** An area in which one thing is dominant. **3.** One of the three main divisions (animal, vegetable, and mineral) of the natural world. **4.** *Biol.* The highest taxonomic classification into which organisms are grouped, based on fundamental similarities and common ancestry.

king·fish·er (kĭng′fĭsh′ər) ►*n.* Any of a family of crested, large-billed birds that feed on fish.

King James Bible ►*n.* An English translation of the Bible published in 1611.

king·pin (kĭng′pĭn′) ►*n.* **1.** See **headpin. 2.** The most important person or element. **3.** See **kingbolt.**

King's English (kĭngz) ►*n.* Standard English in England.

king-size (kĭng′sīz′) or **king-sized** (-sīzd′) ►*adj.* **1.** Larger or longer than the usual size. **2.** Very large.

King·ston (kĭng′stən) The capital of Jamaica, in the SE part on the Caribbean Sea.

Kings·town (kĭngz′toun′) The capital of St. Vincent and the Grenadines, West Indies, on the SW coast of St. Vincent I.

kink (kĭngk) ►*n.* **1.** A tight curl or twist in a length of thin material. **2.** A muscle cramp. **3.** A difficulty that is likely to impede operation. **4.** A mental peculiarity; quirk. ►*v.* To form a kink (in). [Du., a twist in rope.]

kink·a·jou (kĭng′kə-jōō′) ►*n.* A furry long-tailed arboreal mammal of tropical America. [Fr. *quincajou,* wolverine, of Algonquian orig.]

kink·y (kĭng′kē) ►*adj.* **-i·er, -i·est 1.** Tightly twisted or curled. **2.** *Slang* Of or relating to eccentric sexual practices. —**kink′i·ness** *n.*

kins·folk (kĭnz′fōk′) ►*pl.n.* Var. of **kinfolk.**

Kin·sha·sa (kĭn-shä′sə) The capital of Dem. Rep. of the Congo, in the W part on the Congo R.

kin·ship (kĭn′shĭp′) ►*n.* **1.** Connection by heredity, marriage, or adoption; family relationship. **2.** Likeness; affinity.

kins·man (kĭnz′mən) ►*n.* A male relative.

kins·wom·an (kĭnz′wŏom′ən) ►*n.* A female relative.

ki·osk (kē′ŏsk′, kē-ŏsk′) ►*n.* A small, usu. free-standing structure used as a newsstand or booth. [< Turk. *köşk.*]

Ki·o·wa (kī′ə-wô′, -wä′, -wä′) ►*n., pl.* **-wa** or **-was 1.** A member of a Native American people formerly inhabiting the S Great Plains, now chiefly in SW Oklahoma. **2.** The Kiowa-Tanoan language of the Kiowa.

Kiowa Apache ►*n.* A member of an Athabaskan-speaking Native American people closely associated with the Kiowa.

Ki·o·wa-Ta·no·an (kī′ə-wô′tä′nō-ən) ►*n.* An American Indian language family of New Mexico, NE Arizona, and the S Great Plains. —**Ki′·o·wa-Ta′no·an** *adj.*

kip (kĭp) ►*n., pl.* **kip** See table at **currency.** [Thai.]

Kip·ling (kĭp′lĭng), **(Joseph) Rudyard** 1865–1936. Indian-born British writer.

kip·per (kĭp′ər) ►*n.* A split, salted, and smoked herring or salmon. [< OE *cypera,* spawning male salmon.] —**kip′per** *v.*

Kir·ghiz (kĭr-gēz′) ►*adj. & n.* Var. of **Kyrgyz.**

Ki·ri·ba·ti (kĕr′ə-bä′tē, kĭr′ə-băs′) An island country of the W-central Pacific near the equator. Cap. Tarawa.

kir·i·ga·mi (kĭr′ĭ-gä′mē) ►*n.* The Japanese art of cutting and folding paper into ornamental objects or designs. [J.]

kirk (kûrk) ►*n. Scots* A church. [< OE *cirice,* CHURCH.]

kirsch (kĭrsh) ►*n.* A cherry brandy. [< Ger. *Kirschwasser : Kirsch,* cherry + *Wasser,* water (< OHGer. *wassar*).]

Ki·shi·nev (kĭsh′ə-nĕf′, -nôf′) See **Chişinău.**

Kis·lev (kĭs′ləv, kēs-lĕv′) ►*n.* The 9th month of the Jewish calendar. See table at **calendar.** [Heb. *kislēw.*]

kis·met (kĭz′mĕt′, -mĭt) ►*n.* Fate; fortune. [Turk.]

kiss (kĭs) ►*v.* **1.** To touch or caress with the lips, as in affection or greeting. **2.** To touch lightly or gently. ►*n.* **1.** A caress or touch with the lips. **2.** A slight touch. **3.** A small piece of candy, esp. of chocolate. [< OE *cyssan.*]

kiss·er (kĭs′ər) ►*n.* **1.** One that kisses. **2.** *Slang* The mouth. **3.** *Slang* The face.

Kis·sin·ger (kĭs′ĭn-jər), **Henry Alfred** b. 1923. German-born Amer. diplomat.

kit (kĭt) ►*n.* **1a.** A set of articles or implements: *a shaving kit.* **b.** A container for such a set. **2.** A set of parts to be assembled: *a model airplane kit.* **3.** A packaged set of related materials: *a sales kit.* —*idiom:* **the (whole) kit and caboodle** The entire collection or lot. [ME *kitte,* wooden tub.]

kitch·en (kĭch′ən) ►*n.* A room or area for preparing and cooking food. [< LLat. *coquīna.*]

kitch·en·ette (kĭch′ə-nĕt′) ►*n.* A small kitchen.

kitchen police ►*n.* **1.** Enlisted military personnel assigned to work in a kitchen. **2.** Military duty assisting cooks.

kitch·en·ware (kĭch′ən-wâr′) ►*n.* Utensils for use in a kitchen.

kite (kīt) ►*n.* **1a.** A light framework covered with cloth, plastic, or paper, designed to be flown in the wind at the end of a long string. **b.** A parafoil flown in a similar manner for recreation.

2. Any of various predatory birds having long pointed wings and often a forked tail. [< OE *cyta,* bird of prey.]

kith and kin (kĭth) ►*pl.n.* One's acquaintances and relatives. [< OE *cȳth,* kinsfolk.]

kitsch (kĭch) ►*n.* Pieces of art or other objects that appeal to popular or uncultivated taste, as in being garish or overly sentimental. [Ger.]

kit·ten (kĭt′n) ►*n.* A young cat. [ME *kitoun.*]

kit·ten·ish (kĭt′n-ĭsh) ►*adj.* Playfully coy and frisky. —**kit′ten·ish·ly** *adv.*

kit·ty¹ (kĭt′ē) ►*n., pl.* **-ties** A pool of money, esp. one to which a number of people have contributed. [Prob. < KIT.]

kit·ty² (kĭt′ē) ►*n., pl.* **-ties** A cat, esp. a kitten.

Kitty Hawk A town of NE NC, site of the Wright brothers' first two successful flights (December 17, 1903).

ki·va (kē′və) ►*n.* A usu. underground ceremonial chamber located in a Pueblo village. [Hopi *kíva.*]

ki·wi (kē′wē) ►*n., pl.* **-wis 1.** A flightless New Zealand bird having vestigial wings and a long slender bill. **2a.** A woody Chinese vine having fuzzy fruit with an edible pulp. **b.** The fruit of this plant. [Maori.]

KKK ►*abbr.* Ku Klux Klan

Klam·ath (klăm′əth) ►*n., pl.* **-ath** or **-aths 1.** A member of a Native American people of S-central Oregon and N California. **2.** The language of the Klamath.

Klee (klā), **Paul** 1879–1940. Swiss artist.

klep·to·ma·ni·a (klĕp′tə-mā′nē-ə, -mān′yə) ►*n.* An obsessive impulse to steal regardless of economic need. [Gk. *kleptein,* steal + -MANIA.] —**klep′to·ma′ni·ac′** *n.*

klieg light (klēg) ►*n.* A powerful lamp used esp. in making movies. [Alteration of *Klieglight,* trademark for such a lamp, after J.H. *Kliegl* (1869–1959) and A.T. *Kliegl* (1872–1927).]

Klon·dike (klŏn′dīk′) A region of Yukon Terr., Canada, E of AK.

klutz (klŭts) ►*n.* A clumsy or inept person. [Yiddish *klots.*] —**klutz′i·ness** *n.* —**klutz′y** *adj.*

km ►*abbr.* kilometer

kmph ►*abbr.* kilometers per hour

knack (năk) ►*n.* **1.** A clever, expedient way of doing something. **2.** A specific talent for something. [< MDu. *cnacken,* to crack.]

knack·wurst or **knock·wurst** (nŏk′wûrst′, -wŏorst′) ►*n.* A short, thick, highly seasoned sausage. [Ger.]

knap·sack (năp′săk′) ►*n.* A sturdy bag with shoulder straps for carrying articles on the back. [LGer. *Knappsack.*]

knave (nāv) ►*n.* **1.** An unprincipled, crafty fellow. **2.** See jack (sense 2). [< OE *cnafa,* boy.] —**knav′er·y** *n.* —**knav′ish** *adj.*

knead (nēd) ►*v.* **1.** To mix and work into a uniform mass, esp. with the hands: *kneading dough.* **2.** To massage. [< OE *cnedan.*]

knee (nē) ►*n.* The joint between the thigh and the lower leg. ►*v.* **kneed, knee·ing** To strike with the knee. [< OE *cnēo.*]

knee·cap (nē′kăp′) ►*n.* See **patella.**

kneel (nēl) ►*v.* **knelt** (nĕlt) or **kneeled, kneel·ing** To go down or rest on one or both knees. [< OE *cnēowlian.*]

knell (nĕl) ►*v.* **1.** To ring slowly and solemnly, esp. for a funeral; toll. **2.** To signal or proclaim by or as if by tolling. ►*n.* **1.** A solemn or mournful toll. **2.** A signal of disaster or destruction. [< OE *cnyllan*.]

knew (nōō, nyōō) ►*v.* P.t. of **know.**

knick·ers (nĭk′ərz) ►*pl.n.* **1.** Full breeches gathered and banded just below the knee. **2.** *Chiefly Brit.* Panties. [< *knickerbockers*.]

knick·knack (nĭk′năk′) ►*n.* A small ornamental article; trinket. [< KNACK.]

knife (nīf) ►*n., pl.* **knives** (nīvz) **1.** A cutting instrument consisting of a sharp blade attached to a handle. **2.** A cutting edge; blade. ►*v.* **knifed, knif·ing 1.** To use a knife on, esp. to stab. **2.** *Informal* To betray. —*idiom:* **under the knife** *Informal* Undergoing surgery. [< ON *knīfr*.]

knight (nīt) ►*n.* **1a.** A medieval gentleman-soldier. **b.** A man holding a nonhereditary title conferred by a sovereign. **2.** A member of certain fraternal orders. **3.** A noble defender or champion. **4.** A chess piece, usu. in the shape of a horse's head. ►*v.* To raise (a person) to knighthood. [< OE *cniht*.] —**knight′ly** *adj.*

knight-errant (nīt′ĕr′ənt) ►*n., pl.* **knights-errant** (nīts′-) A knight who wanders in search of adventures to prove his chivalry.

knight·hood (nīt′hōōd′) ►*n.* **1.** The rank or vocation of a knight. **2.** Knights considered as a group.

knish (kə-nĭsh′) ►*n.* A piece of dough stuffed with potato, meat, or cheese and baked or fried. [Yiddish < Ukrainian *knysh*.]

knit (nĭt) ►*v.* **knit** or **knit·ted, knit·ting 1.** To make (a fabric or garment) by intertwining yarn or thread in a series of connected loops. **2.** To join closely. **3.** To draw (the brows) together in wrinkles; furrow. ►*n.* A fabric or garment made by knitting. [< OE *cnyttan*, tie in a knot.] —**knit′ter** *n.*

knob (nŏb) ►*n.* **1.** A rounded protuberance. **2a.** A rounded handle. **b.** A rounded control switch or dial. [ME *knobbe*.] —**knobbed** *adj.* —**knob′by** *adj.*

knock (nŏk) ►*v.* **1.** To strike with a hard or sharp blow: *knocked him on the head.* **2.** To cause to be displaced or unengaged; force: *a blunder that knocked him out of the job.* **3.** To collide or cause to collide. **4.** To produce by hitting: *knocked a hole in the wall.* **5.** *Slang* To disparage; criticize. **6.** To make the rattling noise of a misfiring engine. —*phrasal verbs:* **knock around** (or **about**) **1.** To be rough or brutal with. **2.** To wander from place to place. **knock down 1.** To fell; topple. **2.** To disassemble into parts. **3.** To declare sold at an auction. **4.** *Informal* To reduce in amount or intensity. **knock off 1.** *Informal* To take a break; stop. **2.** *Informal* To complete or accomplish easily; finish. **3.** *Slang* To kill. **4.** *Slang* To hold up or rob. **knock out 1.** To render unconscious. **2.** To defeat (a boxing opponent) by a knockout. **3.** To render useless. **4.** *Informal* To excite or overwhelm, esp. by being sexually attractive. —*idiom:* **knock dead** *Slang* To affect strongly and positively. [< OE *cnocian*.] —**knock** *n.*

knock·down (nŏk′doun′) ►*adj.* **1.** Strong enough to knock down or overwhelm: *a knockdown blow.* **2.** Easily assembled or disassembled: *knockdown furniture.*

knock·er (nŏk′ər) ►*n.* A hinged fixture used for knocking on a door.

knock-knee (nŏk′nē′) ►*n.* A deformity of the legs in which the knees are abnormally close together. —**knock′-kneed′** *adj.*

knock·out (nŏk′out′) ►*n.* **1.** A victory in boxing in which one's opponent is unable to rise from the canvas within a specified time. **2.** *Slang* A strikingly attractive or impressive person or thing.

knock·wurst (nŏk′wûrst′, -wōōrst′) ►*n.* Var. of **knackwurst.**

knoll (nōl) ►*n.* A small rounded hill; hillock. [< OE *cnoll*.]

Knos·sos (nŏs′əs) An ancient city of N Crete.

knot (nŏt) ►*n.* **1a.** A compact intersection of interlaced material, such as rope. **b.** A fastening made by tying together lengths of material. **2.** A decorative bow. **3.** A unifying bond, esp. a marriage bond. **4.** A tight cluster of persons or things. **5.** A feeling of tightness: *a knot in my stomach.* **6.** A complex problem. **7a.** A hard node on a tree trunk at a point from which a branch grows. **b.** The round, often darker cross section of such a node in cut lumber. **8.** A protuberant growth or swelling in a tissue. **9.** A unit of speed, one nautical mile per hour. ►*v.* **knot·ted, knot·ting 1.** To tie or fasten with a knot. **2.** To make or become snarled or entangled. [< OE *cnotta*.] —**knot′ti·ness** *n.* —**knot′ty** *adj.*

knot·hole (nŏt′hōl′) ►*n.* A hole in a piece of lumber where a knot once was.

know (nō) ►*v.* **knew** (nōō, nyōō), **known** (nōn), **know·ing 1.** To perceive directly with the mind or senses. **2.** To regard as true beyond doubt. **3.** To be capable of or skilled in: *knows how to cook.* **4.** To have learned: *knows her Latin verbs.* **5.** To have experience of. **6a.** To recognize: *I know that face.* **b.** To be acquainted with. **7.** To be able to distinguish: *knows right from wrong.* —*idiom:* **in the know** Possessing special or secret information. [< OE *cnāwan*.] —**know′a·ble** *adj.* —**know′er** *n.*

know-how (nō′hou′) ►*n.* Practical knowledge or skill.

know·ing (nō′ĭng) ►*adj.* **1.** Possessing knowledge, information, or understanding. **2.** Clever; shrewd. **3.** Suggestive of private knowledge: *a knowing glance.* **4.** Deliberate; conscious. —**know′ing·ly** *adv.*

knowl·edge (nŏl′ĭj) ►*n.* **1.** The state or fact of knowing. **2.** Familiarity, awareness, or understanding gained through experience or study. **3.** The sum or range of what has been perceived, discovered, or learned. [ME *knowleche*.] —**knowl′edge·a·ble** *adj.* —**knowl′edge·a·bly** *adv.*

Knox (nŏks), **Henry** 1750–1806. Amer. Revolutionary soldier.

Knox, John 1514?–72. Scottish religious reformer.

Knt. ►*abbr.* knight

knuck·le (nŭk′əl) ►*n.* The rounded prominence of a joint, esp. of one of the joints connecting the fingers to the hand. ►*v.* **-led, -ling** To press, rub, or hit with the knuckles. —*phrasal verbs:* **knuckle down** To apply oneself earnestly. **knuckle under** To yield to pressure; give in. [ME *knokel*.]

knuck·le·bone (nŭk′əl-bōn′) ►*n.* A knobbed bone, as of a knuckle or joint.

knurl (nûrl) ►*n.* **1.** A knob or knot. **2.** One of a set of small ridges, as on a thumbscrew, to

aid in gripping. [Prob. < ME *knor*, a swelling.]
—**knurled** *adj.* —**knurl′y** *adj.*

KO (kā′ō′) *Slang* ▸*v.* **KO′d, KO′ing** To knock
out in boxing. ▸*n.* (kā-ō′, kā′ō′) A knockout
in boxing.

ko·a·la (kō-ä′lə) ▸*n.* A furry, bearlike arboreal
Australian marsupial. [Dharuk (Australian)
gulawan⁷.]

koala

Ko·be (kō′bē′, -bā′) A city of S Honshu, Japan,
SW of Kyoto.

Ko·di·ak bear (kō′dē-äk′) ▸*n.* A large brown
bear inhabiting a cluster of islands in Alaska.
[After KODIAK (ISLAND).]

Kodiak Island An island of S AK in the Gulf
of Alaska.

Koest·ler (kĕst′lər, kĕs′-), **Arthur** 1905–83.
Hungarian-born British writer.

kof·te (kōf′tə) ▸*n.* A dish of the Middle East and
South Asia made of ground meat, onions, and
spices. [Turk. *köfte*, Ar. *kufta*, and Hindi and
Urdu *koftā*, all < Pers. *kūfta*, pounded, kofta.]

kohl (kōl) ▸*n.* A cosmetic preparation used to
darken the rims of the eyelids. [Ar. *kuḥl*.]

Kohl, Helmut b. 1930. German politician; chancellor of West Germany (1982–90) and of
Germany (1990–98).

kohl·ra·bi (kōl-rä′bē, -räb′ē) ▸*n., pl.* **-bies** A
plant whose thick basal stem is eaten as a vegetable. [< Ital. *cavoli rape*.]

ko·la or **co·la** *kō′lə* ▸*n.* Either of two African
evergreens having nutlike seeds used in carbonated beverages and pharmaceuticals. [Of
West African orig.]

Kol·ka·ta (kōl-kä′tə) A city of E India in the
Ganges delta, formerly known as Calcutta.

kom·bu·cha (kŏm′boō′chä′) ▸*n.* A lightly sparkling beverage made by fermenting black or
green tea and sugar with a culture of various
bacteria and yeasts. [Prob. < J., tea made from
kelp.]

kook (koōk) ▸*n.* *Slang* An eccentric or crazy
person. [Poss. < CUCKOO.] —**kook′i·ness** *n.*
—**kook′y** *adj.*

kook·a·bur·ra (koōk′ə-bûr′ə, -bûr′ə) ▸*n.* A
large kingfisher of S and E Australia, having a
call like raucous laughter. [Wiradhuri (Australian) *gugubarra*, of imit. orig.]

ko·pek or **ko·peck** (kō′pĕk) ▸*n.* A coin equal to
¹⁄₁₀₀ of the Russian ruble. [Russ. *kopeĭka*.]

Ko·ran or **Qur·'an** also **Qur·an** (kə-răn′, -rän′,
kô-, kō-) ▸*n.* The sacred text of Islam, considered by Muslims to contain the revelations

of God to Muhammad. [Ar. *qurăn*.] —**Ko·**
ran′ic *adj.*

Ko·re·a (kə-rē′ə, kô-, kō-) A peninsula and
former country of E Asia between the Yellow
Sea and the Sea of Japan.

Ko·re·an (kə-rē′ən, kô-, kō-) ▸*n.* **1.** A native
or inhabitant of Korea. **2.** The language of the
Koreans. —**Ko·re·an** *adj.*

ko·ru·na (kôr′ə-nä′) ▸*n.* See table at **currency**.
[Czech.]

Kos·ci·uśz·ko (kôsh-choōsh′kō) or **Kos·ci·us·**
ko (kŏs′ē-ŭs′kō, kŏs′kē-), **Thaddeus** 1746–
1817. Polish general who fought with the colonists in the American Revolution.

ko·sher (kō′shər) ▸*adj.* **1.** Conforming to or
prepared in accordance with Jewish dietary
laws. **2.** *Slang* Legitimate; permissible. [< Heb.
kāšēr, proper.]

Ko·so·vo (kô′sə-vō′, kŏ′-) A republic of the W
Balkan Peninsula. Cap. Priština. —**Ko′so·var′**
(-vär′) *adj. & n.*

Ko·sy·gin (kə-sē′gən), **Aleksei Nikolayevich**
1904–80. Soviet premier (1964–80).

Kow·loon (kou′loōn′) A city of SE China on
Kowloon Peninsula opposite Hong Kong I.

kow·tow (kou-tou′, kou′tou′) ▸*v.* **1.** To kneel
and touch the forehead to the ground in expression of deep respect, worship, or submission.
2. To show servile deference. See Synonyms at
fawn¹. [Mandarin *kòu tóu*.] —**kow′tow′** *n.*

KP ▸*abbr.* kitchen police

kraal (krôl, kräl) ▸*n.* *South African* **1.** A rural
village. **2.** An enclosure for livestock. [Afr. <
Port. *curral*, pen.]

Kra·ka·tau (krăk′ə-tou′, krä′kə-) or **Kra·ka·**
to·a (-tō′ə) A volcanic island of Indonesia
between Sumatra and Java.

Kra·ków (krăk′ou, krä′kou, -koōf) A city of S
Poland on the Vistula R. SSW of Warsaw.

Krem·lin (krĕm′lĭn) ▸*n.* **1.** The citadel of Moscow, housing the offices of the Russian and
formerly the Soviet government. **2.** The government of Russia and formerly that of the
Soviet Union. [< ORuss. *kremlĭnŭ*, separate.]

Krem·lin·ol·o·gy (krĕm′lə-nŏl′ə-jē) ▸*n.* The
study of the policies of the Soviet or Russian
government. —**Krem′lin·ol′o·gist** *n.*

krill (krĭl) ▸*n., pl.* **krill** Small marine crustaceans
that are the principal food of baleen whales.
[Norw. *kril*, young fry of fish.]

Krish·na (krĭsh′nə) ▸*n.* *Hinduism* The 8th and
principal avatar of Vishnu.

kro·na¹ (krō′nə) ▸*n., pl.* **-nur** (-nər) See table at
currency. [Icel. *krōna*.]

kro·na² (krō′nə) ▸*n., pl.* **-nor** (-nôr′, -nər) See
table at **currency**. [Swed.]

kro·ne (krō′nə) ▸*n., pl.* **-ner** (-nər) See table at
currency. [Norw. and Dan.]

kroon (krōn) ▸*n., pl.* **kroon·i** (krō′nē) The
primary unit of currency in Estonia before the
adoption of the euro. [Estonian.]

kryp·ton (krĭp′tŏn′) ▸*n. Symbol* **Kr** A colorless,
largely inert gaseous element used chiefly in
fluorescent lamps. At. no. 36. See table at **ele-**
ment. [< Gk. *kruptos*, hidden.]

KS ▸*abbr.* **1.** Kansas **2.** Kaposi's sarcoma

Kt ▸*abbr.* knight (chess)

kt. ▸*abbr.* **1.** karat **2.** *Naut.* knot

Kt. ▸*abbr.* knight (title)

Kua·la Lum·pur (kwä′lə loōm-poōr′) The
capital of Malaysia, on the southwestern Malay

Peninsula northwest of Singapore.

Ku·blai Khan (koo'blī kän') also **Ku·bla Khan** (-blə) 1215–94. Mongol emperor (1260–94) and founder of the Mongol dynasty in China.

ku·dos (koo'dōz', -dōs', -dŏs', kyoo'-) ►*n.* Acclaim or praise for exceptional achievement. [Gk.]

   Usage: Since it comes from a Greek singular noun, *kudos* should be viewed as singular. Correctness requires *Kudos is* (not *are*) *due her for her brilliant work on the score.* However, use of the plural form, as in *She received many kudos for her work,* is common.

ku·du (koo'doo) ►*n., pl.* **-du** or **-dus** A large striped African antelope with spirally curved horns in the male. [< Xhosa *i-qudu.*]

kud·zu (kood'zoo, kŭd'-) ►*n.* A fast-growing vine native to E Asia and grown for fodder, forage, and erosion control. [J. *kuzu.*]

Kui·per belt (kī'pər) ►*n.* A region in the solar system beyond Neptune's orbit, containing thousands of small icy bodies, some having highly elliptical orbits that sometimes reach the inner solar system as comets. [After Gerard *Kuiper* (1905–73).]

Kuiper belt object ►*n.* Any of the small icy bodies orbiting the sun in the Kuiper belt, generally having a diameter less than Pluto's. [After Gerard *Kuiper* (1905–73).]

ku·lak (koo-läk', koo'läk', -läk') ►*n.* A prosperous landed peasant in czarist Russia. [Russ.]

kul·fi (kool'fē) ►*n.* A dense ice cream of S Asian origin, gen. made with boiled milk, sugar, cardamom, pistachios, and other ingredients. [Hindi and Urdu *qulfī.*]

kum·quat (kŭm'kwŏt') ►*n.* **1.** A tree or shrub bearing small edible orangelike fruit. **2.** The fruit itself. [Cantonese *gam¹ gwat¹.*]

ku·na (koo'nə) ►*n.* See table at **currency.** [Serbo-Croatian.]

kung fu (kŭng' foo', koong') ►*n.* The Chinese martial arts, esp. those forms similar to karate. [Mandarin *gōngfu,* skill, art, labor.]

Kurd (kûrd, koord) ►*n.* A member of a people inhabiting the transnational region of Kurdistan.

Kurd·ish (kûr'dĭsh, koor'-) ►*adj.* Of or relating to the Kurds or their language. ►*n.* The Iranian language of the Kurds.

Kurd·i·stan (kûr'dĭ-stän', koor'dĭ-stän') An extensive plateau region of SW Asia.

Ku·ril Islands also **Ku·rile Islands** (koor'ĭl, koo-rēl') An island chain of extreme E Russia extending about 1,210 km (750 mi) in the Pacific between Kamchatka Peninsula and E Hokkaido, Japan. —**Ku·ril'i·an** *adj.*

Ku·ro·sa·wa (koor'ə-sä'wə), **Akira** 1910–98. Japanese filmmaker.

kur·ta (kûr'tə) ►*n.* A long-sleeved shirt, often

extending to the knees. [Hindi and Urdu *kurtā.*]

kurta

Ku·wait (koo-wät') **1.** A country of NE Arabia at the head of the Persian Gulf. Cap. Kuwait. **2.** The capital of Kuwait, in the E-central part. —**Ku·wait'i** (-wä'tē) *adj. & n.*

kW ►*abbr.* kilowatt

kwa·cha (kwä'chə) ►*n.* See table at **currency.** [Indigenous word in Zambia.]

kwan·za (kwän'zə) ►*n., pl.* **-za** or **-zas** See table at **currency.** [Bantu or Swahili.]

Kwan·zaa also **Kwan·za** (kwän'zə) ►*n.* An African-American cultural festival celebrated from December 26 to January 1. [< Swahili *(matunda ya) kwanza,* first (fruits).]

kwa·shi·or·kor (kwä'shē-ôr'kôr') ►*n.* Severe protein malnutrition, esp. in children, marked by anemia, potbelly, reduced pigmentation, and growth retardation. [Indigenous word in Ghana.]

kWh ►*abbr.* kilowatt-hour

KY ►*abbr.* Kentucky

kyat (chät) ►*n.* See table at **currency.** [Burmese.]

Kyo·to (kē-ō'tō, kyō'-) A city of W-central Honshu, Japan, NNE of Osaka.

Kyr·gyz or **Kir·ghiz** (kîr-gēz') ►*adj.* Of or relating to Kyrgyzstan or its people or language. ►*n., pl.* **-gyz** or **-gyz·es** or **-ghiz** or **-ghiz·es** **1a.** A native or inhabitant of Kyrgyzstan. **b.** A member of a traditionally nomadic people living principally in Kyrgyzstan. **2.** The Turkic language of the Kyrgyz.

Kyr·gyz·stan (kîr'gē-stän') A country of central Asia bordering on NW China. Cap. Bishkek.

Kyu·shu (kē-oo'shoo, kyoo'-) An island of SW Japan on the East China Sea and the Pacific.

L

l¹ or **L** (ĕl) ►*n., pl.* **l's** or **L's** also **ls** or **Ls** The 12th letter of the English alphabet.

l² ►*abbr.* length

L¹ also **l** The symbol for the Roman numeral 50.

L² ►*abbr.* **1.** large **2.** left **3.** or **l** liter **4.** *Sports* loss

L. ►*abbr.* **1.** lake **2.** Latin

la (lä) ►*n. Mus.* The 6th tone of the diatonic scale. [< Med.Lat.]

LA ►*abbr.* **1.** Los Angeles **2.** Louisiana

lab (lăb) ►*n.* A laboratory.

la·bel (lā'bəl) ►*n.* **1.** Something, such as a small piece of paper or cloth, attached to an article to identify its owner, contents, or destination. **2.** A descriptive term; epithet. ►*v.* **-beled, -bel·ing** or **-belled, -bel·ling 1.** To attach a label to. **2.** To identify or classify. [< OFr., strip of cloth.] **—la′bel·er, la′bel·ler** *n.*

la·bi·al (lā′bē-əl) ►*adj.* **1.** Of the lips or labia. **2.** *Ling.* Articulated mainly with the lips, as (b), (m), or (w). ►*n. Ling.* A labial consonant. [< Lat. *labium,* lip.] **—la′bi·al·ly** *adv.*

la·bi·um (lā′bē-əm) ►*n., pl.* **-bi·a** (-bē-ə) *Anat.* Any of four folds of tissue of the female external genitals. [Lat., lip.]

la·bor (lā′bər) ►*n.* **1.** Physical or mental exertion. **2.** A specific task. **3.** Work for wages. **4a.** Workers collectively. **b.** The trade union movement. **5.** The physical efforts of childbirth. ►*v.* **1.** To work; toil. **2.** To strive painstakingly. **3.** To proceed with effort; plod. **4.** To suffer from distress or a disadvantage. [< Lat.] **—la′bor·er** *n.*

lab·o·ra·to·ry (lăb′rə-tôr′ē) ►*n., pl.* **-ries 1.** A place equipped for scientific experimentation, research, or testing. **2.** A place where drugs and chemicals are manufactured.

Labor Day ►*n.* The 1st Monday in September, observed as a holiday in honor of working people.

la·bored (lā′bərd) ►*adj.* **1.** Produced or done with effort. **2.** Lacking natural ease; strained.

la·bo·ri·ous (lə-bôr′ē-əs) ►*adj.* Marked by or requiring hard or tedious work. **—la·bo′ri·ous·ly** *adv.* **—la·bo′ri·ous·ness** *n.*

labor union ►*n.* An organization of workers formed to promote the members' interests with respect to wages and working conditions.

Lab·ra·dor (lăb′rə-dôr′) The mainland territory of the province of Newfoundland and Labrador, Canada, on NE **Labrador Peninsula** E of Quebec. **—Lab′ra·dor′e·an, Lab′ra·dor′i·an** *adj. & n.*

la·bret (lā′brĭt) ►*n.* An ornament inserted into a perforation in the lip. [Latin *labrum,* lip + -ET.]

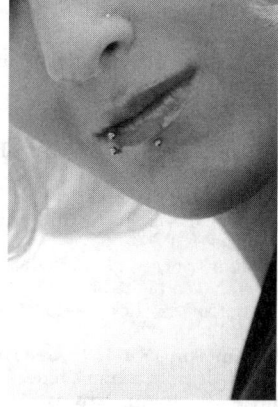

labret

la·bur·num (lə-bûr′nəm) ►*n.* A poisonous tree or shrub cultivated for its drooping clusters of yellow flowers. [< Lat.]

lab·y·rinth (lăb′ə-rĭnth′) ►*n.* **1.** An intricate structure of interconnecting passages through which it is difficult to find one's way; maze. **2.**

Labyrinth *Gk. Myth.* The maze in which the Minotaur was confined. [< Gk. *laburinthos.*] **—lab′y·rin′thine** (-rĭn′thĭn, -thēn′) *adj.*

lac (lăk) ►*n.* A resinous secretion of an Asian insect, used in making shellac. [< Hindi *lākh* < Skt. *lākṣā,* resin.]

lace (lās) ►*n.* **1.** A cord used to draw and tie together two opposite edges, as of a shoe. **2.** A delicate fabric made of yarn or thread in an open weblike pattern. ►*v.* **laced, lac·ing 1.** To draw together and tie the laces of. **2.** To intertwine: *lace garlands through a trellis.* **3a.** To add a touch of flavor to. **b.** To add a substance, esp. an intoxicant or narcotic, to. [< OFr. *las,* noose < Lat. *laqueus.*] **—lac′er** *n.* **—lac′y** *adj.*

lac·er·ate (lăs′ə-rāt′) ►*v.* **-at·ed, -at·ing 1.** To rip, cut, or tear (e.g., the skin). **2.** To cause deep emotional pain to; distress. [< Lat. *lacer,* torn.] **—lac′er·a′tion** *n.*

lach·ry·mose also **lac·ri·mose** (lăk′rə-mōs′) ►*adj.* Tearful. [Lat. *lacrimōsus.*] **—lach′ry·mose′ly** *adv.*

lack (lăk) ►*n.* **1.** Deficiency or absence: *Lack of funding ended the project.* A particular deficiency or absence: *a lack of supporters.* ►*v.* **1.** To be without any or much of: *lacked strength.* **2.** To be missing or deficient. **3.** To be in need of something: *does not lack for friends.* [ME.]

lack·a·dai·si·cal (lăk′ə-dā′zĭ-kəl) ►*adj.* Lacking spirit, liveliness, or interest. [< *lackaday,* an exclamation of regret.] **—lack′a·dai′si·cal·ly** *adv.*

lack·ey (lăk′ē) ►*n., pl.* **-eys 1.** A footman. **2.** A servile follower; toady. [< OFr. *laquais.*]

lack·lus·ter (lăk′lŭs′tər) ►*adj.* Lacking brightness, luster, or vitality. See Synonyms at **dull.**

la·con·ic (lə-kŏn′ĭk) ►*adj.* Using few words; terse. [< Gk. *Lakōnikos,* Spartan.] **—la·con′i·cal·ly** *adv.*
Syns: *reticent, taciturn, tightlipped adj.*

lac·quer (lăk′ər) ►*n.* Any of various clear or colored synthetic or resinous coatings used to impart a high gloss to surfaces. [< Ar. *lakk,* LAC.] **—lac′quer** *v.*

lac·ri·mal also **lach·ry·mal** (lăk′rə-məl) ►*adj.* Of tears or the tear-producing glands. [< Lat. *lacrima,* tear.]

la·crosse (lə-krôs′, -krŏs′) ►*n.* A game played on a rectangular field by two teams of ten players each, in which participants use a long-handled stick that has a webbed pouch on one end to maneuver a ball into the opposing team's goal. [< Fr. *(jeu de) la crosse,* (game of) the hooked stick.]

lac·tate (lăk′tāt′) ►*v.* **-tat·ed, -tat·ing** To secrete or produce milk. **—lac·ta′tion** *n.*

lac·tic (lăk′tĭk) ►*adj.* Relating to or derived from milk.

lactic acid ►*n.* A syrupy liquid, $C_3H_6O_3$, present in sour milk, molasses, various fruits, and wines.

lacto– or **lact–** ►*pref.* Milk: *lactate.* [< Lat. *lac, lact-,* milk.]

lac·tose (lăk′tōs′) ►*n.* A white crystalline sugar, $C_{12}H_{22}O_{11}$, found in milk that may be hydrolyzed to yield glucose and galactose. Lactose is used in infant foods, bakery products, confections, and pharmaceuticals.

lac·to-veg·e·tar·i·an (lăk′tō-vĕj′ĭ-târ′ē-ən) ►*n.* A vegetarian whose diet includes dairy products.

la·cu·na (lə-kyōō'nə) ►*n., pl.* **-nae** (-nē) or **-nas**
1. An empty space. **2.** *Anat.* A cavity. [Lat.
lacūna, pool.] **—la·cu'nal** *adj.*

lad (lăd) ►*n.* A boy or young man. [ME *ladde*.]

lad·der (lăd'ər) ►*n.* **1.** A structure consisting of
two long sides crossed by parallel rungs, used to
climb up and down. **2.** A series of ranked stages
or levels. [< OE *hlǣder*.]

lad·der·back (lăd'ər-băk') ►*n.* A chair back
made of two upright posts connected by horizontal slats.

lade (lād) ►*v.* **lad·ed, lad·en** (lād'n) or **lad·ed,
lad·ing** **1.** To load or be loaded with or as if
with cargo. **2.** To burden; weigh down. [< OE
hladan.] **—lad'en** *adj.*

lad·ing (lā'dĭng) ►*n.* Cargo; freight.

La·di·no (lə-dē'nō) ►*n.* A Romance language
descended from medieval Spanish, spoken by
Sephardic Jews esp. in the Balkans. [Sp. < Lat.
Latīnus.]

la·dle (lād'l) ►*n.* A long-handled spoon with a
deep bowl for serving liquids. [< OE *hlǣdel*.]
—la'dle *v.* **—la'dler** *n.*

Lad·o·ga (lăd'ə-gə), **Lake** A lake of NW Russia
NE of St. Petersburg.

la·dy (lā'dē) ►*n., pl.* **-dies** **1.** A woman, esp. one
who is well-mannered. **2.** A woman who is
the head of a household. **3. Lady** *Chiefly Brit.*
A general feminine title of nobility and other
rank. [< OE *hlǣfdige*.] **—la'dy·like'** *adj.*

la·dy·bird (lā'dē-bûrd') ►*n.* See **ladybug.**

la·dy·bug (lā'dē-bŭg') ►*n.* A small, rounded,
usu. brightly colored beetle, often reddish with
black spots.

la·dy·fin·ger (lā'dē-fĭng'gər) ►*n.* A small finger-shaped sponge cake.

lady in waiting ►*n., pl.* **ladies in waiting** A
lady of a court appointed to attend a queen
or princess.

la·dy·ship also **La·dy·ship** (lā'dē-shĭp') ►*n.*
Used with *Your* or *Her* as a title for a woman
holding the rank of lady.

la·dy's slipper (lā'dēz) ►*n.* An orchid having
showy flowers with the lip modified into a
slipperlike pouch.

lady's slipper

La·fay·ette (läf'ē-ĕt', lä'fē-), Marquis de. 1757–
1834. French soldier and politician.

La Fon·taine (lə fŏn-tān', lä fôn-tĕn'), **Jean de**
1621–95. French writer.

lag (lăg) ►*v.* **lagged, lag·ging** **1.** To fail to keep
up a pace; straggle. **2.** To weaken or slacken
gradually: *My attention lagged as the lecture
progressed.* ►*n.* **1.** An interval between one
event and another. **2.** A condition of weakness
or slackening. [< *lag*, last person.] **—lag'ger** *n.*

la·ger (lä'gər) ►*n.* A beer with a relatively small
amount of hops and aged from six weeks to six
months to allow sedimentation. [< Ger. *Lager-
bier* < *lagern*, to store.]

lag·gard (lăg'ərd) ►*n.* One that lags; straggler.
—lag'gard·ly *adv.*

la·gniappe (lăn'yəp, lăn-yăp') ►*n. Regional* **1.**
A small gift presented by a storeowner to a
customer with the customer's purchase. **2.**
An extra or unexpected gift or benefit. [<
Am.Sp. *(la) ñapa*, (the) gift < Quechua *yapay*,
give more.]

la·goon (lə-gōōn') ►*n.* A shallow body of water,
esp. one separated from a sea by sandbars or
coral reefs. [< Lat. *lacūna*, pool.]

La·gos (lā'gŏs', lä'gōs) A city of SW Nigeria on
the Gulf of Guinea.

La·hore (lə-hôr') A city of NE Pakistan SE of
Rawalpindi.

laid (lād) ►*v.* P.t. and p.part. of **lay¹.**

laid-back (lād'băk') ►*adj. Informal* Relaxed and
casual; easygoing.

lain (lān) ►*v.* P.part. of **lie¹.**

lair (lâr) ►*n.* The den or dwelling of a wild animal. [< OE *leger*.]

lais·sez faire also **lais·ser faire** (lĕs'ā fâr')
►*n.* Noninterference, esp. an economic doctrine that opposes governmental involvement
in commerce. [< Fr., let (people) do (as they
choose).] **—lais'sez-faire'** *adj.*

la·i·ty (lā'ĭ-tē) ►*n.* **1.** Laypeople collectively. **2.**
Nonprofessionals.

lake (lāk) ►*n.* **1.** A large inland body of water.
A large pool of liquid. [< Lat. *lacus*.]

La·ko·ta (lə-kō'tə) ►*n., pl.* **-ta** or **-tas** **1.** A member of the largest and westernmost of the Sioux.
2. The Siouan language of the Lakota.

lam (lăm) *Slang* ►*v.* **lammed, lam·ming** To
escape, as from prison. ►*n.* Flight, esp. from the
law: *on the lam.* [?]

la·ma (lä'mə) ►*n.* In Tibetan Buddhism, one
who is a religious teacher or a leader in a
monastic community. [Tibetan *bla-ma*.]

La·marck (lə-märk', lä-), Chevalier de. **Jean
Baptiste Pierre Antoine de Monet** 1744–
1829. French naturalist.

lamb (lăm) ►*n.* **1a.** A young sheep. **b.** The flesh
of a young sheep used as meat. **2.** A sweet,
mild-mannered person. [< OE.]

Lamb, Charles "Elia." 1775–1834. British critic
and essayist.

lam·baste (lăm-bāst') ►*v.* **-bast·ed, -bast·ing**
Informal **1.** To give a thrashing to. **2.** To scold
sharply. [Perh. *lam*, beat + BASTE³.]

lamb·da (lăm'də) ►*n.* The 11th letter of the
Greek alphabet. [Gk.]

lam·bent (lăm'bənt) ►*adj.* **1.** Flickering or
glowing gently. **2.** Light or brilliant: *lambent
wit.* [< Lat. *lambere*, lick.] **—lam'ben·cy** *n.*
—lam'bent·ly *adv.*

lamb·skin (lăm'skĭn') ►*n.* **1.** The hide of a lamb.
2. Leather made from a lamb's hide.

lame (lām) ►*adj.* **lam·er, lam·est** **1.** Disabled
so that movement, esp. walking, is difficult. **2.**
Weak and ineffectual: *a lame excuse.* **3.** *Informal* Dull or unsatisfactory: *a lame movie.* ►*v.*
lamed, lam·ing To make lame. [< OE *lama*.]
—lame'ly *adv.* **—lame'ness** *n.*

la·mé (lă-mā') ►*n.* A fabric woven with metallic
threads. [Fr., ult. < Lat. *lamina*, thin plate.]

lame duck ►*n.* **1.** An elected officeholder continuing in office during the period between the election and inauguration of a successor. **2.** An ineffective person. **—lame′-duck′** *adj.*

la·mel·la (lə-mĕl′ə) ►*n., pl.* **-mel·lae** (-mĕl′-ē′) or **-mel·las** One of the thin scales, plates, layers, or membranes in an organism. [Lat. *lāmella.*] **—la·mel′lar, la·mel′late′** (lə-mĕl′-āt′, lăm′ə-lāt′) *adj.*

la·ment (lə-mĕnt′) ►*v.* **1.** To express grief for or about; mourn. See Synonyms at **grieve. 2.** To regret deeply; deplore. ►*n.* **1.** An expression of grief; lamentation. **2.** A dirge or elegy. [< Lat. *lāmentārī.*] **—la·men′ta·ble** *adj.* **—la·men′-ta·bly** *adv.* **—la·ment′er** *n.*

lam·en·ta·tion (lăm′ən-tā′shən) ►*n.* **1.** The act of lamenting. **2.** A lament. **3. Lamentations** *(takes sing. v.)* See table at **Bible.**

lam·i·na (lăm′ə-nə) ►*n., pl.* **-nae** (-nē′) or **-nas 1.** A thin plate, sheet, or layer. **2.** *Bot.* **a.** The expanded area of a leaf or petal; blade. **b.** The bladelike part of a kelp. [Lat. *lāmina.*] **—lam′i·nar, lam′i·nal** *adj.*

lam·i·nate (lăm′ə-nāt′) ►*v.* **-nat·ed, -nat·ing 1.** To cover with a thin sheet of material. **2.** To divide into thin layers. **3.** To make by uniting several layers. ►*adj.* (-nĭt, -nāt′) also **lam·i·nat·ed** (-nā′tĭd) Consisting of thin layers. ►*n.* (-nāt′, -nĭt) **1.** A laminated product. **2.** A thin sheet of material used to laminate something. **—lam′i·na′tion** *n.* **—lam′i·na′tor** *n.*

lamp (lămp) ►*n.* A device that generates light and often heat, such as a light bulb, lantern, or vessel containing oil or alcohol burned through a wick. [< Gk. *lampas,* torch.]

lamp·black (lămp′blăk′) ►*n.* Fine soot used as a pigment and in matches, explosives, and fertilizers.

lam·poon (lăm-pōōn′) ►*n.* A written attack ridiculing a person, group, or institution. [Poss. < Fr. *lampons,* let us drink.] **—lam·poon′** *v.* **—lam·poon′er** *n.* **—lam·poon′er·y** *n.*

lam·prey (lăm′prē) ►*n., pl.* **-preys** A primitive elongated fish having a jawless sucking mouth. [< Med.Lat. *lampreda.*]

LAN (lăn) ►*n.* A system that links computers and related equipment to form a network, as within an office. [*l(ocal) a(rea) n(etwork).*]

la·nai (lə-nī′) ►*n., pl.* **-nais** A veranda or patio. [Hawaiian.]

lance (lăns) ►*n.* **1.** A thrusting weapon with a long shaft and a sharp metal head. **2.** A similar implement for spearing fish. **3.** *Med.* See **lancet.** ►*v.* **lanced, lanc·ing 1.** To pierce with a lance. **2.** *Med.* To cut into: *lance a boil.* [< Lat. *lancea.*]

lance corporal ►*n.* A rank in the US Marine Corps below corporal.

Lan·ce·lot (lăn′sə-lət, -lŏt′, län′-) ►*n.* In Arthurian legend, a Knight of the Round Table whose love affair with Queen Guinevere resulted in a war with King Arthur.

lanc·er (lăn′sər) ►*n.* A cavalryman armed with a lance.

lan·cet (lăn′sĭt) ►*n.* A surgical knife with a short, wide, pointed double-edged blade.

land (lănd) ►*n.* **1.** The solid ground of the earth. **2.** A distinct area or region: *desert land.* **3.** A nation, country, or realm. **4.** Public or private landed property; real estate. ►*v.* **1.** To put or arrive on land after traveling by water or air. **2.** *Informal* To arrive or cause to arrive in a place

or condition: *land in jail.* **3.** To catch by or as if by fishing. **4.** To come to rest; alight. [< OE.]

land·ed (lăn′dĭd) ►*adj.* **1.** Owning land. **2.** Consisting of land.

land·fall (lănd′fôl′) ►*n.* **1.** The act or an instance of sighting or reaching land. **2.** The land sighted or reached.

land·fill (lănd′fĭl′) ►*n.* A site for disposing waste in which refuse is buried between layers of dirt. **—land′fill′** *v.*

land grant ►*n.* A government grant of public land for a railroad, highway, or state college.

land·hold·er (lănd′hōl′dər) ►*n.* One who owns land. **—land′hold′ing** *n.*

land·ing (lăn′dĭng) ►*n.* **1.** The act or site of coming to land or rest. **2.** A platform at the top, bottom, or between flights of stairs.

landing gear ►*n.* The structure supporting an aircraft on the ground.

landing strip ►*n.* An airstrip.

land·la·dy (lănd′lā′dē) ►*n.* A woman who owns and rents land, buildings, or dwelling units.

land·line (lănd′līn′) ►*n.* A traditional telephone line in which a telephone is connected to the public network by cables.

land·locked (lănd′lŏkt′) ►*adj.* **1.** Surrounded or almost surrounded by land. **2.** Confined to inland waters, as certain fish.

land·lord (lănd′lôrd′) ►*n.* One who owns and rents land, buildings, or dwelling units.

land·lub·ber (lănd′lŭb′ər) ►*n.* A person unfamiliar with the sea or seamanship. [LAND + *lubber,* clumsy person.] **—land′lub′ber·ly** *adj.*

land·mark (lănd′märk′) ►*n.* **1.** A prominent identifying feature of a landscape. **2.** A fixed marker indicating a boundary line. **3.** A historically significant event or site.

land·mass (lănd′măs′) ►*n.* A large area of land.

land mine ►*n.* An explosive mine laid usu. just below the surface of the ground.

land-poor (lănd′pōōr′) ►*adj.* Owning much land but lacking the capital to improve it.

land·scape (lănd′skāp′) ►*n.* **1.** A view or vista of scenery on land. **2.** A picture depicting such a view. ►*v.* **-scaped, -scap·ing** To improve (a section of ground) by contouring and decorative planting. [< MDu. *landscap,* region.] **—land′scap′er** *n.*

land·slide (lănd′slīd′) ►*n.* **1.** The downward sliding of a mass of earth and rock. **2.** An overwhelming victory, esp. in an election.

land·ward (lănd′wərd) ►*adv. & adj.* To or toward land. **—land′wards** *adv.*

lane (lān) ►*n.* **1.** A narrow way or road. **2.** A set passage or course, as for vehicles or ships. [< OE.]

lan·guage (lăng′gwĭj) ►*n.* **1a.** Communication of thoughts and feelings through a system of arbitrary signals, such as voice sounds, gestures, or written symbols. **b.** Such a system, including rules for combining components, such as words. **c.** Such a system used by a particular group or community. **2.** *Comp.* A system of symbols and rules used for communication with or between computers. **3.** The special vocabulary of a scientific, professional, or other group. **4.** A particular style of speech or writing. **5.** Communication between nonhumans. [< OFr. *langue,* tongue < Lat. *lingua.*]

Lan·gue·doc (läng-dôk′, läng-) A former province of S France on the Mediterranean Sea W of the Rhone R.

lan·guid (lăng′gwĭd) ►*adj.* **1.** Lacking energy; listless: *a languid wave of the hand.* **2.** Lacking force; slow: *languid waves.* [< Lat. *languidus.*] —**lan′guid·ly** *adv.* —**lan′guid·ness** *n.*

lan·guish (lăng′gwĭsh) ►*v.* **1.** To lose strength or vigor. **2.** To exist in miserable conditions. **3.** To become downcast; pine. **4.** To be unattended or neglected. [< Lat. *languēre.*]

lan·guor (lăng′gər, lăng′ər) ►*n.* **1.** Lack of physical or mental energy; lethargy. **2.** Oppressive stillness, as of the air. **3.** A dreamy or sensual quality. [< Lat. < *languēre,* languish.] —**lan′guor·ous** *adj.* —**lan′guor·ous·ly** *adv.*

La Ni·ña (lä nēn′yä) ►*n.* A periodic cooling of the ocean surface off the W coast of South America that affects Pacific and other weather patterns. [Am.Sp., the girl (to distinguish it from El Niño).]

lank (lăngk) ►*adj.* **-er, -est 1.** Long and lean. **2.** Long, straight, and limp: *lank hair.* [< OE *hlanc.*] —**lank′ly** *adv.* —**lank′ness** *n.*

lank·y (lăng′kē) ►*adj.* **-i·er, -i·est** Tall and thin and often ungainly. —**lank′i·ly** *adv.* —**lank′i·ness** *n.*

lan·o·lin (lăn′ə-lĭn) ►*n.* A fatty substance obtained from wool and used in soaps, cosmetics, and ointments. [< Lat. *lāna,* wool.]

Lan·sing (lăn′sĭng) The capital of MI, in the S-central part NW of Detroit.

lan·tern (lăn′tərn) ►*n.* An often portable case with transparent or translucent sides for holding and protecting a light. [< Gk. *lamptēr.*]

lan·tha·nide (lăn′thə-nīd′) ►*n.* See **rare-earth element.** [LANTHAN(UM) + -IDE.]

lan·tha·num (lăn′thə-nəm) ►*n. Symbol* **La** A soft, silvery-white rare-earth element used esp. in glass manufacture. At. no. 57. See table at **element.** [< Gk. *lanthanein,* escape notice.]

lan·yard also **lan·iard** (lăn′yərd) ►*n.* **1.** *Naut.* A short rope used for securing rigging. **2.** A cord worn around the neck for carrying something, such as a whistle. [< OFr. *laniere,* strap.]

Lao (lou) ►*n., pl.* **Lao** or **Laos** (louz) **1.** A member of a Buddhist people of Laos and Thailand. **2.** The Tai language of the Lao.

La·os (lous, lä′ŏs′) A country of SE Asia. Cap. Vientiane. —**La·o′tian** (lā-ō′shən, lou′shən) *adj. & n.*

Lao Tzu also **Lao-tse** (lou′dzŭ′) fl. 6th cent. BC? Chinese philosopher.

lap¹ (lăp) ►*n.* **1.** The front area from the waist to the knees of a seated person. **2.** The portion of a garment that covers the lap. [< OE *læppa,* flap of a garment.] —**lap′ful′** *n.*

lap² (lăp) ►*v.* **lapped, lap·ping 1.** To place or lay (something) so as to overlap another. **2.** To fold or wrap or wind around (something); encircle. **3.** To get ahead of (an opponent) in a race by one or more laps. ►*n.* **1.** A part that overlaps. **2.** One complete circuit, as of a racetrack, or length of a straight course, esp. a swimming pool. **3.** A segment or stage, as of a trip. [ME *lappen* < *lappe,* LAP¹.]

lap³ (lăp) ►*v.* **lapped, lap·ping 1.** To take in (a liquid or food) with the tongue. **2.** To wash against with soft liquid sounds: *waves that were lapping the shore.* —*phrasal verb:* **lap up** To receive eagerly: *lapped up praise.* [< OE *lapian.*] —**lap** *n.*

La Paz (lə päz′, lä päs′) The administrative capital of Bolivia, in the W part.

lap belt ►*n.* A seat belt that fastens across the lap.

lap·board (lăp′bôrd′) ►*n.* A flat board held on the lap and used as a table or desk.

lap dog ►*n.* A small, easily held pet dog.

la·pel (lə-pĕl′) ►*n.* The part of a garment that is an extension of the collar and folds back against the breast. [< LAP¹.] —**la·peled′, la·pelled′** *adj.*

lap·i·dar·y (lăp′ĭ-dĕr′ē) ►*n., pl.* **-ies** One who cuts and polishes gems. ►*adj.* **1.** Of precious stones or the art of working with them. **2.** Concise and polished: *lapidary prose.* [< Lat. *lapis, lapid-,* stone.]

lap·in (lăp′ĭn, lä-păɴ′) ►*n.* Rabbit fur. [Fr.]

lap·is laz·u·li (lăp′ĭs lăz′ə-lē, -yə-, lăzh′ə-) ►*n.* An opaque blue semiprecious gemstone. [< Med.Lat. *lapis lazulī.*]

La·place (lə-pläs′, lä-), Marquis. **Pierre Simon de** 1749–1827. French mathematician and astronomer.

Lap·land (lăp′lănd′, -lənd) A region of extreme N Europe including N Norway, Sweden, and Finland and part of NW Russia. —**Lap′land·er** *n.*

Lapp (lăp) ►*n. Often Offensive* A Sami.

lapse (lăps) ►*v.* **lapsed, laps·ing 1.** To fall from a previous standard, as of quality. **2.** To pass or come to an end, esp. gradually. **3.** To be no longer valid or active; expire. ►*n.* **1.** A minor or temporary failure; slip. **2.** A deterioration or decline. **3.** A period of time; interval. **4.** A pause: *a lapse in the conversation.* [< Lat. *lābī, lāps-.*] —**laps′er** *n.*

lap·top (lăp′tŏp′) ►*n.* A portable computer with a display screen hinged to a keyboard, small enough to use on one's lap.

lap·wing (lăp′wĭng′) ►*n.* A medium-sized shorebird, esp. the northern lapwing. [< OE *hlēapewince.*]

La Ra·za (lä rä′sä) ►*n.* Mexicans or Mexican Americans considered as a group, sometimes extending to all Spanish-speaking people of the Americas. [Am.Sp., the people.]

lar·board (lär′bərd) ►*n. Naut.* See **port².** [< ME *laddebord.*] —**lar′board** *adj.*

lar·ce·ny (lär′sə-nē) ►*n., pl.* **-nies** The stealing of another's personal property; theft. [< Lat. *latrōcinium* < *latrō,* robber.] —**lar′ce·nous** (-nəs) *adj.*

larch (lärch) ►*n.* A deciduous, cone-bearing tree having needlelike leaves and heavy durable wood. [< Lat. *larix.*]

lard (lärd) ►*n.* The white rendered fat of a hog. ►*v.* **1.** To cover with lard or a similar fat. **2.** To insert strips of fat in (meat) before cooking. **3.** To embellish throughout: *larded the report with unnecessary quotations.* [< Lat. *lārdum.*] —**lard′y** *adj.*

lar·der (lär′dər) ►*n.* A place, such as a pantry, where food is stored.

large (lärj) ►*adj.* **larg·er, larg·est 1.** Of greater than average size or amount; big. **2.** Broad; comprehensive. **3.** Tolerant; liberal. —*idiom:* **at large 1.** Not in captivity; at liberty. **2.** As a whole; in general. **3.** Not representing a particular country, state, or district. [< Lat. *largus.*] —**large′ness** *n.*

Syns: *big, great* **Ant:** *small* **adj.**

large calorie ►*n.* See **calorie** (sense 2a).

large intestine ►*n.* The portion of the intestine from the ileum to the anus.

large·ly (lärj′lē) ►*adv.* **1.** For the most part; mainly. **2.** On a large scale; amply.

large-scale (lärj′skāl′) ►*adj.* **1.** Large in scope or extent. **2.** Drawn or made large to show detail.

lar·gess also **lar·gesse** (lär-zhĕs′, -jĕs′, lär′jĕs′) ►*n.* **1.** Liberality in giving. **2.** Money or gifts bestowed. [< OFr. *largesse.*]

lar·go (lär′gō) ►*adv. & adj. Mus.* In a slow, solemn tempo. [Ital.] —**lar′go** *n.*

la·ri (lä′rē) ►*n.* See table at **currency.** [Georgian.]

lar·i·at (lăr′ē-ət) ►*n.* A lasso. [Sp.]

lark¹ (lärk) ►*n.* **1.** A songbird found almost worldwide and having a melodious song, esp. the skylark. **2.** Any of several similar birds, such as the meadowlark. [< OE *lāwerce.*]

lark² (lärk) ►*n.* A carefree adventure or prank. ►*v.* To engage in fun or pranks. [Perh. < ON *leikr,* play.] —**lark′er** *n.* —**lark′ish** *adj.*

lark·spur (lärk′spûr′) ►*n.* See **delphinium.**

lar·va (lär′və) ►*n., pl.* **-vae** (-vē) or **-vas 1.** The newly hatched, wingless, often wormlike form of many insects before metamorphosis. **2.** The newly hatched stage of any of various animals that differ markedly in form and appearance from the adult. [Lat. *lārva,* specter, mask.] —**lar′val** *adj.*

lar·yn·gi·tis (lăr′ĭn-jī′tĭs) ►*n.* Inflammation of the larynx. —**lar′yn·git′ic** (-jĭt′ĭk) *adj.*

lar·ynx (lăr′ĭngks) ►*n., pl.* **la·ryn·ges** (lə-rĭn′jēz) or **lar·ynx·es** The part of the respiratory tract between the pharynx and the trachea, containing the vocal cords. [< Gk. *larunx.*] —**la·ryn′ge·al** (lə-rĭn′jē-əl) *adj.*

la·sa·gna also **la·sa·gne** (lə-zän′yə) ►*n.* **1.** Pasta in flat, very wide strips. **2.** A dish made by baking such pasta with layers of sauce and fillings such as cheese or meat. [Ital.]

La Salle (lə săl′, lä), Sieur de. Title of Robert Cavelier. 1643–87. French explorer in North America.

las·civ·i·ous (lə-sĭv′ē-əs) ►*adj.* **1.** Lustful; lecherous. **2.** Arousing sexual desire; salacious. [< Lat. *lascīvus.*] —**las·civ′i·ous·ly** *adv.*

la·ser (lā′zər) ►*n.* A device that emits highly amplified radiation of one or more discrete wavelengths. [*l(ight) a(mplification by) s(timulated) e(mission of) r(adiation).*]

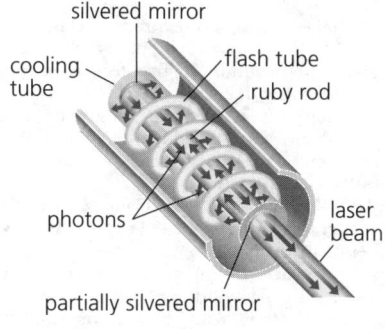

silvered mirror
cooling tube
flash tube
ruby rod
photons
laser beam
partially silvered mirror

laser

laser disc or **laser disk** ►*n.* See **optical disc.**

laser printer ►*n.* A printer that uses a laser to produce an image on a rotating drum before electrostatically transferring the image to paper.

lash¹ (lăsh) ►*n.* **1.** A stroke or blow with or as if with a whip. **2.** A whip or its thong. **3.** An eyelash. ►*v.* **1.** To strike with or as if with a whip. **2.** To strike against with force or violence: *sleet lashing the roof.* **3.** To beat or swing rapidly; thrash. **4.** To attack verbally: *lashed out at her critics.* **5.** To goad; sting. [ME.] —**lash′er** *n.*

lash² (lăsh) ►*v.* To secure or bind, as with a rope. [< Lat. *laqueāre,* ensnare.]

LA·SIK (lā′sĭk) ►*n.* Eye surgery to correct certain refractive disorders, such as myopia, in which a surface layer of the cornea is temporarily separated and folded back to expose the inner surface for reshaping with a laser. [*la(ser-assisted in) si(tu) k(eratomileusis).*]

Las Pal·mas (läs päl′mäs) The chief city of the Canary Is. of Spain.

lass (lăs) ►*n.* **1.** A girl or young woman. **2.** A sweetheart. [ME *las.*]

las·sie (lăs′ē) ►*n.* A lass.

las·si·tude (lăs′ĭ-to͞od′, -tyo͞od′) ►*n.* A state of weariness, lethargy, or listlessness. [< Lat. *lassus,* weary.]

las·so (lăs′ō, lă-so͞o′) ►*n., pl.* **-sos** or **-soes** A long rope with a noose at one end, used esp. to catch horses and cattle. [Sp. *lazo;* see LACE.] —**las′so** *v.* —**las′so·er** *n.*

last¹ (lăst) ►*adj.* **1.** Being, coming, or placed after all others; final. **2.** Most recent; latest. **3.** Most authoritative or conclusive. **4.** Least likely or expected. ►*adv.* **1.** After all others. **2.** Most recently. **3.** At the end; finally. ►*n.* **1.** One that is last. **2.** The end. —*idiom:* **at last** Finally. [< OE *latost.*] —**last′ly** *adv.*

last² (lăst) ►*v.* **1.** To continue; go on: *The song lasted three minutes.* **2.** To remain adequate or sufficient. [< OE *lǣstan.*]

last³ (lăst) ►*n.* A foot-shaped block or form used in making or repairing shoes. [< OE *lǣst,* sole of the foot.]

last-ditch (lăst′dĭch′) ►*adj.* Done as a final recourse; desperate.

last-in, first-out (lăst′ĭn′ fûrst′out′) ►*n.* A method of inventory accounting in which the cost of the latest units to enter the inventory is matched with the income from the first units sold.

last·ing (lăs′tĭng) ►*adj.* Continuing or remaining for a long time; enduring: *a lasting peace.* —**last′ing·ly** *adv.*

Last Judgment ►*n. Theol.* In Christianity and certain other religious traditions, the final judgment by God of all humankind.

last rites ►*pl.n.* Religious rites performed for one in danger of dying or for a burial.

last straw ►*n.* The last of a series of annoyances or setbacks that leads to a final loss of patience or hope.

Last Supper ►*n.* In the Bible, Jesus's supper with the Apostles on the night before his crucifixion.

Las Ve·gas (läs vā′gəs) A city of SE NV near the CA and AZ borders.

Lat. ►*abbr.* Latin

latch (lăch) ►*n.* **1.** A fastening, as for a door or gate, typically consisting of a movable bar that fits into a notch. **2.** A spring lock opened by a key. ►*v.* To close with a latch. —*idiom:* **latch**

on to (or **onto**) **1.** To get hold of; obtain. **2.** To cling to. [< OE *læccan*, seize.]

late (lāt) ►*adj.* **lat·er, lat·est 1.** Coming, occurring, or remaining after the proper or expected time. See Synonyms at **tardy. 2.** Occurring at an advanced hour, esp. well into the night: *a late movie.* **3.** Of or toward the end. **4.** Recent: *a late development.* **5.** Recently deceased: *in memory of the late explorer.* ►*adv.* **later, latest 1.** After the expected or usual time. **2.** At or into an advanced period or stage. **3.** Recently. —*idiom:* **of late** Recently. [< OE *læt.*] —**late′ness** *n.*

late·com·er (lāt′kŭm′ər) ►*n.* **1.** One who arrives late. **2.** A recent arrival or participant.

Late Greek ►*n.* The Greek language in late antiquity and the early Byzantine period.

Late Latin ►*n.* The Latin language as used from the 3rd to the 7th cent. AD.

late·ly (lāt′lē) ►*adv.* Not long ago; recently.

la·tent (lāt′nt) ►*adj.* **1.** Present or potential but not evident or active. See Synonyms at **inactive. 2.** *Psychol.* Present in the unconscious mind but not consciously expressed. See Synonyms at **inactive.** [< Lat. *latēre,* lie hidden.] —**la′ten·cy** *n.* —**la′tent·ly** *adv.*

lat·er·al (lāt′ər-əl) ►*adj.* **1.** Of or situated at or on the side. **2.** Relating to a change within an organization to a position at a similar level, as in salary or responsibility, to the one being left. ►*n. Football* A pass thrown sideways or backward. [< Lat. *latus, later-,* side.] —**lat′er·al** *v.* —**lat′er·al·ly** *adv.*

la·tex (lā′tĕks′) ►*n.* **1.** The milky sap of certain plants that coagulates on exposure to air. **2.** An emulsion of such sap, used to manufacture thin elastic products such as balloons, disposable gloves, and contraceptive devices. Some people are allergic to this natural rubber latex. **3.** A similar material made from polymers derived from petroleum, used to make paints and thin elastic products; synthetic latex. [Lat., fluid.] —**la′tex′** *adj.*

lath (lāth) ►*n., pl.* **laths** (lā*th*z, lāths) **1.** A thin strip of wood or metal, usu. nailed in rows as a substructure for plaster, shingles, or tiles. **2.** A similarly used building material. [< OE *lætt.*]

lathe (lā*th*) ►*n.* A machine on which a piece of material, such as wood or metal, is spun and shaped against a fixed cutting tool. [ME.] —**lathe** *v.*

lath·er (lā*th*′ər) ►*n.* **1.** A foam formed esp. by soap agitated in water. **2.** Frothy sweat. **3.** *Informal* An agitated state; dither. ►*v.* To produce or coat with lather. [< OE *lēthran,* to lather.] —**lath′er·er** *n.* —**lath′er·y** *adj.*

Lat·in (lāt′n) ►*n.* **1.** The Indo-European language of the ancient Romans. **2.** A member of a Latin people, esp. a native or inhabitant of Latin America. ►*adj.* **1.** Relating to ancient Rome or its language or culture. **2.** Relating to the Romance languages or to the peoples that speak them. **3.** Relating to Latinos or their culture. **4.** Relating to the Roman Catholic Church. [< Lat. *Latīnus.*]

La·ti·na (lə-tē′nə, lă-) ►*n.* A Latino woman or girl.

Latin America The countries of the Western Hemisphere S of the US, esp. those speaking Spanish, Portuguese, or French. —**Latin American** *n.* —**Lat′in-A·mer′i·can** *adj.*

La·ti·no (lə-tē′nō, lă-) ►*n., pl.* **-nos 1.** A Latin American. **2.** A person of Latin-American ancestry, esp. one living in the US. See Usage Note at **Hispanic.** —**La·ti′no** *adj.*

lat·i·tude (lăt′ĭ-tōōd′, -tyōōd′) ►*n.* **1a.** The angular distance north or south of the equator, measured in degrees along a meridian. **b.** A region that is considered in relation to this distance. **2.** Freedom from limitations. See Synonyms at **room.** [< Lat. *lātitūdō < lātus,* wide.] —**lat′i·tu′di·nal** *adj.* —**lat′i·tu′di·nal·ly** *adv.*

lat·i·tu·di·nar·i·an (lăt′ĭ-tōōd′n-âr′ē-ən, -tyōōd′-) ►*adj.* Holding or expressing tolerant views, esp. in religious matters. —**lat′i·tu′di·nar′i·an** *n.* —**lat′i·tu′di·nar′i·an·ism** *n.*

La·ti·um (lā′shē-əm, -shəm) An ancient country of W-central Italy bordering on the Tyrrhenian Sea.

lat·ke (lăt′kə) ►*n.* A pancake, esp. one made of grated potato. [Yiddish.]

la·trine (lə-trēn′) ►*n.* A communal toilet. [< Lat. *lavātrīna,* bath.]

lats (lăts) ►*n., pl.* **la·ti** (lä′tē′) See table at **currency.** [Latvian.]

lat·te (lä′tā) ►*n.* A caffe latte.

lat·ter (lăt′ər) ►*adj.* **1.** Being the second of two persons or things mentioned. **2.** Near the end. [< OE *lætra.*] —**lat′ter·ly** *adv.*

lat·ter-day (lăt′ər-dā′) ►*adj.* Belonging to present or recent times; modern.

Latter-day Saint ►*n.* See **Mormon.**

lat·tice (lăt′ĭs) ►*n.* **1a.** An open framework made of interwoven strips, of metal or wood. **b.** A structure, such as a window, made of or containing a lattice. **2.** *Phys.* A regular, periodic configuration of points throughout an area or space. [< OFr. *lattis.*] —**lat′ticed** *adj.* —**lat′tice·work′** *n.*

Lat·vi·a (lăt′vē-ə) A country of N Europe on the Baltic Sea. Cap. Riga.

Lat·vi·an (lăt′vē-ən) ►*adj.* Relating to Latvia or its people, language, or culture. ►*n.* **1.** A native or inhabitant of Latvia. **2.** Their Baltic language.

laud (lôd) ►*v.* To praise highly. ►*n.* Praise. [< Lat. *laudāre.*] —**laud·a′tion** *n.* —**laud′er** *n.*

laud·a·ble (lô′də-bəl) ►*adj.* Praiseworthy; commendable. —**laud′a·bil′i·ty, laud′a·ble·ness** *n.* —**laud′a·bly** *adv.*

lau·da·num (lôd′n-əm) ►*n.* A tincture of opium, formerly used as a drug. [NLat.]

laud·a·to·ry (lô′də-tôr′ē) ►*adj.* Expressing or conferring praise.

laugh (lăf) ►*v.* **1.** To express certain emotions, esp. mirth or delight, by a series of unarticulated sounds. **2.** To affect by laughter: *laughed them off the stage.* ►*n.* **1.** The sound or act of laughing. **2.** *Informal* Something amusing or absurd. **3.** often **laughs** *Informal* Fun; amusement. [< OE *hlæhhan.*] —**laugh′er** *n.* —**laugh′ing·ly** *adv.*

laugh·a·ble (lăf′ə-bəl) ►*adj.* Causing or deserving laughter or derision. —**laugh′a·ble·ness** *n.* —**laugh′a·bly** *adv.*

laugh·ing·stock (lăf′ĭng-stŏk′) ►*n.* An object of jokes or ridicule; a butt.

laugh·ter (lăf′tər) ►*n.* The act or sound of laughing. [< OE *hleahtor.*]

launch¹ (lônch, länch) ►*v.* **1a.** To propel with force; hurl. **b.** To set or thrust in motion. **2.** To put (a boat) into the water. **3.** To set going;

initiate. [< Lat. *lanceāre,* wield a lance < *lancea,* lance.] —**launch** *n.* —**launch′er** *n.*

launch² (lônch, länch) ►*n.* **1.** A large ship's boat. **2.** An open motorboat. [< Malay *lancha.*]

launch pad or **launch·ing pad** (lôn′chĭng, län′-) ►*n.* The base or platform from which a rocket or space vehicle is launched.

laun·der (lôn′dər, län′-) ►*v.* **1.** To wash or wash and iron (clothes or linens). **2.** To make (illegally obtained money) appear lawfully obtained, esp. by transferring it through legitimate accounts or businesses. [< Lat. *lavandāria,* things to be washed < *lavāre,* wash.] —**laun′der·er** *n.* —**laun′dress** (-drĭs) *n.*

Laun·dro·mat (lôn′drə-măt′, län′-) A service mark for a commercial establishment with washing machines and dryers.

laun·dry (lôn′drē, län′-) ►*n., pl.* **-dries 1.** Soiled or laundered clothes. **2.** A place where laundering is done.

lau·re·ate (lôr′ē-ĭt, lŏr′-) ►*n.* One awarded a prize for great achievements esp. in the arts or sciences. [< Lat. *laureātus,* adorned with laurel.] —**lau′re·ate** *adj.* —**lau′re·ate·ship′** *n.*

lau·rel (lôr′əl, lŏr′-) ►*n.* **1.** A Mediterranean evergreen tree with aromatic leaves. **2.** Any of several similar shrubs or trees, such as the mountain laurel. **3.** often **laurels a.** A wreath of laurel that is conferred as a mark of honor in ancient times. **b.** Honor and glory. [< Lat. *laurus.*]

la·va (lä′və, lăv′ə) ►*n.* **1.** Molten rock that reaches the earth's surface through a volcano or fissure. **2.** Rock formed by the cooling and solidifying of lava. [Ital.]

lav·age (lăv′ĭj, lä-väzh′) ►*n.* A washing, esp. of a hollow bodily organ, with repeated injections of water. [< Lat. *lavāre,* wash.]

lav·a·liere (lăv′ə-lîr′) ►*n.* **1.** A pendant worn on a chain around the neck. **2.** A small microphone worn around the neck. [Fr. *lavallière,* type of necktie, after the Duchesse de *la Vallière* (1644–1710).]

la·vash (lə-väsh′) ►*n.* A thin leavened bread of Armenian origin. [Ult. < Turk. *lavaç.*]

lav·a·to·ry (lăv′ə-tôr′ē) ►*n., pl.* **-ries 1.** A room equipped with washing and toilet facilities; bathroom. **2.** A flush toilet. [< LLat. *lavātōrium* < Lat. *lavāre,* wash.]

lave (lāv) ►*v.* **laved, lav·ing** To wash; bathe. [< Lat. *lavāre.*]

lav·en·der (lăv′ən-dər) ►*n.* **1.** An aromatic plant having small purplish flowers, widely cultivated for its essential oil. **2.** A pale to light purple. [< Med.Lat. *lavendula.*] —**lav′en·der** *adj.*

lav·ish (lăv′ĭsh) ►*adj.* **1.** Extravagant. See Synonyms at **profuse. 2.** Immoderate in giving. ►*v.* To give or bestow in abundance; shower. [< OFr. *lavasse,* downpour < *laver,* LAVE.] —**lav′-ish·er** *n.* —**lav′ish·ly** *adv.* —**lav′ish·ness** *n.*

La·voi·sier (lə-vwä′zē-ā′, lä-vwä-zyā′), **Antoine Laurent** 1743–94. French chemist.

law (lô) ►*n.* **1a.** A rule of conduct established by custom, agreement, or authority. **b.** A body of such rules. **2.** A piece of enacted legislation. **3.** A judicial system or its workings. **4.** The science and study of law; jurisprudence. **5.** A code of ethics or behavior. **6.** A formulation or generalization based on observed phenomena or consistent experience: *the law of gravity.* [< OE *lagu.*]

law·a·bid·ing (lô′ə-bī′dĭng) ►*adj.* Adhering to the law.

law·ful (lô′fəl) ►*adj.* Allowed or recognized by law. —**law′ful·ly** *adv.* —**law′ful·ness** *n.*

law·less (lô′lĭs) ►*adj.* **1.** Unrestrained by or contrary to the law. **2.** Not governed by law. —**law′less·ly** *adv.* —**law′less·ness** *n.*

law·mak·er (lô′mā′kər) ►*n.* One who drafts laws; a legislator. —**law′mak′ing** *n.*

lawn¹ (lôn) ►*n.* A plot of grass, usu. tended or mowed. [< OFr. *launde,* pasture.]

lawn² (lôn) ►*n.* A fine light cotton or linen. [After *Laon,* France.]

Law·rence (lôr′əns, lŏr-), **D(avid) H(erbert)** 1885–1930. British writer.

Lawrence, T(homas) E(dward) "Lawrence of Arabia." 1888–1935. British soldier and writer.

law·ren·ci·um (lô-rĕn′sē-əm, lō-) ►*n. Symbol* **Lr** A short-lived, synthetic radioactive element. At. no. 103. See table at **element.** [After E.O. *Lawrence* (1901–58).]

law·suit (lô′sōōt′) ►*n.* An action or proceeding other than a criminal prosecution brought before a court for settlement.

law·yer (loi′yər) ►*n.* One whose profession is to give legal advice to clients and represent them in court. [ME *lauier* < *law,* LAW.] —**law′-yer·ly** *adj.*

lax (lăks) ►*adj.* **-er, -est 1.** Lacking in rigor, strictness, or firmness. See Synonyms at **negligent. 2.** Not taut; slack. See Synonyms at **loose.** [< Lat. *laxus,* loose.] —**lax·a′tion** *n.* —**lax′i·ty, lax′ness** *n.* —**lax′ly** *adv.*

lax·a·tive (lăk′sə-tĭv) ►*n.* A food or drug that stimulates evacuation of the bowels. [< Lat. *laxāre,* relax.] —**lax′a·tive** *adj.*

lay¹ (lā) ►*v.* **laid** (lād), **lay·ing 1.** To cause to lie down. **2.** To place in or bring to a specified condition. **3.** To bury. **4.** To put or set down: *lay railroad track.* **5.** To produce and deposit (eggs). **6.** To put against: *laid an ear to the door.* **7.** To put forward or impose: *lay the blame on us.* **8.** To devise; contrive. **9.** To spread: *lay paint on a canvas.* **10.** To prepare: *lay the table for lunch.* **11.** To present; submit: *laid the case before us.* —*phrasal verbs:* **lay aside 1.** To give up; abandon. **2.** To save for the future. **lay away** To reserve for the future; save. **lay by** To save. **lay down 1.** To give up; surrender. **2.** To specify: *laid down the rules.* **lay in** To store for future use. **lay off 1.** To dismiss or suspend from a job. **2.** *Slang* To cease; quit. **lay out 1.** To make a plan for. **2.** To knock to the ground. **lay over** To make a stopover. **lay up 1.** To store for future needs. **2.** *Informal* To confine with an illness or injury. —*idioms:* **lay low 1.** To keep oneself or one's plans hidden. **2.** To cause to be dead or unable to get up from a lying position. **lay of the land** The nature, arrangement, or disposition of something. **lay waste** To destroy. [< OE *lecgan.*]

lay² (lā) ►*adj.* **1.** Of or relating to the laity. **2.** Nonprofessional: *a lay opinion.* [< Gk. *laos,* the people.]

lay³ (lā) ►*n.* **1.** A narrative poem, such as one sung by medieval minstrels; ballad. **2.** A song; tune. [< OFr. *lai.*]

lay⁴ (lā) ►*v.* P.t. of **lie¹.**

lay·a·way (lā′ə-wā′) ►*n.* A payment plan in which merchandise is reserved with a down payment until the balance is paid in full.

lay·er (lā′ər) ►*n.* **1.** One that lays, esp. a hen. **2.** A single thickness or level of material. **3.** An item of clothing that is worn over or under another. ►*v.* **1.** To divide or form into layers. **2.** To cut hair into different, usu. overlapping lengths.

lay·ette (lā-ĕt′) ►*n.* Clothing and bedding for a newborn child. [Fr. < OFr. *laie*, box.]

lay·man (lā′mən) ►*n.* **1.** One who is not a cleric. **2.** One who is a nonprofessional in a given field. See Usage Note at **man.**

lay·off (lā′ôf′, -ŏf′) ►*n.* Dismissal of employees, esp. for lack of work.

lay·out (lā′out′) ►*n.* **1.** An arrangement or plan. **2.** *Print.* The overall design of a page, spread, or book.

lay·o·ver (lā′ō′vər) ►*n.* A short stop or break in a journey, usu. imposed by scheduling requirements, as of airline flights.

lay·per·son (lā′pûr′sən) ►*n.* **1.** One who is not a cleric. **2.** One who is not a professional in a given field. —**lay′peo′ple** *n.*

lay·wom·an (lā′woom′ən) ►*n.* **1.** A woman who is not a cleric. **2.** A woman who is a nonprofessional in a given field. See Usage Note at **man.**

Laz·a·rus (lăz′ər-əs) In the Bible, the man whom Jesus miraculously raised from the dead.

Lazarus, Emma 1849–87. Amer. poet.

laze (lāz) ►*v.* **lazed, laz·ing** To be idle; loaf.

la·zy (lā′zē) ►*adj.* **-zi·er, -zi·est 1.** Not willing to work or be energetic. **2.** Slow-moving; sluggish: *a lazy river.* **3.** Conducive to inactivity or indolence: *a lazy summer day.* [Prob. of LGer. orig.] —**la′zi·ly** *adv.* —**la′zi·ness** *n.*
  Syns: *indolent, slothful* **adj.**

lazy Su·san (soo′zən) ►*n.* A revolving tray for condiments or food.

lb. ►*abbr.* **1.** libra (ancient Roman weight) **2.** pound (modern weight)

lc ►*abbr.* lowercase

lcd ►*abbr.* least common denominator

LCD ►*abbr.* liquid-crystal display

lcm ►*abbr.* least common multiple

LCpl ►*abbr.* lance corporal

LD ►*abbr.* **1a.** learning disability **b.** learning-disabled **2.** lethal dose

LDL cholesterol (ĕl′dē-ĕl′) ►*n.* A lipoprotein with high concentrations of lipids and low concentrations of protein that transports cholesterol in the blood and is associated at high levels with an increased risk of heart disease. [*l(ow-)d(ensity) l(ipoprotein).*]

L-do·pa (ĕl-dō′pə) ►*n.* An amino acid that is converted in the brain to dopamine, used in synthetic form to treat Parkinson's disease.

lea (lē, lā) ►*n.* A meadow. [< OE *lēah.*]

leach (lēch) ►*v.* To remove or be removed from by the action of a percolating liquid. [< OE *lece*, muddy stream.] —**leach′er** *n.*

lead¹ (lēd) ►*v.* **led** (lĕd), **lead·ing 1.** To guide, conduct, escort, or direct. See Synonyms at **guide. 2.** To influence; induce. **3.** To be ahead or be at the head of: *My name led the list.* **4.** To pursue; live: *lead an independent life.* **5.** To begin or open with, as in games: *lead an ace.* **6.** To tend toward a certain goal or result: *policies that led to disaster.* ►*n.* **1.** The first or foremost position. **2.** The margin by which one is ahead. **3.** A clue. **4.** Command; leadership. **5.** An example; precedent. **6.** The principal role in a play. **7.** *Games* **a.** The prerogative or turn to make the first play. **b.** A card played first in a round. **8.** A leash. —*phrasal verbs:* **lead off** To begin; start. **lead on** To lure; entice. **lead up to** To proceed toward (a main topic) with preliminary remarks. [< OE *lǣdan.*] —**lead′er** *n.* —**lead′er·ship′** *n.*

lead² (lĕd) ►*n.* **1.** *Symbol* **Pb** A malleable, bluish-white, dense metallic element used in solder, radiation shields, glass, and alloys. At. no. 82. See table at **element. 2.** Any of various, often graphitic compositions used as the writing substance in pencils. **3.** A weight used to make soundings. **4.** Bullets; shot. **5.** *Print.* A thin strip of metal used to separate lines of type. ►*v.* **1.** To cover, line, weight, or fill with lead. **2.** To secure (window glass) with lead. **3.** To treat (e.g., gasoline or paint) with lead. [< OE *lēad.*] —**lead** *adj.*

lead·en (lĕd′n) ►*adj.* **1.** Made of lead. **2.** Heavy and inert. **3.** Downcast; depressed. **4.** Dark gray: *a leaden sky.* —**lead′en·ly** *adv.*

lead·ing¹ (lē′dĭng) ►*adj.* **1.** In the first or front position. **2.** Chief; principal. **3.** Performing a lead in a theatrical production. **4.** Encouraging a desired response: *a leading question.*

lead·ing² (lĕd′ĭng) ►*n.* **1.** A border of lead, as around a windowpane. **2.** *Print.* The spacing between lines.

lead-time (lĕd′tīm′) ►*n.* The time between the initial stage of a project and the appearance of results.

leaf (lēf) ►*n., pl.* **leaves** (lēvz) **1.** A usu. green, flattened plant structure attached to a stem and functioning as a principal organ of photosynthesis. **2.** A leaflike part. **3.** Any of the sheets of paper that are bound in a book. **4.** A very thin sheet of metal. **5.** A hinged or removable section for a table top. **6.** A movable section of a folding door, shutter, or gate. ►*v.* **1.** To produce leaves. **2.** To turn pages: *leafed through the catalog.* [< OE *lēaf.*] —**leaf′less** *adj.* —**leaf′y** *adj.*

leaf·age (lē′fĭj) ►*n.* Foliage.

leaf·let (lē′flĭt) ►*n.* **1.** A small leaf or leaflike part. **2.** A printed handbill or flier. ►*v.* To hand out leaflets (to).

leaf spring ►*n.* A spring consisting of several layers of flexible metallic strips.

leaf·stalk or **leaf stalk** (lēf′stôk′) ►*n.* See **petiole.**

league¹ (lēg) ►*n.* **1.** An association or alliance for common action. **2.** An association of sports teams. **3.** A level of competition. [< Lat. *ligāre*, tie together.] —**league** *v.*

league² (lēg) ►*n.* A unit of distance equal to 3.0 mi (4.8 km). [< Lat. *leuga*, a unit of distance, of Celt. orig.]

League of Nations A world organization (1920–46) to promote international cooperation and peace.

Le·ah (lē′ə) In the Bible, the first wife of Jacob.

leak (lēk) ►*v.* **1.** To escape or permit the escape of something through a breach or flaw. **2.** To disclose or become known through a breach of secrecy. ►*n.* **1.** A crack or flaw that permits something to escape from or enter a container or conduit. **2a.** The act or instance of leaking. **b.** An amount leaked. **3.** A disclosure of confidential information. [ME *leken.*] —**leak′er** *n.* —**leak′i·ness** *n.* —**leak′y** *adj.*

leak·age (lē′kĭj) ▸*n.* **1.** The process of leaking. **2.** Something that escapes by leaking.

lean¹ (lēn) ▸*v.* **1.** To bend or cause to bend away from the vertical. See Synonyms at **slant. 2.** To incline one's weight so as to be supported: *I leaned against the wall to rest.* **3.** To rely for assistance or support. **4.** To have a tendency or preference. **5.** *Informal* To exert pressure. [< OE *hleonian.*]

lean² (lēn) ▸*adj.* **-er, -est 1.** Not fleshy or fat; thin. **2.** Containing little or no fat: *a lean steak.* **3.** Not productive or prosperous: *lean years.* ▸*n.* Meat with little or no fat. [< OE *hlǽne.*] **—lean′ly** *adv.* **—lean′ness** *n.*

lean·ing (lē′nĭng) ▸*n.* A tendency; preference. See Synonyms at **predilection.**

lean-to (lēn′tōo′) ▸*n., pl.* **-tos 1.** A structure with a single-pitch roof attached to the side of a building. **2.** A shelter having a roof with a single pitch.

leap (lēp) ▸*v.* **leaped** or **leapt** (lĕpt, lēpt), **leap·ing 1a.** To propel oneself upward or a long way; spring or jump. **b.** To move quickly or suddenly. **2.** To change quickly from one subject to another. **3.** To act quickly or eagerly. ▸*n.* **1.** The act of leaping; jump. **2.** An abrupt transition. [< OE *hlēapan.*] **—leap′er** *n.*

leap·frog (lēp′frôg′, -frŏg′) ▸*n.* A game in which a player bends over while the next in line leaps over him or her. **—leap′frog′** *v.*

leap year ▸*n.* A year having 366 days, with February 29 being the extra day.

Lear (lîr), **Edward** 1812–88. British artist and writer.

learn (lûrn) ▸*v.* **learned** also **learnt** (lûrnt), **learn·ing 1.** To gain knowledge, comprehension, or mastery of through experience or study. **2.** To memorize. **3.** To become informed. See Synonyms at **discover.** [< OE *leornian.*] **—learn′er** *n.*

learn·ed (lûr′nĭd) ▸*adj.* Possessing systematic knowledge. **—learn′ed·ly** *adv.*
> *Syns: erudite, scholarly* **adj.**

learn·ing (lûr′nĭng) ▸*n.* **1.** The act of gaining knowledge or skill. **2.** Acquired knowledge or skill.

learning disability ▸*n.* A cognitive or neurological disorder that impedes academic skills. **—learn′ing-dis·a′bled** *adj.*

lease (lēs) ▸*n.* A contract granting use or occupation of property during a specified period for a specified rent. ▸*v.* **leased, leas·ing 1.** To grant use of by lease. **2.** To hold under lease. [< Lat. *laxāre,* let go.]

lease·hold (lēs′hōld′) ▸*n.* **1.** Possession by lease. **2.** Property held by lease. **—lease′hold′er** *n.*

leash (lēsh) ▸*n.* A restraining chain, rope, or strap attached to the collar or harness of an animal. [< Lat. *laxāre,* let go.] **—leash** *v.*

least (lēst) ▸*adj.* Superl. of **little. 1.** Lowest in importance or rank. **2.** Smallest. ▸*adv.* Superl. of **little.** To or in the lowest or smallest degree. ▸*n.* The lowest or smallest. **—idioms: at least 1.** Not less than. **2.** In any event. **in the least** At all. [< OE *lǽst.*]

least common denominator ▸*n.* The least common multiple of the denominators of a set of fractions.

least common multiple ▸*n.* The smallest quantity exactly divisible by two or more given quantities.

leath·er (lĕth′ər) ▸*n.* The dressed or tanned hide of an animal. [< OE *lether-.*] **—leath′er** *adj.* **—leath′er·y** *adj.*

leath·er·neck (lĕth′ər-nĕk′) ▸*n. Slang* A US Marine.

leave¹ (lēv) ▸*v.* **left** (lĕft), **leav·ing 1.** To go out of or away (from). **2a.** To go without taking: *left my book on the bus.* **b.** To omit: *left out the best part.* **3.** To have as a remainder or result. **4.** To allow to remain in a specified state. **5.** To bequeath. **6.** To abandon; forsake. **—phrasal verb: leave off** To stop; cease. [< OE *lǽfan.*]

leave² (lēv) ▸*n.* **1.** Permission. See Synonyms at **permission. 2.** Official permission to be absent from work or duty. **3.** Departure; farewell. [< OE *lēaf.*]

leav·en (lĕv′ən) ▸*n.* **1.** An agent, such as yeast, that causes batter or dough to rise, esp. by fermentation. **2.** An element that lightens or enlivens. ▸*v.* **1.** To add a rising agent to. **2.** To lighten or enliven. [< Lat. *levāre,* raise.] **—leav′ened** *adj.*

leav·en·ing (lĕv′ə-nĭng) ▸*n.* An agent that causes rising or fermentation; leaven.

leaves (lēvz) ▸*n.* Pl. of **leaf.**

leave-tak·ing (lēv′tā′kĭng) ▸*n.* A departure or farewell.

leav·ings (lē′vĭngz) ▸*pl.n.* Scraps or remains.

Leb·a·non (lĕb′ə-nən, -nŏn′) A country of SW Asia on the Mediterranean Sea. Cap. Beirut. **—Leb′a·nese′** (-nēz′, -nēs′) *adj. & n.*

lech·er (lĕch′ər) ▸*n.* A man given to lewd or lascivious behavior. [< OFr. *lechier,* lick.] **—lech′er·ous** *adj.* **—lech′er·ous·ly** *adv.* **—lech′er·y** *n.*

lec·i·thin (lĕs′ə-thĭn) ▸*n.* Any of a group of phospholipids found in plant and animal tissues, used as an emulsifier in a range of products such as food, paints, and plastics. [< Gk. *lekithos,* egg yolk + -IN.]

Le Cor·bu·sier (lə kôr-bōo-zyā′, -bü-) Charles Édouard Jeanneret. 1887–1965. Swiss-born French architect and writer.

lec·tern (lĕk′tərn) ▸*n.* A reading stand for a public speaker. [< Med.Lat. *lēctrīnum.*]

lec·ture (lĕk′chər) ▸*n.* **1.** A speech on a given subject delivered before an audience or class, as for the purpose of instruction. **2.** An earnest admonition; reprimand. [< Lat. *legere, lēct-,* read.] **—lec′ture** *v.*

lec·tur·er (lĕk′chər-ər) ▸*n.* **1.** One who delivers lectures. **2.** A member of the faculty of a college or university, usu. without rank or tenure.

led (lĕd) ▸*v.* P.t. and p.part. of **lead¹.**

LED (ĕl′ē-dē′, lĕd) ▸*n.* A semiconductor diode that converts applied voltage to light, used in lamps and digital displays. [*l(ight-)e(mitting) d(iode).*]

ledge (lĕj) ▸*n.* **1.** A horizontal projection forming a narrow shelf on a wall. **2.** A shelflike projection on a cliff or rock wall. **3.** An underwater ridge or rock shelf. [ME, crossbar.]

ledg·er (lĕj′ər) ▸*n.* A book in which the monetary transactions of a business are posted. [ME *legger,* breviary.]

lee (lē) ▸*n.* **1.** *Naut.* The side away from the wind; the sheltered side. **2.** Cover; shelter. [< OE *hlēo,* shelter.]

Lee, Ann "Mother Ann." 1736–84. British founder (1776) of the Shakers in America.

Lee, Henry "Light Horse Harry." 1756–1818. Amer. Revolutionary politician and soldier.

Lee, Robert Edward 1807–70. Amer. Confederate general.

Robert E. Lee
c. 1864 photograph

leech (lēch) ►*n.* **1.** Any of various aquatic bloodsucking worms, of which one species was formerly used by physicians to bleed patients. **2.** One that preys on others; parasite. [< OE *lǣce*.] —**leech** *v.*

Leeds (lēdz) A borough of N-central England NE of Manchester.

leek (lēk) ►*n.* An edible plant related to the onion, having a white slender bulb and dark-green leaves. [< OE *lēac*.]

leer (lîr) ►*v.* To give a lewd or malicious look. [< OE *hlēor*, cheek.] —**leer** *n.* —**leer′ing·ly** *adv.*

leer·y (lîr′ē) ►*adj.* **-i·er, -i·est** Suspicious; wary. To glance with sexual desire or malicious intent. —**leer′i·ly** *adv.* —**leer′i·ness** *n.*

lees (lēz) ►*pl.n.* Dregs. [< Med.Lat. *lia*.]

Leeu·wen·hoek (lā′vən-hōōk′), **Anton van** 1632–1723. Dutch microscopy pioneer.

lee·ward (lōō′ərd, lē′wərd) ►*adv. & adj. Naut.* On or toward the side to which the wind is blowing. —**lee′ward** *n.*

Lee·ward Islands (lē′wərd) **1.** The N group of the Lesser Antilles in the West Indies, from the Virgin Is. SE to Dominica. **2.** A chain of small islets of HI in the central Pacific WNW of the main islands.

lee·way (lē′wā′) ►*n.* **1.** The drift of a ship or aircraft to leeward of the course being steered. **2.** A margin of freedom or variation; latitude. See Synonyms at **room.**

left¹ (lĕft) ►*adj.* **1.** Of, located on, or corresponding to the side of the body to the north when one is facing east. **2.** Located on the left side of a person facing downstream. **3.** often **Left** Of or belonging to the political left. ►*n.* **1a.** The direction or position on the left side. **b.** The left side or hand. **c.** A turn in this direction: *make a left.* **2.** often **Left** The people and groups who pursue liberal or egalitarian political goals. ►*adv.* Toward or on the left. [ME.]

left² (lĕft) ►*v.* P.t. and p.part. of **leave¹.**

left field ►*n.* **1.** *Baseball* The third of the outfield to the left, looking from home plate. **2.** *Informal* A position far from the mainstream, as of opinion. —**left fielder** *n.*

left-hand (lĕft′hănd′) ►*adj.* **1.** Of or on the left. **2.** Designed for or done with the left hand.

left-hand·ed (lĕft′hăn′dĭd) ►*adj.* **1.** Using the left hand more skillfully or easily than the right. **2.** Done with or made for the left hand. **3.** Of doubtful sincerity; dubious. **4.** Counterclockwise. ►*adv.* With the left hand. —**left′-hand′-ed·ly** *adv.* —**left′-hand′ed·ness** *n.*

left-hand·er (lĕft′hăn′dər) ►*n.* One who is left-handed.

left·ism also **Left·ism** (lĕf′tĭz′əm) ►*n.* The ideology of the political left. —**left′ist** *adj. & n.*

left·o·ver (lĕft′ō′vər) ►*adj.* Remaining as an unused portion. ►*n.* **1.** A remnant or unused portion. **2. leftovers** Food remaining from a previous meal.

left wing ►*n.* **1.** The leftist faction of a group. **2.** See **left¹** (sense 2). —**left′-wing′** *adj.* —**left′-wing′er** *n.*

left·y (lĕf′tē) ►*n., pl.* **-ies** *Informal* A left-handed person.

leg (lĕg) ►*n.* **1.** A limb or appendage used for locomotion or support. **2.** A part resembling a leg in shape or function. **3.** The part of a pair of trousers that covers the leg. **4.** A stage of a journey or course. ►*v.* **legged, leg·ging** *Informal* To go on foot; walk or run: *legged it home.* [< ON *leggr*.]

leg·a·cy (lĕg′ə-sē) ►*n., pl.* **-cies 1.** Money or property bequeathed to another by will. **2.** Something handed down from an ancestor or predecessor. See Synonyms at **heritage.** [< Lat. *lēgāre*, bequeath.]

le·gal (lē′gəl) ►*adj.* **1.** Of or relating to law or lawyers. **2a.** Authorized by or based on law. **b.** Established by law; statutory. **3.** In conformity with or permitted by law. **4.** Acceptable under official rules: *a legal forward pass.* [< Lat. *lēx, lēg-,* law.] —**le·gal′i·ty** (lē-găl′ĭ-tē) *n.* —**le′gal·i·za′tion** *n.* —**le′gal·ize′** *v.* —**le′gal·ly** *adv.*

le·gal·ism (lē′gə-lĭz′əm) ►*n.* Overly strict, literal adherence to the law or to a religious or moral code. —**le′gal·ist** *n.* —**le′gal·is′tic** *adj.*

leg·ate (lĕg′ĭt) ►*n.* An official emissary, esp. of the pope. [< Lat. *lēgātus,* p.part. of *lēgāre,* depute.]

leg·a·tee (lĕg′ə-tē′) ►*n.* The inheritor of a legacy.

le·ga·tion (lĭ-gā′shən) ►*n.* A diplomatic mission in a foreign country ranking below an embassy. —**le·ga′tion·ar·y** *adj.*

le·ga·to (lĭ-gä′tō) ►*adv. & adj. Mus.* In a smooth, even style. [Ital.]

leg·end (lĕj′ənd) ►*n.* **1.** An unverified popular story, esp. one believed to be historical. **2.** One of great fame or popular renown. **3.** An inscription on an object. **4.** An explanatory caption. **5.** An explanatory table or list of the symbols on a map or chart. [< Med.Lat. *(lectiō) legenda,* (lesson) to be read.] —**leg′en·dar′y** *adj.*

leg·er·de·main (lĕj′ər-də-mān′) ►*n.* Sleight of hand. [< OFr. *leger de main,* light of hand.]

leg·ged (lĕg′ĭd, lĕgd) ►*adj.* Having a specified kind or number of legs.

leg·ging (lĕg′ĭng) ►*n.* **1.** A leg covering usu. extending from the ankle to the knee. **2. leggings** A tight-fitting, stretchable garment extending from the waist to the ankle.

leg·gy (lĕg′ē) ►*adj.* **-gi·er, -gi·est 1.** Having long slender legs. **2.** Having long, often leafless stems: *a leggy houseplant.* —**leg′gi·ness** *n.*

leg·horn or **Leg·horn** (lĕg′hôrn′, -ərn) ►*n.* A breed of hardy domestic fowl noted for prolific production of eggs.

leg·i·ble (lĕj′ə-bəl) ►*adj.* Possible to read or decipher. [< Lat. *legere,* read.] —**leg′i·bil′i·ty, leg′i·ble·ness** *n.* —**leg′i·bly** *adv.*

le·gion (lē′jən) ►*n.* **1.** A unit of the Roman army consisting of 3,000 to 6,000 infantry and 100 to 200 cavalry. **2.** A large number; multitude. [< Lat. *legere,* gather.] —**le′gion·ar′y** *adj. & n.* —**le′gion·naire′** *n.*

leg·is·late (lĕj′ĭ-slāt′) ►*v.* **-lat·ed, -lat·ing 1.** To create or pass laws. **2.** To bring about by legislation. [< Lat. *lēgis lātor,* proposer of a law.] —**leg′is·la′tor** *n.* —**leg′is·la·to′ri·al** (-lə-tôr′ē-əl) *adj.*

leg·is·la·tion (lĕj′ĭ-slā′shən) ►*n.* **1.** The act or process of legislating; lawmaking. **2.** A proposed or enacted law or group of laws.

leg·is·la·tive (lĕj′ĭ-slā′tĭv) ►*adj.* **1.** Of or relating to the enactment of laws. **2.** Having the power to create laws.

leg·is·la·ture (lĕj′ĭ-slā′chər) ►*n.* A body of people empowered to make laws.

le·git·i·mate (lə-jĭt′ə-mĭt) ►*adj.* **1.** Lawful. **2.** Being in accordance with accepted standards. **3.** Reasonable: *a legitimate doubt.* **4.** Born of legally married parents. **5.** Valid or justifiable: *a legitimate complaint.* ►*v.* (-māt′) **-mat·ed, -mat·ing** To make legitimate. [< Lat. *lēgitimus* < *lēx,* law.] —**le·git′i·ma·cy** (-mə-sē) *n.* —**le·git′i·mate·ly** *adv.*

le·git·i·mize (lə-jĭt′ə-mīz′) ►*v.* **-mized, -miz·ing** To legitimate. —**le·git′i·mi·za′tion** *n.*

leg·ume (lĕg′yōōm′, lə-gyōōm′) ►*n.* **1.** Any of various plants in the same family as the pea and bean. **2.** A pod of such a plant that splits into two valves with the seeds attached. [< Lat. *legūmen,* bean.] —**le·gu′mi·nous** *adj.*

leg·work (lĕg′wûrk′) ►*n. Informal* Work, such as collecting information, that involves walking or traveling about.

Le Ha·vre (lə hä′vrə, häv′) A city of N France on the English Channel WNW of Paris.

lei[1] (lā, lā′ē) ►*n., pl.* **leis** A wreath of flowers and other objects, esp. one worn around the neck. [Hawaiian.]

lei[2] (lā) ►*n.* Pl. of **leu.**

Leib·niz or **Leib·nitz** (līb′nĭts, līp′-), Baron **Gottfried Wilhelm von.** 1646–1716. German philosopher and mathematician.

Leices·ter (lĕs′tər) A borough of central England ENE of Birmingham.

Leip·zig (līp′sĭg, -sĭk) A city of E-central Germany SSW of Berlin.

lei·sure (lē′zhər, lĕzh′ər) ►*n.* Free time when one is not working or attending to other duties. —*idiom:* **at (one's) leisure** At one's convenience. [< OFr. *leisir,* be permitted.]

lei·sure·ly (lē′zhər-lē, lĕzh′ər-) ►*adj.* Done without haste; unhurried. ►*adv.* In an unhurried manner. —**lei′sure·li·ness** *n.*

leit·mo·tif also **leit·mo·tiv** (līt′mō-tēf′) ►*n.* **1.** *Mus.* A melodic passage or phrase associated with a specific character or element. **2.** A dominant and recurring theme, as in a novel. [Ger. *Leitmotiv.*]

lek (lĕk) ►*n.* See table at **currency.** [Albanian, after *Lek* Dukagjini.]

lem·ming (lĕm′ĭng) ►*n.* A small rodent inhabit-

ing northern regions and known for periodic mass migrations. [Norw.]

lem·on (lĕm′ən) ►*n.* **1a.** A spiny evergreen tree native to Asia, cultivated for its oval yellow fruit. **b.** The fruit of this tree, having a juicy, acid pulp. **2.** *Informal* One that is unsatisfactory or defective: *That used car was a lemon.* [< Pers. *līmūn.*] —**lem′on·y** *adj.*

lem·on·ade (lĕm′ə-nād′) ►*n.* A drink made of lemon juice, water, and sugar.

lem·pi·ra (lĕm-pîr′ə) ►*n.* See table at **currency.** [After *Lempira* (1497–1537), Honduran leader.]

le·mur (lē′mər) ►*n.* A primate that is native to Madagascar and adjacent islands, having long lower incisors and nails. [< Lat. *lemurēs,* ghosts.]

Le·na (lē′nə, lyĕ′-) A river of E Russia rising near Lake Baikal and flowing about 4,300 km (2,670 mi) to the Arctic Ocean.

lend (lĕnd) ►*v.* **lent** (lĕnt), **lend·ing 1.** To give or allow the use of temporarily. **2.** To provide (money) temporarily, usu. at interest. **3.** To contribute; impart: *Books lent a feeling of warmth to the room.* **4.** To make available for another's use: *The neighbors lent us help after the storm.* [< OE *lǣnan.*] —**lend′er** *n.*

L'En·fant (län-fänt′, län-fäɴ′), **Pierre Charles** 1754–1825. French-born architect.

L'En·gle (lĕng′gəl), **Madeleine** 1918–2007. Amer. writer.

length (lĕngkth, lĕngth, lĕnth) ►*n.* **1.** The measurement of something along its greatest dimension. **2.** Extent or distance from beginning to end: *the length of a novel.* **3.** The amount of time between specified moments; duration: *the length of a journey.* **4.** often **lengths** The degree to which an action or policy is carried. —*idiom:* **at length 1.** Eventually. **2.** For a considerable time; fully: *spoke at length about the ruling.* [< OE *lengthu.*] —**length′y** *adj.*

length·en (lĕngk′thən, lĕng′-, lĕn′-) ►*v.* To make or become longer.

length·ways (lĕngkth′wāz′, lĕngth′-, lĕnth′-) ►*adv.* Lengthwise.

length·wise (lĕngkth′wīz′, lĕngth′-, lĕnth′-) ►*adv. & adj.* Along the direction of the length.

le·ni·ent (lē′nē-ənt, lēn′yənt) ►*adj.* **1.** Not harsh or strict; indulgent: *lenient parents* **2.** Not harsh or strict; merciful: *lenient rules.* [< Lat. *lēnīre,* pacify < *lēnis,* soft.] —**le′ni·en·cy, le′ni·ence** *n.* —**le′ni·ent·ly** *adv.*

Le·nin (lĕn′ĭn), **Vladimir Ilich** 1870–1924. Russian revolutionary and first head of the USSR (1922–24).

Len·in·grad (lĕn′ĭn-grăd′) See **Saint Petersburg.**

Len·in·ism (lĕn′ə-nĭz′əm) ►*n.* The theory and practice of proletarian revolution as developed by Lenin. —**Len′in·ist** *adj. & n.*

Len·non (lĕn′ən), **John** 1940–80. British musician and composer.

lens (lĕnz) ►*n., pl.* **lens·es 1.** A piece of glass or other transparent material with opposite surfaces either or both of which are curved, by means of which light rays are refracted so that they converge or diverge to form an image. **2.** A combination of two or more such pieces used to form an image for viewing or photographing. **3.** A transparent part of the eye between the iris and vitreous humor that focuses light rays entering the pupil to form an image on the retina. [< Lat. *lēns,* lentil.]

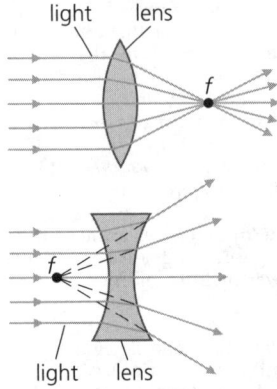

lens
Light rays converge when passing through a biconvex lens *(top)* and diverge when passing through a biconcave lens *(bottom).*
f indicates the focus.

lent (lĕnt) ►*v.* P.t. and p.part. of **lend.**

Lent ►*n.* The 40 weekdays from Ash Wednesday until Easter, observed by Christians as a season of penitence. [< OE *lencten,* spring.]

len·til (lĕn′təl) ►*n.* The flat, rounded, edible seed of a pealike plant native to SW Asia. [< Lat. *lenticula,* dim. of *lēns,* lentil.]

len·to (lĕn′tō) ►*adv. & adj. Mus.* In a slow tempo. [Ital. < Lat. *lentus.*]

Le·o (lē′ō) ►*n.* **1.** A constellation in the Northern Hemisphere. **2.** The 5th sign of the zodiac. [< Lat. *leō,* LION.]

Le·ón (lā-ōn′) **1.** A region and former kingdom of NW Spain. **2.** A city of central Mexico ENE of Guadalajara.

Le·o·nar·do da Vin·ci (lē′ə-när′dō də vĭn′chē, dä, lā′-) 1452–1519. Italian painter, engineer, and scientist.

le·one (lē-ōn′) ►*n.* See table at **currency.** [< SIERRA LEONE.]

le·o·nine (lē′ə-nīn′) ►*adj.* Of or characteristic of a lion. [< Lat. *leō, leōn-,* LION.]

leop·ard (lĕp′ərd) ►*n.* A large wild cat of Africa and S Asia, having either tawny fur with dark spots or black fur. [< Gk. *leopardos.*]

Le·o·pold II (lē′ə-pōld′) 1835–1909. King of the Belgians (1865–1909) and ruler of the Congo Free State (now Dem. Rep. of the Congo) (1876–1908).

le·o·tard (lē′ə-tärd′) ►*n.* A snug one-piece garment that covers the torso, worn esp. by dancers. [After Jules *Léotard* (1830–70).] —**le′o·tard′ed** *adj.*

lep·er (lĕp′ər) ►*n.* **1.** A person affected by leprosy. **2.** A pariah; outcast. [< Gk. *lepros,* scaly.]

lep·i·dop·ter·ist (lĕp′ĭ-dŏp′tər-ĭst) ►*n.* An entomologist specializing in the study of butterflies and moths. [< Gk. *lepis,* scale.] —**lep′i·dop′ter·y** (-tə-rē) *n.*

lep·re·chaun (lĕp′rĭ-kŏn′, -kôn′) ►*n.* In Irish folklore, a mischievous creature or fairy. [Ir. Gael. *luprachán.*]

lep·ro·sy (lĕp′rə-sē) ►*n.* A chronic bacterial disease marked by skin lesions and damage

to nerves and other organs that, if untreated, can lead to disfigurement, lack of sensation, and blindness. [ME *lepruse* < *leprus,* leprous.] —**lep′rous** *adj.*

lep·ton (lĕp′tŏn′) ►*n.* Any of a class of six elementary fermions. Leptons participate in weak interactions and have masses generally less than those of mesons and baryons. [Gk. *leptos,* thin + -ON¹.]

les·bi·an (lĕz′bē-ən) ►*n.* A woman whose sexual orientation is to women. [After *Lesbos,* Gk. island.] —**les′bi·an** *adj.* —**les′bi·an·ism** *n.*

le·sion (lē′zhən) ►*n.* A pathological or traumatic change in a body tissue or organ, such as a tumor or wound. [< Lat. *laesiō.*]

Le·so·tho (lə-sō′tō, -sōō′tōō) A country of S Africa forming an enclave within E-central South Africa. Cap. Maseru.

less (lĕs) ►*adj.* Comp. of **little. 1.** Not as great in amount or quantity. **2.** Lower in importance, esteem, or rank. **3.** Consisting of a smaller number. See Usage Note at **few.** ►*adv.* Comp. of **little.** To a smaller extent, degree, or frequency. ►*n.* A smaller amount: *She got less than she asked for.* [< OE *lǣssa* and *lǣs.*]

–less ►*suff.* **1.** Without; lacking: *blameless.* **2.** Unable to act or be acted on in a specified way: *dauntless.* [< OE *lēas,* without.]

les·see (lĕ-sē′) ►*n.* One that holds a lease. [< AN < p.part. of *lesser,* to let out, lease; see LEASE.]

less·en (lĕs′ən) ►*v.* To make or become less.

less·er (lĕs′ər) ►*adj.* Comp. of **little.** Smaller in size or importance.

Lesser Antilles An island group of the E West Indies extending in an arc from Aruba to the Virgin Is.

Les·sing (lĕs′ĭng), **Doris May Taylor** b. 1919. British writer.

Doris Lessing
photographed in 2006

les·son (lĕs′ən) ►*n.* **1.** Something to be learned. **2a.** A period of instruction. **b.** An instructional exercise. **3.** An experience or observation that imparts new knowledge or understanding. [< Lat. *lēctiō,* a reading.]

les·sor (lĕs′ôr′, lĕ-sôr′) ►*n.* One who leases property; a landlord. [< AN *lesser,* LEASE.]

lest (lĕst) ►*conj.* **1.** For fear that: *tiptoed lest they should hear.* **2.** In case someone might: *Lest you forget, please lock the door now.* [< OE *thȳ lǣs the,* so that not.]

let¹ (lĕt) ►*v.* **let, let·ting 1.** To give permission or opportunity to; allow: *I let them borrow the car.* **2.** To cause to; make: *Let the news be known.* **3.** Used as an auxiliary in the imperative to express: **a.** A command, request, or proposal: *Let's finish the job!* **b.** A warning or threat: *Just let her try!* **4.** To release or give forth: *let out a yelp.* **5.** To rent or lease. —*phrasal verbs:* **let down 1.** To lower. **2.** To disappoint. **let on** To allow to be known; admit. **let out 1.** To come to a close. **2.** To reveal: *Who let the story out?* **let up** To diminish: *The rain let up.* —*idiom:* **let alone** Not to mention; much less: *I don't have a dime, let alone a dollar.* [< OE *lætan.*]

let² (lĕt) ►*n.* **1.** Something that hinders; obstacle. **2.** *Sports* An invalid stroke in tennis and other net games that must be repeated. [< OE *lettan,* hinder.]

–let ►*suff.* **1.** Small: *booklet.* **2.** Something worn on: *armlet.* [< OFr. *-elet.*]

let·down (lĕt′doun′) ►*n.* **1.** A decrease, decline, or relaxation, as of effort or energy. **2.** A disappointment.

le·thal (lē′thəl) ►*adj.* Causing or capable of causing death. [< Lat. *lētum,* death.] —**le·thal′i·ty** (lē-thăl′ĭ-tē) *n.* —**le′thal·ly** *adv.*

leth·ar·gy (lĕth′ər-jē) ►*n., pl.* **-gies** A state of decreased energy; sluggishness. [< Gk. *lēthargos,* forgetful : *lēthē,* forgetfulness + *argos,* idle (A–¹ + *ergon,* work).] —**le·thar′gic** (lə-thär′jĭk) *adj.* —**le·thar′gi·cal·ly** *adv.*

Le·the (lē′thē) ►*n. Gk. Myth.* The river of forgetfulness in Hades. [Gk. *lēthē.*]

let's (lĕts) Let us.

Lett (lĕt) ►*n.* A member of a Baltic people constituting the main population of Latvia.

let·ter (lĕt′ər) ►*n.* **1.** A written character representing a speech sound and being a unit of an alphabet. **2.** A written or printed communication. **3.** Literal meaning. **4. letters** (takes sing. v.) Learning or knowledge, esp. of literature. ►*v.* To write letters on. [< Lat. *littera.*] —**let′ter·er** *n.*

let·tered (lĕt′ərd) ►*adj.* **1.** Literate. **2.** Learned. **3.** Inscribed with letters.

let·ter·head (lĕt′ər-hĕd′) ►*n.* **1.** Stationery with a printed or engraved heading. **2.** The heading itself.

let·ter·ing (lĕt′ər-ĭng) ►*n.* **1.** The act of forming letters. **2.** Letters inscribed, as on a sign.

let·ter-per·fect (lĕt′ər-pûr′fĭkt) ►*adj.* Correct to the last detail.

let·ter·press (lĕt′ər-prĕs′) ►*n.* The process of printing from a raised inked surface.

Let·tish (lĕt′ĭsh) ►*n.* See **Latvian** (sense 2).

let·tuce (lĕt′əs) ►*n.* A plant cultivated for its edible leaves, eaten esp. as salad. [< Lat. *lactūca.*]

let·up (lĕt′ŭp′) ►*n.* **1.** A reduction; slowdown. **2.** A pause.

le·u (lĕ′ōō) ►*n., pl.* **lei** (lā) See table at **currency.** [Rom. < Lat. *leō,* LION.]

leu·ke·mi·a (lōō-kē′mē-ə) ►*n.* A neoplastic disease of the bone marrow in which unrestrained proliferation of white blood cells occurs, marked usu. by anemia, impaired blood clotting and enlargement of the lymph nodes, liver, and spleen. —**leu·ke′mic** *adj. & n.*

leuko– or **leuk–** also **leuco–** or **leuc–** ►*pref.* **1.** White; colorless: *leukocyte.* **2.** Leukocyte: *leukemia.* [< Gk. *leukos.*]

leu·ko·cyte also **leu·co·cyte** (lōō′kə-sīt′) ►*n.* A white blood cell. —**leu′ko·cyt′ic** (-sĭt′ĭk) *adj.*

lev (lĕf) ►*n., pl.* **lev·a** (lĕv′ə) See table at **currency.** [Bulgarian, ult. < Lat. *leō,* LION.]

Le·vant (lə-vănt′) The countries bordering on the E Mediterranean Sea. —**Le′van·tine′** (lĕv′ən-tīn′, -tēn′, lə-văn′-) *adj. & n.*

lev·ee (lĕv′ē) ►*n.* **1.** An embankment raised to prevent a river from overflowing. **2.** A landing place on a river. [< OFr. *lever,* raise.]

lev·el (lĕv′əl) ►*n.* **1.** Relative position or rank on a scale. **2.** A natural or proper position, place, or stage. **3.** Position along a vertical axis; height or depth. **4a.** A horizontal line or plane at right angles to the plumb. **b.** The position or height of such a line or plane. **5.** A flat horizontal surface. **6.** A land area of uniform elevation. **7.** An instrument for ascertaining whether a surface is horizontal. ►*adj.* **1.** Having a flat smooth surface. **2.** Horizontal. **3.** At the same height or position as another; even. **4.** Consistent; steady. **5.** Rational; sensible. **6.** Filled evenly to the top. ►*v.* **-eled, -el·ing** or **-elled, -el·ling 1a.** To make horizontal, flat, or even. **b.** To place on the same rank; equalize. **2.** To tear down; raze. **3.** To aim a weapon horizontally. See Synonyms at **aim. 4.** To direct emphatically toward someone: *leveled charges of dishonesty.* **5.** To measure the different elevations of (a tract of land) with a level. **6.** *Informal* To be frank and open. —*phrasal verb:* **level off** To move toward stability or consistency. —*idiom:* **on the level** *Informal* Without deception; honest. [< VLat. **lībellum,* leveling tool < *lībra,* a balance.] —**lev′el·er** *n.* —**lev′el·ly** *adv.*

lev·el·head·ed (lĕv′əl-hĕd′ĭd) ►*adj.* Characteristically self-composed and sensible. —**lev′el·head′ed·ness** *n.*

lev·er (lĕv′ər, lē′vər) ►*n.* **1.** A simple machine consisting of a rigid bar pivoted on a fixed point and used to transmit force. **2.** A projecting handle used to adjust or operate a mechanism. **3.** A means of accomplishing; tool. ►*v.* To move or lift with or as if with a lever. [< OFr. *lever,* raise < Lat. *levāre.*]

lev·er·age (lĕv′ər-ĭj, lē′vər-) ►*n.* **1.** The action or mechanical advantage of a lever. **2.** Positional advantage; power to act effectively. **3.** The use of credit or borrowed funds, often for a speculative investment. —**lev′er·age** *v.*

Le·vi (lē′vī′) In the Bible, a son of Jacob and Leah.

le·vi·a·than (lə-vī′ə-thən) ►*n.* **1.** Something unusually large of its kind. **2.** *Bible* A monstrous sea creature mentioned in the Bible. [< Heb. *liwyātān,* a sea monster.]

Le·vi's (lē′vīz′) A trademark for denim pants.

lev·i·tate (lĕv′ĭ-tāt′) ►*v.* **-tat·ed, -tat·ing** To rise or raise into the air and float in apparent defiance of gravity. [Lat. *levis,* light + (GRAVI)-TATE.] —**lev′i·ta′tion** *n.*

Le·vit·i·cus (lə-vĭt′ĭ-kəs) ►*n.* See table at **Bible.**

lev·i·ty (lĕv′ĭ-tē) ►*n., pl.* **-ties** Lightness of manner or speech; frivolity. [< Lat. *levitās.*]

lev·y (lĕv′ē) ►*v.* **-ied, -y·ing 1.** To impose or collect (a tax or fine). **2.** To draft into military service. **3.** To wage (a war). **4.** To confiscate property. ►*n., pl.* **-ies 1.** The act or process of levying. **2.** Money, property, or troops levied. [< OFr. *lever,* raise; see LEVER.] —**lev′i·er** *n.*

lewd (lōōd) ►*adj.* **-er, -est 1.** Lustful. **2.** Obscene; indecent. [< OE *lǣwede,* ignorant.] —**lewd′ly** *adv.* —**lewd′ness** *n.*

Lew·is (lōō′ĭs), **C(live) S(taples)** 1898–1963. British writer and critic.

Lewis, Frederick Carlton "Carl." b. 1961. Amer. athlete.

Lewis, (Harry) Sinclair 1885–1951. Amer. novelist.

Lewis, Meriwether 1774–1809. Amer. soldier and explorer.

lex·i·cog·ra·phy (lĕk′sĭ-kŏg′rə-fē) ►*n.* The work of writing or compiling a dictionary. —**lex′i·cog′ra·pher** *n.* —**lex′i·co·graph′ic** (-kə-grăf′ĭk), **lex′i·co·graph′i·cal** *adj.*

lex·i·con (lĕk′sĭ-kŏn′) ►*n.* **1.** A dictionary. **2.** A specialized vocabulary. [< Gk. *lexikon (biblion)*, (book) of words.] —**lex′i·cal** *adj.*

Lex·ing·ton (lĕk′sĭng-tən) **1.** A city of N-central KY E of Louisville. **2.** A town of NE MA; site of the first battle of the American Revolution (April 19, 1775).

lf ►*abbr.* lightface

LF ►*abbr.* **1.** left field **2.** low frequency

lg. ►*abbr.* **1.** large **2.** long

LGBT ►*abbr.* lesbian, gay, bisexual, transgender

Lha·sa (lä′sə, lăs′ə) A city of SW China, the capital of Tibet.

li·a·bil·i·ty (lī′ə-bĭl′ĭ-tē) ►*n., pl.* **-ties 1.** Something for which one is liable; an obligation, responsibility, or debt. **2.** Something that holds one back; handicap.

li·a·ble (lī′ə-bəl) ►*adj.* **1.** Legally obligated; responsible. **2.** Subject; susceptible. **3.** Likely; apt. [Prob. < OFr. *lier*, bind.]

li·ai·son (lē′ā-zŏn′, lē-ā′-) ►*n.* **1a.** Communication between groups or units. **b.** One that maintains communication. **2.** A sexual relationship, esp. when at least one partner is married or sexually involved with someone else. [< Lat. *ligātiō*, binding < *ligāre*, bind.]

li·an·a (lē-ä′nə, -ăn′ə) ►*n.* Any climbing, woody, usu. tropical vine. [< Fr. *liane*, prob. < *lier*, bind.]

li·ar (lī′ər) ►*n.* One that tells lies.

li·ba·tion (lī-bā′shən) ►*n.* **1.** The ritual pouring of a liquid offering or the liquid so poured. **2.** *Informal* A beverage, esp. one that contains alcohol. [< Lat. *lībāre*, pour out as an offering.]

li·bel (lī′bəl) ►*n.* **1.** The legally indefensible publication or broadcast of words or images that are degrading to a person or injurious to his or her reputation. **2.** An incidence of this. ►*v.* **-beled, -bel·ing** or **-belled, -bel·ling** To make a libel about (a person). [< Lat. *libellus*, petition < *liber*, book.] —**li′bel·er, li′bel·ist** *n.* —**li′bel·ous** *adj.* —**li′bel·ous·ly** *adv.*

lib·er·al (lĭb′ər-əl, lĭb′rəl) ►*adj.* **1a.** Favoring reform, open to new ideas, and tolerant of the ideas and behavior of others; not bound by traditional thinking. See Synonyms at **broadminded**. **b.** Favoring civil and political liberties, democratic reforms, and protection from arbitrary authority. **2a.** Tending to give freely; generous. **b.** Abundant; ample. **3.** Not strict or literal; approximate. **4.** Of or based on the traditional arts and sciences of a college or university curriculum: *a liberal education.* ►*n.* A person with liberal ideas or opinions. [< Lat. *liber*, free.] —**lib′er·al·ism** *n.* —**lib′er·al′i·ty** (lĭb′ə-răl′ĭ-tē) *n.* —**lib′er·al·i·za′tion** *n.* —**lib′er·al·ize** *v.* —**lib′er·al·ly** *adv.*

Syns: *freehanded, generous, munificent, openhanded* **Ant:** *stingy adj.*

lib·er·ate (lĭb′ə-rāt′) ►*v.* **-at·ed, -at·ing** To set free, as from oppression, confinement, or foreign control. [Lat. *līberāre* < *līber*, free.] —**lib′er·a′tion** *n.* —**lib′er·a′tion·ist** *n.* —**lib′er·a′tor** *n.*

Li·be·ri·a (lī-bîr′ē-ə) A country of W Africa on the Atlantic. Cap. Monrovia. —**Li·be′ri·an** *adj. & n.*

lib·er·tar·i·an (lĭb′ər-târ′ē-ən) ►*n.* One who advocates maximizing individual rights and minimizing the role of the state. [< LIBERTY.] —**lib′er·tar′i·an·ism** *n.*

lib·er·tine (lĭb′ər-tēn′) ►*n.* **1.** A dissolute or licentious person. **2.** One who defies established religious precepts; freethinker. [< Lat. *līber*, free.] —**lib′er·tine′** *adj.* —**lib′er·tin·ism′** *n.*

lib·er·ty (lĭb′ər-tē) ►*n., pl.* **-ties 1a.** The condition of being free from restriction or control; freedom. **b.** The right to act or believe as one chooses. **2.** Permission; authorization. **3.** often **liberties a.** Undue familiarity. **b.** Latitude; license. **4.** Authorized leave from naval duty. [< Lat. *lībertās* < *līber*, free.]

li·bi·do (lī-bē′dō, -bī′-) ►*n., pl.* **-dos 1.** The psychic and emotional energy associated with biological drives. **2.** Sexual desire. [Lat. *libīdō*, desire.] —**li·bid′i·nal** (-bĭd′n-əl) *adj.* —**li·bid′i·nous** *adj.*

Li·bra (lē′brə, lī′-) ►*n.* **1.** A constellation in the Southern Hemisphere near Scorpius and Virgo. **2.** The 7th sign of the zodiac. [< Lat. *lībra*, scales.]

li·brar·i·an (lī-brâr′ē-ən) ►*n.* A specialist in library work. —**li·brar′i·an·ship′** *n.*

li·brar·y (lī′brĕr′ē) ►*n., pl.* **-ies 1.** A place in which reading materials, such as books, periodicals, and newspapers, and often other materials such as musical and video recordings, are kept for use or lending. **2.** A collection of such materials. [< Lat. *librārium*, bookcase.]

li·bret·to (lī-brĕt′ō) ►*n., pl.* **-bret·tos** or **-bret·ti** (-brĕt′ē) The text of a dramatic musical work, such as an opera. [Ital., dim. of *libro*, book.] —**li·bret′tist** *n.*

Li·bre·ville (lē′brə-vĭl′, -vēl′) The capital of Gabon, in the NW part on the Gulf of Guinea.

Lib·y·a (lĭb′ē-ə) A country of N Africa on the Mediterranean Sea. Cap. Tripoli. —**Lib′y·an** *adj. & n.*

lice (līs) ►*n.* Pl. of **louse** (sense 1).

li·cense (lī′səns) ►*n.* **1a.** Official or legal permission to engage in a regulated activity. See Synonyms at **permission**. **b.** A document, card, plate, or tag issued as proof of official or legal permission. **c.** A contract allowing someone to use a proprietary product or service. **2.** Freedom of action or permission to act. **3.** Lack of due restraint in behavior. **4.** An excuse to do something wrong: *people who see low-fat labels as a license to eat larger amounts.* ►*v.* **-censed, -cens·ing 1.** To give permission to or for. **2.** To grant a license to or for. See Synonyms at **authorize**. [< Lat. *licentia*, permission < *licēre*, be permitted.] —**li′cens·a·ble** *adj.* —**li′cens·ee′** *n.* —**li′cens·er** *n.*

li·censed practical nurse (lī′sənst) ►*n.* A nurse who has completed a practical nursing program and is licensed by a state to provide routine patient care under the direction of a registered nurse or physician.

li·cen·tious (lī-sĕn′shəs) ►*adj.* Lacking moral, esp. sexual restraint. [< Lat. *licentia,* LICENSE.] —**li·cen′tious·ly** *adv.* —**li·cen′tious·ness** *n.*

li·chee (lē′chē) ►*n.* Var. of **lychee.**

li·chen (lī′kən) ►*n.* An organism made up of a fungus that grows symbiotically with either an alga or a photosynthetic bacterium and forms a crustlike or branching growth on rocks or tree trunks. [< Gk. *leikhēn.*] —**li′chen·ous** *adj.*

Lich·ten·stein (lĭk′tən-stīn′, -stēn′), **Roy** 1923–97. Amer. pop artist.

lic·it (lĭs′ĭt) ►*adj.* Legal. [< Lat. *licēre,* be permitted.] —**lic′it·ly** *adv.* —**lic′it·ness** *n.*

lick (lĭk) ►*v.* **1.** To pass the tongue over or along. **2.** To lap up. **3.** To lap or flicker at like a tongue. **4.** *Slang* To defeat soundly. ►*n.* **1.** The act of licking. **2.** A small quantity. **3.** A deposit of exposed natural salt licked by passing animals. **4.** *Slang* A blow. [< OE *liccian.*] —**lick′er** *n.*

lick·e·ty-split (lĭk′ĭ-tē-splĭt′) ►*adv. Informal* With great speed. [< LICK, fast + SPLIT.]

lick·ing (lĭk′ĭng) ►*n. Slang* **1.** A beating or spanking. **2.** A severe loss or defeat.

lic·o·rice (lĭk′ər-ĭs, -ĭsh) ►*n.* **1.** A plant having a sweet, distinctively flavored root. **2.** A candy made from or flavored with this root. [< Gk. *glukurrhiza : glukus,* sweet + *rhiza,* root.]

lid (lĭd) ►*n.* **1.** A removable cover for a hollow receptacle. **2.** An eyelid. [< OE *hlid.*]

li·do·caine (lī′də-kān′) ►*n.* A synthetic drug used as a local anesthetic and to treat arrhythmia. [(*acetani*)*lide,* a compound + (CO)CAINE.]

lie[1] (lī) ►*v.* **lay** (lā), **lain** (lān), **ly·ing** (lī′ĭng) **1.** To be or place oneself at rest in a flat, horizontal, or recumbent position; recline. **2.** To be placed on a surface that is usu. horizontal: *Dirty dishes lay on the table.* **3.** To be or remain in a specified condition. **4.** To occupy a position or place. ►*n.* The manner or position in which something is situated. —*idiom:* **lie low** To keep oneself or one's plans hidden. [< OE *licgan.*]

lie[2] (lī) ►*n.* A false statement deliberately presented as true. ►*v.* **lied, ly·ing** (lī′ĭng) **1.** To tell a lie. **2.** To convey a false image or impression: *Appearances often lie.* [< OE *lyge.*]

Liech·ten·stein (lĭk′tən-stīn′, lĭкн′tən-shtīn′) A small Alpine principality in central Europe between Austria and Switzerland. Cap. Vaduz.

lied (lēt) ►*n.,* pl. **lie·der** (lē′dər) A German lyric song. [< OHGer. *liod.*]

lie detector ►*n.* An instrument designed to detect when a person has answered a question falsely.

lief (lēf) ►*adv.* **-er, -est** Readily; willingly. [< OE *lēof,* dear.]

liege (lēj) ►*n.* **1.** A feudal lord. **2.** A vassal. ►*adj.* Loyal; faithful. [< LLat. *læticus,* of a serf < *lætus,* serf.]

lien (lēn, lē′ən) ►*n.* The right to hold another's property as security for a debt owed. [< Lat. *ligāmen,* bond.]

lieu (lōō) ►*n. Archaic* Place; stead. —*idiom:* **in lieu of** In place of; instead of. [< OFr.]

lieu·ten·ant (lōō-tĕn′ənt) ►*n.* **1a.** A rank, as in the US Navy, above lieutenant junior grade and below lieutenant commander. **b.** A first lieutenant. **c.** A second lieutenant. **2.** An officer in a police or fire department ranking below a captain. **3.** One who acts in place of a superior. [< OFr., deputy.] —**lieu·ten′an·cy** *n.*

lieutenant colonel ►*n.* A rank, as in the US Army, above major and below colonel.

lieutenant commander ►*n.* A rank, as in the US Navy, above lieutenant and below commander.

lieutenant general ►*n.* A rank, as in the US Army, above major general and below general.

lieutenant governor ►*n.* An elected official ranking just below the governor of a state in the US.

lieutenant junior grade ►*n.,* pl. **lieutenants junior grade** A rank, as in the US Navy, above ensign and below lieutenant.

life (līf) ►*n.,* pl. **lives** (līvz) **1.** *Biol.* The quality that distinguishes living organisms from dead organisms and inanimate matter, manifested in functions such as metabolism, growth, reproduction, and response to stimuli. **2.** Living organisms collectively: *marine life.* **3.** A living being, esp. a person: *A fire that claimed many lives.* **4.** The interval between birth and death. **5.** The time for which something exists or functions: *the useful life of a car.* **6.** A biography. **7.** Human existence, relationships, or activities: *everyday life.* **8.** A manner of living: *led a hard life.* **9.** A source of vitality. [< OE *līf.*] —**life′less** *adj.* —**life′less·ly** *adv.*

life·blood (līf′blŭd′) ►*n.* An indispensable or vital part.

life·boat (līf′bōt′) ►*n.* A boat used for abandoning ship or for rescue services.

life buoy ►*n.* A usu. ringlike cork or polystyrene life preserver.

life care ►*n.* The provision of services, such as housing and social activities, for the elderly.

life·guard (līf′gärd′) ►*n.* An expert swimmer employed to safeguard other swimmers.

life insurance ►*n.* Insurance that guarantees a specific sum of money to a designated beneficiary upon the death of the insured.

life·like (līf′līk′) ►*adj.* Accurately representing real life. See Synonyms at **vivid.**

life·line (līf′līn′) ►*n.* **1.** A line thrown to someone falling or drowning. **2.** A means or route by which necessary supplies are transported.

life·long (līf′lông′, -lŏng′) ►*adj.* Continuing for a lifetime.

life preserver ►*n.* A buoyant device designed to keep a person afloat in the water.

life-size (līf′sīz′) also **life-sized** (-sīzd′) ►*adj.* Being of the same size as an original.

life·style (līf′stīl′) ►*n.* A way of life or living of a person or group.

life-sup·port (līf′sə-pôrt′) ►*adj.* Relating to the methods, equipment, or conditions needed to sustain life. —**life support** *n.*

life·time (līf′tīm′) ►*n.* The period of time during which an individual is alive.

life·work (līf′wûrk′) ►*n.* The chief or entire work of a person's lifetime.

lift (lĭft) ►*v.* **1.** To direct or carry from a lower to a higher position; raise: *lifted a box.* **2a.** To revoke; rescind: *lift an embargo.* **b.** To bring an end to by removing forces: *lift a blockade.* **3a.** To raise in condition, rank, or esteem. **b.** To uplift; elate: *lifted her spirits.* **4.** *Informal* To steal or plagiarize. **5.** To disappear by or as if by rising: *The fog lifted an hour ago.* ►*n.* **1.** The act or process of rising or raising. **2.** Power or force that is available for raising. **3.** The extent or height to which something is raised or rises. **4.** An elevation of the spirits. **5.** A machine or device designed to raise or carry something. **6.** *Chiefly Brit.* An elevator. **7.** A ride in a vehicle that is given to help someone. **8.** An act of assistance: *gave her a lift with the heavy boxes.* **9.** The component of the total aerodynamic force acting on an aircraft, perpendicular to the relative wind and normally exerted in an upward direction. —*phrasal verb:* **lift off** To begin flight. [< ON *lypta*.] —**lift′a·ble** *adj.* —**lift′er** *n.*

lift·off (lĭft′ôf′, -ŏf′) ►*n.* The moment in which a rocket or other craft leaves the ground.

lig·a·ment (lĭg′ə-mənt) ►*n.* A sheet or band of tough, fibrous tissue connecting bones or cartilages at a joint or supporting an organ. [< Med.Lat. *ligāmentum*.]

lig·a·ture (lĭg′ə-chŏŏr′, -chər) ►*n.* **1.** The act of tying or binding. **2.** A cord, wire, or bandage used for binding. **3.** A character, such as æ, combining two or more letters. **4.** *Mus.* A slur. [< Lat. *ligāre*, bind.]

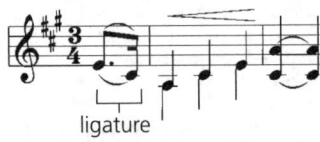

ligature
opening notes of "The Star-Spangled Banner"

light¹ (līt) ►*n.* **1.** Electromagnetic radiation that is visible to the human eye. **2.** The sensation of perceiving light; brightness. **3a.** A source of light, esp. a lamp or electric fixture. **b.** The illumination that is derived from such a source. **4.** Daylight: *departed at first light.* **5.** A source of fire, such as a match or cigarette lighter. **6.** A mechanical device that uses illumination as a signal or warning, esp. a traffic signal. **7.** Something that provides information or clarification: *research that produced new light on the issue.* **8.** A state of awareness or understanding: *in the light of experience.* **9.** Public attention. **10.** A way of looking at or considering a matter; aspect: *saw the situation in a different light.* **11.** A person who inspires or is adored by another: *You are the light of my life.* ►*v.* **light·ed** or **lit** (līt), **light·ing 1.** To set or be set on fire; ignite. **2.** To cause to give out light: *lit a lamp.* **3.** To illuminate. ►*adj.* **-er, -est 1.** Not dark; bright. **2.** Not dark in color. —*idiom:* **in (the) light of** In consideration of. [< OE *lēoht.*] —**light′ness** *n.*

Usage: Lighted and lit are equally acceptable as past tense and past participle of *light*. Both forms are well established as adjectives also: *a lit (or lighted) candle.*

light² (līt) ►*adj.* **-er, -est 1a.** Not heavy: *a light load.* **b.** Of relatively little weight for its size or bulk. **2a.** Having a structure that is slim and has little weight for its type or class: *light aircraft.* **b.** Carrying little equipment or armament: *light cavalry.* **3.** Low in quantity or intensity: *light snow.* **4.** Exerting little force; gentle: *light pat.* **5.** Indistinct; faint: *light type that's hard to see.* **6.** Not harsh or severe; gentle: *a light punishment.* **7.** Easy to perform or accomplish: *light chores.* **8.** Not serious or having little significance:

light comedy; light conversation. **9.** Containing a relatively small amount of an undesirable ingredient, such as alcohol: *light beer.* **10.** Free from worries or troubles; blithe: *a light heart.* **11.** Mildly dizzy or faint. **12.** Moving easily and quickly; nimble: *light on his feet.* **13.** Easily disturbed: *a light sleeper.* ►*adv.* **-er, -est 1.** Lightly. **2.** With little weight and few burdens: *traveling light.* ►*v.* **light·ed** or **lit** (līt), **light·ing 1.** To get down; alight. **2.** To land. —*phrasal verb:* **light into** *Informal* To assail. —*idiom:* **go light on** To use, acquire, or consume in small or moderate amounts: *went light on the garlic.* **2.** To treat leniently. [< OE *lēoht.*] —**light′ly** *adv.* —**light′ness** *n.*

light bulb ►*n.* A light-emitting device consisting of a gas-filled glass tube or bulb, used inside electric light fixtures and flashlights.

light-e·mit·ting diode (līt′ĭ-mĭt′ĭng) ►*n.* LED.

light·en¹ (līt′n) ►*v.* To make or become light or lighter; illuminate or brighten.

light·en² (līt′n) ►*v.* **1.** To make or become less heavy. **2.** To make or become less oppressive, troublesome, or severe.

light·er¹ (lī′tər) ►*n.* **1.** One that ignites. **2.** A device for lighting a cigarette, cigar, or pipe.

light·er² (lī′tər) ►*n.* A barge used to deliver goods to or from a cargo ship. [ME.]

light·face (līt′fās′) ►*n.* A typeface with relatively thin, light lines. —**light′faced′** *adj.*

light·head·ed (līt′hĕd′ĭd) ►*adj.* Faint or dizzy: *was lightheaded after standing so long.* —**light′-head′ed·ly** *adv.* —**light′head′ed·ness** *n.*

light·heart·ed (līt′här′tĭd) ►*adj.* Happy and carefree. —**light′heart′ed·ly** *adv.* —**light′-heart′ed·ness** *n.*

light heavyweight ►*n.* A boxer weighing from 161 to 175 lbs., between a middleweight and a heavyweight.

light·house (līt′hous′) ►*n.* A tall structure topped by a powerful light that guides ships.

light·ing (lī′tĭng) ►*n.* **1.** The state of being lighted; illumination. **2.** The method or equipment used to provide artificial illumination. **3.** The act or process of igniting.

light·ning (līt′nĭng) ►*n.* An abrupt, powerful natural electric discharge in the atmosphere, accompanied by a flash of light. ►*adj.* Very fast or sudden. [ME < *lightnen*, light up.] —**light′-ning** *v.*

lightning bug ►*n.* See **firefly.**

lightning rod ►*n.* **1.** A metal rod placed high on a structure to prevent damage by conducting lightning to the ground. **2.** One that elicits strong, usu. negative reactions, esp. to divert attention from more serious issues: *a comment that was a lightning rod for criticism.*

light·weight (līt′wāt′) ►*n.* **1.** One that weighs relatively little or less than average. **2.** A boxer weighing from 127 to 135 lbs., between a featherweight and a welterweight. **3.** A person of little intelligence, influence, or importance. —**light′weight′** *adj.*

light year ►*n.* **1.** The distance that light travels in a vacuum in one year, approx. 9.46 trillion km or 5.88 trillion mi. **2.** often **light years** *Informal* A long way.

lig·nin (lĭg′nĭn) ►*n.* A complex polymer that hardens and strengthens the cell walls of plants. [Lat. *lignum*, wood + -IN.]

lig·nite (lĭg′nīt′) ►*n.* A soft, brownish-black coal. [Lat. *lignum*, wood + –ITE¹.] —**lig·nit′ic** (-nĭt′ĭk) *adj.*

lig·num vi·tae (lĭg′nəm vī′tē) ►*n., pl.* **-taes** A tropical American tree having heavy durable wood. [NLat. *lignum vītae*, wood of life.]

lig·ro·in (lĭg′rō-ĭn) ►*n.* See **naphtha.** [Ger.]

Li·gu·ri·a (lĭ-gyŏŏr′ē-ə) A region of NW Italy on the **Ligurian Sea,** an arm of the Mediterranean Sea between NW Italy and Corsica. —**Li·gu′ri·an** *adj. & n.*

lik·a·ble also **like·a·ble** (lī′kə-bəl) ►*adj.* Pleasing; attractive. —**lik′a·ble·ness** *n.*

like¹ (līk) ►*v.* **liked, lik·ing 1.** To find pleasant; enjoy. **2.** To want, wish, or prefer. **3.** To feel about; regard: *How do you like these seats?* ►*n.* Something that is liked; preference. [< OE *lícian*, please.]

like² (līk) ►*prep.* **1.** Resembling closely; similar to: *Your house is like mine.* **2.** In the typical manner of: *It's not like you to do that.* **3.** Inclined to: *felt like running away.* **4.** As if the probability exists for: *looks like rain.* **5.** Such as: *saved things like old newspapers.* ►*adj.* Similar: *on this and like occasions.* ►*adv.* **1.** As if: *ran like crazy.* **2.** *Informal* Probably; likely: *Like as not, he'll probably change his mind.* **3.** Approximately: *The price is more like ten dollars.* ►*n.* One similar to or like another: *bolts, screws, and the like.* ►*conj. Informal* **1.** In the same way that; as: *To dance like she does takes practice.* **2.** As if: *It looks like we'll finish on time.* —*idioms:* **be like** *Informal* To say: *And he's like, "Leave me alone!"* **like so:** In the manner indicated: *You apply the paint like so.* [< OE *gelíc*, similar.]

Usage: Writers since the time of Chaucer have used *like* as a conjunction, but this usage has received so much criticism that many people prefer to restrict *like* to its function as a preposition, at least in formal writing, thus requiring *The dogs howled as* (not *like*) *we expected them to.* The use of *like* as a conjunction when the following verb is not expressed, as in *He took to politics like a duck to water,* is less likely to provoke objections, in part because it so closely resembles a preposition in these instances.

–like ►*suff.* Resembling or characteristic of: *ladylike.* [< LIKE².]

like·li·hood (līk′lē-hŏŏd′) ►*n.* **1.** The state of being probable; probability. **2.** Something probable.

like·ly (līk′lē) ►*adj.* **-li·er, -li·est 1.** Having a tendency or likelihood. **2.** Credible; plausible: *a likely excuse.* **3.** Apparently suitable: *a likely candidate for the job.* **4.** Promising: *a likely topic for investigation.* ►*adv. Informal* Probably.

like·mind·ed (līk′mīn′dĭd) ►*adj.* Of the same turn of mind.

lik·en (lī′kən) ►*v.* To see, mention, or show as similar; compare.

like·ness (līk′nĭs) ►*n.* **1.** Similarity; resemblance. **2.** An imitative appearance; semblance. **3.** A copy or picture of something; image.

like·wise (līk′wīz′) ►*adv.* **1.** In the same way; similarly. **2.** As well; also.

lik·ing (lī′kĭng) ►*n.* **1.** A feeling of attraction; fondness. **2.** Preference or taste: *The climate is not to my liking.*

li·lac (lī′lək, -lŏk, -lăk) ►*n.* **1.** A shrub that is widely cultivated for its clusters of fragrant, usu. purplish or white flowers. **2.** A pale purple. [< Ar. *līlak,* ult. < Skt. *nīla-,* dark blue.] —**li′lac** *adj.*

lilac

li·lan·ge·ni (lĭ-läng′gĕ-nē) ►*n., pl.* **em·a·lan·ge·ni** (ĕm′ə-läng-gĕn′ē) See table at **currency.** [Of Bantu orig.]

Li·li·u·o·ka·la·ni (lē-lē′ŏŏ-ō-kä-lä′nē), **Lydia Kamekaeha Paki** 1838–1917. Queen of the Hawaiian Islands (1891–93).

Li·long·we (lĭ-lông′wä) The capital of Malawi, in the S-central part.

lilt (lĭlt) ►*n.* **1.** A cheerful or lively manner of speaking. **2.** A light, happy tune or song. [< ME *lilten,* sound an alarm.]

lil·y (lĭl′ē) ►*n., pl.* **-ies 1.** Any of a genus of plants having variously colored, often trumpet-shaped flowers. **2.** A similar plant, such as the daylily. [< Lat. *līlium.*]

lil·y-liv·ered (lĭl′ē-lĭv′ərd) ►*adj.* Cowardly.

lily of the valley ►*n., pl.* **lilies of the valley** A plant having a cluster of small, fragrant, bell-shaped white flowers.

lily pad ►*n.* One of the floating leaves of a water lily.

Li·ma (lē′mə) The capital of Peru, in the west-central part.

li·ma bean (lī′mə) ►*n.* **1.** A plant having flat pods containing large, light green, edible seeds. **2.** The seed of this plant. [After LIMA, Peru.]

limb (lĭm) ►*n.* **1.** A large tree branch. **2.** One of the jointed appendages of an animal, such as an arm, leg, wing, or flipper. [< OE *lim.*]

lim·ber (lĭm′bər) ►*adj.* **1.** Bending or flexing readily; pliable. **2.** Capable of moving, bending, or contorting easily; supple. ►*v.* To make or become limber: *limbered up before the game.* [?] —**lim′ber·ness** *n.*

lim·bic system (lĭm′bĭk) ►*n.* A group of deep brain structures associated with emotion, behavior, and various functions of the autonomic nervous system. [< Lat. *limbus,* border.] —**lim′bic** *adj.*

lim·bo¹ (lĭm′bō) ►*n., pl.* **-bos 1.** often **Limbo** In the Roman Catholic Church, the abode of souls excluded from heaven but not condemned to further punishment. **2.** A condition of prolonged uncertainty or neglect. [< Lat. *limbus,* border.]

lim·bo² (lĭm′bō) ►*n., pl.* **-bos** A West Indian dance in which the dancers bend over backward and pass under a pole lowered slightly each time. [Prob. ult. of African orig.]

Lim·burg·er (lĭm′bûr′gər) ►*n.* A soft white cheese with a very strong odor and flavor. [After *Limburg,* Belgium.]

lime¹ (līm) ►*n.* **1.** A spiny evergreen citrus tree that is cultivated for its green, egg-shaped fruit. **2.** The fruit of this tree. [Prob. < Ar. *līmūn,* lemon.]

lime² (līm) ►*n.* See **linden.** [< OE *lind.*]

lime³ (līm) ►*n.* **1.** Calcium oxide. **2.** Birdlime. ►*v.* **limed, lim·ing** To treat with lime. [< OE *līm,* birdlime.] —**lim′y** *adj.*

lime·light (līm′līt′) ►*n.* **1.** A focus of public attention. **2.** An early type of stage light in which lime was heated to incandescence producing brilliant illumination.

lim·er·ick (lĭm′ər-ĭk) ►*n.* A humorous or nonsensical verse of five anapestic lines usu. with the rhyme scheme *aabba.* [After *Limerick,* Ireland.]

lime·stone (līm′stōn′) ►*n.* A common sedimentary rock consisting mostly of calcium carbonate.

lim·it (lĭm′ĭt) ►*n.* **1.** The point, edge, or line beyond which something cannot or may not proceed. **2. limits** A boundary: *city limits.* **3.** The greatest or least amount or number allowed. ►*v.* To confine or restrict within a boundary. [< Lat. *līmes, līmit-.*] —**lim′it·a·ble** *adj.* —**lim′i·ta′tion** *n.* —**lim′it·less** *adj.*

lim·it·ed (lĭm′ĭ-tĭd) ►*adj.* **1.** Confined within certain limits. **2.** Mediocre or qualified: *a limited success.* **3.** Designating trains or buses that make few stops. —**lim′i·ted·ly** *adv.*

limn (lĭm) ►*v.* **limned, limn·ing 1.** To describe by painting or drawing. **2.** To describe with words. [< Lat. *lūmināre,* illuminate.] —**limn′er** (lĭm′nər) *n.*

lim·o (lĭm′ō) ►*n., pl.* **lim·os** *Informal* A limousine.

lim·ou·sine (lĭm′ə-zēn′, lĭm′ə-zēn′) ►*n.* **1.** A large, luxurious passenger vehicle, esp. one that is driven by a chauffeur. **2.** A small bus that is used to carry passengers esp. to airports and hotels. [After *Limousin,* a region of France.]

limp (lĭmp) ►*v.* **1.** To walk lamely, favoring one leg. **2.** To proceed haltingly. ►*n.* An irregular, jerky, or awkward gait. ►*adj.* **-er, -est 1.** Lacking rigidity: *limp, wet hair.* **2.** Weak or spiritless: *limp opposition.* [Prob. < OE *lemphealt,* lame.] —**limp′ly** *adv.* —**limp′ness** *n.*

lim·pet (lĭm′pĭt) ►*n.* A marine gastropod mollusk having a conical shell and adhering to rocks in tidal areas. [Poss. ME *lempet.*]

lim·pid (lĭm′pĭd) ►*adj.* **1.** Characterized by transparent clearness. See Synonyms at **clear. 2.** Free from clouds or haze: *a limpid sky.* [Lat. *limpidus.*] —**lim·pid′i·ty, lim′pid·ness** *n.* —**lim′pid·ly** *adv.*

Lim·po·po (lĭm-pō′pō) A river of SE Africa rising near Johannesburg in NE South Africa and flowing about 1,770 km (1,100 mi) to the Indian Ocean in S Mozambique.

lin·age also **line·age** (lī′nĭj) ►*n.* The number of lines of printed or written material.

linch·pin (lĭnch′pĭn′) ►*n.* **1.** A locking pin that is inserted in the end of a shaft, as in an axle, to prevent a wheel from slipping off. **2.** A central cohesive element. [< OE *lynis,* linchpin + PIN.]

Lin·coln (lĭng′kən) The capital of NE, in the SE part SW of Omaha.

Lincoln, Abraham 1809–65. The 16th US president (1861–65).

Abraham Lincoln
1865 portrait

Lincoln, Mary Todd 1818–82. First lady of the US (1861–65) as the wife of President Abraham Lincoln.

Lind·bergh (lĭnd′bûrg′, lĭn′-), **Anne Spencer Morrow** 1906–2001. Amer. aviator and writer.

Lindbergh, Charles Augustus 1902–74. Amer. pioneer aviator.

lin·den (lĭn′dən) ►*n.* A shade tree having heart-shaped leaves and drooping clusters of yellowish, often fragrant flowers. [< OE *lind.*]

Lind·say (lĭn′zē), **(Nicholas) Vachel** 1879–1931. Amer. poet.

line¹ (līn) ►*n.* **1.** A geometric figure that is formed by a point moving along a fixed direction and the reverse direction. **2.** A thin continuous mark, as that made by a pen, pencil, or brush. **3.** A crease on the skin, esp. on the face; wrinkle. **4.** A border or boundary. **5.** A contour or outline. **6.** A cable, rope, string, cord, or wire. **7.** A clothesline. **8.** A pipe or pipes for conveying a fluid. **9.** An electric-power transmission line. **10.** A telephone connection. **11.** A system of transportation, usu. over a definite route. **12.** A course of progress or movement: *a line of flight.* **13.** A general manner or course of procedure: *different lines of thought.* **14.** An official policy: *the party line.* **15a.** Alignment: *brought the front wheels into line.* **b.** Correspondence: *a policy that is in line with reality.* **16.** One's trade or occupation: *What line of work on you in?* **17.** Merchandise of a similar nature: *a line of small tools.* **18.** A group of persons or things arranged in a row: *long lines at the box office.* **19.** A horizontal row of printed or written words or symbols. **20.** A series of persons, esp. from one family, who succeed each other: *a line of monarchs.* **21.** A brief letter; note. **22a.** A unit of verse ending in a textual or typographic break. **b.** often **lines** The dialogue of a theatrical presentation, such as a play. **23.** *Informal* Glib or insincere talk. **24.** The combat troops or warships at the front of a battle area. **25.** *Football* **a.** A line of scrimmage. **b.** The linemen. ►*v.* **lined, lin·ing 1.** To mark with lines. **2.** To place in a series or row. **3.** To form a bordering line along. —***phrasal verb:*** **line up 1.** To form a line. **2.** *Football* To take one's position in a formation before a snap or kickoff. **3.** To engage, schedule, or organize:

line up a speaker for graduation; line up support. **—idioms: down the line 1.** Throughout. **2.** In the future. **in line for** Next in order for. **on the line** In jeopardy. **out of line 1.** Uncalled for; improper. **2.** Out of control. [< Lat. *līnum*, linen, thread.]

line² (līn) ►v. **lined, lin·ing 1.** To fit or sew a covering to the inside surface of. **2.** To cover the inner surface of. [< OE *līn*, flax < Lat. *līnum*.]

lin·e·age¹ (lĭn′ē-ĭj) ►n. Direct descent from a particular ancestor; ancestry. [< OFr. *lignage* < *ligne*, LINE.]

line·age² (lī′nĭj) ►n. Var. of **linage**.

lin·e·al (lĭn′ē-əl) ►adj. **1.** In the direct line of descent from an ancestor. **2.** Linear. **—lin′e·al·ly** adv.

lin·e·a·ment (lĭn′ē-ə-mənt) ►n. A distinctive shape, contour, or line, esp. of the face. [< Lat. *līnea*, LINE.]

lin·e·ar (lĭn′ē-ər) ►adj. **1.** Of or resembling a line; straight. **2.** Having only one dimension. [< Lat. *līnea*, LINE¹.] **—lin′e·ar·ly** adv.

linear equation ►n. An algebraic equation involving only terms of the first degree.

line·back·er (līn′băk′ər) ►n. Football A defensive player forming a second line of defense behind the players on the line of scrimmage.

line drive ►n. Baseball A batted ball hit sharply in a roughly straight line.

line-i·tem veto (līn′ī′təm) ►n. The power of a governmental executive, usu. a governor, to veto some parts of a bill while signing other parts into law.

line·man (līn′mən) ►n. **1.** One who installs or repairs telephone, telegraph, or electric power lines. **2.** One who inspects and repairs railroad tracks. **3.** Football A player positioned on the forward line.

lin·en (lĭn′ən) ►n. **1.** Thread or cloth made from flax. **2.** also **linens** Garments or household articles, such as bed sheets, made from linen or a similar cloth. [< OE *līnen*, flaxen, ult. < Lat. *līnum*, flax.] **—lin′en** adj.

line of scrimmage ►n. Football Either of two imaginary lines parallel to the goal line at the ends of the ball as it rests prior to being snapped and at which each team lines up for a new play.

line printer ►n. A high-speed printer that prints an entire line of type at one time.

lin·er¹ (lī′nər) ►n. **1.** One that makes lines. **2.** A large commercial ship or airplane, esp. one carrying passengers on a regular route.

lin·er² (lī′nər) ►n. **1.** One who puts in linings. **2.** Material used as a lining.

lines·man (līnz′mən) ►n. **1a.** Football An official who marks the downs and the position of the ball. **b.** Sports An official in various court games who calls shots that fall out of bounds. **2.** See **lineman** (sense 1).

line·up also **line-up** (līn′ŭp′) ►n. A group of people or things arrayed for a purpose, esp.: **a.** An array or sequential display of persons or photographs of persons shown to a potential witness to identify a suspect in a crime. **b.** Sports The members of a team who are chosen to start a game. **c.** A sequence of broadcasts or events for entertainment: the fall lineup of new TV shows.

–ling ►suff. **1.** One connected with: hireling. **2.** One having a specified quality: underling. **3.**

One that is young, small, or inferior: duckling. [< OE.]

lin·ger (lĭng′gər) ►v. **1.** To be slow in leaving, esp. out of reluctance; tarry. **2.** To persist: an aftertaste that lingers. [ME lengeren < lengen, prolong.] **—lin′ger·er** n. **—lin′ger·ing·ly** adv.

lin·ge·rie (län′zhə-rā′, län′zhə-rē) ►n. Women's undergarments or sleepwear designed to be sexually alluring. [< OFr. < linge, linen.]

lin·go (lĭng′gō) ►n., pl. **-goes** The specialized vocabulary of a particular group, esp. when unfamiliar. [< Lat. lingua, language.]

lin·gua fran·ca (lĭng′gwə frăng′kə) ►n., pl. **lingua fran·cas** (-kəz) A medium of communication between peoples of different languages. [Ital.]

lin·gual (lĭng′gwəl) ►adj. Of or pronounced with the tongue. [< Lat. lingua, tongue.] **—lin′gual** n. **—lin′gual·ly** adv.

lin·gui·ne also **lin·gui·ni** (lĭng-gwē′nē) ►n. Pasta in long, flat, thin strands. [Ital., pl. dim. of lingua, tongue.]

lin·guist (lĭng′gwĭst) ►n. **1.** A specialist in linguistics. **2.** A polyglot. [Lat. lingua, language + –IST.]

lin·guis·tics (lĭng-gwĭs′tĭks) ►n. (takes sing. v.) The study of the nature and structure of human speech. **—lin·guis′tic** adj. **—lin·guis′ti·cal·ly** adv.

lin·i·ment (lĭn′ə-mənt) ►n. A liquid medication that is rubbed into the skin to relieve pain or irritation. [< LLat. linīmentum < Lat. linere, anoint.]

lin·ing (lī′nĭng) ►n. A covering or coating for an inside surface.

link (lĭngk) ►n. **1.** One of the rings or loops forming a chain. **2a.** One of a connected series of units: links of sausage. **b.** A unit in a transportation or communications system. **c.** A tie or bond. **3a.** An association: My only link with the school is through the alumni group. **b.** A causal, parallel, or reciprocal relationship; a correlation: Researchers have found a link between obesity and diabetes. **4.** Comp. A text segment or graphical item that serves as a cross-reference, as between or within hypertext documents. ►v. **1.** To connect with a link or links. **2.** To associate: The detective linked the suspect to the crime. **3.** To make a hypertext link in. [ME linke, of Scand. orig.]

link·age (lĭng′kĭj) ►n. **1.** The act or process of linking or the condition of being linked. **2.** A system of connected elements used to transmit power or motion.

linking verb (lĭng′kĭng) ►n. See **copula**.

links (lĭngks) ►pl.n. A golf course. [< OE hlinc, ridge.]

Lin·nae·us (lĭ-nē′əs, -nā′-), **Carl** or **Carolus** 1707–78. Swedish botanist.

lin·net (lĭn′ĭt) ►n. A small brownish Old World finch. [< OFr. linette < lin, flax.]

li·no·le·um (lĭ-nō′lē-əm) ►n. A durable, washable material made in sheets, used as a covering esp. for floors. [Orig. a trademark.]

lin·seed (lĭn′sēd′) ►n. The seed of flax, esp. when used as the source of linseed oil. [< OE līnsǣd.]

lint (lĭnt) ►n. Clinging bits of fiber and fluff; fuzz. [< Lat. linteum, linen.] **—lint′y** adj.

lin·tel (lĭn′tl) ►n. The horizontal beam over the

top of a window or door. [< VLat. *līmitāris,* of a threshold.]

lintel

li·on (lī′ən) ►*n.* **1.** A large carnivorous feline mammal, of Africa and NW India, having a short tawny coat and, in the male, a heavy mane. **2.** A celebrity. —*idiom:* **lion's share** The greatest or best part. [< Gk. *leōn.*]

li·on·ess (lī′ə-nĭs) ►*n.* A female lion.

li·on·heart·ed (lī′ən-här′tĭd) ►*adj.* Extraordinarily courageous.

li·on·ize (lī′ə-nīz′) ►*v.* **-ized, -iz·ing** To treat (a person) as a celebrity. —**li′on·i·za′tion** *n.*

lip (lĭp) ►*n.* **1.** Either of two fleshy folds that surround the opening of the mouth. **2a.** A structure or part that encircles an orifice. **b.** A protruding part of certain flowers. **3a.** The tip of a pouring spout. **b.** A rim. **4.** *Slang* Insolent talk. [< OE *lippa.*]

lip·id (lĭp′ĭd) ►*n.* Any of a group of organic compounds that includes fats, oils, waxes, sterols, and triglycerides. [LIPO– + –IDE.] —**lip·id′ic** *adj.*

lipo– or **lip–** ►*pref.* **1.** Fat: *liposuction.* **2.** Lipid: *lipoprotein.* [< Gk. *lipos,* fat.]

lip·o·pro·tein (lĭp′ō-prō′tēn′, -tē-ĭn, lī′pō-) ►*n.* A lipid-protein complex by which lipids are transported in the bloodstream.

lip·o·suc·tion (lĭp′ō-sŭk′shən, lī′pō-) ►*n.* A surgical procedure that uses suction to remove excess fat from an area of the body.

lip reading ►*n.* A technique for understanding unheard speech by interpreting the lip and facial movements of the speaker. —**lip′-read′** *v.* —**lip reader** *n.*

lip service ►*n.* Insincere agreement or allegiance; hypocritical respect.

lip·stick (lĭp′stĭk′) ►*n.* A small stick of waxy lip coloring enclosed in a cylindrical case.

lip-synch also **lip-sync** (lĭp′sĭngk′) ►*v.* **-synched, -synch·ing** also **-synced, -sync·ing** To move the lips in synchronization with recorded speech or song.

liq·ue·fy also **liq·ui·fy** (lĭk′wə-fī′) ►*v.* To make or become liquid, esp.: **a.** To melt a solid by heating. **b.** To condense a gas by cooling. [< Lat. *liquefacere.*] —**liq′ue·fac′tion** *n.*

li·queur (lĭ-kûr′, -kyoor′) ►*n.* A strongly flavored alcoholic beverage, usu. served after dinner. [Fr., LIQUOR.]

liq·uid (lĭk′wĭd) ►*n.* A substance capable of flowing or of being poured. ►*adj.* **1.** Of or being a liquid. **2.** Liquefied, esp.: **a.** Melted by heating: *liquid wax.* **b.** Condensed by cooling: *liquid oxygen.* **3.** Readily convertible into cash: *liquid assets.* **4.** Having a flowing quality without abrupt breaks: *liquid prose.* [< Lat. *liquēre,* be liquid.] —**liq′uid·ness** *n.*

liq·ui·date (lĭk′wĭ-dāt′) ►*v.* **-dat·ed, -dat·ing** **1a.** To pay off (e.g., a debt); settle. **b.** To settle the affairs of (e.g., a business). **2.** To convert (assets) into cash. **3.** To eliminate, esp. by killing. —**liq′ui·da′tion** *n.* —**liq′ui·da′tor** *n.*

liquid crystal ►*n.* Any of various liquids in which the atoms or molecules are regularly arrayed along one or two dimensions, the order giving rise to optical properties associated with the crystals.

liq·uid-crys·tal display (lĭk′wĭd-krĭs′təl) ►*n.* A flat-panel display, made of an array of cells containing liquid crystals that align to block or transmit light in response to an electric current.

li·quid·i·ty (lĭ-kwĭd′ĭ-tē) ►*n.* **1.** The state of being liquid. **2.** The quality of being readily convertible into cash.

liq·uor (lĭk′ər) ►*n.* **1.** An alcoholic beverage made by distillation rather than by fermentation. **2.** A liquid substance or solution. ►*v.* To steep (e.g., malt). [< Lat., a liquid.]

li·ra (lîr′ə, lē′rä) ►*n., pl.* **li·re** (lîr′ā, lē′rĕ) or **li·ras** **1.** See table at **currency.** **2.** The primary unit of currency in Italy, Malta, and San Marino before the adoption of the euro. [< Lat. *lībra,* pound.]

Lis·bon (lĭz′bən) The capital of Portugal, in the W part on an inlet of the Atlantic Ocean.

lisle (līl) ►*n.* A fine, smooth, tightly twisted thread spun from long-stapled cotton. [After *Lisle* (Lille), France.]

lisp (lĭsp) ►*n.* A speech defect or mannerism in which the sounds (s) and (z) are pronounced as (th) and (th). [< OE *wlisp.*] —**lisp** *v.* —**lisp′er** *n.*

lis·some also **lis·som** (lĭs′əm) ►*adj.* **1.** Moving with ease; graceful. **2.** Easily bent; supple. [Alteration of LITHESOME.] —**lis′some·ly** *adv.* —**lis′some·ness** *n.*

list¹ (lĭst) ►*n.* A series of names, words, or other items written, printed, or imagined one after the other. ►*v.* **1.** To make a list of; itemize. **2.** To have a stated list price. [< OItal. *lista.*]

list² (lĭst) ►*n.* An inclination to one side, as of a ship; tilt. ►*v.* To lean or cause to lean to the side. [?]

lis·ten (lĭs′ən) ►*v.* **1.** To make an effort to hear something. **2.** To pay attention: *Listen to your teacher.* [< OE *hlysnan.*] —**lis′ten·er** *n.*

list·ing (lĭs′tĭng) ►*n.* **1.** An entry in a list. **2.** A list.

list·less (lĭst′lĭs) ►*adj.* Lacking energy or enthusiasm; lethargic. [Poss. ME *liste,* desire + –NESS.] —**list′less·ly** *adv.* —**list′less·ness** *n.*

list price ►*n.* A basic published price, often subject to discount.

list·serv·er (lĭst′sûr′vər) ►*n.* A computer program that automatically handles subscription requests and e-mail delivery for members of a discussion group.

Liszt (lĭst), **Franz** 1811–86. Hungarian composer and pianist.

lit¹ (lĭt) ►*v.* P.t. and p.part. of **light¹**. See Usage Note at **light¹**.

lit² (lĭt) ►*v.* P.t. and p.part. of **light²**.

lit. ►*abbr.* **1.** liter **2a.** literal **b.** literally **3.** literary **4.** literature

lit·a·ny (lĭt′n-ē) ►*n., pl.* **-nies 1.** A prayer consisting of petitions recited by a leader alternating with responses by the congregation. **2.** A repetitive series. [< Gk. *litaneia*, entreaty.]

lit·as (lĭt′äs) ►*n.* See table at **currency**. [Lithuanian.]

li·ter (lē′tər) ►*n.* See table at **measurement**. [< Gk. *litra*, a unit of weight.]

lit·er·a·cy (lĭt′ər-ə-sē) ►*n.* **1.** The ability to read and write. **2.** The condition of being knowledgeable in a certain field: *cultural literacy.*

lit·er·al (lĭt′ər-əl) ►*adj.* **1.** Limited to the simplest or most obvious meaning of a word or words. **2.** Word for word; verbatim: *a literal translation.* **3.** Consisting of or expressed by letters: *literal notation.* [< Lat. *littera*, letter.] —**lit′er·al·ly** *adv.* —**lit′er·al·ness** *n.*

lit·er·ar·y (lĭt′ə-rĕr′ē) ►*adj.* **1.** Of or relating to literature. **2a.** Relating to writers or the profession of literature. **b.** Bookish; pedantic. [Lat. *litterārius.*] —**lit′er·ar′i·ly** (-râr′ə-lē) *adv.*

lit·er·ate (lĭt′ər-ĭt) ►*adj.* **1.** Able to read and write. **2.** Knowledgeable in a given field: *computer literate.* **3.** Well-written. [< Lat. *litterātus*, lettered.] —**lit′er·ate** *n.* —**lit′er·ate·ly** *adv.*

lit·er·a·ti (lĭt′ə-rä′tē) ►*pl.n.* The literary intelligentsia. [Lat. *litterāti*, lettered people.]

lit·er·a·ture (lĭt′ər-ə-chŏor′, -chər) ►*n.* **1.** The body of written works of a particular language, period, culture, or field of study. **2.** Imaginative or creative writing. **3.** Printed material. [< Lat. *litterātūra.*]

–lith ►*suff.* Rock; stone: *megalith.* [< Gk. *lithos*, stone.]

lithe (līth) ►*adj.* **lith·er, lith·est 1.** Graceful. **2.** Readily bent; supple. [< OE *līthe.*] —**lithe′ly** *adv.* —**lithe′ness** *n.*

lithe·some (līth′səm) ►*adj.* Lithe; lissome.

–lithic ►*suff.* Stone Age: *Paleolithic.* [Gk. *lithos*, stone + –IC.]

lith·i·um (lĭth′ē-əm) ►*n.* **1.** *Symbol* **Li** A soft, silvery, highly reactive metallic element used in ceramics, alloys, and thermonuclear weapons. At. no. 3. See table at **element**. **2.** This element in the form of a carbonate salt, used as a drug primarily to treat bipolar disorder.

litho– or **lith–** ►*pref.* Stone: *lithography.* [< Gk. *lithos*, stone.]

lith·o·graph (lĭth′ə-grăf′) ►*n.* A print produced by lithography. —**lith′o·graph′** *v.* —**li·thog′raph·er** (lĭ-thŏg′rə-fər) *n.* —**lith′o·graph′ic, lith′o·graph′i·cal** *adj.*

li·thog·ra·phy (lĭ-thŏg′rə-fē) ►*n.* A printing process in which the image is rendered on a flat surface and treated to retain ink while the nonimage areas are treated to repel ink.

lith·o·sphere (lĭth′ə-sfîr′) ►*n.* The outer part of the earth; the earth's crust and upper mantle.

Lith·u·a·ni·a (lĭth′ŏo-ā′nē-ə) A country of N Europe on the Baltic Sea. Cap. Vilnius.

Lith·u·a·ni·an (lĭth′ŏo-ā′nē-ən) ►*n.* **1.** A native or inhabitant of Lithuania. **2.** The Baltic language of the Lithuanians. —**Lith′u·a′ni·an** *adj.*

lit·i·gant (lĭt′ĭ-gənt) ►*n.* A party in a lawsuit.

lit·i·gate (lĭt′ĭ-gāt′) ►*v.* **-gat·ed, -gat·ing** To prosecute or defend a legal case. [Lat. *lītigāre, lītigāt-* : *līs, līt-*, lawsuit + *agere*, pursue.] —**lit′i·ga′tion** *n.* —**lit′i·ga′tor** *n.*

li·ti·gious (lĭ-tĭj′əs) ►*adj.* **1.** Of or marked by litigation. **2.** Tending to engage in lawsuits. —**li·ti′gious·ly** *adv.* —**li·ti′gious·ness** *n.*

lit·mus (lĭt′məs) ►*n.* A water-soluble blue powder derived from lichens that changes to red with increasing acidity and to blue with increasing basicity. [Of Scand. orig.]

litmus paper ►*n.* White paper saturated with litmus, used as a pH or acid/base indicator.

litmus test ►*n.* **1.** A test for chemical acidity or basicity using litmus paper. **2.** A test that uses a single indicator to prompt a decision.

li·tre (lē′tər) ►*n. Chiefly Brit.* Var. of **liter**.

lit·ter (lĭt′ər) ►*n.* **1a.** Carelessly discarded refuse, such as wastepaper. **b.** A disorderly accumulation; pile. **2.** The offspring produced at one birth by a mammal. **3a.** Straw or other material used as bedding for animals. **b.** A material used to absorb an animal's excretions. ►*v.* To make untidy by discarding rubbish carelessly. [< Med. Lat. *lectāria* < Lat. *lectus*, bed.] —**lit′ter·er** *n.*

lit·ter·bug (lĭt′ər-bŭg′) ►*n. Informal* One who litters public areas.

lit·tle (lĭt′l) ►*adj.* **lit·tler** or **less** (lĕs) also **less·er** (lĕs′ər), **lit·tlest** or **least** (lēst) **1.** Small in size, quantity, or degree. See Synonyms at **small**. **2.** Short in extent or duration; brief: *little time.* **3.** Unimportant; trivial. **4.** Narrow; petty: *mean little comments.* **5.** Without much power or influence. **6.** Young. **7.** Younger: *my little brother.* ►*adv.* **less, least** Not much: *slept little.* ►*n.* A small quantity: *Give me a little.* —*idiom:* **little by little** Gradually. [< OE *lȳtel.*] —**lit′tle·ness** *n.*

Little Dipper ►*n.* A cluster of seven stars in Ursa Minor having the shape of a ladle with Polaris at the tip of its handle.

Little Rock The capital of Arkansas, in the central part on the Arkansas R.

lit·to·ral (lĭt′ər-əl) ►*adj.* Of or on a shore, esp. a seashore. ►*n.* A coastal region; shore. [< Lat. *lītus, lītor-*, shore.]

lit·ur·gy (lĭt′ər-jē) ►*n., pl.* **-gies 1.** A prescribed form for public worship. **2.** often **Liturgy** The Christian Eucharist. [< Gk. *leitourgia*, public service : *lēiton*, town hall + *ergon*, work.] —**li·tur′gi·cal** (lĭ-tûr′jĭ-kəl) *adj.*

liv·a·ble also **live·a·ble** (lĭv′ə-bəl) ►*adj.* **1.** Suitable to live in; habitable. **2.** Endurable. —**liv′a·ble·ness** *n.*

live¹ (lĭv) ►*v.* **lived, liv·ing 1.** To be alive; exist. **2.** To continue to be alive. **3.** To subsist. **4.** To reside. **5.** To conduct one's life in a particular manner: *lived frugally.* **6.** To remain in memory or usage: *an event that lives on in our minds.* —*phrasal verbs:* **live down** To overcome the shame or effect of over time. **live with** To resign oneself to. [< OE *libban.*]

live² (līv) ►*adj.* **1.** Having life; alive. See Synonyms at **living**. **2.** Of current interest. **3.** Glowing; burning: *live coals.* **4.** Not yet exploded: *live ammunition.* **5.** Carrying an electric current. **6.** Broadcast while being performed. [Alteration of ALIVE.]

live·blog (līv′blŏg′) ►*v.* **-blogged, -blog·ging** To write or maintain a blog about an event as the event is happening. —**live′blog′ger** *n.*

live-in (lĭv′ĭn′) ►*adj.* **1.** Residing in the place

where one is employed. **2.** Residing together with another esp. in a sexual relationship. —**live′·in′** *n.*

live·li·hood (līv′lē-ho͝od′) ►*n.* Means of support; subsistence. [< OE *līflād,* course of life.]

live·long (līv′lông′) ►*adj.* Complete; whole: *the livelong day.* [ME : OE *lēof,* dear + LONG¹.]

live·ly (līv′lē) ►*adj.* **-li·er, -li·est 1.** Full of energy; vigorous or animated. **2.** Quick-paced: *a lively tune.* ►*adv.* With energy or vigor; briskly: *Step lively!* —**live′li·ly** *adv.* —**live′li·ness** *n.*

li·ven (lī′vən) ►*v.* To make or become more lively.

live oak (līv) ►*n.* Any of several American evergreen oaks.

liv·er (līv′ər) ►*n.* A large, reddish-brown, glandular vertebrate organ that secretes bile and is active in the formation of certain blood proteins and the metabolism of carbohydrates, fats, and proteins. [< OE *lifer.*]

Liv·er·pool (līv′ər-po͞ol′) A city of NW England WSW of Manchester.

liver spot ►*n.* A benign brownish patch on the skin, often occurring in old age and usu. in fair-skinned people with sun-damaged skin.

liv·er·wort (līv′ər-wûrt′, -wôrt′) ►*n.* Any of various small, green, nonvascular plants that grow in moist environments and are related to the mosses.

liv·er·wurst (līv′ər-wûrst′, -wo͝orst′) ►*n.* A sausage made of or containing ground liver.

liv·er·y (līv′ə-rē, līv′rē) ►*n., pl.* **-ies 1.** A distinctive uniform worn by the male servants of a household. **2a.** The boarding and care of horses for a fee. **b.** The hiring out of horses and carriages. **3.** A business that rents out vehicles such as automobiles or boats. [< OFr. *livree,* delivery.] —**liv′er·ied** *adj.* —**liv′er·y·man** *n.*

lives (līvz) ►*n.* Pl. of **life.**

live·stock (līv′stŏk′) ►*n.* Domestic animals, such as cattle or horses, raised for home use or for profit.

live wire (līv) ►*n.* **1.** A wire carrying electric current. **2.** *Informal* A vivacious, alert, or energetic person.

liv·id (līv′ĭd) ►*adj.* **1.** Discolored, as from a bruise; black-and-blue. **2.** Ashen or pallid. **3.** Extremely angry. [< Lat. *līvidus.*] —**li·vid′i·ty, liv′id·ness** *n.* —**liv′id·ly** *adv.*

liv·ing (līv′ĭng) ►*adj.* **1.** Possessing life. **2.** In active function or use: *a living language.* **3.** Relating to the routine conduct or maintenance of life: *abhorrent living conditions.* **4.** True to life; realistic. ►*n.* **1.** The condition or action of maintaining life: *the high cost of living.* **2.** A manner or style of life: *plain living.* **3.** A livelihood.
Syns: *alive, live, animate, vital* **adj.**

living room ►*n.* A room in a private residence intended for social and leisure activities.

Liv·ing·stone (līv′ĭng-stən), **David** 1813–73. British missionary and explorer.

living will ►*n.* A document in which the signer states his or her wishes regarding medical treatment that sustains or prolongs life, esp. by invasive or extraordinary means.

li·vre (lē′vər, -vrə) ►*n.* See table at **currency.** [Fr.]

Liv·y (līv′ē) 59 BC–AD 17. Roman historian.

liz·ard (līz′ərd) ►*n.* **1.** Any of numerous reptiles having a scaly elongated body, movable eyelids,

four legs, and a tapering tail. **2.** Leather made from the skin of a lizard. [< Lat. *lacerta.*]

Lju·blja·na (lo͞o′blē-ä′nə) The capital of Slovenia, in the central part.

lla·ma (lä′mə) ►*n.* A long-necked South American mammal related to the camel, raised for its warm wool and used as a beast of burden. [< Quechua.]

Lloyd George (loid′ jôrj′), **David** 1863–1945. British prime minister (1916–22).

lm ►*abbr.* Phys. lumen

LNG ►*abbr.* liquefied natural gas

lo (lō) ►*interj.* Used to attract attention or to show surprise. [< OE *lā.*]

load (lōd) ►*n.* **1a.** A supported weight or mass. **b.** The force to which a structure is subjected. **2.** Something that is carried, as by a vehicle, person, or animal. **3.** The share of work allocated to or required of a person, machine, group, or organization. **4.** A heavy responsibility; burden. **5.** often **loads** *Informal* A great number or amount. ►*v.* **1.** To put (something) into or onto a structure or conveyance. **2.** To fill nearly to overflowing. **3.** To weigh down; burden. **4.** To charge (a firearm) with ammunition. **5.** To insert material into: *loaded the camera with film.* **6.** *Games* To make (dice) heavier on one side. **7.** To charge with meanings or implications. **8.** *Comp.* To transfer (data) from storage into a computer's memory. [< OE *lād.*] —**load′er** *n.*

load·ed (lō′dĭd) ►*adj.* **1.** Carrying a load. **2.** Having great seriousness or implication. **3.** *Slang* Intoxicated; drunk. **4.** *Slang* Rich.

loaf¹ (lōf) ►*n., pl.* **loaves** (lōvz) A shaped mass of bread or other food baked in one piece. [< OE *hlāf.*]

loaf² (lōf) ►*v.* To pass time idly. [< obsolete *landloafer,* vagabond.] —**loaf′er** *n.*

loam (lōm) ►*n.* Soil composed of sand, clay, silt, and organic matter. [< OE *lām,* clay.] —**loam′y** *adj.*

loan (lōn) ►*n.* **1.** An instance of lending. **2.** A sum of money that is lent, usu. with an interest fee. ►*v.* To lend (money or property). [< ON *lān.*] —**loan′er** *n.*

loan·word (lōn′wûrd′) ►*n.* A word, such as *honcho,* adopted from another language and at least partly naturalized.

loath (lōth, lō*th*) ►*adj.* Unwilling or reluctant. [< OE *lāth,* loathsome.]

loathe (lō*th*) ►*v.* **loathed, loath·ing** To dislike greatly; abhor. [< OE *lāthian.*]

loath·ing (lō′*th*ĭng) ►*n.* Great dislike; abhorrence. —**loath′ing·ly** *adv.*

loath·some (lōth′səm, lō*th*′-) ►*adj.* Causing loathing; abhorrent. See Synonyms at **offensive.** —**loath′some·ness** *n.*

lob (lŏb) ►*v.* **lobbed, lob·bing** To hit, throw, or propel in a high arc. [Earlier *lob,* lump, hang heavily, prob. ult. of imit. orig.] —**lob** *n.*

lob·by (lŏb′ē) ►*n., pl.* **-bies 1.** A hall, foyer, or waiting room at or near the entrance to a building, such as a hotel. **2.** A group of persons engaged in trying to influence legislators. ►*v.* **-bied, -by·ing** To try to influence public officials for or against a specific cause. [Med. Lat. *lobia,* cloister, of Gmc. orig.] —**lob′by·er, lob′by·ist** *n.*

lobe (lōb) ►*n.* **1.** A rounded part or projection, esp. of an organic structure: *the lobe of an ear.*

2. A subdivision of a bodily organ bounded by structural boundaries. [< Gk. *lobos*.] —**lobed** *adj.*

lo·bot·o·my (lə-bŏt′ə-mē, lō-) ►*n., pl.* **-mies** Surgery on the frontal lobe of the brain to sever one or more nerve tracts, formerly performed to treat certain mental disorders.

lob·ster (lŏb′stər) ►*n.* **1.** An edible marine crustacean having a pair of pincers and a cylindrical body. **2.** Any of several related crustaceans. [< OE *loppestre*.]

lo·cal (lō′kəl) ►*adj.* **1.** Of or relating to a particular place: *a local custom.* **2.** Not widespread: *local outbreaks of flu.* **3.** Of or affecting a specific part of the body: *a local infection; local anesthetic.* **4.** Making many stops on a route: *a local train.* ►*n.* **1.** A public conveyance that stops at all stations. **2.** A local chapter or branch of an organization, esp. of a labor union. **3.** *Informal* A person from a particular locality. [< Lat. *locus*, place.] —**lo′cal·ly** *adv.*

lo·cale (lō-kăl′) ►*n.* A place, esp. with reference to an event. [< OFr. *local*, LOCAL.]

lo·cal·i·ty (lō-kăl′ĭ-tē) ►*n., pl.* **-ties** A particular neighborhood, place, or district.

lo·cal·ize (lō′kə-līz′) ►*v.* **-ized, -iz·ing 1.** To make local. **2.** To confine or restrict to a locality. —**lo′cal·i·za′tion** *n.*

lo·cate (lō′kāt′, lō-kāt′) ►*v.* **-cat·ed, -cat·ing 1.** To determine the position of. **2.** To find by searching. **3.** To place; situate. **4.** To become established; settle. [Lat. *locāre*, to place.] —**lo′cat′er, lo′cat′or** *n.*

lo·ca·tion (lō-kā′shən) ►*n.* **1.** The act or process of locating. **2.** A place where something is located. **3.** A site away from a studio at which part or all of a movie is shot. —**lo·ca′tion·al** *adj.*

loc. cit. ►*abbr. Lat.* loco citato (in the place cited)

loch (lŏкн, lŏk) ►*n. Scots* **1.** A lake. **2.** An arm of the sea similar to a fjord. [< Sc.Gael. *loch*.]

lo·ci (lō′sī′, -kē, -kī′) ►*n.* Pl. of **locus.**

lock¹ (lŏk) ►*n.* **1.** A device operated by a key, combination, or keycard and used, as on a door, for holding, closing, or securing. **2.** A section of a canal closed off with gates for raising or lowering the water level. **3.** A mechanism in a firearm for exploding the charge. ►*v.* **1.** To fasten or become fastened with a lock. **2.** To confine or exclude by or as if by means of a lock. **3.** To clasp or link firmly: *lock arms.* **4.** To bind in close struggle or battle. **5.** To become entangled; interlock. **6.** To become rigid or immobile. [< OE *loc*, bolt, bar.] —**lock′a·ble** *adj.*

lock² (lŏk) ►*n.* A length or curl of hair; tress. [< OE *locc*.]

Locke (lŏk), **John** 1632–1704. English philosopher.

lock·er (lŏk′ər) ►*n.* **1.** A small, usu. metal compartment that can be locked, esp. one at a public place for the safekeeping of clothing and valuables. **2.** A flat trunk for storage. **3.** A refrigerated cabinet or room for storing frozen foods.

locker room ►*n.* A room with lockers, as in a gymnasium, in which to change clothes and store equipment.

lock·et (lŏk′ĭt) ►*n.* A small ornamental case for a keepsake, usu. worn as a pendant.

locket
top: closed
bottom: open

lock·jaw (lŏk′jô′) ►*n.* **1.** See **tetanus. 2.** A symptom of tetanus, in which the jaw is held tightly closed by a spasm of muscles.

lock·out (lŏk′out′) ►*n.* The closing down of a workplace by an employer during a labor dispute.

lock·smith (lŏk′smĭth′) ►*n.* One who makes or repairs locks.

lock·step (lŏk′stĕp′) ►*n.* A way of marching in which the marchers follow each other closely.

lo·co (lō′kō) ►*adj. Slang* Mentally deranged. [Sp.]

lo·co·mo·tion (lō′kə-mō′shən) ►*n.* The act of moving or ability to move from place to place. [Lat. *locus*, place + MOTION.]

lo·co·mo·tive (lō′kə-mō′tĭv) ►*n.* A self-propelled vehicle, usu. electric or diesel-powered, that moves railroad cars. ►*adj.* Of or involved in locomotion.

lo·co·mo·tor (lō′kə-mō′tər) ►*adj.* Locomotive.

lo·co·weed (lō′kō-wēd′) ►*n.* Any of several plants of W North America that are poisonous to livestock.

lo·cus (lō′kəs) ►*n., pl.* **-ci** (-sī′, -kē, -kī′) **1.** A place. **2.** A focus of intense concentration. **3.** *Math.* The set of all points that satisfy specified conditions. **4.** The position that a given gene occupies on a chromosome. [Lat.]

lo·cust (lō′kəst) ►*n.* **1.** A grasshopper that travels in destructive swarms that devour vegetation. **2.** The periodical cicada. **3.** Any of several trees bearing long pods, such as the carob. [< Lat. *locusta*.]

lo·cu·tion (lō-kyōō′shən) ►*n.* **1.** A particular word, phrase, or expression. **2.** Style of speaking; phraseology. [< Lat. *loquī, locūt-*, speak.]

lode (lōd) ►*n.* A vein of mineral ore deposited between layers of rock. [< OE *lād*, way.]

lo·den (lōd′n) ►*n.* **1.** A durable, water-repellent, coarse woolen fabric. **2.** A deep olive green. [Ger., coarse fabric.]

lode·star (lōd′stär′) ►*n.* **1.** A star, esp. Polaris, used as a point of reference. **2.** A principle or person that serves as a guide. [ME *lodesterre*.]

lode·stone (lōd′stōn′) ►*n.* A magnetized piece of magnetite. [Obsolete *lode,* course + STONE.]

lodge (lŏj) ►*n.* **1a.** A cottage or cabin used as a temporary abode or shelter. **b.** An inn. **2.** Any of various Native American dwellings, such as a hogan, wigwam, or longhouse. **3a.** A local chapter of certain fraternal organizations. **b.** The meeting hall of such a chapter. **4.** The den of certain animals, such as the dome-shaped one built by beavers. ►*v.* **lodged, lodg·ing 1.** To provide with or rent quarters temporarily, esp. for sleeping. **2.** To live in a place temporarily. **3.** To register (e.g., a complaint) before an authority. **4.** To vest (authority). **5.** To be or become embedded. [< OFr. *loge.*]

lodg·er (lŏj′ər) ►*n.* One that lodges, esp. one who rents and lives in a furnished room.

lodg·ing (lŏj′ĭng) ►*n.* **1.** often **lodgings** Sleeping accommodations. **2.** Rented rooms.

Łódź (lŏdz, wŏŏch) A city of central Poland WSW of Warsaw.

lo·ess (lō′əs, lĕs, lŭs) ►*n.* A windblown deposit of fine-grained silt or clay. [Ger. *Löss.*]

loft (lôft, lŏft) ►*n.* **1a.** A large, usu. unpartitioned floor in a commercial building. **b.** A loft converted into an apartment or studio. **2.** An open space under a roof; attic. **3.** A gallery or balcony, as in a church. **4.** A high arc given to a struck or thrown object, such as a golf ball or baseball. ►*v.* **1.** To put, store, or keep in a loft. **2.** To propel in a high arc. [< ON *lopt,* upstairs room.]

loft·y (lôf′tē, lŏf′-) ►*adj.* **-i·er, -i·est 1.** Of imposing height. **2.** Exalted; noble. **3.** Arrogant; haughty. —**loft′i·ly** *adv.* —**loft′i·ness** *n.*

log¹ (lôg, lŏg) ►*n.* **1.** A section of a trunk or limb of a fallen or felled tree. **2.** A device trailed from a ship to determine its speed through water. **3.** A record of a ship's or aircraft's speed, progress, and navigation. **4.** A regularly kept record; journal. ►*v.* **logged, log·ging 1a.** To cut down timber (on). **b.** To cut (trees) into logs. **2.** To enter in a log. **3.** To travel (a specified distance, time, or speed). —*phrasal verbs:* **log in** or **on** To enter into a computer the information required to begin a session. **log out** or **off** To enter into a computer the command to end a session. [ME *logge.*] —**log′ger** *n.*

log² (lôg, lŏg) ►*n. Math.* A logarithm.

lo·gan·ber·ry (lō′gən-bĕr′ē) ►*n.* An edible blackberrylike red fruit. [After James H. *Logan* (1841–1928).]

log·a·rithm (lô′gə-rĭth′əm, lŏg′ə-) ►*n.* The power to which a base must be raised to produce a given number. [Gk. *logos,* reason + *arithmos,* number.] —**log′a·rith′mic, log′a·rith′mi·cal** *adj.* —**log′a·rith′mi·cal·ly** *adv.*

loge (lōzh) ►*n.* **1.** A small compartment, esp. a box in a theater. **2.** The front rows of the mezzanine in a theater. [< OFr. *lodge.*]

log·ger·head (lô′gər-hĕd′, lŏg′ər-) ►*n.* A marine turtle having a large head with powerful jaws. —*idiom:* **at loggerheads** Engaged in a head-on dispute. [Prob. dial. *logger,* wooden block + HEAD.]

log·ic (lŏj′ĭk) ►*n.* **1.** The study of the principles of reasoning. **2.** Valid reasoning, esp. as distinguished from invalid or irrational argumentation. **3.** The mathematical operations performed by a computer, such as sorting and comparing, that involve yes-no decisions. [<

Gk. *logos,* reason.] —**lo·gi′cian** (lō-jĭsh′ən) *n.*

log·i·cal (lŏj′ĭ-kəl) ►*adj.* **1.** Of, using, or in accordance with logic. **2.** Reasonable. **3.** Showing consistency of reasoning. —**log′i·cal·ly** *adv.* —**log′i·cal·ness** *n.*

Syns: *analytic, ratiocinative, rational adj.*

log·in (lôg′ĭn′, lŏg′-) also **log·on** (-ŏn′) ►*n.* The process of identifying oneself to a computer, as by entering one's username and password.

lo·gis·tics (lō-jĭs′tĭks, lə-) ►*n. (takes sing. or pl. v.)* The procurement, distribution, maintenance, and replacement of materiel and personnel. [< Gk. *logistikos,* skilled in calculating.] —**lo·gis′tic, lo·gis′ti·cal** *adj.* —**lo·gis′ti·cal·ly** *adv.*

log·jam (lôg′jăm′, lŏg′-) ►*n.* **1.** An immovable mass of floating logs crowded together. **2.** A deadlock; impasse.

lo·go (lō′gō′) ►*n., pl.* **-gos** A symbol or design that identifies a brand. [< LOGOTYPE.]

lo·go·type (lô′gə-tīp′, lŏg′ə-) ►*n.* **1.** A piece of type bearing two or more usu. separate elements. **2.** A logo. [< Gk. *logos,* word.]

log·roll·ing (lôg′rō′lĭng, lŏg′-) ►*n.* The trading of influence or votes among legislators to achieve passage of projects of interest to one another. —**log′roll′er** *n.*

–logue or **–log** ►*suff.* Speech; discourse: *travelogue.* [< Gk. *-logos < legein,* speak.]

lo·gy (lō′gē) ►*adj.* **-gi·er, -gi·est** Lethargic; sluggish. [Perh. < Du. *log,* heavy.]

–logy ►*suff.* **1.** Discourse; expression: *phraseology.* **2.** Science; theory; study: *geology.* [< Gk. *-logia < legein,* speak.]

loin (loin) ►*n.* **1a.** *Anat.* The part of the side and back between the ribs and pelvis. **b.** A cut of meat from this part of an animal. **2. loins a.** The region of the thighs and groin. **b.** The genitals. [< VLat. **lumbea,* of the loin < Lat. *lumbus,* loin.]

loin·cloth (loin′klôth′, -klŏth′) ►*n.* A strip of cloth worn around the loins.

Loire (lwär) A river, about 1,015 km (630 mi), rising in SE France and flowing to the Bay of Biscay.

loi·ter (loi′tər) ►*v.* **1a.** To stand idly about; linger aimlessly. **b.** To violate a law or ordinance prohibiting persons from remaining in an area without a clear purpose. **2.** To hover over or remain near an area. **3.** To proceed slowly or with many stops. **4.** To act slowly; take one's time. [Prob. < MDu. *loteren,* be loose.] —**loi′ter·er** *n.*

loll (lŏl) ►*v.* **1.** To recline in an indolent or relaxed way. **2.** To hang or droop laxly. [Prob. < MDu. *lollen,* doze.] —**loll′er** *n.*

lol·li·pop also **lol·ly·pop** (lŏl′ē-pŏp′) ►*n.* A piece of hard candy on the end of a small stick. [Perh. dial. *lolly,* tongue + POP¹.]

Lom·bar·dy (lŏm′bər-dē, lŭm′-) A region of N Italy bordering on Switzerland. —**Lom′bard** *adj. & n.*

Lo·mé (lō-mā′) The capital of Togo, in the S part on the Bight of Benin.

lo mein (lō′ mān′) ►*n.* A Chinese dish of wheat noodles boiled then seasoned and stir-fried. [Cantonese *lou⁴ min⁶.*]

Lon·don (lŭn′dən) The capital of the United Kingdom, on the Thames R. in SE England.

London, John Griffith "Jack." 1876–1916. Amer. writer.

lone (lōn) ►*adj.* **1.** Solitary: *a lone tree.* **2.** Isolated; unfrequented: *the lone prairie.* **3.** Sole: *the lone school in town.* [< ALONE.]

lone·ly (lōn′lē) ▸*adj.* **-li·er, -li·est 1a.** Sad at being alone. **b.** Producing such sadness. **2.** Without companions; solitary. **3.** Unfrequented by people; desolate. —**lone′li·ness** *n.*

lon·er (lō′nər) ▸*n.* One who avoids the company of other people.

lone·some (lōn′səm) ▸*adj.* **1.** Sad at feeling alone. **2.** Offering solitude; secluded. **3.** Solitary; lone. —**lone′some·ly** *adv.* —**lone′some·ness** *n.*

long¹ (lông, lŏng) ▸*adj.* **-er, -est 1.** Having great length. **2.** Of relatively great duration: *a long time.* **3.** Of a specified length or duration: *a mile long; an hour long.* **4.** Concerned with distant issues; far-reaching: *a long view of the plan.* **5.** Risky; chancy: *long odds.* **6.** Having an abundance or excess: *long on hope.* **7.** Having a comparatively great duration. Used of a vowel or consonant. ▸*adv.* **1.** For an extended period of time. **2.** For or throughout a specified period: *all night long.* **3.** At a distant point of time: *long before we were born.* ▸*n.* A long time. —*idioms:* **any longer** For more time: *can't wait any longer.* **as** (or **so**) **long as** Inasmuch as; since. **no longer** Not now as formerly: *We no longer smoke.* [< OE *lang.*]

long² (lông, lŏng) ▸*v.* To have an earnest desire; yearn. [< OE *langian.*]

long·bow (lông′bō′, lŏng′-) ▸*n.* A wooden, hand-drawn bow, often 6 ft or longer.

long distance ▸*n.* Telephone service between distant points. —**long′-dis′tance** *adj. & adv.*

lon·gev·i·ty (lŏn-jĕv′ĭ-tē, lôn-) ▸*n.* **1.** Long life. **2.** Long duration. [< Lat. *longaevus,* ancient.]

Long·fel·low (lông′fĕl′ō, lŏng′-), **Henry Wadsworth** 1807–82. Amer. poet.

long·hand (lông′hănd′, lŏng′-) ▸*n.* Cursive writing.

long·horn (lông′hôrn′, lŏng′-) ▸*n.* A Texas Longhorn.

long·house (lông′hous′) ▸*n.* A long communal dwelling, esp. of certain Native American, Polynesian, and Indonesian peoples.

long·ing (lông′ĭng, lŏng′-) ▸*n.* A persistent yearning or desire. —**long′ing** *adj.* —**long′ing·ly** *adv.*

Long Island An island of SE NY separated from CT by **Long Island Sound,** an arm of the Atlantic.

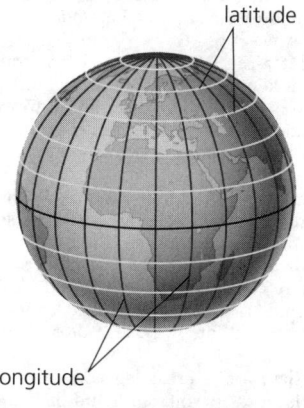

latitude

longitude

longitude

lon·gi·tude (lŏn′jĭ-tōōd′, -tyōōd′, lôn′-) ▸*n.* Angular distance east or west, measured with respect to the Prime Meridian at Greenwich, England. [< Lat. *longitūdō* < *longus,* long.] —**lon′gi·tu′di·nal** *adj.* —**lon′gi·tu′di·nal·ly** *adv.*

long jump ▸*n. Sports* A jump in track and field that is made for distance, usu. from a moving start.

long-lived (lông′līvd′, -lĭvd′, lŏng′-) ▸*adj.* Having a long life. —**long′-lived′ness** *n.*

long-play·ing (lông′plā′ĭng, lŏng′-) ▸*adj.* Of or being a phonograph record that turns at 33⅓ revolutions per minute.

long-range (lông′rānj′, lŏng′-) ▸*adj.* **1.** Of or designed for great distances: *long-range missiles.* **2.** Involving an extended span of time: *long-range planning.*

long·shore·man (lông′shôr′mən, lŏng′-) ▸*n.* A dockworker.

long shot ▸*n.* An entry, as in a horserace, with only a slight chance of winning.

long-stand·ing or **long·stand·ing** (lông′-stăn′dĭng, lŏng′-) ▸*adj.* Of long duration or existence.

long-suf·fer·ing (lông′sŭf′ər-ĭng, lŏng′sŭf′-ər-ĭng) ▸*adj.* Patiently enduring pain or difficulties.

long-term (lông′tûrm′, lŏng′-) ▸*adj.* Involving or being in effect for a long time.

long ton ▸*n.* See table at **measurement.**

long-wind·ed (lông′wĭn′dĭd, lŏng′-) ▸*adj.* Wearisomely talkative. See Synonyms at **wordy.** —**long′-wind′ed·ly** *adv.*

loo·fah (lōō′fə) ▸*n.* **1.** A tropical vine having cylindrical fruit with a fibrous interior. **2.** The interior of this fruit, used esp. as a sponge. [Ar. *lūfa.*]

look (lōōk) ▸*v.* **1.** To use the eyes to see. **2.** To search. **3.** To focus one's gaze or attention: *look toward the river.* **4.** To seem or appear to be: *look ripe.* **5.** To face in a specified direction. **6.** To have an appearance of conformity with: *look one's age.* ▸*n.* **1.** The act or instance of looking; gave or glance. **2.** Appearance or aspect. **3.** **looks** Physical appearance, esp. when pleasing. —*phrasal verbs:* **look after** To take care of. **look into** To investigate. **look on (**or **upon)** To consider; regard. **look out** To be on guard. **look over** To inspect, esp. in a casual way. **look up 1.** To search for and find, as in a reference book. **2.** To visit: *look up an old friend.* **3.** To improve. —*idioms:* **look down on (**or **upon)** To regard with contempt or condescension. **look up to** To admire. [< OE *lōcian.*] —**look′er** *n.*

look·ing glass (lōōk′ĭng) ▸*n.* See **mirror** (sense 1).

look·out (lōōk′out′) ▸*n.* **1.** The act of observing or keeping watch. **2.** A high place commanding a wide view for observation. **3.** One who keeps watch.

loom¹ (lōōm) ▸*v.* **1.** To come into view as a massive, distorted, or indistinct image. **2.** To appear imminent and usu. threatening. [Perh. of Scand. orig.]

loom² (lōōm) ▸*n.* An apparatus that is used for making thread or yarn into cloth by weaving strands together at right angles. [< OE *gelōma,* tool.]

loon¹ (lōōn) ▸*n.* A diving bird having mottled

plumage and an eerie, laughlike cry. [Of Scand. orig.]

loon² (lo͞on) ▸*n. Informal* One who is crazy or simple-minded. [ME *louen*, rogue.]

loon·y or **loon·ey** (lo͞o′nē) ▸*adj.* **-i·er, -i·est** *Slang* **1.** Extremely foolish or silly. **2.** Crazy. —**loon′i·ness** *n.* —**loon′y** *n.*

loop (lo͞op) ▸*n.* **1.** A length of line, ribbon, or other thin material doubled over and joined at the ends. **2.** Something having a shape, order, or path of motion that is circular or curved over on itself. ▸*v.* **1.** To form, or form into, a loop. **2.** To fasten, join, or encircle with a loop or loops. [ME *loupe.*]

loop·hole (lo͞op′hōl′) ▸*n.* **1.** A means of evasion. **2.** A small hole or slit in a wall, esp. one through which small arms may be fired. [ME *loupe* + HOLE.]

loop·y (lo͞o′pē) ▸*adj.* **-i·er, -i·est** *Slang* Offbeat; crazy.

loose (lo͞os) ▸*adj.* **loos·er, loos·est** **1.** Not tightly fastened or secured. **2.** Not taut, fixed, or rigid. **3.** Free from confinement. **4.** Not tight-fitting. **5.** Not bound, bundled, or gathered together. **6.** Lacking restraint or responsibility: *loose talk.* **7.** Licentious; immoral. **8.** Not literal or exact: *a loose translation.* ▸*adv.* In a loose manner. ▸*v.* **loosed, loos·ing** **1.** To set free; release. **2.** To undo, untie, or unwrap. **3.** To cast loose; detach. **4.** To let fly; discharge: *loosed an arrow.* **5.** To relax. [< ON *lauss.*] —**loose′ly** *adv.* —**loose′ness** *n.*

Syns: *lax, slack* **Ant:** *tight* **adj.**

loos·en (lo͞o′sən) ▸*v.* **1.** To make or become loose or looser. **2.** To free from restraint, pressure, or strictness.

loot (lo͞ot) ▸*n.* **1.** Valuables pillaged in war; spoils. **2.** Stolen goods or money. ▸*v.* **1.** To take goods from (a place) by force, esp. in time of war or lawlessness. **2.** To take without right; steal: *looted the tomb.* [Hindi *lūṭ* < Skt. *lotram*, plunder.] —**loot′er** *n.*

lop (lŏp) ▸*v.* **lopped, lop·ping** **1.** To cut off (a part) from, esp. with a single swift blow. **2.** To cut off branches or twigs from; trim. **3.** To eliminate or excise as superfluous. [Perh. < ME *loppe*, small branches.]

lope (lōp) ▸*v.* **loped, lop·ing** To run or ride with a steady, easy gait. ▸*n.* A steady, easy gait. [< ON *hlaupa*, leap.] —**lop′er** *n.*

lop·sid·ed (lŏp′sī′dĭd) ▸*adj.* **1.** Heavier, larger, or higher on one side than on the other. **2.** Marked by the domination of one competitor over another. —**lop′sid·ed·ly** *adv.*

lo·qua·cious (lō-kwā′shəs) ▸*adj.* Very talkative. [< Lat. *loquāx, loquāc-* < *loquī*, speak.] —**lo·qua′cious·ly** *adv.* —**lo·qua′cious·ness, lo·quac′i·ty** (-kwăs′ĭ-tē) *n.*

lord (lôrd) ▸*n.* **1.** The owner of a feudal estate. **2. Lord** *Chiefly Brit.* The general masculine title of nobility and other rank. **3. Lord a.** God. **b.** Jesus. **4.** A man of renowned power, authority, or mastery in a given field or activity. ▸*v.* To domineer. [< OE *hlāford.*]

lord·ly (lôrd′lē) ▸*adj.* **-li·er, -li·est** **1.** Of or characteristic of a lord. **2.** Dignified and noble. **3.** Arrogant and overbearing. —**lord′li·ness** *n.*

lord·ship (lôrd′shĭp′) ▸*n.* **1.** often **Lordship** Used with *Your, His,* or *Their* as a title for a man holding the rank of lord. **2.** The position or domain of a lord.

Lord's Prayer (lôrdz prâr′) ▸*n.* The prayer taught by Jesus to his disciples.

lore (lôr) ▸*n.* Accumulated facts, traditions, or beliefs about a specific subject. [< OE *lār.*]

lor·gnette (lôrn-yĕt′) ▸*n.* Eyeglasses or opera glasses with a short handle. [< OFr. < *lorgne*, squinting.]

lorn (lôrn) ▸*adj.* Bereft; forlorn. [< OE *-loren*, p.part. of *-lēosan*, lose.]

Lor·raine (lō-rān′, lô-, lô-rĕn′) A region and former province of NE France.

lor·ry (lôr′ē, lŏr′ē) ▸*n., pl.* **-ries** *Chiefly Brit.* A motor truck. [?]

Los An·ge·les (lôs ăn′jə-ləs, -lēz′, ăng′gə-ləs) A city of S CA on the Pacific.

lose (lo͞oz) ▸*v.* **lost** (lôst, lŏst), **los·ing** **1.** To be unable to find; mislay. **2.** To be deprived of: *lost a friend.* **3.** To be unable to maintain or keep. **4.** To fail to win; be defeated. **5.** To fail to take advantage of. **6.** To let (oneself) become engrossed. **7.** To rid oneself of: *lost five pounds.* **8.** To cause the loss of: *Politics lost her the job.* **9.** To suffer loss. —**phrasal verb: lose out** To fail or be defeated. [< OE *losian*, be lost.] —**los′er** *n.*

loss (lôs, lŏs) ▸*n.* **1.** The act or an instance of losing or having lost. **2.** One that is lost. **3. losses** People killed, wounded, or captured in wartime; casualties. —**idiom: at a loss** Perplexed; puzzled. [< OE *los.*]

loss leader ▸*n.* A commodity offered at or below cost to attract customers.

lost (lôst, lŏst) ▸*v.* P.t. and p.part. of **lose.** ▸*adj.* **1.** Unable to find one's way. **2a.** No longer in one's possession or control. **b.** No longer known or practiced: *a lost art.* **3a.** Absorbed or rapt. **b.** Bewildered or confused.

lot (lŏt) ▸*n.* **1. a lot** or **lots** *Informal* **a.** A large amount or number: *a lot of people; lots of problems.* **b.** Used adverbially to mean "to a great degree or extent" or "frequently": *felt a lot better; ran lots faster.* **c.** A number of associated people or things. **d.** Miscellaneous articles sold as one unit. **2a.** A piece of land having fixed boundaries. **b.** A piece of land used for a given purpose: *a parking lot.* **3a.** An object used in making a determination at random. **b.** The use of lots for selection. **c.** One's fate in life. [< OE *hlot.*]

lo·ti (lō′tē) ▸*n., pl.* **ma·lo·ti** (mä-) See table at **currency.** [Sotho.]

lo·tion (lō′shən) ▸*n.* A liquid medicine or cosmetic applied to the skin. [< Lat. *lōtiō*, a washing < *lavere*, wash.]

lot·ter·y (lŏt′ə-rē) ▸*n., pl.* **-ies** **1.** A contest in which tokens are distributed or sold and winners are selected in a random drawing. **2.** A selection made by lot from a number of applicants or competitors. [Prob. < Du. *loterije* < MDu. *lot*, lot.]

lo·tus (lō′təs) ▸*n.* **1a.** An aquatic plant having large round leaves, a round perforated seed-pod, and fleshy rhizomes. **b.** The edible seed, leaf, or rhizome of this plant. **c.** Any of several similar or related plants. **2.** *Gk. Myth.* A fruit that was said to produce a drugged, indolent state in those who ate it. [< Gk. *lōtos*, name of several plants.]

lotus position ▸*n.* A cross-legged sitting position that is used in yoga and Buddhist meditation.

lotus position

loud (loud) ►*adj.* **-er, -est 1.** Marked by high volume and intensity of sound: *a loud whistle.* **2.** Producing sound of high volume and intensity: *a loud construction work site.* **3.** Having strikingly bright colors: *a loud necktie.* See Synonyms at **garish.** [< OE *hlūd.*] —**loud, loud′ly** *adv.* —**loud′ness** *n.*

loud·mouth (loud′mouth′) ►*n. Informal* One given to loud, irritating, or indiscreet talk. —**loud′mouthed′** (-mouthd′, -moutht′) *adj.*

loud·speak·er (loud′spē′kər) ►*n.* A device that converts electric signals to sound and projects it, esp. one that is freestanding.

Lou·is XIV (lōō′ē, lōō-ē′) "the Sun King." 1638– 1715. King of France (1643–1715).

Louis XV 1710–74. King of France (1715–74).

Louis XVI 1754–93. King of France (1774–92).

Lou·i·si·an·a (lōō-ē′zē-ăn′ə, lōō′zē-) A state of the S US on the Gulf of Mexico. Cap. Baton Rouge.

Louisiana French ►*n.* French as spoken by the descendants of the original French settlers of Louisiana.

Louisiana Purchase A former territory of the W US from the Mississippi R. to the Rocky Mts. between the Gulf of Mexico and the Canadian border; purchased from France in 1803.

Lou·is Phi·lippe (lōō′ē fĭ-lēp′, lōō-ē′ fē-lēp′) "the Citizen King." 1773–1850. King of France (1830–48).

Lou·is·ville (lōō′ē-vĭl′, -ə-vəl) A city of N-central KY on the Ohio R. W of Lexington.

lounge (lounj) ►*v.* **lounged, loung·ing** To stand, sit, or lie in a lazy, relaxed way. ►*n.* **1.** A comfortably furnished waiting room, as in a hotel or theater. **2.** A bar serving cocktails. **3.** A long couch. [Perh. < Fr. *s'allonger,* stretch out.] —**loung′er** *n.*

lour (lour) ►*v. & n.* Var. of **lower¹.**

louse (lous) ►*n.* **1.** *pl.* **lice** (līs) Any of numerous small wingless insects parasitic on various animals, including humans. **2.** *pl.* **lous·es** *Slang* A mean or despicable person. ►*v.* **loused, lous·ing** *Slang* To bungle. Often used with *up: louse up a deal.* [< OE *lūs.*]

lous·y (lou′zē) ►*adj.* **-i·er, -i·est 1.** Infested with lice. **2.** Mean; nasty. **3.** Inferior or worthless. **4.** Very bad or painful: *a lousy headache.* —**lous′i·ly** *adv.* —**lous′i·ness** *n.*

lout (lout) ►*n.* An awkward, stupid person; oaf. [Perh. < OE *lūtan,* bend.] —**lout′ish** *adj.* —**lout′ish·ly** *adv.*

lou·ver also **lou·vre** (lōō′vər) ►*n.* **1.** An opening fitted with fixed or movable horizontal slats for admitting air and light and shedding rain. **2.** One of the slats of a louver. **3.** A slatted, ventilating opening. [< OFr. *lover,* skylight.] —**lou′vered** *adj.*

love (lŭv) ►*n.* **1.** Deep affection and warm feeling for another. **2.** A strong feeling of affection for another person accompanied by sexual attraction. **3.** A beloved person. **4.** A strong fondness or enthusiasm. **5.** *Sports* A zero score in tennis. ►*v.* **loved, lov·ing 1.** To feel love (for). **2.** To like or desire enthusiastically. —*idiom:* **in love** Feeling love; enamored. [< OE *lufu.*] —**lov′a·ble, love′a·ble** *adj.* —**love′less** *adj.*

love·bird (lŭv′bûrd′) ►*n.* A small parrot often kept as a cage bird.

love·lorn (lŭv′lôrn′) ►*adj.* Deprived of love or one's lover.

love·ly (lŭv′lē) ►*adj.* **-li·er, -li·est 1.** Having pleasing or attractive qualities; beautiful. **2.** Enjoyable; delightful. —**love′li·ness** *n.*

love·mak·ing (lŭv′mā′kĭng) ►*n.* **1.** Sexual activity between lovers. **2.** Courtship.

lov·er (lŭv′ər) ►*n.* **1.** One who loves another, esp. one who feels sexual love. **2. lovers** A couple in love with each other. **3.** A sexual partner. **4.** One who is fond of or devoted to something. —**lov′er·ly** *adv. & adj.*

love seat ►*n.* A small sofa that seats two.

love·sick (lŭv′sĭk′) ►*adj.* **1.** Pining with love. **2.** Exhibiting or expressing a lover's yearning. —**love′sick′ness** *n.*

lov·ing (lŭv′ĭng) ►*adj.* Feeling or showing love; affectionate. —**lov′ing·ly** *adv.*

loving cup ►*n.* A large ornamental vessel, usu. with two or more handles, often given as an award in sporting contests.

low¹ (lō) ►*adj.* **-er, -est 1a.** Having little height. **b.** Of less than usual height or depth. **2a.** Below average or standard in degree, intensity, or amount. **b.** Relatively small, as a price or other value. **3a.** Not loud; soft. **b.** Having a pitch corresponding to a relatively small number of sound-wave cycles per second. **4.** Humble or inferior in status. **5.** Morally base. **6.** Emotionally or mentally depressed; sad. **7.** Depreciatory; disparaging: *a low opinion.* ►*adv.* **1.** At, in, or to a low position, level, or space. **2.** Softly; quietly: *speak low.* **3.** With a deep pitch. ►*n.* **1.** A low level, position, or degree. **2.** *Meteorol.* A region of atmospheric air that exerts less pressure than the air around it. **3.** The low gear configuration of a transmission. [< ON *lāgr.*] —**low′ness** *n.*

low² (lō) ►*n.* A moo. [< OE *hlōwan.*] —**low** *v.*

low beam ►*n.* The beam of a vehicle's headlight that provides short-range illumination.

low·born (lō′bôrn′) ►*adj.* Of humble birth.

low·boy (lō′boi′) ►*n.* A low tablelike chest of drawers.

low·bred (lō′brĕd′) ►*adj.* Coarse; vulgar.

low·brow (lō′brou′) ►*n.* One having uncultivated tastes. ►*adj.* Uncultivated; vulgar.

low-cal (lō′kăl′) ►*adj.* Having fewer calories than what is typical: *low-cal foods.*

low-carb (lō′kärb′) ►*adj.* Having fewer carbohydrates than what is typical: *low-carb diets.*

Low Countries Belgium, the Netherlands, and Luxembourg.

low-down or **low·down** (lō′doun′) ►*adj.*

Despicable; mean. ►*n.* Correct information or details.

Low·ell (lō′əl), **James Russell** 1819–91. Amer. editor, poet, and diplomat.

Lowell, Robert Traill Spence, Jr. 1917–77. Amer. poet.

low·er[1] (lou′ər, lour) also **lour** (lour) ►*v.* **1.** To look angry; scowl. See Synonyms at **frown**. **2.** To appear dark or stormy, as the sky. [ME *louren.*] —**low′er** *n.*

low·er[2] (lō′ər) ►*adj.* Comp. of **low**[1]. **1.** Below another in rank, position, or authority. **2.** Physically situated below something comparable: *the lower back.* **3. Lower** *Geol. & Archaeol.* Being an earlier division of the period named. **4.** Denoting the larger and usu. more representative house of a bicameral legislature. ►*v.* **1.** To let, bring, or move something down to a lower level. **2.** To make or become less; reduce or diminish.

low·er·case (lō′ər-kās′) ►*adj.* Of or relating to letters that are smaller and often in a form differing from their corresponding capital letters. —**low′er·case′** *n. & v.*

lower class (lō′ər) ►*n.* The socioeconomic class or classes of lower than middle rank in a society. —**low′er-class′** *adj.*

low·est common denominator (lō′ĭst) ►*n.* See **least common denominator**.

low frequency ►*n.* A radio-wave frequency in the range from 30 to 300 kilohertz.

low-grade (lō′grād′) ►*adj.* **1.** Of inferior quality. **2.** Reduced in degree or intensity: *a low-grade fever.*

low-key (lō′kē′) also **low-keyed** (-kēd′) ►*adj.* Restrained, as in style or quality.

low·land (lō′lənd) ►*n.* An area of relatively low land. ►*adj.* Relating to low, usu. level land. —**low′land·er** *n.*

low·ly (lō′lē) ►*adj.* **-li·er, -li·est 1.** Having a low rank or position. **2.** Humble or meek in manner. —**low′li·ness** *n.* —**low′ly** *adv.*

low-mind·ed (lō′mīn′dĭd) ►*adj.* Exhibiting a coarse, vulgar character. —**low′-mind′ed·ly** *adv.* —**low′-mind′ed·ness** *n.*

low profile ►*n.* Unobtrusive, restrained behavior or activity.

low relief ►*n.* Sculptural relief that projects very little from the background; bas-relief.

low road ►*n.* Deceitful, immoral behavior or practice.

low-tech (lō′tĕk′) ►*adj.* Relating to technology that does not involve highly advanced systems or devices.

low tide ►*n.* **1.** The lowest level of the tide. **2.** The time of this level.

lox (lŏks) ►*n., pl.* **lox** or **-es** Salmon that is cured in brine and often smoked. [Yiddish *laks* < OHGer. *lahs,* salmon.]

LOX ►*abbr.* liquid oxygen

loy·al (loi′əl) ►*adj.* **1.** Steadfast in allegiance, as to one's homeland. **2.** Faithful to a person, ideal, cause, or duty. [< Lat. *lēgālis,* LEGAL.] —**loy′al·ly** *adv.* —**loy′al·ty** *n.*

loy·al·ist (loi′ə-lĭst) ►*n.* One who maintains loyalty to the lawful government during a revolt.

loz·enge (lŏz′ĭnj) ►*n.* **1.** A small medicated candy dissolved slowly in the mouth to soothe irritated throat tissues. **2.** A flat diamond-shaped figure. [< OFr. *losenge.*]

LP (ĕl′pē′) ►*n.* A long-playing record.

LPN ►*abbr.* licensed practical nurse

LSAT (ĕl′săt′) A trademark used for a standardized law school entrance examination.

LSD (ĕl′ĕs-dē′) ►*n.* A powerful drug, lysergic acid diethylamide, $C_{20}H_{25}N_3O$, that induces hallucinations.

LT or **Lt.** ►*abbr.* lieutenant

lt. ►*abbr.* light

LTC or **Lt Col** ►*abbr.* lieutenant colonel

Ltd. or **ltd.** ►*abbr.* limited

LTG or **Lt Gen** ►*abbr.* lieutenant general

Lt. Gov. ►*abbr.* lieutenant governor

Lu·an·da (lōō-än′də) The capital of Angola, in the NW part on the Atlantic.

lu·au (lōō-ou′, lōō′ou′) ►*n.* A traditional Hawaiian feast. [Hawaiian *lū'au.*]

lube (lōōb) *Informal* ►*v.* **lubed, lub·ing** To lubricate (e.g., a car's joints). ►*n.* A lubricant.

lu·bri·cant (lōō′brĭ-kənt) ►*n.* A substance, such as grease or oil, that reduces friction when applied as a surface coating to moving parts. —**lu′bri·cant** *adj.*

lu·bri·cate (lōō′brĭ-kāt′) ►*v.* **-cat·ed, -cat·ing** To apply a lubricant to. [< Lat. *lūbricus,* slippery.] —**lu′bri·ca′tion** *n.*

lu·bri·cious (lōō-brĭsh′əs) also **lu·bri·cous** (lōō′brĭ-kəs) ►*adj.* **1.** Slippery. **2.** Shifty or tricky. **3a.** Lewd; wanton. **b.** Salacious. [< Lat. *lūbricus.*] —**lu·bri′cious·ness** *n.* —**lu·bric′i·ty** (-brĭs′ĭ-tē) *n.*

Luce (lōōs), **Clare Boothe** 1903–87. Amer. writer and public official.

Luce, Henry Robinson 1898–1967. Amer. editor and publisher.

Lu·cerne (lōō-sûrn′, -sĕrn′) A city of central Switzerland on the N shore of **Lake Lucerne**.

lu·cid (lōō′sĭd) ►*adj.* **1.** Easily understood: *a lucid explanation.* **2.** Clear-minded; rational. **3.** Brightly lit; luminous. **4.** Clear; translucent: *a lucid stream.* [Lat. *lūcidus* < *lūcēre,* shine.] —**lu·cid′i·ty, lu′cid·ness** *n.* —**lu′cid·ly** *adv.*

Lu·ci·fer (lōō′sə-fər) ►*n.* In Christian tradition, the archangel cast from heaven for leading the revolt of the angels; Satan.

Lu·cite (lōō′sīt′) A trademark for a transparent thermoplastic acrylic resin.

luck (lŭk) ►*n.* **1.** The chance happening of good or bad events; fortune. **2.** Good fortune; success. ►*v.* To gain success or something desirable by chance: *lucked into a good apartment.* [< MDu. *gheluc.*]

luck·less (lŭk′lĭs) ►*adj.* Unlucky. See Synonyms at **unfortunate**.

luck·y (lŭk′ē) ►*adj.* **-i·er, -i·est** Having, bringing, or attended by good luck. See Synonyms at **fortunate**. —**luck′i·ly** *adv.* —**luck′i·ness** *n.*

lu·cra·tive (lōō′krə-tĭv) ►*adj.* Producing wealth; profitable. [< Lat. *lucrārī,* make a profit.] —**lu′cra·tive·ly** *adv.*

lu·cre (lōō′kər) ►*n.* Money or profits. [< Lat. *lucrum.*]

Lu·cre·tius (lōō-krē′shəs, -shē-əs) 96?–55? BC. Roman philosopher and poet. —**Lu·cre′tian** (-shən) *adj.*

lu·cu·brate (lōō′kyōō-brāt′) ►*v.* **-brat·ed, -brat·ing** To study or write in a scholarly fashion. [Lat. *lūcubrāre,* work by lamplight.]

lu·di·crous (lōō′dĭ-krəs) ►*adj.* Laughable because of obvious absurdity or incongruity. See Synonyms at **foolish**. [< Lat. *lūdicrus,* playful.] —**lu′di·crous·ly** *adv.*

lug¹ (lŭg) ►*n.* **1.** A handle or projection used as a hold or support. **2.** A lug nut. **3.** *Slang* A clumsy fool. [ME *lugge*, earflap.]

lug² (lŭg) ►*v.* **lugged, lug·ging** To drag or haul with difficulty. [ME *luggen.*]

luge (lo͞ozh) ►*n. Sports* **1.** A sport in which a small open sled is ridden by one or two people lying face-up with the feet pointed downhill. **2.** The sled used in this sport. [< Med.Lat. *sludia.*]

lug·gage (lŭg′ĭj) ►*n.* Baggage, esp. suitcases. [Prob. LUG² + (BAG)GAGE.]

lug nut ►*n.* A heavy rounded nut that fits over a bolt.

lu·gu·bri·ous (lo͞o-go͞o′brē-əs, -gyo͞o′-) ►*adj.* Mournful or gloomy, esp. to a ludicrous degree. [< Lat. *lūgubris* < *lūgēre*, mourn.] —**lu·gu′bri·ous·ly** *adv.* —**lu·gu′bri·ous·ness** *n.*

Luke (lo͞ok) ►*n.* See table at **Bible.**

Luke, Saint. fl. 1st cent. AD. Companion of Saint Paul and the traditionally accepted author of the third Gospel.

luke·warm (lo͞ok′wôrm′) ►*adj.* **1.** Mildly warm. **2.** Half-hearted: *lukewarm support for the candidate.* [ME *leukwarm.*] —**luke′warm′ly** *adv.*

lull (lŭl) ►*v.* **1.** To cause to sleep or rest; soothe. **2.** To deceive into trustfulness. ►*n.* A relatively calm or inactive interval or period. [ME *lullen.*]

lull·a·by (lŭl′ə-bī′) ►*n., pl.* **-bies** A soothing song with which to lull a child to sleep. [< ME *lullen*, to lull + (GOOD)BY(E).]

lum·ba·go (lŭm-bā′gō) ►*n.* A painful condition of the lower back, as one resulting from muscle strain or a slipped disk. [LLat. *lumbāgō.*]

lum·bar (lŭm′bər, -bär′) ►*adj.* Of, near, or situated in the part of the back and sides between the lowest ribs and the hips. [< Lat. *lumbus.*]

lum·ber¹ (lŭm′bər) ►*n.* **1.** Timber sawed into boards and planks. **2.** Something useless or cumbersome. ►*v.* To cut down (trees) and prepare as marketable timber. [Perh. < LUMBER².] —**lum′ber·er** *n.*

lum·ber² (lŭm′bər) ►*v.* To walk or move clumsily or heavily. See Synonyms at **blunder.** [ME *lomeren.*]

lum·ber·jack (lŭm′bər-jăk′) ►*n.* One who fells trees and transports the timber to a mill.

lum·ber·yard (lŭm′bər-yärd′) ►*n.* An establishment that sells lumber and other building materials from a yard.

lu·men (lo͞o′mən) ►*n., pl.* **-mens** or **-mi·na** (-mə-nə) *Anat.* The inner open space or cavity of a tubular organ. [Lat., light, an opening.] —**lu′men·al, lu′min·al** *adj.*

lu·mi·nar·y (lo͞o′mə-nĕr′ē) ►*n., pl.* **-ies 1.** An object, such as a celestial body, that gives light. **2.** A notable person in a specific field. See Synonyms at **celebrity.** [< Lat. *lūmen*, light.] —**lu′mi·nar′y** *adj.*

lu·mi·nes·cence (lo͞o′mə-nĕs′əns) ►*n.* **1.** The production of light without heat, as in fluorescence. **2.** The light so produced. [< Lat. *lūmen*, light.] —**lu′mi·nes′cent** *adj.*

lu·mi·nous (lo͞o′mə-nəs) ►*adj.* **1.** Emitting light, esp. in the dark. **2.** Reflecting light; illuminated. **3.** Presented or perceived clearly or vividly. [< Lat. *lūmen, lūmin-*, light.] —**lu′mi·nos′i·ty** (-nŏs′ĭ-tē) *n.* —**lu′mi·nous·ness** *n.* —**lu′mi·nous·ly** *adv.*

luminous flux ►*n.* The rate of flow of light per unit of time.

lum·mox (lŭm′əks) ►*n. Informal* An oaf. [?]

lump¹ (lŭmp) ►*n.* **1.** An irregularly shaped mass or piece. **2.** *Med.* A swelling or small palpable mass. **3. lumps** *Informal* Punishment or criticism: *take one's lumps.* ►*adj.* **1.** Formed into lumps: *lump sugar.* **2.** Not divided into parts: *a lump payment.* ►*v.* To put together in a single group or pile. [ME *lumpe.*] —**lump′i·ness** *n.* —**lump′y** *adj.*

lump² (lŭmp) ►*v.* To tolerate: *like it or lump it.* [Perh. < dial. *lump*, look sullen.]

lump·ec·to·my (lŭm-pĕk′tə-mē) ►*n., pl.* **-mies** Surgical excision of a tumor from the breast.

lu·na·cy (lo͞o′nə-sē) ►*n., pl.* **-cies 1.** Mental derangement; craziness. **2.** Foolish conduct. [< LUNATIC.]

lu·nar (lo͞o′nər) ►*adj.* **1.** Of, involving, caused by, or affecting the moon. **2.** Measured by the revolution of the moon. [< Lat. *lūna*, moon.]

lu·na·tic (lo͞o′nə-tĭk) ►*n.* **1.** A person who is affected by lunacy; a mentally deranged person. **2.** A very foolish person. ►*adj.* **1.** Mentally deranged. **2.** Of or for the mentally deranged. **3.** Wildly or giddily foolish. [< Lat. *lūnāticus* < *lūna*, moon.]

lunch (lŭnch) ►*n.* A meal eaten at midday. [Short for LUNCHEON.] —**lunch** *v.*

lunch·eon (lŭn′chən) ►*n.* A lunch, esp. a party at which lunch is served. [Poss. < ME *nonshench*, a drink at noon.]

lunch·eon·ette (lŭn′chə-nĕt′) ►*n.* A small restaurant that serves simple meals.

lung (lŭng) ►*n.* Either of two spongy, saclike thoracic organs in most vertebrates where the exchange of carbon dioxide for oxygen occurs. [< OE *lungen*, lungs.]

lunge (lŭnj) ►*n.* **1.** A sudden thrust or pass, as with a sword. **2.** A sudden forward movement. ►*v.* **lunged, lung·ing** To move with a lunge. [< OFr. *alongier*, lengthen.] —**lung′er** *n.*

lung·fish (lŭng′fĭsh′) ►*n.* Any of several tropical freshwater fishes that have a lunglike organ that enables them to breathe air.

lu·pine also **lu·pin** (lo͞o′pən) ►*n.* A plant having tall spikes of variously colored flowers. [< Lat. *lupīnus*, wolflike.]

lu·pus (lo͞o′pəs) ►*n.* An autoimmune disease of the connective tissue, usu. involving multiple organ systems. [< Lat., wolf.]

lurch¹ (lûrch) ►*v.* **1.** To make an abrupt sudden movement. **2.** To move with abrupt movements. See Synonyms at **blunder. 3.** To roll or pitch suddenly or erratically: *The ship lurched in the storm.* [?] —**lurch** *n.* —**lurch′ing·ly** *adv.*

lurch² (lûrch) ►*n.* A difficult position. [Perh. < ME *lurching*, total victory in a game.]

lure (lo͝or) ►*n.* **1.** Something that tempts or attracts with the promise of pleasure or reward: *the lure of the open road.* **2.** An artificial bait used in catching fish. [< AN, of Gmc. orig.] —**lure** *v.*

lu·rid (lo͝or′ĭd) ►*adj.* Marked by vivid description or explicit details that are meant to provoke or shock. [Lat. *lūridus*, pale.] —**lu′rid·ly** *adv.* —**lu′rid·ness** *n.*

lurk (lûrk) ►*v.* **1.** To lie in wait, as in ambush. **2.** To move furtively; sneak. **3.** To read but not contribute to the discussion in an online forum. [ME *lurken*, poss. of Scand. orig.]

Lu·sa·ka (lo͞o-sä′kə) The capital of Zambia, in the S-central part.

lus·cious (lŭsh′əs) ▸*adj.* **1.** Sweet and pleasant to taste or smell. See Synonyms at **delicious. 2.** Having strong sensual or sexual appeal. [ME *lucius.*] —**lus′cious·ly** *adv.*

lush¹ (lŭsh) ▸*adj.* **-er, -est 1a.** Marked by luxuriant vegetation. **b.** Abundant; plentiful. See Synonyms at **profuse. 2.** Luxurious; opulent. [ME *lush,* soft.] —**lush′ly** *adv.* —**lush′ness** *n.*

lush² (lŭsh) ▸*n. Slang* A drunkard. [?]

lust (lŭst) ▸*n.* **1.** Intense sexual desire. **2.** An overwhelming craving. **3.** Intense eagerness or enthusiasm. ▸*v.* To have an intense desire, esp. sexual desire. [< OE, desire.] —**lust′ful** *adj.* —**lust′ful·ly** *adv.* —**lust′ful·ness** *n.*

lus·ter (lŭs′tər) ▸*n.* **1.** Soft, reflected light; sheen. **2.** Brilliance or radiance. **3.** Glory, distinction, or splendor. [< Lat. *lūstrāre,* brighten.] —**lus′trous** (-trəs) *adj.* —**lus′trous·ly** *adv.*

lus·tre (lŭs′tər) ▸*n. Chiefly Brit.* Var. of **luster.**

lust·y (lŭs′tē) ▸*adj.* **-i·er, -i·est** Full of vigor; robust. —**lust′i·ly** *adv.* —**lust′i·ness** *n.*

lute (lo͞ot) ▸*n.* A stringed instrument having a fretted fingerboard and a body shaped like half a pear. [< Ar. *al-'ud.*] —**lu′te·nist, lu′ta·nist** (lo͞ot′n-ĭst), **lut′ist** *n.*

lu·te·ti·um (lo͞o-tē′shē-əm) ▸*n. Symbol* **Lu** A silvery-white rare-earth element. At. no. 71. See table at **element.** [< Lat. *Lutetia,* ancient name of Paris.]

Lu·ther (lo͞o′thər), **Martin** 1483–1546. German theologian and Reformation leader.

Martin Luther
1529 portrait

Lu·ther·an (lo͞o′thər-ən) ▸*adj.* Of or relating to the branch of the Protestant Church adhering to the views of Martin Luther. —**Lu′ther·an** *n.* —**Lu′ther·an·ism** *n.*

Lux·em·bourg also **Lux·em·burg** (lŭk′səm-bûrg′) **1.** A country of NW Europe. Cap. Luxembourg. **2.** Also **Luxembourg City** The capital of Luxembourg, in the S part.

Lux·em·burg (lŭk′səm-bûrg′), **Rosa** 1870?– 1919. Polish-born German socialist; murdered.

lux·u·ri·ant (lŭg-zho͝or′ē-ənt, lŭk-sho͝or′-) ▸*adj.* **1.** Marked by rich or profuse growth: *luxuriant hair.* See Synonyms at **profuse. 2.** Excessively florid or elaborate; ornate. —**lux·u′ri·ance** *n.* —**lux·u′ri·ant·ly** *adv.*

lux·u·ri·ate (lŭg-zho͝or′ē-āt′, lŭk-sho͝or′-) ▸*v.* **-at·ed, -at·ing** To take luxurious pleasure; indulge oneself.

lux·u·ry (lŭg′zhə-rē, lŭk′shə-) ▸*n., pl.* **-ries 1.** Sumptuous living or surroundings: *lives in luxury.* **2.** Something that is not essential but provides pleasure and comfort. **3.** Something that is desirable and expensive or hard to obtain or do. [< Lat. *luxuria < luxus.*] —**lux·u′ri·ous** (-zho͝or′ēəs, -sho͝or′-) *adj.* —**lux·u′ri·ous·ly** *adv.*

Syns: extravagance, frill **Ant:** *necessity* **n.**

Lu·zon (lo͞o-zŏn′) An island of the NW Philippines, the largest island of the archipelago.

L'viv (lə-vĭv′, -vēo͞o′) or **L'vov** (lə-vôv′, -vôf′) A city of W-central Ukraine near the Polish border.

-ly¹ ▸*suff.* **1.** Like; having the characteristics of: *sisterly.* **2.** Recurring at a specified interval of time: *hourly.* [< OE *-līc.*]

-ly² ▸*suff.* **1.** In a specified manner; in the manner of: *gradually.* **2.** At a specified interval of time: *weekly.* **3.** With respect to: *partly.* [< OE *-līce.*]

ly·chee also **li·chee** (lē′chē) ▸*n.* **1.** An evergreen tree native to China with bright red fruits surrounding a large seed. **2.** The fruit of this tree. [Mandarin *lì zhī.*]

Lyd·i·a (lĭd′ē-ə) An ancient country of W-central Asia Minor on the Aegean Sea. —**Lyd′i·an** *adj. & n.*

lye (lī) ▸*n.* **1.** The liquid obtained by leaching wood ashes. **2.** See **potassium hydroxide. 3.** See **sodium hydroxide.** [< OE *lēag.*]

Lyme disease (līm) ▸*n.* An inflammatory disease that is caused by a spirochete transmitted by ticks. [After *Lyme,* CT.]

lymph (lĭmf) ▸*n.* A clear watery fluid that contains white blood cells and acts to remove bacteria and certain proteins from the tissues, transport fat from the small intestine, and supply mature lymphocytes to the blood. [Lat. *lympha,* water < Gk. *numphē,* water spirit.]

lym·phad·e·nop·a·thy (lĭm-făd′n-ŏp′ə-thē, lĭm′fə-dn-) ▸*n., pl.* **-thies** An enlargement of the lymph nodes, usu. associated with disease. [LYMPH + Greek *adēn,* gland + –PATHY.]

lym·phat·ic (lĭm-făt′ĭk) ▸*adj.* Of or relating to lymph or the lymphatic system. ▸*n.* A vessel that conveys lymph.

lymphatic system ▸*n.* The system of spaces and vessels between tissues and organs by which lymph is circulated.

lymph node ▸*n.* Any of numerous oval or round bodies that supply lymphocytes to the bloodstream and remove bacteria and foreign particles from the lymph.

lym·pho·cyte (lĭm′fə-sīt′) ▸*n.* A white blood cell formed in lymphoid tissue.

lym·phoid (lĭm′foid′) ▸*adj.* Of lymph, lymphatic tissue, or the lymphatic system.

lynch (lĭnch) ▸*v.* To punish without legal process or authority, esp. by hanging. [Prob. after Charles *Lynch* (1736–96).] —**lynch′ing** *n.*

lynx (lĭngks) ▸*n., pl.* **lynx** or **-es** A wildcat with soft thick fur, a short tail, and tufted ears. [< Gk. *lunx.*]

lynx-eyed (lĭngks′īd′) ▸*adj.* Keen of vision.

Ly·on or **Ly·ons** (lē-ōN′, lyôN) A city of E-central France on the Rhone R.

lyre (līr) ▸*n.* A stringed instrument of the harp family used esp. in ancient Greece. [< Gk. *lura.*]

lyr·ic (lĭr′ĭk) ▸*adj.* **1.** Of or relating to poetry that expresses subjective thoughts and feelings, often in a songlike style or form. **2.** Lyrical. ►*n.* **1.** A lyric poem. **2.** often **lyrics** The words of a song. [< Gk. *lurikos*, of a lyre.] —**lyr′i·cism** (-sĭz′əm) *n.*

lyr·i·cal (lĭr′ĭ-kəl) ►*adj.* **1.** Expressing deep personal emotion or observations. **2.** Highly enthusiastic; rhapsodic. **3.** Lyric. —**lyr′i·cal·ly** *adv.*

lyr·i·cist (lĭr′ĭ-sĭst) ►*n.* A person who is a writer of song lyrics.

ly·ser·gic acid (lĭ-sûr′jĭk, lī-) ►*n.* A crystalline alkaloid, $C_{16}H_{16}N_2O_2$, derived from ergot and used in medical research. [< Gk. *lusis*, loosening + ERG(OT) + –IC.]

lysergic acid di·eth·yl·am·ide (dī′ĕth-əl-ăm′-īd′) ►*n.* See **LSD.**

ly·sin (lī′sĭn) ►*n.* An antibody that acts to destroy red blood cells, bacteria, or other cellular elements. [< Gk. *lusis*, a loosening.]

ly·sis (lī′sĭs) ►*n., pl.* **-ses** (-sēz) **1.** The dissolution or destruction of cells. **2.** The gradual subsiding of the symptoms of an acute disease. [< Gk. *lusis*, a loosening.]

–lysis ►*suff.* Decomposition; dissolving: *hydrolysis.* [< Gk. *lusis*, a loosening.]

–lyte ►*suff.* A substance that can be decomposed by a specified process: *electrolyte.* [< Gk. *lutos*, soluble < *luein*, loosen.]

M

m¹ or **M** (ĕm) ►*n., pl.* **m's** or **M's** also **ms** or **Ms** The 13th letter of the English alphabet.

m² ►*abbr.* **1.** *Gram.* masculine **2.** *Phys.* mass **3.** meter (measurement) **4.** mile

M¹ also **m** The symbol for the Roman numeral 1,000.

M² ►*abbr.* **1.** *Print.* em **2.** Mach number **3.** male **4.** married **5.** medium **6.** metal **7.** million **8.** Monsieur **9.** month

M. ►*abbr.* master

mA ►*abbr.* milliampere

Ma (mä), **Yo-Yo** b. 1955. Amer. cellist.

Yo-Yo Ma
photographed in 2006

MA ►*abbr.* **1.** *Lat.* Magister Artium (Master of Arts) **2.** Massachusetts

ma'am (măm) ►*n.* Used as a form of polite address for a woman: *Is that all, ma'am?* [< MADAM.]

ma·ca·bre (mə-kä′brə, mə-käb′, -kä′bər) ►*adj.* Upsetting or horrifying by association with death or injury; gruesome. [< OFr. *(danse) Macabre,* (dance) of death.]

mac·ad·am (mə-kăd′əm) ►*n.* Pavement made of layers of compacted broken stone, now usu. bound with tar or asphalt. [After J.L. *McAdam* (1756–1836).] —**mac·ad′am·ize** *v.*

Ma·cao (mə-kou′) See **Macau.**

ma·caque (mə-kăk′, -käk′) ►*n.* Any of various usu. short-tailed monkeys of Asia, Gibraltar, and N Africa. [Of Bantu orig.]

mac·a·ro·ni (măk′ə-rō′nē) ►*n., pl.* **-ni** Pasta in any of various hollow shapes, esp. short curved tubes. [Ital. dial. *maccaroni.*]

mac·a·roon (măk′ə-roon′) ►*n.* A chewy cookie made with sugar, egg whites, and almond paste or coconut. [< Ital. dial. *maccarone,* dumpling.]

Mac·Ar·thur (mĭk-är′thər), **Douglas** 1880–1964. Amer. general.

Ma·cau also **Ma·cao** (mə-kou′) A city and administrative region of SE China.

Ma·cau·lay (mə-kô′lē), **Thomas Babington** 1800–59. British historian, writer, and politician.

ma·caw (mə-kô′) ►*n.* A large, usu. brilliantly colored tropical American parrot. [Port. *macaú.*]

Mac·ca·bees (măk′ə-bēz′) ►*pl.n. Bible* **1.** A family of Jewish patriots of the 2nd and 1st cent. BC. **2.** See table at **Bible.** —**Mac′ca·be′an** *adj.*

Mac·don·ald (mĭk-dŏn′əld), Sir **John Alexander** 1815–91. Scottish-born Canadian prime minister (1867–73 and 1878–91).

MacDonald, (James) Ramsay 1866–1937. British prime minister (1924 and 1929–35).

mace¹ (mās) ►*n.* **1.** A ceremonial staff used as a symbol of authority. **2.** A heavy medieval war club with a spiked head. [< OFr.]

mace² (mās) ►*n.* An aromatic spice made from the dried seed covering of the nutmeg. [< Gk. *makir,* a kind of spice.]

Mace A trademark for an aerosol used to immobilize an attacker temporarily.

Mac·e·do·ni·a (măs′ĭ-dō′nē-ə, -dōn′yə) **1.** Also **Mac·e·don** (-dən, -dŏn′) An ancient kingdom of N Greece. **2.** A historical region of SE Europe on the Balkan Peninsula. **3.** A country of the S-central Balkan Peninsula. Cap. Skopje.

Mac·e·do·ni·an (măs′ĭ-dō′nē-ən) ►*adj.* Of or relating to ancient or modern Macedonia. ►*n.* **1.** A native or inhabitant of ancient or modern Macedonia. **2.** The language of ancient Macedonia, of uncertain affiliation within Indo-European. **3.** The Slavic language of modern Macedonia, closely related to Bulgarian.

mac·er·ate (măs′ə-rāt′) ►*v.* **-at·ed, -at·ing** **1.** To soften or separate by soaking or steeping. **2.** To emaciate, usu. by starvation. [Lat. *mācerāre.*] —**mac′er·a′tion** *n.*

Mach also **mach** (mäk) ►*n.* Mach number.

Mach (mäk, mäкн), **Ernst** 1838–1916. Austrian physicist and philosopher.

ma·chet·e (mə-shĕt′ē, -chĕt′ē) ►*n.* A large, broad-bladed knife used for cutting vegetation and as a weapon. [Sp., ult. < VLat. **mattea,* mace.]

Ma·chi·a·vel·li (măk′ē-ə-vĕl′ē, mä′kyä-), **Niccolò** 1469–1527. Italian political theorist.

Ma·chi·a·vel·li·an (măk′ē-ə-vĕl′ē-ən) ►*adj.*

Relating to Machiavelli's political doctrine that craft and deceit are justified in pursuing and maintaining power. —**Ma′chi·a·vel′li·an** *n.* —**Ma′chi·a·vel′li·an·ism** *n.*

mach·i·na·tion (măk′ə-nā′shən, măsh′-) ▸*n.* A scheme or secret plot usu. meant to achieve an evil end. —**mach′i·nate′** *v.*

ma·chine (mə-shēn′) ▸*n.* **1a.** A device or system consisting of fixed and moving parts that alters, directs, or modifies mechanical energy and transmits it to accomplish a specific objective. **b.** A simple device, such as a lever, pulley, or screw, that alters an applied force. **2.** A system or device, such as a computer, that performs or assists with a human task. **3.** An organized political group under the control of a strong leader or faction. ▸*v.* **-chined, -chin·ing** To shape or finish by machine. [< Gk. *mēkhanē.*]

machine gun ▸*n.* A gun that fires rapidly and continuously. —**ma·chine′-gun** *v.* —**machine gunner** *n.*

machine language ▸*n.* A set of coded instructions that a computer can use directly without further translation.

ma·chin·er·y (mə-shē′nə-rē, -shēn′rē) ▸*n., pl.* **-ies 1.** Machines or machine parts collectively. **2.** The working parts of a particular machine. **3.** A system of related elements that operate together: *diplomatic and political machinery.*

ma·chin·ist (mə-shē′nĭst) ▸*n.* One who makes, operates, or repairs machines.

ma·chis·mo (mä-chēz′mō) ▸*n.* A strong or exaggerated sense of masculinity. [Sp. < *macho,* MACHO.]

Mach number also **mach number** (mäk) ▸*n.* The ratio of the speed of an object to the speed of sound in the surrounding medium. [After Ernst MACH.]

ma·cho (mä′chō) ▸*adj.* Marked by machismo. ▸*n., pl.* **-chos** Machismo. [Sp., male < Lat. *masculus.*]

Ma·chu Pic·chu (mä′chōō pēk′chōō, pē′-) An ancient Inca fortress city in the Andes NW of Cuzco, Peru.

Mac·ken·zie River (mə-kĕn′zē) A river of NW Canada flowing about 1,740 km (1,080 mi) to **Mackenzie Bay,** an arm of the Beaufort Sea.

mack·er·el (măk′ər-əl, măk′rəl) ▸*n., pl.* **-el** or **-els** Any of several marine food fishes having dark bars on the back and a silvery belly. [< OFr. *maquerel.*]

mack·i·naw (măk′ə-nô′) ▸*n.* A short double-breasted coat of heavy, usu. plaid, woolen material. [< *Mackinaw City,* Michigan.]

mack·in·tosh also **mac·in·tosh** (măk′ĭn-tŏsh′) ▸*n. Chiefly Brit.* A raincoat. [After Charles *Macintosh* (1766–1843).]

Mac·mil·lan (mĭk-mĭl′ən), **(Maurice) Harold** 1st Earl of Stockton. 1894–1986. British prime minister (1957–63).

mac·ra·mé (măk′rə-mā′) ▸*n.* Coarse lace work made by weaving and knotting cords. [< Ar. *miqrama,* embroidered veil.]

mac·ro (măk′rō′) ▸*n., pl.* **-ros** *Comp.* A single, user-defined command that is part of an application and executes a series of commands. [< MACROINSTRUCTION.]

macro- or **macr-** ▸*pref.* **1.** Large: *macroscopic.* **2.** Long: *macrobiotics.* **3.** Inclusive: *macroeconomics.* [< Gk. *makros,* large.]

mac·ro·bi·ot·ics (măk′rō-bī-ŏt′ĭks) ▸*n. (takes*

sing. v.) The theory or practice of promoting well-being and longevity esp. by means of a diet chiefly of whole grains and beans. —**mac′ro·bi·ot′ic** *adj.*

mac·ro·ceph·a·ly (măk′rō-sĕf′ə-lē) ▸*n.* Abnormal largeness of the head. —**mac′ro·ce·phal′-ic** (-sə-făl′ĭk), **mac′ro·ceph′a·lous** *adj.*

mac·ro·cosm (măk′rə-kŏz′əm) ▸*n.* **1.** The entire world; universe. **2.** A system that contains subsystems. [Med.Lat. *macrocosmus.*] —**mac′ro·cos′mic** *adj.*

mac·ro·ec·o·nom·ics (măk′rō-ĕk′ə-nŏm′ĭks, -ē′kə-) ▸*n. (takes sing. v.)* The study of the overall workings of a national economy. —**mac′ro·e·con′o·mist** *n.*

mac·ro·in·struc·tion (măk′rō-ĭn-strŭk′shən) ▸*n.* A macro.

ma·cron (mā′krŏn′, -krən, măk′rŏn′) ▸*n.* A symbol (ˉ) placed over a vowel to show that it has a long sound. [< Gk. *makros,* long.]

mac·ro·phage (măk′rə-fāj′) ▸*n.* A large phagocytic cell.

mac·ro·scop·ic (măk′rə-skŏp′ĭk) also **mac·ro·scop·i·cal** (-ĭ-kəl) ▸*adj.* Large enough to be seen or examined by the unaided eye.

mad (măd) ▸*adj.* **mad·der, mad·dest 1.** Feeling anger or resentment. See Synonyms at **angry. 2.** Mentally deranged. **3.** Lacking restraint, reason, or judgment. **4.** Feeling or showing strong liking or enthusiasm: *mad about sports.* **5.** Marked by extreme excitement, confusion, or agitation; frantic: *a mad scramble.* **6.** Exhibiting uncharacteristic aggressiveness, esp. when caused by rabies or another disease: *a mad dog.* [< OE *gemād,* insane.] —**mad′ly** *adv.* —**mad′man** *n.* —**mad′ness** *n.* —**mad′wom′an** *n.*

Mad·a·gas·car (măd′ə-găs′kər) An island country in the Indian Ocean off SE Africa. Cap. Antananarivo. —**Mad′a·gas′can** *adj. & n.*

Mad·am (măd′əm) ▸*n., pl.* **Mes·dames** (mā-dăm′, -däm′) Used formerly as a courtesy title before a woman's given name. **2.** Used as a salutation in a letter. **3. madam** Used as a form of polite address for a woman. **4. madam** A woman who manages a brothel. [< OFr. *ma dame* : *ma,* my + *dame,* lady (< Lat. *domina*).]

Ma·dame (mə-dăm′, măd′əm) ▸*n., pl.* **Mes·dames** (mā-dăm′, -däm′) A French courtesy title for a woman. [Fr.]

mad·cap (măd′kăp′) ▸*adj.* Behaving or acting impulsively or rashly. [MAD + CAP, head.] —**mad′cap′** *n.*

mad·den (măd′n) ▸*v.* **1.** To make or become angry. **2.** To cause (someone) to go mad; drive to madness. —**mad′den·ing·ly** *adv.*

mad·der (măd′ər) ▸*n.* **1.** Any of several Eurasian plants having small yellow flowers and a fleshy red root. **2.** A red dye obtained from the roots of the madder. [< OE *mædere.*]

made (mād) ▸*v.* P.t. and p.part. of **make.**

Ma·dei·ra (mə-dîr′ə) ▸*n.* A fortified dessert wine, esp. from the Madeira Is.

Madeira Islands An archipelago of Portugal in the NE Atlantic W of Morocco. —**Ma·dei′-ran** *adj. & n.*

Mad·e·moi·selle (măd′ə-mə-zĕl′, măd-mwä-zĕl′) ▸*n., pl.* **Mad·e·moi·selles** (-zĕlz) or **Mes·de·moi·selles** (mād′mwä-zĕl′) A French courtesy title for a girl or young woman. [< OFr. *ma demoiselle* : *ma,* my + *damisele,* young lady; see DAMSEL.]

made-to-or·der (mād′tōō-ôr′dər) ►*adj.* **1.** Made according to particular instructions. **2.** Very suitable.

made-up (mād′ŭp′) ►*adj.* **1.** Fictitious: *a made-up story.* **2.** Wearing makeup.

mad·house (măd′hous′) ►*n.* **1.** *Offensive* An institution for the mentally ill. **2.** *Informal* A place of disorder and confusion.

Mad·i·son (măd′ĭ-sən) The capital of WI, in the S-central part.

Madison, Dolley Payne Todd 1768–1849. First lady of the US (1809–17).

Madison, James 1751–1836. The 4th US president (1809–17). —**Mad′i·so′ni·an** (-sō′nē-ən) *adj.*

James Madison

Ma·don·na (mə-dŏn′ə) ►*n.* **1.** The Virgin Mary. **2.** An image or figure of the Virgin Mary. [Ital. : *ma*, my + *donna*, lady (< Lat. *domina*).]

mad·ras (măd′rəs, mə-drăs′, -dräs′) ►*n.* A fine cotton cloth, usu. with a plaid, striped, or checked pattern. [< MADRAS.]

Ma·dras (mə-drăs′, -dräs′) See **Chennai.**

Ma·drid (mə-drĭd′) The capital of Spain, in the central part.

mad·ri·gal (măd′rĭ-gəl) ►*n.* **1.** A polyphonic song written for four to six voices and usu. unaccompanied. **2.** An unaccompanied vocal composition for two or three voices in simple harmony. [Ital. *madrigale*.]

ma·dro·ne or **ma·dro·na** (mə-drō′nə) also **ma·dro·ño** (-drō′nyō) ►*n., pl.* **-nes** or **-nas** also **-ños** An evergreen tree of W North America, having flaky bark and orange or red edible berries. [Am.Sp.]

mael·strom (māl′strəm) ►*n.* **1.** A violent or turbulent situation. **2.** A large and violent whirlpool. [Obsolete Du. : Du. *malen*, grind + *stroom*, stream.]

maes·tro (mīs′trō) ►*n., pl.* **-tros** or **-tri** (-trē) A master in an art, esp. a composer, conductor, or music teacher. [< Lat. *magister*, master.]

Ma·fi·a (mä′fē-ə) ►*n.* **1a.** A secret criminal organization active esp. in Sicily. **b.** A secret criminal organization active esp. in the United States and Italy. **2.** Any of various criminal organizations dominated by members of the same nationality. [Ital.]

Ma·fi·o·so (mä′fē-ō′sō) ►*n., pl.* **-si** (-sē) or **-sos** A member of the Mafia. [Ital.]

mag·a·zine (măg′ə-zēn′, măg′ə-zēn′) ►*n.* **1.** A periodical containing articles, stories, pictures, or other features. **2.** A place where goods are stored, esp. ammunition. **3.** A usu. detachable compartment in some types of firearms, in which cartridges are held. **4.** A compartment on a machine in which a necessary material is kept. [< Ar. *maḫzan*, storehouse.]

Ma·gel·lan (mə-jĕl′ən), **Ferdinand** 1480?–1521. Portuguese navigator.

Magellan, Strait of A channel separating South America from Tierra del Fuego and connecting the Atlantic and Pacific.

ma·gen·ta (mə-jĕn′tə) ►*n.* A vivid purplish red. [After *Magenta*, Italy.] —**ma·gen′ta** *adj.*

mag·got (măg′ət) ►*n.* The legless, soft-bodied larva of any of various flies, often found in decaying matter. [ME *magot*.] —**mag′got·y** *adj.*

ma·gi (mā′jī′) ►*n.* Pl. of **magus.**

mag·ic (măj′ĭk) ►*n.* **1.** The art that purports to control or forecast natural events, effects, or forces by invoking the supernatural through the use of charms, spells, or rituals. **2.** The exercise of sleight of hand or conjuring, as in making something seem to disappear, for entertainment. **3.** A mysterious quality of enchantment. [< Gk. *magos*, MAGUS.] —**mag′ic, mag′i·cal** *adj.* —**mag′i·cal·ly** *adv.* —**ma·gi′cian** (mə-jish′ən) *n.*

mag·is·te·ri·al (măj′ĭ-stîr′ē-əl) ►*adj.* **1a.** Authoritative; commanding. **b.** Dogmatic; overbearing. **2.** Of a magistrate or a magistrate's official functions. [< Lat. *magister*, master.] —**mag′is·te′ri·al·ly** *adv.*

mag·is·trate (măj′ĭ-strāt′, -strĭt) ►*n.* A judge or justice having power at the local level or over minor offences. [< Lat. *magistrātus*.]

mag·ma (măg′mə) ►*n., pl.* **-ma·ta** (-mä′tə) or **-mas** The molten rock material under the earth's crust that cools and hardens to form igneous rock. [< Gk., unguent.] —**mag·mat′ic** (-măt′ĭk) *adj.*

Mag·na Car·ta or **Mag·na Char·ta** (măg′nə kär′tə) ►*n.* The charter of English political and civil liberties granted by King John in 1215.

mag·nan·i·mous (măg-năn′ə-məs) ►*adj.* Showing generosity of spirit, esp. in overlooking insults or not seeking revenge. [< Lat. *magnanimus*.] —**mag′na·nim′i·ty** (-nə-nĭm′ĭ-tē) *n.* —**mag·nan′i·mous·ly** *adv.*

mag·nate (măg′nāt′, -nĭt) ►*n.* A powerful or influential person. [< LLat. *magnās, magnāt-*.]

mag·ne·sia (măg-nē′zhə, -shə) ►*n.* A white powdery compound, MgO, used in refractories, in electric insulation, and as an antacid. [< Gk. *Magnēsia*, ancient city-state in Asia Minor.]

mag·ne·si·um (măg-nē′zē-əm, -zhəm) ►*n.* Symbol **Mg** A light, silvery, moderately hard metallic element that burns with a brilliant white flame, used in structural alloys and pyrotechnics. At. no. 12. See table at **element.** [< MAGNESIA.]

mag·net (măg′nĭt) ►*n.* **1.** An object that is surrounded by a magnetic field and attracts iron or steel. **2.** An electromagnet. **3.** A person, place, or object that attracts. [< Gk. *Magnēs (lithos)*, (stone) of Magnesia.]

mag·net·ic (măg-nĕt′ĭk) ►*adj.* **1a.** Of or relating to magnetism or magnets. **b.** Having the properties of a magnet. **c.** Capable of being magnetized or attracted by a magnet. **2.** Relating to the magnetic poles of the earth. **3.** Exerting attraction. —**mag·net′i·cal·ly** *adv.*

magnetic disk ►*n.* *Comp.* A memory device

covered with a magnetic coating on which digital information is stored by magnetization of microscopically small regions.

magnetic field ►*n.* A detectable force that exists at every point in the region around a magnet or electric current.

magnetic north ►*n.* The direction of the earth's magnetic pole to which the north-seeking pole of a magnetic needle points.

magnetic pole ►*n.* **1.** Either of two points on a magnet where the magnet's field is most intense. **2.** Either of two variable points on the earth, close to but not coinciding with the geographic poles, where the earth's magnetic field is most intense.

magnetic resonance imaging ►*n.* The use of the magnetic properties of atomic nuclei to produce images of the inner structure of solids, esp. human cells, tissues, and organs.

magnetic tape ►*n.* A plastic tape coated with iron oxide for use in magnetic recording.

mag·net·ism (măg′nĭ-tĭz′əm) ►*n.* **1.** The properties and effects associated with a magnetic field. **2.** The force exerted by a magnetic field. **3.** Unusual power to attract or influence: *the magnetism of money.*

mag·net·ite (măg′nĭ-tīt′) ►*n.* A black iron ore often occurring in naturally magnetized form.

mag·net·ize (măg′nĭ-tīz′) ►*v.* **-ized, -iz·ing 1.** To make magnetic. **2.** To attract, charm, or influence: *a speech that magnetized the crowd.* —**mag′net·i·za′tion** *n.* —**mag′net·iz′er** *n.*

mag·ne·to (măg-nē′tō) ►*n., pl.* **-tos** A device that produces alternating current for distribution to the spark plugs, used in the ignition systems of some internal-combustion engines. [Short for *magnetoelectric machine.*]

mag·ne·tom·e·ter (măg′nĭ-tŏm′ĭ-tər) ►*n.* A device that measures the strength and direction esp. of the earth's magnetic field.

magnet school ►*n.* A public school for students of high ability that attracts its student body from all parts of a city.

mag·nif·i·cent (măg-nĭf′ĭ-sənt) ►*adj.* **1.** Splendid in appearance; grand: *a magnificent palace.* **2.** Grand or noble in thought or deed; exalted: *a magnificent notion.* **3.** Outstanding or exceptional; superlative: *a magnificent place for sailing.* [< Lat. *magnificus.*] —**mag·nif′i·cence** *n.* —**mag·nif′i·cent·ly** *adv.*

mag·ni·fy (măg′nə-fī′) ►*v.* **-fied, -fy·ing 1.** To increase the apparent size of, esp. by means of a lens or other device. **2.** To make greater in size, extent, or effect; enlarge. **3.** To cause to appear greater or more important. See Synonyms at **exaggerate. 4.** *Archaic* To glorify or praise. [< Lat. *magnificāre.*] —**mag′ni·fi·ca′tion** *n.* —**mag′ni·fi′er** *n.*

mag·ni·fy·ing glass (măg′nə-fī′ĭng) ►*n.* A lens or system of lenses that enlarges the image of an object.

mag·ni·tude (măg′nĭ-tōōd′, -tyōōd′) ►*n.* **1.** Greatness, esp. in size or extent. **2.** Greatness in significance or influence. **3.** *Astron.* The relative brightness of a celestial body, esp. as seen from Earth, designated on a numerical scale. [< Lat. *magnus,* great.]

mag·no·lia (măg-nōl′yə) ►*n.* Any of various trees having large, usu. white, pink, or purple flowers. [After Pierre *Magnol* (1638–1715).]

mag·num (măg′nəm) ►*n.* **1.** A bottle for wine

or liquor holding approx. ⅖ gal. **2.** A cartridge or firearm having high power for its caliber. [< Lat., neuter of *magnus,* great.]

magnum opus ►*n.* The greatest single work of an artist, writer, or composer. [Lat.]

mag·pie (măg′pī′) ►*n.* **1.** A long-tailed, loud-voiced, chiefly black and white bird related to the crows and jays. **2.** A person who chatters constantly. [*Mag,* a nickname for Margaret + *pie,* magpie.]

Ma·gritte (mä-grēt′), **René** 1898–1967. Belgian painter.

ma·guey (mə-gā′, măg′wā) ►*n., pl.* **-gueys 1.** Any of various agaves or related plants. **2.** The fiber obtained from a maguey. [Sp., of Cariban orig.]

ma·gus (mā′gəs) ►*n., pl.* **ma·gi** (mā′jī′) **1. Magus** In the New Testament, one of the wise men from the East who paid homage to the infant Jesus. **2.** A sorcerer; magician. [< Pers. *maguš.*]

Mag·yar (măg′yär′, mäg′-) ►*n.* A member of the principal ethnic group of Hungary. [Hung.] —**Mag′yar** *adj.*

ma·ha·ra·ja or **ma·ha·ra·jah** (mä′hə-rä′jə, -zhə) ►*n.* A king or prince in India ranking above a raja. [< Skt. *mahārājaḥ.*]

ma·ha·ra·ni or **ma·ha·ra·nee** (mä′hə-rä′nē) ►*n., pl.* **-nis** or **-nees 1.** The wife of a maharaja. **2.** A princess in India ranking above a rani. [< Skt. *mahārājñī.*]

ma·ha·ri·shi (mä′hə-rē′shē, mə-här′ə-shē) ►*n., pl.* **-shis** *Hinduism* A teacher of spiritual knowledge. [Skt. *mahārṣiḥ.*]

ma·hat·ma (mə-hät′mə, -hăt′-) ►*n. Hinduism* A person venerated for spirituality and high-mindedness. [Skt. *mahātmā.*]

Mah·di (mä′dē) ►*n., pl.* **-dis** *Islam* The messiah expected to appear at the world's end and establish a reign of peace. [Ar. *mahdī,* rightly guided (one), Mahdi.] —**Mah′dism** *n.* —**Mah′dist** *n.*

Ma·hi·can (mə-hē′kən) also **Mo·hi·can** (mō-, mə-) ►*n., pl.* **-can** or **-cans 1.** A member of a Native American confederacy formerly inhabiting the upper Hudson R. valley, now in Oklahoma and Wisconsin. **2.** The Algonquian language of the Mahican.

mah·jong (mä′zhŏng′) ►*n.* A Chinese game usu. played by four persons with rectangular tiles bearing various designs. [Mandarin *má jiàng.*]

Mah·ler (mä′lər), **Gustav** 1860–1911. Austrian composer.

ma·hog·a·ny (mə-hŏg′ə-nē) ►*n., pl.* **-nies 1a.** Any of a genus of tropical American trees valued for their hard, reddish-brown wood. **b.** The wood of such a tree. **2.** Any of several similar trees or their wood. [?]

maid (mād) ►*n.* **1.** *Archaic* An unmarried girl or woman; maiden. **2.** A woman servant. [< OE *mægden.*]

maid·en (mād′n) ►*n. Archaic* An unmarried girl or woman. ►*adj.* **1.** Of or befitting a maiden. **2.** First or earliest: *a maiden voyage.* [< OE *mægden.*] —**maid′en·hood′** *n.*

maid·en·hair fern (mād′n-hâr′) ►*n.* A fern having feathery fronds with slender dark stalks. [From the fineness of its stems.]

maiden name ►*n.* The surname given to a girl at birth, sometimes changed at marriage.

maid of honor ►*n., pl.* **maids of honor** The

chief unmarried woman attendant of a bride.

mail¹ (māl) ►*n.* **1.** Materials, such as letters and packages, handled in a postal system. **2.** A postal system: *sent the package through the mail.* **3.** *Comp.* Messages sent electronically; e-mail. ►*v.* To send by mail. [< OFr. *male,* bag, of Gmc. orig.] —**mail′er** *n.*

mail² (māl) ►*n.* Flexible armor composed of small overlapping metal rings, loops of chain, or scales. [< Lat. *macula,* mesh.] —**mailed** *adj.*

mail·box (māl′bŏks′) ►*n.* **1.** A public container for deposit of outgoing mail. **2.** A private box for the delivery of mail. **3.** A computer file for collecting and storing e-mail.

mail carrier ►*n.* A person, esp. a postal worker, who delivers mail.

Mail·er (mā′lər), **Norman Kingsley** 1923–2007. Amer. writer.

mail·man (māl′măn′, -mən) ►*n.* A man who carries and delivers mail.

mail order ►*n.* An order for goods to be shipped through the mail. —**mail′-or′der** *adj.*

maim (mām) ►*v.* **1.** To disable, mutilate, or cripple. See Synonyms at **mangle¹**. **2.** To impair. [< OFr. *mahaignier.*] —**maim′er** *n.*

Mai·mon·i·des (mī-mŏn′ĭ-dēz′) Moses ben Maimon. 1135?–1204. Spanish-born Egyptian rabbi, philosopher, and physician.

main (mān) ►*adj.* **1.** Most important; principal; chief. **2.** Exerted to the utmost; sheer: *by main strength.* **3.** Relating to or being the principal clause or verb of a complex sentence. ►*n.* **1.** The chief or largest part: *ideas that are in the main, impractical.* **2.** The principal pipe or conduit in a system for conveying water, gas, oil, or other utility. **3.** Physical strength: *fought with might and main.* [< OE *mægen,* strength.] —**main′ly** *adv.*

Maine (mān) A state of the NE US. Cap. Augusta.

main·frame (mān′frām′) ►*n.* A large, powerful computer, often serving many connected terminals.

main·land (mān′lănd′, -lənd) ►*n.* A major landmass, esp. considered in relation to nearby islands or attached peninsulas.

main·line (mān′līn′) ►*v.* **-lined, -lin·ing** *Slang* To inject (an illegal or addictive drug) into a vein.

main·mast (mān′məst, -măst′) ►*n.* The principal mast of a sailing vessel.

main·sail (mān′səl, -sāl′) ►*n.* The principal sail of a sailing vessel.

main·spring (mān′sprĭng′) ►*n.* **1.** The principal spring mechanism in a device, esp. a timepiece. **2.** The chief motivating force.

main·stay (mān′stā′) ►*n.* **1.** A chief support. **2.** A rope that steadies and supports the mainmast of a sailing ship.

main·stream (mān′strēm′) ►*n.* The prevailing current of thought, influence, or activity. ►*v.* **1.** To integrate (a disadvantaged student) into regular classes. **2.** To incorporate into the mainstream. —**main′stream′** *adj.*

main·tain (mān-tān′) ►*v.* **1.** To carry on; continue: *maintain good relations.* **2.** To preserve or retain: *maintain one's composure.* **3.** To keep in good repair: *maintain an engine.* **4.** To provide for; support: *maintain a family.* **5.** To declare to be true: *maintain one's innocence.* [< Lat. *manū tenēre,* hold in the hand.] —**main·tain′a·ble**

adj. —**main′te·nance** (-tə-nəns) *n.*

mai·tre d′ (mā′trə dē′, mā′tər) ►*n., pl.* **mai·tre d′s** (dēz′) *Informal* A maître d'hôtel.

maî·tre d′hô·tel (mā′trə dō-tĕl′) ►*n., pl.* **maî·tres d′hôtel** (-trə) **1.** A headwaiter. **2.** A major-domo. [Fr.]

maize (māz) ►*n.* See **corn¹** (sense 1). [< Cariban *mahiz.*]

Maj. or **Maj** or **MAJ** ►*abbr.* major

maj·es·ty (măj′ĭ-stē) ►*n., pl.* **-ties 1.** Sovereign power, dignity, or grandeur. **2. Majesty** Used with *His, Her,* or *Your* as a title for a sovereign. **3.** Magnificence or splendor: *the majesty of the Rockies.* [< Lat. *māiestās.*] —**ma·jes′tic** (mə-jĕs′tĭk) *adj.* —**ma·jes′ti·cal·ly** *adv.*

Maj Gen ►*abbr.* major general

ma·jor (mā′jər) ►*adj.* **1.** Great in importance, rank, or extent. **2.** Of great concern; very serious: *a major illness.* **3.** *Mus.* Of or based on a major scale. ►*n.* **1.** A rank, as in the US Army, above captain and below lieutenant colonel. **2a.** A field of study chosen as an academic specialty. **b.** A student specializing in such studies. ►*v.* To pursue studies in a major field. [< Lat. *māior.*]

Major, John Roy b. 1943. British prime minister (1990–97).

Ma·jor·ca (mə-jôr′kə, -yôr′-) An island of Spain in the W Mediterranean off the E-central coast of the mainland. —**Ma·jor′can** *adj. & n.*

ma·jor-do·mo (mā′jər-dō′mō) ►*n., pl.* **-mos** A head steward or butler. [< Lat. *māior,* chief + *domus,* house.]

major general ►*n.* A rank, as in the US Army, above brigadier general and below lieutenant general.

ma·jor·i·ty (mə-jôr′ĭ-tē, -jŏr′-) ►*n., pl.* **-ties 1.** A number more than half of the total number of a given group. **2.** The amount by which the greater number of votes cast, as in an election, exceeds the total number of remaining votes. **3.** The age at which one is legally recognized as an adult.

major league ►*n.* A league of major importance in professional sports, esp. baseball. —**ma′jor-league′** *adj.*

major medical ►*n.* Insurance that covers all or most medical bills for major illnesses.

major scale ►*n. Mus.* A diatonic scale having half steps between the 3rd and 4th and the 7th and 8th degrees.

major scale
C major scale

Ma·ju·ro (mə-jŏor′ō) The capital of the Marshall Islands, an atoll in the E part.

make (māk) ►*v.* **made** (mād), **mak·ing 1.** To bring about; create: *make a fuss.* **2.** To form or construct: *made a dress.* **3.** To cause to be or become: *made him happy.* **4a.** To cause to act in a specified manner: *made her smile.* **b.** To compel: *made us leave.* **5.** To prepare; fix: *make dinner.* **6.** To carry out; perform. **7.** To achieve or attain: *make peace.* **8.** To arrive at. **9.** To gain or earn: *make money.* **10.** To constitute: *made a good team.* **11.** To act or behave in a specified manner: *made merry.* **12.** To proceed: *made for home.* ►*n.* **1.** The style or manner in which a thing is made. **2.** A specific line of manufactured goods. —*phrasal verbs:* **make out 1.** To see, esp. with difficulty. **2.** To understand. **3.** To write out or draw up. **4.** To fare: *made out well on the deal.* **5.** *Informal* To neck; pet. **make up 1.** To put together; construct or compose. **2.** To constitute. **3.** To apply cosmetics. **4.** To invent. **5.** To compensate, as for an omission. **6.** To resolve a quarrel. —*idioms:* **make believe** To pretend. **make do** To get along with the means available. **make good 1.** To carry out successfully. **2.** To pay back. **make it** To be successful. **make light of** To treat as unimportant. **make love 1.** To court; woo. **2.** To engage in sexual intercourse. **make no bones about** To be completely frank about. **make the most of** To use to the greatest advantage. **make time** To move or travel fast. **make way** To give room for passage. [< OE *macian.*] —**mak′er** *n.*

make-be·lieve (māk′bĭ-lēv′) ►*n.* Playful or fanciful pretense. —**make′-be·lieve′** *adj.*

make·shift (māk′shĭft′) ►*adj.* Suitable as a temporary or expedient substitute.

make·up or **make-up** (māk′ŭp′) ►*n.* **1.** The way in which something is composed, constructed, or arranged. **2.** The qualities or temperament that constitute a personality. **3.** Cosmetics applied esp. to the face.

mak·ings (mā′kĭngz) ►*pl.n.* The material or ingredients needed for making something.

ma·ko (mä′kō) ►*n.*, *pl.* -kos A shark having a large heavy body and a nearly symmetrical tail. [Maori.]

mal– ►*pref.* Bad; badly: *malformation.* [< Lat. *malus,* bad, and *male,* badly.]

Mal·a·bo (măl′ə-bō′, mä-lä′bō) The capital of Equatorial Guinea, on an island in the Gulf of Guinea.

Ma·lac·ca (mə-lăk′ə, -lä′kə), **Strait of** A channel between Sumatra and the Malay Peninsula connecting the Andaman Sea with the South China Sea.

Mal·a·chi (măl′ə-kī′) ►*n.* **1.** A Hebrew prophet of the 5th cent. BC. **2.** See table at **Bible.**

mal·a·chite (măl′ə-kīt′) ►*n.* A green carbonate mineral used as a source of copper and for ornamental purposes. [< Gk. *molokhitis < malakhē,* mallow.]

mal·ad·just·ment (măl′ə-jŭst′mənt) ►*n.* Faulty or poor adjustment. —**mal′ad·just′ed** *adj.*

mal·a·droit (măl′ə-droit′) ►*adj.* Marked by a lack of dexterity; clumsy; inept. —**mal′a·droit′ly** *adv.* —**mal′a·droit′ness** *n.*

mal·a·dy (măl′ə-dē) ►*n.*, *pl.* -dies A disease, disorder, or ailment. [< Lat. *male habitus,* in poor condition.]

Mal·a·gas·y (măl′ə-găs′ē) ►*n.*, *pl.* -gas·y or -gas·ies **1.** A native or inhabitant of Madagascar. **2.** The Austronesian language of the Malagasy. —**Mal′a·gas′y** *adj.*

mal·aise (mă-lāz′, -lĕz′) ►*n.* **1.** A vague feeling of illness. **2.** A general depression or unease. [< OFr.]

mal·a·mute (măl′ə-myōōt′) ►*n.* A powerful dog developed in Alaska as a sled dog and hav-

ing a thick coat and a bushy tail. [< *Malemute,* an Alaskan Eskimo people.]

mal·a·prop·ism (măl′ə-prŏp-ĭz′əm) ►*n.* A ludicrous misuse of a word. [After Mrs. *Malaprop,* a character in *The Rivals,* a play by Richard B. Sheridan.]

mal·a·pro·pos (măl′ăp-rə-pō′) ►*adj.* Out of place; inappropriate; inopportune. [Fr. *mal à propos.*] —**mal′a·pro·pos′** *adv.*

ma·lar·i·a (mə-lâr′ē-ə) ►*n.* An infectious disease marked by fever and anemia, caused by a protozoan that invades red blood cells and is transmitted by the bite of a mosquito. [Ital. < *mal′ aria,* foul air.] —**ma·lar′i·al** *adj.*

ma·lar·key also **ma·lar·ky** (mə-lär′kē) ►*n.* *Slang* Exaggerated or foolish talk, usu. intended to deceive. [?]

mal·a·thi·on (măl′ə-thī′ŏn′) ►*n.* The organic compound $C_{10}H_{19}O_6PS_2$, used as an insecticide.

Ma·la·wi (mə-lä′wē) A country of SE Africa. Cap. Lilongwe. —**Ma·la′wi·an** *adj.* & *n.*

Ma·lay (mə-lā′, mā′lā′) ►*n.* **1.** A member of a people inhabiting the Malay Peninsula and parts of the W Malay Archipelago. **2.** The Austronesian language of the Malays. —**Ma·lay′an, Ma·lay′** *adj.* & *n.*

Mal·a·ya·lam (măl′ə-yä′ləm) ►*n.* A Dravidian language spoken in SW India.

Malay Archipelago An island group of SE Asia between Australia and the Asian mainland.

Malay Peninsula also **Ma·la·ya** (mə-lä′ə, mā-) A peninsula of SE Asia comprising SW Thailand, W Malaysia, and the island of Singapore.

Ma·lay·sia (mə-lä′zhə, -shə) A country of SE Asia consisting of the S Malay Peninsula and the N part of Borneo. Cap. Kuala Lumpur. —**Ma·lay′sian** *adj.* & *n.*

Mal·colm X (măl′kəm ĕks′) Malcolm Little. 1925–65. Amer. activist.

mal·con·tent (măl′kən-tĕnt′) ►*adj.* Discontented. ►*n.* A discontented person.

Mal·dives (môl′dīvz, -dēvz, măl′-) An island country in the Indian Ocean SW of Sri Lanka. Cap. Male. —**Mal·div′i·an** (-dĭv′ē-ən), **Mal·di′van** *adj.* & *n.*

male (māl) ►*adj.* **1a.** Of or being the sex that has organs to produce spermatozoa for fertilizing ova. **b.** Consisting of members of this sex. **2.** *Bot.* **a.** Of or being an organ, as an anther, that produces gametes capable of fertilizing those produced by female organs. **b.** Bearing stamens but not pistils. **3.** Made for insertion into a fitted bore or socket: *a male plug.* ►*n.* A member of the male sex. [< Lat. *masculus.*] —**male′ness** *n.*

Ma·le (mä′lē) The capital of the Maldives, on **Male,** the chief atoll of the island country.

Mal·e·cite (măl′ə-sīt′) ►*n.* Var. of **Maliseet.**

mal·e·dic·tion (măl′ĭ-dĭk′shən) ►*n.* A curse. [< Lat. *maledīcere,* to curse.]

mal·e·fac·tor (măl′ə-făk′tər) ►*n.* **1.** A criminal. **2.** An evildoer. [< Lat. < *malefacere,* do wrong.] —**mal′e·fac′tion** *n.*

ma·lef·ic (mə-lĕf′ĭk) ►*adj.* **1.** Exerting a malignant influence. **2.** Malicious. [Lat. *maleficus.*]

ma·lef·i·cence (mə-lĕf′ĭ-səns) ►*n.* **1.** The doing of evil or harm; mischief. **2.** Harmful or evil nature or quality. [Lat. *maleficentia.*] —**ma·lef′i·cent** *adj.*

ma·lev·o·lence (mə-lĕv′ə-ləns) ►*n.* **1.** The

quality or state of being malevolent. **2.** Malicious behavior. [ME < OFr. *malivolence* < Lat. *malevolentia* < *malevolēns*, *malevolent*-, malevolent : *male*, badly + *volēns*, pr.part. of *velle*, to want.]

ma·lev·o·lent (mə-lĕv′ə-lənt) ►*adj.* Having or exhibiting ill will; malicious. [Lat. *malevolēns*, *malevolent*-.] —**ma·lev′o·lence** *n.* —**ma·lev′o·lent·ly** *adv.*

mal·fea·sance (măl-fē′zəns) ►*n. Law* Misconduct or wrongdoing, esp. by a public official. [AN *malfaisance* < Lat. *malefacere*, do wrong.]

mal·for·ma·tion (măl′fôr-mā′shən) ►*n.* Abnormal or anomalous formation or structure; deformity. —**mal·formed′** *adj.*

mal·func·tion (măl-fŭngk′shən) ►*v.* To fail to function normally. —**mal·func′tion** *n.*

Ma·li (mä′lē) A country of W Africa. Cap. Bamako. —**Ma′li·an** *adj. & n.*

mal·ice (măl′ĭs) ►*n.* **1.** A desire to harm others or to see others suffer; spite. **2.** *Law* The intent to commit an unlawful act without justification or excuse. [< Lat. *malitia* < *malus*, bad.] —**ma·li′cious** (mə-lĭsh′əs) *adj.* —**ma·li′cious·ly** *adv.* —**ma·li′cious·ness** *n.*

ma·lign (mə-līn′) ►*v.* To speak evil of; defame. ►*adj.* **1.** Evil or harmful in influence or effect; injurious. **2.** Malevolent. [< Lat. *malignus*, evil, harmful.] —**ma·lign′er** *n.*

ma·lig·nant (mə-lĭg′nənt) ►*adj.* **1.** *Med.* **a.** Tending to metastasize: *a malignant tumor.* **b.** Virulent or threatening to life: *a malignant disease.* **2.** Having or showing ill will; malicious. —**ma·lig′nan·cy** *n.* —**ma·lig′nant·ly** *adv.*

ma·lig·ni·ty (mə-lĭg′nĭ-tē) ►*n., pl.* -**ties 1a.** Intense ill will or hatred; great malice. **b.** An act or feeling of great malice. **2.** The condition of being evil or injurious.

ma·lin·ger (mə-lĭng′gər) ►*v.* To feign illness or other incapacity to avoid work. [< Fr. *malingre*, sickly.] —**ma·lin′ger·er** *n.*

Mal·i·seet (măl′ə-sēt′) or **Mal·e·cite** (-sīt′) ►*n., pl.* -**seet** or -**seets** or -**cite** or -**cites 1.** A member of a Native American people inhabiting New Brunswick and NE Maine. **2.** The Algonquian language of the Maliseet.

mall (môl, măl) ►*n.* **1.** A large, often enclosed shopping complex with stores, businesses, and restaurants. **2.** A street lined with shops and closed to vehicles. **3.** A shady public walk or promenade. [After *The Mall*, London.]

mal·lard (măl′ərd) ►*n., pl.* -**lard** or -**lards** A wild duck, the male of which has a green head and neck. [< OFr. *mallart*, perh. < *male*, MALE.]

mal·le·a·ble (măl′ē-ə-bəl) ►*adj.* **1.** Capable of being shaped or formed; pliable. **2.** Easily controlled; tractable. **3.** Able to adjust to changing circumstances; adaptable. [< Lat. *malleus*, hammer.] —**mal′le·a·bil′i·ty** *n.* —**mal′le·a·bly** *adv.*

mal·let (măl′ĭt) ►*n.* **1.** A short-handled hammer, usu. with a cylindrical head of wood. **2.** *Sports* A similar long-handled implement used to strike a ball, as in croquet and polo. [< OFr. *maillet*, dim. of *mail*, MAUL.]

mal·le·us (măl′ē-əs) ►*n., pl.* -**le·i** (-ē-ī′) A hammer-shaped bone that is the outermost bone in the middle ear. [Lat., hammer.]

mal·low (măl′ō) ►*n.* A plant having showy pink or white flowers. [< Lat. *malva*.]

mal·nour·ished (măl-nûr′ĭsht, -nŭr′-) ►*adj.*

Affected by improper or poor nutrition.

mal·nu·tri·tion (măl′nōō-trĭsh′ən, -nyōō-) ►*n.* Insufficient or unhealthy nutrition.

mal·oc·clu·sion (măl′ə-klōō′zhən) ►*n.* Faulty closure between the upper and lower teeth.

mal·o·dor (măl-ō′dər) ►*n.* A bad odor. See Synonyms at **stench.** —**mal·o′dor·ous** *adj.* —**mal·o′dor·ous·ly** *adv.*

Mal·o·ry (măl′ə-rē), Sir **Thomas** fl. 1470. English writer.

ma·lo·ti (mä-lō′tē) ►*n.* Pl. of **loti.**

mal·prac·tice (măl-prăk′tĭs) ►*n.* Substandard performance, as by a physician or lawyer, esp. when resulting in injury or loss. —**mal′prac·ti′tion·er** *n.*

malt (môlt) ►*n.* **1.** Grain, usu. barley, that has been allowed to sprout, used chiefly in brewing and distilling. **2.** An alcoholic beverage, such as beer, brewed from malt. **3.** See **malted milk** (sense 2). [< OE *mealt.*] —**malt** *v.* —**malt′y** *adj.*

Mal·ta (môl′tə) An island country in the Mediterranean S of Sicily. Cap. Valletta. —**Mal·tese′** *adj. & n.*

malt·ed milk (môl′tĭd) ►*n.* **1.** A soluble powder made of dried milk, malted barley, and wheat flour. **2.** A beverage made by mixing milk with this powder and often ice cream and flavoring; malt.

Mal·thus (măl′thəs), **Thomas Robert** 1766–1834. British economist. —**Mal·thu′sian** (-thōō′zhən, -zē-ən) *adj. & n.*

mal·tose (môl′tōs′, -tōz′) ►*n.* A sugar. $C_{12}H_{22}O_{11}$, formed in the digestion of starch.

mal·treat (măl-trēt′) ►*v.* To treat in a rough or cruel way; abuse. —**mal·treat′ment** *n.*

mal·ware (măl′wâr′) ►*n.* Malicious computer software that interferes with normal computer functions or sends personal data about the user to unauthorized parties. [MAL(ICIOUS) + –WARE.]

ma·ma or **mam·ma** (mä′mə, mə-mä′) ►*n. Informal* Mother. [Of baby-talk orig.]

mam·ba (mäm′bə) ►*n.* A venomous snake of tropical Africa. [Zulu *i-mâmbà*.]

mam·bo (mäm′bō) ►*n., pl.* -**bos** A dance of Latin-American origin, resembling the rumba. [Am.Sp.] —**mam′bo** *v.*

Mam·et (măm′ĭt), **David** b. 1947. Amer. playwright, screenwriter, and film director.

mam·mal (măm′əl) ►*n.* Any of various warm-blooded vertebrate animals, including humans, marked by a covering of hair on the skin and, in the female, milk-producing glands. [< Lat. *mamma*, breast.] —**mam·ma′li·an** (mă-mā′lē-ən) *adj. & n.*

mam·mal·o·gy (mă-măl′ə-jē, -mŏl′-) ►*n.* The branch of zoology that deals with mammals. —**mam·mal′o·gist** *n.*

mam·ma·ry (măm′ə-rē) ►*adj.* Of or relating to a breast or milk-producing organ. [< Lat. *mamma*, breast.]

mam·mo·gram (măm′ə-grăm′) ►*n.* An x-ray image produced by mammography.

mam·mog·ra·phy (mă-mŏg′rə-fē) ►*n., pl.* -**phies** Radiological examination of the breasts to detect tumors. [< Lat. *mamma*, breast.]

Mam·mon or **mam·mon** (măm′ən) ►*n.* Material wealth, personified as a false god or regarded as having an evil influence. [< Aram. *māmōnā*, riches.]

mam·moth (măm′əth) ►*n.* Any of various prehistoric elephants often having long coats of hair. ►*adj.* Of enormous size; huge. [Obsolete Russ. *mamut.*]

mam·my (măm′ē) ►*n., pl.* **-mies 1.** A mother. **2.** *Offensive* A Black nursemaid, esp. formerly in the S US. [< Dialectal *mam,* var. of MAMA.]

man (măn) ►*n., pl.* **men** (měn) **1.** An adult male human. **2.** A human regardless of sex or age; person. **3.** The human race: *man's quest for peace.* **4.** A male human having qualities considered characteristic of manhood. **5.** *Informal* A husband, lover, or sweetheart. **6.** *Games* A piece that is used in a board game, such as chess or checkers. ►*v.* **manned, man·ning 1.** To supply with men or persons: *man a ship.* **2.** To take one's station at; attend or operate. —*idiom:* **to a man** Without exception. [< OE *mann.*]
　　Usage: The use of *man* to mean "a human, regardless of sex" has a long history, but many feel that the sense of "male" is predominant over that of "person." Accordingly, many occupational titles in which *man* occurs as an element are being replaced, sometimes officially, by terms that are neutral. For example, *firefighter* is often used instead of *fireman, member of Congress* instead of *congressman,* and *chair* or *chairperson* instead of *chairman.* In addition, compounds formed with *woman,* as in *businesswoman, policewoman,* and *chairwoman,* are increasingly used as parallel terms to the corresponding compounds formed with *man.* See Usage Note at **-ess.**

Man, Isle of An island in the Irish Sea off NW England, governed as a British crown dependency.

man about town ►*n., pl.* **men about town** A sophisticated, socially active man who frequents fashionable places.

man·a·cle (măn′ə-kəl) ►*n.* **1.** A device for shackling the hands. **2.** Something that confines or restrains. ►*v.* **-cled, -cling** To restrain with or as if with manacles. See Synonyms at **hobble.** [< Lat. *manicula* < *manus,* hand.]

man·age (măn′ĭj) ►*v.* **-aged, -ag·ing 1.** To direct, control, or handle. **2.** To direct the business affairs of. **3.** To contrive or arrange. **4.** To get along; get by. [Ital. *maneggiare,* ult. < Lat. *manus,* hand.] —**man′age·a·bil′i·ty, man′age·a·ble·ness** *n.* —**man′age·a·bly** *adv.*

man·aged care (măn′ĭjd) ►*n.* A health care arrangement in which an organization, such as an HMO, acts as an intermediary between patient and physician.

man·age·ment (măn′ĭj-mənt) ►*n.* **1.** The act, manner, or practice of managing. **2.** The person or persons who manage an organization.

man·ag·er (măn′ĭ-jər) ►*n.* **1.** One who manages. **2.** One in charge of the training and performance of an athlete or team. —**man′a·ge′ri·al** (-ĭ-jîr′ē-əl) *adj.* —**man′a·ge′ri·al·ly** *adv.* —**man′ag·er·ship′** *n.*

Ma·na·gua (mä-nä′gwä) The capital of Nicaragua, in the W part on **Lake Managua.** —**Ma·na′guan** *adj. & n.*

Ma·na·ma (mə-năm′ə, -nä′mə) The capital of Bahrain, on the Persian Gulf.

ma·ña·na (mä-nyä′nə) ►*adv.* **1.** Tomorrow. **2.** At some future time. [Sp., morning, tomorrow < Lat. *māne.*] —**ma·ña′na** *n.*

ma·nat (mä-nät′) ►*n.* See table at **currency.** [Azerbaijani and Turkmen.]

man·a·tee (măn′ə-tē′) ►*n.* A large aquatic herbivorous mammal of warm Atlantic coastal waters. [Sp. *manatí* < Cariban.]

manatee

Ma·naus (mə-nous′, mä-) A city of NW Brazil on the Río Negro near its junction with the Amazon R.

Man·ches·ter (măn′chĕs′tər, -chĭ-stər) A city of NW England ENE of Liverpool.

Man·chu (măn′chōō, măn-chōō′) ►*n., pl.* **-chu** or **-chus 1.** A member of a people native to Manchuria who ruled China during the Qing dynasty (1644–1912). **2.** The Tungusic language of the Manchu. —**Man′chu** *adj.*

Man·chu·ri·a (măn-chŏŏr′ē-ə) A region of NE China. —**Man·chu′ri·an** *adj. & n.*

man·da·la (mŭn′də-lə) ►*n.* Any of various ritualistic geometric designs used in Hinduism and Buddhism as an aid to meditation. [Skt. *maṇḍalam,* circle.]

Man·da·lay (măn′dl-ā′) A city of central Myanmar on the Irrawaddy R. N of Yangon.

man·da·mus (măn-dā′məs) ►*n.* A writ issued by a court requiring a public official or entity to perform a duty associated with that office or entity. [Lat. *mandāmus,* we order.]

Man·dan (măn′dăn′) ►*n., pl.* **-dan** or **-dans 1.** A member of a Native American people formerly living along the Missouri R. in S-central North Dakota. **2.** The Siouan language of the Mandan.

man·da·rin (măn′də-rĭn) ►*n.* **1.** A high-ranking public official in the Chinese Empire. **2.** A member of an intellectual or cultural elite. **3.** A mandarin orange. [< Skt. *mantrin-,* counselor < *mantraḥ,* counsel.] —**man′da·rin** *adj.*

Man·da·rin (măn′də-rĭn) ►*n.* The official standard language of China, based on the dialect of Beijing.

mandarin orange ►*n.* A small, loose-skinned orange citrus fruit. [Fr. *mandarine* < Sp. *mandarín,* MANDARIN.]

man·date (măn′dāt′) ►*n.* **1.** An authoritative command or instruction. **2a.** A commission from the League of Nations authorizing a member nation to administer a territory. **b.** A region under administration. [< Lat. *mandāre,* to order.] —**man′date′** *v.*

man·da·to·ry (măn′də-tôr′ē) ►*adj.* **1.** Required or obligatory. **2.** Of, relating to, or containing a mandate.

Man·de (măn′dā′) ►*n., pl.* **Mande** or **-des 1.** A group of Niger-Congo languages spoken in the upper Niger R. valley. **2.** A member of a Mande-speaking people.

Man·de·la (măn-dĕl′ə), **Nelson Rolihlahla** b. 1918. South African president (1994–99).

Nelson Mandela
photographed in 2004

man·di·ble (mănʹdə-bəl) ►*n.* **1.** The lower jaw of a vertebrate animal. **2.** Either part of a bird's beak. **3.** A jawlike part of an insect or other invertebrate. [< LLat. *mandibula* < *mandere*, chew.] —**man·dib'u·lar** (-dĭbʹyə-lər) *adj.*

Man·din·go (măn-dĭngʹgō) ►*n., pl.* **-gos** or **-goes** See **Mande.**

man·do·lin (mănʹdə-lĭnʹ, mănʹdl-ĭn) ►*n.* A stringed musical instrument with a usu. pear-shaped body and a fretted neck. [< Ital. *mandola*, lute < Gk. *pandoura.*]

man·drake (mănʹdrāk') ►*n.* **1.** A S European plant having a branched root thought to resemble the human body, once widely believed to have magical powers. **2.** The mayapple. [< Gk. *mandragoras.*]

man·drel or **man·dril** (mănʹdrəl) ►*n.* **1.** A spindle or axle used to secure or support material being machined. **2.** A metal rod or bar around which material, such as metal or glass, may be shaped. [Poss. < Fr. *mandrin*, lathe.]

man·drill (mănʹdrəl) ►*n.* A large African monkey having a colorful face and rump, esp. in the adult male. [MAN + *drill*, a baboon.]

mane (mān) ►*n.* **1.** The long hair growing from the neck of certain animals, such as the horse and male lion. **2.** A long thick growth of human hair. [< OE *manu.*]

ma·nège also **ma·nege** (mă-nĕzhʹ) ►*n.* The art of training or riding horses. [Fr. < Ital. *maneggio* < *maneggiare*, MANAGE.]

ma·nes or **Ma·nes** (māʹnēzʹ, mäʹnāsʹ) ►*pl.n.* In ancient Roman religion, the spirits of the dead. [< Lat. *mānēs.*]

Ma·net (mə-nāʹ, mă-), **Édouard** 1832–83. French painter.

ma·neu·ver (mə-nōōʹvər, -nyōōʹ-) ►*n.* **1a.** A physical movement involving skill and dexterity. **b.** A controlled change in the direction of a moving vehicle such as an aircraft. **2a.** A strategic or tactical military or naval movement. **b.** often **maneuvers** A large-scale tactical exercise that simulates combat. **3.** A skillful or cunning action undertaken to gain an end. ►*v.* **1.** To move or direct through a series of movements or changes in course. **2.** To carry out a military maneuver. **3.** To use stratagems in gaining an end. **4.** To manipulate or guide adroitly to a desired position or goal. [< Lat.

manū operārī, work by hand.] —**ma·neuʹver·a·bilʹi·ty** *n.* —**ma·neuʹver·a·ble** *adj.*

man·ful (mănʹfəl) ►*adj.* Displaying traditionally masculine traits such as courage or resolve. —**manʹful·ly** *adv.* —**manʹful·ness** *n.*

man·ga (mängʹgə) ►*n.* A style of comic strip or comic book characterized by stylized colorful art and often adult themes. [J.]

man·ga·nese (măngʹgə-nēzʹ, -nēsʹ) ►*n. Symbol* **Mn** A brittle metallic element used chiefly in making alloys of steel. At. no. 25. See table at **element.** [< Ital. < Med.Lat. *magnēsia*, MAGNESIA.]

mange (mānj) ►*n.* A contagious skin disease esp. of domestic animals, marked by itching and loss of hair. [< OFr. *manjue* < *mangier*, eat; see MANGER.] —**mangʹy** *adj.*

man·ger (mānʹjər) ►*n.* A trough or an open box in which feed for livestock is placed. [< Lat. *mandūcāre*, eat.]

man·gle¹ (măngʹgəl) ►*v.* **-gled, -gling** **1.** To mutilate or disfigure by battering or hacking. **2.** To ruin or botch. [< AN *mangler.*] —**manʹgler** *n.*
Syns: *maim, maul, mutilate* **v.**

man·gle² (măngʹgəl) ►*n.* A laundry machine for pressing fabrics. [Du. *mangel.*]

man·go (măngʹgō) ►*n., pl.* **-goes** or **-gos** **1.** A tropical Asian evergreen tree cultivated for its edible fruit. **2.** The sweet juicy fruit of the mango. [< Tamil *mānkāy.*]

man·grove (mănʹgrōvʹ, măngʹ-) ►*n.* Any of various tropical or subtropical trees or shrubs having stiltlike roots and forming dense thickets in tidal regions. [< Taino *mangue.*]

man·han·dle (mănʹhăn'dəl) ►*v.* To handle roughly.

Man·hat·tan¹ (măn-hătʹn) A borough of New York City in SE NY, mainly on **Manhattan Island.** —**Man·hatʹtan·ite'** (-īt') *n.*

Man·hat·tan² (măn-hătʹn, mən-) ►*n.* A cocktail made of sweet vermouth and whiskey. [< MANHATTAN¹.]

man·hole (mănʹhōl') ►*n.* A hole, usu. with a cover, through which an underground structure, such as a sewer, can be entered.

man·hood (mănʹhŏŏd') ►*n.* **1.** The state of being an adult male. **2.** The qualities, such as courage and vigor, often thought to be appropriate to a man. **3.** Men collectively.

man·hour (mănʹour') ►*n.* An industrial unit of production equal to the work one person can produce in one hour.

man·hunt (mănʹhŭnt') ►*n.* An organized search esp. for a fugitive criminal.

ma·ni·a (māʹnē-ə, mānʹyə) ►*n.* **1.** An excessive enthusiasm, interest, or desire. **2.** *Psychiat.* A manifestation of bipolar disorder, marked esp. by high energy, racing thoughts, irritability, and rapid speech. [< Gk.]

–mania ►*suff.* An exaggerated desire or enthusiasm for: *pyromania.* [< MANIA.]

ma·ni·ac (māʹnē-ăk') ►*n.* **1.** A mentally ill person whose behavior is violent or bizarre. Not used in psychiatric diagnosis. **2.** One with an excessive enthusiasm for something. **3.** One who acts in a wildly irresponsible way. [< Gk. *maniakos*, mad < *mania*, madness.] —**maʹni·ac'**, **ma·ni'a·cal** (mə-nīʹə-kəl) *adj.*

man·ic (mănʹĭk) ►*adj.* Of, affected by, or marked by mania.

man·ic·de·pres·sive disorder (măn′ĭk-dĭ-prĕs′ĭv) ►*n.* See **bipolar disorder.**

man·i·cot·ti (măn′ĭ-kŏt′ē) ►*n.* A dish of large pasta tubes with a filling. [Ital.]

man·i·cure (măn′ĭ-kyŏŏr′) ►*n.* A cosmetic treatment of the fingernails. ►*v.* **-cured, -cur·ing 1.** To give a manicure to. **2.** To trim evenly. [Fr.] —**man′i·cur′ist** *n.*

man·i·fest (măn′ə-fĕst′) ►*adj.* Clearly apparent to the sight or understanding; obvious. See Synonyms at **apparent.** ►*v.* **1.** To show plainly; reveal. **2.** To become manifest; be revealed. ►*n.* A list of cargo or passengers. [< Lat. *manifestus.*] —**man′i·fest′ly** *adv.*

man·i·fes·ta·tion (măn′ə-fĕ-stā′shən) ►*n.* An indication of the existence or presence of something.

man·i·fes·to (măn′ə-fĕs′tō) ►*n., pl.* **-toes** or **-tos** A public declaration of principles or intentions, esp. political ones. [Ital., MANIFEST.]

man·i·fold (măn′ə-fōld′) ►*adj.* **1.** Of many and diverse kinds. **2.** Having many features or forms. ►*n.* A pipe having several openings for making multiple connections.

man·i·kin or **man·ni·kin** (măn′ĭ-kĭn) ►*n.* **1.** *Derogatory* A short man. **2.** A mannequin. [< MDu. *mannekijn,* little man.]

Ma·nil·a (mə-nĭl′ə) The capital of the Philippines, on Luzon I. by **Manila Bay,** an inlet of the South China Sea.

Manila hemp ►*n.* The fiber of the abaca, a Philippine plant related to the banana, used to make cordage and paper.

Manila paper ►*n.* A strong paper or thin cardboard, usu. buff in color.

man·i·oc (măn′ē-ŏk′) ►*n.* See **cassava.** [< Tupí *mandioca.*]

ma·nip·u·late (mə-nĭp′yə-lāt′) ►*v.* **-lat·ed, -lat·ing 1.** To operate or control, esp. by skilled use of the hands; handle. **2.** To influence or manage shrewdly or deviously. **3.** To tamper with or falsify for personal gain. [< Lat. *manipulus,* handful.] —**ma·nip′u·la′tion** *n.* —**ma·nip′u·la′tive** *adj.* —**ma·nip′u·la′tor** *n.* —**ma·nip′u·la·to′ry** (-lə-tôr′ē) *adj.*

Man·i·to·ba (măn′ĭ-tō′bə) A province of S-central Canada. Cap. Winnipeg. —**Man′i·to′ban** *adj. & n.*

man·i·tou (măn′ĭ-tŏŏ′) ►*n., pl.* **-tous** In Algonquian religious belief, a supernatural power that permeates the world. [< Ojibwa *manitoo.*]

man·kind (măn′kīnd′) ►*n.* **1.** The human race. **2.** Men as opposed to women.

man·ly (măn′lē) ►*adj.* **-li·er, -li·est 1.** Having qualities traditionally attributed to a man. **2.** Of a man; masculine. —**man′li·ness** *n.* —**man′ly** *adj.*

man·made or **man-made** (măn′mād′) ►*adj.* Made by humans; synthetic.

Mann (măn), **Horace** 1796–1859. Amer. educator.

Mann (măn, män), **Thomas** 1875–1955. German writer.

man·na (măn′ə) ►*n.* **1.** In the Bible, the food miraculously provided for the Israelites in the wilderness during their flight from Egypt. **2.** Something of value that comes unexpectedly. [< Heb. *mān.*]

manned (mănd) ►*adj.* Transporting or operated by a human: *a manned spacecraft.*

man·ne·quin (măn′ĭ-kĭn) ►*n.* **1.** A life-size representation of the human body, used to fit or display clothes; dummy. **2.** One who models clothes. [Fr. < MDu. *mannekijn,* manikin.]

man·ner (măn′ər) ►*n.* **1.** A way of doing something or the way in which a thing is done or happens. **2.** Bearing or behavior. **3. manners a.** Socially proper behavior. **b.** The prevailing customs of a society or period, esp. as the subject of a literary work. **4.** Practice, style, or method in the arts. **5.** Kind; sort. —*idiom:* **in a manner of speaking** In a way; so to speak. [< Lat. *manuārius,* of the hand.]

man·nered (măn′ərd) ►*adj.* **1.** Having manners of a specific kind: *ill-mannered.* **2.** Artificial or affected. **3.** Of or exhibiting mannerisms.

man·ner·ism (măn′ə-rĭz′əm) ►*n.* **1.** A distinctive behavioral trait. **2.** Exaggerated or affected style or habit.

man·ner·ly (măn′ər-lē) ►*adj.* Having good manners. —**man′ner·li·ness** *n.*

man·ni·kin (măn′ĭ-kĭn) ►*n.* Var. of **manikin.**

man·nish (măn′ĭsh) ►*adj.* **1.** Relating to men; masculine. **2.** Resembling or suggestive of a man rather than a woman. —**man′nish·ly** *adv.*

man-of-war (măn′ə-wôr′) ►*n., pl.* **men-of-war** (mĕn′-) **1.** See **warship. 2.** A Portuguese man-of-war.

ma·nom·e·ter (mă-nŏm′ĭ-tər) ►*n.* An instrument for measuring the pressure of liquids and gases. [Gk. *manos,* sparse + –METER.] —**man′o·met′ric** (măn′ə-mĕt′rĭk), **man′o·met′ri·cal** *adj.* —**ma·nom′e·try** *n.*

man·or (măn′ər) ►*n.* **1a.** A landed estate. **b.** The main house on an estate. **2.** The district over which a feudal lord had domain. [< Lat. *manēre,* dwell.] —**ma·no′ri·al** (mə-nôr′ē-əl) *adj.*

man·pow·er (măn′pou′ər) ►*n.* **1.** The power of human physical strength. **2.** Power in terms of the workers available, as for a particular task.

man·qué (mäN-kā′) ►*adj.* Unfulfilled; frustrated: *an artist manqué.* [Fr. < Lat. *mancus,* maimed.]

man·sard (măn′särd′) ►*n.* A roof having a double slope on all sides, with the lower slope much steeper than the upper. [After François *Mansart* (1598–1666).]

manse (măns) ►*n.* A cleric's house and land, esp. a Presbyterian minister's residence. [< Med.Lat. *mānsa,* dwelling < Lat. *manēre,* dwell.]

Mans·field (mănz′fēld′), **Katherine** 1888–1923. New Zealand–born British writer.

man·sion (măn′shən) ►*n.* A large stately house. [< Lat. *mānsiō,* dwelling.]

man-sized (măn′sīzd′) also **man-size** (-sīz′) ►*adj. Informal* Very large.

man·slaugh·ter (măn′slô′tər) ►*n.* The killing of a person without premeditated malice, either with murderous intent partly extenuated by circumstances or as the unintended result of another crime.

man·ta (măn′tə) ►*n.* A large ray of tropical and subtropical seas having winglike pectoral fins and two hornlike fins on the head. [Sp., blanket.]

man·tel also **man·tle** (măn′tl) ►*n.* **1.** An ornamental facing around a fireplace. **2.** The protruding shelf over a fireplace. [ME < var. of MANTLE.]

man·tel·piece (măn′tl-pēs′) ►*n.* A mantle.

man·til·la (măn-tē′yə, -tĭl′ə) ►*n.* A lace or silk

scarf traditionally worn over the head and shoulders by women in Spain and Latin America. [Sp.]

man·tis (măn′tĭs) ►*n., pl.* **-es** or **-tes** (-tēz) A predatory insect having two pairs of walking legs and powerful grasping forelimbs. [Gk., seer.]

man·tis·sa (măn-tĭs′ə) ►*n.* The decimal part of a logarithm. [Lat., counterweight.]

man·tle (măn′tl) ►*n.* **1.** A loose sleeveless outer garment; cloak. **2.** Something that covers, envelops, or conceals. **3.** Var. of **mantel. 4.** A device in gas lamps consisting of a sheath of threads that glows brightly when heated by the flame. **5.** The layer of the earth between the crust and the core. ►*v.* **-tled, -tling** To cover with or as if with a mantle. [< Lat. *mantellum.*]

Mantle, Mickey Charles 1931–95. Amer. baseball player.

man·tra (măn′trə, mŭn′-) ►*n.* **1.** *Hinduism* A sacred verbal formula repeated in prayer, meditation, or incantation. **2.** A commonly repeated word or phrase. [Skt. *mantraḥ.*] —**man′tric** *adj.*

man·u·al (măn′yōō-əl) ►*adj.* **1.** Of or relating to the hands. **2.** Done by or operated with the hands. **3.** Employing human rather than mechanical energy: *manual labor.* ►*n.* **1.** A small reference book, esp. one giving instructions. **2.** An organ keyboard. [< Lat. *manus,* hand.] —**man′u·al·ly** *adv.*

manual alphabet ►*n.* An alphabet used by hearing-impaired people in which finger positions represent the letters.

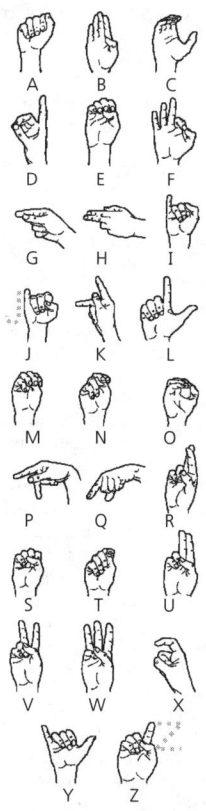

manual alphabet

man·u·fac·to·ry (măn′yə-făk′tə-rē) ►*n., pl.* **-ries** A factory.

man·u·fac·ture (măn′yə-făk′chər) ►*v.* **-tured, -tur·ing 1.** To make or process from raw materials, esp. by means of a large-scale industrial operation. **2.** To make up; fabricate. ►*n.* **1.** The act or process of manufacturing. **2.** A manufactured product. [< Med.Lat. *manūfactūra,* making by hand.] —**man′u·fac′tur·er** *n.*

man·u·mit (măn′yə-mĭt′) ►*v.* **-mit·ted, -mit·ting** To free from slavery or bondage. [< Lat. *manūmittere.*] —**man′u·mis′sion** (-mĭsh′ən) *n.*

ma·nure (mə-nŏŏr′, -nyŏŏr′) ►*n.* **1.** Dung, esp. of livestock. **2.** Dung or other material used to fertilize soil. ►*v.* **-nured, -nur·ing** To fertilize (soil) by applying manure. [< AN *mainouverer,* cultivate; see MANEUVER.]

man·u·script (măn′yə-skrĭpt′) ►*n.* **1.** A book or other document written by hand. **2.** A version of a text prepared and submitted for publication. [< Med.Lat. *manūscrīptus,* written by hand.]

Manx (măngks) ►*n.* **1.** (*takes. pl. v.*) The people of the Isle of Man. **2.** The extinct Celtic language of the Manx. —**Manx** *adj.* —**Manx′-man** *n.* —**Manx′wom′an** *n.*

man·y (měn′ē) ►*adj.* **more** (môr, mōr), **most** (mōst) **1.** Amounting to a large indefinite number: *many friends.* **2.** Being one of a large indefinite number: *many a day.* ►*n.* (*takes pl. v.*) A large indefinite number. ►*pron.* (*takes pl. v.*) A large number of persons or things. [< OE *manig.*]

man·y-sid·ed (měn′ē-sī′dĕd) ►*adj.* Having many sides or aspects: *a many-sided polygon.*

man·za·ni·ta (măn′zə-nē′tə) ►*n.* An evergreen shrub of the Pacific coast of North America. [Sp. < *manzana,* apple.]

Mao·ism (mou′ĭz′əm) ►*n.* Marxism-Leninism as developed in China chiefly by Mao Zedong. —**Mao′ist** *adj. & n.*

Mao·ri (mou′rē) ►*n., pl.* **-ri** or **-ris 1.** A member of a people of New Zealand, of Polynesian-Melanesian descent. **2.** Their Austronesian language. —**Mao′ri** *adj.*

Mao Ze·dong (mou′ dzə′dŏng′) also **Mao Tse-tung** (tsə′-tŏŏng′) 1893–1976. Chinese Communist leader and theorist.

Mao Zedong

map (măp) ►*n.* **1.** A representation, usu. on a plane surface, of a region. **2.** Something resembling a map, as in schematic representation. ►*v.* **mapped, map·ping 1.** To make a map of. **2.** To plan in detail: *map out the future.* [< Lat. *mappa.*] —**map′mak′er** *n.* —**map′pa·ble** *adj.* —**map′per** *n.*

ma·ple (mā′pəl) ►*n.* **1.** Any of a genus of deciduous trees having palmate leaves and long-winged fruits borne in pairs. **2.** The wood of a maple. **3.** The flavor of maple syrup. [< OE *mapul.*]

maple sugar ►*n.* A sugar made by boiling down maple syrup.

maple syrup ►*n.* A sweet syrup made by boiling the sap of the sugar maple.

Ma·pu·to (mə-pōō′tō) The capital of Mozambique, in the extreme S part.

mar (mär) ►*v.* **marred, mar·ring** To damage, disfigure, or spoil. [< OE *mierran*, impede.]

mar·a·bou (măr′ə-bōō′) ►*n.* **1.** A large African stork that scavenges for carrion. **2.** The soft white down of the marabou. [< Ar. *murābiṭ*, Muslim hermit.]

ma·ra·ca (mə-rä′kə) ►*n.* A percussion instrument consisting of a gourdlike rattle containing pebbles or beans. [Port. *maracá.*]

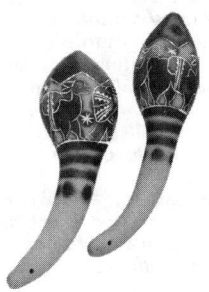

maraca

Ma·ra·cai·bo (mä′rä-kī′bō) A city of NW Venezuela on **Lake Maracaibo,** the largest lake of South America.

mar·a·schi·no (măr′ə-skē′nō, -shē′-) ►*n., pl.* **-nos** A cordial made from the fermented juice and crushed pits of a bitter cherry. [Ital. < *marasca*, sour cherry.]

maraschino cherry ►*n.* A cherry preserved in a sweet red syrup.

Ma·rat (mə-rä′, mä-), **Jean Paul** 1743–93. Swiss-born French revolutionary and scientist.

Ma·ra·thi (mə-rä′tē, -răt′ē) ►*n.* The principal Indic language of the state of Maharashtra, India.

mar·a·thon (măr′ə-thŏn′) ►*n.* **1.** A cross-country footrace of 26 mi, 385 yd (42.195 km). **2.** A test or contest of endurance. [After *Marathon*, Greece.] —**mar′a·thon′er** *n.*

ma·raud (mə-rôd′) ►*v.* To rove in search of plunder. [Fr. *marauder.*] —**ma·raud′er** *n.*

mar·ble (mär′bəl) ►*n.* **1.** A metamorphic, often streaked rock formed by alteration of limestone or dolomite, used esp. in architecture and sculpture. **2.** A sculpture carved from this rock. **3a.** A small hard ball, usu. of glass, used in children's games. **b. marbles** *(takes sing. v.)* A game played with marbles. **4. marbles** *Slang* Common sense; sanity: *lost his marbles.* [< Gk. *marmaros.*] —**mar′ble** *adj.* —**mar′bly** *adj.*

mar·bled (mär′bəld) ►*adj.* **1.** Made of or cov-

ered with marble. **2.** Mottled or streaked: *meat marbled with fat.* —**mar′bling** *n.*

march[1] (märch) ►*v.* **1.** To walk or cause to walk steadily and rhythmically forward, usu. in step with others. **2a.** To proceed directly and purposefully. **b.** To advance steadily: *Time marches on.* **3.** To participate in an organized walk. ►*n.* **1.** The act of marching. **2.** Steady forward movement or progression: *the march of progress.* **3.** A measured, even step. **4.** The distance covered by marching: *a week's march.* **5.** *Mus.* A composition in usu. duple meter that is appropriate for marching. **6.** An organized walk, as for a public cause. —*idiom:* **on the march** Advancing steadily. [< OFr. *marchier*, of Gmc. orig.] —**march′er** *n.*

march[2] (märch) ►*n.* A border region; frontier. [< OFr. *marche*, of Gmc. origin.]

March (märch) ►*n.* The 3rd month of the Gregorian calendar. See table at **calendar.** [< Lat. *Mārtius (mēnsis)*, (month) of Mars.]

mar·chio·ness (mär′shə-nĭs, mär′shə-nĕs′) ►*n.* **1.** The wife or widow of a marquis. **2.** A noblewoman ranking above a countess and below a duchess. [Med.Lat. *marchiōnissa.*]

Mar·co·ni (mär-kō′nē), **Guglielmo** 1874–1937. Italian engineer and inventor.

Mar·cos (mär′kōs), **Ferdinand Edralin** 1917–89. Philippine president (1965–86).

Mar·cus Au·re·li·us An·to·ni·nus (mär′kəs ô-rē′lē-əs ăn′tə-nī′nəs) AD 121–180. Roman philosopher and emperor (161–180).

Mar·di Gras (mär′dē grä′) ►*n.* The day before Ash Wednesday, celebrated in many places with carnivals and parades of costumed merrymakers. [Fr.]

mare[1] (mâr) ►*n.* A female horse or related animal. [< OE *mēre.*]

ma·re[2] (mä′rā) ►*n., pl.* **-ri·a** (-rē-ə) Any of the large dark areas on the moon or planets, esp. Mars. [Lat., sea.]

Mar·gar·et of Anjou (mär′gə-rət, -grət) 1430?–82. French-born queen consort of Henry VI of England.

mar·ga·rine (mär′jər-ĭn) ►*n.* A fatty solid butter substitute consisting of hydrogenated vegetable oils mixed with emulsifiers, vitamins, and coloring matter. [Fr.]

mar·ga·ri·ta (mär′gə-rē′tə) ►*n.* A cocktail made with tequila, an orange-flavored liqueur, and lemon or lime juice. [Sp.]

mar·gin (mär′jĭn) ►*n.* **1.** An edge and the area immediately adjacent to it; border. **2.** The blank space bordering the written or printed area on a page. **3.** An allowance beyond what is needed: *a margin of safety.* See Synonyms at **room. 4.** A measure or degree of difference: *a margin of 500 votes.* **5.** The difference between cost and selling price, as of securities. [< Lat. *margō, margin-.*]

mar·gin·al (mär′jə-nəl) ►*adj.* **1.** Of, at, or constituting a margin. **2.** Barely within a lower standard or limit: *marginal writing ability.* —**mar′gin·al·ly** *adv.*

mar·gi·na·li·a (mär′jə-nā′lē-ə) ►*pl.n.* Notes in the margin or margins of a book. [< Med.Lat. *marginālis*, marginal.]

ma·ri·a·chi (mä′rē-ä′chē) ►*n., pl.* **-chis** A street band in Mexico, usu. featuring violin, guitar, and trumpet players. [Am.Sp., perh. < Fr. *mariage*, marriage.]

Mar·i·an·a Islands (măr′ē-ăn′ə, mâr′-) A US-administered island group in the W Pacific E of the Philippines, comprising Guam, an independent commonwealth, and the **Northern Mariana Islands.**

Ma·rie An·toi·nette (mə-rē′ ăn′twə-nĕt′) 1755–93. Queen of France (1774–93) as the wife of Louis XVI.

Marie Antoinette
detail of an 1868 painting

Marie de Mé·di·cis (də mä′dē-sēs′) 1573–1642. Italian-born queen of France as the wife (1600–10) of Henry IV and regent (1610–17) for her son Louis XIII.

mar·i·gold (măr′ĭ-gōld′, mâr′-) ►*n.* An American annual plant cultivated for its showy yellow or orange flowers. [ME.]

mar·i·jua·na also **mar·i·hua·na** (măr′ə-wä′nə) ►*n.* **1.** The cannabis plant. **2.** The dried flower clusters and leaves of this plant, smoked or ingested as an illicit recreational drug or as an unconventional treatment of certain disease symptoms. [Sp. *marihuana.*]

ma·rim·ba (mə-rĭm′bə) ►*n.* A large wooden percussion instrument with resonators, resembling a xylophone. [Of Bantu orig.]

ma·ri·na (mə-rē′nə) ►*n.* A waterside facility offering docks, moorings, and supplies for small boats. [< Lat. *marīnus,* MARINE.]

mar·i·nade (măr′ə-nād′) ►*n.* A usu. seasoned liquid in which food is soaked before cooking. [Fr. < *mariner,* MARINATE.]

mar·i·nate (măr′ə-nāt′) ►*v.* **-nat·ed, -nat·ing** To soak (e.g., meat) in a marinade. [Fr. *mariner* < *marine,* seawater, brine (obs.); see MARINE.]

ma·rine (mə-rēn′) ►*adj.* **1.** Of or relating to the sea: *marine exploration.* **2.** Of shipping or maritime affairs. **3.** Of sea navigation. See Synonyms at **nautical.** ►*n.* **1. Marine** A member of the US Marine Corps. **2.** A soldier serving on a ship. [< Lat. *mare,* sea.]

Marine Corps ►*n.* A branch of the US armed forces composed chiefly of amphibious troops.

mar·i·ner (măr′ə-nər) ►*n.* A sailor.

mar·i·o·nette (măr′ē-ə-nĕt′) ►*n.* A jointed puppet manipulated by strings. [Fr. *marionnette.*]

mar·i·tal (măr′ĭ-tl) ►*adj.* Of or relating to marriage. [< Lat. *marītus,* married.] —**mar′i·tal·ly** *adv.*

mar·i·time (măr′ĭ-tīm′) ►*adj.* **1.** Of or adjacent to the sea. **2.** Of marine shipping or navigation. See Synonyms at **nautical.** [Lat. *maritimus* < *mare,* sea.]

Maritime Provinces The Canadian provinces of Nova Scotia, New Brunswick, and Prince Edward Island. —**Mar′i·tim′er** *n.*

mar·jo·ram (mär′jər-əm) ►*n.* An aromatic plant in the mint family having leaves used as seasoning. [< Med.Lat. *maiorana.*]

mark¹ (märk) ►*n.* **1.** A visible trace or impression, such as a line or spot. **2.** A symbol, name, or other identifier, esp. one placed on merchandise, as to signify ownership or origin. **3.** A punctuation mark. **4.** An academic grade or other appraisal: *earned high marks in geometry.* **5a.** A distinctive trait or property: *a mark of good breeding.* **b.** A recognized standard of quality: *not up to the mark.* **c.** A lasting effect: *The experience had left its mark.* **6.** Importance; note. **7.** A target, aim, or goal. **8.** *Slang* An intended victim. ►*v.* **1a.** To make a mark (on). **b.** To form, make, or depict by making a mark. **2a.** To single out or identify by or as if by a mark. **b.** To distinguish or characterize. **3.** To set off or separate, as with a line: *marked off the property.* **4.** To grade (academic work). —*phrasal verbs:* **mark down** To reduce in price. **mark up 1.** To deface by covering with marks. **2.** To increase the price of. [< OE *mearc.*] —**mark′er** *n.*

mark² (märk) ►*n.* The deutsche mark. [< OE *marc,* unit of weight.]

Mark (märk) ►*n.* See table at **Bible.**

Mark, Saint. fl. 1st cent. AD. A disciple of Saint Peter and the traditionally accepted author of the second Gospel.

mar·ka (mär′kä) ►*n.* See table at **currency.** [Serbo-Croatian.]

Mark An·to·ny (ăn′tə-nē) or **Mark An·tho·ny** (ăn′thə-nē) 83?–30 BC. Roman orator, politician, and soldier.

mark·down (märk′doun′) ►*n.* A reduction in price.

marked (märkt) ►*adj.* **1.** Having a distinguishing mark. **2.** Clearly defined; noticeable. **3.** Singled out, esp. for a dire fate: *a marked man.* —**mark′ed·ly** (mär′kĭd-lē) *adv.*

mar·ket (mär′kĭt) ►*n.* **1.** A public gathering held for buying and selling merchandise. **2.** A place where goods are sold. **3.** A shop that sells a particular type of merchandise: *a meat market.* **4.** A system of exchange in which prices are determined by the interaction of buyers and sellers: *the soybean market.* **5.** A specific group of buyers: *the student market.* **6.** The extent of demand for merchandise: *a big market for gourmet foods.* ►*v.* **1.** To offer for sale. **2.** To promote (a product or service) to particular groups of consumers. [< Lat. *mercārī, mercāt-,* buy.] —**mar′ket·a·bil′i·ty** *n.* —**mar′ket·a·ble** *adj.* —**mar′ket·er** *n.*

mar·ket·place (mär′kĭt-plās′) ►*n.* **1.** An open area in which a public market is set up. **2.** The world of business and commerce.

market price ►*n.* The prevailing price at which a commodity is sold.

market value ►*n.* The amount a seller may expect to obtain in the open market.

mark·ing (mär′kĭng) ►*n.* The characteristic pattern or coloration of a plant or animal.

marks·man (märks′mən) ►*n.* A man skilled in shooting. —**marks′man·ship′** *n.*

marks·wom·an (märks′wŏŏm′ən) ►*n.* A woman skilled in shooting.

mark·up (märk′ŭp′) ►*n.* **1.** A raise in price. **2.** An amount added to a cost price in calculating a selling price. **3a.** The set of typesetting instructions written on a manuscript. **b.** *Comp.* The set of tags describing an electronic document's formatting specifications.

markup language ►*n.* A coding system, such as HTML, used to structure and link text files.

marl (märl) ►*n.* Clay containing calcium carbonate, used as fertilizer. [< Med.Lat. *margila* < Lat. *marga.*] —**marl′y** *adj.*

mar·lin (mär′lĭn) ►*n.* A large saltwater game fish, having an elongated spearlike upper jaw. [< MARLINESPIKE.]

mar·line·spike also **mar·lin·spike** (mär′lĭn-spīk′) ►*n.* A pointed metal spike, used to separate strands of rope or wire in splicing. [*marline*, two-strand rope + SPIKE¹.]

Mar·lowe (mär′lō), **Christopher** 1564–93. English playwright and poet.

mar·ma·lade (mär′mə-lād′) ►*n.* A preserve made from the pulp and rind esp. of citrus fruits. [< Gk. *melimēlon*, a kind of apple.]

Mar·ma·ra (mär′mər-ə), **Sea of** A sea of NW Turkey between Europe and Asia, forming part of the connection between the Mediterranean and the Black Sea.

mar·mo·re·al (mär-môr′ē-əl) ►*adj.* Resembling marble, as in smoothness or hardness. [< Lat. *marmoreus* < *marmor*, marble.]

mar·mo·set (mär′mə-sĕt′, -zĕt′) ►*n.* Any of various small tropical American monkeys having soft fur, tufted ears, and long tails. [< OFr. *marmouset*, grotesque figurine.]

mar·mot (mär′mət) ►*n.* Any of various stocky, short-legged burrowing rodents of the Northern Hemisphere. [Fr. *marmotte.*]

ma·roon¹ (mə-rōōn′) ►*v.* **1.** To abandon on a deserted island or coast. **2.** To leave helpless. [< Fr. *marron*, fugitive slave.]

ma·roon² (mə-rōōn′) ►*n.* A dark purplish red. [< Ital. *marrone.*] —**ma·roon′** *adj.*

mar·quee (mär-kē′) ►*n.* **1.** A rooflike structure, often bearing a signboard, projecting over an entrance, as to a theater. **2.** A large, often open-sided tent used chiefly for outdoor entertainment. [Fr. *marquise*, marquise.]

marquee

Mar·que·sas Islands (mär-kā′zəz, -səz, -səs) A volcanic archipelago in the S Pacific, part of French Polynesia. —**Mar·que′san** *adj. & n.*

mar·quess also **marquis** (mär′kwĭs) ►*n.* A British nobleman ranking below a duke and above an earl or a count. [ME *marques* < OFr. *marquis*, MARQUIS.]

mar·que·try (mär′kĭ-trē) ►*n., pl.* **-tries** Material that is inlaid into a veneer in an intricate design. [< OFr. *marqueter*, to checker, of Gmc. orig.]

mar·quis (mär-kē′) ►*n., pl.* **-quis** (-kēz′) **1.** A French nobleman ranking below a duke and above an earl or count. **2.** (mär′kwĭs) Variant of **marquess.** [< OFr. *marche*, border country, of Gmc. orig.]

mar·quise (mär-kēz′) ►*n.* **1.** The wife or widow of a marquis. **2.** A noblewoman ranking above a countess and below a duchess. [Fr.]

Mar·ra·kesh or **Mar·ra·kech** (mär′ə-kĕsh′, mə-rä′kĕsh) A city of W-central Morocco in the Atlas Mts. foothills.

mar·riage (mär′ĭj) ►*n.* **1.** The legal union of a man and woman as husband and wife, or in some jurisdictions a legal union between two persons of the same sex. **2.** A wedding. **3.** A close union: *a marriage of comedy and tragedy.* —**mar′riage·a·ble** *adj.*

mar·row (mär′ō) ►*n.* **1.** The soft fatty tissue that fills most bone cavities and is the source of red and many white blood cells. **2.** The inmost, choicest, or most important part. [< OE *mearg.*]

mar·ry (mär′ē) ►*v.* **-ried, -ry·ing 1a.** To take as a spouse. **b.** To give in marriage. **c.** To perform a marriage ceremony for. **2.** To obtain by marriage: *marry money.* **3.** To unite in a close, usu. permanent way. [< Lat. *marītus*, married.] —**mar′ried** *adj.*

Mars (märz) ►*n.* **1.** *Rom. Myth.* The god of war. **2.** The 4th planet from the sun, at a mean distance of 227.9 million km (141.6 million mi) and a mean diameter of approx. 6,794 km (4,222 mi).

Mar·sal·is (mär-săl′ĭs), **Wynton Learson** b. 1961. Amer. trumpeter.

Mar·seille or **Mar·seilles** (mär-sā′) A city of SE France on the Mediterranean Sea.

marsh (märsh) ►*n.* A usu. grassy or reedy wetland. [< OE *mersc.*] —**marsh′y** *adj.*

mar·shal (mär′shəl) ►*n.* **1.** A military officer of the highest rank in some countries. **2a.** A US federal or city officer who carries out court orders. **b.** The head esp. of a fire department. **3.** A person in charge of a parade or ceremony. **4.** A high official in a royal court. ►*v.* **-shaled, -shal·ing** also **-shalled, -shal·ling 1.** To place or set in position or order. See Synonyms at **arrange. 2.** To enlist and organize. **3.** To guide ceremoniously; usher. [< OFr. *mareschal*, military commander.]

Mar·shall (mär′shəl), **George Catlett** 1880–1959. Amer. soldier, diplomat, and politician.

Marshall, John 1755–1835. Amer. jurist and politician; chief justice of the US Supreme Court (1801–35).

Marshall, Thurgood 1908–93. Amer. jurist; US Supreme Court justice (1967–91).

Marshall Islands An island country in the central Pacific. Cap. Majuro.

marsh·mal·low (märsh′mĕl′ō, -măl′ō) ►*n.* **1.** A light spongy confection made of corn syrup, gelatin, sugar, and starch. **2.** often **marsh mallow** A perennial wetland plant having showy pink flowers and a root sometimes used in confectionery.

marsh marigold ►*n.* A wetland plant having bright yellow flowers; cowslip.

mar·su·pi·al (mär-sōō′pē-əl) ►*n.* Any of numerous mammals, including kangaroos, opossums, and wombats, marked by an abdominal pouch in the female in which the newly born young are sheltered and fed. [< Gk. *marsipion*, pouch.]

mart (märt) ►*n.* A store or market. [Ult. < VLat. **marcātus*, MARKET.]

mar·ten (mär′tn) ►*n., pl.* **-ten** or **-tens 1.** A weasellike, chiefly arboreal mammal of northern forests. **2.** The fur of the marten. [< OFr. *martre* and Med.Lat. *martrīna*, both of Gmc. orig.]

Mar·tí (mär-tē′), **José Julián** 1853–95. Cuban revolutionary leader and poet.

mar·tial (mär′shəl) ►*adj.* Of or relating to war or to military life. [< Lat. *Mārs*, Mars.] —**mar′tial·ly** *adv.*

Martial AD 40?–c. 100. Roman poet.

martial art ►*n.* Any of various arts of self-defense, such as karate or judo, usu. practiced as sport.

martial law ►*n.* Rule by military authorities, imposed on a civilian population esp. in time of war or when civil authority has broken down.

Mar·tian (mär′shən) ►*adj.* Of or relating to the planet Mars. ►*n.* A hypothetical inhabitant of the planet Mars.

mar·tin (mär′tn) ►*n.* Any of several birds of the swallow family. [Prob. < *Martin*.]

mar·ti·net (mär′tn-ĕt′) ►*n.* A rigid disciplinarian. [After Jean *Martinet* (d. 1672).]

mar·ti·ni (mär-tē′nē) ►*n., pl.* **-nis** A cocktail of gin or vodka and dry vermouth. [?]

Mar·ti·nique (mär′tĭ-nēk′, -tn-ēk′) An island and overseas department of France in the Windward Is. of the West Indies. Cap. Fort-de-France.

Martin Luther King Day ►*n.* The 3rd Monday in January, observed in the US in commemoration of the birthday of Martin Luther King, Jr.

mar·tyr (mär′tər) ►*n.* **1.** One who chooses to suffer death rather than renounce religious principles. **2.** One who makes great sacrifices for a cause. **3.** One who makes a show of enduring great suffering. [< Gk. *martus, martur-*, witness.] —**mar′tyr** *v.* —**mar′tyr·dom** *n.*

mar·vel (mär′vəl) ►*n.* One that evokes surprise, admiration, or wonder. See Synonyms at **wonder.** ►*v.* **-veled, -vel·ing** also **-velled, -vel·ling** To become filled with wonder. [< Lat. *mīrābilis*, wonderful.]

mar·vel·ous also **mar·vel·lous** (mär′və-ləs) ►*adj.* **1.** Causing wonder or astonishment. **2.** Excellent; superb. —**mar′vel·ous·ly** *adv.*

Marx (märks), **Karl** 1818–83. German philosopher, economist, and revolutionary. —**Marx′i·an** *adj. & n.*

Marx·ism (märk′sĭz′əm) ►*n.* The political and economic doctrine of Karl Marx and Friedrich Engels that society inevitably develops through class struggle from oppression under capitalism to eventual classlessness. —**Marx′ist** *n. & adj.*

Marx·ism-Len·in·ism (märk′sĭz′əm-lĕn′ĭ-nĭz′-əm) ►*n.* The expansion of Marxism to include the concepts of Leninism. —**Marx′ist-Len′in·ist** *adj. & n.*

Mar·y (mâr′ē) ►*n.* In the New Testament, the mother of Jesus.

Mary I or **Mary Tu·dor** (tōō′dər, tyōō′-) "Bloody Mary." 1516–58. Queen of England and Ireland (1553–58).

Mary II 1662–94. Queen of England, Scotland, and Ireland (1689–94) with her husband William III.

Mar·y·land (mĕr′ə-lənd) A state of the E US. Cap. Annapolis. —**Mar′y·land·er** *n.*

Mary Mag·da·lene (măg′də-lən, -lēn′) In the New Testament, a woman whom Jesus cured of evil spirits; also identified with the repentant prostitute who washed Jesus' feet.

Mary Queen of Scots Mary Stuart. 1542–87. Queen of Scotland (1542–67).

mar·zi·pan (mär′zə-păn′, märt′sə-pän′) ►*n.* A confection made of ground almonds, egg whites, and sugar. [< Ital. *marzapane*.]

Ma·sai (mä-sī′, mä′sī) ►*n., pl.* **-sai** or **-sais 1.** A member of a people of Kenya and parts of Tanzania. **2.** The Nilotic language of this people. —**Ma·sai′** *adj.*

ma·sa·la (mä-sä′lä) ►*n.* Any of various mixtures of spices that are used in South Asian cuisine. [Hindi and Urdu *masālā*.]

masc. ►*abbr.* masculine

mas·car·a (mă-skăr′ə) ►*n.* A cosmetic applied to accentuate the eyelashes. [Prob. < Sp. *máscara*, MASK.]

mas·cot (măs′kŏt′, -kət) ►*n.* A person, animal, or object believed to bring good luck or used as a distinguishing symbol, as of a sports team. [< Prov. *mascoto*, fetish < Med.Lat. *masca*, mask.]

mas·cu·line (măs′kyə-lĭn) ►*adj.* **1.** Of or relating to men or boys. **2.** Marked by qualities gen. attributed to a man. **3.** *Gram.* Of or being the gender of words referring to things classified as male. ►*n. Gram.* The masculine gender. [< Lat. *masculus* < *mās.*] —**mas′cu·line·ly** *adv.* —**mas′cu·line·ness** *n.* —**mas′cu·lin′i·ty** *n.*

ma·ser (mā′zər) ►*n.* Any of several devices that amplify or generate electromagnetic waves, esp. microwaves. [*m(icrowave) a(mplification by) s(timulated) e(mission of) r(adiation).*]

Mas·e·ru (măz′ə-rōō′) The capital of Lesotho, in the W part.

mash (măsh) ►*n.* **1.** A fermentable starchy mixture from which alcohol can be distilled. **2.** A mixture of ground grain and nutrients fed to livestock and fowl. **3.** A soft pulpy mixture or mass. ►*v.* **1.** To convert (malt or grain) into mash. **2.** To convert into a soft pulpy mass: *mash potatoes.* See Synonyms at **crush.** —*phrasal verb:* **mash up** To combine (two or more audio or video recordings) to produce a composite recording. [< OE **mǣsc.*] —**mash′er** *n.*

MASH ►*abbr.* Mobile Army Surgical Hospital

mask (măsk) ►*n.* **1.** A covering worn on the face to conceal one's identity. **2.** Such a covering adorned with a representation of a face, worn esp. for theatrical or ritual purposes. **3a.** A protective covering for the face or head. **b.** A covering for the nose and mouth that is used for inhaling oxygen or an anesthetic. **4.** A dark facial marking, as on a raccoon. **5.** Something that disguises or conceals. **6.** Var. of **masque.** ►*v.* **1.** To cover with a mask. **2.** To make indistinct or blurred to the senses. **3.** To conceal, protect, or disguise. See Synonyms at **disguise.** [< Med.Lat. *masca*, specter, witch, mask.]

mas·och·ism (măs′ə-kĭz′əm) ►*n.* **1.** The tendency to derive sexual gratification from being physically or emotionally abused. **2.** A willingness to subject oneself to unpleasant or trying experiences. [After Leopold von Sacher-*Masoch* (1836–1895).] —**mas·och·ist** *n.* —**mas·och·is·tic** *adj.* —**mas·och·is·ti·cal·ly** *adv.*

ma·son (mā′sən) ►*n.* **1.** One who builds or works with stone or brick. **2. Mason** A Freemason. [< OFr. *masson.*]

Ma·son-Dix·on Line (mā′sən-dĭk′sən) The boundary between PA and MD, regarded as the division between free and slave states before the Civil War.

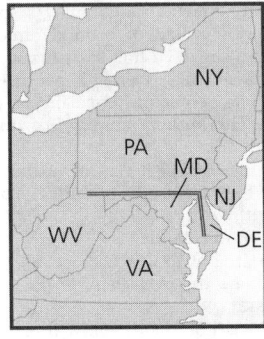

Mason-Dixon Line
The original line extended from the southeast corner of the colony of Pennsylvania 233 miles west and 82 miles south.

Ma·son·ic (mə-sŏn′ĭk) ►*adj.* Of or relating to Freemasonry.

Mason jar ►*n.* A wide-mouthed glass jar with a screw top, used for preserving food. [After John L. *Mason* (1832–1902).]

ma·son·ry (mā′sən-rē) ►*n., pl.* **-ries 1.** Stonework or brickwork. **2.** The trade or work of a mason. **3. Masonry** Freemasonry.

masque also **mask** (măsk) ►*n.* **1.** An allegorical dramatic entertainment, popular in the 1500s and early 1600s. **2.** See **masquerade** (sense 1). [Fr.; see MASK.]

mas·quer·ade (măs′kə-rād′) ►*n.* **1.** A costume party or ball at which masks are worn. **2.** A disguise or false outward show. ►*v.* **-ad·ed, -ad·ing 1.** To wear a mask or disguise. **2.** To have a deceptive appearance. [< Ital. *mascherata* < *maschera,* MASK.] —**mas′quer·ad′er** *n.*

mass (măs) ►*n.* **1.** A unified body of matter with no specific shape. **2.** A large but nonspecific amount or number. **3.** The principal part; majority. **4.** *Phys.* The quantity of matter that a body contains, not dependent on gravity and therefore different from but proportional to its weight. **5. masses** The body of common people. ►*v.* To gather or form into a mass. [< Gk. *maza.*]

Mass also **mass** ►*n.* In certain Christian churches, the celebration of the Eucharist. [< LLat. *missa.*]

Mas·sa·chu·sett also **Mas·sa·chu·set** (măs′ə-chōō′sĭt, -zĭt) ►*n., pl.* **-sett** or **-setts** also **-set** or **-sets 1.** A member of a Native American people formerly located along Massachusetts Bay from Plymouth N to Salem. **2.** The Algonquian language of the Massachusett.

Mas·sa·chu·setts (măs′ə-chōō′sĭts) A state of the NE US. Cap. Boston.

mas·sa·cre (măs′ə-kər) ►*n.* **1.** The act of killing many humans indiscriminately and cruelly. **2.** *Informal* A severe defeat, as in sports. [< OFr. *macecre,* butchery.] —**mas′sa·cre** *v.*

mas·sage (mə-säzh′, -säj′) ►*n.* The rubbing or kneading of parts of the body, as to aid circulation or relax the muscles. [Fr. < Ar. *masaḥa,* to stroke, or *massa,* touch.] —**mas·sage′** *v.*

Mas·sa·soit (măs′ə-soit′) 1580?–1661. Wampanoag leader.

mas·seur (mă-sûr′, mə-) ►*n.* A man who gives massages professionally. [Fr. < *masser,* to massage.]

mas·seuse (mă-sœz′) ►*n.* A woman who gives massages professionally. [Fr. < *masser,* to massage.]

mas·sive (măs′ĭv) ►*adj.* **1.** Consisting of or making up a large mass. **2.** Imposing, as in quantity or scale. —**mas′sive·ly** *adv.*

mass-mar·ket (măs′mär′kĭt) ►*adj.* Of or produced for consumption by a wide range of consumers.

mass medium ►*n., pl.* **mass media** A means of public communication reaching a large audience.

mass number ►*n.* The sum of the number of neutrons and protons in an atomic nucleus.

mass-pro·duce (măs′prə-dōōs′, -dyōōs′) ►*v.* To manufacture in large quantities, esp. by assembly-line techniques. —**mass production** *n.*

mast (măst) ►*n.* **1.** A tall vertical spar that rises from the keel of a sailing vessel to support the sails and rigging. **2.** A vertical pole. [< OE *mæst.*]

mas·tec·to·my (mă-stĕk′tə-mē) ►*n., pl.* **-mies** Surgical removal of all or part of a breast. [Gk. *mastos,* breast + –ECTOMY.]

mas·ter (măs′tər) ►*n.* **1.** One having control or authority over another, esp.: **a.** A male owner of an animal. **b.** A male owner of a slave. **c.** A male employer of a servant. **d.** The captain of a merchant ship. **2.** A male teacher or tutor. **3.** One who holds a master's degree. **4.** An expert. **5. Master** Used as a courtesy title for a boy. **6.** An original recording from which copies can be made. ►*v.* **1.** To make oneself a master of: *master a language.* **2.** To overcome or defeat. [< Lat. *magister.*]

master chief petty officer ►*n.* The highest noncommissioned rank in the US Navy or Coast Guard.

mas·ter·ful (măs′tər-fəl) ►*adj.* **1.** Domineering; imperious. **2.** Skillful; expert. —**mas′ter·ful·ly** *adv.* —**mas′ter·ful·ness** *n.*

master gunnery sergeant ►*n.* A rank in the US Marine Corps equivalent to sergeant major.

master key ►*n.* A key that opens every one of a set of locks.

mas·ter·ly (măs′tər-lē) ►*adj.* Showing the knowledge or skill of a master. ►*adv.* With the skill of a master. —**mas′ter·li·ness** *n.*

mas·ter·mind (măs′tər-mīnd′) ►*n.* One who plans and directs a difficult project. —**mas′ter·mind′** *v.*

master of ceremonies ►*n., pl.* **masters of ceremonies** One who acts as host at a formal event or program of varied entertainment.

mas·ter·piece (măs′tər-pēs′) ►*n.* **1.** An outstanding work of art or craft. **2.** Something superlative of its kind.

mas·ter's degree (măsʹtərz) ►*n.* An academic degree conferred upon those who complete at least one year of study beyond the bachelor's degree.

master sergeant ►*n.* **1.** A rank in the US Army and Marine Corps below sergeant major. **2.** A rank in the US Air Force below senior master sergeant.

mas·ter·stroke (măsʹtər-strōk′) ►*n.* A masterly achievement or action. See Synonyms at **feat.**

mas·ter·work (măsʹtər-wûrk′) ►*n.* A masterpiece.

mas·ter·y (măsʹtə-rē) ►*n., pl.* **-ies 1.** Possession of consummate skill. **2.** The status of master. **3.** Full command of a subject.

mast·head (măstʹhĕd′) ►*n.* **1.** The top of a ship's mast. **2.** The listing in a newspaper or periodical of information about its staff, operation, and circulation.

mas·tic (măsʹtĭk) ►*n.* **1.** The resin of a Mediterranean tree that is used in varnishes and as a flavoring and formerly in chewing gum. **2.** A pastelike cement, esp. one made with powdered lime or brick and tar. [< Gk. *mastikhē,* chewing gum.]

mas·ti·cate (măsʹtĭ-kāt′) ►*v.* **-cat·ed, -cat·ing** To chew. [< Gk. *mastikhan,* grind one's teeth.] —**masʹti·caʹtion** *n.*

mas·tiff (măsʹtĭf) ►*n.* A large dog with a short brownish coat. [< Lat. *mānsuētus,* tamed.]

mas·ti·tis (mă-stīʹtĭs) ►*n.* Inflammation of the breast or udder. [< Gk. *mastos,* breast.]

mas·to·don (măsʹtə-dŏn′) ►*n.* A prehistoric elephantlike mammal. [Gk. *mastos,* nipple + Gk. *odōn,* tooth.]

mas·toid (măsʹtoid′) ►*n.* The mastoid process. [Gk. *mastos,* breast + -OID.]

mastoid process ►*n.* The rear portion of the temporal bone behind the ear.

mas·tur·bate (măsʹtər-bāt′) ►*v.* **-bat·ed, -bat·ing** To excite one's own or another's genitals, esp. by manual contact. [Lat. *māsturbārī.*] —**masʹtur·baʹtion** *n.* —**masʹtur·baʹtor** *n.* —**masʹtur·ba·toʹry** *adj.*

mat¹ (măt) ►*n.* **1.** A flat piece of material used as a floor covering. **2.** A floor pad to protect athletes, as in wrestling. **3.** A thickly tangled mass. ►*v.* **mat·ted, mat·ting 1.** To cover or protect with a mat. **2.** To form into a tangled mass. [< LLat. *matta.*]

mat² (măt) ►*n.* **1.** A border placed around a picture to serve as a frame or provide contrast between the picture and the frame. **2.** also **matte** A dull, often rough finish, as of paint, glass, or paper. ►*adj.* also **matte** Having a dull finish. [< Fr., dull.] —**mat** *v.*

mat·a·dor (mătʹə-dôr′) ►*n.* A bullfighter who performs the final passes and kills the bull. [Sp. < *matar,* kill.]

match¹ (măch) ►*n.* **1.** One equal or similar to another. **2.** A pair, each one of which harmonizes with the other. **3.** *Sports* A game or contest. **4.** A marriage or arrangement of marriage. ►*v.* **1.** To be or make similar or equal to. **2.** To harmonize with. **3.** To join in marriage. **4.** To place in competition with. [< OE *gemœcca,* mate.] —**matchʹer** *n.*

match² (măch) ►*n.* A narrow strip of flammable material coated on one end with a compound that ignites easily, esp. by friction. [< Gk. *muxa,* lamp wick.]

match·book (măchʹbo͝ok′) ►*n.* A small cardboard folder containing safety matches.

match·less (măchʹlĭs) ►*adj.* Having no equal.

match·lock (măchʹlŏk′) ►*n.* **1.** A firearm in which the powder is ignited by a gunlock holding a slow-burning match. **2.** The gunlock of such a firearm.

match·mak·er (măchʹmā′kər) ►*n.* **1.** One who arranges marriages. **2.** *Sports* One who arranges athletic matches. —**matchʹmak′ing** *n.*

match·up (măchʹŭp′) ►*n.* The pairing of two people or things, as for athletic competition or for comparison.

mate¹ (māt) ►*n.* **1.** One of a matched pair: *the mate to this glove.* **2.** A spouse or romantic partner. **3.** Either of a pair of breeding animals. **4.** A close associate. **5.** A deck officer on a merchant ship ranking below the master. ►*v.* **mat·ed, mat·ing 1.** To join closely; pair. **2.** To unite in marriage or romantic partnership. **3.** To pair for breeding. [< MLGer., messmate.]

mate² (māt) ►*n.* A checkmate. ►*v.* **mat·ed, mat·ing** To checkmate. [< Ar. *māt,* dead.]

ma·te³ (mäʹtā) also **ma·té** (mä-tĕʹ) ►*n.* A tealike beverage made from the leaves of a South American tree. [< Quechua *mate,* hollow gourd.]

ma·te·ri·al (mə-tîrʹē-əl) ►*n.* **1.** The substance out of which a thing is or can be made. **2. materials** Tools or apparatus for the performance of a given task. **3.** Cloth; fabric. **4.** One qualified or suited for a position or activity. ►*adj.* **1.** Of or composed of matter. **2.** Of or affecting physical well-being. **3.** Of or concerned with the physical rather than the intellectual or spiritual. **4.** Relevant. [< Lat. *māteria,* matter.] —**ma·teʹri·al·ly** *adv.*

ma·te·ri·al·ism (mə-tîrʹē-ə-lĭz′əm) ►*n.* **1.** *Philos.* The theory that physical matter is the only reality and that everything can be explained in terms of matter and physical phenomena. **2.** Excessive regard for physical possessions. —**ma·teʹri·al·ist** *n.* —**ma·te′ri·al·isʹtic** *adj.*

ma·te·ri·al·ize (mə-tîrʹē-ə-līz′) ►*v.* **-ized, -iz·ing 1.** To take physical form or shape. **2.** To appear, esp. suddenly. **3.** To cause to become real or actual. —**ma·te′ri·al·i·zaʹtion** *n.*

ma·te·ri·el or **ma·té·ri·el** (mə-tîrʹē-ĕlʹ) ►*n.* The equipment and supplies of a military force or other organization. See Synonyms at **equipment.** [< Fr. *matériel,* MATERIAL.]

ma·ter·nal (mə-tûrʹnəl) ►*adj.* **1.** Of, relating to, or characteristic of a mother or motherhood; motherly. **2.** Inherited from or related through one's mother. [< Lat. *māternus* < *māter,* mother.] —**ma·terʹnal·ism** *n.* —**ma·terʹnal·ly** *adv.*

ma·ter·ni·ty (mə-tûrʹnĭ-tē) ►*n.* The state of being a mother; motherhood.

math (măth) ►*n.* Mathematics.

math·e·mat·ics (măth′ə-mătʹĭks) ►*n.* *(takes sing. v.)* The study of the measurement, properties, and relationships of quantities and sets, using numbers and symbols. [< Gk. *mathēma,* science.] —**math′e·matʹi·cal** *adj.* —**math′e·matʹi·cal·ly** *adv.* —**math′e·ma·tiʹcian** (-mə-tĭshʹən) *n.*

Math·er (măthʹər) **Increase** (1639–1723) and **Cotton** (1663–1728). Amer. clerics and writers.

mat·i·nee or **mat·i·née** (măt′n-āʹ) ►*n.* An

entertainment, such as a dramatic performance or movie, that is given during the late morning or the afternoon. [< Lat. *mātūtīnus*, of the morning.]

mat·ins (măt′nz) ►*n.* (*takes sing. or pl. v.*) *Eccles.* The office that formerly constituted the first of the seven canonical hours. [< Med.Lat. *mātūtīnus*, of morning.]

Ma·tisse (mə-tēs′, mä-), **Henri** 1869–1954. French artist.

matri– ►*pref.* Mother; maternal: *matrilineal.* [< Lat. *māter, mātr-.*]

ma·tri·arch (mā′trē-ärk′) ►*n.* **1.** A woman who rules a family, clan, or tribe. **2.** A leading or venerable woman. —**ma′tri·ar′chal, ma′tri·ar′chic** *adj.*

ma·tri·ar·chy (mā′trē-är′kē) ►*n., pl.* **-chies** A social system in which the mother is head of the family.

mat·ri·cide (măt′rĭ-sīd′) ►*n.* **1.** The act of killing one's mother. **2.** One who kills one's mother. —**mat′ri·cid′al** *adj.*

ma·tric·u·late (mə-trĭk′yə-lāt′) ►*v.* **-lat·ed, -lat·ing** To admit or be admitted into a group, esp. a college or university. [< LLat. *mātrīcula*, list < *mātrīx,* MATRIX.] —**ma·tric′u·la′tion** *n.*

mat·ri·lin·e·al (măt′rə-lĭn′ē-əl) ►*adj.* Based on or tracing ancestral descent through the maternal line. —**mat′ri·lin′e·al·ly** *adv.*

mat·ri·mo·ny (măt′rə-mō′nē) ►*n., pl.* **-nies** The act or state of being married. [< Lat. *mātrimōnium.*] —**mat′ri·mo′ni·al** *adj.*

ma·trix (mā′trĭks) ►*n., pl.* **ma·tri·ces** (mā′trĭ-sēz′, măt′rĭ-) or **ma·trix·es** **1.** A situation or surrounding substance in which something else originates, develops, or is contained. **2.** *Math.* A array of numbers or algebraic quantities in rows and columns. [< Lat. *mātrīx,* breeding animal < *māter,* mother.]

ma·tron (mā′trən) ►*n.* **1.** A married woman or widow, esp. a woman in middle age or older. **2.** A woman who acts as a supervisor in a public institution. [< Lat. *mātrōna.*] —**ma′tron·li·ness** *n.* —**ma′tron·ly** *adv.* & *adj.*

matron of honor ►*n., pl.* **matrons of honor** A married woman serving as chief attendant of the bride at a wedding.

matte (măt) ►*n.* Var. of **mat²** (sense 2). ►*adj.* Var. of **mat².**

mat·ter (măt′ər) ►*n.* **1.** That which occupies space and has mass; physical substance. **2.** A specific type of such substance: *organic matter.* **3.** The substance of thought or expression. **4.** A subject of concern or action. **5.** Trouble or difficulty: *What's the matter?* **6.** An approximated quantity: *a matter of years.* **7.** Something printed or written. ►*v.* To be of importance. —*idioms:* **as a matter of fact** In fact; actually. **no matter** Regardless of. [< Lat. *māteria.*]

mat·ter-of-fact (măt′ər-əv-făkt′) ►*adj.* **1.** Relating or adhering to facts. **2.** Straightforward or unemotional. —**mat′ter-of-fact′ly** *adv.*

Mat·thew (măth′yōō) ►*n.* See table at **Bible.**

Matthew, Saint. fl. 1st cent. AD. One of the 12 Apostles and the traditionally accepted author of the first Gospel.

mat·ting (măt′ĭng) ►*n.* A coarse fabric used esp. for covering floors.

mat·tock (măt′ək) ►*n.* A digging tool with a flat blade set at right angles to the handle. [< OE *mattuc.*]

mattock

mat·tress (măt′rĭs) ►*n.* A large pad cushioned with springs or filled with a soft material, used on or as a bed. [< Ar. *maṭraḥ,* mat, cushion.]

ma·ture (mə-tyŏŏr′, -tŏŏr′, -chŏŏr′) ►*adj.* **-tur·er, -tur·est** **1.** Fully grown or developed. **2.** In a desired or final condition; ripe. **3.** Marked by emotional traits, such as patience or prudence, considered characteristic of adulthood. **4.** Payable; due: *a mature bond.* ►*v.* **-tured, -tur·ing** **1.** To bring or come to full development; ripen. **2.** To become due. [< Lat. *mātūrus.*] —**mat′u·ra′tion** (măch′ə-rā′shən) *n.* —**ma·ture′ly** *adv.* —**ma·tur′i·ty, ma·ture′ness** *n.*

mat·zo also **mat·zoh** (măt′sə, -sō) ►*n., pl.* **-zos** also **-zohs** (-səz, -səs, -sōs′) A brittle, flat piece of unleavened bread, eaten esp. during Passover. [< Heb. *maṣṣâ.*]

maud·lin (môd′lĭn) ►*adj.* Effusively or tearfully sentimental. See Synonyms at **sentimental.** [< Mary *Magdalene.*]

Maugham (môm), **W(illiam) Somerset** 1874–1965. British writer.

Mau·i (mou′ē) One of the Hawaiian Is., NW of the island of Hawaii.

maul (môl) ►*n.* A heavy, long-handled hammer used to drive stakes, piles, or wedges. ►*v.* **1.** To injure by or as if by beating. See Synonyms at **mangle¹.** **2.** To handle roughly. [< Lat. *malleus.*] —**maul′er** *n.*

maun·der (môn′dər, män′-) ►*v.* **1.** To talk incoherently or aimlessly. **2.** To move or act aimlessly or vaguely. [Prob. < MEANDER.]

Mau·pas·sant (mō′pə-sänt′, mō-pä-sän′), **(Henri René Albert) Guy de** 1850–93. French writer.

Mau·ri·ta·ni·a (môr′ĭ-tā′nē-ə) A country of NW Africa bordering on the Atlantic. Cap. Nouakchott. —**Mau′ri·ta′ni·an** *adj.* & *n.*

Mau·ri·tius (mô-rĭsh′əs, -ē-əs) An island country in the SW Indian Ocean. Cap. Port Louis. —**Mau·ri′tian** *adj.* & *n.*

mau·so·le·um (mô′sə-lē′əm, -zə-) ►*n., pl.* **-le·ums** or **-le·a** (-lē′ə) A large stately tomb or a building housing such a tomb or tombs. [After *Mausōlos* (d. 353 BC).]

mauve (mōv) ►*n.* A grayish to reddish purple. [< Lat. *malva,* mallow.] —**mauve** *adj.*

ma·ven (mā′vən) ►*n.* An expert. [< Heb. *mēbîn.*]

mav·er·ick (măv′ər-ĭk, măv′rĭk) ►*n.* **1.** One that shows independence of thought or action. **2.** An unbranded range animal, esp. a calf or colt. [Poss. after Samuel A. *Maverick* (1803–70).] —**mav′er·ick** *adj.*

maw (mô) ►*n.* **1.** The mouth or gullet of a voracious animal. **2.** The opening into something deemed insatiable. [< OE *maga*.]

mawk·ish (mô′kĭsh) ►*adj.* Excessively and objectionably sentimental. See Synonyms at **sentimental.** [< ME *mawke*, maggot.] —**mawk′ish·ly** *adv.* —**mawk′ish·ness** *n.*

max. ►*abbr.* maximum

max·il·la (măk-sĭl′ə) ►*n., pl.* **-lae** (-ē) or **-las** *Anat.* Either of two bones forming the upper jaw. [Lat., jawbone.] —**max′il·lar′y** (-sə-lĕr′ē) *adj. & n.*

max·im (măk′sĭm) ►*n.* A succinct formulation of a fundamental principle or rule of conduct. [< Med.Lat. (*prōpositiō) maxima*, greatest (premise).]

max·i·mal (măk′sə-məl) ►*adj.* Of or being a maximum. —**max′i·mal·ly** *adv.*

Max·i·mil·ian (măk′sə-mĭl′yən) 1832–67. Austrian archduke and emperor of Mexico (1864–67).

max·i·mize (măk′sə-mīz′) ►*v.* **-mized, -mizing** To make as great as possible. —**max′i·mi·za′tion** *n.* —**max′i·miz′er** *n.*

max·i·mum (măk′sə-məm) ►*n., pl.* **-mums** or **-ma** (-mə) **1.** The greatest possible quantity, degree, or number. **2.** An upper limit permitted by law or other authority. ►*adj.* The greatest or highest possible or permitted. [< Lat. *maximus*, greatest.]

Max·well (măks′wĕl′, -wəl), **James Clerk** 1831–79. British physicist.

may (mā) ►*aux.v. P.t.* **might** (mīt) **1.** To be allowed to: *May I go? Yes, you may.* **2.** Used to indicate possibility: *It may rain.* **3.** Used to express a fervent wish: *Long may he live!* **4.** Used to express contingency, purpose, or result in clauses introduced by *that* or *so that: displayed so that all may see.* See Usage Note at **can¹.** [< OE *magan*, be able.]

May ►*n.* The 5th month in the Gregorian calendar. See table at **calendar.** [< Lat. *Maia*, an Italic goddess.]

Ma·ya (mä′yə) ►*n., pl.* **-ya** or **-yas** **1.** A member of a Mesoamerican people of SE Mexico, Guatemala, and Belize, whose civilization reached its height around A.D. 300–900. **2.** A modern-day descendant of this people. **3.** Any of the Mayan languages.

Ma·yan (mä′yən) ►*n.* **1.** A Maya. **2.** A linguistic stock of Central America that includes Maya. ►*adj.* **1.** Of or relating to the Maya. **2.** Of the Mayan linguistic stock.

may·ap·ple (mā′ăp′əl) ►*n.* A North American plant having a single white flower, yellow fruit, and poisonous roots, leaves, and seeds.

may·be (mā′bē) ►*adv.* Used to indicate uncertainty or possibility: *Maybe it won't rain.*

may·day (mā′dā′) ►*n.* An international radiotelephone signal word used by aircraft and ships in distress. [< Fr. *m'aidez*, help me!]

May Day ►*n.* **1.** May 1, a traditional holiday in celebration of spring. **2.** May 1, a holiday in some countries in honor of labor.

may·flow·er (mā′flou′ər) ►*n.* Any of various plants that bloom in May.

may·fly (mā′flī′) ►*n.* A winged insect that lives in the adult stage for only a few days.

may·hem (mā′hĕm′, mā′əm) ►*n.* **1.** *Law* The crime of willfully maiming or crippling a person. **2.** Infliction of wanton destruction. **3.** A state of violent disorder or riotous confusion;

havoc. [< OFr. *mahaignier*, maim.]

may·n't (mā′ənt, mānt) May not.

may·on·naise (mā′ə-nāz′, mā′ə-nāz′) ►*n.* A dressing made of egg yolk, oil, lemon juice or vinegar, and seasonings. [Fr.]

may·or (mā′ər, mâr) ►*n.* The head of government of a city, town, or borough. [< Lat. *māior*, superior.] —**may′or·al** *adj.* —**may′or·al·ty** *n.* —**may′or·ship′** *n.*

May·pole also **may·pole** (mā′pōl′) ►*n.* A pole decorated with streamers that May Day celebrants hold while dancing.

Mays (māz), **Willie Howard, Jr.** b. 1931. Amer. baseball player.

maze (māz) ►*n.* **1.** An intricate, usu. confusing network of interconnecting pathways. **2.** Something made up of many confused or conflicting elements; tangle. [< OE *āmasian*, bewilder.]

ma·zur·ka (mə-zûr′kə, -zŏŏr′-) ►*n.* **1.** A lively Polish dance. **2.** Music for a mazurka.

mb ►*abbr.* millibar

Mb ►*abbr.* megabit

MB ►*abbr.* **1.** Manitoba **2.** megabyte

MBA ►*abbr.* Master of Business Administration

Mba·bane (əm-bä-bän′, -bä′nē) The capital of Swaziland, in the NW part.

mbi·ra (ĕm-bîr′ə, əm-) ►*n.* A musical instrument consisting of a hollow gourd and a number of usu. metal strips that vibrate when plucked. [Of Bantu orig.]

MC (ĕm′sē′) ►*n.* A master of ceremonies.

Mc·Clel·lan (mə-klĕl′ən), **George Brinton** 1826–85. Amer. Union general.

Mc·Cor·mick (mə-kôr′mĭk), **Cyrus Hall** 1809–84. Amer. inventor.

Mc·Cul·lers (mə-kŭl′ərz), **Carson Smith** 1917–67. Amer. writer.

Mc·Kin·ley (mə-kĭn′lē), **Mount** Also **De·na·li** (də-nä′lē) The highest mountain in North America, rising to 6,194 m (20,320 ft) in S-central AK.

McKinley, William 1843–1901. The 25th US president (1897–1901).

William McKinley
photographed c. 1900

MD ►*abbr.* **1.** Maryland **2.** *Lat.* Medicinae Doctor (Doctor of Medicine) **3.** muscular distrophy

Mdm. ►*abbr.* Madam

me (mē) ►*pron.* The objective case of **I. 1.** Used as a direct or indirect object: *He saw me; They gave me a ride.* **2.** Used as the object of a preposition: *It's for me.* See Usage Note at **I. 3.** *Informal* Used after a linking verb such as *is: It's me.* [< OE *mē*.]

ME ►*abbr.* **1.** also **Me.** Maine **2.** mechanical engineering **3.** Middle English

mead (mēd) ►*n.* An alcoholic beverage made from fermented honey. [< OE *meodu.*]

Mead, Margaret 1901–78. Amer. anthropologist.

Margaret Mead
photographed in the late 1970s

Meade (mēd), **George Gordon** 1815–72. Amer. Union general.

mead·ow (mĕd′ō) ►*n.* A tract of grassland used as pasture or for growing hay. [< OE *mǣd.*] —**mead′ow·y** *adj.*

mead·ow·lark (mĕd′ō-lärk′) ►*n.* A songbird having brownish plumage, a yellow breast, and a black crescent-shaped marking beneath the throat.

mea·ger also **mea·gre** (mē′gər) ►*adj.* **1.** Deficient in quantity, fullness, or extent. **2.** Thin; lean. [< Lat. *macer.*] —**mea′ger·ly** *adv.* —**mea′ger·ness** *n.*

meal[1] (mēl) ►*n.* **1.** Coarsely ground edible grain. **2.** Any granular substance. [< OE *melu.*] —**meal′i·ness** *n.* —**meal′y** *adj.*

meal[2] (mēl) ►*n.* The food served and eaten in one sitting. [< OE *mǣl.*]

meal·time (mēl′tīm′) ►*n.* The usual time for eating a meal.

meal·y-mouthed (mē′lē-mou*th*d′, -mou*tht*′) ►*adj.* Unwilling to speak simply and directly.

mean[1] (mēn) ►*v.* **meant** (mĕnt), **mean·ing 1a.** To be defined as; denote. **b.** To act as a symbol of; represent. **2.** To intend to convey or indicate. **3.** To have as a consequence: *Friction means heat.* **4.** To be of a specified importance: *She meant so much to me.* [< OE *mǣnan,* tell of.]

mean[2] (mēn) ►*adj.* **-er, -est 1a.** Lacking in kindness; unkind. **b.** Cruel or spiteful. **c.** Expressing spite: *a mean look.* **d.** Tending toward or marked by cruelty or violence: *mean streets.* **e.** Extremely unpleasant. **2.** Ignoble; base. **3.** Miserly. **4.** Low in value, rank, or social status. **5.** *Slang* Hard to cope with. [< OE *gemǣne,* common.] —**mean′ly** *adv.* —**mean′ness** *n.*

mean[3] (mēn) ►*n.* **1.** Something midway between extremes; a medium. **2.** *Math.* The average value of a set of numbers. **3. means** *(takes sing. or pl. v.)* A course of action or instrument by which an end can be achieved. **4. means** *(takes pl. v.)* Money, property, or other wealth. ►*adj.* Occupying a middle position between two

extremes. —*idioms:* **by all means** Without fail; certainly. **by no means** In no sense; certainly not. [< Lat. *mediānus* < *medius,* middle.]

Usage: In the sense of "financial resources," *means* takes a plural verb: *His means are more than adequate.* In the sense of "a way to an end," *means* is singular when referring to a particular strategy or method but plural when it refers to a group of strategies or methods: *Every means was tried. There are several means at our disposal.*

me·an·der (mē-ăn′dər) ►*v.* **1.** To follow a winding and turning course. **2.** To move aimlessly and idly. ►*n.* often **meanders** A bend or winding, as of a path. [< Gk. *Maiandros,* a river in Phrygia.]

mean·ing (mē′nĭng) ►*n.* **1.** Something conveyed or intended, esp. by language; sense or significance. **2.** An interpreted goal, intent, or end. **3.** Inner significance. —**mean′ing·ful** *adj.* —**mean′ing·ful·ly** *adv.* —**mean′ing·less** *adj.*

mean·time (mēn′tīm′) ►*n.* The time between two occurrences. ►*adv.* Meanwhile.

mean·while (mēn′wīl′, -hwīl′) ►*n.* The intervening time. ►*adv.* In the intervening time.

mea·sles (mē′zəlz) ►*n. (takes sing. or pl. v.)* **1.** An acute, contagious viral disease, marked by red spots on the skin, fever, and coughing. **2.** Any of several milder diseases similar to measles. [Of MLGer. orig.]

mea·sly (mēz′lē) ►*adj.* **-sli·er, -sli·est** *Slang* Contemptibly small: *a measly tip.*

meas·ure (mĕzh′ər) ►*n.* **1a.** A reference that is used for the quantitative comparison of properties. **b.** A unit that is specified by a scale, such as an inch, or by variable conditions, such as a day's march. **c.** Dimensions, quantity, or capacity ascertained by a standard. **d.** A device that is used for measuring. **e.** The act of measuring. **2.** A basis of comparison. **3.** Extent or degree. **4.** A limited amount or degree. **5a.** An action taken as a means to an end. **b.** A legislative bill or enactment adopted by a legislature as a remedy for a problem. **6a.** Poetic meter. **b.** *Mus.* The metric unit between two bars on the staff; bar. ►*v.* **-ured, -ur·ing 1a.** To ascertain the dimensions, quantity, or capacity of. **b.** To lay out dimensions by measuring: *measure off an area.* **2.** To compare: *measured our strength against theirs.* **3.** To consider or choose with care; weigh: *He measures his words.* —*phrasal verb:* **measure up 1.** To be the equal of. **2.** To have the necessary qualifications. —*idiom:* **for good measure** In addition to the required amount. [< Lat. *mēnsūra.*] —**meas′ur·a·ble** *adj.* —**meas′ur·a·bly** *adv.* —**meas′ur·er** *n.*

measure
from "Roses of the South," a waltz by
Johann Strauss the Younger

meas·ure·ment (mĕzh′ər-mənt) ►*n.* **1.** The act of measuring or the process of being measured. **2.** A system of measuring: *measurement in miles.* See table on pages 522–523. **3.** The dimension, quantity, or capacity determined by measuring.

meat (mēt) ►*n.* **1.** The edible flesh of animals, esp. mammals. **2.** The edible part, as of a piece of fruit. **3.** The essence, substance, or gist: *the meat of the editorial.* **4.** Food. [< OE *mete*, food.] —**meat′i·ness** *n.* —**meat′y** *adj.*

meat·ball (mēt′bôl′) ►*n.* **1.** A ball of cooked ground meat. **2.** *Slang* A stupid person.

mec·ca (mĕk′ə) ►*n.* A center of interest or attraction: *a mecca for tourists.*

Mecca A city of W Saudi Arabia near the coast of the Red Sea; birthplace of Muhammad.

me·chan·ic (mĭ-kăn′ĭk) ►*n.* A worker skilled in making, using, or repairing machines.

me·chan·i·cal (mĭ-kăn′ĭ-kəl) ►*adj.* **1.** Of or relating to machines or tools. **2.** Operated or produced by a machine. **3.** Of or relating to mechanics. **4.** Performed in a machinelike manner; automatic: *a mechanical task.* [< Gk. *mēkhanē*, machine.] —**me·chan′i·cal·ly** *adv.*

mechanical drawing ►*n.* **1.** Drafting. **2.** A drawing that enables measurements to be interpreted.

me·chan·ics (mĭ-kăn′ĭks) ►*n.* **1.** *(takes sing. v.)* The branch of physics concerned with the analysis of the action of forces on matter or material systems. **2.** *(takes sing. or pl. v.)* Design, construction, and use of machinery or mechanical structures. **3.** *(takes pl. v.)* The functional and technical aspects of an activity.

mech·a·nism (mĕk′ə-nĭz′əm) ►*n.* **1a.** A machine or mechanical appliance. **b.** The arrangement of connected parts in a machine. **2.** A system of parts that operate or interact like those of a machine. **3.** A means or process by which something is done or comes into being. **4.** *Philos.* The doctrine that all natural phenomena are explicable by material causes and mechanical principles.

mech·a·nis·tic (mĕk′ə-nĭs′tĭk) ►*adj.* **1.** *Philos.* Of or relating to the philosophy of mechanism. **2.** Automatic and impersonal. —**mech′a·nis′ti·cal·ly** *adv.*

mech·a·nize (mĕk′ə-nīz′) ►*v.* **-nized, -niz·ing** **1.** To equip with machinery. **2.** To make automatic or routine. —**mech′a·ni·za′tion** *n.*

med·al (mĕd′l) ►*n.* **1.** A flat piece of metal stamped with a design commemorating an event or person, often given as an award. **2.** A piece of metal stamped with a religious device. [< Ital. *medaglia.*]

med·al·ist (mĕd′l-ĭst) ►*n.* **1.** A recipient of a medal. **2.** One who designs medals.

me·dal·lion (mĭ-dăl′yən) ►*n.* **1.** A large medal. **2.** An emblem of registration for a taxicab. **3.** Something resembling a large medal. [< Ital. *medaglione.*]

med·dle (mĕd′l) ►*v.* **-dled, -dling** To intrude into other people's affairs. [< VLat. **miscular̄e*, mix up.] —**med′dler** (mĕd′lər, mĕd′l-ər) *n.* —**med′dle·some** *adj.*

Mede (mēd) ►*n.* A member of an Iranian people inhabiting ancient Media.

Me·del·lín (mĕ′dĕ-yēn′) A city of NW Colombia NW of Bogotá.

med·e·vac (mĕd′ĭ-văk′) ►*n.* Transport of persons, esp. by helicopter, to a place where they can receive medical care. [*med(ical) evac(uation).*]

me·di·a (mē′dē-ə) ►*n.* Pl. of **medium.** See Usage Note at **medium.**

Media An ancient country of SW Asia in NW Iran. —**Me′di·an** *adj. & n.*

me·di·ae·val (mē′dē-ē′vəl, mĕd′ē-) ►*adj.* Var. of **medieval.**

me·di·al (mē′dē-əl) ►*adj.* Of or situated in the middle; median. [< Lat. *medius*, middle.] —**me′di·al·ly** *adv.*

me·di·an (mē′dē-ən) ►*adj.* **1.** Of or located in the middle. **2.** *Statistics* Of or being the middle value in a distribution. ►*n.* **1.** A median point, plane, line, or part. **2.** The paved or landscaped area dividing opposing lanes of traffic on some highways. **3.** *Statistics* The middle value in a distribution, above and below which lie an equal number of values. **4.** *Math.* A line that joins a vertex of a triangle to the midpoint of the opposite side. [< Lat. *medius*, middle.]

median strip ►*n.* See **median** (sense 2).

me·di·ate (mē′dē-āt′) ►*v.* **-at·ed, -at·ing** **1.** To resolve or seek to resolve (differences) by working with all conflicting parties. **2.** To act as an intermediary. **3.** *Phys.* To convey (a force) between subatomic particles. [LLat. *mediāre*, be in the middle.] —**me′di·a′tion** *n.* —**me′di·a′tor** *n.*

med·ic (mĕd′ĭk) ►*n.* **1.** A member of a military medical corps. **2.** A physician or surgeon. [Lat. *medicus*, physician.]

Med·i·caid also **med·i·caid** (mĕd′ĭ-kād′) ►*n.* A US government program that pays for medical care for people who cannot finance their own medical expenses.

med·i·cal (mĕd′ĭ-kəl) ►*adj.* Of or relating to the study or practice of medicine. [< Lat. *medicus*, physician.] —**med′i·cal·ly** *adv.*

me·dic·a·ment (mĭ-dĭk′ə-mənt, mĕd′ĭ-kə-) ►*n.* A medicine. [Lat. *medicāmentum.*]

Med·i·care also **med·i·care** (mĕd′ĭ-kâr′) ►*n.* A US government program that pays for medical care for people over 65.

med·i·cate (mĕd′ĭ-kāt′) ►*v.* **-cat·ed, -cat·ing** **1.** To treat with medicine. **2.** To add a medicinal substance to. [Lat. *medicāre.*]

med·i·ca·tion (mĕd′ĭ-kā′shən) ►*n.* **1.** A medicine. **2.** The act of medicating.

Med·i·ci (mĕd′ə-chē′, mĕd′ĭ-) Italian noble family including **Cosimo** (1389–1464) and **Lorenzo** (1449–92). —**Med′i·ce′an** (-chē′-ən, -sē′-) *adj.*

med·i·cine (mĕd′ĭ-sĭn) ►*n.* **1a.** The science of diagnosing, treating, or preventing disease or bodily injury. **b.** The branch of this science encompassing treatment by means other than surgery. **2.** An agent used to treat disease. **3.** Something serving as a remedy or corrective. **4.** Shamanistic practices or beliefs. [< Lat. *medicīna* < *medicus*, physician.] —**me·di′ci·nal** (mĭ-dĭs′ə-nəl) *adj.* —**me·di′ci·nal·ly** *adv.*

medicine man ►*n.* A male shaman.

medicine woman ►*n.* A female shaman.

med·i·co (mĕd′ĭ-kō′) ►*n., pl.* **-cos** *Informal* A doctor or medical student. [< Lat. *medicus.*]

me·di·e·val also **me·di·ae·val** (mē′dē-ē′vəl, mĕd′ē-, mĭ-dē′vəl) ►*adj.* **1a.** Of or belonging to the Middle Ages. **b.** Of or relating to a historical period roughly coinciding with the

MEASUREMENT TABLE

Conversion between Metric and US Customary Units

From Metric to US Customary

WHEN YOU KNOW	MULTIPLY BY	TO FIND
millimeters	0.04	inches
centimeters	0.39	inches
meters	3.28	feet
	1.09	yards
kilometers	0.62	miles
milliliters	0.03	fluid ounces
liters	1.06	quarts
	0.26	gallons
cubic meters	35.31	cubic feet
grams	0.035	ounces
kilograms	2.20	pounds
metric tons (1,000 kg)	1.10	short tons
square centimeters	0.155	square inches
square meters	1.20	square yards
square kilometers	0.39	square miles
hectares	2.47	acres

From US Customary to Metric

WHEN YOU KNOW	MULTIPLY BY	TO FIND
inches	2.54	centimeters
feet	30.48	centimeters
yards	0.91	meters
miles	1.61	kilometers
fluid ounces	29.57	milliliters
cups	0.24	liters
pints	0.47	liters
quarts	0.95	liters
gallons	3.79	liters
cubic feet	0.028	cubic meters
ounces	28.35	grams
pounds	0.45	kilograms
short tons (2,000 lbs)	0.91	metric tons
square inches	6.45	square centimeters
square feet	0.09	square meters
square yards	0.84	square meters
square miles	2.59	square kilometers
acres	0.40	hectares

Temperature Conversion between Celsius and Fahrenheit

$$°C = (°F - 32) ÷ 1.8$$
$$°F = (°C \times 1.8) + 32$$

Metric Prefixes

A multiple of a unit in the metric system is formed by adding a prefix to its name. The prefixes change the magnitude of the unit by orders of ten. Those for 10^9 to 10^{-9} are given below.

PREFIX	SYMBOL	MULTIPLYING FACTOR	
giga-	G	10^9	= 1,000,000,000
mega-	M	10^6	= 1,000,000
kilo-	k	10^3	= 1,000
hecto-	h	10^2	= 100
deca-	da	10	= 10
deci-	d	10^{-1}	= 0.1
centi-	c	10^{-2}	= 0.01
milli-	m	10^{-3}	= 0.001
micro-	μ	10^{-6}	= 0.000,001
nano-	n	10^{-9}	= 0.000,000,001

MEASUREMENT TABLE, continued
US Customary System

Unit	Relation to Other US Customary Units	Metric Equivalent
Length		
inch	1/12 foot	2.54 centimeters
foot	12 inches or 1/3 yard	0.305 meter
yard	36 inches or 3 feet	0.91 meter
rod	16 1/2 feet or 5 1/2 yards	5.03 meters
furlong	220 yards or 1/8 mile	0.20 kilometer
mile (statute)	5,280 feet or 1,760 yards	1.61 kilometers
mile (nautical)	6,076 feet or 2,025 yards	1.852 kilometers
Volume or Capacity (Liquid Measure)		
ounce	1/16 pint	29.57 milliliters
gill	4 ounces	0.12 liter
cup	8 ounces	0.24 liter
pint	16 ounces	0.47 liter
quart	2 pints or 1/4 gallon	0.95 liter
gallon	128 ounces or 8 pints	3.79 liters
barrel (wine)	31 1/2 gallons	119.24 liters
barrel (beer)	31 gallons	117.35 liters
barrel (oil)	42 gallons	158.99 liters
Volume or Capacity (Dry Measure)		
cup	1/2 pint	0.275 liter
pint	2 cups or 1/2 quart	0.55 liter
quart	4 cups or 2 pints	1.10 liters
peck	8 quarts or 1/4 bushel	8.81 liters
bushel	4 pecks	35.239 liters
Weight		
grain	1/7000 pound	64.799 milligrams
dram	1/16 ounce	1.772 grams
ounce	16 drams	28.350 grams
pound	16 ounces	453.6 grams
ton (short)	2,000 pounds	907.18 kilograms
ton (long)	2,240 pounds	1,016.0 kilograms
Geographic Area		
acre	43,560 square feet or 4,840 square yards	4,047 square meters

British Imperial System

Unit	Relation to Other British Imperial Units	Conversion to US Customary Units	Conversion to Metric Units
Volume or Capacity (Liquid Measure)			
pint	1/2 quart	1.20 pints	0.57 liter
quart	2 pints = 1/4 gallon	1.20 quarts	1.14 liters
gallon	8 pints = 4 quarts	1.20 gallons	4.55 liters
Volume or Capacity (Dry Measure)			
peck	1/4 bushel	1.03 pecks	9.09 liters
bushel	4 pecks	1.03 bushels	36.37 liters

European Middle Ages and marked by feudal or aristocratic social structures, as in Japan or China. **2.** *Informal* Old-fashioned. [< Lat. *medius*, middle + *aevum*, age.] —**me′di·e′val·ist** *n.* —**me′di·e′val·ly** *adv.*

Medieval Greek ▸*n.* The Greek language from about 800 to about 1500.

Medieval Latin ▸*n.* The Latin language from about 700 to about 1500.

Med·i·gap (mĕd′ĭ-găp′) ▸*n.* Private health insurance designed to supplement Medicare. [MEDI(CARE) and MEDI(CAID) + GAP.]

Me·di·na (mĭ-dē′nə) A city of W Saudi Arabia N of Mecca.

me·di·o·cre (mē′dē-ō′kər) ▸*adj.* Of ordinary or undistinguished quality. [< Lat. *mediocris* : *medius*, middle + *ocris*, rugged mountain.] —**me′di·oc′ri·ty** (-ŏk′rĭ-tē) *n.*

med·i·tate (mĕd′ĭ-tāt′) ▸*v.* -**tat·ed**, -**tat·ing 1a.** *Buddhism & Hinduism* To train or empty the mind, as by focusing on one object. **b.** To engage in prayer. **2.** To think or reflect, esp. in a calm and deliberate manner. [Lat. *meditārī.*] —**med′i·ta′tion** *n.* —**med′i·ta·tion·al** *adj.* —**med′i·ta′tive·ly** *adv.* —**med′i·ta′tor** *n.*

Med·i·ter·ra·ne·an (mĕd′ĭ-tə-rā′nē-ən) The region surrounding the Mediterranean Sea. —**Med′i·ter·ra′ne·an** *adj. & n.*

Mediterranean fruit fly ▸*n.* A fruit fly having wings with black markings, the larvae of which destroy fruit crops.

Mediterranean Sea An inland sea surrounded by Europe, Asia, and Africa and connected by narrow straits to the Atlantic and the Black Sea.

me·di·um (mē′dē-əm) ▸*n., pl.* -**di·a** (-dē-ə) or -**di·ums 1.** A position, condition, or course of action midway between extremes. **2.** An intervening substance through which something else is transmitted or carried on. **3.** An agency by which something is accomplished, conveyed, or transferred. **4.** *pl.* **media a.** A means of mass communication. **b. media** *(takes sing. or pl. v.)* The communications industry or profession. **5.** *pl.* **mediums** A person thought to have the power to communicate with the spirits of the dead. **6.** *pl.* **media** An environment in which something functions and thrives. **7.** A means of expression as determined by the materials or the creative methods involved. ▸*adj.* Midway between extremes. [Lat. < *medius*, middle.]
Usage: The plural form *media* is often used as a singular to refer to a particular means of communication, as in *This is the most exciting new media since television.* However, many people prefer *medium* in such contexts. *Media* is standard when used as a collective term for journalists and broadcasters, as in *The media has ignored the issue.*

med·ley (mĕd′lē) ▸*n., pl.* -**leys 1.** A jumbled assortment. **2.** A musical arrangement of several melodies. [< AN *medler*, MEDDLE.]

me·dul·la (mĭ-dŭl′ə) ▸*n., pl.* -**las** or -**dul·lae** (-dŭl′ē) **1.** The inner core of certain organs or body structures, such as the marrow of bone. **2.** The medulla oblongata. [< Lat.] —**me·dul′lar, med′ul·lar′y** (mĕd′l-ĕr′ē, mə-dŭl′ə-rē) *adj.*

medulla ob·lon·ga·ta (ŏb′lông-gä′tə) ▸*n., pl.* -**tas** or **me·dul·lae ob·lon·ga·tae** (mĭ-dŭl′ē ŏb′lông-gä′tē) The lowermost portion of the vertebrate brain that controls respiration, cir-

culation, and certain other bodily functions. [NLat. *medulla oblongāta*, oblong medulla.]

Med·ved·ev (myĕd-vyĕd′ĕv, myĭ-dvyĕ′dyĭf), **Dmitry Anatolyevich** b. 1965. Russian president (2008–12) and prime minister (appointed 2012).

meek (mēk) ▸*adj.* -**er**, -**est 1.** Showing patience and humility. **2.** Submissive; passive. [ME *meke*, of Scand. orig.] —**meek′ly** *adv.* —**meek′ness** *n.*

meer·schaum (mîr′shəm, -shôm′) ▸*n.* **1.** A claylike mineral used esp. to make tobacco pipes. **2.** A pipe made of meerschaum. [Ger. : *Meer*, sea (< OHGer. *mari*) + *Schaum*, foam.]

meer·kat (mîr′kăt′) ▸*n.* An African burrowing mongoose, having brownish gray fur and a long tail. [< MDu. *meercatte*, sea cat, monkey (since monkeys came from overseas).]

meet[1] (mēt) ▸*v.* **met** (mĕt), **meet·ing 1a.** To come into the presence of. **b.** To come into the company of: *I met my colleagues for a meeting.* **c.** To be introduced to; make the acquaintance of: *Have you met my wife?* **2.** To be present at the arrival of: *met the train.* **3.** To come into conjunction with. **4.** To come to the notice of: *more than meets the eye.* **5a.** To fulfill. See Synonyms at **satisfy. b.** To deal or contend with effectively. **6.** To come together: *Let's meet tonight.* ▸*n.* A meeting or contest. [< OE *mētan*.]

meet[2] (mēt) ▸*adj.* Fitting; proper. [< OE *gemēte*.] —**meet′ly** *adv.*

meet·ing (mē′tĭng) ▸*n.* **1.** A coming together. **2.** An assembly or gathering.

mega– ▸*pref.* **1.** Large: *megalith.* **2.** Surpassing other examples of its kind; extraordinary: *megahit.* **3.** One million (10^6): *megaton.* **4.** 1,048,576 (2^{20}): *megaybte.* [< Gk. *megas*, great.]

meg·a·bit (mĕg′ə-bĭt′) ▸*n. Comp.* **1.** One million bits. **2.** 1,048,576 (2^{20}) bits.

meg·a·byte (mĕg′ə-bīt′) ▸*n.* **1.** A unit of computer memory or data storage capacity equal to 1,048,576 (2^{20}) bytes. **2.** One million bytes.

meg·a·church (mĕg′ə-chûrch′) ▸*n.* A large, usu. nondenominational Protestant church.

meg·a·cy·cle (mĕg′ə-sī′kəl) ▸*n.* See **megahertz.**

meg·a·fau·na (mĕg′ə-fô′nə) ▸*n., pl.* **megafauna** or -**nas** Large animals of a particular region, period, or habitat considered as a group.

meg·a·hertz (mĕg′ə-hûrts′) ▸*n.* One million cycles per second.

meg·a·hit (mĕg′ə-hĭt′) ▸*n.* An exceedingly successful product or event.

meg·a·lith (mĕg′ə-lĭth′) ▸*n.* A very large stone used in various prehistoric structures or monuments. —**meg′a·lith′ic** *adj.*

megalo– ▸*pref.* Exaggeratedly large: *megalomania.* [< Gk. *megas, megal-*, great.]

meg·a·lo·ma·ni·a (mĕg′ə-lō-mā′nē-ə, -mān′yə) ▸*n.* A mental disorder characterized by delusions of wealth, power, or omnipotence. —**meg′a·lo·ma′ni·ac′** *n.*

meg·a·lop·o·lis (mĕg′ə-lŏp′ə-lĭs) ▸*n.* **1.** A very large city. **2.** An urban complex made up of several large cities and their surrounding areas. [MEGALO– + Gk. *polis*, city.]

meg·a·phone (mĕg′ə-fōn′) ▸*n.* A funnel-shaped device used to amplify the voice.

meg·a·ton (mĕg′ə-tŭn′) ▸*n.* A unit of explosive force equal to that of one million metric tons of TNT. —**meg′a·ton′nage** (-tŭn′ĭj) *n.*

meg·a·vi·ta·min (mĕg′ə-vī′tə-mĭn) ►*n.* A dose of a vitamin greatly exceeding the recommended daily allowance.

meg·a·watt (mĕg′ə-wŏt′) ►*n.* One million watts. —**meg′a·watt′age** *n.*

mei·o·sis (mī-ō′sĭs) ►*n., pl.* **-ses** (-sēz′) Cell division in sexually reproducing organisms that reduces the number of chromosomes in reproductive cells. [Gk. *meiōsis*, diminution.] —**mei·ot′ic** (-ŏt′ĭk) *adj.* —**mei·ot′i·cal·ly** *adv.*

Me·ir (mī′ər, mā-ēr′), **Golda** 1898–1978. Russian-born Israeli politician.

meit·ner·i·um (mīt-nûr′ē-əm) ►*n. Symbol* **Mt** A short-lived synthetic radioactive element. At. no. 109. See table at **element**. [After Lise *Meitner* (1878–1968).]

Me·kong (mā′kông′, -kŏng′) A river of SE Asia flowing about 4,500 km (2,800 mi) from SE China to the South China Sea through S Vietnam.

mel·an·cho·li·a (mĕl′ən-kō′lē-ə) ►*n.* A mental disorder marked by severe depression and hopelessness. [LLat., MELANCHOLY.]

mel·an·chol·ic (mĕl′ən-kŏl′ĭk) ►*adj.* **1.** Affected with melancholy. **2.** Of or relating to melancholia. —**mel′an·chol′ic** *n.* —**mel′an·chol′i·cal·ly** *adv.*

mel·an·chol·y (mĕl′ən-kŏl′ē) ►*n.* **1.** Sadness; depression. **2.** Pensive reflection. ►*adj.* **1.** Gloomy; sad. **2.** Pensive; thoughtful. [< Gk. *melankholia*.]

Mel·a·ne·sia (mĕl′ə-nē′zhə, -shə) A division of Oceania in the SW Pacific comprising the islands NE of Australia and S of the equator.

Mel·a·ne·sian (mĕl′ə-nē′zhən) ►*adj.* Of Melanesia or its peoples, languages, or cultures. ►*n.* **1.** A member of any of the indigenous peoples of Melanesia. **2.** A subfamily of the Austronesian languages spoken in Melanesia.

mé·lange also **me·lange** (mā-länzh′) ►*n.* A mixture. [< OFr. *meslance* < *mesler*, MEDDLE.]

mel·a·nin (mĕl′ə-nĭn) ►*n.* A dark pigment found esp. in skin, hair, fur, and feathers.

mel·a·nism (mĕl′ə-nĭz′əm) ►*n.* **1.** See **melanosis. 2.** Dark coloration due to a high concentration of melanin. —**mel′a·nis′tic** *adj.*

melano– or **melan–** ►*pref.* Black; dark: *melanosis*. [< Gk. *melas, melan-.*]

mel·a·no·ma (mĕl′ə-nō′mə) ►*n., pl.* **-mas** or **-ma·ta** (-mə-tə) A dark-pigmented, usu. malignant tumor gen. occurring in the skin.

mel·a·no·sis (mĕl′ə-nō′sĭs) ►*n.* Abnormally dark pigmentation resulting from a disorder of pigment metabolism. —**mel′a·not′ic** (-nŏt′ĭk) *adj.*

mel·a·to·nin (mĕl′ə-tō′nĭn) ►*n.* A hormone involved in sleep and reproduction in mammals. [Gk. *melas*, black + TON(E) + –IN.]

Mel·ba toast (mĕl′bə) ►*n.* Very thinly sliced crisp toast. [After Dame Nellie *Melba* (1861–1931).]

Mel·bourne (mĕl′bərn) A city of SE Australia SW of Canberra.

meld¹ (mĕld) ►*v.* To declare or display (a card or combination of cards) for inclusion in one's score in various card games. [Prob. < Ger. *melden*, announce.] —**meld** *n.*

meld² (mĕld) ►*v.* To merge or become merged; blend. [Perh. blend of MELT and WELD.]

me·lee (mā′lā′, mā-lā′) also **mê·lée** (mĕ-lā′) ►*n.* **1.** A confused struggle or fight at close quarters. See Synonyms at **brawl. 2.** A tumultuous mingling, as of a crowd. [< OFr. *meslee* < *mesler*, MEDDLE.]

Me·le·ke·ok (mə-lā′kā-ŏŏk) The capital of Palau, on an island in the NE part of the country.

mel·io·rate (mēl′yə-rāt′, mē′lē-ə-) ►*v.* **-rat·ed, -rat·ing** To make or become better; improve. [< Lat. *melior*, better.] —**mel′io·ra·ble** (-rə-bəl) *adj.* —**mel′io·ra′tion** *n.*

mel·lif·lu·ous (mə-lĭf′lōō-əs) ►*adj.* Flowing in a smooth or sweet manner. [< LLat. *mellifluus*.] —**mel·lif′lu·ous·ly** *adv.*

mel·low (mĕl′ō) ►*adj.* **-er, -est 1.** Soft, sweet, and full-flavored because of ripeness. **2.** Rich and soft in quality: *a mellow wine.* **3.** Having the gentleness often associated with maturity. **4.** Relaxed; easygoing. **5.** *Slang* Slightly and pleasantly intoxicated. ►*v.* To make or become mellow. [ME *melwe.*] —**mel′low·ly** *adv.* —**mel′low·ness** *n.*

me·lo·de·on (mə-lō′dē-ən) ►*n.* A small harmonium. [Alteration of *melodium* < MELODY.]

me·lo·di·ous (mə-lō′dē-əs) ►*adj.* **1.** Tuneful. **2.** Agreeable to hear. —**me·lo′di·ous·ly** *adv.*

mel·o·dra·ma (mĕl′ə-drä′mə, -drăm′ə) ►*n.* **1.** A dramatic work marked by exaggerated emotions, stereotypical characters, and interpersonal conflicts. **2.** Behavior or events having melodramatic characteristics. [< Fr. *mélodrame*, musical drama.]

mel·o·dra·mat·ic (mĕl′ə-drə-măt′ĭk) ►*adj.* **1.** Having the emotional appeal of melodrama. **2.** Exaggeratedly emotional or sentimental. —**mel′o·dra·mat′i·cal·ly** *adv.*

mel·o·dy (mĕl′ə-dē) ►*n., pl.* **-dies 1.** A pleasing succession or arrangement of sounds. **2.** A rhythmic sequence of single tones organized so as to make up a musical phrase. [< Gk. *melōidia*.] —**me·lod′ic** (mə-lŏd′ĭk) *adj.* —**me·lod′i·cal·ly** *adv.*

mel·on (mĕl′ən) ►*n.* Any of several fruits, as cantaloupe or watermelon, having a hard rind and juicy flesh. [< Gk. *mēlopepōn*.]

melt (mĕlt) ►*v.* **1.** To change or be changed from a solid to a liquid state by application of heat or pressure or both. **2.** To dissolve: *Sugar melts in water.* **3.** To disappear or cause to disappear gradually. **4.** To pass imperceptibly into something else. **5.** To become softened in feeling. [< OE *meltan*.] —**melt′a·ble** *adj.*

melt·down (mĕlt′doun′) ►*n.* **1.** A severe overheating of a nuclear reactor core, resulting in escape of radiation. **2.** A disastrous situation; failure.

melt·ing point (mĕl′tĭng) ►*n.* The temperature at which a solid becomes a liquid at standard atmospheric pressure.

melting pot ►*n.* A place where immigrants of different cultures form a single culture.

Mel·ville (mĕl′vĭl), **Herman** 1819–91. Amer. writer. —**Mel·vil′le·an** *adj.*

Melville Island An island of N Northwest Terrs., Canada, N of Victoria I.

mem·ber (mĕm′bər) ►*n.* **1.** A distinct part of a whole. **2.** A part or an organ of a human or animal body. **3.** One that belongs to a group or organization. [< Lat. *membrum*.]

mem·ber·ship (mĕm′bər-shĭp′) ►*n.* **1.** The state of being a member. **2.** All the members in a group.

mem·brane (mĕm′brān′) ►*n.* **1.** A thin pliable layer of plant or animal tissue covering or separating structures or organs. **2.** A thin sheet of natural or synthetic material that is permeable to substances in solution. [Lat. *membrāna*, skin.] —**mem′bra·nal** (-brə-nəl), **mem′bra·nous** *adj.*

me·men·to (mə-mĕn′tō) ►*n., pl.* **-tos** or **-toes** A keepsake. [< Lat. *mementō*, imper. of *meminisse*, remember.]

Mem·ling (mĕm′lĭng), **Hans** 1430?–94. Flemish painter.

mem·o (mĕm′ō) ►*n., pl.* **-os** A memorandum.

mem·oir (mĕm′wär′, -wôr′) ►*n.* **1.** often **memoirs** An autobiography or biography. **2.** **memoirs** The report of the proceedings of a learned society. [< Fr. *mémoire*, memory.] —**mem′oir·ist** *n.*

mem·o·ra·bil·i·a (mĕm′ər-ə-bĭl′ē-ə, -bĭl′yə) ►*pl.n.* **1.** Objects valued for their historical significance. **2.** Events or experiences worthy of remembrance. [< Lat. *memorābilis*, MEMORABLE.]

mem·o·ra·ble (mĕm′ər-ə-bəl) ►*adj.* Worth being remembered or noted. [< Lat. *memor*, mindful.] —**mem′o·ra·bil′i·ty** *n.* —**mem′o·ra·bly** *adv.*

mem·o·ran·dum (mĕm′ə-răn′dəm) ►*n., pl.* **-dums** or **-da** (-də) **1.** A short note written as a reminder. **2.** A written record or communication, as in a business office. [Lat., thing to be remembered.]

me·mo·ri·al (mə-môr′ē-əl) ►*n.* **1.** Something, such as a monument or holiday, intended to honor the memory of a person or event. **2.** A written statement of facts or a formal petition. ►*adj.* Commemorative. —**me·mo′ri·al·ize′** *v.* —**me·mo′ri·al·ly** *adv.*

Memorial Day ►*n.* A US holiday commemorating members of the armed forces killed in war, officially observed on the last Monday in May.

mem·o·rize (mĕm′ə-rīz′) ►*v.* **-rized, -riz·ing** To commit to memory; learn by heart. —**mem′o·ri·za′tion** *n.* —**mem′o·riz′er** *n.*

mem·o·ry (mĕm′ə-rē) ►*n., pl.* **-ries** **1.** The mental faculty of retaining and recalling past experience. **2.** The act of remembering; recollection. **3.** All that a person can remember. **4.** Something remembered: *childhood memories.* **5.** The period of time covered by remembrance or recollection. **6.** *Comp.* **a.** A unit of a computer that preserves data for retrieval. **b.** Capacity for storing information. [< Lat. *memoria* < *memor*, mindful.]

Mem·phis (mĕm′fĭs) **1.** An ancient city of Egypt S of Cairo. **2.** A city of SW TN on the Mississippi R.

mem·sa·hib (mĕm′sä′hĭb, -sä′ĭb, -säb) ►*n.* Used as a form of address for a European woman in colonial India. [MA'AM + SAHIB.]

men (mĕn) ►*n.* Pl. of **man.**

men·ace (mĕn′ĭs) ►*n.* **1.** A threat. **2.** A troublesome or annoying person. ►*v.* **-aced, -ac·ing** To threaten. [< Lat. *mināx, mināc-*, threatening < *minārī*, threaten.] —**men′ac·er** *n.* —**men′ac·ing·ly** *adv.*

mé·nage (mā-näzh′) ►*n.* A household. [< OFr. < *maneir*, REMAIN.]

me·nag·er·ie (mə-năj′ə-rē, -năzh′-) ►*n.* A collection of wild animals on exhibition. [Fr. *ménagerie* < OFr. *menage*, MÉNAGE.]

Me·nan·der (mə-năn′dər) 342–292 BC. Greek dramatist.

me·nar·che (mə-när′kē) ►*n.* The first menstrual period of a girl or woman. [Gk. *mēn*, month + *arkhē*, beginning.] —**me·nar′che·al** *adj.*

Men·chú (mĕn-chōō′), **Rigoberta** b. 1959. Guatemalan human rights activist.

Menck·en (mĕng′kən), **H(enry) L(ouis)** 1880–1956. Amer. editor and critic.

mend (mĕnd) ►*v.* **1.** To make repairs or restoration to; fix. **2.** To reform or correct. **3.** To improve in health; heal. ►*n.* A mended place. —*idiom:* **on the mend** Improving, esp. in health. [< ME *amenden*, AMEND.] —**mend′a·ble** *adj.* —**mend′er** *n.*

men·da·cious (mĕn-dā′shəs) ►*adj.* **1.** Lying; untruthful. **2.** False; untrue. [< Lat. *mendāx, mendāc-*.] —**men·da′cious·ly** *adv.* —**men·dac′i·ty** (-dăs′ĭ-tē) *n.*

Men·del (mĕn′dl), **Gregor Johann** 1822–84. Moravian botanist.

Men·de·le·ev (mĕn′də-lā′əf), **Dmitri Ivanovich** 1834–1907. Russian chemist.

men·de·le·vi·um (mĕn′də-lē′vē-əm) ►*n. Symbol* **Md** A synthetic radioactive element. At. no. 101. See table at **element.** [After Dmitri Ivanovich MENDELEEV.]

Men·dels·sohn (mĕn′dl-sən, -zōn′), **Felix** 1809–47. German composer, pianist, and conductor.

men·di·cant (mĕn′dĭ-kənt) ►*adj.* **1.** Depending on alms for a living. **2.** Relating to religious orders whose members are forbidden to own property and must work or beg for their livings. ►*n.* **1.** A beggar. **2.** A member of a mendicant order. [< Lat. *mendīcāre*, beg.]

Men·e·la·us (mĕn′ə-lā′əs) ►*n. Gk. Myth.* The king of Sparta at the time of the Trojan War.

men·ha·den (mĕn-hād′n) ►*n., pl.* **-den** or **-dens** A fish of North American Atlantic waters, used as fertilizer and bait. [Of Algonquian orig.]

men·hir (mĕn′hîr′) ►*n.* A standing stone. [Fr. < Breton, long stone.]

me·ni·al (mē′nē-əl, mēn′yəl) ►*adj.* **1.** Of or relating to work regarded as servile. **2.** Of or appropriate for a servant. ►*n.* A domestic servant. [< AN *meignee*, household.] —**me′ni·al·ly** *adv.*

men·in·gi·tis (mĕn′ĭn-jī′tĭs) ►*n.* Inflammation of the meninges of the brain and the spinal cord.

me·ninx (mē′nĭngks) ►*n., pl.* **me·nin·ges** (mə-nĭn′jēz) Any of the three membranes enclosing the brain and spinal cord in vertebrates. [Gk. *mēninx*, membrane.] —**me·nin′ge·al** (mə-nĭn′jē-əl)

me·nis·cus (mə-nĭs′kəs) ►*n., pl.* **-nis·ci** (-nĭs′ī, -kī, -kē) or **-es 1.** A crescent-shaped body. **2.** The curved upper surface of a liquid in a container. **3.** A cartilage disk that cushions the ends of bones that meet in a joint. [< Gk. *mēniskos*, crescent.]

men·o·pause (mĕn′ə-pôz′) ►*n.* **1.** The cessation of menstruation, occurring usu. between the ages of 45 and 55. **2.** The period during which such cessation occurs. [Gk. *mēn*, month + PAUSE.] —**men′o·paus′al** *adj.*

me·no·rah (mə-nôr′ə) ►*n. Judaism* A nine-branched candelabrum used in celebration of Hanukkah. [Heb. *mənôrâ*.]

menorah

men·ses (mĕn′sēz) ▸*pl.n. (takes sing. or pl. v.)*
1. See **menstruation. 2.** Blood and cellular
debris from the uterus discharged during menstruation. [Lat. *mēnsēs,* pl. of *mēnsis,* month.]
men·stru·al (mĕn′strōo-əl) ▸*adj.* Relating to
menstruation. [< Lat. *mēnstruus.*]
men·stru·ate (mĕn′strōo-āt′) ▸*v.* **-at·ed,**
-at·ing To experience menstruation. [< Lat.
mēnstrua, menses.]
men·stru·a·tion (mĕn′strōo-ā′shən) ▸*n.* The
monthly flow of blood and cellular debris from
the uterus.
men·su·ra·ble (mĕn′sər-ə-bəl, -shər-) ▸*adj.*
Capable of being measured. [< Lat. *mēnsūra,*
measure.] —**men′su·ra·bil′i·ty** *n.*
men·su·ra·tion (mĕn′sə-rā′shən, -shə-) ▸*n.* **1.**
The act, process, or art of measuring. **2.** Measurement of geometric quantities.
–ment ▸*suff.* Product, means, action, or state:
curtailment. [< Lat. *-mentum,* n. suff.]
men·tal (mĕn′tl) ▸*adj.* **1.** Relating to the mind:
mental illness. **2.** Executed or performed by the
mind. [< Lat. *mēns,* mind.] —**men′tal·ly** *adv.*
mental age ▸*n.* A measure of mental development as determined by intelligence tests, gen.
restricted to children and expressed as the age
of which that level is typical.
men·tal·i·ty (mĕn-tăl′ĭ-tē) ▸*n., pl.* **-ties 1.** Cast
or turn of mind. **2.** Intellectual capabilities or
endowment.
mental retardation ▸*n. Often Offensive*
Impaired intellectual development resulting
from any of various causes, including genetic
disorders and brain injury.
men·thol (mĕn′thôl′) ▸*n.* A fragrant white
crystalline organic compound used in perfumes, flavorings, and inhalants. [< Lat. *men-
tha,* mint + –OL.] —**men′tho·lat′ed** *adj.*
men·tion (mĕn′shən) ▸*v.* To speak or write
about, esp. briefly or incidentally. [< Lat.
mentiō, reference.] —**men′tion** *n.* —**men′-
tion·a·ble** *adj.*
men·tor (mĕn′tôr′, -tər) ▸*n.* A wise and trusted
counselor or teacher. ▸*v.* To serve as a trusted
counselor or teacher. [< Gk. *Mentōr,* counselor
of Odysseus.]
men·u (mĕn′yōō) ▸*n.* **1.** A list of dishes to
be served or available for a meal. **2.** A list of
options, esp. as displayed on a screen. [< OFr.
menut, small; see MINUTE².]
me·ow (mē-ou′) ▸*n. Informal* The cry of a cat.
[Imit.] —**me·ow′** *v.*
me·phi·tis (mə-fī′tĭs) ▸*n.* **1.** An offensive smell.
2. A foul-smelling gas emitted from the earth.
[Lat. *mephītis.*] —**me·phit′ic** (-fĭt′ĭk) *adj.*
–mer ▸*suff.* Polymer: *monomer.* [< Gk. *meros,*
part.]
mer·can·tile (mûr′kən-tēl′, -tīl′, -tĭl) ▸*adj.* Of

or relating to merchants or trade. [< Ital. <
mercante, MERCHANT.]
Mer·ca·tor (mər-kā′tər), **Gerhardus** 1512–94.
Flemish cartographer.
mer·ce·nar·y (mûr′sə-nĕr′ē) ▸*adj.* **1.** Motivated by a desire for monetary or material
gain. **2.** Hired for service in a foreign army. [<
Lat. *mercēnārius < mercēs,* wages.] —**mer′ce·
nar′y** *n.*
mer·cer·ize (mûr′sə-rīz′) ▸*v.* **-ized, -iz·ing** To
treat (cotton thread) with sodium hydroxide
so as to shrink the fiber and increase its luster and affinity for dye. [After John *Mercer*
(1791–1866).]
mer·chan·dise (mûr′chən-dīz′, -dīs′) ▸*n.*
Goods bought and sold in business; commercial wares. ▸*v.* (-dīz′) **-dised, -dis·ing 1.**
To buy and sell (goods). **2.** To promote merchandise sales. [< OFr. *marchand,* MERCHANT.]
—**mer′chan·dis′er** *n.*
mer·chant (mûr′chənt) ▸*n.* **1.** One whose occupation is buying and selling goods for profit. **2.**
A shopkeeper. [< Lat. *mercārī,* to trade.]
mer·chant·man (mûr′chənt-mən) ▸*n.* A ship
used in commerce.
merchant marine ▸*n.* **1.** A nation's commercial ships. **2.** The personnel of the merchant
marine.
mer·ci·ful (mûr′sĭ-fəl) ▸*adj.* Full of mercy; compassionate. —**mer′ci·ful·ly** *adv.*
mer·cu·ri·al (mər-kyoŏr′ē-əl) ▸*adj.* **1.** Containing or caused by the action of the element mercury. **2.** Quick and changeable in temperament;
volatile. [< Lat. *Mercurius,* Mercury.] —**mer·
cu′ri·al·ly** *adv.*
mer·cu·ric (mər-kyoŏr′ĭk) ▸*adj.* Relating to or
containing bivalent mercury.
mer·cu·rous (mər-kyoŏr′əs, mûr′kyər-əs) ▸*adj.*
Of or containing monovalent mercury.
mer·cu·ry (mûr′kyə-rē) ▸*n.* **1.** *Symbol* **Hg** A silvery-white poisonous metallic element, liquid
at room temperature, used in thermometers
and batteries. At. no. 80. See table at **element.
2.** Temperature: *The mercury fell overnight.* [<
Lat. *Mercurius,* Mercury.]
Mercury ▸*n.* **1.** *Rom. Myth.* A god that served as
messenger to the other gods and was himself
the god of commerce, travel, and thievery. **2.**
The smallest of the planets and the one nearest
the sun, at a mean distance of 57.9 million km
(36 million mi) and a mean radius of approx.
2,440 km (1,516 mi).
mer·cy (mûr′sē) ▸*n., pl.* **-cies 1.** Compassionate
treatment, esp. of those under one's power. **2.** A
disposition to be kind and forgiving. **3.** A blessing. [< Lat. *mercēs,* reward.] —**mer′ci·less** *adj.*
—**mer′ci·less·ly** *adv.* —**mer′ci·less·ness** *n.*
mere (mîr) ▸*adj. Superl.* **mer·est 1.** Being no
more than what is specified: *a mere 50 cents.* **2.**
Considered apart from anything else: *shocked
by the mere idea.* [< Lat. *merus,* pure.] —**mere′-
ly** *adv.*
Mer·e·dith (mĕr′ĭ-dĭth), **James Howard** b.
1933. Amer. civil rights advocate.
me·ren·gue (mə-rĕng′gä) ▸*n.* A dance of
Dominican and Haitian origin, marked by a
sliding step. [< Sp., meringue.]
mer·e·tri·cious (mĕr′ĭ-trĭsh′əs) ▸*adj.* Attracting
attention in a vulgar manner. [< Lat. *meretrīx,*
prostitute.] —**mer′e·tri′cious·ly** *adv.*
mer·gan·ser (mər-găn′sər) ▸*n.* A fish-eating

diving duck having a slim hooked bill. [Lat. *mergus*, diver + *ānser*, goose.]

merge (mûrj) ►*v.* **merged, merg·ing** To combine or cause to be combined into a single entity. [Lat. *mergere*, plunge.]

merg·er (mûr′jər) ►*n.* The act or an instance of merging, esp. the absorption of one corporation by another.

me·rid·i·an (mə-rĭd′ē-ən) ►*n.* **1a.** A great circle on the earth's surface passing through the North and South geographic poles. **b.** Either half of such a circle from pole to pole. **2.** *Astron.* A great circle passing through the two poles of the celestial sphere and the point directly overhead. **3.** The highest point or stage; zenith. **4.** *Regional* See **median** (sense 2). [< Lat. *merīdiēs*, midday.]

me·ringue (mə-răng′) ►*n.* A dessert topping or pastry shell made from stiffly beaten egg whites and sugar. [Fr. *meringue*.]

me·ri·no (mə-rē′nō) ►*n., pl.* **-nos 1.** A breed of sheep having long fine wool. **2.** A soft lightweight fabric made of fine wool. [Sp.]

mer·it (mĕr′ĭt) ►*n.* **1.** Superior quality or worth; excellence. **2.** often **merits** An aspect of character or behavior deserving approval or disapproval. **3. merits a.** *Law* The factors to be considered in making a substantive decision in a case. **b.** The factual content of a matter. ►*v.* To earn; deserve. See Synonyms at **earn.** [< Lat. *meritus*, p.part. of *merēre*, deserve.] —**mer′it·less** *adj.*

mer·i·to·ri·ous (mĕr′ĭ-tôr′ē-əs) ►*adj.* Deserving reward or praise; having merit. [< Lat. *meritōrius*, earning money.] —**mer′i·to′ri·ous·ly** *adv.*

Mer·kel (mûr′kəl), **Angela** b. 1954. German politician; became chancellor in 2005.

mer·maid (mûr′mād′) ►*n.* A legendary sea creature having the head and upper body of a woman and the tail of a fish. [ME : OE *mere*, sea + MAID.]

mer·man (mûr′măn′, -mən) ►*n.* A legendary sea creature having the head and upper body of a man and the tail of a fish. [MER(MAID) + MAN.]

mer·ry (mĕr′ē) ►*adj.* **-ri·er, -ri·est 1.** Full of high-spirited gaiety. **2.** Marked by fun and festivity. [< OE *mirige*.] —**mer′ri·ly** *adv.* —**mer′ri·ment** *n.* —**mer′ri·ness** *n.*

mer·ry-go-round (mĕr′ē-gō-round′) ►*n.* **1.** A revolving circular platform fitted with seats, often in the form of animals, ridden for amusement. **2.** A busy round; whirl.

mer·ry·mak·ing (mĕr′ē-mā′kĭng) ►*n.* **1.** Participation in festive activities. **2.** A festivity; revelry. —**mer′ry·mak′er** *n.*

Mer·sey (mûr′zē) A river of NW England flowing about 115 km (70 mi) to the Irish Sea.

Mer·ton (mûr′tn), **Thomas** 1915–68. Amer. Trappist monk and writer.

me·sa (mā′sə) ►*n.* A flat-topped elevation with steep sides. [Sp. < Lat. *mēnsa*, table.]

mes·cal (mĕs-kăl′) ►*n.* **1.** See **peyote** (sense 1). **2a.** A Mexican liquor distilled from fermented agave juice. **b.** An agave, esp. one used for producing food or beverages. [< Nahuatl *mexcalli*, liquor made from agave.]

mes·ca·line (mĕs′kə-lēn′, -lĭn) ►*n.* A hallucinogenic alkaloid drug, obtained from peyote buttons.

mes·clun (mĕs′klən) ►*n.* A mixture of young leafy greens used as salad. [Provençal *mesclom*, mixture.]

Mes·dames (mā-däm′, -dăm′) ►*n.* **1.** Pl. of **Madam** (sense 1). **2.** Pl. of **Madame.**

Mes·de·moi·selles (mād′mwä-zĕl′) ►*n.* Pl. of **Mademoiselle.**

mesh (mĕsh) ►*n.* **1.** Any of the open spaces in a net or network. **2.** A net or network: *a screen made of wire mesh.* **3.** The engagement of gear teeth. ►*v.* **1.** To ensnare. **2.** To engage or cause (gear teeth) to become engaged. **3.** To fit together harmoniously. [Prob. < MDu. *maesche*.]

mes·mer·ize (mĕz′mə-rīz′, mĕs′-) ►*v.* **-ized, -iz·ing** To hypnotize. [After Franz *Mesmer* (1734–1815).] —**mes′mer·ism′** *n.*

meso– or **mes–** ►*pref.* Middle: *mesosphere.* [< Gk. *mesos*.]

Mes·o·a·mer·i·ca (mĕz′ō-ə-mĕr′ĭ-kə, mĕs′-) A region extending S and E from central Mexico to include parts of Guatemala, Belize, Honduras, and Nicaragua. —**Mes′o·a·mer′i·can** *adj.* & *n.*

Mes·o·lith·ic (mĕz′ə-lĭth′ĭk, mĕs′-) ►*adj.* Of or being the Stone Age period between the Paleolithic and Neolithic, marked by the appearance of microlithic tools and weapons. ►*n.* The Mesolithic Period.

mes·on (mĕz′ŏn′, mĕs′-) ►*n.* Any of a class of subatomic particles that participate in strong interactions and are composed of a quark and an antiquark.

Mes·o·po·ta·mi·a (mĕs′ə-pə-tā′mē-ə) An ancient region of SW Asia between the Tigris and Euphrates Rivers in modern-day Iraq. —**Mes′o·po·ta′mi·an** *adj.* & *n.*

mes·o·sphere (mĕz′ə-sfîr′, mĕs′-) ►*n.* The portion of the atmosphere from about 50 to 80 km (31 to 50 mi) above the earth's surface. —**mes′o·spher′ic** (-sfîr′ĭk, -sfĕr′-) *adj.*

Mes·o·zo·ic (mĕz′ə-zō′ĭk, mĕs′-) ►*adj.* Of or being the 3rd geologic era, including the Cretaceous, Jurassic, and Triassic Periods and marked esp. by the appearance and extinction of dinosaurs. ►*n.* The Mesozoic Era.

mes·quite (mĕ-skēt′, mə-) ►*n.* A small spiny tree or shrub native to hot dry regions chiefly of the Americas. [< Nahuatl *mizquitl*.]

mess (mĕs) ►*n.* **1.** An untidy condition. **2.** A confused or troubling condition. **3.** An amount of food, as for a meal: *a mess of fish.* **4a.** A group, as of soldiers, that regularly eats meals together. **b.** Food served to such a group. ►*v.* **1.** To make disorderly or soiled. **2.** To interfere: *messing in our affairs.* —*phrasal verbs:* **mess up** To botch; bungle. **mess with 1.** To use or handle something carelessly. **2.** To fight with. [< Lat. *missus*, course of meal.]

mes·sage (mĕs′ĭj) ►*n.* **1.** A usu. short communication transmitted from one person or group to another. **2.** A lesson or moral. [< Med.Lat. *missāticum* < Lat. *missus*, sent.]

mes·sen·ger (mĕs′ən-jər) ►*n.* One that carries messages or performs errands. [< OFr. *messagier* < *message*, MESSAGE.]

Mes·si·ah (mĭ-sī′ə) ►*n.* **1.** also **Mes·si·as** (mĭ-sī′əs) The anticipated deliverer and king of the Jews. Used with *the.* **2.** also **Messias** *Christianity* Jesus. Used with *the.* **3. messiah** An expected savior or liberator. [< Aram. *məšîḥā* or Heb. *māŝîah*, anointed.] —**Mes'si·an'ic** (mĕs'ē-ăn'ĭk) *adj.*

Mes·sieurs (mā-syœ') ►*n.* Pl. of **Monsieur.**

Messrs.¹ (mĕs'ərz) ►*n.* Pl. of **Mr.**

Messrs.² ►*abbr.* Messieurs

mess·y (mĕs'ē) ►*adj.* **-i·er, -i·est 1a.** Disorderly and dirty: *a messy room.* **b.** Given to making messes: *a messy roommate.* **2.** Unpleasantly difficult to settle or resolve: *a messy court case.* —**mess'i·ly** *adv.* —**mess'i·ness** *n.*

mes·ti·za (mĕs-tē'zə) ►*n.* A woman of mixed racial ancestry, esp. of European and Native American ancestry. [Span., fem. of *mestizo.*]

mes·ti·zo (mĕs-tē'zō) ►*n., pl.* **-zos** or **-zoes** A person of mixed racial ancestry, esp. of European and Native American ancestry. [< LLat. *mixtīcius,* mixed.]

met (mĕt) ►*v.* P.t. and p.part. of **meet¹.**

meta– or **met–** ►*pref.* **1.** Situated behind: *metacarpus.* **2.** Change; transformation: *metastasis.* [< Gk. *meta,* beside, after.]

me·tab·o·lism (mĭ-tăb'ə-lĭz'əm) ►*n.* **1.** The physical and chemical processes occurring within a living cell or organism that are necessary for life. **2.** The functioning of a specific substance within the body: *iodine metabolism.* [< Gk. *metabolē,* change.] —**met'a·bol'ic** (mĕt'ə-bŏl'ĭk) *adj.* —**met'a·bol'i·cal·ly** *adv.* —**me·tab'o·lize'** *v.*

me·tab·o·lite (mĭ-tăb'ə-līt') ►*n.* A substance produced by metabolism. [METABOL(ISM) + –ITE¹.]

met·a·car·pus (mĕt'ə-kär'pəs) ►*n., pl.* **-pi** (-pī) **1.** The part of the human hand that includes the five bones between the fingers and the wrist. **2.** The corresponding part of the forefoot of a quadruped.

Met·a·com (mĕt'ə-kŏm') "Philip." d. 1676. Wampanoag leader.

met·al (mĕt'l) ►*n.* **1.** Any of a category of elements that usu. have a shiny surface, are gen. good conductors of heat and electricity, and can be melted or fused, hammered into thin sheets, or drawn into wires. **2.** An alloy of two or more metals. **3.** Basic character; mettle. **4.** *Mus.* Heavy metal. [< Gk. *metallon.*] —**me·tal'lic** (mə-tăl'ĭk) *adj.* —**me·tal'li·cal·ly** *adv.*

metallic bond ►*n.* The chemical bond characteristic of metals, in which mobile valence electrons are shared among atoms in a usu. stable crystalline structure.

met·al·lur·gy (mĕt'l-ûr'jē) ►*n.* The science that deals with extracting metals from their ores and creating useful objects from them. [< Gk. *metallourgos,* miner : *metallon,* metal + *ergon,* work.] —**met'al·lur'gic, met'al·lur'gi·cal** *adj.* —**met'al·lur'gist** *n.*

met·al·work (mĕt'l-wûrk') ►*n.* Articles, esp. decorative objects, made of metal. —**met'al·work'er** *n.*

met·a·mor·phic (mĕt'ə-môr'fĭk) ►*adj.* **1.** also **met·a·mor·phous** (-fəs) Of metamorphosis. **2.** *Geol.* Changed in structure or composition as a result of metamorphism.

met·a·mor·phism (mĕt'ə-môr'fĭz'əm) ►*n.* *Geol.* The process by which rocks are altered in composition, texture, or structure by heat, pressure, and chemical action.

met·a·mor·phose (mĕt'ə-môr'fōz', -fōs') ►*v.* **-phosed, -phos·ing** To change by metamorphosis. See Synonyms at **convert.**

met·a·mor·pho·sis (mĕt'ə-môr'fə-sĭs) ►*n., pl.* **-ses** (-sēz') **1.** A transformation, as by magic or sorcery. **2.** A marked change in appearance, character, condition, or function. **3.** *Biol.* Change in form and often habits during development after the embryonic stage, as in insects. [< Gk. *metamorphōsis.*]

met·a·phor (mĕt'ə-fôr', -fər) ►*n.* A figure of speech in which a word or phrase that ordinarily designates one thing is used to designate another, thus making an implicit comparison, as in *the evening of life.* [< Gk. *metaphora* : META– + *pherein,* carry.] —**met'a·phor'ic** (-fôr'ĭk), **met'a·phor'i·cal** *adj.* —**met'a·phor'i·cal·ly** *adv.*

met·a·phys·i·cal (mĕt'ə-fĭz'ĭ-kəl) ►*adj.* **1.** Of or relating to metaphysics. **2.** Based on speculative or abstract reasoning. —**met'a·phys'i·cal·ly** *adv.*

met·a·phys·ics (mĕt'ə-fĭz'ĭks) ►*n.* *(takes sing. v.)* The branch of philosophy that examines the nature of reality and the relationship between mind and matter. [< Med.Gk. *metaphusika,* title of Aristotle's treatise on the subject.] —**met'a·phy·si'cian** (-fĭ-zĭsh'ən) *n.*

me·tas·ta·sis (mə-tăs'tə-sĭs) ►*n., pl.* **-ses** (-sēz') The spreading of a disease from an original site to one or more sites elsewhere in the body. —**me·tas'ta·size'** *v.* —**met'a·stat'ic** (mĕt'ə-stăt'ĭk) *adj.* —**met'a·stat'i·cal·ly** *adv.*

met·a·tar·sus (mĕt'ə-tär'səs) ►*n., pl.* **-si** (-sī, -sē) The middle part of the foot, composed of the five bones between the toes and ankle, that forms the instep. —**met'a·tar'sal** *adj.*

mete (mēt) ►*v.* **met·ed, met·ing** To dole; allot: *mete out punishment.* [< OE *metan.*]

me·tem·psy·cho·sis (mə-tĕm'sĭ-kō'sĭs, mĕt'- əm-sī-) ►*n., pl.* **-ses** (-sēz) Reincarnation. [< Gk. *metempsukhōsis.*]

me·te·or (mē'tē-ər, -ôr') ►*n.* **1.** A bright trail or streak that appears in the sky when a meteoroid is heated to incandescence by friction with the earth's atmosphere. **2.** A meteoroid or meteorite. [< Gk. *meteōros,* high in the air.]

me·te·or·ic (mē'tē-ôr'ĭk, -ŏr'-) ►*adj.* **1.** Of or formed by a meteoroid. **2.** Similar to a meteor in speed or brilliance: *a meteoric rise to fame.* —**me'te·or'i·cal·ly** *adv.*

me·te·or·ite (mē'tē-ə-rīt') ►*n.* A stony or metallic mass of matter that has fallen to the earth's surface from outer space. —**me'te·or·it'ic** (-ə-rĭt'ĭk), **me'te·or·it'i·cal** *adj.*

me·te·or·oid (mē'tē-ə-roid') ►*n.* A solid body, moving in space, that is smaller than an asteroid and at least as large as a speck of dust.

me·te·or·ol·o·gy (mē'tē-ə-rŏl'ə-jē) ►*n.* The science that deals with the phenomena of the atmosphere, esp. weather. —**me'te·or·o·log'i·cal** (-ər-ə-lŏj'ĭ-kəl) *adj.* —**me'te·or·o·log'i·cal·ly** *adv.* —**me'te·or·ol'o·gist** *n.*

me·ter¹ (mē'tər) ►*n.* **1a.** The measured arrangement of words in poetry, as by accentual rhythm. **b.** A particular arrangement of words in a poem, such as iambic pentameter. **2.** *Mus.* **a.** Division into measures or bars. **b.** A specific rhythm in a measure. [ME, ult. < Gk. *metron.*]

me·ter² (mē'tər) ►*n.* See table at **measurement.** [Fr. *mètre* < Gk. *metron,* measure.]

me·ter³ (mē'tər) ►*n.* Any of various devices that measure or indicate and record or regulate. ►*v.* **1.** To measure or regulate with a meter. **2.** To imprint with postage by means of a postage meter or similar device. [< –METER.]

–meter ▸*suff.* Measuring device: *thermometer* [< Gk. *metron*, measure.]

me·ter·kil·o·gram-sec·ond (mē′tər-kĭl′ə-grăm-sĕk′ənd) ▸*adj.* Of or being a system of units for mechanics, using the meter, the kilogram, and the second as basic units of length, mass, and time.

meth·a·done (mĕth′ə-dōn′) ▸*n.* A potent synthetic narcotic drug, $C_{21}H_{27}NO$, used in addiction treatment programs.

meth·am·phet·a·mine (mĕth′ăm-fĕt′ə-mēn′, -mĭn) ▸*n.* An amine derivative of amphetamine used in the form of its crystalline hydrochloride as a stimulant.

meth·ane (mĕth′ān′) ▸*n.* An odorless, colorless, flammable gas, CH_4, the major constituent of natural gas, used as a fuel and an important source of organic compounds. [METH(YL) + –ANE.]

meth·a·nol (mĕth′ə-nôl′, -nōl′, -nŏl′) ▸*n.* A colorless, toxic, flammable liquid, CH_3OH, used as an antifreeze, solvent, fuel, and denaturant for ethyl alcohol.

meth·od (mĕth′əd) ▸*n.* **1.** A systematic means or manner of procedure. **2.** Orderly arrangement of parts or steps to accomplish an end. [< Gk. *methodos*.] —**me·thod′i·cal** (mə-thŏd′ĭ-kəl), **me·thod′ic** *adj.* —**me·thod′i·cal·ly** *adv.*

Meth·od·ist (mĕth′ə-dĭst) ▸*n.* A member of an evangelical Protestant church founded on the principles of John Wesley. —**Meth′od·ism** *n.* —**Meth′od·is′tic** *adj.*

meth·od·ol·o·gy (mĕth′ə-dŏl′ə-jē) ▸*n., pl.* -**gies 1.** A body of practices, procedures, and rules used in a discipline. **2.** The branch of logic that deals with the general principles of the formation of knowledge. —**meth′od·o·log′i·cal** (-ə-də-lŏj′ĭ-kəl) *adj.* —**meth′od·o·log′i·cal·ly** *adv.*

Me·thu·se·lah (mə-thōō′zə-lə) A biblical patriarch said to have lived 969 years.

meth·yl (mĕth′əl) ▸*adj.* Relating to or being a hydrocarbon unit, CH_3. [Ult. < Gk. *methu*, wine.] —**me·thyl′ic** (mə-thĭl′ĭk) *adj.*

methyl alcohol ▸*n.* See **methanol.**

meth·yl·at·ed spirit (mĕth′ə-lā′tĭd) ▸*n.* A denatured alcohol consisting of a mixture of ethanol and methanol.

met·i·cal (mĕt′ĭ-kăl′, mĕt′ĭ-käl′) ▸*n.* See table at **currency.** [< Ar. *miṭqāl*, a unit of weight.]

me·tic·u·lous (mĭ-tĭk′yə-ləs) ▸*adj.* Acting with excessive concern for details; extremely precise. [< Lat. *metīculōsus*, timid < *metus*, fear.] —**me·tic′u·lous·ness** *n.* —**me·tic′u·lous·ly** *adv.*

mé·tier (mē-tyā′, mā-) ▸*n.* **1.** A trade or profession. **2.** One's specialty. [< Lat. *ministērium*, ministry.]

me·ton·y·my (mə-tŏn′ə-mē) ▸*n., pl.* -**mies** A figure of speech in which one word or phrase is substituted for another with which it is closely associated, as in the use of *Washington* for *the US government.* [Gk. *metōnumia*.] —**met′o·nym′** (mĕt′ə-nĭm′) *n.* —**met′o·nym′ic, met′o·nym′i·cal** *adj.*

me·tre (mē′tər) ▸*n. Chiefly Brit.* **1.** Var. of **meter¹**. **2.** Var. of **meter²**.

met·ric (mĕt′rĭk) ▸*adj.* Of or relating to the metric system.

met·ri·cal (mĕt′rĭ-kəl) ▸*adj.* **1.** Of or composed in poetic meter: *metrical verse.* **2.** Of or relating to measurement. [< Gk. *metrikos*.] —**met′ri·cal·ly** *adv.*

met·ri·ca·tion (mĕt′rĭ-kā′shən) ▸*n.* Conversion to the metric system of weights and measures.

met·rics (mĕt′rĭks) ▸*n. (takes sing. v.)* The study of poetic meter; prosody.

metric system ▸*n.* A decimal system of units based on the meter as a unit length, the kilogram as a unit mass, and the second as a unit time. See table at **measurement.**

metric ton ▸*n.* See table at **measurement.**

met·ro·nome (mĕt′rə-nōm′) ▸*n. Mus.* An adjustable device used to mark time at precise intervals. [Gk. *metron*, measure + *nomos*, division.] —**met′ro·nom′ic** (mĕt′rə-nŏm′ĭk) *adj.*

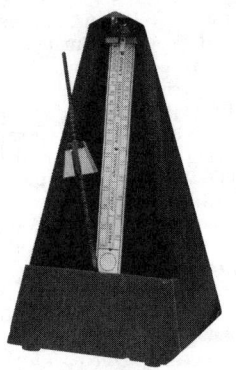

metronome

me·trop·o·lis (mĭ-trŏp′ə-lĭs) ▸*n.* **1.** A major city, esp. the chief city of a country or region. **2.** A city or an urban area regarded as the center of a specific activity. [< Gk. *mētropolis*, mother city.] —**met′ro·pol′i·tan** (mĕt′rə-pŏl′ĭ-tən) *adj. & n.*

–metry ▸*suff.* Process or science of measuring: *photometry.* [< Gk. *metron*, measure.]

met·tle (mĕt′l) ▸*n.* The ability to meet a challenge or persevere under demanding circumstances. [< METAL.] —**met′tle·some** *adj.*

Meuse (myōōz, mœz) A river of W Europe flowing about 900 km (560 mi) from NE France through E Belgium and the S Netherlands to the North Sea.

MeV ▸*abbr.* **1.** mega-electron volt **2.** or **mev** million electron volts

mew (myōō) ▸*v.* To make a high-pitched, crying sound, as that of a cat. [ME *meuen*.] —**mew** *n.*

mews (myōōz) ▸*pl.n. (takes sing. or pl. v.)* A small street or alley orig. with private stables, often converted into residential apartments. [< OFr. *mue* < *muer*, molt.]

Mexican American ▸*n.* A US citizen or resident of Mexican ancestry. —**Mex′i·can-A·mer′i·can** *adj.*

Mex·i·co (mĕk′sĭ-kō′) A country of S-central North America. Cap. Mexico City. —**Mex′i·can** (-kən) *adj. & n.*

Mexico, Gulf of An arm of the Atlantic in SE North America bordering on E Mexico, the SE US, and Cuba.

Mexico City The capital of Mexico, at the S end of the central plateau.

mez·za·nine (mĕz′ə-nēn′, mĕz′ə-nēn′) ▸*n.* **1.**

A partial story between two main stories of a building. **2.** The lowest balcony in a theater or its first few rows. [< Ital. *mezzanino* < Lat. *mediānus*, in the middle.]

mez·zo·so·pran·o (mĕt′sō-sə-prăn′ō, -prä′nō, mĕd′zō-) ►*n., pl.* **-os 1.** A voice having a range between soprano and contralto. **2.** A woman having a mezzo-soprano voice. [Ital.]

MFA ►*abbr.* Master of Fine Arts

mg ►*abbr.* milligram

mgt. ►*abbr.* management

MHz ►*abbr.* megahertz

mi (mē) ►*n. Mus.* The 3rd tone of the diatonic scale. [< Med.Lat.]

MI ►*abbr.* **1.** Michigan **2.** military intelligence **3.** myocardial infarction

mi. or **mi** ►*abbr.* mile

MIA (ĕm′ī-ā′) ►*n.* A member of the armed services reported missing in action. [*m(issing) i(n) a(ction).*]

Mi·am·i (mī-ăm′ē, -ăm′ə) A city of SE FL on Biscayne Bay.

mi·as·ma (mī-ăz′mə, mē-) ►*n., pl.* **-mas** or **-ma·ta** (-mə-tə) **1.** A noxious atmosphere or influence. **2.** A poisonous vapor formerly thought to rise from swamps and putrid matter and cause disease. [Gk. < *miainein*, pollute.] —**mi·as′mal, mi·as′mic** *adj.*

mi·ca (mī′kə) ►*n.* Any of a group of chemically and physically related silicate minerals, common in igneous and metamorphic rocks. [< Lat. *mīca*, grain.]

Mi·cah (mī′kə) also **Mi·che·as** (mī-kē′əs) ►*n.* **1.** A Hebrew prophet of the 8th cent. BC. **2.** See table at **Bible.**

mice (mīs) ►*n.* Pl. of **mouse.**

Mi·chel·an·ge·lo Buo·nar·ro·ti (mī′kəl-ăn′-jə-lō′ bwôn′ə-rô′tē, mĭk′-) 1475–1564. Italian sculptor, painter, architect, and poet.

Mich·i·gan (mĭsh′ĭ-gən) A state of the N-central US. Cap. Lansing.

Michigan, Lake The third largest of the Great Lakes, between WI and MI.

Mic·mac (mĭk′măk′) ►*n.* Var. of **Mi′kmaq.**

mi·cra (mī′krə) ►*n.* Pl. of **micron.**

mi·cro (mī′krō) ►*adj.* **1.** Very small or microscopic. **2.** Basic or small-scale: *the economy's performance at the micro level.* [< MICRO–.]

micro– or **micr–** ►*pref.* **1a.** Small: *microcircuit.* **b.** Abnormally small: *microcephaly.* **c.** Requiring or involving microscopy: *microsurgery.* **2.** One-millionth (10⁻⁶): *microsecond.* [< Gk. *mikros*, small.]

mi·crobe (mī′krōb′) ►*n.* A microorganism. [Fr. : MICRO– + Gk. *bios*, life.] —**mi·cro′bi·al** (-krō′-bē-əl) *adj.*

mi·cro·bi·ol·o·gy (mī′krō-bī-ŏl′ə-jē) ►*n.* The branch of biology that deals with microorganisms. —**mi′cro·bi′o·log′i·cal** (-bī′ə-lŏj′ĭ-kəl) *adj.* —**mi′cro·bi′o·log′i·cal·ly** *adv.* —**mi′cro·bi·ol′o·gist** *n.*

mi·cro·brew (mī′krō-brōō′) ►*n.* A beer or ale brewed in a microbrewery.

mi·cro·brew·er·y (mī′krō-brōō′ə-rē, -brōōr′ē) ►*n.* A small brewery, often selling its products on the premises. —**mi′cro·brew′er** *n.*

mi·cro·ceph·a·ly (mī′krō-sĕf′ə-lē) ►*n.* Abnormal smallness of the head. [MICRO– + Gk. *kephalē*, head + -Y².] —**mi′cro·ce·phal′ic** (-sə-făl′ĭk) *adj. & n.* —**mi′cro·ceph′a·lous** *adj.*

mi·cro·chip (mī′krə-chĭp′) ►*n. Comp.* See **chip** (sense 4).

mi·cro·cir·cuit (mī′krō-sûr′kĭt) ►*n.* An electric circuit consisting of miniaturized components. —**mi′cro·cir′cuit·ry** *n.*

mi·cro·cosm (mī′krə-kŏz′əm) ►*n.* A small, representative system having analogies to a larger system in constitution, configuration, or development. [< Gk. *mikros kosmos*, small world.] —**mi′cro·cos′mic** (-kŏz′mĭk), **mi′cro·cos′mi·cal** *adj.*

mi·cro·dot (mī′krə-dŏt′) ►*n.* A copy or photograph reduced to an extremely small size.

mi·cro·ec·o·nom·ics (mī′krō-ĕk′ə-nŏm′ĭks, -ēk′ə-) ►*n.* (takes sing. v.) The study of how businesses, households, and individuals within an economy allocate limited resources. —**mi′-cro·ec′o·nom′ic** *adj.*

mi·cro·e·lec·tron·ics (mī′krō-ĭ-lĕk-trŏn′ĭks) ►*n. (takes sing. v.)* The branch of electronics that deals with miniature components. —**mi′cro·e·lec·tron′ic** *adj.*

mi·cro·fiche (mī′krō-fēsh′) ►*n., pl.* **-fiche** or **-fich·es** A sheet of microfilm containing rows of pages in reduced form. [Fr.]

mi·cro·film (mī′krə-fĭlm′) ►*n.* A film on which printed materials are photographed greatly reduced in size. —**mi′cro·film′** *v.*

mi·cro·lith (mī′krō-lĭth′) ►*n. Archaeol.* A very small blade made of flaked stone and used as a tool. —**mi′cro·lith′ic** (-lĭth′ĭk) *adj.*

mi·cro·man·age (mī′krō-măn′ĭj) ►*v.* To direct or control in a detailed, often meddlesome manner.

mi·crom·e·ter¹ (mī-krŏm′ĭ-tər) ►*n.* A device for measuring very small distances.

mi·cro·me·ter² (mī′krō-mē′tər) ►*n.* See **micron.**

mi·cron (mī′krŏn′) ►*n., pl.* **-crons** or **-cra** (-krə) A unit of length equal to one millionth (10⁻⁶) of a meter. [< Gk. *mikros*, small.]

Mi·cro·ne·si·a (mī′krō-nē′zhə, -shə) The islands of the W Pacific, E of the Philippines and N of the equator.

Mi·cro·ne·sian (mī′krə-nē′zhən) ►*n.* **1.** A member of any of the peoples inhabiting Micronesia. **2.** A subfamily of the Austronesian language family. —**Mi′cro·ne′sian** *adj.*

mi·cro·or·gan·ism (mī′krō-ôr′gə-nĭz′əm) ►*n.* An organism or parasitic agent of microscopic size, esp. a bacterium or protozoan.

mi·cro·phone (mī′krə-fōn′) ►*n.* An instrument that converts sound waves into an electric current, usu. fed into an amplifier, recorder, or broadcast transmitter.

mi·cro·proc·es·sor (mī′krō-prŏs′ĕs-ər) ►*n.* An integrated circuit that contains a major processing unit of a computer on a single chip.

mi·cro·scope (mī′krə-skōp′) ►*n.* An optical instrument that uses a combination of lenses to produce magnified images of small objects, esp. of objects too small to be seen by the unaided eye.

mi·cro·scop·ic (mī′krə-skŏp′ĭk) also **mi·cro·scop·i·cal** (-ĭ-kəl) ►*adj.* **1.** Relating to microscopes. **2a.** So small as to require a microscope for viewing. **b.** Tiny; minute. —**mi′cro·scop′i·cal·ly** *adv.*

mi·cros·co·py (mī-krŏs′kə-pē) ►*n.* **1.** The study or use of microscopes. **2.** Investigation employing a microscope.

mi·cro·sec·ond (mī′krō-sĕk′ənd) ►*n.* One millionth (10⁻⁶) of a second.

mi·cro·sur·ger·y (mī′krō-sûr′jə-rē) ►*n.* Surgery on minute body structures or cells performed with the aid of microscopes. —**mi′cro·sur′gi·cal** *adj.*

mi·cro·wave (mī′krə-wāv′, -krō-) ►*adj.* Relating to electromagnetic radiation between radio waves and infrared waves in the electromagnetic spectrum. ►*n.* **1.** A wave of microwave radiation. **2.** *Informal* A microwave oven. —**mi′cro·wav′a·ble, mi′cro·wave′a·ble** *adj.* —**mi′cro·wave′** *v.*

microwave oven ►*n.* An oven in which food is cooked, warmed, or thawed by the heat produced as microwaves cause water molecules in the foodstuff to vibrate.

mid (mĭd) ►*adj.* Middle; central. [< OE *midd.*]

mid– ►*pref.* Middle: *midsummer.* [< MID.]

mid·air (mĭd′âr′) ►*n.* A point or region in the air. ►*adj.* Occurring in midair.

Mi·das (mī′dəs) ►*n.* A fabled king who turned all that he touched to gold.

mid·day (mĭd′dā′) ►*n.* Noon. —**mid′day′** *adj.*

mid·den (mĭd′n) ►*n.* A refuse heap. [ME *midding,* of Scand. orig.]

mid·dle (mĭd′l) ►*adj.* **1.** Equally distant from extremes or limits. **2.** Intermediate; in-between. **3.** Intervening between an earlier and a later period of time. ►*n.* **1.** An area or a point equidistant between extremes. **2.** The waist. [< OE *middel.*]

middle age ►*n.* The time of human life gen. between 40 and 60. —**mid′dle-aged′** *adj.*

Middle Ages ►*pl.n.* The period in European history between antiquity and the Renaissance, often dated from AD 476 to 1453.

Middle America ►*n.* **1.** That part of the US middle class thought of as being conservative in values and attitudes. **2.** The American heartland thought of as being made up of small towns, small cities, and suburbs.

middle class ►*n.* The members of society occupying a socioeconomic position between the lower working classes and the wealthy.

Middle Dutch ►*n.* Dutch from the mid-1100s through the 1400s.

middle ear ►*n.* The space between the eardrum and the inner ear that contains the malleus, incus, and stapes.

Middle East also **Mid·east** (mĭd-ēst′) An area comprising the countries of SW Asia and NE Africa. —**Middle Eastern** *adj.* —**Middle Easterner** *n.*

Middle English ►*n.* English from about 1100 to 1500.

middle ground ►*n.* A point of view midway between extremes.

Middle High German ►*n.* High German from the 1000s through the 1400s.

Middle Low German ►*n.* Low German from the mid-1200s through the 1400s.

mid·dle·man (mĭd′l-măn′) ►*n.* **1.** A trader who buys from producers and sells to retailers or consumers. **2.** A go-between.

middle management ►*n.* A group of persons occupying intermediate managerial positions. —**middle manager** *n.*

mid·dle-of-the-road (mĭd′l-əv-thə-rōd′) ►*adj.* Pursuing a course of action midway between extremes, esp. in politics.

middle school ►*n.* A school typically including grades five or six through eight. —**mid′dle-school′** *adj.* —**mid′dle-school′er** *n.*

mid·dle·weight (mĭd′l-wāt′) ►*n.* A boxer weighing from 148 to 160 lbs., between a welterweight and a light heavyweight.

Middle West See **Midwest.**

mid·dling (mĭd′lĭng, -lĭn) ►*adj.* **1.** Of medium size, position, or quality. **2.** Mediocre. ►*adv. Informal* Fairly; moderately. [ME *midlin.*] —**mid′dling·ly** *adv.*

mid·dy (mĭd′ē) ►*n., pl.* **-dies 1.** A midshipman. **2.** A loose blouse with a sailor collar.

Mid·east (mĭd-ēst′) See **Middle East.** —**Mid·east′ern** *adj.* —**Mid·east′ern·er** *n.*

mid·field·er (mĭd′fēld′ər) ►*n.* A player who plays just behind the forwards in certain sports like soccer.

midge (mĭj) ►*n.* A small nonbiting fly often forming large swarms near ponds and lakes. [< OE *mycg.*]

midg·et (mĭj′ĭt) ►*n.* **1.** *Offensive* An unusually small or short person of otherwise normal proportions. **2.** A miniature version of something. —**midg′et** *adj.*

mid·land (mĭd′lənd) ►*n.* The middle part of a country or region. —**mid′land** *adj.*

Mid·lands (mĭd′ləndz) A region of central England.

mid·line (mĭd′līn′) ►*n.* A medial line, esp. the medial line of the body.

mid·night (mĭd′nīt′) ►*n.* The middle of the night; 12 o'clock at night.

midnight sun ►*n.* The sun as seen at midnight during the summer within the Arctic and Antarctic Circles.

mid·point (mĭd′point′) ►*n.* A point or position at or near the middle.

mid·riff (mĭd′rĭf) ►*n.* **1.** See **diaphragm** (sense 1). **2.** The outer part of the human body from below the breast to the waist. [< OE *midhrif.*]

mid·ship·man (mĭd′shĭp′mən, mĭd-shĭp′mən) ►*n.* A student at a naval academy training to be a commissioned officer.

midst (mĭdst, mĭtst) ►*n.* **1.** The middle position or part; center. **2.** The condition of being surrounded by something: *the midst of chaos.* ►*prep.* Among. [< ME *middes.*]

mid·sum·mer (mĭd′sŭm′ər) ►*n.* **1.** The middle of the summer. **2.** The summer solstice, about June 21 in the Northern Hemisphere. —**mid′sum′mer** *adj.*

mid·term (mĭd′tûrm′) ►*n.* **1.** The middle esp. of an academic or political term. **2.** An examination given at the middle of a school term. —**mid′term′** *adj.*

mid·town (mĭd′toun′) ►*n.* A central portion of a city. —**mid′town′** *adj.*

mid·way (mĭd′wā′) ►*n.* The area of a fair, carnival, or circus where sideshows and other amusements are located. ►*adv.* In the middle; halfway. —**mid′way′** *adj.*

Midway A US territory consisting of a coral atoll with two small islands in the NW Hawaiian Is.

mid·week (mĭd′wēk′) ►*n.* The middle of the week. —**mid′week′** *adj.* —**mid′week′ly** *adj. & adv.*

Mid·west (mĭd-wĕst′) or **Middle West** A region of the N-central US around the Great Lakes and the upper Mississippi Valley. —**Mid·**

west′ern adj. —**Mid·west′ern·er** n.

mid·wife (mĭd′wīf′) ►n., pl. **-wives** (-wīvz′) A person, usu. a woman, trained to assist women in childbirth. [ME midwif : prob. mid, with + wif, woman.] —**mid·wife′ry** (-wĭf′ə-rē, mĭd′wīf′rē) n.

mid·win·ter (mĭd′wĭn′tər) ►n. 1. The middle of the winter. 2. The winter solstice, about December 22 in the Northern Hemisphere. —**mid′win′ter** adj.

mid·year (mĭd′yîr′) ►n. 1. The middle of the calendar or academic year. 2. An examination given in the middle of a school year. —**mid′year′** adj.

mien (mēn) ►n. Bearing or manner; appearance. [< ME demeine, DEMEANOR.]

Mies Van Der Ro·he (mēz′ văn dər rō′ə, rō′, fän, mēs′), **Ludwig** 1886–1969. German-born Amer. architect. —**Mies′i·an** (mē′sē-ən) adj.

miff (mĭf) ►v. To offend; annoy. [?]

might[1] (mīt) ►n. 1. Great power or force, as of a nation or army. 2. Physical strength. [< OE miht.]

might[2] (mīt) ►aux.v. P.t. of **may**. Used to indicate a condition contrary to fact, a possibility weaker than may, or to express a higher degree of politeness than may. [< OE magan, be able.]

might·y (mī′tē) ►adj. **-i·er, -i·est 1.** Having great power. 2. Imposing or awesome. ►adv. Regional Very. —**might′i·ly** adv. —**might′i·ness** n.

mi·graine (mī′grān′) ►n. A severe, recurring headache, usu. affecting only one side of the head. [< Gk. hēmikrania, pain in half the head.]

mi·grant (mī′grənt) ►n. 1. One that migrates. 2. A worker who travels from one area to another in search of work. 3. One who leaves one country to settle permanently in another; immigrant. —**mi′grant** adj.

mi·grate (mī′grāt′) ►v. **-grat·ed, -grat·ing 1.** To move from one country or region and settle in another. 2. To move periodically from one region or climate to another. 3. Comp. To move (e.g., an application) from one system to another. [Lat. migrāre.] —**mi·gra′tion** n. —**mi′gra·to′ry** (-grə-tôr′ē) adj.

Usage: Migrate sometimes implies a lack of permanent settlement, esp. as a result of seasonal or periodic movement. *Emigrate* and *immigrate* imply a permanent move, generally across a political boundary. *Emigrate* describes the move relative to the point of departure, while *immigrate* describes the move relative to the destination.

mi·ka·do (mĭ-kä′dō) ►n., pl. **-dos** An emperor of Japan. [J.]

mike (mīk) Informal ►n. A microphone. ►v. **miked, mik·ing** To supply with or transmit through a microphone.

Mi′k·maq (mĭk′măk′) or **Mic·mac** (mĭk′măk′) ►n., pl. **-maq** or **-maqs** or **-mac** or **-macs 1.** A member of a Native American people of E Canada and NE Maine. 2. The Algonquian language of the Mi′kmaq.

mil (mĭl) ►n. A unit of length equal to one thousandth (10⁻³) of an inch. [< Lat. mĭllēsimus, thousandth < mĭlle, thousand.]

Mi·lan (mĭ-lăn′, -län′) A city of N Italy NE of Genoa. —**Mil′a·nese′** (mĭl′ə-nēz′, -nēs′) adj. & n.

mild (mīld) ►adj. **-er, -est 1.** Gentle or kind in disposition or behavior. 2. Not harsh, severe, or strong; moderate. [< OE milde.] —**mild′ly** adv. —**mild′ness** n.

mil·dew (mĭl′dōō′, -dyōō′) ►n. Any of various fungi that form a usu. whitish growth on plants and other organic materials. [< OE mildēaw.] —**mil′dew′** v.

mile (mīl) ►n. 1. See table at **measurement**. 2. A nautical mile. 3. An air mile. [< Lat. mīlia (passuum), a thousand (paces).]

mile·age (mī′lĭj) ►n. 1. Distance that is measured or expressed in miles. 2. Service or wear estimated by miles used or traveled. 3. An allowance for travel expenses at a specified rate per mile.

mile·post (mīl′pōst′) ►n. A post indicating distance in miles, as along a highway.

mil·er (mī′lər) ►n. One who competes in one-mile races.

mile·stone (mīl′stōn′) ►n. 1. A stone milepost. 2. A turning point.

Mi·le·tus (mī-lē′təs) An ancient Ionian city of W Asia Minor in present-day Turkey.

mi·lieu (mĭl-yōō′, mē-lyœ′) ►n., pl. **-lieus** or **-lieux** (-lyœ′) An environment; setting. [< OFr., center.]

mil·i·tant (mĭl′ĭ-tənt) ►adj. **1.** Fighting or warring. 2. Combative or aggressive esp. for a cause. ►n. A militant person or party. [< Lat. mīlitāre, serve as a soldier.] —**mil′i·tance, mil′i·tan·cy** n. —**mil′i·tant·ly** adv.

mil·i·ta·rism (mĭl′ĭ-tə-rĭz′əm) ►n. 1. Glorification of the ideals of a professional military class. 2. Predominance of the armed forces in state policies. —**mil′i·ta·rist** n. —**mil′i·ta·ris′tic** adj.

mil·i·ta·rize (mĭl′ĭ-tə-rīz′) ►v. **-rized, -riz·ing 1.** To equip, train, or prepare for war. 2. To imbue with militarism. —**mil′i·ta·ri·za′tion** n.

mil·i·tar·y (mĭl′ĭ-tĕr′ē) ►adj. Of or relating to the armed forces or war. ►n., pl. **-y** also **-ies** Armed forces. [< Lat. mīles, mīlit-, soldier.] —**mil′i·tar′i·ly** (-târ′ə-lē) adv.

mil·i·tate (mĭl′ĭ-tāt′) ►v. **-tat·ed, -tat·ing** To bring about an effect or change. [Lat. mīlitāre, serve as a soldier.]

mi·li·tia (mə-lĭsh′ə) ►n. An army that is composed of ordinary citizens rather than professional soldiers, on call for service in an emergency. [Lat. mīlitia, military service.] —**mi·li′tia·man** n.

milk (mĭlk) ►n. 1. A nourishing whitish liquid that is produced by the mammary glands of female mammals after they have given birth and used to feed their young. 2. The milk of cows or other animals, used as food by humans. 3. A liquid that resembles milk: coconut milk. ►v. 1. To draw milk from (a female mammal). 2. To draw or extract a liquid from as if by milking. [< OE milc.] —**milk′i·ness** n. —**milk′y** adj.

milk·maid (mĭlk′mād′) ►n. A girl or woman who milks cows.

milk·man (mĭlk′măn′) ►n. A man who sells or delivers milk to customers.

milk of magnesia ►n. A milky white liquid suspension of magnesium hydroxide, $Mg(OH)_2$, used as an antacid and laxative.

milk shake ►n. A whipped beverage made of milk, flavoring, and usu. ice cream.

milk tooth ►*n.* See **primary tooth.**

milk·weed (mĭlk′wēd′) ►*n.* A plant having milky juice and pods that split open to release downy seeds.

Milky Way ►*n.* **1.** The galaxy containing the sun, solar system, and all of the individually visible stars in the night sky. **2.** The broad meandering band of faint light that consists of stars from this galaxy, often visible in the night sky.

mill¹ (mĭl) ►*n.* **1.** A building equipped with machinery for grinding grain. **2.** A device for crushing or grinding. **3.** A building equipped with machinery for processing materials; factory. **4.** A place that turns out something routinely in the manner of a factory: *a diploma mill.* ►*v.* **1.** To grind or crush in or as if in a mill. **2.** To move around in churning confusion. [< LLat. *molīna.*] —**mill′er** *n.*

mill² (mĭl) ►*n.* A monetary unit equal to ¹⁄₁₀₀₀ of a US dollar. [< Lat. *mīllēsimus*; see MIL.]

Mill, James (1773–1836) and **John Stuart** (1806–73). British philosophers and economists.

Mil·lay (mĭ-lā′), **Edna Saint Vincent** 1892–1950. Amer. poet.

mill·dam (mĭl′dăm′) ►*n.* A dam to make a millpond.

mil·len·ni·um (mə-lĕn′ē-əm) ►*n.*, *pl.* **-ni·ums** or **-ni·a** (-ē-ə) **1.** A span of 1,000 years. **2.** In the New Testament, a thousand-year period in which Jesus is to rule on earth. **3.** A hoped-for period of joy, serenity, and justice. **4.** A thousandth anniversary. [< Lat. *mīlle*, thousand + *annus*, year.] —**mil·len′ni·al** (-əl) *adj.* —**mil·len′ni·al·ism** *n.* —**mil·len′ni·al·ist** *n.* —**mil·len′ni·al·ly** *adv.*

mil·le·pede (mĭl′ə-pēd′) ►*n.* Var. of **millipede.**

Mil·ler (mĭl′ər), **Arthur Asher** 1915–2005. Amer. playwright.

mil·let (mĭl′ĭt) ►*n.* **1.** A grass grown for its small edible whitish grains and for hay. **2.** The grain itself. [< OFr. *mil* < Lat. *milium.*]

Mil·let (mĭ-lā′, mē-), **Jean François** 1814–1875. French painter.

milli– ►*pref.* One thousandth (10⁻³): *millisecond.* [< Lat. *mīlle*, thousand.]

mil·liard (mĭl′yərd, -yärd′, mĭl′ē-ärd′) ►*n.* *Chiefly Brit.* A billion. [Fr.]

mil·li·bar (mĭl′ə-bär′) ►*n.* A unit of atmospheric pressure equal to 100 newtons per square meter.

mil·li·gram (mĭl′ĭ-grăm′) ►*n.* See table at **measurement.**

mil·li·li·ter (mĭl′ə-lē′tər) ►*n.* See table at **measurement.**

mil·li·me·ter (mĭl′ə-mē′tər) ►*n.* See table at **measurement.**

mil·li·ner (mĭl′ə-nər) ►*n.* One who makes or sells esp. women's hats. [< ME *Milener*, a native of Milan.] —**mil′li·ner′y** (-něr′ē) *n.*

mil·lion (mĭl′yən) ►*n.*, *pl.* **-lion** or **-lions** The cardinal number equal to 10⁶. [< OItal. *milione* < Lat. *mīlle*, thousand.] —**mil′lion** *adj. & pron.*

mil·lion·aire (mĭl′yə-nâr′) ►*n.* A person whose wealth amounts to at least a million dollars, pounds, or the equivalent in other currency. [Fr. *millionnaire.*]

mil·lionth (mĭl′yənth) ►*n.* **1.** The ordinal number matching the number million in a series. **2.** One of a million equal parts. —**mil′lionth** *adv. & adj.*

mil·li·pede or **mil·le·pede** (mĭl′ə-pēd′) ►*n.* A plant-eating arthropod having a cylindrical segmented body with two pairs of legs attached to most of its body segments. [Lat. *mīlipeda*, a kind of insect : *mīlle*, thousand + *pēs, ped-*, foot.]

mil·li·sec·ond (mĭl′ĭ-sĕk′ənd) ►*n.* One thousandth (10⁻³) of a second.

mill·pond (mĭl′pŏnd′) ►*n.* A pond formed by a dam to provide power for turning a mill wheel.

mill·race (mĭl′rās′) ►*n.* **1.** The fast stream of water that drives a mill wheel. **2.** The channel in which this stream flows.

mill·stone (mĭl′stōn′) ►*n.* **1.** One of a pair of large circular stones used for grinding grain. **2a.** A source of worry or distress. **b.** An obstacle to success.

mill·stream (mĭl′strēm′) ►*n.* The rapid stream of water in a millrace.

mill wheel ►*n.* A wheel, typically driven by water, that powers a mill.

Milne (mĭln), **A(lan) A(lexander)** 1882–1956. British writer.

Mi·losz (mē′lŏsh, -wŏsh), **Czeslaw** 1911–2004. Polish-born Amer. writer.

milque·toast (mĭlk′tōst′) ►*n.* One who has a timid, unassertive nature. [After Caspar *Milquetoast*, a meek comic-strip character.]

milt (mĭlt) ►*n.* Fish sperm. [< ME, spleen, milt.]

Mil·ton (mĭl′tən), **John** 1608–74. English poet and scholar.

Mil·wau·kee (mĭl-wô′kē) A city of SE WI on Lake Michigan.

mime (mīm) ►*n.* **1.** Pantomime. **2.** A modern performer who specializes in silent comic mimicry. ►*v.* **mimed, mim·ing 1.** To mimic. **2.** To pantomime. [< Gk. *mimos*, actor, mimic.] —**mim′er** *n.*

mim·e·o·graph (mĭm′ē-ə-grăf′) ►*n.* A duplicator that makes copies of written, drawn, or typed material from a stencil fitted around an inked drum. [Originally a trademark.] —**mim′e·o·graph′** *v.*

mi·me·sis (mĭ-mē′sĭs, mī-) ►*n.* The representation of aspects of the sensible world, esp. human actions, in literature and art. [Gk. *mimēsis*, mimicry < *mimeisthai*, imitate.]

mi·met·ic (mĭ-mĕt′ĭk, mī-) ►*adj.* Of or exhibiting mimicry. [< Gk. *mimēsis*, mimicry; see MIMESIS.] —**mi·met′i·cal·ly** *adv.*

mim·ic (mĭm′ĭk) ►*v.* **-icked, -ick·ing 1.** To imitate closely, esp. in speech or gesture. **2.** To ridicule by imitating; mock. **3.** To reproduce or simulate. **4.** To appear similar to or affect the body similarly: *an insect that mimics a twig; a drug that mimics a compound.* ►*n.* One that copies others. ►*adj.* Of mimicry. [< Gk. *mimikos*, of mimicry < *mimos*, mime.] —**mim′ick·er** *n.*

mim·ic·ry (mĭm′ĭ-krē) ►*n.*, *pl.* **-ries** The act or practice of mimicking; imitation.

mi·mo·sa (mĭ-mō′sə, -zə) ►*n.* **1.** Any of various mostly tropical plants usu. having leaves sensitive to touch or light. **2.** A drink consisting of champagne and orange juice. [< Lat. *mīmus*, MIME.]

min. ►*abbr.* **1.** minimum **2. Min.** minister **3.** minor **4.** minute

min·a·ret (mĭn′ə-rĕt′) ►*n.* A tall slender tower attached to a mosque, from which a call to prayer is issued. [< Ar. *manāra*, lamp.]

minaret
Maltepe Mosque, Ankara, Turkey

min·a·to·ry (mĭn′ə-tôr′ē) also **min·a·to·ri·al** (-tôr′ē-əl) ►*adj.* Menacing or threatening. [< Lat. *minārī*, threaten.]

mince (mĭns) ►*v.* **minced, minc·ing 1.** To cut into very small pieces. **2.** To pronounce in an affected way. **3.** To moderate (words) for the sake of decorum; euphemize. **4.** To walk with exaggerated primness. [< VLat. **minūtiāre* < Lat. *minūtus,* MINUTE².] —**minc′er** *n.* —**minc′-ing** *adj.*

mince·meat (mĭns′mēt′) ►*n.* A mixture, as of finely chopped apples, raisins, spices, and rum or brandy, used esp. as a pie filling. —*idiom:* **make mincemeat of** *Slang* To destroy utterly.

mind (mīnd) ►*n.* **1.** The part or faculty of a person by which one feels, perceives, thinks, remembers, desires, and imagines. **2.** A person of great mental ability. **3.** Memory; recollection. **4.** Opinion or sentiment. **5.** Sanity. ►*v.* **1.** To be careful about. **2.** To obey. **3.** To look after. See Synonyms at **tend²**. **4.** To be careful about. **5.** To care or be concerned about. **6.** To object (to); dislike. [< OE *gemynd.*]

Min·da·na·o (mĭn′də-nä′ō, -nou′) An island of the S Philippines NE of Borneo.

mind-blow·ing (mīnd′blō′ĭng) ►*adj. Informal* **1.** Producing hallucinatory effects. **2.** Mind-boggling. —**mind′blow′er** *n.*

mind-bog·gling (mīnd′bŏg′lĭng) ►*adj. Informal* Intellectually or emotionally overwhelming.

mind·ful (mīnd′fəl) ►*adj.* Attentive; heedful. See Synonyms at **careful**. —**mind′ful·ly** *adv.*

mind·less (mīnd′lĭs) ►*adj.* **1.** Lacking intelligence or sense. **2.** Careless; heedless. —**mind′-less·ly** *adv.* —**mind′less·ness** *n.*

mind·set or **mind-set** (mīnd′sĕt′) ►*n.* A fixed mental attitude that determines one's responses to and interpretations of situations.

mine¹ (mīn) ►*n.* **1a.** A hole or tunnel from which ore or minerals are extracted. **b.** A surface excavation where the earth is removed for extracting its ore or minerals. **c.** The site of such a hole, tunnel, or excavation, including its surface buildings and equipment. **2.** A deposit of ore or minerals. **3.** An abundant source. **4a.** A tunnel dug under an enemy position. **b.** An explosive device, often buried or submerged and designed to be detonated by contact or a time fuse. ►*v.* **mined, min·ing 1.** To extract (ore or minerals) from the earth. **2.** To dig a mine in. **3.** To lay explosive mines in or under. **4.** To undermine; subvert. [< VLat. **mīna,* of Celt. orig.] —**min′a·ble, mine′a·ble** *adj.* —**min′er** *n.*

mine² (mīn) ►*pron. (takes sing. or pl. v.)* Used to indicate the one or ones belonging to me: *The green gloves are mine.* [< OE *mīn.*]

mine·field (mīn′fēld′) ►*n.* An area in which explosive mines have been placed.

min·er·al (mĭn′ər-əl) ►*n.* **1.** A natural inorganic substance having a definite chemical composition and characteristic crystalline structure. **2a.** An element, such as gold or silver. **b.** An organic derivative, such as coal or petroleum. **3.** A substance that is neither animal nor vegetable; inorganic matter. **4.** A nutritionally important inorganic element, such as calcium or zinc. **5.** An ore. [< Med.Lat. *minerāle,* of a mine.] —**min′er·al** *adj.* —**min′er·al·ize** *v.*

min·er·al·o·gy (mĭn′ə-rŏl′ə-jē, -răl′-) ►*n.* The study of minerals. —**min′er·a·log′i·cal** (-ər-ə-lŏj′ĭ-kəl) *adj.* —**min′er·a·log′i·cal·ly** *adv.* —**min′er·al′o·gist** *n.*

mineral oil ►*n.* Any of various oils, esp. a distillate of petroleum used as a laxative.

mineral water ►*n.* Water that contains dissolved mineral salts or gases.

mineral wool ►*n.* A fibrous insulating material made by steam blasting and cooling molten glass or rock.

Mi·ner·va (mĭ-nûr′və) ►*n. Rom. Myth.* The goddess of wisdom, the arts, and warfare. [Lat.]

min·e·stro·ne (mĭn′ĭ-strō′nē, -strōn′) ►*n.* A thick soup containing vegetables, beans, and pasta. [Ital. < *minestrare,* serve.]

mine·sweep·er (mīn′swēp′ər) ►*n.* A ship equipped for detecting, removing, or neutralizing marine mines.

min·gle (mĭng′gəl) ►*v.* **-gled, -gling** To mix together in close association. [< OE *mengan,* mix.] —**min′gler** *n.*

min·i (mĭn′ē) ►*n., pl.* **min·is 1.** Something distinctively smaller than others of its class. **2.** A miniskirt. —**min′i** *adj.*

mini– ►*pref.* Small; miniature: *minibike.* [< MINIATURE and MINIMUM.]

min·i·a·ture (mĭn′ē-ə-choŏr′, -chər, mĭn′ə-) ►*n.* **1.** A very small copy or model. **2.** A very small, detailed painting. ►*adj.* Very small. See Synonyms at **small**. [Ital. *miniatura,* illumination of manuscripts.] —**min′i·a·tur′ist** *n.* —**min′i·a·tur·i·za′tion** *n.* —**min′i·a·tur·ize′** *v.*

min·i·bike (mĭn′ē-bīk′) ►*n.* A small motorbike. [Originally a trademark.]

min·i·bus (mĭn′ē-bŭs′) ►*n.* A small bus.

min·im (mĭn′əm) ►*n.* **1.** A unit of fluid measure equal to ⅟₆₀ of a fluid dram. **2.** A small portion. [< Lat. *minimus,* least.]

min·i·mal (mĭn′ə-məl) ►*adj.* Smallest in amount or degree. —**min′i·mal·ly** *adv.*

min·i·mal·ism (mĭn′ə-mə-lĭz′əm) ►*n.* **1.** A school of abstract painting and sculpture that emphasizes extreme simplification of form. **2.** Use of the fewest and barest essentials or elements, as in the arts, literature, or design.

min·i·mal·ist (mĭn′ə-mə-lĭst) ►*n.* **1.** One who advocates a moderate or conservative policy. **2.** A practitioner of minimalism. —**min′i·mal·ist** *adj.*

min·i·mize (mĭn′ə-mīz′) ►*v.* **-mized, -miz·ing** To reduce to or represent as having minimal importance or value. —**min′i·mi·za′tion** *n.* —**min′i·miz′er** *n.*

min·i·mum (mĭn′ə-məm) ►*n., pl.* **-mums** or **-ma** (-mə) **1.** The least possible quantity or degree. **2.** The lowest quantity reached or

permitted. [Lat., neuter of *minimus*, least.]
—**min′i·mum** *adj.*

minimum wage ►*n.* The lowest wage, determined by law or contract, that can be paid for a specified job.

min·ion (mĭn′yən) ►*n.* An obsequious follower or dependent. [< OFr. *mignot*, darling.]

min·i·se·ries (mĭn′ē-sîr′ēz) ►*n.* **1.** A televised drama shown in a number of episodes. **2.** A short series of athletic contests.

min·i·skirt (mĭn′ē-skûrt′) ►*n.* A very short skirt. —**min′i·skirt′ed** *adj.*

min·is·ter (mĭn′ĭ-stər) ►*n.* **1.** One authorized to perform religious functions in a Christian church. **2.** The head of a governmental department. **3.** A diplomat ranking below an ambassador. **4.** A person serving as an agent for another. ►*v.* To attend to the wants and needs of others. See Synonyms at **tend²**. [< Lat., servant.] —**min′is·te′ri·al** (-stîr′ē-əl) *adj.* —**min′is·te′ri·al·ly** *adv.* —**min′is·trant** *n.* —**min′is·tra′tion** *n.* —**min′is·tra′tive** *adj.*

min·is·try (mĭn′ĭ-strē) ►*n., pl.* **-tries 1.** The act of serving; ministration. **2a.** The profession and services of a minister. **b.** The clergy. **c.** The period of service of a minister. **3a.** A governmental department presided over by a minister. **b.** The building in which it is housed. **c.** The duties, functions, or term of a governmental minister.

min·i·van (mĭn′ē-văn′) ►*n.* A small passenger van, typically with removable rear seats.

mink (mĭngk) ►*n., pl.* **mink** or **minks 1.** A semiaquatic weasellike mammal having a pointed snout and partly webbed toes, and bred for its commercially valuable fur. **2.** The fur of the mink. [ME, mink fur.]

Min·ne·ap·o·lis (mĭn′ē-ăp′ə-lĭs) A city of SE MN on the Mississippi R. adjacent to St. Paul.

Min·ne·so·ta (mĭn′ĭ-sō′tə) A state of the N US bordering on Lake Superior and Canada. Cap. St. Paul. —**Min′ne·so′tan** *adj. & n.*

min·now (mĭn′ō) ►*n., pl.* **-now** or **-nows** Any of various small freshwater fishes widely used as bait. [ME *meneu.*]

Mi·no·an (mĭ-nō′ən) ►*adj.* Of or relating to the Bronze Age culture in Crete from about 3000 to 1100 BC. [< Gk. *Minōs*, Minos, Crete.] —**Mi·no′an** *n.*

mi·nor (mī′nər) ►*adj.* **1.** Lesser or smaller in amount, size, or importance. **2.** Lesser in seriousness or danger. **3.** *Law* Not having reached legal adulthood. **4.** *Mus.* Of or being a minor scale. ►*n.* **1.** *Law* One who has not reached legal adulthood. **2a.** A secondary area of academic study. **b.** One studying a minor: *She is a chemistry minor.* **3.** *Mus.* A minor key, scale, or interval. **4. minors** *Sports* The minor leagues. ►*v.* To pursue academic studies in a minor field. [< Lat.]

Mi·nor·ca (mĭ-nôr′kə) A Spanish island in the Balearics of the W Mediterranean Sea. —**Mi·nor′can** *adj. & n.*

mi·nor·i·ty (mə-nôr′ĭ-tē, -nŏr′-, mī-) ►*n., pl.* **-ties 1.** The smaller of two groups forming a whole. **2a.** A racial, religious, or other group different from the larger group of which it is part. **b.** A member of such a group. **3.** The state or period of being younger than the age for legal adulthood.

minor league ►*n.* A league of professional

sports clubs not belonging to the major leagues. —**mi′nor-league′** *adj.*

minor scale ►*n. Mus.* A diatonic scale having a semitone between the 2nd and 3rd degrees.

minor scale
C minor scale

Min·o·taur (mĭn′ə-tôr′, mī′nə-) ►*n. Gk. Myth.* A monster who was half man and half bull.

Minsk (mĭnsk) The capital of Belarus, in the central part.

min·ster (mĭn′stər) ►*n. Chiefly Brit.* **1.** A monastery church. **2.** A large church, esp. a collegiate church or a cathedral. [< VLat. **monistērium*, MONASTERY.]

min·strel (mĭn′strəl) ►*n.* **1.** A medieval traveling entertainer. **2.** A performer in a minstrel show. [< LLat. *ministeriālis*, official in the imperial household.]

minstrel show ►*n.* A comic variety show of the 1800s and early 1900s, usu. featuring white actors in blackface.

mint¹ (mĭnt) ►*n.* **1.** A place where money is manufactured by a government. **2.** An abundant amount, esp. of money. ►*v.* **1.** To produce (money) by stamping metal. **2.** To invent or fabricate (e.g., a phrase). ►*adj.* New or as if new: *mint condition.* [< Lat. *monēta*, coin.] —**mint′er** *n.*

mint² (mĭnt) ►*n.* **1.** Any of various related plants, many of which are cultivated for their aromatic oil and foliage. **2.** A candy flavored with natural or artificial mint flavoring. [< Lat. *menta*.] —**mint′y** *adj.*

mint julep ►*n.* A drink made of bourbon, sugar, crushed mint leaves, and shaved ice.

min·u·end (mĭn′yōō-ĕnd′) ►*n.* The quantity from which another quantity is to be subtracted. [< Lat. *minuendum*, thing to be diminished.]

min·u·et (mĭn′yōō-ĕt′) ►*n.* **1.** A stately dance in 3/4 time originating in 17th-cent. France. **2.** Music for a minuet. [< OFr., dainty < *menu*, MINUTE².]

Min·u·it (mĭn′yōō-ĭt), **Peter** 1580–1638. Dutch colonial administrator.

mi·nus (mī′nəs) ►*prep.* **1.** Reduced by; less: *Nine minus three is six.* **2.** *Informal* Without: *I went to work minus my keys.* ►*adj.* **1.** Negative or on the negative part of a scale: *a minus value.* **2.** Ranking on the lower end of a designated scale: *a grade of A minus.* ►*n.* **1a.** The minus sign (−). **b.** A negative quantity. **2.** A deficiency or defect. [< Lat. < *minor*, less.]

min·us·cule (mĭn′ə-skyōōl′, mĭ-nŭs′kyōōl′) ►*adj.* Very small; tiny. See Synonyms at **small**. [< Lat. *minusculus*, very small.]

minus sign ►*n. Math.* The symbol −, as in 4 − 2 = 2, used to indicate subtraction or a negative quantity.

min·ute¹ (mĭn′ĭt) ►*n.* **1.** A unit of time equal to ⅟₆₀ of an hour or 60 seconds. **2.** A unit of angular measurement equal to ¹⁄₆₀ of a degree or 60 seconds. **3.** A moment. **4.** A specific point in time. **5. minutes** An official record of the proceedings at a meeting. [< Lat. *minūtus*, small; see MINUTE².]

mi·nute² (mī-nōot', -nyōot', mĭ-) ►*adj.* **1.** Exceptionally small; tiny. See Synonyms at **small. 2.** Beneath notice; insignificant. **3.** Marked by careful examination; detailed. [< Lat. *minūtus*, p.part. of *minuere*, lessen.] —**mi·nute'ly** *adv.* —**mi·nute'ness** *n.*

min·ute·man (mĭn'ĭt-măn') ►*n.* An armed man ready to fight on a minute's notice during the American Revolutionary War.

mi·nu·ti·ae (mĭ-nōo'shē-ē', -nyōo'-) ►*pl.n.* Small or trivial details. [< pl. of LLat. *minūtia*, smallness.]

minx (mĭngks) ►*n.* An impudent young woman. [?] —**minx'ish** *adj.*

Mi·o·cene (mī'ə-sēn') *Geol.* ►*adj.* Of or being the 4th epoch of the Tertiary Period, marked by the development of grasses and grazing mammals. ►*n.* The Miocene Epoch. [Gk. *meiōn*, less + –CENE.]

mir·a·cle (mĭr'ə-kəl) ►*n.* **1.** An event inexplicable by the laws of nature and so held to be supernatural in origin or an act of God. **2.** A marvel. See Synonyms at **wonder.** [< Lat. *mīrāculum.*] —**mi·rac'u·lous** (mĭ-răk'yə-ləs) *adj.* —**mi·rac'u·lous·ly** *adv.*

mi·rage (mĭ-räzh') ►*n.* **1.** An optical phenomenon that creates the illusion of water, often with inverted reflections of distant objects. **2.** Something illusory or insubstantial. [Fr. < Lat. *mīrārī*, wonder at.]

mire (mīr) ►*n.* **1.** A bog. **2.** Deep slimy soil or mud. **3.** A difficult situation. ►*v.* **mired, mir·ing 1.** To sink or stick in or as if in mire. **2.** To soil with mud. [< ON *mȳrr.*] —**mir'y** *adj.*

mir·in (mĭr'ĭn) ►*n.* A sweet Japanese rice wine, used esp. in cooking. [J.]

Mi·ró (mē-rō'), **Joan** 1893–1983. Spanish artist.

mir·ror (mĭr'ər) ►*n.* **1.** A surface capable of reflecting sufficient undiffused light to form a image of an object placed in front of it. **2.** Something that gives a true picture of something else. ►*v.* To reflect in or as in a mirror. [< OFr. *mireor < mirer*, look at.]

mirth (mûrth) ►*n.* Gladness and gaiety. [< OE *myrgth.*] —**mirth'ful** *adj.* —**mirth'ful·ly** *adv.*

mis- ►*pref.* **1.** Bad; badly; wrong; wrongly: *misconduct.* **2.** Failure; lack: *misfire.* [< OE and OFr. *mes-.*]

mis·ad·ven·ture (mĭs'əd-věn'chər) ►*n.* A misfortune; mishap.

mis·al·li·ance (mĭs'ə-lī'əns) ►*n.* An unsuitable marriage.

mis·an·thrope (mĭs'ən-thrōp', mĭz'-) also **mis·an·thro·pist** (mĭs-ăn'thrə-pĭst, mĭz'-) ►*n.* One who hates humankind. [< Gk. *misanthrōpos*, hating people.] —**mis'an·throp'ic** (-thrŏp'-ĭk) *adj.* —**mis'an·throp'i·cal·ly** *adv.* —**mis·an'thro·py** *n.*

mis·ap·pre·hend (mĭs-ăp'rĭ-hěnd') ►*v.* To misunderstand. —**mis·ap'pre·hen'sion** *n.*

mis·be·got·ten (mĭs'bĭ-gŏt'n) ►*adj.* **1.** Of illegitimate birth. **2.** Of dubious origin. **3.** Deserving of contempt.

misc. ►*abbr.* miscellaneous

mis·car·riage (mĭs'kăr'ĭj, mĭs-kăr'-) ►*n.* **1.** The spontaneous, premature expulsion of a non-

viable embryo or fetus from the uterus. **2.** Mismanagement.

mis·car·ry (mĭs'kăr'ē, mĭs-kăr'ē) ►*v.* **1.** To have a miscarriage. **2.** To go wrong.

mis·ceg·e·na·tion (mĭ-sěj'ə-nā'shən, mĭs'ĭ-jə-) ►*n.* Cohabitation, sexual relations, or marriage between persons of different races. [< Lat. *miscēre*, mix + *genus*, race.]

mis·cel·la·ne·ous (mĭs'ə-lā'nē-əs) ►*adj.* Consisting of various kinds; varied. [< Lat. *miscellāneus < miscēre*, mix.] —**mis'cel·la·ne·ous·ly** *adv.*

mis·cel·la·ny (mĭs'ə-lā'nē) ►*n.*, pl. **-nies 1.** A collection of various items or ingredients. **2.** A collection of diverse literary works.

mis·chance (mĭs-chăns') ►*n.* **1.** A mishap. **2.** Bad luck.

mis·chief (mĭs'chĭf) ►*n.* **1.** A cause of discomfiture or annoyance. **2.** Damage caused by a specific person. **3.** An inclination to play pranks. [< OFr. *meschief*, misfortune.]

mis·chie·vous (mĭs'chə-vəs) ►*adj.* **1.** Causing mischief. **2.** Playful in a naughty or teasing way. —**mis'chie·vous·ly** *adv.* —**mis'chie·vous·ness** *n.*

mis·ci·ble (mĭs'ə-bəl) ►*adj. Chem.* Capable of being mixed in all proportions. [< Lat. *miscēre*, mix.] —**mis'ci·bil'i·ty** *n.*

mis·con·ceive (mĭs'kən-sēv') ►*v.* To misunderstand. —**mis'con·cep'tion** *n.*

mis·con·duct (mĭs-kŏn'dŭkt) ►*n.* **1.** Improper or immoral behavior. **2.** Dishonest or bad management. **3.** Deliberate wrongdoing, esp. by an official. ►*v.* (mĭs'kən-dŭct') **1.** To mismanage. **2.** To behave (oneself) badly.

mis·con·strue (mĭs'kən-strōo') ►*v.* To misinterpret. —**mis'con·struc'tion** *n.*

mis·cre·ant (mĭs'krē-ənt) ►*n.* One who behaves badly, often by breaking the law. [< OFr. *mescroire*, disbelieve : MIS– + *croire*, believe (< Lat. *crēdere*).] —**mis'cre·ant** *adj.*

mis·cue (mĭs-kyōo') ►*n.* A mistake. —**mis·cue'** *v.*

mis·deed (mĭs-dēd') ►*n.* A wrongdoing.

mis·de·mean·or (mĭs'dĭ-mē'nər) ►*n.* **1.** A misdeed. **2.** *Law* A criminal offense that is less serious than a felony.

mise en scène (mēz' än sěn') ►*n.*, pl. **mise en scènes** (sěn') The arrangement and setting for a play or film. [Fr., putting on stage.]

mi·ser (mī'zər) ►*n.* A stingy person, esp. one who hoards money. [< Lat., wretched.] —**mi'ser·li·ness** *n.* —**mi'ser·ly** *adj.*

mis·er·a·ble (mĭz'ər-ə-bəl, mĭz'rə-) ►*adj.* **1.** Very unhappy; wretched. **2.** Causing discomfort or distress. **3.** Wretchedly poor; squalid. **4.** Of poor quality. [< Lat. *miserābilis*, pitiable < *miser*, wretched.] —**mis'er·a·bly** *adv.*

mis·er·y (mĭz'ə-rē) ►*n.*, pl. **-ies 1.** Great physical or emotional suffering. **2.** An affliction or trial. [< Lat. *miseria.*]

mis·fire (mĭs-fīr') ►*v.* **1.** To fail to ignite, fire, or discharge when expected. **2.** To fail to achieve an anticipated result. —**mis'fire'** *n.*

mis·fit (mĭs'fĭt', mĭs-fĭt') ►*n.* **1.** A poor fit. **2.** A maladjusted person.

mis·for·tune (mĭs-fôr'chən) ►*n.* **1.** Bad fortune. **2.** A mishap.

mis·giv·ing (mĭs-gĭv'ĭng) ►*n.* **1.** Doubt, distrust, or apprehension. **2.** often **misgivings** A feeling of misgiving.

mis·guide (mĭs-gīd′) ▸*v.* To lead in the wrong direction; lead astray. —**mis·guid′ance** *n.* —**mis·guid′ed** *adj.* —**mis·guid′ed·ly** *adv.*

mis·han·dle (mĭs-hăn′dl) ▸*v.* To deal with clumsily or inefficiently.

mis·hap (mĭs′hăp′, mĭs-hăp′) ▸*n.* An unfortunate accident.

mish·mash (mĭsh′măsh′) ▸*n.* A hodgepodge. [< MASH.]

mis·in·ter·pret (mĭs′ĭn-tûr′prĭt) ▸*v.* To interpret or explain inaccurately. —**mis′in·ter′pre·ta′tion** *n.* —**mis′in·ter′pret·er** *n.*

mis·lay (mĭs-lā′) ▸*v.* To put in a place that is afterward forgotten; lose.

mis·lead (mĭs-lēd′) ▸*v.* **1.** To lead in the wrong direction. **2.** To give a wrong impression or lead toward a wrong conclusion, esp. intentionally.

mis·like (mĭs-līk′) ▸*v.* To dislike. ▸*n.* Dislike.

mis·no·mer (mĭs-nō′mər) ▸*n.* A wrong or inappropriate name. [< OFr. *mesnomer,* call by a wrong name.]

mi·so (mē′sō) ▸*n., pl.* -**sos** A thick fermented paste made of cooked soybeans, salt, and often rice or barley. [J.]

mi·sog·a·my (mĭ-sŏg′ə-mē) ▸*n.* Hatred of marriage. [Gk. *misein,* to hate + –GAMY.] —**mi·sog′a·mist** *n.*

mi·sog·y·ny (mĭ-sŏj′ə-nē) ▸*n.* Hatred or distrust of women. [< Gk. *misein,* to hate + *gunē,* woman.] —**mi·sog′y·nist** *n.* —**mi·sog′y·nis′tic, mi·sog′y·nous** *adj.*

mis·place (mĭs-plās′) ▸*v.* **1a.** To put in a wrong place. **b.** To mislay. **2.** To bestow (e.g., confidence) on an unsuitable or unworthy person. —**mis·place′ment** *n.*

mis·play (mĭs-plā′, mĭs′plā′) ▸*n. Sports & Games* A mistaken play. —**mis·play′** *v.*

mis·read (mĭs-rēd′) ▸*v.* **1.** To read inaccurately. **2.** To misinterpret.

mis·rep·re·sent (mĭs-rĕp′rĭ-zĕnt′) ▸*v.* To give a false or misleading representation of. —**mis·rep′re·sen·ta′tion** *n.*

miss¹ (mĭs) ▸*v.* **1.** To fail to hit, reach, catch, meet, or make contact with. **2.** To fail to perceive or understand. **3.** To fail to achieve or attain. **4.** To fail to attend or perform. **5.** To omit. **6.** To avoid. **7.** To discover or feel the absence of. **8.** To misfire. ▸*n.* **1.** A failure to hit or succeed. **2.** A misfire. [< OE *missan.*]

miss² (mĭs) ▸*n.* **1. Miss** Used as a courtesy title for a young woman or girl. **2.** Used as a polite address for a girl or young woman. [< MISTRESS.]

mis·sal (mĭs′əl) ▸*n. Rom. Cath. Ch.* A book containing all the prayers and responses necessary for celebrating the Mass. [< Med.Lat. *missālis,* of the Mass.]

mis·sile (mĭs′əl, -īl′) ▸*n.* **1.** An object or weapon fired or projected at a target. **2.** A guided missile. **3.** A ballistic missile. [< Lat. *missilis,* throwable < *mittere,* let go.] —**mis′sile·ry** *n.*

miss·ing (mĭs′ĭng) ▸*adj.* Absent; lost; lacking.

mis·sion (mĭsh′ən) ▸*n.* **1.** A special assignment given to a person or group. **2.** An ambition or purpose that is assumed by a person or group. **3a.** A body of envoys to a foreign country. **b.** A permanent diplomatic office abroad. **4.** A body of missionaries, or the building housing them. [< Lat. *mittere, miss-,* send off.]

mis·sion·ar·y (mĭsh′ə-nĕr′ē) ▸*n., pl.* -**ies 1.** One who is sent on a mission, esp. a religious or charitable mission in a foreign country. **2.** One who attempts to convert others to a particular doctrine or set of principles. —**mis′sion·ar′y** *adj.*

Mis·sis·sip·pi (mĭs′ĭ-sĭp′ē) A state of the SE US. Cap. Jackson. —**Mis′sis·sip′pi·an** *adj. & n.*

Mis·sis·sip·pi·an (mĭs′ĭ-sĭp′ē-ən) *Geol.* ▸*adj.* Of or being the 5th period of the Paleozoic Era, marked by widespread shallow seas. ▸*n.* The Mississippian Period.

Mississippi River The chief river of the US, rising in N MN and flowing about 3,700 km (2,300 mi) to the Gulf of Mexico.

mis·sive (mĭs′ĭv) ▸*n.* A written message. [< Med.Lat. *(littere) missīve,* (letter) sent.]

Mis·sou·ri¹ (mĭ-zoŏr′ē) ▸*n., pl.* -**ri** or -**ris 1.** A member of a Native American people formerly of N-central Missouri, now in Oklahoma. **2.** The Siouan language of the Missouri.

Mis·sou·ri² (mĭ-zoŏr′ē, -zoŏr′ə) A state of the central US. Cap. Jefferson City. —**Mis·sou′ri·an** *adj. & n.*

Missouri River A river of the US rising in the Rocky Mts. and flowing about 3,750 km (2,350 mi) to the Mississippi R. N of St. Louis, MO.

mis′al·ly′ *v.*	**mis′di·rec′tion** *n.*	**mis′print′** *n.*
mis′ap·ply′ *v.*	**mis′do′ing** *n.*	**mis′print′** *v.*
mis′ap·pro′pri·ate′ *v.*	**mis·ed′u·cate′** *v.*	**mis′pro·nounce′** *v.*
mis′at·trib′ute *v.*	**mis·es′ti·mate′** *v.*	**mis·quote′** *v.*
mis′be·have′ *v.*	**mis·file′** *v.*	**mis·reck′on** *v.*
mis′be·hav′ior *n.*	**mis·gov′ern** *v.*	**mis′re·mem′ber** *v.*
mis′be·lieve′ *v.*	**mis·hear′** *v.*	**mis′re·port′** *v. & n.*
mis·cal′cu·late′ *v.*	**mis′i·den′ti·fy** *v.*	**mis·rule′** *n. & v.*
mis·call′ *v.*	**mis′im·pres′sion** *n.*	**mis·shape′** *v.*
mis·cast′ *v.*	**mis·in·form′** *v.*	**mis·shap′en** *adj.*
mis·char′ac·ter·ize′ *v.*	**mis′in·for·ma′tion** *n.*	**mis·shap′en·ly** *adv.*
mis·clas′si·fy′ *v.*	**mis·judge′** *v.*	**mis·spell′** *v.*
mis′com·mu′ni·ca′tion *n.*	**mis·judg′ment** *n.*	**mis·spel′ling** *n.*
mis·count′ *v.*	**mis·la′bel** *v.*	**mis·spend′** *v.*
mis·count′ *n.*	**mis·man′age** *v.*	**mis·state′** *v.*
mis·date′ *v.*	**mis·man′age·ment** *n.*	**mis·time′** *v.*
mis·deal′ *v.*	**mis·match′** *v.*	**mis′trans·late′** *v.*
mis·di′ag·nose′ *v.*	**mis′match′** *n.*	**mis′trans·la′tion** *n.*
mis′di·ag·no′sis *n.*	**mis·mate′** *v.*	**mis·val′ue** *v.*
mis·di′al *v.*	**mis·name′** *v.*	**mis·word′** *v.*
mis′di·rect′ *v.*	**mis′per·ceive′** *v.*	**mis·write′** *v.*
	mis′per·cep′tion *n.*	

mis·speak (mĭs-spēk′) ►*v*. To speak mistakenly, inappropriately, or rashly.

mis·step (mĭs-stĕp′) ►*n*. **1.** A misplaced step. **2.** A social or procedural blunder.

mist (mĭst) ►*n*. **1.** A mass of fine droplets of water in the atmosphere. **2.** Water vapor condensed on and clouding a surface. **3.** Fine drops of a liquid sprayed into the air. **4.** Something that dims or conceals. ►*v*. To become obscured or misty. [< OE.]

mis·take (mĭ-stāk′) ►*n*. **1.** An error or fault. **2.** A misconception or misunderstanding. [< ON *mistaka*, take in error.] —**mis·tak′a·ble** *adj*. —**mis·take′** *v*.

mis·tak·en (mĭ-stā′kən) ►*adj*. **1.** Wrong in opinion, understanding, or perception. **2.** Based on error. —**mis·tak′en·ly** *adv*.

Mis·ter (mĭs′tər) ►*n*. **1.** Used as a courtesy title for a man, usu. written in its abbreviated form *Mr*. **2. mister** *Informal* Used in addressing a man. [Alteration of MASTER.]

mis·tle·toe (mĭs′əl-tō′) ►*n*. **1.** Any of various semiparasitic plants that grow on the branches of other plants and have leathery evergreen leaves and waxy white berries. **2.** A sprig of mistletoe, often used as a Christmas decoration. [< OE *misteltān*, sprig of mistletoe.]

mis·treat (mĭs-trēt′) ►*v*. To treat roughly or wrongly; abuse. —**mis·treat′ment** *n*.

mis·tress (mĭs′trĭs) ►*n*. **1.** A woman having control or authority over another, esp.: **a.** A female owner of an animal. **b.** A female owner of a slave. **c.** A female employer of a servant. **2.** A woman who has a continuing sexual relationship with a man who is married to someone else. **3.** Something personified as female that has supremacy or control: *a country that is mistress of the seas*. **4. Mistress** Used formerly as a courtesy title for a woman. [< OFr. *maistresse*, feminine of *maistre*, MASTER.]

mis·tri·al (mĭs′trī′əl, mĭs′trīl′, mĭs-trī′əl, mĭs-trīl′) ►*n*. A trial that is rendered void and of no legal effect because of a procedural irregularity or because the jury is unable to reach a verdict.

mis·trust (mĭs-trŭst′) ►*n*. Lack of trust; suspicion. ►*v*. **1.** To regard without trust or confidence. **2.** To doubt the truth or sincerity of. —**mis·trust′ful** *adj*.

mist·y (mĭs′tē) ►*adj*. **-i·er, -i·est** **1.** Consisting of or resembling mist. **2.** Obscured or clouded by or as if by mist. **3.** Vague or hazy. —**mist′i·ly** *adv*. —**mist′i·ness** *n*.

mis·un·der·stand (mĭs′ŭn-dər-stănd′) ►*v*. To understand incorrectly; misinterpret.

mis·un·der·stand·ing (mĭs′ŭn-dər-stăn′dĭng) ►*n*. **1.** A failure to understand correctly. **2.** A disagreement or quarrel.

mis·use (mĭs-yōōz′) ►*v*. **1.** To use incorrectly. **2.** To mistreat or abuse. ►*n*. (-yōōs′) Improper, unlawful, or incorrect use.

mite¹ (mīt) ►*n*. Any of various small, often parasitic arachnids. [< MDu.]

mite² (mīt) ►*n*. **1.** A very small contribution or amount of money. **2.** A tiny object or amount. [< MDu. *mite*, a small coin.]

mi·ter (mī′tər) ►*n*. **1.** *Eccles*. A tall pointed hat with peaks in front and back, worn esp. by bishops. **2.** A miter joint. ►*v*. To fit together with or meet in a miter joint. [< Gk. *mitra*, headdress.]

miter

miter joint ►*n*. A joint made by fitting together two beveled edges to form a 90° corner.

mit·i·gate (mĭt′ĭ-gāt′) ►*v*. **-gat·ed, -gat·ing** To make or become less in force or intensity; moderate. [< Lat. *mītigāre* : *mītis*, soft + *agere*, do.] —**mit′i·ga·ble** (-gə-bəl) *adj*. —**mit′i·ga′-tion** *n*.

mi·to·chon·dri·on (mī′tə-kŏn′drē-ən) ►*n*., *pl*. **-dri·a** (-drē-ə) A microscopic structure in nearly all living cells, containing genetic material and enzymes important for cell metabolism. [< Gk. *mitos*, warp thread + *khondrion*, granule.] —**mi′to·chon′dri·al** *adj*.

mi·to·sis (mī-tō′sĭs) ►*n*. *Biol*. **1.** The process in cell division by which the nucleus divides, normally resulting in two new nuclei, each of which contains a complete copy of the parental chromosomes. **2.** The entire process of cell division including division of the nucleus and the cytoplasm. [Gk. *mitos*, thread + -OSIS.] —**mi·tot′ic** (-tŏt′ĭk) *adj*. —**mi·tot′i·cal·ly** *adv*.

mitt (mĭt) ►*n*. **1.** A woman's glove that extends over the hand and only partially covers the fingers. **2.** A mitten. **3.** A baseball glove, esp. one used by catchers and first basemen. **4.** *Slang* A hand. [< MITTEN.]

mit·ten (mĭt′n) ►*n*. A covering for the hand that encases the thumb separately and the four fingers together. [< OFr. *mitaine*.]

Mit·ter·rand (mē′tə-ränd′, -räɴ′), **François Maurice** 1916–96. French president (1981–95).

mitz·vah (mĭts′və) ►*n*., *pl*. **-voth** (-vōt′, -vōs′) or **-vahs** **1.** A commandment of the Jewish law. **2.** A worthy deed. [Heb. *miṣwâ* < *ṣiwwâ*, to command.]

mix (mĭks) ►*v*. **1a.** To combine or blend into one mass or mixture. **b.** To create or form by combining ingredients. **2.** To combine or join: *mix joy with sorrow*. **3.** To associate socially. **4.** To crossbreed. **5a.** To combine (audio tracks or channels) to make an audio recording. **b.** To make in this manner. ►*n*. A mixture, esp. of ingredients packaged and sold commercially. —*phrasal verb:* **mix up 1.** To confuse. **2.** To involve: *got mixed up in the scandal*. [< Lat.

miscēre, mixt-.] **—mix′a·ble** *adj.*

mixed bag (mĭkst) ▸*n.* A varied assortment.

mixed drink ▸*n.* A drink made of one or more kinds of liquor combined with other ingredients, usu. shaken or stirred.

mixed number ▸*n.* A number, such as 7¼, consisting of an integer and a fraction or decimal.

mix·er (mĭk′sər) ▸*n.* **1.** One that mixes, esp. a device that mixes substances or ingredients. **2.** A sociable person. **3.** A party affording people an opportunity to get acquainted. **4.** A nonalcoholic beverage, such as soda water, used in mixed drinks.

Mix·tec (mēs′tĕk) ▸*n.*, *pl.* **-tec** or **-tecs** **1.** A member of a Mesoamerican Indian people of S Mexico whose civilization was overthrown by the Aztecs in the 1500s. **2.** Any of the languages spoken by the Mixtec.

mix·ture (mĭks′chər) ▸*n.* **1.** The act of mixing or the state of being mixed. **2.** Something made by mixing, as: **a.** One that consists of diverse elements. **b.** *Chem.* A blend of substances not chemically bound to each other. [< Lat. *mixtūra* < *miscēre,* mix.]

mix-up also **mix·up** (mĭks′ŭp′) ▸*n.* A state or instance of confusion; muddle.

miz·zen or **miz·en** (mĭz′ən) ▸*n.* **1.** A fore-and-aft sail set on the mizzenmast. **2.** A mizzenmast. [Ult. < Lat. *mediānus,* middle.] **—miz′-zen** *adj.*

miz·zen·mast or **miz·en·mast** (mĭz′ən-məst, -măst′) ▸*n.* **1.** The third mast aft on a sailing vessel having three or more masts. **2.** The mast aft of the mainmast on a ketch or yawl.

mks ▸*abbr.* meter-kilogram-second

mL also **ml** ▸*abbr.* milliliter

MLB ▸*abbr.* Major League Baseball

Mlle. ▸*abbr.* Mademoiselle

Mlles. ▸*abbr.* Mesdemoiselles

mm ▸*abbr.* millimeter

Mme. ▸*abbr.* Madame

Mmes. ▸*abbr.* Mesdames

MMR ▸*abbr.* measles, mumps, rubella

MN ▸*abbr.* Minnesota

mne·mon·ic (nĭ-mŏn′ĭk) ▸*adj.* Assisting or intended to assist the memory. ▸*n.* A device, such as a formula or rhyme, used as a mnemonic aid. [< Gk. *mnēmōn,* mindful.] **—mne·mon′i·cal·ly** *adv.*

MO ▸*abbr.* **1.** mail order **2.** Missouri **3.** modus operandi **4.** money order

mo. ▸*abbr.* month

Mo·ab (mō′ăb) An ancient kingdom E of the Dead Sea in SW Jordan. **—Mo′ab·ite′** *adj.* & *n.*

moan (mōn) ▸*n.* **1.** A low, sustained, mournful cry, as of sorrow or pain. **2.** A whining complaint. [ME *mone.*] **—moan** *v.* **—moan′er** *n.*

moat (mōt) ▸*n.* A deep wide ditch, usu. filled with water, esp. one surrounding a medieval town, fortress, or castle as a defense. [< OFr. *mote,* mound.]

mob (mŏb) ▸*n.* **1.** A large disorderly throng. See Synonyms at **crowd. 2.** The mass of common people. **3.** *Informal* An organized gang of criminals. ▸*v.* **mobbed, mob·bing 1.** To crowd around and jostle, annoy, or attack. **2.** To crowd into (a place). [< Lat. *(vulgus) mōbile,* fickle (crowd).]

mo·bile (mō′bəl, -bēl′, -bīl′) ▸*adj.* **1a.** Capable of moving or of being moved readily. **b.** Of or

relating to wireless communications devices. **2.** Changing quickly from one condition to another. ▸*n.* (mō′bēl′) **1.** A sculpture consisting of parts that move, esp. in response to air currents. **2.** A cell phone. [< Lat. *mōbilis.*] **—mo·bil′i·ty** (-bĭl′ĭ-tē) *n.*

mobile home ▸*n.* A house trailer installed on a site and used as a home.

mo·bi·lize (mō′bə-līz′) ▸*v.* **-lized, -liz·ing 1.** To make mobile or capable of movement. **2.** To assemble and prepare for or as if for war. **—mo′bi·li·za′tion** *n.*

mob·ster (mŏb′stər) ▸*n.* A member of a criminal gang.

moc·ca·sin (mŏk′ə-sĭn) ▸*n.* **1.** A soft leather slipper or shoe. **2.** A water moccasin. [Of Virginia Algonquian orig.]

mo·cha (mō′kə) ▸*n.* **1a.** A rich pungent Arabian coffee. **b.** A coffee beverage flavored with milk, sugar, and cocoa. **2.** A flavoring of coffee mixed with chocolate. **3.** A dark olive brown. [After *Mocha,* Yemen.]

mock (mŏk) ▸*v.* **1.** To treat with ridicule or contempt; deride. **2.** To imitate in derision. **3.** To resemble closely. ▸*adj.* Simulated; sham. [< OFr. *mocquer.*] **—mock′er** *n.* **—mock′er·y** *n.* **—mock′ing·ly** *adv.*

mock-he·ro·ic (mŏk′hĭ-rō′ĭk) ▸*n.* A satirical imitation or burlesque of the heroic manner or style. **—mock′-he·ro′ic** *adj.*

mock·ing·bird (mŏk′ĭng-bûrd′) ▸*n.* A gray and white songbird of N America and the Caribbean that mimics the sounds of other birds.

mock orange ▸*n.* Any of numerous deciduous shrubs having white, usu. fragrant flowers.

mock·up also **mock-up** (mŏk′ŭp′) ▸*n.* A usu. full-sized scale model of a machine or structure, used for demonstration or testing.

mod (mŏd) ▸*n.* Fashionable style of dress. ▸*adj.* Fashionably up-to-date. [< MODERN.]

mode (mōd) ▸*n.* **1a.** A manner, way, or method of doing or acting. **b.** A particular form or kind. **c.** A given condition of functioning; status. **2.** The current fashion or style. **3.** *Mus.* Any of certain arrangements of the diatonic tones of an octave. **4.** *Statistics* The number in a distribution that occurs the most frequently. [< Lat. *modus.*] **—mod′al** *adj.*

mod·el (mŏd′l) ▸*n.* **1.** A small representation of an existing object, usu. built to scale. **2.** A preliminary pattern. **3.** A schematic description of a system that accounts for its known properties. **4.** A style or design. **5.** An example to be emulated. **6.** One who poses for an artist. **7.** One who models clothes. ▸*adj.* **1.** Being or used as a model. **2.** Worthy of imitation; exemplary. ▸*v.* **-eled, -el·ing** also **-elled, -el·ling 1.** To plan or construct a model (of). **2.** To display (clothes) by wearing or posing. **3.** To serve or work as a model. [< Lat. *modus,* measure.] **—mod′el·er** *n.*

mo·dem (mō′dəm) ▸*n.* A device that transmits and receives data using a modulated carrier wire. [*mo(dulator-)dem(odulator).*]

mod·er·ate (mŏd′ər-ĭt) ▸*adj.* **1.** Not excessive or extreme. **2.** Temperate. **3.** Average or mediocre. **4.** Opposed to radical views or measures. ▸*n.* One who holds moderate views or opinions. ▸*v.* (mŏd′ə-rāt′) **-at·ed, -at·ing 1.** To make or become less extreme, intense, or violent. **2.** To preside over as a moderator. [< Lat. *moderātus,*

p.part. of *moderārī,* to moderate.] —**mod′er·**
ate·ly *adv.* —**mod′er·a′tion** *n.*
   Syns: qualify, temper **v.**
mod·er·a·tor (mŏd′ə-rā′tər) ►*n.* **1.** One that
moderates. **2.** A presiding officer.
mod·ern (mŏd′ərn) ►*adj.* **1a.** Of or relating to
recent times or the present. **b.** Characteristic
of the present; up-to-date. **2.** Of or relating to a
recently advanced style or technology. [< LLat.
modernus.] —**mod′ern** *n.* —**mod·ern′i·ty**
(mŏ-dûr′nĭ-tē, mō-) *n.* —**mod′ern·i·za′tion**
n. —**mod′ern·ize′** *v.*
Modern English ►*n.* English since about 1500.
Modern Greek ►*n.* Greek since the early
1500s.
Modern Hebrew ►*n.* The Hebrew language
as used from the 1700s on, and an official
language of Israel.
mod·ern·ism (mŏd′ər-nĭz′əm) ►*n.* **1.** Modern thought, character, or practice. **2.** often
Modernism The use of innovative forms of
expression that distinguish many styles in the
arts and literature of the 1900s. —**mod′ern·ist**
n. —**mod′ern·is′tic** *adj.*
mod·est (mŏd′ĭst) ►*adj.* **1.** Having or showing
a moderate estimation of oneself. **2a.** Retiring;
shy. **b.** Observing conventional proprieties;
decent. **3a.** Free from ostentation. See Synonyms at **plain. b.** Not extreme; moderate: *a*
modest price. [Lat. *modestus.*] —**mod′est·ly**
adv. —**mod′es·ty** *n.*
mod·i·cum (mŏd′ĭ-kəm) ►*n.* A small or token
amount. [< Lat. *modicus,* moderate.]
mod·i·fy (mŏd′ə-fī′) ►*v.* **-fied, -fy·ing 1.** To
change or become changed; alter. **2.** To make
or become less extreme, severe, or strong. **3.**
Gram. To qualify or limit the meaning of. [<
Lat. *modificāre,* to limit.] —**mod′i·fi·ca′tion** *n.*
—**mod′i·fi·er** *n.*
mod·ish (mō′dĭsh) ►*adj.* Conforming to the
current fashion: stylish. —**mod′ish·ly** *adv.*
mo·diste (mō-dēst′) ►*n.* One who produces,
designs, or deals in women's fashions. [Fr.]
mod·u·late (mŏj′ə-lāt′) ►*v.* **-lat·ed, -lat·ing 1.**
To regulate or adjust to a certain degree. **2.** To
change or vary the pitch, intensity, or tone of.
3. *Mus.* To pass from one tonality to another
by harmonic progression. **4.** *Electron.* To vary
the frequency, amplitude, phase, or other characteristic of (electromagnetic waves). **5.** *Chem.*
To act on (a receptor) as an agonist, antagonist,
or both. [< Lat. *modulus,* measure.] —**mod′u·**
la′tion *n.* —**mod′u·la·tor** *n.*
mod·ule (mŏj′ōol) ►*n.* **1.** A standardized component of a system designed for easy assembly
or flexible use. **2.** A self-contained assembly of
electronic components and circuitry. **3.** A self-
contained unit of a spacecraft that performs
a specific task. [Lat. *modulus,* dim. of *modus,*
measure.] —**mod′u·lar** *adj.*
mo·dus op·er·an·di (mō′dəs ŏp′ə-răn′dē, -dī′)
►*n., pl.* **mo·di operandi** (mō′dē, -dī) A method
of operating or functioning. [NLat.]
Mo·ga·di·shu (mō′gə-dē′shōo, -dĭsh′ōo, mō′-)
The capital of Somalia, on the Indian Ocean.
mo·gul¹ (mō′gəl) ►*n.* A hard mound or bump
on a ski slope. [Prob. of Scand. orig.]
mo·gul² (mō′gəl, mō-gül′) ►*n.* **1.** A rich or
powerful person. **2. Mogul** Var. of **Mughal.**
[< Urdu *Mugal,* MUGHAL.]
mo·hair (mō′hâr′) ►*n.* **1.** The long silky hair of

the Angora goat. **2.** Fabric or yarn made from
this hair. [< Ar. *muḫayyar.*]
Mo·ham·med (mō-hăm′ĭd, -hä′mĭd, mōō-) See
Muhammad.
Mo·hawk (mō′hôk′) ►*n., pl.* **-hawk** or **-hawks**
1. A member of a Native American people
formerly of NE New York, now in S Ontario
and extreme N New York. **2.** The Iroquoian
language of the Mohawk.
Mo·he·gan (mō-hē′gən) ►*n., pl.* **-gan** or **-gans**
1. A member of a Native American people formerly of E Connecticut, now in SE Connecticut
and Wisconsin. **2.** The Algonquian language of
the Mohegan.
Mo·hi·can (mō-hē′kən) ►*n.* Var. of **Mahican.**
Mohs scale (mōz) ►*n.* A scale for classifying
minerals based on relative hardness, ranging
from 1 for the softest to 10 for the hardest.
[After Friedrich *Mohs* (1773–1839).]
moi·e·ty (moi′ĭ-tē) ►*n., pl.* **-ties 1.** A half. **2.** A
portion or share. [< LLat. *medietās.*]
moil (moil) ►*v.* To work hard; toil. [< OFr. *moil-*
lier, moisten.] —**moil** *n.* —**moil′er** *n.*
moi·ré (mwä-rā′, mô-) ►*n.* **1.** Fabric, esp. silk,
with a wavy or rippled pattern. **2.** A similar
pattern pressed on cloth by engraved rollers.
[Fr. < p.part. of *moirer,* to water.] —**moi·ré′** *adj.*
moist (moist) ►*adj.* **-er, -est 1.** Slightly wet;
damp. **2.** Humid. **3.** Marked by considerable
rainfall. **4.** Juicy or succulent. [< Lat. *mūcidus,*
moldy.] —**mois′ten** (moi′sən) *v.* —**moist′ly**
adv. —**moist′ness** *n.*
mois·ture (mois′chər) ►*n.* Diffused or condensed liquid; dampness. —**mois′tur·ize′** *v.*
—**mois′tur·iz′er** *n.*
Mo·ja·ve Desert (mō-hä′vē) An arid region of
S CA and NV SE of the Sierra Nevada.
mo·jo (mō′jō′) ►*n., pl.* **-jos** or **-joes 1.** A
magic charm or spell. **2.** An amulet worn by
adherents of hoodoo or voodoo. **3.** An ability
or quality that causes one to excel. [Perh. of
African orig.]
mol ►*abbr. Chem.* mole
mo·lal (mō′ləl) ►*adj.* Being a solution having
one mole of solute in 1,000 grams of solvent.
—**mo·lal′i·ty** (mō-lăl′ĭ-tē) *n.*
mo·lar (mō′lər) ►*n.* A tooth with a broad crown
for grinding food, located behind the bicuspids.
[< Lat. *molāris,* of a mill, grinding.] —**mo′**
lar *adj.*
mo·las·ses (mə-lăs′ĭz) ►*n.* A thick brownish
syrup produced in refining raw sugar. [< LLat.
mellāceum, must.]
mold¹ (mōld) ►*n.* **1.** A hollow form or matrix for
shaping a fluid or plastic substance. **2.** A frame
or model for forming or shaping something. **3.**
Something made in or shaped on a mold. **4.**
General shape or form. **5.** Distinctive shape,
character, or type. ►*v.* To shape in or on a mold.
[< Lat. *modulus,* dim. of *modus,* measure.]
—**mold′a·ble** *adj.* —**mold′er** *n.*
mold² (mōld) ►*n.* **1a.** Any of various fungi that
contribute to the decay of organic matter. **b.**
The growth of such fungi. **2.** Any of various
other organisms that resemble fungi. ►*v.* To
become moldy. [ME *moulde.*]
mold³ (mōld) ►*n.* Loose soil rich in humus and
fit for planting. [< OE *molde.*]
Mol·da·vi·a (mŏl-dā′vē-ə, -dāv′yə) **1.** A historical region of E Romania E of Transylvania. **2.**
See **Moldova.** —**Mol·da′vi·an** *adj. & n.*

mold·er (mōl′dər) ►*v.* To decay or crumble into dust. See Synonyms at **decay.** [Poss. < MOLD³.]

mold·ing (mōl′dĭng) ►*n.* **1.** The act or process of molding. **2.** Something molded. **3.** An ornamental strip, as of wood, used to decorate or finish a surface, such as a wall or door.

Mol·do·va (mŏl-dō′və, môl-) A country of E Europe bordering on Romania. Cap. Chișinău. —**Mol′do′van** *adj. & n.*

mold·y (mōl′dē) ►*adj.* **-i·er, -i·est 1.** Covered with or containing mold. **2.** Musty or stale, as from decay. —**mold′i·ness** *n.*

mole¹ (mōl) ►*n.* A small congenital growth on the human skin, usu. dark and slightly raised. [< OE *māl.*]

mole² (mōl) ►*n.* A small mammal having silky fur, strong forefeet for burrowing, and often rudimentary eyes. [ME *molle.*]

mole³ (mōl) ►*n.* A massive jetty or breakwater built to protect a harbor. [< Lat. *mōlēs.*]

mole⁴ (mōl) ►*n. Chem.* The amount of a substance that contains Avogadro's number of atoms, molecules, ions, or other elementary units. [Ger. *Mol.*]

mo·le⁵ (mō′lā′) ►*n.* A spicy sauce of Mexican origin, usu. having a base of onions, chilies, nuts or seeds, and unsweetened chocolate. [< Nahuatl *mōlli.*]

molecular biology ►*n.* The branch of biology dealing with the structure and function of essential molecules, such as nucleic acids, and esp. their role in heredity.

molecular weight ►*n.* The sum of the atomic weights of the atoms in a molecule.

mol·e·cule (mŏl′ĭ-kyo͞ol′) ►*n.* **1.** The smallest particle into which an element or compound can be divided without changing its chemical and physical properties. **2.** A small particle; tiny bit. [< Lat. *mōlēs,* mass.] —**mo·lec′u·lar** *adj.*

mole·hill (mōl′hĭl′) ►*n.* A small mound of loose earth raised by a burrowing mole. —*idiom:* **make a mountain out of a molehill** To exaggerate a minor problem.

mole·skin (mōl′skĭn′) ►*n.* **1.** The fur of a mole. **2.** A heavy-napped cotton fabric.

mo·lest (mə-lĕst′) ►*v.* **1.** To disturb or annoy. **2a.** To subject (a child) to sexual contact. **b.** To subject (an adult) to unwanted sexual contact. [< Lat. *molestāre.*] —**mo′les·ta′tion** (mō′lĕ-stā′shən) *n.* —**mo·lest′er** *n.*

Mo·lière (mōl-yâr′) Jean Baptiste Poquelin. 1622–73. French playwright.

moll (mŏl) ►*n. Slang* A girlfriend of a gangster. [< *Moll,* nickname for *Mary.*]

mol·li·fy (mŏl′ə-fī′) ►*v.* **-fied, -fy·ing 1.** To placate; soothe. **2.** To lessen, as in intensity. [< LLat. *mollificāre,* make soft.] —**mol′li·fi·ca′tion** *n.*

mol·lusk also **mol·lusc** (mŏl′əsk) ►*n.* Any of a phylum of chiefly marine invertebrates typically having a soft body and a protective shell and including the snails, clams, and squids. [< Lat. *molluscus,* thin-shelled < *mollis,* soft.]

mol·ly·cod·dle (mŏl′ē-kŏd′l) ►*v.* **-dled, -dling** To spoil by pampering. ►*n.* A pampered person. [*molly,* milksop + CODDLE.]

Mo·lo·kai (mŏl′ə-kī′, mō′lə-) An island of central HI between Oahu and Maui.

Mo·lo·tov cocktail (mŏl′ə-tôf′, môl′-, mō′lə-) ►*n.* A makeshift incendiary bomb made of a bottle filled with flammable liquid and a usu. rag wick. [After V.M. *Molotov* (1890–1986).]

molt (mōlt) ►*v.* To shed an outer covering, such as feathers or skin, for replacement by a new growth. ►*n.* The act of molting. [< Lat. *mūtāre,* to change.]

mol·ten (mōl′tən) ►*adj.* Made liquid and glowing by heat; melted. [P.part. of MELT.]

Mo·luc·cas (mə-lŭk′əz) A group of islands of E Indonesia between Sulawesi and New Guinea. —**Mo·luc′can** *adj. & n.*

mol. wt. ►*abbr.* molecular weight

mo·lyb·de·num (mə-lĭb′də-nəm) ►*n. Symbol* **Mo** A hard, silvery-white metallic element used to toughen alloy steels. At. no. 42. See table at **element.** [< Gk. *molubdos,* lead.]

mom (mŏm) ►*n. Informal* Mother. [< MAMA.]

Mom·ba·sa (mŏm-bäs′ə, -bä′sä) A city of SE Kenya mainly on **Mombasa Island,** in the Indian Ocean.

mo·ment (mō′mənt) ►*n.* **1.** A brief interval of time. **2.** A specific point in time: *not here at the moment.* **3.** A particular period of importance or excellence. **4.** Importance. [< Lat. *mōmentum* < *movēre,* move.]

mo·men·tar·i·ly (mō′mən-târ′ə-lē) ►*adv.* **1.** For a moment. **2.** In a moment; shortly.

mo·men·tar·y (mō′mən-tĕr′ē) ►*adj.* **1.** Lasting for only a moment. **2.** Occurring or present at every moment. —**mo′men·tar′i·ness** *n.*

mo·ment·ly (mō′mənt-lē) ►*adv.* From moment to moment.

mo·men·tous (mō-mĕn′təs) ►*adj.* Of utmost importance or significance. —**mo·men′tous·ly** *adv.* —**mo·men′tous·ness** *n.*

mo·men·tum (mō-mĕn′təm) ►*n., pl.* **-ta** (-tə) or **-tums 1.** The product of a body's mass and velocity. **2a.** The force exhibited by a moving body. **b.** The impetus for a development. [Lat. *mōmentum,* movement < *movēre,* move.]

mom·my ►*n., pl.* **-mies** *Informal* A mother. [Alteration of MAMMY.]

mommy track ►*n.* A career path in which mothers relinquish certain professional opportunities in favor of benefits such as shorter or flexible hours.

mon– ►*pref.* Var. of **mono–.**

Mon·a·co (mŏn′ə-kō′, mə-nä′kō) A principality on the Mediterranean Sea consisting of an enclave in SE France. Cap. **Monaco** or **Monaco-Ville.** —**Mon′a·can** *adj. & n.*

mon·arch (mŏn′ərk, -ärk′) ►*n.* **1.** A usu. hereditary sovereign, such as a king or queen. **2.** One that commands or rules. **3.** A large orange and black butterfly. [< Gk. *monarkhos.*] —**mo·nar′chal** (mə-när′kəl), **mo·nar′chic** *adj.*

mon·ar·chism (mŏn′ər-kĭz′əm, -är′-) ►*n.* **1.** The system or principles of monarchy. **2.** Belief in or advocacy of monarchy. —**mon′ar·chist** *n.* —**mon′ar·chis′tic** *adj.*

mon·ar·chy (mŏn′ər-kē, -är′-) ►*n., pl.* **-chies 1.** Government by a monarch. **2.** A state ruled or headed by a monarch.

mon·as·ter·y (mŏn′ə-stĕr′ē) ►*n., pl.* **-ries** The dwelling place of a community of monks. [< LGk. *monastērion* < Gk. *monazein,* live alone.] —**mon′as·te′ri·al** (-stîr′ē-əl, -stĕr′-) *adj.*

mo·nas·tic (mə-năs′tĭk) also **mo·nas·ti·cal** (-tĭ-kəl) ►*adj.* **1.** Of a monastery. **2.** Characteristic of life in a monastery or convent, esp.: **a.** Secluded and contemplative. **b.** Strictly disciplined. **c.** Self-abnegating; austere. [< LGk. *monastikos.*] —**mo·nas′ti·cal·ly** *adv.* —**mo·nas′ti·cism** *n.*

mon·au·ral (mŏn-ôr′əl) ►*adj.* **1.** Of or designating sound reception by one ear. **2.** Using a single channel to record or reproduce sound; monophonic. —**mon·au′ral·ly** *adv.*

Mon·day (mŭn′dē, -dā′) ►*n.* The 2nd day of the week. [< OE *Mōnandæg.*]

Mo·net (mō-nā′, mô-), **Claude** 1840–1926. French painter.

mon·e·ta·rism (mŏn′ĭ-tə-rĭz′əm, mŭn′-) ►*n.* A policy of regulating an economy by altering the money supply, esp. by increasing it moderately but steadily. —**mon′e·ta·rist** *adj. & n.*

mon·e·tar·y (mŏn′ĭ-tĕr′ē, mŭn′-) ►*adj.* **1.** Of or relating to money. **2.** Of or relating to a nation's currency or coinage. [< Lat. *monēta*, money.] —**mon′e·tar′i·ly** *adv.*

mon·e·tize (mŏn′ĭ-tīz′, mŭn′-) ►*v.* **-tized, -tiz·ing 1.** To convert (an asset) into cash. **2.** To convert into a source of income. **3.** To establish (a metal) as a currency, esp. by minting coins. —**mon′e·ti·za′tion** *n.*

mon·ey (mŭn′ē) ►*n., pl.* **-eys** or **-ies** A medium that can be exchanged for goods and services and is used as a measure of their values on the market. **2.** The official currency issued by a government. **3.** Assets and property considered in terms of monetary value; wealth. **4.** Profit or loss: *made money on the sale.* **5.** often **moneys** or **monies** Sums of money; funds: *state tax monies.* [< Lat. *monēta.*]

mon·eyed also **mon·ied** (mŭn′ēd) ►*adj.* **1.** Wealthy. See Synonyms at **rich. 2.** Representing or arising from money or wealth.

mon·ey·lend·er (mŭn′ē-lĕn′dər) ►*n.* One that lends money at an interest rate.

mon·ey·mak·ing (mŭn′ē-mā′kĭng) ►*n.* Acquisition of money. ►*adj.* **1.** Engaged in acquiring wealth. **2.** Profitable. —**mon′ey·mak′er** *n.*

money market ►*n.* **1.** The trade in short-term, low-risk debt securities, such as US Treasury bills. **2.** A mutual fund that sells its shares in order to purchase short-term securities.

money order ►*n.* An order for the payment of a specified amount of money, usu. issued and payable at a bank or post office.

mon·ger (mŭng′gər, mŏng′-) ►*n.* **1.** A dealer. **2.** A person promoting something undesirable. [< Lat. *mangō.*]

Mon·gol (mŏng′gəl, -gōl′, mŏn′-) ►*n.* **1.** A member of any of the traditionally nomadic peoples of Mongolia. **2.** See **Mongolian** (sense 4). **3.** *Anthro.* A member of the Mongoloid racial division. —**Mon′gol** *adj.*

Mon·go·li·a (mŏng-gō′lē-ə, -gōl′yə, mŏn-) **1.** An ancient region of E-central Asia comprising modern-day Inner Mongolia and the country of Mongolia. **2.** A country of N-central Asia between Russia and China. Cap. Ulaanbaatar.

Mon·go·li·an (mŏng-gō′lē-ən, -gōl′yən, mŏn-) ►*n.* **1.** A native or inhabitant of Mongolia. **2.** A Mongol. **3.** *Anthro.* A member of the Mongoloid racial division. **4a.** A subfamily of the Altaic language family including Mongolian. **b.** Any of the languages of the Mongols. —**Mon·go′li·an** *adj.*

mon·gol·ism also **Mon·gol·ism** (mŏng′gə-lĭz′-əm, mŏn′-) ►*n. Offensive* Down syndrome.

Mon·gol·oid (mŏng′gə-loid′, mŏn′-) ►*adj.* **1.** *Anthro.* Of or being a human racial classification traditionally distinguished by yellowish-brown skin color and straight black hair and including peoples indigenous to central and E Asia. Not in scientific use. See Usage Note at **Negroid. 2.** Of or like a Mongol. **3.** also **mongoloid** *Offensive* Relating to Down syndrome. —**Mon′gol·oid′** *n.*

mon·goose (mŏng′gōōs′, mŏn′-) ►*n., pl.* **-goos·es** Any of various agile carnivorous mammals having a long tail and noted for their ability to kill snakes. [Marathi *mangūs.*]

mon·grel (mŭng′grəl, mŏng′-) ►*n.* A plant or animal, esp. a dog, of mixed breed. ►*adj.* **1.** Of mixed origin or character. **2.** Being a mongrel organism. [Prob. < ME *mong*, mixture.]

mon·ied (mŭn′ēd) ►*adj.* Var. of **moneyed.**

mon·ies (mŭn′ēz) ►*n.* Pl. of **money.**

mon·ick·er or **mon·ick·er** (mŏn′ĭ-kər) ►*n. Slang* A nickname. [< Ir. dial. *munik.*]

mo·nism (mō′nĭz′əm, mŏn′ĭz′əm) ►*n.* The view in metaphysics that all reality is composed of and reducible to one substance. —**mo′nist** *n.* —**mo·nis′tic** (mō-nĭs′tĭk, mŏ-) *adj.*

mo·ni·tion (mō-nĭsh′ən, mə-) ►*n.* A warning or admonition. [< Lat. *monēre, monit-*, warn.]

mon·i·tor (mŏn′ĭ-tər) ►*n.* **1.** A pupil who assists a teacher. **2a.** A usu. electronic device used to record or control a process or system. **b.** A screen used to check the picture being broadcast or picked up by a camera. **c.** *Comp.* A device that accepts video signals from a computer and displays information on a screen; video display. ►*v.* To check, watch, or keep track of, often by means of an electronic device. [Lat., one who warns < *monēre*, warn.]

mon·i·to·ry (mŏn′ĭ-tôr′ē) ►*adj.* Conveying an admonition or warning.

monk (mŭngk) ►*n.* A man who is a member of a religious community living in a monastery. [< LGk. *monakhos* < Gk. *monos*, single.] —**monk′ish** *adj.* —**monk′ish·ly** *adv.*

mon·key (mŭng′kē) ►*n., pl.* **-keys** Any of various tailed primates, including the macaques, baboons, capuchins, and marmosets, and excluding the apes. ►*v. Informal* To play or tamper with something. [?]

monkey business ►*n. Slang* Mischievous or deceitful behavior.

monkey wrench ►*n.* **1.** A hand tool with adjustable jaws for turning nuts. **2.** *Informal* Something that hinders or disrupts.

monks·hood (mŭngks′hŏŏd′) ►*n.* **1.** See **aconite. 2.** A poisonous aconite native to Europe, having racemes of blue or purple flowers.

Mon·mouth (mŏn′məth), Duke of. James Scott. 1649–85. English pretender to the throne.

mon·o¹ (mŏn′ō) ►*n. Informal* Infectious mononucleosis.

mon·o² (mŏn′ō) ►*adj. Informal* Monaural.

mono– or **mon–** ►*pref.* One; single; alone: *monofilament.* [< Gk. *monos*, single.]

mon·o·chro·mat·ic (mŏn′ə-krō-măt′ĭk) ►*adj.* **1.** Of only one color. **2.** Of or composed of radiation of only one wavelength.

mon·o·chrome (mŏn′ə-krōm′) ►*n.* **1.** A painting or drawing done in different shades of a single color. **2.** The technique of executing a monochrome. [< Gk. *monokhrōmos*, of one color.] —**mon′o·chro′mic** *adj.*

mon·o·cle (mŏn′ə-kəl) ►*n.* An eyeglass for one

eye. [< LLat. *monoculus,* one-eyed.]

mon·o·cline (mŏn′ə-klīn′) ►*n.* A geologic structure in which all layers are inclined in the same direction. —**mon′o·cli′nal** *adj.*

mon·o·clo·nal (mŏn′ə-klō′nəl) ►*adj.* Derived as clones from a single cell or produced by the clones of a single cell: *a monoclonal tumor.*

mon·o·cot·y·le·don (mŏn′ə-kŏt′l-ēd′n) also **mon·o·cot** (mŏn′ə-kŏt′) ►*n.* A plant having a single embryonic seed leaf that appears at germination. —**mon′o·cot′y·le′don·ous** *adj.*

mo·noc·u·lar (mŏ-nŏk′yə-lər, mə-) ►*adj.* **1.** Having one eye. **2.** Of or intended for use by only one eye.

mon·o·cul·ture (mŏn′ə-kŭl′chər) ►*n.* **1.** The cultivation of a single crop in an area or region. **2.** A single homogeneous society or culture. —**mon′o·cul′tur·al** *adj.*

mon·o·dy (mŏn′ə-dē) ►*n., pl.* **-dies** An ode or elegy. [< Gk. *monōidia.*] —**mo·nod′ic** (mə-nŏd′ĭk) *adj.* —**mon′o·dist** *n.*

mon·o·fil·a·ment (mŏn′ə-fĭl′ə-mənt) ►*n.* A single strand of untwisted synthetic fiber used esp. for fishing line.

mo·nog·a·my (mə-nŏg′ə-mē) ►*n.* **1.** The condition or practice of being sexually faithful to one partner during a relationship. **2.** Marriage to only one person at a time. —**mo·nog′a·mist** *n.* —**mo·nog′a·mous** *adj.* —**mo·nog′a·mous·ly** *adv.*

mon·o·gram (mŏn′ə-grăm′) ►*n.* A design composed of one or more initials of a name. ►*v.* **-grammed, -gram·ming** also **-gramed, -gram·ing** To mark with a monogram. —**mon′o·gram·mat′ic** (-grə-măt′ĭk) *adj.*

mon·o·graph (mŏn′ə-grăf′) ►*n.* A scholarly book or article on a specific, often limited subject. —**mon′o·graph′ic** *adj.*

mon·o·lin·gual (mŏn′ə-lĭng′gwəl) ►*adj.* Using or knowing only one language. —**mon′o·lin′gual** *n.* —**mon′o·lin′gual·ism** *n.*

mon·o·lith (mŏn′ə-lĭth′) ►*n.* **1.** A large block of stone, esp. one used in architecture or sculpture. **2.** A large organization that acts as a powerful unit. —**mon′o·lith′ic** *adj.*

mon·o·logue also **mon·o·log** (mŏn′ə-lôg′, -lŏg′) ►*n.* **1.** A soliloquy. **2.** A series of jokes delivered by a comedian. **3.** A long speech by one person, often monopolizing a conversation. —**mon′o·logu′ist, mo·nol′o·gist** (mə-nŏl′ə-jĭst, mŏn′ə-lôg′ĭst, -lŏg′-) *n.*

mon·o·ma·ni·a (mŏn′ə-mā′nē-ə, -mān′yə) ►*n.* **1.** Obsession with one idea. **2.** Intent concentration on one subject. —**mon′o·ma′ni·ac′** *n.* —**mon′o·ma·ni′a·cal** (-mə-nī′ə-kəl) *adj.*

mon·o·mer (mŏn′ə-mər) ►*n.* A molecule that can combine with other molecules to form a polymer. —**mon′o·mer′ic** (-mĕr′ĭk) *adj.*

mo·no·mi·al (mŏ-nō′mē-əl, mə-) ►*n.* **1.** An algebraic expression consisting of only one term. **2.** *Biol.* A taxonomic name consisting of a single word. [MON(O)– + (BIN)OMIAL.] —**mo·no′mi·al** *adj.*

mon·o·mor·phism (mŏn′ō-môr′fĭz′əm) ►*n.* **1.** *Biol.* The occurrence of only one form, as only one allele of a particular gene. **2.** *Chem.* Crystallization of a compound in only one form. —**mon′o·mor′phic** *adj.*

Mo·non·ga·he·la River (mə-nŏng′gə-hē′lə, mə-nŏng′gə-hā′lə) A river rising in N WV and flowing about 200 km (125 mi) to join the Allegheny R. and form the Ohio R.

mon·o·nu·cle·o·sis (mŏn′ō-noō′klē-ō′sĭs, -nyoō-) ►*n.* Infectious mononucleosis.

mon·o·phon·ic (mŏn′ə-fŏn′ĭk) ►*adj.* Monaural. —**mon′o·phon′i·cal·ly** *adv.*

mon·o·plane (mŏn′ə-plān′) ►*n.* An airplane with only one pair of wings.

mo·nop·o·lize (mə-nŏp′ə-līz′) ►*v.* **-lized, -liz·ing 1.** To acquire or maintain a monopoly of. **2.** To dominate or use to the exclusion of others: *monopolized the conversation.* —**mo·nop′o·li·za′tion** *n.* —**mo·nop′o·liz′er** *n.*

mo·nop·o·ly (mə-nŏp′ə-lē) ►*n., pl.* **-lies 1.** Exclusive control or ownership, as of a commodity or service. **2a.** A company or group having such control. **b.** A commodity or service so controlled. [< Gk. *monopōlion,* sole selling rights.] —**mo·nop′o·list** *n.* —**mo·nop′o·lis′tic** *adj.*

mon·o·rail (mŏn′ə-rāl′) ►*n.* A railway system using a single rail.

mon·o·sac·cha·ride (mŏn′ə-săk′ə-rīd′, -rĭd) ►*n.* A carbohydrate that cannot be decomposed by hydrolysis; simple sugar.

mon·o·so·di·um glu·ta·mate (mŏn′ə-sō′dē-əm gloō′tə-māt′) ►*n.* A white crystalline compound used as a flavor enhancer.

mon·o·syl·la·ble (mŏn′ə-sĭl′ə-bəl) ►*n.* A word or an utterance of one syllable. —**mon′o·syl·lab′ic** (-sĭ-lăb′ĭk) *adj.*

mon·o·the·ism (mŏn′ə-thē-ĭz′əm) ►*n.* The belief that there is only one God. —**mon′o·the′ist** *n.* —**mon′o·the·is′tic** *adj.*

mon·o·tone (mŏn′ə-tōn′) ►*n.* A succession of sounds or words uttered in a single tone of voice or sung at a single pitch.

mo·not·o·nous (mə-nŏt′n-əs) ►*adj.* **1.** Unvarying in tone or pitch. **2.** Repetitiously dull. —**mo·not′o·nous·ly** *adv.* —**mo·not′o·ny** *n.*

mon·o·type (mŏn′ə-tīp′) ►*n.* **1.** *Biol.* The sole member of its group, such as a single species that constitutes a genus. **2.** A unique print made by pressing paper against a painted or inked surface. —**mon′o·typ′ic** (-tĭp′ĭk) *adj.*

mon·o·un·sat·u·rat·ed (mŏn′ō-ŭn-săch′ə-rā′tĭd) ►*adj.* Being an unsaturated fat composed esp. of fatty acids having only one double bond in the carbon chain.

mon·o·va·lent (mŏn′ə-vā′lənt) ►*adj.* Univalent. —**mon′o·va′lence, mon′o·va′len·cy** *n.*

mon·ox·ide (mə-nŏk′sīd′) ►*n.* An oxide with each molecule containing one oxygen atom.

mon·o·zy·got·ic (mŏn′ō-zī-gŏt′ĭk) ►*adj.* Derived from a single fertilized ovum.

James Monroe
c. 1820 portrait

Mon·roe (mən-rōʹ), **James** 1758–1831. The 5th US president (1817–25).

Monroe, Marilyn Norma Jean Baker. 1926–62. Amer. actress.

Mon·ro·vi·a (mən-rōʹvē-ə) The capital of Liberia, in the NW.

Mon·sieur (mə-syœʹ) ►*n., pl.* **Mes·sieurs** (mā-syœʹ, mĕsʹərz) A French courtesy title for a man. [< OFr., my lord.]

Mon·si·gnor also **mon·si·gnor** (mŏn-sēnʹyər) ►*n. Rom. Cath. Ch.* A title and office conferred on a cleric by the pope. [Ital. < Fr. *Monseigneur.*]

mon·soon (mŏn-sōōnʹ) ►*n.* A wind system that influences large climatic regions and reverses direction seasonally, esp. the Asiatic system producing dry and wet seasons in India and S Asia. [< Ar. *mawsim,* season.]

mon·ster (mŏnʹstər) ►*n.* **1.** A creature having a strange or frightening appearance. **2.** An organism having structural defects or deformities. **3.** Something unusually large. **4.** One who inspires horror or disgust. [< Lat. *mōnstrum,* portent < *monēre,* warn.] —**mon·stros′i·ty** (-strŏsʹĭ-te) *n.* —**mon′strous** *adj.* —**mon′strous·ly** *adv.* —**mon′strous·ness** *n.*

mon·strance (mŏnʹstrəns) ►*n. Rom. Cath. Ch.* A receptacle in which the host is held. [< Lat. *mōnstrāre,* show < *mōnstrum,* MONSTER.]

monstrance

mon·tage (mŏn-täzhʹ, môN-) ►*n.* **1.** A single pictorial composition made by juxtaposing several pictures or designs. **2.** A relatively rapid succession of different shots in a movie. [Fr. < *monter,* MOUNT¹.]

Mon·tag·nais (mŏnʹtən-yāʹ) ►*n., pl.* **-nais 1.** A member of a Native American people inhabiting Quebec and Labrador. **2.** The Algonquian language of the Montagnais.

Mon·taigne (mŏn-tānʹ), **Michel Eyquem de** 1533–92. French essayist.

Mon·tan·a (mŏn-tănʹə) A state of the NW US bordering on Canada. Cap. Helena. —**Mon·tan′an** *adj. & n.*

mon·tane (mŏn-tānʹ, mŏnʹtānʹ) ►*adj.* Of, growing in, or inhabiting mountain areas. [Lat. *montānus.*]

Mon·te Car·lo (mŏnʹtē kärʹlō) A town of Monaco on the Mediterranean Sea.

Mon·te·neg·ro (mŏnʹtə-nĕgʹrō, -nēʹgrō) A country of SE Europe on the Adriatic Sea. Cap. Podgorica. —**Mon′te·neg′rin** *adj. & n.*

Monterey jack ►*n.* A mild semisoft cheese with a high moisture content.

Mon·tes·quieu (mŏnʹtə-skyōōʹ) Baron de la Brede et de Montesquieu. Title of Charles de Secondat. 1689–1755. French philosopher and jurist.

Mon·tes·so·ri (mŏnʹtĭ-sôrʹē), **Maria** 1870–1952. Italian physician and educator.

Montessori method ►*n.* A method of educating children that stresses development of a child's own initiative.

Mon·te·vi·de·o (mŏnʹtə-vĭ-dāʹō) The capital of Uruguay, in the S part on the Río de la Plata estuary.

Mon·te·zu·ma II (mŏnʹtĭ-zōōʹmə) 1466?–1520. Last Aztec emperor in Mexico (1502–20).

Mont·gom·er·y (mŏnt-gŭmʹə-rē, -gŭmʹrē) The capital of AL, in the SE-central part SSE of Birmingham.

Montgomery, Sir **Bernard Law.** First Viscount Montgomery. 1887–1976. British army officer.

month (mŭnth) ►*n.* **1.** A unit of time corresponding approximately to one cycle of the moon's phases, or about 30 days or 4 weeks. **2.** One of the usu. 12 divisions of a calendar year. **3.** A period extending from a date in one calendar month to the corresponding date in the next month. [< OE *mōnath.*]

month·ly (mŭnthʹlē) ►*adj.* **1.** Occurring, appearing, or payable every month. **2.** Continuing or lasting for a month. ►*adv.* Once a month; every month. ►*n., pl.* **-lies** A publication appearing once each month.

Mont·pel·ier (mŏnt-pēlʹyər) The capital of VT, in the N-central part.

Mon·tre·al (mŏnʹtrē-ôlʹ) A city of S Quebec, Canada, on **Montreal Island** in the St. Lawrence R.

mon·u·ment (mŏnʹyə-mənt) ►*n.* **1.** A structure erected as a memorial. **2.** A tombstone. **3.** Something preserved for its historic or aesthetic significance. **4a.** An outstanding or enduring achievement. **b.** An exceptional example. [< Lat. *monumentum* < *monēre,* remind.]

mon·u·men·tal (mŏnʹyə-mĕnʹtl) ►*adj.* **1.** Of or serving as a monument. **2.** Impressively large and sturdy. **3.** Of outstanding significance. **4.** Astounding: *monumental cowardice.* —**mon′u·men′tal·ly** *adv.*

moo (mōō) ►*v.* To emit the deep bellowing sound made by a cow. [Imit.] —**moo** *n.*

mooch (mōōch) *Informal* ►*v.* To obtain free; beg. See Synonyms at **cadge.** ►*n.* One who begs or cadges; sponge. [< OFr. *muchier,* skulk.] —**mooch′er** *n.*

mood¹ (mōōd) ►*n.* **1.** A state of mind or emotion. **2.** Inclination; disposition. [< OE *mōd.*]

mood² (mōōd) ►*n.* A set of verb forms or inflections used to indicate the factuality or likelihood of the action or condition expressed. [< MODE.]

mood disorder ►*n.* A psychiatric disorder marked by a pervasive disturbance of mood.

mood·y (mōōʹdē) ►*adj.* **-i·er, -i·est 1.** Given to changeable moods; temperamental. **2.** Subject to periods of depression; gloomy. —**mood′i·ly** *adv.* —**mood′i·ness** *n.*

moon (mōōn) ►*n.* **1.** often **Moon** The natural satellite of Earth, approx. 356,000 km (221,600 mi) distant at perigee and 406,997 km (252,950 mi) at apogee, and having a mean diameter of 3,475 km (2,160 mi), mass approx. one eightieth that of Earth, and an average period of revolution around Earth of 29 days 12 hours 44 minutes. **2.** A natural satellite revolving around a planet. **3.** The moon as it appears at a particular phase: *the full moon.* **4.** A month. **5.** A disk, globe, or crescent resembling the moon. ►*v.* To wander about or pass time in a dreamy or aimless way. [< OE *mōna.*] —**moon′y** *adj.*

moon·beam (mōōn′bēm′) ►*n.* A ray of moonlight.

moon·light (mōōn′līt′) ►*n.* The light of the moon. ►*v. Informal* To work at a second job, often at night. —**moon′light′er** *n.*

moon·lit (mōōn′lĭt′) ►*adj.* Lighted by moonlight.

moon·shine (mōōn′shīn′) ►*n.* **1.** Moonlight. **2.** *Informal* Foolish talk; nonsense. **3.** Illegally distilled whiskey. —**moon′shin′er** *n.*

moon·stone (mōōn′stōn′) ►*n.* A form of feldspar valued for its pearly translucence.

moon·struck (mōōn′strŭk′) ►*adj.* **1.** Dazed or distracted with romantic sentiment. **2.** Mentally deranged; crazed. [From the belief that the moon caused insanity.]

moor¹ (mōōr) ►*v.* **1.** To secure in place with or as if with lines, cables, or anchors. See Synonyms at **fasten. 2.** To provide with an abiding emotional attachment. [ME *moren.*] —**moor′age** *n.*

moor² (mōōr) ►*n.* An often high but poorly drained area, usu. covered with low shrubs. [< OE *mōr.*]

Moor ►*n.* **1.** A member of a Muslim people of mixed Berber and Arab ancestry, now living chiefly in NW Africa. **2.** One of the Muslims who invaded Spain in the 8th cent. [< Gk. *Mauros.*] —**Moor′ish** *adj.*

moor·ing (mōōr′ĭng) ►*n.* **1.** A place at which a vessel or aircraft can be moored. **2.** often **moorings** Elements providing stability or security.

moose (mōōs) ►*n., pl.* **moose** A large deer of N North America, having broad flattened antlers in the male. [Of Algonquian orig.]

moot (mōōt) ►*adj.* **1a.** Subject to debate; arguable. **b.** Irrelevant. **2.** *Law* Without legal significance. ►*v.* To bring up as a subject for discussion or debate. See Synonyms at **broach.** [< OE *mōt,* assembly.]

moot court ►*n.* A mock court where hypothetical cases are tried by law students as an exercise.

mop (mŏp) ►*n.* **1.** A household implement made of absorbent material attached to a handle and used for cleaning floors. **2.** A tangled mass, esp. of hair. ►*v.* **mopped, mop·ping** To wash or wipe with or as if with a mop. —*phrasal verb:* **mop up 1.** To clear (an area) of remaining enemy troops after a victory. **2.** To conclude a project or activity. [ME *mappe,* ult. < Lat. *mappa,* cloth.] —**mop′per** *n.*

mope (mōp) ►*v.* **moped, mop·ing** To be gloomy or dejected. See Synonyms at **brood.** [?] —**mop′er** *n.* —**mop′ish·ly** *adv.*

mo·ped (mō′pĕd′) ►*n.* **1.** A motorbike that can be pedaled as well as driven by a low-powered gasoline engine. **2.** A motor scooter.

mop·pet (mŏp′ĭt) ►*n.* A young child. [< ME *moppe,* child.]

mop-up (mŏp′ŭp′) ►*n.* The act of disposing of final or remaining details.

mo·raine (mə-rān′) ►*n.* An accumulation of

boulders, stones, or other debris carried and deposited by a glacier. [Fr.]

moraine
Wrangell–St. Elias National Park and Preserve, Alaska

mor·al (môr′əl, mŏr′-) ►*adj.* **1.** Of or concerned with the judgment of right or wrong of human action and character. **2.** Conforming to standards of what is right or just in behavior. **3.** Arising from conscience. **4.** Having psychological rather than tangible effects. **5.** Based on likelihood rather than evidence. ►*n.* **1.** The principle taught by a story or event. **2. morals** Rules or habits of conduct, esp. of sexual conduct. [< Lat. *mōrālis* < *mōs, mōr-,* custom.] —**mor′al·ly** *adv.*

mo·rale (mə-răl′) ►*n.* The state of mind of a person or group as exhibited by confidence, cheerfulness, and discipline. [Fr.]

mor·al·ist (môr′ə-lĭst, mŏr′-) ►*n.* **1.** A teacher or student of ethics. **2.** One who follows a system of moral principles. —**mor′a·lis′tic** *adj.* —**mor′a·lis′ti·cal·ly** *adv.*

mo·ral·i·ty (mə-răl′ĭ-tē, mô-) ►*n., pl.* **-ties 1.** The quality of being moral. **2.** A system of ideas of right and wrong conduct. **3.** Virtuous conduct.

mor·al·ize (môr′ə-līz′, mŏr′-) ►*v.* **-ized, -iz·ing** To think about or discuss moral issues. —**mor′al·i·za′tion** *n.* —**mor′al·iz′er** *n.*

mo·rass (mə-răs′, mô-) ►*n.* **1.** An area of low-lying, soggy ground. **2.** A difficult, perplexing, or overwhelming situation. [< OFr. *marais.*]

mor·a·to·ri·um (môr′ə-tôr′ē-əm, mŏr′-) ►*n., pl.* **-to·ri·ums** or **-to·ri·a** (-tôr′ē-ə) **1.** *Law* A lawful suspension of the payment of certain debt during a period of financial or civil distress. **2.** A suspension or delay of any action or activity. [< LLat. *mōrātōrius,* delaying < Lat. *mora,* delay.]

Mo·ra·vi·a (mə-rā′vē-ə, mô-) A region of central and E Czech Republic. —**Mo·ra′vi·an** *adj. & n.*

mo·ray (môr′ā, mə-rā′) ►*n.* Any of numerous often brightly colored marine eels, having a large mouth with sharp teeth. [< Gk. *muraina.*]

mor·bid (môr′bĭd) ►*adj.* **1.** Given to or marked by unwholesome thoughts or feelings, esp. of death. **2.** Of or caused by disease. [Lat. *morbidus* < *morbus,* disease.] —**mor′bid·ly** *adv.* —**mor′bid·ness** *n.*

mor·bid·i·ty (môr-bĭd′ĭ-tē) ►*n., pl.* **-ties 1.** The

condition or quality of being morbid. **2.** The rate of incidence of a disease.

mor·da·cious (môr-dā′shəs) ►*adj.* **1.** Given to biting. **2.** Caustic; sarcastic. [< Lat. *mordāx, mordāc-* < *mordēre,* bite.] —**mor·da′cious·ly** *adv.* —**mor·dac′i·ty** (-dăs′ĭ-tē) *n.*

mor·dant (môr′dnt) ►*adj.* **1.** Bitingly sarcastic. **2.** Incisive and trenchant. **3.** Serving to fix colors in dyeing. ►*n.* A reagent, such as tannic acid, that fixes dyes to tissues or other materials. [< Lat. *mordēre,* bite.] —**mor′dan·cy** *n.* —**mor′dant·ly** *adv.*

more (môr) ►*adj.* Comp. of **many, much. 1a.** Greater in number. **b.** Greater in size, amount, extent, or degree. **2.** Additional; extra: *She needs some more time.* ►*n.* A greater or additional quantity, number, degree, or amount. ►*pron. (takes pl. v.)* A greater or additional number of persons or things. ►*adv.* Comp. of **much. 1a.** To or in a greater extent or degree: *loved him even more.* **b.** Used to form the comparative of many adjectives and adverbs: *more difficult; more softly.* **2.** In addition: *phoned twice more.* —*idiom:* **more or less 1.** Approximately. **2.** To an undetermined degree. [< OE *māra.*]

More, Sir **Thomas.** 1477?–1535. English politician, scholar, and writer.

mo·rel (mə-rĕl′, mô-) ►*n.* An edible mushroom having a cap with irregular pits and ridges. [< OFr. *morille.*]

more·o·ver (môr-ō′vər, môr′ō′vər) ►*adv.* Furthermore; besides.

mo·res (môr′āz′, -ēz) ►*pl.n.* The accepted customs and rules of a particular social group. [Lat. *mōrēs,* customs.]

Mor·gan (môr′gən), **John Pierpont** 1837–1913. Amer. financier and philanthropist.

morgue (môrg) ►*n.* A place in which the bodies of persons found dead are temporarily kept. [Fr.]

mor·i·bund (môr′ə-bŭnd′, mŏr′-) ►*adj.* At the point of death. [Lat. *moribundus* < *morī,* die.] —**mor′i·bun′di·ty** *n.* —**mor′i·bund′ly** *adv.*

Mor·mon (môr′mən) ►*n.* A member of the Mormon Church. —**Mor′mon** *adj.* —**Mor′mon·ism** *n.*

Mormon Church ►*n.* A church founded by Joseph Smith in 1830 and having its headquarters in Salt Lake City, Utah.

morn (môrn) ►*n.* Morning. [< OE *morgen.*]

morn·ing (môr′nĭng) ►*n.* The first or early part of the day, esp. from sunrise to noon.

morning glory ►*n.* Any of various usu. twining vines having trumpet-shaped, variously colored flowers that gen. are open for only a day.

mo·roc·co (mə-rŏk′ō) ►*n., pl.* **-cos** A soft fine leather of goatskin. [< Morocco.]

Morocco A country of NW Africa on the Mediterranean and the Atlantic. Cap. Rabat. —**Mo·roc′can** *adj. & n.*

mo·ron (môr′ŏn′) ►*n.* A stupid person. [< Gk. *mōros,* stupid.] —**mo·ron′ic** (mə-rŏn′ĭk, mô-) *adj.*

Mo·ro·ni (mə-rō′nē, mô-) The capital of the Comoros, on Grand Comoro I.

mo·rose (mə-rōs′, mô-) ►*adj.* Sullenly melancholy; gloomy. [Lat. *mōrōsus,* peevish.] —**mo·rose′ly** *adv.* —**mo·rose′ness** *n.*

morph (môrf) ►*v.* **1.** To transform (an image) by computer: *morphed the villain into a snake.* **2.** To be transformed. [< metamorphose.]

–morph ►*suff.* **1.** Form; shape; structure: *isomorph.* **2.** Morpheme: *allomorph.* [< Gk. *morphē,* shape.]

mor·pheme (môr′fēm′) ►*n.* A linguistic unit, such as *man,* or *-ed* in *walked,* that has meaning and cannot be divided into smaller meaningful parts. [Fr. *morphème.*] —**mor·phem′ic** *adj.* —**mor·phem′i·cal·ly** *adv.*

mor·phine (môr′fēn′) ►*n.* A powerfully addictive narcotic drug extracted from opium, used in medicine as an anesthetic or sedative. [Fr. < Lat. *Morpheus,* god of dreams.]

morpho– or **morph–** ►*pref.* **1.** Form; shape; structure: *morphogenesis.* **2.** Morpheme: *morphology.* [< Gk. *morphē,* shape.]

mor·pho·gen·e·sis (môr′fō-jĕn′ĭ-sĭs) ►*n.* Evolutionary or embryological development of the structure of an organism or part. —**mor′pho·ge·net′ic** (-jə-nĕt′ĭk), **mor′pho·gen′ic** *adj.*

mor·phol·o·gy (môr-fŏl′ə-jē) ►*n., pl.* **-gies 1.** The biological study of the form and structure of organisms. **2.** *Ling.* The study of word formation, including inflection, derivation, and compounds. —**mor′pho·log′i·cal** (-fə-lŏj′ĭ-kəl), **mor′pho·log′ic** *adj.* —**mor′pho·log′i·cal·ly** *adv.* —**mor·phol′o·gist** *n.*

mor·ris (môr′ĭs, mŏr′-) ►*n.* An English folk dance in which a story is enacted by costumed dancers. [< ME *moreys,* Moorish.]

Morris, Robert 1734–1806. Amer. Revolutionary politician and financier.

Morris, William 1834–96. British poet, artist, and social reformer.

Morris chair ►*n.* A large easy chair with an adjustable back and removable cushions. [After William Morris.]

Morris Jes·up (jĕs′əp), **Cape** A cape of N Greenland on the Arctic Ocean; the world's northernmost point of land.

Mor·ris·on (môr′ĭ-sən, mŏr′-), **Toni** b. 1931. Amer. writer.

Toni Morrison
photographed in 2004

mor·row (môr′ō, mŏr′ō) ►*n.* The following day. [ME *morwe* < OE *morgen.*]

Morse (môrs), **Samuel Finley Breese** 1791–1872. Amer. painter and inventor.

Morse code ►*n.* A code, used esp. in telegraphy, in which sequences of dots and dashes or short and long signals represent letters and numbers. [After Samuel F. B. Morse.]

mor·sel (môr′səl) ►*n.* **1.** A small piece of food. **2.** A tasty tidbit. **3.** A bit or item: *a morsel of* *wisdom.* [< Lat. *mordēre*, to bite.]

mor·tal (môr′tl) ►*adj.* **1.** Liable or subject to death. **2.** Of or accompanying death. **3.** Causing death; fatal. **4a.** Fought to the death: *mortal combat.* **b.** Unrelentingly antagonistic: *mortal foes.* **5.** Of great intensity or severity; dire: *mortal terror.* ►*n.* A human. [< Lat. *mors, mort-,* death.] —**mor′tal·ly** *adv.*

mor·tal·i·ty (môr-tăl′ĭ-tē) ►*n.* **1.** The condition of being mortal. **2.** Death rate.

mor·tar (môr′tər) ►*n.* **1.** A vessel in which substances are crushed or ground with a pestle. **2a.** A muzzleloading cannon used to fire shells in high trajectories. **b.** A shell fired by such a cannon. **3.** A bonding material used in building, esp. a mixture of cement or lime with sand and water. [< Lat. *mortārium.*]

mor·tar·board (môr′tər-bôrd′) ►*n.* **1.** A square board with a handle used for holding and carrying mortar. **2.** An academic cap topped by a flat square and a tassel.

mort·gage (môr′gĭj) ►*n.* **1.** A loan for the purchase of real property, secured by a lien on the property. **2.** The document specifying the terms and conditions of the repayment of such a loan. ►*v.* **-gaged, -gag·ing** To pledge (real property) as the security for a loan. [< OFr.] —**mort′ga·gee′** (-gĭ-jē′) *n.* —**mort′ga·gor′** (-jôr′, -jər) *n.*

mor·ti·cian (môr-tĭsh′ən) ►*n.* See **funeral director.** [Lat. *mors, mort-,* death + –ICIAN.]

mor·ti·fy (môr′tə-fī′) ►*v.* **-fied, -fy·ing 1.** To shame; humiliate. **2.** To discipline (one's body and appetites) by self-denial. [< Lat. *mortificāre,* cause to die.] —**mor′ti·fi·ca′tion** *n.*

mor·tise (môr′tĭs) ►*n.* A usu. rectangular cavity in a piece of wood, stone, or other material, prepared to receive a tenon and thus form a joint. [< OFr. *mortaise.*]

mort·main (môrt′mān′) ►*n.* A legal arrangement in which a property owner such as a church cannot transfer or sell it. [< OFr. *mortemain.*]

mor·tu·ar·y (môr′chŏŏ-ĕr′ē) ►*n., pl.* **-ies** A place where dead bodies are kept before burial or cremation. [< Lat. *mortuus,* dead.]

mos. ►*abbr.* months

mo·sa·ic (mō-zā′ĭk) ►*n.* A picture or decorative design made by setting small colored pieces, as of stone, glass, or tile, onto a surface. [< Med. Lat. *mūsāicus,* of the Muses < *Musa,* MUSE.]

mosaic

Mos·cow (mŏs′kou, -kō) The capital of Russia, in the W-central part.

Mo·selle (mō-zĕl′) also **Mo·sel** (mō′zəl) A river rising in NE France and flowing about 545 km (340 mi) to the Rhine R. in W Germany.

Mos·es (mō′zĭz, -zĭs) In the Bible, the Hebrew prophet and lawgiver who led the Israelites out of Egypt. —**Mo·sa′ic** (mō-zā′ĭk) *adj.*

Moses, Anna Mary Robertson "Grandma Moses." 1860–1961. Amer. painter.

mo·sey (mō′zē) ►*v. Informal* To move in a leisurely manner; saunter. [?]

mosh (mŏsh) ►*v.* To knock against others intentionally while dancing at a rock concert; slamdance. [Perh. alteration of MASH.]

mosh pit ►*n.* An area in front of a concert stage in which audience members mosh.

Mos·lem (mŏz′ləm, mŏs′-) ►*n. & adj.* Var. of **Muslim.**

mosque (mŏsk) ►*n.* A Muslim house of worship. [< Ar. *masjid* < *sajada,* to worship.]

mos·qui·to (mə-skē′tō) ►*n., pl.* **-toes** or **-tos** Any of various two-winged insects, the females of which suck blood. Some species transmit diseases. [< Lat. *musca,* fly.]

moss (môs, mŏs) ►*n.* Any of various green nonvascular plants having leaflike structures arranged around the stem. [< OE *mos,* bog, and Med.Lat. *mossa,* moss (of Gmc. orig.).] —**moss′i·ness** *n.* —**moss′y** *adj.*

most (mōst) ►*adj.* Superl. of **many, much. 1a.** Greatest in number. **b.** Greatest in amount, extent, or degree. **2.** In the greatest number of instances: *Most fish have fins.* ►*n.* The greatest amount or degree: *She has the most to gain.* ►*pron.* (*takes sing. or pl. v.*) The greatest part or number: *Most of the town was destroyed.* ►*adv.* Superl. of **much. 1.** In or to the highest degree, quantity, or extent. Used with many adjectives and adverbs to form the superlative: *most honest; most impatiently.* **2.** Very: *a most impressive book.* **3.** *Informal* Almost: *Most everyone agrees.* —*idiom:* **at (the) most** At the maximum: *two miles at most.* [< OE *mǣst.*]

-most ►*suff.* **1.** Most: *innermost.* **2.** Nearest to: *endmost.* [< OE *-mest.*]

most·ly (mōst′lē) ►*adv.* **1.** For the greatest part; mainly. **2.** Generally; usually.

Mo·sul (mō-sōōl′, mō′səl) A city of N Iraq on the Tigris R.

mot (mō) ►*n.* A short witty saying or remark. [< OFr., word, saying.]

mote (mōt) ►*n.* A speck, esp. of dust. [< OE *mot.*]

mo·tel (mō-tĕl′) ►*n.* A hotel for motorists providing rooms usu. having direct access to an open parking area. [Blend of MOTOR and HOTEL.]

mo·tet (mō-tĕt′) ►*n. Mus.* A polyphonic composition based on a religious text. [< OFr. < *mot,* word.]

moth (môth, mŏth) ►*n., pl.* **moths** (môthz, mŏthz, môths, mŏths) Any of numerous insects related to and resembling butterflies but gen. night-flying and having hairlike or feathery antennae. [< OE *moththe.*]

moth·ball (môth′bôl′, mŏth′-) ►*n.* **1.** A marble-sized ball, orig. of camphor but now of naphthalene, stored with clothes to repel moths. **2.** **mothballs** Protective storage: *put the battleship into mothballs.*

moth·er (mŭ*th*′ər) ►*n.* **1.** A female parent. **2.** A woman having some of the authority or responsibility of a mother: *a den mother.* **3.** A creative source; origin: *Philosophy is the mother of the sciences.* ►*adj.* **1.** Being a mother: *a mother hen.* **2.** Characteristic of a mother: *mother love.* **3.** Native: *one's mother language.* ►*v.* **1.** To give birth to; create and produce. **2.** To watch over, nourish, and protect; care for. [< OE *mōdor.*] —**moth′er·hood′** *n.* —**moth′er·less** *adj.* —**moth′er·li·ness** *n.* —**moth′er·ly** *adj.*

moth·er·board (mŭ*th*′ər-bôrd′) ►*n.* The main printed circuit board in a complex electronic device, usu. containing the central processing unit, the main system memory, and other components essential to the device's operation.

moth·er-in-law (mŭ*th*′ər-ĭn-lô′) ►*n., pl.* **moth·ers-in-law** (-ərz-) The mother of one's spouse.

moth·er·land (mŭ*th*′ər-lănd′) ►*n.* **1.** One's native land. **2.** The land of one's ancestors.

moth·er-of-pearl (mŭ*th*′ər-əv-pûrl′) ►*n.* The pearly internal layer of certain mollusk shells, used to make decorative objects.

mother superior ►*n., pl.* **mothers superior** or **mother superiors** A woman in charge of a religious community of women.

mo·tif (mō-tēf′) ►*n.* A recurrent thematic element in a musical, artistic, or literary work. See Synonyms at **figure**. [< OFr., MOTIVE.]

mo·tile (mōt′l, mō′tīl′) ►*adj. Biol.* Moving or having the power to move spontaneously. [Lat. *movēre, mōt-*, move + –ILE.] —**mo·til′i·ty** (mō-tĭl′ĭ-tē) *n.*

mo·tion (mō′shən) ►*n.* **1.** The act or process of changing position or place. **2.** A meaningful or expressive change in the position of a part of the body; gesture. **3.** A formal proposal put to the vote under parliamentary procedures. ►*v.* To signal to or direct by making a gesture. [< Lat. *movēre, mōt-*, move.] —**mo′tion·less** *adj.* —**mo′tion·less·ly** *adv.*

motion picture ►*n.* **1.** A movie. **2. motion pictures** The movie industry.

motion sickness ►*n.* Nausea and dizziness caused by motion, as in travel by aircraft, car, or ship.

mo·ti·vate (mō′tə-vāt′) ►*v.* **-vat·ed, -vat·ing** To provide with an incentive; move to action; impel. —**mo′ti·va′tion** *n.* —**mo′ti·va′tion·al** *adj.* —**mo′ti·va′tor** *n.*

mo·tive (mō′tĭv) ►*n.* An emotion, desire, need, or similar impulse that causes one to act in a particular way. ►*adj.* Causing or able to cause motion. [< LLat. *mōtīvus*, of motion < Lat. *movēre*, move.]

mot·ley (mŏt′lē) ►*adj.* **1.** Having elements of great variety; heterogenous; varied. **2.** Multicolored. [ME *motlei.*]

mo·to·cross (mō′tō-krôs′, -krŏs′) ►*n.* A cross-country motorcycle race. [Fr. *moto-cross* : moto, motorcycle + CROSS(-COUNTRY).]

mo·tor (mō′tər) ►*n.* **1.** Something that produces or imparts motion. **2.** A device that converts any form of energy into mechanical energy, esp. an internal-combustion engine or a device that converts electric current into mechanical power. ►*adj.* **1.** Causing or producing motion. **2.** Driven by or having a motor. **3.** Of or for motors or motor vehicles: *motor oil.* **4.** Relating to movements of the muscles. ►*v.* To travel in a motor vehicle. [< Lat. *mōtor.*]

—**mo′tor·i·za′tion** *n.* —**mo′tor·ize′** *v.*

mo·tor·bike (mō′tər-bīk′) ►*n.* A motorcycle.

mo·tor·boat (mō′tər-bōt′) ►*n.* A boat propelled by an internal-combustion engine.

mo·tor·cade (mō′tər-kād′) ►*n.* A procession of motor vehicles. [< CAVALCADE.]

mo·tor·car (mō′tər-kär′) ►*n.* An automobile.

mo·tor·cy·cle (mō′tər-sī′kəl) ►*n.* A two-wheeled vehicle resembling a heavy bicycle, propelled by a gasoline engine. —**mo′tor·cy′cle** *v.* —**mo′tor·cy′clist** *n.*

motor home ►*n.* A large motor vehicle having self-contained living quarters, used for recreational travel.

motor inn ►*n.* An urban motel usu. having several stories and a guest parking lot.

mo·tor·ist (mō′tər-ĭst) ►*n.* One who drives or rides in an automobile.

motor lodge ►*n.* See **motel**.

mo·tor·man (mō′tər-mən) ►*n.* One who drives a streetcar or subway train.

motor scooter ►*n.* A small two-wheeled vehicle with a low-powered gasoline engine.

motor vehicle ►*n.* A self-propelled wheeled vehicle that does not run on rails.

Mott (mŏt), **Lucretia Coffin** 1793–1880. Amer. feminist and social reformer.

mot·tle (mŏt′l) ►*v.* **-tled, -tling** To mark with spots or blotches of different shades or colors. [Prob. < MOTLEY.]

mot·to (mŏt′ō) ►*n., pl.* **-toes** or **-tos** A brief statement used to express a principle, goal, or ideal. [Ital. < VLat. **mōttum*, utterance.]

moue (mōō) ►*n.* A grimace; pout. [Fr.]

mould (mōld) ►*n. & v. Chiefly Brit.* Var. of **mold**.

mound (mound) ►*n.* **1.** A raised mass, as of earth, sand, or rocks. **2.** A natural elevation, such as a small hill. **3.** A pile; heap. See Synonyms at **heap**. **4.** *Archaeol.* A large artificial pile of earth or stones often marking a burial site. **5.** *Baseball* The slightly elevated pitcher's area in the center of the diamond. [?] —**mound** *v.*

Mound Builder ►*n.* **1.** A Native American culture flourishing from the 5th cent. BC to the 16th cent. AD esp. in the Ohio and Mississippi Valleys, known for its large burial and effigy mounds. **2.** A member of a people associated with this culture.

mount¹ (mount) ►*v.* **1.** To climb or ascend. **2.** To get up on: *mount a horse.* **3.** To increase in amount, extent, or intensity. **4a.** To fix securely to a support: *mount an engine in a car.* **b.** To place or fix in an appropriate setting for display, study, or use. **5.** To prepare and set in motion. **6.** To set (guns) in position. ►*n.* **1.** A horse or other animal on which to ride. **2.** An object to which another is affixed for accessibility, display, or use. [< VLat. **montāre* < Lat. *mōns, mont-*, hill.] —**mount′a·ble** *adj.*

mount² (mount) ►*n.* A mountain or hill: *Mount Everest.* [< Lat. *mōns, mont-.*]

moun·tain (moun′tən) ►*n.* A natural elevation of the earth's surface greater in height than a hill. [< VLat. **montānea.*]

mountain ash ►*n.* Any of various deciduous trees having clusters of small white flowers and bright orange-red berries.

mountain bike ►*n.* A sturdy bicycle designed for use on hills and rough surfaces and usu.

equipped with knobby tires and shock absorbers. —**mountain biking** *n.*

mountain bike

moun·tain·eer (moun′tə-nîr′) ►*n.* **1.** An inhabitant of a mountainous area. **2.** One who climbs mountains for sport. ►*v.* To climb mountains for sport.

mountain goat ►*n.* A goat antelope of the N Rocky Mountains, having curved black horns and a yellowish-white coat and beard.

mountain laurel ►*n.* An evergreen shrub of E North America, having glossy leaves and clusters of pink or white flowers.

mountain lion ►*n.* See **cougar.**

moun·tain·ous (moun′tə-nəs) ►*adj.* **1.** Having many mountains. **2.** Massive; huge.

mountain range ►*n.* A series of mountain ridges alike in form, direction, and origin.

moun·tain·side (moun′tən-sīd′) ►*n.* The sloping side of a mountain.

moun·tain·top (moun′tən-tŏp′) ►*n.* The summit of a mountain.

moun·te·bank (moun′tə-băngk′) ►*n.* **1.** A peddler of quack medicines. **2.** A flamboyant charlatan. [< Ital. *monta im banco,* he gets up onto the bench.]

Mount·ie also **Mount·y** (moun′tē) ►*n., pl.* **-ies** *Informal* A member of the Royal Canadian Mounted Police.

mount·ing (moun′tĭng) ►*n.* A supporting structure or frame: *a mounting for a gem.*

mourn (môrn) ►*v.* To feel or express grief or sorrow (for). See Synonyms at **grieve.** [< OE *murnan.*] —**mourn′er** *n.*

mourn·ful (môrn′fəl) ►*adj.* **1.** Feeling or expressing grief. **2.** Causing or suggesting sadness. —**mourn′ful·ly** *adv.* —**mourn′ful·ness** *n.*

mourn·ing (môr′nĭng) ►*n.* **1.** Expression of grief. **2.** Outward signs of grief for the dead, such as wearing black clothes. **3.** The period during which a death is mourned.

mourning dove ►*n.* A wild dove of North and Central America, noted for its mournful call.

mouse (mous) ►*n., pl.* **mice** (mīs) **1.** Any of numerous small, usu. long-tailed rodents, having a pointed snout and rounded ears. **2.** A handheld, button-activated input device that controls the movement of an indicator on a computer screen. ►*v.* (mouz) **moused, mous·ing** To hunt or catch mice. [< OE *mūs.*] —**mous′er** (mou′zər, -sər) *n.*

mouse·pad (mous′păd′) ►*n. Comp.* A flat pad that provides a surface on which to use a mouse.

mouse·trap (mous′trăp′) ►*n.* A trap for catching mice.

mous·sa·ka (mōō-sä′kə, mōō′sä-kä′) ►*n.* A Greek baked dish of ground meat, sliced eggplant, and cheese. [< Ar. dial. *musaqqa′a.*]

mousse (mōōs) ►*n.* **1.** A chilled dessert made with whipped cream, gelatin, eggs, and flavoring. **2.** A foam for styling the hair. [< OFr., foam.]

mous·tache (mŭs′tăsh′, mə-stăsh′) ►*n.* Var. of **mustache.**

mous·y (mou′sē, -zē) ►*adj.* **-i·er, -i·est 1.** Of a drab, mouselike color. **2.** Timid or shy. —**mous′i·ness** *n.*

mouth (mouth) ►*n., pl.* **mouths** (mou*th*z) **1.** The body opening and related organs through which food is taken in, chewed, and swallowed and sounds and speech are articulated. **2.** A natural opening, as the part of a river that empties into a larger body of water or the entrance to a harbor, valley, or cave. **3.** The opening by which a container is filled or emptied. ►*v.* (mou*th*) **1.** To declare in a pompous manner; declaim. **2.** To put, take, or move around in the mouth. —***phrasal verb:*** **mouth off** *Slang* To criticize, brag, or talk back loudly. [< OE *mūth.*] —**mouth′ful′** *n.*

mouth organ ►*n.* See **harmonica.**

mouth·part (mouth′pärt′) ►*n.* Any of the parts of the mouth of an insect or other arthropod.

mouth·piece (mouth′pēs′) ►*n.* **1.** A part, as of a musical instrument, used in or near the mouth. **2.** A protective device worn over the teeth by athletes. **3.** A spokesperson.

mouth-to-mouth resuscitation ►*n.* A technique of artificial resuscitation in which the rescuer's mouth is placed over the victim's and air is forced into the victim's lungs.

mouth·wash (mouth′wŏsh′, -wôsh′) ►*n.* A flavored, usu. antiseptic solution used for cleaning the mouth and freshening the breath.

mouth·wa·ter·ing (mouth′wô′tər-ĭng) ►*adj.* Appealing to the sense of taste; appetizing.

mouth·y (mou′*th*ē, -thē) ►*adj.* **-i·er, -i·est** Annoyingly talkative; bombastic. —**mouth′i·ness** *n.*

mov·a·ble also **move·a·ble** (mōō′və-bəl) ►*adj.* **1.** Possible to move: *a movable rock.* **2.** *Law* Of or relating to personal property (that is, property that can be moved). —**mov′a·bil′i·ty** *n.* —**mov′a·ble** *adj.* —**mov′a·bly** *adv.*

move (mōōv) ►*v.* **moved, mov·ing 1a.** To change in position from one point to another. **b.** To transfer (a piece) in a board game. **c.** To go from one residence or location to another. **2.** To be disposed of by sale: *Coats move slowly in the summer.* **3.** To take action; act. **4.** To stir the emotions (of). **5.** To make a formal motion in parliamentary procedure. **6.** To evacuate (the bowels). ►*n.* **1.** The act of moving. **2.** A change of residence or location. **3a.** The act of transferring a piece in board games. **b.** A participant's turn to make a play. **4.** A calculated action taken to achieve an end. —***idioms:*** **get a move on** To get going. **move in on** To attempt to seize control of. **on the move** Busily moving about or progressing. [< Lat. *movēre*.]

move·ment (mōōv′mənt) ►*n*. **1.** The act of moving or a change in position. **2.** A change in the location of troops, ships, or aircraft for strategic purposes. **3.** A large-scale organized effort: *the labor movement.* **4.** An evacuation of the bowels. **5.** *Mus.* A self-contained section of an extended composition. **6.** A mechanism, such as the works of a watch, that produces or transmits motion.

mov·er (mōō′vər) ►*n*. **1.** One that moves. **2.** One that transports furnishings as an occupation.

mov·ie (mōō′vē) ►*n*. **1a.** A sequence of filmed images projected onto a screen in rapid succession to create the illusion of motion and continuity. **b.** Any work, as of art or entertainment, having this form. **2. movies** The movie industry. [< MOVING PICTURE.]

mov·ing (mōō′vĭng) ►*adj*. **1.** Of or causing motion or transfer. **2.** Arousing deep emotion. —**mov′ing·ly** *adv.*

moving picture ►*n*. A movie.

mow[1] (mou) ►*n*. A place, usu. a barn, where hay or grain is stored. [< OE *mūga*.]

mow[2] (mō) ►*v*. **mowed, mowed** or **mown** (mōn), **mow·ing 1.** To cut down (grass or grain) with a scythe or machine. **2.** To cut (grass or grain) from. —*phrasal verb:* **mow down** To destroy in great numbers, as in battle. [< OE *māwan*.] —**mow′er** *n*.

mox·ie (mŏk′sē) ►*n*. *Slang* Courage in adversity. [< *Moxie*, a trademark for a soft drink.]

Mo·zam·bique (mō′zəm-bēk′, -zăm-) A country of SE Africa. Cap. Maputo. —**Mo′zam·bi′can** (-bē′kən) *adj. & n.*

Mozambique Channel An arm of the Indian Ocean between Madagascar and SE Africa.

Mo·zart (mōt′särt), **Wolfgang Amadeus** 1756–91. Austrian composer.

moz·za·rel·la (mŏt′sə-rĕl′ə, mōt′-) ►*n*. A mild white Italian cheese, often melted, as on pizza. [Ital. < *mozzare*, slice off.]

MP ►*abbr*. **1.** member of Parliament **2.** military police **3.** mounted police

MP3 (ĕm′pē-thrē′) ►*n*. **1.** An MPEG standard used esp. for digitally transmitting music over the Internet. **2.** An audio file with data encoded using this standard. [< MP(EG-1 layer) 3.]

MPEG (ĕm′pĕg′) ►*n*. **1.** A set of standards for the compression of digital video and audio data. **2.** A data file that has been so compressed. [*m(oving) p(ictures) e(xperts) g(roup).*]

mpg ►*abbr*. miles per gallon

mph ►*abbr*. miles per hour

Mr. (mĭs′tər) ►*n., pl.* **Messrs.** (mĕs′ərz) Used as a courtesy title before the surname or full name of a man. [< MASTER.]

MRE ►*abbr*. meal ready to eat

MRI ►*abbr*. magnetic resonance imaging

Mrs. (mĭs′ĭz) ►*n., pl.* **Mmes.** (mā-däm′, -dăm′) Used as a courtesy title for a married or widowed woman. [< MISTRESS.]

ms ►*abbr*. **1.** or **ms.** manuscript **2.** millisecond

MS ►*abbr*. **1.** *Lat.* Magister Scientiae (Master of Science) **2.** Mississippi **3.** multiple sclerosis

Ms. also **Ms** (mĭz) ►*n., pl.* **Mses.** also **Mss.** (mĭz′ĭz) Used as a courtesy title for a woman or girl. [Blend of *Miss*, form of address, and MRS.]

MSG ►*abbr*. **1.** master sergeant **2.** monosodium glutamate

Msgr. ►*abbr*. Monsignor

MSGT or **MSgt** ►*abbr*. master sergeant

MST ►*abbr*. Mountain Standard Time

Mt The symbol for **meitnerium.**

MT ►*abbr*. **1.** megaton **2.** metric ton **3.** Montana **4.** Mountain Time

Mt. ►*abbr*. **1.** mount **2.** mountain

Mts. ►*abbr*. mountains

mu (myōō, mōō) ►*n*. The 12th letter of the Greek alphabet. [Gk.]

Mu·bar·ak (mōō-bär′ək), **(Muhammad) Hosni Said** b. 1928. Egyptian military leader and politician.

much (mŭch) ►*adj*. **more** (môr, mōr), **most** (mōst) Great in quantity, degree, or extent: *not much rain.* ►*n*. **1.** A large quantity or amount. **2.** Something great or remarkable: *I've never been much to look at.* ►*adv*. **more, most 1.** To a great degree or extent: *much smarter.* **2.** Just about; almost: *much the same.* [< OE *mycel.*]

mu·ci·lage (myōō′sə-lĭj) ►*n*. A sticky substance used as an adhesive. [< Lat. *mūcus*, mucus.] —**mu′ci·lag′i·nous** (-lăj′ə-nəs) *adj.*

muck (mŭk) ►*n*. **1.** A moist sticky mixture, esp. of mud and filth. **2.** Moist farmyard dung. **3.** Dark fertile soil that is rich in humus. ►*v*. To soil or make dirty with or as if with muck. —*phrasal verb:* **muck up** *Informal* To botch. [ME *muk*, of Scand. orig.] —**muck′y** *adj.*

muck·rake (mŭk′rāk′) ►*v*. **-raked, -rak·ing** To search for and expose misconduct in public life. —**muck′rak′er** *n*.

mu·co·sa (myōō-kō′sə) ►*n., pl.* **-sae** (-sē) or **-sas** See **mucous membrane.** [< Lat. *mūcōsus*, mucous.]

mu·cous (myōō′kəs) ►*adj*. Containing or secreting mucus. [< Lat. *mūcōsus.*]

mucous membrane ►*n*. A membrane lining all body passages that communicate with the air, the glands of which secrete mucus.

mu·cus (myōō′kəs) ►*n*. The viscous substance secreted as a protective lubricant coating by glands of the mucous membranes. [Lat. *mūcus.*]

mud (mŭd) ►*n*. **1.** Wet, sticky, soft earth. **2.** Slanderous or defamatory charges. [ME *mudde.*] —**mud′di·ly** *adv*. —**mud′di·ness** *n*. —**mud′dy** *adj. & v.*

mud·dle (mŭd′l) ►*v*. **-dled, -dling 1.** To mix confusedly; jumble. **2.** To confuse or befuddle (a person or the mind, e.g.). See Synonyms at **befuddle. 3.** To mix (a drink or the ingredients of a drink), esp. with a muddler. **4.** To botch; bungle. **5.** To make turbid or muddy. ►*n*. A mess or jumble. —*phrasal verb:* **muddle through** To persist successfully in a disorganized way. [Poss. < MDu. *moddelen.*]

mud·dler (mŭd′lər) ►*n*. **1.** A small pestlelike baton used to prepare mixed drinks. **2.** One who muddles.

mud·guard (mŭd′gärd′) ►*n*. A shield over or behind a vehicle's wheel.

mud·sling·er (mŭd′slĭng′ər) ►*n*. One who makes malicious charges in hopes of discrediting an opponent. —**mud′sling′ing** *n*.

mues·li (myōōz′lē) ►*n*. A mixture of rolled oats, nuts, and dried fruit, often used as a breakfast cereal. [Ger. dialectal, dim. of Ger. *Mus*, mash.]

mu·ez·zin (myōō-ĕz′ĭn, mōō-) ►*n*. *Islam* The

crier who calls the faithful to prayer five times a day. [< Ar. *mu'aḏḏin*.]

muff¹ (mŭf) ►*v.* To perform clumsily; bungle. See Synonyms at **botch.** [?] —**muff** *n.*

muff² (mŭf) ►*n.* A small, cylindrical, usu. fur cover, open at both ends, used to keep the hands warm. [< Med.Lat. *muffula.*]

muf·fin (mŭf′ĭn) ►*n.* A small, cup-shaped bread, often sweetened. [Poss. < LGer. *Muffen,* cakes.]

muf·fle (mŭf′əl) ►*v.* **-fled, -fling 1.** To wrap up snugly for warmth, protection, or secrecy. **2.** To wrap or pad in order to deaden a sound. **3.** To deaden (a sound). **4.** To suppress; stifle: *muffle political opposition.* [ME *muflen,* poss. < OFr. *mofle,* MUFF².]

muf·fler (mŭf′lər) ►*n.* **1.** A heavy scarf worn around the neck for warmth. **2.** A device that absorbs noise, esp. one used with an internal-combustion engine.

muf·ti¹ (mŭf′tē, mōōf′-) ►*n.* A Muslim scholar who interprets the Islamic system of law. [Ar. *muftī,* one who gives legal opinions.]

muf·ti² (mŭf′tē) ►*n.* Civilian dress, esp. when worn by one usu. in uniform. [Prob. < Ar. *muftī,* judge.]

mug¹ (mŭg) ►*n.* A heavy cylindrical drinking cup usu. having a handle. [Perh. of Scand. orig.]

mug² (mŭg) ►*n.* **1.** *Informal* **a.** The human face. **b.** A grimace. **2.** A hoodlum. ►*v.* **mugged, mug·ging 1.** *Informal* To take a photograph of for police files. **2.** To threaten and assault with intent to rob. **3.** To grimace, esp. for humorous effect. [Prob. < MUG¹.] —**mug′ger** *n.*

Mu·ga·be (mōō-gä′bē), **Robert Gabriel** b. 1924. Zimbabwean political leader.

mug·gy (mŭg′ē) ►*adj.* **-gi·er, -gi·est** Warm and extremely humid. [Prob. < ME *mugen,* to drizzle.] —**mug′gi·ness** *n.*

Mu·ghal (mōō-gŭl′) or **Mo·gul** (mō′gəl, mō-gŭl′) ►*n.* **1.** A member of the force that invaded India in 1526. **2.** A member of the Muslim dynasty that ruled India until 1857. [Urdu *mugal* < Pers. *mugul* < Mongolian *moṅgol,* Mongol.] —**Mu·ghal′** *adj.*

mug shot ►*n. Informal* A photograph of a person's face, esp. for police files.

Mu·ham·mad (mōō-hăm′ĭd, -hä′mĭd) also **Mo·ham·med** (mō-, mōō-) 570?–632. Arab prophet of Islam.

Mu·ham·mad·an (mōō-hăm′ĭ-dən) ►*adj.* **1.** Relating to Muhammad. **2.** *Offensive* Relating to Islam; Muslim. ►*n. Offensive* A Muslim.

Mu·ham·mad·an·ism (mōō-hăm′ĭ-də-nĭz′əm) ►*n. Offensive* Islam.

Mu·har·ram (mōō-hăr′əm) ►*n.* The 1st month of the Islamic calendar. See table at **calendar.** [Ar. *Muḥarram.*]

Muir (myōōr), **John** 1838–1914. Scottish-born Amer. naturalist.

mu·ja·hid (mōō-jä′hĭd′) ►*n., pl.* **mu·ja·hi·deen** or **mu·ja·hi·din** (mōō-jä′hĕ-dēn′) One engaged in a jihad, esp. as a guerrilla warrior. [< Ar. *mujāhid.*]

muk·luk (mŭk′lŭk′) ►*n.* **1.** A soft Eskimo boot made of reindeer skin or sealskin. **2.** A slipper similar to a mukluk. [Yupik *maklak,* bearded seal (species of seal from whose skin mukluks are made).]

mu·lat·to (mōō-lăt′ō, -lä′tō, myōō-) ►*n., pl.* **-tos** or **-toes** *Often Offensive* A person of mixed

white and black ancestry, esp. one having one white and one black parent. [Sp. *mulato,* person of mixed race.]

mul·ber·ry (mŭl′bĕr′ē, -bə-rē) ►*n.* **1.** A tree bearing sweet reddish or purplish berrylike fruit. **2.** The fruit itself. [< OE *mōrberie.*]

mulch (mŭlch) ►*n.* A protective covering, as of leaves or hay, placed around plants to prevent evaporation of moisture, freezing of roots, and growth of weeds. ►*v.* To cover with mulch. [Prob. < ME *melsh,* soft.]

mulct (mŭlkt) ►*n.* A penalty such as a fine. ►*v.* **1.** To penalize by fining. **2.** To take something from (another) by means of unseemly or deceptive methods. [< Lat. *mulcta.*]

mule¹ (myōōl) ►*n.* **1.** The sterile hybrid offspring of a male donkey and female horse. **2.** *Informal* A stubborn person. [< Lat. *mūlus.*] —**mul′ish** *adj.* —**mul′ish·ly** *adv.* —**mul′ish·ness** *n.*

mule² (myōōl) ►*n.* A backless slipper or shoe, often with a closed toe. [Ult. < Lat. *mulleus (calceus),* reddish-purple (shoe).]

mule deer ►*n.* A long-eared deer of W North America, having a black-tipped tail.

mule·skin·ner (myōōl′skĭn′ər) ►*n. Informal* A driver of mules.

mu·le·teer (myōō′lə-tîr′) ►*n.* A driver of mules. [< OFr. *mulet,* mule.]

mull¹ (mŭl) ►*v.* To heat and spice (e.g., wine). [?]

mull² (mŭl) ►*v.* To ponder or ruminate: *mull over a plan.* [?]

mul·lah also **mul·la** (mŭl′ə, mōōl′ə) ►*n. Islam* A religious teacher or leader, esp. in Shiite practice. [< Ar. *mawlā,* master.]

mul·lein (mŭl′ən) ►*n.* Any of various tall plants having closely clustered yellow flowers and downy leaves. [< AN *moleine.*]

mul·let (mŭl′ĭt) ►*n., pl.* **-let** or **-lets 1.** Any of various stout-bodied, edible fishes that are widely cultivated for food. **2.** A hairstyle formed by cutting hair short on the top and sides of the head and allowing it to grow longer in back. [Ult. < Gk. *mullos.*]

mul·li·ga·taw·ny (mŭl′ĭ-gə-tô′nē) ►*n., pl.* **-nies** A South Asian soup made with meat or chicken and curry. [Tamil *miḷagutaṇṇī.*]

mul·lion (mŭl′yən) ►*n.* A vertical strip, as of wood or stone, dividing the panes of a window. [< AN *moynel,* perh. < Lat. *mediānus,* middle.] —**mul′lioned** *adj.*

mullion
mullioned windows

multi– ►*pref.* **1.** Many; much; multiple: *multicolored.* **2a.** More than one: *multiparous.* **b.**

More than two: *multilateral.* [< Lat. *multus,* much, many.]

mul·ti·cel·lu·lar (mŭl′tē-sĕl′yə-lər, -tĭ-) ►*adj.* Having many cells. —**mul′ti·cel′lu·lar′i·ty** (-lăr′ĭ-tē) *n.*

mul·ti·col·ored (mŭl′tĭ-kŭl′ərd) also **mul·ti·col·or** (-kŭl′ər) ►*adj.* Having many colors.

mul·ti·cul·tur·al (mŭl′tē-kŭl′chər-əl, -tĭ-) ►*adj.* Of or including several cultures or ethnic groups.

mul·ti·cul·tur·al·ism (mŭl′tē-kŭl′chər-ə-lĭz′-əm, -tĭ-) ►*n.* The belief that a society should respect and promote all the various cultures or ethnic groups of which it is composed.

mul·ti·di·men·sion·al (mŭl′tĭ-dĭ-mĕn′shə-nəl) ►*adj.* Having several dimensions. —**mul′ti·di·men′sion·al′i·ty** (-shə-năl′ĭ-tē) *n.*

mul·ti·di·rec·tion·al (mŭl′tē-dĭ-rĕk′shə-nəl, -dī-, -tĭ-) ►*adj.* Reaching out or operating in several directions.

mul·ti·dis·ci·pli·nar·y (mŭl′tē-dĭs′ə-plə-nĕr′ē, -tĭ-) ►*adj.* Involving or making use of several academic disciplines at once.

mul·ti·eth·nic (mŭl′tē-ĕth′nĭk, -tĭ-) ►*adj.* Of or including a variety of ethnic groups.

mul·ti·fac·et·ed (mŭl′tē-făs′ĭ-tĭd, -tĭ-) ►*adj.* Having many facets or aspects: *a multifaceted approach to solving the problem.*

mul·ti·fam·i·ly (mŭl′tē-făm′ə-lē, -tĭ-) ►*adj.* Of or intended for use by several families.

mul·ti·far·i·ous (mŭl′tə-fâr′ē-əs) ►*adj.* Having great variety: *a job with multifarious duties.* [< LLat. *multifārius.*] —**mul′ti·far′i·ous·ly** *adv.*

mul·ti·form (mŭl′tə-fôrm′) ►*adj.* Occurring in or having many forms or shapes. —**mul′ti·for′mi·ty** *n.*

mul·ti·lat·er·al (mŭl′tĭ-lăt′ər-əl) ►*adj.* **1.** Having many sides. **2.** Involving more than two nations or parties. —**mul′ti·lat′er·al·ly** *adv.*

mul·ti·lay·ered (mŭl′tē-lā′ərd, -tĭ-) ►*adj.* Consisting of several layers or levels.

mul·ti·lev·el (mŭl′tə-lĕv′əl) ►*adj.* Having several levels: *a multilevel parking garage.*

mul·ti·lin·gual (mŭl′tē-lĭng′gwəl, -tĭ-) ►*adj.* **1.** Of, including, or expressed in several languages. **2.** Fluent in several languages.

mul·ti·me·di·a (mŭl′tē-mē′dē-ə, -tĭ-) ►*pl.n.* (takes sing. v.) The combined use of media, such as movies and the Internet, as for education or entertainment. ►*adj.* **1.** Relating to the combined use of media. **2.** *Comp.* Relating to an application that integrates different media, such as text, graphics, video, and sound.

mul·ti·mil·lion·aire (mŭl′tē-mĭl′yə-nâr′, -tĭ-) ►*n.* One whose financial assets equal at least two million dollars.

mul·ti·na·tion·al (mŭl′tē-năsh′ə-nəl, -năsh′-nəl, -tĭ-) ►*adj.* **1.** Having operations, subsidiaries, or investments in more than two countries. **2.** Of or involving more than two countries. ►*n.* A company or corporation operating in more than two countries.

mul·tip·a·rous (mŭl-tĭp′ər-əs) ►*adj.* **1.** Having given birth two or more times. **2.** Giving birth to more than one offspring at a time.

mul·ti·ple (mŭl′tə-pəl) ►*adj.* Of, having, or consisting of more than one individual, element, or part. ►*n. Math.* A number into which another number may be divided with no remainder. [< Lat. *multipulus.*]

mul·ti·ple-choice (mŭl′tə-pəl-chois′) ►*adj.* Offering several answers from which the correct one is to be chosen.

multiple fruit ►*n.* A fruit, such as a fig or pineapple, derived from the ovaries of several flowers that are combined into one structure.

multiple personality disorder ►*n.* A psychiatric disorder in which two or more distinct personalities exist in the same person, each of which prevails at a particular time.

multiple sclerosis ►*n.* An autoimmune disease of the central nervous system in which destruction of myelin causes weakness, loss of coordination, and speech and visual disturbances.

multiple star ►*n.* A system of three or more stars orbiting around a common mass that appear as one to the naked eye.

mul·ti·plex (mŭl′tə-plĕks′) ►*adj.* **1.** Multiple; manifold. **2.** Of or being a system of simultaneous communication of two or more messages on the same wire or radio channel. ►*n.* A movie theater or dwelling with multiple separate units. [Lat.] —**mul′ti·plex′** *v.*

mul·ti·pli·cand (mŭl′tə-plĭ-kănd′) ►*n.* A number to be multiplied by another. [Lat. *multiplicandum,* thing to be multiplied.]

mul·ti·pli·ca·tion (mŭl′tə-plĭ-kā′shən) ►*n.* **1.** The act of multiplying or the condition of being multiplied. **2.** The reproduction of plants and animals. **3.** *Math.* The operation of adding a number to itself a certain number of times. —**mul′ti·pli′ca·tive** *adj.*

multiplication sign ►*n.* The sign used to indicate multiplication, either a times sign (×) or a centered dot (·).

mul·ti·plic·i·ty (mŭl′tə-plĭs′ĭ-tē) ►*n., pl.* **-ties** **1.** The state of being various or multiple. **2.** A large number. [< LLat. *multiplicitās.*]

mul·ti·pli·er (mŭl′tə-plī′ər) ►*n.* The number by which another number is multiplied.

mul·ti·ply (mŭl′tə-plī′) ►*v.* **-plied, -ply·ing 1.** To increase in amount, number, or degree. **2.** *Math.* To perform multiplication (on). **3.** To breed; reproduce. [< Lat. *multiplicāre.*]

mul·ti·pur·pose (mŭl′tē-pûr′pəs, -tĭ-) ►*adj.* Designed or used for several purposes.

mul·ti·ra·cial (mŭl′tē-rā′shəl, -tĭ-) ►*adj.* **1.** Made up of, involving, or acting on behalf of various races: *a multiracial society.* **2.** Having ancestors of several or various races.

mul·ti·stage (mŭl′tĭ-stāj′) ►*adj.* Functioning by stages: *a multistage rocket.*

mul·ti·sto·ry (mŭl′tĭ-stôr′ē) ►*adj.* Having several stories: *a multistory hotel.*

mul·ti·task·ing (mŭl′tē-tăs′kĭng, -tĭ-) ►*n.* **1.** The concurrent operation by one central processing unit of two or more processes. **2.** Engagement in more than one activity at the same time or serially. —**mul′ti·task′** *v.*

mul·ti·tude (mŭl′tĭ-tōōd′, -tyōōd′) ►*n.* A very great number. [< Lat. *multitūdō < multus,* many.] —**mul′ti·tu′di·nous** *adj.* —**mul′ti·tu′di·nous·ly** *adv.*

mul·ti·va·lent (mŭl′tĭ-vā′lənt, mŭl-tĭv′ə-lənt) ►*adj.* Polyvalent. —**mul′ti·va′lence** *n.*

mul·ti·vi·ta·min (mŭl′tə-vī′tə-mĭn) ►*adj.* Containing many vitamins. ►*n.* A preparation containing many vitamins.

mum[1] (mŭm) ►*adj.* Not talking. [ME.]

mum[2] (mŭm) ►*n.* A chrysanthemum.

Mum·bai (mŭm′bī′) A city of W-central India, formerly known as Bombay.

mum·ble (mŭm′bəl) ►*v.* **-bled, -bling** To speak or utter indistinctly by lowering the voice or partially closing the mouth. [< MDu. *mommelen.*] —**mum′ble** *n.* —**mum′bler** *n.* —**mum′bly** *adj.*

mum·bo jum·bo (mŭm′bō jŭm′bō) ►*n.* **1.** Unintelligible or incomprehensible language; gibberish. **2.** An obscure ritual or incantation. [Prob. < Mandinka (Mande language of West Africa) *maamajomboo,* masked dancer with prophetic powers.]

mum·mer (mŭm′ər) ►*n.* One who acts or plays in a mask or costume. [< OFr. *momer,* to pantomime.] —**mum′mer·y** *n.*

mum·my (mŭm′ē) ►*n., pl.* **-mies** A body embalmed after death, as by the ancient Egyptians. [< Ar. *mūmiyā',* medicinal resin from mummies.] —**mum′mi·fi·ca′tion** *n.* —**mum′mi·fy** *v.*

mumps (mŭmps) ►*pl.n.* *(takes sing. or pl. v.)* A contagious viral disease marked by painful swelling esp. of the salivary glands and sometimes of the ovaries or testes. [< dial. *mump,* grimace.]

munch (mŭnch) ►*v.* To chew (food) noisily or with pleasure. [ME *monchen.*]

Munch (mŏŏngk), **Edvard** 1863–1944. Norwegian artist.

mun·dane (mŭn-dān′, mŭn′dān′) ►*adj.* **1.** Of this world; worldly. **2.** Of or concerned with the ordinary. [< LLat. *mundānus* < *mundus,* world.] —**mun·dane′ly** *adv.*

mung bean (mŭng) ►*n.* An Asian plant cultivated for its edible seeds and pods and the chief source of bean sprouts. [< Skt. *mudgaḥ.*]

Mu·nich (myŏŏ′nĭk) A city of SE Germany SE of Frankfurt.

mu·nic·i·pal (myŏŏ-nĭs′ə-pəl) ►*adj.* **1.** Of or typical of a municipality. **2.** Having local self-government. [< Lat. *mūnicipium,* town.] —**mu·nic′i·pal·ly** *adv.*

mu·nic·i·pal·i·ty (myŏŏ-nĭs′ə-păl′ĭ-tē) ►*n., pl.* **-ties** A political unit, such as a city or town, that is incorporated for local self-government.

mu·nif·i·cent (myŏŏ-nĭf′ĭ-sənt) ►*adj.* Extremely liberal in giving; very generous. See Synonyms at **liberal.** [Lat. *mūnificēns* < *mūnus,* gift.] —**mu·nif′i·cence** *n.* —**mu·nif′i·cent·ly** *adv.*

mu·ni·tions (myŏŏ-nĭsh′ənz) ►*pl.n.* War materiel. [< Lat. *mūnīre, mūnīt-,* defend.]

Mu·ñoz Ma·rín (mōō-nyōs′ mä-rēn′), **Luis** 1898–1980. Puerto Rican politician; the first elected governor of Puerto Rico (1949–65).

mu·on (myŏŏ′ŏn′) ►*n.* A negatively charged lepton having a mass 207 times that of an electron. [< earlier *mu meson* < *mu* (used as an abbreviation for the particle's orig. name, *mesotron*).]

mu·ral (myŏŏr′əl) ►*n.* A very large image painted on or applied directly to a wall or ceiling. [< Lat. *mūrus,* wall.] —**mu′ral·ist** *n.*

Mu·ra·sa·ki Shi·ki·bu (mōō′rä-sä′kē shē′kē-bōō′), Baroness. 978?–1031? Japanese writer.

mur·der (mûr′dər) ►*n.* The killing of another person without justification, esp. by an act that was premeditated, deliberate, or so reckless as to show indifference to the value of human life. ►*v.* **1.** To kill (another human) in an act of murder. **2.** To mar or spoil by ineptness: *murder the English language.* **3.** *Slang* To defeat decisively. [< OE *morthor.*] —**mur′der·er** *n.* —**mur′der·ess** *n.*

mur·der·ous (mûr′dər-əs) ►*adj.* **1.** Capable of, guilty of, or intending murder. **2.** Characteristic of murder; brutal. **3.** *Informal* Very difficult or dangerous: *a murderous exam.* —**mur′der·ous·ly** *adv.* —**mur′der·ous·ness** *n.*

mu·rex (myŏŏr′ĕks) ►*n., pl.* **mu·ri·ces** (myŏŏr′ĭ-sēz′) or **mu·rex·es** Any of various predatory marine gastropods having rough spiny shells. [< Lat. *mūrex,* mollusk yielding purple dye.]

murk (mûrk) ►*n.* Partial or total darkness; gloom. [< ON *myrkr* or OE *mirce.*] —**murk′i·ly** *adv.* —**murk′i·ness** *n.* —**murk′y** *adj.*

mur·mur (mûr′mər) ►*n.* **1.** A low, indistinct, continuous sound. **2.** A grumbled complaint. **3.** *Med.* An abnormal sound, usu. in the heart. [< Lat.] —**mur′mur** *v.* —**mur′mur·er** *n.* —**mur′mur·ous** *adj.*

mus·cat (mŭs′kăt′, -kət) ►*n.* A sweet red, white, or black grape used for making wine or raisins. [< LLat. *muscus,* MUSK.]

Muscat The capital of Oman, in the N on the Gulf of Oman.

mus·ca·tel (mŭs′kə-tĕl′) ►*n.* A rich sweet wine made chiefly from muscat grapes. [ME *muscadelle* < LLat. *muscus,* MUSK.]

mus·cle (mŭs′əl) ►*n.* **1.** A tissue composed of fibers capable of contracting and relaxing to effect bodily movement. **2.** A contractile organ consisting of muscle tissue. **3.** Muscular strength. **4.** *Informal* Power or authority. ►*v.* **-cled, -cling** *Informal* To force one's way. [< Lat. *mūsculus,* dim. of *mūs,* mouse.]

mus·cle·bound also **mus·cle-bound** (mŭs′-əl-bound′) ►*adj.* Having stiff, overdeveloped muscles, usu. from excessive exercise.

Mus·co·vite (mŭs′kə-vīt′) ►*adj.* A native or resident of Moscow or Muscovy. —**Mus′co·vite′** *adj.*

Mus·co·vy (mŭs′kə-vē) A former principality of W-central Russia centered on Moscow.

mus·cu·lar (mŭs′kyə-lər) ►*adj.* **1.** Of or consisting of muscle. **2.** Having well-developed muscles. [< Lat. *mūsculus,* MUSCLE.] —**mus′cu·lar′i·ty** (-lăr′ĭ-tē) *n.* —**mus′cu·lar·ly** *adv.*
Syns: *brawny, burly, sinewy* ***adj.***

muscular dystrophy ►*n.* Any of a group of inherited muscle disorders marked by progressive, irreversible destruction of skeletal muscle.

mus·cu·la·ture (mŭs′kyə-lə-chŏŏr′) ►*n.* The system of muscles in a body or a body part. [Fr. < Lat. *mūsculus,* MUSCLE.]

muse (myŏŏz) ►*v.* **mused, mus·ing** To consider or say thoughtfully. [< OFr. *muser.*] —**mus′er** *n.*

Muse ►*n.* **1.** *Gk. Myth.* Any of the nine daughters of Zeus, each of whom presided over a different art or science. **2. muse** A source of inspiration. [< Gk. *Mousa.*]

mu·se·um (myŏŏ-zē′əm) ►*n.* A place devoted to the acquisition, study, and exhibition of objects of scientific, historical, or artistic value. [< Gk. *Mouseion,* shrine of the Muses < *Mousa,* MUSE.]

mush¹ (mŭsh, mŏŏsh) ►*n.* **1.** Cornmeal boiled in water or milk. **2.** Something thick, soft, and pulpy. **3.** *Informal* Mawkish sentimentality. [Prob. alteration of MASH.]

mush² (mŭsh) ►*v.* To drive (a team of dogs) over snow. [Poss. < Fr. *marchons,* let's go.]

mush·room (mŭsh′rōōm′, -rŏōm′) ►*n.* Any of various fleshy fungi having an umbrella-shaped cap borne on a stalk. ►*v.* To grow or spread rapidly. [< Med.Lat. *musariō.*]
mush·y (mŭsh′ē, mŏōsh′ē) ►*adj.* -i·er, -i·est **1.** Thick, soft, and pulpy. **2.** Excessively tender or romantic. See Synonyms at sentimental. —mush′i·ness *n.*
mu·sic (myōō′zĭk) ►*n.* **1.** The art of arranging sounds in time to produce a composition that elicits an aesthetic response in a listener. **2.** Vocal or instrumental sounds having some degree of melody, harmony, or rhythm. **3.** A musical composition. **4.** Aesthetically pleasing or harmonious sound or combination of sounds. [< Gk. *(hē) mousikē (tekhnē)*, (the art) of the Muses < *Mousa*, MUSE.]
mu·si·cal (myōō′zĭ-kəl) ►*adj.* **1.** Of or producing music. **2.** Melodious. **3.** Set to or accompanied by music. **4.** Devoted to or skilled in music. ►*n.* A play or movie having musical numbers. —mu′si·cal·ly *adv.*
mu·si·cale (myōō′zĭ-kăl′) ►*n.* A program of music performed at a social gathering. [Fr. < *(soirée) musicale*, musical (evening).]
music box ►*n.* A box containing a mechanical device that produces music.
mu·si·cian (myōō-zĭsh′ən) ►*n.* One who composes, conducts, or performs music. —mu·si′cian·ship′ *n.*
mu·si·col·o·gy (myōō′zĭ-kŏl′ə-jē) ►*n.* The historical and scientific study of music. —mu′si·col′o·gist *n.*
musk (mŭsk) ►*n.* An odorous substance secreted by an Asian deer or produced synthetically. [< Pers. *mušk.*] —musk′i·ness *n.* —musk′y *adj.*
mus·keg (mŭs′kĕg′) ►*n.* A peaty bog, esp. in N North America. [Cree *maskek.*]
mus·kel·lunge (mŭs′kə-lŭnj′) ►*n., pl.* -lunge or -lung·es A large pike of the N US and S Canada. [< Ojibwa *maashkinoozhe.*]
mus·ket (mŭs′kĭt) ►*n.* A smoothbore shoulder gun used from the late 1500s through the 1700s. [< Ital. *moschetto* < Lat. *musca*, fly.] —mus′ket·eer *n.*
mus·ket·ry (mŭs′kĭ-trē) ►*n.* **1.** Muskets collectively. **2.** Musketeers collectively.
musk·mel·on (mŭsk′mĕl′ən) ►*n.* Any of several edible melons, such as the cantaloupe, having a rough rind and juicy flesh.
Mus·ko·ge·an (mŭs-kō′gē-ən) ►*n.* A family of Native American languages of the SE US that includes Choctaw, Chickasaw, and Creek.
Mus·ko·gee (mŭs-kō′gē) ►*n.* See Creek.
musk·ox or **musk ox** (mŭsk′ŏks′) ►*n.* A large oxlike mammal of Alaska, Canada, and Greenland, with broad flat horns and a shaggy coat.
musk·rat (mŭs′krăt′) ►*n., pl.* -rat or -rats **1.** A large semiaquatic rodent native to North America and naturalized in Eurasia. **2.** The dense brown fur of the muskrat.
Mus·lim (mŭz′ləm, mŏōz′-, mŭs′-, mŏōs′-) or **Mos·lem** (mŏz′ləm, mŏs′-) ►*n.* A believer or adherent of Islam. —Mus′lim *adj.*
mus·lin (mŭz′lĭn) ►*n.* Any of various sturdy cotton fabrics of plain weave. [< Ital. *mussolina*, of Mosul, Iraq.]
muss (mŭs) ►*v.* To make messy or untidy; rumple. ►*n.* A state of disorder; mess. [Prob. < MESS.] —muss′i·ly *adv.* —muss′y *adj.*
mus·sel (mŭs′əl) ►*n.* Any of various narrow-

shelled bivalve mollusks, esp. an edible marine species. [< Med.Lat. *mŭscula* < Lat. *mŭsculus*, muscle.]
Mus·so·li·ni (mŏō′sə-lē′nē), **Benito Amilcare Andrea** "Il Duce." 1883–1945. Italian Fascist dictator and prime minister (1922–43).
Mus·sorg·sky (mə-zôrg′skē, -sôrg′-), **Modest Petrovich** 1839–81. Russian composer.
must[1] (mŭst) ►*aux.v.* Used to indicate: **a.** Necessity or obligation: *Citizens must register in order to vote.* **b.** Insistence: *You must not go there alone.* **c.** Inevitability or certainty: *We all must die.* **d.** Probability: *It must be almost midnight.* ►*n.* An absolute requirement. [< OE *mōste*, p.t. of *mōtan*, be allowed.]
must[2] (mŭst) ►*n.* Staleness. [< MUSTY.]
must[3] (mŭst) ►*n.* Unfermented or fermenting fruit juice, usu. grape. [< Lat. *mustum.*]
mus·tache also **mous·tache** (mŭs′tăsh′, mə-stăsh′) ►*n.* The hair growing on the human upper lip. [< Gk. *mustax.*]
mus·ta·chio (mə-stăsh′ō, -stăsh′ē-ō′) ►*n., pl.* -chios A mustache, esp. a luxuriant one. [< Ital. dial. *mustaccio*, MUSTACHE.]
mus·tang (mŭs′tăng′) ►*n.* A small, hardy wild horse of the W North American plains. [Am. Sp. *mesteño*, stray animal.]
mus·tard (mŭs′tərd) ►*n.* **1.** Any of various Eurasian plants cultivated for their pungent seeds and edible leaves. **2.** A condiment made from mustard seeds. [< OFr. *mustarde* < Lat. *mustum*, new wine.] —mus′tard·y *adj.*
mustard gas ►*n.* An oily volatile liquid used in warfare as a blistering agent.
mus·ter (mŭs′tər) ►*v.* **1.** To summon or assemble (troops). **2.** To gather or summon up: *mustering up her strength for the ordeal.* See Synonyms at call. ►*n.* A gathering, esp. of troops, for service, inspection, or roll call. —*phrasal verbs:* muster in To enlist (someone) in military service. muster out To discharge (someone) from military service. [< Lat. *mōnstrāre*, show < *mōnstrum*, portent; see MONSTER.]
mustn't (mŭs′ənt) Must not.
must·y (mŭs′tē) ►*adj.* -i·er, -i·est Stale or moldy in odor or taste. [Alteration of obsolete *moisty* < MOIST.] —must′i·ness *n.*
mu·ta·ble (myōō′tə-bəl) ►*adj.* **1.** Subject to change. **2.** Fickle. —mu′ta·bil′i·ty, mu′ta·ble·ness *n.* —mu′ta·bly *adv.*
mu·ta·gen (myōō′tə-jən, -jĕn′) ►*n.* An agent, such as ultraviolet light or a radioactive element, that can induce mutation in an organism. —mu′ta·gen′ic *adj.*
mu·tant (myōōt′nt) ►*n.* An organism, cell, virus, or gene resulting from genetic mutation. —mu′tant *adj.*
mu·tate (myōō′tāt, myōō-tāt′) ►*v.* -tat·ed, -tat·ing To undergo or cause to undergo mutation. [Lat. *mūtāre.*] —mu′ta·tive (-tā′-tĭv, -tə-tĭv) *adj.*
mu·ta·tion (myōō-tā′shən) ►*n.* **1.** A change, as in nature, form, or quality. **2.** Any heritable alteration of an organism.
mute (myōōt) ►*adj.* mut·er, mut·est **1.** Refraining from speech. **2.** Incapable of producing speech or vocal sound. **3.** *Offensive* Unable to speak. **4.** Expressed without speech; unspoken. ►*n.* **1.** *Offensive* One who is incapable of speech. **2.** *Mus.* A device used to muffle or soften the tone of an instrument. ►*v.* mut·ed, mut·ing

To soften the sound, color, or shade of. [< Lat. *mūtus*.] —**mute′ly** *adv.* —**mute′ness** *n.*

Usage: In reference to people who are unable to use language orally, *mute* and *deaf-mute* are considered objectionable. These terms imply that a person who is incapable of oral speech is necessarily deprived of the use of language. In fact, many deaf people communicate fully through the use of a sign language.

mu·ti·late (myoōt′l-āt′) ►*v.* **-lat·ed, -lat·ing 1.** To injure severely or disfigure, esp. by cutting off tissue or body parts. See Synonyms at **mangle**[1]. **2.** To damage or mar. [< Lat. *mutilus*, maimed.] —**mu′ti·la′tion** *n.* —**mu′ti·la′tive** *adj.* —**mu′ti·la′tor** *n.*

mu·ti·ny (myoōt′n-ē) ►*n.*, *pl.* **-nies** Open rebellion against constituted authority, esp. by military personnel against superior officers. [< VLat. **movita*, a revolt.] —**mu′ti·neer′** *n.* —**mu′ti·nous** *adj.* —**mu′ti·nous·ly** *adv.* —**mu′ti·ny** *v.*

mutt (mŭt) ►*n. Informal* A mongrel dog. [< *muttonhead*, fool.]

mut·ter (mŭt′ər) ►*v.* **1.** To speak or utter indistinctly in low tones. **2.** To complain or grumble. ►*n.* A low, indistinct utterance. [ME *muttren*.] —**mut′ter·er** *n.*

mut·ton (mŭt′n) ►*n.* The flesh of a fully grown sheep. [< OFr. *moton*.]

mut·ton·chops (mŭt′n-chŏps′) ►*pl.n.* Side whiskers narrow at the temple and broad along the lower jawline.

mu·tu·al (myoō′choo-əl) ►*adj.* **1.** Directed and received by each toward the other: *mutual respect.* **2.** Having the same relationship each to the other: *mutual predators.* **3.** Possessed in common: *mutual interests.* [< Lat. *mūtuus*, borrowed.] —**mu′tu·al′i·ty** (-ăl′ĭ-tē) *n.* —**mu′tu·al·ly** *adv.*

mutual fund ►*n.* An investment company that by the sale of its shares acquires funds to invest in diversified securities.

muu·muu (moō′moō′) ►*n.* A long loose dress. [Hawaiian *mu'umu'u*.]

Mu·zak (myoō′zăk′) A trademark for background music or television transmitted esp. to businesses by subscription.

muz·zle (mŭz′əl) ►*n.* **1.** The usu. projecting nose and jaws of certain animals; snout. **2.** A device fitted over an animal's snout to prevent biting or eating. **3.** The front end of the barrel of a firearm. ►*v.* **-zled, -zling 1.** To put a muzzle on (an animal). **2.** To restrain from expressing opinions. [< Med.Lat. *mūsellum* < Lat. *mūsum*.]

muz·zle·load·er (mŭz′əl-lō′dər) ►*n.* A firearm loaded at the muzzle. —**muz′zle·load′ing** *adj.*

MVP ►*abbr.* most valuable player

my (mī) ►*adj.* The possessive form of **I.** Used as a modifier before a noun: *my boots; my brother.* ►*interj.* Used as an exclamation of surprise, pleasure, or dismay: *Oh, my! What a day!* [< OE *mīn.*]

my·al·gia (mī-ăl′jə) ►*n.* Pain or tenderness in one or more muscles. [Gk. *mus*, muscle + –ALGIA.] —**my·al′gic** (-jĭk) *adj.*

Myan·mar (myän-mär′) or **Bur·ma** (bûr′mə) A country of SE Asia on the Bay of Bengal and the Andaman Sea. Cap. Yangon.

my·as·the·ni·a grav·is (mī′əs-thē′nē-ə grăv′ĭs) ►*n.* A disease marked by progressive muscular weakness and fatigue caused by impaired transmission of nerve impulses. [Gk. *mus*, muscle + Gk. *asthenia*, weakness + Lat. *gravis*, serious.]

my·ce·li·um (mī-sē′lē-əm) ►*n.*, *pl.* **-li·a** (-lē-ə) The vegetative part of a fungus, consisting of a mass of branching, threadlike filaments that forms its main growing structure. [MYC(O)– + Gk. *hēlos*, wart.] —**my·ce′li·al** *adj.*

My·ce·nae (mī-sē′nē) An ancient Greek city in the NE Peloponnesus. —**My′ce·nae′an** (-sə-nē′ən) *adj. & n.*

–mycin ►*suff.* A substance derived from a bacterium in the order Actinomycetales: *erythromycin.* [MYC(O)– + –IN.]

myco– or **myc–** ►*pref.* Fungus: *mycology.* [< Gk. *mukēs.*]

my·col·o·gy (mī-kŏl′ə-jē) ►*n.* The branch of botany that deals with fungi. —**my′co·log′i·cal** (-kə-lŏj′ĭ-kəl) *adj.* —**my·col′o·gist** *n.*

my·co·tox·in (mī′kō-tŏk′sĭn) ►*n.* A toxin produced by a fungus.

my·e·lin (mī′ə-lĭn) also **my·e·line** (-lĭn, -lēn) ►*n.* A white fatty material that encloses certain axons and nerve fibers.

my·e·li·tis (mī′ə-lī′tĭs) ►*n.* Inflammation of the spinal column or bone marrow.

myelo– or **myel–** ►*pref.* **1.** Spinal cord: *myelitis.* **2.** Bone marrow: *myeloma.* [< Gk. *muelos*, marrow, poss. < *mus*, muscle.]

my·e·lo·ma (mī′ə-lō′mə) ►*n.*, *pl.* **-mas** or **-ma·ta** (-mə-tə) A malignant tumor formed by the cells of the bone marrow.

my·na or **my·nah** (mī′nə) ►*n.* An Asian starling. Certain species can mimic human speech. [Hindi *mainā*, perh. < Skt. *madana-*, joyful.]

my·o·car·di·um (mī′ō-kär′dē-əm) ►*n.*, *pl.* **-di·a** (-dē-ə) The muscular tissue of the heart. [Gk. *mus*, muscle + *kardia*, heart.] —**my′o·car′di·al** *adj.*

my·o·pi·a (mī-ō′pē-ə) ►*n.* **1.** A visual defect in which distant objects appear blurred because their images are focused in front of the retina rather than on it; nearsightedness. **2.** Shortsightedness in thinking or planning. [< Gk. *muōps*, nearsighted.] —**my·op′ic** (-ŏp′ĭk, -ō′-pĭk) *adj.* —**my·op′i·cal·ly** *adv.*

my·o·sin (mī′ə-sĭn) ►*n.* The most common protein in muscle cells. [Gk. *muos*, genitive of *mus*, muscle + –IN.]

myr·i·ad (mĭr′ē-əd) ►*adj.* Constituting a very large, indefinite number. ►*n.* A vast number. [Gk. *murias*, *muriad-*, ten thousand.]

myr·i·a·pod (mĭr′ē-ə-pŏd′) ►*n.* Any of several arthropods, such as the centipede, having at least nine pairs of legs. [Gk. *murias*, ten thousand + –POD.]

My·ron (mī′rən) 5th cent. BC. Greek sculptor.

myrrh (mûr) ►*n.* An aromatic gum resin obtained from several Asian or African trees and shrubs and used in perfume and incense. [< Gk. *murrha.*]

myr·tle (mûr′tl) ►*n.* **1.** An evergreen shrub or tree, esp. an aromatic Mediterranean shrub having white flowers and blue-black berries. **2.** See **periwinkle**[2]. [< Gk. *murtos.*]

my·self (mī-sĕlf′) ►*pron.* **1.** That one identical with me. Used as: **a.** Reflexively: *I hurt myself.* **b.** For emphasis: *I myself was certain of the facts.* **2.** My normal or healthy state: *I'm feeling myself again.* [< OE *mē selfum.*]

mys·te·ri·ous (mĭ-stîr′ē-əs) ►*adj.* **1.** Of, relating

to, or being a religious mystery. **2.** Arousing wonder or curiosity, esp. by being difficult to explain or understand: *a mysterious disappearance.* —**mys·te′ri·ous·ly** *adv.*
   Syns: *esoteric, arcane, occult, cryptic, enigmatic* **adj.**

mys·ter·y (mĭs′tə-rē) ►*n., pl.* **-ies 1.** Something that cannot be explained or fully understood; enigma. **2.** One whose identity is unknown and who arouses curiosity. **3.** A mysterious character or quality. **4.** A work of fiction, a drama, or a film dealing with a puzzling crime. **5.** A religious truth that is knowable only through divine revelation. [< Gk. *mustērion,* secret rite.]

mystery play ►*n.* A medieval drama based on episodes in the life of Jesus. [< Med.Lat. *misterium,* craft guild (mystery plays being sponsored by such guilds).]

mys·tic (mĭs′tĭk) ►*adj.* **1a.** Relating to mysticism or mystics. **b.** Deeply spiritual; mystical. **c.** Relating to religious mysteries or occult rites and practices. **2.** Inspiring a sense of mystery. ►*n.* One who practices or believes in mysticism. [< Gk. *mustikos* < *mustērion,* MYSTERY.]

mys·ti·cal (mĭs′tĭ-kəl) ►*adj.* Of or relating to mysticism, mystic rites, or mystic practices. —**mys′ti·cal·ly** *adv.* —**mys′ti·cal·ness** *n.*

mys·ti·cism (mĭs′tĭ-sĭz′əm) ►*n.* Belief in direct experience of the transcendent reality of God, esp. by means of contemplation and asceticism instead of rational thought.

mys·ti·fy (mĭs′tə-fī′) ►*v.* **-fied, -fy·ing 1.** To confuse or bewilder. See Synonyms at **perplex. 2.** To make obscure or mysterious. [Fr. *mystifier.*] —**mys′ti·fi·ca′tion** *n.* —**mys′ti·fi′er** *n.* —**mys′ti·fy′ing·ly** *adv.*

mys·tique (mĭ-stēk′) ►*n.* An aura of mystery or reverence surrounding a particular person, thing, or idea. [Fr. < Lat. *mysticus,* MYSTIC.]

myth (mĭth) ►*n.* **1.** A traditional story dealing with supernatural beings, ancestors, or heroes that serves as a primordial type in the world view of a people. **2.** A fiction or half-truth. **3.** A fictitious story, person, or thing. [< Gk. *muthos.*] —**myth′i·cal, myth′ic** *adj.* —**myth′i·cal·ly** *adv.*

myth·mak·er (mĭth′mā′kər) ►*n.* One that creates myths or mythical situations. —**myth′-mak·ing** *n.*

my·thol·o·gy (mĭ-thŏl′ə-jē) ►*n., pl.* **-gies 1.** A body of myths about the origin, history, deities, ancestors, and heroes of a people. **2.** The study of myths. —**myth′o·log′i·cal** (mĭth′ə-lŏj′-ĭ-kəl) *adj.* —**myth′o·log′i·cal·ly** *adv.* —**my·thol′o·gist** *n.* —**my·thol′o·gize′** *v.*

N

n¹ or **N** (ĕn) ►*n., pl.* **n′s** or **N′s** also **ns** or **Ns** The 14th letter of the English alphabet.

n² ►*abbr.* **1.** *Gram.* neuter **2.** neutron

N ►*abbr.* **1.** *Print.* en **2.** knight (chess) **3.** newton **4a.** north **b.** northern

n. ►*abbr.* noun

NA ►*abbr.* **1.** North America **2.** also **n/a** not applicable

NAACP ►*abbr.* National Association for the Advancement of Colored People

nab (năb) ►*v.* **nabbed, nab·bing** *Informal* **1.** To seize; arrest. **2.** To grab; snatch. [Perh. var. of dial. *nap,* seize.]

na·bob (nā′bŏb′) ►*n.* A person of wealth and prominence. [< Ar. *nuwwāb,* deputies.]

Na·bo·kov (nə-bô′kəf, nä′bə-kôf′), **Vladimir** 1899–1977. Russian-born Amer. writer.

na·celle (nə-sĕl′) ►*n.* **1.** A streamlined enclosure on an aircraft for housing the crew or an engine. **2.** A similar enclosure on a wind turbine that houses the energy-generating components. [< LLat. *nāvicella,* boat.]

na·cho (nä′chō′) ►*n., pl.* **-chos** A small fried tortilla chip topped with cheese and often chili-pepper sauce and broiled. [Am.Sp.]

na·cre (nā′kər) ►*n.* See **mother-of-pearl.** [< Ar. *naqqāra,* drum.]

Na-De·ne also **Na-Dé·né** (nä-dā′nē, -dā-nä′) ►*n.* A North American Indian language family including Athabaskan and Tlingit.

na·dir (nā′dər, -dĭr′) ►*n.* **1.** A point on the celestial sphere diametrically opposite the zenith. **2.** The lowest point. [< Ar. *nazīr (as-samt),* opposite (the zenith).]

NAFTA ►*abbr.* North American Free Trade Agreement

nag¹ (năg) ►*v.* **nagged, nag·ging 1.** To annoy by constant scolding, complaining, or urging. **2.** To torment persistently, as with anxiety or pain. **3.** To scold, complain, or find fault constantly: *nagging at the children.* ►*n.* One who nags. [Prob. of Scand. orig.] —**nag′ger** *n.* —**nag′ging·ly** *adv.*

nag² (năg) ►*n.* A horse, esp. an old or worn-out horse. [ME *nagge.*]

Na·ga·sa·ki (nä′gə-sä′kē) A city of W Kyushu, Japan, on **Nagasaki Bay,** an inlet of the East China Sea.

Na·go·ya (nə-goi′ə, nä′gô-yä′) A city of central Honshu, Japan, E of Kyoto.

Na·hua·tl (nä′wät′l) ►*n., pl.* **-tl** or **-tls 1.** A member of any of various Indian peoples of central Mexico, including the Aztecs. **2.** The Uto-Aztecan language of the Nahuatl.

Na·hum (nā′həm, nā′əm) ►*n.* **1.** A Hebrew prophet of the 7th cent. BC. **2.** See table at **Bible.**

nai·ad (nā′əd, -ăd′, nī′-) ►*n., pl.* **-a·des** (-ə-dēz′) or **-ads** *Gk. Myth.* One of the nymphs living in brooks, springs, and fountains. [< Gk. *naias.*]

nail (nāl) ►*n.* **1.** A slim, pointed piece of metal hammered into material as a fastener. **2a.** A thin, horny, transparent plate covering the upper surface of the tip of each finger and toe. **b.** A claw or talon. ►*v.* **1.** To fasten with or as if with a nail. **2.** To cover, enclose, or shut by fastening with nails: *nail up a window.* **3.** *Slang* To seize; catch: *nail a suspect.* **4.** *Slang* To strike or hit. —*phrasal verb:* **nail down** To settle conclusively. [< OE *nægl,* fingernail, toenail.]

Nai·paul (nī′pôl), Sir **V(idiadhar) S(urajprasad)** b. 1932. Trinidadian-born British writer.

nai·ra (nī′rə) ►*n.* See table at **currency.** [Alteration of NIGERIA.]

Nai·ro·bi (nī-rō′bē) The capital of Kenya, in the S-central part.

na·ive or **na·ïve** (nī-ēv′, nä-) also **na·if** or **na·ïf** (-ēf′) ►*adj.* **1.** Lacking worldliness and sophistication. **2.** Simple and credulous; ingenuous. [< Lat. *nātīvus*, native, rustic.] —**na·ive′ly** *adv.*

na·ive·té or **na·ïve·té** (nī′ēv-tā′, nä′-, nī-ē′vĭ-tā′, nä-) ►*n.* **1.** The state of being naive. **2.** A naive statement or act. [Fr. *naïveté*.]

na·ked (nā′kĭd) ►*adj.* **1.** Without clothing; nude. **2.** Having no covering; bare. **3.** Being without addition, disguise, or embellishment: *naked ambition*. [< OE *nacod*.] —**na′ked·ly** *adv.* —**na′ked·ness** *n.*

naked eye ►*n.* The eye unassisted by an optical instrument.

nak·fa (näk′fä′) ►*n.* See table at **currency**. [Tigrinya (Eritrea) *naqfa*.]

nam·by-pam·by (năm′bē-păm′bē) ►*adj.* **1.** Weak or unrealisitc. **2.** Indecisive; spineless. [< *Namby-Pamby*, satire on Ambrose Philips (1674–1749) by Henry Carey (1687?–1743).]

name (nām) ►*n.* **1.** A word or words by which an entity is designated. **2.** A disparaging designation: *called me names*. **3.** Appearance rather than reality: *a democracy in name only*. **4a.** A reputation: *a bad name*. **b.** A distinguished reputation. **5.** An illustrious person. See Synonyms at **celebrity**. ►*v.* **named, nam·ing** **1.** To give a name to. **2.** To mention, specify, or cite by name. **3.** To nominate or appoint. See Synonyms at **appoint**. **4.** To specify or fix: *name the time and date*. ►*adj.* Informal Well-known by a name: *a name performer*. —**idiom: in the name of** By the authority of. [< OE *nama*.] —**nam′a·ble, name′a·ble** *adj.* —**nam′er** *n.*

name day ►*n.* The feast day of the saint after whom one is named.

name-drop (nām′drŏp′) ►*v.* To mention casually the names of famous or important people to create the impression that one is familiar with them in an attempt to impress or influence others. —**name′-drop′per** *n.*

name·less (nām′lĭs) ►*adj.* **1.** Having no name. **2.** Unknown by name; obscure. **3.** Anonymous: *a nameless benefactor*. **4.** Defying description: *nameless horror*. —**name′less·ly** *adv.*

name·ly (nām′lē) ►*adv.* That is to say; specifically.

name·sake (nām′sāk′) ►*n.* One who is named after another.

Na·mib·i·a (nə-mĭb′ē-ə) A country of SW Africa on the Atlantic. Cap. Windhoek. —**Na·mib′i·an** *adj. & n.*

Nan·jing (nän′jĭng′) also **Nan·king** (nän′kĭng′, nän′-) A city of E-central China on the Yangtze R. NW of Shanghai.

nan·keen (nän-kēn′) ►*n.* A sturdy yellow or buff cotton cloth. [< NANJING.]

nan·ny (năn′ē) ►*n., pl.* **-nies** A person, usu. a woman, employed to take care of a child. [Alteration of *nana*.]

nanny goat ►*n.* A female goat. [< *Nanny*, nickname for *Anne*.]

nano– ►*pref.* **1.** Extremely small: *nanostructure*. **2.** One billionth (10^{-9}): *nanosecond*. [< Gk. *nanos*, dwarf.]

nan·o·me·ter (năn′ə-mē′tər) ►*n.* One billionth (10^{-9}) of a meter.

nan·o·scale (năn′ə-skāl′) ►*adj.* Relating to or

occurring on a scale of nanometers.

nan·o·sec·ond (năn′ə-sĕk′ənd) ►*n.* One billionth (10^{-9}) of a second.

nan·o·struc·ture (năn′ō-strŭk′chər) ►*n.* **1.** An object of nanoscale proportions. **2.** The structure of such an object.

nan·o·tech·nol·o·gy (năn′ə-tĕk-nŏl′ə-jē) ►*n.* The science of building electronic circuits and devices from single atoms and molecules.

nan·o·tube (năn′ə-tōōb′, -tyōōb′) ►*n.* A hollow cylindrical tube composed of atoms of a single element, usu. carbon.

Nan·tuck·et (năn-tŭk′ĭt) An island of SE MA S of Cape Cod. —**Nan·tuck′et·er** *n.*

nap¹ (năp) ►*n.* A brief sleep, often during the day. ►*v.* **napped, nap·ping** **1.** To take a nap. **2.** To be unaware of imminent danger or trouble. [< OE *hnappian*, doze.]

nap² (năp) ►*n.* A soft or fuzzy surface on fabric or leather. [< MDu. *noppe*.]

nap·a cabbage (năp′ə, nä′pə) ►*n.* A plant related to the common cabbage, having an elongated head of overlapping, crinkled edible leaves. [Prob. J. *nappa*, greens.]

na·palm (nā′päm′) ►*n.* A highly incendiary jelly used in bombs and flamethrowers. [*na(phthenate)* + *palm(itate)*, substances used in its composition.] —**na′palm′** *v.*

nape (nāp, năp) ►*n.* The back of the neck. [ME.]

na·per·y (nā′pə-rē) ►*n.* Household linen, esp. table linen. [< OFr. *nape*, tablecloth.]

naph·tha (năf′thə, năp′-) ►*n.* A highly volatile, flammable liquid distilled esp. from petroleum and used as a fuel or solvent and in making chemicals. [< Gk.]

naph·tha·lene (năf′thə-lēn′, năp′-) ►*n.* A white crystalline compound used in making dyes, moth repellents, and explosives and as a solvent. [NAPHTH(A) + AL(COHOL) + –ENE.]

Na·pi·er (nā′pē-ər, nə-pîr′), **John** Laird of Merchiston. 1550–1617. Scottish mathematician.

nap·kin (năp′kĭn) ►*n.* **1.** A piece of cloth or absorbent paper used at table to protect the clothes or wipe the lips and fingers. **2.** A cloth or towel. [< OFr. *nape*, tablecloth.]

Na·ples (nā′pəlz) A city of S-central Italy on the **Bay of Naples,** an arm of the Tyrrhenian Sea.

Na·po·le·on I (nə-pō′lē-ən, -pōl′yən) Napoleon Bonaparte. 1769–1821. Emperor of the French and King of Italy (1804–14). —**Na·po′le·on′ic** (-ŏn′ĭk) *adj.*

Napoleon I

Napoleon III Charles Louis Napoleon Bonaparte. 1808–73. Emperor of the French (1852–70).

narc (närk) ►*n. Slang* A narcotics agent.

nar·cis·sism (när′sĭ-sĭz′əm) ►*n.* Excessive preoccupation with or admiration of oneself. See Synonyms at **conceit.** [< NARCISSUS.] —**nar′·cis·sist** *n.* —**nar′cis·sis′tic** *adj.*

nar·cis·sus (när-sĭs′əs) ►*n., pl.* **narcissus** or **-cis·si** (-sĭs′ī′, -sĭs′ē) or **-cis·sus·es** A daffodil, esp. one with small flowers. [< Gk. *narkissos.*]

Narcissus ►*n. Gk. Myth.* A youth who fell in love with his own image in a pool of water and was transformed into a flower.

nar·co·lep·sy (när′kə-lĕp′sē) ►*n.* A disorder marked by sudden and uncontrollable, often brief, attacks of deep sleep. [Gk. *narkē,* numbness + *lēpsis,* seizure.] —**nar′co·lep′tic** (-lĕp′tĭk) *adj. & n.*

nar·co·sis (när-kō′sĭs) ►*n., pl.* **-ses** (-sēz) Deep stupor or unconsciousness produced by a drug. [< Gk. *narkōsis,* a numbing.]

nar·cot·ic (när-kŏt′ĭk) ►*n.* An addictive drug that reduces pain, alters mood and behavior, and usu. induces sleep or stupor. [< Gk. *narkōtikos,* numbing.] —**nar·cot′ic** *adj.*

nar·co·tism (när′kə-tĭz′əm) ►*n.* **1.** Addiction to narcotics. **2.** Narcosis.

nar·co·tize (när′kə-tīz′) ►*v.* **-tized, -tiz·ing 1.** To place under the influence of a narcotic. **2.** To put to sleep. **3.** To dull; deaden.

nar·co·traf·fick·ing (när′kō-trăf′ĭ-kĭng) ►*n.* The smuggling and distribution of illegal drugs.

nar·is (nâr′ĭs) ►*n., pl.* **-es** (-ēz) A nostril. [Lat. *nāris.*]

Nar·ra·gan·sett (năr′ə-găn′sĭt) ►*n., pl.* **-sett** or **-setts 1.** A member of a Native American people inhabiting parts of Rhode Island. **2.** The Algonquian language of the Narragansett.

nar·rate (năr′āt′, nă-rāt′) ►*v.* **-rat·ed, -rat·ing 1.** To give an account of; tell. See Synonyms at **describe. 2.** To supply a descriptive commentary for a movie or performance. [Lat. *narrāre.*] —**nar·ra′tion** *n.* —**nar′ra′tor** *n.*

nar·ra·tive (năr′ə-tĭv) ►*n.* **1.** A narrated account; story. **2.** The act or process of narrating. —**nar′ra·tive** *adj.*

nar·row (năr′ō) ►*adj.* **-er, -est 1.** Of small or limited width. **2.** Limited in area or scope; cramped. **3.** Lacking flexibility; rigid: *narrow opinions.* **4.** Barely sufficient; close: *a narrow margin of victory.* **5.** Painstakingly thorough; meticulous: *narrow scrutiny.* ►*v.* To reduce in width or extent; make narrower. ►*n.* **narrows** *(takes sing. or pl. v.)* A narrow body of water that connects two larger ones. [< OE *nearu.*] —**nar′row·ly** *adv.* —**nar′row·ness** *n.*

nar·row-mind·ed (năr′ō-mīn′dĭd) ►*adj.* Lacking tolerance or breadth of view; petty. —**nar′·row-mind′ed·ly** *adv.*

nar·thex (när′thĕks′) ►*n.* A portico or lobby to the nave of a church. [LGk. *narthēx.*]

nar·whal (när′wəl) ►*n.* An Arctic whale marked in the male by a long spirally twisted tusk. [< ON *nāhvalr.*]

nar·y (nâr′ē) ►*adj.* Not one. [< *ne'er a.*]

NASA (năs′ə) ►*abbr.* National Aeronautics and Space Administration

na·sal (nā′zəl) ►*adj.* **1.** Of or relating to the nose. **2.** Marked by or resembling a resonant sound

produced through the nose: *a nasal whine.* [< Lat. *nāsus,* nose.] —**na·sal′i·ty** (nā-zăl′ĭ-tē) *n.* —**na′sal·ly** *adv.*

NASCAR (năs′kär′) ►*abbr.* National Association for Stock Car Auto Racing

nas·cent (năs′ənt, nā′sənt) ►*adj.* Coming into existence; emergent. [< Lat. *nāscī,* be born.] —**nas′cence** *n.*

Nash (năsh), **(Frederic) Ogden** 1902–71. Amer. writer.

Nash·ville (năsh′vĭl′) The capital of TN, in the N-central part NE of Memphis.

Nas·sau (năs′ô′) The capital of the Bahamas, on an island in the NW part of the archipelago.

Nas·ser (năs′ər, nä′sər), **Gamal Abdel** 1918–70. Egyptian army officer and politician.

nas·tur·tium (nə-stûr′shəm, nă-) ►*n.* A plant of S and Central America having edible spurred flowers. [< Lat., a kind of cress.]

nas·ty (năs′tē) ►*adj.* **-ti·er, -ti·est 1a.** Disgusting or repellent. See Synonyms at **offensive. b.** Unpleasantly cold or wet: *nasty weather.* **2.** Offensive; indecent. **3.** Mean or spiteful. **4.** Painful or dangerous: *a nasty accident.* [ME *nasti.*] —**nas′ti·ly** *adv.* —**nas′ti·ness** *n.*

na·tal (nāt′l) ►*adj.* **1.** Of or accompanying birth. **2.** Of the time or place of one's birth. [< Lat. *nātus,* p.part. of *nāscī,* be born.]

na·tal·i·ty (nā-tăl′ĭ-tē, nə-) ►*n.* See **birthrate.**

Natch·ez (năch′ĭz) ►*n., pl.* **Natchez 1.** A member of an extinct Native American people formerly living along the lower Mississippi R. **2.** The language of the Natchez.

Na·tick (nā′tĭk) ►*n.* A dialect of Massachusett.

na·tion (nā′shən) ►*n.* **1.** A relatively large group of people organized under a single government. **2.** A people; nationality. **3.** A federation or tribe. [< Lat. *nātiō < nāscī,* be born.] —**na′tion·hood′** *n.*

Nation, Carry Amelia Moore 1846–1911. Amer. temperance crusader.

na·tion·al (năsh′ə-nəl, năsh′nəl) ►*adj.* **1.** Of or relating to a nation: *a national anthem.* **2.** Of or relating to nationality: *national origin.* **3.** Of or maintained by the government of a nation: *a national landmark.* ►*n.* A citizen of a particular nation. —**na′tion·al·ly** *adv.*

National Guard ►*n.* The military reserve units controlled by each US state and subject to the call of either the federal or the state government.

na·tion·al·ism (năsh′ə-nə-lĭz′əm) ►*n.* **1.** Devotion, esp. excessive or undiscriminating devotion, to the interests or culture of a particular nation. **2.** The belief that a particular group constitutes a distinct people deserving of political self-determination. —**na′tion·al·ist** *n.* —**na′tion·al·is′tic** *adj.*

na·tion·al·i·ty (năsh′ə-năl′ĭ-tē) ►*n., pl.* **-ties 1.** The status of belonging to a particular nation by origin, birth, or naturalization. **2.** A people having common origins or traditions and often constituting a nation.

na·tion·al·ize (năsh′ə-nə-līz′) ►*v.* **-ized, -iz·ing 1.** To convert from private to governmental ownership and control. **2.** To make national in scope. —**na′tion·al·i·za′tion** *n.*

national monument ►*n.* A landmark or site of historic interest set aside by a national government for public enjoyment.

national park ►*n.* A tract of public land maintained by a national government for recreational and cultural use.

na·tion·wide (nā′shən-wīd′) ▸*adv. & adj.* Throughout a whole nation.

na·tive (nā′tĭv) ▸*adj.* **1a.** Being such by birth or origin: *a native Scot.* **b.** Being one's own by birth: *our native land.* **2.** Originating or produced in a certain place; indigenous. **3.** Inborn; innate: *native ability.* ▸*n.* **1a.** One born in a specified place. **b.** An original or lifelong inhabitant of a place. **2.** An animal or plant that originated in a particular place. [< Lat. *nātīvus* < *nāscī*, be born.]

Usage: When used to refer to a member of an indigenous people, the noun *native,* like its synonym *aborigine,* can evoke unwelcome stereotypes of cultural backwardness. But, as is often the case with words that categorize people, the use of the noun is more problematic than the use of the corresponding adjective. Thus, *the peoples native to northern Europe* or *the aboriginal inhabitants of the South Pacific* is preferable to *the natives of northern Europe* or *the aborigines of the South Pacific.*

Native Alaskan ▸*n.* See **Alaska Native.**

Native American ▸*n.* A member of any of the peoples indigenous to the Western Hemisphere before European contact. **—Native American** *adj.*

Usage: Many people now prefer *Native American* to Columbus's misnomer *Indian* in referring to the earliest inhabitants of the Western Hemisphere. However, it should not be assumed that the latter is necessarily offensive or out of date. *Indian* is often used in combinations, such as *American Indian* or *Pueblo Indian,* that cannot reasonably be formed with *Native American.* Of the two terms, only *Native American* is customarily held to include the Eskimo and Aleut peoples.

Native Hawaiian ▸*n.* A member of the indigenous Polynesian people of the Hawaiian Islands.

na·tiv·i·ty (nə-tĭv′ĭ-tē, nā-) ▸*n., pl.* **-ties 1.** Birth, esp. the conditions or circumstances of being born. **2. Nativity a.** The birth of Jesus. **b.** Christmas. [< Lat. *nātīvitās.*]

natl. ▸*abbr.* national

NATO (nā′tō) ▸*abbr.* North Atlantic Treaty Organization

nat·ty (năt′ē) ▸*adj.* **-ti·er, -ti·est** Neat, trim, and smart; dapper. [Perh. < ME *net,* good.] **—nat′-ti·ly** *adv.* **—nat′ti·ness** *n.*

nat·u·ral (năch′ər-əl, năch′rəl) ▸*adj.* **1.** Present in or produced by nature. **2.** Of or relating to nature. **3.** Conforming to the usual course of nature: *a natural death.* **4.** Having a particular character by nature: *a natural leader.* **5.** Free from affectation or inhibitions. **6.** Not altered or treated: *natural coloring.* **7.** Expected and accepted: *the natural course of events.* **8.** *Math.* Of or relating to positive integers. **9.** *Mus.* Not sharped or flatted. ▸*n.* **1.** One esp. suited by nature or qualifications: *a natural for the job.* **2.** *Mus.* The sign (♮) placed before a note to cancel a preceding sharp or flat. **—nat′u·ral·ness** *n.*

natural gas ▸*n.* A mixture of hydrocarbon gases, chiefly methane, occurring with petroleum deposits and used esp. as a fuel.

natural history ▸*n.* The study of organisms and natural objects, esp. their origins, evolution, and relationships.

nat·u·ral·ism (năch′ər-ə-lĭz′əm) ▸*n.* **1.** Factual or realistic representation in art or literature. **2.** The view that all phenomena can be explained in terms of natural causes and laws.

nat·u·ral·ist (năch′ər-ə-lĭst) ▸*n.* **1.** A person who is versed in natural history, esp. in zoology or botany. **2.** A person who is an adherent of naturalism.

nat·u·ral·is·tic (năch′ər-ə-lĭs′tĭk) ▸*adj.* Lifelike; realistic. **—nat′u·ral·is′ti·cal·ly** *adv.*

nat·u·ral·ize (năch′ər-ə-līz′) ▸*v.* **-ized, -iz·ing 1.** To grant full citizenship to. **2.** To adopt into general use. **3.** To introduce and establish (a species) in an environment to which it is not native. **—nat′u·ral·i·za′tion** *n.*

nat·u·ral·ly (năch′ər-ə-lē) ▸*adv.* **1.** In a natural manner. **2.** By nature; inherently. **3.** Without a doubt; surely.

natural resource ▸*n.* A material source of wealth, such as timber or a mineral deposit, that occurs in a natural state.

natural science ▸*n.* A science, such as biology, chemistry, or physics, that deals with the objects, phenomena, or laws of nature and the physical world.

natural selection ▸*n.* The process in nature by which organisms that are better adapted to their environment survive longer and transmit more of their genetic characteristics to succeeding generations than do those that are less well adapted.

na·ture (nā′chər) ▸*n.* **1a.** The material world and its phenomena. **b.** The forces that produce and control such phenomena: *the balance of nature.* **2.** The world of living things and the outdoors. **3.** A primitive state of existence. **4.** The basic character or qualities of humanity: *human nature.* **5.** Disposition; temperament: *a sweet nature.* **6.** A kind or sort. [< Lat. *nātūra* < *nāscī*, be born.] **—na′tured** *adj.*

na·tur·op·a·thy (nā′chə-rŏp′ə-thē) ▸*n., pl.* **-thies** A system of therapy that relies on natural remedies, such as sunlight, diet, and massage, to treat illness. **—na′tur·o·path′** (-ə-păth′) *n.* **—na′tur·o·path′ic** *adj*

naught also **nought** (nôt) ▸*n.* **1.** Nonexistence; nothingness. **2.** The figure 0; zero. [< OE *nāwiht,* not a thing.]

naugh·ty (nô′tē) ▸*adj.* **-ti·er, -ti·est 1.** Disobedient; mischievous. **2.** Indecent; improper. **—naugh′ti·ly** *adv.* **—naugh′ti·ness** *n.*

Na·u·ru (nä-ōō′rōō) An island country of the central Pacific S of the equator and W of Kiribati. Cap. Yaren. **—Na·u′ru·an** *adj. & n.*

nau·se·a (nô′zē-ə, -zhə, -sē-ə, -shə) ▸*n.* **1.** A feeling of sickness in the stomach marked by an urge to vomit. **2.** Strong aversion; disgust. [< Lat. *nausiē,* seasickness.]

nau·se·ate (nô′zē-āt′, -zhē-, -sē-, -shē-) ▸*v.* **-at·ed, -at·ing** To feel or cause to feel nausea. See Synonyms at **disgust. —nau′se·at′ing·ly** *adv.* **—nau′se·a′tion** *n.*

nau·seous (nô′shəs, -zē-əs) ▸*adj.* **1.** Causing nausea; sickening. **2.** Affected with nausea.

nau·ti·cal (nô′tĭ-kəl) ▸*adj.* Of or characteristic of ships, shipping, sailors, or navigation. [< Gk. *nautēs,* sailor.] **—nau′ti·cal·ly** *adv.*

Syns: marine, maritime **adj.**

nautical mile ▸*n.* A unit of length used in

sea and air navigation, usu. equal to 1,852 m (about 6,076 ft).

nau·ti·lus (nôt′l-əs) ►*n., pl.* **-es** or **-li** (-lī′) A cephalopod mollusk having a partitioned spiral shell. [< Gk. *nautilos*, sailor.]

Nav·a·jo also **Nav·a·ho** (năv′ə-hō′, nä′və-) ►*n., pl.* **-jo** or **-jos** also **-ho** or **-hos 1.** A member of a Native American people inhabiting reservation lands in Arizona, New Mexico, and SE Utah. **2.** The Athabaskan language of the Navajo. —**Nav′a·jo′** *adj.*

na·val (nā′vəl) ►*adj.* Of or relating to a navy.

Na·varre (nə-vär′, nä-) A former kingdom of SW Europe in the Pyrenees of N Spain and SW France.

nave (nāv) ►*n.* The central part of a church, extending from the narthex to the chancel and flanked by the aisles. [< Lat. *nāvis*, ship.]

na·vel (nā′vəl) ►*n.* The mark on the abdomen of mammals where the umbilical cord was attached during gestation. [< OE *nafela*.]

navel orange ►*n.* A usu. seedless orange having at its apex a navellike formation enclosing a small secondary fruit.

nav·i·ga·ble (năv′ĭ-gə-bəl) ►*adj.* **1.** Sufficiently deep or wide to provide passage for vessels. **2.** Capable of being steered. —**nav′i·ga·bil′i·ty** *n.*

nav·i·gate (năv′ĭ-gāt′) ►*v.* **-gat·ed, -gat·ing 1a.** To plan and direct the course of a vessel or vehicle. **b.** To know or determine a migratory course. Used of an animal. **2a.** To travel over a planned course, esp. over water. **b.** To make sequential progress through: *navigated the website.* [Lat. *nāvigāre : nāvis*, ship + *agere*, drive.] —**nav′i·ga′tion** *n.* —**nav′i·ga′tion·al** *adj.* —**nav′i·ga′tor** *n.*

Nav·ra·ti·lo·va (năv′rə-tĭ-lō′və, nä′vrə-), **Martina** b. 1956. Czechoslovakian-born Amer. tennis player.

Martina Navratilova
photographed in 2007

na·vy (nā′vē) ►*n., pl.* **-vies 1.** All of a nation's warships. **2.** A nation's entire military organization for sea warfare and defense. **3.** Navy blue. [< Lat. *nāvigia*, ships.]

navy bean ►*n.* A variety of the kidney bean cultivated for its edible white seeds.

navy blue ►*n.* A dark grayish blue. [From the color of the British naval uniform.]

nay (nā) ►*adv.* **1.** No: *voted nay.* **2.** And moreover: *He was ill-favored, nay, hideous.* ►*n.* **1.** A

denial or refusal. **2.** A negative vote or voter. [< ON *nei*.]

Nay·pyi·daw (nĕ′pyē-dô′) The capital of Myanmar (Burma), in the south-central part of the country north of Yangon (Rangoon).

Naz·a·reth (năz′ər-əth) A town of N Israel SE of Haifa.

Na·zi (nät′sē, năt′-) ►*n., pl.* **-zis** A member of the fascist political party that held power (1933–45) in Germany under Adolf Hitler. —**Na′zi** *adj.* —**Na′zism, Na′zi·ism** *n.*

NB ►*abbr.* **1.** New Brunswick **2.** nota bene

NBA ►*abbr.* National Basketball Association

NbE ►*abbr.* north by east

NbW ►*abbr.* north by west

NC ►*abbr.* **1.** no charge **2.** North Carolina

NCAA ►*abbr.* National Collegiate Athletic Association

NCC ►*abbr.* National Council of Churches

NCO ►*abbr.* noncommissioned officer

ND ►*abbr.* **1.** no date **2.** North Dakota

N'Dja·me·na (ən-jä′mə-nə) The capital of Chad, in the SW part.

NE ►*abbr.* **1.** Nebraska **2.** New England **3a.** northeast **b.** northeastern

NEA ►*abbr.* **1.** National Education Association **2.** National Endowment for the Arts

Ne·an·der·thal (nē-ăn′dər-thôl′, -tôl′, nā-än′-dər-täl′) ►*adj.* **1.** also **Ne·an·der·tal** (-tôl′, -täl′) Of or being a species of extinct hominins of the late Pleistocene Epoch, living esp. in Europe and associated with Middle Paleolithic tools. **2.** *Slang* Crude, boorish, or slow-witted. —**Ne·an′der·thal′** *n.*

neap tide (nēp) ►*n.* A tide occurring during the first and third quarters of the moon, when the difference between high and low tides is least. [< OE *nēp(flōd)*, neap (tide).]

near (nîr) ►*adv.* **-er, -est 1.** To, at, or within a short distance or interval in space or time: *moved the box nearer to the table.* **2.** Almost; nearly: *was near exhausted from the work.* **3.** With or in a close relationship. ►*adj.* **-er, -est 1.** Close in time, space, position, or degree: *near equals.* **2.** Closely related. See Synonyms at **close. 3.** Nearly so: *a near victory.* **4.** Closely resembling an original: *a near likeness.* **5.** Closer of two or more. ►*prep.* Close to: *an inn near Tokyo.* ►*v.* To come close or closer to; draw near. [< OE *nēar*, comp. of *nēah*.] —**near′ness** *n.*

near·by (nîr′bī′) ►*adj.* Located a short distance away. ►*adv.* Not far away: *lives downtown and works nearby.*

Near East A region of SW Asia including Asia Minor, the Levant, and Mesopotamia and sometimes defined also as including the Arabian Peninsula and NE Africa. —**Near Eastern** *adj.*

near·ly (nîr′lē) ►*adv.* Almost but not quite.

near·sight·ed (nîr′sī′tĭd) ►*adj.* Unable to see distant objects clearly. —**near′sight′ed·ly** *adv.* —**near′sight′ed·ness** *n.*

neat (nēt) ►*adj.* **-er, -est 1.** Clean and tidy. **2.** Orderly and precise; systematic. **3.** Marked by ingenuity and skill; adroit: *a neat turn of phrase.* **4.** Not diluted: *neat whiskey.* **5.** *Slang* Wonderful; terrific: *a neat party.* [< Lat. *nitidus*, elegant.] —**neat′ly** *adv.* —**neat′ness** *n.*

neat·en (nēt′n) ►*v.* To make neat or tidy.

neath or **'neath** (nēth) ►*prep.* Beneath.

neat's-foot oil (nēts′fŏŏt′) ►*n.* A light yellow

oil obtained from the feet and shinbones of cattle, used chiefly to dress leather. [< *neat*, cow < OE *nēat*.]

neb·bish (nĕb′ĭsh) ►*n.* A weak-willed or timid person. [< Yiddish *nebekh*, poor.]

Ne·bras·ka (nə-brăs′kə) A state of the central US in the Great Plains. Cap. Lincoln. —**Ne·bras′kan** *adj. & n.*

Neb·u·chad·nez·zar II (nĕb′ə-kəd-nĕz′ər, nĕb′yə-) 630?–562 BC. King of Babylonia (605–562).

neb·u·la (nĕb′yə-lə) ►*n., pl.* **-lae** (-lē′) or **-las** A diffuse mass of interstellar dust or gas. [< Lat., cloud.] —**neb′u·lar** *adj.*

neb·u·lize (nĕb′yə-līz′) ►*v.* **-lized, -liz·ing** To convert (a liquid) to a fine spray; atomize. —**neb′u·li·za′tion** *n.* —**neb′u·liz′er** *n.*

neb·u·los·i·ty (nĕb′yə-lŏs′ĭ-tē) ►*n., pl.* **-ties 1.** The quality or condition of being nebulous. **2.** A nebula.

neb·u·lous (nĕb′yə-ləs) ►*adj.* **1.** Cloudy, misty, or hazy. **2.** Lacking definite form or limits; vague: *nebulous assurances of future cooperation.* **3.** Of or characteristic of a nebula. —**neb′u·lous·ly** *adv.* —**neb′u·lous·ness** *n.*

nec·es·sar·i·ly (nĕs′ĭ-sâr′ə-lē, -sĕr′-) ►*adv.* Of necessity; inevitably.

nec·es·sar·y (nĕs′ĭ-sĕr′ē) ►*adj.* **1.** Needed or required. See Synonyms at **indispensable**. **2.** Unavoidably determined; inevitable: *the necessary results of overindulgence.* **3.** Required by obligation, compulsion, or convention. ►*n., pl.* **-ies** Something indispensable. [< Lat. *necesse*.]

ne·ces·si·tate (nə-sĕs′ĭ-tāt′) ►*v.* **-tat·ed, -tat·ing** To make necessary or unavoidable. —**ne·ces′si·ta′tion** *n.*

ne·ces·si·tous (nə-sĕs′ĭ-təs) ►*adj.* **1.** Needy; indigent. **2.** Urgent.

ne·ces·si·ty (nə-sĕs′ĭ-tē) ►*n., pl.* **-ties 1a.** The condition or quality of being necessary. **b.** Something necessary. **2.** The force exerted by circumstance. **3.** Pressing or urgent need, esp. that arising from poverty. [< Lat. *necessitās*.]

neck (nĕk) ►*n.* **1.** The part of the body joining the head to the trunk. **2.** The part of a garment around or near the neck. **3.** A narrow elongation, projection, or connecting part: *a neck of land; the neck of a flask.* **4.** A narrow margin: *won by a neck.* ►*v. Informal* To kiss and caress amorously. —*idiom:* **neck and neck** Very close together, as in a race. [< OE *hnecca*.] —**necked** *adj.*

neck·er·chief (nĕk′ər-chĭf, -chēf′) ►*n.* A kerchief worn around the neck.

neck·lace (nĕk′lĭs) ►*n.* An ornament worn around the neck.

neck·line (nĕk′līn′) ►*n.* The line formed by the edge of a garment at the neck.

neck·tie (nĕk′tī′) ►*n.* A narrow fabric band worn around the neck and tied in a knot or bow close to the throat.

necro– or **necr–** ►*pref.* Death; the dead: *necrosis.* [< Gk. *nekros*, corpse.]

ne·crol·o·gy (nə-krŏl′ə-jē, nĕ-) ►*n., pl.* **-gies 1.** A list of people who have died, esp. in the recent past. **2.** An obituary. —**nec′ro·log′ic** (nĕk′rə-lŏj′ĭk), **nec′ro·log′i·cal** *adj.* —**ne·crol′o·gist** *n.*

nec·ro·man·cy (nĕk′rə-măn′sē) ►*n.* **1.** The art

that professes to communicate with the spirits of the dead so as to predict the future. **2.** Black magic; sorcery. [NECRO– + Gk. *manteia*, divination.] —**nec′ro·man′cer** *n.*

ne·crop·o·lis (nə-krŏp′ə-lĭs, nĕ-) ►*n., pl.* **-lis·es** or **-leis** (-lās′) A cemetery, esp. a large and elaborate one in an ancient city. [Gk. *nekropolis* : NECRO– + *polis*, city.]

ne·cro·sis (nə-krō′sĭs, nĕ-) ►*n., pl.* **-ses** (-sēz′) Death of cells or tissues through injury or disease. —**ne·crot′ic** (-krŏt′ĭk) *adj.*

nec·tar (nĕk′tər) ►*n.* **1.** A sweet liquid secreted esp. by flowers. **2.** *Gk. & Rom. Myth.* The drink of the gods. **3.** A delicious or invigorating drink. [< Gk. *nektar*.]

nec·tar·ine (nĕk′tə-rēn′) ►*n.* A variety of peach having a smooth waxy skin. [< obsolete *nectarine*, sweet as nectar.]

née also **nee** (nā) ►*adj.* Born. [Fr., feminine p.part. of *naître*, be born.]

need (nēd) ►*n.* **1.** A condition in which something must be supplied in order for a desired state to be achieved. **2.** Something required or wanted; requisite. **3.** Necessity; obligation. **4.** Poverty or misfortune: *in dire need.* —*aux.* To be under the necessity of or the obligation to: *They need not come.* ►*v.* **1.** To have need of; require: *The family needs money.* **2.** To be in need or want. [< OE *nēod*, necessity.]

need·ful (nēd′fəl) ►*adj.* **1.** Necessary; required: *needful repairs.* **2.** Being in need of something. —**need′ful·ly** *adv.*

nee·dle (nēd′l) ►*n.* **1a.** A small slender implement used for sewing, made usu. of steel and having an eye at one end through which a thread is passed. **b.** A similarly shaped implement, such as one used in knitting. **2.** A stylus used to transmit vibrations from the grooves of a phonograph record. **3.** A slender pointer or indicator, as on a dial. **4.** A hypodermic needle. **5.** A narrow stiff leaf, as those of conifers. **6.** A fine sharp projection, as a spine of a sea urchin. ►*v.* **-dled, -dling** *Informal* To goad, provoke, or tease. [< OE *nǣdl.*]

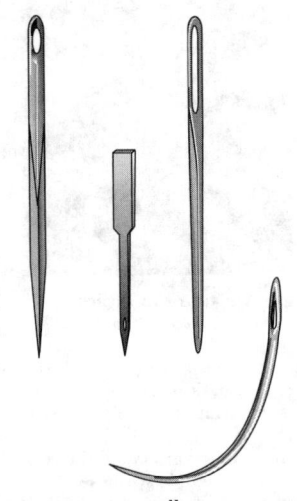

needle
left to right: sailmaking, sewing machine, and tapestry needles
bottom right: spring needle

nee·dle·point (nēd′l-point′) ▸*n.* Decorative needlework on canvas.

need·less (nēd′lĭs) ▸*adj.* Not needed or wished for; unnecessary. —**need′less·ly** *adv.*

nee·dle·work (nēd′l-wûrk′) ▸*n.* Work, such as embroidery, that is done with a needle.

need·n't (nēd′nt) Need not.

needs (nēdz) ▸*adv.* Of necessity; necessarily: *We must needs go.* [< OE *nēde.*]

need·y (nē′dē) ▸*adj.* **-i·er, -i·est 1.** Being in need; impoverished. **2.** Wanting or needing affection, esp. to an excessive degree. —**need′i·ness** *n.*

ne'er (nâr) ▸*adv.* Never.

ne'er-do-well (nâr′dōō-wĕl′) ▸*n.* An idle, irresponsible person. —**ne'er′-do-well′** *adj.*

ne·far·i·ous (nə-fâr′ē-əs) ▸*adj.* Extremely wicked. [< Lat. *nefās,* crime.] —**ne·far′i·ous·ly** *adv.* —**ne·far′i·ous·ness** *n.*

Nef·er·ti·ti (nĕf′ər-tē′tē) 14th cent. BC. Queen of Egypt as the wife of Akhenaten.

neg. ▸*abbr.* Negative.

ne·gate (nĭ-gāt′) ▸*v.* **-gat·ed, -gat·ing 1.** To make ineffective or invalid. **2.** To make negative. [Lat. *negāre,* deny.] —**ne·ga′tion** *n.*

neg·a·tive (nĕg′ə-tĭv) ▸*adj.* **1a.** Expressing negation, refusal, or denial. **b.** Indicating opposition or resistance: *a negative reaction.* **2.** Not positive or constructive: *negative criticism.* **3.** *Med.* Not indicating the presence of a disease or specific condition. **4.** *Math.* **a.** Of or being a quantity less than zero. **b.** Of or being a quantity, number, angle, velocity, or direction in a sense opposite to another understood to be positive. **5.** *Phys.* Of or being an electric charge of the same sign as that of an electron, indicated by the symbol (−). ▸*n.* **1.** A negative word, statement, or act. See Usage Note at **double negative. 2.** A feature or aspect that is not positive or affirmative. **3.** The side in a debate that opposes the question being debated. **4a.** An image in which the light areas of the object rendered appear dark and the dark areas appear light. **b.** A film, plate, or other photographic material containing such an image. ▸*v.* **-tived, -tiv·ing 1.** To veto. **2.** To deny. —**neg′a·tive·ly** *adv.* —**neg′a·tiv′i·ty** (-tĭv′ĭ-tē) *n.*

neg·a·tiv·ism (nĕg′ə-tĭ-vĭz′əm) ▸*n.* A habitual attitude of skepticism or resistance to the suggestions or instructions of others. —**neg′a·tiv·ist** *n.* —**neg′a·tiv·is′tic** *adj.*

Ne·gev (nĕg′ĕv) A hilly desert region of S Israel.

ne·glect (nĭ-glĕkt′) ▸*v.* **1.** To ignore; disregard. **2.** To fail to care for or attend to properly: *neglects her appearance.* **3.** To fail to do through carelessness or oversight. ▸*n.* **1.** The act or an instance of neglecting something. **2.** The state of being neglected. [Lat. *neglegere, neglēct-.*] —**ne·glect′er** *n.*

ne·glect·ful (nĭ-glĕkt′fəl) ▸*adj.* Marked by neglect. See Synonyms at **negligent.** —**ne·glect′ful·ly** *adv.*

neg·li·gee also **neg·li·gée** (nĕg′lĭ-zhā′, nĕg′-lĭ-zhā′) ▸*n.* A woman's loose dressing gown. [Fr. *négligée.*]

neg·li·gence (nĕg′lĭ-jəns) ▸*n.* **1.** The state or quality of being negligent. **2.** *Law* Failure to use the degree of care appropriate to the circumstances, resulting in an unintended injury to another.

neg·li·gent (nĕg′lĭ-jənt) ▸*adj.* **1.** Given to or characterized by negligence. **2.** *Law* Acting with or done through negligence. [< Lat. *neglegere,* neglect.] —**neg′li·gent·ly** *adv.*

   Syns: *derelict, lax, neglectful, remiss, slack* **adj.**

neg·li·gi·ble (nĕg′lĭ-jə-bəl) ▸*adj.* Not worth considering; trifling. —**neg′li·gi·bil′i·ty** *n.* —**neg′li·gi·bly** *adv.*

ne·go·ti·ate (nĭ-gō′shē-āt′) ▸*v.* **-at·ed, -at·ing 1.** To confer with another in order to come to terms. **2.** To arrange or settle by agreement: *negotiate a contract.* **3.** To transfer (an instrument, such as a promissory note) to another party by signing the back of it. **4.** To succeed in coping with: *negotiate a sharp curve.* [< Lat. *negōtium,* business.] —**ne·go′tia·bil′i·ty** *n.* —**ne·go′tia·ble** (-shə-bəl, -shē-ə-) *adj.* —**ne·go′ti·a′tion** *n.* —**ne·go′ti·a′tor** *n.*

ne·gri·tude or **Ne·gri·tude** (nē′grĭ-tōōd′, -tyōōd′, nĕg′rĭ-) ▸*n.* Awareness of and pride in black culture. [Fr. *négritude.*]

Ne·gro (nē′grō) ▸*n., pl.* **-groes** *Often Offensive* A black person. [< Sp. and Port. *negro,* black < Lat. *niger.*] —**Ne′gro** *adj.*

Ne·gro (nē′grō, -grōō), **Río 1.** A river rising in S Brazil and flowing about 805 km (500 mi) to the Uruguay R. in SW Uruguay. **2.** A river of NW South America flowing about 2,255 km (1,400 mi) from E Colombia to the Amazon R. near Manaus, Brazil.

Ne·groid (nē′groid′) ▸*adj.* Of or being a human racial classification traditionally distinguished by physical characteristics such as brown to black pigmentation and tightly curled hair and including peoples indigenous to sub-Saharan Africa. Not in scientific use. —**Ne′groid′** *n.*

   Usage: *Negroid, Caucasoid, Mongoloid,* and similar words were coined as racial categorizations in the 1800s. These words, once widely used in anthropology, are now rarely used scientifically. The general nonscientific use of these words is often considered offensive and should be avoided.

Ne·he·mi·ah (nē′hə-mī′ə, nē′ə-) ▸*n.* **1.** A Hebrew leader of the 5th cent. BC. **2.** See table at **Bible.**

Neh·ru (nā′rōō), **Jawaharlal** 1889–1964. Indian prime minister (1947–64).

neigh (nā) ▸*n.* The long, high-pitched sound made by a horse. [< OE *hnǣgan,* to neigh.] —**neigh** *v.*

neigh·bor (nā′bər) ▸*n.* **1.** One that lives or is located near another. **2.** A fellow human. ▸*v.* **1.** To lie close to or border on. **2.** To live or be situated close by. [< OE *nēahgebūr : nēah,* near + *gebūr,* dweller.]

neigh·bor·hood (nā′bər-hood′) ▸*n.* **1.** A district or area with distinctive characteristics. **2.** The people who live in a particular district. **3.** The surrounding area; vicinity. **4.** *Informal* Approximate amount or range: *in the neighborhood of a million dollars.*

neigh·bor·ly (nā′bər-lē) ▸*adj.* Having or exhibiting the qualities of a friendly neighbor. —**neigh′bor·li·ness** *n.*

nei·ther (nē′thər, nī′-) ▸*adj.* Not one or the other; not either: *Neither shoe feels comfortable.* ▸*pron.* Not either one: *Neither of them fits.* ▸*conj.* **1.** Not either. Used with *nor: I got neither the gift nor the card.* **2.** Also not: *If he won't go, neither will she.* [< OE *nāhwæther.*]

Usage: As a conjunction *neither* is properly followed by *nor*, not *or*, in formal style: *Neither prayers nor curses did any good.*

nel·son (nĕl′sən) ►*n.* A wrestling hold in which the user places an arm under the opponent's arm and presses the wrist or the palm of the hand against the opponent's neck.

Nelson, Horatio Viscount Nelson. 1758–1805. British admiral.

nem·a·tode (nĕm′ə-tōd′) ►*n.* Any of numerous worms having unsegmented cylindrical bodies often narrowing at each end. [Gk. *nēma,* thread + –OID.]

nem·e·sis (nĕm′ĭ-sĭs) ►*n., pl.* **-ses** (-sēz′) **1.** A source of downfall or ruin. **2.** An implacable or unbeatable foe. **3.** One that inflicts just retribution; avenger. **4. Nemesis** *Gk. Myth.* The goddess of retributive justice or vengeance. [Gk., retribution.]

Nen·ets (nĕn′ĕts) ►*n., pl.* **Nenets 1.** A member of a nomadic people of extreme NW Russia. **2.** The Uralic language of the Nenets. [Nenets, human being, Nenets.]

neo– ►*pref.* New; recent: *Neolithic.* [< Gk. *neos,* new.]

ne·o·clas·si·cism (nē′ō-klăs′ĭ-sĭz′əm) ►*n.* A revival of classical aesthetics and forms, esp. in art, architecture, or music. **—ne′o·clas′sic, ne′o·clas′si·cal** *adj.* **—ne′o·clas′si·cist** *n.*

ne·o·co·lo·ni·al·ism (nē′ō-kə-lō′nē-ə-lĭz′əm) ►*n.* The policy or practice of a powerful nation in extending its influence into a less developed one. **—ne′o·co·lo′ni·al** *adj.* **—ne′o·co·lo′ni·al·ist** *n.*

ne·o·dym·i·um (nē′ō-dĭm′ē-əm) ►*n. Symbol* **Nd** A bright, silvery rare-earth element used esp. for coloring glass. At. no. 60. See table at **element.** [NEO– + (*di*)*dymium,* a mixture of rare-earth elements.]

Ne·o·lith·ic (nē′ə-lĭth′ĭk) ►*adj.* Of or being the Stone Age period beginning in the Middle East around 10,000 BC, marked by the development of agriculture and the making of polished stone implements. ►*n.* The Neolithic Period.

ne·ol·o·gism (nē-ŏl′ə-jĭz′əm) ►*n.* A new word, expression, or usage.

ne·on (nē′ŏn′) ►*n.* **1.** *Symbol* **Ne** A rare, inert gaseous element that glows reddish orange in an electric discharge and is used in cathode-ray tubes and other display devices. At. no. 10. See table at **element. 2.** An extremely bright shade of a color. [< Gk. *neos,* new.]

ne·o·nate (nē′ə-nāt′) ►*n.* A newborn infant. [NEO– + Lat. *nātus,* born.] **—ne′o·na′tal** *adj.*

Ne·o·pa·gan (nē′ō-pā′gən) ►*adj.* Of or relating to a religious movement combining worship of pagan nature deities, particularly of the earth, with benign witchcraft. ►*n.* An adherent of such a religion. **—Ne′o·pa′gan·ism** *n.*

ne·o·phyte (nē′ə-fīt′) ►*n.* **1.** A recent convert. **2.** A beginner or novice. [< Gk. *neophutos* : NEO– + -*phutos,* planted (< *phuein,* bring forth).]

ne·o·plasm (nē′ə-plăz′əm) ►*n.* An abnormal new growth of tissue; tumor. **—ne′o·plas′tic** *adj.*

ne·o·prene (nē′ə-prēn′) ►*n.* A tough synthetic rubber used esp. in weather-resistant products, adhesives, shoe soles, paints, and rocket fuels. [NEO– + (*chloro*)*prene.*]

Ne·pal (nə-pôl′, -päl′, nä-) A country of S Asia in the Himalayas between India and SW China. Cap. Kathmandu. **—Nep·al·ese′** (nĕp′ə-lēz′, -lēs′), **Ne·pal′i** *adj. & n.*

ne·pen·the (nĭ-pĕn′thē) ►*n.* **1.** A legendary drug of ancient times, used as a remedy for grief. **2.** Something that eases sorrow or pain. [< Gk. *nēpenthes (pharmakon),* grief-banishing (drug).]

neph·ew (nĕf′yoō) ►*n.* A son of one's brother or sister or of the brother or sister of one's spouse. [< Lat. *nepōs.*]

neph·rite (nĕf′rīt′) ►*n.* A white to dark green variety of jade. [Gk. *nephros,* kidney + –ITE¹.]

ne·phrit·ic (nə-frĭt′ĭk) ►*adj.* **1.** Of the kidneys. **2.** Of or affected with nephritis.

ne·phri·tis (nə-frī′tĭs) ►*n.* Inflammation of the kidneys.

nephro– or **nephr–** ►*pref.* Kidney: *nephritis.* [< Gk. *nephros.*]

nep·o·tism (nĕp′ə-tĭz′əm) ►*n.* Favoritism shown or patronage granted to relatives. [< Lat. *nepōs,* nephew.] **—nep′o·tist** *n.*

Nep·tune (nĕp′toōn′, -tyoōn′) ►*n.* **1.** *Rom. Myth.* The god of the sea. **2.** The 8th planet from the sun, at a mean distance of 4.5 billion km (2.8 billion mi) and with a mean diameter of 49,528 km (30,775 mi). **—Nep·tu′ni·an** *adj.*

nep·tu·ni·um (nĕp-toō′nē-əm, -tyoō′-) ►*n. Symbol* **Np** A naturally radioactive metallic element. At. no. 93. See table at **element.** [< NEPTUNE.]

nerd (nûrd) ►*n. Slang* An unpopular or socially inept person, esp. one regarded as excessively studious. [?] **—nerd′y** *adj.*

Ne·ro (nîr′ō, nē′rō) AD 37–68. Emperor of Rome (54–68). **—Ne·ro′ni·an** *adj.*

Ne·ru·da (nĕ-roō′də), **Pablo** Ricardo Eliezer Neftali Reyes. 1904–73. Chilean poet.

nerve (nûrv) ►*n.* **1.** Any of the cordlike bundles of fibers made up of neurons through which sensory stimuli and motor impulses pass between the central nervous system and other parts of the body. **2.** The sensitive tissue in the pulp of a tooth. **3.** A sore point: *The criticism touched a nerve.* **4a.** Courage: *lost my nerve.* **b.** Fortitude; stamina. **c.** Brazen boldness; cheek. **5. nerves** Nervous agitation caused by fear, anxiety, or stress. ►*v.* **nerved, nerv·ing** To give strength or courage to. [< Lat. *nervus.*]

nerve cell ►*n.* See **neuron.**

nerve center ►*n.* A source of power or control.

nerve gas ►*n.* A poisonous compound that interferes with the functioning of nerves.

nerve·less (nûrv′lĭs) ►*adj.* **1.** Lacking strength or energy. **2.** Lacking courage. **3.** Calm and controlled. **—nerve′less·ly** *adv.* **—nerve′less·ness** *n.*

nerve-rack·ing or **nerve-wrack·ing** (nûrv′-răk′ĭng) ►*adj.* Intensely distressing.

nerv·ous (nûr′vəs) ►*adj.* **1.** Of or affecting the nerves or nervous system. **2.** High-strung; jumpy. **3.** Uneasy; apprehensive. **4.** Restless; lively: *nervous energy.* **—nerv′ous·ly** *adv.* **—nerv′ous·ness** *n.*

nervous breakdown ►*n.* An episode of severe or incapacitating emotional disorder.

nervous system ►*n.* The system of cells, tissues, and organs that regulates the body's responses to internal and external stimuli.

nerv·y (nûr′vē) ►*adj.* **-i·er, -i·est 1.** Arrogantly

impudent; brazen. **2.** Bold; daring. **3.** *Chiefly Brit.* Jumpy; nervous.

Ness (nĕs), **Loch** A lake of N-central Scotland.

–ness ►*suff.* State; quality; condition; degree: *brightness.* [< OE *-nes.*]

nest (nĕst) ►*n.* **1a.** A shelter made by a bird to hold its eggs and young. **b.** A similar structure built by fish, insects, or other animals. **2.** A snug, cozy place. **3.** A hotbed: *a nest of criminal activity.* **4.** A set of objects that can be stacked together: *a nest of tables.* ►*v.* **1.** To build or occupy a nest. **2.** To fit or stack snugly together. [< OE.]

nest
nesting Japanese figures

nest egg ►*n.* A reserve sum of money.

nes·tle (nĕs′əl) ►*v.* **-tled, -tling** **1.** To settle snugly and comfortably. **2.** To lie in a sheltered location. **3.** To snuggle. [< OE *nestlian,* make a nest.] —**nes′tler** *n.*

nest·ling (nĕst′lĭng, nĕs′-) ►*n.* A bird too young to leave its nest.

net¹ (nĕt) ►*n.* **1.** An openwork meshed fabric. **2.** Something made of net, as a device used to capture animals or act as a barrier: *a fishing net; a mosquito net.* **3a.** A barrier strung between two posts to divide a court in half, as in tennis. **b.** The cord meshwork attached to the hoop of a basket in basketball. **4.** *Comp.* **a.** A complex, interconnected group or system. **b. Net** The Internet. ►*v.* **net·ted, net·ting** To catch or ensnare in or as if in a net. [< OE.] —**net′ting** *n.*

net² (nĕt) ►*adj.* **1.** Remaining after all deductions or adjustments have been made: *net profit.* **2.** Ultimate; final: *the net result.* ►*n.* A net amount. ►*v.* **net·ted, net·ting** To bring in as profit. [ME < OFr., NEAT.]

Ne·tan·ya·hu (nĕt′n-yä′hōō, nĕ′tän-), **Benjamin** or **Binyamin** b. 1949. Israeli prime minister (1996–99 and 2009–).

neth·er (nĕth′ər) ►*adj.* Located beneath or below. [< OE *neother,* down.]

Neth·er·lands (nĕth′ər-ləndz) Often called **Holland** A country of NW Europe on the North Sea. Caps. Amsterdam and The Hague. —**Neth′er·land′ish** *adj.*

net·i·quette (nĕt′ĭ-kĕt′, -kĭt) ►*n.* Etiquette advocated in communication over a computer network. [Blend of (INTER)NET and ETIQUETTE.]

net·tle (nĕt′l) ►*n.* A plant with toothed leaves and stinging hairs. ►*v.* **-tled, -tling** To irritate; vex. [< OE *netele.*] —**net′tle·some** *adj.*

net·work (nĕt′wûrk′) ►*n.* **1.** An openwork fabric or structure in which cords, threads, or wires cross at regular intervals. **2.** A complex, interconnected group or system: *a spy network.* **3.** A chain of radio or television broadcasting stations with shared or coordinated program-

ming. **4.** A system of computers that is interconnected so as to share information. ►*v.* **1.** To interact with others for mutual assistance or support. **2.** To connect (computers) into a network.

Ne·tza·hual·có·yotl (nĕ-tsä′wäl-kō-yōt′l) A city of S-central Mexico, a suburb of Mexico City.

neu·ral (nŏŏr′əl, nyŏŏr′-) ►*adj.* Of or relating to a nerve or the nervous system.

neu·ral·gia (nŏŏ-răl′jə, nyŏŏ-) ►*n.* Intense pain extending along a nerve. [< NEUR(O)– + Gk. *algos,* pain.] —**neu·ral′gic** *adj.*

neu·ri·tis (nŏŏ-rī′tĭs, nyŏŏ-) ►*n.* Inflammation of a nerve. —**neu·rit′ic** (-rĭt′ĭk) *adj.*

neuro– or **neur–** ►*pref.* Nerve; nervous system: *neuritis.* [< Gk. *neuron,* sinew, string.]

neu·rol·o·gy (nŏŏ-rŏl′ə-jē, nyŏŏ-) ►*n.* The study of diseases and disorders of the nervous system. —**neu′ro·log′ic** (nŏŏr′ə-lŏj′-ĭk, nyŏŏr′-), **neu′ro·log′i·cal** (-ĭ-kəl) *adj.* —**neu′ro·log′i·cal·ly** *adv.* —**neu·rol′o·gist** *n.*

neu·ron (nŏŏr′ŏn′, nyŏŏr′-) also **neu·rone** (-ōn′) ►*n.* Any of the impulse-conducting cells that make up the nervous system, consisting of a nucleated cell body with dendrites and a single axon. [Gk., sinew, nerve.] —**neu·ron′ic** *adj.*

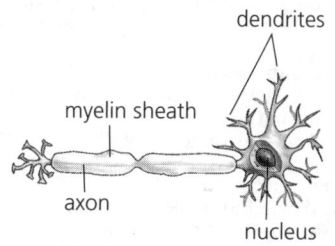

neuron

neu·ro·sis (nŏŏ-rō′sĭs, nyŏŏ-) ►*n.,* pl. **-ses** (-sēz) A mental state marked by excessive anxiety or insecurity compensated for by various defense mechanisms. No longer used in psychiatric diagnosis.

neu·ro·sur·ger·y (nŏŏr′ō-sûr′jə-rē, nyŏŏr′-) ►*n.* Surgery on a part of the nervous system. —**neu′ro·sur′geon** *n.*

neu·rot·ic (nŏŏ-rŏt′ĭk, nyŏŏ-) ►*adj.* **1.** Relating to or affected with a neurosis. No longer used in psychiatric diagnosis. **2.** *Informal* Extremely anxious: *neurotic about money.* ►*n.* **1.** A person suffering from a neurosis. No longer used in psychiatric diagnosis. **2.** *Informal* A person who is chronically anxious. —**neu·rot′i·cal·ly** *adv.*

neu·ro·trans·mit·ter (nŏŏr′ō-trăns′mĭt-ər, -trănz′-, nyŏŏr′-) ►*n.* A chemical substance, such as dopamine, that transmits nerve impulses across a synapse.

neut. ►*abbr.* **1.** neuter **2.** neutral

neu·ter (nŏŏ′tər, nyŏŏr′-) ►*adj.* **1.** *Gram.* Neither masculine nor feminine in gender. **2a.** Having undeveloped or nonfunctional sexual organs. **b.** Having pistils and stamens that are nonfunctional or absent. ►*n.* **1.** *Gram.* **a.** The neuter gender. **b.** A neuter word. **2.** A castrated or spayed animal. **3.** An insect that has undeveloped or nonfunctional sexual organs, such as a worker bee. ►*v.* To castrate or spay. [< Lat., neither.]

neu·tral (nōō′trəl, nyōō′-) ►*adj.* **1.** Not aligned with or supporting a side in a war, dispute, or contest. **2.** Belonging to neither kind or side. **3.** *Chem.* Neither acidic nor alkaline. **4.** *Phys.* Having a net electric charge of zero. **5.** Of or indicating a color that lacks hue; achromatic. ►*n.* **1.** A neutral nation or person. **2.** A neutral color. **3.** A position in which a set of gears is disengaged. [< Lat. *neutrālis,* grammatically neutral.] —**neu′tral·ly** *adv.*

neu·tral·ism (nōō′trə-lĭz′əm, nyōō′-) ►*n.* Neutrality. —**neu′tral·ist** *adj. & n.*

neu·tral·i·ty (nōō-trăl′ĭ-tē, nyōō-) ►*n.* The state or policy of being neutral, esp. in war.

neu·tral·ize (nōō′trə-līz′, nyōō′-) ►*v.* **-ized, -iz·ing** **1.** To make neutral. **2.** To render ineffective. —**neu′tral·i·za′tion** *n.* —**neu′tral·iz′er** *n.*

neutral spirits ►*pl.n.* *(takes sing. or pl. v.)* Ethyl alcohol distilled at or above 190 proof and used in blended alcoholic beverages.

neu·tri·no (nōō-trē′nō, nyōō-) ►*n., pl.* **-nos** Any of three electrically neutral leptons that have small or very small masses. [Ital.]

neu·tron (nōō′trŏn′, nyōō′-) ►*n.* An electrically neutral nucleon, stable when bound in an atomic nucleus and having a mean lifetime of 886 seconds as a free particle. [NEUTR(AL) + -ON[1].]

neutron bomb ►*n.* A nuclear bomb that produces many neutrons but little blast and thus destroys life but spares property.

Ne·va (nē′və) A river of NW Russia flowing about 74 km (46 mi) from Lake Ladoga to the Gulf of Finland.

Ne·vad·a (nə-văd′ə) A state of the W US. Cap. Carson City. —**Ne·vad′an** *adj. & n.*

Nev·el·son (nĕv′əl-sən) **Louise** 1899–1988. Russian-born Amer. sculptor.

nev·er (nĕv′ər) ►*adv.* **1.** Not ever; at no time. **2.** Not at all; in no way. [< OE *næfre.*]

nev·er·more (nĕv′ər-môr′) ►*adv.* Never again.

nev·er·the·less (nĕv′ər-*th*ə-lĕs′) ►*adv.* In spite of that; however.

ne·vus (nē′vəs) ►*n., pl.* **-vi** (-vī′) A lesion of the skin or oral mucosa that is usu. pigmented and raised. [Lat. *naevus.*]

new (nōō, nyōō) ►*adj.* **-er, -est** **1.** Not old; recent. **2.** Never used or worn before: *a new car.* **3.** Just found or learned: *new information.* **4.** Unfamiliar. **5.** Different from the former or the old. **6.** Recently arrived or established: *a new president.* **7.** Rejuvenated. **8.** Currently fashionable. **9.** New In the most recent form, period, or development. ►*adv.* Freshly; recently. [< OE *nīwe.*] —**new′ness** *n.*

New Age ►*adj.* **1.** Relating to a complex of spiritual and consciousness-raising movements originating in the 1970s. **2.** Of or being a style of modern music marked esp. by quiet harmonies and drones.

New Amsterdam A settlement estab. by the Dutch on S Manhattan I. in 1624 and renamed New York after its capture by the English in 1664.

New·ark (nōō′ərk, nyōō′-) A city of NE NJ on **Newark Bay,** an inlet of the Atlantic.

new·bie (nōō′bē, nyōō′-) ►*n.* One that is new

to something, esp. a novice at using computer technology or the Internet. [< NEW.]

new·born (nōō′bôrn′, nyōō′bôrn′) ►*adj.* **1.** Very recently born. **2.** Born anew. ►*n.* A neonate.

New Brunswick A province of E Canada on the Gulf of St. Lawrence. Cap. Fredericton.

New·cas·tle or **New·cas·tle upon Tyne** (nōō′kăs′əl, nyōō′-) A borough of NE England on the Tyne R. N of Leeds.

new·com·er (nōō′kŭm′ər, nyōō′-) ►*n.* One who has only recently arrived.

New Deal ►*n.* The programs and policies to promote economic recovery and social reform introduced in the 1930s by President Franklin Roosevelt. —**New Dealer** *n.*

New Delhi The capital of India, in the N-central part S of Delhi.

new·el (nōō′əl, nyōō′-) ►*n.* **1.** A vertical support at the center of a circular staircase. **2.** A post for a handrail at the bottom or landing of a staircase. [< Lat. *nōdulus,* little knot, nodule.]

New England A region of the NE US comprising ME, NH, VT, MA, CT, and RI. —**New Eng′land·er** *n.*

new·fan·gled (nōō′făng′gəld, nyōō′-) ►*adj.* New and often needlessly novel. [< ME *neufangel,* fond of novelty.]

new·found (nōō′found′, nyōō′-) ►*adj.* Recently discovered.

New·found·land (nōō′fən-lənd, -lănd′, -fənd-, nyōō′-) An island of E Canada, part of the province of Newfoundland and Labrador. Cap. St. John's. —**New′found·land·er** *n.*

Newfoundland and Labrador *Abbr.* **NL** A province of E Canada including the island of Newfoundland and nearby islands and the mainland area of Labrador with its adjacent islands. Cap. St. John's.

New Guinea An island in the SW Pacific N of Australia; divided politically between Indonesia and Papua New Guinea. —**New Guinean** *adj. & n.*

New Hamp·shire (hămp′shər, -shîr′, hăm′-) A state of the NE US between VT and ME. Cap. Concord. —**New Hamp′shir·ite′** *n.*

New Jersey A state of the E US on the Atlantic. Cap. Trenton. —**New Jer′sey·ite′** *n.*

New Latin ►*n.* Latin as used since about 1500.

new·ly (nōō′lē, nyōō′-) ►*adv.* **1.** Not long ago; recently. **2.** Once more; anew. **3.** In a new or different way; freshly.

new·ly·wed (nōō′lē-wĕd′, nyōō′-) ►*n.* A person recently married.

new math ►*n.* Mathematics taught in elementary and secondary schools that is based on set theory.

New Mexico A state of the SW US on the Mexican border. Cap. Santa Fe. —**New Mexican** *adj. & n.*

new moon ►*n.* The phase of the moon at which the moon, as viewed from Earth, does not appear to be illuminated by the sun.

New Neth·er·land (nĕth′ər-lənd) A Dutch colony in North America along the Hudson and lower Delaware Rivers; annexed by England and renamed New York in 1664.

New Or·leans (nōō ôr′lē-ənz, ôr′lənz, ôr-lēnz′, ô′lənz, nyōō, nô′lənz) A city of SE LA on the Mississippi R.

news (nōōz, nyōōz) ►*pl.n.* *(takes sing. v.)* **1a.**

Information about recent events. **b.** A presentation of such information, as in a newspaper. **2.** New information of any kind.

news·cast (nōōz′kăst′, nyōōz′-) ►*n.* A radio or television broadcast of the news. [NEWS + (BROAD)CAST.] —**news′cast′er** *n.*

news·group (nōōz′grōōp′, nyōōz′-) ►*n.* An area on a computer network, esp. the Internet, devoted to discussion of a specified topic.

news·let·ter (nōōz′lĕt′ər, nyōōz′-) ►*n.* A printed report giving news or information of interest to a special group.

news·pa·per (nōōz′pā′pər, nyōōz′-) ►*n.* **1.** A publication, usu. issued daily or weekly, containing current news, editorials, feature articles, and advertising. **2.** See **newsprint.**

news·print (nōōz′prĭnt′, nyōōz′-) ►*n.* Inexpensive paper used esp. for newspapers.

news·reel (nōōz′rēl′, nyōōz′-) ►*n.* A short film dealing with recent events.

news·stand (nōōz′stănd′, nyōōz′-) ►*n.* A stand at which newspapers and periodicals are sold.

news·wor·thy (nōōz′wûr′thē, nyōōz′-) ►*adj.* Interesting or important enough to warrant news coverage. —**news′wor′thi·ness** *n.*

news·y (nōō′zē, nyōō′-) ►*adj.* **-i·er, -i·est** *Informal* Full of news; informative.

newt (nōōt, nyōōt) ►*n.* Any of several small aquatic or semiaquatic salamanders. [< ME *an eute*, an eft < *evete*, EFT.]

New Testament ►*n.* The Gospels, Acts, Epistles, and the Book of Revelation. See table at **Bible.**

new·ton (nōōt′n, nyōōt′n) ►*n.* The unit of force required to accelerate a mass of 1 kilogram 1 meter per second. [After Sir Isaac NEWTON.]

Newton, Sir Isaac. 1642–1727. English mathematician and scientist. —**New·to′ni·an** *adj.*

New World The Western Hemisphere.

New Year's Day ►*n.* January 1, the first day of the year, celebrated as a holiday in many countries.

New Year's Eve ►*n.* The eve of New Year's Day, celebrated with merrymaking.

New York 1. A state of the NE US. Cap. Albany. **2.** or **New York City** A city of S NY at the mouth of the Hudson R. —**New York′er** *n.*

New Zea·land (zē′lənd) An island country in the S Pacific SE of Australia. Cap. Wellington. —**New Zea′land·er** *n.*

next (nĕkst) ►*adj.* **1.** Nearest in space or position; adjacent. **2.** Immediately following, as in time or sequence. ►*adv.* **1.** In the time, order, or place nearest or immediately following. **2.** On the first subsequent occasion: *when next I write.* ►*n.* The next person or thing. —*idiom:* **next to 1.** Adjacent to. **2.** Almost; practically. [< OE *nīehsta*, superl. of *nēah*, near.]

nex·us (nĕk′səs) ►*n., pl.* **-us** or **-us·es 1.** A means of connection; link or tie. **2.** A connected series or group. **3.** The core or center. [Lat. < *nectere*, bind.]

Nez Perce (nĕz′ pûrs′, nĕs′) ►*n., pl.* **Nez Perce** or **-ces** (pûr′sĭz) **1.** A member of a Native American people inhabiting W Idaho and NE Washington. **2.** The language of the Nez Perce.

NFL ►*abbr.* National Football League

NGO ►*abbr.* nongovernmental organization

ngul·trum (əng-gŭl′trəm) ►*n.* See table at **currency.** [Bhutanese.]

NH ►*abbr.* New Hampshire

NHL ►*abbr.* National Hockey League

ni·a·cin (nī′ə-sĭn) ►*n.* A white crystalline acid that is a component of the vitamin B complex. [< NICOTINIC ACID.]

Ni·ag·a·ra Falls (nī-ăg′rə, -ər-ə) Two waterfalls WNW of Buffalo, NY, on the **Niagara River**, a waterway flowing about 55 km (35 mi) N from Lake Erie to Lake Ontario along the US–Canada border.

Nia·mey (nē-ä′mā, nyä-mā′) The capital of Niger, in the SW part on the Niger R.

nib (nĭb) ►*n.* The point of a pen.

nib·ble (nĭb′əl) ►*v.* **-bled, -bling 1.** To bite at gently and repeatedly. **2.** To take small or hesitant bites. ►*n.* A morsel. [ME *nebyllen.*]

Ni·cae·a (nī-sē′ə) An ancient city of NW Asia Minor. —**Ni·cae′an** *adj.*

Nic·a·ra·gua (nĭk′ə-rä′gwə) A country of Central America on the Caribbean Sea and the Pacific. Cap. Managua. —**Ni′ca·ra′guan** *adj. & n.*

Nicaragua, Lake The largest lake of Central America, in SW Nicaragua.

nice (nīs) ►*adj.* **nic·er, nic·est 1.** Pleasing; agreeable. **2.** Pleasant; attractive. **3.** Courteous; polite. **4.** Of good character; respectable. **5.** Fastidious; fussy. **6.** Showing or requiring sensitive discernment; subtle. **7.** Done with skill. [< Lat. *nescius*, ignorant.] —**nice′ly** *adv.* —**nice′ness** *n.*

Nice (nēs) A city of SE France on the Mediterranean Sea.

ni·ce·ty (nī′sĭ-tē) ►*n., pl.* **-ties 1.** Precision or accuracy. **2.** Delicacy of character; scrupulousness. **3.** A fine point or subtle distinction. **4.** An elegant or refined feature.

niche (nĭch, nēsh) ►*n.* **1.** A recess in a wall, as for holding a statue. **2.** A situation or activity specially suited to one's interests or abilities. [< Lat. *nīdus*, nest.]

Nich·o·las (nĭk′ə-ləs), Saint. 4th cent. AD. Bishop of Myra in Asia Minor; often associated with Santa Claus.

Nicholas II 1868–1918. The last czar of Russia (1894–1917).

nick (nĭk) ►*n.* A shallow notch, cut, or chip on an edge or surface. ►*v.* **1.** To cut a nick or notch in. **2.** To cut short; check. —*idiom:* **in the nick of time** Just at the critical moment. [ME *nik.*]

nick·el (nĭk′əl) ►*n.* **1.** *Symbol* **Ni** A silvery, hard, ductile ferromagnetic metallic element used in corrosion-resistant alloys, stainless steel, and batteries, and for electroplating. At. no. 28. See table at **element. 2.** A US coin worth five cents. [< Ger. *Kupfernickel*, a nickel ore.]

nick·el·o·de·on (nĭk′ə-lō′dē-ən) ►*n.* **1.** An early movie theater charging an admission of five cents. **2.** A player piano. **3.** A jukebox. [NICKEL + (*Mel*)*odeon*, music hall.]

nick·er (nĭk′ər) ►*v.* To neigh softly. [Perh. < *neigher* < *neigh.*]

Nick·laus (nĭk′ləs), **Jack William** b. 1940. Amer. golfer.

nick·name (nĭk′nām′) ►*n.* **1.** A descriptive name added to or replacing the actual name of a person, place, or thing. **2.** A familiar or shortened form of a proper name. ►*v.* To give a nickname to. [< ME *an ekename*, an additional name : OE *ēaca*, addition + NAME.]

Nic·o·bar Islands (nĭk′ə-bär′) An island group in the Bay of Bengal NW of Sumatra.

Nic·o·si·a (nĭk′ə-sē′ə) The capital of Cyprus, in the N-central part.

nic·o·tine (nĭk′ə-tēn′) ►*n.* A colorless, poisonous alkaloid, $C_{10}H_{14}N_2$, derived from the tobacco plant and used as an insecticide. [Fr., after Jean *Nicot,* (1530?-1600).]

nic·o·tin·ic acid (nĭk′ə-tĭn′ĭk, -tē′nĭk) ►*n.* See **niacin.**

nic·ti·tate (nĭk′tĭ-tāt′) ►*v.* **-tat·ed, -tat·ing** To wink. [Med.Lat. *nictitāre.*] —**nic′ti·ta′tion** *n.*

Nie·buhr (nē′boŏr′, -bər), **Reinhold** 1892-1971. Amer. theologian.

niece (nēs) ►*n.* The daughter of one's brother or sister or of the brother or sister of one's spouse. [< Lat. *neptis.*]

Nie·tzsche (nē′chə, -chē), **Friedrich Wilhelm** 1844-1900. German philosopher. —**Nie′-tzsche·an** *adj. & n.*

nif·ty (nĭf′tē) ►*adj.* **-ti·er, -ti·est** *Slang* First-rate; great. [?]

Ni·ger (nī′jər, nē-zhâr′) A country of W-central Africa. Cap. Niamey.

Ni·ger-Con·go (nī′jər-kŏng′gō) ►*n.* A large language family of sub-Saharan Africa.

Ni·ge·ri·a (nī-jîr′ē-ə) A country of W Africa on the Gulf of Guinea. Cap. Abuja. —**Ni·ge′ri·an** *adj. & n.*

Niger River A river of W Africa rising in Guinea and flowing about 4,180 km (2,600 mi) through Mali, Niger, and Nigeria to the Gulf of Guinea.

nig·gard (nĭg′ərd) ►*n.* A stingy person; miser. ►*adj.* Stingy; miserly. [ME *nigard,* of Scand. orig.]

nig·gard·ly (nĭg′ərd-lē) ►*adj.* **1.** Grudging and petty; stingy. **2.** Scanty; meager. —**nig′gard·li·ness** *n.* —**nig′gard·ly** *adv.*

nig·gling (nĭg′lĭng) ►*adj.* **1.** Petty; trifling: *niggling details.* **2.** Annoying, troubling, or irritating in a petty way. [?] —**nig′gling·ly** *adv.*

nigh (nī) ►*adv.* **-er, -est 1.** Near in time, place, or relationship. **2.** Nearly; almost: *talked for nigh onto two hours.* ►*adj.* **-er, -est** Close; near. ►*prep.* Near. [< OE *nēah.*]

night (nīt) ►*n.* **1.** The period between sunset and sunrise, esp. the hours of darkness. **2.** Nightfall. **3.** Darkness. **4.** A time or condition of gloom, obscurity, ignorance, or despair. [< OE *niht.*]

night blindness ►*n.* Abnormally weak vision at night or in dim light. —**night′blind′** *adj.*

night·cap (nīt′kăp′) ►*n.* **1.** A usu. alcoholic drink taken just before bedtime. **2.** A cloth cap worn esp. in bed.

night·clothes (nīt′klōz′, -klō*th*z′) ►*pl.n.* See **sleepwear.**

night·club (nīt′klŭb′) ►*n.* An establishment that stays open late at night and provides food, drink, and entertainment.

night·crawl·er or **night crawler** (nīt′krô′lər) ►*n.* An earthworm that crawls out from the ground at night.

night·dress (nīt′drĕs′) ►*n.* A nightgown.

night·fall (nīt′fôl′) ►*n.* The approach of darkness; dusk.

night·gown (nīt′goun′) ►*n.* A loose garment worn in bed by women and girls.

night·hawk (nīt′hôk′) ►*n.* **1.** An insectivorous, chiefly nocturnal bird having grayish-brown plumage that mimics leaves on the forest floor. **2.** *Informal* A night owl.

night·ie or **night·y** (nīt′ē) ►*n., pl.* **-ies** *Informal* A nightgown.

night·in·gale (nīt′n-gāl′, nī′tĭng-gāl′) ►*n.* A reddish-brown songbird noted for the melodious song of the male during the breeding season, most often heard at night. [< OE *nihtegale* : *niht,* NIGHT + *galan,* sing.]

Nightingale, Florence 1820-1910. British nursing pioneer.

Florence Nightingale

night·jar (nīt′jär′) ►*n.* Any of various chiefly nocturnal, insectivorous birds, such as the whip-poor-will. [NIGHT + JAR² (< their harsh calls).]

night·life (nīt′līf′) ►*n.* Social activities or entertainment available in the evening.

night·ly (nīt′lē) ►*adj.* Of or occurring during the night or every night. —**night′ly** *adv.*

night·mare (nīt′mâr′) ►*n.* **1.** A very frightening dream. **2.** A very distressing event or experience. [ME, female incubus : NIGHT + *mare,* goblin.] —**night′mar′ish** *adj.*

night owl ►*n. Informal* A person who habitually stays up late at night.

night school ►*n.* A school that holds classes in the evening.

night·shade (nīt′shād′) ►*n.* Any of several related, sometimes poisonous plants, such as belladonna. [< OE *nihtscada.*]

night·shirt (nīt′shûrt′) ►*n.* A long loose shirt worn in bed.

night·stick (nīt′stĭk′) ►*n.* A club carried by a police officer.

night·time (nīt′tīm′) ►*n.* The time between sunset and sunrise.

ni·hil·ism (nī′ə-lĭz′əm, nē′-) ►*n.* **1.** The doctrine that nothing actually exists or that existence or values are meaningless. **2.** Political belief that advocates violence without discernible constructive goals. [< Lat. *nihil,* nothing.] —**ni′hil·ist** *n.* —**ni′hil·is′tic** *adj.*

Ni·jin·sky (nĭ-zhĭn′skē, -jĭn′-), **Vaslav** 1890-1950. Russian-born dancer and choreographer.

-nik ►*suff.* One associated with or characterized by: *beatnik.* [Of Slav. orig.]

Ni·ke (nī′kē) ►*n. Gk. Myth.* The goddess of victory.

nil (nĭl) ►*n.* Nothing; zero. [Lat. *nihil, nīl.*] —**nil** *adj.*

Nile (nīl) The longest river in the world, flowing about 6,675 km (4,150 mi) through E Africa from its sources in Burundi to a delta on the Mediterranean Sea in NE Egypt.

Ni·lo-Sa·har·an (nī′lō-sə-här′ən, -hâr′ən) ►*n.*

A language family of sub-Saharan Africa.

Ni·lot·ic (nī-lŏt′ĭk) ►*n.* A subfamily within the Nilo-Saharan languages.

Nils·son (nĭl′sən), **Birgit** 1918–2006. Swedish operatic soprano.

nim·ble (nĭm′bəl) ►*adj.* **-bler, -blest 1.** Quick and light in movement or action; deft. **2.** Quick and clever in devising or understanding. [< OE *næmel* and *numol.*] —**nim′bly** *adv.*

nim·bus (nĭm′bəs) ►*n., pl.* **-bi** (-bī′) or **-es 1.** A radiant light usu. in the form of a halo about or over the head in a representation, as of a deity or saint. **2.** A uniformly gray rain cloud. [Lat., cloud.]

NIMBY ►*abbr.* not in my backyard

Nim·itz (nĭm′ĭts), **Chester William** 1885–1966. Amer. admiral.

nin·com·poop (nĭn′kəm-po͞op′, nĭng′-) ►*n.* A silly or foolish person. [?]

nine (nīn) ►*n.* **1.** The cardinal number equal to 8 + 1. **2.** The 9th in a set or sequence. [< OE *nigon.*] —**nine** *adj. & pron.*

9/11 (nīn′ĭ-lĕv′ən) ►*n.* September 11, 2001, the date on which two hijacked airliners were flown into the World Trade Center in New York City and another into the Pentagon. A 4th hijacked airliner crashed in open land in PA.

nine·teen (nīn-tēn′) ►*n.* **1.** The cardinal number equal to 18 + 1. **2.** The 19th in a set or sequence. —**nine·teen′** *adj. & pron.*

nine·teenth (nīn-tēnth′) ►*n.* **1.** The ordinal number matching the number 19 in a series. **2.** One of 19 equal parts. —**nine·teenth′** *adv. & adj.*

nine·ti·eth (nīn′tē-ĭth) ►*n.* **1.** The ordinal number matching the number 90 in a series. **2.** One of 90 equal parts. —**nine′ti·eth** *adv. & adj.*

nine·ty (nīn′tē) ►*n., pl.* **-ties** The cardinal number equal to 9 × 10. —**nine′ty** *adj. & pron.*

Nin·e·veh (nĭn′ə-və) An ancient city of Assyria on the Tigris R. opposite the site of present-day Mosul, Iraq.

nin·ja (nĭn′jə) ►*n.* A medieval Japanese mercenary trained in the martial arts. [J.]

nin·ny (nĭn′ē) ►*n., pl.* **-nies** A fool; simpleton. [Perh. < alteration of INNOCENT.]

ninth (nīnth) ►*n.* **1.** The ordinal number matching the number 9 in a series. **2.** One of nine equal parts. —**ninth** *adv. & adj.*

ni·o·bi·um (nī-ō′bē-əm) ►*n. Symbol* **Nb** A silvery, soft, ductile metallic element used in steel alloys, arc welding, and superconductive materials. At. no. 41. See table at **element.** [< *Niobe,* in Greek myth.]

nip[1] (nĭp) ►*v.* **nipped, nip·ping 1.** To seize and pinch or bite. **2.** To sever by pinching or snipping. **3.** To sting with the cold. **4.** To check or cut off the growth or development of: *a conspiracy that was nipped in the bud.* **5.** *Slang* **a.** To snatch up hastily. **b.** To steal. ►*n.* **1.** A small pinch or bite. **2.** A small amount. **3.** Sharp stinging cold. [Perh. < MDu. *nipen.*]

nip[2] (nĭp) ►*n.* A small amount of liquor. ►*v.* **nipped, nip·ping** To sip (liquor) in small amounts. [Prob. of Du. or LGer. orig.]

nip·per (nĭp′ər) ►*n.* **1.** often **nippers** A tool, such as pliers, used for grasping or nipping. **2.** A pincerlike claw.

nip·ple (nĭp′əl) ►*n.* **1.** The small projection of a mammary gland containing the outlets of the milk ducts. **2.** Something resembling a nipple, esp. the rubber cap on a baby's bottle. [< obsolete *neble,* dim. of ME *neb,* beak, nose < OE.]

nip·py (nĭp′ē) ►*adj.* **-pi·er, -pi·est 1.** Sharp or biting. **2.** Bitingly cold.

nir·va·na (nĭr-vä′nə, nər-) ►*n.* **1.** often **Nirvana** *Buddhism* A state in which the mind, enlightened as to the illusory nature of the self, transcends all suffering and attains peace. **2.** An ideal condition of harmony, stability, or joy. [Skt. *nirvāṇam.*]

Ni·san (nĭs′ən, nē-sän′) ►*n.* The 1st month of the Jewish calendar. See table at **calendar.** [Heb. *nîsān.*]

Ni·sei (nē-sā′, nē′sā′) ►*n., pl.* **-sei** or **-seis** A person born in America of parents who emigrated from Japan. [J.]

nit (nĭt) ►*n.* The egg of certain parasitic insects, esp. a head louse. [< OE *hnitu.*] —**nit′ty** *adj.*

ni·ter (nī′tər) ►*n.* See **potassium nitrate.** [< Gk. *nitron,* soda, of Semitic orig.]

nit·pick (nĭt′pĭk′) ►*v.* To be concerned with insignificant details. See Synonyms at **quibble.** —**nit′pick′er** *n.*

ni·trate (nī′trāt′, -trĭt) ►*n.* **1.** The univalent anionic group NO_3, derived from nitric acid, or a compound containing this group. **2.** Fertilizer consisting of sodium nitrate or potassium nitrate. ►*v.* **-trat·ed, -trat·ing** To treat with nitric acid or a nitrate, usu. to change (an organic compound) into a nitrate. —**ni·tra′tion** *n.*

ni·tric acid (nī′trĭk) ►*n.* A colorless to yellowish corrosive liquid, HNO_3, used in the production of fertilizers, explosives, and rocket fuels.

ni·tride (nī′trīd′) ►*n.* A compound of nitrogen, esp. a binary compound of nitrogen.

ni·tri·fy (nī′trə-fī′) ►*v.* **-fied, -fy·ing 1.** To oxidize (an ammonia compound) into a nitrite or (a nitrite) into a nitrate, esp. by the action of nitrifying bacteria. **2.** To treat or combine with nitrogen or compounds containing nitrogen. —**ni′tri·fi·ca′tion** *n.*

nit·ri·fy·ing bacterium (nī′trə-fī′ĭng) ►*n.* Any of various soil bacteria that oxidize ammonium compounds into nitrites or nitrites into nitrates.

ni·trite (nī′trīt′) ►*n.* The univalent anionic group NO_2, or a compound containing it.

nitro- or **nitr-** ►*pref.* **1.** Nitrate; niter: *nitric acid.* **2a.** Nitrogen: *nitrify.* **b.** Containing the univalent group NO_2: *nitrite.* [< Gk. *nitron,* NITER.]

ni·tro·cel·lu·lose (nī′trō-sĕl′yə-lōs′, -lōz′) ►*n.* Any of various cottonlike polymers derived from cellulose treated with sulfuric and nitric acids and used in explosives and plastics.

ni·tro·gen (nī′trə-jən) ►*n. Symbol* **N** A colorless, odorless, almost inert gaseous element that constitutes nearly four-fifths of the air by volume. At. no. 7. See table at **element.** —**ni·tric** (nī′trĭk) *adj.* —**ni·trog′e·nous** (nī-trŏj′ə-nəs) *adj.* —**ni·trous** (nī′trəs) *adj.*

ni·tro·glyc·er·in also **ni·tro·glyc·er·ine** (nī′trō-glĭs′ər-ĭn, -trə-) ►*n.* A thick, pale yellow, explosive liquid, used in dynamite and as a vasodilator in medicine.

ni·trous oxide (nī′trəs) ►*n.* A colorless, sweet-tasting gas, N_2O, used as a mild anesthetic.

nit·ty-grit·ty (nĭt′ē-grĭt′ē) ►*n. Informal* The specific or practical details. [?]

nit·wit (nĭt′wĭt′) ►*n.* A stupid, silly person.

nix (nĭks) *Slang* ▸*n.* Nothing. ▸*adv.* No. ▸*v.* To forbid; veto. [Ger. dial.]

Nix·on (nĭk′sən), **Richard Milhous** 1913–94. The 37th US president (1969–74); resigned.

Richard Nixon

Nizh·niy Nov·go·rod (nĭzh′nē nŏv′gə-rŏd′, -rət) A city of W Russia on the Volga R.

NJ ▸*abbr.* New Jersey

Nkru·mah (ən-krōō′mə, əng-), **Kwame** 1909–72. Ghanaian politician.

NL ▸*abbr.* **1.** National League **2.** Newfoundland & Labrador **3.** New Latin

NLRB ▸*abbr.* National Labor Relations Board

nm ▸*abbr.* **1.** nanometer **2.** nautical mile

NM ▸*abbr.* New Mexico

NNE ▸*abbr.* north-northeast

NNW ▸*abbr.* north-northwest

no¹ (nō) ▸*adv.* **1.** Used to express refusal, denial, disbelief, or disagreement. **2.** Not at all. Used with the comparative: *no better.* **3.** Not: *whether or no.* ▸*n., pl.* **noes** (nōz) A negative response or vote. [< OE *nā.*]

no² (nō) ▸*adj.* **1.** Not any; not one. **2.** Not at all: *He is no child.* [< OE *nān,* none.]

No or **Noh** (nō) ▸*n.* The classical drama of Japan, with elaborate costumes and highly stylized music and dance. [J. *nō.*]

no. or **No.** ▸*abbr.* **1a.** north **b.** northern **2.** number

No·ah (nō′ə) In the Bible, the patriarch who was chosen by God to build an ark to save human and animal life from a flood.

No·bel (nō-bĕl′), **Alfred Bernhard** 1833–96. Swedish chemist and philanthropist.

no·bel·i·um (nō-bĕl′ē-əm) ▸*n. Symbol* **No** A radioactive element artificially produced in trace amounts. At. no. 102. See table at **element.** [After Alfred Bernhard NOBEL.]

Nobel Prize ▸*n.* Any of the international prizes awarded annually by the Nobel Foundation for outstanding achievements in physics, chemistry, physiology or medicine, literature, economics, and for the promotion of world peace. —**No·bel′ist** *n.*

no·bil·i·ty (nō-bĭl′ĭ-tē) ▸*n., pl.* **-ties 1.** A class of persons distinguished by high birth or rank. **2.** Noble rank or status. **3.** High moral character. [< Lat. *nōbilitās.*]

no·ble (nō′bəl) ▸*adj.* **-bler, -blest 1.** Of or belonging to the nobility. **2a.** Having or showing high moral character. **b.** Lofty; exalted: *a noble ideal.* **3.** Majestic; grand. **4.** *Chem.* Inert: *a noble gas.* ▸*n.* A member of the nobility. [< Lat. *nōbilis.*] —**no′ble·ness** *n.* —**no′bly** *adv.*

no·ble·man (nō′bəl-mən) ▸*n.* A man of noble rank.

no·blesse o·blige (nō-blĕs′ ō-blēzh′) ▸*n.* Benevolent, honorable behavior considered to be the duty of persons of high birth or rank. [Fr., nobility is an obligation.]

no·ble·wom·an (nō′bəl-wŏŏm′ən) ▸*n.* A woman of noble rank.

no·bod·y (nō′bŏd′ē, -bŭd′ē, -bə-dē) ▸*pron.* No person; not anyone. ▸*n., pl.* **-ies** A person of no importance or influence.

no-brain·er (nō′brā′nər) ▸*n. Informal* Something, esp. a decision, that is so obvious as to require little or no thought.

noc·tur·nal (nŏk-tûr′nəl) ▸*adj.* **1.** Of or occurring in the night. **2.** Most active at night: *nocturnal animals.* [< Lat. *nocturnus* < *nox,* night.] —**noc·tur′nal·ly** *adv.*

noc·turne (nŏk′tûrn′) ▸*n.* **1.** A painting of a night scene. **2.** A musical composition of a pensive, dreamy mood, esp. one for the piano. [Fr. < OFr., NOCTURNAL.]

nod (nŏd) ▸*v.* **nod·ded, nod·ding 1.** To lower and raise the head quickly, as in agreement or acknowledgment. **2.** To express with a nod: *nodded agreement.* **3.** To let the head fall forward when sleepy. **4.** To be momentarily inattentive. **5.** To sway or bend, as flowers in the wind. ▸*n.* **1.** A nodding movement. **2.** An indication of assent. [ME *nodden.*] —**nod′der** *n.*

node (nōd) ▸*n.* **1a.** A protuberance or swelling. **b.** *Med.* A small mass of tissue in the form of a swelling or knot that is either normal or pathological, such as a lymph node. **2.** A focal point. **3a.** *Bot.* The point on a stem where a leaf is attached. **b.** See **knot** (sense 7). **4.** *Phys.* A point or region of virtually zero amplitude in a periodic system. [< Lat. *nōdus,* knot.] —**nod′al** *adj.*

nod·ule (nŏj′ŏŏl) ▸*n.* **1.** A small knotlike protuberance. **2.** *Med.* A small, abnormal but usu. benign mass of tissue, as on the thyroid gland. —**nod′u·lar** (nŏj′ə-lər) *adj.*

No·ël also **No·el** (nō-ĕl′) ▸*n.* Christmas. [< Lat. *nātālis (diēs),* (day) of birth.]

noes (nōz) ▸*n.* Pl. of **no¹.**

no-fault (nō′fôlt′) ▸*adj.* **1.** Related to a form of state-mandated automobile insurance that compensates a policyholder who becomes an accident victim, regardless of who is at fault. **2.** Related to a type of divorce granted without requiring proof of fault on the part of either spouse.

no-fly zone (nō′flī′) ▸*n.* Airspace in which certain, esp. military, aircraft are forbidden to fly.

nog·gin (nŏg′ĭn) ▸*n.* **1.** A small mug or cup. **2.** A unit of liquid measure equal to ¼ pint. **3.** *Slang* The human head. [?]

Noh (nō) ▸*n.* Var. of **No.**

noise (noiz) ▸*n.* **1a.** Sound or a sound that is loud, unpleasant, or unexpected. **b.** Sound of any kind. **2.** A loud outcry or commotion. **3.** *Phys.* A usu. persistent disturbance that obscures or reduces the clarity of a signal. **4.** *Comp.* Irrelevant or meaningless data. ▸*v.* **noised, nois·ing** To spread the rumor or report of. [< OFr., poss. < Lat. *nausea.*] —**noise′less** *adj.* —**noise′less·ly** *adv.* —**nois′i·ly** *adv.* —**nois′i·ness** *n.* —**nois′y** *adj.*

Syns: *clamor, din, hubbub, hullabaloo, pandemonium, racket, uproar* **n.**

noise·mak·er (noiz′mā′kər) ►*n.* One that makes noise, esp. a device such as a horn used to make noise at a party.

noi·some (noi′səm) ►*adj.* **1.** Offensive; foul. **2.** Harmful or dangerous. [ME *noiesom.*] —**noi′some·ly** *adv.* —**noi′some·ness** *n.*

no·lo con·ten·de·re (nō′lō kən-těn′də-rē) ►*n.* A plea made by the defendant in a criminal action that is equivalent to an admission of guilt but permits denial of the alleged facts in other proceedings. [Lat. *nōlō contendere*, I do not wish to contest.]

no·mad (nō′măd′) ►*n.* **1.** A member of a group of people who have no fixed home and move or migrate from place to place. **2.** A wanderer. [< Gk. *nomas*, wandering in search of pasture.] —**no·mad′ic** *adj.*

no man's land ►*n.* **1.** Land under dispute by two opposing entrenched armies. **2.** An area of uncertainty or ambiguity. **3.** An unclaimed or unowned piece of land.

nom de guerre (nŏm′ də gâr′) ►*n., pl.* **noms de guerre** (nŏm′) A fictitious name; pseudonym. [Fr., war name.]

nom de plume (plo͞om′) ►*n., pl.* **noms de plume** See **pen name.** [Fr.]

Nome (nōm) A city of W AK on Seward Peninsula.

no·men·cla·ture (nō′mən-klā′chər, nō-měn′klə-) ►*n.* A system of names used in an art or science. [Lat. *nōmenclātūra.*]

nom·i·nal (nŏm′ə-nəl) ►*adj.* **1.** Of or like a name or names. **2.** Existing in name only. **3.** *Gram.* Of or relating to a noun. **4.** Trifling: *a nominal sum.* [< Lat. *nōmen*, name.] —**nom′i·nal·ly** *adv.*

nom·i·nate (nŏm′ə-nāt′) ►*v.* **-nat·ed, -nat·ing** **1.** To propose as a candidate for election or for consideration for an honor or prize. **2.** To designate or appoint to an office or responsibility. See Synonyms at **appoint.** [Lat. *nōmināre*, to name.] —**nom′i·na′tion** *n.* —**nom′i·na′tor** *n.*

nom·i·na·tive (nŏm′ə-nə-tĭv) ►*adj.* Of or belonging to a grammatical case that usu. indicates the subject of a verb. ►*n.* The nominative case.

nom·i·nee (nŏm′ə-nē′) ►*n.* One who has been nominated. [NOMIN(ATE) + -EE¹.]

-nomy ►*suff.* A system of laws governing or a body of knowledge about a specified field: *astronomy.* [< Gk. *nomos*, law.]

non– ►*pref.* Not: *nonfat.* [< Lat. *nōn.*]

non·age (nŏn′ĭj, nō′nĭj) ►*n.* **1.** The state or condition of being under legal age. **2.** The period during which one is under legal age. **3.** A period of immaturity. [< OFr. *nonaage* : NON- + *aage*, AGE.]

non·a·ge·nar·i·an (nŏn′ə-jə-nâr′ē-ən, nō′nə-) ►*n.* A person between 90 and 100 years of age. [< Lat. *nōnāgēnārius.*] —**non′a·ge·nar′i·an** *adj.*

non·a·gon (nŏn′ə-gŏn′, nō′nə-) ►*n.* A polygon having nine sides.

non·a·ligned (nŏn′ə-līnd′) ►*adj.* Not allied with any other nation or bloc; neutral.

nonce (nŏns) ►*n.* The present or particular occasion: *for the nonce.* [< ME *for then anes,* for the one.]

non·cha·lant (nŏn′shə-länt′) ►*adj.* Casually unconcerned or indifferent. [< OFr. *nonchaloir*, be unconcerned.] —**non′cha·lance′** *n.* —**non′cha·lant·ly** *adv.*

non·com (nŏn′kŏm′) ►*n. Informal* A noncommissioned officer.

non·com·bat·ant (nŏn′kəm-băt′nt, -kŏm′bə-tnt) ►*n.* **1.** A member of the armed forces whose duties lie outside combat. **2.** A civilian in wartime.

non·com·mis·sioned officer (nŏn′kə-mĭsh′ənd) ►*n.* An enlisted member of the armed forces, such as a corporal or sergeant, appointed to a rank over other enlisted personnel.

non·com·mit·tal (nŏn′kə-mĭt′l) ►*adj.* Refusing commitment to a particular opinion or course of action.

non com·pos men·tis (nŏn kŏm′pəs měn′tĭs) ►*adj.* Not of sound mind and hence not legally competent. [Lat. *nōn compos mentis*, not in control of the mind.]

---

non′ab·ra′sive *adj.*
non′ab·sorb′ent *adj. & n.*
non′ac·a·dem′ic *adj.*
non·ac′id *n.*
non′ad·dict′ing *adj.*
non′ad·her′ence *n.*
non′ad·he′sive *adj.*
non′ad·just′a·ble *adj.*
non′ag·gres′sion *n.*
non′ag·ri·cul′tur·al *adj.*
non′al·co·hol′ic *adj.*
non′an·a·lyt′ic *adj.*
non′ap·pear′ance *n.*
non′as·ser′tive *adj.*
non′be·liev′er *n.*
non·bind′ing *adj.*
non′ca·lor′ic *adj.*
non·car′bon·at′ed *adj.*
non′car·niv′o·rous *adj.*
non′cat·e·gor′i·cal *adj.*
non-Cath′o·lic *adj. & n.*
non′-Cau·ca′sian *adj. & n.*
non·caus′al *adj.*

non·cit′i·zen *n.*
non·com′bat′ *n.*
non′com·mer′cial *adj.*
non′com·mu′ni·ca·ble *adj.*
non′com·mu′ni·ca·tive *adj.*
non′com·pet′i·tive *adj.*
non′com·pli′ance *n.*
non′com·pli′ant *adj. & n.*
non′con·clu′sive *adj.*
non′con·cur′rent *adj.*
non′con·fi·den′tial *adj.*
non′con·sec′u·tive *adj.*
non′con·ta′gious *adj.*
non′con·tig′u·ous *adj.*
non′con·tin′u·ous *adj.*
non′co·op′er·a′tion *n.*
non′co·op′er·a·tive *adj.*
non′cor·ro′sive *adj. & n.*
non·crim′i·nal *adj. & n.*
non·cur′rent *adj.*
non·dair′y *adj.*
non′de·duct′i·ble *adj.*
non′de·struc′tive *adj.*
non′·di·gest′i·ble *adj.*

non′dis·crim′i·na·to′ry *adj.*
non·drink′er *n.*
non·du′ra·ble *adj.*
non·ed′i·ble *adj. & n.*
non′ed·u·ca′tion·al *adj.*
non′ef·fec′tive *adj.*
non′e·las′tic *adj.*
non′e·lect′ed *adj.*
non·el′i·gi·ble *adj.*
non′en·force′a·ble *adj.*
non′en·force′ment *n.*
non′es·sen′tial *adj.*
non′-Eu·clid′e·an *adj.*
non′ex·ist′ence *n.*
non′ex·ist′ent *adj.*
non′ex·pend′a·ble *adj.*
non′ex·per′i·men′tal *adj.*
non′ex·plo′sive *adj. & n.*
non′ex·tinct′ *adj.*
non·fac′tu·al *adj.*
non·fas′cist *adj. & n.*
non·fer′rous *adj.*
non·fic′tion *n.*

non·con·duc·tor (nŏn′kən-dŭk′tər) ►*n.* A material that conducts little or no electricity, heat, or sound.

non·con·form·ist (nŏn′kən-fôr′mĭst) ►*n.* One who does not conform to accepted beliefs, customs, or practices. —**non′con·form′i·ty** *n.*

non·de·script (nŏn′dĭ-skrĭpt′) ►*adj.* Lacking distinctive qualities. [NON– + Lat. *dēscrīptus*, p.part. of *dēscrībere*, DESCRIBE.]

none (nŭn) ►*pron.* **1.** No one; nobody. **2.** Not any. **3.** No part: *none of your business.* ►*adv.* Not at all; in no way. [< OE *nān.*]

Usage: Although *none* often occurs as a singular pronoun, as in *None of the pizza was left,* it can sometimes be used with either a singular or plural verb: *None of the conspirators has* (or *have*) *been brought to trial. None* can only be plural in sentences such as *None but his most loyal supporters believe his story.*

non·en·ti·ty (nŏn-ĕn′tĭ-tē) ►*n., pl.* **-ties 1.** A person of no importance or significance. **2.** Something that does not exist or that exists only in the imagination.

nones (nōnz) ►*pl.n.* In the ancient Roman calendar, the 7th day of March, May, July, or October and the 5th day of the other months. [< Lat. *nōnus,* ninth.]

none·such (nŭn′sŭch′) ►*n.* A person or thing without equal. —**none′such′** *adj.*

none·the·less (nŭn′thə-lĕs′) ►*adv.* Nevertheless; however.

non·e·vent (nŏn′ĭ-vĕnt′) ►*n. Informal* An anticipated event that does not occur or proves anticlimactic.

non·fat (nŏn′făt′) ►*adj.* Lacking fat solids or having the fat content removed.

non·fea·sance (nŏn-fē′zəns) ►*n. Law* Failure to perform an official or contractual duty. [< *misfeasance,* legal term.]

no·nil·lion (nō-nĭl′yən) ►*n.* **1.** The cardinal number equal to 10³⁰. **2.** *Chiefly Brit.* The cardinal number equal to 10⁵⁴. [Fr. < Lat. *nōnus,* ninth.] —**no·nil′lion** *adj.* —**no·nil′lionth** *n.* & *adj.*

non·in·ter·ven·tion (nŏn′ĭn-tər-vĕn′shən) ►*n.* Failure or refusal to intervene, esp. in the affairs of another nation. —**non′in·ter·ven′-tion·ist** *n.*

non·met·al (nŏn-mĕt′l) ►*n.* Any of a number of elements, such as oxygen or sulfur, that lack the properties of metals. —**non′me·tal′lic** (-mə-tăl′ĭk) *adj.*

no-no (nō′nō′) ►*n., pl.* **-noes** *Informal* Something unacceptable or impermissible.

non·pa·reil (nŏn′pə-rĕl′) ►*adj.* Having no equal; peerless. ►*n.* **1.** One that has no equal. **2.** A small flat chocolate drop covered with white pellets of sugar. [< OFr.]

non·per·son (nŏn-pûr′sən) ►*n.* A person whose obliteration from the memory of the public is sought, esp. for political reasons.

non·plus (nŏn-plŭs′) ►*v.* **-plused, -plus·ing** also **-plussed, -plus·sing** To put at a loss; bewilder. [< Lat. *nōn plūs,* no more.]

non·pro·lif·er·a·tion (nŏn′prə-lĭf′ə-rā′shən) ►*adj.* Of or calling for an end to the proliferation of nuclear weapons.

non·rep·re·sen·ta·tion·al (nŏn-rĕp′rĭ-zĕn-tā′-shə-nəl) ►*adj.* Not representing natural objects realistically.

non·re·stric·tive (nŏn′rĭ-strĭk′tĭv) ►*adj. Gram.* Of or being a subordinate clause or phrase that describes but does not identify or restrict the meaning of the modified term. See Usage Note at **that.**

non·self (nŏn-sĕlf′) ►*n.* That which the immune system identifies as foreign to the body.

non·sense (nŏn′sĕns′, -səns) ►*n.* **1.** Foolish or absurd language or behavior. **2.** Matter of little or no importance or use. —**non·sen′si·cal** *adj.* —**non·sen′si·cal·ly** *adv.*

non se·qui·tur (nŏn sĕk′wĭ-tər, -tŏŏr′) ►*n.* A statement that does not follow logically from what preceded it. [Lat. *nōn sequitur,* it does not follow.]

non·stan·dard (nŏn-stăn′dərd) ►*adj.* **1.** Varying from or not adhering to the standard. **2.** *Ling.* Associated with a language variety used by uneducated speakers or socially disfavored groups.

non·stop (nŏn′stŏp′) ►*adj.* Made or done without a stop. —**non′stop′** *adv.*

---

non·flam′ma·ble *adj.*	**non′ne·go′tia·ble** *adj.*	**non′re·turn′a·ble** *adj.* & *n.*
non·flex′i·ble *adj.*	**non·nu′cle·ar** *adj.*	**non′rig′id** *adj.*
non·fluc′tu·at′ing *adj.*	**non′ob·ser′vant** *adj.*	**non·ru′ral** *adj.*
non′food′ *adj.*	**non′·par′ti·san** *adj.*	**non′sec·tar′i·an** *adj.*
non·haz′ard·ous *adj.*	**non·pa′ter·nal** *adj.*	**non·seg′re·gat′ed** *adj.*
non·he′red·i·tar′y *adj.*	**non·per′ma·nent** *adj.*	**non·sex′ist** *adj.*
non·hu′man *adj.* & *n.*	**non·per′me·a·ble** *adj.*	**non′sig·nif′i·cance** *n.*
non′i·den′ti·cal *adj.*	**non′per·sis′tent** *adj.*	**non′sig·nif′i·cant** *adj.*
non′in·crim′i·nat′ing *adj.*	**non·poi′son·ous** *adj.*	**non′skid′** *adj.*
non′in·duc′tive *adj.*	**non′pre·scrip′tion** *adj.*	**non′smok′er** *n.*
non′in·dus′tri·al *adj.*	**non′pro·duc′tive** *adj.*	**non′smok′ing** *adj.*
non′in·fect′ed *adj.*	**non′pro·fes′sion·al** *n.*	**non·spher′i·cal** *adj.*
non′in·form′a·tive *adj.*	& *adj.*	**non·ste·roi′dal** *adj.* & *n.*
non′in·hab′it·a·ble *adj.*	**non·prof′it** *adj.*	**non′stick′** *adj.*
non′in·stinc′tive *adj.*	**non′pro·tec′tive** *adj.*	**non·sub·mis′sive** *adj.*
non′judg·men′tal *adj.*	**non′ra·di·o·ac′tive** *adj.*	**non·talk′a·tive** *adj.*
non·lin′e·ar *adj.*	**non·read′er** *n.*	**non·ten′ured** *adj.*
non′mag·net′ic *adj.*	**non′re·cov′er·a·ble** *adj.*	**non·think′ing** *adj.*
non′ma·li′·cious *adj.*	**non′re·li′gious** *adj.*	**non·triv′i·al** *adj.*
non·mar′ket·a·ble *adj.*	**non′re·sem′blance** *n.*	**non·u′ni·fied′** *adj.*
non·meas′ur·a·ble *adj.*	**non′res′i·dent** *n.*	**non·ur′ban** *adj.*
non·med′i·cal *adj.*	**non′re·sis′tance** *n.*	**non·us′er** *n.*
non·mem′ber *n.*	**non′re·sis′tant** *adj.*	**non·vot′er** *n.*
non·mil′i·tar′y *adj.*	**non′re·solv′a·ble** *adj.*	**non·ze′ro** *adj.*

non·sup·port (nŏn′sə-pôrt′) ▸*n.* Failure to provide for the maintenance of one's dependents.

non trop·po (nŏn trô′pō, nōn) ▸*adv. & adj. Mus.* In moderation. [Ital., not too much.]

non·un·ion (nŏn-yōōn′yən) ▸*adj.* **1.** Not belonging to a labor union. **2.** Not recognizing a labor union or employing union members.

non·vi·o·lence (nŏn-vī′ə-ləns) ▸*n.* The doctrine or practice of rejecting violence in favor of peaceful tactics as a means of gaining political objectives. —**non·vi′o·lent** *adj.* —**non·vi′o·lent·ly** *adv.*

non·white (nŏn′wīt′, -hwīt′) ▸*n.* A person belonging to a racial group other than white; person of color. —**non′white′** *adj.*

noo·dle[1] (nōōd′l) ▸*n.* A narrow ribbonlike strip of dough, usu. made of flour, eggs, and water. [Ger. *Nudel.*]

noo·dle[2] (nōōd′l) ▸*n. Slang* The human head. [Alteration of *noddle*, back of head.]

nook (nōōk) ▸*n.* **1.** A small corner or recess in a room. **2.** A hidden or secluded spot. [ME *nok*, prob. of Scand. orig.]

noon (nōōn) ▸*n.* Twelve o'clock in the daytime; midday. See Usage Note at **AM.** [< OE *nōn*, ninth hour after sunrise < Lat. *nōnus*, ninth.]

noon·day (nōōn′dā′) ▸*n.* Midday; noon.

no one ▸*pron.* No person; nobody.

noon·time (nōōn′tīm′) ▸*n.* Noon.

noose (nōōs) ▸*n.* **1.** A loop formed in a rope by a slipknot so that it binds tighter as the rope is pulled. **2.** A similar loop of wire or other material, used to snare animals. [ME *nose.*]

Noot·ka (nōōt′kə, nōōt′-) ▸*n., pl.* **-ka** or **-kas 1.** A member of a Native American people inhabiting Vancouver Island in British Columbia and an adjacent area in NW Washington. **2.** The language of the Nootka.

nope (nōp) ▸*adv. Informal* No. [Alteration of NO[1].]

nor (nôr; nər *when unstressed*) ▸*conj.* And not; or not; not either: *has neither phoned nor written us.* [ME.]

　　Usage: When a noun phrase of the type *this* or *that* is introduced by *no*, *or* is more common than *nor*: *He has no experience or interest. Or* is also more common than *nor* when such a noun phrase, adjective phrase, or adverb phrase is introduced by *not*: *He is not a philosopher or a statesman.* See Usage Note at **neither.**

nor·a·dren·a·line (nôr′ə-drĕn′ə-lĭn) ▸*n.* Norepinephrine.

Nor·dic (nôr′dĭk) ▸*adj.* **1.** Scandinavian. **2.** Of a human physical type exemplified by the light-skinned, blond-haired peoples of Scandinavia. Not in scientific use. **3.** Of a ski competition featuring cross-country racing, ski jumping, and biathlon. [< Fr. *nord*, NORTH.] —**Nor′dic** *n.*

nor·ep·i·neph·rine (nôr′ĕp-ə-nĕf′rĭn) ▸*n.* A substance, both a hormone and neurotransmitter, secreted by the adrenal gland and the nerve endings of the sympathetic nervous system, that causes increased heart rate and constriction of blood vessels. Used also as a drug in synthetic form. [*nor*-, pref. for parent substances (< NORMAL) + EPINEPHRINE.]

Nor·gay (nôr′gā), **Tenzing** 1914–86. Sherpa mountaineer; with Sir Edmund Hillary made the first ascent of Mount Everest (1953).

Tenzing Norgay
photographed in 1953

norm (nôrm) ▸*n.* A standard, model, or pattern regarded as typical. [< Lat. *norma*, carpenter's square.]

nor·mal (nôr′məl) ▸*adj.* **1.** Conforming to a norm or standard; typical: *normal room temperature.* **2a.** Of average intelligence or development. **b.** Free from mental illness. ▸*n.* The usual state, amount, or degree. —**nor′mal·cy** *n.* —**nor·mal′i·ty** (-mǎl′ĭ-tē) *n.* —**nor′mal·ly** *adv.*

normal curve ▸*n.* See **bell curve.**

nor·mal·ize (nôr′mə-līz′) ▸*v.* **-ized, -iz·ing** To make normal or regular. —**nor′mal·i·za′tion** *n.* —**nor′mal·iz′er** *n.*

normal school ▸*n.* A school that trains teachers, chiefly for the elementary grades.

Nor·man (nôr′mən) ▸*n.* **1a.** A member of a Scandinavian people who settled in N France in the 10th cent. **b.** A member of a people of Norman and French blood who invaded England in 1066. **2.** A native or inhabitant of Normandy. —**Nor′man** *adj.*

Nor·man·dy (nôr′mən-dē) A historical region and former province of NW France on the English Channel.

Norman French ▸*n.* The dialect of Old French used in medieval Normandy.

nor·ma·tive (nôr′mə-tĭv) ▸*adj.* Of or prescribing a norm or standard. —**nor′ma·tive·ly** *adv.*

nor·o·vi·rus (nôr′ō-vī′rəs) ▸*n.* Any of a group of RNA viruses, formerly called Norwalk viruses, that cause acute gastroenteritis. [< *Nor(walk) virus*, after *Norwalk*, Ohio.]

Norse (nôrs) ▸*adj.* **1.** Of or relating to medieval Scandinavia. **2.** Norwegian. **3.** Of or relating to the branch of the Germanic languages that includes Norwegian and Icelandic. —**Norse** *n.*

Norse·man (nôrs′mən) ▸*n.* A member of any of the peoples of medieval Scandinavia.

north (nôrth) ▸*n.* **1a.** The direction along a meridian 90° counterclockwise from east. **b.** The compass point located at 0°. **2.** often **North a.** The northern part of the earth. **b.** The northern part of a region or country. ▸*adj.* **1.** To, toward, of, or in the north. **2.** Coming from the north: *a north wind.* ▸*adv.* In, from, or toward the north. [< OE.] —**north′ward** *adj. & adv.* —**north′ward·ly** *adj. & adv.* —**north′wards** *adv.*

North America The N continent of the Western Hemisphere, extending northward from the Colombia-Panama border and including Central America, Mexico, the islands of the Caribbean Sea, the continental US, Canada, and Greenland. —**North American** *adj. & n.*

North Car·o·li·na (kär′ə-lī′nə) A state of the SE US bordering on the Atlantic. Cap. Raleigh. —**North Car·o·lin′i·an** (-lĭn′ē-ən) *adj. & n.*

North Dakota A state of the N-central US bordering on Canada. Cap. Bismarck. —**North Dakotan** *adj. & n.*

north·east (nôrth-ēst′, nôr-ēst′) ►*n.* **1.** The direction halfway between due north and due east. **2.** An area or region lying in the northeast. —**north·east′** *adj. & adv.* —**north·east′er·ly** *adj. & adv.* —**north·east′ern** *adj.* —**north·east′ward** *adj. & adv.* —**north·east′ward·ly** *adj. & adv.* —**north·east′wards** *adv.*

north·east·er (nôrth-ē′stər, nôr-ē′-) ►*n.* A storm or gale blowing from the northeast.

north·er·ly (nôr′thər-lē) ►*adj.* **1.** In or toward the north. **2.** Coming from the north: *northerly winds.* —**north′er·ly** *adv.*

north·ern (nôr′thərn) ►*adj.* **1.** Of, in, or toward the north. **2.** From the north: *northern breezes.*

north·ern·er also **North·ern·er** (nôr′thər-nər) ►*n.* A native or inhabitant of a northern region.

Northern Hemisphere ►*n.* The half of the earth north of the equator.

Northern Ireland A division of the United Kingdom in the NE section of the island of Ireland. Cap. Belfast.

northern lights ►*pl.n.* See **aurora borealis.**

North Island An island of New Zealand separated from South I. by Cook Strait.

North Korea A country of NE Asia on the Korean Peninsula. Cap. Pyongyang. —**North Korean** *adj. & n.*

North Pole ►*n.* **1.** The northern end of the earth's axis of rotation. **2.** The celestial zenith of this terrestrial point.

North Sea An arm of the Atlantic between Great Britain and NW Europe.

North Star ►*n.* See **Polaris.**

North Vietnam A former country (1954–75) of SE Asia; now part of Vietnam.

north·west (nôrth-wĕst′, nôr-wĕst′) ►*n.* **1.** The direction halfway between due north and due west. **2.** An area or region lying in the northwest. —**north·west′** *adj. & adv.* —**north·west′er·ly** *adj. & adv.* —**north·west′ern** *adj.* —**north·west′ward** *adj. & adv.* —**north·west′ward·ly** *adj. & adv.* —**north·west′wards** *adv.*

Northwest Passage A water route from the Atlantic to the Pacific through the Arctic Archipelago of N Canada and along the N coast of AK.

Northwest Territories A territory of N Canada between Yukon Territory and Nunavut including islands of the W Arctic Archipelago. Cap. Yellowknife.

Northwest Territory A historical region of N-central US from the Ohio and Mississippi Rivers to the Great Lakes.

Nor·way (nôr′wā′) A country of N Europe in the W part of the Scandinavian Peninsula. Cap. Oslo.

Nor·we·gian (nôr-wē′jən) ►*n.* **1.** A native or inhabitant of Norway. **2.** Either of the Ger-

manic languages of the Norwegians. —**Nor·we′gian** *adj.*

nos. or **Nos.** ►*abbr.* numbers

nose (nōz) ►*n.* **1.** The part of the face that contains the nostrils and organs of smell and forms the beginning of the respiratory tract. **2.** The sense of smell. **3.** The ability to detect, as if by smell: *has a nose for gossip.* **4.** Something, such as the forward end of an aircraft, that resembles a nose. ►*v.* **nosed, nos·ing 1.** To find out by or as if by smell. **2.** To touch with the nose; nuzzle. **3.** To move or advance carefully. **4.** *Informal* To snoop or pry. —*idioms:* **on the nose** Exactly; precisely. **under (someone's) nose** In plain view. [< OE *nosu*.]

nose·bleed (nōz′blēd′) ►*n.* Bleeding from the nose.

nose cone ►*n.* The forwardmost, usu. separable section of a rocket or guided missile.

nose·dive (nōz′dīv′) ►*n.* **1.** A very steep dive of an aircraft. **2.** A sudden plunge. —**nose′-dive′** *v.*

nose·gay (nōz′gā′) ►*n.* A small bouquet of flowers. [ME.]

nosh (nŏsh) ►*v. Informal* To eat a snack or light meal. [Yiddish *nash, naschen,* to nibble.] —**nosh** *n.* —**nosh′er** *n.*

nos·tal·gi·a (nŏ-stăl′jə, nə-) ►*n.* **1.** A bittersweet longing for the past. **2.** Homesickness. [Gk. *nostos,* a return home + –ALGIA.] —**nos·tal′gic** *adj.* —**nos·tal′gi·cal·ly** *adv.*

Nos·tra·da·mus (nŏs′trə-dä′məs, -dä′-, nō′-strə-) 1503–66. French physician and astrologer.

nos·tril (nŏs′trəl) ►*n.* Either of the external openings of the nose. [< OE *nosthyrl.*]

nos·trum (nŏs′trəm) ►*n.* A quack medicine or remedy. [Lat. *nostrum (remedium),* our (remedy).]

nos·y or **nos·ey** (nō′zē) ►*adj.* **-i·er, -i·est** *Informal* Prying; inquisitive. —**nos′i·ly** *adv.* —**nos′i·ness** *n.*

not (nŏt) ►*adv.* In no way; to no degree. Used to express negation, denial, refusal, or prohibition: *I will not go. You may not have any.* [ME, alteration of *naught,* NAUGHT.]

Usage: In formal writing the *not only . . . but also* construction should be used in such a way that each of its elements is followed by a construction of the same type. Instead of *I not only bought a new car but a new mower,* write *I bought not only a new car but a new mower.*

no·ta be·ne (nō′tə bĕn′ē, bē′nē) Used to direct attention to something particularly important. [Lat. *notā bene,* note well.]

no·ta·ble (nō′tə-bəl) ►*adj.* **1.** Worthy of note or notice; remarkable. **2.** Distinguished; eminent. See Synonyms at **famous. 3.** Perceptible; noticeable. ►*n.* A person of distinction. See Synonyms at **celebrity.** —**no′ta·bil′i·ty** *n.* —**no′ta·bly** *adv.*

no·ta·rize (nō′tə-rīz′) ►*v.* **-rized, -riz·ing** To certify or attest to as a notary public. —**no′ta·ri·za′tion** *n.*

no·ta·ry (nō′tə-rē) ►*n., pl.* **-ries** A notary public. [< Lat. *notārius,* stenographer.]

notary public ►*n., pl.* **notaries public** A person legally empowered to witness and authenticate documents and to take affidavits and depositions.

no·ta·tion (nō-tā′shən) ►*n.* **1a.** A system of

figures or symbols used to represent numbers, quantities, tones, or values. **b.** The act or process of using such a system. **2.** A brief note; annotation.

notch (nŏch) ►*n.* **1.** A V-shaped cut. **2.** A narrow pass between mountains. **3.** *Informal* A level or degree. ►*v.* **1.** To cut a notch in. **2.** To record by or as if by making notches. [Prob. < *an otch < OFr. oche < ochier*, to notch.]

note (nōt) ►*n.* **1a.** A brief written record. **b.** A comment or explanation, as on a passage in a text. **2.** A brief informal letter. **3.** A formal written diplomatic or official communication. **4a.** A piece of paper currency. **b.** A promissory note. **5.** *Mus.* **a.** A tone of definite pitch. **b.** A symbol for such a tone. **6.** The vocal sound made by a songbird or other animal. **7.** The sign of a particular quality or emotion: *a note of despair.* **8.** Importance; consequence. **9.** Notice; observation: *took note of the scene.* ►*v.* **not·ed, not·ing 1.** To observe carefully; notice. **2.** To make a note of; write down. **3.** To make mention of; remark. [< Lat. *nota*, a mark.]

note·book (nōt′bŏŏk′) ►*n.* **1.** A book of blank pages for notes. **2.** A portable computer, gen. thinner than a laptop.

not·ed (nō′tĭd) ►*adj.* Well-known; famous. See **famous.**

note·wor·thy (nōt′wûr′thē) ►*adj.* Deserving notice or attention; notable. —**note′wor′thi·ness** *n.*

noth·ing (nŭth′ĭng) ►*pron.* **1.** No thing; not anything. **2.** No part; no portion: *Nothing remains of the old house.* **3.** One of no consequence or interest. ►*n.* **1.** Absence of anything perceptible; nonexistence. **2.** Zero. **3.** A nonentity. ►*adv.* Not at all: *She looks nothing like me.* [< OE *nāthing.*]

noth·ing·ness (nŭth′ĭng-nĭs) ►*n.* **1.** The condition or quality of being nothing; nonexistence. **2.** Empty space; void.

no·tice (nō′tĭs) ►*n.* **1.** Observation; attention. **2.** Respectful attention or consideration. **3.** A written or printed announcement. **4.** A formal announcement or warning. **5.** A critical review. ►*v.* **-ticed, -tic·ing** To observe. [< Lat. *nōtitia*, knowledge < *nōscere*, come to know.]

no·tice·a·ble (nō′tĭ-sə-bəl) ►*adj.* **1.** Evident; observable. **2.** Worthy of notice; significant. —**no′tice·a·bly** *adv.*

no·ti·fy (nō′tə-fī′) ►*v.* **-fied, -fy·ing 1.** To give notice to; inform. **2.** *Chiefly Brit.* To make known; proclaim. [< Lat. *nōtificāre.*] —**no′ti·fi·ca′tion** *n.* —**no′ti·fi′er** *n.*

no·tion (nō′shən) ►*n.* **1.** A belief or opinion. **2.** An idea or conception. **3.** A fanciful impulse. **4.** **notions** Small items for household use, such as needles, buttons, and thread. [< Lat. *nōtiō < nōscere*, come to know.] —**no′tion·al** *adj.*

no·to·ri·ous (nō-tôr′ē-əs) ►*adj.* Known widely and usu. unfavorably; infamous. [< Med.Lat. *nōtōrius < Lat. nōtus*, known.] —**no′to·ri′e·ty** (-tə-rī′ĭ-tē) *n.* —**no·to′ri·ous·ly** *adv.*

not·with·stand·ing (nŏt′wĭth-stăn′dĭng, -wĭth-) ►*prep.* In spite of. ►*adv.* All the same; nevertheless. ►*conj.* Although.

Nouak·chott (nwäk-shŏt′) The capital of Mauritania, in the W part on the Atlantic Ocean.

nou·gat (nōō′gət) ►*n.* A candy made from a sugar or honey paste and nuts. [< Prov.]

nought (nôt) ►*n.* Var. of **naught.**

noun (noun) ►*n.* A word used to name a person, place, thing, quality, or action. [< Lat. *nōmen*, name.]

nour·ish (nûr′ĭsh) ►*v.* **1.** To provide with food or other substances necessary for life and growth. **2.** To foster the development of; promote. [< Lat. *nūtrīre.*] —**nour′ish·ing** *adj.* —**nour′ish·ment** *n.*

nou·veau riche (nōō′vō rēsh′) ►*n., pl.* **nou·veaux riches** (nōō′vō rēsh′) One who has recently become rich. [Fr., new rich.]

no·va (nō′və) ►*n., pl.* **-vae** (-vē) or **-vas** A star that suddenly increases in luminosity and gradually returns to its original brightness over a period of weeks to years. [< Lat. *novus*, new.]

Nova Sco·tia (skō′shə) A province of E Canada comprising a mainland peninsula and the adjacent Cape Breton I. Cap. Halifax. —**No′va Sco′tian** *adj. & n.*

nov·el[1] (nŏv′əl) ►*n.* A fictional prose narrative of considerable length, typically having a plot that is unfolded by the actions, speech, and thoughts of the characters. [< VLat. **novella*, new things < Lat. *novellus*, NOVEL[2].] —**nov′el·is′tic** *adj.*

nov·el[2] (nŏv′əl) ►*adj.* Strikingly new, unusual, or different. [< Lat. *novellus*, dim. of *novus*, new.] —**nov′el·ly** *adv.*

nov·el·ette (nŏv′ə-lĕt′) ►*n.* A short novel.

nov·el·ist (nŏv′ə-lĭst) ►*n.* A writer of novels.

nov·el·ize (nŏv′ə-līz′) ►*v.* **-ized, -iz·ing** To convert into a novelistic format. —**nov′el·i·za′tion** *n.*

no·vel·la (nō-vĕl′ə) ►*n.* A short novel. [Ital., NOVEL[1].]

nov·el·ty (nŏv′əl-tē) ►*n., pl.* **-ties 1.** The quality of being novel; newness. **2.** Something new and unusual. **3.** A small mass-produced article, such as a trinket.

No·vem·ber (nō-vĕm′bər) ►*n.* The 11th month of the Gregorian calendar. See table at **calendar.** [< Lat., ninth month.]

no·ve·na (nō-vē′nə) ►*n. Rom. Cath. Ch.* A recitation of devotions for nine consecutive days. [Med.Lat. < Lat. *novem*, nine.]

nov·ice (nŏv′ĭs) ►*n.* **1.** A beginner. **2.** One who has entered a religious order but has not yet taken vows. [< Med.Lat. *novīcius.*]

no·vi·ti·ate (nō-vĭsh′ē-ĭt, -āt′) ►*n.* **1.** The period of being a religious novice. **2.** A place where novices live. **3.** See **novice** (sense 2). [< Med.Lat. *novīcius*, novice.]

No·vo·cain (nō′və-kān′) A trademark for an anesthetic preparation of procaine.

No·vo·si·birsk (nō′və-sə-bîrsk′) A city of S-central Russia on the Ob R. E of Omsk.

now (nou) ►*adv.* **1.** At the present time. **2.** At once: *Stop now.* **3.** Very recently: *left the room just now.* **4.** At this point in the series of events; then. **5.** In these circumstances; as things are. **6.** Used to introduce a command, reproof, or request: *Now pay attention.* ►*conj.* Seeing that; since. ►*n.* The present time or moment. ►*adj.* **1.** Current. **2.** *Slang* Fashionable; trendy. [< OE *nū.*]

NOW ►*abbr.* National Organization for Women

now·a·days (nou′ə-dāz′) ►*adv.* During the present time; now. [ME *nouadaies.*]

no·way (nō′wā′) also **no·ways** (-wāz′) ►*adv. Informal* Nowise.

no·where (nō′wâr′, -hwâr′) ►*adv.* **1.** Not anywhere. **2.** To no place or result. ►*n.* A remote or unknown place.

no·wise (nō′wīz′) ►*adv.* In no way, manner, or degree; not at all.

nox·ious (nŏk′shəs) ►*adj.* Injurious to health or morals. [< Lat. *noxius* < *noxa*, damage.] —**nox′ious·ly** *adv.*

noz·zle (nŏz′əl) ►*n.* A projecting part with an opening for regulating a flow of fluid. [Dim. of NOSE.]

NP ►*abbr.* **1.** notary public **2.** noun phrase

NRA ►*abbr.* National Rifle Association

ns ►*abbr.* nanosecond

NS ►*abbr.* **1.** or **N/S** New Style **2.** Nova Scotia

N/S ►*abbr.* **1.** nonsmoking **2.** not sufficient

NSC ►*abbr.* National Security Council

NSFW ►*abbr.* not safe for work

NT ►*abbr.* **1.** New Testament **2.** Northwest Territories

nth (ĕnth) ►*adj.* **1.** Relating to an unspecified ordinal number. **2.** Highest; utmost: *to the nth degree.*

nt. wt. ►*abbr.* net weight

nu (nōō, nyōō) ►*n.* The 13th letter of the Greek alphabet. [Gk.]

nu·ance (nōō′äns′, nyōō′-) ►*n.* A subtle or slight degree of difference, as in meaning or feeling; gradation. [< OFr. *nuer*, to shade < VLat. **nūba*, cloud.] —**nu·anced′** *adj.*
   Syns: gradation, shade **n.**

nub (nŭb) ►*n.* **1.** A lump or knob. **2.** The essence; core. [< MLGer. *knubbe*.] —**nub′by** *adj.*

Nu·bi·a (nōō′bē-ə, nyōō′-) A desert region and ancient kingdom in the Nile valley of S Egypt and N Sudan. —**Nu′bi·an** *adj. & n.*

nu·bile (nōō′bĭl, -bīl′, nyōō′-) ►*adj.* Of marriageable age or condition. [< Lat. *nūbere*, take a husband.]

nu·cle·ar (nōō′klē-ər, nyōō′-) ►*adj.* **1.** *Biol.* Of or forming a nucleus of a cell. **2.** *Phys.* Of or relating to atomic nuclei. **3.** Of, using, or derived from nuclear energy. **4.** Drastic or extreme; radical: *Legislators threatened to use the nuclear option to block the nominee.*

nuclear energy ►*n.* The energy released by a nuclear reaction, esp. by fission or fusion.

nuclear family ►*n.* A family unit consisting of a mother and father and their children.

nuclear reaction ►*n.* A reaction, as in fission, that alters the energy, composition, or structure of an atomic nucleus.

nuclear reactor ►*n.* A device in which nuclear fission initiates a controlled chain reaction.

nu·cle·ate (nōō′klē-ĭt, nyōō′-) ►*adj.* Having a nucleus or nuclei. ►*v.* (-āt′) **-at·ed, -at·ing 1.** To bring together into or form a nucleus. **2.** To act as a nucleus for. —**nu′cle·a′tion** *n.*

nu·cle·ic acid (nōō-klē′ĭk, -klā′-, nyōō-) ►*n.* Any of a group of complex compounds that are found in all living cells and viruses and that control cellular function and heredity.

nucleo– or **nucle–** ►*pref.* **1.** Nucleus: *nucleon.* **2.** Nucleic acid: *nucleotide.* [< NUCLEUS.]

nu·cle·o·lus (nōō-klē′ə-ləs, nyōō-) ►*n.,* pl. **-li** (-lī′) A small body in the nucleus of a cell that contains protein and RNA. [Lat., dim. of *nucleus,* NUCLEUS.] —**nu·cle′o·lar** (-lər) *adj.*

nu·cle·on (nōō′klē-ŏn′, nyōō′-) ►*n.* A proton or a neutron. —**nu′cle·on′ic** *adj.*

nu·cle·on·ics (nōō′klē-ŏn′ĭks, nyōō′-) ►*n.* (takes sing. v.) The study of the behavior of

nucleons or atomic nuclei.

nu·cle·o·tide (nōō′klē-ə-tīd′, nyōō′-) ►*n.* Any of various compounds that form the basic constituents of DNA and RNA. [Alteration of *nucleoside.*]

nu·cle·us (nōō′klē-əs, nyōō′-) ►*n.,* pl. **-cle·i** (-klē-ī′) or **-es 1.** A central or essential part around which other parts are gathered or grouped; core. **2.** *Biol.* A membrane-bound organelle within a eukaryotic cell that contains most of the cell's genetic material. **3.** *Phys.* The positively charged central region of an atom, composed of protons and neutrons and containing almost all of the mass of the atom. [Lat., kernel < *nux*, nut.]

nu·clide (nōō′klīd′, nyōō′-) ►*n.* A type of atom specified by its atomic number, atomic mass, and energy state. —**nu·clid′ic** (-klĭd′ĭk) *adj.*

nude (nōōd, nyōōd) ►*adj.* **nud·er, nud·est** Being without clothing; naked. ►*n.* **1.** An unclothed human figure, esp. in artistic representation. **2.** The condition of being unclothed. [Lat. *nūdus.*] —**nu′di·ty** *n.*

nudge (nŭj) ►*v.* **nudged, nudg·ing** To push against gently, esp. in order to gain attention. [Prob. of Scand. orig.] —**nudge** *n.*

nud·ism (nōō′dĭz′əm, nyōō′-) ►*n.* The belief in or practice of going nude, esp. as part of a conscious choice of lifestyle. —**nud′ist** *adj. & n.*

nu·ga·to·ry (nōō′gə-tôr′ē, nyōō′-) ►*adj.* **1.** Insignificant; trifling. **2.** Unavailing; futile. [< Lat. *nūgae*, jokes.]

nug·get (nŭg′ĭt) ►*n.* A small solid lump, esp. of gold. [< dial. *nug*, lump.]

nui·sance (nōō′səns, nyōō′-) ►*n.* One that is inconvenient, annoying, or vexatious; bother. [< OFr., ult. < Lat. *nocēre*, to harm.]

nuke (nōōk, nyōōk) *Slang* ►*n.* **1.** A nuclear device or weapon. **2.** A nuclear power plant. ►*v.* **nuked, nuk·ing** To attack with nuclear weapons.

Nu·ku·'a·lo·fa (nōō′kōō-ə-lô′fə) The capital of Tonga, in the SW Pacific.

null (nŭl) ►*adj.* **1.** Having no legal force; invalid. **2.** Of no consequence; insignificant. **3.** Amounting to nothing. ►*n.* Zero; nothing. [< Lat. *nūllus.*] —**nul′li·ty** *n.*

null character ►*n.* *Comp.* A data control character used as a filler between blocks of data.

nul·li·fy (nŭl′ə-fī′) ►*v.* **-fied, -fy·ing 1.** To make null; invalidate. **2.** To counteract the force or effectiveness of. —**nul′li·fi·ca′tion** *n.*

numb (nŭm) ►*adj.* **-er, -est 1.** Unable to feel or move normally. **2.** Stunned, as from shock. [< ME *nomin*, seized.] —**numb** *v.* —**numb′ly** *adv.* —**numb′ness** *n.*

num·ber (nŭm′bər) ►*n.* **1.** *Math.* **a.** A member of the set of positive integers. **b.** A member of any of the further sets of objects that can be derived from the positive integers. **2. numbers** Arithmetic. **3.** A numeral or series of numerals used for reference or identification: *a telephone number.* **4.** A total; sum. **5.** An indefinite quantity: *a number of people.* **6. numbers** A multitude. **7.** *Gram.* The indication of the singularity or plurality of a linguistic form. **8. Numbers** (takes sing. v.) See table at **Bible. 9.** An item in a program of entertainment. ►*v.* **1.** To assign a number to. **2.** To count or enumerate. **3.** To add up to. **4.** To include in a group or category. **5.** To limit in number. [< Lat. *numerus.*]

Usage: As a collective noun *number* may take either a singular or a plural verb. It takes a singular verb when it is preceded by *the: The number of skilled workers is small.* It takes a plural verb when preceded by *a: A number of the workers are unskilled.*

num·ber·less (nŭm′bər-lĭs) ►*adj.* Innumerable; countless.

nu·mer·a·ble (no͞o′mər-ə-bəl, nyo͞o′-) ►*adj.* Capable of being counted; countable.

nu·mer·al (no͞o′mər-əl, nyo͞o′-) ►*n.* A symbol or mark used to represent a number. [< Lat. *numerus,* number.] —**nu′mer·al** *adj.*

nu·mer·ate (no͞o′mə-rāt′, nyo͞o′-) ►*v.* **-at·ed, -at·ing** To enumerate. [Lat. *numerāre < numerus,* number.] —**nu′mer·a′tion** *n.*

nu·mer·a·tor (no͞o′mə-rā′tər, nyo͞o′-) ►*n.* The expression written above the line in a common fraction to indicate the number of parts.

nu·mer·i·cal (no͞o-mĕr′ĭ-kəl, nyo͞o-) also **nu·mer·ic** (-mĕr′ĭk) ►*adj.* Of, represented by, or being a number or numbers. [< Lat. *numerus,* number.] —**nu·mer′i·cal·ly** *adv.*

nu·mer·ol·o·gy (no͞o′mə-rŏl′ə-jē, nyo͞o′-) ►*n.* The study of occult meanings of numbers. [< Lat. *numerus,* number.] —**nu′mer·ol′o·gist** *n.*

nu·mer·ous (no͞o′mər-əs, nyo͞o′-) ►*adj.* Amounting to a large number; many. [< Lat. *numerōsus.*] —**nu′mer·ous·ly** *adv.* —**nu′mer·ous·ness** *n.*

Nu·mid·i·a (no͞o-mĭd′ē-ə, nyo͞o-) An ancient country of NW Africa corresponding roughly to modern Algeria. —**Nu·mid′i·an** *adj. & n.*

nu·mi·nous (no͞o′mə-nəs, nyo͞o′-) ►*adj.* **1.** Filled with a sense of a supernatural presence. **2.** Spiritually elevated; sublime. [< Lat. *nūmen, nūmin-,* spirit.]

nu·mis·mat·ics (no͞o′mĭz-mă′tĭks, nyo͞o′-) ►*n.* (*takes sing. v.*) The study or collection of money, coins, and medals. [< Gk. *nomisma,* coin in circulation.] —**nu′mis·mat′ic** *adj.* —**nu·mis′ma·tist** (-mĭz′mə-tĭst) *n.*

num·skull also **numb·skull** (nŭm′skŭl′) ►*n.* A stupid person. [NUM(B) + SKULL.]

nun (nŭn) ►*n.* A woman who belongs to a religious order. [< LLat. *nonna.*]

Nu·na·vut (no͞o′nə-vo͞ot′) A territory of N Canada including part of the mainland W of Hudson Bay and most of the Arctic Archipelago. Cap. Iqaluit.

nun·ci·o (nŭn′sē-ō′, no͞on′-) ►*n., pl.* **-os** A papal ambassador or representative. [Ital. < Lat. *nūntius,* messenger.]

nun·ner·y (nŭn′ə-rē) ►*n., pl.* **-ies** A convent of nuns.

nup·tial (nŭp′shəl, -chəl) ►*adj.* **1.** Of marriage or the wedding ceremony. **2.** Of or occurring during the mating season: *the nuptial plumage of male birds.* ►*n.* often **nuptials** A wedding ceremony. [< Lat. *nūptiae,* wedding < *nūbere,* take a husband.]

Nu·rem·berg (no͝or′əm-bûrg′, nyo͝or′-) A city of SE Germany NNW of Munich.

nurse (nûrs) ►*n.* **1.** A person trained to provide medical care for the sick or disabled, esp. one who is licensed and works in a hospital or physician's office. **2a.** A wet nurse. **b.** A nursemaid. ►*v.* **nursed, nurs·ing 1.** To serve as a nurse for. **2.** To suckle. **3.** To treat: *nurse a cough.* **4.** To take special care of. **5.** To assist; attend. See Synonyms at **nurture. 6.** To bear

privately in the mind: *nursing a grudge.* **7.** To consume slowly: *nurse a drink.* [< Lat. *nūtrīx,* wet nurse.]

nurse·maid (nûrs′mād′) ►*n.* A woman employed to take care of infants or young children.

nurse practitioner ►*n.* A registered nurse with special training for providing primary health care.

nurs·er·y (nûr′sə-rē, nûrs′rē) ►*n., pl.* **-ies 1.** A room set apart for children. **2a.** A place for the temporary care of children. **b.** A nursery school. **3.** A place where plants are grown, esp. for sale.

nursery school ►*n.* A school for children, usu. between the ages of three and five.

nurs·ing (nûr′sĭng) ►*n.* The profession or tasks of a nurse.

nursing home ►*n.* A residential establishment that provides care for the elderly or the chronically ill.

nurs·ling (nûrs′lĭng) ►*n.* A nursing infant or young animal.

nur·ture (nûr′chər) ►*n.* **1a.** The process of caring for offspring. **b.** *Biol.* The sum of environmental influences acting on an organism. **c.** The fostering of something. **2.** Upbringing; rearing. ►*v.* **-tured, -tur·ing 1.** To nourish; feed. **2.** To educate; train. **3.** To foster; cultivate. [< Lat. *nūtrīre,* suckle.] —**nur′tur·er** *n.*

Syns: cultivate, foster, nurse *v.*

nut (nŭt) ►*n.* **1a.** A fruit having a single seed enclosed in a hard shell. **b.** The usu. edible seed of such a fruit. **2.** *Slang* **a.** A crazy or eccentric person. **b.** An enthusiast: *a movie nut.* **3.** *Mus.* A ridge of wood at the top of the fingerboard or neck of a stringed instrument, over which the strings pass. **4.** A small block of metal or wood with a central threaded hole that is designed to fit around and secure a bolt or screw. [< OE *hnutu.*]

nut·crack·er (nŭt′krăk′ər) ►*n.* An implement used to crack nuts.

nut·meat (nŭt′mēt′) ►*n.* The edible kernel of a nut.

nut·meg (nŭt′mĕg′) ►*n.* The hard aromatic seed of an East Indian tree, grated or ground as a spice. [Prob. < OFr. *nois mugede.*]

nu·tri·a (no͞o′trē-ə, nyo͞o′-) ►*n., pl.* **nutria** or **-as 1.** A semiaquatic South American rodent. **2.** Its thick brownish fur. [Sp. < VLat., var. of Lat. *lutra.*]

nu·tri·ent (no͞o′trē-ənt, nyo͞o′-) ►*n.* A source of nourishment. ►*adj.* Providing nourishment. [< Lat. *nūtrīre,* nourish.]

nu·tri·ment (no͞o′trə-mənt, nyo͞o′-) ►*n.* A source of nourishment, esp. food.

nu·tri·tion (no͞o-trĭsh′ən, nyo͞o-) ►*n.* **1.** The process of nourishing or being nourished, esp. the process by which a living organism assimilates and uses food. **2.** The study of food and nourishment. [< Lat. *nūtrīre,* nourish.] —**nu·tri′tion·al** *adj.* —**nu·tri′tion·al·ly** *adv.* —**nu·tri′tion·ist** *n.* —**nu′tri·tive** (-trĭ-tĭv) *adj.*

nu·tri·tious (no͞o-trĭsh′əs, nyo͞o-) ►*adj.* Providing nourishment or nutrition. [< Lat. *nūtrīx,* nurse.] —**nu·tri′tious·ly** *adv.* —**nu·tri′tious·ness** *n.*

nuts (nŭts) *Slang* ►*adj.* **1.** Crazy or foolish. **2.** Extremely enthusiastic. ►*interj.* Used to express contempt, disappointment, or refusal. [< NUT.]

nut·shell (nŭt′shĕl′) ►*n.* The shell of a nut. —*idiom:* **in a nutshell** In a few words.

nut·ty (nŭt′ē) ►*adj.* **-ti·er, -ti·est 1.** Full of or tasting like nuts. **2.** *Slang* Crazy: *a nutty idea.* —**nut′ti·ly** *adv.* —**nut′ti·ness** *n.*

Nuuk (nook) The capital of Greenland, on the SW coast.

nuz·zle (nŭz′əl) ►*v.* **-zled, -zling 1.** To rub or push against gently with the nose or snout. **2.** To nestle together. [< NOSE.]

NV ►*abbr.* Nevada

NW ►*abbr.* **1.** northwest **2.** northwestern

NWT ►*abbr.* Northwest Territories

n. wt. ►*abbr.* net weight

NY ►*abbr.* New York

Ny·as·a (nī-ăs′ə), **Lake** A lake of SE Africa between Tanzania, Mozambique, and Malawi.

NYC ►*abbr.* New York City

ny·lon (nī′lŏn′) ►*n.* **1a.** Any of a family of high-strength, resilient synthetic resins. **b.** Cloth or yarn made from nylon. **2. nylons** Stockings made of nylon. [Coined by E.I. Du Pont de Nemours and Co., Inc.]

nymph (nĭmf) ►*n.* **1.** *Gk. & Rom. Myth.* Any of numerous female spirits dwelling in woodlands and waters. **2.** A larva of certain insects, usu. resembling the adult but smaller and lacking fully developed wings. [< Gk. *numphē.*]

nym·pho·ma·ni·a (nĭm′fə-mā′nē-ə, -mān′yə) ►*n.* Unrestrained sexual behavior by a woman. [Gk. *numphē*, nymph + –MANIA.] —**nym′pho·ma′ni·ac** (-nē-ăk) *n.*

NYSE ►*abbr.* New York Stock Exchange

NZ ►*abbr.* New Zealand

O

o or **O** (ō) ►*n., pl.* **o's** or **O's** also **os** or **Os 1.** The 15th letter of the English alphabet. **2.** A zero. **3.** **O** A type of blood in the ABO system.

O[1] (ō) ►*interj.* **1.** Used before the name of a person or thing being formally addressed. **2.** Used to express surprise or strong emotion.

O[2] ►*abbr.* **1.** *Sports* offense **2.** office telephone number **3.** *Baseball* out **4.** outstanding

O. ►*abbr.* ocean

oaf (ōf) ►*n.* A stupid, clumsy person. [ON *alfr*, elf.] —**oaf′ish** *adj.* —**oaf′ish·ly** *adv.*

O·a·hu (ō-ä′hoo) An island of central HI between Molokai and Kauai.

oak (ōk) ►*n.* **1.** Any of numerous trees bearing acorns as fruit. **2.** The durable wood of these trees. [< OE *āc.*] —**oak′en** *adj.*

Oak·land (ōk′lənd) A city of N CA on San Francisco Bay opposite San Francisco.

Oak·ley (ōk′lē), **Annie** 1860–1926. Amer. sharpshooter.

oa·kum (ō′kəm) ►*n.* Loose hemp or jute fiber, sometimes treated with tar, used chiefly for caulking ships. [< OE *ācumba.*]

oar (ôr) ►*n.* A long pole with a blade at one end, used to row or steer a boat. [< OE *ār.*]

oar·lock (ôr′lŏk′) ►*n.* A usu. U-shaped metal hoop used as a fulcrum in rowing and to hold an oar in place.

OAS ►*abbr.* Organization of American States

o·a·sis (ō-ā′sĭs) ►*n., pl.* **-ses** (-sēz) **1.** A fertile or green spot in a desert. **2.** A place of refuge from surrounding unpleasantness. [< Gk.]

oat (ōt) ►*n.* often **oats** (*takes sing. or pl. v.*) **1.** A cereal grass widely cultivated for its edible grains. **2.** The grain of this plant. [< OE *āte.*] —**oat′en** *adj.*

oat·cake (ōt′kāk′) ►*n.* A flattened cake of baked oatmeal.

oath (ōth) ►*n., pl.* **oaths** (ō*th*z, ōths) **1.** A formal promise to fulfill a pledge, often calling on God or a god as witness. **2.** A blasphemous use of a sacred name. [< OE *āth.*]

oat·meal (ōt′mēl′) ►*n.* **1.** A porridge made from rolled or ground oats. **2.** Meal made from oats; rolled or ground oats.

Ob (ŏb, ôb) A river, about 3,700 km (2,300 mi), of central Russia flowing to the **Gulf of Ob**, an arm of the Arctic Ocean.

O·ba·di·ah (ō′bə-dī′ə) ►*n.* **1.** A Hebrew prophet of the 6th cent. BC. **2.** See table at **Bible.**

O·ba·ma (ō-bä′mə), **Barack Hussein, Jr.** b. 1961. The 44th US president (took office in 2009).

Barack Obama
photographed in 2009

ob·bli·ga·to (ŏb′lĭ-gä′tō) ►*n., pl.* **-tos** or **-ti** (-tē) *Mus.* An accompaniment that is an indispensable part of a piece. [Ital.]

ob·du·rate (ŏb′doo-rĭt, -dyoo-) ►*adj.* **1.** Obstinate or intractable. **2.** Hardened against feeling; hardhearted: *an obdurate miser.* [< LLat. *obdūrāre*, harden.] —**ob′du·ra·cy** *n.* —**ob′du·rate·ly** *adv.*

o·be·di·ent (ō-bē′dē-ənt) ►*adj.* Dutifully complying with the orders or instructions of one in authority. [< Lat. *oboedīre*, obey.] —**o·be′di·ence** *n.* —**o·be′di·ent·ly** *adv.*

o·bei·sance (ō-bā′səns, ō-bē′-) ►*n.* **1.** A gesture or body movement expressing deference. **2.** An attitude of deference. [< OFr. *obeir, obeiss-*, OBEY.] —**o·bei′sant** *adj.*

ob·e·lisk (ŏb′ə-lĭsk) ►*n.* **1.** A tall, four-sided shaft of stone, usu. tapered, that rises to a pointed pyramidal top. **2.** *Print.* The dagger sign (†), used esp. as a reference mark. [< Gk. *obeliskos.*]

o·bese (ō-bēs′) ►*adj.* Extremely fat; grossly

overweight. [Lat. *obēsus* < p.part. of **obedere*, devour.] **—o·bese′ly** *adv.* **—o·be′si·ty** *n.*

o·bey (ō-bā′) ►*v.* **1.** To carry out the command of. **2.** To comply with (a command). [< Lat. *oboedīre*.] **—o·bey′er** *n.*

ob·fus·cate (ŏb′fə-skāt′, ŏb-fŭs′kāt′) ►*v.* **-cat·ed, -cat·ing 1.** To make so confused as to be difficult to understand. **2.** To render indistinct or dim. [Lat. *obfuscāre*.] **—ob′fus·ca′tion** *n.* **—ob·fus′ca·to·ry** (ŏb-fŭs′kə-tôr′ē, əb-) *adj.*

o·bi (ō′bē) ►*n.* A wide sash worn by Japanese women as part of the traditional dress. [J.]

o·bit (ō′bĭt, ō-bĭt′) ►*n. Informal* An obituary.

o·bi·ter dic·tum (ō′bĭ-tər dĭk′təm) ►*n., pl.* **obiter dic·ta** (dĭk′tə) *Law* See **dictum** (sense 2). [Lat., something said in passing.]

o·bit·u·ar·y (ō-bĭch′ōō-ĕr′ē) ►*n., pl.* **-ies** A published notice of a death, usu. with a brief biography of the deceased. [Med.Lat. *obituārius*, (report) of death.]

ob·ject (ŏb′jĭkt, -jĕkt′) ►*n.* **1.** Something perceptible by the senses; a material thing. **2.** A focus of attention or action. **3.** The purpose of a specific action. **4.** *Gram.* A noun that receives or is affected by the action of a verb or that follows and is governed by a preposition. **5.** *Comp.* A discrete item that can be selected and maneuvered, such as an onscreen graphic. ►*v.* (əb-jĕkt′) **1.** To present a dissenting or opposing argument. **2.** To feel or express disapproval. [< Lat. *obiectus*, p.part. of *obicere*, to put forward, oppose.] **—ob·jec′tion** *n.* **—ob·jec′tor** *n.*

ob·jec·tion·a·ble (əb-jĕk′shə-nə-bəl) ►*adj.* Meriting disapproval; offensive. **—ob·jec′tion·a·bil′i·ty** *n.* **—ob·jec′tion·a·bly** *adv.*

ob·jec·tive (əb-jĕk′tĭv) ►*adj.* **1.** Existing independent of the mind: *objective reality.* **2.** Uninfluenced by emotions or personal prejudices: *an objective critic.* **3.** *Gram.* Of or being the case of a noun or pronoun that serves as the object of a verb. ►*n.* **1.** Something worked toward or striven for. **2.** *Gram.* The objective case or a word in the objective case. **3.** The lens or mirror in an optical instrument that first receives light rays from the object. **—ob·jec′tive·ly** *adv.* **—ob′jec·tiv′i·ty** (ŏb′jĕk-tĭv′ĭ-tē) *n.*

object lesson ►*n.* A concrete illustration of a moral or principle.

ob·jet d'art (ŏb′zhĕ där′) ►*n., pl.* **ob·jets d'art** (ŏb′zhĕ där′) An object of artistic merit. [Fr.]

ob·late (ŏb′lāt′, ŏ-blāt′) ►*adj.* Flattened at the poles: *an oblate spheroid.* [NLat. *oblātus.*] **—ob′late′ly** *adv.* **—ob′late′ness** *n.*

ob·la·tion (ə-blā′shən, ō-blā′-) ►*n.* The act of offering something to a deity. [< Lat. *offerre*, *oblāt-*, to offer.] **—ob·la′tion·al, ob′la·to′ry** (ŏb′lə-tôr′ē) *adj.*

ob·li·gate (ŏb′lĭ-gāt′) ►*v.* **-gat·ed, -gat·ing** To compel or constrain by a social, legal, or moral requirement. [Lat. *obligāre.*]

ob·li·ga·tion (ŏb′lĭ-gā′shən) ►*n.* **1.** A requirement, such as a contract or promise, that compels one to a particular course of action. **2.** The constraining power of a promise, contract, law, or sense of duty. **3.** The fact or condition of being indebted to another for a favor received.

o·blig·a·to·ry (ə-blĭg′ə-tôr′ē, ŏb′lĭ-gə-) ►*adj.* Of the nature of an obligation; compulsory. **—o·blig′a·to′ri·ly** *adv.*

o·blige (ə-blīj′) ►*v.* **o·bliged, o·blig·ing 1.** To

constrain. **2.** To make indebted or grateful. **3.** To do a service or favor (for). [< Lat. *obligāre.*] **—o·blig′ing·ly** *adv.*

Syns: accommodate, favor **Ant:** *disoblige* **v.**

o·blique (ō-blēk′, ə-blēk′) ►*adj.* **1a.** Slanting or sloping. **b.** *Math.* Neither parallel nor perpendicular. **2.** Indirect or evasive. **3.** *Gram.* Designating any noun case except the nominative or vocative. ►*n.* Something oblique. ►*adv.* (ō-blīk′, ə-blīk′) At an angle of 45°. [< Lat. *oblīquus.*] **—o·blique′ly** *adv.* **—o·blique′ness, o·bliq′ui·ty** (ō-blĭk′wĭ-tē, ə-blĭk′-) *n.*

ob·lit·er·ate (ə-blĭt′ə-rāt′, ō-blĭt′-) ►*v.* **-at·ed, -at·ing 1.** To do away with completely. **2.** To erase or cover over. [Lat. *oblitterāre*, erase.] **—o·blit′er·a′tion** *n.* **—o·blit′er·a′tive** (-ə-rā′tĭv, -ər-ə-tĭv) *adj.*

o·bliv·i·on (ə-blĭv′ē-ən) ►*n.* **1.** The condition of being completely forgotten. **2.** Forgetfulness. [< Lat. *oblīvīscī*, forget.]

o·bliv·i·ous (ə-blĭv′ē-əs) ►*adj.* **1.** Lacking conscious awareness; unmindful. **2.** *Archaic* Lacking all memory; forgetful. **—o·bliv′i·ous·ly** *adv.* **—o·bliv′i·ous·ness** *n.*

Usage: The adjective *oblivious* can be followed by either *to* or *of*: *The party appeared oblivious to* (or *of*) *the mounting pressures for political reform.*

ob·long (ŏb′lông′, -lŏng′) ►*adj.* Deviating from a square, circular, or spherical form by being elongated in one direction. [< Lat. *oblongus.*] **—ob′long′** *n.*

ob·lo·quy (ŏb′lə-kwē) ►*n., pl.* **-quies 1.** Abusively detractive language. **2.** Disgrace; ill repute. [< Lat. *oblouī*, speak against.]

ob·nox·ious (ŏb-nŏk′shəs, əb-) ►*adj.* Very objectionable; odious. [< Lat. *obnoxius*, punishable.] **—ob·nox′ious·ly** *adv.* **—ob·nox′ious·ness** *n.*

o·boe (ō′bō) ►*n.* A woodwind instrument with a conical bore and a double reed mouthpiece. [< Fr. *hautbois.*] **—o′bo·ist** *n.*

ob·scene (ŏb-sēn′, əb-) ►*adj.* **1.** Offensive to accepted standards of decency. **2.** Morally repulsive. **3.** Outrageously or objectionably extreme: *an obscene credit card bill.* [Lat. *obscēnus.*] **—ob·scene′ly** *adv.* **—ob·scen′i·ty** (-sĕn′ĭ-tē) *n.*

ob·scur·ant·ism (ŏb-skyŏŏr′ən-tĭz′əm, əb-, ŏb′skyŏŏ-răn′-) ►*n.* **1.** A policy of withholding information from the public. **2.** The practice of deliberate vagueness or obscurity, as in literature. **—ob·scur′ant·ist** *n.*

ob·scure (ŏb-skyŏŏr′, əb-) ►*adj.* **-scur·er, -scur·est 1.** Dim; dark: *the obscure depths of a cave.* **2.** Indistinctly heard or perceived. **3.** Out of sight; hidden. **4.** Of undistinguished station or reputation. **5.** Ambiguous or vague; unclear. ►*v.* **-scured, -scur·ing 1.** To make dim or unclear. See Synonyms at **block. 2.** To make difficult to discern mentally or understand. **3.** To conceal or cover. [< Lat. *obscūrus.*] **—ob·scure′ly** *adv.* **—ob·scure′ness, ob·scu′ri·ty** *n.*

ob·se·qui·ous (ŏb-sē′kwē-əs, əb-) ►*adj.* Full of or exhibiting servile compliance. [< Lat. *obsequī*, comply.] **—ob·se′qui·ous·ly** *adv.*

ob·se·quy (ŏb′sĭ-kwē) ►*n., pl.* **-quies** A funeral rite or ceremony. [< Lat. *obsequium*, compliance.]

ob·ser·vance (əb-zûr′vəns) ►*n.* **1.** The act or practice of complying with a law, custom, command, or rule. **2.** The custom of celebrating a holiday or other ritual occasion. **3.** A customary rite or ceremony.

ob·ser·vant (əb-zûr′vənt) ►*adj.* **1.** Having or showing a perceptive awareness. **2.** Diligent in observing a law, custom, or principle: *observant of the speed limit.* —**ob·ser′vant·ly** *adv.*

ob·ser·va·tion (ŏb′zər-vā′shən) ►*n.* **1.** The act of observing or the fact of being observed. **2.** The act of noting and recording something with instruments. **3.** An inference, judgment, or remark that is made by observing: *a sharp observation.* —**ob′ser·va′tion·al** *adj.*

ob·ser·va·to·ry (əb-zûr′və-tôr′ē) ►*n.,* pl. **-ries** A place designed for making observations of astronomical esp. meteorological phenomena.

ob·serve (əb-zûrv′) ►*v.* **-served, -serv·ing 1a.** To be or become aware of, esp. through careful attention; notice. **b.** To watch attentively. **c.** To make a scientific or systematic study of. **2.** To say casually; remark. **3.** To adhere to or abide by. **4.** To keep or celebrate (e.g., a holiday). [< Lat. *observāre,* abide by.] —**ob·serv′a·ble** *adj.* —**ob·serv′a·bly** *adv.* —**ob·serv′er** *n.*

ob·sess (əb-sĕs′, ŏb-) ►*v.* **1.** To have the mind excessively preoccupied with a single topic. **2.** To preoccupy the mind of excessively. [Lat. *obsidēre, obsess-*: *ob-,* on + *sedēre,* sit.]

ob·ses·sion (əb-sĕsh′ən, ŏb-) ►*n.* **1.** Compulsive preoccupation with a fixed idea or unwanted emotion. **2.** A compulsive, often unreasonable idea or emotion. —**ob·ses′sion·al** *adj.* —**ob·ses′sive** *adj.* —**ob·ses′sive·ly** *adv.* —**ob·ses′sive·ness** *n.*

ob·sid·i·an (ŏb-sĭd′ē-ən) ►*n.* A hard, usu. black or banded volcanic glass. [Lat. *obsidiānus.*]

ob·so·les·cent (ŏb′sə-lĕs′ənt) ►*adj.* Becoming obsolete. [< Lat. *obsolēscere,* go out of use.] —**ob′so·les′cence** *n.* —**ob′so·les′cent·ly** *adv.*

ob·so·lete (ŏb′sə-lēt′, ŏb′sə-lēt′) ►*adj.* **1.** No longer in use or in effect. **2.** Outmoded in style or construction. [Lat. *obsolētus,* p.part. of *obsolēscere,* fall into disuse.] —**ob′so·lete′ly** *adv.* —**ob′so·lete′ness** *n.* —**ob′so·let′ism** *n.*

ob·sta·cle (ŏb′stə-kəl) ►*n.* Something that opposes, stands in the way of, or delays progress. [< Lat. *obstāculum* < *obstāre,* impede : *ob-,* against + *stāre,* stand.]

ob·ste·tri·cian (ŏb′stĭ-trĭsh′ən) ►*n.* A physician who specializes in obstetrics.

ob·stet·rics (ŏb-stĕt′rĭks, əb-) ►*n.* (takes sing. or pl. v.) The branch of medicine that deals with the care of women during and after pregnancy and childbirth. [< Lat. *obstetrīx,* midwife : *ob-,* opposite + *stāre,* stand.] —**ob·stet′ric, ob·stet′ri·cal** *adj.*

ob·sti·nate (ŏb′stə-nĭt) ►*adj.* **1.** Stubbornly adhering to an attitude or course of action. **2.** Difficult to manage, control, or treat: *an obstinate problem.* [< Lat. *obstināre,* persist.] —**ob′sti·na·cy** (-nə-sē) *n.* —**ob′sti·nate·ly** *adv.*

ob·strep·er·ous (ŏb-strĕp′ər-əs, əb-) ►*adj.* Noisily unruly or defiant. [< Lat. *obstrepere,* make a noise against.] —**ob·strep′er·ous·ly** *adv.* —**ob·strep′er·ous·ness** *n.*

ob·struct (əb-strŭkt′, ŏb-) ►*v.* **1.** To block (a passage) with obstacles. **2.** To impede; retard: *obstructed my progress.* See Synonyms at **hinder.** **3.** To get in the way of; hide from sight. See Synonyms at **block.** [Lat. *obstruere, obstrūct-,*

pile up against.] —**ob·struct′er, ob·struc′tor** *n.* —**ob·struc′tive** *adj.* —**ob·struc′tive·ly** *adv.* —**ob·struc′tive·ness** *n.*

ob·struc·tion (əb-strŭk′shən, ŏb-) ►*n.* **1.** An obstacle. **2.** The act of obstructing. **3.** The condition of being obstructed.

ob·struc·tion·ist (əb-strŭk′shə-nĭst, ŏb-) ►*n.* One who systematically blocks or delays a process. —**ob·struc′tion·ism** *n.*

ob·tain (əb-tān′, ŏb-) ►*v.* **1.** To succeed in gaining possession of; acquire. **2.** To be in existence or effect: *physical laws that obtain at the subatomic level.* [< Lat. *obtinēre.*] —**ob·tain′a·ble** *adj.* —**ob·tain′er** *n.*

ob·trude (ŏb-trōōd′, əb-) ►*v.* **-trud·ed, -trud·ing 1.** To impose (oneself or one's ideas) on others. **2.** To thrust out; push forward. [Lat. *obtrūdere.*] —**ob·trud′er** *n.* —**ob·tru′sion** (-trōō′zhən) *n.* —**ob·tru′sive** (-trōō′sĭv, -zĭv) *adj.* —**ob·tru′sive·ly** *adv.*

ob·tuse (ŏb-tōōs′, -tyōōs′, əb-) ►*adj.* **-tus·er, -tus·est 1.** Lacking quickness of perception or intellect. **2.** Not sharp, pointed, or acute in form; blunt. [< Lat. *obtūsus,* p.part. of *obtundere,* to blunt.] —**ob·tuse′ly** *adv.* —**ob·tuse′ness** *n.*

obtuse angle ►*n.* An angle greater than 90° and less than 180°.

ob·verse (ŏb-vûrs′, əb-, ŏb′vûrs′) ►*adj.* **1.** Facing the observer. **2.** Serving as a counterpart or complement. ►*n.* (ŏb′vûrs′, ŏb-vûrs′, əb-) **1.** The side of a coin or medal that bears the principal stamp or design. **2.** A counterpart or complement. [Lat. *obversus,* p.part. of *obvertere,* turn toward.] —**ob·verse′ly** *adv.*

ob·vi·ate (ŏb′vē-āt′) ►*v.* **-at·ed, -at·ing** To keep from happening or render unnecessary. [Lat. *obviāre,* hinder.] —**ob′vi·a′tion** *n.* —**ob′vi·a′tor** *n.*

ob·vi·ous (ŏb′vē-əs) ►*adj.* **1.** Easily perceived or understood; apparent. See Synonyms at **apparent. 2.** Easily seen through because of a lack of subtlety; transparent. [< Lat. *obviam,* in the way.] —**ob′vi·ous·ly** *adv.* —**ob′vi·ous·ness** *n.*

oc·a·ri·na (ŏk′ə-rē′nə) ►*n.* A small bulb-shaped wind instrument with finger holes and a mouthpiece. [< Ital. *oca,* goose.]

O'Ca·sey (ō-kā′sē), **Sean** 1880–1964. Irish playwright.

oc·ca·sion (ə-kā′zhən) ►*n.* **1.** An event or happening, or the time of an event or happening. **2.** A significant event, esp. a large or important social gathering. **3.** A cause of or reason for something. ►*v.* To provide occasion for; cause. —*idiom:* **on occasion** From time to time. [< Lat. *occidere,* fall down.]

oc·ca·sion·al (ə-kā′zhə-nəl) ►*adj.* **1.** Occurring from time to time. **2.** Created for a special occasion: *occasional verse.* —**oc·ca′sion·al·ly** *adv.*

oc·ci·dent (ŏk′sĭ-dənt, -dĕnt′) ►*n.* **1.** The west. **2. Occident** Europe and the Western Hemisphere. [< Lat. *occidere,* to set.] —**oc′ci·den′tal, Oc′ci·den′tal** *adj. & n.*

oc·cip·i·tal (ŏk-sĭp′ĭ-tl) ►*adj.* Of the occiput or the occipital bone. ►*n.* The occipital bone.

occipital bone ►*n.* A cranial bone that forms the lower posterior part of the skull.

oc·ci·put (ŏk′sə-pŭt′, -pət) ►*n.,* pl. **oc·cip·i·ta** (ŏk-sĭp′ĭ-tə) or **-puts** The back part of the head or skull. [< Lat.]

oc·clude (ə-klōōd′) ►*v.* **-clud·ed, -clud·ing 1.** To close or shut off; obstruct. **2.** *Chem.* To absorb or adsorb and retain (a substance). **3.** To close (the jaw) so that the opposing tooth surfaces fit together. [Lat. *occlūdere.*] —**oc·clu′sion** *n.*

oc·cult (ə-kŭlt′, ŏk′ŭlt′) ►*adj.* **1.** Relating to supernatural influences, agencies, or phenomena. **2.** Available only to the initiate; secret. See Synonyms at **mysterious. 3.** Beyond human comprehension. [< Lat. *occulere,* conceal.] —**oc·cult′** *n.* —**oc·cult′ly** *adv.*

oc·cult·ism (ə-kŭl′tĭz′əm, ŏk′ŭl-) ►*n.* The belief in and study of hidden supernatural powers. —**oc·cult′ist** *n.*

oc·cu·pan·cy (ŏk′yə-pən-sē) ►*n., pl.* **-cies 1.** The act of occupying or the condition of being occupied. **2.** The period during which one occupies a place or position. —**oc′cu·pant** *n.*

oc·cu·pa·tion (ŏk′yə-pā′shən) ►*n.* **1.** An activity that serves as one's regular source of livelihood. **2.** The act or process of holding a place. **3.** Invasion, conquest, and control of a nation or territory by foreign armed forces. —**oc′cu·pa′tion·al** *adj.*

occupational therapy ►*n.* The use of productive or creative activity in the treatment of disabled people. —**occupational therapist** *n.*

oc·cu·py (ŏk′yə-pī′) ►*v.* **-pied, -py·ing 1.** To fill up (time or space). **2.** To dwell or reside in. **3.** To hold or fill (an office or position). **4.** To seize possession of and maintain control over, esp. forcibly. **5.** To engage or busy (oneself). [< Lat. *occupāre,* seize.] —**oc′cu·pi′er** *n.*

oc·cur (ə-kûr′) ►*v.* **-curred, -cur·ring 1.** To take place. See Synonyms at **happen. 2.** To be found to exist or appear. **3.** To come to mind. [Lat. *occurrere,* run toward.] —**oc·cur′rence** *n.*

o·cean (ō′shən) ►*n.* **1.** The entire body of salt water that covers more than 70 percent of the earth's surface. **2.** often **Ocean** Any of the principal divisions of the ocean: *the Indian Ocean.* **3.** A great expanse or amount. [< Gk. *Ōkeanos,* a great river encircling the earth.] —**o′ce·an′ic** (ō′shē-ăn′ĭk) *adj.*

o·cean·ar·i·um (ō′shə-nâr′ē-əm) ►*n., pl.* **-i·ums** or **-i·a** (-ē-ə) A large aquarium for the study or display of marine life.

O·ce·an·i·a (ō′shē-ăn′ē-ə, -ä′nē-ə, -ä′nē-ə) The islands of the S, W, and central Pacific, including Melanesia, Micronesia, Polynesia, and sometimes Australia, New Zealand, and the Malay Archipelago. —**O′ce·an′i·an** *adj. & n.*

o·cean·og·ra·phy (ō′shə-nŏg′rə-fē) ►*n.* The exploration and scientific study of the ocean. —**o′cean·og′ra·pher** *n.* —**o′cean·o·graph′ic** (-nə-grăf′ĭk) *adj.*

oc·e·lot (ŏs′ə-lŏt′, ō′sə-) ►*n.* A spotted wildcat of the SW US and Central and South America. [< Nahuatl *ocelotl.*]

o·cher or **o·chre** (ō′kər) ►*n.* **1.** Any of several earthy mineral oxides of iron occurring in yellow, brown, or red and used as pigments. **2.** A moderate orange yellow. [< Gk. *ōkhros,* pale yellow.] —**o′cher·ous, o′cher·y** (ō′krē) *adj.*

o·clock (ə-klŏk′) ►*adv.* **1.** Of or according to the clock: *three o'clock.* **2.** Positioned relative to the numbers on an imaginary clock dial with the observer at the center: *enemy fighters at ten o'clock.* [< *of the clock.*]

O'Con·nor (ō-kŏn′ər), **(Mary) Flannery** 1925–64. Amer. writer.

O'Connor, Sandra Day b. 1930. Amer. jurist; US Supreme Court justice (1981–2006).

OCR ►*abbr.* optical character recognition

oc·ta·gon (ŏk′tə-gŏn′) ►*n.* A polygon with 8 sides. —**oc·tag′o·nal** (ŏk-tăg′ə-nəl) *adj.*

oc·ta·he·dron (ŏk′tə-hē′drən) ►*n., pl.* **-drons** or **-dra** (-drə) A polyhedron having eight faces.

oc·tal (ŏk′təl) ►*adj.* Of or based on the number eight.

oc·tane (ŏk′tān′) ►*n.* **1.** Any of various hydrocarbons with the formula C_8H_{18}. **2.** An octane number.

octane number ►*n.* A number representing the antiknock properties of motor fuel compared with a reference fuel with a rating of 100.

oc·tant (ŏk′tənt) ►*n.* One eighth of a circle. [Lat. *octāns.*] —**oc·tan′tal** (ŏk-tăn′təl) *adj.*

oc·tave (ŏk′tĭv, -tāv′) ►*n.* **1.** *Mus.* The interval of eight diatonic degrees between two tones of the same name. **2.** A group or series of eight. [< Lat. *octāvus,* eighth.]

Oc·ta·vi·an (ŏk-tā′vē-ən) See **Augustus.**

oc·ta·vo (ŏk-tā′vō, -tä′-) ►*n., pl.* **-vos** *Print.* **1.** The page size, from 5 by 8 inches to 6 by 9.5 inches, of a book that is composed of printer's sheets folded into eight leaves. **2.** A book that is composed of octavo pages. [< Lat. *octāvus,* eighth.]

oc·tet (ŏk-tĕt′) ►*n.* **1.** *Mus.* A composition written for eight voices or eight instruments. **2.** A group of eight. [Ital. *ottetto.*]

oc·til·lion (ŏk-tĭl′yən) ►*n.* **1.** The cardinal number equal to 10^{27}. **2.** *Chiefly Brit.* The cardinal number equal to 10^{48}. [OCT(O)- + (M)ILLION.] —**oc·til′lion** *adj.* —**oc·til′lionth** *n. & adj.*

octo– or **octa–** or **oct–** ►*pref.* Eight: *octagon.* [< Gk. *oktō* and Lat. *octō-,* eight.]

Oc·to·ber (ŏk-tō′bər) ►*n.* The 10th month of the Gregorian calendar. See table at **calendar.** [< Lat. *Octōber,* eighth month.]

oc·to·ge·nar·i·an (ŏk′tə-jə-nâr′ē-ən) ►*n.* A person between 80 and 90 years of age. [< Lat. *octōgēnārius,* containing eighty.]

oc·to·pus (ŏk′tə-pəs) ►*n., pl.* **-pus·es** or **-pi** (-pī′) A marine mollusk with a soft body and eight sucker-bearing arms. [< Gk. *oktōpous,* eight-footed : *oktō,* eight + *pous,* foot.]

oc·tu·plet (ŏk-tŭp′lĭt, -tōō′plĭt, -tyōō′-) ►*n.* One of eight offspring born in a single birth. [*octu(ple),* multiply by eight + (TRI)PLET.]

oc·u·lar (ŏk′yə-lər) ►*adj.* **1.** Of or relating to the eye. **2.** Visual. ►*n.* The eyepiece of an optical instrument. [< Lat. *oculus,* eye.]

OD¹ (ō′dē′) *Slang* ►*v.* **OD′ed, OD′·ing** To take an overdose: *OD'ed on barbiturates.* ►*n.* An overdose of a drug.

OD² ►*abbr.* **1.** Doctor of Optometry **2.** also **o/d** overdraft **3.** overdrawn

odd (ŏd) ►*adj.* **-er, -est 1.** Strange or peculiar. **2.** In excess of a given number: *invited 30-odd guests.* **3.** Being one of an incomplete pair or set. **4.** *Math.* Designating an integer not divisible by 2. [< ON *oddi,* odd number.] —**odd′ly** *adv.* —**odd′ness** *n.*

odd·ball (ŏd′bôl′) ►*n. Informal* An eccentric person.

odd·i·ty (ŏd′ĭ-tē) ►*n., pl.* **-ties 1.** One that is odd. **2.** The state of being odd.

odd job ►*n.* A usu. temporary unskilled or menial job.

odd·ment (ŏd′mənt) ►*n.* Something left over.

odds (ŏdz) ►*pl.n.* **1.** A ratio expressing the amount by which the stake of one bettor differs from that of an opposing bettor. **2.** A ratio expressing the probability of an outcome. **3.** Chances: *The odds are that it will rain.* —*idiom:* **at odds** In disagreement.

odds and ends ►*pl.n.* Miscellaneous items.

odds-on (ŏdz′ŏn′, -ôn′) ►*adj. Informal* Considered most likely to win.

ode (ōd) ►*n.* A lyric poem, usu. serious or meditative in nature and having an elevated style and formal structure. [< Gk. *aoidē*, song.]

–ode ►*suff.* **1.** Way; path: *electrode.* **2.** Electrode: *diode.* [< Gk. *hodos.*]

O·der (ō′dər) A river of central Europe flowing about 900 km (560 mi) from the NE Czech Republic through Poland and Germany to the Baltic Sea.

O·des·sa (ō-dĕs′ə) A city of S Ukraine on **Odessa Bay,** an arm of the Black Sea.

O·dets (ō-dĕts′), **Clifford** 1906–63. Amer. playwright.

O·din (ō′dĭn) ►*n. Myth.* The Norse god of wisdom, war, and art.

Odin
from a 1760 Icelandic illuminated manuscript by
Ólafur Brynjúlfsson

o·di·ous (ō′dē-əs) ►*adj.* Arousing strong dislike or intense displeasure. —**o′di·ous·ly** *adv.* —**o′di·ous·ness** *n.*

o·di·um (ō′dē-əm) ►*n.* **1.** The state or quality of being odious. **2.** Disgrace resulting from hateful conduct. [Lat., hatred.]

o·dom·e·ter (ō-dŏm′ĭ-tər) ►*n.* An instrument that indicates distance traveled by a vehicle. [Fr. *odomètre.*]

o·don·tol·o·gy (ō′dŏn-tŏl′ə-jē) ►*n.* The study of the structure and abnormalities of the teeth. [Gk. *odous, odont-,* tooth + –LOGY.] —**o·don′-to·log′i·cal** (-tə-lŏj′ĭ-kəl) *adj.* —**o′don·tol′o·gist** *n.*

o·dor (ō′dər) ►*n.* **1.** A quality of something that is perceived by the sense of smell. See Synonyms at **smell.** **2.** Esteem; repute: *a doctrine that is no longer in good odor.* [< Lat.] —**o′dor·less** *adj.* —**o′dor·less·ly** *adv.* —**o′dor·ous** *adj.* —**o′dor·ous·ly** *adv.* —**o′dor·ous·ness** *n.*

o·dor·if·er·ous (ō′də-rĭf′ər-əs) ►*adj.* Having or giving off an odor. —**o′dor·if′er·ous·ly** *adv.*

O·dys·seus (ō-dĭs′yŏōs′, ō-dĭs′ē-əs) ►*n. Gk.*

Myth. The hero of Homer's *Odyssey.*

od·ys·sey (ŏd′ĭ-sē) ►*n., pl.* **-seys** A long adventurous voyage. [< ODYSSEUS.]

Oed·i·pus (ĕd′ə-pəs, ē′də-) ►*n. Gk. Myth.* A Theban prince who unwittingly killed his father and then married his mother.

Oedipus complex ►*n. Psychiat.* A subconscious sexual desire in a child, esp. a male child, for the parent of the opposite sex. —**oed′i·pal** *adj.*

oe·nol·o·gy (ē-nŏl′ə-jē) ►*n.* **enology.**

o′er (ôr) ►*prep. & adv.* Over.

oeu·vre (œ′vrə) ►*n., pl.* **oeu·vres** (œ′vrə) **1.** A work of art. **2.** The lifework of an artist. [Fr. < Lat. *opera,* works.]

of (ŭv, ŏv) ►*prep.* **1.** Derived or coming from: *languages of Africa.* **2.** Owing to: *died of cholera.* **3.** Away from: *east of here.* **4.** So as to be separated from: *robbed of one's dignity.* **5.** From the total or group comprising: *two of my friends.* **6.** Composed or made from: *a dress of silk.* **7.** Associated with: *the habitat of the panda.* **8.** Belonging or connected to: *the wings of a dove.* **9.** Possessing: *a person of honor.* **10.** Containing or carrying: *a glass of water.* **11.** Specified as: *a depth of ten feet.* **12.** Centering on; directed toward: *fear of heights.* **13.** Produced by: *fruit of the vine.* **14.** With reference to; about: *spoke of her plans.* **15.** Set aside for: *a day of rest.* **16.** Before: *five minutes of two.* **17.** During or on: *of recent years.* [< OE.]

Usage: The so-called double genitive construction, as in *a friend of my father's* or *a book of mine,* is well supported by literary precedent, and serves a useful purpose. *Bob's photograph* could be either a picture of Bob or one that he has in his possession. *A photograph of Bob's* can only refer to a picture Bob has in his possession.

off (ôf, ŏf) ►*adv.* **1.** From a place or position: *ran off.* **2.** At a certain distance in space or time: *a mile off.* **3.** So as to be no longer operating or functioning: *turned off the radio.* **4.** So as to be smaller, fewer, or less: *tapered off.* **5.** So as to be away from work or duty: *take the day off.* **6.** Into a state of sudden activity: *set the alarm off.* ►*adj.* **1.** Remote: *the off chance of finding him at home.* **2.** Not on, attached, or connected: *with my shoes off.* **3.** Not operating or operational: *The oven is off.* **4.** No longer taking place; canceled: *The party is off.* **5.** Not at a normal or satisfactory level: *Your pitching is off today.* **6.** Going: *She's off to Tibet.* **7.** Absent or away from work or duty: *He's off today.* ►*prep.* **1.** So as to be removed or distant from: *fell off the sofa.* **2.** Away or relieved from: *off duty.* **3.** With the means provided by: *living off my pension.* **4.** Extending or branching out from: *a street off the village green.* **5.** Not up to the usual standard of: *off her game.* **6.** So as to abstain from: *went off caffeine.* **7.** To seaward of: *a mile off Sandy Hook.* ►*v. Slang* To murder. —*idiom:* **off and on** Intermittently. [< OE *of.*]

Usage: In Modern English the compound preposition *off of* is generally regarded as informal and is best avoided in formal speech and writing: *He stepped off* (not *off of*) *the platform.*

of·fal (ô′fəl, ŏf′əl) ►*n.* **1.** Waste parts, esp. of a butchered animal. **2.** Rubbish. [ME.]

off·beat (ôf′bēt′, ŏf′-) ►*n. Mus.* An unaccented beat in a measure. ►*adj.* (ôf′bēt′, ŏf′-) *Slang* Unconventional.

off·col·or (ôf′kŭl′ər, ŏf′-) ►*adj.* **1.** Risqué: *an off-color joke.* **2.** Varying from the expected or required color.

of·fend (ə-fĕnd′) ►*v.* **1.** To cause anger, resentment, or wounded feelings in. **2.** To be displeasing or disagreeable to. **3.** To violate; transgress. [< Lat. *offendere.*] —**of·fend′er** *n.*

of·fense (ə-fĕns′) ►*n.* **1a.** The act of offending. **b.** The state of being offended. **2.** A violation of a moral or social code. **3.** A crime. **4.** (ŏf′ĕns′) The act of attacking or assaulting. **5.** (ŏf′ĕns′) *Sports* **a.** The means or tactics used in attempting to score. **b.** A team in possession of the ball or puck. [< Lat. *offendere, offens-,* offend.]

of·fen·sive (ə-fĕn′sĭv) ►*adj.* **1.** Causing anger, resentment, or affront. **2.** Disagreeable to the senses. **3.** Making an attack. **4.** (ŏf′ĕn-) *Sports* Relating to the offense. ►*n.* A concerted attack or assault. —**of·fen′sive·ly** *adv.* —**of·fen′sive·ness** *n.*
Syns: disgusting, loathsome, nasty, repellent, repulsive, revolting adj.

of·fer (ô′fər, ŏf′ər) ►*v.* **1.** To present for acceptance or rejection. **2.** To present as an act of worship. **3.** To propose as payment. **4.** To present for sale. **5.** To make available: *a seat that offers a better view.* **6.** To put up; mount: *offered no resistance to his attackers.* [< Lat. *offerre : ob-,* to + *ferre,* bring.] —**of′fer** *n.* —**of′fer·er** *n.*

of·fer·ing (ô′fər-ĭng, ŏf′ər-) ►*n.* **1.** The act of making an offer. **2.** Something offered. **3.** A presentation made to a deity as an act of worship.

of·fer·to·ry (ô′fər-tôr′ē, ŏf′ər-) ►*n., pl.* **-ries** *often* **Offertory** **1.** The part of the Eucharist at which bread and wine are offered to God. **2.** A musical setting for this part of the liturgy. [< Lat. *offerre,* OFFER.]

off-guard (ôf′gärd′, ŏf′-) ►*adj.* Off one's guard; unprepared.

off·hand (ôf′hănd′, ŏf′-) ►*adv. & adj.* Without preparation or forethought. —**off′hand′ed·ly** *adv.* —**off′hand′ed·ness** *n.*

of·fice (ô′fĭs, ŏf′ĭs) ►*n.* **1a.** A place in which business, clerical, or professional activities are conducted. **b.** The staff working in such a place. **2.** A subdivision of a governmental department. **3.** A position of authority given to a person, as in a government or corporation. **4.** A duty or function assigned to or assumed by someone. See Synonyms at **function.** **5.** *often* **offices** A service or beneficial act done for another. **6.** *Eccles.* A service, esp. liturgical prayer. [< Lat. *officium,* duty.]

of·fice·hold·er (ô′fĭs-hōl′dər, ŏf′ĭs-) ►*n.* One who holds public office.

of·fi·cer (ô′fĭ-sər, ŏf′ĭ-) ►*n.* One who holds an office of authority or trust in an organization, esp.: **a.** One who holds a commission in the armed forces. **b.** A person licensed in the merchant marine as master, mate, chief engineer, or assistant engineer. **c.** A police officer.

of·fi·cial (ə-fĭsh′əl) ►*adj.* **1.** Of or relating to an office of authority. **2.** Authorized by a proper authority. **3.** Holding office in a public capacity. **4.** Formal: *an official banquet.* ►*n.* **1.** One who holds an office or a position. **2.** *Sports* A referee or umpire. —**of·fi′cial·dom** *n.* —**of·fi′cial·ly** *adv.*

of·fi·ci·ate (ə-fĭsh′ē-āt′) ►*v.* **-at·ed, -at·ing** **1.** To perform the functions of an office or posi-

tion of authority, esp. at a religious service. **2.** *Sports* To serve as a referee or umpire. —**of·fi′ci·a′tor** *n.*

of·fi·cious (ə-fĭsh′əs) ►*adj.* Overly eager in offering unwanted services or advice. [Lat. *officiōsus,* obliging, dutiful.] —**of·fi′cious·ly** *adv.* —**of·fi′cious·ness** *n.*

off·ing (ô′fĭng, ŏf′ĭng) ►*n.* The near future: *new developments in the offing.*

off·ish (ô′fĭsh, ŏf′ĭsh) ►*adj.* Distant; aloof. —**off′ish·ly** *adv.* —**off′ish·ness** *n.*

off-key (ôf′-kē′, ŏf′-) ►*adj.* **1.** *Mus.* Out of tune; sharp or flat. **2.** Inappropriate; improper. —**off′key′** *adv.*

off-lim·its (ôf-lĭm′ĭts, ŏf-) ►*adj.* Forbidden to a designated group.

off·line or **off-line** (ôf′līn′, ŏf′-) ►*adj.* **1.** *Comp.* **a.** Not connected to a central computer or to a computer network. **b.** Inaccessible via a computer network. **2.** Not in production or operation, esp. as part of a supply chain: *refineries that went offline during the hurricane.*

off·load or **off-load** (ôf′lōd′, ŏf′-) ►*v.* **1.** To unload (e.g., a vehicle). **2.** *Comp.* To transfer (data) to a peripheral device.

off·print (ôf′prĭnt′, ŏf′-) ►*n.* A reproduction of an article from a publication. —**off′print′** *v.*

off-road (ôf′rōd′, ŏf′-) ►*adj.* Taking place or designed for use off public roads. —**off′-road′** *adv.*

off-sea·son (ôf′-sē′zən, ŏf′-) ►*n.* A part of the year marked by a cessation or lessening of activity. —**off′-sea′son** *adv. & adj.*

off·set (ôf′sĕt′, ŏf′-) ►*n.* **1.** One that balances, counteracts, or compensates. **2.** *Archit.* A ledge or recess in a wall. **3.** A bend made in a pipe or bar to allow it to pass around an obstruction. **4.** Printing by indirect image transfer. ►*v.* (ôf′sĕt′, ŏf′-, ôf-sĕt′, ŏf-) **-set, -set·ting** **1.** To counterbalance or compensate for. **2.** To produce by offset printing. **3.** To make or form an offset in (a wall, bar, or pipe). —**off′set′** *adv. & adj.*

off·shoot (ôf′shōōt′, ŏf′-) ►*n.* Something that branches out or derives its origin from a particular source, as a shoot from a plant stem. See Synonyms at **branch.**

off·shore (ôf′shôr′, ŏf′-) ►*adj.* **1.** Away from the shore. **2.** At a distance from the shore. —**off′shore′** *adv.*

off·side (ôf′sīd′, ŏf′-) *also* **off·sides** (-sīdz′) ►*adv. & adj. Sports* Illegally ahead of the ball or puck.

off·spring (ôf′sprĭng′, ŏf′-) ►*n., pl.* **-spring** **1.** Progeny; young. **2.** A result; product. [< OE *ofspring.*]

off·stage (ôf′stāj′, ŏf′-) ►*adj. & adv.* Away from the area of a stage visible to the audience.

off-the-cuff (ôf′thə-kŭf′, ŏf′-) ►*adv. & adj.* Without preparation; impromptu.

off-the-rec·ord (ôf′thə-rĕk′ərd, ŏf′-) ►*adv. & adj.* Not for publication or attribution.

off-the-wall (ôf′thə-wôl′, ŏf′-) ►*adj. Informal* Very unconventional or unusual.

off-track betting (ôf′trăk′, ŏf′-) ►*n.* A system of placing bets away from a racetrack.

off-white (ôf′wīt′, -hwīt′, ŏf′-) ►*n.* A grayish or yellowish white. —**off′-white′** *adj.*

off year ►*n.* **1.** A year in which no major political elections occur. **2.** A year of reduced activity or production.

oft (ôft, ŏft) ►*adv.* Often. [< OE.]

of·ten (ô′fən, ŏf′ən, ôf′tən, ŏf′-) ►*adv.* Many times; frequently. [< OE *oft.*]

of·ten·times (ô′fən-tīmz′, ôf′tən-, ŏf′ən-, ŏf′tən-) also **oft·times** (ôf′tīmz′, ŏf′-) ►*adv.* Often.

O·gla·la (ō-glä′lə) ►*n., pl.* **-la** or **-las** A member of a Lakota people inhabiting SW South Dakota.

o·gle (ō′gəl, ô′gəl) ►*v.* **o·gled, o·gling** To look or stare at, esp. in a lecherous manner. [Poss. < LGer. *oegeln.*] —**o′gler** *n.*

O·gle·thorpe (ō′gəl-thôrp′), **James Edward** 1696–1785. English philanthropist and colonizer.

o·gre (ō′gər) ►*n.* **1.** A fabled giant that eats humans. **2.** A brutish or cruel person. [Fr.] —**o′gre·ish** (ō′gər-ĭsh, ō′grĭsh) *adj.*

o·gress (ō′grĭs) ►*n.* **1.** A female ogre. **2.** A brutish or cruel woman.

oh (ō) ►*interj.* **1.** Used to express strong emotion, such as surprise, fear, anger, or pain. **2.** Used to indicate understanding.

OH ►*abbr.* Ohio

O. Henry See William Sydney **Porter.**

O·hi·o (ō-hī′ō) A state of the N-central US. Cap. Columbus. —**O·hi′o·an** *adj. & n.*

Ohio River A river formed by the confluence of the Allegheny and Monongahela Rivers in W Pennsylvania and flowing about 1,580 km (980 mi) to the Mississippi R. in S IL.

ohm (ōm) ►*n.* A unit of electrical resistance equal to that of a conductor in which a current of one ampere is produced by a potential of one volt. [After Georg S. *Ohm* (1787–1854).]

ohm·me·ter (ōm′mē′tər) ►*n.* An instrument that measures electrical resistance in ohms.

Ohr·mazd also **Or·mazd** or **Or·muzd** (ôr′-məzd, ôr-mŭzd′) ►*n.* See **Ahura Mazda.** [< OPers. *Auramazda.*]

–oid ►*suff.* Resembling; having the appearance of: *humanoid.* [< Gk. *eidos,* shape.]

oil (oil) ►*n.* **1.** Any of numerous natural or synthetic substances that are gen. slippery, combustible, viscous, liquid at room temperatures, soluble in organic solvents such as ether but not in water, and used in a great variety of products, esp. lubricants and fuels. **2.** Petroleum. **3.** A substance with an oily consistency. **4.** Oil paint. **5.** An oil painting. ►*v.* To lubricate, supply, or cover with oil. [< Gk. *elaion,* olive oil.] —**oil′er** *n.*

oil·cloth (oil′klôth′, -klŏth′) ►*n.* **1.** A heavy cotton fabric waterproofed with linseed oil. **2.** Fabric coated with a waterproof layer of vinyl.

oil color ►*n.* See **oil paint.**

oil field ►*n.* An area with reserves of recoverable petroleum.

oil paint ►*n.* A paint in which the vehicle is a drying oil.

oil painting ►*n.* **1.** A painting done in oil paints. **2.** The art of painting with oils.

oil shale ►*n.* A black or dark brown shale containing hydrocarbons that yield petroleum by distillation.

oil·skin (oil′skĭn′) ►*n.* **1.** Cloth treated with oil to make it waterproof. **2.** A garment made of oilskin or synthetic waterproof fabric.

oil slick ►*n.* A layer of oil on water.

oil well ►*n.* A hole drilled or dug in the earth from which petroleum flows or is pumped.

oil·y (oi′lē) ►*adj.* **-i·er, -i·est 1.** Of or relating to

oil. **2.** Impregnated with oil; greasy. **3.** Excessively suave or ingratiating. See Synonyms at **unctuous.** —**oil′i·ly** *adv.* —**oil′i·ness** *n.*

oink (oingk) ►*n.* The characteristic grunting noise of a hog. [Imit.] —**oink** *v.*

oint·ment (oint′mənt) ►*n.* A highly viscous or semisolid substance used on the skin as a cosmetic or salve. [< Lat. *unguentum.*]

OJ ►*abbr.* orange juice

O·jib·wa (ō-jĭb′wä′, -wə) also **O·jib·way** (-wā′) ►*n., pl.* **-wa** or **-was** also **-way** or **-ways 1.** A member of a Native American people inhabiting a region of the US and Canada around Lake Superior. **2.** The Algonquian language of the Ojibwa.

OK¹ or **o·kay** (ō-kā′) *Informal* ►*n.* Approval; agreement. ►*v.* **OK′ed, OK′·ing** or **OK′d, OK′·ing** or **o·kayed, o·kay·ing** To approve of or agree to; authorize. ►*interj.* Used to express approval or agreement. [Abbr. of *oll korrect,* slang respelling of *all correct.*] —**OK** *adv. & adj.*

OK² ►*abbr.* Oklahoma

O·kee·cho·bee (ō′kĭ-chō′bē), **Lake** A lake of SE FL N of the Everglades.

O′Keeffe (ō-kēf′), **Georgia** 1887–1986. Amer. painter.

Georgia O'Keeffe

O·ke·fe·no·kee Swamp (ō′kə-fə-nō′kē, -kē-) A large swampy area of SE GA and NE FL.

O·khotsk (ō-kŏtsk′), **Sea of** An arm of the NW Pacific W of the Kamchatka Peninsula.

O·ki·na·wa (ō′kĭ-nä′wə, -nou′-) An island and island group of the central Ryukyu Is. in the W Pacific SW of Japan.

O·kla·ho·ma (ō′klə-hō′mə) A state of the S-central US. Cap. Oklahoma City. —**O′kla·ho′man** *adj. & n.*

Oklahoma City The capital of OK, in the central part.

o·kra (ō′krə) ►*n.* **1.** A tall tropical African plant cultivated for its edible green pods. **2.** The pods of this plant, used esp. in soups. **3.** See **gumbo** (sense 2). [Of West African orig.]

–ol ►*suff.* An alcohol or phenol: *glycerol.* [< (ALCOH)OL.]

O·laf II (ō′läf, ō′ləf, ōō′läf) or **O·lav II** (ō′läv) Saint Olaf. 995?–1030. Patron saint and king of Norway (1016–28).

old (ōld) ►*adj.* **-er, -est 1.** Having lived or existed for a long time; far advanced in years or life. **2.** Made or acquired long ago; not new. **3.** Wise; mature. **4.** Having a specified age. **5.** Belonging

to or being of an earlier time: *her old classmates.*
6. Known through long acquaintance: *an old friend.* **7.** Used as an intensive or to express affection: *any old time; good old Fido.* ►*n.* **1.** An individual of a specified age. Used in combination: *a five-year-old.* See Usage Note at **elder**[1]. **2.** Old people collectively. **3.** Former times; yore: *days of old.* [< OE *eald.*] —**old′ness** *n.*

old·en (ōl′dən) ►*adj.* Old. [ME.]

Old English ►*n.* English from the middle of the 5th to the beginning of the 12th cent.

old-fash·ioned (ōld′făsh′ənd) ►*adj.* **1.** Outdated. **2.** Attached to the values or customs of an earlier time: *old-fashioned parents.* ►*n.* A cocktail made of whiskey, bitters, and fruit.

Old French ►*n.* French from the 9th through the 16th cent.

old guard ►*n.* A conservative, often reactionary element of a class or group.

old hand ►*n.* One who is skilled from long experience.

old hat ►*adj.* **1.** Behind the times; out of fashion. **2.** Trite from overuse.

Old High German ►*n.* High German from the middle of the 9th to the late 11th cent.

old·ie (ōl′dē) ►*n.* Something old, esp. a song that was once popular.

Old Irish ►*n.* Irish from the early 8th to the middle of the 10th cent.

Old Italian ►*n.* Italian until the middle of the 16th cent.

old-line (ōld′līn′) ►*adj.* **1.** Conservative; reactionary. **2.** Long established.

old master ►*n.* **1.** A distinguished European artist from about 1500 to the early 1700s. **2.** A work by such an artist.

Old Norse ►*n.* The Germanic language of the Scandinavians until the mid-14th cent.

Old North French ►*n.* The northern dialects of Old French.

Old Persian ►*n.* An ancient Iranian language attested in inscriptions dating from the 6th to the 5th cent. BC.

Old Provençal ►*n.* Provençal before the middle of the 16th cent.

old school ►*n.* A group that adheres to traditional ideas or practices. —**old′-school′** *adj.*

Old Spanish ►*n.* Spanish before the middle of the 16th cent.

old·ster (ōld′stər) ►*n. Informal* An elderly person.

Old Testament ►*n.* The first division of the Christian Bible, corresponding to the Hebrew Scriptures. See table at **Bible.**

old-tim·er (ōld′tī′mər) ►*n. Informal* **1a.** An elderly person. **b.** One with long tenure or experience. **2.** Something very old.

old wives' tale ►*n.* A superstitious or spurious belief belonging to traditional folklore.

Old World The Eastern Hemisphere; often used to refer to Europe.

o·le·ag·i·nous (ō′lē-ăj′ə-nəs) ►*adj.* **1.** Of or relating to oil. **2.** Unctuous. [< Lat. *oleāginus,* of the olive tree.]

o·le·an·der (ō′lē-ăn′dər, ō′lē-ăn′dər) ►*n.* A poisonous Eurasian shrub having fragrant white, rose, or purple flowers. [Med.Lat.]

o·le·ic acid (ō-lē′ĭk) ►*n.* An oily liquid occurring in animal and vegetable oils.

o·le·o (ō′lē-ō′) ►*n., pl.* **-os** Margarine. [< OLEO-MARGARINE.]

oleo– or **ole–** ►*pref.* Oil: *oleomargarine.* [< Lat. *oleum.*]

o·le·o·mar·ga·rine (ō′lē-ō-mär′jə-rĭn, -rēn′) ►*n.* Margarine.

ol·fac·tion (ōl-făk′shən, ōl-) ►*n.* **1.** The sense of smell. **2.** The act of smelling. [< Lat. *olfacere,* to smell.]

ol·fac·to·ry (ōl-făk′tə-rē, -trē, ōl-) ►*adj.* Of or relating to the sense of smell. [Lat. *olfactōrius.*]

ol·i·gar·chy (ōl′ĭ-gär′kē, ō′lĭ-) ►*n., pl.* **-chies 1a.** Government by a few. **b.** Those making up such a government. **2.** A state governed by oligarchy. —**ol′i·garch′** *n.* —**ol′i·gar′chic,** **ol′i·gar′chi·cal** *adj.*

oligo– or **olig–** ►*pref.* Few: *oligarchy.* [< Gk. *oligos.*]

Ol·i·go·cene (ōl′ĭ-gō-sēn′, ō′lĭ-) *Geol.* ►*adj.* Of or being the 3rd epoch of the Tertiary Period, marked by the rise of true carnivores. ►*n.* The Oligocene Epoch.

ol·ive (ōl′ĭv) ►*n.* **1.** A Mediterranean evergreen tree having fragrant white flowers, leathery leaves, and edible fruit. **2.** The small ovoid fruit of the olive, an important food and source of oil. **3.** A dull yellowish green. [< Gk. *elaia.*] —**ol′ive** *adj.*

olive branch ►*n.* A branch of an olive tree regarded as an emblem of peace.

O·liv·i·er (ō-lĭv′ē-ā′), Sir **Laurence Kerr.** Baron Olivier. 1907–89. British actor and director.

ol·la (ōl′ə, ō′yä) ►*n. Regional* A rounded earthenware pot, used esp. for cooking or to hold water. [Sp., ult. < Lat. *aula,* jar.]

Ol·mec (ōl′měk, ōl′-) ►*n., pl.* **-mec** or **-mecs 1.** An early Mesoamerican Indian civilization of SE Mexico that flourished around 1300–400 BC. **2.** A member of a people sharing the Olmec culture.

O·lym·pi·a[1] (ō-lĭm′pē-ə, ə-lĭm′-) A plain of S Greece in the NW Peleponnesus.

O·lym·pi·a[2] (ō-lĭm′pē-ə, ə-lĭm′-) The capital of WA, in the W part of Puget Sound.

O·lym·pi·an (ō-lĭm′pē-ən) ►*adj.* **1.** *Gk. Myth.* Of or relating to the gods and goddesses of Mount Olympus. **2.** Surpassing all others in scope. ►*n.* **1.** *Gk. Myth.* One of the gods or goddesses of Mount Olympus. **2.** A contestant in the ancient or modern Olympic Games. —**O·lym′pic** *adj.*

O·lym·pic Games (ō-lĭm′pĭk) ►*pl.n.* **1.** A group of modern international athletic contests, including separate summer and winter events each held every four years. **2.** An ancient Greek festival of athletic games and contests of choral poetry and dance. —**O·lym′pic** *adj.*

O·lym·pics (ō-lĭm′pĭks) ►*pl.n.* See **Olympic Games** (sense 1).

O·lym·pus (ə-lĭm′pəs, ō-lĭm′-) A range of N Greece near the Aegean coast; rises to 2,919 m (9,577 ft) at **Mount Olympus,** home of the mythical Greek gods.

Om (ōm) ►*n. Hinduism & Buddhism* A sacred Sanskrit syllable uttered as a mantra. [Skt.]

–oma ►*suff.* Tumor: *melanoma.* [< Gk. *-ōma,* n. suff.]

O·ma·ha[1] (ō′mə-hô′, -hä′) ►*n., pl.* **-ha** or **-has 1.** A member of a Native American people inhabiting NE Nebraska. **2.** The Siouan language of the Omaha.

O·ma·ha[2] (ō′mə-hô′, -hä′) A city of E NE on the Missouri R.

O·man (ō-män′) A sultanate of the SE Arabian

Peninsula on the **Gulf of Oman,** an arm of the Arabian Sea. Cap. Muscat. —**O·man′i** *adj. & n.*

O·mar Khay·yám (ō′mär kī-yäm′, -ăm′) 1050?–1123? Persian poet and mathematician.

OMB ►*abbr.* Office of Management and Budget

om·buds·man (ŏm′bŭdz′mən, -bədz-, -bŏŏdz′-) ►*n.* One who investigates complaints, as from consumers, and mediates grievances and disputes. [< ON *umbodhsmadhr,* deputy.] —**om′buds′man·ship′** *n.*

o·me·ga (ō-mĕg′ə, ō-mē′gə, ō-mā′-) ►*n.* **1.** The 24th letter of the Greek alphabet. **2.** The last of a series; the end. [Gk. *ō mega,* large o.]

o·me·ga-3 fatty acid (ō-mĕg′ə-thrē′, -mē′gə-, -mā′-) ►*n.* Any of several polyunsaturated fatty acids found in leafy green vegetables, vegetable oils, and fish.

om·e·let also **om·e·lette** (ŏm′ə-lĭt, ŏm′lĭt) ►*n.* A dish of beaten eggs cooked and folded, often around a filling. [< Lat. *lāmella,* thin metal plate.]

o·men (ō′mən) ►*n.* Something believed to be a sign of future good or evil. [Lat. *ōmen.*]

om·i·cron (ŏm′ĭ-krŏn′, ō′mĭ-) ►*n.* The 15th letter of the Greek alphabet. [Gk. *o mikron,* small o.]

om·i·nous (ŏm′ə-nəs) ►*adj.* **1.** Menacing; threatening. **2.** Of or being an evil omen. [Lat. *ōminōsus.*] —**om′i·nous·ly** *adv.* —**om′i·nous·ness** *n.*

o·mit (ō-mĭt′) ►*v.* **o·mit·ted, o·mit·ting** **1.** To fail to include or mention; leave out. **2.** To neglect to do (something). [< Lat. *omittere.*] —**o·mis′sion** (ō-mĭsh′ən) *n.*

omni– ►*pref.* All: *omnidirectional.* [< Lat. *omnis.*]

om·ni·bus (ŏm′nĭ-bŭs′, -bəs) ►*n.* A bus. ►*adj.* Covering many things or classes: *an omnibus trade bill.* [< Lat., for all.]

om·ni·di·rec·tion·al (ŏm′nē-dĭ-rĕk′shə-nəl, -dī-) ►*adj.* Capable of transmitting or receiving signals in all directions.

om·nip·o·tent (ŏm-nĭp′ə-tənt) ►*adj.* Having unlimited power, authority, or force. —**om·nip′o·tence** *n.*

om·ni·pres·ent (ŏm′nĭ-prĕz′ənt) ►*adj.* Present everywhere. —**om′ni·pres′ence** *n.*

om·nis·cient (ŏm-nĭsh′ənt) ►*adj.* Having total knowledge; knowing everything. [Med.Lat. *omnisciēns* : OMNI– + Lat. *scīre,* know.] —**om·nis′cience** *n.* —**om·nis′cient·ly** *adv.*

om·ni·um-gath·er·um (ŏm′nē-əm-găth′ər-əm) ►*n.* A miscellaneous collection; hodgepodge. [< Lat. *omnium,* of all.]

om·niv·o·rous (ŏm-nĭv′ər-əs) ►*adj.* **1.** Eating food of any kind, including animals and plants. **2.** Taking in everything available: *an omnivorous mind.* —**om′ni·vore′** (ŏm′nə-vôr′) *n.* —**om·niv′o·rous·ly** *adv.*

Omsk (ômsk) A city of S-central Russia on the Irtysh River.

on (ŏn, ôn) ►*prep.* **1.** Used to indicate: **a.** Position above: *a book on the table.* **b.** Contact with: *a fly on the wall.* **c.** Location at or along: *pebbles on the shore.* **d.** Attachment to or suspension from: *beads on a string.* **2.** Used to indicate motion toward or against: *marched on the capital.* **3.** Used to indicate: **a.** Occurrence during: *on July 3rd.* **b.** The particular occasion or circumstance: *On entering the room, she saw him.* **4.** Used to indicate: **a.** The object affected by an action: *The spotlight fell on the actress.* **b.** The agent or agency of a specified action: *cut my foot on the broken glass.* **5.** Used to indicate a source or basis: *live on bread and water.* **6.** Used to indicate: **a.** The state or process of: *on leave; on fire.* **b.** The purpose of: *travel on business.* **c.** A means of conveyance: *ride on a train.* **d.** Availability by means of: *beer on tap.* **7.** Used to indicate belonging: *a nurse on the hospital staff.* **8.** Used to indicate addition or repetition: *heaped error on error.* **9.** Concerning: *a book on dogs.* **10.** *Informal* With: *I haven't a cent on me.* **11.** At the expense of: *drinks on the house.* ►*adv.* **1.** In or into a position of being in contact with something: *Put the coffee on.* **2.** In or into a position of covering something: *Put your clothes on.* **3.** In the direction of something: *He looked on while the ship docked.* **4.** Toward a point lying ahead in space or time: *moved on to the next city.* **5.** Continuously: *talked on and on.* **6.** In or into operation: *turned the radio on.* [< OE.]

Usage: In constructions where *on* is an adverb attached to a verb, it should not be joined with *to* to form the single word *onto*: *move on to* (not *onto*) *new subjects.*

ON ►*abbr.* Ontario

–on[1] ►*suff.* **1.** Subatomic particle: *baryon.* **2.** Unit; quantum: *photon.* [< ION.]

–on[2] ►*suff.* Inert gas: *radon.* [< (ARG)ON.]

once (wŭns) ►*adv.* **1.** One time only: *once a day.* **2.** At one time in the past. **3.** At any time. ►*n.* A single occurrence; one time: *You can go this once.* ►*conj.* As soon as; when. —*idiom:* **at once** **1.** All at one time; simultaneously. **2.** Immediately. [ME *ones* < OE *ān,* one.]

once-o·ver (wŭns′ō′vər) ►*n.* A quick but comprehensive survey or performance.

on·co·gene (ŏn′kə-jēn, ŏng′-) ►*n.* A gene that causes normal cells to become cancerous. [Gk. *onkos,* mass, tumor + GENE.] —**on′co·gen′ic** (-jĕn′ĭk) *adj.* —**on′co·ge·nic′i·ty** (-jə-nĭs′ĭ-tē) *n.*

on·co·gen·e·sis (ŏn′kō-jĕn′ĭ-sĭs, ŏng′-) ►*n.* The formation and development of tumors. [Gk. *onkos,* mass, tumor + –GENESIS.]

on·col·o·gy (ŏn-kŏl′ə-jē, ŏng-) ►*n.* The scientific study of tumors. [Gk. *onkos,* mass, tumor + –LOGY.] —**on′co·log′i·cal** (-kə-lŏj′ĭ-kəl), **on′co·log′ic** *adj.* —**on·col′o·gist** *n.*

on·com·ing (ŏn′kŭm′ĭng, ôn′-) ►*adj.* Approaching.

one (wŭn) ►*adj.* **1.** Being a single entity, unit, object, or living being; not two or more. **2.** United: *They spoke with one voice.* **3.** Being something indefinite, as in time or position: *One day you'll be sorry.* ►*n.* **1.** The cardinal number, represented by the symbol 1, designating the first such unit in a series. **2.** A single person or thing: *This is the one I like best.* ►*pron.* **1.** An indefinitely specified individual: *met one of the crew.* **2.** An unspecified individual; anyone. [< OE *ān.*] —**one′ness** *n.*

Usage: When a construction headed by *one* appears as the subject of a sentence or relative clause, there may be a question whether the verb should be singular or plural, as in *One of every ten rotors was found defective.* The Usage Panel prefers a singular verb in such cases. Constructions using *one or more* or *one or two* take a plural verb: *One or more cars were usually parked in front of his house. One or two students from our department have won prizes.*

O·nei·da (ō-nī′də) ►*n.*, *pl.* **-da** or **-das 1.** A member of a Native American people formerly inhabiting central New York, now in Wisconsin, New York, and Ontario. **2.** The Iroquoian language of the Oneida.

O'Neill (ō-nēl′), **Eugene Gladstone** 1888–1953. Amer. playwright.

on·er·ous (ŏn′ər-əs, ō′nər-) ►*adj.* Troublesome or oppressive; burdensome. [< Lat. *onerōsus.*] **—on′er·ous·ly** *adv.*

one·self (wŭn-sĕlf′) ►*pron.* One's own self. Used: **a.** Reflexively: *One can congratulate oneself on one's victories.* **b.** In an absolute construction: *When in charge oneself, one may do as one pleases.*

one-shot (wŭn′shŏt′) ►*adj. Informal* **1.** Effective after only one attempt. **2.** Being the only one and unlikely to be repeated.

one-sid·ed (wŭn′-sī′dĭd) ►*adj.* **1.** Biased: *a one-sided view.* **2.** Unequal: *a one-sided contest.* **—one′-sid′ed·ness** *n.*

one-time or **one·time** (wŭn′tīm′) ►*adj.* **1.** Occurring only once: *a one-time winner in 1970.* **2.** Former: *his one-time neighbor.*

one-to-one (wŭn′tə-wŭn′) ►*adj.* Allowing the pairing of each member of a class uniquely with a member of another class.

one-track (wŭn′trăk′) ►*adj.* Obsessed with a single idea or purpose.

one-up (wŭn′ŭp′) ►*v.* **-upped, -up·ping** *Informal* To practice one-upmanship on.

one-up·man·ship (wŭn-ŭp′mən-shĭp′) ►*n.* The art of outdoing or showing up a rival.

one-way (wŭn′wā′) ►*adj.* Moving or permitting movement in one direction only: *a one-way street; a one-way ticket.*

on·go·ing (ŏn′gō′ĭng, ôn′-) ►*adj.* Currently taking place.

on·ion (ŭn′yən) ►*n.* **1.** A bulbous plant widely cultivated as a vegetable. **2.** The pungent bulb of this plant. [< Lat. *uniō.*]

on·ion·skin (ŭn′yən-skĭn′) ►*n.* A thin, strong, translucent paper.

on·line (ŏn′līn′, ôn′-) ►*adj.* **1.** *Comp.* **a.** Connected to a central computer or to a computer network. **b.** Accessible via a computer network. **c.** Conducted by means of a computer network: *online dating.* **2.** In production or operation, esp. as part of a supply chain: *new factories going online.*

on·look·er (ŏn′lŏŏk′ər, ôn′-) ►*n.* One who looks on; a bystander or spectator.

on·ly (ŏn′lē) ►*adj.* Alone in kind or class; sole. ►*adv.* **1.** Without anyone or anything else; alone. **2a.** At the very least. **b.** And nothing else or more. **3.** Exclusively; solely. ►*conj.* But; except. [< OE *ānlīc.*] *Usage:* Generally the adverb *only* should adjoin the word or words that it limits. Variation in the placement of *only* can change the meaning of the sentence, as the following examples show: *Dictators respect only force; they are not moved by words. Dictators only respect force; they do not worship it.* See Usage Note at **not.**

on·o·mat·o·poe·ia (ŏn′ə-măt′ə-pē′ə, -mä′tə-) ►*n.* The formation or use of words such as *buzz* or *murmur* that imitate the sounds associated with the objects or actions they refer to. [< Gk. *onomatopoiia.*] **—on′o·mat′o·poe′ic,**

on′o·mat′o·po·et′ic (-pō-ĕt′ĭk) *adj.* **—on′o·mat′o·poe′i·cal·ly, on′o·mat′o·po·et′i·cal·ly** *adv.*

On·on·da·ga (ŏn′ən-dô′gə, -dä′-, -dä′-) ►*n.*, *pl.* **-ga** or **-gas 1.** A member of a Native American people inhabiting W-central New York, now also in SE Ontario. **2.** Their Iroquoian language. **—On′on·da′gan** *adj.*

on·rush (ŏn′rŭsh′, ôn′-) ►*n.* **1.** A forward rush. **2.** An assault. **—on′rush′ing** *adj.*

on·set (ŏn′sĕt′, ôn′-) ►*n.* **1.** The beginning of something. **2.** A military attack.

on·shore (ŏn′shôr′, ôn′-) ►*adj.* **1.** Moving or directed toward the shore. **2.** Located on the shore. **—on′shore′** *adv.*

on·slaught (ŏn′slôt′, ôn′-) ►*n.* A violent attack. [< Du. *aanslag,* a striking at.]

On·tar·i·o (ŏn-târ′ē-ō′) **1.** A province of E-central Canada. Cap. Toronto. **2.** A city of S CA E of Los Angeles.

Ontario, Lake The smallest of the Great Lakes, between SE Ontario, Canada, and NW NY.

on·to (ŏn′tōo′, -tə, ôn′-) ►*prep.* **1.** On top of; upon. See Usage Note at **on. 2.** *Informal* Aware of: *I'm onto your plans.*

onto– or **ont–** ►*pref.* **1.** Existence; being: *ontology.* **2.** Organism: *ontogeny.* [< Gk. *ōn*, *ont-*, pr.part. of *einai,* to be.]

on·tog·e·ny (ŏn-tŏj′ə-nē) ►*n.*, *pl.* **-nies** The origin and development of an individual organism. **—on′to·ge·net′ic** (ŏn′tō-jə-nĕt′ĭk) *adj.* **—on′to·ge·net′i·cal·ly** *adv.*

on·tol·o·gy (ŏn-tŏl′ə-jē) ►*n.* The branch of metaphysics that deals with the nature of being. **—on′to·log′i·cal** (ŏn′tə-lŏj′ĭ-kəl) *adj.* **—on′-to·log′i·cal·ly** *adv.* **—on·tol′o·gist** *n.*

o·nus (ō′nəs) ►*n.* **1.** A burden. **2.** Blame. [Lat.]

on·ward (ŏn′wərd, ôn′-) ►*adv.* also **on·wards** (-wərdz) In a direction or toward a position that is ahead. **—on′ward** *adj.*

–onym ►*suff.* Word; name: *acronym.* [< Gk. *onuma,* name.]

on·yx (ŏn′ĭks) ►*n.* A chalcedony that occurs in bands of different colors. [< Gk. *onux.*]

oo– ►*pref.* Egg; ovum: *oogenesis.* [< Gk. *ōion,* egg.]

o·o·cyte (ō′ə-sīt′) ►*n.* A cell from which an egg or ovum develops by meiosis; a female germ cell.

oo·dles (ōod′lz) ►*pl.n. Informal* A great amount. [?]

o·o·gen·e·sis (ō′ə-jĕn′ĭ-sĭs) ►*n.* The formation, development, and maturation of an ovum. **—o′o·ge·net′ic** (-jə-nĕt′ĭk) *adj.*

o·o·go·ni·um (ō′ə-gō′nē-əm) ►*n.*, *pl.* **-ni·a** (-nē-ə) or **-ni·ums 1.** A cell that differentiates into an oocyte in the ovary. **2.** A female reproductive structure in certain fungi and algae. [oo– + Gk. *gonos,* seed.]

o·o·lite (ō′ə-līt′) ►*n.* A sedimentary rock, usu. limestone, consisting of small round calcareous grains cemented together. [< Gk. *lithos,* stone.] **—o′o·lit′ic** (-lĭt′ĭk) *adj.*

o·ol·o·gy (ō-ŏl′ə-jē) ►*n.* The branch of zoology that deals with eggs, esp. birds' eggs. **—o′o·log′ic** (ō′ə-lŏj′ĭk), **o′o·log′i·cal** *adj.* **—o′o·log′i·cal·ly** *adv.* **—o·ol′o·gist** *n.*

oomph (ŏŏmf) ►*n. Slang* Spirited vigor. [Of expressive orig.]

oops (ōops) ►*interj.* Used to acknowledge a minor accident or mistake.

ooze¹ (ōōz) ►*v.* **oozed, ooz·ing** To flow or leak out slowly. [< OE *wōs*, juice.] —**ooze** *n.* —**ooz′i·ness** *n.* —**ooz′y** *adj.*

ooze² (ōōz) ►*n.* Soft mud or slime, as on the floor of oceans and lakes. [< OE *wāse.*] —**ooz′i·ness** *n.* —**ooz′y** *adj.*

o·pal (ō′pəl) ►*n.* A translucent mineral of hydrated silica, often used as a gem. [< Skt. *upalaḥ.*] —**o′pal·ine′** (ō′pə-līn′, -lēn′) *adj.*

o·pal·es·cent (ō′pə-lĕs′ənt) ►*adj.* Exhibiting a milky iridescence like that of an opal. —**o′pal·esce′** *v.* —**o′pal·es′cence** *n.*

o·paque (ō-pāk′) ►*adj.* **1a.** Impenetrable by light. **b.** Not reflecting light; dull. **2.** Unintelligible. **3.** Obtuse; dense. [< Lat. *opācus,* dark.] —**o·pac′i·ty** (ō-păs′ĭ-tē), **o·paque′ness** *n.* —**o·paque′ly** *adv.*

op art also **Op Art** (ŏp) ►*n.* Abstract art marked by the use of geometric shapes and brilliant colors to create optical illusions.

op. cit. ►*abbr.* Lat. opere citato (in the work cited)

OPEC (ō′pĕk′) ►*abbr.* Organization of Petroleum Exporting Countries

op-ed or **Op-Ed** (ŏp′ĕd′) ►*adj.* Of or being a newspaper page that features signed articles expressing personal viewpoints.

o·pen (ō′pən) ►*adj.* **1.** Affording unobstructed entrance and exit; not shut or closed. **2.** Having no protecting cover. **3.** Not sealed, tied, or folded. **4.** Having gaps, spaces, or intervals. **5.** Accessible to all; unrestricted. **6.** Susceptible; vulnerable. **7.** Ready to transact business. **8.** Not filled, engaged, or in use. **9.** Frank; candid. ►*v.* **1a.** To make no longer closed or fastened. **b.** To remove obstructions from; clear. **2.** To make or force an opening in. **3.** To remove the cover or wrapping from; undo. **4.** To spread out or apart. **5.** To begin or form the start of; initiate. **6.** To make available. **7.** To make or become more responsive or understanding. **8.** To make known to the public. **9.** To come into view. ►*n.* **1.** The outdoors. **2.** A tournament or contest for both professional and amateur players. —*phrasal verb:* **open up** *Informal* To speak freely and candidly. [< OE.] —**o′pen·er** *n.* —**o′pen·ly** *adv.* —**o′pen·ness** *n.*

o·pen-air (ō′pən-âr′) ►*adj.* Outdoor: *an open-air concert.*

o·pen-and-shut (ō′pən-ən-shŭt′) ►*adj.* Easily settled or determined.

o·pen-end (ō′pən-ĕnd′) ►*adj.* Unlimited.

o·pen-end·ed (ō′pən-ĕn′dĭd) ►*adj.* **1.** Not limited; open-end. **2.** Allowing for change. **3.** Inconclusive or indefinite. **4.** Allowing for an unstructured response: *an open-ended question.*

o·pen-eyed (ō′pən-īd′) ►*adj.* **1.** Having the eyes wide open. **2.** Watchful and alert.

o·pen·hand·ed (ō′pən-hăn′dĭd) ►*adj.* Giving freely; generous. See Synonyms at **liberal.** —**o′pen·hand′ed·ly** *adv.* —**o′pen·hand′ed·ness** *n.*

o·pen-hearth (ō′pən-härth′) ►*adj.* Of a furnace with a heat-reflecting roof used in the production of high-quality steel.

open house ►*n.* **1.** A social event with a general invitation to all. **2.** An occasion when an institution is open for visiting by the public. **3.** An occasion when a residence for sale or rent is held open for public viewing.

o·pen·ing (ō′pə-nĭng) ►*n.* **1.** The act of becom-

ing open or being made to open. **2.** A gap, breach, or aperture. **3a.** The first part or stage. **b.** The first performance. **c.** A series of beginning moves, esp. in chess. **4a.** An opportunity. **b.** An unfilled job or position.

o·pen-mind·ed (ō′pən-mīn′dĭd) ►*adj.* Receptive to new ideas or to reason. See Synonyms at **broad-minded.** —**o′pen-mind′ed·ly** *adv.* —**o′pen-mind′ed·ness** *n.*

open shop ►*n.* A business that does not discriminate against employees based on membership or nonmembership in a union.

o·pen·work (ō′pən-wûrk′) ►*n.* Ornamental or structural work having many openings, usu. in set patterns.

op·er·a¹ (ŏp′ər-ə, ŏp′rə) ►*n.* **1.** A theatrical presentation in which a dramatic performance is set to music. **2.** A theater designed primarily for operas. [< Lat., work.] —**op′er·at′ic** (ŏp′ə-răt′ĭk) *adj.* —**op′er·at′i·cal·ly** *adv.*

o·pe·ra² (ō′pər-ə, ŏp′ər-ə) ►*n.* Pl. of **opus.**

op·er·a·ble (ŏp′ər-ə-bəl, ŏp′rə-) ►*adj.* **1.** Capable of or suitable for use. **2.** Treatable by surgery. [< OPERATE.] —**op′er·a·bil′i·ty** *n.* —**op′er·a·bly** *adv.*

op·er·a glasses (ŏp′ər-ə, ŏp′rə) ►*pl.n.* Small binoculars for use esp. at the theater.

op·er·and (ŏp′ər-ənd) ►*n.* *Math.* A quantity on which an operation is performed. [< Lat. *operandum.*]

op·er·ate (ŏp′ə-rāt′) ►*v.* **-at·ed, -at·ing 1.** To perform a function; work. **2.** To perform surgery. **3.** To exert an influence. **4.** To control the functioning of. **5.** To conduct the affairs of. **6.** To supply with power: *a car that is operated by electricity.* [Lat. *operāre, operāt-,* to work.]

op·er·at·ing system (ŏp′ə-rā′tĭng) ►*n.* Software designed to control the hardware of a specific computer system in order to allow users and application programs to make use of it.

op·er·a·tion (ŏp′ə-rā′shən) ►*n.* **1.** The act or process of operating. **2.** The state of being operative. **3.** *Med.* A surgical procedure for remedying an injury or ailment. **4.** *Math.* A process, such as addition, performed in accordance with specific rules. **5.** *Comp.* An action resulting from a single instruction. **6.** A military action or campaign. —**op′er·a′tion·al** *adj.* —**op′er·a′tion·al·ly** *adv.*

op·er·a·tive (ŏp′ər-ə-tĭv, -ə-rā′tĭv, ŏp′rə-) ►*adj.* **1.** Being in effect; having force. **2.** Functioning effectively. **3.** Of or relating to a surgical operation. ►*n.* **1.** A skilled worker, esp. in industry. **2a.** A spy. **b.** A private detective. **3.** One who works for a political organization. —**op′er·a·tive·ly** *adv.*

op·er·a·tor (ŏp′ə-rā′tər) ►*n.* **1.** One who operates a machine or system. **2.** The owner or manager of a business. **3.** *Informal* A person adept at accomplishing goals shrewdly or unscrupulously. **4.** *Math.* A symbol that represents an operation.

op·er·et·ta (ŏp′ə-rĕt′ə) ►*n.* A theatrical production that has elements of opera but is lighter and more popular in subject and style. [Ital.]

oph·thal·mic (ŏf-thăl′mĭk, ŏp-) ►*adj.* Relating to the eye; ocular.

ophthalmo– or **ophthalm–** ►*pref.* Eye: *opthalmology.* [< Gk. *ophthalmos,* eye.]

oph·thal·mol·o·gy (ŏf′thəl-mŏl′ə-jē, -thăl-, ŏp′-) ►*n.* The study of diseases and disorders of the eye. **—oph·thal′mo·log′i·cal** (-thăl′-mə-lŏj′ĭ-kəl) *adj.* **—oph′thal·mol′o·gist** *n.*

o·pi·ate (ō′pē-ĭt, -āt′) ►*n.* **1.** A narcotic containing opium or one of its derivatives. **2.** A narcotic. **3.** Something that dulls the senses and induces relaxation. ►*adj.* **1.** Containing opium or an opium derivative. **2.** Inducing sleep or sedation. [< Lat. *opium,* OPIUM.]

o·pine (ō-pīn′) ►*v.* **o·pined, o·pin·ing** To hold or state as an opinion. [< Lat. *opīnārī,* suppose.]

o·pin·ion (ə-pĭn′yən) ►*n.* **1.** A belief or conclusion held with confidence but not substantiated by proof. **2.** A judgment based on special knowledge. **3.** A judgment or estimation. [< Lat. *opīniō.*]

o·pin·ion·at·ed (ə-pĭn′yə-nā′tĭd) ►*adj.* Holding stubbornly to one's opinions.

o·pi·um (ō′pē-əm) ►*n.* A bitter, yellowish-brown, addictive narcotic drug prepared from the pods of an Old World poppy. [< Gk. *opion.*]

o·pos·sum (ə-pŏs′əm, pŏs′əm) ►*n., pl.* **-sum** or **-sums** Any of various nocturnal, usu. arboreal marsupials of the Western Hemisphere. [Of Virginia Algonquian orig.]

Op·pen·hei·mer (ŏp′ən-hī′mər), **J(ulius) Robert** 1904–67. Amer. physicist.

op·po·nent (ə-pō′nənt) ►*n.* **1.** One that opposes another or others. See Synonyms at **enemy. 2.** One who is hostile to an idea or cause. [< Lat. *oppōnere,* OPPOSE.] **—op·po′nent** *adj.*

op·por·tune (ŏp′ər-tōon′, -tyōon′) ►*adj.* Occurring at a fitting or advantageous time. [< Lat. *opportūnus.*] **—op′por·tune′ly** *adv.*

op·por·tun·ist (ŏp′ər-tōo′nĭst, -tyōo′-) ►*n.* One who takes advantage of any opportunity to achieve an end, often with no regard for principles or consequences. **—op′por·tun′ism** *n.* **—op′por·tun·is′tic** *adj.*

op·por·tu·ni·ty (ŏp′ər-tōo′nĭ-tē, -tyōo′-) ►*n., pl.* **-ties 1.** A favorable or advantageous circumstance or combination of circumstances. **2.** A chance for progress or advancement.

op·pose (ə-pōz′) ►*v.* **-posed, -pos·ing 1.** To be in contention or conflict with. **2.** To be resistant to. **3.** To place opposite, esp. in contrast or counterbalance. [< Lat. *oppōnere, oppōs-,* set against.] **—op·pos′a·bil′i·ty** *n.* **—op·pos′a·ble** *adj.* **—op′po·si′tion** (ŏp′ə-zĭsh′ən) *n.* **—op′po·si′tion·al** *adj.* **—op·pos′er** *n.*

op·po·site (ŏp′ə-zĭt) ►*adj.* **1.** Placed or located directly across from. **2.** Facing or moving away from each other. **3.** Sharply contrasting: *opposite views.* ►*n.* One that is opposite to another. ►*adv.* In an opposite position. ►*prep.* Across from or facing. [< Lat. *oppositus,* p.part. of *oppōnere,* OPPOSE.] **—op′po·site·ly** *adv.*

op·press (ə-prĕs′) ►*v.* **1.** To keep down by unjust use of force or authority. **2.** To cause to feel worried or depressed. [< Lat. *opprimere, oppress-,* press against.] **—op·pres′sion** *n.* **—op·pres′sor** *n.*

op·pres·sive (ə-prĕs′ĭv) ►*adj.* **1.** Tyrannical. **2.** Difficult to cope with. **3.** Hot and humid; sweltering. **—op·pres′sive·ly** *adv.* **—op·pres′-sive·ness** *n.*

op·pro·bri·ous (ə-prō′brē-əs) ►*adj.* **1.** Expressing contemptuous reproach. **2.** Shameful or infamous. **—op·pro′bri·ous·ly** *adv.*

op·pro·bri·um (ə-prō′brē-əm) ►*n.* **1.** Disgrace arising from shameful conduct. **2.** Scorn; contempt. [Lat. < *opprobrāre,* reproach : *ob-,* intensive pref. + *probrum,* a reproach.]

–opsy ►*suff.* Examination: *biopsy.* [< Gk. *opsis,* sight.]

opt (ŏpt) ►*v.* To choose. **—*phrasal verb:* opt out** To choose not to participate in something. [< Lat. *optāre.*]

op·tic (ŏp′tĭk) ►*adj.* Of or relating to the eye or vision. [< Gk. *optikos.*]

op·ti·cal (ŏp′tĭ-kəl) ►*adj.* **1.** Of or relating to sight. **2.** Designed to assist sight. **3.** Of or relating to optics. **—op′ti·cal·ly** *adv.*

optical art ►*n.* Op art.

optical disc or **optical disk** ►*n. Comp.* A plastic-coated disk that stores digital data as microscopic regions of varying reflectivity and is read by scanning the surface with a laser; laser disc.

optical illusion ►*n.* A deceptive visual image.

op·ti·cian (ŏp-tĭsh′ən) ►*n.* One that makes or sells lenses, eyeglasses, and other optical instruments.

op·tics (ŏp′tĭks) ►*n. (takes sing. v.)* The scientific study of light and vision.

op·ti·mal (ŏp′tə-məl) ►*adj.* Most favorable or desirable. **—op′ti·mal·ly** *adv.*

op·ti·mism (ŏp′tə-mĭz′əm) ►*n.* **1.** A tendency to expect the best possible outcome or dwell on the most hopeful aspects of a situation. **2.** *Philos.* The doctrine that this world is the best of all possible worlds. [< Lat. *optimus,* best.] **—op′ti·mist** *n.* **—op′ti·mis′tic** *adj.* **—op′ti·mis′ti·cal·ly** *adv.*

op·ti·mize (ŏp′tə-mīz′) ►*v.* **-mized, -miz·ing 1.** To make as perfect or effective as possible. **2.** To make the most of. **—op′ti·mi·za′tion** *n.*

op·ti·mum (ŏp′tə-məm) ►*n., pl.* **-ma** (-mə) or **-mums** The point at which the condition, degree, or amount of something is the most favorable. [Lat., best.] **—op′ti·mum** *adj.*

op·tion (ŏp′shən) ►*n.* **1.** The act of choosing; choice. **2.** The power or freedom to choose. **3.** The right to buy or sell an asset within a specified time at a set price. **4.** Something available as a choice. [Lat. *optiō.*] **—op′tion·al** *adj.* **—op′tion·al·ly** *adv.*

op·tom·e·try (ŏp-tŏm′ĭ-trē) ►*n.* The profession of examining eyes and prescribing corrective lenses or other treatments for visual defects. [Gk. *optos,* visible + –METRY.] **—op′to·met′ric** (ŏp′tə-mĕt′rĭk) *adj.* **—op·tom′e·trist** *n.*

op·u·lent (ŏp′yə-lənt) ►*adj.* **1.** Possessing great wealth. **2.** Lavish. [Lat. *opulentus.*] **—op′u·lence** *n.* **—op′u·lent·ly** *adv.*

o·pus (ō′pəs) ►*n., pl.* **o·pe·ra** (ō′pər-ə, ŏp′ər-ə) or **o·pus·es** A creative work, esp. a musical composition. [Lat.]

or (ôr; ər *when unstressed*) ►*conj.* Used to indicate: **a.** An alternative. **b.** The second of two alternatives: *either right or wrong.* **c.** A synonymous or equivalent expression: *acrophobia, or fear of heights.* **d.** Indefiniteness: *two or three.* [< OE *oththe.*]

Usage: When all the elements in a series connected by *or* are singular, the verb they govern is singular: *Tom or Jack is coming.* When all the elements are plural, the verb is plural. When the elements do not agree in number, some usage commentators have suggested that the verb be governed by the element to which it is nearer: *Tom or his sisters are coming.* Other commentators, however, have argued that these sentences must be revised to avoid the problem: *Either Tom is coming or his sisters are.* See Usage Notes at **neither, nor.**

OR ►*abbr.* **1.** operating room **2.** Oregon

–or¹ ►*suff.* One that performs a specified action: *detector.* [< Lat.]

–or² ►*suff.* State; activity: *behavior.* [< Lat.]

or·a·cle (ôr′ə-kəl, ŏr′-) ►*n.* **1a.** A shrine consecrated to a prophetic deity. **b.** A priest or priestess at such a shrine. **c.** A prophecy made known at such a shrine. **2.** A wise person. [< Lat. *ōrāculum.*] —**o·rac′u·lar** (ô-răk′yə-lər, ō-) *adj.*

o·ral (ôr′əl) ►*adj.* **1.** Spoken rather than written. **2.** Of the mouth: *oral surgery.* **3.** Used in or taken through the mouth. **4.** Relating to the first stage of psychosexual development in psychoanalytic theory. [< Lat. *ōs, ōr-,* mouth.] —**o′ral·ly** *adv.*

O·ran (ō-rän′, ô-rän′) A city of NW Algeria on the **Gulf of Oran,** an inlet of the Mediterranean Sea.

or·ange (ôr′ĭnj, ŏr′-) ►*n.* **1a.** Any of several citrus trees having white flowers and round, reddish-yellow fruit. **b.** The sectioned pulpy fruit of an orange, having a sweetish acidic juice. **2.** The hue of the visible spectrum lying between red and yellow. [< Skt. *nāraṅgaḥ.*] —**or′ange** *adj.*

or·ange·ade (ôr′ĭn-jād′, ŏr′-) ►*n.* A beverage of orange juice, sugar, and water.

o·rang·u·tan (ô-răng′ə-tăn′, ə-răng′-) also **o·rang·ou·tang** (-ə-tăng′) ►*n.* An arboreal anthropoid ape having a shaggy reddish-brown coat and very long arms. [Malay *ōrang hūtan.*]

O·ran·je·stad (ō-rän′yə-stät′) The capital of Aruba, on the W coast.

o·rate (ô-rāt′, ôr′āt′) ►*v.* **o·rat·ed, o·rat·ing** To speak in a formal, often pompous manner. [Lat. *ōrāre.*]

o·ra·tion (ô-rā′shən) ►*n.* A formal speech. [< Lat. *ōrāre,* speak.]

or·a·tor (ôr′ə-tər, ŏr′-) ►*n.* **1.** One who delivers an oration. **2.** An eloquent and skilled public speaker. —**or′a·tor′i·cal** (-tôr′ĭ-kəl) —**or′a·tor′i·cal·ly** *adv.*

or·a·to·ri·o (ôr′ə-tôr′ē-ō′, ŏr′-) ►*n., pl.* **-os** *Mus.* A composition for voices and orchestra, usu. on a religious theme, without costumes, scenery, or dramatic action. [After the *Oratorio,* the Oratory of Saint Philip Neri at Rome.]

or·a·to·ry¹ (ôr′ə-tôr′ē, ŏr′-) ►*n.* **1.** The art of public speaking. **2.** Eloquence or skill in making public speeches.

or·a·to·ry² (ôr′ə-tôr′ē, ŏr′-) ►*n., pl.* **-ries** A small private chapel. [< Lat. *ōrāre,* pray.]

orb (ôrb) ►*n.* **1.** A sphere. **2.** A celestial body. **3.** An eye or eyeball. [< Lat. *orbis.*] —**or·bic′u·lar** (ôr-bĭk′yə-lər) *adj.*

or·bit (ôr′bĭt) ►*n.* **1.** The path of a celestial body or artificial satellite as it revolves around another body due to their mutual gravitational attraction. **2.** The path of a body in a field of force surrounding another body. **3.** A range of activity or influence. See Synonyms at **range. 4.** An eye socket. ►*v.* **1.** To revolve around (a body or center of attraction). **2.** To put into an orbit. [< Lat. *orbita.*] —**or′bit·er** *n.*

or·bi·tal (ôr′bĭ-tl) ►*adj.* Of or relating to an orbit. ►*n.* The wave function of an electron in an atom or molecule, indicating the electron's probable location.

or·ca (ôr′kə) ►*n.* A black-and-white toothed whale that feeds esp. on large fish and squid. [< Lat. *orca,* whale.]

orca

or·chard (ôr′chərd) ►*n.* **1.** An area of land devoted to the cultivation of fruit or nut trees. **2.** The trees cultivated in an orchard. [< OE *ortgeard.*]

or·ches·tra (ôr′kĭ-strə, -kĕs′trə) ►*n.* **1.** A group of musicians who play together on various instruments. **2a.** The front section of seats nearest the stage in a theater. **b.** The entire main floor of a theater. [< Gk. *orkhēstra,* space in front of a stage.] —**or·ches′tral** (-kĕs′trəl) *adj.* —**or·ches′tral·ly** *adv.*

or·ches·trate (ôr′kĭ-strāt′) ►*v.* **-trat·ed, -trat·ing 1.** To compose or arrange (music) for an orchestra. **2.** To arrange or organize; direct. —**or′ches·tra′tion** *n.* —**or′ches·tra′tor** *n.*

or·chid (ôr′kĭd) ►*n.* **1a.** Any of a large family of chiefly tropical plants with showy flowers having an enlarged central petal. **b.** The flower itself. **2.** A light reddish purple. [< Gk. *orkhis.*] —**or′chid** *adj.*

or·dain (ôr-dān′) ►*v.* **1.** To install as a minister, priest, or rabbi. **2.** To order or decree by virtue of superior authority. **3.** To predestine. [< Lat. *ōrdināre,* organize.] —**or·dain′er** *n.* —**or·dain′ment** *n.*

or·deal (ôr-dēl′) ►*n.* A difficult or painful experience. See Synonyms at **trial.** [< OE *ordāl.*]

or·der (ôr′dər) ►*n.* **1.** A condition of logical or comprehensible arrangement among the separate elements of a group. **2.** The condition or state of something: *a machine in good working order.* **3a.** The established system of social organization. **b.** A condition in which freedom from disorder is maintained through established authority. **4.** A sequence or arrangement of successive things. **5.** The prescribed form or customary procedure. **6.** A command or direction. **7.** A commission or instruction to buy, sell, or supply something. **8.** A request made by a customer at a restaurant for food. **9.** *Eccles.* **a.** Any of several grades of the Christian ministry. **b.** often **orders** Ordination. **10.** A group of persons living under a religious rule. **11.** A group of people upon whom a government or sovereign has formally conferred honor: *the Order of the Garter.* **12.** Degree of quality or importance; rank. **13.** *Archit.* Any of several classical styles marked by the type of column employed. **14.** *Biol.* A taxonomic category of organisms ranking above a family and below a class. ►*v.* **1.** To issue a command or instruction.

2. To request to be supplied with. **3.** To put into a systematic arrangement. See Synonyms at **arrange.** —*idioms:* **in order to** For the purpose of. **on the order of** Similar to; like. **to order** According to the buyer's specifications. [< Lat. *ōrdō.*] —**or′der·er** *n.*

or·der·ly (ôr′dər-lē) ►*adj.* **1.** Having a systematic arrangement; neat. **2.** Devoid of disruption; peaceful. ►*n., pl.* **-lies 1.** An attendant in a hospital. **2.** A soldier assigned to attend a superior officer. —**or′der·li·ness** *n.*

or·di·nal (ôr′dn-əl) ►*adj.* Being of a specified position in a numbered series. [< Lat. *ōrdō, ōrdin-,* order.]

ordinal number ►*n.* A number, such as *second* or *tenth,* indicating position in a series.

or·di·nance (ôr′dn-əns) ►*n.* **1.** An authoritative command or order. **2.** A municipal statute or regulation. [< Lat. *ōrdināre,* ordain.]

or·di·nar·i·ly (ôr′dn-âr′ə-lē, ôr′dn-ĕr′-) ►*adv.* As a general rule; usually.

or·di·nar·y (ôr′dn-ĕr′ē) ►*adj.* **1.** Commonly encountered; usual. **2.** Of no exceptional ability, degree, or quality; average. [< Lat. *ōrdinārius.*] —**or′di·nar′i·ness** *n.*

or·di·nate (ôr′dn-ĭt, -āt′) ►*n. Symbol* **y** *Math.* The plane Cartesian coordinate representing the distance from a specified point to the *x*-axis, measured parallel to the *y*-axis. [< Lat. *ōrdinātus,* ordered.]

or·di·na·tion (ôr′dn-ā′shən) ►*n.* The act or ceremony of ordaining, as to the ministry.

ord·nance (ôrd′nəns) ►*n.* **1.** Military materiel, such as weapons and ammunition. **2.** Cannon; artillery. [< Lat. *ordināre,* put in order.]

Or·do·vi·cian (ôr′də-vĭsh′ən) *Geol.* ►*adj.* Of or being the 2nd period of the Paleozoic Era, marked by the appearance of primitive fishes. ►*n.* The Ordovician Period. [< Lat. *Ordovicēs,* an ancient Welsh tribe.]

or·dure (ôr′jər) ►*n.* Excrement; dung. [< Lat. *horridus,* frightful.]

ore (ôr) ►*n.* A mineral or rock from which a valuable constituent, esp. a metal, can be mined or extracted. [< OE *ōra.*]

o·re·ad (ôr′ē-ăd′) ►*n. Gk. Myth.* A mountain nymph. [< Gk. *Oreias.*]

o·reg·a·no (ə-rĕg′ə-nō′, ô-rĕg′-) ►*n.* An herb having aromatic leaves used as a seasoning. [< Gk. *origanon.*]

Or·e·gon (ôr′ĭ-gən, -gŏn′, ŏr′-) A state of the NW US on the Pacific. Cap. Salem. —**Or′e·go′ni·an** (-gō′nē-ən) *adj. & n.*

or·gan (ôr′gən) ►*n.* **1.** A musical instrument consisting of a set of pipes that sound tones when supplied with air and a keyboard that controls the flow of air to the pipes; pipe organ. **2.** An instrument resembling or suggestive of a pipe organ. **3.** *Biol.* A differentiated part of an organism that performs a specific function. **4.** An instrument or agency performing specified functions: *a government organ.* **5.** A periodical. [< Gk. *organon,* instrument.]

or·gan·dy (ôr′gən-dē) ►*n., pl.* **-dies** A sheer, stiff cotton fabric, used for curtains and light apparel. [Fr. *organdi.*]

or·gan·elle (ôr′gə-nĕl′) ►*n.* A structure within a cell, such as a vacuole, that performs a specific function. [NLat. *organella,* small organ.]

or·gan·ic (ôr-găn′ĭk) ►*adj.* **1.** Of or affecting an organ of the body. **2.** Of or derived from living organisms. **3.** Cultivated or raised without the use of synthetic chemicals, such as pesticides, or drugs, such as hormones. **4.** Resembling a living organism in organization or development: *an organic whole.* **5.** Constituting an integral part of a whole; fundamental. **6.** *Chem.* Of or designating carbon compounds. —**or·gan′i·cal·ly** *adv.* —**or′gan·ic′i·ty** (ôr′gə-nĭs′ĭ-tē) *n.*

or·gan·ism (ôr′gə-nĭz′əm) ►*n.* **1.** A living being. **2.** A system similar to a living body: *the social organism.*

or·gan·ist (ôr′gə-nĭst) ►*n.* One who plays the organ.

or·gan·i·za·tion (ôr′gə-nĭ-zā′shən) ►*n.* **1a.** The act of organizing or process of being organized. **b.** A manner of accomplishing something in an efficient way. **2.** A group of persons organized for a particular purpose; association. —**or′gan·i·za′tion·al** *adj.*

or·gan·ize (ôr′gə-nīz′) ►*v.* **-ized, -iz·ing 1.** To put together into an orderly, functional, structured whole. **2.** To arrange in a coherent form; systematize. **3.** To arrange systematically for united action. See Synonyms at **arrange. 4.** To establish as an organization. See Synonyms at **establish. 5.** To persuade to form or join a labor union. [< Lat. *organum,* instrument; see ORGAN.] —**or′gan·iz′er** *n.*

or·gan·za (ôr-găn′zə) ►*n.* A sheer stiff fabric of silk or synthetic material. [Prob. < *Organzi* (Urgench), Uzbekistan.]

or·gasm (ôr′găz′əm) ►*n.* The highest point of sexual excitement; climax. [< Gk. *orgasmos.*] —**or·gas′mic, or·gas′tic** *adj.*

or·gy (ôr′jē) ►*n., pl.* **-gies 1.** A social gathering involving unrestrained indulgence, esp. sexual activity. **2.** Uncontrolled indulgence in an activity. [< Gk. *orgia.*] —**or′gi·ast** *n.* —**or′gi·as′tic** *adj.* —**or′gi·as′ti·cal·ly** *adv.*

o·ri·el (ôr′ē-əl) ►*n.* A projecting bay window supported by a bracket. [< Med.Lat. *oriolum,* porch.]

o·ri·ent (ôr′ē-ənt, -ĕnt′) ►*n.* **Orient** The countries of Asia, esp. E Asia. ►*v.* (ôr′ē-ĕnt′) **1.** To align or position in a particular relation to the points of the compass. **2.** To make familiar with a new situation. [< Lat. *oriēns,* pr.part. of *orīrī,* rise.] —**o′ri·en·tate′** *v.*

O·ri·en·tal also **o·ri·en·tal** (ôr′ē-ĕn′tl) ►*adj.* Of or designating the Orient. ►*n. Often Offensive* An Asian person.

o·ri·en·ta·tion (ôr′ē-ĕn-tā′shən) ►*n.* **1.** The act of orienting or the state of being oriented. **2.** Location or position relative to the points of the compass. **3.** A tendency of thought; a general inclination: *a Marxist orientation.* **4.** Sexual orientation. **5.** Introductory instruction concerning a new situation: *orientation for incoming students.*

or·i·fice (ôr′ə-fĭs, ŏr′-) ►*n.* An opening, esp. to a cavity or passage of the body. [< LLat. *ōrificium.*] —**or′i·fi′cial** (-fĭsh′əl) *adj.*

orig. ►*abbr.* originally

o·ri·ga·mi (ôr′ĭ-gä′mē) ►*n.* The Japanese art of folding paper. [J.]

or·i·gin (ôr′ə-jĭn, ŏr′-) ►*n.* **1.** The point at which something comes into existence. **2.** Ancestry. **3.** The fact of originating. **4.** *Math.* The point of intersection of coordinate axes. [< Lat. *orīgō* < *orīrī,* arise.]

o·rig·i·nal (ə-rĭj′ə-nəl) ▸*adj.* **1.** Preceding all others; first. **2.** Fresh and unusual; new. **3.** Inventive. ▸*n.* **1.** A first form from which other forms are made or developed. **2.** An authentic work of art. —**o·rig′i·nal′i·ty** (-năl′ĭ-tē) *n.* —**o·rig′i·nal·ly** *adv.*

o·rig·i·nate (ə-rĭj′ə-nāt′) ▸*v.* **-nat·ed, -nat·ing** To come or bring into being. See Synonyms at **stem¹.** —**o·rig′i·na′tion** *n.* —**o·rig′i·na′tor** *n.*

O·ri·no·co (ôr′ə-nō′kō) A river rising in SE Venezuela and flowing more than 2,415 km (1,500 mi) to the Atlantic.

o·ri·ole (ôr′ē-ōl′) ▸*n.* A songbird with black and bright yellow or green plumage in the male. [< Lat. *aureolus,* golden.]

O·ri·on (ō-rī′ən, ə-rī′-) ▸*n.* A constellation in the celestial equator near Gemini and Taurus.

or·i·son (ôr′ĭ-sən, -zən, ŏr′-) ▸*n.* A prayer. [< LLat. *ōrātiō,* a speech.]

Ork·ney Islands (ôrk′nē) An archipelago in the Atlantic Ocean and the North Sea off the NE coast of Scotland.

Or·lan·do (ôr-lăn′dō) A city of central FL ENE of Tampa.

Or·lé·ans (ôr-lā-äN′) A city of N-central France on the Loire R. SSW of Paris.

Or·lon (ôr′lŏn′) A trademark for an acrylic fiber.

Or·mazd (ôr′məzd) ▸*n.* Var. of **Ohrmazd.**

or·mo·lu (ôr′mə-lōō′) ▸*n.* An alloy resembling gold, used to ornament furniture. [Fr. *or moulu,* ground gold.]

Or·muz (ôr′mŭz′, ôr-mōōz′), **Strait of** See Strait of **Hormuz.**

or·na·ment (ôr′nə-mənt) ▸*n.* Something that decorates or adorns; embellishment. ▸*v.* (-měnt′) To decorate. [< Lat. *ōrnāre,* adorn.] —**or′na·men′tal** *adj.* —**or′na·men′tal·ly** *adv.* —**or′na·men·ta′tion** *n.*

or·nate (ôr-nāt′) ▸*adj.* Elaborately, often excessively ornamented. [< Lat. *ōrnātus,* adorned.] —**or·nate′ly** *adv.* —**or·nate′ness** *n.*

or·ner·y (ôr′nə-rē) ▸*adj.* **-i·er, -i·est** Mean and stubborn. [< ORDINARY.] —**or′ner·i·ness′** *n.*

or·ni·thol·o·gy (ôr′nə-thŏl′ə-jē) ▸*n.* The branch of zoology that deals with birds. [< Gk. *ornis, ornith-,* bird.] —**or′ni·tho·log′i·cal** (-thə-lŏj′ĭ-kəl) *adj.* —**or′ni·thol′o·gist** *n.*

o·rog·e·ny (ô-rŏj′ə-nē) ▸*n.* The process of mountain formation, esp. by a folding of the earth's crust. [Gk. *oros,* mountain + –GENY.]

o·ro·tund (ôr′ə-tŭnd′) ▸*adj.* **1.** Pompous and bombastic. **2.** Sonorous. [< Lat. *ōre rotundō,* with a round mouth.]

or·phan (ôr′fən) ▸*n.* **1.** A child whose parents are dead. **2.** A child who has been deprived of parental care and has not been adopted. [< Gk. *orphanos,* orphaned.] —**or′phan** *v.* —**or′phan·hood′** *n.*

or·phan·age (ôr′fə-nĭj) ▸*n.* An institution for the care of orphans.

Or·phe·us (ôr′fē-əs, -fyōōs′) ▸*n.* Gk. Myth. A poet and musician who almost succeeded in rescuing his wife Eurydice from Hades. —**Or′phic** *adj.*

Orr (ôr), **Robert Gordon** "Bobby." b. 1948. Canadian-born hockey player.

Or·te·ga y Gas·set (ôr-tā′gə ē gä-sĕt′), **José** 1883–1955. Spanish philosopher.

ortho– or **orth–** ▸*pref.* **1.** Straight; correct:

orthodontics. **2.** Perpendicular: orthogonal. [< Gk. *orthos,* straight.]

or·tho·don·tia (ôr′thə-dŏn′shə) or **or·tho·don·ture** (-dŏn′chər) ▸*n.* Orthodontics.

or·tho·don·tics (ôr′thə-dŏn′tĭks) ▸*n. (takes sing. v.)* The dental specialty dealing with correction of irregularities of the teeth. —**or′tho·don′tic** *adj.* —**or′tho·don′tist** *n.*

or·tho·dox (ôr′thə-dŏks′) ▸*adj.* **1.** Adhering to a traditional and established doctrine, esp. in religion. **2. Orthodox** Of or relating to the Eastern Orthodox Church. **3.** Commonly accepted; customary. [< LGk. *orthodoxos.*] —**or′tho·dox′ly** *adv.* —**or′tho·dox′y** *n.*

or·thog·o·nal (ôr-thŏg′ə-nəl) ▸*adj. Math.* Relating to or composed of right angles. —**or·thog′o·nal·ly** *adv.*

or·thog·ra·phy (ôr-thŏg′rə-fē) ▸*n., pl.* **-phies** The study of correct spelling according to established usage. —**or′tho·graph′ic** (ôr′thə-grăf′ĭk) *adj.* —**or′tho·graph′i·cal·ly** *adv.*

or·tho·pe·dics (ôr′thə-pē′dĭks) ▸*n. (takes sing. v.)* The branch of medicine that deals with injuries or disorders of the skeletal system. [< ORTHO– + Gk. *pais, paid-,* child.] —**or′tho·pe′dic** *adj.* —**or′tho·pe′di·cal·ly** *adv.* —**or′tho·pe′dist** *n.*

or·thot·ic (ôr-thŏt′ĭk) ▸*n.* An orthopedic appliance designed to straighten or support a body part. ▸*adj.* Of or relating to orthotics. [< Gk. *orthōsis, orthōt-,* straightening.]

or·thot·ics (ôr-thŏt′ĭks) ▸*n. (takes sing. v.)* The science that deals with the use of mechanical devices to support or supplement impaired joints or limbs. —**or·thot′ist** *n.*

ORV ▸*abbr.* off-road vehicle

Or·well (ôr′wĕl′, -wəl), **George** Eric Arthur Blair. 1903–50. British writer.

–ory ▸*suff.* **1.** Of, relating to, or characterized by: advisory. **2.** A place or thing used for or connected with: crematory. [< Lat. *-ōrius,* adj. suff., and *-ōrium,* n. suff.]

o·ryx (ôr′ĭks, ŏr′-) ▸*n., pl.* **oryx** or **-es** An antelope of Africa or Arabia having slightly curved horns. [< Gk. *orux,* pickax, gazelle.]

OS ▸*abbr.* **1.** operating system **2.** ordinary seaman

O·sage (ō′sāj′, ō-sāj′) ▸*n., pl.* **O·sage** or **O·sag·es** **1.** A member of a Native American people formerly inhabiting W Missouri, now in N-central Oklahoma. **2.** The Siouan language of the Osage. —**O′sage′** *adj.*

O·sa·ka (ō-sä′kə) A city of S Honshu, Japan, on **Osaka Bay,** an inlet of the Pacific.

Osceola
1838 portrait

Os·ce·o·la (ŏs′ē-ō′lə, ō′sē-) 1804?–38. Seminole leader.

os·cil·late (ŏs′ə-lāt′) ►v. **-lat·ed, -lat·ing 1.** To swing back and forth steadily. **2.** To waver; vacillate. **3.** *Phys.* To vary between alternate extremes, usu. within a definable period of time. [< Lat. *ōscillum*, a swing.] —**os′cil·la′-tion** n. —**os′cil·la′tor** n.

os·cil·lo·scope (ə-sĭl′ə-skōp′) ►n. An electronic instrument that produces an instantaneous trace on the screen of a cathode-ray tube corresponding to oscillations of voltage and current. [OSCILL(ATION) + –SCOPE.] —**os·cil′lo·scop′ic** (-skŏp′ĭk) adj.

os·cu·late (ŏs′kyə-lāt′) ►v. **-lat·ed, -lat·ing 1.** To kiss. **2.** To come together; contact. [< Lat. *ōsculum*, a kiss.] —**os′cu·la′tion** n.

–ose¹ ►suff. Possessing; having the characteristics of: *comatose*. [< Lat. *-ōsus*.]

–ose² ►suff. Carbohydrate: *fructose*. [< GLU-COSE.]

o·sier (ō′zhər) ►n. **1.** A willow having long rodlike twigs used in basketry. **2.** A twig of such a willow. [< Med.Lat. *osera*.]

O·si·ris (ō-sī′rĭs) ►n. *Myth.* The ancient Egyptian god of the underworld, the brother and husband of Isis.

–osis ►suff. **1.** Condition; process; action: *osmosis*. **2.** Diseased or abnormal condition: *cyanosis*. [< Gk. *-ōsis*, n. suff.]

Os·lo (ŏz′lō, ŏs′-) The capital of Norway, in the SE part.

os·mi·um (ŏz′mē-əm) ►n. *Symbol* **Os** A bluish-white, hard, dense metallic element used as a platinum hardener. At. no. 76. See table at **element.** [< Gk. *osmē*, odor.]

os·mo·sis (ŏz-mō′sĭs, ŏs-) ►n. **1.** Diffusion of fluid through a semipermeable membrane until there is an equal concentration of fluid on both sides of the membrane. **2.** A gradual process of assimilation or absorption. [< Gk. *ōsmos*, a push.] —**os·mot′ic** (-mŏt′ĭk) adj. —**os·mot′i·cal·ly** adv.

os·prey (ŏs′prē, -prā) ►n., pl. **-preys** A large fish-eating raptor having dark plumage on the back and white below. [< Med.Lat. *avis prede*, bird of prey : Lat. *avis*, bird + Lat. *praeda*, prey.]

os·si·fy (ŏs′ə-fī′) ►v. **-fied, -fy·ing 1.** To change into bone. **2.** To become set in a rigidly conventional pattern. [Lat. *os*, bone + –FY.] —**os′si·fi·ca′tion** n.

os·te·i·tis (ŏs′tē-ī′tĭs) ►n. Inflammation of bone or bony tissue.

os·ten·si·ble (ŏ-stĕn′sə-bəl) ►adj. Represented or appearing as such; apparent. [< Lat. *ostendere*, *ostēns-*, show.] —**os·ten′si·bly** adv.

os·ten·ta·tion (ŏs′tĕn-tā′shən, -tən-) ►n. Pretentious display. [< Lat. *ostentāre*, show off.]

os·ten·ta·tious (ŏs′tĕn-tā′shəs, -tən-) ►adj. Pretentious. See Synonyms at **showy.** —**os′-ten·ta′tious·ly** adv.

osteo– or **oste–** ►pref. Bone: *osteopathy*. [< Gk. *osteon*, bone.]

os·te·op·a·thy (ŏs′tē-ŏp′ə-thē) ►n. A system that emphasizes manipulation as the basis of the bones for treating disease. —**os′te·o·path′** (ŏs′tē-ə-păth′) n. —**os′te·o·path′ic** adj. —**os′te·o·path′i·cal·ly** adv.

os·te·o·po·ro·sis (ŏs′tē-ō-pə-rō′sĭs) ►n. A disease marked by a decrease in bone mass and density, occurring esp. in women following menopause. [OSTEO– + Gk. *poros*, pore + –OSIS.] —**os′te·o·po·rot′ic** (-rŏt′ĭk) adj.

os·tra·cize (ŏs′trə-sīz′) ►v. **-cized, -ciz·ing** To banish or exclude from a group. [Gk. *ostrakizein*.] —**os′tra·cism** n.

os·trich (ŏs′trĭch, ŏs′-) ►n., pl. **-trich** or **-trich·es** A large, swift-running flightless bird of Africa, having a long bare neck and two-toed feet. [< Lat. *avis*, bird + Gk. *strouthos*, ostrich.]

Os·tro·goth (ŏs′trə-gŏth′) ►n. One of a tribe of eastern Goths that conquered and ruled Italy from AD 493 to 555.

Os·wald (ŏz′wôld′), **Lee Harvey** 1939–63. Amer. alleged assassin of President John F. Kennedy (1963).

OT ►abbr. **1.** occupational therapy **2.** Old Testament **3.** overtime

OTB ►abbr. off-track betting

OTC ►abbr. over-the-counter

oth·er (ŭth′ər) ►adj. **1a.** Being the remaining one of two or more. **b.** Being the remaining ones of several. **2.** Different from that or those implied or specified. **3.** Additional; extra. **4.** Opposite; reverse. **5.** Alternate; second: *every other day.* **6.** Of the recent past: *the other day.* ►n. **1a.** The remaining one of two or more. **b. others** The remaining ones of several. **2a.** A different one: *one storm after the other.* **b.** An additional one: *How many others will come later?* ►pron. A different person or thing. ►adv. In another way. [< OE *ōther*.]

oth·er·wise (ŭth′ər-wīz′) ►adv. **1.** In another way; differently. **2.** Under other circumstances. **3.** In other respects. ►adj. Other than supposed; different: *The facts are otherwise.*

oth·er·world·ly (ŭth′ər-wûrld′lē) ►adj. **1.** Of or characteristic of another world, esp. a mystical world. **2.** Relating to or concerned with intellectual or imaginative things. —**oth′er·world′li·ness** n.

–otic ►suff. **1.** Of or characterized by a specified condition or process: *mitotic.* **2.** Having a specified disease or abnormality: *sclerotic.* [< Gk. *-ōtikos*, adj. suff.]

o·ti·ose (ō′shē-ōs′, ō′tē-) ►adj. **1.** Lazy. **2.** Of no use; pointless or superfluous. **3.** Futile. See Synonyms at **vain.** [Lat. *otiōsus.*]

o·ti·tis (ō-tī′tĭs) ►n. Inflammation of the ear. [Gk. *ous, ōt-*, ear + –ITIS.]

OTS ►abbr. Officers' Training School

Ot·ta·wa¹ (ŏt′ə-wə, -wä′, -wô′) ►n., pl. **-wa** or **-was 1.** A member of a Native American people of S Ontario and N Michigan. **2.** The Ojibwa dialect spoken by the Ottawa.

Ot·ta·wa² (ŏt′ə-wə) The capital of Canada, in SE Ontario on the Ottawa R.

Ottawa River A river, about 1,270 km (780 mi), rising in SW Quebec, Canada, and flowing to the St. Lawrence R. near Montreal.

ot·ter (ŏt′ər) ►n., pl. **-ter** or **-ters 1.** Any of various aquatic or semiaquatic carnivorous mammals having webbed feet and dense brown fur. **2.** The fur of an otter. [< OE *otor*.]

Ot·to I (ŏt′ō, ôt′ō) "the Great." 912–973. King of Germany (936–973) and first Holy Roman emperor (962–973).

ot·to·man (ŏt′ə-mən) ►n., pl. **-mans 1.** A backless upholstered sofa. **2.** An upholstered footstool. [< Fr. *ottoman*, Turk.]

Ottoman ►n., pl. **-mans** A Turk, esp. of the

Ottoman Empire. ▸*adj.* **1.** Of the Ottoman Empire. **2.** Turkish.

Ottoman Empire A Turkish sultanate (1299?–1922) of SW Asia, NE Africa, and SE Europe.

Oua·ga·dou·gou (wä′gə-dōō′gōō) The capital of Burkina Faso, in the central part.

ouch (ouch) ▸*interj.* Used to express sudden pain.

ought[1] (ôt) ▸*aux.v.* Used to indicate: **a.** Obligation or duty: *You ought to work harder than that.* **b.** Advisability or prudence: *You ought to wear a raincoat.* **c.** Probability or likelihood: *She ought to finish by next week.* [< OE *āhte,* p.t. of *āgan,* to possess.]

ought[2] (ôt) ▸*pron.* Var. of **aught**[1].

ought[3] (ôt) ▸*n.* Var. of **aught**[2].

ou·gui·ya (ōō-gē′yə) ▸*n.* See table at **currency.** [Indigenous word in Mauritania.]

ounce (ouns) ▸*n.* **1a.** See table at **measurement. b.** A unit of apothecary weight, equal to 480 grains (31.103 grams). **2.** A fluid ounce. **3.** A tiny bit. [< Lat. *ūncia,* a twelfth.]

our (our) ▸*adj.* The possessive form of **we.** Used as a modifier before a noun: *our deeds; our hometown.* [< OE *ūre.*]

ours (ourz) ▸*pron.* (*takes sing. or pl. v.*) Used to indicate the one or ones belonging to us: *The victory is ours. If your car doesn't start, take ours.* [< OE *ūre,* our.]

our·self (our-sĕlf′, är-) ▸*pron.* Myself. Used as a reflexive, as in a royal proclamation.

our·selves (our-sĕlvz′, är-) ▸*pron.* **1.** Those ones identical with us. Used: **a.** Reflexively as a direct or indirect object or the object of a preposition: *We bought ourselves a new camera.* **b.** For emphasis. **2.** Our normal or healthy condition: *We're feeling ourselves again.*

–ous ▸*suff.* **1.** Possessing; full of: *joyous.* **2.** Having a valence lower than in compounds or ions named with adjectives ending in *-ic: ferrous.* [< Lat. *-ōsus.*]

oust (oust) ▸*v.* To eject; force out. [< Lat. *obstāre,* to hinder.]

oust·er (ous′tər) ▸*n.* Eviction; expulsion. [< AN, to oust.]

out (out) ▸*adv.* **1.** Away from the inside. **2.** Away from the center or middle. **3.** Away from a usual place. **4.** Outside: *went out to play.* **5a.** To exhaustion or depletion: *The supplies have run out.* **b.** Into extinction: *The fire has gone out.* **c.** To a finish or conclusion: *Play the game out.* **6.** In or into a state of unconsciousness: *The drug put him out for hours.* **7.** Into view: *The moon came out.* **8.** Into distribution: *giving out free passes.* **9.** Into disuse. **10.** *Baseball* So as to be retired: *He grounded out.* **11.** On strike. ▸*adj.* **1.** Exterior; external. **2.** Outgoing: *the out doorway.* **3.** Not operating or operational: *The power was out.* **4.** Not to be considered or permitted. **5.** No longer fashionable. **6.** No longer possessing or supplied with something: *I can't offer you coffee because we're out.* **7.** *Informal* Openly gay, lesbian, or bisexual. **8.** *Baseball* Not allowed to continue to bat or run. ▸*prep.* **1.** Forth from; through. **2.** Within the area of: *a house with a garden out back.* ▸*n.* **1.** One that is out, esp. one who is out of power. **2.** A means of escape. **3.** *Baseball* A play in which a batter or base runner is retired. ▸*v.* **1.** To be disclosed or revealed: *Truth will out.* **2.** To expose (someone) as being gay, lesbian, or bisexual. **—idiom:**

on the outs *Informal* Not on friendly terms. [< OE *ūt.*]

out– ▸*pref.* In a way that surpasses or exceeds: *outdistance.* [< OUT.]

out·age (ou′tĭj) ▸*n.* A temporary suspension of operation, esp. of electric power.

out-and-out (out′n-out′) ▸*adj.* Complete; thoroughgoing.

out·back (out′băk′) ▸*n.* The wild, remote part esp. of Australia or New Zealand.

out·bid (out-bĭd′) ▸*v.* To bid higher than.

out·board (out′bôrd′) ▸*adj.* **1.** Situated outside the hull of a vessel. **2.** Situated toward or nearer the end of an aircraft wing. **—out′board′** *adv.*

out·bound (out′bound′) ▸*adj.* Outward bound.

out·break (out′brāk′) ▸*n.* A sudden eruption.

out·build·ing (out′bĭl′dĭng) ▸*n.* A subsidiary building associated with a main building.

out·burst (out′bûrst′) ▸*n.* A sudden violent display, as of activity or emotion.

out·cast (out′kăst′) ▸*n.* One that has been excluded from a society. **—out′cast′** *adj.*

out·class (out-klăs′) ▸*v.* To surpass decisively, so as to appear of a higher class.

out·come (out′kŭm′) ▸*n.* A result.

out·crop (out′krŏp′) or **out·crop·ping** (-krŏp′ĭng) ▸*n.* A portion of bedrock protruding through the soil level. [< *crop,* appear on the surface.] **—out·crop′** *v.*

out·cry (out′krī′) ▸*n.* **1.** A loud cry or clamor. **2.** A strong protest.

out·dat·ed (out-dā′tĭd) ▸*adj.* Out-of-date; old-fashioned.

out·dis·tance (out-dĭs′təns) ▸*v.* To surpass by a wide margin.

out·do (out-dōō′) ▸*v.* To do better than.

out·door (out′dôr′) also **out-of-door** (out′-əv-dôr′) ▸*adj.* Located in, done in, or suited to the open air.

out·doors (out-dôrz′) also **out-of-doors** (out′-əv-dôrz′) ▸*n.* The open air; the area away from buildings. ▸*adv.* In or into the outdoors.

out·er (ou′tər) ▸*adj.* **1.** Located on the outside. **2.** Farther from the center or middle.

outer ear ▸*n.* See **external ear.**

out·er·most (ou′tər-mōst′) ▸*adj.* Farthest out.

outer planet ▸*n.* Any of the four planets, Jupiter, Saturn, Uranus, and Neptune, with orbits outside that of Mars.

outer space ▸*n.* Space beyond the limits of a celestial body or system.

out·face (out-fās′) ▸*v.* **1.** To overcome with a bold or self-assured look. **2.** To defy.

out·fall (out′fôl′) ▸*n.* The place where a sewer, drain, or stream discharges.

out·field (out′fēld′) ▸*n.* *Baseball* The playing area extending outward from the diamond. **—out′field′er** *n.*

out·fit (out′fĭt′) ▸*n.* **1.** Clothing or equipment for a specialized purpose. See Synonyms at **equipment. 2.** *Informal* An association of persons who work together. ▸*v.* To provide with an outfit. **—out′fit′ter** *n.*

out·flank (out-flăngk′) ▸*v.* **1.** To maneuver around the flank of (an opposing force). **2.** To gain a tactical advantage over.

out·flow (out′flō′) ▸*n.* **1.** The act of flowing out. **2.** Something that flows out.

out·fox (out-fŏks′) ▸*v.* To outsmart.

out·go (out′gō′) ▸*n.,* pl. **-goes** Something that goes out, esp. money.

out·go·ing (out′gō′ĭng) ►*adj.* **1.** Going out; departing. **2.** Sociable; friendly.

out·grow (out-grō′) ►*v.* **1.** To grow too large for. **2.** To grow too mature for: *outgrow childish games.* **3.** To surpass in growth.

out·growth (out′grōth′) ►*n.* **1.** A product of growing out; offshoot. **2.** A consequence.

out·guess (out-gĕs′) ►*v.* To anticipate correctly the actions of.

out·house (out′hous′) ►*n.* **1.** A toilet housed in a small outdoor structure. **2.** An outbuilding.

out·ing (ou′tĭng) ►*n.* **1.** An excursion. **2.** A walk outdoors. **3a.** The exposing of someone as being gay, lesbian, or bisexual. **b.** The disclosure of a person's secret, esp. when thought to be embarrassing.

out·land (out′lănd′, -lənd) ►*n.* **1.** A foreign land. **2. outlands** The outlying areas of a country. —**out′land′** *adj.* —**out′land·er** *n.*

out·land·ish (out-lăn′dĭsh) ►*adj.* Conspicuously unconventional; bizarre. —**out·land′ish·ly** *adv.* —**out·land′ish·ness** *n.*

out·last (out-lăst′) ►*v.* **1.** To last longer than. **2.** To overcome by enduring for a longer period.

out·law (out′lô′) ►*n.* **1.** A fugitive from the law. **2.** A person excluded from normal legal protection and rights. ►*v.* **1.** To declare illegal. **2.** To deprive of the protection of the law. —**out′law′** *adj.* —**out′law′ry** *n.*

out·lay (out′lā′) ►*n.* **1.** The spending or disbursement of money. **2.** An amount spent.

out·let (out′lĕt′, -lĭt) ►*n.* **1a.** A passage for escape or exit; vent. **b.** A means of release or gratification, as for energies or desires. **2.** A commercial market for goods or services. **3.** A receptacle connected to a power supply and having a socket for a plug.

out·line (out′līn′) ►*n.* **1.** A line indicating the outer contours or boundaries of a figure. **2.** A style of drawing in which objects are delineated in contours without shading. **3.** A short description, account, or summary. ►*v.* **-lined, -lin·ing 1.** To draw an outline of. **2.** To give the main features of; summarize.
    Syns: contour, profile, silhouette **n.**

out·live (out-lĭv′) ►*v.* To live longer than.

out·look (out′lo͝ok′) ►*n.* **1.** A point of view; attitude. **2.** Expectation for the future; prospect. **3a.** A place where something can be viewed. **b.** The view seen.

out·ly·ing (out′lī′ĭng) ►*adj.* Relatively distant or remote from a center.

out·ma·neu·ver (out′mə-no͞o′vər, -nyo͞o′-) ►*v.* **1.** To overcome by more artful maneuvering. **2.** To excel in maneuverability.

out·mod·ed (out-mō′dĭd) ►*adj.* **1.** Not in fashion. **2.** Obsolete.

out·num·ber (out-nŭm′bər) ►*v.* To be more numerous than.

out of ►*prep.* **1a.** From within to the outside of: *got out of the car.* **b.** From a given condition: *came out of her trance.* **c.** From a source or cause: *made out of wood.* **2a.** In a position or situation beyond the range, boundaries, or sphere of: *flew out of sight.* **b.** In a state away from the expected or usual: *out of practice.* **3.** From among: *five out of six votes.* **4.** Because of: *did it out of spite.* **5.** In a condition of no longer having: *We're out of coffee.*

out-of-bounds (out′əv-boundz′) ►*adv. & adj.* **1.** Beyond the designated boundaries, as of the

playing area in a sport. **2.** Violating acceptable standards, as of behavior.

out-of-date (out′əv-dāt′) ►*adj.* Out of style.

out-of-door (out′əv-dôr′) ►*adj.* Var. of **outdoor.**

out-of-doors (out′əv-dôrz′) ►*adv. & n.* Var. of **outdoors.**

out-of-pock·et (out′əv-pŏk′ĭt) ►*adj.* **1.** Calling for the spending of cash: *out-of-pocket expenses.* **2.** Individually responsible for an amount of money. **3.** Lacking funds.

out-of-the-way (out′əv-*th*ə-wā′) ►*adj.* **1.** Remote; secluded. **2.** Unusual.

out·pace (out-pās′) ►*v.* To surpass; outstrip.

out·pa·tient (out′pā′shənt) ►*n.* A patient whose treatment does not require an overnight stay in a hospital. ►*adj.* Relating to outpatients or their care.

out·place·ment (out′plās′mənt) ►*n.* The process of assisting a terminated employee find a new job.

out·play (out-plā′) ►*v.* To play better than.

out·post (out′pōst′) ►*n.* **1a.** A detachment of troops stationed at a distance from a main force. **b.** The station occupied by such troops. **2.** An outlying settlement.

out·pour·ing (out′pôr′ĭng) ►*n.* The act, action, or result of pouring out or producing: *an outpouring of profanity; the outpouring of lava.*

out·put (out′po͝ot′) ►*n.* **1.** An amount produced or manufactured during a certain time. **2.** The energy, power, or work produced by a system. **3.** *Comp.* The information produced by a program or process from a specific input. —**out′put′** *v.*

out·rage (out′rāj′) ►*n.* **1.** An act of extreme violence or viciousness. **2.** An act grossly offensive to decency or good taste. **3.** Resentful anger. ►*v.* **-raged, -rag·ing 1.** To commit an outrage on. **2.** To produce anger or indignity in. [< OFr. *outre,* OUTRÉ.]

out·ra·geous (out-rā′jəs) ►*adj.* **1a.** Grossly offensive. **b.** Beyond the bounds of good taste. **2a.** Extremely unconventional: *outrageous clothing.* **b.** Extravagant; immoderate: *an outrageous amount of money.* —**out·ra′geous·ly** *adv.* —**out·ra′geous·ness** *n.*

out·rank (out-răngk′) ►*v.* To rank higher than.

ou·tré (o͞o-trā′) ►*adj.* Eccentric; bizarre. [< Lat. *ultrā,* beyond.]

out·reach (out-rēch′) ►*v.* **1.** To surpass in reach. **2.** To exceed. ►*n.* (out′rēch′) **1.** Extent of reach. **2.** A systematic attempt to provide services to a community.

out·rid·er (out′rī′dər) ►*n.* A mounted attendant.

outrigger

out·rig·ger (out′rĭg′ər) ►*n.* **1.** A long thin float attached parallel to a seagoing canoe to prevent it from capsizing. **2.** A vessel fitted with an outrigger.

out·right (out′rīt′, -rīt′) ►*adv.* **1.** Without reservation or qualification. **2.** Completely; wholly. **3.** At once; straightway. ►*adj.* (out′rīt′) **1.** Unqualified: *an outright gift.* **2.** Thoroughgoing; out-and-out.

out·run (out-rŭn′) ►*v.* **1.** To run faster than. **2.** To exceed.

out·sell (out-sĕl′) ►*v.* To surpass in sales or selling.

out·set (out′sĕt′) ►*n.* Beginning; start.

out·shine (out-shīn′) ►*v.* **1.** To shine brighter than. **2.** To outdo.

out·side (out-sīd′, out′sīd′) ►*n.* **1.** The outer surface or side. **2.** The space beyond a boundary or limit. **3.** The utmost limit: *We'll be leaving in ten days at the outside.* ►*adj.* **1.** Of, restricted to, or situated on the outer side: *an outside door lock.* **2.** Acting, occurring, originating, or being at a place beyond certain limits: *outside assistance.* **3.** Extreme; uttermost: *exceeded even our outside estimates.* **4.** Unlikely; remote: *an outside chance.* ►*adv.* **1.** On or to the outer side. **2.** Outdoors. ►*prep.* **1.** On or to the outer side of. **2.** Beyond the limits of: *outside the city.* **3.** Except: *no information outside the figures given.*

outside of ►*prep.* Outside.

out·sid·er (out-sī′dər) ►*n.* One who is not part of a group or community.

out·size (out′sīz′) ►*n.* An unusual size, esp. a very large size. —**out′size′, out′sized′** *adj.*

out·skirts (out′skûrts′) ►*pl.n.* The peripheral parts, as of a city.

out·smart (out-smärt′) ►*v.* To outwit.

out·spend (out-spĕnd′) ►*v.* **1.** To spend beyond the limits of. **2.** To outdo in spending.

out·spo·ken (out-spō′kən) ►*adj.* **1.** Spoken without reserve; candid. **2.** Frank in speech. —**out·spo′ken·ly** *adv.* —**out·spo′ken·ness** *n.*

out·spread (out-sprĕd′) ►*v.* To spread out; extend. —**out′spread′** *adj.*

out·stand·ing (out-stăn′dĭng, out′stăn′-) ►*adj.* **1.** Excellent or exceptionally good. **2.** Noticeable or conspicuous. **3.** Not settled or resolved. —**out·stand′ing·ly** *adv.*

out·stretch (out-strĕch′) ►*v.* To extend.

out·strip (out-strĭp′) ►*v.* **1.** To move past or ahead of. **2.** To exceed; surpass.

out·take (out′tāk′) ►*n.* A shot or scene, as of a movie, that is filmed but not used in the final version.

out·ward (out′wərd) ►*adj.* **1.** Of or moving toward the outside or exterior. **2.** Purely exter-

nal; superficial. ►*adv.* also **out·wards** (-wərdz) Toward the outside. —**out′ward·ly** *adv.*

out·wear (out-wâr′) ►*v.* **1.** To outlast. **2.** To use up or exhaust.

out·weigh (out-wā′) ►*v.* **1.** To weigh more than. **2.** To be more significant than.

out·wit (out-wĭt′) ►*v.* **-wit·ted, -wit·ting** To best or defeat by cleverness or cunning: *outwitted her opponents.*

out·work (out-wûrk′) ►*v.* To work better or faster than.

ou·zo (ōō′zō) ►*n.* A Greek liqueur flavored with anise. [Mod.Gk.]

o·va (ō′və) ►*n.* Pl. of **ovum.**

o·val (ō′vəl) ►*adj.* **1.** Egg-shaped. **2.** Shaped like an ellipse; elliptical. [< Lat. *ōvum,* egg.] —**o′val** *n.*

o·va·ry (ō′və-rē) ►*n., pl.* **-ries 1.** One of the paired female reproductive organs that produces eggs and female sex hormones in vertebrates. **2.** *Bot.* The ovule-bearing part of a pistil. [< Lat. *ōvum,* egg.] —**o·var′i·an** (ō-vâr′ē-ən) *adj.*

o·vate (ō′vāt′) ►*adj.* Egg-shaped. —**o′vate′-ly** *adv.*

o·va·tion (ō-vā′shən) ►*n.* Enthusiastic, prolonged applause. [< Lat. *ovāre,* rejoice.]

ov·en (ŭv′ən) ►*n.* A compartment for heating or baking food, as in a stove. [< OE *ofen.*]

o·ver (ō′vər) ►*prep.* **1.** Above: *a sign over the door.* **2.** Above and across: *a jump over the fence.* **3.** On the other side of: *over the border.* **4.** Upon: *put paint over the woodwork.* **5.** All through: *looked over the report.* **6.** So as to cover: *put a shawl over my shoulders.* **7.** Higher than: *water that was over my shoulders.* **8.** Through the duration of: *maintained records over two years.* **9.** More than: *over ten miles.* **10.** With reference to: *an argument over methods.* ►*adv.* **1.** Above. **2a.** Across to another or the opposite side. **b.** Across the edge or brim: *The coffee spilled over.* **3.** Across an intervening distance. **4.** To a different opinion or allegiance. **5.** To a different person, condition, or title: *sign the property over.* **6.** So as to be completely enclosed or covered: *The river froze over.* **7.** Thoroughly: *Think the problem over.* **8a.** From an upright position. **b.** From an upward position to an inverted or reversed position. **9.** Again. **10.** In repetition: *ten times over.* **11.** In addition or excess. **12.** At an end: *The war is over.* —**idioms: over against** Contrasted with. **over and above** In addition to. [< OE *ofer.*]

over– ►*pref.* **1.** Above; upon: *overpass.* **2.** Superior: *overlord.* **3.** Into a reverse position: *overturn.* **4.** Excessively: *overpay.*

o′ver·a·bun′dance *n.*
o′ver·a·bun′dant *adj.*
o′ver·ac′tive *adj.*
o′ver·ag·gres′sive *adj.*
o′ver·am·bi′tion *n.*
o′ver·am·bi′tious *adj.*
o′ver·anx′ious *adj.*
o′ver·bid′ *v.*
o′ver·bur′den *v.*
o′ver·buy′ *v.*
o′ver·ca·pac′i·ty *n.*
o′ver·cap′i·tal·ize′ *v.*
o′ver·cau′tious *adj.*
o′ver·com′pen·sate′ *v.*
o′ver·con′fi·dence *n.*
o′ver·con′fi·dent *adj.*
o′ver·crit′i·cal *adj.*
o′ver·crowd′ *v.*
o′ver·de·vel′op *v.*
o′ver·de·vel′op·ment *n.*
o′ver·dress′ *v.*
o′ver·ea′ger *adj.*
o′ver·eat′ *v.*
o′ver·eat′er *n.*
o′ver·em′pha·sis *n.*
o′ver·em′pha·size′ *v.*
o′ver·es′ti·mate′ *v.*
o′ver·ex·ert′ *v.*
o′ver·ex·tend′ *v.*
o′ver·fed′ *adj.*
o′ver·feed′ *v.*
o′ver·fill′ *v.*
o′ver·graze′ *v.*
o′ver·heat′ *v.*
o′ver·in·dulge′ *v.*
o′ver·in·dul′gence *n.*
o′ver·load′ *v.*
o′ver·load′ *n.*
o′ver·long′ *adj. & adv.*
o′ver·med′i·cate′ *v.*
o′ver·med′i·ca′tion *n.*
o′ver·op′ti·mism *n.*
o′ver·op′ti·mis′tic *adj.*
o′ver·pay′ *v.*
o′ver·pop′u·late′ *v.*

o·ver·act (ō′vər-ăkt′) ►v. To act with unnecessary exaggeration.

o·ver·age¹ (ō′vər-ĭj) ►n. A surplus; excess.

o·ver·age² (ō′vər-āj′) ►adj. Beyond the proper or required age.

o·ver·all (ō′vər-ôl′) ►adj. **1.** From one end to the other. **2.** Including everything; comprehensive. ►adv. (ō′vər-ôl′) Generally. ►n. **overalls** Loose-fitting trousers with a bib front and shoulder straps.

o·ver·arm (ō′vər-ärm′) ►adj. Sports Executed with the arm raised above the shoulder.

o·ver·awe (ō′vər-ô′) ►v. To overcome or subdue by inspiring awe.

o·ver·bal·ance (ō′vər-băl′əns) ►v. **1.** To have greater weight or importance than. **2.** To lose one's balance.

o·ver·bear (ō′vər-bâr′) ►v. **1.** To press down on or overwhelm with physical force. **2.** To dominate or overcome.

o·ver·bear·ing (ō′vər-bâr′ĭng) ►adj. **1.** Domineering and arrogant. **2.** Predominant.

o·ver·bite (ō′vər-bīt′) ►n. A condition in which the front upper teeth project over the lower.

o·ver·blown (ō′vər-blōn′) ►adj. **1.** Excessive; overdone. **2.** Full of bombastic language.

o·ver·board (ō′vər-bôrd′) ►adv. Over the side of a boat or ship. —**idiom: go overboard** To go to extremes.

o·ver·build (ō′vər-bĭld′) ►v. **1.** To build over or on top of. **2.** To build beyond the demand or need of (an area).

o·ver·cast (ō′vər-kăst′, ō′vər-kăst′) ►adj. **1.** Clouded over. **2.** Gloomy; melancholy. **3.** Sewn with long overlaying stitches.

o·ver·charge (ō′vər-chärj′) ►v. **1.** To charge too much. **2.** To fill too full. —**o′ver·charge′** n.

o·ver·cloud (ō′vər-kloud′) ►v. To make or become cloudy.

o·ver·coat (ō′vər-kōt′) ►n. A heavy coat worn over clothing in cold weather.

o·ver·come (ō′vər-kŭm′) ►v. **1.** To defeat in competition or conflict. **2.** To prevail over; surmount. **3.** To overpower, as with emotion.

o·ver·do (ō′vər-dōō′) ►v. **1.** To do or use to excess; exaggerate. **2.** To cook too long.

o·ver·dose (ō′vər-dōs′) ►v. To take or cause to take too large a dose. —**o′ver·dose′** n.

o·ver·draft (ō′vər-drăft′) ►n. **1.** The act of overdrawing a bank account. **2.** The amount overdrawn.

o·ver·draw (ō′vər-drô′) ►v. **1.** To draw against (a bank account) in excess of credit. **2.** To exaggerate or overstate.

o·ver·drive (ō′vər-drīv′) ►n. An automotive transmission gear that transmits to the drive shaft a speed greater than engine speed.

o·ver·due (ō′vər-dōō′, -dyōō′) ►adj. **1.** Being unpaid when due. **2.** Past due; late. See Synonyms at **tardy.**

o·ver·ex·pose (ō′vər-ĭk-spōz′) ►v. **-posed, -pos·ing** To expose too long or too much. —**o′ver·ex·po′sure** n.

o·ver·flow (ō′vər-flō′) ►v. **1.** To flow over the top, brim, or banks (of). **2.** To spread or cover over. **3.** To teem; abound. See Synonyms at **teem.** ►n. (ō′vər-flō′) **1.** A flood. **2.** An excess; surplus. **3.** An outlet through which excess liquid may escape.

o·ver·grow (ō′vər-grō′, ō′vər-grō′) ►v. **1.** To grow over with foliage. **2.** To grow too large for. **3.** To grow beyond normal size. —**o′ver·grown′** adj. —**o′ver·growth′** n.

o·ver·hand (ō′vər-hănd′) also **o·ver·hand·ed** (ō′vər-hăn′dĭd) ►adj. Executed with the hand higher than the shoulder. —**o′ver·hand′** adv. & n.

o·ver·hang (ō′vər-hăng′) ►v. **1.** To project or extend beyond. **2.** To loom over. —**o′ver·hang′** n.

o·ver·haul (ō′vər-hôl′, ō′vər-hôl′) ►v. **1a.** To examine carefully. **b.** To repair thoroughly. **2.** To overtake. —**o′ver·haul′** n.

o·ver·head (ō′vər-hĕd′) ►adj. **1.** Located or functioning from above. **2.** Of or relating to the operating expenses of a business. ►n. The operating expenses of a business, including rent, utilities, and taxes. —**o′ver·head′** adv.

o·ver·hear (ō′vər-hîr′) ►v. To hear without the speaker's awareness or intent.

o·ver·joy (ō′vər-joi′) ►v. To fill with joy; delight. —**o′ver·joyed′** (-joid′) adj.

o·ver·kill (ō′vər-kĭl′) ►n. **1.** The destructive use of military force beyond the amount needed to destroy an enemy. **2.** An excessive action.

o·ver·land (ō′vər-lănd′, -lənd) ►adj. Over or across land. —**o′ver·land′** adv.

o·ver·lap (ō′vər-lăp′) ►v. **1.** To extend over and cover part of. **2.** To have something in common with. —**o′ver·lap′** n.

o·ver·lay (ō′vər-lā′) ►v. To lay or spread over or on. —**o′ver·lay′** n.

o·ver·look (ō′vər-lōōk′) ►v. **1a.** To look over from above. **b.** To afford a view over: The tower overlooks the sea. **2a.** To fail to notice or consider: overlooked an error. **b.** To ignore deliberately or indulgently; disregard. ►n. (ō′vər-lōōk′) An elevated spot that affords a broad view.

o·ver·lord (ō′vər-lôrd′) ►n. A lord having supremacy over other lords.

o′ver·pop′u·lat′ed adj.
o′ver·pop′u·la′tion n.
o′ver·pow′er·ful adj.
o′ver·praise′ v.
o′ver·pre·scribe′ v.
o′ver·price′ v.
o′ver·pro·duce′ v.
o′ver·pro·duc′tion n.
o′ver·pro·tect′ v.
o′ver·pro·tec′tion n.
o′ver·pro·tec′tive adj.
o′ver·re·act′ v.
o′ver·re·ac′tion n.
o′ver·re·fine′ v.
o′ver·reg′u·late v.

o′ver·reg′u·la′tion n.
o′ver·rep′re·sent′ed adj.
o′ver·ripe′ adj.
o′ver·rip′en v.
o′ver·sell′ v.
o′ver·sen′si·tive adj.
o′ver·sim′pli·fi·ca′tion n.
o′ver·sim′pli·fy′ v.
o′ver·sized′ adv.
o′ver·spe′cial·ize′ v.
o′ver·spend′ v.
o′ver·staff′ v.
o′ver·stock′ v.
o′ver·strain′ v.

o′ver·stress′ v.
o′ver·stretch′ v.
o′ver·sup·ply′ n. & v.
o′ver·tax′ v.
o′ver·tax·a′tion n.
o′ver·use′ v. & n.
o′ver·val′u·a′tion n.
o′ver·val′ue v.
o′ver·wea′ry adj. & v.
o′ver·weight′ adj.
o′ver·wind′ v.
o′ver·work′ v.
o′ver·writ′ten adj.
o′ver·zeal′ous adj.

o·ver·ly (ō′vər-lē) ►*adv.* Excessively.

o·ver·mas·ter (ō′vər-măs′tər) ►*v.* To overcome.

o·ver·match (ō′vər-măch′) ►*v.* **1.** To be more than a match for. **2.** To match with a superior opponent.

o·ver·much (ō′vər-mŭch′) ►*adj.* Too much. ►*adv.* In excess.

o·ver·night (ō′vər-nīt′) ►*adj.* **1.** Lasting for or remaining during a night. **2.** Sudden: *an overnight success.* ►*adv.* (ō′vər-nīt′) **1.** During or for the length of the night. **2.** Suddenly. —**o′ver·night′** *n.*

o·ver·pass (ō′vər-păs′) ►*n.* A roadway or bridge that crosses above another.

o·ver·play (ō′vər-plā′) ►*v.* **1.** To overact. **2.** To overestimate the strength of (one's position).

o·ver·pow·er (ō′vər-pou′ər) ►*v.* **1.** To overcome by superior force. **2.** To overwhelm.

o·ver·qual·i·fied (ō′vər-kwŏl′ə-fīd′) ►*adj.* Educated or skilled beyond what is necessary for a particular job.

o·ver·rate (ō′vər-rāt′) ►*v.* To overestimate the merits of.

o·ver·reach (ō′vər-rēch′) ►*v.* **1.** To reach or extend over or beyond. **2.** To miss by reaching too far or attempting too much. **3.** To defeat (oneself) by going too far. —**o′ver·reach′** *n.* —**o′ver·reach′er** *n.*

o·ver·ride (ō′vər-rīd′) ►*v.* **1.** To ride across. **2.** To trample on. **3.** To prevail over. **4.** To declare null and void; set aside.

o·ver·rid·ing (ō′vər-rī′dĭng) ►*adj.* More important than all others: *an overriding concern.* —**o′ver·rid′ing·ly** *adv.*

o·ver·rule (ō′vər-rōōl′) ►*v.* **1a.** To declare (e.g., a court ruling) as superseded and no longer accurate. **b.** To disallow as contrary to rules of law. **2.** To reject or annul.

o·ver·run (ō′vər-rŭn′) ►*v.* **1.** To spread or swarm over destructively. **2.** To spread swiftly throughout. **3.** To overflow. **4.** To run or extend beyond; exceed. ►*n.* (ō′vər-rŭn′) **1.** An act of overrunning. **2.** The amount by which something overruns.

o·ver·scale (ō′vər-skāl′) or **o·ver·scaled** (-skāld′) ►*adj.* Unusually large or extensive.

o·ver·seas (ō′vər-sēz′, ō′vər-sēz′) ►*adv.* Beyond the sea; abroad. —**o′ver·seas′** *adj.*

o·ver·see (ō′vər-sē′) ►*v.* To watch over and direct; supervise. —**o′ver·se′er** *n.*

o·ver·sexed (ō′vər-sĕkst′) ►*adj.* Having an excessive sexual appetite.

o·ver·shad·ow (ō′vər-shăd′ō) ►*v.* **1.** To cast a shadow over. **2.** To surpass; dominate.

o·ver·shoe (ō′vər-shōō′) ►*n.* An outer shoe worn as protection from water or snow.

o·ver·shoot (ō′vər-shōōt′) ►*v.* **1.** To shoot or go over or beyond. **2.** To miss by or as if by shooting or going too far.

o·ver·sight (ō′vər-sīt′) ►*n.* **1.** An unintentional omission or mistake. **2.** Supervision.

o·ver·size (ō′vər-sīz′) also **o·ver·sized** (-sīzd′) ►*adj.* Larger in size than usual.

o·ver·skirt (ō′vər-skûrt′) ►*n.* A skirt worn over another.

o·ver·sleep (ō′vər-slēp′) ►*v.* To sleep beyond one's intended time for waking.

o·ver·state (ō′vər-stāt′) ►*v.* To state in exaggerated terms. See Synonyms at **exaggerate.** —**o′ver·state′ment** *n.*

o·ver·stay (ō′vər-stā′) ►*v.* To stay beyond the limits or duration of.

o·ver·step (ō′vər-stĕp′) ►*v.* To go beyond.

o·ver·stuff (ō′vər-stŭf′) ►*v.* **1.** To stuff too much into. **2.** To upholster thickly.

o·ver·sub·scribe (ō′vər-səb-skrīb′) ►*v.* To subscribe for in excess of available supply. —**o′ver·sub·scrip′tion** (-skrĭp′shən) *n.*

o·vert (ō-vûrt′, ō′vûrt′) ►*adj.* Open and observable; not concealed. [< OFr., p.part. of *ovrir,* to open.] —**o·vert′ly** *adv.* —**o·vert′ness** *n.*

o·ver·take (ō′vər-tāk′) ►*v.* To catch up with.

o·ver-the-count·er (ō′vər-thə-koun′tər) ►*adj.* **1.** Not listed or available on an officially recognized stock exchange. **2.** Sold legally without a doctor's prescription.

o·ver-the-top (ō′vər-thə-tŏp′) ►*adj.* Exceeding the normal bounds; extravagant.

o·ver·throw (ō′vər-thrō′) ►*v.* **1.** To bring about the downfall of; topple. **2.** To throw over and beyond. **3.** To overturn. —**o′ver·throw′** *n.* **Syns:** *overturn, subvert, topple, upset* **v.**

o·ver·time (ō′vər-tīm′) ►*n.* **1.** Working hours in addition to those of a regular schedule. **2.** Payment for such work. **3.** *Sports* A period of playing time added after the expiration of the set time limit.

o·ver·tone (ō′vər-tōn′) ►*n.* **1.** An implication; hint: *an overtone of anger; overtones of jealousy.* **2.** See **harmonic** (sense 1).

o·ver·top (ō′vər-tŏp′) ►*v.* **1.** To tower above. **2.** To take precedence over.

o·ver·ture (ō′vər-chŏor′) ►*n.* **1.** *Mus.* **a.** An instrumental introduction to an extended work. **b.** An independent instrumental composition of similar form. **2.** A first offer or proposal. [< Lat. *apertūra,* opening.]

o·ver·turn (ō′vər-tûrn′) ►*v.* **1.** To turn over; upset. **2a.** To overthrow. See Synonyms at **overthrow. b.** To invalidate or reverse.

o·ver·view (ō′vər-vyōō′) ►*n.* A comprehensive view; survey.

o·ver·ween·ing (ō′vər-wē′nĭng) ►*adj.* **1.** Arrogant; overbearing. **2.** Immoderate.

o·ver·whelm (ō′vər-wĕlm′, -hwĕlm′) ►*v.* **1.** To submerge; engulf. **2.** To defeat completely. **3.** To affect deeply in mind or emotion: *Grief overwhelmed me.* **4.** To turn over; upset.

o·ver·wrought (ō′vər-rôt′) ►*adj.* **1.** Nervous or excited. **2.** Extremely elaborate.

ovi– or **ovo–** or **ov–** ►*pref.* Egg; ovum: *oviduct.* [< Lat. *ōvum,* egg.]

Ov·id (ŏv′ĭd) 43 BC–AD 17. Roman poet. —**O·vid′i·an** (ō-vĭd′ē-ən) *adj.*

o·vi·duct (ō′vĭ-dŭkt′) ►*n.* See **fallopian tube.**

o·vip·a·rous (ō-vĭp′ər-əs) ►*adj.* Producing eggs that hatch outside the body.

o·void (ō′void′) also **o·voi·dal** (ō-void′l) ►*adj.* Egg-shaped. —**o′void** *n.*

o·vo·vi·vip·a·rous (ō′vō-vī-vĭp′ər-əs) ►*adj.* Producing eggs that hatch within the female's body.

o·vu·late (ō′vyə-lāt′, ŏv′yə-) ►*v.* **-lat·ed, -lat·ing** To produce or discharge ova. [< OVULE.] —**o′vu·la′tion** *n.*

o·vule (ō′vyōol, ŏv′yōol) ►*n.* A minute structure in seed plants that develops into a seed after fertilization. [< Lat. *ōvum,* egg.] —**o′vu·lar** (ō′vyə-lər, ŏv′yə-) *adj.*

o·vum (ō′vəm) ►*n., pl.* **o·va** (ō′və) The mature female gamete of animals. [Lat. *ōvum,* egg.]

owe (ō) ►*v.* **owed, ow·ing 1.** To have to pay or repay: *He owes me five dollars.* **2.** To be in debt to. **3.** To have a moral obligation to: *I owe them an apology.* **4.** To be indebted for. [< OE *āgan*, possess.]

Ow·ens (ō′ĭnz), **James Cleveland** "Jesse." 1913–80. Amer. athlete.

ow·ing (ō′ĭng) ►*adj.* Still to be paid; due.

owl (oul) ►*n.* Any of various usu. nocturnal birds of prey having large heads, short hooked beaks, and large eyes set forward. [< OE *ūle.*] —**owl′ish** *adj.*

owl·et (ou′lĭt) ►*n.* A young owl.

own (ōn) ►*adj.* Of or belonging to oneself. ►*n.* That which belongs to one. ►*v.* **1.** To have or possess. **2.** To admit or acknowledge. —*idiom:* **on (one's) own** Completely independent. [< OE *āgen.*] —**own′er** *n.* —**own′er·ship′** *n.*

ox (ŏks) ►*n., pl.* **ox·en** (ŏk′sən) **1.** An adult castrated bull. **2.** A bovine mammal, esp. a domesticated one. [< OE *oxa.*]

ox·al·ic acid (ŏk-săl′ĭk) ►*n.* A poisonous, crystalline organic acid used as a bleach and rust remover. [< Lat. *oxalis*, a plant.]

ox·blood red (ŏks′blŭd′) ►*n.* A deep reddish brown.

ox·bow (ŏks′bō′) ►*n.* **1.** A U-shaped collar for an ox. **2.** A U-shaped bend in a river.

ox·ford (ŏks′fərd) ►*n.* **1.** A low shoe that laces over the instep. **2.** A cotton cloth used primarily for shirts.

Oxford A city of S-central England on the Thames R. WNW of London.

ox·i·dant (ŏk′sĭ-dənt) ►*n.* An oxidizing agent.

ox·i·da·tion (ŏk′sĭ-dā′shən) ►*n.* **1.** The combination of a substance with oxygen. **2.** A reaction in which the atoms in an element lose electrons and the valence of the element is correspondingly increased. —**ox′i·da′tive** *adj.*

ox·ide (ŏk′sīd′) ►*n.* Divalent anionic oxygen or a compound of oxygen. —**ox·id′ic** (ŏk-sĭd′-ĭk) *adj.*

ox·i·dize (ŏk′sĭ-dīz′) ►*v.* **-dized, -diz·ing 1.** To combine with oxygen. **2.** To increase the positive charge or valence of (an element) by removing electrons. **3.** To coat with oxide. —**ox′i·di·za′tion** *n.* —**ox′i·diz′er** *n.*

Ox·o·ni·an (ŏk-sō′nē-ən) ►*adj.* Of or relating to Oxford or Oxford University. [< Med.Lat. *Oxōnia*, Oxford.] —**Ox·o′ni·an** *n.*

oxy– ►*pref.* Oxygen, esp. additional oxygen: *oxyacetylene.* [< OXYGEN.]

ox·y·a·cet·y·lene (ŏk′sē-ə-sĕt′l-ĭn, -ēn′) ►*adj.* Of or using a mixture of acetylene and oxygen: *an oxyacetylene torch.*

ox·y·gen (ŏk′sĭ-jən) ►*n. Symbol* **O** A nonmetallic element that constitutes 21 percent of the atmosphere by volume, is essential for plant and animal respiration, and is required for nearly all combustion. At. no. 8. See table at **element.** [Fr. *oxygène* : Gk. *oxus*, acid + –GEN.] —**ox′y·gen′ic** (-jĕn′ĭk) *adj.* —**ox·yg′e·nous** (ŏk-sĭj′ə-nəs) *adj.*

ox·y·gen·ate (ŏk′sĭ-jə-nāt′) ►*v.* **-at·ed, -at·ing** To treat, combine, or infuse with oxygen. —**ox′y·gen·a′tion** *n.*

oxygen mask ►*n.* A masklike device placed over the mouth and nose and through which oxygen is supplied from an attached tank.

oxygen tent ►*n.* A canopy placed usu. over the head and shoulders of a patient to provide oxygen at a higher level than normal.

ox·y·mo·ron (ŏk′sē-môr′ŏn′) ►*n., pl.* **-mo·rons** or **-mo·ra** (-môr′ə) A rhetorical figure in which incongruous or contradictory terms are combined, as in *a deafening silence.* [Gk. *oxumōron* : *oxus*, sharp + *mōros*, dull.] —**ox′y·mo·ron′ic** (-mə-rŏn′ĭk) *adj.*

oys·ter (oi′stər) ►*n.* Any of several edible bivalve mollusks that have a rough, irregularly shaped shell. [< Gk. *ostreon.*]

oz also **oz.** ►*abbr.* ounce

oz. ap. ►*abbr.* apothecaries' ounce

O·zark Plateau or **O·zark Mountains** (ō′zärk′) An upland region of the S-central US in SW MO, NW AR, and E OK.

oz. av. ►*abbr.* avoirdupois ounce

o·zone (ō′zōn′) ►*n.* An unstable, poisonous allotrope of oxygen, O_3, formed naturally from atmospheric oxygen by electric discharge or ultraviolet radiation, used to purify water and treat industrial wastes. [< Gk. *ozein*, to smell.]

ozone hole ►*n.* An area of the ozone layer periodically depleted of ozone, gen. occurring over the polar regions.

ozone layer ►*n.* A region of the atmosphere lying mostly in the stratosphere, between about 15 and 30 km (10 and 20 mi) in altitude, containing a relatively high concentration of ozone that absorbs solar ultraviolet radiation.

o·zo·no·sphere (ō-zō′nə-sfîr′) ►*n.* See **ozone layer.**

oz. t. ►*abbr.* troy ounce

P

p¹ or **P** (pē) ►*n., pl.* **p's** or **P's** also **ps** or **Ps** The 16th letter of the English alphabet.

p² ►*abbr.* proton

P ►*abbr.* **1.** pass **2.** pawn (chess) **3.** *Phys.* pressure

p. ►*abbr.* **1.** page **2.** part **3.** participle **4.** past **5.** penny **6.** pint

PA ►*abbr.* **1.** or **Pa.** Pennsylvania **2.** physician's assistant **3.** power of attorney **4.** production assistant **5.** prosecuting attorney **6.** public-address system

p.a. ►*abbr.* per annum

pa·an·ga (päng′gə, pä-äng′-) ►*n.* See table at **currency.** [Tongan.]

PABA (pä′bə) ►*n.* A compound used in some sunscreens to absorb ultraviolet light. [*p(ara)-a(mino)b(enzoic) a(cid)*.]

pab·u·lum (păb′yə-ləm) ►*n.* A substance that gives nourishment, esp. a soft food. [Lat. *pābulum.*]

PAC ►*abbr.* political action committee

pace (pās) ►*n.* **1.** A step that is made in walking. **2.** The distance spanned by such a step. **3.** Rate of movement or progress. **4.** A manner of walking or running: *a jaunty pace.* **5.** A gait of a horse in which both feet on one side leave and return to the ground together. ►*v.* **paced,**

pac·ing 1. To walk or stride back and forth. **2.** To measure by counting the number of steps needed to cover a distance. **3.** To set or regulate the rate of speed for. **4.** To train (a horse) in a particular gait, esp. the pace. [< Lat. *passus*.] —**pac′er** *n*.

pace·mak·er (pās′mā′kər) ►*n*. **1.** One who sets the pace in a race. **2.** A leader in a field. **3.** A surgically implanted electronic device used to regulate the heartbeat. —**pace′mak′-ing** *adj. & n.*

pach·y·derm (păk′ĭ-dûrm′) ►*n*. A large, thick-skinned, hoofed mammal such as the elephant or rhinoceros. [< Gk. *pakhudermos*, thick-skinned.]

pach·y·san·dra (păk′ĭ-săn′drə) ►*n*. An evergreen creeping plant often planted as a ground cover. [< Gk. *pakhus*, thick + Gk. *aner, andr-*, man, male.]

pa·cif·ic (pə-sĭf′ĭk) ►*adj*. **1.** Tending to diminish conflict. **2.** Of a peaceful nature; tranquil. —**pa·cif′i·cal·ly** *adv*.

Pacific Islander ►*n*. A native or inhabitant of any of the islands of Oceania.

Pacific Islands, Trust Territory of the A group of islands and islets of the NW Pacific administered by the US from 1947 to 1978.

Pacific Northwest A region consisting of the US states of WA and OR and sometimes defined as also including SW British Columbia, Canada.

Pacific Ocean The largest of the world's oceans, divided into the **North Pacific** and the **South Pacific** and extending from the W Americas to E Asia and Australia.

pac·i·fi·er (păs′ə-fī′ər) ►*n*. A rubber or plastic nipple for a baby to suck or chew on.

pac·i·fism (păs′ə-fĭz′əm) ►*n*. Opposition to war or violence as a means of resolving disputes. —**pac′i·fist** *n*. —**pac′i·fis′tic** *adj*.

pac·i·fy (păs′ə-fī′) ►*v*. **-fied, -fy·ing 1.** To ease the agitation of; calm. **2a.** To subdue war or violence in. **b.** To cause (a group) to end a rebellion. [< Lat. *pāx, pāc-*, peace.] —**pac′i·fi·ca′tion** *n*.

pack (păk) ►*n*. **1a.** A collection of items tied up or wrapped; bundle. **b.** A container made to be carried on the back. **2.** A small package containing a standard number of identical or similar items: *a pack of matches*. **3.** A complete set of related items: *a pack of cards*. **4a.** A group of animals, such as wolves. **b.** A gang or group of people. **5.** A material, such as gauze, that is applied to the body for therapeutic purposes. ►*v*. **1.** To fold, roll, or combine into a bundle. **2a.** To put into a receptacle for transporting or storing. **b.** To fill up with items: *pack one's trunk*. **3a.** To crowd together tightly. **b.** To fill up tight; cram. **4.** To wrap tightly, as for protection. **5.** To press together; compact firmly. **6.** *Informal* To carry: *pack a pistol*. **7.** To send unceremoniously: *packed the children off to bed*. **8.** To rig (a voting panel) to be favorable to one's purposes. [ME.]

pack·age (păk′ĭj) ►*n*. **1.** A wrapped or boxed object; parcel. **2.** A combination of items that are offered as a unit: *a benefits package*. ►*v*. **-aged, -ag·ing** To place or make into a package.

package store ►*n*. A store that sells alcoholic beverages for consumption off the premises.

pack·ag·ing (păk′ə-jĭng) ►*n*. **1.** Material used for making packages. **2.** The manner in which something is presented to the public.

pack animal ►*n*. An animal, such as a mule, used to carry loads.

pack·er (păk′ər) ►*n*. **1.** One that packs. **2.** One who processes and packs goods, usu. meat products.

pack·et (păk′ĭt) ►*n*. **1.** A small package or bundle. **2.** A regularly scheduled passenger and cargo boat.

pack·ing (păk′ĭng) ►*n*. **1.** The processing and packaging of manufactured products, esp. food products. **2.** Material used to prevent breakage or seepage.

pack rat ►*n*. **1.** Any of various small North or Central American rodents that collect a great variety of small objects. **2.** *Slang* A collector of miscellaneous objects.

pack·sad·dle (păk′săd′l) ►*n*. A saddle on which loads can be secured.

pact (păkt) ►*n*. **1.** A formal agreement; treaty. **2.** An arrangement between people; compact. See **agreement**. [< Lat. *pactum*.]

pad¹ (păd) ►*n*. **1.** Soft material used esp. to fill, give shape, or protect against injury. **2.** A number of sheets of paper glued together at one end; tablet. **3.** The broad floating leaf of an aquatic plant such as the water lily. **4.** The cushionlike flesh on the underpart of the feet of many animals. **5.** A launch pad. **6.** *Slang* One's apartment or room. ►*v*. **pad·ded, pad·ding 1.** To line or stuff with soft material. **2.** To lengthen or fill out with extraneous material. [?]

pad² (păd) ►*v*. **pad·ded, pad·ding** To go about quietly on foot. [Prob. of LGer. orig.]

pad·ding (păd′ĭng) ►*n*. Material that is used to pad.

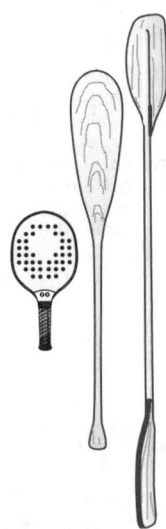

paddle¹
left to right: paddleball, canoe, and kayak paddles

pad·dle¹ (păd′l) ►*n*. **1.** A wooden implement having a blade at one end or at both ends, used to propel a canoe or small boat. **2.** Any of various implements resembling a paddle, used esp. for stirring, mixing, or beating. **3.** A light wooden racket used in playing table tennis. **4.** A board on a paddle wheel. ►*v.* **-dled, -dling 1.** To move or propel through water with or as if with a paddle. **2.** To stir or beat with a paddle. [ME *padell*, cleaning implement.] —**pad′dler** *n.*

pad·dle² (păd′l) ►*v.* **-dled, -dling** To dabble about in shallow water; splash gently with the hands or feet. [Perh. of LGer. orig.]

pad·dle·board (păd′l-bôrd′) ►*n.* A long narrow floatable board that a rider propels over the water, often in a standing position by means of a paddle.

paddle wheel ►*n.* A wheel with boards or paddles around its rim, used to propel a ship.

pad·dock (păd′ək) ►*n.* **1.** A fenced area, usu. near a stable, used chiefly for grazing horses. **2.** An enclosure at a racetrack where horses are saddled and paraded before a race. [< OE *pearroc*.]

pad·dy (păd′ē) ►*n., pl.* **-dies** An irrigated or flooded field where rice is grown. [Malay *padi*.]

paddy wagon ►*n. Slang* A van used by police for taking suspects into custody. [?]

pad·lock (păd′lŏk′) ►*n.* A lock with a U-shaped bar that is passed through the staple of a hasp or a link in a chain and then snapped shut. [ME *padlok*.] —**pad′lock′** *v.*

Pa·de·rew·ski (păd′ə-rĕf′skē, -rĕv′-, pä′də-), **Ignace** (or **Ignacy**) **Jan** 1860–1941. Polish pianist and politician.

pad thai (păd′ tī′, päd′) ►*n.* A Thai dish of stir-fried rice noodles, egg, peanuts, and other ingredients. [Thai *phàd thaj*, Thai fried dish.]

Pad·u·a (păj′ōō-ə, păd′yōō-ə) A city of NE Italy W of Venice.

pae·an (pē′ən) ►*n.* A song of joyful praise or exultation. [< Gk. *Paian*, Apollo.]

pa·el·la (pä-ĕl′ə, pä-ā′yä) ►*n.* A Spanish dish made with rice, vegetables, meat, and seafood. [< Lat. *patella*, pan.]

Paes·tum (pĕs′təm, pē′stəm) An ancient city of S Italy on the Gulf of Salerno.

pa·gan (pā′gən) ►*n.* One who is not a Christian, Muslim, or Jew. [< Lat. *pāgānus*, country dweller.] —**pa′gan** *adj.* —**pa′gan·ism** *n.*

Pa·ga·ni·ni (păg′ə-nē′nē, pä′gä-), **Niccolò** 1782–1840. Italian violinist and composer.

page¹ (pāj) ►*n.* **1.** A sheet of paper or one side of a sheet, as of a book, letter, or manuscript. **2.** *Comp.* A webpage. ►*v.* **paged, pag·ing 1.** To number the pages of. **2.** To turn pages: *page through a magazine.* [< Lat. *pāgina*.]

page² (pāj) ►*n.* **1.** A youth in attendance at court. **2.** One who is employed to run errands, carry messages, or act as a guide, as in a hotel. **3.** One who is similarly employed in the US Congress or another legislature. ►*v.* **paged, pag·ing 1.** To summon or call (a person) by name. **2.** To contact (someone) by sending a message to his or her pager: *The doctor was paged during dinner.* [< OFr.]

pag·eant (păj′ənt) ►*n.* **1.** An elaborate public spectacle depicting a historical event. **2a.** A spectacular procession or celebration. **b.** A contest in which a number of people are judged with regard to their physical beauty. **3.** A usu. pompous or ostentatious display. [< Med.Lat. *pāgina*, mystery play.] —**pag′eant·ry** *n.*

page·boy (pāj′boi′) ►*n.* **1.** A person, usu. a

boy, who serves as a page. **2.** A usu. shoulder-length hairstyle, with the ends of the hair curled under.

page·jack (pāj′jăk′) ►*v.* **1.** To copy material from (a website) and insert it into another website so that a search engine will direct unwitting users to that site. **2.** To control the contents of (a website) by fraud, as by inducing the domain provider to transfer the site's ownership. [(WEB)PAGE + (HI)JACK.]

pag·er (pā′jər) ►*n.* A simple wireless communications device that receives text messages or alerts.

pag·i·na·tion (păj′ə-nā′shən) ►*n.* **1.** The system by which pages are numbered. **2.** The arrangement and number of pages in a book. —**pag′i·nate** *v.*

pa·go·da (pə-gō′də) ►*n.* A multistory Buddhist tower with overhanging eaves at each level, built as a memorial or shrine. [Port. *pagode*.]

Pa·go Pa·go (päng′ō päng′ō, päng′gō päng′gō) The capital of American Samoa, on an island in the SW part.

Pah·la·vi (pä′lə-vē′), **Mohammad Reza** 1919–80. Shah of Iran (1941–79).

paid (pād) ►*v.* P.t. and p.part. of **pay.**

pail (pāl) ►*n.* A watertight cylindrical vessel with a handle; bucket. [ME *paile*.]

pain (pān) ►*n.* **1.** An unpleasant feeling symptomatic of injury or disease. **2.** Suffering or distress. **3. pains** Great care or effort: *take pains with one's work.* **4.** *Informal* A source of annoyance. ►*v.* To cause or suffer pain. —*idiom:* **on (or under) pain of** Subject to the penalty of a specified punishment, such as death. [< Gk. *poinē*, penalty.] —**pain′ful** *adj.* —**pain′ful·ly** *adv.* —**pain′less** *adj.* —**pain′less·ly** *adv.*

　　Syns: ache, pang, throe, twinge **n.**

Paine (pān), **Thomas** 1737–1809. British-born writer and Amer. Revolutionary leader.

pain·kill·er (pān′kĭl′ər) ►*n.* An agent, such as an analgesic drug, that relieves pain. —**pain′kill′ing** *adj.*

pains·tak·ing (pānz′tā′kĭng, pān′stā′kĭng) ►*adj.* Acting with, showing, or involving great care. —**pains′tak′ing·ly** *adv.*

paint (pānt) ►*n.* **1a.** A liquid mixture, usu. of a solid pigment in a liquid vehicle, used as a decorative or protective coating. **b.** The dry film formed by such a mixture when applied to a surface. **2.** Cosmetics applied esp. to the face. ►*v.* **1a.** To represent with paints. **b.** To depict vividly in words. **2.** To coat or decorate with paint. **3.** To apply cosmetics to. [< Lat. *pingere*, to paint.] —**paint′er** *n.*

paint·brush (pānt′brŭsh′) ►*n.* A brush for applying paint.

Paint·ed Desert (pān′tĭd) A plateau region of N-central AZ SE of the Grand Canyon.

paint·ing (pān′tĭng) ►*n.* **1.** The process, art, or occupation of working with paint. **2.** A picture or design in paint.

pair (pâr) ►*n., pl.* **pair** or **pairs 1.** Two corresponding persons or items similar in form or function: *a pair of shoes.* **2.** One object composed of two joined, similar parts: *a pair of pliers.* **3.** Two persons or animals considered together. ►*v.* **1.** To arrange in sets of two; couple. **2.** To form pairs or a pair. [< Lat. *paria*, equals.]

pais·ley (pāz′lē) ►*adj.* Having a colorful swirled

pattern of abstract curved shapes. [After *Paisley*, Scotland.]

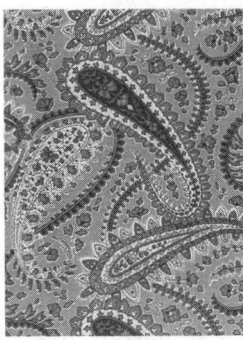

paisley

Pai·ute (pī′yo͞ot′) ►*n.*, *pl.* **-ute** or **-utes** A member of either of two distinct Native American peoples, the Northern Paiute and the Southern Paiute, of the W US.

pa·ja·mas (pə-jä′məz, -jăm′əz) ►*pl.n.* A loose-fitting garment consisting of trousers and a shirt or top, worn for sleeping or lounging. [Hindi *pāijāma*, loose-fitting trousers.]

Pak·i·stan (păk′ĭ-stăn′, pä′kĭ-stän′) A country of S Asia on the Arabian Sea. Cap. Islamabad. —**Pak′i·stan′i** (-stăn′ē, -stä′nē) *adj. & n.*

pa·kor·a (pə-kôr′ə) ►*n.* A traditionally South Asian deep-fried fritter having a chickpea batter. [Hindi and Urdu *pakorā* < Skt. *pakvavaṭaḥ.*]

pal (păl) *Informal* ►*n.* A friend; chum. ►*v.* **palled, pal·ling** To spend time with a friend. [Romany *phral, phal.*]

pal·ace (păl′ĭs) ►*n.* **1.** The official residence of a royal personage. **2.** A large or splendid residence. [< Lat. *Palātium* (Palatine Hill), Rome.]

pal·a·din (păl′ə-dĭn) ►*n.* A paragon of chivalry; heroic champion. [< LLat. *palātīnus*, palatine.]

pal·an·quin (păl′ən-kēn′, păl′ən-kwĭn′) ►*n.* A covered litter carried on poles on the shoulders of multiple bearers. [< Skt. *palyaṅkaḥ*, couch.]

pal·at·a·ble (păl′ə-tə-bəl) ►*adj.* **1.** Agreeable to the taste. **2.** Acceptable to the mind or sensibilities: *a palatable solution.*

pal·ate (păl′ĭt) ►*n.* **1.** The roof of the mouth, consisting of the hard palate and the soft palate. **2.** The sense of taste. [< Lat. *palātum.*] —**pal′a·tal** *adj.*

pa·la·tial (pə-lā′shəl) ►*adj.* **1.** Of or suitable for a palace. **2.** Of the nature of a palace, as in spaciousness or ornateness. [< Lat. *Palātium*, imperial residence.]

pa·lat·i·nate (pə-lăt′n-āt′, -ĭt) ►*n.* The office or territory of a palatine.

pal·a·tine (păl′ə-tīn′) ►*n.* **1.** A title for various officials of the late Roman and Byzantine empires. **2.** A feudal lord exercising sovereign power over his lands. ►*adj.* **1.** Belonging to or fit for a palace. **2.** Of a palatine or palatinate. [< Lat. *Palātium*, imperial residence.]

Pa·lau (pä-lou′, pə-) A nation consisting of about 200 islands in the Caroline Is. of the W Pacific. Cap. Melekeok.

pa·lav·er (pə-lăv′ər, -lä′vər) ►*n.* Long and idle chatter. [< LLat. *parabola*, speech, parable.] —**pa·lav′er** *v.*

pale¹ (pāl) ►*n.* **1.** A stake or pointed stick; picket. **2.** A fence enclosing an area. **3.** The area enclosed by a fence or boundary. —*idiom:* **beyond the pale** Irrevocably unacceptable or unreasonable. [< Lat. *pālus.*]

pale² (pāl) ►*adj.* **pal·er, pal·est 1.** Whitish in complexion; pallid. **2.** Of a low intensity of color; light. **3.** Of a low intensity of light; dim or faint. [< Lat. *pallēre*, be pale.] —**pale** *v.* —**pale′ness** *n.*

paleo– or **pale–** ►*pref.* Ancient or prehistoric: *paleography.* [< Gk. *palaios*, ancient.]

pa·le·o·bi·ol·o·gy (pā′lē-ō-bī-ŏl′ə-jē) ►*n.* The study of ancient organisms by means of their fossils. —**pa′le·o·bi·ol′o·gist** *n.*

Pa·le·o·cene (pā′lē-ə-sēn′) *Geol.* ►*adj.* Of or being the 1st epoch of the Tertiary Period, marked by the appearance of placental mammals. ►*n.* The Paleocene Epoch.

pa·le·og·ra·phy (pā′lē-ŏg′rə-fē) ►*n.* The study of ancient written documents. —**pa′le·og′ra·pher** *n.* —**pa′le·o·graph′ic** (-ə-grăf′ĭk), **pa′le·o·graph′i·cal** *adj.*

Pa·le·o·lith·ic (pā′lē-ə-lĭth′ĭk) ►*adj.* Of or being the Stone Age period beginning with the earliest chipped stone tools, about 2.4 million years ago, until the beginning of the Mesolithic, about 15,000 to 11,500 years ago. ►*n.* The Paleolithic Period.

pa·le·on·tol·o·gy (pā′lē-ŏn-tŏl′ə-jē) ►*n.* The study of the forms of life existing in prehistoric or geologic times. —**pa′le·on′to·log′i·cal** (-ŏn′tə-lŏj′ĭ-kəl) *adj.* —**pa′le·on·tol′o·gist** *n.*

Pa·le·o·zo·ic (pā′lē-ə-zō′ĭk) ►*adj.* Of or being the 2nd geologic era, including the Cambrian, Ordovician, Silurian, Devonian, Mississippian, Pennsylvanian, and Permian Periods. ►*n.* The Paleozoic Era.

Pa·ler·mo (pə-lâr′mō, pä-lĕr′-) A city of NW Sicily, Italy, on the Tyrrhenian Sea.

Pal·es·tine (păl′ĭ-stīn′) A region of SW Asia on the E Mediterranean shore, roughly coextensive with modern Israel and the West Bank. —**Pal′es·tin′i·an** (-stĭn′ē-ən) *adj. & n.*

pal·ette (păl′ĭt) ►*n.* **1.** A board, usu. with a hole for the thumb, on which the artist mixes colors. **2.** The range of colors on a palette. [< OFr., small spade.]

pal·i·mo·ny (păl′ə-mō′nē) ►*n.* *Informal* An allowance for support made under court order and given by one partner to the other after they have separated.

pal·imp·sest (păl′ĭmp-sĕst′) ►*n.* A manuscript, usu. of papyrus or parchment, that has been written on more than once, with the earlier writing incompletely erased. [< Gk. *palimpsēstos*, scraped again.]

pal·in·drome (păl′ĭn-drōm′) ►*n.* A word, phrase, verse, or sentence that reads the same backward or forward, as *A man, a plan, a canal, Panama!* [< Gk. *palindromos*, running back again.]

pal·ing (pā′lĭng) ►*n.* **1.** A pale; picket. **2.** A fence made of pales or pickets.

pal·i·sade (păl′ĭ-sād′) ►*n.* A fence of pales forming a defense barrier or fortification. [< OProv. *palissa*, stake.]

pall¹ (pôl) ►*n.* **1.** A cover for a coffin, bier, or tomb, often made of velvet. **2.** A coffin. **3.** A covering that darkens or obscures: *a pall of smoke.* [< Lat. *pallium*, cloak.]

pall² (pôl) ►*v.* **1.** To become insipid, boring, or wearisome. **2.** To cloy; satiate. [ME *pallen*, grow feeble.]

Pal·la·dio (pə-lä′dē-ō), **Andrea** 1508–80. Italian architect. —**Pal·la′di·an** (-lä′dē-ən) *adj.*

pal·la·di·um (pə-lä′dē-əm) ►*n. Symbol* **Pd** A ductile, lustrous gray-white, tarnish-resistant, metallic element alloyed for use in electric contacts, jewelry, nonmagnetic watch parts, and surgical instruments. At. no. 46. See table at **element.** [< the asteroid *Pallas.*]

pall·bear·er (pôl′bâr′ər) ►*n.* One carrying or attending a coffin at a funeral.

pal·let¹ (păl′ĭt) ►*n.* A portable platform used for storing or moving cargo or freight. [< OFr. *palete*, small spade.]

pal·let² (păl′ĭt) ►*n.* A narrow, hard bed or straw-filled mattress. [< LLat. *palea*, straw.]

pal·li·ate (păl′ē-āt′) ►*v.* **-at·ed, -at·ing 1.** To make less severe or intense; mitigate. **2.** To alleviate the symptoms of. **3.** To make (an offense or crime) seem less serious. [< Lat. *pallium*, cloak.] —**pal′li·a′tion** *n.* —**pal′li·a′tive** *adj. & n.*

pal·lid (păl′ĭd) ►*adj.* **1.** Pale or wan in color or complexion. **2.** Lacking in vitality; dull. [Lat. *pallidus* < *pallēre*, be pale.]

pal·lor (păl′ər) ►*n.* Extreme or unnatural paleness. [< Lat. < *pallēre*, be pale.]

palm¹ (päm) ►*n.* The inner surface of the hand, extending from the wrist to the base of the fingers. ►*v.* To conceal (something) in the palm of the hand. —*phrasal verb:* **palm off** To dispose of or pass off by deception. [< Lat. *palma.*]

palm² (päm) ►*n.* **1.** Any of numerous chiefly tropical evergreen trees, shrubs, or woody vines usu. having an unbranched trunk with a crown of large pinnate or palmate leaves. **2.** An emblem of victory, success, or joy. [< Lat. *palma.*]

pal·mate (păl′māt′, päl′-, päl′māt′) also **pal·mat·ed** (-mā′tĭd) ►*adj.* **1.** Shaped like a hand with the fingers extended. **2.** *Zool.* Webbed. —**pal′mate·ly** *adv.*

pal·met·to (păl-mĕt′ō) ►*n., pl.* **-tos** or **-toes** Any of several palms with fan-shaped leaves, esp. a small one of the SE US having leaf stalks with sharp spines. [Sp. *palmito.*]

palm·is·try (pä′mĭ-strē) ►*n.* The practice or art of telling fortunes from the patterns on the palms of the hands. —**palm′ist** *n.*

Palm Sunday ►*n.* The Sunday before Easter, observed by Christians in commemoration of Jesus's entry into Jerusalem.

palm·y (pä′mē) ►*adj.* **-i·er, -i·est 1.** Of, relating to, or covered with palm trees. **2.** Prosperous; flourishing.

pal·o·mi·no (păl′ə-mē′nō) ►*n., pl.* **-nos** A horse with a golden or tan coat and a white or cream-colored mane and tail. [< Sp., young dove.]

pal·pa·ble (păl′pə-bəl) ►*adj.* **1.** Capable of being touched or felt; tangible. **2.** Easily perceived; obvious. [< LLat. *palpāre*, touch.] —**pal′pa·bly** *adv.*

pal·pate (păl′pāt′) ►*v.* **-pat·ed, -pat·ing** To examine by touching (an area of the body). [Lat. *palpāre*, touch.] —**pal·pa′tion** *n.*

pal·pi·tate (păl′pĭ-tāt′) ►*v.* **-tat·ed, -tat·ing**

1. To tremble, shake, or quiver. **2.** To beat with excessive rapidity; throb. [< Lat. *palpāre*, touch.] —**pal′pi·ta′tion** *n.*

pal·sy (pôl′zē) ►*n., pl.* **-sies** Complete or partial muscle paralysis. [< OFr. *paralisie*, PARALYSIS.] —**pal′sied** *adj.*

pal·try (pôl′trē) ►*adj.* **-tri·er, -tri·est 1.** Lacking in importance or worth; trivial. **2.** Inadequate; negligible: *a paltry sum.* **3.** Marked by lack of generosity; contemptible. [< obsolete *paltry*, trash.] —**pal′tri·ness** *n.*

pam·pa (păm′pə, păm′-) or **pam·pas** (păm′-pəs, păm′pəz) ►*n.* A treeless grassland area of South America south of the Amazon River. [< Quechua, flat field.]

pam·per (păm′pər) ►*v.* To treat with excessive indulgence. [ME *pamperen.*]

pam·phlet (păm′flĭt) ►*n.* An unbound printed work, usu. with a paper cover. [< *Pamphilus*, a short Latin poem of the 1100s.] —**pam′phlet·eer′** (-flĭ-tîr′) *n.*

pan¹ (păn) ►*n.* **1.** A shallow, wide, open container, usu. of metal and used for holding liquids, cooking, and other domestic purposes. **2.** A vessel similar in form to a pan. **3a.** A basin or depression in the earth. **b.** Hardpan. ►*v.* **panned, pan·ning 1.** To wash (e.g., gravel) in a pan for gold or other precious metal. **2.** *Informal* To criticize or review harshly. —*phrasal verb:* **pan out** To turn out well; be successful. [< OE *panne.*]

pan² (păn) ►*v.* **panned, pan·ning** To pivot a movie camera along a horizontal plane to follow an object or create a panoramic effect.

Pan ►*n. Gk. Myth.* The god of woods, fields, and flocks.

pan– ►*pref.* All: *panchromatic.* [Gk. < *pas*, all.]

pan·a·ce·a (păn′ə-sē′ə) ►*n.* A remedy for all diseases, evils, or difficulties; cure-all. [< Gk. *panakēs*, all-healing.]

pa·nache (pə-năsh′, -näsh′) ►*n.* **1.** Dash; verve. **2.** A bunch of feathers or a plume, esp. on a helmet. [< Ital. *pinnacchio*, plume.]

Pan·a·ma (păn′ə-mä′) **1.** A country of SE Central America. Cap. Panama. **2.** Also **Panama City** The capital of Panama, in the central part. —**Pan′a·ma′ni·an** (-mä′nē-ən) *adj. & n.*

Panama, Isthmus of An isthmus of Central America connecting North and South America.

Panama Canal A ship canal, about 82 km (51 mi), crossing the Isthmus of Panama between the Caribbean Sea and the Pacific.

Panama hat ►*n.* A natural-colored hat made from leaves of a palmlike tropical plant of South and Central America.

Pan-A·mer·i·can (păn′ə-mĕr′ĭ-kən) ►*adj.* Of North, South, and Central America.

pan·a·tel·a (păn′ə-tĕl′ə) ►*n.* A long, slender cigar. [Sp.]

pan-broil (păn′broil′) ►*v.* To cook over direct heat in an uncovered, usu. ungreased skillet.

pan·cake (păn′kāk′) ►*n.* A thin cake made of batter that is cooked on both sides.

pan·chro·mat·ic (păn′krō-măt′ĭk) ►*adj.* Sensitive to all colors, as film.

pan·cre·as (păng′krē-əs, păn′-) ►*n.* A long, irregularly shaped gland that produces insulin and secretes pancreatic juice into the intestine. [Gk. *pankreas.*] —**pan′cre·at′ic** (păng′krē-ăt′-ĭk, păn′-) *adj.*

pan·cre·a·ti·tis (păng′krē-ə-tī′tĭs, păn′-) ►*n.* Inflammation of the pancreas.

pan·da (păn′də) ►*n.* **1.** A black and white bear of the mountains of central China. **2.** An arboreal raccoonlike mammal of NE Asia. [Fr.]

panda

pan·dem·ic (păn-dĕm′ĭk) ►*adj.* **1.** Widespread; general. **2.** Epidemic over a wide geographic area. ►*n.* A pandemic disease. [< Gk. *pandēmos*, of all the people.]

pan·de·mo·ni·um (păn′də-mō′nē-əm) ►*n.* A condition or scene of noisy confusion. See Synonyms at **noise**. [< *Pandæmonium*, capital of Hell in Milton's *Paradise Lost.*]

pan·der (păn′dər) ►*v.* **1.** To act as a go-between or liaison in sexual intrigues. **2.** To cater to the lower tastes and desires of others. [< *Pandare*, character in Chaucer's *Troilus and Criseyde.*] —**pan′der, pan′der·er** *n.*

P and L ►*abbr.* profit and loss

Pan·do·ra (păn-dôr′ə) ►*n.* Gk. Myth. The first woman, who opened a box containing all the evils of human life.

pan·dow·dy (păn-dou′dē) ►*n., pl.* **-dies** Sliced fruit baked with sugar and spices in a deep dish, with a thick top crust.

pane (pān) ►*n.* **1.** A framed, glass-filled division of a window or door. **2.** The glass itself. [< Lat. *pannus*, cloth.]

pan·e·gyr·ic (păn′ə-jĭr′ĭk, -jī′rĭk) ►*n.* **1.** A speech or written composition of commendation or praise. **2.** Elaborate praise; encomium. [< Gk. *panēguris*, public assembly.] —**pan′e·gyr′i·cal** *adj.* —**pan′e·gyr′ist** *n.*

pan·el (păn′əl) ►*n.* **1.** A flat, usu. rectangular piece forming a raised, recessed, or framed part of the surface in which it is set. **2.** A vertical section of fabric. **3.** A thin wooden board, used as a painting surface. **4.** A board with switches or buttons to control an electric device. **5.** A list or group of persons for jury duty. **6.** A group of people gathered to discuss a topic, judge a contest, or act as a team on a quiz program. ►*v.* **-eled, -el·ing** or **-elled, -el·ling 1.** To cover, decorate, or furnish with panels. **2.** To separate into panels. [< Lat. *pannus*, cloth.]

pan·el·ing (păn′ə-lĭng) ►*n.* A section of panels or paneled wall.

pan·el·ist (păn′ə-lĭst) ►*n.* A member of a panel.

panel truck ►*n.* A small delivery truck with a fully enclosed body.

pang (păng) ►*n.* **1.** A sudden sharp bodily pain. See Synonyms at **pain**. **2.** A sudden, sharp feeling of emotional distress. [?]

Pan·gae·a (păn-jē′ə) ►*n.* A supercontinent that included all the world's landmasses in the late Paleozoic Era. [PAN– + Gk. *gaia*, earth.]

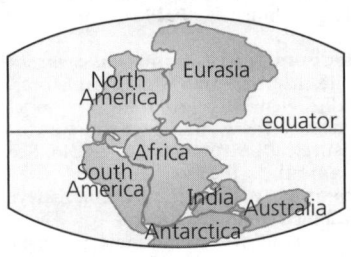

Pangaea

pan·han·dle[1] (păn′hăn′dl) ►*v.* **-dled, -dling** *Informal* To beg for money or food. See Synonyms at **cadge.** —**pan′han′dler** *n.*

pan·han·dle[2] (păn′hăn′dl) ►*n.* A narrow strip of territory projecting from a larger, broader area.

pan·ic (păn′ĭk) ►*n.* **1.** A sudden, overpowering terror, often affecting many people at once. **2.** A state of extreme anxiety. [< Gk. *Panikos*, of Pan (a source of terror, as in flocks or herds).] —**pan′ic** *v.* —**pan′ick·y** *adj.*

pan·i·cle (păn′ĭ-kəl) ►*n.* A loosely branched cluster of flowers, esp. a branching raceme. [Lat. *pānicula.*] —**pan′i·cled** *adj.*

Pan·ja·bi (pŭn-jä′bē, -jăb′ē) ►*n. & adj.* Var. of **Punjabi.**

Pank·hurst (păngk′hûrst′), **Emmeline Goulden** 1858–1928. British suffrage leader.

pan·nier (păn′yər, păn′ē-ər) ►*n.* **1.** A large wicker basket, esp. one carried on the back. **2.** One of a pair of baskets or packs carried on either side of an animal or vehicle, such as a bicycle. [< Lat. *pānārium*, breadbasket.]

pan·o·ply (păn′ə-plē) ►*n., pl.* **-plies 1.** A splendid or striking array: *a panoply of flags.* **2.** Something that covers and protects. **3.** The complete arms and armor of a warrior. [Gk. *panoplia.*]

pan·o·ram·a (păn′ə-răm′ə, -rä′mə) ►*n.* **1.** An unbroken view of a wide area. **2.** A picture or series of pictures representing a continuous scene. [PAN– + Gk. *horāma*, sight.] —**pan′o·ram′ic** *adj.*

pan·pipe (păn′pīp′) ►*n.* A wind instrument consisting of a series of pipes or reeds of graduated length bound together.

pan·sy (păn′zē) ►*n., pl.* **-sies** Any of various plants having flowers with velvety petals of various colors. [< OFr. *pensee*, thought, pansy.]

pant (pănt) ►*v.* **1.** To breathe rapidly in short gasps, as after exertion. **2.** To utter hurriedly or breathlessly. **3.** To long demonstratively; yearn. ►*n.* A short, labored breath; gasp. [ME *panten.*] —**pant′ing·ly** *adv.*

pan·ta·loon (păn′tə-lōōn′) ►*n.* often **pantaloons** Trousers, esp. tight trousers extending from waist to ankle. [< OItal. *Pantalone*, a comic character portrayed as an old man in tight trousers.]

pan·the·ism (păn′thē-ĭz′əm) ►*n.* A doctrine identifying the deity with the universe. —**pan′the·ist** *n.* —**pan′the·is′tic** *adj.*

pan·the·on (păn′thē-ŏn′, -ən) ►*n.* **1.** A temple

dedicated to all gods. **2.** All the gods of a people. **3.** A public building commemorating and dedicated to the heroes and heroines of a nation. [< Gk. *Pantheion.*]

pan·ther (păn′thər) ►*n.* **1.** A large wild cat such as a jaguar, esp. one having black fur. **2.** See **cougar.** [< Gk. *panthēr.*]

pant·ies (păn′tēz) ►*pl.n.* Short underpants for women or children.

pan·to·mime (păn′tə-mīm′) ►*n.* **1.** Communication by means of gesture and facial expression. **2.** A play, dance, or other theatrical performance presented in pantomime. [< Gk. *pantomimos,* pantomimic actor.] —**pan′to·mime** *v.* —**pan′to·mim′ic** (-mĭm′ĭk) *adj.* —**pan′to·mim′ist** (-mī′mĭst) *n.*

pan·try (păn′trē) ►*n., pl.* **-tries** A small room or closet where food, tableware, linens, and similar items are stored. [< OFr. *paneterie,* bread closet.]

pants (pănts) ►*pl.n.* **1.** Trousers. **2.** Underpants. [< PANTALOON.]

pant·suit also **pants suit** (pănt′so͞ot′) ►*n.* A woman's suit having trousers instead of a skirt.

pant·y·hose or **pant·y hose** (păn′tē-hōz′) ►*pl.n.* A woman's one-piece undergarment consisting of underpants and stockings.

pant·y·waist (păn′tē-wāst′) ►*n. Slang* A sissy.

pap (păp) ►*n.* **1.** Soft or semiliquid food, as for infants. **2.** Material lacking real value or substance. [ME < Lat. *pappa.*]

pa·pa (pä′pə, pə-pä′) ►*n. Informal* Father. [Fr.]

pa·pa·cy (pā′pə-sē) ►*n., pl.* **-cies 1.** The office and jurisdiction of a pope. **2.** The period of time during which a pope is in office. **3. Papacy** The system of church government headed by the pope. [< LLat. *pāpa,* POPE.]

pa·pal (pā′pəl) ►*adj.* Of or issued by a pope. [< LLat. *pāpa,* POPE.]

Papal States A group of territories in central Italy ruled by the popes (754–1870).

pa·paw (pô′pô) ►*n.* Var. of **pawpaw.**

pa·pa·ya (pə-pä′yə) ►*n.* **1.** An evergreen tropical American tree widely cultivated for its large yellow edible fruit. **2.** The fruit of this tree. [Sp., of Arawakan orig.]

Pa·pe·e·te (pä′pē-ā′tā, pə-pē′tē) The capital of French Polynesia, on the NW coast of Tahiti in the S Pacific.

pa·per (pā′pər) ►*n.* **1.** A material made of cellulose pulp, derived mainly from wood, rags, and certain grasses, processed into flexible sheets or rolls, and used for writing, printing, drawing, wrapping, and covering walls. **2.** A sheet of this material. **3.** A written work such as an essay or a treatise. **4.** often **papers** An official document, esp. one establishing the identity of the bearer. **5.** A newspaper. **6.** Wallpaper. ►*v.* To cover, wrap, or line with paper. [< Gk. *papuros,* papyrus.] —**pa′per·er** *n.* —**pa′per·y** *adj.*

pa·per·back (pā′pər-băk′) ►*n.* A book having a flexible paper binding.

pa·per·board (pā′pər-bôrd′) ►*n.* Cardboard; pasteboard.

pa·per·bound (pā′pər-bound′) ►*adj.* Bound in paper; paperback.

pa·per·hang·er (pā′pər-hăng′ər) ►*n.* One whose occupation is hanging wallpaper.

pa·per·less (pā′pər-lĭs) ►*adj.* Not requiring paper to record, convey, and store information.

paper tiger ►*n.* One that is seemingly dangerous and powerful but is in fact weak.

paper trail ►*n. Informal* A series of documents providing evidence of one's actions.

pa·per·weight (pā′pər-wāt′) ►*n.* A small, heavy object for holding down papers.

pa·per·work (pā′pər-wûrk′) ►*n.* Work involving the handling of reports, letters, and forms.

pa·pier-mâ·ché (pā′pər-mə-shā′, pă-pyā′-) ►*n.* A material, made from paper pulp or shreds of paper mixed with glue or paste, that can be molded into various shapes when wet. [Fr.] —**pa′pier-mâ·ché′** *adj.*

pa·pil·la (pə-pĭl′ə) ►*n., pl.* **-pil·lae** (-pĭl′ē) A small nipplelike projection, such as a protuberance on the tongue. [Lat., nipple.] —**pap′il·lar′y** (păp′ə-lĕr′ē, pə-pĭl′ə-rē) *adj.*

pa·pist (pā′pĭst) ►*n. Offensive* A Roman Catholic. [< LLat. *pāpa,* POPE.] —**pa′pist·ry** *n.*

pa·poose (pă-po͞os′, pə-) ►*n.* **1.** *Often Offensive* A Native American infant or very young child. **2.** A cradleboard. [Narragansett *papoòs.*]

pa·pri·ka (pă-prē′kə, pə-, păp′rĭ-kə) ►*n.* A powdered seasoning made from sweet red peppers. [Hung., ult. < Gk. *peperi,* pepper.]

Pap smear ►*n.* A test for cancer, esp. of the female genital tract. [After George *Papanicolaou* (1883–1962).]

Pap·u·a New Guinea (păp′yo͞o-ə, pä′po͞o-ä′) An island country of the SW Pacific comprising the E half of New Guinea and adjacent islands. Cap. Port Moresby. —**Pap′u·an** *adj. & n.* —**Pap′u·a New Guin′e·an** *adj. & n.*

pa·py·rus (pə-pī′rəs) ►*n., pl.* **-rus·es** or **-ri** (-rī′) **1.** A tall, aquatic, grasslike plant of Africa. **2.** A material made from the pith or stem of this plant, used esp. to write on. [< Gk. *papuros.*]

par (pär) ►*n.* **1.** An amount or a level considered to be average; standard. **2.** An equality of status, level, or value; equal footing. **3.** The established value of a monetary unit of a country. **4.** The face value of a stock or bond. **5.** The number of golf strokes considered necessary to complete a hole or course. [< Lat. *pār,* equal.]

para. ►*abbr.* paragraph

para– or **par–** ►*pref.* **1.** Beside; near: *parathyroid gland.* **2.** Beyond: *paranormal.* **3.** Subsidiary; assistant: *paralegal.* [< Gk. *para,* beside.]

par·a·ble (păr′ə-bəl) ►*n.* A simple story illustrating a moral or religious lesson. [< Gk. *parabolē.*]

pa·rab·o·la (pə-răb′ə-lə) ►*n.* A plane curve formed by the intersection of a right circular cone and a plane parallel to an element of the cone. [< Gk. *parabolē.*] —**par′a·bol′ic** (păr′ə-bŏl′ĭk) *adj.*

parabolic antenna ►*n.* An antenna that receives or sends electromagnetic signals such as radio waves or microwaves by using a parabolic surface.

Par·a·cel·sus (păr′ə-sĕl′səs) Theophrastus Bombastus von Hohenheim. 1493–1541. German-Swiss alchemist and physician.

par·a·chute (păr′ə-sho͞ot′) ►*n.* A light, usu. hemispherical apparatus used to retard free fall from an aircraft. ►*v.* **-chut·ed, -chut·ing** To drop by means of a parachute. [Fr.] —**par′a·chut′ist** *n.*

pa·rade (pə-rād′) ►*n.* **1.** An organized public procession on a festive or ceremonial occasion. **2.** A ceremonial review of troops. **3.** An extended, usu. showy succession. **4.** An osten tatious show; exhibition: *a parade of wealth.* ►*v.* **-rad·ed, -rad·ing 1.** To take part or cause to take part in a parade. **2.** To assemble for a ceremonial military review. **3.** To stroll in public; promenade. **4.** To exhibit ostentatiously; flaunt. [< Lat. *parāre*, prepare.]

par·a·digm (păr′ə-dīm′, -dĭm′) ►*n.* **1.** An example that serves as a pattern or a model. **2.** A list of all the inflectional forms of a word taken as an illustrative example. [< Gk. *paradeigma*.] —**par′a·dig·mat′ic** (-dĭg-măt′-ĭk) *adj.*

par·a·dise (păr′ə-dīs′, -dīz′) ►*n.* **1.** often **Paradise** Heaven. **2.** A place of ideal beauty or loveliness. [< Avestan (ancient Iranian language) *pairi-daēza-*, enclosure.] —**par′a·di·si′a·cal** (-dĭ-sī′ə-kəl, -zī′-) *adj.*

par·a·dox (păr′ə-dŏks′) ►*n.* **1.** A statement that seems to contradict itself but may nonetheless be true. **2.** One exhibiting inexplicable or contradictory aspects. [< Gk. *paradoxos*, conflicting with expectation.] —**par′a·dox′i·cal** *adj.* —**par′a·dox′i·cal·ly** *adv.*

par·af·fin (păr′ə-fĭn) ►*n.* **1.** A waxy white or colorless solid hydrocarbon mixture used to make candles, wax paper, lubricants, and sealing materials. **2.** *Chiefly Brit.* Kerosene. [< Lat. *parum*, little + Lat. *affīnis*, associated with.] —**par′af·fin′ic** *adj.*

par·a·foil (păr′ə-foil′) ►*n.* A nonrigid, parachutelike airfoil of ribbed or cellular construction. [PARA(CHUTE) + (AIR)FOIL.]

par·a·glid·er (păr′ə-glī′dər) ►*n.* A recreational aircraft consisting of a large parafoil from which a harnessed rider hangs. [PARA(FOIL) + GLIDER.]

par·a·gon (păr′ə-gŏn′, -gən) ►*n.* A model of excellence or perfection. [< OItal. *paragonare*, test on a touchstone.]

par·a·graph (păr′ə-grăf′) ►*n.* **1.** A distinct division of written or printed matter that consists of one or more sentences and typically deals with a single thought or topic. **2.** A mark (¶) used to indicate where a new paragraph should begin. **3.** A brief article, notice, or announcement, as in a newspaper. ►*v.* To divide or arrange into paragraphs. [< Gk. *paragraphein*, write beside : PARA– + *graphein*, write.]

Par·a·guay (păr′ə-gwī′, -gwā′) A country of S-central South America. Cap. Asunción. —**Par′a·guay′an** *adj. & n.*

par·a·keet (păr′ə-kēt′) ►*n.* Any of various small slender parrots, usu. having long tapering tails. [Sp. *periquito*.]

par·a·le·gal (păr′ə-lē′gəl) ►*n.* A person who assists a lawyer in the performance of various legal tasks. ►*adj.* Of or relating to the tasks performed by a paralegal.

par·al·lax (păr′ə-lăks′) ►*n.* A change in the apparent position of an object relative to more distant objects, caused by a change in the viewer's position. [< Gk. *parallassein*, change direction.]

par·al·lel (păr′ə-lĕl′) ►*adj.* **1.** Being an equal distance apart everywhere. **2a.** Having comparable parts or analogous aspects. **b.** Having the same tendency or direction. ►*adv.* In a parallel relationship or manner. ►*n.* **1a.** One that closely resembles another. **b.** A comparison indicating likeness; analogy. **2.** Any of the imaginary lines representing degrees of latitude

that encircle the earth parallel to the plane of the equator. **3.** *Electron.* An arrangement of components in a circuit that splits the current into two or more paths. ►*v.* **-leled, -lel·ing** also **-lelled, -lel·ling 1.** To make parallel. **2.** To be or extend parallel to. **3.** To be similar or analogous to. [< Gk. *parallēlos*.] —**par′al·lel·ism** *n.*

parallel bars ►*pl.n.* A piece of gymnastic equipment consisting of two horizontal bars, usu. set at the same height, on adjustable supports.

par·al·lel·e·pi·ped (păr′ə-lĕl′ə-pī′pĭd, -pĭp′ĭd) ►*n.* A solid with 6 faces, each a parallelogram and each being parallel to the opposite face. [Gk. *parallēlepipedon* : *parallēlos*, parallel + *epipedon*, plane surface : EPI– + *pedon*, ground.]

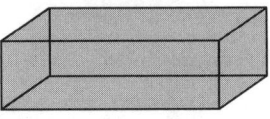

parallelepiped

par·al·lel·o·gram (păr′ə-lĕl′ə-grăm′) ►*n.* A four-sided plane figure with opposite sides parallel.

pa·ral·y·sis (pə-răl′ĭ-sĭs) ►*n., pl.* **-ses** (-sēz′) **1a.** Loss or impairment of the ability to move a body part. **b.** Loss of sensation over a region of the body. **2.** Total stoppage or severe impairment of activity. [< Gk. *paralusis*.] —**par′a·lyt′ic** (păr′ə-lĭt′ĭk) *adj. & n.*

par·a·lyze (păr′ə-līz′) ►*v.* **-lyzed, -lyz·ing 1.** To affect with paralysis. **2.** To make inoperative or powerless.

Par·a·mar·i·bo (păr′ə-măr′ə-bō′) The capital of Suriname, on the Suriname R. near its mouth on the Atlantic.

par·a·me·ci·um (păr′ə-mē′sē-əm, -shē-əm) ►*n., pl.* **-ci·a** (-sē-ə, -shē-ə) or **-ci·ums** Any of various freshwater, usu. slipper-shaped protozoans that move by means of cilia. [< Gk. *paramēkēs*, oblong.]

par·a·med·ic (păr′ə-mĕd′ĭk) ►*n.* A person who is trained to give emergency medical treatment or assist medical professionals.

pa·ram·e·ter (pə-răm′ĭ-tər) ►*n.* **1.** *Math.* A constant in an equation that can be varied to represent a family of curves or surfaces, such as the radius in a family of concentric circles. **2.** A measurable factor, such as temperature, that helps define a system and its behavior. **3.** *Informal* A limiting or restrictive factor. —**par′a·met′ric** (păr′ə-mĕt′rĭk) *adj.*

par·a·mil·i·tar·y (păr′ə-mĭl′ĭ-tĕr′ē) ►*adj.* Of or being a group of civilians organized in a military fashion.

par·a·mount (păr′ə-mount′) ►*adj.* **1.** Of chief concern or importance. **2.** Highest in rank or power. [AN *paramont*, above.]

par·a·mour (păr′ə-mōōr′) ►*n.* A lover, esp. a lover of a person who is married to someone else. [< AN *par amour*, by way of love.]

Pa·ra·ná (păr′ə-nä′, pä′rä-) A river rising in E-central Brazil and flowing about 2,895 km (1,800 mi) to E Argentina.

par·a·noi·a (păr′ə-noi′ə) ►*n.* A psychotic disorder characterized by delusions of persecution or grandeur. [Gk., madness.] —**par′a·noi′ac′** (-ăk′, -ĭk) *n.* —**par′a·noid′** *adj. & n.*

par·a·nor·mal (păr′ə-nôr′məl) ►*adj.* Beyond

the range of normal experience or scientific explanation.

par·a·pet (păr′ə-pĭt, -pĕt′) ►*n.* **1.** A low protective wall or railing along the edge of a raised structure such as a roof or balcony. **2.** An embankment protecting soldiers from enemy fire. [< Ital. *parapetto.*]

par·a·pher·na·lia (păr′ə-fər-nāl′yə, -fə-nāl′yə) ►*pl.n. (takes sing. or pl. v.)* **1.** The articles used in a particular activity. See Synonyms at **equipment. 2.** *Law* Personal property used by a married woman that, although actually owned by her husband and subject to creditors' claims, become her property after his death. [< Gk. *parapherna*, a married woman's property exclusive of her dowry : PARA– + *phernē*, dowry.]

par·a·phrase (păr′ə-frāz′) ►*n.* **1.** A restatement of a text or passage in another form or other words, often to clarify meaning. **2.** The adaptation of a text to serve a different purpose from that of the original. [< Gk. *paraphrasis.*] —**par′a·phrase′** *v.*

par·a·ple·gi·a (păr′ə-plē′jē-ə, -jə) ►*n.* Paralysis of the lower half of the body including both legs. [< Gk. *paraplēssein*, strike on one side.] —**par′a·ple′gic** (-jĭk) *adj. & n.*

par·a·pro·fes·sion·al (păr′ə-prə-fĕsh′ə-nəl) ►*n.* One trained to assist a professional.

par·a·psy·chol·o·gy (păr′ə-sī-kŏl′ə-jē) ►*n.* The study of paranormal phenomena, such as telepathy and clairvoyance.

par·a·site (păr′ə-sīt′) ►*n.* **1.** An organism that lives and feeds on or in an organism of a different species and causes harm to its host. **2.** One who habitually takes advantage of the generosity of others. [< Gk. *parasitos.*] —**par′a·sit·ism** (-sī-tīz′əm, -sī-) *n.* —**par′a·sit·ize′** (-sī-tīz′, -sī-) *v.*

par·a·sit·ic (păr′ə-sĭt′ĭk) also **par·a·sit·i·cal** (-ĭ-kəl) ►*adj.* **1.** Of or characteristic of a parasite. **2.** Caused by a parasite.

par·a·si·tol·o·gy (păr′ə-sī-tŏl′ə-jē, -sī-) ►*n.* The scientific study of parasites or parasitic populations. —**par′a·si·tol′o·gist** *n.*

par·a·sol (păr′ə-sôl′, -sŏl′) ►*n.* A light, usu. small umbrella carried as protection from the sun. [< Ital. *parasole.*]

par·a·sym·pa·thet·ic nervous system (păr′ə-sĭm′pə-thĕt′ĭk) ►*n.* The part of the autonomic nervous system that inhibits the effects of the sympathetic nervous system, resulting in decreased heart rate, dilation of blood vessels, and increased digestive secretions.

par·a·thy·roid gland (păr′ə-thī′roid) ►*n.* Any of four small kidney-shaped glands that lie in pairs near or within the thyroid gland and secrete a hormone necessary for the metabolism of calcium and phosphorus.

par·a·troops (păr′ə-trōōps′) ►*pl.n.* Infantry trained and equipped to parachute. —**par′a·troop′er** *n.*

par·a·ty·phoid fever (păr′ə-tī′foid′) ►*n.* An acute food poisoning, similar to typhoid fever but less severe.

par·boil (pär′boil′) ►*v.* To cook partially by boiling for a brief period. [< LLat. *perbullīre*, boil thoroughly.]

par·cel (pär′səl) ►*n.* **1.** Something wrapped up or packaged; package. **2.** A plot of land, usu. a division of a larger area. **3.** A quantity of merchandise offered for sale. **4.** A group

or company; pack. ►*v.* **-celed, -cel·ing** also **-celled, -cel·ling** **1.** To divide into parts and distribute. **2.** To make into a parcel; package. [< Lat. *particula*, portion.]

parcel post ►*n.* A postal service or department that handles and delivers packages.

parch (pärch) ►*v.* **1.** To make or become extremely dry, esp. by exposure to heat. See Synonyms at **dry. 2.** To make or become thirsty. [ME *parchen.*]

parch·ment (pärch′mənt) ►*n.* **1.** The skin of a sheep or goat prepared as a material on which to write or paint. **2.** A written text or drawing on a sheet of this material. [< Lat. *pergamēna.*]

par·don (pär′dn) ►*v.* **1.** To release (a person) from punishment. **2.** To let (an offense) pass without punishment. **3.** To forgive; excuse. ►*n.* **1.** Exemption of a convicted person from the penalties of an offense or a crime. **2.** Allowance or forgiveness for an offense or a discourtesy. [< VLat. *perdōnāre, give wholeheartedly : PER– + Lat. dōnāre, give (< dōnum, gift).] —**par′don·a·ble** *adj.* —**par′don·er** *n.*

pare (pâr) ►*v.* **pared, par·ing** **1.** To remove the outer covering or skin of: *pare apples.* **2.** To reduce, as in quantity or size; trim: *pare expenses.* [< Lat. *parāre*, prepare.] —**par′er** *n.*

par·e·gor·ic (păr′ə-gôr′ĭk, -gŏr′-) ►*n.* A camphorated tincture of opium, taken internally for the relief of diarrhea and intestinal pain. [< Gk. *parēgoros*, consoling.]

par·ent (pâr′ənt, păr′-) ►*n.* **1.** A father or mother. **2.** An ancestor; progenitor. **3.** An organism that produces or generates offspring. **4.** A source or cause; origin. ►*v.* To act as a parent (to). [< Lat. *parēns, parent-* < Lat. *parere*, give birth.] —**par′ent·age** *n.* —**pa·ren′tal** (pə-rĕn′tl) *adj.* —**par′ent·hood′** *n.*

pa·ren·the·sis (pə-rĕn′thĭ-sĭs) ►*n., pl.* **-ses** (-sēz′) **1.** Either or both of the upright curved lines, ( ), used to mark off explanatory or qualifying remarks or enclose a mathematical expression. **2.** A qualifying or amplifying word, phrase, or sentence inserted within a passage. [< Gk., insertion.] —**par′en·thet′i·cal** (păr′-ən-thĕt′ĭ-kəl), **par′en·thet′ic** (-ĭk) *adj.*

pa·re·sis (pə-rē′sĭs, păr′ĭ-sĭs) ►*n.* Slight or partial paralysis. [Gk.] —**pa·ret′ic** (pə-rĕt′ĭk) *adj. & n.*

pa·re·ve (pä′rə-və) also **par·ve** (pär′və) ►*adj.* Prepared without meat or milk and thus permissible to be eaten with meat or dairy dishes according to Jewish dietary laws. [Yiddish *pareve.*]

par ex·cel·lence (pär ĕk-sə-läns′) ►*adj.* Being of the highest degree; quintessential. [Fr.]

par·fait (pär-fā′) ►*n.* **1.** A dessert made of cream, eggs, sugar, and flavoring. **2.** A dessert made of several layers of different flavors of ice cream or ices, variously garnished. [< Lat. *perfectus*, perfect.]

par·he·li·on (pär-hē′lē-ən, -hēl′yən) ►*n., pl.* **-he·li·a** (-hē′lē-ə, -hēl′yə) A bright spot appearing on either side of the sun, often on a luminous ring or halo. [< Gk. *parēlios*, beside the sun.]

pa·ri·ah (pə-rī′ə) ►*n.* **1.** A social outcast. **2.** A Dalit. [Tamil *paṟaiyar.*]

pa·ri·e·tal (pə-rī′ĭ-təl) ►*adj.* **1.** *Anat.* **a.** Of or forming the wall of a body part, organ, or cavity. **b.** Of or in the region of the sides of the skull. **2.** Dwelling or having authority within the walls or buildings of a college. [< Lat. *pariēs,* wall.]

par·i·mu·tu·el (păr′ĭ-myōō′chōō-əl) ►*n.* A system of betting on races whereby the winners divide the total amount bet, less management expenses, in proportion to the sums they have wagered individually. [Fr. *pari-mutuel.*]

par·ing (pâr′ĭng) ►*n.* Something, such as a peel, that has been pared off.

pa·ri pas·su (păr′ē păs′ōō) ►*adv.* At an equal pace; side by side. [Lat. *parī passū.*]

Par·is¹ (păr′ĭs) ►*n.* Gk. Myth. The prince of Troy whose abduction of Helen provoked the Trojan war.

Par·is² (păr′ĭs) The capital of France, in the N-central part on the Seine R.

par·ish (păr′ĭsh) ►*n.* **1a.** An administrative part of a diocese having its own church. **b.** The members of such a parish. **2.** An administrative subdivision in Louisiana that corresponds to a county in other US states. [< LGk. *paroikia,* diocese < Gk. *paroikos,* neighboring.]

pa·rish·ion·er (pə-rĭsh′ə-nər) ►*n.* A member of a parish.

par·i·ty (păr′ĭ-tē) ►*n., pl.* **-ties 1.** Equality, as in amount, status, or value. **2.** The equivalent in value of a sum of money in a different currency at a fixed rate of exchange. **3.** A level for farm-product prices maintained by governmental support. [< Lat. *pār,* equal.]

park (pärk) ►*n.* **1.** An area of land set aside for public use, as for recreation. **2.** *Sports* A stadium or an enclosed playing field: *a baseball park.* **3.** An area in or near a town designed and usu. zoned for a certain purpose: *a commercial park.* ►*v.* **1.** To put or leave (a vehicle) for a time in a certain location. **2.** *Informal* To place or leave temporarily. [< OFr. *parc,* enclosure.]

par·ka (pär′kə) ►*n.* **1.** A hooded outer garment worn in the Arctic with the fur on the inside. **2.** A coat or jacket with a hood and usu. a warm lining. [Alaskan Russ., pelt.]

Par·ker (pär′kər), **Dorothy Rothschild** 1893–1967. Amer. writer.

Par·kin·son's disease (pär′kĭn-sənz) ►*n.* A progressive nervous disease chiefly of later life, marked by muscular tremor and slowing of movement. [After James *Parkinson* (1755–1824).]

par·kour (pär-kōōr′) ►*n.* A sport in which participants move quickly through a usu. urban area by surmounting obstacles and leaping across open spaces. [Fr., alteration of *parcours,* course.]

Rosa Parks
photographed in 1998

Parks (pärks), **Rosa** 1913–2005. Amer. civil rights leader.

park·way (pärk′wā′) ►*n.* A broad landscaped highway.

par·lance (pär′ləns) ►*n.* A particular manner of speaking; idiom: *legal parlance.* [< OFr. *parler,* speak; see PARLEY.]

par·lay (pär′lā′, -lē) ►*n.* A bet comprising the sum of a prior wager plus its winnings or a series of bets made in such a manner. [< Fr. *paroli.*] —**par′lay′** *v.*

par·ley (pär′lē) ►*n., pl.* **-leys** A discussion or conference, esp. between opponents. ►*v.* To have a discussion, esp. with an opponent. [< LLat. *parabolāre,* speak.]

par·lia·ment (pär′lə-mənt) ►*n.* **1.** A legislative body. **2. Parliament** The national legislature of various countries, esp. the United Kingdom. [< OFr. *parler,* talk.] —**par′lia·men′ta·ry** (-mən′tə-rē, -men′trē) *adj.*

par·lia·men·tar·i·an (pär′lə-měn-târ′ē-ən) ►*n.* **1.** One who is expert in parliamentary procedures, rules, or debate. **2.** A member of a parliament.

par·lor (pär′lər) ►*n.* **1.** A room in a private home set apart for the entertainment of visitors. **2.** A business establishment: *a funeral parlor.* [< OFr. *parlur < parler,* to talk.]

par·lous (pär′ləs) ►*adj.* Perilous; dangerous. [ME < *perilous,* PERILOUS.]

Par·ma (pär′mə) A city of N-central Italy SE of Milan.

Par·me·san (pär′mə-zän′, -zən, -zhän′) ►*n.* A hard Italian cheese usu. served grated as a garnish. [< Ital. *parmigiano,* of Parma.]

par·mi·gia·na (pär′mĭ-zhä′nə, -jä′-) ►*adj.* Made or covered with Parmesan cheese: *eggplant parmigiana.*

Par·na·í·ba (pär′nə-ē′bə, -nä-ē′bä) A river, about 1,290 km (800 mi), of NE Brazil flowing to the Atlantic.

Par·nas·sus (pär-năs′əs) A mountain, about 2,457 m (8,061 ft), of central Greece N of the Gulf of Corinth.

Par·nell (pär-něl′, pär′nəl), **Charles Stewart** 1846–91. Irish nationalist leader.

pa·ro·chi·al (pə-rō′kē-əl) ►*adj.* **1.** Of, supported by, or located in a parish. **2.** Narrowly restricted in scope or outlook; provincial: *parochial attitudes.* [< LLat. *parochia,* diocese; see PARISH.] —**pa·ro′chi·al·ism** *n.* —**pa·ro′chi·al·ly** *adv.*

parochial school ►*n.* A school supported by a religious organization.

par·o·dy (păr′ə-dē) ►*n., pl.* **-dies 1.** A satirical imitation, as of a literary work. **2.** Travesty: *a parody of justice.* [< Gk. *parōidia.*] —**par′o·dist** *n.* —**par′o·dy** *v.*

pa·role (pə-rōl′) ►*n.* **1.** Early release of a prisoner who is then subject to continued monitoring and other restrictions. **2.** Word of honor. ►*v.* **-roled, -rol·ing** To release on parole. [Fr., promise.] —**pa·rol·ee′** *n.*

pa·rot·id gland (pə-rŏt′ĭd) ►*n.* Either of the pair of salivary glands situated below and in front of each ear. [< Gk. *parōtis,* tumor near the ear : PARA- + *ous, ōt-,* ear.]

–parous ►*suff.* Giving birth to; bearing: *multiparous.* [< Lat. *parere,* give birth.]

par·ox·ysm (păr′ək-sĭz′əm) ►*n.* **1.** A sudden outburst, as of emotion. **2a.** A sudden attack or intensification of a disease. **b.** A spasm or fit;

convulsion. [< Gk. *paroxusmos* : PARA– + *oxu-nein*, sharpen, goad (< *oxus*, sharp).] —**par′ox·ys′mal** (-ək-sĭz′məl) *adj.*

par·quet (pär-kā′) ►*n.* **1.** A floor made of parquetry. **2.** The art or process of making parquetry. **3a.** The part of the main floor of a theater in front of the balcony. **b.** The entire main floor of a theater. [< OFr. *parc*, enclosure.]

par·quet·ry (pär′kĭ-trē) ►*n., pl.* **-ries** Inlay of wood, often of different colors, that is used esp. for floors.

Parr (pär), **Catherine** 1512–48. Queen of England as the sixth wife of Henry VIII.

par·ri·cide (pär′ĭ-sīd′) ►*n.* **1.** The killing of one's father, mother, or other near relative. **2.** The killing of the ruler of one's country. **3.** One who commits parricide. [Lat. *parricīda*.] —**par′ri·cid′al** (-sīd′l) *adj.*

par·rot (pär′ət) ►*n.* **1.** Any of numerous chiefly tropical and semitropical birds, marked by a short hooked bill, brightly colored plumage, and, in some species, the ability to mimic human speech. **2.** One who imitates the words or actions of another, esp. without understanding them. ►*v.* To repeat or imitate, esp. without understanding. [Prob. < Fr. dial. *Perrot*, dim. of *Pierre*, Peter.]

parrot fever ►*n.* See psittacosis.

par·ry (pär′ē) ►*v.* **-ried, -ry·ing 1.** To deflect or ward off. **2.** To evade skillfully; avoid. [< Ital. *parare*, defend.] —**par′ry** *n.*

parse (pärs) ►*v.* **parsed, pars·ing 1.** To provide a grammatical description of a word, group of words, or sentence. **2.** To examine or analyze closely. **3.** *Comp.* To analyze or separate (e.g., input) into more easily processed components. [< Lat. *pars*, part (of speech).] —**pars′er** *n.*

par·sec (pär′sĕk′) ►*n.* A unit of astronomical length equal to 3.258 light-years. [PAR(ALLAX) + SEC(OND)¹.]

par·si·mo·ny (pär′sə-mō′nē) ►*n.* Unusual or excessive frugality; stinginess. [< Lat. *parcere, pars-*, spare.] —**par′si·mo′ni·ous** *adj.* —**par′si·mo′ni·ous·ly** *adv.*

pars·ley (pär′slē) ►*n.* An herb having flat or curled leaves that are used for seasoning or as a garnish. [< Gk. *petroselinon*.]

pars·nip (pär′snĭp) ►*n.* **1.** A plant cultivated for its long, white, edible root. **2.** Its root. [< Lat. *pastināca*.]

par·son (pär′sən) ►*n.* **1.** An Anglican cleric in charge of a parish. **2.** A Protestant minister. [< Lat. *persōna*, character.]

par·son·age (pär′sə-nĭj) ►*n.* The official residence provided by a church for its parson.

part (pärt) ►*n.* **1.** A portion, division, or segment of a whole. **2.** A component of a system; detachable piece: *spare parts for cars.* **3.** often **parts** A region, area, land, or territory. **4a.** A role, as in a play. **b.** One's responsibility, duty, or obligation; share. **5.** *Mus.* **a.** The music or score for a particular instrument. **b.** One of the melodic divisions or voices of a composition. **6.** The line where the hair on the head is parted. ►*v.* **1.** To divide into two or more parts. **2.** To break up the relationship or association of: *The dispute parted the two partners.* **3.** To comb (e.g., hair) into a part. **4.** To go away from another; depart or take leave: *parted as friends.* ►*adv.* Partially; in part: *part blue, part green.* ►*adj.* Not full or complete; partial: *a part owner.* —**phrasal**

verb: **part with** To give up or let go of; relinquish. —*idioms:* **in part** To some extent; partly. **take part** To join in. [< Lat. *pars.*]

part. ►*abbr.* participle

par·take (pär-tāk′) ►*v.* **-took** (-tŏŏk′), **-tak·en** (-tā′kən), **-tak·ing 1.** To take or have a part or share; participate. **2.** To take or be given part or portion. [< ME *part-taker*, one who takes part.] —**par·tak′er** *n.*

par·terre (pär-târ′) ►*n.* A flower garden whose beds form a pattern. [< OFr. *par terre*, on the ground : *par*, on + *terre*, ground (< Lat. *terra*, earth).]

parterre

par·the·no·gen·e·sis (pär′thə-nō-jĕn′ĭ-sĭs) ►*n.* **1.** Reproduction in which an unfertilized egg develops into a new individual. **2.** The artificial activation of an unfertilized usu. mammalian egg, resulting in an embryolike cell cluster from which stem cells can be harvested. [< Gk. *parthenos*, virgin.] —**par′the·no·ge·net′ic** (-jə-nĕt′ĭk), **par′the·no·gen′ic** (-jĕn′ĭk) *adj.*

Par·thi·a (pär′thē-ə) An ancient country of SW Asia corresponding to modern NE Iran. —**Par′thi·an** *adj. & n.*

par·tial (pär′shəl) ►*adj.* **1.** Not total; incomplete. **2.** Favoring one person or side over another or others. **3.** Particularly fond: *partial to roses.* [< Lat. *pars*, part.] —**par′tial·ly** *adv.*

par·ti·al·i·ty (pär′shē-ăl′ĭ-tē, pär-shăl′-) ►*n., pl.* **-ties 1.** Prejudice or bias in favor of something. **2.** A special fondness. See Synonyms at predilection.

par·tic·i·pate (pär-tĭs′ə-pāt′) ►*v.* **-pat·ed, -pat·ing** To take part or share in something. [< Lat. *particeps*, partaker.] —**par·tic′i·pant** (-pənt), **par·tic′i·pa′tor** *n.* —**par·tic′i·pa′tion** *n.* —**par·tic′i·pa·to′ry** (-pə-tôr′ē) *adj.*

par·ti·ci·ple (pär′tĭ-sĭp′əl) ►*n.* A form of a verb that can function independently as an adjective and can be used with an auxiliary verb to indicate tense, aspect, or voice. [< Lat. *participium*.] —**par′ti·cip′i·al** (-ē-əl) *adj.*

Usage: The "dangling participle" is common in speech, but its use in writing can lead to unintentional absurdities, as in *He watched his horse take a turn around the track carrying a racing sheet under his arm.* Sometimes the solution lies in moving the participial phrase to be adjacent to the noun or pronoun it logically modifies. In this case, moving the phrase to the start of the sentence would work. In other cases, such as *Turning the corner, the view was quite different,* the sentence must be recast in different form: *When we turned the corner, the view was quite different.*

par·ti·cle (pär′tĭ-kəl) ►*n.* **1.** A very small piece or part; speck. **2.** A very small or the smallest possible amount. **3a.** An elementary particle. **b.** A subatomic particle. **4.** *Ling.* A word (e.g., a preposition) that has little meaning but specifies, connects, or limits the meanings of other words. [< Lat. *particula,* small part.]

particle accelerator ►*n.* A device, such as a cyclotron, that accelerates charged subatomic particles or nuclei to high energies.

particle decay ►*n.* Spontaneous disintegration of a subatomic particle with the emission of energetic particles or radiation.

par·ti-col·ored (pär′tē-kŭl′ərd) ►*adj.* Having parts or sections colored differently from each other. [< OFr. *parti,* divided, striped.]

par·tic·u·lar (pər-tĭk′yə-lər, pə-tĭk′-) ►*adj.* **1.** Belonging to or associated with a specific person, group, thing, or category. **2.** Distinctive among others; noteworthy. **3.** Attentive to or concerned with details, often excessively so; fussy. ►*n.* An individual item, fact, or detail. [< Lat. *particula,* small part.] **—par·tic′u·lar′i·ty** (lär′ĭ-tē) *n.* **—par·tic′u·lar·ly** *adv.*

par·tic·u·lar·ize (pər-tĭk′yə-lə-rīz′, pə-tĭk′-) ►*v.* **-ized, -iz·ing 1.** To mention, describe, or treat individually; itemize or specify. **2.** To go into or give details or particulars.

par·tic·u·late (pər-tĭk′yə-lĭt, -lāt′, pär-) ►*adj.* Of or formed of separate particles. **—par·tic′u·late** *n.*

part·ing (pär′tĭng) ►*n.* **1.** The act or process of separating or dividing. **2.** A departure or leave-taking. ►*adj.* Given, received, or done on departing or separating.

par·ti·san (pär′tĭ-zən) ►*n.* **1.** A strong supporter of a party, cause, faction, person, or idea. **2.** A guerrilla. [< OItal. *parte,* PART.] **—par′ti·san** *adj.* **—par′ti·san·ship′** *n.*

par·tite (pär′tīt′) ►*adj.* Divided into parts. [< Lat. *partīre,* divide.]

par·ti·tion (pär-tĭsh′ən) ►*n.* **1a.** The act or process of dividing something into parts. **b.** The state of being so divided. **2.** Something that divides or separates, as a wall dividing one room or cubicle from another. **3.** A part or section into which something has been divided. ►*v.* **1.** To divide into parts, pieces, or sections. **2.** To divide or separate by means of a partition.

part·ly (pärt′lē) ►*adv.* In part; not completely.

part·ner (pärt′nər) ►*n.* **1.** One associated with another in an activity or a sphere of common interest. **2.** A member of a business partnership. **3a.** A spouse. **b.** A domestic partner. **4.** Either of two persons who are dancing together. **5.** One of a pair or team in a sport or game. [< AN *parcen,* partition.] **—part′ner·ship′** *n.*

part of speech ►*n., pl.* **parts of speech** Any of the traditional grammatical classes of words according to their functions in context, such as the noun, verb, or adjective.

par·took (pär-tŏŏk′) ►*v.* P.t. of **partake.**

par·tridge (pär′trĭj) ►*n., pl.* **-tridge** or **-tridg·**

es Any of several plump-bodied game birds. [< Gk. *perdix.*]

part-time (pärt′tīm′) ►*adj.* For or during less than the customary or standard time: *a part-time job.* **—part′-time′** *adv.*

par·tu·ri·tion (pär′tyŏŏ-rĭsh′ən, -tŏŏ-, pär′-chə-) ►*n.* The act of giving birth; childbirth. [< Lat. *parturīre,* be in labor.]

part·way (pärt′wā′) ►*adv. Informal* To a certain degree or distance; in part.

par·ty (pär′tē) ►*n., pl.* **-ties 1a.** A social gathering. **b.** A group of people who have gathered to participate in a specific task or activity. **2.** A political group organized to promote and support its principles and candidates. **3a.** A participant or accessory: *I refuse to be a party to your scheme.* **b.** A person or group involved in a legal proceeding. ►*adj.* **1.** Of or relating to a political organization. **2.** Of or for use at a social gathering. ►*v.* **-tied, -ty·ing** *Informal* To celebrate or carouse at or as if at a party. [< OFr. *parti,* divided.]

party line ►*n.* **1.** One or more of the policies of a political party to which loyal members are expected to adhere. **2.** A telephone circuit connecting two or more subscribers with the same exchange.

par·ve (pär′və) ►*adj.* Var. of **pareve.**

par·ve·nu (pär′və-nōō′, -nyōō′) ►*n.* One who has risen to a higher social and economic class and has not yet gained acceptance by others in that class. [Fr. < *parvenir,* arrive : *par,* along + *venir,* come (< Lat. *venīre*).]

pas (pä) ►*n., pl.* **pas** (pä) A step or dance. [Fr. < Lat. *passus,* step.]

Pas·cal (pă-skăl′, pä-skäl′), **Blaise** 1623–62. French philosopher, mathematician, and inventor.

pas de deux (də dœ) ►*n., pl.* **pas de deux** A dance for two, esp. in ballet. [Fr.]

pa·sha (pä′shə, păsh′ə, pə-shä′) ►*n.* Used formerly as a title for military and civil officers, esp. in Turkey and N Africa. [Turk. *paşa.*]

pash·mi·na (păsh-mē′nə) ►*n.* **1.** Fine, downy wool growing beneath the outer hair of Himalayan goats. **2.** A soft fabric that is made of this wool. [Persian *pašmīne,* woolen garment, pashmina < *pašmīn,* made of wool < *pašm,* wool, down.]

Pash·to (pŭsh′tō) also **Push·tu** (pŭsh′tōō) ►*n.* The Iranian language spoken by the Pashtuns.

Pash·tun (pŭsh′tōōn) ►*n.* A member of an ethnic group of Afghanistan and parts of W Pakistan. [Pashto *Pəštūn.*]

pass (păs) ►*v.* **1.** To move on or ahead; proceed. **2.** To extend; run: *The river passes through town.* **3.** To move by or past. **4.** To elapse or allow to elapse. **5.** To cause to move: *passed her hand over the curtain.* **6a.** To transfer or be transferred from one to another. **b.** To hand over to someone else: *pass the bread.* **c.** To transfer (a ball or puck) to a teammate. **7.** To be communicated or exchanged. **8.** To come to an end. **9.** To happen; take place. **10.** To be allowed to happen without challenge: *let the remark pass.* **11.** *Games* To decline one's turn to play or bid. **12.** To undergo or cause to undergo a course or test with favorable results. **13.** To serve as a barely acceptable substitute. **14.** To approve or be approved, as by a legislature. **15.** *Law* To

make a decision: *to pass upon a legal question.* **16.** To discharge (bodily wastes); excrete. ►*n.* **1.** The act of passing. **2.** A narrow passage between mountains; way. **3.** A permit, ticket, or authorization to come or go at will. **4.** A sweep or run by a military aircraft over a target area. **5.** A complete cycle of operations, as by a computer program. **6.** A critical situation; predicament. **7.** A sexual invitation or overture. —*phrasal verbs:* **pass away** To end or die. **pass out** To lose consciousness. **pass up** To reject; turn down. [< Lat. *passus*, step.] —**pass′er** *n.*
Usage: The past tense and past participle of *pass* is *passed*: *They passed* (or *have passed*) *our home. Past* is the corresponding adjective (*in centuries past*), adverb (*drove past*), preposition (*past midnight; past the crisis*), and noun (*lived in the past*).

pass. ►*abbr.* passive

pass·a·ble (păs′ə-bəl) ►*adj.* **1.** Capable of being passed, traversed, or crossed; navigable. **2.** Satisfactory but not outstanding; adequate. —**pass′a·bly** *adv.*

pas·sage (păs′ĭj) ►*n.* **1.** The act or process of passing. **2.** Enactment into law of a legislative measure. **3a.** A journey, esp. by air or water. **b.** The right to travel as a passenger, esp. on a ship. **4a.** A path, channel, or duct through, over, or along which something may pass. **b.** A corridor. **5.** A segment of a written work or musical composition.

pas·sage·way (păs′ĭj-wā′) ►*n.* A corridor.

Pas·sa·ma·quod·dy (păs′ə-mə-kwŏd′ē) ►*n., pl.* **-dy** or **-dies 1.** A member of a Native American people inhabiting parts of coastal Maine and New Brunswick. **2.** The Algonquian language of the Passamaquoddy.

pass·book (păs′bŏŏk′) ►*n.* See **bankbook.**

pas·sé (pă-sā′) ►*adj.* **1.** No longer current or in fashion; out-of-date. **2.** Past the prime; faded or aged. [Fr. < *passer,* PASS.]

pas·sen·ger (păs′ən-jər) ►*n.* A person who travels in a conveyance, such as a car or train. [< OFr. *passageor.*]

passe-par·tout (păs-pär-tōō′) ►*n.* Something, such as a master key, that permits one to pass or go at will. [Fr.]

pas·ser·by (păs′ər-bī′, -bī′) ►*n., pl.* **pas·sers·by** (păs′ərz-) A person who passes by, esp. casually or by chance.

pas·ser·ine (păs′ə-rīn′) ►*adj.* Of the order of birds that includes perching birds and songbirds. [< Lat. *passer,* sparrow.]

pass-fail (păs′fāl′) ►*adj.* Of being a system of grading in which a student simply passes or fails instead of receiving a letter grade.

pas·sim (păs′ĭm) ►*adv.* Throughout or frequently; used to indicate that a word, a passage, or an idea occurs frequently in the work cited. [Lat.]

pass·ing (păs′ĭng) ►*adj.* **1.** Moving by; going past. **2.** Of brief duration: *a passing fancy.* **3.** Cursory or superficial: *a passing glance.* **4.** Satisfactory: *received a passing grade.* ►*n.* **1.** The act of one that passes. **2.** Death. —**pass′ing·ly** *adv.*

pas·sion (păsh′ən) ►*n.* **1a.** Strong or powerful emotion: *a crime of passion.* **b.** A powerful emotion, such as anger or joy. **2a.** A state of strong sexual desire or love. **b.** The object of such love or desire. **3a.** Boundless enthusiasm: *a passion for sports.* **b.** The object of such enthusiasm. **4. Passion** The sufferings of Jesus after the Last Supper, including the Crucifixion. [< Lat. *patī, pass-,* suffer.] —**pas′sion·ate** (ə-nĭt) *adj.* —**pas′sion·ate·ly** *adv.* —**pas′sion·less** *adj.*

pas·sive (păs′ĭv) ►*adj.* **1.** Receiving or subjected to an action without acting in return. **2.** Accepting or submitting without resistance; compliant. **3.** Existing, conducted, or experienced without active or concerted effort. **4.** *Gram.* Of or being a verb form or voice used to indicate that the grammatical subject is the object of the action. ►*n. Gram.* **1.** The passive voice. **2.** A verb or construction in the passive voice. [< Lat. *patī, pass-,* suffer.] —**pas′sive·ly** *adv.* —**pas′sive·ness** *n.* —**pas·siv′i·ty** *n.*

passive restraint ►*n.* An automatic safety device, such as an airbag, in a motor vehicle that protects a person during a crash.

pass·key (păs′kē′) ►*n.* **1.** See **master key. 2.** See **skeleton key. 3.** An electronic password.

Pass·o·ver (păs′ō′vər) ►*n. Judaism* A holiday celebrated in the spring to commemorate the exodus of the Hebrews from Egypt.

pass·port (păs′pôrt′) ►*n.* An official government document identifying a citizen, certifying his or her nationality, and requesting admittance from foreign countries. [Fr. *passeport.*]

pass·word (păs′wûrd′) ►*n.* A secret word, phrase, or sequence of characters that must be presented in order to gain access or admittance.

past (păst) ►*adj.* **1.** No longer current; over. **2.** Having existed or occurred in an earlier time; bygone. **3a.** Earlier than the present time; ago: *40 years past.* **b.** Just gone by or elapsed: *in the past few days.* **4.** Having served formerly in a given capacity: *a past president.* **5.** *Gram.* Of or being a verb tense or form used to express an action or a condition prior to the time it is expressed. ►*n.* **1.** The time before the present. **2.** Previous background, experiences, and activities. **3.** *Gram.* **a.** The past tense. **b.** A verb form in the past tense. ►*adv.* So as to pass by or go beyond: *He waved as he walked past.* ►*prep.* **1.** Beyond in time, position, extent, or amount. **2.** Beyond in position; farther than. See Usage Note at **pass.** [ME < p.part. of *passen,* PASS.]

pas·ta (päs′tə) ►*n.* **1.** Unleavened dough molded into any of a variety of shapes and boiled. **2.** A prepared dish of pasta. [Ital. < LLat.]

paste (pāst) ►*n.* **1.** A soft, smooth, thick mixture, as: **a.** A smooth viscous mixture, as of flour and water, that is used as an adhesive. **b.** The moist clay or clay mixture used in making porcelain or pottery. **c.** A smooth dough used in making pastry. **d.** A food that has been pounded until smooth: *anchovy paste.* **2.** A hard, brilliant glass used in making artificial gems. ►*v.* **past·ed, past·ing 1.** To cause to adhere by applying paste. **2.** *Comp.* To insert (e.g., text or a graphic) into a document or file. [< LLat. *pasta.*]

paste·board (pāst′bôrd′) ►*n.* A thin, firm board made of sheets of paper pasted together or pressed paper pulp.

pas·tel (pă-stĕl′) ►*n.* **1a.** A drawing medium of dried paste made of ground pigments and a water-based binder. **b.** A crayon of this material. **2a.** A picture or sketch drawn with this type of crayon. **b.** The art of drawing with pastels. **3.** A soft, delicate hue; a pale color. [< LLat. *pastellus*, woad dye < *pasta*, paste.] **—pas·tel'** *adj.*

pas·tern (păs**'**tərn) ►*n.* The part of a horse's foot between the fetlock and hoof. [< OFr. *pasturon* < *pasture*, pasture.]

Pas·ter·nak (păs**'**tər-năk**'**), **Boris Leonidovich** 1890–1960. Russian writer.

Pas·teur (păs-tûr**'**, pä-stœr**'**), **Louis** 1822–95. French chemist and microbiologist.

Louis Pasteur

pas·teur·i·za·tion (păs**'**chər-ĭ-zā**'**shən, păs**'**-tər-) ►*n.* The process of heating a beverage or other food, such as milk or beer, in order to kill microorganisms that could cause disease, spoilage, or undesired fermentation. [After Louis PASTEUR.] **—pas'teur·ize'** *v.* **—pas'-teur·iz'er** *n.*

pas·tiche (pă-stēsh**'**, pä-) ►*n.* A dramatic, literary, or musical piece openly imitating the works of other artists. [< Ital. *pasticcio*.]

pas·tille (pă-stēl**'**) also **pas·til** (păs**'**tĭl) ►*n.* **1.** A small medicated or flavored tablet. **2.** A tablet containing aromatic substances that is burned to fumigate or deodorize the air. [< Lat. *pastillus*.]

pas·time (păs**'**tīm**'**) ►*n.* An activity that occupies one's spare time pleasantly.

pas·tor (păs**'**tər) ►*n.* A Christian minister or priest who is the leader of a congregation. [< Lat. *pāstor*, shepherd.]

pas·tor·al (păs**'**tər-əl, pă-stôr**'**-) ►*adj.* **1.** Of or relating to shepherds or herders. **2a.** Of or relating to rural life. **b.** Charmingly simple and serene; idyllic. **3.** Of or relating to a pastor or the duties of a pastor. ►*n.* A literary or other artistic work that portrays or evokes rural life, usu. in an idealized manner. **—pas'tor·al·ly** *adv.*

pas·to·rale (păs**'**tə-räl**'**, -răl**'**, pä**'**stə-) ►*n.* A musical composition with a pastoral theme. [Ital.]

past participle ►*n.* A verb form indicating past or completed action or time that is used as an adjective and with auxiliaries to form the passive voice or perfect and pluperfect tenses.

past perfect ►*n.* See **pluperfect** (sense 1).

pas·tra·mi (pə-strä**'**mē) ►*n.* A highly seasoned smoked cut of beef, usu. from the shoulder. [Ult. < Turk. *pastırma*, dried beef.]

pas·try (pā**'**strē) ►*n.*, *pl.* **-tries 1.** Dough or paste

of flour, water, and shortening that is baked and used as a crust for foods such as pies. **2a.** Baked foods made with pastry. **b.** One of these foods.

pas·tur·age (păs**'**chər-ĭj) ►*n.* **1.** The grass or other vegetation eaten by grazing animals. **2.** Land suitable for grazing animals.

pas·ture (păs**'**chər) ►*n.* **1.** A tract of land that supports grass or other vegetation eaten by domestic grazing animals. **2.** Such vegetation. ►*v.* **-tured, -tur·ing 1.** To herd (animals) into a pasture to graze. **2.** To graze. [< Lat. *pāscere*, *pāst-*, feed.]

past·y (pā**'**stē) ►*adj.* **-i·er, -i·est 1.** Resembling paste in consistency. **2.** Having a pale, lifeless appearance; pallid.

pat¹ (păt) ►*v.* **pat·ted, pat·ting 1a.** To tap gently with the open hand or with something flat. **b.** To stroke lightly as a gesture of affection. **2.** To mold by tapping gently with the hands or a flat implement. ►*n.* **1.** A light stroke or tap. **2.** The sound made by a pat. **3.** A small mass: *a pat of butter.* **—idiom: pat on the back** An expression or gesture of praise or approval. [< ME, a blow.]

pat² (păt) ►*adj.* **1.** Suitable; fitting. **2.** Satisfactory in a superficial or contrived way, esp. in being trite or glib: *a pat answer.* ►*adv. Informal* Readily, as a result of memorization: *has the lesson down pat.* [< PAT¹.] **—pat'ly** *adv.* **—pat'-ness** *n.*

pat. ►*abbr.* patent

Pat·a·go·ni·a (păt**'**ə-gō**'**nē-ə, -gōn**'**yə) An upland region of South America in S Argentina and Chile N of the Straits of Magellan. **—Pat'a·go'ni·an** *adj. & n.*

patch (păch) ►*n.* **1a.** A small piece of material affixed to another, larger piece to conceal, reinforce, or repair a worn area, hole, or tear. **b.** A small piece of cloth used for patchwork. **2.** A cloth badge affixed to a garment as a decoration or an insignia, as of a military unit. **3a.** A dressing or covering applied to a wound. **b.** A pad or shield of cloth, esp. one worn over an injured eye. **4a.** A small area that differs from the whole. **b.** A small plot or piece of land: *a bean patch.* **5.** A temporary, removable electronic connection. **6.** *Comp.* A piece of code added to software in order to fix a bug. ►*v.* **1.** To put a patch or patches on. **2.** To make by sewing scraps of material together: *patch a quilt.* **3.** To mend, repair, or put together, esp. hastily. **4.** *Electron.* To connect temporarily. [ME *pacche*.]

patch test ►*n.* A test for allergic sensitivity in which a suspected allergen is applied to the skin on a small surgical pad.

patch·work (păch**'**wûrk**'**) ►*n.* Needlework consisting of varicolored patches of material sewn together, as in a quilt.

patch·y (păch**'**ē) ►*adj.* **-i·er, -i·est 1.** Made up of or marked by patches. **2.** Uneven in quality or performance: *patchy work.* **—patch'i·ness** *n.*

pate (pāt) ►*n.* The human head, esp. the top of the head. [ME.]

pâ·té (pä-tā**'**) ►*n.* A meat paste. [< OFr. *paste*, PASTE.]

pa·tel·la (pə-tĕl**'**ə) ►*n.*, *pl.* **-tel·lae** (-tĕl**'**ē) A flat triangular bone located at the front of the knee joint. [Lat.] **—pa·tel'lar** *adj.*

pat·en (păt**'**n) ►*n.* **1.** A plate used to hold the host during the celebration of the Eucharist.

2. A thin disk of or resembling metal. [< Gk. *patanē*, platter.]

pat·ent (păt′nt) ▸*n.* **1.** A grant made by a government that confers upon the creator of an invention the sole right to make, use, and sell that invention for a set period of time. **2.** A document granting a patent for an invention. **3.** An invention protected by such a grant. ▸*adj.* **1a.** Protected or conferred by a patent. **b.** Of or relating to patents: *patent law.* **2.** (*also* păt′nt) Obvious; plain. See Synonyms at **apparent.** ▸*v.* **1.** To obtain a patent on. **2.** To grant a patent to. [< Lat. *patēns,* open.] —**pat′ent·ee′** *n.* —**pat′ent·ly** *adv.*

patent leather ▸*n.* Black leather finished to a hard, glossy surface. [So called because it is made by a once-patented process.]

pa·ter·fa·mil·i·as (pä′tər-fə-mĭl′ē-əs, pä′-) ▸*n., pl.* **pa·tres·fa·mil·i·as** (pä′trēz-, pä′-) A man who is the head of a household or the father of a family. [Lat. *paterfamiliās* : *pater,* father + *familiās,* of the family.]

pa·ter·nal (pə-tûr′nəl) ▸*adj.* **1.** Relating to or characteristic of a father or fatherhood; fatherly. **2.** Inherited from or related through one's father. [< Lat. *pater,* father.] —**pa·ter′nal·ly** *adv.*

pa·ter·nal·ism (pə-tûr′nə-lĭz′əm) ▸*n.* A policy or practice of treating or governing people in a fatherly manner, esp. by providing for their needs without giving them rights or responsibilities. —**pa·ter′nal·is′tic** *adj.*

pa·ter·ni·ty (pə-tûr′nĭ-tē) ▸*n.* The state of being a father; fatherhood.

pa·ter·nos·ter *also* **Pa·ter·nos·ter** (pä′tər-nŏs′tər, pä′-, păt′ər-) ▸*n.* The Lord's Prayer. [< LLat. : Lat. *pater,* father + *noster,* our.]

path (păth) ▸*n., pl.* **paths** (păthz, păths) **1.** A trodden track or way. **2.** A course; route. [< OE *pæth.*]

pa·thet·ic (pə-thĕt′ĭk) ▸*adj.* **1.** Arousing sympathetic sadness and compassion. **2.** Arousing scornful pity. [< Gk. *pathos,* suffering.] —**pa·thet′i·cal·ly** *adv.*

path·find·er (păth′fīn′dər, päth′-) ▸*n.* One that discovers a new course or way, esp. through or into unexplored regions.

path·name (păth′nām′, päth′-) ▸*n.* The full name of a computer file, including its position in the directory structure.

patho– *or* **path–** ▸*pref.* Disease; suffering: *pathogen.* [< Gk. *pathos,* suffering.]

path·o·gen (păth′ə-jən) ▸*n.* An agent that causes disease, esp. a living microorganism such as a bacterium or fungus. —**path′o·gen′ic** (-jĕn′ĭk) *adj.* —**path′o·ge·nic′i·ty** (-jə-nĭs′ĭ-tē) *n.*

path·o·gen·e·sis (păth′ə-jĕn′ĭ-sĭs) ▸*n.* The development of a diseased or morbid condition.

pa·thol·o·gy (pă-thŏl′ə-jē) ▸*n., pl.* **-gies 1.** The scientific study of disease. **2.** The anatomic or functional manifestations of a disease. **3.** A departure or deviation from a normal condition. —**path′o·log′i·cal** (păth′ə-lŏj′ĭ-kəl) *adj.* —**path′o·log′i·cal·ly** *adv.* —**pa·thol′o·gist** *n.*

pa·thos (pā′thŏs′, -thôs′) ▸*n.* A quality, as of an experience or a work of art, that arouses pity, sympathy, tenderness, or sorrow. [Gk., suffering.]

path·way (păth′wā′, päth′-) ▸*n.* A path.

–pathy ▸*suff.* **1.** Feeling; perception: *telepathy.* **2a.** Disease: *idiopathy.* **b.** A system of treating disease: *homeopathy.* [< Gk. *pathos,* suffering.]

pa·tience (pā′shəns) ▸*n.* **1.** The capacity, quality, or fact of being patient. **2.** *Chiefly Brit.* The game solitaire.

pa·tient (pā′shənt) ▸*adj.* **1.** Enduring pain or difficulty with calmness. **2.** Tolerant; understanding. **3.** Persevering; constant. **4.** Capable of calmly awaiting an outcome; not hasty or impulsive. ▸*n.* One who receives medical treatment. [< Lat. *patī,* endure.] —**pa′tient·ly** *adv.*

pat·i·na (păt′n-ə, pə-tē′nə) ▸*n.* **1.** A thin greenish layer that forms on copper or copper alloys as a result of corrosion or chemical treatment. **2.** The sheen on any surface, produced by age and use. [< Lat., plate.]

pat·i·o (păt′ē-ō′) ▸*n., pl.* **-os 1.** An outdoor space for dining or recreation that adjoins a residence and is often paved. **2.** A roofless inner courtyard. [< OSpan.]

pat·ois (păt′wä′, pă-twä′) ▸*n., pl.* **pat·ois** (păt′-wäz′, pă-twä′) **1a.** A regional dialect. **b.** Nonstandard speech. **2.** Jargon; cant. [< OFr.]

patri– *or* **patr–** ▸*pref.* Father, paternal: *patrilineal.* [< Lat. *pater* and Gk. *patēr,* father.]

pa·tri·arch (pā′trē-ärk′) ▸*n.* **1.** A man who rules a family, clan, or tribe. **2.** A leading or venerable man. **3.** A bishop of high rank, esp. in an Eastern Christian church. —**pa′tri·ar′chal, pa′tri·ar′chic** *adj.*

pa·tri·ar·chy (pā′trē-är′kē) ▸*n., pl.* **-chies** A social system in which the father is the head of the family.

pa·tri·cian (pə-trĭsh′ən) ▸*n.* A person of high rank; aristocrat. —**pa·tri′cian** *adj.*

pat·ri·cide (păt′rĭ-sīd′) ▸*n.* **1.** The act of murdering one's father. **2.** One who commits this act. —**pat′ri·cid′al** (-sīd′l) *adj.*

Pat·rick (păt′rĭk), Saint. AD 389?–461? Christian missionary and patron saint of Ireland.

pat·ri·lin·e·al (păt′rə-lĭn′ē-əl) ▸*adj.* Relating to, based on, or tracing ancestral descent through the paternal line.

pat·ri·mo·ny (păt′rə-mō′nē) ▸*n., pl.* **-nies** An inheritance, esp. from a father or other male ancestor. [< Lat. *patrimōnium* < *pater,* father.] —**pat′ri·mo′ni·al** *adj.*

pa·tri·ot (pā′trē-ət, -ŏt′) ▸*n.* One who loves, supports, and defends one's country. [< Gk. *patrios,* of one's fathers < *patēr,* father.] —**pa′tri·ot′ic** (-ŏt′ĭk) *adj.* —**pa′tri·ot′i·cal·ly** *adv.* —**pa′tri·ot·ism** (-ə-tĭz′əm) *n.*

pa·tris·tic (pə-trĭs′tĭk) *also* **pa·tris·ti·cal** (-tĭ-kəl) ▸*adj.* Of or relating to the fathers of the early Christian church or their writings.

pa·trol (pə-trōl′) ▸*n.* **1.** The act of moving about an area for observation, inspection, or security. **2.** A person or group of persons who perform such an act. **3.** A military unit sent out on a reconnaissance or combat mission. ▸*v.* **-trolled, -trol·ling** To engage in a patrol (of). [< OFr. *patouiller,* paddle about in mud.]

pa·trol·man (pə-trōl′mən) ▸*n.* A policeman who patrols or polices an assigned area.

patrol wagon ▸*n.* An enclosed police truck used to convey prisoners.

pa·trol·wom·an (pə-trōl′wŏŏm′ən) ▸*n.* A policewoman who patrols or polices an assigned area.

pa·tron (pā′trən) ►*n.* **1.** One that supports, protects, or champions someone or something. **2.** A customer, esp. a regular customer. [< Lat. *patrōnus* < *pater*, father.]

pa·tron·age (pā′trə-nĭj, păt′rə-) ►*n.* **1.** Support from a patron. **2.** The trade given to a commercial establishment by its customers. **3.** Customers considered as a group; clientele. **4.** The power to appoint people to political positions.

pa·tron·ess (pā′trə-nĭs) ►*n.* A woman who supports, protects, or champions someone or something.

pa·tron·ize (pā′trə-nīz′, păt′rə-) ►*v.* **-ized, -iz·ing** **1.** To act as a patron to; support or sponsor. **2.** To go to as a customer, esp. on a regular basis. **3.** To treat in a condescending manner. —**pa′tron·iz′ing·ly** *adv.*

patron saint ►*n.* A saint who is regarded as the advocate in heaven for a nation, place, craft, activity, class, or person.

pat·ro·nym·ic (păt′rə-nĭm′ĭk) ►*n.* A name derived from the name of one's father or a paternal ancestor. [< Gk. *patrōnumos*, named after one's father : *patēr*, father + *onuma*, name.] —**pat′ro·nym′ic** *adj.*

pa·troon (pə-trōōn′) ►*n.* A landholder in New York under Dutch colonial rule who was granted proprietary rights to a large tract of land. [Du. < Fr. *patron*, PATRON.]

pat·sy (păt′sē) ►*n., pl.* **-sies** *Slang* A person easily taken advantage of, blamed, or ridiculed. [?]

pat·ter[1] (păt′ər) ►*v.* To make a quick succession of light, soft tapping sounds. ►*n.* A quick succession of light, soft tapping sounds. [< PAT[1].]

pat·ter[2] (păt′ər) ►*v.* To speak or chatter glibly or mechanically. ►*n.* **1.** The jargon of a particular group; cant. **2.** Glib, rapid speech, as of an auctioneer. [ME *patren.*]

pat·tern (păt′ərn) ►*n.* **1.** A usu. repeating artistic or decorative design. See Synonyms at **figure**. **2a.** A plan, diagram, or model to be followed in making things. **b.** A model or an original used as an archetype. **3.** A composite of traits or features. ►*v.* To make, mold, or design by following a pattern. [< OFr. *patron*, PATRON.]

Pat·ton (păt′n), **George Smith, Jr.** 1885–1945. Amer. general.

pat·ty (păt′ē) ►*n., pl.* **-ties** **1.** A small rounded, flattened cake of food, esp. chopped food. **2.** A small pie. [Fr. *pâté*, PÂTÉ.]

pau·ci·ty (pô′sĭ-tē) ►*n.* **1.** Smallness of number. **2.** Scarcity. [< Lat. *paucus*, few.]

Paul (pôl), **Saint.** AD 5?–67? Early Christian missionary. —**Paul′ine** (-īn, -ēn) *adj.*

Pau·ling (pô′lĭng), **Linus Carl** 1901–94. Amer. chemist.

paunch (pônch, pänch) ►*n.* **1.** The belly, esp. a protruding one; potbelly. **2.** See **rumen**. [< Lat. *pantex.*] —**paunch′y** *adj.*

pau·per (pô′pər) ►*n.* One who is extremely poor, esp. one on public charity. [< Lat., poor.] —**pau′per·ism** *n.* —**pau′per·ize** *v.*

pause (pôz) ►*v.* **paused, paus·ing** **1.** To stop moving along or doing an action for a brief period: *He paused in the middle of his speech.* **2.** To stop or suspend the action of (e.g., a device) temporarily. ►*n.* **1a.** A break, stop, or rest, often for an intended purpose or effect. **b.** A hesita-

tion. **c.** Reason for hesitation. **2.** *Mus.* A sign indicating that a note or rest is to be held. [< Gk. *pausis*, a pause.]

Syns: intermission, recess, respite, suspension n.

Pav·a·rot·ti (păv′ə-rŏt′ē, pä′vä-rôt′tē), **Luciano** 1935–2007. Italian tenor.

pave (pāv) ►*v.* **paved, pav·ing** To cover with pavement. —*idiom:* **pave the way** To make progress easier. [< Lat. *pavīre*, tread down.]

pave·ment (pāv′mənt) ►*n.* **1.** A hard smooth surface, esp. of a thoroughfare, that will bear travel. **2.** The material with which such a surface is made.

pa·vil·ion (pə-vĭl′yən) ►*n.* **1.** An ornate tent. **2.** A light, often open structure, used for amusement or shelter. **3.** An annex of a building. **4.** One of a group of related buildings forming a complex. [< Lat. *pāpiliō.*]

pav·ing (pā′vĭng) ►*n.* **1.** The act or technique of laying pavement. **2.** Pavement.

Pav·lov (păv′lôv′, päv′ləf), **Ivan Petrovich** 1849–1936. Russian physiologist. —**Pav·lo′vi·an** (păv-lō′vē-ən, -lô′-) *adj.*

Pav·lo·va (păv-lō′və, păv′lə-, päv′-), **Anna** 1882–1931. Russian ballerina.

paw (pô) ►*n.* **1.** The clawed foot esp. of a quadruped animal. **2.** *Informal* A human hand. ►*v.* **1.** To strike with the paw. **2.** To scrape (e.g., the ground) with a paw or foot. **3a.** To touch clumsily. **b.** To touch (another) in an annoying or unwanted way. [< OFr. *powe.*]

pawl (pôl) ►*n.* A hinged or pivoted device adapted to fit into a notch of a ratchet wheel to impart forward motion or prevent backward motion. [Perh. var. of PALE[1] or POLE[2].]

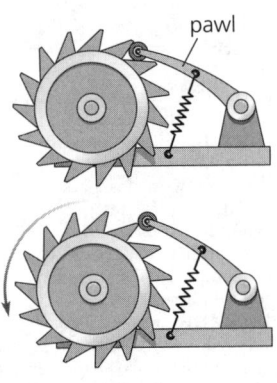

pawl

pawn[1] (pôn) ►*n.* **1.** Something given as security for a loan; pledge. **2.** The condition of being held as a pledge. ►*v.* To give or deposit (personal property) as security for money borrowed. [< OFr. *pan.*]

pawn[2] (pôn) ►*n.* **1.** A chess piece of lowest value. **2.** One used to further the purposes of another. [< Med.Lat. *pedō*, foot soldier < Lat. *pēs*, foot.]

pawn·bro·ker (pôn′brō′kər) ►*n.* One that lends money at interest in exchange for personal property deposited as security.

Paw·nee (pô-nē′) ►*n., pl.* **-nee** or **-nees** **1.** A member of a Native American people formerly of Kansas and Nebraska, now in Oklahoma. **2.** The Caddoan language of the Pawnee.

pawn·shop (pôn′shŏp′) ►*n.* The shop of a pawnbroker.

paw·paw also **pa·paw** (pô′pô) ►*n.* **1.** Any of various deciduous trees and shrubs having maroon flowers and fleshy edible fruit. **2.** The fruit of any of these plants. **3.** See **papaya.** [Orig. a var. of PAPAYA.]

pay (pā) ►*v.* **paid** (pād), **pay·ing 1.** To recompense for goods or services. **2.** To discharge or settle (a debt or obligation). **3.** To bear (a cost or penalty): *pay the price for nonconformity.* **4.** To yield as a return. **5.** To give or bestow: *pay compliments.* **6.** To make (a visit or call). **7.** To be profitable or worthwhile: *Crime doesn't pay.* ►*adj.* Requiring payment to operate: *a pay telephone.* ►*n.* **1.** The act of paying or state of being paid. **2.** Something paid, as a salary or wages. —*phrasal verbs:* **pay down** To reduce (a debt) through payment. **pay off 1.** To pay the full amount on (a debt). **2.** To be profitable. **3.** *Informal* To bribe. —*idiom:* **pay the piper** To bear the consequences of something. [< LLat. *pācāre,* appease < Lat. *pāx,* peace.] —**pay′a·ble** *adj.* —**pay·ee′** *n.* —**pay′er** *n.*

pay·check (pā′chĕk′) ►*n.* **1.** A check issued to an employee in payment of salary or wages. **2.** Salary or wages.

pay dirt ►*n.* **1.** Earth, ore, or gravel that is profitable to mine. **2.** *Informal* A profitable discovery or venture.

pay·load (pā′lōd′) ►*n.* **1.** The part of a cargo that produces revenue. **2.** The total weight of passengers and cargo that can be carried by an aircraft or spacecraft. **3.** The explosive charge carried by a missile or contained in a bomb.

pay·mas·ter (pā′mǎs′tər) ►*n.* A person in charge of paying wages and salaries.

pay·ment (pā′mənt) ►*n.* **1.** The act of paying. **2.** An amount paid.

pay·off (pā′ôf′, -ŏf′) ►*n.* **1.** The return on an investment. **2.** The discharge of a debt or obligation. **3.** The benefit gained as a result of a previous action. **4.** The climax of a narrative or sequence of events. **5.** A bribe.

pay·roll (pā′rōl′) ►*n.* **1.** A list of employees with the wages due to each. **2.** The total sum of wages paid during a pay period.

PBS ►*abbr.* Public Broadcasting Service

PC ►*abbr.* **1.** personal computer **2.** politically correct

p.c. ►*abbr.* **1.** percent **2.** *Lat.* post cibum (after meals)

p/c or **P/C** ►*abbr.* **1.** petty cash **2.** prices current

PCB (pē′sē-bē′) ►*n.* An industrial compound and environmental pollutant, banned in the US in 1979. [*p(oly)c(hlorinated) b(iphenyl).*]

PCP (pē′sē-pē′) ►*n.* A drug, $C_{17}H_{25}N$, used in veterinary medicine as an anesthetic and illegally as a hallucinogen. [*p(henyl)c(yclohexyl) p(iperidine).*]

pct. ►*abbr.* percent

pd. ►*abbr.* paid

p.d. ►*abbr.* per diem

PDT ►*abbr.* Pacific Daylight Time

PE ►*abbr.* **1.** physical education **2.** Prince Edward Island **3.** *Statistics* probable error

pea (pē) ►*n.* **1.** A vine having edible seeds enclosed in green pods. **2.** The round seed of this plant. **3.** Any of several related or similar plants. [< Gk. *pison.*]

peace (pēs) ►*n.* **1.** The absence of war or other hostilities. **2.** An agreement or treaty to end hostilities. **3.** Freedom from quarrels and disagreement; harmony. **4.** Public security and order: *disturbing the peace.* **5.** Serenity: *peace of mind.* [< Lat. *pāx.*] —**peace′a·ble, peace′ful** *adj.* —**peace′a·bly, peace′ful·ly** *adv.* —**peace′ful·ness** *n.*

peace·keep·ing (pēs′kē′pǐng) ►*n.* The preservation of peace, esp. the supervision by international forces of a truce between hostile nations. —**peace′keep′ing** *adj.*

peace·mak·er (pēs′mā′kər) ►*n.* One who makes peace, esp. by settling disputes. —**peace′mak′ing** *adj.* & *n.*

peace officer ►*n.* A law enforcement officer responsible for maintaining civil peace.

peace pipe ►*n.* A calumet.

Peace River A river, about 1,920 km (1,195 mi), of British Columbia and Alberta, Canada.

peace·time (pēs′tīm′) ►*n.* A time free from war. —**peace′time′** *adj.*

peach (pēch) ►*n.* **1.** A small tree having pink flowers and edible fruit. **2.** The soft juicy fruit of this tree, usu. having yellow flesh, downy red-tinted yellow skin, and a deeply ridged pit. [< Lat. *persicus,* Persian.] —**peach′y** *adj.*

pea coat or **pea·coat** (pē′kōt′) ►*n.* A short, warm, double-breasted coat of heavy wool. [< earlier *pee,* jacket of coarse woolen fabric < MDu. *pij.*]

pea·cock (pē′kŏk′) ►*n.* A male peafowl, having brilliant blue or green plumage and long back feathers that can be spread in a fanlike form. [< Lat. *pāvō,* peacock + COCK¹.]

pea·fowl (pē′foul′) ►*n.* A large Asian pheasant. [PEA(COCK) + FOWL.]

pea·hen (pē′hĕn′) ►*n.* A female peafowl.

peak (pēk) ►*n.* **1.** A tapering, projecting point. **2a.** The pointed summit of a mountain. **b.** The mountain itself. **3.** The point of greatest development, value, or intensity. ►*v.* **1.** To bring to or form a peak. **2.** To achieve a maximum of development or intensity. [Prob. ME *pike.*]

peak·ed (pē′kĭd) ►*adj.* Having a sickly appearance. [< *peak,* become sickly.]

peak oil ►*n.* The point at which peak output of all of Earth's petroleum is reached, calculated as the time when 50 percent of reserves have been depleted.

peal (pēl) ►*n.* **1.** A ringing of bells. **2.** A set of tuned bells. **3.** A loud burst of noise: *peals of laughter.* ►*v.* To ring, as bells. [< ME *apel,* appeal.]

Peale (pēl) Amer. family of painters, including **Charles Wilson** (1741–1827), **James** (1749–1831), and **Rembrandt** (1778–1860).

pea·nut (pē′nŭt′) ►*n.* **1.** A widely cultivated plant having seedpods that ripen underground. **2.** The edible, nutlike, oily seed of this plant. **3. peanuts** *Informal* A very small amount of money.

peanut butter ►*n.* A paste made from ground roasted peanuts.

pear (pâr) ►*n.* **1.** A widely cultivated tree having white flowers and edible fruit. **2.** The fruit of this tree, spherical at the base and narrow at the stem. [< Lat. *pirum.*]

pearl (pûrl) ►*n.* **1.** A smooth, lustrous mass formed in the shells of certain mollusks and valued as a gem. **2.** Mother-of-pearl. **3.** One highly valued or esteemed. **4.** A yellowish

white. [< Lat. *perna*, seashell.] —**pearl′y** *adj.*
Pearl Harbor An inlet of the Pacific on the S
coast of Oahu, HI, W of Honolulu.

Pearl Harbor
USS Shaw exploding in the
attack on Pearl Harbor
December 7, 1941

peas·ant (pĕz′ənt) ▸*n.* **1.** A member of a class
made up of agricultural workers, including
small or tenant farmers and laborers on the
land. **2.** A country person; rustic. **3.** A crude or
ill-bred person. [< LLat. *pāgēnsis*, inhabitant of
a district.] —**peas′ant·ry** *n.*
peat (pēt) ▸*n.* Partially decomposed vegetable
matter, usu. mosses, found in bogs and used
as fertilizer and fuel. [ME *pete.*] —**peat′y** *adj.*
peat moss ▸*n.* **1.** Sphagnum. **2.** Peat composed
of moss, usu. sphagnum.
peb·ble (pĕb′əl) ▸*n.* A small stone, esp. one
worn smooth by erosion. ▸*v.* -**bled, -bling 1.**
To pave with pebbles. **2.** To impart a rough
grainy surface to (leather or paper). [< OE
papol-.] —**peb′bly** *adj.*
pe·can (pĭ-kän′, -kăn′, pē′kăn) ▸*n.* **1.** A tree of
the central and S US, having deeply furrowed
bark and edible nuts. **2.** The smooth oval nut of
this tree. [< Illinois *pakani.*]
pec·ca·dil·lo (pĕk′ə-dĭl′ō) ▸*n., pl.* -**loes** or -**los**
A minor sin or fault. [< Lat. *peccātum*, sin.]
pec·ca·ry (pĕk′ə-rē) ▸*n., pl.* -**ries** Any of several
piglike American mammals having stiff bristles
and short tusks. [< Carib *pakira.*]
peck[1] (pĕk) ▸*v.* **1.** To strike or make strokes
with the beak or a pointed instrument. **2.** To
pick up with the beak. **3.** *Informal* To kiss
briefly and casually. **4.** To eat sparingly: *pecked
at his dinner.* ▸*n.* **1.** A stroke or mark made
with the beak. **2.** *Informal* A light, quick kiss.
[ME *pecken.*]
peck[2] (pĕk) ▸*n.* **1.** See table at **measurement.**
2. A unit of dry volume or capacity equal to 8
qt. or approx. 554.8 cu. in. [ME.]
peck·ing order (pĕk′ĭng) ▸*n.* **1.** A hierarchy
among a group, as of people, classes, or nations.
2. The social hierarchy in a flock of domestic
fowl in which each bird pecks subordinate
birds and submits to being pecked by dominant birds.
Pe·cos River (pā′kəs) A river of E NM and W
TX flowing about 1,450 km (900 mi) to the
Rio Grande.
pec·tin (pĕk′tĭn) ▸*n.* Any of a group of water-
soluble colloids found in ripe fruits and used to
jell various drugs and cosmetics. [< Gk. *pēktos*,
coagulated.] —**pec′tic, pec′tin·ous** *adj.*
pec·to·ral (pĕk′tər-əl) ▸*adj.* **1.** Of or situated
in the breast or chest. **2.** Worn on the chest or
breast: *a pectoral cross.* [< Lat. *pectus*, breast.]

pec·u·late (pĕk′yə-lāt′) ▸*v.* -**lat·ed, -lat·ing** To
embezzle. [< Lat. *pecūlium*, private property.]
—**pec′u·la′tion** *n.*
pe·cu·liar (pĭ-kyōōl′yər) ▸*adj.* **1.** Not ordinary
or usual; odd or strange. **2.** Belonging distinctively to one person, group, or kind; unique.
[< Lat. *pecūlium*, private property.] —**pe·cu′li·
ar′i·ty** (-kyōō′lē-ăr′ĭ-tē, -kyōōl-yăr′-) *n.*
pe·cu·ni·ar·y (pĭ-kyōō′nē-ĕr′ē) ▸*adj.* Of or
relating to money. [< Lat. *pecūnia*, wealth.]
ped– ▸*pref.* Var. of **pedo–.**
–ped or **–pede** ▸*suff.* Foot: *biped.* [< Lat. *pēs*,
foot.]
ped·a·gogue (pĕd′ə-gŏg′, -gôg′) ▸*n.* A school-
teacher; educator. [< Gk. *paidagōgos* : *pais*, child
+ *agōgos*, leader (< *agein*, to lead).]
ped·a·go·gy (pĕd′ə-gō′jē, -gŏj′ē) ▸*n.* The art or
profession of teaching. —**ped′a·gog′ic** (-gŏj′-
ĭk, -gō′jĭk), **ped′a·gog′i·cal** *adj.* —**ped′a·
gog′i·cal·ly** *adv.*
ped·al (pĕd′l) ▸*n.* A foot-operated lever, as on a
piano or bicycle. ▸*adj.* Of or relating to a foot or
footlike part. ▸*v.* -**aled, -al·ing** or -**alled, -al·
ling 1.** To use or operate a pedal or pedals. **2.**
To ride a bicycle. [< Lat. *pēs, ped-*, foot.]
ped·ant (pĕd′nt) ▸*n.* One who ostentatiously
exhibits academic knowledge or pays undue
attention to minor details. [Prob. < Gk. *paid-
euein*, instruct.]
pe·dan·tic (pə-dăn′tĭk) ▸*adj.* Marked by a narrow, often ostentatious concern for book learning and formal rules. —**pe·dan′ti·cal·ly** *adv.*
—**ped′ant·ry** (pĕd′n-trē) *n.*
ped·dle (pĕd′l) ▸*v.* -**dled, -dling** To travel about
selling (wares). [< ME *pedlere*, peddler < Lat.
pēs, foot.] —**ped′dler** *n.*
ped·er·ast (pĕd′ə-răst′) ▸*n.* A man who has
sexual relations with a boy. [Gk. *paiderastēs.*]
—**ped′er·as′ty** *n.*
ped·es·tal (pĕd′ĭ-stəl) ▸*n.* A support or base,
as for a column or statue. [< Ital. *piedestallo.*]
pe·des·tri·an (pə-dĕs′trē-ən) ▸*n.* A person traveling on foot. ▸*adj.* **1.** Relating to or made for
pedestrians: *a pedestrian bridge.* **2.** Going or
performed on foot. **3.** Dull; ordinary: *pedestrian
prose.* See Synonyms at **dull.** [< Lat. *pedester*,
going on foot < *pēs*, foot.]
pe·di·at·rics (pē′dē-ăt′rĭks) ▸*n.* (*takes sing. v.*)
The branch of medicine that deals with the care
of infants and children and the treatment of
their diseases. —**pe′di·at′ric** *adj.* —**pe′di·a·
tri′cian** (-ə-trĭsh′ən) *n.*
ped·i·cure (pĕd′ĭ-kyōōr′) ▸*n.* A cosmetic treatment of the feet and toenails. [Fr. *pédicure* : Lat.
pēs, foot + *cūra*, care.] —**ped′i·cur′ist** *n.*
ped·i·gree (pĕd′ĭ-grē′) ▸*n.* **1.** A line of ancestors; ancestry or lineage. **2.** A list of ancestors,
as of a purebred animal. [< AN *pe de grue*,
crane's foot (from the shape of the lines on a
family tree).] —**ped′i·greed′** *adj.*
ped·i·ment (pĕd′ə-mənt) ▸*n.* A gablelike, usu.
triangular architectural element, as on the
façade of a Greek temple. [Prob. < PYRAMID.]
pedo– or **ped–** ▸*pref.* Child; children: *pediatrics.*
[< Gk. *pais, paid-*, child.]
pe·dom·e·ter (pĭ-dŏm′ĭ-tər) ▸*n.* An instrument
that gauges the approximate distance traveled
on foot by registering the number of steps
taken. [Lat. *pēs, ped-*, foot + –METER.]
ped·o·phile (pĕd′ə-fīl′, pē′də-) ▸*n.* A person
who derives sexual gratification from fantasies

or sexual acts involving a child. **—ped′o·phil′-ia** (-fĭl′ē-ə) *n.*

pe·dun·cle (pĭ-dŭng′kəl, pē′dŭng′kəl) ►*n.* **1.** *Bot.* A stalk bearing a flower. **2.** *Zool.* A stalk-like part or structure. [NLat. *pedunculus*, dim. of Lat. *pēs*, foot.]

peek (pēk) ►*v.* **1.** To glance quickly. **2.** To look or peer furtively. [ME *piken*.] **—peek** *n.*

peel (pēl) ►*n.* The skin or rind of certain fruits and vegetables. ►*v.* **1.** To strip or cut away the skin, rind, or bark from; pare. **2.** To strip away; pull off. **3.** To lose or shed skin, bark, or other covering. **4.** To come off in thin strips or pieces, as paint. [< Lat. *pilāre*, deprive of hair.] **—peel′er** *n.*

peen (pēn) ►*n.* The end of a hammerhead opposite the flat striking surface, often wedge-shaped or ball-shaped. [Prob. of Scand. orig.]

peep¹ (pēp) ►*v.* To utter short high-pitched sounds, like those of a baby bird; cheep. [ME **pepen*, to peep; see PIPE.] **—peep** *n.* **—peep′-er** *n.*

peep² (pēp) ►*v.* **1.** To peek furtively, as through a small aperture. **2.** To become partly visible. ►*n.* **1.** A quick or furtive look. **2.** A first glimpse or appearance. [ME *pepen*.] **—peep′er** *n.*

peep·hole (pēp′hōl′) ►*n.* A small hole or crevice through which one may look.

peer¹ (pîr) ►*v.* To look intently, searchingly, or with difficulty. [ME *piren*.]

peer² (pîr) ►*n.* **1.** One who has equal standing with another. **2a.** A nobleman. **b.** A British duke, marquis, earl, viscount, or baron. [< Lat. *pār*, equal.]

peer·age (pîr′ĭj) ►*n.* The rank or title of a peer or peeress.

peer·ess (pîr′ĭs) ►*n.* A British duchess, marchioness, countess, viscountess, or baroness.

peer·less (pîr′lĭs) ►*adj.* Having no match or equal; incomparable. **—peer′less·ly** *adv.*

peeve (pēv) ►*v.* **peeved, peev·ing** To annoy or vex. See Synonyms at **annoy.** ►*n.* **1.** A vexation; grievance. **2.** A resentful mood. [< PEEVISH.]

pee·vish (pē′vĭsh) ►*adj.* **1.** Querulous or discontented. **2.** Ill-tempered. [ME *pevish.*] **—pee′vish·ly** *adv.* **—pee′vish·ness** *n.*

pee·wee (pē′wē) ►*n. Informal* One that is unusually small. [Prob. reduplication of WEE.]

peg (pĕg) ►*n.* **1.** A small cylindrical or tapered pin, as of wood, usu. used to fasten things or plug a hole. **2.** A degree or notch: *Our opinion of him went up a few pegs after he did the dishes.* **3.** A straight throw of a ball. ►*v.* **pegged, peg·ging 1.** To fasten or plug with a peg or pegs. **2.** To mark with a peg or pegs. **3.** To fix (a price) at a certain level. **4.** *Informal* To classify; categorize: *pegged the new boss as a blowhard.* **5.** To hit, esp. with a thrown object: *pegged me in the head with a snowball.* **6.** To work steadily; plug. [< MDu. *pegge.*]

peg·ma·tite (pĕg′mə-tīt′) ►*n.* A coarse-grained granite. [< Gk. *pēgma*, solid mass.]

Pei (pā), **I(eoh) M(ing)** b. 1917. Chinese-born Amer. architect.

PEI ►*abbr.* Prince Edward Island

pei·gnoir (pān-wär′, pĕn-) ►*n.* A woman's loose-fitting dressing gown. [Fr.]

pe·jor·a·tive (pĭ-jôr′ə-tĭv, -jôr′-, pĕj′ə-rā′tĭv) ►*adj.* Disparaging; belittling. ►*n.* A disparaging word or expression. [< Lat. *peior*, worse.] **—pe·jor′a·tive·ly** *adv.*

Pe·king (pē′kĭng′, pā′-) See **Beijing.**

Pe·king·ese (pē′kĭng-ēz′, -ēs′) also **Pe·kin·ese** (pē′kə-nēz′, -nēs′) ►*n., pl.* **-ese 1.** A native or resident of Peking (Beijing). **2.** The Chinese dialect of Peking. **3.** (pē′kə-nēz′, -nēs′) A small, short-legged, long-haired dog with a flat nose.

pe·koe (pē′kō) ►*n.* Black tea made of the leaves around the buds. [Chin. dial. *pek ho.*]

pe·lag·ic (pə-lăj′ĭk) ►*adj.* Of or relating to open oceans or seas. [< Gk. *pelagos*, sea.]

Pe·lé (pā′lā) Edson Arantes do Nascimento. b. 1940. Brazilian soccer player.

pelf (pĕlf) ►*n.* Wealth or riches. [< OFr. *pelfre*, booty.]

pel·i·can (pĕl′ĭ-kən) ►*n.* A large, web-footed bird with an expandable pouch under the lower bill used for catching and holding fish. [< Gk. *pelekan.*]

pel·la·gra (pə-lăg′rə, -lā′grə, -lä′-) ►*n.* A disease caused by a deficiency of niacin and protein in the diet and marked by skin eruptions and digestive and nervous system disturbances. [Ital.] **—pel·lag′rous** *adj.*

pel·let (pĕl′ĭt) ►*n.* **1.** A small, solid or densely packed ball or mass, as of medicine. **2.** A bullet or piece of small shot. [< Lat. *pila*, ball.]

pell-mell also **pell·mell** (pĕl′mĕl′) ►*adv.* **1.** In a jumbled, confused manner. **2.** In frantic, disorderly haste; headlong. [< OFr. *pesle mesle.*]

pel·lu·cid (pə-lōō′sĭd) ►*adj.* **1.** Transparent or translucent. See Synonyms at **clear. 2.** Very clear in style or meaning. [< Lat. *pellūcēre*, shine through.] **—pel·lu′cid·ly** *adv.*

Pel·o·pon·ne·sus (pĕl′ə-pə-nē′səs) A peninsula forming the S part of Greece S of the Gulf of Corinth. **—Pel′o·pon·ne′sian** (-nē′zhən, -shən) *adj. & n.*

pelt¹ (pĕlt) ►*n.* The skin of an animal with the fur or hair still on it. [ME.]

pelt² (pĕlt) ►*v.* **1.** To strike or assail repeatedly with thrown objects. See Synonyms at **barrage. 2.** To hurl or throw (missiles): *pelted stones at the windows.* [ME *pelten.*]

pel·vis (pĕl′vĭs) ►*n., pl.* **-vis·es** or **-ves** (-vēz) A basin-shaped structure of the vertebrate skeleton that rests on the lower limbs and supports the spinal column. [Lat. *pēlvis*, basin.] **—pel′vic** *adj.*

pem·mi·can also **pem·i·can** (pĕm′ĭ-kən) ►*n.* A food made of dried meat pounded into paste and mixed with fat. [Cree *pimihkaam.*]

pen¹ (pĕn) ►*n.* An instrument for writing or drawing with ink. ►*v.* **penned, pen·ning** To write, esp. with a pen. [< Lat. *penna*, feather.]

pen² (pĕn) ►*n.* **1.** A fenced enclosure for animals. **2.** A confining room or space. ►*v.* **penned** or **pent** (pĕnt), **pen·ning** To confine in or as if in a pen. See Synonyms at **enclose.** [< OE *penn.*]

pen³ (pĕn) ►*n. Informal* A prison.

pe·nal (pē′nəl) ►*adj.* Of or relating to punishment, esp. for breaking the law. [< Gk. *poinē*, penalty.] **—pe′nal·ly** *adv.*

pe·nal·ize (pē′nə-līz′, pĕn′ə-) ►*v.* **-ized, -iz·ing 1.** To subject to a penalty. **2.** To hinder; handicap. **—pe′nal·i·za′tion** *n.*

pen·al·ty (pĕn′əl-tē) ►*n., pl.* **-ties 1.** A punishment for a crime or offense. **2.** Something, esp. a sum of money, required as a forfeit for an offense. **3.** *Sports* A punishment or handicap imposed for infraction of a rule.

penalty kick ►*n.* In soccer, a free kick on the goal awarded when the defense has committed a foul in the area in front of the goal.

pen·ance (pĕn′əns) ►*n.* **1.** A voluntary act of contrition for a sin or other wrongdoing. **2. Penance** A sacrament in some Christian churches for the forgiveness of one's sins. [< Lat. *paenitēns*, PENITENT.]

Pe·na·tes (pə-nā′tēz, -nä′-) ►*pl.n.* The ancient Roman gods of the household.

pence (pĕns) ►*n. Chiefly Brit.* Pl. of **penny**.

pen·chant (pĕn′chənt) ►*n.* A definite liking; strong inclination. See Synonyms at **predilection**. [Fr. < *pencher*, incline.]

pen·cil (pĕn′səl) ►*n.* **1.** A writing or drawing implement consisting of a thin rod esp. of graphite encased in wood or held in a mechanical holder. **2.** Something shaped or used like a pencil: *an eyebrow pencil.* ►*v.* **-ciled, -cil·ing** also **-cilled, -cil·ling** To write, draw, or mark with a pencil. [< Lat. *pēniculus*, small brush.]

pen·dant also **pen·dent** (pĕn′dənt) ►*n.* Something suspended from something else, esp. an ornament. ►*adj.* Var. of **pendent**. [< Lat. *pendēre*, hang.]

pen·dent also **pen·dant** (pĕn′dənt) ►*adj.* **1.** Hanging down; dangling. **2.** Projecting; overhanging. **3.** Awaiting settlement; pending. ►*n.* Var. of **pendant**. [< Lat. *pendēre*, hang.]

pend·ing (pĕn′dĭng) ►*adj.* **1.** Not yet decided or settled. **2.** Impending; imminent. ►*prep.* **1.** While in the process of; during. **2.** While awaiting; until. [< Fr. *pendant*, during.]

pen·du·lar (pĕn′jə-lər, pĕn′dyə-, -də-) ►*adj.* Swinging back and forth like a pendulum.

pen·du·lous (pĕn′jə-ləs, pĕn′dyə-, -də-) ►*adj.* Hanging loosely; sagging. [< Lat. *pendēre*, hang.]

pen·du·lum (pĕn′jə-ləm, pĕn′dyə-, pĕn′də-) ►*n.* A body suspended from a fixed support so that it swings freely back and forth under the influence of gravity. [< Lat. *pendulus*, hanging.]

pe·ne·plain also **pe·ne·plane** (pē′nə-plān′) ►*n.* A nearly flat land surface resulting from long erosion. [Lat. *paene*, almost + PLAIN.]

pen·e·trate (pĕn′ĭ-trāt′) ►*v.* **-trat·ed, -trat·ing** **1.** To enter or force a way into; pierce. **2.** To grasp the nature of; understand: *penetrate the workings of the immune system.* **3.** To see through: *keen eyes that penetrate the darkness.* **4.** To enter and gain a share of (a market). [Lat. *penetrāre*.] —**pen′e·tra·ble** (-trə-bəl) *adj.* —**pen′e·tra′tion** *n.*

pen·e·trat·ing (pĕn′ĭ-trā′tĭng) ►*adj.* **1.** Able or seeming to penetrate; piercing. **2.** Keenly perceptive or understanding; acute: *a penetrating mind.* —**pen′e·trat′ing·ly** *adv.*

pen·guin (pĕng′gwĭn, pĕn′-) ►*n.* Any of various stout, flightless aquatic birds of the Southern Hemisphere, having flipperlike wings, webbed feet, and white underparts with a dark back. [Poss. < Welsh *pen gwyn*, white head : *pen*, chief, head + *gwynn*, white.]

pen·i·cil·lin (pĕn′ĭ-sĭl′ĭn) ►*n.* An antibiotic drug obtained from molds or made synthetically, used esp. to treat infections caused by gram-positive bacteria. [< Lat. *pēnicillus*, small brush.]

pen·in·su·la (pə-nĭn′syə-lə, -sə-lə) ►*n.* A piece of land that juts from a larger land mass and is mostly surrounded by water. [Lat. *paenīnsula*.] —**pen·in′su·lar** *adj.*

pe·nis (pē′nĭs) ►*n., pl.* **-nis·es** or **-nes** (-nēz) The male organ of copulation and, in mammals, of urination. [Lat. *pēnis*.] —**pe′nile′** (-nīl′, -nəl) *adj.*

pen·i·tence (pĕn′ĭ-təns) ►*n.* The condition or quality of being penitent.

Syns: compunction, contrition, remorse, repentance n.

pen·i·tent (pĕn′ĭ-tənt) ►*adj.* Feeling or expressing remorse for one's misdeeds or sins. ►*n.* One who is penitent. [< Lat. *paenitēre*, repent.] —**pen′i·ten′tial** (-tĕn′shəl) *adj.* —**pen′i·tent·ly** *adv.*

pen·i·ten·tia·ry (pĕn′ĭ-tĕn′shə-rē) ►*n., pl.* **-ries** A prison for those convicted of major crimes.

pen·knife (pĕn′nīf′) ►*n.* A small pocketknife.

pen·man·ship (pĕn′mən-shĭp′) ►*n.* The art, skill, or style of handwriting.

Penn (pĕn), **William** 1644–1718. English Quaker colonizer in America.

pen name also **pen·name** (pĕn′nām′) ►*n.* A pseudonym used by a writer.

pen·nant (pĕn′ənt) ►*n.* **1.** A long, tapering, usu. triangular flag, used on ships for signaling or identification. **2.** A flag or emblem similar to a pennant. **3.** *Sports* A flag that symbolizes the championship of a league. [Blend of PENDANT and PENNON.]

pen·ne (pĕn′ā) ►*n., pl.* **penne** Pasta in small short tubes with diagonally cut ends. [Ital., pl. of *penna*, feather.]

pen·ni·less (pĕn′ē-lĭs, pĕn′ə-) ►*adj.* **1.** Entirely without money. **2.** Very poor.

Pen·nines (pĕn′īnz′) also **Pen·nine Chain** (pĕn′īn′) A range of hills extending about 260 km (160 mi) from S Scotland to central England.

pen·non (pĕn′ən) ►*n.* A long narrow banner borne on a lance. [< Lat. *penna*, feather.]

Penn·syl·va·nia (pĕn′səl-vān′yə, -vā′nē-ə) A state of the E US. Cap. Harrisburg.

Pennsylvania Dutch ►*n.* **1.** *(takes pl. v.)* The descendants of German and Swiss immigrants who settled in Pennsylvania in the 1600s and 1700s. **2.** The dialect of High German spoken by the Pennsylvania Dutch. [< Ger. *Deutsch*, German.]

Penn·syl·va·nian (pĕn′səl-vān′yən, pĕn′səl-vā′nē-ən) *Geol.* ►*adj.* Of or being the 6th period of the Paleozoic Era, marked by the formation of coal-bearing rock. ►*n.* The Pennsylvanian Period.

pen·ny (pĕn′ē) ►*n., pl.* **-nies** **1.** A US or Canadian coin worth one cent. **2.** *pl.* **pence** (pĕns) A coin used in Great Britain, worth ¹⁄₁₀₀ of a pound. **3.** Any of various coins of small denomination. —*idiom:* **pretty penny** A considerable sum of money. [< OE *penig*, a coin.]

penny pincher ►*n. Informal* One who is very frugal in spending money. —**pen′ny-pinch′ing** *adj. & n.*

pen·ny·roy·al (pĕn′ē-roi′əl) ►*n.* Either of two plants whose leaves yield an aromatic oil.

pen·ny·weight (pĕn′ē-wāt′) ►*n.* A unit of troy weight equal to 24 grains, ¹⁄₂₀ of a troy ounce, or approx. 1.555 grams.

pen·ny-wise (pĕn′ē-wīz′) ►*adj.* Careful in

dealing with small sums of money or small matters.

Pe·nob·scot (pə-nŏb′skət, -skŏt′) ►*n., pl.* **-scot** or **-scots 1.** A member of a Native American people inhabiting central Maine. **2.** The Algonquian language of the Penobscot.

pe·nol·o·gy (pē-nŏl′ə-jē) ►*n.* The study, theory, and practice of prison management and criminal rehabilitation. [Lat. *poena*, penalty + –LOGY.] —**pe·nol′o·gist** *n.*

pen pal ►*n.* A person with whom one becomes acquainted through regular correspondence.

pen·sion (pĕn′shən) ►*n.* A sum of money paid regularly, esp. as a retirement benefit. ►*v.* To grant a pension to. [< Lat. *pēnsiō*, payment.]

pen·sion·er (pĕn′shə-nər) ►*n.* One who receives a pension.

pen·sive (pĕn′sĭv) ►*adj.* **1.** Engaged in deep and serious thought. **2.** Expressing deep, often melancholy thought. [< Lat. *pēnsāre*, think over.] —**pen′sive·ness** *n.*

pent (pĕnt) ►*v.* P.t. and p.part. of **pen²**. ►*adj.* Penned or shut up; closely confined.

penta– or **pent–** ►*pref.* Five: *pentameter*. [< Gk. *pente*, five.]

pen·ta·cle (pĕn′tə-kəl) ►*n.* A five-pointed star formed by five straight lines connecting the vertices of a pentagon. [Med.Lat. **pentāculum* < Gk. *pente*, five.]

pen·ta·gon (pĕn′tə-gŏn′) ►*n.* **1.** A polygon having five sides. **2. Pentagon** A five-sided building near Washington, DC, housing the US Department of Defense. —**pen·tag′o·nal** (pĕn-tăg′ə-nəl) *adj.*

pen·tam·e·ter (pĕn-tăm′ĭ-tər) ►*n.* Verse composed in lines of five metrical feet.

Pen·ta·teuch (pĕn′tə-tōōk′, -tyōōk′) ►*n.* The first five books of the Hebrew Scriptures. [< Gk. *Pentateukhos* : PENTA– + *teukhos*, scroll case.]

pen·tath·lon (pĕn-tăth′lən, -lŏn′) ►*n.* An athletic contest in which each participant competes in five track and field events. [Gk. : PENTA– + *athlon*, contest.]

Pen·te·cost (pĕn′tĭ-kôst′, -kŏst′) ►*n.* A Christian festival celebrated the 7th Sunday after Easter to commemorate the descent of the Holy Spirit upon the disciples. [< Gk. *pentēkostē (hēmera)*, fiftieth (day) < *pentēkonta*, fifty.]

pent·house (pĕnt′hous′) ►*n.* **1.** An apartment on the top floor or roof of a building. **2.** A structure attached to the side of a building or wall. [< OFr. *apendre*, be attached to.]

pent-up (pĕnt′ŭp′) ►*adj.* Not given expression; repressed: *pent-up emotions.*

pe·nul·ti·mate (pĭ-nŭl′tə-mĭt) ►*adj.* Next to last. [< Lat. *paenultimus*.] —**pe·nul′ti·mate** *n.*

pe·num·bra (pĭ-nŭm′brə) ►*n., pl.* **-brae** (-brē) or **-bras** A partial shadow, as in an eclipse, between regions of complete shadow and complete illumination. [< Lat. *paene*, almost + *umbra*, shadow.]

pe·nu·ri·ous (pə-nŏŏr′ē-əs, -nyŏŏr′-) ►*adj.* **1.** Impoverished. **2.** Miserly; stingy.

pen·u·ry (pĕn′yə-rē) ►*n.* Extreme poverty; destitution. [< Lat. *pēnūria*.]

pe·on (pē′ŏn′, pē′ən) ►*n.* **1.** A menial worker. **2a.** An unskilled laborer or farm worker, esp. of Latin America. **b.** Such a worker bound in servitude to a landlord creditor. [< Med.Lat. *pedō*, foot soldier; see PIONEER.] —**pe′on·age** (-ə-nĭj) *n.*

pe·o·ny (pē′ə-nē) ►*n., pl.* **-nies** A garden plant having large, variously colored flowers. [< Gk. *paiōnia*.]

peo·ple (pē′pəl) ►*n., pl.* **-ple 1.** Humans collectively. **2.** A body of persons living in the same political unit, esp. a country. **3.** *pl.* **-ples** A body of persons sharing a common religion, culture, or language. **4. the people** The mass of ordinary persons; populace. **5.** Family, relatives, or ancestors. ►*v.* **-pled, -pling** To populate. [< Lat. *populus*.]

pep (pĕp) *Informal* ►*n.* Energy; vim. ►*v.* **pepped, pep·ping** To impart pep to; invigorate. [< PEPPER.] —**pep′py** *adj.*

pep·per (pĕp′ər) ►*n.* **1a.** A tropical Asian vine bearing small berrylike fruit. **b.** A pungent spice produced from the dried fruit of this plant, used as a condiment. **2a.** Any of several tropical American plants, such as the bell pepper, having podlike, variously colored fruit. **b.** The mild to pungent fruit of any of these plants. ►*v.* **1.** To season or sprinkle with or as if with pepper. **2.** To strike with small missiles or gunfire. See Synonyms at **barrage**. [< Skt. *pippalī*.]

pep·per·corn (pĕp′ər-kôrn′) ►*n.* A preserved or dried berry of the pepper vine.

pep·per·mint (pĕp′ər-mĭnt′) ►*n.* **1.** An aromatic plant having leaves that yield a pungent oil. **2.** A candy flavored with this oil.

pep·per·y (pĕp′ə-rē) ►*adj.* **1.** Of, containing, or like pepper; pungent. **2.** Sharp-tempered; feisty. **3.** Fiery: *a peppery speech.*

pep·sin (pĕp′sĭn) ►*n.* **1.** A digestive enzyme found in gastric juice that catalyzes the breakdown of protein to peptides. **2.** A substance containing pepsin and used as a digestive aid. [< Gk. *pepsis*, digestion.]

pep talk ►*n. Informal* A speech meant to instill enthusiasm or bolster morale.

pep·tic (pĕp′tĭk) ►*adj.* **1.** Of or assisting digestion. **2.** Induced by or associated with the action of digestive secretions: *a peptic ulcer.* [< Gk. *peptein*, digest.]

pep·tide (pĕp′tīd′) ►*n.* Any of various natural or synthetic compounds consisting of two or more amino acids linked end to end. [< Gk. *peptein*, digest.]

Pepys (pēps, pĕp′ĭs), **Samuel** 1633–1703. English diarist. —**Pepys′i·an** *adj.*

Pe·quot (pē′kwŏt′) ►*n., pl.* **-quot** or **-quots 1.** A member of a Native American people of E Connecticut. **2.** The Algonquian language of the Pequot.

per (pûr) ►*prep.* **1.** To, for, or by each: *miles per hour.* **2.** According to: *per your instructions.* [Lat.]

per– ►*pref.* Containing a large or the largest possible proportion of an element: *peroxide.* [< Lat. *per*, through.]

per·am·bu·late (pə-răm′byə-lāt′) ►*v.* **-lat·ed, -lat·ing** To walk about; stroll. [Lat. *perambulāre*.] —**per·am′bu·la′tion** *n.*

per·am·bu·la·tor (pə-răm′byə-lā′tər) ►*n. Chiefly Brit.* A baby carriage.

per an·num (pər ăn′əm) ►*adv.* By the year; annually. [Lat.]

per·cale (pər-kāl′) ►*n.* A closely woven cotton fabric. [< Pers. *pargālah*, rag.]

per cap·i·ta (pər kăp′ĭ-tə) ►*adv. & adj.* Per person. [Med.Lat., by heads.]

per·ceive (pər-sēv′) ►*v.* **-ceived, -ceiv·ing 1.**

To become aware of through the senses. **2.** To become aware of or have knowledge of by using the mind; apprehend. **3.** To regard or consider; deem: *perceived a friendly gesture as a threat.* [< Lat. *percipere.*] —**per·ceiv′a·ble** *adj.*

per·cent also **per cent** (pər-sĕnt′) ▸*adv.* Out of each hundred; per hundred. ▸*n., pl.* **percent** also **per cent 1.** One part in a hundred. **2.** A percentage or portion. [< Lat. *per centum,* by the hundred.]

per·cent·age (pər-sĕn′tĭj) ▸*n.* **1.** A fraction or ratio with 100 understood as the denominator. **2.** A proportion or share in relation to a whole; part. **3.** *Informal* Advantage.

    Usage: Percentage, when preceded by *the,* takes a singular verb: *The percentage of unskilled workers is small.* When preceded by *a,* it takes either a singular or plural verb, depending on the number of the noun in the prepositional phrase that follows: *A small percentage of the workers are unskilled. A large percentage of the crop has spoiled.*

per·cen·tile (pər-sĕn′tīl′) ▸*n.* A number representing the percentage of data points in a set that have values at or below a given value.

per·cep·ti·ble (pər-sĕp′tə-bəl) ▸*adj.* Capable of being perceived. —**per·cep′ti·bil′i·ty** *n.*

per·cep·tion (pər-sĕp′shən) ▸*n.* **1.** The process, act, or result of perceiving. **2a.** Insight or knowledge gained by perceiving. **b.** The capacity for such insight. **3.** An interpretation or impression. [< Lat. *percipere, percept-,* perceive.]

per·cep·tive (pər-sĕp′tĭv) ▸*adj.* **1.** Of or relating to perception. **2a.** Having the ability to perceive. **b.** Marked by discernment; insightful. —**per·cep′tive·ly** *adv.*

per·cep·tu·al (pər-sĕp′chōō-əl) ▸*adj.* Of or involving perception.

perch[1] (pûrch) ▸*n.* **1.** A rod or branch serving as a roost for a bird. **2a.** A place for resting or sitting. **b.** A secure position. [< Lat. *pertica,* stick, pole.] —**perch** *v.*

perch[2] (pûrch) ▸*n., pl.* **perch** or **-es 1.** An edible freshwater fish. **2.** Any of various similar or related fishes. [< Gk. *perkē.*]

per·chance (pər-chăns′) ▸*adv.* Perhaps.

per·cip·i·ent (pər-sĭp′ē-ənt) ▸*adj.* Having the power of perceiving. [< Lat. *percipere,* perceive.] —**per·cip′i·ence** *n.*

per·co·late (pûr′kə-lāt′) ▸*v.* **-lat·ed, -lat·ing 1.** To pass or cause to pass through a porous substance. **2.** To make (coffee) in a percolator. [Lat. *percōlāre.*] —**per′co·la′tion** *n.*

per·co·la·tor (pûr′kə-lā′tər) ▸*n.* A coffeepot in which boiling water is filtered repeatedly through a basket of ground coffee.

per·cus·sion (pər-kŭsh′ən) ▸*n.* **1.** The striking together of two bodies, esp. when noise is produced. **2.** The sound, vibration, or shock caused by percussion. **3.** The act of detonating a percussion cap in a firearm. **4.** *Mus.* Percussion instruments or their players. [< Lat. *percutere, percuss-,* strike hard.] —**per·cus′sive** *adj.*

percussion cap ▸*n.* A thin metal cap explosive that is triggered by being struck.

percussion instrument ▸*n.* An instrument, such as a drum, gong, or maraca, in which sound is produced by one object striking another or by being scraped or shaken. —**per·cus′sion·ist** *n.*

per di·em (pər dē′əm, dī′əm) ▸*adv.* Per day. ▸*n.* An allowance for daily expenses. [Lat., by the day.]

per·di·tion (pər-dĭsh′ən) ▸*n.* **1.** Eternal damnation. **2.** Hell. [< Lat. *perdere,* lose : *per-,* completely + *dare,* give.]

per·e·gri·nate (pĕr′ĭ-grə-nāt′) ▸*v.* **-nat·ed, -nat·ing** To journey or travel from place to place. [< Lat. *peregrīnus,* foreigner.] —**per′e·gri·na′tion** *n.*

per·e·grine falcon (pĕr′ə-grĭn, -grēn′) ▸*n.* A large, widely distributed falcon much used in falconry.

per·emp·to·ry (pə-rĕmp′tə-rē) ▸*adj.* **1.** Precluding further debate or action: *a peremptory decree.* **2.** Not allowing contradiction or refusal; imperative. **3.** Imperious; dictatorial. [Lat. *perēmptōrius.*] —**per·emp′to·ri·ly** *adv.* —**per·emp′to·ri·ness** *n.*

per·en·ni·al (pə-rĕn′ē-əl) ▸*adj.* **1.** Lasting through the year or many years. **2a.** Lasting indefinitely; enduring. **b.** Recurring regularly. **3.** *Bot.* Living three or more years. ▸*n. Bot.* A perennial plant. [< Lat. *perennis.*] —**per·en′ni·al·ly** *adv.*

Per·es (pâr′ĕs), **Shimon** b. 1923. Polish-born Israeli prime minister (1984–86 and 1995–96).

per·fect (pûr′fĭkt) ▸*adj.* **1.** Lacking nothing essential. **2.** Being without defect or blemish: *a perfect specimen.* **3.** Completely suited for a particular purpose. **4.** Accurate; exact. **5.** Complete; utter: *a perfect fool.* **6.** *Gram.* Of or constituting a verb form expressing action completed prior to a particular point in time. ▸*n. Gram.* **1.** The perfect tense. **2.** A verb in this tense. ▸*v.* (pər-fĕkt′) To bring to perfection. [< Lat. *perfectus,* p.part. of *perficere,* finish.] —**per·fect′i·bil′i·ty** *n.* —**per·fect′i·ble** *adj.* —**per′fect·ly** *adv.*

    Syns: consummate, faultless, flawless, impeccable **Ant:** *imperfect* **adj.**

    Usage: Perfect has often been described as an absolute term, hence not allowing modification by *quite* and other qualifiers of degree. But the qualification of *perfect* meets with the approval of 74 percent of the Usage Panel. *Perfect* freely allows comparison in examples such as *There could be no more perfect spot for the picnic,* where it is used to mean "ideal for the purposes."

per·fec·tion (pər-fĕk′shən) ▸*n.* **1.** The quality or condition of being perfect. **2.** The act or process of perfecting. **3.** One considered perfect.

per·fec·tion·ism (pər-fĕk′shə-nĭz′əm) ▸*n.* A tendency to be displeased with anything not perfect or not meeting very high standards. —**per·fec′tion·ist** *adj. & n.*

per·fi·dy (pûr′fĭ-dē) ▸*n., pl.* **-dies** Deliberate breach of faith; treachery. [< Lat. *perfidus,* treacherous.] —**per·fid′i·ous** (pər-fĭd′ē-əs) *adj.* —**per·fid′i·ous·ly** *adv.*

per·fo·rate (pûr′fə-rāt′) ▸*v.* **-rat·ed, -rat·ing 1.** To pierce, punch, or bore a hole or holes in. **2.** To pierce or stamp with rows of holes to allow easy separation. [Lat. *perforāre.*] —**per′fo·ra′tion** *n.*

per·force (pər-fôrs′) ▸*adv.* By necessity; by force of circumstance.

per·form (pər-fôrm′) ▸*v.* **1.** To begin and carry through to completion; do. **2.** To function as expected or required: *workers not performing up to standard.* **3.** To give a public performance (of). [< OFr. *parfornir*.] —**per·form′er** *n.*

per·for·mance (pər-fôr′məns) ►*n.* **1.** The act or manner of performing. **2.** A presentation, as of a play or dance, before an audience. **3.** Something performed; accomplishment.

per·fume (pûr′fyo͞om′, pər-fyo͞om′) ►*n.* **1.** A fragrant substance, esp. a volatile liquid distilled from flowers or prepared synthetically. **2.** A pleasing scent or odor. See Synonyms at **fragrance.** ►*v.* (pər-fyo͞om′) **-fumed, -fum·ing** To fill with fragrance. [< OItal. *parfumare,* fill with smoke.]

per·fum·er·y (pər-fyo͞o′mə-rē) ►*n., pl.* **-ies 1.** Perfumes. **2.** An establishment that makes or sells perfume.

per·func·to·ry (pər-fŭngk′tə-rē) ►*adj.* Done routinely and with little care. [< Lat. *perfungī,* get through with.] —**per·func′to·ri·ly** *adv.* —**per·func′to·ri·ness** *n.*

per·go·la (pûr′gə-lə) ►*n.* An arbor or passageway of columns supporting a roof of trelliswork. [< Lat. *pergula*.]

per·haps (pər-hăps′) ►*adv.* Maybe; possibly.

peri- ►*pref.* **1.** Around; about: *periodontal.* **2.** Near: *perigee.* [< Gk. *peri,* around, near.]

per·i·anth (pĕr′ē-ănth′) ►*n.* The outer parts of a flower, usu. including the calyx and corolla. [PERI– + Gk. *anthos,* flower.]

per·i·car·di·um (pĕr′ĭ-kär′dē-əm) ►*n., pl.* **-di·a** (-dē-ə) The membranous sac that encloses the heart. [PERI– + Gk. *kardia,* heart.] —**per′i·car′di·al** *adj.*

Per·i·cles (pĕr′ĭ-klēz′) c. 495–429 BC. Athenian leader. —**Per′i·cle′an** *adj.*

per·i·gee (pĕr′ə-jē) ►*n.* The point in an orbit around the planet Earth where the orbiting body is closest to the planet. [PERI– + Gk. *gē,* earth.]

per·i·he·li·on (pĕr′ə-hē′lē-ən, -hēl′yən) ►*n., pl.* **-he·li·a** (-hē′lē-ə, -hēl′yə) The point in a solar orbit where the orbiting body is closest to the sun. [PERI– + Gk. *hēlios,* sun.]

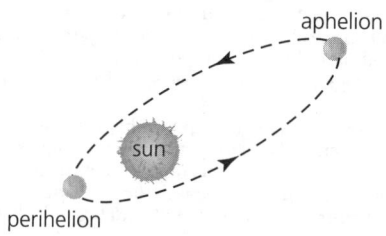

aphelion

sun

perihelion

perihelion

per·il (pĕr′əl) ►*n.* **1.** Danger. **2.** Something that endangers or involves risk. [< Lat. *perīculum*.] —**per′il·ous** *adj.*

pe·rim·e·ter (pə-rĭm′ĭ-tər) ►*n.* **1.** *Math.* A closed line bounding a plane area. **2.** The outer limits of an area. See Synonyms at **circumference.**

per·i·ne·um (pĕr′ə-nē′əm) ►*n., pl.* **-ne·a** (-nē′-ə) The portion of the body extending from the anus to the genitals. [< Gk. *perinaion* : PERI– + *inan,* excrete.]

pe·ri·od (pîr′ē-əd) ►*n.* **1.** An interval of time characterized by the occurrence of a certain condition or event. **2.** *Geol.* A unit of time longer than an epoch and shorter than an era.

3. An arbitrary unit of time, as of an academic day. **4.** An instance of menstruation. **5.** A punctuation mark (.) indicating the end of a declarative sentence and usu. a pause. **6.** *Math.* The interval between sets of repeating values in a wave or similar function. ►*adj.* Of or representing a historical time. [< Gk. *periodos,* circuit.]

pe·ri·od·ic (pîr′ē-ŏd′ĭk) ►*adj.* **1.** Having or marked by repeated cycles. **2.** Happening or appearing at regular intervals. **3.** Occasional; intermittent. —**pe·ri·od′i·cal·ly** *adv.* —**pe′ri·o·dic′i·ty** (-ə-dĭs′ĭ-tē) *n.*

pe·ri·od·i·cal (pîr′ē-ŏd′ĭ-kəl) ►*adj.* **1.** Periodic. **2a.** Published at regular intervals of more than one day. **b.** Of a publication issued at such intervals. ►*n.* A periodical publication.

periodical cicada ►*n.* A cicada of the E US that spends most of its 17- or 13-year life cycle underground as a nymph.

Periodic Table ►*n.* A table of the elements arranged by atomic number such that elements with similar properties are in the same column. See table on pages 276-277.

per·i·o·don·tal (pĕr′ē-ə-dŏn′tl) ►*adj.* Of or relating to tissue and structures surrounding and supporting the teeth. —**per′i·o·don′tist** *n.*

per·i·pa·tet·ic (pĕr′ə-pə-tĕt′ĭk) ►*adj.* Walking about from place to place. [< Gk. *peripatein,* walk about.]

pe·riph·er·al (pə-rĭf′ər-əl) ►*adj.* **1.** Of or on an outer boundary or periphery. **2.** Of minor relevance or importance. ►*n.* An auxiliary device, such as a printer or modem, that works in conjunction with a computer. —**pe·riph′er·al·ly** *adv.*

pe·riph·er·y (pə-rĭf′ə-rē) ►*n., pl.* **-ies 1.** A line that forms the boundary of an area; perimeter. See Synonyms at **circumference. 2.** The area along a boundary; margin. **3.** An area of secondary status or lesser importance: *the periphery of literary studies.* [< Gk. *periphereia* : PERI– + *pherein,* carry.]

pe·riph·ra·sis (pə-rĭf′rə-sĭs) ►*n., pl.* **-ses** (-sēz′) Circumlocution. [< Gk.] —**per′i·phras′tic** (pĕr′ə-frăs′tĭk) *adj.*

per·i·scope (pĕr′ĭ-skōp′) ►*n.* An optical instrument in which mirrors or prisms allow observation of objects not in a direct line of sight. —**per′i·scop′ic** (-skŏp′ĭk) *adj.*

per·ish (pĕr′ĭsh) ►*v.* **1.** To die, esp. in a violent or untimely manner. **2.** To disappear gradually. [< Lat. *perīre*.]

per·ish·a·ble (pĕr′ĭ-shə-bəl) ►*adj.* Subject to decay or spoilage. ►*n.* **perishables** Items, esp. foodstuffs, that are perishable. —**per′ish·a·bil′i·ty** *n.* —**per′ish·a·bly** *adv.*

per·i·stal·sis (pĕr′ĭ-stôl′sĭs, -stăl′-) ►*n., pl.* **-ses** (-sēz) The wavelike muscular contractions of the digestive tract or other tubular structures by which contents are forced onward toward the opening. [< Gk. *peristellein,* wrap around.] —**per′i·stal′tic** *adj.*

per·i·style (pĕr′ĭ-stīl′) ►*n.* A series of columns surrounding a building or enclosing a court. [< Gk. *peristulon* : PERI– + *stulos,* pillar.]

per·i·to·ne·um (pĕr′ĭ-tn-ē′əm) ►*n., pl.* **-to·ne·a** (-tn-ē′ə) The membrane that lines the walls of the abdominal cavity. [< Gk. *peritonaios,* stretched across.]

per·i·to·ni·tis (pĕr′ĭ-tn-ī′tĭs) ►*n.* Inflammation of the peritoneum.

per·i·wig (pĕr′ĭ-wĭg′) ►*n.* A wig; peruke. [< OFr. *perruque,* PERUKE.]

per·i·win·kle[1] (pĕr′ĭ-wĭng′kəl) ►*n.* A small, often edible marine snail having a cone-shaped shell. [Prob. < OE *pīnewincle.*]

per·i·win·kle[2] (pĕr′ĭ-wĭng′kəl) ►*n.* A trailing evergreen plant having glossy, dark green leaves and blue flowers. [< Lat. *pervinca.*]

per·ju·ry (pûr′jə-rē) ►*n., pl.* -ries *Law* The crime of deliberately testifying falsely under oath. [< Lat. *periūrium.*] —**per′jure** *v.* —**per′jur·er** *n.*

perk[1] (pûrk) ►*v.* To raise (e.g., the head or ears) smartly or attentively. —*phrasal verb:* **perk up 1.** To regain or cause to regain one's good spirits or liveliness. **2.** To add to or refresh the appearance of. [Poss. < ME *perken,* to perch.] —**perk′i·ness** *n.* —**perk′y** *adj.*

perk[2] (pûrk) ►*n. Informal* A perquisite.

perk[3] (pûrk) ►*v.* To percolate.

Per·kins (pûr′kĭnz), **Frances** 1882–1965. Amer. social reformer and public official.

Frances Perkins

per·lite (pûr′līt′) ►*n.* A natural volcanic glass used in a fluffy heat-expanded form for fire-resistant insulation and in soil for potting plants. [< Fr. *perle* or Ger. *Perle,* pearl.]

perm (pûrm) *Informal* ►*n.* A permanent. ►*v.* To give (hair) a permanent.

Perm (pĕrm) A city of W-central Russia in the foothills of the Ural Mts.

per·ma·frost (pûr′mə-frôst′, -frŏst′) ►*n.* Permanently frozen subsoil occurring in perennially frigid areas.

per·ma·nent (pûr′mə-nənt) ►*adj.* Lasting or fixed. ►*n.* A long-lasting hair wave. [< Lat. *permanēre,* endure.] —**per′ma·nence, per′ma·nen·cy** *n.* —**per′ma·nent·ly** *adv.*

permanent press ►*n.* A chemical process in which fabrics are permanently treated for wrinkle resistance. —**per′ma·nent-press′** *adj.*

per·me·a·ble (pûr′mē-ə-bəl) ►*adj.* Capable of being permeated, esp. by liquids or gases. —**per′me·a·bil′i·ty** *n.*

per·me·ate (pûr′mē-āt′) ►*v.* -at·ed, -at·ing **1.** To pass through openings or small gaps of. **2.** To spread or flow throughout; pervade. See Synonyms at **imbue.** [Lat. *permeāre.*] —**per′me·a′tion** *n.* —**per′me·a′tive** *adj.*

Per·mi·an (pûr′mē-ən, pĕr′-) *Geol.* ►*adj.* Of or being the 7th and last period of the Paleozoic Era, ending with the largest known mass extinction in the history of life. ►*n.* The Permian Period. [After PERM.]

per·mis·si·ble (pər-mĭs′ə-bəl) ►*adj.* Permitted or allowable. —**per·mis′si·bil′i·ty** *n.*

per·mis·sion (pər-mĭsh′ən) ►*n.* Consent, esp. formal consent. [< Lat. *permittere,* permit.]
 Syns: *authorization, consent, leave, license, sanction* **Ant:** *prohibition* n.

per·mis·sive (pər-mĭs′ĭv) ►*adj.* Tending to grant permission; tolerant or lenient. —**per·mis′sive·ly** *adv.* —**per·mis′sive·ness** *n.*

per·mit (pər-mĭt′) ►*v.* -mit·ted, -mit·ting **1.** To allow the doing of; consent to. **2.** To afford opportunity or possibility (for): *weather that permits sailing.* ►*n.* (pûr′mĭt, pər-mĭt′) A document granting permission. [< Lat. *permittere.*] —**per′mit·tee′** *n.* —**per·mit′ter** *n.*

per·mu·ta·tion (pûr′myōō-tā′shən) ►*n.* **1.** The act of altering a given set of objects in a group. **2.** *Math.* An ordered arrangement of the elements of a set. **3.** A complete change; a transformation: *the country's permutation into a modern democracy.* [< Lat. *permūtāre,* change completely.] —**per′mu·ta′tion·al** *adj.*

per·ni·cious (pər-nĭsh′əs) ►*adj.* **1.** Deadly: *a pernicious virus.* **2.** Destructive: *pernicious rumors.* [< Lat. *perniciēs,* destruction.] —**per·ni′cious·ness** *n.*

pernicious anemia ►*n.* An anemia caused by failure to absorb vitamin B_{12}, marked by a decreased amount and increased size of red blood cells and neurological and gastrointestinal disturbances.

Pe·rón (pə-rōn′, pĕ-) Argentinian popular and political leaders, including **Juan Domingo** (1895–1974), **(Maria) Eva Duarte de Perón** ("Evita," 1919–52), and **Maria Estela Martínez de Perón** ("Isabelita," b. 1931).

per·o·rate (pĕr′ə-rāt′) ►*v.* -rat·ed, -rat·ing **1.** To conclude a speech, esp. with a formal recapitulation. **2.** To speak at great length; declaim. [Lat. *perōrāre,* speak at length.] —**per′o·ra′tion** *n.*

per·ox·ide (pə-rŏk′sīd′) ►*n.* **1.** Any of several compounds containing the O_2 group, often used as oxidizing compounds or bleaches. **2.** Hydrogen peroxide. ►*v.* -id·ed, -id·ing To treat or bleach with peroxide.

per·pen·dic·u·lar (pûr′pən-dĭk′yə-lər) ►*adj.* **1.** Intersecting at or forming right angles. **2.** At right angles to the horizontal; vertical. [< Lat. *perpendiculum,* plumb line.] —**per′pen·dic′u·lar** *n.* —**per′pen·dic′u·lar′i·ty** (-lăr′ĭ-tē) *n.*

per·pe·trate (pûr′pĭ-trāt′) ►*v.* -trat·ed, -trat·ing To be guilty of or responsible for; commit. [Lat. *perpetrāre,* accomplish < *patrāre,* bring about < *pater,* father.] —**per′pe·tra′tion** *n.* —**per′pe·tra′tor** *n.*

per·pet·u·al (pər-pĕch′ōō-əl) ►*adj.* **1.** Lasting for eternity. **2.** Lasting for an indefinitely long time. **3.** Continuing without interruption. [< Lat. *perpetuus,* continuous.] —**per·pet′u·al·ly** *adv.*

per·pet·u·ate (pər-pĕch′ōō-āt′) ►*v.* -at·ed, -at·ing **1.** To make perpetual. **2.** To prolong the existence of. —**per·pet′u·ance, per·pet′u·a′tion** *n.* —**per·pet′u·a′tor** *n.*

per·pe·tu·i·ty (pûr′pĭ-tōō′ĭ-tē, -tyōō′-) ►*n., pl.* -ties The quality or condition of being perpetual. —*idiom:* **in perpetuity** Forever.

per·plex (pər-plĕks′) ►*v.* **1.** To confuse or trouble with uncertainty or doubt. **2.** To complicate. [< Lat. *perplexus*, confused.] —**per·plex′ing·ly** *adv.* —**per·plex′i·ty** *n.*
   Syns: *bewilder, confound, confuse, mystify, puzzle* v.

per·qui·site (pûr′kwĭ-zĭt) ►*n.* **1.** A payment or profit received in addition to a regular wage or salary. **2.** A tip; gratuity. **3.** Something claimed as an exclusive right. [< Lat. *perquīrere*, search for.]

Per·ry (pĕr′ē), **Matthew Calbraith** 1794–1858. Amer. naval officer.

Perry, Oliver Hazard 1785–1819. Amer. naval officer.

pers. ►*abbr.* person

per se (pər sā′, sē′) ►*adv.* In or by itself or oneself; as such. [Lat. *per sē.*]

per·se·cute (pûr′sĭ-kyōōt′) ►*v.* **-cut·ed, -cut·ing** To oppress or harass, esp. because of race, religion, gender, sexual orientation, or beliefs. [< Lat. *persequī, persecūt-*, pursue.] —**per′se·cu′tion** *n.* —**per′se·cu′tor** *n.*

Per·sep·o·lis (pər-sĕp′ə-lĭs) An ancient city of Persia in present-day SW Iran.

per·se·vere (pûr′sə-vîr′) ►*v.* **-vered, -ver·ing** To persist in or remain constant to a purpose, idea, or task in spite of obstacles. [< Lat. *persevērus*, very serious.] —**per′se·ver′ance** *n.*

Per·shing (pûr′shĭng, -zhĭng), **John Joseph** "Black Jack." 1860–1948. Amer. general.

Per·sia (pûr′zhə, -shə) **1.** also **Persian Empire** An ancient empire of SW Asia. **2.** See **Iran.**

Per·sian (pûr′zhən, -shən) ►*n.* **1.** A native or inhabitant of Persia or Iran. **2.** Any of the W Iranian dialects or languages of ancient or medieval Persia and modern Iran. **3.** A domestic cat having a long coat and a broad head with a snub nose.

Persian Gulf An arm of the Arabian Sea between Arabia and SW Iran.

per·si·flage (pûr′sə-fläzh′) ►*n.* Light good-natured talk; banter. [Fr. < *persifler*, to banter.]

per·sim·mon (pər-sĭm′ən) ►*n.* **1.** Any of several Asian and North American trees having hard wood and edible orange-red fruit. **2.** The fruit of a persimmon tree. [Of Algonquian orig.]

per·sist (pər-sĭst′, -zĭst′) ►*v.* **1.** To be obstinately repetitious, insistent, or tenacious. **2.** To hold steadfastly to a purpose or undertaking. **3.** To continue in existence; last. [Lat. *persistere* < *sistere*, stand.] —**per·sis′tence** *n.* —**per·sis′tent** *adj.* —**per·sis′tent·ly** *adv.*

per·snick·e·ty (pər-snĭk′ĭ-tē) ►*adj.* Very particular about details; fastidious. [?]

per·son (pûr′sən) ►*n.* **1.** A human. See Usage Note at **man. 2.** An individual of specified character: *a person of importance.* **3.** The personality of a human; self. **4.** The living body of a human. **5.** *Christianity* Any of the three members of the Trinity (Father, Son, and Holy Spirit). **6.** *Gram.* Any of three groups of pronouns with corresponding verb inflections that distinguish the speaker (first person), the individual addressed (second person), and the individual or thing spoken of (third person). —*idiom:* **in person** Being physically present: *went in person to request the favor.* [< Lat. *persōna*, mask, role, person.]

per·so·na (pər-sō′nə) ►*n., pl.* **-nas** or **-nae** (-nē) **1.** The character represented by the voice of the speaker in a literary work. **2.** *pl.* **-nas** One's public image or personality. [Lat. *persōna*, mask, role, person.]

per·son·a·ble (pûr′sə-nə-bəl) ►*adj.* Having a pleasantly sociable manner. —**per′son·a·ble·ness** *n.* —**per′son·a·bly** *adv.*

per·son·age (pûr′sə-nĭj) ►*n.* A person of distinction. See Synonyms at **celebrity.**

per·son·al (pûr′sə-nəl) ►*adj.* **1.** Of a particular person; private. **2.** Done in person: *a personal appearance.* **3.** Aimed pointedly at an individual, esp. in a critical or hostile manner. **4.** Of the body or physical being. **5.** *Law* Relating to a person's movable property. **6.** Having the nature of a person: *didn't believe in a personal god.* **7.** Indicating grammatical person. ►*n.* A personal item or notice in a newspaper. —**per′son·al·ly** *adv.*

personal computer ►*n.* A computer built around a microprocessor for use by an individual.

personal effects ►*pl.n.* Items generally carried or worn on one's person, such as clothing, jewelry, keys, and a wallet or purse.

per·son·al·i·ty (pûr′sə-năl′ĭ-tē) ►*n., pl.* **-ties 1.** The totality of distinctive behavioral traits of a specific person. **2.** The quality or condition of being a person. **3.** The personal traits that make one socially appealing. **4.** *Informal* A celebrity.

per·son·al·ize (pûr′sə-nə-līz) ►*v.* **-ized, -iz·ing 1.** To make or alter so as to meet individual specifications. **2.** To have printed, engraved, or monogrammed with one's name or initials. **3.** To personify. —**per′son·al·i·za′tion** *n.*

personal property ►*n. Law* Property owned by a person that is not real estate.

personal watercraft ►*n.* A motorized recreational water vehicle usu. ridden by straddling a seat.

persona non gra·ta (nŏn grä′tə, grăt′ə) ►*adj.* Unacceptable or unwelcome, esp. to a foreign government. [Lat. *persōna nōn grāta*, unacceptable person.]

per·son·i·fy (pər-sŏn′ə-fī′) ►*v.* **-fied, -fy·ing 1.** To think of or represent (e.g., an inanimate object) as a person. **2.** To be the embodiment or perfect example of. —**per·son′i·fi·ca′tion** *n.* —**per·son′i·fi′er** *n.*

per·son·nel (pûr′sə-nĕl′) ►*n.* **1.** The body of persons employed by or active in an organization, business, or service. **2.** The department of human resources in an organization. [Fr.]

per·spec·tive (pər-spĕk′tĭv) ►*n.* **1a.** The relationship of aspects of a subject to each other and to a whole. **b.** A point of view. **2.** The technique of representing three-dimensional objects and depth relationships on a two-dimensional surface. **3.** A vista. [< Lat. *perspicere*, inspect : *per-*, through + *specere*, look.]

per·spi·cac·i·ty (pûr′spĭ-kăs′ĭ-tē) ►*n.* Acuteness of perception or understanding. [< Lat. *perspicere*, see through.] —**per·spi·ca′cious** (-kā′shəs) *adj.*

per·spic·u·ous (pər-spĭk′yōō-əs) ►*adj.* Clearly expressed or presented; lucid. [< Lat. *perspicere*, see through.] —**per′spi·cu′i·ty** (-kyōō′ĭ-tē) *n.* —**per·spic′u·ous·ness** *n.*

per·spi·ra·tion (pûr′spə-rā′shən) ►*n.* **1.** The saline moisture excreted through the pores of the skin by the sweat glands; sweat. **2.** The act or process of perspiring.

per·spire (pər-spīr′) ▸*v.* **-spired, -spir·ing** To excrete through the pores of the skin. [< Lat. *perspīrāre*, breathe through.]

per·suade (pər-swād′) ▸*v.* **-suad·ed, -suad·ing** To induce to undertake a course of action or embrace a point of view by means of argument, reasoning, or entreaty. [Lat. *persuādēre* < *suādēre*, urge.] —**per·suad′a·ble** *adj.* —**per·suad′er** *n.* —**per·sua′sive** *adj.* —**per·sua′sive·ly** *adv.* —**per·sua′sive·ness** *n.*

per·sua·sion (pər-swā′zhən) ▸*n.* **1.** The act of persuading or state of being persuaded. **2.** The ability to persuade. **3.** A strongly held opinion. **4.** A body of religious beliefs.

pert (pûrt) ▸*adj.* **-er, -est 1.** High-spirited. **2.** Impudently bold. **3.** Trim and stylish; jaunty. [< Lat. *apertus,* p.part. of *aperīre,* to open.] —**pert′ly** *adv.* —**pert′ness** *n.*

per·tain (pər-tān′) ▸*v.* **1.** To have reference; relate. **2.** To belong as an adjunct or accessory. [< Lat. *pertinēre.*]

Perth (pûrth) A city of SW Australia near the Indian Ocean.

per·ti·na·cious (pûr′tn-ā′shəs) ▸*adj.* **1.** Holding tenaciously to a purpose, belief, opinion, or course of action. **2.** Extremely persistent. [< Lat. *pertināx.*] —**per′ti·na′cious·ly** *adv.* —**per′ti·na′cious·ness** *n.* —**per′ti·nac′i·ty** (-ăs′ĭ-tē) *n.*

per·ti·nent (pûr′tn-ənt) ▸*adj.* Clearly related to a matter at hand. [< Lat. *pertinēre,* pertain.] —**per′ti·nence, per′ti·nen·cy** *n.*

per·turb (pər-tûrb′) ▸*v.* To disturb greatly; make uneasy or anxious. [< Lat. *perturbāre.*] —**per·turb′a·ble** *adj.* —**per·tur·ba′tion** *n.*

per·tus·sis (pər-tŭs′ĭs) ▸*n.* See **whooping cough.** [Lat. *per-,* intensive pref. + *tussis,* cough.] —**per·tus′sal** *adj.*

Pe·ru (pə-rōō′) A country of W South America on the Pacific. Cap. Lima. —**Pe·ru′vi·an** (-vē-ən) *adj. & n.*

pe·ruke (pə-rōōk′) ▸*n.* A wig, esp. one worn by men in the 1600s and 1700s; a periwig. [< OItal. *perrucca.*]

pe·ruse (pə-rōōz′) ▸*v.* **-rused, -rus·ing** To read or examine, esp. with great care. [ME *perusen,* use up.] —**pe·rus′al** *n.*

per·vade (pər-vād′) ▸*v.* **-vad·ed, -vad·ing** To spread throughout; permeate. See Synonyms at **imbue.** [Lat. *pervādere.*] —**per·va′sion** (-vā′zhən) *n.* —**per·va′sive** (-vā′sĭv, -zĭv) *adj.* —**per·va′sive·ness** *n.*

per·verse (pər-vûrs′, pûr′vûrs′) ▸*adj.* **1.** Directed away from what is right; perverted. **2.** Willfully opposing what is reasonable. **3.** Having an effect opposite to what is intended or expected. [< Lat. *perversus,* p.part. of *pervertere,* pervert.] —**per·verse′ness, per·ver′si·ty** *n.*

per·ver·sion (pər-vûr′zhən, -shən) ▸*n.* **1.** The act of perverting or the state of being perverted. **2.** A sexual practice considered deviant.

per·vert (pər-vûrt′) ▸*v.* **1.** To cause to turn away from what is right, proper, or good; debase: *accused of perverting justice.* **2.** To corrupt (someone) morally. See Synonyms at **corrupt. 3.** To interpret incorrectly. ▸*n.* (pûr′vûrt′) One who practices sexual perversion. [< Lat. *pervertere.*] —**per·vert′ed** *adj.*

per·vi·ous (pûr′vē-əs) ▸*adj.* **1.** Open to passage;

permeable. **2.** Open to arguments, ideas, or change. [< Lat. *pervius.*] —**per′vi·ous·ly** *adv.* —**per′vi·ous·ness** *n.*

pes·ce·tar·i·an also **pes·ca·tar·i·an** (pĕs′kə-târ′ē-ən) ▸*n.* A person whose diet is primarily vegetarian but also includes fish. [Perhaps Italian *pesce,* fish (< Latin *piscis*) or a kindred Romance word such as Spanish *pescado,* fish + (VEGE)TARIAN.]

pe·se·ta (pə-sā′tə) ▸*n.* The primary unit of currency in Spain and Andorra before the adoption of the euro. [Sp., dim. of *peso,* PESO.]

pes·ky (pĕs′kē) ▸*adj.* **-ki·er, -ki·est** *Informal* Troublesome; annoying. [Prob. < PEST.] —**pes′ki·ly** *adv.* —**pes′ki·ness** *n.*

pe·so (pā′sō) ▸*n., pl.* **-sos** See table at **currency.** [Sp. < Lat. *pēnsum,* weight.]

pes·si·mism (pĕs′ə-mĭz′əm) ▸*n.* **1.** A tendency to take the gloomiest possible view of a situation. **2.** The doctrine or belief that the evil in the world outweighs the good. [< Lat. *pessimus,* worst.] —**pes′si·mist** *n.* —**pes′si·mis′tic** *adj.*

pest (pĕst) ▸*n.* **1.** An annoying person or thing; nuisance. **2.** An injurious organism, esp. an insect. [< Lat. *pestis,* plague.]

pes·ter (pĕs′tər) ▸*v.* To annoy, as with repeated demands or questions. [Prob. < OFr. *empestrer,* hobble.] —**pes′ter·er** *n.*

pes·ti·cide (pĕs′tĭ-sīd′) ▸*n.* A chemical used to kill pests, esp. insects.

pes·tif·er·ous (pĕ-stĭf′ər-əs) ▸*adj.* **1.** Producing, causing, or contaminated with an infectious disease. **2.** Bothersome or annoying. [< Lat. *pestis,* plague.] —**pes·tif′er·ous·ly** *adv.* —**pes·tif′er·ous·ness** *n.*

pes·ti·lence (pĕs′tə-ləns) ▸*n.* A usu. fatal epidemic disease, esp. bubonic plague.

pes·ti·lent (pĕs′tə-lənt) ▸*adj.* **1.** Tending to cause death. **2.** Likely to cause an epidemic disease. [< Lat. *pestis,* plague.] —**pes′ti·len′tial** (-lĕn′shəl) *adj.*

pes·tle (pĕs′əl, pĕs′təl) ▸*n.* A club-shaped, hand-held tool for grinding or mashing substances in a mortar. [< Lat. *pistillum.*]

pes·to (pĕs′tō) ▸*n.* A sauce usu. made of fresh basil, garlic, pine nuts, olive oil, and grated cheese. [Ital. < *pistare,* pound.]

pet¹ (pĕt) ▸*n.* **1.** An animal kept for amusement or companionship. **2.** An object of the affections. **3.** A favorite: *the teacher's pet.* ▸*adj.* **1.** Kept as a pet. **2.** Particularly cherished or indulged. ▸*v.* **pet·ted, pet·ting 1.** To stroke or caress gently. See Synonyms at **caress. 2.** To fondle and caress amorously. [< OIr. *peata.*]

pet² (pĕt) ▸*n.* A fit of bad temper or pique. [?]

Pé·tain (pā-tăN′), Marshal **Henri Philippe** 1856–1951. French soldier and politician.

pet·al (pĕt′l) ▸*n.* One of the often brightly colored parts surrounding the reproductive organs of a flower. [< Gk. *petalon,* leaf.] —**pet′aled, pet′alled** *adj.*

pe·tard (pĭ-tärd′) ▸*n.* A small bell-shaped bomb used to breach a gate or wall. —*idiom:* **be hoist with one's own petard** To be undone by one's own schemes. [< OFr. *peter,* break wind.]

pet·cock (pĕt′kŏk′) ▸*n.* A small valve used to drain pipes. [Perh. PET¹ + COCK¹.]

pe·ter (pē′tər) ▸*v.* To come to an end slowly; diminish: *Their enthusiasm slowly petered out.* [?]

Peter ►*n.* See table at **Bible.**
Peter, Saint. d. c. AD 67. The chief of the 12 Apostles.
Peter I "the Great." 1672–1725. Russian czar (1682–1725).

Peter I

pet·i·ole (pĕt′ē-ōl′) ►*n. Bot.* The stalk by which a leaf is attached to a stem; leafstalk. [Prob. < Lat. *pediculus,* little foot.]
pet·it also **pet·ty** (pĕt′ē) ►*adj. Law* Lesser in seriousness or scale. [< OFr.]
pe·tite (pə-tēt′) ►*adj.* Small, slender, and trim. See Synonyms at **small.** [Fr.]
petit four ►*n., pl.* **pe·tits fours** or **pet·it fours** (pĕt′ē) A small, square-cut, frosted tea cake. [Fr.]
pe·ti·tion (pə-tĭsh′ən) ►*n.* **1.** A solemn request; entreaty. **2.** A formal document containing such a request. ►*v.* **1.** To address a petition to. **2.** To request formally. **3.** To make a request, esp. formally: *petitioned for retrial.* [< Lat. *petere, petīt-,* request.] —**pe·ti′tion·ar′y** (-tĭsh′ə-nĕr′ē) *adj.* —**pe·ti′tion·er** *n.*
petit jury also **petty jury** ►*n.* See **jury** (sense 1).
petit mal (mäl, măl) ►*n.* A mild form of epilepsy, marked by transient lapses of consciousness and the absence of convulsions. [Fr.]
petit point ►*n.* Needlepoint done with a small stitch. [Fr.]
Pe·trarch (pē′trärk′, pĕt′rärk′), **Francesco** 1304–74. Italian poet, scholar, and humanist. —**Pe·trarch′an** (pĭ-trär′kən) *adj.*
pe·tri dish (pē′trē) ►*n.* A shallow dish with a loose cover, used to culture microorganisms. [After J.R. *Petri* (1852–1921).]
pet·ri·fy (pĕt′rə-fī′) ►*v.* **-fied, -fy·ing 1.** To convert (wood or other organic matter) into a stony replica by impregnation with dissolved minerals. **2.** To cause to lose vitality or become impervious to change; deaden: *a routine that petrified her thinking.* **3.** To stun or paralyze with terror. [< Gk. *petra,* rock.] —**pet′ri·fac′tion** (-făk′shən), **pet′ri·fi·ca′tion** *n.*
petro– or **petri–** or **petr–** ►*pref.* **1.** Rock; stone: *petroglyph.* **2.** Petroleum: *petrochemical.* [< Gk. *petros,* stone.]
pet·ro·chem·i·cal (pĕt′rō-kĕm′ĭ-kəl) ►*n.* A chemical derived from petroleum or natural gas. —**pet′ro·chem′i·cal** *adj.*
pet·ro·glyph (pĕt′rə-glĭf′) ►*n. Archaeol.* A carving or incised drawing on rock, esp. one made by prehistoric people. [< Gk. *gluphē,* carving.] —**pet′ro·glyph′ic** *adj.*

petroglyph
McKee Springs, Dinosaur National Monument, Colorado

pe·trog·ra·phy (pə-trŏg′rə-fē) ►*n.* The description and classification of rocks. —**pe·trog′ra·pher** *n.*
pet·rol (pĕt′rəl) ►*n. Chiefly Brit.* Gasoline. [Fr. *(essence de) pétrole,* (essence of) petroleum.]
pet·ro·la·tum (pĕt′rə-lā′təm, -lä′təm) ►*n.* See **petroleum jelly.** [< PETROL.]
pe·tro·le·um (pə-trō′lē-əm) ►*n.* A thick, flammable, yellow-to-black liquid hydrocarbon mixture that occurs naturally beneath the earth's surface and is processed for fractions including natural gas, gasoline, naphtha, kerosene, paraffin wax, and asphalt. [< Med.Lat. *petrōleum.*]
petroleum jelly ►*n.* A colorless-to-amber gelatinous semisolid, obtained from petroleum and used in lubricants and medicinal ointments.
pe·trol·o·gy (pə-trŏl′ə-jē) ►*n.* The study of the origin, composition, structure, and alteration of rocks. —**pe·trol′o·gist** *n.*
pet·ti·coat (pĕt′ē-kōt′) ►*n.* A garment worn under a dress or skirt, often decorated with ruffles or lace. [ME *peticote.*]
pet·ti·fog·ger (pĕt′ē-fŏg′ər, -fô′gər) ►*n.* A petty, quibbling, or unscrupulous lawyer. —**pet′ti·fog′** *v.* —**pet′ti·fog′ger·y** *n.*
pet·tish (pĕt′ĭsh) ►*adj.* Petulant or ill-tempered. [Prob. < PET².]
pet·ty (pĕt′ē) ►*adj.* **-ti·er, -ti·est 1.** Of small importance; trivial. **2.** Narrow-minded or ungenerous, esp. in trifling matters. **3.** Secondary in importance or rank. **4.** *Law* Var. of **petit.** [< OFr. *petit,* small.] —**pet′ti·ly** *adv.* —**pet′ti·ness** *n.*
petty cash ►*n.* A small fund of money for incidental expenses, as in an office.
petty jury ►*n.* Var. of **petit jury.**
petty officer ►*n.* A noncommissioned officer in the US Navy or Coast Guard.
pet·u·lant (pĕch′ə-lənt) ►*adj.* Unreasonably irritable or ill-tempered; peevish. [Lat. *petulāns.*] —**pet′u·lance, pet′u·lan·cy** *n.* —**pet′u·lant·ly** *adv.*
pe·tu·nia (pĭ-tōōn′yə, -tyōōn′-) ►*n.* A garden plant having funnel-shaped, variously colored flowers. [Of Tupí-Guaraní orig.]
pew (pyōō) ►*n.* A bench for the congregation in a church. [< Lat. *podium,* balcony.]
pe·wee (pē′wē) ►*n.* A small brownish North American flycatcher. [Imit. of its call.]
pew·ter (pyōō′tər) ►*n.* An alloy of tin with

various amounts of antimony, copper, and sometimes lead, used for kitchen utensils and tableware. [< VLat. *peltrum*.] **—pew′ter** *adj.*

pe·yo·te (pā-ō′tē) ►*n.* **1.** A spineless cactus of Mexico and the SW US, having buttonlike tubercles that are the source of mescaline. **2.** Peyote buttons. [< Nahuatl *peyotl*.]

PF ►*abbr.* personal foul

PFC ►*abbr.* private first class

pfen·nig (fĕn′ĭg) ►*n., pl.* **pfennig** or **-nigs** A coin formerly used in Germany, worth ¹⁄₁₀₀ of a deutsche mark. [Ger.]

PG (pē′jē′) A trademark for a movie rating granting admission to persons of all ages but advising parental guidance in the case of children.

pg. ►*abbr.* page

PG-13 (pē′jē′thûr-tēn′) A trademark for a movie rating granting admission to persons of all ages but advising parental guidance for children under 13.

PGA ►*abbr.* Professional Golfers' Association

pH (pē′āch′) ►*n.* A measure of the acidity or alkalinity of a solution, numerically equal to 7 for neutral solutions, increasing with increasing alkalinity and decreasing with increasing acidity. [*p(otential of) h(ydrogen)*.]

pha·e·ton (fā′ĭ-tn) ►*n.* A light, four-wheeled open carriage, usu. drawn by a pair of horses. [Fr. *phaéton*.]

–phage ►*suff.* One that eats: *bacteriophage*. [< Gk. *phagein*, to eat.]

phago– ►*pref.* Eating; consuming: *phagocyte*. [< Gk. *phagein*, eat.]

phag·o·cyte (făg′ə-sīt′) ►*n.* A cell, such as a white blood cell, that engulfs and absorbs foreign bodies in the bloodstream and tissues. **—phag′o·cyt′ic** (-sĭt′ĭk) *adj.*

pha·lanx (fā′lăngks, făl′ăngks′) ►*n., pl.* **-es** or **pha·lan·ges** (fə-lăn′jēz, fā-) **1.** A compact or close-knit group. **2.** A formation of infantry carrying overlapping shields and long spears, developed in Greece in the 4th cent. BC. **3.** *pl.* **phalanges** *Anat.* A bone of a finger or toe. [< Gk.]

phal·a·rope (făl′ə-rōp′) ►*n.* Any of several small wading shorebirds. [< Gk. *phalaris*, coot + *pous*, foot.]

phal·lus (făl′əs) ►*n., pl.* **phal·li** (făl′ī′) or **-es 1.** The penis. **2.** A representation of an erect penis. [< Gk. *phallos*.] **—phal′lic** *adj.*

Phan·e·ro·zo·ic (făn′ər-ə-zō′ĭk) ►*n.* Of or being the geologic time period from approx. 542 million years ago to the present, including the Paleozoic, Mesozoic, and Cenozoic Eras. [Gk. *phaneros*, visible + –ZOIC.]

phan·tasm (făn′tăz′əm) ►*n.* A phantom. [< Gk. *phantasma*.] **—phan·tas′mal** (făn-tăz′məl), **phan·tas′mic** (-tăz′mĭk) *adj.*

phan·tas·ma·go·ri·a (făn-tăz′mə-gôr′ē-ə) ►*n.* A fantastic sequence of haphazardly associative imagery, as in dreams. [Poss. OFr. *fantasme*, PHANTASM + *allegorie*, ALLEGORY.] **—phan·tas′ma·gor′ic** *adj.*

phan·tom (făn′təm) ►*n.* **1.** Something apparently seen, heard, or sensed, but having no physical reality; a ghost or apparition. **2.** An illusory mental image. ►*adj.* Resembling or being a phantom; illusive. [< Gk. *phantasma*.]

Phar·aoh also **phar·aoh** (fâr′ō, fā′rō) ►*n.* A king of ancient Egypt. **—Phar′a·on′ic** (fâr′-ā-ŏn′ĭk) *adj.*

phar·i·see (făr′ĭ-sē) ►*n.* **1. Pharisee** A member of an ancient Jewish group that emphasized observance of the Mosaic law in both oral and written forms. **2.** A hypocritical, self-righteous person. [< Aram. *pərišayyā*, pl. of *pəriš*, separate.] **—phar′i·sa′ic** (-sā′ĭk) *adj.*

phar·ma·ceu·ti·cal (făr′mə-sōō′tĭ-kəl) also **phar·ma·ceu·tic** (-tĭk) ►*adj.* Of pharmacy or pharmacists. ►*n.* A medicinal drug. [< Gk. *pharmakeutikos*.]

phar·ma·cist (făr′mə-sĭst) ►*n.* A person trained and licensed in pharmacy.

pharmaco– ►*pref.* Drug: *pharmacology*. [< Gk. *pharmakon*, drug.]

phar·ma·col·o·gy (făr′mə-kŏl′ə-jē) ►*n.* The science of drugs, including their composition, uses, and effects. **—phar′ma·co·log′-ic** (-kə-lŏj′ĭk), **phar′ma·co·log′i·cal** *adj.* **—phar′ma·col′o·gist** *n.*

phar·ma·co·poe·ia also **phar·ma·co·pe·ia** (făr′mə-kə-pē′ə) ►*n.* **1.** A book containing an official list of medicinal drugs together with articles on their preparation and use. **2.** A stock of drugs. [PHARMACO– + Gk. *poiein*, make.]

phar·ma·cy (făr′mə-sē) ►*n., pl.* **-cies 1.** The art of preparing and dispensing drugs. **2.** A place where drugs are sold; a drugstore. [< Gk. *pharmakeia*, use of drugs.]

pharyngo– or **pharyng–** ►*pref.* Pharynx: *pharyngoscope*. [< Gk. *pharunx*.]

phar·yn·gol·o·gy (făr′ĭn-gŏl′ə-jē, făr′ĭng-) ►*n.* The medical study of the pharynx.

pha·ryn·go·scope (fə-rĭng′gə-skōp′) ►*n.* An instrument used in examining the pharynx.

phar·ynx (făr′ĭngks) ►*n., pl.* **pha·ryn·ges** (fə-rĭn′jēz) or **-ynx·es** The section of the digestive tract that extends from the nasal cavities to the larynx, where it becomes continuous with the esophagus. [< Gk. *pharunx*.] **—pha·ryn′-ge·al** (fə-rĭn′jē-əl, făr′ĭn-jē′əl) *adj.*

phase (fāz) ►*n.* **1.** A distinct stage of development. **2.** A temporary pattern of behavior: *just a passing phase*. **3.** An aspect or facet; part: *every phase of the operation*. **4.** One of the cyclically recurring apparent forms of the moon or a planet. **5.** Any of the forms (solid, liquid, gas, and plasma) in which matter can exist. ►*v.* **phased, phas·ing** To plan or carry out systematically in phases. **—phrasal verbs: phase in** To introduce in stages. **phase out** To eliminate in stages. [< Gk. *phasis*, appearance.] **—pha′sic** (fā′zĭk) *adj.*

phase-in (fāz′ĭn′) ►*n.* A gradual introduction.

phase-out (fāz′out′) ►*n.* A gradual discontinuation.

PhD ►*abbr. Lat.* Philosophiae Doctor (Doctor of Philosophy)

pheas·ant (fĕz′ənt) ►*n., pl.* **-ants** or **-ant** Any of various chickenlike birds having long tails and, in the males, often brilliantly colored plumage. [< Gk. *phasianos*, of the Phasis River in the Caucasus.]

pheno– or **phen–** ►*pref.* **1.** Showing; displaying: *phenotype*. **2.** Derived from benzene: *phenol*. [< Gk. *phainein*, show.]

phe·no·bar·bi·tal (fē′nō-bär′bĭ-tôl′, -tăl′) ►*n.* A crystalline barbiturate used medicinally as a sedative, hypnotic, and anticonvulsant.

phe·nol (fē′nôl′, -nōl′, -nŏl′) ►*n.* A caustic, poisonous, white crystalline compound, C₆H₅OH, derived from benzene and used in plastics, disinfectants, and drugs. **—phe·no′lic** (-nô′-lĭk, -nŏ′-, -nŏl′ĭk) *adj.*

phe·nom·e·non (fĭ-nŏm′ə-nŏn′, -nən) ▸*n.*, *pl.* **-na** (-nə) **1.** An occurrence or fact that is perceptible by the senses. **2.** *pl.* **-nons a.** An unusual fact or occurrence; marvel. **b.** A remarkable or outstanding person; paragon. See Synonyms at **wonder.** [< Gk. *phainomenon.*] **—phe·nom′e·nal** *adj.* **—phe·nom′e·nal·ly** *adv.*

Usage: *Phenomenon* is the only acceptable singular form of this noun; *phenomena* is the usual plural. *Phenomenons* may be used as the plural in nonscientific writing when the meaning is "extraordinary things, occurrences, or persons": *They were phenomenons in the history of music.*

phe·no·type (fē′nə-tīp′) ▸*n.* **1.** The environmentally and genetically determined observable characteristics of an organism. **2.** An individual or group of organisms exhibiting a particular phenotype. **—phe′no·typ′ic** (-tĭp′-ĭk), **phe′no·typ′i·cal** *adj.*

pher·o·mone (fĕr′ə-mōn′) ▸*n.* A chemical secreted by an animal that influences the behavior or development of others of the same species. [Gk. *pherein*, carry + (HOR)MONE.]

phi (fī) ▸*n.* The 21st letter of the Greek alphabet. [< Gk. *phei.*]

phi·al (fī′əl) ▸*n.* A vial. [< Gk. *phialē*, shallow vessel.]

Phi Beta Kappa ▸*n.* An honorary society, founded in 1776, of college students and graduates whose members are chosen on the basis of high academic standing. [< the initials of the Gk. motto *philosophia biou kubernētēs*, philosophy the guide of life.]

Phid·i·as (fĭd′ē-əs) fl. 5th cent. BC. Athenian sculptor.

Phil·a·del·phi·a (fĭl′ə-dĕl′fē-ə) A city of SE PA on the Delaware R. **—Phil′a·del′phi·an** *adj. & n.*

phi·lan·der (fĭ-lăn′dər) ▸*v.* To engage in casual, esp. adulterous sexual affairs. Used esp. of a man. [< Gk. *philandros*, loving men.] **—phi·lan′der·er** *n.*

phil·an·throp·ic (fĭl′ən-thrŏp′ĭk) also **phil·an·throp·i·cal** (-ĭ-kəl) ▸*adj.* Of, relating to, or marked by philanthropy or charitable assistance. See Synonyms at **benevolent.** **—phil′an·throp′i·cal·ly** *adv.*

phi·lan·thro·py (fĭ-lăn′thrə-pē) ▸*n.*, *pl.* **-pies** **1.** The effort to increase the well-being of humankind, as by charitable donations. **2.** Love of humankind in general. **3.** A charitable activity or institution. [< Gk. *philanthrōpos*, loving humankind.] **—phi·lan′thro·pist** *n.*

phi·lat·e·ly (fĭ-lăt′l-ē) ▸*n.* The collection and study of postage stamps, postmarks, and related materials. [Fr. *philatélie*.] **—phil′a·tel′ic** (fĭl′ə-tĕl′ĭk) *adj.* **—phi·lat′e·list** *n.*

–phile or **–phil** ▸*suff.* One that loves or has a strong affinity or preference for: *audiophile.* [< Gk. *philos*, loving.]

Phi·le·mon (fĭ-lē′mən, fī-) ▸*n.* See table at **Bible.**

phil·har·mon·ic (fĭl′här-mŏn′ĭk, fĭl′ər-) ▸*n.* A symphony orchestra or group that supports it. [< Ital. *filarmonico*.]

–philia ▸*suff.* **1.** Tendency toward: *hemophilia.* **2.** Preference for: *Anglophilia.* **3.** Abnormal attraction to: *necrophilia.* [< Gk. *philos*, loving.]

Phil·ip (fĭl′ĭp), Prince. Duke of Edinburgh. b. 1921. Husband of Elizabeth II of Great Britain.

Philip, Saint. fl. 1st cent. AD. One of the 12 Apostles.

Philip II[1] 382–336 BC. King of Macedon (359–336).

Philip II[2] 1527–98. King of Spain (1556–98), of Naples and Sicily (1554–98), and of Portugal (1580–98) as Philip I.

Philip IV 1268–1314. King of France (1285–1314) and of Navarre (1284–1305) as the husband of Joan I of Navarre (c. 1271–1305).

Phi·lip·pi (fĭ-lĭp′ī) An ancient town of NE Greece, near the Aegean Sea. **—Phi·lip′pi·an** (-lĭp′ē-ən) *adj. & n.*

Phi·lip·pi·ans (fĭ-lĭp′ē-ənz) ▸*pl.n.* (takes sing. v.) See table at **Bible.**

phi·lip·pic (fĭ-lĭp′ĭk) ▸*n.* A passionate speech intended to arouse opposition; tirade. [After PHILIP II[1].]

Phil·ip·pines (fĭl′ə-pēnz′, fĭl′ə-pēnz′) A country of E Asia comprising an archipelago in the W Pacific SE of China. Cap. Manila. **—Phil′ip·pine′** *adj.*

Phil·is·tine (fĭl′ĭ-stēn′, fĭ-lĭs′tĭn, -tēn′) ▸*n.* **1.** A member of an ancient people in Palestine. **2.** often **philistine** A person who is smugly indifferent or hostile to art and culture. ▸*adj.* **1.** Of the ancient Philistines. **2.** often **philistine** Boorish or uncultured.

phil·o·den·dron (fĭl′ə-dĕn′drən) ▸*n.*, *pl.* **-drons** or **-dra** (-drə) Any of various climbing tropical American plants often cultivated as houseplants. [< Gk. *philodendros*, fond of trees.]

philodendron

phi·lol·o·gy (fĭ-lŏl′ə-jē) ▸*n.* **1.** Literary study or classical scholarship. **2.** The study of linguistic change over time. [< Gk. *philologos*, fond of learning or of words.] **—phil′o·log′i·cal** (fĭl′-ə-lŏj′ĭ-kəl) *adj.* **—phi·lol′o·gist** *n.*

phi·los·o·pher (fĭ-lŏs′ə-fər) ▸*n.* **1.** A specialist in philosophy. **2.** One who lives by a particular philosophy. **3.** One who takes a calm and rational approach toward life. [< Gk. *philosophos*, lover of wisdom.]

phi·los·o·phize (fĭ-lŏs′ə-fīz′) ▸*v.* **-phized, -phiz·ing** To speculate in a philosophical manner. **—phi·los′o·phiz′er** *n.*

phi·los·o·phy (fĭ-lŏs′ə-fē) ▸*n.*, *pl.* **-phies 1a.** The study of the nature, causes, or principles of reality, knowledge, or values, based on logical reasoning. **b.** A system of thought based on or involving such inquiry: *the philosophy of Plato.* **2.** The study of the theoretical underpinnings

of a particular field: *the philosophy of science.*
3. An underlying theory or set of ideas: *an unusual philosophy of life.* —**phil′o·soph′i·cal** (fĭl′ə-sŏf′ĭ-kəl), **phil′o·soph′ic** *adj.*

phil·ter also **phil·tre** (fĭl′tər) ►*n.* **1.** A love potion. **2.** A magic potion or charm. [< Gk. *philtron < philein*, to love.]

phle·bi·tis (flĭ-bī′tĭs) ►*n.* Inflammation of a vein. —**phle·bit′ic** (-bĭt′ĭk) *adj.*

phlebo– or **phleb–** ►*pref.* Vein: *phlebotomy.* [< Gk. *phleps, phleb-*, blood vessel.]

phle·bot·o·my (flĭ-bŏt′ə-mē) ►*n., pl.* **-mies** The removal of blood from a vein for diagnostic or therapeutic purposes.

phlegm (flĕm) ►*n.* Thick, sticky mucus produced in the respiratory tract. [< Gk. *phlegma,* humor caused by heat.]

phleg·mat·ic (flĕg-măt′ĭk) also **phleg·mat·i·cal** (-ĭ-kəl) ►*adj.* Having or suggesting a calm, stolid temperament; unemotional. [< Gk. *phlegma,* the humor phlegm.]

phlo·em (flō′ĕm′) ►*n.* The food-conducting tissue of vascular plants. [< Gk. *phloios,* bark.]

phlox (flŏks) ►*n., pl.* **phlox** or **-es** Any of various garden plants with white, pink, or purple flowers. [< Gk., wallflower.]

Phnom Penh (pə-nôm′ pĕn′, nŏm′) The capital of Cambodia, in the S part on the Mekong R.

pho (fō) ►*n.* A Vietnamese soup consisting of rice noodles in a clear broth, usu. with thinly sliced beef or chicken. [Vietnamese *phở,* perhaps < French *(pot-au-)feu,* beef stew.]

–phobe ►*suff.* One who fears or is averse to something: *Anglophobe.* [< Gk. *phobos,* fear.]

pho·bi·a (fō′bē-ə) ►*n.* A persistent, abnormal, and irrational fear of a thing or situation. [< Gk. *phobos,* fear.] —**pho′bic** (-bĭk) *adj.*

–phobia ►*suff.* An intense, abnormal, or illogical fear or aversion: *claustrophobia.* [< Gk. *phobos,* fear.]

phoe·be (fē′bē) ►*n.* Any of various North American flycatchers. [Imit. of its song.]

Phoe·ni·cia (fĭ-nĭsh′ə, -nē′shə) An ancient maritime country of SW Asia consisting of city-states along the E Mediterranean.

Phoe·ni·cian (fĭ-nĭsh′ən, -nē′shən) ►*n.* **1.** A native or inhabitant of ancient Phoenicia. **2.** The Semitic language of ancient Phoenicia.

phoe·nix (fē′nĭks) ►*n.* A bird in Egyptian mythology that consumed itself by fire after 500 years and rose renewed from its ashes. [< Gk. *phoinix.*]

Phoenix The capital of AZ, in the S-central part NW of Tucson.

phone (fōn) *Informal* ►*n.* A telephone. ►*v.* **phoned, phon·ing** To telephone.

–phone ►*suff.* **1.** Sound: *homophone.* **2.** Device that receives or emits sound: *megaphone.* **3.** Speaker of a language: *Anglophone.* [< Gk. *phōnē,* sound, voice.]

pho·neme (fō′nēm′) ►*n.* The smallest unit of speech that is capable of conveying a distinction in meaning, as the *m* of *mat* and the *b* of *bat* in English. [< Gk. *phōnēma,* utterance.] —**pho·ne′mic** (fə-nē′mĭk, fō-) *adj.* —**pho·ne′mi·cal·ly** *adv.*

pho·net·ic (fə-nĕt′ĭk) ►*adj.* **1.** Of or relating to phonetics. **2.** Representing the sounds of speech with a set of distinct symbols, each designating a single sound. [< Gk. *phōnētos,* to be spoken.] —**pho·net′i·cal·ly** *adv.*

pho·net·ics (fə-nĕt′ĭks) ►*n. (takes sing. v.)* The branch of linguistics that deals with the study of the sounds of speech. —**pho′ne·ti′cian** (fō′nĭ-tĭsh′ən) *n.*

phon·ics (fŏn′ĭks) ►*n. (takes sing. v.)* **1.** A method of teaching reading and spelling based on phonetics. **2.** Phonetics.

phono– or **phon–** ►*pref.* Sound; voice; speech: *phonology.* [< Gk. *phōnē.*]

pho·no·graph (fō′nə-grăf′) ►*n.* A machine that reproduces sound recorded on a grooved disk. —**pho′no·graph′ic** *adj.*

pho·nol·o·gy (fə-nŏl′ə-jē, fō-) ►*n.* The study of the distribution and pronunciation of speech sounds in a language. —**pho′no·log′ic** (fō′nə-lŏj′ĭk), **pho′no·log′i·cal** *adj.* —**pho·nol′o·gist** *n.*

pho·ny also **pho·ney** (fō′nē) ►*adj.* **-ni·er, -ni·est** **1.** Not genuine or real; fake: *a phony diploma.* **2.** Fraudulent, deceitful, or dishonest: *a phony investment adviser.* [< Ir.Gael. *fáinne,* gilt brass ring.] —**pho′ni·ness** *n.* —**pho′ny** *n.*

–phony ►*suff.* Sound: *telephony.* [Gk. *-phōnia.*]

–phore ►*suff.* Bearer; carrier: *semaphore.* [< Gk. *pherein,* carry.]

–phoresis ►*suff.* Transmission: *electrophoresis.* [< Gk. *phorēsis,* a carrying < *pherein,* carry.]

phos·gene (fŏs′jēn′, fŏz′-) ►*n.* A colorless gas, $COCl_2$, used as a poison gas and in making dyes, resins, and plastics. [< Gk. *phōs,* light.]

phos·phate (fŏs′fāt′) ►*n.* **1.** A salt, ester, or anion of phosphoric acid. **2.** A fertilizer containing phosphorus compounds. —**phos·phat′ic** (-făt′ĭk) *adj.*

phos·pho·lip·id (fŏs′fō-lĭp′ĭd) ►*n.* Any of various lipids, such as lecithin, that contain a phosphate group and one or more fatty acids.

phos·phor (fŏs′fər, -fôr′) ►*n.* **1.** A substance that exhibits phosphorescence. **2.** The phosphorescent coating inside the screen of a cathode-ray tube. [< PHOSPHORUS.]

phos·pho·res·cence (fŏs′fə-rĕs′əns) ►*n.* **1.** Persistent emission of light following exposure to and removal of incident radiation. **2.** Emission of light without heat. —**phos′pho·resce′** *v.* —**phos′pho·res′cent** *adj.*

phosphoric acid ►*n.* A clear colorless solid or syrupy liquid, H_3PO_4, used in fertilizers, detergents, and food flavorings.

phos·pho·rus (fŏs′fər-əs) ►*n.* **1.** *Symbol* **P** A highly reactive, poisonous, nonmetallic element used in safety matches, pyrotechnics, incendiary shells, and fertilizers. At. no. 15. See table at **element.** **2.** A phosphorescent substance. [< Gk. *phōsphoros,* light-bearing : *phōs,* light + *pherein,* carry.] —**phos·phor′ic** (fŏs-fôr′ĭk) *adj.* —**phos′pho·rous** (fŏs′fər-əs, fŏs-fôr′əs) *adj.*

pho·tic (fō′tĭk) ►*adj.* **1.** Of or relating to light. **2.** Penetrated by light, esp. by sunlight: *the photic zone of the ocean.*

pho·to (fō′tō) ►*n., pl.* **-tos** *Informal* A photograph. —**pho′to** *v.*

photo– or **phot–** ►*pref.* **1.** Light: *photosynthesis.* **2.** Photographic: *photomontage.* **3.** Photoelectric: *photoemission.* [< Gk. *phōs,* light.]

pho·to·cell (fō′tō-sĕl′) ►*n.* A photoelectric cell.

pho·to·chem·is·try (fō′tō-kĕm′ĭ-strē) ►*n.* The study of the effects of light on chemical systems. —**pho′to·chem′i·cal** *adj.*

pho·to·cop·y (fō′tə-kŏp′ē) ►*v.* To make a photographic reproduction of (printed or pictorial material), esp. by xerography. ►*n.* A photographic reproduction. —**pho′to·cop′i·er** *n.*

pho·to·e·lec·tric (fō′tō-ĭ-lĕk′trĭk) also **pho·to·e·lec·tri·cal** (-trĭ-kəl) ►*adj.* Of or relating to electric effects caused by light. —**pho′to·e·lec′tri·cal·ly** *adv.*

photoelectric cell ►*n.* An electronic device having an electrical output that varies in response to the intensity of incident radiation.

pho·to·e·mis·sion (fō′tō-ĭ-mĭsh′ən) ►*n.* Photoelectric emission of electrons, esp. from a metallic surface.

pho·to·en·grav·ing (fō′tō-ĕn-grā′vĭng) ►*n.* **1.** The process of reproducing graphic material by photographing it on a metal plate and then etching the plate for printing. **2.** A reproduction made by this process. —**pho′to·en·grave′** *v.* —**pho′to·en·grav′er** *n.*

pho·to·es·say (fō′tō-ĕs′ā′) ►*n.* A story told chiefly through photographs usu. supplemented by a written commentary.

photo finish ►*n.* A race so closely contested that the winner must be determined by a photograph taken at the finish.

pho·to·gen·ic (fō′tə-jĕn′ĭk) ►*adj.* Attractive as a subject for photography.

pho·to·graph (fō′tə-grăf′) ►*n.* An image, esp. a positive print, recorded by exposing a photosensitive surface to light, esp. in a camera. ►*v.* **1.** To take a photograph of. **2.** To be the subject for photographs. —**pho·tog′ra·pher** (fə-tŏg′rə-fər) *n.*

pho·to·graph·ic (fō′tə-grăf′ĭk) also **pho·to·graph·i·cal** (-ĭ-kəl) ►*adj.* **1.** Of or relating to photography or a photograph. **2.** Used in photography. **3.** Like a photograph, esp. in representing with accuracy and detail. —**pho′to·graph′i·cal·ly** *adv.*

pho·tog·ra·phy (fə-tŏg′rə-fē) ►*n.* The art or process of recording or producing images on light-sensitive surfaces.

pho·to·gra·vure (fō′tə-grə-vyŏŏr′) ►*n.* The process of printing from an intaglio plate, etched according to a photographic image.

pho·to·jour·nal·ism (fō′tō-jûr′nə-lĭz′əm) ►*n.* Journalism in which pictorial matter, esp. photographs, takes precedence over written copy. —**pho′to·jour′nal·ist** *n.*

pho·tom·e·try (fō-tŏm′ĭ-trē) ►*n.* Measurement of the properties of light, esp. luminous intensity. —**pho′to·met′ric** (fō′tə-mĕt′rĭk), **pho′·to·met′ri·cal** *adj.*

pho·to·mi·cro·graph (fō′tō-mī′krə-grăf′) ►*n.* A photograph made through a microscope.

pho·to·mon·tage (fō′tō-mŏn-tăzh′, -mŏn-) ►*n.* **1.** The technique of making a picture by assembling pieces of photographs, often with other graphic material. **2.** A composite picture produced by this technique.

pho·ton (fō′tŏn′) ►*n.* The elementary particle of light and other electromagnetic radiation, having zero mass and no electric charge; the quantum of electromagnetic energy. —**pho·ton′ic** *adj.*

pho·ton·ics (fō-tŏn′ĭks) ►*n.* (takes sing. v.) The study of the behavior and properties of photons, esp. as applied to communications, materials science, and information processing.

pho·to·re·cep·tor (fō′tō-rĭ-sĕp′tər) ►*n.* **1.** A nerve ending, cell, or group of cells specialized to sense or receive light. **2.** A device that converts light energy into electrical signals.

pho·to·re·con·nais·sance (fō′tō-rĭ-kŏn′ə-səns, -zəns) ►*n.* Photographic aerial reconnaissance esp. of military targets.

pho·to·sen·si·tive (fō′tō-sĕn′sĭ-tĭv) ►*adj.* Sensitive to light. —**pho′to·sen′si·tiv′i·ty** *n.*

pho·to·sphere (fō′tə-sfîr′) ►*n.* The directly visible outer layer or atmosphere of a star.

pho·to·syn·the·sis (fō′tō-sĭn′thĭ-sĭs) ►*n.* The process by which chlorophyll-containing cells in green plants and certain other organisms use light as an energy source to synthesize carbohydrates from carbon dioxide and water, usu. producing oxygen as a byproduct. —**pho′to·syn′the·size** *v.* —**pho′to·syn·thet′ic** (-sĭn-thĕt′ĭk) *adj.* —**pho′to·syn·thet′i·cal·ly** *adv.*

pho·tot·ro·pism (fō-tŏt′rə-pĭz′əm, fō′tō-trō′-) ►*n. Biol.* Growth or movement toward or away from light. —**pho′to·tro′pic** (fō′tə-trō′pĭk) *adj.*

pho·to·vol·ta·ic (fō′tō-vŏl-tā′ĭk, -vōl-) ►*adj.* Capable of producing a voltage when exposed to radiant energy, esp. light.

photovoltaic cell ►*n.* See **photoelectric cell.**

phrase (frāz) ►*n.* **1.** A sequence of words, esp. when forming a grammatical unit in a sentence. **2.** A brief, cogent expression. **3.** *Mus.* A short passage, often of four measures, usu. forming part of a larger melodic unit. ►*v.* **phrased, phras·ing** **1.** To express orally or in writing. **2.** *Mus.* To render in phrases. [< Gk. *phrasis,* diction.] —**phras′al** *adj.*

phra·se·ol·o·gy (frā′zē-ŏl′ə-jē) ►*n., pl.* **-gies** The way in which words and phrases are used in speech or writing; style. —**phra′se·o·log′i·cal** (-ə-lŏj′ĭ-kəl) *adj.*

phreak (frēk) ►*v. Slang* To manipulate a telephone system illicitly to allow one to make calls without paying for them. [Alteration of FREAK (influenced by PHONE).]

phre·net·ic (frə-nĕt′ĭk) or **phre·net·i·cal** (-ĭ-kəl) ►*adj.* Vars. of **frenetic.**

–phrenia ►*suff.* Mental disorder: *schizophrenia.* [< Gk. *phrēn,* mind.]

phre·nol·o·gy (frĭ-nŏl′ə-jē) ►*n.* The study of the shape and irregularities of the human skull, based on the now discredited belief that they reveal character and mental capacity. [< Gk. *phrēn,* mind.] —**phren′o·log′ic** (frĕn′ə-lŏj′-ĭk, frē′nə-), **phren′o·log′i·cal** *adj.* —**phre·nol′o·gist** *n.*

Phryg·i·a (frĭj′ē-ə) An ancient region of central Asia Minor in modern-day central Turkey. —**Phryg′i·an** *adj. & n.*

phy·lac·ter·y (fĭ-lăk′tə-rē) ►*n., pl.* **-ies** *Judaism* Either of two small leather boxes containing quotations from the Hebrew Scriptures, worn strapped to the forehead and the left arm esp. by orthodox Jewish men during weekday morning worship. [< Gk. *phulaktērion,* safeguard.]

phyl·lo·tax·is (fĭl′ə-tăk′sĭs) also **phyl·lo·tax·y** (fĭl′ə-tăk′sē) ►*n., pl.* **-tax·es** also **-tax·ies** The arrangement of leaves on a stem. [Gk. *phyllon,* leaf + *taxis,* arrangement.]

phy·log·e·ny (fī-lŏj′ə-nē) ►*n., pl.* **-nies** The evolutionary development of an animal or plant species. [Gk. *phulon,* race + –GENY.] —**phy′·lo·ge·net′ic** (fī′lō-jə-nĕt′ĭk), **phy′lo·gen′ic** (-jĕn′ĭk) *adj.*

phy·lum (fī′ləm) ►*n., pl.* **-la** (-lə) **1.** *Biol.* A category ranking below a kingdom and above a class in the hierarchy of taxonomic classification. **2.** *Ling.* A large division of possibly genetically related families of languages or linguistic stocks. [< Gk. *phulon*, class.]

phys– or **physi–** ►*pref.* Vars. of **physio–**.

phys·ic (fĭz′ĭk) ►*n.* A medicine or drug, esp. a cathartic. ►*v.* **-icked, -ick·ing 1.** To act on as a cathartic. **2.** To cure or heal. [< Gk. *phusikē*, natural science < *phusis*, nature.]

phys·i·cal (fĭz′ĭ-kəl) ►*adj.* **1a.** Of or relating to the body. See Synonyms at **bodily. b.** Having a physiological basis or origin. **c.** Involving sexual interest or activity: *physical attraction.* **2.** Of material things. **3.** Of or relating to matter and energy or the sciences dealing with them, esp. physics. ►*n.* A physical examination. —**phys′i·cal·ly** *adv.*

physical education ►*n.* Education in the care and development of the human body, stressing athletics and including hygiene.

physical examination ►*n.* A medical examination to determine the condition of a person's health or physical fitness.

physical geography ►*n.* The study of the natural features, structure, and phenomena of the earth's surface.

physical science ►*n.* Any of the sciences, such as physics, chemistry, astronomy, and geology, that analyze the nature and properties of energy and nonliving matter.

physical therapy ►*n.* The treatment of physical injury or dysfunction with exercise and other nonsurgical interventions such as massage and the application of heat. —**physical therapist** *n.*

phy·si·cian (fĭ-zĭsh′ən) ►*n.* A medical doctor.

phys·i·cist (fĭz′ĭ-sĭst) ►*n.* A scientist who specializes in physics.

phys·ics (fĭz′ĭks) ►*n.* **1.** *(takes sing. v.)* The science of matter and energy and of interactions between the two. **2.** *(takes pl. v.)* Physical properties, processes, or laws.

physio– or **physi–** or **phys–** ►*pref.* **1.** Nature: *physiography.* **2.** Physical: *physiotherapy.* [< Gk. *phusis*, nature.]

phys·i·og·no·my (fĭz′ē-ŏg′nə-mē, -ŏn′ə-mē) ►*n., pl.* **-mies 1.** The art of judging human character from facial features. **2.** Facial features; the face. [< Gk. *phusiognōmonia.*]

phys·i·og·ra·phy (fĭz′ē-ŏg′rə-fē) ►*n.* See **physical geography.** —**phys′i·og′ra·pher** *n.* —**phys′i·o·graph′ic** (-ə-grăf′ĭk), **phys′i·o·graph′i·cal** *adj.*

phys·i·ol·o·gy (fĭz′ē-ŏl′ə-jē) ►*n.* **1.** The biological study of the functions of living organisms and their parts. **2.** All the functions of an organism. —**phys′i·o·log′i·cal** (-ə-lŏj′ĭ-kəl) *adj.* —**phys′i·o·log′i·cal·ly** *adv.* —**phys′i·ol′o·gist** *n.*

phys·i·o·ther·a·py (fĭz′ē-ō-thĕr′ə-pē) ►*n.* See **physical therapy.** —**phys′i·o·ther′a·peu′tic** (-ə-pyōō′tĭk) *adj.* —**phys′i·o·ther′a·pist** *n.*

phy·sique (fĭ-zēk′) ►*n.* The body considered with reference to its proportions, muscular development, and appearance. [Fr., physical, physique < Gk. *phusis*, nature.]

–phyte ►*suff.* A plant with a specified character or habitat: *epiphyte.* [< Gk. *phuton*, plant.]

phyto– or **phyt–** ►*pref.* Plant: *phytochemical.* [< Gk. *phuton.*]

phy·to·chem·i·cal (fī′tō-kĕm′ĭ-kəl) ►*adj.* Relating to plant chemistry. ►*n.* A nonnutritive plant substance thought to have health benefits.

phy·to·plank·ton (fī′tō-plăngk′tən) ►*n.* Plankton consisting of minute plants and other photosynthetic organisms.

pi¹ (pī) ►*n.* **1.** The 16th letter of the Greek alphabet. **2.** *Math.* A transcendental number, approx. 3.14159, expressing the ratio of the circumference to the diameter of a circle. [< Gk. *pei.*]

pi² also **pie** (pī) ►*n., pl.* **pis** also **pies** *Print.* Jumbled type. [?]

pi·a·nis·si·mo (pē′ə-nĭs′ə-mō′) ►*adv. & adj. Mus.* In a very soft or quiet tone. [Ital.]

pi·an·ist (pē-ăn′ĭst, pē′ə-nĭst) ►*n.* One who plays the piano.

pi·an·o¹ (pē-ăn′ō, pyăn′ō) ►*n., pl.* **-os** A keyboard musical instrument with hammers that strike wire strings. [Ital. < *pianoforte*, PIANOFORTE.]

pi·a·no² (pē-ä′nō, pyä′-) ►*adv. & adj. Mus.* In a soft or quiet tone. [Ital.]

pi·an·o·for·te (pē-ăn′ō-fôr′tā, -tē, pē-ăn′ō-fôrt′) ►*n.* A piano. [Ital. < *piano (e) forte*, soft (and) loud.]

pi·az·za (pē-ăz′ə, -ä′zə) ►*n.* **1.** *(also* pē-ät′sə, pyät′sä*)* A public square in an Italian town. **2.** *Regional* A veranda; porch. [Ital. < Gk. *plateia*, broad.]

pi·ca (pī′kə) ►*n. Print.* A unit of type size, equal to 12 points or about ⅙ of an inch. [Prob. < Med.Lat. *pīca*, list of church services.]

pic·a·dor (pĭk′ə-dôr′) ►*n.* A horseman in a bullfight who lances the bull's neck muscles so as to weaken them. [Sp. < *picar*, to prick.]

pic·a·resque (pĭk′ə-rĕsk′, pē′kə-) ►*adj.* Of or involving clever rogues or adventurers, esp. in prose fiction. [< Sp. *pícaro*, rogue.]

Pi·cas·so (pĭ-kä′sō, -kăs′ō), **Pablo** 1881–1973. Spanish artist.

pic·a·yune (pĭk′ə-yōōn′) ►*adj.* **1.** Of little value or importance; paltry. **2.** Petty; mean. [< Prov. *picaioun*, small coin.]

pic·co·lo (pĭk′ə-lō′) ►*n., pl.* **-los** A small flute pitched an octave above a regular flute. [Ital.]

pick¹ (pĭk) ►*v.* **1.** To select from among various options: *picked a vacation destination.* **2.** To gather, esp. from growing plants: *picked a bushel of apples.* **3.** To remove small pieces: *picked at his meal.* **4.** To steal the contents of (a pocket or purse). **5.** To open (a lock) without the use of a key. **6.** To provoke: *pick a fight.* **7.** *Mus.* To pluck (a string or stringed instrument). ►*n.* **1.** The act of selecting; choice. **2.** The best or choicest part. —*phrasal verbs:* **pick on** To tease or bully. **pick out** To choose or select. **pick up 1.** To take on (e.g., passengers or freight). **2.** To learn without great effort. **3.** To receive or intercept: *pick up a radio signal.* **4.** *Informal* To take into custody; arrest. **5.** *Informal* To improve in condition or activity. **6.** *Informal* To make casual acquaintance with (someone), esp. in anticipation of sexual relations. —*idioms:* **pick and choose** To select or decide with great care. **pick (one's) way** To make one's way carefully. [< VLat. **piccāre*, to pierce.] —**pick′er** *n.*

pick² (pĭk) ►*n.* **1.** A tool for breaking hard surfaces, consisting of a curved bar sharpened at both ends and fitted to a long handle. **2.** *Mus.* A plectrum. [ME *pik.*]

pick·ax or **pick·axe** (pĭk′ăks′) ►*n.* A pick, esp. with one end of the head pointed and the other having a chisel edge. [< OFr. *picois.*]

pick·er·el (pĭk′ər-əl, pĭk′rəl) ►*n., pl.* **-el** or **-els** A North American freshwater fish related to the pike. [ME *pikerel,* dim. of *pike,* PIKE²*.*]

pick·et (pĭk′ĭt) ►*n.* **1.** A pointed stake driven into the ground to support a fence, secure a tent, tether animals, mark surveying points, or serve as a defense. **2.** A detachment of one or more troops, ships, or aircraft on guard against an enemy's approach. **3.** A person or persons stationed outside a place of employment, usu. during a strike, to express grievance or protest. ►*v.* **1.** To enclose, secure, mark out, or fortify with pickets. **2.** *Military* To guard with a picket. **3.** To post a picket or pickets at a strike or demonstration. **4.** To act or serve as a picket. [< OFr. *piquet.*] —**pick′et·er** *n.*

picket fence ►*n.* A fence made of upright pointed boards.

picket fence

picket line ►*n.* A line or procession of people picketing a place of business or otherwise staging a public protest.

pick·ing (pĭk′ĭng) ►*n.* **1. pickings** Something that is or may be picked. **2.** often **pickings a.** Leftovers. **b.** A share of spoils.

pick·le (pĭk′əl) ►*n.* **1.** An edible product, such as a cucumber, preserved and flavored in a solution of brine or vinegar. **2.** A solution of brine or vinegar, often spiced, for preserving and flavoring food. **3.** *Informal* A disagreeable, difficult, or troublesome situation; plight. ►*v.* **-led, -ling** To preserve or flavor in a solution of brine or vinegar. [Prob. < MDu. *pekel,* brine.]

pick·pock·et (pĭk′pŏk′ĭt) ►*n.* One who steals from pockets or purses.

pick·up (pĭk′ŭp′) ►*n.* **1.** The act or process of picking up. **2.** Ability to accelerate rapidly. **3.** One that is picked up. **4.** A pickup truck. **5.** *Electron.* **a.** A device that receives vibrations, as of a guitar string, and converts them to an electrical signal. **b.** A device that receives light or sound waves and converts them to an electrical signal. ►*adj.* Informally organized for a particular occasion: *a pickup basketball game.*

pickup truck ►*n.* A light truck with an open body and low sides.

pick·y (pĭk′ē) ►*adj.* **-i·er, -i·est** *Informal* Excessively meticulous; fussy.

pic·nic (pĭk′nĭk) ►*n.* **1.** A meal eaten outdoors, as on an excursion. **2.** *Slang* An easy task. ►*v.* **-nicked, -nick·ing** To go on a picnic. [Fr. *piquenique.*] —**pic′nick·er** *n.*

pi·cot (pē′kō, pē-kō′) ►*n.* A small embroidered loop forming an edging, as on ribbon. [< OFr.]

pic·to·graph (pĭk′tə-grăf′) ►*n.* **1.** A picture representing a word, phrase, or idea, esp. one that is used in early writing systems. **2.** A pictorial representation of numerical data or relationships. [< Lat. *pictus,* painted.] —**pic′to·graph′ic** *adj.*

pic·to·ri·al (pĭk-tôr′ē-əl) ►*adj.* **1.** Of or composed of pictures. **2.** Illustrated by pictures. ►*n.* An illustrated periodical. [< Lat. *pictor,* painter.] —**pic·to′ri·al·ly** *adv.*

pic·ture (pĭk′chər) ►*n.* **1.** A visual representation or image painted, drawn, photographed, or otherwise rendered on a flat surface. **2.** A vivid verbal description. **3.** One that bears a marked resemblance to another. **4.** One that typifies or embodies an emotion, state of mind, or mood. **5.** The chief circumstances of an event or time; situation. **6.** A movie. ►*v.* **-tured, -tur·ing** **1.** To make a picture of. **2.** To visualize. **3.** To describe vividly in words. [< Lat. *pictūra* < *pingere, pict-,* to paint.]

pic·tur·esque (pĭk′chə-rĕsk′) ►*adj.* **1.** Of or suggesting a picture. **2.** Unusually or quaintly attractive. **3.** Strikingly expressive or vivid: *picturesque language.* —**pic′tur·esque′ly** *adv.* —**pic′tur·esque′ness** *n.*

picture tube ►*n.* A cathode-ray tube in a television that converts electrical signals into a visible picture on a luminescent screen.

picture window ►*n.* A large, usu. single-paned window that provides a broad view.

pid·dling (pĭd′lĭng) ►*adj.* Trifling or trivial. [?]

pidg·in (pĭj′ən) ►*n.* A simplified mixture of two or more languages, used for communication between groups speaking different languages. [< PIDGIN ENGLISH.]

Pidgin English ►*n.* Any of several pidgins based on English and now spoken mostly in the Pacific islands and in W Africa. [Perh. < *business English.*]

pie¹ (pī) ►*n.* A baked pastry shell filled with fruit or other ingredients, and usu. covered with a crust. —**idiom: pie in the sky** An empty wish or promise. [ME.]

pie² (pī) ►*n.* *Print.* Var. of **pi².**

pie·bald (pī′bôld′) ►*adj.* Spotted or patched in color, esp. in black and white. ►*n.* A piebald animal, esp. a horse. [*pie,* magpie + BALD.]

piece (pēs) ►*n.* **1.** A unit or element of a larger quantity or class; portion. **2.** An artistic or musical work. **3.** An instance; specimen. **4.** What one has to say about something; opinion: *speak one's piece.* **5.** A coin. **6.** A counter or figure used in a game. **7.** *Slang* A firearm, esp. a rifle. **8.** *Informal* A given distance: *down the road a piece.* ►*v.* **pieced, piec·ing** **1.** To mend by adding a piece to. **2.** To join the pieces of. —**idiom: of a piece** Of the same class or kind. [< VLat. **pettia.*]

pièce de ré·sis·tance (pyĕs də rā-zē-stäNs′) ►*n., pl.* **pièces de résistance** (pyĕs) **1.** An outstanding accomplishment. **2.** The principal dish of a meal. [Fr.]

piece goods ►*pl.n.* Fabrics made and sold in standard lengths.

piece·meal (pēs′mēl′) ►*adv.* By a small amount at a time; in stages. ►*adj.* Made or done in stages. [ME *pecemeale.*]

piece of eight ►*n., pl.* **pieces of eight** An old Spanish silver coin.

piece·work (pēs′wûrk′) ►*n.* Work paid for by the number of units made. —**piece′work′-er** *n.*

pie chart ►*n.* A circular graph divided into sectors proportional to the relative size of the quantities represented.

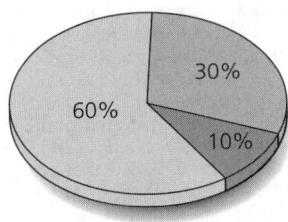

pie chart

pied (pīd) ►*adj.* Patchy in color; piebald. [< ME *pie,* magpie.]

pied·mont (pēd′mŏnt′) ►*n.* An area of land at the foot of a mountain or mountain range.

Piedmont 1. A historical region of NW Italy bordering on France and Switzerland. **2.** A plateau region of the E US extending from NY to AL between the Appalachian Mts. and the Atlantic coastal plain. —**Pied′mon·tese′** (-tēz′, -tēs′) *adj. & n.*

pier (pîr) ►*n.* **1.** A platform extending from a shore over water, used to secure, protect, and provide access to ships or boats. **2.** A supporting structure for the spans of a bridge. **3.** *Archit.* Any of various vertical supporting or reinforcing structures. [< OFr. *puier,* support, and ONFr. *piere,* breakwater.]

pierce (pîrs) ►*v.* **pierced, pierc·ing 1.** To cut or pass through with or as if with a sharp instrument. **2.** To perforate. **3.** To make a way through. [< Lat. *pertundere, pertūs-,* bore through.] —**pierc′ing·ly** *adv.*

Pierce, Franklin 1804–69. The 14th US president (1853–57).

Franklin Pierce

Pie·ro del·la Fran·ce·sca (pyâr′ō dĕl′ə frän-chĕs′kə, frän-) 1420?–92. Italian painter.

Pierre (pîr) The capital of SD, in the central part on the Missouri R.

pi·e·ty (pī′ĭ-tē) ►*n., pl.* **-ties 1.** Devotion and reverence, esp. to God and family. **2.** A pious act or thought. [< Lat. *pietās.*]

pi·e·zo·e·lec·tric·i·ty (pē-ā′zō-ĭ-lĕk-trĭs′ĭ-tē, pī-ē′-) ►*n.* Electricity or polarity induced in certain crystals, such as quartz, by mechanical stress. [Gk. *piezein,* squeeze + ELECTRICITY.] —**pi·e′zo·e·lec′tric, pi·e′zo·e·lec′tri·cal** *adj.*

pif·fle (pĭf′əl) ►*v.* **-fled, -fling** To talk or act feebly or futilely. ►*n.* Nonsense. [?]

pig (pĭg) ►*n.* **1.** A mammal having short legs, cloven hooves, bristly hair, and a blunt snout used for digging, esp. one of a kind raised for meat. **2a.** *Informal* A slovenly, greedy, or gross person. **b.** *Derogatory Slang* A police officer. **3.** A crude block of metal, chiefly iron or lead, poured from a smelting furnace. ►*v.* **pigged, pig·ging** To bear pigs; farrow. —*phrasal verb:* **pig out** *Slang* To eat ravenously; gorge. [ME *pigge.*]

pi·geon (pĭj′ən) ►*n.* **1.** Any of various birds having a plump body, small head, and short legs, esp. a common, often domesticated species. **2.** *Slang* One easily swindled; dupe. [< LLat. *pīpiō,* young chirping bird.]

pi·geon·hole (pĭj′ən-hōl′) ►*n.* A small compartment, as in a desk. ►*v.* **-holed, -hol·ing 1.** To place or file in a pigeonhole. **2.** To categorize. **3.** To put aside and ignore.

pi·geon-toed (pĭj′ən-tōd′) ►*adj.* Having the toes turned inward.

pig·gish (pĭg′ĭsh) ►*adj.* Resembling or characteristic of a pig, as in being greedy.

pig·gy (pĭg′ē) *Informal* ►*n., pl.* **-gies** A little pig. ►*adj.* **-gi·er, -gi·est** Piggish.

pig·gy·back (pĭg′ē-băk′) ►*adv. & adj.* **1.** On the shoulders or back. **2.** By or of a method of transportation in which truck trailers are carried on trains. **3.** In connection with something larger or more important. [< *pickaback.*]

piggy bank ►*n.* A coin bank shaped like a pig.

pig·head·ed (pĭg′hĕd′ĭd) ►*adj.* Stupidly obstinate. —**pig′head·ed·ness** *n.*

pig iron ►*n.* Crude iron cast in blocks.

pig Latin ►*n.* A jargon formed by the transposition of the initial consonant to the end of the word and the suffixion of an additional syllable, as *igpay atinlay* for *pig Latin.*

pig·let (pĭg′lĭt) ►*n.* A young pig.

pig·ment (pĭg′mənt) ►*n.* **1.** A coloring substance or matter, usu. a powder to be mixed with water, oil, or another base. **2.** A substance, such as chlorophyll or melanin, that produces a color in plant or animal tissue. [< Lat. *pigmentum.*] —**pig′men·tar′y** (-mən-tĕr′ē) *adj.*

pig·men·ta·tion (pĭg′mən-tā′shən) ►*n.* Coloration of animal or plant tissues by pigment.

Pig·my (pĭg′mē) ►*n. & adj.* Var. of **Pygmy.**

pig·pen (pĭg′pĕn′) ►*n.* **1.** A pen for pigs. **2.** *Informal* A dirty or very untidy place.

pig·skin (pĭg′skĭn′) ►*n.* **1.** The skin of a pig or leather made from it. **2.** *Sports* A football.

pig·sty (pĭg′stī′) ►*n.* A pigpen.

pig·tail (pĭg′tāl′) ►*n.* **1.** A braid or ponytail, esp. one of a pair worn one on each side of the head. **2.** A short length of wire used to connect other wires to each other or to an electrical device. —**pig′tailed′** *adj.*

pi·ka (pī′kə, pē′-) ►*n.* A small, tailless, furry

mammal of the mountains or grasslands of North America and Eurasia. [Evenki (Siberia) *piika*.]

pike¹ (pīk) ►*n.* A long spear formerly used by infantry. [< *piquer*, to prick.] —**piked** *adj.*

pike² (pīk) ►*n., pl.* **pike** or **pikes** A freshwater game and food fish having a narrow body and long snout. [ME.]

pike³ (pīk) ►*n.* A turnpike.

pike⁴ (pīk) ►*n.* A spike or sharp point. [< OE *pīc.*]

pik·er (pī′kər) ►*n. Slang* A petty or stingy person. [?]

pi·laf or **pi·laff** (pĭ-läf′, pē′läf′) ►*n.* A steamed rice dish with bits of meat, shellfish, or vegetables. [< Turk. *pilâv.*]

pi·las·ter (pĭ-lăs′tər) ►*n.* A rectangular column projecting slightly from a wall as an ornamental motif. [< Med.Lat. *pīlaster.*]

Pi·late (pī′lət), **Pontius** fl. 1st cent. AD. Roman prefect who ordered the crucifixion of Jesus.

pil·chard (pĭl′chərd) ►*n.* A small edible marine fish, esp. a commercially important European species that is often canned. [?]

pile¹ (pīl) ►*n.* **1.** A quantity of objects heaped or thrown together in a stack. See Synonyms at **heap. 2.** *Informal* A large accumulation or quantity. **3.** A nuclear reactor. **4.** A funeral pyre. ►*v.* **piled, pil·ing 1a.** To stack in or form a pile. **b.** To load with a pile: *pile a plate with food.* **2.** To move in a disorderly mass or group: *pile into a car.* [< Lat. *pīla,* pillar.]

pile² (pīl) ►*n.* A heavy timber, concrete, or steel beam driven into the earth as a structural support. [< Lat. *pīlum,* spear.]

pile³ (pīl) ►*n.* Cut or uncut loops of yarn forming the surface of certain fabrics, such as velvet and carpeting. [< Lat. *pilus,* hair.] —**piled** *adj.*

pi·le·at·ed woodpecker (pī′lē-ā′tĭd) ►*n.* A large North American woodpecker having black and white plumage and a red crest. [< Lat. *pīleus,* felt cap.]

pile driver ►*n.* A machine that drives piles into the ground.

piles (pīlz) ►*pl.n.* See **hemorrhoid** (sense 2). [< Lat. *pila,* ball.]

pile·up or **pile-up** (pīl′ŭp′) ►*n.* **1.** *Informal* A serious collision of several motor vehicles. **2.** An accumulation.

pil·fer (pĭl′fər) ►*v.* To steal or filch. [< OFr. *pelfre,* spoils.] —**pil′fer·age** (-ĭj) *n.*

pil·grim (pĭl′grəm) ►*n.* **1.** One who goes on a pilgrimage. **2.** A traveler. **3. Pilgrim** One of the English Puritans who migrated to New England in 1620. [< Lat. *peregrīnus,* foreigner.]

pil·grim·age (pĭl′grə-mĭj) ►*n.* **1.** A journey to a sacred place. **2.** A long journey or search, esp. one of exalted purpose.

pil·ing (pī′lĭng) ►*n.* A number of piles supporting a structure.

Pil·i·pi·no (pĭl′ə-pē′nō) ►*n.* The Filipino language.

pill (pĭl) ►*n.* **1.** A small pellet or tablet of medicine. **2. the pill** *Informal* An oral contraceptive. **3.** Something both distasteful and necessary. **4.** *Slang* An ill-natured person. [< Lat. *pilula,* little ball.]

pil·lage (pĭl′ĭj) ►*v.* **-laged, -lag·ing** To rob of goods by force; plunder. ►*n.* **1.** The act of pillaging. **2.** Spoils. [< OFr. *piller.*]

pil·lar (pĭl′ər) ►*n.* **1.** A slender, freestanding,

vertical support; column. **2.** One occupying a central or responsible position. [< Lat. *pīla.*]

pill·box (pĭl′bŏks′) ►*n.* **1.** A small box for pills. **2.** A low-roofed concrete emplacement, esp. for a machine gun or antitank gun.

pil·lion (pĭl′yən) ►*n.* A seat for an extra rider behind the saddle on a horse or motorcycle. [< Sc.Gael. *pillean.*]

pil·lo·ry (pĭl′ə-rē) ►*n., pl.* **-ries** A wooden framework with holes for the head and hands, in which offenders were formerly locked to be exposed to public scorn as punishment. ►*v.* **-ried, -ry·ing 1.** To expose to ridicule and abuse. **2.** To put in a pillory as punishment. [< OFr. *pilori.*]

pil·low (pĭl′ō) ►*n.* **1.** A cloth case stuffed with soft material and used to cushion the head, esp. during sleep. **2.** A decorative cushion. ►*v.* To serve as a pillow for. [< Lat. *pulvīnus.*]

pil·low·case (pĭl′ō-kās′) ►*n.* A removable covering for a pillow.

pil·low·slip (pĭl′ō-slĭp′) ►*n.* See **pillowcase.**

pi·lose (pī′lōs) also **pi·lous** (-ləs) ►*adj.* Covered with fine soft hair. [< Lat. *pilus,* hair.] —**pi·los′i·ty** (-lŏs′ĭ-tē) *n.*

pi·lot (pī′lət) ►*n.* **1.** One who flies or is licensed to fly an aircraft. **2a.** A licensed specialist who conducts a ship in and out of port or through dangerous waters. **b.** A ship's helmsman. **3.** A guide or leader. **4.** A television program produced as a prototype for a series. ►*v.* **1.** To serve as the pilot of. **2.** To steer or control the course of. See Synonyms at **guide.** ►*adj.* **1.** Serving as a small-scale experimental model. **2.** Serving or leading as guide. [< OItal. *pilota* < Gk. *pēdon,* steering oar.] —**pi′lot·age** (-lə-tĭj) *n.*

pilotfish or **pilot fish** (pī′lət-fĭsh′) ►*n., pl.* **-fish** or **-fish·es** A small slender marine fish that often swims with larger fishes, esp. sharks and mantas.

pi·lot·house (pī′lət-hous′) ►*n. Naut.* An enclosed area, usu. on the bridge of a vessel, from which the vessel is controlled.

pilot light ►*n.* A small jet of gas kept burning in order to ignite a gas burner, as in a stove.

pilot whale ►*n.* Either of two toothed whales having black skin and a bulbous head.

pils·ner (pĭlz′nər, pĭls′-) ►*n.* **1.** A light lager with a strong hops flavor. **2.** A tall, thin, footed beer glass. [Ger.]

Pilt·down man (pĭlt′doun′) ►*n.* A proposed species of extinct humans postulated from a skull uncovered in 1912 but proved in 1953 to be a fake. [After *Piltdown* Common in southeast England.]

Pi·ma (pē′mə) ►*n., pl.* **-ma** or **-mas 1.** A member of a Native American people of S Arizona. **2.** The Uto-Aztecan language of the Pima. —**Pi′man** *adj.*

pi·men·to (pĭ-měn′tō) ►*n., pl.* **-tos 1.** See **allspice. 2.** Var. of **pimiento.** [< LLat. *pigmentum,* pigment.]

pi·mien·to (pĭ-měn′tō, -myěn′tō) also **pi·men·to** (-měn′tō) ►*n., pl.* **-tos** A capsicum pepper having a mild, sweet, red fruit. [Sp.; see PIMENTO.]

pimp (pĭmp) ►*n.* One who procures customers for a prostitute. ►*v.* **1.** To be a pimp. **2.** To compromise one's principles, esp. to further the interests of another, for personal gain. **3.** To customize or adorn, often garishly. [?]

pim·per·nel (pĭm′pər-nĕl′, -nəl) ►*n.* A plant having opposite leaves and flowers with a five-lobed calyx. [< LLat. *pimpinella.*]

pim·ple (pĭm′pəl) ►*n.* A small inflamed swelling of the skin, usu. caused by acne. [ME.] —**pim′-pled, pim′ply** *adj.*

pin (pĭn) ►*n.* **1.** A short, straight, stiff piece of wire with a blunt head and a sharp point, used esp. for fastening. **2.** Something, such as a safety pin or hairpin, that resembles a pin in shape or use. **3.** A slender, usu. cylindrical piece of wood or metal for holding, fastening, or supporting. **4.** An ornament fastened to clothing by means of a clasp. **5.** One of the clubs at which the ball is aimed in bowling. **6.** The pole bearing a pennant to mark a hole in golf. **7. pins** *Informal* The legs. ►*v.* **pinned, pin·ning 1.** To fasten or secure with or as if with a pin. **2.** To make completely dependent: *pinning all our hopes on winning.* **3.** To hold fast; immobilize. —*phrasal verbs:* **pin down 1.** To fix or establish clearly. **2.** To oblige to make a definite response. **pin on** To attribute (a wrongdoing or crime) to. [< OE *pinn.*]

PIN ►*abbr.* personal identification number

pin·a·fore (pĭn′ə-fôr′) ►*n.* A sleeveless apron-like garment. [PIN + *afore*, in front.]

pi·ña·ta (pĭn-yä′tə, pēn-) ►*n.* **1.** A decorated container filled with candy and toys and hung from a height to be broken by blindfolded children with sticks. **2.** *Informal* A frequent object of ongoing abuse. [Sp.]

pin·ball (pĭn′bôl′) ►*n.* A game in which the player activates a lever to keep a ball in play, moving among obstacles and targets on a slanted surface.

pince-nez (păns′nā′, pĭns′-) ►*n., pl.* **pince-nez** (-nāz′, -nā′) Eyeglasses clipped to the bridge of the nose. [Fr.]

pince-nez

pin·cers (pĭn′sərz) *also* **pinch·ers** (pĭn′chərz) ►*pl.n.* (takes sing. or pl. v.) **1.** A grasping tool having a pair of jaws and handles pivoted together to work in opposition. **2.** A pair of appendages used by certain arthropods for grasping, such as the curved parts of a lobster's claw. [< OFr. *pincier*, pinch.]

pinch (pĭnch) ►*v.* **1.** To squeeze between the thumb and a finger, the jaws of a tool, or other edges. **2.** To cause discomfort to (a part of the body) by pressing or being too tight. **3.** To wither or shrivel. **4.** To cause to be in difficulty or financial distress. **5.** *Slang* To take (money or property) wrongfully. **6.** *Slang* To take into

custody; arrest. ►*n.* **1.** The act or an instance of pinching. **2.** An amount that can be held between thumb and forefinger. **3.** An emergency. [< OFr. *pincier.*] —**pinch′er** *n.*

pinch-hit (pĭnch′hĭt′) ►*v.* **1.** *Baseball* To bat in place of a scheduled player. **2.** *Informal* To substitute for another. —**pinch hitter** *n.*

pin·cush·ion (pĭn′kŏŏsh′ən) ►*n.* **1.** A cushion into which pins are stuck when not in use. **2.** An object of frequent criticism or hurtful treatment.

Pin·dar (pĭn′dər) 522?–443? BC. Greek lyric poet. —**Pin·dar′ic** (-dăr′ĭk) *adj.*

pine¹ (pīn) ►*n.* **1.** Any of various cone-bearing evergreen trees having needle-shaped leaves in clusters. **2.** The wood of any of these trees. [< Lat. *pīnus.*]

pine² (pīn) ►*v.* **pined, pin·ing 1.** To feel longing; yearn. **2.** To wither away from longing or grief. [< Gk. *poinē*, punishment.]

pin·e·al gland (pĭn′ē-əl, pī′nē-) ►*n.* A small, cone-shaped organ in the brain of most vertebrates that secretes melatonin. [< Lat. *pīnea*, pine cone.]

pine·ap·ple (pīn′ăp′əl) ►*n.* **1.** A tropical American plant having swordlike leaves and a large, fleshy, edible fruit. **2.** The fruit of the pineapple. [ME *pinappel*, pine cone.]

pine needle ►*n.* The needle-shaped leaf of a pine tree.

pine nut ►*n.* The edible seed of certain pines.

pin·e·y (pī′nē) ►*adj.* Var. of **piny.**

pin·feath·er (pĭn′fĕth′ər) ►*n.* A growing feather, esp. one just emerging through the skin.

ping (pĭng) ►*n.* **1.** A sharp, high-pitched sound, as that made by a bullet striking metal. **2.** A pounding or clanking noise made by an engine, often as a result of faulty fuel combustion. **3.** A protocol that sends a message to another computer and waits for acknowledgment. [Imit. Sense 3 < sonar pings.] —**ping** *v.*

Ping-Pong (pĭng′pông′, -pŏng′) A trademark for table tennis.

pin·head (pĭn′hĕd′) ►*n.* **1.** The head of a pin. **2.** Something small or insignificant. **3.** *Slang* A stupid person. —**pin′head′ed** *adj.*

pin·hole (pĭn′hōl′) ►*n.* A tiny puncture made by or as if by a pin.

pin·ion¹ (pĭn′yən) ►*n.* A bird's wing. ►*v.* **1.** To restrain or immobilize by binding the wings or arms. **2.** To bind fast, hold down, or fix in one place. [< Lat. *pinna*, feather.]

pin·ion² (pĭn′yən) ►*n.* A small cogwheel that engages or is engaged by a larger cogwheel or a rack. [< Lat. *pecten*, comb.]

pink¹ (pĭngk) ►*n.* **1.** A light or pale red. **2.** Any of various plants related to the carnation, often cultivated for their showy, fragrant flowers. **3.** The highest degree of excellence: *in the pink of health.* [?] —**pink** *adj.* —**pink′ish** *adj.*

pink² (pĭngk) ►*v.* **1.** To stab lightly; prick. **2.** To decorate with a perforated pattern. **3.** To cut with pinking shears. [ME *pinken.*]

pink·eye (pĭngk′ī′) ►*n.* An acute, very contagious form of conjunctivitis.

pink·ie *also* **pink·y** (pĭng′kē) ►*n., pl.* **-ies** *Informal* The little finger. [Prob. < Du. *pinkje.*]

pink·ing shears (pĭng′kĭng) ►*pl.n.* Shears with notched blades, used to finish edges of cloth with a zigzag cut for decoration or to prevent raveling or fraying.

pink·o (pĭng′kō) ►*n.*, *pl.* **-os** *Slang* One who holds moderately leftist political views.

pin money ►*n.* Money for incidental expenses.

pin·na·cle (pĭn′ə-kəl) ►*n.* **1.** A small turret or spire on a roof or buttress. **2.** A tall, pointed formation. **3.** The highest point; acme. [< LLat. *pinnāculum*, dim. of Lat. *pinna*, feather.]

pin·nate (pĭn′āt′) ►*adj.* Having parts or branches arranged on each side of a common axis: *pinnate leaves.* [< Lat. *pinna*, feather.]

pi·noch·le or **pi·noc·le** (pē′nŭk′əl, -nŏk′əl) ►*n.* A card game for two to four persons, played with a deck of 48 cards. [Perh. < Ger. dial. *Binokel*, card game.]

pi·ñon also **pin·yon** (pĭn′yōn′, -yən) ►*n.* Any of several pine trees bearing edible, nutlike seeds. [< Lat. *pīnea*, pine cone.]

pin·point (pĭn′point′) ►*n.* An extremely small thing or spot; particle. ►*v.* To locate, identify, or target with precision.

pin·prick (pĭn′prĭk′) ►*n.* **1.** A slight puncture made by a pin. **2.** A minor annoyance.

pins and needles ►*pl.n.* Tingling felt in a part of the body numbed from lack of circulation. **—idiom: on pins and needles** In a state of tense anticipation.

pin·stripe (pĭn′strīp′) ►*n.* **1.** A thin stripe, esp. on a fabric. **2.** A fabric with pinstripes.

pint (pīnt) ►*n.* **1.** See table at **measurement. 2.** A unit of volume or capacity used in dry and liquid measure, equal to 0.568 liter. [< VLat. **pīncta*, mark on a container.]

pin·tail (pĭn′tāl′) ►*n.*, *pl.* **-tail** or **-tails** A duck of the Northern Hemisphere having a sharply pointed tail.

Pin·ter (pĭn′tər), **Harold** 1930–2008. British playwright. **—Pin′ter·esque′** *adj.*

pin·to (pĭn′tō) ►*n.*, *pl.* **-tos** or **-toes** A horse with patchy spots or markings. [Sp.]

pinto bean ►*n.* A form of kidney bean having mottled seeds.

pint·size (pīnt′sīz′) also **pint·sized** (-sīzd′) ►*adj. Informal* Diminutive.

pin·up (pĭn′ŭp′) ►*n.* A picture to be pinned up on a wall, esp. of an attractive person.

pin·wheel (pĭn′wēl′, -hwēl′) ►*n.* **1.** A toy consisting of vanes of colored paper or plastic pinned to a stick so that they revolve when blown on. **2.** A firework that forms a rotating wheel of colored flames.

pin·worm (pĭn′wûrm′) ►*n.* Any of various small parasitic nematode worms, esp. one that infests the human intestines and rectum.

pin·y also **pine·y** (pī′nē) ►*adj.* **-i·er, -i·est** Of or abounding in pines.

Pin·yin or **pin·yin** (pĭn′yĭn′, -yĭn′) ►*n.* A system for transcribing the pronunciation of the standard variety of Mandarin using the Roman alphabet.

pin·yon (pĭn′yōn′, -yən) ►*n.* Var. of **piñon.**

pi·on (pī′ŏn′) ►*n.* Any of the three least massive mesons, having a positive, neutral, or negative electric charge. [< *pi meson.*]

pi·o·neer (pī′ə-nîr′) ►*n.* **1.** One who ventures into unknown or unclaimed territory to settle. **2.** An innovator, esp. in research and development. [< OFr. *peonier*, foot soldier < Lat. *pēs, ped-*, foot.] **—pi′o·neer′** *v.*

pi·ous (pī′əs) ►*adj.* **1a.** Reverently observant of religion; devout. **b.** Devotional: *pious readings.* **2a.** Done for the benefit of others or with the intention of encouraging good. **b.** Sincere but wishful or far-fetched: *a pious hope.* **3.** *Archaic* High-minded. [< Lat. *pius.*] **—pi′ous·ly** *adv.*

pip¹ (pĭp) ►*n.* A small fruit seed, as that of an apple or orange. [< PIPPIN.]

pip² (pĭp) ►*n.* **1.** A dot indicating numerical value on dice or dominoes. **2.** See **blip** (sense 1). [?]

pip³ (pĭp) ►*n.* **1.** A disease of birds. **2.** *Slang* A minor, unspecified human ailment. [< Lat. *pītuīta.*]

pipe (pīp) ►*n.* **1.** A hollow cylinder or tube used to conduct a liquid, gas, or finely divided solid. **2.** A device for smoking, consisting of a tube of wood, clay, or other material with a small bowl at one end. **3.** *Informal* A tubular part or organ of the body. **4a.** A tubular musical wind instrument, such as a fife. **b.** Any of the tubes in an organ. **c. pipes** A small wind instrument, consisting of tubes of different lengths bound together. **d.** A bagpipe. **5. pipes** The vocal cords; the voice, esp. as used in singing. ►*v.* **piped, pip·ing 1.** To convey or transmit by or as if by pipes. **2.** To play (a tune) on a pipe or pipes. **3.** To make a shrill sound. **—phrasal verbs: pipe down** *Slang* To be quiet. **pipe up** To speak up. [< Lat. *pīpāre*, chirp.] **—pip′er** *n.*

pipe dream ►*n.* A fantastic notion or vain hope. [From opium fantasies.]

pipe fitter ►*n.* One that installs and repairs piping systems.

pipe·line (pīp′līn′) ►*n.* **1.** A conduit of pipe for the conveyance of water, gas, or petroleum products. **2.** A channel by which information is privately transmitted. **3.** A line of supply.

pipe organ ►*n. Mus.* See **organ** (sense 1).

pipe·stone (pīp′stōn′) ►*n.* A red or pink clay stone used by Native American peoples for making tobacco pipes.

pi·pette also **pi·pet** (pī-pĕt′) ►*n.* A narrow, usu. calibrated tube used for transferring or measuring liquids.

pipe wrench ►*n.* A wrench with two serrated jaws for gripping and turning pipe.

pip·ing (pī′pĭng) ►*n.* **1.** A system of pipes. **2.** Music made by a pipe or pipes. **3.** A narrow band of material, used for trimming a fabric. **—idiom: piping hot** Very hot.

pip·pin (pĭp′ĭn) ►*n.* Any of several varieties of apple. [< OFr. *pepin.*]

pip-squeak (pĭp′skwēk′) ►*n. Informal* One that is small or insignificant.

pi·quant (pē′kənt, -känt′, pē-känt′) ►*adj.* **1.** Pleasantly pungent; spicy. **2.** Appealingly provocative. [< OFr. *piquer*, to prick.] **—pi′quan·cy, pi′quant·ness** *n.*

pique (pēk) ►*n.* Resentment or vexation from wounded pride; huff. ►*v.* **piqued, piqu·ing 1.** To cause to feel resentment. **2.** To provoke; arouse: *The box piqued her curiosity.* [< OFr. *piquer*, to prick.]

pi·qué (pĭ-kā′, pē-) ►*n.* A fabric with various raised patterns. [< OFr. *piquer*, to prick.]

Pi·ran·del·lo (pĭr′ən-dĕl′ō, pē′rän-dĕl′lō), **Luigi** 1867–1936. Italian writer.

pi·ra·nha also **pi·ra·ña** (pĭ-rän′yə, -rän′yə) ►*n.* A sharp-toothed tropical American freshwater fish known for attacking and feeding on live animals. [Port. < Tupí *pirá*, fish + *ánha*, to cut.]

pi·rate (pī′rĭt) ►*n.* **1.** One who robs at sea or plunders the land from the sea. **2.** One who makes use of or reproduces the work of another illicitly or without authorization. [< Gk. *peiratēs*.] —**pi′ra·cy** *n.* —**pi′rate** *v.* —**pi·rat′ic** (-răt′ĭk), **pi·rat′i·cal** *adj.*

pi·rogue (pĭ-rōg′, pîr′ō) ►*n.* A canoe made from a hollowed tree trunk. [< Carib *piragua*.]

pir·ou·ette (pĭr′ōō-ĕt′) ►*n.* A full turn of the body on the tip of the toe or the ball of the foot, esp. in ballet. [< OFr. *pirouet*, spinning top.] —**pir′ou·ette′** *v.*

Pi·sa (pē′zə, -zä) A city of W Italy on the Arno R. near the Tyrrhenian Sea. —**Pi′san** *adj. & n.*

pis·ca·to·ri·al (pĭs′kə-tôr′ē-əl) ►*adj.* Of or relating to fish or fishing. [< Lat. *piscis*, fish.]

Pi·sces (pī′sēz) ►*pl.n. (takes sing. v.)* **1.** A constellation in the equatorial region of the Northern Hemisphere. **2.** The 12th sign of the zodiac.

pi·so (pē′sō) ►*n., pl.* **-sos** See table at **currency.** [Tagalog < Span. *peso.*]

pis·ta·chi·o (pĭ-stăsh′ē-ō′, -stä′shē-ō′) ►*n., pl.* **-os** **1.** An Asian tree bearing hard-shelled edible nuts with a green kernel. **2.** The nut of this tree. [< Gk. *pistakē*.]

pis·til (pĭs′təl) ►*n.* The seed-bearing reproductive organ of a flower. [< Lat. *pistillum*, pestle.]

pis·tol (pĭs′təl) ►*n.* A firearm designed to be held and fired with one hand. [< Czech *pišťala*, pipe.]

pis·tol-whip (pĭs′təl-wĭp′, -hwĭp′) ►*v.* To beat with a pistol.

pis·ton (pĭs′tən) ►*n.* A solid cylinder or disk that fits snugly into a cylinder and moves back and forth under fluid pressure. [< Ital. *pistone*, large pestle.]

pit¹ (pĭt) ►*n.* **1.** A relatively deep hole in the ground. **2.** A trap or pitfall. **3a.** A natural depression in the body or an organ. **b.** A small indented scar left in the skin by disease or injury; pockmark. **4.** An enclosed area in which animals are placed for fighting. **5.** The musicians' section directly in front of the stage of a theater. **6.** The section of an exchange where trading in a specific commodity is carried on. **7.** A refueling area beside an auto racecourse. **8a.** Hell. **b. the pits** *Slang* A very bad thing or situation. ►*v.* **pit·ted, pit·ting** **1.** To mark or scar with pits. **2.** To set in opposition: *pitted brother against brother.* [< OE *pytt.*]

pit² (pĭt) ►*n.* The single, hard-shelled seed of certain fruits, such as a peach or cherry; stone. ►*v.* **pit·ted, pit·ting** To extract the pit from (a fruit). [< MDu.]

pi·ta (pē′tə) ►*n.* A round, flat bread that opens to form a pocket for filling. [Mod.Gk., bread.]

pit·a·pat (pĭt′ə-păt′) ►*v.* **-pat·ted, -pat·ting** To make a repeated tapping sound. ►*n.* A series of quick steps, taps, or beats. [Imit.]

Pit·cairn Island (pĭt′kârn′) A volcanic island of the S Pacific ESE of Tahiti, administered by Britain.

pitch¹ (pĭch) ►*n.* Any of various thick, dark, sticky substances obtained from the distillation residue of coal tar, wood tar, or petroleum and used for waterproofing, roofing, caulking, and paving. [< Lat. *pix.*]

pitch² (pĭch) ►*v.* **1.** To throw, usu. with careful aim. **2.** To throw (a baseball) from the mound to the batter. **3.** To put up or in position: *pitched a tent; pitch camp.* **4.** To set firmly; implant. **5.** To fix the level of. **6.** *Mus.* To set at a specified pitch or key. **7.** To hit (a golf ball) in a high arc

with backspin. **8.** To fall headlong; plunge. **9.** To dip bow and stern alternately, as a ship in rough seas. ►*n.* **1.** The act or an instance of pitching. **2a.** A downward slant. **b.** The degree of such a slant, as of the angle of a roof. **3.** A level or degree, as of intensity or development. **4.** Lowness or highness of a complex sound, such as a musical tone, that is dependent primarily on frequency. **5.** *Informal* A line of talk designed to persuade. —*phrasal verb:* **pitch in** *Informal* To set to work vigorously, esp. in cooperation with others. [ME *pichen.*]

pitch-black (pĭch′blăk′) ►*adj.* Extremely black.

pitch·blende (pĭch′blĕnd′) ►*n.* A brownish-black mineral, the principal ore of uranium. [< Ger. *Pechblende.*]

pitch-dark (pĭch′därk′) ►*adj.* Extremely dark.

pitched roof (pĭcht) ►*n.* A two-sided sloped roof having a gable at both ends.

pitch·er¹ (pĭch′ər) ►*n.* *Baseball* The player who pitches.

pitch·er² (pĭch′ər) ►*n.* A container for liquids, usu. having a handle and a lip or spout for pouring. [< Med.Lat. *bicārium*, drinking cup.]

pitcher plant ►*n.* Any of various carnivorous plants having tubular fluid-filled leaves that absorb nutrients from trapped insects.

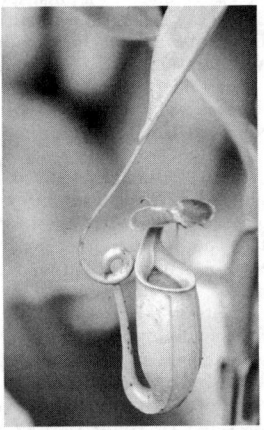

pitcher plant

pitch·fork (pĭch′fôrk′) ►*n.* A large, long-handled fork with widely spaced prongs for lifting and pitching hay. [< ME *pikforke.*]

pitch pipe ►*n.* A small pipe sounded to give the pitch for a piece of music or the standard pitch for tuning an instrument.

pit·e·ous (pĭt′ē-əs) ►*adj.* Arousing pity; pathetic. —**pit′e·ous·ness** *n.*

pit·fall (pĭt′fôl′) ►*n.* **1.** An unapparent difficulty or danger. **2.** A concealed hole in the ground that serves as a trap.

pith (pĭth) ►*n.* **1.** The soft, spongelike substance in the center of stems and branches of many plants. **2.** The essential or central part; heart. **3.** Strength; force. [< OE *pitha.*]

pith helmet ►*n.* A lightweight hat of dried pith worn for protection from the sun.

pith·y (pĭth′ē) ►*adj.* **-i·er, -i·est** **1.** Precise and meaningful. **2.** Of or resembling pith. —**pith′i·ly** *adv.* —**pith′i·ness** *n.*

pit·i·a·ble (pĭt′ē-ə-bəl) ►*adj.* Arousing pity. —**pit′i·a·ble·ness** *n.* —**pit′i·a·bly** *adv.*

pit·i·ful (pĭt′ĭ-fəl) ►*adj.* **1.** Inspiring or deserving pity. **2.** Arousing contemptuous pity, as through ineptitude or inadequacy. —**pit′i·ful·ly** *adv.* —**pit′i·ful·ness** *n.*

pit·i·less (pĭt′ĭ-lĭs) ►*adj.* Having no pity; merciless. —**pit′i·less·ness** *n.*

pi·ton (pē′tŏn′) ►*n.* A spike with an eye or ring for securing a support rope in mountain climbing. [< OFr., nail.]

pit stop ►*n.* **1.** A stop at a pit for refueling or service during an automobile race. **2.** *Informal* A rest stop during a trip.

Pitt¹ (pĭt), **William** 1st Earl of Chatham. 1708–78. British political leader and orator.

Pitt² (pĭt), **William** 2nd Earl of Chatham. 1759–1806. British prime minister (1783–1801 and 1804–06).

pit·tance (pĭt′ns) ►*n.* A small amount or portion, esp. of money. [< Med.Lat. *pietantia,* handout to the poor.]

pit·ter-pat·ter (pĭt′ər-păt′ər) ►*n.* Repeated light, tapping sounds. [Imit.]

Pitts·burgh (pĭts′bûrg′) A city of SW PA at the point where the Allegheny and Monongahela Rivers join to form the Ohio R.

pi·tu·i·tar·y gland (pĭ-tōō′ĭ-tĕr′ē, -tyōō′-) ►*n.* A small oval endocrine gland attached to the base of the vertebrate brain, the secretions of which control the other endocrine glands and influence growth, metabolism, and maturation. [< Lat. *pītuīta,* phlegm.]

pit viper ►*n.* Any of various venomous snakes, such as the rattlesnake, having a small sensory pit below each eye.

pit·y (pĭt′ē) ►*n., pl.* **-ies 1.** Sympathy and sorrow aroused by the misfortune or suffering of another. **2.** A matter of regret: *It's a pity she can't go.* ►*v.* **-ied, -y·ing** To feel pity (for). [< Lat. *pietās,* piety.]

Pi·us V (pī′əs), Saint. 1504–72. Pope (1566–72).

Pius IX 1792–1878. Pope (1846–78).

Pius X, Saint. 1835–1914. Pope (1903–14).

Pius XII 1876–1958. Pope (1939–58).

piv·ot (pĭv′ət) ►*n.* **1.** A short rod or shaft on which a related part rotates or swings. **2.** One that determines the direction or effect of something. **3.** The act of turning on a pivot. ►*v.* To turn or cause to turn on a pivot. [< OFr.] —**piv′ot·al** *adj.* —**piv′ot·al·ly** *adv.*

pix (pĭks) ►*n.* Var. of **pyx.**

pix·el (pĭk′səl, -sĕl′) ►*n.* The basic unit of a digital image, representing a single color or level of brightness. [PIC(TURE) + EL(EMENT).]

pix·ie or **pix·y** (pĭk′sē) ►*n., pl.* **-ies** A fairylike or elfin creature. [?] —**pix′y·ish** *adj.*

Pi·zar·ro (pĭ-zär′ō, -sär′-), **Francisco** 1475?–1541. Spanish explorer.

piz·za (pēt′sə) ►*n.* An Italian baked pie consisting of a crust covered usu. with seasoned tomato sauce and cheese. [Ital.]

piz·zazz or **piz·zaz** (pĭ-zăz′) ►*n. Informal* **1.** Dazzling style; flamboyance. **2.** Energy or excitement. [?]

piz·ze·ri·a (pēt′sə-rē′ə) ►*n.* A place where pizzas are made and sold.

piz·zi·ca·to (pĭt′sĭ-kä′tō) ►*adj. Mus.* Played by plucking the strings. [Ital.] —**piz′zi·ca′to** *adv.*

pk. ►*abbr.* **1.** park **2.** also **Pk.** peak **3.** peck

pkg. ►*abbr.* package

pl. ►*abbr.* **1.** or **Pl.** place **2.** plural

plac·ard (plăk′ärd′, -ərd) ►*n.* **1.** A sign or notice for public display. **2.** A nameplate, as on a door. [< OFr., official document.] —**plac′ard** *v.*

pla·cate (plā′kāt′, plăk′āt′) ►*v.* **-cat·ed, -cat·ing** To allay the anger of; appease. [Lat. *plācāre.*] —**plac′a·ble** *adj.* —**pla·ca′tion** *n.*

place (plās) ►*n.* **1.** An area with or without definite boundaries; a portion of space. **2.** An area occupied by or allocated to a person or thing. **3.** A definite location. **4.** often **Place** A public square or short street in a town. **5.** A table setting. **6.** A position regarded as belonging to someone or something else; stead: *She was chosen in his place.* **7.** Relative position in a series; standing: *fourth place.* ►*v.* **placed, plac·ing 1.** To put in or as if in a particular position; set. **2.** To put or rank in a specified relation, order, or sequence. **3.** To appoint to a post. **4a.** To give an order for: *place a bet.* **b.** To arrange for; make: *place a telephone call.* **5.** To arrive among the first three finishers in a race, esp. to finish second. —*idiom:* **in place of** Instead of. [< Gk. *plateia (hodos),* broad (street).]

pla·ce·bo (plə-sē′bō) ►*n., pl.* **-bos** or **-boes 1.** A substance that has positive effects as a result of a patient's perception that it is beneficial rather than as a result of a causative ingredient. **2.** An inactive substance used as a control in an experiment. [< LLat. *placēbō,* I shall please.]

place kick ►*n. Football* A kick, as for a field goal, for which the ball is held or propped up in a fixed position. —**place′-kick′** *v.*

place mat ►*n.* A table mat for a single setting of dishes and flatware.

place·ment (plās′mənt) ►*n.* **1a.** The act of placing or arranging. **b.** The state of being placed or arranged. **2.** The finding of jobs, lodgings, or other positions for applicants.

pla·cen·ta (plə-sĕn′tə) ►*n., pl.* **-tas** or **-tae** (-tē) A membranous vascular organ that develops in female mammals during pregnancy, lining the uterine wall and partially enveloping the fetus, to which it is attached by the umbilical cord. [< Lat., flat cake.] —**pla·cen′tal** *adj.*

plac·er (plăs′ər) ►*n.* A sand or gravel deposit left by a river or glacier, containing valuable minerals. [Sp. < Med.Lat. *placea,* PLACE.]

plac·id (plăs′ĭd) ►*adj.* Undisturbed by tumult or disorder; calm or composed. [< Lat. *placēre,* please.] —**pla·cid′i·ty** (plə-sĭd′ĭ-tē), **plac′id·ness** *n.* —**plac′id·ly** *adv.*

plack·et (plăk′ĭt) ►*n.* An opening or slit in a garment, as at the collar of a shirt, that makes the garment easy to put on. [?]

pla·gia·rize (plā′jə-rīz′) ►*v.* **-rized, -riz·ing** To use (the ideas or work of another) as one's own or without attribution. [< Lat. *plagiārius,* kidnapper.] —**pla′gia·rism, pla′gia·ry** *n.* —**pla′gia·rist, pla′gia·riz′er** *n.*

plague (plāg) ►*n.* **1.** A virulent infectious disease, esp. bubonic plague, that is caused by a bacterium and is transmitted to humans primarily by the bite of a flea from an infected rat. **2.** A widespread affliction or calamity. **3.** Something that causes persistent hardship or annoyance. ►*v.* **plagued, plagu·ing** To harass, pester, or annoy. [< Lat. *plāga,* blow, calamity.]

plaid (plăd) ►*n.* **1.** A rectangular woolen scarf of a checked or tartan pattern worn over the left shoulder by Scottish Highlanders. **2.** A pattern of this kind, esp. in cloth. [Sc.Gael. *plaide.*] —**plaid, plaid′ed** *adj.*

plain (plān) ►*adj.* **-er, -est 1.** Free from obstructions; open to view; clear. **2.** Easily understood; clearly evident. See Synonyms at **apparent. 3a.** Uncomplicated; simple. **b.** Having little or no ornamentation or decoration. **c.** Straightforward. **d.** Unattractive. **4.** Not mixed with other substances; pure. **5.** Common in rank or station; ordinary. ►*n.* An extensive, level, usu. treeless area of land. ►*adv. Informal* Clearly; simply. [< Lat. *plānus*, flat.] —**plain′ly** *adv.* —**plain′ness** *n.*
    Syns: *modest, simple, unpretentious* **Ant:** *ornate adj.*

plain·clothes (plān′klōz′, -klō*th*z′) ►*adj.* Wearing civilian clothes while on duty to avoid being identified as police or security.

Plains Indian (plānz) ►*n.* A member of any of the Native American peoples inhabiting the Great Plains of North America.

plain·song (plān′sông′, -sŏng′) ►*n.* Medieval liturgical music traditionally sung without accompaniment.

plain·spo·ken (plān′spō′kən) ►*adj.* Frank; straightforward. —**plain′spo′ken·ness** *n.*

plaint (plānt) ►*n.* **1.** A complaint. **2.** A lamentation. [< Lat. *plangere, plānct-*, lament.]

plain·text (plān′tĕkst′) ►*n.* The unencrypted form of an encrypted message.

plain·tiff (plān′tĭf) ►*n. Law* The party instituting a suit in a court. [< OFr. *plaintif*, aggrieved.]

plain·tive (plān′tĭv) ►*adj.* Expressing sorrow; mournful or melancholy. —**plain′tive·ly** *adv.*

plait (plāt, plăt) ►*n.* A braid, esp. of hair. ►*v.* To braid. [< Lat. *plicāre*, fold.]

plan (plăn) ►*n.* **1.** A detailed scheme or method for the accomplishment of an objective. **2.** A proposed or tentative project or goal. **3.** An outline or sketch, esp. a drawing or diagram made to scale. **4.** A program or policy stipulating a service or benefit: *a pension plan.* ►*v.* **planned, plan·ning 1.** To formulate, draw up, or make a plan or plans. **2.** To intend. [< Lat. *plantāre*, to plant.] —**plan′ner** *n.*
    Syns: *blueprint, design, project, scheme, strategy n.*

pla·nar (plā′nər, -när′) ►*adj.* **1.** Of or in a plane. **2.** Flat. —**pla·nar′i·ty** (plā-năr′ĭ-tē) *n.*

Planck (plängk), **Max Karl Ernst Ludwig** 1858–1947. German physicist.

plane[1] (plān) ►*n.* **1.** A surface containing all the straight lines that connect any two points on it. **2.** A flat or level surface. **3.** A level of development. **4.** An airplane. **5.** A supporting surface of an airplane. ►*adj.* Of or being a figure lying in a plane. [Lat. *plānum*.]

plane[2] (plān) ►*n.* A carpenter's tool for smoothing and leveling wood. [< Lat. *plānus*, flat.] —**plane** *v.* —**plan′er** *n.*

plane[3] (plān) ►*n.* A plane tree. [< Gk. *platanos*.]

plane geometry ►*n.* The geometry of two-dimensional figures.

plan·et (plăn′ĭt) ►*n.* **1.** In the traditional model of solar systems, a celestial body larger than an asteroid or comet, illuminated by light from a star, such as the sun, around which it revolves. **2.** A celestial body that orbits the sun, has sufficient mass to assume a nearly round shape, clears out dust and debris from the neighborhood around its orbit, and is not a satellite of another planet. [< Gk. *planētēs*, wanderer.]

plan·e·tar·i·um (plăn′ĭ-târ′ē-əm) ►*n., pl.* **-i·**

ums or **-i·a** (-ē-ə) **1.** An apparatus or model representing the solar system. **2a.** A device for projecting images of celestial bodies onto the inner surface of a dome. **b.** A building housing such a device.

plan·e·tar·y (plăn′ĭ-tĕr′ē) ►*adj.* **1.** Of or resembling a planet. **2.** Worldwide; global.

plane tree ►*n.* A sycamore or related tree having ball-shaped seed clusters and usu. bark that flakes off in patches.

plan·gent (plăn′jənt) ►*adj.* **1.** Loud and resounding. **2.** Plaintive. [< Lat. *plangere*, strike.] —**plan′gen·cy** *n.*

plank (plăngk) ►*n.* **1.** A thick piece of lumber. **2.** One of the articles of a political platform. ►*v.* **1.** To cover with planks. **2.** To bake or broil and serve (fish or meat) on a board. **3.** To put or set down with force. [< LLat. *plancus*, flat.]

plank·ton (plăngk′tən) ►*n.* Small or microscopic organisms that drift or swim weakly in bodies of water. [< Gk. *planktos*, wandering.] —**plank·ton′ic** (-tŏn′ĭk) *adj.*

plant (plănt) ►*n.* **1.** *Bot.* **a.** An organism characteristically having cellulose cell walls, growing by synthesis of food from inorganic substances, and lacking the power of locomotion. **b.** A plant having no permanent woody stem, as distinguished from a tree or shrub. **2a.** A factory. **b.** The buildings, equipment, and fixtures of an institution. ►*v.* **1a.** To place in the ground to grow. **b.** To sow or supply with or as if with seeds or plants. **2a.** To fix in a certain position. **b.** To implant in the mind. **3.** To establish or found. **4.** To (place) for the purpose of spying, deception, or influencing behavior. [< Lat. *planta*, shoot.] —**plant′a·ble** *adj.*

plan·tain[1] (plăn′tən) ►*n.* A plant with a dense spike of small greenish flowers. [< Lat. *plantāgō*.]

plan·tain[2] (plăn′tən) ►*n.* **1.** Any of several varieties of banana having edible, elongated fruit. **2.** The fruit of this plant, usu. eaten cooked. [Sp. *plátano*, plane tree.]

plan·ta·tion (plăn-tā′shən) ►*n.* **1.** A group of cultivated trees or plants. **2.** A large estate or farm on which crops are raised and harvested, often by resident workers.

plant·er (plăn′tər) ►*n.* **1.** One that plants. **2.** The owner or manager of a plantation. **3.** A decorative container for a plant.

plaque (plăk) ►*n.* **1.** An ornamented or engraved plate, slab, or disk used for decoration or on a monument for information. **2.** A small ornament or badge of membership. **3.** A deposit that builds up on a tooth or the inner lining of a blood vessel. **4.** A waxy deposit found in the brain tissue of people with Alzheimer's disease, consisting mainly of protein and degenerating nerve tissue. [< OFr., metal plate.]

plash (plăsh) ►*n.* A light splash or the sound it makes. [Poss. < OE *plæsc*, pool of water.]

–plasm ►*suff.* Material forming cells or tissue: *cytoplasm.* [< PLASMA.]

plas·ma (plăz′mə) ►*n.* **1.** The clear yellowish fluid portion of blood, lymph, or intramuscular fluid in which cells are suspended. **2.** Protoplasm or cytoplasm. **3.** *Phys.* An electrically neutral, highly ionized gas composed of ions, electrons, and neutral particles. ►*adj.* Of or relating to a flat-panel display made up of tiny cells each containing a gaseous mixture that is changed into a plasma state to illuminate a phosphor coating on the inside of the cell. [< Gk., image.] —**plas·mat·ic** (-măt′ĭk), **plas′mic** *adj.*

plas·min (plăz′mĭn) ►*n.* An enzyme in plasma that dissolves the fibrin in blood clots.

plasmo– or **plasm–** ►*pref.* Plasma: *plasmin.*

plas·mol·y·sis (plăz-mŏl′ĭ-sĭs) ►*n., pl.* **-ses** (-sēz′) Shrinkage or contraction of the protoplasm in a cell, caused by loss of water through osmosis. —**plas′mo·lyt·ic** (-mə-lĭt′ĭk) *adj.*

plas·ter (plăs′tər) ►*n.* **1.** A paste that hardens to a smooth solid and is used for coating walls and ceilings. **2.** Plaster of Paris. **3.** A pastelike mixture that is applied to a part of the body, as for healing. ►*v.* **1.** To cover with or as if with plaster. **2.** To cover conspicuously or to excess. [< Gk. *emplastron,* medical dressing.] —**plas′ter·er** *n.*

plas·ter·board (plăs′tər-bôrd′) ►*n.* Drywall.

plaster of Paris ►*n.* A quick-setting paste of white gypsum powder and water, used esp. for casts and statuary molds.

plas·tic (plăs′tĭk) ►*adj.* **1.** Capable of being shaped or formed: *plastic material such as clay.* **2.** Relating to or dealing with shaping or modeling. **3.** Made of a plastic. ►*n.* **1.** Any of various complex organic compounds produced by polymerization, capable of being molded, extruded, cast into various shapes and films, or drawn into filaments used as textile fibers. **2.** *Informal* A credit card or credit cards. [< Gk. *plassein,* mold.] —**plas·tic·i·ty** (plăs-tĭs′ĭ-tē) *n.* —**plas′ti·cize** (-tĭ-sīz′) *v.*

plastic explosive ►*n.* A moldable doughlike explosive substance.

plastic surgery ►*n.* Surgery to remodel, repair, or restore the appearance and sometimes the function of body parts, such as repair of congenital defects. —**plastic surgeon** *n.*

plastic wrap ►*n.* A thin, clear, flexible sheet of plastic used as a moistureproof wrapping.

plas·tid (plăs′tĭd) ►*n.* Any of several pigmented organelles found in plant cells and having various functions, such as the synthesis and storage of food. [< Gk. *plastos,* molded.]

plas·tique (plă-stēk′) ►*n.* See **plastic explosive.** [Fr.]

plat. ►*abbr.* **1.** plateau **2.** platoon

Pla·ta (plä′tə, -tä), **Río de la** A wide estuary of SE South America between Argentina and Uruguay formed by the Paraná and Uruguay Rivers.

plate (plāt) ►*n.* **1.** A smooth, flat, relatively thin, rigid body of uniform thickness. **2a.** A sheet of hammered, rolled, or cast metal. **b.** A flat piece of metal on which something is engraved. **3.** *Print.* **a.** A sheet of material converted into a printing surface, such as an electrotype. **b.** An impression taken from such a surface. **c.** A full-page book illustration, often in color. **4.** A light-sensitive sheet of glass or metal on which a photographic image can be recorded. **5.** A thin metallic or plastic support fitted to the gums to anchor artificial teeth. **6.** *Baseball* Home plate. **7.** A shallow dish from which food is served or eaten. **8.** Service and food for one person at a meal. **9.** Household articles or utensils made of or with a precious metal. **10.** *Geol.* In plate tectonics, one of the sections of the earth's lithosphere, constantly moving in

relation to the other sections. ►*v.* **plat·ed, plat·ing 1.** To cover with a thin layer of metal. **2.** To armor. [< Gk. *platus,* flat.] —**plat′ed** *adj.*

pla·teau (plă-tō′) ►*n., pl.* **-teaus** or **-teaux** (-tōz′) **1.** An elevated, level expanse of land; tableland. **2.** A stable level, period, or state. ►*v.* To reach a stable level; level off. [< OFr. *platel,* platter.]

plate glass ►*n.* A strong rolled and polished glass used for mirrors and large windows.

plate·let (plāt′lĭt) ►*n.* A small, disklike body found in the blood plasma of mammals that promotes blood clotting.

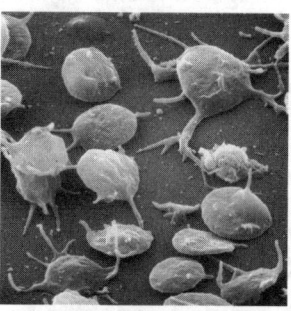

platelet
photomicrograph of blood platelets

plat·en (plăt′n) ►*n.* **1.** The roller in a typewriter or printer. **2.** A flat metal plate in a printing press that positions the paper and holds it against the inked type. [< OFr. *platine,* metal plate.]

plate tectonics ►*n.* A theory that explains the global distribution of geological phenomena in terms of the formation, destruction, and movement of the earth's lithospheric plates.

plat·form (plăt′fôrm′) ►*n.* **1.** A horizontal surface higher than an adjacent area. **2.** A formal declaration of the policy of a group, as of a political party. **3.** The basic technology of a computer system's hardware and software that defines how a computer is operated. [< OFr. *plate-forme,* diagram.]

Plath (plăth), **Sylvia** 1932–63. Amer. writer.

plat·ing (plā′tĭng) ►*n.* **1.** A thin layer or coating of metal, such as gold or silver. **2.** A covering or layer of metal plates.

plat·i·num (plăt′n-əm) ►*n.* **1.** *Symbol* **Pt** A malleable, silver-white, corrosion-resistant metallic element used in electrical components, jewelry, dentistry, and electroplating. At. no. 78. See table at **element. 2.** A medium to light gray. [< Sp. *platina < plata,* silver.]

plat·i·tude (plăt′ĭ-tōōd′, -tyōōd′) ►*n.* A trite or banal remark or idea. See Synonyms at **cliché.** [Fr. < *plat,* flat.] —**plat′i·tu′di·nous** *adj.*

Pla·to (plā′tō) 427?–347? BC. Greek philosopher.

Pla·ton·ic (plə-tŏn′ĭk, plā-) ►*adj.* **1.** Of or characteristic of Plato or his philosophy. **2.** often **platonic** Affectionate without involving sexual relations. —**Pla·ton′i·cal·ly** *adv.*

pla·toon (plə-tōōn′) ►*n.* **1.** A subdivision of a military company usu. consisting of two or more squads. **2.** A group of people working together. [< OFr. *peloton.*]

plat·ter (plăt′ər) ►*n.* **1.** A large shallow dish or

plate. **2.** *Slang* A phonograph record. [< OFr. *plate*, PLATE.]

Platte River (plăt) A river, about 500 km (310 mi), of central NE flowing to the Missouri R. at the IA border.

plat·y·pus (plăt′ĭ-pəs) ►*n., pl.* **-pus·es** A semi-aquatic, egg-laying Australian mammal with webbed feet and a snout like a duck's bill. [< Gk. *platupous*, flat-footed : *platus*, flat + *pous*, foot.]

plau·dit (plô′dĭt) ►*n.* An expression of praise or approval. [< Lat. *plaudere*, applaud.]

plau·si·ble (plô′zə-bəl) ►*adj.* **1.** Apparently true or likely; credible. **2.** Fast-talking or persuasive, esp. in an effort to deceive. [< Lat. *plaudere, plaus-*, applaud.] —**plau′si·bil′i·ty** *n.*
    Syns: *believable, credible* **Ant:** *implausible adj.*

Plau·tus (plô′təs), **Titus Maccius** 254?–184 BC. Roman comic playwright.

play (plā) ►*v.* **1.** To occupy oneself in amusement, sport, or other recreation. **2.** To act in jest. **3.** To behave carelessly; toy. **4.** To act in a specified way: *play fair.* **5a.** To engage in (a game or sport). **b.** To compete against in a game or sport. **c.** To occupy (a position) in a game or sport. **d.** To use (a card, piece, or ball) in a game or sport. **6a.** To act or perform (a role). **b.** To pretend to be: *play cowboy.* **7.** To be performed, as a theatrical work. **8.** *Mus.* **a.** To perform on (an instrument). **b.** To perform (a piece). **9.** To perform or put into effect: *play a joke.* **10.** To manipulate: *played the rivals against each other.* **11.** To cause (e.g., a recorded tape) to be presented in audible or visible form. **12.** To move lightly or irregularly: *The breeze played on the water.* **13.** To bet or wager. ►*n.* **1a.** A literary work for the stage. **b.** The performance of such a work. **2.** Activity engaged in for enjoyment or recreation. **3.** Fun. **4.** The act or manner of playing a game or sport. **5.** A move in a game: *a close play.* **6.** Manner or conduct: *fair play.* **7.** Action or use: *the play of the imagination.* **8.** Freedom for action; scope: *give full play to an artist's talents.* **9.** Free movement, as of mechanical parts. —*phrasal verbs:* **play back** To replay (e.g., a recorded tape). **play down** To minimize the importance of. **play on** or **upon** To take advantage of (another's feelings). **play up** To emphasize or publicize. —*idioms:* **in play** *Sports* In a position to be legitimately played. **play ball** *Slang* To cooperate. **play both ends against the middle** To set opponents against one another so as to advance one's goals. **play fast and loose** To behave irresponsibly or deceitfully. **play it by ear** *Informal* To improvise. **play up to** To curry favor with. **play with fire** To take part in a dangerous or risky undertaking. [< OE *plegian*.] —**play′a·ble** *adj.*

pla·ya (plī′ə) ►*n.* A flat area at the bottom of a desert basin, sometimes temporarily covered with water. [Sp. < LLat. *plagia*, shore.]

play·act (plā′ăkt′) ►*v.* **1.** To play a role in a dramatic performance. **2.** To make believe. **3.** To behave affectedly or artificially.

play·back (plā′băk′) ►*n.* The act or process of replaying a recording.

play·bill (plā′bĭl′) ►*n.* A poster announcing a theatrical performance.

play·boy (plā′boi′) ►*n.* A usu. wealthy man who spends much of his time pursuing romance.

play-by-play (plā′bī-plā′) ►*adj.* Being a detailed running commentary, as of the action of a sports event. —**play′-by-play′** *n.*

play·date (plā′dāt′) ►*n.* A scheduled time for a child to visit and play with another.

play·er (plā′ər) ►*n.* **1.** One who participates in a game or sport. **2.** An actor. **3.** A musician. **4.** A device for playing recorded sound or images.

player piano ►*n.* A mechanically operated piano that uses a perforated paper roll to move the keys.

play·ful (plā′fəl) ►*adj.* **1.** Full of fun; frolicsome. **2.** Humorous; jesting. —**play′ful·ly** *adv.* —**play′ful·ness** *n.*

play·girl (plā′gûrl′) ►*n.* A usu. wealthy woman who spends much of her time pursuing romance.

play·ground (plā′ground′) ►*n.* An outdoor area for recreation and play.

play·ing card (plā′ĭng) ►*n.* A card marked with its rank and suit belonging to a deck and used in playing various games.

play·mate (plā′māt′) ►*n.* A companion in play.

play·off also **play-off** (plā′ôf′, -ŏf′) ►*n.* A final game or series of games played to determine a championship or break a tie.

play·pen (plā′pĕn′) ►*n.* A portable enclosure in which a baby can be left to play.

play·room (plā′ro͞om′, -ro͝om′) ►*n.* A room designed for recreation or play.

play·thing (plā′thĭng′) ►*n.* A toy.

play·wright (plā′rīt′) ►*n.* One who writes plays.

pla·za (plä′zə, plăz′ə) ►*n.* **1.** A public square or similar open area in a town or city. **2.** A parking or service area next to a highway. **3.** A shopping center. [< Lat. *platea*, broad street; see PLACE.]

plea (plē) ►*n.* **1.** An earnest request; appeal. **2.** An excuse; pretext. **3.** *Law* The defendant's answer to a formal criminal charge. [< LLat. *placitum*, decree.]

plea bargain also **plea-bar·gain** (plē′bär′gən) ►*v. Law* To agree to plead guilty, esp. to a lesser criminal offense, in exchange for some concession from the prosecution. —**plea′ bar′gain·ing** *n.*

plead (plēd) ►*v.* **plead·ed** or **pled** (plĕd) or **plead, plead·ing 1.** To appeal earnestly; beg. **2.** To argue for or against something. **3.** To respond to a criminal charge. **4.** To assert as defense, vindication, or excuse. **5.** To set forth the cause of action or the defense of a party to a lawsuit in a formal statement. [< LLat. *placitum*, decree.] —**plead′er** *n.* —**plead′ing·ly** *adv.*
    Usage: In strict legal usage, one is said to *plead guilty* or *plead not guilty* but not to *plead innocent.* In nonlegal contexts, however, *plead innocent* is well established. • The Usage Panel prefers the past tense *pleaded* over *pled* outside of legal contexts.

pleas·ant (plĕz′ənt) ►*adj.* **-er, -est 1.** Pleasing or agreeable; delightful. **2.** Pleasing in manner; amiable. —**pleas′ant·ness** *n.*

pleas·ant·ry (plĕz′ən-trē) ►*n., pl.* **-ries 1.** A pleasant or humorous remark. **2.** A polite social utterance.

please (plēz) ►*v.* **pleased, pleas·ing 1.** To give enjoyment or satisfaction (to). **2.** To be the will or desire of: *may it please the court.* **3.** To like; wish: *Do as you please.* ►*adv.* If it is your desire or pleasure; if you please. Used in polite

requests: *Please stand back.* [< Lat. *placēre.*]
—pleas′ing *adj.*
　Syns: *delight, gladden, gratify* **v.**
pleas·ur·a·ble (plĕzh′ər-ə-bəl) ►*adj.* Agreeable;
gratifying. **—pleas′ur·a·bly** *adv.*
pleas·ure (plĕzh′ər) ►*n.* **1.** Enjoyment or satisfaction. **2.** A source of enjoyment. **3.** One's
preference, wish, or choice.
pleat (plēt) ►*n.* A fold in cloth made by doubling
the material upon itself. [< PLAIT.] **—pleat** *v.*
plebe (plēb) ►*n.* A freshman at a military academy. [Prob. < PLEBEIAN.]
ple·be·ian (plĭ-bē′ən) ►*adj.* Common or vulgar:
plebeian tastes. ►*n.* One who is common and
crude. [< Lat. *plēbs*, common people.]
pleb·i·scite (plĕb′ĭ-sīt′, -sĭt) ►*n.* A direct vote by
the entire electorate on an important issue. [<
Lat. *plēbiscītum.*]
plebs (plĕbz) ►*n., pl.* **ple·bes** (plē′bēz) **1.** The
common people of ancient Rome. **2.** The populace. [Lat. *plēbs.*]
plec·trum (plĕk′trəm) ►*n., pl.* **-trums** or **-tra**
(-trə) A thin piece of metal, plastic, or similar
material, used to pluck the strings of certain
musical instruments, such as the guitar or
harpsichord. [< Gk. *plēktron.*]
pled (plĕd) ►*v.* P.t. and p.part. of **plead.**
pledge (plĕj) ►*n.* **1.** A formal promise. **2.**
Something that is considered as security to
guarantee payment of a debt or obligation. **3.**
A person who has been accepted for membership in a club, fraternity, or sorority. ►*v.*
pledged, pledg·ing 1. To promise solemnly.
See Synonyms at **promise. 2.** To bind by a
pledge. **3.** To deposit as security. **4.** To promise
to join (e.g., a club). [Prob. < LLat. *plevium.*]
—pledg′er *n.*
Ple·ia·des (plē′ə-dēz′, plī′-) ►*pl.n.* An open star
cluster in the constellation Taurus, consisting of
several hundred stars, of which six are visible to
the naked eye.
Pleis·to·cene (plī′stə-sēn′) *Geol.* ►*adj.* Of or
being the 1st epoch of the Quaternary Period,
marked by the appearance of humans. ►*n.*
The Pleistocene Epoch. [Gk. *pleistos*, most +
−CENE.]
ple·na·ry (plē′nə-rē, plĕn′ə-) ►*adj.* **1.** Unlimited
or full: *a diplomat with plenary powers.* **2.** Fully
attended by all qualified members. [< Lat.
plēnus, full.] **—ple′na·ri·ly** *adv.*
plen·i·po·ten·ti·ar·y (plĕn′ə-pə-tĕn′shē-ĕr′ē,
-shə-rē) ►*adj.* Invested with full powers. ►*n.,
pl.* **-ies** A diplomatic agent fully authorized
to represent his or her government. [< LLat.
plēnipotēns.]
plen·i·tude (plĕn′ĭ-tōōd′, -tyōōd′) ►*n.* An
abundance; fullness. [< Lat. *plēnus*, full.]
plen·te·ous (plĕn′tē-əs) ►*adj.* Abundant; copious. See Synonyms at **plentiful.**
plen·ti·ful (plĕn′tĭ-fəl) ►*adj.* **1.** Existing in great
quantity or ample supply. **2.** Providing or
producing an abundance. **—plen′ti·ful·ly** *adv.*
—plen′ti·ful·ness *n.*
　Syns: *abundant, ample, copious, plenteous* **Ant:**
scant **adj.**
plen·ty (plĕn′tē) ►*n.* **1.** A full or more than
adequate amount: *plenty of time; goods in plenty.*
2. A condition of general abundance or prosperity. ►*adv. Informal* Sufficiently: *It's plenty hot.*
[< Lat. *plēnitās.*]
ple·si·o·sau·rus (plē′sē-ə-sôr′əs, plē′zē-) also

ple·si·o·saur (plē′sē-ə-sôr′, plē′zē-) ►*n.* A
large extinct marine reptile of the Mesozoic Era
having paddlelike limbs. [Gk. *plēsios*, near to +
sauros, lizard.]
pleth·o·ra (plĕth′ər-ə) ►*n.* An abundance or
excess of something. [< Gk. *plēthōra.*]
pleu·ri·sy (plŏŏr′ĭ-sē) ►*n.* Inflammation of the
membranous sacs that enclose the lungs. [< Gk.
pleura, rib, side.]
Plex·i·glas (plĕk′sĭ-glăs′) A trademark for a
light, transparent, strong thermoplastic.
plex·us (plĕk′səs) ►*n., pl.* **-us** or **-us·es** A structure in the form of a network, esp. of nerves,
blood vessels, or lymphatics. [< Lat. *plectere*,
plect-, plait.]
pli·a·ble (plī′ə-bəl) ►*adj.* **1.** Easily bent or
shaped. **2.** Easily influenced, persuaded, or
swayed. [< OFr. *plier*, bend.] **—pli′a·bil′i·ty,
pli′a·ble·ness** *n.* **—pli′a·bly** *adv.*
pli·ant (plī′ənt) ►*adj.* **1.** Easily bent or flexed. **2.**
Receptive to change; adaptable. [< OFr. *plier*,
fold, bend.] **—pli′an·cy** *n.*
pli·ers (plī′ərz) ►*pl.n.* A tool having a pair of
pivoted jaws, used for holding or bending.
plight[1] (plīt) ►*n.* A difficult or adverse situation.
[< Lat. *plicitum*, a wrinkle.]
plight[2] (plīt) ►*v.* To promise or bind by a solemn pledge, esp. to betroth. [< OE *pliht*, risk.]
—plight′er *n.*
plinth (plĭnth) ►*n.* A block or slab on which a
pedestal, column, or statue is placed. [< Gk.
plinthos, tile.]
Plin·y[1] (plĭn′ē) "the Elder." AD 23–79. Roman
scholar and naturalist.
Plin·y[2] (plĭn′ē) "the Younger." AD 62?–113?
Roman consul and writer.
Pli·o·cene (plī′ə-sēn′) *Geol.* ►*adj.* Of or being
the 5th and last epoch of the Tertiary Period,
marked by the appearance of modern animals.
►*n.* The Pliocene Epoch. [Gk. *pleiōn*, more
+ −CENE.]
PLO ►*abbr.* Palestine Liberation Organization
plod (plŏd) ►*v.* **plod·ded, plod·ding 1.** To
walk heavily or laboriously; trudge. **2.** To work
or act in a persevering or monotonous way;
drudge. [Perh. imit.] **—plod′der** *n.*
plop (plŏp) ►*v.* **plopped, plop·ping 1.** To fall
with a sound like that of an object falling into
water without splashing. **2.** To drop or set heavily. [Imit.] **—plop** *n. & adv.*
plot (plŏt) ►*n.* **1.** A small piece of ground. **2.**
The sequence of events in a narrative. **3.** A
secret plan; scheme. ►*v.* **plot·ted, plot·ting
1.** To represent graphically, as on a chart. **2.** To
locate by means of coordinates. **3.** To conspire.
[< OE.] **—plot′ter** *n.*
plov·er (plŭv′ər, plō′vər) ►*n., pl.* **-er** or **-ers** Any
of various smallish, short-billed shorebirds. [<
Lat. *pluvia*, rain < *pluere*, to rain.]
plow also **plough** (plou) ►*n.* **1.** A farm implement used for breaking up soil and cutting
furrows. **2.** An implement of similar function,
such as a snowplow. ►*v.* **1.** To break and turn
over (earth) with a plow. **2.** To move or clear
(e.g., snow) by means of a plow. **3.** To move
or progress with driving force: *plowed through
the crowd.* **—phrasal verbs: plow back** To
reinvest (e.g., profits) in one's business. **plow
into** *Informal* To strike with force. **plow under**
To overwhelm. [< OE *plōh*, plow, plowland.]
—plow′a·ble *adj.* **—plow′er** *n.*

plow·share (plou′shâr′) ►*n.* The cutting blade of a plow.

ploy (ploi) ►*n.* A strategem to gain an advantage. [?]

pluck (plŭk) ►*v.* **1.** To pull off or out; pick. **2.** To pull out the hair or feathers of. **3.** To remove abruptly: *plucked their child from school in the middle of the term.* **4.** *Mus.* To sound (the strings of an instrument) by pulling and releasing them. ►*n.* **1.** The act or an instance of plucking. **2.** Resourceful courage; spirit. [< OE *pluccian.*]

pluck·y (plŭk′ē) ►*adj.* **-i·er, -i·est** Courageous; brave. **—pluck′i·ness** *n.*

plug (plŭg) ►*n.* **1.** An object used to fill a hole tightly; stopper. **2a.** A fitting, usu. with metal prongs for insertion in a fixed socket, used to make electrical connections. **b.** A spark plug. **3.** A hydrant. **4.** A piece of chewing tobacco. **5.** *Informal* A favorable public mention, esp. of a person or product. **6.** *Slang* An old, worn-out horse. **7.** An artificial fishing lure. ►*v.* **plugged, plug·ging 1.** To fill (a hole) tightly with or as if with a plug. **2.** *Slang* To hit with a bullet. **3.** *Informal* To make favorable public mention of (e.g., a product). **4.** *Informal* To work doggedly and persistently. **—phrasal verb: plug in 1.** To connect to an electrical outlet by means of a plug. **2.** *Slang* To cause (someone) to use a computer network, the Internet, or an electronic device. **3.** *Slang* To become informed about or involved with. [< MDu. *plugge.*]

plug-in (plŭg′ĭn′) ►*n.* An accessory software program that extends the capabilities of an existing application.

plum (plŭm) ►*n.* **1a.** A smooth-skinned, fleshy, edible fruit with a hard-shelled pit. **b.** A tree bearing such fruit. **2.** An esp. desirable position, assignment, or reward. [< Lat. *prūnum.*]

plum·age (plōō′mĭj) ►*n.* The feathers of a bird.

plumb (plŭm) ►*n.* **1.** A weight on the end of a line, used to determine water depth. **2.** Such a device used to establish true vertical. ►*adv.* **1.** Straight up and down. **2.** *Informal* Directly; squarely. **3.** *Informal* Utterly; completely: *plumb worn out.* ►*adj.* **1.** Exactly vertical. **2.** *Informal* Utter; sheer: *a plumb fool.* ►*v.* **1.** To determine the depth of; sound. **2.** To test the alignment or angle of with a plumb. **3.** To examine closely; probe. [< Lat. *plumbum,* lead.] **—plumb′a·ble** *adj.*

plumb·er (plŭm′ər) ►*n.* One who installs and repairs pipes and plumbing.

plumb·ing (plŭm′ĭng) ►*n.* **1.** The pipes, fixtures, and other apparatus of a water or sewage system in a building. **2.** The work or trade of a plumber.

plumb line ►*n.* A line from which a weight is suspended to determine verticality or depth.

plume (plōōm) ►*n.* **1.** A feather, esp. a large and showy one. **2.** Something that resembles a long feather: *a plume of smoke.* **3.** An area containing pollutants released from a point source. ►*v.* **plumed, plum·ing 1.** To decorate with a plume or plumes. **2.** To pride (oneself) in a self-satisfied way. [< Lat. *plūma.*]

plum·met (plŭm′ĭt) ►*v.* **1.** To fall or drop straight down. **2.** To decline suddenly and steeply. [< Lat. *plumbum,* lead.]

plump¹ (plŭmp) ►*adj.* **-er, -est** Well-rounded and full in form; chubby. ►*v.* To make or become plump. [Prob. < MLGer. *plomp,* thick.] **—plump′ness** *n.*

plump² (plŭmp) ►*v.* **1.** To drop abruptly or heavily. **2.** To give full support or praise. ►*n.* **1.** A heavy or abrupt fall. **2.** The sound of such a fall. ►*adv.* **1.** With a heavy or abrupt drop. **2.** With a sudden or full impact. [< MLGer. *plumpen.*]

plun·der (plŭn′dər) ►*v.* To rob of goods by force, esp. in time of war; pillage. ►*n.* Property stolen by fraud or force. [< MLGer., household goods.] **—plun′der·er** *n.*

plunge (plŭnj) ►*v.* **plunged, plung·ing 1.** To dive, jump, or throw oneself: *We plunged into the lake.* **2.** To undertake an activity earnestly: *She plunged into her studies.* **3.** To slope steeply downward: *The cliff plunges toward the sea.* **4.** To become suddenly lower; decrease dramatically. **5.** To use a plunger to try to unblock (e.g., a drain). [< VLat. **plumbicāre,* heave a sounding lead.] **—plunge** *n.*

plung·er (plŭn′jər) ►*n.* **1.** A device consisting of a rubber suction cup attached to the end of a stick, used to unclog drains and pipes. **2.** A part of a device that operates with a thrusting or plunging movement.

plunk (plŭngk) ►*v.* **1.** To throw, place, or drop heavily or abruptly. **2.** To strum or pluck (a stringed instrument). **3.** To emit a hollow, twanging sound. [Imit.] **—plunk** *n.*

plu·per·fect (plōō-pûr′fĭkt) ►*adj.* Of or relating to a verb tense used to express action completed before a specified or implied past time. ►*n.* **1.** The pluperfect tense. **2.** A verb or form in this tense. [< Lat. *plūs quam perfectum,* more than perfect.]

plu·ral (plŏŏr′əl) ►*adj.* **1.** Relating to or composed of more than one member, set, or kind. **2.** Of or being a grammatical form that designates more than one of the things specified. ►*n.* **1.** The plural number or form. **2.** A word or term in the plural form. [ME *plurel* < OFr. < Lat. *plūrālis* < *plūs, plūr-,* more.] **—plu′ral·ize′** *v.* **—plu′ral·i·za′tion** *n.*

plu·ral·ism (plŏŏr′ə-lĭz′əm) ►*n.* A condition of society in which numerous distinct ethnic, religious, or cultural groups coexist within one nation. **—plu′ral·ist** *n.* **—plu′ral·is′tic** *adj.*

plu·ral·i·ty (plŏŏ-răl′ĭ-tē) ►*n., pl.* **-ties 1a.** In a contest of more than two choices, the number of votes cast for the winner if this number is not more than one half of the total votes cast. **b.** The number by which the vote of a winning choice in such a contest exceeds that of the closest opponent. **2.** The larger or greater part.

plus (plŭs) ►*conj.* **1.** *Math.* Increased by: *Two plus two is four.* **2.** Added to; along with. ►*adj.* **1.** Positive or on the positive part of a scale. **2.** Added or extra. ►*n., pl.* **plus·es** or **plus·ses 1.** *Math.* A symbol (+) used to indicate addition or a positive quantity. **2.** A favorable factor. [Lat. *plūs,* more.]

Usage: When mathematical equations are pronounced as English sentences, the verb is usu. in the singular: *Two plus two is* (or equals*) four.*

plush (plŭsh) ►*n.* A fabric having a thick, deep pile. ►*adj.* **-er, -est** Luxurious. [< OFr. *peluchier,* pluck.] **—plush′i·ly, plush′ly** *adv.* **—plush′i·ness, plush′ness** *n.* **—plush′y** *adj.*

Plu·tarch (plōō′tärk′) AD 46?–120? Greek biographer and philosopher.

plu·ti·no (ploo-tē′nō) ▸*n., pl.* **-nos** A trans-Neptunian Kuiper belt object that orbits the sun in the same time period as Pluto, making exactly two orbits for every three orbits of Neptune. [PLUT(O) + It. *-ino,* dim. suffix.]

Plu·to (ploo′tō) ▸*n.* **1.** *Rom. Myth.* The god of the dead and the ruler of the underworld. **2.** A dwarf planet that is 4.4 billion km (2.8 billion mi) distant at perihelion and 7.4 billion km (4.6 billion mi) at aphelion from the sun, with a diameter less than half that of Earth. [< Gk. *ploutos,* wealth.]

plu·toc·ra·cy (ploo-tŏk′rə-sē) ▸*n., pl.* **-cies 1.** Government by the wealthy. **2.** A wealthy class that controls a government. [Gk. *ploutos,* wealth + –CRACY.] **—plu′to·crat′** (ploo′tə-krăt′) *n.* **—plu′to·crat′ic, plu′to·crat′i·cal** *adj.*

plu·toid (ploo′toid′) ▸*n.* A dwarf planet that orbits the sun at a greater distance on average than Neptune. [PLUTO + –OID.]

plu·ton·ic (ploo-tŏn′ĭk) ▸*adj.* Of deep igneous or magmatic origin: *plutonic rocks.*

plu·to·ni·um (ploo-tō′nē-əm) ▸*n. Symbol* **Pu** A radioactive, silvery metallic element used as a reactor fuel and in nuclear weapons. At. no. 94. See table at **element.**

plu·vi·al (ploo′vē-əl) ▸*adj.* Of or caused by rain. [< Lat. *pluvia,* rain < *pluere,* to rain.]

ply¹ (plī) ▸*v.* **plied** (plīd), **ply·ing 1.** To join together, as by molding or twisting. **2.** To double over (e.g., cloth). ▸*n., pl.* **plies 1.** A layer, as of cloth or wood. **2.** One of the strands twisted together to make yarn, rope, or thread. [< Lat. *plicāre,* fold.]

ply² (plī) ▸*v.* **plied** (plīd), **ply·ing 1.** To use diligently; wield. **2.** To engage in (e.g., a trade); practice. **3.** To traverse or sail over regularly. **4.** To continue supplying: *plied their guests with food.* [< APPLY.]

Plym·outh (plĭm′əth) **1.** A city of SW England on **Plymouth Sound,** an inlet of the English Channel. **2.** A town of SE MA on **Plymouth Bay,** an inlet of the Atlantic SE of Boston; founded (1620) by Pilgrims from the *Mayflower.*

ply·wood (plī′wood′) ▸*n.* A structural material made of layers of wood glued together.

PM ▸*abbr.* **1.** also **PM** or **pm** post meridiem See Usage Note at **AM. 2.** prime minister

PMS ▸*abbr.* premenstrual syndrome

pneu·mat·ic (noo-măt′ĭk, nyoo-) also **pneu·mat·i·cal** (-ĭ-kəl) ▸*adj.* **1.** Of or relating to air or other gases. **2.** Filled with or operated by compressed air. [< Gk. *pneuma,* wind.]

pneu·mo·coc·cus (noo′mə-kŏk′əs, nyoo′-) ▸*n., pl.* **-coc·ci** (-kŏk′sī′, -kŏk′ī′) A bacterium that is a cause of pneumonia, meningitis, and other infectious diseases. [Gk. *pneuma,* breath + –COCCUS.] **—pneu′mo·coc′cal** *adj.*

pneu·mo·nia (noo-mōn′yə, nyoo-) ▸*n.* A disease marked by inflammation of the lungs, usu. caused by a bacterium, virus, or other infectious agent. [< Gk. *pleumōn,* lung.] **—pneu·mon′ic** (-mŏn′ĭk) *adj.*

Po (pō) A river of N Italy flowing about 650 km (405 mi) to the Adriatic Sea.

PO ▸*abbr.* **1.** petty officer **2.** post office

poach¹ (pōch) ▸*v.* To cook in a simmering liquid. [< OFr. *pochier,* put in pockets.]

poach² (pōch) ▸*v.* To take (fish or game) illegally, esp. by trespassing on another's property.

[< OFr. *pochier,* poke, gouge.] **—poach′er** *n.*

Po·ca·hon·tas (pō′kə-hŏn′təs) Matoaka. 1595?–1617. Powhatan princess.

Pocahontas

pock (pŏk) ▸*n.* **1.** A pustule caused by smallpox or a similar eruptive disease. **2.** A mark or scar left in the skin by such a pustule; pockmark. [< OE *pocc.*] **—pock** *v.*

pock·et (pŏk′ĭt) ▸*n.* **1.** A pouch with an open edge sewn into or onto a garment and used to carry small items. **2.** A receptacle or cavity. **3.** Financial means. **4.** A small isolated or protected area or group. ▸*adj.* **1.** Suitable for being carried in one's pocket. **2.** Small; miniature. ▸*v.* **1.** To place in a pocket. **2.** To take possession of for oneself, esp. dishonestly. [< ONFr. *poke,* bag, of Gmc. orig.] **—pock′et·ful′** *n.*

pock·et·book (pŏk′ĭt-book′) ▸*n.* **1.** A wallet; billfold. **2.** A handbag. **3.** Financial means.

pock·et·knife (pŏk′ĭt-nīf′) ▸*n.* A small knife with a blade or blades that fold into the handle when not in use.

pocket veto ▸*n.* An executive's indirect veto of a bill by retaining the bill unsigned until the legislature adjourns.

pock·mark (pŏk′märk′) ▸*n.* A pitlike scar left on the skin by smallpox or another eruptive disease. **—pock′mark′** *v.*

po·co (pō′kō) ▸*adv. Mus.* To a slight degree; somewhat. [Ital. < Lat. *paucus,* little.]

pod¹ (pŏd) ▸*n.* **1.** *Bot.* A seed vessel, as of the pea, that splits open. **2.** An external or detachable housing, as for instruments or personnel, forming part of a vehicle. [?]

pod² (pŏd) ▸*n.* A school of animals, esp. marine mammals, such as seals or whales. [?]

–pod or **–pode** ▸*suff.* Foot; footlike part: *gastropod.* [< Gk. *pous,* foot.]

Pod·go·ri·ca (pŏd′gə-rēt′sə) The capital of Montenegro, in the S part.

po·di·a·try (pə-dī′ə-trē) ▸*n.* The study of diseases and disorders of the foot. [Gk. *pous,* pod-, foot + –IATRY.] **—po′di·at′ric** (pō′dē-ăt′rĭk) *adj.* **—po·di′a·trist** *n.*

po·di·um (pō′dē-əm) ▸*n., pl.* **-di·a** (-dē-ə) or **-di·ums** An elevated platform, as for a speaker or orchestra conductor. [< Gk. *podion,* base, dim. of *pous,* foot.]

Poe (pō), **Edgar Allan** 1809–49. Amer. writer.

po·em (pō′əm) ▸*n.* A verbal composition characterized by the use of condensed language chosen for its sound and suggestive power and by the use of literary techniques such as meter and metaphor. [< Gk. *poiēma,* a creation.]

po·e·sy (pō′ĭ-zē, -sē) ►*n.* Poetry. [< Gk. *poiēsis*, creation.]

po·et (pō′ĭt) ►*n.* A writer of poems. [< Gk. *poiētēs*, maker.]

po·et·as·ter (pō′ĭt-ăs′tər) ►*n.* An inferior poet. [POET + Lat. *-aster*, pejorative suff.]

po·et·ess (pō′ĭ-tĭs) ►*n. Derogatory* A woman who writes poems. See Usage Note at **–ess**.

po·et·ic (pō-ĕt′ĭk) also **po·et′i·cal** ►*adj.* Of or characteristic of poetry or poets.

poetic justice ►*n.* The rewarding of virtue and the punishment of vice, often in an appropriate or ironic manner.

poetic license ►*n.* The liberty taken by an artist or a writer in deviating from conventional form or fact to achieve a desired effect.

poet laureate ►*n., pl.* **poets laureate** or **poet laureates 1.** A poet appointed for life by a British monarch as chief poet of the kingdom. **2.** A poet appointed to a similar honorary position.

po·et·ry (pō′ĭ-trē) ►*n.* **1.** The art or practice of composing poems. **2a.** Poems regarded as forming a division of literature. **b.** The poetic works of a given author, group, or kind.

po·grom (pə-grŏm′, pō′grəm) ►*n.* An organized massacre of a minority group, esp. Jews. [Russ.]

poi (poi) ►*n.* A food made from cooked taro root pounded to a paste and fermented. [Hawaiian.]

poign·ant (poin′yənt) ►*adj.* **1.** Arousing deep emotion, esp. pity or sorrow: *poignant anxiety.* **2.** Profoundly moving; touching: *a poignant memory.* [< Lat. *pungere*, to prick.] **—poign′ance, poign′an·cy** *n.*

poi·ki·lo·therm (poi-kĭl′ə-thûrm′) ►*n.* An organism, such as a reptile, having a body temperature that varies with the temperature of its surroundings. [Gk. *poikilos*, various + *thermē*, heat.] **—poi′ki·lo·ther′mic** (-kə-lō-thûr′mĭk) *adj.*

poin·ci·an·a (poin′sē-ăn′ə, -ä′nə) ►*n.* See **royal poinciana.** [< M. De *Poinci* (fl. 17th cent.).]

poin·set·ti·a (poin-sĕt′ē-ə, -sĕt′ə) ►*n.* A Mexican shrub having a cluster of small yellow flowers surrounded by showy, usu. scarlet petallike bracts. [After J.R. *Poinsett* (1779–1851).]

point (point) ►*n.* **1a.** A sharp or tapered end. **b.** A mark formed by or as if by a sharp end. **2.** A tapering extension of land projecting into water. **3.** *Math.* A dimensionless geometric object having no properties except location. **4.** A place or position. **5.** A specified degree, condition, or limit. **6.** A specific moment in time. **7.** An objective or purpose to be achieved. **8.** A significant or outstanding idea or suggestion. **9.** A distinctive quality or characteristic. **10.** A single unit, as in counting, rating, or measuring. **11.** An electrical contact, esp. one in the distributor of an automobile engine. ►*v.* **1.** To direct or aim. See Synonyms at **aim. 2.** To bring to notice: *point out an error.* **3.** To indicate the position or direction of. **4.** To give emphasis to; stress: *pointed up the difference between them.* **—idioms: beside the point** Irrelevant. **in point of** With reference to. **stretch a point** To make an exception. **to the point** Closely concerning the matter at hand. [< Lat. *pūnctus*, p.part. of *pungere*, to prick.] **—point′y** *adj.*

point-blank (point′blăngk′) ►*adj.* **1a.** Aiming straight at a target. **b.** So close that missing the target is unlikely. **2.** Straightforward; blunt. **—point′-blank′** *adv.*

point·ed (poin′tĭd) ►*adj.* **1.** Having a point. **2.** Sharp; incisive. **3.** Obviously directed at a particular thing: *a pointed comment.* **4.** Clearly evident; marked: *a pointed lack of interest.* **—point′ed·ly** *adv.*

point·er (poin′tər) ►*n.* **1.** One that indicates, esp.: **a.** A long, tapered stick or a laser beacon for indicating objects, as on a chart or blackboard. **b.** A scale indicator on a watch or scale. **2.** A usu. short-haired hunting dog bred to indicate game with an immobile stance. **3.** A piece of advice; suggestion.

poin·til·lism (pwăN′tē-ĭz′-əm, point′l-ĭz′-) ►*n.* A painting technique characterized by the application of paint in small dots and brush strokes. [< OFr. *point*, dot.] **—poin′til·list** *adj. & n.* **—poin′til·lis′tic** *adj.*

point·ing device (poin′tĭng) ►*n. Comp.* An input device, such as a mouse, for manipulating a cursor or pointer on a GUI.

point·less (point′lĭs) ►*adj.* Meaningless; irrelevant. **—point′less·ness** *n.*

point-of-sale (point′əv-sāl′) ►*adj.* Of or being the place where an item is purchased.

point of view ►*n.* **1.** A manner of viewing things; attitude. **2.** A position from which something is observed or considered.

poise (poiz) ►*v.* **poised, pois·ing** To balance or be balanced. ►*n.* **1.** Balance; stability. **2.** Composure. **3.** Dignity of manner. [< Lat. *pēnsāre*.]

poi·son (poi′zən) ►*n.* A substance that causes injury, illness, or death, esp. by chemical means. ►*v.* **1.** To kill or harm with poison. **2.** To put poison on or into. **3a.** To pollute. See Synonyms at **contaminate. b.** To have a harmful influence on; corrupt. [< Lat. *pōtiō*, a drink.] **—poi′son·er** *n.* **—poi′son·ous** *adj.* **—poi′son·ous·ly** *adv.*

poison hemlock ►*n.* A highly poisonous European plant, widely naturalized in North America, having small white flowers.

poison ivy ►*n.* **1.** A North American plant having compound leaves with three leaflets and causing a rash on contact. **2.** The rash itself.

poison oak ►*n.* **1.** Either of two plants of the SE and W US related to poison ivy and causing a rash on contact. **2.** The rash itself.

poison sumac ►*n.* **1.** A shrub or small tree of the E US, having compound leaves and causing a rash on contact. **2.** The rash itself.

poke¹ (pōk) ►*v.* **poked, pok·ing 1.** To push or jab at, as with a finger; prod. **2.** To make (a hole or pathway) by or as if by prodding or jabbing. **3.** To push; thrust. **4.** To pry or meddle. **5.** To search curiously; rummage. ►*n.* A push, thrust, or jab. **—idiom: poke fun at** To ridicule. [ME *poken*.]

poke² (pōk) ►*n. Regional* A sack. [Prob. < ONFr.; see POCKET.]

pok·er¹ (pō′kər) ►*n.* A metal rod used to stir a fire.

pok·er² (pō′kər) ►*n.* Any of various card games played by two or more players who bet on the value of their hands. [Prob. ult. < Ger. *pochen*, knock, rap (as on a table when opening in a traditional Ger. card game).]

poke·weed (pōk′wēd′) ►*n.* A tall poisonous plant of E North America, having small white flowers and dark purple berries. [< dial. *pocan*, of Algonquian orig.]

po·key also **po·ky** (pō′kē) ►*n., pl.* **-keys** also **-kies** *Slang* A jail. [?]

pok·y also **poke·y** (pō′kē) ►*adj.* **-i·er, -i·est** *Informal* Dawdling; slow. [< POKE¹.] —**pok′i·ly** *adv.* —**pok′i·ness** *n.*

pol (pŏl) ►*n. Informal* A politician.

Po·land (pō′lənd) A country of central Europe bordering on the Baltic Sea. Cap. Warsaw.

po·lar (pō′lər) ►*adj.* **1.** Of, measured from, or referred to a pole. **2.** Of or near the North or South Pole. **3.** Occupying or characterized by opposite extremes.

polar bear ►*n.* A large white bear of Arctic regions.

polar bear

Po·lar·is (pə-lăr′ĭs) ►*n.* A star at the end of the handle of the Little Dipper, in the constellation Ursa Minor, and almost at the north celestial pole.

po·lar·i·ty (pō-lăr′ĭ-tē, pə-) ►*n., pl.* **-ties 1.** Intrinsic polar separation, alignment, or orientation, esp. of a physical property. **2.** An indicated polar extreme. **3.** The manifestation of two opposing tendencies.

po·lar·ize (pō′lə-rīz′) ►*v.* **-ized, -iz·ing 1.** To impart polarity to. **2.** To acquire polarity. **3.** To cause to divide into two conflicting groups. —**po′lar·i·za′tion** *n.*

Po·lar·oid (pō′lə-roid′) **1.** A trademark for a transparent plastic capable of polarizing light, used in glare-reducing optical devices. **2.** A trademark for an instant camera.

pole¹ (pōl) ►*n.* **1.** Either extremity of an axis through a sphere. **2.** The North Pole or the South Pole. **3.** *Phys.* See **magnetic pole. 4.** Either of two oppositely charged terminals, as in an electric cell or battery. **5.** Either of two opposing forces. [< Gk. *polos*, axis.]

pole² (pōl) ►*n.* A long slender piece of wood or other material. ►*v.* **poled, pol·ing** To propel (e.g., a boat) with a pole. [< Lat. *pālus*, stake.]

Pole ►*n.* **1.** A native or inhabitant of Poland. **2.** A person of Polish ancestry.

pole·ax or **pole·axe** (pōl′ăks′) ►*n.* A long-handled battle-ax. [ME *pollax*.]

pole·cat (pōl′kăt′) ►*n.* **1.** A weasellike European mammal. **2.** See **skunk** (sense 1). [ME *polcat*.]

po·lem·ic (pə-lĕm′ĭk) ►*n.* **1.** A controversy or refutation. **2. polemics** *(takes sing. or pl. v.)* The art or practice of debate or controversy. [< Gk. *polemos*, war.] —**po·lem′ic, po·lem′i·cal** *adj.* —**po·lem′i·cist** *n.*

po·len·ta (pō-lĕn′tə) ►*n.* A thick mush made of boiled cornmeal. [Ital. < Lat., barley meal.]

pole·star (pōl′stär′) ►*n.* See **Polaris.**

pole vault ►*n.* A field event in which an athlete jumps over a high crossbar with the aid of a

long pole. —**pole′-vault′** *v.* —**pole′-vault′-er** *n.*

po·lice (pə-lēs′) ►*n., pl.* **-lice 1a.** A body of government employees trained to enforce the law, detect and prevent crime, and maintain order in the community. **b.** A body of persons with a similar organization and function: *campus police.* **2.** The soldiers assigned to a specified maintenance duty. ►*v.* **-liced, -lic·ing 1.** To regulate, control, or keep in order with or as if with police. **2.** To make (e.g., a military area) neat in appearance. [< Lat. *polītīa*, the State.]

police dog ►*n.* **1.** A dog trained to aid the police, as in tracking criminals or detecting controlled substances. **2.** See **German shepherd.**

police force ►*n.* See **police** (sense 1).

po·lice·man (pə-lēs′mən) ►*n.* A man who is a member of a police force. See Usage Note at **man.**

police officer ►*n.* A policeman or policewoman.

police state ►*n.* A state in which the government exercises rigid and repressive controls, esp. by means of a secret police force.

police station ►*n.* The headquarters of a police force.

po·lice·wom·an (pə-lēs′wŏom′ən) ►*n.* A woman who is a member of a police force. See Usage Note at **man.**

pol·i·cy¹ (pŏl′ĭ-sē) ►*n., pl.* **-cies** A plan or course of action, as of a government or business, intended to influence and determine decisions and actions. [< Gk. *politeia*, government.]

pol·i·cy² (pŏl′ĭ-sē) ►*n., pl.* **-cies** A written contract or certificate of insurance. [< Gk. *apodeixis*, proof.] —**pol′i·cy·hol′der** *n.*

pol·i·cy·mak·ing (pŏl′ĭ-sē-mā′kĭng) ►*n.* High-level development of policy, esp. government policy. —**pol′i·cy·mak′er** *n.*

po·li·o (pō′lē-ō′) ►*n.* Poliomyelitis.

po·li·o·my·e·li·tis (pō′lē-ō-mī′ə-lī′tĭs) ►*n.* An infectious viral disease that chiefly affects children and in its acute forms attacks the central nervous system, leading to paralysis and muscular atrophy. [Gk. *polios*, gray + MYE-LITIS.]

pol·ish (pŏl′ĭsh) ►*v.* **1.** To make smooth and shiny by rubbing or chemical action. **2.** To remove the outer layers from (grains of rice). **3.** To refine; perfect or complete. ►*n.* **1.** Smoothness or shininess of surface. **2.** A substance used to shine a surface. **3.** Elegance of style or manner. —**phrasal verb: polish off** *Informal* To finish or dispose of quickly. [< Lat. *polīre*.] —**pol′ish·er** *n.*

Po·lish (pō′lĭsh) ►*adj.* Of or relating to Poland or its people or language. ►*n.* The Slavic language of the Poles.

pol·it·bu·ro (pŏl′ĭt-byŏor′ō, pə-lĭt′-) ►*n., pl.* **-ros** The chief political and executive committee of a Communist party. [Russ.]

po·lite (pə-līt′) ►*adj.* **-lit·er, -lit·est 1.** Marked by consideration, tact, and courtesy. **2.** Refined; elegant. [< Lat. *polītus*, polished.] —**po·lite′ly** *adv.* —**po·lite′ness** *n.*

pol·i·tesse (pŏl′ĭ-tĕs′, pô′lē-) ►*n.* Courteous formality. [Fr.]

pol·i·tic (pŏl′ĭ-tĭk) ►*adj.* Showing sound judgment; prudent. [< Gk. *politēs*, citizen.]

po·lit·i·cal (pə-lĭt′ĭ-kəl) ►*adj.* **1.** Of or relating to the affairs of government, politics, or the state.

2. Characteristic of politics, parties, or politicians. —**po·lit′i·cal·ly** adv.

politically correct ►adj. Conforming to a particular social and political ideology, esp. to a liberal point of view concerned with promoting tolerance and avoiding offense in matters such as race and gender. —**political correctness** n.

political science ►n. The study of the processes, principles, and structure of government and political institutions.

pol·i·ti·cian (pŏl′ĭ-tĭsh′ən) ►n. One actively involved in politics, esp. one who holds a political office.

po·lit·i·cize (pə-lĭt′ĭ-sīz′) ►v. **-cized, -ciz·ing** To make political. —**po·lit′i·ci·za′tion** n.

po·li·tick (pŏl′ĭ-tĭk) ►v. To engage in or discuss politics. —**pol′i·tick′er** n.

po·lit·i·co (pə-lĭt′ĭ-kō′) ►n., pl. **-cos** A politician. [< Ital. and Sp. político.]

pol·i·tics (pŏl′ĭ-tĭks) ►n. **1.** (takes sing. v.) The art or science of government. **2.** (takes sing. or pl. v.) The activities or affairs engaged in by a government. **3.** (takes sing. or pl. v.) Intrigue or maneuvering within a group: office politics. **4.** (takes sing. or pl. v.) Political positions.

pol·i·ty (pŏl′ĭ-tē) ►n., pl. **-ties** An organized society, such as a nation, having a specific form of government. [< LLat. polītīa, government.]

Polk (pōk), **James Knox** 1795–1849. The 11th US president (1845–49).

James K. Polk
1846 portrait

pol·ka (pōl′kə, pō′kə) ►n. **1.** A lively dance in duple meter performed by couples. **2.** Music for this dance. [Prob. < Pol.] —**pol′ka** v.

polka dot ►n. One of a number of dots forming a pattern on cloth.

poll (pōl) ►n. **1.** The casting and registering of votes in an election. **2.** The number of votes cast or recorded. **3. polls a.** The places where votes are cast and registered: The polls closed at 8:00. **b.** One of these places: I went to the polls before work. **4.** A survey of the public or of a sample of public opinion to acquire information. ►v. **1.** To receive (a given number of votes). **2.** To receive or record the votes of. **3.** To question in a survey; canvass. **4.** To cut off or trim (e.g., hair or horns). [< MLGer. or MDu. polle, head.] —**poll′er** n.

pol·len (pŏl′ən) ►n. The powderlike material produced by the anthers of seed plants and functioning as the male agent in fertilization. [Lat., fine flour.]

pol·li·nate (pŏl′ə-nāt′) ►v. **-li·nat·ed, -li·nat·**ing To transfer pollen to (the female part of a plant). —**pol′li·na′tion** n. —**pol′li·na′tor** n.

pol·li·no·sis (pŏl′ə-nō′sĭs) ►n. See **hay fever.**

pol·li·wog also **pol·ly·wog** (pŏl′ē-wŏg′, -wôg′) ►n. See **tadpole.** [< ME polwigle.]

pol·lock or **pol·lack** (pŏl′ək) ►n., pl. **-lock** or **-locks** also **-lack** or **-lacks** A codlike marine food fish, often used for manufactured fish products. [ME poullok < ?]

Pol·lock (pŏl′ək), **Jackson** 1912–56. Amer. artist.

poll·ster (pōl′stər) ►n. One that takes public-opinion surveys.

poll tax ►n. A tax levied on all persons in a certain area, esp. as a condition of voting.

pol·lute (pə-lōōt′) ►v. **-lut·ed, -lut·ing 1.** To make unfit for or harmful to living things, esp. by the addition of waste matter. See Synonyms at **contaminate. 2.** To render impure; corrupt. [< Lat. polluere, pollūt-.] —**pol·lut′ant** n. —**pol·lut′er** n. —**pol·lu′tion** n.

Pol·lux (pŏl′əks) ►n. A double star in Gemini.

po·lo (pō′lō) ►n. A game played by two teams on horseback equipped with long-handled mallets for driving a wooden ball. [Of Tibeto-Burman orig.]

polo

Polo, Marco 1254–1324. Venetian traveler in Asia.

pol·o·naise (pŏl′ə-nāz′, pō′lə-) ►n. **1.** A stately Polish dance in triple meter. **2.** Music for this dance. [Fr. < Med.Lat. Polonia, Poland.]

po·lo·ni·um (pə-lō′nē-əm) ►n. Symbol **Po** A radioactive metallic element that occurs naturally as a product of radium decay and is also produced artificially. At. no. 84. See table at **element.** [< Med.Lat. Polōnia, Poland.]

polo shirt ►n. A usu. knitted pullover sport shirt with a collar and an open neck.

pol·ter·geist (pōl′tər-gīst′) ►n. A noisy, usu. mischievous ghost. [Ger.]

pol·troon (pŏl-trōōn′) ►n. An utter coward. [< OItal. poltrone.] —**pol·troon′er·y** n.

poly- ►pref. **1.** More than one; many; much: polyatomic. **2.** More than usual; excessive; abnormal: polydipsia. **3.** Polymer; polymeric: polyethylene. [< Gk. polus, many.]

pol·y·an·dry (pŏl′ē-ăn′drē) ►n. The condition or practice of having more than one husband at one time. —**pol′y·an′drous** adj.

pol·y·chrome (pŏl′ē-krōm′) ►adj. Having

or decorated in many colors. **—pol′y·chro·mat′ic** (-krō-măt′ĭk), **pol′y·chro′mic, pol′y·chro′mous** *adj.*

pol·y·clin·ic (pŏl′ē-klĭn′ĭk) ►*n.* A clinic that treats various diseases and injuries.

pol·y·dip·si·a (pŏl′ē-dĭp′sē-ə) ►*n.* Excessive or abnormal thirst. [< POLY– + Gk. *dipsa,* thirst.] **—pol′y·dip′sic** *adj.*

pol·y·es·ter (pŏl′ē-ĕs′tər, pŏl′ē-ĕs′tər) ►*n.* Any of numerous synthetic resins used esp. in fabric and molded parts.

pol·y·eth·yl·ene (pŏl′ē-ĕth′ə-lēn′) ►*n.* A synthetic resin, used esp. in the form of films and sheets.

po·lyg·a·my (pə-lĭg′ə-mē) ►*n.* The condition or practice of having more than one spouse at one time. **—po·lyg′a·mist** *n.* **—po·lyg′a·mous** *adj.* **—po·lyg′a·mous·ly** *adv.*

pol·y·glot (pŏl′ē-glŏt′) ►*n.* One with a speaking, reading, or writing knowledge of several languages. [POLY– + Gk. *glōtta,* tongue.]

pol·y·gon (pŏl′ē-gŏn′) ►*n.* A closed plane figure bounded by three or more line segments. **—po·lyg′o·nal** (pə-lĭg′ə-nəl) *adj.*

pol·y·graph (pŏl′ē-grăf′) ►*n.* An instrument that measures an individual's physiological responses to questions, the results of which can be analyzed to indicate the likelihood that he or she is answering truthfully.

po·lyg·y·ny (pə-lĭj′ə-nē) ►*n.* The condition or practice of having more than one wife at one time. [< POLY– + Gk. *gunē,* woman.] **—po·lyg′y·nous** *adj.*

pol·y·he·dron (pŏl′ē-hē′drən) ►*n., pl.* **-drons** or **-dra** (-drə) A solid whose faces are polygons. **—pol′y·he′dral** *adj.*

pol·y·math (pŏl′ē-măth′) ►*n.* A person of great or varied learning. [Gk. *polumathēs.*] **—pol′y·math′, pol′y·math′ic** *adj.*

pol·y·mer (pŏl′ə-mər) ►*n.* Any of numerous natural and synthetic compounds of usu. high molecular weight consisting of repeated linked units, each a relatively light and simple molecule. **—pol′y·mer′ic** (-měr′ĭk) *adj.*

pol·y·mer·ase (pə-lĭm′ə-rās′, -rāz′, pŏl′ə-mə-) ►*n.* Any of various enzymes that catalyze the formation of DNA or RNA.

pol·y·mer·ize (pŏl′ə-mə-rīz′, pə-lĭm′ə-) ►*v.* **-ized, -iz·ing** To bond two or more monomers to form a polymer. **—po·lym′er·i·za′tion** *n.*

pol·y·mor·phism (pŏl′ē-môr′fĭz′əm) ►*n.* **1.** *Biol.* The occurrence of more than one form, as of alleles of a particular gene. **2.** *Chem.* Crystallization of a compound in at least two distinct forms. **—pol′y·mor′phic** *adj.*

Pol·y·ne·sia (pŏl′ə-nē′zhə, -shə) A division of Oceania including islands of the central and S Pacific roughly between New Zealand, Hawaii, and Easter I.

Pol·y·ne·sian (pŏl′ə-nē′zhən, -shən) ►*n.* **1.** A native or inhabitant of Polynesia. **2.** A subfamily of the Austronesian language family spoken in Polynesia. **—Pol′y·ne′sian** *adj.*

pol·y·no·mi·al (pŏl′ē-nō′mē-əl) ►*adj.* Of or consisting of more than two names or terms. ►*n. Math.* An algebraic expression of one or more summed terms, each term consisting of a constant multiplier and one or more variables raised to integral powers. [POLY– + (BI)NOMIAL.]

pol·yp (pŏl′ĭp) ►*n.* **1.** A cylindrical organism,

such as a hydra or coral, that has a mouth usu. surrounded by tentacles at one end and is often attached to something at the other end. **2.** *Med.* A growth protruding from the mucous lining of an organ. [< Gk. *polupous,* cuttlefish.]

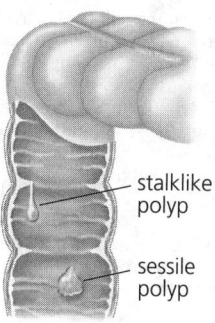

stalklike polyp

sessile polyp

polyp
stalklike polyp *(top)* and sessile polyp *(bottom)* in a section of large intestine

pol·y·pep·tide (pŏl′ē-pĕp′tīd′) ►*n.* A peptide containing many molecules of amino acids.

po·lyph·o·ny (pə-lĭf′ə-nē) ►*n., pl.* **-nies** Music with two or more independent melodic parts sounded together. **—pol′y·phon′ic** (pŏl′ē-fŏn′ĭk), **po·lyph′o·nous** *adj.*

pol·y·sac·cha·ride (pŏl′ē-săk′ə-rīd′) ►*n.* Any of a class of carbohydrates, such as starch and cellulose, consisting of a number of monosaccharides.

pol·y·sty·rene (pŏl′ē-stī′rēn) ►*n.* A rigid, clear thermoplastic polymer used esp. in molded parts or as an insulating foam. [< Lat. *styrax,* a tree.]

pol·y·syl·la·ble (pŏl′ē-sĭl′ə-bəl) ►*n.* A word of more than two and usu. more than three syllables. **—pol′y·syl·lab′ic** (-sĭ-lăb′ĭk) *adj.*

pol·y·tech·nic (pŏl′ē-tĕk′nĭk) ►*adj.* Offering or dealing with instruction in many industrial arts and applied sciences.

pol·y·the·ism (pŏl′ē-thē-ĭz′əm, pŏl′ē-thē′ĭz-əm) ►*n.* The worship of or belief in more than one god. **—pol′y·the′ist** *n.*

pol·y·un·sat·u·rat·ed (pŏl′ē-ŭn-săch′ə-rā′-tĭd) ►*adj.* Relating to long-chain carbon compounds, esp. fats, having multiple double bonds between the carbon atoms.

pol·y·u·re·thane (pŏl′ē-yoŏr′ə-thān′) ►*n.* Any of various thermoplastic polymers used in tough chemical-resistant coatings, adhesives, and foams. [< POLY– + UR(O)– + ETH(YL).]

pol·y·va·lent (pŏl′ē-vā′lənt) ►*adj.* **1.** *Chem.* **a.** Having more than one valence. **b.** Having a valence of 3 or higher. **2.** *Immunol.* **a.** Having more than one site of attachment. Used of an antibody or antigen. **b.** Containing antigens from more than one strain of a microorganism or virus. Used of a vaccine or serum. **—pol′y·va′lence, pol′y·va′len·cy** *n.*

pol·y·vi·nyl chloride (pŏl′ē-vī′nəl) ►*n.* A common thermoplastic resin used in a wide variety of manufactured products.

po·made (pō-mād′, pŏ-) ►*n.* A perfumed hair ointment. [< LLat. *pōmum,* apple.] **—po′made** *v.*

pom·e·gran·ate (pŏm′ĭ-grăn′ĭt, pŏm′grăn′ĭt,

pŭm′ĭ-, pŭm′-) ►*n.* **1.** A shrub or small tree widely cultivated for its edible fruit. **2.** The fruit of this tree, having a tough reddish rind and many seeds. [< OFr. *pome grenate* : *pome*, apple + *grenate*, having many seeds (< Lat. *grānum*, grain, seed).]

Pom·er·a·ni·a (pŏm′ə-rā′nē-ə, -rān′yə) A historical region of N-central Europe bordering on the Baltic Sea in present-day NW Poland and NE Germany.

Pom·er·a·ni·an (pŏm′ə-rā′nē-ən, -rān′yən) ►*adj.* Of or relating to Pomerania or its people. ►*n.* **1.** A native or inhabitant of Pomerania. **2.** A small dog having long silky hair and a foxlike face.

pom·mel (pŭm′əl, pŏm′-) ►*v.* **-meled, -mel·ing** also **-melled, -mel·ling** To beat; pummel. ►*n.* **1.** The upper front part of a saddle. **2.** A knob on the hilt of a sword. [< Lat. *pōmum*, fruit.]

pommel horse ►*n.* A padded piece of gymnastic equipment having two handles on top and adjustable legs.

pomp (pŏmp) ►*n.* **1.** Magnificent display; splendor. **2.** Ostentatious display. [< Gk. *pompē*, procession.]

pom·pa·dour (pŏm′pə-dôr′) ►*n.* A hairstyle formed by sweeping the hair up from the forehead.

pom·pa·no (pŏm′pə-nō′) ►*n.*, *pl.* **-no** or **-nos** A marine food fish of W Atlantic waters. [< Lat. *pampinus*, vine tendril.]

Pom·pe·ii (pŏm-pā′, -pā′ē) An ancient city of S Italy SE of Naples; destroyed by an eruption of Mount Vesuvius (A.D. 79). —**Pom·pe′ian, Pom·pei′ian** *adj. & n.*

Pom·pey (pŏm′pē) 106–48 BC. Roman general and political leader.

Pom·pi·dou (pŏm′pĭ-dōō′, pôN-pē-dōō′), **Georges Jean Raymond** 1911–74. French prime minister (1962–68) and president (1969–74).

pom·pom (pŏm′pŏm′) also **pom·pon** (-pŏn′) ►*n.* **1.** A fluffy ball of wool or other material that is used as a decoration. **2.** A buttonlike flower of some chrysanthemums and dahlias. [Fr.]

pom·pous (pŏm′pəs) ►*adj.* **1.** Self-important; pretentious. **2.** *Archaic* Marked by pomp or stately display. —**pom·pos′i·ty** (-pŏs′ĭ-tē), **pom′pous·ness** *n.* —**pom′pous·ly** *adv.*

Ponce de Le·ón (pŏns′ də lē-ōn′, pōn′sĕ), **Juan** 1460–1521. Spanish explorer.

pon·cho (pŏn′chō) ►*n.*, *pl.* **-chos 1.** A blanketlike cloak having a hole in the center for the head. **2.** A similar hooded garment used as a raincoat. [Am.Sp.]

pond (pŏnd) ►*n.* A still body of water smaller than a lake. ►*v.* To form or cause to form ponds or large puddles. [< OE *pund*, enclosure.]

pon·der (pŏn′dər) ►*v.* **1.** To think about (something) carefully. **2.** To reflect on; meditate. [< Lat. *ponderāre.*] —**pon′der·a·ble** *adj.*

pon·der·o·sa pine (pŏn′də-rō′sə) ►*n.* A tall timber tree of W North America, having long needles. [< Lat. *ponderōsus*, massive.]

pon·der·ous (pŏn′dər-əs) ►*adj.* **1.** Having great weight. **2.** Difficult to maneuver, control, or manage; slow. **3.** Lacking fluency; dull. [< Lat. *pondus, ponder-*, weight.] —**pon′der·ous·ly** *adv.* —**pon′der·ous·ness** *n.*

pone (pōn) ►*n. Regional* See **johnnycake.** [< Virginia Algonquian *poan.*]

pon·gee (pŏn-jē′, pŏn′jē) ►*n.* A light, plainwoven fabric, usu. of raw silk. [Mandarin *běn zhī* : *běn*, one's own + *zhī*, to weave, spin.]

pon·iard (pŏn′yərd) ►*n.* A dagger. [Fr. *poignard* < Lat. *pugnus*, fist.]

pons (pŏnz) ►*n.*, *pl.* **pon·tes** (pŏn′tēz) A slender tissue joining two parts of an organ. [Lat. *pōns*, bridge.]

Pon·ti·ac (pŏn′tē-ăk′) 1720?–69. Ottawa leader.

pon·tiff (pŏn′tĭf) ►*n.* **1.** The pope. **2.** A bishop. [< Lat. *pontifex*, high priest.]

pon·tif·i·cal (pŏn-tĭf′ĭ-kəl) ►*adj.* **1.** Of or suitable for a pontiff. **2.** Pompously dogmatic; pretentious. ►*n.* **pontificals** The vestments and insignia of a pontiff.

pon·tif·i·cate (pŏn-tĭf′ĭ-kĭt, -kāt′) ►*n.* The office or term of office of a pontiff. ►*v.* (-kāt′) **-cat·ed, -cat·ing 1.** To express opinions or judgments in a dogmatic way. **2.** To administer the office of a pontiff. —**pon·tif′i·ca′tion** *n.*

pon·toon (pŏn-tōōn′) ►*n.* **1.** A floating structure, such as a flat-bottomed boat, used to support a bridge. **2.** A float on a seaplane. [< Lat. *pontō*, floating bridge.]

Pon·tus (pŏn′təs) An ancient country of NE Asia Minor along the S coast of the Black Sea. —**Pon′tic** *adj.*

po·ny (pō′nē) ►*n.*, *pl.* **-nies 1.** A small horse. **2.** A word-for-word translation of a foreign language text, esp. one used secretly in studying or test taking. [Prob. < obsolete Fr. *poulenet*, foal.]

po·ny·tail (pō′nē-tāl′) ►*n.* A gathering of hair that is fastened close to the head so that the hair hangs down like a pony's tail.

pon·zu (pŏn′zōō′) ►*n.* A Japanese sauce typically made from mirin, rice vinegar, bonito flakes, citrus juice, and sometimes soy sauce, often used as a condiment for seafood. [J., ult. < E., PUNCH³.]

pooch (pōōch) ►*n. Slang* A dog. [?]

poo·dle (pōōd′l) ►*n.* A dog bred to retrieve game from the water, having thick curly hair and found in various sizes. [< LGer. *pūdel*, puddle.]

pooh (pōō) ►*interj.* Used to express disdain.

Pooh-Bah or **pooh-bah** (pōō′bä′) ►*n.* **1.** A pompous ineffectual official. **2.** A person in high office. [After the character in Gilbert and Sullivan's *The Mikado.*]

pooh-pooh (pōō′pōō′) ►*v. Informal* To express contempt for; make light of.

pool¹ (pōōl) ►*n.* **1.** A small pond. **2.** A puddle. **3.** A deep or still place in a stream. **4.** A swimming pool. [< OE *pōl.*] —**pool** *v.*

pool² (pōōl) ►*n.* **1.** A fund containing all the money bet in a game of chance or on the outcome of an event. **2.** A grouping of resources for the common advantage of the participants. **3.** An agreement between competing business concerns to establish certain controls for common profit. **4.** Any of several games played on a six-pocket billiard table. ►*v.* **1.** To put into a fund for use by all. **2.** To join or form a pool. [Fr. *poule*, hen, stakes.]

pool·room (pōōl′rōōm′, -rŏŏm′) ►*n.* A place for the playing of pool or billiards.

pool table ►*n.* A six-pocket billiards table on which pool is played.

poop¹ (pōōp) ►*n. Naut.* **1.** A superstructure

at the stern of a ship. **2.** A poop deck. [< Lat. *puppis*.]

poop² (poop) ►*v. Slang* To become or cause to become fatigued. [?]

poop³ (poop) ►*n. Slang* Inside information. [?]

poop deck ►*n.* The deck of a ship nearest the stern.

poor (poor) ►*adj.* **-er, -est 1.** Having insufficient wealth to meet the necessities or comforts of life. **2.** Lacking a specified resource or quality. **3.** Not adequate in quality or quantity; inferior: *a poor performance; poor wages.* **4.** Negative, unfavorable, or disapproving: *a poor opinion.* **5.** Humble. **6.** Pitiable. [< Lat. *pauper*.] —**poor′ly** *adv.* —**poor′ness** *n.*

poor box ►*n.* A box in a church used for collecting alms.

poor boy ►*n. Regional* A sandwich of meat or seafood and often lettuce, tomatoes, and condiments, served on French bread.

poor·house (poor′hous′) ►*n. Derogatory* An establishment maintained at public expense as housing for the homeless.

poor·mouth (poor′mouth′, -mouth′) ►*v.* To claim poverty as an excuse or defense.

pop¹ (pŏp) ►*v.* **popped, pop·ping 1.** To make or cause to make a short, sharp, explosive sound. **2.** To burst open with such a sound. **3.** To appear abruptly. **4.** To open wide suddenly. **5.** To shoot a firearm, such as a pistol. **6.** To put or thrust suddenly. ►*n.* **1.** A sudden sharp, explosive sound. **2.** A shot with a firearm. **3.** *Regional* See **soft drink.** [ME *poppen*.]

pop² (pŏp) ►*n. Informal* Father. [< PAPA.]

pop³ (pŏp) ►*adj. Informal* **1.** Of or for the general public; popular: *pop psychology.* **2.** Of or specializing in popular music: *a pop singer.* **3.** Suggestive of pop art. [Short for POPULAR.] —**pop** *n.*

pop. ►*abbr.* population

pop art ►*n.* A form of art that depicts objects from everyday life and employs techniques of commercial art.

pop·corn (pŏp′kôrn′) ►*n.* A variety of corn having hard kernels that burst to form small white puffs when heated.

pope (pŏp) ►*n.* often **Pope** The bishop of Rome and head of the Roman Catholic Church. [< Gk. *pappas*, father.]

Pope, Alexander 1688–1744. English writer.

pop·eyed (pŏp′īd′) ►*adj.* **1.** Having bulging eyes. **2.** Amazed.

pop fly ►*n. Baseball* A short high fly ball.

pop·gun (pŏp′gŭn′) ►*n.* A toy gun that makes a popping noise.

pop·in·jay (pŏp′ĭn-jā′) ►*n.* A vain, talkative person. [< Ar. *babaġā'*, parrot.]

pop·lar (pŏp′lər) ►*n.* **1.** Any of several trees having unisexual flowers borne in catkins. **2.** See **tulip tree.** [< Lat. *pōpulus*.]

pop·lin (pŏp′lĭn) ►*n.* A ribbed fabric used in making clothing and upholstery. [Poss. < OProv. *papalin*, papal.]

pop·o·ver (pŏp′ō′vər) ►*n.* A very light, hollow muffin made with eggs, milk, and flour.

pop·py (pŏp′ē) ►*n., pl.* **-pies** Any of various plants having colorful flowers usu. with four delicate petals and milky sap. [< Lat. *papāver*.]

pop·py·cock (pŏp′ē-kŏk′) ►*n.* Senseless talk. [Prob. < Dutch *poppekak*, doll's excrement.]

pop·u·lace (pŏp′yə-lĭs) ►*n.* **1.** The general public; masses. **2.** A population. [< Ital. *popolaccio*, rabble.]

pop·u·lar (pŏp′yə-lər) ►*adj.* **1.** Widely liked or appreciated. **2.** Of, representing, or carried on by the people at large. **3.** Accepted by or prevalent among the people in general. [< Lat. *populus*, the people.] —**pop′u·lar′i·ty** (-lăr′ĭ-tē) *n.* —**pop′u·lar·ly** *adv.*

popular front ►*n.* A political coalition of leftist parties against fascism.

pop·u·lar·ize (pŏp′yə-lə-rīz′) ►*v.* **-ized, -iz·ing** To make popular. —**pop′u·lar·i·za′tion** *n.* —**pop′u·lar·iz′er** *n.*

pop·u·late (pŏp′yə-lāt′) ►*v.* **-lat·ed, -lat·ing 1.** To supply with inhabitants. **2.** To inhabit. **3.** *Comp.* To fill (an empty field or array) with data. [< Lat. *populus*, the people.]

pop·u·la·tion (pŏp′yə-lā′shən) ►*n.* **1.** All of the people inhabiting a specified area. **2.** All the organisms of the same kind living in a specified habitat. **3.** The set of data from which a statistical sample is taken.

population explosion ►*n.* Great expansion of a biological population, esp. the unchecked growth in human population resulting from a decrease in infant mortality and an increase in longevity.

pop·u·lism (pŏp′yə-lĭz′əm) ►*n.* A political philosophy supporting the rights and power of the people in their struggle against the privileged elite. —**pop′u·list** *n.*

pop·u·lous (pŏp′yə-ləs) ►*adj.* Containing many inhabitants; having a large population.

pop-up (pŏp′ŭp′) ►*n.* **1.** A device or illustration that pops up. **2.** *Comp.* A webpage or advertisement that opens automatically in a new window of a web browser. **3.** *Baseball* See **pop fly.**

por·ce·lain (pôr′sə-lĭn) ►*n.* **1.** A hard white translucent ceramic. **2.** An object made of porcelain. [< OItal. *porcellana*.]

porch (pôrch) ►*n.* **1.** A covered platform, usu. having a separate roof, at an entrance to a building. **2.** An open or enclosed gallery or room attached to the outside of a building. [< Lat. *porticus*, portico.]

por·cine (pôr′sīn′) ►*adj.* Of or resembling swine or a pig. [< Lat. *porcus*, pig.]

por·cu·pine (pôr′kyə-pīn′) ►*n.* Any of various rodents having long sharp quills. [< OFr. *porc espin*, spiny pig.]

pore¹ (pôr) ►*v.* **pored, por·ing 1.** To read or study carefully and attentively. **2.** To meditate deeply; ponder. [ME *pouren*.]

pore² (pôr) ►*n.* A minute opening, as in an animal's skin or a plant leaf, for the passage of fluid. [< Gk. *poros*, passage.]

pork (pôrk) ►*n.* The flesh of a pig or hog used as food. [< Lat. *porcus*, pig.]

pork barrel ►*n. Slang* A government project or appropriation that benefits a specific locale and a legislator's constituents.

pork·er (pôr′kər) ►*n.* A fattened young pig.

porn (pôrn) also **por·no** (pôr′nō) ►*n. Slang* Pornography. —**porn** *adj.*

por·nog·ra·phy (pôr-nŏg′rə-fē) ►*n.* Pictures, writing, video or other material that is sexually explicit and intended to arouse sexual passion. [< LGk. *pornē*, prostitute + –GRAPHY.] —**por·nog′ra·pher** *n.* —**por′no·graph′ic** (-nə-grăf′ĭk) *adj.*

po·rous (pôr′əs) ►*adj.* **1.** Admitting the passage of gas or liquid through pores or interstices. **2.** Easily crossed or penetrated: *a porous border.* —**po·ros′i·ty** (pə-rŏs′ĭ-tē) *n.* —**po′rous·ly** *adv.* —**po′rous·ness** *n.*

por·phy·ry (pôr′fə-rē) ►*n., pl.* **-ries** A fine-grained igneous rock containing large crystals, esp. of feldspar. [< Gk. *porphura*, purple.]

por·poise (pôr′pəs) ►*n., pl.* **-poise** or **-pois·es** Any of various marine, toothed whales usu. having a blunt snout and a triangular dorsal fin. [< OFr. *porpeis*.]

por·ridge (pôr′ĭj, pŏr′-) ►*n.* A soft food made by boiling oatmeal or another meal in water or milk. [< POTTAGE.]

por·rin·ger (pôr′ĭn-jər, pŏr′-) ►*n.* A shallow cup or bowl with a handle. [< OFr. *potager*.]

port¹ (pôrt) ►*n.* **1.** A city or town on a waterway with facilities for loading and unloading ships. **2.** A harbor. [< Lat. *portus*.]

port² (pôrt) ►*n.* The left-hand side of a ship or aircraft facing forward. ►*adj.* Of or relating to the port. [Prob. < PORT¹.]

port³ (pôrt) ►*n.* **1.** A porthole. **2.** An opening, as in a cylinder, for the passage of steam or fluid. **3.** *Comp.* A connection point for a peripheral device. [< Lat. *porta*, gate.]

port⁴ also **Port** (pôrt) ►*n.* A rich sweet fortified wine. [< *Oporto*, city of NW Portugal.]

Port. ►*abbr.* Portuguese

por·ta·ble (pôr′tə-bəl) ►*adj.* Carried or moved with ease. [< Lat. *portāre*, carry.] —**por′ta·bil′i·ty, por′ta·ble·ness** *n.* —**por′ta·ble** *n.* —**por′ta·bly** *adv.*

port·age (pôr′tĭj, pôr-täzh′) ►*n.* **1.** The carrying of boats and supplies overland between two waterways. **2.** A track or route used for such carrying. ►*v.* **-aged, -ag·ing** To transport or travel by portage. [< Lat. *portāre*, carry.]

por·tal (pôr′tl) ►*n.* **1.** A doorway or entrance, esp. a large and imposing one. **2.** *Comp.* A website considered as an entry point to other websites, often by being or providing access to a search engine. [< Med.Lat. *portāle*, city gate.]

portal tomb ►*n.* A Neolithic tomb consisting of two or more upright stones with a capstone.

Port-au-Prince (pôrt′ō-prĭns′) The capital of Haiti, in the SW part.

port·cul·lis (pôrt-kŭl′ĭs) ►*n.* A grating suspended in the gateway of a fortified place and lowered to block passage. [< OFr. *porte coleice*, sliding gate.]

portcullis
Bodiam Castle
East Sussex, England

porte-co·chère or **porte-co·chere** (pôrt′kō-shâr′) ►*n.* An enclosure over a driveway at the entrance of a building to provide shelter. [Fr. *porte cochère*, coach door.]

por·tend (pôr-tĕnd′) ►*v.* **1.** To serve as an omen or warning of; presage. **2.** To indicate; forecast. [< Lat. *portendere*.]

por·tent (pôr′tĕnt′) ►*n.* An indication of something about to occur; omen. [Lat. *portentum*.]

por·ten·tous (pôr-tĕn′təs) ►*adj.* **1.** Of or constituting a portent. **2.** Exciting wonder and awe. **3.** Pompous; pretentiously weighty. —**por·ten′tous·ness** *n.*

por·ter¹ (pôr′tər) ►*n.* **1.** A person employed to carry travelers' baggage. **2.** A railroad employee who waits on passengers. **3.** A maintenance worker. [< Lat. *portātor* < Lat. *portāre*, carry.]

por·ter² (pôr′tər) ►*n. Chiefly Brit.* One in charge of a gate or door. [< LLat. *portārius* < Lat. *porta*, gate.]

por·ter³ (pôr′tər) ►*n.* A dark beer made from browned or charred malt. [< *porter's ale*.]

Porter, William Sydney O. Henry. 1862–1910. Amer. writer.

por·ter·house (pôr′tər-hous′) ►*n.* A cut of beef having a T-bone and a sizable piece of tenderloin.

port·fo·li·o (pôrt-fō′lē-ō′) ►*n., pl.* **-os** **1.** A portable case for holding loose papers or drawings. **2.** The office or post of a cabinet member or minister of state. **3.** A group of investments. [Ital. *portafoglio*.]

port·hole (pôrt′hōl′) ►*n.* A small, usu. circular window in a ship's side.

por·ti·co (pôr′tĭ-kō′) ►*n., pl.* **-coes** or **-cos** A porch or walkway with a roof supported by columns, often leading to the entrance of a building. [< Lat. *porticus*.]

por·tière or **por·tiere** (pôr-tyâr′) ►*n.* A heavy curtain hung across a doorway. [Fr.]

por·tion (pôr′shən) ►*n.* **1.** A part of a whole. **2.** A part allotted to a person or group. **3.** A person's lot or fate. ►*v.* **1.** To distribute in portions. **2.** To provide with a share. [< Lat. *portiō*.]

Port·land (pôrt′lənd) **1.** A city of S ME. **2.** A city of NW OR near the Columbia R. —**Port′land·er** *n.*

Portland cement or **portland cement** ►*n.* A hydraulic cement made by heating and pulverizing a mixture of limestone and clay. [After *Portland*, England.]

Port Lou·is (lōō′ĭs, lōō′ē, lōō-ē′) The capital of Mauritius, in the NW part.

port·ly (pôrt′lē) ►*adj.* **-li·er, -li·est** Having a round, stout body. [< *port*, bearing.] —**port′li·ness** *n.*

port·man·teau (pôrt-măn′tō, pôrt′măn-tō′) ►*n., pl.* **-teaus** or **-teaux** (-tōz, -tōz′) A large leather suitcase with two hinged compartments. [Fr. *portemanteau*.]

Port Mores·by (môrz′bē) The capital of Papua New Guinea, on SE New Guinea.

port of call ►*n.* A port where ships dock in the course of voyages to load or unload cargo, obtain supplies, or undergo repairs.

port of entry ►*n.* A place where travelers or goods may enter or leave a country under official supervision.

Port of Spain or **Port-of-Spain** (pôrt′əv-spān′) The capital of Trinidad and Tobago, on the NW coast of Trinidad on an arm of the Atlantic.

Por·to-No·vo (pôr′tō-nō′vō) The capital of Benin, in the SE part on an inlet of the Bight of Benin.

por·trait (pôr′trĭt, -trāt′) ►*n.* A likeness of a person, esp. one showing the face, created by a painter or photographer. [< OFr. *portraire,* portray.] —**por′trait·ist** *n.*

por·trai·ture (pôr′trĭ-chŏŏr′) ►*n.* The art or practice of making portraits.

por·tray (pôr-trā′) ►*v.* **1.** To depict pictorially. **2.** To describe in words. **3.** To describe in a certain way: *The book portrays her as hardworking.* **4.** To represent dramatically, as on the stage. [< OFr. *portraire.*] —**por·tray′al** *n.* —**por·tray′er** *n.*

Por·tu·gal (pôr′chə-gəl) A country of SW Europe on the W Iberian Peninsula. Cap. Lisbon.

Por·tu·guese (pôr′chə-gēz′, -gēs′) ►*adj.* Of or relating to Portugal or its people or language. ►*n., pl.* **-guese 1.** A native or inhabitant of Portugal. **2.** The Romance language of Portugal and Brazil.

Portuguese man-of-war ►*n.* A complex marine organism of warm seas, having a bluish, bladderlike float from which hang numerous long stinging tentacles.

por·tu·lac·a (pôr′chə-lăk′ə) ►*n.* A succulent South American plant having showy flowers. [< Lat. *portulāca,* purslane.]

Port Vi·la (pôrt′ vē′lə, pôr vē-lä′) The capital of Vanuatu, on an island in the SW Pacific.

POS ►*abbr.* point of sale

pose (pōz) ►*v.* **posed, pos·ing 1.** To assume or cause to assume a particular position or posture, as in sitting for a portrait. **2.** To present or constitute: *pose a threat.* **3.** To place in a specific position. **4.** To represent oneself falsely. ►*n.* **1.** A bodily attitude or position, esp. one assumed for an artist. See Synonyms at **posture. 2.** A studied attitude assumed for effect. [< Lat. *pausa,* PAUSE.] —**pos′a·ble** *adj.* —**pos′er** *n.*

Po·sei·don (pō-sīd′n, pə-) ►*n. Gk. Myth.* The god of the sea and brother of Zeus.

po·seur (pō-zœr′) ►*n.* One who affects a particular attitude or manner to impress others. [Fr. < *poser,* pose.]

posh (pŏsh) ►*adj.* **1.** Fashionable: *a posh hotel.* **2.** Typical of the upper class, esp. in the United Kingdom: *a posh upbringing.* **3.** Imitatiing upper-class characteristics; pretentious: *a posh accent.* [Perh. < Romany *pâsh,* money.]

pos·it (pŏz′ĭt) ►*v.* To assume or put forward, as for consideration. [< Lat. *pōnere, posit-,* place.]

po·si·tion (pə-zĭsh′ən) ►*n.* **1.** A place or location. **2.** The right or appropriate place. **3.** The way in which something or someone is placed. **4.** A situation relative to circumstances: *in a position to bargain.* **5.** A point of view. **6.** Status; rank. **7.** A post of employment; job. ►*v.* To put in position. [< Lat. *pōnere, posit-,* place.] —**po·si′tion·al** *adj.* —**po·si′tion·er** *n.*

pos·i·tive (pŏz′ĭ-tĭv) ►*adj.* **1.** Marked by or displaying certainty or affirmation: *a positive answer.* **2a.** Admirable; beneficial: *positive qualities.* **b.** Optimistic or constructive: *a positive attitude.* **3.** Very confident; certain. **4.** Explicitly expressed: *a positive demand.* **5.** Admitting of no doubt; irrefutable. **6.** *Math.* Of or designating: **a.** A quantity greater than zero. **b.** A quantity, number, angle, or direction opposite to another designated as negative. **7.** *Phys.* Of or

designating electric charge of a sign opposite to that of an electron. **8.** Having the areas of light and dark in their original and normal relationship, as in a photographic print. **9.** *Gram.* Of or being the simple uncompared degree of an adjective or adverb. ►*n.* **1.** A photographic image in which the lights and darks appear as they do in nature. **2.** *Gram.* The positive degree of an adjective or adverb. [< Lat. *positīvus,* formally laid down.] —**pos′i·tive·ly** *adv.* —**pos′i·tive·ness, pos′i·tiv′i·ty** *n.*

pos·i·tron (pŏz′ĭ-trŏn′) ►*n.* The antiparticle of the electron. [POSI(TIVE) + (ELEC)TRON.]

pos·se (pŏs′ē) ►*n.* **1.** A group of civilians called upon by a law enforcement official for assistance. **2.** *Slang* A group of friends. [< Lat. *posse comitātūs,* power of the county.]

pos·sess (pə-zĕs′) ►*v.* **1a.** To have as property; own: *possess great wealth.* **b.** *Law* To have under one's power or control: *possess illegal drugs.* **2.** To have as an attribute. **3.** To gain control or power over. Used of a demon or spirit. [< Lat. *possidēre : pos-,* as master + *sedēre,* sit.] —**pos·ses′sor** *n.*

pos·sessed (pə-zĕst′) ►*adj.* **1a.** Controlled by a spirit or other force. **b.** Controlled by a strong inner drive; obsessed. **2.** Calm; collected.

pos·ses·sion (pə-zĕsh′ən) ►*n.* **1a.** The act or fact of possessing. **b.** The state of being possessed. **2a.** Something owned or possessed. **b.** A territory subject to foreign control. **3.** *Law* **a.** Power or control over something: *possession of a firearm.* **b.** Occupation or control of a piece of property, with or without ownership. **c.** The crime of possessing an illegal drug. **4a.** The state of being dominated by a spirit. **b.** The state of being obsessed with something, such as an idea. **5.** *Sports* Physical control of the ball or puck.

pos·ses·sive (pə-zĕs′ĭv) ►*adj.* **1.** Having or manifesting a desire to control or dominate: *a possessive parent.* **2.** *Gram.* Of or being a noun or pronoun case that indicates possession. ►*n. Gram.* **1.** The possessive case. **2.** A possessive form or construction. —**pos·ses′sive·ly** *adv.* —**pos·ses′sive·ness** *n.*

pos·si·ble (pŏs′ə-bəl) ►*adj.* **1.** Capable of happening, existing, or being true. **2.** Capable of becoming or being made to be so: *a possible building site.* **3.** Capable of happening but of uncertain likelihood: *possible side effects.* [< Lat. *possibilis.*] —**pos′si·bil′i·ty** *n.*

pos·si·bly (pŏs′ə-blē) ►*adv.* **1.** Perhaps. **2.** Conceivably. **3.** Under any circumstances.

pos·sum (pŏs′əm) ►*n.* An opossum.

post¹ (pōst) ►*n.* **1.** A stake set upright into the ground to serve as a marker or support. **2.** Something similar to a post. **3.** *Comp.* An electronic message displayed on a website. ►*v.* **1.** To display in a place of public view. **2.** To announce by posters. **3.** *Comp.* To make (an electronic message) available on a website. **4.** To put up signs on (property) warning against trespassing. **5.** To publish (a name) on a list. [< Lat. *postis.*]

post² (pōst) ►*n.* **1.** A military base. **2.** An assigned station, as of a sentry. **3.** A position of employment. **4.** A trading post. ►*v.* **1.** To assign to a position or station. **2.** To put forward; present: *post bail.* [< Lat. *positum,* p.part. of *pōnere,* place.]

post³ (pōst) ►*n. Chiefly Brit.* **1.** A postal system. **2.** A post office. **3.** A delivery of mail: *a letter in the morning post.* ►*v.* **1.** *Chiefly Brit.* To mail (a letter or package). **2.** To inform of the latest news. **3.** To make entries in (a ledger). **4.** To travel with speed. [< OItal. *posta,* relay station, ult. < Lat. *pōnere,* place.]

post– ►*pref.* **1.** After; later: *postdate.* **2.** Behind; posterior to: *postnasal.* [< Lat. *post,* after.]

post·age (pō'stĭj) ►*n.* **1.** The charge for mailing an item. **2.** The stamps, labels, or printing placed on an item indicating payment of this charge.

post·al (pō'stəl) ►*adj.* Of or relating to a post office or mail service. —**post'al·ly** *adv.*

postal card ►*n.* An unadorned card printed with the image of a postage stamp, issued by a government.

post·card also **post card** (pōst'kärd') ►*n.* **1.** A printed card used for sending a short message through the mail. **2.** See **postal card.**

post·date (pōst-dāt', pōst'-) ►*v.* **1.** To put a date on (e.g., a check) that is later than the actual date. **2.** To occur later than.

post·doc·tor·al (pōst-dŏk'tər-əl) also **post·doc·tor·ate** (-ĭt) ►*adj.* Of or engaged in academic study beyond the doctorate.

post·er (pō'stər) ►*n.* A large, usu. printed placard, bill, or announcement posted to advertise or publicize something.

pos·te·ri·or (pŏ-stîr'ē-ər, pō-) ►*adj.* **1.** Located behind a part or toward the rear of a structure. **2.** Relating to the hind or back part of a body. **3.** Following in time; subsequent. ►*n.* The buttocks. [Lat. < *posterus,* coming after.] —**pos·te'ri·or·ly** *adv.*

pos·ter·i·ty (pŏ-stĕr'ĭ-tē) ►*n.* **1.** Future generations. **2.** All of a person's descendants. [< Lat. *posterus,* coming after.]

pos·tern (pō'stərn, pŏs'tərn) ►*n.* A rear gate, esp. in a fort or castle. [< LLat. *posterula.*]

Post Exchange A service mark for a store on a military base that sells goods to military personnel and their families.

post·grad·u·ate (pōst-grăj'ōō-ĭt, -āt') ►*adj.* Of or relating to advanced study after graduation from college. ►*n.* One engaged in postgraduate study.

post·haste (pōst'hāst') ►*adv.* With great speed; rapidly. [< *post, haste,* a direction on letters.]

post·hu·mous (pŏs'chə-məs) ►*adj.* **1.** Occurring or continuing after one's death. **2.** Published after the writer's death. [< Lat. *postumus.*] —**post'hu·mous·ly** *adv.*

pos·til·ion also **pos·til·lion** (pō-stĭl'yən, pŏ-) ►*n.* One who rides the near horse of the leaders to guide the horses drawing a coach. [< Ital. *postiglione.*]

post·lude (pōst'lōōd') ►*n.* An organ voluntary played at the end of a church service. [POST– + (PRE)LUDE.]

post·man (pōst'mən) ►*n.* See **mailman.**

post·mark (pōst'märk') ►*n.* An official mark stamped on mail that cancels the stamp and records the date and place of mailing. —**post'mark'** *v.*

post·mas·ter (pōst'măs'tər) ►*n.* A person in charge of a post office.

postmaster general ►*n., pl.* **postmasters general** The executive head of a national postal service.

post me·rid·i·em (mə-rĭd'ē-əm) ►*adv. & adj.* After noon. Used chiefly in the abbreviated form to specify the hour: *10:30 PM; a PM appointment.* See Usage Note at **PM.** [Lat. *post merīdiem.*]

post·mis·tress (pōst'mĭs'trĭs) ►*n.* A woman in charge of a post office.

post·mor·tem (pōst-môr'təm) ►*adj.* **1.** Occurring or done after death. **2.** Of or relating to a postmortem. ►*n.* **1.** See **autopsy. 2.** *Informal* An analysis or review of a completed event. [Lat. *post mortem,* after death.] —**post mor'tem** *adv.*

post·na·sal (pōst-nā'zəl) ►*adj.* Located or occurring posterior to the nose.

post·na·tal (pōst-nāt'l) ►*adj.* Of or occurring after birth. —**post·na'tal·ly** *adv.*

post office ►*n.* **1.** The public department responsible for the transportation and delivery of the mails. **2.** A local office where mail is processed and stamps are sold.

post·op·er·a·tive (pōst-ŏp'ər-ə-tĭv, -ŏp'rə-, -ŏp'ə-rā'-) ►*adj.* Happening or done after surgery. —**post·op'er·a·tive·ly** *adv.*

post·paid (pōst'pād') ►*adj.* With the postage paid in advance.

post·par·tum (pōst-pär'təm) ►*adj.* Of or occurring after childbirth. [Lat. *post partum,* after birth.]

post·pone (pōst-pōn', pōs-pōn') ►*v.* **-poned, -pon·ing** To cause to take place later than originally scheduled. See Synonyms at **defer¹.** [Lat. *postpōnere.*] —**post·pone'ment** *n.*

post·script (pōst'skrĭpt', pōs'skrĭpt') ►*n.* A message added to a letter after the writer's signature. [< Lat. *postscrīptum.*]

post·trau·mat·ic (pōst'trô-măt'ĭk, -trou-) ►*adj.* Following injury or resulting from it: *posttraumatic amnesia.*

posttraumatic stress disorder ►*n.* An anxiety disorder resulting from severe trauma, marked by recurrent flashbacks, nightmares, and social withdrawal.

pos·tu·lant (pŏs'chə-lənt) ►*n.* A candidate for admission into a religious order. [< Lat. *postulāre,* request.]

pos·tu·late (pŏs'chə-lāt') ►*v.* **-lat·ed, -lat·ing 1.** To assume or assert the truth or reality of, esp. as a basis of an argument. **2.** To propose as a hypothesis. ►*n.* (pŏs'chə-lĭt, -lāt') Something assumed without proof as being self-evident or generally accepted. [< Lat. *postulāre,* request.] —**pos'tu·la'tion** *n.*

pos·ture (pŏs'chər) ►*n.* **1a.** A position of a person's body or body parts. **b.** A characteristic way of bearing one's body: *stooped posture.* **2a.** An attitude, esp. when adopted to have an effect on others: *a posture of defiance.* **b.** A policy with regard to something: *a government's defense posture.* ►*v.* **-tured, -tur·ing 1.** To assume a certain, often exaggerated body position. **2.** To assume a certain attitude, esp. to make an impression. [< Lat. *positūra,* position.] —**pos'tur·al** *adj.* —**pos'tur·er, pos'tur·ist** *n.*
Syns: *attitude, carriage, pose, stance n.*

po·sy (pō'zē) ►*n., pl.* **-sies** A flower or bunch of flowers. [< POESY.]

pot¹ (pŏt) ►*n.* **1.** A round cooking vessel with a handle. **2.** Something resembling a pot in appearance or function. **3.** *Games* The total amount staked by all the players in one hand at cards. **4.** *Informal* A common fund. ►*v.* **pot·ted, pot·ting 1.** To place or plant in a pot. **2.** To cook or preserve in a pot. [< VLat. **pottus.*]

pot² (pŏt) ►*n. Slang* Marijuana. [?]

po·ta·ble (pō′tə-bəl) ►*adj.* Fit to drink. [< Lat. *pōtāre*, drink.]

pot·ash (pŏt′ăsh′) ►*n.* **1.** See **potassium carbonate. 2.** See **potassium hydroxide. 3.** Any of several compounds containing potassium, esp. soluble compounds used chiefly in fertilizers. [< obsolete *pot ashes.*]

po·tas·si·um (pə-tăs′ē-əm) ►*n. Symbol* **K** A soft, silver-white, extremely reactive metallic element found naturally only in compounds and used in fertilizers and soaps. At. no. 19. See table at **element.** [< POTASH.] —**po·tas′sic** *adj.*

potassium bromide ►*n.* A white crystalline solid or powder, used as a sedative and in lithography.

potassium carbonate ►*n.* A white granular powder used in making glass, enamels, and soaps.

potassium cyanide ►*n.* An extremely poisonous white compound used in electroplating, photography, and as an insecticide.

potassium hydroxide ►*n.* A caustic white solid used as a bleach and in making soaps, dyes, and alkaline batteries; lye.

potassium nitrate ►*n.* A white or colorless crystalline compound used to pickle meat and in making explosives and fertilizers; saltpeter.

po·ta·to (pə-tā′tō) ►*n., pl.* **-toes 1.** A perennial plant widely cultivated for its starchy edible tubers. **2.** A tuber of this plant. [< Taíno *batata.*]

potato chip ►*n.* A thin slice of potato fried in deep fat until crisp and then salted.

Pot·a·wat·o·mi (pŏt′ə-wŏt′ə-mē) ►*n., pl.* **-mi** or **-mis 1.** A member of a Native American people with populations in Oklahoma, Kansas, Michigan, and Ontario. **2.** The Algonquian language of the Potawatomi.

pot·bel·ly (pŏt′bĕl′ē) ►*n.* A protruding belly. —**pot′bel′lied** *adj.*

pot·boil·er (pŏt′boi′lər) ►*n.* A literary or artistic work produced quickly for profit.

po·tent (pōt′nt) ►*adj.* **1.** Possessing strength; powerful. **2.** Exerting or capable of exerting strong effects. **3.** Able to achieve and maintain an erection that allows for sexual intercourse. Used of a male. [< Lat. *potēns.*] —**po′ten·cy** *n.* —**po′tent·ly** *adv.*

po·ten·tate (pōt′n-tāt′) ►*n.* One who has the power and position to rule over others; monarch. [< Lat. *potentātus*, power.]

po·ten·tial (pə-tĕn′shəl) ►*adj.* Capable of being but not yet in existence; latent. ►*n.* **1.** Capacity for growth, development, or future success. **2.** *Elect.* The work per unit of charge required to move a charge from a reference point to a specified point. —**po·ten′ti·al·i·ty** (-shē-ăl′ĭ-tē) *n.* —**po·ten′tial·ly** *adv.*

potential energy ►*n.* The energy of a body or system derived from position or condition rather than motion.

pot·head (pŏt′hĕd′) ►*n. Slang* One who habitually smokes marijuana.

pot·hold·er (pŏt′hōl′dər) ►*n.* A small pad made of fabric, silicone, or other material used to handle hot cooking utensils.

pot·hole (pŏt′hōl′) ►*n.* A large hole, esp. in a road surface. —**pot′holed′** *adj.*

po·tion (pō′shən) ►*n.* A liquid dose, esp. of medicinal, magic, or poisonous content. [< Lat. *pōtiō.*]

pot·luck (pŏt′lŭk′) ►*n.* **1.** Whatever food happens to be available for a meal. **2.** A meal at which each guest brings food that is then shared by all.

Po·to·mac River (pə-tō′mək) A river of the E US rising in NE WV and flowing about 600 km (370 mi) to Chesapeake Bay.

pot pie ►*n.* Meat or poultry and vegetables covered with a pastry crust and baked in a deep dish.

pot·pour·ri (pō′pŏŏ-rē′) ►*n., pl.* **-ris 1.** A combination of incongruous things. **2.** A mixture of dried flower petals and spices. [Fr. *pot pourri.*]

pot roast ►*n.* Beef that is browned and then cooked until tender in a covered pot.

pot·sherd (pŏt′shûrd′) also **pot·shard** (-shärd′) ►*n.* A fragment of broken pottery.

pot·shot also **pot shot** (pŏt′shŏt′) ►*n.* **1.** A random or easy shot. **2.** A criticism made without careful thought.

pot·tage (pŏt′ĭj) ►*n.* A thick soup or stew of vegetables and sometimes meat. [< OFr. *potage.*]

pot·ted (pŏt′ĭd) ►*adj.* Placed or grown in a pot.

pot·ter¹ (pŏt′ər) ►*n.* One who makes pottery.

pot·ter² (pŏt′ər) ►*v. Chiefly Brit.* Var. of **putter².**

Potter, (Helen) Beatrix 1866–1943. British writer and illustrator.

pot·ter·y (pŏt′ə-rē) ►*n., pl.* **-ies 1.** Ware, such as vases, pots, bowls, or plates, shaped from moist clay and hardened by heat. **2.** The craft or occupation of a potter. **3.** The place where a potter works.

pouch (pouch) ►*n.* **1.** A small bag used esp. for carrying loose items. **2.** A bag used to carry mail or diplomatic dispatches. **3.** A sealed container used in packaging food or drink. **4.** *Zool.* A saclike structure, such as the external abdominal pocket in which marsupials carry their young. [< OFr., of Gmc. orig.]

poul·tice (pōl′tĭs) ►*n.* A soft, moist, usu. heated mass spread on cloth and applied to a sore or inflamed part of the body. [< Med.Lat. *pultēs*, thick paste.] —**poul′tice** *v.*

poul·try (pōl′trē) ►*n.* Domesticated fowl, such as chickens, turkeys, ducks, or geese, raised for meat or eggs. [< OFr. *pouletrie.*]

pounce (pouns) ►*v.* **pounced, pounc·ing 1.** To spring or swoop suddenly so as to seize someone or something. **2.** To turn the attention to and try to take advantage of: *pounced on his mistake.* [< ME, hawk's talon.] —**pounce** *n.* —**pounc′er** *n.*

pound¹ (pound) ►*n., pl.* **pound** or **pounds 1a.** See table at **measurement. b.** A unit of apothecary weight equal to 12 oz. (373.242 gr). **2.** A unit of weight differing in various countries and times. **3.** See table at **currency. 4.** The primary unit of currency in Ireland and Cyprus before the adoption of the euro. [< Lat. *pondō*, by weight.]

pound² (pound) ►*v.* **1.** To strike repeatedly and forcefully. See Synonyms at **beat. 2.** To beat to a powder or pulp; pulverize or crush. **3.** To instill by persistent, emphatic repetition. **4.**

To pulsate rapidly and heavily. [< OE *pūnian.*]
—**pound′er** *n.*

pound³ (pound) ►*n.* A public enclosure for confining stray animals. [< OE *pund-.*]

Pound, Ezra Loomis 1885–1972. Amer. writer.

pound·age (poun′dĭj) ►*n.* Weight measured in pounds.

pound cake ►*n.* A rich yellow cake containing eggs, flour, butter, and sugar.

pound sign ►*n.* **1.** The symbol (£) for a unit of currency, esp. the pound sterling. **2.** The symbol (#) for a pound as a unit of weight.

pour (pôr) ►*v.* **1.** To flow or cause to flow in a steady stream. **2.** To send forth or produce copiously, as if in a stream or flood. **3.** To rain heavily. [ME *pouren.*] —**pour′er** *n.*

pout (pout) ►*v.* **1.** To exhibit displeasure or disappointment; sulk. **2.** To protrude the lips in an expression of displeasure. [ME *pouten.*] —**pout** *n.* —**pout′y** *adj.*

pou·tine (pōō-tēn′) ►*n.* A dish of Québécois origin consisting of French fries topped with cheese curds and gravy. [Fr. dial. (Quebec).]

POV ►*abbr.* point of view

pov·er·ty (pŏv′ər-tē) ►*n.* **1.** The state of being poor; lack of money or material goods. **2.** Deficiency in amount; scantiness. **3.** Unproductiveness. [< Lat. *paupertās.*]

pov·er·ty-strick·en (pŏv′ər-tē-strĭk′ən) ►*adj.* Destitute; miserably poor.

POW (pē′ō-dŭb′əl-yōō, -yōō) ►*n.* A prisoner of war.

pow·der (pou′dər) ►*n.* **1.** A substance consisting of ground, pulverized, or otherwise finely dispersed solid particles. **2.** Any of various preparations in the form of powder, as certain cosmetics and medicines. **3.** A dry explosive mixture, such as gunpowder. **4.** Light dry snow. ►*v.* **1.** To turn into or produce as a powder. **2.** To put powder on. [< Lat. *pulvis, pulver-.*] —**pow′der·y** *adj.*

powder keg ►*n.* **1.** A small cask for holding gunpowder or other explosives. **2.** A potentially explosive situation.

powder puff ►*n.* A soft pad for applying powder to the skin.

powder room ►*n.* A lavatory for women.

pow·er (pou′ər) ►*n.* **1a.** The ability or capacity to act or do something effectively. **b.** often **powers** A specific capacity, faculty, or aptitude: *her powers of concentration.* **2.** Physical strength or force exerted or capable of being exerted. **3a.** The ability or official capacity to exercise control; authority. **b.** A political unit having great influence or control over others. **4a.** The energy or motive force by which a physical system or machine is operated. **b.** Electricity. **5.** *Phys.* The rate at which work is done, commonly measured in units such as the watt and horsepower. **6.** *Math.* See **exponent** (sense 2). **7.** A measure of the magnification of an optical instrument. ►*v.* To supply with power, esp. mechanical power. [< VLat. **potēre,* be able.] —**pow′er·ful** *adj.* —**pow′er·ful·ly** *adv.* —**pow′er·ful·ness** *n.* —**pow′er·less** *adj.* —**pow′er·less·ly** *adv.*

pow·er·boat (pou′ər-bōt′) ►*n.* See **motorboat.**

pow·er·house (pou′ər-hous′) ►*n.* One that possesses great force or energy.

power of attorney ►*n.* **1.** The authority to act

on behalf of a person. **2.** A legal instrument granting such authority.

power plant ►*n.* **1.** A complex of structures and machinery for generating electric energy from another source of energy. **2.** All the equipment that constitutes a unit power source.

power shovel ►*n.* A large earthmoving machine used for excavating.

power train ►*n.* An assembly of gears and associated parts by which power is transmitted from an engine to a driving axle.

Pow·ha·tan¹ (pou′ə-tăn′, pou-hăt′n) Wahunsonacock. 1550?–1618. Algonquian leader.

Pow·ha·tan² (pou′ə-tăn′, pou-hăt′n) ►*n., pl.* **-tan** or **-tans** **1.** A member of a confederacy of Native American peoples formerly inhabiting E Virginia, now living there and in New Jersey. **2.** The Algonquian language of the Powhatan.

pow·wow (pou′wou′) ►*n.* **1a.** A council or meeting of Native Americans, sometimes with people from other communities. **b.** *Informal* A conference or gathering. **2.** A ceremony during which a shaman performs healing or hunting rituals. [< Narragansett *powwaw,* shaman.] —**pow′wow′** *v.*

pox (pŏks) ►*n.* A disease such as smallpox, marked by purulent skin eruptions. [< POCK.]

pp. ►*abbr.* **1.** pages **2.** postpaid **3.** prepaid

p.p. ►*abbr.* **1.** parcel post **2.** past participle

PPO ►*abbr.* preferred provider organization

PPV ►*abbr.* pay-per-view

PR ►*abbr.* **1.** public relations **2.** Puerto Rico

pr. ►*abbr.* **1.** pair **2.** *Gram.* present **3.** pronoun

prac·ti·ca·ble (prăk′tĭ-kə-bəl) ►*adj.* **1.** Capable of being effected, done, or put into practice; feasible. **2.** Usable. —**prac′ti·ca·bil′i·ty** *n.* —**prac′ti·ca·bly** *adv.*

prac·ti·cal (prăk′tĭ-kəl) ►*adj.* **1.** Of or acquired through practice or action, rather than theory or speculation: *practical experience.* **2.** Manifested in or involving practice: *practical applications.* **3.** Capable of or suitable to being used or put into effect; useful. **4.** Having or showing good judgment; sensible. **5.** Being actually so in almost every respect; virtual. [< Gk. *praktikos.*] —**prac′ti·cal′i·ty** (-kăl′ĭ-tē), **prac′ti·cal·ness** *n.*

practical joke ►*n.* A prank played on a person, esp. one that embarrasses the victim.

prac·ti·cal·ly (prăk′tĭk-lē) ►*adv.* **1.** Nearly; almost. **2.** In a practical way.

prac·tice (prăk′tĭs) ►*v.* **-ticed, -tic·ing** **1.** To do or perform habitually or customarily; make a habit of: *practice restraint.* **2.** To do or perform repeatedly in order to acquire or polish a skill. **3.** To work at, esp. as a profession: *practice law.* **4.** To carry out; observe. ►*n.* **1.** A habitual or customary action or way of doing something. **2a.** Repeated performance of an activity in order to learn or perfect a skill. **b.** Proficiency gained through repeated exercise. **3.** The act or process of doing something; performance. **4.** Exercise of an occupation or profession. **5.** The business of a professional person. **6.** A habitual action. [< Gk. *praktikos,* practical.] —**prac′tic·er** *n.*

   Syns: exercise, rehearse *v.*

prac·ti·tion·er (prăk-tĭsh′ə-nər) ►*n.* One who practices an occupation, profession, or technique. [< OFr. *practicien.*]

prae·tor (prē′tər) ►*n.* An ancient Roman magistrate below a consul. [< Lat.] **—prae·to′ri·an** (-tôr′ē-ən) adj. & n.

prag·mat·ic (prăg-măt′ĭk) ▸adj. **1.** Concerned with facts or actual events; practical. **2.** Relating to pragmatism. [< Gk. *pragma,* deed.] **—prag·mat′i·cal·ly** adv.

prag·ma·tism (prăg′mə-tĭz′əm) ▸n. A practical, matter-of-fact way of approaching or assessing situations or of solving problems. **—prag′ma·tist** n.

Prague (präg) The capital of the Czech Republic, in the W part.

Prai·a (prī′ə) The capital of Cape Verde, on an island in the S of the archipelago.

prai·rie (prâr′ē) ▸n. An extensive area of flat or rolling grassland, esp. in central North America. [< Lat. *prāta,* meadow.]

prairie dog ▸n. A burrowing rodent of W-central North America, having light brown fur and a barklike call.

prairie schooner ▸n. A covered wagon used by pioneers crossing the North American plains.

praise (prāz) ▸n. **1.** Expression of approval, commendation, or admiration. **2.** The extolling or exaltation of a deity, ruler, or hero. [< LLat. *pretiāre,* to prize.] **—praise** v.

praise·wor·thy (prāz′wûr′thē) ▸adj. Meriting praise; highly commendable.

pra·line (prä′lēn′, prā′-) ▸n. A crisp confection made of nut kernels stirred in boiling sugar syrup. [After the Comte du Plessis-*Praslin* (1598–1675).]

pram (prăm) ▸n. *Chiefly Brit.* A perambulator.

prance (prăns) ▸v. **pranced, pranc·ing 1.** To spring forward on the hind legs, as a spirited horse. **2.** To move about in a spirited manner; strut. [ME *prauncen.*] **—pranc′er** n.

prank (prăngk) ▸n. A mischievous trick or practical joke. [?] **—prank′ster** n.

pra·se·o·dym·i·um (prā′zē-ō-dĭm′ē-əm, prā′-sē-) ▸n. *Symbol* **Pr** A soft, silvery, malleable, rare-earth element used to color glass yellow and in metallic alloys. At. no. 59. See table at **element.** [Gk. *prasios,* leek-green + E. *didymium,* mixture of neodymium and praseodymium once considered an element (< Gk. *didumos,* twin).]

prate (prāt) ▸v. **prat·ed, prat·ing** To talk idly and at length; chatter. [< MDu. *prāten.*]

prat·fall (prăt′fôl′) ▸n. A fall on the buttocks. [*prat,* buttocks + FALL.]

prat·tle (prăt′l) ▸v. **-tled, -tling** To talk idly; babble. [< PRATE.] **—prat′tle** n.

prawn (prôn) ▸n. Any of various shrimps, esp. one that is large or inhabits fresh water. [ME *praine.*]

prax·is (prăk′sĭs) ▸n., pl. **-es** (-sēz′) Practical application of a branch of learning. [< Gk. < *prassein,* do.]

pray (prā) ▸v. **1.** To address a prayer to a deity. **2.** To use prayer to request (that something may happen). **3.** To say (a prayer or group of prayers). **4.** To make a devout request for. [< Lat. *precārī.*] **—pray′er** (prā′ər) n.

prayer (prâr) ▸n. **1.** A reverent petition made to a deity. **2.** An act of praying. **3.** A specially worded form of praying. **4. prayers** A religious observance in which praying predominates. **5.** A fervent request. **6.** The slightest chance or hope. [< Med.Lat. *precāria.*]

prayer·ful (prâr′fəl) ▸adj. **1.** Inclined to praying frequently. **2.** Typical of prayer, as a mannerism. **—prayer′ful·ly** adv.

prayer rug (prâr) ▸n. A small rug used by Muslims to kneel upon during devotions.

prayer wheel (prâr) ▸n. A revolving cylinder inscribed with prayers and used in devotions, esp. by Tibetan Buddhists.

pray·ing mantis (prā′ĭng) ▸n. A green or brownish predatory insect that while at rest folds its front legs as if in prayer.

pre– ▸pref. **1a.** Earlier; before: *prehistoric.* **b.** Preparatory; preliminary: *preoperative.* **c.** In advance: *prepay.* **2.** Anterior; in front of: *premolar.* [< Lat. *prae,* before.]

preach (prēch) ▸v. **1.** To proclaim or deliver in a sermon. **2.** To advocate or urge: *preach tolerance.* **3.** To give moral instruction, esp. in a tedious manner. [< Lat. *praedicāre,* proclaim.] **—preach′er** n. **—preach′y** adj.

pre·ad·o·les·cence (prē′ăd-l-ĕs′əns) ▸n. The period between childhood and puberty. **—pre′ad·o·les′cent** adj. & n.

pre·am·ble (prē′ăm′bəl, prē-ăm′-) ▸n. A preliminary statement, esp. to a formal document, explaining its purpose. [< Med.Lat. *praeambulus,* walking in front.] **—pre·am′bu·lar′y** (-byə-lĕr′ē) adj.

pre′a·dapt′ v.	**pre·in·dus′tri·al** adj.	**pre·pu·bes′cent** adj. & n.
pre′ag·ri·cul′tur·al adj.	**pre·judge′** v.	**pre·pub′li·ca′tion** adj.
pre·ar·range′ v.	**pre·judg′ment** n.	**pre′reg·is·ter** v.
pre·ar·range′ment n.	**pre′launch′** adj.	**pre′reg·is·tra′tion** n.
pre′built′ adj.	**pre′men·o·paus′al** adj.	**pre′re·lease′** n. & adj.
pre·can′cer·ous adj.	**pre′mi·gra′tion** n.	**pre′re·tire′ment** adj. & n.
pre-Chris′tian adj.	**pre′mix′** n. & v.	**pre′sci·en·tif′ic** adj.
pre′co·lo′ni·al adj.	**pre·mod′ern** adj.	**pre′screen′** v.
pre·con′scious adj. & n.	**pre′no·ti·fi·ca′tion** n.	**pre′sea′son** n.
pre·cook′ v.	**pre·no′ti·fy** v.	**pre′se·lect′** v.
pre·cool′ v.	**pre·nup′tial** adj.	**pre·set′** v.
pre′cut′ adj.	**pre·or·dain′** v.	**pre·sig′ni·fy′** v.
pre′dawn′ n. & adj.	**pre·or′di·na′tion** n.	**pre·sort′** v.
pre′de·cease′ v.	**pre′owned′** adj.	**pre′tax′** adj.
pre·des′ig·nate′ v.	**pre·pay′** v.	**pre′term′** adj. & n.
pre′flight′ adj.	**pre·pay′ment** n.	**pre·treat′** v.
pre·gla′cial adj.	**pre′pro·fes′sion·al** adj.	**pre·treat′ment** n.
pre·heat′ v.	**pre·pro′gram′** v.	**pre·tri′al** n.
pre·hom′i·nid n.	**pre·pu′ber·ty** n.	**pre′war′** adj.
& adj.	**pre′pu·bes′cence** n.	**pre′washed′** adj.

pre·am·pli·fi·er (prē-ăm′plə-fī′ər) ►*n.* An electronic circuit or device that detects and strengthens weak signals, as from a radio receiver, for subsequent amplification.

pre·ap·prove (prē′ə-proōov′) ►*v.* To approve (e.g., an applicant) at an earlier point in the approval process than is usual, sometimes even before an application is submitted.

preb·end (prĕb′ənd) ►*n.* **1.** A stipend historically drawn esp. from a cathedral's endowment by a member of the clergy. **2.** The property or tithe providing a prebend. [< Lat. *praebēre*, to grant.]

preb·en·dar·y (prĕb′ən-dĕr′ē) ►*n., pl.* **-ies** An Anglican cleric who receives a prebend.

Pre·cam·bri·an (prē-kăm′brē-ən, -kăm′-) ►*adj.* Of or being the 1st geologic era and oldest and largest division of geologic time, marked by the appearance of early forms of life. ►*n.* The Precambrian Era.

pre·car·i·ous (prĭ-kâr′ē-əs) ►*adj.* **1.** Dangerously lacking in stability. **2.** Subject to chance or unknown conditions. [< Lat. *precārius*, obtained by entreaty.] **—pre·car′i·ous·ly** *adv.* **—pre·car′i·ous·ness** *n.*

pre·cau·tion (prĭ-kô′shən) ►*n.* An action taken to protect against possible danger or failure. [< Lat. *praecavēre*, guard against.] **—pre·cau′tion·ar·y** (-shə-nĕr′ē) *adj.*

pre·cede (prĭ-sēd′) ►*v.* **-ced·ed, -ced·ing** To come to or be before in time, place, or position. [< Lat. *praecēdere*, go before.]

prec·e·dence (prĕs′ĭ-dəns, prĭ-sēd′ns) ►*n.* The fact, state, or right of preceding; priority.

prec·e·dent (prĕs′ĭ-dənt) ►*n.* **1.** An act or instance that may be used as an example in dealing with later similar instances. **2.** Convention or custom.

pre·ced·ing (prĭ-sē′dĭng) ►*adj.* Existing or coming before; previous.

pre·cen·tor (prĭ-sĕn′tər) ►*n.* A cleric who directs the choir of a church. [< Lat. *praecinere*, *praecent-*, sing before.]

pre·cept (prē′sĕpt′) ►*n.* A rule or principle prescribing a particular course of action or conduct. [< Lat. *praeceptum*.]

pre·cep·tor (prĭ-sĕp′tər, prē′sĕp′tər) ►*n.* A teacher; instructor. **—pre′cep·to′ri·al** (prē′-sĕp-tôr′ē-əl) *adj.*

pre·cinct (prē′sĭngkt′) ►*n.* **1.** A district of a city that is patrolled by a specific unit of its police force. **2.** An election district of a city or town. **3.** often **precincts** A place or enclosure that is marked off by definite limits. **4. precincts** Neighborhood; environs. [< Lat. *praecingere*, encircle.]

pre·ci·os·i·ty (prĕsh′ē-ŏs′ĭ-tē, prĕs′-) ►*n., pl.* **-ties** Overrefinement, esp. in one's language.

pre·cious (prĕsh′əs) ►*adj.* **1.** Of high cost or worth; valuable. **2.** Dear; beloved. **3.** Affectedly dainty or overrefined. [< Lat. *pretiōsus*.] **—pre′cious·ness** *n.*

prec·i·pice (prĕs′ə-pĭs) ►*n.* **1.** An overhanging or extremely steep cliff. **2.** The brink of a dangerous situation. [< Lat. *praeceps*, headlong.]

pre·cip·i·tant (prĭ-sĭp′ĭ-tənt) ►*adj.* **1.** Rushing or falling headlong. **2.** Impulsive in thought or action; rash. **3.** Abrupt or unexpected; sudden. **—pre·cip′i·tance, pre·cip′i·tan·cy** *n.*

pre·cip·i·tate (prĭ-sĭp′ĭ-tāt′) ►*v.* **-tat·ed, -tat·ing 1.** To cause to happen, esp. suddenly or

prematurely: *an announcement that precipitated a crisis.* **2.** To hurl downward. **3.** To put suddenly into a certain state or condition. **4.** To condense and fall as rain or snow. **5.** *Chem.* To cause (a solid substance) to be separated from a solution. ►*adj.* (-tĭt) **1.** Moving rapidly and heedlessly; speeding headlong. **2.** Acting with excessive haste and lack of deliberation. See Synonyms at **impetuous**. **3.** Occurring suddenly or unexpectedly. ►*n.* (-tāt′, -tĭt) *Chem.* A solid or solid phase that is separated from a solution. [< Lat. *praeceps*, headlong.] **—pre·cip′i·tate·ly** (-tĭt-lē) *adv.* **—pre·cip′i·tate·ness** *n.* **—pre·cip′i·ta′tive** *adj.* **—pre·cip′i·ta′tor** *n.*

pre·cip·i·ta·tion (prĭ-sĭp′ĭ-tā′shən) ►*n.* **1.** A headlong fall or rush. **2.** Abrupt or impulsive haste. **3a.** Water that falls as rain or snow. **b.** The quantity of such water falling in a specific area within a specific period. **4.** *Chem.* The production of precipitate.

pre·cip·i·tous (prĭ-sĭp′ĭ-təs) ►*adj.* **1.** Resembling a precipice; extremely steep. See Synonyms at **steep**[1]. **2.** Having precipices: *a precipitous bluff.* **3.** *Informal* Headlong, precipitate. **—pre·cip′i·tous·ly** *adv.* **—pre·cip′i·tous·ness** *n.*

pré·cis (prā′sē, prā-sē′) ►*n., pl.* **pré·cis** (prā′sēz, prā-sēz′) A concise summary of a text; abstract. [< OFr. *precis*, condensed.] **—pré′cis** *v.*

pre·cise (prĭ-sīs′) ►*adj.* **1.** Clearly expressed or delineated; definite. **2.** Exact, as in performance or amount; correct. **3.** Strictly distinguished from others; very: *at that precise moment.* **4.** Conforming strictly to rule or proper form. [< Lat. *praecīsus*, p.part. of *praecīdere*, cut short.] **—pre·cise′ly** *adv.* **—pre·cise′ness** *n.*

pre·ci·sion (prĭ-sĭzh′ən) ►*n.* The state or quality of being precise.

pre·clude (prĭ-kloōd′) ►*v.* **-clud·ed, -clud·ing 1.** To make impossible; prevent. **2.** To exclude; debar. [Lat. *praeclūdere*.] **—pre·clu′sion** (-kloō′zhən) *n.*

pre·co·cious (prĭ-kō′shəs) ►*adj.* Marked by development, aptitude, or interests considered advanced for a given age. [< Lat. *praecox*, premature.] **—pre·co′cious·ly** *adv.* **—pre·coc′i·ty** (-kŏs′ĭ-tē), **pre·co′cious·ness** *n.*

pre·cog·ni·tion (prē′kŏg-nĭsh′ən) ►*n.* Knowledge of something before it occurs; clairvoyance. **—pre·cog′ni·tive** *adj.*

pre-Co·lum·bi·an (prē′kə-lŭm′bē-ən) ►*adj.* Of or originating in the Americas before the arrival of Columbus.

pre·con·ceive (prē′kən-sēv′) ►*v.* **-ceived, -ceiv·ing** To form an opinion or a conception of before having adequate knowledge. **—pre′con·cep′tion** (-sĕp′shən) *n.*

pre·con·di·tion (prē′kən-dĭsh′ən) ►*n.* A prerequisite. ►*v.* To condition, train, or accustom in advance.

pre·cur·sor (prĭ-kûr′sər, prē′kûr′sər) ►*n.* **1.** One that precedes and indicates or announces another. **2.** One that precedes another; predecessor. [< Lat. *praecursor*.]

pre·da·ceous also **pre·da·cious** (prĭ-dā′shəs) ►*adj.* Predatory. [< Lat. *praedārī*, plunder.]

pre·date (prē-dāt′) ►*v.* Antedate.

pre·da·tion (prĭ-dā′shən) ►*n.* **1.** The capturing of prey as a means of maintaining life. **2.** The act of robbing, victimizing, or exploiting others. [< Lat. *praedārī*, plunder.]

pred·a·to·ry (prĕd′ə-tôr′ē) ►*adj.* **1.** Living or marked by preying on other organisms. **2a.** Living or marked by plundering or marauding. **b.** Living or marked by exploiting others for one's own gain. [< Lat. *praedārī,* plunder.] —**pred′a·tor** (-tər, -tôr′) *n.*

pred·e·ces·sor (prĕd′ĭ-sĕs′ər, prē′dĭ-) ►*n.* One who precedes another, esp. in an office or position. [< LLat. *praedēcessor.*]

pre·des·ti·na·tion (prē-dĕs′tə-nā′shən) ►*n.* **1.** *Theol.* **a.** The doctrine that God has foreordained all things. **b.** The divine decree foreordaining all souls to either salvation or damnation. **2.** Destiny; fate.

pre·des·tine (prē-dĕs′tĭn) ►*v.* To decide or decree in advance.

pre·de·ter·mine (prē′dĭ-tûr′mĭn) ►*v.* To determine or decide in advance. —**pre′de·ter′mi·na′tion** *n.*

pred·i·ca·ble (prĕd′ĭ-kə-bəl) ►*adj.* Capable of being stated or predicated.

pre·dic·a·ment (prĭ-dĭk′ə-mənt) ►*n.* A troublesome or unpleasant situation. [< LLat. *praedicāmentum.*]

pred·i·cate (prĕd′ĭ-kāt′) ►*v.* **-cat·ed, -cat·ing** **1.** To base or establish: *predicate an argument on the facts.* **2.** To affirm as an attribute or quality: *predicate the perfectibility of humankind.* ►*n.* (-kĭt) *Gram.* The part of a sentence or clause, including the verb, that expresses what the subject is or does. [< Lat. *praedicāre,* proclaim.] —**pred′i·ca′tion** *n.* —**pred′i·ca′tive** *adj.*

pre·dict (prĭ-dĭkt′) ►*v.* To state, tell about, or make known in advance; foretell. [Lat. *praedīcere,* foretell.] —**pre·dict′a·bil′i·ty** *n.* —**pre·dict′a·ble** *adj.* —**pre·dic′tion** *n.* —**pre·dic′tive** *adj.* —**pre·dic′tor** *n.*

pre·di·gest (prē′dĭ-jĕst′, -dĭ-) ►*v.* To subject to partial digestion. —**pre′di·ges′tion** *n.*

pred·i·lec·tion (prĕd′l-ĕk′shən, prēd′-) ►*n.* A special liking for something; preference. [< Med.Lat. *praedīligere,* prefer.]

*Syns: leaning, partiality, penchant **n.***

pre·dis·pose (prē′dĭ-spōz′) ►*v.* **-posed, -pos·ing** **1.** To make (someone) inclined to something in advance. **2.** To make susceptible or liable. —**pre′dis·po·si′tion** (-dĭs-pə-zĭsh′ən) *n.*

pre·dom·i·nant (prĭ-dŏm′ə-nənt) ►*adj.* **1.** Having the most importance, influence, or force. **2.** Most common or conspicuous; prevalent. —**pre·dom′i·nance, pre·dom′i·nan·cy** *n.* —**pre·dom′i·nant·ly** *adv.*

pre·dom·i·nate (prĭ-dŏm′ə-nāt′) ►*v.* **-nat·ed, -nat·ing** **1.** To have controlling power or influence; prevail. **2.** To be of or have greater quantity or importance. ►*adj.* Predominant. [Med.Lat. *praedomīnārī, praedomināt-* : PRE– + Lat. *dominus,* master.] —**pre·dom′i·nate·ly** (-nĭt-lē) *adv.* —**pre·dom′i·na′tion** *n.* —**pre·dom′i·na′tor** *n.*

pree·mie (prē′mē) ►*n. Informal* A prematurely born infant. [< PREMATURE.]

pre·em·i·nent or **pre-em·i·nent** (prē-ĕm′ə-nənt) ►*adj.* Superior to all others; outstanding. See Synonyms at **famous.** [< Lat. *praeēminēre,* excel.] —**pre·em′i·nence** *n.* —**pre·em′i·nent·ly** *adv.*

pre·empt or **pre-empt** (prē-ĕmpt′) ►*v.* **1.** To take the place of or take precedence over. **2.** To take action to prevent (another action)

from happening. **3a.** To appropriate for oneself before others. **b.** To settle on (public land) so as to obtain the right to buy before others. [PRE– + Lat. *emere, ēmpt-,* buy.] —**pre·emp′tion** *n.* —**pre·emp′tive** *adj.*

preen (prēn) ►*v.* **1.** To smooth or clean (feathers) with the beak or bill. **2.** To dress or groom (oneself) with care; primp. **3.** To take pride or satisfaction in (oneself). [ME *preinen.*]

pre·ex·ist (prē′ĭg-zĭst′) ►*v.* To exist before. —**pre′ex·is′tence** *n.* —**pre′ex·is′tent** *adj.*

pref. ►*abbr.* **1.** preface **2.** prefix

pre·fab (prē′făb′) ►*n. Informal* Something prefabricated, esp. a building or section of a building. —**pre′fab′** *adj. & v.*

pre·fab·ri·cate (prē-făb′rĭ-kāt′) ►*v.* To manufacture in advance, esp. in standard sections that can be easily shipped and assembled. —**pre·fab′ri·ca′tion** *n.*

pref·ace (prĕf′ĭs) ►*n.* A preliminary statement introducing a book, usu. written by the author. ►*v.* **-aced, -ac·ing** To introduce by or provide with a preface. [< Lat. *praefātiō.*]

pref·a·to·ry (prĕf′ə-tôr′ē) ►*adj.* Of or being a preface; introductory. [< Lat. *praefārī, praefāt-,* say before.]

pre·fect (prē′fĕkt′) ►*n.* **1.** A high administrative official, as in ancient Rome. **2.** A student monitor, esp. in a private school. [< Lat. *praefectus.*]

pre·fec·ture (prē′fĕk′chər) ►*n.* **1.** An administrative district of some countries, such as Japan or China. **2.** The office or authority of a prefect.

pre·fer (prĭ-fûr′) ►*v.* **-ferred, -fer·ring** **1.** To choose as more desirable. **2.** *Law* To present (a charge) against a defendant before a court: *prefer an indictment.* [< Lat. *praeferre* : PRE– + *ferre,* carry.]

pref·er·a·ble (prĕf′ər-ə-bəl, prĕf′rə-) ►*adj.* More desirable. —**pref′er·a·bly** *adv.*

pref·er·ence (prĕf′ər-əns, prĕf′rəns) ►*n.* **1a.** The exercise of choice. **b.** One so chosen. **2.** The state of being preferred; favor over others. **3.** The granting of an advantage to one country in matters of international trade. —**pref′er·en′tial** (-ə-rĕn′shəl) *adj.*

pre·fer·ment (prĭ-fûr′mənt) ►*n.* Selection for promotion or favored treatment.

pre·ferred stock (prĭ-fûrd′) ►*n.* Capital stock that has priority over a corporation's common stock in the distribution of dividends and often of assets.

pre·fig·ure (prē-fĭg′yər) ►*v.* **1.** To presage; foreshadow. **2.** To imagine in advance. —**pre·fig′u·ra·tive** (-fĭg′yər-ə-tĭv) *adj.* —**pre·fig′ure·ment** *n.*

pre·fix (prē′fĭks′) ►*v.* To put or attach before. ►*n. Gram.* An affix attached to the front of a word to produce a derivative word or an inflected form. [< OFr. *prefixer.*]

pre·fron·tal (prē-frŭn′tl) ►*adj.* Of or situated in the anterior part of the frontal lobe.

preg·na·ble (prĕg′nə-bəl) ►*adj.* Vulnerable to seizure or capture: *a pregnable fort.* [< OFr. *prendre, pregn-,* seize.] —**preg′na·bil′i·ty** *n.*

preg·nant (prĕg′nənt) ►*adj.* **1.** Carrying developing offspring within the body. **2.** Weighty or significant; full of meaning. [< Lat. *praegnāns.*] —**preg′nan·cy** *n.*

pre·hen·sile (prē-hĕn′səl, prē-hĕn′sīl′) ►*adj.* Able to seize or hold, esp. by wrapping around:

a prehensile tail. [< Lat. *prehendere, prehēns-,* grasp.]

prehensile
prehensile tail of an opossum

pre·his·tor·ic (prē′hĭ-stôr′ĭk, -stŏr′-) also **pre·his·tor·i·cal** (-ĭ-kəl) ►*adj.* Of or belonging to an era before recorded history. —**pre·his′to·ry** (-hĭs′tə-rē) *n.*

pre·in·stall (prē′ĭn-stôl′) ►*v.* To install software on a computer or other device before selling it to a consumer. —**pre·in′stal·la′tion** (-stə-lā′shən) *n.*

prej·u·dice (prĕj′ə-dĭs) ►*n.* **1.** An adverse judgment or opinion formed unfairly or without knowledge of the facts. **2.** Irrational suspicion or hatred of a particular social group. **3.** Harm caused to a person, esp. in a legal case. ►*v.* **-diced, -dic·ing 1.** To fill with prejudice or cause to judge with prejudice. See Synonyms at **bias. 2.** To do harm to: *a mistake that prejudiced the outcome.* [< Lat. *praeiūdicium.*] —**prej′u·di′cial** (-dĭsh′əl) *adj.*

prel·ate (prĕl′ĭt) ►*n.* A high-ranking member of the clergy, esp. a bishop. [< Med.Lat. *praelātus.*] —**prel′a·cy** (-ə-sē) *n.*

pre·lim·i·nar·y (prĭ-lĭm′ə-nĕr′ē) ►*adj.* Prior to the main matter, action, or business; introductory. ►*n., pl.* **-ies** Something that precedes, prepares for, or introduces the main matter or action. [< PRE– + Lat. *līmen*, threshold.] —**pre·lim′i·nar′i·ly** (-nâr′ə-lē) *adv.*
Syns: *introductory, preparatory **adj.***

prel·ude (prĕl′yood′, prā′lood′, prē′-) ►*n.* **1.** An introductory performance, event, or action. **2.** *Mus.* A piece or movement serving as an introduction to another section or composition. [< Lat. *praelūdere,* play beforehand.]

pre·mar·i·tal (prē-măr′ĭ-tl) ►*adj.* Taking place or existing before marriage.

pre·ma·ture (prē′mə-tyoor′, -toor′, -choor′) ►*adj.* **1.** Occurring, growing, or existing before the customary, correct, or assigned time; early. **2.** Born after a gestation period of less than the normal time. —**pre′ma·ture′ly** *adv.*

pre·med (prē′mĕd′) *Informal* ►*adj.* Premedical. ►*n.* **1.** A premedical student. **2.** A premedical program of study.

pre·med·i·cal (prē-mĕd′ĭ-kəl) ►*adj.* Preparing for or leading to the study of medicine.

pre·med·i·tate (prē-mĕd′ĭ-tāt′) ►*v.* To form an intent to carry out (an action, such as a crime). —**pre·med′i·ta′tion** *n.* —**pre·med′i·ta′tive** *adj.*

pre·men·stru·al (prē-mĕn′stroo-əl) ►*adj.* Of or occurring in the period just before menstrua-

tion. —**pre·men′stru·al·ly** *adv.*

pre·mier (prĭ-mîr′, -myîr′, prē′mîr′) ►*adj.* **1.** First in status or importance. **2.** First to occur or exist; earliest. ►*n.* (prĭ-mîr′) A prime minister. [< Lat. *prīmārius.*] —**pre·mier′ship′** *n.*

pre·miere or **pre·mière** (prĭ-mîr′, -myâr′) ►*n.* The first public performance, as of a play. ►*v.* **-miered** or **-mièred, -mier·ing** or **-mièr·ing** To present or receive a first public performance. [Fr.]

prem·ise (prĕm′ĭs) ►*n.* **1.** A proposition upon which an argument is based or from which a conclusion is drawn. **2. premises** Land and the buildings on it. [< Lat. *praemittere, praemiss-*, set in front.] —**prem′ise** *v.*

pre·mi·um (prē′mē-əm) ►*n.* **1.** The amount paid, often in installments, for an insurance policy. **2.** A sum of money paid in addition to a regular amount. **3.** A prize or award. **4.** An unusual or high value: *put a premium on honesty.* ►*adj.* Of superior quality or value: *premium gasoline.* —*idiom:* **at a premium** More valuable than usual, as from scarcity. [Lat. *praemium,* reward.]

pre·mo·lar (prē-mō′lər) ►*n.* One of eight bicuspid teeth located in pairs between the canines and molars. —**pre·mo′lar** *adj.*

prem·o·ni·tion (prĕm′ə-nĭsh′ən, prē′mə-) ►*n.* **1.** A presentiment of the future; foreboding. **2.** An advance warning; forewarning. [< Lat. *praemonēre,* forewarn : PRE– + *monēre,* warn.] —**pre·mon′i·to′ry** (-mŏn′ĭ-tôr′ē) *adj.*

pre·na·tal (prē-nāt′l) ►*adj.* Existing or occurring before birth. —**pre·na′tal·ly** *adv.*

pre·oc·cu·py (prē-ŏk′yə-pī′) ►*v.* To occupy completely the mind or attention of. See Synonyms at **engross.** —**pre·oc′cu·pa′tion** (-pā′shən) *n.*

pre·op·er·a·tive (prē-ŏp′ər-ə-tĭv, -ŏp′rə-, -ŏp′-ə-rā′-) ►*adj.* Happening or done before surgery. —**pre·op′er·a·tive·ly** *adv.*

prep. ►*abbr. Gram.* preposition

pre·pack·age (prē-păk′ĭj) ►*v.* To wrap or package (a product) before marketing.

prep·a·ra·tion (prĕp′ə-rā′shən) ►*n.* **1.** The act or process of preparing. **2.** Readiness. **3.** often **preparations** An action done to prepare for something. **4.** A prepared substance, such as a medicine.

pre·par·a·to·ry (prĭ-păr′ə-tôr′ē, -pâr′-, prĕp′-ər-ə-) ►*adj.* Serving to make ready or prepare. See Synonyms at **preliminary.**

preparatory school ►*n.* A usu. private secondary school that prepares students for college.

pre·pare (prĭ-pâr′) ►*v.* **-pared, -par·ing 1.** To make ready. **2.** To put together by combining various elements or ingredients. **3.** To fit out; equip. [< Lat. *praeparāre.*]

pre·par·ed·ness (prĭ-pâr′ĭd-nĭs) ►*n.* The state of being prepared, esp. for combat.

pre·pon·der·ate (prĭ-pŏn′də-rāt′) ►*v.* **-at·ed, -at·ing** To be greater than something else, as in power, weight, or importance. [Lat. *praeponderāre.*] —**pre·pon′der·ance** *n.* —**pre·pon′der·ant** *adj.*

prep·o·si·tion (prĕp′ə-zĭsh′ən) ►*n.* A word placed before a substantive indicating its relation to a verb, an adjective, or another substantive, as English *at, by,* or *with.* [< Lat. *praepōnere, praeposit-*, put in front.] —**prep′o·si′tion·al** *adj.*

Usage: Despite the widespread notion that a preposition may not be used to end a sentence, sentences ending with prepositions can be found in the works of most of the great writers. English syntax allows final placement of the preposition, as in *I asked her which course she had signed up for,* and efforts to place the preposition elsewhere can have stilted results.

pre·pos·sess (prē′pə-zĕs′) ►*v.* **1.** To influence beforehand; prejudice. **2.** To impress favorably in advance.

pre·pos·sess·ing (prē′pə-zĕs′ĭng) ►*adj.* Serving to impress favorably; pleasing: *a prepossessing appearance.*

pre·pos·ter·ous (prĭ-pŏs′tər-əs) ►*adj.* Contrary to reason or common sense; absurd. See Synonyms at **foolish.** [< Lat. *praeposterus,* topsy-turvy.] —**pre·pos′ter·ous·ness** *n.*

prep·py or **prep·pie** (prĕp′ē) ►*n., pl.* **-pies** *Informal* **1.** A student of a preparatory school. **2.** A person whose manner and dress are deemed typical of preparatory schools. —**prep′pi·ness** *n.* —**prep′py** *adj.*

prep school ►*n.* A preparatory school.

pre·puce (prē′pyo͞os′) ►*n.* See **foreskin.** [< Lat. *praepūtium.*] —**pre·pu′tial** (-pyo͞o′shəl) *adj.*

pre·req·ui·site (prē-rĕk′wĭ-zĭt) ►*adj.* Required as a prior condition. —**pre·req′ui·site** *n.*

pre·rog·a·tive (prĭ-rŏg′ə-tĭv) ►*n.* An exclusive right or privilege. [< Lat. *praerogāre,* ask before.]

pres. ►*abbr.* **1.** *Gram.* present **2.** president

pres·age (prĕs′ĭj) ►*n.* **1.** An indication or warning of a future occurrence; omen. **2.** A presentiment; foreboding. ►*v.* (prĭ-sāj′, prĕs′ĭj) **-saged, -sag·ing 1.** To indicate or warn of in advance; portend. **2.** To have a presentiment of. [< Lat. *praesāgium.*]

pres·by·ter (prĕz′bĭ-tər, prĕs′-) ►*n.* **1.** A priest in various hierarchical churches. **2.** An elder in the Presbyterian Church. [< Gk. *presbuteros,* elder.]

pres·by·te·ri·an (prĕz′bĭ-tîr′ē-ən, prĕs′-) ►*adj.* **1.** Relating to ecclesiastical government by presbyters. **2. Presbyterian** Of or relating to a Protestant church governed by presbyters and traditionally Calvinist in doctrine. —**Pres′by·te′ri·an** *n.* —**pres′by·te′ri·an·ism** *n.*

pres·by·ter·y (prĕz′bĭ-tĕr′ē, prĕs′-) ►*n., pl.* **-ies** **1.** A court composed of Presbyterian Church ministers and representative elders of a particular locality. **2.** The section of a church reserved for the clergy.

pre·school (prē′sko͞ol′) ►*adj.* Of or intended for the years of childhood that precede elementary school. —**pre′school′** *n.* —**pre′school′er** *n.*

pre·science (prĕsh′əns, -ē-əns, prē′shəns, -shē-əns) ►*n.* Knowledge of actions or events before they occur. [< Lat. *praescīre,* know before.] —**pre′scient** *adj.*

pre·scribe (prĭ-skrīb′) ►*v.* **-scribed, -scrib·ing** **1.** To set down as a rule or direction: *prescribed the terms of the surrender.* **2.** To order the use of (a medicine or other treatment). [< Lat. *praescrībere.*] —**pre·scrib′er** *n.* —**pre·scrip′tive** (-skrĭp′tĭv) *adj.* —**pre·scrip′tive·ness** *n.*

pre·scrip·tion (prĭ-skrĭp′shən) ►*n.* **1.** The act of prescribing. **2a.** A written order, esp. by a physician, for the preparation and administration of a medicine. **b.** A prescribed medicine.

pres·ence (prĕz′əns) ►*n.* **1.** The state or fact of being present. **2.** The area immediately surrounding someone. **3.** A person who is present. **4a.** A person's bearing. **b.** The quality of self-assurance and effectiveness.

pres·ent¹ (prĕz′ənt) ►*n.* **1.** A moment or period in time intermediate between past and future; now. **2.** *Gram.* The present tense. **3. presents** *Law* The document or instrument in question. ►*adj.* **1.** Existing or happening now: *present trends.* **2.** Being at hand. **3.** *Gram.* Designating a verb tense or form that expresses current time. [< Lat. *praesēns,* pr.part. of *praeesse,* be present.] —**pres′ent·ness** *n.*

pre·sent² (prĭ-zĕnt′) ►*v.* **1a.** To make a gift or award of. **b.** To make a gift to. **2a.** To offer for examination or consideration. **b.** To offer (e.g., a play) for public entertainment. **3.** To represent or depict in a certain manner. **4.** To introduce, esp. formally. **5.** To salute with (a weapon). **6.** To make a presentation. ►*n.* **present** (prĕz′ənt) Something presented; gift. [< Lat. *presentāre.*] —**pre·sent′a·ble** *adj.* —**pres′en·ta′tion** (prĕz′ən-tā′shən, prē′zən-) *n.*

pres·ent-day (prĕz′ənt-dā′) ►*adj.* Current.

pre·sen·ti·ment (prĭ-zĕn′tə-mənt) ►*n.* A sense that something is about to occur; premonition. [< Lat. *praesentīre,* feel beforehand.]

pres·ent·ly (prĕz′ənt-lē) ►*adv.* **1.** In a short time; soon. **2.** Currently.

Usage: An original meaning of *presently,* "at the present time; currently," has survived in popular use, but it is often frowned upon. Sentences like *He is presently the United States ambassador to the United Nations* was acceptable to only 47–50 percent of the Usage Panel in four surveys from 1965 to 1999.

present participle (prĕz′ənt) ►*n.* A participle expressing present action, in English formed by adding *-ing* to the infinitive and used to express present action, to form progressive tenses, and to function as a verbal adjective.

present perfect (pûr′fĭkt) ►*n.* The verb tense expressing action completed at the present time, formed in English by combining the present tense of *have* with a past participle, as in *He has spoken.*

pres·er·va·tion·ist (prĕz′ər-vā′shə-nĭst) ►*n.* One who advocates preservation, esp. of natural areas or endangered species. —**pres′er·va′tion·ism** *n.*

pre·ser·va·tive (prĭ-zûr′və-tĭv) ►*n.* Something used to preserve, esp. a chemical added to foods to inhibit spoilage. —**pre·ser′va·tive** *adj.*

pre·serve (prĭ-zûrv′) ►*v.* **-served, -serv·ing** **1.** To protect from injury or peril. **2.** To keep or maintain intact. **3.** To treat fruit or other foods so as to prevent decay. ►*n.* **1.** often **preserves** Fruit cooked with sugar to protect against decay or fermentation. **2.** An area maintained for the protection of wildlife or natural resources. [< Med.Lat. *praeservāre.*] —**pres′er·va′tion** (prĕz′ər-vā′shən) *n.* —**pre·serv′er** *n.*

pre·shrunk also **pre·shrunk** (prē′shrŭngk′) ►*adj.* Shrunk during manufacture to minimize subsequent shrinkage.

pre·side (prĭ-zīd′) ►*v.* **-sid·ed, -sid·ing** **1.** To hold the position of authority; act as chairperson. **2.** To possess or exercise authority or control. [< Lat. *praesidēre* : PRE– + *sedēre,* sit.]

pres·i·dent (prĕz′ĭ-dənt, -dĕnt′) ►*n.* **1.** One appointed or elected to preside over an assembly or meeting. **2.** often **President** The chief executive of a republic, esp. of the US. **3.** The chief officer of an organization, as a corporation. **—pres′i·den·cy** *n.* **—pres′i·den′tial** (-děn′shəl) *adj.* **—pres′i·dent·ship′** *n.*

Pres·i·dents′ Day or **Pre·si·dents Day** (prĕz′ĭ-dənts, -dĕnts) ►*n.* The 3rd Monday in February, a US legal holiday in honor of US presidents, esp. George Washington and Abraham Lincoln, who were born in February.

Pres·ley (prĕs′lē, prĕz′-), **Élvis Aron** or **Aaron** "the King." 1935–77. Amer. rock musician.

Elvis Presley
photographed in 1963

press (prĕs) ►*v.* **1a.** To exert steady weight or force against; bear down on. **b.** To move by applying pressure: *press a piano key.* **2.** To squeeze the juice or other contents from. **3a.** To reshape or make compact by applying steady force: *press the clay in a mold.* **b.** To iron (e.g., clothing). **4.** To bear down on or attack: *The army pressed the rebels for months.* **5.** To insist upon or put forward insistently: *press a claim.* **6.** To try to influence or persuade, as by insistent arguments; pressure or entreat: *pressed her for a reply.* **7.** To advance eagerly; move forward urgently: *We pressed through the crowd to get to the bus.* **8.** To assemble in large numbers; crowd: *Fans pressed around the movie star.* **9.** To continue a course of action, esp. in spite of difficulties. ►*n.* **1.** Any of various machines or devices that apply pressure. **2.** A printing press. **3.** A place or establishment where matter is printed. **4.** The art, method, or business of printing. **5a.** The communications media considered as a whole, esp. the agencies that collect, publish, transmit, or broadcast news to the public. **b.** News disseminated to the public in printed, broadcast, or electronic form: *kept the scandal out of the press.* **c.** The people involved in the media, as news reporters and broadcasters. **6.** A large gathering; crowd: *lost our friend in the press of people.* **7.** An act of applying pressure: *the press of a button.* **8.** The urgency of business or matters. [< Lat. *premere, press-.*]

press agent ►*n.* A person employed to arrange advertising and publicity, as for a performer or business. **—press a′gent·ry** *n.*

press conference ►*n.* An interview held for news reporters by a political figure or famous person.

press·ing (prĕs′ĭng) ►*adj.* Demanding immediate attention; urgent. **—press′ing·ly** *adv.*

press·room (prĕs′ro͞om′, -ro͝om′) ►*n.* The room in a printing or newspaper publishing estab-

lishment that contains the presses.

pres·sure (prĕsh′ər) ►*n.* **1.** The act of pressing or the condition of being pressed. **2.** The application of continuous force by one body on another that it is touching. **3.** *Phys.* Force applied uniformly over a surface, measured as force per unit of area. **4.** Force exerted by the weight of the atmosphere. **5a.** A constraining influence: *pressure to conform.* **b.** An influence acting as a source of distress or hardship: *economic pressures.* **6.** A physical sensation produced by compression of a part of the body. ►*v.* **-sured, -sur·ing** To exert pressure on. [< Lat. *premere,* press.]

pressure group ►*n.* A group that endeavors to influence public policy.

pressure suit ►*n.* A garment worn in high-altitude aircraft or in spacecraft to compensate for low-pressure conditions.

pres·sur·ize (prĕsh′ə-rīz′) ►*v.* **-ized, -iz·ing** To maintain normal air pressure in (an enclosure, as an aircraft or submarine). **—pres′sur·i·za′-tion** *n.* **—pres′sur·iz′er** *n.*

pres·ti·dig·i·ta·tion (prĕs′tĭ-dĭj′ĭ-tā′shən) ►*n.* Sleight of hand. [Fr.] **—pres′ti·dig′i·ta′tor** *n.*

pres·tige (prĕ-stēzh′, -stēj′) ►*n.* **1.** The level of respect at which one is regarded by others; standing. **2.** Good reputation; honor. [< Lat. *praestīgiae,* tricks.] **—pres′ti·gious** (-stē′jəs, -stĭj′əs) *adj.*

pres·to (prĕs′tō) ►*adv.* **1.** *Mus.* In rapid tempo. **2.** Suddenly; right away. [Ital.] **—pres′to** *adj.*

pre·sume (prĭ-zo͞om′) ►*v.* **-sumed, -sum·ing** **1.** To take for granted; assume. **2.** To act presumptuously or take unwarranted advantage of something. [< LLat. *praesūmere,* anticipate.] **—pre·sum′a·ble** *adj.* **—pre·sum′a·bly** *adv.*

pre·sump·tion (prĭ-zŭmp′shən) ►*n.* **1.** Behavior or attitude that is boldly arrogant or offensive; effrontery. **2.** A condition or basis for accepting or presuming. **—pre·sump′tive** *adj.*

pre·sump·tu·ous (prĭ-zŭmp′cho͞o-əs) ►*adj.* Going beyond what is right or proper; excessively forward. **—pre·sump′tu·ous·ly** *adv.* **—pre·sump′tu·ous·ness** *n.*

pre·sup·pose (prē′sə-pōz′) ►*v.* **-posed, -pos·ing** **1.** To believe or suppose in advance. **2.** To require or involve necessarily as an antecedent condition. **—pre·sup′po·si′tion** (-sŭp′-ə-zĭsh′ən) *n.*

pre·teen (prē′tēn′) ►*adj.* Of or designed for preadolescent children. **—pre′teen′** *n.*

pre·tend (prĭ-tĕnd′) ►*v.* **1.** To give a false appearance of; feign. **2.** To claim or allege insincerely or falsely. **3.** To make believe. **4.** To lay claim to: *pretends to gourmet tastes.* [< Lat. *praetendere.*] **—pre·tend′er** *n.*

pre·tense (prē′tĕns′, prĭ-tĕns′) ►*n.* **1a.** A false appearance or action intended to deceive. **b.** A feigned reason or excuse; pretext. **2a.** Pretentiousness; ostentation. **b.** A studied show; affectation. **3.** A claim to a right, esp. a false one. [< Lat. *praetendere,* assert.]

pre·ten·sion (prĭ-tĕn′shən) ►*n.* **1.** A specious allegation; pretext. **2.** A claim to something, such as a skill. **3.** The unwarranted assumption that one is deserving of merit; pretentiousness.

pre·ten·tious (prĭ-tĕn′shəs) ►*adj.* **1.** Claiming that or behaving as if one is deserving of merit when such is not the case. **2.** Showing or betraying an attitude of superiority. **3.** Extravagantly showy; ostentatious. See Synonyms at **showy.** —**pre·ten′tious·ly** *adv.* —**pre·ten′tious·ness** *n.*

pret·er·ite or **pret·er·it** (prĕt′ər-ĭt) ►*adj.* Of or being the verb tense that describes a past action or state. [< Lat. *praeterīre,* go by.] —**pret′er·ite** *n.*

pre·ter·nat·u·ral (prē′tər-năch′ər-əl, -năch′rəl) ►*adj.* **1.** Extraordinary. **2.** Supernatural. [< Lat. *praeter nātūrām,* beyond nature.] —**pre′ter·nat′u·ral·ly** *adv.* —**pre′ter·nat′u·ral·ness** *n.*

pre·text (prē′tĕkst′) ►*n.* An excuse given to hide the real reason for something. [Lat. *praetextum* < *praetexere,* disguise : PRE– + *texere,* weave.]

pre·text·ing (prē′tĕk′stĭng) ►*n.* Impersonating another person or otherwise engaging in misrepresentation in order to obtain someone's private personal information. —**pre′text′er** *n.*

Pre·to·ri·a (prĭ-tôr′ē-ə) The administrative capital of South Africa, in the NE part N of Johannesburg.

pret·ti·fy (prĭt′ĭ-fī′) ►*v.* **-fied, -fy·ing** To make pretty. —**pret′ti·fi·ca′tion** *n.*

pret·ty (prĭt′ē) ►*adj.* **-ti·er, -ti·est 1.** Pleasing or attractive in a graceful or delicate way. **2.** Clever; adroit: *a pretty maneuver.* **3.** Very bad; terrible: *in a pretty predicament.* **4.** Superficially attractive but lacking substance: *full of pretty phrases.* **5.** *Informal* Considerable in size or extent: *a pretty fortune.* ►*adv.* To a fair degree; moderately: *a pretty good student.* ►*v.* **-tied, -ty·ing** To make pretty. [< OE *prættig,* cunning.] —**pret′ti·ly** *adv.* —**pret′ti·ness** *n.*

pret·zel (prĕt′səl) ►*n.* A glazed, often salted biscuit usu. baked in the form of a loose knot or stick. [Ger.]

pre·vail (prĭ-vāl′) ►*v.* **1.** To be victorious or most powerful: *Shouldn't the public interest prevail over an individual?* **2.** To be most common or frequent. **3.** To use persuasion or inducement successfully. [< Lat. *praevalēre,* be stronger.] —**pre·vail′er** *n.* —**pre·vail′ing** *adj.* —**pre·vail′ing·ly** *adv.*

prev·a·lent (prĕv′ə-lənt) ►*adj.* Widely or commonly occurring or practiced. [< Lat. *praevalēre,* be stronger.] —**prev′a·lence** *n.*

pre·var·i·cate (prĭ-văr′ĭ-kāt′) ►*v.* **-cat·ed, -cat·ing 1.** To behave evasively; equivocate. **2.** To behave indecisively, usu. in delay. [Lat. *praevāricārī.*] —**pre·var′i·ca′tion** *n.* —**pre·var′i·ca′tor** *n.*

pre·vent (prĭ-vĕnt′) ►*v.* **1.** To keep from happening: *took steps to prevent the strike.* **2.** To keep (a person or thing) from doing something; impede: *prevented us from winning.* [< Lat. *praevenīre, praevent-* : PRE– + *venīre,* come.] —**pre·vent′a·ble, pre·vent′i·ble** *adj.* —**pre·ven′tion** *n.*

pre·ven·tive (prĭ-vĕn′tĭv) also **pre·ven·ta·tive** (-tə-tĭv) ►*adj.* **1.** Intended or used to prevent or hinder; acting as an obstacle. **2.** Preventing or slowing the course of illness or disease; prophylactic. —**pre·ven′tive** *n.*

pre·view also **pre·vue** (prē′vyoo′) ►*n.* **1.** An advance showing, as of a movie, before public presentation begins. **2.** The presentation of several scenes advertising a forthcoming movie. **3.** An introductory sample or overview; foretaste. —**pre′view′** *v.*

pre·vi·ous (prē′vē-əs) ►*adj.* Existing or occurring before something else; prior. [< Lat. *prae-*

vius, going before.] —**pre′vi·ous·ly** *adv.*

pre·vi·sion (prĭ-vĭzh′ən) ►*n.* **1.** A knowing in advance; foresight. **2.** A prediction.

prey (prā) ►*n.* **1a.** An animal hunted or caught by another for food. **b.** The collection of animals typically hunted by a predator. **2.** A victim. ►*v.* **1.** To hunt, catch, or eat as prey. **2.** To victimize. **3.** To exert an injurious effect. [< Lat. *praeda.*]

price (prīs) ►*n.* **1.** The sum of money asked or given for something. **2.** The cost at which something is obtained. **3.** The cost of bribing someone: *everyone has a price.* ►*v.* **priced, pric·ing 1.** To fix or establish a price for. **2.** To find out the price of. [< Lat. *pretium.*]

price·less (prīs′lĭs) ►*adj.* Of inestimable worth; invaluable.

price support ►*n.* Maintenance of prices, as of a raw material, at a certain level usu. through government intervention.

price war ►*n.* A period of intense competition in which each competitor tries to cut retail prices below those of the others.

pric·ey also **pric·y** (prī′sē) ►*adj.* **-i·er, -i·est** *Informal* Expensive.

prick (prĭk) ►*n.* **1a.** The act of pricking. **b.** The sensation of being pricked. **2.** A small mark or puncture made by a pointed object. **3.** A pointed object, such as a thorn. ►*v.* **1.** To puncture lightly. **2.** To affect with a mental or emotional pang, as of remorse. **3.** To mark or delineate on a surface by means of small punctures. —*idiom:* **prick up (one's) ears** To listen with attentive interest. [< OE *prica,* puncture.]

prick·er (prĭk′ər) ►*n.* A prickle or thorn.

prick·le (prĭk′əl) ►*n.* **1a.** A pointed outgrowth of the epidermis of a plant. **b.** A spine, thorn, or other small sharp structure. **2.** A tingling sensation. ►*v.* **-led, -ling** To tingle. [< OE *pricel.*]

prick·ly (prĭk′lē) ►*adj.* **-li·er, -li·est 1.** Having prickles. **2.** Marked by tingling. **3.** Causing trouble; thorny. —**prick′li·ness** *n.*

prickly heat ►*n.* See **heat rash.**

prickly pear ►*n.* **1.** Any of various cacti having bristly, flattened stem segments, often colorful flowers, and ovoid prickly fruit. **2.** The edible fruit of a prickly pear.

pride (prīd) ►*n.* **1.** A sense of one's proper dignity or value; self-respect. **2.** Pleasure or satisfaction taken in achievement, possession, or association. **3.** Arrogance; conceit. **4.** The best of a group or class. **5.** A group of lions. ►*v.* **prid·ed, prid·ing** To indulge (oneself) in a feeling of satisfaction. [< OE *prūd,* PROUD.] —**pride′ful** *adj.* —**pride′ful·ly** *adv.* —**pride′ful·ness** *n.*

prie-dieu (prē-dyœ′) ►*n., pl.* **-dieus** or **-dieux** (-dyœz′) A narrow, desklike kneeling bench for use at prayer. [Fr. *prie-Dieu.*]

priest (prēst) ►*n.* **1.** In many Christian churches, a member of the clergy ranking below a bishop but above a deacon. **2.** A person having the authority to perform and administer religious rites. [< OE *prēost.*] —**priest′hood′** *n.* —**priest′li·ness** *n.* —**priest′ly** *adj.*

priest·ess (prē′stĭs) ►*n.* A woman who presides over religious rites, esp. in paganism.

Priest·ley (prēst′lē), **Joseph** 1733–1804. British chemist.

prig (prĭg) ►*n.* A smugly proper or prudish person. [?] —**prig′gish** *adj.*

prim (prĭm) ▸*adj.* **prim·mer, prim·mest** Precise or proper to the point of affectation. [?] —**prim′ly** *adv.* —**prim′ness** *n.*

pri·ma·cy (prī′mə-sē) ▸*n., pl.* **-cies 1.** The state of being first or foremost. **2.** *Eccles.* The office or rank of primate. [< Med.Lat. *prīmātia,* office of primate.]

pri·ma don·na (prē′mə dŏn′ə, prĭm′ə) ▸*n.* **1.** The leading woman soloist in an opera company. **2.** A temperamental, conceited person. [Ital.]

pri·ma fa·cie (prī′mə fā′shē, -shē-ē, fā′shə) ▸*adv.* At first sight; before closer inspection. [< Lat. *prīmā faciē.*] —**pri′ma fa′cie** *adj.*

pri·mal (prī′məl) ▸*adj.* **1.** Being first in time; original. **2.** Of first importance; primary.

pri·mar·i·ly (prī-mâr′ə-lē, -mĕr′-) ▸*adv.* **1.** Chiefly; mainly. **2.** At first; originally.

pri·mar·y (prī′mĕr′ē, -mə-rē) ▸*adj.* **1.** First in rank, quality, or importance. **2.** Occurring first in time or sequence; earliest. **3a.** Not derived from anything else; original. **b.** Immediate; direct. ▸*n., pl.* **-ies 1.** One that is first in time, order, or importance. **2.** A preliminary election in which voters nominate candidates for office. [< Lat. *prīmārius.*]

primary care ▸*n.* Initial medical care given esp. by a family physician, internist, or pediatrician, usu. as part of regular, nonemergency care.

primary color ▸*n.* Any of a group of colors, such as red, yellow, and blue, which can be regarded as generating all colors.

primary school ▸*n.* **1.** A school including the first three or four grades and sometimes kindergarten. **2.** See **elementary school.**

primary tooth ▸*n.* Any of the temporary first teeth of a young mammal.

pri·mate (prī′mĭt, -māt′) ▸*n.* **1.** (prī′māt′) One of the group of mammals that includes monkeys and apes and is marked by nails on the hands and feet, a short snout, and a large brain. **2.** A bishop of highest rank in a province or country. [< Lat. *prīmus,* first.]

prime (prīm) ▸*adj.* **1.** First in quality, importance, rank, or time. **2.** *Math.* Of or being a prime number. ▸*n.* **1.** The period or phase of ideal or peak condition. See Synonyms at **bloom. 2.** *Math.* A prime number. ▸*v.* **primed, prim·ing 1.** To make ready; prepare. **2.** To load (a gun or mine) for firing. **3.** To prepare for operation, as by pouring water into a pump. **4.** To prepare (a surface) for painting by covering with an undercoat. **5.** To instruct beforehand; coach. [< Lat. *prīmus.*] —**prime′ness** *n.*

prime meridian ▸*n.* **1.** A meridian used as a reference line from which longitude east and west is measured. **2. Prime Meridian** The meridian passing through Greenwich, England, designated as the zero meridian by an international conference in 1884.

prime minister ▸*n.* **1.** A chief minister appointed by a ruler. **2.** The chief executive of a parliamentary democracy. —**prime ministership, prime ministry** *n.*

prime number ▸*n.* A positive integer that is greater than 1 and has itself and 1 as its only factors.

prim·er¹ (prĭm′ər) ▸*n.* **1.** An elementary reading textbook. **2.** A book that covers the basic elements of a subject. [< Lat. *prīmārius,* first.]

prim·er² (prī′mər) ▸*n.* **1.** A device used to detonate an explosive charge. **2.** An undercoat of paint or size applied to prepare a surface.

prime rate ▸*n.* The lowest rate of interest on bank loans at a given time and place, offered to preferred borrowers.

prime time ▸*n.* The evening hours, esp. with respect to programming on television and cable networks. —**prime′-time′** *adj.*

pri·me·val (prī-mē′vəl) ▸*adj.* Belonging to the first or earliest age or ages; original. [< Lat. *prīmaevus,* early in life.]

prim·i·tive (prĭm′ĭ-tĭv) ▸*adj.* **1.** Of or relating to an earliest or original stage or state; primeval. **2.** Simple or crude; unsophisticated. **3.** Of a nonindustrial, often tribal culture. **4.** Of or created by an artist without formal training. ▸*n.* **1.** A person belonging to a nonindustrial society. **2a.** A self-taught artist. **b.** A work of art by a primitive artist. [< Lat. *prīmitus,* at first.] —**prim′i·tive·ly** *adv.* —**prim′i·tive·ness** *n.*

prim·i·tiv·ism (prĭm′ĭ-tĭ-vĭz′əm) ▸*n.* The style characteristic of a primitive artist. —**prim′i·tiv·ist** *adj. & n.*

pri·mo·gen·i·tor (prī′mō-jĕn′ĭ-tər) ▸*n.* The earliest ancestor. [LLat. *prīmōgenitor.*]

pri·mo·gen·i·ture (prī′mō-jĕn′ĭ-chŏŏr′) ▸*n.* **1.** The state of being the firstborn or eldest child of the same parents. **2.** *Law* The right of the eldest child, esp. a son, to inherit the entire estate of one or both parents. [LLat. *prīmōgenitūra.*]

pri·mor·di·al (prī-môr′dē-əl) ▸*adj.* Being or happening first in sequence of time; original. [< Lat. *prīmōrdium,* origin.]

primp (prĭmp) ▸*v.* To dress or groom (oneself) with excessive care. [Perh. < PRIM.]

prim·rose (prĭm′rōz′) ▸*n.* Any of numerous plants having variously colored flowers. [< Med.Lat. *prīma rosa,* first rose.]

prince (prĭns) ▸*n.* **1.** A boy or man in a royal family. **2.** A hereditary ruler; king. **3.** An outstanding man in a group or class: *a merchant prince.* [< Lat. *prīnceps.*] —**prince′dom** *n.* —**prince′li·ness** *n.* —**prince′ly** *adj.*

Prince Edward Island A province of SE Canada consisting of **Prince Edward Island** in the S Gulf of St. Lawrence. Cap. Charlottetown.

prin·cess (prĭn′sĭs, -sĕs′, prĭn-sĕs′) ▸*n.* **1.** A female member of a royal family. **2.** A hereditary ruler; queen. **3.** The wife of a prince.

prin·ci·pal (prĭn′sə-pəl) ▸*adj.* First or highest in rank or importance. ▸*n.* **1a.** The head of a school. **b.** A main participant, esp. in a financial transaction. **c.** A person having a leading or starring role. **2a.** An amount of capital orig. borrowed or invested, as opposed to the interest paid or accruing on it. **b.** The most significant part of an estate. **3.** *Law* **a.** The person on behalf of whom an agent acts. **b.** The person having prime responsibility for an obligation. [< Lat. *prīnceps,* prince.] —**prin′ci·pal·ly** *adv.*

Usage: *Principal* and *principle* have no meanings in common. *Principle* is only a noun, and most of its senses refer to that which is basic or to rules and standards. *Principal* is both a noun and an adjective. As a noun it generally denotes a person who holds a high position or plays an important role. As an adjective it has the sense of "chief" or "leading."

prin·ci·pal·i·ty (prĭn′sə-păl′ĭ-tē) ▸*n., pl.* **-ties** A territory, position, or jurisdiction of a prince.

principal parts ▸*pl.n.* In traditional grammars,

the forms of the verb from which all other forms are derived.

prin·ci·ple (prĭn′sə-pəl) ►*n.* **1.** A basic truth, law, or assumption. **2a.** A rule or standard, esp. of good behavior. **b.** Moral or ethical standards or judgments. **3.** A fixed or predetermined policy. **4.** A rule or law concerning the functioning of natural phenomena or mechanical processes. **5.** A basic source. See Usage Note at **principal.** [< Lat. *prīncipium.*]

prin·ci·pled (prĭn′sə-pəld) ►*adj.* Based on, marked by, or manifesting principle.

print (prĭnt) ►*n.* **1a.** A mark or impression made by pressure. **b.** A fingerprint. **2.** Something marked with an impression. **3a.** Lettering or other impressions produced in ink. **b.** Printed state or form. **4.** A design or picture reproduced by printing. **5.** A photographic image transferred to a surface. **6.** A copy of a movie made on film or in a high resolution digital format. **7.** A fabric with a stamped dyed pattern. ►*v.* **1.** To press (e.g., a mark or design) onto a surface. **2.** To make an impression on or in (a surface). **3a.** To produce by means of pressed type, an electronic printer, or similar means, on a paper surface. **b.** To publish. **4.** To convert (a digital document or image) into a file format designed for publication. **5.** To write in characters similar to those commonly used in print. **6.** To produce a photographic image from by passing light through film onto sensitized paper. [< Lat. *premere,* press.]

print·a·ble (prĭn′tə-bəl) ►*adj.* **1.** Capable of being printed or of producing a print. **2.** Fit for publication.

print·ed circuit (prĭn′tĭd) ►*n.* An electric circuit in which the conducting connections have been printed in predetermined patterns on an insulating base.

print·er (prĭn′tər) ►*n.* **1.** One whose occupation is printing. **2.** A device that prints text or graphics on paper.

print·ing (prĭn′tĭng) ►*n.* **1.** The art, process, or business of producing printed material. **2.** Matter that is printed. **3.** All the copies of a publication, such as a book, that are printed at one time.

printing press ►*n.* A machine that transfers images onto paper or similar material.

print·mak·ing (prĭnt′mā′kĭng) ►*n.* The artistic design and making of prints, such as woodcuts. —**print′mak′er** *n.*

print·out (prĭnt′out′) ►*n.* *Comp.* Printed output.

pri·or[1] (prī′ər) ►*adj.* **1.** Preceding in time or order. **2.** Preceding in importance or value. [Lat.]

pri·or[2] (prī′ər) ►*n.* A monastic officer in charge of a priory. [< Lat., superior.]

pri·or·ess (prī′ər-ĭs) ►*n.* A nun in charge of a priory.

pri·or·i·tize (prī-ôr′ĭ-tīz′, -ŏr′-) ►*v.* **-tized, -tiz·ing** To arrange or deal with in order of importance. [PRIORIT(Y) + –IZE.] —**pri·or′i·ti·za′tion** *n.*

Usage: Although *prioritize* is often criticized for being associated with corporate or bureaucratic jargon, resistance to this verb has eroded, probably because it offers a useful way of saying "arrange according to priority." In 2008, 66 percent of the Usage Panel approved the word in

the sentence *Overwhelmed with work, the lawyer was forced to prioritize his caseload.*

pri·or·i·ty (prī-ôr′ĭ-tē, -ŏr′-) ►*n., pl.* **-ties 1.** Precedence, esp. by order of importance. **2.** An established right to precedence. **3.** Something deserving prior attention.

prior to ►*prep.* Before.

pri·or·y (prī′ə-rē) ►*n., pl.* **-ies** A monastery governed by a prior or a convent governed by a prioress.

prism (prĭz′əm) ►*n.* **1.** A polyhedron with parallel, congruent polygons as ends and parallelograms as sides. **2.** A transparent solid, usu. with triangular ends, used for separating white light passed into a spectrum. **3.** A cut-glass object, such as a pendant of a chandelier. [< Gk. *prisma.*] —**pris·mat′ic** (prĭz-măt′ĭk) *adj.*

pris·on (prĭz′ən) ►*n.* A place where persons convicted or accused of crimes are confined; jail. [< Lat. *prēnsiō,* a seizing.]

pris·on·er (prĭz′ə-nər, prĭz′nər) ►*n.* **1.** A person held in custody or captivity, esp. in a prison. **2.** One deprived of freedom of expression or action.

prisoner of war ►*n., pl.* **prisoners of war** A person taken by or surrendering to enemy forces in wartime.

pris·sy (prĭs′ē) ►*adj.* **-si·er, -si·est** Excessively prim and proper. [Perh. blend of PRI(M) and (SI)SSY.] —**pris′si·ness** *n.*

Priš·ti·na (prĭsh′tə-nä′) The capital of Kosovo, in the east-central part.

pris·tine (prĭs′tēn′, prĭ-stēn′) ►*adj.* **1.** Remaining in a pure state; uncorrupted. **2.** Of or typical of the earliest time or condition; primitive or original. [Lat. *prīstinus.*]

prith·ee (prĭth′ē, prĭth′ē) ►*interj. Archaic* Please. [< (*I*) *pray thee.*]

pri·va·cy (prī′və-sē) ►*n.* **1.** The condition of being secluded from others. **2.** The state of being free from public attention or unsanctioned intrusion.

pri·vate (prī′vĭt) ►*adj.* **1.** Secluded from the sight, presence, or intrusion of others. **2.** Of or confined to the individual; personal. **3.** Not available for public use, control, or participation. **4.** Belonging to a particular person or persons. **5.** Not holding an official or public position. **6.** Intimate; secret. ►*n.* Any of the lowest enlisted ranks, as in the US Army. [< Lat. *prīvātus,* not in public life.] —**pri′vate·ly** *adv.* —**pri′vate·ness** *n.*

private enterprise ►*n.* Business activities unregulated by state ownership or control.

pri·va·teer (prī′və-tîr′) ►*n.* **1.** A ship privately owned and manned but authorized to attack and capture enemy vessels. **2.** Such a ship's commander or one of its crew.

pri·va·tion (prī-vā′shən) ►*n.* **1.** Lack of the basic necessities or comforts of life. **2.** The condition resulting from such lack. [< Lat. *prīvāre,* deprive.]

pri·va·tize (prī′və-tīz′) ►*v.* **-tized, -tiz·ing** To change (e.g., an industry) from governmental or public ownership to private enterprise. —**pri′va·ti·za′tion** *n.*

priv·et (prĭv′ĭt) ►*n.* A shrub having opposite leaves and clusters of white flowers, widely used for hedges. [?]

priv·i·lege (prĭv′ə-lĭj, prĭv′lĭj) ►*n.* **1.** A special advantage, immunity, or benefit granted to or enjoyed by an individual, class, or caste. **2.** Protection from being forced to disclose confidential communications in certain relationships, as between attorney and client. ▸*v.* **-leged, -leg·ing** To grant a privilege to. [< Lat. *prīvilēgium.*]

priv·i·leged (prĭv′ə-lĭjd, prĭv′lĭjd) ▸*adj.* **1.** Having privileges. **2.** Entailing or carrying certain privileges: *a reporter who has a privileged relationship with the actor.*

priv·y (prĭv′ē) ▸*adj.* **1.** Made a participant in something secret. **2.** Belonging to a person, such as the British sovereign, in a private rather than official capacity. ▸*n., pl.* **-ies** An outhouse. [< Lat. *prīvātus,* private.]

prize¹ (prīz) ▸*n.* **1.** Something offered or won as an award for superiority or victory, as in a contest or competition. **2.** Something worth striving for or aspiring to. ▸*adj.* **1.** Offered or given as a prize. **2.** Given or worthy of a prize. **3.** Outstanding. ▸*v.* **prized, priz·ing** To value highly; esteem. [< ME *pris,* PRICE.]

prize² (prīz) ▸*n.* Something, esp. an enemy ship captured during wartime. [< OFr. *prise.*]

prize³ (prīz) ▸*v.* **prized, priz·ing** To move with a lever; pry. [< ME *prise,* instrument for prying.]

prize·fight (prīz′fīt′) ▸*n.* A match fought between professional boxers for money. —**prize′fight′er** *n.* —**prize′fight′ing** *n.*

prize·win·ner (prīz′wĭn′ər) ▸*n.* One that wins a prize. —**prize′win′ning** *adj.*

pro¹ (prō) ▸*n., pl.* **pros 1.** An argument in favor of something. **2.** One who takes an affirmative position. ▸*adv.* In favor; affirmatively. [< Lat. *prō,* for.]

pro² (prō) *Informal* ▸*n., pl.* **pros 1.** A professional. **2.** An expert. ▸*adj.* Professional.

pro-¹ ▸*pref.* **1.** Acting in place of: *pronoun.* **2.** Supporting; favoring: *prorevolutionary.* [< Lat. *prō,* for.]

pro-² ▸*pref.* **1.** Precursor of: *procaine* **2.** Anterior; in front of: *prognathous.* [< Gk. *pro.*]

prob·a·bil·i·ty (prŏb′ə-bĭl′ĭ-tē) ▸*n., pl.* **-ties 1.** The quality or condition of being probable; likelihood. **2.** A probable situation, condition, or event. **3.** *Statistics* A number, ranging from 0 to 1, expressing either the projected likelihood that a specific event will occur or the ratio of the number of actual occurrences to the number of possible observances.

prob·a·ble (prŏb′ə-bəl) ▸*adj.* **1.** Likely to happen or to be true. **2.** Likely but uncertain; plausible. [< Lat. *probāre,* prove.] —**prob′a·bly** *adv.*

pro·bate (prō′bāt′) *Law* ▸*n.* The process of establishing the validity of a will. ▸*v.* **-bat·ed, -bat·ing** To establish the validity of (a will). [< Lat. *probāre,* prove.]

pro·ba·tion (prō-bā′shən) ▸*n.* **1.** A trial period in which a person's fitness, as for membership in a group, is tested. **2.** *Law* A criminal sentence consisting of a term of imprisonment that is suspended provided certain conditions are met. [< Lat. *probāre,* test.] —**pro·ba′tion·al** *adj.* —**pro·ba′tion·ar′y** *adj.*

pro·ba·tion·er (prō-bā′shə-nər) ▸*n.* A person on probation.

pro·ba·tive (prō′bə-tĭv) ▸*adj.* **1.** Furnishing evidence or proof. **2.** Serving to test or prove.

probe (prōb) ▸*n.* **1.** A slender, flexible instrument used to explore a wound or body cavity. **2a.** An exploratory action, esp., one designed to investigate a remote or unknown region. **b.** The act of searching with an instrument. **c.** A penetrating inquiry. See Synonyms at **inquiry.** ▸*v.* **probed, prob·ing 1.** To explore with or as if with a probe. **2.** To delve into; investigate. [< Lat. *probāre,* test.]

pro·bi·ty (prō′bĭ-tē) ▸*n.* Integrity; honesty. [< Lat. *probus,* upright.]

prob·lem (prŏb′ləm) ▸*n.* **1.** A question to be considered, solved, or answered. **2.** A situation, matter, or person that is hard to deal with or understand. ▸*adj.* Difficult to deal with or control: *a problem child.* [< Gk. *problēma.*]

prob·lem·at·ic (prŏb′lə-măt′ĭk) also **prob·lem·at·i·cal** (-ĭ-kəl) ▸*adj.* **1.** Posing a problem. **2.** Open to doubt; dubious or unsettled. —**prob′lem·at′i·cal·ly** *adv.*

pro bo·no (prō bō′nō) ▸*adj.* Provided free or at a low cost to serve the public good. [Lat. *prō bonō (publicō),* for the (public) good.]

pro·bos·cis (prō-bŏs′ĭs, -kĭs) ▸*n., pl.* **-cis·es** or **-bos·ci·des** (-bŏs′-ĭ-dēz′) **1.** A long flexible snout or trunk, as of an elephant. **2.** A human nose, esp. a prominent one. [< Gk. *proboskis.*]

pro·caine (prō′kān′) ▸*n.* A white crystalline powder, $C_{13}H_{20}N_2O_2$, used chiefly in its hydrochloride form as a local anesthetic. [PRO-² + (CO)CAINE.]

pro·ce·dure (prə-sē′jər) ▸*n.* **1.** A way of doing something. **2.** A series of steps to an end. **3.** A set of established forms or methods for conducting legal or business affairs. [< OFr. *proceder,* PROCEED.] —**pro·ce′dur·al** *adj.* —**pro·ce′dur·al·ly** *adv.*

pro·ceed (prō-sēd′, prə-) ▸*v.* **1.** To continue, esp. after an interruption. **2.** To begin to carry on an action or a process. **3.** To progress in an orderly manner. **4.** To come from a source; originate. See Synonyms at **stem¹. 5.** To institute and pursue legal action. ▸*n.* **pro·ceeds** (prō′sēdz′) The amount of money derived from a commercial or fundraising venture. [< Lat. *prōcēdere.*]

pro·ceed·ing (prō-sē′dĭng, prə-) ▸*n.* **1.** A course of action; procedure. **2. proceedings a.** Events; doings. **b.** A record of business carried on by an organization. **3.** often **proceedings** Legal action; litigation.

proc·ess¹ (prŏs′ĕs′, prō′sĕs′) ▸*n.* **1.** A series of actions, changes, or functions bringing about a result. **2.** Progress; passage: *the process of time.* **3.** *Law* **a.** The use of the law courts as a means of seeking redress. **b.** The set of events that constitute a legal proceeding. **4.** *Law* The means of compelling a person to appear in court. **5.** *Biol.* An outgrowth of tissue: *a bony process.* ▸*v.* **1.** To put through the steps of a prescribed procedure. **2.** To prepare, treat, or convert by subjecting to a special process. **3.** *Comp.* To perform operations on (data). [< Lat. *prōcēdere, prōcess-,* advance.]

proc·ess² (prə-sĕs′) ▸*v.* To move along in a procession. [< PROCESSION.]

pro·ces·sion (prə-sĕsh′ən) ▸*n.* A group of persons, vehicles, or objects moving along in an orderly, formal manner.

pro·ces·sion·al (prə-sĕsh′ə-nəl) ▸*n.* Music intended to be played or sung when the clergy enter a church at the beginning of a service.

proc·es·sor (prŏs′ĕs′ər, prō′sĕs′-) ►*n.* **1.** One that processes, esp. an apparatus for preparing, treating, or converting material. **2.** *Comp.* **a.** A computer. **b.** A central processing unit.

pro-choice (prō-chois′) ►*adj.* Favoring legalized abortion as an option for an unwanted pregnancy.

pro·claim (prō-klām′, prə-) ►*v.* **1.** To announce officially and publicly; declare. See Synonyms at **announce. 2.** To state emphatically; affirm. [< Lat. *prōclāmāre.*] —**proc′la·ma′tion** (prŏk′-lə-mā′shən) *n.*

pro·cliv·i·ty (prō-klĭv′ĭ-tē) ►*n., pl.* **-ties** A natural propensity or inclination. [< Lat. *prōclīvis,* inclined : PRO–[1] + *clīvus,* slope.]

pro·con·sul (prō-kŏn′səl) ►*n.* **1.** An ancient Roman provincial governor of consular rank. **2.** A high administrator in certain modern colonial empires. [< Lat. *prō cōnsule,* in place of the consul.] —**pro·con′su·lar** (-sə-lər) *adj.*

pro·cras·ti·nate (prō-krăs′tə-nāt′, prə-) ►*v.* **-nat·ed, -nat·ing** To put off doing something, esp. out of habitual carelessness or laziness. [Lat. *prōcrāstināre.*] —**pro·cras′ti·na′tion** *n.* —**pro·cras′ti·na′tor** *n.*

pro·cre·ate (prō′krē-āt′) ►*v.* **-at·ed, -at·ing** To beget offspring; reproduce. [Lat. *prōcreāre.*] —**pro′cre·a′tion** *n.* —**pro′cre·a′tive** *adj.* —**pro′cre·a′tor** *n.*

Pro·crus·te·an also **pro·crus·te·an** (prō-krŭs′tē-ən) ►*adj.* Showing no regard for individual differences or special circumstances. [After *Procrustes,* a mythical Greek giant.]

proc·tor (prŏk′tər) ►*n.* A dormitory and examination supervisor in a school. ►*v.* To supervise (an examination). [< Lat. *prōcūrātor,* PROCURA-TOR.] —**proc·to′ri·al** (-tôr′ē-əl) *adj.*

proc·u·ra·tor (prŏk′yə-rā′tər) ►*n.* **1.** One who is authorized to act on behalf of another. **2.** An administrator, esp. a civil or provincial administrator of ancient Rome. [< Lat. *prōcūrāre,* take care of.]

pro·cure (prō-kyŏŏr′, prə-) ►*v.* **-cured, -cur·ing 1.** To get by special effort; obtain or acquire. **2.** To bring about; effect. **3.** To obtain (a sexual partner) for another. [< Lat. *prōcūrāre,* manage.] —**pro·cur′a·ble** *adj.* —**pro·cure′ment** *n.* —**pro·cur′er** *n.*

prod (prŏd) ►*v.* **prod·ded, prod·ding 1.** To jab or poke, as with a pointed object. **2.** To goad to action; incite. ►*n.* **1.** A pointed object used to prod. **2.** An incitement; stimulus. [?] —**prod′der** *n.*

prod·i·gal (prŏd′ĭ-gəl) ►*adj.* **1.** Rashly or wastefully extravagant. **2.** Profuse; lavish. See Synonyms at **profuse.** [< Lat. *prōdigus* : *prō-,* forth + *agere,* drive.] —**prod′i·gal** *n.* —**prod′i·gal′i·ty** (-găl′ĭ-tē) *n.* —**prod′i·gal·ly** *adv.*

pro·di·gious (prə-dĭj′əs) ►*adj.* **1.** Impressively great in size, force, or extent. **2.** Extraordinary; marvelous. —**pro·di′gious·ly** *adv.*

prod·i·gy (prŏd′ə-jē) ►*n., pl.* **-gies 1.** A person with exceptional talents or powers. **2.** Something extraordinary or rare; marvel. [< Lat. *prōdigium,* portent.]

pro·duce (prə-dōōs′, -dyōōs′, prō-) ►*v.* **-duced, -duc·ing 1.** To bring forth; yield. **2a.** To create by physical or mental effort. **b.** To manufacture. **3.** To cause; give rise to. **4.** To bring forth; exhibit. **5.** To supervise and finance the making of: *produce a play.* **6.** *Math.* To extend (an area or volume) or lengthen (a line). ►*n.* (prŏd′-ōōs, prō′dōōs) Farm products, esp. fresh fruits and vegetables, considered as a group. [< Lat. *prōdūcere.*] —**pro·duc′er** *n.*
    Syns: bear, yield v.

prod·uct (prŏd′əkt) ►*n.* **1.** Something produced naturally or by human effort. **2.** A direct result; consequence. **3.** *Math.* The result obtained by performing multiplication. [< Lat. *prōductus,* p.part. of *prōdūcere,* produce.]

pro·duc·tion (prə-dŭk′shən, prō-) ►*n.* **1.** The act or process of producing. **2.** Something produced; product. **3.** An amount or quantity produced; output. **4.** A presentation of a theatrical work.

pro·duc·tive (prə-dŭk′tĭv, prō-) ►*adj.* **1.** Producing or capable of producing: *a productive farm; a productive employee.* **2.** Marked by abundant production or achievement. See Synonyms at **fertile.** —**pro·duc′tive·ly** *adv.* —**pro′duc·tiv′i·ty** (prō′dŭk-tĭv′ĭ-tē, prŏd′-ək-), **pro·duc′tive·ness** *n.*

pro·em (prō′ĕm′) ►*n.* An introduction; preface. [< Gk. *prooimion.*]

pro·fane (prō-fān′, prə-) ►*adj.* **1.** Marked by contempt or irreverence for what is sacred. **2.** Nonreligious; secular. **3.** Vulgar; coarse. ►*v.* **-faned, -fan·ing 1.** To treat with irreverence. **2.** To put to an improper, unworthy, or degrading use; abuse. [< Lat. *profānus.*] —**prof′a·na′tion** (prŏf′ə-nā′shən) *n.* —**pro·fan′a·to′ry** (-făn′ə-tôr′ē) *adj.* —**pro·fane′ness** *n.*

pro·fan·i·ty (prō-făn′ĭ-tē, prə-) ►*n., pl.* **-ties 1.** The condition or quality of being profane. **2.** Obscene or irreverent language.

pro·fess (prə-fĕs′, prō-) ►*v.* **1.** To affirm openly; declare. **2.** To make a pretense of. **3.** To claim skill in or knowledge of. **4.** To affirm belief in. [< Lat. *profitērī.*] —**pro·fess′ed·ly** *adv.*

pro·fes·sion (prə-fĕsh′ən) ►*n.* **1.** An occupation requiring training and specialized study. **2.** The body of qualified persons in an occupation or field: *the teaching profession.* **3.** An act of professing; declaration.

pro·fes·sion·al (prə-fĕsh′ə-nəl) ►*adj.* **1.** Of or engaged in a profession. **2.** Engaging in a given activity as a source of livelihood. ►*n.* A person following a profession. —**pro·fes′sion·al·ly** *adv.*

pro·fes·sion·al·ism (prə-fĕsh′ə-nə-lĭz′əm) ►*n.* Professional status, methods, character, or standards.

pro·fes·sion·al·ize (prə-fĕsh′ə-nə-līz′) ►*v.* **-ized, -iz·ing** To make professional. —**pro·fes′sion·al·i·za′tion** *n.*

pro·fes·sor (prə-fĕs′ər) ►*n.* **1.** A college or university teacher of the highest rank. **2.** A teacher or instructor. —**pro′fes·so′ri·al** (prō′fĭ-sôr′ē-əl, prŏf′ĭ-) *adj.* —**pro′fes·so′ri·al·ly** *adv.* —**pro·fes′sor·ship′** *n.*

prof·fer (prŏf′ər) ►*v.* To offer for acceptance. [< OFr. *profrir.*] —**prof′fer** *n.*

pro·fi·cient (prə-fĭsh′ənt) ►*adj.* Expert in an art, vocation, or area of learning. [< Lat. *prōficere,* progress.] —**pro·fi′cien·cy** *n.*

pro·file (prō′fīl′) ►*n.* **1.** A side view of an object or a structure, esp. of the human head. **2.** An outline; silhouette. See Synonyms at **outline. 3.** Degree of exposure to public notice; visibility: *kept a low profile.* **4.** A brief biographical essay. [< Ital. *profilare,* draw in outline.] —**pro′file** *v.*

prof·it (prŏf′ĭt) ►*n.* **1.** An advantageous gain or return; benefit. **2.** often **profits** Financial gain from a transaction, investment, or business activity, usu. calculated as income in excess of costs. ►*v.* **1.** To make a gain or profit. **2.** To derive advantage; benefit. [< Lat. *prōfectus.*] **—prof′it·a·bil′i·ty** *n.* **—prof′it·a·ble** *adj.* **—prof′it·a·bly** *adv.*

prof·it·eer (prŏf′ĭ-tîr′) ►*n.* One who makes excessive profits on goods in short supply. **—prof′it·eer′** *v.*

prof·li·gate (prŏf′lĭ-gĭt, -gāt′) ►*adj.* **1.** Given to or marked by licentiousness: *a profligate nightlife.* **2.** Given to or marked by reckless waste: *a profligate spender.* ►*n.* A profligate person. [< Lat. *prōflīgāre,* to ruin.] **—prof′li·ga·cy** (-gə-sē) *n.*

pro for·ma (prō fôr′mə) ►*adj.* Done as a formality; perfunctory. [NLat. *prō formā.*]

pro·found (prə-found′, prō-) ►*adj.* **-er, -est** **1.** Having great insight: *a profound thinker.* **2.** Deeply felt; intense: *profound contempt.* **3.** Thoroughgoing; far-reaching. **4.** Penetrating beyond what is superficial or obvious. **5.** Unqualified: *a profound silence.* **6.** Situated at, extending to, or coming from a great depth; deep. [< Lat. *profundus.*] **—pro·found′ly** *adv.* **—pro·fun′di·ty** (-fŭn′dĭ-tē) *n.*

pro·fuse (prə-fyōōs′, prō-) ►*adj.* **1.** Plentiful; copious. **2.** Giving or given freely and abundantly. [< Lat. *profūsus,* p.part. of *profundere,* pour forth.] **—pro·fuse′ly** *adv.* **—pro·fuse′ness** *n.* **—pro·fu′sion** (-fyōō′zhən) *n.*

Syns: exuberant, lavish, lush, luxuriant, prodigal Ant: spare adj.

pro·gen·i·tor (prō-jĕn′ĭ-tər) ►*n.* **1.** A direct ancestor. See Synonyms at **ancestor. 2.** An originator of a line of descent. **3.** An originator; founder. [< Lat. *prōgenitor.*]

prog·e·ny (prŏj′ə-nē) ►*n.* Offspring or descendants. [< Lat. *prōgeniēs.*]

pro·ges·ter·one (prō-jĕs′tə-rōn′) ►*n.* A steroid hormone secreted by the ovary before implantation of the fertilized ovum. [PRO-¹ + GES(TATION) + STER(OL) + -*one,* suff.]

prog·na·thous (prŏg′nə-thəs, prŏg-nā′-) ►*adj.* Having jaws or mouthparts that project forward to a marked degree. [< PRO-² + Gk. *gnathos,* jaw.] **—prog′na·thism** *n.*

prog·no·sis (prŏg-nō′sĭs) ►*n., pl.* **-ses** (-sēz) A prediction, esp. of the probable course and outcome of a disease. [< Gk.]

prog·nos·tic (prŏg-nŏs′tĭk) ►*adj.* Of or useful in prognosis. ►*n.* **1.** A forecast or prediction. **2.** A portent; omen. [< Gk. *prognōstikos,* foreknowing.]

prog·nos·ti·cate (prŏg-nŏs′tĭ-kāt′) ►*v.* **-cat·ed, -cat·ing** To predict according to present indications or signs; foretell. [< PRO-² + Gk. **—prog·nos′ti·ca′tion** *n.* **—prog·nos′ti·ca′tor** *n.*

pro·gram (prō′grăm′, -grəm) ►*n.* **1a.** A listing of the order of events and other information for a public presentation. **b.** The presentation itself. **2.** A scheduled radio or television show. **3.** An ordered list of events or procedures to be followed; schedule. **4.** A system of services, usu. designed to meet a social need: *a mentorship program.* **5.** A course of academic study; curriculum. **6.** A set of coded instructions that enables a machine, esp. a computer, to perform a desired sequence of operations.

►*v.* **-grammed, -gram·ming** or **-gramed, -gram·ing 1.** To include or schedule in a program. **2.** To design a program for. **3.** To provide (a computer) with a set of instructions. [< Gk. *programma,* public notice : PRO-² + *graphein,* write.] **—pro′gram′ma·ble** *adj.* **—pro′gram·mat′ic** (-grə-măt′ĭk) *adj.*

pro·gramme (prō′grăm′, -grəm) ►*n. & v. Chiefly Brit.* Var. of **program.**

pro·gram·mer or **pro·gram·er** (prō′grăm′ər) ►*n.* One who programs, esp. one who writes computer programs.

pro·gram·ming language (prō′grăm′ĭng, -grə-mĭng) ►*n.* An artificial language that can be translated into machine language and executed by a computer.

prog·ress (prŏg′rĕs′, -rəs, prō′grĕs′) ►*n.* **1.** Forward or onward movement, as toward a destination. **2.** Development or advancement, as toward a goal. ►*v.* **pro·gress** (prə-grĕs′) **1.** To move forward or onward. **2.** To develop or advance. **—*idiom:* in progress** Going on; under way: *a work in progress.* [< Lat. *prōgressus.*]

pro·gres·sion (prə-grĕsh′ən) ►*n.* **1.** Movement or change from one member of a continuous series to the next. **2.** *Math.* A series of numbers or quantities in which there is always the same relation between each quantity and the one succeeding it.

pro·gres·sive (prə-grĕs′ĭv) ►*adj.* **1.** Moving forward; advancing. **2.** Proceeding in steps. **3.** Open to or favoring new policies or methods. **4.** Increasing in rate as the taxable amount increases. **5.** Tending to spread or become more severe. **6.** *Gram.* Designating a verb form that expresses an action or condition in progress. ►*n.* A person who is open to or favors new policies or methods. **—pro·gres′sive·ly** *adv.* **—pro·gres′sive·ness** *n.* **—pro′gres·siv′i·ty** (prō′grĕ-sĭv′ĭ-tē, prŏg′rə-) *n.*

pro·hib·it (prō-hĭb′ĭt) ►*v.* **1.** To forbid by authority. See Synonyms at **forbid. 2.** To prevent; preclude. [< Lat. *prohibēre, prohibit-.*]

pro·hi·bi·tion (prō′ə-bĭsh′ən) ►*n.* **1.** The act of prohibiting. **2.** The forbidding by law of making, transporting, or selling alcoholic beverages. **—pro′hi·bi′tion·ist** *n.*

pro·hib·i·tive (prō-hĭb′ĭ-tĭv) also **pro·hib·i·to·ry** (-tôr′ē) ►*adj.* **1.** Prohibiting; forbidding. **2.** So high or burdensome as to discourage purchase or use. **—pro·hib′i·tive·ly** *adv.*

proj·ect (prŏj′ĕkt′, -ĭkt) ►*n.* **1.** An undertaking requiring concerted effort. **2.** A plan or proposal for accomplishing something. See Synonyms at **plan.** ►*v.* **pro·ject** (prə-jĕkt′) **1.** To thrust or extend outward or forward. See Synonyms at **bulge. 2.** To throw forward; hurl. **3.** To cause (an image) to appear on a surface by the controlled direction of light. **4.** To direct (one's voice) so as to be heard clearly at a distance. **5.** To estimate based on present data: *project next year's expenses.* [< Lat. *prōiectus,* p.part. of *prōicere,* throw out.] **—pro·jec′tion** *n.*

pro·jec·tile (prə-jĕk′təl, -tīl′) ►*n.* **1.** A fired, thrown, or otherwise propelled object, such as a bullet. **2.** A self-propelled missile, such as a rocket.

pro·jec·tor (prə-jĕk′tər) ►*n.* A device that projects an image onto a screen or other surface. **—pro·jec′tion·ist** *n.*

pro·kar·y·ote (prō-kăr′ē-ōt′) ►*n.* A single-celled organism that lacks a nuclear membrane, such as a bacterium. [< PRO-² + Gk. *karuon,* kernel.] —**pro·kar′y·ot′ic** (-ŏt′ĭk) *adj.*

Pro·kof·iev (prə-kôf′ē-ĕf, -kôf′yĭf), **Sergei Sergeyevich** 1891–1953. Russian composer.

pro·lapse (prō-lăps′) ►*v.* **-lapsed, -laps·ing** To fall or slip out of place, as a bodily organ. [Lat. *prōlābī, prōlāps-,* fall down.] —**pro′lapse′** *n.*

pro·le·gom·e·non (prō′lĭ-gŏm′ə-nŏn′, -nən) ►*n., pl.* **-na** (-nə) An introductory essay or remark. [Gk.]

pro·le·tar·i·an (prō′lĭ-târ′ē-ən) ►*n.* A member of the proletariat. [< Lat. *prōlētārius,* of the lowest class of Roman citizens.] —**pro′le·tar′i·an** *adj.* —**pro′le·tar′i·an·ism** *n.*

pro·le·tar·i·at (prō′lĭ-târ′ē-ĭt) ►*n.* The class of industrial wage earners who must earn their living by selling their labor. [Fr. *prolétariat.*]

pro-life (prō-līf′) ►*adj.* Advocating legal protection of human embryos or fetuses, esp. by opposing legalized abortion. —**pro-lif′er** *n.*

pro·lif·er·ate (prə-lĭf′ə-rāt′) ►*v.* **-at·ed, -at·ing** **1.** To grow or multiply by rapidly producing new parts, cells, or offspring. **2.** To increase or spread. [< Fr. *prolifère,* procreative.] —**pro·lif′er·a′tion** *n.*

pro·lif·ic (prə-lĭf′ĭk) ►*adj.* **1.** Producing offspring or fruit in abundance. **2.** Producing or marked by abundant works or results. See Synonyms at **fertile.** [< Lat. *prōlēs,* offspring.]

pro·lix (prō-lĭks′, prō′lĭks′) ►*adj.* Tediously long and wordy. See Synonyms at **wordy.** [< Lat. *prōlixus,* abundant.] —**pro·lix′i·ty** *n.*

pro·logue (prō′lôg′, -lŏg′) ►*n.* **1.** An introduction or preface, as to a play. **2.** An introductory chapter, as to a novel. **3.** An introductory act or event. [< Gk. *prologos.*]

pro·long (prə-lông′, -lŏng′) ►*v.* To lengthen in duration; protract. [< LLat. *prōlongāre.*] —**pro′lon·ga′tion** (prō′lông-gā′shən, -lŏng-) *n.*

prom (prŏm) ►*n.* A formal dance held for a high-school or college class. [< PROMENADE.]

prom·e·nade (prŏm′ə-nād′, -näd′) ►*n.* **1a.** A leisurely walk; stroll. **b.** A public place for such walking. **2.** A march of all the guests at the opening of a ball. [< Fr. *promener,* take for a walk.] —**prom′e·nade′** *v.*

Pro·me·the·us (prə-mē′thē-əs, -thyŏŏs′) ►*n.* *Gk. Myth.* A Titan who stole fire from Olympus and gave it to humankind.

pro·me·thi·um (prə-mē′thē-əm) ►*n.* *Symbol* **Pm** A radioactive rare-earth element. At. no. 61. See table at **element.** [< PROMETHEUS.]

prom·i·nence (prŏm′ə-nəns) ►*n.* **1.** The quality or condition of being prominent. **2.** Something prominent; projection.

prom·i·nent (prŏm′ə-nənt) ►*adj.* **1.** Projecting outward or upward. **2.** Immediately noticeable; conspicuous. **3.** Widely known; eminent. [< Lat. *prōminēre,* jut out.]

pro·mis·cu·ous (prə-mĭs′kyŏŏ-əs) ►*adj.* **1.** Indiscriminate in the choice of sexual partners. **2a.** Showing little forethought or critical judgment. **b.** Consisting of diverse, unrelated parts; confused. [< Lat. *prōmiscuus.*] —**prom′is·cu′i·ty** (prŏm′ĭs-kyŏŏ′ĭ-tē, prō′mĭ-) *n.* —**pro·mis′cu·ous·ly** *adv.*

prom·ise (prŏm′ĭs) ►*n.* **1a.** A declaration assuring that one will or will not do something; vow. **b.** Something promised. **2.** Indication

of something favorable to come, esp. future excellence or success. ►*v.* **-ised, -is·ing** **1.** To commit oneself by a promise to do or give; pledge. **2.** To afford a basis for expecting: *clouds that promise rain.* [< Lat. *prōmittere, prōmiss-,* promise.] —**prom′is·er** *n.*
  Syns: pledge, swear, vow **v.**

prom·is·ing (prŏm′ĭ-sĭng) ►*adj.* Likely to develop favorably. —**prom′is·ing·ly** *adv.*

prom·is·so·ry (prŏm′ĭ-sôr′ē) ►*adj.* Containing or involving a promise.

promissory note ►*n.* A negotiable written promise to pay a specified sum of money on demand or at a particular time.

prom·on·to·ry (prŏm′ən-tôr′ē) ►*n., pl.* **-ries** A high ridge of land or rock jutting out into a body of water. [Lat. *prōmontorium.*]

pro·mote (prə-mōt′) ►*v.* **-mot·ed, -mot·ing** **1.** To raise in position or rank. **2.** To contribute to the progress or growth of; further. See Synonyms at **advance.** **3.** To advocate: *promote a constitutional amendment.* **4.** To attempt to sell or popularize: *promote a new product.* [< Lat. *prōmovēre, prōmōt-.*] —**pro·mo′tion** *n.* —**pro·mo′tion·al** *adj.*

pro·mot·er (prə-mō′tər) ►*n.* **1.** An active supporter or advocate. **2.** A financial and publicity organizer, as of a boxing match.

prompt (prŏmpt) ►*adj.* **-er, -est** **1.** On time; punctual. **2.** Done without delay. ►*v.* **1.** To move to act; spur or incite. **2.** To give rise to; inspire. **3.** To give a cue to, as in a theatrical performance. ►*n.* **1.** A reminder or cue. **2.** *Comp.* A symbol that appears on a monitor to indicate that the computer is ready to receive input. [< Lat. *prōmptus,* ready.] —**prompt′er** *n.* —**prompt′ness** *n.*

prom·ul·gate (prŏm′əl-gāt′, prō-mŭl′gāt′) ►*v.* **-gat·ed, -gat·ing** **1.** To make known to the public; popularize. See Synonyms at **announce.** **2.** To put (e.g., a law) into effect by formal public announcement. [Lat. *prōmulgāre.*] —**prom′ul·ga′tion** *n.* —**prom′ul·ga′tor** *n.*

pron. ►*abbr.* **1.** pronoun **2.** pronunciation

prone (prōn) ►*adj.* **1.** Lying with the front or face downward. **2.** Having a tendency; inclined. [< Lat. *prōnus,* leaning forward.] —**prone** *adv.*

prong (prông, prŏng) ►*n.* **1.** A thin, pointed, projecting part. **2.** A branch or division. [ME *pronge,* forked instrument.]

prong·horn (prông′hôrn′, prŏng′-) ►*n., pl.* **-horn** or **-horns** A small mammal of W North American plains that resembles an antelope and has small forked horns.

pro·noun (prō′noun′) ►*n.* One of a class of words, such as *she* or *whom,* that function as substitutes for nouns or noun phrases.

pro·nounce (prə-nouns′) ►*v.* **-nounced, -nounc·ing** **1.** To utter or articulate (a word or speech sound). **2.** To declare officially or formally. [< Lat. *prōnūntiāre.*] —**pro·nounce′a·ble** *adj.* —**pro·nun′ci·a′tion** (-nŭn′sē-ā′shən) *n.*

pro·nounced (prə-nounst′) ►*adj.* Strongly marked; distinct. —**pro·nounc′ed·ly** (-noun′-sĭd-lē) *adv.*

pro·nounce·ment (prə-nouns′mənt) ►*n.* A formal or authoritative declaration or statement.

pron·to (prŏn′tō) ►*adv.* *Informal* Without delay; quickly. [Sp. < Lat. *prōmptus.*]

pro·nun·ci·a·men·to (prō-nŭn′sē-ə-mĕn′tō)

▸*n., pl.* **-tos** or **-toes** An official declaration; proclamation. [Sp.]

proof (pro͞of) ▸*n.* **1.** The evidence or argument that establishes an assertion as true. **2.** Convincing demonstration of something. **3.** Determination of the quality of something by testing; trial. **4.** The alcoholic strength of a liquor, expressed as twice the percentage of alcoholic content. **5a.** A trial sheet of printed material. **b.** A trial impression, as of an engraved plate. **6.** A trial photographic print. ▸*adj.* **1.** Fully resistant; impervious: *bulletproof.* **2.** Of standard alcoholic strength. ▸*v.* **1.** To make a trial impression of. **2.** To proofread (copy). [< LLat. *proba.*]

proof·read (pro͞of′rēd′) ▸*v.* To read (copy or proof) in order to find errors and mark corrections. —**proof′read′er** *n.*

prop[1] (prŏp) ▸*n.* A support, esp. one placed under or against something to keep it from falling. [ME *proppe.*] —**prop** *v.*

prop[2] (prŏp) ▸*n.* A theatrical property.

prop[3] (prŏp) ▸*n. Informal* A propeller.

prop·a·gan·da (prŏp′ə-găn′də) ▸*n.* **1.** The systematic propagation of a doctrine or cause. **2.** Material disseminated by the advocates of a doctrine or cause. [< Lat. *prōpāgāre,* propagate.] —**prop′a·gan′dist** *n.* —**prop′a·gan′dize′** *v.*

prop·a·gate (prŏp′ə-gāt′) ▸*v.* **-gat·ed, -gat·ing** **1.** To reproduce or cause to reproduce; breed. **2.** To make known; publicize. **3.** *Phys.* To cause (e.g., a wave) to move in some direction or through a medium. [Lat. *prōpāgāre.*] —**prop′·a·ga′tion** *n.* —**prop′a·ga′tive** *adj.* —**prop′a·ga′tor** *n.*

pro·pane (prō′pān′) ▸*n.* A colorless gas, C_3H_8, found in natural gas and petroleum and widely used as a fuel.

pro·pel (prə-pĕl′) ▸*v.* **-pelled, -pel·ling** **1.** To cause to move forward or onward. See Synonyms at **push.** **2.** To cause to develop or progress. [< Lat. *prōpellere.*]

pro·pel·lant also **pro·pel·lent** (prə-pĕl′ənt) ▸*n.* Something, such as an explosive charge or a rocket fuel, that propels. —**pro·pel′lant** *adj.*

pro·pel·ler also **pro·pel·lor** (prə-pĕl′ər) ▸*n.* A machine for propelling an aircraft or boat, consisting of a revolving power-driven shaft with radiating blades.

pro·pen·si·ty (prə-pĕn′sĭ-tē) ▸*n., pl.* **-ties** An innate inclination; tendency. [< Lat. *prōpendēre,* be inclined.]

prop·er (prŏp′ər) ▸*adj.* **1.** Suitable; appropiate. **2.** Called for by rules or conventions; correct. **3.** Strictly following rules or conventions; seemly. **4.** Characteristically belonging to a person or thing: *regained its proper shape.* **5.** Strictly speaking: *the city proper.* [< Lat. *proprius,* one's own.] —**prop′er·ly** *adv.* —**prop′er·ness** *n.*

proper fraction ▸*n.* A fraction in which the numerator is less than the denominator.

proper noun ▸*n.* A noun that is the name of a particular person, place, or thing.

prop·er·tied (prŏp′ər-tēd) ▸*adj.* Owning land or securities as a principal source of revenue.

prop·er·ty (prŏp′ər-tē) ▸*n., pl.* **-ties 1a.** Something owned; a possession. **b.** A piece of real estate. **2.** An article, except costumes and scenery, that is used in a play or movie. **3.** An attribute, characteristic, or quality. [< Lat. *proprietās,* ownership.]

proph·e·cy (prŏf′ĭ-sē) ▸*n., pl.* **-cies 1.** An inspired utterance of a prophet. **2.** A prediction. [< Gk. *prophēteia.*]

proph·e·sy (prŏf′ĭ-sī′) ▸*v.* **-sied, -sy·ing 1.** To reveal by divine inspiration. **2.** To predict. See Synonyms at **foretell.** [< OFr. *prophecie,* PROPHECY.] —**proph′e·si′er** *n.*

proph·et (prŏf′ĭt) ▸*n.* **1.** A person who speaks by divine inspiration. **2.** A predictor; soothsayer. **3. Prophets** See table at **Bible. 4. Prophet** *Islam* Muhammad. Used with *the.* [< Gk. *prophētēs.*]

proph·et·ess (prŏf′ĭ-tĭs) ▸*n.* **1.** A woman who speaks by divine inspiration. **2.** A woman predictor.

proph·et·ic (prə-fĕt′ĭk) also **pro·phet·i·cal** (-ĭ-kəl) ▸*adj.* Of or characteristic of a prophet or prophecy. —**pro·phet′i·cal·ly** *adv.*

pro·phy·lac·tic (prō′fə-lăk′tĭk, prŏf′ə-) ▸*adj.* Acting to defend against or prevent something, esp. disease; protective. ▸*n.* A prophylactic agent or device, such as a condom. [< Gk. *prophulaktikos.*] —**pro′phy·lac′ti·cal·ly** *adv.*

pro·phy·lax·is (prō′fə-lăk′sĭs, prŏf′ə-) ▸*n., pl.* **-lax·es** (-lăk′sēz′) Prevention of or protective treatment for disease. [< Gk. *prophulaktikos,* prophylactic.]

pro·pin·qui·ty (prə-pĭng′kwĭ-tē) ▸*n.* Proximity; nearness. [< Lat. *propinquus,* near.]

pro·pi·ti·ate (prō-pĭsh′ē-āt′) ▸*v.* **-at·ed, -at·ing** To conciliate; appease. [Lat. *propitiāre.*] —**pro·pi′ti·a′tion** *n.* —**pro·pi′ti·a′tor** *n.* —**pro·pi′ti·a·to′ry** (-ə-tôr′ē) *adj.*

pro·pi·tious (prə-pĭsh′əs) ▸*adj.* **1.** Favorable; auspicious. **2.** Merciful or kindly: *a propitious deity.* [< Lat. *propitius.*] —**pro·pi′tious·ly** *adv.*

pro·po·nent (prə-pō′nənt) ▸*n.* One who argues in support of something; advocate. [< Lat. *prōpōnere,* propose.]

pro·por·tion (prə-pôr′shən) ▸*n.* **1.** A part or amount considered in relation to the whole. **2.** A relationship between things or parts of things with respect to comparative magnitude, quantity, or degree. **3.** A relationship between quantities such that if one varies then another varies as a multiple of the first. **4.** Harmonious relation; symmetry. **5.** often **proportions** Dimensions; size. ▸*v.* **1.** To adjust so that proper relations between parts are attained. **2.** To form with symmetry. [< Lat. *prōportiō.*] —**pro·por′tion·al** *adj.* —**pro·por′tion·al·ly** *adv.* —**pro·por′tion·ate** *adj.*

pro·pose (prə-pōz′) ▸*v.* **-posed, -pos·ing 1.** To put forward for consideration; suggest. **2.** To nominate (a person) for a position, office, or membership. **3.** To offer (a toast to be drunk). **4.** To make known as one's intention. **5.** To make an offer, esp. of marriage. [< Lat. *prōpōnere.*] —**pro·pos′al** *n.*

prop·o·si·tion (prŏp′ə-zĭsh′ən) ▸*n.* **1.** A plan suggested for acceptance; proposal. **2.** A matter to be dealt with; task. **3.** An offer of a private bargain, esp. a request for sexual relations. **4.** A subject for discussion or analysis. —**prop′o·si′tion·al** *adj.*

pro·pound (prə-pound′) ▸*v.* To put forward for consideration; set forth. [< Lat. *prōpōnere.*]

pro·pri·e·tar·y (prə-prī′ĭ-tĕr′ē) ▸*adj.* **1.** Relating to a proprietor or to ownership. **2.** Privately owned, as a business. **3.** Owned by a private individual or corporation under a trademark or patent. [< LLat. *proprietārius.*]

pro·pri·e·tor (prə-prī′ĭ-tər) ►*n.* An owner, as of a business. —**pro·pri′e·tor·ship′** *n.*

pro·pri·e·tress (prə-prī′ĭ-trĭs) ►*n.* A woman who is an owner, as of a business.

pro·pri·e·ty (prə-prī′ĭ-tē) ►*n., pl.* **-ties 1a.** Conformity to conventional standards of behavior or morality. **b. proprieties** Socially correct usages or behaviors. **2.** The quality of being proper; appropriateness. [< OFr. *propriete,* property.]

props (prŏps) ►*pl.n. Slang* Due respect; proper recognition. Often used in expressions of gratitude: *Props to my friends for helping me out.* [African American Vernacular English, short for *propers,* proper respect, recognition.]

pro·pul·sion (prə-pŭl′shən) ►*n.* **1.** The process of driving or propelling. **2.** A driving or propelling force. [< Lat. *prōpellere,* drive forward.] —**pro·pul′sive** *adj.*

pro ra·ta (prō rä′tə, răt′ə, rä′tə) ►*adv.* In proportion. [Lat. *prō ratā (parte),* according to the calculated (share).]

pro·rate (prō-rāt′, prō′rāt′) ►*v.* **-rat·ed, -rat·ing** To divide, distribute, or assess proportionately. [< PRO RATA.] —**pro·ra′tion** *n.*

pro·rogue (prō-rōg′) ►*v.* **-rogued, -rogu·ing** To discontinue a session of (e.g., a parliament). [< Lat. *prōrogāre,* postpone.] —**pro′ro·ga′tion** *n.*

pro·sa·ic (prō-zā′ĭk) ►*adj.* **1.** Matter-of-fact; straightforward. **2.** Lacking in imagination and spirit; dull. [LLat. *prōsaīcus,* in prose.] —**pro·sa′i·cal·ly** *adv.*

pro·sce·ni·um (prō-sē′nē-əm, prə-) ►*n.* The area of a modern theater located between the curtain and the orchestra. [< Gk. *proskēnion.*]

pro·sciut·to (prō-shōō′tō) ►*n., pl.* **-ti** (-tē) **-tos** An aged Italian ham that is salted, cured by drying, and usu. served in thin slices. [Ital. < VLat. **perexsūctus,* thoroughly dried out.]

pro·scribe (prō-skrīb′) ►*v.* **-scribed, -scrib·ing** **1.** To prohibit. See Synonyms at **forbid. 2.** To denounce or condemn. **3.** To outlaw (a person). [< Lat. *prōscrībere.*] —**pro·scrip′tion** (-skrĭp′shən) *n.*

pro se (prō sā) ►*adv.* Without representation by an attorney. [Lat. *prō sē,* for himself, for herself, for themselves.]

prose (prōz) ►*n.* Ordinary speech or writing, without metrical structure. [< Lat. *prōsa (ōrātiō),* straightforward (discourse).]

pros·e·cute (prŏs′ĭ-kyōōt′) ►*v.* **-cut·ed, -cut·ing** **1a.** To initiate or conduct a criminal case against. **b.** To initiate or conduct a (civil case or legal action). **2.** To pursue (e.g., a task) until completion. [< Lat. *prōsequī, prōsecūt-,* follow up.] —**pros′e·cu′tion** *n.* —**pros′e·cu′tor** *n.*

pros·e·lyte (prŏs′ə-līt′) ►*n.* A new convert to a doctrine or religion. ►*v.* **-lyt·ed, -lyt·ing** To proselytize. [< Gk. *prosēlutos.*]

pros·e·ly·tize (prŏs′ə-lĭ-tīz′) ►*v.* **-tized, -tiz·ing** To convert (a person) from one belief or faith to another. —**pros′e·ly·ti·za′tion** *n.* —**pros′e·ly·tiz′er** *n.*

pro·sim·i·an (prō-sĭm′ē-ən) ►*n.* Any of various primates of the suborder that includes lemurs, lorises, and tarsiers. —**pro·sim′i·an** *adj.*

pros·o·dy (prŏs′ə-dē) ►*n.* The study of the metrical structure of verse. [< Gk. *prosōidia,* song sung to music.] —**pro·sod′ic** (prə-sŏd′ĭk) *adj.*

pros·pect (prŏs′pĕkt′) ►*n.* **1.** Something expected; possibility. **2. prospects** Chances, esp. of success. **3a.** A potential customer or purchaser. **b.** A candidate likely to succeed. **4.** The direction in which an object faces. **5.** Something presented to the eye; scene. ►*v.* To search about or explore (a region) for mineral deposits or oil. [< Lat. *prōspectus,* view : *prō-,* forward + *specere,* look at.] —**pros′pec′tor** *n.*

pro·spec·tive (prə-spĕk′tĭv) ►*adj.* Likely to happen or become. —**pro·spec′tive·ly** *adv.*

pro·spec·tus (prə-spĕk′təs) ►*n.* A formal summary of a proposed venture or project, sent out to prospective buyers, investors, or participants. [Lat. *prōspectus,* view; see PROSPECT.]

pros·per (prŏs′pər) ►*v.* To be successful, esp. financially. [< Lat. *prosperāre.*]

pros·per·i·ty (prŏ-spĕr′ĭ-tē) ►*n.* The condition of being prosperous.

pros·per·ous (prŏs′pər-əs) ►*adj.* **1.** Successful. **2.** Well-to-do; well-off. **3.** Propitious; favorable. —**pros′per·ous·ly** *adv.*

pros·tate (prŏs′tāt′) ►*n.* A gland in male mammals at the base of the bladder that controls release of urine and secretes a fluid which is a major constituent of semen. [< Gk. *prostatēs* : *pro-,* in front + *histanai,* set, place.]

pros·the·sis (prŏs-thē′sĭs) ►*n., pl.* **-ses** (-sēz) An artificial device used to replace a missing body part, such as a limb. [Gk., addition.] —**pros·thet′ic** (-thĕt′ĭk) *adj.*

prosthesis
athlete wearing a prosthetic leg used for running

pros·ti·tute (prŏs′tĭ-tōōt′, -tyōōt′) ►*n.* One who engages in sex acts in exchange for money. ►*v.* **-tut·ed, -tut·ing** **1.** To offer (oneself or another) for sexual hire. **2.** To sell (oneself or one's talent) for an unworthy purpose. [Lat. *prōstitūta* : *prō-,* in front + *statuere,* cause to stand.] —**pros′ti·tu′tion** *n.*

pros·trate (prŏs′trāt′) ►*adj.* **1.** Lying face down, as in submission or adoration. **2.** Stretched at full length. **3.** Physically or emotionally incapacitated; overcome. ►*v.* **-trat·ed, -trat·ing** **1.** To place (oneself) in a prostrate position. **2.** To throw down flat. **3.** To crush or enervate; overcome. [< Lat. *prōstrātus,* p.part. of *prōsternere,* throw down.] —**pros·tra′tion** *n.*

pros·y (prō′zē) ►*adj.* **-i·er, -i·est 1.** Prosaic. **2.** Dull; commonplace. —**pros′i·ness** *n.*

prot- ►*pref.* Var. of **proto-**.

pro·tac·tin·i·um (prō′tăk-tĭn′ē-əm) ►*n. Symbol* **Pa** A rare, extremely toxic, radioactive metallic element. At. no. 91. See table at **element.** [< PROT(O)–.]

pro·tag·o·nist (prō-tăg′ə-nĭst) ►*n.* **1.** The main character in a drama or other literary work. **2.** A leading or principal figure, as of a cause. [Gk. *prōtagōnistēs* : PROT(O)– + *agōnistēs*, actor (< *agein*, to drive, lead).]

Pro·tag·o·ras (prō-tăg′ər-əs) fl. 5th cent. BC. Greek philosopher. —**Pro·tag′o·re′an** (-ə-rē′- ən) *adj.*

pro·te·an (prō′tē-ən, prō-tē′-) ►*adj.* Readily taking on varied shapes, forms, or meanings. [< PROTEUS.]

pro·tect (prə-tĕkt′) ►*v.* **1.** To keep from damage, attack, theft, or injury. **2.** To keep from being exposed to risk. [< Lat. *prōtegere*.] —**pro·tec′tive** *adj.*

pro·tec·tion (prə-tĕk′shən) ►*n.* **1.** The act of protecting or the condition of being protected. **2.** One that protects.

pro·tec·tion·ism (prə-tĕk′shə-nĭz′əm) ►*n.* The protection of domestic producers by impeding or limiting, as by tariffs, the importation of foreign goods and services. —**pro·tec′tion·ist** *n.*

pro·tec·tor (prə-tĕk′tər) ►*n.* **1.** One that protects; guard or guardian. **2. Protector** One who rules a kingdom during the minority of a sovereign. —**pro·tec′tor·ship′** *n.*

pro·tec·tor·ate (prə-tĕk′tər-ĭt) ►*n.* **1a.** A relationship of protection and partial control by a superior power over a dependent country or region. **b.** The protected country or region. **2. Protectorate** The government, office, or term of a protector.

pro·té·gé also **pro·te·ge** (prō′tə-zhā′, prō′- tə-zhā′) ►*n.* One whose welfare, training, or career is promoted by an influential person. [Fr. < p.part. of *protéger*, protect.]

pro·tein (prō′tēn′, -tē-ĭn) ►*n.* Any of a group of complex organic compounds that are made of amino acids, occur in all living cells, and are essential for the growth and repair of animal tissue. [< LGk. *prōteios*, of the first quality.]

pro tem (prō tĕm′) ►*adv.* Pro tempore.

pro tem·po·re (tĕm′pə-rē) ►*adv.* For the time being. [Lat. *prō tempore*.]

pro·te·ome (prō′tē-ōm′) ►*n.* The set of proteins present in an organism under a given set of environmental conditions. [PROTE(IN) + (GEN)OME.]

pro·test (prə-tĕst′, prō-, prō′tĕst′) ►*v.* **1.** To express a strong objection to (something). **2.** To participate in a public demonstration in opposition to (something). **3.** To promise or affirm (something) earnestly, as after being doubted. ►*n.* (prō′tĕst′) **1.** A formal declaration of disapproval or objection issued by a person or group. **2.** An organized effort to show disapproval of something, esp. a government policy. [< Lat. *prōtestārī*.] —**prot′es·ta′tion** (prŏt′ĭ-stā′shən, prō′tĭ-) *n.* —**pro·test′er** *n.*

Prot·es·tant (prŏt′ĭ-stənt) ►*n.* **1.** A Christian belonging to a denomination descending from those that broke away from the Roman Catholic Church in the 16th cent. **2.** (*also* prə-tĕs′- tənt) **protestant** One who makes a declaration or avowal. —**Prot′es·tant·ism** *n.*

Pro·te·us (prō′tē-əs, -tyōōs′) ►*n.* Gk. Myth. A sea god able to change his shape at will.

pro·ti·um (prō′tē-əm, prō′shē-) ►*n.* The most

abundant isotope of hydrogen, having one proton in the nucleus.

proto– or **prot–** ►*pref.* Earliest; original: *proto-type.* [< Gk. *prōtos*, first.]

pro·to·col (prō′tə-kôl′, -kōl′, -kŏl′) ►*n.* **1a.** The forms of ceremony and etiquette observed by diplomats and heads of state. **b.** A code of correct conduct. **2.** The first copy of a treaty or other such document before its ratification. **3.** A preliminary draft or record of a transaction. **4.** The plan for a course of medical treatment or for a scientific experiment. **5.** A standard procedure for regulating data transmission between computers. [< LGk. *prōtokollon*, table of contents.]

Pro·to-In·do-Eur·o·pe·an (prō′tō-ĭn′dō- yŏor′ə-pē′ən) ►*n.* The earliest reconstructed stage of Indo-European.

pro·ton (prō′tŏn′) ►*n.* A stable, positively charged subatomic particle found in all atomic nuclei. [Gk. *prōton.*]

pro·to·plasm (prō′tə-plăz′əm) ►*n.* The complex, semifluid substance that constitutes the living matter of plant and animal cells. —**pro′- to·plas′mic** (-plăz′mĭk) *adj.*

pro·to·type (prō′tə-tīp′) ►*n.* **1.** An original type or form serving as a basis or standard. **2.** An original, full-scale, and usu. working model of a new or redesigned product. **3.** A typical example of a class or category. ►*v.* To make a prototype of (a product). —**pro′to·typ′ic** (-tĭp′ĭk), **pro′to·typ′i·cal** *adj.*

pro·to·zo·an (prō′tə-zō′ən) ►*n.*, *pl.* **-zo·ans** or **-zo·a** (-zō′ə) Any of numerous chiefly single-celled eukaryotic organisms, most of which move about freely and ingest food, such as amoebas. —**pro′to·zo′an, pro′to·zo′ic** *adj.*

pro·tract (prō-trăkt′, prə-) ►*v.* To draw out or lengthen; prolong. [Lat. *prōtrahere, prōtract-*.] —**pro·trac′tion** *n.*

pro·trac·tile (prō-trăk′təl, -tīl′, prə-) ►*adj.* Capable of being protracted; extensible.

pro·trac·tor (prō′trăk′tər, prə-trăk′-) ►*n.* A semicircular instrument for measuring and constructing angles.

pro·trude (prō-trōōd′) ►*v.* **-trud·ed, -trud·ing** To push or jut outward; project. See Synonyms at **bulge.** [Lat. *prōtrūdere*.] —**pro·tru′sion** *n.* —**pro·tru′sive** *adj.*

pro·tu·ber·ance (prō-tōō′bər-əns, -tyōō′-, prə-) ►*n.* Something, such as a bulge, knob, or swelling, that protrudes. [< Lat. *prōtūberāre*, swell out.] —**pro·tu′ber·ant** *adj.*

proud (proud) ►*adj.* **-er, -est 1.** Feeling pleasurable satisfaction. **2.** Occasioning pride. **3.** Feeling or showing self-respect. **4.** Filled with or showing excessive self-esteem. **5.** Of great dignity; honored. **6.** Majestic; magnificent. [< LLat. *prōde*, advantageous.] —**proud′ly** *adv.*

Prou·dhon (prōō-dôN′), **Pierre Joseph** 1809– 65. French anarchist.

Proust (prōōst), **Marcel** 1871–1922. French writer. —**Proust′i·an** *adj.*

Prov. ►*abbr.* province

prove (prōōv) ►*v.* **proved** or **prov·en** (prōō′- vən), **prov·ing 1.** To establish the truth or validity of by argument or evidence. **2.** To be shown to be such; turn out. [< Lat. *probāre*, test.] —**prov′a·ble** *adj.*

Usage: Both *proved* and *proven* are now well

established in written English as participles: *He has proved* (or *proven*) *his point. Proven* is more common as an adjective before a noun: *a proven talent.*

prov·e·nance (prŏv′ə-nəns, -näns′) ►*n.* Place of origin. [< Lat. *prōvenīre*, originate : *prō-*, forth + *venīre*, come.]

Pro·ven·çal (prō′vən-säl′, -vän-, prŏv′ən-) ►*n.* **1.** The Romance language traditionally spoken in S France, esp. the dialect spoken in Provence. **2.** A native or inhabitant of Provence. —**Pro′ven·çal** *adj.*

Pro·vence (prə-väns′, prô-väns′) A historical region and former province of SE France bordering the Mediterranean Sea.

prov·en·der (prŏv′ən-dər) ►*n.* **1.** Dry food, such as hay, for livestock. **2.** Food or provisions. [< LLat. *praebenda*, stipend.]

pro·ve·nience (prə-vēn′yəns, -vē′nē-əns) ►*n.* A source or origin. [< PROVENANCE.]

prov·erb (prŏv′ûrb′) ►*n.* **1.** A short pithy saying in widespread use that expresses a basic truth or practical precept. **2.** **Proverbs** *(takes sing. v.)* See table at **Bible.** [< Lat. *prōverbium.*] —**pro·ver′bi·al** (prə-vûr′bē-əl) *adj.*

pro·vide (prə-vīd′) ►*v.* **-vid·ed, -vid·ing 1.** To make available (something needed or desired). **2.** To have as an available or desirable feature. **3.** To set down as a stipulation. **4.** To take meas-ures in preparation: *provide against emergencies.* **5.** To supply means of subsistence: *provide for one's family.* [< Lat. *prōvidēre*, provide for : *prō-*, forward + *vidēre*, see.] —**pro·vid′er** *n.*

pro·vid·ed (prə-vī′dĭd) ►*conj.* On the condition; if.

prov·i·dence (prŏv′ĭ-dəns, -dĕns′) ►*n.* **1.** Care or preparation in advance; foresight. **2.** Prudent management; economy. **3.** Divine care and guardianship. **4. Providence** God.

Providence The capital of RI, in the NE part.

prov·i·dent (prŏv′ĭ-dənt, -dĕnt′) ►*adj.* **1.** Providing for future needs or events. **2.** Frugal; economical. —**prov′i·dent·ly** *adv.*

prov·i·den·tial (prŏv′ĭ-dĕn′shəl) ►*adj.* **1.** Of or resulting from divine providence. **2.** Fortunate; opportune.

pro·vid·ing (prə-vī′dĭng) ►*conj.* On the condition; provided.

prov·ince (prŏv′ĭns) ►*n.* **1.** A territory governed as an administrative or political unit of a country or empire. **2. provinces** Areas of a country situated away from the capital or population center. **3.** An area of knowledge, activity, or interest. See Synonyms at **field.** [< Lat. *prōvincia.*]

pro·vin·cial (prə-vĭn′shəl) ►*adj.* **1.** Of or relating to a province. **2.** Limited in perspective; narrow and self-centered. —**pro·vin′cial·ism** *n.* —**pro·vin′cial·ly** *adv.*

prov·ing ground (prōō′vĭng) ►*n.* A place for testing new devices or theories.

pro·vi·sion (prə-vĭzh′ən) ►*n.* **1a.** The act of providing or supplying something: *the provision of rations.* **b.** The act of making preparations for a future event: *The provision for retirement requires planning.* **2a.** Something provided: *A fire escape is an important provision in a building.* **b. provisions** Necessary supplies, such as food and clothing, as for a journey. **3.** A preparatory action or measure: *made provisions for riding out the storm.* **4.** A particular requirement in a

law, rule, agreement, or document. ►*v.* To supply with provisions. [< Lat. *prōvidēre, prōvīs-*, PROVIDE.] —**pro·vi′sion·er** *n.*

pro·vi·sion·al (prə-vĭzh′ə-nəl) ►*adj.* Provided or serving only for the time being. See Synonyms at **temporary.**

pro·vi·so (prə-vī′zō) ►*n., pl.* **-sos** or **-soes** A clause in a document imposing a qualification, condition, or restriction. [< Med.Lat. *prōvīsō (quod)*, provided (that).]

Pro·vo (prō′vō) A city of N-central UT SSE of Salt Lake City.

prov·o·ca·tion (prŏv′ə-kā′shən) ►*n.* **1.** The act of provoking or inciting. **2.** Something that provokes.

pro·voc·a·tive (prə-vŏk′ə-tĭv) ►*adj.* Tending to provoke. —**pro·voc′a·tive·ness** *n.*

pro·voke (prə-vōk′) ►*v.* **-voked, -vok·ing 1.** To incite to anger or resentment. **2.** To stir to action or feeling. **3.** To give rise to; evoke: *provoke laughter.* [< Lat. *prōvocāre*, call out.]

pro·vo·lo·ne (prō′və-lō′nē, prō′və-lōn′) ►*n.* A hard, usu. smoked Italian cheese. [Ital.]

pro·vost (prō′vōst′, -vəst, prŏv′əst) ►*n.* A high administrative officer, as of a university. [< Lat. *praepositus*, superintendent.]

pro·vost marshal (prō′vō) ►*n.* The head of a unit of military police.

prow (prou) ►*n.* The forward part of a ship's hull; bow. [< Gk. *prōira.*]

prow·ess (prou′ĭs) ►*n.* **1.** Superior skill or ability. **2.** Superior strength and courage, esp. in battle. [< OFr. *prou*, brave.]

prowl (proul) ►*v.* To roam (through) stealthily, as in search of prey. —**idiom: on the prowl** Actively looking for something. [ME *prollen.*] —**prowl** *n.* —**prowl′er** *n.*

prox·i·mate (prŏk′sə-mĭt) ►*adj.* **1.** Direct or immediate: *a proximate cause.* **2.** Close in space, time, or order; near. See Synonyms at **close.** [< Lat. *proximāre*, come near.]

prox·im·i·ty (prŏk-sĭm′ĭ-tē) ►*n.* Nearness; closeness. [< Lat. *proximus*, nearest.]

prox·y (prŏk′sē) ►*n., pl.* **-ies 1.** One appointed or authorized to act for another. **2.** Written authorization to act in place of another. [< Med. Lat. *prōcūrātia.*]

prude (prōōd) ►*n.* One who is too concerned with being or seeming to be proper, modest, or righteous. [Fr.] —**prud′er·y** *n.* —**prud′ish** *adj.* —**prud′ish·ly** *adv.* —**prud′ish·ness** *n.*

pru·dent (prōōd′nt) ►*adj.* **1.** Wise in practical matters; exercising good judgment: *a prudent manager of money.* **2.** Marked by care and foresight: *a prudent investment.* [< Lat. *prūdēns.*] —**pru′dence** *n.* —**pru·den′tial** (prōō-dĕn′shəl) *adj.* —**pru′dent·ly** *adv.*

prune¹ (prōōn) ►*n.* A partially dried plum. [< Lat. *prūnum*, plum.]

prune² (prōōn) ►*v.* **pruned, prun·ing 1.** To cut off parts or branches of (a plant) to improve shape or growth. **2.** To remove or cut out as superfluous. [< OFr. *proignier.*]

pru·ri·ent (prōōr′ē-ənt) ►*adj.* Appealing to or arousing immoderate sexual desire. [< Lat. *prūrīre*, itch.] —**pru′ri·ence** *n.*

Prus·sia (prŭsh′ə) A historical region and former kingdom of N-central Europe including present-day N Germany and Poland. —**Prus′sian** *adj. & n.*

pry¹ (prī) ►*v.* **pried** (prīd), **pry·ing** To look

or inquire closely or curiously; snoop. [ME *prien*.]

pry² (prī) ►*v.* **pried** (prīd), **pry·ing 1.** To raise, move, or force open with a lever. **2.** To obtain with difficulty. ►*n., pl.* **pries** (prīz) A tool, as a crowbar, for prying. [< PRIZE³.]

PS ►*abbr.* **1.** postscript **2.** public school

psalm (säm) ►*n.* **1.** A sacred song; hymn. **2. Psalms** *(takes sing. v.)* See table at **Bible.** [< Gk. *psalmos.*] —**psalm′ist** *n.*

psalm·o·dy (sä′mə-dē, săl′mə-) ►*n., pl.* **-dies 1.** The singing of psalms in divine worship. **2.** A collection of psalms. [< Gk. *psalmōidia*, singing to the harp : *psalmos*, psalm + *ōidē*, *aoidē*, SONG.]

Psal·ter also **psal·ter** (sôl′tər) ►*n.* A book containing the book of Psalms or a particular version of, musical setting for, or selection from it. [< Gk. *psaltērion*, harp.]

pseudo– or **pseud–** ►*pref.* False or counterfeit: *pseudonym.* [< Gk. *pseudēs*, false.]

pseu·do·nym (sŏod′n-ĭm′) ►*n.* A fictitious name. —**pseu·don′y·mous** (sōō-dŏn′ə-məs) *adj.*

psf ►*abbr.* pounds per square foot

psi¹ (sī, psī) ►*n.* The 23rd letter of the Greek alphabet. [< Gk. *psei.*]

psi² ►*abbr.* pounds per square inch

psit·ta·co·sis (sĭt′ə-kō′sĭs) ►*n.* An infectious disease of parrots and related birds that is communicable to humans. [< Gk. *psittakos*, parrot + –OSIS.]

pso·ri·a·sis (sə-rī′ə-sĭs) ►*n.* A skin disease marked by recurring inflammation and scaly patches. [Gk. *psōriasis.*]

PST ►*abbr.* Pacific Standard Time

psych (sīk) *Informal* ►*v.* **1.** To put into the right frame of mind. **2.** To undermine psychologically. ►*n.* Psychology.

psy·che (sī′kē) ►*n.* **1.** The spirit or soul. **2.** In psychoanalysis, the mind functioning as the center of thought, emotion, and behavior. [< Gk. *psukhē.*]

psy·che·del·ic (sī′kĭ-dĕl′ĭk) ►*adj.* Marked by or generating hallucinations and distortions of perception. [< PSYCHE + Gk. *dēloun*, make visible.] —**psy′che·del′ic** *n.*

psy·chi·a·try (sĭ-kī′ə-trē, sī-) ►*n.* The branch of medicine that deals with the diagnosis, treatment, and prevention of mental and emotional disorders. —**psy′chi·at′ric** (sī′kē-ăt′rĭk) *adj.* —**psy·chi′a·trist** *n.*

psy·chic (sī′kĭk) ►*n.* See **medium** (sense 5). ►*adj.* **1.** Of the human mind or psyche: *psychic trauma.* **2.** Of or possessing extraordinary mental powers, such as ESP or mental telepathy.

psycho– or **psych–** ►*pref.* Mind; mental: *psychology.* [< Gk. *psukhē*, spirit.]

psy·cho·ac·tive (sī′kō-ăk′tĭv) ►*adj.* Affecting the mind or mental processes.

psy·cho·a·nal·y·sis (sī′kō-ə-năl′ĭ-sĭs) ►*n.* **1.** A method of psychological therapy in which free association, dream interpretation, and analysis of feelings and behavior are used to investigate mental and emotional disorders. **2.** Psychotherapy incorporating the techniques of psychoanalysis. —**psy′cho·an′a·lyst** (-ăn′ə-lĭst) *n.* —**psy′cho·an′a·lyt′ic** (-ăn′ə-lĭt′ĭk), **psy′cho·an′a·lyt′i·cal** *adj.* —**psy′cho·an′a·lyze′** (-līz′) *v.*

psy·cho·dra·ma (sī′kə-drä′mə, -drăm′ə) ►*n.* A

psychotherapeutic technique in which people are assigned roles to be played spontaneously within a dramatic context in order to understand the behavior of people with whom they have difficult interactions.

psy·cho·gen·ic (sī′kə-jĕn′ĭk) ►*adj.* Originating in the mind or in mental or emotional processes. —**psy′cho·gen′i·cal·ly** *adv.*

psy·chol·o·gist (sī-kŏl′ə-jĭst) ►*n.* **1.** A specialist in psychology. **2.** See **clinical psychologist.**

psy·chol·o·gy (sī-kŏl′ə-jē) ►*n., pl.* **-gies 1.** The science that deals with mental processes and behavior. **2.** The emotional and behavioral characteristics of an individual or group. —**psy′cho·log′i·cal** (sī′kə-lŏj′ĭ-kəl) *adj.* —**psy′cho·log′i·cal·ly** *adv.*

psy·cho·met·rics (sī′kə-mĕt′rĭks) ►*n. (takes sing. v.)* The branch of psychology that deals with testing and measuring psychological variables such as intelligence.

psy·chom·e·try (sī-kŏm′ĭ-trē) ►*n.* See **psychometrics.**

psy·cho·mo·tor (sī′kō-mō′tər) ►*adj.* Of or relating to movement or muscular activity associated with mental processes.

psy·cho·path (sī′kə-păth′) ►*n.* A person who engages repeatedly in criminal and antisocial behavior without remorse or empathy for those victimized. —**psy′cho·path′ic** *adj.* —**psy′cho·path′i·cal·ly** *adv.* —**psy·chop′a·thy** (sī-kŏp′ə-thē) *n.*

psy·cho·pa·thol·o·gy (sī′kō-pə-thŏl′ə-jē, -pă-) ►*n.* The study of the origin, growth, and symptoms of mental or behavioral disorders. —**psy′cho·path′o·log′i·cal** (-păth′ə-lŏj′ĭ-kəl), **psy′cho·path′o·log′ic** *adj.* —**psy′cho·pa·thol′o·gist** *n.*

psy·cho·phar·ma·col·o·gy (sī′kō-fär′mə-kŏl′ə-jē) ►*n.* The study of the actions, effects, and development of psychoactive drugs. —**psy′cho·phar′ma·col′o·gist** *n.*

psy·cho·sex·u·al (sī′kō-sĕk′shōō-əl) ►*adj.* Of or relating to the mental and emotional aspects of sexuality.

psy·cho·sis (sī-kō′sĭs) ►*n., pl.* **-ses** (-sēz) A mental state marked by loss of contact with reality, disorganized speech and behavior, and often by hallucinations or delusions, seen in certain mental illnesses and other medical disorders. —**psy·chot′ic** (-kŏt′ĭk) *adj. & n.*

psy·cho·so·mat·ic (sī′kō-sō-măt′ĭk) ►*adj.* **1.** Of or relating to a disorder having physical symptoms but originating from mental or emotional causes. **2.** Of or concerned with the influence of the mind on the body, esp. with respect to disease.

psy·cho·ther·a·py (sī′kō-thĕr′ə-pē) ►*n.* The treatment of mental and emotional disorders through the use of psychological techniques. —**psy′cho·ther′a·peu′tic** (-pyōō′tĭk) *adj.* —**psy′cho·ther′a·pist** *n.*

psy·cho·tro·pic (sī′kə-trō′pĭk, -trŏp′ĭk) ►*adj.* Having an altering effect on perception, emotion, or behavior. Used esp. of a drug.

PT ►*abbr.* **1.** Pacific Time **2.** part-time **3.** physical therapy

pt. ►*abbr.* **1.** part **2.** pint **3.** point **4.** also **Pt.** port

PTA ►*abbr.* Parent Teacher Association

ptar·mi·gan (tär′mĭ-gən) ►*n., pl.* **-gan** or **-gans**

A grouse of northern regions having feathered legs and feet. [< Sc.Gael. *tarmachan*.]

PT boat (pē-tē′) ►*n.* A fast, lightly armed vessel used to torpedo enemy shipping. [P(ATROL) + t(*orpedo*) *boat*.]

pter·o·dac·tyl (tĕr′ə-dăk′təl) ►*n.* An extinct flying reptile of the Mesozoic Era. [Gk. *pteron*, feather, wing + *daktulos*, finger.]

pter·o·saur (tĕr′ə-sôr′) ►*n.* Any of an order of extinct flying reptiles that includes the pterodactyls. [Gk. *pteron*, wing + *sauros*, lizard.]

Ptol·e·ma·ic system (tŏl′ə-mā′ĭk) ►*n.* The astronomical system of Ptolemy, in which Earth is at the center of the universe.

Ptol·e·my¹ (tŏl′ə-mē) An Egyptian dynasty of Macedonian kings (323–30 BC), including **Ptolemy I** (367?–283?) and **Ptolemy XV** (47–30).

Ptol·e·my² (tŏl′ə-mē) fl. 2nd cent. AD. Alexandrian Greek astronomer, mathematician, and geographer.

pto·maine (tō′mān′, tō-mān′) ►*n.* A basic nitrogenous organic compound produced by bacterial putrefaction of protein. [< Gk. *ptōma*, corpse.]

PTSD ►*abbr.* posttraumatic stress disorder

pub (pŭb) ►*n.* A tavern; bar. [< PUBLIC HOUSE.]

pu·ber·ty (pyōō′bər-tē) ►*n.* The stage of adolescence in which an individual becomes physiologically capable of sexual reproduction. [< Lat. *pūbertās*.] —**pu′ber·tal** *adj.*

pu·bes·cent (pyōō-bĕs′ənt) ►*adj.* **1.** Reaching or having recently reached puberty. **2.** Covered with short hairs or soft down. [< Lat. *pūbēscere*, reach puberty.] —**pu·bes′cence** *n.*

pu·bic (pyōō′bĭk) ►*adj.* Of or located in the region of the pubis or the pubes.

pu·bis (pyōō′bĭs) ►*n., pl.* **-bes** (-bēz) The forward portion of either of the hipbones, at the juncture forming the front arch of the pelvis. [< Lat. *pūbēs*, groin.]

pub·lic (pŭb′lĭk) ►*adj.* **1.** Of or affecting the community or the people. **2.** Maintained for or used by the people or community. **3.** Participated in or attended by the people or community: *public worship.* **4.** Connected with or acting on behalf of the people, community, or government: *public office.* **5.** Generally or widely known. ►*n.* **1.** The community or the people as a whole. **2.** A group of people sharing a common interest: *the reading public.* See Usage Note at **collective noun.** [< Lat. *pūblicus*.] —**pub′lic·ly** *adv.*

pub·lic-ad·dress system (pŭb′lĭk-ə-drĕs′) ►*n.* An electronic amplification apparatus used for broadcasting in public areas.

pub·li·can (pŭb′lĭ-kən) ►*n.* **1.** *Chiefly Brit.* The keeper of a public house or tavern. **2.** A tax collector in the Roman Empire. [< Lat. *pūblicānus*, tax collector.]

pub·li·ca·tion (pŭb′lĭ-kā′shən) ►*n.* **1.** The act or process of publishing. **2.** An issue of printed or electronic material.

public defender ►*n.* An attorney employed by the government to represent indigent defendants in criminal cases.

public domain ►*n.* **1.** Land owned and controlled by the state or federal government. **2.** The condition of not being protected by a patent or copyright and therefore being available to the public for use without charge.

public house ►*n.* *Chiefly Brit.* A licensed tavern or bar.

pub·li·cist (pŭb′lĭ-sĭst) ►*n.* One who publicizes, esp. a press or publicity agent.

pub·lic·i·ty (pŭ-blĭs′ĭ-tē) ►*n.* **1.** Public interest, notice, or notoriety. **2.** Information disseminated to attract public notice.

pub·li·cize (pŭb′lĭ-sīz′) ►*v.* **-cized, -ciz·ing** To give publicity to or draw public attention to.

public relations ►*pl.n.* **1.** The methods and activities employed to establish a favorable relationship with the public. **2.** *(takes sing. or pl. v.)* The degree of success obtained in achieving favor with the public.

public school ►*n.* **1.** A tax-supported school in the US providing free education for children of a community or district. **2.** A private boarding school in Great Britain for pupils between the ages of 13 and 18.

pub·lish (pŭb′lĭsh) ►*v.* **1.** To prepare and issue (a book, music, or other material) for public distribution, esp. for sale. **2.** To bring to the public attention; announce. See Synonyms at **announce.** [< Lat. *pūblicāre*, make public.] —**pub′lish·a·ble** *adj.* —**pub′lish·er** *n.*

Puc·ci·ni (pōō-chē′nē), **Giacomo** 1858–1924. Italian operatic composer.

puck (pŭk) ►*n.* A hard rubber disk used in ice hockey. [Perh. < dial. *puck*, strike.]

Puck ►*n.* A mischievous sprite in English folklore.

puck·er (pŭk′ər) ►*v.* To gather into small wrinkles or folds. ►*n.* **1.** A wrinkle or fold. **2.** A facial expression in which the lips are tightly pulled together and pushed outward. [Prob. < dial. *pock*, bag.]

puck·ish (pŭk′ĭsh) ►*adj.* Mischievous; impish.

pud·ding (pŏŏd′ĭng) ►*n.* A sweet dessert, usu. with a soft smooth consistency, that has been boiled, steamed, or baked. [< OFr. *boudin*, sausage.]

pud·dle (pŭd′l) ►*n.* A small amount of liquid, esp. rainwater, collected on a surface. [< OE *pudd*, ditch.]

pud·dling (pŭd′lĭng) ►*n.* Purification of impure metal, esp. pig iron, by heating and stirring in an oxidizing atmosphere.

pu·den·dum (pyōō-dĕn′dəm) ►*n., pl.* **-da** (-də) The external genitals of a human, esp. a woman. [Lat. < *pudēre*, be ashamed.]

pudg·y (pŭj′ē) ►*adj.* **-i·er, -i·est** Somewhat fat; chubby. [< *pudge*, something thick and short.] —**pudg′i·ness** *n.*

Pue·blo (pwĕb′lō) ►*n., pl.* **Pueblo** or **-los 1.** A member of certain Native American peoples, such as the Hopi or Zuni, living in pueblos in N and W New Mexico and NE Arizona. **2. pueb·lo** *pl.* **-los** A community of a Pueblo people, typically consisting of multilevel adobe dwellings around a plaza. [< Lat. *populus*, people.]

pu·er·ile (pyŏŏr′īl′, pwĕr′, pyōō′ər-, -əl) ►*adj.* Immature; childish. [< Lat. *puer*, boy.] —**pu′er·il′i·ty** (-ĭl′ĭ-tē) *n.*

pu·er·per·al (pyōō-ûr′pər-əl) ►*adj.* Relating to or occurring during or immediately after childbirth. [< Lat. *puerper*, a woman in childbed.]

Puer·to Ri·co (pwĕr′tə rē′kō, pôrt′ə, pwĕr′tō) A self-governing US commonwealth on an island in the Caribbean Sea E of Hispaniola. Cap. San Juan. —**Puer′to Ri′can** *adj. & n.*

puff (pŭf) ►*n.* **1a.** A short forceful discharge,

as of air or smoke. **b.** A short sibilant sound produced by a puff. **2.** An act of drawing in and expelling the breath, as in smoking tobacco. **3.** A swelling or rounded protuberance. **4.** A light flaky pastry. **5.** A soft pad for applying powder or lotion. **6.** An expression of exaggerated praise. ►*v.* **1.** To blow in puffs. **2.** To breathe forcefully and rapidly. **3.** To emit puffs. **4.** To take puffs on smoking material. **5.** To swell or seem to swell. **6.** To fill with pride or conceit. **7.** To publicize with exaggerated praise. [< OE *pyff*.] **—puff′i·ness** *n.* **—puff′y** *adj.*

puff·ball (pŭf′bôl′) ►*n.* Any of various fungi having a ball-shaped fruiting body that when pressed or struck releases small spores.

puff·er (pŭf′ər) ►*n.* **1.** See **pufferfish. 2.** A quilted, fitted jacket filled with down or other material for warmth.

puff·er·fish (pŭf′ər-fĭsh′) ►*n., pl.* **-fish** or **-fish·es** Any of various often poisonous fishes that puff themselves up when threatened by swallowing air or water.

puff·er·y (pŭf′ə-rē) ►*n.* Exaggerated praise, esp. when used in publicity.

puf·fin (pŭf′ĭn) ►*n.* A black and white seabird of northern regions having a flattened triangular bill. [ME *poffoun*.]

pug[1] (pŭg) ►*n.* **1.** A dog of a small sturdy breed developed in China, having a short muzzle, wrinkled face, and tightly curled tail. **2.** A short, turned-up nose. [?]

pug[2] (pŭg) ►*n. Slang* A boxer. [< PUGILIST.]

Pu·get Sound (pyō͞o′jĭt) A deep inlet of the Pacific in W WA.

pug·gle (pŭg′əl) ►*n.* A hybrid dog that is a cross between a pug and a beagle. [Blend of PUG[1] and BEAGLE.]

puggle

pu·gi·lism (pyō͞o′jə-lĭz′əm) ►*n. Sports* Boxing. [< Lat. *pugil*, pugilist.] **—pu′gi·list** *n.* **—pu′gi·lis′tic** *adj.*

pug·na·cious (pŭg-nā′shəs) ►*adj.* Combative in nature; belligerent. [< Lat. *pugnus*, fist.] **—pug·na′cious·ness, pug·nac′i·ty** (-năs′ĭ-tē) *n.*

puis·sance (pwĭs′əns, pyō͞o′ĭ-səns) ►*n.* Power; might. [< OFr.] **—puis′sant** *adj.*

puke (pyō͞ok) ►*v.* **puked, puk·ing** *Slang* To vomit. [Perh. imit.] **—puke** *n.*

pu·la (pō͞o′lä) ►*n.* See table at **currency.** [Tswana.]

Pu·las·ki (pō͞o-lăs′kē, pə-), **Casimir** 1747–79. Polish patriot and general in the Amer. Revolution.

pul·chri·tude (pŭl′krĭ-tō͞od′, -tyō͞od′) ►*n.* Physical beauty. [< Lat. *pulcher*, beautiful.] **—pul′chri·tu′di·nous** (-tō͞od′n-əs, -tyō͞od′-) *adj.*

pule (pyō͞ol) ►*v.* **puled, pul·ing** To whine; whimper. [Perh. < Fr. *piauler*.] **—pul′er** *n.*

Pu·lit·zer (pō͞ol′ĭt-sər, pyō͞o′lĭt-), **Joseph**

1847–1911. Hungarian-born Amer. newspaper publisher.

Joseph Pulitzer

pull (pō͞ol) ►*v.* **1.** To apply force to so as to cause motion toward the source of the force. **2a.** To move in a certain direction or toward a certain goal. **b.** To gain a position closer to an objective. **3.** To remove from a fixed position; extract. **4.** To tug at; jerk or tweak. **5.** To rip or tear; rend. **6.** To stretch (e.g., taffy) repeatedly. **7.** To strain (e.g., a muscle) injuriously. **8.** *Informal* To attract; draw: *pull a large crowd.* **9.** *Slang* To draw out (a weapon). **10.** *Informal* To remove. **11.** To row a boat. ►*n.* **1.** The act or process of pulling. **2.** Force exerted in pulling. **3.** Something, such as a knob, that is used for pulling. **4.** A deep inhalation or draft, as of smoke or liquor. **5.** *Slang* A means of gaining special advantage; influence. **6.** *Informal* Ability to draw or attract; appeal. **—phrasal verbs: pull off** *Informal* To do or accomplish in spite of difficulties. **pull out** To leave or depart. **pull through** To come or bring successfully through difficulty. **pull up** To bring or come to a halt. [< OE *pullian*.] **—pull′er** *n.*
Syns: drag, draw, haul, tow, tug Ant: push v.

pull·back (pō͞ol′băk′) ►*n.* An orderly troop withdrawal.

pul·let (pō͞ol′ĭt) ►*n.* A young domestic hen. [< Lat. *pullus*.]

pul·ley (pō͞ol′ē) ►*n., pl.* **-leys 1.** A simple machine consisting essentially of a wheel with a grooved rim in which a pulled rope or chain can run to change the direction of the pull and thereby lift a load. **2.** A wheel turned by or driving a belt. [< OFr. *polie*.]

Pull·man (pō͞ol′mən) ►*n.* **1.** A railroad parlor car or sleeping car. **2.** A large suitcase. [After G.M. *Pullman* (1831–97).]

pull·out (pō͞ol′out′) ►*n.* A withdrawal, esp. of troops.

pull·o·ver (pō͞ol′ō′vər) ►*n.* A garment that is put on by being drawn over the head.

pul·mo·nar·y (pō͞ol′mə-nĕr′ē, pŭl′-) ►*adj.* Of or involving the lungs. [< Lat. *pulmō*, lung.]

pulp (pŭlp) ►*n.* **1.** A soft, moist, shapeless mass of matter. **2.** The soft, moist part of a vegetable or fruit. **3.** A mixture of cellulose material, such as wood, paper, and rags, ground up and moistened to make paper. **4.** The soft inner structure of a tooth, containing nerves and blood vessels. **5.** A publication, such as a magazine, containing lurid subject matter. ►*v.* To reduce to pulp.

[< Lat. *pulpa*.] —**pulp′i·ness** *n.* —**pulp′y** *adj.*

pul·pit (pŏŏl′pĭt, pŭl′-) ▸*n.* An elevated platform, lectern, or stand used in preaching a religious service. [< Lat. *pulpitum*, platform.]

pulp·wood (pŭlp′wŏŏd′) ▸*n.* Soft wood used in making paper.

pul·sar (pŭl′sär′) ▸*n.* Any of several celestial objects emitting periodic, short, intense bursts, as of radio waves or x-rays. [*puls(ating st)ar* (on the model of QUASAR).]

pul·sate (pŭl′sāt′) ▸*v.* **-sat·ed, -sat·ing 1.** To expand and contract rhythmically; beat. **2.** To produce rhythmic sounds. [Lat. *pulsāre*.] —**pul·sa′tion** *n.*

pulse (pŭls) ▸*n.* **1.** The rhythmical throbbing of arteries produced by the regular contractions of the heart. **2.** *Phys.* A brief sudden change in a normally constant quantity: *a pulse of current.* **3.** The perceptible emotions or sentiments of a group of people. ▸*v.* **pulsed, puls·ing** To pulsate. [< Lat. *pulsus* < *pellere*, beat.]

pul·ver·ize (pŭl′və-rīz′) ▸*v.* **-ized, -iz·ing 1.** To reduce or be reduced to a powder or dust. **2.** To overwhelm or defeat utterly. [< Lat. *pulvis*, dust.]

pu·ma (pŏŏ′mə, pyŏŏ′-) ▸*n.* See **cougar.** [< Quechua.]

pum·ice (pŭm′ĭs) ▸*n.* A light porous lava, used in solid form as an abrasive and in powdered form as a polish. [< Lat. *pūmex*.] —**pum′ice** *v.*

pum·mel (pŭm′əl) ▸*v.* **-meled, -mel·ing** also **-melled, -mel·ling 1.** To beat, as with the fists. See Synonyms at **beat. 2.** To cause to undergo harm or loss. [< POMMEL.]

pump¹ (pŭmp) ▸*n.* A device for raising, compressing, or transferring fluids. ▸*v.* **1.** To raise or cause to flow by means of a pump. **2.** To draw, deliver, or pour forth. **3.** To propel, eject, or insert. **4.** To cause to move with an up-and-down or back-and-forth motion. **5.** To move gas or liquid with a pump or a pumplike device. **6.** To question closely or persistently. —*phrasal verb:* **pump up 1.** To inflate with gas by means of a pump. **2.** *Slang* To fill with enthusiasm and energy. —*idiom:* **pump iron** To lift weights. [ME *pumpe*.] —**pump′er** *n.*

pump² (pŭmp) ▸*n.* A woman's shoe that has medium or high heels and no fastenings. [?]

pum·per·nick·el (pŭm′pər-nĭk′əl) ▸*n.* A dark coarse rye bread. [Ger.]

pump·kin (pŭmp′kĭn, pŭm′-, pŭng′-) ▸*n.* A round squash with coarse, strongly flavored yellow to orange flesh, numerous seeds, and a moderately hard, usu. orange rind. [< Gk. *pepōn*, ripe melon.]

pun (pŭn) ▸*n.* A play on words, sometimes on different senses of the same word and sometimes on the similar sense or sound of different words. [?] —**pun** *v.*

punch¹ (pŭnch) ▸*n.* **1.** A tool for piercing or stamping. **2.** A tool for forcing a pin, bolt, or rivet in or out of a hole. [< PUNCHEON¹.] —**punch** *v.*

punch² (pŭnch) ▸*v.* **1.** To hit with a sharp blow of the fist. **2a.** To poke or prod with a stick. **b.** To herd (cattle). **3.** To depress (e.g., a key or button). ▸*n.* **1.** A blow with the fist. **2.** Impressive or effective force. See Synonyms at **vigor.** [ME *punchen*.] —**punch′er** *n.*

punch³ (pŭnch) ▸*n.* A beverage of fruit juices,

often spiced and mixed with wine or liquor. [Perh. < Skt. *pañca*, five.]

punch card ▸*n.* A card punched with holes or notches to represent data for a computer.

pun·cheon¹ (pŭn′chən) ▸*n.* **1.** A short wooden upright used in structural framing. **2.** A piece of broad, roughly dressed timber. [< Lat. *pungere, pūnct-,* to prick.]

pun·cheon² (pŭn′chən) ▸*n.* A cask with a capacity of from 72 to 120 gal. (273 to 454 l). [< OFr. *poinçon,* cask.]

punch line ▸*n.* The climactic phrase of a joke, producing a sudden humorous effect.

punch·y (pŭn′chē) ▸*adj.* **-i·er, -i·est 1.** Marked by vigor or drive. **2.** Groggy or dazed from or as if from a blow.

punc·til·i·o (pŭngk-tĭl′ē-ō′) ▸*n., pl.* **-os 1.** A fine point of etiquette. **2.** Precise observance of formalities. [Obsolete Italian *punctiglio*.] —**punc·til′i·ous** *adj.* —**punc·til′i·ous·ly** *adv.*

punc·tu·al (pŭngk′chŏŏ-əl) ▸*adj.* Acting or arriving exactly at the time appointed; prompt. [< Lat. *pūnctum,* point.] —**punc′tu·al′i·ty** (-ăl′ĭ-tē) *n.* —**punc′tu·al·ly** *adv.*

punc·tu·ate (pŭngk′chŏŏ-āt′) ▸*v.* **-at·ed, -at·ing 1.** To provide (a text) with punctuation marks. **2.** To occur or interrupt periodically. **3.** To emphasize. [< Lat. *pūnctum,* point.]

punc·tu·a·tion (pŭngk′chŏŏ-ā′shən) ▸*n.* **1.** The use of standard marks and signs in writing and printing to separate words into sentences, clauses, and phrases in order to clarify meaning. **2.** The marks so used.

punc·ture (pŭngk′chər) ▸*v.* **-tured, -tur·ing 1.** To pierce with a pointed object. **2.** To depreciate or deflate. ▸*n.* **1.** The act or an instance of puncturing. **2.** A hole made by a sharp object. [< LLat. *pūnctūra,* a pricking.]

pun·dit (pŭn′dĭt) ▸*n.* **1.** A source of opinion; critic. **2.** A learned person. [< Skt. *paṇḍitaḥ.*]

pun·gent (pŭn′jənt) ▸*adj.* **1.** Having a sharp, acrid taste or smell. **2.** Penetrating, biting, or caustic: *pungent satire.* [< Lat. *pungere,* sting.] —**pun′gen·cy** *n.* —**pun′gent·ly** *adv.*

Pu·nic (pyŏŏ′nĭk) ▸*adj.* Of or relating to ancient Carthage. ▸*n.* The dialect of Phoenician spoken in Carthage.

pun·ish (pŭn′ĭsh) ▸*v.* **1.** To subject to a penalty for an offense or fault. **2.** To inflict a penalty for (an offense). **3.** To handle roughly; hurt. [< Lat. *poenīre*.] —**pun′ish·a·ble** *adj.*

pun·ish·ment (pŭn′ĭsh-mənt) ▸*n.* **1.** The imposition of a penalty for wrongdoing. **2.** A penalty for wrongdoing. **3.** Rough treatment or use.

pu·ni·tive (pyŏŏ′nĭ-tĭv) ▸*adj.* Inflicting or aiming to inflict punishment. [< Lat. *pūnīre,* punish.]

Pun·jab (pŭn′jăb′, pŭn-jäb′) A historical region of NW India and N Pakistan.

Pun·ja·bi also **Pan·ja·bi** (pŭn-jä′bē, -jäb′ē) ▸*n., pl.* **-bis 1.** A native or inhabitant of the Punjab. **2.** An Indic language spoken in the Punjab. —**Pun·ja′bi** *adj.*

punk¹ (pŭngk) ▸*n.* **1.** *Slang* **a.** An often aggressive young man. **b.** An inexperienced young person. **2.** *Mus.* **a.** Punk rock. **b.** A punk rocker. ▸*v.* **1.** To act in a cowardly manner. **2.** To humiliate (someone). **3.** To dupe or deceive. **4.** To play a practical joke on. [?]

punk² (pŭngk) ▸*n.* **1.** Dry decayed wood, used as tinder. **2.** A substance that smolders when ignited. ►*adj.* Of poor quality; worthless. [Prob. of Algonquian orig.]

punk rock ►*n.* Rock music marked by fast tempos and lyrics expressing emotional isolation and antisocial attitudes. —**punk rocker** *n.*

pun·ster (pŭn'stər) ►*n.* A maker of puns.

punt[1] (pŭnt) ►*n.* An open flat-bottom boat with squared ends, usu. propelled by a long pole. ►*v.* To propel (a boat) with a pole. [< Lat. *pontō*, PONTOON.]

punt[2] (pŭnt) ►*n. Football* A kick in which the ball is dropped from the hands and kicked before it touches the ground. ►*v.* **1.** To execute a punt. **2.** *Informal* To cease doing something; give up. [?]

pu·ny (pyoō'nē) ►*adj.* **-ni·er, -ni·est** Of inferior size, strength, or significance; weak. [< OFr. *puisne*, second-rank.]

pup (pŭp) ►*n.* **1.** A puppy. **2.** One of the young of certain other animals, such as seals.

pu·pa (pyoō'pə) ►*n., pl.* **-pae** (-pē) or **-pas** An insect (among insects that undergo complete metamorphosis) in the nonfeeding stage between the larva and adult. [Lat., girl, doll.] —**pu'pal** *adj.*

pu·pil[1] (pyoō'pəl) ►*n.* A student under the supervision of a teacher or professor. [< Lat. *pūpillus*, little boy.]

pu·pil[2] (pyoō'pəl) ►*n.* The dark circular opening in the center of the iris of the eye. [< Lat. *pūpilla*, little doll.]

pup·pet (pŭp'ĭt) ►*n.* **1.** A small figure of a person or animal designed to be fitted over and manipulated by the hand. **2.** A marionette. **3.** A doll. **4.** One whose behavior is determined by the will of others. [ME *poppet*, doll.]

pup·pet·eer (pŭp'ĭ-tîr') ►*n.* One who operates and entertains with puppets. —**pup'pet·ry** *n.*

pup·py (pŭp'ē) ►*n., pl.* **-pies** A young dog; pup. [ME *popi*.]

pur·blind (pûr'blīnd') ►*adj.* **1.** Nearly or partly blind. **2.** Slow in understanding or discernment; dull. [ME *pur blind*, totally blind.]

pur·chase (pûr'chĭs) ►*v.* **-chased, -chas·ing** To obtain in exchange for money or its equivalent; buy. ►*n.* **1a.** The act or an instance of buying. **b.** Something bought. **2a.** A hold or position that allows the application of power. **b.** A device, such as a pulley, used to obtain mechanical advantage. [< OFr. *purchacier*, hunt down.] —**pur'chas·a·ble** *adj.* —**pur'chas·er** *n.*

pur·dah (pûr'də) ►*n.* The Hindu or Muslim system of sex segregation, esp. of keeping women in seclusion. [< Pers. *pardah*, veil.]

pure (pyoor) ►*adj.* **pur·er, pur·est 1.** Having a uniform composition; not mixed: *pure oxygen.* **2.** Free of dirt, pollutants, infectious agents, or other unwanted elements. **3.** Complete; utter: *pure folly.* **4.** Having no faults; perfect. **5.** Chaste; virgin. **6.** Of unmixed blood or ancestry. **7.** Theoretical: *pure science.* [< Lat. *pūrus.*] —**pure'ly** *adv.* —**pu'ri·ty** *n.*
　　Syns: absolute, sheer, unadulterated adj.

pure·bred (pyoor'brĕd') ►*adj.* Of or relating to an animal having both parents of the same breed or variety. —**pure'bred'** *n.*

pu·rée (pyoo-rā', pyoor'ā) ►*v.* **-réed, -rée·ing** To rub (food) through a strainer or process in a blender to a thick pulpy consistency. ►*n.* Food prepared by puréeing. [< OFr. *purer*, strain.]

pur·ga·tion (pûr-gā'shən) ►*n.* The act of purging or purifying.

pur·ga·tive (pûr'gə-tĭv) ►*adj.* Tending to cleanse or purge, esp. causing evacuation of the bowels. —**pur'ga·tive** *n.*

pur·ga·to·ry (pûr'gə-tôr'ē) ►*n., pl.* **-ries 1.** In certain Christian doctrines, a temporary state in which the souls of those who have died in grace must expiate their sins. **2.** A place or condition of suffering, expiation, or remorse. —**pur'ga·to'ri·al** (-tôr'ē-əl) *adj.*

purge (pûrj) ►*v.* **purged, purg·ing 1.** To clear (e.g., a container or pipe) of something unclean or unwanted. **2.** To rid (a person or thing) of something unwanted. **3.** To remove or eliminate. **4.** To rid of undesirable people. **5.** To undergo or cause evacuation of (the bowels). **6.** To vomit or force oneself to vomit, esp. as a symptom of an eating disorder. **7.** *Comp.* To clear (a storage device) of unwanted data. ►*n.* **1.** The act of purging. **2.** Something that purges, esp. a medicinal purgative. [< Lat. *pūrgāre.*]

pu·ri·fy (pyoor'ə-fī') ►*v.* **-fied, -fy·ing** To make or become pure. [< Lat. *pūrificāre.*] —**pu'ri·fi·ca'tion** *n.* —**pu'ri·fi'er** *n.*

Pu·rim (poor'ĭm, poo-rēm') ►*n. Judaism* The 14th of Adar, observed in commemoration of Esther's deliverance of the Jews of Persia from massacre. [Heb. *pûrîm.*]

pu·rine (pyoor'ēn') ►*n.* **1.** A colorless crystalline organic base, $C_5H_4N_4$. **2.** Any of a group of organic compounds structurally related to purine, including uric acid and guanine. [Ger. *Purin.*]

pur·ism (pyoor'ĭz'əm) ►*n.* Strict observance of correctness, esp. of language. —**pur'ist** *n.*

Pu·ri·tan (pyoor'ĭ-tn) ►*n.* **1.** A member of a group of English Protestants who in the 1500s and 1600s advocated strict discipline and simplification of religious ceremonies. **2. puritan** One who regards pleasure or luxury as sinful. [< LLat. *pūritās,* purity.] —**pu'ri·tan'i·cal** (-tăn'ĭ-kəl) *adj.*

purl[1] (pûrl) ►*v.* To flow or ripple with a murmuring sound. ►*n.* The sound made by rippling water. [Prob. of Scand. orig.]

purl[2] (pûrl) ►*n.* An inverted knitting stitch. [?] —**purl** *v.*

pur·lieu (pûrl'yoō, pûr'loō) ►*n.* **1.** An outlying or neighboring area. **2. purlieus** Outskirts; environs. [< OFr. *poraler,* traverse.]

pur·loin (pər-loin', pûr'loin') ►*v.* To steal, esp. stealthily. [< AN *purloigner,* remove.]

pur·ple (pûr'pəl) ►*n.* **1.** Any of a group of colors with a hue between violet and red. **2.** Purple cloth, formerly worn as a symbol of royalty or high office. ►*adj.* **1.** Of the color purple. **2.** Elaborate and ornate: *purple prose.* [< Gk. *porphura,* a shellfish yielding purple dye.] —**pur'ple** *v.* —**pur'plish** *adj.*

pur·port (pər-pôrt') ►*v.* To profess to be, often falsely. ►*n.* (pûr'pôrt) **1.** Meaning; import. See Synonyms at **substance. 2.** Intention; purpose. [< AN *purporter.*]

pur·pose (pûr'pəs) ►*n.* **1.** An aim or goal. **2.** Determination; resolution: *a man of purpose.* ►*v.* **-posed, -pos·ing** To intend or resolve. —**idiom: on purpose** Intentionally; deliberately. [< AN *purposer,* intend.] —**pur'pose·ful** *adj.* —**pur'pose·less** *adj.* —**pur'pose·ly** *adv.*

purr (pûr) ►*n.* A soft vibrant sound like that

made by a contented cat. [Imit.] —**purr** v.

purse (pûrs) ►n. **1.** A bag used for carrying personal items, esp. by women; handbag. **2.** A small bag or pouch for carrying money. **3.** An available amount of money or resources. **4.** A sum of money collected as a present or offered as a prize. ►v. **pursed, purs·ing** To pucker. [< LLat. *bursa*; see BURSA.]

purs·er (pûr′sər) ►n. The officer in charge of money matters on board a ship or aircraft.

purs·lane (pûrs′lĭn, -lān′) ►n. A trailing plant having small yellow flowers and fleshy leaves that can be cooked as a vegetable or used in salads. [< Lat. *portulāca*.]

pur·su·ance (pər-sōō′əns) ►n. A carrying out or putting into effect.

pur·su·ant to (pər-sōō′ənt) ►prep. In accordance with.

pur·sue (pər-sōō′) ►v. **-sued, -su·ing 1.** To follow so as to overtake or capture. **2.** To strive to accomplish. **3.** To proceed along the course of; follow: *pursue a course.* **4a.** To take action regarding (something). **b.** To be engaged in (e.g., a hobby). [< Lat. *prōsequī*, prosecute.] —**pur·su′er** n.

pur·suit (pər-sōōt′) ►n. **1.** The act of pursuing. **2.** An activity, such as a hobby, engaged in regularly. [< AN *pursuite*.]

pu·ru·lent (pyōōr′ə-lənt, pyōōr′yə-) ►adj. Containing or secreting pus. [< Lat. *pūrulentus*.] —**pu′ru·lence** n.

pur·vey (pər-vā′, pûr′vā′) ►v. To supply or sell (e.g., food). [< Lat. *prōvidēre*, PROVIDE.] —**pur·vey′ance** n. —**pur·vey′or** n.

pur·view (pûr′vyōō′) ►n. **1.** The extent of function, power, or competence; scope. See Synonyms at **range. 2a.** Range of vision. **b.** Range of understanding or experience. [< AN *purveu*, provided.]

pus (pŭs) ►n. A usu. viscous, yellowish-white fluid formed in infected tissue, consisting of white blood cells, cellular debris, and necrotic tissue. [Lat. *pūs*.]

push (pŏŏsh) ►v. **1a.** To apply pressure against (something), esp. for the purpose of moving it. **b.** To move (something) by exerting force against it; thrust or shove. **c.** To exert a downward pressure on (e.g., a button or keyboard); press. **2.** To force (one's way). **3.** To urge forward insistently; pressure: *push a child to study harder.* **4a.** *Informal* To promote or sell (a product). **b.** *Slang* To sell (a narcotic) illegally. ►n. **1a.** The act of pushing; thrust. **b.** The act of pressing. **2.** A vigorous or insistent effort; drive. **3.** A provocation to action; stimulus. [< Lat. *pulsāre*.]
Syns: propel, shove, thrust **v.**

push·but·ton (pŏŏsh′bŭt′n) ►n. also **push button** A small button that activates an electric circuit when pushed. ►adj. also **push-but·ton** (pŏŏsh′bŭt′n) Equipped with or operated by a pushbutton.

push·cart (pŏŏsh′kärt′) ►n. A light cart pushed by hand.

push·er (pŏŏsh′ər) ►n. **1.** One that pushes: *a pusher of boundaries.* **2.** *Slang* One who sells drugs illegally.

Push·kin (pŏŏsh′kĭn, pŏŏsh′-), **Aleksandr Sergeyevich** 1799–1837. Russian writer.

push·o·ver (pŏŏsh′ō′vər) ►n. **1.** One easily defeated or deceived. **2.** Something easily done. See Synonyms at **breeze.**

Push·tu (pŭsh′tōō) ►n. Var. of **Pashto.**

push·up (pŏŏsh′ŭp′) ►n. An exercise performed by lying face down with the palms on the floor and pushing the body up and down with the arms.

push·y (pŏŏsh′ē) ►adj. **-i·er, -i·est** Disagreeably aggressive or forward. —**push′i·ly** adv. —**push′i·ness** n.

pu·sil·lan·i·mous (pyōō′sə-lăn′ə-məs) ►adj. Lacking courage; cowardly. [< LLat. *pusillanimis*.] —**pu′sil·la·nim′i·ty** (-lə-nĭm′ĭ-tē) n. —**pu′sil·lan′i·mous·ly** adv.

puss[1] (pŏŏs) ►n. *Informal* A cat. [Prob. of Gmc. orig.]

puss[2] (pŏŏs) ►n. *Slang* The human face. [< Middle Irish *bus*, lip.]

puss·y[1] (pŏŏs′ē) ►n., pl. **-ies** *Informal* A cat.

pus·sy[2] (pŭs′ē) ►adj. **-si·er, -si·est** Containing or resembling pus.

puss·y·cat (pŏŏs′ē-kăt′) ►n. **1.** A cat. **2.** *Informal* An easygoing, amiable person.

puss·y·foot (pŏŏs′ē-fŏŏt′) ►v. **1.** To move stealthily or cautiously. **2.** *Informal* To avoid committing oneself.

puss·y willow (pŏŏs′ē) ►n. A North American shrub or small tree with silky catkins.

pus·tule (pŭs′chōōl, pŭs′tyōōl) ►n. A small inflammation of the skin filled with pus. [< Lat. *pūstula*.] —**pus′tu·lar** adj.

put (pŏŏt) ►v. **put, put·ting 1.** To place in a specified position; set. **2.** To cause to be in a specified condition. **3.** To subject: *put him to a lot of trouble.* **4.** To attribute: *put a false interpretation on events.* **5.** To estimate: *put the time at five o'clock.* **6.** To impose or levy (a tax). **7.** To hurl with an overhand pushing motion: *put the shot.* **8.** To bring up for consideration or judgment: *put a question.* **9.** To express; state. **10.** To render in a specified language; translate. **11.** To adapt. **12.** To apply: *put our minds to it.* **13.** To proceed: *The ship put into the harbor.* —**phrasal verbs: put across** To state so as to be understood or accepted. **put down 1.** To write down. **2.** To suppress: *put down a rebellion.* **3.** *Slang* To criticize or belittle. **put off 1.** To delay or postpone. **2.** To offend or repel. **put on 1.** To clothe oneself with. **2.** *Slang* To tease or mislead. **put out 1.** To extinguish. **2.** To inconvenience. **3.** To anger or irritate. —**idiom: put up with** To endure. [ME *putten*.]

pu·ta·tive (pyōō′tə-tĭv) ►adj. Generally regarded as such. See Synonyms at **supposed.** [< Lat. *putāre*, think.]

put·down (pŏŏt′doun′) ►n. *Informal* A critical, disparaging, or humiliating remark.

Put·in (pōō′tn), **Vladimir Vladimirovich** b. 1952. Russian president (2000–08) and prime minister (2008–12), reelected president in 2012.

put-on (pŏŏt′ŏn′, -ôn′) ►adj. Pretended; feigned. ►n. *Slang* **1.** The act of teasing or misleading someone, esp. for amusement. **2.** Something intended as a hoax or joke.

pu·tre·fy (pyōō′trə-fī′) ►v. **-fied, -fy·ing 1.** To decay or cause to decay and have a foul odor. See Synonyms at **decay. 2.** To make or become gangrenous. [< Lat. *puter*, rotten.] —**pu′tre·fac′tion** (-făk′shən) n.

pu·tres·cent (pyōō-trĕs′ənt) ►adj. Becoming putrid; putrefying. [< Lat. *puter*, rotten.] —**pu·tres′cence** n.

pu·trid (pyōo′trĭd) ►*adj.* **1.** Decomposed and foul-smelling. **2.** Vile; corrupt. **3.** Of extremely poor quality; atrocious. [< Lat. *putridus.*] —**pu·trid′i·ty** (-trĭd′ĭ-tē), **pu′trid·ness** *n.*

putsch (pōoch) ►*n.* A sudden attempt by a group to overthrow a government. [Ger.]

putt (pŭt) ►*n.* A short light golf stroke. [Var. of PUT.] —**putt** *v.*

put·tee (pŭ-tē′, pŭt′ē) ►*n.* **1.** A strip of cloth wound spirally around the lower leg. **2.** A gaiter covering the lower leg. [< Skt. *paṭṭikā.*]

put·ter[1] (pŭt′ər) ►*n.* A short golf club used for putting.

put·ter[2] (pŭt′ər) ►*v.* To occupy oneself with minor or unimportant tasks. [< POTTER[2].]

put·ty (pŭt′ē) ►*n., pl.* **-ties** **1.** A doughlike cement made by mixing whiting and linseed oil. **2.** A substance with a similar consistency or function. [< OFr. *potee*, a potful.] —**put′ty** *v.*

puz·zle (pŭz′əl) ►*n.* **1.** Something, such as a toy or game, that tests one's ingenuity. **2.** Something that baffles or confuses. **3.** Bewilderment. ►*v.* **-zled, -zling** **1.** To baffle or confuse by presenting a difficult problem or matter. See Synonyms at **perplex. 2.** To clarify or solve by reasoning or study: *puzzled out the answer.* **3.** To ponder over a problem in an effort to solve or understand it. [?] —**puz′zle·ment** *n.*

PVC ►*abbr.* **1.** photovoltaic cell **2.** polyvinyl chloride

PVT or **Pvt.** ►*abbr.* private

Pyg·my also **Pig·my** (pĭg′mē) ►*n., pl.* **-mies** **1.** also **pygmy** A member of any of several African or Asian peoples of gen. short stature. **2. pygmy** One of unusually small size or of little importance. [< Gk. *pugmē*, cubit.] —**Pyg′my, pyg′my** *adj.*

py·ja·mas (pə-jä′məz, -jăm′əz) ►*pl.n.* Chiefly *Brit.* Var. of **pajamas.**

pylon
top: electric power transmission lines
bottom: Temple of Horus, Edfu, Egypt

py·lon (pī′lŏn′) ►*n.* **1.** A movable, brightly colored cone used to signal something to be avoided, such as a hazard on a roadway. **2.** A vertical supporting structure, esp. a steel tower supporting high-tension wires. **3.** A monumental gateway, esp. a pair of truncated pyramids serving as the entrance to an Egyptian temple. **4.** A structure that attaches an aircraft engine to the plane's wing or fuselage. [Gk. *pulōn*, gateway.]

Pyong·yang (pyŭng′yäng′, -yăng′, pyông′-) The capital of North Korea, in the SW-central part.

py·or·rhe·a (pī′ə-rē′ə) ►*n.* **1.** Inflammation of the gums and tooth sockets, often leading to loosening of the teeth. **2.** A discharge of pus. [Gk. *puon*, pus + *rhein*, flow.]

pyr·a·mid (pĭr′ə-mĭd) ►*n.* **1.** A solid figure with a polygonal base and triangular faces that meet at a common point. **2a.** A massive monument of ancient Egypt having a rectangular base and four triangular faces meeting at an apex, built over or around a tomb. **b.** A flat-topped Mesoamerican temple of similar shape. ►*v.* **1.** To place or build in the shape of a pyramid. **2.** To increase rapidly and on a widening base. [< Gk. *pūramis.*] —**py·ram′i·dal** (pĭ-răm′-ĭ-dl) *adj.*

pyre (pīr) ►*n.* A combustible pile for burning a corpse as a funeral rite. [< Gk. *pur*, fire.]

Pyr·e·nees (pĭr′ə-nēz′) A mountain range of SW Europe along the border between SW France and NE Spain. —**Pyr′e·ne′an** *adj.*

py·re·thrum (pī-rē′thrəm, -rĕth′rəm) ►*n.* **1.** A Eurasian plant cultivated for its colorful flower heads. **2.** An insecticide made from the dried flower heads of these plants. [< Gk. *purethron*, a kind of plant.]

py·rim·i·dine (pī-rĭm′ĭ-dēn′, pĭ-) ►*n.* **1.** A crystalline organic base, $C_4H_4N_2$. **2.** Any of several basic compounds derived from or structurally related to pyrimidine, esp. uracil, cytosine, and thymine.

py·rite (pī′rīt′) ►*n.* A brass-colored mineral form of iron sulfide, used as an iron ore and in producing sulfuric acid. [< Lat. *pyrītēs*, flint.] —**py·rit′ic** (-rĭt′ĭk) *adj.*

py·ri·tes (pī-rī′tēz, pī′rīts′) ►*n., pl.* **pyrites** Any of various natural metallic sulfide minerals, esp. of iron. [< Gk. *purītēs (lithos)*, fire (stone).]

pyro– or **pyr–** ►*pref.* Fire; heat: *pyromania.* [< Gk. *pur*, fire.]

py·rol·y·sis (pī-rŏl′ĭ-sĭs) ►*n.* Decomposition or transformation of a compound caused by heat. —**py′ro·lyt′ic** (-rə-lĭt′ĭk) *adj.*

py·ro·ma·ni·a (pī′rō-mā′nē-ə, -mān′yə) ►*n.* The irresistible urge to start fires. —**py′ro·ma′ni·ac′** (-mā′nē-ăk′) *n.*

py·rom·e·ter (pī-rŏm′ĭ-tər) ►*n.* A thermometer used for measuring high temperatures.

py·ro·tech·nics (pī′rə-tĕk′nĭks) ►*n.* (takes sing. *v.*) **1.** A fireworks display. **2.** A brilliant display, as of wit. —**py′ro·tech′nic, py′ro·tech′ni·cal** *adj.*

Pyr·rhic victory (pĭr′ĭk) ►*n.* A victory offset by excessive losses. [< the victory of *Pyrrhus* (319–272 BC) over the Romans in 279 BC.]

Py·thag·o·ras (pĭ-thăg′ər-əs) fl. 6th cent. BC. Greek philosopher and mathematician.

Py·thag·o·re·an theorem (pĭ-thăg′ə-rē′ən) ►*n.* The theorem that the sum of the squares of the lengths of the sides of a right triangle is equal to the square of the length of the hypotenuse. [After PYTHAGORAS.]

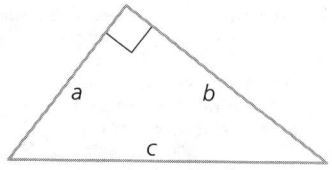

Pythagorean theorem
The Pythagorean theorem is $a^2 + b^2 = c^2$.

py·thon (pī′thŏn′, -thən) ►*n.* Any of various nonvenomous snakes found chiefly in Asia, Africa, and Australia, that coil around and asphyxiate their prey. [< Lat. *Pȳthōn*, mythical serpent.]

pyx also **pix** (pĭks) ►*n.* **1.** A container in which wafers for the Eucharist are kept. **2.** A container in which the Eucharist is carried to the sick. [< Gk. *puxis*, box.]

Q

q or **Q** (kyōō) ►*n., pl.* **q's** or **Q's** also **qs** or **Qs** The 17th letter of the English alphabet.

Q ►*abbr.* **1.** quarter (of a year) **2.** *Games* queen **3.** question

q. ►*abbr.* **1.** quart **2.** also **Q.** quarto

Qad·da·fi or **Kha·da·fy** (kə-dä′fē), **Muammar al-** 1942–2011. Libyan political leader.

Q and A ►*abbr.* question and answer

Qa·tar (kä′tär′, KHŭt′ər, kə-tär′) A country of E Arabia on a peninsula in the SW Persian Gulf. —**Qa·tar′i** *adj. & n.*

QB ►*abbr.* quarterback

QC ►*abbr.* **1.** quality control **2.** Quebec

QED ►*abbr. Lat.* quod erat demonstrandum (which was to be demonstrated)

qi (chē) ►*n.* Variant of **chi².**

QM ►*abbr.* quartermaster

qt. or **qt** ►*abbr.* quart

qto. ►*abbr.* quarto

qty. ►*abbr.* quantity

quack¹ (kwăk) ►*n.* The characteristic sound of a duck. [ME *quek.*] —**quack** *v.*

quack² (kwăk) ►*n.* **1.** An untrained person who pretends to have medical knowledge. **2.** A charlatan. [< obsolete Du. *quacksalver.*] —**quack′er·y** *n.*

quad¹ (kwŏd) ►*n.* A quadrangle.

quad² (kwŏd) ►*n.* **1.** Something having four identifiable parts or members. **2.** A quadruplet.

quad·ran·gle (kwŏd′răng′gəl) ►*n.* **1.** A quadrilateral. **2.** A rectangular area surrounded on all four sides by buildings. [< LLat. *quadrangulum.*] —**quad·ran′gu·lar** (-răng′gyə-lər) *adj.*

quad·rant (kwŏd′rənt) ►*n.* **1.** *Math.* **a.** A circular arc of 90°; one fourth of the circumference of a circle. **b.** The plane area bounded by such an arc and two perpendicular radii. **c.** Any of the four areas into which a plane is divided by the reference axes in a Cartesian coordinate system. **2.** An early instrument for measuring the altitude of celestial bodies. [< Lat. *quadrāns*, quarter.]

quad·ra·phon·ic also **quad·ri·phon·ic** (kwŏd′rə-fŏn′ĭk) ►*adj.* Of or for a four-channel sound system.

quad·rat·ic (kwŏ-drăt′ĭk) ►*adj. Math.* Of or containing quantities of the second degree. [< Lat. *quadrum*, square.] —**quad·rat′ic** *n.*

quad·ren·ni·al (kwŏ-drĕn′ē-əl) ►*adj.* **1.** Happening once in four years. **2.** Lasting for four years. [< Lat. *quadrennium*, period of four years.] —**quad·ren′ni·al·ly** *adv.*

quadri– or **quadru–** or **quadr–** ►*pref.* Four: *quadrilateral.* [< Lat.]

quad·ri·ceps (kwŏd′rĭ-sĕps′) ►*n.* The large four-part extensor muscle at the front of the thigh. [QUADRI– + (BI)CEPS.]

quad·ri·lat·er·al (kwŏd′rə-lăt′ər-əl) ►*n.* A polygon having four sides. ►*adj.* Having four sides.

qua·drille (kwō-drĭl′, kwə-, kə-) ►*n.* **1.** A square dance performed by four couples. **2.** Music for this dance. [< Sp. *cuadrilla*, squad of horsemen < Lat. *quadrum*, square.]

quad·ril·lion (kwŏ-drĭl′yən) ►*n.* **1.** The cardinal number equal to 10¹⁵. **2.** *Chiefly Brit.* The cardinal number equal to 10²⁴. [QUADR(I)– + (M)ILLION.] —**quad·ril′lion** *adj.* —**quad·ril′lionth** *n. & adj.*

quad·ri·par·tite (kwŏd′rə-pär′tīt′) ►*adj.* **1.** Consisting of or divided into four parts. **2.** Involving four participants.

quad·ri·ple·gia (kwŏd′rə-plē′jə) ►*n.* Complete paralysis of the body from the neck down. [QUADRI– + (PARA)PLEGIA.] —**quad′ri·ple′gic** *adj. & n.*

quad·ru·ped (kwŏd′rə-pĕd′) ►*n.* A four-footed animal.

quad·ru·ped·al (kwŏd′rə-pĕd′l, kwŏ-drōō′pə-dl) ►*adj.* Having or walking on four feet.

quad·ru·ple (kwŏ-drōō′pəl, -drŭp′əl, kwŏd′rōō-pəl) ►*adj.* **1.** Having four parts. **2.** Four times as many or as much. ►*n.* A fourfold amount or number. ►*v.* **-pled, -pling** To multiply or be multiplied by four. [< Lat. *quadruplus*, fourfold.]

quad·ru·plet (kwŏ-drŭp′lĭt, -drōō′plĭt, kwŏd′rə-plĭt) ►*n.* **1.** One of four offspring born in a single birth. **2.** A group or combination of four.

quad·ru·pli·cate (kwŏ-drōō′plĭ-kĭt) ►*n.* One of a group of four identical things. [< Lat. *quadruplicāre*, multiply by four.] —**quad·ru′pli·cate′** (-kāt′) *v.* —**quad·ru′pli·ca′tion** *n.*

quaff (kwŏf, kwăf, kwôf) ►*v.* To drink heartily. [?] —**quaff** *n.* —**quaff′er** *n.*

quag·mire (kwăg′mīr′, kwŏg′-) ►*n.* **1.** Land with a soft muddy surface. **2.** A difficult or precarious situation; predicament. [*quag*, marsh + MIRE.]

qua·hog (kō′hôg′, -hŏg′, kwô′-, kwō′-) ►*n.* An edible clam of the Atlantic coast of North America, having a hard rounded shell. [Narragansett *poquaûhock.*]

quail¹ (kwāl) ►*n., pl.* **quail** or **quails** Any of various small, primarily ground-dwelling birds having mottled brown plumage and a short tail. [Perh. < VLat. **coacula.*]

quail² (kwāl) ►*v.* To shrink back in fear; cower. [ME *quailen*, give way.]

quaint (kwānt) ►*adj.* **-er, -est 1.** Odd, esp. in an old-fashioned way. **2.** *Archaic* Unfamiliar or unusual. [< Lat. *cognitus,* p.part. of *cognōscere,* learn.] —**quaint′ly** *adv.* —**quaint′ness** *n.*

quake (kwāk) ►*v.* **quaked, quak·ing 1.** To shake or tremble. **2.** To shiver, as with cold or from fear. ►*n.* **1.** An instance of quaking. **2.** An earthquake. [< OE *cwacian.*] —**quak′y** *adj.*

Quak·er (kwā′kər) ►*n.* A member of the Society of Friends. —**Quak′er·ism** *n.*

qual·i·fi·ca·tion (kwŏl′ə-fĭ-kā′shən) ►*n.* **1.** The act of qualifying or the condition of being qualified. **2.** A quality or an ability that makes a person suitable for a particular position or task. **3.** A restriction or modification.

qual·i·fy (kwŏl′ə-fī′) ►*v.* **-fied, -fy·ing 1a.** To make competent or eligible for an office, position, or task. **b.** To declare competent, as to practice a profession; certify. **c.** To be deserving of something by having certain necessary characteristics: *qualify for a tax credit.* **2a.** To modify, limit, or restrict. **b.** To make less harsh or severe. See Synonyms at **moderate. 3.** *Gram.* To modify the meaning of (e.g., a noun). [< Med.Lat. *quālificāre,* attribute a quality to.] —**qual′i·fi′er** *n.*

qual·i·ta·tive (kwŏl′ĭ-tā′tĭv) ►*adj.* Of or concerning quality. —**qual′i·ta′tive·ly** *adv.*

qual·i·ty (kwŏl′ĭ-tē) ►*n., pl.* **-ties 1.** A trait or characteristic; property. **2.** Essential character; nature. **3.** Degree or grade of excellence. **4.** High social position. [< Lat. *quālis,* of what kind.] —**qual′i·ty** *adj.*

qualm (kwäm, kwôm) ►*n.* **1.** A pang of conscience about a course of action. **2.** A sudden disturbing feeling. **3.** A sudden feeling of sickness, faintness, or nausea. [?]

quan·da·ry (kwŏn′də-rē, -drē) ►*n., pl.* **-ries** A state of uncertainty or perplexity. [?]

quan·ti·fy (kwŏn′tə-fī′) ►*v.* **-fied, -fy·ing** To determine or express the quantity of. [< Lat. *quantus,* how much.] —**quan′ti·fi′a·ble** *adj.*

quan·ti·ta·tive (kwŏn′tĭ-tā′tĭv) ►*adj.* Relating to or expressed as a quantity. —**quan′ti·ta′-tive·ly** *adv.*

quan·ti·ty (kwŏn′tĭ-tē) ►*n., pl.* **-ti·ties 1.** A specified or indefinite number or amount. **2.** A considerable amount or number. [< Lat. *quantus,* how much.]

quan·tum (kwŏn′təm) ►*n., pl.* **-ta** (-tə) **1.** *Phys.* A discrete quantity of electromagnetic radiation. **2.** A quantity or amount. [< Lat. *quantus,* how much.]

quantum physics ►*n.* *(takes sing. v.)* The branch of physics that uses quantum theory to describe and predict the properties of a physical system.

quantum theory ►*n.* *Phys.* The theory that radiant energy is transmitted in the form of discrete units.

quar·an·tine (kwôr′ən-tēn′, kwŏr′-) ►*n.* **1.** A condition, period of time, or place in which one suspected of carrying an infectious agent is kept in confinement. **2.** An action to isolate another nation, such as trade sanctions or a naval blockade. **3.** *Comp.* The isolation of data or data transmissions in order to keep malware from infecting a computer or computer network. ►*v.* **-tined, -tin·ing** To isolate in quarantine. [< Lat. *quadrāgintā,* forty.]

quark (kwôrk, kwärk) ►*n.* Any of a class of six fundamental fermions with fractional electric

charges, regarded as the basic components of all hadrons. [Coined by Murray Gell-Mann (b. 1929).]

quar·rel (kwôr′əl, kwŏr′-) ►*n.* **1.** An angry dispute; altercation. **2.** A reason for a dispute or argument. ►*v.* **-reled, -rel·ing** or **-relled, -rel·ling 1.** To engage in a quarrel; argue. **2.** To find fault. [< Lat. *querēla,* complaint.] —**quar′rel·er, quar′rel·ler** *v.*

quar·rel·some (kwôr′əl-səm, kwŏr′-) ►*adj.* Given to quarreling; contentious. See Synonyms at **argumentative.**

quar·ry[1] (kwôr′ē, kwŏr′ē) ►*n., pl.* **-ries 1.** A hunted animal; prey. **2.** An object of pursuit. [< OFr. *cuiriee,* entrails of a deer given to hounds < Lat. *cor,* heart.]

quar·ry[2] (kwôr′ē, kwŏr′ē) ►*n., pl.* **-ries** An open excavation or pit from which stone is obtained. [< Lat. *quadrum,* square.] —**quar′ri·er** *n.* —**quar′ry** *v.*

quart (kwôrt) ►*n.* **1.** A unit of volume or capacity in both liquid and dry measure. See table at **measurement. 2.** A container having a capacity of one quart. [< Lat. *quārtus,* fourth.]

quar·ter (kwôr′tər) ►*n.* **1.** One of four equal parts. **2.** A coin equal to one fourth of the dollar of the US and Canada. **3.** One fourth of an hour; 15 minutes. **4a.** One fourth of a year; three months: *the second quarter.* **b.** An academic term lasting approximately three months. **5.** One leg of an animal's carcass. **6. quarters** A place of residence. **7.** often **Quarter** A specific district or section, as of a city. **8.** often **quarters** An unspecified direction, person, or group: *information from the highest quarters.* **9.** Mercy or clemency. ►*adj.* Equal to or being a quarter. ►*v.* **1.** To divide into four equal or equivalent parts. **2.** To dismember (a human body) into four parts. **3.** To furnish with housing. [< Lat. *quārtārius < quārtus,* fourth.]

quar·ter·back (kwôr′tər-băk′) ►*n.* *Football* The offensive backfield player who usu. calls the signals for the plays and receives the ball when snapped. —**quar′ter·back′** *v.*

quar·ter·deck (kwôr′tər-dĕk′) ►*n.* The after part of the upper deck of a ship.

quarter horse ►*n.* A strong saddle horse developed in the W US. [From its formerly being trained for quarter-mile races.]

quar·ter·ly (kwôr′tər-lē) ►*adj.* Occurring at three-month intervals. ►*n., pl.* **-lies** A publication issued regularly every three months.

quar·ter·mas·ter (kwôr′tər-măs′tər) ►*n.* **1.** An officer responsible for the food, clothing, and equipment of troops. **2.** A petty officer responsible for the steering of a ship.

quarter note ►*n.* *Mus.* A note having one-fourth the time value of a whole note.

quar·tet also **quar·tette** (kwôr-tĕt′) ►*n.* **1.** *Mus.* A composition for four voices or instruments. **2.** A group or set of four. [< Lat. *quārtus,* fourth.]

quar·tile (kwôr′tīl′, -tĭl) ►*n.* *Statistics* The portion of a frequency distribution containing one fourth of the total sample. [< Lat. *quārtus,* fourth.]

quar·to (kwôr′tō) ►*n., pl.* **-tos 1.** The page size obtained by folding a whole sheet into four leaves. **2.** A book composed of pages of this size. [< Lat. *quārtus,* fourth.]

quartz (kwôrts) ►*n.* A hard silica mineral found

worldwide in many different types of rocks, including sandstone and granite. [Ger. *Quarz*.]

quartz·ite (kwôrt′sīt′) ►*n.* A rock formed from the metamorphism of quartz sandstone.

qua·sar (kwā′zär′, -sär′, -zər, -sər) ►*n.* A compact, extremely bright celestial object whose power output can be hundreds to several thousand times that of the entire Milky Way galaxy. [*quas(i-stell)ar (radio source)*.]

quash[1] (kwŏsh) ►*v.* To annul (a court order, indictment, or court proceedings). [< Med. Lat. *cassare*.]

quash[2] (kwŏsh) ►*v.* **1.** To put down or suppress (e.g., a rebellion). **2.** To put an end to or destroy. [< Med.Lat. *quassāre*, shatter.]

qua·si (kwā′zī′, kwä′zē) ►*adj.* Having a likeness to something; resembling. [< Lat., as if.]

quasi– ►*pref.* Almost; somewhat: *quasi-stellar object.* [Lat. *quasi*, as if.]

qua·si-stel·lar object (kwā′zī-stĕl′ər, kwä′zē-) ►*n.* A quasar.

Quaternary (kwŏt′ər-nĕr′ē, kwə-tûr′nə-rē) *Geol.* ►*adj.* Of or being the 2nd period of the Cenozoic Era, including the Pleistocene and Holocene Epochs. ►*n.* The Quaternary Period. [< Lat. *quater*, four times.]

quat·rain (kwŏt′rān′, kwŏ-trān′) ►*n.* A stanza or poem of four lines. [< Lat. *quattuor*, four.]

quat·re·foil (kăt′ər-foil′, kăt′rə-) ►*n.* A representation of a flower with four petals or a leaf with four leaflets. [< OFr. *quatre*, four; see QUATRAIN + *foil*, leaf.]

qua·ver (kwā′vər) ►*v.* **1.** To quiver, as from weakness; tremble. **2.** To speak in a shaky or tremulous voice. [ME *quaveren*.] —**qua′ver** *n.* —**qua′ver·y** *adj.*

quay (kē, kā, kwā) ►*n.* A wharf. [< ONFr. *cai*.]

quay

quea·sy (kwē′zē) ►*adj.* **-si·er, -si·est 1.** Experiencing nausea; nauseated. **2.** Uneasy; troubled. **3.** Ill at ease; squeamish. [ME *coisy*.] —**quea′si·ly** *adv.* —**quea′si·ness** *n.*

Que·bec (kwĭ-bĕk′) or **Qué·bec** (kā-) **1.** A province of E Canada. Cap. Quebec. **2.** also **Quebec City** The capital of Quebec, Canada, in the S part on the St. Lawrence R. —**Que·beck′er, Que·bec′er** *n.*

Qué·bé·cois (kā′bĕ-kwä′) ►*n., pl.* **-cois** A native or inhabitant of Quebec, esp. a French-speaking one. —**Qué′bé·cois′** *adj.*

Quech·ua (kĕch′wə, -wä′) ►*n., pl.* **-ua** or **-uas**

1. The Quechuan language of the Inca empire, now widely spoken in the Andes highlands. **2.** A speaker of the Quechua language.

Quech·uan (kĕch′wən) ►*n.* **1.** A member of a Native American people of Arizona and California. **2.** A subgroup of languages, the most important being Quechua.

queen (kwēn) ►*n.* **1a.** The wife or widow of a king. **b.** A woman sovereign. **2.** Something eminent or supreme in a given domain and personified as a woman: *Paris is the queen of cities.* **3.** *Games* **a.** The most powerful chess piece. **b.** A playing card bearing the figure of a queen. **4.** A reproductive female in a colony of social insects, such as wasps or ants. [< OE *cwēn*.] —**queen′li·ness** *n.* —**queen′ly** *adj.*

queen mother ►*n.* A dowager queen who is the mother of a reigning monarch.

Queens (kwēnz) A borough of New York City in SE NY on W Long I.

Queen's English ►*n.* Standard English in England.

queer (kwîr) ►*adj.* **-er, -est 1.** Deviating from the expected or normal; strange. **2.** Eccentric. **3.** *Offensive Slang* Gay or lesbian. ►*n.* *Offensive Slang* Used as a disparaging term for a gay man or a lesbian. ►*v.* *Slang* To ruin or thwart. [Poss. of LGer. orig.] —**queer′ly** *adv.* —**queer′ness** *n.*

quell (kwĕl) ►*v.* **1.** To put down forcibly; suppress. **2.** To pacify; quiet. [< OE *cwellan*, kill.]

quench (kwĕnch) ►*v.* **1.** To put out; extinguish. **2.** To suppress; squelch. **3.** To slake (thirst). **4.** To cool (hot metal) by thrusting into liquid. [< OE *ācwencan*.] —**quench′a·ble** *adj.*

quer·u·lous (kwĕr′ə-ləs, kwĕr′yə-) ►*adj.* **1.** Given to complaining; peevish. **2.** Expressing a complaint or grievance. [< Lat. *querulus*.] —**quer′u·lous·ly** *adv.* —**quer′u·lous·ness** *n.*

que·ry (kwîr′ē) ►*n., pl.* **-ries 1.** A question; inquiry. **2.** A doubt in the mind; reservation. **3.** A notation, usu. a question mark. ►*v.* **-ried, -ry·ing** To question. [< Lat. *quaerere*, ask.]

que·sa·dil·la (kā′sə-dē′yə) ►*n.* A flour tortilla folded over a filling, then fried or toasted. [Am. Sp., ult. < Lat. *cāseus*, cheese.]

quest (kwĕst) ►*n.* **1.** The act or an instance of seeking. **2.** An expedition undertaken in medieval romance by a knight. ►*v.* To search. [< Lat. *quaerere*, *quaest-*, seek.] —**quest′er** *n.*

ques·tion (kwĕs′chən) ►*n.* **1.** A sentence, phrase, or gesture that seeks information through a reply. **2a.** A subject or point that is under discussion or open to controversy. **b.** A difficult matter; problem. **3.** Uncertainty; doubt. ►*v.* **1a.** To ask a question or questions of (someone). **b.** To interrogate (e.g., a suspect). **2.** To express doubt about; dispute. —*idiom:* **out of the question** Not to be considered; impossible. [< Lat. *quaerere*, *quaest-*, ask.] —**ques′tion·er** *n.* —**ques′tion·ing·ly** *adv.*

ques·tion·a·ble (kwĕs′chə-nə-bəl) ►*adj.* **1.** Open to doubt; uncertain. **2.** Of dubious morality or respectability. —**ques′tion·a·bil′i·ty** *n.* —**ques′tion·a·bly** *adv.*

question mark ►*n.* A punctuation symbol (?) written at the end of a sentence or phrase to indicate a direct question.

ques·tion·naire (kwĕs′chə-nâr′) ►*n.* A set of questions usu. intended to gather information for a survey. [Fr.]

quet·zal (kĕt-säl′) ►*n., pl.* **-zals** or **-za·les** (-sä′- läs) **1.** A tropical American bird with brilliant green and red plumage and long tail feathers in the male. **2.** See table at **currency.** [< Nahuatl *quetzalli,* large brilliant tail feather.]

queue (kyōō) ►*n.* **1.** A line of waiting people or vehicles. **2.** A long braid of hair worn hanging down the back of the neck. **3a.** A sequence of stored data awaiting processing. **b.** A data structure from which the first item that can be retrieved is the one stored earliest. ►*v.* **queued, queu·ing 1.** To get in line: *queue up for tickets.* **2.** To place in a sequence. [< Lat. *cauda,* tail.]

Que·zon City (kā′sôn′, -sōn′) A city of central Luzon, Philippines, adjoining Manila.

quib·ble (kwĭb′əl) ►*v.* **-bled, -bling** To find fault over minor concerns; cavil. [Prob. < obsolete *quib,* equivocation.] **—quib′ble** *n.* **—quib′bler** *n.*

Syns: *carp, cavil, nitpick* **v.**

quiche (kēsh) ►*n.* A rich unsweetened custard pie, often with additional savory ingredients. [< Ger. *Kuchen,* cake.]

quick (kwĭk) ►*adj.* **-er, -est 1.** Moving or functioning rapidly; speedy. **2.** Learning, thinking, or understanding with speed and dexterity; bright. **3.** Hasty or sharp in reacting. **4.** Occurring or achieved in a brief period of time. ►*n.* **1.** Sensitive flesh, as under the fingernails. **2.** The most personal and sensitive aspect: *an insult that cut to the quick.* **3.** The living. **4.** The vital core; essence. ►*adv.* Quickly. [< OE *cwicu,* alive.] **—quick′ly** *adv.* **—quick′ness** *n.*

quick·en (kwĭk′ən) ►*v.* **1.** To make more rapid; accelerate. **2.** To come or return to life, as a soul. **3.** To excite and stimulate; stir.

quick·ie (kwĭk′ē) ►*n. Informal* Something made or done rapidly.

quick·lime (kwĭk′līm′) ►*n.* Calcium oxide.

quick·sand (kwĭk′sănd′) ►*n.* Sand that is mixed with water in a collected mass and yields easily to pressure so that objects on its surface tend to sink and become engulfed.

quick·sil·ver (kwĭk′sĭl′vər) ►*n.* See **mercury** (sense 1). [< OE *cwicseolfor : cwicu,* alive + *seolfor,* silver.]

quick·step (kwĭk′stĕp′) ►*n.* A march for accompanying quick time.

quick-tem·pered (kwĭk′tĕm′pərd) ►*adj.* Easily aroused to anger.

quick time ►*n.* A military marching pace of 120 steps per minute.

quick-wit·ted (kwĭk′wĭt′ĭd) ►*adj.* Mentally alert and sharp; keen. **—quick′-wit′ted·ly** *adv.*

quid¹ (kwĭd) ►*n.* A cut, as of chewing tobacco. [< OE *cwidu,* cud.]

quid² (kwĭd) ►*n., pl.* **quid** or **quids** *Chiefly Brit.* A pound sterling. [Poss. < Lat., something.]

quid pro quo (kwĭd′ prō kwō′) ►*n.* Something that is given in return for something else. [Lat. *quid prō quō,* what for what?]

qui·es·cent (kwē-ĕs′ənt, kwī-) ►*adj.* **1.** Quiet, still, or inactive. **2.** Marked by an absence of upheaval. [< Lat. *quiēscere,* be quiet.] **—qui·es′cence** *n.* **—qui·es′cent·ly** *adv.*

qui·et (kwī′ĭt) ►*adj.* **-er, -est 1.** Making little or no noise. **2a.** Free of turmoil; calm. **b.** Allowing relaxation; restful. **3.** Understated; restrained. ►*n.* The quality or condition of being quiet. ►*v.* To become or cause to become quiet. [< Lat. *quiētus.*] **—qui′et·ly** *adv.* **—qui′et·ness** *n.*

qui·e·tude (kwī′ĭ-tōōd′, -tyōōd′) ►*n.* Tranquility.

qui·e·tus (kwī-ē′təs) ►*n.* **1.** Death. **2.** A final discharge, as of a debt. [< Lat. *quiētus (est),* (he is) at rest.]

quill (kwĭl) ►*n.* **1.** The hollow main shaft of a feather. **2.** A large stiff feather. **3.** A writing pen made from a quill. **4.** A sharp hollow spine, as of a porcupine. [ME *quil.*]

quilt (kwĭlt) ►*n.* A coverlet made by stitching two layers of fabric with padding in between. [< Lat. *culcita,* mattress.] **—quilt** *v.* **—quilt′ed** *adj.* **—quilt′er** *n.* **—quilt′ing** *n.*

quince (kwĭns) ►*n.* **1.** A shrub or small tree having white or pink flowers and hard yellow pear-shaped fruit. **2.** The many-seeded fruit of this plant, used esp. for jelly. [< Lat. *cotōneum.*]

qui·nine (kwī′nīn′) ►*n.* A bitter, colorless, amorphous powder or crystalline alkaloid derived from certain cinchona barks and used to treat malaria. [< Sp. *quina,* cinchona bark.]

qui·no·a (kĭ-nō′ə, kēn′wä) ►*n.* **1.** A weedy Andean plant cultivated for its edible seeds. **2.** The seeds of this plant, used as food. [Am.Sp. *quínoa* < Quechua *kinwa.*]

quin·quen·ni·al (kwĭn-kwĕn′ē-əl, kwĭng-) ►*adj.* **1.** Happening once every five years. **2.** Lasting for five years. [< Lat. *quīnquennium,* period of five years.] **—quin·quen′ni·al** *n.* **—quin·quen′ni·al·ly** *adv.*

quin·sy (kwĭn′zē) ►*n.* Acute inflammation of the tonsils and the surrounding tissue. [< Gk. *kunankhē,* dog collar.]

quint (kwĭnt) ►*n.* A quintuplet.

quin·tal (kwĭnt′l) ►*n.* **1.** A metric unit of mass equal to 100 kg. **2.** See **hundredweight** (sense 2). [< Ar. *qinṭār,* a unit of weight < Lat. *centēnārius,* of a hundred.]

quin·tes·sence (kwĭn-tĕs′əns) ►*n.* **1.** The purest, most essential element of a thing. **2.** The purest or most typical instance. [< Med.Lat. *quīnta essentia,* fifth essence.] **—quin′tes·sen′tial** (kwĭn′tə-sĕn′shəl) *adj.*

quin·tet also **quin·tette** (kwĭn-tĕt′) ►*n.* **1.** *Mus.* A composition for five voices or instruments. **2.** A group or set of five. [< Lat. *quīntus,* fifth.]

quin·tile (kwĭn′tīl′, kwĭnt′l) ►*n. Statistics* The portion of a frequency distribution containing one fifth of the total sample. [< Lat. *quīntus,* fifth.]

Quin·til·ian (kwĭn-tĭl′yən, -ē-ən) 1st cent. AD. Roman rhetorician.

quin·til·lion (kwĭn-tĭl′yən) ►*n.* **1.** The cardinal number equal to 10^{18}. **2.** *Chiefly Brit.* The cardinal number equal to 10^{30}. [Lat. *quīntus,* fifth + (M)ILLION.] **—quin·til′lion** *adj.* **—quin·til′lionth** *n. & adj.*

quin·tu·ple (kwĭn-tōō′pəl, -tyōō′-, -tŭp′əl, kwĭn′tə-pəl) ►*adj.* **1.** Having five parts. **2.** Five times as many or as much. ►*n.* A fivefold amount or number. ►*v.* **-pled, -pling** To multiply or be multiplied by five. [< Lat. *quīntus,* fifth.]

quin·tu·plet (kwĭn-tŭp′lĭt, -tōō′plĭt, -tyōō′-, kwĭn′tə-plĭt) ►*n.* **1.** One of five offspring born in a single birth. **2.** A group or combination of five.

quin·tu·pli·cate (kwĭn-tōō′plĭ-kĭt, -tyōō′-) ►*n.* One of a set of five identical things. [< Lat. *quīntus,* fifth; see QUINTUPLE + (QUADRU)PLICATE.] **—quin·tup′li·cate′** (-kāt′) *v.*

quip (kwĭp) ►*n.* A clever, witty, often sarcastic remark. ►*v.* **quipped, quip·ping** To make quips or a quip. [Perh. < Lat. *quippe*, indeed.]

quire (kwīr) ►*n.* A set of 24 or sometimes 25 sheets of paper of the same size and stock. [< Lat. *quaternī*, set of four < *quater*, four times.]

quirk (kwûrk) ►*n.* **1.** A peculiarity of behavior; idiosyncrasy. **2.** A sudden sharp turn or twist. [?] —**quirk′i·ness** *n.* —**quirk′y** *adj.*

quirt (kwûrt) ►*n.* A riding whip with a short, stiff handle and a lash made of two or more loose thongs. [Prob. < Am.Sp. *cuarta*, whip; see QUART.]

quis·ling (kwĭz′lĭng) ►*n.* A traitor who serves as the puppet of the enemy occupying his or her country. [After Vidkun *Quisling* (1887–1945).]

quit (kwĭt) ►*v.* **quit** also **quit·ted, quit·ting 1.** To cease or discontinue. See Synonyms at **stop. 2.** To resign from; relinquish. **3.** To depart from; leave. [< Lat. *quiētus*, at rest.]

quit·claim (kwĭt′klām′) ►*n. Law* The transfer of a title or deed to another, without warranty as to the extent of ownership on the part of the seller. [< AN *quiteclamer*, release.] —**quit′-claim′** *v.*

quite (kwīt) ►*adv.* **1.** Altogether; completely. **2.** Actually; really. **3.** To a degree; rather: *quite tasty.* [< Lat. *quiētus*, freed.]

Qui·to (kē′tō) The capital of Ecuador, in the N-central part.

quits (kwĭts) ►*adj.* On even terms with, as by payment. [Prob. < Lat. *quiētus*, at rest.]

quit·tance (kwĭt′ns) ►*n.* **1.** Release or discharge from debt or obligation. **2.** Payment of a debt or obligation. [< OFr. *quiter*, to free.]

quit·ter (kwĭt′ər) ►*n.* One who gives up easily.

quiv·er¹ (kwĭv′ər) ►*v.* **1.** To shake with a tremulous movement. **2.** To tremble, as from cold or strong emotion. [ME *quiveren*.] —**quiv′er** *n.* —**quiv′er·y** *adj.*

quiv·er² (kwĭv′ər) ►*n.* A case for holding arrows. [< OFr. *cuivre*, of Gmc. orig.]

qui vive (kē vēv′) ►*n.* A sentry's challenge. [Fr., (long) live who?]

quix·ot·ic (kwĭk-sŏt′ĭk) ►*adj.* **1.** Idealistic or romantic without regard to practicality. **2.** Capricious; impulsive. [After *Don Quixote*, hero of a romance by Miguel de Cervantes.] —**quix·ot′i·cal·ly** *adv.*

quiz (kwĭz) ►*v.* **quizzed, quiz·zing** To question (someone), esp. closely. ►*n., pl.* **quiz·zes** A short oral or written test. [?]

quiz·zi·cal (kwĭz′ĭ-kəl) ►*adj.* **1.** Suggesting puzzlement; questioning. **2.** Teasing; mocking. **3.** Eccentric; odd. —**quiz′zi·cal·i·ty** (-kăl′ĭ-tē) *n.* —**quiz′zi·cal·ly** *adv.*

quoin (koin, kwoin) ►*n.* **1a.** An exterior angle of a wall or building. **b.** A stone forming a quoin; cornerstone. **2.** A keystone. [Var. of COIN, corner.]

quoit (kwoit, koit) ►*n.* **1. quoits** (takes sing. *v.*) A game in which players toss rings at a stake, trying to get each ring to land with the stake through its center or closest to the stake. **2.** One of the rings used in this game. [< Lat. *culcita*, cushion.]

quon·dam (kwŏn′dəm, -dăm′) ►*adj.* That once was; former. [Lat.]

quo·rum (kwôr′əm) ►*n.* The minimum number of members of a committee or an organization needed for valid transaction of business. [< Lat. *quōrum*, of whom.]

quo·ta (kwō′tə) ►*n.* **1.** A proportional share; allotment. **2.** A production assignment. **3a.** A number or percentage, esp. of people, constituting an upper limit: *strict immigration quotas.* **b.** A number or percentage, esp. of people, constituting a required minimum: *quotas for hiring minority applicants.* [< Lat. *quotus*, of what number.]

quot·a·ble (kwō′tə-bəl) ►*adj.* Worth quoting.

quo·ta·tion (kwō-tā′shən) ►*n.* **1.** The act of quoting. **2.** A passage quoted. **3.** The quoting of current prices and bids for securities and goods.

quotation mark ►*n.* Either of a pair of punctuation marks (" " or ' ') used to mark the beginning and end of a passage attributed to another and repeated word for word.

quote (kwōt) ►*v.* **quot·ed, quot·ing 1.** To repeat or copy the words of (another), usu. with acknowledgment of the source. **2.** To cite for illustration or proof. **3.** To state (a price) for securities, goods, or services. ►*n.* **1.** *Informal* A quotation. **2.** A quotation mark. [< Lat. *quotus*, of what number.] —**quot′er** *n.*

Usage: People have been using the noun *quote* as a truncation of *quotation* for over one hundred years, and its use in less formal contexts is widespread today. Language critics have objected to this usage, however, as unduly journalistic or breezy. It may therefore be best to avoid it in more formal situations.

quoth (kwōth) ►*v. Archaic* Uttered; said. [< OE *cwæth.*]

quo·tid·i·an (kwō-tĭd′ē-ən) ►*adj.* **1.** Everyday; commonplace. **2.** Recurring daily. [< Lat. *quōtīdiānus.*]

quo·tient (kwō′shənt) ►*n.* The number obtained by dividing one quantity by another. [< Lat. *quotiēns*, how many times.]

Qur′an or **Qur·an** (kə-rän′, -răn′, kô-, kō-) ►*n.* Var. of **Koran.**

q.v. ►*abbr. Lat.* quod vide (which see)

R

r¹ or **R** (är) ►*n., pl.* **r's** or **R's** also **rs** or **Rs** The 18th letter of the English alphabet.

r² ►*abbr.* **1.** radius **2.** or **R** *Elect.* resistance

R¹ (är) A trademark for a movie rating granting admission only to persons of or over a certain age, usu. 17, unless accompanied by a parent or guardian.

R² ►*abbr.* **1.** registered trademark **2.** Republican **3.** right **4.** or **r** roentgen **5.** rook (chess) **6.** *Baseball* run

r. ►*abbr.* **1.** retired **2.** rod (unit of length)

R. ►*abbr.* **1.** rabbi **2.** rector **3.** river

Ra (rä) ►*n. Myth.* The ancient Egyptian sun god.

RA ►*abbr.* residence assistant

Ra·bat (rə-bät′, rä-) The capital of Morocco, on the Atlantic NE of Casablanca.

rab·bet (răb′ĭt) ►*n.* **1.** A cut or groove along or near the edge of a piece of wood that allows another piece to fit into it to form a joint. A joint that is so made. ►*v.* **1.** To cut a rabbet in. **2.** To join by a rabbet. [< *rabattre*, beat down.]

rabbet

rab·bi (răb′ī) ►*n.*, *pl.* **-bis 1.** A person ordained for leadership of a Jewish congregation. **2.** A scholar qualified to interpret Jewish law. [< Heb. *rabbî*.] —**rab·bin·i·cal** (rə-bĭn′ĭ-kəl), **rab·bin′ic** *adj.*

rab·bin·ate (răb′ə-nāt′, -nĭt) ►*n.* **1.** The office or function of a rabbi. **2.** Rabbis collectively.

rab·bit (răb′ĭt) ►*n.*, *pl.* **-bits** or **-bit 1.** A long-eared, short-tailed, burrowing mammal with soft fur. **2.** A hare. **3.** The fur of a rabbit or hare. [ME *rubet.*]

rabbit punch ►*n.* A chopping blow to the back of the neck. —**rab′bit-punch′** *v.*

rab·ble (răb′əl) ►*n.* **1.** A tumultuous crowd; mob. **2.** The lowest or least refined part of society. [ME.]

rab·ble-rous·er (răb′əl-rou′zər) ►*n.* One who stirs up the passions of the masses.

Ra·be·lais (răb′ə-lā′), **François** 1494?–1553. French writer. —**Rab′e·lai′si·an** (răb′ə-lā′zē-ən, -zhən) *adj.*

Ra·bi (rŭ′bē) also **Ra·bi·a** (rə-bē′ə) ►*n.* Either the 3rd or 4th month of the Islamic calendar. See table at **calendar.** [Ar. *rabī*ʿ, spring.]

rab·id (răb′ĭd) ►*adj.* **1.** Of or affected by rabies. **2.** Raging; uncontrollable: *rabid thirst.* **3.** Extremely zealous; fanatical. [Lat. *rabidus.*] —**ra·bid′i·ty** (rə-bĭd′ĭ-tē, ră-) *n.* —**rab′id·ly** *adv.*

ra·bies (rā′bēz) ►*n.* An acute, infectious, often fatal viral disease of most mammals that attacks the central nervous system and is transmitted by the bite of infected animals. [Lat. *rabiēs*, rage < *rabere*, rave.]

Ra·bin (rä-bēn′, rä′bēn), **Yitzhak** or **Itzhak** 1922–95. Israeli military leader and prime minister (1974–77 and 1992–95).

rac·coon (ră-kōōn′) ►*n.*, *pl.* **-coons** or **-coon 1.** An omnivorous mammal native to the Americas and introduced elsewhere, having black masklike facial markings and a black-ringed bushy tail. **2.** The fur of this mammal. [Of Virginia Algonquian orig.]

race¹ (rās) ►*n.* **1.** A group of people identified as distinct from other groups because of supposed physical or genetic traits shared by the group. **2.** A group of people united by a common history, nationality, or tradition. **3.** A genealogical line; lineage. **4.** A subspecies, breed, or strain of a plant or animal. [< OItal. *razza.*]

race² (rās) ►*n.* **1.** A competition of speed. **2.** A contest for supremacy: *the presidential race.* **3.** Rapid onward movement: *the race of time.* **4a.** A strong or swift current of water. **b.** The channel of such a current. ►*v.* **raced, rac·ing 1.** To compete in a race. **2.** To move rapidly or at top speed. **3.** To cause (an engine) to run too rapidly. [< ON *rās*, running.] —**rac′er** *n.*

race·course (rās′kôrs′) ►*n.* A course laid out for racing.

race·horse (rās′hôrs′) ►*n.* A horse bred and trained to race.

ra·ceme (rā-sēm′, rə-) ►*n.* An inflorescence having flowers arranged singly along a common stem. [Lat. *racēmus*, bunch of grapes.]

race·track (rās′trăk′) ►*n.* A usu. oval course on which races are held.

race·way (rās′wā′) ►*n.* A racetrack.

Ra·chel (rā′chəl) In the Bible, the second wife of Jacob.

ra·chi·tis (rə-kī′tĭs) ►*n.* See **rickets.** [< Gk. *rhakhis*, spine.] —**ra·chit′ic** (-kĭt′ĭk) *adj.*

ra·cial (rā′shəl) ►*adj.* **1.** Of or determined by race. **2.** Between or among distinct human racial groups: *racial discrimination.* —**ra′cial·ly** *adv.*

Ra·cine (rə-sēn′, rä-), **Jean Baptiste** 1639–99. French playwright.

rac·ism (rā′sĭz′əm) ►*n.* **1.** The belief that a particular race is superior to others. **2.** Discrimination or prejudice based on race. —**rac′ist** *adj. & n.*

rack¹ (răk) ►*n.* **1.** A framework or stand in or on which to hold, hang, or display something. **2.** *Slang* A bed. **3.** A toothed bar that meshes with a gearwheel or pinion. **4.** An instrument of torture on which the victim's body was stretched. **5.** A pair of antlers. ►*v.* **1.** To place (e.g., billiard balls) in a rack. **2.** To cause great suffering to; torment. See Synonyms at **afflict. 3.** To torture on a rack. **4.** To strain to the utmost: *rack one's brains.* —**phrasal verb: rack up** *Informal* To accumulate or score: *rack up points.* [Prob. < MDu. *rec*, framework.]

rack² (răk) ►*n.* A rib cut of lamb or veal. [Prob. < RACK¹.]

rack·et¹ also **rac·quet** (răk′ĭt) ►*n.* **1.** A device consisting of an oval or circular frame with a tight network of strings and a handle, used to strike a ball or shuttlecock. **2.** A table tennis paddle. [< Ar. *rāḥat*, palm.]

rack·et² (răk′ĭt) ►*n.* **1.** A loud distressing noise. See Synonyms at **noise. 2.** A fraudulent or dishonest business or practice. **3.** *Slang* A business or occupation. [?]

rack·et·eer (răk′ĭ-tîr′) ►*n.* A person who engages in an illegal business or other organized illegal activities. —**rack′et·eer′** *v.*

rac·on·teur (răk′ŏn-tûr′) ►*n.* One who tells stories with skill and wit. [< OFr. *raconter*, relate.]

rac·quet·ball (răk′ĭt-bôl′) ►*n.* **1.** A court game similar to handball but played with short-handled rackets and a softer, larger ball. **2.** The ball used in this game.

rac·y (rā′sē) ►*adj.* **-i·er, -i·est 1.** Strong and sharp in flavor or odor. **2.** Risqué; ribald. [< RACE¹.] —**rac′i·ly** *adv.* —**rac′i·ness** *n.*

rad¹ (răd) ►*n.* A unit of energy absorbed from ionizing radiation, equal to 0.01 joule per kilogram. [< RADIATION.]

rad² ►*abbr.* radian

rad. ►*abbr.* **1.** radical **2.** radius

ra·dar (rā′där) ►*n.* A device used for detecting distant objects and determining such features as position or velocity by analysis of radio waves reflected from their surfaces. [*ra(dio) d(etecting) a(nd) r(anging).*]

ra·dar·scope (rā′där-skōp′) ►*n.* The viewing screen of a radar receiver.

ra·di·al (rā′dē-əl) ►*adj.* **1a.** Of or arranged like rays or radii. **b.** Having or marked by parts radiating from a common center. **2.** Moving or directed along a radius. [< Lat. *radius*, ray.] —**ra′di·al·ly** *adv.*

radial symmetry ►*n.* Symmetrical arrangement of constituents, esp. of radiating parts, about a central point.

radial tire ►*n.* A pneumatic tire in which the ply cords are laid at right angles to the center line of the tread.

ra·di·an (rā′dē-ən) ►*n.* A unit of angular measure equal to approx. 57°17′44.62″ [< RADIUS.]

ra·di·ant (rā′dē-ənt) ►*adj.* **1.** Emitting heat or light. **2.** Consisting of or emitted as radiation. **3.** Filled with light shining esp. as rays. [< Lat. *radiāre*, RADIATE.] —**ra′di·ance, ra′di·an·cy** *n.*

radiant energy ►*n.* Energy transferred by radiation, esp. by an electromagnetic wave.

ra·di·ate (rā′dē-āt′) ►*v.* -**at·ed, -at·ing 1.** To send out or issue in rays or waves. **2.** To spread out in straight lines from a center. **3.** To irradiate. **4.** To manifest glowingly: *radiate confidence.* ►*adj.* (-ĭt) **1.** *Bot.* Having rays or raylike parts. **2.** Marked by radial symmetry. [< Lat. *radius*, ray.] —**ra′di·a′tive** *adj.*

ra·di·a·tion (rā′dē-ā′shən) ►*n.* **1.** The act or process of radiating. **2.** *Phys.* **a.** Emission of energy in the form of waves or particles. **b.** Energy emitted in this form. **c.** A stream of particles. **3.** Radiotherapy.

radiation sickness ►*n.* An often fatal illness induced by overexposure to ionizing radiation, marked by nausea, diarrhea, and loss of hair and teeth.

ra·di·a·tor (rā′dē-ā′tər) ►*n.* A device that radiates heat, esp.: **a.** A heating device through which steam or hot water is circulated. **b.** A cooling device that dissipates engine heat.

rad·i·cal (răd′ĭ-kəl) ►*adj.* **1.** Fundamental; basic. **2.** Departing markedly from the usual; extreme. **3.** Advocating fundamental or revolutionary changes. ►*n.* **1.** One who advocates fundamental or revolutionary changes. **2.** *Math.* The root of a quantity as indicated by the radical sign. **3.** An atom or a group of atoms with one unpaired electron. [< Lat. *rādīx*, root.]

rad·i·cal·ism (răd′ĭ-kə-lĭz′əm) ►*n.* The doctrines or practices of political radicals.

rad·i·cal·ize (răd′ĭ-kə-līz′) ►*v.* -**ized, -iz·ing** To make radical or more radical. —**rad′i·cal·i·za′tion** *n.*

radical sign ►*n.* The sign √ placed before a quantity, indicating either the square root or the root designated by a raised integer.

ra·di·i (rā′dē-ī′) ►*n.* Pl. of **radius.**

ra·di·o (rā′dē-ō) ►*n., pl.* -**os 1.** Electromagnetic radiation with lower frequencies and longer wavelengths than those of microwaves. **2a.** The transmission and reception of electromagnetic waves within this range, esp. when convertible to audio sounds. **b.** A device that transmits or receives such signals. **3a.** The industry that broadcasts programs of audio content to listeners by means of radio waves. **b.** An electronic device for listening to radio programming. ►*v.* **1.** To transmit by radio. **2.** To communicate with by radio. [< *radiotelegraphy.*]

radio– or **radi–** ►*pref.* **1.** Radiation; radiant energy: *radiometer.* **2.** Radioactive: *radiocarbon.* **3.** Radio: *radiotelephone.* [< RADIATION.]

radioactive decay ►*n.* Spontaneous disintegration of a radioactive nuclide with the emission of energetic particles or radiation.

ra·di·o·ac·tiv·i·ty (rā′dē-ō-ăk-tĭv′ĭ-tē) ►*n.* **1.** Spontaneous emission of radiation, as from unstable atomic nuclei. **2.** The radiation, such as alpha particles, emitted by a radioactive source. —**ra′di·o·ac′tive** *adj.*

radio astronomy ►*n.* The branch of astronomy that uses observations of emissions in the radio part of the electromagnetic spectrum to study extraterrestrial sources.

ra·di·o·car·bon (rā′dē-ō-kär′bən) ►*n.* A radioactive isotope of carbon, esp. carbon-14.

radiocarbon dating ►*n.* A form of radiometric dating used to determine the age of organic remains in ancient objects on the basis of the half-life of carbon-14 and a comparison between the ratio of carbon-12 to carbon-14 in a sample of the remains to the known ratio in living organisms.

radio frequency ►*n.* A frequency within the range at which radio waves are transmitted, gen. from about 3 hertz to about 300 megahertz.

ra·di·o·gram (rā′dē-ō-grăm′) ►*n.* A message transmitted by wireless telegraphy.

ra·di·o·graph (rā′dē-ō-grăf′) ►*n.* An image produced by radiation, usu. by x-rays, and recorded on a surface such as photographic film. ►*v.* To make a radiograph of. —**ra′di·og′ra·pher** (-ŏg′rə-fər) *n.* —**ra′di·o·graph′ic** *adj.* —**ra′di·og′ra·phy** *n.*

ra·di·o·i·so·tope (rā′dē-ō-ī′sə-tōp′) ►*n.* A radioactive isotope.

ra·di·o·lo·ca·tion (rā′dē-ō-lō-kā′shən) ►*n.* Detection of distant objects by radar.

ra·di·ol·o·gy (rā′dē-ŏl′ə-jē) ►*n.* **1.** The branch of medicine that diagnoses conditions through use of electromagnetic radiation or sound waves and treats disease through the use of radioactive compounds. **2.** The use of radiation for the scientific examination of material structures. —**ra′di·o·log′i·cal** (-ə-lŏj′ĭ-kəl), **ra′di·o·log′ic** *adj.* —**ra′di·ol′o·gist** *n.*

ra·di·om·e·ter (rā′dē-ŏm′ĭ-tər) ►*n.* A device that measures the intensity of radiant energy. —**ra′di·om′e·try** *n.*

ra·di·o·met·ric dating (rā′dē-ō-mĕt′rĭk) ►*n.* A method for determining the age of an object based on the concentration of a particular radioactive isotope contained within it and the half-life of that isotope.

ra·di·o·paque (rā′dē-ō-pāk′) ►*adj.* Not allowing the passage of x-rays or other radiation. —**ra′di·o·pac′i·ty** (-ō-păs′ĭ-tē) *n.*

ra·di·o·phone (rā′dē-ō-fōn′) ►*n.* A radiotelephone. —**ra′di·o·phon′ic** (-fŏn′ĭk) *adj.*

ra·di·o·sonde (rā′dē-ō-sŏnd′) ►*n.* An instrument carried aloft, as by balloon, to gather and transmit meteorological data. [RADIO + Fr. *sonde*, sounding line.]

ra·di·o·tel·e·graph (rā′dē-ō-tĕl′ĭ-grăf′) ►*n.*

Radio transmission of telegraphic messages. —**ra·di·o·tel·e·graph·ic** *adj.* —**ra·di·o·te·leg·ra·phy** (-tə-lĕg′rə-fē) *n.*

ra·di·o·tel·e·phone (rā′dē-ō-tĕl′ə-fōn′) ►*n.* A telephone that sends and receives messages by radio. —**ra′di·o·tel′e·phon′ic** (-fŏn′ĭk) *adj.* —**ra′di·o·te·leph′o·ny** (-tə-lĕf′ə-nē) *n.*

radio telescope ►*n.* A device used for detecting and recording radio waves coming from celestial objects.

radio telescope
at the Very Large Array near Socorro, New Mexico

ra·di·o·ther·a·py (rā′dē-ō-thĕr′ə-pē) ►*n.* Treatment of disease with radiation.

radio wave ►*n.* An electromagnetic wave within the range of radio frequencies.

rad·ish (răd′ĭsh) ►*n.* **1.** A Eurasian plant having an edible root. **2.** The pungent root of this plant. [< Lat. *rādīx*, root.]

ra·di·um (rā′dē-əm) ►*n.* *Symbol* **Ra** A rare, white, highly radioactive metallic element, used in cancer radiotherapy and as a neutron source. At. no. 88. See table at **element.** [< Lat. *radius*, ray.]

ra·di·us (rā′dē-əs) ►*n., pl.* **-di·i** (-dē-ī′) or **-es 1a.** A line segment that joins the center of a circle with any point on its circumference. **b.** A line segment that joins the center of a sphere with any point on its surface. **c.** The length of any such line segment. **2.** A circular area measured by a given radius. **3.** The shorter and thicker of the two forearm bones. [Lat., ray.]

ra·don (rā′dŏn) ►*n.* *Symbol* **Rn** A radioactive, inert gaseous element formed by radium decay, used in radiotherapy. At. no. 86. See table at **element.** [< RADIUM.]

RAF ►*abbr.* Royal Air Force

raf·fi·a (răf′ē-ə) ►*n.* **1.** An African palm tree having large fibrous leaves. **2.** The leaf fibers of this plant. [Malagasy *rafia*.]

raff·ish (răf′ĭsh) ►*adj.* **1.** Vulgar; tawdry. **2.** Jaunty; rakish. [Prob. < ME *raf*, rubbish.] —**raff′ish·ly** *adv.* —**raff′ish·ness** *n.*

raf·fle (răf′əl) ►*n.* A lottery in which a number of persons buy chances to win a prize. ►*v.* **-fled, -fling** To award as a prize in a raffle: *raffle off a new car.* [< OFr. *rafle*, act of seizing.]

raft¹ (răft) ►*n.* **1.** A floating platform, as of planks or logs fastened together, used for transport, travel, or recreation. **2.** A flat-bottomed inflatable boat. [< ON *raptr*, beam.] —**raft** *v.*

raft² (răft) ►*n.* *Informal* A great number or amount. [< ME *raf*, rubbish.]

raf·ter (răf′tər) ►*n.* One of the sloping beams that support a pitched roof. [< OE *ræfter*.]

rag¹ (răg) ►*n.* **1.** A scrap of cloth. **2. rags** Threadbare or tattered clothing. **3.** *Slang* A newspaper. [ME *ragge*.]

rag² (răg) ►*v.* **ragged, rag·ging** *Slang* **1.** To scold. **2.** To criticize or complain about. **3.** To tease or taunt. [?]

rag³ (răg) ►*n.* A ragtime jazz composition.

rag·a·muf·fin (răg′ə-mŭf′ĭn) ►*n.* A dirty, shabbily clothed child. [ME *Ragamuffyn*.]

rage (rāj) ►*n.* **1.** Violent, explosive anger. **2.** Furious intensity. **3.** A fad or craze. ►*v.* **raged, rag·ing 1.** To speak or act in violent anger. **2.** To spread or prevail forcefully. [< LLat. *rabia*.]

rag·ged (răg′ĭd) ►*adj.* **1.** Tattered, frayed, or torn. **2.** Dressed in tattered clothes. **3.** Having an uneven surface or edge. **4.** Imperfect; uneven: *a ragged performance.* —**rag′ged·ness** *n.* —**rag′ged·y** *adj.*

rag·lan (răg′lən) ►*adj.* Having or being a sleeve with slanted seams and extending in one piece to the neckline. [After the First Baron *Raglan* (1788–1855).] —**rag′lan** *n.*

ra·gout (ră-gōo′) ►*n.* A spicy meat or fish stew. [< Fr. *ragoûter*, revive the taste.]

rag·tag (răg′tăg′) ►*adj.* **1.** Unkempt; ragged. **2.** Diverse and disorderly.

rag·time (răg′tīm′) ►*n.* A style of jazz in which a syncopated melody is played against a steadily accented accompaniment.

rag·weed (răg′wēd′) ►*n.* Any of various weeds whose abundant pollen is one of the chief causes of hay fever.

raid (rād) ►*n.* A surprise attack, invasion, or forcible entry. ►*v.* To make a raid on. [< OE *rād*, a riding.] —**raid′er** *n.*

rail¹ (rāl) ►*n.* **1.** A bar extending horizontally between supports, as in a fence. **2.** A steel bar used as a track for railroad cars or other vehicles. **3.** The railroad: *goods transported by rail.* ►*v.* To supply or enclose with rails or a rail. [< Lat. *rēgula*, rod.]

rail² (rāl) ►*n.* A marsh bird having brownish plumage and short wings. [< OFr. *raale*.]

rail³ (rāl) ►*v.* To complain bitterly or abusively. [< VLat. **ragulāre*, bray.] —**rail′er** *n.*

rail·ing (rā′lĭng) ►*n.* A structure made of a rail, often connecting a series of upright members, that is used as a barrier or support.

rail·ler·y (rā′lə-rē) ►*n., pl.* **-ies** Good-natured teasing or ridicule. [< OFr. *railler*, RAIL³.]

rail·road (rāl′rōd′) ►*n.* **1.** A road composed of parallel steel rails supported by ties and providing a track for trains. **2.** A system of railroad tracks, together with the land, stations, rolling stock, and other assets. ►*v.* **1.** To transport by railroad. **2.** *Informal* **a.** To push through quickly in order to prevent careful consideration: *railroad a bill through Congress.* **b.** To convict without a fair trial or on false charges. —**rail′road′er** *n.*

rail·way (rāl′wā′) ►*n.* **1.** A railroad. **2.** A track providing a runway for wheeled equipment.

rai·ment (rā′mənt) ►*n.* Clothing; garments. [< OFr. *areement*, ARRAY.]

rain (rān) ►*n.* **1a.** Water condensed from atmospheric vapor and falling in drops. **b.** A rainfall. **2.** A heavy or abundant fall. ►*v.* **1.** To fall as or like rain. **2.** To release rain. —*phrasal verb:* **rain out** To postpone or interrupt

because of rain. [< OE *rēn*.] **—rain′i·ness** *n.*
—rain′y *adj.*

rain·bow (rān′bō′) ►*n.* An arc of color appearing opposite the sun as a result of the refraction of sunlight in rain or mist.

rain check ►*n.* **1.** A ticket stub entitling the holder to admission to a future event if the scheduled event is canceled because of rain. **2.** An assurance that an offer will be honored or renewed at a later date.

rain·coat (rān′kōt′) ►*n.* A waterproof or water-resistant coat.

rain·drop (rān′drŏp′) ►*n.* A drop of rain.

rain·fall (rān′fôl′) ►*n.* **1.** A shower or fall of rain. **2.** The quantity of water that falls over a specified area during a given time.

rainforest or **rain forest** (rān′fôr′ĭst, fôr′-) ►*n.* A dense evergreen forest usu. in a tropical region with a heavy annual rainfall.

rain·mak·ing (rān′mā′kĭng) ►*n.* The process of producing or attempting to produce rain, as through magical or ritual actions. **—rain′-mak′er** *n.*

rain·storm (rān′stôrm′) ►*n.* A storm accompanied by rain.

rain·wa·ter (rān′wô′tər, -wŏt′ər) ►*n.* Water that has fallen as rain.

raise (rāz) ►*v.* **raised, rais·ing 1.** To move to a higher position; elevate. **2.** To erect or build. **3.** To cause to arise or exist. **4.** To increase, as in size or worth. **5.** To improve in rank or status. **6a.** To grow or breed, esp. in quantity. **b.** To bring up; rear: *raise children.* **7.** To put forward for consideration. See Synonyms at **broach. 8.** To voice; utter: *raise a shout.* **9.** To arouse or stir up. **10.** To collect: *raise money.* **11.** To cause (dough) to puff up. **12.** To end (a siege). **13.** To bet more than (a preceding bettor in poker). ►*n.* **1.** The act of raising or increasing. **2.** An increase in salary. **—idioms: raise Cain** To behave in a rowdy or disruptive fashion. **raise eyebrows** To cause surprise or mild disapproval. [< ON *reisa.*] **—rais′er** *n.*

rai·sin (rā′zĭn) ►*n.* A dried sweet grape. [< Lat. *racēmus,* bunch of grapes.]

rai·son d'ê·tre (rā′zōn dĕt′rə, rĕ-zôN) ►*n., pl.* **rai·sons d'être** (rā′zōn, rĕ-zôN) Reason for existing. [Fr.]

raj (räj) ►*n.* Dominion or rule, esp. the British rule over India (1757–1947). [< Skt. *rājā,* king.]

Raj·ab (rŭj′əb) ►*n.* The 7th month of the Islamic calendar. See table at **calendar.** [Ar.]

ra·ja or **ra·jah** (rä′jə) ►*n.* A prince or ruler in India or the East Indies. [< Skt. *rājā,* king.]

rake¹ (rāk) ►*n.* A long-handled tool with a row of projecting teeth at its head. ►*v.* **raked, rak·ing 1.** To gather, smooth, loosen, or move with or as if with a rake. **2.** *Informal* To acquire in abundance: *raking in money.* **3.** To conduct a thorough search: *raked through the files.* **4.** To aim heavy gunfire along the length of. [< OE *raca.*] **—rak′er** *n.*

rake² (rāk) ►*n.* A usu. well-to-do man who is dissolute or promiscuous. [< *rakehell,* scoundrel.]

rake³ (rāk) ►*v.* **raked, rak·ing** To slant or cause to incline from the perpendicular. [?] **—rake** *n.*

rake-off (rāk′ôf′, -ŏf′) ►*n. Informal* A share of the profits of an enterprise, esp. one accepted as a bribe.

rak·ish¹ (rā′kĭsh) ►*adj.* **1.** Having a trim, streamlined appearance. **2.** Dashing or sporting; jaunty. [Prob. < RAKE³.]

rak·ish² (rā′kĭsh) ►*adj.* Morally corrupt.

Ra·leigh (rô′lē, rä′-) The capital of NC, in the E-central part SE of Durham.

Raleigh (rô′lē, rä′-), Sir **Walter** 1552?–1618. English courtier, navigator, and writer.

Sir Walter Raleigh

ral·ly (rǎl′ē) ►*v.* **-lied, -ly·ing 1.** To call or come together for a common purpose; assemble. **2.** To restore to order. **3.** To rouse or recover from inactivity or decline. **4.** *Sports* To engage in a rally. ►*n., pl.* **-lies 1.** The act of rallying. **2.** A mass gathering, esp. to inspire enthusiasm: *a political rally.* **3.** A notable rise in stock market prices and trading volume after a decline. **4.** *Sports* **a.** An extended volley, as in tennis. **b.** A race in which vehicles are driven over public roads. [< OFr. *ralier,* reunite.]

ram (rǎm) ►*n.* **1.** A male sheep. **2.** A device used to drive, batter, or crush by forceful impact. ►*v.* **rammed, ram·ming 1.** To strike or drive against with a heavy impact. **2.** To force into place. **3.** To cram; stuff. [< OE *ramm.*]

RAM (rǎm) ►*n. Comp.* A memory device in which information can be accessed in any order. [R(ANDOM-)A(CCESS) M(EMORY).]

Ra·ma (rä′mə) ►*n. Hinduism* A deified hero worshiped as an incarnation of Vishnu.

Ram·a·dan (rǎm′ə-dän′, rǎm′ə-dän′) ►*n.* **1.** The 9th month of the Islamic calendar. See table at **calendar. 2.** The fast held from sunrise to sunset during this period. [Ar. *ramaḍān.*]

ram·ble (rǎm′bəl) ►*v.* **-bled, -bling 1.** To wander aimlessly. **2.** To digress at length. ►*n.* A leisurely stroll. [Prob. < MDu. **rammelen.*] **—ram′bler** *n.*

ram·bunc·tious (rǎm-bŭngk′shəs) ►*adj.* Boisterous and disorderly. [Prob. ult. < alteration of ROBUST.] **—ram·bunc′tious·ness** *n.*

ra·men (rä′mən) ►*n.* **1.** A Japanese dish of noodles in broth. **2.** A thin white noodle. [J. *rāmen.*]

Ram·es·ses II also **Ram·e·ses II** (rǎm′ĭ-sēz′) or **Ram·ses II** (rǎm′sēz′) 14th–13th cent. BC. King of Egypt (1304–1237 BC).

ram·ie (rǎm′ē, rä′mē) ►*n.* A flaxlike fiber obtained from the stem of an Asian plant and used in textiles. [Malay *rami.*]

ram·i·fy (rǎm′ə-fī′) ►*v.* **-fied, -fy·ing 1.** To have complicating consequences or developments.

2. To branch out; divide. [< Lat. *rāmus*, branch.] —**ram′i·fi·ca′tion** *n.*

ram·jet (răm′jĕt′) ►*n.* A jet engine that propels aircraft by igniting fuel mixed with air taken in and compressed by the engine.

ramp (rămp) ►*n.* An inclined surface or roadway connecting different levels. [< OFr. *ramper*, rise up.]

ram·page (răm′pāj′) ►*n.* A course of violent, frenzied action or behavior. ►*v.* (also răm-pāj′) **-paged, -pag·ing** To move about wildly or violently. [Sc.] —**ram·pa′geous** *adj.* —**ram·pag′er** *n.*

ram·pant (răm′pənt) ►*adj.* **1.** Extending unchecked: *a rampant growth of weeds.* **2.** Occurring without restraint; rife: *rampant corruption.* [< OFr. *ramper*, rear up.] —**ram′pan·cy** *n.* —**ram′pant·ly** *adv.*

ram·part (răm′pärt′, -pərt) ►*n.* A defensive embankment, often with a parapet on top. [< OFr. *remparer*, fortify.]

ram·rod (răm′rŏd′) ►*n.* **1.** A rod used to force the charge into a muzzleloading firearm. **2.** A rod used to clean the barrel of a firearm.

Ram·ses II (răm′sēz′) See **Ramesses II.**

ram·shack·le (răm′shăk′əl) ►*adj.* Poorly constructed; rickety. [< ME *ransaken*, RANSACK.]

ran (răn) ►*v.* P.t. of **run.**

ranch (rănch) ►*n.* **1.** A large farm, esp. one where livestock is raised. **2.** A ranch house. ►*v.* To manage or work on a ranch. [< OFr. *se ranger*, be arranged.] —**ranch′er** *n.*

ranch house ►*n.* **1.** The main house on a ranch. **2.** A rectangular, one-story house with a low-pitched roof.

ran·cid (răn′sĭd) ►*adj.* Having the disagreeable odor or taste of decomposing oils or fats; rank. [Lat. *rancidus.*] —**ran·cid′i·ty** *n.*

ran·cor (răng′kər) ►*n.* Bitter, long-lasting resentment. [< LLat., rancid smell.] —**ran′cor·ous** *adj.* —**ran′cor·ous·ly** *adv.*

rand (rănd, ränd) ►*n.* See table at **currency.** [Afr.]

Rand, Ayn Alisa Rosenbaum. 1905–82. Russian-born Amer. writer.

R & B ►*abbr.* rhythm and blues

R & D ►*abbr.* research and development

ran·dom (răn′dəm) ►*adj.* **1.** Having no specific pattern or purpose. **2.** *Statistics* Of or relating to equal probability of selection or occurrence for each member of a group. [< OFr. *randon.*] —**ran′dom·ly** *adv.* —**ran′dom·ness** *n.*

ran·dom-ac·cess memory (răn′dəm-ăk′sĕs) ►*n.* RAM.

random coil ►*n.* A protein structure marked by irregular coils or folds.

ran·dom·ize (răn′də-mīz′) ►*v.* **-ized, -iz·ing** To make random in arrangement. —**ran′dom·i·za′tion** *n.*

R & R ►*abbr.* rest and recreation

ran·dy (răn′dē) ►*adj.* **-di·er, -di·est** Desirous of sexual activity. [?]

rang (răng) ►*v.* P.t. of **ring².**

range (rānj) ►*n.* **1a.** A grouping of things in the same category or within specified limits: *different pay ranges.* **b.** An amount or extent of variation: *a wide price range.* **2.** Extent of perception, knowledge, experience, or ability. **3.** The maximum extent or distance of operation, action, or effectiveness. **4.** A place for shooting at targets. **5.** Open land on which livestock wander and

graze. **6.** A group of things extending in a line, esp. a row or chain of mountains. **7.** A stove for cooking. ►*v.* **ranged, rang·ing 1.** To vary within limits. **2.** To extend in a direction. **3.** To wander freely; roam. **4.** To arrange in a particular order, esp. in rows or lines. **5.** To classify. **6.** To determine the distance of (a target). [< OFr. *rangier*, put in a row.]

Syns: *ambit, compass, orbit, purview, reach, scope, sweep* **n.**

rang·er (rān′jər) ►*n.* **1.** A wanderer; rover. **2. Ranger** A member of a group of US soldiers trained for making raids. **3.** A warden employed to maintain and protect a forest or other natural area.

Ran·goon (răn-gōon′, răng-) See **Yangon.**

rang·y (rān′jē) ►*adj.* **-i·er, -i·est** Having long slender limbs.

ra·ni also **ra·nee** (rä′nē) ►*n., pl.* **-nis** also **-nees 1.** The wife of a raja. **2.** A princess or queen in India or the East Indies. [< Skt. *rājñī.*]

rank¹ (răngk) ►*n.* **1a.** A relative position or status in a group. **b.** An official position or grade. **c.** High station or position. **2.** A row, line, or series. **3a.** A line, esp. of soldiers, standing side by side in close order. **b. ranks** Personnel, esp. enlisted military personnel. **4. ranks** A body of people classed together; numbers. ►*v.* **1.** To place in a row or rows. **2.** To classify. **3.** To take precedence over. **4.** To hold a particular rank: *ranked first in the class.* [< OFr. *renc.*]

rank² (răngk) ►*adj.* **-er, -est 1.** Growing profusely or with excessive vigor. **2.** Strong and offensive in odor or flavor. **3.** Absolute; complete: *a rank amateur.* [< OE *ranc*, strong.] —**rank′ly** *adv.* —**rank′ness** *n.*

rank and file ►*n.* **1.** The common soldiers of an army. **2.** The ordinary members of a group, excluding the leaders and officers.

Ran·kin (răng′kĭn), **Jeannette** 1880–1973. Amer. reformer and politician.

Jeannette Rankin
photographed in 1916

rank·ing (răng′kĭng) ►*adj.* Of a high or the highest rank. ►*n.* **rankings** A listing of items in a group according to a system of rating.

ran·kle (răng′kəl) ►*v.* **-kled, -kling 1.** To cause irritation or resentment. **2.** To become sore or inflamed; fester. [< OFr. *rancler.*]

ran·sack (răn′săk′) ►*v.* **1.** To search thoroughly and often roughly. **2.** To pillage. [< ON *rannsaka.*]

ran·som (răn′səm) ►*n.* **1.** The release of a

captive in return for payment of a demanded price. **2.** The price demanded or paid for such a release. [< Lat. *redēmptiō*, a buying back.] —**ran′som** *v.* —**ran′som·er** *n.*

rant (rănt) ▸*v.* To speak or write in an emotionally charged manner. ▸*n.* Emotionally charged speech or writing. [Prob. < Du. *ranten*.] —**rant′er** *n.*

rap¹ (răp) ▸*v.* **rapped, rap·ping 1.** To hit sharply and swiftly. **2.** To utter sharply. **3.** To criticize or blame. ▸*n.* **1.** A quick sharp blow. **2.** A knocking or tapping sound. **3.** *Slang* **a.** A reprimand. **b.** A prison sentence. [ME *rappen*.]

rap² (răp) ▸*n.* **1.** *Slang* A talk or conversation. **2.** A form of popular music marked by spoken or chanted rhyming lyrics with a rhythmic accompaniment. ▸*v.* **rap·ped, rap·ping 1.** *Slang* To discuss freely. **2.** To perform rap music. [Poss. < RAP¹.]

ra·pa·cious (rə-pā′shəs) ▸*adj.* **1.** Having or showing an excessive desire to acquire money or possess things; greedy. **2.** Subsisting on live prey. [< Lat. *rapāx*.] —**ra·pac′i·ty** (rə-păs′ĭ-tē), **ra·pa′cious·ness** *n.*

rape¹ (rāp) ▸*n.* **1.** The crime of using force or the threat of force to compel a person to submit to sexual intercourse or some other sexual penetration. **2.** Seizing and carrying off by force; abduction. **3.** Abusive or improper treatment: *rape of the land by polluters.* [< Lat. *rapere*, seize.] —**rape** *v.* —**rap′ist** *n.*

rape² (rāp) ▸*n.* A plant cultivated as fodder and for its seed oil. [< Lat. *rāpa*, turnip.]

Raph·a·el (răf′ē-əl, rä′fē-ĕl′) 1483–1520. Italian painter.

rap·id (răp′ĭd) ▸*adj.* **-er, -est** Very fast; swift. ▸*n.* often **rapids** A fast-moving part of a river. [Lat. *rapidus*.] —**ra·pid′i·ty** (rə-pĭd′ĭ-tē), **rap′id·ness** *n.* —**rap′id·ly** *adv.*

rapid eye movement ▸*n.* REM.

rapid transit ▸*n.* An urban passenger rail system.

ra·pi·er (rā′pē-ər, răp′yər) ▸*n.* A long slender sword with a double-edged blade. [< OFr. *rapiere*.]

rap·ine (răp′ĭn) ▸*n.* Forcible seizure of property; plunder. [< Lat. *rapīna*.]

rap·pel (ră-pĕl′) ▸*v.* **-pelled, -pel·ling** To descend from a steep height by means of a belayed rope that is passed under one thigh and over the opposite shoulder. [< OFr. *rapeler*, recall.] —**rap·pel′** *n.*

rap·port (ră-pôr′, rə-) ▸*n.* A relationship, esp. one of mutual trust or affinity. [< OFr. *raporter*, bring back.]

rap·proche·ment (rä′prôsh-mäɴ′) ▸*n.* **1.** The establishment of cordial relations, as between two countries. **2.** Cordial relations. [< Fr. *rapprocher*, bring together.]

rap·scal·lion (răp-skăl′yən) ▸*n.* A rascal; scamp. [< RASCAL.]

rapt (răpt) ▸*adj.* **1.** Deeply moved or delighted; enraptured. **2.** Deeply absorbed. [< Lat. *raptus*, p.part. of *rapere*, seize.] —**rapt′ly** *adv.*

rap·tor (răp′tər) ▸*n.* A bird of prey. [< Lat. *rapere*, seize.] —**rap·to′ri·al** (-tôr′ē-əl) *adj.*

rap·ture (răp′chər) ▸*n.* A state of ecstasy. [< Lat. *raptus*, RAPT.] —**rap′tur·ous** *adj.*

ra·ra a·vis (râr′ə ā′vĭs) ▸*n.*, *pl.* **ra·ra a·vis·es** or **ra·rae a·ves** (râr′ē ā′vēz) A rare person or thing. [Lat. *rāra avis*, rare bird.]

rare¹ (râr) ▸*adj.* **rar·er, rar·est 1.** Infrequently occurring; uncommon. **2.** Excellent; extraordinary. **3.** Thin in density; rarefied. [< Lat. *rārus*.] —**rare′ness** *n.* —**rar′i·ty** *n.*

rare² (râr) ▸*adj.* **rar·er, rar·est** Cooked a short time: *a rare steak.* [< OE *hrēr*.]

rare-earth element (râr′ûrth′) ▸*n.* Any of the metallic elements of atomic number 57 through 71.

rar·e·fied also **rar·i·fied** (râr′ə-fīd′) ▸*adj.* **1.** Not dense; thin: *the rarefied mountain air.* **2.** Of or reserved for a small, select group; exclusive: *the most rarefied social circles.* **3.** Refined or esoteric: *rarefied academic theorizing.*

rar·e·fy also **rar·i·fy** (râr′ə-fī′) ▸*v.* **-fied, -fy·ing 1.** To make or become thin or less dense, as air. **2.** To purify or refine. [< Lat. *rārēfacere*.] —**rar′e·fac′tion** *n.* —**rar′e·fi′a·ble** *adj.*

rare·ly (râr′lē) ▸*adv.* Not often; infrequently. See Usage Note at **hardly.**

ras·cal (răs′kəl) ▸*n.* **1.** One that is playfully mischievous. **2.** An unscrupulous person; scoundrel. [< OFr. *rascaille*, rabble.] —**ras·cal′i·ty** (-kăl′ĭ-tē) *n.*

rash¹ (răsh) ▸*adj.* **-er, -est** Imprudently hasty or bold. [ME *rasche*, active.] —**rash′ness** *n.*

rash² (răsh) ▸*n.* **1.** A visible lesion or group of lesions on the skin. **2.** An outbreak of many instances within a brief period: *a rash of burglaries.* [Poss. < OFr. *raschier*, scratch.]

rash·er (răsh′ər) ▸*n.* **1.** A thin slice of fried or broiled bacon. **2.** A serving of thin slices of bacon. [?]

rasp (răsp) ▸*n.* **1.** A coarse file having sharp projections. **2.** The act of filing with a rasp. **3.** A harsh grating sound. [< OFr. *rasper*.] —**rasp** *v.*

rasp·ber·ry (răz′bĕr′ē) ▸*n.* **1.** A shrubby, usu. prickly plant in the rose family that bears edible fruit. **2.** The fruit of this plant, consisting of many small, fleshy, usu. red drupelets. [Obsolete *raspis*, raspberry + BERRY.]

rasp·y (răs′pē) ▸*adj.* **-i·er, -i·est** Rough; grating.

rat (răt) ▸*n.* **1.** Any of various long-tailed rodents similar to but larger than mice. **2.** *Slang* A despicable person, esp. one who betrays or informs on associates. ▸*v.* **rat·ted, rat·ting 1.** To hunt for or catch rats. **2.** *Slang* To reveal incriminating or embarrassing information about someone, esp. to a person in authority. [< OE *ræt.*]

ra·ta·tou·ille (răt′ə-tōō′ē, rä′tä-) ▸*n.* A vegetable stew made with eggplant, tomatoes, zucchini, peppers, onions, and spices. [Fr.]

ratch·et (răch′ĭt) ▸*n.* A mechanism consisting of a pawl that engages the sloping teeth of a wheel or bar, permitting motion in one direction only. ▸*v.* To increase or decrease by increments. [< OFr. *rocquet*, head of a lance.]

rate¹ (rāt) ▸*n.* **1.** A quantity measured with respect to another measured quantity. **2.** A measure of a part with respect to a whole; proportion. **3.** A charge or payment calculated in relation to a sum or quantity. **4.** Level of quality. ▸*v.* **rat·ed, rat·ing 1.** To place or be placed in a rank or grade. **2.** To regard or consider as having a certain value. **3.** *Informal* To merit or deserve. See Synonyms at **earn. 4.** *Informal* To have status or importance. —**idiom: at any rate 1.** Whatever the case may be. **2.** At least. [< Lat. *(prō) ratā (parte)*, (according to a) fixed (part).]

rate² (rāt) ►*v.* **rat·ed, rat·ing** To berate. [ME *raten*.]

rate of exchange ►*n.* An exchange rate.

rath·er (răth′ər, rä′thər) ►*adv.* **1.** Preferably. **2.** More exactly or accurately. **3.** Somewhat: *rather cold.* **4.** On the contrary. [ME < OE *hrathor.*]

raths·kel·ler (rät′skĕl′ər, răt′-, răth′-) ►*n.* A restaurant, usu. below street level, that serves beer. [Ger., restaurant in the city hall basement.]

rat·i·fy (răt′ə-fī′) ►*v.* **-fied, -fy·ing** To approve and give formal sanction to. [< Med.Lat. *ratificāre.*] —**rat′i·fi·ca′tion** *n.*

rat·ing (rā′tĭng) ►*n.* **1.** A position assigned on a scale; a standing. **2.** An evaluation of financial status.

ra·tio (rā′shō, rā′shē-ō′) ►*n., pl.* **-tios 1.** Relation in degree or number between two things. **2.** *Math.* A relationship between two quantities, usu. expressed as the quotient of one divided by the other. [Lat. *ratiō*, calculation.]

ra·ti·oc·i·nate (răsh′ē-ŏs′ə-nāt′) ►*v.* **-nat·ed, -nat·ing** To reason methodically and logically. [Lat. *ratiōcinārī.*] —**ra′ti·oc′i·na′tion** *n.* —**ra′-ti·oc′i·na·tive** *adj.* —**ra′ti·oc′i·na′tor** *n.*

ra·tion (răsh′ən, rā′shən) ►*n.* **1.** A fixed portion, esp. of food. **2. rations** Food issued or available to group members. ►*v.* **1.** To supply with rations. **2.** To distribute as rations. [< Lat. *ratiō*, calculation.]

ra·tion·al (răsh′ə-nəl) ►*adj.* **1.** Having or exercising the ability to reason. See Synonyms at **logical. 2.** Consistent with or based on reason. **3.** Of sound mind; sane. **4.** *Math.* Capable of being expressed as a quotient of integers. [< Lat. *ratiō*, reason.] —**ra′tion·al·ly** *adv.*

ra·tion·ale (răsh′ə-năl′) ►*n.* A fundamental reason; rational basis.

ra·tion·al·ism (răsh′ə-nə-lĭz′əm) ►*n.* Reliance on reason as the best guide for belief and action. —**ra′tion·al·ist** *n.*

ra·tion·al·i·ty (răsh′ə-năl′ĭ-tē) ►*n., pl.* **-ties** The quality or condition of being rational.

ra·tion·al·ize (răsh′ə-nə-līz′) ►*v.* **-ized, -iz·ing 1.** To explain rationally. **2.** To justify (one's behavior) with incorrect reasons, often without conscious awareness. —**ra′tion·al·i·za′tion** *n.*

rational number ►*n.* A number capable of being expressed as an integer or a quotient of integers, excluding zero as a denominator.

rat·line also **rat·lin** (răt′lĭn) ►*n.* Any of the small ropes fastened horizontally to the shrouds of a ship and forming a ladder for going aloft. [ME *rathelinge.*]

rat race ►*n. Informal* A frantic, often competitive activity or routine.

rat·tan (ră-tăn′, rə-) ►*n.* **1.** Any of various climbing palms of tropical Africa and Asia, having long, tough, slender stems. **2.** The stems of any of these palms, used to make furniture and other wickerwork. [Malay *rōtan.*]

rat·tle (răt′l) ►*v.* **-tled, -tling 1.** To make or cause to make a quick succession of short percussive sounds. **2.** To speak rapidly, usu. at length and without much thought or effort. **3.** *Informal* To fluster; unnerve: *The accident rattled me.* ►*n.* **1.** A rapid succession of short percussive sounds. **2.** A device, such as a baby's toy, that rattles when shaken. **3.** The series of

horny segments at the end of a rattlesnake's tail. [ME *ratelen.*]

rat·tler (răt′lər) ►*n.* **1.** One that rattles. **2.** A rattlesnake.

rat·tle·snake (răt′l-snāk′) ►*n.* Any of various venomous pit vipers of the Americas having a series of horny segments at the end of the tail that can be vibrated to produce a rattling or buzzing sound.

rat·tle·trap (răt′l-trăp′) ►*n.* A rickety, worn-out vehicle.

rat·ty (răt′ē) ►*adj.* **-ti·er, -ti·est 1.** Characteristic of or infested with rats. **2.** Dilapidated; shabby.

rau·cous (rô′kəs) ►*adj.* **1.** Rough-sounding; harsh. **2.** Boisterous and disorderly. [< Lat. *raucus.*] —**rau′cous·ness** *n.*

raun·chy (rôn′chē, rän′-) ►*adj.* **-chi·er, -chi·est** *Slang* **1.** Obscene, lewd, or vulgar. **2.** Grimy; unkempt. [?] —**raun′chi·ly** *adv.* —**raun′chi·ness** *n.*

rav·age (răv′ĭj) ►*v.* **-aged, -ag·ing 1.** To destroy. **2.** To pillage; sack. ►*n.* **1.** The act or practice of ravaging. **2. ravages** Destructive or harmful effects. [< OFr. *ravir*, RAVISH.]

rave (rāv) ►*v.* **raved, rav·ing 1.** To speak wildly or irrationally. **2.** To move with great violence or intensity. **3.** To speak with wild enthusiasm. ►*n.* **1.** The act or an instance of raving. **2.** *Informal* An extravagantly enthusiastic opinion or review. **3.** An all-night dance party. ►*adj. Informal* Extravagantly enthusiastic: *a rave review.* [< ONFr. *resver*, dream, wander.]

rav·el (răv′əl) ►*v.* **-eled, -el·ing** also **-elled, -el·ling 1.** To separate the fibers or threads of (e.g., cloth); unravel. **2.** To tangle or complicate. ►*n.* **1.** A raveling. **2.** A loose thread. **3.** A tangle. [< obsolete Du. *ravel*, loose thread.] —**rav′el·er** *n.*

Ra·vel (rə-vĕl′, rä-), **(Joseph) Maurice** 1875–1937. French composer.

rav·el·ing also **rav·el·ling** (răv′ə-lĭng) ►*n.* A thread or fiber that has become separated from a woven material.

ra·ven (rā′vən) ►*n.* A large bird having black plumage and a croaking cry. ►*adj.* Black and shiny. [< OE *hræfn.*]

rav·en·ous (răv′ə-nəs) ►*adj.* **1.** Extremely hungry. **2.** Predatory. **3.** Eager for gratification or extremely desirous. [< OFr. *raviner*, take by force.] —**rav′en·ous·ness** *n.*

ra·vine (rə-vēn′) ►*n.* A deep narrow valley, esp. one worn by running water. [< Lat. *rapīna*, rapine.]

rav·i·o·li (răv′ē-ō′lē) ►*n., pl.* **ravioli** or **-lis** A small casing of pasta with a filling. [Ital.]

rav·ish (răv′ĭsh) ►*v.* **1.** To force (another) to have sexual intercourse; rape. **2.** To overwhelm with emotion; enrapture. [< Lat. *rapere*, seize.] —**rav′ish·er** *n.* —**rav′ish·ment** *n.*

rav·ish·ing (răv′ĭ-shĭng) ►*adj.* Extremely attractive; entrancing. —**rav′ish·ing·ly** *adv.*

raw (rô) ►*adj.* **-er, -est 1a.** Uncooked: *raw meat.* **b.** In a natural condition; not refined or finished: *raw wool.* **c.** Not subjected to adjustment, treatment, or analysis: *raw data.* **2.** Untrained; inexperienced. **3a.** Having subcutaneous tissue exposed: *a raw wound.* **b.** Inflamed; sore: *a raw throat.* **4.** Unpleasantly damp and chilly: *raw weather.* **5.** Crude; coarse. —**idiom: in the raw 1.** In a crude or unrefined state. **2.** Nude;

naked. [< OE *hrēaw*.] —**raw′ness** *n.*

Ra·wal·pin·di (rä′wəl-pĭn′dē) A city of NE Pakistan NNW of Lahore.

raw·boned (rô′bōnd′) ►*adj.* Having a lean, gaunt frame with prominent bones.

raw·hide (rô′hīd′) ►*n.* **1.** The untanned hide of cattle or other animals. **2.** A whip or rope made of rawhide.

ray¹ (rā) ►*n.* **1.** A narrow stream of radiant energy, esp. visible light, traveling in a straight or nearly straight line. **2.** A small amount; trace: *a ray of hope.* **3a.** A straight line extending from a point. **b.** A structure or part having the form of such a line. [< Lat. *radius.*]

ray² (rā) ►*n.* Any of various cartilaginous fishes having enlarged pelvic fins that are fused to the sides of the head and a flattened body. [< Lat. *raia.*]

ray·on (rā′ŏn) ►*n.* **1.** Any of several synthetic textile fibers produced by forcing a cellulose solution through fine spinnerets and solidifying the resulting filaments. **2.** A fabric woven or knit with this fiber. [Poss. < Fr. *rayon*, RAY¹.]

raze (rāz) ►*v.* **razed, raz·ing** To level to the ground; demolish. [< VLat. **rāsāre*, scrape.]

ra·zor (rā′zər) ►*n.* A sharp-edged cutting instrument used esp. for shaving. [< OFr. *raser*, scrape; see RAZE.]

razor clam ►*n.* Any of various clams having long narrow shells, many of which are edible.

razz (răz) ►*v. Slang* To deride, heckle, or tease. [< RASPBERRY.]

RB ►*abbr.* running back

RBI ►*abbr.* Baseball run batted in

RC ►*abbr.* **1.** radio controlled **2.** Red Cross **3.** Roman Catholic

rd ►*abbr.* rod (unit of measure)

RD ►*abbr.* rural delivery

Rd. ►*abbr.* road

RDA ►*abbr.* **1.** recommended daily allowance **2.** recommended dietary allowance

re¹ (rā) ►*n. Mus.* The 2nd tone of the diatonic scale. [< Med.Lat.]

re² (rē) ►*prep.* In reference to; concerning. [Lat. *rē*, ablative of *rēs*, thing.]

RE ►*abbr.* real estate

re– ►*pref.* **1.** Again: *rebuild.* **2.** Back: *react.* **3.** Used as an intensive: *refine.* [< Lat.]

reach (rēch) ►*v.* **1.** To stretch out (a body part); extend. **2.** To touch or grasp by extending. **3.** To arrive at or get to. **4.** To succeed in communicating with. **5.** To extend or carry as far as. **6.** To aggregate or amount to. ►*n.* **1.** The act of stretching or thrusting out. **2.** The extent something can reach. See Synonyms at **range**. **3.** An unbroken expanse. [< OE *rǣcan.*]

re·act (rē-ăkt′) ►*v.* **1.** To act in response to a stimulus or prompting. **2.** To act in opposition to a former condition or act. **3.** To undergo a chemical reaction.

re·ac·tance (rē-ăk′təns) ►*n.* Opposition to the flow of alternating electric current caused by the inductance and capacitance in a circuit.

re·ac·tant (rē-ăk′tənt) ►*n.* A substance that is altered or incorporated into another substance in a chemical reaction.

re·ac·tion (rē-ăk′shən) ►*n.* **1a.** A response to a stimulus. **b.** The state resulting from such a response. **2.** A reverse or opposing action. **3.** Opposition to progress or liberalism. **4.** A chemical change or transformation. **5.** A nuclear reaction.

re·ac·tion·ar·y (rē-ăk′shə-něr′ē) ►*adj.* Opposed to progress or liberalism. ►*n., pl.* **-ar·ies** An opponent of progress or liberalism.

re·ac·tive (rē-ăk′tĭv) ►*adj.* **1.** Tending to be responsive or to react to a stimulus. **2.** Marked by reaction. **3.** Tending to participate readily in chemical or physical reactions.

re·ac·tor (rē-ăk′tər) ►*n.* **1.** One that reacts. **2.** *Electron.* A circuit element, such as a coil, used to introduce reactance. **3.** A chemical or nuclear reactor.

read (rĕd) ►*v.* **read** (rĕd), **read·ing** **1.** To comprehend the meaning of (written or printed characters, words, or symbols). **2.** To speak aloud (written or printed material). **3.** To determine the intent or mood of. **4.** To attribute a certain interpretation or meaning to. **5.** To foretell or predict. **6.** To receive or comprehend (e.g., a radio message). **7.** To study: *read law.* **8.** To learn by reading. **9.** To indicate or register: *The dial reads 32°.* **10.** *Comp.* To obtain information from (a storage medium). **11.** To have

re·ab·sorb′ *v.*	**re′com·mis′sion** *v.*	**re·en′ter** *v.*
re·ab·sorp′tion *n.*	**re′com·mit′** *v.*	**re·en′trance** *n.*
re·ac′ti·vate′ *v.*	**re′com·mit′ment** *n.*	**re′ex·am′i·na′tion** *n.*
re′ad·just′ *v.*	**re′com·pose′** *v.*	**re′ex·am′ine** *v.*
re′af·firm′ *v.*	**re′con·di′tion** *v.*	**re′fin·ance′** *v.*
re′a·lign′ *v.*	**re′con·duct′** *v.*	**re·fin′ish** *v.*
re·an′i·mate′ *v.*	**re′con·firm′** *v.*	**re·fit′** *v.*
re′ap·por′tion *v.*	**re′con·nect′** *v.*	**re·freeze′** *v.*
re′ap·prais′al *n.*	**re′con·vert′** *v.*	**re·fry′** *v.*
re′ap·praise′ *v.*	**re·dec′o·rate′** *v.*	**re·fu′el** *v.*
re·arm′ *v.*	**re·dec′o·ra′tion** *n.*	**re·hear′** *v.*
re·ar′ma·ment *n.*	**re′de·liv′er** *v.*	**re·hear′ing** *n.*
re′ar·range′ *v.*	**re′de·ploy′** *v.*	**re·house′** *v.*
re′ar·range′ment *n.*	**re′de·sign′** *v.*	**re′im·port′** *v.*
re′as·sem′ble *v.*	**re′di·rect′** *v.*	**re′im·press′** *v.*
re′as·sign′ *v.*	**re′dis·trib′ute** *v.*	**re′im·pris′on** *v.*
re·broad′cast′ *v.* & *n.*	**re·do′** *v.*	**re′in·fect′** *v.*
re·cal′cu·late′ *v.*	**re·dou′ble** *v.*	**re′in·fec′tion** *n.*
re·cap′i·tal·ize′ *v.*	**re·ed′u·cate′** *v.*	**re′in·sure′** *v.*
re·cast′ *v.*	**re′e·lect′** *v.*	**re·in′te·grate′** *v.*
re·charge′ *v.*	**re′e·lec′tion** *n.*	**re′in·ter′pret** *v.*
re·charge′a·ble *adj.*	**re′en·act′** *v.*	**re′in·vent′** *v.*
	re′en·act′ment *n.*	**re′in·vest′** *v.*

a particular wording. **12.** To contain a specific meaning. —*idiom:* **read between the lines** To perceive an implicit meaning. [< OE *rǣdan,* advise.] —**read′a·bil′i·ty** *n.* —**read′a·ble** *adj.* —**read′er** *n.* —**read′er·ship′** *n.*

read·i·ly (rĕd′ə-lē, rĕd′l-ē) ►*adv.* **1.** Willingly. **2.** Easily.

read·ing (rē′dĭng) ►*n.* **1.** The act or activity of a reader. **2.** An official or public recitation of written material. **3.** The specific form of a particular passage in a text. **4.** An interpretation or appraisal. **5.** Written or printed material. **6.** The information indicated by a gauge.

read-on·ly memory (rĕd′ōn′lē) ►*n.* ROM.

read·out or **read-out** (rĕd′out′) ►*n.* Presentation of computer data, from calculations or storage.

read·y (rĕd′ē) ►*adj.* **-i·er, -i·est 1.** Prepared or available for service or action. **2.** Inclined; willing. **3.** Prompt in apprehending or reacting. ►*v.* **read·ied, read·y·ing** To make ready. [< OE *rǣde.*] —**read′i·ness** *n.*

read·y-made (rĕd′ē-mād′) ►*adj.* Already made or available: *ready-made clothes.*

Rea·gan (rā′gən), **Ronald Wilson** 1911–2004. The 40th US president (1981–89).

Ronald Reagan
photographed in 1981

re·a·gent (rē-ā′jənt) ►*n.* A substance used in a chemical reaction to detect, measure, examine, or produce other substances.

re·al¹ (rē′əl, rēl) ►*adj.* **1.** Being or occurring in fact or actuality; not imaginary or ideal. **2.** Genuine; not artificial. See Synonyms at **authentic. 3.** Serious: *in real trouble.* **4.** *Law* Of or relating to stationary or fixed property. [< LLat. *reālis.*] —**real′ness** *n.*

re·al² (rā-äl′) ►*n., pl.* **re·ais** (-īsh′) See table at **currency.** [Sp. *royal, real.*]

re·al estate (rē′əl, rēl) ►*n.* Land, including all the resources in and on it. —**re′al-es·tate′** *adj.*

re·al·ism (rē′ə-lĭz′əm) ►*n.* **1.** An inclination toward objective truth and pragmatism. **2.** The representation in art or literature of objects, actions, or social conditions as they actually are. —**re′al·ist** *n.*

re·al·is·tic (rē′ə-lĭs′tĭk) ►*adj.* **1.** Tending to or expressing an awareness of things as they are. **2.** Relating to the representation of objects, actions, or social conditions as they are: *a realistic novel.* See Synonyms at **vivid.** —**re′al·is′ti·cal·ly** *adv.*

re·al·i·ty (rē-ăl′ĭ-tē) ►*n., pl.* **-ties 1.** The quality or state of being actual or true. **2.** One that exists objectively. ►*adj.* Relating to a genre of television or film in which a storyline is created by editing footage of people interacting with one another in unscripted situations.

re·al·ize (rē′ə-līz′) ►*v.* **-ized, -iz·ing 1.** To comprehend completely or correctly. **2.** To make real; fulfill. **3.** To obtain or achieve as gain or profit. —**re′al·iz′a·ble** *adj.* —**re′al·i·za′tion** *n.*

re·al·ly (rē′ə-lē, rē′lē) ►*adv.* **1.** In truth or fact. **2.** To a great degree; very much. **3.** Very; utterly. **4.** Indeed. ►*interj.* Used to express surprise, skepticism, displeasure, or interest.

realm (rĕlm) ►*n.* **1.** A kingdom. **2.** An area, as of knowledge or activity: *the realm of science.* See Synonyms at **field.** [< Lat. *regimen,* government.]

re·al number (rē′əl, rēl) ►*n.* A number that is either rational or the limit of a sequence of rational numbers.

re′in·vig′o·rate′ *v.*
re·is′sue *v. & n.*
re·kin′dle *v.*
re·line′ *v.*
re·lo′cate′ *v.*
re·lo·ca′tion *n.*
re·made′ *adj.*
re·make′ *v.*
re·match′ *n.*
re·mil′i·ta·rize′ *v.*
re·mon′e·tize′ *v.*
re·mount′ *v.*
re′ne·go′ti·ate′ *v.*
re·nom′i·nate′ *v.*
re·num′ber *v.*
re·or′gan·i·za′tion *n.*
re·or′gan·ize′ *v.*
re·pack′ *v.*
re·pack′age *v.*
re·pass′ *v.*
re·phrase′ *v.*
re·plant′ *v.*
re·proc′ess *v.*

re·pub′li·ca′tion *n.*
re·pub′lish *v.*
re·pur′chase *v.*
re·ra′di·ate′ *v.*
re′re·cord′ *v.*
re·sale′ *n.*
re·sched′ule *v.*
re·seg′re·gate′ *v.*
re·seg′re·ga′tion *n.*
re·set′ *v.*
re·shape′ *v.*
re·shuf′fle *v.*
re·sole′ *v.*
re·start′ *v.*
re·state′ *v.*
re·stock′ *v.*
re′strike′ *n.*
re·struc′ture *v.*
re′sup·ply′ *v. & n.*
re·sur′face *v.*
re′sur·vey′ *v.*
re·tell′ *v.*
re′test′ *v. & n.*

re·think′ *v.*
re·train′ *v.*
re′train·ee′ *n.*
re·trans′late *v.*
re′tri′al *n.*
re·try′ *v.*
re·u′ni·fy′ *v.*
re·u′nite′ *v.*
re·us′a·ble *adj. & n.*
re·use′ *v. & n.*
re·val′i·date′ *v.*
re·val′i·da′tion *n.*
re·val′u·ate′ *v.*
re·val′u·a′tion *n.*
re·val′ue *v.*
re·vis′it *v.*
re·vi′tal·i·za′tion *n.*
re·vi′tal·ize′ *v.*
re·wak′en *v.*
re·wind′ *v.*
re·wire′ *v.*
re·work′ *v.*
re·zone′ *v.*

re·al·po·li·tik (rā-äl′pō′lĭ-tēk′) ►*n.* Politics based upon practical, not theoretical or ethical, considerations. [Ger.]

re·al time (rē′əl, rēl) ►*n.* **1.** The actual time in which a physical process under computer study or control occurs. **2.** The time required for a computer to solve a problem. **3.** The timing or arrangement allowing a process to occur normally, without delay.

Re·al·tor (rē′əl-tər, -tôr′) A service mark for a real-estate agent affiliated with the National Association of Realtors.

re·al·ty (rē′əl-tē) ►*n., pl.* **-ties** Real estate.

ream¹ (rēm) ►*n.* **1.** A quantity of paper, usu. 500 or 516 sheets. **2.** often **reams** A large amount. [< Ar. *rizma*, bundle.]

ream² (rēm) ►*v.* **1.** To form, shape, taper, or enlarge (e.g., a hole) with a reamer or similar tool. **2.** To remove (material) with a reamer. [Poss. < ME *remen*, make room.]

ream·er (rē′mər) ►*n.* A tool used to shape or enlarge holes.

reap (rēp) ►*v.* **1.** To cut and gather (grain or a similar crop). **2.** To harvest a crop (from). **3.** To obtain as a result of effort: *reap profits.* [< OE *rīpan.*]

reap·er (rē′pər) ►*n.* One that reaps, esp. a machine for harvesting grain.

rear¹ (rîr) ►*n.* **1.** A back or hind part. **2.** The part of a military deployment farthest from the fighting front. ►*adj.* Of, at, or located in the rear. [< ME *rerewarde*, rear guard.]

rear² (rîr) ►*v.* **1.** To care for (children or a child) during the early stages of life. **2.** To tend (growing plants or animals). **3.** To build; erect. **4.** *Archaic* To lift upright. **5.** To rise on the hind legs, as a horse. [< OE *rǣran*, raise.]

rear admiral ►*n.* A rank, as in the US Navy, above captain and below vice admiral.

rear guard ►*n.* A detachment of troops that protects the rear of a military force.

rear·most (rîr′mōst′) ►*adj.* Farthest in the rear.

rear·ward (rîr′wərd) also **rear·wards** (-wərdz) ►*adv.* Toward, to, or at the rear. —**rear′ward** *adj.*

rea·son (rē′zən) ►*n.* **1a.** The basis or motive for an action, decision, or conviction. **b.** A fact or cause that explains why something exists or has occurred. **2a.** The capacity for logical, rational, and analytic thought. **b.** A normal mental state; sanity: *lost his reason.* ►*v.* **1.** To determine or conclude by logical thinking. **2.** To use the faculty of reason; think logically. **3.** To talk or argue logically and persuasively. —*idioms:* **by reason of** Because of. **within reason** Within the bounds of good sense or practicality. [< Lat. *ratiō* < *rērī*, think.] —**rea′son·er** *n.* —**rea′son·ing** *n.*

rea·son·a·ble (rē′zə-nə-bəl) ►*adj.* **1.** Capable of reasoning; rational. **2.** In accordance with reason or sound thinking. **3.** Not excessive or extreme. —**rea′son·a·bil′i·ty** *n.*

re·as·sure (rē′ə-shoor′) ►*v.* **-sured, -sur·ing** **1.** To restore confidence to. **2.** To assure again. —**re′as·sur′ance** *n.*

re·bate (rē′bāt′) ►*n.* A deduction from an amount to be paid or a return of part of an amount paid. ►*v.* (rē′bāt′, rĭ-bāt′) **-bat·ed, -bat·ing** To deduct or return (an amount) from a payment or bill. [< OFr. *rabattre*, reduce.] —**re′bat·er** *n.*

Re·bec·ca (rĭ-bĕk′ə) In the Bible, the wife of Isaac and the mother of Jacob and Esau.

re·bel (rĭ-bĕl′) ►*v.* **-belled, -bel·ling** **1.** To refuse allegiance to and oppose by force an established government or ruling authority. **2.** To resist or defy an authority or a convention. **3.** To feel or express strong unwillingness or repugnance. ►*n.* **reb·el** (rĕb′əl) **1.** One who rebels. **2.** A person who resists or defies authority or convention. [< Lat. *rebellāre* < *bellum*, war.]

re·bel·lion (rĭ-bĕl′yən) ►*n.* **1.** Open, armed, and organized resistance to a government. **2.** Defiance toward an authority or convention. —**re·bel′lious** *adj.* —**re·bel′lious·ness** *n.*

re·birth (rē-bûrth′, rē′bûrth′) ►*n.* **1.** A second or new birth. **2.** A revival.

re·born (rē-bôrn′) ►*adj.* Emotionally or spiritually revived.

re·bound (rē′bound′, rĭ-) ►*v.* **1.** To spring or bounce back after hitting or colliding with something. **2.** To recover, as from disappointment. **3.** *Basketball* To retrieve the ball as it bounces off the backboard or rim after an unsuccessful shot. ►*n.* (rē′bound′, rĭ-bound′) **1.** A springing or bounding back; recoil. **2a.** A rebounding or caroming ball or hockey puck. **b.** *Basketball* The act or an instance of taking possession of a rebounding ball. **3.** A recovery, as from a disappointment.

re·buff (rĭ-bŭf′) ►*n.* A blunt or abrupt repulse or refusal. ►*v.* **1.** To reject bluntly, often disdainfully; snub. **2.** To repel or drive back. [< Ital. *ribuffo*, reprimand.]

re·buke (rĭ-byook′) ►*v.* **-buked, -buk·ing** To criticize sharply; reprimand. [< ONFr. *rebuker*.] —**re·buke′** *n.*

re·bus (rē′bəs) ►*n., pl.* **-bus·es** A representation of words in the form of pictures or symbols, often presented as a puzzle. [Lat. *rēbus*, by things, ablative pl. of *rēs*, thing.]

re·but (rĭ-bŭt′) ►*v.* **-but·ted, -but·ting** To refute by offering opposing evidence or arguments. [< OFr. *rebouter*.] —**re·but′tal** *n.*

rec (rĕk) ►*n. Informal* Recreation.

re·cal·ci·trant (rĭ-kăl′sĭ-trənt) ►*adj.* Stubbornly resistant to and defiant of authority or guidance. [< LLat. *recalcitrāre*, be disobedient.] —**re·cal′ci·trance, re·cal′ci·tran·cy** *n.*

re·call (rĭ-kôl′) ►*v.* **1.** To ask or order to return; call back. **2.** To remember; recollect. **3.** To cancel, take back, or revoke. **4.** To bring back; restore. ►*n.* (*also* rē′kôl′) **1.** The act of recalling. **2.** The ability to remember information or experiences. **3.** The act of revoking. **4.** The procedure by which a public official may be removed from office by popular vote. **5.** A request by the manufacturer of a defective product to return it, as for repairs.

re·cant (rĭ-kănt′) ►*v.* To make a formal denial of (e.g., an earlier statement). [Lat. *recantāre*.] —**re·can·ta′tion** *n.*

re·cap¹ (rē-kăp′) ►*v.* **1.** To cap again. **2.** To restore (a used automobile tire) by bonding new rubber onto the worn tread. ►*n.* (rē′kăp′) A recapped tire.

re·cap² (rē′kăp′) *Informal* ►*v.* **-capped, -cap·ping** To recapitulate. ►*n.* A summary or recapitulation, as of a news report.

re·ca·pit·u·late (rē′kə-pĭch′ə-lāt′) ►*v.* **-lat·ed, -lat·ing** To repeat in concise form. [< Lat. *capit-*

ulum, main point.] **—re′ca·pit′u·la′tion** *n.*

re·cap·ture (rē-kăp′chər) ►*v.* **1.** To capture again. **2.** To recall: *recapture the past.* **—re·cap′ture** *n.*

recd. ►*abbr.* received

re·cede (rĭ-sēd′) ►*v.* **-ced·ed, -ced·ing** **1.** To move back or away from a limit or point. **2.** To slope backward. **3.** To become or seem to become more distant. [< Lat. *recēdere.*]

Syns: *ebb, retract, retreat* **Ant:** *advance v.*

re·ceipt (rĭ-sēt′) ►*n.* **1.** The act of receiving or being received. **2.** often **receipts** A quantity or amount received: *cash receipts.* **3.** A written acknowledgment that a specified article has been received. **4.** A recipe. ►*v.* **1.** To mark (a bill) as having been paid. **2.** To give a receipt for. [< Lat. *receptus,* received.]

re·ceiv·a·ble (rĭ-sē′və-bəl) ►*adj.* **1.** Suitable for being received. **2.** Awaiting or requiring payment. **—re·ceiv′a·ble** *n.*

re·ceive (rĭ-sēv′) ►*v.* **-ceived, -ceiv·ing** **1a.** To take or acquire (something given); be given: *receive a present.* **b.** To be the person who gets (something sent or transmitted): *receive an e-mail.* **2.** To hear or see: *receive bad news.* **3.** To be subjected to; meet with. **4a.** To take in, hold, or contain. **b.** To welcome or be visited by: *receive guests.* **5.** To convert incoming electromagnetic signals into sound, light, or electrical signals. [< Lat. *recipere.*]

re·ceiv·er (rĭ-sē′vər) ►*n.* **1.** One that receives something. **2.** A device, as part of a television set or telephone, that converts incoming electromagnetic signals into perceptible forms. **3.** A person appointed by a court to receive and administer funds or property connected with ongoing litigation.

re·ceiv·er·ship (rĭ-sē′vər-shĭp′) ►*n. Law* **1.** The office or functions of a receiver. **2.** The state of being held by a receiver.

re·cent (rē′sənt) ►*adj.* **1.** Of or occurring at a time immediately before the present. **2.** Modern; new. [< Lat. *recēns,* fresh.] **—re′cen·cy, re′cent·ness** *n.* **—re′cent·ly** *adv.*

re·cep·ta·cle (rĭ-sĕp′tə-kəl) ►*n.* **1.** Something that holds or contains. **2.** *Electron.* A fitting connected to a power supply and equipped to receive a plug. [< Lat. *receptāculum.*]

re·cep·tion (rĭ-sĕp′shən) ►*n.* **1.** The act of receiving or of being received. **2.** A welcome or acceptance: *a friendly reception.* **3.** A social function: *a wedding reception.* **4a.** Conversion of transmitted electromagnetic signals into perceptible forms. **b.** The condition or quality of the signals so received. [< Lat. *receptiō.*]

re·cep·tion·ist (rĭ-sĕp′shə-nĭst) ►*n.* One employed chiefly to receive visitors and answer the telephone.

re·cep·tive (rĭ-sĕp′tĭv) ►*adj.* **1.** Capable of receiving. **2.** Ready or willing to receive favorably: *receptive to the proposal.* **—re′cep·tiv′i·ty** *n.*

re·cep·tor (rĭ-sĕp′tər) ►*n.* **1.** A specialized cell or group of nerve endings that responds to sensory stimuli. **2.** A site on or in a cell that binds with substances such as drugs.

re·cess (rē′sĕs′, rĭ-sĕs′) ►*n.* **1a.** A temporary cessation of customary activities. See Synonyms at **pause. b.** A period in the school day during which students are given time to play or relax. **2.** often **recesses** A remote, secret, or secluded place. **3a.** An indentation or hollow. **b.** An alcove. ►*v.* **1.** To create a recess in: *recessed a portion of the wall.* **2.** To suspend (e.g., a session) for a recess. [< Lat. *recēdere, recess-,* recede.]

re·ces·sion (rĭ-sĕsh′ən) ►*n.* **1.** The act of withdrawing. **2.** The period of economic decline from the peak to a trough of the business cycle. **3.** A ceremonial exit, esp. of clerics and choir members after a church service. [< Lat. *recēdere, recess-,* recede.]

re·ces·sion·al (rĭ-sĕsh′ə-nəl) ►*n.* A hymn that accompanies a ceremonial recession.

re·ces·sive (rĭ-sĕs′ĭv) ►*adj.* **1.** Tending to go backward or recede. **2.** *Genet.* Incapable of being manifested when occurring with a dominant form of a gene. **—re·ces′sive·ly** *adv.*

re·cid·i·vism (rĭ-sĭd′ə-vĭz′əm) ►*n.* The repeating of or returning to criminal behavior by the same offender or type of offender. [< Lat. *recidere,* fall back.] **—re·cid′i·vist** *n.* **—re·cid′i·vis′tic, re·cid′i·vous** *adj.*

Re·ci·fe (rə-sē′fə) A city of NE Brazil on the Atlantic S of Natal.

rec·i·pe (rĕs′ə-pē′) ►*n.* A set of directions for making or preparing something, esp. food. [Lat., imper. of *recipere,* take.]

re·cip·i·ent (rĭ-sĭp′ē-ənt) ►*n.* One that receives or is given something. ►*adj.* Receptive. [< Lat. *recipere,* receive.]

re·cip·ro·cal (rĭ-sĭp′rə-kəl) ►*adj.* **1.** Done or owed in return: *a reciprocal invitation to lunch.* **2.** Experienced or done on both sides: *reciprocal admiration between friends.* ►*n.* **1.** Something reciprocal to something else. **2.** *Math.* Either of a pair of numbers whose product is 1. [< Lat. *reciprocus,* alternating.] **—re·cip′ro·cal′i·ty** (-kăl′ĭ-tē) *n.* **—re·cip′ro·cal·ly** *adv.*

re·cip·ro·cate (rĭ-sĭp′rə-kāt′) ►*v.* **-cat·ed, -cat·ing** **1.** To give or take mutually; interchange. **2.** To show or give in return. **3.** To make a return for something given or done. **—re·cip′ro·ca′tion** *n.* **—re·cip′ro·ca′tive** *adj.* **—re·cip′ro·ca′tor** *n.*

rec·i·proc·i·ty (rĕs′ə-prŏs′ĭ-tē) ►*n., pl.* **-ties** **1.** A reciprocal condition or relationship. **2.** A mutual or cooperative interchange of favors, esp. the exchange of rights or privileges of trade between nations.

re·cit·al (rĭ-sīt′l) ►*n.* **1.** The act of reciting publicly. **2.** A detailed account of something. **3.** A performance of music or dance, esp. by a solo performer. **—re·ci′tal·ist** *n.*

rec·i·ta·tion (rĕs′ĭ-tā′shən) ►*n.* **1.** The act of reciting. **2.** Oral delivery of prepared lessons by a pupil.

rec·i·ta·tive (rĕs′ĭ-tə-tēv′, rĕch′-) ►*n.* **1.** A style used in operas, oratorios, and cantatas in which the text is declaimed in the rhythm of natural speech. **2.** A passage rendered in this style. [Ital. *recitativo.*]

re·cite (rĭ-sīt′) ►*v.* **-cit·ed, -cit·ing** **1.** To repeat or utter aloud (something memorized or rehearsed), often before an audience. **2.** To relate in detail. [< Lat. *recitāre.*] **—re·cit′er** *n.*

reck·less (rĕk′lĭs) ►*adj.* Acting or done with a lack of care; irresponsible. [< OE *rēcelēas.*] **—reck′less·ly** *adv.* **—reck′less·ness** *n.*

reck·on (rĕk′ən) ►*v.* **1.** To count or compute: *reckon the cost.* **2.** To regard as. **3.** *Informal* To think or conclude. **—phrasal verb: reckon**

with To settle accounts with. [< OE *gerecenian*, recount.]

reck·on·ing (rĕk′ə-nĭng) ►*n.* **1.** The act of counting or computing. **2.** A statement of a sum due. **3.** A settlement of accounts: *a day of reckoning.* **4.** The calculation of the position of a ship or aircraft.

re·claim (rĭ-klām′) ►*v.* **1.** To demand the restoration or return of (e.g., a possession). **2.** To make (e.g., land) suitable for cultivation or habitation. **3.** To procure (usable substances) from waste products. **4.** To reform. [< Lat. *reclāmāre,* entreat.] —**re·claim′a·ble** *adj.* —**re·claim′ant, re·claim′er** *n.* —**rec′la·ma′tion** (rĕk′lə-mā′shən) *n.*

re·cline (rĭ-klīn′) ►*v.* **-clined, -clin·ing** **1.** To lean back or lie down on one's back. **2.** To be adjustable so that the occupant may recline rather than sit up: *a seat that reclines.* [< Lat. *reclīnāre.*]

re·clin·er (rĭ-klī′nər) ►*n.* **1.** A person who reclines. **2.** An armchair, bicycle, or other apparatus that can be adjusted so that the occupant assumes a reclining position.

re·cluse (rĕk′lōōs′, rĭ-klōōs′) ►*n.* One who lives in seclusion. [< Lat. *reclūsus,* p.part. of *reclūdere,* close off.] —**re·clu′sive** (rĭ-klōō′sĭv, -zĭv) *adj.*

rec·og·ni·tion (rĕk′əg-nĭsh′ən) ►*n.* **1.** The act of recognizing or condition of being recognized. **2.** An acknowledgment, as of a claim. **3.** Attention or favorable notice.

re·cog·ni·zance (rĭ-kŏg′nĭ-zəns, -kŏn′ĭ-) ►*n.* *Law* An obligation of record to perform a particular action, such as appearing in court, without the posting of a bond. —**re·cog′ni·zant** *adj.*

rec·og·nize (rĕk′əg-nīz′) ►*v.* **-nized, -niz·ing** **1.** To know or identify from past experience or knowledge. **2.** To acknowledge or accept. **3.** To approve of or appreciate. [< Lat. *recognōscere.*] —**rec′og·niz′a·ble** *adj.*

re·coil (rĭ-koil′) ►*v.* **1.** To spring back, as a gun upon firing. **2.** To shrink back, as in fear. [< OFr. *reculer.*] —**re′coil′** (rē′koil′) *n.* —**re·coil′er** *n.*

rec·ol·lect (rĕk′ə-lĕkt′) ►*v.* To recall to mind; remember. [< Lat. *recolligere,* gather up.] —**rec′ol·lec′tion** *n.*

re·com·bi·nant DNA (rē-kŏm′bə-nənt) ►*n.* Genetically engineered DNA prepared by transplanting or splicing genes from one species into the cells of a different species.

re·com·bi·na·tion (rē′kŏm-bə-nā′shən) ►*n.* The natural or artificial rearrangement of genetic material in living organisms or viruses.

rec·om·mend (rĕk′ə-mĕnd′) ►*v.* **1.** To commend to another as worthy or desirable; endorse. **2.** To advise or counsel. [< Med.Lat. *recommendāre.*] —**rec′om·men·da′tion** *n.*

rec·om·mend·ed daily allowance also **rec·om·mend·ed dietary allowance** (rĕk′ə-mĕn′dĭd) ►*n.* The amount of a nutrient or the amount of calories recommended for a person to consume daily.

rec·om·pense (rĕk′əm-pĕns′) ►*v.* **-pensed, -pens·ing** To award compensation to or for. ►*n.* **1.** Amends made, as for damage or loss. **2.** Payment in return for something. [< LLat. *recompēnsāre.*]

rec·on·cile (rĕk′ən-sīl′) ►*v.* **-ciled, -cil·ing** **1.** To reestablish a close relationship between. **2.**

To settle or resolve. **3.** To bring (oneself) to accept. **4.** To make compatible or consistent: *reconcile opposing views.* [< Lat. *reconciliāre.*] —**rec′on·cil′a·bil′i·ty** *n.* —**rec′on·cil′a·ble** *adj.* —**rec′on·cile′ment, rec′on·cil′i·a′tion** (-sĭl′ē-ā′shən) *n.* —**rec′on·cil′er** *n.*

rec·on·dite (rĕk′ən-dīt′, rĭ-kŏn′dīt′) ►*adj.* **1.** Not easily understood. **2.** Concealed; hidden. [Lat. *reconditus,* p.part. of *recondere,* put away.]

re·con·nais·sance (rĭ-kŏn′ə-səns, -zəns) ►*n.* An inspection or exploration of an area, esp. to gather military information. [< OFr. *reconnoistre,* RECOGNIZE.]

re·con·noi·ter (rē′kə-noi′tər, rĕk′ə-) ►*v.* To make a preliminary examination of (e.g., an area) in order to gather information, esp. for military purposes. [< OFr. *reconnoistre,* RECOGNIZE.] —**re′con·noi′ter·er** *n.*

re·con·sid·er (rē′kən-sĭd′ər) ►*v.* To consider again, esp. with intent to modify a previous decision. —**re′con·sid′er·a′tion** *n.*

re·con·struct (rē′kən-strŭkt′) ►*v.* **1.** To construct again; make over. **2.** To build again mentally; re-create. —**re′con·struct′i·ble** *adj.* —**re′con·struc′tive** *adj.*

re·con·struc·tion (rē′kən-strŭk′shən) ►*n.* **1.** The act or result of reconstructing. **2. Reconstruction** The period (1865–77) during which the states of the Confederacy were controlled by the federal government before being readmitted to the Union.

re·cord (rĭ-kôrd′) ►*v.* **1.** To set down for preservation, esp. in writing. **2.** To register or indicate. **3.** To render (sound or images) into permanent form, as by mechanical or digital means. ►*n.* **rec·ord** (rĕk′ərd) **1a.** A usu. written account of events or facts. **b.** Something on which such an account is made. **2.** Information on a particular subject collected and preserved: *the coldest day on record.* **3.** The known history of performance: *your academic record.* **4.** An unsurpassed measurement: *a world record in weightlifting.* **5a.** A disk designed for a phonograph. **b.** A musical recording that is issued on a medium of some kind. —***idioms:*** **off the record** Not for publication. **on record** Known to have taken a certain position. [< Lat. *recordārī,* remember : RE- + *cor, cord-,* heart.]

re·cord·er (rĭ-kôr′dər) ►*n.* **1.** One that records: *a video recorder.* **2.** A flute with eight finger holes and a whistlelike mouthpiece.

re·cord·ing (rĭ-kôr′dĭng) ►*n.* **1.** Something on which sound or images have been recorded. **2.** A recorded sound or picture.

re·count (rĭ-kount′) ►*v.* To narrate the facts or particulars of. See Synonyms at **describe**. [< OFr. *reconter.*]

re-count (rē-kount′) ►*v.* To count again. ►*n.* (*also* rē′kount′) An additional count.

re·coup (rĭ-kōōp′) ►*v.* **1.** To recover or regain. **2.** To reimburse (someone) for a loss or expenditure. [< OFr. *recouper,* cut back.]

re·course (rē′kôrs′, rĭ-kôrs′) ►*n.* **1.** The act or an instance of turning to a person or thing in an effort to achieve something: *have recourse to the courts.* **2.** One that is turned to for aid or security. [< Lat. *recursus,* a running back.]

re·cov·er (rĭ-kŭv′ər) ►*v.* **1.** To get back, esp. by making an effort. **2.** To regain a usual condition, as of health. **3.** To procure (usable substances) from unusable substances, such as waste. **4.** To receive a favorable judgment in a lawsuit. [< Lat. *recuperāre*.] —**re·cov′er·a·ble** *adj.* —**re·cov′er·y** *n.*

rec·re·ant (rĕk′rē-ənt) ►*adj.* **1.** Unfaithful or disloyal. **2.** *Archaic* Craven or cowardly. [< OFr. < *recroire*, remember : RE– + Lat. *crēdere*, believe.] —**rec′re·ance, rec′re·an·cy** *n.* —**rec′re·ant** *n.*

re·cre·ate (rē′krē-āt′) ►*v.* To create anew. —**re′-cre·a′tion** *n.*

rec·re·a·tion (rĕk′rē-ā′shən) ►*n.* Refreshment of one's mind or body through activity that amuses or stimulates. [< Lat. *recreāre*, refresh.] —**rec′re·ate′** *v.* —**rec′re·a′tion·al** *adj.*

recreational vehicle ►*n.* A vehicle, such as a motor home, used for recreation.

re·crim·i·nate (rĭ-krĭm′ə-nāt′) ►*v.* **-nat·ed, -nat·ing** To counter one accusation with another. [Med.Lat. *recrīminārī*.] —**re·crim′i·na′tion** *n.* —**re·crim′i·na′tive, re·crim′i·na·to′ry** (-nə-tôr′ē) *adj.*

re·cru·desce (rē′krōō-dĕs′) ►*v.* **-desced, -desc·ing** To break out anew, as after an inactive period. [Lat. *recrūdēscere*.] —**re′cru·des′cence** *n.* —**re′cru·des′cent** *adj.*

re·cruit (rĭ-krōōt′) ►*v.* **1a.** To enlist (persons) in military service. **b.** To strengthen or raise (an armed force) by enlistment. **2.** To hire or enroll, or seek to hire or enroll (e.g., new employees). ►*n.* A newly engaged member of a military force or other organization. [< OFr. *recroistre*, grow again.] —**re·cruit′er** *n.* —**re·cruit′ment** *n.*

rec·tal (rĕk′təl) ►*adj.* Of or situated near the rectum. —**rec′tal·ly** *adv.*

rec·tan·gle (rĕk′tăng′gəl) ►*n.* A parallelogram with four right angles. [< Med.Lat. *rēctangulum*.] —**rec·tan′gu·lar** *adj.* —**rec·tan′gu·lar′i·ty** (-lăr′ĭ-tē) *n.*

rec·ti·fy (rĕk′tə-fī′) ►*v.* **-fied, -fy·ing** To set right; correct. [< Lat. *rēctus*, right.] —**rec′ti·fi′a·ble** *adj.* —**rec′ti·fi·ca′tion** *n.*

rec·ti·lin·e·ar (rĕk′tə-lĭn′ē-ər) ►*adj.* Moving in, bounded by, or characterized by a straight line or lines. [< LLat. *rēctilīneus*.]

rec·ti·tude (rĕk′tĭ-tōōd′, -tyōōd′) ►*n.* Moral uprightness. [< LLat. *rēctitūdō*.]

rec·to (rĕk′tō) ►*n., pl.* **-tos** A right-hand page. [< Lat. (folio) *rēctō*, (the leaf) being right.]

rec·tor (rĕk′tər) ►*n.* **1.** A cleric in charge of a parish. **2.** A Roman Catholic priest serving as the managerial and spiritual head of a church or other institution. **3.** The principal of certain schools, colleges, and universities. [< Lat. *rēctor*, director.]

rec·to·ry (rĕk′tə-rē) ►*n., pl.* **-ries** The house in which a rector lives.

rec·tum (rĕk′təm) ►*n., pl.* **-tums** or **-ta** (-tə) The terminal portion of the large intestine, extending from the most distal section of the colon to the anal canal. [< Lat. (intestīnum) *rēctum*, straight (intestine).]

re·cum·bent (rĭ-kŭm′bənt) ►*adj.* Lying down; reclining. [< Lat. *recumbere*, lie down.]

re·cu·per·ate (rĭ-kōō′pə-rāt′, -kyōō′-) ►*v.* **-at·ed, -at·ing 1.** To return to health or strength; recover. **2.** To recover (a financial loss). [Lat. *recuperāre*.] —**re·cu′per·a′tion** *n.* —**re·cu′per·a′tive** (-pə-rā′tĭv, -pər-ə-tĭv) *adj.*

re·cur (rĭ-kûr′) ►*v.* **-curred, -cur·ring** To happen, come up, or show up again or repeatedly.

[Lat. *recurrere*.] —**re·cur′rence** *n.* —**re·cur′-rent** *adj.* —**re·cur′rent·ly** *adv.*

re·curve (rē-kûrv′) ►*v.* To curve backward or downward.

re·cy·cle (rē-sī′kəl) ►*v.* **-cled, -cling 1.** To put or pass through a cycle again; reuse in a cycle. **2.** To extract and reuse (useful substances found in waste): *recycle steel from old cars.* **3.** To use again: *recycle old jokes.* —**re·cy′cla·ble** *adj.* & *n.* —**re·cy′cler** *n.*

red (rĕd) ►*n.* **1.** Any of a group of colors whose hue resembles that of blood, lying at the long-wave end of the visible spectrum. **2.** often **Red** A revolutionary, esp. a Communist. **3.** The condition of being in debt or operating at a loss: *The firm has been in the red all year.* ►*adj.* **red·der, red·dest 1.** Of the color red. **2a.** Having a red or reddish color: *red hair.* **b.** Ruddy or flushed: *red with embarrassment.* **3.** often **Red** Communist. [< OE *rēad.*] —**red′ness** *n.*

red blood cell ►*n.* A cell in the blood of vertebrates that transports oxygen and carbon dioxide to and from the tissues.

red-blood·ed (rĕd′blŭd′ĭd) ►*adj.* Strong and highly spirited.

red·breast (rĕd′brĕst′) ►*n.* A bird, such as the robin, with a red or reddish breast.

red card ►*n.* A red-colored card shown by a referee, esp. in soccer, to eject a player from the game. —**red′-card′** *v.*

Red Cloud Makhpyia-luta. 1822–1909. Oglala leader.

Red Cloud
photographed c. 1880

red·coat (rĕd′kōt′) ►*n.* A British soldier, esp. during the American Revolution.

red·den (rĕd′n) ►*v.* To make or become red.

red·dish (rĕd′ĭsh) ►*adj.* Mixed or tinged with red; somewhat red. —**red′dish·ness** *n.*

re·deem (rĭ-dēm′) ►*v.* **1.** To recover ownership of by paying a specified sum. **2.** To pay off (e.g., a promissory note). **3.** To turn in (e.g., coupons) and receive something in exchange. **4a.** To set free, as from slavery or kidnapping, by providing compensation. **b.** To save from sinfulness. **c.** To restore the worth or reputation of. **5.** To make up for: *redeem an earlier mistake.* [< Lat. *redimere.*] —**re·deem′a·ble** *adj.*

re·demp·tion (rĭ-dĕmp′shən) ►*n.* The act of redeeming or state of being redeemed. [< Lat.

redimere, redēmpt-, buy back.] —**re·demp′-tion·al, re·demp′tive** *adj.*

red-faced (rĕd′fāst′) ►*adj.* Embarrassed.

red flag ►*n.* **1.** A warning signal. **2.** Something that provokes an irritated reaction.

red giant ►*n.* A low-mass star of great size and luminosity that has a relatively low surface temperature, giving it a reddish or orange hue.

red-hand·ed (rĕd′hăn′dĭd) ►*adv. & adj.* In the act of committing something wrong.

red·head (rĕd′hĕd′) ►*n.* A person with red hair.

red herring ►*n.* Something that draws attention away from the central issue.

red-hot (rĕd′hŏt′) ►*adj.* **1.** Glowing hot; very hot. **2.** Very recent: *red-hot information.*

re·dis·trict (rē-dĭs′trĭkt) ►*v.* To divide again into administrative or election districts.

red-let·ter (rĕd′lĕt′ər) ►*adj.* Memorably happy: *a red-letter day.* [From marking in red the holy days in church calendars.]

red·line (rĕd′līn′) ►*v.* **-lined, -lin·ing** To refuse to provide mortgages, insurance, or other goods to areas deemed a poor economic risk, esp. when the residents are nonwhite.

red·o·lent (rĕd′l-ənt) ►*adj.* **1.** Having or emitting an odor. **2.** Suggestive; reminiscent. [< Lat. *redolēre,* smell.] —**red′o·lence** *n.*

re·doubt (rĭ-dout′) ►*n.* A small, often temporary defensive fortification. [< Med.Lat. *reductus,* concealed place.]

re·doubt·a·ble (rĭ-dou′tə-bəl) ►*adj.* **1.** Arousing fear or awe; formidable. **2.** Worthy of respect or honor. [< OFr. *redouter,* to dread.] —**re·doubt′a·bly** *adv.*

re·dound (rĭ-dound′) ►*v.* To have an effect or consequence. [< Lat. *redundāre,* overflow; see REDUNDANT.]

red pepper ►*n.* **1.** The ripe red fruit of a bell pepper. **2.** See **cayenne pepper.**

re·dress (rĭ-drĕs′) ►*v.* **1.** To set right; remedy or rectify. **2.** To make amends to. ►*n.* (*also* rē′drĕs) **1.** Satisfaction for wrong or injury; reparation. **2.** Rectification or reformation. [< OFr. *redrecier,* rearrange.]

Red River A river of the S-central US rising in two branches in the Texas Panhandle and flowing about 2,100 km (1,300 mi) to the Mississippi R.

Red Sea A sea between NE Africa and the Arabian Peninsula.

red shift ►*n.* An increase in the wavelength of radiation emitted by a celestial body due to the Doppler effect.

red snapper ►*n.* Any of several marine food fishes with red or reddish bodies.

red tape ►*n.* Official forms and procedures, esp. when oppressively complex and time-consuming. [From its former use in tying British official documents.]

red tide ►*n.* A usu. reddish discoloration of coastal ocean waters caused by a bloom of plankton, esp. plankton that produce toxins that contaminate shellfish and can kill fish.

re·duce (rĭ-do͞os′, -dyo͞os′) ►*v.* **-duced, -duc·ing 1.** To bring down, as in extent, amount, or degree. **2.** To bring to a humbler, weaker, or more difficult state or condition. **3.** To lower in rank or grade. **4.** To put in a simpler or more systematic form. **5.** *Chem.* **a.** To decrease the valence of (an atom) by adding electrons. **b.**

To remove oxygen from. **c.** To add hydrogen to. **d.** To change to a metallic state; smelt. **6.** *Math.* To simplify the form of (e.g., a fraction) without changing the value. **7.** To lose weight, as by dieting. [< Lat. *redūcere,* bring back.] —**re·duc′i·bil′i·ty** *n.* —**re·duc′i·ble** *adj.* —**re·duc′tion** (-dŭk′shən) *n.* —**re·duc′tive** *adj.*

re·dun·dan·cy (rĭ-dŭn′dən-sē) ►*n., pl.* **-cies 1.** The state of being redundant. **2.** An excess. **3.** Unnecessary repetition.

re·dun·dant (rĭ-dŭn′dənt) ►*adj.* **1.** Exceeding what is necessary or natural; superfluous. **2.** Needlessly repetitive; verbose. [< Lat. *redundāre,* overflow : RE– + *unda,* wave.] —**re·dun′dant·ly** *adv.*

re·du·pli·cate (rĭ-do͞o′plə-kāt′, -dyo͞o′-) ►*v.* **-cat·ed, -cat·ing 1.** To redouble. **2.** *Ling.* To double (the initial syllable or all of a root word) to form a new word. [LLat. *reduplicāre.*] —**re·du′pli·ca′tion** *n.*

red·wood (rĕd′wo͝od′) ►*n.* **1a.** A tall evergreen coniferous tree of S Oregon and N California. **b.** Its soft reddish wood. **2.** A sequoia.

reed (rēd) ►*n.* **1a.** Any of various tall, hollow-stemmed aquatic grasses. **b.** The stalk of a reed. **2a.** A flexible strip of cane or metal used in the mouthpiece of certain musical instruments to produce tone by vibrating in response to a stream of air. **b.** An instrument fitted with a reed. [< OE *hrēod.*] —**reed′y** *adj.*

Reed, John Silas 1887–1920. Amer. writer.

Reed, Walter 1851–1902. Amer. army surgeon.

reef[1] (rēf) ►*n.* A strip or ridge of rocks, sand, or coral at or near the surface of a body of water. [Obsolete Du. *rif,* poss. < ON, ridge.]

reef[2] (rēf) ►*n.* A portion of a sail rolled and tied down to lessen the area exposed to the wind. ►*v.* To reduce the size of (a sail) by tucking in a part. [< ON *rif,* ridge.]

reef·er (rē′fər) ►*n. Slang* Marijuana, esp. a marijuana cigarette. [?]

reek (rēk) ►*v.* **1.** To give off a strong, unpleasant odor. **2.** To be pervaded by something unpleasant. **3.** *Chiefly Brit.* To smoke, steam, or fume. ►*n.* **1.** A stench. See Synonyms at **stench. 2.** *Chiefly Brit.* Smoke or vapor. [< OE *rēocan.*]

reel[1] (rēl) ►*n.* **1.** A device, such as a spool, that turns on an axis and is used for winding rope, tape, or similar materials. **2.** The quantity of material wound on one reel. ►*v.* **1.** To wind on a reel. **2.** To recover by winding on a reel: *reel in a fish.* —**phrasal verb: reel off** To recite fluently: *reeled off a list of names.* [< OE *hrēol.*]

reel[2] (rēl) ►*v.* **1.** To be thrown off balance or fall back. **2.** To stagger or sway, as from drunkenness. **3.** To feel dizzy, as with confusion. ►*n.* **1.** A staggering or whirling movement. **2a.** A moderately fast dance of Scottish origin. **b.** The music for this dance. [ME *relen,* whirl about.]

re·en·try *also* **re-en·try** (rē-ĕn′trē) ►*n.* **1.** The act or action of reentering. **2.** The return of a missile or spacecraft into the atmosphere.

re·fec·to·ry (rĭ-fĕk′tə-rē) ►*n., pl.* **-ries** A room where meals are served. [< Lat. *reficere, refect-,* refresh.]

re·fer (rĭ-fûr′) ►*v.* **-ferred, -fer·ring 1.** To direct to a source for help or information. **2.** To direct the attention of. **3.** To pertain; concern. **4.** To speak or write about something briefly. **5.** To turn one's attention, as in seeking information: *refer to a dictionary.* [< Lat. *referre* :

698

RE– + *ferre*, carry.] **—ref'er·a·ble** (rĕf'ər-ə-bəl, rĭ-fûr'-) *adj.* **—re·fer'ral** *n.*

ref·e·ree (rĕf'ə-rē') ►*n.* **1.** One to whom something is referred, esp. for settlement or decision. **2.** *Sports* An official who supervises play. ►*v.* **-reed, -ree·ing** To act as referee (at or for).

ref·er·ence (rĕf'ər-əns, rĕf'rəns) ►*n.* **1.** An act of referring to something. **2.** A mention or an allusion. **3a.** A note in a publication referring the reader to another passage or source. **b.** A work frequently used as a source. **4a.** A person who is in a position to recommend another, as for a job. **b.** A statement about a person's qualifications and character. **—idiom: in (or with) reference to** In connection with; in relation to. **—ref'er·en'tial** (-ə-rĕn'shəl) *adj.*

ref·er·en·dum (rĕf'ə-rĕn'dəm) ►*n.*, *pl.* **-dums** or **-da** (-də) **1.** The submission of a proposed public measure or actual statute to a direct popular vote. **2.** Such a vote. [Lat., thing to be referred.]

re·fill (rē-fĭl') ►*v.* To fill again. ►*n.* (rē'fĭl') **1.** A replacement for the used contents of a container. **2.** An additional filling.

re·fine (rĭ-fīn') ►*v.* **-fined, -fin·ing 1.** To reduce to a pure state. **2.** To free from coarse characteristics: *refined his manners.* **—re·fin'er** *n.*

re·fined (rĭ-fīnd') ►*adj.* **1.** Free from coarseness or vulgarity. **2.** Free of impurities. **3.** Precise to a fine degree.

re·fine·ment (rĭ-fīn'mənt) ►*n.* **1.** The act of refining or the condition of being refined. **2.** An improvement. **3.** Fineness, as of expression or taste. **4.** A subtle distinction.

re·fin·er·y (rĭ-fī'nə-rē) ►*n.*, *pl.* **-ies** An industrial plant for purifying a crude substance, such as petroleum or sugar.

re·flect (rĭ-flĕkt') ►*v.* **1.** To throw or bend back (e.g., light) from a surface. See Synonyms at **echo. 2.** To form an image of; mirror. **3.** To manifest; show: *Her work reflects intelligence.* **4.** To think seriously. [< Lat. *reflectere*, bend back.] **—re·flec'tion** *n.* **—re·flec'tive** *adj.* **—re·flec'tive·ly** *adv.*

re·flec·tor (rĭ-flĕk'tər) ►*n.* Something, such as a surface, that reflects.

re·flex (rē'flĕks') ►*adj.* **1.** Involuntary or automatic: *a reflex response.* **2.** Bent, turned, or thrown back. ►*n.* **1a.** An involuntary response to a stimulus. **b. reflexes** A person's ability to respond to new or changing stimuli: *an athlete's quick reflexes.* **2a.** Something reflected. **b.** An image produced by reflection. [< Lat. *reflexus*, p.part. of *reflectere*, bend back.]

re·flex·ive (rĭ-flĕk'sĭv) ►*adj.* **1.** Directed back on itself. **2.** *Gram.* **a.** Of or being a verb having an identical subject and direct object, as *dressed* in the sentence *She dressed herself.* **b.** Of or being the pronoun used as the direct object of a reflexive verb, as *herself* in *She dressed herself.* **3.** Of or relating to a reflex. **4.** Elicited automatically; spontaneous. **—re·flex'ive** *n.* **—re·flex'ive·ly** *adv.* **—re·flex'ive·ness, re'flex·iv'i·ty** (rē'flĕk-sĭv'ĭ-tē) *n.*

re·for·est (rē-fôr'ĭst, -fŏr'ĭst) ►*v.* To replant (an area) with trees. **—re'for·es·ta'tion** *n.*

re·form (rĭ-fôrm') ►*v.* **1.** To improve by correcting errors or removing defects. **2.** To abolish abuse or malpractice in. **3.** To give up harmful or immoral practices. ►*n.* **1.** Action to improve what is wrong or defective in something: *health care reform.* **2.** An instance of this; improvement. ►*adj.* **Reform** Of a branch of Judaism that does not require strict observance of traditional religious law and ritual. [< Lat. *refōrmāre.*] **—re·form'a·ble** *adj.* **—re·for'ma·tive** *adj.* **—re·formed'** *adj.* **—re·form'er** *n.*

ref·or·ma·tion (rĕf'ər-mā'shən) ►*n.* **1.** The act of reforming or the state of being reformed. **2. Reformation** A 16th-cent. movement in Western Europe for the reform of the Roman Catholic Church that resulted in the establishment of the Protestant and other churches. **—ref'or·ma'tion·al** *adj.*

re·for·ma·to·ry (rĭ-fôr'mə-tôr'ē) ►*n.*, *pl.* **-ries** A penal institution for young offenders.

re·fract (rĭ-frăkt') ►*v.* **1.** To deflect (e.g., light) from a straight path by refraction. **2.** To determine the refraction of (e.g., an eye). [Lat. *refringere, refrāct-,* break up.]

re·frac·tion (rĭ-frăk'shən) ►*n.* **1.** The turning or bending of a wave when it passes from one medium into another of different density. **2a.** The ability of the eye to bend light so that an image is focused on the retina. **b.** Determination of this ability in an eye. **—re·frac'tion·al, re·frac'tive** *adj.* **—re·frac'tive·ly** *adv.* **—re'·frac·tiv'i·ty** (rē'frăk-tĭv'ĭ-tē) *n.*

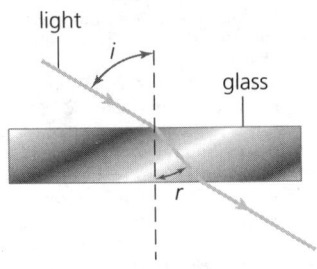

refraction
refraction of light
i: angle of incidence
r: angle of refraction

re·frac·to·ry (rĭ-frăk'tə-rē) ►*adj.* **1.** Showing obstinate resistance to authority. **2.** Difficult to melt or work. ►*n.*, *pl.* **-ries** A material that has a high melting point. **—re·frac'to·ri·ly** *adv.*

re·frain¹ (rĭ-frān') ►*v.* To hold oneself back; forbear: *refrained from swearing.* [< Lat. *refrēnāre,* restrain.]
 Syns: *abstain, forbear* **v.**

re·frain² (rĭ-frān') ►*n.* A phrase or verse repeated at intervals throughout a song or poem. [< OFr. *refraindre,* repeat.]

re·fresh (rĭ-frĕsh') ►*v.* **1a.** To revive, as with rest or food. **b.** To renew by stimulation: *refresh one's memory.* **2.** To make cool, clean, or moist; freshen up. **3.** To replenish: *refresh a drink.* **4.** *Comp.* To update (the information on a screen), as to reflect the most recent changes to a webpage. **—re·fresh'er** *n.* **—re·fresh'ing** *adj.*

re·fresh·ment (rĭ-frĕsh'mənt) ►*n.* **1.** The act of refreshing or the state of being refreshed. **2.** Something that refreshes. **3. refreshments** A snack or light meal.

re·frig·er·ant (rĭ-frĭj'ər-ənt) ►*n.* A substance, such as air, ammonia, water, or carbon dioxide, used to provide cooling.

re·frig·er·ate (rĭ-frĭj'ə-rāt') ►*v.* **-at·ed, -at·ing**

1. To cool or chill (a substance). **2.** To preserve (food) by chilling. [Lat. *refrīgerāre.*] —**re·frig′-er·a′tion** *n.*

re·frig·er·a·tor (rĭ-frĭj′ə-rā′tər) ►*n.* An appliance for storing food or other substances at a low temperature.

ref·uge (rĕf′yōōj) ►*n.* **1.** Protection or shelter, as from danger or hardship. **2a.** A place providing protection or shelter: *a refuge for religious nonconformists.* **b.** An undeveloped area for the preservation of animals and plants. [< Lat. *refugere,* flee.]

ref·u·gee (rĕf′yōō-jē′) ►*n.* One who flees, esp. to another country, seeking refuge, as from war.

re·ful·gent (rĭ-fōōl′jənt, -fŭl′-) ►*adj.* Shining radiantly; resplendent. [< Lat. *refulgēre,* flash back.] —**re·ful′gence** *n.*

re·fund (rĭ-fŭnd′, rē′fŭnd′) ►*v.* To give back (esp. money); repay. ►*n.* (rē′fŭnd′) **1.** A repayment of funds. **2.** An amount repaid. [< Lat. *refundere,* pour back.] —**re·fund′a·ble** *adj.*

re·fur·bish (rē-fûr′bĭsh) ►*v.* To make clean, bright, or fresh again; restore. —**re·fur′bish·ment** *n.*

re·fuse[1] (rĭ-fyōōz′) ►*v.* **-fused, -fus·ing** To decline to do, accept, give, or allow. [< VLat. **refūsāre.*] —**re·fus′al** *n.*

ref·use[2] (rĕf′yōōs) ►*n.* Anything discarded or rejected as useless or worthless; trash. [< OFr. *refus.*]

re·fute (rĭ-fyōōt′) ►*v.* **-fut·ed, -fut·ing** To prove to be false or erroneous. [Lat. *refūtāre.*] —**re·fut′a·ble** (rĭ-fyōō′tə-bəl, rĕf′yə-tə-) *adj.* —**re·fut′a·bly** *adv.* —**ref′u·ta′tion** *n.* —**re·fut′er** *n.*

re·gain (rē-gān′) ►*v.* **1.** To recover possession of. **2.** To reach again.

re·gal (rē′gəl) ►*adj.* Of a monarch; royal. [< Lat. *rēgālis.*] —**re′gal·ly** *adv.*

re·gale (rĭ-gāl′) ►*v.* **-galed, -gal·ing 1.** To delight or entertain. **2.** To entertain sumptuously. [< OFr. *regal,* feast.]

re·ga·lia (rĭ-gāl′yə, -gā′lē-ə) ►*pl.n.* (*takes sing. or pl. v.)* **1.** The emblems and symbols of royalty. **2.** The distinguishing symbols of a rank, office, order, or society. **3.** Magnificent attire; finery. [< Lat. *rēgālis,* regal.]

re·gard (rĭ-gärd′) ►*v.* **1.** To look upon or consider: *I regard him as my best friend.* **2.** To look at attentively; observe. **3.** To relate or refer to; concern. **4.** *Archaic* To take into account. ►*n.* **1.** Careful thought or attention; heed. **2a.** Respect, affection, or esteem. **b. regards** Good wishes: *Give her my regards.* **3.** Respect: *lucky in that regard.* **4.** A look or gaze. —*idiom:* **in (or with) regard to** In reference or relation to. [< OFr. *regarder.*] —**re·gard′ful** *adj.*

re·gard·ing (rĭ-gär′dĭng) ►*prep.* In reference to; concerning.

re·gard·less (rĭ-gärd′lĭs) ►*adv.* In spite of everything; anyway. ►*adj.* Heedless; unmindful. —**re·gard′less·ly** *adv.*

re·gat·ta (rĭ-gä′tə, -găt′ə) ►*n.* A boat race or a series of boat races. [Ital.]

re·gen·cy (rē′jən-sē) ►*n., pl.* **-cies 1.** A person or group governing in place of a monarch who is absent, disabled, or still in minority. **2.** The period during which a regent governs. **3.** The office, region, or government of regents or a regent.

re·gen·er·ate (rĭ-jĕn′ə-rāt′) ►*v.* **-at·ed, -at·**

ing **1.** *Biol.* To replace (e.g., a lost part) by the formation of new tissue. **2.** To form, construct, or create anew. **3.** To give new life or energy to; revitalize. **4.** To reform spiritually or morally. ►*adj.* (-ər-ĭt) **1.** Spiritually or morally reformed. **2.** Formed or created anew. —**re·gen′er·a′tion** *n.* —**re·gen′er·a′tive** *adj.* —**re·gen′er·a′tor** *n.*

re·gent (rē′jənt) ►*n.* **1.** One who rules during the minority, absence, or disability of a monarch. **2.** One acting as a ruler or governor. **3.** A member of a governing board of an institution. [< Lat. *regere,* to rule.]

reg·gae (rĕg′ā) ►*n.* Popular music of Jamaican origin, usu. having a strongly accentuated offbeat. [Jamaican E.]

reg·gae·tón (rĕ-gä-tōn′) ►*n.* A style of popular dance music of Caribbean origin that incorporates dancehall, hip-hop, and various Caribbean musical elements. [Am.Sp. *reggaetón, reguetón.*]

reg·i·cide (rĕj′ĭ-sīd′) ►*n.* **1.** The killing of a king. **2.** One who kills a king. [Lat. *rēx,* king + –CIDE.] —**reg′i·cid′al** *adj.*

re·gime (rā-zhēm′, rĭ-) ►*n.* **1.** A government, esp. an oppressive or undemocratic one. **2.** A regulated system, as of diet and exercise; regimen. [< Lat. *regimen.*]

reg·i·men (rĕj′ə-mən, -mĕn′) ►*n.* A regulated system, as of diet or exercise. [< Lat.]

reg·i·ment (rĕj′ə-mənt) ►*n.* A military unit of ground troops consisting of at least two battalions. ►*v.* (rĕj′ə-mĕnt′) **1.** To put (things) into systematic order. **2.** To subject (people) to strict control and rigid order. [< LLat. *regimentum,* rule.] —**reg′i·men′tal** *adj.* —**reg′i·men·ta′tion** *n.*

Re·gi·na (rĭ-jī′nə) The capital of Saskatchewan, Canada, in the S part.

re·gion (rē′jən) ►*n.* **1a.** A large, usu. continuous segment of a surface or space: *the upper regions of the atmosphere.* **b.** A portion of the earth's surface distinguished from others by some characteristic: *the coastal region.* **c.** A political district or unit. **2.** An area of the body: *the abdominal region.* [< Lat. *regiō.*]

re·gion·al (rē′jə-nəl) ►*adj.* **1.** Of or relating to a large geographic region. **2.** Of or characteristic of a particular region: *a regional accent.* —**re′gion·al·ly** *adv.*

reg·is·ter (rĕj′ĭ-stər) ►*n.* **1a.** An official recording of items, names, or actions. **b.** A book for such entries. **2.** A device that automatically records a quantity or number. **3.** A grill-like device through which heated or cooled air is released into a room. **4.** A state of proper alignment. **5.** *Mus.* The range or part of the range of an instrument or voice. ►*v.* **1a.** To enter in an official register. **b.** To enroll, esp. in order to vote or attend classes. **2.** To indicate (data). Used of an instrument or scale. **3.** To reveal; express: *Her face registered surprise.* **4.** To cause (mail) to be officially recorded by payment of a fee. **5.** To make an impression in the mind: *The warning failed to register.* [< Lat. *regestus,* recorded.] —**reg′is·tra·ble** (-ĭ-strə-bəl) *adj.* —**reg′is·trant** *n.*

reg·is·tered nurse (rĕj′ĭ-stərd) ►*n.* A graduate trained nurse who has passed a state registration examination and has been licensed to practice nursing.

reg·is·trar (rĕj′ĭ-strär′, rĕj′ĭ-strär′) ►*n.* An official, as of a university or corporation, who is in charge of keeping records.

reg·is·tra·tion (rĕj′ĭ-strā′shən) ►*n.* **1.** The act or process of registering. **2.** The number of persons registered; enrollment. **3.** A document certifying registering.

reg·is·try (rĕj′ĭ-strē) ►*n., pl.* **-tries 1.** Registration. **2.** A place where official records are kept.

reg·nant (rĕg′nənt) ►*adj.* Reigning; ruling. [< Lat. *rēgnāre*, reign.]

re·gress (rĭ-grĕs′) ►*v.* **1.** To return to a previous, usu. worse or less developed state. **2.** To move backward or away from a reference point. [Lat. *regredī, regress-*.] —**re′gress′** *n.*

re·gres·sion (rĭ-grĕsh′ən) ►*n.* The process or an instance of regressing.

re·gres·sive (rĭ-grĕs′ĭv) ►*adj.* **1.** Tending to regress. **2.** Marked by regression. **3.** Relating to or being a tax that places a proportionately higher burden on lower-income taxpayers. —**re·gres′sive·ly** *adv.* —**re·gres′sive·ness** *n.*

re·gret (rĭ-grĕt′) ►*v.* **-gret·ted, -gret·ting 1.** To feel sorry, disappointed, or distressed about. **2.** To mourn. ►*n.* **1.** Distress about something that one wishes could be different. **2.** A sense of loss and longing for someone or something gone. **3. regrets** A courteous refusal of an invitation. [< OFr. *regreter*, lament.] —**re·gret′ful** *adj.* —**re·gret′ful·ly** *adv.* —**re·gret′ta·ble** *adj.* —**re·gret′ta·bly** *adv.* —**re·gret′ter** *n.*

re·group (rē-grōōp′) ►*v.* **1.** To arrange in a new grouping. **2a.** To reorganize for renewed effort, as after a setback. **b.** To recollect one's composure and focus for a renewed effort.

regt. ►*abbr.* regiment

reg·u·lar (rĕg′yə-lər) ►*adj.* **1.** Customary, usual, or normal. **2.** Orderly, even, or symmetrical. **3.** Conforming to a fixed procedure, principle, or discipline. **4.** Well-ordered; methodical. **5.** Occurring at fixed intervals; periodic. **6.** Not varying; constant. **7.** Formally correct; proper. **8.** *Informal* Complete; thorough: *a regular scoundrel.* **9.** *Informal* Good; nice: *a regular guy.* **10.** *Gram.* Conforming to the usual pattern of inflection, derivation, or word formation. **11.** *Math.* **a.** Having equal sides and angles. **b.** Having faces that are congruent regular polygons and congruent polyhedral angles. **12.** Belonging to or constituting the permanent army of a nation. ►*n.* **1.** A soldier in a regular army. **2.** A dependable, loyal person. **3.** A habitual customer. [< Lat. *rēgula*, rule.] —**reg′u·lar′i·ty** (-lăr′ĭ-tē) *n.* —**reg′u·lar·ly** *adv.*

reg·u·lar·ize (rĕg′yə-lə-rīz′) ►*v.* **-ized, -iz·ing** To make regular. —**reg′u·lar·i·za′tion** *n.*

reg·u·late (rĕg′yə-lāt′) ►*v.* **-lat·ed, -lat·ing 1.** To control or direct according to rule, principle, or law. **2.** To adjust to a specification or requirement: *regulate temperature.* **3.** To adjust for accurate and proper functioning. [< Lat. *rēgula*, rule.] —**reg′u·la′tive, reg′u·la·to′ry** (-lə-tôr′ē) *adj.* —**reg′u·la′tor** *n.*

reg·u·la·tion (rĕg′yə-lā′shən) ►*n.* **1.** The act of regulating or the state of being regulated. **2.** A principle, rule, or law for controlling or governing conduct. **3.** A governmental order having the force of law.

re·gur·gi·tate (rē-gûr′jĭ-tāt′) ►*v.* **-tat·ed, -tat·ing 1.** To vomit. **2.** To repeat from memory with little reflection. [Med.Lat. *regurgitāre*,

overflow.] —**re·gur′gi·ta′tion** *n.*

re·ha·bil·i·tate (rē′hə-bĭl′ĭ-tāt′) ►*v.* **-tat·ed, -tat·ing 1.** To restore to health or useful life, as through therapy and education: *rehabilitate a patient.* **2.** To restore to good condition: *rehabilitate the economy.* **3.** To reestablish esteem for: *rehabilitate a reputation.* **4.** To restore the former rank, privileges, or rights of: *Under the new regime, disgraced party members were rehabilitated.* [Med.Lat. *rehabilitāre*.] —**re′ha·bil′i·ta′tion** *n.* —**re′ha·bil′i·ta′tive** *adj.*

re·hash (rē-hăsh′) ►*v.* To bring forth in another form but without significant alteration: *rehash old ideas.* —**re′hash′** *n.*

re·hears·al (rĭ-hûr′səl) ►*n.* **1.** The act of practicing in preparation for a public performance. **2.** A session of practice for a performance, as of a play.

re·hearse (rĭ-hûrs′) ►*v.* **-hearsed, -hears·ing 1a.** To practice in preparation for a public performance. See Synonyms at **practice. b.** To perfect (an action) by repetition. **2.** To repeat or recite. [< OFr. *rehercier*, repeat.]

Rehn·quist (rĕn′kwĭst′), **William Hubbs** 1924–2005. Amer. jurist; associate justice of the US Supreme Court (1972–86) and the chief justice (1986–2005).

reign (rān) ►*n.* **1.** Exercise of sovereign power, as by a monarch. **2.** The period during which a monarch rules. **3.** Dominance or widespread influence. [< Lat. *rēgnum*.] —**reign** *v.*

re·im·burse (rē′ĭm-bûrs′) ►*v.* **-bursed, -burs·ing** To pay back. [RE– + *imburse*, pay.] —**re′im·burs′a·ble** *adj.* —**re′im·burse′ment** *n.*

rein (rān) ►*n.* **1.** often **reins** Either of two long narrow leather straps attached to each end of the bit of a bridle and used by a rider or driver to control a horse or other animal. **2.** A means of restraining or checking. ►*v.* **1.** To check or hold back by the use of reins. **2.** To restrain or control. —*idiom:* **give (free) rein to** To release from restraints. [< Lat. *retinēre*, retain.]

re·in·car·na·tion (rē′ĭn-kär-nā′shən) ►*n.* **1.** Rebirth of the soul in another body. **2.** A new embodiment. —**re′in·car′nate** *v.*

rein·deer (rān′dîr′) ►*n., pl.* **-deer** or **-deers** A large deer of arctic regions, having branched antlers. North American subspecies are usu. called caribou. [ON *hreinn* + DEER.]

re·in·force (rē′ĭn-fôrs′) ►*v.* **-forced, -forc·ing 1.** To strengthen or support. **2.** To strengthen with additional personnel or equipment. **3.** *Psychol.* To reward (e.g., a desired response) in order to encourage its repetition. [RE– + *inforce* (var. of ENFORCE).] —**re′in·force′ment** *n.* —**re′in·forc′er** *n.*

re·in·forced concrete (rē′ĭn-fôrst′) ►*n.* Poured concrete containing steel bars or metal netting to increase strength.

re·in·state (rē′ĭn-stāt′) ►*v.* **-stat·ed, -stat·ing** To restore to a previous condition or position. —**re′in·state′ment** *n.*

re·it·er·ate (rē-ĭt′ə-rāt′) ►*v.* **-at·ed, -at·ing** To say again or repeatedly. See Synonyms at **repeat.** —**re·it′er·a′tion** *n.* —**re·it′er·a′tive** (-ə-rā′tĭv, -ər-ə-tĭv) *adj.*

re·ject (rĭ-jĕkt′) ►*v.* **1.** To refuse to accept, submit to, believe, or make use of. **2.** To refuse to consider or grant; deny. ►*n.* (rē′jĕkt) One that has been rejected. [< Lat. *rēicere, rēiect-*, throw back.] —**re·jec′tion** *n.*

re·joice (rĭ-jois′) ►*v.* **-joiced, -joic·ing** To feel joyful or be delighted. [< OFr. *rejoir.*]

re·join[1] (rĭ-join′) ►*v.* To say in reply; answer. [< OFr. *rejoindre.*]

re·join[2] (rē-join′) ►*v.* To come or join together again.

re·join·der (rĭ-join′dər) ►*n.* An answer, esp. to a reply. [< OFr. *rejoindre,* answer.]

re·ju·ve·nate (rĭ-jōō′və-nāt′) ►*v.* **-nat·ed, -nat·ing** To restore to youthful vigor or appearance. [< RE- + Lat. *iuvenis,* young.] **—re·ju′ve·na′tion** *n.* **—re·ju′ve·na′tor** (-tər) *n.*

re·lapse (rĭ-lăps′) ►*v.* **-lapsed, -laps·ing 1.** To return to a former state. **2a.** To become sicker after partial recovery from an illness. **b.** To recur. Used of an illness. ►*n.* (rē′lăps, rĭ-lăps′) A return to a former state, esp. after improvement. [< Lat. *relābī, relāps-,* slip back.]

re·late (rĭ-lāt′) ►*v.* **-lat·ed, -lat·ing 1.** To give an account of (e.g., an occurrence). See Synonyms at **describe. 2.** To establish or demonstrate a connection between. **3.** To have a connection, relation, or reference. **4.** To interact with others. **5.** To react favorably to. [< Lat. *referre, relāt-.*] **—re·lat′a·ble** *adj.*

re·lat·ed (rĭ-lā′tĭd) ►*adj.* **1.** Connected; associated. **2.** Connected by kinship, common origin, or marriage. **—re·lat′ed·ness** *n.*

re·la·tion (rĭ-lā′shən) ►*n.* **1.** A logical or natural association between two or more things. **2.** The connection of people by blood or marriage; kinship. **3.** A relative. **4. relations a.** Mutual dealings or connections, as among persons, groups, or nations. **b.** Sexual intercourse. **5.** The act of telling or narrating. **—idiom: in relation to** In reference to; in connection with. **—re·la′tion·ship′** *n.*

rel·a·tive (rĕl′ə-tĭv) ►*adj.* **1.** Considered in comparison to or dependent on something else. **2.** Connected or related. **3.** *Gram.* Referring to or qualifying an antecedent, as the pronoun *who* in *the man who was on TV.* ►*n.* **1.** A person related to another by heredity, adoption, or marriage. **2.** Something related or connected to something else. **—rel′a·tive·ly** *adv.*

relative clause ►*n.* A dependent clause introduced by a relative pronoun, as *which is downstairs* in *The dining room, which is downstairs, is too dark.*

relative humidity ►*n.* The ratio of the amount of water vapor in the air at a specific temperature to the maximum capacity of the air at that temperature.

rel·a·tiv·ism (rĕl′ə-tĭ-vĭz′əm) ►*n. Philos.* The theory that conceptions of truth, beauty, or morality have no universal validity but are valid only for the persons holding them.

rel·a·tiv·ist (rĕl′ə-tĭ-vĭst) ►*n.* **1.** *Philos.* A proponent of relativism. **2.** A physicist who specializes in the theories of relativity.

rel·a·tiv·i·ty (rĕl′ə-tĭv′ĭ-tē) ►*n.* **1.** The quality or state of being relative. **2.** *Phys.* **a.** Special relativity. **b.** General relativity.

re·lax (rĭ-lăks′) ►*v.* **1.** To make or become less tight. **2.** To make or become less severe or strict. **3.** To relieve from tension or strain. **4.** To take one's ease; rest. [< Lat. *relaxāre.*] **—re′lax·a′tion** (rē′lăk-sā′shən) *n.* **—re·lax′er** *n.*

re·lax·ant (rĭ-lăk′sənt) ►*n.* **1.** A drug that causes muscles to relax. **2.** Something, such as soft music, that helps one to relax.

re·lay (rē′lā) ►*n.* **1.** An act of passing something along, as from one person to another. **2.** A relay race. **3.** *Electron.* A device that responds to a small current or voltage change by activating switches or other devices in an electric circuit. **4.** A fresh team or crew that relieves another. ►*v.* (rē′lā, rĭ-lā′) **1.** To pass or send along. **2.** To supply with fresh relays. [< OFr. *relai,* fresh team of hunting dogs.]

relay race ►*n.* A race between two or more teams in which each team member participates in a part of the race and is then relieved by a teammate.

re·lease (rĭ-lēs′) ►*v.* **-leased, -leas·ing 1a.** To set free from confinement or bondage: *released the prisoner.* **b.** To set free from physical restraint or binding: *released the brake.* **2.** To set free from obligations or debt. **3.** To issue for performance, sale, publication, or distribution. **4.** *Law* To surrender (a right, claim, or title). ►*n.* **1.** Deliverance or liberation, as from confinement. **2.** A device or catch for locking or releasing a mechanism. **3.** Something issued or made public. **4.** *Law* The surrender of a right, title, or claim, esp. to one against whom the right, title, or claim would be enforced. [< Lat. *relaxāre,* relax.] **—re·leas′a·ble** *adj.* **—re·leas′er** *n.*

rel·e·gate (rĕl′ĭ-gāt′) ►*v.* **-gat·ed, -gat·ing 1.** To confine to an inferior or obscure place, rank, category, or condition. **2.** To refer or assign (e.g., a task) for decision or action. [< Lat. *relēgāre,* send away.] **—rel′e·ga′tion** *n.*

re·lent (rĭ-lĕnt′) ►*v.* To become more lenient or forgiving. [< AN *relenter.*]

re·lent·less (rĭ-lĕnt′lĭs) ►*adj.* **1.** Unyielding; pitiless. **2.** Steady and persistent. **—re·lent′less·ly** *adv.* **—re·lent′less·ness** *n.*

rel·e·vant (rĕl′ə-vənt) ►*adj.* **1.** Having to do with the matter at hand. **2.** Meaningful or purposeful in current society or culture. [< *relevāre,* raise up.] **—rel′e·vance, rel′e·van·cy** *n.* **—rel′e·vant·ly** *adv.*

re·li·a·ble (rĭ-lī′ə-bəl) ►*adj.* Capable of being relied on; dependable. **—re·li′a·bil′i·ty, re·li′a·ble·ness** *n.* **—re·li′a·bly** *adv.*

    Syns: *dependable, responsible, trustworthy, trusty* **adj.**

re·li·ant (rĭ-lī′ənt) ►*adj.* Having or exhibiting trust in or dependence on something. **—re·li′ance** *n.* **—re·li′ant·ly** *adv.*

rel·ic (rĕl′ĭk) ►*n.* **1.** Something that has survived from an extinct culture or bygone period. **2.** A memento; keepsake. **3.** An object of religious veneration. **4.** or **relics** A corpse; remains. [< Lat. *reliquus,* remaining.]

re·lief (rĭ-lēf′) ►*n.* **1a.** The easing of a pain or distress. **b.** Something that alleviates pain or distress. **2.** Aid, as given to the needy or disaster victims. **3a.** Release from a post or duty. **b.** One who takes over a post or duty for another. **4.** The projection of figures or forms from a flat background, as in sculpture. **5.** The variations in elevation of an area of the earth's surface. [< OFr. *relever,* relieve.]

relief map ►*n.* A map that depicts land configuration, usu. with contour lines.

re·lieve (rĭ-lēv′) ►*v.* **-lieved, -liev·ing 1a.** To lessen or alleviate. **b.** To make less tedious or unpleasant. **2.** To free from pain, anxiety, or distress. **3.** To assist; aid. **4.** To free from a specified duty or obligation. **5.** *Archaic* To make distinct by contrast; set off. [< Lat. *relevāre*, lift up.] —**re·liev′er** *n.*

re·li·gion (rĭ-lĭj′ən) ►*n.* **1a.** Belief in and reverence for a supernatural power or powers regarded as creator or governor of the universe. **b.** A particular variety of such belief, esp. when organized into a system of doctrine and practice. **2.** A cause or activity pursued with zeal or conscientious devotion. [< Lat. *religiō*.]

re·li·gious (rĭ-lĭj′əs) ►*adj.* **1.** Having belief in and reverence for a deity. **2.** Of or relating to religion. **3.** Scrupulous or conscientious. ►*n.*, *pl.* **-gious** A member of a monastic order. —**re·li′gious·ly** *adv.* —**re·li′gious·ness** *n.*

re·lin·quish (rĭ-lĭng′kwĭsh) ►*v.* **1.** To give up or abandon. **2.** To put aside; stop adhering to. **3.** To surrender. **4.** To release. [< Lat. *relinquere,* leave behind.] —**re·lin′quish·er** *n.* —**re·lin′quish·ment** *n.*

rel·i·quar·y (rĕl′ĭ-kwĕr′ē) ►*n.*, *pl.* **-ies** A receptacle for keeping or displaying sacred relics. [< LLat. *reliquiae,* relics.]

rel·ish (rĕl′ĭsh) ►*n.* **1.** An appetite for something. **2a.** Hearty enjoyment. See Synonyms at **zest. b.** Something that lends pleasure or zest. **3.** A spicy or savory condiment, as of chopped sweet pickles. **4.** The flavor of a food, esp. when appetizing. ►*v.* **1.** To take keen or zestful pleasure in. **2.** To be pleased with or look forward to. [< OFr. *relaissier,* leave behind; see RELEASE.]

re·live (rē-lĭv′) ►*v.* To undergo or experience again, esp. in the imagination.

re·luc·tant (rĭ-lŭk′tənt) ►*adj.* **1.** Unwilling; disinclined: *reluctant to help.* **2.** Hesitant; grudging: *reluctant cooperation.* [< Lat. *reluctārī,* be reluctant.] —**re·luc′tance** *n.* —**re·luc′tant·ly** *adv.*

re·ly (rĭ-lī′) ►*v.* **-lied, -ly·ing 1.** To depend: *relies on her parents for tuition.* **2.** To have faith or confidence: *relied on them to tell the truth.* [< Lat. *religāre,* bind fast.]

rem (rĕm) ►*n. Phys.* The amount of ionizing radiation required to produce the same biological effect as one rad of high-penetration x-rays. [*r(oentgen) e(quivalent in) m(an).*]

REM sleep (rĕm) ►*n.* A period of sleep during which dreaming takes place, marked by rapid periodic twitching of the eye muscles and other physiological changes. [*r(apid) e(ye) m(ovement).*]

re·main (rĭ-mān′) ►*v.* **1.** To continue in the same state, condition, or place. **2.** To be left after the removal, loss, passage, or destruction of others. **3.** To be left as still to be dealt with: *A cure remains to be found.* **4.** To endure or persist. [< Lat. *remanēre,* stay behind.]

re·main·der (rĭ-mān′dər) ►*n.* **1.** Something left over after other parts have been taken away. **2a.** The number left over when one integer is divided by another. **b.** The number obtained when one number is subtracted from another; difference. **3.** A book that remains with a publisher after sales have fallen off. ►*v.* To sell (books) as a remainder, usu. at a reduced price. [< OFr. *remaindre,* REMAIN.]

re·mains (rĭ-mānz′) ►*pl.n.* **1.** All that is left after other parts have been taken away, used up, or destroyed. **2.** A corpse.

re·mand (rĭ-mănd′) ►*v.* **1.** To send back into legal custody or to a lower court for additional proceedings. **2.** To send (a legal case) from a higher to a lower court. [< LLat. *remandāre,* send back word.] —**re·mand′ment** *n.*

re·mark (rĭ-märk′) ►*v.* **1.** To express briefly and casually as a comment. **2.** To take notice of; observe. ►*n.* **1.** The act of noticing or observing. **2.** A casual or brief statement. [< Fr. *remarquer,* notice.]

re·mark·a·ble (rĭ-mär′kə-bəl) ►*adj.* Worthy of notice, esp. for being unusual or extraordinary. —**re·mark′a·bly** *adv.*

Re·marque (rə-märk′), **Erich Maria** 1898– 1970. German-born Amer. writer.

Rem·brandt van Rijn or **Rem·brandt van Ryn** (rĕm′brănt′ vän rīn′, -bränt′) 1606–69. Dutch painter.

re·me·di·a·ble (rĭ-mē′dē-ə-bəl) ►*adj.* Possible to remedy.

re·me·di·al (rĭ-mē′dē-əl) ►*adj.* Intended to correct or improve something, esp. deficient skills. —**re·me′di·al·ly** *adv.*

rem·e·dy (rĕm′ĭ-dē) ►*n.*, *pl.* **-dies 1.** Something that is used to treat a symptom, disease, injury, or other condition. **2.** Something that corrects an evil, fault, or error. ►*v.* **-died, -dy·ing 1.** To relieve or cure. **2.** To set right; rectify. [< Lat. *remedium.*]

re·mem·ber (rĭ-mĕm′bər) ►*v.* **1.** To recall to the mind; think of again. **2.** To retain in the memory. **3.** To keep (someone) in mind. **4.** To give greetings from. [< Lat. *rememorārī.*] —**re·mem′ber·a·ble** *adj.*

re·mem·brance (rĭ-mĕm′brəns) ►*n.* **1.** The act of remembering or the state of being remembered. **2.** A memorial. **3.** The length of time over which one's memory extends. **4.** Something remembered. **5.** A souvenir.

re·mind (rĭ-mīnd′) ►*v.* To cause (someone) to remember. —**re·mind′er** *n.*

rem·i·nisce (rĕm′ə-nĭs′) ►*v.* **-nisced, -nisc·ing** To think about or tell of the past. [< REMINISCENCE.]

rem·i·nis·cence (rĕm′ə-nĭs′əns) ►*n.* **1.** The act or process of recalling the past. **2.** A memory. **3.** often **reminiscences** A narration of past experiences.

rem·i·nis·cent (rĕm′ə-nĭs′ənt) ►*adj.* **1.** Of or containing reminiscence. **2.** Suggestive of something in the past. [< Lat. *reminīscī,* recollect.]

re·miss (rĭ-mĭs′) ►*adj.* Lax in attending to duty. See Synonyms at **negligent.** [< Lat. *remissus,* slack.] —**re·miss′ness** *n.*

re·mis·si·ble (rĭ-mĭs′ə-bəl) ►*adj.* Able to be forgiven. —**re·mis′si·bil′i·ty** *n.* —**re·mis′si·bly** *adv.*

re·mis·sion (rĭ-mĭsh′ən) ►*n.* **1.** The act of remitting or the condition of being remitted. **2.** A lessening of intensity or seriousness, as of a disease. **3.** The period during which the symptoms of a disease abate or subside. **4.** Release, as from a debt or obligation.

re·mit (rĭ-mĭt′) ►*v.* **-mit·ted, -mit·ting 1.** To transmit (money) in payment. **2a.** To cancel (e.g., a tax or penalty). **b.** To pardon; forgive. **3.** To slacken. **4.** To diminish; abate. [< Lat. *remittere,* send back.] —**re·mit′ta·ble** *adj.* —**re·mit′tal** *n.* —**re·mit′ter** *n.*

re·mit·tance (rĭ-mĭt′ns) ►*n.* Credit or money sent to someone.

re·mit·tent (rĭ-mĭt′nt) ►*adj.* Marked by temporary abatement in severity.

re·mix (rē-mĭks′) ►*v.* To recombine recorded audio tracks or channels so as to produce a new recording. ►*n.* (rē′mĭks′) A recording produced by remixing.

rem·nant (rĕm′nənt) ►*n.* **1.** Something left over; remainder. **2.** A surviving trace or vestige. [< OFr. *remaindre*, REMAIN.]

re·mod·el (rē-mŏd′l) ►*v.* To make over in structure or style; renovate. —**re·mod′el·er** *n.*

re·mon·strance (rĭ-mŏn′strəns) ►*n.* The act or an instance of remonstrating.

re·mon·strate (rĭ-mŏn′strāt′, rĕm′ŏn-) ►*v.* **-strat·ed, -strat·ing** To say or plead in protest, objection, or reproof. [Med.Lat. *remōnstrāre*, demonstrate.] —**re′mon·stra′tion** (rē′mŏn-strā′shən, rĕm′ən-) *n.* —**re·mon′stra·tive** (-strə-tĭv) *adj.* —**re·mon′stra·tor** *n.*

re·mor·a (rĭ-môr′ə, rĕm′ər-ə) ►*n.* Any of a family of marine fishes having a sucking disk on the head with which they attach themselves to other animals or the hulls of ships. [Lat., delay.]

re·morse (rĭ-môrs′) ►*n.* Bitter regret for past misdeeds. See Synonyms at **penitence.** [< Lat. *remordēre, remors-*, torment.] —**re·morse′ful** *adj.* —**re·morse′ful·ly** *adv.*

re·morse·less (rĭ-môrs′lĭs) ►*adj.* Having no pity or compassion. —**re·morse′less·ly** *adv.*

re·mote (rĭ-mōt′) ►*adj.* **-mot·er, -mot·est 1.** Located far away. **2.** Distant in time. **3.** Faint; slight: *a remote possibility.* **4.** Distantly related: *a remote cousin.* **5.** Distant in manner; aloof. **6.** Operating or controlled from a distance. **7.** *Comp.* Located at a distance from another computer that is accessible by communications links: *a remote terminal.* ►*n.* **1.** A radio or television broadcast from outside a studio. **2.** Remote control. [< Lat. *remōtus*, p.part. of *removēre*, remove.] —**re·mote′ly** *adv.* —**re·mote′ness** *n.*

remote control ►*n.* **1.** The control of an activity, process, or machine from a distance, as by radioed instructions or coded signals. **2.** A device used to control an apparatus from a distance.

re·move (rĭ-mōōv′) ►*v.* **-moved, -mov·ing 1.** To move from a place or position occupied. **2.** To take off: *removed her jewelry.* **3.** To take away; eliminate. **4.** To dismiss from office. **5.** To change one's residence; move. ►*n.* **1.** The act of removing. **2.** Distance or degree of separation. [< Lat. *removēre.*] —**re·mov′a·ble** *adj.* —**re·mov′a·bly** *adv.* —**re·mov′al** *n.* —**re·mov′er** *n.*

re·moved (rĭ-mōōvd′) ►*adj.* **1.** Distant in space, time, or nature; remote. **2.** Separated in relationship by a given degree of descent: *first cousin once removed.*

re·mu·ner·ate (rĭ-myōō′nə-rāt′) ►*v.* **-at·ed, -at·ing** To pay for goods provided, services rendered, or losses incurred. [Lat. *remūnerārī.*] —**re·mu′ner·a′tion** *n.* —**re·mu′ner·a·tive** (-nər-ə-tĭv, -nə-rā′tĭv) *adj.*

ren·ais·sance (rĕn′ĭ-säns′, -zäns′, rĭ-nā′səns) ►*n.* **1.** A rebirth or revival. **2. Renaissance a.** The humanistic revival of classical art, architecture, literature, and learning in Europe. **b.** The period of this revival, roughly the 14th through the 16th cent. **3.** often **Renaissance** A revival of intellectual or artistic achievement. [< OFr.]

re·nal (rē′nəl) ►*adj.* Relating to or near the kidneys. [< Lat. *rēnēs*, kidneys.]

re·nas·cent (rĭ-năs′ənt, -nā′sənt) ►*adj.* Showing renewed growth or vigor. [< Lat. *renāscī*, be born again.] —**re·nas′cence** *n.*

rend (rĕnd) ►*v.* **rent** (rĕnt) or **rend·ed, rend·ing 1.** To tear or split apart or into pieces violently. **2.** To pull away forcibly; wrest. **3a.** To pierce or disturb with sound. **b.** To cause pain or distress to. [< OE *rendan.*]

ren·der (rĕn′dər) ►*v.* **1a.** To submit or present. **b.** To give; provide: *render assistance.* **c.** To give in return or by obligation. **2.** To make: *The news rendered her speechless.* **3.** To represent in verbal or artistic form; depict. **4.** *Comp.* To convert (graphics) from a file into visual form. **5.** To translate. **6.** To liquefy (fat) by heating. [< OFr. *rendre* < Lat. *reddere* : RE- + *dare*, give.]

ren·dez·vous (rän′dā-vōō′, -də-) ►*n., pl.* **-vous** (-vōōz′) **1.** A meeting at a set time and place. **2.** A set meeting place. **3.** A popular gathering place. ►*v.* To meet at a set time and place. [< OFr. *rendez vous*, present yourselves.]

ren·di·tion (rĕn-dĭsh′ən) ►*n.* **1.** The act of rendering. **2.** An interpretation or performance of a musical or dramatic work. **3.** A translation. **4a.** Surrender, as to an authority. **b.** The transfer of a prisoner from one country to another, often to avoid legal restrictions on interrogation or prosecution. [< OFr. *rendre*, RENDER.]

ren·e·gade (rĕn′ĭ-gād′) ►*n.* **1.** One who rejects a religion, cause, allegiance, or group for another; deserter. **2.** An outlaw. [< Med.Lat. *renegāre*, deny.] —**ren′e·gade′** *adj.*

re·nege (rĭ-nĕg′, -nĭg′) ►*v.* **-neged, -neg·ing 1.** To fail to carry out a promise or commitment. **2.** To fail to follow suit in card games when able and required to do so. [Med.Lat. *renegāre*, deny.] —**re·neg′er** *n.*

re·new (rĭ-nōō′, -nyōō′) ►*v.* **1.** To make new or as if new again; restore. **2.** To take up again; resume. **3.** To repeat so as to reaffirm: *renew a promise.* **4.** To arrange for the extension of. —**re·new′a·ble** *adj.* —**re·new′al** *n.*

ren·net (rĕn′ĭt) ►*n.* **1.** An extract made from the inner lining of the fourth stomach of a young ruminant, used in cheesemaking to curdle milk. **2.** A similar substance obtained from certain other animals, plants, fungi, or bacteria. [ME.]

ren·nin (rĕn′ĭn) ►*n.* A milk-coagulating enzyme produced from rennet.

Re·no (rē′nō′) A city of W NV near the CA border.

Ren·oir (rĕn′wär′, rən-wär′), **Pierre Auguste** 1841–1919. French impressionist painter.

re·nounce (rĭ-nouns′) ►*v.* **-nounced, -nounc·ing 1.** To give up, esp. by formal announcement. **2.** To disclaim one's association with (e.g., a country). [< Lat. *renūntiāre*, report.] —**re·nounce′ment** *n.*

ren·o·vate (rĕn′ə-vāt′) ►*v.* **-vat·ed, -vat·ing** To restore to an earlier state. [Lat. *renovāre.*] —**ren′o·va′tion** *n.* —**ren′o·va′tor** *n.*

re·nown (rĭ-noun′) ►*n.* The quality of being widely known or acclaimed; fame. [< AN *renomer*, make famous.] —**re·nowned′** *adj.*

rent¹ (rĕnt) ►*n.* Periodic payment made by a tenant in return for the right to use the property of another. ►*v.* **1.** To use (another's property) in return for regular payments. **2.** To be for rent. [< VLat. *rendita.*] —**rent'a·ble** *adj.* —**rent'er** *n.*

rent² (rĕnt) ►*v.* P.t. and p.part. of **rend.** ►*n.* An opening made by rending; rip.

rent·al (rĕn'tl) ►*n.* **1.** An amount paid out or taken in as rent. **2.** Property available for renting. **3.** The act of renting. —**rent'al** *adj.*

rent control ►*n.* Governmental regulation of the amounts charged for rented housing.

re·nun·ci·a·tion (rĭ-nŭn'sē-ā'shən) ►*n.* The act or an instance of renouncing. [< Lat. *renūntiāre,* renounce.] —**re·nun'ci·a'tive, re·nun'ci·a·to'ry** (-ə-tôr'ē) *adj.*

re·or·der (rē-ôr'dər) ►*v.* **1.** To order (the same goods) again. **2.** To rearrange. —**re·or'der** *n.*

rep¹ (rĕp) ►*n.* A ribbed or corded fabric. [< Fr. *reps* < E. *ribs.*]

rep² (rĕp) ►*n. Informal* A representative.

rep³ (rĕp) ►*n. Informal* Reputation.

rep⁴ (rĕp) ►*n. Informal* A repetition of a particular movement, as in weightlifting.

Rep. ►*abbr.* **1.** representative **2.** republic **3.** Republican

re·pair¹ ►*v.* **1.** To restore to sound condition after damage or injury; fix. **2.** To set right; remedy. **3.** To restore or renew. ►*n.* **1.** The work or act of repairing. **2.** General condition after use or repairing: *in good repair.* [< Lat. *reparāre.*] —**re·pair'a·ble** *adj.* —**re·pair'man** *n.* —**re·pair'wom'an** *n.*

re·pair² (rĭ-pâr') ►*v.* To betake oneself; go. [< LLat. *repatriāre,* return to one's country; see REPATRIATE.]

rep·a·ra·ble (rĕp'ər-ə-bəl) ►*adj.* Possible to repair. —**rep'a·ra·bly** *adv.*

rep·a·ra·tion (rĕp'ə-rā'shən) ►*n.* **1.** The act or process of making amends for a wrong. **2.** Something done or money paid to make amends. **3. reparations** Compensation, as for damage, required from a nation defeated in war. [< Lat. *reparāre,* repair.] —**re·par'a·tive** (rĭ-păr'ə-tĭv), **re·par'a·to'ry** (-tôr'ē) *adj.*

rep·ar·tee (rĕp'ər-tē', -tā', -är-) ►*n.* **1.** A swift, witty reply. **2.** Conversation marked by witty retorts. [< OFr. *repartir,* to retort.]

re·past (rĭ-păst') ►*n.* A meal or the food eaten or provided at a meal. ►*v.* To eat or feast. [< Lat. *repāscere,* feed.]

re·pa·tri·ate (rē-pā'trē-āt') ►*v.* **-at·ed, -at·ing** To return (a person) to the country of birth, citizenship, or origin. ►*n.* (-ĭt, -āt') One who has been repatriated. [LLat. *repatriāre,* return to one's country : RE– + *patria,* native country; see EXPATRIATE.] —**re·pa'tri·a'tion** *n.*

re·pay (rĭ-pā') ►*v.* **1.** To pay back: *repaid a debt.* **2.** To give in return for. —**re·pay'a·ble** *adj.* —**re·pay'ment** *n.*

re·peal (rĭ-pēl') ►*v.* To revoke or rescind, esp. by legislative action. [< OFr. *rapeler.*] —**re·peal'** *n.* —**re·peal'er** *n.*

re·peat (rĭ-pēt', rē'pēt') ►*v.* **1.** To say or do again. **2.** To tell to another. **3.** To express (oneself) in the same way or words. ►*n.* **1.** An act of repeating. **2.** Something repeated. [< Lat. *repetere,* seek again.] —**re·peat'a·ble** *adj.* —**re·peat'er** *n.*

Syns: *iterate, reiterate* v.

re·peat·ed (rĭ-pē'tĭd) ►*adj.* Said, done, or occurring again and again. —**re·peat'ed·ly** *adv.*

re·peat·ing decimal (rĭ-pē'tĭng) ►*n.* A decimal in which a pattern of one or more digits is repeated indefinitely.

re·pel (rĭ-pĕl') ►*v.* **-pelled, -pel·ling 1.** To ward off or keep away: *repel insects.* **2.** To drive back: *repel an invasion.* **3.** To cause aversion or distaste in. See Synonyms at **disgust.** See Usage Note at **repulse. 4.** To be incapable of absorbing or mixing with: *Oil repels water.* **5.** To present an opposing force to: *Electric charges of the same sign repel one another.* [< Lat. *repellere.*]

re·pel·lent also **re·pel·lant** (rĭ-pĕl'ənt) ►*adj.* **1.** Repulsive. See Synonyms at **offensive. 2.** Resistant or impervious to a substance. **3.** Serving or tending to repel something, esp. insects. ►*n.* **1.** A substance used to repel insects. **2.** A substance for making a surface resistant to something. —**re·pel'lence, re·pel'len·cy** *n.*

re·pent (rĭ-pĕnt') ►*v.* **1.** To feel regret or self-reproach for what one has done or failed to do. **2.** To become a more moral or religious person as a result of remorse or contrition for one's sins. [< OFr. *repentir.*] —**re·pent'er** *n.*

re·pen·tance (rĭ-pĕn'təns) ►*n.* Remorse for past conduct or sin. See Synonyms at **penitence.** —**re·pen'tant** *adj.* —**re·pen'tant·ly** *adv.*

re·per·cus·sion (rē'pər-kŭsh'ən, rĕp'ər-) ►*n.* **1.** An often indirect effect of an event or action. **2.** A reciprocal motion after impact. **3.** A reflection, esp. of sound. [< Lat. *repercutere,* cause to rebound.] —**re'per·cus'sive** *adj.*

rep·er·toire (rĕp'ər-twär') ►*n.* **1.** The stock of songs, plays, or other works that a player or company is prepared to perform. **2.** The range of skills, aptitudes, or accomplishments of a person or group. [< LLat. *repertōrium.*]

rep·er·to·ry (rĕp'ər-tôr'ē) ►*n., pl.* **-ries 1.** A repertoire. **2.** A theater in which a resident company presents works from a specified repertoire, usu. in alternation. [LLat. *repertōrium.*] —**rep'er·to'ri·al** *adj.*

re·pe·tend (rĕp'ĭ-tĕnd', rĕp'ĭ-tĕnd') ►*n.* The digit or group of digits that repeats infinitely in a repeating decimal. [< Lat. *repetendum,* thing to be repeated.]

rep·e·ti·tion (rĕp'ĭ-tĭsh'ən) ►*n.* **1.** The act or an instance of repeating. **2.** Something repeated. [< Lat. *repetere,* repeat.]

rep·e·ti·tious (rĕp'ĭ-tĭsh'əs) ►*adj.* Filled esp. with needless repetition. —**rep'e·ti'tious·ly** *adv.* —**rep'e·ti'tious·ness** *n.*

re·pet·i·tive (rĭ-pĕt'ĭ-tĭv) ►*adj.* Given to or marked by repetition. —**re·pet'i·tive·ly** *adv.* —**re·pet'i·tive·ness** *n.*

re·pine (rĭ-pīn') ►*v.* **-pined, -pin·ing** To be discontented or low in spirits; fret. —**re·pin'er** *n.*

re·place (rĭ-plās') ►*v.* **1.** To put back in place. **2.** To take the place of. **3.** To provide a substitute for (e.g., something broken). —**re·place'a·ble** *adj.* —**re·place'ment** *n.* —**re·plac'er** *n.*

re·play (rē-plā') ►*v.* To play (e.g., a game or recording) over again. —**re'play'** *n.*

re·plen·ish (rĭ-plĕn'ĭsh) ►*v.* To fill or make complete again. [< OFr. *replenir.*] —**re·plen'ish·er** *n.* —**re·plen'ish·ment** *n.*

re·plete (rĭ-plēt') ►*adj.* **1.** Abundantly supplied; abounding: *a report replete with errors.* **2.** Filled to satiation; gorged. [< Lat. *replētus,* p.part. of *replēre,* refill.] —**re·ple'tion, re·plete'ness** *n.*

rep·li·ca (rĕp'lĭ-kə) ►*n.* A copy or close reproduction. [< LLat. *replicāre,* repeat.]

rep·li·cate (rĕp'lĭ-kāt') ►*v.* **-cat·ed, -cat·ing 1.**

To duplicate, copy, reproduce, or repeat. **2.** To fold over or bend back. [< Lat. *replicāre*, fold back.] —**rep′li·ca′tion** *n.*

re·ply (rĭ-plī′) ►*v.* **-plied, -ply·ing 1.** To say or give as an answer. **2.** To respond by an action or gesture. ►*n., pl.* **-plies** A response; answer. [< Lat. *replicāre*, fold back.] —**re·pli′er** *n.*

re·port (rĭ-pôrt′) ►*n.* **1.** A formal account of a group's proceedings or transactions. **2.** Reputation: *a person of bad report.* **3.** An explosive noise. ►*v.* **1.** To make or present an account of. **2.** To relate or present. See Synonyms at **describe. 3.** To make known, esp. to an authority: *reported the incident to the police.* **4.** To serve as a reporter. **5.** To present oneself: *report for duty.* [< Lat. *reportāre*, carry back.]

report card ►*n.* A periodic report of a student's progress.

re·port·ed·ly (rĭ-pôr′tĭd-lē) ►*adv.* Supposedly.

re·port·er (rĭ-pôr′tər) ►*n.* A writer or investigator of news stories. —**rep′or·to′ri·al** (rĕp′ər-tôr′ē-əl, rē′pər-) *adj.*

re·pose¹ (rĭ-pōz′) ►*n.* **1.** The act of resting or the state of being at rest. **2.** Calmness; tranquility. ►*v.* **-posed, -pos·ing 1.** To lie at rest; relax. **2.** To lie supported by something. [< LLat. *repausāre*, make rest.] —**re·pose′ful** *adj.* —**re·pose′ful·ly** *adv.*

re·pose² (rĭ-pōz′) ►*v.* **-posed, -pos·ing** To put or place: *Reposed our hopes in a single man.* [< Lat. *repōnere, repos-,* put away.]

re·pos·i·to·ry (rĭ-pŏz′ĭ-tôr′ē) ►*n., pl.* **-ries 1.** A place where things may be put, esp. for safekeeping. **2.** One possessing or entrusted with something. [< Lat. *repōnere, reposit-,* put away.]

re·pos·sess (rē′pə-zĕs′) ►*v.* **1.** To regain possession of. **2.** To reclaim possession of for failure to make payments due. —**re′pos·ses′sion** *n.*

rep·re·hend (rĕp′rĭ-hĕnd′) ►*v.* To reprove or blame; censure. [< Lat. *reprehendere.*] —**rep′re·hen′sion** *n.*

rep·re·hen·si·ble (rĕp′rĭ-hĕn′sə-bəl) ►*adj.* Deserving rebuke or censure. —**rep′re·hen′si·bil′i·ty** *n.* —**rep′re·hen′si·bly** *adv.*

rep·re·sent (rĕp′rĭ-zĕnt′) ►*v.* **1.** To stand for; symbolize. **2.** To depict; portray. **3.** To describe (a person or thing) as having a specified quality. **4.** To serve as the delegate, spokesperson, or agent for. **5.** To serve as an example of. [< Lat. *repraesentāre,* show.] —**rep′re·sent′a·ble** *adj.*

rep·re·sen·ta·tion (rĕp′rĭ-zĕn-tā′shən, -zən-) ►*n.* **1.** The act of representing or the state of being represented. **2.** Something that represents. **3.** A statement, as of facts or arguments.

rep·re·sen·ta·tion·al (rĕp′rĭ-zĕn-tā′shə-nəl, -zən-) ►*adj.* Of or relating to realistic graphic representation.

rep·re·sen·ta·tive (rĕp′rĭ-zĕn′tə-tĭv) ►*n.* **1.** A typical example, esp. of a class or group. **2.** A delegate or agent acting on behalf of another. **3a.** A member of a legislative body chosen by popular vote. **b.** A member of the US House of Representatives or of the lower house of a state legislature. ►*adj.* **1.** Of or based on political representation: *representative government.* **2.** Serving as a typical example. —**rep′re·sen′ta·tive·ly** *adv.* —**rep′re·sen′ta·tive·ness** *n.*

re·press (rĭ-prĕs′) ►*v.* **1.** To hold back: *repress a laugh.* **2.** To put down by force: *repress a rebellion.* **3.** *Psychol.* To exclude from the conscious mind. [< Lat. *reprimere, repress-.*] —**re·press′i·**

ble *adj.* —**re·pres′sion** *n.* —**re·pres′sive** *adj.* —**re·pres′sive·ly** *adv.* —**re·pres′sor** *n.*

re·prieve (rĭ-prēv′) ►*v.* **-prieved, -priev·ing** To prevent or suspend the punishment of. ►*n.* **1.** Prevention or suspension of a punishment. **2.** Temporary relief, as from pain. [< Lat. *reprehendere,* hold back.]

rep·ri·mand (rĕp′rə-mănd′) ►*v.* To reprove severely; admonish. ►*n.* A severe or formal rebuke. [< Lat. *reprimere,* restrain.]

re·print (rē′prĭnt′) ►*n.* **1.** A new or additional printing of a book. **2.** A printed excerpt; offprint. —**re·print′** *v.* —**re·print′er** *n.*

re·pri·sal (rĭ-prī′zəl) ►*n.* The act or an instance of retaliating for a loss or injury. [< OItal. *ripreso* < *riprendere,* take back; see REPREHEND.]

re·prise (rĭ-prēz′) ►*n.* **1.** *Mus.* A repetition of a theme or verse. **2.** (*often* rĭ-prīz′) A recurrence or resumption. [< OFr. *reprendre,* take back; see REPREHEND.]

re·proach (rĭ-prōch′) ►*v.* To express disapproval or criticism. ►*n.* Blame; rebuke. [< OFr. *reprochier.*] —**re·proach′a·ble** *adj.* —**re·proach′ful** *adj.* —**re·proach′ful·ly** *adv.*

rep·ro·bate (rĕp′rə-bāt′) ►*n.* A morally unprincipled person. [< LLat. *reprobāre,* disapprove.] —**rep′ro·bate′** *adj.* —**rep′ro·ba′tion** *n.*

re·pro·duce (rē′prə-dōos′, -dyōos′) ►*v.* **-duced, -duc·ing 1.** To produce again or anew; recreate. **2.** To produce a counterpart, image, or copy of. **3.** To produce offspring. **4.** To undergo copying: *graphics that reproduce well.* —**re′pro·duc′er** *n.* —**re′pro·duc′i·ble** *adj.* —**re′pro·duc′tion** (-dŭk′shən) *n.* —**re′pro·duc′tive** (-dŭk′tĭv) *adj.* —**re′pro·duc′tive·ly** *adv.*

re·proof (rĭ-prōof′) ►*n.* Censure; rebuke.

re·prove (rĭ-prōov′) ►*v.* **-proved, -prov·ing 1.** To express disapproval to (someone). **2.** To express disapproval about (something). [< LLat. *reprobāre,* disapprove.] —**re·prov′ing·ly** *adv.*

rep·tile (rĕp′tīl′, -tĭl) ►*n.* Any of various usu. cold-blooded egg-laying vertebrates having dry skin covered with scales or horny plates and including the snakes, lizards, and turtles. [< Lat. *rēptilis,* creeping < *rēpere,* creep.] —**rep·til′i·an** (-tĭl′ē-ən, -tĭl′yən) *adj. & n.*

re·pub·lic (rĭ-pŭb′lĭk) ►*n.* **1.** A government whose head of state is not a monarch and is usu. a president. **2.** A country governed by the elected representatives of its people. [< Lat. *rēspūblica.*]

re·pub·li·can (rĭ-pŭb′lĭ-kən) ►*adj.* **1.** Of or advocating a republic. **2. Republican** Of or belonging to the Republican Party. ►*n.* **1.** One who favors a republican form of government. **2. Republican** A member of the Republican Party. —**re·pub′li·can·ism** *n.*

Republican Party ►*n.* One of the two major US political parties.

re·pu·di·ate (rĭ-pyōo′dē-āt′) ►*v.* **-at·ed, -at·ing 1.** To reject the validity of. **2.** To refuse to recognize, acknowledge, or pay. [Lat. *repudiāre.*] —**re·pu′di·a′tion** *n.*

re·pug·nant (rĭ-pŭg′nənt) ►*adj.* **1.** Arousing disgust or aversion; repulsive. **2.** *Logic* Contradictory. [< Lat. *repugnāre,* fight against.] —**re·pug′nance** *n.*

re·pulse (rĭ-pŭls′) ►*v.* **-pulsed, -puls·ing 1.** To drive back; repel. **2.** To reject with rudeness, coldness, or denial. **3.** *Informal* To cause repulsion in. ►*n*. **1.** The act of repulsing. **2.** Rejection; refusal. [< Lat. *repellere, repuls-.*]

Usage: A number of critics have maintained that *repulse* should not be used to mean "to cause repulsion in." Reputable literary precedent exists for this usage, but writers who want to stay on the safe side may prefer to use only *repel* when the intended sense is "to cause repulsion in."

re·pul·sion (rĭ-pŭl′shən) ►*n*. **1.** The act of repulsing. **2.** Extreme aversion. **3.** *Phys.* A force, esp. an electric or magnetic force, causing particles or bodies to repel one another.

re·pul·sive (rĭ-pŭl′sĭv) ►*adj*. **1.** Causing repugnance or disgust. See Synonyms at **offensive**. **2.** Tending to repel or drive off. —**re·pul′sive·ly** *adv.* —**re·pul′sive·ness** *n.*

rep·u·ta·ble (rĕp′yə-tə-bəl) ►*adj*. Having a good reputation. —**rep′u·ta·bly** *adv.*

rep·u·ta·tion (rĕp′yə-tā′shən) ►*n*. **1.** The general opinion or judgment of the public about a person or thing. **2.** The state of being held in high esteem.

re·pute (rĭ-pyōōt′) ►*v*. **-put·ed, -put·ing** To consider; suppose. ►*n*. Reputation; esteem. [< Lat. *reputāre,* think over.]

re·put·ed (rĭ-pyōō′tĭd) ►*adj*. Generally supposed. —**re·put′ed·ly** *adv.*

re·quest (rĭ-kwĕst′) ►*v*. **1.** To ask for, esp. politely. **2.** To ask (a person) to do something. ►*n*. **1.** An act of asking for something. **2.** Something asked for. —*idiom:* **on** (or **upon**) **request** When asked for: *References are available on request.* [< Lat. *requīrere.*]

req·ui·em (rĕk′wē-əm, rē′kwē-) ►*n*. **1.** **Requiem** *Rom. Cath. Ch.* **a.** A mass for a deceased person. **b.** A musical composition for such a mass. **2.** A hymn, composition, or service for the dead. [< Lat. *requiēs,* rest.]

re·quire (rĭ-kwīr′) ►*v*. **-quired, -quir·ing** **1.** To need: *required water.* **2.** To impose an obligation on; compel. [< Lat. *requīrere.*] —**re·quire′ment** *n.*

re·quired (rĭ-kwīrd′) ►*adj*. **1.** Needed; essential. **2.** Obligatory: *required reading.*

req·ui·site (rĕk′wĭ-zĭt) ►*adj*. Required; essential. See Synonyms at **indispensable**. ►*n*. A necessity. [< Lat. *requīsītus,* p.part. of *requīrere,* require.]

req·ui·si·tion (rĕk′wĭ-zĭsh′ən) ►*n*. **1.** A formal request for something needed. **2.** The state of being needed or in use. ►*v*. To demand, as for military needs.

re·quite (rĭ-kwīt′) ►*v*. **-quit·ed, -quit·ing** **1.** To make a return for (something done or felt) in a similar fashion. **2.** To avenge (an insult or wrongdoing). [RE– + ME *quiten,* pay.] —**re·quit′a·ble** *adj.* —**re·quit′al** *n.*

re·run (rē′rŭn′) ►*n*. A second or subsequent presentation of a movie or television program. —**re·run′** *v.*

re·scind (rĭ-sĭnd′) ►*v*. To repeal or annul. [Lat. *rescindere.*] —**re·scind′a·ble** *adj.* —**re·scis′sion** (-sĭzh′ən) *n.*

res·cue (rĕs′kyōō) ►*v*. **-cued, -cu·ing** To save, as from danger. [< OFr. *rescourre.*] —**res′cue** *n.* —**res′cu·er** *n.*

re·search (rĭ-sûrch′, rē′sûrch′) ►*n*. Careful investigation or study, esp. of a scholarly or scientific nature. [< OFr. *recercher,* search closely.] —**re·search′** *v.* —**re·search′er** *n.*

re·sec·tion (rĭ-sĕk′shən) ►*n*. Surgical removal of all or part of an organ, tissue, or structure.

re·sem·blance (rĭ-zĕm′bləns) ►*n*. A similarity, esp. in appearance.

re·sem·ble (rĭ-zĕm′bəl) ►*v*. **-bled, -bling** To exhibit similarity or likeness to. [< OFr. *resembler.*]

re·sent (rĭ-zĕnt′) ►*v*. To feel angry or bitter about. [< OFr. *resentir,* feel strongly.] —**re·sent′ful** *adj.* —**re·sent′ful·ly** *adv.* —**re·sent′ment** *n.*

res·er·va·tion (rĕz′ər-vā′shən) ►*n*. **1.** The act of reserving. **2.** A limiting qualification or condition. **3.** A tract of public land set apart for a special purpose, esp. one for the use of a Native American people. **4.** An arrangement by which accommodations are secured in advance.

re·serve (rĭ-zûrv′) ►*v*. **-served, -serv·ing** **1.** To keep back, as for future use. **2.** To set apart for a particular person or use. **3.** To retain; defer: *reserve judgment.* ►*n*. **1a.** Something kept back, as for future use. **b.** An amount of capital that is not invested or otherwise used in order to meet probable demands. **2.** Self-restraint; reticence. **3.** A reservation of public land. **4.** An amount of a resource known to exist in a particular location: *oil reserves.* **5.** often **reserves** The part of a country's armed forces not on active duty but subject to call up in an emergency. [< Lat. *reservāre,* keep back.] —**re·serv′a·ble** *adj.*

re·served (rĭ-zûrvd′) ►*adj*. **1.** Set aside, as for a particular person or use. **2.** Marked by self-restraint and reticence. —**re·serv′ed·ly** (-zûr′vĭd-lē) *adv.* —**re·serv′ed·ness** *n.*

re·serv·ist (rĭ-zûr′vĭst) ►*n*. A member of a military reserve.

res·er·voir (rĕz′ər-vwär′, -vwôr′, -vôr′) ►*n*. **1.** A body of water stored for public use. **2.** A chamber for storing a fluid. **3.** A large or extra supply. [Fr. *réservoir.*]

re·side (rĭ-zīd′) ►*v*. **-sid·ed, -sid·ing** **1.** To live in a place; dwell. **2.** To be inherently present: *the power that resides in the electorate.* [< Lat. *residēre* : RE– + *sedēre,* sit.] —**re·sid′er** *n.*

res·i·dence (rĕz′ĭ-dəns, -dĕns′) ►*n*. **1.** The place in which one lives. **2.** The act or a period of residing in a place.

res·i·den·cy (rĕz′ĭ-dən-sē, -dĕn′-) ►*n., pl.* **-cies** A period of specialized clinical training for a physician.

res·i·dent (rĕz′ĭ-dənt, -dĕnt′) ►*n*. **1.** One who resides in a particular place. **2.** A physician serving a period of residency. —**res′i·dent** *adj.*

res·i·den·tial (rĕz′ĭ-dĕn′shəl) ►*adj*. **1.** Of or having residence. **2.** Of or limited to homes: *residential zoning.* —**res′i·den′tial·ly** *adv.*

re·sid·u·al (rĭ-zĭj′ōō-əl) ►*adj*. Of or remaining as a residue. ►*n*. **1.** A residue; remainder. **2.** A payment made, as to a performer, for each rerun of a television show. —**re·sid′u·al·ly** *adv.*

res·i·due (rĕz′ĭ-dōō′, -dyōō′) ►*n*. The remainder of something after removal of parts or a part. [< Lat. *residuus,* remaining < *residēre,* RESIDE.]

re·sign (rĭ-zīn′) ►*v*. **1.** To submit (oneself) passively. **2.** To give up (a position); quit **3.** To relinquish (a privilege, right, or claim). [< Lat. *resignāre,* unseal.]

res·ig·na·tion (rĕz′ĭg-nā′shən) ►*n*. **1.** The act

of resigning. **2.** A formal statement that one is resigning. **3.** Acceptance; submission.

re·signed (rĭ-zīnd′) ►*adj.* Acquiescent; accepting. —**re·sign′ed·ly** (-zī′nĭd-lē) *adv.*

re·sil·ient (rĭ-zĭl′yənt) ►*adj.* **1.** Capable of returning to an original shape or position, as after having been compressed. **2.** Able to recover readily, as from misfortune. [< Lat. *resilīre*, leap back.] —**re·sil′ience, re·sil′ien·cy** *n.* —**re·sil′ient·ly** *adv.*

res·in (rĕz′ĭn) ►*n.* **1.** A viscous substance of plant origin, such as rosin or amber, used in varnishes, adhesives, and pharmaceuticals. **2.** Any of various synthetic substances similar to natural resins, used in plastics. ►*v.* To treat with resin. [< Lat. *rēsīna.*] —**res′in·ous** *adj.*

re·sist (rĭ-zĭst′) ►*v.* **1.** To take action in opposition to; try to eliminate. **2.** To remain unaltered or undamaged. [< Lat. *resistere* : RE– + *sistere*, place.] —**re·sist′er** *n.* —**re·sist′i·ble** *adj.*

re·sis·tance (rĭ-zĭs′təns) ►*n.* **1.** The act of resisting or the capacity to resist. **2.** A force that opposes or retards motion. **3.** An underground organization engaged in a struggle against the military or totalitarian occupation of a country. **4.** *Elect.* The opposition of a body or substance to current passing through it. —**re·sis′tant** *adj.*

re·sis·tor (rĭ-zĭs′tər) ►*n.* A device used to provide resistance in an electric circuit.

res·o·lute (rĕz′ə-lōōt′, rĕz′ə-lōōt′) ►*adj.* Firm or determined. [Lat. *resolūtus*, p.part. of *resolvere*, resolve.] —**res′o·lute′ly** *adv.*

res·o·lu·tion (rĕz′ə-lōō′shən) ►*n.* **1.** The state or quality of being resolute. **2.** A course of action determined or decided on. **3.** A formal statement of a decision, as by a legislature. **4.** An explanation, as of a problem; solution. **5.** The fineness of detail that can be distinguished in an image.

re·solve (rĭ-zŏlv′) ►*v.* **-solved, -solv·ing 1a.** To make a firm decision about. **b.** To decide or express by formal vote. **2.** To find a solution to. **3.** To dispel: *resolve a doubt.* ►*n.* **1.** Firmness of purpose; resolution. **2.** A determination or decision. [< Lat. *resolvere*, untie, loosen.] —**re·solv′a·ble** *adj.*

res·o·nance (rĕz′ə-nəns) ►*n.* **1.** The quality or condition of being resonant. **2.** Intensification of sound, esp. of a musical tone, by sympathetic vibration. **3.** *Phys.* The increase in amplitude of oscillation of an electric or mechanical system exposed to a periodic force whose frequency is equal or very close to the natural frequency of the system.

res·o·nant (rĕz′ə-nənt) ►*adj.* **1a.** Strong and deep in tone; resounding. **b.** Having a lasting presence or effect: *resonant words.* **2.** Producing, exhibiting, or resulting from resonance. —**res′o·nant·ly** *adv.*

res·o·nate (rĕz′ə-nāt′) ►*v.* **-nat·ed, -nat·ing 1.** To exhibit or produce resonance. **2.** To evoke a feeling of shared emotion or belief. [Lat. *resonāre*, resound.]

res·o·na·tor (rĕz′ə-nā′tər) ►*n.* A hollow chamber designed to permit internal resonant oscillation of electromagnetic or acoustical waves of specific frequencies.

re·sort (rĭ-zôrt′) ►*v.* **1.** To turn to or make use of (something or someone) for help or as a means of achieving something: *resorted to violence.* **2.**

To go customarily or frequently. ►*n.* **1.** A place frequented by people for relaxation or recreation: *a ski resort.* **2.** Recourse. **3.** One turned to for aid or relief: *would ask her for help only as a last resort.* [< OFr. *resortir*, go out again.]

re·sound (rĭ-zound′) ►*v.* **1.** To make a loud or prolonged sound. See Synonyms at **echo. 2.** To be filled with sound. [< Lat. *resonāre.*] —**re·sound′ing** *adj.* —**re·sound′ing·ly** *adv.*

re·source (rē′sôrs′, -zôrs′, rĭ-sôrs′, -zôrs′) ►*n.* **1.** A source of support or help. **2.** often **resources** An available supply. **3.** The ability to deal with a situation effectively. **4.** Means; assets. **5.** A natural resource. [< Lat. *resurgere*, rise again.]

re·source·ful (rĭ-sôrs′fəl, -zôrs′-) ►*adj.* Clever and imaginative, esp. in difficult situations. —**re·source′ful·ly** *adv.* —**re·source′ful·ness** *n.*

re·spect (rĭ-spĕkt′) ►*v.* **1.** To have regard for; esteem. **2a.** To avoid interfering with or intruding upon: *respected his privacy.* **b.** To avoid violating: *respected the law.* **3.** To concern. ►*n.* **1.** High, often deferential regard; esteem. **2. respects** Expressions of consideration or deference: *pay one's respects.* **3.** A particular aspect, feature, or detail. **4.** Relation; reference. [< Lat. *respectus*, p.part. of *respicere*, regard : RE– + *specere*, look at.] —**re·spect′er** *n.* —**re·spect′ful** *adj.* —**re·spect′ful·ly** *adv.* —**re·spect′ful·ness** *n.*

re·spect·a·ble (rĭ-spĕk′tə-bəl) ►*adj.* **1.** Meriting respect or esteem. **2.** Good or proper in behavior or conventional conduct. **3.** Of moderately good quality. **4.** Considerable in amount, number, or size: *a respectable sum of money.* **5.** Acceptable in appearance; presentable. —**re·spect′a·bil′i·ty** *n.* —**re·spect′a·bly** *adv.*

re·spec·tive (rĭ-spĕk′tĭv) ►*adj.* Individual; particular: *They took their respective seats.*

re·spec·tive·ly (rĭ-spĕk′tĭv-lē) ►*adv.* Singly in the order designated or mentioned.

res·pi·ra·tion (rĕs′pə-rā′shən) ►*n.* **1.** The act or process of inhaling and exhaling. **2.** The act or process by which a cell or organism without lungs exchanges gases with its environment. **3.** The process by which living cells convert the chemical energy of organic molecules into usable energy in the form of ATP, involving the consumption of oxygen and the production of carbon dioxide and water as byproducts. —**res′pi·ra·to·ry** (-pər-ə-tôr′ē, rĭ-spīr′ə-) *adj.*

res·pi·ra·tor (rĕs′pə-rā′tər) ►*n.* **1.** *Med.* A machine that supplies oxygen or a mixture of oxygen and air, used in artificial respiration to control or assist breathing. **2.** A device worn over the mouth or nose or both to protect the respiratory tract from harmful dust or fumes.

respiratory system ►*n.* The system of organs involved in the exchange of oxygen and carbon dioxide between an organism and the environment.

re·spire (rĭ-spīr′) ►*v.* **-spired, -spir·ing** To engage in respiration. [< Lat. *respīrāre*, breathe again.]

res·pite (rĕs′pĭt) ►*n.* **1.** A short interval of rest or relief. See Synonyms at **pause. 2.** A reprieve. ►*adj.* Relating to or being a respite: *respite care.* [< Lat. *respectus*, refuge; see RESPECT.]

re·splen·dent (rĭ-splĕn′dənt) ►*adj.* Splendid or dazzling in appearance. [< Lat. *resplendēre*,

shine brightly.] **—re·splen′dence, re·splen′-
den·cy** *n.* **—re·splen′dent·ly** *adv.*

re·spond (rĭ-spŏnd′) ►*v.* **1.** To reply; answer. **2.**
To act in return. **3.** To react positively or favorably. [< Lat. *respondēre.*]

re·spon·dent (rĭ-spŏn′dənt) ►*n.* One who
responds, esp. the defending party in certain
legal proceedings. **—re·spon′dent** *adj.*

re·sponse (rĭ-spŏns′) ►*n.* **1.** The act of responding. **2.** A reply; answer. **3.** A reaction to a
specific stimulus. [< Lat. *respōnsum.*]

re·spon·si·bil·i·ty (rĭ-spŏn′sə-bĭl′ĭ-tē) ►*n., pl.*
-ties **1.** The state or fact of being responsible. **2.**
Something for which one is responsible.

re·spon·si·ble (rĭ-spŏn′sə-bəl) ►*adj.* **1.** Liable to
be required to give account for something. **2.**
Involving important duties: *a responsible position.* **3.** Being a source or cause. **4.** Dependable;
reliable. See Synonyms at **reliable. 5.** Based
on or marked by good judgment: *responsible
journalism.* **—re·spon′si·bly** *adv.*

re·spon·sive (rĭ-spŏn′sĭv) ►*adj.* **1.** Readily
reacting. **2.** Containing responses: *responsive
liturgy.* **—re·spon′sive·ly** *adv.* **—re·spon′-
sive·ness** *n.*

rest[1] (rĕst) ►*n.* **1.** A period of inactivity, relaxation, or sleep. **2.** The state of being motionless;
the absence of motion. **3.** *Mus.* **a.** An interval of
silence having a specified length. **b.** The symbol
indicating such a pause. **4.** A device used as a
support: *a back rest.* ►*v.* **1a.** To cease motion or
work, esp. in order to become refreshed. **b.** To
lie down and sleep. **2.** To be in or come to a
motionless state. **3a.** To be supported or based:
The ladder rests against the wall. **b.** To place, lay,
or lean. **c.** To be imposed as a responsibility:
The decision rests with you. **d.** To depend or rely.
[< OE.] **—rest′er** *n.*

rest[2] (rĕst) ►*n.* **1.** Something left over; remainder. **2.** That or those remaining: *The rest are
arriving later.* ►*v.* To remain: *Rest assured that
we'll be there.* [< Lat. *restāre,* stay behind : RE- +
stāre, stand.]

res·tau·rant (rĕs′-tə-ränt′, -tər-ənt) ►*n.* A place
where meals are served to the public. [< Fr.
restaurer, RESTORE.]

res·tau·ra·teur (rĕs′tər-ə-tûr′) also **res·tau·
ran·teur** (-tə-rän-tûr′) ►*n.* The manager or
owner of a restaurant. [Fr.]

rest·ful (rĕst′fəl) ►*adj.* Affording, marked by,
or suggesting rest; tranquil. **—rest′ful·ly** *adv.*
—rest′ful·ness *n.*

rest home ►*n.* A private establishment where
elderly or disabled persons are cared for.

res·ti·tu·tion (rĕs′tĭ-tōo′shən, -tyōo′-) ►*n.* **1.**
The act of restoring something to the rightful
owner. **2.** The act of compensating for loss,
damage, or injury. [< Lat. *restituere,* restore :
RE- + *statuere,* set up.]

res·tive (rĕs′tĭv) ►*adj.* Uneasily impatient or
hard to control. [< Lat. *restāre,* keep back : RE-
+ *stāre,* stand.] **—res′tive·ly** *adv.*

rest·less (rĕst′lĭs) ►*adj.* **1.** Marked by a lack of
quiet, repose, or rest. **2.** Not able to rest, relax,
or be still. **3.** Having a persistent desire for
action. **4.** Never still: *the restless sea.* **—rest′-
less·ly** *adv.* **—rest′less·ness** *n.*

res·to·ra·tion (rĕs′tə-rā′shən) ►*n.* **1.** An act
of restoring or the state of being restored. **2.**
Something that has been restored.

re·stor·a·tive (rĭ-stôr′ə-tĭv) ►*adj.* Tending or

having the power to restore. ►*n.* Something that
restores health or strength.

re·store (rĭ-stôr′) ►*v.* **-stored, -stor·ing 1.** To
bring back into existence or use. **2.** To bring
back to an original condition. **3.** To make resti-
tution of; give back. [< Lat. *restaurāre.*]

re·strain (rĭ-strān′) ►*v.* **1.** To hold back; control.
2. To secure so as to prevent or limit movement. [< Lat. *restringere,* bind back.] **—re·
strain′a·ble** *adj.* **—re·strain′er** *n.*

re·straint (rĭ-strānt′) ►*n.* **1.** The act of restraining or the condition of being restrained. **2.**
Something that restrains. **3.** Control or repres-
sion of feelings.

re·strict (rĭ-strĭkt′) ►*v.* **1.** To keep or confine
within physical limits. **2.** To prevent or prohibit
beyond a certain limit. [Lat. *restringere, restrict-,*
bind up.] **—re·stric′tion** *n.*

re·stric·tive (rĭ-strĭk′tĭv) ►*adj.* **1.** Tending or
serving to restrict. **2.** *Gram.* Of or being a
subordinate clause that restricts the meaning of
the noun, phrase, or clause it modifies, as the
clause *who live in glass houses* in *People who live
in glass houses shouldn't throw stones.* See Usage
Note at **that. —re·stric′tive·ly** *adv.* **—re·
stric′tive·ness** *n.*

rest·room (rĕst′rōom′, -rŏŏm′) ►*n.* A room
with toilets and sinks for public use.

re·sult (rĭ-zŭlt′) ►*v.* **1.** To come about as a consequence. **2.** To end in a particular way. ►*n.* **1.**
A consequence; outcome. **2.** *Math.* The quantity
or expression obtained by calculation. [< Lat.
resultāre, leap back.] **—re·sul′tant** *adj.* & *n.*

re·sume (rĭ-zōom′) ►*v.* **-sumed, -sum·ing
1.** To begin or take up again after interruption. **2.** To take or occupy again. [< Lat.
resūmere.] **—re·sum′a·ble** *adj.* **—re·sump′-
tion** (-zŭmp′shən) *n.*

re·su·mé or **re·su·me** or **ré·su·mé** (rĕz′ŏŏ-
mā′, rĕz′ŏŏ-mā′) ►*n.* A summary of one's work
experience and qualifications, often submitted
when applying for a job. [Fr., summarized.]

re·sur·gent (rĭ-sûr′jənt) ►*adj.* Undergoing or
tending to bring about renewal or revival. **—re·
sur′gence** *n.*

re·sur·rect (rĕz′ə-rĕkt′) ►*v.* **1.** To raise from the
dead. **2.** To bring back, as into notice or use.

re·sur·rec·tion (rĕz′ə-rĕk′shən) ►*n.* **1.** A reviv-
al; rebirth. **2. Resurrection** *Christianity* **a.**
The rising of Jesus on the third day after the
Crucifixion. **b.** The rising of the dead at the
Last Judgment. [< Lat. *resurrēctus,* p.part. of
resurgere, to rise again.]

re·sus·ci·tate (rĭ-sŭs′ĭ-tāt′) ►*v.* **-tat·ed, -tat·
ing** To restore consciousness or other signs of
life to one who appears dead. [Lat. *resuscitāre.*]
—re·sus′ci·ta′tion *n.* **—re·sus′ci·ta′tive** *adj.*
—re·sus′ci·ta′tor *n.*

res·ver·a·trol (rĕz-vîr′ĭ-trôl′, -trŏl′, -trōl′) ►*n.*
A compound found in red wine, grapes, and
other foods that has antioxidant and anti-
inflammatory properties and may protect
against cancer and heart disease. [RES(INOUS) +
NLat. *Vērātrum,* hellebore genus + -OL.]

ret. ►*abbr.* **1.** retired **2.** return

re·tail (rē′tāl′) ►*n.* The sale of goods directly to
consumers. [< OFr. *retaillier,* cut up.] **—re′tail′**
adj., adv., & *v.* **—re′tail′er** *n.*

re·tain (rĭ-tān′) ►*v.* **-tained, -tain·ing 1a.** To
maintain possession of. **b.** To keep in a particular
place or condition. **2.** To keep in mind; remember.
3a. To keep in

one's service or pay. **b.** To hire (e.g., a lawyer) by paying a fee. [< Lat. *retinēre*, hold back.] —**re·tain'a·ble** *adj.* —**re·tain'ment** *n.*

re·tain·er¹ (rĭ-tā'nər) ►*n.* **1.** One that retains. **2.** A dental appliance that holds teeth in position after orthodontic treatment. **3.** A servant or attendant, esp. in a noble or wealthy household.

re·tain·er² (rĭ-tā'nər) ►*n.* A fee paid to retain a professional adviser.

re·take (rē-tāk') ►*v.* **1.** To take back or again. **2.** To recapture. **3.** To photograph, film, or record again. —**re'take'** *n.*

re·tal·i·ate (rĭ-tăl'ē-āt') ►*v.* **-at·ed, -at·ing** To respond to an action done to oneself or an associate, esp. to attack someone as a response to a hurtful action. [LLat. *retāliāre.*] —**re·tal'i·a'tion** *n.* —**re·tal'i·a'tive, re·tal'i·a·to'ry** (-ə-tôr'ē) *adj.*

re·tard (rĭ-tärd') ►*v.* To cause to move or develop slowly; delay or impede. [< Lat. *retardāre.*]

re·tar·dant (rĭ-tär'dnt) ►*adj.* Acting or tending to retard. ►*n.* A substance that retards a process: *a flame retardant.* —**re·tar'dant** *n.*

re·tar·da·tion (rē'tär-dā'shən) ►*n.* **1.** The act or the state of being retarded. **2.** The extent to which something is held back or delayed. **3.** *Often Offensive* Impaired intellectual development.

re·tard·ed (rĭ-tär'dĭd) ►*adj.* **1.** *Often Offensive* Affected with impaired intellectual development. **2.** Occurring later than desired or expected; delayed.

retch (rĕch) ►*v.* To vomit or try to vomit. [< OE *hrǣcan.*] —**retch** *n.*

re·ten·tion (rĭ-tĕn'shən) ►*n.* **1.** The act of retaining or the state of being retained. **2.** The practice of requiring a student to repeat a class or a grade because of lack of academic progress. **3.** The ability to recall what has been learned or experienced; memory. [< Lat. *retentus*, p.part. of *retinēre*, retain.] —**re·ten'tive** *adj.* —**re·ten'tive·ness** *n.*

ret·i·cent (rĕt'ĭ-sənt) ►*adj.* **1.** Inclined to keep one's personal affairs to oneself. See Synonyms at **laconic. 2.** Restrained or reserved. **3.** Reluctant; unwilling. [< Lat. *reticēre*, keep silent.] —**ret'i·cence** *n.* —**ret'i·cent·ly** *adv.*

Usage: Reticent is generally used to indicate a reluctance to speak. Its extended use as an all-purpose synonym for *reluctant*, as in *My friends are reticent to drive so far,* is rejected by 83 percent of the Usage Panel.

ret·i·na (rĕt'n-ə) ►*n., pl.* **-nas** or **-nae** (rĕt'n-ē') A delicate, light-sensitive membrane lining the inner eyeball and connected by the optic nerve to the brain. [< Med.Lat. *rētina.*] —**ret'i·nal** *adj.*

ret·i·nue (rĕt'n-ōō', -yōō') ►*n.* The attendants accompanying a high-ranking person. [< OFr. *retenir*, retain.]

re·tire (rĭ-tīr') ►*v.* **-tired, -tir·ing 1.** To withdraw from one's occupation or position. **2.** To withdraw, as for rest or seclusion. **3.** To go to bed. **4.** To take out of use or circulation. **5.** *Baseball* To put out (a batter). [< OFr. *retirer*, draw back.] —**re·tire'ment** *n.*

re·tired (rĭ-tīrd') ►*adj.* **1.** Withdrawn from one's occupation. **2.** Withdrawn; secluded.

re·tir·ee (rĭ-tīr'ē') ►*n.* One who has retired from active working life.

re·tir·ing (rĭ-tīr'ĭng) ►*adj.* Shy and reserved.

re·tool (rē-tōōl') ►*v.* **1.** To provide (e.g., a factory) with new machinery and tools. **2.** To revise and reorganize.

re·tort¹ (rĭ-tôrt') ►*v.* **1.** To reply or answer, esp. in a quick, caustic, or witty manner. **2.** *Archaic* To return in kind; pay back. ►*n.* A quick, witty reply. [Lat. *retorquēre*, *retort-*, bend back.]

re·tort² (rĭ-tôrt', rē'tôrt') ►*n.* A closed laboratory vessel with an outlet tube, used for distillation or decomposition by heat. [< Med.Lat. *retorta* < Lat. *retorquēre*, bend back.]

re·touch (rē-tŭch') ►*v.* **1.** To add new details or touches to. **2.** To improve or change (a photograph) as by removing flaws. —**re'touch'** *n.*

re·trace (rē-trās') ►*v.* To trace again or back. —**re·trace'a·ble** *adj.*

re·tract (rĭ-trăkt') ►*v.* **1.** To take back. **2.** To draw back or in. See Synonyms at **recede.** [Lat. *retractāre*, revoke.] —**re·tract'a·ble, re·tract'i·ble** *adj.* —**re'trac'tion** *n.*

re·trac·tile (rĭ-trăk'tĭl, -tīl') ►*adj.* Capable of being drawn back or in.

re·tread (rē-trĕd') ►*v.* To fit (a worn tire) with a new tread. ►*n.* (rē'trĕd') A tire that has been retreaded.

re·treat (rĭ-trēt') ►*n.* **1a.** The act or process of moving back or away, esp. from something formidable or unpleasant. **b.** Withdrawal of a military force from an enemy attack. **2.** A place affording peace, privacy, or security. **3.** A period of retirement or solitude, esp. for prayer or meditation. **4a.** The signal for a military withdrawal. **b.** A bugle call or drumbeat signaling the lowering of the flag at sunset. ►*v.* To fall or draw back; withdraw. See Synonyms at **recede.** [< Lat. *retrahere*, draw back.]

re·trench (rĭ-trĕnch') ►*v.* To reduce (e.g., expenses); cut down. [< OFr. *retrenchier.*] —**re·trench'ment** *n.*

ret·ri·bu·tion (rĕt'rə-byōō'shən) ►*n.* Punishment administered in return for a wrong committed. [< Lat. *retribuere*, pay back.] —**re·trib'u·tive** (rĭ-trĭb'yə-tĭv), **re·trib'u·to'ry** (-tôr'ē) *adj.*

re·trieve (rĭ-trēv') ►*v.* **-trieved, -triev·ing 1.** To get back into one's possession or control, esp. from a known place or a place of storage. **2.** To find and carry back; fetch. **3.** To gain access to (stored information). [< OFr. *retrover.*] —**re·triev'a·ble** *adj.* —**re·triev'al** *n.*

re·triev·er (rĭ-trē'vər) ►*n.* One that retrieves, esp. any of several breeds of dog developed and trained to retrieve game.

ret·ro (rĕt'rō) ►*adj.* **1.** Retroactive. **2.** Involving or reminiscent of an earlier time.

retro– ►*pref.* Backward; back: *retroactive* [< Lat. *retrō.*]

ret·ro·ac·tive (rĕt'rō-ăk'tĭv) ►*adj.* Applying to a period before enactment. —**ret'ro·ac'tive·ly** *adv.*

ret·ro·fire (rĕt'rō-fīr') ►*v.* To fire (a retrorocket).

ret·ro·fit (rĕt'rō-fĭt') ►*v.* **1.** To outfit with newly developed or previously unavailable parts or equipment. **2.** To fit for use in or on an existing structure. —**ret'ro·fit'** *n.*

ret·ro·grade (rĕt'rə-grād') ►*adj.* **1.** Moving or tending backward. **2.** Reverting to an earlier or inferior condition. ►*v.* **-grad·ed, -grad·ing 1.** To move backward. **2.** To deteriorate; degenerate. [< Lat. *retrōgradī*, go back.]

ret·ro·gress (rĕt'rə-grĕs', rĕt'rə-grĕs') ►*v.* **1.** To return to an earlier, inferior, or less complex condition. **2.** To go or move backward. [Lat. *retrōgradī, retrōgress-*, go backward.] —**ret'ro·gres'sion** *n.* —**ret'ro·gres'sive** *adj.* —**re'tro·gres'sive·ly** *adv.*

ret·ro·rock·et (rĕt'rō-rŏk'ĭt) ►*n.* A rocket used to retard, arrest, or reverse motion.

ret·ro·spect (rĕt'rə-spĕkt') ►*n.* A review or contemplation of things in the past. [< Lat. *retrōspicere*, look back at : RETRO– + *specere*, look at.] —**ret'ro·spec'tion** *n.* —**ret'ro·spec'tive** *n. & adj.*

ret·ro·vi·rus (rĕt'rō-vī'rəs, rĕt'rə-vī'-) ►*n.* A virus that contains RNA and an enzyme that can create DNA using RNA as a template.

re·turn (rĭ-tûrn') ►*v.* **1.** To go or come back, as to an earlier condition or place. **2.** To answer or respond. **3.** To send, put, or carry back. **4.** To give in reciprocation. **5.** To yield (profit or interest). **6.** *Law* To deliver (e.g., a verdict) to a court of law. **7.** To reelect to an office. ►*n.* **1.** The act of returning. **2a.** Something returned. **b. returns** Merchandise returned. **3.** A periodic recurrence. **4.** Something exchanged for that received; repayment. **5.** A reply; response. **6.** A profit or yield. **7.** An official report: *a tax return.* **8.** *Comp.* A key used to begin a new line or paragraph in a text editor. ►*adj.* **1.** Of or bringing about a return. **2.** Given, sent, or done in reciprocation: *return mail.* [< OFr. *retourner.*] —**re·turn'a·ble** *adj. & n.* —**re·turn'er** *n.*

re·turn·ee (rĭ-tûr'nē') ►*n.* One who returns, as from military duty overseas.

re·un·ion (rē-yōōn'yən) ►*n.* **1.** The act of reuniting or the state of being reunited. **2.** A gathering of the members of a group who have been separated.

Reu·ther (rōō'thər), **Walter Philip** 1907–70. Amer. labor leader.

rev (rĕv) *Informal* ►*n.* A revolution, as of a motor. ►*v.* **revved, rev·ving 1.** To increase the speed of (e.g., a motor). **2.** To make livelier.

rev. ►*abbr.* **1.** revenue **2.** reverse **3.** review **4.** revised **5.** revision

Rev. ►*abbr.* Reverend

re·vamp (rē-vămp') ►*v.* To make over; revise. —**re·vamp'** *n.*

re·veal (rĭ-vēl') ►*v.* **1.** To make known. **2.** To cause to be seen; show. [< Lat. *revēlāre.*]

rev·eil·le (rĕv'ə-lē) ►*n.* A signal, as on a bugle, given in the morning to awaken soldiers. [< OFr. *resveiller*, awaken.]

rev·el (rĕv'əl) ►*v.* **-eled, -el·ing** also **-elled, -el·ling 1.** To take great pleasure or delight. **2.** To engage in boisterous festivities. ►*n.* A boisterous festivity or celebration. [< Lat. *rebellāre*, to rebel.] —**rev'el·er, rev'el·ler** *n.* —**rev'el·ry** *n.*

rev·e·la·tion (rĕv'ə-lā'shən) ►*n.* **1a.** An act of revealing. **b.** Something revealed, esp. a dramatic disclosure. **2. Revelation** See table at **Bible.** [< Lat. *revēlāre*, reveal.] —**rev'e·la·to'ry** (-lə-tôr'ē) *adj.*

re·venge (rĭ-vĕnj') ►*v.* **-venged, -veng·ing** To inflict punishment in return for (injury or insult). ►*n.* **1.** The act of revenging. **2.** A desire for revenge. **3.** An opportunity to retaliate or get even. [< OFr. *revengier.*] —**re·venge'ful** *adj.* —**re·veng'er** *n.*

rev·e·nue (rĕv'ə-nōō, -nyōō) ►*n.* **1.** The income of a government. **2.** Yield from property or investment. [< OFr. < Lat. *revenīre*, return : RE– + *venīre*, come.]

re·ver·ber·ate (rĭ-vûr'bə-rāt') ►*v.* **-at·ed, -at·ing** To echo repeatedly; resound. See Synonyms at **echo.** [Lat. *reverberāre.*] —**re·ver'ber·a'tion** *n.*

re·vere (rĭ-vîr') ►*v.* **-vered, -ver·ing** To regard with deference and devotion. [< Lat. *reverērī.*]

Re·vere (rĭ-vîr'), **Paul** 1735–1818. Amer. Revolutionary hero.

Paul Revere

rev·er·ence (rĕv'ər-əns) ►*n.* **1.** Profound awe and respect. **2.** An act of respect, esp. a bow or curtsy. **3. Reverence** Used as a form of address for certain members of the Christian clergy. ►*v.* **-enced, -enc·ing** To consider or treat with reverence.

rev·er·end (rĕv'ər-ənd) ►*adj.* **1.** Deserving reverence. **2. Reverend** A title of respect for certain Christian clerics. ►*n.* *Informal* A cleric or minister. [< Lat. *reverendus.*]

rev·er·ent (rĕv'ər-ənt) ►*adj.* Feeling or expressing reverence. —**rev'er·ent·ly** *adv.*

rev·er·en·tial (rĕv'ə-rĕn'shəl) ►*adj.* **1.** Reverent. **2.** Inspiring reverence.

rev·er·ie (rĕv'ə-rē) ►*n.* **1.** A state of abstracted musing. **2.** A daydream. [< OFr. *rever*, to dream.]

re·ver·sal (rĭ-vûr'səl) ►*n.* **1.** The act or an instance of reversing. **2.** A usu. adverse change in fortune.

re·verse (rĭ-vûrs') ►*adj.* **1.** Turned backward in position, direction, or order. **2.** Moving, acting, or organized in a manner contrary to the usual. **3.** Causing backward movement: *a reverse gear.* ►*n.* **1.** The opposite or contrary. **2.** The back or rear part. **3.** A change to an opposite position, condition, or direction esp. for the worse. **4.** A mechanism, such as a gear in a motor vehicle, used to reverse movement. ►*v.* **-versed, -vers·ing 1.** To turn around to the opposite direction or position. **2.** To exchange the positions of; transpose. **3.** *Law* To change or set aside (a lower court's decision). **4.** To turn or move in the opposite direction. **5.** To reverse the action of an engine. [< Lat. *revertere, revers-*, turn back.] —**re·vers'er** *n.* —**re·vers'i·ble** *adj. & n.*

reverse osmosis ►*n.* A method of purifying water with a membrane across which salts or impurities cannot pass.

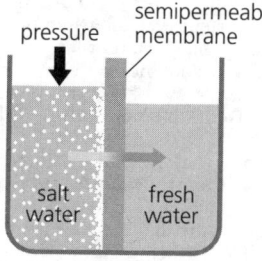

pressure | semipermeable membrane

salt water | fresh water

reverse osmosis

re·vert (rĭ-vûrt′) ►v. **1.** To go back to a former condition, practice, or belief. **2.** *Law* To be returned to the former owner or to the former owner's heirs. [< Lat. *revertere.*] —**re·ver′sion** *n.* —**re·ver′sion·ar·y** *adj.*

re·view (rĭ-vyōō′) ►v. **1.** To look over, study, or examine again. **2.** To look back on. **3.** To examine critically or for correction. **4.** To write or give a critical report on. **5.** *Law* To evaluate a lower court's decision or action for possible errors. **6.** To subject to a formal inspection. ►n. **1.** A reexamination or reconsideration. **2.** A restudying of subject matter. **3a.** A critical estimate of a work or performance. **b.** A periodical devoted esp. to critical articles and essays. **4a.** An inspection or examination for evaluation. **b.** A formal military inspection. **5.** *Law* A higher court's evaluation of a lower court's decision or action that seeks to determine whether any error was made. [< Lat. *revidēre* : RE– + *vidēre,* see.]

re·view·er (rĭ-vyōō′ər) ►n. One who reviews, esp. one who writes reviews.

re·vile (rĭ-vīl′) ►v. **-viled, -vil·ing** To assail with or use scornful language. [< OFr. *reviler.*] —**re·vile′ment** *n.* —**re·vil′er** *n.*

re·vise (rĭ-vīz′) ►v. **-vised, -vis·ing 1.** To alter or edit (a text). **2.** To reconsider and modify. [Lat. *revīsere,* visit again : RE– + *vidēre, vīs-,* see.] —**re·vis′er, re·vi′sor** *n.* —**re·vi′sion** (-vĭzh′ən) *n.*

re·vi·sion·ism (rĭ-vĭzh′ə-nĭz′əm) ►n. Advocacy of the revision of an accepted view, theory, or doctrine. —**re·vi′sion·ist** *adj. & n.*

re·viv·al (rĭ-vī′vəl) ►n. **1.** The act of reviving or the state of being revived. **2.** A new presentation, as of a play. **3.** A meeting or series of meetings for reawakening religious faith.

re·vive (rĭ-vīv′) ►v. **-vived, -viv·ing 1.** To return or bring back to life or consciousness. **2.** To give new health, strength, or spirit to. **3a.** To restore to use, currency, or notice. **b.** To present (e.g., an old play) again. [< Lat. *revīvere,* live again : RE– + *vīvere,* live.] —**re·viv′a·ble** *adj.* —**re·viv′er** *n.*

re·viv·i·fy (rē-vĭv′ə-fī′) ►v. **-fied, -fy·ing** To give new life to. —**re·viv′i·fi·ca′tion** *n.*

rev·o·ca·ble (rĕv′ə-kə-bəl) also **re·vok·a·ble** (rĭ-vō′-) ►adj. Capable of being revoked.

re·voke (rĭ-vōk′) ►v. **-voked, -vok·ing** To invalidate, as by voiding or canceling. [< Lat. *revocāre,* call back.] —**rev′o·ca′tion** (rĕv′ə-kā′shən) *n.* —**re·vok′er** *n.*

re·volt (rĭ-vōlt′) ►v. **1.** To attempt to overthrow the authority of the state; rebel. **2.** To oppose or refuse to accept something. **3.** To fill with disgust or abhorrence; repel. See Synonyms at

disgust. ►n. An uprising, especially against state authority. [< VLat. **revolvitāre,* overturn.]

re·volt·ing (rĭ-vōl′tĭng) ►adj. Causing abhorrence or disgust. See Synonyms at **offensive.**

rev·o·lu·tion (rĕv′ə-lōō′shən) ►n. **1a.** Orbital motion about a point, esp. as distinguished from axial rotation. **b.** A turning or rotation about an axis. **c.** A single complete cycle of such orbital or axial motion. **2.** The overthrow of one government and its replacement with another. **3.** A sudden or momentous change in a situation. [< Lat. *revolūtus,* p.part. of *revolvere,* turn over.]

rev·o·lu·tion·ar·y (rĕv′ə-lōō′shə-nĕr′ē) ►adj. **1.** Of or relating to a revolution: *revolutionary war.* **2.** Marked by or resulting in radical change. ►n., pl. **-ies** One who supports or engages in revolution.

rev·o·lu·tion·ist (rĕv′ə-lōō′shə-nĭst) ►n. A revolutionary. —**rev′o·lu′tion·ist** *adj.*

rev·o·lu·tion·ize (rĕv′ə-lōō′shə-nīz′) ►v. **-ized, -iz·ing** To bring about a radical change in.

re·volve (rĭ-vŏlv′) ►v. **-volved, -volv·ing 1.** To orbit a central point. **2.** To turn on an axis; rotate. [< Lat. *revolvere,* turn over.] —**re·volv′a·ble** *adj.*

re·volv·er (rĭ-vŏl′vər) ►n. A pistol having a revolving cylinder with several cartridge chambers that may be fired in succession.

re·vue (rĭ-vyōō′) ►n. A musical show consisting of often satirical skits, songs, and dances. [Fr. < OFr., REVIEW.]

re·vul·sion (rĭ-vŭl′shən) ►n. A sudden strong feeling of disgust or loathing. [< Lat. *revulsus,* p.part. of *revellere,* tear back.]

re·ward (rĭ-wôrd′) ►n. **1.** A consequence of worthy or unworthy behavior: *the rewards of exercise; the rewards of lying.* **2.** Money offered or given for some special service, such as the return of a lost article. ►v. To give a reward to or for. [< AN.]

re·word (rē-wûrd′) ►v. To state or express again in different words.

re·write (rē-rīt′) ►v. To write again, esp. in a different or improved form. —**re′write′** *n.*

Rey·kja·vík (rā′kyə-vēk′, -vĭk′) The capital of Iceland, in the SW.

RF ►abbr. **1.** radio frequency **2.** right field

RFD ►abbr. rural free delivery

Rh (är′āch′) ►adj. Of or relating to the Rh factor: *an Rh antigen.*

Rhae·ti·a (rē′shē-ə, -shə) An ancient Roman province in present-day E Switzerland and W Austria. —**Rhae′tian** *adj. & n.*

Rhae·to-Ro·mance (rē′tō-rō-mäns′) ►n. A group of Romance dialects spoken in S Switzerland, N Italy, and the Tyrol.

rhap·so·dy (răp′sə-dē) ►n., pl. **-dies 1.** Exalted or excessively enthusiastic expression of feeling. **2.** *Mus.* A usu. instrumental composition of irregular form, often incorporating improvisation. [< Gk. *rhapsōidein,* recite poems.] —**rhap·sod′ic** (-sŏd′ĭk) *adj.* —**rhap·sod′i·cal·ly** *adv.* —**rhap′so·dize** *v.*

rhe·a (rē′ə) ►n. A large flightless South American bird having three-toed feet. [< *Rhea,* a character in Roman myth.]

rhe·ni·um (rē′nē-əm) ►n. *Symbol* **Re** A rare, dense, silvery-white metallic element used for electrical contacts and high-temperature thermocouples. At. no. 75. See table at **element.** [< Lat. *Rhēnus,* the Rhine.]

rhe·o·stat (rē′ə-stăt′) ►*n.* A variable electrical resistor used to regulate current. [< Gk. *rheos,* current.] —**rhe′o·stat′ic** *adj.*

rhe·sus monkey (rē′səs) ►*n.* A brown to grayish Asian monkey, often used in scientific research. [< Gk. *Rhēsos,* a mythical king of Thrace.]

rhet·o·ric (rĕt′ər-ĭk) ►*n.* **1.** The art or study of using language effectively and persuasively. **2.** A style of speaking or writing: *political rhetoric.* **3.** Language that is pretentious or insincere. [< Gk. *rhētōr,* public speaker.] —**rhe·tor′i·cal** (rĭ-tôr′ĭ-kəl) *adj.* —**rhe·tor′i·cal·ly** *adv.* —**rhet′o·ri′cian** (rĕt′ə-rĭsh′ən) *n.*

rhetorical question ►*n.* A question to which no answer is expected.

rheum (ro͞om) ►*n.* A watery mucous discharge from the eyes or nose. [< Gk. *rheuma.*] —**rheum′y** *adj.*

rheu·mat·ic (ro͞o-măt′ĭk) ►*adj.* Of or suffering from rheumatism. ►*n.* One who is affected by rheumatism.

rheumatic fever ►*n.* An inflammatory disease occurring as a result of a streptococcal infection, marked by fever, joint pain, and often scarring of the heart valves.

rheu·ma·tism (ro͞o′mə-tĭz′əm) ►*n.* **1.** Any of several pathological conditions of the muscles, tendons, joints, bones, or nerves, marked by pain and disability. **2.** Rheumatoid arthritis. [< Gk. *rheuma,* RHEUM.]

rheu·ma·toid arthritis (ro͞o′mə-toid′) ►*n.* A chronic disease marked by stiffness, inflammation, and deformity of the joints.

Rh factor ►*n.* Any of several substances on the surface of red blood cells that induce a strong antigenic response in individuals lacking the substance. [< RH(ESUS MONKEY).]

Rhine (rīn) A river of W Europe rising in E Switzerland and flowing about 1,320 km (820 mi) through Germany and the Netherlands to the North Sea.

Rhine·land (rīn′lănd′, -lənd) A region along the Rhine R. in W Germany.

rhine·stone (rīn′stōn′) ►*n.* A colorless artificial gem of paste or glass. [< the *Rhine* River.] —**rhine′stoned′** *adj.*

rhi·ni·tis (rī-nī′tĭs) ►*n.* Inflammation of the nasal mucous membranes. [< Gk. *rhis, rhin-,* nose.]

rhi·no (rī′nō) ►*n., pl.* -**nos** A rhinoceros.

rhi·noc·er·os (rī-nŏs′ər-əs) ►*n., pl.* -**os** or -**os·es** A large thick-skinned hoofed mammal of Africa and Asia, having one or two upright horns on the snout. [< Gk. *rhinokerōs.*]

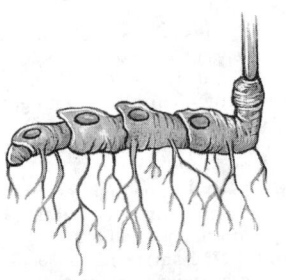

rhizome

rhi·zome (rī′zōm′) ►*n.* A horizontal, usu. underground stem that often sends out roots and shoots. [< Gk. *rhiza,* root.]

Rh-neg·a·tive (är′ăch-nĕg′ə-tĭv) ►*adj.* Lacking an Rh factor.

rho (rō) ►*n.* The 17th letter of the Greek alphabet. [Gk. *rhō.*]

Rhode Island (rōd) A state of the NE US on the Atlantic. Cap. Providence. —**Rhode Is′land·er** *n.*

Rhodes (rōdz) An island of SE Greece, in the Aegean off SW Turkey.

Rho·de·sia (rō-dē′zhə) See **Zimbabwe.** —**Rho·de′sian** *adj. & n.*

rho·di·um (rō′dē-əm) ►*n. Symbol* **Rh** A hard, durable, silvery-white metallic element used to form high-temperature alloys with platinum. At. no. 45. See table at **element.** [< Gk. *rhodon,* rose.]

rho·do·den·dron (rō′də-dĕn′drən) ►*n.* A usu. evergreen ornamental shrub having clusters of variously colored, often bell-shaped flowers. [< Gk., oleander.]

rhom·boid (rŏm′boid′) ►*n.* A parallelogram with unequal adjacent sides.

rhom·bus (rŏm′bəs) ►*n., pl.* -**bus·es** or -**bi** (-bī) An equilateral parallelogram. [< Gk. *rhombos.*]

Rhone or **Rhône** (rōn) A river of SW Switzerland and SE France, flowing about 815 km (505 mi) to the Mediterranean Sea.

rhp ►*abbr.* rated horsepower

Rh-pos·i·tive (är′ăch-pŏz′ĭ-tĭv) ►*adj.* Containing an Rh factor.

rhu·barb (ro͞o′bärb′) ►*n.* **1.** A plant with long edible leafstalks that are usu. cooked and sweetened. **2.** *Informal* A heated dispute; fray. [Prob. < LLat. *rhabarbarum,* foreign rhubarb.]

rhyme (rīm) ►*n.* **1.** Correspondence of terminal sounds of words or of lines of verse. **2.** A poem or poems having such correspondence. **3.** A word that corresponds with another in terminal sound. ►*v.* **rhymed, rhym·ing 1.** To form a rhyme. **2.** To compose rhymes or verse. **3.** To use as a rhyme. [< OFr. *rime.*]

rhythm (rĭth′əm) ►*n.* **1.** Movement or action marked by the regular recurrence of different quantities or conditions. **2.** The patterned, recurring alternations of contrasting elements of sound. **3.** *Mus.* The patterning of musical sound, as by differences in timing, duration, or stress of consecutive notes. **4.** Metrical movement as regulated by the alternation of long and short or accented and unaccented syllables. [< Gk. *rhuthmos.*] —**rhyth′mic, rhyth′mi·cal** *adj.* —**rhyth′mi·cal·ly** *adv.*

rhythm and blues ►*pl.n.* (takes sing. or pl. v.) A kind of music that combines blues and jazz, marked by a strong backbeat.

rhythm method ►*n.* A birth-control method based on abstinence during ovulation.

RI ►*abbr.* Rhode Island

ri·al (rē-ôl′, -äl′) ►*n.* See table at **currency.** [Pers. < Ar. *riyāl.*]

rib (rĭb) ►*n.* **1.** One of a series of long, curved bones extending from the spine to or toward the sternum in most vertebrates. **2.** A cut of meat with one or more rib bones. **3.** Something similar to a rib and serving to shape or support. **4.** *Naut.* A curved member extending upward and outward from a boat or ship's keel to form the framework of the hull. **5.** A raised ridge or wale in fabric. ►*v.* **ribbed, rib·bing 1.** To shape, support, or provide with a rib or ribs. **2.** To make with ridges. **3.** *Informal* To tease or make fun of. [< OE *ribb.*]

rib·ald (rĭb′əld, rĭ′bôld′) ►*adj.* Marked by vulgar, lewd humor. ►*n.* A vulgar, lewdly funny person. [< OFr. *riber,* be wanton.] —**rib′ald·ry** *n.*

rib·bing (rĭb′ĭng) ►*n.* **1.** An arrangement of ribs, as in a boat. **2.** *Informal* The act or an instance of joking or teasing.

rib·bon (rĭb′ən) ►*n.* **1.** A narrow strip or band of fabric, finished at the edges and used for trimming or tying. **2.** Something resembling a ribbon in shape. **3. ribbons** Tattered or ragged strips. **4.** An inked band used for making an impression, as in a typewriter. [< OFr. *ruban,* prob. of Gmc. orig.]

rib cage ►*n.* The structure formed by the ribs and the bones to which they are attached.

ri·bo·fla·vin (rī′bō-flā′vĭn, -bə-) ►*n.* An orange-yellow crystalline compound, the principal growth-promoting factor in the vitamin B complex, found in milk, leafy vegetables, fresh meat, and egg yolks. [RIBO(SE) + Lat. *flāvus,* yellow.]

ri·bo·nu·cle·ic acid (rī′bō-nōō-klē′ĭk, -klā′-, -nyōō-) ►*n.* See **RNA.** [RIBO(SE) + NUCLEIC ACID.]

ri·bose (rī′bōs′) ►*n.* A sugar, $C_5H_{10}O_5$, occurring as a component of riboflavin, nucleotides, and nucleic acids. [Ger.]

ri·bo·some (rī′bə-sōm′) ►*n.* A structure composed of RNA and protein, present in large numbers in the cytoplasm of living cells and active in the synthesis of proteins. [RIBO(SE) + -SOME³.] —**ri′bo·so′mal** *adj.*

Ri·car·do (rĭ-kär′dō), **David** 1772–1823. British economist.

rice (rīs) ►*n.* **1.** A cereal grass cultivated extensively in warm climates. **2.** The starchy edible grain of this plant. [< Gk. *oruza.*]

Rice, Condoleezza b. 1954. Amer. public official; US secretary of state (2005–09).

rich (rĭch) ►*adj.* **-er, -est 1.** Having great material wealth. **2.** Having great worth or value: *a rich harvest.* **3.** Magnificent; sumptuous. **4a.** Abundant: *rich in ideas.* **b.** Abounding, esp. in natural resources: *a rich land.* **5.** Very productive: *rich soil.* **6a.** Containing a large amount of choice ingredients, such as butter, sugar, or eggs. **b.** Strongly aromatic: *a rich coffee.* **7a.** Pleasantly full and mellow: *a rich tenor voice.* **b.** Warm and strong in color. **8.** Containing a large proportion of fuel to air: *a rich gas mixture.* **9.** *Informal* Highly amusing. [< OFr. *riche* and OE *rīce.*] —**rich′ly** *adv.* —**rich′ness** *n.*

Syns: affluent, moneyed, wealthy adj.

Rich·ard I (rĭch′ərd) "the Lion-Hearted." 1157–99. King of England (1189–99).

Richard II 1367–1400. King of England (1377–99); deposed.

Richard III 1452–85. King of England (1483–85).

Ri·che·lieu (rĭsh′ə-lōō′, rē-shə-lyœ′), Duc de. 1585–1642. French cardinal and politician.

rich·es (rĭch′ĭz) ►*pl.n.* Valuable or precious possessions. [< OFr. *richesse.*]

Rich·mond (rĭch′mənd) The capital of VA, in the E-central part on the James R.

Rich·ter scale (rĭk′tər) ►*n.* A logarithmic scale usu. ranging from 0 to 9, used to express an

earthquake's magnitude. [After Charles F. *Richter* (1900–1985).]

rick (rĭk) ►*n.* A stack, as of hay or straw, esp. when covered. [< OE *hrēac.*]

rick·ets (rĭk′ĭts) ►*n. (takes sing. or pl. v.)* A disease of children marked by bone loss and defective bone growth, caused usu. by a deficiency of vitamin D. [?]

rick·et·y (rĭk′ĭ-tē) ►*adj.* **-i·er, -i·est 1.** Likely to break or fall apart; shaky. **2.** Of, having, or resembling rickets. [< RICKETS.] —**rick′et·i·ness** *n.*

rick·ey (rĭk′ē) ►*n., pl.* **-eys** A drink of soda water, lime or lemon juice, sugar, and usu. gin. [Prob. < the name *Rickey.*]

rick·sha or **rick·shaw** (rĭk′shô) ►*n.* A jinriksha.

ric·o·chet (rĭk′ə-shā′, rĭk′ə-shā′) ►*v.* **-cheted** (-shād′), **-chet·ing** (-shā′ĭng) To rebound from a surface. [Fr.] —**ric′o·chet′** *n.*

ri·cot·ta (rĭ-kŏt′ə) ►*n.* A soft, unripened cheese made from whey. [Ital.]

rid (rĭd) ►*v.* **rid** or **rid·ded, rid·ding** To cause (someone) to be free from something; relieve. —*idiom:* **get rid of** To discard or get free of (something). [< ON *rydhja,* clear land.] —**rid′dance** *n.*

rid·dle¹ (rĭd′l) ►*v.* **-dled, -dling 1.** To pierce with numerous holes; perforate. **2.** To spread throughout. [< OE *hriddel,* sieve.]

rid·dle² (rĭd′l) ►*n.* **1.** A puzzling question or statement requiring thought to answer or understand. **2.** One that is perplexing; enigma. ►*v.* **-dled, -dling** To solve or explain. [< OE *rǣdels.*] —**rid′dler** *n.*

ride (rīd) ►*v.* **rode** (rōd), **rid·den** (rĭd′n), **rid·ing 1a.** To be carried or conveyed, as in a vehicle or on horseback. **b.** To participate in a board sport such as snowboarding. **2.** To travel over a surface: *This car rides well.* **3.** To move on water. **4.** To be sustained or supported as on a pivot or an axle. **5.** To be contingent; depend. **6.** To continue without interference: *Let the matter ride.* **7.** To sit on and control the movement of: *rode my bike to town.* **8.** To take part in or do by riding: *He rode his last race.* **9.** To cause to be carried. ►*n.* **1.** The act or an instance of riding. **2.** A path made for riding. **3.** A device, as at an amusement park, that one rides for pleasure or excitement. **4.** A means of transportation: *waiting for my ride to come.* —*phrasal verb:* **ride out** To survive or outlast. [< OE *rīdan.*]

Ride, Sally Kristen 1951–2012. Amer. astronaut; the first US woman in space (1983).

Sally Ride
photographed in 1984

rid·er (rī′dər) ►*n.* **1.** One that rides. **2.** An unrelated provision added to a legislative bill.

rid·er·ship (rī′dər-shĭp′) ►*n.* The number of people who ride a public transport system.

ridge (rĭj) ►*n.* **1.** A long narrow upper section or crest: *the ridge of a wave.* **2.** A long narrow elevated section of the earth's surface, such as a chain of hills or mountains. **3.** A long, narrow or crested part of the body: *the ridge of the nose.* **4.** The horizontal line formed by the juncture of two sloping planes, esp. the line formed by the surfaces at the top of a roof. **5.** A narrow, raised strip, as in cloth or on plowed ground. ►*v.* **ridged, ridg·ing** To mark with, form into, or provide with ridges. [< OE *hrycg.*]

ridge·pole (rĭj′pōl′) ►*n.* A horizontal beam at the ridge of a roof to which the rafters are attached.

rid·i·cule (rĭd′ĭ-kyool′) ►*n.* **1.** The act of using words, gestures, images, or other products of expression to evoke contemptuous feelings regarding a person or thing. **2.** The words or other products of expression used in this way. ►*v.* **-culed, -cul·ing** To make fun of. [< Lat. *ridiculus,* laughable.]

ri·dic·u·lous (rĭ-dĭk′yə-ləs) ►*adj.* Deserving or inspiring ridicule. See Synonyms at **fool·ish.** —**ri·dic′u·lous·ly** *adv.* —**ri·dic′u·lous·ness** *n.*

ri·el (rē-ĕl′) ►*n.* See table at **currency.** [?]

rife (rīf) ►*adj.* **rif·er, rif·est 1.** Widespread; prevalent. **2.** Abounding; full. [< OE *rȳfe.*]

riff (rĭf) ►*n. Mus.* A short rhythmic phrase, esp. one repeated in improvisation. [?]

riff·raff (rĭf′răf′) ►*n.* **1.** Disreputable or worthless people. **2.** Rubbish; trash. [< AN *rif et raf,* one and all.]

ri·fle[1] (rī′fəl) ►*n.* A firearm with a rifled bore, designed to be fired from the shoulder. ►*v.* **-fled, -fling** To cut spiral grooves within. [< OFr. *rifler,* scratch.]

ri·fle[2] (rī′fəl) ►*v.* **-fled, -fling 1.** To search (e.g., an area or container), esp. with the intent to steal or remove something. **2.** To rob: *rifle a safe.* [< OFr. *rifler,* plunder.] —**ri′fler** *n.*

ri·fle·ry (rī′fəl-rē) ►*n.* The skill and practice of shooting a rifle.

ri·fling (rī′flĭng) ►*n.* Grooves cut in a rifle barrel.

rift (rĭft) ►*n.* **1.** A fissure or opening, as in rock. **2.** A break in friendly relations. ►*v.* To split or cause to split open. [ME, of Scand. orig.]

rig (rĭg) ►*v.* **rigged, rig·ging 1.** To equip; fit out. **2.** To equip (a ship) with rigging. **3.** *Informal* To dress, clothe, or adorn. **4.** To construct in haste or in a makeshift manner. **5.** To manipulate dishonestly for personal gain: *rig a prizefight.* ►*n.* **1.** The arrangement of masts, spars, and sails on a sailing vessel. **2.** Gear used for a particular purpose. **3a.** A truck, tractor, or tractor-trailer. **b.** A vehicle with its horses. [ME *riggen.*]

Ri·ga (rē′gə) The capital of Latvia, in the central part on the **Gulf of Riga,** an inlet of the Baltic Sea.

rig·a·ma·role (rĭg′ə-mə-rōl′) ►*n.* Var. of **rig·marole.**

rig·ging (rĭg′ĭng) ►*n.* **1.** The system of ropes, chains, and tackle used to support and control the masts, sails, and yards of a sailing vessel. **2.** The supporting material for construction work.

right (rīt) ►*adj.* **-er, -est 1.** Conforming with justice or morality. **2.** In accordance with fact, reason, or truth; correct. **3.** Fitting, proper, or appropriate. **4.** Favorable, desirable, or convenient. **5.** In or into a satisfactory state or condition. **6.** Intended to be worn or positioned facing outward: *the right side of the medallion.* **7.** Of, located on, or corresponding to the side of the body to the south when one is facing east. **8.** Located on the right side of a person facing downstream: *the right bank of the river.* **9.** often **Right** Of or belonging to the political right. **10.** *Math.* **a.** Formed by or in reference to a line or plane that is perpendicular to another line or plane. **b.** Having a right angle: *a right triangle.* ►*n.* **1.** That which is just, moral, or proper. **2a.** The direction or position on the right side. **b.** The right side. **c.** The right hand. **d.** A turn in this direction: *make a right.* **3.** often **Right** The people and groups who pursue conservative or reactionary political goals. **4.** Something due to a person or governmental body by law, tradition, or nature. ►*adv.* **1.** Toward or on the right. **2.** In a straight line; directly. **3.** In the proper or desired manner. **4.** Exactly; just: *right over there.* **5.** Immediately: *right after dinner.* **6.** Used as an intensive: *kept right on going.* **7.** Used in titles: *The Right Reverend Pat Smith.* ►*v.* **1.** To put in or restore to an upright or proper position. **2.** To put in order or set right; correct. **3.** To redress: *right a wrong.* —*idioms:* **by rights** In a just or proper manner; justly. **to rights** In a satisfactory or orderly condition. [< OE *riht.*] —**right′er** *n.* —**right′ness** *n.*

right angle ►*n.* An angle of 90° formed by two intersecting perpendicular lines. —**right′-an′gled** *adj.*

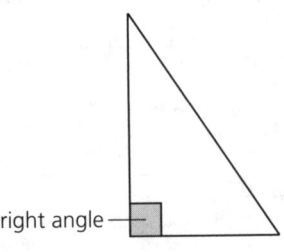

right angle

right angle

right-click (rīt′klĭk′) *Comp.* ►*v.* To click the secondary button of (a mouse).

right·eous (rī′chəs) ►*adj.* Morally upright; just. [< OE *rihtwīs.*] —**right′eous·ly** *adv.* —**right′eous·ness** *n.*

right field ►*n. Baseball* The third of the outfield that is to the right as viewed from home plate. —**right field′er** *n.*

right·ful (rīt′fəl) ►*adj.* **1.** Right or proper; just. **2.** Having or held by a rightful claim. —**right′ful·ly** *adv.* —**right′ful·ness** *n.*

right-hand (rīt′hănd′) ►*adj.* **1.** Relating to or located on the right. **2.** Designed for or done with the right hand. **3.** Indispensable; reliable.

right-hand·ed (rīt′hăn′dĭd) ►*adj.* **1.** Using the right hand more skillfully or easily than the left. **2.** Done with or made for the right hand. **3.** Clockwise. ►*adv.* With the right hand. —**right′-hand′ed·ly** *adv.* —**right′-hand′ed·ness** *n.*

right-hand·er (rīt′hăn′dər) ►*n.* One who is right-handed.

right·ism also **Right·ism** (rī′tĭz′əm) ►*n.* The ideology of the political right. —**right′ist** *n.*

right·ly (rīt′lē) ►*adv.* **1.** In a correct manner; properly. **2.** With honesty; justly.

right of way also **right-of-way** (rīt′əv-wā′) ►*n., pl.* **rights of way** or **right of ways** **1a.** The right to pass over property owned by another. **b.** The path or thoroughfare on which such passage is made. **2.** The strip of land over which facilities such as highways, railroads, or power lines are built. **3.** The customary or legal right of a person, vessel, or vehicle to pass in front of another.

right-on (rīt′ŏn′, -ôn′) ►*adj. Slang* **1.** Up-to-date and sophisticated. **2.** Absolutely right.

right-to-life (rīt′tə-līf′) ►*adj.* Pro-life.

right whale ►*n.* Any of several large baleen whales, marked by a large head with an arched upper jaw and no dorsal fin.

right wing ►*n.* **1.** The conservative or reactionary faction of a group. **2.** See **right** (sense 3). —**right′-wing′** *adj.* —**right′-wing′er** *n.*

rig·id (rĭj′ĭd) ►*adj.* **1.** Not flexible or pliant; stiff. **2.** Not moving; fixed. **3.** Rigorous or harsh. [Lat. *rigidus.*] —**rig′id·ly** *adv.* —**ri·gid′i·ty** *n.*

rig·ma·role (rĭg′mə-rōl′) also **rig·a·ma·role** (-ə-mə-rōl′) ►*n.* **1.** Confused or rambling discourse; nonsense. **2.** A complicated, petty procedure. [< ME *ragmane rolle*, scroll used in a game of chance.]

rig·or (rĭg′ər) ►*n.* **1.** Strictness or severity, as in action or judgment. **2.** A harsh or trying circumstance; hardship. See Synonyms at **difficulty. 3.** Strictness in adhering to standards or a method; exactitude. **4.** Shivering or trembling, as caused by a chill. [< Lat.] —**rig′or·ous** *adj.* —**rig′or·ous·ly** *adv.*

rigor mor·tis (môr′tĭs) ►*n.* Muscular stiffening after death. [Lat., stiffness of death.]

rile (rīl) ►*v.* **riled, ril·ing** To stir to anger; irritate. See Synonyms at **annoy.** [Var. of ROIL.]

Ril·ke (rĭl′kə), **Rainer Maria** 1875–1926. German poet.

rill (rĭl) ►*n.* A small brook. [LGer. *rille.*]

rim (rĭm) ►*n.* **1.** The border or edge of an object. **2.** The circular outer part of a wheel. ►*v.* **rimmed, rim·ming** To furnish with a rim. [< OE *rima.*]

rime (rīm) ►*n.* A white incrustation of ice formed when supercooled water droplets freeze. [< OE *hrīm.*] —**rime** *v.* —**rim′y** *adj.*

Rim·sky-Kor·sa·kov (rĭm′skē-kôr′sə-kôf′), **Nikolai Andreyevich** 1844–1908. Russian composer.

rind (rīnd) ►*n.* A tough outer covering such as bark or the skin of some fruits. [< OE.]

ring¹ (rĭng) ►*n.* **1.** A circular object, form, line, or arrangement. **2.** A small circular band, often of precious metal, worn on the finger. **3.** An enclosed area in which exhibitions or contests take place. **4.** A group of people acting to advance their interests. ►*v.* **1.** To surround with or as if with a ring; encircle. **2.** To form into a ring or rings. [< OE *hring.*]

ring² (rĭng) ►*v.* **rang** (răng), **rung** (rŭng), **ring·ing 1.** To give forth a clear, resonant sound. **2.** To cause something to ring. **3.** To sound a bell to summon someone. **4.** To have a character suggestive of a particular quality: *a story that rings true.* **5.** To be filled with sound; resound. **6.** To hear a persistent humming or buzzing: *My ears were ringing from the blast.* **7.** To call (someone) on the telephone. ►*n.* **1.** The sound created by or as if by a bell. **2.** A loud sound that is repeated or continued. **3.** A telephone call. **4.** A suggestion of a quality. —*phrasal verb:* **ring up** To record, esp. by means of a cash register. —*idiom:* **ring a bell** *Informal* To arouse an often indistinct memory. [< OE *hringan.*]

ring·er (rĭng′ər) ►*n.* **1.** One that rings, esp. one that sounds a bell or chime. **2.** *Slang* A contestant entered dishonestly into a competition. **3.** *Slang* One who bears a striking resemblance to another.

ring·git (rĭng′gĭt) ►*n.* See table at **currency.** [Malay.]

ring·lead·er (rĭng′lē′dər) ►*n.* A leader, esp. of a group involved in illicit activities.

ring·let (rĭng′lĭt) ►*n.* **1.** A curled lock of hair. **2.** A small circle or ring.

ring·mas·ter (rĭng′măs′tər) ►*n.* A person in charge of the performances in a circus ring.

ring·side (rĭng′sīd′) ►*n.* The area or seats immediately outside an arena or a ring.

ring·worm (rĭng′wûrm′) ►*n.* A contagious skin disease caused by a fungi and marked by ring-shaped, scaly, itching patches.

rink (rĭngk) ►*n.* **1.** An area surfaced with smooth ice for skating. **2.** A smooth floor suited for roller-skating. [< OFr. *renc*, line, of Gmc. orig.]

rinse (rĭns) ►*v.* **rinsed, rins·ing 1.** To wash lightly, as with water. **2.** To remove (e.g., soap) by flushing with water. ►*n.* **1.** The act of rinsing. **2.** The liquid used in rinsing. **3.** A solution used in coloring or conditioning the hair. [< Lat. *recēns*, fresh.]

Ri·o de Ja·nei·ro (rē′ō dā zhə-nâr′ō, dē-) A city of SE Brazil on an inlet of the Atlantic.

Ri·o Grande (rē′ō grănd′, grän′dē) A river, about 3,000 km (1,900 mi), rising in SW CO and flowing to the Gulf of Mexico, forming much of the US-Mexico border.

ri·ot (rī′ət) ►*n.* **1.** A public uproar or disturbance. **2.** An unrestrained outbreak, as of laughter or passions. **3.** A profusion. **4.** *Slang* An irresistibly funny person or thing. ►*v.* **1.** To take part in a riot. **2.** To engage in uncontrolled revelry. [< OFr. *rioter*, quarrel.] —**ri′ot·er** *n.*

ri·ot·ous (rī′ət-əs) ►*adj.* **1.** Of or resembling a riot. **2.** Participating in or inciting to riot. **3.** Uproarious; boisterous. **4.** Dissolute; wanton: *riotous living.* **5.** Abundant or luxuriant: *a riotous growth.* —**ri′ot·ous·ly** *adv.* —**ri′ot·ous·ness** *n.*

rip (rĭp) ►*v.* **ripped, rip·ping 1.** To tear apart or become torn apart, esp. roughly or energetically. **2.** To split or saw (wood) along the grain. **3.** *Informal* To move quickly or violently. ►*n.* **1.** The act of ripping. **2.** A torn or split place; tear. —*phrasal verb:* **rip off** *Slang* **1.** To steal or steal from. **2.** To exploit, swindle, or defraud. [< Flem. *rippen.*] —**rip′per** *n.*

RIP ►*abbr. Lat.* requiescat in pace (may he rest in peace; may she rest in peace.)

ri·par·i·an (rĭ-pâr′ē-ən) ►*adj.* Of or relating to the banks of a natural course of water. [< Lat. *rīpa*, bank.]

rip·cord (rĭp′kôrd′) ►*n.* A cord pulled to release a parachute from its pack.

ripe (rīp) ►*adj.* **rip·er, rip·est 1.** Fully developed; mature: *ripe peaches.* **2.** Fully prepared; ready. **3.** Sufficiently advanced. [< OE *rīpe.*] —**ripe′ly** *adv.* —**rip′en** *v.* —**ripe′ness** *n.*

rip-off (rĭp′ôf′, -ŏf′) ►*n. Slang* **1.** A product or service that is overpriced or of poor quality. **2.** Something clearly imitative of or based on something else. **3.** A theft. **4.** An act of exploitation.

ri·poste (rĭ-pōst′) ►*n.* **1.** A quick thrust given after parrying an opponent's lunge in fencing. **2.** A retaliatory action or retort. [< Ital. *risposta,* an answer.] —**ri·poste** *v.*

rip·ple (rĭp′əl) ►*v.* **-pled, -pling 1.** To form or display small waves on the surface. **2.** To rise and fall gently in tone or volume. ►*n.* **1.** A small wave or wavelike motion. **2.** A sound like that made by rippling water: *a ripple of laughter.* [ME *ripplen,* wrinkle.]

rip·saw (rĭp′sô′) ►*n.* A coarse-toothed saw used for cutting wood along the grain.

rip tide ►*n.* A strong surface current flowing away from shore.

rise (rīz) ►*v.* **rose** (rōz), **ris·en** (rĭz′ən), **ris·ing 1.** To stand up after lying, sitting, or kneeling. **2.** To get out of bed. **3.** To move from a lower to a higher position. **4.** To increase in size, volume, or level. **5.** To increase in number, amount, or value. **6.** To increase in intensity, force, or speed. **7.** To increase in pitch or volume. **8.** To ascend above the horizon. **9.** To slope or extend upward. **10.** To come into existence; originate. See Synonyms at **stem**[1]. **11.** To attain a higher status. **12.** To return to life. **13.** To rebel. ►*n.* **1.** The act of rising; ascent. **2.** The first appearance of a celestial object as it ascends above the horizon. **3.** An increase in height, as of the level of water. **4.** A gently sloped hill. **5.** An origin, beginning, or source. See Synonyms at **beginning. 6.** An increase in price, worth, quantity, or degree. **7.** An increase in intensity, volume, or pitch. **8.** Elevation in status, prosperity, or importance. **9.** *Informal* An angry or irritated reaction. [< OE *rīsan.*]

ris·er (rī′zər) ►*n.* **1.** One who rises, esp. from sleep. **2.** The vertical part of a stair step.

ris·i·ble (rĭz′ə-bəl) ►*adj.* **1.** Eliciting laughter. **2.** Capable of laughing or inclined to laugh. [< Lat. *rīsus,* p.part. of *rīdēre,* laugh.] —**ris′i·bil′i·ty** (-bĭl′ĭ-tē) *n.* —**ris′i·bly** *adv.*

risk (rĭsk) ►*n.* **1.** The possibility of suffering harm or loss; danger. **2.** A factor, element, or course involving uncertain danger. ►*v.* **1.** To expose to a chance of loss or damage. **2.** To incur the risk of. See Synonyms at **endanger.** [< Ital. *risco.*] —**risk′i·ness** *n.* —**risk′y** *adj.*

ri·sot·to (rĭ-sô′tō, rē-zôt′tō) ►*n., pl.* **-tos** A dish of rice cooked in stock, often with mushrooms and Parmesan cheese. [Ital. < *riso,* rice.]

ris·qué (rĭs-kā′) ►*adj.* Suggestive of or bordering on indelicacy or impropriety. [Fr. < *risquer,* risk.]

ri·stra (rē′strə) ►*n.* A string on which foodstuffs, such as chilies, are threaded for storage. [< Lat. *restis,* cord.]

rite (rīt) ►*n.* **1.** The prescribed form for conducting a religious or other solemn ceremony. **2.** A ceremonial act. [< Lat. *rītus.*]

rit·u·al (rĭch′ōō-əl) ►*n.* **1.** The prescribed form of a ceremony. **2.** A set of actions that are conducted routinely in the same manner: *a*

morning ritual. [< Lat. *rītuālis,* of rites.] —**rit′u·al·ism** *n.* —**rit′u·al·is′tic** *adj.* —**rit′u·al·ize′** *v.* —**rit′u·al·ly** *adv.*

ritz·y (rĭt′sē) ►*adj.* **-i·er, -i·est** *Informal* Elegant; fancy. [After the *Ritz,* hotels.]

ri·val (rī′vəl) ►*n.* **1.** One who attempts to equal or surpass another; competitor. **2.** One that equals another in a particular respect. ►*v.* **-valed, -val·ing** or **-valled, -val·ling 1.** To attempt to equal or surpass. **2.** To be the equal of; match. [Lat. *rīvālis,* one who shares a stream.] —**ri′val** *adj.* —**ri′val·ry** *n.*

rive (rīv) ►*v.* **rived, riv·en** (rĭv′ən) also **rived, riv·ing 1.** To rend or tear apart. **2.** To cleave or split into pieces. [< ON *rīfa.*]

riv·er (rĭv′ər) ►*n.* A large natural stream of water. [< Lat. *rīpāria.*]

Ri·ve·ra (rĭ-vĕr′ə, rē-vĕ′rä), **Diego** 1886–1957. Mexican painter.

riv·er·bed (rĭv′ər-bĕd′) ►*n.* The area between the banks of a river ordinarily covered by water.

riv·er·boat (rĭv′ər-bōt′) ►*n.* A boat for use on a river.

riv·er·side (rĭv′ər-sīd′) ►*n.* The bank or area alongside a river. —**riv′er·side** *adj.*

riv·et (rĭv′ĭt) ►*n.* A metal bolt or pin having a head on one end, inserted through the pieces to be joined and then hammered on the plain end to form a second head. ►*v.* **1.** To fasten or secure with or as if with a rivet. **2.** To engross or hold (e.g., the attention). [< OFr. *river,* attach.] —**riv′et·er** *n.*

Riv·i·er·a (rĭv′ē-ĕr′ə, rē-vyĕ′rä) A coastal region between the Alps and the Mediterranean from SE France to NW Italy.

riv·u·let (rĭv′yə-lĭt) ►*n.* A small brook or stream. [< Lat. *rīvulus,* small stream.]

Ri·yadh (rē-yäd′) The capital of Saudi Arabia, in the E-central part.

ri·yal (rē-ôl′, -äl′) ►*n.* See table at **currency.** [Ar. *riyāl.*]

rm. ►*abbr.* room

RN ►*abbr.* **1.** registered nurse **2.** Royal Navy

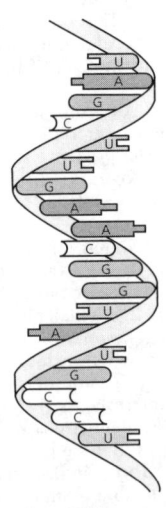

RNA
A. adenine; U. uracil;
C. cytosine; G. guanine

RNA (är′ĕn-ā′) ►*n.* A nucleic acid that is involved in protein synthesis and sometimes in the transmission of genetic information in cells and many viruses, consisting of a long usu. single-stranded chain of nucleotides. [R(IBO) N(UCLEIC) A(CID).]

roach[1] (rōch) ►*n., pl.* **roach** or **-es** An edible freshwater fish of N Europe. [< OFr. *roche*.]

roach[2] (rōch) ►*n., pl.* **roach·es** A cockroach.

road (rōd) ►*n.* **1.** An open, usu. public way for the passage of vehicles, people, and animals. **2.** A course or path. —*idiom:* **on the road** Traveling. [< OE *rād*, a riding.]

road·bed (rōd′bĕd′) ►*n.* **1.** The foundation upon which railroad tracks are laid. **2.** The foundation and surface of a road.

road·block (rōd′blŏk′) ►*n.* **1.** A blockade set across a road. **2.** Something that prevents progress; obstacle.

road·house (rōd′hous′) ►*n.* An inn, restaurant, or nightclub located on a road outside a city.

road·kill (rōd′kĭl′) ►*n.* An animal or animals killed by a car.

road·run·ner (rōd′rŭn′ər) ►*n.* A swift-running, ground-dwelling bird of North and Central America, having streaked brownish plumage and a brown and black crest.

road show ►*n.* A show presented by traveling performers.

road·side (rōd′sīd′) ►*n.* The area bordering a road. —**road′side′** *adj.*

road·ster (rōd′stər) ►*n.* An often roofless or convertible automobile having a single seat in the front for two or three people and a rumble seat or luggage compartment in the back.

Road Town The capital of the British Virgin Is., on Tortola I. in the West Indies.

road·way (rōd′wā′) ►*n.* A road, esp. the part over which vehicles travel.

road·work (rōd′wûrk′) ►*n.* **1.** Road construction or repair. **2.** Outdoor long-distance running as a form of exercise or conditioning.

roam (rōm) ►*v.* To move about without purpose; wander. [ME *romen*.] —**roam′er** *n.*

roan (rōn) ►*adj.* Having a chestnut, bay, or sorrel coat thickly sprinkled with white or gray: *a roan horse.* ►*n.* A roan animal. [< OSpan. *roano*.]

Ro·a·noke Island (rō′ə-nōk′) An island off the NE coast of NC, where Sir Walter Raleigh attempted to found the first English settlement in North America (1585).

roar (rôr) ►*v.* **1.** To utter a loud, deep, prolonged sound, as in rage or excitement. See Synonyms at **yell. 2.** To laugh loudly or excitedly. **3.** To make or produce a loud noise or din: *The engines roared.* [< OE *rārian*.] —**roar** *n.*

roast (rōst) ►*v.* **1.** To cook with dry heat, as in an oven. **2.** To expose to great or excessive heat. **3.** To heat (ores) in order to dehydrate, purify, or oxidize. **4.** *Informal* To ridicule or criticize harshly. ►*n.* **1.** A cut of meat suitable for roasting. **2.** An outing at which food is roasted. ►*adj.* Roasted. [< OFr. *rostir*.] —**roast′er** *n.*

rob (rŏb) ►*v.* **robbed, rob·bing 1.** To steal (from) esp. by using or threatening to use force. **2.** To deprive of something. [< OFr. *rober.*] —**rob′ber** *n.* —**rob′ber·y** *n.*

robe (rōb) ►*n.* **1.** A long, loose, flowing outer garment, esp. one worn to show office or rank. **2.** A dressing gown or bathrobe. **3.** A blanket for the lap or legs. ►*v.* **robed, rob·ing** To dress in or as if in a robe. [< OFr., of Gmc. orig.]

Rob·ert I (rŏb′ərt) "the Bruce." 1274–1329. King of Scotland (1306–29).

Rob·erts (rŏb′ərts), **John Glover, Jr.** b. 1955. Amer. jurist; chief justice of the US Supreme Court (appointed 2005).

Robe·son (rōb′sən), **Paul Bustill** 1898–1976. Amer. actor and singer.

rob·in (rŏb′ĭn) ►*n.* **1.** A North American songbird having a rust-red breast and gray and black upper plumage. **2.** A small songbird of Eurasia and Africa having an orange breast and face. [< the name *Robin*.]

Robinson, Jack Roosevelt "Jackie." 1919–72. Amer. baseball player.

Jackie Robinson

ro·bot (rō′bŏt′) ►*n.* **1.** A mechanical device, sometimes resembling a human, capable of performing often complex tasks. **2.** A device that operates automatically or by remote control. **3.** A person who works or follows orders mechanically. [Czech < *robota*, drudgery.] —**ro·bot′ic** *adj.*

ro·bot·ics (rō-bŏt′ĭks) ►*n. (takes sing. v.)* The science and technology of robotic design.

ro·bust (rō-bŭst′, rō′bŭst′) ►*adj.* **1.** Full of health and strength; vigorous. **2.** Powerfully built; sturdy: *a robust body.* **3a.** Active or dynamic: *a robust debate.* **b.** Working in an effective way. **4.** Marked by richness and fullness: *a robust wine.* **5.** Substantial in amount: *robust gains in stock prices.* [< Lat. *rōbus*, oak, strength.] —**ro·bust′ly** *adv.* —**ro·bust′ness** *n.*

Roch·es·ter (rŏch′ĭ-stər, -ĕs′tər) A city of W NY ENE of Buffalo.

rock[1] (rŏk) ►*n.* **1.** Relatively hard, naturally formed mineral or petrified matter. **2.** A fragment or body of such material. **3.** A naturally formed aggregate of mineral matter making up much of the earth's crust. **4.** One that is stable, firm, or dependable. **5.** *Slang* A large gem, esp. a diamond. —*idiom:* **on the rocks 1.** In a state of difficulty or ruin. **2.** Served over ice cubes. [< VLat. **rocca*.]

rock[2] (rŏk) ►*v.* **1.** To move back and forth or from side to side, esp. gently or rhythmically. **2.** To shake or cause to shake violently. See Synonyms at **agitate. 3.** To play or dance to rock music. ►*n.* **1.** A rocking motion. **2.** A form of popular music arising esp. from rhythm and blues, country music, and gospel and marked by amplified instrumentation and a heavily accented beat. [< OE *roccian*.]

rock-and-roll (rŏk′ən-rōl′) or **rock 'n' roll** (rŏk′ən-rōl′) ►*n.* See **rock**[2] (sense 2).

rock bottom ▸*n.* The lowest possible level.

rock·bound also **rock-bound** (rŏk′bound′) ▸*adj.* Hemmed in by or bordered with rocks.

Rock·e·fel·ler (rŏk′ə-fĕl′ər) Amer. family of business executives, politicians, and philanthropists, including **John Davison** (1839–1937), **John Davison, Jr.** (1874–1960), and **Nelson Aldrich** (1908–79).

rock·er (rŏk′ər) ▸*n.* **1.** A rocking chair. **2.** One of the two curved pieces upon which something rocks. **3.** A rock song, fan, or musician. —*idiom:* **off (one's) rocker** *Slang* Out of one's mind; crazy.

rock·et¹ (rŏk′ĭt) ▸*n.* **1.** An engine that propels by the ejection of matter, esp. by the high-velocity ejection of gaseous combustion products. **2.** A device, such as a craft or projectile weapon, propelled by one or more rocket engines. ▸*v.* To move swiftly and powerfully, as a rocket. [Ital. *rocchetta,* dim. of *rocca,* spindle.]

rock·et² (rŏk′ĭt) ▸*n.* See **arugula.** [< Ital. *rochetta.*]

rock·et·ry (rŏk′ĭ-trē) ▸*n.* The science and technology of rocket design, construction, and flight.

rocket ship ▸*n.* A spacecraft propelled by rockets.

rock·ing chair (rŏk′ĭng) ▸*n.* A chair mounted on rockers or springs.

rocking horse ▸*n.* A toy horse mounted on rockers or springs.

rock 'n' roll (rŏk′ən-rōl′) ▸*n.* Var. of **rock-and-roll.**

rock salt ▸*n.* Rock containing sodium chloride as its main constituent.

Rock·well (rŏk′wĕl′), **Norman** 1894–1978. Amer. illustrator.

rock wool ▸*n.* See **mineral wool.**

rock·y¹ (rŏk′ē) ▸*adj.* **-i·er, -i·est 1.** Consisting of or abounding in rocks. **2.** Resembling or suggesting rock; unyielding. **3.** Marked by difficulties. —**rock′i·ness** *n.*

rock·y² (rŏk′ē) ▸*adj.* **-i·er, -i·est** Inclined to sway or totter; unsteady or shaky.

Rocky Mountains A mountain system of W North America extending more than 4,800 km (3,000 mi) from NW Alaska to the Mexican border.

ro·co·co also **Ro·co·co** (rə-kō′kō, rō′kə-kō′) ▸*n.* A style of art, esp. architecture and decorative art, originating in France in the early 18th cent. and marked by elaborate and fanciful ornamentation. ▸*adj.* **1.** Of the rococo. **2.** Overly elaborate or complicated. [Fr.]

rod (rŏd) ▸*n.* **1.** A thin straight stick or bar, such as: **a.** A fishing rod. **b.** A lightning rod. **c.** A stick used for measuring. **2a.** A stick used to punish by whipping. **b.** Punishment. **3.** A scepter or wand symbolizing authority. **4.** See table at **measurement. 5.** A rod-shaped cell in the retina that responds to dim light. **6.** *Slang* A handgun. [< OE *rodd.*]

rode (rōd) ▸*v.* P.t. of **ride.**

ro·dent (rōd′nt) ▸*n.* Any of an order of mammals, including the mouse, rat, squirrel, and beaver, with large incisors used for gnawing or nibbling. [< Lat. *rōdere,* gnaw.]

ro·de·o (rō′dē-ō′, rō-dā′ō) ▸*n., pl.* **-os 1.** A competition or exhibition of skills such as riding broncos or roping calves. **2.** A cattle roundup. [Sp. < *rodear,* surround.]

rodeo

Rod·gers (rŏj′ərz), **Richard** 1902–79. Amer. composer.

Ro·din (rō-dăn′, -dăɴ′), **François Auguste René** 1840–1917. French sculptor.

roe (rō) ▸*n.* The eggs or spawn of a fish. [ME *row.*]

roe deer ▸*n.* A small Eurasian deer having a brownish coat, a black nose, and three- to four-tiered antlers in the male. [< OE *rā.*]

roent·gen (rĕnt′gən, -jən, rŭnt′-) ▸*n.* A unit of exposure to ionizing radiation, such as x-rays or gamma rays. [After Wilhelm Konrad Roentgen.] —**roent′gen** *adj.*

Roentgen, Wilhelm Konrad 1845–1923. German physicist.

roent·gen·i·um (rĕnt-gĕn′ē-əm, -jĕn′- rŭnt-) ▸*n. Symbol* **Rg** A short-lived, synthetic radioactive element. At. no. 111. See table at **element.** [After Wilhelm Konrad Roentgen.]

Roeth·ke (rĕt′kē, -kə, rĕth′-), **Theodore** 1908–63. Amer. poet.

rog·er (rŏj′ər) ▸*interj.* Used esp. in radio communications to indicate receipt of a message. [< *Roger,* spoken representation of the letter *r,* short for *received.*]

Rog·ers (rŏj′ərz), **Ginger** Virginia McMath. 1911–95. Amer. dancer and actress.

Ro·get (rō-zhā′, rō′zhā), **Peter Mark** 1779–1869. British physician and scholar.

rogue (rōg) ▸*n.* **1.** An unprincipled person. **2.** One who is playfully mischievous. ▸*adj.* **1.** Large and unpredictable: *rogue tornado.* **2.** Operating outside normal or desirable controls. [?] —**rogu′er·y** *n.* —**rogu′ish** *adj.*

roil (roil) ▸*v.* **1.** To make muddy or cloudy by stirring up sediment. **2.** To be or cause to be in a state of agitation or disorder. **3.** To put in a state of emotional agitation; rile or upset. [?]

role also **rôle** (rōl) ▸*n.* **1.** A character or part played by a performer. **2.** A function: *his role in the coup.* See Synonyms at **function.** [< OFr. *rolle,* roll of parchment.]

role model ▸*n.* A person whose behavior serves as a model for another person.

roll (rōl) ▸*v.* **1.** To move or cause to move by repeatedly turning over. **2.** To move or push on wheels or rollers. **3.** To start to move or operate: *The cameras were rolling.* **4.** To gain momentum. **5.** To turn around; revolve or rotate. **6.** To advance with a rising and falling motion, as waves. **7.** To move or rock from side to side, as a ship. **8.** To make a deep rumbling sound, as thunder. **9.** To pronounce with a trill: *roll one's r's.* **10.** To wrap something around itself or something else: *roll up a rug.* **11.** To envelop or enfold in a covering. **12.** To spread or flatten by applying pressure with a roller. **13.** *Games* To throw (dice), as in craps. ▸*n.* **1.**

The act or an instance of rolling. **2.** Something rolled up: *a roll of tape.* **3.** A quantity, as of cloth, rolled into a cylinder. **4.** A piece of parchment or paper that can be or is rolled up; scroll. **5.** A list of names of persons belonging to a group. **6a.** A small rounded portion of bread. **b.** A portion of food shaped like a tube with a filling. **7.** A rolling, swaying, or rocking motion. **8.** A gentle undulation of a surface. **9.** A deep reverberation or rumble. **10.** A rapid succession of short sounds: *a drum roll.* —*phrasal verb:* **roll back** To reduce (e.g., prices or wages) to a previous level. —*idiom:* **on a roll** *Informal* Having sustained success. [< Lat. *rotula,* small wheel.]

roll·back (rōl′băk′) ▸*n.* A reduction, esp. in prices or wages, to a previous level.

roll call ▸*n.* The reading aloud of a list of names to determine who is present.

roll·er (rō′lər) ▸*n.* **1.** One that rolls. **2.** A small spokeless wheel, as on a caster. **3.** An elongated cylinder on which something is wound. **4.** A heavy cylinder used to level, crush, or smooth. **5.** A cylinder used to apply ink or paint to a surface. **6.** A heavy, breaking wave.

Rol·ler·blade (rō′lər-blād′) A trademark for an inline skate.

roller coaster or **roll·er·coast·er** (rōl′ər-kō′-stər) ▸*n.* **1.** A steep, sharply banked elevated railway with open cars, operated as a ride. **2.** Something marked by abrupt, extreme changes.

roller skate ▸*n.* A shoe or boot with a set of wheels attached to its sole for skating on hard surfaces. —**rol′ler-skate′** *v.*

rol·lick (rōl′ĭk) ▸*v.* To romp or frolic boisterously. [?] —**rol′lick·ing** *adj.*

roll·ing pin (rō′lĭng) ▸*n.* A smooth cylinder used for rolling out dough.

ro·ly-po·ly (rō′lē-pō′lē) ▸*adj.* Short and plump. [< ROLL.]

Rom (rŏm) ▸*n.* A Romani, esp. a Romani man or boy. [Romany, man.]

ROM (rŏm) ▸*n. Comp.* Memory hardware that allows access to stored data but prevents modification of the data. [R(EAD-)O(NLY) M(EMORY).]

rom. ▸*abbr. Print.* roman

Ro·ma (rō′mə) ▸*n.* A subgroup of the Romani people primarily inhabiting Central and E Europe. [Romany, men.]

ro·maine (rō-mān′) ▸*n.* A variety of lettuce having a slender head of long dark-green leaves. [< Fr., Roman.]

Ro·man (rō′mən) ▸*adj.* **1a.** Of or relating to Rome or its people or culture. **b.** Of the Roman Empire. **2.** Of or relating to Latin. **3.** Of the Roman Catholic Church. **4. roman** Of or being a style of printing type with upright letters having serifs. ▸*n.* **1.** A native or inhabitant of ancient or modern Rome. **2. roman** Roman print or typestyle. **3. Romans** (*takes sing. v.*) See table at **Bible.**

Roman candle ▸*n.* A cylindrical firework that emits balls of fire.

Roman Catholic ▸*adj.* Relating to the Roman Catholic Church. ▸*n.* A member of the Roman Catholic Church. —**Roman Catholicism** *n.*

Roman Catholic Church ▸*n.* The Christian church having the Bishop of Rome as its head.

ro·mance (rō-măns′, rō′măns′) ▸*n.* **1a.** A love

affair. **b.** Romantic involvement; love. **2.** A mysterious or fascinating quality or appeal, as of something adventurous. **3a.** A medieval narrative telling of the adventures of chivalric heroes. **b.** A long fictitious tale of heroes and extraordinary or mysterious events. **4.** A story or film dealing with a love affair. **5. Romance** The Romance languages. ▸*adj.* **Romance** Of or being any of the languages that developed from Latin, including Italian, French, Portuguese, Romanian, and Spanish. ▸*v.* (rō-măns′) **-manced, -manc·ing** *Informal* To have a love affair with; woo. [< OFr. *romans* < Lat. *Rōmānicus,* Roman.] —**ro·manc′er** *n.*

Roman Empire An empire (27 BC–AD 476) centered in Rome and stretching from Britain and Germany to N Africa and the Persian Gulf.

Ro·man·esque (rō′mə-nĕsk′) ▸*adj.* Of or being a style of European architecture containing both Roman and Byzantine elements, prevalent esp. in the 11th and 12th cent. —**Ro′man·esque′** *n.*

Rom·a·ni also **Rom·a·ny** (rŏm′ə-nē, rō′mə-) ▸*n., pl.* **-ni** or **-nis** also **-ny** or **-nies 1.** A member of a nomadic people orig. migrating from N India to Europe around the 1300s, now also living in North America and Australia. **2.** The Indic language of the Romani. [Romani < *rom,* man.] —**Rom′a·ni** *adj.*

Ro·ma·ni·a (rō-mā′nē-ə, -mān′yə) or **Ru·ma·ni·a** (rōō-) A country of SE Europe with a short coastline on the Black Sea. Cap. Bucharest.

Ro·ma·ni·an (rō-mā′nē-ən, -mān′yən) also **Ru·ma·ni·an** (rōō-) ▸*n.* **1.** A native or inhabitant of Romania. **2.** Their Romance language. —**Ro·ma′ni·an** *adj.*

Roman numeral ▸*n.* Any of the numerical symbols formed with the Roman letters I, V, X, L, C, D, and M, representing respectively the numbers 1, 5, 10, 50, 100, 500, and 1,000.

Ro·mansch also **Ro·mansh** (rō-mänsh′, -mănsh′) ▸*n.* The Rhaeto-Romance language that is an official language of Switzerland.

ro·man·tic (rō-măn′tĭk) ▸*adj.* **1.** Having, showing, expressive of, or conducive to feelings of love. **2.** Imaginative but impractical. **3.** often **Romantic** Of or relating to romanticism in the arts. ▸*n.* **1.** A romantic person. **2.** often **Romantic** A romanticist. —**ro·man′ti·cal·ly** *adv.*

ro·man·ti·cism (rō-măn′tĭ-sĭz′əm) ▸*n.* often **Romanticism** An artistic and intellectual movement originating in Europe in the late 1700s and marked by emphasis on emotion and imagination, departure from classical forms, and rebellion against social conventions. —**ro·man′ti·cist** *n.*

ro·man·ti·cize (rō-măn′tĭ-sīz′) ▸*v.* **-cized, -ciz·ing 1.** To view or interpret romantically. **2.** To think in a romantic way.

Rom·a·ny (rŏm′ə-nē, rō′mə-) ▸*n., pl.* **-nies** Var. of **Romani.**

Rome (rōm) The capital of Italy, in the W-central part.

Ro·me·o (rō′mē-ō′) ▸*n., pl.* **-os** An attractive or romantic male lover. [After *Romeo,* in Shakespeare's *Romeo and Juliet.*]

romp (rŏmp) ▸*v.* **1.** To play or frolic boisterously. **2.** *Slang* To win a race or game easily. [< OFr. *ramper,* rear up.] —**romp** *n.*

romp·er (rŏm′pər) ►*n.* **1.** One that romps. **2. rompers** A loosely fitted, one-piece garment worn esp. by small children for play.

ron·do (rŏn′dō, rŏn-dō′) ►*n., pl.* **-dos** A musical work with a recurring main theme. [Ital. < Fr. *rondeau.*]

rood (rōōd) ►*n.* **1.** A crucifix or cross. **2.** A measure of land equal to ¼ acre, or 40 square rods (0.10 hectare). [< OE *rōd.*]

roof (rōōf, rŏŏf) ►*n.* **1.** The exterior top surface of a building and its supporting structures. **2.** The top covering of something: *the roof of a car.* **3.** The upper surface of the mouth. **4.** The highest point or limit. ►*v.* To cover with a roof. [< OE *hrōf.*] —**roof′er** *n.*

roof·ing (rōō′fĭng, rŏŏf′ĭng) ►*n.* **1.** Materials used in building a roof. **2.** A roof.

roof·tree (rōōf′trē′, rŏŏf′-) ►*n.* The ridgepole of a roof.

rook¹ (rŏŏk) ►*n.* A Eurasian bird having black plumage and nesting in colonies near the tops of trees. ►*v.* To swindle; cheat. [< OE *hrōc.*]

rook² (rŏŏk) ►*n.* A chess piece that may move in a rank or file over any number of empty squares. [< Pers. *ruḫḫ.*]

rook·er·y (rŏŏk′ə-rē) ►*n., pl.* **-ies** A place where large numbers of rooks or certain seabirds or marine animals nest or breed.

rook·ie (rŏŏk′ē) ►*n.* **1.** *Slang* **a.** An untrained or inexperienced recruit. **b.** A novice. **2.** A first-year professional athlete. [< RECRUIT.]

room (rōōm, rŏŏm) ►*n.* **1.** A space that is or can be occupied: *That chair takes up too much room.* **2a.** An interior area of a building set off by walls or partitions. **b.** The people present in such an area: *The whole room laughed.* **3. rooms** Living quarters. **4.** Opportunity or scope: *no room for error.* ►*v.* To occupy a room; lodge. [< OE *rūm.*] —**room′ful** *n.* —**room′y** *adj.*

Syns: *elbowroom, latitude, leeway, margin, scope* **n.**

room·er (rōō′mər, rŏŏm′ər) ►*n.* A lodger.

room·ing house (rōō′mĭng, rŏŏm′ĭng) ►*n.* A house where lodgers may rent rooms.

room·mate (rōōm′māt′, rŏŏm′-) ►*n.* A person with whom one shares a room or rooms.

room·y (rōō′mē, rŏŏm′ē) ►*adj.* **-i·er, -i·est** Having plenty of room; spacious. See Synonyms at **spacious.** —**room′i·ness** *n.*

Roo·se·velt (rō′zə-vĕlt′, rōō′-), **(Anna) Eleanor** 1884–1962. Amer. diplomat, writer, and first lady of the US (1933–45).

Eleanor Roosevelt
photographed in 1957

Franklin Delano Roosevelt
c. 1940 photograph

Roosevelt, Franklin Delano 1882–1945. The 32nd US president (1933–45).

Roosevelt, Theodore 1858–1919. The 26th US president (1901–09).

Theodore Roosevelt
photographed c. 1905

roost (rōōst) ►*n.* A place where winged animals rest or sleep. ►*v.* To rest or sleep on a perch. —*idioms:* **come home to roost** To have repercussions, esp. unfavorable ones. **rule the roost** *Informal* To be in charge; dominate. [< OE *hrōst.*]

roost·er (rōō′stər) ►*n.* An adult male chicken.

root¹ (rōōt, rŏŏt) ►*n.* **1a.** The usu. underground portion of a plant that serves as support, draws minerals and water from the soil, and sometimes stores food. **b.** A similar underground plant part, such as a rhizome. **2a.** The part of an organ or structure, such as a hair, that is embedded in other tissue. **b.** A base or support. **3.** The essential part; core. **4.** A source; origin. **5.** often **roots** The condition of belonging to a particular place or society. **6.** *Ling.* The element that carries the meaning in a word and provides the base for inflection. **7.** *Math.* A number that when multiplied by itself an indicated number of times forms a specified product. ►*v.* **1.** To grow roots or a root. **2.** To become firmly established or settled. **3a.** To dig or pull out by the roots. **b.** To remove or get rid of. [< ON *rōt.*] —**root′er** *n.* —**root′less** *adj.*

root² (rōōt, rŏŏt) ►*v.* **1.** To turn up by digging with the snout or nose. **2.** To cause to appear or be known: *rooted out the source of the problem.* **3.** To rummage for something. [< OE *wrōtan.*] —**root′er** *n.*

root³ (rōōt, rŏŏt) ►*v.* To encourage by applause; cheer. [Poss. alteration of *rout,* bellow.] —**root′er** *n.*

root beer ►*n.* A carbonated soft drink flavored with extracts of certain plant roots and herbs and usu. artificial flavorings.

root canal ►*n.* **1.** A pulp-filled channel in the root of a tooth. **2.** A treatment in which diseased tissue from the root canal is removed.

root cellar ►*n.* An underground pit or cellar used for storing vegetables.

root·stock (rōōt′stŏk′, rŏŏt′-) ►*n.* **1.** A root system of a plant to which a shoot or bud is grafted. **2.** See **rhizome.**

rope (rōp) ►*n.* **1.** A flexible heavy cord of tightly intertwined hemp or other fiber. **2.** A string of items attached in one line, esp. by twisting or braiding: *a rope of onions.* **3. ropes** *Informal* Specialized procedures or details: *learn the ropes.* ►*v.* **roped, rop·ing** **1.** To tie or fasten with a rope or other cord. **2.** To enclose with a rope: *rope off the area.* **3.** To lasso. —*idioms:* **on the ropes** On the verge of defeat or collapse. **the end of (one's) rope** The limit of one's patience, endurance, or resources. [< OE *rāp.*]

Roque·fort (rōk′fərt) A trademark for a sheep's milk cheese ripened in caves.

ror·qual (rôr′kwəl) ►*n.* Any of a family of baleen whales with a grooved throat and a small, pointed dorsal fin. [< Norw. *rørhval* : ON *raudhr*, red + *hvalr*, whale.]

Ror·schach test (rôr′shäk′, -shäкн′) ►*n.* A psychological test in which a subject's interpretations of ten standard inkblots are used to measure emotional and intellectual functioning and integration. [After Hermann *Rorschach* (1884–1922).]

ro·sa·ry (rō′zə-rē) ►*n., pl.* **-ries** *Rom. Cath. Ch.* **1.** A series of prayers dedicated to the Virgin Mary. **2.** A string of beads on which these prayers are counted. [< Med.Lat. *rosārium.*]

rose[1] (rōz) ►*n.* **1a.** Any of a genus of shrubs or vines having prickly stems and variously colored, often fragrant flowers. **b.** The flower of any of these plants. **2.** A rosette. **3.** A dark pink. [< Lat. *rosa.*] **—rose** *adj.*

rose[2] (rōz) ►*v.* P.t. of **rise.**

ro·sé (rō-zā′) ►*n.* A light pink wine made from purple grapes. [Fr.]

ro·se·ate (rō′zē-ĭt, -āt′) ►*adj.* **1.** Rose-colored. **2.** Cheerful or bright; optimistic.

rose·bud (rōz′bŭd′) ►*n.* The bud of a rose.

rose·bush (rōz′bŏŏsh′) ►*n.* A shrub that bears roses.

rose-col·ored (rōz′kŭl′ərd) ►*adj.* Cheerfully, often unduly optimistic.

rose·mar·y (rōz′mâr′ē) ►*n., pl.* **-ies** An aromatic evergreen shrub having grayish-green leaves that are used in cooking and perfumery. [< Lat. *rōs marīnus*, sea dew.]

ro·sette (rō-zĕt′) ►*n.* An ornament, as of ribbon or silk, that resembles a rose.

rose water ►*n.* A fragrant preparation made by steeping or distilling rose petals in water, used in cosmetics and cookery.

rose window ►*n.* A circular window with radiating tracery suggesting a rose.

rose·wood (rōz′wŏŏd′) ►*n.* **1.** Any of various tropical trees having hard brown to purplish wood. **2.** The wood itself, used in cabinetwork.

Rosh Ha·sha·nah (rôsh′ hə-shô′nə, hä-shä-nä′) ►*n.* The Jewish New Year, observed on the 1st or 1st and 2nd days of Tishri. [Heb. *rōš haš-šānâ*, head of the year.]

Ro·si·cru·cian (rō′zĭ-krōō′shən, rŏz′ĭ-) ►*n.* A member of an international organization devoted to the study of ancient mysticism and its application to modern life. **—Ro′si·cru′cian·ism** *n.*

ros·in (rŏz′ĭn) ►*n.* A translucent resin derived from the stumps or sap of pine trees, used to increase sliding friction, as on the bows of stringed instruments, and as an ingredient in various products including varnishes, inks, and adhesives. ►*v.* To coat or rub with rosin. [< RESIN.] **—ros′in·y** *adj.*

Ross (rôs, rŏs), **Betsy Griscom** 1752–1836. Amer. seamstress and patriot.

Ros·set·ti (rō-zĕt′ē), **Dante Gabriel** (1828–82), British poet and painter, and **Christina Georgina** (1830–94), British poet.

Ross Ice Shelf A vast area in Antarctica bordering on the **Ross Sea,** an arm of the S Pacific.

Ros·si·ni (rō-sē′nē), **Gioacchino Antonio**

1792–1868. Italian composer.

Ros·tand (rôs-tän′), **Edmond** 1868–1918. French playwright.

ros·ter (rŏs′tər, rô′stər) ►*n.* A list, esp. of the names of the personnel in a military unit. [Du. *rooster.*]

ros·trum (rŏs′trəm, rô′strəm) ►*n., pl.* **-trums** or **-tra** (-trə) An elevated platform for public speaking. [Lat. *rōstrum*, beak.]

ros·y (rō′zē) ►*adj.* **-i·er, -i·est 1a.** Having a rose color. **b.** Flushed: *rosy cheeks.* **2.** Bright; optimistic. **—ros′i·ness** *n.*

rot (rŏt) ►*v.* **rot·ted, rot·ting 1.** To decompose; decay. See Synonyms at **decay. 2.** To languish: *rot in jail* ►*n.* **1.** The process of rotting or the condition of being rotten. **2.** A plant or animal disease marked by the breakdown of tissue. **3.** Foolish talk; nonsense. [< OE *rotian.*]

ro·ta·ry (rō′tə-rē) ►*adj.* Of, causing, or marked by rotation, esp. around an axis. ►*n., pl.* **-ries 1.** A rotary part or device. **2.** A traffic circle. [< Lat. *rota*, wheel.]

ro·tate (rō′tāt) ►*v.* **-tat·ed, -tat·ing 1.** To turn on an axis. **2.** To alternate in sequence. [< Lat. *rota*, wheel.] **—ro′ta′tor** *n.* **—ro′ta·to′ry** (-tə-tôr′ē) *adj.*

ro·ta·tion (rō-tā′shən) ►*n.* **1a.** The act or process of turning around a center or an axis **b.** A single complete cycle of such motion. **2.** Regular and uniform variation in a sequence or series. **—ro·ta′tion·al** *adj.*

ROTC ►*abbr.* Reserve Officer's Training Corps

rote (rōt) ►*n.* **1.** Memorization through repetition, often without understanding. **2.** Mechanical routine. [ME.] **—rote** *adj.*

Roth IRA (rôth) ►*n.* A modified IRA in which contributions are made from after-tax income, and withdrawals after age 59½ are untaxed. [After William Victor *Roth*, Jr. (1921–2003).]

Roth·schild (rôth′chīld, rŏths′-) German family of bankers, including **Mayer Amschal** (1744–1812), **Salomon Mayer** (1774–1855), and **Nathan Mayer** (1777–1836).

ro·tis·se·rie (rō-tĭs′ə-rē) ►*n.* A device with a rotating spit on which meat or other food is roasted. [< OFr. *rostir*, roast.]

ro·to·gra·vure (rō′tə-grə-vyŏŏr′) ►*n.* **1.** An intaglio printing process in which the impression is transferred from an etched copper cylinder in a rotary press. **2.** Material produced by this process. [Lat. *rota*, wheel + GRAVURE.]

ro·tor (rō′tər) ►*n.* **1.** A rotating part of a machine or device. **2.** An assembly of rotating airfoils, as of a helicopter. [< ROTATOR.]

ro·to·till·er (rō′tə-tĭl′ər) ►*n.* A motorized rotary cultivator. [ROT(ARY) + TILLER[1].] **—ro′to·till′** *v.*

rot·ten (rŏt′n) ►*adj.* **-er, -est 1.** Being in a state of decay. **2.** Having a foul odor; putrid. **3.** Morally corrupt or despicable. **4.** Very bad; wretched. [< ON *rotinn.*] **—rot′ten·ness** *n.*

Rot·ter·dam (rôt′ər-däm′) A city of SW Netherlands on the Rhine-Meuse delta SE of The Hague.

Rott·wei·ler (rŏt′wī′lər, rôt′-) ►*n.* A dog having a stocky body, short black fur, and tan face markings. [After *Rottweil*, Germany.]

ro·tund (rō-tŭnd′) ►*adj.* Rounded in figure; plump. [Lat. *rotundus.*] **—ro·tun′di·ty** *n.*

ro·tun·da (rō-tŭn′də) ►*n.* **1.** A circular building, esp. one with a dome. **2.** A large, often round room with a high ceiling. [< Lat. *rotundus,* round.]

rotunda
Radcliffe Camera
Oxford, England

rou·ble (roo′bəl) ►*n.* Var. of **ruble.**

rou·é (roo-ā′) ►*n.* A man who recklessly indulges in sensual pleasure. [Fr. < *rouer,* break on a wheel.]

rouge (roozh) ►*n.* **1.** A red or pink cosmetic for coloring the cheeks or lips. **2.** A reddish powder used to polish metals or glass. [< Lat. *rubeus,* red.] **—rouge** *v.*

rough (rŭf) ►*adj.* **-er, -est 1a.** Having a bumpy or irregular surface; not smooth. **b.** Coarse or shaggy to the touch. **2a.** Stormy; turbulent: *rough seas.* **b.** Unpleasant or difficult. **3a.** Marked by or done with violence or forcefulness: *rough handling.* **b.** Boisterous, disorderly, or given to violence: *a rough crowd.* **c.** Marked by violence or crime: *a rough neighborhood.* **4.** Not polished or refined. **5.** Harsh to the ear. **6.** Not complete, exact, or perfect: *a rough drawing.* ►*n.* **1.** The part of something that is uneven or coarse. **2a.** Rugged, overgrown terrain. **b.** The area of a golf hole in which the grass is kept longer than that of the fairway. **3.** A disorderly, unrefined, or unfinished state: *a diamond in the rough.* **4.** A rowdy; tough. ►*v.* **1.** To treat roughly or with physical violence. **2.** To prepare or make in an unfinished form: *rough out a house plan.* ►*adv.* In a rough manner. **—idiom: rough it** To live without comforts and conveniences. [< OE *rūh.*] **—rough′ly** *adv.* **—rough′ness** *n.*

rough·age (rŭf′ĭj) ►*n.* See **fiber** (sense 6).

rough·en (rŭf′ən) ►*v.* To make or become rough.

rough-hew (rŭf′hyoo′) ►*v.* **1.** To hew or shape (e.g., timber) roughly, without finishing. **2.** To make in rough form. **—rough′hewn′** *adj.*

rough·house (rŭf′hous′) ►*n.* Rowdy, rough behavior. **—rough′house′** (-houz′) *v.*

rough·neck (rŭf′nĕk′) ►*n.* A rowdy; tough.

rough·shod (rŭf′shŏd′) ►*adj.* Shod with horseshoes having projecting points to prevent slipping. **—idiom: ride roughshod over** To treat with brutal force.

rou·lade (roo-läd′) ►*n.* A slice of meat rolled around a filling and cooked. [Fr. < *rouler,* to roll.]

rou·lette (roo-lĕt′) ►*n.* A gambling game in

which the players bet on which slot of a rotating disk a small ball will come to rest in. [< OFr. *ruelete,* small wheel.]

round (round) ►*adj.* **-er, -est 1a.** Spherical; ball-shaped. **b.** Circular or curved. **c.** Cylindrical. **2.** Complete; full: *a round dozen.* **3.** *Math.* Not exact, esp. when expressed as a multiple of 10: *a round estimate* ►*n.* **1.** Something round, such as a globe. **2.** A cut of beef between the rump and the shank. **3a.** A complete course, succession, or series: *a round of negotiations.* **b.** often **rounds** A course of customary or prescribed actions, duties, or places: *physicians' rounds.* **4.** One drink for each person in a gathering. **5a.** A single shot or volley. **b.** A single cartridge or shell. **6.** An interval of play or action in various sports and games. **7.** *Mus.* A short canon written to be sung several times in continuous succession. ►*v.* **1.** To make or become round. **2.** To surround. **3.** To fill out; make plump. **4.** To bring to completion or perfection; finish. **5.** To express as a round number. **6.** To go or pass around. **7.** To make a turn about or to the other side of: *rounded a bend in the road.* ►*adv. & prep.* Around. **—phrasal verb: round up 1.** To bring together. **2.** To herd (cattle) in a roundup. **—idiom: in the round 1.** With the stage in the center of the audience. **2.** Fully shaped and freestanding, as a sculpture. [< Lat. *rotundus.*] **—round′ish** *adj.* **—round′ness** *n.*

round·a·bout (round′ə-bout′) ►*adj.* **1.** Indirect; circuitous. **2.** Marked by indirectness, evasiveness, or vagueness.

roun·de·lay (roun′də-lā′) ►*n.* A poem or song with a recurring refrain. [< OFr. *rondelet.*]

round·house (round′hous′) ►*n.* **1.** A circular building for housing and switching locomotives. **2.** *Slang* A punch or kick delivered with a sweeping movement to one side.

round·ly (round′lē) ►*adv.* Fully; thoroughly.

round robin ►*n.* A tournament in which each contestant is matched in turn against every other contestant.

round·ta·ble (round′tā′bəl) ►*n.* **1.** often **round table** A conference or discussion involving several participants. **2. Round Table** In Arthurian legend, the circular table of King Arthur and his knights.

round-the-clock (round′thə-klŏk′) ►*adj.* Twenty-four hours a day; continuous.

round trip ►*n.* A trip to a place and back. **—round′-trip′, round′trip′** *adj. & adv.*

round·up (round′ŭp′) ►*n.* **1.** A herding together of cattle. **2.** A gathering up, as of suspects by the police. **3.** A summary.

round·worm (round′wûrm′) ►*n.* See **nematode.**

rouse (rouz) ►*v.* **roused, rous·ing 1.** To awaken. **2.** To become active, attentive, or excited. [ME *rousen,* shake the feathers.]

rous·ing (rou′zĭng) ►*adj.* Inducing enthusiasm or excitement; stirring.

Rous·seau (roo-sō′), **Jean Jacques** 1712–78. Swiss philosopher and writer.

roust (roust) ►*v.* **1.** To cause to get out of bed. **2.** To cause to leave. [Alteration of ROUSE.]

roust·a·bout (roust′ə-bout′) ►*n.* An unskilled laborer, as in an oil field.

rout¹ (rout) ►*n.* **1.** A disorderly retreat or flight following defeat. **2.** An overwhelming defeat. ►*v.* **1.** To put to disorderly flight or retreat. **2.**

To defeat overwhelmingly. [< VLat. *rupta* < Lat. *rumpere*, break.]

rout² (rout) ►*v.* **1.** To dig with the snout; root. **2.** To rummage. **3.** To gouge out. **4.** To drive or force out: *rout out an informant.* [Var. of ROOT².] —**rout′er** *n.*

route (rōōt, rout) ►*n.* **1.** A road or way from one place to another. **2.** A means of reaching a goal. ►*v.* **rout·ed, rout·ing** To send by a route. See Synonyms at **send.** [< OFr.]

rou·tine (rōō-tēn′) ►*n.* **1.** A set of customary and often mechanically performed procedures or activities. **2.** A scripted piece of entertainment. **3.** *Comp.* A set of programming instructions for a specific task. ►*adj.* **1.** In accord with established procedure. **2.** Not special; ordinary. [Fr. < *route*, ROUTE.] —**rou·tine′ly** *adv.*

roux (rōō) ►*n., pl.* **roux** A mixture of flour and fat cooked together, used as a thickening. [Fr. (*beurre*) *roux*, browned (butter), ult. < Lat. *russus*, red.]

rove (rōv) ►*v.* **roved, rov·ing** To wander about at random; roam. [ME *roven*, shoot arrows at a mark.] —**rov′er** *n.*

row¹ (rō) ►*n.* **1.** A series of objects or persons placed next to each other, usu. in a straight line. **2.** A continuous line of buildings along a street. [< OE *rāw.*]

row² (rō) ►*v.* **1.** To propel (a boat) with oars. **2.** To travel or carry by rowboat. ►*n.* A trip by rowboat. [< OE *rōwan.*] —**row′er** *n.*

row³ (rou) ►*n.* **1.** A noisy fight or quarrel. **2.** A loud noise. [?] —**row** *v.*

row·boat (rō′bōt′) ►*n.* A small boat propelled by oars.

row·dy (rou′dē) ►*adj.* **-di·er, -di·est** Disorderly; rough. ►*n., pl.* **-dies** A rough, disorderly person. [Prob. < ROW³.] —**row′di·ly** *adv.* —**row′di·ness** *n.* —**row′dy·ism** *n.*

row·el (rou′əl) ►*n.* A sharp-toothed wheel inserted into the end of the shank of a spur. [< OFr. *roelle*, little wheel.] —**row′el** *v.*

row house (rō) ►*n.* One of a series of similar or identical houses built side by side and joined by common walls.

roy·al (roi′əl) ►*adj.* **1.** Of or relating to a monarch. **2.** Befitting royalty; stately. [< Lat. *rēgālis* < *rēx*, king.] —**roy′al·ly** *adv.*

royal blue ►*n.* A deep to strong blue. —**roy′al-blue′** *adj.*

roy·al·ist (roi′ə-lĭst) ►*n.* A supporter of government by a monarch.

royal poinciana ►*n.* A tree native to Madagascar and widely cultivated for its showy scarlet flowers.

roy·al·ty (roi′əl-tē) ►*n., pl.* **-ties 1a.** A person of royal rank or lineage. **b.** Monarchs and their families collectively. **2.** The power, status, or authority of a monarch. **3.** Royal quality or bearing. **4a.** A share paid to a writer or composer out of the proceeds resulting from the sale or performance of his or her work. **b.** A share paid to an inventor or a proprietor for the right to use his or her invention or services.

rpm ►*abbr.* revolutions per minute

RR ►*abbr.* **1.** railroad **2.** rural route

–rrhea ►*suff.* Flow; discharge: *pyorrhea.* [< Gk. *rhoia*, a flowing < *rhein*, flow.]

rRNA ►*abbr.* ribosomal RNA

RSI ►*abbr.* repetitive strain injury

RSV ►*abbr.* Revised Standard Version

RSVP ►*abbr. French* répondez s'il vous plaît (please reply)

Rte. ►*abbr.* route

Rt. Hon. ►*abbr.* Right Honorable

rub (rŭb) ►*v.* **rubbed, rub·bing 1.** To apply friction and pressure to (a surface). **2.** To move or cause to move along a surface, esp. repeatedly. **3.** To become or cause to become worn, chafed, or irritated. **4.** To be transferred: *Her luck rubbed off on me.* ►*n.* **1.** The act of rubbing. **2.** A difficulty or obstacle. —*phrasal verbs:* **rub down** To massage. **rub out 1.** To obliterate by or as if by rubbing. **2.** *Slang* To murder. [ME *rubben.*]

rub·ber¹ (rŭb′ər) ►*n.* **1.** A yellowish elastic material obtained from the milky sap of various tropical plants and used in products such as tires. **2.** Any of numerous synthetic materials similar to natural rubber. **3.** A low overshoe made of rubber. **4.** An eraser. **5.** *Slang* A condom. [< RUB.] —**rub·ber·y** *adj.*

rub·ber² (rŭb′ər) ►*n. Games* **1.** A series of games of which a majority must be won to terminate the play. **2.** An odd game played to break a tie. [?]

rubber band ►*n.* An elastic loop of rubber used to hold objects together.

rubber cement ►*n.* An adhesive of nonvulcanized rubber.

rub·ber·ize (rŭb′ə-rīz′) ►*v.* **-ized, -iz·ing** To coat, treat, or impregnate with rubber.

rub·ber·neck (rŭb′ər-nĕk′) ►*v. Slang* To stare or gawk. —**rub′ber·neck′er** *n.*

rubber stamp ►*n.* A piece of rubber with raised letters or designs, used to make ink impressions.

rub·ber-stamp (rŭb′ər-stămp′) ►*v.* To endorse or approve without question or deliberation.

rub·bing (rŭb′ĭng) ►*n.* An image of a raised or indented surface made by placing paper over the surface and rubbing the paper gently with a marking agent.

rub·bish (rŭb′ĭsh) ►*n.* **1.** Refuse; garbage. **2.** Foolish discourse; nonsense. [ME *robishe.*]

rub·ble (rŭb′əl) ►*n.* **1.** Fragments of rock or masonry. **2.** Irregular pieces of rock used in masonry. [ME *rubel.*] —**rub′bly** *adj.*

rub·down (rŭb′doun′) ►*n.* A massage.

rube (rōōb) ►*n. Slang* An unsophisticated rustic. [Prob. < *Rube*, nickname for *Reuben.*]

ru·bel (rōō′bəl) ►*n.* See table at **currency.** [Belarusian.]

ru·bel·la (rōō-bĕl′ə) ►*n.* A mild, contagious viral disease capable of producing congenital defects in infants born to mothers infected during early pregnancy. [< Lat. *rubellus*, reddish < *ruber*, red.]

Ru·ben·esque (rōō′bə-nĕsk′) ►*adj.* **1.** Of, relating to, or in the style of painting of Peter Paul Rubens. **2.** Plump or fleshy and voluptuous. Used of a woman.

Ru·bens (rōō′bənz), **Peter Paul** 1577–1640. Flemish painter.

ru·bi·cund (rōō′bĭ-kənd) ►*adj.* Rosy in complexion; ruddy. [Lat. *rubicundus.*]

ru·bid·i·um (rōō-bĭd′ē-əm) ►*n. Symbol* **Rb** A soft, alkali metallic element used in photocells. At. no. 37. See table at **element.** [< Lat. *rūbidus*, red.]

ru·ble also **rou·ble** (rōō′bəl) ►*n.* See table at **currency.** [Russ. *rubl′.*]

ru·bric (rōō′brĭk) ►*n.* **1a.** A class or category. **b.** A title or heading, as of a chapter in a code of law. **2.** A heading or initial letter printed distinctively, usu. in red lettering. [< Lat. *rūbrīca*, red chalk < *ruber*, red.]

ru·by (rōō′bē) ►*n., pl.* **-bies 1.** A deep red, translucent corundum, highly valued as a precious stone. **2.** A deep purplish red. [< Lat. *rubeus*, red.] —**ru′by** *adj.*

ruck·sack (rŭk′săk′, rŏŏk′-) ►*n.* A knapsack. [Ger.]

ruck·us (rŭk′əs) ►*n.* A disturbance; commotion. [Blend of *ruction*, disturbance, and RUMPUS.]

rud·der (rŭd′ər) ►*n.* **1.** A vertically hinged plate mounted at the stern of a vessel or aircraft for steering. **2.** A controlling agent or influence. [< OE *rōther*, steering oar.]

rud·dy (rŭd′ē) ►*adj.* **-di·er, -di·est 1.** Having a healthy reddish color. **2.** Reddish; rosy. [< OE *rudig*.] —**rud′di·ness** *n.*

rude (rōōd) ►*adj.* **rud·er, rud·est 1.** Ill-mannered; discourteous. **2a.** Undeveloped or uncivilized. **b.** Crude or unfinished. **3.** Unpleasantly forceful or harsh: *a rude shock*. [< Lat. *rudis*.] —**rude′ly** *adv.* —**rude′ness** *n.*

ru·di·ment (rōō′də-mənt) ►*n.* often **rudiments 1.** A fundamental element, principle, or skill. **2.** Something in an incipient or undeveloped form. [< Lat. *rudis*, rough, unformed.] —**ru′di·men′ta·ry** (-měn′tə-rē, -měn′trē) *adj.*

Ru·dolf I (rōō′dŏlf) 1218–91. Holy Roman emperor and king of Germany (1273–91) and founder of the Habsburg dynasty.

Ru·dolph (rōō′dŏlf), **Wilma Glodean** 1940–94. Amer. athlete.

rue[1] (rōō) ►*v.* To feel regret, remorse, or sorrow for. [< OE *hrēowian*.] —**rue′ful** *adj.* —**rue′ful·ness** *n.*

rue[2] (rōō) ►*n.* Any of various aromatic Eurasian plants that yield an acrid oil. [< Gk. *rhutē*.]

ruff (rŭf) ►*n.* **1.** A stiffly starched circular collar worn in the 1500s and 1600s. **2.** A collarlike projection around the neck, as of feathers on a bird. [Perh. < RUFFLE.] —**ruffed** *adj.*

ruf·fi·an (rŭf′ē-ən, rŭf′yən) ►*n.* A tough or rowdy person. [< OItal. *ruffiano*.]

ruf·fle (rŭf′əl) ►*n.* **1.** A strip of frilled or closely pleated fabric used for trimming or decoration. **2.** A ruff on a bird. **3.** A ripple. ►*v.* **-fled, -fling 1.** To disturb the smoothness or regularity of. **2.** To pleat or gather (fabric) into a ruffle. **3.** To erect (the feathers). **4.** To discompose or annoy; fluster. [< ME *ruffelen*, roughen.]

ru·fi·yaa (rōō′fē-yä′) ►*n.* See table at **currency.** [< Hindi *rupiyā*.]

ru·fous (rōō′fəs) ►*adj.* Reddish to reddish-orange. [< Lat. *rūfus*, red.]

rug (rŭg) ►*n.* A floor covering consisting of a piece of heavy fabric. [Of Scand. orig.]

Rug·by (rŭg′bē) ►*n.* A game similar to football in which forward passing, substitution of players, and time-outs are not permitted. [After *Rugby* School, England.]

rug·ged (rŭg′ĭd) ►*adj.* **1.** Having a rough, irregular surface. **2.** Strong and sturdy. **3.** Foul; stormy. **4.** Demanding great effort or endurance. [ME, shaggy, of Scand. orig.] —**rug′ged·ly** *adv.* —**rug′ged·ness** *n.*

Ruhr (rŏŏr) A region of NW Germany along and N of the **Ruhr River,** which flows about 235 km (145 mi) to the Rhine R.

ru·in (rōō′ĭn) ►*n.* **1.** often **ruins a.** The state of being physically destroyed, collapsed, or decayed. **b.** The state of being extensively harmed or damaged. **c.** Poverty or bankruptcy. **2.** often **ruins a.** A destroyed, collapsed, or decayed building or other physical entity. **b.** One that has been extensively damaged or harmed. **3.** A cause of destruction: *Gambling will be his ruin*. ►*v.* **1.** To cause to be in a destroyed, collapsed, or decayed state. **2.** To harm or damage irreparably. **3.** To reduce to poverty or bankruptcy. [< Lat. *ruīna*.] —**ru′in·a·ble** *adj.* —**ru′in·a′tion** *n.* —**ru′in·ous** *adj.*

rule (rōōl) ►*n.* **1.** Governing power; authority. **2.** An authoritative direction for conduct or procedure. **3.** A usual or customary course of action or behavior. **4.** A statement that describes what is true in most or all cases. **5.** *Math.* A standard method or procedure. **6.** See **ruler** (sense 2). ►*v.* **ruled, rul·ing 1.** To exercise control (over); govern. **2.** To dominate by powerful influence. **3.** To decide judicially; decree. **4.** To mark with straight parallel lines. —*phrasal verb:* **rule out** To exclude. [< Lat. *rēgula*, ruler, straightedge.]

rule of thumb ►*n., pl.* **rules of thumb** A useful principle having wide application but not intended to be strictly accurate.

rul·er (rōō′lər) ►*n.* **1.** One that rules or governs. **2.** A straightedge strip for drawing straight lines and measuring lengths.

rul·ing (rōō′lĭng) ►*adj.* **1.** Exercising control or authority. **2.** Predominant. ►*n.* An official decision: *a court ruling*.

rum (rŭm) ►*n.* An alcoholic liquor distilled from fermented molasses or sugar cane. [Prob. short for obsolete *rumbullion*.]

Ru·ma·ni·a (rōō-mā′nē-ə, -mān′yə) See **Romania.** —**Ru·ma′ni·an** *adj. & n.*

rum·ba (rŭm′bə, rōōm′-, rŏŏm′-) ►*n.* **1.** A complex rhythmical dance of Cuban origin. **2.** Music for this dance. [Am.Sp.] —**rum′ba** *v.*

rum·ble (rŭm′bəl) ►*v.* **-bled, -bling 1.** To make a deep long rolling sound. **2.** To move or proceed with a rumble. **3.** *Slang* To engage in a gang fight. ►*n.* **1.** A deep long rolling sound. **2.** *Slang* **a.** Murmurous discontent. **b.** A gang fight. [ME *romblen*.] —**rum′bler** *n.* —**rum′bly** *adj.*

ru·men (rōō′mən) ►*n., pl.* **-mi·na** (-mə-nə) or **-mens** The first division of the stomach of a ruminant. [Lat. *rūmen*.] —**ru′mi·nal** *adj.*

ru·mi·nant (rōō′mə-nənt) ►*n.* Any of various hoofed, usu. horned mammals, such as cattle, sheep, and deer, having a divided stomach and chewing a cud. ►*adj.* **1.** Chewing cud. **2.** Meditative; contemplative.

ru·mi·nate (rōō′mə-nāt′) ►*v.* **-nat·ed, -nat·ing 1.** To consider a matter at length. **2.** To chew cud. [Lat. *rūmināre* < *rūmen*, throat.] —**ru′mi·na′tion** *n.* —**ru′mi·na′tive** *adj.* —**ru′mi·na′tor** *n.*

rum·mage (rŭm′ĭj) ►*v.* **-maged, -mag·ing** To make a thorough, often disorderly search (of). [< OFr. *arumer*, stow.]

rummage sale ►*n.* A sale of assorted second-hand objects.

rum·my (rŭm′ē) ►*n.* A card game in which the object is to obtain sets of three or more cards of the same rank or suit. [?]

ru·mor (rōō′mər) ►*n.* A report of uncertain

origin and accuracy; hearsay. [< Lat. *rūmor.*]
—ru′mor *v.*

rump (rŭmp) ►*n.* **1.** The fleshy hindquarters of an animal. **2.** A cut of beef from the rump. **3.** The buttocks. **4.** The last or inferior part. [ME *rumpe,* of Scand. orig.]

rum·ple (rŭm′pəl) ►*v.* **-pled, -pling 1.** To wrinkle or form into folds or creases. **2.** To make unkempt or untidy. [Poss. < MDu. *rumpelen.*] **—rum′ply** *adj.*

rum·pus (rŭm′pəs) ►*n.* A noisy ruckus. [?]

rumpus room ►*n.* A playroom.

run (rŭn) ►*v.* **ran** (răn), **run, run·ning 1a.** To move swiftly on foot so that both or all feet are not on the ground during each stride. **b.** To flee. **2.** To swim in large numbers, as in migrating. **3a.** To move without hindrance or restraint. **b.** To hurry; hasten. **c.** To make a short, quick trip. **4.** To cause to move quickly: *ran her finger along the keyboard.* **5a.** To take part in a race by running. **b.** To compete for elected office: *ran for mayor.* **6.** To move freely, as on wheels. **7.** To travel over a regular route. **8.** *Naut.* To sail or steer before the wind or on an indicated course. **9a.** To flow or cause to flow, esp. in a steady stream: *Run the water into the tub.* **b.** To melt and flow. **c.** To emit pus, mucus, or serous fluid. **d.** To spread and dissolve, as dye in fabric. **10a.** To extend: *This road runs into the next town.* **b.** To spread or climb, as a vine. **c.** To spread rapidly, as a disease. **d.** To unravel, as a nylon stocking. **11a.** To continue in effect or operation. **b.** To accumulate or accrue. **12.** To cause to collide or penetrate. **13a.** To function or cause to function. **b.** To control or manage. **14a.** To pass; elapse. **b.** To persist or recur. **15a.** To pass into a specified condition: *run into debt.* **b.** To have a particular form or expression. **c.** To tend or incline. **d.** To exist in a certain range: *sizes run from small to large.* **16.** *Comp.* To process or execute (a program or instruction). ►*n.* **1a.** An act or period of running. **b.** A pace faster than a walk. **2a.** A distance covered by running or traveling. **b.** A quick trip or visit. **c.** Unrestricted freedom or use: *free run of the library.* **3a.** A running race. **b.** A campaign for public office. **4.** *Baseball* A point scored by reaching home plate safely. **5.** The migration of fish, esp. in order to spawn. **6a.** A conduit or channel. **b.** An outdoor enclosure for domestic animals or poultry. **7a.** A continuous length or extent. **b.** The direction, configuration, or lie of something. **c.** A length of unraveled stitches in a knitted fabric. **8.** A continuous period of operation, as by a machine or factory. **9a.** A movement or flow. **b.** *Regional* See **creek. 10a.** A continuous set or sequence, as of playing cards. **b.** An unbroken series or sequence, as of theatrical performances. **c.** A successful sequence of shots or points. **d.** A series of unexpected and urgent demands, as by customers: *a run on a bank.* **11a.** A sustained state or condition: *a run of good luck.* **b.** A trend or tendency. **12.** An average type or category: *the broad run of voters.* **—phrasal verbs: run along** To go away; leave. **run down 1.** To stop because of lack of force or power. **2.** To become tired. **3.** To collide with and knock down. **4.** To chase and capture. **5.** To trace the source of. **6.** To disparage. **run out** To become used up. **run over 1.** To collide

with and knock down. **2.** To go beyond a limit. **run through 1.** To pierce. **2.** To use up. **3.** To rehearse quickly. **—idioms: in the long run** In the final analysis or outcome. **in the short run** In the immediate future. **on the run 1.** In rapid retreat. **2.** In hiding. **3.** Hurrying busily from place to place. **run out of** To exhaust the supply of. [< OE *rinnan* and ON *rinna.*]

run·a·bout (rŭn′ə-bout′) ►*n.* A small open automobile, carriage, or motorboat.

run·a·round (rŭn′ə-round′) ►*n.* *Informal* Deception, usu. in the form of evasive excuses.

run·a·way (rŭn′ə-wā′) ►*n.* **1.** One who has run away. **2.** *Informal* An easy victory. ►*adj.* **1.** Escaping or having escaped confinement. **2.** Out of control. **3.** Easily won.

run·down (rŭn′doun′) ►*n.* A point-by-point summary. ►*adj.* also **run-down** (rŭn′doun′) **1a.** Weak or exhausted. **b.** Dirty and dilapidated. **2.** Unwound and not running.

rune (rōōn) ►*n.* **1.** One of the letters of an alphabet used by ancient Germanic peoples. **2.** A magic charm. [< OE *rūn.*]

rung¹ (rŭng) ►*n.* **1.** A bar forming a step of a ladder. **2.** A crosspiece between the legs of a chair. **3.** A spoke of a wheel. [< OE *hrung.*]

rung² (rŭng) ►*v.* P.part. of **ring².**

run-in (rŭn′ĭn′) ►*n.* A quarrel or argument.

run·nel (rŭn′əl) ►*n.* **1.** A rivulet; brook. **2.** A narrow channel, as for water. [< OE *rynel.*]

run·ner (rŭn′ər) ►*n.* **1a.** One who runs, as in a race. **b.** *Baseball* One who runs the bases. **c.** *Football* One who carries the ball. **2.** A messenger. **3a.** A smuggler. **b.** A vessel engaged in smuggling. **4.** A device in or on which something slides or moves, as the blade of a skate. **5.** A long narrow carpet. **6.** A stem that produces roots and shoots at widely spaced nodes.

run·ner-up (rŭn′ər-ŭp′) ►*n., pl.* **run·ners-up** (rŭn′ərz-) One that takes second place.

run·ning (rŭn′ĭng) ►*n.* The act or sport of running. ►*adj.* Ongoing; continuous. ►*adv.* Consecutively.

running board ►*n.* A footboard extending under and along the doors of some vehicles.

running light ►*n.* One of several lights on a ship or aircraft to indicate position and size.

run·ny (rŭn′ē) ►*adj.* **-ni·er, -ni·est** Inclined to run or flow: *a runny nose.*

run·off (rŭn′ôf′, -ŏf′) ►*n.* **1.** An overflow of fluid. **2.** A competition held to break a tie.

run-of-the-mill (rŭn′əv-thə-mĭl′) ►*adj.* Not special; average.

runt (rŭnt) ►*n.* **1.** An undersized animal, esp. the smallest of a litter. **2.** *Derogatory* A short person. [?] **—runt′y** *adj.*

run-through (rŭn′thrōō′) ►*n.* **1.** An uninterrupted rehearsal. **2.** A brief outline.

run·way (rŭn′wā′) ►*n.* **1.** A usu. paved strip of level ground on which aircraft take off and land. **2.** A path, channel, or track over which something runs. **3.** A narrow walkway from a stage into an auditorium.

ru·pee (rōō-pē′, rōō′pē) ►*n.* See table at **currency.** [< Skt. *rūpya-,* silver.]

ru·pi·ah (rōō-pē′ə) ►*n., pl.* **-ah** or **-ahs** See table at **currency.** [Hindi *rupiyā,* rupee.]

rup·ture (rŭp′chər) ►*n.* **1.** The process of breaking open or bursting. **2.** *Med.* A hernia, esp. of the groin or intestines. [< Lat. *rumpere, rupt-,* break.] **—rup′ture** *v.*

ru·ral (rŏŏr′əl) ▸*adj.* Of or relating to the country as opposed to the city. [< Lat. *rūs, rūr-*, country.] —**ru′ral·ly** *adv.*

Rus. or **Russ.** ▸*abbr.* Russian

ruse (rōoz, rōos) ▸*n.* A crafty stratagem; subterfuge. [< OFr. *ruser*, drive back.]

rush¹ (rŭsh) ▸*v.* **1.** To move or cause to move swiftly; hurry. **2.** To attack suddenly. **3.** To perform with haste. **4.** To transport with urgent speed. ▸*n.* **1.** A sudden movement toward something. **2a.** Urgent movement to or from a place. **b.** A sudden widespread demand: *a rush for gold coins.* **3.** General haste or busyness. **4.** A sudden attack. **5.** A rapid, often noisy flow. See Synonyms at **flow. 6.** A sudden brief exhilaration. ▸*adj.* Performed with or requiring great haste or urgency. [< Lat. *recūsāre*, reject.] —**rush′er** *n.*

rush² (rŭsh) ▸*n.* **1.** A grasslike wetland plant having stiff hollow or pithy stems. **2.** The stem itself, used in wickerwork. [< OE *rysc.*]

Rush·more (rŭsh′môr′), **Mount** A mountain, 1,745 m (5,725 ft), in the Black Hills of W SD; site of a national memorial.

Mount Rushmore

rusk (rŭsk) ▸*n.* Sweet raised bread dried and browned in an oven. [Sp. or Port. *rosca*, coil, bread ring.]

Rus·kin (rŭs′kĭn), **John** 1819–1900. British writer and art critic. —**Rus′kin′i·an** *adj.*

rus·set (rŭs′ĭt) ▸*n.* **1.** A reddish brown. **2.** A coarse, usu. brownish homespun cloth. **3.** A winter apple with a reddish-brown skin. **4.** A potato with reddish-brown skin. [< Lat. *russus*, red.] —**rus′set** *adj.*

Rus·sia (rŭsh′ə) A country of E Europe and N Asia extending from the Baltic Sea to the Pacific and reaching N to the Arctic Ocean. Cap. Moscow.

Rus·sian (rŭsh′ən) ▸*n.* **1.** A native or inhabitant of Russia. **2.** The Slavic language of the Russians. —**Rus′sian** *adj.*

rust (rŭst) ▸*n.* **1a.** Any of various reddish-brown oxides formed on iron and iron-containing materials by low-temperature oxidation in the presence of water. **b.** Any of various metallic coatings formed by corrosion. **2.** A plant disease caused by various fungi, marked by reddish or brownish spots on leaves and stems. **3.** A strong brown. ▸*v.* **1.** To corrode. **2.** To deteriorate through inactivity or neglect. [< OE *rūst.*] —**rust** *adj.* —**rust′i·ness** *n.* —**rust′y** *adj.*

rus·tic (rŭs′tĭk) ▸*adj.* **1.** Typical of country life. **2a.** Lacking the refinement or elegance associated with urban life. **b.** Charmingly simple or unsophisticated. ▸*n.* **1.** A rural person. **2.** A person regarded as guileless or coarse from having been raised in the country. [< Lat. *rūs*, country.] —**rus·tic′i·ty** (-tĭs′ĭ-tē) *n.*

rus·ti·cate (rŭs′tĭ-kāt′) ▸*v.* **-cat·ed, -cat·ing** To go to or live in the country. —**rus′ti·ca′tion** *n.*

rus·tle (rŭs′əl) ▸*v.* **-tled, -tling 1.** To move or cause to move with soft fluttering or crackling sounds. **2.** To obtain in an enterprising manner: *rustle up supper.* **3.** To steal (livestock). [ME *rustlen.*] —**rus′tler** *n.*

rut¹ (rŭt) ▸*n.* **1.** A sunken track or groove made by the passage of vehicles. **2.** An uninspired routine that one continues unthinkingly or because change is difficult. ▸*v.* **rut·ted, rut·ting** To make ruts in (e.g., a path). [Poss. < ROUTE.] —**rut′ty** *adj.*

rut² (rŭt) ▸*n.* A regularly recurring condition of fertility during which breeding occurs, esp. in deer. [< Lat. *rūgīre*, roar.] —**rut** *v.*

ru·ta·ba·ga (rōo′tə-bā′gə, rōot′ə-) ▸*n.* A turniplike plant having a thick, bulbous, edible root. [Swed. dial. *rotabagge* : ON *rōt*, root + *baggi*, bag.]

Ruth (rōoth) ▸*n.* See table at **Bible.**

Ruth, George Herman "Babe." 1895–1948. Amer. baseball player.

Ru·the·nia (rōo-thēn′yə, -thē′nē-ə) A region of W Ukraine S of the Carpathian Mts. —**Ru·the′ni·an** *adj. & n.*

ru·the·ni·um (rōo-thē′nē-əm) ▸*n.* *Symbol* **Ru** A hard, white, acid-resistant metallic element used to harden platinum and palladium. At. no. 44. See table at **element.** [< Med.Lat. *Ruthenia*, Russia.]

Ruth·er·ford (rŭth′ər-fərd, rŭth′-), **Ernest** 1871–1937. New Zealand physicist.

ruth·er·for·di·um (rŭth′ər-fôr′dē-əm) ▸*n.* *Symbol* **Rf** A short-lived, synthetic radioactive element. At. no. 104. See table at **element.** [After Ernest RUTHERFORD.]

ruth·less (rōoth′lĭs) ▸*adj.* Having no compassion or pity; merciless. [< ME *ruthe*, compassion.] —**ruth′less·ly** *adv.* —**ruth′less·ness** *n.*

RV ▸*abbr.* **1.** recreational vehicle **2.** reentry vehicle **3.** Revised Version

R-val·ue (är′văl′yōo) ▸*n.* A measure of the capacity of a material, such as insulation, to impede heat flow. [*r(esistance) value.*]

Rwan·da (rōo-än′də) A country of E-central Africa. Cap. Kigali. —**Rwan′dan** *adj. & n.*

rwy. ▸*abbr.* railway

Rx (är′ĕks′) ▸*n.* A medical prescription. [< ℞, symbol used in prescriptions, abbr. of Lat. *recipe*, take.]

–ry ▸*suff.* Var. of **–ery.**

rye (rī) ▸*n.* **1.** A widely cultivated cereal grass. **2.** The grain of this plant, ground into flour or used in making whiskey and for livestock feed. **3.** Whiskey made from this grain. [< OE *ryge.*]

Ryu·kyu Islands (rē-ōō′kyōō′, ryōō′-kyōō) An island group of SW Japan extending between Kyushu and Taiwan.

S

s¹ or **S** (ĕs) ►*n., pl.* **s's** or **S's** also **ss** or **Ss** The 19th letter of the English alphabet.

s² ►*abbr.* **1.** second (unit of time) **2.** *Math.* second (of arc) **3.** stere

S ►*abbr.* **1.** *Football* safety **2.** satisfactory **3.** small **4.** soprano **5.** south **6.** *Baseball* strike

s. ►*abbr.* **1.** shilling **2.** singular **3.** son

S. ►*abbr.* **1.** saint **2.** sea

–s¹ or **–es** ►*suff.* Used to form plural nouns: *letters; ashes.* [< OE *-es, -as.*]

–s² or **–es** ►*suff.* Used to form the 3rd person singular present tense of all regular and most irregular verbs: *looks; goes.* [< OE *-es, -as.*]

–s³ ►*suff.* Used to form adverbs: *caught unawares; works nights.* [< OE *-es,* genitive suff.]

–'s ►*suff.* Used to form the possessive case: *nation's; women's.* [< OE *-es,* genitive suff.]

Saar (sär, zär) A river, about 245 km (150 mi), flowing from NE France to the Moselle R. in W Germany.

Saar·land (sär′länd′, zär′-) A region of SW Germany on the border with France.

Sab·bath (săb′əth) ►*n.* **1.** The 7th day of the week, Saturday, observed as the day of rest and worship by Jews and some Christians. **2.** The 1st day of the week, Sunday, observed as the day of rest and worship by most Christians. [< Heb. *šabbāt.*]

sab·bat·i·cal (sə-băt′ĭ-kəl) ►*n.* A usu. paid leave of absence for research, rest, or recreation, as for a professor. [< Gk. *sabbatikos,* of the sabbath.]

sa·ber (sā′bər) ►*n.* **1.** A heavy cavalry sword with a one-edged, slightly curved blade. **2.** A light dueling or fencing sword having a tapered flexible blade. [< Hung. *száblya.*]

Sa·bin (sā′bĭn), **Albert Bruce** 1906–93. Polish-born Amer. microbiologist and physician.

Sa·bine (sā′bīn′) ►*n.* **1.** A member of an ancient people of central Italy. **2.** The Italic language of the Sabines. —**Sa′bine′** *adj.*

Sabin vaccine ►*n.* An oral vaccine used to immunize against poliomyelitis. [After Albert B. Sabin.]

sa·ble (sā′bəl) ►*n.* **1a.** A carnivorous mammal of N Eurasia, having soft dark commercially valuable fur. **b.** The fur of this animal. **2a.** The color black. **b.** sables Black garments worn in mourning. [< ORuss. *sobol′.*] —**sa′ble** *adj.*

sab·o·tage (săb′ə-täzh′) ►*n.* **1.** The deliberate destruction of property or obstruction of normal operations, as by civilians or enemy agents in time of war. **2.** The deliberate attempt to hinder a cause. [< OFr. *saboter,* bungle.] —**sab′o·tage′** *v.*

sab·o·teur (săb′ə-tûr′) ►*n.* One who commits sabotage. [Fr.]

sac (săk) ►*n.* A pouchlike structure in an organism. [< Lat. *saccus,* bag.]

Sac (săk, sôk) ►*n.* Var. of **Sauk.**

SAC ►*abbr.* Strategic Air Command

Sac·a·ga·we·a (săk′ə-gə-wē′ə, sä-kä′gä-wē′ä) or **Sac·a·ja·we·a** (săk′ə-jə-wē′ə) 1787?–1812? Shoshone guide and interpreter for the Lewis and Clark expedition.

sacchar– ►*pref.* Sugar: *saccharine.* [< Gk. *sakkhar* < Skt. *śarkarā.*]

sac·cha·rin (săk′ər-ĭn) ►*n.* A very sweet, white crystalline powder, $C_7H_5NO_3S$, that is used as a calorie-free sweetener.

sac·cha·rine (săk′ər-ĭn, -ə-rēn′, -ə-rīn′) ►*adj.* **1.** Of or characteristic of sugar or saccharin; sweet. **2.** Cloyingly sweet.

sac·er·do·tal (săs′ər-dōt′l, săk′-) ►*adj.* Of or relating to priests or the priesthood. [< Lat. *sacerdōs,* priest.]

sa·chem (sā′chəm) ►*n.* A chief of a Native American, esp. Algonquian tribe or confederation. [Of Massachusett orig.]

sa·chet (să-shā′) ►*n.* A packet of perfumed powder used to scent clothes. [< OFr.]

sack¹ (săk) ►*n.* **1.** A bag, esp. one made of strong material for holding objects in bulk. **2.** A short loose-fitting garment. **3.** *Slang* Dismissal from employment. **4.** *Informal* A bed. ►*v.* **1.** To place into a sack. **2.** *Slang* To dismiss; fire. See Synonyms at **dismiss.** [< Gk. *sakkos.*]

sack² (săk) ►*v.* To plunder; pillage. [< Fr. *(mettre à) sac,* (put in) a sack.] —**sack** *n.*

sack·cloth (săk′klôth′, -klŏth′) ►*n.* **1.** Sacking. **2a.** A rough cloth. **b.** Garments made of sackcloth, worn as a symbol of mourning or penitence.

sack·ing (săk′ĭng) ►*n.* A coarse woven cloth used for making sacks.

sa·cra (sā′krə, săk′rə) ►*n.* Pl. of **sacrum.**

sac·ra·ment (săk′rə-mənt) ►*n.* *Christianity* **1.** A rite that was instituted by Jesus that confers sanctifying grace. **2.** often **Sacrament** The consecrated elements of the Eucharist. [< Lat. *sacrāmentum,* oath.] —**sac′ra·men′tal** (-měn′tl) *n. & adj.*

Sac·ra·men·to (săk′rə-měn′tō) The capital of CA, in the N-central part.

sa·cred (sā′krĭd) ►*adj.* **1.** Dedicated to or set apart for worship. **2.** Worthy of religious veneration. **3.** Made or declared holy. **4.** Dedicated or devoted exclusively to a single use or person. **5.** Worthy of respect. **6.** Of or relating to religious objects or practices. [< Lat. *sacrāre,* consecrate.] —**sa′cred·ly** *adv.* —**sa′cred·ness** *n.*

sacred cow ►*n.* One immune from criticism.

sac·ri·fice (săk′rə-fīs′) ►*n.* **1.** The offering of something to a deity. **2a.** The act of giving up something highly valued for the sake of something else considered to have a greater value or claim. **b.** Something given up in this way. **3.** Relinquishment of something at less than its presumed value. ►*v.* **-ficed, -fic·ing 1.** To offer as a sacrifice. **2.** To forfeit (one thing) for another thing considered of greater value. **3.** To sell or give away at a loss. [< Lat. *sacrificium.*] —**sac′ri·fic′er** *n.* —**sac′ri·fi′cial** (-fĭsh′əl) *adj.* —**sac′ri·fi′cial·ly** *adv.*

sac·ri·lege (săk′rə-lĭj) ►*n.* Desecration, profanation, misuse, or theft of something regarded as sacred. [< Lat. *sacrilegium.*]

sac·ri·le·gious (săk′rə-lĭj′əs, -lē′jəs) ►*adj.* Committing sacrilege or marked by sacrilege. —**sac′ri·le′gious·ly** *adv.*

Usage: *Sacrilegious,* the adjective of *sacrilege,* is often misspelled through confusion with *religious.*

sac·ris·tan (săk′rĭ-stən) ►n. **1.** One who is in charge of a sacristy. **2.** A sexton. [< Med.Lat. *sacristānus*.]

sac·ris·ty (săk′rĭ-stē) ►n., pl. **-ties** A room in a church housing the sacred vessels and vestments. [< Med.Lat. *sacristia*.]

sac·ro·il·i·ac (săk′rō-ĭl′ē-ăk′, sā′krō-) ►adj. Relating to the sacrum and the ilium, esp. where they join. [< SACRUM + ILIUM.] —**sac′-ro·il′i·ac′** n.

sac·ro·sanct (săk′rō-săngkt′) ►adj. Inviolably sacred. [Lat. *sacrōsānctus*, consecrated with religious ceremonies.] —**sac′ro·sanc′ti·ty** n.

sa·crum (sā′krəm, săk′rəm) ►n., pl. **sa·cra** (sā′-krə, săk′rə) A triangular bone that forms the posterior section of the pelvis. [< LLat., sacred.] —**sa′cral** adj.

sad (săd) ►adj. **sad·der, sad·dest 1.** Sorrowful; unhappy. **2.** Causing sorrow or gloom. **3.** Deplorable; sorry. [< OE *sæd*, sated, weary.] —**sad′ly** adv. —**sad′ness** n.

SAD ►abbr. seasonal affective disorder

Sa·dat (sə-dăt′, -dät′), **(Muhammad) Anwar el-** 1918–81. Egyptian politician.

sad·den (săd′n) ►v. To make or become sad.

sad·dle (săd′l) ►n. **1a.** A leather seat for a rider, secured on an animal's back. **b.** The seat of a bicycle or similar vehicle. **2.** A cut of meat consisting of part of the backbone and both loins. ►v. **-dled, -dling 1.** To put a saddle onto. **2.** To load or burden; encumber. [< OE *sadol*.]

sad·dle·bag (săd′l-băg′) ►n. **1.** A pouch that hangs across the back of a horse. **2.** A similar pouch on a motorcycle or bicycle.

Sad·du·cee (săj′ə-sē′, săd′yə-) ►n. A member of a priestly Jewish sect (2nd cent. BC–1st cent. AD) that accepted only the written Mosaic law. —**Sad′du·ce′an** (-sē′ən) adj.

Sade (săd, săd), Comte **Donatien Alphonse François de** "Marquis de Sade." 1740–1814. French writer.

sa·dism (sā′dĭz′əm, săd′ĭz′-) ►n. **1.** The tendency to derive sexual gratification from inflicting pain or emotional abuse on others. **2.** The tendency to derive pleasure from cruelty. [After the Marquis de SADE.] —**sa′dist** n. —**sa·dis′-tic** (sə-dĭs′tĭk) adj. —**sa·dis′ti·cal·ly** adv.

sa·do·mas·o·chism (sā′dō-măs′ə-kĭz′əm, săd′-ō-) ►n. The tendency to derive pleasure, esp. sexual gratification, from inflicting or submitting to physical or emotional abuse. [SAD(ISM) + MASOCHISM.] —**sa′do·mas′o·chist** n. —**sa′do·mas′o·chis′tic** adj.

Sa·far also **Sa·phar** (sə-fär′) ►n. The 2nd month of the Islamic calendar. See table at **calendar.** [Ar. *ṣafar*.]

sa·fa·ri (sə-fär′ē) ►n., pl. **-ris** An overland expedition, esp. in E Africa. [Ar. *safarīya*, journey.]

safe (sāf) ►adj. **saf·er, saf·est 1a.** Free from danger or injury; undamaged. **b.** Not exposed to the threat of danger or harm. **2.** Free from risk: *a safe bet.* **3.** Affording protection: *a safe place.* **4.** *Baseball* Reaching a base without being put out. ►n. A strong container for storing valuables. [< Lat. *salvus*, healthy.] —**safe′ly** adv.

safe-con·duct (sāf′kŏn′dŭkt) ►n. A document or an escort assuring unmolested passage, as through enemy territory.

safe·crack·er (sāf′krăk′ər) ►n. One who breaks into safes. —**safe′crack′ing** n.

safe-de·pos·it box (sāf′dĭ-pŏz′ĭt) ►n. A fireproof box, usu. in a bank vault, for the safe storage of valuables.

safe·guard (sāf′gärd′) ►n. A precautionary measure or device. ►v. To ensure the safety of; protect.

safe·keep·ing (sāf′kē′pĭng) ►n. Protection; care.

safe·light (sāf′līt′) ►n. A lamp that allows darkroom illumination without affecting photosensitive film or paper.

safe sex also **safer sex** ►n. Sexual activity with safeguards, such as a condom, used to avoid acquiring or spreading a sexually transmitted disease. —**safe′-sex′** adj.

safe·ty (sāf′tē) ►n., pl. **-ties 1.** Freedom from danger, risk, or injury. **2.** A protective device, as a lock on a firearm. **3.** *Football* A play in which the offensive team downs the ball behind its own goal line, resulting in two points for the defensive team.

safety belt ►n. A strap or belt worn as a safety precaution, esp. a seat belt.

safety glass ►n. Glass that resists shattering, esp. a composite of two sheets of glass with an intermediate layer of plastic.

safety match ►n. A match that can be lighted only by being struck against a chemically prepared friction surface.

safety pin ►n. A pin in the form of a clasp, with a sheath to cover and hold the point.

safety razor ►n. A razor with guards around the blade to prevent deep cuts.

safety valve ►n. A valve, as in a steam boiler, that automatically opens when pressure reaches a dangerous level.

saf·flow·er (săf′lou′ər) ►n. A plant with flowers that yield a dye and seeds that yield a cooking oil. [Ult. < Ar. *ʿuṣfur*.]

saf·fron (săf′rən) ►n. **1.** The dried stigmas of a kind of crocus, used to color and flavor food and as a dye. **2.** A moderate or strong orange yellow. [< Ar. *zaʿfarān*.]

sag (săg) ►v. **sagged, sag·ging 1.** To sink, droop, or settle from pressure or weight. **2.** To lose vigor, firmness, or resilience. **3.** To decline, as in value or price. [ME *saggen*.] —**sag** n.

sa·ga (sä′gə) ►n. **1.** An Icelandic prose narrative written between the 12th and 14th cent. **2.** A long heroic narrative. [ON.]

sa·ga·cious (sə-gā′shəs) ►adj. Shrewd and wise. [< Lat. *sagāx*.] —**sa·ga′cious·ly** adv. —**sa·gac′i·ty** (-găs′ĭ-tē) n.

sage[1] (sāj) ►n. A venerated, wise person. ►adj. **sag·er, sag·est** Judicious; wise. [< VLat. *sapi-us* < Lat. *sapere*, be wise.] —**sage′ly** adv.

sage[2] (sāj) ►n. **1.** An aromatic plant that has grayish-green leaves and is used as a seasoning. **2.** Sagebrush. [< Lat. *salvia*.]

sage·brush (sāj′brŭsh′) ►n. An aromatic shrub of arid regions of W North America.

Sag·it·tar·i·us (săj′ĭ-târ′ē-əs) ►n. **1.** A constellation in the Southern Hemisphere. **2.** The 9th sign of the zodiac in astrology.

sa·go (sā′gō) ►n., pl. **-gos** A powdery edible starch obtained from the pith of an Asian palm. [Malay *sagu*, mealy pith.]

sa·gua·ro (sə-gwär′ō, -wär′ō) also **sa·hua·ro** (sə-wär′ō) ►n., pl. **-ros 1.** A large branching cactus of the SW US and N Mexico. **2.** Its edible fruit. [Am.Sp.]

saguaro

Sa·hap·tin (sä-hăp′tĭn) ►*n., pl.* **-tin** or **-tins 1.** A member of a Native American people of Idaho, Washington, and Oregon. **2.** The dialectally diverse language of the Sahaptin.

Sa·har·a (sə-hâr′ə, -hăr′ə, -hä′rə) A desert of N Africa extending from the Atlantic coast to the Red Sea and S from the Atlas Mts. to the Sahel. —**Sa·har′an** *adj.*

Sa·hel (sə-hāl′, -hēl′) A semiarid region of N-central Africa S of the Sahara Desert. —**Sa·hel′i·an** *adj.*

sa·hib (sä′hĭb, -ĭb, säb) ►*n.* Used as a form of respectful address for a European man in colonial India. [Hindi *sāhab*, master.]

said (sĕd) ►*v.* P.t. and p.part. of **say.** ►*adj. Law* Aforementioned.
Usage: The adjective *said* is seldom appropriate to any but legal or business writing, where it is equivalent to *aforesaid: the said tenant* (named in a lease).

Sai·gon (sī-gŏn′) See **Ho Chi Minh City.**

sail (sāl) ►*n.* **1.** A piece of shaped fabric that catches the wind and propels or aids in maneuvering a vessel. **2.** A sailing vessel. **3.** A trip in a sailing craft. **4.** Something resembling a sail. ►*v.* **1a.** To move across the surface of water, esp. by means of a sail. **b.** To travel by water in a vessel. **c.** To start out on such a voyage. **d.** To operate a sailing craft, esp. for sport. **2.** To navigate or manage (a vessel). **3.** To progress smoothly. **4.** To glide through the air. [< OE *segl*.]

sail·board (sāl′bôrd′) ►*n.* A modified surfboard having a sail mounted on a pivoting mast, ridden while standing up. —**sail′board′** *v.* —**sail′board′er** *n.*

sail·boat (sāl′bōt′) ►*n.* A relatively small boat propelled by a sail or sails.

sail·fish (sāl′fĭsh′) ►*n.* A large marine fish with a large saillike dorsal fin and an elongated, spearlike upper jaw.

sail·or (sā′lər) ►*n.* One who sails, esp. one who serves in a navy or works on a ship.

sail·plane (sāl′plān′) ►*n.* A light glider used esp. for soaring. —**sail′plane′** *v.*

saint (sānt) ►*n.* **1.** A person considered holy and worthy of public veneration, esp. one who has been canonized. **2.** An extremely virtuous person. [< Lat. *sānctus*, holy.] —**saint** *v.* —**saint′-dom** *n.* —**saint′ed** *adj.* —**saint′hood′** *n.*

—**saint′li·ness** *n.* —**saint′ly** *adj.*

Saint Au·gus·tine (ô′gə-stēn′) A city of NE FL on the Atlantic; the oldest permanent European settlement in the US.

Saint Ber·nard (bər-närd′) ►*n.* A large strong dog orig. used in the Swiss Alps to rescue lost travelers.

Saint Chris·to·pher-Ne·vis (krĭs′tə-fər-nē′vĭs, -nĕv′ĭs) See **Saint Kitts and Nevis.**

Saint Croix (kroi) An island of the US Virgin Is. in the West Indies E of Puerto Rico.

Saint El·mo's fire (ĕl′mōz) ►*n.* A visible electric discharge on a pointed object during an electrical storm. [After *Saint Elmo*, 4th-cent. AD patron saint of sailors.]

Saint George's (jôr′jəz) The capital of Grenada, on the SW coast.

Saint George's Channel A strait between W Wales and SE Ireland.

Saint He·le·na (hə-lē′nə) A volcanic island in the S Atlantic W of Angola; part of the British dependency of **Saint Helena.**

Saint Hel·ens (hĕl′ənz), **Mount** An active volcanic peak of the Cascade Range in SW WA.

Mount Saint Helens
volcanic eruption May 18, 1980

Saint John's (jŏnz) **1.** The capital of Antigua and Barbuda, on the N coast of Antigua. **2.** The capital of Newfoundland and Labrador, Canada, on the E coast of Newfoundland.

Saint John's wort ►*n.* Any of a genus of herbs or shrubs used in medicinal preparations esp. as an antidepressant.

Saint Kitts and Ne·vis (kĭts; nē′vĭs, nĕv′ĭs) also **Saint Chris·to·pher-Ne·vis** (krĭs′tə-fər-nē′-vĭs, -nĕv′ĭs) An island country in the Leeward Is. of the West Indies ESE of Puerto Rico comprising **Saint Kitts** and the smaller island of Nevis. Cap. Basseterre.

Saint Lawrence River A river of SE Canada flowing about 1,200 km (740 mi) NE from Lake Ontario along the Ontario–NY border and through S Quebec to the **Gulf of Saint Lawrence,** an arm of the NW Atlantic. The river forms part of the **Saint Lawrence Seaway,** an international waterway, about 3,750 km (2,350 mi) long, between Lake Superior and the Atlantic.

Saint Lou·is (lōo′ĭs) A city of E MO on the Mississippi R.

Saint Lu·cia (lōo′shə, lōo-sē′ə) An island country of the West Indies in the Windward Is. S of Martinique. Cap. Castries.

Saint Mar·tin or **Saint Maar·ten** (mär′tn) An island of the West Indies in the W Leeward Is., administered by France and the Netherlands.

Saint Paul The capital of MN, in the SE part on the Mississippi R. adjacent to Minneapolis.

Saint Pe·ters·burg (pē′tərz-bûrg′) Formerly **Leningrad** (lĕn′ĭn-grăd′). A city of NW Russia at the head of the Gulf of Finland.

Saint Thomas An island of the US Virgin Is. in the West Indies E of Puerto Rico.

Saint Valentine's Day ►*n.* See **Valentine's Day.**

Saint Vincent and the Grenadines An island country in the central Windward Is. of the West Indies. Cap. Kingstown.

saith (sĕth, sā′ĭth) ►*v.* Archaic 3rd pers. sing. pr.t. of **say.**

sake[1] (sāk) ►*n.* **1.** Purpose: *for the sake of argument.* **2.** Advantage; good: *for the sake of your health.* [< OE *sacu.*]

sa·ke[2] also **sa·ki** (sä′kē, -kĕ) ►*n.* A Japanese liquor made from fermented rice. [J.]

Sa·kha·lin (săk′ə-lēn′) An island of SE Russia in the Sea of Okhotsk N of Hokkaido, Japan.

sal (săl) ►*n.* Salt. [< Lat. *sāl.*]

sa·laam (sə-läm′) ►*n.* **1.** An act of deference or obeisance, esp. a low bow performed while placing the right palm on the forehead. **2.** A greeting in various Muslim cultures. [Ar. *salām,* peace.] —**sa·laam′** *v.*

sa·la·cious (sə-lā′shəs) ►*adj.* Appealing to or stimulating sexual desire. [< Lat. *salāx.*] —**sa·la′cious·ly** *adv.* —**sa·la′cious·ness** *n.*

sal·ad (săl′əd) ►*n.* **1.** A dish usu. made of leafy greens or raw vegetables served with a dressing. **2.** A cold dish of vegetables, fruit, or other food. [< VLat. **salāta* < Lat. *sāl,* salt.]

Sal·a·din (săl′ə-dĭn) 1137?–93. Sultan of Egypt and Syria.

sal·a·man·der (săl′ə-măn′dər) ►*n.* A small, tailed amphibian. [< Gk. *salamandra.*]

sa·la·mi (sə-lä′mē) ►*n.* A highly spiced sausage. [< VLat. **salāmen* < Lat. *sāl,* salt.]

sal·a·ry (săl′ə-rē, săl′rē) ►*n., pl.* **-ries** Fixed compensation for services, paid to a person on a regular basis. [< Lat. *salārium,* money given to Roman soldiers to buy salt.] —**sal′a·ried** *adj.*

sale (sāl) ►*n.* **1a.** The exchange of goods or services for money. **b.** An auction. **2.** An offer or arrangement in which goods are sold at a discount. —***idioms:* for sale** Available to customers: *a store where pets are for sale.* **on sale 1.** Available to customers: *That product should be on sale at your local store.* **2.** Available to customers at a special discount: *Bathing suits are on sale.* [< ON *sala.*]

Sa·lem (sā′ləm) **1.** A city of NE MA NE of Boston; site of witchcraft trials (1692). **2.** The capital of OR, in the NW part SSW of Portland.

sales·clerk (sālz′klûrk′) ►*n.* One employed to sell goods in a store.

sales·man (sālz′mən) ►*n.* A man who is a salesperson. See Usage Note at **man.** —**sales′man·ship′** *n.*

sales·per·son (sālz′pûr′sən) ►*n.* One employed to sell products or services. —**sales′peo′ple** *pl.n.*

sales tax (sālz) ►*n.* A tax levied on the price of goods and services.

sales·wom·an (sālz′wŏŏm′ən) ►*n.* A woman who is a salesperson. See Usage Note at **man.**

sal·i·cyl·ic acid (săl′ĭ-sĭl′ĭk) ►*n.* A white crystalline acid used in making aspirin. [< Fr. *salicyle,* the radical of salicylic acid.]

sa·li·ent (sā′lē-ənt, săl′yənt) ►*adj.* **1.** Strikingly conspicuous. **2.** Projecting or jutting beyond a line or surface. [< Lat. *salīre,* leap.] —**sa′li·ence, sa′li·en·cy** *n.*

sa·line (sā′lēn′, -lĭn′) ►*adj.* Of or containing salt. [Lat. *salīnus.*] —**sa·lin′i·ty** (sə-lĭn′ĭ-tē) *n.*

Sal·in·ger (săl′ĭn-jər), **J(erome) D(avid)** 1919–2010. Amer. writer.

Sa·lish (sā′lĭsh) also **Sa·lish·an** (-lĭ-shən) ►*n.* **1.** A family of Native American languages of the NW US and British Columbia. **2.** The group of Native American peoples speaking languages of this family. **3.** The Flathead people. —**Sa′lish·an** *adj.*

sa·li·va (sə-lī′və) ►*n.* The watery mixture of secretions from glands in the mouth that lubricates chewed food and aids in digestion. [Lat. *salīva.*] —**sal′i·var′y** (săl′ə-vĕr′ē) *adj.*

sal·i·vate (săl′ə-vāt′) ►*v.* **-vat·ed, -vat·ing 1.** To secrete or produce saliva. **2.** *Informal* To be full of desire or eagerness for something. —**sal′i·va′tion** *n.*

Salk (sôlk), **Jonas Edward** 1914–95. Amer. microbiologist.

Jonas Salk
photographed in the mid-1950s

Salk vaccine ►*n.* A vaccine consisting of inactivated polioviruses, used to immunize against poliomyelitis. [After Jonas **Salk.**]

sal·low (săl′ō) ►*adj.* **-er, -est** Of a sickly yellowish color. [< OE *salo.*] —**sal′low·ness** *n.*

sal·ly (săl′ē) ►*n., pl.* **-lies 1.** A sudden assault from a defensive position. **2.** A quick witticism; quip. **3.** A venturing forth; jaunt. [< Lat. *salīre,* leap.] —**sal′ly** *v.*

salm·on (săm′ən) ►*n., pl.* **-on** or **-ons 1.** Any of various large food and game fishes of northern waters, usu. with pinkish flesh. **2.** A yellowish pink to reddish orange. [< Lat. *salmō.*] —**salm′on** *adj.*

sal·mo·nel·la (săl′mə-nĕl′ə) ►*n., pl.* **-nel·lae** (-nĕl′ē) or **-las** or **-la** Any of various rod-shaped bacteria, many of which cause food poisoning or other diseases in humans and other infectious diseases in domestic animals. [After Daniel E. *Salmon* (1850–1914).]

sa·lon (sə-lŏn′, să-lôɴ′) ►*n.* **1.** A large room, such as a drawing room, used for receiving and entertaining guests. **2.** A periodic gathering of people of social or intellectual distinction. **3.** A commercial establishment offering a product or service related to fashion: *a beauty salon.* [< Ital. *sala*, hall.]

Sa·lo·ni·ka (sə-lŏn′ĭ-kə, săl′ə-nē′kə) See **Thessaloníki.**

sa·loon (sə-lōōn′) ►*n.* A bar; tavern. [Fr. *salon*, SALON.]

sal·sa (säl′sə) ►*n.* **1.** A spicy saucelike condiment that is usu. made of tomatoes, onions, and chili peppers. **2a.** A popular form of Latin-American music. **b.** A dance for couples performed to this music. [< Sp., SAUCE.]

salt (sôlt) ►*n.* **1.** A colorless or white crystalline solid, chiefly sodium chloride, used extensively as a food seasoning and preservative. **2.** A chemical compound formed by replacing all or part of the hydrogen ions of an acid with metal ions or other cations. **3. salts** Any of various mineral salts used as laxatives or cathartics. **4.** An element that gives flavor or zest. **5.** Sharp, lively wit. **6.** *Informal* A veteran sailor. ►*adj.* **1.** Salty. **2.** Preserved in salt. ►*v.* **1.** To add salt to. **2.** To preserve with salt. —*phrasal verb:* **salt away** To put aside; save. —*idiom:* **worth (one's) salt** Efficient and capable. [< OE *sealt.*] —**salt′i·ly** *adv.* —**salt′i·ness** *n.* —**salt′y** *adj.*

SALT ►*abbr.* Strategic Arms Limitation Talks

salt·cel·lar (sôlt′sĕl′ər) ►*n.* A small dish for dispensing salt. [< ME *salt saler.*]

sal·tine (sôl-tēn′) ►*n.* A thin salted cracker.

Salt Lake City The capital of UT, in the N-central part near Great Salt Lake.

salt lick ►*n.* A block or deposit of exposed salt that animals lick.

salt marsh ►*n.* Low coastal grassland frequently overflowed by the tide.

salt·pe·ter (sôlt′pē′tər) ►*n.* See **potassium nitrate.** [< Med.Lat. *sālpetrae.*]

salt·shak·er (sôlt′shā′kər) ►*n.* A container for sprinkling table salt.

salt·wa·ter (sôlt′wô′tər, -wŏt′ər) ►*adj.* Consisting of or inhabiting salt water.

sa·lu·bri·ous (sə-lōō′brē-əs) ►*adj.* Conducive or favorable to health or well-being. [< Lat. *salūbris.*] —**sa·lu′bri·ty** (-brĭ-tē) *n.*

sal·u·tar·y (săl′yə-tĕr′ē) ►*adj.* **1.** Beneficial: *salutary advice.* **2.** Wholesome. [< Lat. *salūs*, health.] —**sal′u·tar′i·ly** (-târ′ə-lē) *adv.*

sal·u·ta·tion (săl′yə-tā′shən) ►*n.* An expression of greeting, goodwill, or courtesy.

sa·lu·ta·to·ri·an (sə-lōō′tə-tôr′ē-ən) ►*n.* The student with the second highest academic rank in a class who delivers the opening address at graduation.

sa·lute (sə-lōōt′) ►*v.* **-lut·ed, -lut·ing 1.** To greet. **2.** To recognize (a military superior) with a prescribed gesture. **3.** To honor formally. [< Lat. *salūtāre* < *salūs*, health.] —**sa·lute′** *n.*

Sal·va·dor (săl′və-dôr′) A city of E Brazil on the Atlantic SSW of Recife.

Sal·va·do·ran (săl′və-dôr′ən) or **Sal·va·do·ri·an** (-dôr′ē-ən) ►*n.* A native or inhabitant of El Salvador. —**Sal′va·do′ran, Sal′va·do′ri·an** *adj.*

sal·vage (săl′vĭj) ►*n.* **1a.** The rescue of a ship. **b.** Award given to those who aid in such a rescue when under no obligation to do so. **2a.** The act of saving imperiled property from loss. **b.** The property so saved. **3.** Something saved from destruction or waste and put to further use. ►*v.* **-vaged, -vag·ing 1.** To save from loss or destruction. **2.** To save (discarded or damaged

material) for further use. [< LLat. *salvāre*, save.] —**sal′vage·a·ble** *adj.* —**sal′vag·er** *n.*

sal·va·tion (săl-vā′shən) ►*n.* **1a.** Deliverance from difficulty or evil. **b.** A means or cause of such deliverance. **2.** Deliverance from sin; redemption. [< Lat. *salvāre*, save.]

salve (săv, säv) ►*n.* An ointment that soothes or heals. ►*v.* **salved, salv·ing** To soothe or heal with or as if with salve. [< OE *sealf.*]

sal·ver (săl′vər) ►*n.* A serving tray. [< Sp. *salva*, tasting of food.]

sal·vi·a (săl′vē-ə) ►*n.* Any of various plants having opposite leaves, a two-lipped corolla, and two stamens. [Lat., sage.]

sal·vo (săl′vō) ►*n., pl.* **-vos** or **-voes 1.** A simultaneous discharge of firearms. **2.** A sudden outburst. [Ital. *salva.*]

sal·war (săl′vär) ►*n.* Loose pajamalike trousers, typically having a drawstring waist and legs that narrow at the bottom, worn chiefly in South Asia. [Ult. < Pers. *šalvār.*]

salwar

SAM ►*abbr.* surface-to-air missile

Sa·mar·i·a (sə-mâr′ē-ə, -mâr′-) An ancient city of Palestine in the N part of the West Bank.

Sa·mar·i·tan (sə-mâr′ĭ-tn) ►*n.* **1.** A native or inhabitant of Samaria. **2.** often **samaritan** A Good Samaritan. —**Sa·mar′i·tan** *adj.*

sa·mar·i·um (sə-mâr′ē-əm, -măr′-) ►*n. Symbol* **Sm** A silvery or pale gray metallic rare-earth element used in laser materials, in infrared absorbing glass, and as a neutron absorber. At. no. 62. See table at **element.** [After Colonel M. von *Samarski*, 19th-cent. Russian mining official.]

sam·ba (săm′bə, säm′-) ►*n.* **1.** A Brazilian dance of African origin. **2.** Music for this dance. [Port.] —**sam′ba** *v.*

same (sām) ►*adj.* **1.** Being the very one; identical. **2.** Similar or corresponding. ►*adv.* In the same way. ►*pron.* **1.** One identical with another. **2.** The one previously mentioned: *When you have filled out the form, please remit same to this office.* —*idiom:* **all** (or **just**) **the same** Nevertheless. [< ON *samr.*] —**same′ness** *n.*

same-sex (sām′sĕks′) ►*adj.* Involving or restricted to members of the same sex: *same-sex schools.*

Sa·mi (sä′mē) ►*n., pl.* **Sami** or **-mis 1.** A member of a people of nomadic herding tradition in N Norway, Sweden, and Finland, and extreme NW Russia. **2.** Any of the Uralic languages of the Sami. [Sami.]

Sa·mo·a (sə-mō′ə) **1.** An island group of the S Pacific ENE of Fiji, divided between the sovereign nation of **Samoa** and **American Samoa. 2.** An island country of the S Pacific comprising the W part of the island group of Samoa. Cap. Apia. —**Sa·mo′an** *adj. & n.*

Sam·o·set (săm′ə-sĕt′) d. c. 1653. Abenaki leader and friend of the early colonists.

sam·o·var (săm′ə-vär′) ►*n.* A metal urn with a spigot, used to boil water for tea. [Russ.]

Sam·o·yed (săm′oi-ĕd′, sə-moi′ĭd) ►*n.* **1.** See **Nenets. 2.** A working dog orig. developed in N Eurasia. —**Sam′o·yed′** *adj.*

sam·pan (săm′păn′) ►*n.* A flat-bottomed Asian skiff. [Cantonese *saam¹ baan²* : *saam¹,* three + *baan²,* board, plank.]

sam·ple (săm′pəl) ►*n.* **1a.** A portion, piece, or segment representative of a whole. **b.** A specimen taken for analysis or testing. **2.** *Statistics* A set of data or elements analyzed to estimate the characteristics of a given population. ►*v.* **-pled, -pling** To take a sample of, esp. in order to test or examine. ►*adj.* Serving as a representative or example. [< Lat. *exemplum,* EXAMPLE.]

sam·pler (săm′plər) ►*n.* **1.** One employed to appraise samples. **2.** A piece of cloth embroidered with various designs.

sam·pling (săm′plĭng) ►*n.* See **sample** (sense 2).

Sam·son (săm′sən) In the Bible, a warrior betrayed to the Philistines by Delilah.

Sam·u·el (săm′yoo-əl) ►*n.* **1.** Hebrew judge and prophet of the 11th cent. BC. **2.** See table at **Bible.**

sam·u·rai (săm′ə-rī′) ►*n., pl.* **-rai** or **-rais** The Japanese feudal military aristocracy or one of its members. [J., warrior.]

San (sän) ►*n., pl.* **San** or **Sans 1.** A member of a nomadic hunting people of SW Africa. **2.** Any of the Khoisan languages of the San.

Sa·n'a also **Sa·na** (sä-nä′) The capital of Yemen, in the W part.

San An·to·ni·o (săn ăn-tō′nē-ō′) A city of S-central TX SW of Austin.

san·a·to·ri·um (săn′ə-tôr′ē-əm) also **san·a·tar·i·um** (-târ′-) ►*n., pl.* **-to·ri·ums** or **-to·ri·a** (-tôr′ē-ə) also **-tar·i·ums** or **-tar·i·a** (-târ′ē-ə) **1.** An institution for the treatment of chronic diseases. **2.** A resort for improvement of health, esp. for convalescents. [< Lat. *sānāre,* heal.]

sanc·ti·fy (săngk′tə-fī′) ►*v.* **-fied, -fy·ing 1.** To set apart for sacred use; consecrate. **2.** To make holy; purify. **3.** To give social or moral sanction to. [< Lat. *sānctus,* holy.] —**sanc′ti·fi·ca′tion** *n.*

sanc·ti·mo·ny (săngk′tə-mō′nē) ►*n.* Smug or hypocritical righteousness. [< Lat. *sānctimōnia,* sacredness.] —**sanc′ti·mo′ni·ous** *adj.*

sanc·tion (săngk′shən) ►*n.* **1.** Authoritative permission or approval. See Synonyms at **permission. 2a.** A penalty that is intended to enforce compliance or conformity. **b.** A coercive measure adopted usu. by several nations against a nation violating international law. ►*v.* To authorize, approve, or encourage. [< Lat. *sānctus,* holy.]

sanc·ti·ty (săngk′tĭ-tē) ►*n., pl.* **-ties 1.** Holiness

of life; saintliness. **2.** Sacredness or inviolability. [< Lat. *sānctus,* sacred.]

sanc·tu·ar·y (săngk′choo-ĕr′ē) ►*n., pl.* **-ies 1.** A sacred place, such as a church, temple, or mosque. **2a.** A place of refuge, asylum, or protection. **b.** A reserved area in which wild animals are protected from hunting or disturbance. [< LLat. *sānctuārium.*]

sanc·tum (săngk′təm) ►*n., pl.* **-tums** or **-ta** (-tə) **1.** A sacred or holy place. **2.** A private room or study. [LLat. *sānctum.*]

sand (sănd) ►*n.* Small loose grains of worn or disintegrated rock, finer than a granule and coarser than silt. ►*v.* To polish or scrape with sand or sandpaper. [< OE.] —**sand′er** *n.* —**sand′i·ness** *n.* —**sand′y** *adj.*

Sand, George Amandine Aurore Lucie Dupin, Baroness Dudevant. 1804–76. French writer.

san·dal (săn′dl) ►*n.* **1.** A shoe consisting of a sole fastened to the foot by thongs or straps. **2.** A low-cut shoe with an ankle strap. [< Gk. *sandalon.*] —**san′daled** *adj.*

san·dal·wood (săn′dl-wood′) ►*n.* **1.** An Asian tree with aromatic wood used in carving and perfumery. **2.** The wood of this tree. [< Ar. *ṣandal.*]

sand·bag (sănd′băg′) ►*n.* A bag filled with sand and used esp. to form protective walls. ►*v.* **1.** To put sandbags in or around. **2.** *Slang* **a.** To deal a heavy blow to. **b.** To coerce.

sand·bar (sănd′bär′) ►*n.* A ridge of sand formed in a river or along a shore.

sand·blast (sănd′blăst′) ►*n.* A blast of air carrying sand at high velocity, as for cleaning stone or glass. —**sand′blast′** *v.*

sand·board (sănd′bôrd′) ►*n.* A board resembling a snowboard and equipped with bindings, used for descending sand dunes on one's feet. ►*v.* To use a sandboard. —**sand′board′er** *n.*

sand·box (sănd′bŏks′) ►*n.* A box filled with sand for children to play in.

Sand·burg (sănd′bûrg′, săn′-), **Carl August** 1878–1967. Amer. writer.

sand dollar ►*n.* **1.** Any of various thin circular echinoderms of coastal N Atlantic and Pacific waters. **2.** The internal skeleton of a sand dollar, having five radially symmetric markings.

sand·hog (sănd′hôg′, -hŏg′) ►*n. Slang* One who works in a caisson, as in the construction of underwater tunnels.

San Di·e·go (dē-ā′gō) A city of S CA on **San Diego Bay,** an inlet of the Pacific near the Mexican border.

S & L ►*abbr.* savings and loan association

sand·lot (sănd′lŏt′) ►*n.* A vacant lot used esp. by children for games. —**sand′lot′** *adj.*

sand·man (sănd′măn′) ►*n.* A character in folklore who puts children to sleep by sprinkling sand in their eyes.

sand·pa·per (sănd′pā′pər) ►*n.* Heavy paper coated on one side with an abrasive material, used for smoothing surfaces. —**sand′pa′per** *v.*

sand·pi·per (sănd′pī′pər) ►*n.* Any of various small, usu. long-billed shorebirds.

sand·stone (sănd′stōn′) ►*n.* A sedimentary rock formed by the compaction of sand with a natural cement, such as silica.

sand·storm (sănd′stôrm′) ►*n.* A strong wind carrying clouds of sand and dust.

sand trap ►*n.* A sand-filled depression that

serves as a hazard on a golf course.

sand·wich (sănd′wĭch, săn′-) ►*n.* Two or more slices of bread with a filling placed between them. ►*v.* To insert (one thing) tightly between two other things. [After the 4th Earl of *Sandwich* (1718–92).]

sane (sān) ►*adj.* **san·er, san·est 1.** Mentally healthy. **2.** Reasonable. [Lat. *sānus*, healthy.] —**sane′ly** *adv.* —**sane′ness** *n.*

San Fran·cis·co (frən-sĭs′kō) A city of N CA on a peninsula between the Pacific and **San Francisco Bay,** an inlet of the Pacific. —**San Fran·cis′can** *n.*

sang (săng) ►*v.* P.t. of **sing.**

Sang·er (săng′ər), **Margaret Higgins** 1879–1966. Amer. nurse and social reformer.

Margaret Sanger
photographed c. 1922

sang-froid (sän-frwä′) ►*n.* Coolness and composure. [Fr.]

san·gri·a (săng-grē′ə, săn-) ►*n.* A cold drink usu. made of wine, brandy, sugar, fruit juice, and soda water. [< Sp. *sangría* < *sangre*, blood.]

san·gui·nar·y (săng′gwə-nĕr′ē) ►*adj.* **1.** Accompanied by bloodshed. **2.** Bloodthirsty. —**san′gui·nar′i·ly** (-nâr′ə-lē) *adv.*

san·guine (săng′gwĭn) ►*adj.* **1.** Cheerful; optimistic. **2a.** Of the color of blood; red. **b.** Ruddy: *a sanguine complexion.* [< Lat. *sanguīs*, blood.] —**san′guine·ly** *adv.* —**san′guine·ness, san·guin′i·ty** *n.* —**san·guin′e·ous** *adj.*

san·i·tar·i·um (săn′ĭ-târ′ē-əm) ►*n., pl.* **-i·ums** or **-i·a** (-ē-ə) See **sanatorium.** [< Lat. *sānitās*, health.]

san·i·tar·y (săn′ĭ-tĕr′ē) ►*adj.* **1.** Relating to health. **2.** Clean; hygienic. [< Lat. *sānitās*, health.] —**san′i·tar′i·ly** (-târ′ə-lē) *adv.*

sanitary landfill ►*n.* Rehabilitated land in which garbage and trash have been buried.

sanitary napkin ►*n.* A disposable pad of absorbent material worn to absorb menstrual flow.

san·i·ta·tion (săn′ĭ-tā′shən) ►*n.* **1.** Study and application of public health measures, as in the provision of clean water. **2.** Disposal of sewage and garbage.

san·i·tize (săn′ĭ-tīz′) ►*v.* **-tized, -tiz·ing 1.** To make sanitary. **2.** To remove unpleasant or offensive features from: *sanitized the novel.*

san·i·ty (săn′ĭ-tē) ►*n.* The quality or condition of being sane.

San Jo·se (hō-zā′) A city of N CA SE of San Francisco.

San Jo·sé (sän′ hō-sě′) The capital of Costa Rica, in the central part.

San Juan (săn wän′, hwän′) The capital of Puerto Rico, in the NE part on the Atlantic.

sank (săngk) ►*v.* P.t. of **sink.**

San Ma·ri·no (săn mə-rē′nō) A country in the Apennines near the Adriatic Sea. Cap. **San Marino.**

sans (sănz, sän) ►*prep.* Without. [< OFr.]

San Sal·va·dor (săn săl′və-dôr′) The capital of El Salvador, in the W-central part.

San·skrit (săn′skrĭt′) ►*n.* An ancient Indic language that is the classical language of India.

San·ta An·a (săn′tə ăn′ə) ►*n.* A hot desert wind of S California blowing toward the Pacific coast usu. in winter. [After the *Santa Ana* Canyon of S California.]

San·ta An·na or **San·ta An·a** (săn′tə ăn′ə), **Antonio López de** 1794–1876. Mexican military and political leader.

Santa Claus (klôz′) ►*n.* The personification of the spirit of Christmas, usu. represented as a jolly fat old man with a white beard and red suit. [Prob. < Du. *Sinterklaas.*]

San·ta Fe (săn′tə fā′) The capital of NM, in the N-central part NE of Albuquerque.

Santa Fe Trail A historic trade route extending about 1,270 km (790 mi) between Independence, MO, and Santa Fe, NM

San·ta·ya·na (săn′tē-än′ə), **George** 1863–1952. Spanish-born Amer. philosopher.

San·tee (săn-tē′) ►*n., pl.* **-tee** or **-tees** A member of the eastern branch of the Sioux, with populations in Nebraska, Minnesota, the Dakotas, and Canada.

San·te·ri·a (săn′tə-rē′ə, săn′-) ►*n.* A religion originating in Cuba that combines worship of traditional Yoruban deities with worship of Roman Catholic saints. [Am.Sp. *santería*, worship of saints < Sp. *santo*, SAINT.]

San·ti·a·go (săn′tē-ä′gō, sän′-) The capital of Chile, in the central part.

San·to Do·min·go (săn′tō də-mǐng′gō) The capital of the Dominican Republic, in the SE part on the Caribbean Sea.

São Pau·lo (soun pou′lō) A city of SE Brazil WSW of Rio de Janeiro.

São To·mé (tə-mā′) The capital of São Tomé and Príncipe, on the NE coast of **São Tomé,** the larger of the country's two main islands.

São Tomé and Prín·ci·pe (prĭn′sə-pə) An island country in the Gulf of Guinea off W Africa. Cap. São Tomé.

sap[1] (săp) ►*n.* **1.** The watery fluid that circulates through a plant, carrying food and other substances to the tissues. **2.** Health and energy; vitality. **3.** *Slang* A foolish person. ►*v.* **sapped, sap·ping 1.** To drain of sap. **2.** To deplete. [< OE *sæp.*]

sap[2] (săp) ►*v.* **sapped, sap·ping** To undermine the foundations of (a fortification). [< LLat. *sappa*, hoe.]

Sa·phar (sə-fär′) ►*n.* Var. of **Safar.**

sa·pi·ent (sā′pē-ənt) ►*adj.* Wise and discerning. [< Lat. *sapere*, be wise.] —**sa′pi·ence** *n.* —**sa′pi·ent′ial** (-ĕn′chəl) *adj.* —**sa′pi·ent·ly** *adv.*

sap·ling (săp′lĭng) ►*n.* A young tree.

sap·o·dil·la (săp′ə-dĭl′ə, -dē′yə) ►*n.* **1.** An evergreen tree of Mexico and Central America having an edible fruit. **2.** The fruit of this plant. [< Nahuatl *tzapotl.*]

sa·pon·i·fi·ca·tion (sə-pŏn′ə-fĭ-kā′shən) ►*n.* A reaction in which an ester is heated with an alkali, producing a free alcohol and an acid salt, esp. alkaline hydrolysis of a fat or oil to make soap.

sa·pon·i·fy (sə-pŏn′ə-fī′) ►*v.* **-fied, -fy·ing 1.** To convert (an ester) by saponification. **2.** To convert (a fat or oil) into soap. [< Lat. *sāpō,* hair dye.]

sap·per (săp′ər) ►*n.* A military engineer.

sap·phire (săf′īr′) ►*n.* **1.** A clear, hard, usu. blue variety of corundum that is used as a gemstone. **2.** A corundum gem. **3.** The blue color of a gem sapphire. [Gk. *sapheiros,* of Semitic orig.]

Sap·pho (săf′ō) fl. c. 600 BC. Greek lyric poet. —**Sap′phic** *adj.*

sap·py (săp′ē) ►*adj.* **-pi·er, -pi·est 1.** Excessively sentimental. **2.** *Slang* Silly; foolish. **3.** Full of sap.

sap·ro·phyte (săp′rə-fīt′) ►*n.* An organism that derives its nourishment from dead or decaying organic matter. [Gk. *sapros,* rotten + –PHYTE.] —**sap′ro·phyt′ic** (-fĭt′ĭk) *adj.*

sap·suck·er (săp′sŭk′ər) ►*n.* An American woodpecker that drills holes in trees to feed on sap and insects.

Sar·a·cen (săr′ə-sən) ►*n.* **1.** A member of a preIslamic nomadic people of the Syrian-Arabian Deserts. **2.** A Muslim, esp. of the time of the Crusades.

Sar·ah (sâr′ə) In the Bible, the wife of Abraham and mother of Isaac.

Sa·ra·je·vo (săr′ə-yā′vō) The capital of Bosnia and Herzegovina, in the S-central part.

sa·ran (sə-rǎn′) ►*n.* Any of various thermoplastic resins used to make packaging films and in various heavy fabrics. [< *Saran,* a former US trademark.]

sa·ra·pe (sə-rä′pē, -răp′ē) ►*n.* Var. of **serape.**

Sa·ra·wak (sə-rä′wäk, -wä) A region of Malaysia on NW Borneo.

sar·casm (sär′kăz′əm) ►*n.* **1.** A cutting, often ironic remark. **2.** A form of wit marked by the use of such remarks. [< Gk. *sarkasmos.*] —**sar·cas′tic** (-kăs′tĭk) *adj.* —**sar·cas′ti·cal·ly** *adv.*

sar·co·ma (sär-kō′mə) ►*n., pl.* **-mas** also **-ma·ta** (-mə-tə) A malignant tumor arising from connective tissues. [< Gk. *sarkōma,* fleshy excrescence.]

sar·coph·a·gus (sär-kŏf′ə-gəs) ►*n., pl.* **-gi** (-jī′) or **-gus·es** A stone coffin. [< Gk. *sarkophagos,* coffin.]

sar·dine (sär-dēn′) ►*n.* An edible herring or related fish that is often canned. [< Lat. *sardīna.*]

Sar·din·i·a (sär-dĭn′ē-ə) An island of Italy in the Mediterranean S of Corsica. —**Sar·din′i·an** *adj. & n.*

sar·don·ic (sär-dŏn′ĭk) ►*adj.* **1.** Scornfully mocking. **2.** Given to making sardonic remarks. [< Gk. *sardonios.*] —**sar·don′i·cal·ly** *adv.*

sar·gas·so (sär-găs′ō) ►*n., pl.* **-sos** See **gulfweed.** [Port. *sargaço.*]

Sar·gas·so Sea (sär-găs′ō) A part of the N Atlantic between the West Indies and the Azores, noted for its masses of floating seaweed.

Sar·gent (sär′jənt), **John Singer** 1856–1925. Amer. painter.

sa·ri (sä′rē) ►*n., pl.* **-ris** A lightweight, wrapped outer garment worn chiefly by women of South Asia. [< Skt. *śāṭī.*]

sa·rong (sə-rông′, -rŏng′) ►*n.* A length of brightly colored cloth wrapped about the waist, worn by men and women in Malaysia, Indonesia, and the Pacific islands. [Malay.]

SARS (särz) ►*n.* A viral pneumonia that can progress to respiratory failure and is often marked by high fever, malaise, dry cough, and shortness of breath. [*s(evere) a(cute) r(espiratory) s(yndrome).*]

sar·sa·pa·ril·la (săs′pə-rĭl′ə, särs′-) ►*n.* **1.** The dried roots of a tropical American plant, used as a flavoring. **2.** A carbonated soft drink flavored with extracts of these roots or artificial flavorings having a similar flavor. [Sp. *zarzaparrilla.*]

sar·to·ri·al (sär-tôr′ē-əl) ►*adj.* Relating to tailors or tailoring. [< LLat. *sartor,* tailor.] —**sar·to′ri·al·ly** *adv.*

Sar·tre (sär′trə, särt), **Jean Paul** 1905–80. French writer and philosopher.

SASE ►*abbr.* self-addressed stamped envelope

sash¹ (săsh) ►*n.* A band or ribbon worn about the waist or over the shoulder. [Ar. *šāš,* muslin.]

sash² (săsh) ►*n.* A frame in which the panes of a window or door are set. [< Fr. *châssis,* frame.]

sa·shay (să-shā′) ►*v. Informal* To strut or flounce in a showy manner. [< Fr. *chassé,* a dance step.]

Sas·katch·e·wan (să-skăch′ə-wän′, -wən) A province of S-central Canada. Cap. Regina.

Sas·ka·toon (săs′kə-tōōn′) A city of S-central Saskatchewan, Canada, NW of Regina.

Sas·quatch (săs′kwŏch, -kwăch) ►*n.* See **Bigfoot.**

sass (săs) ►*n. Informal* Impertinence; back talk. [< SASSY.] —**sass** *v.*

sas·sa·fras (săs′ə-frăs′) ►*n.* **1.** A North American tree with irregularly lobed leaves and aromatic bark. **2.** The dried root bark of this plant, formerly used as a flavoring. [< LLat. *saxifragia.*]

sas·sy (săs′ē) ►*adj.* **-si·er, -si·est** Rude and disrespectful; impudent. [< SAUCY.] —**sas′si·ly** *adv.* —**sas′si·ness** *n.*

sat (săt) ►*v.* P.t. and p.part. of **sit.**

SAT (ĕs′ā-tē′) A trademark used for a set of standardized college entrance examinations.

Sa·tan (sāt′n) ►*n.* The Devil. [< Heb. *śāṭān.*]

sa·tan·ic (sə-tăn′ĭk, sā-) or **sa·tan·i·cal** (-ĭ-kəl) ►*adj.* **1.** Relating to or suggestive of Satan. **2.** Fiendishly cruel or evil. —**sa·tan′i·cal·ly** *adv.*

satch·el (săch′əl) ►*n.* A small bag for carrying books or clothing. [< LLat. *saccellus.*]

sate (sāt) ►*v.* **sat·ed, sat·ing 1.** To satisfy (an appetite) fully. **2.** To provide (someone) with more than enough. [< OE *sadian.*]

sa·teen (să-tēn′) ►*n.* A usu. cotton fabric that has a satinlike finish. [< SATIN.]

sat·el·lite (săt′l-īt′) ►*n.* **1.** An object launched to orbit a celestial body, esp. as a device for relaying radio signals. **2.** *Astron.* A celestial body, such as a moon, planet, or other solar system body, that orbits a larger celestial body. **3.** A nation dominated politically and economically by another. **4.** A community located near a big city. **5.** A subservient follower; sycophant. ►*adj.* Of or relating to the transmission of electromagnetic signals by communications satellite. [< Lat. *satelles,* attendant.]

satellite dish ►*n.* A dish antenna that receives and transmits satellite signals.

satellite radio ►*n.* **1.** Radio broadcast of digital radio content via a satellite. **2.** A radio receiver capable of playing such broadcasts.

sa·ti·ate (sā′shē-āt′) ►*v.* **-at·ed, -at·ing 1.** To satisfy (e.g., an appetite) fully. **2.** To provide (someone) with more than enough. [< Lat. *satis,* sufficient.] —**sa′ti·a′tion** *n.*

sa·ti·e·ty (sə-tī′ĭ-tē) ►*n.* The condition of being sated. [< Lat. *satietās.*]

sat·in (săt′n) ►*n.* **1.** A smooth, often silk fabric woven with a glossy face and a dull back. **2.** A kind of paint that dries to a smooth shiny finish. [< OFr.] —**sat′in·y** *adj.*

sat·in·wood (săt′n-wood′) ►*n.* A deciduous tree of South Asia having hard yellow wood.

sat·ire (săt′īr′) ►*n.* **1.** A literary work in which human foolishness or vice is attacked through irony, derision, or wit. **2.** Irony, sarcasm, or caustic wit used to expose or attack human foolishness. [Lat. *satira.*] —**sa·tir′i·cal** (sə-tĭr′ĭ-kəl), **sa·tir′ic** *adj.* —**sa·tir′i·cal·ly** *adv.* —**sat′ir·ist** (săt′ər-ĭst) *n.*

sat·i·rize (săt′ə-rīz′) ►*v.* **-rized, -riz·ing** To ridicule or attack by satire.

sat·is·fac·tion (săt′ĭs-făk′shən) ►*n.* **1a.** The gratification of a desire, need, or appetite. **b.** Pleasure derived from such gratification. **2.** Compensation for injury or loss; reparation.

sat·is·fac·to·ry (săt′ĭs-făk′tə-rē) ►*adj.* Giving satisfaction; adequate. —**sat′is·fac′to·ri·ly** *adv.* —**sat′is·fac′to·ri·ness** *n.*

sat·is·fy (săt′ĭs-fī′) ►*v.* **-fied, -fy·ing 1.** To fulfill the need, desire, or expectation of: *was satisfied with the service.* **2.** To fulfill (a need or desire): *The lemonade satisfied my thirst.* **3.** To free from doubt or question; assure. **4.** To fulfill or discharge (an obligation). **5.** To conform to the requirements of. **6.** To give satisfaction. [< Lat. *satisfacere.*]
Syns: answer, fill, fulfill, meet **v.**

sa·trap (sā′trăp′, săt′răp′) ►*n.* A subordinate ruler. [< OPers. *khshathrapāvā,* protector of the province.]

sat·u·rate (săch′ə-rāt′) ►*v.* **-rat·ed, -rat·ing 1.** To soak or fill so that no more liquid may be absorbed: *a rag that was saturated with water.* **2.** To supply with the maximum that can be held or contained; fill thoroughly. See Synonyms at **imbue. 3.** *Chem.* To cause (a substance) to unite with the greatest possible amount of another substance. **4.** To supply (a market) with a good or service in an amount that consumers are able and willing to purchase. ►*adj.* (-rĭt) Saturated. [< Lat. *satur,* sated.] —**sat′u·ra·ble** (săch′ər-ə-bəl) *adj.* —**sat′u·ra′tion** *n.*

sat·u·rat·ed fat (săch′ə-rā′tĭd) ►*n.* A fat, usu. of animal origin, composed predominantly of fatty acids having only single bonds in the carbon chain.

Sat·ur·day (săt′ər-dē, -dā′) ►*n.* The 7th day of the week. [< OE *Sæternesdæg.*]

Saturday night special ►*n. Informal* A cheap handgun easily obtained and concealed.

Sat·urn (săt′ərn) ►*n.* **1.** *Rom. Myth.* The god of agriculture. **2.** The 2nd largest planet in the solar system and the 6th from the sun at a mean distance of about 1.4 billion km (891 million mi), and having a mean diameter of approx. 121,000 km (75,000 mi).

sat·ur·nine (săt′ər-nīn′) ►*adj.* Morose and sardonic.

sa·tyr (sā′tər, săt′ər) ►*n.* **1.** often **Satyr** *Gk. Myth.* A woodland creature depicted as having the ears, legs, and horns of a goat and a fondness for unrestrained revelry. **2.** A lecher. [< Gk. *saturos.*]

sauce (sôs) ►*n.* **1.** A liquid dressing served with food. **2.** Stewed fruit. **3.** *Informal* Impudence. **4.** *Slang* Alcoholic liquor. ►*v.* **sauced, sauc·ing 1.** To flavor with sauce. **2.** To add zest to. **3.** *Informal* To be impudent to. [< Lat. *salsa,* salted.]

sauce·pan (sôs′păn′) ►*n.* A deep cooking pan with a handle.

sau·cer (sô′sər) ►*n.* **1.** A small shallow dish for holding a cup. **2.** An object resembling a saucer. [< OFr. *saussier,* sauce dish.]

sauc·y (sô′sē) ►*adj.* **-i·er, -i·est 1.** Impertinent or disrespectful, esp. in a playful or lively way. **2.** Attractive, esp. in being sexually alluring. —**sau′ci·ly** *adv.* —**sau′ci·ness** *n.*

Sau·di Arabia (sou′dē, sô′dē, sä-oo′dē) A country occupying most of the Arabian Peninsula. Cap. Riyadh. —**Sau′di, Sau′di Arabian** *adj. & n.*

sau·er·bra·ten (sour′brät′n) ►*n.* A pot roast of beef marinated in vinegar, water, wine, and spices before cooking. [Ger.]

sau·er·kraut (sour′krout′) ►*n.* Shredded cabbage salted and fermented in its own juice. [Ger.]

Sauk (sôk) also **Sac** (săk, sôk) ►*n., pl.* **Sauk** or **Sauks** also **Sac** or **Sacs 1.** A member of a Native American people formerly of Wisconsin, Illinois, and Iowa, now mainly in Oklahoma. **2.** The Algonquian language of the Sauk.

Saul (sôl) In the Bible, the first king of Israel.

Sault Sainte Ma·rie (soo′ sănt′ mə-rē′) A city of S Ontario, Canada, located near the **Sault Sainte Marie Canals,** a shipping route between Lake Superior and Lake Huron.

sau·na (sô′nə, sou′-) ►*n.* **1.** A structure that provides dry heat for refreshing the body. **2.** A period of time spent in a sauna. [Finn.]

saun·ter (sôn′tər) ►*v.* To walk at a leisurely pace. ►*n.* A leisurely stroll. [Prob. < ME *santren,* muse.] —**saun′ter·er** *n.*

sau·sage (sô′sĭj) ►*n.* Finely chopped and seasoned meat stuffed into a casing. [< LLat. *salsīcius,* prepared by salting.]

sau·té (sō-tā′, sô-) ►*v.* **-téed, -té·ing** To fry lightly in fat. [< Lat. *saltāre,* leap.]

sav·age (săv′ĭj) ►*adj.* **1.** Not domesticated or cultivated; wild. **2.** Not civilized; barbaric. ►*n.* A primitive or uncivilized person. ►*v.* **-aged, -ag·ing** To assault ferociously. [< Lat. *silvāticus,* of the woods.] —**sav′age·ly** *adv.* —**sav′age·ry** *n.*

sa·van·na also **sa·van·nah** (sə-văn′ə) ►*n.* A flat grassland of tropical or subtropical regions. [< Taíno *zabana.*]

Sa·van·nah (sə-văn′ə) A city of SE GA near the mouth of the 500 km (310 mi) long **Savannah River,** which forms the border between GA and SC.

sa·vant (să-vänt′) ►*n.* A learned person. [< OFr. < *savoir,* know.]

save¹ (sāv) ►*v.* **saved, sav·ing 1a.** To rescue from danger. **b.** To deliver from sin. **2.** To keep in a safe or healthy condition: *God save King Richard!* **3.** To hold back for future use. **4.** To prevent waste. **5.** To keep from harm; spare: *save one's eyesight.* **6.** *Comp.* To copy (a file) from main memory to a storage medium. [< LLat. *salvāre.*] —**sav′er** *n.*

save² (sāv) ►*prep.* With the exception of; except. ►*conj.* Except; but. [< Lat. *salvō.*]

sav·ing (sā′vĭng) ►*n.* **1.** Preservation or rescue. **2.** Economy. **3. savings** Money saved. ►*prep.* With the exception of. ►*conj.* Except; save.

savings account ►*n.* A bank account that draws interest.

savings and loan association ►*n.* A financial institution that invests deposits chiefly in home mortgage loans.

savings bank ►*n.* A bank that invests and pays interest on savings accounts.

sav·ior (sāv′yər) ►*n.* **1.** A person who rescues another from harm, danger, or loss. **2. Savior** *Christianity* Jesus. [< LLat. *salvātor.*]

sa·voir-faire (săv′wär-fâr′) ►*n.* Social skill or tact. [Fr.]

Sa·vo·na·ro·la (săv′ə-nə-rō′lə, sä′vō-nä-), **Girolamo** 1452–98. Italian reformer.

sa·vor (sā′vər) ►*n.* **1.** A specific taste or smell: *the savor of mint.* **2.** The quality of something that is perceived as taste or smell. **3.** A distinctive quality. ►*v.* **1.** To have a particular savor. **2.** To appreciate fully; relish. [< Lat. *sapor.*]

sa·vor·y¹ (sā′və-rē) ►*adj.* **1.** Appetizing to the taste or smell. **2.** Piquant, pungent, or salty to the taste. —**sa′vor·i·ness** *n.*

sa·vor·y² (sā′və-rē) ►*n., pl.* -**ies** An aromatic herb used as a seasoning. [< Lat. *saturēia.*]

Sa·voy (sə-voi′) A historical region and former duchy of SE France, W Switzerland, and NW Italy. —**Sa·voy′ard** (sə-voi′ärd′, săv′oi-yärd′) *adj. & n.*

sav·vy (săv′ē) *Informal* ►*adj.* -**vi·er, -vi·est** Well informed and perceptive; shrewd. ►*n.* Practical understanding. ►*v.* **sav·vied** (săv′ēd), **sav·vy·ing** To understand. [< Sp. *sabe (usted),* (you) know.]

saw¹ (sô) ►*n.* A cutting tool having a thin metal blade or disk with a sharp-toothed edge. ►*v.* **sawed, sawed** or **sawn** (sôn), **saw·ing** To cut or divide with a saw. [< OE *sagu.*]

saw² (sô) ►*n.* A familiar and often trite saying. [< OE *sagu,* speech.]

saw³ (sô) ►*v.* P.t. of **see¹.**

saw·buck (sô′bŭk′) ►*n.* A sawhorse, esp. one with x-shaped legs.

saw·dust (sô′dŭst′) ►*n.* The small waste particles that result from sawing.

sawed-off (sôd′ôf′, -ŏf′) ►*adj.* **1.** Having one end sawed off: *a sawed-off shotgun.* **2.** *Slang* Short; runty.

saw·fish (sô′fĭsh′) ►*n.* A fish having a sharklike body and a snout with teeth along both sides.

saw·horse (sô′hôrs′) ►*n.* A frame used to support pieces of wood being sawed.

saw·mill (sô′mĭl′) ►*n.* A mill where timber is sawed into boards.

sawn (sôn) ►*v.* P.part. of **saw¹.**

saw·yer (sô′yər) ►*n.* One employed in sawing wood. [ME *sawier.*]

sax (săks) ►*n.* A saxophone.

sax·i·frage (săk′sə-frĭj, -frāj′) ►*n.* Any of various plants with small flowers and leaves that often form a basal rosette. [< Lat. *saxifragus,* rock-breaking.]

Sax·on (săk′sən) ►*n.* **1.** A member of a Ger-

manic tribal group that invaded Britain in the 5th cent. AD. **2.** A native or inhabitant of Saxony. **3.** The Germanic language of any of the Saxons. —**Sax′on** *adj.*

Sax·o·ny (săk′sə-nē) A historical region of N Germany.

sax·o·phone (săk′sə-fōn′) ►*n.* A woodwind instrument with a single-reed mouthpiece and a usu. curved conical metal tube. [After the *Sax* family of 19th cent. Belgian instrument makers.] —**sax′o·phon′ist** *n.*

say (sā) ►*v.* **said** (sĕd), **say·ing** **1.** To utter aloud. **2.** To express in words. **3a.** To state; declare. **b.** To allege. **4.** To recite. **5.** To indicate; show: *The clock says noon.* **6.** To suppose; assume. ►*n.* A turn or chance to speak. ►*adv.* **1.** Approximately. **2.** For instance. [< OE *secgan.*]

say·ing (sā′ĭng) ►*n.* An adage or maxim.

sa·yo·na·ra (sī′ə-när′ə) ►*interj.* Good-bye. [J.]

say-so (sā′sō′) ►*n., pl.* -**sos** *Informal* **1.** An unsupported statement or assurance. **2.** An expression of permission or approval. **3.** The authority to decide.

SB ►*abbr.* **1.** *Lat.* Scientiae Baccalaureus (Bachelor of Science) **2.** stolen base

SBA ►*abbr.* Small Business Administration

SbE ►*abbr.* south by east

SbW ►*abbr.* south by west

sc ►*abbr.* small capital

SC ►*abbr.* **1.** South Carolina **2.** Supreme Court

sc. ►*abbr.* **1.** scale **2.** scene **3.** scruple (unit of weight)

scab (skăb) ►*n.* **1.** A crust discharged from and covering a healing wound. **2.** A person who takes the place of a striking worker. ►*v.* **scabbed, scab·bing** **1.** To become covered with a scab. **2.** To work as a scab. [< ON *skabb.*]

scab·bard (skăb′ərd) ►*n.* A sheath, as for a dagger or sword. [< OFr. *escauberc.*]

scab·by (skăb′ē) ►*adj.* -**bi·er, -bi·est** **1.** Having or covered with scabs. **2.** Affected with scabies.

sca·bies (skā′bēz) ►*n.* A contagious skin disease caused by a mite and characterized by intense itching. [< Lat. *scabiēs,* itch.]

scab·rous (skăb′rəs, skā′brəs) ►*adj.* Rough or harsh. [LLat. *scabrōsus.*]

scads (skădz) ►*pl.n. Informal* A large number or amount. [?]

scaf·fold (skăf′əld, -ōld′) ►*n.* **1.** A temporary platform on which workers perform tasks at heights above the ground. **2.** A platform used in the execution of condemned prisoners. [< Med.Lat. *scaffaldus.*]

sca·lar (skā′lər, -lär′) ►*n.* A quantity, such as length, that is completely specified by its magnitude and has no direction. [< Lat. *scālae,* ladder.]

scal·a·wag (skăl′ə-wăg′) ►*n. Informal* A scoundrel; rascal. [?]

scald (skôld) ►*v.* **1.** To burn (e.g., a person) with hot liquid or steam. **2.** To subject to or treat with boiling water. **3.** To heat (e.g., milk) almost to the boiling point. ►*n.* An injury caused by scalding. [< LLat. *excaldāre,* wash in hot water.]

scale¹ (skāl) ►*n.* **1a.** One of the small hard structures forming the external covering of fishes, reptiles, and certain mammals. **b.** A similar structure or part, such as one of the thin, flat structures on the cone of a conifer. **2.** A dry thin flake of epidermis shed from the skin. **3.** A scale insect. **4.** A flaky oxide film formed on a metal. ►*v.* **scaled, scal·ing 1.** To clear or strip of scale or scales. **2.** To remove or come off in layers or scales. **3.** To become encrusted. [< OFr. *escale.*] —**scal′i·ness** *n.* —**scal′y** *adj.*

scale¹
cone of a white pine

scale² (skāl) ►*n.* **1a.** A system of ordered marks at fixed intervals used in measurement. **b.** An instrument or device bearing such marks. **2.** A progressive classification, as of size, importance, or rank. **3.** A relative level or degree. **4.** *Mus.* An ascending or descending series of tones proceeding by a specified scheme of intervals. ►*v.* **scaled, scal·ing 1.** To climb up or over; ascend. **2.** To make in accord with a particular proportion or scale. **3.** To adjust in calculated amounts: *scaled down their demands.* [< Lat. *scālae,* ladder.] —**scal′a·ble** *adj.*

scale³ (skāl) ►*n.* often **scales** An instrument or machine for weighing. [< ON *skāl,* bowl.]

scale insect ►*n.* A plant-feeding insect that secretes a waxy substance covering the body and is often an agricultural pest.

sca·lene (skā′lēn′, skā-lēn′) ►*adj.* Having three unequal sides. Used of triangles. [< Gk. *skalēnos.*]

scal·lion (skăl′yən) ►*n.* A young onion before the development of the bulb. [< Lat. *(caepa) Ascalōnia,* (onion) of Ascalon, a city in Palestine.]

scal·lop (skŏl′əp, skăl′-) ►*n.* **1a.** A bivalve marine mollusk with a fan-shaped ridged shell. **b.** The edible muscle of a scallop. **2.** One of a series of curved projections forming an ornamental border. **3.** A thin, boneless slice of meat. ►*v.* **-loped, -lop·ing 1.** To edge (e.g., cloth) with scallops. **2.** To bake in a casserole with milk or a sauce and often with bread crumbs. [< OFr. *escalope,* shell.] —**scal′lop·er** *n.*

scalp (skălp) ►*n.* The skin covering the top of the human head. ►*v.* **1.** To cut or tear the scalp from. **2.** To resell (tickets) at an excessively high price. [ME.] —**scalp′er** *n.*

scal·pel (skăl′pəl) ►*n.* A small surgical knife with a thin sharp blade. [Lat. *scalpellum.*]

scam (skăm) ►*n. Slang* A fraudulent business scheme; swindle. [?] —**scam** *v.*

scamp (skămp) ►*n.* A rogue; rascal.

scam·per (skăm′pər) ►*v.* To run nimbly. [Prob. < Flem. *schampeeren.*] —**scam′per** *n.*

scan (skăn) ►*v.* **scanned, scan·ning 1a.** To look at thoroughly, esp. in search of something; examine. **b.** To look over quickly or read hastily. **2.** *Comp.* To search (stored data) automatically for specific data. **3.** *Electron.* To direct a beam of energy in a systematic pattern over (a surface) in order to create an image. **4.** To encode (e.g., text) in digital format by means of a scanner. **5.** *Med.* To examine (e.g., a body part) with a scanner. **6.** To analyze (verse) into metrical patterns. [< Lat. *scandere,* climb.] —**scan** *n.*

scan·dal (skăn′dl) ►*n.* **1.** Public disgrace. **2.** A person, thing, or circumstance that causes disgrace or outrage. **3.** Malicious gossip. [< Gk. *skandalon,* snare.] —**scan′dal·ous** *adj.* —**scan′dal·ous·ly** *adv.*

scan·dal·ize (skăn′dl-īz′) ►*v.* **-ized, -iz·ing** To offend the moral sensibilities of.

scandal sheet ►*n.* A newspaper that habitually prints scandalous stories.

Scan·di·na·vi·a (skăn′də-nā′vē-ə, -nāv′yə) A region of N Europe consisting of Norway, Sweden, and Denmark, and sometimes Finland, Iceland, and the Faroe Is.

Scan·di·na·vi·an (skăn′də-nā′vē-ən, -nāv′yən) ►*n.* **1.** A native or inhabitant of Scandinavia. **2.** A branch of Germanic including Norwegian, Swedish, Danish, and Icelandic. —**Scan′di·na′vi·an** *adj.*

Scandinavian Peninsula A peninsula of N Europe comprising Norway and Sweden.

scan·di·um (skăn′dē-əm) ►*n. Symbol* **Sc** A soft, silvery-white metallic element found in various rare minerals and in certain uranium ores. At. no. 21. See table at **element.** [< Lat. *Scandia,* Scandinavia.]

scan·ner (skăn′ər) ►*n.* **1.** One that scans. **2.** A receiver that broadcasts signals from specified radio frequencies. **3.** A device that converts printed images and text into digital information stored as computer file. **4.** A device, such as a CAT scanner, for observing internal body structures.

scan·sion (skăn′shən) ►*n.* Analysis of verse into metrical patterns. [< Lat. *scandere, scāns-,* climb.]

scant (skănt) ►*adj.* **-er, -est 1.** Barely sufficient: *paid scant attention to me.* **2.** Falling just short of a specific measure. ►*v.* **1.** To skimp. **2.** To limit, as in amount; stint. [< ON *skamt,* short.] —**scant′ly** *adv.*

scant·y (skăn′tē) ►*adj.* **-i·er, -i·est 1.** Small, as in size or extent. **2.** Not covering a considerable amount of the body. —**scant′i·ly** *adv.* —**scant′i·ness** *n.*

scape·goat (skāp′gōt′) ►*n.* One bearing blame for others. ►*v.* To make a scapegoat of. [*(e)scape* + GOAT.]

scap·u·la (skăp′yə-lə) ►*n., pl.* **-las** or **-lae** (-lē′) Either of two large flat bones forming the back part of the shoulder; shoulder blade. [LLat.] —**scap′u·lar** *adj.*

scar (skär) ►*n.* **1.** A mark left on the skin after a surface injury or wound has healed. **2.** A lingering sign of damage or injury. ►*v.* **scarred, scar·ring** To mark with or form a scar. [< Gk. *eskhara,* scab.]

scar·ab (skăr′əb) ►*n.* **1.** A large black beetle regarded as sacred by the ancient Egyptians. **2.** A representation of this beetle. [< Lat. *scarabaeus.*]

scarce (skârs) ►*adj.* **scarc·er, scarc·est 1.** Insufficient to meet a demand or requirement; short in supply. **2.** Hard to find; absent or rare. [< VLat. **excarpere, excarps-,* pluck out.] —**scarce′ness, scar′ci·ty** *n.*

scarce·ly (skârs′lē) ►*adv.* **1.** By a small margin; barely. **2.** Almost not; hardly. **3.** Certainly not. *Usage:* Scarcely has the force of a negative and is therefore regarded as incorrectly used with another negative, as in *I couldn't scarcely believe it.* A clause following *scarcely* is correctly

introduced by *when* or *before* but not by *than:*
The meeting had scarcely begun when (or *before*
but not *than*) *it was interrupted.* See Usage Note
at **hardly.**

scare (skâr) ►*v.* **scared, scar·ing** To frighten or
become frightened. ►*n.* **1.** A fright. **2.** A panic.
[< ON *skjarr,* timid.]

scare·crow (skâr′krō′) ►*n.* A crude figure set up
in a cultivated area to scare birds away.

scarf[1] (skärf) ►*n., pl.* **scarfs** or **scarves** (skärvz)
1. A piece of cloth worn about the head, neck,
or shoulders. **2.** A runner, as for a bureau. [<
ONFr. *escarpe,* sash.]

scarf[2] (skärf) ►*n., pl.* **scarfs** (skärfs) A joint
made by cutting the ends of two pieces correspondingly and strapping or bolting them
together. [ME *skarf.*] —**scarf** *v.*

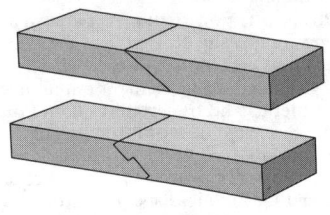

scarf[2]
top: plain scarf
bottom: hooked scarf

scar·i·fy (skăr′ə-fī′) ►*v.* **-fied, -fy·ing 1.** To
make shallow cuts in (the skin). **2.** To distress
deeply, as with severe criticism. [< Gk. *skari-
phos,* pencil, stylus.] —**scar′i·fi·ca′tion** *n.*

scar·la·ti·na (skär′lə-tē′nə) ►*n.* See **scarlet
fever.** [< Ital. *scarlattina* < dim. of *scarlatto,*
SCARLET.]

Scar·lat·ti (skär-lä′tē), **Alessandro** (1660–
1725) and **Domenico** (1685–1757). Italian
composers.

scar·let (skär′lĭt) ►*n.* A strong to vivid red or
reddish orange. [< Pers. *saqirlāt,* rich cloth.]
—**scar′let** *adj.*

scarlet fever ►*n.* An infectious disease caused
by a streptococcus and marked by a scarlet skin
eruption and high fever.

scarp (skärp) ►*n.* An escarpment. [Ital. *scarpa,*
slope.]

scar·y (skâr′ē) ►*adj.* **-i·er, -i·est 1.** Frightening.
2. Easily scared; very timid. —**scar′i·ly** *adv.*
—**scar′i·ness** *n.*

scat[1] (skăt) ►*v.* **scat·ted, scat·ting** *Informal* To
go away hastily. [?]

scat[2] (skăt) ►*n.* Jazz singing in which improvised, meaningless syllables are sung to a melody. [?] —**scat** *v.*

scath·ing (skā′thĭng) ►*adj.* **1.** Harshly critical. **2.**
Harmful or painful; injurious. [< ON *skadha.*]
—**scath′ing·ly** *adv.*

sca·tol·o·gy (skă-tŏl′ə-jē, skə-) ►*n.* Obscene
language or literature, esp. that dealing humorously with excrement and excretory functions.
[< Gk. *skōr, skat-,* excrement.] —**scat′o·log′i·
cal** (skăt′l-ŏj′ĭ-kəl), **scat′o·log′ic** *adj.*

scat·ter (skăt′ər) ►*v.* **1.** To disperse. **2.** To distribute loosely; strew. **3.** To diffuse or deflect
(radiation or particles). [ME *scateren.*]

scat·ter·brain (skăt′ər-brān′) ►*n.* A flighty or
disorganized person. —**scat′ter·brained′** *adj.*

scatter rug ►*n.* A small rug.

scat·ter·shot (skăt′ər-shŏt′) ►*adj.* Indiscriminate and wide-ranging: *scattershot criticism.*

scav·en·ger (skăv′ən-jər) ►*n.* **1.** An animal that
feeds on dead or decaying matter. **2.** One who
searches, as through refuse, for useful material.
[< AN *scawage,* tax on the goods of foreign
merchants.] —**scav′enge** *v.*

sce·nar·i·o (sĭ-nâr′ē-ō′, -när′-, -năr′-) ►*n., pl.*
-os 1. A supposed sequence of events. **2.** An
outline for a screenplay. [< Ital. *scena,* SCENE.]

scene (sēn) ►*n.* **1.** A prospect; view. **2.** The setting of an action. **3.** A subdivision of an act of
a play. **4.** A shot or series of related shots in a
movie. **5.** The scenery for a dramatic presentation. **6.** A public display of passion or temper.
7. A sphere of activity: *the arts scene.* [< Gk.
skēnē, tent, stage.]

scen·er·y (sē′nə-rē) ►*n., pl.* **-ies 1.** A landscape.
2. The painted backdrops on a theatrical stage.
—**sce′nic** *adj.* —**sce′ni·cal·ly** *adv.*

sce·nog·ra·phy (sē-nŏg′rə-fē) ►*n.* **1.** The art of
representing objects in perspective, esp. in theatrical scenery. **2.** Visual design for theatrical
productions. —**sce·nog′raph·er** *n.*

scent (sĕnt) ►*n.* **1.** A distinctive odor. See
Synonyms at **fragrance, smell. 2.** A perfume.
3. The trail of a hunted animal or fugitive. ►*v.*
1. To smell, esp. to hunt by smell. **2.** To detect
as if by smelling: *scented danger.* **3.** To fill with
a scent. [< Lat. *sentīre,* feel.] —**scent′ed** *adj.*

scep·ter (sĕp′tər) ►*n.* A staff held by a sovereign
as an emblem of authority. [< Gk. *skēptron.*]

scep·tic (skĕp′tĭk) ►*n.* Var. of **skeptic.**

scep·ti·cism (skĕp′tĭ-sĭz′əm) ►*n.* Var. of **skepticism.**

sched·ule (skĕj′ool, -oo-əl, skĕj′əl) ►*n.* **1.** A
timetable. **2.** A production plan. **3.** A list of
items. **4.** A program of events or appointments.
►*v.* **-uled, -ul·ing 1.** To enter on a schedule.
2. To make up a schedule for. **3.** To plan for a
certain time. [< LLat. *schedula,* small piece of
paper.] —**sched′u·ler** *n.*

sche·ma (skē′mə) ►*n., pl.* **sche·ma·ta** (skē-
mä′tə, skĭ-mät′ə) or **-mas** A plan, outline, or
model. [< Gk. *skhēma.*]

sche·mat·ic (skē-măt′ĭk, skĭ-) ►*adj.* Relating
to or in the form of a scheme or diagram. ►*n.*
A structural diagram, esp. of an electrical or
mechanical system. —**sche·mat′i·cal·ly** *adv.*

scheme (skēm) ►*n.* **1.** A systematic plan or
design. See Synonyms at **plan. 2.** A plot. See
Synonyms at **plan. 3.** An orderly plan or
arrangement of related parts. ►*v.* **schemed,
schem·ing 1.** To contrive a plan or scheme for.
2. To plot. [< Gk. *skhēma,* figure.] —**schem′-
er** *n.*

scher·zo (skĕr′tsō) ►*n., pl.* **-zos** or **-zi** (-tsē)
Mus. A lively movement commonly in 3/4
time. [Ital.]

Schick test (shĭk) ►*n.* A skin test to determine
immunity to diphtheria. [After Béla *Schick*
(1877–1967).]

Schil·ler (shĭl′ər), **Johann Christoph Friedrich von** 1759–1805. German writer.

schil·ling (shĭl′ĭng) ►*n.* The primary unit of
currency in Austria before the adoption of the
euro. [Ger.]

schism (skĭz′əm, sĭz′-) ►*n.* A separation or division into factions, esp. within a religious body.
[< Gk. *skhisma.*] —**schis·mat′ic** *adj.*

schist (shĭst) ►*n.* A metamorphic rock composed of laminated, often flaky parallel layers. [< Gk. *skhistos*, split.]

schis·to·so·mi·a·sis (shĭs′tə-sə-mī′ə-sĭs) ►*n.* A tropical disease caused by infestation with parasitic worms, usu. acquired through contaminated water. [< *schistosome*, a parasitic worm.]

schizo– or **schiz–** ►*pref.* **1.** Split: *schizophrenia.* **2.** Schizophrenia: *schizoid.* [< Gk. *skhizein*, split.]

schiz·oid (skĭt′soid′) ►*adj.* Relating to a personality disorder marked by reclusiveness and an inability to form close relationships. ►*n.* A schizoid person.

schiz·o·phre·ni·a (skĭt′sə-frē′nē-ə, -frĕn′ē-ə) ►*n.* A psychiatric illness marked usu. by psychosis, including hallucinations, delusions, and disorganized thoughts and speech. —**schiz′o·phren′ic** (-frĕn′ĭk) *adj. & n.*

schle·miel (shlə-mēl′) ►*n. Slang* A habitual bungler; dolt. [Yiddish *shlemíl.*]

schlep (shlĕp) ►*v.* **schlepped, schlep·ping** *Slang* To carry clumsily or with difficulty; lug. ►*n.* **1.** An arduous journey. **2.** An unappealing person. [Yiddish *shlepn*, drag, pull.] —**schlep** *n.*

schlock (shlŏk) ►*n. Slang* Something that is inferior or poorly made. [Poss. < Yiddish *shlak*, stroke, nuisance.] —**schlock, shlock′y** *adj.*

schmaltz also **schmalz** (shmälts) ►*n. Informal* Excessively sentimental art or music. [Yiddish *shmalts*, animal fat.] —**schmaltz′y** *adj.*

schmuck (shmŭk) ►*n. Slang* An oaf. [Yiddish *shmok*, penis, fool.]

schnapps (shnäps, shnăps) ►*n., pl.* **schnapps** Any of various strong, often flavored liquors. [Ger. *Schnaps.*]

schnau·zer (shnou′zər, shnou′tsər) ►*n.* A dog with a wiry coat and blunt muzzle and found in various sizes. [Ger. < *Schnauze*, snout.]

Schoen·berg (shûrn′bûrg, shœn′bĕrk′), **Arnold** 1874–1951. Austrian composer.

schol·ar (skŏl′ər) ►*n.* **1.** A learned person. **2.** A pupil or student. **3.** A student holding a scholarship. [< LLat. *scholāris*, of a school.] —**schol′ar·li·ness** *n.* —**schol′ar·ly** *adj.*

schol·ar·ship (skŏl′ər-shĭp′) ►*n.* **1.** The methods and attainments of a scholar. **2.** A grant awarded to a student.

scho·las·tic (skə-lăs′tĭk) ►*adj.* **1.** Of or relating to schools; academic. **2.** Overly subtle or pedantic. [< Gk. *skholastikos.*] —**scho·las′ti·cal·ly** *adv.*

school¹ (skōol) ►*n.* **1.** An institution for instruction and learning. **2.** The student body of an educational institution. **3.** The process of being educated. **4.** A group of people who are under a common influence or who share a unifying belief. ►*v.* **1.** To educate. **2.** To train or discipline. [< Gk. *skholē.*] —**school′boy′** *n.* —**school′girl′** *n.*

school² (skōol) ►*n.* A large group of aquatic animals, esp. fish, swimming together. [< MDu. *scole.*] —**school** *v.*

school·ing (skōo′lĭng) ►*n.* **1.** Instruction given at school. **2.** Education obtained through experience.

school·marm (skōol′märm′) ►*n.* A woman teacher, esp. a strict or old-fashioned one. [SCHOOL¹ + dial. *marm* (var. of MA′AM).]

school·mas·ter (skōol′măs′tər) ►*n.* A man who is a teacher.

school·mis·tress (skōol′mĭs′trĭs) ►*n.* A woman who is a teacher.

school·room (skōol′rōom′, -rŏom′) ►*n.* A classroom.

school·teach·er (skōol′tē′chər) ►*n.* One who teaches in a school below the college level.

schoo·ner (skōo′nər) ►*n.* **1.** A fore-and-aft rigged sailing vessel with at least two masts. **2.** A large beer glass, usu. holding a pint or more. [?]

Scho·pen·hau·er (shō′pən-hou′ər), **Arthur** 1788–1860. German philosopher.

Schu·bert (shōo′bərt, -bĕrt′), **Franz Peter** 1797–1828. Austrian composer.

Schulz (shŏolts), **Charles Monroe** 1922–2000. Amer. cartoonist.

Schu·mann (shōo′män′, -mən), **Robert** 1810–56. German composer.

schuss (shŏos, shōos) ►*v.* **1.** To ski or snowboard rapidly in a straight downhill course. **2.** *Informal* To ski, esp. at a fast pace. [Ger., shot < OHGer. *scuz.*] —**schuss** *n.*

schwa (shwä) ►*n.* **1.** A neutral vowel sound typically occurring in unstressed syllables, as the final vowel of English *sofa.* **2.** The symbol (ə) used to represent schwa. [< Heb. *šəwā′.*]

Schweit·zer (shwīt′sər, shvīt′-), **Albert** 1875–1965. Alsatian philosopher, physician, and musician.

Albert Schweitzer
photographed in the 1950s

sci·at·i·ca (sī-ăt′ĭ-kə) ►*n.* Nerve pain in the thigh and buttocks, usu. caused by a herniated disk of the lumbar region of the spine. [< Med. Lat. *sciaticus*, of the hip.]

sci·ence (sī′əns) ►*n.* **1.** The observation, identification, description, experimental investigation, and theoretical explanation of phenomena. **2.** A systematic method or body of knowledge in a given experience. **3.** *Archaic* Knowledge gained through experience. [< Lat. *scientia*, knowledge.] —**sci′en·tif′ic** (sī′ən-tĭf′ĭk) *adj.* —**sci′en·tif′i·cal·ly** *adv.*

science fiction ►*n.* Fiction in which the plot is based on speculative scientific discoveries, drastic environmental changes, or space travel. —**sci′ence-fic′tion** *adj.*

scientific notation ►*n.* A method of writing or displaying numbers in terms of a decimal number between 1 and 10 multiplied by a power of 10.

sci·en·tist (sī′ən-tĭst) ►*n.* A person having

expert knowledge of one or more sciences.

sci-fi (sī'fī') ►*n. Informal* Science fiction.

scim·i·tar (sĭm'ĭ-tər, -tär') ►*n.* A broad curved sword with the edge on the convex side. [Ital. *scimitarra.*]

scin·til·la (sĭn-tĭl'ə) ►*n.* A minute amount; trace. [Lat., spark.] —**scin'til·lant** *adj.*

scin·til·late (sĭn'tl-āt') ►*v.* -**lat·ed, -lat·ing 1.** To send forth light in flashes; sparkle. **2.** To be animated and brilliant. [< Lat. *scintilla,* spark.] —**scin'til·la'tion** *n.*

sci·on (sī'ən) ►*n.* **1.** A descendant or heir. **2.** A detached plant shoot used in grafting. [< OFr. *cion.*]

Scip·i·o Af·ri·ca·nus (sĭp'ē-ō' ăf'rĭ-kā'nəs, skĭp'-), **Publius Cornelius** "the Elder." 236?– 183? BC. Roman general.

scis·sors (sĭz'ərz) ►*n. (takes sing. or pl. v.)* A cutting implement of two blades joined by a swivel pin that allows the cutting edges to be opened and closed. [< LLat. *cīsōrium,* cutting instrument.] —**scis'sor** *v.*

scissors kick or **scissor kick** ►*n.* A kick in which the legs are moved apart and brought together like scissors, as in swimming, soccer, or martial arts.

SCLC ►*abbr.* Southern Christian Leadership Conference

scle·ra (sklîr'ə) ►*n.* The tough fibrous tissue covering all of the eyeball except the cornea. [< Gk. *sklēros,* hard.] —**scle'ral** *adj.*

scle·ro·sis (sklə-rō'sĭs) ►*n., pl.* -**ses** (-sēz) A thickening or hardening of a body part, as of an artery, esp. from tissue overgrowth or disease. [< Gk. *sklēros,* hard.] —**scle·rot'ic** (-rŏt'ĭk) *adj.*

scoff (skŏf, skôf) ►*v.* To express derision or scorn: *scoffed at their threats.* [ME *scoffen.*] —**scoff** *n.* —**scoff'er** *n.*

scoff·law (skŏf'lô', skôf'-) ►*n.* One who habitually violates the law.

scold (skōld) ►*v.* To reprimand harshly. ►*n.* A persistent nag or critic. [< ME *scolde,* an abusive person.] —**scold'er** *n.*

sco·li·o·sis (skō'lē-ō'sĭs) ►*n.* Abnormal lateral curvature of the spine. [< Gk. *skolios,* crooked.]

sconce (skŏns) ►*n.* A wall bracket for candles or lights. [< Med.Lat. *scōnsa,* hiding place.]

scone (skōn, skŏn) ►*n.* A rich, biscuitlike pastry. [Perh. < Du. *schoonbrood,* fine white bread.]

scoop (skōōp) ►*n.* **1.** A small shovellike serving utensil. **2.** The bucket or shovel, as of a dredge or backhoe. **3.** *Informal* An exclusive news story acquired by luck or initiative. ►*v.* **1.** To take up and often reposition with a scoop. **2.** To hollow out. **3.** *Informal* To top or outmaneuver (a competitor) in acquiring a news story. [< MDu. *scope.*] —**scoop'er** *n.*

scoot (skōōt) ►*v.* To go suddenly and speedily. [Prob. of Scand. orig.]

scoot·er (skōō'tər) ►*n.* **1.** A child's vehicle consisting of a long footboard between two end wheels, controlled by an upright steering handle. **2.** A motor scooter.

scope (skōp) ►*n.* **1.** The range of one's perceptions, thoughts, or actions. **2.** The possibility to be active. See Synonyms at **room. 3.** The extent of a given activity that is treated or relevant. See Synonyms at **range. 4.** *Informal* A viewing instrument. [< Gk. *skopos,* target, aim.]

–scope ►*suff.* An instrument for observing: *telescope.* [< Gk. *skopein,* see.]

scor·bu·tic (skôr-byōō'tĭk) also **scor·bu·ti·cal** (-tĭ-kəl) ►*adj.* Of, resembling, or affected by scurvy. [< NLat. *scorbūtus,* scurvy.]

scorch (skôrch) ►*v.* **1.** To burn superficially. **2.** To dry out with intense heat. ►*n.* A slight burn. [ME *scorchen.*] —**scorch'er** *n.*

score (skôr) ►*n.* **1.** A record of points made in a competitive event. **2.** A result of a test or examination. **3.** A debt. **4.** A ground; reason. **5.** A group of 20 items. **6.** The written form of a musical composition. **7.** A notch or incision. ►*v.* **scored, scor·ing 1.** To achieve: *score a success.* **2a.** To gain or achieve in a game or contest. **b.** To keep the score of a game or contest. **3.** To evaluate and assign a grade to. **4.** *Mus.* **a.** To orchestrate. **b.** To arrange for a specific instrument. **5.** To mark with lines or notches. [< ON *skor.*] —**score'less** *adj.* —**scor'er** *n.*

sco·ri·a (skôr'ē-ə) ►*n.* **1.** *Geol.* Porous cinderlike fragments of dark lava. **2.** The refuse of a smelted metal or ore; slag. [< Gk. *skōr,* dung.]

scorn (skôrn) ►*n.* **1.** Contempt or disdain. **2.** Derision. **3.** The state of being despised or dishonored: *held in scorn.* ►*v.* **1.** To consider or treat as contemptible or unworthy. **2.** To reject or refuse with derision. See Synonyms at **despise. 3.** To consider or reject (doing something) as beneath one's dignity. [< OFr. *escarn,* of Gmc. orig.] —**scorn'ful** *adj.* —**scorn'ful·ly** *adv.* —**scorn'ful·ness** *n.*

Scor·pi·o (skôr'pē-ō') ►*n.* **1.** Var. of **Scorpius. 2.** The 8th sign of the zodiac.

scor·pi·on (skôr'pē-ən) ►*n.* Any of various arachnids with a segmented tail tipped with a venomous sting. [< Gk. *skorpios.*]

Scor·pi·us (skôr'pē-əs) also **Scor·pi·o** (pē ō') ►*n.* A constellation in the Southern Hemisphere.

Scot (skŏt) ►*n.* **1.** A native or inhabitant of Scotland. **2.** A member of a Gaelic tribe that migrated to N Britain from Ireland in about the 6th cent. AD.

scotch (skŏch) ►*v.* **1.** To put an abrupt end to. **2.** To injure so as to render harmless. **3.** To cut or score. [ME *scocchen,* cut.]

Scotch ►*adj.* Scottish. ►*n.* **1.** The people of Scotland. **2.** Scots English. **3.** Scotch whisky. —**Scotch'man** *n.* —**Scotch'wom'an** *n.*

Scotch-I·rish (skŏch'ī'rĭsh) ►*n.* The people of Scotland who settled in N Ireland or their descendants. —**Scotch'-I'rish** *adj.*

Scotch whisky ►*n.* A whiskey distilled in Scotland from malted barley.

scot-free (skŏt'frē') ►*adv. & adj.* Free from obligation or penalty. [< ME *scot,* tax.]

Scot·land (skŏt'lənd) A constituent country of the United Kingdom, in N Great Britain. Cap. Edinburgh. —**Scots'man** *n.* —**Scots'- wom'an** *n.*

Scott (skŏt), **Dred** 1795?–1858. Amer. slave; subject of a US Supreme Court decision supporting slavery (1857).

Scott, Sir Walter 1771–1832. British writer.

Scott, Winfield 1786–1866. Amer. general.

Scot·tish (skŏt'ĭsh) ►*adj.* Of or relating to Scotland or its people or language. ►*n.* **1.** Scots English. **2.** The people of Scotland.

Scottish Gaelic ►*n.* The Celtic language of Scotland.

scoun·drel (skoun′drəl) ►*n.* A villain; rogue. [?]

scour¹ (skour) ►*v.* **1.** To clean by scrubbing vigorously, as with an abrasive. **2.** To scrub something in order to clean or polish it. [< LLat. *excūrāre*, clean out.]

scour² (skour) ►*v.* **1.** To search through or over thoroughly. **2.** To move swiftly; scurry. [ME *scouren*, move swiftly.]

scourge (skûrj) ►*n.* **1.** A source of great suffering or harm. **2.** A means of inflicting severe suffering or punishment. **3.** A small whip. ►*v.* **scourged, scourg·ing 1.** To devastate; ravage. **2.** To chastise severely. **3.** To flog. [< OFr. *escorgier*, to whip.]

scout (skout) ►*v.* **1.** To reconnoiter. **2.** To observe and evaluate (a talented person) for possible hiring. ►*n.* **1.** One that is sent out to gather information. **2.** A sentinel. **3.** One who seeks out talented persons, esp. in sports and entertainment. **4.** often **Scout** A Boy Scout or Girl Scout. [< Lat. *auscultāre*, listen.]

scout·mas·ter (skout′măs′tər) ►*n.* The adult leader of a troop of Boy Scouts.

scow (skou) ►*n.* A large flat-bottomed boat with square ends. [< MDu. *scouwe*.]

scowl (skoul) ►*v.* To wrinkle or contract the brow as in anger or disapproval. See Synonyms at **frown.** ►*n.* A look of anger or strong disapproval. [ME *scoulen*.] —**scowl′er** *n.*

scrab·ble (skrăb′əl) ►*v.* **-bled, -bling 1.** To grope or scratch frantically. **2.** To clamber. **3.** To struggle. **4.** To scribble. [< MDu. *schrabben*, scrape.] —**scrab′ble** *n.*

scrag·gly (skrăg′lē) ►*adj.* **-gli·er, -gli·est** Ragged; unkempt. [< *scrag*, a scrawny animal.]

scrag·gy (skrăg′ē) ►*adj.* **-gi·er, -gi·est 1.** Jagged; rough. **2.** Bony and lean. [< *scrag*, a scrawny animal.] —**scrag′gi·ness** *n.*

scram (skrăm) ►*v.* **scrammed, scram·ming** *Slang* To leave at once. [< SCRAMBLE.]

scram·ble (skrăm′bəl) ►*v.* **-bled, -bling 1.** To move or climb hurriedly. **2.** To compete frantically. **3.** To mix haphazardly. **4.** To take off with all possible haste. Used of a warplane. **5.** To cook (beaten eggs) while stirring. **6.** *Electron.* To distort (a signal) so as to render it unintelligible without a special receiver. [Perh. blend of obsolete *scamble*, struggle for, and *cramble*, crawl.] —**scram′ble** *n.* —**scram′bler** *n.*

scrap¹ (skrăp) ►*n.* **1.** A small bit or fragment. **2. scraps** Leftover food. **3.** Discarded waste material, esp. metal suitable for reprocessing. ►*v.* **scrapped, scrap·ping 1.** To break down into parts for disposal or salvage. **2.** To abandon as useless; cancel. [< ON *skrap*, trifles.] —**scrap′py** *adj.*

scrap² (skrăp) ►*v.* **scrapped, scrap·ping** To fight, often with the fists. ►*n.* A fight or scuffle. See Synonyms at **brawl.** [Perh. < SCRAPE.] —**scrap′per** *n.*

scrap·book (skrăp′book′) ►*n.* A book with blank pages for mounting pictures, clippings, or other mementos.

scrape (skrāp) ►*v.* **scraped, scrap·ing 1.** To abrade, smooth, injure, or remove by forceful strokes of an edged, sharp, or rough instrument. **2.** To rub (a surface) with considerable pressure. **3.** To draw (a hard or abrasive object) forcefully over a surface. **4.** To come into abrasive contact. **5.** To rub or move with a harsh

grating noise. **6.** To amass or produce with difficulty: *scrape together some cash.* **7.** To manage with difficulty: *scraped through by a narrow margin.* ►*n.* **1.** The act or sound of scraping. **2.** An abrasion on the skin. **3a.** A predicament. **b.** A scuffle. See Synonyms at **brawl.** [< ON *skrapa.*] —**scrap′er** *n.*

scrap·py (skrăp′ē) ►*adj.* **-pi·er, -pi·est 1.** Quarrelsome; contentious. See Synonyms at **argumentative. 2.** Full of fighting spirit. —**scrap′pi·ly** *adv.* —**scrap′pi·ness** *n.*

scratch (skrăch) ►*v.* **1.** To make a shallow cut or mark with something sharp. **2.** To use the nails or claws to dig or scrape at. **3.** To rub (the skin) to relieve itching. **4.** To strike out or cancel (e.g., a word) by or as if by drawing lines through. ►*n.* A mark or wound produced by scratching. ►*adj.* **1.** Done haphazardly or by chance. **2.** Assembled hastily or at random. —*idioms:* **from scratch** From the very beginning. **up to scratch** *Informal* Meeting the requirements. [ME *scracchen.*] —**scratch′er** *n.* —**scratch′i·ly** *adv.* —**scratch′i·ness** *n.* —**scratch′y** *adj.*

scrawl (skrôl) ►*v.* To write hastily or sloppily. [Perh. < obsolete *scrawl*, gesticulate.] —**scrawl** *n.* —**scrawl′y** *adj.*

scraw·ny (skrô′nē) ►*adj.* **-ni·er, -ni·est** Gaunt and bony. [< dial. *scranny.*] —**scraw′ni·ness** *n.*

scream (skrēm) ►*v.* **1.** To utter a long loud piercing cry, as from pain or fear. **2.** To produce a startling effect. ►*n.* **1.** A long loud piercing cry or sound. **2.** *Informal* One that is hilariously funny. [ME *screamen.*] —**scream′er** *n.*

scree (skrē) ►*n.* Loose rock debris covering a slope. [Prob. < ON *skridha*, landslide.]

screech (skrēch) ►*n.* **1.** A high shrill cry. **2.** A similar sound, as of scraping metal. [< ME *scrichen*, to screech.] —**screech** *v.* —**screech′y** *adj.*

screech owl ►*n.* Any of various small owls of the Americas having ear tufts and a quavering whistlelike call.

screen (skrēn) ►*n.* **1.** Something serving to divide, conceal, or protect, such as a movable room partition. **2.** A coarse sieve. **3.** A window or door insertion of framed mesh used to keep out insects. **4a.** A surface or device on which an image, such as a movie, is displayed for viewing. **b.** The medium in which movies are shown: *a star of stage and screen.* **5.** *Sports* A block, set with the body, that impedes the vision or movement of an opponent. ►*v.* **1.** To provide with a screen. **2.** To show (e.g., a movie) on a screen. **3.** To conceal or protect. See Synonyms at **block. 4a.** To separate or sift out by means of a sieve or screen. **b.** To sort through and eliminate unwanted examples of (something): *a filter that screens email.* **c.** To test or examine, as for suitability. [< MDu. *scherm*, shield.] —**screen′er** *n.*

screen·cap (skrēn′kăp′) or **screen capture** ►*n.* **1.** A copy of the image displayed by a computer screen. **2.** A still image taken from a movie or television program.

screen·play (skrēn′plā′) ►*n.* The script for a movie.

screen saver ►*n.* A software program that protects a display screen from having an image etched onto its surface, as by displaying constantly shifting images.

screen test ►*n.* A recorded sequence of an actor, as when auditioning for a role, to evaluate the actor's presence on the screen. —**screen′-test′** *v.*

screen·writ·er (skrēn′rī′tər) ►*n.* A writer of screenplays. —**screen′writ′ing** *n.*

screw (skrōō) ►*n.* **1.** A cylindrical rod with incised threads, having a slotted head so that it can be driven as a fastener by turning it with a screwdriver. **2.** A propeller. ►*v.* **1.** To fasten, tighten, or attach by means of a screw or similar fastener. **2.** To turn or twist. —*phrasal verb:* **screw up** *Slang* To make a mess of. [< OFr. *escrove*, nut.]

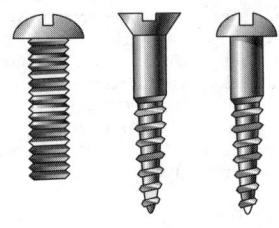

screw
left to right: round-head machine, flat-head wood, and round-head wood screws

screw·ball (skrōō′bôl′) ►*n.* **1.** *Baseball* A pitched ball curving in the direction opposite to a normal curve ball. **2.** *Slang* An eccentric or irrational person.

screw·driv·er (skrōō′drī′vər) ►*n.* **1.** A tool used for turning screws. **2.** A cocktail of vodka and orange juice.

screw·y (skrōō′ē) ►*adj.* **-i·er, -i·est** *Slang* **1.** Eccentric; crazy. **2.** Ludicrously odd.

scrib·ble (skrĭb′əl) ►*v.* **-bled, -bling 1.** To write hastily or carelessly. **2.** To make meaningless marks. [< Lat. *scrībere*, write.] —**scrib′ble** *n.*

scribe (skrīb) ►*n.* **1.** A public clerk. **2.** A professional copyist of manuscripts. **3.** A writer or journalist. [< LLat. *scrība* < Lat. *scrībere*, write.] —**scrib′al** *adj.*

scrim·mage (skrĭm′ĭj) ►*n.* **1.** *Sports* A practice game. **2.** *Football* Play between the two teams from the time the ball is snapped until it is declared dead. **3.** A rough-and-tumble struggle; tussle. [ME < *scrimish,* SKIRMISH.] —**scrim′mage** *v.*

scrimp (skrĭmp) ►*v.* To be very frugal and sparing. [Perh. of Scand. orig.] —**scrimp′er** *n.*

scrim·shaw (skrĭm′shô′) ►*n., pl.* **-shaw** or **-shaws 1.** The art of carving on whalebone or whale ivory. **2.** An article made in this way. [?]

scrip¹ (skrĭp) ►*n.* **1.** A form of money issued by a local government or private organization. **2.** A certificate or receipt used to redeem a credit. [Poss. < SCRIPT.]

scrip² (skrĭp) ►*n. Chiefly Brit.* A fractional share of stock issued to existing shareholders. [< *subscription receipt,* receipt for a portion of a loan.]

script (skrĭpt) ►*n.* **1a.** Handwriting. **b.** A style of writing in cursive. **2.** The text of a play, broadcast, or movie. **3.** *Comp.* A simple program in a language that the computer must convert to machine language each time the program is run. ►*v.* To prepare (a text) for filming or broadcasting. [< Lat. *scrīptum.*] —**script′writ′-er** *n.* —**script′writ′ing** *n.*

scrip·ture (skrĭp′chər) ►*n.* **1a.** A sacred writing or book. **b.** A passage from such a writing or book. **2.** often **Scripture** or **Scriptures** The Bible. **3.** An authoritative statement. [< Lat. *scrīptūra,* writing.] —**scrip′tur·al** *adj.*

scriv·en·er (skrĭv′ə-nər, skrĭv′nər) ►*n.* A scribe or author. [< OFr. *escrivein.*]

scrod (skrŏd) ►*n., pl.* **scrod** A small cod or similar fish. [Poss. < obsolete Du. *schrood,* shred.]

scroll (skrōl) ►*n.* **1.** A roll, as of papyrus, used esp. for writing a document. **2.** Ornamentation that resembles a scroll. **3.** *Mus.* The curved head on an instrument, esp. a violin. ►*v. Comp.* To cause displayed text or graphics to move up, down, or across the screen. [< OFr. *escroue,* strip of parchment.]

Scrooge also **scrooge** (skrōōj) ►*n.* A mean-spirited miserly person; skinflint. [After Ebenezer *Scrooge,* a character in Dickens's *A Christmas Carol.*]

scro·tum (skrō′təm) ►*n., pl.* **-ta** (-tə) or **-tums** The external sac of skin enclosing the testes. [Lat. *scrōtum.*] —**scro′tal** (skrōt′l) *adj.*

scrounge (skrounj) ►*v.* **scrounged, scroung·ing** *Slang* **1.** To beg; mooch. See Synonyms at **cadge. 2.** To obtain by salvaging or foraging. [< dial. *scrunge,* steal.] —**scroung′er** *n.*

scrub¹ (skrŭb) ►*v.* **scrubbed, scrub·bing 1.** To rub hard in order to clean. **2.** To clean or wash something by hard rubbing. **3.** *Slang* To cancel. [< MDu. *schrobben.*] —**scrub** *n.* —**scrub′ber** *n.*

scrub² (skrŭb) ►*n.* **1.** Vegetation consisting chiefly of shrubs and small trees. **2.** An area covered with such vegetation. **3.** A domestic animal that is feral or not purebred. **4.** *Sports* A player not on the first team. [ME.] —**scrub′-by** *adj.*

scruff (skrŭf) ►*n.* The back of the neck; the nape. [< dial. *scuff.*]

scruff·y (skrŭf′ē) ►*adj.* **-i·er, -i·est** Shabby; untidy. [< obsolete *scruff,* SCURF.] —**scruff′i·ly** *adv.* —**scruff′i·ness** *n.*

scrump·tious (skrŭmp′shəs) ►*adj.* Pleasing to the taste; delectable. See Synonyms at **delicious.** [Perh. < SUMPTUOUS.]

scrunch (skrŭnch, skrōōnch) ►*v.* **1.** To crush or crunch. **2.** To hunch. **3.** To make a crunching sound. [< CRUNCH.] —**scrunch** *n.*

scru·ple (skrōō′pəl) ►*n.* **1.** An uneasy feeling arising from conscience or principle. **2.** A unit of apothecary weight equal to about 1.3 grams, or 20 grains. [< Lat. *scrūpus,* rough stone.] —**scru′ple** *v.*

scru·pu·lous (skrōō′pyə-ləs) ►*adj.* **1.** Conscientious; painstaking. **2.** Having scruples; principled. —**scru′pu·lous·ly** *adv.*

scru·ti·nize (skrōōt′n-īz′) ►*v.* **-nized, -niz·ing** To examine carefully.

scru·ti·ny (skrōōt′n-ē) ►*n., pl.* **-nies** Close, careful examination. [< Lat. *scrūtinium.*]

SCSI ►*abbr.* small computer system interface

scu·ba (skōō′bə) ►*n.* A portable apparatus having a container with compressed air, a device that adjusts the pressure of the released air to match the surrounding pressure, and a mouthpiece, used for breathing under water. [*s(elf-)c(ontained)* *u(nderwater)* *b(reathing)* *a(pparatus).*]

scud (skŭd) ►*v.* **scud·ded, scud·ding** To skim along swiftly and easily: *dark clouds scudding by.*

▸*n.* Wind-driven clouds, mist, or rain. [Poss. < ME *scut,* rabbit.]

scuff (skŭf) ▸*v.* **1.** To scrape with the feet. **2.** To scrape and roughen the surface of. ▸*n.* **1.** The act or sound of scuffing. **2.** A flat, backless slipper. [Prob. of Scand. orig.]

scuf·fle (skŭf′əl) ▸*v.* **-fled, -fling 1.** To fight confusedly at close quarters. **2.** To shuffle. ▸*n.* A disorderly struggle at close quarters. See Synonyms at **brawl.** [Prob. < SCUFF.]

scull (skŭl) ▸*n.* **1.** An oar used for rowing a boat from the stern. **2.** One of a pair of short-handled oars used by a single rower. **3.** A small light boat for racing. [ME *sculle.*] —**scull** *v.* —**scull′er** *n.*

scul·ler·y (skŭl′ə-rē) ▸*n., pl.* **-ies** A room adjoining a kitchen for dishwashing and other chores. [< OFr. *escuele,* dish.]

sculpt (skŭlpt) ▸*v.* To sculpture. [< Lat. *sculpere, sculpt-,* carve.]

sculp·tor (skŭlp′tər) ▸*n.* One who sculptures.

sculp·tress (skŭlp′trĭs) ▸*n.* A woman who sculptures. See Usage Note at **-ess.**

sculp·ture (skŭlp′chər) ▸*n.* **1.** The art or practice of shaping three-dimensional figures or forms, as by chiseling marble, modeling clay, or casting in metal. **2.** A work of art that is created by sculpture. ▸*v.* **-tured, -tur·ing 1.** To fashion (e.g., stone or clay) into sculpture. **2.** To represent in sculpture. **3.** To ornament with sculpture. [< Lat. *sculptūra.*] —**sculp′tur·al** *adj.*

scum (skŭm) ▸*n.* **1.** A filmy layer of matter on the surface of a liquid or on a hard surface. **2.** Refuse or worthless matter. **3.** *Slang* A worthless or disreputable person or element of society. [< MDu. *schūm.*] —**scum′my** *adj.*

scup·per (skŭp′ər) ▸*n.* A deck-level opening in the side of a ship to allow water to run off. [ME *scoper.*]

scurf (skûrf) ▸*n.* **1.** Flaking dry skin, such as dandruff. **2.** A loose crust coating a surface, esp. of a plant. **3.** A fungal disease of plants marked by scaly lesions esp. on underground parts, such as potato tubers. [ME, prob. of Scand. orig.] —**scurf′i·ness** *n.* —**scurf′y** *adj.*

scur·ri·lous (skûr′ə-ləs, skŭr′-) ▸*adj.* **1.** Vulgar; abusive. **2.** Malicious or slanderous. [< Lat. *scurrīlis,* jeering.] —**scur·ril′i·ty** (skə-rĭl′ĭ-tē) *n.* —**scur·ril′ous·ly** *adv.*

scur·ry (skûr′ē, skŭr′ē) ▸*v.* **-ried, -ry·ing 1.** To scamper. **2.** To flurry or swirl about. [Prob. < *hurry-scurry.*]

scur·vy (skûr′vē) ▸*n.* A disease caused by deficiency of vitamin C, marked by bleeding gums, subcutaneous bleeding, and weakness. ▸*adj.* **-vi·er, -vi·est** Contemptible. [< *scurf.*]

scut·tle¹ (skŭt′l) ▸*n.* A small hatch in a ship's deck or hull. ▸*v.* **-tled, -tling 1.** To sink (a ship) by cutting or opening holes in the hull. **2.** To thwart or ruin. [< OFr. *escoutille.*]

scut·tle² (skŭt′l) ▸*n.* A metal pail for carrying coal. [< Lat. *scutella,* dish.]

scut·tle³ (skŭt′l) ▸*v.* **-tled, -tling** To run hastily; scurry. [ME *scottlen.*] —**scut′tle** *n.*

scut·tle·butt (skŭt′l-bŭt′) ▸*n. Slang* Gossip; rumor. [SCUTTLE¹ + *butt,* cask.]

scythe (sīth) ▸*n.* A tool with a long curved blade and a bent handle, used for mowing or reaping. [< OE *sīthe.*] —**scythe** *v.*

Scyth·i·a (sĭth′ē-ə, sĭth′-) An ancient region of SW Asia and SE Europe. —**Scyth′i·an** *adj. & n.*

SD ▸*abbr.* **1.** South Dakota **2.** special delivery **3.** standard deviation

SE ▸*abbr.* **1a.** southeast **b.** southeastern **2.** *Football* split end

sea (sē) ▸*n.* **1a.** The continuous body of salt water covering most of the earth's surface. **b.** A tract of water within an ocean. **c.** A large body of water completely or partially enclosed by land. **2.** The condition of the ocean's surface: *a high sea.* **3.** Something that suggests the ocean in its vastness: *a sea of controversy.* —*idiom:* **at sea 1.** On the ocean. **2.** At a loss; perplexed. [< OE *sǣ.*]

sea anemone ▸*n.* Any of various marine organisms with a flexible cylindrical body and numerous tentacles.

sea·bird (sē′bûrd′) ▸*n.* A bird that frequents the ocean, esp. far from shore.

sea·board (sē′bôrd′) ▸*n.* **1.** A seacoast. **2.** Land near the sea. [SEA + obsolete *board,* border.]

sea·bor·gi·um (sē-bôr′gē-əm) ▸*n. Symbol* **Sg** A synthetic radioactive element. At. no. 106. See table at **element.** [After Glenn Theodore *Seaborg* (1912–99).]

sea·coast (sē′kōst′) ▸*n.* Land bordering the sea.

sea·far·er (sē′fâr′ər) ▸*n.* A sailor. —**sea′far′-ing** *adj.*

sea·food (sē′food′) ▸*n.* Edible fish or shellfish from the sea.

sea·go·ing (sē′gō′ĭng) ▸*adj.* Made or used for ocean voyages.

sea·gull also **sea gull** (sē′gŭl′) ▸*n.* A gull, esp. one found near coastal areas.

sea horse ▸*n.* A small marine fish with a prehensile tail, a horselike head, and a body covered with bony plates.

seal¹ (sēl) ▸*n.* **1.** A sealant. **2.** An airtight closure. **3a.** A die or signet with a raised or incised emblem used to stamp an impression on a substance such as wax or lead. **b.** The impression so made. **c.** A small disk or wafer bearing such an imprint and affixed to a document to prove authenticity or to secure it. **4.** A design used to identify a person or thing or to show that something is authentic, accurate, or of good quality: *The committee gave the new product its seal of approval.* ▸*v.* **1a.** To close with a seal. **b.** To cover or fill up an opening. **2.** To apply a waterproof coating to. **3.** To affix a seal to, esp. in order to prove authenticity or attest to accuracy or quality. **4.** To determine irrevocably: *His fate was sealed.* [< Lat. *sigillum.*] —**seal′er** *n.*

seal² (sēl) ▸*n.* **1.** Any of various aquatic mammals with a sleek, torpedo-shaped body and limbs in the form of flippers. **2.** The pelt or fur of a seal. ▸*v.* To hunt seals. [< OE *seolh.*] —**seal′er** *n.*

sea-lane (sē′lān′) ▸*n.* A sea route.

seal·ant (sē′lənt) ▸*n.* A substance used to seal a surface to prevent passage of a liquid or gas.

sea level ▸*n.* The level of the ocean's surface, esp. the level halfway between mean high and low tide.

sea lion ▸*n.* A large seal having a blunter muzzle and thinner coat than the fur seals.

seam (sēm) ▸*n.* **1a.** A line formed by sewing together two pieces of material. **b.** A similar line, ridge, or groove. **2.** A line across a surface, as a crack or wrinkle. **3.** A thin layer or stratum, as of coal. ►*v.* **1.** To join with or as if with a seam. **2.** To mark with a wrinkle or crack: *a face seamed with age.* [< OE *sēam.*]

sea·man (sē′mən) ►*n.* **1.** A sailor. **2.** Any of the three lowest ranks in the US Navy or Coast Guard.

sea·man·ship (sē′mən-shĭp′) ►*n.* Skill in navigating or managing a boat or ship.

seam·stress (sēm′strĭs) ►*n.* A woman who sews, esp. as an occupation.

seam·y (sē′mē) ►*adj.* **-i·er, -i·est 1.** Sordid; base. **2.** Having a seam. **—seam′i·ness** *n.*

sé·ance (sā′äns′) ►*n.* A meeting of people to receive spiritualistic messages. [< OFr. *seoir,* sit < Lat. *sedēre.*]

sea otter ►*n.* A large marine otter of N Pacific coastal waters.

sea·plane (sē′plān′) ►*n.* An aircraft designed for landing on and taking off from a body of water.

sea·port (sē′pôrt′) ►*n.* A harbor or town with facilities for seagoing ships.

sea power ►*n.* **1.** A nation having significant naval strength. **2.** Naval strength.

sea·quake (sē′kwāk′) ►*n.* An earthquake originating under the sea floor.

sear¹ (sîr) ►*v.* **1.** To scorch or burn the surface of. **2.** To brown (meat) quickly using very high heat. **3.** To wither or parch. [< OE *sēarian.*]

sear² (sîr) ►*adj.* Var. of **sere.**

search (sûrch) ►*v.* **1.** To look through in order to find something. **2.** To investigate; probe: *search one's conscience.* **3.** *Law* To examine (a person or property) in order to find evidence of a crime. [< Lat. *circāre,* go around.] **—search** *n.* **—search′er** *n.*

search engine ►*n.* A software program that searches a database for information about specified terms.

search·light (sûrch′līt′) ►*n.* **1.** A powerful light source with a reflector for projecting a high-intensity beam. **2.** The beam itself.

search warrant ►*n.* A legal order allowing a law enforcement officer to search certain premises for evidence of a crime.

sea·scape (sē′skāp′) ►*n.* A view or picture of the sea. [SEA + (LAND)SCAPE.]

sea·shell (sē′shĕl′) ►*n.* The shell of a marine organism, esp. a mollusk.

sea·shore (sē′shôr′) ►*n.* Land by the sea.

sea·sick·ness (sē′sĭk′nĭs) ►*n.* Nausea and dizziness resulting from the motion of a vessel at sea. **—sea′sick′** *adj.*

sea·side (sē′sīd′) ►*n.* The seashore.

sea snake ►*n.* Any of various venomous tropical saltwater snakes.

sea·son (sē′zən) ►*n.* **1a.** One of the four natural divisions of the year, spring, summer, fall, and winter. **b.** The two divisions of the year, rainy and dry, in some tropical regions. **2.** A recurrent period marked by certain occurrences or festivities: *the holiday season; tomato season.* ►*v.* **1.** To enhance the flavor of (food) by adding salt or other flavorings. **2.** To add zest or interest to. **3.** To treat or dry (e.g., lumber) until usable; cure. **4.** To render competent through experience. **5.** To inure. See Synonyms at **harden.** [< Lat. *satiō,* act of sowing.]

sea·son·a·ble (sē′zə-nə-bəl) ►*adj.* Suitable for a given season or time of year. **—sea′son·a·bly** *adv.*

sea·son·al (sē′zə-nəl) ►*adj.* Relating to or occurring in a particular season. **—sea′son·al·ly** *adv.*

sea·son·ing (sē′zə-nĭng) ►*n.* Something used to flavor food.

season ticket ►*n.* A ticket good for a specified period, as for a series of events.

seat (sēt) ►*n.* **1a.** Something, such as a chair or bench, on which one may sit. **b.** The part on which one rests in sitting: *a bicycle seat.* **2.** A place where one may sit: *took a seat on the floor.* **3a.** The buttocks. **b.** The part of a garment covering the buttocks. **4a.** The place where something is located or based: *the seat of intelligence.* **b.** A center of authority; capital: *a county seat.* **5.** Membership, as in a legislature. ►*v.* **1.** To place in or on a seat. **2.** To have or provide seats for: *an arena that seats 2,000.* [< ON *sæti.*]

seat belt ►*n.* A safety strap that holds a person securely in a seat, as in a car.

seat·ing (sē′tĭng) ►*n.* **1.** The act of providing with seats. **2.** The seats so provided.

SEATO ►*abbr.* Southeast Asia Treaty Organization

Se·at·tle¹ (sē-ăt′l) 1786?–1866. Native Amer. leader of several allied peoples in the Pacific Northwest.

Se·at·tle² (sē-ăt′l) A city of W-central WA on Puget Sound.

sea urchin ►*n.* Any of various echinoderms having a soft body enclosed in a skeleton covered with spines.

sea·wall also **sea wall** (sē′wôl′) ►*n.* An embankment to prevent erosion of a shoreline.

sea·ward (sē′wərd) ►*adv. & adj.* Toward or at the sea. **—sea′wards** (-wərdz) *adv.*

sea·wa·ter (sē′wô′tər, -wŏt′ər) ►*n.* The salt water of the ocean.

sea·way (sē′wā′) ►*n.* **1.** A sea route. **2.** An inland waterway for ocean shipping.

sea·weed (sē′wēd′) ►*n.* Any of numerous marine algae, such as kelp or gulfweed.

sea·wor·thy (sē′wûr′thē) ►*adj.* Fit to traverse the seas. **—sea′wor′thi·ness** *n.*

se·ba·ceous (sĭ-bā′shəs) ►*adj.* Relating to or secreting fat or sebum. [< Lat. *sēbum,* tallow.]

seb·or·rhe·a (sĕb′ə-rē′ə) ►*n.* A disease of the sebaceous glands of the skin marked by excessive secretion of oil. [Lat. *sēbum,* fat, tallow + –RRHEA.] **—seb′or·rhe′ic** *adj.*

sec¹ (sĕk) ►*adj.* Dry. Used of wines. [Fr.]

sec² ►*abbr.* secant

SEC ►*abbr.* Securities and Exchange Commission

sec. ►*abbr.* **1.** second **2.** secretary **3.** section

se·cant (sē′kănt′, -kənt) ►*n.* The reciprocal of the cosine of an angle in a right triangle. [< Lat. *secāre,* cut.]

se·cede (sĭ-sēd′) ►*v.* **-ced·ed, -ced·ing** To withdraw formally from membership in an organization, association, or alliance. [Lat. *sēcēdere,* withdraw.]

se·ces·sion (sĭ-sĕsh′ən) ►*n.* The act of seceding. [Lat. *sēcessiō.*] **—se·ces′sion·ism** *n.* **—se·ces′sion·ist** *n.*

se·clude (sĭ-klood′) ►*v.* **-clud·ed, -clud·ing** To set apart from others. See Synonyms at **isolate.** [< Lat. *sēclūdere,* shut away.] **—se·clu′sion** *n.*

sec·ond¹ (sĕk′ənd) ►*n.* **1.** A unit of time equal

to ¹⁄₆₀ of a minute. **2.** A brief interval of time. **3.** *Math.* A unit of angular measure equal to ¹⁄₆₀ of a minute. [< Med.Lat. *(pars minūta) secunda,* second (small part).]

sec·ond² (sĕk′ənd) ►*adj.* **1.** Coming next after the first. **2.** Inferior to another; subordinate: *a leader second to none.* ►*n.* **1a.** The ordinal number matching the number 2 in a series. **b.** One of two equal parts. **2.** One that is next after the first. **3.** often **seconds** Merchandise of inferior quality. **4.** The official attendant of a contestant in a duel or boxing match. **5.** The second lowest forward gear in a motor vehicle. ►*v.* **1.** To attend as an aide or assistant. **2.** To promote or encourage. **3.** To endorse (a motion or nomination). [< Lat. *secundus.*] —**sec′ond, sec′ond·ly** *adv.*

sec·ond·ar·y (sĕk′ən-dĕr′ē) ►*adj.* **1.** Second or lower in rank or importance; not primary. **2.** Following what is first in time or sequence. **3.** Relating to education between elementary school and college. **4.** Derived from what is original: *a secondary source.* ►*n., pl.* **-ies** One that acts in an auxiliary or subordinate capacity. —**sec′ond·ar′i·ly** (-dâr′ə-lē) *adv.*

secondary sex characteristic ►*n.* Any of various physical characteristics that appear at puberty and that differentiate the sexes without having a reproductive function.

second base ►*n.* *Baseball* The base across the diamond from home plate, touched second by a runner. —**second baseman** *n.*

second class ►*n.* **1.** The class or category ranking below the first or best. **2.** Travel accommodations ranking next below the highest or first class. —**sec′ond-class′** *adj.*

sec·ond-de·gree burn (sĕk′ənd-dĭ-grē′) ►*n.* A burn that blisters the skin.

second fiddle ►*n.* *Informal* A secondary role.

sec·ond-gen·er·a·tion (sĕk′ənd-jĕn′ə-rā′-shən) ►*adj.* Relating to one whose parents are immigrants.

sec·ond-guess (sĕk′ənd-gĕs′) ►*v.* **1.** To criticize (a decision) after an outcome is known. **2.** To outguess. **3.** To predict or anticipate.

sec·ond·hand (sĕk′ənd-hănd′) ►*adj.* **1.** Previously used; not new. **2.** Dealing in used merchandise. **3.** Not primary or original. —**sec′ond·hand′** *adv.*

second lieutenant ►*n.* The lowest commissioned rank, as in the US Army.

second nature ►*n.* A deeply ingrained behavior or trait.

second person ►*n.* The form of a pronoun or verb used to designate the person addressed.

sec·ond-rate (sĕk′ənd-rāt′) ►*adj.* Inferior.

sec·ond-string (sĕk′ənd-strĭng′) ►*adj.* Of or being a substitute, as on a sports team.

second thought ►*n.* A reconsideration of a decision or opinion.

second wind (wĭnd) ►*n.* Restored energy or strength.

se·cre·cy (sē′krĭ-sē) ►*n., pl.* **-cies 1.** The quality or condition of being secret. **2.** The ability or habit of keeping secrets.

se·cret (sē′krĭt) ►*adj.* **1.** Concealed from knowledge or view. **2.** Operating covertly: *a secret agent.* **3a.** Known only by the initiated: *secret rites.* **b.** Beyond ordinary understanding; mysterious. ►*n.* **1.** Something concealed from others. **2.** Something beyond understanding or

explanation; mystery. [< Lat. *sēcrētus.*] —**se′-cret·ly** *adv.*

sec·re·tar·i·at (sĕk′rĭ-târ′ē-ĭt) ►*n.* **1.** The department administered by a governmental secretary. **2.** The position of a governmental secretary. [Fr. *secrétariat.*]

sec·re·tar·y (sĕk′rĭ-tĕr′ē) ►*n., pl.* **-ies 1.** One employed to handle correspondence and do clerical work. **2.** An officer in charge of records, minutes of meetings, and correspondence, as for a company. **3.** An official presiding over an administrative department of state. **4.** A desk with a small bookcase on top. [< Med.Lat. *sēcrētārius,* confidential officer.] —**sec′re·tar′i·al** (-târ′ē-əl) *adj.*

secretary
c. 1800 American Hepplewhite secretary

sec·re·tar·y-gen·er·al (sĕk′rĭ-tĕr′ē-jĕn′ər-əl) ►*n., pl.* **sec·re·tar·ies-gen·er·al** A principal executive officer, as in the United Nations.

se·crete¹ (sĭ-krēt′) ►*v.* **-cret·ed, -cret·ing** To generate and release (a substance) from a cell or gland. [< Lat. *sēcernere, sēcrēt-,* set aside.] —**se·cre′tion** *n.* —**se·cre′to·ry** *adj.*

se·crete² (sĭ-krēt′) ►*v.* **-cret·ed, -cret·ing** To conceal; hide. [Prob. < SECRET.] —**se·cre′tion** *n.*

se·cre·tive (sē′krĭ-tĭv, sĭ-krē′tĭv) ►*adj.* Inclined to or done in secrecy. —**se′cre·tive·ly** *adv.* —**se′cre·tive·ness** *n.*

secret service ►*n.* **1.** A government agency engaged in intelligence-gathering activities. **2. Secret Service** A branch of the US Treasury Department concerned esp. with protection of the President.

sect (sĕkt) ►*n.* **1.** A group of people forming a distinct unit within a larger group by virtue of common beliefs. **2.** A religious body, esp. one that has separated from a larger denomination. [< Lat. *sequī, sect-,* follow.]

–sect ►*suff.* To cut; divide: *trisect.* [< Lat. *secāre, sect-,* cut.]

sec·tar·i·an (sĕk-târ′ē-ən) ►*adj.* **1.** Of a sect. **2.** Partisan. **3.** Narrow-minded; parochial. ►*n.* **1.** A member of a sect. **2.** One who is narrow-minded. —**sec·tar′i·an·ism** *n.*

sec·tion (sĕk′shən) ►*n.* **1.** One of several components; piece. **2.** A distinct portion, as of a newspaper. **3.** *Law* A distinct portion or provision of a legal code or set of laws. **4.** Representation of a solid object as it would appear if cut by an intersecting plane, so that the internal structure is displayed. ►*v.* To divide into parts. [< Lat. *secāre, sect-*, cut.]

sec·tion·al (sĕk′shə-nəl) ►*adj.* **1.** Of or relating to a particular district. **2.** Composed of or divided into component sections. ►*n.* A piece of furniture made up of sections that can be used separately or together. —**sec′tion·al·ly** *adv.*

sec·tion·al·ism (sĕk′shə-nə-lĭz′əm) ►*n.* Excessive devotion to local interests and customs. —**sec′tion·al·ist** *n.*

sec·tor (sĕk′tər, -tôr′) ►*n.* **1.** *Math.* The part of a circle bounded by two radii and the included arc. **2.** A military zone of action. **3.** A division, as of a city or economy. [< Lat., cutter.]

sec·u·lar (sĕk′yə-lər) ►*adj.* **1.** Worldly rather than spiritual. **2.** Not related to religion. **3.** *Eccles.* Not belonging to a religious order. Used of the clergy. [< LLat. *saeculāris.*] —**sec′u·lar·i·ty** (-lăr′ĭ-tē) *n.* —**sec′u·lar·ly** *adv.*

sec·u·lar·ize (sĕk′yə-lə-rīz′) ►*v.* **-ized, -iz·ing** **1.** To transfer from ecclesiastical to civil use or ownership. **2.** To make secular. —**sec′u·lar·i·za′tion** *n.*

se·cure (sĭ-kyoŏr′) ►*adj.* **-cur·er, -cur·est** **1.** Free from danger; safe. **2.** Free from fear or doubt. **3.** Free from interception or being listened to by unauthorized persons: *a secure telephone.* **4.** Free from risk; dependable: *secure investments.* ►*v.* **-cured, -cur·ing** **1.** To guard from danger or risk of loss. **2.** To make firm. See Synonyms at **fasten. 3.** To make certain; guarantee. **4.** To bring about: *secured release of the hostages.* [Lat. *secūrus.*] —**se·cure′ly** *adv.* —**se·cure′ment** *n.*

se·cu·ri·ty (sĭ-kyoŏr′ĭ-tē) ►*n., pl.* **-ties 1.** Safety. **2.** Confidence. **3.** Something that gives or assures safety: *called building security.* **4.** Something deposited or given as assurance of the fulfillment of an obligation; pledge. **5.** A financial instrument, such as a stock or bond. **6.** Measures adopted to guard against attack, theft, escape, or disclosure.

se·dan (sĭ-dăn′) ►*n.* **1.** A closed car with two or four doors and a front and rear seat. **2.** also **sedan chair** An enclosed chair carried on poles by two bearers. [?]

se·date¹ (sĭ-dāt′) ►*adj.* Serenely deliberate in character or manner. [< Lat. *sēdāre*, settle.] —**se·date′ly** *adv.* —**se·date′ness** *n.*

se·date² (sĭ-dāt′) ►*v.* **-dat·ed, -dat·ing** To administer a sedative to. [< SEDATIVE.] —**se·da′tion** *n.*

sed·a·tive (sĕd′ə-tĭv) ►*n.* Something, esp. a drug, having a calming or tranquilizing effect. [< Lat. *sēdāre*, settle, calm.] —**sed′a·tive** *adj.*

sed·en·tar·y (sĕd′n-tĕr′ē) ►*adj.* **1.** Marked by or requiring little physical activity. **2.** Attached or rooted; sessile. [< Lat. *sedēns*, pr.part. of *sedēre*, sit.]

Se·der (sā′dər) ►*n. Judaism* The ritual feast commemorating the exodus of the Jews from Egypt, held on the first night or the first two nights of Passover. [Heb. *sēder.*]

sedge (sĕj) ►*n.* Any of numerous grasslike plants with solid triangular stems and leaves arranged in three rows. [< OE *secg.*]

sed·i·ment (sĕd′ə-mənt) ►*n.* **1.** Material that settles to the bottom of a liquid; lees. **2.** *Geol.* Solid fragments of rock that are carried and deposited by wind, water, or ice. [Lat. *sedimentum*, settling < *sedēre*, settle.] —**sed′i·men·ta′tion** *n.*

sed·i·men·ta·ry (sĕd′ə-mĕn′tə-rē, -mĕn′trē) ►*adj.* **1.** Of or resembling sediment. **2.** *Geol.* Of rocks formed from sediment.

se·di·tion (sĭ-dĭsh′ən) ►*n.* Conduct or language inciting rebellion against the authority of a state. [< Lat. *sēditiō*, faction.] —**se·di′tious** *adj.*

se·duce (sĭ-doōs′, -dyoōs′) ►*v.* **-duced, -duc·ing 1.** To lead away from proper conduct. **2.** To induce to engage in sex. **3.** To entice into a different state or position. [< Lat. *sēdūcere*, lead away.] —**se·duc′er** *n.* —**se·duc′tion** (-dŭk′shən) *n.* —**se·duc′tive** *adj.*

sed·u·lous (sĕj′ə-ləs) ►*adj.* Persevering; assiduous. [< Lat. *sēdulus.*] —**sed′u·lous·ly** *adv.*

see¹ (sē) ►*v.* **saw** (sô), **seen** (sēn), **see·ing 1a.** To perceive with the eye. **b.** To refer to or look at: *For directions, see page 2.* **2.** To understand; comprehend. **3a.** To take note of: *We see the good in him.* **b.** To regard; view: *I see this as an improvement.* **4a.** To have a mental image of; visualize. **b.** To foresee or imagine. **5.** To undergo: *The broom does not see a lot of use here.* **6.** To find out; ascertain. **7a.** To visit or be in the company of. **b.** To meet regularly, as in dating. **c.** To visit for consultation: *see a doctor.* **8.** To escort; attend: *I'll see you home.* **9.** To make sure: *Please see that it gets done.* —***phrasal verb:* see through** To understand the true character of. [< OE *sēon.*]

see² (sē) ►*n.* The seat or jurisdiction of a bishop. [< Lat. *sēdēs*, seat.]

seed (sēd) ►*n., pl.* **seeds** or **seed 1.** A ripened plant ovule containing an embryo. **2.** Seeds collectively. **3.** A source or germ: *The seed of an idea.* **4.** A player who has been seeded for a tournament, often at a given rank: *a top seed.* ►*v.* **1.** To plant seeds in. **2.** To remove seeds from. **3a.** To arrange (the drawing for positions in a tournament) so that the more skilled contestants compete in the later rounds. **b.** To rank (a contestant) in this way. ►*adj.* Intended to help in early stages: *Provided seed capital for a fledgling business.* —***idiom:* go** (or **run**) **to seed 1.** To pass into the seed-bearing stage. **2.** To deteriorate. [< OE *sǣd.*]

seed·ling (sēd′lĭng) ►*n.* A young plant, esp. one that grows from a seed.

seed·pod (sēd′pŏd′) ►*n.* See **pod¹** (sense 1).

seed·y (sē′dē) ►*adj.* **-i·er, -i·est 1.** Having many seeds. **2.** Shabby; run-down. —**seed′i·ly** *adv.* —**seed′i·ness** *n.*

see·ing (sē′ĭng) ►*conj.* Inasmuch as.

seek (sēk) ►*v.* **sought** (sôt), **seek·ing 1.** To search for. **2.** To try to obtain or reach. **3.** To try; endeavor: *seek to do good.* [< OE *sēcan.*] —**seek′er** *n.*

seem (sēm) ►*v.* **1.** To give the impression of being: *The dog seems sick.* **2.** To appear to one's own mind. **3.** Used to indicate one's understanding of something: *I can't seem to get the rules straight.* **4.** To appear to be true or evident. [< ON *sœma*, conform to.]

seem·ing (sē′mĭng) ►*adj.* Apparent; ostensible. —**seem′ing** *n.* —**seem′ing·ly** *adv.*

seem·ly (sēm′lē) ►*adj.* **-li·er, -li·est 1.** Proper;

suitable. **2.** Of pleasing appearance. [< ON *sœmiligr.*] —**seem′li·ness** *n.*

seen (sēn) ►*v.* P.part. of **see¹.**

seep (sēp) ►*v.* **1.** To pass slowly through small openings. **2.** To enter, depart, or spread gradually. [< dial. *sipe.*] —**seep′age** *n.*

seer (sîr) ►*n.* **1.** A clairvoyant. **2.** A prophet.

seer·suck·er (sîr′sŭk′ər) ►*n.* A light thin fabric with a crinkled surface and a usu. striped pattern. [< Pers. *shīroshakar*, milk and sugar.]

see·saw (sē′sô′) ►*n.* **1.** A long plank balanced on a central fulcrum so that with a person riding on each end, one end goes up as the other goes down. **2.** A back-and-forth or up-and-down movement. **3.** A process in which one condition or situation repeatedly changes to another. [< SAW¹.] —**see′saw′** *v.*

seethe (sēth) ►*v.* **seethed, seeth·ing 1.** To churn and foam as if boiling. **2.** To be violently agitated. [< OE *sēothan.*]

seg·ment (sĕg′mənt) ►*n.* **1.** A part into which something can be divided; section. **2a.** *Math.* The part of a line between any two points on the line. **b.** In a circle, the region bounded by a chord and the arc that is between the chord's endpoints. ►*v.* (sĕg-mĕnt′) To divide into segments. [Lat. *segmentum.*] —**seg·men′tal** *adj.* —**seg′men·ta′tion** *n.*

seg·re·gate (sĕg′rĭ-gāt′) ►*v.* **-gat·ed, -gat·ing 1.** To separate or isolate from others or from a main body or group. See Synonyms at **isolate. 2.** To cause (e.g., people or institutions) to be separated on the basis of differences such as race, sex, or religion. [Lat. *sēgregāre.*] —**seg′re·ga′tion** *n.* —**seg′re·ga′tion·ist** *adj. & n.* —**seg′re·ga′tor** *n.*

se·gue (sĕg′wā′, sā′gwā′) ►*v.* **-gued, -gue·ing 1.** *Mus.* To make a transition directly from one section or theme to another. **2.** To move smoothly from one situation or element to another. ►*n.* An act or instance of segueing. [< Ital., there follows.]

seign·ior (sān-yôr′, sān′yôr′) ►*n.* A feudal lord. [< VLat. **senior.*] —**sei·gnio′ri·al** *adj.*

seine (sān) ►*n.* A large fishing net made to hang vertically in the water by weights and floats. ►*v.* **seined, sein·ing** To fish with a seine. [< Gk. *sagēnē.*] —**sein′er** *n.*

Seine (sān, sĕn) A river of N France flowing about 770 km (480 mi) to the English Channel.

seis·mic (sīz′mĭk) ►*adj.* Of or caused by an earthquake. —**seis′mi·cal·ly** *adv.*

seismo– or **seism–** ►*pref.* Earthquake: *seismograph.* [< *seismos.*]

seis·mo·graph (sīz′mə-grăf′) ►*n.* An instrument for automatically detecting and recording the intensity and duration of ground movements, esp. of earthquakes. —**seis·mog′ra·pher** (-mŏg′rə-fər) *n.* —**seis′mo·graph′ic** *adj.* —**seis·mog′ra·phy** *n.*

seis·mol·o·gy (sīz-mŏl′ə-jē) ►*n.* The geophysical science of earthquakes and the mechanical properties of the earth. —**seis′mo·log′ic** (-mə-lŏj′ĭk), **seis′mo·log′i·cal** *adj.* —**seis·mol′o·gist** *n.*

sei·tan (sā′tăn′) ►*n.* A chewy, protein-rich food made from wheat gluten. [?]

seize (sēz) ►*v.* **seized, seiz·ing 1.** To grasp suddenly and forcibly. **2.** To capture or conquer. **3.** To take by authority; confiscate. [< OFr. *seisir.*]

sei·zure (sē′zhər) ►*n.* **1.** The act of seizing or being seized. **2.** A sudden attack or spasm, as in epilepsy or another disorder.

sel·dom (sĕl′dəm) ►*adv.* Not often; rarely. [< OE *seldan.*] —**sel′dom·ness** *n.*

se·lect (sĭ-lĕkt′) ►*v.* To choose from among several; pick out. ►*adj.* **1.** Singled out; chosen. **2.** Of special quality; choice. [Lat. *sēligere, sēlēct-.*] —**se·lec′tive** *adj.* —**se·lec′tive·ly** *adv.* —**se·lec′tiv·i·ty** *n.* —**se·lec′tor** *n.*

se·lect·ee (sĭ-lĕk′tē′) ►*n.* One selected, esp. for military service.

se·lec·tion (sĭ-lĕk′shən) ►*n.* **1a.** The act of selecting or the fact of being selected. **b.** One selected. **2.** A carefully chosen collection. **3.** A literary or musical text chosen for reading or performance. **4.** *Biol.* A natural or artificial process that involves the survival and reproduction of some kinds of organisms instead of others, resulting in changes in traits of a species or population.

selective service ►*n.* A system for calling up people for compulsory military service.

se·lect·man (sĭ-lĕkt′măn′, -mən) ►*n.* One of a board of town officers chosen annually in New England communities. See Usage Note at **man.**

se·lect·wom·an (sĭ-lĕkt′woom′ən) ►*n.* A woman who is one of a board of town officers chosen annually in New England communities. See Usage Note at **man.**

se·le·ni·um (sĭ-lē′nē-əm) ►*n.* *Symbol* **Se** A nonmetallic element resembling sulfur, used as a semiconductor and in photocells. At. no. 34. See table at **element.** [< Gk. *selēnē*, moon.]

self (sĕlf) ►*n., pl.* **selves** (sĕlvz) **1.** One's total being. **2.** Individuality. **3.** One's own interests or advantage. **4.** *Immunol.* That which the immune system identifies as belonging to the body. ►*pron.* Myself, yourself, himself, or herself. [< OE, selfsame.]

self– ►*pref.* **1.** Oneself: *self-control.* **2.** Automatic; automatically: *self-loading.* [< OE.]

self-ab·sorbed (sĕlf′əb-sôrbd′, -zôrbd′) ►*adj.* Excessively self-involved. —**self′-ab·sorp′tion** *n.*

self-ad·dressed (sĕlf′ə-drĕst′) ►*adj.* Addressed to oneself.

self-ap·point·ed (sĕlf′ə-poin′tĭd) ►*adj.* Designated by oneself.

self-as·ser·tion (sĕlf′ə-sûr′shən) ►*n.* Determined advancement of one's own personality, wishes, or views. —**self′-as·ser′tive** *adj.* —**self′-as·ser′tive·ness** *n.*

self-as·sured (sĕlf′ə-shoord′) ►*adj.* Confident and poised. —**self′-as·sur′ance** *n.*

self-cen·tered (sĕlf′sĕn′tərd) ►*adj.* Engrossed in oneself; selfish. —**self′-cen′tered·ly** *adv.*

self-con·scious (sĕlf′kŏn′shəs) ►*adj.* **1.** Aware of oneself as an individual. **2.** Socially ill at ease. —**self′-con′scious·ly** *adv.* —**self′-con′scious·ness** *n.*

self-con·tained (sĕlf′kən-tānd′) ►*adj.* **1.** Complete in itself. **2a.** Self-sufficient. **b.** Reserved. —**self′-con·tain′ment** *n.*

self-con·trol (sĕlf′kən-trōl′) ►*n.* Control of one's emotions, desires, or actions. —**self′-con·trolled′** *adj.*

self-de·fense (sĕlf′dĭ-fĕns′) ►*n.* **1.** Defense of oneself, one's property, or one's reputation. **2.** *Law* The right to protect oneself against violence or threatened violence with whatever means reasonably necessary.

self·de·ni·al (sĕlf'dĭ-nī'əl) ►*n.* Sacrifice of one's own desires or interests.

self-de·struct (sĕlf'dĭ-strŭkt') ►*n.* A mechanism for causing a device to destroy itself. ►*v.* To destroy oneself or itself.

self-de·struc·tion (sĕlf'dĭ-strŭk'shən) ►*n.* The act of destroying oneself, esp. suicide. —**self'-de·struc'tive** *adj.* —**self'-de·struc'tive·ly** *adv.* —**self'-de·struc'tive·ness** *n.*

self-de·ter·mi·na·tion (sĕlf'dĭ-tûr'mə-nā'shən) ►*n.* **1.** Determination of one's course of action without compulsion. **2.** Freedom of the people to determine their political status; independence.

self-dis·ci·pline (sĕlf'dĭs'ə-plĭn) ►*n.* Training and control of oneself, usu. for personal improvement.

self-ef·fac·ing (sĕlf'ĭ-fā'sĭng) ►*adj.* Not drawing attention to oneself; modest.

self-es·teem (sĕlf'ĭ-stēm') ►*n.* Confidence; self-respect.

self-ev·i·dent (sĕlf'ĕv'ĭ-dənt) ►*adj.* Requiring no proof or explanation. —**self'-ev'i·dence** *n.* —**self'-ev'i·dent·ly** *adv.*

self-ex·plan·a·to·ry (sĕlf'ĭk-splăn'ə-tôr'ē) ►*adj.* Needing no explanation.

self-ex·pres·sion (sĕlf'ĭk-sprĕsh'ən) ►*n.* Expression of one's own personality, as through speech or art. **self'-ex·pres'sive** *adj.* —**self'-ex·pres'sive·ness** *n.*

self-fer·til·i·za·tion (sĕlf'fûr'tl-ĭ-zā'shən) ►*n.* Fertilization of a plant or animal by itself.

self-ful·fill·ing (sĕlf'fŏŏl-fĭl'ĭng) ►*adj.* **1.** Achieving fulfillment as a result of having been expected or foretold: *a self-fulfilling prophecy.* **2.** Achieving self-fulfillment.

self-ful·fill·ment (sĕlf'fŏŏl-fĭl'mənt) ►*n.* Fulfillment of one's goals and potential.

self-gov·ern·ment (sĕlf'gŭv'ərn-mənt) ►*n.* **1.** Political independence; autonomy. **2.** Democracy. —**self'-gov'erned** *adj.* —**self'-gov'ern·ing** *adj.*

self-hard·en·ing (sĕlf'här'dn-ĭng) ►*adj.* Of or relating to materials that harden without special treatment.

self-im·age (sĕlf'ĭm'ĭj) ►*n.* One's conception of oneself.

self-im·por·tance (sĕlf'ĭm-pôr'tns) ►*n.* Excessively high regard for one's own importance. —**self'-im·por'tant** *adj.* —**self'-im·por'tant·ly** *adv.*

self-im·posed (sĕlf'ĭm-pōzd') ►*adj.* Imposed by oneself on oneself; voluntarily assumed.

self-in·crim·i·na·tion (sĕlf'ĭn-krĭm'ə-nā'shən) ►*n.* Incrimination of oneself, esp. by one's own testimony in a criminal prosecution. —**self'-in·crim'i·nat'ing** *adj.*

self-in·duced (sĕlf'ĭn-dōōst', -dyōōst') ►*adj.* **1.** Induced by oneself. **2.** *Elect.* Produced by self-induction.

self-in·duc·tion (sĕlf'ĭn-dŭk'shən) ►*n.* The generation by a changing current of an electromotive force in the same circuit. —**self'-in·duc'tive** *adj.*

self-in·dul·gence (sĕlf'ĭn-dŭl'jəns) ►*n.* Excessive indulgence of one's own appetites and desires. —**self'-in·dul'gent** *adj.* —**self'-in·dul'gent·ly** *adv.*

self-in·ter·est (sĕlf'ĭn'trĭst) ►*n.* **1.** Selfish regard for one's own advantage or interest. **2.** Personal interest. —**self'-in'ter·est·ed** *adj.*

self·ish (sĕl'fĭsh) ►*adj.* Concerned chiefly or excessively with oneself. —**self'ish·ly** *adv.* —**self'ish·ness** *n.*

self·less (sĕlf'lĭs) ►*adj.* Having no concern for oneself; unselfish. —**self'less·ly** *adv.* —**self'less·ness** *n.*

self-love (sĕlf'lŭv') ►*n.* Regard for one's self. —**self'-lov'ing** *adj.*

self-made (sĕlf'mād') ►*adj.* Successful as a result of one's own efforts.

self-mail·er (sĕlf'mā'lər) ►*n.* A folder that can be mailed without being enclosed in an envelope. —**self'-mail'ing** *adj.*

self-pit·y (sĕlf'pĭt'ē) ►*n.* Exaggerated pity for oneself. —**self'-pit'y·ing** *adj.*

self-pol·li·na·tion (sĕlf'pŏl'ə-nā'shən) ►*n.* Transfer of pollen from an anther to a stigma of the same flower or to a stigma of a different flower on the same plant. —**self'-pol'li·nate'** *v.*

self-pos·ses·sion (sĕlf'pə-zĕsh'ən) ►*n.* Full

---

self'-a·ban'don·ment *n.*
self'-a·base'ment *n.*
self'-ab·sorp'tion *n.*
self'-a·buse' *n.*
self'-act'ing *adj.*
self'-ac'tu·al·i·za'tion *n.*
self'-ac'tu·al·ize' *v.*
self'-ad·min'is·ter *v.*
self'-ad·min'i·stra'ting *adj.*
self'-ag·gran'dize·ment *n.*
self'-a·nal'y·sis *n.*
self'-ap·prov'al *n.*
self'-ap·proved *adj.*
self'-ap·prov'ing *adj.*
self'-as·sert'ing *adj.*
self'-a·ware' *adj.*
self'-a·ware'ness *n.*
self'-clean'ing *adj.*
self'-com·pla'cen·cy *n.*
self'-com·pla'cent. *adj.*
self'-con'cept *n.*

self'-con·cep'tion *n.*
self'-con·cern' *n.*
self'-con·cerned' *adj.*
self'-con·duct'ed *adj.*
self'-con·fessed' *adj.*
self'-con'fi·dence *n.*
self'-con'fi·dent *adj.*
self'-con·tent' *adj. & n.*
self'-con'tra·dic'tion *n.*
self'-con'tra·dic'to·ry *adj.*
self'-cor·rect'ing *adj.*
self'-crit'i·cal *adj.*
self'-crit'i·cal·ly *adv.*
self'-crit'i·cism *n.*
self'-de·ceit' *n.*
self'-de·ceived' *adj.*
self'-de·ceiv'ing *adj.*
self'-de·cep'tion *n.*
self'-de·cep'tive *adj.*
self'-de·cep'tive·ly *adv.*
self'-de·feat'ing *adj.*
self'-de·fin'ing *adj.*
self'-def'i·ni'tion *n.*

self'-dep're·cat'ing *adj.*
self'-dep're·ca·to'ry *adj.*
self'-de·vel'op·ment *n.*
self'-di'ag·no'sis *n.*
self'-di·rect'ed *adj.*
self'-di·rect'ing *adj.*
self'-di·rec'tion *n.*
self'-dis·cov'er·y *n.*
self'-dis·trust' *n.*
self'-ed'u·cat'ed *adj.*
self'-ed'u·ca'tion *n.*
self'-e·lect'ed *adj.*
self'-em·ployed' *adj.*
self'-em·ploy'ment *n.*
self'-en·rich'ment *n.*
self'-e·val'u·a'tion *n.*
self'-ex·am'i·na'tion *n.*
self'-ex'ile *n.*
self'-ex'iled *adj.*
self'-ex·plain'ing *adj.*
self'-fer'tile *adj.*
self'-fer'til·ized' *adj.*
self'-fer'til·iz'ing *adj.*

command of one's faculties, feelings, and behavior. —**self′-pos·sessed′** *adj.*

self·pres·er·va·tion (sĕlf′prĕz′ər-vā′shən) ►*n.* Protection of oneself from harm or destruction.

self-pro·claimed (sĕlf′prō-klāmd′, -prə-) ►*adj.* Self-styled.

self-re·al·i·za·tion (sĕlf′rē′ə-lĭ-zā′shən) ►*n.* The fulfillment of one's potential.

self-ref·er·en·tial (sĕlf′rĕf′ə-rĕn′shəl) ►*adj.* Referring to oneself. —**self′-ref′er·ence** *n.*

self-re·spect (sĕlf′rĭ-spĕkt′) ►*n.* Due respect for oneself. —**self′-re·spect′ing** *adj.*

self-right·eous (sĕlf′rī′chəs) ►*adj.* Smugly or unduly sure of one's own righteousness. —**self′-right′eous·ly** *adv.* —**self′-right′-eous·ness** *n.*

self-sac·ri·fice (sĕlf′săk′rə-fīs′) ►*n.* Sacrifice of one's own interests or well-being for the sake of others. —**self′-sac′ri·fic′ing** *adj.*

self·same (sĕlf′sām′) ►*adj.* Being the very same; identical.

self-sat·is·fac·tion (sĕlf′săt′ĭs-făk′shən) ►*n.* Smug satisfaction with oneself. —**self′-sat′-is·fied′** *adj.*

self-seal·ing (sĕlf′sē′lĭng) ►*adj.* **1.** Capable of sealing itself. **2.** Sealable without moisture: *a self-sealing envelope.*

self-search·ing (sĕlf′sûr′chĭng) ►*n.* Examination of one's feelings and actions and their motivation. —**self′-search′ing** *adj.*

self-seek·ing (sĕlf′sē′kĭng) ►*adj.* Pursuing only one's own ends or interests. —**self′-seek′-ing** *n.*

self-ser·vice (sĕlf′sûr′vĭs) ►*adj.* Requiring customers or users to help themselves: *a self-service elevator.* —**self′-ser′vice** *n.*

self-serv·ing (sĕlf′sûr′vĭng) ►*adj.* Serving one's own interests, esp. without concern for others. —**self′-serv′ing·ly** *adv.*

self-start·er (sĕlf′stär′tər) ►*n.* One who displays an unusual amount of initiative. —**self′-start′ing** *adj.*

self-styled (sĕlf′stīld′) ►*adj.* As characterized by oneself, often without justification. See Usage Note at **so-called.**

self-suf·fi·cient (sĕlf′sə-fĭsh′ənt) ►*adj.* Able to provide for oneself without help. —**self′-suf·fi′cien·cy** *n.*

self-will (sĕlf′wĭl′) ►*n.* Willfulness; obstinacy. —**self′-willed′** *adj.*

Sel·juk (sĕl′jook′, sĕl-jook′) A Turkish dynasty in central and W Asia (11th–13th cent.).

sell (sĕl) ►*v.* **sold** (sōld), **sell·ing 1.** To exchange for money or its equivalent. **2.** To offer for sale: *a firm that sells textiles.* **3.** To promote successfully. **4.** To convince: *They sold me on the idea.* **5.** To be sold or be on sale. —*phrasal verb:* **sell out** *Slang* To betray. [< OE *sellan,* give.] —**sell′er** *n.*

sell·off (sĕl′ôf′, -ŏf′) ►*n.* A period of widespread selling in a securities market, causing a sharp decline in prices.

sell·out (sĕl′out′) ►*n.* **1.** An event for which all the tickets are sold. **2.** *Slang* One who has betrayed one's principles.

selt·zer (sĕlt′sər) ►*n.* **1.** A natural effervescent spring water of high mineral content. **2.** See **carbonated water.** [< Ger. *Selterser (Wasser),* (water) of Selters, Germany.]

sel·vage also **sel·vedge** (sĕl′vĭj) ►*n.* The edge of a fabric woven to prevent raveling. [ME.]

selves (sĕlvz) ►*n.* Pl. of **self.**

se·man·tic (sĭ-măn′tĭk) ►*adj.* Relating to meaning, esp. in language. [< Gk. *sēmantikos,* significant < *sēma,* sign.] —**se·man′ti·cal·ly** *adv.*

se·man·tics (sĭ-măn′tĭks) ►*n. (takes sing. or pl. v.)* The study of meaning in language.

sem·a·phore (sĕm′ə-fôr′) ►*n.* **1.** A visual signaling apparatus with flags, lights, or mechanically moving arms. **2.** A system for alphabetic signaling using hand-held flags. ►*v.* -**phored, -phor·ing** To send (a message) by semaphore. [Gk. *sēma,* sign + –PHORE.]

sem·blance (sĕm′bləns) ►*n.* **1.** An outward or token appearance. **2.** A likeness. **3.** The barest trace. [< OFr. *sembler,* resemble.]

se·men (sē′mən) ►*n.* A whitish secretion of the male reproductive organs, containing spermatozoa. [< Lat. *sēmen,* seed.]

se·mes·ter (sə-mĕs′tər) ►*n.* One of two divisions of an academic year. [< Lat. *(cursus) sēmēstris,* (course) of six months.]

sem·i (sĕm′ī, sĕm′ē) ►*n., pl.* **sem·is** *Informal* **1.**

self′-giv·ing *adj.*
self′-gov·ern·ing *adj.*
self′-grat′i·fi·ca′tion *n.*
self′-guid′ance *n.*
self′-hate′ *n.*
self′-ha′tred *n.*
self′-help′ *n.*
self′-hyp·no′sis *n.*
self′-i·den′ti·fy′ *v.*
self′-i·den′ti·ty *n.*
self′-im·prove′ment *n.*
self′-in·flict′ed *adj.*
self′-in·struct′ed *adj.*
self′-in·volved′ *adj.*
self′-in·volve′ment *n.*
self′-knowl′edge *n.*
self′-lim′it·ed *adj.*
self′-lim′it·ing *adj.*
self′-load′ing *adj.*
self′-loath′ing *n.*
self′-lock′ing *adj.*

self′-mas′ter·y *n.*
self′-med′i·ca′tion *n.*
self′-ob·ser·va′tion *n.*
self′-or·dain′ed *adj.*
self′-per·cep′tion *n.*
self′-per·pet′u·at′ing *adj.*
self′-por′trait *n.*
self′-pow′ered *adj.*
self′-pro·mot′er *n.*
self′-pro·mo′tion *n.*
self′-pro·pelled′ *adj.*
self′-pro·pul′sion *n.*
self′-pro·tec′tion *n.*
self′-pro·tec′tive *adj.*
self′-pro·tec′tive·ly *adv.*
self′-pub′lished *adj.*
self′-re·cord′ing *adj.*
self′-ref′er·en′tial·ly *adv.*
self′-re·flec′tion *n.*
self′-re·gard′ *n.*
self′-reg′u·lat′ing *adj.*
self′-reg·u·la′tion *n.*
self′-re·li′ance *n.*

self′-re·li′ant *adj.*
self′-rep′li·cat′ing *adj.*
self′-rep′li·ca′tion *n.*
self′-re·proach′ *n.*
self′-re·proach′ful *adj.*
self′-re·straint′ *n.*
self′-re·veal′ing *adj.*
self′-rev′e·la′tion *n.*
self′-rule′ *n.*
self′-scru′ti·ny *n.*
self′-seal′ing *adj.*
self′-stud′y *n.*
self′-sup·port′ *n.*
self′-sup·port′ing *adj.*
self′-sus·tain′ing *adj.*
self′-sus·tain′ing·ly *adv.*
self′-taught′ *adj.*
self′-treat′ment *n.*
self′-trust′ *n.*
self′-un′der·stand′ing *n.*
self′-val′i·dat′ing *adj.*
self′-wind′ing *adj.*
self′-worth′ *n.*

A semitrailer. **2.** A semifinal. **3.** A semiformal dance.

semi– ►*pref.* **1.** Half: *semicircle.* **2.** Partial; partially: *semiconscious.* **3.** Occurring twice during: *semimonthly.* See Usage Note at **bi–**. [< Lat. *sēmi-,* half.]

sem·i·an·nu·al (sĕm′ē-ăn′yōō-əl, sĕm′ī-) ►*adj.* Occurring or issued twice a year. —**sem′i·an′nu·al·ly** *adv.*

sem·i·cir·cle (sĕm′ī-sûr′kəl) ►*n.* A half of a circle as divided by a diameter. —**sem′i·cir′cu·lar** (-kyə-lər) *adj.*

semicircular canal ►*n.* Any of three tubular and looped structures of the inner ear, together functioning in maintenance of the sense of balance in the body.

sem·i·co·lon (sĕm′ī-kō′lən) ►*n.* A mark of punctuation (;) used to connect independent clauses and indicating a closer relationship between the clauses than a period does.

sem·i·con·duc·tor (sĕm′ē-kən-dŭk′tər, sĕm′ī-) ►*n.* Any of various solid crystalline substances, such as germanium or silicon, having electrical conductivity greater than insulators but less than good conductors. —**sem′i·con·duct′ing** *adj.*

sem·i·fi·nal (sĕm′ē-fī′nəl, sĕm′ī-) ►*n.* A competition or examination that precedes the final one. —**sem′i·fi′nal** *adj.* —**sem′i·fi′nal·ist** *n.*

sem·i·for·mal (sĕm′ē-fôr′məl, sĕm′ī-) ►*adj.* Moderately formal: *semiformal attire.* ►*n.* Something moderately formal in nature, such as a school dance.

sem·i·month·ly (sĕm′ē-mŭnth′lē, sĕm′ī-) ►*adj.* Occurring or issued twice a month. See Usage Note at **bi–**.

sem·i·nal (sĕm′ə-nəl) ►*adj.* **1.** Of or relating to semen. **2.** Creative. **3.** Providing a basis or stimulus for further development: *seminal research in a new field.* [< Lat. *sēmen, sēmin-,* seed.] —**sem′i·nal·ly** *adv.*

sem·i·nar (sĕm′ə-närʹ) ►*n.* **1.** A course of advanced study or research for a small group of students in a school. **2.** A conference. [< Lat. *sēminārium,* seed plot.]

sem·i·nar·y (sĕm′ə-nĕr′ē) ►*n., pl.* **-ies 1.** A school that trains clergy. **2.** A school of higher education, esp. a private school for girls. —**sem′i·nar′i·an** (-nâr′ē-ən) *n.*

Sem·i·nole (sĕm′ə-nōl′) ►*n., pl.* **-nole** or **-noles 1.** A member of a Native American people of primarily Creek origin, now living in Oklahoma and S Florida. **2.** Either of the Muskogean languages of the Seminole.

se·mi·ot·ics (sē′mē-ŏt′ĭks, sĕm′ē-, sē′mī-) ►*n.* *(takes sing. v.)* The theory and study of signs and symbols, esp. as elements of language. [< Gk. *sēma,* sign.] —**se′mi·o·ti′cian** (-ə-tĭsh′ən) *n.*

sem·i·pre·cious stone (sĕm′ē-prĕsh′əs) ►*n.* A gem, such as an opal, that is not as rare or expensive as a precious stone.

sem·i·pri·vate (sĕm′ē-prī′vĭt, sĕm′ī-) ►*adj.* Shared with other hospital patients.

sem·i·pro·fes·sion·al (sĕm′ē-prə-fĕsh′ə-nəl, sĕm′ī-) ►*adj. Sports* **1.** Playing a sport for pay but not on a full-time basis. **2.** Composed of or engaged in by semiprofessional players. —**sem′i·pro·fes′sion·al** *n.*

sem·i·skilled (sĕm′ē-skĭld′, sĕm′ī-) ►*adj.* Possessing or requiring intermediate skills.

sem·i·sol·id (sĕm′ē-sŏl′ĭd, sĕm′ī-) ►*adj.* Inter-

mediate in properties, esp. in rigidity, between solids and liquids. ►*n.* (sĕm′ē-sŏl′ĭd, sĕm′ī-) A semisolid substance.

Sem·ite (sĕm′īt′) ►*n.* **1.** A member of a people speaking a Semitic language, such as the Arabs, Phoenicians, or ancient Hebrews. **2.** A Jew.

Se·mit·ic (sə-mĭt′ĭk) ►*adj.* **1.** Of or relating to a subgroup of the Afro-Asiatic languages that includes Arabic and Hebrew. **2.** Of or relating to the Semites. ►*n.* The Semitic languages.

sem·i·tone (sĕm′ē-tōn′, sĕm′ī-) ►*n. Mus.* An interval equal to a half tone in the standard diatonic scale. —**sem′i·ton′ic** (-tŏn′ĭk) *adj.*

sem·i·trail·er (sĕm′ē-trā′lər, sĕm′ī-) ►*n.* A trailer having rear wheels only, with the forward portion supported by the truck tractor.

sem·i·vow·el (sĕm′ĭ-vou′əl) ►*n.* A sound having a vowel quality but functioning as a consonant, as the initial sounds of *yell* and *well.*

sem·i·week·ly (sĕm′ē-wēk′lē, sĕm′ī-) ►*adj.* Issued or occurring twice a week. See Usage Note at **bi–**.

sem·i·year·ly (sĕm′ē-yîr′lē, sĕm′ī-) ►*adj.* Issued or occurring twice a year.

sem·o·li·na (sĕm′ə-lē′nə) ►*n.* The coarser particles produced by milling durum wheat, used esp. for making pasta and hot cereals. [< Lat. *simila,* fine flour.]

sen·ate (sĕn′ĭt) ►*n.* **1a.** often **Senate** The upper house in a bicameral legislature, such as the US Congress. **b.** The supreme council of state of the ancient Roman Republic and Empire. **2.** The building in which a senate meets. **3.** A governing or advisory body of some colleges. [< Lat. *senātus.*]

sen·a·tor (sĕn′ə-tər) ►*n.* A member of a senate. —**sen′a·to′ri·al** (-tôr′ē-əl) *adj.*

send (sĕnd) ►*v.* **sent** (sĕnt), **send·ing 1.** To cause to be conveyed to a destination: *send goods by plane.* **2.** To dispatch, as by a communications medium: *send a message by radio.* **3a.** To direct to go on a mission: *sent troops overseas.* **b.** To enable to go: *sent her kid to college.* **4.** To emit: *sends forth warmth.* **5.** To direct or propel with force: *a slap that sent me staggering.* **6.** To cause to take place or occur. **7.** To put into a given state or condition: *sent me into a panic.* [< OE *sendan.*] —**send′er** *n.*

 Syns: dispatch, forward, route, ship, transmit v.

Sen·dak (sĕn′dăk′), **Maurice** b. 1928–2012. Amer. illustrator and writer.

Maurice Sendak
photographed in 2004

send·off (sĕnd′ôf′, -ŏf′) ►*n.* A demonstration of affection and good wishes, as for a person beginning a journey.

Sen·e·ca (sĕn′ĭ-kə) ►*n., pl.* **-ca** or **-cas** **1.** A member of a Native American people of W New York, now also in SE Ontario. **2.** The Iroquoian language of the Seneca.

Seneca, Lucius Amaeus "the Younger." 4? BC–AD 65. Roman Stoic philosopher and writer.

Sen·e·gal (sĕn′ĭ-gôl′, -gäl′) A country of W Africa on the Atlantic. Cap. Dakar. **—Sen′e·ga·lese′** (-gô-lēz′, -lēs′) *adj. & n.*

Senegal River A river of W Africa rising in W Mali and flowing about 1,640 km (1,020 mi) to the Atlantic.

se·nes·cent (sĭ-nĕs′ənt) ►*adj.* Growing old; aging. [< Lat. *senēscere,* grow old.] **—se·nes′cence** *n.*

se·nile (sē′nīl′, sĕn′īl′) ►*adj.* Related to diminished cognitive function because of old age. [Lat. *senīlis.*] **—se·nil′i·ty** (sĭ-nĭl′ĭ-tē) *n.*

sen·ior (sēn′yər) ►*adj.* **1.** Of or being the older of two persons having the same name. **2.** Of or relating to senior citizens. **3.** Above others of the same set or class. **4.** Of the fourth and last year of high school or college. ►*n.* **1.** A person who is older than another. **2.** A senior citizen. **3.** A fourth-year student in a US high school or college. [Lat., older.]

senior chief petty officer ►*n.* A rank, as in the US Navy, below master chief petty officer.

senior citizen ►*n.* A person of relatively advanced age, esp. one who has retired. **—sen′ior-cit′i·zen** *adj.*

senior high school ►*n.* A high school usu. including grades 9, 10, 11, and 12.

sen·ior·i·ty (sēn-yôr′ĭ-tē, -yŏr′-) ►*n.* **1.** The state of being senior. **2.** Precedence over others because of length of service.

senior master sergeant ►*n.* A rank in the US Air Force below chief master sergeant.

sen·na (sĕn′ə) ►*n.* **1.** Any of various plants having compound leaves and yellow flowers. **2.** A preparation of the dried leaves of a senna plant, used as a laxative. [< Ar. *sanā.*]

Sen·nach·er·ib (sĭ-năk′ər-ĭb) d. 681 BC. King of Assyria (705–681).

se·ñor (sĕ-nyôr′) ►*n., pl.* **se·ño·res** (sĕ-nyō′rĕs) A Spanish courtesy title for a man. [< Lat. *senior,* senior.]

se·ño·ra (sĕ-nyō′rä) ►*n.* A Spanish courtesy title for a married woman.

se·ño·ri·ta (sē′nyō-rē′tä) ►*n.* A Spanish courtesy title for a girl or unmarried woman.

sen·sa·tion (sĕn-sā′shən) ►*n.* **1.** A perception associated with stimulation of a sense organ. **2.** An indefinite, generalized body feeling. **3a.** A state of heightened interest or emotion. **b.** A cause of such interest and excitement. **—sen·sa′tion·al** *adj.* **—sen·sa′tion·al·ly** *adv.*

sen·sa·tion·al·ism (sĕn-sā′shə-nə-lĭz′əm) ►*n.* The use of lurid or exaggerated matter, esp. in writing, journalism, or politics. **—sen·sa′tion·al·ist** *n.* **—sen·sa′tion·al·is′tic** *adj.* **—sen·sa′tion·al·ize** *v.*

sense (sĕns) ►*n.* **1.** Any of the faculties of hearing, sight, smell, touch, taste, and equilibrium. **2. senses** The faculties of sensation as means of providing physical gratification and pleasure. **3.** Intuitive or acquired perception. **4.** often **senses** Correct judgment. **5a.** A meaning;

signification. **b.** One of the meanings of a word or phrase. ►*v.* **sensed, sens·ing** **1.** To become aware of; perceive. **2.** To understand. **3.** To detect automatically: *sense radioactivity.* [< Lat. *sēnsus.*]

sense·less (sĕns′lĭs) ►*adj.* **1.** Lacking sense or meaning; meaningless. **2.** Foolish. **3.** *Informal* Unconscious, usu. due to physical trauma. **—sense′less·ly** *adv.* **—sense′less·ness** *n.*

sen·si·ble (sĕn′sə-bəl) ►*adj.* **1.** Acting with or showing good sense: *a sensible choice.* **2.** Having a perception of something; cognizant. **3.** Perceptible or appreciable by the senses or the mind. **—sen′si·ble·ness** *n.* **—sen′si·bly** *adv.*

sen·si·tive (sĕn′sĭ-tĭv) ►*adj.* **1.** Capable of perceiving. **2.** Responsive to external conditions or stimulation; having sensation. **3a.** Susceptible to slight differences or changes in the environment. **b.** Readily altered: *film that is sensitive to light.* **c.** Registering slight differences or changes of condition. **4a.** Easily irritated: *sensitive skin.* **b.** Predisposed to inflammation as a result of preexisting allergy or disease. **5a.** Aware of the attitudes, feelings, or circumstances of others. **b.** Easily hurt or offended. **6.** Of or relating to classified information. [< Lat. *sēnsus,* sense.] **—sen′si·tive·ly** *adv.* **—sen′si·tive·ness, sen′si·tiv′i·ty** *n.*

sen·si·tize (sĕn′sĭ-tīz′) ►*v.* **-tized, -tiz·ing** To make or become more sensitive or more sensitive. **—sen′si·ti·za′tion** *n.*

sen·sor (sĕn′sər, -sôr′) ►*n.* A device, such as a photoelectric cell, that receives and responds to a signal or stimulus.

sen·so·ry (sĕn′sə-rē) ►*adj.* **1.** Of the senses. **2.** Transmitting impulses from sense organs to nerve centers; afferent.

sen·su·al (sĕn′shōō-əl) ►*adj.* **1a.** Relating to gratification of the senses, esp. sexual gratification. **b.** Sexually attractive: *a sensual mouth.* **2.** Of or affecting the senses; sensory **—sen′su·al·ness, sen′su·al′i·ty** (-ăl′ĭ-tē) *n.* **—sen′su·al·ize** *v.*

sen·su·ous (sĕn′shōō-əs) ►*adj.* **1a.** Relating to or involving gratification of the senses. **b.** Sexually attractive. **2.** Relating to or affecting the senses; sensory. **—sen′su·os′i·ty** (-ŏs′ĭ-tē), **sen′su·ous·ness** *n.* **—sen′su·ous·ly** *adv.*

sent (sĕnt) ►*v.* P.t. and p.part. of **send.**

sen·tence (sĕn′təns) ►*n.* **1.** An independent grammatical unit that has a subject and a predicate with a finite verb. **2.** *Law* The penalty imposed by a law court upon someone found guilty of a crime. ►*v.* **-tenced, -tenc·ing** *Law* To pronounce sentence upon. [< Lat. *sententia,* opinion.] **—sen·ten′tial** (sĕn-tĕn′shəl) *adj.* **—sen·ten′tial·ly** *adv.*

sen·ten·tious (sĕn-tĕn′shəs) ►*adj.* **1.** Terse and energetic in expression; pithy. **2.** Given to pompous moralizing. [< Lat. *sententia,* opinion.] **—sen·ten′tious·ness** *n.*

sen·tient (sĕn′shənt, -shē-ənt) ►*adj.* **1.** Having sense perception; conscious. **2.** Experiencing sensation. [< Lat. *sentīre,* feel.] **—sen′tience** *n.* **—sen′tient·ly** *adv.*

sen·ti·ment (sĕn′tə-mənt) ►*n.* **1.** A thought, view, or attitude, esp. one based mainly on emotion. **2a.** Emotion; feeling. **b.** Maudlin emotion; sentimentality. **3.** The thought or emotion underlying a behavior. [< Lat. *sentīre,* feel.]

sen·ti·men·tal (sĕn′tə-mĕn′tl) ►*adj.* **1.** Having, showing, or caused by emotion, esp. tender or affectionate feeling. **2.** Having, showing, or caused by strong or extravagant tenderness or sadness, often in an idealized way. —**sen′ti·men′tal·ism, sen′ti·men·tal′i·ty** (-tăl′ĭ-tē) *n.* —**sen′ti·men′tal·ize** *v.* —**sen′ti·men′tal·ly** *adv.*
Syns: *maudlin, mawkish, mushy* **adj.**

sen·ti·nel (sĕn′tə-nəl) ►*n.* A guard; sentry. [< Ital. *sentinella.*]

sen·try (sĕn′trē) ►*n., pl.* **-tries 1.** A guard, esp. a soldier posted to prevent the passage of unauthorized persons. **2.** The duty of a sentry. [Perh. < obsolete *sentrinel,* var. of SENTINEL.]

Seoul (sōl) The capital and largest city of South Korea, in the NW part.

se·pal (sē′pəl) ►*n.* One of the usu. green leaflike structures composing the outermost part of a flower. [< Gk. *skepē,* covering.]

sep·a·ra·ble (sĕp′ər-ə-bəl, sĕp′rə-) ►*adj.* Possible to separate. —**sep′a·ra·bil′i·ty** *n.*

sep·a·rate (sĕp′ə-rāt′) ►*v.* **-rat·ed, -rat·ing 1a.** To set, keep, or come apart: *separated the slices of bread.* **b.** To sort. **2.** To differentiate between; distinguish. **3.** To remove from a mixture or combination; isolate. **4.** To stop living together as spouses. **5.** To part company; disperse. ►*adj.* (sĕp′ər-ĭt, sĕp′rĭt) **1.** Not touching or adjoined; detached: *a house with a separate garage.* **2.** Existing or considered as an independent entity: *The clinic is separate from the hospital.* **3.** Dissimilar; distinct or individual. See Synonyms at **distinct.** [< Lat. *sēparāre.*] —**sep′a·rate·ly** *adv.* —**sep′a·rate·ness** *n.*

sep·a·ra·tion (sĕp′ə-rā′shən) ►*n.* **1a.** The act or process of separating. **b.** The condition of being separated. **2.** An interval that separates; gap. **3.** *Law* A formal agreement that severs relations between spouses but does not terminate a marriage.

sep·a·ra·tist (sĕp′ər-ə-tĭst, sĕp′rə-, sĕp′ə-rā′-) ►*n.* One who advocates political, religious, or cultural separation. —**sep′a·ra·tism** *n.* —**sep′a·ra·tist** *adj.*

sep·a·ra·tor (sĕp′ə-rā′tər) ►*n.* One that separates, as a device for separating cream from milk.

Se·phar·di (sə-fär′dē) ►*n., pl.* **-dim** (-dĭm) A descendent of the Jews who lived in Spain and Portugal during the Middle Ages. —**Se·phar′dic** (-dĭk) *adj.*

se·pi·a (sē′pē-ə) ►*n.* **1.** A dark brown pigment. **2.** A drawing or photograph done in this pigment. [< Gk. *sēpia,* cuttlefish.] —**se′pi·a** *adj.*

sep·pu·ku (sĕp′ōō-kōō, sĕ-pōō′-) ►*n.* Ritual suicide by disembowelment, formerly practiced by Japanese samurai. [J.: *setsu,* to cut + *fuku,* stomach.]

sep·sis (sĕp′sĭs) ►*n., pl.* **-ses** (-sēz) The systemic condition of widespread infection by pathogenic microorganisms, esp. bacteria, that have invaded the bloodstream, usu. from a local source. [Gk. *sēpsis,* putrefaction.]

Sep·tem·ber (sĕp-tĕm′bər) ►*n.* The 9th month of the Gregorian calendar. See table at **calendar.** [< Lat., the seventh month.]

sep·tic (sĕp′tĭk) ►*adj.* Of or causing sepsis. [< Gk. *sēptos,* rotten.]

sep·ti·ce·mi·a (sĕp′tĭ-sē′mē-ə) ►*n.* Systemic infection of the blood by pathogenic microorganisms, esp. bacteria. —**sep′ti·ce′mic** (-mĭk) *adj.*

septic tank ►*n.* A sewage-disposal tank in which waste material is decomposed by anaerobic bacteria.

sep·til·lion (sĕp-tĭl′yən) ►*n.* **1.** The cardinal number equal to 10²⁴. **2.** *Chiefly Brit.* The cardinal number equal to 10⁴². [Fr.] —**sep·til′lion** *adj.* —**sep·til′lionth** *n. & adj.*

Sep·tu·a·gint (sĕp′tōō-ə-jĭnt′, sĕp-tōō′ə-jənt, -tyōō′-) ►*n.* A Greek translation of the Hebrew Bible made in the 3rd cent. BC. [Lat. *septuāgintā,* seventy (from the traditional number of its translators).]

sep·tum (sĕp′təm) ►*n., pl.* **-ta** (-tə) A thin partition or membrane between two cavities or soft masses of tissue in an organism. [Lat. *saeptum,* partition.]

sep·tu·plet (sĕp-tŭp′lĭt, -tōō′plĭt, -tyōō′-) ►*n.* One of seven offspring born in a single birth. [*septu(ple),* multiply by seven + (TRI)PLET.]

sep·ul·cher (sĕp′əl-kər) ►*n.* **1.** A burial vault. **2.** A receptacle for sacred relics. ►*v.* **-chered, -cher·ing** To place into a sepulcher. [< Lat. *sepulcrum.*] —**se·pul′chral** (sə-pŭl′krəl) *adj.*

seq. ►*abbr. Lat.* sequens (the following)

se·quel (sē′kwəl) ►*n.* Something that follows as a continuation, esp. a literary, dramatic, or cinematic work whose narrative continues that of a preexisting work. [< Lat. *sequēla.*]

se·quence (sē′kwəns, -kwĕns′) ►*n.* **1.** A following of one thing after another; succession. **2.** An order of succession; arrangement. **3.** A related or continuous series. **4.** A series of related shots that make up a complete unit of action in a movie. **5.** *Chem.* The order of constituents in a chemical compound, esp. DNA or a protein. [< Lat. *sequēns,* following.] —**se′quence** *v.* —**se·quen′tial** (sĭ-kwĕn′shəl) *adj.* —**se·quen′tial·ly** *adv.*

se·ques·ter (sĭ-kwĕs′tər) ►*v.* **1.** To set apart; segregate. **2.** To cause to withdraw into seclusion. See Synonyms at **isolate. 3.** *Law* To confiscate (property) as security against legal claims. [< Lat., trustee.] —**se′ques·tra′tion** *n.*

se·quin (sē′kwĭn) ►*n.* A small shiny ornamental disk, usu. sewn on cloth; spangle. [< Ital. *zecchino,* a Venetian coin.] —**se′quined** *adj.*

se·quoi·a (sĭ-kwoi′ə) ►*n.* **1.** A very tall evergreen coniferous tree of the Sierra Nevada, having a massive trunk and reddish wood. **2.** A redwood. [After SEQUOYA.]

Se·quoy·a or **Se·quoy·ah** (sĭ-kwoi′ə) 1770?–1843. Cherokee scholar.

se·ra (sîr′ə) ►*n.* Pl. of **serum.**

se·ra·glio (sə-răl′yō, -răl′-) ►*n., pl.* **-glios 1.** A harem. **2.** A sultan's palace. [Ital. *serraglio.*]

se·ra·pe also **sa·ra·pe** (sə-rä′pē, -răp′ē) ►*n.* A long blanketlike shawl worn esp. by Mexican men. [Am.Sp. *sarape.*]

ser·aph (sĕr′əf) ►*n., pl.* **-a·phim** (-ə-fĭm) or **-aphs** *Christianity* An angel of the highest order. [< Heb. *śārāp,* fiery serpent, seraph.]

Serb (sûrb) ►*n.* A native or inhabitant of Serbia.

Ser·bi·a (sûr′bē-ə) A country of SE Europe. Cap. Belgrade.

Ser·bi·an (sûr′bē-ən) ►*n.* **1.** A native or inhabitant of Serbia. **2.** The Slavic language of the Serbs. —**Ser′bi·an** *adj.*

Ser·bo-Cro·a·tian (sûr′bō-krō-ā′shən) ►*n.* The closely related languages of Serbia, Croatia,

Bosnia and Herzegovina, and Montenegro, when considered as a single language. —**Ser′-bo-Cro·a′tian** *adj.*

sere also **sear** (sîr) ►*adj.* Withered; dry. [< OE *sēar.*]

ser·e·nade (sĕr′ə-nād′, sĕr′ə-nād′) ►*n.* A musical performance given to honor or express love for someone, often by one person. ►*v.* **-nad·ed, -nad·ing** To perform a serenade (for). [< Ital. *serenata.*] —**ser′e·nad′er** *n.*

ser·en·dip·i·ty (sĕr′ən-dĭp′ĭ-tē) ►*n.* The faculty of making fortunate discoveries by accident. [After the Persian fairy tale *The Three Princes of Serendip.*] —**ser′en·dip′i·tous** *adj.* —**ser′en·dip′i·tous·ly** *adv.*

se·rene (sə-rēn′) ►*adj.* **1.** Calm and unruffled; tranquil. **2.** Unclouded; fair: *serene blue skies.* [< Lat. *serēnus.*] —**se·rene′ly** *adv.* —**se·ren′i·ty** (-rĕn′ĭ-tē) *n.*

serf (sûrf) ►*n.* **1.** A member of the lowest feudal class, legally bound to an estate and required to work for the landowner. **2.** A slave. [< Lat. *servus,* slave.] —**serf′dom** *n.*

serge (sûrj) ►*n.* A twilled cloth of worsted or worsted and wool. [< Lat. *sērica,* silken.]

ser·geant (sär′jənt) ►*n.* **1.** Any of several ranks of noncommissioned officers, as in the US Army. **2.** A police officer ranking next below a captain, lieutenant, or inspector. [< LLat. *serviēns,* public official.]

sergeant at arms ►*n., pl.* **sergeants at arms** An officer appointed to keep order within an organization, such as a legislature.

sergeant first class ►*n., pl.* **sergeants first class** A rank in the US Army below master sergeant.

sergeant major ►*n., pl.* **sergeants major** or **sergeant majors** **1.** Any of the highest noncommissioned ranks in the US Army and Marine Corps. **2.** *Chiefly Brit.* A noncommissioned officer of the highest rank.

se·ri·al (sîr′ē-əl) ►*adj.* **1.** Of, forming, or arranged in a series. **2.** Published or produced in installments. **3.** Relating to or engaging in a series of similar acts or behaviors: *serial arson; serial procrastinator.* ►*n.* A work published or produced in installments. —**se′ri·al·i·za′tion** *n.* —**se′ri·al·ize′** *v.* —**se′ri·al·ly** *adv.*

se·ries (sîr′ēz) ►*n., pl.* **series** **1.** A number of objects or events arranged one after the other. **2.** A succession of regularly broadcast television programs. **3.** A succession of publications having similar subjects or formats. **4.** *Sports* A number of games played by the same two teams, often in succession. [Lat. *seriēs* < *serere,* join.]

Usage: When *series* has the singular sense of "one set," it takes a singular verb, even when followed by *of* and a plural noun: *A series of lectures is scheduled.* When *series* has the plural sense of "one or more sets," it takes a plural verb: *Two series of lectures are scheduled.*

ser·if (sĕr′ĭf) ►*n. Print.* A fine line finishing off the main strokes of a letter. [Perh. < Du. *schreef,* line.]

se·ri·o·com·ic (sîr′ē-ō-kŏm′ĭk) ►*adj.* Both serious and comic.

se·ri·ous (sîr′ē-əs) ►*adj.* **1.** Grave in quality or manner. **2.** Carried out with careful thought: *a serious effort.* **3.** Concerned with important rather than trivial matters. **4.** Causing

great concern; critical. **5.** Deeply interested or involved: *a serious relationship.* **6.** Not joking or trifling: *He's serious about his plan.* [< LLat. *sēriōsus.*] —**se′ri·ous·ly** *adv.* —**se′ri·ous·ness** *n.*

ser·mon (sûr′mən) ►*n.* **1.** A homily delivered as part of a liturgy. **2.** A lengthy and tedious reproof or exhortation. [< Lat. *sermō,* discourse.] —**ser′mon·ize′** *v.*

se·rol·o·gy (sĭ-rŏl′ə-jē) ►*n.* The characteristics of a disease or organism indicated by properties of blood serum. —**se′ro·log′ic** (sîr′ə-lŏj′ĭk), **se′ro·log′i·cal** *adj.* —**se·rol′o·gist** *n.*

se·ro·neg·a·tive (sîr′ō-nĕg′ə-tĭv) ►*adj.* Showing a negative reaction to a serological blood test, esp. one testing for the presence of antibodies.

se·ro·pos·i·tive (sîr′ō-pŏz′ĭ-tĭv) ►*adj.* Showing a positive reaction to a serological blood test, esp. one testing for the presence of antibodies.

se·ro·to·nin (sĕr′ə-tō′nĭn, sîr′-) ►*n.* An organic compound found primarily in the brain, blood, and stomach of humans and other mammals that acts as a neurotransmitter and vasoconstrictor. [SER(UM) + TON(E) + –IN.]

se·rous (sîr′əs) ►*adj.* Containing, secreting, or resembling serum.

ser·pent (sûr′pənt) ►*n.* **1.** A snake. **2.** In the Bible, the creature that tempted Eve, identified as Satan in Christian tradition. [< Lat. *serpēns* < *serpere,* creep.]

ser·pen·tine (sûr′pən-tēn′, -tīn′) ►*adj.* Of or like a serpent, as in form or movement.

ser·rate (sĕr′āt′) or **ser·rat·ed** (sĕr′ā′tĭd, sə-rā′-) ►*adj.* Edged with sharp toothlike projections. [< Lat. *serra,* saw.] —**ser·ra′tion** (sə-rā′shən) *n.* —**ser′rate′** *v.*

ser·ried (sĕr′ēd) ►*adj.* Pressed together, esp. in rows. [< Fr. *serrer,* to crowd.]

se·rum (sîr′əm) ►*n., pl.* **se·rums** or **se·ra** (sîr′ə) **1.** The clear yellowish fluid obtained upon separating whole blood into its solid and liquid components after clotting. **2.** Blood serum from the tissues of immunized animals, containing antibodies and used to transfer immunity to another individual. [Lat.]

ser·vant (sûr′vənt) ►*n.* One employed to perform domestic services.

serve (sûrv) ►*v.* **served, serv·ing** **1.** To work for; be a servant to. **2.** To place food before (someone); wait on: *served the guests.* **3.** To provide goods and services for (customers): *a hotel that mostly serves tourists.* **4.** To meet the needs of; satisfy: *The tent served us well in the storm.* **5.** To be of assistance to. **6.** To work through or complete (a period of service). **7.** To be in prison for (a period or term). **8.** To undergo military service for. **9.** To give homage to. **10.** *Law* To deliver or present (a summons or court order, e.g.) to a person who is legally entitled to receive it or required to obey it. **11.** *Sports* To put (a ball) in play, as in tennis. ►*n. Sports* The right or act of serving in many court games. [< Lat. *servīre* < *servus,* slave.]

serv·er (sûr′vər) ►*n.* **1.** One who serves food or drink. **2.** Something, as a tray, used in serving food and drink. **3.** *Sports* The player who serves, as in court games. **4a.** A file server. **b.** A computer that processes HTML requests.

ser·vice (sûr′vĭs) ►*n.* **1a.** Work that is done for others as an occupation or business. **b.**

The occupation or duties of a servant. **2a.** Help or assistance. **b.** An act of help or assistance. **3a.** The serving of food. **b.** A set of dishes or utensils. **4.** A government branch or department and its employees. **5.** The armed forces of a nation, or any branch thereof. **6a.** Installation or repairs provided by a dealer or manufacturer. **b.** The provision to the public of something, esp. a utility: *phone service.* **7.** A religious rite or formal ceremony. **8.** *Sports* A serve. ►*v.* **-viced, -vic·ing 1.** To repair or maintain: *service a car.* **2.** To provide services to. **3.** To make interest payments on (a debt). [< Lat. *servitium*, slavery.]

ser·vice·a·ble (sûr′vĭ-sə-bəl) ►*adj.* **1.** Ready for service; usable. **2.** Able to give long service; durable. **—ser′vice·a·bil′i·ty, ser′vice·a·ble· ness** *n.* **—ser′vice·a·bly** *adv.*

ser·vice·man (sûr′vĭs-măn′, -mən) ►*n.* **1.** A man who is a member of the armed forces. **2.** also **service man** A man whose work is the maintenance and repair of equipment.

service mark ►*n.* A mark used to identify and distinguish services.

service station ►*n.* A gas station, esp. one that services and repairs motor vehicles.

ser·vice·wom·an (sûr′vĭs-wŏom′ən) ►*n.* **1.** A woman who is a member of the armed forces. **2.** also **service woman** A woman whose work is the maintenance and repair of equipment.

ser·vile (sûr′vəl, -vīl′) ►*adj.* Abjectly submissive; slavish. [< Lat. *servīlis* < *servus*, slave.] **—ser′vile·ly** *adv.* **—ser′vile·ness, ser·vil′i· ty** (sər-vĭl′ĭ-tē) *n.*

serv·ing (sûr′vĭng) ►*n.* A helping of food or drink.

ser·vi·tor (sûr′vĭ-tər, -tôr′) ►*n.* An attendant. [< Lat. *servītor.*]

ser·vi·tude (sûr′vĭ-tōod′, -tyōod′) ►*n.* **1.** Subjection to an owner or master. **2.** Forced labor imposed as a punishment. [< LLat. *servitūdō.*]

ser·vo (sûr′vō) ►*n., pl.* **-vos 1.** A servomechanism. **2.** A servomotor.

ser·vo·mech·a·nism (sûr′vō-měk′ə-nĭz′əm) ►*n.* A feedback system used in the automatic control of a mechanical device.

ser·vo·mo·tor (sûr′vō-mō′tər) ►*n.* A motor that controls the action of the mechanical device in a servomechanism. [< Lat. *servus*, slave + MOTOR.]

ses·a·me (sĕs′ə-mē) ►*n.* **1.** A tropical Asian plant bearing small, edible, oil-rich seeds. **2.** The seed of this plant. [< Gk. *sēsamē.*]

ses·qui·cen·ten·ni·al (sĕs′kwĭ-sĕn-tĕn′ē-əl) ►*adj.* Relating to a period of 150 years. ►*n.* A 150th anniversary or its celebration. [Lat. *sesqui-*, one and a half + CENTENNIAL.]

ses·qui·pe·da·lian (sĕs′kwĭ-pĭ-dāl′yən) ►*n.* A long word. ►*adj.* **1.** Given to the use of long words. **2.** Polysyllabic. [< Lat. *sesquipedālis*, of a foot and a half in length.]

ses·sile (sĕs′īl′, -əl) ►*adj.* **1.** Permanently attached, as a barnacle. **2.** Attached directly at the base, stalkless: *sessile leaves.* [< Lat. *sedēre*, *sess-*, sit.]

ses·sion (sĕsh′ən) ►*n.* **1a.** A meeting of a legislative or judicial body. **b.** A series of such meetings. **c.** The duration of such a series of meetings. **2.** The part of a year or of a day during which a school holds classes. [< Lat. *sedēre*, *sess-*, sit.]

ses·tet (sĕ-stĕt′) ►*n.* **1.** The last six lines of a sonnet. **2.** A poem or stanza containing six lines. [Ital. *sestetto.*]

set¹ (sĕt) ►*v.* **set, set·ting 1.** To put in a specified position or arrangement. **2.** To put in a specified state. **3.** To incite to hostile action: *a dispute that set them against each other.* **4.** To put into a stable or fixed position: *set the fence post in cement.* **5.** To put in a mounting. **6.** To arrange for the eating of a meal: *set the table.* **7.** To calibrate (a device): *set an alarm.* **8.** To spread open to the wind: *set the sails.* **9.** To restore to a proper and normal state when injured: *set a broken arm.* **10.** To apply curlers and clips to (hair) in order to style. **11.** To concentrate on a purpose or goal. **12.** To arrange (type) into words and sentences preparatory to printing; compose. **13.** To compose (music) to fit a given text. **14.** To prescribe or establish: *set a precedent.* **15.** To establish (e.g., a computer password) to allow future use. **16.** To establish as a model: *set a good example.* **17.** To prescribe as a time for: *set the meeting for Friday afternoon.* **18.** To prescribe the unfolding of (e.g., a drama) in a specific place: *a play that is set in Venice.* **19.** To determine (a price or value). **20.** To disappear below the horizon. **21.** To sit on eggs, as a hen. **22.** To become fixed or hard. ►*adj.* **1.** Fixed or established. **2.** Established by convention. **3.** Fixed and rigid. **4.** Unwilling to change: *set in his ways.* **5.** Ready: *we are set to leave* ►*n.* **1.** The act or process of setting. **2.** The condition resulting from setting. **3.** A session of performed instrumental or vocal music. **—*phrasal verbs:* set about** To begin. **set aside 1.** To reserve for a special purpose. **2.** To annul or invalidate. **set back** To slow down the progress of. **set down 1.** To seat: *Set the dog down.* **2.** To put into writing. **set forth 1.** To present for consideration. **2.** To express in words. **3.** To begin a journey. **set off 1.** To cause to occur. **2.** To cause to explode. **3.** To distinguish. **4.** To direct attention to by contrast. **5.** To start a journey. **set out 1.** To display for exhibition or sale. **2.** To start a journey. **3.** To undertake or begin something. **set up 1.** To place in an upright position. **2.** To invest with power. **3.** To assemble and erect. **4.** To establish; found: *set up a charity.* **5.** To put (someone else) into a compromising situation by deceit or trickery: *Swindlers set me up.* **—*idioms:* set against** Strongly opposed to. **set sail** Begin a voyage on water. [< OE *settan.*]

Usage: Set is now in most cases a transitive verb: *He sets the table. Sit* is generally an intransitive verb: *He sits at the table.* There are some exceptions: *The sun sets* (not *sits*). *A hen sets* (or *sits*) *on her eggs.*

set² (sĕt) ►*n.* **1.** A group of persons or things of the same kind that belong together: *a chess set.* **2.** A group of books or periodicals published as a unit. **3a.** The scenery constructed for a theatrical performance. **b.** The enclosure in which a movie is filmed. **4a.** A session of music performed usu. for dancing. **b.** The music so played. **5.** The receiving apparatus assembled to operate a radio or television. **6.** *Math.* A collection of distinct elements. **7.** *Sports* A group of tennis games constituting one division or unit of a match. [< Lat. *secta*, faction.]

set·back (sĕt′băk′) ►*n.* **1.** An unanticipated

check in progress; reverse. **2.** A steplike recession, as in a wall or the rise of a tall building.

Se·ton (sēt′n), Saint **Elizabeth Ann Bayley** "Mother Seton." 1774–1821. Amer. religious leader.

set piece ▸*n.* **1.** A piece of freestanding stage scenery. **2.** An artistic or literary work marked by a formal pattern. **3.** A carefully planned and executed military operation.

set·screw (sĕt′skrōō′) ▸*n.* **1.** A usu. headless screw used to hold two parts together. **2.** A screw used to regulate the tension of a spring.

set·tee (sĕ-tē′) ▸*n.* **1.** A long wooden bench with a back. **2.** A small sofa. [Perh. < SETTLE.]

set·ter (sĕt′ər) ▸*n.* Any of several breeds of long-haired hunting dogs.

set theory ▸*n. Math.* The study of the properties of sets.

set·ting (sĕt′ĭng) ▸*n.* **1.** The position in which something, such as an automatic control, is set. **2.** A context or background. **3.** A mounting, as for a jewel.

set·tle (sĕt′l) ▸*v.* **-tled, -tling** **1.** To put into order; arrange or fix definitely as desired. **2.** To establish residence (in). **3.** To restore calmness or comfort to. **4a.** To sink, become compact, or come to rest: *Dust settled on the road.* **b.** To cause (a liquid) to become clear by forming a sediment. **5.** To stabilize. **6a.** To make compensation for (a claim). **b.** To pay (a debt). **7.** To conclude (a dispute). **8.** To decide (a lawsuit) by mutual agreement without court action. ▸*n.* A long wooden bench with a high back. [< OE *setlan* < *setl*, seat.] —**set′tler** *n.*

settle
c. 1865 English settle

set·tle·ment (sĕt′l-mənt) ▸*n.* **1.** The act or process of settling. **2a.** Establishment, as of a person in a business or of people in a new region. **b.** A newly colonized region. **3.** A small community. **4.** An arrangement or other understanding reached.

set-to (sĕt′tōō′) ▸*n., pl.* **-tos** A brief, usu. heated conflict.

set·up (sĕt′ŭp′) ▸*n.* **1.** An arrangement or plan, esp. an initial organization. **2.** *Slang* **a.** A contest prearranged to result in an easy or faked victory. **b.** A deceptive scheme, such as a fraud. **3.** *Sports* A play or pass that creates an opportunity to score. **4.** often **setups** *Informal* The collective ingredients for serving alcoholic drinks.

Seu·rat (sə-rä′, sœ-), **Georges Pierre** 1859–91. French painter.

Seuss (sōōs), Doctor. See Theodor Seuss **Geisel.**

Se·vas·to·pol (sə-văs′tə-pōl′, sĕv′ə-stō′pəl) A city of S Ukraine on the Black Sea W of Yalta.

sev·en (sĕv′ən) ▸*n.* **1.** The cardinal number equal to 6 + 1. **2.** The 7th in a set or sequence. [< OE *seofon.*] —**sev′en** *adj. & pron.*

sev·en·teen (sĕv′ən-tēn′) ▸*n.* **1.** The cardinal number equal to 16 + 1. **2.** The 17th in a set or sequence. [< OE *seofontīne.*] —**sev′en·teen′** *adj. & pron.*

sev·en·teenth (sĕv′ən-tēnth′) ▸*n.* **1.** The ordinal number matching the number 17 in a series. **2.** One of 17 equal parts. —**sev′en·teenth′** *adv. & adj.*

sev·enth (sĕv′ənth) ▸*n.* **1.** The ordinal number matching the number 7 in a series. **2.** One of seven equal parts. **3.** *Mus.* A tone seven degrees above or below a given tone in a diatonic scale. —**sev′enth** *adv. & adj.*

seventh heaven ▸*n.* A state of great joy.

sev·en·ti·eth (sĕv′ən-tē-ĭth) ▸*n.* **1.** The ordinal number matching the number 70 in a series. **2.** One of 70 equal parts. —**sev′en·ti·eth** *adv. & adj.*

sev·en·ty (sĕv′ən-tē) ▸*n., pl.* **-ties** The cardinal number equal to 7 × 10. [< OE *hundseofontig.*] —**sev′en·ty** *adj. & pron.*

sev·er (sĕv′ər) ▸*v.* **1.** To cut off (a part) from a whole. **2.** To divide into parts. **3.** To break up (e.g., a relationship); dissolve. [< Lat. *sēparāre.*]

sev·er·al (sĕv′ər-əl, sĕv′rəl) ▸*adj.* **1.** Being of a number more than two or three but not many. **2.** Respectively different; various: *They parted and went their several ways.* See Synonyms at **distinct.** ▸*pron. (takes pl. v.)* An indefinite but small number; a few. [< Lat. *sēpar*, distinct.] —**sev′er·al·ly** *adv.*

sev·er·al·ty (sĕv′ər-əl-tē, sĕv′rəl-) ▸*n., pl.* **-ties** *Law* **1.** A separate and individual right to possession or ownership. **2.** Property owned in severalty.

sev·er·ance (sĕv′ər-əns, sĕv′rəns) ▸*n.* **1a.** The act or process of severing. **b.** The condition of being severed. **2.** Extra pay given an employee upon leaving a position.

se·vere (sə-vîr′) ▸*adj.* **-ver·er, -ver·est** **1.** Unsparing or harsh, as in treatment of others; strict. **2.** Marked by rigorous standards. **3.** Austere or dour; forbidding. **4.** Extremely plain in substance or style. **5.** Causing great discomfort, damage, or distress: *severe pain; a severe storm.* [Lat. *sevērus.*] —**se·vere′ly** *adv.* —**se·vere′ness, se·ver′i·ty** (-vĕr′ĭ-tē) *n.*

Se·ville (sə-vĭl′) A city of SW Spain NNE of Cádiz.

sew (sō) ▸*v.* **sewed, sewn** (sōn) or **sewed, sew·ing** **1.** To make, repair, or fasten by stitching, as with a needle and thread. **2.** To close, fasten, or attach with stitches. —*phrasal verb:* **sew up** *Informal* To complete successfully. [< OE *seowian.*] —**sew′er** *n.*

sew·age (sōō′ĭj) ▸*n.* Liquid and solid waste carried off in sewers or drains.

Sew·ard (sōō′ərd), **William Henry** 1801–72. Amer. public official.

sew·er (sōō′ər) ▸*n.* An artificial, usu. underground conduit for carrying off sewage or rainwater. [< VLat. *exaquāria* : Lat. *ex-*, out + Lat. *aqua*, water.]

sew·er·age (sōō′ər-ĭj) ▸*n.* **1.** A system of sewers. **2.** Removal of waste materials by sewers. **3.** Sewage.

sew·ing (sō′ĭng) ►*n.* **1.** The act of one who sews. **2.** An article being sewn.

sewing machine ►*n.* A machine for sewing usu. with attachments for special stitching.

sex (sĕks) ►*n.* **1.** Sexual activity, esp. sexual intercourse. **2.** Either of the two divisions, female and male, by which most organisms are classified on the basis of their reproductive organs and functions. **3.** The condition or character of being female or male: *a study that takes sex into account.* **4.** Females or males considered collectively: *dormitories that house only one sex.* [< Lat. *sexus.*]

sex·a·ge·nar·i·an (sĕk′sə-jə-nâr′ē-ən) ►*n.* A person between the ages of 60 and 70. [< Lat. *sexāgēnārius.*] —**sex′a·ge·nar′i·an** *adj.*

sex·a·ges·i·mal (sĕk′sə-jĕs′ə-məl) ►*adj.* Of or based on the number 60. [< Lat. *sexāgēsimus,* sixtieth.]

sex chromosome ►*n.* Either of a pair of chromosomes in diploid cells, or a single chromosome in haploid cells, carrying genes that determine the sex and sex-linked characteristics of an organism. Most mammals have one pair of sex chromosomes in diploid cells, designated XX in females and XY in males.

sex hormone ►*n.* Any of various hormones, such as estrogen and androgen, affecting the growth or function of the reproductive organs.

sex·ism (sĕk′sĭz′əm) ►*n.* Discrimination based on gender, esp. discrimination against women. —**sex′ist** *adj. & n.*

sex·less (sĕks′lĭs) ►*adj.* **1.** Lacking sexual characteristics; neuter. **2.** Lacking in sexual activity.

sex-linked (sĕks′lĭngkt′) ►*adj.* **1.** Carried by a sex chromosome, esp. an X chromosome. Used of genes. **2.** Sexually determined. Used esp. of inherited traits. —**sex linkage** *n.*

sex·tant (sĕk′stənt) ►*n.* A navigational instrument used to measure the altitudes of celestial bodies. [< Lat. *sextāns,* sixth part.]

sex·tet (sĕk-stĕt′) ►*n.* **1a.** A group composed of six musicians. **b.** A composition written for six performers. **2.** A group of six persons or things. [Alteration of SESTET.]

sex·til·lion (sĕk-stĭl′yən) ►*n.* **1.** The cardinal number equal to 10^{21}. **2.** *Chiefly Brit.* The cardinal number equal to 10^{36}. [Fr.] —**sex·til′lion** *adj. & pron.* —**sex·til′lionth** *n. & adj.*

sex·ton (sĕk′stən) ►*n.* One responsible for the care and upkeep of church property. [< Med. Lat. *sacristānus.*]

Sexton, Anne 1928–74. Amer. poet.

Anne Sexton
photographed c. 1967

sex·tu·ple (sĕk-stōo′pəl, -styōo′-, -stŭp′əl) ►*v.* **-pled, -pling** To multiply or be multiplied by six. ►*adj.* **1.** Having six parts. **2.** Multiplied by six; sixfold. ►*n.* A sixfold amount or number. [Prob. Lat. *sextus,* sixth + (QUINT)UPLE.]

sex·tup·let (sĕk-stŭp′lĭt, -stōo′plĭt, -styōo′-) ►*n.* One of six offspring born in a single birth. [SEXTU(PLE) + (TRI)PLET.]

sex·u·al (sĕk′shōo-əl) ►*adj.* **1.** Of sex, sexuality, or the sex organs and their functions. **2.** Relating to the sexes or gender. **3.** Of or involving the union of male and female gametes: *sexual reproduction.* —**sex′u·al·ly** *adv.*

sexual harassment ►*n.* Inappropriate behavior of a sexual nature, such as repeated sexual advances, esp. by a person in authority.

sexual intercourse ►*n.* **1.** Sexual activity between a male and a female that includes insertion of the penis into the vagina. **2.** Sexual union between two people in which the penis is inserted into the mouth or anus.

sex·u·al·i·ty (sĕk′shōo-ăl′ĭ-tē) ►*n.* **1.** The quality of being sexual, esp. sexual orientation and behavior. **2.** A manner of being sexual or engaging in sexual activity. **3.** The condition of reproducing sexually or being divided into sexes.

sexually transmitted disease ►*n.* Any of various diseases usu. contracted through intimate sexual contact.

sexual orientation ►*n.* The direction of one's sexual interest toward members of the same, opposite, or both sexes.

sex·y (sĕk′sē) ►*adj.* **-i·er, -i·est 1.** Arousing sexual desire or interest. **2.** *Slang* Highly appealing or interesting. —**sex′i·ly** *adv.* —**sex′i·ness** *n.*

Sey·chelles (sā-shĕl′, -shĕlz′) An island country in the W Indian Ocean N of Madagascar. Cap. Victoria.

Sey·mour (sē′môr′), **Jane** 1508?–37. Queen of England (1536–37) as the third wife of Henry VIII.

SF ►*abbr.* **1.** sacrifice fly **2.** science fiction

Sg The symbol for **seaborgium.**

SGML (ĕs′jē-ĕm-ĕl′) ►*n.* A markup language for describing the logical structure of a computer document. [*S(tandard) G(eneralized) M(arkup) L(anguage).*]

Sgt. or **Sgt** or **SGT** ►*abbr.* sergeant

Sha'·ban also **Shaa·ban** (shə-bän′, shä-, shô-) ►*n.* The 8th month of the Muslim calendar. See table at **calendar.** [Ar. *ša'bān.*]

Shab·bat (shə-bät′, shä′bəs) ►*n.* The Jewish Sabbath, observed from sundown on Friday until sundown on Saturday. [Heb. *šabbāt.*]

shab·by (shăb′ē) ►*adj.* **-bi·er, -bi·est 1a.** Threadbare or worn-out. **b.** Dilapidated or deteriorated; seedy. **2.** Wearing threadbare clothing. **3.** Disgraceful: *shabby treatment.* [< obsolete *shab,* scab.] —**shab′bi·ly** *adv.*

shack (shăk) ►*n.* A small, crudely built cabin. [Poss. < Nahuatl *xacalli,* adobe hut.]

shack·le (shăk′əl) ►*n.* **1.** A metal fastening, usu. one of a pair, for encircling and confining the ankle or wrist of a prisoner or captive; fetter; manacle. **2.** A device consisting of a U-shaped metal piece and a bolt, used to fasten or restrain a rope or chain. **3.** often **shackles** Something that confines or restrains. ►*v.* **-led, -ling 1.** To confine with shackles. **2.** To restrict. See Synonyms at **hobble.** [< OE *sceacel.*]

shackle
anchor shackle

shad (shăd) ►*n., pl.* **shad** or **shads** A herringlike food fish that swims up streams from marine waters to spawn. [< OE *sceadd*.]

shade (shād) ►*n.* **1.** Light diminished in intensity; partial darkness. **2.** Cover or shelter from the sun or its rays: *sat in the shade under the tree.* **3a.** A gradation of a color: *shades of gray.* **b.** A slight difference or variation; nuance: *shades of meaning.* **c.** A small amount; trace. **4.** Any of various devices used to reduce light or heat: *closed the window shades.* **5. shades** *Informal* Sunglasses. **6.** A disembodied spirit; ghost. ►*v.* **shad·ed, shad·ing 1.** To screen from light or heat. **2.** To darken or obscure. **3.** To represent degrees of shade or shadow in. **4.** To vary by slight degrees: *shade the meaning.* [< OE *sceadu*.]

shad·ow (shăd′ō) ►*n.* **1.** A dark area or shape made by an object blocking rays of light. **2.** A shaded area in a picture. **3.** A cause or feeling of gloom or unhappiness: *The argument cast a shadow on their friendship.* **4a.** A nearby or adjoining region; vicinity: *lived in the shadow of the ballpark.* **b.** A dominating presence or influence: *in her sister's shadow.* **5a.** An imitation or inferior version. **b.** A phantom. **6.** A faint indication; trace: *a shadow of things to come.* ►*v.* **1.** To cast a shadow on; shade. **2.** To make gloomy or dark. **3.** To represent vaguely or mysteriously; foreshadow. **4.** To follow, esp. in secret; trail. ►*adj.* Not having official status: *a shadow government.* [< OE *sceaduwe*.] —**shad′-ow·i·ness** *n.* —**shad′ow·y** *adj.*

shad·ow·box (shăd′ō-bŏks) ►*v.* To spar with an imaginary opponent. —**shad′ow·box′-ing** *n.*

shad·y (shā′dē) ►*adj.* -**i·er, -i·est 1.** Full of or casting shade. **2.** Of dubious character or honesty. —**shad′i·ly** *adv.* —**shad′i·ness** *n.*

shaft (shăft) ►*n.* **1a.** The long narrow body of a spear or arrow. **b.** A spear or arrow. **c.** A long handle as of certain tools. **2.** The midsection of a long bone. **3.** A column or columnlike part. **4.** A ray or beam of light. **5a.** A long cylindrical bar or pole. **b.** A drive shaft. **6.** A long, often vertical passage or duct: *an elevator shaft.* **7.** A scornful remark; barb. **8.** *Slang* Harsh, unfair treatment. Often used with *the*: *Management gave unions the shaft.* ►*v. Slang* To treat in a harsh, unfair way. [< OE *sceaft*.]

shag (shăg) ►*n.* **1.** A tangle or mass, esp. of matted hair. **2.** Cloth having a coarse, long nap. **3.** A rug with a thick, rough pile. [< OE *sceacga*, matted hair.]

shag·gy (shăg′ē) ►*adj.* -**gi·er, -gi·est 1.** Having long rough hair or wool. **2.** Bushy and matted. **3.** Poorly groomed; unkempt. —**shag′gi·ness** *n.*

shah (shä) ►*n.* Used formerly as a title for the hereditary monarch of Iran. [Pers. *shāh*.]

Shah Ja·han (jə-hän′) 1592–1666. Mughal emperor of India (1628–58).

shake (shāk) ►*v.* **shook** (sho͝ok), **shak·en** (shā′-kən), **shak·ing 1a.** To move or cause to move from side to side or up and down with short jerky movements. See Synonyms at **agitate**. **b.** To tremble, vibrate, or rock. **c.** To brandish or wave: *shook his fist.* **2.** To cause to waver or become unstable. **3.** To remove or dislodge by or as if by jerky movements: *shook the dust from the cushions.* **4.** To scatter or strew by jerky movements: *shakes salt onto the popcorn.* **5.** To clasp (hands) in greeting or leave-taking or as a sign of agreement. ►*n.* **1.** The act or an instance of shaking. **2.** See **milk shake. 3. shakes** *Informal* Uncontrollable trembling. —**phrasal verbs: shake down** *Slang* **1.** To extort money from. **2.** *Slang* To make a thorough search of. **shake off** To free oneself from. **shake out 1.** To come to pass; transpire. **2.** To straighten or extend by jerky movements. **shake up 1.** To unnerve; shock. **2.** To rearrange drastically. —**idioms: no great shakes** *Slang* Unexceptional; ordinary. **shake a leg** *Informal* To hurry. [< OE *sceacan*.]

shake·down (shāk′doun′) ►*n.* **1.** *Slang* Extortion of money, as by blackmail. **2.** *Slang* A thorough search. **3.** A period of appraisal followed by adjustments to improve efficiency or functioning. ►*adj.* Serving to test performance: *a shakedown cruise.*

shak·er (shā′kər) ►*n.* **1.** One that impels or encourages action. **2.** A container used for shaking. **3. Shaker** A member of a Christian group practicing communal living and observing celibacy.

Shake·speare (shāk′spîr), **William** 1564–1616. English playwright and poet. —**Shake·spear′e·an, Shake·spear′i·an** *adj. & n.*

shake·up (shāk′ŭp′) ►*n.* A thorough reorganization.

shak·o (shăk′ō, shā′kō, shä′-) ►*n., pl.* -**os** or -**oes** A stiff cylindrical military dress hat with a short visor and a plume. [< Hung. *csákós (süveg)*, pointed (cap).]

shak·y (shā′kē) ►*adj.* -**i·er, -i·est 1.** Trembling or quivering. **2.** Unsteady or weak. **3.** Precarious: *a shaky existence.* —**shak′i·ly** *adv.* —**shak′i·ness** *n.*

shale (shāl) ►*n.* A rock composed of layers of claylike, fine-grained sediments. [< OE *scealu*.] —**shal′ey** *adj.*

shale oil ►*n.* A crude oil obtained from oil shale by heating and distillation.

shall (shăl) ►*aux.v. p.t.* **should** (sho͝od) Used before a verb in the infinitive to show: **a.** Simple futurity: *We shall arrive tomorrow.* **b.** An order, promise, or obligation: *You shall leave now.* **c.** Inevitability: *That day shall come.* [< OE *sceal.*]

Usage: The traditional rules require that *shall* be used with the first person to indicate simple futurity and that *will* be used for that same purpose with the second and third persons. These rules are rarely observed in American English, however, even at the most formal levels, and the widespread practice of using *will* to indicate futurity with all three persons is both widespread and acceptable in American English.

shal·lot (shăl′ət, shə-lŏt′) ►*n.* **1.** A type of onion with pear-shaped bulbs. **2.** The mild-flavored edible bulb of this plant. [< VLat. *escalōnia*, SCALLION.]

shal·low (shăl′ō) ►*adj.* **-er, -est 1.** Measuring little from bottom to top or surface; lacking physical depth. **2.** Lacking depth of intellect, emotion, or knowledge. **3.** Marked by insufficient inhalation of air: *shallow breaths.* ►*n.* often **shallows** A part of a body of water of little depth; shoal. [ME *shalowe.*] —**shal′low·ly** *adv.* —**shal′low·ness** *n.*

sha·lom (shä-lōm′, shə-) ►*interj.* Used to express greeting or farewell. [Heb. *šālôm*, peace.]

shalt (shălt) ►*aux.v. Archaic* 2nd pers. sing. pr.t. of **shall.**

sham (shăm) ►*n.* **1.** Something false or empty purported to be genuine. **2.** An imposter. **3.** A decorative fabric cover, as on a pillow. ►*adj.* Not genuine; fake. ►*v.* **shammed, sham·ming** To put on a false appearance; feign. [Perh. < SHAME.] —**sham′mer** *n.*

sha·man (shä′mən, shā′-) ►*n.* A member of certain tribal societies who acts as a medium between the visible world and an invisible spirit world and who uses magic or sorcery usu. for healing. [< Skt. *śramaṇaḥ*, Buddhist monk.] —**sha′man·ism** *n.* —**sha′man·is′tic** *adj.*

sham·ble (shăm′bəl) ►*v.* **-bled, -bling** To walk in an awkward, lazy, or unsteady manner, shuffling the feet. [< *shamble*, ungainly.]

sham·bles (shăm′bəlz) ►*pl.n. (takes sing. v.)* A scene or condition of complete disorder or ruin. [< ME *shamel*, place where meat is butchered and sold.]

shame (shām) ►*n.* **1a.** A painful emotion caused by a strong sense of guilt, embarrassment, unworthiness, or disgrace. **b.** Capacity for such a feeling: *Have you no shame?* **2.** One that brings dishonor, disgrace, or condemnation. **3.** Disgrace; ignominy. **4.** A great disappointment. ►*v.* **shamed, sham·ing 1.** To cause to feel shame. **2.** To bring dishonor or disgrace on. **3.** To force by making ashamed: *He was shamed into an apology.* [< OE *sceamu.*] —**shame′ful** *adj.* —**shame′ful·ly** *adv.* —**shame′ful·ness** *n.*

shame·faced (shām′fāst′) ►*adj.* **1.** Indicative of shame: *a shamefaced excuse.* **2.** Shy; bashful. [< OE *sceamfæst.*] —**shame′fac′ed·ly** (-fā′sĭd-lē) *adv.* —**shame′fac′ed·ness** *n.*

shame·less (shām′lĭs) ►*adj.* **1.** Feeling no shame or disgrace. **2.** Marked by a lack of shame: *a shameless lie.* —**shame′less·ly** *adv.*

sham·my (shăm′ē) ►*n.* Var. of **chamois** (sense 2).

sham·poo (shăm-po͞o′) ►*n., pl.* **-poos 1.** A preparation of soap or detergent used to wash the hair and scalp. **2.** Any of various cleaning agents for rugs or upholstery. **3.** The act or process of washing or cleaning with shampoo. [< Hindi *cāpnā*, press.] —**sham·poo′** *v.*

sham·rock (shăm′rŏk) ►*n.* **1.** A plant having leaves with three leaflets, such as a clover. **2.** A depiction of this plant, used as an emblem of Ireland. [Ir.Gael. *seamróg.*]

shang·hai (shăng-hī′, shăng′hī′) ►*v.* **-haied, -hai·ing 1.** To kidnap (a man) for service aboard a ship, esp. after drugging him. **2.** To compel (someone) to do something, esp. by fraud or force. [< SHANGHAI.]

Shang·hai (shăng-hī′, shäng′-) A city of E China at the mouth of the Yangtze R. SE of Nanjing.

Shan·gri-la (shăng′grĭ-lä′) ►*n.* An imaginary, remote paradise on earth. [After *Shangri-La*, in James Hilton's *Lost Horizon*.]

shank (shăngk) ►*n.* **1.** The part of the human leg between the knee and ankle or the corresponding part in other vertebrates. **2.** A cut of meat from the leg of an animal. **3.** The section of a tool or instrument connecting the functioning part and handle. **4.** A long narrow part; shaft. [< OE *sceanca.*]

Shan·non (shăn′ən) A river, about 386 km (240 mi), rising in N-central Ireland and flowing to the Atlantic.

shan't (shănt, shänt) Shall not.

shan·ty (shăn′tē) ►*n., pl.* **-ties** A shack. [Prob. < Canadian Fr. *chantier.*]

shape (shāp) ►*n.* **1a.** The characteristic surface configuration of a thing; form: *a lake in the shape of an hourglass.* **b.** Spatial form or appearance: *The coastline changes shape.* **2.** The contour of a person's body; figure. **3.** A definite, distinctive form. **4.** Assumed or false appearance; guise: *a god who assumed a swan's shape.* **5a.** The condition of something esp; with regard to its effectiveness: *What shape is the car in?* **b.** Bodily condition, esp. in regard to muscle tone or endurance: *a runner who is in great shape.* ►*v.* **shaped, shap·ing 1.** To give a particular form to. **2.** To cause to conform to a particular form: *a bone that is shaped to bear weight.* —*phrasal verb:* **shape up 1.** *Informal* To turn out; develop. **2.** To improve. [< OE *gesceap*, creation.] —**shaped** *adj.* —**shap′er** *n.*

shape·less (shāp′lĭs) ►*adj.* **1.** Lacking a definite shape. **2.** Lacking symmetrical or attractive form; not shapely. —**shape′less·ly** *adv.* —**shape′less·ness** *n.*

shape·ly (shāp′lē) ►*adj.* **-li·er, -li·est** Having a pleasing shape. —**shape′li·ness** *n.*

shard (shärd) ►*n.* A broken piece or fragment, as of pottery or glass. [< OE *sceard*, notch.]

share¹ (shâr) ►*n.* **1.** A part or portion belonging to a person or group. **2.** An equitable portion. **3.** Any of the equal parts into which the capital stock of a corporation or company is divided. ►*v.* **shared, shar·ing 1.** To divide and parcel out in shares; apportion. **2.** To use or experience in common: *share a responsibility.* [< OE *scearu.*] —**shar′er** *n.*

share² (shâr) ►*n.* A plowshare. [< OE *scēar.*]

share·crop·per (shâr′krŏp′ər) ►*n.* A tenant farmer who gives a share of the crops raised to the landlord as rent.

share·hold·er (shâr′hōl′dər) ►*n.* One that holds a share or shares of a company or investment fund. —**share′hold′ing** *n.*

share·ware (shâr′wâr′) ►*n.* Copyrighted software that is available free of charge on a trial basis.

shark (shärk) ►*n.* **1.** Any of numerous carnivorous, chiefly marine, cartilaginous fishes having a streamlined body, oil-filled liver, and tough skin covered with toothlike scales. **2.** A ruthless, greedy, or dishonest person. [?]

shark·skin (shärk′skĭn′) ►*n.* **1.** A shark's skin or leather made from it. **2.** A synthetic fabric having a smooth shiny surface.

Sha·ron (shə-rōn′), **Ariel** b. 1928. Israeli military leader and prime minister (2001–06).

sharp (shärp) ►*adj.* **-er, -est 1.** Having a thin edge or a fine point. **2a.** Having clear form and distinct detail. **b.** Not rounded or blunt; pointed: *a sharp nose.* **3.** Abrupt or acute: *a sharp turn.* **4.** Shrewd; astute. **5.** Crafty or deceitful. **6.** Alert: *a sharp eye.* **7.** Harsh or biting. **8.** Intense; severe: *a sharp pain.* **9.** Sudden and shrill. **10.** *Mus.* **a.** Raised in pitch by a semitone: *a C sharp.* **b.** Being above the proper pitch. **11.** *Informal* Attractive or stylish. See Synonyms at **fashionable.** ▸*adv.* **1.** In a sharp manner. **2.** Punctually; exactly. **3.** *Mus.* Above the proper pitch. ▸*n.* **1.** *Mus.* **a.** A note or tone raised one semitone above its normal pitch. **b.** A sign (#) indicating this. **2.** A shrewd cheater. [< OE *scearp,* slope.] —**sharp′ly** *adv.* —**sharp′ness** *n.*

sharp·en (shär′pən) ▸*v.* To make or become sharp or sharper. —**sharp′en·er** *n.*

sharp·shoot·er (shärp′shōo′tər) ▸*n.* One who is highly proficient at shooting.

Shatt al Ar·ab or **Shatt-al-Ar·ab** (shät′ ăl ăr′əb, shät′) A river channel, about 195 km (120 mi) long, of SE Iraq formed by the confluence of the Tigris and Euphrates Rivers and flowing to the Persian Gulf.

shat·ter (shăt′ər) ▸*v.* **1.** To break or burst suddenly into pieces, as with a violent blow. **2.** To disable or destroy. [< OE *scaterian,* scatter.]

shat·ter·proof (shăt′ər-proof′) ▸*adj.* Resistant to shattering.

shave (shāv) ▸*v.* **shaved, shaved** or **shav·en** (shā′vən), **shav·ing 1.** To remove the beard or other body hair (from) with a razor or shaver. **2.** To remove thin slices of or from. **3.** To come close to or graze in passing. See Synonyms at **brush¹. 4.** To reduce by a small amount. ▸*n.* The act, process, or result of shaving. [< OE *sceafan.*]

shav·er (shā′vər) ▸*n.* **1.** A device, esp. an electric razor, used in shaving. **2.** *Informal* A small child, esp. a boy.

shav·ing (shā′vĭng) ▸*n.* A thin slice or sliver, as of wood.

Shaw (shô), **George Bernard** 1856–1950. Irish-born British playwright, essayist, and critic.

sha·war·ma (shə-wär′mə) ▸*n.* Meat that is roasted slowly on a spit and wrapped in pita bread, traditionally served with lettuce, tomato, and garlic sauce. [Ar. *šawurma, šawirma* < Turk. *çevirme,* turn (on a spit).]

shawl (shôl) ▸*n.* A piece of cloth worn as a covering for the head, neck, and shoulders. [< Pers. *šāl.*]

Shaw·nee (shô-nē′) ▸*n., pl.* -**nee** or -**nees 1.** A member of a Native American people formerly of the central Ohio Valley, now in Oklahoma. **2.** The Algonquian language of the Shawnee.

Shaw·wal (shə-wäl′) ▸*n.* The 10th month of the Islamic calendar. See table at **calendar.** [Ar. *šawwāl.*]

she (shē) ▸*pron.* **1.** Used to refer to the female previously mentioned or implied. See Usage Note at **I. 2.** Used to refer to a person or animal whose gender is unspecified or unknown. **3.** Used in place of *it* to refer to certain inanimate things, such as ships and nations. ▸*n.* A female animal or person: *Is the cat a she?* [Prob. < OE *sēo,* feminine of *sē,* that one.]

sheaf (shēf) ▸*n., pl.* **sheaves** (shēvz) **1.** A bound bundle of cut stalks, esp. of grain. **2.** A collection of items held or bound together. [< OE *scēaf.*]

shear (shîr) ▸*v.* **sheared, sheared** or **shorn** (shôrn), **shear·ing 1.** To remove (fleece or hair) by cutting or clipping. **2.** To remove the hair or fleece from. **3.** To cut with or as if with shears: *shear a hedge.* **4.** To divest or deprive. ▸*n.* also **shears 1.** A pair of scissors. **2.** Any of various implements or machines that cut with a scissorlike action. [< OE *sceran.*]

sheath (shēth) ▸*n., pl.* **sheaths** (shēthz, shēths) **1a.** A case for a blade, as of a sword or knife. **b.** Any of various similar coverings. **2.** *Biol.* An enveloping tubular structure, as the base of a grass leaf. **3.** A close-fitting dress. [< OE *scēath.*] —**sheath** *v.*

sheath
Persian sheath *(left)* and dagger *(right)*

sheathe (shēth) ▸*v.* **sheathed, sheath·ing** To insert into or provide with a sheath. [ME *shethen.*]

sheath·ing (shē′thĭng) ▸*n.* A layer esp. of boards applied to a building to serve as a base for weatherproof cladding.

she·bang (shə-băng′) ▸*n. Slang* A situation or organization: *ran the whole shebang.* [?]

She·bat (shə-bät′, -vät′) ▸*n.* Var. of **Shevat.**

shed¹ (shĕd) ▸*v.* **shed, shed·ding 1a.** To lose (a growth or covering) by a natural process: *The snake shed its skin.* **b.** To take off (an article of clothing). **2.** To produce or release (a tear or tears.) **3.** To repel without allowing penetration: *A duck's feathers shed water.* **4.** To radiate; cast: *shed light.* —*idiom:* **shed blood** To kill. [< OE *scēadan,* divide.] —**shed′der** *n.*

shed² (shĕd) ▸*n.* A small roofed structure for storage or shelter. [< ME *shadde.*]

she'd (shĕd) **1.** She had. **2.** She would.

sheen (shēn) ▸*n.* Glistening brightness; luster. [< OE *scīene.*]

sheep (shēp) ▸*n., pl.* **sheep 1.** Any of various usu. horned ruminant mammals raised for wool, meat, or skin. **2.** One who is easily swayed or led. [< OE *scēap.*]

sheep·dog also **sheep dog** (shēp′dôg′, -dŏg′) ▸*n.* A dog bred or trained to herd sheep.

sheep·ish (shē′pĭsh) ▸*adj.* Embarrassed, as by consciousness of a fault: *a sheepish grin.* —**sheep′ish·ly** *adv.* —**sheep′ish·ness** *n.*

sheep·skin (shēp′skĭn′) ▸*n.* **1.** The tanned skin of a sheep, with or without the fleece. **2.** *Informal* A diploma.

sheer¹ (shîr) ▸*v.* To swerve from a course. [Prob. < LGer. *scheren.*] —**sheer** *n.*

sheer² (shîr) ►*adj.* **-er, -est 1.** Thin and transparent: *sheer curtains.* **2.** Completely such, without qualification or exception: *sheer happiness.* See Synonyms at **pure. 3.** Almost perpendicular: *a sheer cliff.* See Synonyms at **steep¹.** [< ME *shir,* clear, and *skir,* clean.]

sheet¹ (shēt) ►*n.* **1.** A rectangular piece of fabric serving as a basic article of bedding. **2.** A broad, thin, usu. rectangular piece, as of paper or metal. **3.** A flat, continuous surface: *a sheet of ice.* [< OE *scēte.*]

sheet² (shēt) ►*n.* **1.** A rope or chain attached to a lower corner of a sail, serving to move or extend it. **2. sheets** The spaces at either end of an open boat in front of and behind the seats. [< OE *scēata,* corner of a sail.]

sheet metal ►*n.* Metal rolled into a relatively thin sheet. —**sheet′-met′al** *adj.*

sheet music ►*n.* Musical compositions printed on unbound sheets of paper.

Sheet·rock (shēt′rŏk′) A trademark for drywall.

sheikh or **sheik** (shēk, shāk) ►*n.* **1.** The leader of an Arab or Muslim tribe, village, or family. **2.** A wealthy or influential man in an Arab society. [Ar. *šayḫ,* old man.] —**sheikh′dom** *n.*

shek·el (shĕk′əl) ►*n.* **1a.** Any of several ancient units of weight, esp. a Hebrew unit equal to about a half ounce. **b.** The chief silver coin of the ancient Hebrews. **2. shekels** *Slang* Money. [Heb. *šeqel.*]

shelf (shĕlf) ►*n., pl.* **shelves** (shĕlvz) **1.** A flat, usu. rectangular structure, as of wood or metal, fixed horizontally to a wall or in a frame and used to hold or store objects. **2.** Something, such as a projecting ledge of rock, that resembles a shelf. [ME.]

shelf life ►*n.* The length of time a product can be safely used or consumed.

shell (shĕl) ►*n.* **1a.** The usu. hard outer covering that encases certain organisms, such as insects and most mollusks. **b.** A similar outer covering of a nut, seed, or certain eggs. **2.** Something resembling a shell, esp.: **a.** An external, usu. hard, protective cover. **b.** A framework or exterior, as of a building. **c.** A thin layer of pastry. **3.** A long narrow racing boat propelled by rowers. **4.** A projectile or piece of ammunition. **5.** *Phys.* **a.** A set of electron orbitals having nearly the same energy. **b.** Any of the stable series of other particles at a given energy level. **6.** *Comp.* A program that works with the operating system as a command processor. **7.** A thin usu. outer garment for the upper body that repels wind or water. ►*v.* **1.** To remove the shell of; shuck. **2.** To fire shells at; bombard. **3.** To look for or collect shells, as on a shore. —*phrasal verb:* **shell out** To pay (money). [< OE *scell.*]

she'll (shĕl) She will.

shel·lac (shə-lăk′) ►*n.* **1.** A purified lac formed into flakes and used in varnishes, paints, inks, and sealants. **2.** A thin varnish made by dissolving this substance in denatured alcohol. ►*v.* **-lacked, -lack·ing 1.** To coat or finish with shellac. **2.** *Slang* To defeat decisively. [SHEL(L) + LAC.]

Shel·ley (shĕl′ē), **Mary Wollstonecraft Godwin** 1797–1851. British writer.

Shelley, Percy Bysshe 1792–1822. British poet.

shell·fire (shĕl′fīr′) ►*n.* The shooting of artillery shells.

shell·fish (shĕl′fĭsh′) ►*n.* Any of various edible aquatic invertebrate animals having a shell, esp. mollusks and crustaceans. —**shell′fish′ing** *n.*

shell shock ►*n.* Posttraumatic stress disorder. —**shell′-shocked′** *adj.*

shel·ter (shĕl′tər) ►*n.* **1a.** Something that provides cover or protection, as from the weather. **b.** An establishment that provides temporary housing for homeless people. **2.** The state of being covered or protected. ►*v.* **1.** To provide shelter for. **2.** To take cover or refuge. **3.** To invest (income) to protect it from taxation. [?]

shelve (shĕlv) ►*v.* **shelved, shelv·ing 1.** To place on a shelf. **2.** To put aside; postpone. See Synonyms at **defer¹.**

shelves (shĕlvz) ►*n.* Pl. of **shelf.**

shelv·ing (shĕl′vĭng) ►*n.* A set of shelves.

Shen·an·do·ah Valley (shĕn′ən-dō′ə) A valley of N VA between the Allegheny Mts. and the Blue Ridge.

she·nan·i·gan (shə-năn′ĭ-gən) ►*n. Informal* **1.** Mischief. **2.** An underhanded act. [?]

Shep·ard (shĕp′ərd), **Alan Bartlett, Jr.** 1923–98. First Amer. astronaut in space (1961).

shep·herd (shĕp′ərd) ►*n.* **1.** One who herds, guards, and tends sheep. **2.** One who cares for and guides a group of people. ►*v.* **1.** To herd or tend as a shepherd. See Synonyms at **guide. 2.** To guide or lead on a course. [< OE *scēaphierde.*]

shep·herd·ess (shĕp′ər-dĭs) ►*n.* A girl or woman who herds or guards sheep.

shep·herd's pie (shĕp′ərdz) ►*n.* A meat pie baked under a crust of mashed potatoes.

sheq·el (shĕk′əl) ►*n., pl.* **sheq·al·im** (shĕk′-ə-lĭm) See table at **currency.** [Heb. *šeqel,* SHEKEL.]

sher·bet (shûr′bĭt) also **sher·bert** (-bûrt′) ►*n.* A frozen dessert made mainly of fruit juice or fruit purée, usu. with sugar and milk or cream. [< Ar. *šarba,* drink.]

Sher·i·dan (shĕr′ĭ-dn), **Philip Henry** 1831–88. Amer. Union general.

sher·iff (shĕr′ĭf) ►*n.* A public officer with responsibility for law enforcement and administrative legal duties, usu. for a US county. [< OE *scīrgerēfa,* royal representative in a shire.]

Sher·man (shûr′mən), **Roger** 1721–93. Amer. Revolutionary patriot and politician.

Sherman, William Tecumseh 1820–91. Amer. Union general.

Sher·pa (shûr′pə) ►*n., pl.* **-pa** or **-pas** A member of a Tibetan people living in Nepal and Sikkim, known in modern times as porters and guides on mountaineering expeditions.

sher·ry (shĕr′ē) ►*n., pl.* **-ries** A fortified Spanish wine. [< *Xeres* (Jerez), Spain.]

Sher·wood Forest (shûr′wŏŏd′) A forest of central England; site of the legendary exploits of Robin Hood.

Shet·land (shĕt′lənd) ►*n.* A fine yarn made from the wool of sheep raised in the Shetland Islands.

Shetland Islands An archipelago of N Scotland in the Atlantic NE of the Orkney Is.

Shetland pony ►*n.* A small sturdy pony originating in the Shetland Islands.

She·vat (shə-vät′) also **She·bat** (shə-bät′, -vät′)

►*n.* The 11th month of the Jewish calendar. See table at **calendar**. [Heb. *šəbāṭ*.]

shi·at·su (shē-ät′sōō) ►*n.* Therapeutic massage in which the thumbs and palms are used to apply pressure to the same areas of the body treated with acupuncture. [< J. *shiatsuryōhō*.]

shi·ba i·nu (shē′bə ē′nōō) ►*n.* A small dog developed in Japan, having a thick coat of various colors, including red or black and tan. [J. : *shiba*, of unknown orig. + *inu*, dog.]

shiba inu

shib·bo·leth (shĭb′ə-lĭth, -lĕth′) ►*n.* A word or phrase closely identified with a particular group or cause. [< Heb. *šibbōlet*.]

shied (shīd) ►*v.* P.t. and p.part. of **shy**.

shield (shēld) ►*n.* **1.** A broad piece of armor strapped to the arm for protection against weapons. **2.** A protective device or structure. **3.** Something that resembles a shield, such as a policeman's badge. ►*v.* **1.** To protect or defend with or as if with a shield; guard. **2.** To cover up; conceal. [< OE *scield*.] —**shield′er** *n.*

shi·er (shī′ər) ►*adj.* Comp. of **shy**[1].

shi·est (shī′ĭst) ►*adj.* Superl. of **shy**[1].

shift (shĭft) ►*v.* **1.** To exchange (one thing) for another. **2.** To move or transfer from one place or position to another. **3.** To change position, direction, or place. **4.** To change (gears), as in an automobile. **5.** To provide for one's own needs; get along. ►*n.* **1.** A change from one person or configuration to another; substitution. **2a.** A group of workers that relieve another on a regular schedule. **b.** The working period of such a group: *the night shift.* **3.** A change in direction or position. **4.** A gearshift. **5a.** A loosely fitting dress that hangs straight from the shoulder. **b.** A woman's undergarment; slip or chemise. [< OE *sciftan*, arrange.]

shift·less (shĭft′lĭs) ►*adj.* Lacking ambition or purpose. —**shift′less·ness** *n.*

shift·y (shĭf′tē) ►*adj.* **-i·er, -i·est** Suggestive of deceitful character; evasive or untrustworthy. —**shift′i·ly** *adv.* —**shift′i·ness** *n.*

Shi·ite also **Shi′ite** (shē′īt′) ►*n.* A member of the branch of Islam that regards the caliph Ali and his descendants as the legitimate successors to Muhammad. —**Shi′ism** *n.* —**Shi′ite′** *adj.*

shil·in (shĭl′ĭn) ►*n.* See table at **currency**. [Somali < E. *shilling*.]

shill (shĭl) ►*n. Slang* One who poses as an enthusiastic customer or gambler to dupe bystanders into participating in a swindle. [?] —**shill** *v.*

shil·le·lagh (shə-lā′lē, -lə) ►*n.* A cudgel of oak or other hardwood. [After *Shillelagh*, Ireland.]

shil·ling (shĭl′ĭng) ►*n.* **1.** See table at **currency**. **2.** A coin formerly used in the United Kingdom, worth one twentieth of a pound. [< OE *scilling*.]

shil·ly-shal·ly (shĭl′ē-shăl′ē) ►*v.* **-lied** (-lēd), **-ly·ing 1.** To procrastinate; dawdle. **2.** To vacillate. [< *shall I*.] —**shil′ly-shal′li·er** *n.*

shim (shĭm) ►*n.* A thin piece or wedge used to make something level or to adjust something to fit properly. [?] —**shim** *v.*

shim·mer (shĭm′ər) ►*v.* To shine with or be reflected as a subdued flickering light. ►*n.* A flickering or tremulous light; glimmer. [< OE *scimerian*.] —**shim′mer·y** *adj.*

shim·my (shĭm′ē) ►*n., pl.* **-mies 1.** Abnormal vibration or wobbling, as of the wheels of an automobile. **2.** A dance popular in the 1920s, marked by rapid shaking of the body. [Prob. < CHEMISE.] —**shim′my** *v.*

shin (shĭn) ►*n.* The front part of the leg between the knee and the ankle. ►*v.* **shinned, shin·ning** To climb (e.g., a pole) by gripping and pulling alternately with the hands and legs. [< OE *scinu*.]

shin·dig (shĭn′dĭg′) ►*n.* A festive party or celebration. [Prob. < *shindy*, commotion.]

shine (shīn) ►*v.* **shone** (shōn) or **shined, shin·ing 1.** To emit light. **2.** To reflect light; glint or glisten. **3.** To distinguish oneself; excel. **4.** To aim or cast the beam of (a light). **5.** *p.t. and p.part.* **shined** To make glossy or bright by polishing. ►*n.* **1.** Brightness; radiance. **2.** A shoeshine. **3.** Fair weather: *rain or shine.* —*idiom:* **take a shine to** *Informal* To like spontaneously. [< OE *scīnan*.]

shin·er (shī′nər) ►*n.* **1.** *Slang* A black eye. **2.** Any of numerous small silvery fishes.

shin·gle[1] (shĭng′gəl) ►*n.* **1.** A thin oblong piece of material, such as wood, laid in overlapping rows to cover the roofs or sides of a house. **2.** *Informal* A small signboard, as one indicating a professional office. ►*v.* To cover (e.g., a roof) with shingles. [< Lat. *scandula*.] —**shin′gler** *n.*

shin·gle[2] (shĭng′gəl) ►*n.* **1.** Beach gravel consisting of large smooth pebbles. **2.** A beach covered with such gravel. [ME.]

shin·gles (shĭng′gəlz) ►*pl.n. (takes sing. or pl. v.)* An acute viral infection marked by skin eruption along a nerve path on one side of the body. [< Lat. *cingulum*, girdle.]

shin·ny (shĭn′ē) ►*v.* **-nied** (-nēd), **-ny·ing** To climb by shin: *shinny up a pole.* [< SHIN.]

Shin·to (shĭn′tō) ►*n.* A religion native to Japan, marked by worship of nature spirits and ancestors. [J. *shintō*.] —**Shin′to** *adj.* —**Shin′to·ism** *n.* —**Shin′to·ist** *adj. & n.*

shin·y (shī′nē) ►*adj.* **-i·er, -i·est** Bright; glistening. —**shin′i·ness** *n.*

ship (shĭp) ►*n.* **1.** A large vessel built for deepwater navigation. **2.** A sailing vessel having three or more square-rigged masts. **3.** An aircraft or spacecraft. ►*v.* **shipped, ship·ping 1.** To place or receive on board a ship. **2.** To cause to be transported; send. See Synonyms at **send**. **3.** To take in (water) over the side of a ship. [< OE *scip*.] —**ship′per** *n.*

–ship ►*suff.* **1.** Quality or condition: *friendship.* **2.** Rank, status, or office: *professorship.* **3.** Art or skill: *penmanship.* [< OE *-scipe*.]

ship·board (shĭp′bôrd′) ►*n.* The condition of being aboard a ship.

ship·build·ing (shĭp′bĭl′dĭng) ►*n.* The business

of designing and constructing ships. **—ship'-build'er** *n.*

ship·mas·ter (shĭp′măs′tər) ►*n.* The officer in command of a merchant ship.

ship·mate (shĭp′māt′) ►*n.* A fellow sailor.

ship·ment (shĭp′mənt) ►*n.* **1.** The act of shipping goods. **2.** A quantity of goods or cargo shipped together.

ship·ping (shĭp′ĭng) ►*n.* **1.** The act or business of transporting goods. **2.** The body of ships belonging to one port or country.

ship·shape (shĭp′shāp′) ►*adj.* Orderly and neat.

ship·wreck (shĭp′rĕk′) ►*n.* **1.** The destruction of a ship, as by storm or collision. **2.** The remains of a wrecked ship. **3.** A complete failure or ruin. ►*v.* To cause to suffer shipwreck.

ship·yard (shĭp′yärd′) ►*n.* A yard where ships are built or repaired.

shire (shīr) ►*n.* A former division of Great Britain, equivalent to a county. [< OE *scīr*, district.]

shirk (shûrk) ►*v.* To avoid or neglect (a duty or responsibility). [?] **—shirk'er** *n.*

shirr (shûr) ►*v.* **1.** To gather (cloth) into parallel rows. **2.** To cook (eggs) by baking until set. [?]

shirt (shûrt) ►*n.* **1.** A garment for the upper part of the body, usu. having a collar, sleeves, and a front opening. **2.** An undershirt. [< OE *scyrte*, skirt.]

shirt·waist (shûrt′wāst′) ►*n.* A woman's blouse styled like a tailored shirt.

shish ke·bab also **shish ke·bob** or **shish ka·bob** (shĭsh′ kə-bŏb′) ►*n.* A dish of pieces of seasoned meat and often vegetables roasted and served on skewers. [< Turk. *şiş kebabı.*]

Shi·va (shē′və) ►*n.* A principal Hindu god, the destroyer and restorer of worlds.

shiv·er[1] (shĭv′ər) ►*v.* To shake, as with cold or fear; tremble. [ME *chiveren.*] **—shiv'er** *n.*

shiv·er[2] (shĭv′ər) ►*v.* To break into fragments or splinters. [< ME *shivere*, splinter.]

Sho·ah (shō′ə) ►*n.* The Holocaust. [Heb. *šôå*, calamity.]

shoal[1] (shōl) ►*n.* **1.** A shallow place in a body of water. **2.** A sandy elevation at the bottom of a body or water; sandbar. [< OE *sceald*, shallow.]

shoal[2] (shōl) ►*n.* **1.** A large school of fish or other aquatic animals. **2.** A large group; crowd. [Prob. MLGer. or MDu. *schōle.*]

shoat (shōt) ►*n.* A young pig. [ME *shote.*]

shock[1] (shŏk) ►*n.* **1.** A violent collision or impact. **2.** Something that causes a sudden emotional disturbance. **3.** A sudden emotional disturbance. **4.** A massive, acute physical reaction usu. to trauma, infection, or allergy, marked by a loss of blood pressure resulting in a decreased blood flow to body tissues. **5.** The sensation and muscular spasm caused by an electric current passing through the body. ►*v.* **1.** To surprise and disturb greatly. **2.** To induce a state of shock in (a person). **3.** To subject (an animal or person) to an electric shock of the heart or brain. [< OFr. *chuquier*, collide with.]

shock[2] (shŏk) ►*n.* **1.** A number of sheaves of grain stacked upright in a field for drying. **2.** A thick heavy mass: *a shock of white hair.* [ME *shok.*]

shock absorber ►*n.* A device used to absorb mechanical shocks, esp. in a motor vehicle.

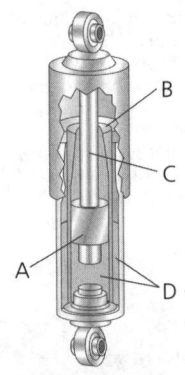

shock absorber
A. piston; B. cylinder;
C. piston rod; D. oil

shock·er (shŏk′ər) ►*n.* One that startles or horrifies, as a sensational story.

shock·ing (shŏk′ĭng) ►*adj.* **1.** Highly disturbing emotionally. **2.** Highly distasteful. **3.** Vivid or intense: *shocking pink.* **—shock'ing·ly** *adv.*

shock therapy ►*n.* See **electroconvulsive therapy.**

shock troops ►*pl.n.* Soldiers specially chosen, trained, and armed to lead an attack.

shock wave ►*n.* **1.** A large-amplitude compression wave, as that produced by an explosion or by supersonic motion of a body in a medium. **2.** A violent or extreme disruption or reaction.

shod·dy (shŏd′ē) ►*adj.* **-di·er, -di·est 1.** Made of or containing inferior material. **2.** Dishonest or unscrupulous. **3.** Cheaply imitative. [?] **—shod'di·ly** *adv.* **—shod'di·ness** *n.*

shoe (shoo) ►*n.* **1.** A durable covering for the human foot. **2.** A horseshoe. **3.** The casing of a pneumatic tire. **4.** The part of a brake that presses against the wheel or drum to retard motion. ►*v.* **shod** (shŏd), **shod** or **shod·den** (shŏd′n), **shoe·ing** To furnish or fit with shoes. [< OE *scōh.*]

shoe·horn (shoo′hôrn′) ►*n.* A curved implement inserted at the heel to help put on a shoe. **—shoe'horn'** *v.*

shoe·lace (shoo′lās′) ►*n.* A string or cord used for lacing and fastening shoes.

shoe·mak·er (shoo′mā′kər) ►*n.* One that makes or repairs shoes. **—shoe'mak'ing** *n.*

shoe·string (shoo′strĭng′) ►*n.* **1.** See **shoelace. 2.** A small sum of money; capital that is barely adequate. ►*adj.* Cut long and slender: *shoestring potatoes.*

shoe·tree (shoo′trē′) ►*n.* A form made of inflexible material inserted into a shoe to preserve its shape.

sho·gun (shō′gən) ►*n.* One of the military commanders who from 1192 until 1867 ruled Japan while being nominally subordinate to the emperor. [J. *shōgun*, general.]

shone (shōn) ►*v.* P.t. and p.part. of **shine.**

shoo (shoo) ►*interj.* Used to frighten away animals. **—shoo** *v.*

shoo-in (shoo′ĭn′) ►*n. Informal* A sure winner.

shook (shook) ►*v.* P.t. of **shake.**

shook-up (shook-ŭp′) ►*adj. Slang* Emotionally upset; shaken.

shoot (shoot) ►*v.* **shot** (shŏt), **shoot·ing 1.**

To hit, wound, or kill with a missile. **2.** To fire (a missile) from a weapon. **3.** To discharge (a weapon). **4.** To send forth swiftly. **5.** To pass over or through swiftly: *shooting the rapids.* **6.** To record on film. **7.** To project or cause to project or protrude. **8.** To begin to grow or produce; put forth. **9.** *Sports & Games* To propel (e.g., a ball) toward its objective. **10.** *Informal* To spend, exhaust, or waste: *shot their savings on a new boat.* ▸*n.* **1.** The young growth arising from a germinating seed; sprout. **2.** An organized shooting activity, such as a hunt. **3.** A session in which something is photographed or filmed. —*phrasal verb:* **shoot up 1.** *Informal* To grow or get taller rapidly. **2.** *Slang* To inject a drug with a hypodermic syringe. [< OE *scēotan.*] —**shoot′er** *n.*

shoot·ing star (shoo′tĭng) ▸*n.* See **meteor.**

shoot·out (shoot′out′) ▸*n.* **1.** A gunfight. **2.** *Sports* **a.** A high-scoring period or game. **b.** A means of resolving a tie in sports such as soccer and hockey, in which selected players from each team alternately take individual shots on a goal defended only by a goalie.

shop (shŏp) ▸*n.* **1.** A small retail store. **2.** A place for manufacturing or repairing goods or machinery. **3.** The industrial arts as a technical science or course of study. **4.** A commercial or industrial establishment. ▸*v.* **shopped, shop·ping** To visit stores to buy or examine goods. [< OE *sceoppa,* workshop.] —**shop′per** *n.*

shop·keep·er (shŏp′kē′pər) ▸*n.* One who owns or manages a shop.

shop·lift (shŏp′lĭft′) ▸*v.* To steal merchandise from a store. —**shop′lift′er** *n.*

shop·ping center (shŏp′ĭng) ▸*n.* A group of retail stores and other businesses having a common parking lot.

shopping mall ▸*n.* **1.** An urban shopping area limited to pedestrians. **2.** A shopping center with stores facing enclosed walkways for pedestrians.

shop steward ▸*n.* A union member elected to represent coworkers in dealings with management.

shop·talk (shŏp′tôk′) ▸*n.* Talk or conversation concerning one's work or business.

shop·worn (shŏp′wôrn′) ▸*adj.* **1.** Frayed, faded, or defective from being on display in a store. **2.** Hackneyed; trite.

shore¹ (shôr) ▸*n.* The land along the edge of an ocean, sea, lake, or river; coast. [< OE *scora.*]

shore² (shôr) ▸*v.* **shored, shor·ing** To support by or as if by a prop: *shore up a sagging wall.* [ME *shoren.*]

shore·bird (shôr′bûrd′) ▸*n.* A bird that frequents the shores of coastal or inland waters.

shore·line (shôr′līn′) ▸*n.* The edge of a body of water.

shorn (shôrn) ▸*v.* P.part. of **shear.**

short (shôrt) ▸*adj.* **-er, -est 1.** Having little length. **2.** Having little height. **3.** Lasting a brief time. **4.** Not lengthy; succinct. **5.** Rudely brief; abrupt. **6.** Inadequate; insufficient: *oil in short supply.* **7.** Lacking in length or amount. **8.** Containing shortening. **9.** *Ling.* Of or being a speech sound of relatively brief duration, as the sound of (ă) in *pat.* ▸*adv.* **1.** Abruptly; quickly. **2.** At a point before a given limit or goal. **3.** At a disadvantage: *caught short.* ▸*n.* **1.** Anything short. **2. shorts a.** Short pants extending to

the knee or above. **b.** Men's undershorts. **3.** A short circuit. **4.** A short subject. ▸*v.* To cause a short circuit in. [< OE *scort.*] —**short′ness** *n.*

short·age (shôr′tĭj) ▸*n.* A deficiency in amount.

short·bread (shôrt′brĕd′) ▸*n.* A cookie made with much butter or other shortening.

short·cake (shôrt′kāk′) ▸*n.* A dessert consisting of a biscuit or cake served with fruit and topped with cream.

short·change (shôrt′chānj′) ▸*v.* **1.** To give less than the correct change to. **2.** To treat deceitfully; cheat.

short circuit ▸*n.* A low-resistance connection between two points in an electric circuit through which current flows instead of along the intended path. —**short′-cir′cuit** *v.*

short·com·ing (shôrt′kŭm′ĭng) ▸*n.* A deficiency; flaw.

short·cut (shôrt′kŭt′) ▸*n.* **1.** A more direct route than the customary one. **2.** A means of saving time or effort. —**short′cut′** *v.*

short·en (shôr′tn) ▸*v.* To make or become short or shorter. —**short′en·er** *n.*

  Syns: *abbreviate, abridge, curtail, truncate* **Ant:** *lengthen* v.

short·en·ing (shôr′tn-ĭng, shôrt′nĭng) ▸*n.* **1.** A fat, such as butter or lard, used to make cake or pastry light and flaky. **2.** A shortened form of something, as a word.

short·fall (shôrt′fôl′) ▸*n.* **1.** A shortage. **2.** The amount by which a supply falls short of expectation, need, or demand.

short·hand (shôrt′hănd′) ▸*n.* A system of rapid handwriting employing symbols to represent words, phrases, and letters.

short·hand·ed (shôrt′hăn′dĭd) ▸*adj.* **1.** Lacking the necessary number of workers. **2.** Having fewer players than the opposing team, usu. because of a penalty.

short·list (shôrt′lĭst′) ▸*n.* A list of preferable items or candidates selected for final consideration. —**short′-list′** *v.*

short-lived (shôrt′līvd′, -lĭvd′) ▸*adj.* Living or lasting only a short time.

short·ly (shôrt′lē) ▸*adv.* **1.** Soon. **2.** In a few words; concisely. **3.** Abruptly; curtly.

short order ▸*n.* An order of food prepared and served quickly. —**short′-or′der** *adj.*

short-range (shôrt′rānj′) ▸*adj.* **1.** Designed for short distances. **2.** Relating to the near future.

short shrift ▸*n.* **1.** Careless treatment. **2.** Quick work.

short·sight·ed (shôrt′sī′tĭd) ▸*adj.* **1.** Nearsighted; myopic. **2.** Lacking foresight. —**short′sight′ed·ness** *n.*

short·stop (shôrt′stŏp′) ▸*n.* *Baseball* **1.** The field position between 2nd and 3rd base. **2.** The infielder who plays this position.

short story ▸*n.* A short piece of prose fiction, having few characters and aiming at unity of effect.

short subject ▸*n.* A brief film shown before a feature-length film.

short-tem·pered (shôrt′tĕm′pərd) ▸*adj.* Easily moved to anger.

short-term (shôrt′tûrm′) ▸*adj.* **1.** Involving or lasting a relatively brief time. **2.** Payable or reaching maturity within a relatively brief time.

short ton ▸*n.* See table at **measurement.**

short wave ►*n.* A radio wave with a wavelength of approx. 200 m or less. —**short′wave′** *adj.*

Sho·sho·ne also **Sho·sho·ni** (shō-shō′nē) ►*n.,* *pl.* **-ne** or **-nes** also **-ni** or **-nis** **1.** A member of a Native American people inhabiting an area from W Wyoming and SE Idaho to S Nevada. **2.** Any of the Uto-Aztecan languages of the Shoshone. —**Sho·sho′ne·an** *adj.*

Shos·ta·ko·vich (shŏs′tə-kō′vĭch), **Dmitri** 1906–75. Russian composer.

shot¹ (shŏt) ►*n.* **1.** The firing or discharge of a weapon. **2.** The distance over which something is shot; range. **3.** *Sports* A throw, hit, or stroke in any of several games. **4.** A pointed or critical remark. **5.** *Informal* **a.** An attempt; try. **b.** An opportunity. **6a.** A projectile designed to be discharged from a gun. **b.** One of a group of pellets discharged esp. from a shotgun. **7.** *Sports* A shot put. **8a.** A photograph. **b.** A single cinematic take. **9.** A hypodermic injection. **10.** A drink, esp. a jigger of liquor. [< OE *scot.*]

shot² (shŏt) ►*v.* P.t. and p.part. of **shoot.**

shot·gun (shŏt′gŭn′) ►*n.* A smooth-bore gun that fires shot over short ranges. ►*interj.* Used to claim the front passenger seat of a vehicle.

shot put ►*n.* **1.** An athletic event in which a heavy metal ball is thrown for distance. **2.** The ball used in this competition. —**shot′-put′ter** *n.*

should (shŏŏd) ►*aux.v.* P.t. of **shall.** Used to express obligation, necessity, probability, or contingency.
   Usage: *Should have* is sometimes incorrectly written *should of* by writers who have mistaken the source of the spoken contraction *should've.*

shoul·der (shōl′dər) ►*n.* **1a.** The joint connecting the arm with the torso. **b.** The part of the human body between the neck and upper arm. **2.** often **shoulders** The area of the back from one shoulder to the other. **3.** The edge along either side of a roadway. ►*v.* **1.** To carry or place on the shoulders. **2.** To take on; assume. **3.** To push with or as if with the shoulder. [< OE *sculdor.*]

shoulder blade ►*n.* See **scapula.**

should·n't (shŏŏd′nt) Should not.

shout (shout) ►*n.* A loud cry. ►*v.* To utter a shout. See Synonyms at **yell.** [ME *shoute.*] —**shout′er** *n.*

shove (shŭv) ►*v.* **shoved, shov·ing 1.** To push quickly, forcefully, or roughly. **2.** To put (something) roughly in place: *shoved the key into my purse.* —*phrasal verb:* **shove off 1.** To push (a boat) away from shore in leaving. **2.** *Informal* To leave. [< OE *scūfan.*] —**shove** *n.*

shov·el (shŭv′əl) ►*n.* **1.** A tool with a handle and scoop for digging and moving material, such as dirt or snow. **2.** A large mechanical device for heavy digging or excavation. ►*v.* **-eled, -el·ing** also **-elled, -el·ling 1.** To move or remove with a shovel. **2.** To convey roughly or hastily: *shoveled his food down.* [< OE *scofl.*]

show (shō) ►*v.* **showed, shown** (shōn) or **showed, show·ing 1.** To cause or allow to be seen; display. **2.** To conduct; guide. **3.** To point out. **4.** To manifest; reveal. **5.** To demonstrate by reasoning or procedure. **6.** To grant; bestow. **7.** To be visible or evident. **8.** *Sports* To finish third or better, as in a horserace. ►*n.* **1.** A display; manifestation. **2.** A false appearance; pretense. **3.** A striking display; spectacle. **4.** A

public exhibition or entertainment. **5.** A radio or television program. **6.** *Informal* An undertaking: *ran the whole show.* **7.** *Sports* Third place esp. in a horserace. —*phrasal verb:* **show off** To behave or display in an ostentatious or boasting manner. [< OE *scēawian,* look at.]

show·boat (shō′bōt′) ►*n.* **1.** A river steamboat having a troupe of performers and a theater. **2.** A showoff. ►*v.* To show off.

show business ►*n.* The entertainment industry.

show·case (shō′kās′) ►*n.* **1.** A display case, as in a store or museum. **2.** A setting for advantageous display. ►*v.* **-cased, -cas·ing** To display or feature prominently.

show·down (shō′doun′) ►*n.* An event that forces an issue to a conclusion.

show·er (shou′ər) ►*n.* **1.** A brief fall of rain, hail, or sleet. **2.** An outpouring: *a shower of praise.* **3.** A party held to honor and present gifts to someone. **4.** A bath in which the water is sprayed on the bather. ►*v.* **1.** To pour down in a shower. **2.** To bestow abundantly or liberally. **3.** To take a shower. [< OE *scūr.*]

show·ing (shō′ĭng) ►*n.* **1.** A presentation or display. **2.** Performance: *a poor showing.*

show·man (shō′mən) ►*n.* **1.** A theatrical producer. **2.** One with a flair for dramatic behavior. —**show′man·ship′** *n.*

show·off (shō′ôf′, -ŏf′) ►*n.* One who shows off.

show·piece (shō′pēs′) ►*n.* Something exhibited as an outstanding example of its kind.

show place also **show·place** (shō′plās′) ►*n.* A place viewed and frequented for its beauty or historical noteworthiness.

show room ►*n.* A large room in which merchandise is displayed.

show·stop·per (shō′stŏp′ər) ►*n.* A performance evoking so much audience applause that the show is temporarily interrupted.

show·y (shō′ē) ►*adj.* **-i·er, -i·est 1.** Making a striking or aesthetically pleasing display: *showy flowers.* **2.** Marked by extravagant, often tasteless display. —**show′i·ly** *adv.* —**show′i·ness** *n.*
   Syns: flamboyant, ostentatious, pretentious adj.

shrank (shrăngk) ►*v.* P.t. of **shrink.**

shrap·nel (shrăp′nəl) ►*n., pl.* **-nel 1.** Shell fragments from a high-explosive shell. **2.** A 19th-cent. artillery shell containing metal balls designed to explode in the air above enemy troops. [After Gen. Henry *Shrapnel* (1761–1842).]

shred (shrĕd) ►*n.* **1.** A long irregular strip cut or torn off. **2.** A small amount; particle: *not a shred of evidence.* ►*v.* **shred·ded** or **shred, shred·ding 1.** To cut or tear into shreds. **2.** To use a shredder to shred (e.g., paper documents). [< OE *scrēade.*]

shred·der (shrĕd′ər) ►*n.* **1.** One that shreds. **2.** A device used for shredding documents, often to prevent unauthorized persons from reading them.

shrew (shrōō) ►*n.* **1.** A small, mouselike, chiefly insectivorous mammal with a pointed snout. **2.** A nagging or scolding woman. [< OE *scrēawa.*] —**shrew′ish** *adj.* —**shrew′ish·ly** *adv.*

shrewd (shrōōd) ►*adj.* **-er, -est 1.** Having or showing a clever awareness, esp. in practical matters. **2.** Artful; cunning. [< ME *shrew,* rascal.] **—shrewd′ly** *adv.* **—shrewd′ness** *n.*

shriek (shrēk) ►*n.* A shrill, often frantic cry. [ME *shriken,* to shriek.] **—shriek** *v.*

shrift (shrĭft) ►*n. Archaic* The act of shriving. [< OE *scrift* < Lat. *scrīptum,* something written.]

shrike (shrīk) ►*n.* A carnivorous bird having a strong hooked bill and often impaling its prey on thorns. [< OE *scrīc,* thrush.]

shrill (shrĭl) ►*adj.* **-er, -est** High-pitched and piercing. ►*v.* To produce a shrill sound. [ME *shrille.*] **—shrill′ness** *n.* **—shril′ly** *adv.*

shrimp (shrĭmp) ►*n., pl.* **shrimp** or **shrimps** **1a.** Any of various small, often edible marine crustaceans. **b.** The flesh of one of these crustaceans, used as food. **2.** *Derogatory Slang* A person who is small in stature. [ME *shrimpe.*] **—shrimp′er** *n.*

shrine (shrīn) ►*n.* **1.** A container for sacred relics. **2.** The tomb of a saint. **3.** A site or object revered for its associations. [< Lat. *scrīnium,* case for books or papers.]

shrink (shrĭngk) ►*v.* **shrank** (shrăngk) or **shrunk** (shrŭngk), **shrunk** or **shrunk·en** (shrŭng′kən), **shrink·ing 1.** To become smaller, esp. from exposure to heat, moisture, or cold. **2.** To dwindle. **3.** To draw back; recoil. ►*n. Slang* A psychotherapist. [< OE *scrincan.*] **—shrink′a· ble** *adj.* **—shrink′age** *n.* **—shrink′er** *n.*

shrink-wrap (shrĭngk′răp′) ►*n.* A protective plastic film wound about articles of merchandise and then shrunk by heat to form a sealed package. **—shrink′-wrap′** *v.*

shrive (shrīv) ►*v.* **shrove** (shrōv) or **shrived, shriv·en** (shrĭv′ən) or **shrived, shriv·ing** To hear the confession of and give absolution to (a penitent). [< Lat. *scrībere,* write.]

shriv·el (shrĭv′əl) ►*v.* **-eled, -el·ing** or **-elled, -el·ling 1.** To become or make shrunken and wrinkled, often by drying. **2.** To lose or cause to lose vitality. [?]

shroud (shroud) ►*n.* **1.** A cloth used to wrap a body for burial. **2.** Something that conceals, protects, or screens: *a shroud of fog.* **3.** One of a set of ropes or cables stretched from the masthead to a vessel's sides to support the mast. ►*v.* **1.** To wrap (a corpse) in burial clothing. **2.** To shut off from sight; screen. See Synonyms at **block. 3.** To envelop and make difficult to understand. [< OE *scrūd,* garment.]

shrub (shrŭb) ►*n.* A low woody plant having several stems but no single trunk. [< OE *scrybb.*] **—shrub′bi·ness** *n.* **—shrub′by** *adj.*

shrub·ber·y (shrŭb′ə-rē) ►*n., pl.* **-ies** A group or planting of shrubs.

shrug (shrŭg) ►*v.* **shrugged, shrug·ging** To raise (the shoulders), esp. as a gesture of doubt, disdain, or indifference. **—phrasal verb: shrug off 1.** To minimize. **2.** To get rid of. [ME *shruggen.*] **—shrug** *n.*

shrunk (shrŭngk) ►*v.* P.t. and p.part. of **shrink.**

shrunk·en (shrŭng′kən) ►*v.* P.part. of **shrink.**

shuck (shŭk) ►*n.* **1.** A husk, pod, or shell of a seed, nut, or fruit. **2.** A shell of a bivalve. ►*v.* **1.** To remove the husk or shell from: *shuck corn.* **2.** To open the shell of (a bivalve): *shuck oysters.* **3.** *Informal* To cast off: *shucked their coats and cooled off.* ►*interj.* **shucks** (shŭks) Used to express mild disappointment, disgust, or annoyance. [?] **—shuck′er** *n.*

shud·der (shŭd′ər) ►*v.* **1.** To shiver convulsively,

as from fear or revulsion. **2.** To vibrate; quiver. [ME *shodderen.*] **—shud′der** *n.*

shuf·fle (shŭf′əl) ►*v.* **-fled, -fling 1.** To move with short, sliding steps, without lifting the feet. **2.** To dance casually with sliding and tapping steps. **3.** To move (something) from one place to another. **4.** *Games* To mix together (playing cards, tiles, or dominoes) in random order. **5.** To present, play, or display (music or video files) in random order. [ME *shovelen.*] **—shuf′-fle** *n.* **—shuf′fler** *n.*

shuf·fle·board (shŭf′əl-bôrd′) ►*n.* A game in which disks are pushed along a smooth level surface toward numbered scoring areas. [< obsolete *shove-board.*]

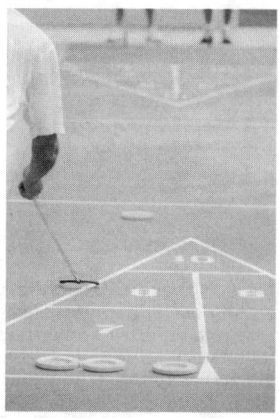

shuffleboard

shun (shŭn) ►*v.* **shunned, shun·ning** To avoid using, accepting, or engaging in: *shunned advice; shun fatty foods.* [< OE *scunian,* abhor.]

shunt (shŭnt) ►*n.* **1.** The act of turning aside or moving to an alternate course. **2.** A railroad switch. **3.** *Elect.* A low-resistance alternative path for a portion of the current. ►*v.* **1.** To turn onto another course: *shunting traffic around an accident.* **2.** To evade by putting aside or ignoring. **3.** *Elect.* To provide or divert (current) by means of a shunt. [ME *shunten,* flinch.]

shush (shŭsh) ►*interj.* Used to demand silence. ►*v.* To silence by saying "shush."

shut (shŭt) ►*v.* **shut, shut·ting 1.** To move or be moved so as to block an opening: *Shut the window. The door shut by itself.* **2.** To block entrance to or exit from. **3.** To confine. **4.** To stop or cause to stop operating: *shut down a club.* **—phrasal verbs: shut off** To stop the flow of. **shut out 1.** To prevent (a team) from scoring any points or runs. **2.** To keep from entering. **shut up 1.** To become or cause to become silent. **2.** To confine. [< OE *scyttan.*]

shut·down (shŭt′doun′) ►*n.* A cessation of operations, as at a factory.

shut·eye (shŭt′ī′) ►*n. Slang* Sleep.

shut-in (shŭt′ĭn′) ►*n.* One confined indoors by illness or disability. **—shut-in′** *adj.*

shut·out (shŭt′out′) ►*n.* **1.** See **lockout. 2.** *Sports* A game in which one side does not score.

shut·ter (shŭt′ər) ►*n.* **1.** A hinged cover or screen for a window. **2.** A device that opens and closes the lens aperture of a camera. ►*v.* To furnish or close with shutters.

shut·ter·bug (shŭt'ər-bŭg') ►*n. Informal* An enthusiastic amateur photographer.

shut·tle (shŭt'l) ►*n.* **1a.** A vehicle used for regular travel between two points. **b.** A space shuttle. **2a.** A device used in weaving to carry the weft thread back and forth. **b.** A device for holding the thread in tatting or in a sewing machine. ►*v.* **-tled, -tling** To move or travel back and forth, esp. by a shuttle. [< OE *scytel*, dart.]

shut·tle·cock (shŭt'l-kŏk') ►*n.* A conical array of feathers or a conical plastic mesh attached to a small rounded end of cork or rubber, used in badminton.

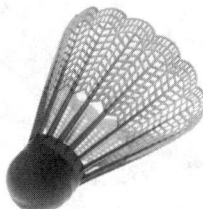

shuttlecock

shy¹ (shī) ►*adj.* **shi·er** (shī'ər), **shi·est** (shī'ĭst) or **shy·er, shy·est** **1.** Easily startled; timid. **2.** Tending to avoid or distrust others; reserved or wary. **3.** Short; lacking: *was shy $100 on his rent.* ►*v.* **shied** (shīd), **shy·ing** **1.** To move suddenly or draw back, as if startled or afraid. **2.** To avoid treating or discussing something. [< OE *scēoh*.] **—shy'ly** *adv.* **—shy'ness** *n.*

shy² (shī) ►*v.* **shied** (shīd), **shy·ing** To throw with a swift motion; fling. [Perh. < SHY¹.]

shy·ster (shī'stər) ►*n. Slang* An unethical, unscrupulous practitioner, esp. of law. [Poss. < Ger. *Scheisser*, scoundrel.]

SI ►*abbr.* French Système International [d'Unités] (International System [of Units])

Si·am (sī-ăm') See Thailand. **—Si'a·mese'** (-ə-mēz, -mēs') *adj. & n.*

Siamese cat ►*n.* A domestic cat having blue eyes and a pale coat with darker ears, tail, and feet.

Siamese twin ►*n.* A conjoined twin. Not in scientific use.

Si·be·li·us (sĭ-bā'lē-əs, -bāl'yəs), **Jean** 1865–1957. Finnish composer.

Si·be·ri·a (sī-bîr'ē-ə) A region of central and E Russia stretching from the Urals to the Pacific. **—Si·be'ri·an** *adj. & n.*

sib·i·lant (sĭb'ə-lənt) *Ling.* ►*adj.* Producing a hissing sound. ►*n.* A sibilant speech sound, such as English (s) or (z). [< Lat. *sībilāre*, hiss.] **—sib'i·lance** *n.* **—sib'i·lant·ly** *adv.*

sib·ling (sĭb'lĭng) ►*n.* One of two or more individuals having one or both parents in common; a brother or sister. [< OE.]

sib·yl (sĭb'əl) ►*n.* A woman prophet. [< Gk. *Sibulla*.]

sic¹ (sĭk, sēk) ►*adv.* Thus; so. Used to indicate that a quoted passage, esp. one containing an error or unconventional spelling, has been retained in its original form or written intentionally. [Lat. *sīc*.]

sic² also **sick** (sĭk) ►*v.* **sicced, sic·cing** also **sicked, sick·ing** To urge (e.g., a dog) to attack or chase. [Var. of SEEK.]

Si·chuan also **Sze·chwan** or **Sze·chuan** (sĕch'wän') A province of S-central China.

Si·ci·ly (sĭs'ə-lē) An island of S Italy in the Mediterranean off the S end of the Italian peninsula. **—Si·cil'ian** (sĭ-sĭl'yən) *adj. & n.*

sick (sĭk) ►*adj.* **-er, -est** **1a.** Suffering from a physical illness. **b.** Of or for sick persons: *sick wards.* **c.** Nauseated. **2a.** Mentally ill or disturbed. **b.** Unwholesome; morbid: *a sick joke.* **3.** Defective; unsound. **4a.** Deeply distressed; upset. **b.** Disgusted; revolted. **c.** Weary; tired: *sick of it all.* **d.** Pining; longing. [< OE *sēoc*.] **—sick'ness** *n.*

sick·bay (sĭk'bā') ►*n.* The hospital and dispensary of a ship.

sick·bed (sĭk'bĕd') ►*n.* A sick person's bed.

sick·en (sĭk'ən) ►*v.* To make or become sick. See Synonyms at **disgust.**

sick·en·ing (sĭk'ə-nĭng) ►*adj.* **1.** Revolting or disgusting. **2.** Causing sickness. **—sick'en·ing·ly** *adv.*

sick·le (sĭk'əl) ►*n.* A tool having a curved blade attached to a short handle, used for cutting grain or tall grass. [< Lat. *sēcula*.]

sickle cell anemia ►*n.* A chronic, sometimes fatal anemia marked by crescent-shaped blood cells and by fever, joint pain, and jaundice.

sick·ly (sĭk'lē) ►*adj.* **-li·er, -li·est** **1.** Prone to sickness. **2.** Of or associated with sickness: *a sickly pallor.* **—sick'li·ness** *n.*

sick·out (sĭk'out') ►*n.* An organized job action in which employees absent themselves from work on the pretext of illness.

side (sīd) ►*n.* **1a.** A surface of an object, esp. a surface joining a top and bottom. **b.** Either of the two surfaces of a very thin, flat object, such as a piece of paper. **2.** The left or right half in reference to a vertical axis, as of the body. **3.** The space immediately next to someone or something: *stood at her father's side.* **4.** An area separated from another area by an intervening feature, such as a line or barrier: *on this side of the Atlantic.* **5.** One of two or more opposing individuals, groups, teams, or sets of opinions. **6.** A distinct aspect: *showed his kinder side.* **7.** Line of descent. ►*adj.* **1.** Located on a side: *a side door.* **2.** From or to one side; oblique: *a side view.* **3.** Minor; incidental: *a side interest.* **4.** Supplementary: *a side benefit.* ►*v.* **sid·ed, sid·ing** To align oneself in a disagreement: *sided with the liberals.* **—idioms: on the side** In addition to the main portion, occupation, or activity. **side by side** Next to each other. **this side of** *Informal* Verging on: *just this side of criminal.* [< OE *sīde*.]

side·arm (sīd'ärm') ►*adj.* Thrown with a sideways motion of the arm between shoulder and hip height. **—side'arm'** *adv.*

side arm ►*n.* A small weapon, such as a pistol, carried at the side or waist.

side·board (sīd'bôrd') ►*n.* A piece of furniture having drawers for linens and tableware.

side·burns (sīd'bûrnz') ►*pl.n.* Growths of hair down the sides of a man's face in front of the ears. [After Ambrose E. *Burnside* (1824–81).]

side·car (sīd'kär') ►*n.* A one-wheeled passenger car attached to the side of a motorcycle.

side effect ►*n.* A secondary, usu. undesirable effect, esp. of a drug or therapy.

side·kick (sīd'kĭk') ►*n. Slang* A close companion.

side·light (sīd′līt′) ►*n.* Incidental information.

side·line (sīd′līn′) ►*n.* **1.** *Sports* A line along either side of a playing court or field, marking its limits. **2.** A secondary job, activity, or line of merchandise. ►*v.* *Informal* To remove from active participation.

side·long (sīd′lông′, -lŏng′) ►*adj.* Directed to one side; sideways: *a sidelong glance.*

side·man (sīd′măn′) ►*n.* A member of a jazz band who is not the leader.

si·de·re·al (sī-dîr′ē-əl) ►*adj.* **1.** Of or concerned with the stars. **2.** Measured in reference to the apparent motion of the stars: *sidereal time.* [< Lat. *sīdus, sīder-,* star.]

SI-de·rived unit (ĕs′ī′-dĭ-rīvd′) ►*n.* A unit of measurement, such as the newton, that is derived from a basic unit in the International System.

side·sad·dle (sīd′săd′l) ►*n.* A saddle designed so that the rider sits with both legs on one side of the horse. —**side′sad·dle** *adv.*

side·show (sīd′shō′) ►*n.* **1.** A minor show offered in addition to the main attraction. **2.** An incidental spectacle.

side·step (sīd′stĕp′) ►*v.* **1.** To step out of the way of. **2.** To evade; skirt. —**side′step′** *n.*

side·stroke (sīd′strōk′) ►*n.* A swimming stroke in which a person swims on one side and thrusts the arms forward alternately while performing a scissors kick. —**side′stroke′** *v.*

side·swipe (sīd′swīp′) ►*v.* To strike along the side in passing. ►*n.* A glancing blow.

side·track (sīd′trăk′) ►*v.* **1.** To divert from a main issue or course. **2.** To switch (a railroad car) to a siding. ►*n.* A railroad siding.

side·walk (sīd′wôk′) ►*n.* A paved walkway along the side of a street.

side·wall (sīd′wôl′) ►*n.* A side surface of an automobile tire.

side·ways (sīd′wāz′) ►*adv. & adj.* **1.** Toward or from one side. **2.** With one side forward.

side·wind·er (sīd′wīn′dər) ►*n.* A small rattlesnake that moves by a lateral looping motion of its body.

sid·ing (sī′dĭng) ►*n.* **1.** Material, such as shingles, used for surfacing a frame building. **2.** A short section of railroad track connected by switches with a main track.

si·dle (sīd′l) ►*v.* **-dled, -dling** **1.** To move sideways. **2.** To advance in a furtive or coy way. [< *sideling,* oblique.]

Si·don (sīd′n) An ancient city of Phoenicia on the Mediterranean in present-day SW Lebanon.

SIDS ►*abbr.* sudden infant death syndrome

siege (sēj) ►*n.* **1.** The surrounding and blockading of a city, town, or fortress by an army attempting to capture it. **2.** A prolonged period, as of illness. ►*v.* **sieged, sieg·ing** To lay siege to. [< VLat. **sedicum,* a sitting < Lat. *sedēre,* sit.]

si·er·ra (sē-ĕr′ə) ►*n.* A rugged range of mountains having a jagged profile. [Sp. < Lat. *serra,* saw.] —**si·er′ran** *adj.*

Sierra Le·one (lē-ōn′, -ō′nē) A country of W Africa on the coast of the Atlantic Ocean. Cap. Freetown.

Sierra Ma·dre (mä′drā) ►*n.* A mountain system of Mexico comprising three ranges: **Sierra Madre del Sur,** in the S along the Pacific; **Sierra Madre Occidental,** in the W along the Pacific and the Gulf of California; and **Sierra Madre Oriental,** roughly paralleling the Gulf of Mexico.

Sierra Nevada A mountain range of E CA.

si·es·ta (sē-ĕs′tə) ►*n.* A rest after the midday meal. [Sp. < Lat. *sexta (hōra),* sixth (hour).]

sieve (sĭv) ►*n.* A utensil of wire mesh or closely perforated metal, used for straining, sifting, or puréeing. [< OE *sife.*] —**sieve** *v.*

sift (sĭft) ►*v.* **1.** To put through a sieve to separate fine from coarse particles. **2.** To examine and sort carefully: *sift the evidence.* [< OE *siftan.*]

sigh (sī) ►*v.* **1.** To exhale audibly in a long deep breath, as in weariness or relief. **2.** To feel longing or grief. ►*n.* The act or sound of sighing. [< OE *sīcan.*] —**sigh′er** *n.*

sight (sīt) ►*n.* **1.** The ability to see. **2a.** The act or fact of seeing. **b.** Something seen. **c.** Something worth seeing. **d.** *Informal* Something unsightly. **3.** often **sights** A device used to assist aim by guiding the eye, as on a firearm. ►*v.* **1.** To perceive with the eyes: *sighted land after 40 days at sea.* **2.** To adjust the sights of. [< OE *sihth,* something seen.]

sight·ed (sī′tĭd) ►*adj.* Having sight.

sight·less (sīt′lĭs) ►*adj.* Unable to see; blind. —**sight′less·ly** *adv.* —**sight′less·ness** *n.*

sight·ly (sīt′lē) ►*adj.* **-li·er, -li·est** Pleasing to see; attractive. —**sight′li·ness** *n.*

sight-read (sīt′rēd′) ►*v.* To read or perform (e.g., music) without preparation or prior acquaintance. —**sight′-read′er** *n.*

sight·see·ing (sīt′sē′ĭng) ►*n.* The act of visiting sights of interest.

sig·ma (sĭg′mə) ►*n.* The 18th letter of the Greek alphabet. [Gk.]

sign (sīn) ►*n.* **1.** Something that suggests the existence of a fact, condition, or quality. **2.** An act or gesture that is used to convey an idea. **3.** A posted notice bearing a designation, direction, or command. **4.** A figure or device that stands for a word, phrase, or operation: *a minus sign.* **5.** A portentous event; omen. **6.** One of the 12 divisions of the zodiac. ►*v.* **1.** To affix one's signature to. **2.** To write (one's signature). **3.** To approve or ratify (a document) by affixing a signature or seal. **4.** To hire by obtaining a signature on a contract. **5.** To relinquish or transfer title to by signature. **6.** To communicate with a sign or by sign language. —***phrasal verbs:* sign off** To stop broadcasting. **sign up** To enlist. [< Lat. *signum.*] —**sign′er** *n.*

sig·nal (sĭg′nəl) ►*n.* **1.** An indicator that serves as a means of communication: *a traffic signal; a smoke signal.* **2.** *Electron.* **a.** An impulse or fluctuating electric quantity whose variations represent coded information. **b.** The sound, image, or message transmitted by such coded information. ►*adj.* Notable; remarkable. ►*v.* **-naled, -nal·ing** or **-nalled, -nal·ling** **1.** To make a signal (to). **2.** To relate or make known by signals: *signaled their approval.* [< LLat. *signālis,* of a sign.] —**sig′nal·er, sig′nal·ler** *n.*

sig·nal·ize (sĭg′nə-līz′) ►*v.* **-ized, -iz·ing** **1.** To make remarkable or conspicuous. **2.** To point out particularly.

sig·na·to·ry (sĭg′nə-tôr′ē) ►*adj.* Bound by signed agreement. ►*n., pl.* **-ries** **1.** One that has signed a legal document as a party. **2.** A country that is a party to a treaty.

sig·na·ture (sĭg′nə-chər) ►*n.* **1.** One's name as written by oneself. **2.** A distinctive mark, characteristic, or sound. **3.** *Mus.* A sign used to indicate tempo or key. [< Lat. *signāre*, mark with a sign.]

sign·board (sīn′bôrd′) ►*n.* A board bearing a sign.

sig·net (sĭg′nĭt) ►*n.* A seal, esp. one used officially to mark documents. [< OFr.]

sig·nif·i·cance (sĭg-nĭf′ĭ-kəns) ►*n.* **1.** The state or quality of being significant; importance. **2.** A meaning that is expressed or implied: *What was the significance of that smile?*

sig·nif·i·cant (sĭg-nĭf′ĭ-kənt) ►*adj.* **1.** Having or expressing a meaning. **2.** Having or expressing a covert or nonverbal meaning; suggestive: *a significant glance.* **3.** Having a major effect; important. **4.** Fairly large; substantial: *significant losses.* [< Lat. *significāre*, SIGNIFY.] —**sig·nif′i·cant·ly** *adv.*

sig·ni·fy (sĭg′nə-fī′) ►*v.* **-fied, -fy·ing 1.** To denote; mean. **2.** To be a sign or indication of; suggest or imply. **3.** To make known; signal. **4.** To be significant; matter. [< Lat. *significāre < signum*, sign.] —**sig′ni·fi·ca′tion** (-fĭ-kā′shən) *n.* —**sig′ni·fi′er** *n.*

sign language ►*n.* A language that uses a system of manual, facial, and other body movements as the means of communication.

sign·post (sīn′pōst′) ►*n.* **1.** A post supporting a sign. **2.** An indication; guide.

Si·ha·nouk (sē′ə-nōōk′), King **Norodom** 1922–2012. Cambodian prime minister (1955–57), head of state (1960–70 and 1975–76), and king (1941–55 and 1993–2004).

Sikh (sēk) ►*n.* An adherent of a monotheistic religion of India marked by belief in a cycle of reincarnation from which humans can attain freedom by living righteous lives. —**Sikh** *adj.* —**Sikh′ism** *n.*

Sik·kim (sĭk′ĭm) A region and former kingdom of NE India in the E Himalayas between Nepal and Bhutan.

Si·kor·sky (sĭ-kôr′skē), **Igor Ivan** 1889–1972. Russian-born Amer. aviation pioneer.

si·lage (sī′lĭj) ►*n.* Fodder prepared by compressing and fermenting green forage crops in conditions devoid of oxygen, usu. in a silo.

si·lence (sī′ləns) ►*n.* **1.** The absence of sound; stillness. **2.** A period of time without speech or noise. **3.** Refusal or failure to speak out. ►*v.* **-lenced, -lenc·ing 1.** To make silent. **2.** To suppress.

si·lenc·er (sī′lən-sər) ►*n.* A device attached to a firearm to muffle the sound of firing.

si·lent (sī′lənt) ►*adj.* **1.** Marked by the absence of sound; still. **2.** Not inclined to speak; reticent. **3.** Not voiced or expressed; unspoken: *a silent prayer.* **4.** *Ling.* Unpronounced, as the *b* in *subtle.* [< Lat. *silēre*, be silent.] —**si′lent·ly** *adv.*

Si·le·sia (sī-lē′zhə, -shə, sĭ-) A region of central Europe mainly in SW Poland and N Czech Republic. —**Si·le′sian** *adj. & n.*

sil·hou·ette (sĭl′ōō-ĕt′) ►*n.* **1.** A drawing consisting of the outline of something, esp. a human profile, filled in with a solid color. **2.** An outline. See Synonyms at **outline.** ►*v.* **-et·ted, -et·ting** To cause to be seen as a silhouette; outline. [After Étienne de *Silhouette* (1709–67).]

silhouette
Ludwig van Beethoven

sil·i·ca (sĭl′ĭ-kə) ►*n.* A crystalline compound, SiO_2, occurring abundantly as quartz, sand, and other minerals. [< Lat. *silex*, flint.] —**si·li′ceous** (sĭ-lĭsh′əs) *adj.*

sil·i·cate (sĭl′ĭ-kāt′, -kĭt) ►*n.* A compound containing silicon, oxygen, and a metal.

sil·i·con (sĭl′ĭ-kən, -kŏn′) ►*n. Symbol* **Si** A nonmetallic element occurring extensively in the earth's crust and used in glass, semiconductors, and concrete. At. no. 14. See table at **element.** [< SILICA.]

sil·i·cone (sĭl′ĭ-kōn′) ►*n.* Any of a group of synthetic polymers containing chains of silicon and oxygen atoms with organic side groups attached to the silicon atoms, characterized by thermal stability and used in adhesives, lubricants, and synthetic rubber.

sil·i·co·sis (sĭl′ĭ-kō′sĭs) ►*n.* A lung disease caused by continued inhalation of silica dust and marked by progressive fibrosis.

silk (sĭlk) ►*n.* **1a.** A fine lustrous fiber produced by a silkworm to form its cocoon. **b.** Thread or fabric made from this fiber. **2.** A silky, filamentous material, such as the webbing spun by spiders. [< OE *sioloc.*]

silk-cot·ton tree (sĭlk′kŏt′n) ►*n.* A spiny tropical tree cultivated for its leathery fruit that contain the silklike fiber kapok.

silk·en (sĭl′kən) ►*adj.* **1.** Made of silk. **2.** Smooth and lustrous. **3.** Delicately pleasing or soothing: *a silken voice.*

silk-screen also **silk·screen** (sĭlk′skrēn′) ►*n.* A stencil method in which ink is forced through a design-bearing screen of silk or other fine mesh onto the printing surface. —**silk′-screen′** *v.*

silk·worm (sĭlk′wûrm′) ►*n.* Any of various moth caterpillars that produce cocoons of silk.

silk·y (sĭl′kē) ►*adj.* **-i·er, -i·est 1.** Made of silk. **2.** Resembling silk; lustrous. **3.** Pleasantly agreeable, as to the ear: *a silky voice.* —**silk′i·ly** *adv.* —**silk′i·ness** *n.*

sill (sĭl) ►*n.* The horizontal member that bears the upright portion of a frame, esp. the base of a window. [< OE *syll*, threshold.]

Sills (sĭlz), **Beverly** 1929–2007. Amer. operatic soprano and opera manager.

sil·ly (sĭl′ē) ►*adj.* **-li·er, -li·est 1.** Lacking good sense. See Synonyms at **foolish. 2.** Frivolous. **3.** Dazed. [< OE *gesælig*, blessed.] —**sil′li·ness** *n.*

si·lo (sī′lō) ►*n., pl.* **-los 1.** A usu. tall cylindrical structure in which silage is produced and stored. **2.** An underground shelter for a missile. [Sp.]

silt (sĭlt) ►*n.* A fine sediment intermediate in size between sand and clay. ►*v.* To fill or become filled with silt. [ME *cylte.*] —**silt′y** *adj.*

Si·lu·ri·an (sĭ-lŏŏr′ē-ən, sī-) *Geol.* ►*adj.* Of or being the 3rd period of the Paleozoic Era, marked by the development of early invertebrate land animals. ►*n.* The Silurian Period.

sil·ver (sĭl′vər) ►*n.* **1.** *Symbol* **Ag** A lustrous white malleable metallic element highly valued for jewelry, tableware, and other ornamental use and used in coinage, photography, dental and soldering alloys, electrical contacts, and printed circuits. At. no. 47. See table at **element. 2.** Coins made of silver. **3.** Tableware and other articles made of or plated with silver. **4.** A lustrous medium gray. ►*adj.* **1.** Of the color silver. **2.** Eloquent: *a silver voice.* **3.** Of a 25th anniversary. ►*v.* **1.** To cover, plate, or adorn with silver or a silvery substance. **2.** To give a silver color to. [< OE *siolfor.*] —**sil′ver·i·ness** *n.* —**sil′ver·y** *adj.*

silver bromide ►*n.* A pale yellow crystalline compound, AgBr, used as the light-sensitive component on photographic film.

sil·ver·fish (sĭl′vər-fĭsh′) ►*n., pl.* **-fish** or **-fish·es** A silvery wingless insect that often damages bookbindings and clothing.

silver iodide ►*n.* A yellow powder, AgI, used in photography, rainmaking, and medicine.

silver nitrate ►*n.* A poisonous colorless crystalline compound, AgNO₃, used in making photographic film, silvering mirrors, dyeing hair, plating silver, and medicine.

sil·ver·smith (sĭl′vər-smĭth′) ►*n.* One that makes or replates articles of silver.

sil·ver·ware (sĭl′vər-wâr′) ►*n.* Articles made of or plated with silver, esp. tableware.

Sim·birsk (sĭm-bîrsk′) A city of W Russia on the Volga R. ESE of Moscow.

Sim·fer·o·pol (sĭm′fə-rō′pəl) A city of S Ukraine in the S Crimea NE of Sevastopol.

sim·i·an (sĭm′ē-ən) ►*n.* An ape or monkey. [< Lat. *sīmia*, ape.] —**sim′i·an** *adj.*

sim·i·lar (sĭm′ə-lər) ►*adj.* Having a resemblance in appearance or nature; alike though not identical. [< Lat. *similis*, like.] —**sim′i·lar·ly** *adv.*

sim·i·lar·i·ty (sĭm′ə-lăr′ĭ-tē) ►*n., pl.* **-ties** The quality or condition of being similar.

sim·i·le (sĭm′ə-lē) ►*n.* A figure of speech in which two essentially unlike things are compared, often using *like* or *as*, as in *eyes like stars.* [< Lat., like.]

si·mil·i·tude (sĭ-mĭl′ĭ-tōōd′, -tyōōd′) ►*n.* Similarity; resemblance. [< Lat. *similis*, like.]

sim·mer (sĭm′ər) ►*v.* **1.** To be cooked gently just at or below the boiling point. **2a.** To be filled with pent-up emotion; seethe. **b.** To develop in a slow or unexcited way: *I'll let the idea simmer for a few days.* —*phrasal verb:* **simmer down** To become calm after excitement or anger. [< ME *simpire.*] —**sim′mer** *n.*

si·mo·ny (sī′mə-nē, sĭm′ə-) ►*n.* The buying or selling of spiritual things, esp. ecclesiastical offices or indulgences. [After *Simon* Magus, who tried to buy spiritual powers from the Apostle Peter.]

Si·mon Ze·lo·tes (sī′mən zē-lō′tēz) fl. 1st cent. AD. One of the 12 Apostles.

sim·pa·ti·co (sĭm-pä′tĭ-kō′, -păt′ĭ-) ►*adj.* **1.** Compatible. **2.** Attractive; pleasing. [Ital.]

sim·per (sĭm′pər) ►*v.* To smile in a silly or self-conscious manner. [Perh. of Scand. orig.] —**sim′per** *n.* —**sim′per·er** *n.*

sim·ple (sĭm′pəl) ►*adj.* **-pler, -plest 1.** Having only one thing, element, or part: *a simple chemical substance.* **2.** Not involved or complicated; easy: *a simple task.* **3.** Bare; mere: *a simple "yes" or "no."* **4.** Not embellished or adorned: *a simple dress.* **5.** Not elaborate or luxurious. See Synonyms at **plain. 6.** Unassuming or unpretentious. **7.** Simple-minded. **8.** Straightforward; sincere. **9.** Humble or lowly in condition or rank. **10.** Insignificant; trivial. [< Lat. *simplus.*] —**sim′ple·ness** *n.*

simple fraction ►*n.* A fraction in which both the numerator and the denominator are whole numbers.

simple interest ►*n.* Interest paid only on the original principal, not on the interest accrued.

sim·ple-mind·ed (sĭm′pəl-mīn′dĭd) ►*adj.* **1.** Lacking in sophistication; naive. **2.** Stupid or silly. **3.** Mentally impaired. —**sim′ple-mind′ed·ly** *adv.* —**sim′ple-mind′ed·ness** *n.*

simple sentence ►*n.* A sentence having only one clause, as *The cat purred.*

sim·ple·ton (sĭm′pəl-tən) ►*n.* A person deficient in judgment or intelligence; fool.

sim·plic·i·ty (sĭm-plĭs′ĭ-tē) ►*n., pl.* **-ties 1.** The property, condition, or quality of being simple. **2.** Absence of luxury or showiness; plainness. **3.** Absence of affectation or pretense. **4.** Foolishness. [< Lat. *simplicitās.*]

sim·pli·fy (sĭm′plə-fī′) ►*v.* **-fied, -fy·ing** To make simple or simpler. —**sim′pli·fi·ca′tion** *n.* —**sim′pli·fi′er** *n.*

sim·ply (sĭm′plē) ►*adv.* **1.** In a plain and unadorned way. **2.** Merely; only. **3.** Absolutely; altogether: *simply delicious.*

sim·u·late (sĭm′yə-lāt′) ►*v.* **-lat·ed, -lat·ing 1.** To take on the appearance or character of; imitate. **2.** To pretend; feign. **3.** To create a model of. [Lat. *simulāre.*] —**sim′u·la′tion** *n.* —**sim′u·la′tive** *adj.* —**sim′u·la′tor** *n.*

si·mul·cast (sī′məl-kăst′, sĭm′əl-) ►*v.* To broadcast a program simultaneously from two or more locations or on two or more distribution channels. [SIMUL(TANEOUS) + (BROAD)CAST.] —**si′mul·cast′** *n.*

si·mul·ta·ne·ous (sī′məl-tā′nē-əs, sĭm′əl-) ►*adj.* Happening, existing, or done at the same time. [Lat. *simul*, at the same time + (INSTAN)TANEOUS.] —**si′mul·ta′ne·ous·ly** *adv.* —**si′-mul·ta·ne′i·ty** (-tə-nē′ĭ-tē, -nā′-) *n.*

sin¹ (sĭn) ►*n.* **1.** A transgression of a religious or moral law. **2.** Something shameful or wrong. [< OE *synn.*] —**sin** *v.* —**sin′ful** *adj.* —**sin′ful·ness** *n.* —**sin′ner** *n.*

sin² ►*abbr.* sine

Si·nai (sī′nī′), **Mount** A mountain, about 2,285 m (7,500 ft), of the S Sinai Peninsula.

Sinai Peninsula A peninsula at the N end of the Red Sea between the Gulf of Suez and the Gulf of Aqaba.

Si·na·tra (sə-nä′trə), **Francis Albert** "Frank." 1915–98. Amer. singer and actor.

Frank Sinatra
photographed c. 1961

since (sĭns) ►*adv.* **1.** From then until now or between then and now: *They left town and haven't been here since.* **2.** Before now; ago: *long since forgotten.* ►*prep.* From the time of: *friends since school.* ►*conj.* **1.** From the time when or after which: *hasn't worked since she had the accident.* **2.** Inasmuch as; because: *Since you asked, I'll tell you.* [OE *siththan.*]

sin·cere (sĭn-sîr′) ►*adj.* **-cer·er, -cer·est** Not feigned or affected; true. [Lat. *sincērus.*] —**sin·cer′i·ty** (-sĕr′ĭ-tē) *n.* —**sin·cere′ly** *adv.*

Sin·clair (sĭn-klâr′), **Upton Beall** 1878–1968. Amer. writer and reformer.

sine (sīn) ►*n.* In a right triangle, the ratio of the side opposite an acute angle to the hypotenuse. [Med.Lat. *sinus.*]

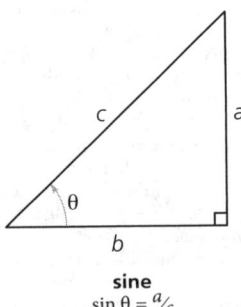

sine
$\sin \theta = {}^{a}/_{c}$

si·ne·cure (sī′nĭ-kyŏŏr′, sĭn′ĭ-) ►*n.* A salaried position requiring little or no work. [< Med.Lat. *sine cūrā*, without care (of souls).]

si·ne di·e (sī′nĭ dī′ē, sĭn′ā dē′ā′) ►*adv.* Without a future time specified; indefinitely. [Med.Lat. *sine diē*, without a day.]

si·ne qua non (sĭn′ĭ kwä nŏn′, nōn′, sī′nĭ) ►*n.* An essential element or condition. [LLat. *sine quā nōn*, without which not.]

sin·ew (sĭn′yŏŏ) ►*n.* **1.** A tendon. **2.** Vigorous strength. [< OE *sinu.*]

sin·ew·y (sĭn′yŏŏ-ē) ►*adj.* **1.** Stringy and tough, as meat. **2.** Lean and muscular. See Synonyms at **muscular.**

sing (sĭng) ►*v.* **sang** (săng) or **sung** (sŭng),

sung, sing·ing 1. To utter a series of words or sounds in musical tones. **2.** To make melodious sounds. **3.** To bring to a specified state by singing: *sang the baby to sleep.* **4.** To proclaim or extol something in verse. **5.** *Slang* To give evidence against someone. ►*n.* A gathering of people for group singing. [< OE *singan.*] —**sing′a·ble** *adj.* —**sing′er** *n.*

sing. ►*abbr.* singular

Sin·ga·pore (sĭng′gə-pôr′, sĭng′ə-) A country of SE Asia comprising **Singapore Island** and adjacent smaller islands. Cap. the city of **Singapore.** —**Sin′ga·por′e·an** *adj. & n.*

singe (sĭnj) ►*v.* **singed, singe·ing 1.** To burn superficially; scorch. **2.** To burn off the feathers or bristles of. [< OE *sengan.*] —**singe** *n.*

Sing·ha·lese (sĭng′gə-lēz′, -lēs′) ►*n. & adj.* Var. of **Sinhalese.**

sin·gle (sĭng′gəl) ►*adj.* **1.** Not accompanied by another or others; solitary. **2.** Consisting of one part or section. **3.** Separate; individual: *every single one of you.* **4.** Designed to accommodate one person: *a single bed.* **5.** Not married or involved in a romantic relationship. ►*n.* **1.** One that is separate and individual. **2.** Something capable of holding one person at a time, as a hotel room. **3.** A person who is not married or involved in a romantic relationship. **4.** A one-dollar bill. **5.** *Baseball* A hit enabling the batter to reach first base. **6. singles** *Sports* A match between two players in tennis and other games. ►*v.* **-gled, -gling** *Baseball* To hit a single. —*phrasal verb:* **single out** To choose or distinguish from others: *singled her out for praise.* [< Lat. *singulus.*] —**sin′gle·ness** *n.*

sin·gle-breast·ed (sĭng′gəl-brĕs′tĭd) ►*adj.* Closing with a narrow overlap and fastened with a single row of buttons.

single file ►*n.* A line of people or things standing or moving one behind the other.

sin·gle-hand·ed also **sin·gle-han·ded** (sĭng′-gəl-hăn′dĭd) ►*adj.* **1.** Working or done without help; unassisted. **2.** Using only one hand. **3.** *Naut.* Being or restricted to a one-person sailing crew. —**sin′gle-hand′ed·ly** *adv.* —**sin′gle-hand′ed·ness** *n.*

sin·gle-mind·ed (sĭng′gəl-mīn′dĭd) ►*adj.* **1.** Having one overriding purpose or goal. **2.** Steadfast. —**sin′gle-mind′ed·ly** *adv.* —**sin′gle-mind′ed·ness** *n.*

sin·gles bar (sĭng′gəlz) ►*n.* A bar patronized esp. by unmarried men and women.

sin·gly (sĭng′glē) ►*adv.* **1.** Alone. **2.** One by one; individually.

sing·song (sĭng′sông′, -sŏng′) ►*n.* A monotonous rising and falling of the voice. —**sing′song′** *adj.*

sin·gu·lar (sĭng′gyə-lər) ►*adj.* **1.** Being only one; individual. **2.** Unique. **3a.** Being beyond what is ordinary, esp. in being exceptionally good; remarkable. **b.** Strange or unusual. **4.** *Gram.* Of or being a single person or thing or several entities considered as a unit. ►*n. Gram.* The singular number or a form designating it. [< Lat. *singulāris.*] —**sin′gu·lar′i·ty** (-lăr′ĭ-tē), **sin′gu·lar·ness** *n.* —**sin′gu·lar·ly** *adv.*

Sin·ha·lese (sĭn′hə-lēz′, -lēs′) or **Sing·ha·lese** (sĭng′gə-lēz′, -lēs′) ►*n., pl.* **-lese 1.** A member of a people constituting the majority of the population of Sri Lanka. **2.** The Indic language of the Sinhalese. —**Sin′ha·lese′** *adj.*

sin·is·ter (sĭn′ĭ-stər) ►*adj.* **1.** Suggesting or threatening harm or evil. **2.** Portending misfortune or disaster; ominous. [< Lat., on the left.]

sink (sĭngk) ►*v.* **sank** (săngk) or **sunk** (sŭngk), **sunk, sink·ing 1a.** To fall toward the bottom of a body of water or other liquid. **b.** To cause to descend beneath the surface or to the bottom of a liquid. **2.** To fall or drop to a lower level. **3.** To force into or penetrate a substance. **4.** To dig or drill (e.g., a well) in the earth. **5.** To pass into a specified condition: *sank into a deep sleep.* **6.** To deteriorate in quality or condition. **7.** To diminish or decline. **8.** To become weaker, quieter, or less forceful. **9.** To become felt or understood: *The lesson sank in.* **10.** To invest. **11.** *Sports* To propel (a ball or shot) into a hole, basket, or pocket. ►*n.* **1.** A basin fixed to a wall or floor and having a drainpipe and a piped water supply. **2.** A sinkhole. [< OE *sincan.*] —**sink′a·ble** *adj.*

sink·er (sĭng′kər) ►*n.* A weight used for sinking fishing lines or nets.

sink·hole (sĭngk′hōl′) ►*n.* A natural depression in a land surface, usu. occurring in limestone regions and formed by solution or collapse of a cavern roof.

Sino- ►*pref.* Chinese: *Sinology.* [< LLat. *Sīnae,* the Chinese, ult. of Chin. orig.; akin to Mandarin *Qín,* the Qin dynasty of China (221–206 BC).]

Si·nol·o·gy (sī-nŏl′ə-jē, sĭ-) ►*n.* The study of Chinese language, literature, or civilization. —**Si′no·log′i·cal** (sī′nə-lŏj′ĭ-kəl, sĭn′ə-) *adj.* —**Si·nol′o·gist** *n.*

Si·no-Ti·bet·an (sī′nō-tĭ-bĕt′n, sĭn′ō-) ►*n.* A language family that includes Chinese and Tibeto-Burman. —**Si′no-Ti·bet′an** *adj.*

sin·u·ous (sĭn′yo͞o-əs) ►*adj.* **1.** Twisting; winding. **2.** Supple and lithe: *the sinuous grace of a dancer.* [< Lat. *sinus,* curve.] —**sin′u·os′i·ty** (-ŏs′ĭ-tē) *n.* —**sin′u·ous·ly** *adv.*

si·nus (sī′nəs) ►*n.* **1.** Any of various air-filled cavities in the bones of the skull, esp. one communicating with the nostrils. **2.** A bodily channel containing chiefly venous blood. [< Lat., curve, hollow.]

si·nus·i·tis (sī′nə-sī′tĭs) ►*n.* Inflammation of a sinus, esp. in the nasal region.

Si·on (sī′ən) ►*n.* Var. of **Zion.**

Siou·an (so͞o′ən) ►*n.* A large North American Indian language family spoken from Lake Michigan to the Rocky Mountains.

Sioux (so͞o) ►*n., pl.* **Sioux** (so͞o, so͞oz) **1.** A member of a group of Native American peoples, comprising the Santee, the Lakota, and the Assiniboin, inhabiting the N Great Plains from Minnesota to E Montana and from S Saskatchewan to Nebraska, and now located mainly in North and South Dakota, Minnesota, Montana, and Nebraska. **2.** Any of their Siouan languages. —**Sioux** *adj.*

sip (sĭp) ►*v.* **sipped, sip·ping** To drink in small quantities. ►*n.* **1.** The act of sipping. **2.** A small quantity of liquid sipped. [ME *sippen.*] —**sip′per** *n.*

si·phon also **sy·phon** (sī′fən) ►*n.* A tube that carries liquid from a higher level over a barrier and then down to a lower level, with the flow maintained by gravity and atmospheric pressure as long as the tube remains filled. ►*v.* To draw off or convey (a liquid) through a siphon. [< Gk. *siphōn.*]

sir (sûr) ►*n.* **1. Sir** Used as an honorific title for baronets and knights. **2.** Used as a form of polite address for a man. **3.** Used as a salutation in a letter: *Dear Sir.* [< SIRE.]

sire (sīr) ►*n.* **1.** A biological father. **2.** The male parent of an animal, esp. a domesticated mammal. **3.** *Archaic* Used as a form of address for a male superior, esp. a king. ►*v.* **sired, sir·ing 1.** To be the biological father of (a child). **2.** To be the male individual producing (an animal's offspring) through sexual reproduction. [< Lat. *senior,* older.]

si·ren (sī′rən) ►*n.* A device for making a loud, usu. wailing sound used as a signal or warning. [< OFr. *sereine,* SIREN.]

Siren ►*n.* **1.** *Gk. Myth.* One of a group of sea nymphs whose sweet singing lured mariners to destruction. **2. siren** A beautiful or alluring woman. [< Gk. *seirēn.*]

Sir·i·us (sîr′ē-əs) ►*n.* A star in Canis Major, the brightest star in the sky.

sir·loin (sûr′loin′) ►*n.* A cut of meat from the upper part of the loin. [< OFr. *surlonge.*]

si·roc·co (sə-rŏk′ō) ►*n., pl.* **-cos** A hot, humid southerly wind of S Europe originating in the Sahara. [< Ar. *šarq,* east.]

sis (sĭs) ►*n. Informal* Sister.

si·sal (sī′səl) ►*n.* The fiber of a widely cultivated agave, used for cordage and rope. [After *Sisal,* Mexico.]

sis·sy (sĭs′ē) ►*n., pl.* **-sies 1.** A timid person. **2.** *Offensive* A boy or man regarded as effeminate. [< SIS.] —**sis′sy·ish** *adj.*

sis·ter (sĭs′tər) ►*n.* **1.** A female having one or both parents in common with another person. **2.** A female who shares a common ancestry or allegiance with another, esp.: **a.** A kinswoman. **b.** A close female friend. **c.** A fellow African-American female. **3. Sister** A nun. ►*adj.* Closely related or associated: *sister ships.* [< OE *sweostor* and ON *systir.*] —**sis′ter·li·ness** *n.* —**sis′ter·ly** *adj.*

sis·ter·hood (sĭs′tər-ho͝od′) ►*n.* **1.** The relationship of being a sister or sisters. **2.** The quality of being sisterly. **3.** Association of women in a common cause.

sis·ter-in-law (sĭs′tər-ĭn-lô′) ►*n., pl.* **sis·ters-in-law** (-tərz-) **1.** The sister of one's spouse. **2.** The wife of one's sibling. **3.** The wife of the sibling of one's spouse.

sit (sĭt) ►*v.* **sat** (săt), **sit·ting 1.** To rest with the body supported on the buttocks or hindquarters. See Usage Note at **set**[1]. **2.** To perch, as a bird. **3.** To cover eggs for hatching; brood. **4.** To maintain a seated position on (a horse). **5.** To be situated or located. **6.** To pose for an artist or photographer. **7.** To be in session. **8.** To remain inactive or unused. **9.** To please: *The idea didn't sit well with me.* **10.** To babysit. —***phrasal verbs:*** **sit down** To take a seat. **sit in on** To attend as a visitor. **sit on** *Informal* To suppress: *sat on the evidence.* **sit up 1.** To rise to a sitting position. **2.** To become suddenly alert. —***idiom:*** **sit tight** *Informal* To patiently await the next move. [< OE *sittan.*] —**sit′ter** *n.*

sit·ar (sĭt′är′, sĭ-tär′) ►*n.* A stringed instrument of India having a seasoned gourd for a body and a hollow wooden neck with movable raised frets. [< Pers. *sitār.*] —**si·tar′ist** *n.*

sit·com (sĭt′kŏm′) ►*n.* A situation comedy.

sit-down (sĭt′doun′) ►*n.* **1.** A work stoppage in

which the workers refuse to leave their place of employment until their demands are met. **2.** An obstruction of normal activity by the act of a large group sitting down to express a grievance or protest.

site (sīt) ▸*n.* **1.** The place where something was, is, or is to be located. **2.** A website. ▸*v.* **sit·ed, sit·ing** To situate or locate. [< Lat. *situs*.]

sit-in (sĭt′ĭn′) ▸*n.* An organized protest in which participants sit down in a place and refuse to move.

sit·ting (sĭt′ĭng) ▸*n.* **1.** A period during which one is seated and occupied with a single activity. **2.** A session, as of a legislature. ▸*adj.* Incumbent: *a sitting governor.*

Sitting Bull Tatanka Iyotanka. 1834?–90. Hunkpapa leader.

Sitting Bull

sit·u·ate (sĭch′ōō-āt′) ▸*v.* **-at·ed, -at·ing** To place in a certain spot; locate. [< Lat. *situs*, location.]

sit·u·a·tion (sĭch′ōō-ā′shən) ▸*n.* **1.** A state of affairs. **2.** Position or status with regard to conditions and circumstances. **3.** A job. —**sit′u·a′tion·al** *adj.*

situation comedy ▸*n.* A humorous television series having a regular cast of characters.

sit-up (sĭt′ŭp′) ▸*n.* A physical exercise in which one uses the abdominal muscles to raise the torso to a sitting position without moving the legs.

Si·van (sĭv′ən) ▸*n.* The 3rd month of the Jewish calendar. See table at **calendar.** [Heb. *sîwān*.]

six (sĭks) ▸*n.* **1.** The cardinal number equal to 5 + 1. **2.** The 6th in a set or sequence. [< OE.] —**six** *adj. & pron.*

six-gun (sĭks′gŭn′) ▸*n.* A six-chambered revolver.

Six Nations ▸*pl.n.* The Iroquois confederacy after the Tuscarora joined it in 1722.

six-pack (sĭks′păk′) ▸*n.* **1.** Six units of a commodity, esp. six containers of a beverage sold in a pack. **2.** *Informal* The six mounds of abdominal muscle visible on a person with low body fat and high muscular definition.

six-shoot·er (sĭks′shōō′tər) ▸*n.* A six-gun.

six·teen (sĭk-stēn′) ▸*n.* **1.** The cardinal number equal to 15 + 1. **2.** The 16th in a set or sequence. —**six·teen′** *adj. & pron.*

six·teenth (sĭk-stēnth′) ▸*n.* **1.** The ordinal number matching the number 16 in a series. **2.** One of 16 equal parts. —**six·teenth′** *adv. & adj.*

sixth (sĭksth) ▸*n.* **1.** The ordinal number matching the number 6 in a series. **2.** One of six

equal parts. **3.** *Mus.* A tone six degrees above or below a given tone in a diatonic scale. —**sixth** *adv. & adj.*

six·ti·eth (sĭk′stē-ĭth) ▸*n.* **1.** The ordinal number matching the number 60 in a series. **2.** One of 60 equal parts. —**six′ti·eth** *adv. & adj.*

six·ty (sĭks′tē) ▸*n., pl.* **-ties** The cardinal number equal to 6 × 10. —**six′ty** *adj. & pron.*

siz·a·ble also **size·a·ble** (sī′zə-bəl) ▸*adj.* Of considerable size; fairly large. —**siz′a·bly** *adv.*

size¹ (sīz) ▸*n.* **1.** The physical dimensions, magnitude, or extent of an object. **2.** Any of a series of graduated dimensions whereby manufactured articles are classified. ▸*v.* **sized, siz·ing** To arrange according to size. —*phrasal verb:* **size up** To make an estimate or judgment of. [ME *sise.*]

size² (sīz) ▸*n.* A gluey substance used as a glaze or filler for materials such as paper, cloth, or wall surfaces. [ME *sise.*] —**size** *v.*

siz·ing (sī′zĭng) ▸*n.* A glaze or filler; size.

siz·zle (sĭz′əl) ▸*v.* **-zled, -zling 1.** To make the hissing sound of frying fat. **2.** To seethe with anger. **3.** To be very hot. **4.** To be very popular, exciting, or interesting. [< ME *sissen*, hiss.] —**siz′zle** *n.* —**siz′zling·ly** *adv.*

SJ ▸*abbr.* Society of Jesus

SK ▸*abbr.* Saskatchewan

ska (skä) ▸*n.* Popular music of Jamaican origin having a fast tempo and a strongly accentuated offbeat. [Perh. < *Love Skavoovie*, greeting used by Cluet Johnson, early ska musician.]

skate¹ (skāt) ▸*n.* **1.** An ice skate, roller skate, or inline skate. **2.** *Informal* A skateboard. ▸*v.* **skat·ed, skat·ing 1.** To glide or move along on skates. **2.** To move or progress in an unconcerned manner. **3.** To ride or perform tricks on a skateboard. [< ONFr. *escache*, stllt.] —**skat′er** *n.*

skate² (skāt) ▸*n.* A ray having a flattened body with greatly expanded pectoral fins that extend around the head. [< ON *skata.*]

skate·board (skāt′bôrd′) ▸*n.* A usu. short narrow board mounted on a set of four wheels, ridden standing or crouching. —**skate′board′** *v.* —**skate′board′er** *n.*

skeet (skēt) ▸*n.* A form of trapshooting in which clay targets are thrown from traps to simulate birds in flight. [< SHOOT.]

skein (skān) ▸*n.* **1.** A length of thread or yarn wound in a loose long coil. **2.** A flock of geese in flight. [< OFr. *escaigne.*]

skel·e·ton (skĕl′ĭ-tn) ▸*n.* **1a.** The internal supporting structure of a vertebrate, usu. composed of bone and cartilage. **b.** The hard external supporting and protecting structure in many invertebrates, such as crustaceans. **2.** A supporting structure or framework. **3.** An outline or sketch. [< Gk. *skeletos*, dried up.] —**skel′e·tal** *adj.*

skeleton key ▸*n.* A key designed or adapted to open many different locks.

skep·tic also **scep·tic** (skĕp′tĭk) ▸*n.* **1.** One who habitually doubts, questions, or disagrees. **2.** One inclined to skepticism in religion or philosophy. [< Gk. *skeptesthai*, examine.] —**skep′ti·cal** *adj.* —**skep′ti·cal·ly** *adv.*

skep·ti·cism also **scep·ti·cism** (skĕp′tĭ-sĭz′əm) ▸*n.* **1.** A doubting or questioning attitude. **2.** *Philos.* The doctrine that absolute knowledge is impossible. **3.** Doubt or disbelief esp. of religious tenets.

sketch (skĕch) ►*n.* **1.** A hasty or undetailed drawing or painting. **2.** A brief outline. **3.** A short, often satirical scene or play; skit. ►*v.* To make a sketch (of). [< Ital. *schizzo*.] —**sketch′-er** *n.* —**sketch′i·ly** *adv.* —**sketch′y** *adj.*

skew (skyoo) ►*v.* **1.** To turn or place at an angle. **2.** To distort. ►*adj.* Turned to one side. ►*n.* A slant. [< ONFr. *eskiuer*, escape.]

skew·er (skyoo′ər) ►*n.* A long pointed rod for impaling and holding food during cooking. [ME *skuer*.] —**skew′er** *v.*

ski (skē) ►*n., pl.* **skis** One of a pair of long flat runners for gliding over snow or water. ►*v.* **skied, ski·ing** To go or glide on skis, esp. as a sport. [< ON *skīdh*.] —**ski′a·ble** *adj.* —**ski′er** *n.* —**ski′ing** *n.*

skid (skĭd) ►*n.* **1.** The act of sliding or slipping over a surface. **2a.** A plank or log used for sliding or rolling heavy objects. **b.** A pallet for loading or handling goods. **3.** A device applying pressure to a wheel to brake a vehicle. **4.** A runner in the landing gear of certain aircraft, such as helicopters. **5.** **skids** *Slang* A path to ruin or failure: *His career hit the skids.* ►*v.* **skid·ded, skid·ding** **1.** To slide sideways while moving due to loss of traction. **2.** To slide from forward momentum, esp. during an attempt to stop: *wheels skidding on oily pavement.* [?]

skid row (rō) ►*n. Slang* A squalid district inhabited by derelicts.

skiff (skĭf) ►*n.* A small, flat-bottomed open boat. [< OItal. *schifo*, of Gmc. orig.]

ski lift ►*n.* A power-driven conveyor used to carry skiers to the top of a slope.

skill (skĭl) ►*n.* **1.** Proficiency; dexterity: *painted with great skill.* **2.** An art, trade, or technique, esp. one requiring use of the hands or body: *the skill of glassmaking.* [< ON *skil*, discernment.] —**skilled** *adj.*

    Syns: **art, craft, expertise, technique** *n.*

skil·let (skĭl′ĭt) ►*n.* See **frying pan.** [ME *skelet.*]

skill·ful also **skil·ful** (skĭl′fəl) ►*adj.* **1.** Possessing or exercising skill. **2.** Marked by or requiring skill. —**skill′ful·ly** *adv.* —**skill′ful·ness** *n.*

skim (skĭm) ►*v.* **skimmed, skim·ming** **1a.** To remove floating matter from (a liquid). **b.** To remove (floating matter): *skimmed the cream off the milk.* **2.** To glide or pass quickly and lightly over. See Synonyms at **brush¹. 3.** To read or glance through quickly or superficially. [ME *skimmen.*]

skim milk ►*n.* Milk from which the cream has been removed.

skimp (skĭmp) ►*v.* **1.** To deal with hastily or carelessly. **2.** To be stingy or sparing; scrimp. [Poss. < SCRIMP.]

skimp·y (skĭm′pē) ►*adj.* **-i·er, -i·est 1.** Inadequate in size or amount; scanty. **2.** Not covering a considerable amount of the body. —**skimp′i·ly** *adv.* —**skimp′i·ness** *n.*

skin (skĭn) ►*n.* **1.** The membranous tissue forming the outer covering of an animal. **2.** An animal hide or pelt. **3.** A usu. thin, closely adhering outer layer: *a peach skin; the skin of an aircraft.* ►*v.* **skinned, skin·ning** **1.** To remove skin from. **2.** To injure the skin of. **3.** *Slang* To cheat; swindle. —*idioms:* **by the skin of (one's) teeth** By the smallest margin. **get under (one's) skin** To provoke. [< ON *skinn.*] —**skin′less** *adj.*

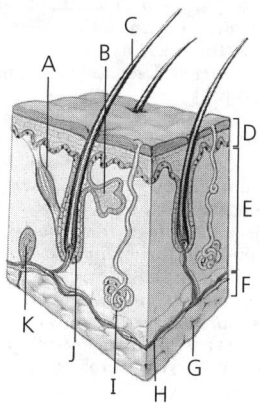

skin
cross section of human skin
A. muscle; B. sebaceous gland;
C. hair; D. epidermis; E. dermis;
F. subcutaneous tissue; G. fat;
H. artery; I. sweat gland;
J. hair follicle; K. corpuscle

skin diving ►*n.* Underwater swimming, with a face mask and fins, usu. with a snorkel. —**skin′-dive′** *v.* —**skin diver** *n.*

skin·flint (skĭn′flĭnt′) ►*n.* A miser.

Skin·ner (skĭn′ər), **B(urrhus) F(rederic)** 1904–90. Amer. psychologist.

skin·ny (skĭn′ē) ►*adj.* **-ni·er, -ni·est 1.** Having very little bodily flesh or fat, often unattractively so. **2.** Having little width: *a skinny island.* —**skin′ni·ness** *n.*

skin·ny-dip (skĭn′ē-dĭp′) ►*v. Informal* To swim in the nude. —**skin′ny-dip′ping** *n.*

skip (skĭp) ►*v.* **skipped, skip·ping 1a.** To move by hopping on one foot and then the other. **b.** To leap or jump lightly (over). **2.** To ricochet. **3.** To pass from point to point omitting what intervenes. **4.** To pass over, omit, or disregard. **5.** To be promoted beyond (the next grade or level). **6.** *Informal* To leave hastily: *skipped town.* ►*n.* **1.** A skipping gait. **2.** A gap or omission. **3.** A control mechanism on an audio or video player that advances or reverses the playing of a recording. [ME *skippen.*] —**skip′per** *n.*

skip·jack tuna (skĭp′jăk′) ►*n.* A commercially important tuna of tropical to warm temperate waters, having dark stripes on the side. [SKIP (<its leaping) + JACK, fellow.]

skip·per (skĭp′ər) ►*n.* The master of a ship. [< MDu. *schipper.*] —**skip′per** *v.*

skir·mish (skûr′mĭsh) ►*n.* **1.** A minor battle in war. **2.** A minor conflict or dispute. [< OItal. *scaramuccia.*] —**skir′mish** *v.*

skirt (skûrt) ►*n.* **1.** The part of a garment, such as a dress or coat, that hangs from the waist down. **2.** A garment hanging from the waist and worn esp. by women and girls. ►*v.* **1.** To lie along the edge (of); border. **2.** To pass around the edge or border (of). **3.** To evade or avoid. [< ON *skyrta*, shirt.]

skit (skĭt) ►*n.* A short, usu. comic theatrical sketch. [?]

skit·ter (skĭt′ər) ►*v.* To skip, glide, or move rapidly or lightly along a surface. [Prob. < dial. *skite*, run rapidly.]

skit·tish (skĭt'ĭsh) ►*adj.* **1.** Excitable or nervous. **2.** Inconstant; capricious. [ME.] —**skit'tish·ly** *adv.* —**skit'tish·ness** *n.*

skoal (skōl) ►*interj.* Used as a drinking toast. [< ON *skāl*, bowl.]

Skop·je (skôp'yĕ) The capital of Macedonia, in the N part of the country.

skulk (skŭlk) ►*v.* **1.** To lie in hiding; lurk. **2.** To move about stealthily. [ME *skulken*, of Scand. orig.] —**skulk'er** *n.*

skull (skŭl) ►*n.* The bony framework that encloses and protects the brain and sense organs; cranium. [ME *skulle*.]

skull·cap (skŭl'kăp') ►*n.* **1.** A light, close-fitting, brimless cap. **2.** A yarmulke.

skull·dug·ger·y (skŭl-dŭg'ə-rē) ►*n.* Crafty deception or trickery. [Prob. < Sc. *sculduddery*, obscenity.]

skunk (skŭngk) ►*n.* **1.** A small mammal of the Americas having a bushy tail and black and white fur and ejecting a foul-smelling secretion when threatened. **2.** *Slang* A despicable person. ►*v. Slang* To defeat overwhelmingly. [Of Massachusett orig.]

skunk cabbage ►*n.* A foul-smelling plant of eastern North American wetlands having small flowers on a spadix enclosed in a greenish or purplish spathe.

sky (skī) ►*n., pl.* **skies** (skīz) **1.** The upper atmosphere, seen as a hemisphere above the earth. **2.** often **skies** Atmospheric conditions: *fair skies.* **3.** The celestial regions. [< ON *skȳ*, cloud.]

sky·cap (skī'kăp') ►*n.* An airport porter.

sky·dive (skī'dīv') ►*v.* To jump from an airplane, performing various maneuvers before opening a parachute. —**sky'div'er** *n.* —**sky'div'ing** *n.*

sky-high (skī'hī') ►*adv.* **1.** To a very high level: *boxes piled sky-high.* **2.** In or to pieces: *blew the bridge sky-high.* ►*adj.* Very high in cost or value.

sky·jack (skī'jăk') ►*v.* To hijack (an aircraft). [SKY + (HI)JACK.] —**sky'jack'ing** *n.*

sky·lark (skī'lärk') ►*n.* A lark of Eurasia and Africa having brownish plumage and noted for its singing while in flight. ►*v.* To romp or frolic.

sky·light (skī'līt') ►*n.* An overhead window, as in a roof, admitting daylight.

sky·line (skī'līn') ►*n.* **1.** The horizon. **2.** An outline, as of buildings, against the sky.

sky·rock·et (skī'rŏk'ĭt) ►*n.* A firework that rises into the air and explodes brilliantly. ►*v.* To rise rapidly and suddenly.

sky·scrap·er (skī'skrā'pər) ►*n.* A very tall building.

sky·ward (skī'wərd) ►*adv. & adj.* At or toward the sky. —**sky'wards** *adv.*

sky·writ·ing (skī'rī'tĭng) ►*n.* The process of writing in the sky by releasing vapor from a flying airplane. —**sky'writ'er** *n.*

slab (slăb) ►*n.* **1.** A broad, flat, thick piece or slice. **2.** An outside piece cut from a log when squaring it for lumber. [ME.]

slack (slăk) ►*adj.* **-er, -est 1.** Not tense, firm, or taut. See Synonyms at **loose. 2a.** Lacking in activity; not busy. **b.** Moving slowly; sluggish. **3.** Lacking in diligence, care, or concern. See Synonyms at **negligent.** ►*v.* **1.** To make or become slack. **2.** To slake (lime). ►*n.* **1.** Something slack or loose. **2.** A period of little activity. **3. slacks** Trousers for informal wear. —*phrasal verb:* **slack off 1.** To decrease in activity or intensity. **2.** To work less intensely than is required or expected. [< OE *slæc.*] —**slack'ly** *adv.* —**slack'ness** *n.*

slack·en (slăk'ən) ►*v.* To make or become slower, looser, or less intense or severe.

slack·er (slăk'ər) ►*n.* One who shirks work or duty, esp. military service in wartime.

slag (slăg) ►*n.* The glassy mass left after smelting metallic ore. [< MLGer. *slagge.*]

slain (slān) ►*v.* P.part. of **slay.**

slake (slāk) ►*v.* **slaked, slak·ing 1.** To cause to lessen or subside; moderate or quench. **2.** To combine (lime) chemically with water or moist air. [< OE *slacian.*]

sla·lom (slä'ləm) ►*n.* **1.** The act or sport of moving along a zigzag course. **2.** A race along a downhill zigzag course, esp. in skiing. [Norw. *slalåm.*] —**sla'lom** *v.*

slam¹ (slăm) ►*v.* **slammed, slam·ming 1.** To shut with force and loud noise. **2.** To put, throw, or hit so as to produce a loud noise. ►*n.* **1.** A loud forceful impact. **2.** A noise so produced. [Perh. of Scand. orig.]

slam² (slăm) ►*n.* The winning of all the tricks or all but one during the play of one hand in bridge and other card games. [?]

slam dancing ►*n.* A style of dancing, usu. performed to punk rock, in which dancers intentionally collide. —**slam'-dance'** *v.*

slam dunk ►*n. Basketball* A dramatic forceful dunk. —**slam'-dunk'** *v.*

slam·mer (slăm'ər) ►*n. Slang* A jail. [< SLAM¹.]

slan·der (slăn'dər) ►*n.* A false and malicious, usu. oral statement that damages the reputation of another. [< Lat. *scandalum,* SCANDAL.] —**slan'der** *v.* —**slan'der·er** *n.* **slan'der·ous** *adj.* —**slan'der·ous·ly** *adv.*

slang (slăng) ►*n.* A vocabulary of casual or playful expressions used esp. for humor, irreverence, or striking effect. [?] —**slang'i·ness** *n.* —**slang'y** *adj.*

slant (slănt) ►*v.* **1.** To slope or cause to slope. **2.** To present in a way that conforms with a particular bias. ►*n.* **1.** A sloping plane, direction, or course. **2.** A particular bias. [< ME *slenten.*] —**slant'ing·ly** *adv.* —**slant'wise'** *adv. & adj.* **Syns:** *incline, lean, slope, tilt, tip* **v.**

slap (slăp) ►*n.* **1a.** A sharp blow made with the open hand or a flat object. **b.** The sound so made. **2.** An insult. ►*v.* **slapped, slap·ping 1.** To give a slap to. **2.** To strike or cause to strike sharply and loudly. —*idiom:* **slap on the wrist** A token punishment. [ME *slappe.*]

slap·dash (slăp'dăsh') ►*adj.* Hasty and careless.

slap·hap·py (slăp'hăp'ē) ►*adj. Slang* Dazed, giddy, or silly, as if from blows to the head.

slap·stick (slăp'stĭk') ►*n.* Comedy marked by loud and boisterous farce.

slash (slăsh) ►*v.* **1.** To cut with forceful sweeping strokes. **2.** To make a gash or slit in. **3.** To reduce drastically. ►*n.* **1a.** A sweeping stroke made with a sharp instrument. **b.** A cut made by slashing. **2.** A diagonal mark (/) used esp. to separate alternatives, as in *and/or,* and to represent the word *per,* as in *miles/hour.* [Poss. < OFr. *esclater,* break.] —**slash'er** *n.*

slat (slăt) ►*n.* A flat narrow strip, as of metal or wood. [< OFr. *esclat,* splinter.]

slate (slāt) ►*n.* **1a.** A fine-grained rock that splits into thin, smooth-surfaced layers. **b.** A piece of this rock cut for use as roofing or surfacing material or as a writing surface. **2.** A list of the candidates of a political party running for various offices. **3.** A dark or bluish gray. ►*v.* **slat·ed, slat·ing 1.** To cover with slate. **2.** To schedule. [< OFr. *esclate*, splinter.] —**slat′y** *adj.*

slath·er (slă*th*′ər) ►*v. Informal* To spread thickly or lavishly. [?]

slat·tern (slăt′ərn) ►*n.* A slovenly woman. [Poss. < dial. *slatter*, to slop.] —**slat′tern·ly** *adj.*

slaugh·ter (slô′tər) ►*n.* **1.** The killing of animals for food. **2.** The killing of a large number of people; massacre. ►*v.* **1.** To butcher (animals) for food. **2.** To kill brutally or in large numbers. [ME, of Scand. orig.] —**slaugh′ter·er** *n.*

slaugh·ter·house (slô′tər-hous′) ►*n.* A place where animals are butchered.

Slav (släv) ►*n.* A member of one of the Slavic-speaking peoples of E Europe.

slave (slāv) ►*n.* **1.** One who is owned as the property of someone else, esp. in involuntary servitude. **2.** One who is subservient to or controlled by a specified person, emotion, or influence. ►*v.* **slaved, slav·ing** To work very hard or doggedly; toil. [< Lat. *Sclāvus*, Slav.]

slav·er¹ (slăv′ər) ►*v.* **1.** To slobber; drool. **2.** To behave obsequiously. See Synonyms at **fawn¹.** [Prob. < ON *slafra*.] —**slav′er** *n.*

slav·er² (slā′vər) ►*n.* One, such as a person or ship, engaged in the trafficking of slaves.

slav·er·y (slā′və-rē, slāv′rē) ►*n., pl.* **-ies 1.** The state of being a slave; bondage. **2.** The practice of owning slaves. **3.** A condition of hard work and subjection.

Slav·ic (slä′vĭk) ►*adj.* Of or relating to the Slavs or their languages. ►*n.* A branch of the Indo-European language family that includes Russian, Polish, and Czech.

slav·ish (slā′vĭsh) ►*adj.* **1.** Of or like a slave; servile: *slavish devotion.* **2.** Showing no originality: *a slavish copy of the original.* —**slav′ish·ly** *adv.*

Sla·vo·ni·a (slə-vō′nē-ə, -vōn′yə) A historical region of NE Croatia. —**Sla·vo′ni·an** *adj. & n.*

Sla·von·ic (slə-vŏn′ĭk) ►*n.* Slavic. —**Sla·von′-ic** *adj.*

slaw (slô) ►*n.* Coleslaw.

slay (slā) ►*v.* **slew** (sloō) or **slayed, slain** (slān) or **slayed, slay·ing** To kill violently. [< OE *slēan.*] —**slay′er** *n.*

slea·zy (slē′zē) ►*adj.* **-zi·er, -zi·est 1a.** Shabby and dirty; tawdry. **b.** Dishonest or corrupt. **2.** Cheap or shoddy. [?] —**sleaze** *n.* —**slea′zi·ly** *adv.* —**slea′zi·ness** *n.*

sled (slĕd) ►*n.* **1.** A vehicle having runners, used for moving over ice and snow. **2.** A light vehicle, often on runners, used by children for coasting over snow or ice. ►*v.* **sled·ded, sled·ding** To ride or convey by a sled. [< MDu. *sledde.*]

sledge (slĕj) ►*n.* A large sled drawn by work animals, used for transporting loads across ice and snow. [Du. dial. *sleedse.*]

sledge·ham·mer (slĕj′hăm′ər) ►*n.* A long heavy hammer usu. wielded with both hands. [< OE *slecg.*]

sleek (slēk) ►*adj.* **-er, -est 1.** Smooth and lustrous as if polished; glossy: *long, sleek, blond hair.* **2.** In good health and having smooth or glossy hair, fur, or skin: *a sleek hound.* **3.** Able to or designed to move efficiently through air

or water; streamlined: *a sleek sedan.* **4.** Polished or smooth in manner, esp. in an unctuous way; slick: *a sleek politician.* [< SLICK.] —**sleek** *v.* —**sleek′ly** *adv.* —**sleek′ness** *n.*

sleep (slēp) ►*n.* **1.** A natural, periodic state of rest in which consciousness is lost and bodily movement and responsiveness to external stimuli decrease. **2.** A state, as of inactivity or unconsciousness, similar to sleep. ►*v.* **slept** (slĕpt), **sleep·ing 1.** To be in or as if in a state of sleep. **2.** To pass by sleeping. —*phrasal verb:* **sleep with** To have sexual relations with. [< OE *slǣp.*]

sleep·er (slē′pər) ►*n.* **1.** One that sleeps. **2.** A sleeping car. **3.** One that achieves unexpected recognition, popularity, or success.

sleep·ing bag (slē′pĭng) ►*n.* A lined, usu. zippered bag for sleeping, esp. outdoors.

sleeping car ►*n.* A railroad car having accommodations for sleeping.

sleeping pill ►*n.* A drug in the form of a pill or capsule that is used to relieve insomnia.

sleeping sickness ►*n.* An often fatal infectious disease of sub-Saharan Africa that is transmitted by tsetse flies and is marked by fever, lethargy, and lymph node swelling.

sleep·less (slēp′lĭs) ►*adj.* **1a.** Marked by a lack of sleep. **b.** Unable to sleep. **2.** Always alert or in motion. —**sleep′less·ly** *adv.*

sleep·walk·ing (slēp′wô′kĭng) ►*n.* The act of walking or performing other activities while asleep or in a sleeplike state. —**sleep′walk′** *v.*

sleep·wear (slēp′wâr′) ►*n.* Clothes, such as pajamas, worn in bed.

sleep·y (slē′pē) ►*adj.* **-i·er, -i·est 1.** Ready for sleep; drowsy. **2.** Inactive; quiet. —**sleep′i·ly** *adv.* —**sleep′i·ness** *n.*

sleet (slēt) ►*n.* **1.** Precipitation consisting of frozen or partially frozen raindrops. **2.** An icy glaze. ►*v.* To shower sleet. [ME *slete.*] —**sleet′y** *adj.*

sleeve (slēv) ►*n.* **1.** A part of a garment that covers the arm. **2.** A case into which an object fits. —*idiom:* **up (one's) sleeve** Hidden but ready to be used. [< OE *slēf.*] —**sleeved** *adj.* —**sleeve′less** *adj.*

sleigh (slā) ►*n.* A light vehicle on runners, usu. drawn by a horse over snow or ice. [< MDu. *slēde.*] —**sleigh** *v.*

sleight (slīt) ►*n.* **1.** Dexterity. **2.** A trick or stratagem. [< ON *slœgdh < slœgr*, sly.]

sleight of hand ►*n.* **1.** The performance of juggling or magic tricks so quickly and deftly that the manner of execution cannot be observed; legerdemain. **2.** A trick performed in this way.

slen·der (slĕn′dər) ►*adj.* **-er, -est 1.** Having little width in proportion to height or length. **2.** Small in amount or extent; meager. [ME *slendre.*] —**slen′der·ly** *adv.* —**slen′der·ness** *n.*

slen·der·ize (slĕn′də-rīz′) ►*v.* **-ized, -iz·ing** To make or become slender.

slept (slĕpt) ►*v.* P.t. and p.part. of **sleep.**

sleuth (sloōth) ►*n.* A detective. [< SLEUTH-HOUND.] —**sleuth** *v.*

sleuth·hound (sloōth′hound′) ►*n.* **1.** A dog used for tracking or pursuing. **2.** A detective. [< ME *sloth, sluth,* track.]

slew¹ also **slue** (sloō) ►*n. Informal* A large amount or number. [< OIr. *slúag.*]

slew² (sloō) ►*v.* P.t. of **slay.**

slew³ also **slue** (sloō) ►*v.* **slewed, slewing** also

slued, slu·ing To turn or twist to the side. ►*n.* The act of slewing. [?]

slice (slīs) ►*n.* **1.** A thin broad piece cut from a larger amount. **2.** A portion or share. **3.** *Sports* A stroke that causes a ball to curve off course to the right or, if the player is left-handed, to the left. ►*v.* **sliced, slic·ing 1.** To cut or divide into slices. **2.** To cut or remove from a larger piece. **3.** *Sports* To hit (a ball) with a slice. [< OFr. *esclicier*, to splinter.] —**slice′a·ble** *adj.* —**slic′er** *n.*

slick (slĭk) ►*adj.* **-er, -est 1.** Smooth, glossy, and slippery: *paths slick with ice.* **2.** Deftly executed; adroit. **3.** Confident and effortlessly effective. **4.** Superficially attractive but lacking depth. ►*n.* A smooth or slippery surface or area: *an oil slick.* ►*v.* To make smooth or glossy. [ME *slike.*] —**slick′ly** *adv.* —**slick′ness** *n.*

slick·er (slĭk′ər) ►*n.* **1.** A long loose raincoat made of a glossy material. **2.** *Informal* A person with stylish clothing and manners.

slide (slīd) ►*v.* **slid** (slĭd), **slid·ing 1a.** To move over a surface while maintaining continuous contact. **b.** To slip or skid. **c.** To pass smoothly and quietly; glide. **2.** To become less favorable or less desirable. ►*n.* **1.** A sliding movement or action. **2a.** A smooth surface or track for sliding. **b.** A playground apparatus for sliding down. **3.** A part that operates by sliding, as the bolt in a lock. **4a.** An image on a transparent base for projection on a screen. **b.** A small glass plate for mounting specimens for a microscope. **5.** A fall of a mass of rock, earth, or snow down a slope. [< OE *slīdan.*]

slid·er (slī′dər) ►*n.* **1.** One that slides. **2.** *Baseball* A fast pitch that breaks in the same direction as a curve ball at the last moment.

slide rule ►*n.* A device consisting of two logarithmically scaled rules arranged to slide along each other, used in performing mathematical operations.

slid·ing scale (slī′dĭng) ►*n.* A scale in which indicated prices, taxes, or wages vary in accordance with another factor, as wages with the cost-of-living index.

sli·er (slī′ər) ►*adj.* Comp. of **sly.**

sli·est (slī′ĭst) ►*adj.* Superl. of **sly.**

slight (slīt) ►*adj.* **-er, -est 1.** Small in size, degree, or amount. **2.** Frail or delicate. **3.** Of small importance; trifling. ►*v.* **1.** To snub or insult. **2.** To treat as if of small importance. **3.** To neglect. ►*n.* An act of deliberate discourtesy or disrespect; snub. [ME, slender, poss. of Scand. orig.] —**slight′ly** *adv.* —**slight′ness** *n.*

slim (slĭm) ►*adj.* **slim·mer, slim·mest 1.** Small in girth or thickness; slender. **2.** Scanty or meager. ►*v.* **slimmed, slim·ming** To make or become slim. [< MDu. *slimp*, bad, crooked.] —**slim′ly** *adv.* —**slim′ness** *n.*

slime (slīm) ►*n.* **1.** A moist, foul, gen. slippery or sticky substance. **2.** A mucous secretion, as of fish or slugs. [< OE *slīm.*] —**slim′y** *adj.*

sling (slĭng) ►*n.* **1.** A weapon made of a looped strap in which a stone is hurled. **2.** A looped belt, rope, strap, or chain for supporting, cradling, or hoisting loads. **3.** A cloth band suspended from the neck to support an injured arm or hand. ►*v.* **slung** (slŭng), **sling·ing 1.** To hurl with a swinging motion; fling. **2.** To place, carry, or move in a sling. [ME *slinge.*]

sling·shot (slĭng′shŏt′) ►*n.* A Y-shaped stick having an elastic strap attached to the prongs, used for shooting stones or pellets.

slink (slĭngk) ►*v.* **slunk** (slŭngk), **slink·ing** To move furtively. [< OE *slincan.*]

slink·y (slĭng′kē) ►*adj.* **-i·er, -i·est** Sinuous and sleek.

slip¹ (slĭp) ►*v.* **slipped, slip·ping 1.** To move quietly and stealthily. **2.** To slide out of place or from one's grasp. **3.** To slide involuntarily and lose one's balance. **4.** To decline from a former or standard level; fall off. **5.** To make a mistake. **6.** To place or insert smoothly and quietly. **7.** To put on or remove easily or quickly: *slip on a sweater.* ►*n.* **1.** The act of slipping. **2.** A slight error or oversight. **3.** A docking place for a ship between two piers. **4.** A woman's undergarment of dress length. **5.** A pillowcase. —*idioms:* **give (someone) the slip** *Slang* To escape the company or pursuit of. **let slip** To say inadvertently or thoughtlessly. [ME *slippen.*] —**slip′page** *n.*

slip² (slĭp) ►*n.* **1.** A plant cutting used for propagation. **2.** A slender, youthful person. **3.** A small piece of paper. [< MLGer. or MDu. *slippe.*]

slip·cov·er (slĭp′kŭv′ər) ►*n.* A fitted, removable, usu. cloth cover for a piece of upholstered furniture. —**slip′cov′er** *v.*

slip·knot (slĭp′nŏt′) ►*n.* A knot made with a loop so that it slips easily along the rope or cord around which it is tied.

slipped disk (slĭpt) ►*n.* An injury due to the shifting out of position of a cushioning disk between the spinal vertebrae.

slip·per (slĭp′ər) ►*n.* A light low shoe that can be slipped on and off easily.

slip·per·y (slĭp′ə-rē) ►*adj.* **-i·er, -i·est 1.** Causing or tending to cause sliding or slipping. **2.** Not trustworthy; elusive or tricky. [< OE *slipor.*] —**slip′per·i·ness** *n.*

slip·shod (slĭp′shŏd′) ►*adj.* Carelessly done or arranged.

slip-up (slĭp′ŭp′) ►*n.* An error; oversight.

slit (slĭt) ►*n.* A long straight narrow cut or opening. [< OE *slītan*, cut up.] —**slit** *v.*

slith·er (slĭth′ər) ►*v.* **1.** To move by twisting the body over a surface, as a snake does. **2.** To slip and slide. [< OE *slidrian.*] —**slith′er·y** *adj.*

sliv·er (slĭv′ər) ►*n.* A thin sharp-ended piece; splinter. [< OE *slīfan*, split.] —**sliv′er** *v.*

slob (slŏb) ►*n.* *Informal* A crude or slovenly person. [Ir.Gael. *slab*, mud.]

slob·ber (slŏb′ər) ►*v.* **1.** To let saliva or food dribble from the mouth. **2.** To express emotion effusively. [ME *sloberen.*] —**slob′ber** *n.*

sloe (slō) ►*n.* **1.** A thorny Eurasian shrub with white flowers and bluish-black, plumlike fruits used as a flavoring. **2.** The tart, blue-black, plumlike fruit of this shrub. [< OE *slā.*]

slog (slŏg) ►*v.* **slogged, slog·ging 1.** To walk with a slow, labored gait. **2.** To work diligently for long hours; toil. [Perh. < SLUG³.]

slo·gan (slō′gən) ►*n.* **1.** A phrase expressing the aims or nature of an enterprise, team, or other group; motto. **2.** A catchword that is used in advertising or promotion. [< Sc. *slogorne*, battle cry.]

sloop (slo͞op) ►*n.* A single-masted, fore-and-aft-rigged sailing boat with a mainsail and a jib. [Du. *sloep* < MDu. *slūpen*, glide.]

sloop

slop (slŏp) ►*n.* **1.** Spilled or splashed liquid. **2.** Soft mud or slush. **3.** Unappetizing watery food. **4.** often **slops** Waste food used esp. to feed pigs. ►*v.* **slopped, slop·ping 1.** To spill or splash messily. **2.** To feed slops to. [ME *sloppe,* muddy place.]

slope (slōp) ►*v.* **sloped, slop·ing** To incline upward or downward. See Synonyms at **slant.** ►*n.* **1.** An inclined line, surface, plane, or stretch of ground. **2a.** A deviation from the horizontal. **b.** The amount of such deviation. [< ME *aslope,* sloping.]

slop·py (slŏp′ē) ►*adj.* **-pi·er, -pi·est 1.** Untidy or messy. **2.** Carelessly done. **3.** Muddy or slushy. —**slop′pi·ly** *adv.* —**slop′pi·ness** *n.*

slosh (slŏsh) ►*v.* **1.** To splash or flounder, as in water. **2.** To splash (a liquid) copiously. [Perh. < SLOP and SLUSH.] —**slosh′y** *adj.*

slot (slŏt) ►*n.* **1.** A narrow groove or opening. **2.** A suitable place, position, or niche, as in a sequence. ►*v.* **slot·ted, slot·ting 1.** To make a slot in. **2.** To put into or assign to a slot. [< OFr. *esclot,* hollow of the breastbone.]

sloth (slôth, slōth, slŏth) ►*n.* **1.** Laziness or indolence. **2.** Any of various slow-moving arboreal mammals of South and Central America. [ME *slowth* < *slow,* SLOW.]

sloth·ful (slôth′fəl, slōth′-, slŏth′-) ►*adj.* Disinclined to work or exertion; lazy. See Synonyms at **lazy.** —**sloth′ful·ly** *adv.*

slot machine ►*n.* A coin-operated vending or gambling machine.

slouch (slouch) ►*n.* **1.** An awkward, drooping posture or gait. **2.** *Slang* A lazy or incompetent person. [?] —**slouch** *v.*

slough¹ (slōō, slou) ►*n.* **1.** A hollow, usu. filled with mud. **2.** A stagnant swamp. **3.** A state of deep despair. [< OE *slōh.*]

slough² (slŭf) ►*n.* **1.** Dead tissue separated from surrounding living tissue, as in a wound. **2.** An outer layer that is shed. ►*v.* To shed or cast off. [ME *slughe.*]

Slo·vak (slō′väk′, -văk′) also **Slo·va·ki·an** (slō-vä′kē-ən, -văk′ē-ən) ►*n.* **1.** A native or inhabitant of Slovakia. **2.** The Slavic language of the Slovaks. —**Slo′vak, Slo·va′ki·an** *adj.*

Slo·va·ki·a (slō-vä′kē-ə, -văk′ē-ə) A country of central Europe. Cap. Bratislava.

slov·en (slŭv′ən) ►*n.* One who is habitually untidy or careless. [ME *slovein.*]

Slo·vene (slō′vēn′) also **Slo·ve·ni·an** (slō-vē′-nē-ən, -vēn′yən) ►*n.* **1.** A native or inhabitant

of Slovenia. **2.** The Slavic language of the Slovenes. —**Slo′vene, Slo·ve′ni·an** *adj.*

Slo·ve·ni·a (slō-vē′nē-ə, -vēn′yə) A country of central Europe SE of Austria. Cap. Ljubljana.

slov·en·ly (slŭv′ən-lē) ►*adj.* **1.** Untidy or messy. **2.** Marked by carelessness; slipshod: *slovenly work.* —**slov′en·li·ness** *n.*

slow (slō) ►*adj.* **-er, -est 1a.** Not moving or able to move quickly. **b.** Marked by a low speed or tempo: *a slow waltz.* **2.** Taking or requiring a long time. **3.** Registering a time or rate behind or below the correct one. **4.** Marked by low sales or activity. **5.** Dull or boring. **6.** Not having or showing mental quickness. ►*adv.* **-er, -est** Slowly. ►*v.* **1.** To make or become slow or slower. **2.** To delay; retard. [< OE *slāw.*] —**slow′ly** *adv.* —**slow′ness** *n.*

Usage: Slow is often used adverbially in speech and informal writing, esp. for brevity and forcefulness: *Drive slow! Slow* is also used with certain senses of common verbs: *The watch runs slow.* Otherwise, in formal writing *slowly* is generally preferred.

slow·down (slō′doun′) ►*n.* A slackening of pace: *a production slowdown.*

slow motion ►*n.* A filmmaking technique in which the action as projected is slower than the original action. —**slow′-mo′tion** *adj.*

slow·poke (slō′pōk′) ►*n. Informal* One who moves, works, or acts slowly.

sludge (slŭj) ►*n.* **1.** Semisolid material such as that precipitated by sewage treatment. **2.** Mud, mire, or ooze. [Perh. < dial. *slutch,* mire.] —**sludg′y** *adj.*

slue¹ ►*v. & n.* Var. of **slew³.**

slue² (slōō) ►*n.* Var. of **slew¹.**

slug¹ (slŭg) ►*n.* **1.** A round bullet larger than buckshot. **2.** *Informal* A shot of liquor. **3.** A small metal disk used in place of a coin. **4.** A lump of metal. [Perh. < SLUG².]

slug² (slŭg) ►*n.* A terrestrial gastropod mollusk having a slow-moving elongated body with no shell. [ME *slugge,* sluggard.]

slug³ (slŭg) ►*v.* **slugged, slug·ging** To strike heavily, esp. with the fist or a bat. [Poss. < SLUG¹.] —**slug** *n.* —**slug′ger** *n.*

slug·gard (slŭg′ərd) ►*n.* A lazy person; idler. [ME *sluggart.*] —**slug′gard·ly** *adj.*

slug·gish (slŭg′ish) ►*adj.* **1.** Slow; inactive. **2.** Lazy or indolent. **3.** Slow to perform or respond. [Prob. ME *slugge,* lazy person.] —**slug′gish·ly** *adv.* —**slug′gish·ness** *n.*

sluice (slōōs) ►*n.* **1a.** An artificial channel for water, with a gate to regulate the flow. **b.** The gate itself. **2.** A sluiceway. **3.** A long inclined trough, as for floating logs or separating gold ore. ►*v.* **sluiced, sluic·ing 1.** To wash with or as if with a sudden flow of water; flush. **2.** To draw off by a sluice. **3.** To send down a sluice. [< Lat. *exclūdere, exclūs-,* shut out.]

sluice·way (slōōs′wā′) ►*n.* An artificial channel, esp. one for carrying off excess water.

slum (slŭm) ►*n.* A poor, squalid, densely populated urban area. ►*v.* **slummed, slum·ming** To visit a slum, esp. from curiosity. [?] —**slum′-my** *adj.*

slum·ber (slŭm′bər) ►*v.* **1.** To sleep or doze. **2.** To be dormant. [Prob. < OE *slūma,* sleep.] —**slum′ber** *n.* —**slum′ber·er** *n.*

slum·ber·ous (slŭm′bər-əs) or **slum·brous** (-brəs) ►*adj.* **1.** Sleepy; drowsy. **2.** Quiet; tranquil. **3.** Causing or inducing sleep.

slum·lord (slŭm′lôrd′) ►*n.* An owner of slum property, esp. one who allows the property to deteriorate.

slump (slŭmp) ►*v.* **1.** To fall, decline, or sink suddenly. **2.** To droop, as in sitting; slouch. **3a.** To decline suddenly; fall off. **b.** To perform poorly or inadequately. [Prob. of Scand. orig.] —**slump** *n.*

slung (slŭng) ►*v.* P.t. and p.part. of **sling.**

slunk (slŭngk) ►*v.* P.t. and p.part. of **slink.**

slur (slûr) ►*v.* **slurred, slur·ring 1.** To pronounce indistinctly. **2.** To disparage. **3.** To pass over lightly or carelessly. **4.** *Mus.* To glide over (a series of notes) smoothly without a break. ►*n.* **1.** A disparaging remark; aspersion. **2.** A slurred sound. **3.** *Mus.* A curved line connecting notes to indicate that they are to be played or sung legato. [Prob. < ME *sloor,* mud.]

slurp (slûrp) ►*v.* To eat or drink noisily. [Du. *slurpen.*] —**slurp** *n.*

slush (slŭsh) ►*n.* **1.** Partially melted snow or ice. **2.** Soft mud; slop. **3.** Sentimental drivel. **4.** A drink made of flavored syrup and crushed ice. [Perh. of Scand. orig.] —**slush′i·ly** *adv.* —**slush′i·ness** *n.* —**slush′y** *adj.*

slush fund ►*n.* A fund for undesignated purposes, esp. one used to finance a corrupt practice.

slut (slŭt) ►*n.* **1a.** *Often Offensive* A sexually promiscuous person. **b.** A woman prostitute. **2.** A slovenly woman. [ME *slutte.*] —**slut′tish** *adj.*

sly (slī) ►*adj.* **sli·er, sli·est** also **sly·er, sly·est 1.** Clever or cunning, esp. in the practice of deceit. **2.** Stealthy or surreptitious. **3.** Playfully mischievous. —*idiom:* **on the sly** Secretly. [< ON *slægr.*] —**sly′ly** *adv.* —**sly′ness** *n.*

SM ►*abbr.* service mark

smack¹ (smăk) ►*v.* **1.** To make a sound by pressing the lips together and pulling them apart quickly. **2.** To kiss or slap noisily. ►*n.* **1.** The loud sharp sound of smacking the lips. **2.** A noisy kiss. **3.** A sharp blow or loud slap. ►*adv.* Directly; straight: *was hit smack in the face.* [Perh. of MFlem. orig.]

smack² (smăk) ►*n.* **1.** A distinctive flavor. **2.** A suggestion or trace. ►*v.* **1.** To have a distinct flavor. **2.** To suggest: *This smacks of foul play.* [< OE *smæc.*]

smack³ (smăk) ►*n.* A fishing boat sailing under various rigs, according to size. [Du. or LGer. *smak.*]

smack⁴ (smăk) ►*n.* *Slang* Heroin. [Prob. < Yiddish *shmek,* a sniff, smell.]

small (smôl) ►*adj.* **-er, -est 1.** Being below the average in size, quantity, or extent. **2.** Insignificant or trivial. **3.** Limited in degree or scope: *a small farmer.* **4.** Not fully grown. **5.** Narrow in outlook; petty: *a small mind.* **6.** Belittled; humiliated. **7.** Lacking force or volume: *a small voice.* ►*adv.* **1.** In small pieces: *Cut the meat up small.* **2.** Softly. **3.** In a small manner. ►*n.* Something smaller than the rest: *the small of the back.* [< OE *smæl.*] —**small′ness** *n.*

  Syns: *diminutive, little, miniature, minuscule, minute, petite, tiny, wee **adj.***

small arm ►*n.* A firearm that can be carried in the hand.

small calorie ►*n.* See **calorie** (sense 1).

small capital ►*n.* A letter having the form of a capital letter but smaller.

small fry ►*n.* **1.** Small children. **2.** People or

things regarded as unimportant.

small intestine ►*n.* The part of the digestive tract between the outlet of the stomach and the large intestine.

small-mind·ed (smôl′mīn′dĭd) ►*adj.* Having a narrow or petty attitude. —**small′-mind′ed·ly** *adv.* —**small′-mind′ed·ness** *n.*

small·pox (smôl′pŏks′) ►*n.* A highly infectious, often fatal viral disease that is characterized by pustules that form pockmarks. The disease has been eradicated worldwide by vaccination.

small talk ►*n.* Casual or light conversation.

small-time or **small-time** (smôl′tīm′) ►*adj.* *Informal* Insignificant or minor.

smarm·y (smär′mē) ►*adj.* **-i·er, -i·est** Excessively ingratiating or insincerely earnest. See Synonyms at **unctuous.** [< *smarm,* smear.]

smart (smärt) ►*adj.* **-er, -est 1a.** Intelligent; bright. **b.** Canny and shrewd in dealings with others. **2a.** Amusingly clever; witty. **b.** Impertinent or insolent. **3.** Quick and energetic: *a smart pace.* **4.** Fashionable; elegant: *a smart restaurant.* See Synonyms at **fashionable. 5.** Capable of making adjustments that resemble those resulting from human decisions, esp. by means of a computer: *smart missiles.* ►*v.* **1.** To cause or feel a sharp stinging pain. **2.** To feel mental distress. [< OE *smeart,* stinging.] —**smart′ly** *adv.* —**smart′ness** *n.*

smart al·eck (ăl′ĭk) ►*n.* *Informal* One who is annoyingly self-assertive, esp. for making impudent displays of knowledge. —**smart′-al′eck, smart′-al′eck·y** *adj.*

smart·en (smär′tn) ►*v.* **1.** To make or become more brisk or lively. **2.** To make or become smart or smarter.

smash (smăsh) ►*v.* **1a.** To break or be broken into pieces. **b.** To render (something) into a mush, as by throwing. See Synonyms at **crush. 2.** To strike with a heavy blow; hit. ►*n.* **1a.** A heavy blow or collision. **b.** *Sports* A powerful overhand stroke, as in tennis. **2.** A violent breaking of something or the noise made by such breaking: *The dishes fell with a loud smash.* **3.** Total destruction; ruin. **4.** *Informal* A resounding success. ►*adj.* *Informal* Very successful. [Prob. imit.] —**smash′er** *n.*

smash·up (smăsh′ŭp′) ►*n.* **1.** A total defeat. **2.** A serious collision between vehicles.

smat·ter·ing (smăt′ər-ĭng) ►*n.* **1.** Superficial or piecemeal knowledge. **2.** A small, scattered amount. [< *smatter,* dabble.]

smear (smîr) ►*v.* **1a.** To spread, cover, or stain with a sticky dirty substance. **b.** To cause to be blurry or spread in unwanted places. **2.** To slander or vilify. ►*n.* **1.** A smudge or blot. **2.** A sample, as of blood, spread on a slide for microscopic examination. **3.** Vilification or slander. [< OE *smerian,* anoint.] —**smear′y** *adj.*

smell (smĕl) ►*n.* **1.** The sense, located in the nasal cavities of mammals, by which odors are perceived. **2.** The act of smelling. **3a.** The odor of something. **b.** A distinctive quality; aura. ►*v.* **smelled** or **smelt** (smĕlt), **smell·ing 1.** To perceive (an odor) by the sense of smell. **2.** To have or emit an odor. **3.** To be suggestive, esp. of dishonesty or corruption. [ME *smellen.*]

  Syns: *aroma, odor, scent **n.***

smell·ing salts (smĕl′ĭng) ►*pl.n.* A preparation based on an ammonia compound, sniffed esp. to relieve faintness.

smell·y (smĕl′ē) ►*adj.* **-i·er, -i·est** *Informal* Having an unpleasant odor.

smelt¹ (smĕlt) ►*v.* To melt or fuse (ores) to separate metallic constituents. [Du. or LGer. *smelten.*]

smelt² (smĕlt) ►*n., pl.* **smelts** or **smelt** A small silvery food fish. [< OE.]

smelt³ (smĕlt) ►*v.* P.t. and p.part. of **smell.**

smelt·er (smĕl′tər) ►*n.* **1.** also **smelt·er·y** (-tə-rē) *pl.* **-ies** An establishment for smelting. **2.** A worker who smelts ore.

smid·gen (smĭj′ən) ►*n.* A very small quantity or portion. [Prob. < dial. *smitch*, particle.]

smi·lax (smī′lăks′) ►*n.* **1.** A slender, glossy-leaved climbing vine used in floral decoration. **2.** Any of several prickly vines having heart-shaped leaves and greenish flowers. [< Gk.]

smile (smīl) ►*n.* A facial expression formed by an upward curving of the corners of the mouth and indicating pleasure, affection, or amusement. ►*v.* **smiled, smil·ing 1.** To have or form a smile. **2.** To express approval. **3.** To express with a smile. [< ME *smilen*, to smile.]

smil·ey (smī′lē) ►*n., pl.* **-eys** An emoticon, esp. one indicating a smiling face [:-)].

smirch (smûrch) ►*v.* **1.** To soil or stain. **2.** To dishonor. [ME *smorchen.*] —**smirch** *n.*

smirk (smûrk) ►*v.* To smile in an annoying self-satisfied manner. [< OE *smercian*, smile.] —**smirk** *n.* —**smirk′er** *n.*

smite (smīt) ►*v.* **smote** (smōt), **smit·ten** (smĭt′n) or **smote, smit·ing 1.** To inflict a heavy blow on. **2.** To kill by or as if by blows. **3.** To afflict. [< OE *smītan*, smear.]

smith (smĭth) ►*n.* **1.** A metalworker, esp. one who works with hot metal. **2.** A blacksmith. [< OE.]

Smith, Adam 1723–90. Scottish economist and philosopher.

Smith, Bessie 1894?–1937. Amer. singer and songwriter.

Bessie Smith
photographed c. 1925

Smith, John 1580?–1631. English colonist, explorer, and writer.

Smith, Joseph 1805–44. Amer. founder (1830) of the Church of Jesus Christ of Latter-day Saints.

Smith, Margaret Chase 1897–1995. Amer. politician.

smith·er·eens (smĭth′ə-rēnz′) ►*pl.n. Informal* Pieces; bits. [< Ir.Gael. *smidirín.*]

Smith·son (smĭth′sən), **James** 1765–1829. British chemist, mineralogist, and philanthropist.

smith·y (smĭth′ē, smĭth′ē) ►*n., pl.* **-ies** A blacksmith's shop; forge. [< ON *smidhja.*]

smock (smŏk) ►*n.* A loose outer garment worn to protect the clothes. ►*v.* To decorate (fabric) with stitched gathers in a honeycomb pattern. [< OE *smoc.*]

smog (smŏg, smôg) ►*n.* **1.** Fog polluted with smoke. **2.** Air pollution produced when sunlight causes hydrocarbons and nitrogen oxides, esp. from automotive exhaust, to combine. [SM(OKE) + (F)OG.] —**smog′gy** *adj.*

smoke (smōk) ►*n.* **1.** The vapor made up of small particles of matter from incomplete burning of materials such as wood or coal. **2.** A cloud of fine particles. **3.** The act of smoking a form of tobacco. **4.** *Informal* A cigarette or cigar. ►*v.* **smoked, smok·ing 1.** To draw in and exhale smoke from a cigarette, cigar, or pipe. **2.** To emit smoke. **3.** To emit smoke excessively. **4.** To preserve (meat or fish) by exposure to smoke. **5.** To fumigate. **6.** *Slang* To perform at the utmost capacity. **7.** *Slang* To kill. —*phrasal verb:* **smoke out** To force out of hiding or as if by the use of smoke. [< OE *smoca.*] —**smoke′less** *adj.* —**smok′er** *n.* —**smok′i·ness** *n.* —**smok′y** *adj.*

smoke detector ►*n.* An alarm device that automatically detects the presence of smoke.

smoke·house (smōk′hous′) ►*n.* A structure where meat or fish is smoked.

smoke screen ►*n.* **1.** Dense smoke used to conceal military operations. **2.** Something used to conceal plans or intentions.

smoke·stack (smōk′stăk′) ►*n.* A large vertical pipe through which combustion gases and smoke are discharged.

smol·der also **smoul·der** (smōl′dər) ►*v.* **1.** To burn with little smoke and no flame. **2.** To exist in a suppressed state. ►*n.* Thick smoke resulting from a slow fire. [ME *smolderen*, suffocate.]

smooch (smōōch) *Slang* ►*n.* A kiss. ►*v.* To kiss. [Perh. of imit. orig.]

smooth (smōōth) ►*adj.* **-er, -est 1.** Free from irregularities, roughness, or projections. **2.** Having a fine texture or consistency. **3.** Having an even or gentle motion. **4.** Having no obstructions or difficulties. **5.** Ingratiating: *smooth talk.* ►*v.* **1.** To make or become smooth. **2.** To rid of obstructions, hindrances, or difficulties. **3.** To make calm; soothe. [< OE *smōth.*] —**smooth′er** *n.* —**smooth′ly** *adv.* —**smooth′ness** *n.*

smooth·bore (smōōth′bôr′) ►*adj.* Having no rifling within the barrel. Used of a firearm.

smor·gas·bord (smôr′gəs-bôrd′) ►*n.* A buffet meal featuring a varied number of dishes. [Swed. *smörgåsbord.*]

smote (smōt) ►*v.* P.t. and p.part. of **smite.**

smoth·er (smŭth′ər) ►*v.* **1.** To kill or extinguish by depriving of oxygen. **2.** To conceal or suppress. **3.** To cover thickly. [< ME *smorther*, dense smoke.]

smudge (smŭj) ►*v.* **smudged, smudg·ing** To smear or blur. ►*n.* **1.** A blotch or smear. **2.** A smoky fire used to protect against insects or frost. [ME *smogen.*] —**smudg′y** *adj.*

smug (smŭg) ►*adj.* **smug·ger, smug·gest** Self-satisfied or complacent. [< MLGer.] —**smug′-ly** *adv.* —**smug′ness** *n.*

smug·gle (smŭg′əl) ►*v.* **-gled, -gling 1a.** To bring a prohibited item into a country. **b.** To bring an item into a country without paying the associated duties or taxes on it. **2.** To convey illicitly or by stealth. [Prob. LGer. *smuggeln.*] —**smug′gler** *n.*

smut (smŭt) ►*n.* **1.** A particle of dirt. **2.** Sexually explicit or prurient material, such as movies. **3.** Any of various plant diseases caused by fungi that form black powdery masses. [< ME *smotten*, defile.] —**smut′ti·ness** *n.* —**smut′ty** *adj.*

snack (snăk) ►*n.* **1.** A light meal. **2.** Food eaten between meals. [< ME *snacche*, bite.] —**snack** *v.*

snaf·fle (snăf′əl) ►*n.* A jointed bit for a horse.

sna·fu (snă-fōō′) ►*n., pl.* **-fus** *Slang* A chaotic or confused situation. [*s(ituation) n(ormal) a(ll) f(ouled) u(p)*.]

snag (snăg) ►*n.* **1.** A sharp or jagged protuberance. **2a.** A dead tree that is still standing. **b.** A tree or limb that protrudes above a water surface. **3.** A break, pull, or tear in fabric. **4.** An unforeseen obstacle. ►*v.* **snagged, snagging 1.** To get caught by a snag. **2.** *Informal* To catch or obtain quickly. **3.** To hinder; impede. [Of Scand. orig.]

snail (snāl) ►*n.* An aquatic or terrestrial mollusk having a spirally coiled shell and distinct head. [< OE *snægl.*]

snail mail ►*n.* *Informal* Mail delivered by a postal system, as distinct from e-mail.

snake (snāk) ►*n.* **1.** Any of numerous scaly, legless, sometimes venomous reptiles having a long, tapering, cylindrical body and flexible jaws. **2.** A treacherous person. **3.** A long flexible wire used for cleaning drains and sewers. ►*v.* **snaked, snak·ing** To move, drag, or pull in a snakelike manner. [< OE *snaca.*] —**snak′i·ly** *adv.* —**snak′y** *adj.*

snake oil ►*n.* A worthless preparation fraudulently peddled as a cure for many ills.

Snake River A river of the NW US rising in NW WY and flowing about 1,670 km (1,040 mi) to the Columbia R. in SE WA.

snap (snăp) ►*v.* **snapped, snap·ping 1.** To make or cause to make a sharp cracking sound. **2.** To break suddenly with a sharp sound. **3a.** To give way abruptly. **b.** To suffer a physical or mental breakdown, esp. while under stress. **4.** To bite or seize with a snatching motion. **5.** To speak abruptly or sharply: *snapped at the child.* **6.** To move swiftly and smartly: *snap to attention.* **7.** *Football* To pass (the ball) from the ground back between the legs to begin a down; hike. **8.** To open or close with a click. **9a.** To take (a photograph). **b.** To photograph (a subject). ►*n.* **1.** A sharp cracking sound. **2.** A sudden breaking or release of something under pressure. **3.** A clasp, catch, or other fastening device. **4.** A sudden attempt to bite or snatch. **5.** A thin crisp cookie: *a ginger snap.* **6.** *Informal* Briskness or energy. **7.** A spell of cold weather. **8.** Something accomplished without effort. See Synonyms at **breeze. 9.** *Football* The act of snapping the ball. [< MLGer. or MDu. *snappen*, seize.] —**snap′pish** *adj.* —**snap′py** *adj.*

snap bean ►*n.* See **string bean.**

snap·drag·on (snăp′drăg′ən) ►*n.* A cultivated plant having showy clusters of two-lipped, variously colored flowers.

snap·per (snăp′ər) ►*n.* **1.** One that snaps. **2.** *pl.* **-per** or **-pers** Any of numerous marine fishes, many of which are important food fishes.

snap·ping turtle (snăp′ĭng) ►*n.* Any of a family of freshwater turtles having a rough shell and powerful hooked jaws.

snap·shot (snăp′shŏt′) ►*n.* A photograph taken with a small camera.

snare[1] (snâr) ►*n.* **1.** A trap, often consisting of a noose, used for capturing birds and small animals. **2.** Something that entangles the unwary. ►*v.* **snared, snar·ing** To trap with or as if with a snare. See Synonyms at **catch.** [< OE *snearu* and ON *snara.*]

snare[2] (snâr) ►*n.* Any of the wires or cords stretched across the lower head of a drum so as to vibrate against it. [Prob. < Du. *snaar*, string.]

snarl[1] (snärl) ►*v.* **1.** To growl while baring the teeth. **2.** To speak angrily or threateningly. [< obsolete *snar.*] —**snarl** *n.* —**snarl′er** *n.*

snarl[2] (snärl) ►*n.* A tangle. ►*v.* **1.** To tangle or knot. **2.** To confuse. [ME *snarle*, trap.]

snatch (snăch) ►*v.* **1.** To grasp or seize suddenly. **2.** To steal, esp. with a sudden movement. ►*n.* **1.** The act of snatching. **2.** A brief period. **3.** A bit or fragment: *a snatch of dialogue.* [ME *snacchen.*] —**snatch′er** *n.*

snaz·zy (snăz′ē) ►*adj.* **-zi·er, -zi·est** *Slang* Fashionable and flashy or showy. [?]

sneak (snēk) ►*v.* **sneaked** or **snuck** (snŭk), **sneak·ing** To move, give, or take in a quiet, stealthy way. ►*n.* **1.** One who is stealthy or underhanded. **2.** An instance of sneaking. [< OE *snīcan.*] —**sneak′i·ly** *adv.* —**sneak′y** *adj.*

sneak·er (snē′kər) ►*n.* A shoe designed for outside activity, usu. made of canvas with a rubber sole.

sneer (snîr) ►*n.* A slight raising of one corner of the upper lip, expressive of contempt. [< OE *fnǣran*, breathe heavily.] —**sneer** *v.*

sneeze (snēz) ►*v.* **sneezed, sneez·ing** To expel air forcibly from the mouth and nose in an explosive involuntary spasm. [< OE *fnēosan.*] —**sneeze** *n.*

snick·er (snĭk′ər) ►*v.* To utter a nasty, partly stifled laugh. [Perh. imit.] —**snick′er** *n.*

snide (snīd) ►*adj.* **snid·er, snid·est** Slyly derogatory. [?] —**snide′ly** *adv.*

sniff (snĭf) ►*v.* **1.** To inhale a short audible breath through the nose. **2.** To indicate ridicule, contempt, or doubt. **3.** To detect by or as if by sniffing. [ME *sniffen.*] —**sniff** *n.*

snif·fle (snĭf′əl) ►*v.* **-fled, -fling 1.** To breathe audibly through a congested nose. **2.** To whimper. [< SNIFF.] —**snif′fle** *n.*

snif·ter (snĭf′tər) ►*n.* A pear-shaped goblet with a narrow top, used esp. in serving brandy. [< ME *snifteren*, sniff.]

snig·ger (snĭg′ər) ►*v.* To snicker. [Perh. < SNICKER.] —**snig′ger** *n.*

snip (snĭp) ►*v.* **snipped, snip·ping** To cut or clip with short quick strokes. ►*n.* **1a.** A small cut made with scissors or shears. **b.** A small piece clipped off. **2.** *Informal* A small person. [Du. or LGer. *snippen.*]

snipe (snīp) ►*n.* **1.** *pl.* **snipe** or **snipes** Any of various long-billed, brownish wading birds. **2.** A shot, esp. a gunshot, from a concealed place. ►*v.* **sniped, snip·ing 1.** To shoot at people from a concealed place. **2.** To make nasty remarks. [ME.] —**snip′er** *n.*

snip·pet (snĭp′ĭt) ►*n.* A tidbit or morsel.

snip·py (snĭp′ē) ►*adj.* **-pi·er, -pi·est** *Informal* Sharp-tongued; impertinent.

snit (snĭt) ►*n. Informal* An agitated state. [?]

snitch (snĭch) ►*v. Slang* **1.** To turn informer. **2.** To steal. [?] —**snitch** *n.*

sniv·el (snĭv′əl) ►*v.* **-eled, -el·ing** or **-elled, -el·ling 1.** To sniffle. **2.** To complain or whine tearfully. [ME *snivelen*.] —**sniv′el** *n.*

snob (snŏb) ►*n.* One who is convinced of his or her superiority in matters of taste or intellect. [< *snob*, lower-class person.] —**snob′ber·y** *n.* —**snob′bish** *adj.* —**snob′bish·ly** *adv.*

snoop (sno͞op) ►*v.* To pry furtively. ►*n.* One who snoops. [Du. *snoepen*, eat on the sly.] —**snoop′er** *n.* —**snoop′i·ly** *adv.* —**snoop′i·ness** *n.* —**snoop′y** *adj.*

snoot (sno͞ot) ►*n. Informal* **1.** A snout or nose. **2.** A snob.

snoot·y (sno͞o′tē) ►*adj.* **-i·er, -i·est** *Informal* Snobbishly aloof; haughty. —**snoot′i·ness** *n.*

snooze (sno͞oz) ►*v.* **snoozed, snooz·ing** To take a light nap; doze. [?] —**snooze** *n.*

snore (snôr) ►*v.* **snored, snor·ing** To breathe with harsh snorting noises while sleeping. [ME *snoren*, snort.] —**snore** *n.* —**snor′er** *n.*

snor·kel (snôr′kəl) ►*n.* **1.** A breathing apparatus used by skin divers, consisting of a long tube held in the mouth. **2.** A retractable tube in a submarine that contains air-intake and exhaust pipes. [Ger. *Schnorchel*.] —**snor′kel** *v.*

snort (snôrt) ►*n.* **1.** A loud rough sound made by breathing forcefully through the nostrils. **2.** *Slang* A drink of liquor, esp. a small one. ►*v.* **1.** To make a snort. **2.** To make an abrupt noise expressive of scorn or anger. **3.** *Slang* To ingest (e.g., a drug) by sniffing. [< ME *snorten*, to snort.] —**snort′er** *n.*

snot (snŏt) ►*n. Slang* **1.** Nasal mucus; phlegm. **2.** An annoying, arrogant, or impertinent person. [< OE *gesnot*.] —**snot′ti·ly** *adv.* —**snot′ti·ness** *n.* —**snot′ty** *adj.*

snout (snout) ►*n.* **1.** The projecting nose or facial part of an animal's head. **2.** *Slang* The human nose. [ME.]

snow (snō) ►*n.* **1.** Frozen precipitation in the form of translucent ice crystals that fall in soft white flakes. **2.** A fall of snow. ►*v.* **1.** To fall to the earth as snow. **2.** To cover or close off with snow. **3.** *Slang* To overwhelm with insincere talk, esp. with flattery. [< OE *snāw*.] —**snow′y** *adj.*

Snow, C(harles) P(ercy) Baron Snow of Leicester. 1905–80. British writer and scientist.

snow·ball (snō′bôl′) ►*n.* A mass of soft wet snow packed into a ball. ►*v.* **1.** To grow or cause to grow rapidly in significance, importance, or size. **2.** To throw snowballs (at).

snow blindness ►*n.* A usu. temporary loss of vision caused by exposure of the eyes to bright sunlight reflected from snow or ice.

snow·board (snō′bôrd′) ►*n.* A board equipped with bindings for the feet and used to maneuver down snow-covered slopes as a sport. —**snow′board′** *v.* —**snow′board′er** *n.*

snow·bound (snō′bound′) ►*adj.* Confined in one place by heavy snow.

snow·drift (snō′drĭft′) ►*n.* A mass or bank of snow piled up by the wind.

snow·drop (snō′drŏp′) ►*n.* A bulbous plant having nodding white spring flowers.

snow·fall (snō′fôl′) ►*n.* **1.** A fall of snow. **2.** The amount of snow that falls in a given period and area.

snow·flake (snō′flāk′) ►*n.* A single flake or crystal of snow.

snow leopard ►*n.* A large wild cat of central and South Asia, having thick, whitish-grayish fur with dark markings.

snow·man (snō′măn′) ►*n.* A figure of a person made from packed snow.

snow·mo·bile (snō′mō-bēl′, -mə-) ►*n.* A small vehicle with skis in front and tanklike treads, used for traveling on snow. —**snow′mo·bile′** *v.*

snowmobile

snow pea ►*n.* A variety of the common pea having a soft thick edible pod.

snow·plow (snō′plou′) ►*n.* A plowlike device or vehicle used to remove snow.

snow·shoe (snō′sho͞o′) ►*n.* An oblong or oval frame with interlaced strips or a taut sheet of material, attached to the foot to facilitate walking on deep snow. —**snow′shoe′** *v.*

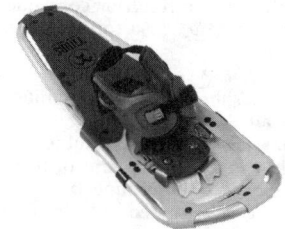

snowshoe

snow·storm (snō′stôrm′) ►*n.* A storm marked by heavy snowfall.

snow tire ►*n.* A tire with a deep tread or studs for traction on snow-covered surfaces.

snub (snŭb) ►*v.* **snubbed, snub·bing 1.** To ignore or behave coldly toward; slight. **2.** To dismiss or turn down in a decisive way. **3.** *Naut.* To check the movement of (e.g., a rope) by turning it quickly about a post. ►*n.* A deliberate slight. [ME *snubben*, rebuke.]

snub-nosed (snŭb′nōzd′) ►*adj.* Having a short, turned-up nose.

snuck (snŭk) ►*v.* P.t. and p.part. of **sneak.**

snuff¹ (snŭf) ►*v.* **1.** To inhale audibly through the nose. **2.** To sniff (at). [ME *snoffen*, sniffle.]

snuff² (snŭf) ►*v.* **1.** To put out; extinguish. **2.** To cut off the charred portion of (a candlewick). [Poss. of LGer. orig.] —**snuff′er** *n.*

snuff³ (snŭf) ►*n.* **1.** A preparation of finely pulverized tobacco for ingesting by sniffing. **2.** See **dip** (sense 9). —*idiom:* **up to snuff** *Informal* Up to standard. [< Du. *snuftabak*.]

snuf·fle (snŭf′əl) ►*v.* **-fled, -fling 1.** To breathe noisily, as through a blocked nose. **2.** To sniff, esp. repeatedly, as a dog. [Prob. < Du. *snuffelen*, sniff about.] —**snuf′fle** *n.* —**snuf′fler** *n.*

snug (snŭg) ►*adj.* **snug·ger, snug·gest 1.** Comfortably sheltered; cozy. **2.** Small but well arranged: *a snug apartment.* **3.** Close-fitting; tight. [Of Scand. orig.] —**snug, snug′ly** *adv.* —**snug′ness** *n.*

snug·gle (snŭg′əl) ►*v.* **-gled, -gling** To nestle or cuddle. [< SNUG.]

so¹ (sō) ►*adv.* **1a.** To such an extent: *She was so happy that she cried.* **b.** To a great extent: *But the idea is so obvious.* **2.** Afterward; then: *to the store and so home.* **3.** Used to signal a new subject: *So what happened?* **4.** Thereabouts: *only $10 or so.* **5.** Likewise: *She is here, and so am I.* **6.** In truth; indeed: *"You can't be right." "I am so!"* **7.** *Informal* Used as an intensive, esp. with verbs or verb phrases: *That is so not going to happen.* **8.** In the manner expressed or indicated; thus: *Hold the brush so.* ►*adj.* True or factual. ►*conj.* **1.** For that reason; therefore: *This is easier, so don't argue.* **2.** With the result or consequence that: *He quit, so I took his place.* **3.** In order that: *I stayed so I could see you.* ►*interj.* Used to express surprise or comprehension. —*idioms:* **so as to** In order to: *Shop early so as to beat the rush.* **so that** In order that. [< OE swā.]

Usage: Many critics have insisted that *so* must be followed by *that* in formal writing when used to introduce a clause giving the reason for or purpose of an action: *He stayed so that he could see the second feature.* But this rule is best regarded as a stylistic preference. • Both *so* and *so that* are acceptably used to introduce clauses that state a result or consequence: *The bridge was still closed, so* (or *so that*) *the drive took an hour.*

so² (sō) ►*n. Mus.* Var. of **sol¹.**

SO ►*abbr.* **1.** *Sports* shootout **2.** significant other **3.** strikeout

so. or **So.** ►*abbr.* **1.** south **2.** southern

soak (sōk) ►*v.* **1a.** To immerse or be immersed in liquid for a period of time. **b.** To make thoroughly wet or saturated. **2a.** To absorb (e.g., liquid): *Use the bread to soak up the gravy.* **b.** To be exposed to: *soaked up the sun.* **c.** *Informal* To take in mentally, esp. easily: *soaked up the music scene.* **3.** To seep into or permeate. **4.** To remove (e.g., a stain) by continued immersion. **5.** *Slang* To charge (a person) an inordinate amount for something: *people were getting soaked during the gas shortage.* ►*n.* The act or process of soaking. [< OE *socian*.] —**soak′er** *n.*

soap (sōp) ►*n.* **1.** A cleansing agent made from an alkali acting on natural oils and fats. **2.** A metallic salt of a fatty acid. **3.** A soap opera. [< OE *sāpe*.] —**soap** *v.* —**soap′i·ly** *adv.* —**soap′i·ness** *n.* —**soap′y** *adj.*

soap·box (sōp′bŏks′) ►*n.* **1.** A box in which soap is packed. **2.** A temporary platform used for impromptu public speaking.

soap opera ►*n.* A serial drama that is usu. performed on daytime television and is character-ized by melodrama and sentimentality.

soap·stone (sōp′stōn′) ►*n.* A soft metamorphic rock composed mostly of talc.

soar (sôr) ►*v.* **1a.** To fly into the air. **b.** To maintain altitude without moving the wings or using an engine; glide. **2.** To increase suddenly: *Sales soared.* [< VLat. *exaurāre*.]

sob (sŏb) ►*v.* **sobbed, sob·bing** To weep aloud with convulsive gasping. [ME *sobben*.] —**sob** *n.*

so·ba (sō′bə) ►*n.* A Japanese noodle made with buckwheat flour. [J.]

so·ber (sō′bər) ►*adj.* **-er, -est 1.** Not intoxicated. **2.** Abstemious or temperate. **3.** Devoid of frivolity, excess, or exaggeration. **4.** Serious; solemn. ►*v.* To make or become sober. [< Lat. *sōbrius*.] —**so′ber·ly** *adv.* —**so′ber·ness** *n.*

so·bri·e·ty (sə-brī′ĭ-tē, sō-) ►*n.* The state or condition of being sober.

so·bri·quet (sō′brĭ-kā′, -kĕt′) ►*n.* **1.** A nickname. **2.** An assumed name. [Fr.]

Soc. ►*abbr.* Socialist

so-called (sō′kôld′) ►*adj.* So named, called, or designated, often incorrectly.

Usage: Quotation marks are not used to set off descriptions that follow expressions such as *so-called* and *self-styled*, which themselves relieve the writer of responsibility for the attribution: *his so-called foolproof method* (not *"foolproof method"*).

soc·cer (sŏk′ər) ►*n.* A game in which two 11-member teams propel a ball into the opposing team's goal by kicking or butting or by using any part of the body except the arms and hands. [< *association football*.]

so·cia·ble (sō′shə-bəl) ►*adj.* **1.** Fond of the company of others: *a sociable party guest.* **2.** Marked by or affording occasion for agreeable conversation and conviviality. See Synonyms at **social.** ►*n.* A social. [< Lat. *sociāre*, share.] —**so′cia·bil′i·ty** *n.* —**so′cia·bly** *adv.*

so·cial (sō′shəl) ►*adj.* **1a.** Of or relating to human society and its organization: *social classes.* **b.** Of or occupied with human welfare: *social programs.* **2a.** Interacting with other people and living in communities. **b.** *Biol.* Living together in organized groups. **3a.** Seeking out or enjoying the company of others. **b.** Marked by friendly relations or companionship. **c.** Intended for convivial activities. ►*n.* An informal social gathering. [< Lat. *socius*, companion.] —**so′cial·ly** *adv.*

Syns: companionable, convivial, gregarious, sociable **Ant:** antisocial *adj.*

so·cial·ism (sō′shə-lĭz′əm) ►*n.* A social system in which the means of producing and distributing goods are owned collectively and political power is exercised by the whole community. —**so′cial·ist** *n.* —**so′cial·is′tic** *adj.*

so·cial·ite (sō′shə-līt′) ►*n.* One prominent in fashionable society.

so·cial·ize (sō′shə-līz′) ►*v.* **-ized, -iz·ing 1.** To place under public ownership or control. **2.** To cause to behave in accordance with social expectations. **3.** To take part in social activities. —**so′cial·i·za′tion** *n.* —**so′cial·iz′er** *n.*

so·cial·ized medicine (sō′shə-līzd′) ►*n.* A system that provides health care all by means of government regulation and tax subsidies.

social science ►*n.* A science, such as sociology, psychology, or anthropology, that studies society and individual relationships in and to society. —**social scientist** *n.*

social security ▸*n.* A government program that provides monthly payments to the elderly and the disabled, financed by assessment of employers and employees.

social studies ▸*pl.n. (takes sing. or pl. v.)* A course of study including geography, history, government, and sociology, taught in elementary and secondary schools.

social work ▸*n.* Organized public work to aid the disadvantaged and counsel those with special problems. —**social worker** *n.*

so·ci·e·ty (sə-sī′ĭ-tē) ▸*n., pl.* **-ties 1.** Humans collectively. **2.** A group of people having mutual interests, shared institutions, and a common culture. **3.** An association of people uniting in a common interest. **4.** The rich and fashionable social class. **5.** Companionship; company. **6.** *Biol.* A community of organisms. [< Lat. *societās*, fellowship.] —**so·ci′e·tal** *adj.*

Society Islands An island group of French Polynesia in the S Pacific E of Samoa.

Society of Friends ▸*n.* A Christian denomination, founded in the mid-17th cent. in England, that rejects formal sacraments, a formal creed, a priesthood, and violence; Quakers.

socio– ▸*pref.* **1.** Society: *sociology.* **2.** Social: *socioeconomic.* [< Lat. *socius*, companion.]

so·ci·o·ec·o·nom·ic (sō′sē-ō-ĕk′ə-nŏm′ĭk, -ē′kə-, -shē-) ▸*adj.* Both social and economic.

so·ci·ol·o·gy (sō′sē-ŏl′ə-jē, -shē-) ▸*n.* The study of the origins, organization, institutions, and development of human society. —**so′ci·o·log′ic** (-ə-lŏj′ĭk), **so·ci·o·log′i·cal** *adj.* —**so′·ci·o·log′i·cal·ly** *adv.* —**so′ci·ol′o·gist** *n.*

so·ci·o·path (sō′sē-ə-păth′, -shē-) ▸*n.* An adult who has a personality disorder marked by antisocial behavior. —**so′ci·o·path′ic** *adj.*

sock¹ (sŏk) ▸*n., pl.* **socks** or **sox** (sŏks) A short stocking. [< Lat. *soccus*, a kind of shoe.]

sock² (sŏk) ▸*v.* To hit forcefully. [?] —**sock** *n.*

sock·et (sŏk′ĭt) ▸*n.* An opening or cavity into which something fits. [< AN *soc*, plowshare.]

socket wrench ▸*n.* A wrench with a usu. interchangeable socket to fit over a nut or bolt.

Soc·ra·tes (sŏk′rə-tēz′) 470?–399 BC. Greek philosopher.

So·crat·ic (sə-krăt′ĭk, sō-) ▸*adj.* Of Socrates or his method of philosophical questioning.

sod (sŏd) ▸*n.* Grass-covered surface soil held together by matted roots. ▸*v.* **sod·ded, sod·ding** To cover with sod. [< MLGer. *sode.*]

so·da (sō′də) ▸*n.* **1a.** Any of various forms of sodium carbonate. **b.** Chemically combined sodium. **2a.** Carbonated water. **b.** *Regional* See **soft drink. 3.** A drink made from carbonated water, ice cream, and usu. flavoring. [< OItal.]

soda fountain ▸*n.* **1.** An apparatus for dispensing soda water. **2.** A counter where soft drinks, ice-cream dishes, or sandwiches are served.

soda pop ▸*n.* See **soft drink.**

soda water ▸*n.* **1a.** Carbonated water. **b.** See **soft drink. 2.** A solution of water, baking soda, and acid.

sod·den (sŏd′n) ▸*adj.* **1.** Thoroughly soaked; saturated. **2.** Soggy and heavy. **3.** Stupid or dull, esp. from drink. [ME *soden*, p.part. of *sethen*, to boil.] —**sod′den·ly** *adv.* —**sod′den·ness** *n.*

so·di·um (sō′dē-əm) ▸*n. Symbol* **Na** A soft, light, extremely malleable metallic element that

is naturally abundant in various compounds, esp. in common salt. At. no. 11. See table at **element.** [SOD(A) + –IUM.]

sodium bicarbonate ▸*n.* Baking soda.

sodium chloride ▸*n.* A colorless or white crystalline compound, NaCl, used in the manufacture of chemicals and as a food preservative and seasoning.

sodium hydroxide ▸*n.* A white deliquescent solid, NaOH, used in chemicals and soaps and in petroleum refining; lye.

sodium nitrate ▸*n.* A white crystalline compound, NaNO₃, used in fertilizers, solid rocket propellants, and glass.

Sod·om (sŏd′əm) A city of ancient Palestine.

sod·om·y (sŏd′ə-mē) ▸*n.* Any of various forms of sexual acts regarded as perverted, esp. anal intercourse, oral-anal contact, or sexual intercourse with an animal. [< SODOM.] —**sod′o·mize′** (-mīz′) *v.*

so·fa (sō′fə) ▸*n.* A long upholstered seat usu. with a back and arms. [< Ar. *ṣuffa*, divan.]

So·fi·a (sō′fē-ə, sō-fē′ə) The capital of Bulgaria, in the W-central part.

soft (sôft, sŏft) ▸*adj.* **-er, -est 1.** Yielding readily to pressure or weight: *a soft melon.* **2.** Out of condition; flabby: *got soft sitting at a desk all day.* **3.** Smooth or fine to the touch. **4a.** Not loud, harsh, or irritating. **b.** Not brilliant or glaring; subdued. **5.** Mild; balmy: *a soft breeze.* **6a.** Tender or affectionate. **b.** Not stern; lenient. **7.** *Informal* Simple; feeble. **8.** *Informal* Easy: *a soft job.* **9.** Having low dissolved mineral content: *soft water.* ▸*adv.* In a soft manner; gently. [< OE *sôfte*, pleasant.] —**soft′en** *v.* —**soft′en·er** *n.* —**soft′ly** *adv.* —**soft′ness** *n.*

soft·ball (sôft′bôl′, sŏft′-) ▸*n. Sports* **1.** A variation of baseball played with a larger, softer ball. **2.** The ball used in this game.

soft-boiled (sôft′boild′, sŏft′-) ▸*adj.* Boiled in the shell to a soft consistency. Used of an egg.

soft coal ▸*n.* See **bituminous coal.**

softcore or **soft-core** (sôft′kôr′, sŏft′-) ▸*adj.* Being less explicit than hard-core material in depicting or describing sexual activity.

soft drink ▸*n.* A nonalcoholic, flavored, carbonated beverage.

soft·heart·ed (sôft′här′tĭd, sŏft′-) ▸*adj.* Easily moved; tender; merciful. —**soft′heart′ed·ly** *adv.* —**soft′heart′ed·ness** *n.*

soft landing ▸*n.* The landing of a space vehicle in such a way as to prevent damage.

soft palate ▸*n.* The movable fold that hangs from the rear of the hard palate and closes off the nasal cavity from the oral cavity during swallowing.

soft-ped·al (sôft′pĕd′l, sŏft′-) ▸*v. Informal* To make less emphatic or obvious.

soft sell ▸*n. Informal* A restrained or relaxed method of selling or promotion.

soft-shell clam (sôft′shĕl′, sŏft′-) ▸*n.* An edible clam having a thin elongated shell.

soft soap ▸*n. Informal* Flattery; cajolery. —**soft′-soap′** *v.*

soft·ware (sôft′wâr′, sŏft′-) ▸*n. Comp.* The programs, routines, and symbolic languages that control the functioning of the hardware and direct its operation.

soft·wood (sôft′wŏŏd′, sŏft′-) ▸*n.* A coniferous tree or its wood.

soft·y or **soft·ie** (sôf′tē, sŏf′-) ▸*n., pl.* **-ies**

Informal One who is overly sentimental, trusting, or lenient.

sog·gy (sŏg′ē, sô′gē) ►*adj.* **-gi·er, -gi·est** Saturated with moisture; soaked. [< dial. *sog*, be soaked.] —**sog′gi·ly** *adv.* —**sog′gi·ness** *n.*

soil¹ (soil) ►*n.* **1.** The top layer of the earth's surface in which plants can grow. **2.** A particular kind of earth or ground. **3.** Country; land: *one's native soil.* [< Lat. *solium*, seat.]

soil² (soil) ►*v.* **1.** To make or become dirty. **2.** To disgrace; tarnish. **3.** To corrupt; defile. ►*n.* **1a.** The state of being soiled. **b.** A stain. **2.** Manure, esp. human excrement, used as fertilizer. [< OFr. *souiller.*]

soi·ree also **soi·rée** (swä-rā′) ►*n.* An evening party or reception. [< OFr. *seir*, evening.]

so·journ (sō′jûrn′, sō-jûrn′) ►*v.* To stay for a time. ►*n.* A temporary stay. [< VLat. **subdiurnāre.*] —**so′journ′er** *n.*

sol¹ (sōl) also **so** (sō) ►*n. Mus.* The 5th tone of the diatonic scale. [< Med.Lat.]

sol² (sōl) ►*n., pl.* **so·les** (sō′lĕs) See table at **currency.** [Fr.]

sol·ace (sŏl′ĭs) ►*n.* **1.** Comfort in sorrow or distress; consolation. **2.** A source of comfort or consolation. ►*v.* **-aced, -ac·ing** To comfort or console in time of trouble. See Synonyms at **comfort.** [< Lat. *sōlācium* < *sōlārī*, console.]

so·lar (sō′lər) ►*adj.* **1.** Of or proceeding from the sun: *solar rays.* **2.** Powered by the energy of sunlight. **3.** Measured in reference to the sun: *a solar year.* [< Lat. *sōl*, sun.]

solar battery ►*n.* An electric battery consisting of a number of connected solar cells.

solar cell ►*n.* A photoelectric semiconductor device that converts solar energy into electric energy.

solar flare ►*n.* A sudden eruption of magnetic energy released on or near the sun's surface, usu. accompanied by bursts of electromagnetic radiation and particles.

so·lar·i·um (sō-lâr′ē-əm, sə-) ►*n., pl.* **-i·a** (-ē-ə) or **-i·ums** A room or glassed-in porch exposed to the sun. [Lat. *sōlārium.*]

solar plexus ►*n.* **1.** The large network of nerves located behind the stomach. **2.** The pit of the stomach.

solar system ►*n.* The sun together with the eight planets and all other celestial bodies that orbit the sun.

solar wind (wĭnd) ►*n.* The stream of charged atomic particles that radiates from the sun.

sold (sōld) ►*v.* P.t. and p.part. of **sell.**

sol·der (sŏd′ər) ►*n.* **1.** Any of various alloys, usu. tin and lead, that can be fused with other metals and are used to join metallic parts. **2.** Something that joins or cements. [< Lat. *solidāre*, make solid.] —**sol′der** *v.*

sol·dier (sōl′jər) ►*n.* **1.** One who serves in an army. **2.** An enlisted person or a noncommissioned officer. **3.** An active follower. ►*v.* To be or serve as a soldier. [< AN *soldeier* < OFr. *sol*, pay.] —**sol′dier·ly** *adj.*

soldier of fortune ►*n.* One who will serve in any army for pay or love of adventure.

sol·dier·y (sōl′jə-rē) ►*n.* **1.** Soldiers collectively. **2.** The profession of soldiering.

sole¹ (sōl) ►*n.* **1.** The underside of the foot. **2.** The underside of a shoe or boot. ►*v.* **soled, sol·ing** To furnish (a shoe or boot) with a sole. [< Lat. *solea*, sandal.]

sole² (sōl) ►*adj.* Being the only one; single. [< Lat. *sōlus.*] —**sole′ly** *adv.*

sole³ (sōl) ►*n., pl.* **sole** or **soles** Any of various chiefly marine flatfishes having both eyes on the right side of the body. [< Lat. *solea*, sandal, flatfish.]

sol·e·cism (sŏl′ĭ-sĭz′əm, sō′lĭ-) ►*n.* **1.** A nonstandard usage or grammatical construction. **2.** A violation of etiquette. [< Gk. *soloikos*, speaking incorrectly.]

sol·emn (sŏl′əm) ►*adj.* **1.** Deeply earnest; grave. **2.** Performed with full ceremony. **3.** Gloomy; somber. [< Lat. *sollemnis*, customary.] —**so·lem′ni·ty** (sə-lĕm′nĭ-tē) *n.* —**sol′emn·ly** *adv.*

sol·em·nize (sŏl′əm-nīz′) ►*v.* **-nized, -niz·ing** **1.** To celebrate or observe with dignity and gravity. **2.** To perform (e.g., a marriage) with formal ceremony. —**sol′em·ni·za′tion** *n.*

so·le·noid (sō′lə-noid′) ►*n.* A coil of wire that acts like a magnet when a current passes through it. [< Gk. *sōlēnoeidēs*, pipe-shaped.]

so·lic·it (sə-lĭs′ĭt) ►*v.* **1.** To seek to obtain: *solicit votes.* **2.** To petition persistently; entreat. **3.** To entice or tempt. [< Lat. *sollicitāre*, to trouble.] —**so·lic′i·ta′tion** *n.*

so·lic·i·tor (sə-lĭs′ĭ-tər) ►*n.* **1.** One who solicits. **2.** An attorney holding a public office that handles cases involving a city, state, or other jurisdiction. **3.** *Chiefly Brit.* An attorney who is not a member of the bar and who may be heard only in the lower courts.

so·lic·i·tous (sə-lĭs′ĭ-təs) ►*adj.* Showing great attention or concern to another. [< Lat. *sollicitus.*] —**so·lic′i·tous·ly** *adv.* —**so·lic′i·tous·ness** *n.*

so·lic·i·tude (sə-lĭs′ĭ-tōōd′, -tyōōd′) ►*n.* The state of being solicitous.

sol·id (sŏl′ĭd) ►*adj.* **-er, -est** **1a.** Of definite shape and volume; not liquid or gaseous: *It was so cold the water in the bucket became solid.* **b.** Of three-dimensional geometric figures or bodies. **c.** Firm or compact in substance: *The floor was solid and would not give way.* **2.** Not hollowed out. **3.** Being the same substance or color throughout. **4.** Of good quality and substance. **5.** Sound; reliable. **6.** Financially sound. **7.** Upstanding and dependable. ►*n.* **1.** A solid substance. **2.** A geometric figure having three dimensions. [< Lat. *solidus.*] —**so·lid′i·ty** (sə-lĭd′ĭ-tē), **sol′id·ness** *n.* —**sol′id·ly** *adv.*

sol·i·dar·i·ty (sŏl′ĭ-dăr′ĭ-tē) ►*n.* Unity of interest or sympathy.

so·lid·i·fy (sə-lĭd′ə-fī′) ►*v.* **-fied, -fy·ing** To make or become solid or united. —**so·lid′i·fi·ca′tion** *n.*

sol·id-state (sŏl′ĭd-stāt′) ►*adj.* Based on or consisting of semiconducting materials.

so·lil·o·quy (sə-lĭl′ə-kwē) ►*n., pl.* **-quies** **1.** A dramatic discourse in which a character reveals his or her thoughts when alone or unaware of the presence of other characters. **2.** The act of speaking to oneself. [LLat. *sōliloquium.*] —**so·lil′o·quize′** *v.*

sol·ip·sism (sŏl′ĭp-sĭz′əm, sō′lĭp-) ►*n.* The view that the self is the only reality. [Lat. *sōlus*, alone + *ipse*, self + -ISM.] —**sol′ip·sist** *n.* —**sol′ip·sis′tic** *adj.*

sol·i·taire (sŏl′ĭ-târ′) ►*n.* **1.** A gemstone set alone, as in a ring. **2.** A card game played by one person. [Fr., SOLITARY.]

sol·i·tar·y (sŏl′ĭ-tĕr′ē) ►*adj.* **1.** Existing or living alone. **2.** Happening or done alone. **3.** Remote or secluded. **4.** Single; sole. [< Lat. *sōlitās,* solitude.] —**sol′i·tar′i·ly** (-târ′ə-lē) *adv.* —**sol′i·tar′i·ness** *n.*

sol·i·tude (sŏl′ĭ-tōōd′, -tyōōd′) ►*n.* **1.** The state of being alone; isolation: *Composers need solitude to work.* **2.** The state of being secluded or uninhabited: *sought out the solitude of the forest.* [< Lat. *sōlus,* alone.]

so·lo (sō′lō) ►*n., pl.* **-los 1.** *Mus.* A composition for an individual voice or instrument, with or without accompaniment. **2.** A performance or accomplishment by a single individual. ►*v.* To perform a solo. [Ital.] —**so′lo** *adj. & adv.* —**so′lo·ist** *n.*

Sol·o·mon (sŏl′ə-mən) fl. 10th cent. BC. King of Israel famous for his wisdom.

Solomon Islands 1. An island group of the W Pacific E of New Guinea divided between Papua New Guinea and the independent Solomon Is. **2.** A country comprising the Solomon Is. SE of Bougainville. Cap. Honiara.

So·lon (sō′lən, -lŏn′) 638?–559? BC. Athenian lawgiver and poet.

sol·stice (sŏl′stĭs, sōl′-, sôl′-) ►*n.* Either of two times of the year when the sun reaches an extreme of its northward or southward motion. [< Lat. *sōlstitium : sōl,* sun + *-stitium,* stoppage.] —**sol·sti′tial** (-stĭsh′əl) *adj.*

sol·u·ble (sŏl′yə-bəl) ►*adj.* **1.** Capable of being dissolved. **2.** Possible to solve or explain. [< Lat. *solvere,* loosen.] —**sol′u·bil′i·ty** *n.* —**sol′u·bly** *adv.*

sol·ute (sŏl′yōōt, sōl′ōōt) ►*n.* A substance dissolved in another substance. ►*adj.* Being in solution; dissolved. [< Lat. *solūtus,* p.part. of *solvere,* loosen.]

so·lu·tion (sə-lōō′shən) ►*n.* **1a.** A method or process of dealing with a problem: *sought a solution to falling enrollments.* **b.** The answer to a problem or the explanation for something: *the solution to the mystery.* **2a.** A homogeneous mixture of two or more substances. **b.** The process of forming such a mixture.

solve (sŏlv, sôlv) ►*v.* **solved, solv·ing** To find a solution to. [< Lat. *solvere,* loosen.] —**solv′a·ble** *adj.* —**solv′er** *n.*

sol·vent (sŏl′vənt, sôl′-) ►*adj.* **1.** Able to meet financial obligations. **2.** Capable of dissolving another substance. ►*n.* A substance, usu. a liquid, capable of dissolving another substance. [< Lat. *solvere,* loosen.] —**sol′ven·cy** *n.*

Sol·zhe·ni·tsyn (sōl′zhə-nēt′sĭn), **Aleksandr Isayevich** 1918–2008. Soviet writer and dissident.

som (sŏm) ►*n., pl.* **som** See table at **currency.** [Kyrgyz.]

So·ma·li (sō-mä′lē) ►*n., pl.* **-li** or **-lis 1.** A native or inhabitant of Somalia. **2.** The Cushitic language of Somalia. —**So·ma′li** *adj.*

So·ma·li·a (sō-mä′lē-ə, -mäl′yə) A country of extreme E Africa on the Gulf of Aden and the Indian Ocean. Cap. Mogadishu. —**So·ma′li·an** *adj. & n.*

So·ma·li·land (sō-mä′lē-lănd′, sə-) A region of E Africa comprising present-day Somalia, Djibouti, and SE Ethiopia.

so·mat·ic (sō-măt′ĭk) ►*adj.* Of the body, esp. as distinguished from a body part, the mind, or the environment; physical. See Synonyms at **bodily.** [< Gk. *sōma,* body.]

somatic cell ►*n.* Any cell of a multicellular organism other than a germ cell.

som·ber (sŏm′bər) ►*adj.* **1.** Dark; gloomy: *a somber room.* **2a.** Melancholy; dismal: *a somber mood.* **b.** Serious; grave: *a somber spokesperson.* [< LLat. *subumbrāre,* cast a shadow.] —**som′ber·ly** *adv.*

som·bre (sŏm′bər) ►*adj. Chiefly Brit.* Var. of **somber.**

som·bre·ro (sŏm-brâr′ō, səm-) ►*n., pl.* **-ros** A large, broad-brimmed hat. [Sp.]

sombrero

some (sŭm) ►*adj.* **1.** Being an unspecified number or quantity: *some people; some sugar.* **2.** Unknown or unspecified by name: *Some man called.* **3.** *Informal* Remarkable: *She is some skier.* ►*pron.* An indefinite or unspecified number or portion. See Usage Note at **every.** ►*adv.* **1.** Approximately; about. **2.** *Informal* Somewhat. [< OE *sum,* a certain one.]

–some[1] ►*suff.* Characterized by a specified quality, condition, or action: *loathsome.* [< OE *-sum.*]

–some[2] ►*suff.* A group of a specified number of members: *threesome.* [< OE *sum,* some.]

–some[3] ►*suff.* Body: *centrosome.* [< Gk. *sōma.*]

some·bod·y (sŭm′bŏd′ē, -bŭd′ē, -bə-dē) ►*pron.* An unspecified or unknown person. ►*n. Informal* A person of importance.

some·day (sŭm′dā′) ►*adv.* At an indefinite time in the future.

   Usage: Someday (adverb) and *sometime* express future time indefinitely. This sense can also be conveyed by *some day* and *some time.* The two-word forms are always used when *some* is an adjective modifying and specifying a more particular day or time: *Come some day* (not *someday*) *soon.*

some·how (sŭm′hou′) ►*adv.* In a way not specified, understood, or known.

some·one (sŭm′wŭn′, -wən) ►*pron.* An unspecified or unknown person; somebody. ►*n. Informal* A somebody.

some·place (sŭm′plās′) ►*adv. & n.* Somewhere.

som·er·sault (sŭm′ər-sôlt′) ►*n.* An acrobatic stunt in which the body rolls in a complete circle, heels over head. [< OFr. *sobresault.*] —**som′er·sault′** *v.*

some·thing (sŭm′thĭng) ►*pron.* An undetermined or unspecified thing. ►*n.* A remarkable or important thing or person. ►*adv.* Somewhat.

—idiom: something else *Informal* One that is special or remarkable.

some·time (sŭm′tīm′) ►*adv.* **1.** At an indefinite or unstated time. **2.** At an indefinite time in the future. See Usage Note at **someday.** ►*adj.* Former.

some·times (sŭm′tīmz′) ►*adv.* Now and then.

some·way (sŭm′wā′) also **some·ways** (-wāz′) ►*adv.* In some way or another.

some·what (sŭm′wŏt′, -hwŏt′, -wŭt′, -hwŭt′) ►*adv.* To some extent or degree. ►*pron.* Something: *The news was somewhat of a surprise.*

some·where (sŭm′wâr′, -hwâr′) ►*adv.* **1.** At, in, or to a place not specified or known. **2.** To a place or state of further development or progress. ►*n.* An unspecified place.

Somme (sŏm, sôm) A river, about 245 km (150 mi) of N France flowing to the English Channel.

som·me·lier (sŭm′əl-yā′, sô′mə-lyā′) ►*n.* A restaurant employee who orders and maintains the wines sold in the restaurant. [Fr.]

som·nam·bu·late (sŏm-năm′byə-lāt′) ►*v.* **-lat·ed, -lat·ing** To walk while asleep. [Lat. *somnus,* sleep + *ambulāre,* walk.]

som·nam·bu·lism (sŏm-năm′byə-lĭz′əm) ►*n.* See **sleepwalking. —som·nam′bu·list** *n.*

som·no·lent (sŏm′nə-lənt) ►*adj.* Drowsy; sleepy. [< Lat. *somnolentus < somnus,* sleep.] **—som′no·lence** *n.* **—som′no·lent·ly** *adv.*

so·mo·ni (so′mo-ne′) ►*n., pl.* **-ni** or **-nis** See table at **currency.** [Tajik.]

son (sŭn) ►*n.* **1.** One's male child. **2.** A man considered as if in a relationship of child to parent: *a son of the soil.* [< OE *sunu.*] **—son′ly** *adj.*

so·nar (sō′när′) ►*n.* A system or apparatus using transmitted and reflected sound waves to detect and locate underwater objects. [*so(und) na(vigation and) r(anging).*]

so·na·ta (sə-nä′tə) ►*n. Mus.* A composition for one or more solo instruments, usu. written in three or four movements. [Ital.]

song (sông, sŏng) ►*n.* **1a.** A brief composition written for singing. **b.** The act or art of singing: *broke into song.* **2.** A melodious utterance, as of a bird. **3a.** Poetry. **b.** A lyric poem. **—idiom: for a song** *Informal* At a low price. [< OE *sang.*]

song·bird (sông′bûrd′, sŏng′-) ►*n.* **1.** A bird having a melodious song or call. **2.** Any of various birds with the ability to learn and produce complicated songs.

Song of Solomon ►*n.* Song of Songs.

Song of Songs ►*n.* See table at **Bible.**

song·ster (sông′stər, sŏng′-) ►*n.* **1.** One who sings. **2.** See **songwriter.**

song·writ·er (sông′rī′tər, sŏng′-) ►*n.* One who writes song lyrics or tunes.

son·ic (sŏn′ĭk) ►*adj.* Of or relating to sound or its speed in air. [< Lat. *sonus,* sound.]

sonic barrier ►*n.* The sudden sharp increase in aerodynamic drag experienced by aircraft approaching the speed of sound.

sonic boom ►*n.* An explosive sound caused by the shock wave preceding an aircraft traveling at a supersonic speed.

son-in-law (sŭn′ĭn-lô′) ►*n., pl.* **sons-in-law** (sŭnz′-) The husband of one's child.

son·net (sŏn′ĭt) ►*n.* A rhymed 14-line poem, usu. in iambic pentameter. [< OProv. *sonet.*]

son·o·gram (sŏn′ə-grăm′, sō′nə-) ►*n.* An image, as of an unborn fetus or an internal body organ, produced by ultrasonography.

son·o·rous (sŏn′ər-əs, sə-nôr′-) ►*adj.* **1.** Having or producing sound. **2.** Having or producing a full, deep, or rich sound. **3.** Impressive in style of speech. [< Lat. *sonor,* sound.] **—so·nor′i·ty** (sə-nôr′ĭ-tē, -nôr′-) *n.* **—son′o·rous·ly** *adv.*

soon (soon) ►*adv.* **-er, -est 1.** In the near future: *The bus should be here soon.* **2.** Within a short time; quickly: *Come as soon as you can.* **3.** Willingly; gladly: *I'd as soon leave right now.* **—idiom: sooner or later** Eventually. [< OE *sōna,* immediately.]

Usage: No sooner, as a comparative adverb, should be followed by *than,* not *when,* as in: *No sooner had she left than he called.*

soot (soot, soot) ►*n.* The fine black particles, chiefly carbon, produced by incomplete combustion of coal, oil, wood, or other fuel. [< OE *sōt.*] **—soot′i·ness** *n.* **—soot′y** *adj.*

sooth (sooth) ►*n. Archaic* Truth; reality. [< OE *sōth.*]

soothe (sooth) ►*v.* **soothed, sooth·ing 1.** To calm or quiet (e.g., a person). **2.** To ease or relieve the pain of. [< OE *sōthian,* verify.] **—sooth′er** *n.* **—sooth′ing·ly** *adv.*

sooth·say·er (sooth′sā′ər) ►*n.* One who foretells events; seer.

sop (sŏp) ►*v.* **sopped, sop·ping 1.** To dip, soak, or drench in a liquid. **2.** To take up by absorption. ►*n.* Something yielded to placate or soothe; bribe. [< OE *sopp,* bread dipped in liquid.] **—sop′py** *adj.*

SOP ►*abbr.* standard operating procedure

soph. ►*abbr.* sophomore

soph·ism (sŏf′ĭz′əm) ►*n.* **1.** A plausible but fallacious argument. **2.** Deceptive or fallacious argumentation. [< Gk. *sophos,* clever.] **—soph′ist** *n.* **—so·phis′tic, so·phis′ti·cal** *adj.* **—so·phis′ti·cal·ly** *adv.*

so·phis·ti·cate (sə-fĭs′tĭ-kāt′) ►*v.* **-cat·ed, -cat·ing 1.** To cause to become less naive and more worldly: *Travel tends to sophisticate a person.* **2.** To refine: *sophisticated the theory to take criticism into account.* ►*n.* (-kĭt) A sophisticated person. **—so·phis′ti·ca′tion** *n.*

so·phis·ti·cat·ed (sə-fĭs′tĭ-kā′tĭd) ►*adj.* **1.** Having or showing much worldly knowledge or cultural refinement. **2.** Very complex or complicated. **3.** Appealing to refined tastes.

soph·is·try (sŏf′ĭ-strē) ►*n., pl.* **-tries** Plausible but faulty or misleading argumentation.

Soph·o·cles (sŏf′ə-klēz′) 496?–406 BC. Greek dramatist. **—Soph′o·cle′an** *adj.*

soph·o·more (sŏf′ə-môr′, sŏf′môr′) ►*n.* A second-year student in a US high school or college. [< obsolete *sophom,* sophism.]

soph·o·mor·ic (sŏf′ə-môr′ĭk, -môr′-) ►*adj.* **1.** Of or like a sophomore. **2.** Exhibiting immaturity and lack of judgment.

sop·o·rif·ic (sŏp′ə-rĭf′ĭk, sō′pə-) ►*adj.* **1.** Inducing sleep. **2.** Drowsy. ►*n.* A drug that induces sleep. [< Lat. *sopor,* sleep.]

so·pran·o (sə-prăn′ō, -prä′nō) ►*n., pl.* **-os 1.** The highest singing voice of a woman or young boy. **2.** The tonal range characteristic of a soprano. **3.** A singer, voice, or instrument having this range. [Ital. < Lat. *suprā,* above.]

sor·bet (sôr′bĭt, sôr-bā′) ►*n.* A frozen dessert made primarily of fruit juice or fruit purée, sugar, and water. [French < Turk. *şerbet,* sweet fruit drink < Ar. *šarba.*]

sor·bi·tol (sôr′bĭ-tôl′, -tōl′, -tŏl′) ►*n.* A white sweetish crystalline alcohol found in fruits, used esp. as a sugar substitute. [*sorb,* rowan + −IT(E)² + −OL.]

sor·cer·y (sôr′sə-rē) ►*n.* Use of supernatural power over others through the assistance of spirits. [< Lat. *sors,* lot.] **—sor′cer·er** *n.* **—sor′cer·ess** *n.*

sor·did (sôr′dĭd) ►*adj.* **1.** Morally degraded; base. **2.** Filthy; foul. **3.** Depressingly squalid; wretched. [< Lat. *sordēre,* be dirty.] **—sor′did·ly** *adv.* **—sor′did·ness** *n.*

sore (sôr) ►*adj.* **sor·er, sor·est 1.** Painful or tender. **2.** Feeling pain; hurting. **3.** Causing sorrow or distress; grievous. **4.** *Informal* Angry; offended. ►*n.* **1.** An open skin lesion, wound, or ulcer. **2.** A source of pain or distress. [< OE *sār.*] **—sore′ly** *adv.* **—sore′ness** *n.*

sor·ghum (sôr′gəm) ►*n.* A cultivated grass native to sub-Saharan Africa, several varieties of which are widely grown for their grain, as forage, or as a source of syrup. [< Ital. *sorgo.*]

so·ror·i·ty (sə-rôr′ĭ-tē) ►*n., pl.* **-ties 1.** A chiefly social organization of women college students. **2.** An association or society of women. [< Lat. *soror,* sister.]

sor·rel¹ (sôr′əl, sŏr′-) ►*n.* Any of several plants with sour leaves. [< OFr. *sur,* sour.]

sor·rel² (sôr′əl, sŏr′-) ►*n.* **1.** A brownish orange to light brown. **2.** A sorrel-colored horse. [< OFr. *sor,* red-brown.]

sor·row (sôr′ō, sŏr′ō) ►*n.* **1.** Mental suffering caused by loss or misfortune, or an instance of this: *tried to assuage her sorrows.* **2.** Something causing sadness or grief. ►*v.* To feel or express sorrow. See Synonyms at **grieve.** [< OE *sorg.*] **—sor′row·ful** *adj.* **—sor′row·ful·ly** *adv.*

sor·ry (sôr′ē, sŏr′ē) ►*adj.* **-ri·er, -ri·est 1a.** Feeling or expressing sorrow. **b.** Feeling or expressing sympathy or pity. **c.** Feeling or expressing regret. **2.** Poor or wretched: *a sorry excuse.* **3.** Grievous or sad. [< OE *sār,* sore.]

sort (sôrt) ►*n.* **1.** A group of similar persons or things; kind. **2.** Type, character, or quality. **3.** *Comp.* An operation that arranges data in a specified way. ►*v.* **1.** To arrange according to class, kind, or size. See Synonyms at **arrange. 2.** To make a search or examination of a collection of things: *sorted through the laundry.* **—phrasal verb: sort out 1.** To separate from others. **2.** To clarify or resolve. **3.** To bring to health or good condition. **4.** To reprimand for a mistake or offense. **—idioms: out of sorts 1.** Slightly ill. **2.** Irritable or cross. **sort of** *Informal* Somewhat. [< Lat. *sors,* lot.]

sor·tie (sôr′tē, sôr-tē′) ►*n.* **1.** An armed attack made from a place surrounded by enemy forces. **2.** A flight of a combat aircraft on a mission. [Fr. < OFr. *sortir,* go out.]

SOS (ĕs′ō-ĕs′) ►*n.* A call or signal for help or rescue. [From the international radiotelegraphic distress signal.]

so-so (sō′sō′) ►*adj.* Mediocre. **—so′-so′** *adv.*

sot (sŏt) ►*n.* A drunkard. [< OFr. *fool.*] **—sot′tish** *adj.* **—sot′tish·ly** *adv.*

sou·brette (soo-brĕt′) ►*n.* A saucy maid in comic drama or opera. [< Prov. *soubret,* conceited < *super,* above.]

souf·flé (soo-flā′) ►*n.* A light fluffy baked dish

made with egg yolks and beaten egg whites. [< Lat. *sufflāre,* puff up.]

soufflé

sough (sŭf, sou) ►*v.* To make a soft murmuring sound. [< OE *swōgan.*] **—sough** *n.*

sought (sôt) ►*v.* P.t. and p.part. of **seek.**

soul (sōl) ►*n.* **1a.** A part of humans regarded as immaterial, immortal, separable from the body at death, capable of moral judgment, and susceptible to happiness or misery in a future state. **b.** The part of a human when disembodied after death. **2a.** A human. **b.** A person considered as the perfect embodiment of an intangible quality: *the very soul of discretion.* **c.** A person's emotional or moral nature. **3.** The central or vital part of something. **4.** A sense of emotional strength or spiritual vitality held to derive from black and esp. African-American cultural experience. **5.** A strong, deeply felt emotion conveyed by a speaker, performer, or artist. **6.** A style of popular music developed by African Americans, combining elements of gospel music and rhythm and blues. [< OE *sāwol.*]

soul·ful (sōl′fəl) ►*adj.* Filled with or expressing deep feeling. **—soul′ful·ly** *adv.*

sound¹ (sound) ►*n.* **1a.** A vibratory disturbance, with frequencies between about 20 and 20,000 hertz, capable of being heard. **b.** The sensation stimulated in the ears by such a disturbance. **c.** Such sensations collectively. **2.** A distinctive noise. **3.** *Ling.* An articulation made by the vocal apparatus. **4.** A conveyed impression; implication. **5.** Auditory material that is recorded, as for a movie. ►*v.* **1.** To make or cause to make a sound. **2.** To convey an impression: *sounds reasonable.* **3.** *Med.* To examine by auscultation. [< Lat. *sonus.*] **—sound′er** *n.* **—sound′less** *adj.* **—sound′less·ly** *adv.*

sound² (sound) ►*adj.* **-er, -est 1.** Free from defect or damage. **2.** Based on valid reasoning. **3a.** Solid. **b.** Financially secure or safe. **4.** Thorough; complete: *a sound thrashing.* **5.** Deep and undisturbed: *a sound sleep.* [< OE *gesund.*] **—sound′ly** *adv.* **—sound′ness** *n.*

sound³ (sound) ►*n.* A long body of water, wider than a strait, usu. connecting larger bodies of water. [< OE *sund,* sea.]

sound⁴ (sound) ►*v.* **1.** To measure the depth of (water). **2.** To try to learn the attitudes or opinions of. **3.** To dive swiftly downward, as a whale. [< OFr. *sonde,* sounding line.] **—sound′er** *n.* **—sound′ing** *n.*

sound barrier ►*n.* See **sonic barrier.**

sound box ►*n.* *Mus.* A hollow chamber, as of a violin or guitar, that intensifies resonance.

sound effect ►*n.* An imitative sound, as of thunder, produced for film, stage, or radio.

sound·ing board (soun′dĭng) ►*n*. **1.** A thin board forming the upper portion of the resonant chamber in an instrument, such as a violin or piano. **2.** A structure placed so as to amplify a speaker's voice. **3.** A means serving to spread or popularize opinions.

sound·proof (sound′proōf′) ►*adj*. Not penetrable by audible sound. **—sound′proof′** *v*.

sound·track (sound′trăk′) ►*n*. **1.** The audio portion of a film or video recording. **2.** A recording of the music from a movie.

soup (soōp) ►*n*. **1.** A liquid food prepared from meat, fish, or vegetable stock with other ingredients. **2.** Dense fog. **—phrasal verb: soup up** *Slang* To modify so as to enhance power or performance. [< OFr. *soupe*, of Gmc. orig.]

soup·çon (soōp-sôN′, soōp′sŏn′) ►*n*. A very small amount; trace. [< OFr. *sospeçon*, SUS-PICION.]

soup kitchen ►*n*. A place where food is offered to the needy.

soup·y (soō′pē) ►*adj*. **-i·er, -i·est** **1.** Having the appearance or consistency of soup. **2.** *Slang* Foggy.

sour (sour) ►*adj*. **-er, -est** **1.** Having a sharp or acid taste. **2.** Spoiled or rancid. **3a.** Bad-tempered. **b.** Displeased, disagreeable, or disenchanted. ►*v*. To make or become sour. [< OE *sūr*.] **—sour′ish** *adj*. **—sour′ly** *adv*. **—sour′ness** *n*.
  Syns: acerbic, acid, tart adj.

sour·ball (sour′bôl′) ►*n*. A round piece of hard tart candy.

source (sôrs) ►*n*. **1.** A point of origin. **2.** The beginning of a stream of water, such as a spring or river. **3.** One that supplies information. [< OFr. *sourse* < *sourdre*, rise; see SURGE.]

sour cream ►*n*. Cream soured and thickened with bacteria that produce lactic acid, used in cooking.

sour·dough (sour′dō′) ►*n*. **1.** Sour fermented dough used as leaven in making bread. **2.** Bread made from such a leaven.

sour·sop (sour′sŏp′) ►*n*. A tropical American tree widely cultivated for its spiny tart fruit.

souse (sous) ►*v*. **soused, sous·ing** **1.** To plunge into a liquid. **2.** To drench or become drenched. **3.** To steep. **4.** *Slang* To make intoxicated. ►*n*. **1.** The act or process of sousing. **2a.** Food steeped in pickle, esp. pork trimmings. **b.** Brine. **3.** *Slang* A drunkard. [< OFr. *sous*, pickled meat, of Gmc. orig.]

south (south) ►*n*. **1a.** The direction along a meridian 90° clockwise from east. **b.** The compass point 180° clockwise from north. **2.** often **South a.** The southern part of the earth. **b.** The southern part of a region or country. ►*adj*. **1.** To, toward, of, or in the south. **2.** Coming from the south: *a south wind.* ►*adv*. In, from, or toward the south. [< OE *sūth*.] **—south′ward** (south′wərd, sŭth′ərd) *adj. & adv.* **—south′-ward·ly** *adj. & adv.* **—south′wards** *adv.*

South Africa A country of S Africa on the Atlantic and Indian Oceans. Caps. Pretoria, Cape Town, and Bloemfontein. **—South African** *adj. & n.*

South America A continent of the S Western Hemisphere SE of North America between the Atlantic and Pacific Oceans. **—South American** *adj. & n.*

South Asia A region of southern Asia consist-ing of Bangladesh, Bhutan, India, the Maldives, Nepal, Pakistan, and Sri Lanka. **—South Asian** *adj. & n.*

South Car·o·li·na (kăr′ə-lī′nə) A state of the SE US bordering on the Atlantic. Cap. Columbia. **—South Car′o·lin′i·an** (-lĭn′ē-ən) *adj. & n.*

South China Sea An arm of the W Pacific bounded by SE China, Taiwan, the Philippines, Borneo, and Vietnam.

South Dakota A state of the N-central US. Cap. Pierre. **—South Dakotan** *adj. & n.*

south·east (south-ēst′, sou-ēst′) ►*n*. **1.** The direction halfway between due south and due east. **2.** An area or region lying in the southeast. **—south·east′** *adj. & adv.* **—south·east′er·ly** *adj. & adv.* **—south·east′ern** *adj.* **—south·east′ward** *adv. & adj.* **—south·east′ward·ly** *adv. & adj.* **—south·east′wards** *adv.*

Southeast Asia A region of Asia including Indochina, the Malay Peninsula, and the Malay Archipelago. **—Southeast Asian** *adj. & n.*

south·east·er (south-ē′stər, sou-ē′-) ►*n*. A storm or gale blowing from the southeast.

south·east·er·ly (south-ē′stər-lē, sou-ē′-) ►*adj*. **1.** Situated toward the southeast. **2.** Coming or being from the southeast. **—south·east′-er·ly** *adv.*

south·er·ly (sŭth′ər-lē) ►*adj*. **1.** In or toward the south. **2.** From the south: *southerly winds.* **—south′er·ly** *adv.*

south·ern (sŭth′ərn) ►*adj*. **1.** Of, in, or toward the south. **2.** From the south: *southern breezes.* [< OE *sūtherne*.] **—south′ern·most′** *adj.*

Southern Alps A mountain range of the W coast of South I., New Zealand.

south·ern·er also **South·ern·er** (sŭth′ər-nər) ►*n*. A native or inhabitant of a southern region.

Southern Hemisphere ►*n*. The half of the earth south of the equator.

southern lights ►*pl.n.* See **aurora australis.**

Southern Ocean The waters surrounding Antarctica, actually the S extensions of the Atlantic, Pacific, and Indian Oceans.

South Island An island of New Zealand SW of North I., from which it is separated by Cook Strait.

South Korea A country of E Asia on the S Korean peninsula. Cap. Seoul. **—South Korean** *adj. & n.*

south·paw (south′pô′) ►*n*. *Slang* A left-handed person, esp. a left-handed baseball pitcher.

South Pole ►*n*. **1.** The southern end of the earth's axis of rotation, a point in Antarctica. **2.** The celestial zenith of this terrestrial pole.

South Seas The oceans S of the equator, esp. the S Pacific.

South Vietnam A former country of SE Asia (1954–75); now part of Vietnam.

south·west (south-wĕst′, sou-wĕst′) ►*n*. **1.** The direction halfway between due south and due west. **2.** An area or region lying in the southwest. **—south·west′** *adj. & adv.* **—south·west′er·ly** *adj. & adv.* **—south·west′ern** *adj.* **—south·west′ward** *adv. & adj.* **—south·west′ward·ly** *adv. & adj.* **—south·west′wards** *adv.*

south·west·er (south-wĕs′tər, sou-wĕs′-) also **sou′·west·er** (sou-wĕs′-) ►*n*. **1.** A storm or gale from the southwest. **2.** A waterproof hat with a broad brim in back.

sou·ve·nir (sōō′və-nîr′, sōō′və-nîr′) ►*n.* A token of remembrance; memento. [< Lat. *subvenīre*, come to mind : *sub-*, under + *venīre*, come.]

souv·la·ki (sōōv-lä′kē) ►*n., pl.* **-ki·a** (-kē-ə) also **-kis** A Greek dish consisting of pieces of seasoned meat roasted on skewers. [Mod. Gk. *souvláki*.]

sov·er·eign (sŏv′ər-ĭn, sŏv′rĭn) ►*n.* **1.** The chief of state in a monarchy. **2.** A gold coin formerly used in Great Britain. ►*adj.* **1.** Independent: *a sovereign state.* **2.** Having supreme rank or power. **3.** Paramount; supreme. **4a.** Excellent. **b.** Unmitigated: *sovereign contempt.* [< VLat. *superānus* < Lat. *super*, above.]

sov·er·eign·ty (sŏv′ər-ĭn-tē, sŏv′rĭn-) ►*n., pl.* **-ties 1.** Supremacy of authority or rule. **2.** Royal rank, authority, or power. **3.** Complete independence and self-government.

so·vi·et (sō′vē-ĕt′, -ĭt, sŏv′ē-) ►*n.* **1.** One of the popularly elected legislative assemblies of the former Soviet Union. **2. Soviet** A native or inhabitant of the former Soviet Union. ►*adj.* often **Soviet** Of or relating to the former Soviet Union. [Russ. *sovet.*]

Soviet Union See **Union of Soviet Socialist Republics. —Soviet** *adj.*

sow¹ (sō) ►*v.* **sowed, sown** (sōn) or **sowed, sow·ing 1.** To plant (seeds) to produce a crop. **2.** To distribute seeds over (land). **3.** To propagate; disseminate: *sow rumors.* [< OE *sāwan.*] **—sow′er** *n.*

sow² (sou) ►*n.* An adult female pig, esp. one that has had at least one litter. [< OE *sugu, sū.*]

So·we·to (sə-wĕt′ō, -wā′tō) A former district of segregated townships on the SW outskirts of Johannesburg, South Africa.

sox (sŏks) ►*n.* Pl. of **sock¹.**

soy (soi) ►*n.* **1.** The soybean. **2.** Soy sauce. [< J. *shō-yu*, soy sauce.]

soy·bean (soi′bēn′) ►*n.* A bean native to E Asia, widely cultivated for its seeds, used for food, as a source of oil, and as animal feed.

So·yin·ka (shô-yĭng′kə), **Wole** b. 1934. Nigerian writer.

Wole Soyinka
photographed in 2009

soy·milk (soi′mĭlk′) ►*n.* A whitish liquid made from soybeans, used as a substitute for milk.

soy sauce ►*n.* A salty brown sauce made by fermenting soybeans and wheat.

sp. ►*abbr.* **1.** species **2.** specimen **3.** spelling

Sp. ►*abbr.* Spanish

spa (spä) ►*n.* **1.** A resort providing therapeutic baths. **2.** A resort area having mineral springs. **3.** A tub for relaxation or invigoration, usu.

with a device that creates whirlpools. [After *Spa*, Belgium.]

space (spās) ►*n.* **1a.** *Math.* A set of elements or points satisfying specified geometric postulates. **b.** The infinite extension of the three-dimensional region in which all matter exists. **2a.** The expanse in which the solar system, stars, and galaxies exist; universe. **b.** The region beyond Earth's atmosphere. **3a.** A blank or empty area: *the spaces between words.* **b.** An area provided for a particular purpose: *a parking space.* **4a.** A period or interval of time. **b.** A little while. ►*v.* **spaced, spac·ing 1.** To organize or arrange with spaces between. **2.** *Slang* To become disoriented from or as if from a drug: *space out.* [< Lat. *spatium.*] **—spac′er** *n.*

space bar ►*n.* A bar of a computer or typewriter keyboard that when pressed introduces a blank space, as between words.

space·craft (spās′krăft′) ►*n., pl.* **-craft** A vehicle designed to be launched into space.

space heater ►*n.* A small, usu. portable appliance that warms a small enclosed area.

space·ship (spās′shĭp′) ►*n.* See **spacecraft.**

space shuttle ►*n.* A reusable spacecraft designed to transport astronauts between Earth and an orbiting space station and to deploy and retrieve satellites.

space station ►*n.* A large satellite equipped to support a human crew and designed to remain in extended orbit around Earth.

space suit ►*n.* A protective pressure suit designed to permit the wearer relatively free movement in space.

space-time (spās′tīm′) ►*n.* *Phys.* The four-dimensional continuum of one temporal and three spatial coordinates in which any event or physical object is located.

space walk ►*n.* Extravehicular activity. **—space walk** *v.* **—space walker** *n.*

spa·cious (spā′shəs) ►*adj.* Large in range, extent, or scope. **—spa′cious·ly** *adv.* **—spa′cious·ness** *n.*
  Syns: *ample, capacious, commodious, roomy adj.*

spac·y or **spac·ey** (spā′sē) ►*adj.* **-i·er, -i·est** *Slang* **1.** Unable to focus adequate attention on serious or necessary matters. **2.** Stupefied or disoriented from drug use.

spade¹ (spād) ►*n.* A digging tool with a long handle and a flat blade. ►*v.* **spad·ed, spad·ing** To dig with a spade. [< OE *spadu.*]

spade² (spād) ►*n.* Any of a suit of playing cards marked with a black, leaf-shaped figure. [< Gk. *spathē*, broad blade.]

spade·work (spād′wûrk′) ►*n.* Preparatory work necessary for a project or activity.

spa·dix (spā′dĭks) ►*n., pl.* **-di·ces** (-dĭ-sēz′) A clublike stalk bearing tiny flowers, usu. enclosed in a sheathlike spathe. [< Gk. *spadix*, broken-off palm branch.]

spa·ghet·ti (spə-gĕt′ē) ►*n.* Pasta in long, often thick strands. [Ital., pl. dim. of *spago*, string.]

Spain (spān) A country of SW Europe on the Iberian Peninsula. Cap. Madrid.

spake (spāk) ►*v. Archaic* P.t. of **speak.**

spam (spăm) ►*n.* Unsolicited e-mail, usu. of a commercial nature. ►*v.* **spammed, spam·ming** To send unsolicited e-mail to. [< *Spam*, trademark for a canned meat product.]

span¹ (spăn) ►*n.* **1.** The distance or extent

between two points or extremities. **2.** The distance between the tips of the wings of an airplane. **3.** The section between two intermediate supports of a bridge. **4.** A unit of measure equal to about 9 in. (23 cm). **5.** A period of time: *a span of life.* ►*v.* **spanned, span·ning 1.** To extend across. **2.** To encircle or cover with the hand or hands. [< OE *spann,* a unit of measurement.]

span² (spăn) ►*n.* A pair of harnessed or matched animals, such as oxen. [< MDu. *spannen,* to harness.]

span·dex (spăn′dĕks) ►*n.* An elastic synthetic fiber or fabric made from a polymer containing polyurethane. [< EXPAND.]

span·gle (spăng′gəl) ►*n.* A small piece of shiny metal or plastic used esp. on garments for decoration. [< MDu. *spange,* clasp.] —**span′gle** *v.* —**span′gly** *adj.*

Span·iard (spăn′yərd) ►*n.* A native or inhabitant of Spain.

span·iel (spăn′yəl) ►*n.* A dog usu. having drooping ears, short legs, and a wavy, silky coat. [< OFr. *espaignol,* Spanish.]

Span·ish (spăn′ĭsh) ►*n.* **1.** The Romance language of the largest part of Spain and most of Central and South America. **2.** The people of Spain. —**Span′ish** *adj.*

Spanish moss ►*n.* A plant that grows on trees from the S US to Argentina, having greenish-gray stems and leaves that droop in long matted clusters.

spank (spăngk) ►*v.* To slap on the buttocks with the open hand. [Perh. imit.] —**spank** *n.*

spank·ing (spăng′kĭng) ►*adj.* **1.** *Informal* Exceptional; remarkable. **2.** Brisk and fresh: *a spanking breeze.* ►*adv.* Used as an intensive: *a spanking clean shirt.* ►*n.* A rapid succession of slaps on the buttocks. [Perh. of Scand. orig.]

spar¹ (spär) ►*n.* A wooden or metal pole used to support sail rigging. [ME *sparre,* rafter.]

spar² (spär) ►*v.* **sparred, spar·ring 1.** To box, esp. for practice. **2.** To bandy words about; wrangle. [ME *sparren,* strike rapidly.]

spare (spâr) ►*v.* **spared, spar·ing 1a.** To refrain from harming, destroying, or killing: *spared the city from bombardment.* **b.** To refrain from denouncing; treat leniently or with consideration. **c.** To allow (someone) to avoid experiencing or doing (something). **2a.** To avoid. **b.** To use or supply with restraint. ►*adj.* **spar·er, spar·est 1a.** Kept in reserve: *a spare part.* **b.** Extra: *spare cash.* **c.** Free for other use; unoccupied: *spare time.* **2a.** Without excess; meager. **b.** Lean and trim: *a runner with a spare figure.* **3.** Simple: *a writer's spare style.* ►*n.* **1.** A replacement, esp. a tire, reserved for future need. **2.** The knocking down of all ten bowling pins with two successive rolls of the ball. [< OE *sparian.*] —**spare′ly** *adv.* —**spare′ness** *n.*

spare·ribs (spâr′rĭbz′) ►*pl.n.* Pork ribs taken from the sides of the belly, with most of the meat trimmed off. [< MLGer. *ribbespēr.*]

spar·ing (spâr′ĭng) ►*adj.* Thrifty or frugal. —**spar′ing·ly** *adv.*

spark (spärk) ►*n.* **1.** A glowing particle, esp. one thrown off from a burning substance or resulting from friction. **2a.** A brief flash of light, esp. one produced by electric discharge. **b.** A short pulse or flow of electric current. **3.** A quality or factor with latent potential; seed: *the spark of genius.* ►*v.* **1.** To give off sparks. **2.** To set in motion; spur: *spark a controversy.* [< OE *spearca.*]

spar·kle (spär′kəl) ►*v.* **-kled, -kling 1.** To give off sparks. **2.** To give off or reflect flashes of light; glitter. **3.** To be brilliant or witty. **4.** To release gas bubbles; effervesce. [ME *sparklen.*] —**spar′kle** *n.* —**spar′kler** *n.*

spark plug ►*n.* A device in a cylinder of an internal-combustion engine that ignites the fuel mixture by an electric spark.

spar·row (spăr′ō) ►*n.* Any of various small brownish or grayish birds found throughout the Americas. [< OE *spearwa.*]

sparrow hawk ►*n.* **1.** A small North American falcon. **2.** A small Old World hawk that preys on small birds.

sparse (spärs) ►*adj.* **spars·er, spars·est** Occurring at widely spaced intervals. [Lat. *sparsus,* p.part. of *spargere,* scatter.] —**sparse′ly** *adv.* —**sparse′ness, spar′si·ty** *n.*

Spar·ta (spär′tə) A city-state of ancient Greece in the SE Peloponnesus.

Spar·ta·cus (spär′tə-kəs) d. 71 BC. Thracian gladiator who led a slave revolt against Rome.

Spar·tan (spär′tn) ►*adj.* **1.** Of Sparta or its people. **2.** also **spartan a.** Rigorously self-disciplined. **b.** Simple, frugal, or austere. —**Spar′tan** *n.*

spasm (spăz′əm) ►*n.* **1.** A sudden involuntary muscular contraction. **2.** A sudden burst of energy, activity, or emotion. [< Gk. *spasmos.*] —**spas·mod′ic** (spăz-mŏd′ĭk) *adj.* —**spas·mod′i·cal·ly** *adv.*

spas·tic (spăs′tĭk) ►*adj.* Of or affected by muscular spasms. ►*n.* A person affected with chronic muscular spasms. [< Gk. *spastikos.*] —**spas′ti·cal·ly** *adv.*

spat¹ (spăt) ►*v.* P.t. and p.part. of **spit¹.**

spat² (spăt) ►*n., pl.* **spat** or **spats** A larva of a bivalve mollusk that has settled by attaching to a surface. [ME.]

spat³ (spăt) ►*n.* A gaiter covering the upper shoe and the ankle. [< *spatterdash.*]

spat⁴ (spăt) ►*n.* A brief quarrel. ►*v.* **spat·ted, spat·ting** To engage in a spat. [?]

spate (spāt) ►*n.* A sudden flood, rush, or outpouring. [ME.]

spathe (spāth) ►*n. Bot.* A leaflike organ that encloses or spreads from the base of a spadix. [< Gk. *spathē,* broad blade.]

spa·tial (spā′shəl) ►*adj.* Relating to space. [< Lat. *spatium,* space.] —**spa′tial·ly** *adv.*

spat·ter (spăt′ər) ►*v.* To scatter or be scattered in drops or small splashes; splatter. ►*n.* **1.** The act or sound of spattering. **2.** A drop or splash of something spattered. [Perh. of LGer. orig.]

spat·u·la (spăch′ə-lə) ►*n.* An implement with a flexible blade used esp. to mix, spread, or lift material. [< Gk. *spathē,* broad blade.]

spav·in (spăv′ĭn) ►*n.* A condition in which the hock joint becomes swollen or painful. [< OFr. *espavain,* swelling.] —**spav′ined** *adj.*

spawn (spôn) ►*n.* **1.** The eggs of aquatic animals such as fishes, oysters, or frogs. **2.** Offspring, esp. when occurring in large numbers. ►*v.* **1.** To produce offspring, esp. in large numbers. **2.** To produce or give rise to. [< Lat. *expandere,* expand.]

spay (spā) ►*v.* To remove the ovaries of (an animal). [< AN *espeier,* cut with a sword.]

SPCA ►*abbr.* Society for the Prevention of Cruelty to Animals

speak (spēk) ►*v.* **spoke** (spōk), **spo·ken** (spō′kən), **speak·ing 1.** To utter words; talk. **2.** To converse. **3.** To deliver a public speech. **4.** To act as spokesperson. **5.** To converse in or be able to converse in (a language). —*phrasal verb:* **speak out** or **up** To speak without fear or hesitation. [< OE *sprecan.*] —**speak′a·ble** *adj.*

speak·eas·y (spēk′ē′zē) ►*n., pl.* **-ies** A place for the illegal sale and consumption of alcoholic drinks.

speak·er (spē′kər) ►*n.* **1.** One who speaks. **2.** One who delivers a public speech. **3.** The presiding officer of a legislative assembly. **4.** A device that converts electric signals to audible sound.

spear[1] (spîr) ►*n.* **1.** A weapon consisting of a long shaft with a sharply pointed end. **2.** A barbed shaft for spearing fish. ►*v.* To pierce or stab with or as if with a spear. [< OE *spere.*]

spear[2] (spîr) ►*n.* A slender stalk, as of asparagus or grass. [< *spire,* whorl.]

spear·fish (spîr′fĭsh′) ►*v.* To fish with a spear or spear gun. —**spear′fish′er** *n.* —**spear′fish′ing** *n.*

spear gun ►*n.* A device for mechanically shooting a spearlike missile under water, as in spearfishing.

spear·head (spîr′hĕd′) ►*n.* **1.** The sharpened head of a spear. **2.** The leading forces in a military attack. **3.** The driving force in an action or endeavor. —**spear′head** *v.*

spear·mint (spîr′mĭnt′) ►*n.* A common mint yielding an oil used widely as a flavoring.

spe·cial (spĕsh′əl) ►*adj.* **1.** Surpassing what is common or usual; exceptional. **2.** Distinct among others of a kind; singular. **3.** Peculiar to a specific person or thing; particular. **4.** Having a limited or specific function, application, or scope. **5.** Additional or extra. ►*n.* **1.** Something issued or produced for a particular service or occasion: *a television special.* **2.** A featured attraction, such as a reduced price: *a special on salmon.* [< Lat. *speciēs,* kind.] —**spe′cial·ly** *adv.*

special delivery ►*n.* Delivery of mail by a special messenger for an additional charge rather than by scheduled delivery.

special education ►*n.* Instruction designed for students whose learning needs cannot be met by a standard school curriculum.

special effect ►*n.* A visual effect added to a movie or a taped television show during processing.

special forces ►*pl.n.* **1.** A military or paramilitary unit trained to carry out special operations. **2.** A division of the US Army composed of soldiers trained in special operations.

spe·cial·ist (spĕsh′ə-lĭst) ►*n.* **1.** One who is devoted to a particular occupation or branch of study. **2.** A physician whose practice is limited to a particular branch of medicine or surgery. **3.** Any of several noncommissioned ranks in the US Army.

spe·cial·ize (spĕsh′ə-līz′) ►*v.* **-ized, -iz·ing 1.** To pursue a special activity, occupation, or field of study. **2.** *Biol.* To adapt or become adapted to a specific function or environment. —**spe′cial·i·za′tion** *n.*

special operation ►*n.* A usu. covert military operation, as for purposes of sabotage, reconnaissance, or personnel recovery, often carried out in hostile territory.

special relativity ►*n.* The physical theory of space and time developed by Albert Einstein.

spe·cial·ty (spĕsh′əl-tē) ►*n., pl.* **-ties 1.** A special pursuit, occupation, aptitude, or skill. **2.** A branch of medicine in which a physician specializes. **3.** An item or product of a distinctive kind or of particular superiority.

spe·cie (spē′shē, -sē) ►*n.* Coined money; coin. [< Lat. *(in) speciē,* (in) kind.]

spe·cies (spē′shēz, -sēz) ►*n., pl.* **-cies 1.** *Biol.* A group of closely related organisms that are very similar to each other and are usu. capable of interbreeding and producing fertile offspring. The species is the fundamental category of taxonomic classification, ranking below a genus. **2.** A kind, variety, or type. [< Lat. *speciēs,* kind, form.]

spe·cif·ic (spĭ-sĭf′ĭk) ►*adj.* **1a.** Explicitly set forth; definite. See Synonyms at **explicit. b.** Clear or detailed in communicating. **2.** Of, characterizing, or distinguishing a species. **3.** Intended for or acting on a particular thing in the treatment of a particular disease. ►*n.* **1.** A remedy for a particular ailment or disorder. **2. specifics** Distinct items or details. [LLat. *specificus* < Lat. *speciēs,* kind.] —**spe·cif′i·cal·ly** *adv.* —**spec′i·fic′i·ty** (spĕs′ə-fĭs′ĭ-tē) *n.*

spec·i·fi·ca·tion (spĕs′ə-fĭ-kā′shən) ►*n.* **1.** Something that is specified. **2. specifications** A detailed statement of particulars, esp. one prescribing materials, dimensions, and quality of work for something to be built, installed, or manufactured.

specific gravity ►*n.* The ratio of the mass of a solid or liquid to the mass of an equal volume of distilled water at 4°C (39°F) or of a gas to an equal volume of air or hydrogen under prescribed conditions of temperature and pressure.

spec·i·fy (spĕs′ə-fī′) ►*v.* **-fied, -fy·ing** To state explicitly, unambiguously, or in detail. [< Med. Lat. *specificāre;* see SPECIFIC.]

spec·i·men (spĕs′ə-mən) ►*n.* An individual, item, or part representative of a class or whole; sample. [Lat., example < *specere,* look at.]

spe·cious (spē′shəs) ►*adj.* **1.** Seemingly true but actually fallacious: *a specious argument.* **2.** Deceptively attractive. [< Lat. *speciōsus,* attractive < *specere,* look at.] —**spe′cious·ly** *adv.* —**spe′cious·ness** *n.*

speck (spĕk) ►*n.* **1.** A small spot or mark. **2.** A tiny amount; bit. ►*v.* To mark with specks. [< OE *specca.*]

speck·le (spĕk′əl) ►*n.* A small spot, esp. a natural dot of color on skin, plumage, or foliage. [ME *spakle.*] —**speck′le** *v.* —**speck′led** *adj.*

spec·ta·cle (spĕk′tə-kəl) ►*n.* **1a.** A remarkable or impressive sight. **b.** A lavish public performance or display. **2. spectacles** A pair of eyeglasses. [< Lat. *spectāculum* < *spectāre,* watch < *specere,* look at.] —**spec′ta·cled** *adj.*

spec·tac·u·lar (spĕk-tăk′yə-lər) ►*adj.* Of the nature of a spectacle; sensational. ►*n.* A lavish spectacle. —**spec·tac′u·lar·ly** *adv.*

spec·ta·tor (spĕk′tā′tər) ►*n.* An observer of an event, esp. a sports contest. [Lat. *spectātor* < *spectāre,* watch; see SPECTACLE.]

spec·ter (spĕk′tər) ►*n.* **1.** A ghostly apparition; phantom. **2.** A haunting or disturbing prospect: *the specter of nuclear war.* [< Lat. *spectrum,* apparition; see SPECTRUM.]

spec·tra (spĕk′trə) ►*n.* Pl. of **spectrum.**

spec·tral (spĕk′trəl) ►*adj.* **1.** Resembling a specter; ghostly. **2.** Of or produced by a spectrum.

spectro– ►*pref.* Spectrum: *spectrograph.* [< SPECTRUM.]

spec·tro·gram (spĕk′trə-grăm′) ►*n.* A graph or photograph of a spectrum.

spec·tro·graph (spĕk′trə-grăf′) ►*n.* **1.** A spectroscope equipped to photograph spectra. **2.** See **spectrogram.** —**spec′tro·graph′ic** *adj.* —**spec′tro·graph′i·cal·ly** *adv.* —**spec·trog′ra·phy** (-trŏg′rə-fē) *n.*

spec·trom·e·ter (spĕk-trŏm′ĭ-tər) ►*n.* A spectroscope equipped to measure wavelengths or indexes of refraction. —**spec′tro·met′ric** (-trə-mĕt′rĭk) *adj.* —**spec·trom′e·try** *n.*

spec·tro·scope (spĕk′trə-skōp′) ►*n.* An instrument used to analyze a sample by separating its components into a spectrum. —**spec′tro·scop′ic** (-skŏp′ĭk), **spec′tro·scop′i·cal** *adj.* —**spec′tros′co·pist** (-trŏs′kə-pĭst) *n.* —**spec·tros′co·py** *n.*

spec·trum (spĕk′trəm) ►*n., pl.* **-tra** (-trə) or **-trums 1.** *Phys.* The range of possible values of some measurable property of a physical system or phenomenon, such as the frequency of sound or the wavelength of electromagnetic radiation. **2.** A broad range: *the spectrum of modern thought.* [Lat., appearance < *specere,* look at.]

spec·u·late (spĕk′yə-lāt′) ►*v.* **-lat·ed, -lat·ing 1.** To assume to be true without conclusive evidence. **2.** To engage in risky business ventures that offer the chance of large profits. [< *specula,* watchtower < *specere,* look at.] —**spec′u·la′tion** *n.* —**spec′u·la·tive** *adj.* —**spec′u·la·tor** *n.*

spec·u·lum (spĕk′yə-ləm) ►*n., pl.* **-la** (-lə) or **-lums 1.** A mirror used in optical instruments. **2.** An instrument for dilating a body cavity for medical examination. [< Lat., mirror < *specere,* look at.]

speech (spēch) ►*n.* **1a.** The act of speaking. **b.** The capacity to speak. **2a.** What is spoken or expressed, as in conversation. **b.** A talk or public address. **3a.** The language or dialect of a nation or region. **b.** One's manner of speaking. [< OE *sprǣc.*]

speech·less (spēch′lĭs) ►*adj.* **1.** Lacking the faculty of speech. **2.** Temporarily unable to speak, as from astonishment. —**speech′less·ly** *adv.* —**speech′less·ness** *n.*

speed (spēd) ►*n.* **1.** The rate or a measure of the rate of motion. **2.** A rate of action, activity, or performance. **3a.** The act of moving rapidly. **b.** Rapidity or swiftness. See Synonyms at **haste. 4.** A transmission gear in a motor vehicle. **5.** *Slang* A stimulant drug. ►*v.* **sped** (spĕd) or **speed·ed, speed·ing 1a.** To move or cause to move rapidly. **b.** To drive at a speed exceeding a legal limit. **2.** To increase the speed or rate of; accelerate. [< OE *spēd,* success.] —**speed′er** *n.* —**speed′i·ly** *adv.* —**speed′y** *adj.*

speed·boat (spēd′bōt′) ►*n.* A fast motorboat.

speed·om·e·ter (spĭ-dŏm′ĭ-tər, spē-) ►*n.* **1.** An instrument for indicating speed, as of an automobile. **2.** An odometer.

speed·up (spēd′ŭp′) ►*n.* Acceleration of production without an increase in pay.

speed·way (spēd′wā′) ►*n.* **1.** A course for automobile or motorcycle racing. **2.** A road designed for fast-moving traffic.

speed·well (spēd′wĕl′) ►*n.* A plant with clusters of small, usu. blue flowers.

spell[1] (spĕl) ►*v.* **spelled** or **spelt** (spĕlt), **spell·ing 1.** To name or write in order the letters of (a word). **2.** To mean; signify: *an event that spells trouble.* —*phrasal verb:* **spell out** To make explicit; specify. [< OFr. *espeller,* read letter by letter, of Gmc. orig.]

spell[2] (spĕl) ►*n.* **1a.** A word or formula believed to have magic power. **b.** A bewitched state; trance: *The sorcerer put the prince under a spell.* **2.** Allure; fascination. [< OE, tale.]

spell[3] (spĕl) ►*n.* **1.** A short, indefinite period of time. **2.** *Informal* A period of weather: *a cold spell.* **3.** One's turn at work; shift. **4.** *Informal* A period of illness or indisposition. ►*v.* To relieve (someone) from work temporarily. [< OE *spelian,* stand in for.]

spell·bind (spĕl′bīnd′) ►*v.* To hold under or as if under a spell; enchant. [Back-formation < *spellbound.*] —**spell′bind′er** *n.*

spell checker ►*n.* An application in a word processing program that checks for spelling errors. —**spell check** *v.*

spell·er (spĕl′ər) ►*n.* **1.** One who spells words. **2.** A book used to teach spelling.

spell·ing (spĕl′ĭng) ►*n.* **1.** The forming of words with letters in an accepted order. **2.** The way in which a word is spelled.

spe·lunk·er (spĭ-lŭng′kər, spē-lŭng′-) ►*n.* One who explores and studies caves; caver. [< Gk. *spēlunx,* cave.] —**spe·lunk′ing** *n.*

spend (spĕnd) ►*v.* **spent** (spĕnt), **spend·ing 1.** To use up or put out; expend. **2.** To pay out (money); disburse. **3.** To wear out; exhaust. **4.** To pass (time). **5.** To waste or squander. [< Lat. *expendere,* expend, and OFr. *despendre,* dispense.] —**spend′er** *n.*

spend·thrift (spĕnd′thrĭft′) ►*n.* One who spends money recklessly or wastefully. [SPEND + THRIFT, accumulated wealth (obs.).]

Spen·ser (spĕn′sər), **Edmund** 1552?–99. English poet. —**Spen·se′ri·an** (-sîr′ē-ən) *adj.*

spent (spĕnt) ►*v.* P.t. and p.part. of **spend.** ►*adj.* Depleted of energy, force, or strength; exhausted.

sperm (spûrm) ►*n., pl.* **sperm** or **sperms 1.** A male gamete. **2.** Semen. [< Gk. *sperma,* sperm.] —**sper·mat′ic** (spər-măt′ĭk) *adj.*

sper·ma·ce·ti (spûr′mə-sē′tē, -sĕt′ē) ►*n., pl.* **-tis** A white waxy substance obtained from the sperm whale and formerly used for making candles, ointments, and cosmetics. [< Med. Lat. *spermacētī* : LLat. *sperma,* SPERM + Lat. *cētī,* of a whale.]

sper·mat·o·zo·on (spər-măt′ə-zō′ŏn′, -ən, spûr′mə-tə-) ►*n., pl.* **-zo·a** (-zō′ə) The mature male gamete of an animal. [*spermato-,* sperm + –ZOON.]

sper·mi·cide (spûr′mĭ-sīd′) ►*n.* A contraceptive agent that kills spermatozoa. —**sper′mi·cid′al** (-sīd′l) *adj.*

sperm whale ►*n.* A large toothed whale with a long narrow jaw, formerly hunted for the spermaceti in its massive head.

spew (spyōō) ►*v.* **1.** To send out or force out in large amounts. **2.** To vomit. [< OE *spīwan.*]

SPF ►*abbr.* sun protection factor

sp gr ►*abbr.* specific gravity

sphag·num (sfăg′nəm) ►*n.* Any of a genus of mosses whose decomposed remains form peat. [< Gk. *sphagnos,* a kind of shrub.]

sphere (sfîr) ►*n.* **1.** *Math.* A three-dimensional surface, all points of which are equidistant from a fixed point. **2.** A spherical object or figure; ball. **3.** A planet, star, or other heavenly body. **4.** An area of power, control, or influence; domain. See Synonyms at **field.** [< Gk. *sphaira.*] —**spher′i·cal** (sfîr′ĭ-kəl, sfĕr′-) *adj.* —**spher′i·cal·ly** *adv.*

spher·oid (sfîr′oid′, sfĕr′oid′) ►*n.* A three-dimensional geometric surface generated by revolving an ellipse around one of its axes. —**sphe·roi′dal** *adj.*

sphinc·ter (sfĭngk′tər) ►*n.* A ringlike muscle that normally maintains constriction of a body passage or orifice. [< Gk. *sphinktēr* < *sphingein,* bind tight.]

sphinx (sfĭngks) ►*n., pl.* **sphinx·es** or **sphin·ges** (sfĭn′jēz′) **1.** A figure in Egyptian myth having the body of a lion and the head of a man, ram, or hawk. **2.** A winged creature in Greek myth having the head of a woman and the body of a lion, noted for killing those who could not answer its riddle. **3.** A puzzling or mysterious person. [< Gk.]

spice (spīs) ►*n.* **1.** A pungent, aromatic plant substance, as nutmeg or pepper, used as flavoring. **2.** Something that adds zest or interest: *The controversy added spice to the political campaign.* [< LLat. *speciēs,* wares < Lat., kind; see SPECIES.] —**spice** *v.* —**spic′y** *adj.*

spick-and-span also **spic-and-span** (spĭk′ən-spăn′) ►*adj.* **1.** Neat and clean; spotless. **2.** Brand-new; fresh. [*spick,* spike + *span-new,* entirely new.]

spic·ule (spĭk′yōōl) ►*n.* **1.** A small needlelike structure or part. **2.** *Astron.* A spike-shaped formation emanating from the ionized gas of the solar photosphere. [Lat. *spīculum.*]

spi·der (spī′dər) ►*n.* **1.** Any of an order of eight-legged arachnids having a body divided into two parts and often spinning webs to trap insects. **2.** *Regional* A frying pan. [< OE *spīthra.*] —**spi′der·y** *adj.*

spider monkey ►*n.* A tropical American monkey having long arms and legs and a long prehensile tail and lacking a thumb.

spider vein ►*n.* A small, dilated vein that is visible just beneath the skin.

spiel (spēl, shpēl) ►*n.* *Informal* A lengthy or extravagant speech or argument usu. intended to persuade. [Ger. *Spiel* or Yiddish *shpil,* play.]

spiff·y (spĭf′ē) ►*adj.* **-i·er, -i·est** *Informal* Stylish in appearance or dress. [Poss. < dial. *spiff,* dandified.] —**spiff′i·ly** *adv.*

spig·ot (spĭg′ət) ►*n.* A faucet. [ME.]

spike¹ (spīk) ►*n.* **1a.** A long, thick, sharp-pointed piece of wood or metal, such as one along the top of a fence or wall. **b.** A large heavy nail. **2.** A sharp-pointed projection such as one in the sole of a shoe for traction. ►*v.* **spiked, spik·ing 1.** To secure or provide with a spike. **2.** To pierce or injure with a spike. **3.** *Informal* To put an end to; block: *spike a rumor.* **4.** *Informal* To add liquor to. [< ON *spīk.*] —**spik′y** *adj.*

spike² (spīk) ►*n.* **1.** An ear of grain. **2.** *Bot.* A usu. elongated cluster of stalkless flowers. [< Lat. *spīca.*]

spike·let (spīk′lĭt) ►*n.* A small or secondary spike, characteristic of grasses and sedges.

spike·nard (spīk′närd′) ►*n.* An aromatic plant from which a fragrant ointment was obtained in ancient times.

spill (spĭl) ►*v.* **spilled** or **spilt** (spĭlt), **spill·ing 1.** To cause or allow to run, flow, or fall out. **2.** To shed (blood). **3.** To fall or cause to fall, as from a horse. ►*n.* **1.** The act or an instance of spilling. **2.** An amount spilled. **3.** A fall. [< OE *spillan,* kill.] —**spill′age** *n.*

spill·way (spĭl′wā′) ►*n.* A channel for an overflow of water, as from a reservoir.

spin (spĭn) ►*v.* **spun** (spŭn), **spin·ning 1.** To rotate or cause to rotate swiftly; twirl. **2.** To have a sensation of whirling, as from dizziness. **3a.** To draw out and twist (fibers) into thread. **b.** To form (thread or yarn) by spinning. **4.** To form (e.g., a web or cocoon) by extruding viscous threads. **5.** To relate or create: *spin tales.* **6.** To play (recorded music), esp. as a disc jockey. **7.** To interpret or distort, esp. so as to sway public opinion. ►*n.* **1.** A swift whirling motion. **2.** A state of confusion. **3.** *Informal* A short drive in a vehicle. **4.** An interpretation or distortion. **5a.** The angular momentum of rotation of a rigid body about its own axis. **b.** The intrinsic angular momentum of a subatomic particle. —*phrasal verb:* **spin out** To rotate out of control, as a skidding car leaving a roadway. [< OE *spinnan.*] —**spin′ner** *n.*

spin·ach (spĭn′ĭch) ►*n.* A plant cultivated for its dark-green edible leaves. [< Pers. *aspanākh.*]

spi·nal (spī′nəl) ►*adj.* Of or near the spine or spinal cord. ►*n.* An anesthetic injected into the spinal cord. —**spi′nal·ly** *adv.*

spinal column ►*n.* The series of vertebrae encasing the spinal cord and forming the main support of the body; spine.

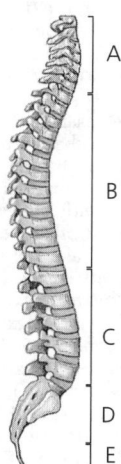

spinal column
right lateral view of an adult
human spinal column
A. cervical vertebrae;
B. thoracic vertebrae;
C. lumbar vertebrae;
D. sacrum; E. coccyx

spinal cord ▸*n.* The part of the central nervous system that extends from the brain through the spinal column.

spin·dle (spĭn′dl) ▸*n.* **1.** A slender rod or pin on which fibers are twisted into thread and then wound. **2.** Any of various slender revolving mechanical parts. **3.** *Biol.* The cellular structure along which the chromosomes are distributed during mitosis and meiosis. [< OE *spinel.*]

spin·dly (spĭnd′lē) ▸*adj.* **-dli·er, -dli·est** Slender, elongated, and often weak.

spin·drift (spĭn′drĭft′) ▸*n.* Windblown sea spray. [< obsolete *spoon,* run before the wind + DRIFT.]

spine (spīn) ▸*n.* **1.** The spinal column of a vertebrate. **2.** A sharp-pointed, projecting plant or animal part such as a thorn or quill. **3.** Courage or willpower; backbone. [< Lat. *spīna.*] —**spine′less** *adj.* —**spin′y** *adj.*

spin·et (spĭn′ĭt) ▸*n.* **1.** A small upright piano. **2.** A small harpsichord with a single keyboard. [< Ital. *spinetta.*]

spin·na·ker (spĭn′ə-kər) ▸*n.* A large triangular sail secured only at the corners. [Poss. < *Sphinx,* a racing yacht of the 1860s.]

spin·ner·et (spĭn′ə-rĕt′) ▸*n.* A structure from which spiders and silkworms secrete silk threads to form webs or cocoons.

spin·ning jenny (spĭn′ĭng) ▸*n.* An early spinning machine having several spindles.

spinning wheel ▸*n.* A device for making yarn or thread, consisting of a foot-driven or hand-driven wheel and a single spindle.

spin·off or **spin-off** (spĭn′ôf′, -ŏf′) ▸*n.* Something, such as a product or enterprise, derived from something larger or more complex.

Spi·no·za (spĭ-nō′zə), **Baruch** 1632–77. Dutch philosopher and theologian.

spin·ster (spĭn′stər) ▸*n. Often Offensive* A woman, esp. an older one, who has not married. [ME *spinnestere.*] —**spin′ster·hood′** *n.*

spir·a·cle (spĭr′ə-kəl, spī′rə-) ▸*n.* **1.** A small respiratory opening, esp. in the exoskeleton of an insect. **2.** A blowhole. [< Lat. *spīrāculum* < *spīrāre,* breathe.]

spi·ral (spī′rəl) ▸*n.* **1.** A curve on a plane that continuously winds around a fixed point at an increasing or decreasing distance. **2.** A three-dimensional curve that turns around an axis; helix. **3.** Something having the form of such a curve. ▸*adj.* **1.** Of or resembling a spiral. **2.** Coiling in a constantly changing plane; helical. ▸*v.* **-raled, -ral·ing** also **-ralled, -ral·ling 1.** To take or cause to take a spiral form or course. **2.** To rise or fall with steady acceleration. [< Gk. *speira,* coil.] —**spi′ral·ly** *adv.*

spiral galaxy ▸*n.* A galaxy consisting of a central cluster of mostly old stars, from which extend two or more spiral arms made up mostly of younger stars, interstellar gas, and dust.

spi·rant (spī′rənt) ▸*n.* See **fricative.** [< Lat. *spīrāre,* breathe.] —**spi′rant** *adj.*

spire (spīr) ▸*n.* A top part or structure that tapers upward, such as a steeple. [< OE *spīr.*]

spi·re·a also **spi·rae·a** (spī-rē′ə) ▸*n.* Any of various shrubs having clusters of white or pink flowers. [< Gk. *speiraia,* privet.]

spir·it (spĭr′ĭt) ▸*n.* **1.** A force or principle believed to animate living beings. **2. Spirit** The Holy Spirit. **3.** A supernatural being; ghost. **4.** The part of a human associated with the mind, will, and feelings. **5.** A pervasive or essential attitude, quality, or principle: *a spirit of rebellion.* **6a.** Enthusiasm, energy, or courage. **b. spirits** A mood or emotional state. **7.** The actual though unstated sense or significance of something: *the spirit of the law.* **8.** often **spirits** *(takes sing. v.)* An alcohol solution of an essential or volatile substance. **9. spirits** An alcoholic beverage. ▸*v.* To carry off mysteriously or secretly. [< Lat. *spīritus,* breath.] —**spir′it·less** *adj.*

spir·it·ed (spĭr′ĭ-tĭd) ▸*adj.* Marked by animation, vigor, or courage. —**spir′it·ed·ly** *adv.*

spir·i·tu·al (spĭr′ĭ-chōō-əl) ▸*adj.* **1.** Relating to or consisting of spirit as opposed to matter. **2.** Ecclesiastical; sacred. **3.** Concerned with spirit rather than with worldly things: *a very spiritual person.* ▸*n.* A religious song of African-American origin. —**spir′i·tu·al′i·ty** (-ăl′ĭ-tē) *n.* —**spir′i·tu·al·ize′** *v.* —**spir′i·tu·al·ly** *adv.*

spir·i·tu·al·ism (spĭr′ĭ-chōō-ə-lĭz′əm) ▸*n.* The belief that the dead communicate with the living, as through a medium. —**spir′i·tu·al·ist** *n.* —**spir′i·tu·al·is′tic** *adj.*

spir·i·tu·ous (spĭr′ĭ-chōō-əs) ▸*adj.* Of or containing alcohol; alcoholic.

spi·ro·chete (spī′rə-kēt′) ▸*n.* Any of an order of slender, spiral bacteria, including those that cause syphilis and yaws. [< Gk. *speira,* coil + *khaitē,* long hair.]

spit¹ (spĭt) ▸*n.* **1.** Saliva, esp. when expectorated. **2.** The act of spitting. ▸*v.* **spat** (spăt) or **spit, spit·ting 1.** To eject (e.g., saliva) from the mouth. **2.** To eject as if from the mouth. —*phrasal verb:* **spit up** To vomit. Used esp. of a baby. [< OE *spittan,* to spit.]

spit² (spĭt) ▸*n.* **1.** A slender pointed rod on which meat is impaled for roasting. **2.** A narrow point of land extending into a body of water. ▸*v.* **spit·ted, spit·ting** To impale on or as if on a spit. [< OE *spitu.*]

spit·ball (spĭt′bôl′) ▸*n.* **1.** A chewed lump of paper to be used as a projectile. **2.** *Baseball* An illegal pitch in which the ball is moistened on one side, as if with saliva.

spite (spīt) ▸*n.* Malicious ill will prompting an urge to hurt. ▸*v.* **spit·ed, spit·ing** To treat with malice. —*idiom:* **in spite of** Regardless of; despite. [ME.] —**spite′ful** *adj.* —**spite′ful·ly** *adv.* —**spite′ful·ness** *n.*

spit·tle (spĭt′l) ▸*n.* Spit; saliva. [< OE *spātl.*]

spit·tle·bug (spĭt′l-bŭg′) ▸*n.* Any of various leaping insects whose nymphs form frothy masses of liquid on plant stems.

spit·toon (spĭ-tōōn′) ▸*n.* A bowl-shaped vessel for spitting into. [< SPIT¹.]

splash (splăsh) ▸*v.* **1.** To propel, dash, or scatter (a fluid) about in masses. **2.** To scatter fluid upon. **3.** To fall into or move through fluid with the sound of splashing. ▸*n.* **1.** The act or sound of splashing. **2.** A flying mass of fluid. **3.** A mark made by or as if by splashing. **4.** A sensation; stir. [Prob. < PLASH.] —**splash′er** *n.*

splash·down (splăsh′doun′) ▸*n.* The landing of a spacecraft or missile in water.

splash·y (splăsh′ē) ▸*adj.* **-i·er, -i·est 1.** Making a splash or splashes. **2.** Extravagant or ostentatious: *a splashy ad campaign.* —**splash′i·ness** *n.*

splat¹ (splăt) ▸*n.* A slat of wood, as one in the middle of a chair back. [Perh. < ME *splatten,* split open.]

splat² (splăt) ►*n.* A smacking noise. [Imit.]

splat·ter (splăt′ər) ►*v.* To spatter or cause to spatter. [Perh. blend of SPLASH and SPATTER.] —**splat′ter** *n.*

splay (splā) ►*adj.* **1.** Spread or turned out. **2.** Clumsy or awkward. ►*v.* **1.** To spread or be spread out or apart, esp. clumsily. **2.** To slant or slope or make slanting or sloping. [< ME *splayen,* display.] —**splay** *n.*

splay·foot (splā′fo͝ot′) ►*n.* A deformity marked by abnormally flat and turned-out feet. —**splay′foot′ed** *adj.*

spleen (splēn) ►*n.* **1.** A large lymphoid organ, lying on the left side of the human body below the diaphragm, that filters and stores blood and produces lymphocytes. **2.** Ill temper. [< Gk. *splēn.*]

splen·did (splĕn′dĭd) ►*adj.* **1.** Brilliant with light or color; radiant. **2.** Magnificent. **3.** Glorious; illustrious. **4.** Excellent. [< Lat. *splendēre,* shine.] —**splen′did·ly** *adv.*

splen·dif·er·ous (splĕn-dĭf′ər-əs) ►*adj.* Splendid. [< Med.Lat. *splendiferus.*]

splen·dor (splĕn′dər) ►*n.* **1.** Great light or luster; brilliance. **2.** Magnificent appearance or display. [< Lat. < *splendēre,* shine.]

splen·dour (splĕn′dər) ►*n. Chiefly Brit.* Var. of **splendor.**

sple·net·ic (splĭ-nĕt′ĭk) ►*adj.* **1.** Of the spleen. **2.** Ill-humored; irritable. [< Gk. *splēn,* spleen.]

splen·ic (splĕn′ĭk) ►*adj.* Of or near the spleen. [< Gk. *splēn,* spleen.]

splice (splīs) ►*v.* **spliced, splic·ing 1a.** To join (e.g., two pieces of film) at the ends. **b.** To join (e.g., ropes) by interweaving strands. **2.** To join (pieces of wood) by overlapping and binding. **3.** To join together or insert (segments of DNA or RNA) so as to form new genetic combinations. [< Du. *splissen.*] —**splice** *n.*

splint (splĭnt) ►*n.* **1.** A rigid device used to prevent motion of a joint or the ends of a fractured bone. **2.** A thin flexible wooden strip, such as one used in making baskets. [< MDu. or MLGer. *splinte.*] —**splint** *v.*

splin·ter (splĭn′tər) ►*n.* A sharp slender piece, as of wood or metal, split or broken off from a main body. ►*v.* To form or cause to form splinters. [< MDu.]

split (splĭt) ►*v.* **split, split·ting 1.** To divide or become divided, esp. into lengthwise sections. **2.** To separate; disunite: *a quarrel that split the family.* **3.** To divide and share: *split a dessert.* **4.** To separate into layers or sections. **5.** *Slang* To leave, esp. abruptly. ►*n.* **1.** The act or a result of splitting. **2.** A breach or rupture in a group. [< MDu. *splitten.*] —**split′ter** *n.*

split end ►*n.* **1.** *Football* A pass receiver who lines up apart from the rest of the formation. **2.** The end of a hair that has split into strands.

split-lev·el (splĭt′lĕv′əl) ►*adj.* Having the floor levels of adjoining rooms separated by about half a story: *a split-level ranch house.*

split second ►*n.* An instant; flash.

split·ting (splĭt′ĭng) ►*adj.* Very severe: *a splitting headache.*

splotch (splŏch) ►*n.* An irregularly shaped spot, stain, or blotch. [Perh. blend of SPOT and BOTCH.] —**splotch** *v.* —**splotch′y** *adj.*

splurge (splûrj) ►*v.* **splurged, splurg·ing** To indulge in an extravagant expense or display. [?] —**splurge** *n.*

splut·ter (splŭt′ər) ►*v.* **1.** To make a spitting sound. **2.** To speak or utter incoherently, as in anger. [Perh. < SPUTTER.] —**splut′ter** *n.*

spoil (spoil) ►*v.* **spoiled** or **spoilt** (spoilt), **spoil·ing 1.** To impair the value or quality of; damage: *spoiled the dish by adding too much salt.* **2.** To harm the character of (a child) by overindulgence or leniency. **3.** To become unfit for use or consumption, as from decay. Used esp. of food. See Synonyms at **decay. 4.** To pillage. ►*n.* **spoils 1.** Goods or property seized by force; plunder. **2.** Political patronage enjoyed by a successful party or candidate. —*phrasal verb:* **spoil for** To be eager for: *spoiling for a fight.* [< Lat. *spolium,* booty.] —**spoil′age** *n.* —**spoil′er** *n.*

spoil·sport (spoil′spôrt′) ►*n.* One who spoils or mars the pleasure of others.

spoke¹ (spōk) ►*n.* **1.** One of the rods connecting the hub and rim of a wheel. **2.** A rung of a ladder. [< OE *spāca.*]

spoke² (spōk) ►*v.* **1.** P.t. of **speak. 2.** *Archaic* P.part. of **speak.**

spo·ken (spō′kən) ►*v.* P.part. of **speak.**

spokes·man (spōks′mən) ►*n.* A man who speaks on behalf of another or others. See Usage Note at **man.**

spokes·per·son (spōks′pûr′sən) ►*n.* A spokesman or spokeswoman.

spokes·wom·an (spōks′wo͝om′ən) ►*n.* A woman who speaks on behalf of another or others. See Usage Note at **man.**

spo·li·a·tion (spō′lē-ā′shən) ►*n.* **1.** The act of plundering. **2.** The state of being plundered. [< Lat. *spoliāre,* despoil; see SPOIL.]

sponge (spŭnj) ►*n.* **1a.** Any of various marine invertebrate animals that have a porous skeleton and feed on small particles in the water. **b.** The flexible, absorbent skeleton of a sponge, used for bathing, cleaning, and other purposes. **c.** A piece of material with similar qualities, made esp. of cellulose or plastic. **2.** A gauze pad used to absorb blood and other fluids, as in surgery. ►*v.* **sponged, spong·ing 1.** To moisten, wipe, or clean with a sponge. **2.** *Informal* To live by relying on another's generosity; freeload. [< Gk. *spongos.*] —**spong′er** *n.* —**spong′y** *adj.*

sponge cake ►*n.* A light porous cake containing no shortening.

sponge rubber ►*n.* A soft porous rubber used in cushions, gaskets, and weather stripping.

spon·sor (spŏn′sər) ►*n.* **1.** One who assumes responsibility for another person or a group. **2.** *Christianity* A godparent. **3.** One that finances a project, event, or organization directed by another person or group. [LLat. *spōnsor.*] —**spon′sor** *v.* —**spon′sor·ship′** *n.*

spon·ta·ne·ous (spŏn-tā′nē-əs) ►*adj.* **1.** Happening or arising without apparent external cause; self-generated. **2.** Voluntary or unpremeditated: *spontaneous applause.* [< Lat. *sponte,* voluntarily.] —**spon′ta·ne′i·ty** (-tə-nē′ĭ-tē, -nā′-) *n.* —**spon·ta′ne·ous·ly** *adv.*

spontaneous abortion ►*n.* See **miscarriage** (sense 1).

spontaneous combustion ►*n.* The breaking into flame of combustible material, such as oily rags or hay, due to heat generated within the material by slow oxidation.

spoof (spo͞of) ►*n.* **1.** A satirical imitation; parody. **2.** A deception or ruse. ►*v.* **1.** To satirize. **2.**

To play a trick on. **3.** *Comp.* To assume the identity of (another user or device) to gain access to a system. [After *Spoof*, name of a game invented by Arthur Roberts (1852–1933), Br. comedian.]

spook (spook) ►*n.* **1.** *Informal* A ghost. **2.** *Slang* A secret agent; spy. ►*v.* **1.** To haunt. **2.** To frighten. [< MDu. *spooc.*] —**spook′i·ly** *adv.* —**spook′i·ness** *n.* —**spook′y** *adj.*

spool (spool) ►*n.* **1.** A cylinder on which yarn, wire, thread, or string is wound. **2.** A reel for magnetic tape. ►*v.* **1.** To wind or be wound on or off a spool. **2.** To store (data sent to a printer) in a buffer. [< MDu. and MLGer. *spoele.*]

spoon (spoon) ►*n.* **1.** A utensil consisting of a small shallow bowl on a handle, used in preparing, serving, or eating food. **2.** A shiny, curved, metallic fishing lure. ►*v.* **1.** To lift, scoop up, or carry with or as if with a spoon. **2.** To engage in amorous kissing or caressing. [< OE *spōn*, chip of wood.] —**spoon′ful′** *n.*

spoon·bill (spoon′bĭl′) ►*n.* Any of several long-legged wading birds having a long flat bill with a broad tip.

spoon·er·ism (spoo′nə-rĭz′əm) ►*n.* A transposition of sounds of two or more words, such as *sew you to your sheet* for *show you to your seat.* [After William A. *Spooner* (1844–1930).]

spoon-feed (spoon′fēd′) ►*v.* **1.** To feed (another) with a spoon. **2.** To treat (another) in a way that discourages independent thought or action.

spoor (spoor) ►*n.* The track or trail of an animal, esp. a wild animal. [Afr. < MDu.]

spo·rad·ic (spə-răd′ĭk, spô-) ►*adj.* Occurring at irregular intervals. [< Gk. *sporas, sporad-*, scattered.] —**spo·rad′i·cal·ly** *adv.*

spore (spôr) ►*n.* A usu. one-celled reproductive body or resting stage, as of a fern, fungus, or bacterium. [Gk. *spora*, seed.]

spor·ran (spôr′ən, spŏr′-) ►*n.* A pouch worn at the front of the kilt by Scottish Highlanders. [< Middle Irish *sparán.*]

sporran

sport (spôrt) ►*n.* **1.** An activity usu. involving physical exertion and having a set form and body of rules; game. **2.** An active pastime; diversion. **3.** Light mockery. **4.** One known for the manner of one's acceptance of defeat or criticism: *a poor sport.* **5.** *Informal* One who lives a jolly, extravagant life. **6.** *Biol.* A mutation. ►*v.* **1.** To play or frolic. **2.** To joke or trifle. **3.** To display or show off. ►*adj.* also **sports 1.** Of or appropriate for sport: *sport fishing.* **2.** Appropriate for outdoor or informal wear: *a sport shirt.* [< OFr. *desport*, pleasure.] —**sport′i·ness** *n.* —**sport′y** *adj.*

sport·ing (spôr′tĭng) ►*adj.* **1.** Used in or appropriate for sports: *sporting goods.* **2.** Marked by sportsmanship. **3.** Of or associated with gambling. —**sport′ing·ly** *adv.*

spor·tive (spôr′tĭv) ►*adj.* Playful or frolicsome. —**spor′tive·ly** *adv.* —**spor′tive·ness** *n.*

sports·cast (spôrts′kăst′) ►*n.* A radio or television broadcast of a sports event or of sports news. —**sports′cast′er** *n.*

sports·man (spôrts′mən) ►*n.* **1.** A man who is active in sports. **2.** A man who exhibits sportsmanship. See Usage Note at **man.** —**sports′man·like′** *adj.*

sports·man·ship (spôrts′mən-shĭp′) ►*n.* Conduct and attitude of participants in sports, esp. when considered commendable as in fair play and courtesy.

sports·wom·an (spôrts′woom′ən) ►*n.* **1.** A woman who is active in sports. **2.** A woman who exhibits sportsmanship. See Usage Note at **man.**

sports·writ·er (spôrts′rī′tər) ►*n.* One who writes about sports, esp. for a newspaper or magazine.

sport-utility vehicle ►*n.* An SUV.

spot (spŏt) ►*n.* **1.** A mark, such as a stain, on a surface differing sharply in color from its surroundings. **2.** A position; location. **3.** *Informal* A situation, esp. a troublesome one. ►*v.* **spot·ted, spot·ting 1.** To mark or become marked with spots. **2.** To locate precisely. **3.** To detect or discern, esp. visually. ►*adj.* Made, paid, or delivered immediately: *a spot sale.* —*idiom:* **on the spot** Under pressure. [< OE.] —**spot′ted** *adj.*

spot check ►*n.* An inspection conducted at random or limited to a few instances. —**spot′-check′** *v.*

spot·less (spŏt′lĭs) ►*adj.* **1.** Perfectly clean: *a spotless kitchen.* **2.** Impeccable. —**spot′less·ly** *adv.* —**spot′less·ness** *n.*

spot·light (spŏt′līt′) ►*n.* **1a.** A strong beam of light that illuminates only a small area, used esp. on a stage. **b.** A lamp that produces such a light. **2.** Public attention, notoriety, or prominence. —**spot′light′** *v.*

spot·ter (spŏt′ər) ►*n.* One that looks for, locates, and reports something, esp. a military lookout.

spot·ty (spŏt′ē) ►*adj.* **-ti·er, -ti·est** Lacking consistency, as in quality; uneven.

spou·sal (spou′zəl, -səl) ►*adj.* **1.** Nuptial. **2.** Of a spouse. ►*n.* often **spousals** Marriage; nuptials. [< Lat. *spōnsālis.*]

spouse (spous, spouz) ►*n.* A husband or wife; marriage partner. [< Lat. *spōnsus*, p.part. of *spondēre*, to pledge, betroth.]

spout (spout) ►*v.* **1.** To gush forth or discharge in a rapid stream or in spurts. **2.** To utter loudly and pompously: *spout nonsense.* ►*n.* **1.** A tube through which liquid is released or discharged. **2.** A continuous stream of liquid. [ME *spouten.*] —**spout′er** *n.*

spp. ►*abbr.* species (plural)

sprain (sprān) ►*n.* A painful wrenching or laceration of the ligaments of a joint. ►*v.* To cause a sprain to (a joint or ligament). [?]

sprang (sprăng) ►*v.* P.t. of **spring.**

sprat (sprăt) ►*n.* **1.** A small food fish, eaten fresh or smoked and often canned as a sardine. **2.** A young herring. [< OE *sprot.*]

sprawl (sprôl) ►*v.* **1.** To sit or lie with the limbs spread out awkwardly. **2.** To spread out haphazardly. [< OE *sprēawlian,* writhe.] —**sprawl** *n.*

spray¹ (sprā) ►*n.* **1.** Liquid moving in a mass of dispersed droplets or mist, as from a wave. **2a.** A fine jet of liquid discharged from a pressurized container. **b.** A pressurized container; atomizer. ►*v.* **1.** To disperse (a liquid) in a spray. **2.** To apply a spray to (a surface). [< MDu. *sprayen,* sprinkle.] —**spray'er** *n.*

spray² (sprā) ►*n.* A small branch bearing buds, flowers, or berries. [< OE **spræg.*]

spread (sprĕd) ►*v.* **spread, spread·ing 1.** To open or be extended more fully; stretch. **2.** To separate or become separated more widely; open out. **3.** To distribute over a surface in a layer; apply. **4.** To distribute widely: *The tornado spread destruction.* **5.** To become or cause to become widely known. ►*n.* **1.** The act or process of spreading: *the spread of disease.* **2.** An open area of land; expanse. **3.** The extent or limit to which something is or can be spread; range. **4.** A cloth covering for a bed or table. **5.** *Informal* An abundant meal laid out on a table. **6.** A food to be spread on bread or crackers. **7.** Two facing pages of a magazine, newspaper, or book, considered as a unit. **8.** A difference, as between two totals. [< OE *sprǣdan.*] —**spread'a·ble** *adj.* —**spread'er** *n.*

spread eagle ►*n.* **1.** The figure of an eagle with wings and legs spread. **2.** A posture or design resembling a spread eagle. —**spread' ea'gle** *adj.*

spread·sheet (sprĕd'shēt') ►*n.* An array of rows and columns for recording and analyzing data.

spree (sprē) ►*n.* A sudden indulgence in or outburst of an activity: *a shopping spree; a crime spree.* [Perh. < Sc. *spreath,* cattle raid.]

spri·er (sprī'ər) ►*adj.* Comp. of **spry.**

spri·est (sprī'ĭst) ►*adj.* Superl. of **spry.**

sprig (sprĭg) ►*n.* A small shoot or twig of a plant. [ME *sprigge.*]

spright·ly (sprīt'lē) ►*adj.* **-li·er, -li·est** Lively and brisk; animated.

spring (sprĭng) ►*v.* **sprang** (sprăng) or **sprung** (sprŭng), **sprung, spring·ing 1.** To move upward or forward suddenly; leap. **2.** To move suddenly, esp. because of being resilient or moved by a spring. **3a.** To emerge suddenly. **b.** To arise from a source; develop. See Synonyms at **stem¹. 4.** To come loose, as parts of a mechanism. **5.** To release from a checked or held position: *spring a trap.* **6.** To present unexpectedly or suddenly: *spring a surprise.* ►*n.* **1.** An elastic device, esp. a coil of wire, that regains its original shape after being compressed or extended. **2.** Elasticity; resilience: *a mattress with a lot of spring.* **3.** The act of springing. **4.** A natural fountain or stream of water. **5.** A source or origin. **6.** The season between winter and summer. [< OE *springan.*] —**spring'i·ly** *adv.* —**spring'i·ness** *n.* —**spring'y** *adj.*

spring·board (sprĭng'bôrd') ►*n.* **1.** A flexible board used by gymnasts. **2.** See **diving board.**

spring fever ►*n.* A feeling of languor or yearn-

ing brought on by the coming of spring.

Spring·field (sprĭng'fēld') The capital of IL, in the central part.

spring-load·ed (sprĭng'lō'dĭd) ►*adj.* Secured or loaded by means of a spring.

spring tide ►*n.* The exceptionally high and low tides that occur at the time of the new moon or the full moon.

spring·time (sprĭng'tīm') ►*n.* The season of spring.

sprin·kle (sprĭng'kəl) ►*v.* **-kled, -kling** To scatter or fall in drops or small particles. ►*n.* **1.** A light rainfall. **2.** A small amount. [ME *sprenklen.*] —**sprin'kler** *n.*

sprinkler system ►*n.* A network of overhead pipes that release water to extinguish fires.

sprin·kling (sprĭng'klĭng) ►*n.* A small or scattered amount.

sprint (sprĭnt) ►*n.* A short race at top speed. [Of Scand. orig.] —**sprint** *v.* —**sprint'er** *n.*

sprite (sprīt) ►*n.* An elf or pixie. [< Lat. *spīritus,* spirit.]

spritz·er (sprĭt'sər, shprĭt'-) ►*n.* A drink made of wine and carbonated water. [Ger. < *spritzen,* spray.]

sprock·et (sprŏk'ĭt) ►*n.* Any of various toothlike projections arranged on a wheel rim to engage the links of a chain. [?]

sprout (sprout) ►*v.* **1.** To begin to grow; give off shoots or buds. **2.** To emerge and develop rapidly. ►*n.* A young plant growth, such as a bud or shoot. [< OE *sprūtan.*]

spruce¹ (sproōs) ►*n.* **1.** Any of various cone-bearing evergreen trees with short pointed needles and soft wood. **2.** The wood of a spruce. [< obsolete *Spruce fir,* Prussian fir.]

spruce² (sproōs) ►*adj.* **spruc·er, spruc·est** Neat and trim in appearance. ►*v.* **spruced, spruc· ing** To neaten. [Perh. < obsolete *spruce leather,* Prussian leather.]

sprung (sprŭng) ►*v.* A p.t. and the p.part. of **spring.**

spry (sprī) ►*adj.* **spri·er** (sprī'ər), **spri·est** (sprī'ĭst) or **spry·er, spry·est** Active; nimble. [Perh. of Scand. orig.] —**spry'ly** *adv.* —**spry'- ness** *n.*

spud (spŭd) ►*n.* **1.** *Informal* A potato. **2.** A sharp spadelike tool. [ME *spudde,* short knife.]

spume (spyoōm) ►*n.* Foam or froth on a liquid. [< Lat. *spūma.*] —**spu'mous, spum'y** *adj.*

spu·mo·ni or **spu·mo·ne** (spoō-mō'nē) ►*n.* Ice cream in layers of different colors or flavors, often with fruits and nuts. [Ital.]

spun (spŭn) ►*v.* P.t. and p.part. of **spin.**

spun glass ►*n.* See **fiberglass.**

spunk (spŭngk) ►*n. Informal* Spirit; pluck. [Sc. Gael. *spong,* tinder.] —**spunk'y** *adj.*

spur (spûr) ►*n.* **1.** A spiked device attached to a rider's heel and used to urge a horse forward. **2.** An incentive. **3.** A spurlike attachment or projection, as on the back of a bird's leg or on certain flowers. **4.** A lateral ridge projecting from a mountain or mountain range. **5.** A short side track connecting with the main railroad track. ►*v.* **spurred, spur·ring 1.** To urge (a horse) on by the use of spurs. **2.** To incite or stimulate. [< OE *spura.*]

spurge (spûrj) ►*n.* Any of various plants with milky juice and small flowers. [< OFr. *espurgier,* purge (from its use as a purgative).]

spu·ri·ous (spyoŏr'ē-əs) ►*adj.* Lacking authenticity or validity. [< Lat. *spurius,* illegitimate.] —**spu′ri·ous·ly** *adv.* —**spu′ri·ous·ness** *n.*

spurn (spûrn) ►*v.* To reject with disdain or contempt. [< OE *spurnan.*] —**spurn′er** *n.*

spurt (spûrt) ►*n.* **1.** A sudden forcible gush or jet. **2.** A sudden short burst of energy or activity. ►*v.* **1.** To gush forth. **2.** To make a brief intense effort. [?]

Sput·nik (spo͝ot′nĭk, spŭt′-, spo͞ot′nyĭk) ►*n.* A Soviet artificial earth satellite. [Russ. *sputnik (zemli),* fellow traveler (of Earth).]

sput·ter (spŭt′ər) ►*v.* **1.** To spit out small particles in noisy bursts. **2.** To utter in an excited or confused manner. **3.** To make sporadic spitting or popping sounds: *The fire sputtered and died.* [Prob. of LGer. orig.] —**sput′ter** *n.* —**sput′ter·er** *n.*

spu·tum (spyo͞o′təm) ►*n., pl.* **-ta** (-tə) Expectorated matter including saliva and substances such as phlegm from the respiratory tract. [Lat. *spūtum < spuere,* to spit.]

spy (spī) ►*n., pl.* **spies** (spīz) **1.** One who secretly collects information concerning the enemies of a government or group. **2.** One who secretly keeps watch on others. ►*v.* **spied** (spīd), **spy·ing 1.** To watch or observe secretly. **2.** To catch sight of. **3.** To engage in espionage. [< OFr. *espier,* watch, of Gmc. orig.]

spy·glass (spī′glăs′) ►*n.* A small telescope.

sq. or **Sq.** ►*abbr.* square

squab (skwŏb) ►*n.* **1.** A young or unfledged pigeon. **2.** A soft, thick cushion. ►*adj.* Young and undeveloped; newly hatched or unfledged. [Prob. of Scand. orig.]

squab·ble (skwŏb′əl) ►*v.* **-bled, -bling** To engage in an argument, usu. over a trivial matter; bicker. ►*n.* A noisy, usu. trivial quarrel. [Prob. of Scand. orig.]

squad (skwŏd) ►*n.* **1.** A small group of people organized in a common activity. **2.** The smallest tactical military unit. **3.** A small police unit. **4.** An athletic team. [< VLat. **exquadra,* SQUARE.]

squad car ►*n.* A police automobile connected by radio with headquarters.

squad·ron (skwŏd′rən) ►*n.* **1.** A naval unit consisting of two or more divisions of a fleet. **2.** A basic tactical air force unit. [Ital. *squadrone,* augmentative of *squadra,* SQUAD.]

squal·id (skwŏl′ĭd) ►*adj.* **1.** Dirty or deteriorated, esp. from poverty or lack of care. **2.** Morally repulsive; sordid. [Lat. *squālidus.*] —**squal′id·ly** *adv.* —**squal′id·ness** *n.*

squall¹ (skwôl) ►*n.* A loud harsh cry. [Prob. of Scand. orig.] —**squall** *v.*

squall² (skwôl) ►*n.* A brief sudden violent windstorm, often with rain or snow. [Prob. of Scand. orig.] —**squall′y** *adj.*

squal·or (skwŏl′ər) ►*n.* A filthy and wretched condition. [Lat. *squālor.*]

squa·mous (skwā′məs, skwä′-) ►*adj.* Covered with or resembling scales. [< Lat. *squāma,* scale.]

squan·der (skwŏn′dər) ►*v.* **1.** To spend or use extravagantly. See Synonyms at **waste. 2.** To fail to take advantage of: *squandered an opportunity.* [?]

Squan·to (skwŏn′tō) also **Ti·squan·tum** (tĭ-skŏn′təm) d. 1622. Wampanoag Native Amer. who aided the Plymouth colony.

square (skwâr) ►*n.* **1.** A plane figure having four equal sides. **2.** Something having an equal-sided rectangular form. **3.** An instrument for drawing or testing right angles. **4.** *Math.* The product of a number or quantity multiplied by itself. **5a.** An open area at the intersection of two or more streets. **b.** A rectangular space enclosed by streets; block. **6.** *Slang* A dull, rigidly conventional person. ►*adj.* **squar·er, squar·est 1.** Having four equal sides and four right angles. **2.** Forming a right angle. **3a.** Expressed in units measuring area: *square feet.* **b.** Having a specified length in each of two equal dimensions. **4.** Like a square in form: *a square house.* **5.** Honest; direct: *a square answer.* **6.** Just; equitable: *a square deal.* **7.** Paid up; settled. **8.** Even; tied. **9.** *Slang* Rigidly conventional. ►*v.* **squared, squar·ing 1.** To cut to a square or rectangular shape. **2.** To conform; agree: *a story that did not square with the facts.* **3.** To bring into balance; settle: *square a debt.* **4.** *Math.* To multiply a number or quantity by itself. [< VLat. **exquadra < Lat. quadrum,* a square.] —**square′ly** *adv.* —**square′ness** *n.*

square bracket ►*n.* One of a pair of marks, [ ], used to enclose written or printed material.

square dance ►*n.* A dance in which sets of four couples form squares. —**square′-dance′** *v.* —**square dancer** *n.*

square knot ►*n.* A double knot in which the loose ends are parallel to the standing parts, usu. used to join the ends of two lines.

square knot

square meal ►*n.* A substantial nourishing meal.

square-rigged (skwâr′rĭgd′) ►*adj. Naut.* Fitted with square sails as the principal sails.

square-rig·ger (skwâr′rĭg′ər) ►*n. Naut.* A square-rigged vessel.

square root ►*n. Math.* A divisor of a quantity that when squared gives the quantity.

squash¹ (skwŏsh, skwôsh) ►*n.* **1.** Any of various plants related to the pumpkins and gourds. **2.** The fleshy fruit of a squash, eaten as a vegetable. [< Narragansett *askútasquash.*]

squash² (skwŏsh, skwôsh) ►*v.* **1.** To beat, squeeze, or flatten into a pulp. See Synonyms at **crush. 2.** To suppress; quash: *squash a revolt.* ►*n.* **1.** The impact or sound of squashing. **2.** A crush or press, as of people. **3.** A game played in a closed walled court with rackets and a hard rubber ball. [< OFr. *esquasser.*] —**squash′i·ness** *n.* —**squash′y** *adj.*

squat (skwŏt) ►v. **squat·ted, squat·ting 1.** To sit in a crouching position with the hams resting on or near the heels. **2.** To settle on unoccupied land without legal claim. **3.** To occupy a given piece of public land in order to acquire title to it. ►adj. **squat·ter, squat·test 1.** Short and thick. **2.** Crouched in a squatting position. ►n. The act or posture of squatting. [< OFr. *esquatir*, crush.] —**squat'ter** n.

squaw (skwô) ►n. *Offensive* A Native American woman. [Massachusett *squa*.]

squawk (skwôk) ►v. **1.** To utter a harsh cry; screech. **2.** *Informal* To complain noisily or peevishly. [Imit.] —**squawk** n.

squeak (skwēk) ►v. To utter or give forth a thin, high-pitched cry or sound. [ME *squeken*.] —**squeak** n. —**squeak'i·ly** adv. —**squeak'i·ness** n. —**squeak'y** adj.

squeal (skwēl) ►v. **1.** To utter with or produce a loud shrill cry or sound. **2.** *Slang* To turn informer. [ME *squelen*.] —**squeal** n. —**squeal'er** n.

squea·mish (skwē'mĭsh) ►adj. **1a.** Easily nauseated or sickened. **b.** Nauseated. **2.** Easily shocked or disgusted. **3.** Excessively fastidious. [< AN *escoymous*.] —**squea'mish·ly** adv. —**squea'mish·ness** n.

squee·gee (skwē'jē) ►n. A tool with a rubber blade set perpendicular to a handle, used to wipe water from a surface, as of a window. [Poss. < alteration of SQUEEZE.] —**squee'gee** v.

squeeze (skwēz) ►v. **squeezed, squeez·ing 1a.** To press together; compress. **b.** To press gently, as in affection: *squeezed her hand.* **c.** To exert pressure. **2.** To extract by applying pressure: *squeeze juice from a lemon.* **3.** To force by pressure; cram. ►n. **1.** An act of squeezing. **2.** An amount squeezed. **3.** Financial pressure caused by narrowing economic margins. [< OE *cwȳsan.*] —**squeez'er** n.

squelch (skwĕlch) ►v. **1.** To subdue forcibly: *squelch a revolt.* **2.** To inhibit or suppress: *squelch a rumor.* **3.** To produce a splashing, squishing, or sucking sound. [Prob. imit.] —**squelch** n.

squib (skwĭb) ►n. **1a.** A small firecracker. **b.** A firecracker that burns but does not explode. **2.** A brief witty writing or speech. [Prob. imit.]

squid (skwĭd) ►n., pl. **squids** or **squid** A marine mollusk with a usu. elongated body and eight arms and two tentacles. [?]

squig·gle (skwĭg'əl) ►n. A small wiggly mark or scrawl. ►v. **-gled, -gling** To squirm and wriggle. [Perh. blend of SQUIRM and WIGGLE.] —**squig'gly** adj.

squint (skwĭnt) ►v. **1.** To look with eyes partly closed, as in bright sunlight. **2.** To close (the eyes) partly while looking. [< ME *asquint*, looking sidelong.] —**squint** n. —**squint'y** adj.

squire (skwīr) ►n. **1.** A man who attends or escorts a woman; gallant. **2.** An English country gentleman. **3.** A young nobleman attendant upon and ranked next below a knight. ►v. **squired, squir·ing** To attend as a squire; escort. [< OFr. *esquier*, ESQUIRE.]

squirm (skwûrm) ►v. **1.** To twist about in a wriggling motion; writhe. **2.** To feel or exhibit signs of humiliation or embarrassment. [?] —**squirm** n. —**squirm'er** n. —**squirm'y** adj.

squir·rel (skwûr'əl, skwŭr'-) ►n. **1.** Any of various arboreal rodents usu. having a long flexible bushy tail. **2.** The fur of a squirrel. [< Gk. *skiouros.*]

squirt (skwûrt) ►v. To eject (liquid) in a thin swift stream or jet. ►n. **1.** A device for squirting. **2.** A squirted jet. **3.** A small or young person; pipsqueak. [ME *squirten.*]

squish (skwĭsh) ►v. **1.** To crush or squash. **2.** To emit the gurgling or sucking sound of soft mud being walked on. [Prob. < SQUASH².] —**squish** n. —**squish'y** adj.

Sr. ►abbr. **1.** or **sr.** senior **2.** señor **3.** *Eccles.* sister (title)

Sri Lan·ka (srē läng'kə) Formerly **Cey·lon** (sĭ-lŏn', sā-). An island country of South Asia in the Indian Ocean off SE India. Cap. Colombo. —**Sri Lan'kan** adj. & n.

SRO ►abbr. **1.** single room occupancy **2.** standing room only

SSA ►abbr. Social Security Administration

SSE ►abbr. south-southeast

SSN ►abbr. Social Security number

SSRI ►abbr. selective serotonin reuptake inhibitor

SSW ►abbr. south-southwest

ST ►abbr. standard time

St. ►abbr. **1.** saint **2.** state **3.** strait **4.** street

-st ►suff. Var. of –est².

stab (stăb) ►v. **stabbed, stab·bing 1.** To pierce or wound with or as if with a pointed weapon. **2.** To thrust with or as if with a pointed weapon. ►n. **1.** An act of stabbing. **2.** A wound inflicted with a pointed weapon. **3.** A sudden piercing pain. **4.** An attempt; try. [ME *stabben.*]

sta·bi·lize (stā'bə-līz') ►v. **-lized, -liz·ing 1.** To make or become stable. **2.** To maintain the stability of. —**sta'bi·li·za'tion** n. —**sta'bi·liz'er** n.

sta·ble¹ (stā'bəl) ►adj. **-bler, -blest 1a.** Resistant to change of position or condition: *a stable platform.* **b.** Not subject to sudden or extreme change: *a stable currency.* **c.** Maintaining equilibrium: *a stable aircraft.* **2.** Long-lasting; enduring: *a stable peace.* **3a.** Consistent or dependable: *stable in her support of the project.* **b.** Not exhibiting erratic or volatile emotions or behavior: *remained stable even after he lost his job.* **4.** *Phys.* Having no known mode of decay. Used of atomic particles. [< Lat. *stabilis.*] —**sta·bil'i·ty** n. —**sta'bly** adv.

sta·ble² (stā'bəl) ►n. **1.** A building for the shelter and feeding of certain domestic animals, esp. horses. **2.** All the racehorses of a single owner. ►v. **-bled, -bling** To put or keep in a stable. [< Lat. *stabulum.*]

stac·ca·to (stə-kä'tō) ►adj. **1.** *Mus.* Cut short crisply; detached. **2.** Made up of short, sharp sounds: *staccato gunfire.* [Ital., p.part. of *staccare*, DETACH.] —**stac·ca'to** n. & adv.

stack (stăk) ►n. **1.** A large, usu. conical pile, as of straw. **2.** An orderly pile, esp. one arranged in layers. See Synonyms at **heap. 3.** A chimney or flue. **4.** A vertical exhaust pipe, as on a ship or locomotive. **5.** often **stacks** The area of a library in which most of the books are shelved. **6.** *Informal* A large quantity. ►v. **1.** To arrange in a stack; pile. **2.** *Games* To prearrange the order of (a deck of cards) so as to cheat. —**phrasal verb: stack up** *Informal* To measure up; compare. [< ON *stakkr.*] —**stack'er** n.

sta·di·um (stā'dē-əm) ►n., pl. **-di·ums** or **-di·**

a (-dē-ə) A large, usu. open structure for sports events. [< Gk. *stadion*, unit of measure, racecourse.]

Staël (stäl), Madame de. Baronne Anne Louise Germaine Necker de Staël-Holstein. 1766–1817. French writer.

Madame de Staël

staff (stăf) ►*n., pl.* **staffs** or **staves** (stāvz) **1.** A stick or cane used as an aid in walking, as a weapon, or as a symbol of authority. **2.** *pl.* **staffs a.** A group of assistants to a person in authority. **b.** The personnel of an enterprise. **3.** A set of horizontal lines on which musical notes are written. ►*v.* To provide with a staff of employees. [< OE *stæf*.]

staff·er (stăf′ər) ►*n.* A member of a staff.

staff sergeant ►*n.* A rank in the US Army, Air Force, and Marine Corps above sergeant.

stag (stăg) ►*n.* An adult male deer. ►*adj.* **1.** Of or for men only: *a stag party*. **2.** Pornographic: *stag films*. ►*adv.* Unaccompanied: *went to the dance stag.* [< OE *stagga*.]

stage (stāj) ►*n.* **1.** A raised and level floor or platform. **2a.** A raised platform on which theatrical performances are presented. **b.** The acting profession: *The stage is her life.* **3.** The scene of a noteworthy event. **4.** A resting place on a journey. **5.** A stagecoach. **6.** A level, degree, or period of time in the course of a process; step. **7.** One of the successive propulsion units of a rocket. ►*v.* **staged, stag·ing 1.** To produce or direct (a theatrical performance). **2.** To arrange and carry out: *stage an invasion.* —*idiom:* **stage left (or right)** The area of a stage to one's left (or right) when facing the audience. [< VLat. **staticum* < Lat. *stāre*, stand.]

stage·coach (stāj′kōch′) ►*n.* A four-wheeled horse-drawn vehicle formerly used to transport mail and passengers.

stage·craft (stāj′krăft′) ►*n.* Skill in the techniques and devices of the theater.

stag·ger (stăg′ər) ►*v.* **1.** To move or cause to move unsteadily; totter. **2.** To cause to falter. **3.** To astonish, shock, or overwhelm. **4.** To arrange in alternating or overlapping times or positions. ►*n.* A tottering or reeling motion. [< ON *stakra* < *staka*, push.] —**stag′ger·er** *n.* —**stag′ger·ing·ly** *adv.*

stag·ing (stā′jĭng) ►*n.* **1.** A temporary platform; scaffolding. **2.** The process of putting on a play.

stag·nant (stăg′nənt) ►*adj.* **1.** Not flowing or moving: *stagnant ponds.* **2.** Showing little or no activity or vitality; inactive or sluggish. [< Lat. *stăgnāre*, STAGNATE.] —**stag′nan·cy** *n.* —**stag′nant·ly** *adv.*

stag·nate (stăg′nāt′) ►*v.* **-nat·ed, -nat·ing** To be or become stagnant. [< Lat. *stăgnum*, swamp.] —**stag·na′tion** *n.*

stag·y also **stag·ey** (stā′jē) ►*adj.* **-i·er, -i·est** Overly theatrical or dramatic. —**stag′i·ly** *adv.* —**stag′i·ness** *n.*

staid (stād) ►*adj.* Marked by sedateness and often a strait-laced sense of propriety; serious and conventional. [< obsolete *staid*, p.part. of STAY[1].] —**staid′ly** *adv.*

stain (stān) ►*v.* **1.** To discolor, soil, or spot. **2.** To corrupt; taint. **3.** To change the color of (e.g., a piece of wood) by applying a stain. ►*n.* **1.** A discolored or soiled spot or smudge. **2.** A diminishment of one's character or reputation by being associated with something disgraceful. **3.** A liquid substance applied esp. to wood that penetrates the surface and imparts a rich color. [< OFr. *desteindre*, deprive of color, and ON *steina*, paint.] —**stain′less** *adj.*
   Syns: *blot, brand, stigma, taint* **n.**

stained glass (stānd) ►*n.* Glass that is colored esp. for use in windows.

stainless steel ►*n.* Any of various steels alloyed with sufficient chromium to be resistant to corrosion or rusting.

stair (stâr) ►*n.* **1.** often **stairs** A staircase. **2.** One of a flight of steps. [< OE *stæger*.]

stair·case (stâr′kās′) ►*n.* A flight of steps and its supporting structure.

stair·way (stâr′wā′) ►*n.* See **staircase.**

stair·well (stâr′wĕl′) ►*n.* A vertical shaft around which a staircase has been built.

stake (stāk) ►*n.* **1.** A pointed piece of wood or metal driven into the ground as a marker, barrier, or support. **2a.** A post to which an offender is bound for execution by burning. **b.** Execution by burning. **3.** often **stakes a.** Money or property risked in a wager or gambling game. **b.** The prize awarded the winner of a contest or race. **4.** A share or interest in an enterprise. **5.** Something, such as a crucial change or grave consequence, that may result from a situation. ►*v.* **staked, stak·ing 1.** To mark the location or limits of with or as if with stakes. **2.** To fasten with or to a stake. **3.** To gamble; risk. **4.** To provide working capital for; finance. [< OE *staca*.]

stake·out (stāk′out′) ►*n.* Surveillance of an area, building, or person, esp. by police.

sta·lac·tite (stə-lăk′tīt′, stăl′ək-) ►*n.* An icicle-shaped mineral deposit hanging from the roof of a cavern. [< Gk. *stalaktos*, dripping.]

sta·lag·mite (stə-lăg′mīt′, stăl′əg-) ►*n.* A conical mineral deposit built up on the floor of a cavern. [< Gk. *stalagma*, a drop.]

stale (stāl) ►*adj.* **stal·er, stal·est 1.** Having lost freshness or flavor: *stale bread.* **2.** Lacking originality or spontaneity; trite. [ME, settled, clear (beer).] —**stale** *v.* —**stale′ly** *adv.* —**stale′ness** *n.*

stale·mate (stāl′māt′) ►*n.* A situation in which further action is blocked; deadlock. [Obsolete *stale* + MATE[2].] —**stale′mate′** *v.*

Sta·lin (stä′lĭn), **Joseph** Iosif Vissarionovich Dzhugashvili. 1879–1953. Soviet politician. —**Sta′lin·ism** *n.* —**Sta′lin·ist** *adj. & n.*

Joseph Stalin
photographed c. 1945

stalk¹ (stôk) ►*n.* A stem that supports a plant or plant part. [ME.]

stalk² (stôk) ►*v.* **1.** To pursue or track (prey) stealthily. **2.** To follow or observe (a person) persistently, esp. out of obsession or derangement. **3.** To walk with a stiff or haughty gait. **4.** To move threateningly or menacingly. [< OE *bestealcian*, move stealthily.] —**stalk′er** *n.*

stall¹ (stôl) ►*n.* **1.** A compartment for one animal in a barn or shed. **2a.** A booth or stand for selling wares. **b.** A small compartment: *a shower stall.* **3.** A pew in a church. ►*v.* **1.** To cause (an engine) accidentally to stop running. **2.** To come to a standstill: *Negotiations stalled.* [< OE *steall*, standing place.]

stall² (stôl) ►*v.* To employ delaying tactics (against). [< ME *stale*, decoy.] —**stall** *n.*

stal·lion (stăl′yən) ►*n.* An uncastrated adult male horse or other equine. [< AN *estaloun*, of Gmc. orig.]

stal·wart (stôl′wərt) ►*adj.* **1.** Loyal and resolute. **2.** Strong and imposing. [< OE *stælwierthe*, serviceable.]

sta·men (stā′mən) ►*n., pl.* **-mens** or **sta·mi·na** (stā′mə-nə, stăm′ə-) The pollen-producing reproductive organ of a flower. [Lat. *stāmen*, thread.]

stam·i·na (stăm′ə-nə) ►*n.* Physical or moral power of endurance. [Lat. *stāmina*, pl. of *stāmen*, thread, thread of life.]

sta·mi·nate (stā′mə-nĭt, -nāt′, stăm′ə-) ►*adj.* Having stamens but no pistils.

stam·mer (stăm′ər) ►*v.* To speak with involuntary pauses or repetitions. [< OE *stamerian*.] —**stam′mer** *n.* —**stam′mer·er** *n.*

stamp (stămp) ►*v.* **1.** To bring down (the foot) forcibly. **2.** To step on heavily, esp. so as to crush or extinguish. **3.** To shape or cut out with a mold, form, or die. **4.** To imprint or impress with a mark. **5.** To affix an adhesive stamp to. **6.** To mark; characterize. ►*n.* **1.** The act of stamping. **2a.** An implement or device used to stamp. **b.** The impression or shape stamped. **3.** A mark indicating ownership, approval, or completion. **4.** A small piece of gummed paper sold by a government for attachment to an article that is to be mailed. **5.** A characterizing mark or quality. [ME *stampen.*]

stam·pede (stăm-pēd′) ►*n.* A sudden frenzied rush of panic-stricken animals or people. ►*v.* **-ped·ed, -ped·ing** To participate in or cause a stampede. [Sp. *estampida*, uproar.]

stance (stăns) ►*n.* **1.** The position of a standing person or animal. See Synonyms at **posture.** **2.** Point of view. [< VLat. **stantia* < Lat. *stāre*, stand.]

stanch¹ (stônch, stănch, stänch) also **staunch** (stônch, stänch) ►*v.* To stop or check the flow of a bodily fluid, esp. blood. See Usage Note at **staunch¹.** [< VLat. **stanticāre*, stop < Lat. *stāre*, stand.]

stanch² (stônch, stänch, stănch) ►*adj.* Var. of **staunch¹.** See Usage Note at **staunch¹.**

stan·chion (stăn′chən, -shən) ►*n.* An upright pole or post. [< OFr. *estanchon* < Lat. *stāre*, stand.]

stand (stănd) ►*v.* **stood** (sto͞od), **stand·ing 1.** To rise to an upright position. **2.** To assume an upright position. **3.** To place upright. **4.** To be placed or situated. **5.** To remain stable, valid, or intact. **6.** To be in a specific state or condition: *stands in awe of the achievement.* **7.** To remain motionless or inactive. **8.** To tolerate; endure. **9.** To undergo: *stand trial.* ►*n.* **1.** The act of standing. **2.** A halt; standstill. **3.** A place designated for standing: *a witness stand.* **4.** A booth or counter for the sale of goods. **5.** A parking space reserved for taxis. **6.** A position or opinion one is prepared to uphold: *take a stand.* **7. stands** Tiers of benches as seating for spectators. **8.** A rack or prop for holding things upright. **9.** A growth of tall plants or trees. —*phrasal verbs:* **stand for 1.** To represent; symbolize. **2.** To tolerate. **stand out** To be prominent or outstanding. **stand up** To remain valid, sound, or durable. —*idioms:* **stand up for** To side with; defend. **stand up to** To confront fearlessly. [< OE *standan.*]

stan·dard (stăn′dərd) ►*adj.* **1.** Serving as an established measurement or value: *a standard unit of volume.* **2.** Recognized as a model of authority or excellence: *a standard reference work.* **3.** Acceptable but of less than top quality: *a standard grade of beef.* **4.** Normal, familiar, or usual: *the standard excuse.* **5.** Conforming to norms of usage admired by educated speakers and writers: *standard pronunciation.* ►*n.* **1.** An acknowledged basis for comparing or measuring; criterion. **2.** A degree or level of requirement, excellence, or attainment. **3.** A set of specifications adopted within an industry to allow compatibility between products. **4.** A flag, banner, or ensign. **5.** A pedestal, stand, or base. [< OFr. *estandard*, rallying place, of Gmc. orig.]

stan·dard-bear·er (stăn′dərd-bâr′ər) ►*n.* One who is in the vanguard of a political or religious movement.

standard deviation ►*n.* A statistic used as a measure of the dispersion or variation in a distribution or set of data.

Standard English ►*n.* The variety of English generally acknowledged as the model for the speech and writing of educated speakers.

stan·dard·ize (stăn′dər-dīz′) ►*v.* **-ized, -iz·ing** To cause to conform to a standard. —**stan′dard·i·za′tion** *n.*

standard of living ►*n.* A measure of the goods and services affordable by and available to a person or country.

standard time ►*n.* The time in any of 24 global

time zones, usually the mean solar time at the central meridian of each zone.

stand·by (stănd′bī′) ►*n., pl.* **-bys 1.** One that can always be relied on, as in an emergency. **2.** One kept in readiness as a substitute. ►*adj.* Waiting to be assigned unfilled travel space, as on an airline. ►*adv.* On a standby basis: *flew standby to Seattle.*

stand·ee (stăn-dē′) ►*n.* One who stands, as in a theater.

stand-in (stănd′ĭn′) ►*n.* **1.** One who substitutes for a movie actor, as during technical adjustments. **2.** A substitute.

stand·ing (stăn′dĭng) ►*n.* **1.** A relative position in a group; rank. **2.** Status; reputation. **3.** Continuance in time; duration. ►*adj.* **1.** Remaining upright. **2.** Performed from a standing position: *a standing jump.* **3.** Permanent: *a standing army.* **4.** Remaining in force indefinitely: *a standing invitation.*

standing stone ►*n.* A prehistoric monument of a class found chiefly in the British Isles and northern France, consisting of a single tall, upright megalith.

Stan·dish (stăn′dĭsh′), **Miles** or **Myles** 1584?–1656. English soldier and colonist in America.

stand·off (stănd′ôf′, -ŏf′) ►*n.* **1.** A tie or draw, as in a contest. **2.** A situation in which one force neutralizes or counterbalances the other.

stand·off·ish (stănd-ô′fĭsh, -ŏf′ĭsh) ►*adj.* Aloof or reserved. —**stand·off′ish·ness** *n.*

stand·out (stănd′out′) ►*n.* *Informal* One that is outstanding or excellent.

stand·pipe (stănd′pīp′) ►*n.* **1.** A large elevated vertical pipe or cylindrical tank that is filled with water to produce a desired pressure. **2.** A pipe or system of pipes through which water can flow, as for the operation of fire hoses on upper floors of a building.

stand·point (stănd′point′) ►*n.* A position from which things are considered; point of view. [Translation of Ger. *Standpunkt.*]

stand·still (stănd′stĭl′) ►*n.* A halt.

stand·up or **stand-up** (stănd′ŭp′) ►*adj.* **1.** Standing erect. **2.** Of or being a performer who delivers a solo comic monologue.

stank (stăngk) ►*v.* P.t. of **stink.**

Stan·ley or **Port Stan·ley** (stăn′lē) The administrative capital of the Falkland Is., in the E part.

Stan·ton (stăn′tən), **Elizabeth Cady** 1815–1902. Amer. feminist and social reformer.

stan·za (stăn′zə) ►*n.* One of the divisions of a poem, composed of two or more lines. [Ital.]

sta·pes (stā′pēz) ►*n., pl.* **-pes** or **sta·pe·des** (stā′pĭ-dēz′) A small stirrup-shaped bone of the middle ear. [< Med.Lat. *stapēs*, stirrup.]

staph·y·lo·coc·cus (stăf′ə-lō-kŏk′əs) ►*n., pl.* **-coc·ci** (-kŏk′sī, -kŏk′ī) A spherical parasitic bacterium usu. occurring in grapelike clusters that causes boils and other infections. [Gk. *staphulē*, bunch of grapes + –COCCUS.] —**staph′y·lo·coc′cal, staph′y·lo·coc′·cic** (-kŏk′sĭk, -kŏk′ĭk) *adj.*

sta·ple¹ (stā′pəl) ►*n.* **1.** A principal raw material or commodity. **2.** A major part, element, or feature. **3.** A basic dietary item. **4.** The fiber of cotton, wool, or flax, graded as to length and fineness. ►*adj.* **1.** Produced or stocked in large quantities. **2.** Principal; main. [Poss. < MDu. *stāpel*, emporium.]

sta·ple² (stā′pəl) ►*n.* **1.** A thin piece of wire shaped as three sides of a square so that it can be driven into thin or soft material, such as paper, and bent to function as a fastener. **2.** A similarly shaped piece of metal with pointed ends, driven into a surface to secure something, such as a bolt or length of wire. [< OE *stapol*, post.] —**sta′ple** *v.* —**sta′pler** *n.*

star (stär) ►*n.* **1a.** A celestial body that generates light and other radiant energy and consists of a mass of hot gas held together by its own gravity. **b.** A celestial body visible at night as a relatively stationary point of light. **2.** A graphic design having five or more radiating points. **3a.** An outstanding performer, esp. a leading actor or actress. **b.** A celebrity; luminary. **4.** An asterisk (*). **5. stars** The future; destiny. ►*v.* **starred, star·ring 1.** To ornament or mark with stars. **2.** To mark with an asterisk. **3.** To play the leading role in a theatrical or film production. [< OE *steorra.*] —**star′dom** *n.* —**star′ry** *adj.*

star·board (stär′bərd) ►*n.* The right-hand side of a ship or aircraft as one faces forward. [< OE *stēorbord.*] —**star′board** *adj. & adv.*

starch (stärch) ►*n.* **1.** A nutrient carbohydrate, $(C_6H_{10}O_5)_n$, found notably in corn, potatoes, wheat, and rice and commonly prepared as a white tasteless powder. **2.** Any of various substances, such as natural starch, used to stiffen cloth, as in laundering. **3.** A food having a high starch content. ►*v.* To stiffen with starch. [< ME *sterchen*, stiffen.] —**starch′i·ness** *n.* —**starch′y** *adj.*

stare (stâr) ►*v.* **stared, star·ing** To look directly and fixedly, often with a wide-eyed gaze. ►*n.* An intent gaze. [< OE *starian.*] —**star′er** *n.*

star·fish (stär′fĭsh′) ►*n.* Any of various, often spiny marine animals having five arms extending from a central disk.

star·gaze (stär′gāz′) ►*v.* **1.** To observe the stars. **2.** To daydream. —**star′gaz′er** *n.*

stark (stärk) ►*adj.* **-er, -est 1.** Clearly delineated: *a stark contrast.* **2a.** Bare or desolate. **b.** Severe or unmitigated; harsh. **3.** Complete or utter; extreme: *stark poverty.* ►*adv.* Utterly: *stark naked.* [< OE *stearc*, severe.] —**stark′ly** *adv.* —**stark′ness** *n.*

star·let (stär′lĭt) ►*n.* A young film actress publicized as a future star.

star·light (stär′līt′) ►*n.* The light from the stars.

star·ling (stär′lĭng) ►*n.* A bird usu. having dark, often iridescent plumage, widely naturalized worldwide. [< OE *stærlinc.*]

star·lit (stär′lĭt′) ►*adj.* Illuminated by starlight.

star·ry-eyed (stär′ē-īd′) ►*adj.* Naively enthusiastic, overoptimistic, or romantic.

Stars and Stripes (stärz) ►*n.* (*takes sing.* or *pl. v.*) The flag of the US.

start (stärt) ►*v.* **1.** To commence; begin. **2.** To set into motion, operation, or activity. **3.** To move suddenly or involuntarily: *started at the noise.* **4.** To begin to attend: *start school.* **5.** To enter in a race or game. **6.** To establish: *start a business.* ►*n.* **1.** A beginning. **2.** A place or time of beginning. **3.** A startled reaction or movement. [< OE *styrtan*, move suddenly.] —**start′er** *n.*

star·tle (stär′tl) ►*v.* **-tled, -tling 1.** To cause to make a quick involuntary movement, as in fright. **2.** To alarm or surprise. ►*n.* A sudden movement in response to something frightening, such as a noise. [< OE *steartlian*, kick.] —**star′tling·ly** *adv.*

start·up or **start-up** (stärt′ŭp′) ►*n.* **1.** The act of setting into operation or motion. **2.** A business that has recently begun operation.

starve (stärv) ►*v.* **starved, starv·ing 1.** To die or cause to die from prolonged lack of food. **2.** *Informal* To be hungry. **3.** To suffer from deprivation: *starving for love.* [< OE *steorfan*, die.] —**star·va′tion** *n.*

starve·ling (stärv′lĭng) ►*n.* One that is starving or being starved.

stash (stăsh) *Slang* ►*v.* To hide or store away in a secret place. ►*n.* A hidden or secret supply. [?]

–stasis ►*suff.* **1.** Stable state: *homeostasis.* **2.** Position: *metastasis.* [< Gk. *stasis*, standstill.]

stat. ►*abbr.* **1.** statistic **2.** statistics **3.** statuary **4.** statute

–stat ►*suff.* One that stabilizes: *rheostat.* [< Gk. *-statēs*, one that causes to stand.]

state (stāt) ►*n.* **1a.** A condition of being. **b.** A mental or emotional condition. **c.** Social position or rank. **2a.** The supreme public power within a sovereign political entity. **b.** A body politic, esp. one constituting a nation. **c.** One of the semiautonomous territorial and political subdivisions of a federated country, such as the US. ►*v.* **stat·ed, stat·ing** To set forth in words; declare. [< Lat. *status.*] —**state′hood′** *n.*

state·craft (stāt′krăft′) ►*n.* The art of leading a country.

state·house (stāt′hous′) ►*n.* A building in which a state legislature holds sessions.

state·less (stāt′lĭs) ►*adj.* Not having citizenship in a state or nation.

state·ly (stāt′lē) ►*adj.* **-li·er, -li·est 1.** Impressive, as in size; majestic: *stately mansions.* **2.** Dignified and slow: *a stately tempo.*

state·ment (stāt′mənt) ►*n.* **1a.** The act of stating. **b.** Something stated. **c.** A formal declaration, esp. with regard to facts or claims. **2.** An abstract of a financial account. **3.** A monthly report sent to a debtor or bank depositor.

Stat·en Island (stăt′n) A borough of New York City coextensive with **Staten Island** in New York Bay SW of Manhattan I.

state·room (stāt′rōōm′, -rōōm′) ►*n.* A private compartment on a ship or train.

state·side (stāt′sīd′) ►*adj.* Of or in esp. the continental US. —**state′side′** *adv.*

states·man (stāts′mən) ►*n.* **1.** A man who is a leader in national or international affairs. **2.** A man noted for disinterested public service. See Usage Note at **man.** —**states′man·like′** *adj.* —**states′man·ship′** *n.*

states·wom·an (stāts′wŏŏm′ən) ►*n.* **1.** A woman who is a leader in national or international affairs. **2.** A woman noted for disinterested public service. See Usage Note at **man.**

stat·ic (stăt′ĭk) ►*adj.* **1a.** Having no motion; being at rest. **b.** Fixed. **2.** *Phys.* Relating to bodies at rest or to balanced forces. **3.** Of or producing stationary electrical charges; electrostatic. ►*n.* **1.** Interference or noise, such as crackling in a receiver, produced when static or atmospheric electricity disturbs signal reception. **2.** *Informal* **a.** Obstruction. **b.** Angry criticism. [< Gk. *statos*, standing.] —**stat′i·cal·ly** *adv.*

sta·tion (stā′shən) ►*n.* **1.** The place where a

person or thing stands or is assigned to stand; post. **2.** The place from which a service is provided or operations are directed: *a police station.* **3.** A stopping place along a route, esp. a depot. **4.** Social position; rank. **5.** An establishment that is equipped for radio or television transmission. ►*v.* To assign to a position. [< Lat. *statiō.*]

sta·tion·ar·y (stā′shə-nĕr′ē) ►*adj.* **1.** Not moving; fixed. **2.** Unchanging.

station break ►*n.* An intermission in a radio or television program for identification of the network or station.

sta·tion·er (stā′shə-nər) ►*n.* One who sells stationery. [Prob. < Lat. *statiō*, shop; see STATION.]

sta·tion·er·y (stā′shə-nĕr′ē) ►*n.* Writing materials, such as paper and envelopes.

station wagon ►*n.* An automobile having an extended interior with a third seat or luggage platform and a tailgate.

sta·tis·tic (stə-tĭs′tĭk) ►*n.* A numerical piece of information. —**sta·tis′ti·cal** *adj.* —**sta·tis′ti·cal·ly** *adv.*

sta·tis·tics (stə-tĭs′tĭks) ►*n.* **1.** (*takes sing. v.*) The mathematics of the collection, organization, and interpretation of numerical data. **2.** (*takes pl. v.*) Numerical data. [< Ger. *Statistik*, political science, ult. < Lat. *status*, state.] —**stat′is·ti′cian** (stăt′ĭ-stĭsh′ən) *n.*

stat·u·ar·y (stăch′ōō-ĕr′ē) ►*n., pl.* **-ies** Statues collectively.

stat·ue (stăch′ōō) ►*n.* A form or likeness produced in material such as stone, clay, or bronze. [< Lat. *statuere*, set up; see STATUE.]

stat·u·esque (stăch′ōō-ĕsk′) ►*adj.* Suggestive of a statue, as in grace or dignity.

stat·u·ette (stăch′ōō-ĕt′) ►*n.* A small statue.

stat·ure (stăch′ər) ►*n.* **1.** The natural height of a human or animal in an upright position. **2.** An achieved level; status. [< Lat. *statūra* < *stāre*, stand.]

stat·us (stăt′əs, stā′təs) ►*n.* **1.** Position relative to that of others; standing. **2.** High standing; prestige. **3.** The legal character or condition of a person or thing: *the status of a minor.* **4.** A state of affairs; situation. [Lat.]

status quo (kwō) ►*n.* The existing state of affairs. [Lat. *status quō*, state in which.]

stat·ute (stăch′ōōt) ►*n.* **1.** A law enacted by a legislature. **2.** A decree, as of a ruler. [< Lat. *statuere, statūt-*, establish < *status*, position.]

statute mile ►*n.* The standard mile, 5,280 ft.

stat·u·to·ry (stăch′ə-tôr′ē) ►*adj.* Enacted, regulated, or authorized by statute.

staunch¹ (stônch, stänch) also **stanch** (stônch, stänch, stănch) ►*adj.* **-er, -est 1.** Firm and steadfast; loyal or true. **2.** Strong; solid. [< OFr. *estanchier*, STANCH¹.] —**staunch′ly** *adv.* —**staunch′ness** *n.*

Usage: *Staunch* is more common than *stanch* as the spelling of the adjective. *Stanch* is more common than *staunch* as the spelling of the verb.

staunch² (stônch, stänch) ►*v.* Var. of **stanch¹.**

stave (stāv) ►*n.* **1.** A narrow strip of wood forming part of the sides of a barrel, tub, or similar structure. **2.** A staff or cudgel. **3.** See **staff** (sense 3). **4.** A stanza. ►*v.* **staved** or **stove** (stōv), **stav·ing** To crush or smash inward, often by making a hole. Often used with *in.*

—*phrasal verb:* **stave off** To keep or hold off. [< STAVES.]

staves (stāvz) ►*n.* Pl. of **staff.**

stay¹ (stā) ►*v.* **1a.** To continue to be in a place or condition: *stay home; stay calm.* **b.** To wait in order to do something: *stay to watch the end of the game.* **2a.** To endure or persist in an action or activity: *stay with a plan.* **b.** To keep up in a race or contest: *tried to stay with the lead runner.* **3.** To suspend (a planned action) by legal order. **4.** To satisfy or appease temporarily. ►*n.* **1.** A brief period of residence or visiting. **2.** The legal order by which a planned action is stayed. [< Lat. *stāre,* stand.]

stay² (stā) ►*v.* To brace, support, or prop up: *The tower is stayed with cables.* ►*n.* **1.** A support or brace. **2.** A strip of bone, plastic, or metal, used to stiffen a garment or part. **3. stays** A corset. [< OFr. *estaie,* a support, of Gmc. orig.]

stay·ca·tion (stā-kā′shən) ►*n.* A vacation in which one does not travel away from home. [Blend of STAY¹ and VACATION.]

STD ►*abbr.* sexually transmitted disease

std. ►*abbr.* standard

stead (stĕd) ►*n.* **1.** The place, position, or function of another person. **2.** Advantage: *stood them in good stead.* [< OE *stede.*]

stead·fast (stĕd′făst′, -fəst) ►*adj.* **1.** Firmly loyal or constant. **2.** Fixed or unchanging: *a steadfast rule.* —**stead′fast′ly** *adv.* —**stead′-fast′ness** *n.*

stead·y (stĕd′ē) ►*adj.* **-i·er, -i·est 1.** Firm in position or place; fixed. **2.** Direct and unfaltering; sure. **3.** Not changing or fluctuating; uniform. **4.** Not easily excited or upset. **5.** Reliable; dependable. ►*v.* **stead·ied, stead·y·ing** To make or become steady. —**stead′i·ly** *adv.* —**stead′i·ness** *n.*

steak (stāk) ►*n.* **1.** A slice or slab of meat, esp. beef, usu. grilled or broiled. **2.** A thick slice of a large fish cut across the body. [< ON *steik.*]

steal (stēl) ►*v.* **stole** (stōl), **sto·len** (stō′lən), **steal·ing 1.** To take (the property of another) without right or permission. **2.** To get or effect surreptitiously or artfully: *steal a kiss.* **3.** To move, carry, or place stealthily. **4.** *Baseball* To advance safely to (another base) during the delivery of a pitch. ►*n.* **1.** The act of stealing. **2.** *Slang* A bargain. [< OE *stelan.*] —**steal′er** *n.*

stealth (stĕlth) ►*n.* **1.** The act of moving, proceeding, or acting in a covert way. **2.** Furtiveness. [ME *stelth.*] —**stealth′i·ly** *adv.* —**stealth′i·ness** *n.* —**stealth′y** *adj.*

steam (stēm) ►*n.* **1a.** The vapor phase of water. **b.** A mist of cooling water vapor. **2.** Pressurized water vapor used for heating, cooking, or to provide mechanical power. **3.** Power; energy. ►*v.* **1.** To produce or emit steam. **2.** To become or rise up as steam. **3.** To become misted or covered with steam. **4.** To move by means of steam power. **5.** *Informal* To become very angry; fume. **6.** To expose to steam, as in cooking. [< OE *stēam.*] —**steam′y** *adj.*

steam·boat (stēm′bōt′) ►*n.* A steamship.

steam engine ►*n.* An engine that converts the heat energy of pressurized steam into mechanical energy, esp. one in which steam drives a piston in a closed cylinder.

steam·er (stē′mər) ►*n.* **1.** A steamship. **2.** A container in which something is steamed. **3.** See **soft-shell clam.**

steam·fit·ter (stēm′fĭt′ər) ►*n.* One who installs and repairs heating, ventilating, refrigerating, and air-conditioning systems.

steam·punk (stēm′pŭngk′) ►*n.* **1.** Science fiction set esp. in an alternate version of 19th-cent. England and involving advanced technologies usu. based on steam power. **2.** An aesthetic style inspired by steampunk fiction.

steam·roll·er (stēm′rō′lər) ►*n.* A machine equipped with a heavy roller for smoothing road surfaces. ►*v.* **1.** To smooth or level (a road) with a steamroller. **2.** To overwhelm or suppress ruthlessly; crush.

steam·ship (stēm′shĭp′) ►*n.* A large vessel propelled by steam-driven screws or paddles.

steam shovel ►*n.* **1.** A large, steam-driven machine for digging. **2.** See **power shovel.**

ste·a·tite (stē′ə-tīt′) ►*n.* See **soapstone.** [< Gk. *steatitis,* a precious stone.]

steed (stēd) ►*n.* A horse, esp. a spirited one. [< OE *stēda,* stallion.]

steel (stēl) ►*n.* **1.** A hard, strong, durable, malleable alloy of iron and carbon. **2.** Something, such as a sword, made of steel. **3.** A quality suggestive of steel: *nerves of steel.* ►*v.* **1.** To cover, plate, edge, or point with steel. **2.** To make hard or strong; brace. [< OE *stўle.*] —**steel′i·ness** *n.* —**steel′y** *adj.*

steel drum ►*n.* A tuned metal percussion instrument fashioned from an oil barrel.

steel wool ►*n.* Fine fibers of steel matted or woven together to form an abrasive.

steep¹ (stēp) ►*adj.* **-er, -est 1.** Having a sharp inclination; precipitous. **2.** Excessive; stiff: *a steep price.* [< OE *stēap.*] —**steep′ly** *adv.* —**steep′ness** *n.*
    Syns: abrupt, precipitous, sheer adj.

steep² (stēp) ►*v.* **1.** To soak or be soaked in liquid in order to cleanse, soften, or extract a given property from. **2.** To saturate: *steeped in history.* [ME *stepen.*]

stee·ple (stē′pəl) ►*n.* **1.** A tall tower rising from the roof of a building, such as a church. **2.** A spire. [< OE *stēpel.*]

stee·ple·chase (stē′pəl-chās′) ►*n.* A horserace across open country or over an obstacle course. —**stee′ple·chas′er** *n.*

stee·ple·jack (stē′pəl-jăk′) ►*n.* A worker on very high structures, such as steeples.

steer¹ (stîr) ►*v.* **1.** To guide, esp. by a device such as a rudder or wheel. **2.** To direct the course or progress of. See Synonyms at **guide. 3.** To follow or move in a set course. [< OE *stēran.*] —**steer′er** *n.* —**steers′man** *n.*

steer² (stîr) ►*n.* A young ox, esp. one castrated before sexual maturity and raised for beef. [< OE *stēor.*]

steer·age (stîr′ĭj) ►*n.* **1.** The act or practice of steering. **2.** The section of a passenger ship providing the cheapest accommodations.

steg·a·nog·ra·phy (stĕg′ə-nŏg′rə-fē) ►*n.* The deliberate concealment of data within other data, as by embedding digitized text in a digitized image. [< Greek *steganos,* covered + –GRAPHY.] —**steg′a·no·graph′ic** (-nə-grăf′-ĭk) *adj.*

steg·o·sau·rus (stĕg′ə-sôr′əs) also **steg·o·saur** (stĕg′ə-sôr′) ►*n.* A herbivorous dinosaur having a double row of upright bony plates along the back. [Gk. *stegos,* roof + *sauros,* lizard.]

stein (stīn) ►*n.* A mug, esp. for beer. [Ger.]

stein

Stein, Gertrude 1874–1946. Amer. writer.
Stein·beck (stīn′běk′), **John Ernst** 1902–68. Amer. writer.
Stein·em (stī′nəm), **Gloria** b. 1934. Amer. feminist, writer, and editor.

Gloria Steinem
photographed in 2008

stel·lar (stěl′ər) ►*adj.* **1.** Of or consisting of stars. **2a.** Of a star performer. **b.** Outstanding. [< Lat. *stēlla*, star.]
stem¹ (stěm) ►*n.* **1a.** The main ascending part of a plant; stalk. **b.** A stalk supporting another plant part, such as a leaf or flower. **2.** A connecting or supporting part, such as the tube of a tobacco pipe or the slender upright support of a wineglass. **3.** The main line of descent of a family. **4.** *Ling.* The main part of a word to which affixes are added. **5.** *Naut.* The prow. ►*v.* **stemmed, stem·ming 1.** To derive or originate. **2.** To make progress against (a force or flow). [< OE *stefn*, ship's stem.]
   Syns: arise, derive, flow, issue, originate, proceed, rise, spring **v.**
stem² (stěm) ►*v.* **stemmed, stem·ming** To stop or hold back by or as if by damming. [< ON *stemma*.]
stem cell ►*n.* An unspecialized cell that gives rise to specialized cells.
stem·ware (stěm′wâr′) ►*n.* Glassware mounted on a stem.
stench (stěnch) ►*n.* A strong, foul odor; stink. [< OE *stenc*, odor.]
   Syns: malodor, reek, stink **n.**
sten·cil (stěn′səl) ►*n.* A sheet, as of plastic, in which a letter or design has been cut so that

ink or paint applied to the sheet will reproduce the pattern on the surface beneath. ►*v.* **-ciled, -cil·ing** or **-cilled, -cil·ling** To mark or produce with a stencil. [< OFr. *estenceler*, adorn brightly.]
Sten·dhal (stěn-däl′) Marie Henri Beyle. 1783–1842. French writer.
ste·nog·ra·phy (stə-nŏg′rə-fē) ►*n.* The art or process of writing in shorthand. [< Gk. *stenos*, narrow.] **—ste·nog′ra·pher** *n.* **—sten′o·graph′ic** (stěn′ə-grăf′ĭk) *adj.* **—sten′o·graph′i·cal·ly** *adv.*
sten·to·ri·an (stěn-tôr′ē-ən) ►*adj.* Extremely loud. [After *Stentor*, a loud herald in the *Iliad*.]
step (stěp) ►*n.* **1a.** The single complete movement of raising one foot and putting it down in another spot, as in walking. **b.** A manner of walking; gait. **c.** A fixed rhythm or pace, as in marching. **2.** A short distance. **3a.** A rest for the foot in ascending or descending. **b. steps** Stairs. **4a.** One of a series of actions or measures taken to achieve a goal. **b.** A stage in a process. **5.** A degree in progress or a grade or rank in a scale. ►*v.* **stepped, step·ping 1.** To put or press the foot down. **2.** To shift or move slightly by taking a step or two: *step back.* **3.** To walk a short distance. **4.** To measure by pacing. **—*phrasal verb:* step up 1.** To increase, esp. in stages: *step up production.* **2.** To come forward. **—*idioms:* in step 1.** Moving in rhythm. **2.** In conformity with one's environment: *in step with the times.* **out of step 1.** Not moving in rhythm. **2.** Not in conformity with one's environment. [< OE *stæpe*.]
step– ►*pref.* Related through remarriage rather than by blood: *stepparent.* [< OE *stēop-*.]
step·broth·er (stěp′brŭth′ər) ►*n.* A son of one's stepparent.
step·child (stěp′chīld′) ►*n.* A spouse's child by a previous union.
step·daugh·ter (stěp′dô′tər) ►*n.* A spouse's daughter by a previous union.
step·fa·ther (stěp′fä′thər) ►*n.* The husband of one's parent and not one's natural father.
Ste·phen (stē′vən), Saint. d. c. AD 36. Christian martyr.
step·lad·der (stěp′lăd′ər) ►*n.* A portable ladder with a hinged supporting frame.
step·moth·er (stěp′mŭth′ər) ►*n.* The wife of one's parent and not one's natural mother.
step·par·ent (stěp′pâr′ənt, -păr′-) ►*n.* A stepfather or stepmother.
steppe (stěp) ►*n.* A vast semiarid grass-covered plain, as found in SE Europe and Siberia. [< Russ. *step′*.]
step·ping·stone (stěp′ĭng-stōn′) ►*n.* An advantageous position for advancement toward a goal.
step·sis·ter (stěp′sĭs′tər) ►*n.* A daughter of one's stepparent.
step·son (stěp′sŭn′) ►*n.* A spouse's son by a previous union.
ster. ►*abbr.* sterling
–ster ►*suff.* **1.** One that is associated with, participates in, makes, or does: *songster.* **2.** One that is: *youngster.* [< OE *-estre.*]
stere (stîr) ►*n.* A unit of volume equal to one cubic meter. [< Gk. *stereos*, solid.]
ster·e·o (stěr′ē-ō′) ►*n., pl.* **-os 1.** A stereophonic sound-reproduction system. **2.** Stereophonic sound. **—ste′re·o′** *adj.*

stereo– ▸*pref.* **1.** Solid: *stereotype.* **2.** Three-dimensional: *stereoscope.* [< Gk. *stereos.*]

ster·e·o·phon·ic (stěr′ē-ə-fŏn′ĭk) ▸*adj.* Of or used in a sound-reproduction system that uses two or more separate channels to give a more natural distribution of sound. **—ster′e·o·phon′i·cal·ly** *adv.*

ster·e·o·scope (stĕr′ē-ə-skōp′) ▸*n.* An optical instrument with two eyepieces used to impart a three-dimensional effect to two photographs of the same scene taken at slightly different angles. **—ster′e·o·scop′ic** *adj.* **—ster′e·o·scop′i·cal·ly** *adv.*

ster·e·os·co·py (stĕr′ē-ŏs′kə-pē) ▸*n.* The viewing of objects as three-dimensional.

ster·e·o·type (stĕr′ē-ə-tīp′) ▸*n.* **1.** A conventional, oversimplified conception, opinion, or image. **2.** One regarded as embodying or conforming to a set image or type. **3.** A metal printing plate cast from a matrix that is molded from a raised printing surface. ▸*v.* **1.** To make a stereotype of or from. **2.** To characterize by a conventional stereotype. **—ster′e·o·typ′ic** (-tĭp′ĭk), **ster′e·o·typ′i·cal** *adj.*

ster·ile (stĕr′əl, -īl′) ▸*adj.* **1a.** Incapable of producing offspring. **b.** Producing little or no vegetation. **2.** Free from microorganisms. **3.** Not productive or effective: *a sterile discussion.* [< Lat. *sterilis.*] **—ste·ril′i·ty** (stə-rĭl′ĭ-tē) *n.*

ster·il·ize (stĕr′ə-līz′) ▸*v.* **-ized, -iz·ing** To make sterile. **—ster′il·i·za′tion** *n.*

ster·ling (stûr′lĭng) ▸*n.* **1.** British money. **2.** Sterling silver. ▸*adj.* **1.** Of or consisting of British money. **2.** Made of sterling silver. **3.** Of the highest quality. [ME, silver penny.]

sterling silver ▸*n.* An alloy of 92.5% silver with copper or another metal.

stern[1] (stûrn) ▸*adj.* **-er, -est 1.** Hard or severe in manner or character. **2.** Firm or unyielding; uncompromising. **3.** Difficult to endure. [< OE *styrne.*] **—stern′ly** *adv.* **—stern′ness** *n.*

stern[2] (stûrn) ▸*n.* The rear part of a ship or boat. [ME *sterne.*]

Sterne (stûrn), **Laurence** 1713–68. British writer.

ster·num (stûr′nəm) ▸*n., pl.* **-nums** or **-na** (-nə) A long flat bone that is situated along the center of the chest and articulates with the ribs; breastbone. [< Gk. *sternon.*]

ster·oid (stĕr′oid′, stîr′-) ▸*n.* Any of numerous natural or synthetic fat-soluble organic compounds having as a basis 17 carbon atoms arranged in four rings, including the sterols and adrenal and sex hormones. [STER(OL) + -OID.]

ster·ol (stîr′ôl′, stĕr′-) ▸*n.* Any of a group of predominantly unsaturated solid alcohols of the steroid group, such as cholesterol, present in the fatty tissues of plants and animals. [< CHOLESTEROL.]

stet (stĕt) ▸*v.* **stet·ted, stet·ting** *Print.* To nullify (a correction or deletion) in printed matter. [Lat., let it stand < *stāre,* stand.]

steth·o·scope (stĕth′ə-skōp′) ▸*n.* An instrument used for listening to sounds produced within the body. [Gk. *stēthos,* chest + -SCOPE.]

Steu·ben (stōō′bən, styōō′-), Baron **Friedrich Wilhelm von.** 1730–94. Prussian-born Amer. Revolutionary leader.

ste·ve·dore (stē′vĭ-dôr′) ▸*n.* A dockworker. [Sp. *estibador* < *estibar,* stow.]

Ste·vens (stē′vənz), **Wallace** 1879–1955. Amer. poet.

Ste·ven·son (stē′vən-sən), **Robert Louis Balfour** 1850–94. British writer.

stew (stōō, styōō) ▸*v.* **1.** To cook (food) by simmering or boiling slowly. **2.** *Informal* To be in a state of anxiety or agitation. ▸*n.* **1.** A dish, as of meat and vegetables, cooked by stewing. **2.** *Informal* Mental agitation. [< OFr. *estuver,* place in hot water.]

stew·ard (stōō′ərd, styōō′-) ▸*n.* **1.** One who manages another's property, finances, or other affairs. **2.** One in charge of the household affairs of a large estate, club, hotel, or resort. **3.** A ship's officer in charge of provisions and dining arrangements. **4.** An attendant on a ship or airplane. [< OE *stigweard.*] **—stew′ard·ship′** *n.*

stew·ard·ess (stōō′ər-dĭs, styōō′-) ▸*n.* A woman flight attendant. See Usage Note at **-ess.**

Stew·art (stōō′ərt, styōō′-), **James Maitland** "Jimmy." 1908–97. Amer. actor.

stick (stĭk) ▸*n.* **1.** A long slender piece of wood, esp. a branch cut from a tree or shrub. **2.** A long thin implement with a blade or net on the end used to propel and control a puck or ball in hockey or lacrosse. **3.** A walking stick. **4.** Something that is long and thin: *a stick of dynamite.* **5.** A poke or thrust. **6. sticks** *Informal* A remote area; backwoods. **7.** *Informal* A stiff, boring, or spiritless person. ▸*v.* **stuck** (stŭk), **stick·ing 1.** To pierce, puncture, or penetrate with a pointed instrument. **2.** To thrust (a pointed instrument) into another object. **3.** To fix or impale on a pointed object. **4a.** To fasten by forcing an end or point into something. **b.** To fasten or attach with an adhesive, such as glue or tape. **5.** To confuse or puzzle. **6.** To be or become fixed or embedded in place. **7.** To persist, endure, or persevere. **8.** To be or become blocked, checked, or obstructed: *The car stuck in the mud.* **9.** To project or protrude. **—phrasal verbs: stick around** *Informal* To remain; linger. **stick up** To rob, esp. at gunpoint. [< OE *sticca.*]

stick·er (stĭk′ər) ▸*n.* **1.** One that sticks, as an adhesive label. **2.** A thorn or prickle.

stick·ler (stĭk′lər) ▸*n.* One who insists on something unyieldingly. [< ME *stightlen,* contend.]

stick shift ▸*n.* An automotive transmission with a shift lever operated by hand.

stick-to-it·ive·ness (stĭk-tōō′ĭ-tĭv-nĭs) ▸*n. Informal* Unwavering tenacity.

stick·up (stĭk′ŭp′) ▸*n. Slang* A robbery, esp. at gunpoint.

stick·y (stĭk′ē) ▸*adj.* **-i·er, -i·est 1.** Sticking or tending to stick to a surface; adhesive. **2.** Warm and humid; muggy. **3.** *Informal* Painful or difficult: *a sticky situation.* **—stick′i·ly** *adv.* **—stick′i·ness** *n.*

stiff (stĭf) ▸*adj.* **-er, -est 1.** Difficult to bend: *a stiff collar.* **2.** Not moving or operating easily or freely: *stiff joints.* **3.** Not loose or fluid; thick: *stiff dough.* **4a.** Rigidly formal. **b.** Lacking ease or grace. **5.** Having a strong, swift, steady force: *a stiff breeze.* **6.** Potent or strong: *a stiff drink.* **7a.** Difficult; arduous. **b.** Harsh or severe: *a stiff penalty.* ▸*n. Slang* A corpse. ▸*v. Slang* To cheat (someone) of something owed. [< OE *stīf.*] **—stiff′en** *v.* **—stiff′ly** *adv.* **—stiff′ness** *n.*

stiff-necked (stĭf′nĕkt′) ▸*adj.* Stubborn and arrogant or aloof.

sti·fle (stī′fəl) ►*v.* **-fled, -fling 1.** To extinguish or cut off: *stifle dissent.* **2.** To keep in or hold back; suppress. **3.** To smother or suffocate. [ME *stifilen.*] —**sti′fling·ly** *adv.*

stig·ma (stĭg′mə) ►*n., pl.* **stig·mas** or **-ma·ta** (stĭg-mä′tə, -mät′ə, stĭg′mə-) **1.** An association of disgrace or public disapproval. See Synonyms at **stain. 2. stigmata** *Christianity* Marks or sores corresponding to the crucifixion wounds of Jesus. **3.** *Bot.* The apex of a flower pistil, on which pollen is deposited. [< Gk., tattoo mark.] —**stig·mat′ic** (-măt′ĭk) *adj.*

stig·ma·tize (stĭg′mə-tīz′) ►*v.* **-tized, -tiz·ing 1.** To characterize as disgraceful; brand. **2.** To mark with stigmata or a stigma. —**stig′ma·ti·za′tion** *n.*

stile (stīl) ►*n.* A set or series of steps for crossing a fence or wall. [< OE *stigel.*]

sti·let·to (stĭ-lĕt′ō) ►*n., pl.* **-tos** or **-toes** A small dagger with a slender tapering blade. [Ital., dim. of *stilo*, dagger.]

still¹ (stĭl) ►*adj.* **-er, -est 1a.** Not moving or in motion. **b.** Free from disturbance or commotion. **2.** Marked by no sound or faint sound. ►*n.* **1.** Silence; quiet. **2.** A still photograph, esp. one from a scene of a movie. ►*adv.* **1.** Without movement: *stand still.* **2.** Now as before: *still unfinished.* **3.** In increasing amount or degree: *and still further complaints.* **4.** All the same; nevertheless. ►*v.* **1.** To make or become still. **2.** To allay; calm. [< OE *stille.*] —**still′ness** *n.*

still² (stĭl) ►*n.* **1.** An apparatus for distilling liquids, such as alcohols. **2.** A distillery. [< ME *distillen,* DISTILL.]

still·birth (stĭl′bûrth′) ►*n.* **1.** The birth of a dead infant. **2.** An infant that is dead at birth. —**still′born** *adj.*

still life ►*n., pl.* **still lifes** A painting, picture, or photograph of inanimate objects.

stilt (stĭlt) ►*n.* **1.** Either of a pair of long slender poles equipped with raised footrests to enable the user to walk elevated above the ground. **2.** A tall supporting post, as for a dock. [ME *stilte.*]

stilt

stilt·ed (stĭl′tĭd) ►*adj.* Stiffly or artificially formal; stiff. —**stilt′ed·ly** *adv.*

stim·u·lant (stĭm′yə-lənt) ►*n.* **1.** An agent, esp. a drug, that temporarily arouses or accelerates physiological activity. **2.** A stimulus or incentive. **3.** An alcoholic drink. —**stim′u·lant** *adj.*

stim·u·late (stĭm′yə-lāt′) ►*v.* **-lat·ed, -lat·ing** To rouse to activity or heightened action; excite. [< Lat. *stimulus*, goad.] —**stim′u·la′tion** *n.* —**stim′u·la′tive** *adj.*

stim·u·lus (stĭm′yə-ləs) ►*n., pl.* **-li** (-lī′) **1.** Something that stimulates. **2.** Government spending designed to generate or increase economic activity. [Latin, goad.]

sting (stĭng) ►*v.* **stung** (stŭng), **sting·ing 1.** To pierce or wound painfully with a sharp-pointed structure or organ. **2.** To cause to feel a sharp, smarting pain. **3.** To cause to suffer keenly. ►*n.* **1.** The act of stinging. **2.** The wound or pain caused by stinging. **3.** A sharp, piercing organ or part, as of a bee or wasp. [< OE *stingan.*] —**sting′er** *n.*

sting·ray (stĭng′rā′) ►*n.* A ray having a whiplike tail armed with one or more venomous spines.

stin·gy (stĭn′jē) ►*adj.* **-gi·er, -gi·est 1.** Giving or spending reluctantly. **2.** Scanty or meager. [Poss. < dial. *stingy*, stinging < STING.] —**stin′gi·ly** *adv.* —**stin′gi·ness** *n.*

stink (stĭngk) ►*v.* **stank** (stăngk) or **stunk** (stŭngk), **stunk, stink·ing 1.** To emit a strong foul odor. **2.** *Slang* To be extremely bad. **3.** To be morally offensive or have the appearance of corruption. ►*n.* **1.** A strong offensive odor. See Synonyms at **stench. 2.** *Slang* A fuss; uproar. [< OE *stincan*, emit a smell.] —**stink′er** *n.*

stink·bug (stĭngk′bŭg′) ►*n.* Any of numerous insects that emit a foul odor.

stint (stĭnt) ►*v.* **1.** To be frugal or sparing. **2.** To restrict or limit, as in amount or number. ►*n.* **1.** A length of time spent in doing a job or fulfilling a duty. **2.** A limitation or restriction. [< OE *styntan,* to blunt.] —**stint′er** *n.*

sti·pend (stī′pĕnd′, -pənd) ►*n.* A fixed and regular payment, such as a salary or allowance. [< Lat. *stipendium,* soldier's pay.]

stip·ple (stĭp′əl) ►*v.* **-pled, -pling 1.** To draw, engrave, or paint in dots or short strokes. **2.** To apply (e.g., paint) in dots or short strokes. [< MDu. *stip*, dot.] —**stip′ple** *n.*

stip·u·late (stĭp′yə-lāt′) ►*v.* **-lat·ed, -lat·ing 1.** To specify or agree to as a condition in an agreement. **2.** To agree to (a fact) in order to reduce the scope of the dispute to be resolved by a court. Used of litigants. [Lat. *stipulārī,* to bargain.] —**stip′u·la′tion** *n.*

stir¹ (stûr) ►*v.* **stirred, stir·ring 1.** To pass an implement through in circular motions so as to mix or cool the contents. **2.** To change or cause to change position slightly. **3a.** To excite strong feelings in or rouse, as from indifference. **b.** To provoke: *stir up trouble.* ►*n.* **1.** An act of stirring. **2.** A slight movement. **3.** A disturbance or commotion. [< OE *styrian,* agitate.] —**stir′rer** *n.*

stir² (stûr) ►*n.* *Slang* Prison. [< Romani *stariben, stirapen* < *astar,* seize.]

stir-fry (stûr′frī′) ►*v.* To fry quickly in a small amount of oil while stirring continuously. ►*n.* Food fried in this manner.

stir·ring (stûr′ĭng) ►*adj.* **1.** Exciting; rousing. **2.** *Archaic* Active; lively. —**stir′ring·ly** *adv.*

stir·rup (stûr′əp, stĭr′-) ►*n.* A loop or ring hung from either side of a horse's saddle to support the rider's foot. [< OE *stīgrāp.*]

stitch (stĭch) ►*n.* **1a.** A link, loop, or knot formed by a threaded needle in sewing or surgical suturing. **b.** A single loop of yarn around a knitting needle. **c.** A way of arranging the threads in sewing, knitting, crocheting, or suturing: *a purl stitch.* **2.** A sudden sharp pain. ►*v.* **1.** To fasten, join, or ornament with or as if with stitches. **2.** To sew. [< OE *stice,* a sting.] —**stitch′er** *n.* —**stitch′er·y** *n.*

stoat (stōt) ►*n., pl.* **stoat** or **stoats** See **ermine** (sense 1). [ME *stote.*]

sto·chas·tic (stō-kăs′tĭk) ►*adj.* Statistics Involving or containing a random variable or process. [< Gk. *stokhastēs,* diviner.]

stock (stŏk) ►*n.* **1.** A supply accumulated for future use; store. **2.** The total merchandise kept on hand by a commercial establishment. **3.** Domestic animals; livestock. **4a.** A kind of financial security granting rights of ownership in a corporation. **b.** The stock issued by a particular company. **5.** *Bot.* A trunk or main stem. **6a.** The original progenitor of a family line. **b.** The descendants of a common ancestor. **c.** Ancestry or lineage. **d.** A group of related languages. **7.** The raw material out of which something is made. **8.** The broth in which meat, fish, bones, or vegetables are simmered, used in preparing soup or sauces. **9.** A supporting structure, block, or frame: *a gun stock.* **10. stocks** A wooden device with holes for confining the ankles and sometimes the wrists, formerly used for punishment. **11.** A company of actors and technicians attached to a single theater and performing in repertory. **12.** Confidence or credence. ►*v.* **1.** To provide with stock. **2.** To keep and store for future sale or use. ►*adj.* **1.** Kept regularly in stock. **2.** Routine: *a stock answer.* [< OE *stocc,* tree trunk.]

stock·ade (stŏ-kād′) ►*n.* A defensive barrier made of strong posts or timbers driven upright side by side into the ground. [< Sp. *estaca,* stake, of Gmc. orig.]

stock·bro·ker (stŏk′brō′kər) ►*n.* One that acts as an agent in buying and selling stocks or other securities. —**stock′bro′ker·age** *n.*

stock car ►*n.* An automobile of a standard make modified for racing.

stock exchange ►*n.* **1.** A place or system in which stocks, bonds, or other securities are bought and sold. **2.** An association of stockbrokers.

stock·hold·er (stŏk′hōl′dər) ►*n.* A shareholder.

Stock·holm (stŏk′hōlm′, -hōm′) The capital of Sweden, in the E part on the Baltic Sea.

stock·ing (stŏk′ĭng) ►*n.* A close-fitting, usu. knitted covering for the foot and leg. [< ME *stokke,* leg covering.]

stocking cap ►*n.* A long tapering knitted cap.

stock market ►*n.* **1.** See **stock exchange. 2.** The buying and selling of stocks.

stock·pile (stŏk′pīl′) ►*n.* A supply stored for future use. —**stock′pile′** *v.*

stock-still (stŏk′stĭl′) ►*adj.* Completely still; motionless.

stock·y (stŏk′ē) ►*adj.* **-i·er, -i·est** Solidly built; thickset. —**stock′i·ness** *n.*

stock·yard (stŏk′yärd′) ►*n.* A large enclosed yard in which livestock are kept until slaughtered or sold.

stodg·y (stŏj′ē) ►*adj.* **-i·er, -i·est 1a.** Dull, unimaginative, and commonplace. See Synonyms at **dull. b.** Old-fashioned and stuffy. **2.** Indigestible; heavy. [< *stodge,* to stuff.] —**stodg′i·ly** *adv.* —**stodg′i·ness** *n.*

sto·ic (stō′ĭk) ►*n.* **1.** One who is seemingly indifferent to or unaffected by pleasure or pain.

2. Stoic A member of a Greek school of philosophy advocating the calm acceptance of all occurrences. ►*adj.* also **sto·i·cal** (-ĭ-kəl) Seemingly indifferent to or unaffected by pleasure or pain; impassive. [< Gk. *Stōikos* < *stoa* (*poikilē*), (Painted) Porch, where Zeno taught.] —**sto′i·cal·ly** *adv.* —**sto′i·cism** *n.*

stoke (stōk) ►*v.* **stoked, stok·ing 1.** To stir up and feed (a fire or furnace). **2.** To tend a furnace. [< MDu. *stōken,* poke.] —**stok′er** *n.*

Sto·ker (stō′kər), **Abraham** "Bram." 1847–1912. Irish-born British writer.

Bram Stoker

STOL ►*abbr.* short takeoff and landing

stole¹ (stōl) ►*n.* **1.** A long scarf worn by some members of the Christian clergy while officiating. **2.** A woman's long scarf of cloth or fur worn about the shoulders. [< Gk. *stolē,* garment.]

stole² (stōl) ►*v.* P.t. of **steal.**

sto·len (stō′lən) ►*v.* P.part. of **steal.**

stol·id (stŏl′ĭd) ►*adj.* **-er, -est** Having or revealing little emotion; impassive. [Lat. *stolidus,* stupid.] —**sto·lid′i·ty** *n.*

sto·ma (stō′mə) ►*n., pl.* **-ma·ta** (-mə-tə) or **-mas** A small opening, esp. one of the pores in a leaf through which gases pass. [< Gk., mouth.]

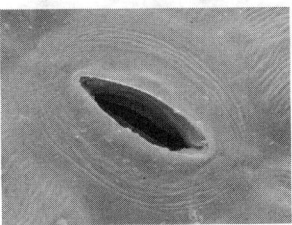

stoma
in a leaf of iceberg lettuce

stom·ach (stŭm′ək) ►*n.* **1.** A large saclike organ of the digestive tract, located in vertebrates between the esophagus and the small intestine. **2.** The abdomen or belly. **3.** An appetite for food. **4.** Desire; inclination. ►*v.* To bear; tolerate. [< Gk. *stomakhos.*]

stom·ach·er (stŭm′ə-kər) ►*n.* A decorative garment formerly worn over the chest and stomach, esp. by women.

sto·mach·ic (stə-măk′ĭk) ►*adj.* Beneficial to or stimulating digestion in the stomach. —**sto·mach′ic** *n.*

stomp (stŏmp, stômp) ►*v.* To tread or trample heavily or violently (on). [< STAMP.]

stone (stōn) ►*n.* **1.** Hardened earthy or mineral matter; rock. **2.** A small piece of rock. **3.** A gem or precious stone. **4.** The hard covering enclosing the seed in certain fruits, such as the cherry. **5.** A mineral concretion in an organ, such as the kidney. **6.** *pl.* **stone** A unit of weight in Great Britain, 14 lbs. (6.4 kg). ►*v.* **stoned, ston·ing** To pelt or kill with stones. [< OE *stān.*]

Stone, Lucy 1818–93. Amer. social reformer.

Stone Age ►*n.* The earliest known period of human culture, marked by the use of stone tools.

stoned (stōnd) ►*adj. Slang* **1.** Intoxicated, esp. by marijuana. **2.** Drunk.

stone·wall (stōn′wôl′) ►*v. Informal* To refuse to answer or cooperate (with).

stone·ware (stōn′wâr′) ►*n.* A heavy, nonporous pottery.

ston·y (stō′nē) ►*adj.* **-i·er, -i·est 1.** Covered with or full of stones. **2.** Resembling stone. **3.** Cold; impassive: *a stony expression.* —**ston′i·ly** *adv.* —**ston′i·ness** *n.*

stood (stŏŏd) ►*v.* P.t. and p.part. of **stand.**

stooge (stōōj) ►*n.* **1.** The straight man to a comedian. **2.** A willing dupe. **3.** *Slang* A stool pigeon. [?]

stool (stōōl) ►*n.* **1.** A backless and armless single seat. **2.** A low bench or support for the feet. **3.** A toilet. **4.** Evacuated fecal matter. [< OE *stōl.*]

stool pigeon ►*n.* **1.** *Slang* A person acting as a decoy or informer, esp. for the police. **2.** A pigeon used as a decoy.

stoop¹ (stōōp) ►*v.* **1.** To bend forward and down. **2.** To walk or stand with the head and upper back bent forward. **3a.** To lower or debase oneself: *I wouldn't stoop to such behavior.* **b.** To descend from a superior social position; condescend. ►*n.* The act, habit, or posture of stooping. [< OE *stūpian.*]

Syns: condescend, deign **v.**

stoop² (stōōp) ►*n.* A small porch or staircase at the entrance of a house or building. [Du. *stoep,* front verandah.]

stop (stŏp) ►*v.* **stopped, stop·ping 1.** To close (an opening) by covering, filling in, or plugging up. **2.** To obstruct or prevent the flow or passage of. **3.** To bring or come to an end or halt. **4.** To desist from; cease. **5.** To restrain or prevent: *The mud stopped us from walking further.* **6.** To make a brief halt, visit, or stay. ►*n.* **1.** The act of stopping or the condition of being stopped. **2.** A stay or visit. **3.** A place stopped at: *a bus stop.* **4.** A stopper. **5.** An f-stop. **6.** A mark of punctuation, esp. a period. **7.** A tuned set of pipes, as in an organ. [Prob. < VLat. **stuppāre,* to caulk < Gk. *stuppē,* tow.] —**stop′page** (stŏp′ĭj) *n.*

Syns: cease, desist, discontinue, halt, quit **Ant:** *start* **v.**

stop·cock (stŏp′kŏk′) ►*n.* A valve that regulates the flow of fluid through a pipe.

stop·gap (stŏp′găp′) ►*n.* A temporary expedient.

stop·light (stŏp′līt′) ►*n.* See **traffic light.**

stop·o·ver (stŏp′ō′vər) ►*n.* A place visited briefly in the course of a journey.

stop·per (stŏp′ər) ►*n.* A device, such as a plug, inserted to close an opening.

stop·watch (stŏp′wŏch′) ►*n.* A watch that can be instantly started and stopped by pushing a button and used to measure an exact duration of time.

stor·age (stôr′ĭj) ►*n.* **1a.** The act of storing or the state of being stored. **b.** A space for storing. **2.** The price charged for keeping goods stored.

storage battery ►*n.* A group of reversible or rechargeable electric cells acting as a unit.

store (stôr) ►*n.* **1.** A place where merchandise is offered for sale; shop. **2.** A stock or supply reserved for future use. **3. stores** Supplies, esp. of food, clothing, or arms. **4.** A storehouse. ►*v.* **stored, stor·ing 1.** To reserve or put away for future use. **2.** To fill, supply, or stock. **3.** To deposit in a storehouse for safekeeping. **4.** To copy (data) into memory or onto a storage device, such as a hard disk. [< Lat. *īnstaurāre,* restore.]

store·front (stôr′frŭnt′) ►*n.* **1.** The side of a store facing a street. **2.** A room in a commercial building at street level.

store·house (stôr′hous′) ►*n.* **1.** A building in which goods are stored; warehouse. **2.** An abundant source or supply.

store·keep·er (stôr′kē′pər) ►*n.* One who keeps a retail store or shop.

store·room (stôr′rōōm′, -rŏŏm′) ►*n.* A room in which things are stored.

sto·rey (stôr′ē) ►*n. Chiefly Brit.* Var. of **story².**

sto·ried (stôr′ēd) ►*adj.* Celebrated or famous in history or story.

stork (stôrk) ►*n.* A large wading bird having long legs and a long straight bill. [< OE *storc.*]

storm (stôrm) ►*n.* **1.** An atmospheric disturbance with strong winds accompanied by rain, snow, or other precipitation. **2.** A violent disturbance or upheaval: *a storm of protest.* **3.** A sudden overwhelming attack. ►*v.* **1.** To blow with strong winds and usu. produce copious rain, snow, or other precipitation. **2.** To behave or shout angrily. **3.** To move or rush violently or angrily: *stormed into the room.* **4.** To assault or overwhelm with sudden force. [< OE.] —**storm′i·ness** *n.* —**storm′y** *adj.*

sto·ry¹ (stôr′ē) ►*n., pl.* **-ries 1.** An account of an event or a series of events. **2.** A prose or verse narrative intended to entertain. **3.** A short story. **4.** A news report. **5.** An explanation: *What's the story on these bills?* **6.** A lie. [< Lat. *historia,* HISTORY.]

sto·ry² (stôr′ē) ►*n., pl.* **-ries 1.** A complete horizontal division of a building. **2.** The set of rooms on the same level of a building. [< Med. Lat. *historia,* picture, story < Lat., HISTORY.]

sto·ry·tell·er (stôr′ē-tĕl′ər) ►*n.* One who tells stories. —**sto′ry·tell′ing** *n.*

stoup (stōōp) ►*n.* A basin for holy water at a church. [< ON *staup,* cup.]

stout (stout) ►*adj.* **-er, -est 1a.** Thickset; fat. **b.** Strong in body; sturdy. **c.** Substantial; solid. **2.** Resolute or bold in character; valiant. ►*n.* A strong, very dark beer or ale. [< OFr. *estout,* of Gmc. orig.] —**stout′ly** *adv.* —**stout′ness** *n.*

stout·heart·ed (stout′här′tĭd) ►*adj.* Brave; courageous. —**stout′heart′ed·ly** *adv.* —**stout′heart′ed·ness** *n.*

stove¹ (stōv) ►*n.* An apparatus in which electricity or a fuel is used to furnish heat, as for cooking or heating. [< MLGer. or MDu., heated room.]

stove² (stōv) ►*v.* P.t. and p.part. of **stave.**

stove·pipe (stōv′pīp′) ►*n.* **1.** A pipe used to conduct smoke from a stove into a chimney flue. **2.** A man's tall silk hat.

stow (stō) ►*v.* **1.** To put or store away compactly. **2.** To fill by packing tightly. —*phrasal verb:* **stow away** To be a stowaway. [< OE *stōw,* place.]

stow·a·way (stō′ə-wā′) ►*n.* A person who hides aboard a vehicle, esp. a ship, to obtain free passage.

Stowe (stō), **Harriet (Elizabeth) Beecher** 1811–96. Amer. writer.

Harriet Beecher Stowe

STP ►*abbr.* standard temperature and pressure
Str. ►*abbr.* strait

stra·bis·mus (strə-bĭz′məs) ►*n.* A visual defect in which one eye cannot focus with the other on an objective because of imbalance of the eye muscles. [< Gk. *strabizein,* squint.] —**stra·bis′mal, stra·bis′mic** *adj.*

strad·dle (străd′l) ►*v.* **-dled, -dling 1.** To stand or sit with a leg on each side of. **2.** To appear to favor both sides of (an issue). [< STRIDE.] —**strad′dle** *n.* —**strad′dler** *n.*

Stra·di·va·ri (străd′ə-vâr′ē, -vär′ē) also **Stra·di·va·ri·us** (-ē-əs) Family of Italian violin makers, including **Antonio** (1644?–1737), **Francesco** (1671–1743), and **Omobono** (1679–1742).

strafe (strāf) ►*v.* **strafed, straf·ing** To attack with machine-gun fire from a low-flying aircraft. [< Ger. *strafen,* punish.]

strag·gle (străg′əl) ►*v.* **-gled, -gling 1a.** To move slowly or in a scattered or irregular group. **b.** To lag behind another or others. **2.** To extend or be spread out: *The vine straggled over the ground.* [ME *straglen,* wander.] —**strag′gler** *n.* —**strag′gly** *adj.*

straight (strāt) ►*adj.* **-er, -est 1.** Extending continuously in the same direction without curving. **2.** Having no waves or bends. **3.** Erect; upright. **4.** Level or even. **5.** Direct and candid: *a straight answer.* **6a.** Honest; fair. **b.** Right; correct. **7.** Neatly arranged; orderly. **8.** Uninterrupted; consecutive: *five straight days.* **9.** Heterosexual. **10.** *Slang* Not being under the influence of alcohol or drugs. **11.** Not deviating from the normal or usual; conventional. **12.** Undiluted: *straight bourbon.* ►*adv.* In a straight course or manner. ►*n.* **1.** Something that is straight. **2.** A straightaway. **3.** *Games* A poker hand containing five cards of various suits in numerical sequence. **4a.** A conventional person. **b.** A heterosexual person. [ME < p.part. of *strecchen,* STRETCH.] —**straight′ly** *adv.* —**straight′ness** *n.*

straight angle ►*n.* An angle of 180°.

straight·a·way (strāt′ə-wā′) ►*n.* A straight course, stretch, or track, esp. the stretch of a racecourse from the last turn to the finish. ►*adv.* (strāt′ə-wā′) At once; immediately.

straight·edge (strāt′ĕj′) ►*n.* A rigid flat rectangular bar with a straight edge for testing or drawing straight lines. ►*adj.* also **straight·edge** (strāt′ĕj′) **1.** Having a level, even edge: *a straightedge ruler.* **2.** Abstaining from alcohol, tobacco, and drugs.

straight·en (strāt′n) ►*v.* To make or become straight or straighter. —*phrasal verb:* **straighten out 1.** To resolve (a confusion or conflict). **2.** To make less confused or troubled. —**straight′en·er** *n.*

straight·for·ward (strāt-fôr′wərd) ►*adj.* **1.** Honest; frank. **2.** Easy to accomplish, identify, or understand: *a straightforward repair.* ►*adv.* In a direct or frank manner. —**straight·for′ward·ly** *adv.* —**straight·for′ward·ness** *n.* —**straight·for′wards** *adv.*

straight man ►*n.* An actor who serves as a foil for a comedian.

straight razor ►*n.* A razor blade hinged to a handle into which it slips when not in use.

straight·way (strāt′wā′, -wā′) ►*adv.* At once.

strain¹ (strān) ►*v.* **1.** To pull, draw, or stretch tight. **2.** To exert or tax to the utmost. **3.** To injure or impair by overuse or overexertion; wrench. **4.** To force beyond the proper or reasonable limit. **5.** To pass through a filtering agent such as a strainer. **6.** To strive hard. ►*n.* **1.** The act of straining. **2a.** A great effort, force, or tension. **b.** A great demand or stress. **3.** A deformation produced by stress. [< Lat. *stringere,* draw tight.]

strain² (strān) ►*n.* **1a.** The collective descendants of a common ancestor. **b.** Ancestry; lineage. **2.** *Biol.* A group of organisms of the same species, having distinctive characteristics but not usu. considered a separate breed or variety. **3.** A kind or sort: *a different strain of leadership.* **4.** An inherent quality or tendency: *a strain of silliness.* **5.** often **strains** *Mus.* A tune or air. [< OE *strēon.*]

strain·er (strā′nər) ►*n.* One that strains, as a device used to separate solids from liquids.

strait (strāt) ►*n.* also **straits 1.** A narrow channel joining two larger bodies of water. **2.** A position of difficulty: *in desperate straits.* [< Lat. *strictus,* p.part. of *stringere,* draw tight.]

strait·en (strāt′n) ►*v.* **1.** To put into difficulties. **2.** *Archaic* To make narrow or restricted.

strait·jack·et also **straight·jack·et** (strāt′jăk′-ĭt) ►*n.* A jacketlike garment used to bind the arms tightly as a means of restraining a violent patient or prisoner.

strait-laced (strāt′lāst′) ►*adj.* Excessively strict in behavior, morality, or opinions.

strand¹ (strănd) ►*n.* A shore; beach. ►*v.* **1.** To drive or be driven aground. **2.** To bring into or leave in a difficult or helpless position. [< OE.]

strand² (strănd) ►*n.* **1.** Any of a number of fibers or filaments that have been twisted together, as to form a cable or rope. **2.** A ropelike length of something: *a strand of pearls.* [ME *strond.*]

strange (strānj) ►*adj.* **strang·er, strang·est 1a.** Not previously known; unfamiliar. **b.** Not of one's own locality or kind; not native. See Synonyms at **foreign. 2.** Out of the ordinary;

unusual or striking. **3.** Not comfortable or at ease. **4.** Not accustomed or conditioned. [< Lat. *extrāneus*, foreign.] —**strange′ly** *adv.* —**strange′ness** *n.*

strang·er (strān′jər) ▸*n.* **1.** One who is neither a friend nor an acquaintance. **2.** A foreigner, newcomer, or outsider.

stran·gle (străng′gəl) ▸*v.* **-gled, -gling 1a.** To kill by choking or suffocating. **b.** To smother. **2.** To suppress or stifle. [< Gk. *strangalē*, halter.] —**stran′gler** *n.*

stran·gu·late (străng′gyə-lāt′) ▸*v.* **-lat·ed, -lat· ing 1.** To strangle. **2.** *Med.* To constrict so as to cut off the flow of blood or other fluid. [Lat. *strangulāre*, STRANGLE.] —**stran′gu·la′tion** *n.*

strap (străp) ▸*n.* A long narrow strip of pliant material, such as leather, often with a fastener for binding or securing objects. ▸*v.* **strapped, strap·ping 1.** To fasten or secure with a strap. **2.** To beat with a strap. **3.** To sharpen (e.g., a razor). [< STROP.]

strap·less (străp′lĭs) ▸*adj.* Having no strap or straps. ▸*n.* A strapless garment.

strapped (străpt) ▸*adj. Informal* In financial need.

strap·ping (străp′ĭng) ▸*adj.* Tall and sturdy; robust.

stra·ta (strā′tə, străt′ə) ▸*n.* Pl. of **stratum.**

strat·a·gem (străt′ə-jəm) ▸*n.* **1.** A scheme designed to achieve an objective, as in surprising an enemy. **2.** The devising or execution of such schemes. [< Gk. *stratēgēma* < *stratēgos*, general : *stratos*, army + *agein*, lead.]

strat·e·gy (străt′ə-jē) ▸*n., pl.* **-gies 1.** The planning and conduct of large-scale military operations. **2.** A plan of action. See Synonyms at **plan. 3.** The art or skill of using stratagems, as in politics and business. —**stra·te′gic** (strə-tē′jĭk) *adj.* —**stra·te′gi·cal·ly** *adv.* —**strat′e· gist** *n.*

Strat·ford-up·on-Av·on (străt′fərd-ə-pŏn-ā′- vən, -pŏn-) also **Strat·ford-on-Av·on** (-ŏn-, -ôn-) A town of central England SSE of Birmingham; birthplace of William Shakespeare (1564).

strat·i·fy (străt′ə-fī′) ▸*v.* **-fied, -fy·ing 1.** To form, arrange, or deposit in layers. **2.** To arrange or separate into social levels. —**strat′i· fi·ca′tion** *n.*

strat·o·sphere (străt′ə-sfîr′) ▸*n.* The region of the atmosphere above the troposphere and below the mesosphere. [Fr. *stratosphère*.] —**strat′o·spher′ic** (-sfîr′ĭk, -sfĕr′-) *adj.*

stra·tum (strā′təm, străt′əm) ▸*n., pl.* **-ta** (-tə) or **-tums 1.** A horizontal layer of material, esp. one of several layers of sedimentary rock. **2.** A level of society composed of people with similar social or economic status. [< Lat. *sternere*, *strāt-*, spread.]

Usage: The standard singular form is *stratum;* the standard plural is *strata* (or sometimes *stratums*) but not *stratas.*

stra·tus (strāt′ī, strā′tī) ▸*n., pl.* **-i** (-ī) A low-altitude cloud formation consisting of a horizontal layer of gray clouds. [< Lat. *strātus*, p.part. of *sternere*, spread.]

Strauss (strous, shtrous), **Johann** (1804–49), "the Elder," and **Johann** (1825–99), "the Younger." Austrian composers.

Strauss, Richard 1864–1949. German composer.

Stra·vin·sky (strə-vĭn′skē), **Igor Fyodorovich** 1882–1971. Russian-born composer.

straw (strô) ▸*n.* **1a.** Stalks of threshed grain. **b.** A single stalk of threshed grain. **2.** A slender tube used for sucking up a liquid. **3.** Something of little value. [< OE *strēaw*.]

straw·ber·ry (strô′bĕr′ē) ▸*n.* **1.** A low-growing plant having white flowers and red, fleshy, edible fruit. **2.** The fruit itself.

straw boss ▸*n. Informal* A temporary boss or crew leader.

straw vote ▸*n.* An unofficial vote or poll.

stray (strā) ▸*v.* **1a.** To move away from or go beyond established limits. **b.** To wander about; roam. **2.** To act contrary to moral behavior, esp. in being sexually unfaithful. **3.** To digress. See Synonyms at **swerve.** ▸*n.* One that has strayed, esp. a loose domestic animal. ▸*adj.* **1.** Straying or having strayed; wandering or lost. **2.** Scattered or separate. [< OFr. *estraier*.]

streak (strēk) ▸*n.* **1.** A line, mark, or band differentiated by color or texture from its surroundings. **2.** A slight contrasting element; trace. **3.** *Informal* An unbroken stretch; run. ▸*v.* **1.** To mark with or form streaks. **2.** To move at high speed; rush. [< OE *strica*.] —**streak′er** *n.* —**streak′y** *adj.*

stream (strēm) ▸*n.* **1.** A flow of water in a channel or bed, as a brook. **2.** A steady current of a fluid. **3.** A steady flow or succession. See Synonyms at **flow.** ▸*v.* **1.** To flow in or as if in a stream. **2.** To pour forth or give off a stream. **3.** To move or arrive in large numbers. **4.** To extend, wave, or float outward. **5.** To leave a continuous trail of light. [< OE *strēam*.]

stream·er (strē′mər) ▸*n.* **1a.** A long narrow flag or banner. **b.** A long narrow strip of material. **2.** A newspaper headline that runs across a full page.

stream·line (strēm′līn′) ▸*v.* **1.** To construct so as to offer the least resistance to fluid flow: *streamline a car's design.* **2.** To improve the efficiency of, often by simplification: *streamline a factory process.* —**stream′lined′** *adj.*

street (strēt) ▸*n.* **1.** A public thoroughfare in a city or town. **2.** The people living, working, or gathering along a street. [< LLat. *strāta*, paved road < Lat. *sternere*, extend.]

street·car (strēt′kär′) ▸*n.* A public vehicle operated on rails along the streets of a city.

street·walk·er (strēt′wô′kər) ▸*n.* A prostitute.

strength (strĕngkth, strĕngth, strĕnth) ▸*n.* **1.** The quality of being strong; physical power or capacity. **2.** The capacity to resist attack; impregnability. **3.** The capacity to resist strain or stress; durability. **4.** Moral or intellectual power. **5.** Capacity or potential for action. **6.** Degree of intensity, force, or potency. **7.** Effective or binding force: *the strength of an argument.* [< OE *strengthu*.]

strength·en (strĕngk′thən, strĕng′-, strĕn′-) ▸*v.* To make or become strong or stronger. —**strength′en·er** *n.*

stren·u·ous (strĕn′yoo-əs) ▸*adj.* **1.** Requiring great effort, energy, or exertion. **2.** Vigorously active. [< Lat. *strēnuus*.] —**stren′u·ous·ly** *adv.* —**stren′u·ous·ness** *n.*

strep throat (strĕp) ▸*n.* A throat infection caused by streptococci and marked by fever, pain, and enlarged lymph nodes. [< STREP- TOCOCCUS.]

strep·to·coc·cus (strĕp′tə-kŏk′əs) ►*n., pl.* **-coc· ci** (-kŏk′sī, -kŏk′ī) A round, gram-positive bacterium that occurs in pairs or chains and can cause various infections including strep throat and erysipelas. [Gk. *streptos*, twisted + –COCCUS.] —**strep′to·coc′cal** *adj.*

stress (strĕs) ►*n.* **1.** Importance, significance, or emphasis placed on something. See Synonyms at **emphasis. 2.** The relative force with which a word or sound is spoken. **3.** An accent or mark representing such force. **4.** *Phys.* The internal distribution of force per unit of area within a body subject to an applied force or system of forces. **5.** A condition of extreme difficulty, pressure, or strain. ►*v.* **1.** To place emphasis on. **2.** To pronounce with a stress. **3.** *Informal* To subject to physiological or mental stress. Often used with *out.* **4.** To subject to mechanical stress. [< VLat. **strictia*, narrowness < Lat. *stringere*, draw tight.] —**stress′ful** *adj.*

stres·sor (strĕs′ər) ►*n.* An agent or condition that causes stress.

stretch (strĕch) ►*v.* **1.** To lengthen, widen, or distend. **2.** To cause to extend across a given space. **3.** To make taut; tighten. **4.** To reach or put forth; extend: *stretched out his hand.* **5.** To extend (oneself) to full length. **6.** To wrench or strain (e.g., a muscle). **7.** To extend or enlarge beyond the usual or proper limits. **8.** To increase the quantity of by admixture or dilution. *stretch a meal.* **9.** To prolong. ►*n.* **1.** The act of stretching or the state of being stretched. **2.** The extent to which something can be stretched. **3.** A continuous length, area, or expanse. **4.** A straight section of a racecourse or track. **5.** A continuous period of time. ►*adj.* Made of an elastic material. [< OE *streccan*.] —**stretch′a·ble** *adj.* —**stretch′y** *adj.*

stretch·er (strĕch′ər) ►*n.* **1.** A litter used to transport the sick, wounded, or dead. **2.** One that stretches.

strew (strōō) ►*v.* **strewed, strewn** (strōōn) or **strewed, strew·ing 1.** To spread here and there; scatter or distribute. **2.** To distribute something over (an area or surface). [< OE *strēowian*.]

stri·a (strī′ə) ►*n., pl.* **stri·ae** (strī′ē) **1.** A narrow groove or channel. **2.** A thin line. [Lat.] —**stri′at′ed** (-ā′tĭd) *adj.* —**stri·a′tion** *n.*

strick·en (strĭk′ən) ►*v.* P.part. of **strike.** ►*adj.* **1.** Struck or wounded, as by a projectile. **2.** Afflicted, as with disease.

strict (strĭkt) ►*adj.* **-er, -est 1.** Rigorous in the imposition of discipline. **2.** Requiring close observance or demanding in expectations: *strict standards.* **3.** Carefully observed or maintained: *strict loyalty.* **4.** Precise; exact: *a strict definition.* [< Lat. *strictus*, p.part. of *stringere*, draw tight.] —**strict′ly** *adv.* —**strict′ness** *n.*

stric·ture (strĭk′chər) ►*n.* **1.** A restraint, limit, or restriction. **2.** An adverse criticism. **3.** *Med.* An abnormal narrowing of a bodily duct or passage. [< LLat. *strictūra*, contraction.]

stride (strīd) ►*v.* **strode** (strōd), **strid·den** (strĭd′n), **strid·ing** To walk with long steps. ►*n.* **1.** The act of striding. **2.** A single long step. **3.** often **strides** An advance. [< OE *strīdan.*] —**strid′er** *n.*

stri·dent (strīd′nt) ►*adj.* **1.** Loud, harsh, grating, or shrill: *a strident voice.* **2.** Forcefully assertive or severely critical: *strident rhetoric.* [< Lat.

strīdēre, make harsh sounds.] —**stri′dence, stri′den·cy** *n.* —**stri′dent·ly** *adv.*

strife (strīf) ►*n.* **1.** Heated, often violent conflict or disagreement. **2.** Contention or competition between rivals. [< OFr. *estrif*, of Gmc. orig.]

strike (strīk) ►*v.* **struck** (strŭk), **struck** or **strick·en** (strĭk′ən), **strik·ing 1a.** To hit sharply, as with a hand, fist, weapon, or implement. **b.** To inflict (a blow). **2.** To collide with or crash into. **3.** To attack or begin an attack. **4.** To afflict suddenly, as with a disease. **5.** To impress by stamping or printing. **6.** To indicate by a percussive sound: *The clock struck nine.* **7.** To produce (a flame or spark) by friction. **8.** To eliminate: *strike a statement from the records.* **9.** To discover: *strike gold.* **10.** To reach; fall upon: *strike a trail.* **11.** To impress: *strikes me as a good idea.* **12.** To cause (an emotion) to penetrate deeply. **13a.** To make or conclude (a bargain). **b.** To achieve (a balance). **14.** To take on or assume (a pose). **15.** To set out: *strike out for new lands.* **16.** To engage in a strike against an employer. ►*n.* **1.** An act of striking. **2.** An attack. **3.** A cessation of work by employees seeking concessions from their employer. **4.** A sudden achievement or discovery. **5.** *Baseball* A pitched ball counted against the batter, esp. one swung at and missed or judged to have passed through the strike zone. **6.** The knocking down of all the pins in bowling with the first bowl of a frame. —*phrasal verbs:* **strike out** *Baseball* **1.** To pitch three strikes to (a batter), putting the batter out. **2.** To be struck out. **strike up 1.** To start to play vigorously. **2.** To initiate or begin. [< OE *strīcan*, stroke.] —**strik′er** *n.*

strike·break·er (strīk′brā′kər) ►*n.* A person who works or is hired during a strike.

strike·out (strīk′out′) ►*n. Baseball* An out made by a batter charged with three strikes and credited to the pitcher who threw the strikes.

strike zone ►*n. Baseball* The area over home plate through which a pitch must pass to be called a strike.

strik·ing (strī′kĭng) ►*adj.* Arrestingly or vividly impressive. —**strik′ing·ly** *adv.*

Strind·berg (strĭnd′bûrg), **(Johan) August** 1849–1912. Swedish writer.

string (strĭng) ►*n.* **1.** A cord usu. made of fiber, used for fastening, tying, or lacing. **2.** *Mus.* **a.** A cord stretched on an instrument and struck, plucked, or bowed to produce tones. **b.** also **strings** Stringed instruments collectively. **3.** Something shaped into a long thin line. **4.** A set of objects threaded together: *a string of beads.* **5.** A series; sequence. **6.** *Comp.* A set of consecutive characters. **7.** also **strings** *Informal* A limiting or hidden condition. ►*v.* **strung** (strŭng), **string·ing 1.** To fit or furnish with strings or a string: *string a guitar.* **2.** To thread on a string. **3.** To arrange in a series. **4.** To fasten, tie, or hang with strings. **5.** To stretch out or extend. [< OE *streng.*] —**string′i·ness** *n.* —**string′y** *adj.*

string bean ►*n.* **1.** A tropical American plant having edible pods. **2.** The narrow green pod of this plant.

strin·gent (strĭn′jənt) ►*adj.* **1.** Imposing rigorous standards; severe. **2.** Constricted; tight. **3.** Marked by scarcity of money or credit. [< Lat. *stringere*, draw tight.] —**strin′gen·cy** *n.* —**strin′gent·ly** *adv.*

string·er (strĭng′ər) ►*n.* **1.** One that strings. **2.**

A heavy horizontal timber used as a support or connector. **3.** A part-time or freelance news correspondent.

string theory ►*n. Phys.* The theory that tiny, vibrating stringlike objects have vibration modes that correspond to elementary particles existing in a space-time that has more than three dimensions.

strip¹ (strĭp) ►*v.* **stripped, strip·ping 1a.** To remove the covering from. **b.** To undress. **2a.** To deprive, as of honors or rank. **b.** To rob or plunder. **3a.** To remove all excess detail from. **b.** To dismantle piece by piece. **4.** To damage the threads of (e.g., a screw) or the teeth of (a gear). [< OE *bestrȳpan,* plunder.] —**strip′per** *n.*

strip² (strĭp) ►*n.* **1.** A long narrow piece. **2.** A comic strip. **3.** An airstrip. **4.** A narrow space or area, as along a highway. [ME.]

stripe (strīp) ►*n.* **1.** A long narrow band distinguished, as by color or texture, from the surrounding material or surface. **2.** A strip of cloth or braid worn on a uniform to indicate rank, awards received, or length of service. **3.** Sort; kind. ►*v.* **striped, strip·ing** To mark with stripes or a stripe. [Poss. < MDu. or MLGer. *stripe.*]

strip·ling (strĭp′lĭng) ►*n.* A male adolescent or young adult. [ME.]

strip mall ►*n.* A shopping complex containing a row of businesses that usu. open onto a common parking lot.

strip mine ►*n.* An open mine, esp. a coal mine, whose seams are exposed by the removal of topsoil. —**strip′-mine′** *v.*

strip search ►*n.* The search of a person for illegal or contraband articles by requiring the removal of clothing. —**strip′-search** *v.*

strip·tease (strĭp′tēz′) ►*n.* A burlesque act in which a person slowly removes clothing, usu. to musical accompaniment.

strive (strīv) ►*v.* **strove** (strōv) or **strived, striv·en** (strĭv′ən) or **strived, striv·ing 1.** To exert much effort or energy. **2.** To struggle; contend. [< OFr. *estriver < estrif,* STRIFE.]

strobe (strōb) ►*n.* **1.** A strobe light. **2.** A stroboscope.

strobe light ►*n.* A flash lamp that produces high-intensity short-duration light pulses. [< STROBOSCOPE.]

stro·bo·scope (strō′bə-skōp′) ►*n.* Any of various instruments used to observe moving objects by making them appear stationary, as by pulsed illumination. [Gk. *strobos,* a whirling + –SCOPE.] —**stro′bo·scop′ic** (-skŏp′ĭk) *adj.*

strode (strōd) ►*v.* P.t. of **stride.**

stroke¹ (strōk) ►*n.* **1.** The act of striking; blow. **2.** A sudden occurrence or result. **3.** A sudden severe attack, as of paralysis. **4.** A sudden loss of brain function caused by a blockage or rupture of a blood vessel to the brain. **5.** An inspired or effective idea or act. **6a.** A single completed movement, as in swimming or rowing. **b.** An act of depressing a computer key. **c.** A movement of a piston from one end of the limit of its motion to another. **7.** A single mark made by a writing implement, such as a pen. [ME.]

stroke² (strōk) ►*v.* **stroked, strok·ing** To rub lightly. See Synonyms at **caress.** ►*n.* A light caressing movement. [< OE *strācian.*]

stroll (strōl) ►*v.* To go for a leisurely walk.

[Prob. Ger. dial. *strollen.*] —**stroll** *n.*

stroll·er (strō′lər) ►*n.* **1.** One who strolls. **2.** A light carriage that is pushed to transport small children.

strong (strông) ►*adj.* **-er, -est 1.** Physically powerful. **2.** In good or sound health. **3.** Capable of withstanding force or wear. **4.** Having force or rapidity of motion: *a strong current.* **5.** Persuasive or forceful. **6.** Extreme; drastic. **7.** Intense in degree or quality. **8.** Having a specified number of members. **9.** Stressed or accented, as a syllable. [< OE *strang.*] —**strong′ly** *adv.*

strong-arm (strông′ärm′) ►*adj. Informal* Coercive: *strong-arm tactics.*

strong·box (strông′bŏks′) ►*n.* A stoutly made safe.

strong force ►*n.* The force that arises from the strong interaction of quarks.

strong·hold (strông′hōld′) ►*n.* **1.** A fortress. **2.** A place of refuge.

strong interaction ►*n.* A fundamental interaction of nature, mediated by gluons and binding quarks together within hadrons.

strong·man (strông′măn′) ►*n.* A political figure who exercises control by force.

stron·ti·um (strŏn′chē-əm, -tē-əm, -shəm) ►*n.* *Symbol* **Sr** A soft, silvery, easily oxidized metallic element, used in fireworks and various alloys. At. no. 38. See table at **element.** [< *Strontian,* Scotland.]

strontium-90 ►*n.* A strontium isotope with a half-life of 28 years, present as a radiation hazard in nuclear fallout.

strop (strŏp) ►*n.* A flexible strip of leather or canvas used to sharpen a razor. ►*v.* **stropped, strop·ping** To sharpen (a razor) on a strop. [< Gk. *strophos,* twisted cord.]

stro·phe (strō′fē) ►*n.* A stanza of a poem. [Gk. *strophē,* a turning.] —**stro′phic** (strō′fĭk, strŏf′ĭk) *adj.*

strove (strōv) ►*v.* P.t. of **strive.**

struck (strŭk) ►*v.* P.t. and p.part. of **strike.** ►*adj.* Affected or shut down by a labor strike.

struc·ture (strŭk′chər) ►*n.* **1.** Something made up of parts that are put together in a particular way. **2.** The way in which parts are arranged or put together to form a whole. **3.** Something constructed, as a building. ►*v.* **-tured, -turing** To give form or arrangement to. [< Lat. *struere, strūct-,* construct.] —**struc′tur·al** *adj.* —**struc′tur·al·ly** *adv.*

stru·del (strōōd′l) ►*n.* A pastry made with fruit or cheese rolled up in layers of thin sheets of dough and baked. [Ger.]

strug·gle (strŭg′əl) ►*v.* **-gled, -gling 1a.** To make a strenuous effort; strive. **b.** To progress with difficulty. **2.** To contend or compete. ►*n.* **1.** Strenuous effort. **2.** Combat; strife. [ME *struglen.*] —**strug′gler** *n.*

strum (strŭm) ►*v.* **strummed, strum·ming** To play (e.g., a guitar) by stroking or brushing the strings. [Perh. imit.] —**strum** *n.*

strum·pet (strŭm′pĭt) ►*n.* A prostitute. [ME.]

strung (strŭng) ►*v.* P.t. and p.part. of **string.**

strung-out (strŭng′out′) ►*adj. Slang* Severely debilitated from long-term drug use.

strut (strŭt) ►*v.* **strut·ted, strut·ting** To walk in an exaggerated, self-important manner. ►*n.* **1.** A strutting gait. **2.** A bar or rod used to brace a structure against forces applied from the side. [< OE *strūtian,* stand out stiffly.] —**strut′ter** *n.*

strych·nine (strĭk′nīn′, -nĭn, -nēn′) ►*n.* A poisonous white crystalline alkaloid, $C_{21}H_{22}O_2N_2$, derived from plants and used as a poison. [< Gk. *strukhnon*, a kind of nightshade.]

Stu·art (stoo′ərt, styoo′-), **Gilbert Charles** 1755–1828. Amer. painter.

stub (stŭb) ►*n.* **1.** A short blunt remaining end. **2a.** The part of a check or receipt retained as a record. **b.** The part of a ticket returned as a voucher of payment. ►*v.* **stubbed, stub·bing** **1.** To strike (one's toe or foot) against something. **2.** To crush out (a lit cigarette). [< OE *stybb*, tree stump.]

stub·ble (stŭb′əl) ►*n.* **1.** Short stiff stalks, as of grain, remaining on a field after harvesting. **2.** Something resembling stubble, such as a short growth of beard. [< Lat. *stipula*, straw.] —**stub′bly** *adj.*

stub·born (stŭb′ərn) ►*adj.* **1a.** Refusing to change one's mind despite pressure to do so; unyielding. **b.** Marked by a refusal to change one's mind. **2.** Difficult to treat or deal with: *a stubborn stain.* [ME *stuborn.*] —**stub′born·ly** *adv.* —**stub′born·ness** *n.*

stub·by (stŭb′ē) ►*adj.* **-bi·er, -bi·est** Short and stocky. —**stub′bi·ness** *n.*

stuc·co (stŭk′ō) ►*n., pl.* **-coes** or **-cos** A durable finish for exterior walls, usu. made of cement, sand, and lime. ►*v.* To finish or decorate with stucco. [Ital., of Gmc. orig.]

stuck (stŭk) ►*v.* P.t. and p.part. of **stick.**

stuck-up (stŭk′ŭp′) ►*adj.* *Informal* Snobbish; conceited.

stud[1] (stŭd) ►*n.* **1.** An upright post in the framework of a wall for supporting sheets of lath or drywall. **2.** A small knob or rivet slightly projecting from a surface. **3a.** A small ornamental button mounted on a short post. **b.** A mounted buttonlike earring. ►*v.* **stud·ded, stud·ding** **1.** To provide with studs. **2.** To strew: *Daisies studded the meadow.* [< OE *studu.*]

stud[2] (stŭd) ►*n.* **1.** A male animal, such as a bull or stallion, kept for breeding. **2.** *Slang* A virile man. [< OE *stōd*, breeding stable.]

stud·book (stŭd′boŏk′) ►*n.* A book registering the pedigrees of thoroughbred animals.

stu·dent (stood′nt, styood′-) ►*n.* **1.** One who attends a school, college, or university. **2.** One who makes a study of something. [< Med.Lat. *studiāre*, STUDY.]

stud·ied (stŭd′ēd) ►*adj.* Carefully contrived; calculated.

stu·di·o (stoo′dē-ō, styoo′-) ►*n., pl.* **-os** **1.** An artist's workroom. **2.** A place where an art is taught: *a dance studio.* **3.** A room or building for audio, movie, television, or radio productions. **4.** A studio apartment. [Ital.]

studio apartment ►*n.* A small apartment usu. consisting of one main living space, a kitchen, and a bathroom.

stu·di·ous (stoo′dē-əs, styoo′-) ►*adj.* **1.** Given to diligent study. **2.** Earnest; purposeful. —**stu′di·ous·ly** *adv.* —**stu′di·ous·ness** *n.*

stud·y (stŭd′ē) ►*n., pl.* **-ies** **1a.** The effort to acquire knowledge, as by reading, observation, or research. **b.** A branch of knowledge. **2a.** Attentive examination: *The new drug is still under study.* **b.** A detailed analysis investigating a subject: *a study of children's reading habits.* **3.** A room intended or equipped for studying or writing. ►*v.* **-ied, -y·ing** **1.** To apply one's mind

purposefully to the acquisition of knowledge or understanding of (a subject). **2.** To take (a course) at a school. **3a.** To inquire into; investigate. **b.** To read or look at closely. [< Lat. *studium* < *studēre*, to study.]

stuff (stŭf) ►*n.* **1.** The material out of which something is made or formed; substance. **2.** *Informal* **a.** Unspecified material: *Put that stuff over there.* **b.** Worthless objects. **3.** *Slang* Foolish or empty words or ideas. **4.** *Chiefly Brit.* Woven material, esp. woolens. ►*v.* **1a.** To pack tightly. **b.** To block (a passage); plug. **2.** To fill with stuffing. **3.** To gorge: *stuffed myself on desserts.* [< OFr. *estoffer*, equip, of Gmc. orig.]

stuff·ing (stŭf′ĭng) ►*n.* **1.** Padding, as for cushions. **2.** Food used as a filling for meat or vegetables.

stuff·y (stŭf′ē) ►*adj.* **-i·er, -i·est** **1.** Lacking sufficient ventilation. **2.** Blocked: *a stuffy nose.* **3.** Stodgy. —**stuff′i·ness** *n.*

stul·ti·fy (stŭl′tə-fī′) ►*v.* **-fied, -fy·ing** **1.** To limit or stifle: *stultify free expression.* **2.** To cause to seem stupid or foolish. [< Lat. *stultus*, foolish.] —**stul′ti·fi·ca′tion** *n.*

stum·ble (stŭm′bəl) ►*v.* **-bled, -bling** **1a.** To trip and almost fall. **b.** To proceed unsteadily; flounder. See Synonyms at **blunder. c.** To act or speak falteringly or clumsily. **2.** To make a mistake. **3.** To come upon accidentally. [ME *stumblen.*] —**stum′ble** *n.*

stum·bling block (stŭm′blĭng) ►*n.* An obstacle or impediment.

stump (stŭmp) ►*n.* **1.** The part of a tree trunk left in the ground after the tree has fallen or been felled. **2.** A part remaining after the main part has been cut off or worn away. **3.** A place or occasion used for political speeches. ►*v.* **1.** To clear stumps from. **2.** To traverse (a district) making political speeches. **3.** To walk in a stiff, heavy manner. **4.** To puzzle; baffle. [ME *stumpe.*] —**stump′er** *n.* —**stump′y** *adj.*

stun (stŭn) ►*v.* **stunned, stun·ning** **1.** To daze or render senseless, as by a blow or loud noise. **2.** To stupefy; astound. [< OFr. *estoner.*]

stung (stŭng) ►*v.* P.t. and p.part. of **sting.**

stunk (stŭngk) ►*v.* P.t. and p.part. of **stink.**

stun·ning (stŭn′ĭng) ►*adj.* **1.** Strikingly attractive. **2a.** Impressive. **b.** Surprising. —**stun′-ning·ly** *adv.*

stunt[1] (stŭnt) ►*v.* To check the growth or development of. [< OE *stunt*, short.]

stunt[2] (stŭnt) ►*n.* **1.** A feat displaying unusual skill or daring. **2.** Something unusual done for publicity. [?]

stu·pa (stoo′pə) ►*n.* A dome-shaped Buddhist shrine or monument. [Skt. *stūpaḥ.*]

stupa
Boudhanath Stupa
Kathmandu, Nepal

stu·pe·fy (stōō′pə-fī′, styōō′-) ►*v.* **-fied, -fy·ing 1.** To cause (someone) to be unable to think clearly or be sensitive to the surroundings; daze. **2.** To amaze; astonish. [< Lat. *stupēre*, be stunned.] —**stu′pe·fac′tion** (-făk′-shən) *n.*

stu·pen·dous (stōō-pĕn′dəs, styōō-) ►*adj.* **1.** So great in scope or importance as to amaze. **2.** Extremely large in amount, extent, or size: *stupendous savings.* [< LLat. *stupendus*, stunning.] —**stu·pen′dous·ly** *adv.*

stu·pid (stōō′pĭd, styōō′-) ►*adj.* **-er, -est 1.** Slow to learn or understand. **2.** Lacking intelligence. **3.** In a dazed or stunned state. **4.** Used to express disparagement or exasperation: *Take your stupid notebook.* [Lat. *stupidus*, stupefied.] —**stu·pid′i·ty** *n.* —**stu′pid·ly** *adv.* —**stu′pid·ness** *n.*

stu·por (stōō′pər, styōō′-) ►*n.* A state of reduced sensibility or consciousness. [< Lat. < *stupēre*, be stunned.] —**stu′por·ous** *adj.*

stur·dy (stûr′dē) ►*adj.* **-di·er, -di·est 1.** Healthy and vigorous; robust. **2.** Substantially built; strong. [< OFr. *estourdi*, dazed, reckless.] —**stur′di·ly** *adv.* —**stur′di·ness** *n.*

stur·geon (stûr′jən) ►*n.* Any of various large food fishes valued as a source of caviar. [< OFr. *estourgeon*, of Gmc. orig.]

stut·ter (stŭt′ər) ►*v.* To speak with a spasmodic repetition or prolongation of sounds. ►*n.* The act or habit of stuttering. [< ME *stutten.*] —**stut′ter·er** *n.*

Stuy·ve·sant (stī′vĭ-sənt), **Peter** 1612?–72. Dutch colonial administrator.

sty¹ (stī) ►*n.,* pl. **sties** (stīz) A pigpen. [< OE *stig.*]

sty² (stī) ►*n.,* pl. **sties** (stīz) Inflammation of one or more sebaceous glands of an eyelid. [< OE *stīgan*, rise.]

style (stīl) ►*n.* **1.** The way in which something is said, done, expressed, or performed. **2.** Sort; type. **3.** Individuality expressed in one's actions and tastes. **4.** Elegance. **5a.** The fashion of the moment. **b.** A particular fashion. **6.** A customary manner of presenting printed material, including usage, punctuation, and spelling. **7.** A slender, pointed writing instrument. **8.** *Bot.* The usu. slender part of a pistil. ►*v.* **styled, styl·ing 1.** To arrange or design. **2.** To call or name; designate. **3.** To make consistent with rules of style. [< Lat. *stilus.*] —**sty·lis′tic** (stī-lĭs′tĭk) *adj.* —**sty·lis′ti·cal·ly** *adv.*

styl·ish (stī′lĭsh) ►*adj.* Conforming to the current fashion. See Synonyms at **fashionable.** —**styl′ish·ly** *adv.* —**styl′ish·ness** *n.*

styl·ist (stī′lĭst) ►*n.* **1.** One who cultivates an artful literary style. **2.** A designer of or consultant on styles. **3.** A hairdresser.

styl·ize (stī′līz′) ►*v.* **-ized, -iz·ing** To restrict or make conform to a particular style.

sty·lus (stī′ləs) ►*n.,* pl. **-lus·es** or **-li** (-lī) **1a.** A sharp, pointed instrument used for writing, marking, or engraving. **b.** *Comp.* A pointed instrument for use on a pressure-sensitive screen. **2.** A phonograph needle. [Lat.]

sty·mie (stī′mē) ►*v.* **-mied, -mie·ing** To be an obstacle to; thwart or stump. [Orig., a golf ball obstructing one's line of play; perh. akin to Scots *stymie*, person with poor vision.]

styp·tic (stĭp′tĭk) ►*adj.* Contracting the tissues

or blood vessels; astringent. [< Gk. *stuphein*, contract.] —**styp′tic** *n.*

Sty·ro·foam (stī′rə-fōm′) A trademark used for a light resilient polystyrene plastic.

suave (swäv) ►*adj.* **suav·er, suav·est** Courteous and elegant. [< Lat. *suāvis.*] —**suave′ly** *adv.* —**suave′ness, suav′i·ty** *n.*

sub¹ (sŭb) ►*n.* **1.** *Naut.* A submarine. **2.** A submarine sandwich.

sub² (sŭb) *Informal* ►*n.* A substitute. ►*v.* **subbed, sub·bing** To act as a substitute.

sub– ►*pref.* **1.** Below; beneath: *subsoil.* **2a.** Subordinate; secondary: *subhead.* **b.** Subdivision: *subatomic.* **3.** Less than; short of: *subnormal.* [< Lat. *sub,* under.]

sub·al·tern (sŭb-ôl′tərn, sŭb′əl-tûrn′) ►*n.* **1.** A subordinate. **2.** One who is marginalized and oppressed by the dominant culture, esp. in a colonial context. **3.** *Chiefly Brit.* An officer holding a military rank just below that of captain. [< LLat. *subalternus.*]

sub·a·tom·ic (sŭb′ə-tŏm′ĭk) ►*adj.* **1.** Of or relating to particles that are smaller than an atom. **2.** Participating in reactions characteristic of the constituents of the atom.

subatomic particle ►*n.* Any of various units of matter smaller than a hydrogen atom.

sub·com·mit·tee (sŭb′kə-mĭt′ē) ►*n.* A subordinate committee composed of members from a main committee.

sub·com·pact (sŭb-kŏm′păkt′) ►*n.* An automobile smaller than a compact.

sub·con·scious (sŭb-kŏn′shəs) ►*adj.* Beneath the threshold of conscious perception. ►*n.* The part of the mind below the level of conscious perception. —**sub·con′scious·ly** *adv.* —**sub·con′scious·ness** *n.*

sub·con·ti·nent (sŭb′kŏn′tə-nənt, sŭb-kŏn′-) ►*n.* A large landmass, such as India, that is part of a continent but is considered either geographically or politically separate.

sub·con·tract (sŭb-kŏn′trăkt′, sŭb′kŏn′trăkt) ►*n.* A contract in which a party agrees to perform part of the work that was originally arranged with the signer of a previous contract. —**sub·con′tract′** *v.* —**sub·con′trac·tor** *n.*

sub·cul·ture (sŭb′kŭl′chər) ►*n.* A cultural subgroup within a larger cultural group.

sub·cu·ta·ne·ous (sŭb′kyōō-tā′nē-əs) ►*adj.* Just beneath the skin. —**sub′cu·ta′ne·ous·ly** *adv.*

sub·di·vide (sŭb′dĭ-vīd′, sŭb′dĭ-vīd′) ►*v.* **1.** To divide into smaller parts. **2.** To divide into parts, esp. to divide (land) into lots. —**sub′di·vid′er** *n.* —**sub′di·vi′sion** (-vĭzh′ən) *n.*

sub·due (səb-dōō′, -dyōō′) ►*v.* **-dued, -du·ing 1.** To conquer and subjugate; vanquish. **2.** To quiet or bring under control. **3.** To make less intense. [< Lat. *subdūcere*, withdraw.] —**sub·du′er** *n.*

sub·head (sŭb′hĕd′) ►*n.* **1.** The heading or title of a subdivision of a printed subject. **2.** A subordinate heading or title.

subj. ►*abbr.* **1.** subject **2.** subjunctive

sub·ject (sŭb′jĕkt′, -jĭkt) ►*adj.* **1.** Under the power or authority of another. **2.** Prone; disposed: *subject to colds.* **3.** Likely to incur or receive: *subject to misinterpretation.* **4.** Contingent or dependent: *subject to approval.* See Synonyms at **dependent.** ►*n.* **1.** One who is under the rule of another, esp. one who owes allegiance to a government or ruler. **2a.** One about which something is said or done; topic. **b.** The main theme of a work of art. **3.** A course or area of study. **4a.** One that experiences or is subjected to something. **b.** One that is the object of study. **5.** *Gram.* The noun, noun phrase, or pronoun in a clause that denotes the doer of the action or what is described by the predicate. ►*v.* (səb-jĕkt′) **1.** To cause to experience, undergo, or be acted upon. **2.** To subjugate. [< Lat. *subiectus,* p.part. of *sūbicere,* to subject.] —**sub·jec′tion** (səb-jĕk′shən) *n.*

sub·jec·tive (səb-jĕk′tĭv) ►*adj.* **1a.** Dependent on or taking place in a person's mind rather than the external world: *The sensation of pain is a subjective experience.* **b.** Based on a given person's experience, understanding, and feelings; personal: *a subjective judgment.* **2.** *Gram.* Of or being the nominative case. —**sub·jec′tive·ly** *adv.* —**sub′jec·tiv′i·ty** (sŭb′jĕk-tĭv′ĭ-tē) *n.*

sub·join (səb-join′) ►*v.* To add at the end; append. [< Lat. *subiungere* : *sub-,* under + *iungere,* join.]

sub·ju·gate (sŭb′jə-gāt′) ►*v.* **-gat·ed, -gat·ing** **1.** To bring under control, esp. by military force; conquer. **2.** To make subordinate or subject to the dominion of something else. [< Lat. *subiugāre* : *sub-,* under + *iugum,* yoke.] —**sub′ju·ga′tion** *n.* —**sub′ju·ga′tor** *n.*

sub·junc·tive (səb-jŭngk′tĭv) ►*adj.* Of or being a mood of a verb used to express an uncertainty, a wish, or an unlikely condition. [< Lat. *subiungere, subiūnct-,* SUBJOIN.] —**sub·junc′tive** *n.*

sub·lease (sŭb′lēs′) ►*n.* A lease of property granted by a lessee. —**sub′lease′** *v.*

sub·let (sŭb′lĕt′) ►*v.* **1.** To rent (property one holds by lease) to another. **2.** To subcontract (work). ►*n.* (sŭb′lĕt′) Property rented by one tenant to another.

sub·li·mate (sŭb′lə-māt′) ►*v.* **-mat·ed, -mat·ing** **1.** *Chem.* To change from a solid to a gaseous state or from a gaseous to a solid state without becoming a liquid. **2.** *Psychol.* To modify the natural expression of (an instinctual impulse) in a socially acceptable manner. [Lat. *sublīmāre,* elevate.] —**sub′li·ma′tion** *n.*

sub·lime (sə-blīm′) ►*adj.* **1.** Of high spiritual, moral, or intellectual worth. **2.** Exalted; lofty. **3.** Inspiring awe. ►*v.* **-limed, -lim·ing** *Chem.* To sublimate. [< Lat. *sublīmis,* uplifted.] —**sub·lime′ly** *adv.* —**sub·lim′i·ty** (sə-blĭm′ĭ-tē) *n.*

sub·lim·i·nal (sŭb-lĭm′ə-nəl) ►*adj. Psychol.* Below the threshold of conscious perception or awareness. [SUB– + Lat. *līmen,* threshold.] —**sub·lim′i·nal·ly** *adv.*

sub·lu·na·ry (sŭb-lōō′nə-rē, sŭb′lōō-nĕr′ē) ►*adj.* **1.** Situated beneath the moon. **2.** Of this world; earthly. [LLat. *sublūnāris.*]

sub·ma·chine gun (sŭb′mə-shēn′) ►*n.* A lightweight automatic or semiautomatic gun fired from the shoulder or hip.

sub·ma·rine (sŭb′mə-rēn′, sŭb′mə-rēn′) ►*n.* **1.** A ship capable of operating under water. **2.** A submarine sandwich. ►*adj.* Beneath the surface of the water; undersea.

submarine sandwich

submarine sandwich ►*n.* A large sandwich consisting of a long roll split lengthwise and filled with layers of ingredients such as meat, cheese, tomatoes, lettuce, and condiments. [From the resemblance of the roll to a submarine.]

---

sub·ab·dom′i·nal *adj.*
sub·a·cute′ *adj.*
sub·a′gen·cy *n.*
sub·al′pine′ *adj.*
sub·ap′i·cal *adj.*
sub·ap′i·cal·ly *adv.*
sub·a′que·ous *adj.*
sub·arc′tic *adj.*
sub·ar′id *adj.*
sub·as·sem′bly *n.*
sub·av′er·age *adj.*
sub·ax′il·lar′y *adj.*
sub·base′ment *n.*
sub′branch′ *n.*
sub·cat·e·go′ry *n.*
sub′class′ *n.*
sub·clas′si·fi·ca′tion *n.*
sub·class′i·fy′ *v.*
sub·clin′i·cal *adj.*
sub′com·mand′er *n.*
sub′com·mis′sion *n.*
sub′con′fer·ence *n.*
sub·coun′cil *n.*
sub·cra′ni·al *adj.*
sub·dea′con *n.*
sub′dean′ *n.*
sub′de·part′ment *n.*
sub′di·rec′tor *n.*
sub′di·rec′to·ry *n.*
sub·dis′ci·pline *n.*

sub′dis′trict *n.*
sub·dur′al *adj.*
sub·en′try *n.*
sub·fam′i·ly *n.*
sub·floor′ *n.*
sub·floor′ing *n.*
sub·freez′ing *adj.*
sub·gen′re *n.*
sub·ge′nus *n.*
sub·gla′cial *adj.*
sub′group′ *n.*
sub·head′ing *n.*
sub·hu′man *adj.*
sub·in′dex *n.*
sub′in·dus′try *n.*
sub′king′dom *n.*
sub·le′thal *adj.*
sub·le′thal·ly *adv.*
sub·lit′er·ate *adj.*
sub·mem′ber *n.*
sub·min′i·mal *adj.*
sub·min′i·mum *adj.*
sub′mo·lec′u·lar *adj.*
sub′o·ce·an′ic *adj.*
sub·of′fi·cer *n.*
sub·par′ *adj.*
sub′per·i·os′te·al *adj.*
sub·phy′lum *n.*
sub′pop·u·la′tion *n.*
sub·prime′ *adj.*

sub·prin′ci·pal *n.*
sub′pro·fes′sion·al *n.*
sub′pro′gram *n.*
sub·re′gion *n.*
sub′sam′ple *n. & v.*
sub′sec′tion *n.*
sub·seg′ment *n.*
sub·sense′ *n.*
sub·se′ries *n.*
sub·spe′cial·ist *n.*
sub·spe′cial·i·za′-
  tion *n.*
sub·spe′cial·ize *v.*
sub·spe′cial·ty *n.*
sub·spe′cies *n.*
sub′stage′ *n.*
sub·strat′o·sphere′ *n.*
sub·sur′face *adj.*
sub·sys′tem *n.*
sub·teen′ *adj.*
sub·tem′per·ate *adj.*
sub·ten′ant *n.*
sub·thresh′old′ *n.*
sub·top′ic *n.*
sub·treas′ur·y *n.*
sub·tribe′ *n.*
sub·type′ *n.*
sub·u′nit *n.*
sub·vo′cal *adj.*
sub·ze′ro *adj.*

sub·merge (səb-mûrj′) ▸v. **-merged, -merg·ing 1.** To place under water. **2.** To cover with water. **3.** To go under or as if under water. [Lat. *submergere.*] —**sub·mer′gence** n. —**sub·mer′gi·ble** adj.

sub·merse (səb-mûrs′) ▸v. **-mersed, -mers·ing** To submerge. [< Lat. *submergere, submers-*, submerged.] —**sub·mer′sion** (-mûr′-zhən, -shən) n.

sub·mers·i·ble (səb-mûr′sə-bəl) ▸adj. Submergible. ▸n. A vessel or vehicle capable of operating under water.

sub·mi·cro·scop·ic (sŭb′mī-krə-skŏp′ĭk) ▸adj. Too small to be resolved by an optical microscope.

sub·mit (səb-mĭt′) ▸v. **-mit·ted, -mit·ting 1.** To yield or surrender (oneself) to the will or authority of another. **2.** To present (something) to the judgment of another. **3.** To offer as a contention. **4.** To allow oneself to be subjected to something: *submit to drug testing.* [< Lat. *submittere*, set under.] —**sub·mis′sion** n. —**sub·mis′sive** adj.

sub·nor·mal (sŭb-nôr′məl) ▸adj. Less than normal; below the average. —**sub′nor·mal′i·ty** (-măl′ĭ-tē) n.

sub·or·bi·tal (sŭb-ôr′bĭ-tl) ▸adj. Having a trajectory of less than one full orbit.

sub·or·di·nate (sə-bôr′dn-ĭt) ▸adj. **1.** Of a lower or inferior class or rank. **2.** Subject to the authority or control of another. ▸n. One that is subordinate. ▸v. (sə-bôr′dn-āt′) **-nat·ed, -nat·ing 1.** To put in a lower or inferior rank or class. **2.** To make subservient. [< Med.Lat. *subōrdināre*, put in lower rank.] —**sub·or′di·nate·ly** adv. —**sub·or′di·na′tion** n. —**sub·or′di·na′tive** adj.

sub·orn (sə-bôrn′) ▸v. To induce to commit an unlawful act, esp. perjury. [Lat. *subōrnāre.*] —**sub′or·na′tion** (sŭb′ôr-nā′shən) n. —**sub·orn′er** n.

sub·plot (sŭb′plŏt′) ▸n. A plot subordinate to the main plot of a literary work or film.

sub·poe·na (sə-pē′nə) ▸n. An order issued by a court commanding a person to appear in court, usu. to give testimony. ▸v. To serve or summon with such a writ. [< Med.Lat., under a penalty.]

sub ro·sa (sŭb rō′zə) ▸adv. In secret. [Lat. *sub rosā*, under the rose.] —**sub-ro′sa** adj.

sub·rou·tine (sŭb′rōō-tēn′) ▸n. *Comp.* A set of instructions that performs a specific task for a main routine.

sub-Sa·har·an (sŭb′sə-hâr′ən, -här′-, -här′-) ▸adj. Of or relating to the region of Africa south of the Sahara.

sub·scribe (səb-scrīb′) ▸v. **-scribed, -scrib·ing 1.** To pledge or contribute (a sum of money). **2.** To sign (one's name). **3.** To sign one's name to in testimony or consent: *subscribe a will.* **4.** To contract to receive and pay for a subscription, as to a publication. **5.** To express approval or agreement: *subscribe to a belief.* [< Lat. *subscrībere*, write under.] —**sub·scrib′er** n.

sub·script (sŭb′skrĭpt′) ▸n. A character or symbol written directly beneath or next to and slightly below a letter or number. [< Lat. *subscrīptus*, p.part. of *subscrībere*, write under.]

sub·scrip·tion (səb-skrĭp′shən) ▸n. **1.** A purchase made by signed order, as for issues of a periodical or a series of events. **2.** The signing of one's name, as to a document.

sub·se·quent (sŭb′sĭ-kwĕnt′, -kwənt) ▸adj. Following in time or order. [< Lat. *subsequī*, follow close after.] —**sub′se·quent′ly** adv.

sub·ser·vi·ent (səb-sûr′vē-ənt) ▸adj. **1.** Subordinate. **2.** Obsequious; servile. [< Lat. *subservīre*, serve, support.] —**sub·ser′vi·ence** n. —**sub·ser′vi·ent·ly** adv.

sub·set (sŭb′sĕt′) ▸n. A set contained within a set.

sub·side (səb-sīd′) ▸v. **-sid·ed, -sid·ing 1.** To become less; abate: *The wind subsided.* **2.** To sink to a lower level. **3.** To sink to the bottom, as a sediment. [Lat. *subsīdere* : *sub-*, down + *sīdere*, settle.] —**sub·si′dence** n.

sub·sid·i·ar·y (səb-sĭd′ē-ĕr′ē) ▸adj. **1.** Serving to assist or supplement. **2.** Subordinate. **3.** Of or like a subsidy. ▸n., pl. **-ar·ies** One that is subsidiary to another, esp. a company owned by another company. —**sub·sid′i·ar′i·ly** (-âr′ə-lē) adv.

sub·si·dize (sŭb′sĭ-dīz′) ▸v. **-dized, -diz·ing** To assist or support with a subsidy. —**sub′si·di·za′tion** n.

sub·si·dy (sŭb′sĭ-dē) ▸n., pl. **-dies** Financial assistance given by one person or government to another. [< Lat. *subsidium*, support : *sub-*, behind + *sedēre*, sit.]

sub·sist (səb-sĭst′) ▸v. **1.** To exist; be. **2.** To maintain life, esp. at a meager level: *subsisted on one meal a day.* [Lat. *subsistere*, support : *sub-*, behind + *sistere*, stand.]

sub·sis·tence (səb-sĭs′təns) ▸n. **1.** The act or state of subsisting. **2.** A means of subsisting. **3.** Existence. —**sub·sis′tent** adj.

sub·soil (sŭb′soil′) ▸n. The layer of earth beneath the topsoil.

sub·son·ic (sŭb-sŏn′ĭk) ▸adj. **1.** Of less than audible frequency. **2.** Having a speed less than that of sound.

sub·stance (sŭb′stəns) ▸n. **1a.** That which has mass and occupies space; matter. **b.** A material of a particular kind or constitution. **2.** The essence; gist. **3.** That which is solid and practical: *a plan without substance.* **4.** Density; body. **5.** Material possessions; wealth. [< Lat. *substāre*, be present : *sub-*, under + *stāre*, stand.]
Syns: core, gist, purport **n.**

substance abuse ▸n. The use of an illegal or unprescribed drug or the inappropriate habitual use of another drug or alcohol, esp. when resulting in addiction.

sub·stan·dard (sŭb-stăn′dərd) ▸adj. Failing to meet a standard; below standard.

sub·stan·tial (səb-stăn′shəl) ▸adj. **1.** Considerable; large: *won by a substantial margin.* **2.** Solidly built; strong. **3.** Ample; sustaining. **4.** Possessing wealth; well-to-do. **5a.** Of or having substance; material. **b.** Not imaginary; real. [< Lat. *substantia*, SUBSTANCE.] —**sub·stan′tial·ly** adv.

sub·stan·ti·ate (səb-stăn′shē-āt′) ▸v. **-at·ed, -at·ing** To support with proof or evidence. —**sub·stan′ti·a′tion** n.

sub·stan·tive (sŭb′stən-tĭv) ▸adj. **1.** Substantial; considerable. **2.** Basic; essential. ▸n. *Gram.* A word or group of words functioning as a noun. —**sub′stan·tive·ly** adv.

sub·sta·tion (sŭb′stā′shən) ▸n. A branch station, as of a post office.

sub·sti·tute (sŭb′stĭ-tōōt′, -tyōōt′) ▸n. One

that takes the place of another. ►*v.* **-tut·ed, -tut·ing 1.** To put or use in place of another. **2.** To take the place of another. [< Lat. *substituere,* stand in : *sub-,* in place of + *statuere,* cause to stand.] —**sub′sti·tu′tion** *n.*

sub·strate (sŭb′strāt′) ►*n.* **1.** The substance on which an enzyme acts. **2.** An underlying layer; substratum. [< SUBSTRATUM.]

sub·stra·tum (sŭb′strā′təm, -străt′əm) ►*n.* **1.** An underlying layer or foundation. **2.** Subsoil.

sub·struc·ture (sŭb′strŭk′chər) ►*n.* The supporting part of a structure; foundation.

sub·sume (səb-sōōm′) ►*v.* **-sumed, -sum·ing** To place in a more comprehensive category. [Med.Lat. *subsūmere.*] —**sub·sum′a·ble** *adj.*

sub·tend (səb-tĕnd′) ►*v. Math.* To be opposite to and delimit: *The hypotenuse subtends a right angle.* [Lat. *subtendere,* extend beneath.]

sub·ter·fuge (sŭb′tər-fyōōj′) ►*n.* A deceptive stratagem or device. [< Lat. *subterfugere,* flee secretly.]

sub·ter·ra·ne·an (sŭb′tə-rā′nē-ən) ►*adj.* **1.** Situated or operating beneath the earth's surface; underground. **2.** Hidden; secret. [Lat. *subterrāneus* : *sub-,* under + *terra,* earth.]

sub·text (sŭb′tĕkst′) ►*n.* An implicit meaning or theme of a literary text.

sub·ti·tle (sŭb′tīt′l) ►*n.* **1.** A secondary, usu. explanatory title, as of a literary work. **2.** A printed translation of the dialogue of a foreign-language film shown at the bottom of the screen. —**sub′ti′tle** *v.*

sub·tle (sŭt′l) ►*adj.* **-tler, -tlest 1a.** So slight as to be difficult to detect. **b.** Not obvious; abstruse. **2.** Able to make fine distinctions: *a subtle mind.* **3.** *Archaic* **a.** Skillful; clever. **b.** Crafty. [< Lat. *subtīlis.*] —**sub′tle·ty, sub′tle·ness** *n.* —**sub′tly** *adv.*

sub·to·tal (sŭb′tōt′l) ►*n.* The total of part of a series of numbers. —**sub′to′tal** *v.*

sub·tract (səb-trăkt′) ►*v.* To take away or deduct, as one number from another. [Lat. *subtrahere, subtrāct-.*] —**sub·trac′tion** *n.*

sub·tra·hend (sŭb′trə-hĕnd′) ►*n. Math.* A quantity to be subtracted from another. [Lat. *subtrahendum,* to be subtracted.]

sub·trop·i·cal (sŭb-trŏp′ĭ-kəl) ►*adj.* Of or being the geographic areas adjacent to the tropics.

sub·trop·ics (sŭb-trŏp′ĭks) ►*pl.n.* Subtropical regions.

sub·urb (sŭb′ûrb′) ►*n.* **1.** A usu. residential area near a city. **2. suburbs** The usu. residential region surrounding a major city. [< Lat. *suburbium.*] —**sub·ur′ban** (sə-bûr′bən) *adj.*

sub·ur·ban·ite (sə-bûr′bə-nīt′) ►*n.* One who lives in a suburb.

sub·ur·bi·a (sə-bûr′bē-ə) ►*n.* **1.** The suburbs. **2.** Suburbanites collectively.

sub·ven·tion (səb-vĕn′shən) ►*n.* An endowment or subsidy. [< Lat. *subvenīre,* come to help : *sub-,* behind + *venīre,* come.]

sub·ver·sive (səb-vûr′sĭv, -zĭv) ►*adj.* Tending to subvert an established order, esp. to undermine an established government. ►*n.* One who advocates subversive means or policies. —**sub·ver′sive·ly** *adv.* —**sub·ver′sive·ness** *n.*

sub·vert (səb-vûrt′) ►*v.* **1.** To overthrow (e.g., a government). See Synonyms at **overthrow. 2.** To render ineffective (a rule or an established notion). **3.** To cause to serve a purpose other than the original or established one; comman-

deer. **4.** To undermine, mislead, or betray. [< Lat. *subvertere.*] —**sub·ver′sion** (-vûr′zhən, -shən) *n.* —**sub·vert′er** *n.*

sub·way (sŭb′wā′) ►*n.* An underground railroad, usu. operated by electricity.

suc·ceed (sək-sēd′) ►*v.* **1.** To come next in time or succession, esp. to replace another in a position. **2.** To accomplish something attempted. [< Lat. *succēdere.*]

suc·cess (sək-sĕs′) ►*n.* **1.** The achievement of something attempted. **2.** The gaining of fame or prosperity. **3.** One that succeeds. [< Lat. *succēdere, success-,* succeed.] —**suc·cess′ful** *adj.* —**suc·cess′ful·ly** *adv.*

suc·ces·sion (sək-sĕsh′ən) ►*n.* **1.** The act of following in order. **2.** A group of people or things following in order. **3.** The sequence, right, or act of succeeding to a title, throne, or estate. —**suc·ces′sion·al** *adj.* —**suc·ces′sion·al·ly** *adv.*

suc·ces·sive (sək-sĕs′ĭv) ►*adj.* Following in uninterrupted order; consecutive. —**suc·ces′sive·ly** *adv.*

suc·ces·sor (sək-sĕs′ər) ►*n.* One that succeeds or follows another.

suc·cinct (sək-sĭngkt′) ►*adj.* Brief and clear in expression; concise. [< Lat. *succīnctus,* p.part. of *succingere,* gird from below.] —**suc·cinct′ly** *adv.* —**suc·cinct′ness** *n.*

suc·cor (sŭk′ər) ►*n.* Assistance in time of distress; relief. [< Lat. *succurrere,* run to the aid of.] —**suc′cor** *v.*

suc·co·tash (sŭk′ə-tăsh′) ►*n.* A stew of kernels of corn, lima beans, and tomatoes. [Narragansett *msíckquatash,* boiled whole-kernel corn.]

Suc·coth (sōō-kôt′, sōō-kōs′, sōōk′əs) ►*n.* Var. of **Sukkot.**

suc·cu·bus (sŭk′yə-bəs) ►*n., pl.* **-bus·es** or **-bi** (-bī′, -bē′) An evil spirit supposed to have sexual intercourse with a sleeping man. [< Lat. *succuba,* paramour.]

suc·cu·lent (sŭk′yə-lənt) ►*adj.* **1.** Full of juice or sap; juicy. **2.** Having thick fleshy leaves or stems. ►*n.* A succulent plant, such as a cactus. [Lat. *succulentus* < *succus,* juice.] —**suc′cu·lence** *n.* —**suc′cu·lent·ly** *adv.*

suc·cumb (sə-kŭm′) ►*v.* **1.** To submit or yield to something overwhelming. **2.** To die, esp. from a disease or injury. [< Lat. *succumbere,* lie down before.]

such (sŭch) ►*adj.* Of this or that kind or extent. ►*adv.* **1.** To so extreme a degree; so: *such beautiful flowers.* **2.** Very; especially. ►*pron.* **1.** Such a one or ones. **2.** Someone or something implied or indicated: *Such are the fortunes of war.* The like: *pins, needles, and such.* —*idiom:* **such as** For example. [< OE *swylc.*]

such·like (sŭch′līk′) ►*adj.* Similar. ►*pron.* One or ones of such a kind.

suck (sŭk) ►*v.* **1.** To draw (liquid) into the mouth by movements that create suction. **2.** To draw something in by suction. **3.** To suckle. ►*n.* The act or sound of sucking. [< OE *sūcan.*]

suck·er (sŭk′ər) ►*n.* **1.** One that sucks. **2.** *Informal* One who is easily deceived. **3.** A lollipop. **4.** A freshwater fish with a thick-lipped mouth used for feeding by suction. **5.** An organ or other structure adapted for sucking nourishment or for clinging by suction. **6.** *Bot.* A secondary shoot produced from the base or roots of a woody plant. ►*v. Informal* To trick; dupe.

suck·le (sŭk′əl) ►v. **-led, -ling 1.** To give or take milk at the breast or udder; nurse. **2.** To nourish; nurture. [ME *suclen.*]

suck·ling (sŭk′lĭng) ►n. A young unweaned mammal. [ME *suklinge.*] —**suck′ling** *adj.*

Su·cre (soo′krā, -krĕ) The constitutional capital of Bolivia, in the S-central part SE of La Paz.

su·crose (soo′krōs′) ►n. A sugar, $C_{12}H_{22}O_{11}$, found in many plants, notably sugar cane and sugar beets. [Fr. *sucre*, sugar + -OSE².]

suc·tion (sŭk′shən) ►n. **1.** The act or process of sucking. **2.** A force that causes a fluid or solid to be drawn into a space or to adhere to a surface because of the difference between external and internal pressures. [< Lat. *sūgere, sūct-*, suck.]

Su·dan (soo-dăn′) **1.** A region of N Africa S of the Sahara and N of the equator. **2.** A country of NE Africa S of Egypt. In 2011, the S part voted to form a separate nation. Cap. Khartoum. —**Su′da·nese′** (sood′n-ēz′, -ēs′) *adj. & n.*

sud·den (sŭd′n) ►*adj.* **1.** Happening without warning; unforeseen. **2.** Happening or done without delay; hasty. **3.** Marked by sharp change in elevation; precipitous. [< Lat. *subitus.*] —**sud′den·ly** *adv.* —**sud′den·ness** *n.*

sudden infant death syndrome ►n. *Abbr.* **SIDS** A fatal syndrome of infants marked by sudden cessation of breathing.

Su·de·ten (soo-dā′tn, zoo-) A series of mountain ranges along the Czech-Polish border between the Elbe and Oder Rivers.

Su·de·ten·land (soo-dāt′n-lănd′, zoo-) A historical region of N Czech Republic.

su·do·ku (soo-dō′koo) ►n. A puzzle in which a grid consisting of several regions is to be filled with numbers so that every row, column, and region contains only one instance of each number. [Japanese *sūdoku*, short for *suu(ji wa) doku(shin ni kagiru)*, the numbers are limited to a single occurrence.]

suds (sŭdz) ►*pl.n.* **1.** Soapy water. **2.** Foam; lather. [Poss. < MDu. *sudse*, marsh.] —**sud′sy** *adj.*

sue (soo) ►v. **sued, su·ing 1.** To initiate or pursue legal proceedings against (another party). **2.** To make an appeal or entreaty: *sue for peace.* [< Lat. *sequī*, follow.] —**su′er** *n.*

suede also **suède** (swād) ►n. **1.** Leather with a soft napped surface. **2.** Fabric made to resemble suede. [< Fr. *Suède*, Sweden.]

su·et (soo′ĭt) ►n. The hard fat around the kidneys of cattle and sheep, used in cooking and making tallow. [< Lat. *sēbum.*]

Sue·to·ni·us (swē-tō′nē-əs) Gaius Suetonius Tranquillus. fl. 2nd cent. AD. Roman historian.

Su·ez (soo-ĕz′, soo′ĕz′) A city of NE Egypt at the head of the **Gulf of Suez,** an arm of the Red Sea W of the Sinai Peninsula.

Suez, Isthmus of An isthmus of NE Egypt connecting Africa and Asia.

Suez Canal A ship canal, about 160 km (100 mi), linking the Red Sea with the Mediterranean.

suff. ►*abbr.* suffix

suf·fer (sŭf′ər) ►v. **1.** To feel pain or distress; sustain loss or harm. **2.** To undergo or be subjected to (a negative experience): *a species that suffered a decline in population.* **3.** To appear at a disadvantage: *suffer by comparison.* **4a.** To put up with; tolerate. **b.** To permit; allow. [< Lat. *sufferre : sub-*, under + *ferre*, carry.] —**suf′fer·a·ble** *adj.* —**suf′fer·a·bly** *adv.* —**suf′fer·er** *n.*

Usage: In general usage *suffer* is preferably used with *from*, rather than *with*, in constructions such as *He suffered from hypertension.*

suf·fer·ance (sŭf′ər-əns, sŭf′rəns) ►n. **1.** Patient endurance. **2.** Sanction or permission implied by failure to prohibit; tacit consent.

suf·fer·ing (sŭf′ər-ĭng, sŭf′rĭng) ►n. Physical or mental pain or distress.

suf·fice (sə-fīs′) ►v. **-ficed, -fic·ing 1.** To be sufficient (for). **2.** To be capable or competent. [< Lat. *sufficere.*]

suf·fi·cient (sə-fĭsh′ənt) ►*adj.* Being as much as is needed. —**suf·fi′cien·cy** *n.* —**suf·fi′cient·ly** *adv.*

Syns: *acceptable, adequate, enough* **adj.**

suf·fix (sŭf′ĭks) ►n. An affix added to the end of a word or stem, serving to form a new word or an inflectional ending. [< Lat. *suffixus*, p.part. of *suffigere*, affix.] —**suf′fix** *v.* —**suf·fix′ion** (sə-fĭk′shən) *n.*

suf·fo·cate (sŭf′ə-kāt′) ►v. **-cat·ed, -cat·ing 1.** To kill or destroy by preventing access to oxygen. **2.** To suppress; stifle. [Lat. *suffōcāre.*] —**suf′fo·ca′tion** *n.*

suf·frage (sŭf′rĭj) ►n. **1.** The right or privilege of voting. **2.** A vote. [< Lat. *suffrāgium.*]

suf·fra·gette (sŭf′rə-jĕt′) ►n. *Chiefly Brit.* A woman advocating suffrage for women.

suf·fra·gist (sŭf′rə-jĭst) ►n. An advocate of the extension of voting rights, esp. to women. —**suf′fra·gism** *n.*

suf·fuse (sə-fyooz′) ►v. **-fused, -fus·ing 1.** To spread through or over, as with liquid or light. **2.** To permeate, as with a quality or emotion. See Synonyms at **imbue.** [Lat. *suffundere, suffūs-.*] —**suf·fu′sion** *n.* —**suf·fu′sive** *adj.*

Su·fi (soo′fē) ►n. *Islam* A Muslim mystic. —**Su′fism** (-fĭz′əm) *n.*

sug·ar (shoog′ər) ►n. **1.** Crystalline or powdered sucrose, used as a sweetener; table sugar. **2.** Any of a class of water-soluble crystalline carbohydrates with a characteristically sweet taste. ►v. **1.** To coat, cover, or sweeten with sugar. **2.** To make less distasteful. [< Skt. *śarkarā.*]

sugar beet ►n. A beet with fleshy white roots from which sugar is obtained.

sugar cane ►n. A tall tropical grass with thick stems that yield sugar.

sug·ar·coat (shoog′ər-kōt′) ►v. **1.** To cause to seem more appealing or pleasant. **2.** To cover with sugar.

sug·ar·less (shoog′ər-lĭs) ►*adj.* **1.** Containing no sugar. **2.** Sweetened with a substance other than sucrose.

sugar maple ►n. A maple tree of E North America, with sap that is the source of maple syrup and maple sugar.

sug·ar·plum (shoog′ər-plŭm′) ►n. A small ball of candy.

sug·ar·y (shoog′ə-rē) ►*adj.* **-i·er, -i·est 1.** Tasting of or resembling sugar. **2.** Excessively or cloyingly sweet.

sug·gest (səg-jĕst′, sə-jĕst′) ►v. **1.** To offer for consideration or action; propose. **2.** To bring or call to mind by association. **3.** To imply. [Lat. *suggerere, suggest-.*]

sug·gest·i·ble (səg-jĕs′tə-bəl, sə-jĕst′-) ►*adj.* Readily influenced by suggestion.

sug·ges·tion (sǝg-jĕs′chǝn, sǝ-jĕs′-) ►*n.* **1.** The act of suggesting. **2.** Something suggested. **3.** A hint or trace.

sug·ges·tive (sǝg-jĕs′tĭv, sǝ-jĕs′-) ►*adj.* **1.** Tending to suggest; evocative. **2.** Conveying a hint or suggestion. **3.** Calling to mind sexual desire or sex acts. —**sug·ges′tive·ly** *adv.* —**sug·ges′tive·ness** *n.*

Su·har·to (sǝ-här′tō, sōō-) 1921–2008. Indonesian military and political leader.

su·i·cide (sōō′ĭ-sīd′) ►*n.* **1.** The act or an instance of intentionally killing oneself. **2.** One who commits suicide. [Lat. *suī,* of oneself + –CIDE.] —**su′i·cid′al** *adj.*

su·i ge·ne·ris (sōō′ī′ jĕn′ǝr-ĭs, sōō′ē) ►*adj.* Unique; singular. [Lat. *suī generis,* of its own kind.]

suit (sōōt) ►*n.* **1.** A set of matching outer garments, esp. a coat with trousers or a skirt. **2.** An outfit for a special activity: *a diving suit.* **3.** A group of related things. **4.** Any of the four sets of playing cards that constitute a deck. **5.** *Law* A lawsuit. **6.** The act or an instance of courtship. ►*v.* **1.** To meet the requirements of. **2.** To make appropriate; adapt. **3.** To be appropriate for; befit: *That color suits you.* **4.** To please; satisfy. [< VLat. **sequita,* following.]

suit·a·ble (sōō′tǝ-bǝl) ►*adj.* Appropriate to a purpose or occasion. —**suit′a·bil′i·ty, suit′a·ble·ness** *n.* —**suit′a·bly** *adv.*

suit·case (sōōt′kās′) ►*n.* A usu. rectangular piece of luggage.

suite (swēt) ►*n.* **1.** A staff of attendants. **2.** A set of matching furniture. **3.** A series of connected rooms. **4.** *Mus.* A composition consisting of a set of dances. [< OFr.; see SUIT.]

suit·or (sōō′tǝr) ►*n.* **1.** A man who is courting a woman. **2.** A petitioner.

Su·kar·no also **Soe·kar·no** (sōō-kär′nō) 1901–70. Indonesian president (1945–67).

su·ki·ya·ki (sōō′kē-yä′kē) ►*n.* A Japanese dish of sliced meat, bean curd, and vegetables fried together. [J.]

Suk·kot or **Suk·koth** (sōō-kôt′) or **Suc·coth** (sōō-kôt′, sōō-kōs′, sōōk′ǝs) ►*n.* A Jewish harvest festival celebrated in Tishri. [< Heb. *sukkâ,* booth.]

Su·la·we·si (sōō′lä-wä′sē) also **Cel·e·bes** (sĕl′ǝ-bēz′, sǝ-lē′bēz′, sĕ-lä′bĕs) An island of central Indonesia on the equator E of Borneo.

Su·lei·man I or **Sü·ley·man I** (sōō′lä-män′, -lǝ-) "the Magnificent" 1494?–1566. Sultan of Turkey (1520–66).

sul·fa drug (sŭl′fǝ) ►*n.* Any of a group of synthetic organic compounds that are used to inhibit bacterial growth and activity. [< *sulfa(nilamide),* a sulfa drug : SULF(UR) + ANIL(INE) + *amide.*]

sul·fate (sŭl′fāt′) ►*n.* The divalent group SO_4 or a compound containing this group. [Fr. < Lat. *sulfur,* sulfur.]

sul·fide (sŭl′fīd′) ►*n.* A compound of sulfur with another element, esp. a metal.

sul·fur also **sul·phur** (sŭl′fǝr) ►*n. Symbol* **S** A pale yellow nonmetallic element occurring widely in nature and used in gunpowder, insecticides, and pharmaceuticals. At. no. 16. See table at **element.** [< Lat. *sulfur.*]

sulfur dioxide ►*n.* A colorless, extremely irritating gas or liquid, SO_2, that is used in the manufacture of sulfuric acid and is a hazard-

ous pollutant resulting from the burning of fossil fuels.

sul·fu·ric (sŭl-fyŏŏr′ĭk) ►*adj.* Of or containing sulfur.

sulfuric acid ►*n.* A highly corrosive, dense oily liquid, H_2SO_4, used to manufacture a wide variety of chemicals and materials.

sul·fur·ous (sŭl′fǝr-ǝs, -fyǝr-, sŭl-fyŏŏr′ǝs) ►*adj.* **1.** Of or containing sulfur. **2.** Characteristic of burning sulfur, as in odor.

sulk (sŭlk) ►*v.* **sulked, sulk·ing** To be sullenly aloof or withdrawn. ►*n.* A mood or display of sulking. [< SULKY.]

sulk·y (sŭl′kē) ►*adj.* **-i·er, -i·est** Sullenly aloof. ►*n.* A light two-wheeled vehicle carrying only the driver and drawn by one horse. [Perh. < obsolete *sulke,* sluggish. N. < its having only one seat.] —**sulk′i·ly** *adv.* —**sulk′i·ness** *n.*

sul·len (sŭl′ǝn) ►*adj.* **-er, -est** **1.** Showing a brooding ill humor or silent resentment. **2.** Gloomy or somber. [< Lat. *sōlus,* alone.] —**sul′len·ly** *adv.* —**sul′len·ness** *n.*

Sul·li·van (sŭl′ǝ-vǝn), Sir **Arthur Seymour** 1842–1900. British composer.

Sullivan, Louis Henry or **Henri** 1856–1924. Amer. architect.

sul·ly (sŭl′ē) ►*v.* **-lied, -ly·ing** **1.** To mar the cleanness or luster of. **2.** To defile; taint. [Prob. < OFr. *souiller.*]

sul·phur (sŭl′fǝr) ►*n.* Var. of **sulfur.**

sul·tan (sŭl′tǝn) ►*n.* A ruler of a Muslim country, esp. of the former Ottoman Empire. [< Ar. *sulṭān.*]

sul·tan·a (sŭl-tăn′ǝ, -tä′nǝ) ►*n.* **1.** The wife, mother, sister, or daughter of a sultan. **2.** A small yellow seedless raisin.

sul·tan·ate (sŭl′tǝ-nāt′) ►*n.* **1.** The office, power, or reign of a sultan. **2.** A country ruled by a sultan.

sul·try (sŭl′trē) ►*adj.* **-tri·er, -tri·est** **1.** Hot and humid. **2.** Sensual; voluptuous. [Poss. < SWELTER.] —**sul′tri·ness** *n.*

Su·lu Sea (sōō′lōō) An arm of the W Pacific between the Philippines and Borneo.

sum (sŭm) ►*n.* **1a.** The result obtained by addition. **b.** An arithmetic problem. **2.** The whole quantity; aggregate. **3.** An amount of money. **4.** A summary. **5.** The gist. ►*v.* **summed, sum·ming** To add. —*phrasal verb:* **sum up** To summarize. [< Lat. *summus,* highest.]

su·mac also **su·mach** (sōō′măk, shōō′-) ►*n.* Any of various shrubs or small trees with compound leaves, greenish flowers, and usu. red fruit. [< Ar. *summāq,* sumac tree.]

Su·ma·tra (sōō-mä′trǝ) An island of W Indonesia in the Indian Ocean S of the Malay Peninsula. —**Su·ma′tran** *adj. & n.*

Su·mer (sōō′mǝr) An ancient country of S Mesopotamia in present-day S Iraq. —**Su·me′ri·an** (-mîr′ē-ǝn, -mĕr′-) *adj. & n.*

sum·ma·rize (sŭm′ǝ-rīz′) ►*v.* **-rized, -riz·ing** To make a summary of. —**sum′ma·ri·za′tion** *n.*

sum·ma·ry (sŭm′ǝ-rē) ►*adj.* **1.** Presented in condensed form; concise. **2.** Performed speedily and without ceremony: *summary justice.* ►*n., pl.* **-ries** A condensed statement of the substance or principal points of a larger work. [< Lat. *summa,* SUM.] —**sum·mar′i·ly** (sǝ-mĕr′ǝ-lē) *adv.*

sum·ma·tion (sǝ-mā′shǝn) ►*n.* A concluding

argument after the presentation of a legal case.

sum·mer (sŭm′ər) ►*n.* The usu. warmest season of the year, occurring between spring and autumn. ►*v.* To pass the summer. [< OE *sumor.*] —**sum′mer·y** *adj.*

sum·mer·house (sŭm′ər-hous′) ►*n.* A small roofed structure in a park or garden.

summer squash ►*n.* A variety of squash, such as zucchini, that is eaten before it develops a hard rind.

sum·mer·time (sŭm′ər-tīm′) ►*n.* The summer season.

sum·mit (sŭm′ĭt) ►*n.* **1.** The highest point. **2.** The highest degree of achievement or status. **3.** A conference or meeting of high-level leaders, usu. called to shape a program of action. [< Lat. *summus,* highest.]

sum·mon (sŭm′ən) ►*v.* **1.** To call together; convene. See Synonyms at **call. 2.** To request to appear; send for. **3.** To order to appear in court. **4.** To bring to mind or remember. Often used with *up.* [< Lat. *summonēre,* remind privately : *sub-,* secretly + *monēre,* warn.]

sum·mons (sŭm′ənz) ►*n., pl.* -**mons·es** **1.** A call to appear or do something. **2.** *Law* An order or process directing a person to report to court. —**sum′mons** *v.*

Sum·ner (sŭm′nər), **Charles** 1811–74. Amer. politician.

su·mo (soō′mō) ►*n.* A Japanese form of wrestling. [J. *sumō.*]

sump (sŭmp) ►*n.* **1.** A pit or hole that receives drainage. **2.** A cesspool. [ME *sompe,* marsh.]

sump·tu·ous (sŭmp′choo-əs) ►*adj.* Of a size or splendor suggesting great expense; lavish. [< Lat. *sūmptus,* expense.] —**sump′tu·ous·ly** *adv.* —**sump′tu·ous·ness** *n.*

Sum·ter (sŭm′tər), **Fort** A garrison at the mouth of the harbor of Charleston, SC; surrendered to Confederate forces in the first battle of the Civil War (April, 12 1861).

sun (sŭn) ►*n.* **1.** often **Sun** The star around which the Earth and other planets orbit. It sustains life on Earth with its light and heat, and has a mean distance from Earth of about 150 million km (93 million mi). **2.** A star that is the center of a planetary system. **3.** The radiant energy, esp. heat and visible light, emitted by the sun; sunshine. ►*v.* **sunned, sun·ning** To expose to or bask in the sun's rays. [< OE *sunne.*] —**sun′less** *adj.*

sun·baked (sŭn′bākt′) ►*adj.* Baked, dried, or hardened by exposure to sunlight.

sun·bathe (sŭn′bāth′) ►*v.* To expose the body to the sun. —**sun′bath′er** *n.*

sun·beam (sŭn′bēm′) ►*n.* A ray of sunlight.

sun·block (sŭn′blŏk′) ►*n.* A sunscreen.

sun·bon·net (sŭn′bŏn′ĭt) ►*n.* A woman's wide-brimmed bonnet for shading the face and neck from the sun.

sun·burn (sŭn′bûrn′) ►*n.* Inflammation or blistering of the skin caused by overexposure to direct sunlight. —**sun′burn′** *v.*

sun·burst (sŭn′bûrst′) ►*n.* A design having a central sunlike disk with radiating spires.

sun·dae (sŭn′dē, -dā′) ►*n.* A dish of ice cream with a topping such as syrup, fruits, nuts, or whipped cream. [Poss. < SUNDAY.]

Sun·da Islands (sŭn′də, soōn′-) A group of islands of the W Malay Archipelago between the South China Sea and the Indian Ocean.

Sun·day (sŭn′dē, -dā′) ►*n.* **1.** The 1st day of the week. **2.** The Sabbath observed on this day in most branches of Christianity. [< OE *sunnandæg.*]

sun·der (sŭn′dər) ►*v.* To break or wrench apart; sever. [< OE *sundrian.*] —**sun′der·ance** *n.*

sun·di·al (sŭn′dī′əl) ►*n.* An instrument that indicates the time of day by the shadow cast by a central projecting pointer on a calibrated dial.

sun·down (sŭn′doun′) ►*n.* Sunset.

sun·dries (sŭn′drēz) ►*pl.n.* Small miscellaneous items. [< SUNDRY.]

sun·dry (sŭn′drē) ►*adj.* Various; miscellaneous. [< OE *syndrig,* separate.]

sun·fish (sŭn′fĭsh′) ►*n.* **1.** Any of various flat-bodied North American freshwater fishes. **2.** Any of various large, round-bodied saltwater fishes.

sun·flow·er (sŭn′flou′ər) ►*n.* Any of various plants with large yellow-rayed flower heads that produce edible seeds rich in oil.

sung (sŭng) ►*v.* A p.t. and the p.part. of **sing.**

sun·glass·es (sŭn′glăs′ĭz) ►*pl.n.* Eyeglasses with tinted lenses to protect the eyes from the sun's glare.

sunk (sŭngk) ►*v.* A p.t. and the p.part. of **sink.**

sunk·en (sŭng′kən) ►*adj.* **1.** Depressed, fallen in, or hollowed: *sunken cheeks.* **2.** Submerged: *a sunken reef.* **3.** Below a surrounding level.

sun·lamp or **sun lamp** (sŭn′lămp′) ►*n.* A lamp that radiates ultraviolet rays used in therapeutic and cosmetic treatments.

sun·light (sŭn′līt′) ►*n.* The light of the sun.

sun·lit (sŭn′lĭt′) ►*adj.* Illuminated by the sun.

Sun·na also **Sun·nah** (soōn′ə) ►*n.* The way of life prescribed as normative in Islam, based on the teachings and practices of Muhammad and on the Koran. [Ar. *sunna.*]

Sun·ni (soōn′ē) ►*n., pl.* -**ni** or -**nis** A member of the branch of Islam that accepts the first four caliphs as rightful successors of Muhammad. [Ar. *sunnī* < *sunna,* Sunna.] —**Sun′ni** *adj.* —**Sun′nite′** *n.*

sun·ny (sŭn′ē) ►*adj.* -**ni·er,** -**ni·est** **1.** Exposed to or abounding in sunshine. **2.** Cheerful; genial. —**sun′ni·ness** *n.*

sun·rise (sŭn′rīz′) ►*n.* The appearance of the sun, usu. above the eastern horizon except for extreme latitudes.

sun·roof (sŭn′roōf′, -roōf′) ►*n.* A roof panel on a motor vehicle that can be slid back or raised.

sun·screen (sŭn′skrēn′) ►*n.* A preparation used to protect skin from the damaging rays of the sun.

sun·set (sŭn′sĕt′) ►*n.* The disappearance of the sun below the horizon.

sun·shade (sŭn′shād′) ►*n.* Something, as a parasol, used as a protection from the sun.

sun·shine (sŭn′shīn′) ►*n.* **1.** The light or the direct rays from the sun. **2.** Cheerfulness; geniality. —**sun′shin′y** *adj.*

sun·spot (sŭn′spŏt′) ►*n.* Any of the relatively cool dark spots appearing in groups on the surface of the sun.

sun·stroke (sŭn′strōk′) ►*n.* Heat stroke caused by exposure to the sun.

sun·tan (sŭn′tăn′) ►*n.* A darkening of the skin resulting from exposure to the sun. —**sun′tanned′** *adj.*

sun·up (sŭn′ŭp′) ►*n.* Sunrise.

Sun Yat-sen (so͞on′ yät′sĕn′) 1866–1925. Chinese politician.

Sun Yat-sen

sup (sŭp) ►*v.* **supped, sup·ping** To have supper; dine. [< OFr. *soupe*, SOUP.]

sup. ►*abbr.* **1.** superior **2.** superlative

su·per (so͞o′pər) *Informal* ►*n.* A superintendent in an apartment or office building. ►*adj.* **1.** Very large or great. **2.** Excellent.

super– ►*pref.* **1.** Above; over; upon: *superimpose.* **2.** Superior, as in size, quality, degree, or ability: *superfine.* **3.** Exceeding a norm: *supersaturate.* [< Lat. *super*, over, above.]

su·per·a·ble (so͞o′pər-ə-bəl) ►*adj.* Possible to overcome; surmountable. [< Lat. *superāre*, overcome < *super*, over.]

su·per·a·bun·dant (so͞o′pər-ə-bŭn′dənt) ►*adj.* Abundant to excess. —**su′per·a·bun′dance** *n.*

su·per·an·nu·at·ed (so͞o′pər-ăn′yo͞o-ā′tĭd) ►*adj.* **1.** Retired or ineffective because of advanced age. **2.** Outmoded; obsolete. [< Med. Lat. *superannuātus*, over one year old : SUPER– + Lat. *annus*, year.]

su·perb (so͞o-pûrb′) ►*adj.* **1.** First-rate; excellent. **2.** Majestic or magnificent. [Lat. *superbus.*] —**su·perb′ly** *adv.*

su·per·bug (so͞o′pər-bŭg′) ►*n.* A strain of bacteria resistant to all antibiotics.

su·per·car·go (so͞o′pər-kär′gō) ►*n., pl.* **-goes** or **-gos** An officer on a merchant ship who has charge of the cargo. [< Sp. *sobrecargo* : SUPER– + *cargo*, CARGO.]

su·per·charge (so͞o′pər-chärj′) ►*v.* To increase the power of (e.g., an engine).

su·per·charg·er (so͞o′pər-chär′jər) ►*n.* A blower or compressor for supplying air under high pressure to the cylinders of an internal-combustion engine.

su·per·cil·i·ous (so͞o′pər-sĭl′ē-əs) ►*adj.* Feeling or showing haughty disdain. [< Lat. *supercilium*, eyebrow : SUPER– + *cilium*, lower eyelid.] —**su′per·cil′i·ous·ly** *adv.* —**su′per·cil′i·ous·ness** *n.*

su·per·col·lid·er (so͞o′pər-kə-lī′dər) ►*n.* A high-energy particle accelerator.

su·per·con·duc·tiv·i·ty (so͞o′pər-kŏn′dŭk-tĭv′ĭ-tē) ►*n.* The property of certain metals, alloys, and ceramics to allow the flow of electric current without resistance at extremely low temperatures. —**su′per·con·duc′tive** *adj.* —**su′per·con·duc′tor** *n.*

su·per·cool (so͞o′pər-ko͞ol′) ►*v.* To cool (a substance) below a transition temperature without the transition occurring; e.g., to cool a liquid below the freezing point without solidification.

su·per·e·go (so͞o′pər-ē′gō) ►*n., pl.* **-gos** In psychoanalysis, the part of the psyche formed through the internalization of moral standards of parents and society.

su·per·e·rog·a·to·ry (so͞o′pər-ĭ-rŏg′ə-tôr′ē) ►*adj.* Superfluous; unnecessary. [< LLat. *superērogāre*, overspend : SUPER– + *ērogāre*, spend.]

su·per·fi·cial (so͞o′pər-fĭsh′əl) ►*adj.* **1.** Of, affecting, or being on the surface. **2.** Concerned with only the obvious; shallow. **3.** Apparent rather than actual or substantial. **4.** Minor or unimportant. [< Lat. *superficiēs*, surface : SUPER– + *faciēs*, face.] —**su′per·fi′ci·al′i·ty** (-fĭsh′ē-ăl′ĭ-tē) *n.* —**su′per·fi′cial·ly** *adv.*

su·per·fine (so͞o′pər-fīn′) ►*adj.* **1.** Of exceptional quality. **2.** Overly delicate or refined. **3.** Of extra fine texture.

su·per·flu·i·ty (so͞o′pər-flo͞o′ĭ-tē) ►*n., pl.* **-ties** **1.** The quality or condition of being superfluous. **2.** Something superfluous. **3.** Overabundance; excess.

su·per·flu·ous (so͞o-pûr′flo͞o-əs) ►*adj.* Beyond what is required or sufficient. [< Lat. *superfluere*, overflow : SUPER– + *fluere*, flow.] —**su·per′flu·ous·ly** *adv.*

Syns: excess, extra, supernumerary, surplus adj.

su·per·gal·ax·y (so͞o′pər-găl′ək-sē) ►*n.* A very large group of galaxies.

su·per·gi·ant (so͞o′pər-jī′ənt) ►*n.* A very large star with a luminosity thousands of times that of the sun.

su·per·he·ro (so͞o′pər-hîr′ō) ►*n.* A fictional figure having superhuman powers or greatly enhanced abilities, usu. portrayed as fighting evil or crime.

su·per·high·way (so͞o′pər-hī′wā′) ►*n.* A broad highway for high-speed traffic.

su·per·hu·man (so͞o′pər-hyo͞o′mən) ►*adj.* **1.** Divine; supernatural. **2.** Beyond ordinary or normal human ability, power, or experience. —**su′per·hu′man·ly** *adv.*

su·per·im·pose (so͞o′pər-ĭm-pōz′) ►*v.* **-posed, -pos·ing** To lay or place on or over something else. —**su′per·im′po·si′tion** (-ĭm′pə-zĭsh′ən) *n.*

su·per·in·tend (so͞o′pər-ĭn-tĕnd′, so͞o′prĭn-) ►*v.* To oversee and manage; supervise. [SUPER– + Lat. *intendere*, INTEND.] —**su′per·in·ten′dence** *n.* —**su′per·in·ten′dent** *n.*

su·pe·ri·or (so͞o-pîr′ē-ər) ►*adj.* **1.** High or higher in order, degree, rank, or quality. **2.** Situated above or over. **3.** Arrogant; haughty. **4.** Indifferent or immune. ►*n.* **1.** One who surpasses another in rank or quality. **2.** The head of a religious order or house. [< Lat. < *super*, over.] —**su·pe′ri·or′i·ty** (-ôr′ĭ-tē, -ŏr′-) *n.*

Superior, Lake The largest of the Great Lakes, between the N-central US and S Ontario, Canada.

su·per·la·tive (so͞o-pûr′lə-tĭv) ►*adj.* **1.** Of the highest order, quality, or degree. **2.** Excessive or exaggerated. **3.** *Gram.* Expressing or involving the extreme degree of comparison of an adjective or adverb. ►*n.* **1.** Something superlative. **2.** *Gram.* **a.** The superlative degree. **b.** An adjective, such as *biggest,* or adverb, such as *most highly,* expressing this degree. [< Lat. *superlātus,* exaggerated.] —**su·per′la·tive·ly** *adv.*

su·per·man (sōō′pər-măn′) ►*n.* A man with more than human powers.

su·per·mar·ket (sōō′pər-mär′kĭt) ►*n.* A large self-service retail market selling food and household goods.

su·per·nal (sōō-pûr′nəl) ►*adj.* **1.** Celestial; heavenly. **2.** Of or from the sky. [< Lat. *supernus.*] —**su·per′nal·ly** *adv.*

su·per·nat·u·ral (sōō′pər-năch′ər-əl) ►*adj.* **1.** Of or relating to existence outside the natural world. **2.** Attributed to divine power. —**su′per·nat′u·ral·ly** *adv.*

su·per·no·va (sōō′pər-nō′və) ►*n.,* pl. **-vae** (-vē) or **-vas** A rare celestial phenomenon in which a star explodes, resulting in an extremely bright, short-lived object.

su·per·nu·mer·ar·y (sōō′pər-nōō′mə-rĕr′ē, -nyōō′-) ►*adj.* **1.** Exceeding a fixed or prescribed number; extra. **2.** Superfluous. See Synonyms at **superfluous.** ►*n.,* pl. **-ies 1.** One that is supernumerary. **2.** An actor or actress without a speaking part; extra. [Lat. *supernumerārius* : SUPER– + *numerus,* number.]

su·per·phos·phate (sōō′pər-fŏs′fāt′) ►*n.* **1.** An acid phosphate. **2.** A fertilizer that is made by the action of sulfuric acid on phosphate rock.

su·per·pow·er (sōō′pər-pou′ər) ►*n.* A powerful and dominant nation, esp. the leader of an international power bloc.

su·per·sat·u·rate (sōō′pər-săch′ə-rāt′) ►*v.* To cause (a chemical solution) to contain more dissolved solute than is normally possible under given conditions of temperature and pressure. —**su′per·sat′u·ra′tion** *n.*

su·per·scribe (sōō′pər-skrīb′) ►*v.* **-scribed, -scrib·ing** To write (something) on the outside or upper part, as of a letter. [SUPER– + Lat. *scrībere,* write.] —**su′per·scrip′tion** (-skrĭp′shən) *n.*

su·per·script (sōō′pər-skrĭpt′) ►*n.* A character placed above and immediately next to another. [Lat. *superscrīptus,* p.part. of *superscrībere,* SUPERSCRIBE.] —**su′per·script** *adj.*

su·per·sede (sōō′pər-sēd′) ►*v.* **-sed·ed, -sed·ing 1.** To take the place of; supplant. **2.** To take the place of (a person), as in an office; succeed. [< OFr. *superceder,* postpone < Lat. *supersedēre,* abstain : SUPER– + *sedēre,* sit.]

su·per·son·ic (sōō′pər-sŏn′ĭk) ►*adj.* Of, caused by, or having a speed greater than the speed of sound. —**su′per·son′i·cal·ly** *adv.*

su·per·star (sōō′pər-stär′) ►*n.* A widely acclaimed star, as in movies or sports, who has great popular appeal.

su·per·sti·tion (sōō′pər-stĭsh′ən) ►*n.* **1.** A belief that an object, action, or circumstance not logically related to a course of events influences its outcome. **2.** A belief or practice irrationally maintained by ignorance or by faith in magic or chance. [< Lat. *superstes, superstit-,* standing over.] —**su′per·sti′tious** *adj.* —**su′per·sti′tious·ly** *adv.*

su·per·struc·ture (sōō′pər-strŭk′chər) ►*n.* A physical or conceptual structure built on top of something else, esp. a ship's structure above the main deck.

su·per·tank·er (sōō′pər-tăng′kər) ►*n.* A very large ship used esp. to transport oil.

supertanker

su·per·vene (sōō′pər-vēn′) ►*v.* **-vened, -ven·ing** To come or occur as something additional or unexpected. [Lat. *supervenīre* : SUPER– + *venīre,* come.]

su·per·vise (sōō′pər-vīz′) ►*v.* **-vised, -vis·ing** To manage and direct; be in charge of. [< Med.Lat. *supervidēre, supervīs-* : SUPER– + Lat. *vidēre,* see.] —**su′per·vi′sor** *n.* —**su′per·vi′so·ry** *adj.*

su·per·vi·sion (sōō′pər-vĭzh′ən) ►*n.* The act or function of supervising. See Synonyms at **care.**

su·pine (sōō-pīn′, sōō′pīn′) ►*adj.* **1.** Lying on the back or having the face upward. **2.** Lethargic; passive. [< Lat. *supīnus.*] —**su·pine′ly** *adv.*

sup·per (sŭp′ər) ►*n.* An evening meal, esp. a light meal when dinner is taken at midday. [< OFr. *souper,* SUP.]

sup·plant (sə-plănt′) ►*v.* To take the place of; supercede. [< Lat. *supplantāre,* trip up.]

sup·ple (sŭp′əl) ►*adj.* **-pler, -plest 1.** Readily folded or manipulated. **2.** Agile; limber: *a supple gymnast.* **3.** Adaptable to changing circumstances. [< Lat. *supplex,* suppliant.] —**sup′ple·ness** *n.* —**sup′ply, sup′ple·ly** *adv.*

sup·ple·ment (sŭp′lə-mənt) ►*n.* Something added to complete a thing or to make up for a deficiency. ►*v.* (-mĕnt′) To provide or form a supplement to. [< Lat. *supplēre,* to complete.] —**sup′ple·men′ta·ry** (-mĕn′tə-rē, -trē), **sup′ple·men′tal** *adj.* —**sup′ple·men·ta′tion** (-mĕn-tā′shən) *n.*

sup·pli·ant (sŭp′lē-ənt) ►*adj.* Asking humbly and earnestly; beseeching. ►*n.* A supplicant. [< Lat. *supplicāre,* SUPPLICATE.] —**sup′pli·ance** *n.* —**sup′pli·ant·ly** *adv.*

sup·pli·cant (sŭp′lĭ-kənt) ►*n.* One who beseeches or supplicates. ►*adj.* Supplicating.

sup·pli·cate (sŭp′lĭ-kāt′) ►*v.* **-cat·ed, -cat·ing 1.** To make a humble, earnest petition; beg. **2.** To beseech. [< Lat. *supplicāre* < *supplex,* suppliant.] —**sup′pli·ca′tion** *n.*

sup·ply (sə-plī′) ►*v.* **-plied, -ply·ing 1.** To make available for use; provide: *Does the hotel supply towels?* **2.** To furnish or equip with: *supplied the team with uniforms.* **3.** To fill sufficiently; satisfy: *supply a need.* ►*n.,* pl. **-plies 1.** The act of supplying: *funds for the supply of the expedition.* **2.** An amount available; stock: *Our supply of milk is low.* **3.** often **supplies** Materials or provisions stored and dispensed when needed. **4.** *Econ.* The amount of a commodity available to meet a demand or for sale at a given price. [< Lat. *supplēre*, to fill up.] —**sup·pli′er** *n.*

sup·port (sə-pôrt′) ►*v.* **1a.** To bear the weight of, esp. from below. **b.** To bear or hold up (an amount of weight). **2.** To keep from weakening or failing. **3.** To provide for or maintain by supplying with money or necessities. **4.** To furnish corroborating evidence for. **5.** To aid the cause or interests of. **6.** To endure; tolerate. **7.** To offer help or advice regarding (a product or service). ►*n.* **1.** The act of supporting or the condition of being supported. **2.** One that supports. **3.** Financial maintenance. [< Lat. *supportāre*, carry.] —**sup·port′a·ble** *adj.* —**sup·port′er** *n.* —**sup·por′tive** *adj.*

sup·pose (sə-pōz′) ►*v.* **-posed, -pos·ing 1.** To assume for the sake of argument. **2a.** To believe, esp. on uncertain grounds. **b.** To consider probable or likely. **3.** To imply as an antecedent condition; presuppose. [< OFr. *supposer*.]

sup·posed (sə-pōzd′) ►*adj.* **1.** (*also* sə-pō′zĭd) Presumed to be true or real without conclusive evidence. **2.** Intended: *medication that is supposed to relieve pain.* **3a.** Required: *He is supposed to go to the store.* **b.** Permitted: *We are not supposed to smoke here.* —**sup·pos′ed·ly** *adv.*
Syns: *conjectural, putative, reputed* **Ant:** *certain* **adj.**

sup·pos·ing (sə-pō′zĭng) ►*conj.* Assuming that: *Supposing I'm right, what can we do?*

sup·po·si·tion (sŭp′ə-zĭsh′ən) ►*n.* **1.** The act of supposing. **2.** An assumption.

sup·pos·i·to·ry (sə-pŏz′ĭ-tôr′ē) ►*n., pl.* **-ries** A small plug of medication designed to melt within a body cavity other than the mouth. [< Lat. *suppositus*, placed beneath.]

sup·press (sə-prĕs′) ►*v.* **1.** To put an end to forcibly. **2.** To keep from being revealed or circulated. **3.** To inhibit the expression of: *suppress a smile.* [< Lat. *supprimere, suppress-*.] —**sup·press′ion** *n.* —**sup·press′ive** *adj.*

sup·pu·rate (sŭp′yə-rāt′) ►*v.* **-rat·ed, -rat·ing** To form or discharge pus. [< Lat. *suppūrāre*.] —**sup′pu·ra′tion** *n.*

su·pra·na·tion·al (soo′prə-năsh′ə-nəl, -năsh′nəl) ►*adj.* Of or extending beyond the boundaries or authority of a nation. [Lat. *suprā*, beyond + NATIONAL.]

su·prem·a·cist (soo-prĕm′ə-sĭst) ►*n.* One who believes that a certain group is or should be supreme.

su·prem·a·cy (soo-prĕm′ə-sē) ►*n.* **1.** The quality or condition of being supreme. **2.** Supreme power.

su·preme (soo-prĕm′) ►*adj.* **1.** Greatest in power, authority, or rank. **2.** Greatest in importance, degree, or achievement. **3.** Ultimate; final: *the supreme sacrifice.* [Lat. *suprēmus* < *super*, over.] —**su·preme′ly** *adv.* —**su·preme′ness** *n.*

Supreme Court ►*n.* **1.** The highest US federal court. **2. supreme court** The highest court in most US states.

Supt. ►*abbr.* superintendent

sur– ►*pref.* **1.** Over; above; upon: *surpass.* **2.** Additional: *surtax.* [< Lat. *super*.]

sur·cease (sûr′sēs′, sər-sēs′) ►*n.* Cessation. [< Lat. *supersedēre*, SUPERSEDE.]

sur·charge (sûr′chärj′) ►*n.* **1.** An additional

sum added to the usual cost. **2.** An excessive amount or burden. ►*v.* **1.** To charge an extra sum. **2.** To overcharge.

sure (shoor, shûr) ►*adj.* **sur·er, sur·est 1.** Impossible to doubt or dispute; certain. **2.** Strong; firm: *sure convictions.* **3.** Confident: *sure of victory.* **4a.** Bound to happen; inevitable: *sure defeat.* **b.** Destined: *sure to succeed.* See Synonyms at **certain. 5.** Trustworthy; reliable. —*idioms:* **for sure** *Informal* Certainly; unquestionably. **make sure** Make certain. **to be sure** Indeed; certainly. [< Lat. *sēcūrus,* SECURE.] —**sure′ness** *n.*

sure-fire (shoor′fīr′) ►*adj. Informal* Bound to be successful.

sure-foot·ed or **sure·foot·ed** (shoor′foot′ĭd) ►*adj.* Not liable to stumble or fall. —**sure′-foot′ed·ly** *adv.*

sure·ly (shoor′lē) ►*adv.* **1.** With confidence; unhesitatingly. **2.** Undoubtedly; certainly.

sure·ty (shoor′ĭ-tē) ►*n., pl.* **-ties 1.** The condition of being sure. **2.** Something beyond doubt. **3.** A guarantee or security. **4.** One who has contracted to be responsible for another.

surf (sûrf) ►*n.* The waves of the sea as they break upon a shore or reef. ►*v.* **1.** To engage in surfing. **2.** *Informal* To look at a variety of things casually, esp. while browsing the Internet. [?] —**surf′er** *n.*

sur·face (sûr′fəs) ►*n.* **1.** The outer or the topmost boundary of an object. **2.** The superficial or external aspect. ►*adj.* **1.** Of or on the surface. **2.** Superficial. ►*v.* **-faced, -fac·ing 1.** To form the surface of. **2.** To rise or come to the surface. **3.** To emerge from concealment. [Fr.]

surf·board (sûrf′bôrd′) ►*n.* A narrow, somewhat rounded board used for surfing.

sur·feit (sûr′fĭt) ►*v.* To feed or supply to excess; satiate. ►*n.* **1a.** Overindulgence in food or drink. **b.** The result of such overindulgence; satiety or disgust. **2.** An excessive amount. [< OFr. *surfaire*, overdo.]

surf·ing (sûr′fĭng) ►*n.* The sport of riding on the crest or along the tunnel of a wave, esp. while on a surfboard.

surge (sûrj) ►*v.* **surged, surg·ing 1.** To move in a billowing or swelling manner. **2.** To increase suddenly. ►*n.* **1.** A sudden rushing motion like that of a great wave. **2.** A sudden onrush: *a surge of joy.* **3.** *Elect.* A sudden increase in current or voltage. [< Lat. *surgere*, rise.]

sur·geon (sûr′jən) ►*n.* A physician specializing in surgery. [< OFr. *cirurgie*, SURGERY.]

surge protector ►*n.* A device that protects equipment plugged into it from a surge in electric current.

sur·ger·y (sûr′jə-rē) ►*n., pl.* **-ies 1.** The treatment of injury, deformity, and disease by the use of instruments. **2.** A procedure that is part of such treatment; an operation. **3.** A surgical operating room or laboratory. [< Gk. *kheirourgos*, working by hand : *kheir*, hand + *ergon*, work.] —**sur′gi·cal** *adj.* —**sur′gi·cal·ly** *adv.*

Su·ri·na·me (soor′ə-nä′mə) *also* **Su·ri·nam** (soor′ə-năm′, -näm′) A country of NE South America on the Atlantic. Cap. Paramaribo. —**Su′ri·na·mese′** (-nä-mēz′, -mēs′) *adj. & n.*

sur·ly (sûr′lē) ►*adj.* **-li·er, -li·est** Sullenly ill-humored; gruff. [ME *sirly*, lordly < *sir*, SIR.] —**sur′li·ly** *adv.* —**sur′li·ness** *n.*

sur·mise (sər-mīz′) ►*v.* **-mised, -mis·ing** To make a judgment about (something) without sufficient evidence; guess. ►*n.* An idea or opinion based on little evidence; conjecture. [< OFr. *surmettre, surmis-.*]

sur·mount (sər-mount′) ►*v.* **1.** To overcome; triumph over: *surmount an obstacle.* **2.** To ascend to the top of: *surmount a hill.* **3.** To be above or on top of: *The lintel was surmounted by a frieze.* [< OFr. *surmonter.*] —**sur·mount′a·ble** *adj.* —**sur·mount′er** *n.*

sur·name (sûr′nām′) ►*n.* A name shared in common to identify the members of a family; last name.

sur·pass (sər-păs′) ►*v.* **1.** To do more than or be superior to: *surpassed her classmates in academic honors.* **2.** To be beyond the limit, powers, or capacity of; transcend: *surpass comprehension.* **3.** To be greater than, as in degree or quality.

sur·pass·ing (sər-păs′ĭng) ►*adj.* Exceptional; exceeding. —**sur·pass′ing·ly** *adv.*

sur·plice (sûr′plĭs) ►*n.* A loose-fitting white ecclesiastical gown worn over a cassock. [< Med.Lat. *superpellīcium* : SUPER– + Lat. *pellis,* skin.]

sur·plus (sûr′pləs, sûr′plŭs′) ►*adj.* Being in excess of what is needed. See Synonyms at **superfluous.** ►*n.* A surplus amount or quantity. [< Med.Lat. *superplūs* : SUPER– + Lat. *plūs,* more.]

sur·prise (sər-prīz′) ►*v.* **-prised, -pris·ing 1.** To astonish by the unanticipated. **2a.** To encounter suddenly or unexpectedly. **b.** To attack or capture suddenly and without warning. ►*n.* **1.** The act of surprising or the condition of being surprised. **2.** Something that surprises. [< OFr. *surprendre,* overcome.] —**sur·pris′ing** *adj.* —**sur·pris′ing·ly** *adv.*

sur·re·al·ism (sə-rē′ə-lĭz′əm) ►*n.* A 20th-century literary and artistic movement that attempts to express the workings of the subconscious by fantastic imagery and incongruous juxtapositions. —**sur·re′al, sur·re′al·is′tic** *adj.* —**sur·re′al·ist** *n.* —**sur·re′al·is′ti·cal·ly** *adv.*

sur·ren·der (sə-rĕn′dər) ►*v.* **1.** To relinquish possession or control of to another because of demand or compulsion. **2.** To give (oneself) up, as to an emotion: *surrendered himself to grief.* **3.** To give oneself up to another. ►*n.* The act of surrendering. [< OFr. *surrendre.*]

sur·rep·ti·tious (sûr′əp-tĭsh′əs) ►*adj.* Secret and stealthy. [< Lat. *surripere,* take away secretly.] —**sur′rep·ti′tious·ly** *adv.*

sur·rey (sûr′ē, sŭr′ē) ►*n., pl.* **-reys** A four-wheeled horse-drawn carriage having two or four seats. [After *Surrey,* England.]

sur·ro·gate (sûr′ə-gĭt, -gāt′, sŭr′-) ►*n.* **1.** A substitute. **2.** *Law* A judge in some US states having jurisdiction over the settlement of estates. [< Lat. *surrogāre,* substitute.] —**sur′ro·gate** (-gĭt, gāt′) *adj.*

sur·round (sə-round′) ►*v.* **1.** To extend on all sides of simultaneously; encircle: *the magnetic field that surrounds the earth.* **2.** To enclose or confine on all sides: *The police surrounded the house.* [< LLat. *superundāre,* inundate : SUPER– + *unda,* wave.]

sur·round·ings (sə-roun′dĭngz) ►*pl.n.* The external circumstances that surround a person or thing.

sur·tax (sûr′tăks′) ►*n.* **1.** An additional tax. **2.** A tax levied after net income has exceeded a certain level.

sur·veil·lance (sər-vā′ləns) ►*n.* Close observation of a person or group, esp. one under suspicion. [< OFr. *surveiller,* watch over.]

sur·vey (sər-vā′, sûr′vā′) ►*v.* **1a.** To look over the parts or features of. **b.** To look at carefully and appraise. **2.** To determine the boundaries, area, or elevations of (part of the earth's surface) by means of measuring angles and distances. ►*n.* (sûr′vā′) *pl.* **-veys 1a.** A comprehensive view. **b.** A careful inspection or appraisal. **2a.** The process of surveying. **b.** A map of what has been surveyed. **3.** A document reporting the results of a survey. [< Med. Lat. *supervidēre* : SUPER– + Lat. *vidēre,* look.] —**sur·vey′or** *n.*

sur·vey·ing (sər-vā′ĭng) ►*n.* The act, practice, or occupation of a surveyor.

sur·vive (sər-vīv′) ►*v.* **-vived, -viv·ing 1.** To remain alive or in existence; endure. **2.** To live longer than; outlive. [< Lat. *supervīvere* : SUPER– + *vīvere,* live.] —**sur·viv′a·ble** *adj.* —**sur·viv′al** *n.* —**sur·vi′vor** *n.*

sus·cep·ti·ble (sə-sĕp′tə-bəl) ►*adj.* **1.** Easily influenced or affected: *susceptible to colds.* **2.** Capable of accepting or permitting: *susceptible of proof.* [< Lat. *susceptus,* p.part. of *suscipere,* receive.] —**sus·cep′ti·bil′i·ty** *n.* —**sus·cep′ti·bly** *adv.*

su·shi (sōo′shē) ►*n.* Cold rice shaped into small pieces and topped with raw or cooked fish. [J.]

sus·pect (sə-spĕkt′) ►*v.* **1.** To consider (something) to be true or probable on little or no evidence. **2.** To have doubts about (something); distrust: *I suspect his motives.* **3.** To consider (a person) guilty without proof. ►*n.* (sŭs′pĕkt′) One who is suspected, esp. of a crime. ►*adj.* (sŭs′pĕkt′, sə-spĕkt′) Open to or viewed with suspicion. [< Lat. *suspectāre* : SUB– + *specere,* look at.]

sus·pend (sə-spĕnd′) ►*v.* **1.** To bar for a period from a privilege, office, or position. **2.** To cause to stop for a period; interrupt. **3a.** To hold in abeyance; defer: *suspend judgment.* See Synonyms at **defer¹. b.** To render temporarily ineffective: *suspend a jail sentence.* **4.** To hang so as to allow free movement. **5.** To support or keep from falling without apparent attachment. [< Lat. *suspendere,* hang up.]

sus·pend·ers (sə-spĕn′dərz) ►*n.* A pair of often elastic straps worn over the shoulders to support trousers.

sus·pense (sə-spĕns′) ►*n.* **1.** Anxiety or apprehension resulting from uncertainty. **2.** The quality in a work of narrative art that evokes pleasurable excitement and anticipation regarding an outcome. [< Lat. *suspēnsus,* p.part. of *suspendere,* suspend.] —**sus·pense′ful** *adj.*

sus·pen·sion (sə-spĕn′shən) ►*n.* **1.** The act of suspending or the condition of being suspended, esp.: **a.** A temporary deferment. See Synonyms at **pause. b.** A postponement of judgment or decision. **2.** A device from which a mechanical part is suspended. **3.** The system of springs and other devices that insulates the chassis of a vehicle from shocks. **4.** *Chem.* A relatively coarse, noncolloidal dispersion of solid particles in a liquid.

suspension bridge ►*n.* A bridge having the

roadway suspended from cables that are usu. supported at intervals by towers.

suspension bridge
Golden Gate Bridge
San Francisco, California

sus·pi·cion (sə-spĭsh′ən) ▸*n.* **1.** The act or an instance of suspecting something on little or no evidence. **2.** A hint or trace. [< Lat. *suspicere*, SUSPECT.]

sus·pi·cious (sə-spĭsh′əs) ▸*adj.* **1.** Arousing or apt to arouse suspicion; questionable. **2.** Tending to suspect; distrustful. **3.** Expressing suspicion. —**sus·pi′cious·ly** *adv.* —**sus·pi′cious·ness** *n.*

Sus·que·han·na River (sŭs′kwə-hăn′ə) A river of the NE US rising in central NY and flowing about 715 km (445 mi) through E PA and NE MD to Chesapeake Bay.

sus·tain (sə-stān′) ▸*v.* **1.** To keep in existence; maintain. **2a.** To supply with necessities or nourishment. **b.** To support the spirits or resolution of; encourage. **3.** To keep from falling or sinking. **4a.** To endure or withstand: *sustain hardships.* **b.** To suffer: *suffered a fatal injury.* **5.** To affirm the validity of: *The judge sustained the objection.* [< Lat. *sustinēre*, hold up.] —**sus·tain′a·ble** *adj.*

sus·te·nance (sŭs′tə-nəns) ▸*n.* **1.** The support of life or health; means of livelihood. **2.** Something, esp. food, that sustains life or health. [< OFr. *sustenir*, SUSTAIN.]

su·tra (soo′trə) ▸*n.* **1.** *Hinduism* Any of various aphoristic doctrinal summaries recorded between 500 and 200 BC. **2.** *Buddhism* A scriptural narrative, esp. a text traditionally regarded as a discourse of the Buddha. [Skt. *sūtram*, thread.]

su·ture (soo′chər) ▸*n.* **1a.** The act of joining together by or as if by sewing. **b.** The material used in this procedure. **2.** The line of junction or an immovable joint between two bones, esp. of the skull. ▸*v.* **-tured, -tur·ing** To join by means of sutures. [< Lat. *sūtūra* < *suere*, sew.]

SUV (ĕs′yoo′vē′) ▸*n.* A four-wheel-drive vehicle with a roomy body, designed for off-road travel. [s(port) u(tility) v(ehicle).]

Su·va (soo′və, -vä) The capital of Fiji, on the SE coast of Viti Levu.

su·ze·rain (soo′zər-ən, -zə-rān′) ▸*n.* **1.** A nation that controls the international affairs of another nation. **2.** A feudal lord. [Fr.] —**su′ze·rain** *adj.* —**su′ze·rain·ty** *n.*

svelte (svĕlt) ▸*adj.* **svelt·er, svelt·est** Slender and graceful in figure or outline. [< Ital. *svelto*, stretched.]

sw ▸*abbr.* short wave

SW ▸*abbr.* **1.** southwest **2.** southwestern

Sw. ▸*abbr.* Swedish

swab (swŏb) ▸*n.* **1.** Absorbent material attached to the end of a stick or wire and used for cleaning, applying medicine, or collecting a sample of a substance. **2.** A mop used for cleaning floors or decks. **3.** *Slang* A sailor. ▸*v.* **swabbed, swab·bing 1.** To use a swab on. **2.** To collect with a swab. [< MDu. *swabble*, mop.]

Swa·bi·a (swā′bē-ə) A historical region of SW Germany. —**Swa′bi·an** *adj. & n.*

swad·dle (swŏd′l) ▸*v.* **-dled, -dling 1.** To wrap, as in cloth. **2.** To wrap (a baby) in strips of cloth. **3.** To swathe. [< OE *swathian.*]

swag (swăg) ▸*n.* *Slang* Stolen property; loot. [Prob. of Scand. orig.]

swag·ger (swăg′ər) ▸*v.* **1.** To walk or behave with an insolent air; strut. **2.** To brag. [Prob. of Scand. orig.] —**swag′ger** *n.*

swagger stick ▸*n.* A short cane carried esp. by military officers.

Swa·hi·li (swä-hē′lē) ▸*n.* A Bantu language of the coast of E Africa from Somalia to Mozambique.

swain (swān) ▸*n.* **1.** A country lad, esp. a young shepherd. **2.** A young male suitor or lover. [< ON *sveinn.*]

swal·low[1] (swŏl′ō) ▸*v.* **1.** To cause to pass through the mouth and throat into the stomach. **2.** To bear humbly or passively: *swallowed the insults.* **3.** To envelop or engulf. **4.** *Slang* To believe without question. ▸*n.* **1.** The act of swallowing. **2.** An amount swallowed. [< OE *swelgan.*]

swal·low[2] (swŏl′ō) ▸*n.* Any of a family of birds with long pointed wings and a usu. notched or forked tail. [< OE *swealwe.*]

swal·low·tail (swŏl′ō-tāl′) ▸*n.* **1.** A deeply forked tail, as of a swallow. **2.** Any of a family of butterflies with a taillike extension at the end of each hind wing.

swam (swăm) ▸*v.* P.t. of **swim.**

swa·mi (swä′mē) ▸*n.*, *pl.* **-mis 1.** A Hindu religious teacher. **2.** A mystic. [< Skt. *svāmī.*]

swamp (swŏmp, swômp) ▸*n.* **1.** A usu. forested wetland that is frequently flooded. **2.** A tangle; morass. ▸*v.* **1.** To drench in or cover with liquid. **2.** To overwhelm. **3.** To fill or sink (a ship) with water. [Perh. of Low Germ. orig.] —**swamp′i·ness** *n.* —**swamp′y** *adj.*

swan (swŏn) ▸*n.* Any of various large waterbirds with webbed feet, a long slender neck, and usu. white plumage. [< OE.]

swan dive ▸*n.* A dive with the legs straight together, the back arched, and the arms stretched out from the sides and then brought together over the head.

swank (swăngk) ▸*n.* **1.** Stylishness or elegance. **2.** Swagger or pretension. ▸*adj.* **-er, -est** Swanky. [Perh. akin to MHGer. *swanken*, swing.]

swank·y (swăng′kē) ▸*adj.* **-i·er, -i·est 1.** Strikingly fashionable or luxurious. See Synonyms at **fashionable. 2.** Ostentatious or pretentious. —**swank′i·ly** *adv.* —**swank′i·ness** *n.*

swan song ▸*n.* A farewell appearance, action, or work.

swap (swŏp) *Informal* ▸*v.* **swapped, swap·**

ping To trade one thing for another. ►*n.* An exchange; trade. [ME *swappen*, strike the hands together in closing a bargain.]

sward (swôrd) ►*n.* Land covered with grassy turf. [< OE *sweard*, skin.]

swarm (swôrm) ►*n.* **1.** A large number of insects or other small organisms, esp. when in motion. **2.** A multitude; throng. ►*v.* **1a.** To move in a swarm. **b.** To leave a hive as a swarm. Used of bees. **2.** To move or gather in large numbers. **3.** To be overrun; teem: *a riverbank swarming with insects.* See Synonyms at **teem.** [< OE *swearm.*]

swarth·y (swôr′*thē*) ►*adj.* **-i·er, -i·est** Having a dark complexion or color. [< OE *sweart.*] —**swarth′i·ness** *n.*

swash (swŏsh, swôsh) ►*v.* To strike, move, or wash with a splashing sound. [Prob. imit.] —**swash** *n.*

swash·buck·ler (swŏsh′bŭk′lər, swôsh′-) ►*n.* A flamboyant soldier or adventurer. —**swash′-buck′ling** *adj.*

swas·ti·ka (swŏs′tĭ-kə) ►*n.* **1.** An ancient cosmic or religious symbol formed by a Greek cross with the ends of the arms bent at right angles. **2.** Such a symbol with a clockwise bend to the arms, used as the emblem of the Nazi Germany. [Skt. *svastikaḥ*, sign of good luck.]

swat (swŏt) ►*v.* **swat·ted, swat·ting** To strike or hit with a sharp blow. [< SQUAT, to squash (obs.).] —**swat** *n.* —**swat′ter** *n.*

swatch (swŏch) ►*n.* **1.** A sample strip cut from a piece of material. **2.** A representative portion; sample. [?]

swath (swŏth, swôth) ►*n.* **1a.** The width of a scythe stroke or a mowing-machine blade. **b.** A path left in mowing. **2.** Something likened to a swath, esp. a strip or path: *cut a swath through the snow.* [< OE *swæth*, track.]

swathe (swŏ*th*, swô*th*, swā*th*) ►*v.* **swathed, swath·ing 1.** To wrap, as in layers of cloth. **2.** To wrap or bind in bandages. [< OE *swathian.*] —**swathe** *n.*

sway (swā) ►*v.* **1.** To move or cause to move with a swinging motion. **2.** To incline or bend to one side. **3.** To vacillate. **4.** To exert influence on or control over. ►*n.* **1.** The act of swaying. **2.** Influence or control. [ME *sweien.*]

sway·back (swā′băk′) ►*n.* Excessive inward or downward curvature of the spine. —**sway′-backed′** *adj.*

Swa·zi (swä′zē) ►*n., pl.* **-zi** or **-zis 1.** A member of a SE African people of Swaziland. **2.** The Bantu language of this people.

Swa·zi·land (swä′zē-lănd′) A country of SE Africa between South Africa and Mozambique. Cap. Mbabane.

swear (swâr) ►*v.* **swore** (swôr), **sworn** (swôrn), **swear·ing 1.** To make a solemn declaration. **2.** To promise; vow. See Synonyms at **promise. 3.** To use obscene or blasphemous language; curse. **4.** To commit oneself by oath to giving truthful evidence or testimony. **5.** To declare or affirm with great conviction. **6.** To administer a legal oath to. —*phrasal verbs:* **swear in** To administer a legal or official oath to. **swear off** *Informal* To renounce; give up. [< OE *swerian.*]

sweat (swĕt) ►*v.* **sweat·ed** or **sweat, sweat·ing 1.** To excrete perspiration through the pores in the skin; perspire. **2.** To exude or become moist with surface droplets. **3.** To

collect moisture in small drops from the air. **4.** *Informal* To work or cause to work long and hard. **5.** *Informal* To fret or worry. ►*n.* **1.** Perspiration. **2.** Condensation of moisture in the form of droplets on a surface. **3.** The process of sweating or the condition of being sweated. **4.** *Informal* An anxious, fretful condition. —*phrasal verb:* **sweat out** *Slang* To endure anxiously. [< OE *swætan.*] —**sweat′i·ness** *n.* —**sweat′y** *adj.*

sweat·er (swĕt′ər) ►*n.* A knitted or crocheted garment worn on the upper body.

sweat gland ►*n.* Any of the numerous small glands in the skin of humans that secrete perspiration externally through pores.

sweat·shirt (swĕt′shûrt′) ►*n.* A usu. long-sleeved pullover made usu. of heavy cotton jersey.

sweat·shop (swĕt′shŏp′) ►*n.* A shop or factory in which employees work long hours at low wages under poor conditions.

Swede (swēd) ►*n.* A native or inhabitant of Sweden.

Swe·den (swēd′n) A country of N Europe E of Norway. Cap. Stockholm.

Swe·den·borg (swēd′n-bôrg′), **Emanuel** 1688–1772. Swedish scientist and theologian. —**Swe′den·bor′gi·an** *adj. & n.*

Swed·ish (swē′dĭsh) ►*adj.* Of or relating to Sweden, the Swedes, or their language. ►*n.* The Germanic language of Sweden.

sweep (swēp) ►*v.* **swept** (swĕpt), **sweep·ing 1.** To clean, as of dirt, with a brush. **2.** To touch or brush lightly. **3.** To clear, drive, or convey with relentless force, as by wind or rain. **4.** To move swiftly or broadly: *The news swept through the country.* **5a.** To win all the stages of (a game or contest). **b.** To win overwhelmingly in. **6.** To extend gracefully, esp. in a long curve. ►*n.* **1.** An act or instance of sweeping. **2a.** A wide curving motion. **b.** A curve or contour that resembles the path of sweeping motion. **3.** An extent or stretch. **4.** Range or scope. See Synonyms at **range. 5.** A chimney sweep. **6a.** The winning of all stages of a contest. **b.** An overwhelming victory. [ME *swepen.*] —**sweep′er** *n.*

sweep·ing (swē′pĭng) ►*adj.* **1.** Having wide-ranging influence or effect. **2.** Curving; contoured. ►*n.* **sweepings** Things swept up; refuse. —**sweep′ing·ly** *adv.*

sweep·stakes (swēp′stāks′) ►*pl.n. (takes sing. or pl. v.)* **1.** A lottery in which the participants' contributions form a fund awarded as a prize to one or several winners. **2.** An event or a contest, esp. a horserace, the result of which determines the winner of such a lottery.

sweet (swēt) ►*adj.* **-er, -est 1.** Having the taste of sugar. **2.** Pleasing to the senses, mind, or feelings. **3.** Having a pleasing disposition; lovable. **4.** Not saline or salted: *sweet butter.* **5.** Not spoiled, sour, or decaying. ►*n.* **1.** Something sweet to the taste. **2. sweets** Sweet foods, esp. candy. **3.** A dear or beloved person. [< OE *swēte.*] —**sweet′ly** *adv.* —**sweet′ness** *n.*

sweet alyssum ►*n.* An herb of the mustard family grown for its small, fragrant flowers.

sweet·bread (swēt′brĕd′) ►*n.* The thymus gland or pancreas of a young animal used for food.

sweet·bri·er also **sweet·bri·ar** (swēt′brī′ər)

►*n.* A rose having prickly stems, fragrant leaves, and bright pink flowers.

sweet corn ►*n.* The common table corn, with kernels that are sweet when young.

sweet·en (swēt′n) ►*v.* **1.** To make sweet or sweeter. **2.** To make more valuable or agreeable. —**sweet′en·er** *n.*

sweet·en·ing (swēt′n-ĭng) ►*n.* **1.** The act or process of making sweet. **2.** Something that sweetens; sweetener.

sweet·heart (swēt′härt′) ►*n.* **1.** A beloved. **2.** *Informal* A generous or dear person.

sweet·meat (swēt′mēt′) ►*n.* A sweet delicacy, as a piece of candy or candied fruit.

sweet pea ►*n.* A climbing plant cultivated for its fragrant flowers.

sweet potato ►*n.* **1.** A tropical American vine cultivated for its fleshy tuberous usu. orange root. **2.** The root of this vine, eaten cooked as a vegetable.

sweet-talk (swēt′tôk′) ►*v. Informal* To coax or cajole with flattery. —**sweet talk** *n.*

sweet tooth ►*n. Informal* A fondness or craving for sweets.

sweet William ►*n.* A widely cultivated plant with flat-topped dense clusters of white, pink, red, or purple flowers.

swell (swĕl) ►*v.* **swelled, swelled** or **swol·len** (swō′lən), **swell·ing 1.** To increase in size or volume. **2.** To increase in force, size, number, or intensity. **3.** To bulge out, as a sail. **4.** To be or become filled or puffed up, as with pride. ►*n.* **1.** A swollen part. **2.** A long smoothly moving wave on water. **3.** *Informal* One who is fashionably elegant. ►*adj.* **-er, -est** *Informal* **1.** Fashionably elegant; stylish. **2.** Excellent; wonderful. [< OE *swellan.*]

swell·ing (swĕl′ĭng) ►*n.* **1.** The state of being swollen. **2.** Something swollen.

swel·ter (swĕl′tər) ►*v.* To suffer from oppressive heat. [< OE *sweltan,* perish.]

swept (swĕpt) ►*v.* P.t. and p.part. of **sweep.**

swerve (swûrv) ►*v.* **swerved, swerv·ing** To turn aside or be turned aside from a straight path or established pattern. ►*n.* The act of swerving. [< OE *sweorfan,* rub.]
   Syns: depart, deviate, digress, diverge, stray, veer **v.**

swift (swĭft) ►*adj.* **-er, -est 1.** Moving or capable of moving with great speed; fast. **2.** Occurring or accomplished quickly. ►*n.* Any of various dark birds having pointed wings and a short forked tail, and noted for their swift flight. [< OE.] —**swift′ly** *adv.* —**swift′ness** *n.*

Swift, Jonathan 1667–1745. Irish-born English writer.

swig (swĭg) ►*n. Informal* A deep swallow or draft, esp. of liquor; gulp. [?] —**swig** *v.*

swill (swĭl) ►*v.* **1.** To drink greedily or grossly. **2.** To feed (animals) with swill. ►*n.* **1.** A mixture of liquid and solid food fed to animals, esp. pigs; slop. **2.** Alcohol of poor quality. [< OE *swilian,* wash out.]

swim (swĭm) ►*v.* **swam** (swăm), **swum** (swŭm), **swim·ming 1.** To move through water by means of the limbs, fins, or tail or by undulating the body. **2.** To cross by swimming. **3.** To be covered or flooded with a liquid: *chicken swimming in gravy.* **4.** To feel dizzy. **5.** To appear to float or spin slowly. ►*n.* The act or a period of swimming. —*idiom:* **in the swim** Active in

the general current of affairs. [< OE *swimman.*] —**swim′mer** *n.*

swim bladder ►*n.* A gas-filled organ in many fishes that regulates buoyancy and, in some species, aids in respiration or in producing sound.

swim·ming·ly (swĭm′ĭng-lē) ►*adv.* Splendidly; excellently.

swim·suit (swĭm′sōōt′) ►*n.* A garment worn while swimming; bathing suit.

swin·dle (swĭn′dl) ►*v.* **-dled, -dling** To cheat or defraud of money or property. ►*n.* The act or an instance of swindling. [< Ger. *schwindeln,* be dizzy.] —**swin′dler** *n.*

swine (swīn) ►*n., pl.* **swine 1.** Any of various even-toed hoofed mammals having thick skin and a movable snout, esp. the domesticated pig. **2.** A brutish or contemptible person. [< OE *swīn.*]

swing (swĭng) ►*v.* **swung** (swŭng), **swing·ing 1.** To move or cause to move back and forth. **2.** To hit at something with a sweeping motion. **3.** To turn in place, as on a hinge or pivot. **4.** To walk or move with a swaying motion. **5.** To hang freely. **6.** *Slang* To be put to death by hanging. **7.** *Informal* To manage or arrange successfully. **8.** To have a compelling or infectious rhythm. **9.** *Slang* **a.** To be lively, trendy, and exciting. **b.** To engage in promiscuous sex. ►*n.* **1.** The act of swinging. **2.** The sweep or scope of something that swings. **3.** A seat suspended from above on which one can ride back and forth. **4.** A popular dance music based on jazz but usu. employing a larger band and less improvisation. [< OE *swingan,* flog.]

swing·er (swĭng′ər) ►*n.* **1.** One that swings. **2.** *Slang* **a.** A sophisticated, socially active person. **b.** One who is sexually promiscuous.

swipe (swīp) ►*n.* **1.** A sweeping blow or stroke. **2.** *Informal* A critical remark. ►*v.* **swiped, swip·ing 1.** To hit with a sweeping motion. **2.** To pass a card containing encoded data through an electronic reader. **3.** *Informal* To steal. [Perh. < SWEEP.]

swirl (swûrl) ►*v.* **1.** To move with a spinning or whirling motion. **2.** To arrange in a spiral or whorl. [< ME *swyrl,* eddy.] —**swirl** *n.* —**swirl′y** *adj.*

swish (swĭsh) ►*v.* **1.** To move with a hissing sound. **2.** To rustle. [Imit.] —**swish** *n.*

Swiss (swĭs) ►*adj.* Of or relating to Switzerland or its people. ►*n.* **1.** *pl.* **Swiss** A native or inhabitant of Switzerland. **2.** See **Swiss cheese.**

Swiss chard ►*n.* A variety of beet having large succulent leaves used as a vegetable.

Swiss cheese ►*n.* A firm, pale yellow cheese with large holes and a nutty flavor.

switch (swĭch) ►*n.* **1a.** An exchange, esp. one done secretly. **b.** A change or shift from one thing to another. **2a.** A device used to break or open an electric circuit. **b.** A device used to transfer rolling stock from one track to another. **3a.** A slender flexible rod, stick, or twig. **b.** A blow given with a switch. ►*v.* **1a.** To exchange: *switch seats.* **b.** To shift, transfer, or divert. **2.** To connect or disconnect by operating a switch. **3.** To move (rolling stock) from one track to another. **4a.** To whip with a switch. **b.** To jerk abruptly or sharply: *The cow switched its tail.* [Prob. of LGer. or Flem. orig.] —**switch′er** *n.*

switch·blade (swĭch′blād′) ►*n.* A pocketknife with a spring-operated blade.

switch·board (swĭch′bôrd′) ►*n.* **1.** A panel with apparatus for operating electric circuits. **2.** See **telephone exchange.**

switch hitter ►*n. Baseball* A player who can bat either right-handed or left-handed.

switch·man (swĭch′mən) ►*n.* One who operates railroad switches.

Swit·zer·land (swĭt′sər-lənd) A country of W-central Europe. Cap. Bern.

swiv·el (swĭv′əl) ►*n.* A device that joins two parts while allowing one part to turn relative to the other. ►*v.* **-eled, -el·ing** or **-elled, -el·ling** To turn or rotate, as on a swivel. [ME *swyvel.*]

swiz·zle stick (swĭz′əl) ►*n.* A small thin rod for stirring mixed drinks.

swol·len (swō′lən) ►*v.* P.part. of **swell.** ►*adj.* Puffed up; distended.

swoon (swōon) ►*v.* To faint. ►*n.* A fainting spell. [Prob. < OE **swōgan,* suffocate.]

swoop (swōop) ►*v.* To move in a sudden sweep, as a bird descending on its prey. [< OE *swāpan,* sweep.] —**swoop** *n.*

sword (sôrd) ►*n.* **1.** A weapon having a long blade with one or two cutting edges. **2.** An instrument of death or destruction. **3.** The use of force, as in war. [< OE *sweord.*]

sword·fish (sôrd′fĭsh′) ►*n.* A large marine food and game fish having a long swordlike extension of the upper jaw.

sword·play (sôrd′plā′) ►*n.* The act or art of using a sword.

swords·man (sôrdz′mən) ►*n.* One skilled in the use of swords. —**swords′man·ship′** *n.*

swore (swôr) ►*v.* P.t. of **swear.**

sworn (swôrn) ►*v.* P.part. of **swear.**

swum (swŭm) ►*v.* P.part. of **swim.**

swung (swŭng) ►*v.* P.t. and p.part. of **swing.**

syb·a·rite (sĭb′ə-rīt) ►*n.* A person devoted to pleasure and luxury. [< *Sybaris,* an ancient Gk. city in Italy.] —**syb′a·rit′ic** (-rĭt′ĭk) *adj.*

syc·a·more (sĭk′ə-môr′) ►*n.* **1.** A deciduous tree, esp. of North America, having palmately lobed leaves and ball-like fruit clusters. **2.** A Eurasian maple tree. [< Gk. *sukomoros,* a kind of fig tree.]

syc·o·phant (sĭk′ə-fənt, sī′kə-) ►*n.* A person who attempts to gain advantage by flattering influential people or behaving in a servile manner. [< Gk. *sukophantēs,* informer.] —**syc′o·phan·cy** *n.* —**syc′o·phan′tic** (-făn′tĭk) *adj.*

Syd·ney (sĭd′nē) A city of SE Australia on an inlet of the Tasman Sea.

syl·lab·i·fy (sĭ-lăb′ĭ-fī′) or **syl·lab·i·cate** (-kāt′) ►*v.* **-fied, -fy·ing** or **-cat·ed, -cat·ing** To form or divide into syllables. —**syl·lab′i·fi·ca′tion, syl·lab′i·ca′tion** *n.*

syl·la·ble (sĭl′ə-bəl) ►*n.* **1.** A unit of spoken language consisting of a single uninterrupted sound forming a word, such as *wit,* or part of a word, such as *per-* in *person.* **2.** One or more letters or phonetic symbols representing a spoken syllable. [< Gk. *sullabē.*] —**syl·lab′ic** (sĭ-lăb′ĭk) *adj.*

syl·la·bus (sĭl′ə-bəs) ►*n., pl.* **-bus·es** or **-bi** (-bī′) An outline or summary of the main points of a text, lecture, or course of study. [Prob. < Gk. *sillubos,* book label.]

syl·lo·gism (sĭl′ə-jĭz′əm) ►*n.* A deductive argument consisting of a major premise, a minor premise, and a conclusion. [< Gk. *sullogismos.*] —**syl′lo·gis′tic** *adj.* —**syl′lo·gis′ti·cal·ly** *adv.*

sylph (sĭlf) ►*n.* **1.** A slim graceful woman or girl. **2.** An imaginary being believed to inhabit the air. [NLat. *sylpha,* sylph (being).]

syl·van (sĭl′vən) ►*adj.* **1.** Of or characteristic of woods or forest regions. **2.** Abounding in trees. [< Lat. *silva,* forest.]

sym·bi·o·sis (sĭm′bē-ō′sĭs, -bī-) ►*n. Biol.* A close association between two or more different organisms, esp. when mutually beneficial. [< Gk. *sumbios,* living together : *sun-,* together + *bios,* life.] —**sym′bi·ot′ic** (-ŏt′ĭk) *adj.* —**sym′bi·ot′i·cal·ly** *adv.*

sym·bol (sĭm′bəl) ►*n.* **1.** Something that represents something else by association, resemblance, or convention. **2.** A printed or written sign used to represent an operation, element, quantity, quality, or relation, as in mathematics or music. [< Gk. *sumbolon,* token for identification.] —**sym·bol′ic** (-bŏl′ĭk) *adj.* —**sym·bol′i·cal·ly** *adv.*

symbolic language ►*n.* A high-level programming language.

sym·bol·ism (sĭm′bə-lĭz′əm) ►*n.* The representation of things by means of symbols.

sym·bol·ize (sĭm′bə-līz′) ►*v.* **-ized, -iz·ing 1.** To serve as a symbol of. **2.** To represent by a symbol. —**sym′bol·i·za′tion** *n.*

sym·me·try (sĭm′ĭ-trē) ►*n., pl.* **-tries 1.** The correspondence of the form and arrangement of elements on opposite sides of a dividing line or plane or about a center or an axis. **2.** A relationship having correspondence or similarity between entities or parts. [< Gk. *summetros,* of like measure.] —**sym·met′ri·cal** (sĭ-mĕt′rĭ-kəl), **sym·met′ric** *adj.* —**sym·met′ri·cal·ly** *adv.*

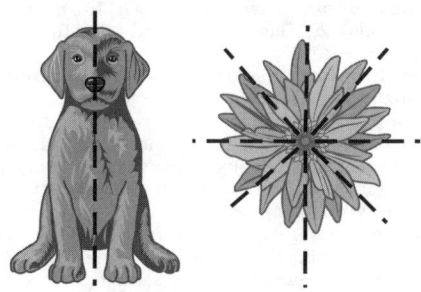

symmetry
left: bilateral symmetry
right: radial symmetry

sym·pa·thet·ic (sĭm′pə-thĕt′ĭk) ►*adj.* **1.** Expressing or resulting from sympathy. **2.** Favorably inclined; agreeable. **3.** Relating to the sympathetic nervous system. —**sym′pa·thet′i·cal·ly** *adv.*

sympathetic nervous system ►*n.* The part of the autonomic nervous system that inhibits the parasympathetic nervous system, resulting in increased heart rate, contraction of blood vessels, and reduction of digestive secretions.

sym·pa·thize (sĭm′pə-thīz′) ►*v.* **-thized, -thiz·ing 1.** To feel or express compassion; commiserate. **2.** To share or understand the feelings or ideas of another. —**sym′pa·thiz′er** *n.*

sym·pa·thy (sĭm′pə-thē) ►*n., pl.* **-thies 1.** A feeling or expression of pity or sorrow for the distress of another. **2a.** Mutual understanding or feeling between people. **b.** Agreement with or support for an opinion or position. **3.** A relationship between things in which whatever affects one correspondingly affects the other. [< Gk. *sumpathēs*, having like feelings.]

sym·phon·ic (sĭm-fŏn′ĭk) ►*adj.* **1.** Relating to or having the form of a symphony. **2.** Harmonious in sound.

sym·pho·ny (sĭm′fə-nē) ►*n., pl.* **-nies 1.** An extended piece for a symphony orchestra. **2.** A symphony orchestra. **3.** Harmony, esp. of sound. [< Gk. *sumphōnos*, harmonious.]

symphony orchestra ►*n.* A large orchestra composed of string, wind, and percussion sections.

sym·po·si·um (sĭm-pō′zē-əm) ►*n., pl.* **-si·ums** or **-si·a** (-zē-ə) **1.** A meeting or conference for discussion of a particular topic. **2.** A collection of writings on a particular topic. [< Gk. *sumposion*, drinking party.]

symp·tom (sĭm′təm, sĭmp′-) ►*n.* **1.** An indication of a disorder or disease, esp. a subjective one such as pain, nausea, or weakness. **2.** An indication; sign. [< Gk. *sumptōma.*] —**symp′-to·mat′ic** *adj.* —**symp′to·mat′i·cal·ly** *adv.*

syn. ►*abbr.* synonym

syn·a·gogue (sĭn′ə-gŏg′, -gôg′) ►*n.* **1.** A building used for worship and religious instruction in the Jewish faith. **2.** A congregation of Jews for the purpose of worship. [< Gk. *sunagōgē*, assembly : *sun-*, together + *agein*, bring.]

syn·apse (sĭn′ăps′, sĭ-năps′) ►*n.* The junction across which a nerve impulse passes to a neuron or other cell. ►*v.* **-apsed, -aps·ing** To form a synapse. [Gk. *sunapsis*, point of contact.] —**syn·ap′tic** *adj.*

sync or **synch** (sĭngk) *Informal* ►*n.* **1.** Synchronization. **2.** Harmony; accord. ►*v.* To synchronize.

syn·chro·nize (sĭng′krə-nīz′, sĭn′-) ►*v.* **-nized, -niz·ing 1.** To occur or cause to occur at the same time. **2.** To operate in unison. **3.** To cause to agree exactly in time or rate. **4.** To represent as occurring at the same time or in the same time period. —**syn′chro·ni·za′tion** *n.* —**syn′chro·niz′er** *n.*

syn·chro·nous (sĭng′krə-nəs, sĭn′-) ►*adj.* **1.** Occurring or existing at the same time. **2.** Moving or operating at the same rate. [< Gk. *sunkhronos.*] —**syn′chro·nous·ly** *adv.* —**syn′chro·ny** *n.*

syn·co·pate (sĭng′kə-pāt′, sĭn′-) ►*v.* **-pat·ed, -pat·ing** To modify (rhythm) by syncopation.

syn·co·pa·tion (sĭng′kə-pā′shən, sĭn′-) ►*n. Mus.* A shift of accent when a normally weak beat is stressed.

syn·co·pe (sĭng′kə-pē, sĭn′-) ►*n.* **1.** *Ling.* The shortening of a word by omitting a sound from the middle; e.g., *bos'n* for *boatswain*. **2.** *Med.* A brief loss of consciousness caused by inadequate blood flow to the brain. [< Gk. *sunkoptein*, cut short.]

syn·di·cate (sĭn′dĭ-kĭt) ►*n.* **1.** An association of people or firms formed to promote a common interest or carry out a business enterprise. **2.** An agency that sells articles or photographs for publication in a number of newspapers or periodicals simultaneously. ►*v.* (-kāt′) **-cat·ed,**

-cat·ing 1. To organize into a syndicate. **2.** To sell or publish through a syndicate. [< Gk. *sundikos*, public advocate.] —**syn′di·ca′tion** *n.*

syn·drome (sĭn′drōm′) ►*n.* A group of symptoms that collectively characterize a disease or disorder. [Gk. *sundromē*, concurrence of symptoms.]

syn·er·gy (sĭn′ər-jē) also **syn·er·gism** (-jĭz′əm) ►*n.* The interaction of two or more agents or forces so that their combined effect is greater than the sum of their individual effects. [< Gk. *sunergos*, working together : *sun-*, together + *ergon*, work.] —**syn′er·gist′ic** *adj.* —**syn′er·gist′ic·al·ly** *adv.*

syn·fu·el (sĭn′fyōō′əl) ►*n.* A fuel derived from coal, shale, or tar sand, or obtained by fermentation, as of grain. [SYN(THETIC) + FUEL.]

syn·od (sĭn′əd) ►*n.* **1.** A council or assembly of Christian church officials. **2.** A council; assembly. [< Gk. *sunodos*, assembly.] —**syn·od′ic** (sĭ-nŏd′ĭk), **syn·od′i·cal** *adj.*

syn·o·nym (sĭn′ə-nĭm′) ►*n.* A word having the same or nearly the same meaning as another word in a language. [< Gk. *sunōnumon.*] —**syn′o·nym′i·ty** *n.* —**syn·on′y·mous** (sĭ-nŏn′ə-məs) *adj.* —**syn·on′y·mous·ly** *adv.*

syn·on·y·my (sĭ-nŏn′ə-mē) ►*n.* The quality of being synonymous.

syn·op·sis (sĭ-nŏp′sĭs) ►*n., pl.* **-ses** (-sēz) A brief outline or general view, as of a written work. [< Gk. *sunopsis*, general view.]

syn·tax (sĭn′tăks′) ►*n.* **1.** The way in which words or other elements of sentence structure are combined to form grammatical sentences. **2.** *Comp.* The rules governing the formation of statements in a programming language. [< Gk. *suntassein*, put in order.] —**syn·tac′-tic** (-tăk′tĭk), **syn·tac′ti·cal** *adj.* —**syn·tac′ti·cal·ly** *adv.*

syn·the·sis (sĭn′thĭ-sĭs) ►*n., pl.* **-ses** (-sēz′) **1.** The combining of separate elements or substances to form a coherent whole. **2.** The complex whole so formed. **3.** *Chem.* Formation of a compound from simpler compounds or elements. [< Gk. *sunthesis < suntithenai*, put together.] —**syn′the·size′** *v.*

syn·the·siz·er (sĭn′thĭ-sī′zər) ►*n.* An electronic instrument that combines simple waveforms to produce more complex sounds, such as those of various other instruments.

syn·thet·ic (sĭn-thĕt′ĭk) ►*adj.* **1.** Of or produced by synthesis. **2.** Not natural or genuine; artificial. ►*n.* A synthetic chemical compound. [< Gk. *sunthetos*, combined.] —**syn·thet′i·cal·ly** *adv.*

syph·i·lis (sĭf′ə-lĭs) ►*n.* A usu. sexually transmitted disease caused by a spirochete, marked initially by a chancre and, if untreated, progressing to widespread organ damage. [< *Syphilus*, protagonist of a 16th-cent. poem.] —**syph′i·lit′ic** *adj.*

sy·phon (sī′fən) ►*n. & v.* Var. of **siphon.**

Syr·i·a (sîr′ē-ə) A country of SW Asia S of Turkey. Cap. Damascus. —**Syr′i·an** *adj. & n.*

sy·ringe (sə-rĭnj′, sîr′ĭnj) ►*n.* **1.** A medical instrument used to inject fluids into the body or draw them from it. **2.** A hypodermic syringe. [< Gk. *surinx*, shepherd's pipe.]

syr·up (sîr′əp, sûr′-) ►*n.* **1.** A thick, sweet, sticky liquid consisting of sugar, flavorings, and water. **2.** A thick, sugary liquid made by concentrating plant sap, juice, or grain extracts. [< Ar. *šarāb*.] —**syr′up·y** *adj.*

sys·tem (sĭs′təm) ►*n.* **1.** A group of interacting elements forming a complex whole, esp.: **a.** An organism as a whole, esp. with regard to its vital processes or functions. **b.** A network of structures and channels, as for communication. **2.** An organized method; procedure. [< Gk. *sustēma* : *sun-*, together + *histanai*, set up.] —**sys′tem·at′ic** *adj.* —**sys′tem·at′i·cal·ly** *adv.*

sys·tem·a·tize (sĭs′tə-mə-tīz′) ►*v.* **-tized, -tiz·ing** To put into a system; arrange according to a plan. See Synonyms at **arrange.** —**sys′tem·a·ti·za′tion** *n.*

sys·tem·ic (sĭ-stĕm′ĭk) ►*adj.* **1.** Of or relating to systems or a system. **2.** Of or affecting the entire body. —**sys·tem′i·cal·ly** *adv.*

sys·tem·ize (sĭs′tə-mīz′) ►*v.* **-ized, -iz·ing** To systematize.

sys·tems analysis (sĭs′təmz) ►*n.* The study of a procedure to determine the most efficient method of executing it to obtain a desired end, esp. by means of a computer. —**systems analyst** *n.*

sys·to·le (sĭs′tə-lē) ►*n.* The rhythmic contraction of the heart, esp. of the ventricles. [Gk. *sustolē*, contraction.] —**sys·tol′ic** (sĭ-stŏl′ĭk) *adj.*

systolic pressure ►*n.* The highest arterial blood pressure reached when the ventricles are contracting.

Sze·chuan or **Sze·chwan** (sĕch′wän′) See **Sichuan.**

T

t¹ or **T** (tē) ►*n., pl.* **t's** or **T's** also **ts** or **Ts** The 20th letter of the English alphabet. —*idiom:* **to a T** Perfectly; precisely.

t² ►*abbr.* teaspoon

T ►*abbr.* **1.** tablespoon **2.** *Football* tackle **3.** temperature **4.** tenor **5.** *Sports* turnover

t. ►*abbr.* **1.** tare **2.** time **3.** transitive **4.** troy (system of weights)

TA ►*abbr.* teaching assistant

tab¹ (tăb) ►*n.* A projection attached to an object to facilitate opening, handling, or identification.

tab² (tăb) ►*n.* **1.** *Informal* A bill or check. **2.** A key on a computer keyboard or typewriter used esp. in indenting text. —*idiom:* **keep tabs on** *Informal* To observe carefully over time. [< TABLET or TABULATION. Sense 2 < TABULATOR.]

tab·bou·leh or **ta·bou·leh** or **ta·bou·li** (tə-bōō′lē) ►*n.* A Lebanese salad of bulgur, scallions, tomatoes, mint, and parsley.

tab·by (tăb′ē) ►*n., pl.* **-bies 1.** A domestic cat with black and grayish striped or mottled fur. **2.** A domestic cat, esp. a female. [< Ar. *'attābī*.]

tab·er·na·cle (tăb′ər-năk′əl) ►*n.* **1.** often **Tabernacle** The portable sanctuary in which the Jews carried the Ark of the Covenant through the desert. **2.** often **Tabernacle** A case or box on a church altar containing the consecrated elements of the Eucharist. **3.** A place of worship. [< LLat. *tabernāculum*.]

ta·ble (tā′bəl) ►*n.* **1.** An article of furniture having a flat horizontal surface that is supported by legs. **2.** An orderly display of data, usu. arranged in rows and columns. **3.** An abbreviated list, as of contents; synopsis. **4.** A slab or tablet bearing an inscription or a device. ►*v.* **-bled, -bling 1.** To put or place on a table. **2.** To postpone consideration of; shelve. [< Lat. *tabula*, board.]

tab·leau (tăb′lō′, tă-blō′) ►*n., pl.* **tab·leaux** or **tab·leaus** (tăb′lōz′, tă-blōz′) **1.** A vivid or graphic description. **2.** A stage technique in which the performers freeze in position simultaneously. **3.** A tableau vivant. [Fr.]

tableau vi·vant (vē-väN′) ►*n., pl.* **tab·leaux vi·vants** (tă-blō′vē-väN′) A scene presented on stage by actors who remain silent and motionless as if in a picture. [Fr., living picture.]

ta·ble·cloth (tā′bəl-klôth′, -klŏth′) ►*n.* A cloth to cover a table, esp. during a meal.

ta·ble d'hôte (tā′bəl dōt′, tä′blə) ►*n., pl.* **ta·bles d'hôte** (tä′bəl, tä′blə) A full-course meal served at a fixed price in a restaurant or hotel. [Fr., host's table.]

ta·ble·land (tā′bəl-lănd′) ►*n.* A plateau or mesa.

ta·ble·spoon (tā′bəl-spōōn′) ►*n.* **1.** A large spoon used for serving food. **2.** A household cooking measure equal to 3 teaspoons or ½ fl. oz. (15 ml). —**ta′ble·spoon′ful′** *n.*

tab·let (tăb′lĭt) ►*n.* **1.** A slab or plaque, as of stone or ivory, bearing an inscription. **2.** A pad of writing paper glued together along one edge. **3.** A lightweight portable computer having a touchscreen as the method by which data is input. **4.** A small flat pellet of oral medication. [< OFr. *table*, TABLE.]

table tennis ►*n.* A game similar to lawn tennis, played on a table with wooden paddles and a small plastic ball.

ta·ble·top (tā′bəl-tŏp′) ►*n.* The flat surface of a table. ►*adj.* Designed or made for use on the top of a table.

ta·ble·ware (tā′bəl-wâr′) ►*n.* Dishes, glassware, and silverware used in setting a table.

tab·loid (tăb′loid′) ►*n.* A newspaper of small format giving the news in condensed form, often with sensational material. [< *Tabloid*, a trademark.]

ta·boo (tă-bōō′, tə-) ►*n., pl.* **-boos 1.** A ban attached to something by social custom. **2.** A prohibition, esp. among certain South Pacific peoples, excluding something from use, approach, or mention because of its sacred and inviolable nature. [Tongan *tabu*, prohibited.] —**ta·boo′** *adj.* —**ta·boo′** *v.*

ta·bor (tā′bər) ►*n.* A small drum used to accompany a fife. [< OFr. *tambur.*]

ta·bou·leh or **ta·bou·li** (tə-bōō′lē) ►*n.* Vars. of **tabbouleh.**

tab·u·lar (tăb′yə-lər) ►*adj.* Organized as a table or list. [< Lat. *tabula*, board.]

tab·u·late (tăb′yə-lāt′) ►*v.* **-lat·ed, -lat·ing** To arrange in tabular form; condense and list. [< Lat. *tabula*, writing.] —**tab′u·la′tion** *n.* —**tab′u·la′tor** *n.*

ta·chom·e·ter (tă-kŏm′ĭ-tər, tə-) ►*n.* An instrument used to measure speed, esp. rotational speed. [Gk. *takhos*, speed + –METER.] —**tach′o·met′ric** (tăk′ə-mĕt′rĭk) *adj.* —**ta·chom′e·try** *n.*

tac·it (tăs′ĭt) ►*adj.* **1.** Not spoken: *gave tacit approval.* **2.** Implied by actions or statements. [Lat. *tacitus*, silent.] —**tac′it·ly** *adv.* —**tac′it·ness** *n.*

tac·i·turn (tăs′ĭ-tûrn′) ►*adj.* **1.** Habitually untalkative. See Synonyms at **laconic. 2.** Characterized by reserve or a lack of expression. [< Lat. *taciturnus.*] —**tac′i·tur′ni·ty** *n.* —**tac′i·turn·ly** *adv.*

Tac·i·tus (tăs′ĭ-təs), **Publius Cornelius** AD 55?–120? Roman historian.

tack¹ (tăk) ►*n.* **1.** A short light nail with a sharp point and a flat head. **2.** The position of a vessel relative to the trim of its sails. **3.** A course of action. **4.** A loose, temporary stitch. ►*v.* **1.** To fasten or attach with a tack. **2.** To add as an extra item: *tacked on a hefty surcharge.* **3.** To change the course of a vessel. [< ONFr. *taque*, fastener.] —**tack′er** *n.*

tack² (tăk) ►*n.* The harness for a horse, including the bridle and saddle. [< TACKLE.]

tack·le (tăk′əl) ►*n.* **1.** The equipment used in a sport or occupation, esp. in fishing; gear. **2.** A system of ropes and blocks for raising and lowering weights. **3.** *Sports* **a.** The act of stopping a player carrying the ball, esp. by forcing the player to the ground, as in football. **b.** The act of obstructing a player so as to cause loss of possession of the ball, as in soccer. **c.** In football, either of the two line players positioned between guard and end. ►*v.* **-led, -ling 1.** To take on and wrestle with (e.g., an opponent or problem). **2.** To stop or obstruct (an opponent) by means of a tackle. [ME *takel.*] —**tack′ler** *n.*

tack·y¹ (tăk′ē) ►*adj.* **-i·er, -i·est** Gummy; sticky. [< TACK¹.] —**tack′i·ness** *n.*

tack·y² (tăk′ē) ►*adj.* **-i·er, -i·est** *Informal* **1.** Neglected and in a state of disrepair: *a tacky old cabin.* **2a.** Lacking style or good taste: *tacky clothes.* **b.** Distasteful or offensive; tasteless: *a tacky remark.* [< *tackey*, an inferior horse.] —**tack′i·ly** *adv.* —**tack′i·ness** *n.*

ta·co (tä′kō) ►*n., pl.* **-cos** A corn tortilla folded around a filling, as of meat or cheese. [Am.Sp. < Sp., wad of bank notes.]

tac·o·nite (tăk′ə-nīt′) ►*n.* A variety of chert mined as an iron ore. [After the *Taconic* Mountains in New York.]

tact (tăkt) ►*n.* Sensitivity in dealing with others. [< Lat. *tāctus*, sense of touch.] —**tact′ful** *adj.* —**tact′less** *adj.*

tac·tic (tăk′tĭk) ►*n.* **1.** A plan or action for achieving a goal; maneuver. **2. tactics** (*takes sing. v.*) The study of the most effective ways of securing objectives set by strategy, esp. in war. [< Gk. *taktika*, tactics.] —**tac′ti·cal** *adj.* —**tac·ti′cian** (-tĭsh′ən) *n.*

tac·tile (tăk′təl, -tīl′) ►*adj.* Of, perceptible to, or proceeding from the sense of touch. [< Lat. *tangere, tāct-*, touch.] —**tac′tile·ly** *adv.* —**tac·til′i·ty** (-tĭl′ĭ-tē) *n.*

tad (tăd) ►*n. Informal* A small amount or degree. [Perh. < TADPOLE.]

tad·pole (tăd′pōl′) ►*n.* The limbless aquatic larval stage of a frog or toad, with gills and a long flat tail. [ME *taddepol.*]

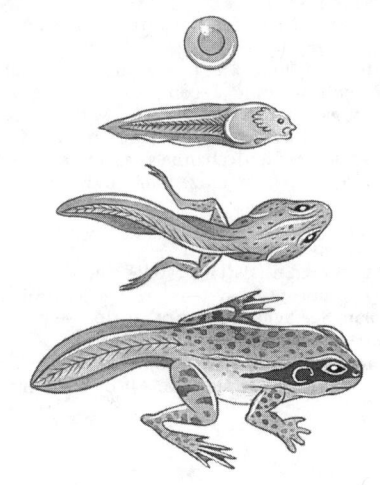

tadpole
from top to bottom: egg and three stages of a tadpole metamorphosing into a frog

tae kwon do (tī′ kwŏn′ dō′) ►*n.* A Korean martial art that emphasizes powerful kicks. [Korean *t'aekwŏndo.*]

taf·fe·ta (tăf′ĭ-tə) ►*n.* A crisp, lustrous, plain-woven fabric of silk, rayon, or nylon. [< Pers. *tāftah*, silk or linen cloth.]

taf·fy (tăf′ē) ►*n., pl.* **-fies** A sweet chewy candy of molasses or brown sugar. [?]

Taft (tăft), **William Howard** 1857–1930. The 27th US president (1909–13); chief justice of the US Supreme Court (1921–30).

William Howard Taft
1911 portrait

tag¹ (tăg) ►*n.* **1.** A strip of paper, metal, or plastic attached to something to identify, classify, or label. **2.** A designation or epithet. **3.** *Comp.* A character sequence in a markup language that gives information, esp. formatting specifications. ►*v.* **tagged, tag·ging 1.** To label or identify with a tag. **2.** To follow closely. **3.** To mark (a surface) with graffiti. [ME *tagge*, dangling piece of cloth on a garment.] —**tag′ger** *n.*

tag² (tăg) ►*n.* **1.** A children's game in which one player pursues the others until he or she touches one of them, who in turn becomes the pursuer. **2.** *Baseball* The act of tagging a player out. ►*v.* **tagged, tag·ging 1.** To touch (another player) in the game of tag. **2.** *Baseball* To touch (a runner) with the ball in order to put that player out. [?]

Ta·ga·log (tə-gä′lôg, -ləg) ►*n., pl.* **-log** or **-logs 1.** A member of a people native to the Philippines. **2.** The Austronesian language of the Tagalog.

Ta·gore (tə-gôr′, tä-), Sir **Rabindranath** 1861–1941. Indian writer.

ta·hi·ni (tə-hē′nē) ►*n.* A paste made from ground sesame seeds. [< Ar. *ṭaḥīna.*]

Ta·hi·ti (tə-hē′tē) An island of the S Pacific in the Society Is. of French Polynesia.

Ta·hi·tian (tə-hē′shən) ►*n.* **1.** A native or inhabitant of Tahiti. **2.** The Polynesian language of Tahiti. —**Ta·hi′tian** *adj.*

Ta·hoe (tä′hō), **Lake** A lake on the CA-NV border W of Carson City, NV.

Tai (tī) ►*n., pl.* **Tai** or **Tais 1.** A family of languages of SE Asia and S China that includes Thai and Lao. **2.** A member of a Tai-speaking people. **3.** Thai. —**Tai** *adj.*

tai chi or **Tai Chi** (tī′ chē′, jē′) ►*n.* A Chinese martial art whose system of physical exercises is often practiced as a way of meditating or improving well-being. [< Mandarin *tai jí (quán),* highest reach (boxing).]

tai·ga (tī′gə) ►*n.* The subarctic forest of N Eurasia and North America just south of the tundra. [Russ. *taïga.*]

tail (tāl) ►*n.* **1.** The hind part of an animal, esp. when extending beyond the main part of the body. **2.** The bottom, rear, or hindmost part of something. **3a.** The rear of an aircraft. **b.** An assembly of stabilizing planes and control surfaces in this rear portion. **4.** An appendage to the rear or bottom: *the tail of a kite.* **5. tails** A formal evening costume worn by men. **6.** often **tails** *(takes sing. v.)* The reverse side of a coin. ►*adj.* Posterior; hindmost. ►*v. Informal* To follow and keep under surveillance. [< OE *tægel.*] —**tail′less** *adj.*

tail·back (tāl′băk′) ►*n. Football* The back on an offensive team who lines up farthest from the line of scrimmage.

tail·gate (tāl′gāt′) ►*n.* A hinged part that extends across the rear of a pickup truck or other vehicle and can be folded down. ►*v.* **-gat·ed, -gat·ing 1.** To drive too closely behind (another vehicle). **2.** To participate in a social gathering taking place next to a parked automobile, as before a sporting event. —**tail′gat′er** *n.*

tail·ings (tā′lĭngz) ►*pl.n.* Refuse or dross remaining after ore has been processed.

tail·light (tāl′līt′) ►*n.* A red light mounted on the rear of a vehicle.

tai·lor (tā′lər) ►*n.* One who makes, repairs, and alters garments. ►*v.* **1.** To make (a garment). **2.** To make or adapt for a particular purpose. [< LLat. *tāliāre,* cut.]

tai·lor-made (tā′lər-mād′) ►*adj.* Made or as if made to order.

tail·pipe (tāl′pīp′) ►*n.* The pipe through which exhaust gases from an engine are discharged.

tail·spin (tāl′spĭn′) ►*n.* **1.** The rapid descent of an aircraft in a nose-down spiral spin. **2.** A sudden steep decline or slump.

Tai·no (tī′nō) ►*n., pl.* **-no** or **-nos 1.** A member of an Arawak people of the West Indies whose

culture was destroyed under Spanish colonization. **2.** The language of this people.

taint (tānt) ►*v.* **1.** To affect or associate with something undesirable or reprehensible: *a reputation tainted by allegations of illegal activity.* **2a.** To expose to an infectious agent or undesirable substance: *water tainted with parasites.* **b.** To subject to decay or putrefaction: *The meat was tainted.* See Synonyms at **contaminate.** ►*n.* **1.** An undesirable association: *the taint of a scandal.* See Synonyms at **stain. 2.** An undesirable quality; shortcoming. [< AN *teint,* tinged, and OFr. *ataint,* touched.]

Tai·pei (tī′pā′, -bā′) The capital of Taiwan, in the N part.

Tai·wan (tī′wän′) Officially **Republic of China.** Formerly **For·mo·sa** (fôr-mō′sə). A country off SE China comprising the island of **Taiwan** and other smaller islands. Cap. Taipei. —**Tai′wan·ese′** (-wä-nēz′, -nēs′) *adj. & n.*

Ta·jik (tä-jĭk′, tə-) ►*n., pl.* **-jik** or **-jiks 1a.** A native or inhabitant of Tajikistan. **b.** A member of a people inhabiting Tajikistan and neighboring areas. **2.** The Iranian language of the Tajik.

Ta·jik·i·stan (tä-jĭk′ĭ-stän′, -stän′) A country of central Asia bordering on Afghanistan and China. Cap. Dushanbe.

ta·ka (tä′kə) ►*n.* See table at **currency.** [Bengali *ṭākā* < Skt. *ṭaṅkaḥ,* stamped coin.]

take (tāk) ►*v.* **took** (tŏŏk), **tak·en** (tā′kən), **tak·ing 1.** To get into one's hands or possession. **2.** To grasp or grip. **3.** To remove or cause to be absent. **4.** To subtract. **5.** To delight or captivate. **6a.** To carry in one's possession. See Usage Note at **bring. b.** To convey by transportation. **c.** To lead or cause to go along to another place. **7.** To eat, drink, consume, or inhale. **8.** To make use of or select for use, esp.: **a.** To occupy: *take a seat.* **b.** To require: *It takes money to do that.* **c.** To use as a means of conveyance or transportation. **d.** To use as a means of safety: *take shelter.* **9a.** To make or perform: *take a decision.* **b.** To commit oneself to the study of: *take a course.* **10a.** To accept (e.g., something given). **b.** To let in; admit: *The boat is taking water.* **c.** To endure: *take criticism.* **d.** To agree to undertake or engage in: *take a job.* **11.** *Gram.* To govern: *Intransitive verbs take no direct object.* **12a.** To follow (e.g., a suggestion). **b.** To interpret or react in a certain manner: *take literally.* **13a.** To determine through measurement or observation. **b.** To write down: *take notes.* **c.** To make by photography: *take a picture.* **14.** To have the intended effect; work. **15.** To become: *take sick.* ►*n.* **1a.** A quantity collected at one time, esp. the money collected as admission to an event. **b.** The number of animals killed or captured at one time. **2.** A scene filmed without interrupting the run of the camera. —*phrasal verbs:* **take after** To follow as an example. **take back** To retract (something stated or written). **take for** To regard as or mistake for: *took him for the boss.* **take in 1.** To include or constitute. **2.** To attend or experience: *She took in the scene.* **3.** To understand. **take off 1.** To remove, as clothing. **2.** To go or leave. **3.** To rise up in flight, as an airplane. **take out 1.** To extract; remove. **2.** *Informal* To escort, as a date. **take over** To assume the control or management of. **take to 1.** To develop as a habit. **2.** To become fond of. **take up 1.** To begin again. **2.** To develop an interest in. —*idioms:* **take effect 1.** To become operative, as a law. **2.** To produce the desired reaction. **take place** To happen; occur. [< ON *taka.*] —**tak′er** *n.*

take·off (tāk′ôf′, -ŏf′) ►*n.* **1.** The act of leaving the ground. **2.** *Informal* An imitative caricature or burlesque.

take·out also **take-out** (tāk′out′) ►*adj.* Intended to be eaten off the premises: *takeout pizza.* —**take′-out′** *n.*

take·o·ver also **take-o·ver** (tāk′ō′vər) ►*n.* The act of assuming control.

ta·la (tä′lə) ►*n.* See table at **currency.** [Samoan < E., DOLLAR.]

talc (tălk) ►*n.* A fine-grained mineral used in making talcum powder. [< Pers. *talk.*]

tal·cum powder (tăl′kəm) ►*n.* A fine powder made from purified talc, for use on the skin. [< Med.Lat. *talcum,* TALC.]

tale (tāl) ►*n.* **1.** A recital of events or happenings. **2.** A narrative of imaginary events; story. **3.** A deliberate lie. [< OE *talu.*]

tale·bear·er (tāl′bâr′ər) ►*n.* One who spreads malicious gossip. —**tale′bear′ing** *adj. & n.*

tal·ent (tăl′ənt) ►*n.* **1a.** An innate ability, as for artistic accomplishment: *a rare talent for music.* **b.** Natural endowment or ability of a superior quality: *a theatrical cast of immense talent.* **c.** A person with such ability. **2.** Any of various ancient units of weight and money. [< Gk. *talanton,* unit of money.] —**tal′ent·ed** *adj.*

Ta·li·ban (tăl′ə-băn′) ►*n. (takes sing. or pl. v.)* A fundamentalist Muslim paramilitary group of Afghanistan and W Pakistan. [Pashto *tālibān,* pl. of *tālib,* student < Arabic *ṭālib.*]

tal·is·man (tăl′ĭs-mən, -ĭz-) ►*n.* An object believed to protect or give supernatural powers to its bearer. [< Gk. *telesma,* consecration.] —**tal′is·man′ic** (-măn′ĭk) *adj.*

talk (tôk) ►*v.* **1a.** To converse by means of spoken language. **b.** To utter or pronounce words. **2.** To converse about: *talk politics.* **3.** To speak (a language or form of language). **4a.** To parley or negotiate. **b.** To consult or confer. **5.** To gossip. **6.** To persuade with arguments: *talked them into joining.* ►*n.* **1.** The act of talking; conversation: *We had a nice talk over lunch.* **2.** A speech or lecture: *He gave a talk on art.* **3.** Hearsay, rumor, or speculation. **4.** A subject of conversation. **5.** often **talks** A conference or negotiation. —*phrasal verbs:* **talk back** To reply rudely. **talk down** To address someone with insulting condescension. **talk over** To discuss. [ME *talken.*] —**talk′er** *n.*

talk·a·tive (tô′kə-tĭv) ►*adj.* Inclined to talk or converse. —**talk′a·tive·ness** *n.*

talk·ing-to (tô′kĭng-tōō′) ►*n., pl.* **-tos** *Informal* A scolding; dressing-down.

talk show ►*n.* A television or radio show in which people participate in discussions or are interviewed.

tall (tôl) ►*adj.* **-er, -est 1.** Having greater than ordinary height. **2.** Having a specified height: *a plant three feet tall.* **3.** *Informal* Fanciful or boastful. **4.** Impressively great or difficult: *a tall order to fill.* ►*adv.* With proud bearing; straight: *stand tall.* [< OE *getæl,* swift.] —**tall′ness** *n.*

Tal·la·has·see (tăl′ə-hăs′ē) The capital of FL, in the NW part.

Tal·ley·rand-Pé·ri·gord (tăl′ē-rănd′pĕr′ĭ-gôr′),

Charles Maurice de 1754–1838. French politician and diplomat.

Tal·linn also **Tal·lin** (tăl′ĭn, tä′lĭn) The capital of Estonia, in the NW part.

tal·low (tăl′ō) ►*n.* Hard fat obtained from cattle, sheep, or horses and used in candles, soaps, and lubricants. [ME *talow.*] —**tal′low·y** *adj.*

tal·ly (tăl′ē) ►*n., pl.* **-lies** **1.** A reckoning or amount: *the final tally of votes.* **2.** A stick on which notches are made to keep a count. ►*v.* **-lied, -ly·ing 1.** To reckon or count: *tallied up the bill.* **2.** To correspond or agree: *The report tallies with your description.* [< Lat. *tālea,* stick.]

tal·ly·ho (tăl′ē-hō′) ►*interj.* Used to urge hounds on during a fox hunt. [Prob. < OFr. *thialau.*]

Tal·mud (tăl′mŏŏd, tăl′məd) ►*n. Judaism* The collection of ancient Rabbinic writings constituting the basis of religious authority in Orthodox Judaism. —**Tal·mu′dic** (-mŏŏ′dĭk, -myŏŏ′-), **Tal·mu′di·cal** *adj.* —**Tal′mud·ist** *n.*

tal·on (tăl′ən) ►*n.* The long curved claw esp. of a bird of prey. [< Lat. *tālus,* ankle.]

ta·lus (tā′ləs) ►*n., pl.* **-li** (-lī) The bone that articulates with the tibia and fibula to form the ankle joint. [Lat. *tālus,* ankle.]

ta·ma·le (tə-mä′lē) ►*n.* A Mexican dish of fried chopped meat and crushed peppers, wrapped in cornmeal dough and cornhusks and steamed. [< Nahuatl *tamalli.*]

tam·a·rack (tăm′ə-răk′) ►*n.* An American larch tree. [Prob. of Algonquian orig.]

ta·ma·ri (tə-mä′rē) ►*n.* Soy sauce made with little or no wheat.

tam·a·rind (tăm′ə-rĭnd′) ►*n.* **1.** A tropical tree widely cultivated for its pods, which contain seeds embedded in an edible pulp. **2a.** The fruit of this tree. **b.** Syrup prepared from the pulp of this fruit. [< Ar. *tamr hindī,* Indian date.]

tam·a·risk (tăm′ə-rĭsk′) ►*n.* A shrub or small tree with scalelike leaves and small pinkish flowers. [< Lat. *tamarīx.*]

tam·bou·rine (tăm′bə-rēn′) ►*n.* A musical instrument consisting of a small drumhead with jingling disks fitted into the rim. [< OFr. *tambourin,* small drum.]

tame (tām) ►*adj.* **tam·er, tam·est 1.** Brought from wildness into a domesticated or tractable state. **2.** Gentle; docile. **3.** Insipid; flat: *a tame party.* [< OE *tam.*] —**tam′a·ble, tame′a·ble** *adj.* —**tame** *v.* —**tame′ly** *adv.* —**tame′ness** *n.* —**tam′er** *n.*

Tam·er·lane (tăm′ər-lān′) or **Tam·bur·laine** (-bər-) Timur. 1336–1405. Mongolian conqueror.

Tam·il (tăm′əl, tŭm′-, tä′məl) ►*n., pl.* **-il** or **-ils 1.** A member of a people of S India and N Sri Lanka. **2.** The Dravidian language of the Tamil. —**Tam′il** *adj.*

Tam·muz (tä′mŏŏz) ►*n.* The 4th month of the Jewish calendar. See table at **calendar.** [Heb. *Tammūz.*]

tam-o'-shan·ter (tăm′ə-shăn′tər) ►*n.* A flat-topped, tight-fitting Scottish cap. [After the hero of Burns's poem "*Tam o' Shanter*".]

tamp (tămp) ►*v.* To pack down tightly by a succession of blows or taps. [Prob. < *tampin,* plug for a gun muzzle.]

Tam·pa (tăm′pə) A city of W-central FL on **Tampa Bay,** an inlet of the Gulf of Mexico.

tam·per (tăm′pər) ►*v.* **1.** To interfere harmfully; meddle. **2.** To make alterations or adjustments, esp. secretly so as to subvert an intended purpose or function: *tamper with a lock.* **3.** To make improper or secret arrangements in an effort to influence an outcome: *tamper with a jury.* [Prob. < TEMPER.] —**tam′per·er** *n.*

tam·pon (tăm′pŏn′) ▸*n.* A plug of absorbent material inserted into a body cavity or wound. [< OFr., of Gmc. orig.]

tan¹ (tăn) ▸*v.* **tanned, tan·ning 1.** To convert (hide) into leather, as by treating with tannin. **2.** To make brown by exposure to the sun. **3.** *Informal* To thrash; beat. ▸*n.* **1.** A light brown. **2.** A suntan. ▸*adj.* **tan·ner, tan·nest 1.** Of the color tan. **2.** Having a suntan. [< Med.Lat. *tannum,* tanbark.]

tan² ▸*abbr. Math.* tangent

tan·a·ger (tăn′ĭ-jər) ▸*n.* Any of various American songbirds often having brightly colored plumage in the male. [< Tupí *tanagorá.*]

tan·bark (tăn′bärk′) ▸*n.* **1.** Tree bark used as a source of tannin. **2.** Shredded bark used to cover a surface such as a circus arena.

tan·dem (tăn′dəm) ▸*n.* **1.** A bicycle built for two riders. **2.** An arrangement of two or more persons or objects placed one behind or adjacent to the other. ▸*adj.* Having two identical parts with one behind or adjacent to the other: *a tandem axle.* [Lat., at last.] —**tan′dem** *adv.*

Ta·ney (tô′nē), **Roger Brooke** 1777–1864. Amer. jurist; chief justice of the US Supreme Court (1836–64).

tang (tăng) ▸*n.* **1.** A distinctively sharp taste, flavor, or odor. **2.** A projection by which a tool is attached to its handle. [ME *tange,* of Scand. orig.] —**tang′i·ness** *n.* —**tang′y** *adj.*

Tan·gan·yi·ka (tăn′gən-yē′kə, tăng′-) A former country of E-central Africa; joined with Zanzibar (1964) to form Tanzania. —**Tan′gan· yi′kan** *adj. & n.*

Tanganyika, Lake A lake of E-central Africa between Dem. Rep. of the Congo and Tanzania.

tan·ge·lo (tăn′jə-lō′) ▸*n., pl.* **-los 1.** A hybrid citrus tree derived from grapefruit and tangerine. **2.** The fruit of this tree. [Blend of TANGERINE and *pomelo,* a kind of grapefruit.]

tan·gent (tăn′jənt) ▸*adj.* **1.** Making contact at a single point or along a line; touching but not intersecting. **2.** Irrelevant. ▸*n.* **1.** A line, curve, or surface meeting another line, curve, or surface at a common point and sharing a common tangent line or tangent plane at that point. **2.** In a right triangle, the ratio of the sine of an acute angle to its cosine. **3.** A sudden digression. [< Lat. *tangēns,* touching.] —**tan′gen· cy** *n.* —**tan·gen′tial** (-jĕn′shəl) *adj.* —**tan· gen′tial·ly** *adv.*

tan·ger·ine (tăn′jə-rēn′, tăn′jə-rēn′) ▸*n.* A mandarin orange with a red-orange skin. [After *Tanger* (Tangier), Morocco.]

tan·gi·ble (tăn′jə-bəl) ▸*adj.* **1a.** Discernible by the touch; palpable. **b.** Real or concrete: *tangible evidence.* **2.** Possible to understand or realize: *tangible benefits.* ▸*n.* **1.** Something palpable or concrete. **2. tangibles** Material assets. [< Lat. *tangere,* touch.] —**tan′gi·bil′i·ty, tan′gi·ble· ness** *n.* —**tan′gi·bly** *adv.*

Tan·gier (tăn-jîr′) also **Tan·giers** (-jîrz′) A city of N Morocco at the W end of the Strait of Gibraltar.

tan·gle (tăng′gəl) ▸*v.* **-gled, -gling 1.** To intertwine in a confused mass; snarl. **2.** To be or become entangled. **3.** To snare; entrap. See Synonyms at **catch. 4.** *Informal* To enter into dispute or conflict: *tangled with the law.* [ME *tangilen,* involve in an embarrassing situation.] —**tan′gle** *n.*

tan·go (tăng′gō) ▸*n., pl.* **-gos 1.** A dance of Argentine origin for couples in 2/4 or 4/4 time. **2.** The music for this dance. [Am.Sp.] —**tan′go** *v.*

tank (tăngk) ▸*n.* **1.** A large container for liquids or gases. **2.** An enclosed, heavily armored combat vehicle mounted with cannon and guns and moving on continuous treads. **3.** A tank top. [< Gujarati (Indic) *tānkh,* cistern, and Port. *tanque,* reservoir.] —**tank′ful** *n.*

tank·ard (tăng′kərd) ▸*n.* A large drinking cup, usu. with a handle and a hinged cover. [ME.]

tank·er (tăng′kər) ▸*n.* A ship, plane, or truck constructed to transport liquids, such as oil, in bulk.

tan·ki·ni (tăng-kē′nē) ▸*n.* **-nis** A two-piece women's swimsuit having a tank top and a bikini bottom. [Blend of TANK (TOP) and BIKINI.]

tankini

tank top ▸*n.* A sleeveless shirt with wide shoulder straps.

tan·ner (tăn′ər) ▸*n.* One who tans hides.

tan·ner·y (tăn′ə-rē) ▸*n., pl.* **-ies** An establishment where hides are tanned.

tan·nic acid (tăn′ĭk) ▸*n.* A lustrous yellowish to light brown substance derived from certain plants and used chiefly in tanning leather and fixing dyes.

tan·nin (tăn′ĭn) ▸*n.* Any of various usu. plant substances that promote tanning of leather, such as tannic acid. [< Med.Lat. *tannum,* tanbark.]

tan·sy (tăn′zē) ▸*n., pl.* **-sies** A plant with buttonlike yellow flower heads and aromatic leaves that are sometimes used medicinally. [< LLat. *tanacētum,* wormwood.]

tan·ta·lize (tăn′tə-līz′) ▸*v.* **-lized, -liz·ing 1.** To excite by exposing something desirable that is difficult or impossible to obtain: *tantalized by the hope of finding a cure.* **2.** To excite the senses of: *The aroma of fresh cookies tantalized us.* [< *Tantalus,* Greek mythological figure.] —**tan′ta·li·za′tion** *n.* —**tan′ta·liz′er** *n.* —**tan′ta· liz′ing·ly** *adv.*

tan·ta·lum (tăn′tə-ləm) ►*n. Symbol* **Ta** A very hard, heavy, gray metallic element used to make capacitors and for aircraft, missile, and nuclear reactor parts. At. no. 73. See table at **element.** [< *Tantalus,* Greek mythological figure.]

tan·ta·mount (tăn′tə-mount′) ►*adj.* Equivalent in effect or value. [< AN *tant amunter,* amount to so much.]

tan·tra (tŭn′trə, tăn′-) ►*n.* Any of a comparatively recent body of Hindu or Buddhist religious literature. [Skt. *tantram.*] —**tan′tric** *adj.*

tan·trum (tăn′trəm) ►*n.* A fit of bad temper. [?]

Tan·za·ni·a (tăn′zə-nē′ə) A country of E-central Africa on the Indian Ocean. Cap. Dodoma. —**Tan·za′ni·an** *adj. & n.*

Tao (dou, tou) also **Dao** (dou) ►*n.* **1.** In Taoism, the basic, eternal principle of the universe. **2.** In Confucianism, the right manner of human activity and virtuous conduct. [Chinese (Mandarin) *dào,* way, Tao.]

Tao·ism (dou′ĭz′əm, tou′-) also **Dao·ism** (dou′-) ►*n.* A Chinese philosophy and system of religion based on the teachings of Lao-tzu and others that advocates conforming one's behavior and thought to the Tao. [< Mandarin *dào,* way.] —**Tao′ist** *n.* —**Tao·is′tic** *adj.*

tap¹ (tăp) ►*v.* **tapped, tap·ping 1.** To strike gently; rap. **2.** To make light clicking sounds. **3.** To select, as for membership in an organization. See Synonyms at **appoint.** ►*n.* **1a.** A gentle blow. **b.** The sound made by such a blow. **2.** A metal plate attached to the toe or heel of a shoe. [ME *tappen.*]

tap² (tăp) ►*n.* **1.** A faucet; spigot. **2.** Liquor drawn from a spigot. **3.** A tool for cutting an internal screw thread. **4.** A makeshift terminal in an electric circuit. ►*v.* **tapped, tap·ping 1.** To furnish with a spigot or tap. **2.** To pierce in order to draw off liquid. **3.** To draw (liquid) from a vessel or container. **4.** To open outlets from: *tap a water main.* **5a.** To wiretap. **b.** To establish an electric connection in (a power line). **6.** To cut screw threads in. [< OE *tæppa.*]

tap dance ►*n.* A dance in which the rhythm is sounded out by the clicking taps on the heels and toes of a dancer's shoes. —**tap′-dance′** *v.* —**tap dancer** *n.*

tape (tāp) ►*n.* **1a.** A continuous narrow flexible strip of material such as adhesive tape or magnetic tape. **b.** A narrow strip of strong woven fabric. **c.** A string stretched across the finish line of a racetrack. **2.** A tape recording. ►*v.* **taped, tap·ing 1.** To fasten, secure, or wrap with tape: *taped the box together.* **2.** To tape-record. [< OE *tæppe.*]

tape deck ►*n.* A tape recorder and player with no amplifier or speaker, used as a component in an audio system.

tape measure ►*n.* A tape marked off in a scale, used for taking measurements.

ta·per (tā′pər) ►*n.* **1.** A slender candle or waxed wick. **2.** A gradual decrease in thickness or width of an elongated object. ►*v.* **1.** To make or become gradually narrower or thinner toward one end. **2.** To diminish gradually; slacken off. [< OE *tapor.*] —**ta′per·ing·ly** *adv.*

tape recorder ►*n.* A device for recording and playing back sound on magnetic tape.

tape recording ►*n.* **1a.** A magnetic tape on which sound or images have been recorded. **b.** The material recorded. **2.** The act of recording

on this tape. —**tape′-re·cord′** *v.*

tap·es·try (tăp′ĭ-strē) ►*n., pl.* **-tries** A heavy cloth woven with varicolored designs, usu. hung on walls. [< Gk. *tapēs,* carpet.]

tape·worm (tāp′wûrm′) ►*n.* A long ribbonlike worm that is parasitic in the intestines of vertebrates.

tap·i·o·ca (tăp′ē-ō′kə) ►*n.* **1.** A starch made from cassava roots. **2.** A pudding made from this starch. [< Tupí *typióca.*]

ta·pir (tā′pər, tə-pîr′, tā′pîr′) ►*n.* A large hoofed mammal of tropical America and Southeast Asia, having a stocky body, short legs, and a fleshy, trunklike proboscis. [< Tupí *tapiira.*]

tap·room (tăp′rōōm′, -rŏŏm′) ►*n.* A barroom.

tap·root (tăp′rōōt′, -rŏŏt′) ►*n.* The main root of a plant, growing straight downward from the stem.

taps (tăps) ►*pl.n. (takes sing. or pl. v.)* A military bugle call sounded at night as an order to put out lights and at funerals and memorial services. [Perh. < *taptoo,* TATTOO¹.]

tar¹ (tär) ►*n.* **1.** A dark, oily, viscous material, consisting mainly of hydrocarbons, produced by the destructive distillation of organic substances such as wood, coal, or peat. **2.** A solid residue of tobacco smoke. ►*v.* **tarred, tar·ring** To coat or surface with tar. [< OE *teru.*]

tar² (tär) ►*n.* A sailor. [Poss. < TARPAULIN.]

tar·an·tel·la (tăr′ən-těl′ə) ►*n.* **1.** A lively, whirling southern Italian dance. **2.** The music for this dance. [Ital. < *Taranto,* a city of SE Italy.]

ta·ran·tu·la (tə-răn′chə-lə) ►*n., pl.* **-las** or **-lae** (-lē′) Any of various large, hairy spiders capable of inflicting a painful bite. [< OItal. *tarantola* < *Taranto,* a city of SE Italy.]

Ta·ra·wa (tə-rä′wə, tär′ə-wä′, tä′rä-) The capital of Kiribati, on an atoll in the W-central Pacific.

tar·dy (tär′dē) ►*adj.* **-di·er, -di·est 1.** Not on time. **2.** Slow; sluggish. [< Lat. *tardus,* slow.] —**tar′di·ly** *adv.* —**tar′di·ness** *n.*
Syns: late, overdue **Ant:** *prompt* **adj.**

tare¹ (târ) ►*n.* Any of several weeds that grow in grain fields. [ME.]

tare² (târ) ►*n.* The weight of a container or wrapper that is deducted from the gross weight to obtain net weight. [< Ar. *ṭarḥ,* subtraction.]

tar·get (tär′gĭt) ►*n.* **1a.** An object that is shot at to test accuracy. **b.** Something aimed or fired at. **2.** An object of criticism or attack. **3.** A goal. [< OFr. *targe,* light shield.] —**tar′get** *v.*

tar·iff (tär′ĭf) ►*n.* **1a.** A list or system of duties imposed on imported or exported goods. **b.** A duty of this kind. **2.** A schedule of prices or fees. [< Ar. *ta′rīf,* notification.]

Tar·king·ton (tär′kĭng′tən), **(Newton) Booth** 1869–1946. Amer. writer.

tar·mac (tär′măk′) ►*n.* A bituminous road or surface, esp. an airport runway. [Originally a trademark.]

tarn (tärn) ►*n.* A small mountain lake. [ME *tarne,* of Scand. orig.]

tar·nish (tär′nĭsh) ►*v.* **1.** To make or become dull or discolored. **2.** To sully or taint. [< OFr. *ternir.*] —**tar′nish** *n.*

ta·ro (tär′ō, tăr′ō) ►*n., pl.* **-ros 1.** A tropical Asian plant with broad leaves and a large, starchy, edible tuber. **2.** The tuber of this plant. [Of Polynesian orig.]

tar·ot (tăr′ō, tə-rō′) ►*n.* Any of a set of playing cards used in fortunetelling. [< Ital. *tarocco.*]

tarp (tärp) ►*n. Informal* A tarpaulin.

tar·pa·per (tär′pā′pər) ►*n.* Heavy paper impregnated with tar, used as a waterproof building material.

tar·pau·lin (tär-pô′lĭn, tär′pə-) ►*n.* Material, such as waterproofed canvas, used to cover and protect things. [?]

tar·pon (tär′pən) ►*n., pl.* **-pon** or **-pons** A large marine game fish having a bluish-green back and silvery sides. [?]

tar·ra·gon (tăr′ə-gŏn′, -gən) ►*n.* An aromatic Eurasian herb with leaves used in seasoning. [< Ar. *ṭarḫūn.*]

tar·ry (tăr′ē) ►*v.* **-ried, -ry·ing 1.** To linger or be late. **2.** To wait or stay temporarily. [ME *tarien.*] —**tar′ri·er** *n.*

tar·sus (tär′səs) ►*n., pl.* **-si** (-sī, -sē) The section of the vertebrate foot between the leg and the metatarsus. [< Gk. *tarsos*, ankle.] —**tar′sal** *adj.*

tart¹ (tärt) ►*adj.* **-er, -est 1.** Having a sharp pungent taste; sour. See Synonyms at **sour. 2.** Caustic; cutting. [< OE *teart*, severe.] —**tart′ly** *adv.* —**tart′ness** *n.*

tart² (tärt) ►*n.* **1.** A pastry shell with shallow sides, no top crust, and any of various fillings. **2.** A prostitute. [< OFr. *tarte.*]

tar·tan (tär′tn) ►*n.* Any of numerous textile patterns consisting of stripes of varying widths and colors crossed at right angles. [Poss. < OFr. *tiretaine*, a kind of fabric.] —**tar′tan** *adj.*

tar·tar (tär′tər) ►*n.* **1.** *Dentistry* A hard yellowish deposit on the teeth. **2.** A reddish acid compound deposited on the sides of casks during winemaking. [< Med.Gk. *tartaron*, a chemical.]

Tartar ►*n.* See **Tatar.**

tartar sauce ►*n.* Mayonnaise mixed with chopped pickles and other ingredients and served as a condiment for fish.

Tar·ta·ry (tär′tə-rē) A region of E Europe and N Asia controlled by the Mongols in the 13th and 14th cent.

Tash·kent (tăsh-kĕnt′, täsh-) The capital of Uzbekistan, in the E part N of Dushanbe.

task (tăsk) ►*n.* **1.** A piece of assigned work. **2.** A difficult or tedious undertaking. —*idiom:* **take to task** To reprimand or censure. [< VLat. **taxa*, tax.]

task·bar (tăsk′bär′) ►*n.* A row of buttons on a computer screen that represent programs that are running.

task force ►*n.* A temporary grouping of forces for achieving a specific goal.

task·mas·ter (tăsk′măs′tər) ►*n.* One who regularly imposes difficult or demanding tasks.

Tas·ma·ni·a (tăz-mā′nē-ə, -mān′yə) An island of SE Australia separated from the mainland by Bass Strait. —**Tas·ma′ni·an** *adj. & n.*

Tas·man Sea (tăz′mən) An arm of the S Pacific between SE Australia and W New Zealand.

tas·sel (tăs′əl) ►*n.* **1.** A bunch of threads or cords bound at one end and hanging free at the other, used as an ornament. **2.** Something resembling this, esp. the male inflorescence of a corn plant. ►*v.* **-seled, -sel·ing** or **-selled, -sel·ling 1.** To fringe or decorate with tassels. **2.** To put forth a tassellike blossom. [ME.]

taste (tāst) ►*v.* **tast·ed, tast·ing 1.** To distinguish the flavor of by taking into the mouth. **2.** To eat or drink a small quantity of. **3.** To experience, esp. for the first time. **4.** To have a distinct flavor: *The stew tastes salty.* ►*n.* **1.** The sense that distinguishes the sweet, sour, salty, and bitter qualities of something placed in the mouth. **2.** The sensation produced by something in the mouth; flavor. **3.** A small quantity eaten or tasted. **4.** A limited or first experience. **5.** A personal preference. **6.** The ability to discern what is aesthetically appropriate: *a room furnished with taste.* [< VLat. **tastāre*, touch.] —**tast′a·ble** *adj.* —**tast′er** *n.*

taste bud ►*n.* Any of numerous clusters of cells on the tongue that are primarily responsible for the sense of taste.

taste·ful (tāst′fəl) ►*adj.* Having, showing, or in keeping with good taste. —**taste′ful·ly** *adv.* —**taste′ful·ness** *n.*

taste·less (tāst′lĭs) ►*adj.* **1.** Lacking flavor; insipid. **2.** Having or showing poor taste. —**taste′less·ly** *adv.* —**taste′less·ness** *n.*

tast·y (tā′stē) ►*adj.* **-i·er, -i·est** Having a pleasing flavor. —**tast′i·ly** *adv.* —**tast′i·ness** *n.*

tat (tăt) ►*v.* **tat·ted, tat·ting** To do or make by tatting. [Prob. < TATTING.] —**tat′ter** *n.*

ta·ta·mi (tä-tä′mē, tə-) ►*n., pl.* **-mi** or **-mis** Straw matting used as a floor covering esp. in a Japanese house. [J.]

Ta·tar (tä′tər) ►*n.* **1a.** A member of a group of Turkic peoples primarily inhabiting W-central Russia and parts of Siberia and central Asia. **b.** Any of the Turkic languages of the Tatars. **2.** A member of any of the Turkic and Mongolian peoples of central Asia who invaded W Asia and E Europe in the Middle Ages.

tat·ter (tăt′ər) ►*n.* A torn and hanging piece of cloth; shred. ►*v.* To make or become ragged. [ME *tater*, of Scand. orig.]

tat·ting (tăt′ĭng) ►*n.* **1.** Handmade lace made by looping and knotting a single strand of heavy thread on a small hand shuttle. **2.** The art of making such lace. [?]

tat·tle (tăt′l) ►*v.* **-tled, -tling 1.** To reveal the plans or activities of another: *tattled on his sister when she snuck out.* **2.** To prattle; prate. [ME *tatelen*, stammer.] —**tat′tler** *n.*

tat·tle·tale (tăt′l-tāl′) ►*n.* One who tells or tattles on others.

tat·too¹ (tă-to͞o′) ►*n., pl.* **-toos 1.** A call sounded to summon soldiers or sailors to quarters at night. **2.** A rhythmic tapping. [< Du. *taptoe.*] —**tat·too′** *v.*

tat·too² (tă-to͞o′) ►*n., pl.* **-toos** A permanent mark or design made on the skin by a process of pricking and ingraining an indelible pigment. ►*v.* To mark (the skin) with a tattoo. [Of Polynesian orig.] —**tat·too′er** *n.*

tau (tou, tô) ►*n.* The 19th letter of the Greek alphabet. [Gk.]

taught (tôt) ►*v.* P.t. and p.part. of **teach.**

taunt (tônt) ►*v.* **1.** To provoke or deride in a jeering manner. **2.** To tease and excite sexually. ►*n.* A jeer or gibe. [?] —**taunt′er** *n.* —**taunt′ing·ly** *adv.*

taupe (tōp) ►*n.* A brownish gray. [< Lat. *talpa*, mole.] —**taupe** *adj.*

Tau·rus (tôr′əs) ►*n.* **1.** A constellation in the Northern Hemisphere. **2.** The 2nd sign of the zodiac.

taut (tôt) ►*adj.* **-er, -est 1.** Tight; not slack. See Synonyms at **tight. 2.** Strained; tense. **3.** Trim; tidy. [ME *tohte*, distended.] —**taut′ly** *adv.* —**taut′ness** *n.*

tau·tol·o·gy (tô-tŏl′ə-jē) ►*n., pl.* **-gies 1.** Needless repetition of the same sense in different words. **2.** *Logic* A statement that includes all logical possibilities and is therefore always true. [< Gk. *tautologos*, redundant.] **—tau·to·log′i·cal** (tôt′l-ŏj′ĭ-kəl), **tau′to·log′ic** *adj.*

tav·ern (tăv′ərn) ►*n.* **1.** A saloon; bar. **2.** A roadside inn. [< Lat. *taberna*.]

taw·dry (tô′drē) ►*adj.* **-dri·er, -dri·est 1.** Gaudy and cheap. See Synonyms at **garish. 2.** Shameful; indecent: *tawdry secrets.* [Ult. after *Saint Audrey* (d. 679).] **—taw′dri·ly** *adv.* **—taw′dri·ness** *n.*

taw·ny (tô′nē) ►*n.* A light brown to brownish orange. [< AN *taune*, tanned.] **—taw′ni·ness** *n.* **—taw′ny** *adj.*

tax (tăks) ►*n.* **1.** A contribution for the support of a government required of persons, groups, or businesses within the domain of that government. **2.** An excessive demand; strain. ►*v.* **1.** To place a tax on (e.g., property). **2.** To exact a tax from. **3.** To make heavy demands upon. **4.** To accuse; confront: *taxed him with ingratitude.* [< Med.Lat. *taxāre*, to tax < Lat. *tangere*, touch.] **—tax′a·ble** *adj.* **—tax·a′tion** *n.* **—tax′er** *n.*

tax·i (tăk′sē) ►*n., pl.* **-is** or **-ies** A taxicab. ►*v.* **tax·ied** (tăk′sēd), **tax·i·ing** or **tax·y·ing 1.** To transport or be transported by taxi. **2.** To move slowly on the ground or water before takeoff or after landing.

tax·i·cab (tăk′sē-kăb′) ►*n.* An automobile that carries passengers for a fare. [< *taxi(meter)* (< Med.Lat. *taxa*, tax) + CAB.]

tax·i·der·my (tăk′sĭ-dûr′mē) ►*n.* The art or operation of stuffing and mounting animal skins in a lifelike state. [< TAX(O)– + Gk. *derma*, skin.] **—tax′i·der′mist** *n.*

tax·ing (tăk′sĭng) ►*adj.* Burdensome.

taxo– or **taxi–** or **tax–** ►*pref.* Order; arrangement: *taxonomy.* [< Gk. *taxis*.]

tax·on·o·my (tăk-sŏn′ə-mē) ►*n., pl.* **-mies 1.** The classification and naming of organisms in an ordered system intended to indicate natural relationships, esp. evolutionary relationships. **2.** The science, laws, or principles of classification. **3.** An ordered arrangement of groups or categories: *a taxonomy of literary genres.* **—tax′o·nom′ic** (tăk′sə-nŏm′ĭk) *adj.* **—tax′o·nom′i·cal·ly** *adv.* **—tax·on′o·mist** *n.*

tax·pay·er (tăks′pā′ər) ►*n.* One who pays taxes.

tax shelter ►*n.* A financial arrangement that reduces taxes on current earnings.

Tay·lor (tā′lər), Dame **Elizabeth Rosemond** 1932–2011. British-born Amer. actress.

Zachary Taylor
1860 portrait

Taylor, Zachary 1784–1850. The 12th US president (1849–50).

TB ►*abbr.* **1.** tailback **2.** terabyte **3.** tuberculosis

Tbi·li·si (tə-bə-lē′sē) The capital of Georgia, in the SE part WNW of Baku.

T-bone (tē′bōn′) ►*n.* A thick steak containing a T-shaped bone.

tbs. or **tbsp.** ►*abbr.* tablespoon

T cell ►*n.* Any of the lymphocytes that mature in the thymus and have the ability to recognize specific peptide antigens through the receptors on their cell surface. [*t(hymus-derived) cell.*]

Tchai·kov·sky (chī-kôf′skē), **Peter Ilich** 1840–93. Russian composer. **—Tchai·kov′sky·an, Tchai·kov′ski·an** *adj.*

TD ►*abbr.* touchdown

TDD ►*abbr.* telecommunications device for the deaf

TE ►*abbr. Football* tight end

tea (tē) ►*n.* **1a.** An Asian evergreen shrub or small tree having cup-shaped white flowers and glossy leaves. **b.** The dried processed leaves of this plant, used to make a beverage, usu. served hot. **2.** An aromatic, slightly bitter beverage made by steeping tea leaves in boiling water. **3.** Any similar drink prepared from the leaves of other plants. **4.** An afternoon reception or social gathering at which tea is served. **5.** *Slang* Marijuana. [< Chin. dial. *te.*]

tea bag ►*n.* A small porous sack holding enough tea leaves to make an individual serving of tea.

teach (tēch) ►*v.* **taught** (tôt), **teach·ing 1.** To impart knowledge or skill (to). **2.** To instruct in. **3.** To cause to learn by example or experience. [< OE *tǣcan.*] **—teach′a·bil′i·ty, teach′a·ble·ness** *n.* **—teach′a·ble** *adj.*

teach·er (tē′chər) ►*n.* One who teaches, esp. one hired to teach.

teach·ing (tē′chĭng) ►*n.* **1.** The work of a teacher. **2.** A precept or doctrine.

teak (tēk) ►*n.* **1.** An Asian tree with hard, durable yellowish-brown wood. **2.** The wood of this tree. [< Malayalam *tēkka.*]

tea·ket·tle (tē′kĕt′l) ►*n.* A covered kettle with a spout, used for boiling water, as for tea.

teal (tēl) ►*n., pl.* **teal** or **teals 1.** Any of several small wild ducks. **2.** A moderate bluish green. [ME *tele.*] **—teal** *adj.*

team (tēm) ►*n.* **1.** A group on the same side, as in a game. **2.** A group organized to work together. **3.** Two or more harnessed draft animals. See Usage Note at **collective noun.** ►*v.* **1.** To harness together to form a team. **2.** To form a team. [< OE *tēam.*]

team·mate (tēm′māt′) ►*n.* A fellow member of a team.

team·ster (tēm′stər) ►*n.* **1.** A truck driver. **2.** One who drives a team of draft animals.

team·work (tēm′wûrk′) ►*n.* Cooperative effort.

tea·pot (tē′pŏt′) ►*n.* A covered pot with a spout, used for making and serving tea.

tear¹ (târ) ►*v.* **tore** (tôr), **torn** (tôrn), **tear·ing 1a.** To pull apart or into pieces; rend. **b.** To lacerate. **2.** To make (an opening) by ripping. **3.** To separate forcefully; wrench: *tore the pipe from the wall.* **4.** To divide or disrupt: *was torn between choices.* **5.** To rush headlong. ►*n.* A rip or rent. **—phrasal verb: tear down** To demolish. **—idiom: tear (one's) hair** To be greatly upset or distressed. [< OE *teran.*]

tear² (tîr) ►*n.* **1.** A drop of the clear salty liquid that lubricates the surface between the eyeball and eyelid. **2. tears** The act of weeping. ►*v.* To become filled with tears. [< OE *tēar.*] —**tear′ful** *adj.* —**tear′ful·ly** *adv.* —**tear′i·ly** *adv.* —**tear′i·ness** *n.* —**tear′y** *adj.*

tear·drop (tîr′drŏp′) ►*n.* A single tear.

tear gas (tîr) ►*n.* Any of various agents that irritate the eyes and cause blinding tears.

tear·jerk·er (tîr′jûr′kər) ►*n. Slang* A very sad or sentimental story, drama, or performance.

tea·room (tē′rōōm′, -rŏŏm′) ►*n.* A restaurant serving tea and other refreshments.

tease (tēz) ►*v.* **teased, teas·ing 1a.** To make fun of (someone) playfully or annoyingly. **b.** To arouse sexual desire in (someone) deliberately with no intention of having sex. **2a.** To disentangle and dress the fibers of (wool). **b.** To ruffle (the hair) by combing toward the scalp. **c.** To raise the nap of (cloth). [< OE *tǣsan,* comb apart.] —**teas′er** *n.* —**teas′ing·ly** *adv.*

tea·sel (tē′zəl) ►*n.* **1.** A plant with prickly stems and flower heads surrounded by spiny bracts. **2.** Its bristly flower head, used to raise a nap on fabrics. [< OE *tǣsel.*]

tea·spoon (tē′spōōn′) ►*n.* **1.** The common small spoon used esp. with tea, coffee, and desserts. **2.** A household cooking measure equal to ⅓ tablespoon (about 5 ml). —**tea′spoon·ful** *n.*

teat (tēt, tĭt) ►*n.* A nipple of the mammary gland. [< OFr. *tete,* of Gmc. orig.]

Te·bal·di (tə-bäl′dē, tĕ-), **Renata** 1922–2004. Italian-born operatic soprano.

tech (tĕk) *Informal* ►*n.* **1.** A technician. **2.** Technology. **3.** Technical work. ►*adj.* Technical.

tech·ne·ti·um (tĕk-nē′shē-əm, -shəm) ►*n. Symbol* **Tc** A silvery-gray radioactive metal, the first synthetically produced element. At. no. 43. See table at **element.** [< Gk. *tekhnētos,* artificial; see TECHNICAL.]

tech·ni·cal (tĕk′nĭ-kəl) ►*adj.* **1.** Of or relating to technique. **2.** Specialized. **3.** Of the practical, mechanical, or industrial arts: *a technical school.* **4.** Relating to technology or technological studies. **5.** Relating to the methodology of science; scientific. **6a.** Strictly or narrowly defined. **b.** Based on analysis or principle; theoretical rather than practical: *a technical distinction.* [< Gk. *tekhnē,* skill.] —**tech′ni·cal·ly** *adv.*

tech·ni·cal·i·ty (tĕk′nĭ-kăl′ĭ-tē) ►*n., pl.* **-ties 1.** The quality or condition of being technical. **2.** Something meaningful only to a specialist: *a legal technicality.*

technical sergeant ►*n.* A rank in the US Air Force above staff sergeant.

tech·ni·cian (tĕk-nĭsh′ən) ►*n.* An expert in a technical field or process.

Tech·ni·col·or (tĕk′nĭ-kŭl′ər) A trademark for a method of making color movies.

tech·nique (tĕk-nēk′) ►*n.* **1.** The basic method for making or doing something, such as an artistic work or scientific procedure. **2.** Skill or command in a particular activity. See Synonyms at **skill.** [Fr. < Gk. *tekhnikos,* TECHNICAL.]

tech·noc·ra·cy (tĕk-nŏk′rə-sē) ►*n., pl.* **-cies** Government by technicians or technical experts. [Gk. *tekhnē,* skill; see TECHNICAL + –CRACY.] —**tech′no·crat** *n.* —**tech′no·crat′ic** *adj.*

tech·nol·o·gy (tĕk-nŏl′ə-jē) ►*n., pl.* **-gies 1.**

The application of science, esp. in industry or commerce. **2.** The scientific methods and materials thus used. [< Gk. *tekhnē,* skill + -LOGY.] —**tech′no·log′i·cal** (-nə-lŏj′ĭ-kəl) *adj.* —**tech′no·log′i·cal·ly** *adv.* —**tech·nol′o·gist** *n.*

tech·no·pho·bi·a (tĕk′nə-fō′bē-ə) ►*n.* Fear of technology, esp. computers. —**tech′no·phobe′** *n.* —**tech′no·pho′bic** *adj.*

tec·ton·ics (tĕk-tŏn′ĭks) ►*n. (takes sing. v.)* **1.** The geology of the earth's structural features. **2.** The art of large-scale construction. [< Gk. *tektōn,* builder.] —**tec·ton′ic** *adj.*

Te·cum·seh (tĭ-kŭm′sə) 1768–1813. Shawnee leader.

ted·dy bear also **Ted·dy bear** (tĕd′ē) ►*n.* A child's toy bear. [After *Teddy,* nickname of Theodore Roosevelt.]

te·di·ous (tē′dē-əs) ►*adj.* Tiresomely long or dull; boring. [< Lat. *taedium,* TEDIUM.] —**te′di·ous·ly** *adv.* —**te′di·ous·ness** *n.*

te·di·um (tē′dē-əm) ►*n.* Boredom; monotony. [Lat. *taedium* < *taedēre,* to weary.]

tee (tē) ►*n.* **1.** A small peg with a concave top for holding a golf ball for an initial drive. **2.** The area of each golf hole from which the initial drive is made. ►*v.* To place (a golf ball) on a tee. —*phrasal verb:* **tee off 1.** To drive a golf ball from the tee. **2.** *Slang* To start. [< obsolete Sc. *teaz.*]

teem (tēm) ►*v.* To abound or swarm. [< OE *tīeman,* beget.] —**teem′ing·ly** *adv.*
    Syns: abound, overflow, swarm **v.**

teen (tēn) ►*n.* **1. teens a.** The numbers 10 through 19 or 13 through 19. **b.** The 10th through 19th items in a series or scale: *temperatures in the low teens.* **c.** The years of life between ages 13 and 19. **2.** A teenager. ►*adj.* Teenage.

teen·age or **teen-age** (tēn′āj′) also **teen·aged** or **teen-aged** (-ājd′) ►*adj.* Of, for, or involving those aged 13 through 19. —**teen′ag′er** *n.*

tee·ny (tē′nē) also **teen·sy** (tēn′sē) ►*adj.* **-ni·er, -ni·est** also **-si·er, -si·est** *Informal* Tiny. [< TINY.]

tee·pee (tē′pē) ►*n.* Var. of **tepee.**

tee shirt ►*n.* Var. of **T-shirt.**

tee·ter (tē′tər) ►*v.* **1.** To move unsteadily; totter. **2.** To seesaw; vacillate. [ME *titeren.*]

tee·ter-tot·ter (tē′tər-tŏt′ər) ►*n.* See **seesaw** (sense 1).

teeth (tēth) ►*n.* Pl. of **tooth.**

teethe (tēth) ►*v.* **teethed, teeth·ing** To have the teeth emerge from the gums. [ME *tethen* < *teth,* teeth.]

tee·to·tal·er (tē′tōt′l-ər) ►*n.* One who abstains completely from alcoholic beverages. [< *tee,* pronunciation of 1st letter in *total* + *total (abstinence).*] —**tee·to′tal·ism** *n.*

TEFL ►*abbr.* teaching English as a foreign language

Tef·lon (tĕf′lŏn′) A trademark for a nonstick material used to coat cooking utensils.

Te·gu·ci·gal·pa (tĕ-gōō′sē-gäl′pä) The capital of Honduras, in the S-central part.

Teh·ran or **Te·he·ran** (tĕ′ə-rän′, -rän′, tĕ-rän′, -rän′) The capital of Iran, in the N-central part.

tek·tite (tĕk′tīt′) ►*n.* A dark glassy rock of possibly meteoric origin. [< Gk. *tēktos,* molten.]

tel. ►*abbr.* telephone

Tel A·viv–Ya·fo (tĕl′ä-vēv′yä′fō) or **Tel A·viv–**

Jaf·fa (-jăf′ə, -yä′fə) A city of W-central Israel on the Mediterranean WNW of Jerusalem.

tele– or **tel–** ►*pref.* **1.** Distance; distant: *telepathy.* **2a.** Telegraph; telephone: *telegram.* **b.** Television: *telecast.* [< Gk. *tēle*, far off.]

tel·e·cast (tĕl′ĭ-kăst′) ►*v.* To broadcast by television. —**tel′e·cast′** *n.*

tel·e·com·mu·ni·ca·tion (tĕl′ĭ-kə-myōō′-nĭ-kā′shən) ►*n.* often **telecommunications** *(takes sing. v.)* The technology of sending messages by electrical or electronic means.

tel·e·com·mute (tĕl′ĭ-kə-myōōt′) ►*v.* **-mut·ed, -mut·ing** To work at home using a computer connected to the network of one's employer. —**tel′e·com·mut′er** *n.*

tel·e·con·fer·ence (tĕl′ĭ-kŏn′fər-əns, -frəns) ►*n.* A conference held among people in different locations by means of a telecommunications network.

tel·e·gen·ic (tĕl′ə-jĕn′ĭk) ►*adj.* Presenting an appealing appearance on television. [TELE– + (PHOTO)GENIC.]

tel·e·gram (tĕl′ĭ-grăm′) ►*n.* A message sent by telegraph.

tel·e·graph (tĕl′ĭ-grăf′) ►*n.* A communications system that transmits and receives simple electric impulses, esp. one in which the transmission and reception stations are directly connected by wires. ►*v.* To transmit (a message) by telegraph. —**te·leg′ra·pher** (tə-lĕg′rə-fər), **te·leg′ra·phist** *n.* —**tel′e·graph′ic** *adj.* —**tel′e·graph′i·cal·ly** *adv.* —**te·leg′ra·phy** *n.*

tel·e·ki·ne·sis (tĕl′ĭ-kĭ-nē′sĭs, -kī-) ►*n.* The supposed inducement of movement of an object by mental or spiritual power. [TELE– + Gk. *kinēsis*, movement.] —**tel′e·ki·net′ic** (-nĕt′ĭk) *adj.*

tel·e·mar·ket·ing (tĕl′ə-mar′ki-ting) ►*n.* The business of marketing goods or services by telephone. —**tel′e·mar′ket·er** *n.*

te·lem·e·try (tə-lĕm′ĭ-trē) ►*n.* The automatic measurement and transmission of data from remote sources. —**tel′e·me′ter** (tĕl′ə-mē′-tər) *n.* —**tel′e·met′ric** (tĕl′ə-mĕt′rĭk), **tel·e·met′ri·cal** *adj.*

te·lep·a·thy (tə-lĕp′ə-thē) ►*n.* The supposed process of communicating through means other than the senses. —**tel′e·path′ic** (tĕl′ə-păth′ĭk) *adj.* —**tel′e·path′i·cal·ly** *adv.* —**te·lep′a·thist** *n.*

tel·e·phone (tĕl′ə-fōn′) ►*n.* An instrument that converts voice and other sound signals into a form that can be transmitted to remote locations. ►*v.* **-phoned, -phon·ing** To try to make a telephone connection with; place a call to: *telephoned the police station.*

telephone exchange ►*n.* A central system of switches and other equipment that establishes connections between telephones.

te·leph·o·ny (tə-lĕf′ə-nē) ►*n.* The transmission of sound between distant stations, esp. by radio or telephone. —**tel′e·phon′ic** (tĕl′-ə-fŏn′ĭk) *adj.*

tel·e·pho·to (tĕl′ə-fō′tō) ►*adj.* Of or relating to a photographic lens or lens system used to produce a large image of a distant object.

tel·e·play (tĕl′ə-plā′) ►*n.* A play written or adapted for television.

tel·e·scope (tĕl′ĭ-skōp′) ►*n.* **1.** An arrangement of lenses or mirrors or both that gathers light, permitting direct observation or photographic recording of distant objects. **2.** Any of various devices used to detect and observe distant objects by their emission, absorption, or reflection of electromagnetic radiation. ►*v.* **-scoped, -scop·ing 1.** To slide inward or outward in overlapping sections, as the cylindrical sections of a small hand telescope do. **2.** To condense. —**tel′e·scop′ic** (-skŏp′ĭk) *adj.*

tel·e·thon (tĕl′ə-thŏn′) ►*n.* A lengthy television program to raise funds for a charity. [TELE– + (MARA)THON.]

tel·e·type·writ·er (tĕl′ĭ-tīp′rī′tər) ►*n.* An electromechanical typewriter that transmits or receives messages coded in electrical signals.

tel·e·vise (tĕl′ə-vīz′) ►*v.* **-vised, -vis·ing** To broadcast by television. [< TELEVISION.]

tel·e·vi·sion (tĕl′ə-vĭzh′ən) ►*n.* **1a.** An electronic broadcast system in which providers transmit video content, often on multiple channels: *a new sitcom in television.* **b.** An electronic device for viewing television programs and movies, consisting of a display screen and speakers: *sat too close to the television.* **2.** The industry of producing and broadcasting television programs: *made her fortune in television.*

tel·ex (tĕl′ĕks′) ►*n.* **1.** A communications system consisting of teletypewriters connected to a telephonic network. **2.** A message sent or received by telex. [TEL(ETYPEWRITER) + EX(CHANGE).] —**tel′ex′** *v.*

tell (tĕl) ►*v.* **told** (tōld), **tell·ing 1a.** To express with words. **b.** To give an account of; narrate. **c.** To notify; inform. **d.** To give instructions to; direct. **2.** To discover by observation; discern: *I can tell that you are upset.* **3.** To have an effect or impact: *In this game every move tells.* —*phrasal verb:* **tell off** *Informal* To rebuke severely; reprimand. [< OE *tellan.*]

tell·er (tĕl′ər) ►*n.* A bank employee who receives and pays out money.

Teller, Edward 1908–2003. Hungarian-born Amer. physicist.

tell·ing (tĕl′ĭng) ►*adj.* Having force or effect; striking. —**tell′ing·ly** *adv.*

tell·tale (tĕl′tāl′) ►*n.* **1.** A tattletale; talebearer. **2.** An indicator; sign.

tel·lu·ri·um (tĕ-lŏŏr′ē-əm) ►*n. Symbol* **Te** A brittle, silvery-white metallic element used in compact discs, semiconductors, ceramics, and thermoelectric devices. At. no. 52. See table at **element.** [< Lat. *tellūs*, earth.]

te·mer·i·ty (tə-mĕr′ĭ-tē) ►*n.* Foolhardiness or recklessness. [< Lat. *temere*, rashly.]

temp. ►*abbr.* **1.** temperature **2.** temporary **3.** *Lat.* tempore (in the time of)

tem·peh (tĕm′pā′) ►*n.* A high-protein food made from partially cooked, fermented soybeans. [Indonesian *tempe.*]

tem·per (tĕm′pər) ►*v.* **1.** To soften or moderate. See Synonyms at **moderate. 2.** To harden or strengthen (e.g., metal), as by alternate heating and cooling. ►*n.* **1.** A state of mind or emotion; disposition. **2.** Calmness; composure. **3a.** A tendency to become angry or irritable. **b.** Anger; rage: *a fit of temper.* **4.** The degree of hardness of a metal. [< Lat. *temperāre.*]

tem·per·a (tĕm′pər-ə) ►*n.* **1.** A painting medium in which pigment is mixed with water-soluble glutinous materials such as size or egg yolk. **2.** Painting done in this medium. [Ital. <

temperare, mingle; see TEMPER.]

tem·per·a·ment (tĕm′prə-mənt, tĕm′pər-ə-) ►*n.* **1.** The manner of thinking, behaving, or reacting characteristic of a particular person. **2.** Excessive irritability or sensitiveness. [< Lat. *temperāre,* temper.] —**tem′per·a·men′tal** *adj.* —**tem′per·a·men′tal·ly** *adv.*

tem·per·ance (tĕm′pər-əns, -prəns) ►*n.* **1.** Abstinence from alcoholic liquors. **2.** Moderation and self-restraint.

tem·per·ate (tĕm′pər-ĭt, -prĭt) ►*adj.* **1a.** Of or occurring in the Temperate Zone: *temperate species.* **b.** Not subject to extreme hot or cold weather. **2a.** Moderate; restrained. **b.** Exercising moderation and self-restraint. —**tem′per·ate·ly** *adv.* —**tem′per·ate·ness** *n.*

Temperate Zone Either of two latitude zones of the earth, the **North Temperate Zone,** between the Arctic Circle and the tropic of Cancer, or the **South Temperate Zone,** between the Antarctic Circle and the tropic of Capricorn.

tem·per·a·ture (tĕm′pər-ə-chŏor′, -chər, tĕm′-prə-) ►*n.* **1.** The hotness or coldness of a body or environment. **2.** Abnormally high body heat; fever. [< Lat. *temperāre,* temper.]

tem·pered (tĕm′pərd) ►*adj.* Having a specified temper or disposition.

tem·pest (tĕm′pĭst) ►*n.* A violent windstorm. [< Lat. *tempestās < tempus,* time.]

tem·pes·tu·ous (tĕm-pĕs′chŏo-əs) ►*adj.* Tumultuous; stormy. —**tem·pes′tu·ous·ly** *adv.* —**tem·pes′tu·ous·ness** *n.*

tem·plate (tĕm′plĭt) ►*n.* **1.** A pattern or gauge, such as a thin metal plate, used as a guide in making something accurately. **2.** *Comp.* A document or file having a format that is set automatically or in advance. [Prob. < OFr. *temple,* device in a loom.]

tem·ple¹ (tĕm′pəl) ►*n.* **1.** A building dedicated to religious ceremonies or worship. **2.** *Judaism* A synagogue, esp. of a Reform congregation. [< Lat. *templum.*]

tem·ple² (tĕm′pəl) ►*n.* **1.** The flat region on either side of the forehead. **2.** The sidepiece of an eyeglass frame. [< Lat. *tempus.*]

tem·po (tĕm′pō) ►*n., pl.* **-pos** or **-pi** (-pē) **1.** The speed at which music is to be played. **2.** A pace. [Ital. < Lat. *tempus,* time.]

tem·po·ral¹ (tĕm′pər-əl, -prəl) ►*adj.* **1.** Of or limited by time. **2.** Worldly; secular. [< Lat. *tempus, tempor-,* time.] —**tem′po·ral·ly** *adv.*

tem·po·ral² (tĕm′pər-əl, -prəl) ►*adj.* Of or near the temples of the skull. [< Lat. *tempus, tempor-,* temple.]

temporal bone ►*n.* Either of two bones that form the sides and base of the skull.

tem·po·rar·y (tĕm′pə-rĕr′ē) ►*adj.* Lasting or used for a limited time. ►*n., pl.* **-ies** One that works or serves for a limited time. —**tem′po·rar′i·ly** *adv.*

*Syns: acting, interim, provisional **Ant:** permanent **adj.***

tem·po·rize (tĕm′pə-rīz′) ►*v.* **-rized, -riz·ing** **1.** To gain time, as by postponing an action or decision. **2.** To yield to current conditions; compromise. [< Lat. *tempus, tempor-,* time.] —**tem′po·ri·za′tion** *n.*

tempt (tĕmpt) ►*v.* **1.** To try to get (someone) to do wrong, esp. by a promise of reward. **2.** To be attractive to. **3.** To risk provoking: *tempt*

fate. **4.** To incline or dispose: *I'm tempted to go.* [< Lat. *temptāre,* try.] —**temp·ta′tion** *n.* —**tempt′er** *n.*

tempt·ress (tĕmp′trĭs) ►*n.* A usu. sexually alluring woman who repeatedly seduces or manipulates others. See Usage Note at **–ess.**

tem·pu·ra (tĕm′pŏo-rə, tĕm-pŏor′ə) ►*n.* A Japanese dish of deep-fried batter-dipped vegetables and shrimp or other seafood. [J.]

ten (tĕn) ►*n.* **1.** The cardinal number equal to 9 + 1. **2.** The 10th in a set or sequence. [< OE *tīen.*] —**ten** *adj. & pron.*

ten·a·ble (tĕn′ə-bəl) ►*adj.* Defensible: *a tenable theory.* [< Lat. *tenēre,* hold.] —**ten′a·bil′i·ty, ten′a·ble·ness** *n.* —**ten′a·bly** *adv.*

te·na·cious (tə-nā′shəs) ►*adj.* **1.** Extremely persistent; stubborn. **2.** Clinging; adhesive. **3.** Tending to retain; retentive: *a tenacious memory.* [< Lat. *tenāx.*] —**te·na′cious·ly** *adv.* —**te·nac′i·ty** (-năs′ĭ-tē), **te·na′cious·ness** *n.*

ten·an·cy (tĕn′ən-sē) ►*n., pl.* **-cies 1.** Possession or occupancy of land or buildings by title, lease, or rent. **2.** The period of a tenant's occupancy or possession.

ten·ant (tĕn′ənt) ►*n.* **1.** One that pays rent to use or occupy property owned by another. **2.** An occupant. [< Lat. *tenēre,* hold.]

Ten Commandments ►*pl.n. Bible* The ten laws given by God to Moses on Mount Sinai.

tend¹ (tĕnd) ►*v.* **1.** To have a tendency. **2.** To be likely. **3.** To move or extend in a certain direction. [< Lat. *tendere.*]

tend² (tĕnd) ►*v.* **1.** To take care of. **2.** To serve at: *tend bar.* **3.** To apply one's attention; attend. [< ME *attenden,* ATTEND.]

*Syns: attend, mind, minister, watch **v.***

ten·den·cy (tĕn′dən-sē) ►*n., pl.* **-cies 1.** An inclination to think, act, or behave in a particular way: *his tendency to exaggerate.* **2.** A characteristic likelihood: *a fabric with a tendency to wrinkle.*

ten·den·tious (tĕn-dĕn′shəs) ►*adj.* Favoring a particular point of view; partisan. [< Lat. *tendēns,* tending.]

ten·der¹ (tĕn′dər) ►*adj.* **-er, -est 1a.** Delicate; fragile. **b.** Easily chewed. **2.** Young and vulnerable. **3.** Sensitive or sore. **4.** Gentle and loving. **5.** Sentimental; soft. [< Lat. *tener.*] —**ten′der·ly** *adv.* —**ten′der·ness** *n.*

ten·der² (tĕn′dər) ►*n.* **1.** A formal offer. **2.** Money: *legal tender.* ►*v.* To offer formally. [< Lat. *tendere,* extend.] —**ten′der·er** *n.*

tend·er³ (tĕn′dər) ►*n.* **1.** One who tends something. **2.** *Naut.* A vessel attendant on other vessels. **3.** A railroad car attached to the locomotive, carrying fuel and water.

ten·der·foot (tĕn′dər-fŏot′) ►*n., pl.* **-foots** or **-feet** An inexperienced person; novice.

ten·der·heart·ed (tĕn′dər-här′tĭd) ►*adj.* Compassionate. —**ten′der·heart′ed·ly** *adv.* —**ten′der·heart′ed·ness** *n.*

ten·der·ize (tĕn′də-rīz′) ►*v.* **-ized, -iz·ing** To make (meat) tender. —**ten′der·iz′er** *n.*

ten·der·loin (tĕn′dər-loin′) ►*n.* The tenderest part of a loin of beef or pork.

ten·di·ni·tis also **ten·do·ni·tis** (tĕn′də-nī′tĭs) ►*n.* Inflammation of a tendon. [< NLat. *tendō, tendin-,* TENDON.]

ten·don (tĕn′dən) ►*n.* A band of tough fibrous tissue that connects a muscle with its bony attachment. [< Gk. *tenōn.*]

ten·dril (tĕn′drəl) ►*n.* **1.** A twisting threadlike structure by which a twining plant clings to a support. **2.** Something resembling this. [< OFr. *tendrillon*, tender young shoot.]

ten·e·ment (tĕn′ə-mənt) ►*n.* **1.** A building to live in, esp. one rented to tenants. **2.** A run-down, low-rental apartment building whose facilities and upkeep barely meet minimum standards. [< Lat. *tenēre*, hold.]

ten·et (tĕn′ĭt) ►*n.* A doctrine, principle, or position held as part of a philosophy, religion, or field of endeavor. [< Lat. *tenēre*, hold.]

ten-gal·lon hat (tĕn′găl′ən) ►*n.* A hat having a high rounded crown and a wide brim.

ten·ge (tĕn-gĕ′) ►*n., pl.* **tenge** See table at **currency.** [Kazakh and Turkmen.]

Ten·nes·see (tĕn′ĭ-sē′, tĕn′ĭ-sē′) A state of the SE US. Cap. Nashville. —**Ten′nes·se′an** *adj.* & *n.*

ten·nis (tĕn′ĭs) ►*n.* A game played with rackets and a light ball by two or four players on a court divided by a net. [< AN *tenetz*, hold!]

tennis shoe ►*n.* See **sneaker.**

Ten·ny·son (tĕn′ĭ-sən), **Alfred.** 1st Baron Tennyson. 1809–92. British poet.

Te·noch·ti·tlán (tĕ-nôch′tē-tlän′) An ancient Aztec capital on the site of present-day Mexico City.

ten·on (tĕn′ən) ►*n.* A projection on a piece of wood that is shaped for insertion into a mortise in order to make a joint. [< OFr. < Lat. *tenēre*, hold.]

ten·or (tĕn′ər) ►*n.* **1.** The general character of something. **2.** Purport or drift: *the tenor of your message.* **3.** *Mus.* **a.** The highest natural adult male voice. **b.** The range between alto and bass. **c.** A singer, voice, or instrument having this range. [< Lat. < *tenēre*, hold.]

ten·pin (tĕn′pĭn′) ►*n.* **1.** One of the bottle-shaped pins used in bowling. **2. tenpins** *(takes sing. v.)* See **bowling** (sense 1a).

tense¹ (tĕns) ►*adj.* **tens·er, tens·est** **1.** Tightly stretched; taut. See Synonyms at **tight. 2a.** Feeling mental or nervous tension: *was very tense before the exam.* **b.** Nerve-racking; suspenseful: *a tense standoff.* ►*v.* **tensed, tens·ing** To make or become tense. [Lat. *tēnsus*, p.part. of *tendere*, stretch.] —**tense′ly** *adv.* —**tense′ness** *n.*

tense² (tĕns) ►*n.* **1.** Any of the inflected forms of a verb that indicate the time and continuance or completion of the action or state. **2.** A set of tense forms indicating a particular time: *How is the future tense made in Spanish?* [< Lat. *tempus*, time.]

ten·sile (tĕn′səl, -sīl′) ►*adj.* **1.** Of or relating to tension. **2.** Capable of being stretched or extended. [< Lat. *tēnsus*, stretched.] —**ten·sil′i·ty** (tĕn-sĭl′ĭ-tē) *n.*

ten·sion (tĕn′shən) ►*n.* **1.** The act of stretching or the condition of being stretched. **2.** A force tending to stretch or elongate something. **3a.** Mental strain. **b.** A strained relationship between people or groups. **4.** The interplay of conflicting elements in a piece of art. **5.** Voltage. [< Lat. *tendere, tēns-*, stretch.]

ten·sor (tĕn′sər, -sôr′) ►*n.* A muscle that tenses a body part.

tent (tĕnt) ►*n.* A portable shelter made of fabric or other material stretched over a supporting framework of poles and usu. secured to the ground with cords and stakes. [< VLat. **tendita*, stretched.]

ten·ta·cle (tĕn′tə-kəl) ►*n.* **1.** An elongated flexible extension, as one of those surrounding the mouth of a sea anemone, used for grasping or locomotion. **2.** One of these structures in a cephalopod, usu. being retractile and having a club with suckers or hooks at the tip. [< Lat. *tentāre*, feel.] —**ten·tac′u·lar** (-tăk′yə-lər) *adj.*

ten·ta·tive (tĕn′tə-tĭv) ►*adj.* **1.** Not fully worked out or concluded; provisional. **2.** Uncertain; hesitant. [< Lat. *tentāre*, try.] —**ten′ta·tive·ly** *adv.* —**ten′ta·tive·ness** *n.*

ten·ter·hook (tĕn′tər-hŏŏk′) ►*n.* A hooked nail for securing cloth on a drying framework. —*idiom:* **on tenterhooks** In a state of suspense or anxiety. [*tenter*, framework for drying + HOOK.]

tenth (tĕnth) ►*n.* **1.** The ordinal number matching the number 10 in a series. **2.** One of ten equal parts. —**tenth** *adv.* & *adj.*

ten·u·ous (tĕn′yōō-əs) ►*adj.* **1.** Insubstantial; flimsy: *a tenuous link between the suspects.* **2.** Precarious: *tenuous survival.* **3.** Long and thin; slender. **4.** Rarefied. [< Lat. *tenuis.*] —**ten′u·ous·ly** *adv.* —**ten′u·ous·ness, te·nu′i·ty** (tĕ-nōō′ĭ-tē, -nyōō′-) *n.*

ten·ure (tĕn′yər, -yŏŏr′) ►*n.* **1a.** The holding of something, as an office or real estate. **b.** A period during which something is held. **2.** The status of holding one's position on a permanent basis. [< Lat. *tenēre*, hold.]

Te·o·ti·hua·cán (tā′ə-tē′wä-kän′) An ancient city of central Mexico.

te·pee also **tee·pee** or **ti·pi** (tē′pē) ►*n.* A portable dwelling of certain Native American peoples, consisting of a conical framework of poles covered with skins or bark. [Sioux *tʰípi*, dwelling.]

tep·id (tĕp′ĭd) ►*adj.* Moderately warm; lukewarm. [< Lat. *tepēre*, be lukewarm.] —**te·pid′i·ty, tep′id·ness** *n.* —**tep′id·ly** *adv.*

te·qui·la (tə-kē′lə) ►*n.* An alcoholic liquor distilled from an agave. [After *Tequila,* Mexico.]

tera– ►*pref.* One trillion (10^{12}): *terabyte.* [< Gk. *teras,* monster.]

ter·a·bit (tĕr′ə-bĭt′) ►*n. Comp.* **1.** One trillion bits. **2.** 1,099,511,627,776 (2^{40}) bits.

ter·a·byte (tĕr′ə-bīt′) ►*n.* **1.** A unit of computer memory or data storage capacity equal to 1,024 gigabytes (2^{40} bytes). **2.** One trillion bytes.

te·rat·o·gen (tə-răt′ə-jən, tĕr′ə-tə-) ►*n.* An agent, such as a drug, that causes malformation of an embryo or fetus. [Gk. *teras, terat-,* monster + –GEN.] —**ter′a·to·gen′ic** *adj.*

ter·bi·um (tûr′bē-əm) ►*n. Symbol* **Tb** A soft, silvery-gray rare-earth element, used in cathode-ray tubes and low-energy lighting applications. At. no. 65. See table at **element.** [After *Ytterby,* Sweden.]

ter·cen·ten·a·ry (tûr′sĕn-tĕn′ə-rē, tər-sĕn′tə-nĕr′ē) ►*n., pl.* **-ries** A 300th anniversary. [Lat. *ter,* thrice + CENTENARY.] —**ter′cen·ten′a·ry** *adj.*

Ter·ence (tĕr′əns) 185?–159? BC. Carthaginian-born Roman playwright.

Te·re·sa (tə-rē′sə, -zə, -rā′-), Mother. 1910–97. Albanian-born Indian nun.

Te·resh·ko·va (tə-rĕsh-kō′və), **Valentina Vladmirovna** b. 1937. Soviet cosmonaut; first woman in space (1963).

Mother Teresa
photographed in 1993

Valentina Tereshkova
photographed in 2005

ter·i·ya·ki (tĕr′ē-yä′kē) ►*n.* A Japanese dish of grilled or broiled slices of marinated meat or shellfish. [J.]

term (tûrm) ►*n.* **1a.** A limited or established period of time that something is supposed to last, as tenure in public office or a prison sentence. **b.** An end or termination. **c.** The end of a normal gestation period: *carried the fetus to term.* **d.** A deadline, as for making a payment. **2a.** A word or phrase having a particular meaning, esp. in a specific field. **b. terms** Language of a certain kind: *praised him in glowing terms.* **3.** often **terms** A stipulation or condition: *peace terms.* **4. terms** The relationship between persons or groups: *on good terms.* **5.** *Math.* One of the quantities in a fraction, equation, or series. ►*v.* To designate; call. [< Lat. *terminus,* boundary.]

ter·ma·gant (tûr′mə-gənt) ►*n.* A quarrelsome or scolding woman; shrew. [ME *Termagaunt,* character in medieval mystery plays.]

ter·mi·nal (tûr′mə-nəl) ►*adj.* **1.** Of or forming a limit, boundary, or end. **2.** Concluding; final. **3.** Of or occurring in a term or each term. **4.** Ending in death; fatal. ►*n.* **1.** A point or part that forms the end. **2.** *Elect.* A position in a circuit at which a connection is normally established or broken. **3a.** A railroad or bus station, esp. a terminus. **b.** A building in an airport where travelers board and get off airplanes. **4.** A device, usu. having a keyboard and video display, through which data can be entered or displayed. [< Lat. *terminus,* boundary.] —**ter′mi·nal·ly** *adv.*

ter·mi·nate (tûr′mə-nāt′) ►*v.* **-nat·ed, -nat·ing** To bring or come to an end; conclude. —**ter′mi·na·ble** *adj.* —**ter′mi·na′tion** *n.* —**ter′mi·na′tive** *adj.* —**ter′mi·na′tor** *n.*

ter·mi·nol·o·gy (tûr′mə-nŏl′ə-jē) ►*n., pl.* **-gies 1.** The technical terms of a particular field, science, or art. **2.** The study of such terms. [< Med. Lat. *terminus,* expression.] —**ter′mi·no·log′i·cal** (-nə-lŏj′ĭ-kəl) *adj.*

ter·mi·nus (tûr′mə-nəs) ►*n., pl.* **-nus·es** or **-ni** (-nī′) **1.** The final point; end. **2.** An endpoint on a transportation line. [Lat.]

ter·mite (tûr′mīt′) ►*n.* Any of numerous antlike social insects that often feed on wood. [< LLat. *termes,* wood-eating worm.]

term limits ►*pl.n.* A restriction on the number of terms an official may serve.

tern (tûrn) ►*n.* Any of various seabirds resembling gulls but usu. smaller and having a forked tail. [Of Scand. orig.]

ter·na·ry (tûr′nə-rē) ►*adj.* **1.** Composed of three or arranged in threes. **2.** *Math.* **a.** Having the base three. **b.** Involving three variables. [< Lat. *ternī,* three each.]

terp·si·cho·re·an (tûrp′sĭ-kə-rē′ən, -kôr′ē-ən) ►*adj.* Of dancing. ►*n.* A dancer. [< *Terpsichore,* Greek Muse of dancing.]

Terr. ►*abbr.* **1.** terrace **2.** territory

ter·race (tĕr′ĭs) ►*n.* **1.** A porch or balcony. **2.** An open area adjacent to a house serving as an outdoor living space. **3.** A raised bank of earth having a flat top. **4.** A row of buildings on raised or sloping ground. **5.** A residential street, esp. along the top or slope of a hill. ►*v.* **-raced, -rac·ing** To form into terraces. [< VLat. **terrācea* < Lat. *terra,* earth.]

ter·ra cot·ta (tĕr′ə kŏt′ə) ►*n.* **1.** A hard ceramic clay used in pottery and construction. **2.** A brownish orange. [Ital.] —**ter′ra-cot′ta** *adj.*

terra fir·ma (fûr′mə) ►*n.* Dry land. [NLat., solid ground.]

ter·rain (tə-rān′) ►*n.* **1.** An area of land; ground. **2.** Topography: *rugged terrain.* [< Lat. *terrēnus,* of the earth.]

ter·ra·pin (tĕr′ə-pĭn) ►*n.* A turtle of coast areas of the E and S US, having a ridged or knobbed carapace. [Of Virginia Algonquian orig.]

ter·rar·i·um (tə-râr′ē-əm) ►*n., pl.* **-i·ums** or **-i·a** (-ē-ə) A closed container in which plants and sometimes small animals, such as turtles and lizards, are kept. [Lat. *terra,* earth + –ARIUM.]

ter·res·tri·al (tə-rĕs′trē-əl) ►*adj.* **1.** Of Earth or its inhabitants. **2.** Living or growing on land or on or in the ground. **3.** Transmitted from structures on the earth and not involving satellites. ►*n.* An inhabitant of Earth. [< Lat. *terrestris* < *terra,* earth.]

ter·ri·ble (tĕr′ə-bəl) ►*adj.* **1.** Causing great fear or alarm; dreadful. **2.** Extreme or severe. **3.** Very bad. [< Lat. *terribilis* < *terrēre,* frighten.] —**ter′ri·bly** *adv.*

ter·ri·er (tĕr′ē-ər) ►*n.* Any of several small dogs orig. developed for driving game from burrows. [< OFr. *(chien) terrier,* ground (dog) < Lat. *terra.*]

ter·rif·ic (tə-rĭf′ĭk) ►*adj.* **1.** Fine; splendid: *a terrific party.* **2.** Awesome; astounding. **3.** Terrifying. **4.** Terrible; severe. [Lat. *terrificus.*] —**ter·rif′i·cal·ly** *adv.*

ter·ri·fy (tĕr′ə-fī′) ►*v.* **-fied, -fy·ing** To fill with terror. [Lat. *terrificāre.*]

ter·ri·to·ri·al (tĕr′ĭ-tôr′ē-əl) ►*adj.* **1.** Of or relating to the geographic area under a given jurisdiction. **2.** Of a particular territory; regional. —**ter′ri·to′ri·al·ly** *adv.*

ter·ri·to·ry (tĕr′ĭ-tôr′ē) ►*n., pl.* **-ries 1a.** An area of land; region. **b.** The land and waters under the jurisdiction of a government. **2.** often **Territory** A usu. self-governing part of a nation not accorded statehood or provincial status. **3.** An area for which a person is responsible. **4.** A sphere of activity. See Synonyms at **field.** [< Lat. *territōrium* < *terra,* earth.]

ter·ror (tĕr′ər) ►*n.* **1.** Intense, overpowering fear. **2.** One that instills intense fear. **3.** Violence committed by a group, esp. against civilians, in the pursuit of political goals. **4.** *Informal* A nuisance; pest. [< Lat. < *terrēre,* frighten.]

ter·ror·ism (tĕr′ə-rĭz′əm) ►*n.* The use of violence, esp. against civilians, in the pursuit of political goals. —**ter′ror·ist** *n.* —**ter′ror·is′tic** *adj.*

ter·ror·ize (tĕr′ə-rīz′) ►*v.* **-ized, -iz·ing 1.** To terrify. **2.** To coerce by intimidation or fear. —**ter′ror·i·za′tion** *n.* —**ter′ror·iz′er** *n.*

ter·ry (tĕr′ē) ►*n.* An absorbent pile fabric with uncut loops on one or both sides. [?]

terse (tûrs) ►*adj.* **ters·er, ters·est** Brief and to the point; concise. [Lat. *tersus,* p.part. of *tergēre,* cleanse.] —**terse′ly** *adv.* —**terse′ness** *n.*

ter·ti·ar·y (tûr′shē-ĕr′ē) ►*adj.* **1.** Third in order, degree, or rank. **2. Tertiary** *Geol.* Of or being the 1st period of the Cenozoic Era, including the Pliocene, Miocene, Oligocene, Eocene, and Paleocene Epochs. ►*n.* **Tertiary** The Tertiary Period. [< Lat. *tertius,* third.]

TESL ►*abbr.* teaching English as a second language

Tes·la (tĕs′lə), **Nikola** 1856–1943. Serbian-born Amer. engineer and physicist.

tes·sel·late (tĕs′ə-lāt′) ►*v.* **-lat·ed, -lat·ing** To form into a mosaic pattern. [< Lat. *tessella,* small cube < Gk. *tessares,* four.] —**tes′sel·la′tion** *n.*

test (tĕst) ►*n.* **1.** A procedure for critical evaluation of the presence, quality, or truth of something; trial. **2.** A series of questions or problems designed to determine knowledge, intelligence, or ability. **3.** A basis for evaluation or judgment. [< Lat. *testū, testum,* pot.] —**test′er** *n.*

tes·ta·ment (tĕs′tə-mənt) ►*n.* **1.** Proof; evidence. **2.** A statement of belief. **3.** A usu. formal, written directive providing for the disposition of a person's property after death; will. **4. Testament** Either of the two main divisions of the Christian Bible. [< Lat. *testis,* witness.] —**tes′ta·men′tar·y** (-mĕn′tə-rē, -mĕn′trē) *adj.*

tes·tate (tĕs′tāt′) ►*adj.* Having made a legally valid will before death. [< Lat. *testārī,* make a will.]

tes·ta·tor (tĕs′tā′tər, tĕ-stā′tər) ►*n.* A deceased person who has left a legally valid will.

tes·ta·trix (tĕ-stā′trĭks) ►*n., pl.* **-tri·ces** (-trĭ-sēz′) A deceased woman who has left a legally valid will.

test ban ►*n.* An agreement between nations to forgo testing of nuclear weapons.

tes·ti·cle (tĕs′tĭ-kəl) ►*n.* A testis, esp. together with the scrotum. [< Lat. *testiculus.*]

tes·ti·fy (tĕs′tə-fī′) ►*v.* **-fied, -fy·ing 1.** To give testimony in a legal case or before a deliberative body. **2.** To declare publicly. **3.** To serve as evidence. [< Lat. *testificārī.*] —**tes′ti·fi′er** *n.*

tes·ti·mo·ni·al (tĕs′tə-mō′nē-əl) ►*n.* **1.** A statement in support of a particular truth or fact. **2.** A written affirmation of another's character or worth. **3.** A tribute. —**tes′ti·mo′ni·al** *adj.*

tes·ti·mo·ny (tĕs′tə-mō′nē) ►*n., pl.* **-nies 1a.** A declaration by a witness under oath, as that given before a court. **b.** All such declarations offered in a legal case or hearing. **2.** Supportive evidence; proof. **3.** A public declaration. [< Lat. *testimōnium.*]

tes·tis (tĕs′tĭs) ►*n., pl.* **-tes** (-tēz) One of the paired male reproductive organs that produces spermatozoa and male sex hormones in vertebrates. [Lat.]

tes·tos·ter·one (tĕs-tŏs′tə-rōn′) ►*n.* A steroid hormone produced mainly in the testes that causes the development of male secondary sex characteristics. [TEST(IS) + STER(OL) + -one, suff.]

test tube ►*n.* A clear cylindrical glass tube used in laboratory experimentation.

tes·ty (tĕs′tē) ►*adj.* **-ti·er, -ti·est** Irritable;

touchy. [< OFr. *teste,* head.] —**tes′ti·ly** *adv.* —**tes′ti·ness** *n.*

Tet (tĕt) ►*n.* The lunar New Year as celebrated in Vietnam. [Vietnamese *tĕt.*]

tet·a·nus (tĕt′n-əs) ►*n.* An often fatal infectious disease marked by spasmodic contraction of voluntary muscles, esp. of the neck and jaw. [< Gk. *tetanos,* rigid.]

tête-à-tête (tāt′ə-tāt′, tĕt′ə-tĕt′) ►*adv. & adj.* Without the intrusion of a third person. ►*n.* A private conversation between two persons. [Fr.]

teth·er (tĕth′ər) ►*n.* **1a.** A rope, chain, strap, or cord for keeping an animal within a certain radius. **b.** A rope, chain, cable, or other line for restraining or securing an object. **2.** The limit of one's resources or endurance. ►*v.* To restrain or secure with a tether. [< ON *tjōdhr.*]

Te·ton or **Te·ton Sioux** (tē′tŏn′) ►*n., pl.* **-ton** or **-tons** or **Teton Sioux** See **Lakota.**

tetra– or **tetr–** ►*pref.* Four: *tetrahedron.* [Gk.]

tet·ra·cy·cline (tĕt′rə-sī′klēn′, -klĭn) ►*n.* A yellow compound derived from bacteria and used as a broad-spectrum antibiotic. [TETRA– + CYCL(IC) + –INE².]

tet·ra·he·dron (tĕt′rə-hē′drən) ►*n., pl.* **-drons** or **-dra** (-drə) A polyhedron having four faces. —**tet′ra·he′dral** *adj.*

te·tram·e·ter (tĕ-trăm′ĭ-tər) ►*n.* Verse composed in lines of four metrical feet.

Teu·ton (tōōt′n, tyōōt′n) ►*n.* **1.** A member of an ancient people, probably of Germanic or Celtic origin, who lived in Jutland until about 100 BC. **2.** A member of a Germanic-speaking people, esp. a German.

Teu·ton·ic (tōō-tŏn′ĭk, tyōō-) ►*adj.* **1.** Of or relating to the Teutons. **2.** Of the Germanic languages. ►*n.* Germanic.

Te·vet (tā′vās, tĕ-vĕt′) ►*n.* The 10th month of the Jewish calendar. See table at **calendar.** [Heb. *tēbēt.*]

Tex·as (tĕk′səs) A state of the S-central US on the Gulf of Mexico. Cap. Austin. —**Tex′an** *adj. & n.*

Texas hold'em (hōld′əm) ►*n.* A poker game in which players each receive two cards and share five cards.

Texas Longhorn ►*n.* A breed of beef cattle having very long horns.

Texas Longhorn

text (tĕkst) ►*n.* **1.** The wording or words of something written or printed. **2.** The body of a printed work as distinct from a preface, footnote, or appendix. **3.** A Scriptural passage to be read and expounded upon in a sermon. **4.** A subject; topic. **5.** A textbook. ►*v.* **1.** To send a text message to. **2.** To communicate by text message. [< Lat. *textus* < p.part. of *texere,* weave.] —**tex′tu·al** *adj.*

text·book (tĕkst'bŏŏk') ►*n.* A book used for the study of a subject.

tex·tile (tĕks'tīl', -təl) ►*n.* **1.** A cloth or fabric, esp. when woven or knitted. **2.** Fiber or yarn for weaving cloth. [< Lat. *textus*, p.part. of *texere*, weave.]

text message ►*n.* A message sent electronically to a cell phone, esp. from another cell phone.

text messaging ►*n.* **1.** The process by which text messages are transmitted. **2.** The service provided by a telecommunications company for transmitting text messages.

tex·ture (tĕks'chər) ►*n.* **1.** A structure of interwoven fibers or other elements. **2.** The basic structure or composition of a substance. **3.** The appearance and feel of a surface. [< Lat. *textūra* < *textus*; see TEXT.] —**tex'tur·al** *adj.* —**tex'tured** *adj.*

TGIF ►*abbr.* thank God it's Friday

–th¹ ►*suff.* Var. of –eth¹.

–th² also **–eth** ►*suff.* Used to form ordinal numbers: *millionth.* [< OE -tha.]

Thack·er·ay (thăk'ə-rē, thăk'rē), **William Makepeace** 1811–63. British writer.

Thai (tī) ►*n., pl.* **Thai** or **Thais 1.** A native or inhabitant of Thailand. **2.** The Tai language of Thailand. —**Thai** *adj.*

Thai·land (tī'lănd', -lənd) Formerly **Siam.** A country of SE Asia on the **Gulf of Thailand** (formerly the Gulf of Siam), an arm of the South China Sea. Cap. Bangkok.

thal·a·mus (thăl'ə-məs) ►*n., pl.* **-mi** (-mī') A large mass of gray matter that relays sensory impulses to the cerebral cortex. [< Gk. *thalamos*, inner chamber.] —**tha·lam'ic** (thə-lăm'ĭk) *adj.*

Tha·les (thā'lēz) 624?–546? BC. Greek philosopher. —**Tha·le'sian** (thā-lē'zhən) *adj.*

tha·lid·o·mide (thə-lĭd'ə-mīd') ►*n.* A sedative drug that was withdrawn from the market because it causes severe birth defects when taken during pregnancy. [(ph)thal(ic acid) + (im)id(e) + (i)mide.]

thal·li·um (thăl'ē-əm) ►*n. Symbol* **Tl** A soft, malleable, highly toxic metallic element used in photocells and infrared detectors. At. no. 81. See table at **element.** [< Lat. *thallus*, green shoot + –IUM.]

Thames (tĕmz) A river of S England flowing about 340 km (210 mi) eastward through London to a wide estuary on the North Sea.

than (thăn, thən) ►*conj.* Used to introduce the second element or clause of an unequal comparison: *She is a better athlete than I.* ►*prep. Informal* In comparison with: *valued no one more than her.* [< OE thanne.]

thane (thān) ►*n.* **1.** A freeman granted land by the king in Anglo-Saxon England. **2.** A feudal lord in Scotland. [< OE thegn.]

thank (thăngk) ►*v.* **1.** To express gratitude to. **2.** To credit. [< OE thancian.]

thank·ful (thăngk'fəl) ►*adj.* Grateful. —**thank'-ful·ly** *adv.* —**thank'ful·ness** *n.*

thank·less (thăngk'lĭs) ►*adj.* **1.** Ungrateful. **2.** Not likely to be appreciated: *a thankless job.* —**thank'less·ly** *adv.* —**thank'less·ness** *n.*

thanks (thăngks) ►*pl.n.* Grateful feelings or thoughts; gratitude. ►*interj.* Used to express thanks. —*idiom:* **thanks to** On account of; because of.

thanks·giv·ing (thăngks-gĭv'ĭng) ►*n.* An act of giving thanks, esp. to God.

Thanksgiving Day ►*n.* The 4th Thursday of November, a legal holiday in the US, during which gratitude is expressed for health and harvest.

that (thăt, thŏt) ►*pron., pl.* **those** (thōz) **1a.** The one designated or implied: *What kind of soup is that?* **b.** The one, thing, or type specified: *The relics found were those of an earlier time.* **2.** Used to introduce a clause, esp. a restrictive clause: *the car that has the flat tire.* **3.** In, on, by, or with which: *She called the day that she arrived.* ►*adj., pl.* **those 1.** Being the one indicated or implied: *that place.* **2.** Being the one further removed or less obvious: *That route is shorter than this one.* ►*adv.* To such an extent: *Is it that difficult?* ►*conj.* **1.** Used to introduce a subordinate clause: *I doubt that you are right.* **2.** Used to introduce an exclamation of desire: *Oh, that I were rich!* [< OE thæt.]

Usage: The standard rule is that *that* should be used only to introduce a restrictive (or "defining") relative clause, which serves to identify the entity being talked about. Thus, we say *The house that Jack built has been torn down,* where the clause *that Jack built* tells which house was torn down. Only *which* is to be used with nonrestrictive (or "nondefining") clauses, which give additional information about an entity that has already been identified in the context. Thus, we say *The students in Chemistry 101 have been complaining about the textbook, which* (not *that*) *is hard to follow.* See Usage Notes at **this, there.**

thatch (thăch) ►*n.* Plant stalks or foliage used for roofing. ►*v.* To cover with or as if with thatch. [< OE thæc.]

Thatch·er (thăch'ər), Baroness **Margaret Hilda** b. 1925. British prime minister (1979–90).

thaw (thô) ►*v.* **1.** To change from a frozen solid to a liquid by gradual warming. **2.** To lose stiffness or numbness by being warmed. **3.** To become warm enough for snow and ice to melt. **4.** To become less reserved. ►*n.* **1.** The process of thawing. **2.** A period during which ice and snow melt. **3.** A relaxation of restraint or tension. [< OE thawian.]

THC (tē'ăch-sē') ►*n.* The primary intoxicant in marijuana and hashish. [t(etra)h(ydro) c(annabinol).]

the¹ (thē *before a vowel; thə before a consonant*) ►*def.art.* **1.** Used before singular or plural nouns and noun phrases that denote particular, specified persons or things: *the shoes I bought.* **2.** Used before a noun or an adjective with generic force: *an animal such as the wolf; the rich.* [< OE.]

the² (thē *before a vowel; thə before a consonant*) ►*adv.* To that extent; by that much. Used before a comparative: *the sooner the better.* [< OE thȳ.]

the·a·ter or **the·a·tre** (thē'ə-tər) ►*n.* **1.** A building for the presentation of plays, films, or other dramatic performances. **2.** A room with tiers of seats used for lectures or demonstrations. **3.** Dramatic literature or performance. **4.** A setting, as for military operations. [< Gk. *theatron.*]

the·at·ri·cal (thē-ăt'rĭ-kəl) ►*adj.* **1.** Of or suitable for the theater. **2.** Overly or affectedly dramatic. ►*n.* A stage performance, esp. by amateurs. —**the·at'ri·cal'i·ty** (-kăl'ĭ-tē), **the·**

at·ri·cal·ness *n.* —**the·at·ri·cal·ly** *adv.*

the·at·rics (thē-ăt′rĭks) ►*n.* **1.** *(takes sing. v.)* The art of the theater. **2.** *(takes pl. v.)* Theatrical effects or mannerisms.

Thebes (thēbz) **1.** An ancient city of Upper Egypt on the Nile R. in present-day central Egypt. **2.** An ancient city of Greece NW of Athens. —**The′ban** (thē′bən) *adj. & n.*

thee (*thē*) ►*pron.* The objective case of **thou.**

theft (thĕft) ►*n.* **1.** The unlawful taking of another's property; larceny. **2.** An instance of such taking. [< OE *thīefth.*]

their (thâr) ►*adj.* The possessive form of **they.** Used as a modifier before a noun: *their house.* [< ON *theira.*]

theirs (thârz) ►*pron.* *(takes sing. or pl. v.)* The one or ones belonging to them: *The red house is theirs.*

the·ism (thē′ĭz′əm) ►*n.* Belief in the existence of a god or gods. —**the′ist** *n.* —**the·is′tic, the·is′ti·cal** *adj.*

them (*thĕm, thəm*) ►*pron.* The objective case of **they. 1.** Used as a direct or indirect object: *He saw them. She gave them a ride.* **2.** Used as the object of a preposition: *We traveled with them.* See Usage Note at **I. 3.** Used after a linking verb such as *is*: *It's them.* [< ON *theim* and OE *thǣm.*]

the·mat·ic (thĭ-măt′ĭk) ►*adj.* Of or being a theme. [Gk. *thematikos.*] —**the·mat′i·cal·ly** *adv.*

theme (thēm) ►*n.* **1.** A topic of discourse or discussion. **2.** The subject of an artistic work. **3.** An implicit or recurrent idea; motif. **4.** A short written composition. **5.** *Mus.* A recurring melodic element in a composition. [< Gk. *thema.*]

them·selves (*thĕm-sĕlvz′, thəm-*) ►*pron.* **1.** Those ones identical with them. **2.** Used reflexively as the direct or indirect object of a verb or as the object of a preposition. **3.** Used for emphasis: *The wind toppled the trees themselves.*

then (*thĕn*) ►*adv.* **1.** At that time. **2.** Next in time, space, or order. **3.** In addition; moreover; besides. **4.** In that case: *If it snows, then bring your skis.* **5.** As a consequence: *The case, then, is closed.* ►*n.* That time or moment. ►*adj.* Being so at that time. [< OE *thenne.*]

thence (thĕns, thĕns) ►*adv.* **1.** From there. **2.** From that circumstance or source. **3.** *Archaic* Thenceforth. [< OE *thanon.*]

thence·forth (thĕns-fôrth′, thĕns-) ►*adv.* From that time forward; thereafter.

thence·for·ward (thĕns-fôr′wərd, thĕns-) also **thence·for·wards** (-wərdz) ►*adv.* From that time or place onward; thenceforth.

theo– or **the–** ►*pref.* God: *theocracy.* [< Gk. *theos,* god.]

the·oc·ra·cy (thē-ŏk′rə-sē) ►*n., pl.* **-cies 1.** Government ruled by or subject to religious authority. **2.** A country or state so governed. —**the′o·crat′** (thē′ə-krăt′) *n.* —**the′o·crat′ic** *adj.* —**the′o·crat′i·cal·ly** *adv.*

The·oc·ri·tus (thē-ŏk′rĭ-təs) fl. 3rd cent. BC. Greek poet.

The·o·do·ra (thē′ə-dôr′ə) AD 508?–548. Byzantine empress (525–548).

The·od·o·ric (thē-ŏd′ər-ĭk) AD 454?–526. King of the Ostrogoths (c. 474–526).

the·ol·o·gy (thē-ŏl′ə-jē) ►*n., pl.* **-gies 1.** The study of the nature of God and religious truth.

2. A system or school of opinions concerning God and religious questions. —**the′o·lo′gi·an** (-ə-lō′jən) *n.* —**the′o·log′i·cal** (-ə-lŏj′ĭ-kəl) *adj.* —**the′o·log′i·cal·ly** *adv.*

the·o·rem (thē′ər-əm, thîr′əm) ►*n.* **1.** An idea that is demonstrably true or is assumed to be so. **2.** *Math.* A proposition that has been or is to be proved. [< Gk. *theōrēma.*]

the·o·ret·i·cal (thē′ə-rĕt′ĭ-kəl) also **the·o·ret·ic** (-rĕt′ĭk) ►*adj.* Of or based on theory. [< Gk. *theōrētikos.*] —**the′o·ret′i·cal·ly** *adv.*

the·o·re·ti·cian (thē′ər-ĭ-tĭsh′ən, thîr′ĭ-) ►*n.* One who formulates, studies, or is expert in the theory of a science or an art.

the·o·rize (thē′ə-rīz′, thîr′īz) ►*v.* **-rized, -riz·ing** To formulate theories or a theory. —**the′o·riz′er, the′o·rist** *n.*

the·o·ry (thē′ə-rē, thîr′ē) ►*n., pl.* **-ries 1.** A set of statements or principles devised to explain a group of facts or phenomena, esp. one that has been repeatedly tested or is widely accepted. **2.** The branch of a science or art consisting of its explanatory statements, accepted principles, and methods of analysis, as opposed to practice. **3.** Abstract reasoning; speculation. **4.** An assumption; conjecture. [< Gk. *theōria.*]

the·os·o·phy (thē-ŏs′ə-fē) ►*n., pl.* **-phies** Mystical philosophy or speculation about the nature of the soul and God. [THEO– + Gk. *sophia,* wisdom.] —**the′o·soph′ic** (thē′ə-sŏf′-ĭk), **the′o·soph′i·cal** *adj.* —**the·os′o·phist** *n.*

ther·a·peu·tic (thĕr′ə-pyōō′tĭk) ►*adj.* **1.** Having healing or curative powers. **2.** Relating to medical treatment of a disease or condition. [< Gk. *therapeuein,* treat medically.] —**ther′a·peu′ti·cal·ly** *adv.*

ther·a·peu·tics (thĕr′ə-pyōō′tĭks) ►*n.* *(takes sing. v.)* Medical treatment of disease. —**ther′a·peu′tist** *n.*

ther·a·py (thĕr′ə-pē) ►*n., pl.* **-pies 1.** Treatment of illness, injury, or disability. **2.** Psychotherapy. [< Gk. *therapeuein,* treat medically.] —**ther′a·pist** *n.*

there (thâr) ►*adv.* **1.** At or in that place. **2.** To, into, or toward that place. **3.** At that stage, moment, or point. ►*pron.* Used to introduce a clause or sentence: *There is hope.* ►*n.* That place or point. [< OE *thǣr.*]

Usage: The demonstrative forms *that there* and *this here* are nonstandard.

there·a·bouts (thâr′ə-bouts′) also **there·a·bout** (-bout′) ►*adv.* **1.** Near that place. **2.** Approximately.

there·af·ter (thâr-ăf′tər) ►*adv.* From a specified time onward; from then on.

there·at (thâr-ăt′) ►*adv.* **1.** At that place; there. **2.** At that event; on account of that.

there·by (thâr-bī′) ►*adv.* By that means.

there·fore (thâr′fôr′) ►*adv.* For that reason; consequently.

there·from (thâr-frŭm′, -frŏm′) ►*adv.* From that place, time, or thing.

there·in (thâr-ĭn′) ►*adv.* **1.** In that place, time, or thing. **2.** In that respect.

there·in·af·ter (thâr′ĭn-ăf′tər) ►*adv.* In a later part.

there·of (thâr-ŭv′, -ŏv′) ►*adv.* **1.** Of this, that, or it. **2.** From that cause or origin.

there·on (thâr-ŏn′, -ôn′) ►*adv.* On or upon this, that, or it.

The·re·sa or **Te·re·sa** (tə-rē′sə, -zə, -rā′-), Saint. 1515–82. Spanish nun and mystic.

there·to (thâr-tōō′) ►*adv.* To that, this, or it.

there·to·fore (thâr′tə-fôr′) ►*adv.* Until that time.

there·un·to (thâr′ŭn-tōō′) ►*adv.* Archaic To that, this, or it; thereto.

there·up·on (thâr′ə-pŏn′, -pôn′) ►*adv.* **1.** Concerning that matter. **2.** Directly following that. **3.** In consequence of that; therefore.

there·with (thâr-wĭth′, -wĭth′) ►*adv.* With that, this, or it.

there·with·al (thâr′wĭth-ôl′, -wĭth-) ►*adv.* With all that, this, or it; besides.

ther·mal (thûr′məl) ►*adj.* Of, using, producing, or caused by heat. ►*n.* A rising current of warm air. —**ther′mal·ly** *adv.*

thermo– or **therm–** ►*pref.* Heat: *thermodynamics.* [< Gk. *thermos*, warm.]

ther·mo·cou·ple (thûr′mə-kŭp′əl) ►*n.* A device used to measure temperatures, consisting of two dissimilar metals joined at the ends so that an electric current flows when the contacts are at different temperatures.

ther·mo·dy·nam·ics (thûr′mō-dī-năm′ĭks) ►*n.* *(takes sing. v.)* Physics that deals with the relationships between heat and other forms of energy. —**ther′mo·dy·nam′ic** *adj.* —**ther′mo·dy·nam′i·cal·ly** *adv.*

ther·mom·e·ter (thər-mŏm′ĭ-tər) ►*n.* An instrument for measuring temperature. —**ther′mo·met′ric** (thûr′mō-mĕt′rĭk) *adj.* —**ther·mom′e·try** *n.*

ther·mo·nu·cle·ar (thûr′mō-nōō′klē-ər, -nyōō′-) ►*adj.* **1.** Of or derived from the fusion of atomic nuclei at high temperatures. **2.** Relating to or being weapons that employ nuclear fusion.

ther·mo·plas·tic (thûr′mə-plăs′tĭk) ►*adj.* Becoming soft when heated and hard when cooled. ►*n.* A thermoplastic material.

Ther·mop·y·lae (thər-mŏp′ə-lē) A narrow pass of E-central Greece; site of a Spartan stand against the Persians (480 BC).

ther·mos (thûr′məs) ►*n.* A bottle or flask having a vacuum between its inner and outer walls, designed to maintain the desired temperature of the contents. [Orig. a trademark.]

ther·mo·set·ting (thûr′mō-sĕt′ĭng) ►*adj.* Permanently hardening or solidifying on being heated.

ther·mo·sphere (thûr′mə-sfîr′) ►*n.* The outermost layer of the atmosphere, between the mesosphere and interplanetary space, where air becomes extremely thin and temperatures increase steadily with altitude. —**ther′mo·spher′ic** (-sfîr′ĭk, -sfĕr′-) *adj.*

ther·mo·stat (thûr′mə-stăt′) ►*n.* A device, as in a heating system, that senses temperature changes and activates switches controlling the equipment. —**ther′mo·stat′ic** *adj.*

the·sau·rus (thĭ-sôr′əs) ►*n.*, *pl.* **-sau·rus·es** or **-sau·ri** (-sôr′ī′) A book of selected words, esp. a dictionary of synonyms and related words. [< Gk. *thēsauros*, treasury.]

these (thēz) ►*pron.* & *adj.* Pl. of **this.**

the·sis (thē′sĭs) ►*n.*, *pl.* **-ses** (-sēz) **1.** A proposition maintained by argument. **2.** A dissertation advancing an original point of view as a result of research. [< Gk.]

thes·pi·an (thĕs′pē-ən) ►*adj.* Of or relating to

drama; dramatic. ►*n.* An actor or actress. [< THESPIS.]

Thes·pis (thĕs′pĭs) fl. 6th cent. BC. Greek poet.

Thes·sa·lo·ni·ans (thĕs′ə-lō′nē-ənz) ►*pl.n.* *(takes sing. v.)* See table at **Bible.**

Thes·sa·lo·ní·ki (thĕ′sä-lô-nē′kē) or **Sa·lo·ni·ka** (sə-lŏn′ĭ-kə, săl′ə-nē′kə) A city of NE Greece on an inlet of the Aegean Sea.

Thes·sa·ly (thĕs′ə-lē) A region of E-central Greece along the Aegean Sea. —**Thes·sa′lian** (thĕ-sā′lē-ən), **Thes′sa·lo′ni·an** *adj.* & *n.*

the·ta (thā′tə, thē′-) ►*n.* The 8th letter of the Greek alphabet. [Gk. *thēta.*]

thew (thyōō) ►*n.* often **thews** Sinew or muscle. [< OE *thēaw*, habit.]

they (thā) ►*pron.* The ones previously mentioned or implied. [< ON *their.*]

Usage: Use of the third-person plural pronoun *they* to refer to a singular noun or pronoun such as *a person* or *somebody* is common in speech and widespread in many mainstream publications. Nevertheless, many people avoid using *they* in this way in order to adhere to the traditional grammatical rule concerning pronoun agreement. Most of the Usage Panel still upholds this practice but in decreasing numbers. In our 1996 survey, 80 percent rejected the use of *they* in the sentence *A person at that level should not have to keep track of the hours they put in.* By 2008, however, only 62 percent of the Panel still held this view. See Usage Note at **I.**

they'd (thād) **1.** They had. **2.** They would.

they'll (thāl) They will.

they're (thâr) They are.

they've (thāv) They have.

thi·a·mine (thī′ə-mĭn, -mēn′) also **thi·a·min** (-mĭn) ►*n.* A vitamin of the vitamin B complex, found in yeast, meat, and bran and necessary for carbohydrate metabolism. [Gk. *theion*, sulfur + (VIT)AMIN.]

thick (thĭk) ►*adj.* **-er, -est 1a.** Relatively great in extent from one surface to the opposite; not thin. **b.** Measuring in this dimension: *two inches thick.* **2.** Thickset. **3.** Dense; concentrated. **4.** Having a heavy or viscous consistency. **5.** Having a great number; abounding. **6.** Very noticeable; pronounced: *a thick accent.* **7.** *Informal* Lacking mental agility; stupid. **8.** *Informal* Very friendly; intimate. **9.** *Informal* Excessive. ►*n.* **1.** The thickest part. **2.** The most intense part: *in the thick of the fighting.* —*idiom:* **thick and thin** Good and bad times. [< OE *thicce.*] —**thick′ly** *adv.* —**thick′ness** *n.*

thick·en (thĭk′ən) ►*v.* To make or become thick or thicker. —**thick′en·er** *n.* —**thick′en·ing** *n.*

thick·et (thĭk′ĭt) ►*n.* A dense growth of shrubs or underbrush. [OE *thiccet.*]

thick·set (thĭk′sĕt′) ►*adj.* **1.** Having a short wide body; stocky. **2.** Placed closely together.

thick·skinned (thĭk′skĭnd′) ►*adj.* **1.** Having a thick skin. **2.** Not easily offended.

thief (thēf) ►*n.*, *pl.* **thieves** (thēvz) One who commits a theft. [< OE *thēof.*]

thieve (thēv) ►*v.* **thieved, thiev·ing** To commit theft. [Perh. < OE *thēofian.*] —**thiev′er·y** *n.*

thigh (thī) ►*n.* The portion of the leg between the hip and the knee. [< OE *thēoh.*]

thigh·bone (thī′bōn′) ►*n.* See **femur.**

thim·ble (thĭm′bəl) ►*n.* A small cup, as of metal or plastic, worn to protect the finger in sewing. [< OE *thūma*, thumb.] —**thim′ble·ful′** *n.*

Thim·phu (thǐm'po͞o', tǐm'-) The capital of Bhutan, in the W part in the E Himalayas.

thin (thǐn) ▸*adj.* **thin·ner, thin·nest 1a.** Relatively small in extent from one surface to the opposite. **b.** Not great in diameter or cross section; fine. **2.** Lean or slender. **3.** Not dense or concentrated; sparse. **4.** Not rich or heavy in consistency. **5.** Lacking force or substance; flimsy. ▸*v.* **thinned, thin·ning** To make or become thin or thinner. [< OE *thynne*.] —**thin'ly** *adv.* —**thin'ness** *n.*

thine (thīn) ▸*pron.* *(takes sing. or pl. v.)* Used to indicate the one or ones belonging to thee. ▸*adj.* A possessive form of **thou.** Used instead of *thy* before an initial vowel or *h*: *thine enemy.* [< OE *thīn.*]

thing (thǐng) ▸*n.* **1.** An individual object. **2.** A creature: *That kitten is the cutest thing!* **3.** An entity or item: *How many things are on the test?* **4. things a.** Possessions; belongings. **b.** Articles of clothing. **5.** An act, deed, or work: *hadn't done a thing all day.* **6.** A means to an end: *just the thing to increase sales.* **7.** A piece of information: *wouldn't tell me a thing.* **8.** A matter of concern: *things on my mind.* **9.** A turn of events: *A funny thing happened today.* **10. things** The general state of affairs. **11a.** A persistent infatuation: *You have a thing for me, don't you?* **b.** A persistent aversion: *He has a thing about cats.* **12.** *Slang* A uniquely suitable and satisfying activity: *doing her own thing.* [< OE *thing.*]

think (thǐngk) ▸*v.* **thought** (thôt), **think·ing 1.** To have or formulate in the mind. **2.** To ponder or decide: *think what to do.* **3.** To believe; suppose: *He thinks he's right.* **4a.** To remember: *I can't think what her name is.* **b.** To imagine: *Think how rich we could be!* **c.** To devise or invent: *think up a plan.* **5.** To consider an idea: *I'm thinking about moving.* [< OE *thencan.*] —**think'a·ble** *adj.* —**think'er** *n.*

think tank ▸*n.* A research group organized for solving complex problems.

thin·ner (thǐn'ər) ▸*n.* A liquid, as turpentine, mixed with paint to reduce viscosity.

thin-skinned (thǐn'skǐnd') ▸*adj.* **1.** Having a thin rind or skin. **2.** Oversensitive.

third (thûrd) ▸*n.* **1.** The ordinal number matching the number 3 in a series. **2.** One of three equal parts. **3.** *Mus.* A tone that is three degrees above or below a given tone in a diatonic scale. [< OE *thridda.*] —**third** *adv. & adj.* —**third'-ly** *adv.*

third base ▸*n. Baseball* The third base reached by a runner moving counterclockwise from home plate. —**third baseman** *n.*

third class ▸*n.* Accommodations of the third and usu. lowest order of luxury and price. —**third'-class'** *adv. & adj.*

third-de·gree burn (thûrd'dĭ-grē') ▸*n.* A severe burn resulting in destruction of skin and sometimes of underlying tissues.

third person ▸*n.* The form of a verb or pronoun used in referring to a person or thing other than the speaker or the one spoken to.

Third World ▸*n.* The developing nations of Africa, Asia, and Latin America.

thirst (thûrst) ▸*n.* **1a.** A sensation of dryness in the mouth related to a desire to drink. **b.** The desire to drink. **2.** An insistent desire; craving. ▸*v.* **1.** To feel a need to drink. **2.** To yearn. [< OE *thurst.*] —**thirst'i·ly** *adv.* —**thirst'y** *adj.*

thir·teen (thûr-tēn') ▸*n.* **1.** The cardinal number equal to 12 + 1. **2.** The 13th in a set or sequence. [< OE *thrēotīne.*] —**thir·teen'** *adj. & pron.*

thir·teenth (thûr-tēnth') ▸*n.* **1.** The ordinal number matching the number 13 in a series. **2.** One of 13 equal parts. —**thir·teenth'** *adv. & adj.*

thir·ti·eth (thûr'tē-ĭth) ▸*n.* **1.** The ordinal number matching the number 30 in a series. **2.** One of 30 equal parts. —**thir·ti·eth** *adv. & adj.*

thir·ty (thûr'tē) ▸*n., pl.* **-ties** The cardinal number equal to 3 × 10. [< OE *thrītig.*] —**thir'ty** *adj. & pron.*

this (thǐs) ▸*pron., pl.* **these** (thēz) **1a.** The person or thing present, nearby, or just mentioned. **b.** What is about to be said. **c.** The present event, action, or time. **2.** The nearer or the more immediate one. ▸*adj., pl.* **these 1.** Being just mentioned or present. **2.** Being nearer or more immediate. **3.** Being about to be stated or described. ▸*adv.* To this extent; so: *never stayed out this late.* [< OE.]

Usage: *This* and *that* are both used as demonstrative pronouns to refer to a thought expressed earlier: *The letter was unopened; that (or this) in itself casts doubt on the inspector's theory. That* is sometimes considered as the better choice in referring to what has gone before. When the referent is yet to be mentioned, only *this* is used: *This* (not *that*) *is what bothers me. We have no time to consider late applications.* See Usage Notes at **that, there.**

this·tle (thǐs'əl) ▸*n.* Any of numerous often weedy plants having prickly leaves and floral bracts. [< OE *thistel.*]

thistle

this·tle·down (thǐs'əl-doun') ▸*n.* The silky down attached to the seeds of a thistle.

thith·er (thǐth'ər, thǐth'-) ▸*adv.* To or toward that place; there. ▸*adj.* Being on the more distant side; farther. [< OE *thider.*]

thole pin (thōl) ▸*n.* A peg set in pairs in the gunwales of a boat to serve as an oarlock. [< OE *thol.*]

Thom·as (tǒm'əs), Saint. fl. 1st cent. AD. One of the 12 Apostles.

Thomas, Dylan Marlais 1914–53. British poet.

Thomas à Kem·pis (ə kěm'pǐs, ä) 1380?–1471. German monk and writer.

Thomp·son (tǒmp'sən), **Benjamin.** Count Rumford. 1753–1814. Amer.-born British physicist.

Thor (thôr) ►*n. Myth.* The Norse god of thunder.

tho·rax (thôr′ăks′) ►*n., pl.* **-es** or **tho·ra·ces** (thôr′ə-sēz′) **1.** The part of the vertebrate body between the neck and the diaphragm, partially encased by the ribs; chest. **2.** The middle region of the body of certain arthropods. [< Gk. *thōrax*, breastplate.] —**tho·rac′ic** (thə-răs′ĭk) *adj.*

Tho·reau (thə-rō′, thôr′ō), **Henry David** 1817–62. Amer. writer. —**Tho·reau′vi·an** *adj.*

tho·ri·um (thôr′ē-əm) ►*n. Symbol* **Th** A radioactive, silvery-white metallic element used in magnesium alloys. At. no. 90. See table at **element.** [< THOR.]

thorn (thôrn) ►*n.* **1a.** A modified branch in the form of a sharp woody structure. **b.** Any of various shrubs, trees, or woody plants bearing such sharp structures. **2.** One that causes pain, irritation, or discomfort. [< OE.] —**thorn′i·ness** *n.* —**thorn′y** *adj.*

thor·ough (thûr′ō, thûr′ō) ►*adj.* **1.** Complete in all respects. **2.** Painstakingly careful. [< OE *thuruh*, through.] —**thor′ough·ly** *adv.* —**thor′ough·ness** *n.*

thor·ough·bred (thûr′ō-brĕd′, thûr′ə-, thûr′-) ►*n.* **1.** A purebred or pedigreed animal. **2.** **Thoroughbred** A horse originating from a cross between Arabian stallions and English mares. ►*adj.* Bred of pure stock; purebred.

thor·ough·fare (thûr′ō-fâr′, thûr′ə-, thûr′-) ►*n.* A main road or public highway.

thor·ough·go·ing (thûr′ō-gō′ĭng, thûr′ə-, thûr′-) ►*adj.* **1.** Very thorough; complete. **2.** Absolute; unqualified.

Thorpe (thôrp), **James Francis** "Jim." 1887?–1953. Amer. athlete.

Jim Thorpe

those (thōz) ►*pron. & adj.* Pl. of **that.**

thou (thou) ►*pron.* Used to indicate the one being addressed, esp. in a religious context. [< OE *thū.*]

though (thō) ►*conj.* **1.** Although; while. **2.** Even if. See Usage Note at **although.** ►*adv.* However; nevertheless. [ME, of Scand. orig.]

thought (thôt) ►*v.* P.t. and p.part. of **think.** ►*n.* **1.** The process or power of thinking. **2.** An idea. **3.** A body of ideas. **4.** Consideration; attention. **5.** Intention; expectation. [< OE *gethōht.*]

thought·ful (thôt′fəl) ►*adj.* **1.** Given to or showing careful thought. **2.** Considerate of others. —**thought′ful·ly** *adv.* —**thought′ful·ness** *n.*

thought·less (thôt′lĭs) ►*adj.* **1.** Careless; unthinking. **2.** Inconsiderate. —**thought′less·ly** *adv.* —**thought′less·ness** *n.*

thou·sand (thou′zənd) ►*n.* The cardinal number equal to 10×100 or 10^3. [< OE *thūsend.*] —**thou′sand** *adj. & pron.*

thou·sandth (thou′zəndth, -zənth) ►*n.* **1.** The ordinal number matching the number 1,000 in a series. **2.** One of 1,000 equal parts. —**thou′sandth** *adv. & adj.*

Thrace (thrās) A region and ancient country of the SE Balkan Peninsula N of the Aegean Sea. —**Thra′cian** (thrā′shən) *adj. & n.*

thrall (thrôl) ►*n.* **1.** The state of being in the power of another person or under the sway of an influence. **2.** One held in bondage; slave. [< ON *thrӕll.*] —**thrall′dom, thral′dom** *n.*

thrash (thrăsh) ►*v.* **1.** To beat, esp. repeatedly, as with a stick. See Synonyms at **beat.** **2.** To defeat soundly or decisively. **3.** To move wildly or violently. [< THRESH.] —**thrash′er** *n.*

thrash·er (thrăsh′ər) ►*n.* Any of various long-tailed songbirds found throughout the Americas. [Perh. < THRUSH.]

thread (thrĕd) ►*n.* **1.** A fine cord made of fibers or filaments twisted together, used in needlework and in weaving cloth. **2.** Something like a thread, as in fineness or length. **3.** A helical or spiral ridge on a screw, nut, or bolt. ►*v.* **1a.** To pass one end of a thread through (e.g., a needle). **b.** To pass a tape or film into or through. **2.** To pass cautiously through. **3.** To machine a thread on (a screw, nut, or bolt). [< OE *thrӕd.*] —**thread′er** *n.* —**thread′y** *adj.*

thread·bare (thrĕd′bâr′) ►*adj.* **1.** Having the nap worn down so that the threads show through. **2.** Shabby; seedy. **3.** Hackneyed.

threat (thrĕt) ►*n.* **1.** An expression of an intention to inflict pain, injury, or evil. **2.** One regarded as a possible danger. [< OE *thrēat,* oppression.]

threat·en (thrĕt′n) ►*v.* **1.** To express a threat against or give indications of taking hostile action against. **2.** To announce the possibility of (something) in a threat or prediction: *Workers threatened to strike.* **3.** To be a source of danger to; endanger. **4.** To portend: *clouds threatening rain.* —**threat′en·ing·ly** *adv.*

three (thrē) ►*n.* **1.** The cardinal number equal to 2 + 1. **2.** The 3rd in a set or sequence. [< OE *thrī.*] —**three** *adj. & pron.*

three-di·men·sion·al (thrē′dĭ-mĕn′shə-nəl, -dī-) ►*adj.* **1.** Of, having, or existing in three dimensions. **2.** Having or appearing to have extension in depth.

three·score (thrē′skôr′) ►*adj.* Sixty. —**three′score** *n. & pron.*

three·some (thrē′səm) ►*n.* A group of three.

thren·o·dy (thrĕn′ə-dē) ►*n., pl.* **-dies** A poem or song of lamentation. [Gk. *thrēnos,* lament + *ōidē,* song; see ODE.]

thresh (thrĕsh) ►*v.* **1.** To beat (e.g., cereal plants) with a machine or flail to separate the grains or seeds from the straw. **2.** To thrash. [< OE *therscan.*] —**thresh′er** *n.*

thresh·old (thrĕsh′ōld′, -hōld′) ►*n.* **1.** A piece of wood or stone placed beneath a door. **2.** Either end of an airport runway. **3.** The beginning; outset. **4.** The lowest level or intensity at which a stimulus can be perceived or can produce a given effect. [< OE *therscold.*]

threw (thrōō) ►*v.* P.t. of **throw.**

thrice (thrīs) ►*adv.* Three times. [Ult. < OE *thrīga.*]

thrift (thrĭft) ►*n.* **1.** Wise economy in managing money and other resources; frugality. **2.** A savings and loan association, credit union, or savings bank. [ME, prosperity.] —**thrift′i·ly** *adv.* —**thrift′i·ness** *n.* —**thrift′y** *adj.*

thrift store ►*n.* A shop that sells used articles, esp. clothing, as to benefit a charity.

thrill (thrĭl) ►*v.* **1.** To cause to feel a sudden sensation of pleasure or delight; excite greatly: *was thrilled to hear that she had won.* **2.** To cause to quiver, tremble, or vibrate. ►*n.* **1.** A sudden feeling of pleasure or excitement. **2.** A source or cause of pleasure or excitement. **3.** A quivering or trembling. [< OE *thȳrlian,* pierce.] —**thrill′er** *n.* —**thrill′ing·ly** *adv.*

thrive (thrīv) ►*v.* **thrived** or **throve** (thrōv), **thrived** or **thriv·en** (thrĭv′ən), **thriv·ing 1.** To flourish. **2.** To make steady progress. [< ON *thrīfask* < *thrīfa,* seize.] —**thriv′er** *n.*

throat (thrōt) ►*n.* **1.** The anterior portion of the neck. **2.** The portion of the digestive tract that lies between the rear of the mouth and the esophagus. [< OE *throte.*]

throat·y (thrō′tē) ►*adj.* **-i·er, -i·est** Uttered or sounding as if uttered deep in the throat. —**throat′i·ly** *adv.* —**throat′i·ness** *n.*

throb (thrŏb) ►*v.* **throbbed, throb·bing 1.** To beat rapidly or violently; pound. **2.** To vibrate rhythmically; pulsate. [ME *throbben.*] —**throb** *n.* —**throb′bing·ly** *adv.*

throe (thrō) ►*n.* **1.** A severe pang or spasm of pain. See Synonyms at **pain. 2. throes** Extreme difficulty: *a country in the throes of economic collapse.* [< OE *thrawu.*]

throm·bo·sis (thrŏm-bō′sĭs) ►*n., pl.* **-ses** (-sēz) The formation or presence of a thrombus.

throm·bus (thrŏm′bəs) ►*n., pl.* **-bi** (-bī) A blood clot formed in a blood vessel or chamber of the heart. [< Gk. *thrombos,* clot.]

throne (thrōn) ►*n.* **1.** A chair occupied by a sovereign or bishop on state or ceremonial occasions. **2.** Sovereign power or rank. [< Gk. *thronos.*]

throng (thrông, thrŏng) ►*n.* A large group of people or things crowded together. See Synonyms at **crowd.** ►*v.* **1.** To crowd into or around: *thronged the subway platform.* **2.** To move in a throng. [< OE *gethrang.*]

throt·tle (thrŏt′l) ►*n.* **1.** A valve that regulates the flow of a fluid, such as the valve in an internal-combustion engine that controls the amount of vaporized fuel entering the cylinders. **2.** A lever or pedal controlling such a valve. ►*v.* **-tled, -tling 1.** To regulate the speed of (an engine) with a throttle. **2.** To suppress: *tried to throttle the press.* **3.** To strangle (a person); choke. [< ME *throtelen,* strangle.]

through (thrōō) ►*prep.* **1.** In one side and out another side of. **2.** In the midst of. **3.** By way of. **4.** By the means or agency of. **5.** Here and there in; around. **6.** From the beginning to the end of. **7.** Done or finished with. ►*adv.* **1.** From one end or side to another end or side. **2.** From beginning to end. **3.** Throughout the whole extent or thickness. **4.** To a conclusion. ►*adj.* **1.** Allowing continuous passage; unobstructed. **2.** Passing or extending from one end, side, or surface to another. **3.** Finished; done. —*idiom:* **through and through 1.** In every part; throughout. **2.** Completely. [< OE *thurh.*]

through·out (thrōō-out′) ►*prep.* In, to, through, or during every part of: *throughout the year.* ►*adv.* **1.** Everywhere. **2.** During the entire time or extent.

throve (thrōv) ►*v.* P.t. of **thrive.**

throw (thrō) ►*v.* **threw** (thrōō), **thrown** (thrōn), **throw·ing 1.** To propel through the air with a swift motion of the hand or arm; fling. **2.** To put with force; hurl. **3.** *Informal* To confuse; perplex. **4.** To put on or off hastily or carelessly: *throw on a jacket.* **5.** To form on a potter's wheel: *throw a vase.* **6.** To cast: *throw a shadow.* **7.** To arrange or give (e.g., a party). **8.** To activate (a lever or switch). **9.** *Informal* To lose (e.g., a contest) purposely. ►*n.* **1.** The act or an instance of throwing. **2.** The distance or height to which something is or can be thrown. **3.** A light coverlet. —*phrasal verbs:* **throw away** or **out** To discard. **throw over** To desert; abandon. **throw up** To vomit. —*idiom:* **throw up (one's) hands** To give up in despair. [< OE *thrāwan.*] —**throw′er** *n.*

throw·back (thrō′băk′) ►*n.* **1.** A reversion to a former type or ancestral characteristic. **2.** One that has characteristics of an earlier time.

thru (thrōō) ►*prep., adv., & adj. Informal* Through.

thrum (thrŭm) ►*v.* **thrummed, thrum·ming** To play (a stringed instrument) idly or monotonously. [Imit.] —**thrum** *n.*

thrush (thrŭsh) ►*n.* Any of various songbirds usu. having brownish upper plumage and a spotted breast. [< OE *thrysce.*]

thrust (thrŭst) ►*v.* **thrust, thrust·ing 1.** To push or drive forcibly. See Synonyms at **push. 2a.** To force into a specified state or condition. **b.** To impose on an unwilling or improper recipient. ►*n.* **1a.** A forceful shove. **b.** A lunge or stab. **2a.** A driving force or pressure. **b.** The forward-directed force developed in a jet or rocket engine as a reaction to the rearward ejection of exhaust gases. **c.** Outward or lateral stress in a structure. **3.** The essence; point. [< ON *thrȳsta.*]

thru·way also **through·way** (thrōō′wā′) ►*n.* See **expressway.**

Thu·cyd·i·des (thōō-sĭd′ĭ-dēz′) 460?–400? BC. Greek historian.

thud (thŭd) ►*n.* **1.** A dull sound. **2.** A blow or fall causing such a sound. [Poss. < OE *thyddan,* strike with a weapon.] —**thud** *v.*

thug (thŭg) ►*n.* A cutthroat or ruffian; hoodlum. [Hindi *thag,* perh. < Skt. *sthagaḥ,* a cheat < *sthagayati,* conceals.] —**thug′ger·y** *n.* —**thug′gish** *adj.*

thu·li·um (thōō′lē-əm) ►*n. Symbol* **Tm** A bright, silvery rare-earth element used in portable x-ray units. At. no. 69. See table at **element.** [< *Thule,* the northernmost part of the ancient world.]

thumb (thŭm) ►*n.* **1.** The short, thick first digit of the human hand, opposable to the other four digits. **2.** The part of a glove or mitten that covers the thumb. ►*v.* **1.** To scan by turning over pages with the thumb. **2.** To soil or wear by handling. **3.** *Informal* To hitchhike. —*idiom:* **all thumbs** Clumsy. [< OE *thūma.*]

thumb·nail (thŭm′nāl′) ►*n.* **1.** The nail of the thumb. **2.** *Comp.* A reduced image of a graphic or a document page. ►*adj.* Brief: *a thumbnail sketch.*

thumb·screw (thŭm′skrōō′) ►*n.* **1.** A screw designed so that it can be turned with the thumb and fingers. **2.** An instrument of torture formerly used to compress the thumb.

thumb·tack (thŭm′tăk′) ►*n.* A smooth-headed tack that can be pressed into place with the thumb. —**thumb′tack′** *v.*

thump (thŭmp) ►*n.* **1.** A blow, as with a blunt object. **2.** A muffled sound, as that produced by a blow from a blunt object; thud. ►*v.* **1.** To beat so as to produce a thump or thumps. **2.** *Informal* To defeat soundly; drub. [Prob. imit.]

thun·der (thŭn′dər) ►*n.* **1.** The booming sound produced by rapidly expanding air along the path of a bolt of lightning. **2.** A sound resembling thunder. ►*v.* **1.** To produce thunder or similar sounds. **2.** To utter loud remarks or threats. [< OE *thunor.*] —**thun′der·ous** *adj.*

thun·der·bolt (thŭn′dər-bōlt′) ►*n.* A discharge of lightning accompanied by thunder.

thun·der·clap (thŭn′dər-klăp′) ►*n.* A single sharp crash of thunder.

thun·der·cloud (thŭn′dər-kloud′) ►*n.* A dark cloud that produces thunder and lightning.

thun·der·head (thŭn′dər-hěd′) ►*n.* The swollen upper portion of a thundercloud.

thun·der·show·er (thŭn′dər-shou′ər) ►*n.* A brief rainstorm accompanied by thunder and lightning.

thun·der·storm (thŭn′dər-stôrm′) ►*n.* An electrical storm with heavy rain.

thun·der·struck (thŭn′dər-strŭk′) ►*adj.* Astonished; stunned.

Thurs·day (thûrz′dē, -dā′) ►*n.* The 5th day of the week. [< OE *thunres dæg,* Thor's day.]

thus (thŭs) ►*adv.* **1.** In this manner. **2.** To a stated degree or extent; so. **3.** Therefore; consequently. [< OE.]

thwack (thwăk) ►*v.* To strike resoundingly with a flat object. [Imit.] —**thwack** *n.*

thwart (thwôrt) ►*v.* To block or hinder; frustrate. ►*n.* A seat across a boat that a rower sits on. ►*adj.* Transverse. [< ON *thvert,* across.]

thy (thī) ►*adj.* The possessive form of **thou.**

thyme (tīm) ►*n.* An aromatic plant with leaves used as seasoning. [< Gk. *thumon.*]

thy·mine (thī′mēn′) ►*n.* A pyrimidine base that is an essential constituent of DNA. [THYM(US) + –INE².]

thy·mus (thī′məs) ►*n.,* *pl.* **-mus·es** A small glandular organ located behind the top of the breastbone that is made up mainly of lymphatic tissue, is involved in producing T cells, and becomes smaller after puberty. [< Gk. *thumos.*]

thy·roid (thī′roid′) ►*n.* **1.** The thyroid gland. **2.** A dried powdered preparation of the thyroid gland of certain animals, used as a drug. [Gk. *thureoeidēs.*]

thyroid gland ►*n.* A two-lobed endocrine gland located in front of and on either side of the trachea in humans and producing various hormones.

thy·self (thī-sĕlf′) ►*pron.* Archaic Yourself.

ti (tē) ►*n. Mus.* The 7th tone of the diatonic scale. [Alteration of *si.*]

Tian Shan (tyän′ shän′) A mountain range of central Asia extending about 2,600 km (1,600 mi).

ti·ar·a (tē-ăr′ə, -âr′ə, -är′ə) ►*n.* **1.** A bejeweled crownlike ornament worn on the head by women. **2.** The triple crown historically worn by the pope. [< Gk., turban.]

Ti·ber (tī′bər) A river of central Italy flowing about 406 km (252 mi) through Rome to the Tyrrhenian Sea.

Ti·be·ri·us (tī-bîr′ē-əs) 42 BC–AD 37. Emperor of Rome (AD 14–37). —**Ti·be′ri·an** *adj.*

Ti·bet (tə-bĕt′) An autonomous region of W China on the **Tibetan Plateau** N of the Himalayas. —**Ti·bet′an** *adj. & n.*

Ti·bet·o-Bur·man (tĭ-bĕt′ō-bûr′mən) ►*n.* A branch of the Sino-Tibetan language family that includes Tibetan and Burmese.

tib·i·a (tĭb′ē-ə) ►*n., pl.* **-i·ae** (-ē-ē′) or **-i·as** The inner and larger of the two bones of the lower leg, extending from the knee to the ankle. [Lat. *tibia,* pipe, shinbone.] —**tib′i·al** *adj.*

tic (tĭk) ►*n.* A spasmodic muscular contraction, usu. of the face or extremities. [Fr.]

tick¹ (tĭk) ►*n.* **1.** A clicking sound made repeatedly by a machine, such as a clock. **2.** A light mark used to check off or call attention to an item. [ME *tek,* light tap.] —**tick** *v.*

tick² (tĭk) ►*n.* Any of numerous small bloodsucking parasitic arachnids. [ME *tik.*]

tick³ (tĭk) ►*n.* **1.** A cloth case for a mattress or pillow. **2.** Ticking. [Prob. ult. < Gk. *thēkē,* receptacle.]

tick·er (tĭk′ər) ►*n.* **1.** A telegraphic instrument that receives news reports and prints them on paper tape. **2.** *Slang* The heart.

ticker tape ►*n.* The paper strip on which a ticker prints.

tick·et (tĭk′ĭt) ►*n.* **1.** A paper slip or card indicating that its holder has paid for admission or a service. **2.** A certificate or license. **3.** An identifying tag; label. **4.** A list of candidates endorsed by a political party; slate. **5.** A legal notice to a person charged with a violation of law, esp. a minor violation. ►*v.* **1.** To tag; label. **2.** To serve with a notice of legal violation. [< OFr. *estiquet,* notice, label.]

tick·ing (tĭk′ĭng) ►*n.* A strong, tightly woven fabric used to make pillow and mattress coverings.

tick·le (tĭk′əl) ►*v.* **-led, -ling** **1.** To touch (the body) lightly so as to cause laughter or twitching movements. **2.** To feel or cause a tingling sensation. **3a.** To tease or excite pleasurably: *tickled my curiosity.* **b.** To please; delight. [ME *tikelen.*] —**tick′le** *n.*

tick·lish (tĭk′lĭsh) ►*adj.* **1.** Sensitive to tickling. **2.** Easily offended or upset. **3.** Requiring tactful handling; delicate. —**tick′lish·ly** *adv.* —**tick′-lish·ness** *n.*

tic-tac-toe also **tick-tack-toe** (tĭk′tăk-tō′) ►*n.* A game for two, each trying to make a line of three X's or three O's in a boxlike figure with nine spaces. [Prob. imit.]

tid·al (tīd′l) ►*adj.* Of or affected by tides.

tidal wave ►*n.* **1.** An unusual, often destructive rise of water along the seashore. **2.** An overwhelming manifestation, as of opinion; flood.

tid·bit (tĭd′bĭt′) ▸*n.* A choice morsel. [Perh. dial. *tid,* tender + BIT¹.]

tid·dly·winks (tĭd′lē-wĭngks′) ▸*pl.n. (takes sing. v.)* A game in which players try to snap small disks into a cup by pressing them on the edge with a larger disk. [Poss. dial. *tiddly,* little + WINK.]

tide (tīd) ▸*n.* **1a.** The periodic variation in the surface level of the oceans, seas, and other open waters of the earth, caused by gravitational attraction of the moon and sun. **b.** A specific occurrence of such a variation. **c.** The water that moves in such a variation. **2.** An onrush; flow: *a tide of immigration.* See Synonyms at **flow. 3.** A time or season. ▸*v.* **tid·ed, tid·ing** To drift with the tide. —*phrasal verb:* **tide over** To support through a difficult period. [< OE *tīd,* division of time.]

tide·land (tīd′lănd′) ▸*n.* Coastal land submerged during high tide.

tide·wa·ter (tīd′wô′tər, -wŏt′ər) ▸*n.* **1.** Water that inundates land at flood tide. **2.** Water affected by the tides, esp. tidal streams. **3.** Low coastal land drained by tidal streams.

tid·ings (tī′dĭngz) ▸*pl.n.* Information; news: *sad tidings.* [Perh. < ON *tīdhendi,* events.]

ti·dy (tī′dē) ▸*adj.* **-di·er, -di·est 1a.** Orderly and clean. **b.** Given to keeping things clean and in order. **2.** *Informal* Substantial; considerable. ▸*v.* **-died, -dy·ing** To put (things) in order. [ME *tīdī,* timely.] —**ti′di·ly** *adv.* —**ti′di·ness** *n.*

tie (tī) ▸*v.* **tied, ty·ing** (tī′ĭng) **1.** To fasten or secure with a cord, rope, or strap. **2.** To draw together and knot with strings or laces. **3.** To make (a knot or bow). **4.** To bring or hold together; unite. **5.** To equal (an opponent) in a contest. ▸*n.* **1.** A length, as of cord or string, used for tying. **2.** Something that unites; bond. **3.** A necktie. **4.** A beam or rod that gives structural support. **5.** A timber or cement slab laid crosswise to support railway tracks. **6.** An equality, as of votes or scores. —*phrasal verbs:* **tie in** To coordinate; connect. **tie up 1.** To moor; dock. **2.** To obstruct. **3.** To keep occupied; engage. [< OE *tīgan.*]

tie
railroad ties

tie-dye (tī′dī′) ▸*v.* To dye (fabric) after tying parts of the fabric so that they will not absorb dye, creating a mottled or streaked look. —**tie′-dye′** *n.*

tie-in (tī′ĭn′) ▸*n.* A connection or association.

tier (tîr) ▸*n.* **1.** One of a series of rows placed one above another. **2.** A rank or class. [< OFr. *tire,* row.] —**tier** *v.*

Ti·er·ra del Fue·go (tē-ĕr′ə dĕl fwā′gō) **1.** An archipelago off S South America separated from the mainland by the Strait of Magellan. **2.** The main island of this archipelago.

tie-up (tī′ŭp′) ▸*n.* A temporary stoppage.

tiff (tĭf) ▸*n.* **1.** A fit of irritation. **2.** A petty quarrel. [?] —**tiff** *v.*

ti·ger (tī′gər) ▸*n.* A large Asian wild cat having a tawny coat with black stripes. [< Gk. *tigris.*] —**ti′gress** *n.*

tiger lily ▸*n.* An lily native to China, having large black-spotted reddish-orange flowers.

tight (tīt) ▸*adj.* **-er, -est 1.** Fixed or fastened firmly in place. **2.** Stretched out fully. **3.** Of such close construction as to be impermeable. **4.** Compact. **5.** Fitting close or too close to the skin. **6.** *Slang* Personally close; intimate. **7.** Constricted. **8.** Stingy. **9.** Difficult: *a tight spot.* **10.** Closely contested. **11.** *Slang* Drunk. ▸*adv.* **-er, -est 1.** Firmly; securely. **2.** Soundly: *sleep tight.* [ME, prob. of Scand. orig.] —**tight′en** *v.* —**tight′ly** *adv.* —**tight′ness** *n.*
Syns: *taut, tense* **adj.**

tight end ▸*n. Football* An offensive end who lines up close to a tackle.

tight·fist·ed (tīt′fĭs′tĭd) ▸*adj.* Stingy.

tight-lipped also **tight-lipped** (tīt′lĭpt′) ▸*adj.* **1.** Having the lips pressed together. **2.** Reluctant to speak. See Synonyms at **laconic.**

tight·rope (tīt′rōp′) ▸*n.* A tightly stretched rope on which acrobats perform.

tights (tīts) ▸*pl.n.* **1.** A snug, stretchable garment covering the body from the neck down generally worn by women or girls. **2.** A similar garment designed for athletic use, worn esp. by dancers and acrobats.

tight·wad (tīt′wŏd′) ▸*n. Slang* A miser.

Ti·gris (tī′grĭs) A river of SW Asia rising in E Turkey and flowing about 1,850 km (1,150 mi) through Iraq to the Euphrates R.

Ti·jua·na (tē′ə-wä′nə, tē-hwä′nä) A city of extreme NW Mexico on the US border.

tik·ka¹ (tĭk′ə) ▸*n.* **1.** A pendant attached by a chain so as to hang to the middle of the forehead, worn esp. by Hindu brides. **2.** A bindi. [Hindi *ţīkā* and Punjabi *ţikkā.*]

tik·ka² (tĭk′ə) ▸*n.* A South Asian dish consisting of pieces of meat, usu. chicken, marinated in yogurt and spices and cooked on a skewer. [Hindi and Urdu *tikkā,* small piece of meat < Persian *tikka,* bit, small piece.]

til·de (tĭl′də) ▸*n.* A diacritical mark (˜) placed over the letter *n* in Spanish and over a vowel in Portuguese to indicate nasalization. [Sp. < Lat. *titulus,* superscription.]

tile (tīl) ▸*n.* **1.** A slab, as of baked clay, laid in rows to cover walls, floors, and roofs. **2.** A short length of clay or concrete pipe, used in sewers and drains. **3.** A marked playing piece, as in mahjong. ▸*v.* **tiled, til·ing** To cover or provide with tiles. [< Lat. *tēgula* < *tegere,* cover.] —**til′er** *n.*

till¹ (tĭl) ▸*v.* To cultivate (land or soil). [< OE *tilian.*] —**till′a·ble** *adj.*

till² (tĭl) ▸*prep. & conj.* Until. [< OE *til* < ON.]

till³ (tĭl) ▸*n.* A drawer or compartment for money, as in a store. [ME *tille.*]

till·age (tĭl′ĭj) ▸*n.* Cultivation of land.

till·er¹ (tĭl′ər) ►*n.* One that tills land.

til·ler² (tĭl′ər) ►*n.* A lever used to turn a boat's rudder. [< Med.Lat. *tēlārium,* weaver's beam < Lat. *tēla.*]

tilt (tĭlt) ►*v.* **1.** To slope or cause to slope, as by raising one end; incline. See Synonyms at **slant. 2.** To thrust (a lance) in a joust. ►*n.* **1.** A slant; slope. **2.** A bias. **3.** A joust. —*idiom:* **at full tilt** *Informal* At full speed. [ME *tilten,* cause to fall.] —**tilt′er** *n.*

tim·ber (tĭm′bər) ►*n.* **1a.** Trees or wooded land considered as a source of wood. **b.** Wood used as a building material. **2a.** A dressed piece of wood, esp. a structural beam. **b.** A rib in a ship's frame. [< OE, trees for building.] —**tim′-bered** *adj.*

tim·ber·line (tĭm′bər-līn′) ►*n.* The elevation in a mountainous region above which trees do not grow.

timber wolf ►*n.* See **gray wolf.**

tim·bre (tăm′bər, tĭm′-) ►*n.* **1.** The quality of a sound that distinguishes it from others of the same pitch and volume. **2.** Distinctive character: *the timbre of the painter's work.* [< OFr., drum.]

Tim·buk·tu (tĭm′bŭk-tōō′, tĭm-bŭk′tōō) A city of central Mali near the Niger R. NE of Bamako.

time (tīm) ►*n.* **1a.** A nonspatial continuum in which events occur in apparently irreversible succession. **b.** An interval separating two points on this continuum; duration. **c.** A number representing a specific point on this continuum, reckoned in hours and minutes. **d.** A system by which such intervals are measured or such numbers are reckoned. **2.** often **times** A period; era: *hard times.* **3.** A suitable or opportune moment. **4.** A period designated for a given activity: *harvest time.* **5.** One of several instances. **6.** *Informal* A prison sentence. **7.** The rate of speed of a measured activity: *marching in double time.* **8.** The characteristic beat of musical rhythm. ►*adj.* **1.** Of or relating to time. **2.** Constructed to operate at a particular moment: *a time release.* **3.** Of or relating to installment buying. ►*v.* **timed, tim·ing 1.** To set the time for (e.g., an event). **2.** To adjust to keep accurate time. **3.** To adjust the timing of. **4.** To record, set, or maintain the speed, tempo, or duration of. —*idioms:* **for the time being** Temporarily. **from time to time** Once in a while. **on time 1.** According to schedule. **2.** By paying in installments. [< OE *tīma.*] —**tim′er** *n.*

time bomb ►*n.* **1.** A bomb that can be set to detonate at a particular time. **2.** Something that threatens eventual disaster.

time clock ►*n.* A clock that records the starting and quitting times of employees.

time deposit ►*n.* A bank deposit that cannot be withdrawn before a specified date.

time-hon·ored (tīm′ŏn′ərd) ►*adj.* Respected because of age or age-old observance.

time·keep·er (tīm′kē′pər) ►*n.* One who records time, as in a sports event.

time-lapse (tīm′lăps′) ►*adj.* Of or being a technique that photographs a slow process at intervals, so that serial projection of the frames gives an accelerated view of the process.

time·less (tīm′lĭs) ►*adj.* **1.** Eternal. **2.** Unaffected by time; ageless. —**time′less·ly** *adv.* —**time′less·ness** *n.*

time·line (tīm′līn′) ►*n.* **1.** A timetable. **2.** A chronology, esp. a representation of key events in a given time period.

time·ly (tīm′lē) ►*adj.* **-li·er, -li·est** Occurring at a suitable or opportune time; well-timed. —**time′li·ness** *n.*

time-out also **time out** (tīm′out′) ►*n.* A brief cessation of play during a game.

time·piece (tīm′pēs′) ►*n.* An instrument that measures, registers, or records time.

times (tīmz) ►*prep. Math.* Multiplied by: *Five times two is ten.*

time-share (tīm′shâr′) ►*n.* An ownership interest or a lease or license agreement granting use and occupancy of a property for a specific time period each year.

times sign ►*n. Math.* The symbol × used to indicate multiplication.

time·ta·ble (tīm′tā′bəl) ►*n.* A schedule of the expected times of events, such as arrivals and departures at a railroad station.

time·worn (tīm′wôrn′) ►*adj.* **1.** Showing the effects of long use or wear. **2.** Trite.

time zone ►*n.* Any of the 24 longitudinal divisions of the earth's surface in which a standard time is kept.

tim·id (tĭm′ĭd) ►*adj.* **-er, -est 1.** Shy. **2.** Fearful and hesitant. [Lat. *timidus.*] —**ti·mid′i·ty, tim′id·ness** *n.* —**tim′id·ly** *adv.*

tim·ing (tī′mĭng) ►*n.* The regulation of occurrence, pace, or coordination to achieve the most desirable effects.

timing belt ►*n.* A belt that drives the camshaft in an internal-combustion engine.

Ti·mor (tē′môr, tē-môr′) An island in the Malay Archipelago E of Java, divided between Indonesia and East Timor.

tim·or·ous (tĭm′ər-əs) ►*adj.* Fearful; timid. [< Lat. *timor,* fear.] —**tim′or·ous·ly** *adv.* —**tim′or·ous·ness** *n.*

Timor Sea An arm of the Indian Ocean between Timor and Australia.

tim·o·thy (tĭm′ə-thē) ►*n.* A grass widely cultivated for hay. [Prob. after *Timothy* Hanson, 18th-cent. American farmer.]

Timothy ►*n.* See table at **Bible.**

Timothy, Saint. fl. 1st cent. AD. Christian leader and companion of Saint Paul.

tim·pa·ni also **tym·pa·ni** (tĭm′pə-nē) ►*pl.n.* A set of tunable kettledrums usu. used in the percussion section of a symphony orchestra. [Ital. < Gk. *tumpanon,* drum.] —**tim′pa·nist** *n.*

tin (tĭn) ►*n.* **1.** *Symbol* **Sn** A malleable, silvery metallic element used to coat other metals to prevent corrosion and in alloys such as soft solder, pewter, type metal, and bronze. At. no. 50. See table at **element. 2.** A tin container or box. **3.** *Chiefly Brit.* A can for preserved food. ►*v.* **tinned, tin·ning 1.** To plate or coat with tin. **2.** *Chiefly Brit.* To pack in tins; can. [< OE.]

tinc·ture (tĭngk′chər) ►*n.* **1.** A dyeing substance; pigment. **2.** An imparted color; tint. **3.** A trace or vestige. **4.** An alcohol solution of a nonvolatile medicine: *tincture of iodine.* ►*v.* **-tured, -tur·ing** To stain or tint with a color. [< Lat. *tingere, tīnct-,* dye.]

tin·der (tĭn′dər) ►*n.* Readily combustible material used for kindling. [< OE *tynder.*]

tin·der·box (tĭn′dər-bŏks′) ►*n.* **1.** A box for holding tinder. **2.** A potentially explosive situation.

tine (tīn) ►*n.* A point or prong, as on a fork. [< OE *tind.*] —**tined** (tīnd) *adj.*

tin·foil also **tin foil** (tĭn′foil′) ►*n.* A thin pliable sheet of aluminum, tin, or a tin alloy.

tinge (tĭnj) ►*v.* **tinged** (tĭnjd), **tinge·ing** or **ting·ing 1.** To color slightly; tint. **2.** To affect slightly. [< Lat. *tingere.*] —**tinge** *n.*

tin·gle (tĭng′gəl) ►*v.* **-gled, -gling** To have the sensation of being poked lightly with needles in a certain area of the body, often caused by the cold, a sharp slap, or excitement. [ME *tinglen.*] —**tin′gle** *n.* —**tin′gler** *n.* —**tin′gly** *adj.*

tin·ker (tĭng′kər) ►*n.* **1.** A traveling mender of metal utensils. **2.** A clumsy worker; meddler. ►*v.* **1.** To work as a tinker. **2.** To make aimless or experimental adjustments. [ME *tinkere.*]

tin·kle (tĭng′kəl) ►*v.* **-kled, -kling** To make or cause to make light metallic sounds, as those of a small bell. [ME *tinklen.*] —**tin′kle** *n.* —**tin′kly** *adj.*

tin·ny (tĭn′ē) ►*adj.* **-ni·er, -ni·est 1.** Of, containing, or suggesting tin. **2.** Having a thin metallic sound. —**tin′ni·ness** *n.*

tin·sel (tĭn′səl) ►*n.* **1.** Very thin sheets or strips of a glittering material used as a decoration. **2.** Something showy but basically valueless. [< OFr. *estincelle,* spangle.] —**tin′sel** *adj.*

tin·smith (tĭn′smĭth′) ►*n.* One who works with light metal, such as tin.

tint (tĭnt) ►*n.* **1.** A shade of a color, esp. a pale or delicate variation. **2.** A trace. **3.** A hair dye. ►*v.* To give a tint to. [< Lat. *tĭnctus,* dyeing.] —**tint′er** *n.*

tin·tin·nab·u·la·tion (tĭn′tĭ-năb′yə-lā′shən) ►*n.* The ringing or sounding of bells. [< Lat. *tintinnābulum,* small bell.]

Tin·to·ret·to (tĭn′tə-rĕt′ō) 1518–94. Italian painter.

tin·type (tĭn′tīp′) ►*n.* See **ferrotype.**

ti·ny (tī′nē) ►*adj.* **-ni·er, -ni·est** Extremely small. See Synonyms at **small.** [< ME *tine.*] —**ti′ni·ness** *n.*

tip¹ (tĭp) ►*n.* **1.** The end of a pointed or projecting object. **2.** A piece meant to be fitted to the end of something. ►*v.* **tipped, tip·ping 1.** To furnish with a tip. **2.** To cover, decorate, or remove the tip of. [ME.]

tip² (tĭp) ►*v.* **tipped, tip·ping 1.** To push or knock over; topple. **2.** To tilt. See Synonyms at **slant. 3.** To raise (one's hat) in greeting. [ME *tipen.*] —**tip** *n.*

tip³ (tĭp) ►*v.* **tipped, tip·ping** To strike gently; tap. [< ME *tippe,* a tap.] —**tip** *n.*

tip⁴ (tĭp) ►*n.* **1.** An extra sum of money given to someone for services rendered; gratuity. **2.** A piece of useful advice or information. [?] —**tip** *v.* —**tip′per** *n.*

ti·pi (tē′pē) ►*n.* Var. of **tepee.**

tip-off (tĭp′ôf′, -ŏf′) ►*n. Informal* A piece of inside information; hint or warning.

tip·pet (tĭp′ĭt) ►*n.* A covering for the shoulders with long ends that hang in front. [ME *tipet.*]

tip·ple (tĭp′əl) ►*v.* **-pled, -pling** To drink (alcoholic liquor), esp. habitually. [Perh. < ME *tipeler,* bartender.] —**tip′pler** *n.*

tip·ster (tĭp′stər) ►*n. Informal* One who sells tips to bettors or speculators.

tip·sy (tĭp′sē) ►*adj.* **-si·er, -si·est** Slightly drunk. [< TIP².] —**tip′si·ly** *adv.* —**tip′si·ness** *n.*

tip·toe (tĭp′tō′) ►*v.* To walk quietly on one's toes. ►*adv.* On one's toes. —**tip′toe′** *n.*

tip·top (tĭp′tŏp′) ►*n.* The highest point; summit. ►*adj.* Excellent; first-rate.

ti·rade (tī′rād′, tĭ-rād′) ►*n.* An angry, often denunciatory speech; diatribe. [< OFr., firing.]

tir·a·mi·su (tĭr′ə-mē′soō, -mē-soō′) ►*n.* A dessert of cake infused with a liquid such as coffee and layered with a cheese filling. [Ital. *tira mi sù,* pick me up.]

Ti·ra·në also **Ti·ra·na** (tə-rä′nə, tē-) The capital of Albania, in the W-central part.

tire¹ (tīr) ►*v.* **tired, tir·ing 1.** To make or become weary. **2.** To make or become bored or impatient. [< OE *tyrian.*]

tire² (tīr) ►*n.* **1.** A covering for a wheel, usu. of hollow rubber filled with compressed air. **2.** A hoop of metal or rubber fitted around a wheel. [ME.]

tired (tīrd) ►*adj.* **1a.** Fatigued. **b.** Impatient; bored. **2.** Trite: *the same tired rhetoric as always.* —**tired′ly** *adv.* —**tired′ness** *n.*

tire iron ►*n.* A tool consisting of a metal bar with a socket wrench at one end, used for changing tires.

tire·less (tīr′lĭs) ►*adj.* Not tiring easily; indefatigable. —**tire′less·ly** *adv.*
    Syns: *indefatigable, unflagging, unwearied, weariless adj.*

tire·some (tīr′səm) ►*adj.* Tedious; wearisome. —**tire′some·ly** *adv.* —**tire′some·ness** *n.*

'tis (tĭz) It is.

Tish·ri (tĭsh′rē, -rä) ►*n.* The 7th month of the Jewish calendar. See table at **calendar.** [Heb. *tišrî.*]

tis·sue (tĭsh′oō, -yoō) ►*n.* **1.** A fine, very thin fabric, such as gauze. **2.** Thin translucent paper used esp. for packing or wrapping. **3.** A soft absorbent piece of paper used as toilet paper or a handkerchief. **4.** A web; network. **5.** *Biol.* **a.** A group of cells that are similar in form or function. **b.** Cellular matter in general. [< OFr. *tissu,* woven < Lat. *texere,* weave.]

tit¹ (tĭt) ►*n.* Any of various insectivorous songbirds, esp. those of Eurasia and Africa. [< TITMOUSE.]

tit² (tĭt) ►*n.* A teat. [< OE *titt.*]

Ti·tan (tīt′n) ►*n.* **1.** *Gk. Myth.* One of a family of giants who were overthrown by the family of Zeus. **2. titan** A person of colossal size, strength, or achievement.

ti·tan·ic (tī-tăn′ĭk) ►*adj.* Of enormous size or strength; colossal. —**ti·tan′i·cal·ly** *adv.*

ti·ta·ni·um (tī-tā′nē-əm, tĭ-) ►*n. Symbol* **Ti** A highly corrosion-resistant, lustrous white metallic element used in alloys for low weight, strength, and high-temperature stability. At. no. 22. See table at **element.**

tithe (tīth) ►*n.* **1.** A portion of one's annual income given voluntarily, esp. a contribution of one tenth of one's income for the support of a church. **2.** A tenth part. ►*v.* **tithed, tith·ing** To pay a tithe. [< OE *tēotha.*] —**tith′er** *n.*

Ti·tian (tĭsh′ən) 1488?–1576. Italian painter. —**Ti′tian·esque′** *adj.*

Ti·ti·ca·ca (tē′tē-kä′kä), **Lake** A freshwater lake of South America in the Andes on the Bolivia-Peru border.

tit·il·late (tĭt′l-āt′) ►*v.* **-lat·ed, -lat·ing** To excite pleasurably; arouse. [Lat. *tītillāre.*] —**tit′·il·lat′ing·ly** *adv.* —**tit′il·la′tion** *n.*

ti·tle (tīt′l) ►*n.* **1.** An identifying name given to a book, film, or other work. **2a.** A formal appellation, as of rank or office. **b.** Such an appellation used to indicate nobility. **3.** A claim or right. **4.** *Law* **a.** A form of ownership free of valid claims by other parties. **b.** The evidence of a right of possession. **c.** The instrument, such as a deed, that constitutes this evidence. **5.** *Sports* A championship. ▸*v.* **-tled, -tling** To give a title to. [< Lat. *titulus.*]

ti·tled (tīt′ld) ▸*adj.* Having a title, esp. of nobility.

tit·mouse (tĭt′mous′) ▸*n., pl.* **-mice** (-mīs′) Any of several small insectivorous songbirds of woodland areas. [< ME *titmose.*]

Ti·to (tē′tō), Marshal. Josip Broz. 1892–1980. Yugoslavian president (1953–80).

ti·tra·tion (tī-trā′shən) ▸*n.* Determination of the concentration of a solute by measuring the amount of an added reagent needed to complete a reaction. [< OFr. *titre,* title.] **—ti′-trate′** *v.*

tit·ter (tĭt′ər) ▸*v.* To laugh in a restrained, nervous giggle. [Prob. imit.] **—tit′ter** *n.*

tit·tle (tĭt′l) ▸*n.* The tiniest bit; iota. [< Med.Lat. *titulus,* diacritical mark.]

tit·u·lar (tĭch′ə-lər) ▸*adj.* **1.** Of or constituting a title. **2.** In name only; nominal. [< Lat. *titulus,* title.]

Ti·tus¹ (tī′təs) AD 39–81. Emperor of Rome (79–81).

Ti·tus² (tī′təs) ▸*n.* See table at **Bible.**

tiz·zy (tĭz′ē) ▸*n., pl.* **-zies** *Slang* A state of nervous confusion; dither. [?]

TKO ▸*abbr.* technical knockout

TLC ▸*abbr.* tender loving care

Tlin·git (tlĭng′gĭt, -kĭt, klĭng′kĭt) ▸*n., pl.* **-git** or **-gits 1.** A member of a Native American people of the coastal and island areas of SE Alaska. **2.** The language of the Tlingit.

TM ▸*abbr.* trademark

TN ▸*abbr.* Tennessee

TNO ▸*abbr.* trans-Neptunian object

Tnpk. ▸*abbr.* turnpike

TNT ▸*n.* A yellow crystalline compound used as an explosive. [*t(ri)n(itro)t(oluene).*]

to (tōō; *when unstressed* tə) ▸*prep.* **1.** In a direction toward. **2.** Reaching as far as. **3.** Toward or reaching a given state. **4.** In contact with; against: *cheek to cheek.* **5.** In front of: *face to face.* **6.** For or of: *the top to the jar.* **7.** Concerning; regarding: *no answer to my letter.* **8.** In a relation with: *parallel to the road.* **9.** As an accompaniment for. **10.** Composing; constituting: *two cups to a pint.* **11.** In accord with: *not to my liking.* **12.** As compared with: *a book superior to his others.* **13a.** Before: *The time is ten to five.* **b.** Up till; until: *worked from nine to five.* **14.** For the purpose of: *went out to lunch.* **15.** Used before a verb to indicate the infinitive: *I'd like to go.* ▸*adv.* **1.** Into a shut or closed position: *pushed the door to.* **2.** Into a state of consciousness: *The patient came to.* **3.** Into a state of action: *sat down for lunch and fell to.* **4.** *Naut.* Into the wind. [< OE *tō.*]

toad (tōd) ▸*n.* Any of various amphibians characteristically living on land and having drier, rougher skin and shorter legs than the frogs. [< OE *tādige.*]

toad·stool (tōd′stōōl′) ▸*n.* A fungus with an umbrella-shaped fruiting body, esp. one thought to be inedible or poisonous.

toad·y (tō′dē) ▸*n., pl.* **-ies** A servile flatterer;

sycophant. ▸*v.* **-ied, -y·ing** To be a toady to. See Synonyms at **fawn¹.** [< TOAD.]

toast¹ (tōst) ▸*v.* **1.** To heat and brown (e.g., bread). **2.** To warm thoroughly. ▸*n.* Sliced bread heated and browned. [< Lat. *torrēre, tost-,* parch.]

toast² (tōst) ▸*n.* **1.** The act of raising a glass and drinking in honor of a person or thing. **2.** The person or thing honored in this way. ▸*v.* To drink to or propose a toast (to). [Poss. < TOAST¹.]

toast·er (tō′stər) ▸*n.* A mechanical device used to toast bread.

toast·y (tō′stē) ▸*adj.* **-i·er, -i·est** Pleasantly warm.

to·bac·co (tə-băk′ō) ▸*n., pl.* **-cos** or **-coes 1a.** A tropical American plant widely cultivated for its leaves, which are used primarily for smoking. **b.** The leaves of this plant processed chiefly for use in cigarettes, cigars, snuff, or pipes. **2.** Such products collectively. [Sp. *tabaco.*]

to·bac·co·nist (tə-băk′ə-nĭst) ▸*n.* A dealer in tobacco and smoking supplies.

To·ba·go (tə-bā′gō) An island of Trinidad and Tobago in the SE West Indies NE of Trinidad.

To·bit (tō′bĭt) ▸*n.* See table at **Bible.**

to·bog·gan (tə-bŏg′ən) ▸*n.* A long, narrow, runnerless sled constructed of thin boards curled upward at the front end. ▸*v.* **1.** To travel on a toboggan. **2.** *Slang* To decline or fall rapidly. [< Micmac *topaghan.*] **—to·bog′gan·er, to·bog′gan·ist** *n.*

toc·ca·ta (tə-kä′tə) ▸*n. Mus.* A virtuoso, free-style composition, usu. for the organ, with brilliant runs and scales. [Ital.]

Tocque·ville (tōk′vĭl), **Alexis Charles Henri Clérel de** 1805–59. French traveler and writer.

toc·sin (tŏk′sĭn) ▸*n.* A warning bell. [< OProv. *tocasenh.*]

to·day (tə-dā′) ▸*n.* The present day, time, or age. ▸*adv.* **1.** During or on the present day. **2.** At the present time. [< OE *tō dæge.*]

tod·dle (tŏd′l) ▸*v.* **-dled, -dling** To walk with short unsteady steps. [?] **—tod′dler** *n.*

tod·dy (tŏd′ē) ▸*n., pl.* **-dies** A hot toddy. [Hindi *tāṛī,* sap of palm.]

to-do (tə-dōō′) ▸*n., pl.* **-dos** (-dōōz′) *Informal* An excited reaction; fuss.

toe (tō) ▸*n.* **1.** One of the digits of the foot. **2.** The forward part of something worn on the foot. **3.** Something resembling a toe in form, function, or location. ▸*v.* **toed, toe·ing** To touch, kick, or reach with the toe. [< OE *tā.*]

toed (tōd) ▸*adj.* Having a toe, esp. of a specified number or kind: *an even-toed ungulate.*

TOEFL (tō′fəl) A trademark for a test of English as a foreign language.

toe·hold (tō′hōld′) ▸*n.* **1.** A space to support the toe in climbing. **2.** A slight or initial advantage.

toe·nail (tō′nāl′) ▸*n.* The nail on a toe.

tof·fee (tô′fē, tŏf′ē) ▸*n.* A chewy candy of brown sugar or molasses and butter. [< TAFFY.]

to·fu (tō′fōō) ▸*n.* A protein-rich food made from ground soybeans. [J. *tōfu,* of Chin. orig.]

tog (tŏg, tôg) *Informal* ▸*n.* **togs** Clothes. ▸*v.* **togged, tog·ging** To dress or clothe. [< Lat. *toga,* TOGA.]

to·ga (tō′gə) ▸*n.* A loose one-piece outer garment worn in public by male citizens in ancient Rome. [Lat.] **—to′gaed** (tō′gəd) *adj.*

to·geth·er (tə-gĕth′ər) ►*adv.* **1.** In or into a single group or place. **2.** In or into contact. **3a.** In relationship to one another. **b.** By joint or cooperative effort. **4.** Regarded collectively. **5.** Simultaneously. **6.** In harmony or accord. [< OE *tōgædere.*] —**to·geth′er·ness** *n.*

Usage: Together with, like *in addition to,* is often employed following the subject of a sentence or clause to introduce an addition. The addition, however, does not alter the number of the verb, which is governed by the subject: *The king* (singular), *together with two aides, is expected in an hour.* The same is true of *along with, besides,* and *in addition to.*

tog·gle switch (tŏg′əl) ►*n.* A switch in which a projecting lever with a spring is used to open or close an electric circuit.

To·go (tō′gō′) A country of W Africa on the Bight of Benin. Cap. Lomé.

tö·grög (tœ′grœg) or **tu·grik** (to͞o′grĭk) ►*n., pl.* **tögrög** See table at **currency.** [Mongolian *tögrög,* circle, tögrög.]

toil¹ (toil) ►*v.* **1.** To work strenuously. **2.** To proceed with difficulty. ►*n.* Tiring labor or effort. [< Lat. *tudiculāre,* stir about.] —**toil′er** *n.*

toil² (toil) ►*n.* often **toils** Something that entangles: *in the toils of despair.* [< Lat. *tēla,* web.]

toi·let (toi′lĭt) ►*n.* **1a.** A disposal apparatus for defecation and urination. **b.** A room or booth containing such an apparatus. **2.** The act of dressing or grooming oneself. [< OFr. *tellette,* cloth, dim. of *teile;* see TOIL².]

toilet paper ►*n.* Thin absorbent paper for cleaning oneself after defecation or urination.

toi·let·ry (toi′lĭ-trē) ►*n., pl.* **-ries** An article used in personal grooming or dressing.

toi·lette (twä-lĕt′) ►*n.* **1.** The process of dressing or grooming oneself; toilet. **2.** A person's dress or style of dress. [Fr.; see TOILET.]

toilet water ►*n.* See **eau de toilette.**

to·ken (tō′kən) ►*n.* **1a.** Something serving as an indication or representation; sign. **b.** Something that signifies or evidences authority, validity, or identity. **2.** One that represents a group. **3.** A keepsake. **4.** A piece of stamped metal used as a substitute for currency. ►*adj.* Done as an indication or a pledge: *a token payment.* [< OE *tācen.*]

to·ken·ism (tō′kə-nĭz′əm) ►*n.* Symbolic gestures rather than effective action toward a goal.

To·ky·o (tō′kē-ō′, -kyō) The capital of Japan, in E-central Honshu on **Tokyo Bay,** an inlet of the Pacific.

told (tōld) ►*v.* P.t. and p.part. of **tell.**

tol·er·a·ble (tŏl′ər-ə-bəl) ►*adj.* **1.** Endurable. **2.** Acceptable but not superior; passable. —**tol′·er·a·bil′i·ty, tol′er·a·ble·ness** *n.* —**tol′er·a·bly** *adv.*

tol·er·ance (tŏl′ər-əns) ►*n.* **1.** The capacity for respecting the beliefs or practices of others. **2.** Leeway for variation from a standard. **3.** The capacity to endure hardship or pain. **4.** Resistance, as to a drug. —**tol′er·ant** *adj.* —**tol′er·ant·ly** *adv.*

tol·er·ate (tŏl′ə-rāt′) ►*v.* **-at·ed, -at·ing** **1.** To refrain from interfering with or prohibiting (something undesirable or outside one's own practice or beliefs); allow. **2.** To recognize and respect (the rights, beliefs, or practices of others). **3.** To be patient regarding (something

unpleasant or undesirable); endure: *tolerated his insults for weeks.* [Lat. *tolerāre,* to bear.] —**tol′·er·a′tion** *n.*

Tol·kien (tōl′kēn′, tŏl′-), **J(ohn) R(onald) R(euel)** 1892–1973. British writer.

J.R.R. Tolkien

toll¹ (tōl) ►*n.* **1.** A fixed tax for a privilege, esp. for passage across a bridge. **2.** A charge for a service, such as a long-distance telephone call. **3.** The amount or extent of loss or destruction, as in a disaster. [< Gk. *telōneion,* tollbooth.]

toll² (tōl) ►*v.* **1.** To sound (a large bell) slowly at regular intervals. **2.** To announce or summon by tolling. ►*n.* The sound of a bell being struck. [ME *tollen.*]

toll·booth (tōl′bo͞oth′) ►*n.* A booth where a toll is collected.

toll·gate (tōl′gāt′) ►*n.* A gate barring passage until a toll is collected.

Tol·stoy (tōl′stoi, tŏl′-), Count **Leo** 1828–1910. Russian writer. —**Tol·stoy′an** *adj.*

Tol·tec (tōl′tĕk′, tŏl′-) ►*n., pl.* **-tec** or **-tecs** A member of a people of central and S Mexico whose empire flourished from the 10th to the 12th cent. —**Tol′tec, Tol′tec′an** *adj.*

tom (tŏm) ►*n.* The male of various animals, esp. a cat or turkey. [< *Tom,* nickname for *Thomas.*]

tom·a·hawk (tŏm′ə-hôk′) ►*n.* A light ax formerly used as a tool or weapon by certain Native American peoples. [Virginia Algonquian *tamahaac.*] —**tom′a·hawk′** *v.*

to·ma·to (tə-mā′tō, -mä′-) ►*n., pl.* **-toes** **1.** A fleshy, smooth-skinned reddish fruit, eaten as a vegetable. **2.** A plant bearing such fruit. [< Nahuatl *tomatl.*]

tomb (to͞om) ►*n.* **1.** A place of burial. **2.** A vault or chamber for burial of the dead. [< Gk. *tumbos.*]

tom·boy (tŏm′boi′) ►*n.* A girl whose behavior is perceived to be stereotypically boyish or masculine.

tomb·stone (to͞om′stōn′) ►*n.* A gravestone.

tom·cat (tŏm′kăt′) ►*n.* A male cat.

tome (tōm) ►*n.* A book, esp. a large or scholarly one. [< Gk. *tomos,* section.]

tom·fool·er·y (tŏm-fo͞o′lə-rē) ►*n., pl.* **-ies** **1.** Foolish behavior. **2.** Nonsense.

to·mog·ra·phy (tə-mŏg′rə-fē) ►*n.* A technique for making detailed x-rays of a predetermined plane section of a solid object. [Gk. *tomos,* section + –GRAPHY.] —**to′mo·gram′** (tō′mə-grăm′) *n.* —**to′mo·graph′** *n.* —**to′mo·graph′ic** *adj.*

to·mor·row (tə-môr′ō, -mŏr′ō) ►*n.* **1.** The day

following today. **2.** The near future. ►*adv.* On or for the day following today. [< OE *tō morgenne*, in the morning.]

tom-tom (tŏm′tŏm′) ►*n.* **1.** A mid-sized drum having a cylindrical body, often used in drum sets. **2.** Any of various small-headed drums that are beaten with the hands. [Hindi *ṭamṭam*.]

–tomy ►*suff.* Cutting; incision: *lobotomy.* [< Gk. *tomos,* cutting < *temnein,* cut.]

ton (tŭn) ►*n.* **1a.** A short ton. **b.** A long ton. **c.** A metric ton. See table at **measurement. 2.** *Informal* A very large quantity: *tons of fan mail.* [< OE *tunne,* large cask.]

to·nal·i·ty (tō-năl′ĭ-tē) ►*n., pl.* **-ties** *Mus.* The arrangement of the tones and chords of a composition in relation to a tonic.

tone (tōn) ►*n.* **1.** *Mus.* **a.** A sound of distinct pitch, quality, and duration; note. **b.** The largest interval between adjacent notes in the diatonic scale. **2.** The quality of sound. **3.** The pitch of a word or phrase. **4.** Manner of expression: *an angry tone of voice.* **5.** A general quality or atmosphere: *a room with an elegant tone.* **6a.** A color or shade of color. **b.** Quality of color. **7.** *Physiol.* **a.** The tension in resting muscles. **b.** Normal tissue firmness. ►*v.* **toned, ton·ing 1.** To give a particular tone or inflection to. **2.** To make firmer or stronger, as muscles. —*phrasal verb:* **tone down** To make less harsh or severe; moderate. [< Gk. *tonos.*] —**ton′al** *adj.* —**ton′al·ly** *adv.*

ton·er (tō′nər) ►*n.* One that tones, esp. a powdery ink used dry or suspended in a liquid to produce a photocopy.

Ton·ga (tŏng′gə) A country in the SW Pacific E of Fiji comprising about 150 islands. Cap. Nukuʻalofa. —**Ton′gan** *adj. & n.*

tongs (tôngz, tŏngz) ►*pl.n.* (takes sing. or pl. v.) A grasping device consisting of two arms joined at one end by a pivot or hinge. [< OE *tong.*]

tongue (tŭng) ►*n.* **1.** The fleshy, movable, muscular organ in the mouth that functions in tasting, chewing, swallowing, and speech. **2.** The tongue of an animal, such as a cow, used as food. **3.** A spoken language. **4.** Quality of utterance: *his sharp tongue.* **5.** Anything resembling a tongue in shape or function. [< OE *tunge.*]

tongue-in-cheek (tŭng′ĭn-chēk′) ►*adj.* Meant ironically or facetiously.

tongue-tied (tŭng′tīd′) ►*adj.* Speechless or confused in expression, as from shyness, embarrassment, or astonishment.

tongue twister ►*n.* **1.** A word or group of words difficult to articulate rapidly. **2.** Something difficult to pronounce.

ton·ic (tŏn′ĭk) ►*n.* **1a.** An agent, such as a medication, that supposedly improves health or well-being. **b.** A liquid preparation for the scalp or hair. **2.** An invigorating, refreshing, or restorative agent or influence: *Laughter was a tonic for the losing team.* **3.** See **tonic water. 4.** *Regional* See **soft drink. 5.** *Mus.* The first note of a diatonic scale; keynote. ►*adj.* **1.** Stimulating physical or mental vigor. **2.** *Mus.* Of or based on the tonic or keynote. **3.** *Med.* Marked by continuous muscle contraction: *a tonic seizure.* [< Gk. *tonos,* tone.]

tonic water ►*n.* A carbonated beverage flavored with quinine.

to·night (tə-nīt′) ►*adv.* On or during the present or coming night. ►*n.* This night or the night of

this day. [< OE *tō niht,* at night; see NIGHT.]

Ton·kin (tŏn′kĭn′, tŏng′-) A historical region of SE Asia on the **Gulf of Tonkin,** an arm of the South China Sea, now forming most of N Vietnam. —**Ton′kin·ese′** (-ēz′, -ēs′) *adj. & n.*

ton·nage (tŭn′ĭj) ►*n.* **1.** The number of tons of water a ship displaces when afloat. **2.** The capacity of a merchant ship in units of 100 cu. ft. **3.** A charge per ton on cargo. **4.** The total shipping of a country or port, figured in tons. **5.** Weight measured in tons.

ton·sil (tŏn′səl) ►*n.* A mass of lymphoid tissue, esp. either of two such masses embedded at the back of the mouth. [< Lat. *tōnsillae,* tonsils.] —**ton′sil·lar** *adj.*

ton·sil·lec·to·my (tŏn′sə-lĕk′tə-mē) ►*n., pl.* **-mies** Surgical removal of tonsils or a tonsil.

ton·sil·li·tis (tŏn′sə-lī′tĭs) ►*n.* Inflammation of the tonsils. —**ton′sil·lit′ic** (-lĭt′ĭk) *adj.*

ton·so·ri·al (tŏn-sôr′ē-əl) ►*adj.* Of barbering or a barber. [< Lat. *tōnsor,* barber.]

ton·sure (tŏn′shər) ►*n.* **1.** The act of shaving the head, esp. as a preliminary to becoming a priest. **2.** The part of the head so shaved. ►*v.* **-sured, -sur·ing** To shave the head of. [< Lat. *tondēre, tōns-,* shear.]

ton·y (tō′nē) ►*adj.* **-i·er, -i·est** *Informal* Expensive, luxurious, or exclusive.

too (to͞o) ►*adv.* **1.** In addition; also. **2.** More than enough; excessively: *She worries too much.* **3.** *Informal* Indeed; so: *You will too do it!* [< OE *tō.*]

took (to͝ok) ►*v.* P.t. of **take.**

tool (to͞ol) ►*n.* **1.** A device, such as a saw, used to perform manual or mechanical work. **2.** A machine, such as a lathe, used to cut and shape machine parts. **3.** A means or instrument. **4.** *Comp.* An application program, esp. one that creates or edits other programs. **5.** A dupe. ►*v.* **1.** To form, work, or decorate with a tool. **2.** *Slang* To drive or ride in a vehicle. —*phrasal verb:* **tool up** To furnish tools or machinery for (an industry or factory). [< OE *tōl.*]

tool·bar (to͞ol′bär′) ►*n.* A row of icons on a computer screen for activating commands and functions.

toot (to͞ot) ►*v.* To sound a horn or whistle in short blasts. ►*n.* A blast, as of a horn. [Ult. imit.] —**toot′er** *n.*

tooth (to͞oth) ►*n., pl.* **teeth** (tēth) **1.** One of a set of hard, bonelike structures rooted in sockets in the jaws, used to bite and chew. **2.** A projecting part resembling a tooth in shape or function, as on a comb. —*idiom:* **to the teeth** Lacking nothing; completely: *armed to the teeth.* [< OE *tōth.*] —**toothed** (to͞otht, to͞othd) *adj.* —**tooth′less** *adj.*

tooth·ache (to͞oth′āk′) ►*n.* An aching pain in or near a tooth.

tooth·brush (to͞oth′brŭsh′) ►*n.* A brush for cleaning teeth.

toothed whale ►*n.* A cetacean having numerous teeth and a single blowhole.

tooth·paste (to͞oth′pāst′) ►*n.* A paste for cleaning teeth.

tooth·pick (to͞oth′pĭk′) ►*n.* A small stick for removing food from between the teeth.

tooth·some (to͞oth′səm) ►*adj.* Delicious; luscious.

top¹ (tŏp) ►*n.* **1.** The uppermost part, point, surface, or end. **2.** A lid or cap. **3a.** The highest position or rank. **b.** The highest degree or pitch. ►*v.* **topped, top·ping 1.** To form, furnish with, or serve as a top. **2.** To reach or go over the top of. **3.** To exceed or surpass. —*idioms:* **off the top of (one's) head** *Informal* In an impromptu way. **on top of** *Informal* **1.** In control of. **2.** Fully informed about. **3.** In addition to. **4.** Following closely on. [< OE.]

top² (tŏp) ►*n.* A toy made to spin on a pointed end. [< OE.]

to·paz (tō′păz′) ►*n.* **1.** A mineral consisting largely of aluminum silicate and valued as a gem. **2.** Any of various yellow gemstones, esp. a yellow variety of sapphire. [< Gk. *topazos.*]

top·coat (tŏp′kōt′) ►*n.* A lightweight overcoat.

top dog ►*n. Slang* One who has the dominant position or highest authority.

top-drawer (tŏp′drôr′) ►*adj.* Of the highest importance, rank, or merit.

To·pe·ka (tə-pē′kə) The capital of KS, in the NE part W of Kansas City.

top·flight (tŏp′flīt′) ►*adj. Informal* First-rate; excellent.

top hat ►*n.* A man's formal hat with a narrow brim and a tall cylindrical crown.

top-heav·y (tŏp′hĕv′ē) ►*adj.* Likely to topple due to being overloaded at the top.

to·pi·ar·y (tō′pē-ĕr′ē) ►*n., pl.* **-ies 1.** The art of trimming live shrubs or trees into decorative shapes. **2.** A plant so trimmed. [< Gk. *topia,* ornamental gardening.]

top·ic (tŏp′ĭk) ►*n.* The subject of a speech, essay, thesis, or conversation. [< Gk. *topos,* place.]

top·i·cal (tŏp′ĭ-kəl) ►*adj.* **1.** Local. **2.** Currently of interest; contemporary. **3.** *Med.* Of or applied to a localized area of the body. —**top′i·cal′i·ty** (-kăl′ĭ-tē) *n.* —**top′i·cal·ly** *adv.*

top·knot (tŏp′nŏt′) ►*n.* **1.** A crest or knot of hair or feathers on the crown of the head. **2.** A decorative ribbon or bow worn as a headdress.

top·less (tŏp′lĭs) ►*adj.* **1.** Having no top. **2.** Not covering the breasts.

top·most (tŏp′mōst′) ►*adj.* Highest; uppermost.

top-notch or **top·notch** (tŏp′nŏch′) ►*adj. Informal* First-rate; excellent.

topo– ►*pref.* Place: *topography.* [< Gk. *topos,* place.]

to·pog·ra·phy (tə-pŏg′rə-fē) ►*n.* **1.** The physical features of a region. **2.** Description or representation of such features. —**to·pog′ra·pher** *n.* —**top′o·graph′ic** (tŏp′ə-grăf′ĭk), **top′o·graph′i·cal** *adj.* —**top′o·graph′i·cal·ly** *adv.*

top·ping (tŏp′ĭng) ►*n.* A sauce, frosting, or garnish for food.

top·ple (tŏp′əl) ►*v.* **-pled, -pling 1.** To knock over. **2.** To bring about the destruction or ending of. See Synonyms at **overthrow. 3.** To defeat, as in a contest: *toppled the league leader.* **4.** To totter and fall. [< TOP¹.]

tops (tŏps) ►*adj. Slang* First-rate; excellent.

top·sail (tŏp′səl, -sāl′) ►*n. Naut.* A square sail set above the lowest sail on the mast of a square-rigged ship.

top-se·cret (tŏp′sē′krĭt) ►*adj.* Of the highest level of security classification.

top·side (tŏp′sīd′) ►*adv. & adj.* On or to the upper parts of a ship; on deck.

top·soil (tŏp′soil′) ►*n.* The upper part of soil.

top·sy-tur·vy (tŏp′sē-tûr′vē) ►*adv.* **1.** Upside-down. **2.** In utter disorder or confusion. ►*adj.* In a disordered state. [Prob. < TOP¹ + obsolete *terve,* overturn.] —**top′sy-tur′vi·ly** *adv.* —**top′sy-tur′vi·ness** *n.*

toque (tōk) ►*n.* A woman's small, brimless, close-fitting hat. [Fr.]

toque
knit toque

tor (tôr) ►*n.* A rocky peak or hill. [< OE *torr,* prob. of Celt. orig.]

To·rah also **to·rah** (tôr′ə, tô-rä′) ►*n. Judaism* **1.** The first five books of the Hebrew Scriptures. See table at **Bible. 2.** The scroll on which these scriptures are written, used in a synagogue during services.

torch (tôrch) ►*n.* **1a.** A portable light produced by the flame of a burning material wound about the end of a stick. **b.** *Chiefly Brit.* A flashlight. **2.** Something that serves to illuminate or guide. **3.** *Slang* An arsonist. **4.** A portable apparatus that produces a very hot flame by the combustion of gases, used in welding. ►*v. Slang* To set on fire. [< Lat. *torquēre,* twist.]

tore (tôr) ►*v.* P.t. of **tear¹.**

tor·e·a·dor (tôr′ē-ə-dôr′) ►*n.* A bullfighter. [Sp.]

tor·ment (tôr′mĕnt′) ►*n.* **1.** Great physical pain or mental anguish. **2.** A source of harassment or pain. ►*v.* (tôr-mĕnt′, tôr′mĕnt′) **1.** To cause to undergo torment. See Synonyms at **afflict. 2.** To pester; annoy. [< Lat. *tormentum.*] —**tor·ment′ing·ly** *adv.* —**tor·men′tor, tor·ment′er** *n.*

torn (tôrn) ►*v.* P.part. of **tear¹.**

tor·na·do (tôr-nā′dō) ►*n., pl.* **-does** or **-dos** A violently rotating column of air extending from a cumulonimbus cloud to the ground and having destructive winds. [< Sp. *tronada,* thunderstorm.]

To·ron·to (tə-rŏn′tō) The capital of Ontario, Canada, in the S part on Lake Ontario.

tor·pe·do (tôr-pē′dō) ►*n., pl.* **-does** A cigar-shaped, self-propelled underwater projectile, designed to detonate on contact with or in the vicinity of a target. ►*v.* **-doed, -do·ing** To attack or destroy with or as if with a torpedo. [Lat. *torpēdō,* electric ray.]

tor·pid (tôr′pĭd) ►*adj.* **1.** Lethargic or inactive. **2.** Conducive to inactivity: *a torpid summer evening.* **3.** Dormant; hibernating. [Lat. *torpidus.*] —**tor·pid′i·ty** *n.*

tor·por (tôr′pər) ►*n.* **1.** A state of inactivity or insensibility. **2.** Lethargy; apathy. [Lat. < *torpēre,* be stiff.] —**tor′po·rif′ic** (-pə-rĭf′ĭk) *adj.*

torque (tôrk) ►*n.* The tendency of a force to produce rotation about an axis. [< Lat. *torquēre,* twist.] —**torque** *v.*

tor·rent (tôr′ənt, tŏr′-) ►*n.* **1.** A turbulent, swift-flowing stream. **2.** A deluge. **3.** A heavy, uncontrolled flow. [< Lat. *torrēre,* burn.] —**tor·ren′tial** (tô-rĕn′shəl, tə-) *adj.*

tor·rid (tôr′ĭd, tŏr′-) ►*adj.* **-er, -est 1.** Very dry and hot. **2.** Passionate. [Lat. *torridus* < *torrēre,* parch.] —**tor·rid′i·ty, tor′rid·ness** *n.* —**tor′-rid·ly** *adv.*

Torrid Zone The central latitude zone of the earth, between the tropic of Cancer and the tropic of Capricorn; the tropics.

tor·sion (tôr′shən) ►*n.* **1.** A twisting or turning. **2.** The stress caused when one end of an object is twisted relative to the other end. [< Lat. *torquēre, tort-,* twist.] —**tor′sion·al** *adj.*

tor·so (tôr′sō) ►*n., pl.* **-sos 1.** The trunk of the human body. **2.** A statue of the human body without the head or limbs. [< Lat. *thyrsus,* stalk.]

tort (tôrt) ►*n. Law* A wrong committed by someone who is legally obligated to provide a certain amount of carefulness in behavior to another, who may seek compensation in a civil suit for damages. [< Lat. *torquēre, tort-,* twist.]

torte (tôrt, tôr′tə) ►*n.* A rich cake made with eggs, flour, and usu. chopped nuts. [Ger.]

tor·til·la (tôr-tē′yə) ►*n.* A thin disk of unleavened bread made from cornmeal or wheat flour. [< LLat. *torta,* a kind of bread.]

tor·toise (tôr′tĭs) ►*n.* Any of various terrestrial turtles. [< Med.Lat. *tortūca.*]

tor·toise·shell (tôr′tĭs-shĕl′) ►*n.* The translucent brownish outer covering of certain turtles, formerly used to make combs and jewelry.

Tor·to·la (tôr-tō′lə) An island of the British Virgin Is. in the West Indies E of Puerto Rico.

tor·tu·ous (tôr′chōō-əs) ►*adj.* **1.** Winding or twisting. **2.** Not straightforward; devious. **3.** Complex. [< Lat. *tortus,* twisted.] —**tor′tu·ous·ly** *adv.* —**tor′tu·ous·ness** *n.*

tor·ture (tôr′chər) ►*n.* **1.** Infliction of severe pain as a means of punishment or coercion. **2.** Pain or mental anguish. ►*v.* **-tured, -tur·ing 1.** To subject to torture. **2.** To bring great physical or mental pain upon. See Synonyms at **afflict. 3.** To overwork, misinterpret, or distort. [< Lat. *torquēre, tort-,* twist.] —**tor′tur·er** *n.* —**tor′tur·ous** *adj.* —**tor′tur·ous·ly** *adv.*

To·ry (tôr′ē) ►*n., pl.* **-ries 1.** A member of the Conservative Party in Great Britain. **2.** An American who favored the British side during the American Revolution. [< Ir.Gael. *tóraidhe,* robber.] —**To′ry** *adj.* —**To′ry·ism** *n.*

Tos·ca·ni·ni (tŏs′kə-nē′nē), **Arturo** 1867–1957. Italian conductor.

toss (tôs, tŏs) ►*v.* **1.** To throw lightly. **2a.** To move or cause to move from side to side or up and down. **b.** To flip (a coin) to decide something. **3.** To mix (food) lightly so as to cover with dressing or sauce: *toss a salad.* **4.** To move or lift (the head) with a sudden motion. ►*n.* **1.** An act of tossing. **2.** An abrupt upward movement, as of the head. [ME *tossen,* poss. of Scand. orig.]

toss·up (tôs′ŭp′, tŏs′-) ►*n. Informal* An even chance or choice.

tot¹ (tŏt) ►*n.* **1.** A small child. **2.** A small amount. [?]

tot² (tŏt) ►*v.* **tot·ted, tot·ting** To total: *totted up the bill.*

to·tal (tōt′l) ►*n.* **1.** An amount obtained by addition; sum. **2.** A whole quantity; entirety. ►*adj.* **1.** Constituting the whole amount; entire. See Synonyms at **whole. 2.** Complete; utter. ►*v.* **-taled, -tal·ing** or **-talled, -tal·ling 1.** To determine the sum of. **2.** To amount to. **3.** *Slang* To destroy: *totaled the car.* [< Lat. *tōtus,* whole.] —**to′tal·ly** *adv.*

to·tal·i·tar·i·an (tō-tăl′ĭ-târ′ē-ən) ►*adj.* Of or being a form of government in which the political authority exercises absolute control over all aspects of life and opposition is outlawed. ►*n.* A practitioner or supporter of such a government. [TOTAL + (AUTHOR)ITARIAN.] —**to·tal′i·tar′i·an·ism** *n.*

to·tal·i·ty (tō-tăl′ĭ-tē) ►*n., pl.* **-ties 1.** The quality or state of being total. **2.** An aggregate amount.

tote (tōt) ►*v.* **tot·ed, tot·ing** To haul; lug. [Poss. of Bantu orig.]

to·tem (tō′təm) ►*n.* **1.** *Anthro.* **a.** An animal, plant, or natural object serving as an emblem of a clan or family. **b.** A representation of this. **2.** A venerated symbol. [Ojibwa *nindoodem,* my totem.] —**to·tem′ic** (-tĕm′ĭk) *adj.*

totem pole ►*n.* A post carved and painted with a series of family or clan crests, as among certain Native American peoples.

tot·ter (tŏt′ər) ►*v.* **1.** To sway as if about to fall. **2.** To walk unsteadily. [ME *toteren.*] —**tot′ter** *n.* —**tot′ter·y** *adj.*

tou·can (tōō′kăn′, -kän′) ►*n.* A tropical American bird with brightly colored plumage and a very large bill. [< Tupí *tucano,* bird.]

touch (tŭch) ►*v.* **1.** To cause or permit a part of the body, esp. the hand or fingers, to come in contact with so as to feel. **2.** To be or bring into contact with. **3.** To tap or nudge lightly. **4.** To partake of: *didn't touch her food.* **5.** To disturb or move by handling. **6a.** To adjoin or border. **b.** To come up to; equal. **7.** To treat briefly or allusively: *remarks touching recent events.* **8.** To be pertinent to. **9.** To affect emotionally; move. ►*n.* **1.** The act or an instance of touching. **2.** The physiological sense by which bodily contact is perceived. **3.** A sensation from a specific contact. **4.** A light push; tap. **5.** A mark or effect left by contact with something. **6.** A small amount; trace. **7.** A characteristic way of doing things. **8.** A facility; knack. **9.** Contact or communication: *Keep in touch.* —*phrasal verbs:* **touch down** To land. **touch off 1.** To cause to explode. **2.** To initiate; trigger. **touch up** To improve by making minor changes. [< OFr. *touchier.*] —**touch′a·ble** *adj.*

touch-and-go (tŭch′ən-gō′) ►*adj.* Precarious and uncertain in nature or outcome.

touch·down (tŭch′doun′) ►*n.* **1.** *Football* A score of six points, made by moving the ball across the opponent's goal line. **2.** The landing of an aircraft or spacecraft.

tou·ché (tōō-shā′) ►*interj.* Used to acknowledge a hit in fencing or a successful criticism in an argument. [Fr. < p.part. of *toucher,* TOUCH.]

touch·ing (tŭch′ĭng) ►*adj.* Eliciting sympathy or tenderness. —**touch′ing·ly** *adv.*

touch·screen (tŭch′skrēn′) ►*n.* A monitor screen that responds to the touch of a finger or stylus.

touch·stone (tŭch′stōn′) ►*n.* **1.** A hard stone used to test the quality of gold or silver. **2.** A test of authenticity or value; standard.

touch·y (tŭch′ē) ►*adj.* **-i·er, -i·est 1.** Easily offended or annoyed; oversensitive. **2.** Delicate; difficult: *a touchy situation.* —**touch′i·ly** *adv.* —**touch′i·ness** *n.*

tough (tŭf) ►*adj.* **-er, -est 1.** Strong and resilient. **2.** Hard to cut or chew. **3a.** Physically rugged. **b.** Strong-minded; resolute. **4.** Aggressive; pugnacious. **5a.** Severe; harsh. **b.** Demanding; difficult. **c.** *Informal* Unfortunate; too bad: *a tough break.* ►*n.* A hoodlum. [< OE *tōh.*] —**tough′ly** *adv.* —**tough′ness** *n.*

tough·en (tŭf′ən) ►*v.* To make or become tough. See Synonyms at **harden.**

Tou·louse-Lau·trec (tōō-lōōz′lō-trĕk′), **Henri de** 1864–1901. French artist.

tou·pee (tōō-pā′) ►*n.* A hairpiece worn to cover a bald spot. [< OFr. *toupe,* tuft.]

tour (tōōr) ►*n.* **1.** A trip with visits to places of interest for business, pleasure, or instruction. **2.** A brief trip to or through a place to see or inspect it. **3.** A journey to fulfill engagements in several places: *a concert tour.* **4.** A period of duty at a single place or job. ►*v.* To make a tour (of). [< Lat. *tornus,* lathe; see TURN.]

tour de force (tōōr′ də fôrs′) ►*n., pl.* **tours de force** (tōōr′) A feat of great virtuosity or strength. [Fr.]

tour·ism (tōōr′ĭz′əm) ►*n.* **1.** The practice of traveling for pleasure. **2.** Tourist travel and accommodation.

tour·ist (tōōr′ĭst) ►*n.* One who travels for pleasure. —**tour′ist·y** *adj.*

tour·ma·line (tōōr′mə-lĭn, -lēn′) ►*n.* A mineral valued, esp. in its green, clear, and blue varieties, as a gemstone. [< Sinhalese *toramalli,* carnelian.]

tour·na·ment (tōōr′nə-mənt, tûr′-) ►*n.* **1.** A contest composed of a series of elimination games or trials. **2.** A medieval jousting or tilting match. [< OFr. *torneier,* TOURNEY.]

tour·ney (tōōr′nē, tûr′-) ►*n., pl.* **-neys** A tournament. [< VLat. **tornizāre,* turn around.]

tour·ni·quet (tōōr′nĭ-kĭt, tûr′-) ►*n.* A device, usu. a tightly encircling bandage, used to check bleeding in an injured limb. [Fr.]

tou·sle (tou′zəl) ►*v.* **-sled, -sling** To disarrange or rumple; dishevel. [ME *touselen.*]

Tous·saint L'Ou·ver·ture (tōō-săN′ lōō-vĕr-tür′), **François Dominique** 1743?–1803. Haitian military and political leader.

tout (tout) ►*v.* **1.** To promote or publicize energetically. **2.** To deal in information on racehorses. ►*n.* One who touts. [ME *tuten,* peer at.] —**tout′er** *n.*

tow¹ (tō) ►*v.* To draw or pull behind by a chain or line. See Synonyms at **pull.** ►*n.* **1.** An act of towing. **2.** Something that tows or is towed. —*idiom:* **in tow 1.** In a condition of being towed. **2.** Under one's charge. **3.** As a companion or follower: *came to dinner with a friend in tow.* [< OE *togian.*] —**tow′age** *n.* —**tow′er** *n.*

tow² (tō) ►*n.* Coarse broken flax or hemp fiber. [ME.]

to·ward (tôrd, tə-wôrd′) ►*prep.* also **to·wards** (tôrdz, tə-wôrdz′) **1.** In the direction of. **2.** In a position facing. **3.** Somewhat before in time. **4.** With regard to. **5.** In partial fulfillment of: *a payment toward the house.* **6.** By way of achiev-

ing: *efforts toward peace.* [< OE *tōweard.*]

tow·el (tou′əl) ►*n.* An absorbent cloth or paper used for wiping or drying. ►*v.* **-eled, -el·ing** or **-elled, -el·ling** To wipe or dry with a towel. [< OFr. *toaille.*]

tow·er (tou′ər) ►*n.* **1.** A tall building or part of a building. **2.** A tall slender structure used for observation, signaling, or pumping. ►*v.* To rise to a conspicuous height. [< Lat. *turris.*]

tow·er·ing (tou′ər-ĭng) ►*adj.* **1.** Of imposing height. **2.** Outstanding; preeminent. **3.** Very great or intense. —**tow′er·ing·ly** *adv.*

tow·head (tō′hĕd′) ►*n.* A person with white-blond hair. —**tow′head′ed** *adj.*

tow·hee (tō′hē, tō-hē′) ►*n.* A songbird of E North America having black, white, and rust-colored plumage in the male. [Imit.]

town (toun) ►*n.* **1.** A population center larger than a village and usu. smaller than a city. **2.** *Informal* A city. [< OE *tūn,* village.]

town·house or **town house** (toun′hous′) ►*n.* A row house, esp. a single-family residence.

town meeting ►*n.* A legislative assembly of townspeople.

town·ship (toun′shĭp′) ►*n.* **1.** A subdivision of a county in most northeastern and Midwestern US states. **2.** A public land surveying unit of 36 square miles.

towns·peo·ple (tounz′pē′pəl) ►*pl.n.* The inhabitants or citizens of a town or city.

tow·path (tō′păth′) ►*n.* A path along a canal or river used by animals towing boats.

tox·e·mi·a (tŏk-sē′mē-ə) ►*n.* A condition in which toxins produced by body cells at a local source of infection are contained in the blood. —**tox·e′mic** *adj.*

toxi- or **tox–** ►*pref.* Poison: *toxemia.* [< Lat. *toxicum.*]

tox·ic (tŏk′sĭk) ►*adj.* **1.** Of or caused by a toxin or poison. **2.** Poisonous. —**tox′i·cal·ly** *adv.* —**tox·ic′i·ty** (-sĭs′ĭ-tē) *n.*

tox·i·col·o·gy (tŏk′sĭ-kŏl′ə-jē) ►*n.* The study of poisons and the treatment of poisoning. —**tox′i·co·log′i·cal** (-kə-lŏj′ĭ-kəl), **tox′i·co·log′ic** *adj.* —**tox′i·col′o·gist** *n.*

toxic shock syndrome ►*n.* An acute infection followed in severe cases by shock, found mainly in girls or women using vaginal tampons.

tox·in (tŏk′sĭn) ►*n.* **1.** A poisonous substance, esp. a protein, produced by organisms and capable of causing bodily disease as well as of inducing neutralizing antibodies or antitoxins. **2.** A poisonous nonorganic substance, such as a chemical dye.

toy (toi) ►*n.* **1.** An object for a child to play with. **2.** A trifle or bauble. **3.** A very small breed of dog. ►*v.* **1.** To amuse oneself idly. **2.** To treat something casually or without seriousness: *toyed with the idea.* See Synonyms at **flirt.** [ME *toye.*]

Tpk. ►*abbr.* turnpike

tr. ►*abbr.* **1.** transitive **2.** translated **3a.** trust **b.** trustee

trace¹ (trās) ►*n.* **1a.** A visible mark made by the passage of a person, animal, or thing. **b.** Evidence of the former presence of something; vestige. **2a.** An extremely small amount or barely perceptible indication. **b.** A constituent, such as a chemical compound or element, present in quantities less than a standard limit. ►*v.* **traced, trac·ing 1.** To follow the course or trail of. **2a.** To ascertain the successive stages in the development of. **b.** To locate or discover through inquiry. **3a.** To draw (a line or figure). **b.** To form (letters) with special care. **4.** To copy by following lines seen through transparent paper. [< Lat. *trahere, tract-,* draw.] —**trace′a·bil′i·ty** *n.* —**trace′a·ble** *adj.* —**trac′er** *n.*

trace² (trās) ►*n.* One of two side straps or chains connecting a harnessed draft animal to a vehicle. [< OFr. *trait* < Lat. *trahere, tract-,* haul.]

tracer bullet ►*n.* A bullet that leaves a luminous or smoky trail.

trac·er·y (trā′sə-rē) ►*n., pl.* **-ies** Ornamental work of interlaced and branching lines.

tracery
exterior view of the rose window at the
Cathedral of Notre-Dame, Paris, France

tra·che·a (trā′kē-ə) ►*n., pl.* **-che·ae** (-kē-ē′) or **-che·as** A thin-walled cartilaginous tube descending from the larynx to the bronchi that carries air to the lungs; windpipe. [< Gk. *(artēria) trakheia,* rough (artery).] —**tra′che·al** *adj.*

tra·che·ot·o·my (trā′kē-ŏt′ə-mē) ►*n., pl.* **-mies** Surgical incision into the trachea through the neck.

track (trăk) ►*n.* **1a.** A mark, such as a footprint, left in passing. **b.** A path or course; trail. **2a.** A course laid out for running or racing. **b.** Track and field. **3.** A rail or set of parallel rails upon which a vehicle runs. **4.** Either of the continuous metal belts with which vehicles such as tanks move. **5.** A groove, ridge, or rail for a moving device or part. ►*v.* **1.** To follow the tracks of; trail. **2.** To leave marks of (e.g., mud) on a surface. **3a.** To observe or monitor, as by radar. **b.** To locate by searching diligently: *track down a story.* —*idioms:* **keep track of** To remain informed about. **lose track of** To fail to keep informed about. [< OFr. *trac.*] —**track′a·ble** *adj.* —**track′er** *n.* —**track′less** *adj.*

track and field ►*n.* Athletic events performed on a running track and the adjacent field. —**track′-and-field′** *adj.*

track·ball (trăk′bôl′) ►*n.* A ball mounted in a stationary housing and rotated to control a pointer on a computer screen.

track·ing (trăk′ĭng) ►*n.* The placing of students in a course of study according to ability, achievement, or needs.

tract¹ (trăkt) ►*n.* **1a.** An expanse of land. **b.** A specified area of land. **2.** *Anat.* A system of organs and tissues that together perform a specialized function. [< Lat. *tractus* < p.part. of *trahere,* draw.]

tract² (trăkt) ►*n.* A propaganda pamphlet, esp. one put out by a religious or political group. [< Lat. *tractātus,* something discussed.]

trac·ta·ble (trăk′tə-bəl) ►*adj.* **1.** Easily managed or controlled; governable. **2.** Easily worked, as

metals; malleable. [< Lat. *tractāre,* manage.] —**trac′ta·bil′i·ty** *n.* —**trac′ta·bly** *adv.*

tract house ►*n.* One of numerous houses of similar or complementary design constructed on a tract of land. —**tract housing** *n.*

trac·tion (trăk′shən) ►*n.* **1.** The act of drawing or pulling or the condition of being drawn or pulled. **2.** Pulling power, as of an engine. **3.** Adhesive friction, as of a wheel on a road. **4.** *Informal* Impetus or advancement. [< Lat. *trahere, tract-,* pull.]

trac·tor (trăk′tər) ►*n.* **1.** An automotive vehicle designed for pulling machinery. **2.** A truck having a cab and no body, used for pulling large vehicles. [< Lat. *trahere, tract-,* pull.]

trac·tor-trail·er (trăk′tər-trā′lər) ►*n.* A truck consisting of a tractor attached to a semitrailer or trailer, used for transporting loads.

trade (trād) ►*n.* **1.** The business of buying and selling commodities, products, or services; commerce. **2.** An exchange of one thing for another. **3.** An occupation, esp. one requiring skilled labor. ►*v.* **trad·ed, trad·ing** **1.** To engage in buying and selling. **2.** To exchange one thing for another. **3.** To shop regularly at a particular store. [< MLGer., track.] —**trad′er** *n.*

trade-in (trād′ĭn′) ►*n.* **1.** Merchandise accepted as partial payment for a new purchase. **2.** A transaction involving such merchandise.

trade·mark (trād′märk′) ►*n.* A name, symbol, or other device identifying a product or service, esp. an officially registered name or symbol that is thereby protected against use by others. ►*v.* **1.** To label (a product) with a trademark. **2.** To register (something) as a trademark.

trade name ►*n.* A name under which a product or service is marketed or under which a business operates.

trade-off or **trade-off** (trād′ôf′, -ŏf′) ►*n.* An exchange in which something desirable is given up for something regarded as more desirable.

trades·man (trādz′mən) ►*n.* **1.** One who practices a manual trade. **2.** A merchant.

trade union ►*n.* A labor union. —**trade unionism** *n.* —**trade unionist** *n.*

trade wind (wĭnd) ►*n.* Any of a system of winds blowing in the tropics from the northeast in the Northern Hemisphere and from the southeast in the Southern Hemisphere.

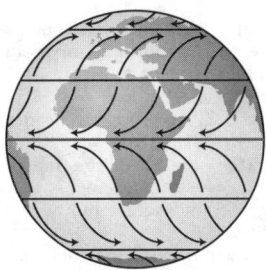

trade winds
As warm, moist air rises along the equator, surface air moves in to take its place, creating trade winds.

trad·ing post (trā′dĭng) ►*n.* A store in a sparsely settled area offering supplies in exchange for local products.

tra·di·tion (trə-dĭsh′ən) ►*n.* **1.** The passing down of a culture from generation to generation, esp. orally. **2a.** A custom handed down. **b.** A set of such customs viewed as a coherent body of precedents influencing the present. See Synonyms at **heritage.** [< Lat. *trādere,* hand over : TRANS– + *dare,* give.] —**tra·di′tion·al** *adj.* —**tra·di′tion·al·ist** *adj. & n.* —**tra·di′tion·al·ly** *adv.*

tra·duce (trə-do͞os′, -dyo͞os′) ►*v.* **-duced, -duc·ing** To slander; defame. [Lat. *trādūcere.*] —**tra·duce′ment** *n.*

Tra·fal·gar (trə-făl′gər), **Cape** A cape on the SW coast of Spain NW of the Strait of Gibraltar.

traf·fic (trăf′ĭk) ►*n.* **1.** The commercial exchange of goods; trade. **2a.** The passage of persons, vehicles, or messages through routes of transportation or communication. **b.** The amount, as of vehicles, in transit. **3.** Dealings; communication. ►*v.* **-ficked, -fick·ing** To carry on trade; deal in. [< OItal. *trafficare,* trade.] —**traf′fick·er** *n.*

traffic circle ►*n.* A circular one-way road at a junction of thoroughfares, facilitating an uninterrupted flow of traffic.

traffic light ►*n.* A road signal for directing vehicular traffic by means of colored lights.

trag·e·dy (trăj′ĭ-dē) ►*n., pl.* **-dies. 1.** A drama or literary work in which the main character is brought to ruin or suffers extreme sorrow. **2.** A disastrous event. [< Gk. *tragōidía.*] —**tra·ge′di·an** (trə-jē′dē-ən) *n.* —**tra·ge′di·enne′** (-ĕn′) *n.*

trag·ic (trăj′ĭk) ►*adj.* **1.** Of or having the nature of tragedy. **2.** Writing or performing in tragedy. **3.** Calamitous; disastrous. [< Gk. *tragikos.*] —**trag′i·cal·ly** *adv.*

trag·i·com·e·dy (trăj′ĭ-kŏm′ĭ-dē) ►*n., pl.* **-dies** A drama combining elements of tragedy and comedy. —**trag′i·com′ic** (-kŏm′ĭk), **trag′i·com′i·cal** *adj.*

trail (trāl) ►*v.* **1.** To drag or allow to drag or stream behind, as along the ground. **2.** To follow the traces or scent of; track. **3.** To lag behind (an opponent). **4.** To extend or grow along the ground or over a surface. **5.** To drift in a thin stream. **6.** To become gradually fainter: *Her voice trailed off.* ►*n.* **1.** A marked or beaten path. **2.** A mark or trace left by a moving body. **3.** Something that follows behind. **4.** Something that hangs loose and long. [ME *trailen.*]

trail bike also **trail·bike** (trāl′bĭk′) ►*n.* **1.** See **dirt bike. 2.** An all-purpose mountain bike designed for groomed trails.

trail·blaz·er (trāl′blā′zər) ►*n.* **1.** One who blazes a trail. **2.** An innovative leader in a field; pioneer. —**trail′blaz′ing** *adj.*

trail·er (trā′lər) ►*n.* **1.** A large transport vehicle hauled by a truck or tractor. **2.** A van drawn by a truck or automobile and used as a dwelling or office.

trailer park ►*n.* An area in which parking space for house trailers is rented.

train (trān) ►*n.* **1.** A series of connected railroad cars. **2.** A long line of moving people, animals, or vehicles. **3.** A part of a gown that trails behind the wearer. **4.** A staff of people following in attendance. **5.** An orderly succession of related events or thoughts. ►*v.* **1.** To coach in or accustom to a mode of behavior or performance. **2.** To make or become proficient with specialized instruction and practice. **3.** To prepare physically, as with a regimen. **4.** To cause (e.g., a plant) to take a desired course or shape. **5.** To direct (e.g., a gun or camera) at something. See Synonyms at **aim.** [< OFr. *trainer,* drag.] —**train′a·ble** *adj.* —**train·ee′** *n.* —**train′er** *n.* —**train′ing** *n.*

traipse (trāps) ►*v.* **traipsed, traips·ing** To walk or tramp about. [Poss. < OFr. *trapasser,* trespass.]

trait (trāt) ►*n.* **1.** A distinguishing feature, as of character. **2.** A genetically determined characteristic or condition. [< Lat. *tractus,* something drawn.]

trai·tor (trā′tər) ►*n.* One who betrays one's country, a cause, or a trust, esp. one who commits treason. [< Lat. *trāditor* < *trādere,* hand over; see TRADITION.] —**trai′tor·ous** *adj.*

Tra·jan (trā′jən) AD 53–117. Roman emperor (98–117).

tra·jec·to·ry (trə-jĕk′tə-rē) ►*n., pl.* **-ries** The path of a projectile or other moving body through space. [< Lat. *trāicere, trāiect-,* throw across.]

tram (trăm) ►*n.* **1.** *Chiefly Brit.* A streetcar. **2.** A cable car, esp. one suspended from an overhead cable. **3.** An open wagon run on tracks in a coal mine. [Sc., shaft of a barrow.]

tram·mel (trăm′əl) ►*n.* **1.** A shackle used in teaching horses. **2.** A hindrance or restraint. ►*v.* **-meled, -mel·ing** or **-melled, -mel·ling** **1.** To trap or enmesh. **2.** To hinder. [< LLat. *trēmaculum,* a kind of net.] —**tram′mel·er** *n.*

tramp (trămp) ►*v.* **1.** To walk with a firm heavy step. **2.** To travel on foot; hike. **3.** To tread down; trample. ►*n.* **1.** The sound of heavy walking or marching. **2.** A walking trip. **3.** One who travels aimlessly about; vagrant. **4.** A prostitute. **5.** A cargo vessel that has no regular schedule but takes on freight whenever it can. [< MLGer. *trampen.*] —**tramp′er** *n.*

tram·ple (trăm′pəl) ►*v.* **-pled, -pling 1.** To beat down with the feet so as to injure or destroy. **2.** To treat harshly or ruthlessly. [ME *tramplen.*] —**tram′ple** *n.*

tram·po·line (trăm′pə-lēn′, -lĭn) ►*n.* A strong, taut fabric attached with springs to a metal frame and used for gymnastic springing and tumbling. [Ital. *trampolino.*] —**tram′po·lin′er, tram′po·lin′ist** *n.*

trance (trăns) ►*n.* **1.** A hypnotic, cataleptic, or ecstatic state. **2.** Detachment from one's physical surroundings, as in contemplation or daydreaming. **3.** A dazed state. [< Lat. *trānsīre,* go across.]

tran·quil (trăng′kwəl, trăn′-) ►*adj.* Free from agitation; calm. [< Lat. *tranquillus.*] —**tran·quil′i·ty, tran·quil′li·ty** *n.* —**tran′quil·ly** *adv.*

tran·quil·ize also **tran·quil·lize** (trăng′kwə-līz′, trăn′-) ►*v.* **-ized, -iz·ing** also **-lized, -liz·ing 1.** To make or become tranquil. **2.** To sedate. —**tran′quil·i·za′tion** *n.*

tran·quil·iz·er (trăng′kwə-līz′ər, trăn′-) ►*n.* A drug used to reduce anxiety.

trans. ►*abbr.* **1.** transaction **2.** transitive **3.** translation **4.** transportation

trans– ►*pref.* **1.** Across; beyond: *transatlantic.* **2.** Through: *transcontinental.* **3.** Change; transfer: *transliterate.* [< Lat. *trāns,* over, across.]

trans·act (trăn-săkt′, -zăkt′) ►*v.* To carry out or conduct (business or affairs). [Lat. *trānsigere*, *trānsāct-* : *trāns-*, over + *agere*, make.] —**trans·ac′tor** *n.*

trans·ac·tion (trăn-săk′shən, -zăk′-) ►*n.* **1.** The act or process of transacting. **2.** Something transacted. —**trans·ac′tion·al** *adj.*

Trans·al·pine Gaul (trăns-ăl′pīn′, trănz-) The part of ancient Gaul NW of the Alps, including modern France and Belgium.

trans·at·lan·tic (trăns′ət-lăn′tĭk, trănz′-) ►*adj.* **1.** On the other side of the Atlantic. **2.** Spanning or crossing the Atlantic.

trans·ax·le (trăns-ăk′səl, trănz-) ►*n.* An automotive part that combines the transmission and the differential, used on vehicles that have front-wheel drive. [TRANS(MISSION) + AXLE.]

Trans·cau·ca·sia (trăns′kô-kā′zhə, -zhē-ə, trănz′-) A region of Georgia, Armenia, and Azerbaijan between the Caucasus Mts. and the borders of Turkey and Iran. —**Trans′cau·ca′sian** *adj. & n.*

tran·scend (trăn-sĕnd′) ►*v.* **1.** To go beyond; exceed. **2.** To surpass. **3.** To exist above and independent of. [< Lat. *trānscendere.*] —**tran·scen′dence** *n.* —**tran·scen′dent** *adj.*

tran·scen·den·tal (trăn′sĕn-dĕn′tl) ►*adj.* **1.** Rising above common thought or ideas; exalted; mystical. *Math.* Of or relating to a real or complex number that is not the root of any polynomial that has positive degree and ration-al coefficients. —**tran′scen·den′tal·ly** *adv.*

tran·scen·den·tal·ism (trăn′sĕn-dĕn′tl-ĭz′əm) ►*n.* A belief or doctrine asserting the existence of an ideal spiritual reality that transcends empirical and scientific reality and is knowable through intuition. —**tran′scen·den′tal·ist** *n.*

trans·con·ti·nen·tal (trăns′kŏn-tə-nĕn′tl) ►*adj.* Spanning or crossing a continent.

tran·scribe (trăn-skrīb′) ►*v.* **-scribed, -scrib·ing** **1.** To write or type a copy of. **2.** To write out fully, as from notes. **3.** To adapt or arrange (a musical composition). [Lat. *trānscrībere.*] —**tran·scrib′er** *n.*

tran·script (trăn′skrĭpt′) ►*n.* Something transcribed; a written or printed copy. [< Lat. *trānscrīptum.*]

tran·scrip·tion (trăn-skrĭp′shən) ►*n.* **1.** The act or process of transcribing. **2.** Something transcribed, esp. an adaptation of a musical composition.

trans·duc·er (trăns-do͞o′sər, -dyo͞o′-, trănz-) ►*n.* A substance or device, such as a microphone, that converts input energy of one form into output energy of another. [< Lat. *trānsdūcere*, transfer.]

tran·sept (trăn′sĕpt′) ►*n.* Either of the two lateral arms of a cruciform church. [TRANS– + Lat. *saeptum*, partition.]

trans fat (trăns) ►*n.* An unsaturated fatty acid produced by the partial hydrogenation of vegetable oils. [< *trans-*, pref. indicating chemical structure.]

trans·fer (trăns-fûr′, trăns′fər) ►*v.* **-ferred, -fer·ring** **1.** To convey, shift, or change from one place, person, or thing to another. **2.** *Law* To give or convey legal title of (e.g., property) to another. **3.** To convey (e.g., a design) from one surface to another. **4.** To change from one public conveyance to another. ►*n.* (trăns′fər) **1.** also **trans·fer·al** (trăns-fûr′əl) The conveyance of something from one place or person to another. **2.** One who transfers or is transferred. **3.** A design that is conveyed by contact from one surface to another. **4.** A ticket entitling a passenger to change from one public conveyance to another. **5.** also **transferal** *Law* A conveyance of title or property from one person to another. [< Lat. *trānsferre* : TRANS– + *ferre*, carry.] —**trans·fer′a·ble, trans·fer′ra·ble** *adj.* —**trans·fer′ence** *n.* —**trans·fer′rer** *n.*

trans·fig·ure (trăns-fĭg′yər) ►*v.* **-ured, -ur·ing** **1.** To change the form or appearance of; transform. See Synonyms at **convert. 2.** To exalt or glorify. [< Lat. *trānsfigūrāre.*] —**trans·fig′u·ra′tion** *n.*

trans·fix (trăns-fĭks′) ►*v.* **1.** To render motionless, as with terror or awe. **2.** To pierce with a pointed weapon. [Lat. *trānsfīgere, trānsfīx-.*] —**trans·fix′ion** *n.*

trans·form (trăns-fôrm′) ►*v.* **1.** To change markedly in appearance or form. **2.** To change in nature or condition. See Synonyms at **convert.** [< Lat. *trānsfōrmāre.*] —**trans·form′a·ble** *adj.* —**trans′for·ma′tion** *n.*

trans·form·er (trăns-fôr′mər) ►*n.* A device used to transfer electric energy from one circuit to another.

trans·fuse (trăns-fyo͞oz′) ►*v.* **-fused, -fus·ing** **1.** To transfer (liquid) from one vessel into another. **2.** To permeate; instill. **3.** To administer a transfusion of or to. [< Lat. *trānsfundere, trānsfūs-*, pour out.] —**trans·fus′er** *n.*

trans·fu·sion (trăns-fyo͞o′zhən) ►*n.* **1.** The act or process of transfusing. **2.** The transfer of whole blood or blood products from one individual to another.

trans·gen·der (trăns-jĕn′dər, trănz-) ►*adj.* **1.** Appearing as, wishing to be considered as, or having undergone surgery to become a member of the opposite sex. **2.** Of or relating to transgender people. ►*n.* A transgender person.

trans·gen·dered (trăns-jĕn′dərd, trănz-) ►*adj.* Transgender.

trans·gress (trăns-grĕs′, trănz-) ►*v.* **1.** To go beyond or over (a limit). **2.** To act in violation of (e.g., the law). [< Lat. *trānsgredī, trānsgress-*, step across.] —**trans·gres′sion** *n.* —**trans·gres′sor** *n.*

tran·ship (trăn-shĭp′) ►*v.* Var. of **transship.**

tran·si·ent (trăn′zē-ənt, -zhənt, -shənt) ►*adj.* **1.** Passing with time; transitory. **2.** Remaining in a place only a brief time. ►*n.* One that is transient, esp. a person staying a single night at a hotel. [< Lat. *trānsīre*, go over.] —**tran′si·ence, tran′si·en·cy** *n.* —**tran′si·ent·ly** *adv.*

tran·sis·tor (trăn-zĭs′tər, -sĭs′-) ►*n.* A semiconductor device with at least three terminals, used in a circuit as an amplifier, detector, or switch. [TRANS(FER) + (RES)ISTOR.] —**tran·sis′tor·ize′** *v.*

tran·sit (trăn′sĭt, -zĭt) ►*n.* **1.** The act of passing over, across, or through; passage. **2.** Conveyance of people or goods from one place to another, esp. on a local public transportation system. **3.** A surveying instrument that measures angles. [< Lat. *trānsitus.*]

tran·si·tion (trăn-zĭsh′ən, -sĭsh′-) ►*n.* Change

from one form, state, or place to another. **—tran·si′tion·al** *adj.* **—tran·si′tion·al·ly** *adv.*

tran·si·tive (trăn′sĭ-tĭv, -zĭ-) ►*adj.* Being or using a verb that requires a direct object to complete its meaning. **—tran′si·tive·ly** *adv.* **—tran′si·tive·ness, tran′si·tiv′i·ty** *n.*

tran·si·to·ry (trăn′sĭ-tôr′ē, trăn′zĭ-) ►*adj.* Existing only briefly. **—tran′si·to′ri·ly** *adv.*

trans·late (trăns′lāt′, trănz′-, trăns-lāt′, trănz-) ►*v.* **-lat·ed, -lat·ing 1.** To render in another language. **2.** To express in different, often simpler words: *translated the technical jargon into ordinary language.* **3.** To convey from one form or style to another. **4.** *Phys.* To move from one place to another without rotation. [< Lat. *trānslātus,* p.part. of *trānsferre,* transfer.] **—trans·lat′a·bil′i·ty** *n.* **—trans·lat′a·ble** *adj.* **—trans·la′tion** *n.* **—trans′la′tor** *n.*

trans·lit·er·ate (trăns-lĭt′ə-rāt′, trănz-) ►*v.* **-at·ed, -at·ing** To represent (letters or words) in the corresponding characters of another alphabet. [TRANS– + Lat. *littera,* letter + –ATE¹.] **—trans·lit′er·a′tion** *n.*

trans·lu·cent (trăns-lōō′sənt, trănz-) ►*adj.* Transmitting light but diffusing it sufficiently to cause images to be blurred. [< Lat. *trānslūcēre,* shine through.] **—trans·lu′cence, trans·lu′cen·cy** *n.*

trans·mi·grate (trăns-mī′grāt′, trănz-) ►*v.* **-grat·ed, -grat·ing** To pass into another body after death. Used of the soul. [Lat. *trānsmigrāre.*] **—trans′mi·gra′tion** *n.*

trans·mis·sion (trăns-mĭsh′ən, trănz-) ►*n.* **1.** The act or process of transmitting. **2.** Something transmitted. **3.** An automotive assembly of gears that links an engine to a driving axle. **4.** The sending of a signal from a transmitter. **—trans·mis′sive** (-mĭs′ĭv) *adj.*

trans·mit (trăns-mĭt′, trănz-) ►*v.* **-mit·ted, -mit·ting 1.** To send from one person, thing, or place to another. See Synonyms at **send. 2.** To cause to spread, as an infection. **3.** To impart by heredity. **4.** To send (a signal), as by radio. **5.** To convey (e.g., force) from one part of a mechanism to another. [< Lat. *trānsmittere.*] **—trans·mis′si·ble, trans·mit′ta·ble** *adj.* **—trans·mit′tal** *n.*

trans·mit·ter (trăns-mĭt′ər, trănz-) ►*n.* **1.** One that transmits. **2.** Any of various electrical devices used to originate signals, as in radio or telegraphy.

trans·mog·ri·fy (trăns-mŏg′rə-fī′, trănz-) ►*v.* **-fied** (-fīd′), **-fy·ing** To change into a different shape or form, esp. one that is fantastic or bizarre. See Synonyms at **convert.** [?]

trans·mute (trăns-myōōt′, trănz-) ►*v.* **-mut·ed, -mut·ing 1.** To change from one form, nature, substance, or state into another; transform. See Synonyms at **convert. 2.** To transfer (an element) into another by nuclear reactions. [< Lat. *trānsmūtāre.*] **—trans·mut′a·bil′i·ty** *n.* **—trans·mut′a·ble** *adj.* **—trans·mut′a·bly** *adv.* **—trans′mu·ta′tion** *n.*

trans·na·tion·al (trăns-năsh′ə-nəl, trănz-) ►*adj.* **1.** Reaching beyond national boundaries. **2.** Of or involving several nations or nationalities.

trans-Nep·tu·ni·an object (trăns′nĕp-tōō′nē-ən, -tyōō′-, trănz′-) ►*n.* A celestial object that orbits the sun at a greater distance on average than Neptune.

trans·o·ce·an·ic (trăns′ō-shē-ăn′ĭk, trănz′-) ►*adj.* **1.** Situated beyond the ocean. **2.** Spanning or crossing the ocean.

tran·som (trăn′səm) ►*n.* **1.** A small hinged window above a door. **2.** A horizontal crosspiece over a door or in a window. [Prob. < Lat. *trānstrum,* cross-beam.]

trans·pa·cif·ic (trăns′pə-sĭf′ĭk, trănz′-) ►*adj.* **1.** On the other side of the Pacific. **2.** Spanning or crossing the Pacific.

trans·par·ent (trăns-pâr′ənt, -păr′-) ►*adj.* **1.** Capable of transmitting light so that objects on the other side can be seen clearly. See Synonyms at **clear. 2.** So fine in texture that it can be seen through; sheer. **3a.** Easily detected; obvious: *transparent lies.* **b.** Free from guile; candid or open. **c.** Open to public scrutiny; not hidden or proprietary. [< Med.Lat. *trānspārēre,* show through.] **—trans·par′en·cy** *n.* **—trans·par′ent·ly** *adv.*

tran·spire (trăn-spīr′) ►*v.* **-spired, -spir·ing 1.** *Biol.* To give off (vapor) through pores or stomata. **2.** To happen; occur. **3.** To become known. [< Med.Lat. *trānspīrāre.*] **—tran′spi·ra′tion** (-spə-rā′shən) *n.*

trans·plant (trăns-plănt′) ►*v.* **1.** To uproot and replant (a growing plant). **2.** To transfer from one place or residence to another. **3.** *Med.* To transfer (tissue or an organ) from one body or body part to another. **—trans′plant′** *n.* **—trans′plan·ta′tion** *n.*

trans·port (trăns-pôrt′) ►*v.* **1.** To carry from one place to another. **2.** To cause to feel strong emotion, esp. joy; enrapture. **3.** To send abroad to a penal colony. ►*n.* (trăns′pôrt′) **1.** The act of transporting; conveyance. **2.** Rapture. **3.** A ship or aircraft used to transport troops or military equipment. **4.** A vehicle, as an aircraft, used to transport passengers or freight. [< Lat. *trānsportāre.*] **—trans·port′a·bil′i·ty** *n.* **—trans·port′a·ble** *adj.* **—trans′por·ta′tion** *n.* **—trans·port′er** *n.*

trans·pose (trăns-pōz′) ►*v.* **-posed, -pos·ing 1.** To reverse or change the order or place of. **2.** *Mus.* To write or perform (a composition) in a key other than the original. [< Lat. *trānspōnere.*] **—trans·pos′er** *n.* **—trans′po·si′tion** (-pə-zĭsh′ən) *n.*

trans·sex·u·al (trăns-sĕk′shōō-əl) ►*adj.* **1.** Identifying as or having undergone medical treatment to become a member of the opposite sex. **2.** Of or relating to transsexual people. ►*n.* One who is transsexual. **—trans·sex′u·al·ism, trans·sex′u·al′i·ty** *n.*

trans·ship (trăns-shĭp′) also **tran·ship** (trăn-shĭp′) ►*v.* To transfer (cargo) from one conveyance to another for reshipment. **—trans·ship′ment** *n.*

tran·sub·stan·ti·ate (trăn′səb-stăn′shē-āt′) ►*v.* **-at·ed, -at·ing 1.** To change (one substance) into another. **2.** *Christianity* To change the substance of (the Eucharistic bread and wine) into the body and blood of Jesus. [Med.Lat. *trānsubstantiāre.*] **—tran′sub·stan′ti·a′tion** *n.*

trans·u·ran·ic (trăns′yōō-răn′ĭk, -rā′nĭk, trănz′-) also **trans·u·ra·ni·um** (-rā′nē-əm) ►*adj.* Having an atomic number greater than 92. [< TRANS– + URAN(IUM).]

Trans·vaal (trăns-väl′, trănz-) A region of NE South Africa.

trans·ver·sal (trăns-vûr′səl, trănz-) ▸*adj.* Transverse. ▸*n. Math.* A line that intersects a system of other lines.

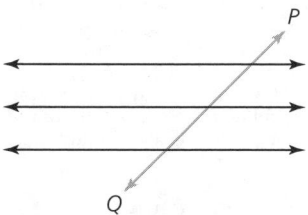

transversal
Line *PQ* is a transversal.

trans·verse (trăns-vûrs′, trănz-, trăns′vûrs′, trănz′-) ▸*adj.* Situated or lying across; crosswise. [< Lat. *trănsvertere,* turn across.] —**transverse′** *n.* —**trans·verse′ly** *adv.*

trans·ves·tite (trăns-vĕs′tīt′, trănz-) ▸*n.* A person who dresses in a style or manner traditionally associated with the opposite sex. [TRANS– + Lat. *vestīre,* dress.] —**trans·ves′tism** *n.*

Tran·syl·va·nia (trăn′sĭl-vān′yə, -vă′nē-ə) A historical region of W Romania bounded by the Carpathian Mts. —**Tran′syl·va′ni·an** *adj. & n.*

Transylvanian Alps A range of the S Carpathian Mts. across central Romania.

trap (trăp) ▸*n.* **1.** A device for catching and holding animals. **2.** Any stratagem for betraying, tricking, or exposing an unsuspecting person or group. **3.** A device, such as a U-shaped bend in a drainpipe, for sealing a passage against the escape of foul gases. **4.** A sand trap. **5. traps** *Mus.* Percussion instruments. **6.** *Slang* The human mouth. ▸*v.* **trapped, trap·ping 1.** To catch in a trap; ensnare. See Synonyms at **catch. 2.** To prevent from escaping or getting free: *was trapped in the attic.* **3.** To trap furbearing animals. [< OE *træppe.*] —**trap′per** *n.*

trap
sink trap

trap·door (trăp′dôr′) ▸*n.* A hinged or sliding door in a floor, roof, or ceiling.

tra·peze (tră-pēz′, trə-) ▸*n.* A short horizontal bar that is suspended from two parallel ropes, used for acrobatics. [< LLat. *trapezium,* TRAPEZOID.]

trap·e·zoid (trăp′ĭ-zoid′) ▸*n.* A quadrilateral with two parallel sides. [< Gk. *trapeza,* table (*tra-,* four + *peza,* foot) + –OID.] —**trap′e·zoi′dal** *adj.*

trap·pings (trăp′ĭngz) ▸*pl.n.* **1.** An ornamental covering for a horse. **2a.** Articles of dress or adornment. **b.** Outward signs; appearance. [< ME *trap.*]

trap·shoot·ing (trăp′shoo′tĭng) ▸*n. Sports* Shooting at clay pigeons that are hurled into the air.

trash (trăsh) ▸*n.* **1.** Discarded material; refuse. **2a.** Something considered worthless, such as a poor piece of writing. **b.** A person or group held in contempt. ▸*v. Slang* **1.** To discard. **2.** To damage, as by vandalism. [Prob. of Scand. orig.] —**trash′y** *adj.*

trashed (trăsht) ▸*adj. Slang* Drunk.

trau·ma (trô′mə, trou′-) ▸*n., pl.* **-mas 1.** Serious injury to the body. **2.** Severe emotional distress caused by an experience. **3.** An experience that causes severe emotional distress, such as combat. [Gk.] —**trau·mat′ic** (-măt′ĭk) *adj.* —**trau′ma·tize′** *v.*

tra·vail (trə-vāl′, trăv′āl′) ▸*n.* **1.** Strenuous work; toil. **2.** Tribulation or agony; anguish. **3.** The labor of childbirth. [< LLat. *tripālium,* instrument of torture.]

trav·el (trăv′əl) ▸*v.* **-eled, -el·ing** or **-elled, -el·ling 1.** To go from one place to another; journey. **2a.** To pass, as from one person to another: *The news traveled quickly.* **b.** To be transmitted, as light or sound. **3.** To move swiftly. **4.** To associate. ▸*n.* **1.** The act of traveling. **2. travels** A series of journeys. [< OFr. *travailler,* to toil.] —**trav′el·er, trav′el·ler** *n.*

trav·e·logue also **trav·e·log** (trăv′ə-lôg′, trăv′-ə-lŏg′) ▸*n.* A film or illustrated lecture on travel.

tra·verse (trə-vûrs′, trăv′ərs) ▸*v.* **-versed, -vers·ing 1a.** To travel or pass across, over, or through. **b.** To move to and fro over. **c.** To cross (a slope) diagonally, as in skiing. **2.** To swivel (e.g., a mounted gun) laterally on a pivot. **3.** To extend across. ▸*n.* **trav·erse** (trăv′ərs, trə-vûrs′) **1.** The act of traversing. **2.** Something, such as a beam, lying crosswise. ▸*adj.* **trav·erse** (trăv′ərs, trə-vûrs′) Transverse. [< OFr. *traverser* < Lat. *trănsversus,* TRANSVERSE.] —**tra·vers′a·ble** *adj.* —**tra·vers′al** *n.* —**tra·vers′er** *n.*

trav·er·tine (trăv′ər-tēn′, -tĭn) ▸*n.* A porous calcite deposited from solution in ground or surface waters. [< Lat. *(lapis) tīburtīnus,* (stone) of Tibur (Tivoli), Italy.]

trav·es·ty (trăv′ĭ-stē) ▸*n., pl.* **-ties** A grotesque imitation or likeness. [< Ital. *travestire,* to disguise, parody.] —**trav′es·ty** *v.*

trawl (trôl) ▸*n.* A large tapered fishing net that is towed along the sea bottom or at a given depth. ▸*v.* To fish with a trawl. [ME *trawelle.*]

trawl·er (trô′lər) ▸*n.* A boat equipped for trawling.

tray (trā) ▸*n.* A shallow flat receptacle with a raised edge, used for carrying, holding, or displaying articles. [< OE *trĕg.*]

treach·er·ous (trĕch′ər-əs) ▸*adj.* **1.** Betraying a trust or confidence. **2.** Marked by unforeseen hazards: *treacherous shoals.* —**treach′er·ous·**

ly *adv.* **—treach′er·ous·ness** *n.*

treach·er·y (trĕch′ə-rē) ►*n., pl.* **-ies** Willful betrayal of trust; perfidy. [< OFr. *trichier,* to trick.]

trea·cle (trē′kəl) ►*n.* **1.** Cloying speech or sentiment. **2.** *Chiefly Brit.* Molasses. [< Gk. *thēriakē (antidotos),* (antidote against) wild animals.] **—trea′cly** (-klē) *adj.*

tread (trĕd) ►*v.* **trod** (trŏd) or **treaded, trodden** (trŏd′n) or **trod** or **treaded, treading 1.** To walk on, over, or along. **2.** To press beneath the feet; trample: *dirt that was trodden into the rug.* **3.** To walk or dance: *tread a measure.* ►*n.* **1.** The act, manner, or sound of treading. **2.** The horizontal part of a step in a staircase. **3.** The grooved face of a tire. **4.** The part of a shoe sole that touches the ground. **5.** Either of the continuous ridged belts with which bulldozers, tanks, and certain other vehicles move over the ground. [< OE *tredan.*] **—tread′er** *n.*

tread·le (trĕd′l) ►*n.* A pedal that is operated by the foot to drive a wheel, as in a sewing machine. [< OE *tredel,* step of a stair.] **—tread′le** *v.*

tread·mill (trĕd′mĭl′) ►*n.* **1.** A device used to power machinery, consisting of a wheel with steps on which a person treads. **2.** An exercise device consisting of a continuous moving belt on which a person or animal can walk or run while remaining in one place. **3.** A monotonous routine.

trea·son (trē′zən) ►*n.* The betrayal of one's country, esp. by aiding an enemy. [< Lat. *trāditiō,* a handing over; see TRADITION.] **—trea′son·a·ble** *adj.* **—trea′son·ous** *adj.*

treas·ure (trĕzh′ər) ►*n.* **1.** Accumulated or stored wealth in the form of money, jewels, or other valuables. **2.** One considered esp. precious or valuable. ►*v.* **-ured, -ur·ing 1.** To value highly. **2.** To store away; hoard. [< Gk. *thēsauros.*] **—treas′ur·a·ble** *adj.*

treas·ur·er (trĕzh′ər-ər) ►*n.* One who is in charge of funds or revenues, as of a government or club.

treas·ure-trove (trĕzh′ər-trōv′) ►*n.* **1.** Treasure found hidden. **2.** A discovery of great value. [AN *tresor trove,* found treasure.]

treas·ur·y (trĕzh′ə-rē) ►*n., pl.* **-ies 1.** A place where treasure is kept. **2.** A place where funds are received, kept, managed, and disbursed. **3.** Such funds or revenues. **4. Treasury** A governmental department in charge of the public revenue.

treat (trēt) ►*v.* **1.** To act or behave toward: *treated me fairly.* **2.** To regard and handle in a certain way: *treated the matter as a joke.* **3.** To deal with, handle, or cover. **4.** To provide with food, entertainment, or gifts at one's own expense. **5.** To subject to a process. **6.** To give medical aid to (someone). ►*n.* **1.** Something paid for by someone else. **2.** A special delight or pleasure. [< Lat. *tractāre.*] **—treat′a·ble** *adj.*

trea·tise (trē′tĭs) ►*n.* A systematic, usu. extensive written discourse on a subject. [< VLat. *tractātīcius,* TRACT[1].]

treat·ment (trēt′mənt) ►*n.* **1.** The act or manner of handling or dealing with someone or something. **2.** The application of remedies to cure or mitigate a disease, condition, or injury.

trea·ty (trē′tē) ►*n., pl.* **-ties** A formal written agreement between two or more nations. [< Lat. *tractātus,* discussion.]

treb·le (trĕb′əl) ►*adj.* **1.** Triple. **2.** *Mus.* Of or having the highest part, voice, or range. **3.** High-pitched; shrill. ►*n.* **1.** *Mus.* The highest part, voice, instrument, or range. **2.** A high shrill sound or voice. ►*v.* **-led, -ling** To triple. [< Lat. *triplus.*] **—treb′ly** *adv.*

treble clef ►*n.* *Mus.* A symbol indicating that the second line from the bottom of a staff represents the pitch of G above middle C.

treble clef

tree (trē) ►*n.* **1.** A perennial woody plant with a main trunk and usu. a distinct crown. **2.** Something resembling a tree, esp. a diagram showing family lineage. ►*v.* To chase and force up a tree. [< OE *trēow.*] **—tree′less** *adj.*

tree frog or **tree·frog** (trē′frôg′, -frŏg′) ►*n.* A usu. small arboreal frog having long toes terminating in adhesive disks.

tree line or **tree·line** (trē′līn′) ►*n.* **1.** The limit of northern or southern latitude beyond which trees will not grow. **2.** See **timberline**.

tree of heaven ►*n.* A deciduous, rapidly growing tree widely planted as a street tree.

tre·foil (trē′foil′, trĕf′oil′) ►*n.* **1.** A plant, such as a clover, having compound leaves with three leaflets. **2.** An ornament resembling such a leaf. [< Lat. *trifolium.*]

trek (trĕk) ►*v.* **trekked, trek·king** To make a long difficult journey. [Afr., travel by ox wagon < MDu. *trecken,* pull.] **—trek** *n.* **—trek′ker** *n.*

trel·lis (trĕl′ĭs) ►*n.* An open latticework used for training climbing plants. [< Lat. *trilīx,* woven with three threads.] **—trel′lised** *adj.*

trem·a·tode (trĕm′ə-tōd′) ►*n.* Any of numerous parasitic flatworms having external suckers or hooks. [< Gk. *trēmatōdē,* having holes.]

trem·ble (trĕm′bəl) ►*v.* **-bled, -bling 1.** To shake involuntarily, as from excitement or anger; quake. **2.** To feel fear or anxiety. **3.** To vibrate or quiver. [< VLat. **tremulāre.*] **—trem′ble** *n.* **—trem′bler** *n.*

tre·men·dous (trĭ-mĕn′dəs) ►*adj.* **1a.** Extremely large; enormous. **b.** Very great in scope or importance. **2.** Remarkable; outstanding. [< Lat. *tremendus,* terrible.] **—tre·men′dous·ly** *adv.*

trem·o·lo (trĕm′ə-lō′) ►*n., pl.* **-los** *Mus.* A tremulous effect produced by rapid repetition of a single tone or by rapid alternation of two tones. [Ital.]

trem·or (trĕm′ər) ►*n.* **1.** A shaking movement, as of the earth. **2.** An involuntary trembling or quivering, as of the hands. [< Lat.]

trem·u·lous (trĕm′yə-ləs) ►*adj.* **1.** Vibrating or quivering; trembling. **2.** Timid; fearful. [<

Lat. *tremulus* < *tremere*, tremble.] —**trem′u·lous·ly** *adv.*

trench (trĕnch) ►*n.* **1.** A deep furrow. **2.** A ditch embanked with its own soil and used for concealment and protection in warfare. **3.** A steep-sided valley on the ocean floor. ►*v.* To dig a trench in. [< OFr. *trenchier,* cut.]

trench·ant (trĕn′chənt) ►*adj.* **1.** Forceful; penetrating: *a trenchant argument.* **2.** Caustic; cutting: *a trenchant wit.* [< OFr. *trenchier,* cut.] —**trench′an·cy** *n.*

trench coat ►*n.* A belted raincoat with straps on the shoulders and deep pockets.

trench·er (trĕn′chər) ►*n.* A wooden serving board. [< AN *trencher,* cut.]

trench fever ►*n.* An acute infectious bacterial disease transmitted by body lice.

trench foot ►*n.* A foot disorder resembling frostbite, often affecting soldiers who must stand in cold flooded trenches.

trench mouth ►*n.* A painful infection of the mouth and throat, marked by ulcers and caused by bacteria and spirochetes.

trend (trĕnd) ►*n.* **1.** A general tendency or course of events. **2.** Current style; vogue: *the latest trend in fashion.* **3.** A general direction of movement. ►*v.* To have a certain direction or tendency. [< OE *trendan,* revolve.]

trend·y (trĕn′dē) ►*adj.* **-i·er, -i·est** *Informal* In accord with the latest fashion. See Synonyms at **fashionable.** —**trend′i·ly** *adv.* —**trend′i·ness** *n.*

Tren·ton (trĕn′tən) The capital of New Jersey, in the W-central part on the Delaware R.

tre·pan (trĭ-păn′) ►*n.* A trephine. ►*v.* **-panned, -pan·ning** To trephine. [< Gk. *trupanon,* borer.]

tre·phine (trĭ-fīn′) ►*n.* A surgical saw for cutting out disks of bone, usu. from the skull, or removing corneal tissue. ►*v.* **-phined, -phin·ing** To operate on with a trephine. [< Lat. *trēs fīnēs,* three ends.] —**treph′i·na′tion** (trĕf′ə-nā′shən) *n.*

trep·i·da·tion (trĕp′ĭ-dā′shən) ►*n.* Dread; apprehension. [< Lat. *trepidus,* anxious.]

tres·pass (trĕs′pəs, -păs′) ►*v.* **1.** To invade the property or rights of another without consent. **2.** To infringe on the privacy or time of another. **3.** To commit an offense or sin. [< OFr. *trespasser.*] —**tres′pass** *n.* —**tres′pass·er** *n.*

tress (trĕs) ►*n.* A lock of hair. [< OFr. *tresse.*]

tres·tle (trĕs′əl) ►*n.* **1.** A horizontal bar held up by two pairs of divergent legs and used as a support. **2.** A framework of vertical slanted supports and horizontal crosspieces supporting a bridge. [< Lat. *trānstrum,* beam.]

T. rex (tē′ rĕks′) ►*n.* See **tyrannosaurus.**

trey (trā) ►*n., pl.* **treys** A card or die with three pips. [< Lat. *tria.*]

tri– ►*pref.* **1.** Three: *trisect.* **2a.** Occurring at intervals of three: *trimonthly.* **b.** Occurring three times during: *triweekly.* [< Lat. *trēs* and Gk. *treis.*]

tri·ad (trī′ăd′, -əd) ►*n.* A group of three. [< Gk. *trias.*] —**tri·ad′ic** *adj.*

tri·age (trē-äzh′, trē′äzh′) ►*n.* **1.** A process for sorting injured people into groups based on their need for medical treatment. **2.** A system used to allocate a scarce commodity, esp. in an emergency. [< OFr. *trier,* sort.]

tri·al (trī′əl) ►*n.* **1.** Examination of evidence and applicable law to determine the issue of specified charges or claims. **2.** The act or process of testing or trying. **3.** An effort or attempt. **4.** A test of patience or endurance. **5.** A nuisance; pain. See Synonyms at **burden. 6.** A qualifying competition, as in a sport. ►*adj.* **1.** Relating to a trial. **2.** Provisional; experimental: *a trial separation.* **3.** Made or done during a test. —*idiom:* **on trial** In the process of being tried, as in a court of law. [< AN *trier,* try.]
Syns: *affliction, crucible, ordeal, tribulation* **n.**

tri·an·gle (trī′ăng′gəl) ►*n.* **1.** The polygon formed by connecting three points not in a straight line by straight line segments. **2.** A musical percussion instrument formed of a metal bar in the shape of a triangle. —**tri·an′gu·lar** *adj.*

tri·an·gu·late (trī-ăng′gyə-lāt′) ►*v.* **-lat·ed, -lat·ing** To measure by using trigonometry. —**tri·an′gu·la′tion** *n.*

Tri·as·sic (trī-ăs′ĭk) *Geol.* ►*adj.* Of or being the 1st period of the Mesozoic Era, marked by the rise of dinosaurs and the appearance of the earliest mammals. ►*n.* The Triassic Period.

tri·ath·lon (trī-ăth′lən, -lŏn′) ►*n.* An athletic contest consisting of three successive events, usu. long-distance swimming, bicycling, and running. [*tri–* + (DEC)ATHLON.] —**tri·ath′lete** *n.*

tribe (trīb) ►*n.* **1.** A unit of social organization consisting of several families, clans, or other groups who share a common ancestry, culture, and usu. impermanent leadership. **2.** A group sharing a common distinguishing characteristic. **3.** A taxonomic category ranking below a family and above a genus and usu. containing several genera. [< Lat. *tribus,* a division of the Roman people.] —**trib′al** *adj.* —**trib′al·ly** *adv.* —**tribes′man** *n.* —**tribes′wom·an** *n.*

trib·u·la·tion (trĭb′yə-lā′shən) ►*n.* **1.** Great affliction or distress. See Synonyms at **trial. 2.** An experience that tests one's endurance, patience, or faith. See Synonyms at **burden.** [< Lat. *trībulāre,* oppress.]

tri·bu·nal (trī-byōō′nəl, trĭ-) ►*n.* **1.** *Law* **a.** A law court. **b.** The place where a session of court is held. **2.** A committee or board appointed to adjudicate in a particular matter. [< Lat. *tribūnus,* tribune.]

trib·une (trĭb′yōōn′, trĭ-byōōn′) ►*n.* **1.** An officer of ancient Rome elected by the plebeians to protect their rights. **2.** A protector or champion of the people. [< Lat. *tribūnus.*] —**trib′u·nar′y** (trĭb′yə-nĕr′ē) *adj.*

trib·u·tar·y (trĭb′yə-tĕr′ē) ►*n., pl.* **-ies 1.** A stream that flows into a larger body of water. **2.** One that pays tribute. ►*adj.* **1.** Contributory. **2.** Paid in tribute. **3.** Paying tribute.

trib·ute (trĭb′yōōt) ►*n.* **1.** A gift or other acknowledgment of gratitude, respect, or admiration. **2a.** A payment made by one ruler or nation to another in acknowledgment of submission or as the price of protection or security. **b.** A forced payment. [< Lat. *tribuere,* pay.]

trice (trīs) ►*n.* A very short period of time; instant. [< MDu. *trīsen,* hoist.]

tri·cen·ten·ni·al (trī′sĕn-tĕn′ē-əl) ►*adj.* Tercentenary. ►*n.* A tercentenary event or celebration.

tri·ceps (trī′sĕps′) ►*n., pl.* **-ceps·es** (-sĕp′sĭz) also **-ceps** A large muscle running along the back of the upper arm and serving to extend the forearm. [< Lat., three-headed.]

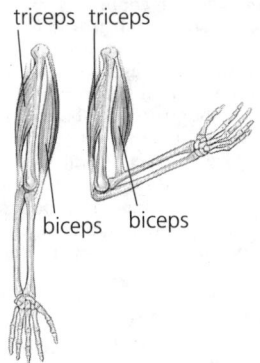

triceps

left: triceps contracted when elbow is extended
right: triceps relaxed when elbow is flexed

tri·cer·a·tops (trī-sĕr′ə-tŏps′) ►*n.* A herbivorous dinosaur with three facial horns and a bony plate covering the neck. [NLat. *Triceratops,* genus name : TRI– + Gk. *keras,* horn + Gk. *ōps,* face.]

trich·i·no·sis (trĭk′ə-nō′sĭs) ►*n.* A disease caused by eating undercooked meat, usu. pork, that is infested with parasitic worms, marked by intestinal pain, fever, nausea, muscular pain, and edema of the face. [*trichina,* a parasitic worm + –OSIS.]

trick (trĭk) ►*n.* **1a.** An act or plan intended to achieve an end by deceptive or fraudulent means. **b.** A mischievous action; prank. **2a.** A peculiar trait; mannerism. **b.** A deceptive or illusive appearance: *a trick of sunlight.* **3a.** A feat requiring special knowledge. **b.** A specialized skill: *the tricks of the trade.* **4a.** A feat of magic or legerdemain. **b.** A clever act. **5.** *Games* All the cards played in a single round. ►*v.* To cheat or deceive. ►*adj.* **1.** Involving tricks; tricky. **2.** Weak, defective, or liable to fail: *a trick knee.* **—idiom: not miss a trick** To be extremely alert. [< ONFr. *trikier,* deceive.] **—trick′er** *n.*

trick·er·y (trĭk′ə-rē) ►*n., pl.* **-ies** The practice or use of tricks; deception.

trick·le (trĭk′əl) ►*v.* **-led, -ling 1.** To flow or fall in drops or in a thin stream. **2.** To proceed slowly or bit by bit. ►*n.* **1.** The act or condition of trickling. **2.** A slow, small, or irregular quantity. [ME *triklen.*]

trick·ster (trĭk′stər) ►*n.* One who plays clever or deceptive tricks.

trick·y (trĭk′ē) ►*adj.* **-i·er, -i·est 1.** Crafty; sly. **2.** Requiring caution or skill. **—trick′i·ly** *adv.* **—trick′i·ness** *n.*

tri·col·or (trī′kŭl′ər) ►*n.* A flag having three colors. ►*adj.* also **tri·col·ored** (-ərd) Having three colors.

tri·corn also **tri·corne** (trī′kôrn′) ►*n.* A hat with the brim turned up on three sides. [< Lat. *tricornis,* three-horned.]

tri·cot (trē′kō) ►*n.* A lightweight knit fabric used esp. for underwear. [Fr. < *tricoter,* knit.]

tri·cy·cle (trī′sĭk′əl, -sĭ-kəl) ►*n.* A three-wheeled vehicle usu. propelled by pedals.

tri·dent (trīd′nt) ►*n.* A long, three-pronged fishing spear or weapon. [< Lat. *tridēns* : TRI– + *dēns,* tooth.]

tried (trīd) ►*v.* P.t. and p.part. of **try.** ►*adj.* Tested and proved to be trustworthy.

tri·en·ni·al (trī-ĕn′ē-əl) ►*adj.* **1.** Occurring every third year. **2.** Lasting three years. ►*n.* A third anniversary. [< Lat. *triennium,* three years.] **—tri·en′ni·al·ly** *adv.*

Tri·este (trē-ĕst′, -ĕs′tĕ) A city of extreme NE Italy on the **Gulf of Trieste,** an inlet of the Gulf of Venice at the head of the Adriatic Sea.

tri·fle (trī′fəl) ►*n.* **1.** Something of little importance or value. **2.** A small amount. ►*v.* **-fled, -fling** To treat flippantly or without seriousness; play or toy: *Don't trifle with my affections.* See Synonyms at **flirt.** [< OFr. *trufle,* trickery.] **—tri′fler** (trī′flər) *n.*

tri·fling (trī′flĭng) ►*adj.* **1.** Of slight worth or importance. **2.** Frivolous or foolish.

tri·fo·cal (trī-fō′kəl, trī′fō′-) ►*adj.* Having three focal lengths. ►*n.* **trifocals** Eyeglasses having trifocal lenses.

trig (trĭg) ►*adj.* Smart and trim, as in appearance. [< ON *tryggr,* true.]

trig·ger (trĭg′ər) ►*n.* **1a.** The lever pressed by the finger to discharge a firearm. **b.** A similar device used to release or activate a mechanism. **2.** An event that precipitates other events. [< MDu. *trecker* < *trecken,* pull.] **—trig′ger** *v.*

tri·glyc·er·ide (trī-glĭs′ə-rīd′) ►*n.* A naturally occurring ester of three fatty acids and glycerol that is the chief constituent of fats and oils.

trig·o·nom·e·try (trĭg′ə-nŏm′ĭ-trē) ►*n.* The study of relationships between the sides and the angles of triangles. [Gk. *trigōnon,* triangle + –METRY.] **—trig′o·no·met′ric** (-nə-mĕt′rĭk), **trig′o·no·met′ri·cal** *adj.*

trill (trĭl) ►*n.* **1.** A fluttering or tremulous sound; warble. **2.** *Mus.* The rapid alternation of two tones either a whole or a half tone apart. **3.** *Ling.* **a.** A rapid vibration of one speech organ against another. **b.** A speech sound so pronounced. [Ital. *trillo.*] **—trill** *v.*

tril·lion (trĭl′yən) ►*n.* **1.** The cardinal number equal to 10^{12}. **2.** *Chiefly Brit.* The cardinal number equal to 10^{18}. [Fr.] **—tril′lion** *adj.* **—tril′lionth** *n. & adj.*

tri·lo·bite (trī′lə-bīt′) ►*n.* An extinct three-lobed marine arthropod of the Paleozoic Era. [< Gk. *trilobos,* three-lobed.]

tril·o·gy (trĭl′ə-jē) ►*n., pl.* **-gies** A group of three related artistic works. [Gk. *trilogia.*]

trim (trĭm) ►*v.* **trimmed, trim·ming 1.** To make neat or tidy by clipping, smoothing, or pruning. **2.** To remove the excess or unwanted parts from. **3.** To decorate, esp. by adding a border or contrasting element. **4.** *Naut.* **a.** To adjust (the sails and yards) relative to the wind. **b.** To balance (a ship) by shifting its cargo or contents. **5.** To balance (an aircraft) in flight. ►*n.* **1a.** State of order or appearance; condition. **b.** A condition of good health or fitness. **2.** Ornamentation. **3.** often **trims** Excised or rejected material. **4a.** The readiness of a vessel for sailing. **b.** The balance of a ship. ►*adj.* **trim·mer, trim·mest 1.** In good or neat order. **2.** Having lines of neat and pleasing simplicity. [< OE *trymman,* strengthen.] **—trim′ly** *adv.* **—trim′mer** *n.* **—trim′ness** *n.*

tri·mes·ter (trī-mĕs′tər, trī′mĕs′-) ►*n.* **1.** A

period of three months. **2.** One of three terms into which an academic year is sometimes divided. [< Lat. *trimēstris*, of three months.]

trim·e·ter (trĭm′ĭ-tər) ►*n.* Verse composed in lines of three metrical feet. —**tri·met′ric** (trī-mĕt′rĭk), **tri·met′ri·cal** *adj.*

trim·ming (trĭm′ĭng) ►*n.* **1.** The act of one that trims. **2.** Something added as decoration. **3. trimmings** Accessories; extras.

trine (trīn) ►*adj.* Threefold; triple. ►*n.* A group of three. [< Lat. *trīnus.*]

Trin·i·dad (trĭn′ĭ-dăd′) An island of Trinidad and Tobago in the Atlantic off NE Venezuela. —**Trin′i·dad′i·an** *adj. & n.*

Trinidad and Tobago A country of the SE West Indies off NE Venezuela, comprising the islands of Trinidad and Tobago. Cap. Port of Spain.

trin·i·ty (trĭn′ĭ-tē) ►*n., pl.* -**ties 1.** A group of three closely related members. **2. Trinity** In Christian theology, the union of the three divine persons in one God. [< Lat. *trīnitās.*]

trin·ket (trĭng′kĭt) ►*n.* **1.** A small ornament or piece of jewelry. **2.** A trifle. [?]

tri·o (trē′ō) ►*n., pl.* -**os 1.** *Mus.* **a.** A composition for three performers. **b.** A group of three performers. **2.** A group of three. [< Ital.]

trip (trĭp) ►*n.* **1.** A going from one place to another; journey. **2.** A stumble or fall. **3.** A maneuver causing someone to stumble or fall. **4.** *Slang* An exciting or hallucinatory experience. **5.** A device for triggering a mechanism. ►*v.* **tripped, trip·ping 1.** To stumble or cause to stumble. **2.** To move nimbly with light rapid steps; skip. **3.** To make or cause to make an error. **4.** To release or be released, as a catch, trigger, or switch. [< OFr. *tripper*, stamp the foot, of Gmc. orig.] —**trip′per** *n.*

tri·par·tite (trī-pär′tīt) ►*adj.* **1.** Composed of or divided into three parts. **2.** Of or executed by three parties: *a tripartite agreement.*

tripe (trīp) ►*n.* **1.** The stomach lining of cattle or other ruminants, used as food. **2.** *Informal* Something of no value; rubbish. [< OFr.]

tri·ple (trĭp′əl) ►*adj.* **1.** Having three parts. **2.** Three times as many or as much. **3.** *Mus.* Having three beats in a measure. ►*n.* **1.** A number or quantity three times as great as another. **2.** Something having three prominent parts or members. **3.** *Baseball* A hit enabling the batter to reach third base. ►*v.* -**pled, -pling 1.** To make or become three times as great. **2.** *Baseball* To make a triple. [< Lat. *triplus.*] —**tri′ply** *adv.*

triple play ►*n. Baseball* A play in which three players are put out.

trip·let (trĭp′lĭt) ►*n.* **1.** A group or set of three. **2.** One of three children born at one birth. [TRIPL(E) + (DOUBL)ET.]

tri·plex (trĭp′lĕks′, trī′plĕks′) ►*adj.* Having three parts or divisions: *a triplex cinema.* [Lat.] —**tri′plex′** *n.*

trip·li·cate (trĭp′lĭ-kĭt) ►*n.* One of a set of three identical objects or copies. ►*v.* (-kāt′) -**cat·ed, -cat·ing** To make three identical copies of. [< Lat. *triplicāre*, to triple.] —**trip′li·ca′tion** *n.*

tri·pod (trī′pŏd′) ►*n.* **1.** A three-legged object, such as a cauldron, stool, or table. **2.** An adjustable three-legged stand, as for supporting a camera or telescope. [< Gk. *tripous*, three-footed : TRI– + *pous*, foot.]

Trip·o·li (trĭp′ə-lē) The capital of Libya, in the

NW part on the Mediterranean Sea. —**Tri·pol′i·tan** (trĭ-pŏl′ĭ-tn) *adj. & n.*

trip·tych (trĭp′tĭk) ►*n.* A three-paneled work of art, such as an altarpiece. [< Gk. *triptukhos*, threefold.]

tri·sect (trī′sĕkt′, trī-sĕkt′) ►*v.* To divide into three equal parts. —**tri′sec′tion** *n.*

trite (trīt) ►*adj.* **trit·er, trit·est** Uninteresting for having been overused; hackneyed. [Lat. *trītus* < p.part. of *terere*, wear out.] —**trite′ly** *adv.* —**trite′ness** *n.*

trit·i·um (trĭt′ē-əm, trĭsh′ē-) ►*n.* A rare radioactive hydrogen isotope with one proton and two neutrons in the nucleus. [< Gk. *tritos*, third.]

tri·umph (trī′əmf) ►*v.* **1.** To be victorious or successful; win. **2.** To rejoice; exult. ►*n.* **1.** The fact or an instance of being victorious; victory. **2.** Exultation. [< Lat. *triumphāre.*] —**tri·um′phal** *adj.* —**tri·um′phant** *adj.*

tri·um·vir (trī-ŭm′vər) ►*n., pl.* -**virs** or -**vi·ri** (-və-rī′) One of three men sharing civil authority in ancient Rome. [< Lat. : *trium*, of three + *vir*, man.] —**tri·um′vi·ral** *adj.* —**tri·um′vi·rate** (-vər-ĭt) *n.*

triv·et (trĭv′ĭt) ►*n.* **1.** A stand with short feet, used under a hot dish on a table. **2.** A three-legged stand. [< Lat. *tripēs*, three-footed : TRI– + *pēs*, foot.]

triv·i·a (trĭv′ē-ə) ►*pl.n.* (takes sing. or pl. v.) **1.** Insignificant or inessential matters. **2.** Miscellaneous facts. [Lat.]

triv·i·al (trĭv′ē-əl) ►*adj.* Of little significance. —**triv′i·al′i·ty** (-ăl′ĭ-tē) *n.* —**triv′i·al·ly** *adv.*

triv·i·al·ize (trĭv′ē-ə-līz′) ►*v.* -**ized, -iz·ing** To reduce to triviality. —**triv′i·al·i·za′tion** *n.*

–**trix** ►*suff.* A woman who is connected with a specified thing: *testatrix.* [Lat. *-trīx.*]

tro·chee (trō′kē) ►*n.* A metrical foot consisting of one long or accented syllable followed by one short or unaccented one. [< Gk. *trokhaios.*] —**tro·cha′ic** (-kā′ĭk) *adj.*

trod (trŏd) ►*v.* P.t. and p.part. of **tread.**

trod·den (trŏd′n) ►*v.* P.part. of **tread.**

trog·lo·dyte (trŏg′lə-dīt′) ►*n.* **1.** A member of a fabulous or prehistoric race that lived in caves. **2.** A reclusive, reactionary, or brutish person. [< Gk. *Trōglodutai*, cave dwellers.] —**trog′lo·dyt′ic** (-dĭt′ĭk) *adj.*

troi·ka (troi′kə) ►*n.* A Russian carriage drawn by three horses abreast. [Russ. *troĭka.*]

Tro·jan (trō′jən) ►*n.* **1.** A native or inhabitant of ancient Troy. **2.** A person of courageous determination. —**Tro′jan** *adj.*

Trojan War ►*n. Gk. Myth.* The ten-year war waged against Troy by the Greeks, resulting in the destruction of Troy.

troll[1] (trōl) ►*v.* **1.** To fish by trailing a baited line from behind a slowly moving boat. **2a.** To sing in succession the parts of (a round). **b.** To sing heartily. ►*n.* **1.** The act of trolling for fish. **2.** A musical round. [< OFr. *troller*, wander.] —**troll′er** *n.*

troll[2] (trōl) ►*n.* A supernatural creature of Scandinavian folklore, often described as living in caves or under bridges. [< ON.]

trol·ley also **trol·ly** (trŏl′ē) ►*n., pl.* -**leys** also -**lies 1.** A streetcar. **2.** A device that collects electric current and transmits it to the motor of an electric vehicle. **3.** A wheeled carriage or basket suspended from an overhead track. [Poss. < TROLL[1].]

trolley bus ►*n.* A bus that is powered by electricity from an overhead wire.

trolley car ►*n.* A streetcar.

trol·lop (trŏl′əp) ►*n.* **1.** A woman prostitute. **2.** A slovenly woman. [Perh. < TROLL¹, roll about.]

Trol·lope (trŏl′əp), **Anthony** 1815–82. British writer.

trom·bone (trŏm-bōn′, trăm-, trŏm′bōn′) ►*n.* A brass musical instrument with a movable U-shaped slide for producing different pitches. [< Ital. < *tromba*, trumpet.] —**trom·bon′ist** *n.*

tromp (trŏmp) ►*v.* **1.** To tramp. **2.** To trample underfoot. **3.** To trounce. [< TRAMP.]

trompe l'oeil (trômp′ loi′) ►*n.* A detailed style of painting that gives an illusion of photographic reality. [Fr.]

–tron ►*suff.* Device for manipulating subatomic particles: *betatron.* [Gk., noun suff.]

troop (trōop) ►*n.* **1.** A group or company of people, animals, or things. **2a.** A group of soldiers. **b. troops** Military units; soldiers. ►*v.* To move or go as a throng. [< OFr. *trope.*]

troop·er (trōo′pər) ►*n.* **1a.** A member of a cavalry unit. **b.** A cavalry horse. **2a.** A mounted police officer. **b.** A state police officer.

trope (trōp) ►*n.* A figure of speech using words in nonliteral ways. [< Gk. *tropos*, a turn.]

tro·phy (trō′fē) ►*n., pl.* **-phies** A prize or memento received as a symbol of victory. [< Gk. *tropaion.*]

–trophy ►*suff.* Nutrition; growth: *hypertrophy.* [< Gk. *trophē.*]

trop·ic (trŏp′ĭk) ►*n.* Either of two parallels of latitude, the tropic of Cancer or the tropic of Capricorn, representing the farthest north and south at which the sun can shine directly overhead. ►*adj.* Of or concerning the tropics; tropical. [< Gk. *tropē*, a turning.]

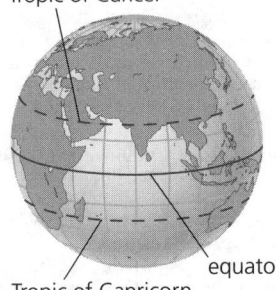

Tropic of Cancer

equator

Tropic of Capricorn

tropic

–tropic ►*suff.* Changing in a specified way or in response to a specified stimulus: *phototropic.* [< Gk. *tropē*, a turning.]

trop·i·cal (trŏp′ĭ-kəl) ►*adj.* **1.** Of or characteristic of the tropics. **2.** Hot and humid; torrid.

tropical storm ►*n.* A cyclonic storm originating in the tropics and having winds ranging from 39 to 73 mph (63 to 117 kph).

Tropic of Cancer ►*n.* The parallel of latitude 23°27′ north of the equator.

Tropic of Capricorn ►*n.* The parallel of latitude 23°27′ south of the equator.

tropics (trŏp′ĭks) ►*pl.n.* The regions of the earth between the Tropic of Cancer and the Tropic of Capricorn.

tro·pism (trō′pĭz′əm) ►*n.* The turning or bending movement of an organism in response to an external stimulus. [< Gk. *tropē*, a turning.]

tro·po·sphere (trō′pə-sfîr′, trŏp′ə-) ►*n.* The lowest region of the earth's atmosphere, marked by decreasing temperature with increasing altitude. [Gk. *tropē*, a turning + SPHERE.] —**tro′po·spher′ic** (-sfîr′ĭk, -sfĕr′-) *adj.*

–tropy ►*suff.* The state of turning in a specified way or from a specified stimulus: *phototropy.* [< Gk. *tropos*, changeable.]

trot (trŏt) ►*n.* **1.** The gait of a four-footed animal in which diagonal pairs of legs move forward together. **2.** A gait of a person, faster than a walk; jog. ►*v.* **trot·ted, trot·ting 1.** To go or move at a trot. **2.** To hurry. [< OFr.] —**trot′ter** *n.*

troth (trôth, trŏth, trōth) ►*n.* **1a.** Betrothal. **b.** One's pledged fidelity. **2.** Good faith; fidelity. [< OE *trēowth*, truth.]

Trot·sky (trŏt′skē, trôt′-), **Leon** Lev Davidovitch Bronstein. 1879–1940. Russian revolutionary theoretician. —**Trot′sky·ite′** *adj. & n.*

trou·ba·dour (trōo′bə-dôr′, -dŏor′) ►*n.* **1.** One of a class of 12th and 13th cent. lyric poets in S France, N Italy, and N Spain. **2.** A strolling minstrel. [< OProv. *trobador.*]

trou·ble (trŭb′əl) ►*n.* **1.** A state of distress, affliction, danger, or need. **2.** A source of distress or difficulty. **3.** Inconvenience or bother. **4.** A condition of pain or malfunction. ►*v.* **-bled, -bling 1.** To afflict with pain or discomfort. **2.** To distress; worry. **3.** To inconvenience; bother. **4.** To agitate; stir up. [< Lat. *turbidus*, confused.] —**trou′bler** *n.* —**trou′ble·some** *adj.*

Syns: *distress, worry* **v.**

trou·ble·mak·er (trŭb′əl-mā′kər) ►*n.* One who stirs up trouble or strife.

trou·ble·shoot·er (trŭb′əl-shōo′tər) ►*n.* One who locates and eliminates sources of trouble.

trough (trôf, trŏf) ►*n.* **1.** A long, narrow, usu. shallow receptacle, esp. for holding water or feed for animals. **2.** A gutter under the edge of a roof for carrying off rainwater. **3.** A long narrow depression, as between waves. **4.** A low point in a cycle or on a graph. [< OE *trog.*]

trounce (trouns) ►*v.* **trounced, trounc·ing 1.** To thrash; beat. **2.** To defeat decisively. [?]

troupe (trōop) ►*n.* A company or group, esp. of touring performers. [Fr., TROOP.]

troup·er (trōo′pər) ►*n.* **1.** A member of a theatrical company. **2.** A veteran actor or performer.

trou·sers (trou′zərz) ►*pl.n.* A garment covering the body from the waist to the ankles, divided into sections to fit each leg separately. [< Sc.Gael. *triubhas.*]

trous·seau (trōo′sō, trōo-sō′) ►*n., pl.* **-seaux** (-sōz, -sōz′) or **-seaus** The possessions that a bride assembles for her marriage. [< OFr.]

trout (trout) ►*n., pl.* **trout** or **trouts** Any of various edible, chiefly freshwater fishes related to the salmon. [< LLat. *tructa.*]

trove (trōv) ►*n.* A treasure-trove.

trow·el (trou′əl) ►*n.* **1.** A flat-bladed hand tool for leveling, spreading, or shaping substances such as cement. **2.** A small digging tool with a scoop-shaped blade. [< LLat. *truella* < Lat. *trua*, ladle.] —**trow′el** *v.*

troy (troi) ►*adj.* Of or expressed in troy weight. [< *Troyes*, France.]

Troy An ancient city of NW Asia Minor near the Dardanelles.

troy weight ►*n.* A system of units of weight in which the grain is the same as in the avoirdupois system and the pound contains 12 ounces, 240 pennyweights, or 5,760 grains.

tru·ant (trōō′ənt) ►*n.* **1.** One absent without permission, esp. from school. **2.** One who shirks work or duty. [< OFr., beggar.] —**tru′ant** *adj.* —**tru′an·cy** *n.*

truce (trōōs) ►*n.* **1.** A temporary cessation of hostilities by agreement; armistice. **2.** A respite from a disagreeable state of affairs. [< OE *trēow*, a pledge.]

truck¹ (trŭk) ►*n.* **1.** A heavy motor vehicle for carrying loads. **2.** A two-wheeled barrow for moving heavy objects by hand. **3.** One of the swiveling frames of wheels under each end of a railroad car or trolley car. ►*v.* **1.** To transport by truck. **2.** To drive a truck. [Poss. < TRUCKLE.] —**truck′er** *n.*

truck² (trŭk) ►*v.* **1.** To have dealings or commerce; traffic. **2.** *Archaic* To exchange; barter. ►*n.* **1.** Barter; exchange. **2.** Garden produce raised for the market. **3.** *Informal* Worthless goods; rubbish. **4.** *Informal* Dealings; business. [< ONFr. *troquer*.]

truck·age (trŭk′ĭj) ►*n.* **1.** Transportation of goods by truck. **2.** A charge for this service.

truck·le (trŭk′əl) ►*n.* A small wheel or roller; caster. ►*v.* **-led, -ling** To be servile or submissive. See Synonyms at **fawn¹**. [< Lat. *trochlea*, system of pulleys.]

truc·u·lent (trŭk′yə-lənt) ►*adj.* **1.** Disposed to engage in hostile opposition. **2.** Showing or expressing hostile opposition. **3.** Disposed to violence. [Lat. *truculentus*.] —**truc′u·lence** *n.*

Tru·deau (trōō-dō′), **Pierre Elliott** 1919–2000. Canadian prime minister (1968–79 and 1980–84).

trudge (trŭj) ►*v.* **trudged, trudg·ing** To walk in a laborious, heavy-footed way; plod. [?] —**trudge** *n.* —**trudg′er** *n.*

true (trōō) ►*adj.* **tru·er, tru·est** **1a.** Consistent with fact or reality; not false or erroneous. **b.** Real or genuine. See Synonyms at **authentic**. **2.** Reliable; accurate. **3.** Faithful; loyal. **4.** Sincerely felt or expressed. **5.** Rightful; legitimate. **6a.** Exactly conforming to a rule, standard, or pattern. **b.** Determined with reference to the earth's axis, not the magnetic poles: *true north.* ►*adv.* **1.** Rightly; truthfully. **2.** Unswervingly; exactly. **3.** So as to conform to a type, standard, or pattern. ►*v.* **trued, tru·ing** or **true·ing** To position (something) so as to make it balanced, level, or square. ►*n.* Proper alignment or adjustment: *out of true.* [< OE *trēowe*, trustworthy.] —**true′ness** *n.*

true-blue (trōō′blōō′) ►*adj.* Loyal or faithful; staunch.

true·love (trōō′lŭv′) ►*n.* One's beloved.

truf·fle (trŭf′əl) ►*n.* **1.** An underground fungus valued as a delicacy. **2.** A rich chocolate confection. [< Lat. *tūber*, lump.]

tru·ism (trōō′ĭz′əm) ►*n.* A statement that is obviously true or that is often presented as true. See Synonyms at **cliché**. —**tru·is′tic** *adj.*

tru·ly (trōō′lē) ►*adv.* **1.** Sincerely; genuinely. **2.** Truthfully; accurately. **3.** Indeed.

Tru·man (trōō′mən), **Harry S.** 1884–1972. The 33rd US president (1945–53).

Harry S. Truman
photographed c. 1945

trump (trŭmp) ►*n.* **1.** often **trumps** A suit in card games that outranks all other suits for the duration of a hand. **2.** A card of such a suit. ►*v.* To play a trump. —**phrasal verb: trump up** To devise fraudulently. [< TRIUMPH.]

trump·er·y (trŭm′pə-rē) ►*n., pl.* **-ies** **1.** Showy but worthless finery. **2.** Nonsense. **3.** Trickery. [< OFr. *tromper*, deceive.]

trum·pet (trŭm′pĭt) ►*n.* **1a.** A soprano brass instrument consisting of a long metal tube ending in a flared bell. **b.** Something shaped or sounding like a trumpet. **2.** A resounding call. ►*v.* To sound or proclaim loudly. [< OHGer. *trumpa*, horn.] —**trum′pet·er** *n.*

trun·cate (trŭng′kāt′) ►*v.* **-cat·ed, -cat·ing** To shorten or reduce. See Synonyms at **shorten**. [Lat. *truncāre*.] —**trun·ca′tion** *n.*

trun·cheon (trŭn′chən) ►*n.* A short stick carried by police; billy club. [< VLat. **trunciō*, club.] —**trun′cheon** *v.*

trun·dle (trŭn′dl) ►*n.* **1.** A small wheel or roller. **2.** A trundle bed. ►*v.* **-dled, -dling** To push on wheels or rollers. [< OE *trendel*, circle.]

trundle bed ►*n.* A low bed on casters that can be rolled under another bed for storage.

trunk (trŭngk) ►*n.* **1.** The main woody axis of a tree. **2.** The human body excluding the head and limbs; torso. **3.** A proboscis, esp. the long prehensile proboscis of an elephant. **4.** A main body, apart from tributaries or appendages. **5a.** A covered compartment for luggage and storage, usu. at the rear of an automobile. **b.** A large packing case or box that clasps shut, used as luggage or for storage. **6. trunks** Shorts worn esp. for swimming. [< Lat. *truncus*.]

truss (trŭs) ►*n.* **1.** A supportive device worn to prevent enlargement of a hernia or the return of a reduced hernia. **2.** A wooden or metal framework designed to support a structure, such as a roof. ►*v.* **1.** To tie up or bind tightly. **2.** To bind the wings or legs of (a fowl) before cooking. **3.** To support or brace with a truss. [< OFr. *trousse*, bundle.]

trust (trŭst) ►*n.* **1a.** Firm belief in the integrity or ability of a person or thing. **b.** The condition and obligation of having confidence placed in one. **2a.** Custody; care. See Synonyms at **care. b.** Something committed into the care of another; charge. **3.** Reliance on something in the future; hope: *We have trust that the future will be better.* **4.** A legal relationship in which one party holds a title to property while another party has the entitlement to the beneficial use of that property. **5.** An institution or organization directed by trustees. **6.** A combination of firms or corporations for the purpose of reducing competition. ►*v.* **1a.** To have or place confidence in; depend on. **b.** To have confidence in allowing (someone) to use, know, or look after something. **2.** To assume: *I trust he'll be ready.* **3.** To believe: *I trust what you say.* **4.** To entrust. **5.** To extend credit to. —*idiom:* **in trust** In the possession or care of a trustee. [ME *truste.*] —**trust′er** *n.*

trus·tee (trŭ-stē′) ►*n.* **1.** A person in a trust relationship who holds title to property for the benefit of another. **2.** A member of a board that directs the funds and policy of an institution. —**trus·tee′ship′** *n.*

trust·ful (trŭst′fəl) ►*adj.* Full of trust. —**trust′ful·ly** *adv.* —**trust′ful·ness** *n.*

trust·wor·thy (trŭst′wûr′thē) ►*adj.* Warranting trust; reliable. See Synonyms at **reliable.** —**trust′wor′thi·ness** *n.*

trust·y (trŭs′tē) ►*adj.* **-i·er, -i·est** Meriting trust; trustworthy. See Synonyms at **reliable.** ►*n., pl.* **-ies** A trusted person, esp. a convict granted special privileges. —**trust′i·ly** *adv.* —**trust′i·ness** *n.*

truth (trooth) ►*n., pl.* **truths** (troothz, trooths) **1a.** Conformity to fact or actuality. **b.** Reality; actuality. **2.** A statement proven to be or accepted as true: *truths about nature.* **3.** Sincerity; honesty. **4.** *Theol. & Philos.* That which is considered to be the ultimate ground of reality. [< OE *trēowth.*]

Truth, Sojourner 1797?–1883. Amer. abolitionist and feminist.

truth·ful (trooth′fəl) ►*adj.* **1.** Consistently telling the truth; honest. **2.** Corresponding to reality. —**truth′ful·ly** *adv.* —**truth′ful·ness** *n.*

try (trī) ►*v.* **tried** (trīd), **try·ing** **1.** To make an effort (to do something). **2.** To test in order to determine strength, effect, worth, or desirability. **3a.** To conduct the trial of (a legal claim). **b.** To put (a defendant) on trial. **4.** To subject to strain or hardship; tax. **5.** To render (fat). ►*n., pl.* **tries** (trīz) An attempt; effort. [< OFr. *trier,* pick out.]

Usage: The phrase *try and* is commonly used as a substitute for *try to,* as in *Could you try and make less noise?* The usage is associated with informal style and strikes an inappropriately conversational note in formal writing.

try·ing (trī′ĭng) ►*adj.* Causing strain, hardship, or distress. —**try′ing·ly** *adv.*

try·out (trī′out′) ►*n.* A test to ascertain the skills of applicants, as for a sports team.

tryst (trĭst) ►*n.* **1.** An agreement between lovers to meet. **2.** A usu. private meeting or meeting place so arranged. [< OFr. *triste,* a waiting place (in hunting).] —**tryst** *v.* —**tryst′er** *n.*

tsar (zär, tsär) ►*n.* Var. of **czar** (sense 1).

tset·se fly (tsĕt′sē, tsē′tsē) ►*n.* A bloodsucking fly of sub-Saharan Africa that transmits microorganisms causing diseases such as sleeping sickness. [Of Bantu orig.]

TSgt ►*abbr.* technical sergeant

T-shirt also **tee shirt** (tē′shûrt′) ►*n.* A short-

sleeved pullover shirt with no collar.

tsp. ►*abbr.* teaspoon

T-square (tē′skwâr′) ►*n.* A T-shaped ruler used for drawing parallel lines.

tsu·na·mi (tsoo-nä′mē) ►*n., pl.* **-mis** or **tsunami** A very large ocean wave caused by an underwater earthquake or volcanic eruption. [J.]

Tswa·na (tswä′nə, swä′-) ►*n., pl.* **-na** or **-nas** **1.** A member of a Bantu people of Botswana and W South Africa. **2.** The Bantu language of the Tswana.

Tu·a·mo·tu Archipelago (too′ə-mō′too) An island group of French Polynesia in the S Pacific E of Tahiti.

tub (tŭb) ►*n.* **1.** A round, open, flat-bottomed vessel used for washing, packing, or storing. **2.** A bathtub. [< MDu. or MLGer.]

tu·ba (too′bə, tyoo′-) ►*n.* A large, valved, brass instrument with a bass pitch. [< Lat., trumpet.]

tu·bal ligation (too′bəl, tyoo′-) ►*n.* A method of female sterilization in which the fallopian tubes are surgically tied.

tub·by (tŭb′ē) ►*adj.* **-bi·er, -bi·est 1.** Having a rounded shape: *a tubby fishing boat.* **2.** *Informal* Short and fat. —**tub′bi·ness** *n.*

tube (toob, tyoob) ►*n.* **1.** A hollow cylinder, esp. one that conveys a fluid or functions as a passage. **2.** A flexible cylindrical container sealed at one end and having a screw cap at the other, for pigments, toothpaste, or other substances. **3a.** An electron tube. **b.** A vacuum tube. **4.** *Chiefly Brit.* A subway. **5.** often **the tube** *Slang* Television. [< Lat. *tubus.*] —**tube′less** *adj.*

tu·ber (too′bər, tyoo′-) ►*n.* **1a.** A swollen, usu. underground outgrowth of the stem of a plant, such as the potato, bearing buds from which new plants sprout. **b.** A similar outgrowth of a plant root. **2.** *Biol.* A tubercle. [Lat. *tūber,* lump.] —**tu′ber·ous** *adj.*

tu·ber·cle (too′bər-kəl, tyoo′-) ►*n.* **1.** A nodule or swelling that is the characteristic lesion of tuberculosis. **2.** A small rounded prominence on the roots of some plants or a knoblike process on a bone or in the skin. [Lat. *tūberculum,* small lump.]

tu·ber·cu·lar (too-bûr′kyə-lər, tyoo-) ►*adj.* **1.** Of or covered with tubercles. **2.** Of or affected with tuberculosis.

tu·ber·cu·lin (too-bûr′kyə-lĭn, tyoo-) ►*n.* A liquid containing proteins derived from tubercle bacilli, used in tests for tuberculosis. [Lat. *tūberculum,* tubercle + –IN.]

tu·ber·cu·lo·sis (too-bûr′kyə-lō′sĭs, tyoo-) ►*n.* An infectious disease caused by a bacillus and characterized by the formation of tubercles, esp. in the lungs. [Lat. *tūberculum,* tubercle + –OSIS.] —**tu·ber′cu·lous** *adj.*

tube·rose (toob′rōz′, tyoob′-, too′bə-) ►*n.* A tuberous Mexican plant cultivated for its fragrant white flowers. [< feminine of Lat. *tūberōsus,* bearing tubers.]

Tub·man (tŭb′mən), **Harriet** 1820?–1913. Amer. abolitionist.

tu·bu·lar (too′byə-lər, tyoo′-) ►*adj.* Of or having the form of a tube.

tuck (tŭk) ►*v.* **1a.** To thrust or fold the edge of so as to confine: *He tucked his shirt into his pants.* **b.** To wrap snugly: *tucked the baby in bed.* **c.** To make one or more folds in: *tucked the pleats before sewing the hem.* **2.** To put in a snug, safe, or concealed place. **3.** To draw in; contract.

1. A flattened pleat or fold, esp. one stitched in place. **2.** *Informal* A cosmetic surgical procedure in which skin or fat is removed to create a slimmer or more youthful appearance. —*phrasal verb:* **tuck in** To make one secure in bed for sleep, esp. by tucking bedclothes into the bed. [ME *tukken*.]

tuck·er (tŭk′ər) ►*v. Informal* To weary; exhaust. [Perh. < TUCK.]

Tuc·son (tōō′sŏn′) A city of SE AZ SSE of Phoenix.

–tude ►*suff.* Condition, state, or quality: *exactitude*. [< Lat. -*tūdō*.]

Tues·day (tōōz′dē, -dā′, tyōōz′-) ►*n.* The 3rd day of the week. [< OE *Tīwesdæg*.]

tuff (tŭf) ►*n.* A rock composed of compacted volcanic ash. [< OItal. *tufo*.]

tuft (tŭft) ►*n.* A short cluster of strands, as of hair or grass, attached at the base or growing close together. [ME.] —**tuft′ed** *adj.*

tug (tŭg) ►*v.* **tugged, tug·ging 1.** To pull vigorously or repeatedly (at). See Synonyms at **pull. 2.** To move by pulling with great effort or exertion. **3.** To tow by tugboat. ►*n.* **1.** A strong pull or pulling force. **2.** A tugboat. [< OE *tēon*.]

tug·boat (tŭg′bōt′) ►*n.* A small powerful boat designed for towing or pushing larger vessels.

tug of war ►*n.* **1.** A contest in which two teams tug on opposite ends of a rope, each trying to pull the other across a dividing line. **2.** A struggle for supremacy.

tu·grik (tōō′grĭk) ►*n.* Var. of **tögrög.**

tu·i·tion (tōō-ĭsh′ən, tyōō-) ►*n.* **1.** A fee for instruction, esp. at a school. **2.** Instruction; teaching. [< Lat. *tuērī, tuit-*, protect.] —**tu·i′tion·al, tu·i′tion·ar′y** *adj.*

tu·lip (tōō′lĭp, tyōō′-) ►*n.* A bulbous plant cultivated for its variously colored, cup-shaped flowers. [< Ottoman Turkish *tülbend*, muslin.]

tulip tree ►*n.* A tall tree with tuliplike green and orange flowers.

tulle (tōōl) ►*n.* A fine starched net of silk, rayon, or nylon, used esp. for veils, tutus, or gowns. [After *Tulle*, France.]

Tul·sa (tŭl′sə) A city of NE OK on the Arkansas R. NE of Oklahoma City.

tum·ble (tŭm′bəl) ►*v.* **-bled, -bling 1.** To perform acrobatic feats, such as somersaults. **2a.** To fall or roll end over end. **b.** To spill or roll out in disorder. **c.** To pitch headlong; fall. **3.** To decline or collapse suddenly. **4.** To cause to fall; bring down. **5.** To toss or whirl in a drum or tumbler. [< OE *tumbian*, dance.] —**tum′ble** *n.*

tum·ble·down (tŭm′bəl-doun′) ►*adj.* Dilapidated or rickety.

tum·bler (tŭm′blər) ►*n.* **1.** An acrobat or gymnast. **2.** A drinking glass without a handle or stem. **3.** The part in a lock that releases the bolt when moved by a key. **4.** The drum of a clothes dryer.

tum·ble·weed (tŭm′bəl-wēd′) ►*n.* A densely branched plant that when withered breaks off from the roots and is rolled about by the wind.

tum·brel or **tum·bril** (tŭm′brəl) ►*n.* A two-wheeled cart, esp. one that can be tilted to dump a load. [< OFr. *tomberel*.]

tu·mes·cence (tōō-mĕs′əns, tyōō-) ►*n.* A swelling or enlarging. [< Lat. *tumēscere*, begin to swell.] —**tu·mes′cent** *adj.*

tu·mid (tōō′mĭd, tyōō′-) ►*adj.* **1.** Swollen; dis-

tended. Used of a body part. **2.** Overblown; bombastic. [Lat. *tumidus*.] —**tu·mid′i·ty** *n.*

tum·my (tŭm′ē) ►*n., pl.* **-mies** *Informal* **1.** The stomach. **2.** The abdomen. [Alteration of STOMACH.]

tu·mor (tōō′mər, tyōō′-) ►*n.* **1.** An abnormal growth of tissue due to uncontrolled, progressive multiplication of cells that serve no physiological function; neoplasm. **2.** A swollen part; swelling. [< Lat.] —**tu′mor·ous** *adj.*

tu·mult (tōō′mŭlt′, tyōō′-) ►*n.* **1.** A great noise, as of a crowd. **2.** A state of agitation of the mind or emotions. [< Lat. *tumultus*.] —**tu·mul′tu·ous** (tōō-mŭl′chōō-əs, tyōō-) *adj.* —**tu·mul′-tu·ous·ness** *n.*

tu·mu·lus (tōō′myə-ləs, tyōō′-) ►*n., pl.* **-li** (-lī′) An ancient grave mound; barrow. [Lat.]

tun (tŭn) ►*n.* A large cask. [< OE *tunne*.]

tu·na (tōō′nə, tyōō′-) ►*n., pl.* **-na** or **-nas 1.** Any of various often large marine food fishes. **2.** also **tuna fish** The canned or processed flesh of tuna. [< Ar. *at-tūn*, TUNNY.]

tun·dra (tŭn′drə) ►*n.* A treeless area in high-latitude regions, characterized by permanently frozen subsoil and low-growing vegetation. [Russ.]

tune (tōōn, tyōōn) ►*n.* **1.** *Mus.* **a.** A melody, esp. a simple one. **b.** A song. **c.** The state of being in correct pitch: *sang out of tune*. **2.** Concord or agreement; harmony: *in tune with the times*. **3.** *Electron.* Adjustment of a receiver or circuit for maximum response to a given signal or frequency. ►*v.* **tuned, tun·ing 1.** *Mus.* To put into tune. **2.** To adjust for maximum performance. **3.** *Electron.* To adjust (a receiver) to a desired frequency. [< TONE.] —**tun′a·ble, tune′a·ble** *adj.* —**tune′less** *adj.* —**tune′less·ly** *adv.* —**tune′less·ness** *n.*

tune·ful (tōōn′fəl, tyōōn′-) ►*adj.* Melodious. —**tune′ful·ly** *adv.* —**tune′ful·ness** *n.*

tun·er (tōō′nər, tyōō′-) ►*n.* **1.** One that tunes. **2.** A device for tuning, esp. an electronic device used to select signals for amplification and conversion to video, sound, or both.

tune-up (tōōn′ŭp′, tyōōn′-) ►*n.* An adjustment of a motor or engine to improve working order or efficiency.

tung·sten (tŭng′stən) ►*n. Symbol* **W** A hard, brittle, corrosion-resistant gray to white metallic element used in high-temperature structural materials and in lamp filaments. At. no. 74. See table at **element.** [Swed.]

Tun·gus·ic (tōōng-gōō′zĭk, tŭn-) ►*n.* A subfamily of the Altaic languages of E Siberia and N Manchuria. —**Tun·gus′ic** *adj.*

tu·nic (tōō′nĭk, tyōō′-) ►*n.* **1.** A loose-fitting, knee-length garment worn in ancient Greece and Rome. **2.** A long, plain, close-fitting military jacket. **3.** A loose-fitting women's garment that falls to the hip or thigh often worn over leggings or pants. [< Lat. *tunica*.]

tun·ing fork (tōō′nĭng, tyōō′-) ►*n.* A small two-pronged metal device that when struck produces a sound of fixed pitch, used for tuning musical instruments.

Tu·nis (tōō′nĭs, tyōō′-) The capital of Tunisia, in the N part on the **Gulf of Tunis,** an inlet of the Mediterranean.

Tu·ni·sia (tōō-nē′zhə, -shə, tyōō-) A country of N Africa bordering on the Mediterranean. Cap. Tunis. —**Tu·ni′sian** *adj. & n.*

tun·nel (tŭn′əl) ►*n.* An underground or underwater passage. ►*v.* **-neled, -nel·ing** or **-nelled, -nel·ling 1.** To make a tunnel (through or under). **2.** To dig in the form of a tunnel. [< OFr. *tonnelle*, tubular net.]

tunnel vision ►*n.* **1.** An extremely narrow outlook; narrow-mindedness. **2.** Vision in which the visual field is severely constricted.

tun·ny (tŭn′ē) ►*n., pl.* **-ny** or **-nies** See **tuna** (sense 1). [< Gk. *thunnos.*]

tu·pe·lo (tōō′pə-lō′, tyōō′-) ►*n., pl.* **-los** Any of several trees of the SE US and Asia having soft light wood. [Prob. Creek *'topilwa.*]

Tu·pí (tōō′pē, tōō-pē′) ►*n., pl.* **-pí** or **-pís 1.** A member of any of a group of Indian peoples living along the coast of Brazil, in the Amazon River Valley, and in Paraguay. **2.** The language of the Tupí. —**Tu′pi·an** *adj.*

tur·ban (tûr′bən) ►*n.* A headdress consisting of a long scarf wound around the head, traditionally worn in N Africa, the Near East, and Central and South Asia. [< Ottoman Turk. *tülbend*, muslin.]

turban

tur·bid (tûr′bĭd) ►*adj.* **1.** Having sediment or foreign particles stirred up or suspended: *turbid water.* **2.** Heavy or dense, as smoke. **3.** In turmoil: *turbid feelings.* [Lat. *turbidus*, disordered.] —**tur′bid·ly** *adv.* —**tur′bid·ness, tur·bid′i·ty** *n.*

tur·bine (tûr′bĭn, -bīn′) ►*n.* A machine in which the kinetic energy of a moving fluid is converted to mechanical power as the fluid turns a series of buckets, paddles, or blades arrayed around the circumference of a wheel or cylinder. [< Lat. *turbō*, spinning top.]

tur·bo·jet (tûr′bō-jĕt′) ►*n.* A jet engine with a turbine-driven compressor.

tur·bo·prop (tûr′bō-prŏp′) ►*n.* A turbojet engine used to drive an external propeller.

tur·bot (tûr′bət) ►*n., pl.* **-bot** or **-bots** An edible European flatfish. [< OFr. *tourbout.*]

tur·bu·lent (tûr′byə-lənt) ►*adj.* **1.** Moving rapidly or violently. **2.** Marked by disorder or unrest. [< Lat. *turbulentus.*] —**tur′bu·lence** *n.* —**tur′bu·lent·ly** *adv.*

tu·reen (tōō-rēn′, tyōō-) ►*n.* A broad, deep, usu. covered dish used esp. for serving soups or stews. [< OFr. *terrin*, earthen < Lat. *terra*, earth.]

turf (tûrf) ►*n.* **1.** Surface earth containing grass and its matted roots; sod. **2.** A piece of cut turf.

3. A piece of peat burned as fuel. **4.** *Informal* **a.** The range of one's authority or influence. **b.** The area claimed by a gang. **5.** A racetrack for horses. [< OE.]

tur·gid (tûr′jĭd) ►*adj.* **1.** Excessively ornate or complex: *turgid prose.* **2.** Swollen or distended. [Lat. *turgidus.*] —**tur·gid′i·ty, tur′gid·ness** *n.*

Tu·rin (tŏŏr′ĭn, tyŏŏr′-) A city of NW Italy on the Po R.

Turk (tûrk) ►*n.* **1.** A native or inhabitant of Turkey. **2.** An Ottoman. **3.** A member of a Turkic-speaking people.

tur·key (tûr′kē) ►*n., pl.* **-keys 1a.** A large, widely domesticated North American bird having brownish plumage and a bare wattled head and neck. **b.** The flesh of this bird. **2.** *Informal* **a.** A disliked person. **b.** A failure; flop. [< TURKEY.]

Turkey A country of SW Asia and SE Europe between the Mediterranean and Black Seas. Cap. Ankara.

turkey vulture ►*n.* A vulture found throughout the Americas, having dark plumage and a bare red head and neck.

Turk·ic (tûr′kĭk) ►*n.* A subfamily of the Altaic languages including Turkish. —**Turk′ic** *adj.*

Turk·ish (tûr′kĭsh) ►*adj.* Of Turkey, the Turks, or the Turkish language. ►*n.* The Turkic language of Turkey.

Turkish bath ►*n.* A steam bath followed by a shower and massage.

Turk·men·i·stan (tûrk′mĕn-ĭ-stăn′, -stän′) A country of W-central Asia E of the Caspian Sea. Cap. Ashgabat. —**Turk′men** (tûrk′mən) *n. & adj.*

Turks and Cai·cos Islands (tûrks; kā′kəs, kī′kōs) Two island groups of the British West Indies in the Atlantic SE of the Bahamas.

tur·mer·ic (tûr′mər-ĭk) ►*n.* An Indian plant with yellow flowers and a rhizome that when powdered is used as a condiment and as a yellow dye. [< Med.Lat. *terra merita* : Lat. *terra*, earth + Lat. *merita*, deserved.]

tur·moil (tûr′moil′) ►*n.* Extreme confusion or agitation. [?]

turn (tûrn) ►*v.* **1.** To move or cause to move around an axis or center; rotate or revolve: *The wheels turned slowly. A motor turns the wheels.* **2.** To change the position of so as to show the other side. **3.** To shape on a lathe. **4.** To give distinctive form to: *turn a phrase.* **5.** To injure by twisting: *turn an ankle.* **6.** To nauseate; upset. **7a.** To change the direction or course of: *turn the car left.* **b.** To direct or change one's way or course. **8.** To make a course around or about: *turn the corner.* **9.** To antagonize or become antagonistic. **10.** To direct (e.g., the attention or interest) toward or away from something. **11.** To send, drive, or let: *turn the dog loose.* **12.** To have recourse; resort: *I turned to him for advice.* **13.** To depend on something for success or failure; hinge. **14.** To become: *a lawyer turned novelist.* **15a.** To transform or become transformed; change. **b.** To change color. **c.** To become sour. ►*n.* **1.** The act of turning; rotation; revolution. **2.** A change of direction: *a left turn.* **3.** A change or deviation, as in a trend. **4.** A chance or opportunity: *took advantage at every turn.* **5.** A momentary shock or scare. **6.** Natural inclination: *a speculative turn of mind.* **7.** A rendering: *a turn of phrase.* **8.** A deed or action: *a good turn.* **9.** A short excursion. **10.** A single wind or convolution, as of wire on a spool. —*phrasal verbs:* **turn down 1.** To diminish, as the volume of. **2.** To reject. **turn in 1.** To hand in. **2.** To inform on or deliver: *The thief turned himself in.* **3.** *Informal* To go to bed. **turn off 1.** To stop the operation of. **2.** *Slang* To displease or disgust. **turn on 1.** To start the operation of: *Turn on the light.* **2.** *Slang* To please or excite. **turn out 1.** To shut off. **2.** To arrive or assemble. **3.** To produce; make. **4.** To result; end up. **turn over 1.** To think about; consider. **2.** To transfer to another. **turn up 1.** To increase, as the volume of. **2.** To find or be found. **3.** To arrive; appear. —*idioms:* **by turns** Alternately. **in turn** In the proper order. **out of turn** Not in the proper order. **turn over a new leaf** To start acting or thinking in a more responsible way. **turn the tables** To reverse a situation and gain the upper hand. [< Gk. *tornos,* lathe.] —**turn′er** *n.*

turn·a·bout (tûrn′ə-bout′) ►*n.* A shift or reversal in fortune, allegiance, or direction.

turn·a·round (tûrn′ə-round′) ►*n.* **1.** A turnabout. **2.** A dramatic, usu. positive change in performance: *Stock prices fell early but rallied in an afternoon turnaround.* **3.** The time needed for performing a task.

turn·buck·le (tûrn′bŭk′əl) ►*n.* A metal coupling device consisting of an oblong piece internally threaded at both ends into which two pieces of threaded rod are screwed.

turn·coat (tûrn′kōt′) ►*n.* One who traitorously switches allegiance.

Tur·ner (tûr′nər), **Joseph Mallord William** 1775–1851. British painter.

Turner, Nat 1800–31. Amer. slave leader.

turn·ing point (tûr′nĭng) ►*n.* A decisive moment.

tur·nip (tûr′nĭp) ►*n.* **1.** A cultivated plant with a large edible whitish root and edible leaves. **2.** The root of this plant. [*tur-,* of unknown orig. + dial. *nepe,* turnip (< Lat. *nāpus*).]

turn·key (tûrn′kē′) ►*n., pl.* **-keys** A jailer.

turn·off (tûrn′ôf′, -ŏf′) ►*n.* **1.** An exit on a highway. **2.** *Slang* Something distasteful.

turn·on (tûrn′ŏn′, -ôn′) ►*n. Slang* Something that causes pleasure or excitement.

turn·out (tûrn′out′) ►*n.* **1.** The number of people participating in a particular activity: *Shopper turnout was enormous.* **2.** An array of equipment, esp. that worn by a firefighter. **3.** A widening in a road.

turn·o·ver (tûrn′ō′vər) ►*n.* **1.** The act or fact of turning over. **2.** An abrupt change or transfer. **3.** A pastry made by covering half of a piece of dough with filling and folding the other half over it. **4a.** The number of times a particular stock of goods is sold and restocked during a given period. **b.** The amount of business transacted during a given period. **5.** The rate of replacement of personnel. **6.** *Sports* A loss of possession of the ball to the opposing team, as by a misplay or an infraction of the rules.

turn·pike (tûrn′pīk′) ►*n.* A toll road, esp. an expressway with tollgates. [ME *turnepike,* spiked barrier.]

turn·stile (tûrn′stīl′) ►*n.* A device for controlling passage from one area to another, usu. consisting of several revolving horizontal arms projecting from a central post.

turn·ta·ble (tûrn′tā′bəl) ►*n.* A circular rotating platform, such as the platform of a phonograph on which the record is placed.

turn·ta·blism (tûrn′tā′bə-lĭz′əm) ►*n.* The technique of manipulating the sounds put out by phonographic turntables, esp. by sliding records back and forth under the needles.

turn·ta·blist (tûrn′tā′bə-lĭst, -blĭst) ►*n.* One who is skilled at turntablism.

tur·pen·tine (tûr′pən-tīn′) ►*n.* A thin volatile oil, $C_{10}H_{16}$, obtained from certain pine trees and used as a paint thinner, solvent, and medicinally as a liniment. [< Gk. *terebinthos,* a kind of tree.]

tur·pi·tude (tûr′pĭ-tōōd′, -tyōōd′) ►*n.* Depravity; baseness. [< Lat. *turpis,* shameful.]

tur·quoise (tûr′kwoiz′, -koiz′) ►*n.* **1.** A blue to blue-green mineral of aluminum and copper, prized as a gemstone. **2.** A light bluish green. [< OFr. *turqueis,* Turkish.] —**tur′quoise′** *adj.*

tur·ret (tûr′ĭt, tŭr′-) ►*n.* **1.** A small tower-shaped projection on a building. **2.** A projecting armored structure, usu. rotating horizontally, containing mounted guns and their gunners, as on a warship or tank. [< OFr. *torete* < *tor,* tower.] —**tur′ret·ed** *adj.*

tur·tle¹ (tûr′tl) ►*n.* Any of an order of aquatic or terrestrial reptiles having beaklike jaws and the body enclosed in a bony or leathery shell. [Perh. < OFr. *tortue.*]

tur·tle² (tûr′tl) ►*n. Archaic* A turtledove. [< Lat. *turtur.*]

tur·tle·dove (tûr′tl-dŭv′) ►*n.* **1.** A small dove of Eurasia and Africa, having a soft purring voice. **2.** See **mourning dove.**

tur·tle·neck (tûr′tl-nĕk′) ►*n.* **1.** A high, close-fitting, often rolled-down collar. **2.** A garment with such a collar.

Tus·ca·ny (tŭs′kə-nē′) A region of W-central Italy between the N Apennines and the Ligurian and Tyrrhenian Seas. —**Tus′can** *adj. & n.*

Tus·ca·ro·ra (tŭs′kə-rôr′ə) ►*n., pl.* **-ra** or **-ras** **1.** A member of a Native American people formerly of North Carolina, now in W New York and SE Ontario. **2.** The Iroquoian language of the Tuscarora.

tusk (tŭsk) ►*n.* A long pointed tooth, as of an elephant, extending outside the mouth. [< OE *tūsc.*] —**tusked** *adj.*

tus·sle (tŭs′əl) ►*v.* **-sled, -sling** To struggle roughly; scuffle. [ME *tussillen.*] —**tus′sle** *n.*

tus·sock (tŭs′ək) ►*n.* A clump or tuft, as of grass. [?]

Tut·ankh·a·mun or **Tut·ankh·a·men** (tōōt′-äng-kä′mən) fl. c. 1350 BC. King of Egypt (1355–46).

tu·te·lage (tōōt′l-ĭj, tyōōt′-) ►*n.* **1.** The function or role of a guardian; guardianship. **2.** The function or role of a tutor; instruction. **3.** The state of being under a guardian or tutor. [< Lat. *tūtēla.*] —**tu′te·lar′y** (-ĕr′ē) *adj.*

tu·tor (tōō′tər, tyōō′-) ►*n.* A private instructor, esp. one giving additional or remedial instruction. [< Lat. *tūtor.*] —**tu′tor** *v.* —**tu·to′ri·al** (-tôr′ē-əl) *adj. & n.*

Tut·si (tōōt′sē) ►*n., pl.* **-si** or **-sis** A member of a Bantu-speaking people of Rwanda and Burundi.

tut·ti-frut·ti (tōō′tē-frōō′tē) ►*n.* A confection or flavoring that contains a variety of chopped candied fruits. [Ital., all fruits.]

tu·tu (tōō′tōō) ►*n.* A short ballet skirt, usu. having layers of gathered sheer fabric. [Fr.]

tutu

Tu·tu (tōō′tōō), **Desmond** b. 1931. South African prelate and antiapartheid leader.

Tu·va·lu (tōō-vä′lōō, tōō′və-lōō′) A country of the W Pacific N of Fiji. Cap. Funafuti.

tux (tŭks) ►*n. Informal* A tuxedo.

tux·e·do (tŭk-sē′dō) ►*n., pl.* **-dos** or **-does** A man's formal or semiformal suit, including a jacket with satin lapels, matching trousers, a bow tie, and often a cummerbund. [After *Tuxedo* Park, New York.]

TV (tē′vē′) ►*n.* Television.

TVA ►*abbr.* Tennessee Valley Authority

TV dinner ►*n.* A frozen precooked meal that needs only to be heated before serving.

twad·dle (twŏd′l) ►*n.* Idle talk; nonsense. [Prob. < dial. *twattle.*] —**twad′dle** *v.*

twain (twān) ►*n., adj.,* & *pron.* Two. [< OE *twēgen.*]

Twain, Mark See Samuel Langhorne **Clemens.**

twang (twăng) ►*n.* **1.** A sharp vibrating sound, as of the plucked string of a banjo or guitar. **2.** A strongly nasal tone of voice. [Imit.] —**twang** *v.* —**twang′y** *adj.*

tweak (twēk) ►*v.* To pinch or twist sharply. [< OE *twiccian.*] —**tweak** *n.*

tweed (twēd) ►*n.* **1.** A coarse woolen fabric usu. woven of several colors. **2. tweeds** Clothing made of tweed. [< Sc. *tweel,* TWILL.] —**tweed′y** *adj.*

tweet (twēt) ►*n.* A high chirping sound, as of a young or small bird. [Imit.] —**tweet** *v.*

tweet·er (twē′tər) ►*n.* A loudspeaker designed to reproduce high-pitched sounds in a high-fidelity audio system.

tweez·ers (twē′zərz) ►*pl.n. (takes sing. or pl. v.)* Small pincers, usu. of metal, used for plucking or handling small objects. [< obsolete *tweezes.*] —**tweeze** *v.*

twelfth (twĕlfth) ►*n.* **1.** The ordinal number matching the number 12 in a series. **2.** One of 12 equal parts. —**twelfth** *adv.* & *adj.*

Twelfth Night ►*n.* January 5, the eve of Epiphany.

twelve (twĕlv) ►*n.* **1.** The cardinal number equal to the sum of 11 + 1. **2.** The 12th in a set or sequence. [< OE *twelf.*] —**twelve** *adj.* & *pron.*

twelve·month (twĕlv′mŭnth′) ►*n.* A year.

twen·ti·eth (twĕn′tē-ĭth) ►*n.* **1.** The ordinal number matching the number 20 in a series. **2.** One of 20 equal parts. —**twen′ti·eth** *adv.* & *adj.*

twen·ty (twĕn′tē) ►*n., pl.* **-ties** The cardinal number equal to 2 × 10. [< OE *twēntig.*] —**twen′ty** *adj.* & *pron.*

twen·ty-twen·ty or **20/20** (twĕn′tē-twĕn′tē) ►*adj.* Having normal visual acuity.

twerp (twûrp) ►*n. Slang* An insignificant and contemptible person. [?]

Twi (chwē, chē) ►*n.* A language of Ghana.

twice (twīs) ►*adv.* **1.** In two cases or on two occasions; two times. **2.** In doubled degree or amount. [< OE *twiga.*]

twid·dle (twĭd′l) ►*v.* **-dled, -dling** **1.** To turn over or around lightly. **2.** To play with; trifle. —*idiom:* **twiddle (one's) thumbs** To do little or nothing; be idle. [Poss. blend of TWIST and FIDDLE.] —**twid′dler** *n.*

twig (twĭg) ►*n.* A small slender branch. [< OE *twigge.*] —**twig′gy** *adj.*

twi·light (twī′līt′) ►*n.* **1.** The time of the day when the sun is below the horizon but is casting diffuse light. **2.** The soft indistinct light of this time, esp. after sunset. **3.** A period or condition of decline. [ME.]

twill (twĭl) ►*n.* A fabric with diagonal parallel ribs. [< OE *twilīc.*]

twin (twĭn) ►*n.* **1.** One of two offspring born at the same birth. **2.** One of two identical or similar things; counterpart. ►*adj.* **1.** Born at the same birth. **2.** Being two or one of two identical or like things. **3.** Consisting of two identical or like parts. [< OE *twinn.*]

twin bed ►*n.* One of a matching pair of single beds.

twine (twīn) ►*v.* **twined, twin·ing** **1.** To twist together; intertwine. **2.** To form by twisting. **3.** To encircle or coil about. **4.** To go in a winding course. ►*n.* A strong string or cord made of two or more threads twisted together. [< OE *twīn,* double thread.]

twinge (twĭnj) ►*n.* A sudden sharp physical or emotional pain. See Synonyms at **pain.** ►*v.* **twinged, twing·ing** To feel or cause to feel a sharp pain. [< OE *twengan,* pinch.]

twin·kle (twĭng′kəl) ►*v.* **-kled, -kling** **1.** To shine with slight intermittent gleams. **2.** To be bright or sparkling: *Their eyes twinkled.* **3.** To wink. ►*n.* **1.** An intermittent gleam of light. **2.** A sparkle of merriment or delight in the eye. [< OE *twinclian.*] —**twink′ly** *adv.*

twin·kling (twĭng′klĭng) ►*n.* A brief interval.

twirl (twûrl) ►*v.* **1.** To rotate or revolve briskly; spin. **2.** To twist or wind (around). [?] —**twirl** *n.* —**twirl′er** *n.*

twist (twĭst) ►*v.* **1.** To entwine (several threads) to produce a single strand. **2.** To wind or coil about something: *twisted the reins around her hand.* **3.** To impart a spiral or coiling shape to. **4a.** To turn or open by turning. **b.** To break by turning: *twist off a small branch.* **5.** To wrench or sprain. **6.** To distort the intended meaning of. **7.** To move in a winding course. **8.** To rotate or turn in another direction. ►*n.* **1.** Something twisted or formed by twisting. **2.** A spin, twirl, or rotation. **3.** A sprain or wrench, as of an ankle. **4.** An unexpected turn of events. [ME *twisten.*] —**twist′er** *n.*

twit (twĭt) ►*n. Informal* An annoying person. ►*v.* **twit·ted, twit·ting** To taunt or tease. [< OE *ætwītan : æt,* at + *wītan,* reproach.]

twitch (twĭch) ►*v.* To move or cause to move jerkily or spasmodically. ►*n.* **1.** A sudden involuntary muscular movement: *a twitch of the eye.* **2.** A sudden jerk or tug. [ME *twicchen.*] —**twitch′y** *adj.*

twit·ter (twĭt′ər) ►*v.* To utter a series of light chirping or tremulous sounds. [ME *twiteren.*] —**twit′ter** *n.* —**twit′ter·y** *adj.*

twixt also **'twixt** (twĭkst) ►*prep.* Betwixt.

two (to͞o) ►*n.* **1.** The cardinal number equal to the sum of 1 + 1. **2.** The 2nd in a set or sequence. [< OE *twā.*] —**two** *adj. & pron.*

two-bit (to͞o′bĭt′) ►*adj. Slang* Worth very little; cheap; insignificant.

two bits ►*pl.n.* **1.** *Informal* Twenty-five cents. **2.** *Slang* A petty sum.

two-by-four (to͞o′bī-fôr′) ►*n.* A length of lumber that is 2 inches thick and 4 inches wide or that is trimmed to slightly smaller dimensions.

two-di·men·sion·al (to͞o′dĭ-mĕn′shə-nəl, -dī-) ►*adj.* **1.** Having only two dimensions, esp. length and width. **2.** Lacking depth: *a movie with two-dimensional characters.*

two-faced (to͞o′fāst′) ►*adj.* **1.** Having two faces. **2.** Hypocritical or double-dealing; deceitful. —**two′-fac·ed·ly** (-fā′sĭd-lē, -fāst′lē) *adv.* —**two′-fac′ed·ness** *n.*

two-ply (to͞o′plī′) ►*adj.* Made of two layers, thicknesses, or strands.

two·some (to͞o′səm) ►*n.* Two people together; a couple.

two-step (to͞o′stĕp′) ►*n.* A ballroom dance in 2/4 time with long sliding steps.

two-time (to͞o′tīm′) ►*v. Slang* **1.** To be unfaithful to. **2.** To deceive; double-cross. —**two′-tim′er** *n.*

two-way (to͞o′wā′) ►*adj.* Affording passage or communication in two directions.

TX ►*abbr.* Texas

–ty ►*suff.* Condition; quality: *novelty.* [< Lat. *-tās.*]

ty·coon (tī-ko͞on′) ►*n.* A wealthy and powerful businessperson; magnate. [J. *taikun,* title of a shogun.]

tyke (tīk) ►*n.* **1.** A small child, esp. a boy. **2.** A mongrel or cur. [< ON *tīk,* bitch.]

Ty·ler (tī′lər), **John** 1790–1862. The 10th US president (1841–45).

John Tyler
detail of an 1859 portrait

tym·pa·ni (tĭm′pə-nē) ►*pl.n.* Var. of **timpani.** —**tym′pa·nist** *n.*

tym·pan·ic membrane (tĭm-păn′ĭk) ►*n.* See **eardrum.**

tym·pa·num (tĭm′pə-nəm) ►*n., pl.* **-na** (-nə) or **-nums 1.** See **middle ear. 2.** See **eardrum.** [< Gk. *tumpanon,* drum.]

Tyn·dale (tĭn′dl), **William** 1494?–1536. English religious reformer and martyr.

type (tīp) ►*n.* **1.** A number of people or things sharing common traits; class; category. **2a.** One having the features of a group or class: *a type of cactus.* **b.** An example or model; embodiment. **3.** *Print.* **a.** A small block bearing a raised character that leaves a printed impression when inked and pressed on paper. **b.** Such pieces collectively. **c.** Printed or typewritten characters; print. ►*v.* **typed, typ·ing 1a.** To write (something) using a typewriter. **b.** To input (something) manually on an electronic device. **2.** To assign to a category; characterize. **3.** To typecast. [< Gk. *tupos,* impression.]

type·cast (tīp′kăst′) ►*v.* To assign (a performer) repeatedly to the same kind of part.

type·face (tīp′fās′) ►*n. Print.* **1.** The surface of a block of type that makes the impression. **2.** The size or style of type.

type·script (tīp′skrĭpt′) ►*n.* A typewritten copy, as of a book.

type·set (tīp′sĕt′) ►*v.* To set (written material) into type; compose. —**type′set′ter** *n.* —**type′set′ting** *n.*

type·write (tīp′rīt′) ►*v.* To write (something) with a typewriter; type.

type·writ·er (tīp′rī′tər) ►*n.* A machine that prints characters by means of a keyboard that moves a set of raised types, which strike the paper through an inked ribbon.

ty·phoid (tī′foid′) ►*n.* Typhoid fever. [TYPH(US) + -OID.] —**ty′phoid′** *adj.*

typhoid fever ►*n.* An acute, highly infectious disease caused by a bacillus transmitted by contaminated food or water and marked by high fever, coughing, and a rash.

ty·phoon (tī-fo͞on′) ►*n.* A tropical cyclone of the W Pacific or Indian Oceans. [Gk. *tuphōn,* whirlwind, Ar. *ṭūfān,* deluge, and Cantonese *toi⁴ fung¹,* great wind.]

ty·phus (tī′fəs) ►*n.* Any of several infectious diseases caused by bacteria, esp. those transmitted by fleas, lice, or mites, marked by sustained high fever, delirium, and a red rash. [< Gk. *tuphos,* stupor.] —**ty′phous** (-fəs) *adj.*

typ·i·cal (tĭp′ĭ-kəl) ►*adj.* **1.** Exhibiting the characteristics peculiar to a kind, group, or category; representative. **2.** Conforming to or serving as a type. **3.** Usual; ordinary: *a typical day at the office.* [< Gk. *tupikos.*] —**typ′i·cal·ly** *adv.* —**typ′i·cal·ness, typ′i·cal′i·ty** (-kăl′ĭ-tē) *n.*

typ·i·fy (tĭp′ə-fī′) ►*v.* **-fied** (-fīd′), **-fy·ing 1.** To serve as a typical example of. **2.** To represent by an image, form, or model; symbolize.

typ·ist (tī′pĭst) ►*n.* One who operates a typewriter.

ty·po (tī′pō) ►*n., pl.* **-pos** *Informal* A typographical error.

typographical error ►*n.* A mistake in printed copy, esp. one caused by striking an incorrect key on a keyboard.

ty·pog·ra·phy (tī-pŏg′rə-fē) ►*n., pl.* **-phies 1.** The composition of printed material from

movable type. **2.** The arrangement and appearance of printed matter. —**ty·pog′ra·pher** *n.*
—**ty′po·graph′i·cal** (tī′pə-grăf′ĭ-kəl), **ty′po·graph′ic** *adj.*

ty·ran·ni·cal (tĭ-răn′ĭ-kəl, tī-) ►*adj.* **1.** Of or relating to a tyrant or tyranny. **2.** Characteristic of a tyrant or tyranny; despotic. See Synonyms at **dictatorial.** —**ty·ran′ni·cal·ly** *adv.*

tyr·an·nize (tĭr′ə-nīz′) ►*v.* **-nized, -niz·ing 1.** To treat tyrannically; oppress. **2.** To rule as a tyrant. —**tyr′an·niz′er** *n.*

ty·ran·no·saur·us (tĭ-răn′ə-sôr′əs, tī-) also **ty·ran·no·saur** (tĭ-răn′ə-sôr′, tī-) ►*n.* A large carnivorous dinosaur with small forelimbs and a large head. [Gk. *turannos*, tyrant + *sauros*, lizard.]

tyr·an·nous (tĭr′ə-nəs) ►*adj.* Despotic; tyrannical. —**tyr′an·nous·ly** *adv.*

tyr·an·ny (tĭr′ə-nē) ►*n., pl.* **-nies 1.** Unjust or oppressive governmental power. **2.** A government in which a single ruler is vested with absolute power. **3.** A tyrannical act: *refused to submit to her husband's tyrannies.* **4.** A harshly limiting condition: *the tyranny of social expectations.* [< Gk. *turannos*, tyrant.]

ty·rant (tī′rənt) ►*n.* **1.** An absolute ruler, esp. an oppressive or cruel one. **2.** A harsh or domineering person. [< Gk. *turannos.*]

tyre (tīr) ►*n. Chiefly Brit.* Var. of **tire²**.

Tyre An ancient Phoenician seaport in present-day S Lebanon.

ty·ro (tī′rō) ►*n., pl.* **-ros** A beginner. [< Lat. *tīrō*, recruit.]

Ty·rol (tə-rōl′, tī-, tī′rōl′) A region of the E Alps in W Austria and N Italy. —**Ty·rol′e·an, Tyr′o·lese′** (tĭr′ə-lēz′, -lēs′, tī′rə-) *adj. & n.*

Tyr·rhe·ni·an Sea (tə-rē′nē-ən) An arm of the Mediterranean between the Italian peninsula and the islands of Corsica, Sardinia, and Sicily.

tzar (zär, tsär) ►*n.* Var. of **czar** (sense 1).

U

u or **U** (yōō) ►*n., pl.* **u's** or **U's** also **us** or **Us** The 21st letter of the English alphabet.

UAE ►*abbr.* United Arab Emirates

UAW ►*abbr.* United Automobile Workers

U·ban·gi (yōō-băng′gē, ōō-bäng′-) A river of central Africa flowing about 1,125 km (700 mi) along the NW border of the Dem. Rep. of the Congo to the Congo R.

u·biq·ui·tous (yōō-bĭk′wĭ-təs) ►*adj.* Being or seeming to be everywhere at the same time; omnipresent. [< Lat. *ubīque*, everywhere.] —**u·biq′ui·tous·ly** *adv.* —**u·biq′ui·ty** *n.*

U-boat (yōō′bōt′) ►*n.* A German submarine. [< Ger. *Unterseeboot* : OHGer. *untar*, under + *See*, sea + *Boot*, boat.]

U-bolt (yōō′bōlt′) ►*n.* A U-shaped bolt, fitted with threads and a nut at each end.

uc also **UC** ►*abbr.* uppercase

ud·der (ŭd′ər) ►*n.* A baglike mammary organ of female cows, sheep, and goats. [< OE *ūder.*]

UFO (yōō′ĕf-ō′) ►*n.* An unidentified flying object.

U·gan·da (yōō-găn′də, ōō-gän′dä) A country of E-central Africa. Cap. Kampala. —**U·gan′dan** *adj. & n.*

ug·ly (ŭg′lē) ►*adj.* **-li·er, -li·est 1.** Displeasing to the eye; unsightly. **2.** Repulsive or offensive; objectionable. **3.** Morally reprehensible; bad. **4.** Threatening or ominous: *ugly black clouds.* **5.** Cross or disagreeable: *an ugly temper.* [< ON *uggligr*, frightful < *uggr*, fear.] —**ug′li·ness** *n.*
Syns: *hideous, ill-favored, unsightly* **Ant:** *beautiful* **adj.**

U·gric (ōō′grĭk, yōō′-) ►*n.* The branch of the Finno-Ugric subfamily of languages that includes Hungarian. —**U′gric** *adj.*

UHF ►*abbr.* ultrahigh frequency

UK ►*abbr.* United Kingdom

u·kase (yōō-kās′, -kāz′, yōō′kās′, -kāz′) ►*n.* An authoritative decree; edict. [< Russ. *ukaz.*]

U·kraine (yōō-krān′) A country of E Europe. Cap. Kiev.

U·krain·i·an (yōō-krā′nē-ən) ►*n.* **1.** A native or inhabitant of Ukraine. **2.** The Slavic language of the Ukrainians. —**U·krain′i·an** *adj.*

u·ku·le·le or **u·ke·le·le** (yōō′kə-lā′lē, ōō′kə-) ►*n.* A small four-stringed guitar popularized in Hawaii. [Hawaiian *'ukulele.*]

U·laan·baa·tar (ōō′län-bä′tär′) The capital of Mongolia, in the N-central part.

ul·cer (ŭl′sər) ►*n.* **1.** A lesion of the skin or a mucous membrane accompanied by formation of pus and necrosis of surrounding tissue. **2.** A corrupting condition or influence. [< Lat. *ulcus, ulcer-.*] —**ul′cer·ous** *adj.*

ul·cer·ate (ŭl′sə-rāt′) ►*v.* **-at·ed, -at·ing** To develop or cause to develop an ulcer. —**ul′cer·a′tion** *n.* —**ul′cer·a′tive** (-sə-rā′tĭv, -sər-ə-tĭv) *adj.*

–ule ►*suff.* Small: *ovule.* [Fr. < Lat. *-ulus*, diminutive suff.]

ULF ►*abbr.* ultralow frequency

ul·na (ŭl′nə) ►*n., pl.* **-nas** or **-nae** (-nē) The bone extending from the elbow to the wrist on the side opposite to the thumb. [Lat., elbow.] —**ul′nar** *adj.*

ul·ster (ŭl′stər) ►*n.* A loose, long, often belted overcoat. [< ULSTER.]

Ulster A historical region of N Ireland.

ult. ►*abbr.* **1.** ultimately **2.** ultimo

ul·te·ri·or (ŭl-tîr′ē-ər) ►*adj.* **1.** Beyond what is evident or admitted: *an ulterior motive.* **2.** Lying beyond a certain area. [Lat., farther.]

ul·ti·mate (ŭl′tə-mĭt) ►*adj.* **1a.** Completing a series, process, or progression. **b.** Eventual: *hoped for ultimate victory.* **2.** Fundamental; elemental. **3.** Greatest; extreme. ►*n.* The maximum: *the ultimate in sophistication.* [< Lat. *ultimus*, last.] —**ul′ti·mate·ly** *adv.*

ul·ti·ma·tum (ŭl′tə-mā′təm, -mä′-) ►*n., pl.* **-tums** or **-ta** (-tə) A final offer or demand made by one party to another expressing or implying the threat of serious consequences if the terms are not accepted. [< Lat. *ultimātus*, last.]

ul·ti·mo (ŭl′tə-mō′) ►*adv.* In or of the month before the present one. [Lat. *ultimō (mēnse)*, in the last (month).]

ul·tra (ŭl′trə) ►*adj.* Going beyond the normal limit; extreme. [< Lat. *ultrā*, ultra-.]

ultra– ►*pref.* **1.** Beyond: *ultraviolet.* **2.** Extreme;

excessive: *ultraconservative*. [< Lat. *ultrā*, beyond.]

ul·tra·con·ser·va·tive (ŭl′trə-kən-sûr′və-tĭv) ►*adj.* Extremely conservative; reactionary.

ul·tra·high frequency (ŭl′trə-hī′) ►*n.* A band of radio frequencies from 300 to 3,000 megahertz.

ul·tra·lib·er·al (ŭl′trə-lĭb′ər-əl, -lĭb′rəl) ►*adj.* Extremely liberal; radical.

ul·tra·ma·rine (ŭl′trə-mə-rēn′) ►*n.* **1.** A blue pigment. **2.** A bright deep blue. ►*adj.* **1.** Of the color ultramarine. **2.** Of or from a place beyond the sea. [< Med.Lat. *ultrāmarīnus*, from beyond the sea : ULTRA– + Lat. *mare*, sea.]

ul·tra·mi·cro·scope (ŭl′trə-mī′krə-skōp′) ►*n.* A microscope with high-intensity illumination used to study very minute objects.

ul·tra·mi·cro·scop·ic (ŭl′trə-mī′krə-skŏp′- ĭk) ►*adj.* **1.** Too minute to be seen with an ordinary microscope. **2.** Of or relating to an ultramicroscope.

ul·tra·mod·ern (ŭl′trə-mŏd′ərn) ►*adj.* Extremely modern in ideas or style. —**ul′tra· mod′ern·ism** *n.* —**ul′tra·mod′ern·ist** *n.*

ul·tra·mon·tane (ŭl′trə-mŏn′tān′, -mŏn-tān′) ►*adj.* **1.** Of or relating to peoples or regions lying beyond the mountains. **2.** Supporting the authority of the pope in ecclesiastical and political matters. [Med.Lat. *ultrāmontānus*.] —**ul′tra·mon′tane′** *n.*

ul·tra·son·ic (ŭl′trə-sŏn′ĭk) ►*adj.* **1.** Relating to acoustic frequencies above the range of human hearing ; or above approx. 20,000 hertz. **2.** Of or involving ultrasound.

ul·tra·so·nog·ra·phy (ŭl′trə-sə-nŏg′rə-fē) ►*n.* The use of high-frequency sound waves to image internal body structures, a fetus, or objects that are underwater. [ULTRASON(IC) + –GRAPHY.] —**ul′tra·son′o·graph** *n.* —**ul′tra· so·nog′ra·pher** *n.* —**ul′tra·son′o·graph′ic** (-sŏn′ə-grăf′ĭk, -sō′nə-) *adj.*

ul·tra·sound (ŭl′trə-sound′) ►*n.* **1.** Ultrasonic sound. **2.** The use of ultrasonic waves for medical diagnosis or therapy. **3.** An image produced by ultrasound.

ul·tra·vi·o·let (ŭl′trə-vī′ə-lĭt) ►*adj.* Of electromagnetic radiation between violet visible light and x-rays in the electromagnetic spectrum. ►*n.* The ultraviolet range of electromagnetic radiation.

ul·u·late (ŭl′yə-lāt′, yōōl′-) ►*v.* **-lat·ed, -lat·ing** To howl, wail, or lament loudly, esp. by alternating rapidly between two high-pitched sounds. [Lat. *ululāre*.] —**ul′u·la′tion** *n.*

U·lys·ses (yōō-lĭs′ēz′) ►*n. Myth.* Odysseus.

u·ma·mi (ōō-mä′mē) ►*n.* A taste sensation produced by the presence of certain chemical compounds in meats and other high-protein foods. [J. : *uma(i)*, delicious + *-mi*, n. suff.]

um·bel (ŭm′bəl) ►*n.* A flat-topped or rounded flower cluster in which the individual flower stalks arise from about the same point. [< Lat. *umbella*, parasol.]

um·ber (ŭm′bər) ►*n.* **1.** A natural brown earth containing ferric and manganese oxides, used as pigment. **2.** Any of the shades of brown produced by umber. ►*adj.* Brownish. [Poss. < UMBRIA.]

um·bil·i·cal (ŭm-bĭl′ĭ-kəl) ►*adj.* Relating to the navel. ►*n.* An umbilical cord.

umbilical cord ►*n.* The flexible structure con-

necting a fetus at the navel with the placenta and containing blood vessels that transport nourishment to the fetus and remove its wastes.

um·bil·i·cus (ŭm-bĭl′ĭ-kəs, ŭm′bə-lī′kəs) ►*n., pl.* **-ci** (-sī′) See **navel**. [Lat. *umbilīcus*.]

um·bra (ŭm′brə) ►*n., pl.* **-bras** or **-brae** (-brē) **1.** A dark area, esp. the darkest part of a shadow. **2.** The completely dark portion of the shadow cast by one body onto another during an eclipse. [Lat., shadow.] —**um′bral** *adj.*

um·brage (ŭm′brĭj) ►*n.* **1.** Offense or resentment: *took umbrage at their rudeness.* **2.** *Archaic* Shadow or shade. [< Lat. *umbra*, shadow.]

um·brel·la (ŭm-brĕl′ə) ►*n.* **1.** A device for protection from the weather consisting of a collapsible canopy mounted on a central rod. **2.** Something that covers or protects. **3.** Something that encompasses many different elements or groups. [< Lat. *umbella*, parasol.]

Um·bri·a (ŭm′brē-ə) A region of central Italy in the Apennines. —**Um′bri·an** *adj. & n.*

u·mi·ak (ōō′mē-ăk′) ►*n.* A large open boat used by Yupik and Inuit people, made of skins stretched on a wooden frame. [Inuit *umiaq*.]

um·laut (ōōm′lout′) ►*n.* **1.** A change in a vowel sound caused by partial assimilation to a sound in the following syllable. **2.** The diacritic mark (¨) placed over a vowel to indicate an umlaut, esp. in German. [Ger.]

um·ma or **um·mah** (ōōm′ə) ►*n.* The worldwide community of Muslims. [Ar. *'umma*.]

um·pire (ŭm′pīr′) ►*n.* **1.** One appointed to rule on plays in various sports, esp. baseball. **2.** One appointed to settle a dispute. [< OFr. *nonper*, impartial mediator.] —**um′pire′** *v.*

ump·teen (ŭmp′tēn′, ŭm′-) ►*adj. Informal* Large but unspecified in number. [Slang *ump(ty)*, dash in Morse code + *-teen* (in numbers).] —**ump′teenth′** *adj.*

UN ►*abbr.* United Nations

un-¹ ►*pref.* Not: *unhappy*. [< OE.]

un-² ►*pref.* **1.** To reverse an action: *unbind.* **2.** To deprive of: *unfrock.* **3.** Used as an intensive: *unloose.* [< OE *ond-*, against.]

un·a·ble (ŭn-ā′bəl) ►*adj.* **1.** Lacking the necessary power, authority, or means. **2.** Incompetent.

un·ac·com·pa·nied (ŭn′ə-kŭm′pə-nēd) ►*adj.* **1.** Going or acting without a companion. **2.** *Mus.* Performed or scored without accompaniment.

un·ac·count·a·ble (ŭn′ə-koun′tə-bəl) ►*adj.* **1.** Impossible to account for; inexplicable. **2.** Not responsible. —**un′ac·count′a·bly** *adv.*

un·ac·cus·tomed (ŭn′ə-kŭs′təmd) ►*adj.* **1.** Not common or usual. **2.** Not habituated: *unaccustomed to a life of stress.*

un·a·dul·ter·at·ed (ŭn′ə-dŭl′tə-rā′tĭd) ►*adj.* Not mingled or diluted; pure. See Synonyms at **pure.**

un·ad·vised (ŭn′əd-vīzd′) ►*adj.* **1.** Not informed. **2.** Rash; imprudent. —**un′ad·vis′· ed·ly** (-vī′zĭd-lē) *adv.*

un·af·fect·ed (ŭn′ə-fĕk′tĭd) ►*adj.* **1.** Not changed or affected. **2.** Unpretentious or sincere. —**un′af·fect′ed·ness** *n.*

un·al·loyed (ŭn′ə-loid′) ►*adj.* **1.** Not in mixture with other metals; pure. **2.** Complete; unqualified. —**un′al·loy′ed·ly** *adv.*

u·nan·i·mous (yōō-năn′ə-məs) ►*adj.* **1.** Sharing

the same opinions or views. **2.** Based on complete agreement. [< Lat. *ūnanimus*, with one mind.] —**u′na·nim′i·ty** (yōō′nə-nĭm′ĭ-tē) *n.* —**u·nan′i·mous·ly** *adv.*

un·armed (ŭn-ärmd′) ►*adj.* Lacking weapons; defenseless.

un·as·sail·a·ble (ŭn′ə-sā′lə-bəl) ►*adj.* **1.** Impossible to dispute or disprove; undeniable. **2.** Impregnable. —**un′as·sail′a·bil′i·ty** *n.*

un·as·sist·ed (ŭn′ə-sĭs′tĭd) ►*adj.* **1.** Not having assistance; unaided. **2.** *Sports* Performed or accomplished by only one player.

un·as·sum·ing (ŭn′ə-sōō′mĭng) ►*adj.* Not pretentious; modest.

un·at·tached (ŭn′ə-tăcht′) ►*adj.* **1.** Not attached or joined. **2.** Not engaged, married, or involved in a serious relationship.

un·a·vail·ing (ŭn′ə-vā′lĭng) ►*adj.* Not availing; useless. See Synonyms at **futile.** —**un′a·vail′ing·ly** *adv.*

un·a·void·a·ble (ŭn′ə-voi′də-bəl) ►*adj.* Impossible to avoid; inevitable. See Synonyms at **certain.** —**un′a·void′a·bil′i·ty** *n.* —**un′a·void′a·bly** *adv.*

un·a·ware (ŭn′ə-wâr′) ►*adj.* Not aware or cognizant. ►*adv.* Unawares.

Usage: Unaware, followed by *of*, is the usual adjectival form modifying a noun or pronoun or following a linking verb: *Unaware of the difficulty, I went ahead.* Unawares is the usual adverbial form: *The rain caught them unawares.*

un·a·wares (ŭn′ə-wârz′) ►*adv.* **1.** By surprise; unexpectedly. **2.** Without forethought or plan. See Usage Note at **unaware.**

un·bal·anced (ŭn-băl′ənst) ►*adj.* **1.** Not in balance or not in proper balance. **2.** Showing or marked by erratic or volatile emotions or behavior. **3.** *Accounting* Not adjusted so that debit and credit correspond.

un·bar (ŭn-bär′) ►*v.* To open.

un·bear·a·ble (ŭn-bâr′ə-bəl) ►*adj.* Unendurable; intolerable. —**un·bear′a·bly** *adv.*

un·beat·a·ble (ŭn-bē′tə-bəl) ►*adj.* Impossible to defeat or surpass.

un·beat·en (ŭn-bēt′n) ►*adj.* **1.** Never defeated. **2.** Not traveled over or trampled down: *an unbeaten path.* **3.** Not beaten or pounded: *unbeaten eggs.*

un·be·com·ing (ŭn′bĭ-kŭm′ĭng) ►*adj.* **1.** Not appropriate, attractive, or flattering. **2.** Not proper; indecorous.

un·be·known (ŭn′bĭ-nōn′) ►*adj.* Occurring or existing without being known: *a crisis unbeknown to us.* [UN-¹ + obsolete *beknown,* known.]

un·be·lief (ŭn′bĭ-lēf′) ►*n.* Lack of belief or faith, esp. in religious matters. —**un′be·liev′er** *n.* —**un′be·liev′ing** *adj.*

un·bend (ŭn-bĕnd′) ►*v.* **1.** To make or become less tense; relax. **2.** To straighten.

un·bend·ing (ŭn-bĕn′dĭng) ►*adj.* **1.** Not yielding; inflexible. **2.** Aloof and often antisocial. —**un·bend′ing·ly** *adv.*

un·bid·den (ŭn-bĭd′n) also **un·bid** (-bĭd′) ►*adj.* Not invited, asked, or requested.

un·blink·ing (ŭn-blĭng′kĭng) ►*adj.* **1.** Without blinking. **2.** Without visible emotion. **3.** Fearless in facing reality. —**un·blink′ing·ly** *adv.*

un·blush·ing (ŭn-blŭsh′ĭng) ►*adj.* Without shame or embarrassment.

un·bolt (ŭn-bōlt′) ►*v.* To release the bolts of (a door or gate); unlock.

un·born (ŭn-bôrn′) ►*adj.* Not yet born.

un·bos·om (ŭn-bōōz′əm, -bōō′zəm) ►*v.* **1.** To confide (one's thoughts). **2.** To relieve (oneself) of thoughts or feelings.

un·bound·ed (ŭn-boun′dĭd) ►*adj.* Having no boundaries or limits.

un·bowed (ŭn-boud′) ►*adj.* **1.** Not bowed; unbent. **2.** Not subdued.

un·bri·dled (ŭn-brīd′ld) ►*adj.* **1.** Unrestrained; uncontrolled. **2.** Not fitted with a bridle.

---

un′a·bashed′ *adj.*
un′a·bat′ed *adj.*
un′abridged′ *adj.*
un′ac·cept′a·bil′i·ty *n.*
un′ac·cept′a·ble *n.*
un′ac·cept′a·bly *adv.*
un′ac·com′plished *adj.*
un′ac·count′a·bil′i·ty *n.*
un′ac·count′ed *adj.*
un′ac·cred′it·ed *adj.*
un′a·cheiv′a·ble *adj.*
un′ac·knowl′edged *adj.*
un′ac·quaint′ed *adj.*
un′ad·ven′tur·ous *adj.*
un′ad·ver′tised′ *adj.*
un′ad·vis′a·ble *adj.*
un′af·ford′a·ble *n.*
un′a·fraid′ *adj.*
un·aid′ed *adj.*
un′a·ligned′ *adj.*
un′al·ter·a·bil′i·ty *n.*
un·al′ter·a·ble *adj.*
un·al′ter·a·bly *adv.*
un′am·big′u·ous *adj.*
un′am·big′u·ous·ly *adv.*
un·an′a·lyz′a·ble *adj.*
un′a·pol′o·get′ic *adj.*
un′ap·peal′ing *adj.*
un′ap·peas′a·ble *adj.*

un′ap·pe·tiz′ing *adj.*
un′ap·pre′ci·at·ed *adj.*
un′ap·proach′a·bil′i·ty *n.*
un′ap·proach′a·ble *adj.*
un′ap·pro′pri·at′ed *adj.*
un′ap·proved′ *adj.*
un·ar′gu·a·ble *adj.*
un·arm′ *v.*
un·as·ser′tive *adj.*
un·as·ser′tive·ness *n.*
un′at·tain′a·bil′i·ty *n.*
un′at·tain′a·ble *adj.*
un·at·test′ed *adj.*
un′at·trac′tive *adj.*
un·at·trib′ut·ed *adj.*
un′a·vail′a·bil′i·ty *n.*
un′a·vail′a·ble *adj.*
un·baked′ *adj.*
un′be·liev′a·ble *adj.*
un′be·liev′ing·ly *adv.*
un·bleached′ *adj.*
un·blem′ished *adj.*
un·blenched′ *adj.*
un·brand′ed *adj.*
un·breath′a·ble *adj.*
un·bridge′a·ble *adj.*
un·caged′ *adj.*
un·ceas′ing *adj.*

un·ceas′ing·ly *adv.*
un·cel′e·brat′ed *adj.*
un·cer′ti·fied′ *adj.*
un·change′a·ble *adj.*
un·change′a·bly *adv.*
un′char·ac·ter·is′tic *adj.*
un·charged′ *adj.*
un·checked′ *adj.*
un·cir′cu·lat′ed *adj.*
un·cir′cum·cised′ *adj.*
un·clas′si·fied′ *adj.*
un·clench′ *v.*
un·clut′tered *adj.*
un·coat′ed *adj.*
un·col·lect′ed *adj.*
un·com′pen·sat′ed *adj.*
un·com·pet′i·tive *adj.*
un·com·plain′ing *adj.*
un·com·plain′ing·ly *adv.*
un·com′pli·cat′ed *adj.*
un′com·pli·men′ta·ry *adj.*
un′com·pre·hend′ing *adj.*
un′com·pre·hend′ing·ly *adv.*
un′com·pro·mis′ing·ly *adv.*
un′con·ceiv′a·ble *adj.*
un′con·ceiv′a·bly *adv.*
un′con·nect′ed *adj.*
un′con·nect′ed·ly *adv.*
un′con·quer·a·ble *adj.*

un·bro·ken (ŭn-brō′kən) ►*adj.* **1.** Not broken; intact. **2.** Uninterrupted; continuous. **3.** Not tamed or broken to harness.

un·bur·den (ŭn-bûr′dn) ►*v.* To free from a burden or trouble.

un·but·ton (ŭn-bŭt′n) ►*v.* To unfasten the buttons (of).

un·called-for (ŭn-kôld′fôr′) ►*adj.* **1.** Not required or requested. **2.** Not justified or deserved; unwarranted.

un·can·ny (ŭn-kăn′ē) ►*adj.* **-ni·er, -ni·est** Mysterious or impossible to explain, esp. when causing uneasiness or astonishment. See Synonyms at **weird.** —**un·can′ni·ly** *adv.* —**un·can′ni·ness** *n.*

un·cer·e·mo·ni·ous (ŭn-sĕr′ə-mō′nē-əs) ►*adj.* **1.** Without the due formalities; abrupt. **2.** Informal. —**un·cer′e·mo′ni·ous·ly** *adv.*

un·cer·tain (ŭn-sûr′tn) ►*adj.* **1.** Not known or established; questionable. **2.** Not determined; undecided. **3.** Not having sure knowledge. **4.** Subject to change. —**un·cer′tain·ly** *adv.*

un·cer·tain·ty (ŭn-sûr′tn-tē) ►*n.* **1.** Lack of certainty. **2.** Something uncertain.

un·char·i·ta·ble (ŭn-chăr′ĭ-tə-bəl) ►*adj.* **1.** Not generous or tolerant. **2.** Unfair or unkind. —**un·char′i·ta·bly** *adv.*

un·chart·ed (ŭn-chär′tĭd) ►*adj.* Not recorded on a map or plan; unexplored; unknown.

un·chaste (ŭn-chāst′) ►*adj.* Not chaste.

un·chris·tian (ŭn-krĭs′chən) ►*adj.* Not believing in or following the doctrines of Christianity.

un·cial also **Un·cial** (ŭn′shəl, -sē-əl) ►*adj.* Of a style of writing characterized by rounded capital letters and found esp. in Greek and Latin manuscripts of the 4th to the 8th cent. AD. [< Lat. *ūnciālis,* inch-high.] —**un′cial** *n.*

un·civ·il (ŭn-sĭv′əl) ►*adj.* Discourteous; rude. —**un·civ′il·ly** *adv.*

un·civ·i·lized (ŭn-sĭv′ə-līzd′) ►*adj.* Not civilized; barbarous.

un·clad (ŭn-klăd′) ►*adj.* Naked.

un·clasp (ŭn-klăsp′) ►*v.* **1.** To release or loosen the clasp of. **2.** To release from a grip or embrace.

un·cle (ŭng′kəl) ►*n.* **1.** The brother of one's mother or father. **2.** The husband of a sibling of one's mother or father. —*idiom:* **cry uncle** *Informal* To surrender or submit. [< Lat. *avunculus,* maternal uncle.]

un·clean (ŭn-klēn′) ►*adj.* **1.** Foul or dirty. **2.** Morally defiled; unchaste. **3.** Ceremonially impure. —**un·clean′ness** *n.*

un·clean·ly (ŭn-klĕn′lē) ►*adj.* Habitually unclean. —**un·clean′li·ness** *n.*

Uncle Sam (săm) ►*n.* The government of the US, often personified as a tall thin man with a white beard. [< *US,* abbreviation of UNITED STATES.]

Uncle Sam
World War I US Army recruitment poster by
James Montgomery Flagg (1877–1960)

un·con′quer·a·bly *adv.*
un′con·sol′i·dat′ed *adj.*
un′con·tam′i·nat′ed *adj.*
un′con·test′ed *adj.*
un′con·trol′la·bil′i·ty *n.*
un′con·trol′la·ble *adj.*
un′con·trol′la·bly *adv.*
un′con·trolled′ *adj.*
un′con·tro·ver′sial *adj.*
un′con·tro·ver′sial·ly *adv.*
un′con·vinc′ing *adj.*
un′con·vinc′ing·ly *adv.*
un′cooked′ *adj.*
un′co·op′er·a·tive *adj.*
un′co·op′er·a·tive·ly *adv.*
un′cor·rect′ed *adj.*
un′cor·rob′o·rat′ed *adj.*
un·crit′i·cal *adj.*
un·crowd′ed *adj.*
un·crowned′ *adj.*
un·cul′ti·vat′ed *adj.*
un·curl′ *v.*
un·dam′aged *adj.*
un·dat′ed *adj.*
un′de·bat′a·ble *adj.*
un′de·bat′a·bly *adv.*
un′de·ceiv′a·ble *adj.*
un′de·ceiv′a·bly *adv.*
un′de·ceive′ *v.*

un′de·clared′ *adj.*
un′de·ni′a·ble *adj.*
un′de·ni′a·bly *adv.*
un′de·pend′a·bil′i·ty *n.*
un′de·pend′a·ble *adj.*
un′de·served′ *adj.*
un′de·serv′ed·ly *adv.*
un′de·serv′ing *adj.*
un′de·sired′ *adj.*
un′di·gest′ed *adj.*
un′dig′ni·fied′ *adj.*
un′dip′lo·mat′ic *adj.*
un′dis·turbed′ *adj.*
un·doubt′ed·ly *adv.*
un·doubt′ing *adj.*
un·ed′u·cat′ed *adj.*
un′e·mo′tion·al *adj.*
un′e·mo′tion·al·ly *adv.*
un′em·ploy′a·ble *adj. & n.*
un·err′ing *adj.*
un·err′ing·ly *adv.*
un·fad′ing *adj.*
un·fad′ing·ly *adv.*
un·fash′ion·a·ble *adj.*
un·fash′ion·a·bly *adv.*
un·fas′ten *v.*
un·fath′om·a·ble *adj.*
un·fa′vor·a·ble *adj.*
un·fa′vor·a·bly *adv.*

un·fin′ished *adj.*
un·fo′cused *adj.*
un′fore·seen′ *adj.*
un′for·get′ta·bil′i·ty *n.*
un·fund′ed *adj.*
un·fuss′y *adj.*
un·gen′er·ous *adj.*
un·gen′er·ous·ly *adv.*
un·grate′ful *adj.*
un·grate′ful·ly *adv.*
un·hes′i·tat′ing *adj.*
un·hes′i·tat′ing·ly *adv.*
un·hoped′-for′ *adj.*
un·hurt′ *adj.*
un′im·por′tance *n.*
un′im·por′tant *adj.*
un′in·form′a·tive *adj.*
un′in·form′a·tive·ly *adv.*
un′in·hab′it·a·bil′i·ty *n.*
un′in·hab′it·a·ble *adj.*
un′in·hab′it·ed *adj.*
un′in·hib′it·ed *adj.*
un′in·i′ti·at′ed *adj.*
un′in·spir′ing *adj.*
un′in·spir′ing·ly *adv.*
un′in·struct′ed *adj.*
un′in·struc′tive *adj.*
un′in·sur′a·ble *adj.*
un′in·sured′ *adj.*

Uncle Tom ►*n.* A black person regarded as being subservient or too deferential to white people. [After *Uncle Tom*, a character in *Uncle Tom's Cabin*, a novel by Harriet Beecher Stowe.]

un·cloak (ŭn-klōk′) ►*v.* **1.** To remove a cloak or cover from. **2.** To expose; reveal.

un·close (ŭn-klōz′) ►*v.* To open.

un·clothe (ŭn-klō*th*′) ►*v.* To remove the clothing or cover from.

un·coil (ŭn-koil′) ►*v.* To unwind or become unwound.

un·com·fort·a·ble (ŭn-kŭmf′fər-tə-bəl, -kŭmf′tə-, -kŭmf′tər-) ►*adj.* **1.** Experiencing discomfort; uneasy. **2.** Causing anxiety; disquieting. —**un·com′fort·a·bly** *adv.*

un·com·mit·ted (ŭn′kə-mĭt′ĭd) ►*adj.* Not pledged to a specific cause or course.

un·com·mon (ŭn-kŏm′ən) ►*adj.* **1.** Not common; rare. **2.** Wonderful; remarkable. —**un·com′mon·ly** *adv.* —**un·com′mon·ness** *n.*

un·com·mu·ni·ca·tive (ŭn′kə-myōō′nĭ-kā′tĭv, -kə-tĭv) ►*adj.* Not communicative; reserved. —**un′com·mu′ni·ca′tive·ness** *n.*

un·com·pro·mis·ing (ŭn-kŏm′prə-mī′zĭng) ►*adj.* Not making concessions; inflexible.

un·con·cern (ŭn′kən-sûrn′) ►*n.* **1.** Lack of interest; indifference. **2.** Lack of worry or apprehensiveness.

un·con·cerned (ŭn′kən-sûrnd′) ►*adj.* **1.** Not interested; indifferent. **2.** Not apprehensive. —**un′con·cern′ed·ly** (-sûr′nĭd-lē) *adv.*

un·con·di·tion·al (ŭn′kən-dĭsh′ə-nəl) ►*adj.* Without conditions or limitations. —**un′con·di′tion·al·ly** *adv.*

un·con·di·tioned (ŭn′kən-dĭsh′ənd) ►*adj.* **1.** Unconditional. **2.** *Psychol.* Not resulting from conditioning; unlearned or natural.

un·con·scion·a·ble (ŭn-kŏn′shə-nə-bəl) ►*adj.* **1.** Not restrained or guided by conscience. **2.** Beyond prudence or reason; excessive. —**un·con′scion·a·bly** *adv.*

un·con·scious (ŭn-kŏn′shəs) ►*adj.* **1.** Lacking awareness and the capacity for sensory perception. **2.** Temporarily lacking consciousness. **3.** Occurring without conscious awareness: *unconscious resentment.* **4.** Involuntary: *an unconscious mannerism.* ►*n. Psychol.* The part of the mind that operates without conscious awareness or control. —**un·con′scious·ly** *adv.* —**un·con′scious·ness** *n.*

un·con·sti·tu·tion·al (ŭn′kŏn-stĭ-tōō′shə-nəl, -tyōō′-) ►*adj.* In violation of the requirements of the constitution of a nation or state. —**un′con·sti·tu′tion·al′i·ty** (-nǎl′ĭ-tē) *n.* —**un′con·sti·tu′tion·al·ly** *adv.*

un·con·ven·tion·al (ŭn′kən-věn′shə-nəl) ►*adj.* Not adhering to convention; out of the ordinary. —**un′con·ven′tion·al′i·ty** (-nǎl′ĭ-tē) *n.* —**un′con·ven′tion·al·ly** *adv.*

un·cork (ŭn-kôrk′) ►*v.* **1.** To draw the cork from. **2.** To free from a constrained state.

un·cou·ple (ŭn-kŭp′əl) ►*v.* To disconnect.

un·couth (ŭn-kōōth′) ►*adj.* **1.** Crude; unrefined. **2.** Awkward or clumsy. [< OE *uncūth*, unknown, strange.] —**un·couth′ly** *adv.*

un·cov·er (ŭn-kŭv′ər) ►*v.* **1.** To remove the cover from. **2.** To disclose; reveal. **3.** To remove the hat from (one's head) in respect.

un·cross (ŭn-krôs′, -krŏs′) ►*v.* To move (e.g., one's legs) from a crossed position.

unc·tion (ŭngk′shən) ►*n.* **1.** The act of anointing as part of a ceremonial or healing ritual. **2.** An ointment or oil; salve. **3.** Something that serves to soothe; balm. **4.** Affected or exaggerated earnestness. [< Lat. *unguere, ūnct-*, anoint.]

unc·tu·ous (ŭngk′chōō-əs) ►*adj.* **1.** Excessively ingratiating or insincerely earnest. **2.** Greasy; oily. [< Lat. *ūnctum*, ointment.] —**unc′tu·ous·ly** *adv.* —**unc′tu·ous·ness** *n.*

   Syns: *fulsome, oily, smarmy* **adj.**

un·cut (ŭn-kŭt′) ►*adj.* **1.** Not cut. **2.** *Print.* Not slit or trimmed: *uncut pages.* **3.** Not shaped by cutting: *uncut gems.* **4.** Not condensed, abridged, or censored.

un·daunt·ed (ŭn-dôn′tĭd, -dän′-) ►*adj.* Not discouraged or disheartened; resolutely courageous. —**un·daunt′ed·ly** *adv.*

un·de·cid·ed (ŭn′dĭ-sī′dĭd) ►*adj.* **1.** Not yet determined or settled. **2.** Not having reached a decision; uncommitted.

---

un′in·tel′li·gence *n.*
un′in·tel′li·gent *adj.*
un′in·tel′li·gent·ly *adv.*
un′in·tel′li·gi·bil′i·ty *n.*
un′in·tel′li·gi·ble *adj.*
un′in·tel′li·gi·bly *adv.*
un′in·ten′tion·al *adj.*
un′in·ten′tion·al·ly *adv.*
un′in·ter·rupt′ed *adj.*
un′in·vit′ing *adj.*
un′in·vit′ing·ly *adv.*
un·just′ *adj.*
un·jus′ti·fi′a·ble *adj.*
un·jus′ti·fi′a·bly *adv.*
un·just′ly *adv.*
un·kind′ *adj.*
un·kind′ly *adv.*
un·know′a·ble *adj.*
un·know′ing *adj.*
un·known′ *adj.*
un·latch′ *v.*
un·law′ful *adj.*
un·leav′ened *adj.*
un·link′ *v.*
un·man′age·a·bil′i·ty *n.*

un·man′age·a·ble *adj.*
un·man′age·a·bly *adv.*
un·man′ner·ly *adj. & adv.*
un·marked′ *adj.*
un·mar′ried *adj. & n.*
un·meet′ *adj.*
un·mixed′ *adj.*
un′mo·lest′ed *adj.*
un·mo′ti·vat′ed *adj.*
un·muf′fle *v.*
un·my′e·lin·at′ed *adj.*
un·name′a·ble *adj.*
un·named′ *adj.*
un·nec′es·sar′i·ly *adv.*
un·nec′es·sar′y *adj.*
un·no′tice·a·ble *adj.*
un·no′tice·a·bly *adv.*
un′ob·jec′tion·a·ble *adj.*
un′ob·struct′ed *adj.*
un·oc′cu·pied′ *adj.*
un·of·fi′cial *adj.*
un·of·fi′cial·ly *adv.*
un′op·posed′ *adj.*
un′o·rig′i·nal *adj.*
un·or′na·ment′ *v.*

un·or′tho·dox′ *adj.*
un·pag′i·nat′ed *adj.*
un·pal′at·a·bil′i·ty *n.*
un·pal′at·a·ble *adj.*
un·pal′at·a·bly *adv.*
un·peo′pled *adj.*
un′per·turbed′ *adj.*
un·pile′ *v.*
un·planned′ *adj.*
un·pleas′ant *adj.*
un·pleas′ant·ly *adv.*
un·pleas′ant·ness *n.*
un·pol′ished *adj.*
un′po·lit′i·cal *adj.*
un·polled′ *adj.*
un·pop′u·lar *adj.*
un·pop′u·lar′i·ty *n.*
un·pop′u·lat′ed *adj.*
un·prac′ticed *adj.*
un′pre·dict′a·bil′i·ty *n.*
un′pre·dict′a·ble *adj.*
un′pre·dict′a·bly *adv.*
un·prej′u·diced *adj.*
un′pre·med′i·tat′ed *adj.*

un·de·mon·stra·tive (ŭn′dĭ-mŏn′strə-tĭv) ▸*adj.* Not given to expressions of feeling; reserved. —**un′de·mon′stra·tive·ness** *n.*

un·der (ŭn′dər) ▸*prep.* **1.** In a lower position or place than. **2.** Beneath the surface of. **3.** Beneath the guise of: *traveled under a false name.* **4.** Less than; smaller than: *under three years of age.* **5.** Less than the required amount or degree of: *under voting age.* **6.** Inferior to in status or rank. **7.** Subject to the authority of: *under a dictatorship.* **8.** Undergoing or receiving the effects of: *under constant care.* **9.** Subject to the obligation of: *under contract.* **10.** Within the group or classification of: *listed under biology.* **11.** In the process of: *under discussion.* **12.** Because of: *under these conditions.* ▸*adv.* **1.** In or into a place below or beneath. **2.** So as to be covered or enveloped: *saw the boat capsize and go under.* **3.** So as to be less than the required amount or degree: *10 degrees or under.* ▸*adj.* **1.** Lower. **2.** Subordinate; inferior. **3.** Less than is required or customary. [< OE.]

under– ▸*pref.* **1.** Beneath; below: *underground.* **2.** Inferior; subordinate: *undersecretary.* **3.** Less than normal: *undersized.* [< OE.]

un·der·a·chieve (ŭn′dər-ə-chēv′) ▸*v.* To perform worse or achieve less success than expected. —**un′der·a·chiev′er** *n.*

un·der·age¹ (ŭn′dər-ĭj) ▸*n.* A deficient amount; shortfall.

un·der·age² (ŭn′dər-āj′) also **un·der·aged** (-ājd′) ▸*adj.* Below the customary or legal age.

un·der·arm (ŭn′dər-ärm′) ▸*adj.* **1.** Located, placed, or used under the arm. **2.** *Sports* Underhand. ▸*adv.* With an underarm motion or delivery. ▸*n.* The armpit.

un·der·bel·ly (ŭn′dər-bĕl′ē) ▸*n.* **1.** The soft underside of an animal's body. **2.** The vulnerable or weak part or aspect. **3.** The corrupt or immoral part or aspect.

un·der·bid (ŭn′dər-bĭd′) ▸*v.* **1.** To bid lower than. **2.** *Games* To bid too low. —**un′der·bid′** *n.*

un·der·bite (ŭn′dər-bīt′) ▸*n.* A condition in which the lower teeth overlap the upper teeth.

un·der·brush (ŭn′dər-brŭsh′) ▸*n.* Small trees or shrubs growing beneath the taller trees in a forest, esp. when thick or tangled.

un·der·car·riage (ŭn′dər-kăr′ĭj) ▸*n.* **1.** A supporting framework, as of a motor vehicle. **2.** The landing gear of an aircraft.

un·der·charge (ŭn′dər-chärj′) ▸*v.* To charge (someone) less than is customary or required. —**un′der·charge′** *n.*

un·der·class·man (ŭn′dər-klăs′mən) ▸*n.* A student in the freshman or sophomore class at a secondary school or college.

un·der·clothes (ŭn′dər-klōz′, -klōthz′) ▸*pl.n.* Clothes worn next to the skin, beneath one's outer clothing.

un·der·coat (ŭn′dər-kōt′) ▸*n.* **1.** A coat worn beneath another coat. **2.** Short hairs or fur underneath the longer outer hairs of an animal's coat. **3.** also **un·der·coat·ing** (-kō′tĭng) **a.** A coat of sealing material applied before a final coat. **b.** A tarlike substance sprayed on the underside of a vehicle to prevent rusting. —**un′der·coat′** *v.*

un·der·cov·er (ŭn′dər-kŭv′ər) ▸*adj.* Conducted in secret or through the use of subterfuge, as in spying.

un·der·cur·rent (ŭn′dər-kûr′ənt, -kŭr′-) ▸*n.* **1.** A current below another current or a surface. **2.** An underlying tendency or force often contrary to what is superficially evident.

un·der·cut (ŭn′dər-kŭt′) ▸*v.* **1.** To diminish or destroy the effectiveness of; undermine. **2.** To sell at a lower price or work for lower wages than (a competitor). **3.** To make a cut under or below. **4.** *Sports* **a.** To impart backspin to (a ball) by striking downward as well as forward. **b.** To slice (a ball) with an underarm stroke. —**un′der·cut′** *n.*

un·der·de·vel·oped (ŭn′dər-dĭ-vĕl′əpt) ▸*adj.* **1.** Not fully developed: *seeds with underdeveloped embryos.* **2.** Having a low level of economic and technological development. —**un′der·de·vel′op·ment** *n.*

un·der·dog (ŭn′dər-dôg′, ŭn′dər-dŏg′) ▸*n.* **1.**

One who is expected to lose a contest or struggle. **2.** One who is at a disadvantage.

un·der·done (ŭn′dər-dŭn′) ►*adj.* Not sufficiently cooked.

un·der·dress (ŭn′dər-drĕs′) ►*n.* Underclothes. ►*v.* (ŭn′dər-drĕs′) To dress too informally for an occasion.

un·der·es·ti·mate (ŭn′dər-ĕs′tə-māt′) ►*v.* **1.** To make too low an estimate of the quantity, degree, or worth of: *Don't underestimate the difficulties involved in the project.* **2.** To consider (someone) to be less effective than is actually the case: *underestimated his rivals and was outmaneuvered.* ►*n.* (-mĭt) An estimate that is too low. —**un′der·es′ti·ma′tion** *n.*

un·der·ex·pose (ŭn′dər-ĭk-spōz′) ►*v.* To expose (film) to light for too short a time. —**un′der·ex·po′sure** *n.*

un·der·foot (ŭn′dər-fŏŏt′) ►*adv.* **1.** Below or under the feet. **2.** In the way.

un·der·gar·ment (ŭn′dər-gär′mənt) ►*n.* A garment worn under outer garments.

un·der·go (ŭn′dər-gō′) ►*v.* To experience or be subjected to: *a person who underwent great difficulty; a house undergoing renovations.*

un·der·grad·u·ate (ŭn′dər-grăj′ŏŏ-ĭt) ►*n.* A college or university student who has not yet received a degree. ►*adj.* Of or relating to undergraduates: *undergraduate courses.*

un·der·ground (ŭn′dər-ground′) ►*adj.* **1.** Below the surface of the earth. **2.** Hidden or concealed; clandestine. **3.** Of or relating to avant-garde or experimental films, publications, and art. ►*n.* **1.** A clandestine, often nationalist, organization working against a government in power. **2.** *Chiefly Brit.* A subway system. **3.** An avant-garde movement. ►*adv.* (ŭn′dər-ground′) **1.** Below the surface of the earth. **2.** In secret; stealthily.

un·der·growth (ŭn′dər-grōth′) ►*n.* Shrubs, saplings, and herbaceous plants growing beneath trees in a forest.

un·der·hand (ŭn′dər-hănd′) ►*adj. Sports* Executed with the hand brought forward and up from below the level of the shoulder; underarm. —**un′der·hand′** *adv.*

un·der·hand·ed (ŭn′dər-hăn′dĭd) ►*adj.* **1.** Done secretly; dishonest and sneaky. **2.** Underhand: *an underhanded toss.* —**un′der·hand′ed** *adv.* —**un′der·hand′ed·ly** *adv.* —**un′der·hand′ed·ness** *n.*

un·der·lie (ŭn′dər-lī′) ►*v.* **-lay, -lain, -ly·ing** **1.** To be located under or below. **2.** To be the support or basis of; account for.

un·der·line (ŭn′dər-līn′, ŭn′dər-līn′) ►*v.* **1.** To draw a line under: *underlined the book's title.* **2.** To emphasize: *The debate underlined the divisions within the party.* —**un′der·line′** *n.*

un·der·ling (ŭn′dər-lĭng) ►*n.* A subordinate.

un·der·ly·ing (ŭn′dər-lī′ĭng) ►*adj.* **1.** Lying under or beneath. **2.** Basic; fundamental: *the underlying cause of the problem.* **3.** Present but not readily noticeable.

un·der·mine (ŭn′dər-mīn′) ►*v.* **1.** To weaken by wearing away gradually or imperceptibly. **2.** To dig a mine or tunnel beneath.

un·der·most (ŭn′dər-mōst′) ►*adj.* Lowest in position, rank, or place; bottom. ►*adv.* Lowest.

un·der·neath (ŭn′dər-nēth′) ►*adv.* **1.** In or to a place beneath; below. **2.** On the lower face or underside. ►*prep.* **1.** Under; below; beneath. **2.** Under the power or control of. ►*adj.* Lower; under. ►*n.* The part or side below or under. [< OE *underneothan* : *under,* UNDER + *neothan,* below.]

un·der·pants (ŭn′dər-pănts′) ►*pl.n.* A lower undergarment, usually having short or no legs, that is worn next to the skin under other clothing.

un·der·pass (ŭn′dər-păs′) ►*n.* A passage underneath something, esp. a road under another road.

un·der·pin·ning (ŭn′dər-pĭn′ĭng) ►*n.* **1.** A supporting structure or part. **2. underpinnings** *Informal* The legs.

un·der·play (ŭn′dər-plā′, ŭn′dər-plā′) ►*v.* **1.** To act (a role) subtly or with restraint. **2.** To minimize the importance of.

un·der·rate (ŭn′dər-rāt′) ►*v.* To rate too low; underestimate.

un·der·score (ŭn′dər-skôr′) ►*v.* **1.** To underline: *The teacher underscores incorrect answers.* **2a.** To emphasize: *The leaders underscored their commitment to peace.* **b.** To cause to appear deserving of attention: *The loss underscored the team's need for improvement.* —**un′der·score′** *n.*

un·der·sea (ŭn′dər-sē′) ►*adj. & adv.* Beneath the surface of the sea. —**un′der·seas′** *adv.*

un·der·sec·re·tar·y (ŭn′dər-sĕk′rə-tĕr′ē) ►*n.* An official directly subordinate to a cabinet member. —**un′der·sec′re·tar′i·at** (-târ′ē-ĭt) *n.*

un·der·sell (ŭn′dər-sĕl′) ►*v.* **1.** To present with little or insufficient enthusiasm. **2.** To sell for a lower price than.

un·der·shirt (ŭn′dər-shûrt′) ►*n.* An undergarment worn under a shirt.

un·der·shoot (ŭn′dər-shŏŏt′) ►*v.* **1.** To shoot a projectile short of (a target). **2.** To land an aircraft short of (a landing area).

un·der·shorts (ŭn′dər-shôrts′) ►*pl.n.* Underpants.

un·der·shot (ŭn′dər-shŏt′) ►*adj.* **1.** Driven by water passing from below, as a water wheel. **2.** Having the lower jaw or teeth projecting beyond the upper.

un·der·side (ŭn′dər-sīd′) ►*n.* The side or surface that is underneath.

un·der·signed (ŭn′dər-sīnd′) ►*n., pl.* **-signed** A signer whose name is at the bottom or end of a document. —**un′der·signed′** *adj.*

un·der·sized (ŭn′dər-sīzd′) also **un·der·size** (-sīz′) ►*adj.* Smaller than normal or sufficient size.

un·der·skirt (ŭn′dər-skûrt′) ►*n.* A skirt worn under another.

un·der·slung (ŭn′dər-slŭng′) ►*adj.* Having springs attached to the axles from below, as on an auto chassis.

un·der·stand (ŭn′dər-stănd′) ►*v.* **-stood** (-stŏŏd′), **-stand·ing** **1a.** To perceive the nature and significance of: *She understands the difficulty involved.* **b.** To perceive the intended meaning of (e.g., a remark): *We understand what they're saying; we just disagree with it.* **c.** To know and be tolerant or sympathetic toward. **2.** To know by close contact or long experience with. **3.** To learn indirectly, as by hearsay. **4.** To assume to be or accept as agreed: *It is understood that the fee will be*

$50. [< OE *understandan* : UNDER– + *standan*, stand.] —**un′der·stand′a·ble** *adj.* —**un′der·stand′a·bly** *adv.*

un·der·stand·ing (ŭn′dər-stăn′dĭng) ►*n.* **1a.** The ability by which one understands; intelligence: *concepts beyond the understanding of a child.* **b.** The quality of discernment; comprehension: *Do you have much understanding of calculus?* **2.** Individual or specified judgment or outlook; opinion: *In my understanding, this is a good plan.* **3.** A usu. implicit agreement between two or more people or groups: *an understanding between neighbors over late-night noise.* ►*adj.* Marked by or having good sense or compassion: *an understanding teacher.*

un·der·state (ŭn′dər-stāt′) ►*v.* **1.** To state with less completeness or truth than seems warranted by the facts. **2.** To express with restraint or lack of emphasis, esp. for rhetorical effect. —**un′der·state′ment** *n.*

un·der·stood (ŭn′dər-sto͝od′) ►*adj.* **1.** Agreed on; assumed. **2.** Implicit or implied.

un·der·sto·ry (ŭn′dər-stôr′ē) ►*n.* An underlying layer of vegetation, as in a forest.

un·der·stud·y (ŭn′dər-stŭd′ē) ►*v.* **1.** To study or know (a role) so as to be able to replace a regular performer. **2.** To act as an understudy to. ►*n.* **1.** A performer who understudies another. **2.** One that can do the work of another.

un·der·take (ŭn′dər-tāk′) ►*v.* **1.** To deliberately begin to do (something): *undertake a task.* **2.** To pledge or commit oneself (to do something): *undertake to fix the roof.*

un·der·tak·er (ŭn′dər-tā′kər) ►*n.* See **funeral director.**

un·der·tak·ing (ŭn′dər-tā′kĭng) ►*n.* **1.** Something that is undertaken; venture: *a dangerous undertaking.* **2.** The profession of a funeral director.

un·der-the-count·er (ŭn′dər-*thə*-koun′tər) ►*adj.* Transacted or sold illicitly.

un·der·tone (ŭn′dər-tōn′) ►*n.* **1.** An underlying or implied tendency or meaning; undercurrent. **2.** A tone of low pitch or volume. **3.** A pale or subdued color.

un·der·tow (ŭn′dər-tō′) ►*n.* The seaward pull of receding waves after they break on a shore.

un·der·wa·ter (ŭn′dər-wô′tər, -wŏt′ər) ►*adj.* Used, done, or existing beneath the surface of water. —**un′der·wa′ter** *adv.*

un·der·wear (ŭn′dər-wâr′) ►*n.* See **underclothes.**

un·der·weight (ŭn′dər-wāt′) ►*adj.* Weighing less than is normal, healthy, or required.

un·der·world (ŭn′dər-wûrld′) ►*n.* **1.** The world of the dead in various religious traditions. **2.** The part of society organized for and engaged in crime and vice.

un·der·write (ŭn′dər-rīt′) ►*v.* **1a.** To assume financial responsibility for. **b.** To supply with funding, esp. as a sponsor: *underwrite a public television show.* **2.** To sign (an insurance policy) so as to assume liability in case of specified losses. **3.** To agree to buy the unsold part of (stock not yet sold publicly) at a fixed time and price. **4.** To write under, esp. to endorse (a document). —**un′der·writ′er** *n.*

un·de·sir·a·ble (ŭn′dĭ-zīr′ə-bəl) ►*adj.* Not wanted; objectionable. ►*n.* An undesirable person. —**un′de·sir′a·bly** *adv.*

un·dies (ŭn′dēz) ►*pl.n.* Informal Underclothes.

un·dis·posed (ŭn′dĭ-spōzd′) ►*adj.* **1.** Not settled, removed, or resolved. **2.** Disinclined; unwilling.

un·do (ŭn-do͞o′) ►*v.* **1.** To reverse or erase; annul. **2.** To untie, disassemble, or loosen. **3.** To open; unwrap. **4a.** To cause the ruin or downfall of. **b.** To throw into confusion.

un·do·ing (ŭn-do͞o′ĭng) ►*n.* **1.** The act of unfastening or loosening. **2a.** The act of bringing to ruin. **b.** A cause or source of ruin. **3.** The act of reversing or annulling something.

un·dress (ŭn-drĕs′) ►*v.* To remove the clothing (of); disrobe. ►*n.* **1.** Informal attire. **2.** Nakedness.

un·due (ŭn-do͞o′, -dyo͞o′) ►*adj.* **1.** Exceeding what is appropriate or normal. **2.** Not just, proper, or legal.

un·du·lant (ŭn′jə-lənt, ŭn′dyə-, -də-) ►*adj.* Undulating.

un·du·late (ŭn′jə-lāt′, ŭn′dyə-, -də-) ►*v.* **-lat·ed, -lat·ing** **1.** To move or cause to move in a smooth, wavelike motion. **2.** To have a wavelike appearance or form: *dunes that undulate toward the sea.* [< LLat. *undula*, small wave, dim. of Lat. *unda*, wave.]

un·du·la·tion (ŭn′jə-lā′shən, ŭn′dyə-, -də-) ►*n.* **1.** A wavelike movement. **2.** A wavelike form, outline, or appearance. **3.** One of a series of waves or wavelike segments.

un·du·ly (ŭn-do͞o′lē, -dyo͞o′-) ►*adv.* Excessively; immoderately: *unduly fearful.*

un·dy·ing (ŭn-dī′ĭng) ►*adj.* Everlasting.

un·earned (ŭn-ûrnd′) ►*adj.* **1.** Not gained by work or service. **2.** Not deserved.

un·earth (ŭn-ûrth′) ►*v.* **1.** To dig up. **2.** To bring to public notice; uncover.

un·earth·ly (ŭn-ûrth′lē) ►*adj.* **1.** Not of the earth; supernatural. **2.** Unnaturally strange and frightening; eerie. See Synonyms at **weird.**

un·eas·y (ŭn-ē′zē) ►*adj.* **1.** Lacking ease, comfort, or a sense of security. **2.** Affording no ease or reassurance: *an uneasy calm.* **3.** Awkward or unsure in manner; constrained. —**un·ease′, un·eas′i·ness** *n.* —**un·eas′i·ly** *adv.*

un·em·ployed (ŭn′ĕm-ploid′, -ĭm-) ►*adj.* **1.** Not having work; jobless. **2.** Not being used; idle. —**un′em·ploy′ment** *n.*

un·e·qual (ŭn-ē′kwəl) ►*adj.* **1.** Not the same in any measurable aspect. **2.** Asymmetric. **3.** Irregular; variable. **4.** Not having the required abilities; inadequate. **5.** Not fair. —**un·e′qual·ly** *adv.*

un·e·qualed also **un·e·qualled** (ŭn-ē′kwəld) ►*adj.* Not matched or paralleled; unrivaled.

un·e·quiv·o·cal (ŭn′ĭ-kwĭv′ə-kəl) ►*adj.* Open to no doubt or misunderstanding; clear. —**un′-e·quiv′o·cal·ly** *adv.*

UNESCO ►*abbr.* United Nations Educational, Scientific, and Cultural Organization

un·e·ven (ŭn-ē′vən) ►*adj.* **1.** Not equal, as in size, length, or quality. **2.** Not consistent or uniform. **3.** Not smooth or level. **4.** Not straight or parallel. —**un·e′ven·ly** *adv.* —**un·e′ven·ness** *n.*

un·e·vent·ful (ŭn′ĭ-vĕnt′fəl) ►*adj.* **1.** Lacking in significant events. **2.** Occurring without disruption. —**un′e·vent′ful·ness** *n.*

un·ex·am·pled (ŭn′ĭg-zăm′pəld) ►*adj.* Without precedent; unparalleled.

un·ex·cep·tion·a·ble (ŭn′ĭk-sĕp′shə-nə-bəl) ►*adj.* Beyond any reasonable objection.

Usage: Unexceptional and *unexceptionable* are sometimes confused. *Unexceptionable* means "not open to any objection," as in *A judge's ethical standards should be unexceptionable.* *Unexceptional* generally means "not exceptional, not varying from the usual," as in *Some judges' ethical standards have been unexceptional.*

un·ex·cep·tion·al (ŭn'ĭk-sĕp'shə-nəl) ►*adj.* **1.** Not varying from a norm; usual. **2.** Not subject to exceptions; absolute. See Usage Note at **unexceptionable.** —**un'ex·cep'tion·al·ly** *adv.*

un·ex·pect·ed (ŭn'ĭk-spĕk'tĭd) ►*adj.* Occurring without warning; unforeseen. —**un'ex·pect'ed·ly** *adv.* —**un'ex·pect'ed·ness** *n.*

un·fail·ing (ŭn-fā'lĭng) ►*adj.* **1.** Not failing or running out; inexhaustible. **2.** Constant; unflagging. **3.** Infallible. —**un·fail'ing·ly** *adv.*

un·fair (ŭn-fâr') ►*adj.* **1.** Not just or evenhanded; biased. **2.** Contrary to laws or conventions, esp. in commerce; unethical. —**un·fair'ly** *adv.* —**un·fair'ness** *n.*

un·faith·ful (ŭn-fāth'fəl) ►*adj.* **1.** Not faithful; disloyal. **2.** Breaking trust in a marriage or relationship by having sexual relations with someone other than one's spouse or sexual partner. **3.** Not justly representing or reflecting the original; inaccurate. —**un·faith'ful·ly** *adv.* —**un·faith'ful·ness** *n.*

un·fa·mil·iar (ŭn'fə-mĭl'yər) ►*adj.* **1.** Not acquainted; not conversant. **2.** Not within one's knowledge; strange. —**un'fa·mil·iar'i·ty** (-mĭl-yăr'ĭ-tē, -mĭl'ē-ăr'ĭ-tē) *n.* —**un'fa·mil'iar·ly** *adv.*

un·feel·ing (ŭn-fē'lĭng) ►*adj.* **1.** Having no sensation; numb. **2.** Not sympathetic; callous. —**un·feel'ing·ly** *adv.*

un·feigned (ŭn'fānd') ►*adj.* Not pretended; genuine.

un·fet·ter (ŭn-fĕt'ər) ►*v.* To free from restrictions or bonds.

un·fit (ŭn-fĭt') ►*adj.* **1.** Inappropriate. **2.** Unqualified. **3.** In poor physical or mental health. ►*v.* To make unfit; disqualify. —**un·fit'ly** *adv.* —**un·fit'ness** *n.*

un·flag·ging (ŭn-flăg'ĭng) ►*adj.* Persistent or untiring. See Synonyms at **tireless.** —**un·flag'ging·ly** *adv.*

un·flap·pa·ble (ŭn-flăp'ə-bəl) ►*adj.* Not easily upset; cool. —**un·flap'pa·bil'i·ty** *n.*

un·fledged (ŭn-flĕjd') ►*adj.* **1.** Not having the feathers necessary to fly. Used of a young bird. **2.** Inexperienced or immature.

un·flinch·ing (ŭn-flĭn'chĭng) ►*adj.* Steadfast; resolute. —**un·flinch'ing·ly** *adv.*

un·fold (ŭn-fōld') ►*v.* **1.** To open and spread out (something folded). **2.** To reveal or be revealed gradually.

un·for·get·ta·ble (ŭn'fər-gĕt'ə-bəl) ►*adj.* Earning a permanent place in the memory; memorable. —**un'for·get'ta·bly** *adv.*

un·formed (ŭn-fôrmd') ►*adj.* **1.** Having no definite shape or structure. **2.** Immature; undeveloped.

un·for·tu·nate (ŭn-fôr'chə-nĭt) ►*adj.* **1.** Having bad luck; unlucky. **2.** Causing misfortune; disastrous. **3.** Regrettable; deplorable: *an unfortunate lack of good manners.* —**un·for'tu·nate·ly** *adv.*

Syns: hapless, ill-fated, ill-starred, luckless, unlucky **Ant:** *fortunate* **adj.**

un·found·ed (ŭn-foun'dĭd) ►*adj.* Not based on fact or sound evidence; groundless. See Synonyms at **baseless.**

un·fre·quent·ed (ŭn-frē'kwən-tĭd, ŭn'frē-kwĕn'tĭd) ►*adj.* Receiving few or no visitors.

un·friend·ly (ŭn-frĕnd'lē) ►*adj.* **1.** Not disposed to friendship. **2.** Not indicative or suggestive of friendliness. —**un·friend'li·ness** *n.*

un·frock (ŭn-frŏk') ►*v.* To defrock.

un·furl (ŭn-fûrl') ►*v.* To spread or open (something) out.

un·gain·ly (ŭn-gān'lē) ►*adj.* **-li·er, -li·est 1.** Awkward; clumsy. **2.** Unwieldy. [< UN-¹ + ME *gain,* straight.] —**un·gain'li·ness** *n.*

Un·ga·va Bay (ŭn-gā'və, -gä'-) An inlet of Hudson Strait in NE Quebec, Canada, W of N Labrador, separated from Husdon Bay by the **Ungava Peninsula.**

un·god·ly (ŭn-gŏd'lē) ►*adj.* **1.** Not revering God; impious. **2.** Sinful; wicked. **3.** Outrageous: *an ungodly hour.* —**un·god'li·ness** *n.*

un·gov·ern·a·ble (ŭn-gŭv'ər-nə-bəl) ►*adj.* Incapable of being governed or controlled.

un·gra·cious (ŭn-grā'shəs) ►*adj.* **1.** Lacking courtesy; rude. **2.** Unattractive —**un·gra'cious·ly** *adv.* —**un·gra'cious·ness** *n.*

un·guard·ed (ŭn-gär'dĭd) ►*adj.* **1.** Lacking protection; vulnerable. **2.** Incautious; imprudent.

un·guent (ŭng'gwənt) ►*n.* A salve; ointment. [< Lat. *unguentum.*]

un·gu·late (ŭng'gyə-lĭt, -lāt') ►*n.* A hoofed mammal, such as a horse, pig, or deer. [< Lat. *ungula,* hoof.] —**un'gu·late** *adj.*

un·hal·lowed (ŭn-hăl'ōd) ►*adj.* **1.** Not hallowed or consecrated. **2.** Irreverent; impious.

un·hand (ŭn-hănd') ►*v.* To remove one's hand from; let go.

un·hap·py (ŭn-hăp'ē) ►*adj.* **1.** Not happy; sad. **2.** Not satisfied; discontented. **3.** Unlucky. **4.** Not suitable; inappropriate: *an unhappy choice of words.* —**un·hap'pi·ly** *adv.* —**un·hap'pi·ness** *n.*

un·health·y (ŭn-hĕl'thē) ►*adj.* **1a.** In ill health; sick. **b.** Symptomatic of ill health. **c.** Conducive to poor health; unwholesome. **2.** Harmful to character; corruptive. —**un·health'i·ly** *adv.* —**un·health'i·ness** *n.*

un·heard (ŭn-hûrd') ►*adj.* **1.** Not heard. **2.** Not given a hearing.

un·heard-of (ŭn-hûrd'ŭv', -ŏv') ►*adj.* **1.** Not previously known. **2.** Without precedent.

un·hinge (ŭn-hĭnj') ►*v.* **1.** To remove from hinges. **2.** To derange; unbalance.

un·ho·ly (ŭn-hō'lē) ►*adj.* **1.** Wicked; immoral. **2.** Not hallowed or consecrated. **3.** Outrageous. —**un·ho'li·ness** *n.*

un·hook (ŭn-hŏŏk') ►*v.* **1.** To remove from a hook. **2.** To unfasten the hooks of.

un·horse (ŭn-hôrs') ►*v.* To cause to fall from a horse.

uni- ►*pref.* One: *unicycle.* [< Lat. *ūnus,* one.]

u·ni·cam·er·al (yōō'nĭ-kăm'ər-əl) ►*adj.* Consisting of a single legislative chamber.

UNICEF ►*abbr.* United Nations Children's Fund (formerly United Nations International Children's Emergency Fund)

u·ni·cel·lu·lar (yōō'nĭ-sĕl'yə-lər) ►*adj.* Consisting of one cell: *unicellular organisms.*

u·ni·corn (yōō'nĭ-kôrn') ►*n.* A fabled horselike creature with a single horn on its forehead. [< Lat. *ūnicornis,* having one horn.]

unicorn
The Lady and the Unicorn: "Sight",
one in a series of six 15th-century tapestries

u·ni·cy·cle (yōō′nĭ-sī′kəl) ►*n.* A single-wheeled vehicle usu. propelled by pedals.

un·i·den·ti·fied flying object (ŭn′ī-dĕn′tə-fīd′) ►*n.* A flying or apparently flying object of an unknown nature, esp. one presumed to be of extraterrestrial origin.

u·ni·form (yōō′nə-fôrm′) ►*adj.* **1.** Always the same; unvarying. **2.** Being the same as or consonant with another or others. ►*n.* A distinctive outfit intended to identify those who wear it as members of a specific group. [< Lat. *ūniformis,* of one form.] —**u′ni·for′mi·ty, u′ni·form′-ness** *n.* —**u′ni·form′ly** *adv.*

u·ni·fy (yōō′nə-fī′) ►*v.* **-fied, -fy·ing** To make into or become a unit; consolidate. [< LLat. *ūnificāre.*] —**u′ni·fi·ca′tion** *n.*

u·ni·lat·er·al (yōō′nə-lăt′ər-əl) ►*adj.* Of, on, involving, or affecting only one side. —**u′ni·lat′er·al·ly** *adv.*

un·im·peach·a·ble (ŭn′ĭm-pē′chə-bəl) ►*adj.* Beyond doubt, question, or reproach. —**un′-im·peach′a·bly** *adv.*

un·in·ter·est·ed (ŭn-ĭn′trĭ-stĭd, -tə-rĕs′tĭd) ►*adj.* Not interested in something; having no interest. See Usage Note at **disinterested.** —**un′in·ter·est·ed·ly** *adv.*

un·ion (yōōn′yən) ►*n.* **1a.** The act of uniting or the state of being united. **b.** A combination so formed, esp. a confederation of people, parties, or political entities for common interest. **2a.** The state of matrimony; marriage. **b.** Sexual intercourse. **3.** A labor union. **4.** A coupling device for connecting parts, such as pipes or rods. **5. Union** The United States of America, esp. during the Civil War. [< LLat. *ūniō* < Lat. *ūnus,* one.]

un·ion·ism (yōōn′yə-nĭz′əm) ►*n.* **1.** The principles, theory, or system of a union, esp. a labor union. **2. Unionism** Loyalty to the federal government during the Civil War. —**un′ion·ist** *n.*

un·ion·ize (yōōn′yə-nīz′) ►*v.* **-ized, -iz·ing** To organize into or cause to join a labor union. —**un′ion·i·za′tion** *n.* —**un′ion·iz′er** *n.*

Union Jack ►*n.* The flag of the United Kingdom.

Union of Soviet Socialist Republics Commonly called **Soviet Union.** A former country of E Europe and N Asia with coastlines on the Baltic and Black Seas and the Arctic and Pacific Oceans.

union shop ►*n.* A business or industrial establishment whose employees are required to be or become union members; closed shop.

u·nique (yōō-nēk′) ►*adj.* **1.** Being the only one of its kind. **2.** Characteristic only of a particular category or entity: *a weather pattern that is unique to coastal areas.* [< Lat. *ūnicus.*] —**u·nique′ly** *adv.* —**u·nique′ness** *n.*

u·ni·sex (yōō′nĭ-sĕks′) ►*adj.* Designed for or suitable to both sexes.

u·ni·sex·u·al (yōō′nĭ-sĕk′shōō-əl) ►*adj.* **1.** Of or for only one sex. **2.** *Bot.* Having either stamens or pistils but not both.

u·ni·son (yōō′nĭ-sən, -zən) ►*n.* **1a.** Identity of musical pitch. **b.** The combination of parts at the same pitch or in octaves. **2.** The action of speaking the same words simultaneously. **3.** Agreement; concord. —*idiom:* **in unison 1.** In complete agreement. **2.** At the same time. [< LLat. *ūnisonus,* with one sound.]

u·nit (yōō′nĭt) ►*n.* **1.** One regarded as a constituent part of a whole. **2a.** A mechanical part or module. **b.** An entire apparatus that performs a specific function. **3.** A precisely specified quantity in terms of which the magnitudes of other quantities of the same kind can be stated. [< UNITY.]

U·ni·tar·i·an (yōō′nĭ-târ′ē-ən) ►*n.* A member of a Christian denomination that rejects the doctrine of the Trinity and emphasizes tolerance in religious belief. —**U′ni·tar′i·an** *adj.* —**U′ni·tar′i·an·ism** *n.*

u·ni·tar·y (yōō′nĭ-tĕr′ē) ►*adj.* **1.** Of or relating to a unit. **2.** Whole. —**u′ni·tar′i·ly** *adv.*

u·nite (yōō-nīt′) ►*v.* **u·nit·ed, u·nit·ing 1.** To bring together so as to form a whole. **2.** To combine (people) in interest, attitude, or action. **3.** To become joined, formed, or combined into a unit. [< Lat. *ūnīre.*]

U·nit·ed Arab Emirates (yōō-nī′tĭd) A country of E Arabia, a federation of seven sheikdoms on the Persian Gulf and the Gulf of Oman. Cap. Abu Dhabi.

United Kingdom or **United Kingdom of Great Britain and Northern Ireland** A country of W Europe comprising England, Scotland, Wales, and Northern Ireland. Cap. London.

United Nations An international organization founded in 1945 to promote peace, security, and development.

United States or **United States of America** A country of central and NW North America with coastlines on the Atlantic and Pacific. Cap. Washington DC.

unit pricing ►*n.* The pricing of goods on the basis of cost per unit of measure.

u·ni·ty (yōō′nĭ-tē) ►*n., pl.* **-ties 1.** The state or quality of being one; singleness. **2.** The condition of being in accord; harmony. **3.** Singleness of purpose or action; continuity. **4.** *Math.* The number 1. [< Lat. *ūnitās.*]

univ. ►*abbr.* **1.** universal **2.** university

u·ni·va·lent (yōō′nĭ-vā′lənt) ►*adj. Chem.* **1.** Having valence 1. **2.** Having only one valence.

u·ni·valve (yōō′nĭ-vălv′) ►*n.* A mollusk having a shell consisting of a single valve or piece. —**u′ni·valve′** *adj.*

u·ni·ver·sal (yōō′nə-vûr′səl) ►*adj.* **1.** Relating to the entire universe. **2.** Relating to all members of a class or group. See Synonyms at **general. 3.** Adapted to many sizes, uses, or devices: *a universal remote control.* **—u′ni·ver′sal·ly** *adv.* **—u′ni·ver·sal′i·ty** *n.*

universal donor ►*n.* A person with group O blood, which is compatible with all other groups in the ABO system.

u·ni·ver·sal·ism (yōō′nə-vûr′sə-lĭz′əm) ►*n.* **1. Universalism** The theological doctrine that everyone will be saved. **2.** The belief that a particular idea has universal application. **—U′ni·ver′sal·ist** *n. & adj.*

universal joint ►*n.* A joint or coupling that allows parts of a machine not in line with each other limited freedom of movement in any direction while transmitting rotary motion.

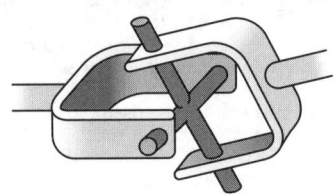

universal joint

Universal Product Code ►*n.* A number and bar code that allow a scanner to identify a particular consumer product.

universal time ►*n.* The time at the Prime Meridian, calculated from the apparent rotation of the celestial sphere and used primarily by astronomers.

u·ni·verse (yōō′nə-vûrs′) ►*n.* **1.** All existing things regarded as a whole. **2.** A hypothetical whole of space-time, matter, and energy existing apart from this universe. [< Lat. *ūniversus,* whole.]

u·ni·ver·si·ty (yōō′nə-vûr′sĭ-tē) ►*n., pl.* **-ties** An institution for higher learning with teaching and research facilities, usu. including undergraduate, graduate, and professional schools. [< Med.Lat. *ūniversitās.*]

un·kempt (ŭn-kĕmpt′) ►*adj.* **1.** Not combed. **2.** Disorderly or untidy. [UN-¹ + ME *kembed,* p.part. of *kemben,* comb.]

un·lead·ed (ŭn-lĕd′ĭd) ►*adj.* Not containing lead: *unleaded gasoline.*

un·learn (ŭn-lûrn′) ►*v.* To put (something learned) out of the mind; forget.

un·learn·ed (ŭn-lûr′nĭd) ►*adj.* **1.** Not educated. **2.** (-lûrnd′) Not acquired by training or studying. **—un·learn′ed·ly** *adv.*

un·leash (ŭn-lēsh′) ►*v.* To release or loose from or as if from a leash.

un·less (ŭn-lĕs′) ►*conj.* Except on the condition that. [< ME *onlesse.*]

un·let·tered (ŭn-lĕt′ərd) ►*adj.* Not educated, esp. unable to read and write.

un·like (ŭn-līk′) ►*adj.* **1.** Not alike; different; dissimilar. **2.** Not equal. ►*prep.* **1.** Different from; not like. **2.** Not typical of: *It's unlike him not to call.* **—un·like′ness** *n.*

un·like·ly (ŭn-līk′lē) ►*adj.* **1.** Not likely; improbable. **2.** Likely to fail. **—un·like′li·hood′** *n.* **—un·like′li·ness** *n.*

un·lim·ber (ŭn-lĭm′bər) ►*v.* To make ready for action.

un·load (ŭn-lōd′) ►*v.* **1a.** To remove the load or cargo from. **b.** To discharge (cargo or a load). **2a.** To relieve (oneself) of something oppressive; unburden. **b.** To pour forth (one's troubles or feelings). **3a.** To remove the charge from (a firearm). **b.** To discharge (a firearm); fire. **4.** To dispose of, esp. by selling in great quantity. **—un·load′er** *n.*

un·lock (ŭn-lŏk′) ►*v.* **1a.** To undo (a lock). **b.** To undo the lock of. **2.** To give access to; open. **3.** To provide a key to: *unlock a mystery.*

un·looked-for (ŭn-lŏokt′fôr′) ►*adj.* Not expected; unforeseen: *unlooked-for riches.*

un·loose (ŭn-lōos′) ►*v.* **1.** To let loose or unfasten; release. **2.** To relax or ease.

un·luck·y (ŭn-lŭk′ē) ►*adj.* **1.** Subjected to or marked by misfortune. **2.** Inauspicious. See Synonyms at **unfortunate. —un·luck′i·ly** *adv.* **—un·luck′i·ness** *n.*

un·make (ŭn-māk′) ►*v.* **1.** To deprive of position, rank, or authority. **2.** To ruin; destroy. **3.** To alter the nature of.

un·man·nered (ŭn-măn′ərd) ►*adj.* **1.** Lacking good manners; rude. **2.** Natural and unaffected. **—un·man′nered·ly** *adv.*

un·mask (ŭn-măsk′) ►*v.* **1.** To remove a mask from. **2.** To disclose the true character of; expose.

un·men·tion·a·ble (ŭn-mĕn′shə-nə-bəl) ►*adj.* **1.** Not fit to be mentioned. **2. unmentionables** Underclothes.

un·mer·ci·ful (ŭn-mûr′sĭ-fəl) ►*adj.* **1.** Having no mercy; merciless. **2.** Excessive: *unmerciful heat.* **—un·mer′ci·ful·ly** *adv.* **—un·mer′ci·ful·ness** *n.*

un·mis·tak·a·ble (ŭn′mĭ-stā′kə-bəl) ►*adj.* Obvious; evident. **—un′mis·tak′a·bly** *adv.*

un·mit·i·gat·ed (ŭn-mĭt′ĭ-ga′tĭd) ►*adj.* **1.** Not diminished or moderated. **2.** Without qualification or exception; absolute.

un·mor·al (ŭn-môr′əl, -mŏr′-) ►*adj.* Amoral.

un·nat·u·ral (ŭn-năch′ər-əl) ►*adj.* **1a.** Not in accordance with what usually occurs in nature. **b.** Not formed by nature; artificial. **2a.** Deviating from social norms. **b.** Brutal or unfeeling. **3.** Stilted, affected, or awkward. **—un·nat′u·ral·ly** *adv.* **—un·nat′u·ral·ness** *n.*

un·nerve (ŭn-nûrv′) ►*v.* To cause to lose courage or firmness of purpose. **—un·nerv′ing·ly** *adv.*

un·num·bered (ŭn-nŭm′bərd) ►*adj.* **1.** Innumerable; countless. **2.** Not marked with an identifying number.

un·or·gan·ized (ŭn-ôr′gə-nīzd′) ►*adj.* **1.** Lacking order or unity. **2.** Not unionized.

un·pack (ŭn-păk′) ►*v.* **1.** To remove the contents of. **2.** To remove (something) from a container.

un·par·al·leled (ŭn-păr′ə-lĕld′) ►*adj.* Without parallel; unequaled.

un·par·lia·men·ta·ry (ŭn′pär-lə-mĕn′tə-rē, -mĕn′trē) ►*adj.* Not in accord with parliamentary procedure.

un·peo·ple (ŭn-pē′pəl) ►*v.* To depopulate (an area).

un·plug (ŭn-plŭg′) ►*v.* **1.** To remove a plug from. **2.** To disconnect (an electric appliance) by removing a plug from an outlet.

un·plugged (ŭn-plŭgd′) ►*adj.* Relating to music played on acoustic rather than electronic instruments. ►*adv.* Acoustically.

un·plumbed (ŭn-plŭmd′) ►*adj.* **1.** Not measured or sounded with a plumb. **2.** Not fully examined or explored. **3.** Not having or being connected to a plumbing system.

un·prec·e·dent·ed (ŭn-prĕs′ĭ-dĕn′tĭd) ►*adj.* Having no previous example.

un·pre·pared (ŭn′prĭ-pârd′) ►*adj.* **1.** Not prepared or ready. **2.** Impromptu. **—un′pre·par′ed·ly** *adv.* **—un′pre·par′ed·ness** *n.*

un·pre·ten·tious (ŭn′prĭ-tĕn′shəs) ►*adj.* Lacking pretention or affectation; modest. See Synonyms at **plain. —un′pre·ten′tious·ly** *adv.* **—un′pre·ten′tious·ness** *n.*

un·print·a·ble (ŭn-prĭn′tə-bəl) ►*adj.* Not proper for publication.

un·pro·fes·sion·al (ŭn′prə-fĕsh′ə-nəl) ►*adj.* **1.** Not conforming to the standards of a profession. **2.** Characteristic of an amateur; inexpert. **—un′pro·fes′sion·al·ly** *adv.*

un·prof·it·a·ble (ŭn-prŏf′ĭ-tə-bəl) ►*adj.* **1.** Bringing in no profit. **2.** Serving no useful purpose. **—un·prof′it·a·bly** *adv.*

un·qual·i·fied (ŭn-kwŏl′ə-fīd′) ►*adj.* **1.** Lacking the proper or required qualifications: *unqualified for the job.* **2.** Not modified by conditions or reservations.

un·quote (ŭn-kwōt′) ►*n.* Used by a speaker to indicate the end of a quotation.

un·rav·el (ŭn-răv′əl) ►*v.* **1.** To separate (entangled threads). **2.** To separate and clarify the elements of (something baffling); solve. **3.** To cause to fail or become ruined or unfulfilled: *Their plans unraveled.*

un·read (ŭn-rĕd′) ►*adj.* **1.** Not read or studied. **2.** Having read little; unlearned.

un·read·a·ble (ŭn-rē′də-bəl) ►*adj.* **1.** Illegible. **2.** Not interesting; dull: *an unreadable book.* **3.** Incomprehensible: *an unreadable look.*

un·re·al (ŭn-rē′əl, -rēl′) ►*adj.* **1.** Not real or substantial. **2.** *Slang* So remarkable as to elicit disbelief. **—un′re·al′i·ty** *n.*

un·rea·son·a·ble (ŭn-rē′zə-nə-bəl) ►*adj.* **1.** Not governed by reason. **2.** Exceeding reasonable limits. **—un·rea′son·a·ble·ness** *n.* **—un·rea′son·a·bly** *adv.*

un·re·gen·er·ate (ŭn′rĭ-jĕn′ər-ĭt) ►*adj.* **1.** Not spiritually renewed or reformed; not repentant. **2.** Not reconciled to change.

un·re·lent·ing (ŭn′rĭ-lĕn′tĭng) ►*adj.* **1.** Relentless; inexorable. **2.** Not diminishing in intensity, pace, or effort.

un·re·mit·ting (ŭn′rĭ-mĭt′ĭng) ►*adj.* Never slackening; persistent.

un·re·served (ŭn′rĭ-zûrvd′) ►*adj.* **1.** Not held back for a particular person. **2.** Given without reservation; unqualified. **—un′re·serv′ed·ly** (-zûr′vĭd-lē) *adv.*

un·rest (ŭn-rĕst′, ŭn′rĕst′) ►*n.* **1.** Uneasiness; disquiet: *voter unrest over the scandal.* **2.** Social disturbance, often involving demonstrations or rioting.

un·ri·valed or **un·ri·valled** (ŭn-rī′vəld) ►*adj.* Unequaled; incomparable.

un·roll (ŭn-rōl′) ►*v.* **1.** To unwind and open (something rolled up). **2.** To unfold; reveal.

un·ruf·fled (ŭn-rŭf′əld) ►*adj.* Not agitated; calm.

un·ru·ly (ŭn-rōō′lē) ►*adj.* **1.** Difficult to discipline, control, or rule. **2.** Difficult to keep in place or in order: *unruly hair.* [ME *unreuli.*] **—un·ru′li·ness** *n.*

un·sad·dle (ŭn-săd′l) ►*v.* **1.** To remove a saddle from. **2.** To unhorse.

un·sat·u·rat·ed (ŭn-săch′ə-rā′tĭd) ►*adj.* **1.** Of or being a fat, usu. of plant origin, composed predominantly of fatty acids having one or more double bonds in the carbon chain. **2.** Capable of dissolving more of a solute.

un·sa·vor·y (ŭn-sā′və-rē) ►*adj.* **1.** Distasteful or disagreeable. **2.** Unappealing in taste or smell: *an unsavory meal.* **3.** Morally offensive.

un·scathed (ŭn-skāthd′) ►*adj.* Not injured or harmed: *escaped the hurricane unscathed.*

un·schooled (ŭn-skōōld′) ►*adj.* **1.** Not educated or instructed. **2.** Not the result of training; natural: *unschooled talents.*

un·scram·ble (ŭn-skrăm′bəl) ►*v.* **1.** To disentangle; resolve. **2.** To restore (a scrambled message) to intelligible form.

un·screw (ŭn-skrōō′) ►*v.* **1.** To take out the screw or screws from. **2.** To loosen, adjust, or remove by rotating.

un·scru·pu·lous (ŭn-skrōō′pyə-ləs) ►*adj.* Devoid of scruples; not honorable. **—un·scru′pu·lous·ly** *adv.* **—un·scru′pu·lous·ness** *n.*

un·sea·son·a·ble (ŭn-sē′zə-nə-bəl) ►*adj.* **1.** Not characteristic of the time of year: *unseasonable weather.* **2.** Poorly timed; inopportune. **—un·sea′son·a·bly** *adv.*

un·seat (ŭn-sēt′) ►*v.* **1.** To remove from a seat, esp. from a saddle. **2.** To remove from office.

un·seem·ly (ŭn-sēm′lē) ►*adj.* **1.** Violating standards of decency or propriety. **2.** Inappropriate.

un·set·tle (ŭn-sĕt′l) ►*v.* **1.** To make unstable: *strikes that unsettled the economy.* **2.** To make uneasy: *news that unsettled us.*

un·set·tled (ŭn-sĕt′ld) ►*adj.* **1.** Disordered; disturbed. **2.** Likely to change or vary; variable: *unsettled weather.* **3.** Not determined or resolved. **4.** Not paid or adjusted. **5.** Having few or no inhabitants. **6.** Not fixed or established: *an unsettled lifestyle.*

un·sight·ly (ŭn-sīt′lē) ►*adj.* Unpleasant or offensive to look at; unattractive. See Synonyms at **ugly. —un·sight′li·ness** *n.*

un·skilled (ŭn-skĭld′) ►*adj.* **1.** Lacking skill or training. **2.** Requiring no training or skill. **3.** Exhibiting a lack of skill; inexpert.

un·so·cia·ble (ŭn-sō′shə-bəl) ►*adj.* Not disposed to seek the company of others. **—un·so′cia·bil′i·ty** *n.* **—un·so′cia·bly** *adv.*

un·sound (ŭn-sound′) ►*adj.* **1.** Not dependably strong or solid. **2.** Not physically or mentally healthy. **3.** Not logically valid; fallacious. **—un·sound′ly** *adv.* **—un·sound′ness** *n.*

un·spar·ing (ŭn-spâr′ĭng) ►*adj.* **1.** Unmerciful; severe. **2.** Generous or unstinting. **—un·spar′ing·ly** *adv.* **—un·spar′ing·ness** *n.*

un·speak·a·ble (ŭn-spē′kə-bəl) ►*adj.* **1.** Beyond description; inexpressible: *unspeakable happiness.* **2.** Inexpressibly bad or objectionable: *unspeakable poverty.* **—un·speak′a·bly** *adv.*

un·sta·ble (ŭn-stā′bəl) ►*adj.* **1.** Tending strongly to change: *unstable weather.* **2a.** Fickle. **b.** Showing or marked by erratic or volatile emotions or behavior. **3.** Unsteady: *an unstable ladder.* **4a.** Decaying with relatively short lifetime. Used of subatomic particles. **b.** Radioactive. **—un·sta′ble·ness** *n.* **—un·sta′bly** *adv.*

un·stead·y (ŭn-stĕd′ē) ►*adj.* **1.** Not securely in place; unstable. **2.** Fluctuating; inconstant.

3. Not even; wavering. —**un·stead′i·ly** *adv.* —**un·stead′i·ness** *n.*

un·stick (ŭn-stĭk′) ►*v.* To free from being stuck.

un·stop (ŭn-stŏp′) ►*v.* **1.** To remove a stopper from. **2.** To remove an obstruction from.

un·stressed (ŭn-strĕst′) ►*adj.* **1.** *Ling.* Not stressed or accented. **2.** Not exposed or subjected to stress.

un·struc·tured (ŭn-strŭk′chərd) ►*adj.* **1.** Lacking structure. **2.** Not regulated or regimented.

un·strung (ŭn-strŭng′) ►*adj.* **1.** Having the strings loosened or removed. **2.** Emotionally upset.

un·stud·ied (ŭn-stŭd′ēd) ►*adj.* Not contrived; natural.

un·sub·stan·tial (ŭn′səb-stăn′shəl) ►*adj.* **1.** Lacking material substance; not real. **2.** Flimsy. **3.** Lacking basis in fact.

un·sung (ŭn-sŭng′) ►*adj.* **1.** Not honored or praised; uncelebrated. **2.** Not sung.

un·tan·gle (ŭn-tăng′gəl) ►*v.* **1.** To disentangle. See Synonyms at **extricate. 2.** To clarify or resolve.

un·taught (ŭn-tôt′) ►*adj.* **1.** Not instructed. **2.** Not acquired by instruction; natural.

un·thank·ful (ŭn-thăngk′fəl) ►*adj.* **1.** Ungrateful. **2.** Disagreeable.

un·think·a·ble (ŭn-thĭng′kə-bəl) ►*adj.* Impossible to imagine; inconceivable.

un·think·ing (ŭn′thĭng′kĭng) ►*adj.* **1.** Thoughtless or heedless. **2.** Exhibiting a lack of thought. —**un·think′ing·ly** *adv.*

un·tie (ŭn-tī′) ►*v.* **1.** To undo or loosen (e.g., a knot). **2.** To free from something that binds or restrains.

un·til (ŭn-tĭl′) ►*prep.* **1.** Up to the time of: *We danced until dawn.* **2.** Before (a specified time): *She can't leave until Friday.* ►*conj.* **1.** Up to the time that: *We walked until it got dark.* **2.** Before: *You cannot leave until we do.* **3.** To the point or extent that: *I talked until I was hoarse.* [ME.]

un·time·ly (ŭn-tīm′lē) ►*adj.* **1.** Occurring or done at an inappropriate time; inopportune. **2.** Occurring too soon; premature. —**un·time′li·ness** *n.* —**un·time′ly** *adv.*

un·to (ŭn′tōō) ►*prep.* To. [ME.]

un·told (ŭn-tōld′) ►*adj.* **1.** Not told or revealed. **2.** Beyond description or enumeration.

un·touch·a·ble (ŭn-tŭch′ə-bəl) ►*adj.* **1.** Not to be touched. **2.** Out of reach; unobtainable. **3.** Beyond criticism, impeachment, or attack. ►*n.* often **Untouchable** *Hinduism* A Dalit.

un·to·ward (ŭn-tôrd′) ►*adj.* **1.** Improper; unseemly. **2.** Unfavorable or adverse.

un·truth (ŭn-trōōth′) ►*n.* **1.** Something false; a lie. **2.** Lack of truth.

un·tu·tored (ŭn-tōō′tərd, -tyōō′-) ►*adj.* **1.** Having had no formal education. **2.** Unsophisticated; unrefined.

un·twist (ŭn-twĭst′) ►*v.* To loosen or separate (something twisted) by turning in the opposite direction; unwind.

un·used (ŭn-yōōzd′) ►*adj.* **1.** Not in use. **2.** Never having been used. **3.** (ŭn-yōōst′) Not accustomed: *unused to city traffic.*

un·u·su·al (ŭn-yōō′zhōō-əl) ►*adj.* Not usual or ordinary. —**un·u′su·al·ly** *adv.*

un·ut·ter·a·ble (ŭn-ŭt′ər-ə-bəl) ►*adj.* **1.** Inexpressible or indescribable. **2.** Impossible to pronounce. —**un·ut′ter·a·bly** *adv.*

un·var·nished (ŭn′vär′nĭsht) ►*adj.* **1.** Not varnished. **2.** Stated with no effort to soften or disguise; plain.

un·veil (ŭn-vāl′) ►*v.* **1.** To remove a veil or covering from. **2.** To disclose; reveal.

un·voiced (ŭn-voist′) ►*adj.* **1.** Not expressed or uttered. **2.** *Ling.* Voiceless.

un·war·rant·ed (ŭn-wôr′ən-tĭd, -wôr′-) ►*adj.* Having no justification; groundless. See Synonyms at **baseless.**

un·wea·ried (ŭn-wîr′ēd) ►*adj.* **1.** Not tired or tiring. **2.** Unrelenting or unremitting. See Synonyms at **tireless.**

un·well (ŭn-wĕl′) ►*adj.* In poor health; sick.

un·whole·some (ŭn-hōl′səm) ►*adj.* **1.** Injurious to health; unhealthy. **2.** Offensive or loathsome. —**un·whole′some·ness** *n.*

un·wield·y (ŭn-wēl′dē) ►*adj.* Difficult to carry or manage because of bulk or shape.

un·will·ing (ŭn-wĭl′ĭng) ►*adj.* **1.** Not willing; hesitant. **2.** Done, given, or said reluctantly. —**un·will′ing·ly** *adv.* —**un·will′ing·ness** *n.*

un·wind (ŭn-wīnd′) ►*v.* **1.** To unroll; uncoil. **2.** To relax.

un·wit·ting (ŭn-wĭt′ĭng) ►*adj.* **1.** Not knowing; unaware. **2.** Not intended; unintentional. [ME : UN-¹ + *witting,* knowing (< OE *witan,* know).] —**un·wit′ting·ly** *adv.*

un·wont·ed (ŭn-wôn′tĭd, -wōn′-, -wŭn′-) ►*adj.* Not usual or accustomed.

un·world·ly (ŭn-wûrld′lē) ►*adj.* **1.** Not worldly-wise; naive. **2.** Concerned with the spirit or soul. **3.** Suggestive of another world. —**un·world′li·ness** *n.*

un·wor·thy (ŭn-wûr′thē) ►*adj.* **1.** Insufficient in worth; undeserving. **2.** Not suiting or befitting. **3.** Vile; despicable. —**un·wor′thi·ly** *adv.* —**un·wor′thi·ness** *n.*

un·writ·ten (ŭn-rĭt′n) ►*adj.* **1.** Not written or recorded. **2.** Based on custom; understood.

up (ŭp) ►*adv.* **1.** In or to a higher position: *looking up.* **2.** In or to an upright position: *sat up in bed.* **3a.** Above a surface: *coming up for air.* **b.** Above the horizon: *as the sun came up.* **4.** Into consideration: *take up a new topic.* **5.** In or toward a position conventionally regarded as higher, as on a map: *up in Canada.* **6.** To or at a higher price: *stocks going up.* **7.** So as to advance, increase, or improve: *Our spirits went up.* **8.** With or to a greater pitch or volume. **9.** Into a state of excitement or turbulence. **10.** Completely; entirely: *drank it up in a gulp; fastened up the coat.* **11.** Used as an intensifier with certain verbs: *typed up a list.* **12.** So as to approach; near: *drove up to the toll booth.* **13.** Apiece: *tied the score at four up.* ►*adj.* **1.** Above a former level; higher: *My grades are up.* **2a.** Out of bed: *was up by seven.* **b.** Standing; erect. **c.** Facing upward. **3.** Raised; lifted: *a switch in the up position.* **4.** Moving or directed upward: *an up elevator.* **5a.** Increasingly excited or agitated; aroused. **b.** *Informal* Cheerful; optimistic. **c.** *Slang* Happily excited; euphoric. **6.** *Informal* Taking place; going on: *wondered what was up back home.* **7.** Being considered; under study: *a contract up for renewal.* **8.** Running as a candidate. **9.** On trial; charged: *up for manslaughter.* **10.** Finished; over: *Your time is up.* ►*prep.* **1.** From a lower to or toward a higher point on: *up the hill.* **2.** Toward or at a point farther along: *up the road.* **3.** Toward the source of: *up the Nile.* ►*n.* **1.** An upward slope; rise. **2.** An upward movement or trend. **3.** *Slang* Excitement or euphoria. ►*v.* **upped, up·ping 1.** To increase: *upped their fees.* **2.** To raise to a higher level. —*idioms:* **on the up-and-up** Open and honest. **up against** Confronted with; facing. **up to 1.** Occupied with, esp. devising or scheming. **2.** Able to do or deal with. **3.** Dependent on: *It's up to us.* **4a.** To the point of: *read up to chapter 12.* **b.** As much or as many as: *allowed up to two hours to finish the test.* [< OE *up*, upward, and *uppe*, on high.]

up– ►*pref.* **1.** Up; upward: *uphill.* **2.** Upper: *upland.* [< OE *ūp-, upp-.*]

up-and-com·ing (ŭp′ən-kŭm′ĭng) ►*adj.* Marked for future success; promising.

U·pan·i·shad (ōō-pä′nĭ-shäd′) ►*n.* Any of a group of philosophical treatises contributing to the theology of ancient Hinduism, elaborating on the earlier Vedas.

up·beat (ŭp′bēt′) ►*n. Mus.* An unaccented beat occurring before the first beat of a measure. ►*adj.* Optimistic; cheerful.

up·braid (ŭp-brād′) ►*v.* To reprove sharply; reproach. [< OE *ūpbrēdan.*]

up·bring·ing (ŭp′brĭng′ĭng) ►*n.* The rearing and training received during childhood.

UPC ►*abbr.* Universal Product Code

up·com·ing (ŭp′kŭm′ĭng) ►*adj.* Occurring soon; forthcoming.

up·coun·try (ŭp′kŭn′trē) ►*n.* The interior of a country. —**up′coun′try** *adj. & adv.*

up·date (ŭp-dāt′) ►*v.* To bring up to date. —**up′date′** *n.*

Up·dike (ŭp′dīk′), **John Hoyer** 1932–2009. Amer. writer.

up·draft (ŭp′drăft′) ►*n.* An upward current of air.

up·end (ŭp-ĕnd′) ►*v.* **1.** To stand, set, or turn on one end. **2.** To overturn or overthrow.

up·front or **up-front** (ŭp′frŭnt′) ►*adj. Informal* **1.** Straightforward; frank. **2.** Paid or due in advance: *upfront cash.* —**up′front′** *adv.*

up·grade (ŭp′grād′) ►*v.* **1.** To raise to a higher grade or standard. **2.** *Comp.* To replace (software or hardware) with a newer or better product. ►*n.* **1.** *Comp.* A hardware or software product that performs better than an earlier version. **2.** An upward incline.

up·heav·al (ŭp-hē′vəl) ►*n.* **1.** The process of being heaved upward. **2.** A sudden violent disruption or upset. **3.** *Geol.* A raising of a part of the earth's crust.

up·hill (ŭp′hĭl′) ►*adj.* **1.** Going up a hill or slope. **2.** Difficult; laborious. ►*adv.* (ŭp′hĭl′) **1.** To or toward higher ground; up a slope. **2.** Against adversity; with difficulty.

up·hold (ŭp-hōld′) ►*v.* **1.** To hold aloft. **2.** To prevent from falling; support. **3.** To maintain or affirm. —**up·hold′er** *n.*

up·hol·ster (ŭp-hōl′stər, ə-pōl′-) ►*v.* To supply (furniture) with stuffing, springs, cushions, and covering fabric. [< ME *upholden*, repair.] —**up·hol′ster·er** *n.*

up·hol·ster·y (ŭp-hōl′stə-rē, -strē, ə-pōl′-) ►*n., pl.* **-ies 1.** Material used in upholstering. **2.** The business of upholstering.

up·keep (ŭp′kēp′) ►*n.* The act or cost of maintaining in proper operation and repair.

up·land (ŭp′lənd, -lănd′) ►*n.* An area of land of high elevation. —**up′land′** *adj.*

up·lift (ŭp-lĭft′) ►*v.* **1.** To raise; elevate. **2.** To

raise to a higher social, intellectual, or moral level. **3.** To raise to spiritual or emotional heights; exalt. —**up′lift′** *n.*

up·load (ŭp′lōd′) ►*v.* To transfer (data or programs), usu. from a peripheral computer or device to a central computer.

up·most (ŭp′mōst′) ►*adj.* Uppermost.

up·on (ə-pŏn′, ə-pôn′) ►*prep.* On.

up·per (ŭp′ər) ►*adj.* **1.** Higher in place, position, or rank. **2. Upper** *Geol. & Archaeol.* Being a later division of the period named. ►*n.* **1.** The part of a shoe or boot above the sole. **2.** *Slang* A drug, esp. an amphetamine, used as a stimulant.

up·per·case (ŭp′ər-kās′) ►*adj.* Of, printed, or formatted in capital letters: *an uppercase A.* —**up′per·case′** *n. & v.*

upper class ►*n.* The highest socioeconomic class in a society. —**up′per-class′** *adj.*

up·per·class·man (ŭp′ər-klăs′mən) ►*n.* A junior or senior in a secondary school or college.

upper crust ►*n. Informal* The highest social class or group. —**up′per-crust′** *adj.*

up·per·cut (ŭp′ər-kŭt′) ►*n. Sports* A swinging blow directed upward, as in boxing.

upper hand ►*n.* A position of control or advantage.

up·per·most (ŭp′ər-mōst′) ►*adv. & adj.* In the highest position, place, or rank.

Upper Vol·ta (vŏl′tə, vōl′-) See **Burkina Faso.**

up·pi·ty (ŭp′ĭ-tē) ►*adj. Informal* **1.** Presumptuous. **2.** Not deferential.

up·raise (ŭp-rāz′) ►*v.* To raise or lift up.

up·right (ŭp′rīt′) ►*adj.* **1.** In a vertical position or direction. **2.** Moral; honorable. ►*adv.* Vertically: *walk upright.* ►*n.* Something, such as a goal post, that stands upright. —**up′right′ly** *adv.* —**up′right′ness** *n.*

upright piano ►*n.* A piano having the strings mounted vertically.

up·ris·ing (ŭp′rī′zĭng) ►*n.* A popular revolt against a government; rebellion.

up·roar (ŭp′rôr′) ►*n.* **1.** A condition of noisy excitement and confusion. See Synonyms at **noise. 2.** A heated protest or controversy. [Prob. < MLGer. *uprōr,* upward motion.]

up·roar·i·ous (ŭp-rôr′ē-əs) ►*adj.* **1.** Causing or accompanied by an uproar. **2.** Hilarious. —**up·roar′i·ous·ly** *adv.* —**up·roar′i·ous·ness** *n.*

up·root (ŭp-rōōt′, -rŏot′) ►*v.* **1.** To remove completely by or as if by pulling up the roots. **2.** To force to leave an accustomed or native location. —**up·root′ed·ness** *n.*

up·scale (ŭp′skāl′) ►*adj.* Intended for or relating to high-income consumers. —**up·scale′** *v.*

up·set (ŭp-sĕt′) ►*v.* **1.** To overturn or cause to overturn. **2.** To disturb the functioning, order, or course of. **3.** To distress mentally or emotionally. **4.** (ŭp′sĕt′) To defeat unexpectedly (an opponent favored to win). ►*n.* (ŭp′sĕt′) **1.** The act of upsetting or the condition of being upset. **2.** A disturbance, disorder, or state of agitation. **3.** A game or contest in which the favorite is defeated. ►*adj.* **1.** Overturned. **2.** Showing symptoms of indigestion. **3.** Emotionally or mentally distressed. [ME *upsetten,* set up.]

up·shot (ŭp′shŏt′) ►*n.* The final result; outcome.

up·side down (ŭp′sīd′) ►*adv.* **1.** With the upper side down. **2.** In great disorder. **3.** Being or holding an asset that is worth less than its purchase price or the debt owed on it. [< ME *up so doun*, up as if down.] —**up′side·down′** *adj.*

up·si·lon (ŭp′sə-lŏn′, yo͞op′-) ►*n.* The 20th letter of the Greek alphabet. [LGk. *u psilon*, simple u.]

up·stage (ŭp′stāj′) ►*adv.* Toward, at, or on the rear part of a stage. ►*adj.* Of the rear part of a stage. ►*v.* (ŭp-stāj′) **1.** To make (another performer) face away from the audience by assuming a position upstage. **2.** To divert attention or praise from. **3.** To treat haughtily.

up·stairs (ŭp′stârz′) ►*adv.* **1.** Up the stairs. **2.** To or on a higher floor. ►*n.* (ŭp′stârz′) *(takes sing. v.)* The upper part of a building. —**up′stairs′** *adj.*

up·stand·ing (ŭp-stăn′dĭng, ŭp′stăn′-) ►*adj.* **1.** Standing erect or upright. **2.** Morally upright; honest.

up·start (ŭp′stärt′) ►*n.* One who attains sudden wealth or importance, esp. one made immodest by the change; parvenu.

up·state (ŭp′stāt′) ►*n.* The northerly section of a US state. —**up′state′** *adv. & adj.*

up·stream (ŭp′strēm′) ►*adv. & adj.* Being or moving closer to the source of a stream; in the direction opposite to that of the current.

up·stroke (ŭp′strōk′) ►*n.* An upward stroke.

up·surge (ŭp′sûrj′) ►*n.* A rapid or abrupt rise: *an upsurge in crime.* **up·surge′** *v.*

up·sweep (ŭp′swēp′) ►*n.* An upward curve or sweep. —**up′sweep′** *v.*

up·swing (ŭp′swĭng′) ►*n.* An upward swing or trend; increase.

up·take (ŭp′tāk′) ►*n.* **1.** A passage for drawing up smoke or air. **2.** Understanding; comprehension: *quick on the uptake.*

up·tem·po also **up·tem·po** (ŭp′tĕm′pō) ►*n., pl.* **-pos** A fast or lively tempo, as in jazz. —**up′tem′po** *adj.*

up·tight (ŭp′tīt′) ►*adj. Slang* **1.** Tense; nervous. **2.** Rigidly conventional.

up-to-date (ŭp′tə-dāt′) ►*adj.* Informed of or reflecting the latest information or styles. —**up′-to-date′ness** *n.*

up·town (ŭp′toun′) ►*n.* The upper part of a town or city. ►*adv.* (ŭp′toun′) To, toward, or in the uptown. —**up′town′** *adj.*

up·turn (ŭp′tûrn′, ŭp-tûrn′) ►*v.* **1.** To turn up or over. **2.** To direct upward. ►*n.* (ŭp′tûrn′) An upward movement or trend, as in business.

up·ward (ŭp′wərd) ►*adv. & adj.* To or toward a higher place, point, or level. —*idiom:* **upward (or upwards) of** More than; in excess of. —**up′ward·ly** *adv.* —**up′wards** *adv.*

upward mobility ►*n.* Advancement in economic and social standing.

up·wind (ŭp′wĭnd′) ►*adv.* In or toward the direction from which the wind blows. —**up′wind′** *adj.*

Ur (ûr, o͝or) A city of ancient Sumer in S Mesopotamia on a site in SE Iraq.

u·ra·cil (yo͝or′ə-sĭl) ►*n.* A pyrimidine base that is an essential constituent of RNA. [< UR(EA) + AC(ETIC).]

U·ral-Al·ta·ic (yo͝or′əl-ăl-tā′ĭk) ►*n.* A hypothetical language group that comprises the Uralic and Altaic families. —**U′ral-Al·ta′ic** *adj.*

U·ral·ic (yo͝o-răl′ĭk) also **U·ra·li·an** (yo͝o-rā′lē-ən) ►*n.* A language family that comprises

the Finno-Ugric and Samoyedic subfamilies. —**U·ral′ic** *adj.*

U·ral Mountains (yo͝or′əl) A range of W Russia forming the traditional boundary between Europe and Asia and extending about 2,365 km (1,470 mi) from the Arctic to Kazakhstan.

Ural River A river of W Russia and W Kazakhstan rising in the S Ural Mts. and flowing about 2,430 km (1,510 mi) to the Caspian Sea.

u·ra·ni·um (yo͝o-rā′nē-əm) ►*n. Symbol* **U** A dense, radioactive, silvery-white metallic element, used in research, nuclear fuels, and nuclear weapons. At. no. 92. See table at **element.** [< URANUS.]

U·ra·nus (yo͝or′ə-nəs, yo͝o-rā′nəs) ►*n.* **1.** *Gk. Myth.* The earliest supreme god, a personification of the sky. **2.** The 7th planet from the sun, at a distance of approx. 2.9 billion km (1.8 billion mi) and with a mean diameter of 51,118 km (31,763 mi).

ur·ban (ûr′bən) ►*adj.* Of, relating to, or located in a city. [< Lat. *urbs*, city.]

Urban II 1042?–99. Pope (1088–99).

ur·bane (ûr-bān′) ►*adj.* **-ban·er, -ban·est** Polite and refined in manner; suave. [Lat. *urbānus*, URBAN.] —**ur·bane′ly** *adv.*

ur·ban·ite (ûr′bə-nīt′) ►*n.* A city dweller.

ur·ban·i·ty (ûr-băn′ĭ-tē) ►*n.* Refinement and elegance of manner.

ur·ban·ize (ûr′bə-nīz′) ►*v.* **-ized, -iz·ing** To make urban in nature. —**ur′ban·i·za′tion** *n.*

urban legend ►*n.* An apocryphal story, often including elements of humor or horror, that spreads quickly and is popularly believed.

ur·chin (ûr′chĭn) ►*n.* **1.** A playful or mischievous youngster; scamp. **2.** A sea urchin. [< Lat. *ēricius*, hedgehog.]

Ur·du (o͝or′do͞o, ûr′-) ►*n.* An Indic language that is an official language of Pakistan and is closely related to Hindi.

–ure ►*suff.* **1.** Act; process; condition: *erasure.* **2a.** Function; office: *judicature.* **b.** Body performing a function: *legislature.* [< Lat. *-ūra.*]

u·re·a (yo͝o-rē′ə) ►*n.* A water-soluble compound that is the chief nitrogenous component of urine in mammals and other organisms. [< Fr. *urée* < *urine*, URINE.]

u·re·mi·a (yo͝o-rē′mē-ə) ►*n.* A toxic condition caused by kidney disease in which waste products normally excreted in the urine are retained in the bloodstream. —**u·re′mic** *adj.*

u·re·ter (yo͝o-rē′tər, yo͝or′ĭ-tər) ►*n.* The duct that conveys urine from the kidney to the urinary bladder or cloaca. [< Gk. *ourētēr.*]

u·re·thra (yo͝o-rē′thrə) ►*n., pl.* **-thras** or **-thrae** (-thrē) The canal through which urine is discharged from the bladder and through which semen is discharged in the male. [< Gk. *ourēthra.*] —**u·re′thral** *adj.*

urge (ûrj) ►*v.* **urged, urg·ing 1.** To force or drive forward or onward; impel. **2.** To entreat earnestly and often repeatedly; exhort. **3.** To advocate earnestly; press for. ►*n.* **1.** The act of urging. **2.** An impulse that prompts action or effort. [Lat. *urgēre.*]

ur·gent (ûr′jənt) ►*adj.* **1.** Requiring immediate action; pressing. **2.** Conveying a sense of pressing importance. —**ur′gen·cy** *n.* —**ur′gent·ly** *adv.*

–urgy ►*suff.* Technique; process: *metallurgy.* [< Gk. *-ourgia* < *ergon*, work.]

u·ric (yŏŏr′ĭk) ►*adj.* Relating to, contained in, or obtained from urine.

uric acid ►*n.* A semisolid compound that is the chief nitrogenous component of urine in birds, terrestrial reptiles, and insects.

u·ri·nal (yŏŏr′ə-nəl) ►*n.* **1.** A place for urinating. **2.** A receptacle for urine.

u·ri·nal·y·sis (yŏŏr′ə-năl′ĭ-sĭs) ►*n.* Chemical analysis of urine.

u·ri·nar·y (yŏŏr′ə-nĕr′ē) ►*adj.* Of urine or its production, function, or excretion.

urinary bladder ►*n.* A muscular sac in the anterior part of the pelvic cavity in which urine collects before excretion.

u·ri·nate (yŏŏr′ə-nāt′) ►*v.* **-nat·ed, -nat·ing** To excrete urine. —**u′ri·na′tion** *n.*

u·rine (yŏŏr′ĭn) ►*n.* The waste product secreted by the kidneys that in mammals is a yellowish, slightly acid fluid discharged through the urethra. [< Lat. *ūrīna.*]

urino– or **urin–** ►*pref.* Urine: *urinalysis.* [< Lat. *ūrīna,* urine.]

URL (yŏŏ′är-ĕl′) ►*n.* An Internet address (e.g., *http://hmhbooks.com/eref/*), usu. consisting of the access protocol (*http*), the domain name (*hmhbooks.com*), and optionally the path to a file (*eref*).

urn (ûrn) ►*n.* **1.** A vase of varying size and shape, usu. having a footed base or pedestal. **2.** A closed metal vessel having a spigot and used for warming or serving tea or coffee. [< Lat. *urna.*]

uro– or **ur–** ►*pref.* **1.** Urine: *uric.* **2.** Urinary tract: *urology.* **3.** Urea: *polyurethane.* [< Gk. *ouron,* urine.]

u·ro·gen·i·tal (yŏŏr′ō-jĕn′ĭ-tl) ►*adj.* Of or involving both the urinary and genital structures or functions.

u·rol·o·gy (yŏŏ-rŏl′ə-jē) ►*n.* The study of diseases and disorders of the urinary tract and urogenital system. —**ur′o·log′ic** (yŏŏr′ə-lŏj′-ĭk), **ur′o·log′i·cal** *adj.* —**u·rol′o·gist** *n.*

Ur·sa Major (ûr′sə) ►*n.* A constellation containing the seven stars that form the Big Dipper.

Ursa Minor ►*n.* A constellation containing the seven stars that form the Little Dipper.

ur·sine (ûr′sīn′) ►*adj.* Of or characteristic of a bear. [< Lat. *ursus,* bear.]

ur·ti·car·i·a (ûr′tĭ-kâr′ē-ə) ►*n.* See **hives.** [< Lat. *urtica,* nettle.]

U·ru·guay (yŏŏr′ə-gwī′, -gwā′) A country of SE South America on the Atlantic and the Río de la Plata. Cap. Montevideo. —**U′ru·guay′an** *adj. & n.*

Uruguay River A river of SE South America rising in S Brazil and flowing about 1,595 km (990 mi) to the Río de la Plata.

us (ŭs) ►*pron.* The objective case of **we. 1.** Used as a direct or indirect object: *She saw us; They offered us free tickets.* See Usage Note at **we. 2.** Used as the object of a preposition: *This letter is addressed to us.* See Usage Note at **I. 3.** *Informal* Used after a linking verb such as *is: It's us.* [< OE *ūs.*]

US ►*abbr.* United States

USA ►*abbr.* **1.** United States Army **2.** United States of America

us·a·ble also **use·a·ble** (yŏŏ′zə-bəl) ►*adj.* **1.** That can be used: *usable byproducts.* **2.** Fit for use; convenient to use: *a usable reference.* —**us′-a·bil′i·ty** *n.* —**us′a·bly** *adv.*

USAF ►*abbr.* United States Air Force

us·age (yŏŏ′sĭj, -zĭj) ►*n.* **1.** The act, manner, or amount of using. **2.** A usual, habitual, or accepted practice. **3.** The way in which words or phrases are actually used in a speech community.

USCG ►*abbr.* United States Coast Guard

USDA ►*abbr.* United States Department of Agriculture

use (yŏŏz) ►*v.* **used, us·ing 1.** To put into service; employ. **2.** To avail oneself of; practice. **3.** To conduct oneself toward; treat. **4.** To exploit. **5.** To take habitually, as alcohol or tobacco. **6.** Used in the past tense with *to* to indicate a former state, habitual practice, or custom: *Mail service used to be faster.* ►*n.* (yŏŏs) **1a.** The act of using; employment. **b.** The fact of being used. **2.** The manner of using. **3a.** The privilege of using something. **b.** The ability to use something. **4.** The need or occasion to employ: *have no use for these old clothes.* **5.** The quality of being suitable to an end; usefulness. **6.** A purpose for which something is used. **7.** Accustomed or usual practice. **8.** *Law* **a.** Enjoyment of property, as by occupying or exercising it. **b.** The benefit or profit of lands and tenements held in trust by another. —*phrasal verb:* **use up** To consume completely. [< Lat. *ūtī, ūs-.*] —**us′er** *n.*

used (yŏŏzd) ►*adj.* **1.** Not new; secondhand. **2.** (also yŏŏst) Accustomed; habituated: *We aren't used to the cold.*

use·ful (yŏŏs′fəl) ►*adj.* Being of use; serviceable. —**use′ful·ly** *adv.* —**use′ful·ness** *n.*

use·less (yŏŏs′lĭs) ►*adj.* **1.** Of no beneficial use; futile; ineffective. **2.** Incapable of functioning; ineffectual. See Synonyms at **futile.** —**use′-less·ly** *adv.* —**use′less·ness** *n.*

Use·net (yŏŏz′nĕt′) ►*n.* A system that uses a computer network, esp. the Internet, to transfer thematically organized messages.

us·er-friend·ly (yŏŏ′zər-frĕnd′lē) ►*adj.* Easy to use or learn to use. —**us′er-friend′li·ness** *n.*

us·er·name (yŏŏ′zər-nām′) ►*n.* A sequence of characters used as identification esp. for logging on to a multiuser computer system.

ush·er (ŭsh′ər) ►*n.* **1.** One who escorts people to their seats, as in a theater. **2.** An official doorkeeper, as in a courtroom. **3.** An official who precedes persons of rank in a procession. ►*v.* **1.** To serve as an usher to; escort. **2.** To lead or conduct. See Synonyms at **guide. 3.** To precede and introduce; inaugurate: *events that ushered in a new era.* [< Lat. *ōstiārius,* doorkeeper.]

USMC ►*abbr.* United States Marine Corps

USN ►*abbr.* United States Navy

USO ►*abbr.* United Service Organizations

USPS ►*abbr.* United States Postal Service

USS ►*abbr.* United States ship

USSR ►*abbr.* Union of Soviet Socialist Republics

usu. ►*abbr.* usually

u·su·al (yŏŏ′zhŏŏ-əl) ►*adj.* **1.** Common; ordinary; normal. **2.** Habitual or customary. [< LLat. *ūsuālis.*] —**u′su·al·ly** *adv.* —**u′su·al·ness** *n.*

> **Syns:** *accustomed, customary, habitual, inveterate* **adj.**

u·su·fruct (yŏŏ′zə-frŭkt′, -sə-) ►*n. Law* The right to the use and profits of something belonging to another. [< Lat. *ūsusfrūctus.*]

u·su·rer (yŏŏ′zhər-ər) ►*n.* One who lends

money at interest, esp. at an exorbitant or unlawfully high rate. [< Lat. *ūsūra*, usury.]

u·su·ri·ous (yoŏ-zhoŏr′ē-əs) ►*adj.* Relating to, practicing, or being usury. —**u·su′ri·ous·ly** *adv.* —**u·su′ri·ous·ness** *n.*

u·surp (yoŏ-sûrp′, -zûrp′) ►*v.* To seize and hold illegally by force. [< Lat. *ūsūrpāre*, take for one's own use.] —**u′sur·pa′tion** (yoŏ′sər-pā′shən, -zər-) *n.* —**u·surp′er** *n.*

u·su·ry (yoŏ′zhə-rē) ►*n., pl.* -**ries 1.** The practice of lending money and charging the borrower interest, esp. at an exorbitant or illegally high rate. **2.** An excessive or illegally high interest rate. [< Lat. *ūsūra.*]

UT or **Ut.** ►*abbr.* Utah

U·tah (yoŏ′tô′, -tä′) A state of the W US. Cap. Salt Lake City. —**U′tahn** *adj. & n.*

Ute (yoŏt) ►*n., pl.* **Ute** or **Utes 1.** A member of a Native American people of Utah, Colorado, and N New Mexico. **2.** The Uto-Aztecan language of the Ute.

u·ten·sil (yoŏ-těn′səl) ►*n.* An implement or container, esp. one used in a kitchen. [< Lat. *ūtēnsilis,* fit for use.]

u·ter·us (yoŏ′tər-əs) ►*n., pl.* **u·ter·i** (yoŏ′tə-rī′) or -**us·es** A hollow muscular organ located in the pelvic cavity of female mammals in which the fertilized egg develops. [< Lat.] —**u′ter·ine** (-tər-ĭn, -tə-rīn′) *adj.*

u·tile (yoŏt′l, yoŏ′tīl′) ►*adj.* Useful. [< Lat. *ūtilis.*]

u·til·i·tar·i·an (yoŏ-tĭl′ĭ-târ′ē-ən) ►*adj.* **1.** Of or in the interests of utility. **2.** Stressing utility over beauty. **3.** Believing in or advocating utilitarianism. ►*n.* One who advocates utilitarianism.

u·til·i·tar·i·an·ism (yoŏ-tĭl′ĭ-târ′ē-ə-nĭz′əm) ►*n.* **1.** The belief that the value of a thing or action is determined by its utility. **2.** The ethical theory that all action should be directed toward achieving the greatest happiness for the greatest number of people.

u·til·i·ty (yoŏ-tĭl′ĭ-tē) ►*n., pl.* -**ties 1.** The quality or condition of being useful; usefulness. **2.** A useful article or device. **3.** An organization, such as a power company, that provides a public service under government regulation. **4.** *Comp.* A program that performs a specific task related to the management of computer func-

tions, resources, or files. [< Lat. *ūtilis,* useful.]

u·til·ize (yoŏt′l-īz′) ►*v.* -**ized, -iz·ing** To put to use. [< Lat. *ūtilis,* useful.] —**u′til·iz′a·ble** *adj.* —**u′til·i·za′tion** *n.* —**u′til·iz′er** *n.*

ut·most (ŭt′mōst′) ►*adj.* **1.** Being at or the most distant limit or point; farthest. **2.** Of the highest or greatest degree, amount, or intensity. [< OE *ūtmest.*] —**ut′most′** *n.*

U·to-Az·tec·an (yoŏ′tō-ăz′těk′ən) ►*n.* **1.** A language family of North and Central America that includes Ute, Hopi, Nahuatl, and Shoshone. **2.** A member of a people speaking a Uto-Aztecan language. —**U′to-Az′tec·an** *adj.*

u·to·pi·a (yoŏ-tō′pē-ə) ►*n.* **1.** often **Utopia** An ideally perfect place, esp. in its social, political, and moral aspects. **2.** An impractical, idealistic scheme for social and political reform. [< *Utopia,* a novel by Sir Thomas More.] —**u·to′pi·an** *adj.*

ut·ter¹ (ŭt′ər) ►*v.* **1.** To send forth with the voice: *uttered a cry.* **2.** To pronounce or speak. [ME *utteren.*] —**ut′ter·a·ble** *adj.*

ut·ter² (ŭt′ər) ►*adj.* Complete; absolute: *utter darkness.* [< OE *ūtera,* outer.]

ut·ter·ance (ŭt′ər-əns) ►*n.* **1a.** The act of uttering. **b.** The power of speaking; speech. **2.** Something expressed; statement.

ut·ter·ly (ŭt′ər-lē) ►*adv.* Completely; absolutely.

ut·ter·most (ŭt′ər-mōst′) ►*adj.* **1.** Utmost. **2.** Outermost. —**ut′ter·most′** *n.*

U-turn (yoŏ′tûrn′) ►*n.* A turn, as by a vehicle, reversing the direction of travel.

UV ►*abbr.* ultraviolet

u·vu·la (yoŏ′vyə-lə) ►*n.* A small, fleshy mass of tissue, esp. that which hangs from the soft palate above the base of the tongue. [< LLat. *ūvula,* little grape.]

ux·o·ri·ous (ŭk-sôr′ē-əs, ŭg-zôr′-) ►*adj.* Excessively submissive or devoted to one's wife. [< Lat. *uxor,* wife.] —**ux·o′ri·ous·ness** *n.*

Uz·bek (oŏz′běk′, ŭz′-) ►*adj.* Of or relating to Uzbekistan or its people or language. ►*n., pl.* -**bek** or -**beks 1.** A native or inhabitant of Uzbekistan. **2.** A member of a Turkic people inhabiting Uzbekistan and neighboring areas. **3.** The Turkic language of the Uzbeks.

Uz·bek·i·stan (oŏz-běk′ĭ-stän′, -stän′, ŭz-) A country of W-central Asia. Cap. Tashkent.

V

v or **V** (vē) ►*n., pl.* **v's** or **V's** also **vs** or **Vs** The 22nd letter of the English alphabet.

V ►*abbr.* **1.** velocity **2.** volt **3.** volume **4.** vowel

v. ►*abbr.* **1.** verb **2.** verse **3.** version **4.** versus **5.** vide **6.** volume (book)

VA ►*abbr.* **1.** Veterans' Administration **2.** Virginia

va·can·cy (vā′kən-sē) ►*n., pl.* -**cies 1.** The condition of being vacant; emptiness. **2.** An empty space; void. **3.** A position, office, or lodging that is unfilled or unoccupied.

va·cant (vā′kənt) ►*adj.* **1a.** Containing nothing; empty. **b.** Unoccupied. **2.** Free from activity; idle. **3a.** Lacking intelligence. **b.** Lacking expression; blank. [< Lat. *vacāre,* be empty.] —**va′cant·ly** *adv.*

va·cate (vā′kāt′, vā-kāt′) ►*v.* -**cat·ed, -cat·ing**

1. To make vacant. **2.** *Law* To make void or annul. [Lat. *vacāre,* be empty.]

va·ca·tion (vā-kā′shən, və-) ►*n.* A period, usu. from several days to weeks, taken as a break from work or study. ►*v.* To take or spend a vacation. —**va·ca′tion·er** *n.*

vac·ci·nate (văk′sə-nāt′) ►*v.* -**nat·ed, -nat·ing** To administer a vaccine. —**vac′ci·na′tion** *n.*

vac·cine (văk-sēn′, văk′sēn′) ►*n.* A preparation of a weakened or killed pathogen, such as a bacterium or virus, that is administered to a person or animal in order to produce immunity to an infectious disease. [< Lat. *vaccīnus,* of cows.]

vac·il·late (văs′ə-lāt′) ►*v.* -**lat·ed, -lat·ing 1.** To be unable to choose between different courses of action or opinions; waver. **2.** To change between one state and another; fluctuate. **3.**

To sway to and fro. [Lat. *vacillāre*.] —**vac′il·la′tion** *n.*

va·cu·i·ty (vă-kyoō′ĭ-tē, və-) ►*n., pl.* **-ties 1.** Total absence of matter; emptiness. **2.** An empty space; vacuum. **3.** Emptiness of mind. **4.** Something, esp. a remark, that is vacuous.

vac·u·ole (văk′yoō-ōl′) ►*n.* A small, usu. fluid-filled cavity in the cytoplasm of a cell. [Fr. < Lat. *vacuus*, empty.]

vac·u·ous (văk′yoō-əs) ►*adj.* **1.** Inane; stupid. **2.** Blank; vacant. **3.** *Archaic* Empty. [< Lat. *vacuus*.] —**vac′u·ous·ness** *n.*

vac·u·um (văk′yoō-əm, -yoōm, -yəm) ►*n., pl.* **-u·ums** or **-u·a** (-yoō-ə) **1a.** Absence of matter. **b.** A space relatively empty of matter. **2.** A state or feeling of emptiness; void. **3.** A vacuum cleaner. ►*v.* To clean with a vacuum cleaner. [Lat. < *vacuus*, empty.]

vacuum bottle ►*n.* A thermos.

vacuum cleaner ►*n.* An electrical appliance that cleans surfaces by suction.

vac·u·um-packed (văk′yoō-əm-păkt′, -yoōm-, -yəm-) ►*adj.* Sealed under a partial vacuum.

vacuum tube ►*n.* An electron tube containing a nearly total vacuum, permitting electrons to move with low interaction with any remaining gas molecules.

va·de me·cum (vā′dē mā′kəm) ►*n., pl.* **-cums** A useful thing that one constantly carries about. [Lat. *vāde mēcum*, go with me.]

Va·duz (vä-doōts′, fä-) The capital of Liechtenstein, in the W part on the Rhine R.

vag·a·bond (văg′ə-bŏnd′) ►*n.* A person who moves from place to place without a permanent home and often without a regular means of support. [< LLat. *vagābundus*, wandering.] —**vag′a·bond′** *adj.* —**vag′a·bond′age** *n.*

va·ga·ry (vā′gə-rē, və-gâr′ē) ►*n., pl.* **-ries 1.** An erratic or capricious happening. **2.** A whim. [< Lat. *vagārī*, wander.]

va·gi·na (və-jī′nə) ►*n.* The passage leading from the vulva to the cervix of the uterus in female mammals. [Lat. *vāgīna*, sheath.] —**vag′i·nal** (văj′ə-nəl) *adj.*

va·grant (vā′grənt) ►*n.* **1.** One who wanders from place to place without a permanent home or livelihood. **2.** One who lives on the streets and constitutes a public nuisance. ►*adj.* **1.** Wandering from place to place; roving. **2.** Moving in a random fashion. [Prob. < OFr. *wacrer*, wander, of Gmc. orig.] —**va′gran·cy** *n.*

vague (vāg) ►*adj.* **vagu·er, vagu·est 1.** Not clearly expressed or outlined. **2.** Lacking definite shape or character; indistinct. **3.** Indistinctly perceived, understood, or recalled. [< Lat. *vagus*.] —**vague′ly** *adv.* —**vague′ness** *n.*

vain (vān) ►*adj.* **-er, -est 1.** Not yielding the desired outcome; fruitless: *a vain attempt.* See Synonyms at **futile. 2.** Lacking substance or worth: *vain talk.* **3.** Excessively proud of one's appearance or accomplishments; conceited. —*idiom:* **in vain 1.** To no avail; without success. **2.** Irreverently or disrespectfully. [< Lat. *vānus*, empty.] —**vain′ly** *adv.*

    Syns: *empty, hollow, idle, otiose* **adj.**

vain·glo·ry (vān′glôr′ē) ►*n., pl.* **-ries 1.** Excessive pride and vanity. **2.** Vain and ostentatious display. —**vain·glo′ri·ous** *adj.*

val·ance (văl′əns, vā′ləns) ►*n.* **1.** An ornamen-

tal drapery hung across a top edge, as of a bed. **2.** A decorative strip mounted esp. across the top of a window. [ME.]

vale (vāl) ►*n.* A valley; dale. [< Lat. *vallēs*.]

val·e·dic·tion (văl′ĭ-dĭk′shən) ►*n.* An act or expression of leave-taking. [< Lat. *valedīcere*, say farewell.] —**val′e·dic′to·ry** (-tə-rē) *adj.*

val·e·dic·to·ri·an (văl′ĭ-dĭk-tôr′ē-ən) ►*n.* The student, usu. with the highest class rank, who delivers the valedictory at graduation.

va·lence (vā′ləns) ►*n.* *Chem.* An integer representing the capacity of an atom or group of atoms to combine in specific proportions with other atoms. [< Lat. *valēre*, be strong.]

Va·len·ci·a (və-lĕn′shē-ə, -sē-ə) **1.** A region and former kingdom of E Spain on the Mediterranean coast S of Catalonia. **2.** A city of E Spain on the **Gulf of Valencia,** a wide inlet of the Mediterranean Sea. **3.** A city of N Venezuela WSW of Caracas on the W shore of **Lake Valencia.**

–valent ►*suff.* Having a specified valence or valences: *polyvalent.* [< VALENCE.]

val·en·tine (văl′ən-tīn′) ►*n.* **1.** A usu. sentimental card sent to a sweetheart or friend on Valentine's Day. **2.** One's chosen sweetheart on Valentine's Day.

Valentine, Saint. fl. 3rd cent. AD. Roman Christian martyr.

Val·en·tine's Day or **Val·en·tines Day** (văl′-ən-tīnz′) ►*n.* February 14, celebrated in various countries by the exchange of valentines.

va·le·ri·an (və-lîr′ē-ən) ►*n.* A plant widely cultivated for its small fragrant flowers and for use in medicine. [< Med.Lat. *valeriāna*.]

Va·le·ri·an (və-lîr′ē-ən) d. c. AD 260. Emperor of Rome (253–260).

val·et (vă-lā′, văl′ā, văl′ĭt) ►*n.* **1.** A man's male servant, who takes care of his clothes and performs other personal services. **2.** An employee, as in a hotel, who performs personal services for guests. **3.** A person who parks and retrieves cars for patrons of a restaurant or other business establishment. [< VLat. **vassellitus*, servant.]

val·e·tu·di·nar·i·an (văl′ĭ-toōd′n-âr′ē-ən, -tyoōd′-) ►*n.* A sickly or weak person, esp. one who is constantly concerned with his or her health. [< Lat. *valētūdō*, health.] —**val′e·tu′di·nar′i·an·ism** *n.*

Val·hal·la (văl-hăl′ə, väl-hä′lə) ►*n.* In Norse mythology, the hall in which Odin received the souls of slain heroes.

val·iant (văl′yənt) ►*adj.* Possessing or exhibiting valor; brave. [< Lat. *valēre*, be strong.] —**val′iance** *n.* —**val′iant·ly** *adv.*

val·id (văl′ĭd) ►*adj.* **1.** Well grounded; just: *a valid objection.* **2.** Having legal force; effective: *a valid passport.* [< Lat. *validus*, strong.] —**va·lid′i·ty, val′id·ness** *n.* —**val′id·ly** *adv.*

val·i·date (văl′ĭ-dāt′) ►*v.* **-dat·ed, -dat·ing 1.** To substantiate; verify. **2.** To make legally valid. —**val′i·da′tion** *n.*

va·lise (və-lēs′) ►*n.* A small piece of hand luggage. [Fr. < Ital. *valigia*.]

Val·i·um (văl′ē-əm) A trademark used for the drug diazepam.

Val·kyr·ie (văl-kîr′ē, -kī′rē, văl′kə-rē) ►*n.* In Norse mythology, any of Odin's handmaidens who conducted the souls of the slain to Valhalla.

Val·let·ta (və-lĕt′ə) The capital of Malta, on the NE coast.

val·ley (văl′ē) ►*n., pl.* **-leys 1.** A long narrow lowland between mountains or hills. **2.** An area drained by a river system. **3.** A V-shaped junction where two slopes of a roof meet. [< Lat. *vallēs.*]

Valley Forge A village of SE PA; site of George Washington's winter headquarters (1777–78).

Valley Forge
George Washington *(standing right)* and the Marquis de Lafayette *(standing left)* at Valley Forge

val·or (văl′ər) ►*n.* Courage and boldness, as in battle; bravery. [< LLat. *valor.*] —**val′or·ize′** *v.* —**val′or·ous** *adj.*

val·u·a·ble (văl′yōō-ə-bəl, văl′yə-) ►*adj.* **1.** Having high monetary or material value. **2.** Of great importance, use, or service. ►*n. often* **valuables** A valuable personal possession, such as a piece of jewelry.

val·u·ate (văl′yōō-āt′) ►*v.* **-at·ed, -at·ing** To set a value for; appraise. —**val′u·a′tor** *n.*

val·u·a·tion (văl′yōō-ā′shən) ►*n.* **1.** The act of assessing value or price; appraisal. **2.** Assessed value or price.

val·ue (văl′yōō) ►*n.* **1.** A fair equivalent or return for something, as goods or services. **2.** Monetary or material worth. **3.** Worth as measured in usefulness or importance; merit. **4.** A principle, standard, or quality considered important or desirable. **5.** Precise meaning, as of a word. **6.** *Math.* A quantity expressed by an algebraic term. **7.** *Mus.* The relative duration of a tone or rest. **8.** The relative darkness or lightness of a color. **9.** *Ling.* The sound quality of a letter or diphthong. ►*v.* **-ued, -u·ing 1.** To determine or estimate the value of; appraise. **2.** To regard highly; esteem. **3.** To rate according to relative worth or desirability; evaluate. [< OFr. *valoir,* be worth.] —**val′ue·less** *adj.*

val·ue-add·ed tax (văl′yōō-ăd′ĭd) ►*n.* A tax on the estimated market value added to a product at each stage of manufacture or distribution.

valve (vălv) ►*n.* **1a.** A device that regulates the flow of gases or liquids by blocking and opening passageways. **b.** The movable control element of such a device. **c.** A device in a brass wind instrument that permits change in pitch by a rapid varying of the air column in a tube. **2.** *Anat.* A membranous structure, as in a vein, that prevents the return flow of a fluid. **3.** A paired, often hinged part, as of a mollusk shell or seed pod. [< Lat. *valva,* leaf of a door.] —**valved** *adj.*

va·moose (vă-mōōs′, və-) ►*v.* **-moosed, -moos·ing** *Slang* To leave hurriedly. [< Sp. *vamos,* let's go.]

vamp¹ (vămp) ►*n.* **1.** The part of a boot or shoe covering the instep and often the toe. **2.** *Mus.*

One or more bars of music repeated indefinitely as an accompaniment. ►*v.* **1.** To provide with a new vamp. **2.** To patch up. **3.** To improvise. [< OFr. *avanpie,* sock : *avaunt,* before + *pie,* foot (< Lat. *pēs*).] —**vamp′er** *n.*

vamp² (vămp) ►*n. Informal* A woman who aggressively seduces men, esp. to exploit them. [< VAMPIRE.] —**vamp** *v.*

vam·pire (văm′pīr′) ►*n.* **1.** In popular folklore, an undead being in human form that survives by sucking the blood of living people, esp. at night. **2.** A person who preys on others. [< Ger. *Vampir,* of Slav. orig.]

vampire bat ►*n.* Any of various tropical American bats that bite mammals and birds to feed on their blood.

van¹ (văn) ►*n.* **1.** A roomy motor vehicle often having between three and five rows of seats. **2.** An enclosed truck or wagon, as for transporting goods or livestock. [< CARAVAN.]

van² (văn) ►*n.* The vanguard.

va·na·di·um (və-nā′dē-əm) ►*n. Symbol* **V** A bright white, soft, ductile metallic element used in some steels and as a catalyst. At. no. 23. See table at **element.** [< ON *Vanadīs,* a goddess.]

Van Allen belt ►*n.* Either of two torus-shaped zones of high-energy ionized particles trapped in Earth's magnetic field and surrounding the planet, extending tens of thousands of kilometers into space. [After J.A. *Van Allen* (1914–2006).]

Van Bu·ren (byŏŏr′ən), **Martin** 1782–1862. The 8th US president (1837–41).

Martin Van Buren

Van·cou·ver (văn-kōō′vər) A city of SW British Columbia, Canada, opposite Vancouver Island.

Vancouver Island An island in the Pacific off SW British Columbia, Canada.

Van·dal (văn′dl) ►*n.* **1. vandal** One who commits vandalism. **2.** A member of a Germanic people that overran Gaul, Spain, and N Africa in the 4th and 5th cent. A.D. and sacked Rome in 455. [Lat. *Vandalus,* of Gmc. orig.]

van·dal·ism (văn′dl-ĭz′əm) ►*n.* Willful or malicious damage or destruction of the property of another. —**van′dal·ize′** *v.*

Van·der·bilt (văn′dər-bĭlt′), **Cornelius** 1794–1877. Amer. financier.

Van·dyke (văn-dīk′) ►*n.* A short pointed beard.

vane (vān) ►*n.* **1.** A weathervane. **2.** A usu. thin rigid surface radially mounted along an axis that is turned by or used to turn a fluid. **3.** A stabilizing fin attached to the tail of a bomb or other missile. [< OE *fana*, flag.]

van Gogh (văn gō′, gôкн′), **Vincent** 1853–90. Dutch painter.

van·guard (văn′gärd) ▸*n.* **1.** Those in the foremost position, as in an army. **2.** Those at the forefront of a trend or movement. [< OFr. *avaunt garde.*]

va·nil·la (və-nĭl′ə) ▸*n.* **1.** A tropical American vine of the orchid family, cultivated for its long narrow seedpods. **2.** The seedpod of this plant. **3.** A flavoring extract prepared from the seedpods of this plant. ▸*adj.* **1.** Flavored with vanilla or vanillin. **2.** Basic, ordinary, or conventional. [Obsolete Sp. *vainilla*, dim. of *vaina*, sheath.]

va·nil·lin (və-nĭl′ĭn, văn′ə-lĭn) ▸*n.* A crystalline compound found in vanilla beans or produced synthetically and used in perfumes, flavorings, and pharmaceuticals.

van·ish (văn′ĭsh) ▸*v.* **1.** To pass out of sight, esp. quickly. See Synonyms at **disappear. 2.** To pass out of existence. [< Lat. *ēvānēscere.*] —**van′ish·er** *n.*

van·i·ty (văn′ĭ-tē) ▸*n., pl.* **-ties 1a.** Excessive pride in one's appearance or accomplishments. See Synonyms at **conceit. b.** Something about which one is vain. **2.** Worthlessness, pointlessness, or futility. **3.** Something vain, futile, or worthless. **4a.** See **vanity case. b.** See **dressing table. c.** A bathroom cabinet that encloses a basin and its water lines and drain, usu. with a cabinet underneath. [< Lat. *vānus*, empty.]

vanity case ▸*n.* **1.** A small handbag or case used for carrying cosmetics or toiletries. **2.** A woman's compact.

vanity plate ▸*n.* A license plate for a motor vehicle bearing a combination of letters or numbers selected by the purchaser.

vanity press ▸*n.* A publisher that publishes a book at the expense of the author.

van·quish (văng′kwĭsh, văn′-) ▸*v.* **1.** To defeat, as in a battle or contest. **2.** To overcome or subdue: *vanquished my fears.* [< Lat. *vincere.*]

van·tage (văn′tĭj) ▸*n.* **1.** An advantage in a competition or conflict. **2.** Something, as a strategic position, that provides superiority. **3.** A position affording a comprehensive view or perspective. [< OFr. *avantage*, ADVANTAGE.]

Van·ua·tu (vän′wä-to͞o′, vä′no͞o-ä′to͞o) Formerly **New Hebrides.** An island country of the S Pacific E of N Australia. Cap. Port Vila. —**Van′ua·tu′an** *adj. & n.*

vap·id (văp′ĭd, vā′pĭd) ▸*adj.* Lacking liveliness, zest, or interest; flat or dull. [Lat. *vapidus.*] —**va·pid′i·ty, vap′id·ness** *n.*

va·por (vā′pər) ▸*n.* **1.** The gaseous state of a substance that is liquid or solid at room temperature. **2.** A faintly visible suspension of fine particles of matter in the air. **3.** *Archaic* Something insubstantial or fleeting. **4. vapors** *Archaic* Depression or hysteria. ▸*v.* **1.** To give off vapor. **2.** To evaporate. [< Lat. *vapor.*]

va·por·ize (vā′pə-rīz′) ▸*v.* **-ized, -iz·ing** To convert or be converted into vapor. —**va′por·i·za′tion** *n.* —**va′por·iz′er** *n.*

va·por·ous (vā′pər-əs) ▸*adj.* **1.** Of or resembling vapor. **2a.** Producing vapors; volatile. **b.** Giving off or full of vapors. **3.** Insubstantial, vague, or ethereal. —**va′por·ous·ness** *n.*

va·pour (vā′pər) ▸*n. & v. Chiefly Brit.* Vapor.

va·que·ro (vä-kâr′ō) ▸*n., pl.* **-ros** *Regional*

See **cowboy.** [Sp. < *vaca*, cow.]

var. ▸*abbr.* **1.** variant **2.** variation **3.** variety

Var·gas Llo·sa (vär′gəs yō′sə), **Mario** b. 1936. Peruvian writer.

var·i·a·ble (vâr′ē-ə-bəl, văr′-) ▸*adj.* **1a.** Likely to vary; changeable. **b.** Inconstant; fickle. **2.** *Biol.* Tending to exhibit genetic variation or variation in a physical trait. ▸*n.* **1.** Something that is variable. **2.** *Math.* **a.** A quantity capable of assuming any of a set of values. **b.** A symbol representing such a quantity. —**var′i·a·bil′i·ty, var′i·a·ble·ness** *n.* —**var′i·a·bly** *adv.*

var·i·ance (vâr′ē-əns, văr′ē-əns) ▸*n.* **1a.** Variation; difference. **b.** The degree of such variation. **2.** A difference of opinion; dispute. **3.** *Law* License to engage in an act contrary to a usual rule.

var·i·ant (vâr′ē-ənt, văr′-) ▸*adj.* Exhibiting variation; differing. ▸*n.* Something exhibiting variation in form from another, as a different spelling of the same word.

var·i·a·tion (vâr′ē-ā′shən, văr′-) ▸*n.* **1.** The act, process, or result of varying. **2.** The extent or degree to which something varies. **3.** Something differing from another of the same type. **4.** *Biol.* The existence of usu. hereditary differences within a species or other group of organisms. **5.** *Mus.* An altered version of a given theme, diverging from it by melodic ornamentation and by changes in harmony, rhythm, or key.

var·i·col·ored (vâr′ĭ-kŭl′ərd, văr′-) ▸*adj.* Having a variety of colors; variegated.

var·i·cose (văr′ĭ-kōs′) ▸*adj.* Abnormally swollen or knotted: *varicose veins.* [< Lat. *varix*, swollen vein.] —**var′i·cos′i·ty** *n.*

var·ied (vâr′ēd, văr′-) ▸*adj.* **1.** Varying; diverse. **2.** Varicolored.

var·i·e·gate (vâr′ē-ĭ-gāt′, vâr′ĭ-gāt′, văr′-) ▸*v.* **-gat·ed, -gat·ing 1.** To change the appearance of, esp. by marking with different colors. **2.** To give variety to. [< LLat. *variegāre* : Lat. *varius*, various + *agere*, do.] —**var′i·e·ga′tion** *n.*

va·ri·e·tal (və-rī′ĭ-tl) ▸*adj.* Of or relating to a variety, esp. a biological variety. ▸*n.* A wine made principally from one variety of grape.

va·ri·e·ty (və-rī′ĭ-tē) ▸*n., pl.* **-ties 1.** The quality or condition of being various. **2.** A number of different things; assortment. **3.** A group that is distinguished from other groups by a specific characteristic or set of characteristics. **4.** *Biol.* A subdivision of a species consisting of a group of individuals that differ from others of the species in certain minor characteristics. [< Lat. *varius*, various.]

variety show ▸*n.* A theatrical entertainment consisting of successive unrelated acts.

variety store ▸*n.* A retail store that carries a variety of usu. inexpensive merchandise.

var·i·o·rum (vâr′ē-ôr′əm, văr′-) ▸*n.* An edition of a written work with notes by various scholars and often with various versions of the text. [< Lat. *(ēditiō cum notīs) variōrum*, (edition with the notes) of various persons.]

var·i·ous (vâr′ē-əs, văr′-) ▸*adj.* **1a.** Of diverse kinds. **b.** Unlike; different. **2.** Being more than one. **3.** Varied in nature or character. [< Lat. *varius.*] —**var′i·ous·ly** *adv.*

var·let (vär′lĭt) ▸*n.* **1.** An attendant or servant. **2.** A rascal; knave. [< OFr.]

var·mint (vär′mĭnt) ▸*n. Informal* A person or

animal considered undesirable or troublesome. [Alteration of VERMIN.]

var·nish (vär′nĭsh) ►*n.* **1a.** A liquid containing a solvent and a binder that is used to give a surface a hard transparent coating. **b.** The smooth coating resulting from the application of this paint. **2.** A deceptively attractive external appearance; gloss. ►*v.* **1.** To cover with varnish. **2.** To gloss: *tried to varnish the truth.* [< OFr. *vernis.*]

var·si·ty (vär′sĭ-tē) ►*n., pl.* **-ties** The main team representing a university, college, or school, as in sports. [Alteration of UNIVERSITY.]

var·y (vâr′ē, văr′ē) ►*v.* **-ied** (-ēd), **-y·ing 1.** To cause or undergo change; modify or alter. **2.** To give variety to; make diverse. **3.** To deviate from a standard or expectation: *behavior that varies from the norm.* [< Lat. *variāre.*]

vas (văs) ►*n., pl.* **va·sa** (vā′zə) *Anat.* A vessel or duct. [Lat. *vās,* vessel.]

Va·sa·ri (və-zär′ē, -sär′ē), **Giorgio** 1511–74. Italian painter, architect, and art historian.

vas·cu·lar (văs′kyə-lər) ►*adj.* Of, characterized by, or containing vessels that carry or circulate fluids, such as blood, lymph, or sap. [< Lat. *vāsculum,* little vessel.]

vas def·er·ens (văs′ dĕf′ər-ənz, -ə-rĕnz′) ►*n.* The duct through which sperm is passed from a testis to the urethra. [NLat., duct that carries away.]

vase (vās, vāz, väz) ►*n.* An open container, as of glass, used for holding flowers or for ornamentation. [< Lat. *vās,* vessel.]

va·sec·to·my (və-sĕk′tə-mē) ►*n., pl.* **-mies** Surgical removal of all or part of the vas deferens, usu. as a means of sterilization.

vaso– or **vas–** ►*pref.* **1.** Blood vessel: *vasoconstriction.* **2.** Vas deferens: *vasectomy.* [< Lat. *vās,* vessel.]

va·so·con·stric·tion (vā′zō-kən-strĭk′shən) ►*n.* Constriction of a blood vessel. —**va′so·con·stric′tor** *n.*

va·so·dil·a·tion (vā′zō-dī-lā′shən, -dĭ-) also **va·so·dil·a·ta·tion** (-dĭl′ə-tā′shən, -dī′lə-) ►*n.* Dilation of a blood vessel. —**va′so·di·la′tor** *n.*

va·so·mo·tor (vā′zō-mō′tər) ►*adj.* Causing or regulating constriction or dilation of blood vessels.

vas·sal (văs′əl) ►*n.* **1.** A person who held land from a feudal lord and received protection in return for homage and allegiance. **2.** A subordinate or dependent. [< VLat. **vassallus,* of Celt. orig.]

vas·sal·age (văs′ə-lĭj) ►*n.* **1.** The condition of being a vassal. **2.** The service, homage, and fealty required of a vassal. **3.** Subordination or subjection; servitude.

vast (văst) ►*adj.* **-er, -est** Very great in size, extent, or quantity. [Lat. *vāstus.*] —**vast′ly** *adv.* —**vast′ness** *n.*

vat (văt) ►*n.* A large vessel, such as a tub, used to hold or store liquids. [< OE *fæt.*]

VAT ►*abbr.* value-added tax

vat·ic (văt′ĭk) ►*adj.* Of or characteristic of a prophet; oracular. [< Lat. *vātēs,* seer.]

Vat·i·can (văt′ĭ-kən) ►*n.* **1.** The official residence of the pope in Vatican City. **2.** The papal government; papacy.

Vatican City An independent papal state on the Tiber River within Rome, Italy.

va·tu (vä′tōō) ►*n.* See table at **currency.** [Indigenous word in Vanuatu.]

vaude·ville (vôd′vĭl′, vôd′-, vô′də-) ►*n.* Stage entertainment offering a variety of short acts such as song-and-dance routines. [< OFr. *vaudevire,* popular song.] —**vaude·vil′lian** *n.*

Vaughan (vôn), **Sarah** 1924–90. Amer. jazz singer.

vault¹ (vôlt) ►*n.* **1.** An arched structure, usu. of masonry, serving to cover a space. **2.** Something resembling a vault. **3.** A room, such as a storeroom, with arched walls and ceiling, esp. when underground. **4.** A room or compartment for the safekeeping of valuables. **5.** A burial chamber. ►*v.* To construct, supply, or cover with a vault. [< VLat. **volvitus,* arched.]

vault² (vôlt) ►*v.* To jump or leap over, esp. with the aid of a support such as the hands or a pole. ►*n.* **1.** The act of vaulting. **2.** A piece of gymnastic equipment with an upholstered body used esp. for vaulting. [< VLat. **volvitāre* < Lat. *volvere,* turn.] —**vault′er** *n.*

vault·ing horse (vôl′tĭng) ►*n.* See **vault²** (sense 2).

vaunt (vônt, vŏnt) ►*v.* To boast; brag. [< LLat. *vānitāre.*] —**vaunt** *n.*

vb. ►*abbr.* verb

V-chip (vē′chĭp′) ►*n.* A computer chip installed in a television to control the display of esp. sexual or violent programs. [V(IEWER) and V(IOLENCE) + CHIP.]

VCR (vē′sē-är′) ►*n.* An electronic device for recording and playing back video images and sound on a videocassette. [V(IDEO)C(ASSETTE) R(ECORDER).]

VD ►*abbr.* venereal disease

veal (vēl) ►*n.* The meat of a calf. [< Lat. *vitellus.*]

Veb·len (vĕb′lən), **Thorstein Bunde** 1857–1929. Amer. economist.

vec·tor (vĕk′tər) ►*n.* **1.** *Math.* A quantity completely specified by a magnitude and a direction. **2.** An organism that carries disease-causing microorganisms from one host to another. [< Lat. *vehere, vect-,* carry.]

vector boson ►*n.* Any of a class of bosons that have one unit of spin, including photons and gluons.

Ve·da (vā′də, vē′-) ►*n. Hinduism* Any of the oldest Hindu sacred texts, composed in Sanskrit. [Skt. *vedaḥ,* knowledge.] —**Ve′dic** *adj.*

Ve·dan·ta (vĭ-dän′tə, -dăn′-) ►*n. Hinduism* The system of philosophy that further develops the implications in the Upanishads that all reality is a single principle. [Skt. *vedāntaḥ* : *vedaḥ,* VEDA + *antaḥ,* completion.] —**Ve·dan′tic** *adj.*

veep (vēp) ►*n. Slang* A vice president. [Pronunciation of *V.P.,* abbr. of *vice president.*]

veer (vîr) ►*v.* To turn aside from a course, direction, or purpose. See Synonyms at **swerve.** [< OFr. *virer.*] —**veer** *n.*

veg (vĕj) ►*v.* **vegged, veg·ging** *Informal* To engage in relaxing or passive activities. Often used with *out.* [< VEGETATE.]

Vega (vā′gə), **Lope de** 1562–1635. Spanish playwright.

ve·gan (vē′gən, vĕj′ən) ►*n.* A vegetarian who eats plant products only. [< VEGETARIAN.]

veg·e·ta·ble (vĕj′tə-bəl, vĕj′ĭ-tə-) ►*n.* **1a.** A usu. herbaceous plant cultivated for an edible part, such as roots, leaves, or flowers. **b.** The edible part of such a plant. **c.** An organism classified as a plant. **2.** *Offensive Slang* One who is severely incapacitated, as by coma. [< LLat. *vegetābilis*, enlivening.] —**veg′e·ta·ble** *adj.*

veg·e·tal (vĕj′ĭ-tl) ►*adj.* **1.** Of or characteristic of plants. **2.** Relating to growth rather than to sexual reproduction; vegetative. [< Lat. *vegetāre*, enliven.]

veg·e·tar·i·an (vĕj′ĭ-târ′ē-ən) ►*n.* One whose diet consists primarily or wholly of plant parts and who eats no meat. —**veg′e·tar′i·an** *adj.* —**veg′e·tar′i·an·ism** *n.*

veg·e·tate (vĕj′ĭ-tāt′) ►*v.* **-tat·ed, -tat·ing 1.** To grow or sprout as a plant. **2.** To be in a state of physical or mental inactivity or insensibility. [Lat. *vegetāre*, enliven.]

veg·e·ta·tion (vĕj′ĭ-tā′shən) ►*n.* **1.** The act or process of vegetating. **2.** The plants of an area or region; plant life.

veg·e·ta·tive (vĕj′ĭ-tā′tĭv) ►*adj.* **1.** Characteristic of plants or their growth. **2.** *Biol.* **a.** Capable of growth. **b.** Functioning in processes such as growth or nutrition rather than sexual reproduction. **c.** Relating to asexual reproduction. **3.** Relating to an impaired level of brain function characterized by response to some stimuli but no cognitive function.

ve·he·ment (vē′ə-mənt) ►*adj.* Characterized by forcefulness of expression or intensity of emotion; fervid. [< Lat. *vehemēns*.] —**ve′he·mence** *n.* —**ve′he·ment·ly** *adv.*

ve·hi·cle (vē′ĭ-kəl) ►*n.* **1.** A device for transporting persons or things; conveyance. **2.** A medium through which something is transmitted, expressed, or accomplished. **3.** A work intended to display the special talents of one performer. **4.** A substance used as the medium in which active ingredients are applied or administered. [Lat. *vehiculum* < *vehere*, carry.] —**ve·hic′u·lar** (vē-hĭk′yə-lər) *adj.*

veil (vāl) ►*n.* **1.** A length of cloth worn over the head, shoulders, and often the face, esp. by women. **2.** The life or vows of a nun: *take the veil.* **3.** Any of various cloth head coverings worn by Muslim women. **4.** A piece of fabric hung to separate or conceal something. **5.** Something that conceals or obscures: *a veil of secrecy.* ►*v.* To cover, conceal, or disguise with or as if with a veil. [< Lat. *vēla*.]

vein (vān) ►*n.* **1.** A vessel through which blood returns to the heart. **2.** One of the branching structures forming the framework of a leaf or an insect's wing. **3.** *Geol.* A long, regularly shaped deposit of an ore; lode. **4.** A long wavy strip of color, as in marble. **5.** A particular turn of mind: *spoke in a serious vein.* ►*v.* To mark, form, or decorate with veins. [< Lat. *vēna*.] —**veined** *adj.*

ve·lar (vē′lər) ►*adj.* **1.** Of a velum, esp. the soft palate. **2.** *Ling.* Articulated with the back of the tongue touching or near the soft palate.

Ve·láz·quez (və-läs′kĕs), **Diego Rodríguez de Silva y** 1599–1660. Spanish painter.

Vel·cro (vĕl′krō) A trademark for a fastening tape used esp. on cloth products.

veld also **veldt** (vĕlt, fĕlt) ►*n.* Any of the open grazing areas of S Africa. [Afr.]

vel·lum (vĕl′əm) ►*n.* **1.** A fine parchment made from calfskin, lambskin, or kidskin and used in making books. **2.** A paper resembling vellum. [< OFr. *velin*.]

ve·loc·i·rap·tor (və-lŏs′ə-răp′tər) ►*n.* A small carnivorous dinosaur having sickle-shaped talons and a long flat snout with sharp teeth. [NLat. *Vēlōciraptor*, genus name : Lat. *vēlōx*, *vē:lōc-*, fast + *raptor*, one who seizes; see RAPTOR.]

ve·loc·i·ty (və-lŏs′ĭ-tē) ►*n., pl.* **-ties 1.** Rapidity of motion; speed. **2.** *Phys.* The combination of a moving body's speed and direction. [< Lat. *vēlōx*, fast.]

ve·lour or **ve·lours** (və-lŏor′) ►*n., pl.* **-lours** (-lŏorz′) A closely napped fabric resembling velvet. [< Lat. *villōsus*, hairy.]

ve·lum (vē′ləm) ►*n., pl.* **-la** (-lə) **1.** A covering or partition of thin membranous tissue. **2.** The soft palate. [Lat., veil.]

vel·vet (vĕl′vĭt) ►*n.* **1.** A soft fabric having a smooth dense pile and a plain underside. **2.** Something suggesting the smooth surface of velvet. **3.** The soft furry covering on the developing antlers of deer. [< VLat. *villūtittus*.] —**vel′vet·y** *adj.*

vel·vet·een (vĕl′vĭ-tēn′) ►*n.* A cotton pile fabric resembling velvet. [< VELVET.]

Ven. ►*abbr.* venerable

ve·na ca·va (vē′nə kā′və) ►*n., pl.* **ve·nae ca·vae** (vē′nē kā′vē) Either of two large veins that empty into the right atrium of the heart. [Lat. *vēna*, vein + *cava*, hollow.]

ve·nal (vē′nəl) ►*adj.* Open to, marked by, or susceptible to bribery; corrupt or corruptible. [< Lat. *vēnum*, sale.] —**ve·nal′i·ty** (-năl′ĭ-tē) *n.* —**ve′nal·ly** *adv.*

ve·na·tion (vē-nā′shən, vĕ-) ►*n.* Distribution or arrangement of veins. [< Lat. *vēna*, vein.]

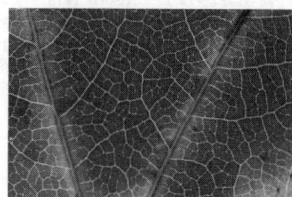

venation
of a sweet gum leaf

vend (vĕnd) ►*v.* To sell, esp. by peddling. [Lat. *vēndere* : *vēnum*, sale + *dare*, give.]

ven·det·ta (vĕn-dĕt′ə) ►*n.* **1.** A bitter feud, esp. between two families. **2.** A series of acts attacking or attempting to injure another. [Ital.]

vend·ing machine (vĕn′dĭng) ►*n.* A self-service machine that dispenses merchandise after payment is made.

ven·dor or **vend·er** (vĕn′dər) ►*n.* **1.** One that sells or vends. **2.** One that provides products or services to a business for a fee.

ve·neer (və-nîr′) ►*n.* **1.** A thin surface layer, as of finely grained wood, glued to a base of inferior material. **2.** A surface show; façade. ►*v.* To overlay with a veneer. [< Ger. *furnieren*, furnish.]

ven·er·a·ble (vĕn′ər-ə-bəl) ►*adj.* **1.** Commanding respect by virtue of age or position. **2.** Worthy of reverence, as by religious association. —**ven′er·a·bil′i·ty** *n.*

ven·er·ate (vĕn′ə-rāt′) ►*v.* To regard with deep respect or reverence. [Lat. *venerārī*.] —**ven′er·a′tion** *n.*

ve·ne·re·al (və-nîr′ē-əl) ►*adj.* Transmitted by

sexual intercourse. [< Lat. *venus, vener-*, love.]

ve·ne·re·al disease ►*n.* A sexually transmitted disease.

ve·ne·tian blind or **Ve·ne·tian blind** (və-nē′-shən) ►*n.* A window blind consisting of thin horizontal adjustable slats that overlap when closed. [< *Venetian*, of Venice.]

Ven·e·zue·la (věn′ə-zwā′lə) A country of N South America on the Caribbean Sea. Cap. Caracas. —**Ven′e·zue′lan** *adj. & n.*

ven·geance (věn′jəns) ►*n.* Infliction of punishment in return for a wrong committed; retribution. —*idiom:* **with a vengeance** To an extreme degree: *December has turned cold with a vengeance.* [< OFr. *vengier*, AVENGE.]

venge·ful (věnj′fəl) ►*adj.* Desiring vengeance; vindictive. —**venge′ful·ly** *adv.* —**venge′ful·ness** *n.*

ve·ni·al (vē′nē-əl, věn′yəl) ►*adj.* Easily excused or forgiven; pardonable; minor: *a venial sin.* [< Lat. *venia*, forgiveness.]

Ven·ice (věn′ĭs) A city of NE Italy on islets within a lagoon in the **Gulf of Venice**, an inlet of the N Adriatic. —**Ve·ne′tian** (və-nē′-shən) *n. & adj.*

ven·i·son (věn′ĭ-sən, -zən) ►*n.* The flesh of a deer used as food. [< Lat. *vēnātiō*, hunting.]

ven·om (věn′əm) ►*n.* **1.** A poisonous secretion of an animal, such as a snake or spider, usu. transmitted by a bite or sting. **2.** Malice; spite. [< Lat. *venēnum*, poison.]

ven·om·ous (věn′ə-məs) ►*adj.* **1.** Secreting venom: *a venomous snake.* **2.** Full of venom. **3.** Malicious; spiteful.

ve·nous (vē′nəs) ►*adj.* **1.** Of or relating to veins. **2.** Having numerous veins. [< Lat. *vēna*, vein.]

vent¹ (věnt) ►*n.* **1.** An opening permitting escape, as of fumes or a gas. **2.** A means of escape; outlet. ►*v.* **1.** To give expression to. **2.** To discharge through an opening. **3.** To provide with a vent. [< OFr. *vent* and *esvent*.]

vent² (věnt) ►*n.* A slit in a garment, as in the seam of a jacket. [< OFr. *fente*, slit.]

ven·ti·late (věn′tl-āt′) ►*v.* **-lat·ed, -lat·ing 1.** To admit or force fresh air into to replace stale or noxious air. **2.** To circulate through and freshen. **3.** To expose to public discussion or examination. **4.** To inhale and exhale; breathe. **5.** To keep (one) breathing by artificial means. [< Lat. *ventulus*, breeze.] —**ven′ti·la′tion** *n.* —**ven′ti·la′tor** *n.*

ven·tral (věn′trəl) ►*adj.* **1.** Of or relating to the abdomen; abdominal. **2.** Of or situated on or close to the front of the human body or the lower surface of the body of an animal. [< Lat. *venter*, belly.]

ven·tri·cle (věn′trĭ-kəl) ►*n.* A cavity or chamber within a body or an organ, esp.: **a.** Either of the chambers of the heart that contract to pump blood into arteries. **b.** Any of the interconnecting cavities of the brain. [< Lat. *ventriculus*.] —**ven·tric′u·lar** (-trĭk′yə-lər) *adj.*

ven·tril·o·quism (věn-trĭl′ə-kwĭz′əm) also **ven·tril·o·quy** (-kwē) ►*n.* The art of projecting one's voice so that it seems to come from another source. [< Lat. *ventriloquus*, speaking from the belly.] —**ven·tril′o·quist** *n.*

ven·ture (věn′chər) ►*n.* **1.** An undertaking that is dangerous or of uncertain outcome. **2.** Something, such as money, at hazard in a risky enterprise. ►*v.* **-tured, -tur·ing 1.** To expose to danger or risk. **2.** To brave the dangers of. **3.** To express at the risk of denial, criticism, or censure. **4.** To take a risk; dare. [< ME *aventure*, ADVENTURE.]

ven·ture·some (věn′chər-səm) ►*adj.* **1.** Disposed to venture or to take risks. See Synonyms at **adventurous. 2.** Risky; hazardous.

ven·tur·ous (věn′chər-əs) ►*adj.* Venturesome.

ven·ue (věn′yōō) ►*n.* **1.** A place where a gathering is held. **2a.** The locality from which a jury is called and in which a trial is held. **b.** The locality where a crime is committed. [< OFr., a coming < Lat. *venīre*, come.]

Ve·nus (vē′nəs) ►*n.* **1.** *Rom. Myth.* The goddess of love and beauty. **2.** The 2nd planet from the sun, at a mean distance of approx. 108.2 million km (67.2 million mi) and with an average radius of 6,052 km (3,761 mi). —**Ve·nu′sian** (vĭ-nōō′zhən, -nyōō′-) *adj.*

Venus fly·trap (flī′trăp′) ►*n.* An insectivorous plant of the coastal Carolinas, having hinged leaf blades that close and entrap insects.

ver. ►*abbr.* **1.** verse **2.** version

ve·ra·cious (və-rā′shəs) ►*adj.* **1.** Honest; truthful. **2.** Accurate; true. [< Lat. *vērāx*.]

ve·rac·i·ty (və-răs′ĭ-tē) ►*n., pl.* **-ties 1.** Adherence to the truth; truthfulness. **2.** Conformity to fact or truth; accuracy. **3.** Something that is true. [< Lat. *vērāx*, true.]

ve·ran·da or **ve·ran·dah** (və-răn′də) ►*n.* A usu. roofed porch or balcony extending along the outside of a building. [Hindi *varaṇḍā*.]

verb (vûrb) ►*n.* The part of speech that expresses existence, action, or occurrence in most languages. [< Lat. *verbum*, word.]

ver·bal (vûr′bəl) ►*adj.* **1.** Of or associated with words. **2.** Concerned with words only rather than with content or ideas. **3.** Spoken rather than written; oral: *a verbal contract.* **4.** Word for word; literal. **5.** Of or derived from a verb. ►*n.* A noun or adjective derived from a verb. [< Lat. *verbum*, word.] —**ver′bal·ly** *adv.*

Usage: Because *verbal* can mean both "concerned with words" and "spoken rather than written," care must be given to avoid ambiguity. The phrase *modern technologies for verbal communication* may refer to devices such as radio and the telephone or to devices such as the telegraph and fax machine. In such contexts the word *oral* is available to convey the narrower sense of communication by spoken means.

ver·bal·ize (vûr′bə-līz′) ►*v.* **-ized, -iz·ing 1.** To express in words. **2.** To convert to use as a verb. —**ver′bal·i·za′tion** *n.*

ver·ba·tim (vər-bā′tĭm) ►*adv. & adj.* In the same words; word for word. [< Med.Lat.]

ver·be·na (vər-bē′nə) ►*n.* Any of various plants cultivated for their showy spikes of variously colored flowers. [Lat. *verbēna*, sacred bough.]

ver·bi·age (vûr′bē-ĭj, -bĭj) ►*n.* **1.** An excess of words for the purpose; wordiness. **2.** Wording; diction. [< OFr. *verbier*, chatter.]

ver·bose (vər-bōs′) ►*adj.* Using more words than is necessary; wordy. See Synonyms at **wordy.** [< Lat. *verbum*, word.] —**ver·bos′i·ty** (-bŏs′ĭ-tē) *n.*

ver·bo·ten (vər-bōt′n, fĕr-) ►*adj.* Forbidden; prohibited. [Ger.]

ver·dant (vûr′dnt) ►*adj.* **1.** Green with vegetation. **2.** Of a green color. [< OFr. *verdoyer*, become green.] —**ver′dan·cy** *n.*

Verde (vûrd), **Cape** A peninsula of W Senegal projecting into the Atlantic; westernmost point of Africa.

Ver·di (vâr′dē), **Giuseppe** 1813–1901. Italian composer.

ver·dict (vûr′dĭkt) ►*n.* **1.** The finding of a jury in a trial. **2.** A judgment; conclusion. [< AN *verdit.*]

ver·di·gris (vûr′dĭ-grēs′, -grĭs′, -grē′) ►*n.* A green patina formed on copper, brass, and bronze after long exposure to air or seawater. [< OFr. *vert-de-Grice,* green of Greece.]

ver·dure (vûr′jər) ►*n.* **1.** The lush greenness of flourishing vegetation. **2.** Vigorous greenery. [< OFr. < *verd,* green.]

verge¹ (vûrj) ►*n.* **1.** An edge, rim, or margin. **2.** The point beyond which an action or a condition is likely to begin or occur; brink. **3.** A rod or staff carried as an emblem of authority or office. ►*v.* **verged, verg·ing** To border on; approach. [< Lat. *virga,* rod.]

verge² (vûrj) ►*v.* **verged, verg·ing 1.** To slope or incline. **2.** To pass or merge gradually. [Lat. *vergere.*]

verg·er (vûr′jər) ►*n. Chiefly Brit.* **1.** One who carries a verge, as before a religious dignitary in a procession. **2.** One who takes care of the interior of a church.

Ver·gil (vûr′jəl) See **Virgil.**

ver·i·fy (vĕr′ə-fī′) ►*v.* **-fied** (-fīd′), **-fy·ing 1.** To prove the truth of; substantiate. **2.** To determine or test the truth or accuracy of. [< Med. Lat. *vērificāre.*] —**ver′i·fi′a·ble** *adj.* —**ver′i·fi·ca′tion** *n.* —**ver′i·fi′er** *n.*

ver·i·ly (vĕr′ə-lē) ►*adv.* **1.** In truth; in fact. **2.** Surely; assuredly. [< ME *verrai,* true; see VERY.]

ver·i·si·mil·i·tude (vĕr′ə-sĭ-mĭl′ĭ-tōōd′, -tyōōd′) ►*n.* **1.** The quality of appearing to be true or real. **2.** Something that appears to be true or real. [< Lat. *vērīsimilis,* appearing to be true.]

ver·i·ta·ble (vĕr′ĭ-tə-bəl) ►*adj.* Being truly so called; real or genuine. [< OFr. *verite,* VERITY.] —**ver′i·ta·bly** *adv.*

ver·i·ty (vĕr′ĭ-tē) ►*n., pl.* **-ties 1.** The quality or condition of being true, factual, or real. **2.** Something, such as a statement or belief, that is true. [< Lat. *vērus,* true.]

Ver·meer (vər-mîr′, -mâr′), **Jan** 1632–75. Dutch painter.

ver·meil (vûr′məl, -māl′) ►*n.* **1.** Vermilion. **2.** (vĕr-mā′) Gilded silver, bronze, or copper. [< OFr. *vermeil.*]

ver·mi·cel·li (vûr′mĭ-chĕl′ē, -sĕl′ē) ►*n.* Pasta in long, very thin strands. [Ital.]

ver·mic·u·lite (vər-mĭk′yə-līt′) ►*n.* Any of a group of minerals resembling mica and used in heat-expanded form esp. as insulation or as a planting medium. [Lat. *vermiculus,* little worm + -ITE¹.]

ver·mi·form (vûr′mə-fôrm′) ►*adj.* Shaped like a worm. [< Lat. *vermis,* worm.]

vermiform appendix ►*n.* A narrow vestigial organ that projects from the cecum.

ver·mi·fuge (vûr′mə-fyōōj′) ►*n.* A medicine that expels intestinal worms. [Lat. *vermis,* worm + *fugāre,* drive out.]

ver·mil·ion also **ver·mil·lion** (vər-mĭl′yən) ►*n.* **1.** A vivid red. **2.** A bright red pigment. [< OFr. *vermeillon < vermeil.*] —**ver·mil′ion** *adj.*

ver·min (vûr′mĭn) ►*pl.n.* Various small animals, such as rats or cockroaches, that are destruc-tive, annoying, or injurious to health. [< Lat. *vermis,* worm.] —**ver′min·ous** *adj.*

Ver·mont (vər-mŏnt′) A state of the NE US bordering on Canada. Cap. Montpelier. —**Ver·mont′er** *n.*

ver·mouth (vər-mōōth′) ►*n.* A fortified wine flavored with aromatic herbs. [< Ger. *Wermut.*]

ver·nac·u·lar (vər-năk′yə-lər) ►*n.* **1.** The everyday language spoken by a people as distinguished from the literary language. **2.** A jargon: *the legal vernacular.* [< Lat. *vernāculus,* native.] —**ver·nac′u·lar** *adj.*

ver·nal (vûr′nəl) ►*adj.* Of or occurring in the spring. [Lat. *vērnālis.*] —**ver′nal·ly** *adv.*

Verne (vûrn, vĕrn), **Jules Gabriel** 1828–1905. French writer.

ver·ni·er (vûr′nē-ər) ►*n.* A small scale attached to a main scale, calibrated to indicate fractional parts of the subdivisions of the larger scale. [After Pierre *Vernier* (1580?–1637).]

Ve·ro·na (və-rō′nə) A city of N Italy W of Venice. —**Ve′ro·nese′** (vĕr′ə-nēz′, -nēs′) *adj. & n.*

Ver·sailles (vər-sī′, vĕr-) A city of N-central France WSW of Paris; site of a palace built by Louis XIV.

ver·sa·tile (vûr′sə-təl, -tīl′) ►*adj.* **1.** Capable of doing many things competently. **2.** Having varied uses or functions. [< Lat. *versāre,* turn.] —**ver′sa·til′i·ty** (-tĭl′ĭ-tē) *n.*

verse (vûrs) ►*n.* **1.** Writing arranged according to a metrical pattern; poetry. **2a.** One line of poetry. **b.** A stanza. **3.** A specific type of metrical composition, such as blank verse. **4.** One of the numbered subdivisions of a chapter in the Bible. [< Lat. *vertere,* turn.]

versed (vûrst) ►*adj.* Practiced or skilled; knowledgeable.

ver·si·fy (vûr′sə-fī′) ►*v.* **-fied, -fy·ing 1.** To change from prose into verse. **2.** To write verses. —**ver′si·fi·ca′tion** *n.* —**ver′si·fi′er** *n.*

ver·sion (vûr′zhən, -shən) ►*n.* **1.** A description or account from one point of view. **2.** A translation, esp. of the Bible or of a part of it. **3.** A form or variation of an earlier or original type. **4.** An adaptation of a work of art or literature into another medium or style. [< Lat. *vertere,* vers-, turn.]

vers li·bre (vĕr lē′brə) ►*n.* Free verse. [Fr.]

ver·so (vûr′sō) ►*n., pl.* **-sos 1.** A left-hand page. **2.** The back of a coin or medal. [NLat. *versō (foliō),* (with the page) turned.]

ver·sus (vûr′səs, -səz) ►*prep.* **1.** Against: *the plaintiff versus the defendant.* **2.** In contrast with: *death versus dishonor.* [< Lat., turned.]

ver·te·bra (vûr′tə-brə) ►*n., pl.* **-brae** (-brā′, -brē′) or **-bras** Any of the bones or cartilaginous segments forming the spinal column. [< Lat.] —**ver′te·bral** *adj.*

ver·te·brate (vûr′tə-brĭt, -brāt′) ►*adj.* **1.** Having a backbone or spinal column. **2.** Of the vertebrates. ►*n.* Any of a group of animals, including the fishes, amphibians, reptiles, birds, and mammals, having a segmented spinal column.

ver·tex (vûr′tĕks′) ►*n., pl.* **-ti·ces** (-tĭ-sēz′) or **-tex·es 1.** The highest point; apex or summit. **2a.** The point at which the sides of an angle intersect. **b.** The point on a triangle opposite to and farthest away from its base. **c.** A point on a polyhedron common to three or more sides. [Lat. < *vertere,* turn.]

ver·ti·cal (vûr′tĭ-kəl) ▸*adj.* **1.** Being or situated at right angles to the horizon; upright. **2.** Situated at the vertex or highest point; directly overhead. ▸*n.* **1.** Something vertical, as a line. **2.** A vertical position. [< Lat. *vertex*, VERTEX.] —**ver′ti·cal·ly** *adv.*

ver·tig·i·nous (vər-tĭj′ə-nəs) ▸*adj.* **1.** Turning about an axis. **2.** Affected by vertigo. **3.** Tending to produce vertigo; dizzying. [< Lat. *vertīgō*, vertigo.]

ver·ti·go (vûr′tĭ-gō′) ▸*n., pl.* **-goes** or **-gos** The sensation of dizziness. [< Lat. *vertīgō*.]

ver·vain (vûr′vān′) ▸*n.* See **verbena.** [< Lat. *verbēna*, sacred foliage.]

verve (vûrv) ▸*n.* **1.** Energy and enthusiasm, as in artistic performance or composition. **2.** Vitality; liveliness. See Synonyms at **vigor.** [< OFr., fanciful expression.]

ver·y (vĕr′ē) ▸*adv.* **1.** In a high degree; extremely: *very happy.* **2.** Truly; absolutely: *the very best advice.* ▸*adj.* **-i·er, -i·est 1.** Complete; absolute: *the very end.* **2.** Identical; selfsame: *the very question she asked yesterday.* **3.** Used for emphasis: *the very mountains shook.* **4.** Precise; exact: *the very center of town.* **5.** Mere: *The very thought is frightening.* [< OFr. *verai*, true < Lat. *vērus.*]

very high frequency ▸*n.* A band of radio frequencies between 30 and 300 megahertz.

very low frequency ▸*n.* A band of radio frequencies between 3 and 30 kilohertz.

ves·i·cant (vĕs′ĭ-kənt) ▸*n.* A blistering agent, esp. mustard gas. [< Lat. *vēsīca*, blister.] —**ves′i·cant** *adj.*

ves·i·cle (vĕs′ĭ-kəl) ▸*n.* **1.** A small bladderlike cell or cavity. **2.** A blister. [< Lat. *vēsīcula.*] —**ve·sic′u·lar** (vĕ-sĭk′yə-lər, və-) *adj.*

Ves·pa·sian (vĕs-pā′zhən, -zhē-ən) AD 9–79. Emperor of Rome (69–79).

ves·per (vĕs′pər) ▸*n.* **1.** A bell that summons worshipers to vespers. **2.** *Archaic* Evening. [< Lat., evening.]

ves·pers (vĕs′pərz) ▸*pl.n.* (*takes sing. or pl. v.*) A worship service held in the late afternoon or evening. [< Lat. *vespera*, evening.]

ves·per·tine (vĕs′pər-tīn′) ▸*adj.* **1.** Of or occurring in the evening. **2.** *Bot.* Opening or blooming in the evening. [< Lat. *vesper*, evening.]

Ves·puc·ci (vĕs-pōō′chē, -pyōō′-), **Amerigo** 1454–1512. Italian explorer.

Amerigo Vespucci

ves·sel (vĕs′əl) ▸*n.* **1.** A hollow container, as a cup, vase, or pitcher; receptacle. **2.** A ship, large boat, or similar craft. **3.** *Anat.* A duct or other

narrow tube that contains or conveys a body fluid. **4.** A person seen as the agent or embodiment, as of a quality. [< Lat. *vāsculum.*]

vest (vĕst) ▸*n.* **1.** A sleeveless garment, often having buttons down the front, worn over a shirt or as part of a three-piece suit. **2.** A waistlength, sleeveless garment worn for protection: *a bulletproof vest; a down vest.* **3.** *Chiefly Brit.* An undershirt. ▸*v.* **1.** To place in the control of a person or group: *vested his estate in his son.* **2.** To invest with power or rights: *vested the council with broad powers.* **3.** To clothe, as in ecclesiastical vestments. [< Lat. *vestis*, garment.]

Ves·ta (vĕs′tə) ▸*n. Rom. Myth.* The goddess of the hearth.

ves·tal (vĕs′təl) ▸*adj.* Chaste; pure. ▸*n.* A woman who is a virgin. [< VESTA.]

vestal virgin ▸*n.* One of the celibate priestesses who tended the sacred fire in the temple of Vesta in ancient Rome.

vest·ed interest (vĕs′tĭd) ▸*n.* **1.** A special interest in protecting or promoting that which is to one's own personal advantage. **2.** A group that has a vested interest.

ves·ti·bule (vĕs′tə-byōōl′) ▸*n.* **1.** A small entrance hall or lobby. **2.** An enclosed area at the end of a passenger car on a train. **3.** *Anat.* A cavity, chamber, or channel that leads to another cavity. [Lat. *vestibulum.*]

ves·tige (vĕs′tĭj) ▸*n.* **1.** A visible trace, evidence, or sign of something that no longer exists or appears. **2.** A remnant. [< Lat. *vestigium.*]

ves·tig·i·al (vĕ-stĭj′ē-əl, -stĭj′əl) ▸*adj.* **1.** Of or constituting a vestige. **2.** *Biol.* Occurring or persisting as a rudimentary or degenerate structure. —**ves·tig′i·al·ly** *adv.*

vest·ment (vĕst′mənt) ▸*n.* **1.** A garment, esp. a robe or gown worn as an indication of office. **2.** Any of the ritual robes worn by the clergy at ecclesiastical services or rites. [< Lat. *vestis*, garment.]

vest-pock·et (vĕst′pŏk′ĭt) ▸*adj.* Small.

ves·try (vĕs′trē) ▸*n., pl.* **-tries 1.** A sacristy. **2.** A meeting room in a church. **3.** A committee elected to administer the temporal affairs of a parish. [< Lat. *vestis*, garment.]

ves·try·man (vĕs′trē-mən) ▸*n.* A man who is a member of a vestry.

ves·ture (vĕs′chər) ▸*n.* Clothing; apparel. [< *vestīre*, clothe.]

Ve·su·vi·us (vĭ-sōō′vē-əs), **Mount** An active volcano, 1,281 m (4,203 ft), of S Italy on the E shore of the Bay of Naples. —**Ve·su′vi·an** *adj.*

vet¹ (vĕt) ▸*n. Informal* A veterinarian. ▸*v.* **vet·ted, vet·ting 1.** To subject to veterinary examination or treatment. **2.** To subject to thorough examination or evaluation: *vetted the manuscript.*

vet² (vĕt) ▸*n. Informal* A veteran.

vetch (vĕch) ▸*n.* A plant having featherlike leaves that end in tendrils and small, variously colored flowers. [< Lat. *vicia.*]

vet·er·an (vĕt′ər-ən, vĕt′rən) ▸*n.* **1.** A person who has served in the armed forces. **2.** A person of long experience in an activity or capacity. [Lat. *veterānus* < *vetus*, old.]

Vet·er·ans Day (vĕt′ər-ənz, vĕt′rənz) ▸*n.* November 11, observed in the US in honor of veterans of the armed services and in commemoration of the armistice that ended World War I in 1918.

vet·er·i·nar·i·an (vĕt′ər-ə-nâr′ē-ən, vĕt′rə-) ►*n.* A person who practices veterinary medicine.
vet·er·i·nar·y (vĕt′ər-ə-nĕr′ē, vĕt′rə-) ►*adj.* Of the medical or surgical treatment of animals. ►*n., pl.* **-ies** A veterinarian. [< Lat. *veterīnae,* beasts of burden.]
ve·to (vē′tō) ►*n., pl.* **-toes 1a.** The constitutional power of the chief executive of a state or nation to prevent or delay the enactment of legislation passed by the legislature. **b.** Exercise of this right. **2a.** Authority to prohibit or reject a proposed or intended act. **b.** Exercise of this authority. ►*v.* **-toed, -to·ing 1.** To prevent (a legislative bill) from becoming law by exercising the power of veto. **2.** To forbid or prohibit authoritatively. [< Lat. *vetō,* I forbid.]
vex (vĕks) ►*v.* **1.** To annoy; bother. See Synonyms at **annoy. 2.** To cause perplexity in; puzzle. **3.** To debate at length. [< Lat. *vexāre.*]
vex·a·tion (vĕk-sā′shən) ►*n.* **1.** The condition of being vexed; annoyance. **2.** One that vexes. —**vex·a′tious** *adj.*
VFW ►*abbr.* Veterans of Foreign Wars
VGA ►*abbr.* video graphics array
VHF ►*abbr.* very high frequency
VHS (vē′āch-ĕs′) A trademark for a videotape format.
VI ►*abbr.* Virgin Islands
vi·a (vī′ə, vē′ə) ►*prep.* By way of. [< Lat. *via,* road.]
vi·a·ble (vī′ə-bəl) ►*adj.* **1.** Feasible; practicable: *a viable plan.* **2.** Capable of living or developing under favorable conditions: *viable seeds.* **3.** Capable of living outside the uterus: *a viable fetus.* [< OFr. *vie,* life < Lat. *vīta.*] —**vi′a·bil′i·ty** *n.*
vi·a·duct (vī′ə-dŭkt′) ►*n.* A series of spans or arches used to carry a road or railroad over something, such as a valley or road. [Lat. *via,* road + (AQUE)DUCT.]

viaduct
train crossing the Landwasser viaduct in Switzerland

vi·al (vī′əl) ►*n.* A small container, esp. for liquids. [< ME *fiol,* PHIAL.]
vi·and (vī′ənd) ►*n.* **1.** An item of food. **2. viands** Provisions; victuals. [Ult. < *vīvere,* live.]
vi·at·i·cum (vī-ăt′ĭ-kəm, vē-) ►*n., pl.* **-ca** (-kə) or **-cums** The Eucharist given to a dying person or one in danger of death. [< Lat. *viāticum,* traveling provisions.]
vibe (vīb) ►*n. Slang* A distinctive emotional quality or atmosphere: *a café with a funky vibe.* [Short for *vibration.*]

vi·brant (vī′brənt) ►*adj.* **1.** Full of vigor or energy. **2.** Produced as a result of vibration; vibrating. **3.** Brightly colored. —**vi′bran·cy** *n.* —**vi′brant·ly** *adv.*
vi·bra·phone (vī′brə-fōn′) ►*n. Mus.* An instrument similar to a marimba but having metal bars and rotating disks in the resonators to produce a vibrato. [Lat. *vibrāre,* shake + –PHONE.] —**vi′bra·phon′ist** *n.*
vi·brate (vī′brāt′) ►*v.* **-brat·ed, -brat·ing 1.** To move or cause to move back and forth rapidly. **2.** To feel a quiver of emotion. **3.** To shake or tremble. **4.** To produce a sound; resonate. [Lat. *vibrāre.*] —**vi′bra′tor** *n.* —**vi′bra·to′ry** (-brə-tôr′ē) *adj.*
vi·bra·tion (vī-brā′shən) ►*n.* **1a.** The act of vibrating. **b.** The condition of being vibrated. **2.** *Phys.* A rapid linear motion of a particle or of an elastic solid about an equilibrium position. **3.** A single complete vibrating motion. **4. vibrations** *Slang* A distinctive emotional aura or atmosphere that is instinctively sensed or experienced.
vi·bra·to (və-brä′tō, vĭ-) ►*n., pl.* **-tos** *Mus.* A tremulous or pulsating effect produced in an instrumental or vocal tone by slight rapid variations in pitch. [Ital.]
vi·bur·num (vī-bûr′nəm) ►*n.* Any of various shrubs or trees having clusters of small white or pink flowers and berrylike red or black fruit. [Lat. *vīburnum.*]
vic·ar (vĭk′ər) ►*n.* **1.** An Anglican parish priest who is not entitled to the tithes of the parish. **2.** *Rom. Cath. Ch.* A priest who acts for another. [< Lat. *vicārius,* a substitute.]
vic·ar·age (vĭk′ər-ĭj) ►*n.* The residence or benefice of a vicar.
vi·car·i·ous (vī-kâr′ē-əs, -kăr′-, vĭ-) ►*adj.* **1.** Felt or undergone as if one were taking part in the experience or feelings of another. **2.** Endured or done by one person substituting for another. **3.** Acting for another. [< Lat. *vicārius,* substitute.] —**vi·car′i·ous·ly** *adv.* —**vi·car′i·ous·ness** *n.*
vice[1] (vīs) ►*n.* **1a.** A habit considered evil, degrading, or immoral. **b.** Wicked or depraved conduct. **2.** Prostitution, the sale of illegal drugs, and certain other forms of usu. nonviolent criminal behavior. **3a.** A personal failing; shortcoming. **b.** A defect; flaw. [< Lat. *vitium.*]
vice[2] (vīs) ►*n.* Var. of **vise.**
vice– ►*pref.* One who acts in the place of another: *vice-chairman.* [Lat. *vice,* in place of.]
vice admiral (vīs) ►*n.* A rank, as in the US Navy, above rear admiral and below admiral.
vice president ►*n.* **1.** An officer ranking next below a president, usu. empowered to assume the president's duties under conditions such as absence, illness, or death. **2.** A deputy to a president, esp. in a corporation, in charge of a specific department. —**vice-pres′i·den·cy** *n.*
vice·re·gal (vīs-rē′gəl) ►*adj.* Of a viceroy.
vice·roy (vīs′roi′) ►*n.* The governor of a country, province, or colony, ruling as the representative of a sovereign. [Fr.] —**vice′roy′al·ty** *n.*
vi·ce ver·sa (vī′sə vûr′sə, vīs′) ►*adv.* With the order or meaning reversed; conversely. [Lat. *vice versā,* the position being reversed.]
vi·chys·soise (vĭsh′ē-swäz′, vē′shē-) ►*n.* A thick creamy potato soup. [Fr. < *Vichy,* a city of central France.]
vi·cin·i·ty (vĭ-sĭn′ĭ-tē) ►*n., pl.* **-ties 1.** A nearby

or surrounding area; neighborhood. **2.** Nearness; proximity. **3.** An approximate degree or amount. [< Lat. *vīcīnus*, neighboring.]

vi·cious (vĭsh′əs) ▸*adj.* **1.** Mean-spirited or deliberately hurtful. **2.** Savage and dangerous. **3.** Violent; intense. **4.** Marked by a tendency to worsen: *a vicious circle.* [< Lat. *vitium*, evil.] —**vi′cious·ly** *adv.* —**vi′cious·ness** *n.*

vi·cis·si·tude (vĭ-sĭs′ĭ-tōōd′, -tyōōd′) ▸*n.* **1.** A change or variation: *the vicissitudes of the oil market.* **2.** A usu. unforeseen change in circumstance or experience that affects one's life. See Synonyms at **difficulty. 3.** The quality of being changeable; mutability. [< Lat. *vicissim*, in turn.]

vic·tim (vĭk′tĭm) ▸*n.* **1.** One who is harmed or killed by another: *the murderer's victims.* **2.** One who is harmed by a circumstance or condition: *victims of poverty.* **3.** One who is tricked, swindled, or injured. [Lat. *victima.*]

vic·tim·ize (vĭk′tə-mīz′) ▸*v.* **-ized, -iz·ing** To make a victim of. —**vic′tim·i·za′tion** *n.* —**vic′tim·iz′er** *n.*

vic·tim·less crime (vĭk′tĭm-lĭs) ▸*n.* An illegal act having no direct victim.

vic·tor (vĭk′tər) ▸*n.* The winner in a fight, battle, contest, or struggle. [< Lat.]

Victor Em·man·u·el II (ĭ-măn′yōō-əl) 1820–78. King of Sardinia (1849–61) and Italy (1861–78).

vic·to·ri·a (vĭk-tôr′ē-ə) ▸*n.* A low, four-wheeled carriage for two with a folding top and an elevated driver's seat in front. [After VICTORIA[1].]

Victoria[1] 1819–1901. Queen of Great Britain and Ireland (1837–1901) and empress of India (1877–1901).

Victoria[1]

Victoria[2] **1.** The capital of British Columbia, Canada, on SE Vancouver I. **2.** The capital of Seychelles, on the NE coast of Mahé I.

Victoria, Lake Also **Victoria Ny·an·za** (nī-ăn′zə, nyän′-) A lake of E-central Africa in Uganda, Kenya, and Tanzania.

Victoria Falls A waterfall, 108 m (354 ft), of S-central Africa in the Zambezi R. between SW Zambia and NW Zimbabwe.

Vic·to·ri·an (vĭk-tôr′ē-ən) ▸*adj.* **1.** Of or belonging to the period of the reign of Queen Victoria. **2.** Displaying the moral standards of this period. **3.** Being in the highly ornamented, eclectic style of architecture, decor, and furnishings popular in 19th-cent. England. ▸*n.* A person of the Victorian period.

vic·to·ri·ous (vĭk-tôr′ē-əs) ▸*adj.* **1.** Being the winner in a contest or struggle. **2.** Characteris-

tic of or expressing victory. —**vic·to′ri·ous·ly** *adv.* —**vic·to′ri·ous·ness** *n.*

vic·to·ry (vĭk′tə-rē) ▸*n., pl.* **-ries 1.** Defeat of an enemy or opponent. **2.** Success in a struggle against difficulties; triumph.

vict·ual (vĭt′l) ▸*n.* **1.** Food fit for human consumption. **2. victuals** Food supplies; provisions. ▸*v.* **-ualed, -ual·ing** or **-ualled, -ual·ling 1.** To provide with food. **2.** To lay in food supplies. [< Lat. *victus*, nourishment < *vīvere*, live.]

vi·cu·ña also **vi·cu·na** (vĭ-kōōn′yə, -kōō′nə, -kyōō′nə, vĭ-) ▸*n.* **1.** A llamalike mammal of the central Andes, having fine silky wool. **2.** The wool of the vicuña. [< Quechua *wikuña.*]

vi·de (vī′dē, wē′dā′) ▸*v.* See. Used to direct a reader's attention. [Lat. *vidē*, sing. imper. of *vidēre*, see.]

vi·del·i·cet (vī-dĕl′ĭ-sĕt′, wĭ-dā′lĭ-kĕt′) ▸*adv.* That is; namely. Used to introduce examples, lists, or items. [Lat. *vidēlicet.*]

vid·e·o (vĭd′ē-ō′) ▸*n., pl.* **-os 1.** A sequence of images displayed in rapid succession on a screen to simulate continuous motion. **2.** A movie recorded electronically. **3.** The electronic medium in which such movies are recorded. **4.** A videotaped rendition of a song. [Lat. *videō*, I see < *vidēre*, see.] —**vid′e·o′** *adj.*

video camera ▸*n.* An electronic camera that captures moving images so that they can be recorded, as on videotape or a hard drive, or viewed on a monitor.

vid·e·o·cas·sette (vĭd′ē-ō-kə-sĕt′, -kă-) ▸*n.* A cassette containing videotape.

videocassette recorder ▸*n.* A VCR.

vid·e·o·disc also **vid·e·o·disk** (vĭd′ē-ō-dĭsk′) ▸*n.* A disc on which sounds and images, as of a movie, are recorded. [Originally a Ger. trademark.]

video display ▸*n.* See **display** (sense 2).

video game ▸*n.* An electronic game played by manipulating moving figures on a screen.

vid·e·o·tape (vĭd′ē-ō-tāp′) ▸*n.* A magnetic tape used to record visual images and associated sound for subsequent playback or broadcasting. —**vid′e·o·tape′** *v.*

vie (vī) ▸*v.* **vied, vy·ing** (vī′ĭng) To strive for superiority; contend. [< Lat. *invītāre*, invite.]

Vi·en·na (vē-ĕn′ə) The capital of Austria, in the NE part on the Danube R. —**Vi′en·nese′** (-ə-nēz′, -nēs′) *adj. & n.*

Vien·tiane (vyĕn-tyän′) The capital of Laos, in the N-central part on the Mekong R. and the Thailand border.

Vi·et·cong (vē-ĕt′kŏng′, -kông′, vyĕt′-) ▸*n., pl.* **-cong** A Vietnamese in or supporting the National Liberation Front of the former South Vietnam. —**Vi·et′cong′** *adj.*

Vi·et·nam (vē-ĕt′näm′, -năm′, vyĕt′-) A country of SE Asia in E Indochina on the South China Sea; divided (1954–1976) into **North Vietnam** and **South Vietnam.** Cap. Hanoi.

Vi·et·nam·ese (vē-ĕt′nə-mēz′, vē′ĭt-, vyĕt′-) ▸*n., pl.* **-ese 1.** A native or inhabitant of Vietnam. **2.** The language of Vietnam. —**Vi′et·nam·ese′** *adj.*

view (vyōō) ▸*n.* **1.** An examination or inspection. **2.** Field of vision: *disappeared from view.* **3.** A scene or vista. **4.** A way of showing or seeing something, as from a particular position or angle: *a side view of the house.* **5.** An opinion; judgment: *my views on politics.* **6.** An aim or intention: *laws enacted with a view to ending discrimination.* ►*v.* **1.** To look at; watch. **2.** To regard; consider. [< Lat. *vidēre*, see.] **—view′er** *n.*

view·find·er (vyōō′fīn′dər) ►*n.* A device on a camera that indicates what will appear in the field of view of the lens.

view·point (vyōō′point′) ►*n.* A point of view.

vig·il (vĭj′əl) ►*n.* **1.** A watch kept during normal sleeping hours. **2.** The eve of a religious festival as observed by devotional watching. **3.** often **vigils** Ritual devotions observed on the eve of a holy day. [< Lat. *vigilia.*]

vig·i·lance (vĭj′ə-ləns) ►*n.* Alert watchfulness.

vig·i·lant (vĭj′ə-lənt) ►*adj.* On the alert; watchful. See Synonyms at **careful. —vig′i·lant·ly** *adv.*

vig·i·lan·te (vĭj′ə-lăn′tē) ►*n.* A person who is not a member of law enforcement but who pursues and punishes persons suspected of lawbreaking. [Sp.] **—vig′i·lan′tism, vig′i·lan′te·ism** *n.*

vi·gnette (vĭn-yĕt′) ►*n.* **1.** A decorative design placed at the beginning or end of a book or chapter. **2.** A picture that shades off into the surrounding color at the edges. **3.** A brief literary or dramatic sketch. [< OFr. *vigne*, vine.]

vig·or (vĭg′ər) ►*n.* **1.** Physical or mental strength or energy. **2.** Strong feeling; enthusiasm or intensity. [< Lat.]

Syns: *dash, punch, verve, vim, vitality* **n.**

vig·or·ous (vĭg′ər-əs) ►*adj.* **1.** Robust; hardy. **2.** Energetic; lively. **—vig′or·ous·ly** *adv.*

vig·our (vĭg′ər) ►*n.* Chiefly Brit. Var. of **vigor.**

Vi·king (vī′kĭng) ►*n.* One of a seafaring Scandinavian people who raided the coasts of N and W Europe from the 8th through the 10th cent.

vile (vīl) ►*adj.* **vil·er, vil·est 1.** Morally depraved; ignoble or wicked. **2.** Disgusting; repulsive. **3.** Unpleasant or objectionable. **4.** Miserably poor; wretched. [< Lat. *vīlis.*] **—vile′ly** *adv.* **—vile′ness** *n.*

vil·i·fy (vĭl′ə-fī′) ►*v.* **-fied, -fy·ing** To speak evil of; defame. [< LLat. *vīlificāre.*] **—vil′i·fi·ca′tion** *n.* **—vil′i·fi′er** *n.*

vil·la (vĭl′ə) ►*n.* An often large and luxurious country house. [Ital.]

Vil·la (vē′ə), **Francisco** "Pancho." 1878?–1923. Mexican revolutionary leader.

vil·lage (vĭl′ĭj) ►*n.* **1.** A usu. rural settlement smaller than a town. **2.** An incorporated community smaller in population than a town. **3.** The inhabitants of a village. [< Lat. *vīllāticum*, farmstead.] **—vil′lag·er** *n.*

vil·lain (vĭl′ən) ►*n.* **1.** A wicked or evil person; scoundrel. **2.** A dramatic or fictional character who is typically at odds with the hero; antagonist. **3.** (also vĭl′ān′, vĭ-lān′) Var. of **villein.** [< VLat. **vīllānus*, serf.]

vil·lain·ous (vĭl′ə-nəs) ►*adj.* **1.** Befitting a villain; wicked. **2.** Unpleasant; vile.

vil·lain·y (vĭl′ə-nē) ►*n., pl.* **-ies 1.** Villainous conduct or action. **2.** A villainous act.

vil·lein also **vil·lain** (vĭl′ən, -ān′, vĭ-lān′) ►*n.* One of a class of feudal serfs who held the legal status of freemen in their dealings with all people except their lord. [ME *vilein.*]

Vil·ni·us (vĭl′nē-əs) or **Vil·na** (-nə) The capital of Lithuania, in the SE part.

vim (vĭm) ►*n.* Liveliness; enthusiasm. See Syn-

onyms at **vigor.** [Lat., accusative of *vīs.*]

VIN ►*abbr.* vehicle identification number

vin·ai·grette (vĭn′ĭ-grĕt′) ►*n.* A dressing of oil and vinegar. [< OFr. < *vinaigre*, VINEGAR.]

Vin·cent de Paul (vĭn′sənt də pôl′), Saint. 1581–1660. French ecclesiastic.

vin·ci·ble (vĭn′sə-bəl) ►*adj.* Capable of being defeated. [< Lat. *vincere*, conquer.]

vin·di·cate (vĭn′dĭ-kāt′) ►*v.* **-cat·ed, -cat·ing 1.** To clear of accusation, blame, suspicion, or doubt with supporting proof. **2.** To demonstrate or prove the value or validity of; justify. [< Lat. *vindex*, avenger.] **—vin′di·ca′tion** *n.* **—vin′di·ca′tor** *n.*

vin·dic·tive (vĭn-dĭk′tĭv) ►*adj.* **1.** Disposed to seek revenge; vengeful. **2.** Intended to cause pain or harm; spiteful. [< Lat. *vindicta*, vengeance.] **—vin·dic′tive·ly** *adv.*

vine (vīn) ►*n.* **1a.** A weak-stemmed plant that derives its support from climbing, twining, or creeping along a surface. **b.** The stem of such a plant. **2.** A grapevine. [< Lat. *vīneus*, of wine.]

vin·e·gar (vĭn′ĭ-gər) ►*n.* A sour liquid containing acetic acid, produced by fermenting a solution such as wine or fermented rice, used as a condiment and preservative. [< OFr. *vinaigre* : *vin*, wine + *aigre*, sour (< Lat. *ācer*).]

vin·e·gar·y (vĭn′ĭ-gə-rē, -grē) ►*adj.* **1.** Of or like vinegar; acid. **2.** Unpleasant and irascible.

vine·yard (vĭn′yərd) ►*n.* A farm where grapes are grown.

vin·i·cul·ture (vĭn′ĭ-kŭl′chər, vī′nĭ-) ►*n.* Viticulture. [Lat. *vīnum*, wine + CULTURE.]

Vin·land (vĭn′lənd) An unidentified coastal region of NE North America visited by Norse voyagers as early as c. 1000.

vin·tage (vĭn′tĭj) ►*n.* **1.** The yield of wine or grapes from a vineyard or district during one season. **2.** The year or place in which a wine is bottled. **3.** A year or period of origin: *a car of 1942 vintage.* ►*adj.* **1.** Of or relating to a vintage. **2.** Characterized by excellence and enduring appeal; classic. [< Lat. *vīndēmia.*]

vint·ner (vĭnt′nər) ►*n.* **1.** A wine merchant. **2.** One who makes wine. [< Lat. *vīnētum*, vineyard.]

vi·nyl (vī′nəl) ►*n.* Any of various typically tough, flexible, shiny plastics, often used for coverings and clothing. [Lat. *vīnum*, wine + –YL.]

vi·ol (vī′əl) ►*n.* Any of a family of stringed instruments, chiefly of the 16th and 17th cent., having a fretted fingerboard, usu. six strings, and played with a bow. [< OProv. *viola.*]

vi·o·la (vē-ō′lə) ►*n.* A stringed instrument of the violin family, slightly larger than a violin, tuned a fifth lower, and having a deeper, more sonorous tone. [< OProv. *viola.*] **—vi·o′list** *n.*

vi·o·la·ble (vī′ə-lə-bəl) ►*adj.* That can be violated.

vi·o·late (vī′ə-lāt′) ►*v.* **-lat·ed, -lat·ing 1.** To break or disregard (e.g., a law). **2.** To assault (a person) sexually. **3.** To desecrate or defile. **4.** To disturb; interrupt. [< Lat. *violāre* < *vīs*, force.] **—vi′o·la′tive** *adj.* **—vi′o·la′tor** *n.*

vi·o·la·tion (vī′ə-lā′shən) ►*n.* The act of violating or the condition of being violated.

vi·o·lence (vī′ə-ləns) ►*n.* **1.** Physical force exerted so as to cause damage or injury. **2.** Vehemence; fervor. **3.** Intensity or severity: *the violence of a hurricane.*

vi·o·lent (vī′ə-lənt) ►*adj.* **1.** Causing or intending to cause damage, injury, or death. **2.** Caused by unexpected force or injury rather than by natural causes: *a violent death.* **3.** Very forceful: *A violent squall.* **4.** Having or showing great emotional force. **5.** Intense; extreme. [< Lat. *violentus* < *vīs*, force.] **—vi·o·lent·ly** *adv.*

vi·o·let (vī'ə-lĭt) ►*n.* **1a.** A low-growing herb having spurred irregular flowers that are characteristically purplish-blue but sometimes yellow or white. **b.** Any of several similar plants. **2.** The hue of the short-wave end of the visible spectrum; reddish blue. [< Lat. *viola.*]

vi·o·lin (vī'ə-lĭn') ►*n.* A small stringed instrument held horizontally at the shoulder and played with a bow, having an unfretted fingerboard and four strings tuned at intervals of a fifth. [Ital. *violino.*] **—vi'o·lin'ist** *n.*

vi·o·lon·cel·lo (vē'ə-lən-chĕl'ō, vī'ə-) ►*n., pl.* **-los** A cello. [Ital.]

VIP (vē'ī-pē') ►*n. Informal* A very important person.

vi·per (vī'pər) ►*n.* **1.** Any of several venomous snakes having a single pair of long hollow fangs. **2.** A harmless but supposedly venomous snake. **3.** A malicious or treacherous person. [< Lat. *vīpera*, snake < *vīviparus*, VIVIPAROUS.] **—vi'per·ous** *adj.*

vi·ra·go (və-rä'gō, -rā'-, vîr'ə-gō') ►*n., pl.* **-goes** or **-gos** A noisy, domineering woman. [Lat. *virāgō* < *vir*, man.]

vi·ral (vī'rəl) ►*adj.* **1.** Of or caused by a virus. **2.** Of or relating to the propagation of ideas or information by means of social networks rather than mass media. **—vi'ral·ly** *adv.*

vir·e·o (vîr'ē-ō') ►*n., pl.* **-os** Any of various small songbirds having grayish or greenish plumage. [Lat. *vireō*, a kind of bird.]

Vir·gil also **Ver·gil** (vûr'jəl) 70–19 BC. Roman poet. **—Vir·gil'i·an** (-jĭl'ē-ən) *adj.*

vir·gin (vûr'jĭn) ►*n.* **1.** A person who has not experienced sexual intercourse. **2.** A female virgin. Used chiefly in historical contexts. **3. Virgin** Mary, the mother of Jesus. ►*adj.* **1.** Of or being a virgin; chaste. **2.** In a pure or natural state. [< Lat. *virgō, virgin-.*] **—vir·gin'i·ty** *n.*

vir·gin·al¹ (vûr'jə-nəl) ►*adj.* **1.** Of or befitting a virgin. **2.** Untouched or unsullied; fresh.

vir·gin·al² (vûr'jə-nəl) ►*n.* A small legless harpsichord popular in the 16th and 17th cent. [< VIRGIN.]

Vir·gin·ia (vər-jĭn'yə) A state of the E US on Chesapeake Bay and the Atlantic. Cap. Richmond. **—Vir·gin'ian** *adj. & n.*

Virginia creeper ►*n.* A North American climbing vine having compound leaves with five leaflets and bluish-black berries.

Virginia reel ►*n.* An American country-dance in which couples perform various steps together to the instructions of a caller.

Virgin Islands 1. A group of islands of the NE West Indies E of Puerto Rico; divided politically into the **British Virgin Islands** to the NE and the Virgin Islands of the United States to the SW. **2.** Officially **Virgin Islands of the United States** A US territory constituting the SW group of the Virgin Is. Cap. Charlotte Amalie.

Vir·go (vûr'gō) ►*n.* **1.** A constellation in the region of the celestial equator between Leo and Libra. **2.** The 6th sign of the zodiac.

vir·gule (vûr'gyool) ►*n.* See **slash** (sense 2). [< LLat. *virgula.*]

vir·ile (vîr'əl, -īl') ►*adj.* **1.** Of or having the characteristics of an adult male, esp. the ability to have sexual intercourse. **2.** Robustly manly. **3.** Energetic or forceful. [< Lat. *vir*, man.] **—vi·ril'i·ty** (və-rĭl'ĭ-tē) *n.*

vi·rol·o·gy (vī-rŏl'ə-jē) ►*n.* The study of viruses and viral diseases. **—vi·rol'o·gist** *n.*

vir·tu·al (vûr'choo-əl) ►*adj.* **1.** Existing in essence or effect though not in actual fact or form: *the virtual extinction of the buffalo.* **2.** Created, simulated, or carried on by means of a computer or computer network: *virtual conversations in a chatroom.* [< Lat. *virtūs*, excellence; see VIRTUE.] **—vir'tu·al'i·ty** (-ăl'ĭ-tē) *n.*

vir·tu·al·ly (vûr'choo-ə-lē) ►*adv.* In effect: *The city was virtually paralyzed by the transit strike.*

virtual reality ►*n.* A computer simulation of a real or imaginary system in real time.

vir·tue (vûr'choo) ►*n.* **1a.** Moral excellence and righteousness; goodness. **b.** An example or kind of moral excellence. **2.** *Archaic* Chastity, esp. in a woman. **3.** A particularly efficacious or beneficial quality; advantage. **4.** Effective force or power. **—idiom: by virtue of** On the basis of. [< Lat. *virtūs* < *vir*, man.]

vir·tu·os·i·ty (vûr'choo-ŏs'ĭ-tē) ►*n., pl.* **-ties** The technical skill or style of a virtuoso.

vir·tu·o·so (vûr'choo-ō'sō, -zō) ►*n., pl.* **-sos** or **si** (sē) **1.** A musician with masterly ability, technique, or style. **2.** A person with masterly skill or technique in any field, esp. the arts. [Ital.] **—vir'tu·o'sic** *adj.*

vir·tu·ous (vûr'choo-əs) ►*adj.* **1.** Having or showing virtue, esp. moral excellence. **2.** *Archaic* Chaste. **—vir'tu·ous·ly** *adv.*

vir·u·lent (vîr'yə-lənt, vĭr'ə-) ►*adj.* **1.** Causing or promoting the rapid onset of severe illness, as an infection or toxin. **2.** Extremely hostile or malicious. [< Lat. *vīrulentus.*] **—vir'u·lence** *n.* **—vir'u·lent·ly** *adv.*

vi·rus (vī'rəs) ►*n.* **1a.** Any of various submicroscopic agents that infect living organisms, often causing disease, and that consist of a single or double strand of RNA or DNA surrounded by a protein coat. **b.** A disease caused by a virus. **2.** *Comp.* A self-replicating program that copies itself into other programs on a computer, usu. having negative effects. [Lat. *vīrus*, poison.]

vi·sa (vē'zə) ►*n.* An official authorization appended to a passport, permitting entry into and travel within a particular country or region. [< Lat. *vīsa* < p.part. of *vidēre*, see.]

vis·age (vĭz'ĭj) ►*n.* **1.** The face or facial expression of a person. **2.** Appearance; aspect. [< OFr. < Lat. *vīsus*, appearance < *vidēre*, see.]

vis-à-vis (vē'zə-vē') ►*prep.* **1.** Compared with. **2.** In relation to. ►*adv.* Face to face. ►*n., pl.* **vis-à-vis** (-vēz', -vē') One opposite or corresponding to another; counterpart. [Fr., face to face.]

Vi·sa·yan Islands (vĭ-sī'ən) An island group of the central Philippines in and around the **Visayan Sea** between Luzon and Mindanao. **—Vi·sa'yan** *adj. & n.*

vis·cer·a (vĭs'ər-ə) ►*pl.n.* The internal body organs, esp. those contained within the abdomen and thorax. [< Lat. *vīscus, vīscer-.*]

vis·cer·al (vĭs'ər-əl) ►*adj.* **1.** Of, situated in, or affecting the viscera. **2.** Arising from impulse or sudden emotion rather than from thought or deliberation. **—vis′cer·al·ly** *adv.*

vis·cid (vĭs′ĭd) ►*adj.* Thick and adhesive. Used of a fluid. [LLat. *viscidus.*] **—vis·cid′i·ty** *n.* **—vis′cid·ly** *adv.*

vis·cose (vĭs′kōs′) ►*n.* A golden-brown viscous solution derived from cellulose, used to make rayon and cellophane. [VISC(OUS) + −OSE².]

vis·cos·i·ty (vĭ-skŏs′ĭ-tē) ►*n., pl.* **-ties** The condition or property of being viscous.

vis·count (vī′kount′) ►*n.* A nobleman ranking below an earl or count and above a baron. [< Med.Lat. *vicecomes.*]

vis·cous (vĭs′kəs) ►*adj.* **1.** Having relatively high resistance to flow. **2.** Viscid. [< LLat. *viscum,* birdlime.] **—vis′cous·ly** *adv.* **—vis′-cous·ness** *n.*

vise also **vice** (vīs) ►*n.* A heavy clamp, usu. mounted on a workbench and operated by a screw or lever, used in carpentry to hold a piece in position. [< OFr. *vis,* screw.]

Vish·nu (vĭsh′nōō) ►*n. Hinduism* A principal Hindu deity, often conceived as a member of the triad including Brahma and Shiva.

vis·i·bil·i·ty (vĭz′ə-bĭl′ĭ-tē) ►*n., pl.* **-ties 1.** The fact, state, or degree of being visible. **2.** The greatest distance under given weather conditions to which it is possible to see without instrumental assistance.

vis·i·ble (vĭz′ə-bəl) ►*adj.* **1.** Capable of being seen. **2.** Manifest; apparent. [< *vidēre, vīs-,* see.] **—vis′i·bly** *adv.*

Vis·i·goth (vĭz′ĭ-gŏth′) ►*n.* A member of the western Goths that invaded the Roman Empire in the 4th cent. A.D. and settled in France and Spain.

vi·sion (vĭzh′ən) ►*n.* **1.** The faculty of sight; eyesight. **2.** Unusual foresight. **3.** A mental image produced by the imagination. **4.** The mystical experience of seeing something that is not present to the eye or is supernatural. **5.** One of extraordinary beauty. [< Lat. *vīsus,* p.part. of *vidēre,* see.]

vi·sion·ar·y (vĭzh′ə-něr′ē) ►*adj.* **1.** Marked by vision or foresight. **2.** Having the nature of fantasies or dreams. **3.** Given to impractical or fanciful ideas. **4.** Not practicable; utopian. ►*n., pl.* **-ies 1.** One given to speculative, often impractical ideas. **2.** A seer; prophet. **3.** One having unusual foresight.

vis·it (vĭz′ĭt) ►*v.* **1.** To go or come to see for reasons of business, duty, or pleasure. **2.** To stay with as a guest. **3a.** To afflict or assail. **b.** To inflict punishment on or for; avenge. **4.** To access (a website). **5.** *Informal* To converse; chat. ►*n.* **1.** An act or instance of visiting. **2.** A stay as a guest. [< Lat. *vīsitāre < vidēre,* see.]

vis·i·tant (vĭz′ĭ-tənt) ►*n.* A visitor; guest.

vis·i·ta·tion (vĭz′ĭ-tā′shən) ►*n.* **1.** A visit, esp. an official inspection or examination. **2.** The right of a divorced or separated parent to visit a child. **3.** An affliction or blessing, esp. regarded as being ordained by God. **4.** The appearance or arrival of a supernatural being. **—vis′i·ta′tion·al** *adj.*

vis·i·tor (vĭz′ĭ-tər) ►*n.* One that visits.

vi·sor (vī′zər) ►*n.* **1.** A projecting part, as on a cap or the windshield of a car, that protects the eyes from sun, wind, or rain. **2.** A movable front piece on a helmet, designed to protect the face from injury. [ME *viser* < AN *vis,* VISAGE.]

vis·ta (vĭs′tə) ►*n.* **1.** A distant view, esp. one

seen through an opening. **2.** A broad mental view, as of a series of events. [Ital. < *vedere,* see < Lat. *vidēre.*]

Vis·tu·la (vĭs′chə-lə, -choo-) A river of central Poland, flowing about 1,050 km (650 mi) north to the Baltic Sea near Gdańsk.

vi·su·al (vĭzh′ōō-əl) ►*adj.* **1.** Of or relating to the sense of sight. **2.** Able to be seen; visible. **3.** Done or executed by sight only. [< Lat. *vīsus,* sight; see VISION.] **—vi′su·al·ly** *adv.*

vi·su·al·ize (vĭzh′ōō-ə-līz′) ►*v.* **-ized, -iz·ing 1.** To form a mental image or vision of. **2a.** To render visible, as in an image or representation. **b.** To produce an image of using radiological technology. **—vi′su·al·i·za′tion** *n.* **—vi′su·al·iz′er** *n.*

vi·ta (vī′tə, vē′-) ►*n., pl.* **vi·tae** (vī′tē, vē′tī) **1.** A curriculum vitae. **2.** A short account of a person's life. [Lat. *vīta,* life; see VITAL.]

vi·tal (vīt′l) ►*adj.* **1.** Relating to or characteristic of life: *vital strength.* See Synonyms at **living. 2.** Necessary to the continuation of life: *vital organs.* **3.** Full of life; animated. **4.** Of great importance; essential. [< Lat. *vīta,* life.] **—vi′tal·ly** *adv.*

vi·tal·i·ty (vī-tăl′ĭ-tē) ►*n., pl.* **-ties 1a.** The capacity to live, grow, or develop. **b.** The principle or force that distinguishes living from nonliving things. **2.** Physical or intellectual vigor; liveliness. See Synonyms at **vigor.**

vi·tal·ize (vīt′l-īz′) ►*v.* **-ized, -iz·ing** To endow with life, vigor, or energy. **—vi′tal·i·za′tion** *n.* **—vi′tal·iz′er** *n.*

vi·tals (vīt′lz) ►*pl.n.* **1.** The vital body organs. **2.** Essential parts, as of a system. **3.** *Informal* Vital signs.

vital signs ►*pl.n.* A person's temperature, heart rate, respiratory rate, and blood pressure.

vital statistics ►*pl.n.* Statistics concerning births, deaths, marriages, and migrations.

vi·ta·min (vī′tə-mĭn) ►*n.* A fat-soluble or water-soluble organic substance that is essential in very small amounts for normal function of living organisms and obtained by animals chiefly from their diet. [< Lat. *vīta,* life + AMINE.]

vitamin A ►*n.* A vitamin or mixture of vitamins found chiefly in fish-liver oils, milk, and some yellow and green vegetables, lack of which causes damage to the skin and mucous membranes.

vitamin B ►*n.* **1.** Vitamin B complex. **2.** A member of this complex, esp. thiamine.

vitamin B₁ ►*n.* See **thiamine.**

vitamin B₂ ►*n.* See **riboflavin.**

vitamin B₁₂ ►*n.* A compound containing cobalt, found esp. in liver and used to treat pernicious anemia.

vitamin B complex ►*n.* A group of vitamins including thiamine, riboflavin, niacin, folic acid, biotin, and vitamin B₁₂, occurring chiefly in yeast, liver, eggs, and some vegetables.

vitamin C ►*n.* See **ascorbic acid.**

vitamin D ►*n.* A vitamin that is required for normal growth of teeth and bones and is produced by ultraviolet irradiation of sterols found in milk, fish, and eggs.

vitamin E ►*n.* A fat-soluble vitamin found in vegetable oils, wheat germ, plant leaves, and milk that acts as an antioxidant in the body.

vitamin K ►*n.* A vitamin occurring in leafy green vegetables, tomatoes, and egg yolks, that promotes blood clotting and prevents hemorrhaging.

vi·ti·ate (vĭsh′ē-āt′) ►*v.* **-at·ed, -at·ing 1.** To reduce the value or impair the quality of. **2.** To corrupt morally; debase. See Synonyms at **corrupt. 3.** To invalidate. [< Lat. *vitium*, fault.] **—vi′ti·a′tion** *n.* **—vi′ti·a′tor** *n.*

vit·i·cul·ture (vĭt′ĭ-kŭl′chər, vī′tĭ-) ►*n.* The cultivation of grapes. [Lat. *vītis*, vine + CULTURE.] **—vit′i·cul′tur·ist** *n.*

Vi·ti Le·vu (vē′tē lĕv′ōō) The largest of the Fiji Is., in the SW Pacific.

vit·re·ous (vĭt′rē-əs) ►*adj.* **1.** Of or resembling glass; glassy. **2.** Of or relating to the vitreous humor. [< Lat. *vitreus.*]

vitreous humor ►*n.* The clear gelatinous substance that fills the eyeball between the retina and the lens.

vit·ri·fy (vĭt′rə-fī′) ►*v.* **-fied, -fy·ing** To change or make into glass or a glassy substance, esp. through heat fusion. [< Lat. *vitrum*, glass.] **—vit′ri·fi·ca′tion** *n.*

vit·ri·ol (vĭt′rē-ōl′, -əl) ►*n.* **1a.** See **sulfuric acid. b.** Any of various sulfates of metals. **2.** Bitterly abusive feeling or expression. [< Lat. *vitreolus*, of glass.]

vit·ri·ol·ic (vĭt′rē-ŏl′ĭk) ►*adj.* **1.** Of or derived from vitriol. **2.** Bitterly scathing; caustic.

vit·tles (vĭt′əlz) ►*pl.n. Nonstandard* Victuals.

vi·tu·per·ate (vī-tōō′pə-rāt′, -tyōō′-, vĭ-) ►*v.* **-at·ed, -at·ing** To criticize harshly or angrily; berate. [Lat. *vituperāre.*] **—vi·tu′per·a′tion** *n.* **—vi·tu′per·a·tive** *adj.*

vi·va (vē′və, -vä′) ►*interj.* Used to express acclamation, salute, or applause. [Ital., (long) live < Lat. *vīvere*, live.]

vi·va·ce (vē-vä′chā) ►*adv. & adj. Mus.* In a lively manner. Used as a direction. [Ital. < Lat. *vīvax*, VIVACIOUS.]

vi·va·cious (vĭ-vā′shəs, vī-) ►*adj.* Full of animation and spirit; lively. [< Lat. *vīvāx < vīvere*, live.] **—vi·va′cious·ly** *adv.* **—vi·vac′i·ty** (-văs′ĭ-tē) *n.*

Vi·val·di (vĭ-väl′dē), **Antonio Lucio** 1678–1741. Italian composer and violinist.

viv·id (vĭv′ĭd) ►*adj.* **1.** Perceived as bright and distinct; brilliant: *a vivid star.* **2.** Having intensely bright colors. **3.** Presented in clear and striking manner: *a vivid account of the accident.* **4.** Perceived or felt with the freshness of immediate experience: *a vivid recollection.* **5.** Active in forming lifelike images: *a vivid imagination.* [Lat. *vīvidus < vīvere*, live.] **—viv′id·ly** *adv.* **—viv′id·ness** *n.*

Syns: graphic, lifelike, realistic adj.

viv·i·fy (vĭv′ə-fī′) ►*v.* **-fied, -fy·ing 1.** To give or bring life to; animate. **2.** To make more lively or intense; enliven. [< Lat. *vīvus*, alive.]

vi·vip·a·rous (vī-vĭp′ər-əs, vĭ-) ►*adj.* Giving birth to living offspring that develop within the mother's body. [Lat. *vīvus*, alive + -PAROUS.] **—vi′vi·par′i·ty** (vī′və-păr′ĭ-tē, vĭv′ə-) *n.* **—vi·vip′a·rous·ly** *adv.*

viv·i·sec·tion (vĭv′ĭ-sĕk′shən) ►*n.* The act of cutting into or otherwise injuring living animals for scientific research. [Lat. *vīvus*, alive + (DIS)SECTION.] **—viv′i·sect′** *v.*

vix·en (vĭk′sən) ►*n.* **1.** A female fox. **2.** A woman regarded as quarrelsome or ill-tempered. [ME *fixen.*] **—vix′en·ish** *adj.*

viz. ►*abbr. Lat.* videlicet (namely)

viz·ard (vĭz′ərd, -ärd′) ►*n.* A mask. [< VISOR.]

vi·zier (vĭ-zîr′, vĭz′yər) ►*n.* A high officer in a Muslim government, esp. in the Ottoman Empire. [< Ar. *wazīr*, minister.]

Vla·di·vos·tok (vlăd′ə-və-stŏk′, -vŏs′tŏk′) A city of extreme SE Russia on an arm of the Sea of Japan.

VLF ►*abbr.* very low frequency

VMD ►*abbr. Lat.* Veterinariae Medicinae Doctor (Doctor of Veterinary Medicine)

vo·ca·ble (vō′kə-bəl) ►*n.* A word considered as a sequence of sounds or letters rather than as a unit of meaning. [< Lat. *vocāre*, call.]

vo·cab·u·lar·y (vō-kăb′yə-lĕr′ē) ►*n., pl.* **-ies 1.** All the words of a language. **2.** The sum of words used by a particular person or group. **3.** A list of words and often phrases, usu. arranged alphabetically and defined or translated; lexicon. [< Lat. *vocābulum*, name.]

vo·cal (vō′kəl) ►*adj.* **1.** Of or for the voice. **2.** Uttered or produced by the voice. **3.** Quick to speak or criticize; outspoken. ►*n.* **1.** A vocal sound. **2.** *Mus.* A singing part: *jazz vocals.* [< Lat. *vōx*, voice.] **—vo′cal·ly** *adv.*

vocal cords ►*pl.n.* A pair of bands or folds of mucous membrane in the throat that vibrate when air from the lungs is forced between them, thereby producing vocal sounds.

vo·cal·ic (vō-kăl′ĭk) ►*adj.* Relating to or having the nature of a vowel.

vo·cal·ist (vō′kə·lĭst) ►*n.* A singer.

vo·cal·ize (vō′kə-līz′) ►*v.* **-ized, -iz·ing 1.** To use the voice, esp. to sing. **2.** To give voice to. **3.** To articulate (a consonant) as a vowel. **—vo′cal·i·za′tion** *n.* **—vo′cal·iz′er** *n.*

vo·ca·tion (vō-kā′shən) ►*n.* **1.** An occupation, esp. one for which a person is particularly suited. **2.** A calling, esp. to a religious career. [< Lat. *vocāre*, call.] **—vo·ca′tion·al** *adj.*

vocational school ►*n.* A school that offers instruction in skilled trades such as mechanics or carpentry.

voc·a·tive (vŏk′ə-tĭv) ►*adj.* Of or being a grammatical case indicating the one being addressed. [< Lat. *vocāre*, call.] **—voc′a·tive** *n.*

vo·cif·er·ate (vō-sĭf′ə-rāt′) ►*v.* **-at·ed, -at·ing** To cry out loudly and vehemently, esp. in protest. [Lat. *vōciferārī* : *vōx*, voice + *ferre*, carry.]

vo·cif·er·ous (vō-sĭf′ər-əs) ►*adj.* Making or marked by noisy and vehement outcry. **—vo·cif′er·ous·ly** *adv.*

vod·ka (vŏd′kə) ►*n.* A clear alcoholic liquor distilled from a mash of fermented wheat, rye, corn, or potatoes. [Russ. < *voda*, water.]

vogue (vōg) ►*n.* **1.** The prevailing fashion, practice, or style. **2.** Popular acceptance or favor; popularity. [< OFr.] **—vogu′ish** *adj.*

voice (vois) ►*n.* **1a.** Sound produced by the vocal organs of a vertebrate, esp. a human. **b.** The ability to produce such sounds: *lost her voice.* **2.** A specified quality, condition, or pitch of vocal sound. **3.** *Ling.* Expiration of air through vibrating vocal cords, used in the production of vowels and voiced consonants. **4.** A sound resembling vocal utterance. **5.** *Mus.* **a.** Musical sound produced by vibration of the vocal cords. **b.** A singer: *a choir of 200 voices.* **c.** One of the individual parts or strands in a composition. **6a.** Expression; utterance. **b.** A medium or agency of expression. **c.** The right or opportunity to express a choice or opinion. **7.** *Gram.* A property of verb forms indicating the relation between the subject and the action expressed by the verb. ▸*v.* **voiced, voic·ing 1.** To give voice to; utter. **2.** *Ling.* To pronounce with vibration of the vocal cords. **3.** *Mus.* To regulate the tone of (e.g., the pipes of an organ). [< Lat. *vōx.*]

voice box ▸*n.* The larynx.

voiced (voist) ▸*adj.* **1.** Having a voice or a specified kind of voice: *harsh-voiced.* **2.** *Ling.* Uttered with vibration of the vocal cords, as the consonant (b).

voice·less (vois′lĭs) ▸*adj.* **1.** Having no voice. **2.** *Ling.* Uttered without vibration of the vocal cords, as the sound (t). —**voice′less·ly** *adv.* —**voice′less·ness** *n.*

voice·mail (vois′māl′) ▸*n.* **1.** A computerized system for leaving and receiving telephone messages. **2.** A message left on such a system.

voice-o·ver or **voice·o·ver** (vois′ō′vər) ▸*n.* The voice of an unseen narrator or an onscreen character not seen speaking, as in a movie, commercial, or documentary.

voice·print (vois′prĭnt′) ▸*n.* An electronically recorded representation of a person's voice.

void (void) ▸*adj.* **1.** Containing no matter; empty. **2.** Not occupied; vacant. **3.** Completely lacking; devoid. **4.** Ineffective; useless. **5.** Having no legal force or validity; null. ▸*n.* **1.** An empty space; vacuum. **2.** A feeling of emptiness, loneliness, or loss. ▸*v.* **1.** To empty. **2.** To excrete (body wastes). **3.** To leave; vacate. **4.** To make void; invalidate. [< Lat. *vacīvus.*]

voi·là (vwä-lä′) ▸*interj.* Used to call attention to something that is presented or something that has been accomplished. [Fr.]

voile (voil) ▸*n.* A sheer fabric used for making lightweight dresses and curtains. [< Lat. *vēlum,* covering.]

vol. ▸*abbr.* volume

vol·a·tile (vŏl′ə-tl, -tīl′) ▸*adj.* **1.** Evaporating readily at normal temperatures and pressures. **2a.** Tending to vary often. **b.** Inconstant; fickle. **3.** Tending to violence; explosive. [< Lat. *volāre,* fly.] —**vol′a·til′i·ty** (-tĭl′ĭ-tē) *n.*

vol·a·til·ize (vŏl′ə-tl-īz′) ▸*v.* **-ized, -iz·ing 1.** To become or make volatile. **2.** To evaporate or cause to evaporate.

vol·can·ic (vŏl-kăn′ĭk, vôl-) ▸*adj.* **1.** Of or relating to volcanoes. **2.** Powerfully explosive: *a volcanic temper.*

vol·ca·nism (vŏl′kə-nĭz′əm) also **vul·ca·nism** (vŭl′-) ▸*n.* Volcanic force or activity.

vol·ca·no (vŏl-kā′nō) ▸*n., pl.* **-noes** or **-nos 1.** An opening in the earth's crust through which molten lava, ash, and gases are ejected. **2.** A mountain formed by the materials ejected from a volcano. [< Lat. *Volcānus,* Vulcan.]

vole (vōl) ▸*n.* Any of various rodents having a short muzzle and tail and small ears. [< obsolete *volemouse.*]

Vol·ga (vŏl′gə) A river of W Russia rising NW of Moscow and flowing about 3,700 km (2,300 mi) to the Caspian Sea.

Vol·go·grad (vŏl′gə-grăd′) Formerly **Stalin-grad.** A city of SW Russia on the Volga R.

vo·li·tion (və-lĭsh′ən) ▸*n.* **1.** The act of making a conscious choice or decision. **2.** The power or faculty of choosing; will. [< Lat. *velle, vol-,* wish.] —**vo·li′tion·al** *adj.*

vol·ley (vŏl′ē) ▸*n., pl.* **-leys 1a.** A simultaneous discharge of a number of projectiles. **b.** The

projectiles thus discharged. **2.** A bursting forth of many things together: *a volley of questions.* **3.** *Sports* An exchange of strokes in a game such as tennis, ending when one side fails to make a good return. ▸*v.* **1.** To discharge or be discharged in or as if in a volley. **2.** *Sports* To strike (a ball) before it touches the ground. [< Lat. *volāre,* fly.] —**vol′ley·er** *n.*

vol·ley·ball (vŏl′ē-bôl′) ▸*n.* **1.** A game played by two teams on a court divided by a high net, in which up to three hits are used to ground the ball on the opposing team's court. **2.** The inflated ball used in this game.

volleyball
Chinese *(left)* and Russian *(right)* volleyball teams at the 2009 World Grand Prix

volt (vōlt) ▸*n.* The unit of electric potential and electromotive force equal to the difference in potential needed to cause a current of one ampere to flow through a resistance of one ohm. [< Count A. VOLTA.]

Vol·ta (vōl′tə) A river of W Africa, flowing about 465 km (290 mi) through Ghana to the Gulf of Guinea.

Vol·ta (vōl′tä), Count **Alessandro** 1745–1827. Italian physicist.

volt·age (vōl′tĭj) ▸*n.* The difference in electric potential between two points, expressed in volts.

vol·ta·ic (vŏl-tā′ĭk, vōl-, vôl-) ▸*adj.* Of or producing electricity by chemical action; galvanic.

Vol·taire (vōl-târ′, vŏl-) François Marie Arouet. 1694–1778. French philosopher and writer.

volt·me·ter (vōlt′mē′tər) ▸*n.* An instrument for measuring electric potential differences in volts.

vol·u·ble (vŏl′yə-bəl) ▸*adj.* Marked by a ready flow of speech; fluent. [< Lat. *volūbilis.*] —**vol′-u·bil′i·ty** *n.* —**vol′u·bly** *adv.*

vol·ume (vŏl′yōōm, -yəm) ▸*n.* **1a.** A collection of written or printed sheets bound together; book. **b.** One of the books of a set. **c.** A series of issues of a periodical, usu. covering one calendar year. **2a.** The amount of space occupied by a three-dimensional object or region of space. **b.** The capacity of such a region or of a specified container. **3.** Amount; quantity: *a low volume of business.* **4a.** The amplitude or loudness of a sound. **b.** A control for adjusting loudness. [< Lat. *volūmen,* roll of writing.]

vol·u·met·ric (vŏl′yōō-mĕt′rĭk) ▸*adj.* Of or relating to measurement by volume. [VOLU(ME) + -METRY + -IC.]

vo·lu·mi·nous (və-lōō′mə-nəs) ▸*adj.* **1.** Having great volume, fullness, size, or number. **2.** Filling or capable of filling many volumes. **3.** Having many coils; winding. [LLat. *volūminōsus,* having many folds.] —**vo·lu′mi·nous·ly** *adv.*

vol·un·tar·y (vŏl′ən-tĕr′ē) ▸*adj.* **1.** Arising from one's own free will. **2.** Acting or done willingly and without constraint or expectation of reward. **3.** Normally controlled by or subject to individual volition. **4.** *Law* **a.** Without obligation or recompense: *voluntary conveyance of property.* **b.** Done intentionally but without premeditation or deliberation: *voluntary manslaughter.* ▸*n., pl.* **-ies** A piece for solo organ played before, during, or after a religious service. [< Lat. *voluntās*, choice.] —**vol′un·tar′i·ly** (-târ′ə-lē) *adv.*

vol·un·teer (vŏl′ən-tîr′) ▸*n.* **1.** A person who performs or offers a service of his or her own free will, esp. without pay. **2.** *Bot.* A cultivated plant growing from self-sown or accidentally dropped seed. ▸*v.* **1.** To give or offer of one's own accord. **2.** To perform or offer to perform a service of one's own free will, esp. without pay.

vo·lup·tu·ar·y (və-lŭp′chōō-ĕr′ē) ▸*n., pl.* **-ies** One who is given over to luxury and sensual pleasures. —**vo·lup′tu·ar′y** *adj.*

vo·lup·tu·ous (və-lŭp′chōō-əs) ▸*adj.* **1.** Of, marked by, or giving sensual pleasure. **2.** Devoted to or indulging in sensual pleasures. **3.** Having a curvaceous figure: *a voluptuous woman.* [< Lat. *voluptās*, pleasure.] —**vo·lup′tu·ous·ly** *adv.* —**vo·lup′tu·ous·ness** *n.*

vo·lute (və-lōōt′) ▸*n.* A spiral, scroll-like formation or decoration. [< Lat. *volūta.*]

vom·it (vŏm′ĭt) ▸*v.* **1.** To eject part or all of the contents of the stomach through the mouth. **2.** To eject or discharge in a gush; spew out. ▸*n.* Matter ejected from the stomach through the mouth. [< Lat. *vomitāre.*]

voo·doo (vōō′dōō) ▸*n.* **1.** A religion of West African origin practiced chiefly in Caribbean countries, in which a supreme God rules a large pantheon of deities, deified ancestors, and saints. **2.** A priest or priestess of voodoo. **3.** Deceptive or delusive nonsense. ▸*adj.* Based on unrealistic or delusive assumptions: *voodoo economics.* [Of West African orig.]

vo·ra·cious (vô-rā′shəs, və-) ▸*adj.* **1.** Consuming or eager to consume great amounts of food; ravenous. **2.** Having or marked by a strong desire for an activity or pursuit: *a voracious reader.* [< Lat. *vorāx.*] —**vo·ra′cious·ly** *adv.* —**vo·rac′i·ty** (-răs′ĭ-tē), **vo·ra′cious·ness** *n.*

-vorous ▸*suff.* Eating; feeding on: *omnivorous.* [< Lat. *vorāre*, devour.]

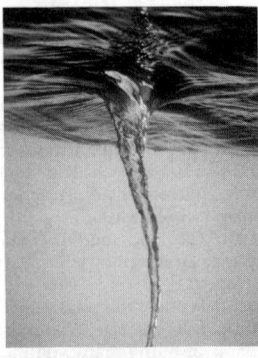

vortex

vor·tex (vôr′tĕks′) ▸*n., pl.* **-es** or **-ti·ces** (-tĭ-sēz′) **1.** A whirling mass of water or air that sucks everything near it toward its center. **2.** Something regarded as drawing into its center all that surrounds it. [Lat. < *vertere*, turn.] —**vor′ti·cal** *adj.*

vo·ta·ry (vō′tə-rē) ▸*n., pl.* **-ries 1a.** One bound by religious vows. **b.** A devout worshiper. **2.** One who is fervently devoted, as to a leader, activity, or ideal. [< Lat. *vōtum*, VOW[1].]

vote (vōt) ▸*n.* **1a.** A formal expression of preference for a candidate for office or for a proposed resolution of an issue. **b.** A means by which such a preference is made known, such as a raised hand or a marked ballot. **2.** The number of votes cast in an election or to resolve an issue. **3.** A group of voters: *the rural vote.* **4.** The result of an election. **5.** Suffrage. ▸*v.* **vot·ed, vot·ing 1.** To cast a vote. **2.** To endorse, bring into existence, or make available by vote. [< Lat. *vōtum*, VOW[1].] —**vot′er** *n.*

vo·tive (vō′tĭv) ▸*adj.* Given or dedicated in fulfillment of a vow. [< Lat. *vōtum*, VOW[1].]

vouch (vouch) ▸*v.* **1.** To give a personal assurance or guarantee: *I can vouch for his integrity.* **2.** To serve as a guarantee. **3.** To substantiate by supplying evidence. [< AN *voucher*, summon.]

vouch·er (vou′chər) ▸*n.* **1.** A piece of substantiating evidence; proof. **2.** A written record, as of an expenditure or transaction. **3.** A certificate representing a credit against future expenditures.

vouch·safe (vouch-sāf′, vouch′sāf′) ▸*v.* **-safed, -saf·ing** To condescend to grant or bestow. [ME *vouchen sauf*, warrant as safe.]

vow[1] (vou) ▸*n.* **1.** An earnest promise that binds one to a specified act or mode of behavior. **2.** A declaration or assertion. ▸*v.* **1.** To promise solemnly; pledge. See Synonyms at **promise**. **2.** To make a vow. —*idiom:* **take vows** To enter a religious order. [< Lat. *vōtum* < *vovēre*, to vow.] —**vow′er** *n.*

vow[2] (vou) ▸*v.* To declare or assert. [< AVOW.]

vow·el (vou′əl) ▸*n.* **1.** A speech sound created by the relatively free passage of breath through the larynx and mouth. **2.** A letter representing a vowel. [< Lat. *vōcālis*, sounding.]

vox pop·u·li (vŏks pŏp′yə-lī′, -lē) ▸*n.* Popular opinion. [Lat. *vōx populī*, voice of the people.]

voy·age (voi′ĭj) ▸*n.* A long journey, esp. by sea, to foreign or distant parts. ▸*v.* **-aged, -ag·ing** To make a voyage. [< LLat. *viāticum*, journey.] —**voy′ag·er** *n.*

voy·eur (voi-yûr′) ▸*n.* **1.** A person who derives sexual gratification from observing the naked bodies or sexual acts of others. **2.** An enthusiastic observer of sordid or sensational subjects. [Fr. < OFr. *voir*, see < Lat. *vidēre.*] —**voy·eur′ism** *n.* —**voy′eur·is′tic** *adj.*

VP ▸*abbr.* **1.** verb phrase **2.** vice president

VS ▸*abbr.* veterinary surgeon

vs. ▸*abbr.* versus

vss. ▸*abbr.* verses

VT ▸*abbr.* Vermont

Vul·can (vŭl′kən) ▸*n. Rom. Myth.* The god of fire and metalworking.

vul·ca·nism (vŭl′kə-nĭz′əm) ▸*n.* Var. of **vol·canism**.

vul·ca·nize (vŭl′kə-nīz′) ▸*v.* **-nized, -niz·ing** To improve the strength, resiliency, and texture of (e.g., rubber) by combining with sulfur or other additives under heat and pressure. —**vul′ca·ni·za′tion** n. —**vul′ca·niz′er** n.

Vulg. ▸abbr. Vulgate

vul·gar (vŭl′gər) ▸adj. **1.** Crudely indecent. **2.** Deficient in taste, cultivation, or refinement. **3.** Of or expressed in language spoken by the common people; vernacular. **4.** Of or associated with the common people. [< Lat. *vulgāris*, of the common people < *vulgus*, common people.] —**vul′gar·ly** adv.

vul·gar·i·an (vŭl-gâr′ē-ən) ▸n. One who displays wealth ostentatiously and is often poorly educated or lacking in refinement. See Synonyms at **boor.**

vul·gar·ism (vŭl′gə-rĭz′əm) ▸n. **1.** Vulgarity. **2a.** A crudely indecent word or phrase; obscenity. **b.** A word, phrase, or manner of expression used chiefly by uneducated people.

vul·gar·i·ty (vŭl-găr′ĭ-tē) ▸n., pl. **-ties 1.** The quality or condition of being vulgar. **2.** Something, such as an act or expression, that offends good taste or propriety.

vul·gar·ize (vŭl′gə-rīz′) ▸v. **-ized, -iz·ing 1.** To make vulgar; debase. **2.** To popularize. —**vul′-gar·i·za′tion** n. —**vul′gar·iz′er** n.

Vulgar Latin ▸n. The common speech of the ancient Romans, which is distinguished from standard literary Latin and is the ancestor of the Romance languages.

vul·gate (vŭl′gāt′, -gĭt) ▸n. **1.** Common speech; vernacular. **2. Vulgate** The Latin edition of the Bible used as the Roman Catholic authorized version. [< LLat. *vulgāta*, popular.]

vul·ner·a·ble (vŭl′nər-ə-bəl) ▸adj. **1.** Not protected against harm or injury. **2.** Susceptible to attack; assailable. **3.** Easily affected or hurt, as by criticism. [< Lat. *vulnerāre*, to wound.] —**vul′ner·a·bil′i·ty** n. —**vul′ner·a·bly** adv.

vul·pine (vŭl′pīn′) ▸adj. **1.** Of a fox. **2.** Cunning. [< Lat. *vulpēs*, fox.]

vul·ture (vŭl′chər) ▸n. **1.** Any of various large, usu. carrion-eating birds characteristically having a featherless head and neck. **2.** A greedy, opportunistic person. [< Lat. *vultur.*]

vul·va (vŭl′və) ▸n., pl. **-vae** (-vē) The external genital organs of the female. [Lat., covering.] —**vul′val, vul′var** adj.

vv. ▸abbr. verses

v.v. ▸abbr. vice versa

W

w¹ or **W** (dŭb′əl-yōō, -yōō) ▸n., pl. **w's** or **W's** also **ws** or **Ws** The 23rd letter of the English alphabet.

w² ▸abbr. **1.** weight **2.** width **3.** *Phys.* work

W ▸abbr. **1.** watt **2.** week **3a.** west **b.** western **4.** *Sports* win

w. ▸abbr. **1.** wife **2.** also **w/** with

WA ▸abbr. Washington

WAAC ▸abbr. Women's Army Auxiliary Corps

WAAF ▸abbr. Women's Auxiliary Air Force

WAC ▸abbr. Women's Army Corps

wack·y (wăk′ē) also **whack·y** (wăk′ē, hwăk′ē) ▸adj. **-i·er, -i·est** *Slang* **1.** Eccentric. **2.** Crazy; silly: *a wacky outfit.* [Prob. < *out of whack.*] —**wack′i·ly** adv. —**wack′i·ness** n.

wad (wŏd) ▸n. **1.** A small mass of soft material. **2.** A compressed ball, roll, or lump, as of tobacco. **3.** A plug, as of cloth, used to hold a powder charge in place, as in a muzzleloading gun. **4.** *Informal* A large amount. **5.** *Informal* A sizable roll of paper money. ▸v. **wad·ded, wad·ding 1.** To compress into a wad. **2.** To pad, pack, line, or plug with wadding. [?]

wad·ding (wŏd′ĭng) ▸n. **1.** Material such as cotton or wool used in layers for padding. **2.** Material for gun wads.

wad·dle (wŏd′l) ▸v. **-dled, -dling** To walk with short steps that tilt the body from side to side. [< WADE.] —**wad′dle** n. —**wad′dler** n.

wade (wād) ▸v. **wad·ed, wad·ing 1.** To walk in or through a substance, such as water, that impedes movement. **2.** To make one's way arduously: *waded through a boring report.* [< OE *wadan.*]

wad·er (wā′dər) ▸n. **1.** See **wading bird. 2. waders** Waterproof hip boots or trousers.

wa·di (wä′dē) ▸n., pl. **-dis** also **-dies 1.** A valley, gully, or streambed in N Africa and SW Asia that remains dry except during the rainy season. **2.** An oasis. [Ar. *wādī.*]

wad·ing bird (wā′dĭng) ▸n. A long-legged bird that frequents shallow water.

WAF ▸abbr. Women in the Air Force

wa·fer (wā′fər) ▸n. **1.** A thin crisp cake, biscuit, or candy. **2.** *Eccles.* A small thin disk of unleavened bread used in the Eucharist. **3.** *Electron.* A thin semiconductor slice on which an integrated circuit can be formed. [< ONFr. *waufre*, of Gmc. orig.]

waf·fle¹ (wŏf′əl) ▸n. A light crisp batter cake baked in a waffle iron. [< MDu. *wāfel.*]

waf·fle² (wŏf′əl) ▸v. **-fled, -fling 1.** To be unable to make a decision. **2.** To speak or write evasively. [Prob. < obsolete *waff*, yelp.]

waffle iron ▸n. An appliance having hinged indented plates that impress a grid pattern into waffle batter as it cooks.

waft (wăft, wäft) ▸v. To float or carry gently and smoothly through the air or over water. ▸n. **1.** A whiff. **2.** A light breeze. [< *wafter*, convoy ship.]

wag¹ (wăg) ▸v. **wagged, wag·ging** To move or cause to move briskly and repeatedly from side to side, to and fro, or up and down. [ME *waggen.*] —**wag** n.

wag² (wăg) ▸n. A humorous or witty person. [Perh. < WAG¹.] —**wag′ger·y** n. —**wag′gish** adj.

wage (wāj) ▸n. **1.** Payment for labor or services to a worker. **2. wages** (takes sing. or pl. v.) A suitable return or reward. ▸v. **waged, wag·ing** To engage in (e.g., a war or campaign). [< ONFr., of Gmc. orig.]

wa·ger (wā′jər) ▸n. Something staked on an uncertain outcome; bet. ▸v. To bet. [< ONFr. *wagier*, pledge.]

wag·gle (wăg′əl) ▸v. **-gled, -gling** To move or wave with short quick motions; wag. [ME *wagelen.*] —**wag′gle** n. —**wag′gly** adj.

Wag·ner (väg′nər), **Richard** 1813–83. German

composer. —**Wag·ner′i·an** *adj. & n.*

wag·on (wăg′ən) ►*n.* **1.** A large, four-wheeled vehicle drawn by draft animals or tractor and used esp. for transporting loads. **2a.** A station wagon. **b.** A police patrol wagon. **3.** A child's low, four-wheeled cart. —*idiom:* **on the wagon** *Slang* Abstaining from alcohol. [< MDu. *wagen*.]

wagon train ►*n.* A line or train of wagons traveling cross-country.

wa·hoo (wä-hōō′, wä′hōō) ►*n., pl.* **-hoo** or **-hoos** A large food and game fish of subtropical and tropical seas. [?]

waif (wāf) ►*n.* **1.** A homeless or forsaken child. **2.** A person, esp. a young woman, who is thin or gaunt. **3.** A stray animal. [< AN, stray.]

Wai·ki·ki (wī′kĭ-kē′) A beach and resort district of Oahu I., HI, SE of Honolulu.

wail (wāl) ►*v.* **1.** To cry loudly and mournfully, as in grief or protest. **2.** To make a mournful, high-pitched sound: *The wind wailed through the trees.* [ME *wailen*, prob. of Scand. orig.] —**wail** *n.* —**wail′er** *n.*

wain (wān) ►*n.* A large open farm wagon. [< OE *wægn*.]

wain·scot (wān′skət, -skŏt′, -skōt′) ►*n.* **1.** A facing or paneling, usu. of wood, on the walls of a room. **2.** The lower part of an interior wall when finished in a material different from that of the upper part. [< MDu. *waghenscot*.] —**wain′scot** *v.*

wain·wright (wān′rīt′) ►*n.* One who builds and repairs wagons.

waist (wāst) ►*n.* **1.** The part of the human trunk between the bottom of the rib cage and the pelvis. **2.** The part of a garment that encircles the waist. **3.** The middle section of an object. [ME *wast*.]

waist·band (wāst′bănd′) ►*n.* A band of material encircling the waist of a garment.

waist·coat (wĕs′kĭt, wāst′kōt′) ►*n. Chiefly Brit.* A vest.

waist·line (wāst′līn′) ►*n.* **1a.** The narrowest part of the waist. **b.** The measurement of this part. **2.** The line at which the skirt and bodice of a dress join.

wait (wāt) ►*v.* **1.** To remain in expectation: *waiting for the bus.* **2.** To stay in one place until another catches up. **3.** To be ready for use. **4.** To be in abeyance. **5.** To work as a waiter, waitress, or salesperson. ►*n.* The act of waiting or the time spent waiting. [< ONFr. *waitier*, watch.]

wait·er (wā′tər) ►*n.* One who serves at a table, as in a restaurant.

wait·ing room (wā′tĭng) ►*n.* A room, as in a doctor's office, for the use of people waiting.

wait·ress (wā′trĭs) ►*n.* A woman who serves at a table. See Usage Note at **–ess.**

waive (wāv) ►*v.* **waived, waiv·ing** To give up (a claim or right) voluntarily. [< AN *weyver*, abandon.]

waiv·er (wā′vər) ►*n.* **1.** Intentional relinquishment of a right, claim, or privilege. **2.** The document that waives a right or claim.

wake¹ (wāk) ►*v.* **woke** (wōk) or **waked** (wākt), **waked** or **wok·en** (wō′kən), **wak·ing** **1.** To become awake: *woke late.* **2.** To stay awake. **3.** To cause to come out of sleep. **4.** To rouse from inactivity. ►*n.* A gathering of people in the presence of the body of a deceased person in order to honor the person and console one another.

[< OE *wacan* and *wacian*.]

wake² (wāk) ►*n.* **1.** The visible track left by something, as a ship, moving through water. **2.** A track or condition left behind; aftermath. [Of Scand. orig.]

wake·ful (wāk′fəl) ►*adj.* **1a.** Not sleeping. **b.** Without sleep; sleepless. **2.** Watchful; alert. —**wake′ful·ness** *n.*

Wake Island An island of the W Pacific between HI and Guam.

wak·en (wā′kən) ►*v.* **1.** To rouse from sleep; awake. **2.** To rouse from an inactive state. [< OE *wæcnan.*] —**wak′en·er** *n.*

wale (wāl) ►*n.* **1.** A raised ridge in the surface of a fabric such as corduroy. **2.** A mark raised on the skin, as by a whip; welt. [< OE *walu*, welt, ridge.]

Wales (wālz) A principality of the United Kingdom W of England on the island of Great Britain. Cap. Cardiff.

Wa·łę·sa (wä-lĕn′sə, vä-wĕn′sä), **Lech** b. 1943. Polish leader.

Wal·cott (wôl′kŏt′, wŏl′-), **Derek Alton** b. 1930. West Indian writer.

Wald·heim (wôld′hīm′, vält′-), **Kurt** 1918–2007. Austrian diplomat and politician.

walk (wôk) ►*v.* **1.** To move or cause to move on foot at a pace slower than a run. **2.** To pass over, on, or through on foot. **3.** *Informal* To quit one's job. **4.** *Informal* To be acquitted. **5.** *Baseball* To give or be given a base on balls. ►*n.* **1a.** A manner of walking. **b.** A gait, esp. a slow gait of a horse in which the feet touch the ground one after another. **2.** The act or an instance of walking. **3.** A distance covered in walking. **4.** A sidewalk or other walkway. **5.** *Baseball* A base on balls. —*phrasal verbs:* **walk out** To go on strike. **walk over** *Informal* To treat badly or contemptuously. [< OE *wealcan*, roll.] —**walk′er** *n.* —**walk′a·ble** *adj.*

walk·a·way (wôk′ə-wā′) ►*n.* An easily won contest or victory.

Wal·ker (wô′kər), **Alice** b. 1944. Amer. writer.

Alice Walker
photographed in 2009

walk·ie-talk·ie (wô′kē-tô′kē) ►*n.* A portable two-way short-range radio.

walk·ing papers (wô′kĭng) ►*pl.n. Slang* A notice of discharge or dismissal.

walking stick ►*n.* **1.** A staff used as an aid in walking. **2.** Any of various insects that have the appearance of twigs or sticks.

walk-on (wôk′ŏn′, -ôn′) ►*n.* A minor, usu. nonspeaking role in a theatrical production.

walk·out (wôk′out′) ►*n.* **1.** A labor strike. **2.** The act of leaving or quitting a meeting or organization as a sign of protest.

walk·o·ver (wôk′ō′vər) ►*n.* Something that is easy and presents no difficulties, esp. an easily won sports contest.

walk·up also **walk-up** (wôk′ŭp′) ►*n.* **1.** A multistory building with no elevator. **2.** An apartment or office in a walkup.

walk·way (wôk′wā′) ►*n.* A passage for walking.

wall (wôl) ►*n.* **1.** A sturdy upright structure, as in a building, that encloses an area or separates two areas. **2.** A defensive embankment or rampart. **3.** Something resembling a wall in appearance or function: *the stomach wall.* ►*v.* To enclose, surround, or fortify with or as if with a wall. See Synonyms at **enclose.** [< Lat. *vallum*, palisade.]

wal·la·by (wŏl′ə-bē) ►*n., pl.* **-bies** or **-by** Any of various Australian marsupials related to the kangaroos but gen. smaller. [Dharuk (Australian) *walaba.*]

wall·board (wôl′bôrd′) ►*n.* See **drywall.**

wal·let (wŏl′ĭt) ►*n.* A flat pocket-sized folding case for holding paper money, cards, or photographs. [ME *walet*, knapsack.]

wall·eye (wôl′ī′) ►*n.* **1.** *pl.* **-eye** or **-eyes** A North American freshwater food and game fish having large silvery eyes. **2a.** An imbalance of the eye muscles in which one or both of the eyes deviate outward. **b.** An eye with a white or opaque cornea. —**wall′eyed′** *adj.*

wall·flow·er (wôl′flou′ər) ►*n.* **1.** A cultivated plant with fragrant yellow, orange, or brownish flowers. **2.** One who does not participate in the activity at a social event because of shyness or unpopularity.

Wal·loon (wŏ-lōōn′) ►*n.* **1.** One of a people of Celtic descent inhabiting S and SE Belgium. **2.** The Romance language traditionally spoken by the Walloons, closely related to French.

wal·lop (wŏl′əp) *Informal* ►*v.* **1.** To beat soundly; thrash. **2.** To strike with a hard blow. **3.** To defeat thoroughly. ►*n.* **1.** A hard blow. **2.** A powerful force or effect. [< ONFr. **waloper*, gallop.] —**wal′lop·er** *n.*

wal·low (wŏl′ō) ►*v.* **-lowed, -low·ing 1.** To lie or roll about in water or mud. **2.** To indulge oneself: *wallowing in self-pity.* **3.** To be plentifully supplied: *wallowing in money.* ►*n.* A muddy pool where animals wallow. [< OE *wealwian.*]

wall·pa·per (wôl′pā′pər) ►*n.* **1.** Paper printed with designs or colors and pasted to a wall as a decorative covering. **2.** A picture or design displayed on the background of an electronic screen. —**wall′pa′per** *v.*

wall-to-wall (wôl′tə-wôl′) ►*adj.* **1.** Completely covering a floor. **2.** *Informal* Present or spreading everywhere.

wal·nut (wôl′nŭt′, -nət) ►*n.* **1a.** Any of several deciduous trees with round sticky fruit that encloses an edible nut. **b.** The nut of a walnut. **2.** The hard, dark brown wood of a walnut. [< OE *wealhhnutu.*]

Wal·pole (wô′pōl′, wŏl′-), **Horace.** 4th Earl of Orford. 1717–97. British writer.

wal·rus (wôl′rəs, wŏl′-) ►*n., pl.* **-rus** or **-rus·es** A large Arctic marine mammal with two long tusks and tough wrinkled skin. [Du.]

walrus

waltz (wôlts, wôls) ►*n.* **1.** A dance in triple time with a strong accent on the first beat. **2.** Music for this dance. ►*v.* **1.** To dance the waltz. **2.** *Slang* To move lightly and easily: *waltzed out of the room.* **3.** *Informal* To accomplish a task, chore, or assignment with little effort. [< OHGer. *walzan*, roll.] —**waltz′er** *n.*

Wam·pa·no·ag (wäm′pə-nō′ăg) ►*n., pl.* **-ag** or **-ags 1.** A member of a Native American people of E Rhode Island and SE Massachusetts. **2.** The Algonquian language of the Wampanoag.

wam·pum (wŏm′pəm, wôm′-) ►*n.* **1.** Small beads made from mollusk shells and fashioned into strings or belts, formerly used by certain Native American peoples as currency and jewelry. **2.** *Informal* Money. [Of Massachusett orig.]

wan (wŏn) ►*adj.* **wan·ner, wan·nest 1.** Unnaturally pale. **2.** Suggestive of weariness, illness, or unhappiness. [< OE *wann*, gloomy, dark.] —**wan′ly** *adv.* —**wan′ness** *n.*

wand (wŏnd) ►*n.* **1.** A slender rod carried as a symbol of office; scepter. **2.** A stick or baton used by a magician, conjurer, or diviner. [< ON *vöndr.*]

wan·der (wŏn′dər) ►*v.* **1.** To move about aimlessly. **2.** To go by an indirect route or at no set pace. **3.** To go astray. **4.** To lose clarity or coherence of thought or expression. [< OE *wandrian.*] —**wan′der·er** *n.*

wan·der·ing Jew (wŏn′dər-ĭng) ►*n.* A trailing plant with usu. variegated foliage, popular as a houseplant.

wan·der·lust (wŏn′dər-lŭst′) ►*n.* A strong or irresistible impulse to travel. [Ger.]

wane (wān) ►*v.* **waned, wan·ing 1.** To decrease gradually in size, amount, intensity, or degree. **2.** To show a decreasing illuminated area, as the moon does in passing from full to new. **3.** To approach an end: *The old year is waning.* ►*n.* **1.** A gradual decrease or decline. **2.** The period of the moon's waning. [< OE *wanian.*]

wan·gle (wăng′gəl) ►*v.* **-gled, -gling** *Informal* To make, achieve, or get by cleverness or deceit. [?] —**wang′ler** *n.*

wan·na·be (wŏn′ə-bē′, wôn′-) *Informal* ►*n.* **1.** One who aspires to a role or position. **2.** One who emulates the customs of an admired individual or group. **3.** An imitative product. ►*adj.* Wishing to be; would-be. [< *want to be.*]

want (wŏnt, wônt) ►*v.* **1.** To wish for. See Synonyms at **desire. 2.** To be without; lack. **3.** To be in need of; require. ►*n.* **1.** The condition of lacking something usual or necessary. **2.** Pressing need; destitution. **3.** Something desired. **4.** A defect; fault. [< ON *vanta*, be lacking.]

want ad ►*n.* A classified advertisement.

want·ing (wŏn′tĭng, wôn′-) ►*adj.* **1.** Absent; lacking. **2.** Not up to standards or expectations. ►*prep.* **1.** Without. **2.** Minus; less.

wan·ton (wŏn′tən) ►*adj.* **1.** Lascivious or promiscuous. Used esp. of women. **2.** Capricious and unjust: *wanton killing.* **3.** Unrestrainedly excessive: *wanton spending.* **4.** Luxuriant; overabundant. **5.** Frolicsome; playful. ►*n.* One, esp. a woman, who is licentious or promiscuous. [ME *wantowen.*] —**wan′ton·ly** *adv.* —**wan′-ton·ness** *n.*

wap·i·ti (wŏp′ĭ-tē) ►*n., pl.* **-ti** or **-tis** See **elk.** [Shawnee *waapiti.*]

war (wôr) ►*n.* **1a.** A state or period of armed conflict between nations, states, or parties. **b.** The techniques of war; military science. **2a.** A condition of antagonism or contention. **b.** A determined struggle or attack. ►*v.* **warred, war·ring 1.** To wage war. **2.** To struggle, contend, or fight. [< ONFr. *werre,* of Gmc. orig.]

war·ble (wôr′bəl) ►*v.* **-bled, -bling** To sing with trills, runs, or other melodic embellishments. ►*n.* The act or sound of warbling. [< ONFr. *werbler,* of Gmc. orig.]

war·bler (wôr′blər) ►*n.* **1.** Any of various small, variously colored New World songbirds. **2.** Any of various small, often brownish or grayish Old World songbirds.

war chest ►*n.* **1.** An accumulation of funds to finance a war effort. **2.** A fund reserved for a particular purpose such as a political campaign.

war cry ►*n.* A battle cry.

ward (wôrd) ►*n.* **1.** A division in a hospital: *a maternity ward.* **2.** An administrative division of a city or town, esp. an electoral district. **3.** A division in a prison. **4.** A minor or a person deemed legally incompetent. **5.** A means of protection. ►*v.* To guard; protect. —*phrasal verb:* **ward off** To avert: *ward off disaster.* [< OE *weard,* a watching.]

–ward or **–wards** ►*suff.* Direction toward: *downward; backwards.* [< OE *-weard.*]

war·den (wôrd′n) ►*n.* **1.** The chief administrative official of a prison. **2.** An official charged with the enforcement of certain regulations: *a game warden.* **3.** A churchwarden. [< ONFr. *wardein,* a guard.]

ward·er (wôr′dər) ►*n.* A guard or watcher of a gate or tower. [< ONFr. *warder,* to guard, of Gmc. orig.]

ward·robe (wôr′drōb′) ►*n.* **1.** A cabinet or closet built to hold clothes. **2.** Garments collectively, esp. all the clothing belonging to one person. **3.** The costumes belonging to a theater. [< ONFr. *warderobe.*]

ward·room (wôrd′rōōm′, -rŏŏm′) ►*n.* The common recreation area and dining room for the commissioned officers on a warship.

ward·ship (wôrd′shĭp′) ►*n.* **1.** The state of being a ward. **2.** Custody; guardianship.

ware (wâr) ►*n.* **1.** An item that is offered for sale. **2.** An attribute or ability, esp. when regarded as an article of commerce. [< OE *waru.*]

–ware ►*suff.* **1.** Articles of the same general kind, material, or use: *silverware.* **2.** Software: *shareware.* [< WARE. Sense 2 < SOFTWARE.]

ware·house (wâr′hous′) ►*n.* A place in which goods or merchandise are stored. —**ware′-house′** (-houz′) *v.*

war·fare (wôr′fâr′) ►*n.* **1.** The act of waging war. **2.** Conflict; strife. [ME.]

war·fa·rin (wôr′fər-ĭn) ►*n.* An anticoagulant drug used also to kill rodents. [*W(isconsin) A(lumni) R(esearch) F(oundation)* + *(coum)arin,* a compound.]

war·head (wôr′hĕd′) ►*n.* The section in the forward part of a projectile, such as a guided missile, that contains the explosive charge.

War·hol (wôr′hôl′), **Andy** 1928–87. Amer. artist.

war·horse (wôr′hôrs′) ►*n.* **1.** A horse used in combat; charger. **2.** *Informal* One who has been through many struggles. **3.** A frequently performed musical or dramatic work.

war·like (wôr′līk′) ►*adj.* **1.** Belligerent; hostile. **2.** Of or relating to war.

war·lock (wôr′lŏk′) ►*n.* A man claiming or believed to practice witchcraft. [< OE *wærloga,* oath-breaker.]

war·lord (wôr′lôrd′) ►*n.* A military commander exercising civil power in a region.

warm (wôrm) ►*adj.* **-er, -est 1.** Moderately hot. **2.** Preserving or imparting heat: *a warm overcoat.* **3.** Having a sensation of unusually high body heat, as from exercise. **4.** Marked by enthusiasm; ardent: *warm support.* **5.** Excited, animated, or emotional: *a warm debate.* **6.** Recently made; fresh: *a warm trail.* **7.** Close to discovering, guessing, or finding something, as in certain games. ►*v.* **1.** To make or become warm. **2.** To make zealous or ardent; enliven. **3.** To fill with pleasant emotions: *warmed by the sight of home.* **4.** To become ardent, enthusiastic, or animated: *began to warm to the subject.* **5.** To become kindly disposed or friendly: *felt the audience warming to her.* —*phrasal verb:* **warm up** To make or become ready for action, as by exercising or practicing beforehand. [< OE *wearm.*] —**warm′er** *n.* —**warm′ish** *adj.* —**warm′ly** *adv.* —**warm′ness** *n.*

warm-blood·ed (wôrm′blŭd′ĭd) ►*adj.* Maintaining a relatively constant and warm body temperature independent of environmental temperature, as a mammal. —**warm′-blood′-ed·ness** *n.*

warm-heart·ed (wôrm′här′tĭd) ►*adj.* Kind; friendly. —**warm′heart′ed·ness** *n.*

war·mon·ger (wôr′mŭng′gər, -mŏng′-) ►*n.* One who advocates or attempts to stir up war. —**war′mon′ger·ing** *n.*

warmth (wôrmth) ►*n.* **1.** The quality or condition of being warm. **2.** Excitement or intensity. [ME.]

warm-up (wôrm′ŭp′) ►*n.* The act, procedure, or period of warming up.

warn (wôrn) ►*v.* **1.** To make aware of present or potential danger; caution. **2.** To admonish as to action or manners. **3.** To notify to go or stay away. [< OE *warnian.*]

warn·ing (wôr′nĭng) ►*n.* **1.** An indication or statement of impending danger. **2.** Advice to beware or desist. **3.** A cautionary or deterrent example. ►*adj.* Acting or serving to warn.

warp (wôrp) ►*v.* **1.** To twist or bend or become twisted or bent out of shape. **2.** To alter or be altered from a normal, proper, or healthy state. **3.** *Naut.* To move (a vessel) by hauling on a line fastened to an anchor or pier. ►*n.* **1.** The state of being twisted or bent out of shape. **2.** A distortion or twist. **3.** The threads that run lengthwise in a woven fabric, crossed at right angles to the woof. [< OE *weorpan*, throw away.]

war·path (wôr′păth′, -päth′) ►*n.* **1.** A course that leads to warfare or battle. **2.** A belligerent course or mood.

war·plane (wôr′plān′) ►*n.* A combat aircraft.

war·rant (wôr′ənt, wŏr′-) ►*n.* **1.** An order that serves as authorization, esp. a judicial writ authorizing a search, seizure, or arrest. **2.** Something that assures, attests to, or guarantees; proof. **3.** Authorization or certification; sanction. **4.** A certificate of appointment given to a warrant officer. ►*v.* **1.** To provide adequate grounds for; justify. **2a.** To guarantee (a product). **b.** To guarantee (a purchaser) indemnification against damage or loss. [< ONFr. *warant*, authorization, of Gmc. orig.] —**war′ran·tee′** *n.* —**war′ran·tor** *n.*

warrant officer ►*n.* A military officer intermediate between a noncommissioned and a commissioned rank.

war·ran·ty (wôr′ən-tē, wŏr′-) ►*n., pl.* **-ties 1.** A legally binding guarantee. **2.** Official authorization or sanction. **3.** Justification for an act or course of action.

war·ren (wôr′ən, wŏr′-) ►*n.* **1.** An area where small game animals, esp. rabbits, live and breed. **2.** An overcrowded living area. **3.** A mazelike place where one may easily become lost. [< ONFr. *warenne*, enclosure.]

Warren, Earl 1891–1974. Amer. jurist; chief justice of the US Supreme Court (1953–69).

war·ri·or (wôr′ē-ər, wŏr′-) ►*n.* One engaged or experienced in battle. [< ONFr. *werreieur*.]

War·saw (wôr′sô′) The capital of Poland, in the E-central part on the Vistula R.

war·ship (wôr′shĭp′) ►*n.* A combat ship.

wart (wôrt) ►*n.* **1.** A hard rough lump on the skin, caused by a virus. **2.** A similar growth, as on a plant. **3.** A flaw or imperfection. [< OE *wearte*.] —**wart′y** *adj.*

wart·hog (wôrt′hôg′, -hŏg′) ►*n.* A wild African hog having prominent upward-curving tusks and wartlike growths on the face.

war·time (wôr′tīm′) ►*n.* A time of war.

war·y (wâr′ē) ►*adj.* **-i·er, -i·est 1.** On guard; watchful. **2.** Characterized by caution. [< OE *wær.*] —**war′i·ly** *adv.* —**war′i·ness** *n.*

was (wŭz, wŏz; wəz *when unstressed*) ►*v.* 1st and 3rd pers. sing. p. indic. of **be.**

wa·sa·bi (wə-sä′bē, wä′sə-) ►*n.* A pungent green Japanese condiment made from the root of a plant similar to horseradish. [Jap.]

wash (wŏsh, wôsh) ►*v.* **1.** To cleanse, using water or other liquid, usu. with soap, detergent, or bleach, by immersing, dipping, rubbing, or scrubbing. **2.** To cleanse oneself. **3.** To make moist or wet. **4.** To flow over, against, or past: *waves washed the beach.* **5.** To carry, erode, or destroy by moving water: *Rain washed the topsoil away.* **6.** To rid of corruption; purify. **7.** To separate constituents of (an ore) by immersion in or agitation with water. **8.** *Informal* To hold up under examination: *Your excuse won't wash.* ►*n.* **1.** The act of washing. **2.** A quantity of articles that are to be or have just been washed. **3.** A liquid used in washing or coating. **4.** A thin layer of watercolor or India ink spread on a drawing. **5.** A rush of water. **6.** An event or activity in which one's gains equal one's losses. —*phrasal verbs:* **wash down** To follow the

swallowing of (food) with a drink. **wash up 1.** To clean one's hands. **2.** To ruin: *He's washed up as a ballplayer.* [< OE *wæscan.*]

wash·a·ble (wŏsh′ə-bəl, wôsh′-) ►*adj.* Capable of being washed without damage.

wash-and-wear (wŏsh′ən-wâr′, wôsh′-) ►*adj.* Treated so as to require little or no ironing after being washed.

wash·ba·sin (wŏsh′bā′sən, wôsh′-) ►*n.* A washbowl.

wash·board (wŏsh′bôrd′, wôsh′-) ►*n.* A board having a corrugated surface on which clothes can be rubbed during laundering.

wash·bowl (wŏsh′bōl′, wôsh′-) ►*n.* A basin that can be filled with water for use in washing oneself.

wash·cloth (wŏsh′klôth′, -klŏth′, wôsh′-) ►*n.* A cloth used for washing the face or body.

washed-out (wŏsht′out′, wôsht′-) ►*adj.* **1.** Carried or eroded away by moving water: *a washed-out road.* **2.** Lacking color or intensity; faded. **3.** Exhausted.

washed-up (wŏsht′ŭp′, wôsht′-) ►*adj.* No longer successful, esp. in a public career.

wash·er (wŏsh′ər, wô′shər) ►*n.* **1.** One that washes, esp. a machine for washing. **2.** A flat disk, as of metal or rubber, placed beneath a nut or bolt to distribute pressure or placed between parts to space the parts properly or prevent leakage in a joint.

wash·ing (wŏsh′ĭng, wô′shĭng) ►*n.* **1.** Articles washed at one time. **2.** The residue after an ore has been washed.

washing soda ►*n.* A hydrated sodium carbonate used as a general cleanser.

Wash·ing·ton (wŏsh′ĭng-tən, wô′shĭng-) **1.** A state of the NW US on the Pacific Ocean. Cap. Olympia. **2.** The capital of the US, on the Potomac R. between VA and MD and coextensive with the District of Columbia. —**Wash′ing·to′ni·an** (-tō′nē-ən) *adj. & n.*

Washington, Booker T(aliaferro) 1856–1915. Amer. educator.

Washington, Dinah Ruth Lee Jones. 1924–63. Amer. jazz and blues singer.

George Washington
1795 portrait

Martha Washington
c. 1853 portrait

Washington, George 1732–99. Amer. military leader and 1st US president (1789–97).

Washington, Martha Dandridge Custis 1731–1802. 1st first lady of the US (1789–97).

wash·out (wŏsh′out′, wôsh′-) ►*n.* **1.** Erosion of a relatively soft surface, such as a roadbed, by a sudden gush of water. **2.** A failure or disappointment, esp. an event canceled due to rain or a person who has failed in a course of study.

wash·room (wŏsh′rōōm′, -rŏŏm′, wôsh′-) ►*n.* A bathroom, esp. one in a public place.

wash·stand (wŏsh′stănd′, wôsh′-) ►*n.* **1.** A stand designed to hold a basin and pitcher of water for washing. **2.** A bathroom sink.

wash·tub (wŏsh′tŭb′, wôsh′-) ►*n.* A tub used for washing clothes.

was·n't (wŭz′ənt, wŏz′-) Was not.

wasp (wŏsp, wôsp) ►*n.* Any of various social or solitary insects having a slender body with a constricted abdomen and often inflicting a painful sting. [< OE *wæps.*]

WASP or **Wasp** (wŏsp, wôsp) ►*n.* A white Protestant of Anglo-Saxon ancestry. [*W(hite) A(nglo-)S(axon) P(rotestant)*.]

wasp·ish (wŏs′pĭsh) ►*adj.* **1.** Of or suggestive of a wasp. **2.** Easily irritated or annoyed; irascible. —**wasp′ish·ly** *adv.*

wasp waist ►*n.* A very slender or tightly corseted waist. —**wasp′-waist′ed** *adj.*

was·sail (wŏs′əl, wŏ-sāl′) ►*n.* **1a.** A toast given in drinking someone's health. **b.** The drink used in such toasting. **2.** A festivity with much drinking and merriment. ►*v.* To drink to the health of; toast. [< ON *ves heill,* be healthy.]

wast (wŏst; wəst *when unstressed*) ►*v. Archaic* 2nd pers. sing. p.t. of **be.**

wast·age (wā′stĭj) ►*n.* **1.** Loss by deterioration or wear. **2.** An amount wasted.

waste (wāst) ►*v.* **wast·ed, wast·ing 1.** To use, consume, or expend thoughtlessly or carelessly. **2.** To lose or cause to lose energy, strength, or vigor: *Disease wasted his body.* **3.** To fail to take advantage of; lose: *waste an opportunity.* **4.** To destroy completely. ►*n.* **1.** The act or an instance of wasting or the condition of being wasted: *a waste of talent; gone to waste.* **2.** A barren or wild area or expanse. **3.** A useless byproduct. **4.** Garbage; trash. **5.** The undigested residue of food eliminated from the body; excrement. [< Lat. *vāstus,* empty.]

   Syns: *dissipate, fritter, squander* **Ant:** *save v.*

waste·bas·ket (wāst′băs′kĭt) ►*n.* A small container for trash.

waste·ful (wāst′fəl) ►*adj.* Marked by or inclined to waste. —**waste′ful·ly** *adv.*

waste·land (wāst′lănd′) ►*n.* Land that is desolate, barren, or ravaged.

waste·pa·per (wāst′pā′pər) ►*n.* Discarded paper.

wast·rel (wā′strəl) ►*n.* **1.** One who wastes. **2.** An idler or loafer. [< WASTE.]

watch (wŏch) ►*v.* **1.** To observe carefully or continuously. **2.** To look and wait expectantly or in anticipation: *watch for an opportunity.* **3.** To stay awake deliberately; keep vigil. **4.** To keep a watchful eye on; guard. **5.** To keep up on or informed about: *watch the price of gold.* **6.** To be careful about, esp. with regard to propriety: *Watch your language!* **7.** To tend (e.g., a flock). See Synonyms at **tend²**. ►*n.* **1.** The act of watching. **2.** A period of close observation. **3.** A person or group of people serving, esp. at night, to guard or protect. **4.** The post or period of duty of a guard or sentinel. **5.** *Naut.* **a.** Any of the periods of time, usu. four hours, into which the day aboard ship is divided. **b.** The members of a ship's crew on duty during a specific watch. **6.** A small portable timepiece, esp. one worn on the wrist. [< OE *wæccan.*] —**watch′er** *n.*

watch·dog (wŏch′dôg′, -dŏg′) ►*n.* **1.** A dog trained to guard people or property. **2.** One serving as a guardian or protector.

watch·ful (wŏch′fəl) ►*adj.* Closely observant or alert; vigilant. See Synonyms at **careful.** —**watch′ful·ly** *adv.* —**watch′ful·ness** *n.*

watch·mak·er (wŏch′mā′kər) ►*n.* One who makes or repairs watches.

watch·man (wŏch′mən) ►*n.* A man employed to stand guard or keep watch.

watch·tow·er (wŏch′tou′ər) ►*n.* An observation tower for a guard or lookout.

watch·word (wŏch′wûrd′) ►*n.* **1.** A prearranged reply to a challenge, as from a guard; password. **2.** A rallying cry; slogan.

wa·ter (wô′tər, wŏt′ər) ►*n.* **1.** A clear, colorless, odorless, and tasteless liquid, H_2O, essential for most plant and animal life and the most widely used of all solvents. **2a.** Any of various forms of water, as rain. **b.** *often* **waters** Naturally occurring mineral water, as at a spa. **3.** A body of water such as a sea, lake, river, or stream. **4.** A body fluid, such as urine, perspiration, or tears. **5.** An aqueous solution of a substance, esp. a gas: *ammonia water.* **6.** A wavy finish or sheen, as of a fabric. **7a.** The transparency and luster of a gem. **b.** A level of excellence: *of the first water.* ►*v.* **1.** To sprinkle, moisten, or supply with water. **2.** To give drinking water to. **3.** To dilute or weaken by adding water. **4.** To give a sheen to the surface of (silk, linen, or metal). **5.** To produce or discharge fluid, as from the eyes. —*idiom:* **water under the bridge** A past occurrence, esp. something unfortunate that cannot be rectified. [< OE *wæter.*]

wa·ter·bed (wô′tər-bĕd′, wŏt′ər-) ►*n.* A bed whose mattress is a large water-filled plastic bag.

wa·ter·bird also **water bird** (wô′tər-bûrd′, wŏt′ər-) ►*n.* A swimming or wading bird.

wa·ter·borne (wô′tər-bôrn′, wŏt′ər-) ►*adj.* **1.** Supported or transported by water: *waterborne freight.* **2.** Transmitted in water: *waterborne diseases.*

water buffalo ►*n.* A large, often domesticated Asian buffalo with large spreading horns, used esp. as a draft animal.

water cannon ►*n.* A truck-mounted apparatus that fires water at high pressure, used esp. to disperse crowds.

water chestnut ►*n.* **1.** An aquatic Asian sedge having cylindrical stems. **2.** The succulent edible corm of this plant.

water closet ►*n.* A room or booth containing a toilet and often a washbowl.

wa·ter·col·or (wô′tər-kŭl′ər, wŏt′ər-) ►*n.* **1.** A paint composed of a water-soluble pigment. **2.** A painting that is made with watercolors. —**wa′ter·col′or·ist** *n.*

wa·ter·course (wô′tər-kôrs′, wŏt′ər-) ►*n.* **1.** A channel through which water flows. **2.** A stream or river.

wa·ter·craft (wô′tər-krăft′, wŏt′ər-) ►*n.* A boat or ship.

wa·ter·cress (wô′tər-krĕs′, wŏt′ər-) ►*n.* A plant growing in freshwater ponds and streams and having pungent edible leaves.

wa·ter·fall (wô′tər-fôl′, wŏt′ər-) ►*n.* A steep descent of water from a height.

wa·ter·fowl (wô′tər-foul′, wŏt′ər-) ►*n.* **1.** A waterbird, esp. a swimming bird. **2.** Swimming birds, such as ducks and geese, collectively.

wa·ter·front (wô′tər-frŭnt′, wŏt′ər-) ►*n.* **1.**

Land abutting a body of water. **2.** The part of a town or city that abuts water.

water gap ►*n.* A break in a chain of mountains or hills through which a river runs.

water hyacinth ►*n.* A tropical American plant forming dense floating masses in ponds and streams.

wa·ter·ing hole (wô′tər-ĭng, wŏt′ər-) or **water hole** ►*n.* **1.** A pool where animals come to drink. **2.** *Informal* A place, such as a bar, where drinks are served.

wa·ter·ish (wô′tər-ĭsh, wŏt′ər-) ►*adj.* Watery.

water lily ►*n.* Any of various aquatic plants with broad floating leaves and showy, variously colored flowers.

water line ►*n.* **1.** The line on the hull of a ship to which the surface of the water rises. **2.** Any of several parallel lines on the hull of a ship that indicate the depth to which the ship sinks under various loads.

wa·ter·logged (wô′tər-lôgd′, -lŏgd′, wŏt′ər-) ►*adj.* **1.** Soaked or saturated with water. **2.** Partly flooded with water. Used of a ship or boat.

Wa·ter·loo¹ (wô′tər-lōō′, wŏt′ər-) A town of central Belgium near Brussels; site of Napoleon's final defeat (1815).

Wa·ter·loo² (wô′tər-lōō, wŏt′ər-) ►*n., pl.* **-loos** A final crushing defeat.

wa·ter·mark (wô′tər-märk′, wŏt′ər-) ►*n.* **1.** A mark showing the height to which water has risen. **2.** A translucent design impressed on paper during manufacture and visible when the paper is held to the light. **3.** *Comp.* Information directly encoded into a digital image, video, or audio file that identifies the copyright owner or a licensed user. ►*v.* **1.** To mark (paper) with a watermark. **2.** *Comp.* To add a digital watermark to.

wa·ter·mel·on (wô′tər-mĕl′ən, wŏt′ər-) ►*n.* **1.** An African vine cultivated for its large edible fruit. **2.** The fruit itself, having a hard green rind and sweet watery reddish flesh.

water moccasin ►*n.* A venomous snake of lowlands and swampy regions of the S US; cottonmouth.

water ou·zel (ōō′zəl) ►*n.* See **dipper** (sense 2). [< OE *ōsle*.]

water pipe ►*n.* **1.** A pipe that conducts water. **2.** An apparatus for smoking in which the smoke is drawn through a vessel of water.

water polo ►*n.* A water sport in which two teams of swimmers try to throw a ball into each other's goal.

wa·ter·pow·er (wô′tər-pou′ər, wŏt′ər-) ►*n.* The energy produced by running or falling water that is used for driving machinery, esp. for generating electricity.

wa·ter·proof (wô′tər-prōōf′, wŏt′ər-) ►*adj.* Impervious to or unaffected by water. ►*n.* *Chiefly Brit.* A raincoat. **—wa′ter·proof′** *v.*

wa·ter·re·pel·lent (wô′tər-rĭ-pĕl′ənt, wŏt′-ər-) ►*adj.* Resistant to water but not entirely waterproof.

wa·ter·re·sis·tant (wô′tər-rĭ-zĭs′tənt, wŏt′ər-) ►*adj.* Resistant to damage by water.

Wa·ters (wô′tərz, wŏt′ərz), **Muddy** McKinley Morganfield. 1915–83. Amer. blues musician.

wa·ter·shed (wô′tər-shĕd′, wŏt′ər-) ►*n.* **1.** The region draining into a body of water. **2.** A ridge of high land dividing two areas drained by different river systems. **3.** A turning point. [Poss.

translation of Ger. *Wasserscheide* : *Wasser*, water + *Scheide*, divide.]

water ski ►*n.* A broad ski used for gliding over water while being towed by a motorboat. **—wa′ter-ski′** *v.* **—wa′ter-ski′er** *n.*

water ski
Anais Amade at the 2009 Mediterranean Games

wa·ter·spout (wô′tər-spout′, wŏt′ər-) ►*n.* **1.** A tornado or lesser whirlwind occurring over water and resulting in a whirling column of air and spray. **2.** A hole or pipe from which water, esp. rainwater, is discharged.

water table ►*n.* The level below which the ground is saturated with water.

wa·ter·tight (wô′tər-tīt′, wŏt′ər-) ►*adj.* **1.** So tightly made that water cannot enter or escape. **2.** Having no flaws or loopholes: *a watertight alibi.*

water tower ►*n.* A standpipe or elevated tank used for storing water.

wa·ter·way (wô′tər-wā′, wŏt′ər-) ►*n.* A navigable body of water, as a river or canal.

water wheel ►*n.* A wheel driven by falling or running water, used to power machinery.

water wings ►*pl.n.* Inflatable floats used to support the arms of a person learning to swim.

wa·ter·works (wô′tər-wûrks′, wŏt′ər-) ►*pl.n.* **1.** The water system, including reservoirs, tanks, buildings, pumps, and pipes, of a city or town. **2.** An exhibition of moving water, such as a fountain. **3.** *Informal* Tears.

wa·ter·y (wô′tə-rē, wŏt′ə-) ►*adj.* **-i·er, -i·est** **1.** Filled with, consisting of, or soaked with water. **2.** Diluted: *watery soup.* **3.** Pale; washed-out: *watery sunshine.* **—wa′ter·i·ness** *n.*

Wat·son (wŏt′sən), **James Dewey** b. 1928. Amer. molecular biologist.

watt (wŏt) ►*n.* A unit of power equal to one joule per second. [After James WATT.]

Watt, James 1736–1819. British engineer and inventor.

watt·age (wŏt′ĭj) ►*n.* **1.** An amount of power, esp. electric power, expressed in watts or kilowatts. **2.** The electric power required by an appliance or device.

wat·tle¹ (wŏt′l) ►*n.* A construction of poles intertwined with twigs, reeds, or branches, used for walls, fences, and roofs. [< OE *watel*.] **—wat′tled** *adj.*

wat·tle² (wŏt′l) ►*n.* A fleshy, often brightly colored fold of skin hanging from the throat of certain birds. [?] **—wat′tled** *adj.*

Waugh (wô), **Evelyn (Arthur Saint John)** 1903–66. British writer.

wave (wāv) ►*v.* **waved, wav·ing 1.** To move or cause to move back and forth or up and down in the air. **2.** To make a signal with a movement of the hand. **3.** To move or swing as in giving a signal. See Synonyms at **flourish. 4.** To curve or curl, as hair. ▸*n.* **1.** A ridge or swell moving along the surface of a body of water. **2.** An undulating surface movement: *waves of wheat.* **3.** A slight curve or curl, as in the hair. **4.** A movement up and down or back and forth: *a wave of the hand.* **5.** A surge or rush: *a wave of nausea.* **6.** A persistent weather condition: *a heat wave.* **7.** *Phys.* **a.** A disturbance traveling through a medium. **b.** A graphic representation of the variation of such a disturbance with time. [< OE *wafian.*]

wave·band (wāv′bănd′) ▸*n.* A range of frequencies, esp. radio frequencies.

wave·form (wāv′fôrm′) ▸*n.* The mathematical representation of a wave, esp. a graph obtained by plotting a characteristic of the wave against time.

wave function ▸*n.* A mathematical function used to describe the propagation of the wave associated with any particle or particle group.

wave·length (wāv′lĕngkth′, -lĕngth′, -lĕnth′) ▸*n.* The distance between one peak or crest of a wave, as of light or sound, and the next corresponding peak or crest.

wave·let (wāv′lĭt) ▸*n.* A small wave; ripple.

wa·ver (wā′vər) ▸*v.* **1.** To move or swing back and forth. **2a.** To show or experience irresolution or indecision; vacillate. **b.** To falter or yield: *His resolve began to waver.* **3.** To tremble or quaver, as a voice. [ME *waveren.*] —**wa′ver·ing·ly** *adv.*

wav·y (wā′vē) ▸*adj.* **-i·er, -i·est 1.** Abounding or rising in waves: *a wavy sea.* **2.** Marked by or moving in a wavelike form. **3.** Having curls, curves, or undulations: *wavy hair.* —**wav′i·ly** *adv.* —**wav′i·ness** *n.*

wax¹ (wăks) ▸*n.* **1a.** Any of various natural, oily or greasy heat-sensitive substances, such as beeswax, consisting of hydrocarbons or fats. **b.** Earwax. **2.** A preparation containing wax used for polishing. ▸*v.* To treat or polish with wax. [< OE *weax.*]

wax² (wăks) ▸*v.* **1.** To increase gradually in size, amount, intensity, or degree. **2.** To show an increasing illuminated area, as the moon does in passing from new to full. **3.** To grow or become: *a speaker waxing eloquent.* [< OE *weaxan.*]

wax bean ▸*n.* A variety of string bean having yellow pods.

wax·en (wăk′sən) ▸*adj.* **1.** Made of wax. **2.** Pale or smooth as wax: *waxen skin.*

wax myrtle ▸*n.* An aromatic evergreen shrub of the SE US, having small berrylike fruit with a waxy coating.

waxwing

wax·wing (wăks′wĭng′) ▸*n.* Any of several crested birds having grayish-brown plumage and usu. waxy red tips on the wing feathers.

wax·work (wăks′wûrk′) ▸*n.* **1.** A figure made of wax, esp. a life-size wax effigy of a famous person. **2. waxworks** *(takes sing. or pl. v.)* An exhibition of wax figures.

wax·y (wăk′sē) ▸*adj.* **-i·er, -i·est 1.** Resembling wax, as in texture. **2.** Full of or covered with wax. —**wax′i·ness** *n.*

way (wā) ▸*n.* **1.** A road, path, or route that leads from one place to another. **2.** Space to proceed: *made way for the procession.* **3.** also **ways** (wāz) *(takes sing. v.) Informal* Distance: *The travelers have come a long way.* **4.** A course of action: *the easy way out.* **5.** A manner or method of doing: *no way to reach him.* **6.** Progress or advancement in accomplishing a goal: *worked her way up.* **7.** A habit, characteristic, or tendency: *Things have a way of happening.* **8.** A specific direction: *He glanced my way.* **9.** An aspect or feature: *resembles his father in many ways.* **10.** Freedom to do as one wishes: *if I had my way.* **11.** An aptitude or a facility: *has a way with words.* **12.** A condition: *in a bad way financially.* **13.** Vicinity: *out our way.* —*idioms:* **by the way** Incidentally. **by way of 1.** Through; via. **2.** As a means of: *by way of apology.* **out of the way 1.** In a remote location. **2.** Improper; amiss. **under way** In progress. [< OE *weg.*]

Usage: In American English *ways* is often used as an equivalent of *way* in phrases such as *a long ways to go.* The usage is not incorrect but is regarded as informal.

way·bill (wā′bĭl′) ▸*n.* A document giving details and instructions relating to a shipment of goods.

way·far·er (wā′fâr′ər) ▸*n.* One who travels, esp. on foot. [ME *weifarere.*] —**way′far′ing** *n. & adj.*

way·lay (wā′lā′) ▸*v.* **-laid** (-lād′), **-lay·ing 1.** To lie in wait for and attack from ambush. See Synonyms at **ambush.** **2.** To approach and speak to (one who is already occupied). **3.** To interrupt the course or progress of. —**way′lay·er** *n.*

Wayne (wān), **Anthony** 1745–96. Amer. Revolutionary general.

Wayne, John Marion Morrison. 1907–79. Amer. film actor.

–ways ▸*suff.* Way, manner, direction, or position: *sideways.* [ME.]

ways and means (wāz) ▸*pl.n.* Methods and resources available to accomplish an end, esp. to meet expenses.

way·side (wā′sīd′) ▸*n.* The side of a road.

way station ▸*n.* A station between principal stations on a route, as of a railroad.

way·ward (wā′wərd) ▸*adj.* **1.** Disobedient; willful: *a wayward child.* **2.** Going somewhere not intended or desired: *a wayward golf ball.* **3.** Capricious. [< ME *awaiward*, turned away.] —**way′ward·ly** *adv.* —**way′ward·ness** *n.*

WBC ▸*abbr.* white blood cell

WbN ▸*abbr.* west by north

WbS ▸*abbr.* west by south

WC ▸*abbr.* **1.** water closet **2.** wind chill

we (wē) ▸*pron.* **1.** Used to indicate the speaker or writer along with another or others as the subject. **2.** Used instead of *I*, esp. by a sovereign or by a writer. [< OE *wē.*]

Usage: When the pronoun is followed by an appositive noun phrase, the form *us* is frequently encountered where grammatical correctness would require *we*, as in *Us owners* (properly *We owners*) *will have something to say about the contract.* Less frequently, *we* is substituted for *us*, as in *For we students, it's a no-win situation.* Avoid both usages. See Usage Note at **I.**

weak (wēk) ▶*adj.* **-er, -est 1.** Lacking physical strength, energy, or vigor; feeble. **2.** Likely to fail under pressure, stress, or strain. **3.** Lacking strength of character or will. **4.** Lacking the proper strength or amount of ingredients: *weak coffee.* **5.** Unable to function normally or fully: *a weak heart.* **6.** Unable to digest food easily; readily nauseated: *a weak stomach.* **7.** Lacking aptitude or skill. **8.** Lacking persuasiveness: *a weak argument.* **9.** Lacking power or intensity: *weak light; a weak voice.* **10.** Unstressed or unaccented, as a syllable. [< ON *veikr*, pliant.]

weak·en (wē′kən) ▶*v.* To make or become weak or weaker.

weak·fish (wēk′fĭsh′) ▶*n.* A marine food and game fish of North American Atlantic waters. [Obsolete Du. *weekvis*.]

weak force ▶*n.* The force that arises from the weak interaction of quarks and leptons.

weak interaction ▶*n.* A fundamental interaction of nature between elementary particles that is responsible for some particle and nuclear decay and for the interaction of neutrinos.

weak-kneed (wēk′nēd′) ▶*adj.* Lacking strength of character or purpose.

weak·ling (wēk′lĭng) ▶*n.* One of weak constitution or character.

weak·ly (wēk′lē) ▶*adj.* **-li·er, -li·est** Feeble; weak. ▶*adv.* In a weak manner.

weak·ness (wēk′nĭs) ▶*n.* **1.** The condition or quality of being weak. **2.** A personal defect or failing. **3.** A special fondness or liking: *a weakness for chocolate.*

weal[1] (wēl) ▶*n.* Prosperity; well-being. [< OE *wela.*]

weal[2] (wēl) ▶*n.* A welt or bump. [< WALE.]

wealth (wĕlth) ▶*n.* **1a.** An abundance of valuable material possessions or resources; riches. **b.** The state of being rich; affluence. **2.** All goods and resources having economic value. [< OE *wela.*]

wealth·y (wĕl′thē) ▶*adj.* **-i·er, -i·est** Having wealth; rich; prosperous. See Synonyms at **rich.**

wean (wēn) ▶*v.* **1.** To accustom (the young of a mammal) to take nourishment other than by suckling. **2.** To rid of a habit or interest, esp. gradually: *weaned herself from cigarettes.* **3.** *Informal* To be raised on: *weaned on good literature.* [< OE *wenian.*]

weap·on (wĕp′ən) ▶*n.* **1.** An instrument of attack or defense in combat. **2.** A means used to defend against or defeat another. [< OE *wæpen.*]

weap·on·ize (wĕp′ə-nīz′) ▶*v.* **-ized, -iz·ing 1.** To equip with weapons: *weaponize outer space.* **2.** To prepare for use as a weapon: *weaponize a virus.* **—weap·on·i·za′tion** *n.*

weap·on·ry (wĕp′ən-rē) ▶*n.* Weapons collectively.

wear (wâr) ▶*v.* **wore** (wôr), **worn** (wôrn), **wear·ing 1.** To carry or have on one's person: *wear a jacket.* **2.** To have habitually on one's person: *wear glasses; wear a beard.* **3.** To display in one's appearance: *wears a smile.* **4.** To bear or maintain in a particular manner: *wears her hair long.* **5a.** To damage, erode, or consume by long or hard use: *shoes worn down at the heels.* **b.** To show the effect of such use: *The tires are starting to wear.* **6.** To produce by constant use or exposure: *wore hollows in the steps.* **7.** To fatigue, weary, or exhaust: *criticism that wore her patience.* **8.** To last under continual or hard use: *a fabric that wears well.* **9.** To pass gradually or tediously: *The hours wore on.* ▶*n.* **1.** The act of wearing or the state of being worn; use. **2.** Clothing, esp. of a particular kind or for a particular use: *men's wear; evening wear.* **3.** Gradual impairment or diminution resulting from use or attrition: *The rug is showing wear.* **4.** The ability to withstand use. **—phrasal verbs: wear down** To break down or exhaust by relentless pressure or resistance. **wear off** To diminish gradually in effect. **wear out 1.** To make or become unusable through long or heavy use. **2.** To use up or consume gradually. [< OE *werian.*] **—wear′a·ble** *adj.* **—wear′er** *n.*

wear and tear (târ) ▶*n.* Damage or depreciation resulting from ordinary use.

wea·ri·less (wîr′ē-lĭs) ▶*adj.* Not tired, tiring, or relenting. See Synonyms at **tireless.**

wea·ri·some (wîr′ē-səm) ▶*adj.* Causing fatigue; tiresome. **—wea′ri·some·ly** *adv.* **—wea′ri·some·ness** *n.*

wea·ry (wîr′ē) ▶*adj.* **-ri·er, -ri·est 1.** Tired. **2.** Expressive of tiredness: *a weary smile.* **3.** Exhausted of tolerance; impatient: *weary of delays.* ▶*v.* **wea·ried** (wîr′ēd), **wea·ry·ing** To make or become weary. [< OE *wērig.*] **—wea′ri·ly** *adv.* **—wea′ri·ness** *n.*

wea·sel (wē′zəl) ▶*n.* **1.** Any of several carnivorous mammals having a long slender body, a long tail, and short legs. **2.** A sneaky or treacherous person. ▶*v.* To be evasive; equivocate. [< OE *wesle.*]

weath·er (wĕth′ər) ▶*n.* **1.** The state of the atmosphere at a given time and place with respect to temperature, moisture, wind, and barometric pressure. **2.** Bad, rough, or stormy atmospheric conditions. ▶*v.* **1.** To expose to or withstand the action of the weather. **2.** To show the effects of exposure to the weather. **3.** To come through safely; survive. [< OE *weder.*] **—weath′ered** *adj.*

weath·er-beat·en (wĕth′ər-bēt′n) ▶*adj.* **1.** Worn by exposure to the weather. **2.** Lined and coarsened from being outdoors: *a weather-beaten face.*

weath·er·board (wĕth′ər-bôrd′) ▶*n.* See **clapboard.**

weath·er·bound (wĕth′ər-bound′) ▶*adj.* Delayed, halted, or kept indoors by bad weather.

weath·er·cock (wĕth′ər-kŏk′) ▶*n.* A weathervane, esp. one in the form of a rooster.

weath·er·ing (wĕth′ər-ĭng) ▶*n.* Any of the chemical or mechanical processes by which objects exposed to the weather break down.

weath·er·ize (wĕth′ə-rīz′) ▶*v.* **-ized, -iz·ing** To protect against cold weather, as with insulation.

weath·er·man (wĕth′ər-mən) ▶*n.* A man who reports and forecasts the weather.

weath·er·proof (wĕ*th*'ər-pro͞of') ►*adj.* Capable of withstanding exposure to weather without damage. —**weath'er·proof'** *v.*

weather stripping ►*n.* Material in narrow strips, as of metal or plastic, installed around doors and windows to insulate a building's interior. —**weath'er-strip'** (wĕ*th*'ər-strĭp') *v.*

weath·er·vane (wĕ*th*'ər-vān') ►*n.* A device that pivots on a vertical spindle to indicate wind direction.

weathervane

weave (wēv) ►*v.* **wove** (wōv), **wo·ven** (wō'vən), **weav·ing 1a.** To make (cloth) by interlacing the threads of the weft and the warp on a loom. **b.** To interlace (e.g., threads) into cloth. **2.** To construct by interlacing or interweaving strips or strands of material: *weave a basket.* **3.** To combine (elements) into a whole. **4.** To interpose (another element) throughout a complex whole: *wove folk tunes into the symphony.* **5.** To spin (a web). **6.** *p.t.* **weaved** To move or progress by winding in and out or from side to side: *weaved through the traffic.* ►*n.* **1.** A pattern or method of weaving: *a twill weave.* **2.** A hairstyle in which hair extensions are attached to existing strands of hair. [< OE *wefan.*] —**weav'er** *n.*

web (wĕb) ►*n.* **1.** A woven fabric, esp. one on a loom or just removed from it. **2.** A latticed or woven structure. **3.** A structure of threadlike filaments spun by spiders. **4.** Something intricately contrived, esp. something that ensnares or entangles: *a web of lies.* **5.** A complex network: *a web of telephone wires.* **6.** often **Web** *Comp.* The World Wide Web. **7.** A membrane or fold of skin connecting the toes, as of certain amphibians and birds. ►*v.* **webbed**, **web·bing 1.** To provide or cover with a web. **2.** To ensnare in or as if in a web. [< OE.] —**webbed** *adj.*

web·bing (wĕb'ĭng) ►*n.* A strong, narrow, closely woven fabric used esp. for seat belts and harnesses or in upholstery.

web·cast (wĕb'kăst') ►*n.* A broadcast of an event over the World Wide Web.

We·ber¹ (vā'bər), **Max** 1864–1920. German sociologist.

We·ber² (wĕb'ər), **Max** 1881–1961. Russian-born Amer. painter.

web-foot·ed (wĕb'fo͝ot'ĭd) ►*adj.* Having feet with webbed toes.

web·i·nar (wĕb'ə-när') ►*n.* A seminar that is conducted over the Internet. [WEB + (SEM)I-NAR.]

web·log (wĕb'lôg', -lŏg') ►*n.* A blog.

web·mas·ter (wĕb'măs'tər) ►*n.* A person who develops, markets, or maintains websites.

web·page or **Web page** (wĕb'pāj') ►*n.* A document on the World Wide Web, often linked to other Web documents.

web·site or **Web site** (wĕb'sīt') ►*n.* A set of interconnected webpages, gen. located on the same server, prepared as a collection of information by a person or organization.

Web·ster (wĕb'stər), **Daniel** 1782–1852. Amer. politician and orator.

Webster, John 1580?–1625? English playwright.

Webster, Noah 1758–1843. Amer. lexicographer.

web·worm (wĕb'wûrm') ►*n.* Any of various caterpillars that construct webs.

wed (wĕd) ►*v.* **wed·ded, wed** or **wed·ded, wed·ding 1.** To take as a spouse; marry. **2.** To perform the marriage ceremony for. **3.** To unite closely. **4.** To cause to adhere devotedly or stubbornly: *wasn't wedded to the idea of building a new school.* [< OE *weddian.*]

wed·ding (wĕd'ĭng) ►*n.* **1.** The ceremony or celebration of a marriage. **2.** A close association or union: *a wedding of ideas.*

wedge (wĕj) ►*n.* **1.** A piece of material, such as metal or wood, tapered for insertion in a narrow crevice and used for splitting, tightening, securing, or levering. **2.** Something shaped like a wedge: *a wedge of pie.* **3.** Something that intrudes and causes division or disruption. ►*v.* **wedged, wedg·ing 1.** To split or force apart with or as if with a wedge. **2.** To fix in place with a wedge. **3.** To crowd or squeeze into a limited space. [< OE *wecg.*]

wed·lock (wĕd'lŏk') ►*n.* The state of being married; matrimony. [< OE *wedlāc.*]

Wednes·day (wĕnz'dē, -dā') ►*n.* The 4th day of the week. [< OE *Wōdnesdæg.*]

wee (wē) ►*adj.* **we·er, we·est** Very small; tiny. See Synonyms at **small.** —*idiom:* **wee hours** The hours between midnight and dawn. [< OE *wǣge,* weight.]

weed (wēd) ►*n.* **1.** A plant considered undesirable, unattractive, or troublesome, esp. one growing where it is not wanted, as in a garden. **2.** *Slang* Marijuana. ►*v.* **1.** To clear of weeds. **2.** To eliminate as unsuitable or unwanted: *weed out unqualified applicants.* [< OE *wēod.*] —**weed'er** *n.* —**weed'y** *adj.*

weeds (wēdz) ►*pl.n.* The black mourning clothes of a widow. [< OE *wǣd,* garment.]

week (wēk) ►*n.* **1.** A period of seven days, esp. a period that begins on a Sunday and continues through the next Saturday. **2.** The part of a calendar week devoted to work, school, or business. [< OE *wicu.*]

week·day (wēk'dā') ►*n.* Any day of the week except Saturday or Sunday.

week·end (wēk'ĕnd') ►*n.* The end of the week, esp. the period from Friday evening through Sunday evening. ►*v.* To spend the weekend.

week·ly (wēk'lē) ►*adv.* **1.** Once a week. **2.** Every week. **3.** By the week. ►*adj.* **1.** Occurring, appearing, or done once a week or every week. **2.** Computed by the week. ►*n.,* pl. **-lies**

A publication issued once a week.

week·night (wĕk′nīt′) ►*n.* Any of the nights of the week other than weekend nights.

ween (wēn) ►*v. Archaic* To think; suppose. [< OE *wēnan.*]

weep (wēp) ►*v.* **wept** (wĕpt), **weep·ing 1.** To shed (tears) as an expression of emotion, esp. grief; cry. **2.** To ooze or exude (moisture). [< OE *wēpan.*] —**weep′er** *n.* —**weep′y** *adj.*

weep·ing (wē′pĭng) ►*adj.* **1.** Shedding tears. **2.** Having slender drooping branches.

wee·vil (wē′vəl) ►*n.* Any of numerous beetles that characteristically have a downward-curving snout and are destructive to nuts, fruits, stems, and roots. [< OE *wifel.*]

weft (wĕft) ►*n.* **1.** The woof in a woven fabric. **2.** Woven fabric. [< OE *wefta.*]

weigh (wā) ►*v.* **1.** To determine the weight of by or as if by using a scale or balance. **2.** To consider or balance in the mind; ponder. **3.** *Naut.* To raise (anchor). **4.** To be of a specific weight. **5.** To have consequence or importance: *The decision weighed heavily against us.* **6.** To burden or be a burden on; oppress. —*phrasal verb:* **weigh in 1.** To be weighed before or after an athletic contest. **2.** *Slang* To contribute to a discussion. [< OE *wegan.*]

weight (wāt) ►*n.* **1.** A measure of the heaviness of an object. **2a.** The force with which an object is attracted to Earth or another celestial body, equal to the product of the object's mass and the acceleration of gravity. **b.** A unit measure of this force. **c.** A system of such measures. **3.** An object used principally to exert a force by virtue of its gravitational attraction to Earth, esp.: **a.** A solid used as a standard in weighing. **b.** An object used to hold something down. **c.** *Sports* A heavy object, such as a dumbbell, used in weightlifting. **4.** Burden: *the weight of responsibility.* **5.** A factor assigned to a piece of statistical data that reflects its overall importance. **6.** The greater part; preponderance. **7.** Influence; importance. ►*v.* **1.** To add heaviness or weight to. **2.** To load down; burden. **3.** To assign a statistical weight to. [< OE *wiht.*]

weight·less (wāt′lĭs) ►*adj.* **1.** Having little or no weight. **2.** Not experiencing the effects of gravity. —**weight′less·ness** *n.*

weight·lift·ing (wāt′lĭf′tĭng) ►*n.* The lifting of heavy weights as an exercise or in athletic competition. —**weight lifter** *n.*

weight·y (wā′tē) ►*adj.* **-i·er, -i·est 1.** Heavy. **2.** Burdensome; oppressive. **3.** Of great consequence; momentous: *a weighty matter.* **4.** Having great power or influence: *a weighty argument.* —**weight′i·ly** *adv.* —**weight′i·ness** *n.*

weir (wîr) ►*n.* **1.** A fence placed in a stream to catch fish. **2.** A dam across a river or canal to raise, regulate, or divert the water. [< OE *wer.*]

weird (wîrd) ►*adj.* **-er, -est 1.** Strikingly odd or unusual, esp. in an unsettling way; strange. **2.** Suggestive of the supernatural. [< OE *wyrd,* fate.] —**weird′ly** *adv.* —**weird′ness** *n.*
    Syns: *eerie, uncanny, unearthly adj.*

weird·o (wîr′dō) ►*n., pl.* **-oes** *Slang* A strange or eccentric person.

wel·come (wĕl′kəm) ►*adj.* **1.** Greeted, received, or accepted with pleasure. **2.** Cordially permitted or invited: *You are welcome to join us.* **3.** Used in the expression *you're welcome* to acknowledge another's thanks. ►*v.* **-comed,**

-com·ing 1. To greet or entertain cordially or hospitably. **2.** To receive or accept gladly. [< OE *wilcuma,* welcome guest.] —**wel′come** *interj. & n.*

weld (wĕld) ►*v.* **1.** To join (metals) by applying heat and sometimes pressure. **2.** To bring into close association or union. ►*n.* A union or joint produced by welding. [< WELL¹, weld (obs.).] —**weld′er** *n.*

wel·fare (wĕl′fâr′) ►*n.* **1.** Health, happiness, or prosperity; well-being. **2.** Financial or other aid provided, esp. by the government, to people in need. [< OE *wel faran,* fare well.]

welfare state ►*n.* A social system whereby the state assumes primary responsibility for the welfare of its citizens.

well¹ (wĕl) ►*n.* **1.** A deep hole or shaft sunk into the earth to obtain water, oil, gas, or brine. **2.** A container or reservoir for a liquid, such as ink. **3.** A spring or fountain. **4.** An abundant source: *a well of information.* **5.** An open space extending vertically through the floors of a building, as for stairs. **6.** An enclosed space for receiving and holding something, such as the wheels of an airplane when retracted. ►*v.* **1.** To rise up. **2.** To pour forth. [< OE *welle.*]

well² (wĕl) ►*adv.* **bet·ter** (bĕt′ər), **best** (bĕst) **1.** In a good or proper manner. See Usage Note at **good. 2.** Skillfully: *dances well.* **3.** Satisfactorily: *slept well.* **4.** Successfully: *gets along well with people.* **5.** In a comfortable or affluent manner: *lived well.* **6.** Advantageously: *married well.* **7.** With reason or propriety: *can't very well say no.* **8.** In all likelihood: *You may well need a coat.* **9.** Prudently: *You would do well to obey.* **10.** In a close or familiar manner: *knew them well.* **11.** Favorably: *spoke well of them.* **12.** Thoroughly: *well cooked.* **13.** Perfectly: *I well understand your fears.* **14.** Considerably: *well past noon.* ►*adj.* **better, best 1.** In a satisfactory condition: *All is well.* **2a.** Healthy. **b.** Cured or healed. **3a.** Advisable: *It would be well not to ask.* **b.** Fortunate: *It is well that you stayed.* ►*interj.* **1.** Used to introduce a remark or fill a pause. **2.** Used to express surprise. —*idiom:* **as well 1.** In addition. **2.** With equal effect: *I might as well go.* [< OE *wel.*]

we'll (wēl) We will.

well-ap·point·ed (wĕl′ə-poin′tĭd) ►*adj.* Fully supplied with suitable equipment or furnishings.

well-bal·anced (wĕl′băl′ənst) ►*adj.* **1.** Evenly proportioned, balanced, or regulated. **2.** Mentally or emotionally stable; well-adjusted.

well-be·ing (wĕl′bē′ĭng) ►*n.* The state of being healthy, happy, or prosperous; welfare.

well-born (wĕl′bôrn′) ►*adj.* Born to a genteel or aristocratic family.

well-bred (wĕl′brĕd′) ►*adj.* Raised to be well-mannered and refined.

well-de·fined (wĕl′dĭ-fīnd′) ►*adj.* **1.** Having definite and distinct lines or features. **2.** Accurately and unambiguously stated or described: *a well-defined concept.*

well-dis·posed (wĕl′dĭ-spōzd′) ►*adj.* Disposed to be kindly, friendly, or sympathetic.

Welles (wĕlz), **(George) Orson** 1915–85. Amer. director, actor, writer, and producer.

well-fixed (wĕl′fĭkst′) ►*adj. Informal* Financially secure; well-to-do.

well-found·ed (wĕl′foun′dĭd) ►*adj.* Based on sound judgment, reasoning, or evidence.

well-groomed (wĕl′grōomd′) ►*adj.* **1.** Neat and clean in dress and personal appearance. **2.** Carefully tended or cared for.

well-ground·ed (wĕl′groun′dĭd) ►*adj.* **1.** Adequately versed in a subject. **2.** Having a sound basis; well-founded.

well-heeled (wĕl′hēld′) ►*adj.* Wealthy.

Wel·ling·ton (wĕl′ĭng-tən) The capital of New Zealand, on S North I.

Wellington, First Duke of. Arthur Wellesley. "the Iron Duke." 1769–1852. British general and politician.

well-in·ten·tioned (wĕl′ĭn-tĕn′shənd) ►*adj.* Marked by or having good intentions.

well-man·nered (wĕl′măn′ərd) ►*adj.* Polite.

well-mean·ing (wĕl′mē′nĭng) ►*adj.* Well-intentioned.

well·ness (wĕl′nĭs) ►*n.* The condition of good physical and mental health, esp. when maintained by proper diet and exercise.

well-nigh (wĕl′nī′) ►*adv.* Nearly; almost.

well-off (wĕl′ôf′, -ŏf′) ►*adj.* **1.** Well-to-do. **2.** In fortunate circumstances.

well-read (wĕl′rĕd′) ►*adj.* Knowledgeable through having read extensively.

well-round·ed (wĕl′roun′dĭd) ►*adj.* Well-balanced in a range or variety of aspects.

Wells (wĕlz), **H(erbert) G(eorge)** 1866–1946. British writer.

Wells, Ida Bell 1862–1931. Amer. journalist and reformer.

Ida B. Wells

well-spo·ken (wĕl′spō′kən) ►*adj.* **1.** Chosen or expressed with aptness or propriety. **2.** Courteous in speech.

well·spring (wĕl′sprĭng′) ►*n.* **1.** The source of a stream or spring. **2.** A source; origin.

well-timed (wĕl′tīmd′) ►*adj.* Occurring at an opportune time.

well-to-do (wĕl′tə-dōo′) ►*adj.* Prosperous; affluent; well-off.

well-turned (wĕl′tûrnd′) ►*adj.* **1.** Shapely: *a well-turned ankle.* **2.** Concisely or aptly expressed: *a well-turned phrase.*

well-wish·er (wĕl′wĭsh′ər) ►*n.* One who extends good wishes to another.

well-worn (wĕl′wôrn′) ►*adj.* **1.** Showing signs of much wear or use. **2.** Trite.

welsh (wĕlsh, wĕlch) ►*v.* **welshed, welsh·ing** *Informal* **1.** To swindle a person by not paying a debt or wager. **2.** To fail to fulfill an obligation. [?] **—welsh′er** *n.*

Welsh ►*n.* **1.** The people of Wales. **2.** The Celtic language of Wales. **—Welsh** *adj.* **—Welsh′man** *n.* **—Welsh′wom′an** *n.*

Welsh cor·gi (kôr′gē) ►*n.* A dog originating in Wales, having a long body, short legs, and a foxlike head. [Welsh.]

Welsh rabbit also **Welsh rare·bit** (râr′bĭt) ►*n.* A dish made of melted cheese and sometimes ale, served hot over toast or crackers.

welt (wĕlt) ►*n.* **1.** A usu. leather strip stitched into a shoe between the sole and the upper. **2.** A tape or covered cord sewn into a seam as reinforcement or trimming. **3.** A ridge or bump on the skin caused by a blow or an allergic reaction. ►*v.* **1.** To reinforce or trim with a welt. **2.** To flog. [ME *welte.*]

wel·ter (wĕl′tər) ►*n.* **1.** A confused mass; jumble. **2.** Confusion; turmoil. ►*v.* **1.** To wallow or toss about, as in mud or high seas. **2.** To lie soaked in a liquid. **3.** To roll and surge, as the sea. [< ME *welteren.*]

wel·ter·weight (wĕl′tər-wāt′) ►*n.* A boxer weighing from 136 to 147 lbs., between a lightweight and a middleweight. [< *welter,* boxer.]

Wel·ty (wĕl′tē), **Eudora** 1909–2001. Amer. writer.

wen (wĕn) ►*n.* A harmless cyst containing sebaceous matter. [< OE.]

wench (wĕnch) ►*n. Archaic* **1.** A young woman or girl. **2.** A woman servant. **3.** A promiscuous woman. [< OE *wencel,* child.]

wend (wĕnd) ►*v.* To proceed on or along (one's way). [< OE *wendan.*]

went (wĕnt) ►*v.* P.t. of **go¹.**

wept (wĕpt) ►*v.* P.t. and p.part. of **weep.**

were (wûr) ►*v.* **1.** 2nd pers. sing. and pl. and 1st and 3rd pers. pl. p.t. of **be. 2.** P. subjunctive of **be.**

we're (wîr) We are.

were·n't (wûrnt, wûr′ənt) Were not.

were·wolf also **wer·wolf** (wâr′wŏŏlf′, wîr′-, wûr′-) ►*n.* In folklore, a person capable of assuming the form of a wolf. [< OE *werewulf* : *wer,* man + *wulf,* wolf.]

wert (wûrt) ►*v. Archaic* 2nd pers. sing. p.t. of **be.**

Wes·ley (wĕs′lē, wĕz′-), **John** 1703–91. British founder of Methodism.

west (wĕst) ►*n.* **1a.** The direction opposite to the earth's axial rotation; the general direction of sunset. **b.** The compass point 270° clockwise from due north. **2.** often **West** The western part of a region or country. **3.** often **West** The economically developed nations of North America and Europe. ►*adj.* **1.** To, toward, of, or in the west. **2.** Coming from the west: *a west wind.* ►*adv.* In, from, or toward the west. [< OE.] **—west′ward** *adj. & adv.* **—west′ward·ly** *adj. & adv.* **—west′wards** *adv.*

West, Benjamin 1738–1820. Amer. painter.

West Bank A disputed territory of SW Asia between Israel and Jordan W of the Jordan R.; occupied by Israel since 1967.

west·er·ly (wĕs′tər-lē) ►*adj.* **1.** Situated toward the west. **2.** From the west: *westerly winds.* **—west′er·ly** *adv.*

west·ern (wĕs′tərn) ►*adj.* **1.** Of, in, or toward the west. **2.** From the west: *western breezes.* **3.** often **Western** Of or characteristic of western regions or the West. ►*n.* often **Western** A novel, film, or television or radio program having themes or settings characteristic of the American West. [< OE *westerne*.]

west·ern·er also **West·ern·er** (wĕs′tər-nər) ►*n.* **1.** A native or inhabitant of a western region. **2.** A native or inhabitant of Europe or the Western Hemisphere.

Western Hemisphere The half of the earth comprising North America, Central America, and South America.

west·ern·ize (wĕs′tər-nīz′) ►*v.* **-ized, -iz·ing** To convert to the customs of Western civilization. —**west′ern·i·za′tion** *n.*

Western Sahara A region of NW Africa on the Atlantic coast.

West Germany A former country (1945–90) of central Europe bordering on the North Sea; reunified with East Germany to form Germany. —**West German** *adj. & n.*

West Indies An archipelago between SE North America and N South America, separating the Caribbean Sea from the Atlantic and including the Greater Antilles, the Lesser Antilles, and the Bahama Is. —**West Indian** *adj. & n.*

West·pha·lia (wĕst-fāl′yə, -fā′lē-ə) A historical region and former duchy of W-central Germany east of the Rhine R. —**West·pha′lian** *adj. & n.*

West Virginia A state of the E-central US. Cap. Charleston. —**West Virginian** *adj. & n.*

wet (wĕt) ►*adj.* **wet·ter, wet·test 1.** Covered or soaked with a liquid, such as water. **2.** Not yet dry or firm: *wet paint.* **3.** Rainy or foggy. **4.** *Informal* Allowing the sale of alcoholic beverages: *a wet county.* ►*n.* **1.** Moisture. **2.** Rainy weather. ►*v.* **wet** or **wet·ted, wet·ting** To make or become wet. —**idiom: all wet** *Slang* Entirely mistaken. [< OE *wǣt.*] —**wet′ly** *adv.* —**wet′ness** *n.*

wet blanket ►*n. Informal* One that discourages enjoyment or enthusiasm.

wet·land (wĕt′lănd′) ►*n.* A lowland area, as a marsh, that is saturated with moisture.

wet nurse ►*n.* A woman who suckles another woman's child.

wet·suit (wĕt′sōōt′) ►*n.* A tight-fitting, usu. rubber suit worn to keep the body warm in water.

wetsuit

we've (wēv) We have.

whack (wăk, hwăk) ►*v.* To strike with a sharp blow; slap. ►*n.* **1.** A sharp resounding blow. **2.** The sound made by a whack. —**idiom: out of whack** *Informal* Not functioning correctly. [Prob. imit.]

whack·y (wăk′ē, hwăk′ē) ►*adj. Slang* Var. of **wacky.**

whale¹ (wāl, hwāl) ►*n.* **1a.** Any of various marine mammals having flippers, a tail with horizontal flukes, and one or two blowholes for breathing. **b.** Any of the larger members of this group, such as a blue whale or a humpback whale, in contrast to the dolphins and porpoises. **2.** *Informal* An impressive example: *a whale of a story.* ►*v.* **whaled, whal·ing** To engage in the hunting of whales. [< OE *hwæl.*]

whale² (wāl, hwāl) ►*v.* **whaled, whal·ing 1.** To strike repeatedly; thrash. **2.** To strike or hit (a ball) with great force. [?]

whale·boat (wāl′bōt′, hwāl′-) ►*n.* A long rowboat, pointed at both ends and formerly used in whaling.

whale·bone (wāl′bōn′, hwāl′-) ►*n.* **1.** The elastic horny material forming the fringed plates that hang from the upper jaw of certain whales and strain plankton from the water. **2.** An object made of this material.

whal·er (wā′lər, hwā′-) ►*n.* **1.** One who hunts whales. **2.** A ship used in hunting whales. **3.** A whaleboat.

wham (wăm, hwăm) ►*n.* **1.** A forceful resounding blow. **2.** The sound of such a blow; thud. ►*v.* **whammed, wham·ming** To strike with resounding impact. [Imit.]

wham·my (wăm′ē, hwăm′ē) ►*n., pl.* **-mies** *Slang* **1.** A supernatural spell for causing misfortune; hex. **2.** A serious or devastating setback. [Perh. < WHAM.]

wharf (wôrf, hwôrf) ►*n., pl.* **wharves** (wôrvz, hwôrvz) or **wharfs** A pier where ships or boats are tied up and loaded or unloaded. [< OE *hwearf.*]

Whar·ton (wôr′tn, hwôr′-), **Edith Newbold Jones** 1862–1937. Amer. writer.

what (wŏt, wŭt, hwŏt, hwŭt; wət, hwət *when unstressed*) ►*pron.* **1a.** Which thing or which particular one of many: *What are you having for dinner?* **b.** Which kind, character, or designation: *What are these objects?* **c.** One of how much value or significance: *What are possessions to a dying man?* **2a.** That which; the thing that: *Listen to what I tell you.* **b.** Whatever thing that: *come what may.* **3.** *Informal* Something: *I'll tell you what.* See Usage Note at **which.** ►*adj.* **1.** Which one or ones: *What train do I take?* **2.** Whatever: *They soon repaired what damage had been done.* **3.** How great: *What a fool!* ►*adv.* How much; how: *What does it matter?* ►*interj.* Used to express surprise or incredulity. —**idiom: what if** What would occur if; suppose that: *What if we were rich?* [< OE *hwæt.*]

what·ev·er (wŏt-ĕv′ər, wŭt-, hwŏt-, hwŭt-) ►*pron.* **1.** Everything or anything that: *Do whatever you please.* **2.** No matter what: *Whatever happens, we'll meet here tonight.* **3.** *Informal* What: *Whatever does he mean?* **4.** *Informal* What remains and need not be mentioned: *Bring something to the party—pretzels, crackers, whatever.* ►*adj.* Of any number or kind; any: *Whatever requests you make will be granted.* ►*interj.*

Used to indicate indifference to or scorn for something, such as a remark or suggestion. *Usage:* Both *whatever* and *what ever* can be used in sentences such as *Whatever* (or *What ever*) *made her say that?* The same is true of the forms *whoever, whenever, wherever,* and *however* when these expressions are used similarly. In adjectival uses only the one-word form is used: *Take whatever* (not *what ever*) *books you need.*

what·not (wŏt′nŏt′, wŭt′-, hwŏt′-, hwŭt′-) ▸*n.* **1.** An unspecified object or article. **2.** A set of open shelves for ornaments.

what·so·ev·er (wŏt′sō-ĕv′ər, wŭt′-, hwŏt′-, hwŭt′-) ▸*pron. & adj.* Whatever.

wheat (wēt, hwēt) ▸*n.* **1.** A cereal grass widely cultivated for its commercially important edible grain. **2.** The grain of this plant, ground to produce flour. [< OE *hwǣte.*] —**wheat′en** *adj.*

wheat germ ▸*n.* The vitamin-rich embryos of wheat kernels, used as a food supplement or animal feed.

Wheat·ley (wēt′lē, hwēt′-), **Phillis** 1753?–84. African-born Amer. poet.

whee·dle (wēd′l, hwēd′l) ▸*v.* **-dled, -dling** To persuade, attempt to persuade, or obtain by flattery or guile; cajole. [?] —**whee′dler** *n.* —**whee′dling·ly** *adv.*

wheel (wēl, hwēl) ▸*n.* **1.** A solid disk or rigid circular ring connected by spokes to a hub, designed to turn around an axle passed through the center. **2.** Something resembling a wheel in appearance or movement. **3.** Something having a wheel as its principal part: *a steering wheel.* **4. wheels** Forces that provide energy, movement, or direction: *the wheels of commerce.* **5.** A revolution or rotation around an axis; turn. **6. wheels** *Slang* A motor vehicle. **7.** *Slang* One with power or influence: *A big wheel at the bank.* ▸*v.* **1.** To roll, move, or transport on or as if on wheels. **2.** To turn around or as if around a central axis; revolve or rotate. **3.** To whirl around, changing direction; pivot. [< OE *hwēol.*]

wheel·bar·row (wēl′băr′ō, hwēl′-) ▸*n.* A one- or two-wheeled vehicle with handles at the rear, used to carry small loads.

wheel·base (wēl′bās′, hwēl′-) ▸*n.* The distance from front to rear axle in a motor vehicle.

wheel·chair (wēl′châr′, hwēl′-) ▸*n.* A chair mounted on large wheels, used primarily by people who cannot walk or have difficulty walking.

wheel·er (wē′lər, hwē′-) ▸*n.* **1.** One that wheels. **2.** Something equipped with wheels: *a three-wheeler.*

wheel·er-deal·er (wē′lər-dē′lər, hwē′-) ▸*n.* *Informal* An aggressive or unscrupulous operator, esp. in business.

wheel·house (wēl′hous′, hwēl′-) ▸*n.* See **pilot-house.**

wheel·wright (wēl′rīt′, hwēl′-) ▸*n.* One who builds and repairs wheels.

wheeze (wēz, hwēz) ▸*v.* **wheezed, wheez·ing** To breathe with difficulty, producing a hoarse whistling sound. ▸*n.* **1.** A wheezing sound. **2.** *Informal* An old joke. [Prob. < ON *hvǣsa,* hiss.] —**wheez′er** *n.* —**wheez′i·ly** *adv.* —**wheez′i·ness** *n.* —**wheez′y** *adj.*

whelk (wělk, hwělk) ▸*n.* Any of various large, mostly edible marine snails. [< OE *weoloc.*]

whelm (wělm, hwělm) ▸*v.* **1.** To submerge. **2.** To overwhelm. [ME *whelmen,* overturn.]

whelp (wělp, hwělp) ▸*n.* **1.** A young offspring of a carnivorous mammal, esp. a dog or wolf. **2.** An impudent boy or young man. ▸*v.* To give birth to whelps. [< OE *hwelp.*]

when (wěn, hwěn) ▸*adv.* At what time: *When will we leave?* ▸*conj.* **1.** At the time that: *in the spring, when the snow melts.* **2.** As soon as: *I'll call you when I get there.* **3.** Whenever: *When the wind blows, all the doors rattle.* **4.** Whereas; although: *playing when she should have been studying.* ▸*pron.* **1.** What or which time: *Since when has this been going on?* **2.** At or during the time that: *Where were you on the night when the murder took place?* ▸*n.* The time or date: *the where and when of the meeting.* [< OE *hwenne.*]

Usage: In informal style *when* is often used after forms of *be* in definitions: *A dilemma is when you don't know which way to turn.* The construction is useful, but it is widely regarded as incorrect or as unsuitable for formal discourse.

whence (wěns, hwěns) ▸*adv.* **1.** From what place: *Whence came this traveler?* **2.** From what origin or source: *Whence comes this feast?* ▸*conj.* By reason of which: *had the same name, whence the error.* [< OE.]

when·ev·er (wěn-ěv′ər, hwěn-) ▸*adv.* **1.** At whatever time. **2.** When. See Usage Note at **whatever.** ▸*conj.* **1.** At whatever time that. **2.** Every time that: *breaks whenever it rains.*

when·so·ev·er (wěn′sō-ěv′ər, hwěn′-) ▸*adv. & conj.* Whenever.

where (wâr, hwâr) ▸*adv.* **1.** At or in what place: *Where is the telephone?* **2.** In what situation or position: *Where would we be without your help?* **3.** From what place or source: *Where did you get this idea?* **4.** To what place or end: *Where is this argument leading?* ▸*conj.* **1a.** At, to, or in a place in which: *We should go where it is quieter.* **b.** At, to, or in a situation in which: *I want to know where you expect the project to be in six months.* **2a.** At, to, or in any place in which; wherever: *Sit where you like.* **b.** Wherever: *Where there's smoke, there's fire.* **3.** Whereas: *That model has an attractive design, where this one is more dependable.* ▸*pron.* **1.** At, to, or in a place in which: *She moved to a city where jobs were more plentiful.* **2.** What place, source, or cause: *Where are you from?* **3.** The place or situation at, in, or to which: *We're already three miles from where we left.* ▸*n.* The place or occasion: *the where and when of the performance.* [< OE *hwǣr.*]

where·a·bouts (wâr′ə-bouts′, hwâr′-) ▸*adv.* About where; in, at, or near what location: *Whereabouts do you live?* ▸*n. (takes sing. or pl. v.)* Approximate location: *Her whereabouts are still unknown.*

where·as (wâr-ăz′, hwâr-) ▸*conj.* **1.** It being the fact that; inasmuch as. **2.** While at the same time. **3.** While on the contrary.

where·at (wâr-ăt′, hwâr-) ▸*conj.* **1.** Toward or at which. **2.** Whereupon.

where·by (wâr-bī′, hwâr-) ▸*conj.* In accordance with which; by or through which.

where·fore (wâr′fôr′, hwâr′-) ▸*adv.* **1.** For what reason; why. **2.** Therefore. ▸*n.* A purpose or cause: *the whys and wherefores of your decision.*

where·in (wâr-ĭn′, hwâr-) ▸*adv.* In what way; how: *Wherein have we sinned?* ▸*conj.* **1.** In which location; where. **2.** During which.

where·of (wâr-ŏv′, -ŭv′, hwâr-) ▸*conj.* **1.** Of what: *I know whereof I speak.* **2.** Of which or when: *ancient lore whereof much is lost.*

where·on (wâr-ŏn′, -ôn′, hwâr-) ►*adv.* *Archaic* On which or what.

where·so·ev·er (wâr′sō-ĕv′ər, hwâr′-) ►*conj.* Wherever.

where·to (wâr′tōō′, hwâr′-) ►*adv.* To what place; toward what end. ►*conj.* To which.

where·up·on (wâr′ə-pŏn′, -pôn′, hwâr′-) ►*conj.* **1.** On which. **2.** Following which.

wher·ev·er (wâr-ĕv′ər, hwâr-) ►*adv.* **1.** In or to whatever place: *used red pencil wherever needed.* **2.** Where. See Usage Note at **whatever.** ►*conj.* In or to whichever place or situation: *goes wherever I go.*

where·with (wâr′wĭth′, -wĭth′, hwâr′-) ►*conj.* By means of which.

where·with·al (wâr′wĭth-ôl′, -wĭth-, hwâr′-) ►*n.* The necessary means, esp. financial means.

whet (wĕt, hwĕt) ►*v.* **whet·ted, whet·ting 1.** To sharpen (e.g., a knife); hone. **2.** To make more keen; stimulate. [< OE *hwettan.*]

wheth·er (wĕth′ər, hwĕth′-) ►*conj.* **1.** Used to introduce: **a.** One alternative: *We should find out whether the museum is open.* **b.** Alternative possibilities: *Whether she wins or loses, she can be proud.* **2.** Either: *He passed the test, whether by skill or luck.* [< OE *hwether.*]

whet·stone (wĕt′stōn′, hwĕt′-) ►*n.* A hard, fine-grained stone for honing tools.

whey (wā, hwā) ►*n.* The watery part of milk that separates from the curds, as in the process of making cheese. [< OE *hwǣg.*]

which (wĭch, hwĭch) ►*pron.* **1.** What particular one or ones: *Which is your house?* **2.** The one or ones previously mentioned or implied: *my room, which is small and dark; the topic on which she spoke.* **3.** Whichever: *Choose which you like best.* **4.** A thing or circumstance that: *He left early, which was wise.* ►*adj.* **1.** What particular one or ones of a number of things or people: *Which part of town do you mean?* **2.** Any one or any number of; whichever: *Use which door you please.* **3.** Being the one or ones previously mentioned or implied: *It started to rain, at which point we ran.* [< OE *hwilc.*]

Usage: In its use to refer to the contents of sentences and clauses, *which* should be used only when it is preceded by its antecedent. When the antecedent follows, *what* should be used, particularly in formal style: *Still, he has not said he will withdraw, which is more surprising* but *Still, what* (not *which*) *is more surprising, he has not said he will withdraw.* See Usage Note at **that.**

which·ev·er (wĭch-ĕv′ər, hwĭch-) ►*pron.* Whatever one or ones. ►*adj.* Being any one or number: *Take whichever items you please.*

which·so·ev·er (wĭch′sō-ĕv′ər, hwĭch′-) ►*pron. & adj.* Whichever.

whiff (wĭf, hwĭf) ►*n.* **1a.** A brief passing odor carried in the air: *a whiff of perfume.* **b.** A very small trace. **2.** An inhalation, as of air or smoke. **3.** A slight gentle gust of air. ►*v.* **1.** To be carried in brief gusts; waft. **2.** To smell or sniff. [Perh. alteration of ME *weffe,* offensive smell.]

Whig (wĭg, hwĭg) ►*n.* **1.** A member of an 18th- and 19th-cent. British political party opposed to the Tories. **2.** A supporter of the war against England during the American Revolution. **3.** A member of a 19th-century American political party formed to oppose the Democratic Party.

[Prob. short for *Whiggamore,* one of a body of 17th-cent. Scottish rebels.] —**Whig′ger·y** *n.* —**Whig′gish** *adj.* —**Whig′gism** *n.*

while (wīl, hwīl) ►*n.* **1.** A period of time: *stay for a while.* **2.** The time, effort, or trouble taken in doing something: *It wasn't worth my while.* ►*conj.* **1.** As long as: *fun while it lasted.* **2.** Although: *While I like opera, I'm not a fanatic.* **3.** But; however: *The soles are leather, while the uppers are canvas.* ►*v.* **whiled, whil·ing** To spend (time) idly or pleasantly: *while away the hours.* [< OE *hwīl.*]

whi·lom (wī′ləm, hwī′-) ►*adj.* Former: *the whilom editor in chief.* ►*adv.* *Archaic* At a past time. [< OE *hwīlum,* at times.]

whilst (wīlst, hwīlst) ►*conj.* *Chiefly Brit.* While. [ME *whilest.*]

whim (wĭm, hwĭm) ►*n.* **1.** A sudden or capricious idea; fancy. **2.** Arbitrary thought or impulse: *governed by whim.* [< *whim-wham,* fanciful object.]

whim·per (wĭm′pər, hwĭm′-) ►*v.* To make soft whining sounds. [Prob. imit.] —**whim′per** *n.*

whim·si·cal (wĭm′zĭ-kəl, hwĭm′-) ►*adj.* **1.** Characterized by, arising from, or subject to whimsy: *a whimsical personality.* **2.** Playful or fanciful, esp. in a humorous way: *whimsical dialogue.* [< WHIMSY.] —**whim′si·cal′i·ty** (-kăl′ĭ-tē) *n.* —**whim′si·cal·ly** *adv.*

whim·sy also **whim·sey** (wĭm′zē, hwĭm′-) ►*n., pl.* -**sies** also -**seys 1.** An unusual, unexpected, or fanciful idea; whim. **2.** Quaint, fanciful, or playful humor: *stories full of whimsy.* [Prob. < *whim-wham,* fanciful object.]

whine (wīn, hwīn) ►*v.* **whined, whin·ing 1.** To produce a sustained, high-pitched, plaintive sound, as in pain, fear, or complaint. **2.** To complain in a childish fashion. **3.** To make a steady, high-pitched noise: *jet engines whining.* [< OE *hwīnan,* make a whizzing sound.] —**whine** *n.* —**whin′er** *n.* —**whin′y** *adj.*

whin·ny (wĭn′ē, hwĭn′ē) ►*v.* **whin·nied** (wĭn′-ēd, hwĭn′-), **whin·ny·ing** To neigh softly, as a horse. —**whin′ny** *n.*

whip (wĭp, hwĭp) ►*v.* **whipped** or **whipt** (wĭpt, hwĭpt), **whip·ping 1.** To strike with a strap or rod; lash. **2.** To afflict, castigate, or reprove severely. **3.** To strike or affect in a manner similar to whipping or lashing: *Icy wind whipped my face.* **4.** To arouse or excite, esp. with words. **5.** To beat (e.g., cream or eggs) into a froth or foam. **6.** *Informal* To snatch or remove in a sudden manner: *He whipped off his cap.* **7.** *Informal* To defeat; beat. **8.** To move swiftly or nimbly. ►*n.* **1.** A flexible instrument, esp. a rod or thong, used for driving animals or administering punishment. **2.** A whipping motion or stroke; lash. **3.** A member of a legislative body charged by his or her party with enforcing party discipline and ensuring attendance. —*phrasal verb:* **whip up** To arouse; excite: *whip up enthusiasm.* **2.** *Informal* To prepare quickly: *whip up a light lunch.* [ME *wippen.*] —**whip′per** *n.*

whip·cord (wĭp′kôrd′, hwĭp′-) ►*n.* **1.** A worsted fabric with a distinct diagonal rib. **2.** A strong twisted or braided cord sometimes used in making whiplashes. **3.** Catgut.

whip·lash (wĭp′lăsh′, hwĭp′-) ►*n.* **1.** The lash of a whip. **2.** An injury to the cervical spine caused by an abrupt jerking motion of the head, either backward or forward.

whip·per·snap·per (wĭp′ər-snăp′ər, hwĭp′-) ►*n.* One who is regarded as insignificant and pretentious. [< dial. *snippersnapper.*]

whip·pet (wĭp′ĭt, hwĭp′-) ►*n.* A swift, short-haired dog resembling the greyhound but smaller. [Prob. < WHIP.]

whip·ping boy (wĭp′ĭng, hwĭp′-) ►*n.* A scapegoat.

whip·poor·will or **whip·poor·will** (wĭp′-ər-wĭl′, hwĭp′-, wĭp′ər-wĭl′, hwĭp′-) ►*n.* An insect-eating bird of North and Central America having brownish feathers that blend in with its woodland habitat. [Imit. of its call.]

whip·saw (wĭp′sô′, hwĭp′-) ►*n.* A narrow two-person crosscut saw. ►*v.* **1.** To cut with a whipsaw. **2.** To cause to move or alternate rapidly in contrasting directions. **3.** To defeat in two ways at once.

whip·stitch (wĭp′stĭch′, hwĭp′-) ►*v.* To sew with overcast stitches, as in finishing a fabric edge or binding two pieces of fabric together. —**whip′stitch′** *n.*

whipt (wĭpt, hwĭpt) ►*v.* P.t. and p.part. of **whip.**

whir (wûr, hwûr) ►*v.* **whirred, whir·ring** To produce a vibrating or buzzing sound or move while making such a sound. ►*n.* A sound of buzzing or vibration: *the whir of turning wheels.* [ME *whirren.*]

whirl (wûrl, hwûrl) ►*v.* **1.** To rotate rapidly about a center or an axis; spin. **2.** To move while rotating or turning about: *The dancer whirled across the stage.* **3.** To turn rapidly, changing direction; wheel. **4.** To have the sensation of spinning; reel. **5.** To move or drive at high speed. ►*n.* **1.** A whirling or spinning motion. **2.** One that whirls or is whirled. **3.** A state of confusion; tumult. **4.** A state of giddiness or dizziness: *My head is in a whirl.* **5.** *Informal* **a.** A short trip or ride. **b.** A try: *give it a whirl.* [< ON *hvirfla.*] —**whirl′er** *n.*

whirl·i·gig (wûr′lĭ-gĭg′, hwûr′-) ►*n.* **1.** A toy, such as a pinwheel, that whirls. **2.** A merry-go-round. [ME *whirlegigge.*]

whirl·pool (wûrl′pool′, hwûrl′-) ►*n.* **1.** A rapidly rotating current of water; vortex. **2.** Something confusing or tumultuous that is easy to be drawn into or difficult to get out of: *a whirlpool of despair.* **3.** A bathtub or pool having submerged jets of warm water.

whirl·wind (wûrl′wĭnd′, hwûrl′-) ►*n.* **1.** A rapidly rotating column of air, such as a tornado, dust devil, or waterspout. **2a.** A tumultuous rush. **b.** A destructive force. ►*adj.* Tumultuous or rapid: *a whirlwind campaign.*

whisk

whisk (wĭsk, hwĭsk) ►*v.* **1.** To move or cause to move with quick light sweeping motions. **2.** To

whip (eggs or cream). **3.** To move lightly, nimbly, and rapidly. ►*n.* **1.** A quick light sweeping motion. **2.** A whiskbroom. **3.** A kitchen utensil for whipping foodstuffs. [ME *wisken.*]

whisk·broom (wĭsk′broom′, -broom′, hwĭsk′-) ►*n.* A small short-handled broom used esp. to brush clothes.

whisk·er (wĭs′kər, hwĭs′-) ►*n.* **1a. whiskers** The hair on a man's cheeks and chin. **b.** A single hair of a beard or mustache. **2.** One of the long stiff tactile bristles that grow near the mouth of most mammals. **3.** *Informal* A narrow margin: *lost by a whisker.* [ME *wisker < wisken,* whisk.] —**whisk′ered, whisk′er·y** *adj.*

whis·key also **-ky** (wĭs′kē, hwĭs′-) ►*n., pl.* **-keys** also **-kies 1.** An alcoholic liquor distilled from grain, such as corn, rye, or barley. **2.** A drink of such liquor. [< Sc.Gael. *uisce beatha,* aqua vitae.]

whis·per (wĭs′pər, hwĭs′-) ►*n.* **1.** Soft speech produced without full voice. **2.** Something uttered very softly. **3.** A rumor or hint: *whispers of scandal.* **4.** A low rustling sound. ►*v.* **1.** To speak softly. **2.** To tell secretly or privately. **3.** To make a soft rustling sound. [< OE *hwisprian.*] —**whis′per·er** *n.* —**whis′per·y** *adj.*

whist (wĭst, hwĭst) ►*n.* A card game similar to bridge. [< obsolete *whisk.*]

whis·tle (wĭs′əl, hwĭs′-) ►*v.* **-tled, -tling 1.** To produce a clear musical sound by forcing air through the teeth or through an aperture formed by pursing the lips. **2.** To produce a clear, shrill, sharp musical sound by passing air over or through an opening. **3.** To make a high-pitched sound when moving swiftly through the air: *The stone whistled past my head.* **4.** To produce by whistling: *whistle a tune.* ►*n.* **1.** A device or instrument for making whistling sounds by means of breath, forced air, or steam. **2.** A sound produced by a whistle or by whistling. —*idiom:* **blow the whistle** *Slang* To expose a wrongdoing in the hope of ending it. [< OE *hwistlian.*] —**whis′tler** *n.*

Whis·tler (wĭs′lər, hwĭs′-), **James Abbott McNeill** 1834–1903. Amer. painter.

whistle stop ►*n.* **1.** A town at which a train stops only if signaled. **2.** An appearance of a political candidate in a small town, traditionally on the rear platform of a train.

whit (wĭt, hwĭt) ►*n.* The least bit; iota: *not a whit afraid.* [< OE *wiht,* thing.]

white (wĭt, hwĭt) ►*n.* **1.** The achromatic color of maximum lightness; the color of objects that reflect nearly all light of all visible wavelengths. **2.** The white or whitish part, as of an egg. **3. whites** White trousers or a white outfit. **4.** also **White** A member of a racial group having light-colored skin, esp. one of European origin. ►*adj.* **whit·er, whit·est 1.** Being of the color white. **2.** Light-colored; pale. **3.** also **White** Of or belonging to a racial group having light-colored skin, esp. one of European origin. **4.** Not written on; blank. **5.** Snowy: *a white Christmas.* **6.** Incandescent. [< OE *hwīt.*] —**whit′en** *v.* —**whit′en·er** *n.* —**white′ness** *n.*

White, E(lwyn) B(rooks) 1899–1985. Amer. writer and humorist.

White, Stanford 1853–1906. Amer. architect.

white ant ►*n.* See **termite.**

white·bait (wĭt′bāt′, hwĭt′-) ►*n.* The young of

various fishes, esp. the herring, considered a delicacy when fried.

white blood cell ►*n.* Any of various white or colorless nucleated blood cells, such as lymphocytes, that help protect the body from infection.

white·board (wīt′bôrd′, hwīt′-) ►*n.* A panel covered with white, glossy plastic for writing on with erasable markers. [WHITE + (BLACK)-BOARD.]

white·cap (wīt′kăp′, hwīt′-) ►*n.* A wave with a crest of foam. —**white′capped′** *adj.*

white-col·lar (wīt′kŏl′ər, hwīt′-) ►*adj.* Of or relating to workers whose work does not involve manual labor.

white dwarf ►*n.* The collapsed remnant core of a low-mass star that has ejected its outer layers and can no longer sustain nuclear fusion.

white elephant ►*n.* **1.** A rare whitish or light-gray form of the Asian elephant. **2.** A possession that provides few benefits and is an inconvenience or a financial burden to maintain.

white·fish (wīt′fĭsh′, hwīt′-) ►*n.* **1.** Any of various white or silvery freshwater food fishes. **2.** See **beluga** (sense 2).

white flag ►*n.* A white cloth or flag signaling truce or surrender.

white gold ►*n.* An alloy of gold and nickel, sometimes also containing palladium or zinc, having a pale platinumlike color.

White·hall (wīt′hôl′, hwīt′-) ►*n.* The British civil service. [After *Whitehall*, a street in London, England.]

White·horse (wīt′hôrs′, hwīt′-) The capital of Yukon Terr., Canada, in the S part on the Yukon R.

White House ►*n.* **1.** The executive branch of the US government. **2.** The executive mansion of the US President.

white lead (lĕd) ►*n.* A heavy white poisonous compound of lead used in paint pigments.

white lie ►*n.* A trivial, harmless, or well-intentioned untruth.

white light ►*n.* Electromagnetic radiation of all the frequencies in the visible range of the spectrum, appearing white to the eye.

white matter ►*n.* Whitish nerve tissue, esp. of the brain and spinal cord, consisting chiefly of nerve fibers with myelin sheaths.

White Nile A section of the Nile R. in E Africa flowing to Khartoum, where it joins the Blue Nile to form the Nile River proper.

white·out (wīt′out′, hwīt′-) ►*n.* **1.** A polar weather condition caused by a heavy cloud cover over the snow, characterized by absence of shadow, invisibility of the horizon, and discernibility of only very dark objects. **2.** A fluid, usu. white, that dries quickly and is applied to printed matter to cover mistakes.

white pine ►*n.* **1.** A timber tree of E North America, having durable, easily worked wood. **2.** The wood of this tree.

white sale ►*n.* A sale of household items, esp. bed sheets, towels, or curtains.

white sauce ►*n.* A sauce made with butter, flour, and milk, cream, or stock.

white·wash (wīt′wŏsh′, -wôsh′, hwīt′-) ►*n.* **1.** A mixture of lime and water, often with whiting, size, or glue added, used to whiten walls and fences. **2.** Concealment or palliation of flaws or failures. ►*v.* **1.** To paint or coat with

whitewash. **2.** To conceal or gloss over (e.g., wrongdoing). —**white′wash′er** *n.*

white whale ►*n.* See **beluga** (sense 1).

whith·er (wĭth′ər, hwĭth′-) *Archaic* ►*adv.* To what place, result, or condition. ►*conj.* **1.** To which specified place or position. **2.** Wherever. [< OE *hwider.*]

whit·ing[1] (wī′tĭng, hwī′-) ►*n.* A pure white chalk ground and washed for use in paints, ink, and putty. [ME < *whiten*, whiten.]

whit·ing[2] (wī′tĭng, hwī′-) ►*n., pl.* **-ing** or **-ings** Any of several marine food fishes having white flesh, esp. certain hakes. [< MDu. *wijting.*]

whit·ish (wī′tĭsh, hwī′-) ►*adj.* Somewhat white.

Whit·man (wĭt′mən, hwĭt′-), **Walter** "Walt." 1819–92. Amer. poet.

Whit·ney (wĭt′nē, hwĭt′-), **Eli** 1765–1825. Amer. inventor of the cotton gin (1793).

Whitney, Mount A peak, 4,417 m (14,491 ft), in the Sierra Nevada of E-central CA, the highest point in the contiguous 48 states.

Whit·sun·day (wĭt′sən-dē, -dā′, hwĭt′-) ►*n.* See **Pentecost.** [< OE *hwīta sunnandæg*, White Sunday.]

Whit·ti·er (wĭt′ē-ər, hwĭt′-), **John Greenleaf** 1807–92. Amer. poet.

whit·tle (wĭt′l, hwĭt′l) ►*v.* **-tled, -tling 1a.** To cut small bits or pare shavings from (a piece of wood). **b.** To fashion in this way. **2.** To reduce gradually: *whittled down my expenses.* [< OE *thwītan.*] —**whit′tler** *n.*

whiz also **whizz** (wĭz, hwĭz) ►*v.* **whizzed, whiz·zing 1.** To make a whirring or hissing sound, as of an object speeding through air. **2.** To move or do something quickly: *The days whizzed by. She whizzed past on her bike.* ►*n., pl.* **whiz·zes 1.** A whizzing sound. **2.** *Informal* One who has remarkable skill: *a math whiz.* [Imit.]

who (hōō) ►*pron.* **1.** What or which person or persons: *Who left?* **2.** The person or persons that: *The boy who came yesterday has gone.* [< OE *hwā.*]

Usage: The traditional rules that determine the use of *who* and *whom* are relatively simple. *Who* is used for a grammatical subject, where a nominative pronoun such as *I* or *he* would be appropriate, and *whom* is used elsewhere: *I met the man who is taking the job. I met the man whom the committee selected for the job.* • The grammatical rules governing the use of *who* and *whom* apply equally to *whoever* and *whomever.* See Usage Note at **else.**

WHO ►*abbr.* World Health Organization

whoa (wō, hwō) ►*interj.* **1.** Used as a command to stop, as to a horse. **2.** Used to express surprise, amazement, or great pleasure.

who'd (hōōd) **1.** Who would. **2.** Who had.

who·dun·it (hōō-dŭn′ĭt) ►*n. Informal* A detective story. [< *who done it?*]

who·ev·er (hōō-ĕv′ər) ►*pron.* **1.** Whatever person or persons: *Whoever comes will be welcomed.* **2.** Who. See Usage Notes at **whatever, who.**

whole (hōl) ►*adj.* **1.** Containing all parts; complete: *the whole series of novels.* **2.** Not divided; in one unit: *a whole loaf.* **3.** Constituting the full amount, extent, or duration: *cried the whole time.* **4.** Not wounded, injured, or impaired. **5.** *Math.* Not fractional; integral. ►*n.* **1.** All of the component parts or elements of a thing. **2.** A complete entity or system. —**idiom: on**

the whole In general. [< OE *hāl*.] —whole'-
ness *n*.
  Syns: *all, entire, total* **adj.**
whole·heart·ed (hōl'här'tĭd) ►*adj*. Without
reservation: *wholehearted approval.* —whole'-
heart'ed·ly *adv.*
whole note ►*n*. A musical note having, in common time, the value of four beats.
whole number ►*n*. **1.** A member of the set of
positive integers and zero. **2.** A positive integer.
3. An integer.
whole·sale (hōl'sāl') ►*n*. The sale of goods in
large quantities, as for resale by a retailer. ►*adj*.
1. Of or engaged in the sale of goods at wholesale. **2.** Performed extensively and indiscriminately: *wholesale destruction.* ►*v*. **-saled, -sal·
ing** To sell or be sold at wholesale. —whole'-
sale' *adv.* —whole'sal'er *n.*
whole·some (hōl'səm) ►*adj*. **-som·er, -som·est**
1. Conducive to or indicative of good health or
well-being: *a wholesome diet; a wholesome complexion.* **2.** Promoting mental, moral, or social
health: *wholesome entertainment.* —whole'-
some·ly *adv.* —whole'some·ness *n.*
whole-wheat (hōl'wēt', -hwēt') ►*adj*. Made
from the entire grain of wheat.
who'll (hōōl) Who will.
whol·ly (hō'lē, hōl'lē) ►*adv*. **1.** Completely;
entirely. **2.** Exclusively; solely.
whom (hōōm) ►*pron*. The objective case of
who. See Usage Note at **who.**
whom·ev·er (hōōm-ĕv'ər) ►*pron*. The objective
case of **whoever.** See Usage Note at **who.**
whom·so·ev·er (hōōm'sō-ĕv'ər) ►*pron*. The
objective case of **whosoever.**
whoop (hōōp, wōōp, hwōōp) ►*n*. **1.** A loud cry
of exultation or excitement. **2.** The paroxysmal
gasp typical of whooping cough. ►*v*. **1.** To
utter with a whoop. See Synonyms at **yell. 2.**
To gasp as with whooping cough. **3.** To chase,
call, urge on, or drive with a whoop. [< OFr.
hopper, to whoop.]
whoop·ing cough (hōō'pĭng, wōō'-, hwōō'-,
hōōp'ĭng) ►*n*. A highly contagious bacterial
disease of the respiratory system, usu. affecting
children and marked by spasms of coughing
interspersed with deep noisy gasps.
whooping crane ►*n*. A large North American
crane having predominantly white plumage
and a loud trumpeting cry.
whoops (wōōps, hwōōps, wŏŏps, hwŏŏps)
►*interj*. Used to express apology or surprise.
whoosh (wōōsh, hwōōsh, wŏŏsh, hwŏŏsh) ►*n*.
1. A soft rushing sound. **2.** A swift movement
or flow; rush. [Imit.] —whoosh *v.*
whop (wŏp, hwŏp) ►*v*. **whopped, whop·ping**
1. To strike with a thudding blow. **2.** To defeat
soundly. [ME *whappen.*] —whop *n.*
whop·per (wŏp'ər, hwŏp'-) ►*n*. Slang **1.** Something exceptionally big or remarkable. **2.** A
gross lie.
whop·ping (wŏp'ĭng, hwŏp'-) ►*adj*. Slang
Exceptionally large.
whore (hôr) ►*n*. A prostitute. [< OE *hōre.*]
—whor'ish *adj.*
whorl (wôrl, hwôrl, wûrl, hwûrl) ►*n*. **1.** A form
that coils or spirals; curl; swirl. **2.** *Bot.* An
arrangement of three or more leaves, petals, or
other organs radiating from a single node. **3.**
One of the circular ridges or convolutions of a
fingerprint. [ME *whorle.*]

whorl

who's (hōōz) **1.** Who is. **2.** Who has.
whose (hōōz) ►*adj*. **1.** The possessive form of
who. 2. The possessive form of **which.** [<
OE *hwæs.*]
who·so·ev·er (hōō'sō-ĕv'ər) ►*pron*. Whoever.
why (wī, hwī) ►*adv*. For what purpose, reason,
or cause: *Why do birds sing?* ►*conj*. **1.** The
reason, cause, or purpose for which: *I know
why you left.* **2.** *Informal* For which: *told me the
reason why he's angry.* ►*n., pl.* **whys** The cause or
reason. ►*interj*. Used to express mild surprise,
indignation, or impatience. [< OE *hwȳ.*]
WI ►*abbr*. **1.** West Indies **2.** Wisconsin
Wic·ca (wĭk'ə) ►*n*. A Neopagan nature religion
typically centering on a mother goddess or a
goddess-god pair and the practice of ceremonial witchcraft. [< OE *wicca,* necromancer.]
—Wic'can *adj. & n.*
Wich·i·ta (wĭch'ĭ-tô') A city of S-central KS on
the Arkansas R.
wick (wĭk) ►*n*. A cord or strand of woven or
twisted fibers, as in a candle, that draws up
fuel to the flame by capillary action. ►*v*. To
convey or be conveyed by capillary action. [<
OE *wēoce.*]
wick·ed (wĭk'ĭd) ►*adj*. **-er, -est 1.** Evil by nature
and in practice. **2.** Playfully mischievous: *a
wicked prank.* **3.** Severe and distressing: *a wicked sunburn.* [< OE *wicca,* sorcerer.] —wick'ed·
ly *adv.* —wick'ed·ness *n.*
wick·er (wĭk'ər) ►*n*. **1.** Long flexible twigs,
plant stems, or other pliable materials used in
weaving baskets or furniture. **2.** Wickerwork.
[ME *wiker.*]
wick·er·work (wĭk'ər-wûrk') ►*n*. Furniture or
other work made of wicker.
wick·et (wĭk'ĭt) ►*n*. **1.** A small door or gate, esp.
one built into or near a larger one. **2.** A small,
often grated window or opening. **3.** In cricket,
either of the two sets of three stumps forming
the bowler's target. **4.** An arch through which
players try to drive their ball in croquet. [<
ONFr. *wiket.*]
wick·i·up (wĭk'ē-ŭp') ►*n*. A frame hut covered
with matting, as of bark or brush, used by
certain nomadic Native Americans. [Fox *wiiki-
yaapi,* wigwam.]
wide (wīd) ►*adj*. **wid·er, wid·est 1a.** Measured
from side to side: *a ribbon two inches wide.* **b.**
Extending over a large area from side to side;
broad: *a wide road.* **2.** Great in extent or range:
a wide selection. **3.** Fully open: *look with wide
eyes.* **4.** Far from a goal or point: *a shot wide of*

the mark. ►*adv.* **-er, -est 1.** Extensively: *traveled far and wide.* **2.** To the full extent; completely. **3.** So as to miss a target; astray. [< OE *wīd.*] —**wide′ly** *adv.* —**wid′en** *v.* —**wide′ness** *n.*

wide·a·wake (wīd′ə-wāk′) ►*adj.* **1.** Completely awake. **2.** Alert; watchful.

wide-eyed (wīd′īd′) ►*adj.* **1.** With the eyes completely open, as in wonder. **2.** Innocent; credulous.

wide·spread (wīd′sprĕd′) ►*adj.* **1.** Spread or scattered over a considerable extent. **2.** Occurring widely.

wid·ow (wĭd′ō) ►*n.* A woman whose spouse has died and who has not remarried. ►*v.* To make a widow or widower of. [< OE *widuwe.*] —**wid′ow·hood′** *n.*

wid·ow·er (wĭd′ō-ər) ►*n.* A man whose spouse has died and who has not remarried. [ME *widewer.*]

width (wĭdth, wĭtth) ►*n.* **1.** The state, quality, or fact of being wide. **2.** The measurement of something from side to side.

wield (wēld) ►*v.* **1.** To handle (e.g., a weapon or tool), esp. capably. **2.** To exercise (e.g., power) effectively. [< OE *wieldan,* rule.]

wie·ner (wē′nər) ►*n.* A frankfurter. [Ger.]

Wie·sel (vē′səl), **Elie(zer)** b. 1928. Romanian-born writer and lecturer.

wife (wīf) ►*n., pl.* **wives** (wīvz) A female spouse. [< OE *wīf.*] —**wife′hood′** *n.* —**wife′ly** *adj.*

Wi-Fi (wī′fī′) A trademark for the certification of products that meet certain standards for transmitting data over wireless networks.

wig (wĭg) ►*n.* A covering of human or synthetic hair worn on the head for personal adornment, as part of a costume, or to conceal baldness. [< PERIWIG.]

wig·gle (wĭg′əl) ►*v.* **-gled, -gling** To move or cause to move from side to side with short irregular twisting motions. [ME *wiglen.*] —**wig′gle** *n.* —**wig′gler** *n.* —**wig′gly** *adj.*

Wight (wīt), **Isle of** An island in the English Channel off S-central England.

wig·wam (wĭg′wŏm′) ►*n.* A Native American dwelling usu. having an arched or conical framework overlaid with bark, hides, or mats. [Eastern Abenaki *wikəwam.*]

wi·ki (wĭk′ē) ►*n., pl.* **-kis** A collaborative website whose content can be edited by anyone who has access to it. [< Hawaiian *wikiwiki,* quick.]

wild (wīld) ►*adj.* **-er, -est 1.** Occurring or living in a natural state; not domesticated or cultivated: *wild geese, wild plants.* **2.** Not inhabited or farmed: *remote, wild country.* **3.** Uncivilized; barbarous. **4.** Unruly: *wild children.* **5.** Full or suggestive of uncontrolled emotion: *wild with jealousy.* **6.** Extravagant; fantastic: *a wild idea.* **7.** Erratic: *a wild pitch.* **8.** Having a value determined by the cardholder's choice: *deuces wild.* ►*adv.* In a wild manner: *roaming wild.* ►*n.* **1.** A natural or undomesticated state: *plants growing in the wild.* **2.** often **wilds** An uninhabited or uncultivated region. [< OE *wilde.*] —**wild′ly** *adv.* —**wild′ness** *n.*

wild·cat (wīld′kăt′) ►*n.* **1.** Any of various wild felines of small to medium size, as the lynx. **2.** A quick-tempered person. **3.** An oil well drilled in an area not known to be productive. ►*adj.* **1.** Risky or unsound. **2.** Undertaken without official union approval: *a wildcat strike.*

Wilde (wīld), **Oscar Fingal O'Flahertie Wills** 1854–1900. Irish writer.

wil·de·beest (wĭl′də-bēst′, vĭl′-) ►*n., pl.* **-beests** or **-beest** See **gnu.** [Obsolete Afr.]

Wil·der (wĭl′dər), **Laura Ingalls** 1867–1957. Amer. writer.

Wilder, Thornton Niven 1897–1975. Amer. writer.

wil·der·ness (wĭl′dər-nĭs) ►*n.* **1.** An unsettled, uncultivated region left in its natural condition. **2.** A bewildering or threatening vastness. [< OE *wilddēor,* wild beast.]

wild-eyed (wīld′īd′) ►*adj.* Glaring in or as if in anger, terror, or madness.

wild·fire (wīld′fīr′) ►*n.* A raging, rapidly spreading fire.

wild·fowl (wīld′foul′) ►*n.* A wild game bird, such as a duck or quail.

wild-goose chase (wīld′gōōs′) ►*n.* A futile pursuit or search.

wild·life (wīld′līf′) ►*n.* Wild animals, esp. when living in a natural environment.

wild rice ►*n.* **1.** A tall aquatic grass of North America, bearing edible grain. **2.** The grain of this plant.

wile (wīl) ►*n.* **1.** A deceitful stratagem or trick. **2.** A disarming or seductive manner, device, or procedure. ►*v.* **wiled, wil·ing 1.** To lure; entice. **2.** To pass (time) agreeably. [< ONFr. *wil,* of Gmc. orig.]

Wil·helm I (vĭl′hĕlm) also **Wil·liam I** (wĭl′yəm) 1797–1888. King of Prussia (1861–88); kaiser of Germany (1871–88).

Wilhelm II 1859–1941. Kaiser of Germany and king of Prussia (1888–1918).

will¹ (wĭl) ►*n.* **1.** The mental faculty by which one deliberately chooses a course of action; volition. **2.** Self-control; self-discipline. **3.** A desire, purpose, or determination, esp. of one in authority. **4.** Deliberate intention or wish: *against my will.* **5.** Bearing or attitude toward others; disposition: *full of good will.* **6.** A legal declaration of how a person wishes his or her possessions to be disposed of after death. ►*v.* **willed, will·ing 1.** To decide on; choose. **2.** To yearn for; desire. **3.** To decree, dictate, or order. **4.** To grant in a legal will; bequeath. —***idiom:*** **at will** Just as or when one wishes. [< OE *willa.*]

will² (wĭl) ►*aux.v. P.t.* **would** (wōōd) **1.** Used to indicate: **a.** Simple futurity: *They will appear later.* **b.** Likelihood or certainty: *You will regret this.* **c.** Willingness: *Will you help me?* **d.** Requirement or command: *You will report to me now.* **e.** Intention: *I will if I feel like it.* **f.** Customary or habitual action: *They would get together on weekends.* **g.** Probability: *That will be Katie calling.* **2.** To wish; desire: *Do what you will.* See Usage Note at **shall.** [< OE *willan.*]

Wil·lem·stad (vĭl′əm-stät′) The capital of Curaçao, on the S coast.

will·ful also **wil·ful** (wĭl′fəl) ►*adj.* **1.** Deliberate; voluntary. **2.** Obstinate; stubborn. —**will′ful·ly** *adv.* —**will′ful·ness** *n.*

Wil·liam (wĭl′yəm) b. 1982. British prince.

William I¹ "the Conqueror." 1027?–87. King of England (1066–87).

William I² Prince of Orange. 1533–84. Dutch aristocrat; led successful revolt against Spanish rule (1568–76).

William I³ See **Wilhelm I.**

William II¹ 1056?–1100. King of England (1087–1100).

William II² See **Wilhelm II.**

William III "William of Orange." 1650–1702. King of England, Scotland, and Ireland (1689–1702), Dutch governor (1672–1702), and prince of Orange.

William IV 1765–1837. King of Great Britain and Ireland (1830–37).

Wil·liams (wĭl′yəmz), **Roger** 1603?–83. English-born cleric; founder of Rhode Island.

Williams, Tennessee 1911–83. Amer. playwright.

wil·lies (wĭl′ēz) ►*pl.n. Slang* Feelings of uneasiness; creeps. [?]

will·ing (wĭl′ĭng) ►*adj.* **1.** Disposed or inclined; prepared. **2.** Acting or ready to act gladly. **3.** Done, given, or borne voluntarily. —**will′ing·ly** *adv.* —**will′ing·ness** *n.*

wil·li·waw (wĭl′ē-wô′) ►*n.* A violent gust of cold wind blowing seaward from a mountainous coast. [?]

will-o′-the-wisp (wĭl′ə-thə-wĭsp′) ►*n.* **1.** See **ignis fatuus** (sense 1). **2.** A delusive or misleading hope. [< *Will* (nickname for *William*).]

wil·low (wĭl′ō) ►*n.* **1.** Any of various trees or shrubs having usu. narrow leaves and slender flexible twigs. **2.** The wood of a willow. [< OE *welig.*]

wil·low·y (wĭl′ō-ē) ►*adj.* **-i·er, -i·est** Slender and graceful; *a willowy figure.*

will·pow·er or **will pow·er** (wĭl′pou′ər) ►*n.* The strength of will to carry out one's decisions, wishes, or plans.

wil·ly-nil·ly (wĭl′ē-nĭl′ē) ►*adv. & adj.* **1.** Whether desired or not. **2.** Without order or plan. [< *will ye, nill ye,* be you willing, be you unwilling.]

Wil·son (wĭl′sən), **(James) Harold** Baron Wilson of Rievaulx. 1916–95. British prime minister (1964–70 and 1974–76).

Wilson, (Thomas) Woodrow 1856–1924. The 28th US president (1913–21). —**Wil·so′ni·an** (-sō′nē-ən) *adj.*

Woodrow Wilson

wilt¹ (wĭlt) ►*v.* **1.** To lose or cause to lose freshness; droop. **2.** To lose or deprive of energy or vigor; weaken; sap. ►*n.* Any of various plant diseases marked by collapse of terminal shoots, branches, or entire plants. [Poss. < ME *welken.*]

wilt² (wĭlt) ►*aux.v. Archaic* 2nd pers. sing. pr.t. of **will².**

wi·ly (wī′lē) ►*adj.* **-li·er, -li·est** Full of wiles; cunning. —**wil′i·ness** *n.*

wimp (wĭmp) ►*n. Slang* A timid or unadventurous person. [Perh. < WHIMPER.] —**wimp′y** *adj.*

wim·ple (wĭm′pəl) ►*n.* A cloth framing the face and drawn into folds beneath the chin, worn by women in medieval times and by certain nuns. [< OE *wimpel.*]

win (wĭn) ►*v.* **won** (wŭn), **win·ning 1.** To achieve victory or finish first in a competition. **2.** To achieve success in an effort. **3.** To receive as a prize or reward. **4.** To obtain or earn. See Synonyms at **earn. 5.** To succeed in gaining the favor or support of. **6.** To succeed in gaining the affection or love of (someone). ►*n.* A victory, esp. in a competition. [< OE *winnan,* strive.] —**win′ner** *n.*

wince (wĭns) ►*v.* **winced, winc·ing** To shrink or start involuntarily, as in pain or distress; flinch. [ME *wincen,* kick.] —**wince** *n.*

winch (wĭnch) ►*n.* **1.** A stationary hoisting machine having a drum around which is wound a rope, cable, or chain attached to the load being lifted. **2.** A crank used to give rotary motion. [< OE *wince,* roller.] —**winch** *v.*

wind¹ (wĭnd) ►*n.* **1.** Moving air, esp. as impelled by natural causes. **2a.** Respiration: *had the wind knocked out of me.* **b.** Flatulence. **3.** often **winds** *Mus.* **a.** The brass and woodwinds sections of an orchestra. **b.** Wind instruments or their players. **4.** An agent of change or disruption: *the winds of war.* **5.** Information, esp. of something concealed; intimation: *got wind of the situation.* **6.** Empty or boastful talk. ►*v.* **1.** To detect the scent of. **2.** To cause to be out of breath. [< OE *wind.*]

wind² (wīnd) ►*v.* **wound** (wound), **wind·ing 1.** To wrap or be wrapped around a center or another object once or repeatedly. **2.** To encircle or be encircled in coils; entwine. **3.** To go along (a twisting course). **4.** To turn (e.g., a crank) in circular motions. ►*n.* A single turn, twist, or curve. —*phrasal verb:* **wind up 1.** To finish; end. **2.** To put in order; settle. **3.** To arrive eventually in a place or situation: *wound up in debt.* [< OE *windan.*] —**wind′er** *n.*

wind³ (wīnd, wĭnd) ►*v.* **wind·ed** (wīn′dĭd, wĭn′-) or **wound** (wound), **wind·ing** *Mus.* To sound by blowing (a wind instrument). [< WIND¹.]

wind·bag (wĭnd′băg′) ►*n. Slang* A tiresomely talkative person.

wind·break (wĭnd′brāk′) ►*n.* A hedge, fence, or row of trees serving to lessen the force of the wind.

wind·burn (wĭnd′bûrn′) ►*n.* Skin irritation caused by exposure to the wind. —**wind′burned′** *adj.*

wind-chill factor (wĭnd′chĭl′) ►*n.* The temperature of still air that would have the same effect on exposed skin as a given combination of wind speed and air temperature.

wind·fall (wĭnd′fôl′) ►*n.* **1.** A sudden, unexpected piece of good fortune. **2.** A fruit blown down by the wind.

wind farm (wĭnd) ►*n.* An arrangement of windmills that generate electricity.

wind·flow·er (wĭnd′flou′ər) ►*n.* See **anemone** (sense 1).

Wind·hoek (vĭnt′hŏŏk′) The capital of Namibia, in the central part.

wind·ing (wīn′dĭng) ►*n.* **1.** Something wound about a center or an object. **2.** A curve or bend, as of a road. ►*adj.* **1.** Twisting or turning; sinuous. **2.** Spiral.

wind·ing-sheet (wīn′dĭng-shēt′) ►*n.* A sheet for wrapping a corpse; shroud.

wind instrument (wĭnd) ►*n. Mus.* **1.** An instrument, such as an oboe or tuba, sounded by a column of air, esp. the breath. **2.** A woodwind, as opposed to a brass instrument.

wind·jam·mer (wĭnd′jăm′ər) ►*n.* A large sailing ship.

wind·lass (wĭnd′ləs) ►*n.* Any of numerous hauling or lifting machines consisting essentially of a horizontal cylinder wound with rope and turned by a crank. [< ON *vindāss*.]

wind·mill (wĭnd′mĭl′) ►*n.* A machine that runs on the energy generated by a wheel of adjustable blades rotated by the wind.

win·dow (wĭn′dō) ►*n.* **1.** An opening constructed in a wall or roof to admit light or air. **2.** A framework enclosing a window. **3.** A windowpane. **4.** An opening that resembles a window. **5.** A temporary period of a specified nature: *a window of opportunity.* **6.** *Comp.* A rectangular area on a display screen that can be viewed independently of other such areas. [< ON *vindauga*.]

window box ►*n.* A usu. long narrow box for plants, placed on a windowsill or ledge.

win·dow-dress·ing also **win·dow dress·ing** (wĭn′dō-drĕs′ĭng) ►*n.* **1.** Decorative exhibition of retail merchandise in store windows. **2.** A means of improving appearances or creating a falsely favorable impression.

win·dow·pane (wĭn′dō-pān′) ►*n.* A piece of glass in a window.

win·dow-shop (wĭn′dō-shŏp′) ►*v.* To look at merchandise in store windows or showcases without buying. —**win′dow-shop′per** *n.*

win·dow·sill (wĭn′dō-sĭl′) ►*n.* The horizontal ledge at the base of a window opening.

wind·pipe (wĭnd′pīp′) ►*n. Anat.* See **trachea.**

wind·row (wĭnd′rō′) ►*n.* A long linear pile, as of cut hay or of wind-blown snow or leaves.

wind·shield (wĭnd′shēld′) ►*n.* A protective pane of transparent shielding located in front of the occupants of a vehicle.

wind·sock (wĭnd′sŏk′) ►*n.* A tapered, open-ended sleeve attached to a stand by a pivot so as to indicate the direction of the wind blowing through it.

windsock

Wind·sor (wĭn′zər) A city of SE Ontario, Canada, opposite Detroit, MI.

Windsor, Duke of. See **Edward VIII.**

wind·storm (wĭnd′stôrm′) ►*n.* A storm with high winds but little or no rain.

wind·surf·ing (wĭnd′sûrf′ĭng) ►*n.* The sport of sailing while standing on a sailboard. —**wind′-surf′** *v.* —**wind′surf′er** *n.*

wind·swept (wĭnd′swĕpt′) ►*adj.* Exposed to or swept by winds.

wind tunnel (wĭnd) ►*n.* A chamber through which air is forced at controlled velocities to study its effect on an object.

wind-up or **wind·up** (wĭnd′ŭp′) ►*n.* **1a.** The act of bringing something to an end. **b.** A conclusion; finish. **2.** The preparatory movements of a baseball pitcher before throwing the ball in certain situations. ►*adj.* Operated by a hand-wound spring.

wind·ward (wĭnd′wərd) ►*adv. & adj.* Toward the wind. —**wind′ward** *n.*

Windward Islands An island group of the SE West Indies, including the S group of the Lesser Antilles.

wind·y (wĭn′dē) ►*adj.* **-i·er, -i·est 1.** Marked by or abounding in wind. **2.** Open to the wind; unsheltered. **3.** Tiresomely talkative. —**wind′i·ly** *adv.* —**wind′i·ness** *n.*

wine (wīn) ►*n.* **1.** The fermented juice of grapes. **2.** The fermented juice or sap of other fruits or plants. ►*v.* **wined, win·ing** To entertain with wine. [< Lat. *vīnum.*]

wine·glass (wīn′glăs′) ►*n.* A glass, usu. with a stem, from which wine is drunk.

wine·grow·er (wīn′grō′ər) ►*n.* One who owns a vineyard and produces wine.

wine·press (wīn′prĕs′) ►*n.* **1.** A vat in which the juice is pressed from grapes. **2.** A device that presses the juice from grapes.

win·er·y (wī′nə-rē) ►*n., pl.* **-ies** An establishment at which wine is made.

wine·skin (wīn′skĭn′) ►*n.* A bag, as of goatskin, used for holding and dispensing wine.

wing (wĭng) ►*n.* **1.** One of a pair of movable organs for flying, as of a bird, bat, or insect. **2.** *Informal* A human arm. **3.** An airfoil whose main function is providing lift, esp. either of two such airfoils positioned on each side of the fuselage of an aircraft. **4. wings** The unseen backstage area on either side of a stage. **5.** A structure that is attached to and connected with a main building. **6.** Either of two groups with opposing views within a larger group; faction. **7a.** Either the left or right flank of an army or a naval fleet. **b.** An air force unit that is larger than a group but smaller than a numbered air force, or division. **8.** *Sports* Either of the forward positions played near the sideline, esp. in hockey. ►*v.* **1.** To move on or as if on wings; fly. **2.** To effect or accomplish by flying. **3.** To wound superficially. —*idioms:* **on the wing** In flight; flying. **under (one's) wing** Under one's protection. **wing it** *Informal* To improvise; ad-lib. [ME *wenge.*] —**wing′less** *adj.*

winged (wĭngd, wĭng′ĭd) ►*adj.* **1.** Having wings or winglike appendages. **2.** Soaring with or as if with wings.

wing nut ►*n.* A nut with winglike projections for thumb and forefinger leverage in turning.

wing·span (wĭng′spăn′) ►*n.* The distance

between the tips of the outspread wings, as of a bird or airplane.

wing·tip (wĭng′tĭp′) ►*n.* **1.** A shoe with a perforated part that covers the toe and extends backward along its sides. **2.** The tip of the wing of a bird, insect, or other animal.

wink (wĭngk) ►*v.* **1.** To close and open one eye deliberately, as to convey a message, signal, or suggestion. **2.** To blink rapidly. **3.** To shine fitfully; twinkle. ►*n.* **1.** The act of winking. **2.** An instant. **3.** *Informal* A brief period of sleep. —*phrasal verb:* **wink at** To pretend not to notice: *wink at corruption.* [< OE *wincian*, close one's eyes.]

Win·ne·ba·go (wĭn′ə-bā′gō) ►*n., pl.* **-go** or **-gos** or **-goes** See **Ho-Chunk.**

win·ning (wĭn′ĭng) ►*adj.* **1.** Successful; victorious. **2.** Attractive; charming. ►*n.* **1.** Victory. **2.** often **winnings** Something won, esp. money.

Win·ni·peg (wĭn′ə-pĕg′) The capital of Manitoba, Canada, in the SE part.

Winnipeg, Lake A lake of S-central Manitoba, Canada.

win·now (wĭn′ō) ►*v.* **1.** To separate the chaff from (grain) by means of a current of air. **2.** To sort into categories, esp. of good and bad. **3.** To separate or get rid of (an undesirable part). [< OE *windwian.*] —**win′now·er** *n.*

win·o (wī′nō) ►*n., pl.* **-os** *Slang* An indigent wine-drinking alcoholic.

win·some (wĭn′səm) ►*adj.* Charming, often in a childlike way. [< OE *wynsum.*] —**win′some·ly** *adv.* —**win′some·ness** *n.*

win·ter (wĭn′tər) ►*n.* The usu. coldest season of the year, occurring between autumn and spring. ►*v.* **1.** To spend the winter. **2.** To keep or feed (e.g., livestock) during the winter. [< OE.]

win·ter·green (wĭn′tər-grēn′) ►*n.* **1.** A low-growing evergreen plant of North America, with aromatic leaves and spicy scarlet berries. **2.** An oil or flavoring derived from this plant or certain other plants or produced synthetically.

win·ter·ize (wĭn′tə-rīz′) ►*v.* **-ized, -iz·ing** To prepare or equip (e.g., an automobile) for winter weather. —**win′ter·i·za′tion** *n.*

win·ter·kill (wĭn′tər-kĭl′) ►*v.* To kill by or die from exposure to cold winter weather. —**win′-ter·kill′** *n.*

winter squash ►*n.* Any of several thick-rinded varieties of squash, such as the butternut squash, that can be stored for long periods.

win·ter·time (wĭn′tər-tīm′) ►*n.* The season of winter.

Win·throp (wĭn′thrəp), **John** 1588–1649. English-born Amer. colonial administrator.

win·try (wĭn′trē) also **win·ter·y** (wĭn′tə-rē) ►*adj.* **-tri·er, -tri·est** also **-ter·i·er, -ter·i·est** **1.** Of or like winter; cold. **2.** Suggestive of winter; cheerless: *a wintry smile.*

wipe (wīp) ►*v.* **wiped, wip·ing** **1.** To rub, as with a cloth or paper, in order to clean or dry. **2.** To remove, clean, or dry by or as if by rubbing. **3.** To rub or pass (e.g., a cloth) over a surface. —*phrasal verb:* **wipe out** **1.** To destroy completely. **2.** *Slang* To murder. **3.** *Slang* To lose one's balance and fall, as while surfing. [< OE *wīpian.*] —**wipe** *n.* —**wip′er** *n.*

wire (wīr) ►*n.* **1.** A usu. pliable metallic strand or rod, used esp. for structural support or insulated and used to conduct electricity. **2.** A group of wire strands bundled or twisted

together; cable. **3.** *Slang* A hidden microphone, as on a person's body. **4a.** A telegraph service. **b.** A telegram or cablegram. **5.** The finish line of a racetrack. ►*v.* **wired, wir·ing** **1.** To bind, connect, or attach with wires or a wire. **2.** To equip with a system of electrical wires. **3.** *Slang* To install electronic eavesdropping equipment in. **4.** To send by telegraph. **5.** To send a telegram to. **6.** To determine (a behavior) genetically; hardwire. [< OE *wīr.*]

wire·haired (wīr′hârd′) ►*adj.* Having a coat of stiff wiry hair, as certain dogs.

wire·less (wīr′lĭs) ►*adj.* **1.** Having no wire or wires. **2.** Relating to the transmission of electromagnetic signals through the air: *a wireless telephone.* ►*n.* **1.** A radiotelegraph or radiotelephone system. **2.** *Chiefly Brit.* Radio.

wire service ►*n.* A news-gathering organization that distributes syndicated copy electronically to subscribers.

wire·tap (wīr′tăp′) ►*n.* **1.** An act of secretly listening to or recording a person's electronic communications, often as part of a police investigation. **2.** A concealed listening or recording device connected to a communications circuit. ►*v.* **1.** To monitor (a communications circuit) by means of a wiretap. **2.** To record the conversations of (a person) or the communications devices in (a place) by means of a wiretap.

wir·ing (wīr′ĭng) ►*n.* A system of electric wires.

wir·y (wīr′ē) ►*adj.* **-i·er, -i·est** **1.** Wirelike, esp. in stiffness. **2.** Sinewy and lean: *a wiry build.* —**wir′i·ness** *n.*

Wis·con·sin (wĭs-kŏn′sĭn) A state of the N-central US. Cap. Madison. —**Wis·con′sin·ite′** *n.*

wis·dom (wĭz′dəm) ►*n.* **1.** Understanding of what is true, right, or lasting. **2.** Common sense; good judgment. **3.** Scholarly learning. [< OE *wīsdōm.*]

Wisdom of Solomon ►*n.* See table at **Bible.**

wisdom tooth ►*n.* One of four rearmost molars on each side of both jaws in humans.

wise¹ (wīz) ►*adj.* **wis·er, wis·est** **1.** Having wisdom; judicious. **2.** Exhibiting common sense; prudent. **3.** Aware; informed: *wise to their tricks.* **4.** *Slang* Rude and disrespectful; impudent. [< OE *wīs.*] —**wise′ly** *adv.*

wise² (wīz) ►*n.* Method or manner of doing; way: *in no wise.* [< OE *wīse.*]

–wise ►*suff.* Manner, direction, or position: *clockwise.* [< OE *-wīse*, WISE².]

wise·a·cre (wīz′ā′kər) ►*n. Slang* A smart aleck. [< MDu. *wijsseggher*, soothsayer < OHGer. *wīssago.*]

wise·crack (wīz′krăk′) ►*n. Informal* A flippant or sarcastic remark. —**wise′crack′** *v.*

wish (wĭsh) ►*n.* **1.** A desire or longing for something. **2.** An expression of a wish. **3.** Something desired or longed for. ►*v.* **1.** To long for; want: *I wish that you could come.* See Synonyms at **desire. 2.** To express wishes for; bid: *wished her good night.* **3.** To invoke upon: *I wish them luck.* **4.** To order or entreat: *I wish you to go.* [< OE *wȳscan*, to wish.] —**wish′er** *n.*

wish·bone (wĭsh′bōn′) ►*n.* The forked bone in front of the breastbone of most birds.

wish·ful (wĭsh′fəl) ►*adj.* Having or expressing a wish or longing. —**wish′ful·ly** *adv.* —**wish′-ful·ness** *n.*

wish·y-wash·y (wĭsh′ē-wŏsh′ē, -wô′shē) ►*adj.* **-i·er, -i·est** *Informal* **1.** Irresolute or indecisive.

2. Weak or ineffective. [< WASH.]

wisp (wĭsp) ►*n.* **1.** A small bunch or bundle, as of hair. **2.** One that is thin, frail, or slight. **3.** A faint streak, as of smoke or clouds. [ME.] —**wisp′y** *adj.*

wis·ter·i·a (wĭ-stîr′ē-ə) also **wis·tar·i·a** (wĭ-stâr′-) ►*n.* A climbing woody vine having racemes of showy purplish or white flowers. [After Caspar *Wistar* (1761–1818).]

wist·ful (wĭst′fəl) ►*adj.* Full of or expressing melancholy longing or wishful yearning. [< obsolete *wistly*, intently.] —**wist′ful·ly** *adv.* —**wist′ful·ness** *n.*

wit (wĭt) ►*n.* **1a.** Perception and understanding; intelligence. **b.** often **wits** Practical intelligence; shrewdness or resourcefulness. **c. wits** Sound mental faculties; sanity. **2a.** The ability to express oneself intelligently in a playful or humorous manner. **b.** One noted for this ability, esp. in conversation. —*idiom:* **at (one's) wits' end** At the limit of one's mental resources; utterly at a loss. [< OE.]

witch (wĭch) ►*n.* **1.** One, esp. a woman, who claims or is believed to practice sorcery. **2.** A follower of Wicca. **3.** A spiteful or overbearing woman. [< OE *wicce*, witch, and *wicca*, sorcerer.] —**witch′er·y** *n.* —**witch′y** *adj.*

witch·craft (wĭch′krăft′) ►*n.* Magic; sorcery.

witch doctor ►*n.* A sorcerer or shamanistic healer, esp. among traditional African peoples.

witch hazel ►*n.* **1.** A deciduous shrub of E North America having yellow flowers. **2.** An alcoholic solution containing an extract of this plant, used as a mild astringent. [Obsolete *wych*, a kind of elm + HAZEL.]

witch-hunt (wĭch′hŭnt′) ►*n.* An investigation whose underlying purpose is to identify and harass those with differing views.

witch·ing (wĭch′ĭng) ►*adj.* **1.** Of or appropriate to witchcraft. **2.** Enchanting.

with (wĭth, wĭth) ►*prep.* **1.** In the company of: *Did you go with her?* **2.** Next to: *stood with the rabbi.* **3.** Having a possession or attribute: *a man with a moustache.* **4.** Having as an accompanying condition: *a patient with a bad back.* **5.** In a manner characterized by: *performed with skill.* **6.** In the charge or keeping of: *left the cat with the neighbors.* **7.** In the opinion of: *if it's all right with you.* **8.** In support of; on the side of: *I'm with you all the way.* **9.** By the means of: *eat with a fork.* **10.** In spite of. **11.** At the same time as: *gets up with the birds.* **12.** In regard to: *pleased with her decision.* **13.** In comparison or contrast to: *a dress identical with the one I had.* **14.** Having received: *With her permission, he left.* **15.** Inclusive of: *comes to $19.95 with sales tax.* **16.** In opposition to; against: *wrestling with an opponent.* **17.** As a result or consequence of: *sick with the flu.* **18.** So as to be touching or joined to: *linked arms with their partners.* **19.** So as to be free of or separated from: *parted with her husband.* **20.** In the course of: *We grow older with the hours.* **21.** In proportion to: *wines that improve with age.* **22.** As well as: *sing with the best of them.* [< OE.]

with·al (wĭth-ôl′, wĭth-) ►*adv.* **1.** In addition; besides. **2.** Despite that; nevertheless. [ME.]

with·draw (wĭth-drô′, wĭth-) ►*v.* **-drew** (-drōō′), **-drawn** (-drôn′), **-draw·ing 1.** To take back or away; remove. **2.** To recall or retract. **3.** To move or draw back; retire. **4.** To leave or return, as from a military position. **5.** To remove oneself from active participation. **6.** To become detached from social or emotional involvement. [ME *withdrawen.*]

with·draw·al (wĭth-drô′əl, wĭth-) ►*n.* **1.** The act or process of withdrawing. **2.** Detachment, as from social or emotional involvement. **3.** A removal of something that has been deposited, as in an account. **4a.** Discontinuation of the use of an addictive substance. **b.** The physiological and mental readjustment that accompanies such discontinuation.

with·drawn (wĭth-drôn′, wĭth-) ►*adj.* Unresponsive or socially detached; aloof.

withe (wĭth, wĭth, wĭth) ►*n.* A tough supple twig, esp. of willow, used for binding things together. [< OE *withthe.*]

with·er (wĭth′ər) ►*v.* **1.** To dry up or shrivel from or as if from loss of moisture. **2.** To cause to shrivel or fade. **3.** To cause to lose force or vitality. See Synonyms at **blast. 4.** To devastate; stun: *withered them with a glance.* [< ME *widderen.*]

with·ers (wĭth′ərz) ►*pl.n.* The high part of the back of a horse or similar animal, located between the shoulder blades. [Prob. < OE *wither-*, against.]

with·hold (wĭth-hōld′, wĭth-) ►*v.* **-held** (-hĕld′), **-hold·ing 1.** To refrain from giving, granting, or permitting. **2.** To keep in check; restrain. **3.** To deduct (withholding tax) from a salary. [ME *witholden.*]

with·hold·ing tax (wĭth-hōl′dĭng, wĭth-) ►*n.* A portion of an employee's wages or salary withheld by the employer as partial payment of the employee's income tax.

with·in (wĭth-ĭn′, wĭth-) ►*adv.* **1.** In or into the inner part; inside. **2.** Inside the mind or body; inwardly. ►*prep.* **1.** In or into the inner part of. **2.** Not beyond the limits or extent of. **3.** In the scope or sphere of. ►*n.* An inner position, place, or area: *treachery from within.*

with-it (wĭth′ĭt′, wĭth-) ►*adj. Slang* **1.** Up-to-date. **2.** Mentally competent.

with·out (wĭth-out′, wĭth-) ►*adv.* **1.** On the outside. **2.** With something absent or lacking: *had to do without.* ►*prep.* **1a.** Not having; lacking. **b.** Not accompanied by. **2.** At, on, to, or toward the outside or exterior of. [< OE *withūtan.*]

with·stand (wĭth-stănd′, wĭth-) ►*v.* **-stood** (-stōōd′), **-stand·ing 1.** To oppose with force or resolution. **2.** To resist successfully. [< OE *withstandan.*]

wit·less (wĭt′lĭs) ►*adj.* Lacking intelligence or wit; foolish. —**wit′less·ly** *adv.*

wit·ness (wĭt′nĭs) ►*n.* **1.** One who can give a firsthand account of something seen, heard, or experienced. **2.** *Law* **a.** One called on to testify in court. **b.** One called on to be present at a transaction to attest to what takes place. **c.** One who signs one's name to a document in attestation of its authenticity. **3a.** An attestation; testimony. **b.** Something serving as evidence; sign. **4.** One who publicly affirms religious faith. ►*v.* **1.** To be present at or have personal knowledge of. **2.** To provide or serve as evidence of. **3.** To testify to; bear witness. **4.** To be the setting or site of. **5.** To attest to the legality or authenticity of by signing one's name. **6.** To testify to one's religious beliefs. [< OE *witness < wit*, WIT.]

Witt·gen·stein (vĭt′gən-shtīn′, -stīn′), **Ludwig**

1889–1951. Austrian philosopher.

wit·ti·cism (wĭt′ĭ-sĭz′əm) ►*n.* A witty remark. [WITT(Y) + (CRIT)ICISM.]

wit·ty (wĭt′ē) ►*adj.* **-ti·er, -ti·est** Having or showing wit; cleverly humorous. —**wit′ti·ly** *adv.* —**wit′ti·ness** *n.*

wives (wīvz) ►*n.* Pl. of **wife.**

wiz·ard (wĭz′ərd) ►*n.* **1.** A sorcerer or magician. **2.** A skilled or clever person: *a wizard at math.* [ME *wisard* < *wise,* WISE¹.] —**wiz′ard·ry** *n.*

wiz·ened (wĭz′ənd) ►*adj.* Withered; shriveled. [< OE *wisnian,* wither.]

wk. ►*abbr.* week

WL ►*abbr.* wavelength

WNW ►*abbr.* west-northwest

WO ►*abbr.* warrant officer

w/o ►*abbr.* without

woad (wōd) ►*n.* **1.** An annual Eurasian plant with leaves that yield a blue dye. **2.** The dye from this plant. [< OE *wād.*]

wob·ble (wŏb′əl) ►*v.* **-bled, -bling 1.** To move or rotate with an uneven or rocking motion from side to side. **2.** To tremble or quaver. **3.** To waver or vacillate in one's opinions. [Prob. < LGer. *wabbeln.*] —**wob′ble** *n.* —**wob′bli·ness** *n.* —**wob′bly** *adj.*

Wode·house (wŏŏd′hous′), **P(elham) G(renville)** 1881–1975. British writer.

woe (wō) ►*n.* **1.** Sorrow or grief; misery. **2.** A cause of sorrow or misery: *economic and political woes.* ►*interj.* Used to express sorrow or dismay. [< OE *wā,* woe!]

woe·be·gone (wō′bĭ-gôn′, -gŏn′) ►*adj.* **1.** Feeling or expressing deep sorrow, grief, or wretchedness. **2.** Of an inferior or deplorable condition.

woe·ful (wō′fəl) ►*adj.* **1.** Affected by woe; mournful. **2.** Causing woe. **3.** Deplorably bad or wretched: *woeful housing conditions.* —**woe′ful·ly** *adv.* —**woe′ful·ness** *n.*

wok (wŏk) ►*n.* A metal pan having a convex bottom, used esp. for frying and steaming in Asian cooking. [Cantonese *wok*⁶.]

wok

woke (wōk) ►*v.* P.t. of **wake**¹.

wok·en (wō′kən) ►*v.* P.part. of **wake**¹.

wolf (wŏŏlf) ►*n., pl.* **wolves** (wŏŏlvz) **1.** A carnivorous mammal, chiefly of northern regions, related to and resembling the dog. **2.** One regarded as predatory, rapacious, and fierce. **3.** *Slang* A man who habitually makes aggressive sexual advances to women. ►*v.* To eat greedily or voraciously. [< OE *wulf.*] —**wolf′ish** *adj.*

Wolfe (wŏŏlf), **James** 1727–59. British general in Canada.

Wolfe, Thomas (Clayton) 1900–38. Amer. writer.

wolf·hound (wŏŏlf′hound′) ►*n.* Any of various large dogs orig. trained to hunt wolves.

wolf·ram (wŏŏl′frəm) ►*n.* See **tungsten.** [Ger.]

Woll·stone·craft (wŏŏl′stən-krăft′, -kräft′), **Mary** 1759–97. British writer.

Wol·sey (wŏŏl′zē), **Cardinal. Thomas** 1475?–1530. English prelate and politician.

wol·ver·ine (wŏŏl′və-rēn′) ►*n.* A carnivorous mammal of northern regions, related to the weasel. [Prob. < WOLF.]

wom·an (wŏŏm′ən) ►*n., pl.* **wom·en** (wĭm′ĭn) **1.** An adult female human. **2.** Womankind. **3.** *Informal* A wife, lover, or sweetheart. [< OE *wīfman.*]

wom·an·hood (wŏŏm′ən-hŏŏd′) ►*n.* **1.** The state of being a woman. **2.** The qualities thought to be appropriate to or representative of women. **3.** Women collectively.

wom·an·ish (wŏŏm′ə-nĭsh) ►*adj.* **1.** Characteristic of or suitable to a woman, esp. when considered inferior to a man. **2.** Suggestive of a woman rather than a man.

wom·an·iz·er (wŏŏm′ə-nī′zər) ►*n.* A man who seduces or attempts to seduce women as a matter of habit. —**wom′an·ize′** *v.*

wom·an·kind (wŏŏm′ən-kīnd′) ►*n.* Women collectively.

wom·an·ly (wŏŏm′ən-lē) ►*adj.* **-li·er, -li·est** Relating to or characteristic of women. —**wom′an·li·ness** *n.*

womb (wŏŏm) ►*n.* **1.** See **uterus.** **2.** A place where something is generated. [< OE *wamb.*]

wom·bat (wŏm′băt′) ►*n.* An Australian marsupial somewhat resembling a small bear. [Indigenous word in Australia.]

wom·en (wĭm′ĭn) ►*n.* Pl. of **woman.**

wom·en·folk (wĭm′ĭn-fōk′) ►*pl.n.* **1.** Women collectively. **2.** The women of a community or family.

won¹ (wŏn) ►*n., pl.* **won** See table at **currency.** [Korean.]

won² (wŭn) ►*v.* P.t. and p.part. of **win.**

won·der (wŭn′dər) ►*n.* **1a.** An emotion of awe, surprise, or admiration. **b.** One that arouses such emotion. **2a.** An extraordinary or remarkable act or achievement. **b.** An event inexplicable by the laws of nature; a miracle. ►*v.* **1.** To have a feeling of awe or admiration; marvel. **2.** To be filled with curiosity or doubt. **3.** To be inquisitive or in doubt about. [< OE *wundor.*] **Syns:** *marvel, miracle, phenomenon n.*

won·der·ful (wŭn′dər-fəl) ►*adj.* **1.** Admirable; excellent. **2.** Capable of eliciting wonder; astonishing. —**won′der·ful·ly** *adv.*

won·der·land (wŭn′dər-lănd′) ►*n.* **1.** A marvelous imaginary realm. **2.** A marvelous real place or scene.

won·der·ment (wŭn′dər-mənt) ►*n.* **1.** Astonishment, awe, or surprise. **2.** A marvel.

won·drous (wŭn′drəs) ►*adj.* Wonderful. —**won′drous·ly** *adv.*

wonk (wŏngk) ►*n. Slang* **1.** A student who studies excessively. **2.** One who studies an issue or topic thoroughly or excessively. [?]

wont (wônt, wōnt, wŭnt) ►*adj.* **1.** Accustomed or used: *was wont to give generously.* **2.** Likely. ►*n.* Customary practice; habit: *left early, as was her wont.* [ME < *wonen,* to be used to.]

won't (wōnt) Will not.

wont·ed (wôn′tĭd, wŏn′-, wŭn′-) ►*adj.* Accustomed; usual: *ate with his wonted appetite.*

won ton or **won·ton** (wŏn′tŏn′) ►*n.* A noodle-dough dumpling filled usu. with spiced pork or other ground meat. [Cantonese *wan⁴ tan¹*.]

woo (wōō) ►*v.* **1.** To seek the affection of, as with the intent to marry. **2.** To seek to influence by means of entreaties or inducements. [< OE *wōgian.*] —**woo′er** *n.*

wood (wŏŏd) ►*n.* **1a.** The tough fibrous supporting and water-conducting tissue beneath the bark of trees and shrubs, consisting largely of cellulose and lignin. **b.** This tissue, often cut and dried esp. for building material and fuel. **2.** often **woods** A forest. [< OE *wudu.*]

Wood, Grant 1892–1942. Amer. artist.

wood alcohol ►*n.* See **methanol.**

wood·bine (wŏŏd′bīn′) ►*n.* **1.** Any of various climbing vines, esp. a European honeysuckle having yellowish flowers. **2.** See **Virginia creeper.** [< OE *wudubinde.*]

wood·block (wŏŏd′blŏk′) ►*n.* See **woodcut.**

wood·chuck (wŏŏd′chŭk′) ►*n.* A large burrowing North American rodent having a short-legged, heavy-set body and brownish fur. [Prob. of New England Algonquian orig.]

wood·cock (wŏŏd′kŏk′) ►*n., pl.* -**cock** or -**cocks** A game bird having brownish plumage, short legs, and a long bill.

wood·craft (wŏŏd′krăft′) ►*n.* **1.** Skill in matters relating to the woods, as hunting or camping. **2.** Skill in working with wood.

wood·cut (wŏŏd′kŭt′) ►*n.* **1.** A block of wood with an engraved design for printing. **2.** A print made from a woodcut.

wood·cut·ter (wŏŏd′kŭt′ər) ►*n.* One who fells trees and chops wood, as for fuel.

wood duck ►*n.* A brightly colored American duck, the male of which has a large crest.

wood·ed (wŏŏd′ĭd) ►*adj.* Covered with trees or woods.

wood·en (wŏŏd′n) ►*adj.* **1.** Made of wood. **2.** Stiff and unnatural; without spirit. **3.** Clumsy and awkward; ungainly. —**wood′en·ly** *adv.*

wood·land (wŏŏd′lənd, -lănd′) ►*n.* Land covered with trees.

wood·peck·er (wŏŏd′pĕk′ər) ►*n.* Any of various birds that cling to and climb trees and have a chisellike bill for drilling through bark and wood.

wood·pile (wŏŏd′pīl′) ►*n.* A pile of wood, esp. for fuel.

wood·ruff (wŏŏd′rəf, -rŭf′) ►*n.* Any of various plants having whorled leaves and small funnel-shaped flowers. [< OE *wudurofe.*]

wood·shed (wŏŏd′shĕd′) ►*n.* A shed in which firewood is stored.

woods·man (wŏŏdz′mən) ►*n.* A man who works or lives in the woods or is versed in woodcraft; forester.

woods·y (wŏŏd′zē) ►*adj.* -**i·er**, -**i·est** Of or suggestive of the woods.

wood·wind (wŏŏd′wĭnd′) ►*n. Mus.* A wind instrument, such as a flute or oboe, in which sound is produced by the vibration of reeds or by air passing across the mouthpiece.

wood·work (wŏŏd′wûrk′) ►*n.* Something made of wood, esp. wooden interior fittings in a house, as moldings or doors.

wood·y (wŏŏd′ē) ►*adj.* -**i·er**, -**i·est** **1.** Forming or consisting of wood: *woody tissue.* **2.** Suggestive of wood. **3.** Wooded.

woof (wŏŏf, wōōf) ►*n.* **1.** The crosswise threads in a woven fabric at right angles to the warp threads. **2.** The texture of a fabric. [< OE *ōwef.*]

woof·er (wŏŏf′ər) ►*n.* A loudspeaker that reproduces bass frequencies. [< *woof*, dog's bark.]

wool (wŏŏl) ►*n.* **1a.** The dense, soft, often curly hair of sheep and certain other mammals, used as a textile fiber. **b.** A yarn or garment made of this hair. **2.** A covering or substance suggestive of the texture of true wool. [< OE *wull.*]

wool·en also **wool·len** (wŏŏl′ən) ►*adj.* Made or consisting of wool. ►*n.* often **woolens** Fabric or clothing made from wool.

Woolf (wŏŏlf), **(Adeline) Virginia (Stephen)** 1882–1941. British writer.

Virginia Woolf

wool·gath·er·ing (wŏŏl′găth′ər-ĭng) ►*n.* Indulgence in fanciful daydreams.

wool·ly also **wool·y** (wŏŏl′ē) ►*adj.* -**li·er**, -**li·est** also -**i·er**, -**i·est 1a.** Made of or covered with wool. **b.** Resembling wool. **2.** Not sharp or clear: *woolly thinking.* ►*n., pl.* -**lies** also -**ies** A garment made of wool. —**wool′li·ness** *n.*

woolly mammoth ►*n.* A Pleistocene mammoth of cold northern regions.

woom·er·a (wŏŏm′ər-ə) ►*n.* A hooked wooden stick used for hurling a spear or dart. [Dharuk (Australian) *wamara.*]

wooz·y (wŏŏ′zē, wŏŏz′ē) ►*adj.* -**i·er**, -**i·est 1.** Dazed or confused. **2.** Dizzy or queasy. [?] —**wooz′i·ness** *n.*

Worces·ter·shire (wŏŏs′tər-shîr, -shər) ►*n.* A piquant sauce of soy, vinegar, and spices.

word (wûrd) ►*n.* **1.** A meaningful sound or combination of sounds, or its representation in writing. **2a.** Something said; a remark or comment. **b.** A command or direction. **c.** An assurance; promise. **d.** A verbal signal; password. **3. words a.** Discourse or talk; speech. **b.** *Mus.* Lyrics; text. **c.** An angry argument. **4a.** News: *Any word on your job?* **b.** Rumor: *Word has it that they're in love.* **5. Word** The Bible. ►*v.* To express in words: *worded the memo carefully.* [< OE.] —**word′less** *adj.* —**word′less·ly** *adv.*

word·age (wûr′dĭj) ►*n.* **1.** Words collectively. **2.** The number of words used. **3.** Wording.

word·book (wûrd′bŏŏk′) ►*n.* A lexicon, vocabulary, or dictionary.

word·ing (wûr′dĭng) ►*n.* The way in which something is expressed in words.

word·play (wûrd′plā′) ►*n.* A witty or clever use of words.

word processing ►*n.* The creation, editing, and

production of documents and texts by means of computer systems. —**word processor** *n.*

Words·worth (wûrdz'wûrth'), **William** 1770–1850. British poet.

word·y (wûr'dē) ►*adj.* **-i·er, -i·est** Using more words than are necessary to convey meaning. —**word'i·ness** *n.*
*Syns: diffuse, long-winded, prolix, verbose **adj.***

wore (wôr) ►*v.* P.t. of **wear.**

work (wûrk) ►*n.* **1.** Physical or mental effort or activity. **2a.** Activity by which one makes a living; employment: *looking for work.* **b.** A trade, profession, or other means of livelihood. **3a.** The part of a day devoted to an occupation: *met her after work.* **b.** One's place of employment: *I'll call you at work.* **4a.** Something produced as the result of effort. **b.** An act; deed: *charitable works.* **c.** An artistic creation, such as a painting. **d. works** Engineering structures. **5.** A duty or task. **6. works** *(takes sing. or pl. v.)* A factory or industrial plant: *a steel works.* **7. works** Internal mechanism: *the works of a watch.* **8.** Workmanship: *sloppy work.* **9.** *Phys.* The transfer of energy from one physical system to another. **10. works** *Informal* Everything: *a pizza with the works.* ►*v.* **1.** To exert oneself physically or mentally. **2.** To be employed. **3.** To operate or cause to operate. **4.** To have an effect or influence. **5.** To reach a specified condition through gradual or repeated movement: *The stitches worked loose.* **6.** To proceed laboriously: *worked through the pile of unpaid bills.* **7.** To move in an agitated manner, as with emotion. **8.** To behave in a specified way when processed: *Gold works easily.* **9.** To bring about: *work miracles.* **10.** To shape or forge. **11.** To solve (a problem) by calculation. **12.** To bring to a specified condition by gradual or repeated effort: *worked the nail out of the board.* **13.** *Informal* To arrange or contrive. **14.** To excite or provoke: *worked the mob into a frenzy.* —*phrasal verb:* **work out 1.** To solve: *worked out their differences.* **2.** To develop: *work out a plan.* **3.** To prove successful or effective. **4.** To engage in strenuous exercise. —*idiom:* **in the works** In preparation; under development. [< OE *weorc.*]

work·a·ble (wûr'kə-bəl) ►*adj.* **1.** Capable of being put into effect; practicable. **2.** Capable of being worked. —**work'a·bil'i·ty** *n.*

work·a·day (wûr'kə-dā') ►*adj.* **1.** Of or suited for working days. **2.** Mundane; commonplace. [< ME *werkeday,* workday.]

work·a·hol·ic (wûr'kə-hô'lĭk, -hŏl'ĭk) ►*n.* One who has a compulsive and unrelenting need to work. [WORK + (ALCO)HOLIC.]

work·bench (wûrk'běnch') ►*n.* A sturdy table or bench at which manual work is done, as by a machinist.

work·book (wûrk'bŏŏk') ►*n.* **1.** A booklet containing problems and exercises with space included for written answers. **2.** An operating manual, as for an appliance. **3.** A book in which a record of work is kept.

work·day (wûrk'dā') ►*n.* **1.** A day on which work is usu. done. **2.** The part of the day during which one works.

work·er (wûr'kər) ►*n.* **1.** One who works. **2.** One who does manual or industrial labor. **3.** A member of a colony of social insects such as ants or bees, usu. a sterile female, that performs specialized work.

work·fare (wûrk'fâr') ►*n.* A form of welfare in which aid recipients are required to perform work, esp. public-service work.

work force ►*n.* **1.** The workers employed in a specific project or activity. **2.** All people working or available to work, as in a nation.

work·horse (wûrk'hôrs') ►*n.* **1.** A horse used for labor rather than for racing or riding. **2.** *Informal* A person who works tirelessly. **3.** Something, such as a machine, that is durable and performs dependably.

work·house (wûrk'hous') ►*n.* **1.** A prison in which limited sentences are served at manual labor. **2.** *Chiefly Brit.* A poorhouse.

work·ing (wûr'kĭng) ►*adj.* **1a.** Of, used for, or spent in work. **b.** Functioning. **2.** Sufficient or adequate for using: *a working knowledge of Spanish.* **3.** Serving as a basis for further work: *a working hypothesis.*

work·load (wûrk'lōd') ►*n.* The amount of work assigned or done in a given time period.

work·man (wûrk'mən) ►*n.* **1.** A man who performs labor for wages. **2.** A craftsman.

work·man·like (wûrk'mən-līk') ►*adj.* Befitting a skilled worker; skillfully done.

work·man·ship (wûrk'mən-shĭp') ►*n.* **1.** The art of a skilled worker or craftsperson. **2.** The quality of something made.

work·out (wûrk'out') ►*n.* **1.** A session of exercise to improve fitness or athletic skill. **2.** A strenuous test of ability and endurance.

work·place (wûrk'plās') ►*n.* **1.** A place where people are employed. **2.** The work setting in general.

work·shop (wûrk'shŏp') ►*n.* **1.** A room, area, or establishment where manual work is done. **2.** An educational seminar in a specified field. ►*v.* **-shopped, -shop·ping** To create or revise (a drama or literary work) based on suggestions or criticism from a group of collaborators.

work·space (wûrk'spās') ►*n.* An area used or allocated for one's work, as in an office.

work·sta·tion (wûrk'stā'shən) ►*n.* **1.** An area, as in an office, equipped for one worker, usu. including a computer. **2.** A powerful computer used for a specific purpose, such as software development or imaging.

work·ta·ble (wûrk'tā'bəl) ►*n.* A table designed for a specific activity, as sewing.

work·week (wûrk'wēk') ►*n.* The hours or days worked in a week.

world (wûrld) ►*n.* **1.** The earth, esp. together with the life it supports. **2.** The universe. **3.** Human society. **4.** A specified part of the earth: *the Western World.* **5.** A realm or domain. **6.** A sphere of human activity or interest: *the world of sports.* **7.** A particular way of life. **8.** Secular life and its concerns: *a woman of the world.* **9.** A large amount: *did him a world of good.* **10.** A celestial body such as a planet. [< OE *weorold.*]

world·ly (wûrld'lē) ►*adj.* **-li·er, -li·est 1.** Relating to the material world, esp. in contrast to spiritual concerns. **2.** Sophisticated; cosmopolitan. —**world'li·ness** *n.*

world·ly-wise (wûrld'lē-wīz') ►*adj.* Experienced in the ways of the world.

world·view (wûrld'vyoo') ►*n.* A set of beliefs about life and the universe held by an individual or a group. [Translation of German *Weltanschauung* : *Welt,* world + *Anschauung,* view.]

world·wide (wûrld'wīd') ►*adj.* Involving or

extending throughout the world; universal.
—**world′wide′** *adv.*

World Wide Web ►*n.* The complete system of interlinked documents that use the HTTP protocol, residing on the Internet and accessible to users via a web browser.

worm (wûrm) ►*n.* **1.** Any of various invertebrates, as an earthworm or tapeworm, having a long, flexible, rounded or flattened body. **2.** Any of various insect larvae having a soft elongated body. **3.** Something, such as the spirally threaded shaft of a worm gear, that resembles a worm. **4.** An insidiously tormenting or devouring force. **5.** A pitiable or contemptible person. **6.** A malicious program that replicates itself until it fills all of the storage space on a drive or network. **7. worms** Infestation, esp. of the intestines, with parasitic worms. ►*v.* **1.** To move with or as if with the sinuous crawling motion of a worm. **2.** To elicit by artful or devious means: *wormed a confession out of the suspect.* **3.** To cure of intestinal worms. [< OE *wyrm.*] —**worm′y** *adj.*

worm-eat•en (wûrm′ēt′n) ►*adj.* Eaten or burrowed into by worms.

worm gear ►*n.* **1.** A gear consisting of a spirally threaded shaft and a wheel with teeth that mesh into it. **2.** A worm wheel.

worm•hole (wûrm′hōl′) ►*n.* **1.** A hole made by a burrowing worm. **2.** *Phys.* A theoretical distortion of space-time in which one location or time is linked with another through a path that is shorter than expected.

worm wheel ►*n.* The toothed wheel of a worm gear.

worm•wood (wûrm′wŏŏd′) ►*n.* Any of several aromatic plants including the species whose bitter extract is used in making absinthe. [< OE *wermōd.*]

worn (wôrn) ►*v.* P.part. of **wear.** ►*adj.* **1.** Affected or impaired by wear or use. **2.** Showing the wearing effects of overwork, worry, or suffering.

worn-out (wôrn′out′) ►*adj.* **1.** Worn or used until no longer usable. **2.** Thoroughly exhausted; spent.

wor•ri•some (wûr′ē-səm, wûr′-) ►*adj.* **1.** Causing worry or anxiety. **2.** Tending to worry.

wor•ry (wûr′ē, wŭr′ē) ►*v.* **-ried, -ry•ing 1.** To feel uneasy or troubled. See Synonyms at **brood. 2.** To cause to feel anxious, distressed, or troubled. See Synonyms at **trouble. 3.** To bother or annoy. **4a.** To pull, bite, or tear at repeatedly. **b.** To touch, move, or handle idly. ►*n., pl.* **-ries 1.** Mental uneasiness or anxiety. **2.** A source of worry. [< OE *wyrgan,* strangle.] —**wor′ri•er** *n.*

wor•ry•wart (wûr′ē-wôrt′, wŭr′-) ►*n.* One who worries excessively and needlessly.

worse (wûrs) ►*adj.* Comp. of **bad, ill. 1.** More inferior, as in quality, condition, or effect. **2.** More severe or unfavorable. ►*adv.* Comp. of **badly, ill.** In a worse manner. [< OE *wyrsa.*]

wors•en (wûr′sən) ►*v.* To make or become worse.

wor•ship (wûr′shĭp) ►*n.* **1a.** Reverent love and devotion for a deity or sacred object. **b.** The ceremonies or prayers by which this love is expressed. **2.** Ardent admiration or love; adoration: *his worship of fame.* **3.** often **Worship** *Chiefly Brit.* Used as a form of address for

magistrates and certain other dignitaries: *Your Worship.* ►*v.* **-shiped, -ship•ing** or **-shipped, -ship•ping 1.** To honor and love as a deity. **2.** To love devotedly. **3.** To participate in religious worship. [< OE *weorthscipe,* worthiness.] —**wor′ship•er** *n.*

wor•ship•ful (wûr′shĭp-fəl) ►*adj.* **1.** Given to or showing worship. **2.** *Chiefly Brit.* Used as a respectful form of address. —**wor′ship•ful•ly** *adv.*

worst (wûrst) ►*adj.* Superl. of **bad, ill. 1.** Most inferior, as in quality, condition, health, or effect. **2.** Most severe or unfavorable. ►*adv.* Superl. of **badly, ill.** In the worst manner or degree. ►*v.* To gain the advantage over; defeat. ►*n.* Something that is worst. [< OE *wyrsta.*]

wor•sted (wŏŏs′tĭd, wûr′stĭd) ►*n.* **1.** Firm-textured, compactly twisted woolen yarn made from long-staple fibers. **2.** Fabric made from such yarn. [< ME *worthstede.*]

wort (wûrt, wôrt) ►*n.* A plant: *liverwort.* [< OE *wyrt.*]

worth (wûrth) ►*n.* **1.** The quality that renders something desirable, useful, or valuable. **2.** A quantity of something that may be purchased for a specified sum: *ten dollars′ worth of gas.* **3.** Wealth; riches: *net worth.* ►*adj.* **1.** Equal in value to something specified. **2.** Deserving of; meriting: *a proposal worth considering.* **3.** Having wealth or riches amounting to. [< OE *weorth.*]

worth•less (wûrth′lĭs) ►*adj.* **1.** Lacking worth; of no use or value. **2.** Low; despicable. —**worth′less•ness** *n.*

worth•while (wûrth′hwīl′, -wīl′) ►*adj.* Sufficiently valuable or important to be worth one's time or effort.

wor•thy (wûr′thē) ►*adj.* **-thi•er, -thi•est 1.** Having worth, merit, or value. **2.** Honorable; admirable. **3.** Deserving: *worthy of acclaim.* ►*n., pl.* **-thies** An eminent or distinguished person. —**wor′thi•ness** *n.*

would (wŏŏd) ►*aux.v.* P.t. of **will[2]. 1.** Used to express repeated or habitual action in the past: *We would get up early and go fishing.* **2.** Used after a statement of desire or request: *I wish you would stay.* **3.** Used for politeness: *Would you go with me?* **4.** Used to indicate uncertainty: *It would seem so.* See Usage Note at **if.**

would-be (wŏŏd′bē′) ►*adj.* Desiring or attempting to be: *a would-be actor.*

would•n't (wŏŏd′nt) Would not.

wouldst (wŏŏdst) or **would•est** (wŏŏd′ĭst) ►*v.* Archaic 2nd pers. sing. p.t. of **will[2].**

wound[1] (wŏŏnd) ►*n.* **1.** An injury, esp. one in which the skin is torn, pierced, cut, or broken. **2.** An injury to the feelings. ►*v.* To inflict a wound on. [< OE *wund.*]

wound[2] (wound) ►*v.* P.t. and p.part. of **wind[2].**

Wound•ed Knee (wŏŏn′dĭd) A creek of SW SD, site of a massacre of Native Americans by US troops (1890).

wove (wōv) ►*v.* P.t. of **weave.**

wo•ven (wō′vən) ►*v.* P.part. of **weave.**

wow (wou) *Informal* ►*interj.* Used to express wonder, amazement, or great pleasure. ►*n.* An outstanding success. ►*v.* To have a strong and usu. pleasurable effect on.

WPA ►*abbr.* Work Projects Administration

wrack[1] (răk) ►*n.* Destruction or ruin. [< OE *wræc,* punishment.]

wrack² (răk) ►*n.* **1.** Wreckage, esp. of a ship cast ashore. **2.** Seaweed that has been cast ashore or dried. [MDu. *wrak.*]

wraith (rāth) ►*n.* **1.** An apparition of a living person. **2.** The ghost of a dead person. **3.** Something faint or insubstantial: *a wraith of smoke.* [?]

wran·gle (răng′gəl) ►*v.* **-gled, -gling 1.** To quarrel noisily or angrily; bicker. **2.** To win or obtain by argument. **3.** To attempt to deal with or understand something. **4.** To herd (horses or other livestock). ►*n.* An angry or noisy dispute. [ME *wranglen.*] —**wran′gler** *n.*

wrap (răp) ►*v.* **wrapped** or **wrapt** (răpt), **wrap·ping 1.** To draw, fold, or wind about in order to cover. **2.** To enclose within a covering; enfold. **3.** To encase and secure (an object), esp. with paper; package. **4.** To envelop or surround, esp. so as to obscure: *The castle was wrapped in fog.* **5.** To absorb; engross: *wrapped in thought.* ►*n.* **1.** An outer garment worn for warmth. **2.** A wrapping or wrapper. **3.** The completion of filming on a movie. **4.** A tortilla or other flatbread rolled around a filling. —*phrasal verb:* **wrap up 1.** To finish; conclude. **2.** To summarize; recapitulate. —*idiom:* **under wraps** Secret or concealed. [ME *wrappen.*]

wrap·a·round (răp′ə-round′) ►*adj.* Shaped to curve around the sides: *a wraparound porch.* ►*n.* **1.** A garment, such as a skirt, that is open to the side and is wrapped around the body. **2.** A feature, as of a word processing program, that moves text that will not fit on one line to the following line.

wrap·per (răp′ər) ►*n.* **1.** A material, such as paper, in which something is wrapped. **2.** The tobacco leaf covering a cigar. **3.** A loose robe or negligee. **4.** One that wraps.

wrap·ping (răp′ĭng) ►*n.* The material in which something is wrapped.

wrap-up (răp′ŭp′) ►*n.* **1.** A brief final summary, as of the news. **2.** A concluding or final action.

wrasse (răs) ►*n.* Any of numerous often brightly colored marine fishes. [Cornish *gwragh.*]

wrath (răth) ►*n.* **1.** Furious, often vindictive anger; rage. **2.** Punishment or vengeance as a manifestation of anger. [< OE *wrǣththu.*] —**wrath′ful** *adj.* —**wrath′ful·ly** *adv.*

wreak (rēk) ►*v.* **1.** To inflict (e.g., vengeance). **2.** To vent (e.g., anger). [< OE *wrecan.*]

wreath (rēth) ►*n., pl.* **wreaths** (rēthz, rēths) **1.** A ring or circular band, as of flowers or leaves. **2.** A curling or circular form: *a wreath of smoke.* [< OE *writha,* band.]

wreathe (rēth) ►*v.* **wreathed, wreath·ing 1.** To twist or entwine into a wreath. **2.** To encircle with or as if with a wreath. **3.** To coil or spiral. [< WREATH.]

wreck (rĕk) ►*n.* **1.** The act of wrecking or the state of being wrecked. **2a.** A shipwreck. **b.** Debris or cargo cast ashore after a shipwreck. **3a.** An automobile or railroad collision or accident. **b.** The damaged remains, esp. a vehicle that has crashed: *walked away unharmed from the wreck.* **4.** One in a shattered, broken-down, or worn-out state. ►*v.* **1.** To destroy in or as if in a collision. **2.** To dismantle or tear down. **3.** To cause to undergo ruin or disaster. See Synonyms at **blast.** [< AN *wrec,* wrecking.]

wreck·age (rĕk′ĭj) ►*n.* The debris or remains of something wrecked.

wreck·er (rĕk′ər) ►*n.* **1.** One that wrecks. **2.** A member of a demolition crew. **3.** A vehicle or piece of equipment employed in recovering or removing wrecks. **4.** One who lures a vessel to destruction in order to plunder it.

wren (rĕn) ►*n.* Any of various small brownish songbirds having a short, often erect tail. [< OE *wrenna.*]

wren

Wren, Sir **Christopher.** 1632–1723. English architect.

wrench (rĕnch) ►*n.* **1.** A tool with fixed or adjustable jaws for gripping, turning, or twisting an object such as a nut or a bolt. **2.** A sudden forcible twist or turn. **3.** An injury produced by twisting or straining. **4.** A sudden surge of emotion. ►*v.* **1a.** To twist or turn suddenly and forcibly. **b.** To twist and sprain: *wrenched my knee.* **2.** To free by pulling at; yank. **3.** To pull at the feelings or emotions of; distress. [< OE *wrencan,* twist.]

wrest (rĕst) ►*v.* **1.** To obtain or remove by pulling with twisting movements. **2.** To gain or take by force. **3.** To obtain with persistent effort. [< OE *wrǣstan.*] —**wrest′er** *n.*

wres·tle (rĕs′əl) ►*v.* **-tled, -tling 1.** To try to throw or immobilize another person, esp. by gripping with the hands. **2.** To engage in the sport of wrestling. **3.** To struggle to deal with something: *wrestle with a problem.* [< OE **wrǣstlian.*] —**wres′tle** *n.* —**wres′tler** *n.*

wres·tling (rĕs′lĭng) ►*n.* A sport in which two competitors attempt to throw or immobilize each other by various holds or maneuvers.

wretch (rĕch) ►*n.* **1.** A miserable, unfortunate, or unhappy person. **2.** A base or despicable person. [< OE *wrecca.*]

wretch·ed (rĕch′ĭd) ►*adj.* **-er, -est 1.** Woeful; miserable. **2.** Contemptible; vile. **3.** Of inferior quality. [< ME *wrecche,* WRETCH.] —**wretch′ed·ly** *adv.* —**wretch′ed·ness** *n.*

wri·er (rī′ər) ►*adj.* Comp. of **wry.**

wri·est (rī′ĭst) ►*adj.* Superl. of **wry.**

wrig·gle (rĭg′əl) ►*v.* **-gled, -gling 1.** To turn or twist with writhing motions; squirm. **2.** To proceed with writhing motions. **3.** To make (e.g., one's way) by or as if by wriggling. [ME *wrigglen.*] —**wrig′gle** *n.* —**wrig′gler** *n.*

Wright (rīt), **Frank Lloyd** 1867–1959. Amer. architect.

Wright, Orville 1871–1948. Amer. aviation pioneer; with his brother **Wilbur** (1867–1912) invented the airplane.

Wright, Richard Nathaniel 1908–60. Amer. writer.

wring (rĭng) ►*v.* **wrung** (rŭng), **wring·ing 1.** To twist and squeeze, esp. to extract liquid. **2.** To wrench or twist forcibly or painfully: *wring someone's neck.* **3.** To twist or squeeze (one's hands) in distress. **4.** To anguish or aggrieve. **5.** To extract by or as if by twisting or compressing; extort: *wring the truth out of a witness.* [< OE *wringan.*]

wring·er (rĭng′ər) ►*n.* One that wrings, esp. a device in which laundry is pressed between rollers to extract water.

wrin·kle (rĭng′kəl) ►*n.* **1.** A small furrow, ridge, or crease on a normally smooth surface, as cloth or the skin. **2.** An unexpected development, action, or idea. **3.** A problem or flaw. ►*v.* **-kled, -kling 1.** To make a wrinkle or wrinkles in. **2.** To form wrinkles. [Prob. < OE *gewrinclian*, crease.] —**wrin′kly** *adj.*

wrist (rĭst) ►*n.* **1.** The joint between the hand and forearm. **2.** The bones of this joint; carpus. [< OE.]

wrist·band (rĭst′bănd′) ►*n.* A band, as on a wristwatch, that encircles the wrist.

wrist·watch (rĭst′wŏch′) ►*n.* A watch worn on a band that fastens about the wrist.

writ (rĭt) ►*n.* **1.** A written order issued by a court, commanding the party to whom it is addressed to perform or cease performing a specified act. **2.** Writings: *holy writ.* [< OE.]

writ·a·ble also **write·a·ble** (rī′tə-bəl) ►*adj. Comp.* Capable of recording data: *writable compact discs.*

write (rīt) ►*v.* **wrote** (rōt), **writ·ten** (rĭt′n), **writ·ing 1a.** To form (letters, words, or symbols) on a surface with an instrument such as a pen. **b.** To spell. **2.** To compose and set down, esp. in literary or musical form. **3.** To relate or communicate in writing. **4.** To send a letter or note to. **5.** To communicate by letter; correspond. **6.** *Comp.* To copy (data) to a storage device. —*phrasal verbs:* **write in** To cast a vote by inserting (a name not listed on a ballot). **write off 1.** To reduce the book value of. **2.** To cancel from accounts as a loss. [< OE *wrītan.*]

write-in (rīt′ĭn′) ►*n.* A vote cast by writing in the name of a candidate not on the ballot.

write-off (rīt′ôf′, -ŏf′) ►*n.* A downward adjustment in earnings or in the value of an asset on account of a loss or expense.

write-pro·tect (rīt′prə-tĕkt′) ►*v. Comp.* To modify (a file or disk) so that its data cannot be edited or erased.

writ·er (rī′tər) ►*n.* One who writes, esp. as an occupation.

write-up (rīt′ŭp′) ►*n.* A published account, review, or notice.

writhe (rīth) ►*v.* **writhed, writh·ing** To twist or squirm, as in pain. [< OE *wrīthan.*]

writ·ing (rī′tĭng) ►*n.* **1.** The activity, occupation, or style of a writer. **2.** Written form: *Put it in writing.* **3.** Handwriting. **4.** Something written, esp. a literary composition. **5. Writings** *(takes sing. or pl. v.) Bible* The third of the

three divisions of the Hebrew Scriptures. See table at **Bible.**

Wro·cław (vrôt′släf′) A city of SW Poland on the Oder R.

wrong (rông, rŏng) ►*adj.* **1.** Not correct; erroneous: *a wrong answer.* **2a.** Contrary to conscience, morality, or law. **b.** Unfair; unjust. **3.** Not required, intended, or wanted: *a wrong turn.* **4.** Not fitting; inappropriate. **5.** Not in accord with established usage, method, or procedure. **6.** Not functioning properly; amiss: *What's wrong with the computer?* ►*adv.* **1.** In a wrong manner; erroneously. **2.** Immorally or unjustly. **3.** In an unfavorable way; amiss. ►*n.* **1.** Something that is wrong. **2.** The condition of being in error or at fault: *in the wrong.* ►*v.* **1.** To treat injuriously or dishonorably. **2.** To discredit unjustly; malign. [ME, of Scand. orig.] —**wrong′ly** *adv.*

wrong·do·er (rông′dōō′ər, rŏng′-) ►*n.* One who does wrong. —**wrong′do′ing** *n.*

wrong·ful (rông′fəl, rŏng′-) ►*adj.* **1.** Wrong; unjust. **2.** Unlawful: *wrongful death.* —**wrong′ful·ly** *adv.* —**wrong′ful·ness** *n.*

wrong-head·ed (rông′hĕd′ĭd, rŏng′-) ►*adj.* Mistaken or misguided, often stubbornly so.

wrote (rōt) ►*v.* P.t. of **write.**

wroth (rôth) ►*adj. Archaic* Angry. [< OE *wrāth.*]

wrought (rôt) ►*adj.* **1.** Fashioned; created. **2.** Shaped by hammering: *wrought silver.*

wrought iron ►*n.* An easily welded and forged form of iron containing 1 to 3% siliceous slag.

wrought-up (rôt′ŭp′) ►*adj.* Agitated; excited.

wrung (rŭng) ►*v.* P.t. and p.part. of **wring.**

wry (rī) ►*adj.* **wri·er** (rī′ər), **wri·est** (rī′ĭst) or **wry·er, wry·est 1.** Humorous in an understated or ironic way. **2.** Temporarily twisted in an expression of distaste or displeasure: *made a wry face.* **3.** Bent to one side; crooked. [< OE *wrīgian*, turn.] —**wry′ly** *adv.* —**wry′ness** *n.*

WSW ►*abbr.* west-southwest

wt. ►*abbr.* weight

WTO ►*abbr.* World Trade Organization

wurst (wûrst, wōōrst) ►*n.* Sausage. [Ger.]

WV ►*abbr.* West Virginia

WWI ►*abbr.* World War I

WWII ►*abbr.* World War II

WWW ►*abbr.* World Wide Web

WY ►*abbr.* Wyoming

Wy·an·dot also **Wy·an·dotte** (wī′ən-dŏt′) ►*n., pl.* **-dot** or **-dots** also **-dotte** or **-dottes 1.** A member of a Native American people of the former Huron confederacy, now in NE Oklahoma. **2.** The Iroquoian language of the Wyandot.

Wy·att or **Wy·at** (wī′ət), Sir **Thomas** 1503–42. English diplomat and poet.

Wyc·liffe (wĭ′klĭf), **John** 1328?–84. English theologian and religious reformer.

Wy·o·ming (wī-ō′mĭng) A state of the W US. Cap. Cheyenne.

WYSIWYG (wĭz′ē-wĭg′) ►*adj.* Relating to a computer system in which the screen displays text and graphics exactly as they will be printed. [*w(hat) y(ou) s(ee) i(s) w(hat) y(ou) g(et).*]

X

x¹ or **X** (ĕks) ►*n., pl.* **x's** or **X's** also **xs** or **Xs** **1.** The 24th letter of the English alphabet. **2.** A mark inscribed to represent the signature of one who cannot sign one's own name. **3.** An unknown or unnamed factor, thing, or person. ►*v.* **x'd, x'ing** or **X'd, X'ing** To delete or cancel with a series of X's: *x'd out the error.*

x² The symbol for **abscissa**.

X¹ (ĕks) ►*n.* A movie rating barring admission to anyone under the age of 17.

X² **1.** also **x** The symbol for the Roman numeral 10. **2.** A symbol for the word *cross*. Used in combination, as in *motoX* for *motocross*.

X³ ►*abbr.* **1.** Christ (Greek Χριστος, *Khristos*) **2.** Christian **3.** or **x** *Bus.* ex **4.** extra

Xan·thus (zăn′thəs) An ancient city of Asia Minor in present-day SW Turkey.

Xa·vi·er (zā′vē-ər, zăv′ē-), Saint **Francis** 1506–52. Spanish Jesuit missionary.

Saint Francis Xavier
18th-century painting

x-ax·is (ĕks′ăk′sĭs) ►*n., pl.* **x-ax·es** (-ăk′sēz) **1.** The horizontal axis of a two-dimensional Cartesian coordinate system. **2.** One of three axes in a three-dimensional Cartesian coordinate system.

X-chro·mo·some (ĕks′krō′mə-sōm′) ►*n.* The sex chromosome associated with female characteristics in most mammals, occurring paired in the female and single in the male sex-chromosome pair.

xe·bec (zē′bĕk′) ►*n.* A small three-masted Mediterranean vessel with both square and triangular sails. [< Ar. dial. *šabbāk*.]

xe·non (zē′nŏn′) ►*n.* *Symbol* **Xe** A colorless, odorless, noble gas element found in minute quantities in the atmosphere. At. no. 54. See table at **element**. [< Gk. *xenos*, strange.]

Xe·noph·a·nes (zə-nŏf′ə-nēz′) 560?–478? BC. Greek philosopher.

xen·o·phobe (zĕn′ə-fōb′, zē′nə-fōb′) ►*n.* A person who is fearful or contemptuous of strangers or foreigners. [Gk. *xenos*, foreign + –PHOBE.] —**xen′o·pho′bi·a** *n.* —**xen′o·pho′bic** *adj.*

Xen·o·phon (zĕn′ə-fən, -fŏn′) 430?–355? BC. Greek soldier and writer.

xer·ic (zĕr′ĭk, zîr′-) ►*adj.* Of or adapted to an extremely dry habitat. [< Gk. *xēros*, dry.]

xe·rog·ra·phy (zĭ-rŏg′rə-fē) ►*n.* A dry photographic or photocopying process in which a negative image formed by a resinous powder on an electrically charged plate is transferred to and thermally fixed on a paper or other surface. [Gk. *xēros*, dry + –GRAPHY.] —**xer′o·graph′ic** (zîr′ə-grăf′ĭk) *adj.*

xer·o·phyte (zîr′ə-fīt′) ►*n.* A plant adapted to surviving with little water. [< Gk. *xēros*, dry.] —**xer′o·phyt′ic** (-fĭt′ĭk) *adj.*

Xer·ox (zîr′ŏks) A trademark for a photocopying process or machine employing xerography.

Xer·xes I (zûrk′sēz) "the Great." 519?–465 BC. King of Persia (486–465).

Xho·sa also **Xo·sa** (kō′sä, -zə) ►*n., pl.* **-sa** or **-sas** **1.** A member of a Bantu people of the E part of Cape Province, South Africa. **2.** The language of this people.

xi (zī, sī, ksē) ►*n.* The 14th letter of the Greek alphabet. [Gk. *xei*.]

Xi'an (shē′än′, shyän) A city of N-central China SW of Beijing.

XL ►*abbr.* **1.** extra large **2.** extra long

X·mas (krĭs′məs, ĕks′məs) ►*n.* Christmas. [< X, the Greek letter chi, abbr. of *Khristos*, Christ.]

x-ray also **X-ray** (ĕks′rā′) ►*n.* **1a.** A relatively high-energy photon with a very short wavelength. **b.** A stream of such photons, used in radiography, radiology, radiotherapy, and scientific research. **2.** A photograph taken with x-rays. ►*v.* **1.** To irradiate with x-rays. **2.** To photograph with x-rays.

xy·lem (zī′ləm) ►*n.* The water-conducting and supporting tissue of vascular plants. Woody tissue is made of xylem. [< Gk. *xulon*, wood.]

xy·lo·phone (zī′lə-fōn′) ►*n.* A percussion instrument consisting of a mounted row of wooden bars graduated in length to sound a chromatic scale, played with two small mallets. —**xy′lo·phon′ist** *n.*

Y

y¹ or **Y** (wī) ►*n., pl.* **y's** or **Y's** also **ys** or **Ys** The 25th letter of the English alphabet.

y² The symbol for **ordinate**.

Y ►*abbr.* year

–y¹ or **–ey** ►*suff.* **1.** Characterized by: *rainy.* **2.** Like: *summery.* **3.** Inclined toward: *sleepy.* [< OE -*ig*.]

–y² ►*suff.* **1.** Condition; quality: *jealousy.* **2a.** Activity: *cookery.* **b.** Instance of a specified action: *entreaty.* **3a.** Place for an activity: *cannery.* **b.** Result or product of an activity: *laundry.* **4.** Group: *soldiery.* [< Lat. -*ia.* Sense 2b < Lat. -*ium*.]

–y³ or **–ie** ►*suff.* **1.** Small one: *doggy.* **2.** Dear one: *sweetie.* **3.** One having to do with or characterized by: *groupie.* [ME -*ie*.]

Y2K (wī′tōō-kā′) ►*adj.* **1.** Relating to the year 2000. **2.** Relating to a programming code defect in which a year represented by its last two digits is misinterpreted as being between 1900–99 instead of 2000–99. [Y(EAR) + *2K*, 2000.]

yacht (yät) ►*n.* Any of various relatively small, streamlined sailing or motor-driven vessels used for pleasure cruises or racing. [< MLGer. *jachtschip.*] —**yacht** *v.* —**yacht′ing** *n.* —**yachts′man** *n.* —**yachts′wom′an** *n.*

ya·hoo (yä′hōō, yä′-) ►*n., pl.* **-hoos** An unrefined, often disruptive person. [< the *Yahoos,* characters in *Gulliver's Travels* by Jonathan Swift.]

Yah·weh (yä′wä, -wě) also **Yah·veh** (-vä, -vě) ►*n.* Used as a proper name for God in the Hebrew Scriptures.

yak¹ (yăk) ►*n.* A shaggy-haired ox of the mountains of central Asia. [Tibetan *gyag.*]

yak² (yăk) ►*v.* **yakked, yak·king** *Slang* To talk or chatter persistently. [Imit.] —**yak** *n.*

y'all (yôl) ►*pron. Regional* Var. of **you-all.**

Yal·ta (yôl′tə) A city of SE Ukraine in the S Crimea on the Black Sea.

Ya·lu (yä′lōō′) A river, about 800 km (500 mi), forming part of the North Korea–China border.

yam (yăm) ►*n.* **1.** The starchy edible root of a tropical vine. **2.** See **sweet potato.** [Port. *inhame,* of West African orig.]

yam·mer (yăm′ər) ►*v. Informal* **1.** To talk volubly and often loudly. **2.** To complain peevishly; whine. [ME *yameren,* lament.]

Ya·mous·sou·kro (yä′mōō-sōō′krō) The official capital of Côte d'Ivoire, in the central part N of Abidjan.

yang (yăng) ►*n.* The active, male cosmic principle in Chinese dualistic philosophy. [Mandarin *yáng,* sun, light.]

Yan·gon (yän′gôn′) or **Ran·goon** (răn-gōōn′, răng-) The capital of Myanmar, in the S part.

Yang·tze (yăng′sě′, -tsě′) or **Chang·jiang** (chäng′jyäng′) The longest river of China and of Asia, flowing about 6,300 km (3,900 mi) from Tibet to the East China Sea.

yank (yăngk) ►*v.* To pull or extract with or as if with a sudden forceful movement. ►*n.* A sudden vigorous pull; jerk. [?]

Yank ►*n. Informal* A Yankee.

Yan·kee (yăng′kē) ►*n.* **1.** A native or inhabitant of New England, esp. one of English descent. **2.** A native of a northern US state. **3.** A US citizen; American. [?]

Ya·oun·dé (yä-ōōn-dā′) The capital of Cameroon, in the S-central part.

yap (yăp) ►*v.* **yapped, yap·ping 1.** To bark sharply or shrilly; yelp. **2.** *Slang* To talk noisily or stupidly; jabber. ►*n.* **1.** A bark; yelp. **2.** *Slang* Chatter; jabber. **3.** *Slang* The mouth. [Prob. imit.] —**yap′per** *n.*

Ya·qui (yä′kē) ►*n., pl.* **-qui** or **-quis 1.** A member of a Native American people of NW Mexico, now also in S Arizona. **2.** The Uto-Aztecan language of the Yaqui.

yard¹ (yärd) ►*n.* **1.** See table at **measurement. 2.** *Naut.* A long tapering spar slung to a mast to support and spread a sail. [< OE *gerd,* stick.]

yard² (yärd) ►*n.* **1.** A tract of ground next to a building. **2.** A tract of ground, often enclosed, used for a specific activity. **3.** An area where railroad trains are made up and cars are switched, stored, and serviced. **4.** An enclosed area for livestock. [< OE *geard.*]

yard·age (yär′dĭj) ►*n.* An amount or length of something measured in yards.

yard·arm (yärd′ärm′) ►*n. Naut.* Either end of a yard of a square sail.

yard·stick (yärd′stĭk′) ►*n.* **1.** A graduated measuring stick one yard in length. **2.** A test or standard used in making a comparison or judgment.

yar·mul·ke (yär′məl-kə, yä′məl-) ►*n.* A skullcap traditionally worn by Jewish men and boys. [Yiddish.]

yarmulke

yarn (yärn) ►*n.* **1.** A continuous strand of twisted threads, as of wool or nylon, used in weaving or knitting. **2.** *Informal* A long, often elaborate story. [< OE *gearn.*]

yar·row (yăr′ō) ►*n.* A plant having finely dissected foliage and flat, usu. white or yellow flower heads. [< OE *gearwe.*]

yaw (yô) ►*v.* **1.** To swerve off course momentarily or temporarily, as a ship. **2.** To turn about the vertical axis, as an aircraft. [Perhaps of Scandinavian origin.] —**yaw** *n.*

yawl (yôl) ►*n.* **1.** A two-masted fore-and-aft-rigged sailing vessel with the smaller mast abaft the rudder. **2.** A ship's small boat. [Du. *jol,* poss. < LGer. *jolle.*]

yawn (yôn) ►*v.* **1.** To open the mouth wide with a deep involuntary inhalation, as when sleepy or bored. **2.** To open wide; gape. ►*n.* The act of yawning. [< OE *geonian.*] —**yawn′er** *n.*

yaws (yôz) ►*pl.n. (takes sing. or pl. v.)* A highly contagious tropical disease caused by a spirochete and marked by raspberrylike sores, esp. on the hands, feet, and face. [< Carib *yaya,* disease.]

y-ax·is (wī′ăk′sĭs) ►*n., pl.* **y-ax·es** (-ăk′sēz) **1.** The vertical axis of a two-dimensional Cartesian coordinate system. **2.** One of three axes in a three-dimensional Cartesian coordinate system.

Y-chro·mo·some (wī′krō′mə-sōm′) ►*n.* The sex chromosome associated with male characteristics in most mammals, occurring with one X-chromosome in the male sex-chromosome pair.

yd. ►*abbr.* yard (measurement)

ye¹ (thē) ►*def.art. Archaic* The. [From the substitution of *y* for *þ* (th).]

ye² (yē) ►*pron. Archaic* You. [< OE *gē.*]

yea (yā) ►*adv.* **1.** Yes; aye. **2.** Indeed; truly. ►*n.* **1.** An affirmative statement or vote. **2.** One who votes affirmatively. [< OE *gēa.*]

yeah (yĕ′ə, yă′ə, yā′ə) ►*adv. Informal* Yes. [< YEA.]

year (yîr) ►*n.* **1a.** The period during which the earth completes one revolution around the sun, equal to 365 days, 5 hours, 49 minutes, and 12 seconds. In the Gregorian calendar, the year begins on January 1 and ends on December 31 and is divided into 12 months, 52 weeks, and 365 days, or 366 days in a leap year. **b.** A corresponding period in other calendars. **2.** A year or part of a year devoted to a special activity: *the academic year.* **3. years** Age, esp. old age. **4. years** A long time. [< OE *gēar.*]

year·book (yîr′bŏŏk′) ►*n.* **1.** A book published every year, containing information about the previous year. **2.** A yearly book published by the graduating class of a school or college.

year·ling (yîr′lĭng) ►*n.* An animal that is one year old or has not completed its second year.

year·long (yîr′lông′, -lŏng′) ►*adj.* Lasting one year.

year·ly (yîr′lē) ►*adj.* Occurring once a year; annual. ►*adv.* Once a year; annually.

yearn (yûrn) ►*v.* To have a strong, often sad longing. [< OE *geornan.*]

yearn·ing (yûr′nĭng) ►*n.* A deep longing.

year-round (yîr′round′) ►*adj.* Existing, active, or continuous throughout the year.

yeast (yēst) ►*n.* **1.** Any of various unicellular fungi capable of fermenting carbohydrates, including several varieties used in leavening baked goods and fermenting alcoholic beverages and as a dietary supplement. **2.** An agent of ferment or activity. [< OE *gist.*] —**yeast′y** *adj.*

Yeats (yāts), **William Butler** 1865–1939. Irish writer. —**Yeats′i·an** *adj.*

Ye·ka·te·rin·burg (yĭ-kăt′ər-ən-bûrg′) A city of W-central Russia in the E foothills of the Ural Mts.

yell (yĕl) ►*v.* To cry out or utter loudly, as in pain, fright, surprise, or enthusiasm. [< OE *giellan.*] —**yell** *n.*

   Syns: *bawl, bellow, holler, howl, roar, shout, whoop* **v.**

yel·low (yĕl′ō) ►*n.* **1.** Any of a group of colors whose hue is that of ripe lemons, lying between orange and green on the visible spectrum. **2.** *Regional* The yolk of an egg. ►*adj.* **-er, -est 1.** Of the color yellow. **2.** Having a yellow-brown skin color. **3.** *Slang* Cowardly. **4.** Exploiting, distorting, or exaggerating; sensational: *yellow journalism.* ►*v.* To make or become yellow. [< OE *geolu.*] —**yel′low·ish** *adj.*

yellow card ►*n.* A yellow-colored card shown by a referee, esp. in soccer, to signal a flagrant foul. —**yel′low-card′** *v.*

yellow fever ►*n.* An infectious tropical disease transmitted by mosquitoes and marked by high fever, jaundice, and gastrointestinal hemorrhaging.

yellow jacket ►*n.* A small wasp with yellow and black markings.

Yel·low·knife (yĕl′ō-nīf′) The capital of Northwest Terrs., Canada, on the N shore of Great Slave Lake.

Yellow River also **Huang He** (hwäng′ hĕ′) A river of N China flowing about 5,400 km (3,350 mi) E to the Bohai Sea.

Yellow Sea An arm of the Pacific between China and the Korean Peninsula.

Yel·low·stone (yĕl′ō-stōn′) A river, about 1,080 km (670 mi), of NW WY and S and E Montana.

yelp (yĕlp) ►*v.* To utter a short sharp bark or cry. [< OE *gielpan*, boast.] —**yelp** *n.*

Yem·en (yĕm′ən, yā′mən) A country of SW Asia at the S tip of the Arabian peninsula; formed when Yemen (or North Yemen) merged with Southern Yemen (1990). Cap. San'a. —**Yem′en·ite′, Yem′e·ni** (-ə-nē) *adj. & n.*

yen[1] (yĕn) ►*n.* A yearning or craving. [Cantonese *jyun*[6].] —**yen** *v.*

yen[2] (yĕn) ►*n., pl.* **yen** See table at **currency.** [J. *en* < Mandarin *yuán*, dollar.]

Ye·ni·sey (yĭ-nĭ-syā′) A river of central Russia flowing about 4,090 km (2,540 mi) to the Arctic Ocean.

yen·ta (yĕn′tə) ►*n.* *Slang* A meddlesome or gossipy person, esp. a woman. [Yiddish *yente.*]

yeo·man (yō′mən) ►*n.* **1.** An attendant, servant, or lesser official in a royal or noble household. **2.** A petty officer performing chiefly clerical duties in the US Navy. **3.** An independent farmer, esp. a member of a former class of small freeholding farmers in England. [ME *yoman.*]

yeo·man·ry (yō′mən-rē) ►*pl.n.* The class of yeomen; small freeholding farmers.

yep (yĕp) ►*adv. Informal* Yes. [< YES.]

yer·ba ma·te (yâr′bə mä′tä) also **yer·ba ma·té** (mä-tā′) ►*n.* See **mate**[3]. [Am.Sp. : *yerba*, herb + *mate*, mate.]

Ye·re·van (yĕ′rə vän′) The capital of Armenia, in the W-central part.

yes (yĕs) ►*adv.* Used to express affirmation, agreement, confirmation, or consent. ►*n., pl.* **yes·es** An affirmative response or vote. [< OE *gēse*, so be it!]

ye·shi·va or **ye·shi·vah** (yə-shē′və) ►*n. Judaism* **1.** A school where students study the Talmud. **2.** An elementary or secondary school with a curriculum that includes religion and culture. [Heb. *yəšîbâ.*]

yes man ►*n. Informal* One who uncritically agrees with a superior.

yes·ter·day (yĕs′tər-dā′, -dē) ►*n.* **1.** The day before the present day. **2.** also **yesterdays** Time in the past, esp. the recent past. ►*adv.* **1.** On the day before the present day. **2.** A short while ago. [< OE *geostran dæg.*]

yes·ter·year (yĕs′tər-yîr′) ►*n.* **1.** Time past. **2.** The year before the present year.

yet (yĕt) ►*adv.* **1.** At this time; for the present. **2.** Up to a specified time; thus far. **3.** At a future time; eventually. **4.** Besides; in addition. **5.** Still more; even: *a yet sadder tale.* **6.** Nevertheless; nonetheless: *young yet wise.* ►*conj.* And despite this; nevertheless. —*idiom:* **as yet** Up to the present time. [< OE *gēt.*]

   Usage: In formal style *yet* in the sense "up to now" requires that the accompanying verb be in the present perfect, rather than in the simple past: *He hasn't started yet,* not *He didn't start yet.*

ye·ti (yĕt′ē) ►*n., pl.* **-tis** See **abominable snowman.** [Of Tibetan dial. (Sherpa) orig.]

yew (yōō) ►*n.* **1.** A poisonous evergreen tree or shrub having scarlet cup-shaped seed coverings and flat, dark green needles. **2.** The durable, fine-grained wood of a yew. [< OE *īw.*]

Yid·dish (yĭd′ĭsh) ►*n.* The language historically of Jews of Central and E Europe, derived principally from medieval German dialects. —**Yid′dish** *adj.*

yield (yēld) ▸v. **1a.** To give forth by a natural process, esp. by cultivation. See Synonyms at **produce**. **b.** To furnish or give in return: *an investment that yields high returns.* **2a.** To give over possession of; surrender. **b.** To give up or concede. **3.** To give way to pressure, force, or persuasion. **4.** To give place, as to one that is superior. ▸n. **1.** An amount yielded, as of a crop. **2.** A profit obtained from an investment; return. [< OE *geldan*, pay.]

yin (yĭn) ▸n. The passive, female cosmic principle in Chinese dualistic philosophy. [Mandarin *yīn*, moon, shade.]

yin
yin *(right)* and yang *(left)* symbol

yip (yĭp) ▸n. A sharp, high-pitched bark; yelp. [Perh. ME *yippe*.] —**yip** v.

yip·pee (yĭp′ē) ▸interj. Informal Used to express joy or elation.

–yl ▸suff. An organic acid radical: *methyl.* [< Gk. *hulē*, wood, matter.]

YMCA ▸abbr. Young Men's Christian Association

YMHA ▸abbr. Young Men's Hebrew Association

yo·del (yōd′l) ▸v. **-deled, -del·ing** or **-delled, -del·ling** To sing so that the voice fluctuates between the normal chest voice and a falsetto. [Ger. *jodeln.*] —**yo′del·er** n.

yo·ga (yō′gə) ▸n. **1.** also **Yoga** A Hindu discipline involving controlled breathing and prescribed body positions, with the goal of attaining a state of deep spiritual insight and tranquility. **2.** A system of positional exercises derived from this discipline to promote fitness and control of the mind. [< Skt. *yogaḥ*, union.]

yo·gi (yō′gē) ▸n., pl. **-gis** One who is adept in yoga. [< Skt. *yogī* < *yogaḥ*, union; see YOGA.]

yo·gurt also **yo·ghurt** (yō′gərt) ▸n. A tart custardlike food prepared from milk curdled by bacteria. [Turk. *yoğurt*.]

yoke (yōk) ▸n. **1a.** A crossbar with two U-shaped pieces that encircle the necks of draft animals. **b.** pl. **yoke** or **yokes** A pair of draft animals joined by a yoke. **2.** A frame carried across a person's shoulders with equal loads suspended from each end. **3.** A clamp or vise that holds two parts together. **4.** A fitted part of a garment, esp. at the shoulders, to which another piece is attached. **5.** A bond or tie. **6.** Subjugation or bondage. ▸v. **yoked, yok·ing** **1.** To fit or join with or as if with a yoke. **2.** To join or bind together. [< OE *geoc.*]

yo·kel (yō′kəl) ▸n. A rustic; bumpkin. [?]

Yo·ko·ha·ma (yō′kə-hä′mə) A city of SE Honshu, Japan, on the W shore of Tokyo Bay.

yolk (yōk) ▸n. The portion of the egg of egg-laying vertebrates, often yellow in color, that provides nourishment for the early embryo. [< OE *geolca*.]

Yom Kip·pur (yôm′ kĭp′ər, kē-poŏr′) ▸n. Judaism A holy day observed on the 10th day of Tishri and marked by fasting and prayer for the atonement of sins.

yon (yŏn) ▸adv. & adj. Yonder. [< OE *geond*.]

yon·der (yŏn′dər) ▸adv. In or at that indicated place. ▸adj. Being at an indicated distance, usu. within sight. [< OE *geond*.]

yoo-hoo (yoō′hoō′) ▸interj. Used to call someone at a distance.

yore (yôr) ▸n. Time long past: *days of yore.* [< OE *geāra*, long ago < *gēar*, YEAR.]

York (yôrk) A city of N England NE of Leeds.

York, Cape 1. The northernmost point of Australia, at the tip of **Cape York Peninsula. 2.** A cape of NW Greenland in N Baffin Bay.

York·town (yôrk′toun′) A village of SE VA; site of British surrender in the Revolutionary War (1781).

Yo·ru·ba (yôr′ə-bə, yō-roō-bä′) ▸n., pl. **-ba** or **-bas 1.** A member of a West African people living chiefly in SW Nigeria. **2.** The language of the Yoruba. —**Yo′ru·ban** adj.

Yo·sem·i·te Valley (yō-sĕm′ĭ-tē) A valley of E-central CA; surrounded by **Yosemite National Park** and including **Yosemite Falls,** 739 m (2,425 ft) high.

you (yoō) ▸pron. **1.** The one or ones being addressed: *Is that you?* **2.** One; anyone: *You can't win them all.* [< OE *ēow*.]

you-all (yoō′ôl′) also **y′all** (yôl) ▸pron. Regional You (plural).

you'd (yoōd) **1.** You had. **2.** You would.

you'll (yoōl, yŏol; yəl when unstressed) You will.

young (yŭng) ▸adj. **-er, -est 1.** Being in an early period of life or development. **2.** Newly begun or formed: *The evening is young.* **3.** Of or suggestive of youth or early life. **4.** Vigorous or fresh; youthful. **5.** Lacking experience; immature. ▸n. **1.** Young persons collectively: *programs for the young.* **2.** Offspring; brood. [< OE *geong*.] —**young′ish** adj.

Young, Brigham 1801–77. Amer. Mormon leader.

Young, Denton True "Cy." 1867–1955. Amer. baseball player.

young·ling (yŭng′lĭng) ▸n. A young living being, esp. a young person.

young·ster (yŭng′stər) ▸n. A young person.

your (yoōr, yôr; yər when unstressed) ▸adj. The possessive form of **you.** Used as a modifier before a noun: *your boots.* [< OE *ēower.*]

you're (yoōr; yər when unstressed) You are.

yours (yoōrz, yôrz) ▸pron. (takes sing. or pl. v.) The one or ones belonging to you: *If I can't find my bike, I'll take yours.*

your·self (yoōr-sĕlf′, yôr-, yər-) ▸pron., pl. **-selves** (-sĕlvz′) That one identical with you. Used as: **a.** Reflexively: *Did you buy yourself a gift?* **b.** For emphasis: *Do it yourself.*

youth (yoōth) ▸n., pl. **youths** (yoōths, yoōthz) **1.** The condition or quality of being young. **2.** An early period of development or existence, esp. the time of life before adulthood. **3a.** A young person, esp. a young man. **b.** Young people collectively. [< OE *geoguth*.]

youth·ful (yoōth′fəl) ▸adj. **1.** Possessing youth; young. **2.** Characteristic of youth; fresh. **3.** In an early stage; new. —**youth′ful·ly** adv.

youth hostel ▸n. A supervised inexpensive lodging place for young travelers.

you've (yo͞ov) You have.

yowl (youl) ►*v.* To utter a long, loud, mournful cry; wail. [ME *yowlen.*] —**yowl** *n.*

yo-yo (yō'yō') ►*n., pl.* **-yos** A toy consisting of a flattened spool wound with string that is spun down from and reeled up to the hand. [Orig. a trademark.]

yr. ►*abbr.* **1.** year **2.** your

yt·ter·bi·um (ĭ-tûr'bē-əm) ►*n. Symbol* **Yb** A soft, bright, silvery rare-earth element used as an x-ray source in some laser materials, and in some special alloys. At. no. 70. See table at **element.** [After *Ytterby,* Sweden.]

yt·tri·um (ĭt'rē-əm) ►*n. Symbol* **Y** A silvery metallic element used to increase the strength of magnesium and aluminum alloys. At. no. 39. See table at **element.** [After *Ytterby,* Sweden.]

yu·an (yo͞o-än') ►*n., pl.* **-an** or **-ans** See table at **currency.** [Mandarin *yuán.*]

Yu·ca·tán (yo͞o'kə-tăn', -tän') A peninsula mostly in SE Mexico between the Caribbean Sea and the Gulf of Mexico.

yuc·ca (yŭk'ə) ►*n.* Any of various evergreen plants native to North America, having stiff sword-shaped leaves and a terminal cluster of white flowers. [Of Taino orig.]

yuck (yŭk) ►*interj. Slang* Used to express rejection or strong disgust. —**yuck'y** *adj.*

Yu·go·sla·vi·a (yo͞o'gō-slä'vē-ə) A former country of SE Europe (1918–91) on the Balkan Peninsula, comprising the republics of Serbia, Montenegro, Croatia, Slovenia, Macedonia, and Bosnia and Herzegovina. —**Yu'go·sla'vi·an** *adj.* & *n.*

Yuk·on River (yo͞o'kŏn) A river flowing about 3,185 km (1,980 mi) from S Yukon Terr., Canada, through AK to the Bering Sea.

Yukon Territory A territory of NW Canada E of AK. Cap. Whitehorse.

Yule (yo͞ol) ►*n.* Christmas, esp. as traditionally celebrated in N Europe with customs influenced by pagan celebrations of the winter solstice. [< OE *gēol.*]

yule log ►*n.* A large log traditionally burned in a fireplace at Yuletide.

Yule·tide (yo͞ol'tīd') ►*n.* The season of Yule.

yum·my (yŭm'ē) ►*adj.* **-mi·er, -mi·est** *Informal* **1.** Delicious. See Synonyms at **delicious. 2.** Pleasant; attractive.

Yu·pik (yo͞o'pĭk) ►*n., pl.* **-pik** or **-piks 1.** A member of a group of Eskimoan peoples of SW Alaska and extreme NE Russia. **2.** The languages of the Yupik.

yup·pie (yŭp'ē) ►*n. Informal* A young, affluent, usu. city-dwelling professional. [< *y(oung) u(rban) p(rofessional).*]

yurt (yûrt) ►*n.* A circular, domed, portable tent used by nomadic peoples of central Asia. [Russ. *yurta.*]

yurt

YWCA ►*abbr.* Young Women's Christian Association

YWHA ►*abbr.* Young Women's Hebrew Association

Z

z or **Z** (zē) ►*n., pl.* **z's** or **Z's** also **zs** or **Zs 1.** The 26th letter of the English alphabet. **2. Z's** *Slang* Sleep.

Z The symbol for **impedance.**

Za·greb (zä'grĕb) The capital of Croatia, in the N part ESE of Ljubljana, Slovenia.

Za·har·i·as (zə-här'ē-əs), **Mildred Ella Didrikson** "Babe." 1911–56. Amer. athlete.

Babe Didrikson Zaharias
photographed in 1946

Za·ire (zī'îr, zä-îr') See **Congo** (sense 1). —**Za·ir'e·an, Za·ir'i·an** *adj.* & *n.*

Zam·be·zi (zăm-bē'zē) A river, about 2,735 km (1,700 mi), of central and S Africa rising in NW Zambia and flowing to the Mozambique Channel.

Zam·bi·a (zăm'bē-ə) A country of S-central Africa. Cap. Lusaka. —**Zam'bi·an** *adj.* & *n.*

za·ny (zā'nē) ►*adj.* **-ni·er, -ni·est** Comical or ludicrous because of incongruity or strangeness. ►*n., pl.* **-nies** A comical person given to extravagant or outlandish behavior. [< Ital. dial. *zanni.*] —**za'ni·ly** *adv.* —**za'ni·ness** *n.*

Zan·zi·bar (zăn'zə-bär') **1.** A region of E Africa, comprising **Zanzibar Island** and several adjacent islands off the NE coast of Tanzania. **2.** A city of Tanzania on the W coast of Zanzibar I.

zap (zăp) ►*v.* **zapped, zap·ping** *Slang* **1.** To strike with a beam of energy, an electric current, or supernatural power. **2.** To expose to radiation. **3.** To destroy or kill. [Imit.] —**zap'per** *n.*

z-ax·is (zē'ăk'sĭs) ►*n., pl.* **z-ax·es** (-ăk'sēz) One of three axes in a three-dimensional Cartesian coordinate system.

za·zen (zä'zĕn') ►*n.* Meditation while sitting cross-legged, as practiced in Zen. [J. : *za,* to sit down + *zen*, silent meditation; see ZEN.]

zeal (zēl) ►*n.* Enthusiastic devotion to a cause, ideal, or goal. [< Gk. *zēlos.*]

zeal·ot (zĕl′ət) ►*n.* One who is zealous, esp. one who is fanatically devoted to a cause. [< Gk. *zēlōtēs.*] —**zeal′ot·ry** *n.*

zeal·ous (zĕl′əs) ►*adj.* Filled with or motivated by zeal; fervent. —**zeal′ous·ly** *adv.*

ze·bra (zē′brə) ►*n.* A swift, wild, horselike African mammal having distinctive overall markings of alternating white and black or brown stripes. [< OPort. *zevro*, wild ass.]

ze·bu (zē′boō, -byoō) ►*n.* A domesticated ox of Asia and E Africa, having a prominent hump and a large dewlap. [Fr. *zébu.*]

Zech·a·ri·ah (zĕk′ə-rī′ə) ►*n.* **1.** A Hebrew prophet of the 6th cent. BC. **2.** See table at **Bible.**

zed (zĕd) ►*n. Chiefly Brit.* The letter *z.* [< Gk. *zēta*, zeta.]

Zed·e·ki·ah (zĕd′ĭ-kī′ə) 6th cent. BC. The last king of Judah (597–586 BC).

Zeit·geist (tsīt′gīst′, zīt′-) ►*n.* The taste and outlook characteristic of a period or generation. [Ger.]

Zen (zĕn) ►*n.* A school of Buddhism practiced esp. in the Far East asserting that enlightenment can be attained through meditation rather than through faith and devotion. [J., ult. < Skt. *dhyānam*, meditation.]

Zend-A·ves·ta (zĕn′də-vĕs′tə) ►*n.* See **Avesta.**

ze·nith (zē′nĭth) ►*n.* **1.** The point on the celestial sphere that is directly above the observer. **2.** The upper region of the sky. **3.** The highest point above the observer's horizon attained by a celestial body. **4.** The point of culmination; acme. [< Ar. *samt (ar-ra's)*, path (over the head).]

Ze·no of Cit·i·um (zē′nō, sĭt′ē-əm) 335?–263? BC. Greek Stoic philosopher.

Zeno of E·le·a (ē-lē′ə) 495?–430? BC. Greek philosopher.

Zeph·a·ni·ah (zĕf′ə-nī′ə) ►*n.* **1.** A Hebrew prophet of the 7th cent. BC. **2.** See table at **Bible.**

zeph·yr (zĕf′ər) ►*n.* **1.** The west wind. **2.** A gentle breeze. [< Gk. *Zephuros*, god of the west wind.]

zep·pe·lin also **Zep·pe·lin** (zĕp′ə-lĭn) ►*n.* A rigid airship having a long cylindrical body supported by internal gas cells. [After Count Ferdinand von *Zeppelin* (1838–1917).]

ze·ro (zîr′ō, zē′rō) ►*n., pl.* **-ros** or **-roes 1.** The numerical symbol 0; cipher. **2.** *Math.* **a.** The identity element for addition. **b.** A cardinal number indicating the absence of any or all units under consideration. **c.** An ordinal number indicating an initial point or origin. **3.** The temperature indicated by the numeral 0 on a thermometer. **4.** *Informal* One having no influence or importance. **5.** The lowest point. ►*adj.* **1.** Of or being zero. **2a.** Having no measurable or otherwise determinable value. **b.** *Informal* Absent, inoperative, or irrelevant. ►*v.* **-roed, -ro·ing** To adjust (an instrument or device) to zero value. —*phrasal verb:* **zero in 1.** To aim or concentrate firepower on an exact target location. **2.** To converge intently; close in: *zero in on the cause.* [< Ar. *şifr*, cipher.]

zero gravity ►*n.* A condition of apparent weightlessness such as that experienced in orbit or in free fall.

zero hour ►*n.* The scheduled time for the start of an action, esp. a military operation.

ze·ro-sum (zîr′ō-sŭm′, zē′rō-) ►*adj.* Of or being a situation in which a gain on one side necessarily entails an equal loss on another.

zest (zĕst) ►*n.* **1a.** Flavor or interest; piquancy. **b.** The outermost part of the rind of an orange, lemon, or other citrus fruit, used as flavoring. **2.** Spirited enjoyment; gusto. ►*v.* To remove small pieces from (a rind from a citrus fruit) for use as a flavoring in cooking. [Obsolete Fr., citrus peel.] —**zest′ful** *adj.* —**zest′ful·ly** *adv.* **Syns:** *gusto, relish* **n.**

ze·ta (zā′tə, zē′-) ►*n.* The 6th letter of the Greek alphabet. [Gk. *zēta.*]

Zeus (zoōs) ►*n. Gk. Myth.* The principal god of the Greek pantheon, ruler of the heavens and father of other gods and mortal heroes.

Zhou En·lai or **Chou En·lai** (jō′ ĕn-lī′) 1898–1976. Chinese revolutionary and politician.

Zhou Enlai
photographed in the 1970s

Zi·dane (zē-dän′), **Zinedine Yazid** b. 1972. French soccer player.

zig·gu·rat (zĭg′ə-răt′) ►*n.* A temple tower of ancient Mesopotamia, having the form of a terraced pyramid. [Assyrian *zigguratu*, summit.]

zig·zag (zĭg′zăg′) ►*n.* **1a.** A line or course that proceeds by sharp turns in alternating directions. **b.** One of a series of such sharp turns. **2.** Something, such as a design, marked by zigzags. ►*adj.* Moving in or having a zigzag. ►*adv.* In a zigzag manner or pattern. ►*v.* **-zagged, -zag·ging** To move in or form a zigzag. [Fr. < Ger. *Zickzack.*]

zilch (zĭlch) ►*n. Slang* Zero; nothing. [?]

zil·lion (zĭl′yən) ►*n. Informal* An indefinitely large number. [Alteration of *million.*]

Zim·bab·we (zĭm-bäb′wē, -wā) Formerly **Rhodesia.** A country of S Africa. Cap. Harare. —**Zim·bab′we·an** *adj. & n.*

zinc (zĭngk) ►*n. Symbol* **Zn** A bluish-white, lustrous metallic element used to form many alloys, including brass, and to galvanize iron and other metals. At. no. 30. See table at **element.** ►*v.* **zinced, zinc·ing** or **zincked, zinck·ing** To coat or treat with zinc; galvanize. [Ger. *Zink.*]

zinc oxide ►*n.* An amorphous white or yellowish powder, ZnO, used as a pigment and in pharmaceuticals and cosmetics.

zine or **'zine** (zēn) ►*n.* **1.** An inexpensive, self-published, underground publication. **2.** An e-zine. [< (MAGA)ZINE.]

zing (zĭng) ►*n.* **1.** A brief high-pitched humming or buzzing sound. **2.** Liveliness; zip. ►*v.* **1.** To make a zing. **2.** To move swiftly. **3.** *Informal* To attack verbally. [Imit.] —**zing′y** *adj.*

zing·er (zĭng′ər) ►*n. Informal* A witty, often caustic remark.

zin·ni·a (zĭn′ē-ə) ►*n.* A widely cultivated plant with showy, variously colored flower heads. [After J.G. *Zinn* (1727–59).]

Zi·on (zī′ən) also **Si·on** (sī′ən) ►*n.* **1a.** The historic land of Israel as a symbol of the Jewish people. **b.** The Jewish people; Israel. **2.** A place or religious community regarded as consecrated to God. **3.** A utopia.

Zi·on·ism (zī′ə-nĭz′əm) ►*n.* A political movement that supports the maintenance and preservation of the state of Israel as a Jewish homeland, originally arising in the late 1800s with the goal of reestablishing a Jewish homeland in the region of Palestine. —**Zi′on·ist** *adj. & n.*

zip (zĭp) ►*n.* **1.** A brief, sharp, hissing sound. **2.** Energy; vim. **3.** *Slang* Nothing; nil; zero. ►*v.* **zipped, zip·ping 1.** To move or act with speed or energy. **2.** To fasten or unfasten with a zipper. [Imit.]

ZIP Code ►*n.* A series of digits designating a specific locality in the United States, appended to a postal address to expedite the sorting and delivery of mail. [Orig. a trademark.]

zip·line (zĭp′līn′) ►*n.* A cable stretched between points of different elevations with a pulley and a harness or bar for attaching a rider, who moves by gravity. —**zip′line′** *v.*

zip·per (zĭp′ər) ►*n.* A fastening device consisting of parallel rows of metal or plastic teeth on adjacent edges of an opening that are interlocked by a sliding tab. [< ZIP.]

zip·py (zĭp′ē) ►*adj.* **-pi·er, -pi·est** Full of energy; lively.

zir·con (zûr′kŏn′) ►*n.* A brown to colorless mineral that is heated, cut, and polished to form a brilliant blue-white gem. [Ult. < Pers. *āzargūn*, fire color.]

zir·co·ni·um (zûr-kō′nē-əm) ►*n. Symbol* **Zr** A lustrous, grayish-white, strong, ductile metallic element used chiefly in ceramic and refractory compounds and as an alloying agent. At. no. 40. See table at **element.**

zit (zĭt) ►*n. Slang* A pimple. [?]

zith·er (zĭth′ər, zĭth′-) ►*n.* A musical instrument composed of a flat sound box set with strings of graded length, played with the fingertips or a plectrum. [< Gk. *kithara*, ancient musical instrument.] —**zith′er·ist** *n.*

zi·ti (zē′tē) ►*n.* Pasta in medium-sized, often ridged tubes. [Ital.]

zlo·ty (zlô′tē) ►*n., pl.* **-ty** or **-tys** See table at **currency.** [Pol. *złoty* < *złoto*, gold.]

zo·di·ac (zō′dē-ăk′) ►*n.* **1a.** A band of the celestial sphere extending about 8° to either side of the ecliptic that represents the path of the principal planets, the moon, and the sun. **b.** In astrology, this band divided into 12 equal parts called signs, each bearing the name of a constellation for which it was orig. named. **2.** A diagram or figure representing the zodiac. [< Gk. *zōidion*, small figure, zodiacal sign < *zōion*, living thing.] —**zo·di′a·cal** (-dī′ə-kəl) *adj.*

–zoic ►*suff.* **1.** Relating to a specified manner of animal existence: *protozoic.* **2.** Of a specified geologic era: *Archeozoic.* [< Gk. *zōion*, living being.]

Zo·la (zō′lə, zō-lä′), **Émile** 1840–1902. French writer and critic.

zom·bie (zŏm′bē) ►*n.* **1.** In voodoo belief and folklore, a corpse that has been reanimated, esp. by means of a supernatural power or spell. **2.** One who looks or behaves like an automaton. **3.** A computer connected to the Internet and controlled by a remote unauthorized user without the owner's knowledge. [< Kimbundu *nzúmbi*, ghost, soul, spirit.]

zon·al (zō′nəl) ►*adj.* **1.** Relating to a zone. **2.** Divided into zones. —**zon′al·ly** *adv.*

zone (zōn) ►*n.* **1.** An area or region distinguished from adjacent parts by a distinctive feature or characteristic. **2.** A section of an area or territory used for a specific purpose: *a residential zone.* ►*v.* **zoned, zon·ing** To divide into zones. [< Gk. *zōnē*, girdle.]

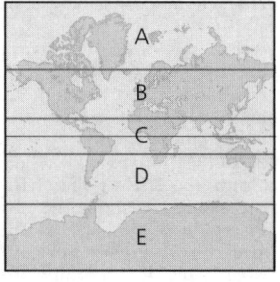

zone
climatic zones
A. North Frigid Zone
B. North Temperate Zone
C. Torrid Zone
D. South Temperate Zone
E. South Frigid Zone

zonk (zôngk, zŏngk) ►*v. Slang* To cause to be asleep or intoxicated. [?]

zoo (zōō) ►*n., pl.* **zoos 1.** A park or institution in which living animals, esp. wild animals, are kept and exhibited to the public. **2.** *Slang* A place or situation marked by confusion or disorder. [< ZOOLOGICAL GARDEN.]

zoo– or **zo–** ►*pref.* **1.** Animal: *zoology.* **2.** Motile: *zoospore.* [< Gk. *zōion*, living being.]

zoological garden ►*n.* See **zoo** (sense 1).

zo·ol·o·gy (zō-ŏl′ə-jē, zōō-) ►*n.* **1.** The branch of biology that deals with animals and animal life. **2.** The animal life of a particular area or period. **3.** The characteristics of a particular animal group or category. —**zo′o·log′i·cal** (-ə-lŏj′ĭ-kəl), **zo′o·log′ic** *adj.* —**zo·ol′o·gist** *n.*

zoom (zōōm) ►*v.* **1.** To move swiftly, esp. with a continuous low-pitched buzzing or humming sound. **2.** To simulate movement away from or toward a subject using a zoom lens. [Imit.]

zoom lens ►*n.* A camera lens whose focal length can be rapidly changed, allowing rapid change in the size of an image.

–zoon ►*suff.* Animal; independently moving organic unit: *spermatozoon.* [< Gk. *zōion*, living being.]

zo·o·plank·ton (zō′ə-plăngk′tən) ►*n.* Plankton that consists of animals.

zo·o·spore (zō′ə-spôr′) ►*n.* A motile, flagellated asexual spore.

Zo·ro·as·ter (zôr′ō-ăs′tər) 6th cent. BC. Iranian prophet who founded Zoroastrianism.

Zo·ro·as·tri·an·ism (zôr′ō-ăs′trē-ə-nĭz′əm) ►*n.* The religious system founded in Persia by Zoroaster, teaching the worship of Ahura Mazda in the context of a universal struggle between the forces of light and of darkness. **—Zo·ro·as′tri·an** *adj. & n.*

zounds (zoundz) ►*interj.* Used to express anger, surprise, or indignation.

zuc·chi·ni (zoo-kē′nē) ►*n., pl.* **-ni** or **-nis** A variety of summer squash having an elongated shape and a smooth, dark green rind. [Ital. < *zucca,* gourd.]

Zu·lu (zoo′loo) ►*n., pl.* **-lu** or **-lus 1.** A member of a people of SE Africa. **2.** The Bantu language of the Zulu. **—Zu′lu** *adj.*

Zu·lu·land (zoo′loo-lănd′) A historical region of E South Africa.

Zu·ni (zoo′nē) also **Zu·ñi** (-nyē, -nē) ►*n., pl.* **-ni** or **-nis** also **-ñi** or **-ñis 1.** A member of a Pueblo people of W New Mexico. **2.** The language of the Zuni.

Zu·rich (zoor′ĭk) A city of NE Switzerland at the N tip of the **Lake of Zurich.**

zwie·back (swē′băk′, swī′-, zwē′-, zwī′-) ►*n.* A usu. sweetened bread baked first as a loaf and later sliced and toasted. [Ger.]

zy·de·co (zī′dĭ-kō′) ►*n.* Popular music of S Louisiana played by small groups featuring a guitar and accordion. [< Louisiana Fr.]

zy·go·sis (zī-gō′sĭs, zĭ-) ►*n., pl.* **-ses** (-sēz) The union of gametes to form a zygote.

zy·gote (zī′gōt′) ►*n.* **1.** The cell formed by the union of two gametes, esp. a fertilized ovum before cleavage. **2.** The organism that develops from a zygote. [< Gk. *zugoun,* to yoke.] **—zy·got′ic** (-gŏt′ĭk) *adj.*

zy·mur·gy (zī′mûr′jē) ►*n.* The branch of chemistry that deals with fermentation processes, as in brewing. [Gk. *zumē,* leaven + –URGY.]

PICTURE CREDITS

The editorial and production staff wishes to thank the many individuals, organizations, and agencies that have contributed to the art program of the Dictionary.

Credits on the following pages are arranged alphabetically by boldface entry word. In cases where two or more illustrations complement an entry, the sources follow the order of the illustrations. The following source abbreviations are used throughout the credits: AGE - age fotostock; AL - Alamy; AP/WWP - AP Images; AR - Art Resource; CI - Carlyn Iverson; CL/AA - Clarinda/Academy Artworks; COR - Corbis; EM - Elizabeth Morales; GI - Getty Images; HM - © Houghton Mifflin Harcourt, School Division; LOC - Library of Congress; PG - Precision Graphics; PR - Photo Researchers, Inc.; and SS - SuperStock, Inc.

Hank Aaron GI – MLB Photos **abscissa** CL-AA **acoustics** UG/GGS Information Services **acupuncture** SS – Tetra Images **John Adams** AR – Réunion des Musées Nationaux **John Quincy Adams** COR – The Corcoran Art Gallery **advection** EM **aerodynamics** CL-AA **Louisa May Alcott** GI – Hulton Archive **Muhammad Ali** GI – Mandel Ngan **alpenhorn** AL – Fabrice Bettex **ampule** PR – Claire Paxton & Jacqui Farrow **angioplasty** PG **anorak** GI – Scott Markewitz **Susan B. Anthony** COR **ao dai** AL – Peter Treanor **apogee** CL-AA **arabesque** SS – SuperStock **Neil Armstrong** NASA – Johnson Space Center **Chester A. Arthur** AR – National Portrait Gallery, Smithsonian Institution **asthma** Garth Glazier **atmosphere** CL-AA **Aung San Suu Kyi** AP/WWP – Myanmar News Agency **avatar** AL – The Print Collector; COR – Stapleton Collection

backboard GI – David Madison **balance beam** GI – Thomas Niedermueller/Bongarts **James Baldwin** GI – Ulf Anderson **bandanna** SS – Imageshop **bar graph** CL-AA **basilica** CL-AA **beak** EM **Simone de Beauvoir** COR – Eric Preau **bedstead** dreamstime – Pferd **belaying pin** AGE – John Burke **Alexander Graham Bell** LOC **Benedict XVI** AP/WWP – Andrew Medichini **bindi** SS – PhotosIndia.com **bit²** CL-AA **Elizabeth Blackwell** US National Library of Medicine **blockhouse** iStockphoto.com – Brian Swartz **boiler** PG **boomerang** HM **Ray Bradbury** GI – Mark Davis **Braille** CL-AA **brisket** Ka Botzis **Elizabeth Barrett Browning** SS – Stock Montage **James Buchanan** LOC – Mathew Brady **burqa** AL – Dave Stamboulis **George H. W. Bush** George Bush Presidential Library and Museum – P00565 **George W. Bush** George W. Bush Presidential Library – White House photo by Eric Draper **butte** COR – moodboard

Saint Frances Xavier Cabrini LOC **cairn** AGE – Bold Stock **calligraphy** AL – Image Source Black **campanile** AGE – Ben Welsh **Annie Jump Cannon** COR – Hulton-Deutsch Collection **canopy** AL – Emil Pozar **Jimmy Carter** LOC **Mary Cassatt** AL – Folio **Fidel Castro** COR – Claudia Daut **cell** CL-AA **chameleon** GI – Michael Dunning **César Chávez** COR – Najlah Feanny **chemical bond** Robin Storesund **Chinese checkers** HM **chord¹** Christopher Granniss **Dame Agatha Christie** GI – Walter Bird **Sir Winston Churchill** COR – Bettmann **circle** CL-AA **claddagh** HM **Grover Cleveland** COR **Bill Clinton** William J. Clinton Presidential Library & Museum – Ralph Alswang **cloverleaf** COR – Lester Lefkowitz **Nat "King" Cole** COR – Bettmann **comb** GI – Chris Hepburn **concentric** EM **cone** CL-AA **Calvin Coolidge** GI – Hulton Archive **Nicolaus Copernicus** AL – The Art Gallery Collection **cosecant** CL-AA **cosine** CL-AA **cotangent** CL-AA **cowl neck** GI – Marc Romanelli **cradleboard** LOC **crater** AL – mediacolor's **cropdusting** GI – Chuck Keeler **Marie Curie** COR – Bettmann **cylinder** CL-AA

Charles Darwin SS – Huntington Library **decahedron** CL-AA **deck chair** GI – Sakis Papadopoulos **dehumidify** PG **desalinize** PG **diacritic** Margaret Anne Miles **diatom** COR – Lester V. Bergman **Charles Dickens** COR – Bettmann **Emily Dickinson** The Granger Collection, New York **dirt bike** AGE – Thomas Schneider **Dorothea Dix** LOC **DNA** EM **dome** COR – Michel Gounot **Frederick Douglass** LOC **dreidel** HM **drumlin** EM

earbud COR – Radius Images **Amelia Earhart** GI – Hulton Archive **eclipse** PG **edelweiss** GI – Norbert Rosing **Dwight Eisenhower** Eisenhower Presidential Library **Elizabeth II** GI – Chris Jackson **El Niño** EM **emphysema** EM **equator** Jerry Malone **espalier** AL – Jim Allan **eye** CI

fanlight AL – Kathy deWitt **featherstitch** CL-AA **figurehead** AGE – ARCO/de Cuveland **Millard Fillmore** LOC **fish ladder** Shutterstock Images – Terry Davis **F. Scott Fitzgerald** GI – Hulton Archive **flamingo** SS – Tetra Images **floodplain** EM **food chain** PG **Gerald Ford** Courtesy Gerald R. Ford Library – David Hume Kennerly **formation** US Navy Photo – Photographer's Mate 3rd Class Leah Wilson **fracture** PG

Benjamin Franklin LOC **fret²** AGE – Tessa Updike **Carlos Fuentes** AP/WWP – Victor R. Caivano **funicular** PG **fuse²** PG

galosh HM **Mahatma Gandhi** GI – Hulton Archive **James Garfield** AR – National Portrait Gallery, Smithsonian Institution **gazebo** dreamstime – Michael Pettigrew **Geronimo** COR – Gerhard Sisters **Althea Gibson** COR – Bettmann **gimbal** PG **glider** AL – Rtimages **goatee** AL – Blend Images **Jane Goodall** GI – Vince Bucci **gooseneck** HM **graft¹** Patrice Rossi Calkin **Martha Graham** GI – Hulton Archive **Ulysses S. Grant** AR – National Portrait Gallery, Smithsonian Institution **greenhouse effect** PG **grizzly bear** AL – franzfoto.com **Johann Gutenberg** AL – Interfoto

hairpin GI – Blaine Franger **halo** PR – George D. Lepp **hang glider** AGE – Dennis MacDonald **Warren Harding** COR – Bettmann **harmonic** EM **Benjamin Harrison** LOC – Pach Brothers **William Henry Harrison** LOC **hatchback** AL – Goddard Automotive **Rutherford Hayes** LOC **headgear** AL – Picture Partners **Ernest Hemingway** Globe Photos, Inc. – IPOL **herringbone** AL – Eric Hernandez/BUILT Images **Hildegard von Bingen** AR – Erich Lessing **Hiroshima** COR – Bettmann **hogan** COR – Buddy Mays **hoodie** GI – Thinkstock Images **Herbert Hoover** LOC **hovercraft** PG **Langston Hughes** GI – Hulton Archive **hurdles** AP/WWP – Kevin Frayer **Zora Neale Hurston** LOC **hydroelectric** PG

inclined plane EM **induction** PG **intercept** CL-AA **Isabella I** AR – Erich Lessing

Andrew Jackson AR – National Portrait Gallery, Smithsonian Institution **javelin** AP/WWP – Ng Han Guan **Thomas Jefferson** AR – Réunion des Musées Nationaux **Andrew Johnson** LOC **Lyndon B. Johnson** Lyndon Baines Johnson Library and Museum – Yoichi R. Okamoto **Chief Joseph** LOC – cph.3a03795 **jug** HM

kangaroo Photodisc **Helen Keller** LOC **John F. Kennedy** SS **kettledrum** GI – C Squared Studios **kimono** AL – Eric Nathan **Martin Luther King, Jr.** GI – AFP **koala** COR **kurta** AGE – Dinodia Photo Library RF

labret COR – Ocean **lady's slipper** COR – Joe McDonald **laser** PG **Robert E. Lee** LOC **lens** PG **Doris Lessing** AP/WWP – Martin Cleaver **ligature** Tech-Graphics **lilac** SS – Pixtal **Abraham Lincoln** SS – Jack Novak **lintel** AL – Per Karlsson-BKWine.com **locket** HM **longitude** Jerry Malone **lotus position** AL – PhotosIndia.com **Martin Luther** GI – Hulton Archive

Yo-Yo Ma AP/WWP – Robert E. Klein **James Madison** AR – Réunion des Musées Nationaux **major scale** Tech-Graphics **manatee** AGE – Andre Seale **Nelson Mandela** AP/WWP – Themba Hadebe **manual alphabet** CL-AA **Mao Zedong** COR – Roman Soumar **maraca** HM **Marie Antoinette** AR – Réunion des Musées Nationaux **marquee** Margaret Anne Miles **Mason-Dixon Line** PG **mattock** IIM **William McKinley** LOC **Margaret Mead** AL – Lewton Cole **measure** Tech-Graphics **menorah** HM **metronome** GI – Photodisc **minaret** AR – SEF **minor scale** Tech-Graphics **miter** AP/WWP – John Giles/PA Wire **James Monroe** AR – Image copyright © The Metropolitan Museum of Art **monstrance** AGE – Dinodia Photo Library **moraine** AGE – Alan Majchrowicz **Toni Morrison** COR – Colin McPherson **mosaic** GI – Richard Cummins **mountain bike** SS – age fotostock **mullion** Peter Chipman

Napoleon I SS – age fotostock **Martina Navratilova** GI – Mark Davis **needle** CL-AA **nest** HM **neuron** CL-AA **Florence Nightingale** Bridgeman Art Library – Florence Nightingale Museum **Richard Nixon** COR **Tenzing Norgay** GI – Baron

Barack Obama The White House – Pete Souza **Odin** AL – The Art Gallery Collection **Georgia O'Keeffe** GI – Joe Munroe/Archive Photos **orca** Shutterstock Images – Xavier Marchant **Osceola** SS **outrigger** AGE – Michel Renaudeau

paddle¹ CL-AA **paisley** HM **panda** GI – Sean Russell **Pangaea** EM **parallelepiped** CL-AA **Rosa Parks** AP/WWP – Carlos Osorio **parterre** AL – CpC Photo **Louis Pasteur** LOC **pawl** PG **Pearl Harbor** National Archives and Records Administration **perihelion** CL-AA **Frances Perkins** COR **Peter I** GI – The Bridgeman Art Library **petroglyph** GI – Toyohiro Yamada **philodendron** HM **picket fence** COR – Comstock **pie chart** UG/GGS Information Services **Franklin Pierce** LOC **pince-nez** GI – George Marks **pitcher plant** AGE – Chua Wee Boo **platelet** PR – NIBSC **Pocahontas** AR – National Portrait Gallery, Smithsonian Institution **polar bear** COR – Jeff Vanuga **James K. Polk** COR – The Corcoran Gallery of Art **polo** GI – Manpreet Romana **polyp** EM **portcullis** GI – Travel Ink **prehensile** COR **Elvis Presley** COR – Sunset Boulevard **prosthesis** GI – Mark Kolbe **puggle** AL – Allison Dinner **Joseph Pulitzer** COR – Bettmann **pylon** GI – Photodisc; AGE – Agency Jon Arnold Images, Ivan Vdovin **Pythagorean theorem** CL-AA

quay AL – Steven May

rabbet CL-AA **radio telescope** AL – Adina Tovy **Sir Walter Raleigh** GI – The Bridgeman Art Library **Jeannette Rankin** LOC **Ronald Reagan** Courtesy Ronald Reagan Library **Red Cloud** LOC **refraction** CL-AA **Paul Revere** SS **reverse osmosis** PG **rhizome** EM **Sally Ride** NASA – Johnson Space Center **right angle** CL-AA **RNA** EM **Jackie Robinson** GI – Hulton Archive **rodeo** COR – Gerhard Egger **Eleanor Roosevelt** COR – Marvin Kroner **Franklin Delano Roosevelt** GI – Stock Montage **Theodore Roosevelt** COR – Bettmann **rotunda** Shutterstock Images – Lesley Rigg **Mount Rushmore** COR